KU-214-237

175 YEARS OF DICTIONARY PUBLISHING

Collins

175 YEARS OF DICTIONARY PUBLISHING

Dictionary & Thesaurus

HarperCollins Publishers
Westerhill Road
Bishopbriggs
Glasgow
G64 2QT
Great Britain

Fifth Edition 2011

Reprint 10 9 8 7 6 5 4 3 2 1 0

ISBN 978-0-00-743519-7

Collins® is a registered trademarks of HarperCollins Publishers Limited

www.collinslanguage.com

A catalogue record for this book is available from the British Library

Text typeset by Davidson Publishing Solutions, Glasgow

Printed in China by Imago

Acknowledgements
We would like to thank those authors and publishers who kindly gave permission for copyright material to be used in the Collins Word Web. We would also like to thank Times Newspapers Ltd for providing valuable data.

Editors
Gerry Breslin
Lorna Gilmour
Paige Weber

For the Publisher
Lucy Cooper
Kerry Ferguson
Elaine Higgleton

Contents

Using this Dictionary & Thesaurus

Collins Dictionary & Thesaurus is two books in one. It provides two kinds of language help, arranged on the same page for quick and easy reference. In the upper section of each page you will find a dictionary text that gives help with spellings and meanings, while the lower section provides a thesaurus with a choice of synonyms. A helpful Ⓣ symbol appears at each dictionary headword that has a matching thesaurus entry below, to link the two texts together in a clear and easy-to-use layout.

Dictionary

In the dictionary text, each word defined is presented as a main entry in a single alphabetical sequence. Every definition is written in concise, straightforward English. Where a word has more than one sense, the one given first is the normal everyday meaning in today's language. Other senses of a word – for instance, historical or technical meanings – are explained after the main present-day meaning. Each sense is separately numbered.

In addition, the dictionary gives help with spelling. The text shows variant spellings, and plurals and verb parts where these are difficult, unusual, or likely to produce problems. It makes it clear, for instance, that in British English there are two '*l*'s in *travelling*, but in American English the correct spelling is *traveling*, and it shows that *sari* and *saree* are both correct spellings. It also advises that the plural of *helix* can be either *helices* or *helixes*. Simple pronunciations are given for words which might be unfamiliar.

Included in the dictionary text are numerous biographical entries, which provide key dates, achievements and biographical facts about fascinating people, from Sir Martin Frobisher to Boris Becker to Margaret Drabble.

Thesaurus

In the lower part of each page is the thesaurus section, which is also arranged in a single alphabetical listing of main words. At each of these main entries, you will find a list or lists of alternative words or phrases of the same or similar meaning. Even if an entry word has more than one meaning, synonyms for the different meanings will be found in the same entry, grouped in lists. The lists for different senses are arranged in the order that they are found in the corresponding dictionary entry, and they are introduced by the same sense numbers.

Not every word or sense in the dictionary section has an entry in the thesaurus. Terms denoting specific things often have no synonyms (*flak jacket*, *histogram*, and *spatula*, for instance). Such items are not included in the thesaurus unless they have an alternative name or give rise to a figurative use.

Dictionary & Thesaurus

The arrangement of the two texts in parallel format enables you to refer from dictionary to thesaurus entries and then back again with ease. ***Collins Dictionary & Thesaurus*** is thus a uniquely helpful book, providing spelling, meaning, and a wide choice of alternative words. The new edition of this comprehensive, all-in-one, practical dictionary and thesaurus is designed to meet a wide range of your everyday language needs.

Dictionary

Main entry words

Main entry words are printed in large bold type, e.g.

academy

All main entry words, including abbreviations and combining forms, are presented in one alphabetical sequence, e.g.

abyss
Ac
AC
a/c
acacia
academic

Ⓣ symbol

A Ⓣ symbol appears after a headword to show that this dictionary entry has a matching entry in the thesaurus text:

modest Ⓣ *adj* **1** having a humble opinion of oneself··· accomplishments **2** not extreme or

Variant spellings

All variant spellings are shown in full, e.g.

griffin, griffon *or* **gryphon** *n* a mythical winged monster with an eagle's head and a lion's body

Pronunciations

Pronunciations are given in brackets for words that are difficult or confusing; the word is re-spelt as it is pronounced, with the stressed syllable in bold type, e.g.

chaperone (**shap**-per-rone) *n* **1** an older person who accompanies and supervises a young person or young people on social occasions

Parts of Speech

Parts of speech are shown in italics as an abbreviation. When a word can be used as more than one part of speech, the change of part of speech is shown after an arrow ▷, e.g.

goodness Ⓣ *n* **1** the quality of being good ▷ *interj* **2** an exclamation of surprise

Parts of speech may be combined for some words, e.g.

gratis *adv, adj* without payment; free

Irregular parts

Irregular parts or confusing forms of verbs, nouns, adjectives, and adverbs are shown in bold type, e.g.

> **begin** ❶ *vb* **-ginning, -gan, -gun**
> **dislodge** *vb* **-lodging, -lodged**
> **filly** *n, pl* **-lies**
> **empty** ❶ *adj* **-tier, -tiest**
> **well**[1] ❶ *adv* **better, best**

Meanings

Different meanings, or senses, for each headword are separated by bold sense numbers, e.g.

> **lark**[2] *informal n* **1** a carefree adventure or frolic **2** a harmless piece of mischief **3** an activity or job viewed with disrespect ...

Examples

Example sentences or phrases appear in italic at the end of some senses to give examples of the word in use, e.g.

> **multipurpose** *adj* having many uses: *a giant multipurpose enterprise*

Phrases and idioms

Phrases and idioms are included immediately after the meanings of the main entry word, e.g.

> **lark**[2] *informal n* **1** a carefree adventure or frolic ... ▷*vb* **4 lark about** to have a good time frolicking or playing pranks ...

Related words

Related words are shown in the same paragraph as the main entry word, e.g.

> **maladroit** (mal-a-**droyt**) *adj* clumsy, awkward, or tactless **maladroitly** *adv* **maladroitness** *n*

Note: where the meaning of a related word is not given, it may be understood from the main entry word, or from another related word.

Word origins

Word origins, or etymologies, appear at the end of some entries, to describe the linguistic origin of the word:

> **nutrition** ❶ (new-**trish**-un) *n* **1** the process of taking in and absorbing nutrients ...
> **WORD ORIGIN** Latin *nutrire* to nourish

Thesaurus

Main entry words

Main entry words are printed in bold type:

> **bewilder** *vb* **= confound**, surprise, stun, confuse, puzzle, baffle, mix up

Senses

Where a word has several senses, the senses are numbered according to their corresponding senses in the dictionary text:

> **interpret** *vb* **1 = explain**, define, clarify, spell out, make sense of, decode, decipher, expound, elucidate, throw light on, explicate **2 = take**, understand, read, explain, regard, construe **3 = portray**, present, perform, render, depict, enact, act out **4 = translate**, convert, paraphrase, adapt, transliterate

Key synonyms

The first synonym to appear in any list is the key synonym, which is in bold and introduced by an = sign. The key synonym is the most commonly used synonym for that entry or for that particular sense of that entry, e.g.

> **nirvana** *n* **= paradise**, peace, joy, bliss, serenity, tranquillity

The synonyms that follow the key synonym appear in Roman font, and they are listed according to common use.

Parts of speech

Parts of speech are shown in italics. If an entry has more than one part of speech, each part of speech (after the first) is introduced by an arrow symbol ▷:

> **blanket** *n* **1 = cover**, rug, coverlet…
> ▷ *vb* **4 = coat**, cover, hide, surround, cloud, mask, conceal, obscure, eclipse, cloak

Opposites

Opposites, or antonyms, appear at the end of an entry or a sense, and they are introduced by the word **OPPOSITE**:

> **cosmopolitan** *adj* **3 = sophisticated**, worldly, cultured, refined, cultivated, urbane, well-travelled, worldly-wise
> **OPPOSITE:** unsophisticated

Abbreviations

adj	adjective	*interj*	interjection
adv	adverb	*intr*	intransitive
anat	anatomy	*masc*	masculine
anthropol	anthropology	*med*	medicine
archaeol	archaeology	*meteorol*	meteorology
archit	architecture	*mil*	military
astrol	astrology	*myth*	mythology
astron	astronomy	*n*	noun
Austral	Australian	*naut*	nautical
bacteriol	bacteriology	*N*	North
biochem	biochemistry	*NZ*	New Zealand
biol	biology	*ornithol*	ornithology
bot	botany	*pathol*	pathology
Brit	British	*pharmacol*	pharmacology
Canad	Canadian	*photog*	photography
cap	capitalised	*physiol*	physiology
chem	chemistry	*pl*	plural
conj	conjugation	*prep*	preposition
crystallog	crystallography	*pron*	pronoun
derog	derogatory	*psycho*	psychology
det	determiner	*RC church*	Roman Catholic church
E	East	*S*	South
econ	economics	*S African*	South African
e.g.	for example	*Scot*	Scottish
esp.	especially	*sing*	singular
Esq.	esquire	*sociol*	sociology
etc.	et cetera	*theol*	theology
fem	feminine	*tr*	transitive
foll.	followed	*US*	United States
geog	geography	*vb*	verb
geol	geology	*W*	West
geom	geometry	*zool*	zoology
i.e.	that is to say		

Aa

DICTIONARY

a *or* **A** *n, pl* **a's, A's** *or* **As** **1** the first letter of the English alphabet **2** **from A to B** from one place to another: *I just want a car that takes me from A to B* **3** **from A to Z** from start to finish

a *adj (indefinite article)* **1** used preceding a singular count noun that has not been mentioned before: *a book; a great shame* **2** used preceding a noun or adjective of quantity: *a litre of wine; a great amount has been written; I swim a lot and walk much more* **3** each or every; per: *I saw him once a week for six weeks*

A **1** *music* the sixth note of the scale of C major **2** ampere(s) **3** atomic: *an A-bomb*

Å angstrom unit

a- *or before a vowel* **an-** *prefix* not or without: *atonal; asexual; anaemia*
WORD ORIGIN Greek

A1, A-1 *or* **A-one** *adj informal* first-class, excellent

A4 *n* a standard paper size, 297 × 210 mm

AA **1** Alcoholics Anonymous **2** (in Britain and South Africa) Automobile Association

AAA *Brit* (formerly) Amateur Athletic Association

Aalto *n* **Alvar** 1898–1976, Finnish architect and furniture designer, noted particularly for his public and industrial buildings, in which wood is much used. He invented bent plywood furniture (1932)

A & R artists and repertoire

aardvark *n* a S African anteater with long ears and snout
WORD ORIGIN obsolete Afrikaans: earth pig

AB **1** able-bodied seaman **2** Alberta

ab- *prefix* away from or opposite to: *abnormal*
WORD ORIGIN Latin

aback *adv* **taken aback** startled or disconcerted

abacus (ab-a-cuss) *n* a counting device consisting of a frame holding beads on metal rods
WORD ORIGIN Latin

abaft *adv, adj naut* closer to the stern of a ship
WORD ORIGIN Old English *be* by + *æftan* behind

abalone (ab-a-lone-ee) *n* an edible sea creature with a shell lined with mother-of-pearl
WORD ORIGIN American Spanish *abulón*

abandon ❶ *vb* **1** to desert or leave: *he had already abandoned his first wife* **2** to give up completely: *did you abandon all attempts at contact with the boy?* **3** to give oneself over completely to an emotion ▷*n* **4** **with abandon** uninhibitedly and without restraint **abandonment** *n*
WORD ORIGIN Old French *a bandon* under one's control

abandoned *adj* **1** no longer used or occupied: *four people were found dead in an abandoned vehicle* **2** wild and uninhibited: *that fluffy abandoned laugh*

abase *vb* **abasing, abased** ▪ **abase oneself** to make oneself humble **abasement** *n*
WORD ORIGIN Old French *abaissier*

abashed *adj* embarrassed and ashamed
WORD ORIGIN Old French *esbair* to be astonished

abate *vb* **abating, abated** to make or become less strong: *the tension has abated in recent months* **abatement** *n*
WORD ORIGIN Old French *abatre* to beat down

abattoir (ab-a-twahr) *n* a slaughterhouse
WORD ORIGIN French *abattre* to fell

Abba[1] *n* Swedish pop group (1972–82): comprised Benny Andersson (born 1946), Agnetha Faltskog (born 1950), Anni-Frid Lyngstad (born 1945), and Bjorn Ulvaeus (born 1945); numerous hit singles included "Waterloo" (1974), "Dancing Queen" (1977), and "The Winner Takes It All" (1980)

Abba[2] *n* **1** *new testament* father (used of God) **2** a title given to bishops and patriarchs in the Syrian, Coptic, and Ethiopian Churches
WORD ORIGIN from Aramaic

abbacy *n, pl* **-cies** the office or jurisdiction of an abbot or abbess
WORD ORIGIN Church Latin *abbatia*

Abbado *n* **Claudio** born 1933, Italian conductor; principal conductor of the London Symphony Orchestra (1979–88); director of the Vienna State Opera (1986–91), and the Berlin Philharmonic (1989–2001)

Abbas *n* **Ferhat** 1899–1985, Algerian nationalist leader: joined the National Liberation Front (1956); president of the provisional government of the Algerian republic (1958–61)

Abbas I *n* called *the Great*. 1557–1628, shah of Persia. He greatly extended Persian territory by defeating the Uzbeks and the Ottomans

Abbe *n* **Ernst** 1840–1905, German physicist, noted for his work in optics and the microscope condenser known as the **Abbe condenser**

abbé (ab-bay) *n* a French abbot or other clergyman

abbess *n* the nun in charge of a convent
WORD ORIGIN Church Latin *abbatissa*

abbey ❶ *n* **1** a church associated with a community of monks or nuns **2** a community of monks or nuns **3** a building inhabited by monks or nuns
WORD ORIGIN Church Latin *abbatia* ABBACY

abbot *n* the head of an abbey of monks
WORD ORIGIN Aramaic *abbā* father

abbreviate *vb* **-ating, -ated** **1** to shorten a word by leaving out some letters **2** to cut short **abbreviation** *n*
WORD ORIGIN Latin *brevis* brief

ABC[1] *n* **1** the alphabet **2** an alphabetical guide **3** the basics of something

ABC[2] Australian Broadcasting Corporation

Abd Allah *n* 1846–99, Sudanese leader; he led the uprising against the Egyptian government of the Sudan; defeated by Kitchener in 1898

Abd al-Malik ibn Marwan *n* ?646–705 AD, fifth caliph (685–705) of the Omayyad Arab dynasty. He pacified the Muslim empire and extended its territory in North Africa

Abdelkader *n* ?1807–83, Algerian nationalist, who resisted the French invasion of Algeria and established (1837) an independent state. He surrendered to the French in 1847

Abd-el-Krim *n* 1882–1963, Moroccan chief who led revolts against Spain and France, surrendered before their combined forces in 1926, but later formed the North African independence movement

abdicate *vb* **-cating, -cated** **1** to give up the throne formally **2** to give up one's responsibilities **abdication** *n*
WORD ORIGIN Latin *abdicare* to disclaim

abdomen *n* the part of the body that contains the stomach and intestines **abdominal** *adj*
WORD ORIGIN Latin

abdominoplasty *n* the surgical removal of excess skin and fat from the abdomen

abduct ❶ *vb* to remove (a person) by force; kidnap **abduction** *n* **abductor** *n*

THESAURUS

abandon *vb* **1 = leave**, strand, ditch, leave behind, walk out on, forsake, jilt, run out on, throw over, turn your back on, desert, dump, leave high and dry, leave in the lurch **2 = stop**, drop, give up, halt, cease, cut out, pack in *(Brit informal)*, discontinue, leave off, desist from
OPPOSITE: continue

abbey *n* **1, 3 = monastery**, convent, priory, cloister, nunnery, friary

abduct *vb* **= kidnap**, seize, carry off,

DICTIONARY

a

WORD ORIGIN Latin *abducere* to lead away

Abdul-Hamid II *n* 1842–1918, sultan of Turkey (1876–1909), deposed by the Young Turks, noted for his brutal suppression of the Armenian revolt (1894–96)

Abdullah *n* 1882–1951, emir of Transjordan (1921–46) and first king of Jordan (1946–51). He joined the Arab revolt against Turkish rule in World War I; assassinated 1951

Abdullah II *n* born 1962, King of Jordan from 1999, son of King **Hussein** ▸ See **Hussein** (sense 1)

Abdul Rahman *n* **Tunku** 1903–90, Malaysian statesman; prime minister of Malaya (1957–63) and of Malaysia (1963–70)

abeam *adv, adj* at right angles to the length of a ship or aircraft

Abelson *n* **Philip** 1913–2004, US physical chemist. He created (with Edwin McMillan) the first transuranic element, neptunium (1940)

Abercrombie *n* Sir (**Leslie**) **Patrick** 1879–1957, British town planner and architect, best known for *The County of London Plan* (1943) and *The Greater London Plan* (1944)

Aberdeen Angus *n* a black hornless breed of beef cattle originating in Scotland

aberrant *adj* not normal, accurate, or correct: *aberrant behaviour*

aberration *n* **1** a sudden change from what is normal, accurate, or correct **2** a brief lapse in control of one's thoughts or feelings: *he suddenly had a mental aberration*

WORD ORIGIN Latin *aberrare* to wander away

abet *vb* **abetting, abetted** to help or encourage in wrongdoing

WORD ORIGIN Old French *abeter* to lure on

abeyance *n* **in abeyance** put aside temporarily

WORD ORIGIN Old French *abeance*, literally: a gaping after

abhor *vb* **-horring, -horred** to detest utterly

WORD ORIGIN Latin *abhorrere* to shudder at

abhorrent *adj* hateful or disgusting **abhorrence** *n*

abide ❶ *vb* **1** to tolerate: *I can't abide stupid people* **2** to last or exist for a long time: *these instincts, while subdued in the individual, may abide in the race* **3 abide by** to act in accordance with: *he must abide by the findings of the report* **4** *archaic* to live

WORD ORIGIN Old English *ābīdan*, from *a-* (intensive) + *bīdan* to wait

abiding ❶ *adj* lasting for ever: *an abiding interest in history*

ability ❶ *n, pl* **-ties 1** possession of the necessary skill or power to do something **2** great skill or competence: *his ability as a speaker was legendary*

WORD ORIGIN Latin *habilitas*

abject *adj* **1** utterly miserable: *one Mexican in five lives in abject poverty* **2** lacking all self-respect **abjectly** *adv*

WORD ORIGIN Latin *abjectus* thrown away

abjure *vb* **-juring, -jured** to renounce or deny under oath **abjuration** *n*

WORD ORIGIN Latin *abjurare*

ablation *n* **1** the surgical removal of an organ or part **2** the wearing away of a rock or glacier **3** the melting of a part, such as the heat shield of a space re-entry vehicle

WORD ORIGIN Latin *ablatus* carried away

ablaze *adj* **1** on fire **2** brightly illuminated: *the sky was ablaze with the stars shining bright* **3** emotionally aroused: *his eyes were ablaze with anger*

able ❶ *adj* **1** having the necessary power, skill, or opportunity to do something **2** capable or talented

WORD ORIGIN Latin *habilis* easy to hold

-able *suffix forming adjectives* able to be acted upon as specified: *washable* **-ably** *suffix forming adverbs* **-ability** *suffix forming nouns*

WORD ORIGIN Latin *-abilis, -ibilis*

able-bodied *adj* strong and healthy

able-bodied seaman *or* **able seaman** *n* a seaman who is trained in certain skills

abled *adj* having a range of physical powers as specified: *less abled; differently abled*

ableism (ay-bel-iz-zum) *n* discrimination against disabled or handicapped people

able rating *n* (in Britain) a seaman of the lowest rank in a navy

ablutions *pl n* the act of washing: *after the nightly ablutions, I settled down to read*

WORD ORIGIN Latin *abluere* to wash away

ably *adv* competently or skilfully

ABM antiballistic missile

abnegation *n* the act of giving something up

WORD ORIGIN Latin *abnegare* to deny

abnormal ❶ *adj* differing from the usual or typical **abnormality** *n* **abnormally** *adv*

aboard *adv, adj, prep* on, in, onto, or into (a ship, plane, or train)

abode *n* one's home

WORD ORIGIN from ABIDE

abolish ❶ *vb* to do away with (laws, regulations, or customs)

WORD ORIGIN Latin *abolere* to destroy

abolition ❶ *n* **1** the act of doing away with something: *the abolition of slavery* **2 Abolition** the ending of slavery **abolitionist** *n, adj*

THESAURUS

run off with, run away with, make off with, snatch *(slang)*

abide *vb* **1 = tolerate**, suffer, accept, bear, endure, brook, hack *(slang)*, put up with, take, stand, stomach, thole *(Scot)*
3 abide by something = obey, follow, agree to, carry out, observe, fulfil, stand by, act on, comply with, hold to, heed, submit to, conform to, keep to, adhere to, mind

abiding *adj* **= enduring**, lasting, continuing, remaining, surviving, permanent, constant, prevailing, persisting, persistent, eternal, tenacious, firm, fast, everlasting, unending, unchanging
OPPOSITE: brief

ability *n* **1 = capability**, power, potential, facility, capacity, qualification, competence, proficiency, competency, potentiality
OPPOSITE: inability
2 = skill, talent, know-how *(informal)*, gift, expertise, faculty, flair, competence, energy, accomplishment, knack, aptitude, proficiency, dexterity, cleverness, potentiality, adroitness, adeptness

able *adj* **2 = capable**, experienced, fit, skilled, expert, powerful, masterly, effective, qualified, talented, gifted, efficient, clever, practised, accomplished, competent, skilful, adept, masterful, strong, proficient, adroit, highly endowed
OPPOSITE: incapable

abnormal *adj* **= unusual**, different, odd, strange, surprising, extraordinary, remarkable, bizarre, unexpected, curious, weird, exceptional, peculiar, eccentric, unfamiliar, queer, irregular, phenomenal, uncommon, erratic, monstrous, singular, unnatural, deviant, unconventional, off-the-wall *(slang)*, oddball *(informal)*, out of the ordinary, left-field *(informal)*, anomalous, atypical, aberrant, untypical, wacko *(slang)*, outré, daggy *(Austral & NZ informal)*
OPPOSITE: normal

abolish *vb* **= do away with**, end, destroy, eliminate, shed, cancel, axe *(informal)*, get rid of, ditch *(slang)*, dissolve, junk *(informal)*, suppress, overturn, throw out, discard, wipe out, overthrow, void, terminate, drop, trash *(slang)*, repeal, eradicate, put an end to, quash, extinguish, dispense with, revoke, stamp out, obliterate, subvert, jettison, repudiate, annihilate, rescind, exterminate, invalidate, bring to an end, annul, nullify, blot out, expunge, abrogate, vitiate, extirpate, kennet *(Austral slang)*, jeff *(Austral slang)* **OPPOSITE:** establish

abolition *n* **1 = eradication**, ending,

DICTIONARY

a

A-bomb *n* ▸ short for **atomic bomb**
abominable *adj* very bad or unpleasant: *I think that what is being done here is utterly abominable*
abominably *adv*
abominable snowman *n* a large creature, like a man or an ape, that is said to live in the Himalayas
WORD ORIGIN translation of Tibetan *metohkangmi* foul snowman
abominate *vb* **-nating, -nated** to dislike intensely **abomination** *n*
WORD ORIGIN Latin *abominari* to regard as an ill omen
aboriginal *adj* existing in a place from the earliest known period
Aboriginal *adj* **1** of or relating to (esp. Australian) Aborigines ▹*n* **2** an Aborigine
aborigine (ab-or-**rij**-in-ee) *n Brit, Austral & NZ* an original inhabitant of a country or region, esp. (**A-**) Australia
WORD ORIGIN Latin *aborigines* the name of the inhabitants of Latium in pre-Roman times
Aborigine *n* a member of a dark-skinned people who were already living in Australia when European settlers arrived
abort ❶ *vb* **1** (of a pregnancy) to end before the fetus is viable **2** to perform an abortion on a pregnant woman **3** to end a plan or process before completion
WORD ORIGIN Latin *abortare*
abortion ❶ *n* **1** an operation to end pregnancy **2** the premature ending of a pregnancy when a fetus is expelled from the womb before it can live independently **3** the failure of a mission or project **4** *informal* something that is grotesque
abortionist *n*
abortion pill *n* a drug used to terminate a pregnancy in its earliest stage
abortive *adj* failing to achieve its purpose
abound ❶ *vb* **1** to exist in large numbers **2 abound in** to have a large number of
WORD ORIGIN Latin *abundare* to overflow
about ❶ *prep* **1** relating to or concerning **2** near to **3** carried on: *I haven't any money about me* **4** on every side of ▹*adv* **5** near in number, time, or degree; approximately **6** nearby **7** here and there: *there were some fifteen other people scattered about on the first floor* **8** all around; on every side **9** in or to the opposite direction **10** in rotation: *turn and turn about* **11** used to indicate understatement: *it's about time somebody told the truth on that subject* **12 about to** on the point of; intending to: *she was about to get in the car* **13 not about to** determined not to: *we're not about to help her out* ▹*adj* **14** active: *he was off the premises well before anyone was up and about*
WORD ORIGIN Old English *abūtan*, *onbūtan* on the outside of
about-turn *or US* **about-face** *n* **1** a complete change of opinion or direction **2** a reversal of the direction in which one is facing
above ❶ *prep* **1** higher than; over **2** greater than in quantity or degree: *above average* **3** superior to or higher than in quality, rank, or ability **4** too high-minded for: *he considered himself above the task of working* **5** too respected for; beyond: *his fleet was above suspicion* **6** too difficult to be understood by: *a discussion that was way above my head* **7** louder or higher than (other noise) **8** in preference to **9 above all** most of all; especially ▹*adv* **10** in or to a higher place: *the hills above* **11** in a previous place (in something written or printed) **12** higher in rank or position ▹*n* **13 the above** something previously mentioned ▹*adj* **14** appearing in a previous place (in something written or printed): *for a copy of the free brochure write to the above address*
WORD ORIGIN Old English *abufan*
above board *adj* completely honest and open
abracadabra *n* a word used in magic spells, which is supposed to possess magic powers
WORD ORIGIN Latin
abrasion *n* **1** a scraped area on the skin; graze **2** *geog* the erosion of rock by rock fragments scratching and scraping it
WORD ORIGIN Latin *abradere* to scrape away
abrasive *adj* **1** rude and unpleasant in manner **2** tending to rub or scrape; rough ▹*n* **3** a substance used for cleaning, smoothing, or polishing
abreast *adj* **1** alongside each other and facing in the same direction: *the two cars were abreast* **2 abreast of** up to date with
abridge *vb* **abridging, abridged** to shorten a written work by taking out parts **abridgment** *or* **abridgement** *n*
WORD ORIGIN Late Latin *abbreviare*
abroad ❶ *adv* **1** to or in a foreign country **2** generally known or felt: *there is a new spirit abroad*
abrogate *vb* **-gating, -gated** to cancel (a law or an agreement) formally
abrogation *n*
WORD ORIGIN from Latin *ab-* away + *rogare* to propose a law
abrupt ❶ *adj* **1** sudden or unexpected: *an abrupt departure* **2** rather rude in speech or manner **abruptly** *adv*
abruptness *n*
WORD ORIGIN Latin *abruptus* broken off

THESAURUS

end, withdrawal, destruction, removal, overturning, wiping out, overthrow, voiding, extinction, repeal, elimination, cancellation, suppression, quashing, termination, stamping out, subversion, extermination, annihilation, blotting out, repudiation, erasure, annulment, obliteration, revocation, effacement, nullification, abrogation, rescission, extirpation, invalidation, vitiation, expunction
abort *vb* **1 = miscarry 2 = terminate** *(a pregnancy)* **3 = stop**, end, finish, check, arrest, halt, cease, bring *or* come to a halt *or* standstill, axe *(informal)*, pull up, terminate, call off, break off, cut short, pack in *(Brit informal)*, discontinue, desist
abortion *n* **1 = termination**, feticide, aborticide, deliberate miscarriage **2 = miscarriage**
abound *vb* **1 = be plentiful**, thrive, flourish, be numerous, proliferate, be abundant, be thick on the ground, superabound
about *prep* **1 = regarding**, on, re, concerning, touching, dealing with, respecting, referring to, relating to, concerned with, connected with, relative to, with respect to, as regards, anent *(Scot)* **2 = near**, around, close to, bordering, nearby, beside, close by, adjacent to, just round the corner from, in the neighbourhood of, alongside of, contiguous to, within sniffing distance of *(informal)*, at close quarters to, a hop, skip and a jump away from *(informal)* ▹*adv* **5 = approximately**, around, almost, nearing, nearly, approaching, close to, roughly, just about, more or less, in the region of, in the vicinity of, not far off
above *prep* **1 = over**, upon, beyond, on top of, higher than, atop **OPPOSITE:** under **2 = exceeding 3 = senior to**, over, ahead of, in charge of, higher than, surpassing, superior to, more powerful than **OPPOSITE:** subordinate to
abroad *adv* **1 = overseas**, out of the country, beyond the sea, in foreign lands
abrupt *adj* **1 = sudden**, unexpected, hurried, rapid, surprising, quick, swift, rash, precipitate, hasty, impulsive, headlong, unforeseen, unanticipated **OPPOSITE:** slow **2 = curt**, direct, brief, sharp, rough, short, clipped, blunt, rude, tart, impatient, brisk, concise, snappy, terse, gruff, succinct, pithy, brusque, offhand, impolite, monosyllabic, ungracious, discourteous, uncivil, unceremonious, snappish **OPPOSITE:** polite

DICTIONARY

a

abs *pl n* abdominal muscles
abscess (ab-sess) *n* **1** a swelling containing pus as a result of inflammation ▷*vb* **2** to form a swelling containing pus **abscessed** *adj*
WORD ORIGIN Latin *abscessus* literally: a throwing off
abscissa *n, pl* **-scissas** *or* **-scissae** *maths* (in a two-dimensional system of Cartesian coordinates) the distance from the vertical axis measured parallel to the horizontal axis
WORD ORIGIN New Latin *linea abscissa* a cut-off line
abscond *vb* to run away unexpectedly
WORD ORIGIN Latin *abscondere* to conceal
abseil (ab-sale) *vb* **1** to go down a steep drop by a rope fastened at the top and tied around one's body ▷*n* **2** an instance of abseiling
WORD ORIGIN German *abseilen*
absence ❶ *n* **1** the state of being away **2** the time during which a person or thing is away **3** the fact of being without something
absent ❶ *adj* **1** not present in a place or situation **2** lacking **3** not paying attention ▷*vb* **4** **absent oneself** to stay away **absently** *adv*
WORD ORIGIN Latin *absens*
absentee *n* a person who should be present but is not
absenteeism *n* persistent absence from work or school
absent-minded *adj* inattentive or forgetful **absent-mindedly** *adv*
absinthe *n* a strong, green, alcoholic drink, originally containing wormwood
WORD ORIGIN Greek *apsinthion* wormwood
absolute ❶ *adj* **1** total and complete: *he ordered an immediate and absolute ceasefire* **2** with unrestricted power and authority: *she has absolute control with fifty per cent of the shares* **3** undoubted or certain: *I was telling the absolute truth* **4** not dependent on or relative to anything else **5** pure; unmixed: *absolute alcohol* ▷*n* **6** a principle or rule believed to be unfailingly correct **7** **the Absolute** *philosophy* that which is totally unconditioned, perfect, or complete
WORD ORIGIN Latin *absolutus*
absolutely ❶ *adv* **1** completely or perfectly ▷*interj* **2** yes indeed, certainly
absolute majority *n* a number of votes totalling over 50 per cent, such as the total number of votes that beats the combined opposition
absolute pitch *n* the ability to identify the pitch of a note, or to sing a given note, without reference to one previously sounded
absolute zero *n physics* the lowest temperature theoretically possible, at which the particles that make up matter would be at rest: equivalent to −273.15°C or −459.67°F
absolution *n Christianity* a formal forgiveness of sin pronounced by a priest
absolutism *n* a political system in which a monarch or dictator has unrestricted power
absolve *vb* **-solving, -solved** to declare to be free from blame or sin
WORD ORIGIN Latin *absolvere*
absorb ❶ *vb* **1** to soak up a liquid **2** to engage the interest of someone **3** to receive the force of an impact **4** *physics* to take in radiant energy and retain it **5** to take in or incorporate: *this country has absorbed almost one million refugees* **absorbent** *adj* **absorbing** *adj*
WORD ORIGIN Latin *absorbere* to suck
absorption ❶ *n* **1** the process of absorbing something or the state of being absorbed **2** *physiol* the process by which nutrients enter the tissues of an animal or a plant **absorptive** *adj*
abstain *vb* **1** (usually foll. by *from*) to choose not to do or partake of something: *you will be asked to abstain from food prior to your general anaesthetic* **2** to choose not to vote **abstainer** *n*
WORD ORIGIN Latin *abstinere*
abstemious (ab-steem-ee-uss) *adj* taking very little alcohol or food **abstemiously** *adv* **abstemiousness** *n*
WORD ORIGIN Latin *abstemius*
abstention *n* **1** the formal act of not voting **2** the act of abstaining from something, such as drinking alcohol
abstinence *n* the practice of choosing not to do something one would like **abstinent** *adj*
abstract ❶ *adj* **1** referring to ideas or qualities rather than material objects: *an abstract noun* **2** not applied or practical; theoretical: *he was frustrated by the highly abstract mathematics being taught* **3** of art in which the subject is represented by shapes and patterns rather than by a realistic likeness ▷*n* **4** a summary **5** an abstract painting or sculpture

THESAURUS

absence *n* **2 = time off**, leave, break, vacation, recess, truancy, absenteeism, nonappearance, nonattendance **3 = lack**, deficiency, deprivation, omission, scarcity, want, need, shortage, dearth, privation, unavailability, nonexistence
absent *adj* **1 = away**, missing, gone, lacking, elsewhere, unavailable, not present, truant, nonexistent, nonattendant **OPPOSITE:** present **3 = absent-minded**, blank, unconscious, abstracted, vague, distracted, unaware, musing, vacant, preoccupied, empty, absorbed, bemused, oblivious, dreamy, daydreaming, faraway, unthinking, heedless, inattentive, unheeding **OPPOSITE:** alert ▷*vb* **4 absent yourself = stay away**, withdraw, depart, keep away, truant, abscond, play truant, slope off *(informal)*, bunk off *(slang)*, remove yourself
absolute *adj* **1 = complete**, total, perfect, entire, pure, sheer, utter, outright, thorough, downright, consummate, unqualified, full-on *(informal)*, out-and-out, unadulterated, unmitigated, dyed-in-the-wool, thoroughgoing, unalloyed, unmixed, arrant, deep-dyed *(usually derogatory)* **2 = supreme**, sovereign, unlimited, ultimate, full, utmost, unconditional, unqualified, predominant, superlative, unrestricted, pre-eminent, unrestrained, tyrannical, peerless, unsurpassed, unquestionable, matchless, peremptory, unbounded
absolutely *adv* **1 = completely**, totally, perfectly, quite, fully, entirely, purely, altogether, thoroughly, wholly, utterly, consummately, every inch, to the hilt, a hundred per cent, one hundred per cent, unmitigatedly, lock, stock and barrel **OPPOSITE:** somewhat
absorb *vb* **1 = soak up**, drink in, devour, suck up, receive, digest, imbibe, ingest, osmose **2 = engross**, hold, involve, fill, arrest, fix, occupy, engage, fascinate, preoccupy, engulf, fill up, immerse, rivet, captivate, monopolize, enwrap
absorption *n* **1 = immersion**, holding, involvement, concentration, occupation, engagement, fascination, preoccupation, intentness, captivation, raptness **2 = soaking up**, consumption, digestion, sucking up, osmosis
abstract *adj* **2 = theoretical**, general, complex, academic, intellectual, subtle, profound, philosophical, speculative, unrealistic, conceptual, indefinite, deep, separate, occult, hypothetical, generalized, impractical, arcane, notional, abstruse, recondite, theoretic, conjectural, unpractical, nonconcrete **OPPOSITE:** actual ▷*n* **4 = summary**, résumé, outline, extract, essence, summing-up, digest, epitome, rundown, condensation, compendium, synopsis, précis, recapitulation, review, abridgment **OPPOSITE:** expansion ▷*vb* **9 = extract**, draw, pull, remove, separate, withdraw, isolate, pull out, take out, take away, detach,

DICTIONARY

a

6 an abstract word or idea **7 in the abstract** without referring to specific circumstances ▹*vb* **8** to summarize **9** to remove or extract
WORD ORIGIN Latin *abstractus* drawn off
abstracted *adj* lost in thought; preoccupied **abstractedly** *adv*
abstraction *n* **1** a general idea rather than a specific example: *these absurd philosophical abstractions continued to bother him* **2** the quality of being abstract or abstracted
abstruse *adj* not easy to understand
WORD ORIGIN Latin *abstrusus* concealed
absurd ❶ *adj* obviously senseless or illogical; ridiculous **absurdity** *n* **absurdly** *adv*
WORD ORIGIN Latin *absurdus*
Abu-Bekr *or* **Abu-Bakr** *n* 573–634 AD, companion and father-in-law of Mohammed; the first caliph of Islam
Abu Hanifah *n* 700–67 AD, Muslim theologian and teacher of jurisprudence
abundance ❶ *n* **1** a great amount **2** degree of plentifulness **3 in abundance** in great amounts: *they had fish and fruit in abundance*
abundant *adj*
WORD ORIGIN Latin *abundare* to abound
abundantly *adv* **1** very: *he made his disagreement with the prime minister abundantly clear* **2** plentifully; in abundance
abuse ❶ *n* **1** prolonged ill-treatment of or violence towards someone: *child abuse* **2** insulting comments **3** improper use: *an abuse of power* ▹*vb* **abusing, abused 4** to take advantage of dishonestly: *these two ministers had abused their position for financial gain* **5** to ill-treat violently: *he had been sexually abused as a child* **6** to speak insultingly or cruelly to
abuser *n*
WORD ORIGIN Latin *abuti* to misuse
abusive ❶ *adj* rude or insulting: *he was alleged to have used abusive language towards spectators* **abusively** *adv*
abut *vb* **abutting, abutted** to be next to or touching
WORD ORIGIN Old French *abouter*
abutment *n* a construction that supports the end of a bridge
abysmal *adj informal* extremely bad
abysmally *adv*
WORD ORIGIN Medieval Latin *abysmus* abyss
abyss *n* **1** a very deep hole in the ground **2** a frightening or threatening situation: *the abyss of revolution and war ahead*
WORD ORIGIN Greek *abussos* bottomless
Ac *chem* actinium
AC 1 alternating current **2** athletic club
a/c 1 account **2** account current
acacia (a-kay-sha) *n* a shrub or tree with small yellow or white flowers
WORD ORIGIN Greek *akakia*
academic ❶ *adj* **1** relating to a college or university **2** (of pupils) having an aptitude for study **3** relating to studies such as languages and pure science rather than technical or professional studies **4** of theoretical interest only: *the argument is academic* ▹*n* **5** a member of the teaching or research staff of a college or university **academically** *adv*
academy *n, pl* **-mies 1** a society for the advancement of literature, art, or science **2** a school for training in a particular skill: *sixteen hundred students would also spend their first year at the military academy* **3** (in Scotland) a secondary school
WORD ORIGIN Greek *akadēmeia* the place where Plato taught
Acadian *adj* **1** denoting or relating to Acadia or its inhabitants ▹*n* **2** any of the early French settlers in Nova Scotia ▸See also **Cajun**
acanthus *n* **1** a plant with large spiny leaves and spikes of white or purplish flowers **2** a carved ornament based on the leaves of the acanthus plant
WORD ORIGIN Greek *akantha* thorn
ACAS (in Britain) Advisory Conciliation and Arbitration Service
ACC (in New Zealand) Accident Compensation Corporation
acc. 1 *grammar* accusative **2** account
Accardo *n* **Salvatore** born 1941, Italian violinist and conductor
accede *vb* **-ceding, -ceded ▪ accede to 1** to agree to **2** to take up (an office or position): *he acceded to the throne after his Irish exile*
WORD ORIGIN Latin *accedere*
accelerando *adv music* with increasing speed
WORD ORIGIN Italian
accelerate ❶ *vb* **-ating, -ated 1** to move or cause to move more quickly **2** to cause to happen sooner than expected
WORD ORIGIN Latin *accelerare*

THESAURUS

dissociate, pluck out **OPPOSITE:** add
absurd *adj* **= ridiculous**, crazy *(informal)*, silly, incredible, outrageous, foolish, unbelievable, daft *(informal)*, hilarious, ludicrous, meaningless, unreasonable, irrational, senseless, preposterous, laughable, funny, stupid, farcical, illogical, incongruous, comical, zany, idiotic, nonsensical, inane, dumb-ass *(slang)* **OPPOSITE:** sensible
abundance *n* **1 = plenty**, heap *(informal)*, bounty, exuberance, profusion, plethora, affluence, fullness, opulence, plenitude, fruitfulness, copiousness, ampleness, cornucopia, plenteousness, plentifulness **OPPOSITE:** shortage
abuse *n* **1 = maltreatment**, wrong, damage, injury, hurt, harm, spoiling, bullying, exploitation, oppression, imposition, mistreatment, manhandling, ill-treatment, rough handling **2 = insults**, blame, slights, curses, put-downs, libel, censure, reproach, scolding, defamation, indignities, offence, tirade, derision, slander, rudeness, vilification, invective, swear words, opprobrium, insolence, upbraiding, aspersions, character assassination, disparagement, vituperation, castigation, contumely, revilement, traducement, calumniation **3 = misuse**, corruption, perversion, misapplication, misemployment, misusage ▹*vb* **5 = ill-treat**, wrong, damage, hurt, injure, harm, mar, oppress, maul, molest, impose upon, manhandle, rough up, brutalize, maltreat, handle roughly, knock about *or* around **OPPOSITE:** care for **6 = insult**, injure, offend, curse, put down, smear, libel, slate *(informal, chiefly Brit)*, slag (off) *(slang)*, malign, scold, swear at, disparage, castigate, revile, vilify, slander, defame, upbraid, slight, inveigh against, call names, traduce, calumniate, vituperate **OPPOSITE:** praise
abusive *adj* **= insulting**, offensive, rude, degrading, scathing, maligning, scolding, affronting, contemptuous, disparaging, castigating, reviling, vilifying, invective, scurrilous, defamatory, insolent, derisive, censorious, slighting, libellous, upbraiding, vituperative, reproachful, slanderous, traducing, opprobrious, calumniating, contumelious **OPPOSITE:** complimentary
academic *adj* **1 = scholastic**, school, university, college, educational, campus, collegiate **4 = theoretical**, ideal, abstract, speculative, hypothetical, impractical, notional, conjectural ▹*n* **5 = scholar**, intellectual, don, student, master, professor, fellow, pupil, lecturer, tutor, scholastic, bookworm, man of letters, egghead *(informal)*, savant, academician, acca *(Austral slang)*, bluestocking *(usually derogatory)*, schoolman *(US rare)*
accelerate *vb* **1a = increase**, grow, advance, extend, expand, build up, strengthen, raise, swell, intensify, enlarge, escalate, multiply, inflate, magnify, proliferate, snowball **OPPOSITE:** fall
1b = speed up, speed, advance,

DICTIONARY

acceleration ● *n* **1** the act of increasing speed **2** the rate of increase of speed or the rate of change of velocity

accelerator *n* **1** a pedal in a motor vehicle that is pressed to increase speed **2** *physics* a machine for increasing the speed and energy of charged particles

accent ● *n* **1** the distinctive style of pronunciation of a person or group from a particular area, country, or social background **2** a mark used in writing to indicate the prominence of a syllable or the way a vowel is pronounced **3** particular emphasis: *there will be an accent on sport and many will enjoy rowing* **4** the stress on a syllable or musical note ▷*vb* **5** to lay particular emphasis on
WORD ORIGIN Latin *accentus*

accentuate *vb* **-ating, -ated** to stress or emphasize **accentuation** *n*

accept ● *vb* **1** to take or receive something offered **2** to agree to **3** to consider something as true **4** to tolerate or resign oneself to **5** to take on the responsibilities of: *he asked if I would become his assistant and I accepted that position* **6** to receive someone into a community or group **7** to receive something as adequate or valid
WORD ORIGIN Latin *acceptare*

acceptable ● *adj* **1** able to be endured; tolerable: *in war killing is acceptable* **2** good enough; adequate: *he found the article acceptable* **acceptability** *n* **acceptably** *adv*

acceptance ● *n* **1** the act of accepting something **2** favourable reception **3** belief or agreement

accepted ● *adj* commonly approved or recognized: *the accepted wisdom about old age*

access ● *n* **1** a means of approaching or entering a place **2** the condition of allowing entry, for example entry to a building by wheelchairs or prams **3** the right or opportunity to use something or enter a place: *the bourgeoisie gained access to political power* **4** the opportunity or right to see or approach someone: *my ex-wife sabotages my access to the children* ▷*vb* **5** to obtain information from a computer
WORD ORIGIN Latin *accedere* to accede

accessible ● *adj* **1** easy to approach, enter, or use **2** easy to understand: *the most accessible opera by Wagner* **accessibility** *n*

accession *n* the act of taking up an office or position: *the 40th anniversary of her accession to the throne*

accessory ● *n, pl* **-ries 1** a supplementary part or object **2** a small item, such as a bag or belt, worn or carried by someone to complete his or her outfit **3** a person who is involved in a crime but who was not present when it took place
WORD ORIGIN Late Latin *accessorius*

access road *n* a road providing a way to a particular place or on to a motorway

access time *n* the time required to retrieve a piece of stored information from a computer

accident ● *n* **1** an unpleasant event that causes damage, injury, or death **2** an unforeseen event or one without apparent cause: *they had met in town by accident*
WORD ORIGIN Latin *accidere* to happen

accidental ● *adj* **1** occurring by chance or unintentionally ▷*n* **2** *music* a symbol denoting a sharp, flat, or natural that is not a part of the key signature **accidentally** *adv*

accident-prone *adj* (of a person) often involved in accidents

acclaim ● *vb* **1** to applaud or praise: *the highly acclaimed children's TV series* **2** to acknowledge publicly: *he was immediately acclaimed the new prime minister* ▷*n* **3** an enthusiastic expression of approval
WORD ORIGIN Latin *acclamare*

acclamation *n* **1** an enthusiastic reception or display of approval **2** *Canad* an instance of being elected without opposition **3 by**

THESAURUS

quicken, get under way, gather momentum, get moving, pick up speed, put your foot down *(informal)*, open up the throttle, put on speed **OPPOSITE:** slow down **2 = expedite**, press, forward, promote, spur, further, stimulate, hurry, step up *(informal)*, speed up, facilitate, hasten, precipitate, quicken **OPPOSITE:** delay

acceleration *n* **1 = hastening**, hurrying, stepping up *(informal)*, expedition, speeding up, stimulation, advancement, promotion, spurring, quickening

accent *n* **1 = pronunciation**, tone, articulation, inflection, brogue, intonation, diction, modulation, elocution, enunciation, accentuation ▷*vb* **5 = emphasize**, stress, highlight, underline, bring home, underscore, accentuate, give emphasis to, call *or* draw attention to

accept *vb* **1 = receive**, take, gain, pick up, secure, collect, have, get, obtain, acquire **3 = acknowledge**, believe, allow, admit, adopt, approve, recognize, yield, concede, swallow *(informal)*, buy *(slang)*, affirm, profess, consent to, buy into *(slang)*, cooperate with, take on board, accede, acquiesce, concur with

acceptable *adj* **2 = satisfactory**, fair, all right, suitable, sufficient, good enough, standard, adequate, so-so *(informal)*, tolerable, up to scratch *(informal)*, passable, up to the mark **OPPOSITE:** unsatisfactory

acceptance *n* **1 = accepting**, taking, receiving, obtaining, acquiring, reception, receipt **2,3 = acknowledgement**, agreement, belief, approval, recognition, admission, consent, consensus, adoption, affirmation, assent, credence, accession, approbation, concurrence, accedence, stamp *or* seal of approval

accepted *adj* **= agreed**, received, common, standard, established, traditional, confirmed, regular, usual, approved, acknowledged, recognized, sanctioned, acceptable, universal, authorized, customary, agreed upon, time-honoured **OPPOSITE:** unconventional

access *n* **1 = entrance**, road, door, approach, entry, path, gate, opening, way in, passage, avenue, doorway, gateway, portal, passageway **2, 3 = admission**, entry, passage, entrée, admittance, ingress

accessible *adj* **1 = handy**, near, nearby, at hand, within reach, at your fingertips, reachable, achievable, get-at-able *(informal)*, a hop, skip and a jump away **OPPOSITE:** inaccessible

accessory *n* **1 = extra**, addition, supplement, convenience, attachment, add-on, component, extension, adjunct, appendage, appurtenance **3 = accomplice**, partner, ally, associate, assistant, helper, colleague, collaborator, confederate, henchman, abettor

accident *n* **1 = crash**, smash, wreck, collision, pile-up *(informal)*, smash-up *(informal)* **2 = chance**, fortune, luck, fate, hazard, coincidence, fluke, fortuity

accidental *adj* **1a = unintentional**, unexpected, incidental, unforeseen, unintended, unplanned, unpremeditated **OPPOSITE:** deliberate **1b = chance**, random, casual, unintentional, unintended, unplanned, fortuitous, inadvertent, serendipitous, unlooked-for, uncalculated, contingent

acclaim *vb* **1 = praise**, celebrate, honour, cheer, admire, hail, applaud, compliment, salute, approve, congratulate, clap, pay tribute to, commend, exalt, laud, extol, crack up *(informal)*, eulogize ▷*n* **3 = praise**, honour, celebration, approval, tribute, applause, cheering, clapping, ovation, accolades, plaudits, kudos, commendation, exaltation, approbation, acclamation,

DICTIONARY

a

acclamation by a majority without a ballot
acclimatize *or* **-tise** *vb* **-tizing, -tized** *or* **-tising, -tised** to adapt to a new climate or environment **acclimatization** *or* **-tisation** *n*
accolade *n* **1** an award, praise, or honour **2** a touch on the shoulder with a sword conferring knighthood **WORD ORIGIN** Latin *ad-* to + *collum* neck
accommodate ❶ *vb* **-dating, -dated** **1** to provide with lodgings **2** to have room for **3** to do a favour for **4** to adjust or become adjusted; to adapt **WORD ORIGIN** Latin *accommodare*
accommodating ❶ *adj* willing to help; obliging
accommodation ❶ *n* a place in which to sleep, live, or work
accommodation address *n Brit* an address on letters to a person who cannot or does not wish to receive mail at a permanent address
accompaniment ❶ *n* **1** something that accompanies something else **2** *music* a supporting part for an instrument, a band, or an orchestra
accompanist *n* a person who plays a musical accompaniment
accompany ❶ *vb* **-nies, -nying, -nied** **1** to go with (someone) **2** to happen or exist at the same time as **3** to provide a musical accompaniment for **WORD ORIGIN** Old French *accompaignier*
accomplice *n* a person who helps someone else commit a crime **WORD ORIGIN** Late Latin *complex* partner
accomplish ❶ *vb* **1** to manage to do; achieve: *most infants accomplish it immediately* **2** to complete **WORD ORIGIN** Latin *complere* to fill up
accomplished ❶ *adj* **1** expert or proficient: *an accomplished liar* **2** successfully completed
accomplishment ❶ *n* **1** the successful completion of something **2** something successfully completed **3** *(often pl)* personal abilities or skills
accord ❶ *n* **1** agreement or harmony **2** a formal agreement between groups or nations: *the Paris peace accords* **3** **of one's own accord** voluntarily or willingly **4** **with one accord** unanimously ▹*vb* **5** to grant: *she was at last accorded her true status* **6** **accord with** to fit in with or be consistent with **WORD ORIGIN** Latin *ad-* to + *cor* heart
accordance *n* **in accordance with** conforming to or according to: *food is prepared in accordance with Jewish laws*
according *adv* **1** **according to** **a** as stated by: *according to her, they were once engaged* **b** in conformity with: *work hours varied according to the tides* **2** **according as** depending on whether
accordingly ❶ *adv* **1** in an appropriate manner **2** consequently
accordion *n* a box-shaped musical instrument played by moving the two sides apart and together, and pressing a keyboard or buttons to produce the notes **accordionist** *n* **WORD ORIGIN** German *Akkordion*
accost *vb* to approach, stop, and speak to **WORD ORIGIN** Latin *ad-* to + *costa* side, rib
account ❶ *n* **1** a report or description **2** a person's money held in a bank **3** a statement of financial transactions with the resulting balance **4** part or behalf: *I am sorry that you suffered on my account* **5** **call someone to account** to demand an explanation from someone **6** **give a good** *or* **bad account of oneself** to perform well or fail to perform well **7** **of no account** of little importance or value **8** **on account of** because of **9** **take account of** *or* **take into account** to take into consideration; allow for ▹*vb* **10** to consider as: *the evening was accounted a major step forward by all concerned* **WORD ORIGIN** Old French *acont*
accountable ❶ *adj* responsible to someone or for some action **accountability** *n*
accountant ❶ *n* a person who maintains and audits business accounts **accountancy** *n*
account for *vb* **1** to give reasons for **2** to explain or count up what has been spent
accounting *n* the skill or practice of maintaining and auditing business accounts
accoutrements (ak-koo-tra-ments)

THESAURUS

eulogizing, panegyric, encomium **OPPOSITE:** criticism
accommodate *vb* **1 = house**, put up, take in, lodge, board, quarter, shelter, entertain, harbour, cater for, billet **3 = help**, support, aid, encourage, assist, befriend, cooperate with, abet, lend a hand to, lend a helping hand to, give a leg up to *(informal)* **4 = adapt**, match, fit, fashion, settle, alter, adjust, modify, compose, comply, accustom, reconcile, harmonize
accommodating *adj* **= obliging**, willing, kind, friendly, helpful, polite, cooperative, agreeable, amiable, courteous, considerate, hospitable, unselfish, eager to please, complaisant **OPPOSITE:** unhelpful
accommodation *n* **= housing**, homes, houses, board, quartering, quarters, digs *(Brit informal)*, shelter, sheltering, lodging(s), dwellings
accompaniment *n* **1 = supplement**, extra, addition, extension, companion, accessory, complement, decoration, frill, adjunct, appendage, adornment **2** *(music)* **= backing music**, backing, support, obbligato
accompany *vb* **1 = go with**, lead, partner, protect, guide, attend, conduct, escort, shepherd, convoy, usher, chaperon **2 = occur with**, belong to, come with, supplement, coincide with, join with, coexist with, go together with, follow, go cheek by jowl with
accomplish *vb* **1, 2 = realize**, produce, effect, finish, complete, manage, achieve, perform, carry out, conclude, fulfil, execute, bring about, attain, consummate, bring off *(informal)*, do, effectuate **OPPOSITE:** fail
accomplished *adj* **1 = skilled**, able, professional, expert, masterly, talented, gifted, polished, practised, cultivated, skilful, adept, consummate, proficient **OPPOSITE:** unskilled
accomplishment *n* **1 = accomplishing**, effecting, finishing, carrying out, achievement, conclusion, bringing about, execution, completion, realization, fulfilment, attainment, consummation **2 = achievement**, feat, attainment, act, stroke, triumph, coup, exploit, deed
accord *n* **1 = sympathy**, agreement, concert, harmony, accordance, unison, rapport, conformity, assent, unanimity, concurrence **OPPOSITE:** conflict **2 = treaty**, contract, agreement, arrangement, settlement, pact, deal *(informal)* ▹*vb* **6 accord with something = agree with**, match, coincide with, fit with, square with, correspond with, conform with, concur with, tally with, be in tune with *(informal)*, harmonize with, assent with
accordingly *adv* **1 = appropriately**, correspondingly, properly, suitably, fitly **2 = consequently**, so, thus, therefore, hence, subsequently, in consequence, ergo, as a result
account *n* **1 = description**, report, record, story, history, detail, statement, relation, version, tale, explanation, narrative, chronicle, portrayal, recital, depiction, narration ▹*vb* **10 = consider**, rate, value, judge, estimate, think, hold, believe, count, reckon, assess, weigh, calculate, esteem, deem, compute, gauge, appraise, regard as
accountable *adj* **= answerable**, subject, responsible, obliged, liable, amenable, obligated, chargeable
accountant *n* **= auditor**, book-keeper,

DICTIONARY

a

or *US* **accouterments** (ak-koo-ter-ments) *pl n* clothing and equipment for a particular activity
WORD ORIGIN Old French *accoustrer* to equip

accredit *vb* **1** to give official recognition to **2** to send (a diplomat) with official credentials to a particular country **3** to certify as meeting required standards **4** to attribute (a quality or an action) to (a person) **accreditation** *n*
WORD ORIGIN French *accréditer*

accretion (ak-kree-shun) *n* **1** a gradual increase in size, through growth or addition **2** something added, such as an extra layer
WORD ORIGIN Latin *accretio*

accrue *vb* **-cruing, -crued 1** (of money or interest) to increase gradually over a period of time **2 accrue to** to fall naturally to: *some advantage must accrue to the weaker party*
WORD ORIGIN Latin *accrescere*

accumulate ➊ *vb* **-lating, -lated** to gather together in an increasing quantity; collect **accumulative** *adj*
WORD ORIGIN Latin *accumulare* to heap up

accumulation ➊ *n* **1** something that has been collected **2** the collecting together of things

accumulator *n* **1** *Austral & Brit* a rechargeable device for storing electrical energy **2** *Brit horse racing* a collective bet on successive races, with both stake and winnings being carried forward to accumulate progressively

accuracy ➊ *n* faithful representation of the truth: *care is taken to ensure the accuracy of the content*

accurate ➊ *adj* faithfully representing the truth: *all the information was accurate* **accurately** *adv*
WORD ORIGIN Latin *accurare* to perform with care

accursed (a-curse-id) *adj* **1** under a curse **2** hateful or detestable

accusation ➊ *n* **1** an allegation that a person is guilty of some wrongdoing **2** a formal charge brought against a person **accusatory** *adj*

accusative *n grammar* a grammatical case in some languages that identifies the direct object of a verb

accuse ➊ *vb* **-cusing, -cused** to charge a person with wrongdoing **accuser** *n* **accusing** *adj* **accusingly** *adv*
WORD ORIGIN Latin *accūsāre*

accused *n* **the accused** *law* the defendant appearing on a criminal charge

accustom *vb* **accustom oneself to** to become familiar with or used to from habit or experience
WORD ORIGIN Old French *acostumer*

accustomed ➊ *adj* **1** usual or customary: *he parked his motorcycle in its accustomed place* **2 accustomed to a** used to **b** in the habit of

ace ➊ *n* **1** a playing card with one symbol on it **2** *informal* an expert: *an American stock car ace* **3** *tennis* a winning serve that the opponent fails to reach **4** a fighter pilot who has destroyed several enemy aircraft ▷ *adj* **5** *informal* superb or excellent: *an ace tennis player*
WORD ORIGIN Latin *as* a unit

acerbic (ass-sir-bik) *adj* harsh or bitter: *an acerbic critic*
WORD ORIGIN Latin *acerbus* sharp, sour

acerbity *n, pl* **-ties 1** bitter speech or temper **2** bitterness of taste

acetaldehyde (ass-it-tal-dee-hide) *n chem* a colourless volatile liquid, used as a solvent

acetate (ass-it-tate) *n* **1** *chem* any salt or ester of acetic acid **2** Also: **acetate rayon** a synthetic textile fibre made from cellulose acetate

acetic (ass-see-tik) *adj chem* of, containing, or producing acetic acid or vinegar
WORD ORIGIN Latin *acetum* vinegar

acetic acid *n chem* a strong-smelling colourless liquid used to make vinegar

acetone (ass-it-tone) *n chem* a strong-smelling colourless liquid used as a solvent for paints and lacquers

acetylene (ass-set-ill-een) *n chem* a colourless soluble flammable gas used in welding metals

ache ➊ *vb* **aching, ached 1** to feel or be the source of a continuous dull pain **2** to suffer mental anguish ▷ *n* **3** a continuous dull pain
WORD ORIGIN Old English *ācan*

Achebe *n* **Chinua** born 1930, Nigerian novelist. His works include *Things Fall Apart* (1958), *A Man of the People* (1966), and *Anthills of the Savannah* (1987)

Acheson *n* **Dean** (**Gooderham**) 1893–1971, US lawyer and statesman: secretary of state (1949–53) under President Truman

achieve ➊ *vb* **achieving, achieved** to gain by hard work or effort **achiever** *n*
WORD ORIGIN Old French *achever* to bring to an end

achievement ➊ *n* **1** something that has been accomplished by hard work, ability, or heroism **2** the successful completion of something

Achilles heel (ak-kill-eez) *n* a small but fatal weakness
WORD ORIGIN *Achilles* in Greek mythology was killed by an arrow in his unprotected heel

Achilles tendon *n* the fibrous cord that connects the muscles of the calf to the heel bone

achromatic *adj* **1** without colour **2** refracting light without breaking it up into its component colours **3** *music* involving no sharps or flats **achromatically** *adv*

acid ➊ *n* **1** *chem* one of a class of compounds, corrosive and sour

THESAURUS

bean counter *(informal)*

accumulate *vb* **= build up**, increase, grow, be stored, collect, gather, pile up, amass, stockpile, hoard, accrue, cumulate **OPPOSITE:** disperse

accumulation *n* **1 = collection**, increase, stock, store, mass, build-up, pile, stack, heap, rick, stockpile, hoard **2 = growth**, collection, gathering, build-up, aggregation, conglomeration, augmentation

accuracy *n* **= exactness**, precision, fidelity, authenticity, correctness, closeness, truth, verity, nicety, veracity, faithfulness, truthfulness, niceness, exactitude, strictness, meticulousness, carefulness, scrupulousness, preciseness, faultlessness, accurateness **OPPOSITE:** inaccuracy

accurate *adj* **= correct**, right, true, exact, faithful, spot-on *(Brit informal)*, faultless, on the money *(US)*

accusation *n* **2 = charge**, complaint, allegation, indictment, impeachment, recrimination, citation, denunciation, attribution, imputation, arraignment, incrimination

accuse *vb* **= charge with**, indict for, impeach for, arraign for, cite, tax with, censure with, incriminate for, recriminate for **OPPOSITE:** absolve

accustomed *adj* **1 = usual**, established, expected, general, common, standard, set, traditional, normal, fixed, regular, ordinary, familiar, conventional, routine, everyday, customary, habitual, wonted **OPPOSITE:** unusual

ace *n* **2** *(informal)* **= expert**, star, champion, authority, winner, professional, master, pro *(informal)*, specialist, genius, guru, buff *(informal)*, wizard *(informal)*, whizz *(informal)*, virtuoso, connoisseur, hotshot *(informal)*, past master, dab hand *(Brit informal)*, maven *(US)* ▷ *adj* **5** *(informal)* **= great**, good, brilliant, mean *(slang)*, fine, champion, expert, masterly, wonderful, excellent, cracking *(Brit informal)*, outstanding, superb, fantastic *(informal)*, tremendous *(informal)*, marvellous *(informal)*, terrific *(informal)*, mega *(slang)*, awesome *(slang)*, dope *(slang)*, admirable, virtuoso, first-rate, brill *(informal)*, bitchin' *(US slang)*, chillin' *(US slang)*, booshit *(Austral slang)*, exo *(Austral slang)*, sik *(Austral slang)*, ka pai *(NZ)*, rad *(informal)*, phat *(slang)*, schmick *(Austral informal)*, beaut

DICTIONARY

when dissolved in water, that combine with a base to form a salt **2** *slang* LSD **3** a sour-tasting substance ▷ *adj* **4** *chem* of, from, or containing acid **5** sharp or sour in taste **6** sharp in speech or manner **acidly** *adv*
WORD ORIGIN Latin *acidus*

Acid House *or* **Acid** *n* a type of funk-based, electronically edited disco music of the late 1980s, which has hypnotic sound effects and which is associated with hippy culture and the use of the drug ecstasy
WORD ORIGIN *acid* (LSD) + *House* music

acidic *adj* containing acid

acidify *vb* **-fies, -fying, -fied** to convert into acid **acidification** *n*

acidity *n* **1** the quality of being acid **2** the amount of acid in a solution

acid rain *n* rain containing pollutants released into the atmosphere by burning coal or oil

acid reflux *n* the regurgitation of stomach acid into the oesophagus, causing heartburn

acid test *n* a rigorous and conclusive test of worth or value
WORD ORIGIN from the testing of gold with nitric acid

acknowledge ❶ *vb* **-edging, -edged** **1** to recognize or admit the truth of a statement **2** to show recognition of a person by a greeting or glance **3** to make known that a letter or message has been received **4** to express gratitude for (a favour or compliment)
WORD ORIGIN Old English *oncnāwan* to recognize

acknowledgment *or* **acknowledgement** *n* **1** the act of acknowledging something or someone **2** something done or given as an expression of gratitude

acme (ak-mee) *n* the highest point of achievement or excellence
WORD ORIGIN Greek *akmē*

acne (ak-nee) *n* a skin disease in which pus-filled spots form on the face
WORD ORIGIN New Latin

acolyte *n* **1** a follower or attendant **2** *Christianity* a person who assists a priest
WORD ORIGIN Greek *akolouthos*

aconite *n* **1** a poisonous plant with hoodlike flowers **2** dried aconite root, used as a narcotic
WORD ORIGIN Greek *akoniton*

acorn *n* the fruit of the oak tree, consisting of a smooth nut in a cuplike base
WORD ORIGIN Old English *æcern*

acoustic *adj* **1** of sound, hearing, or acoustics **2** (of a musical instrument) without electronic amplification **3** designed to absorb sound: *acoustic tiles* **acoustically** *adv*
WORD ORIGIN Greek *akouein* to hear

acoustics *n* **1** the scientific study of sound ▷ *pl n* **2** the characteristics of a room or auditorium determining how well sound can be heard within it

acquaint *vb* **acquaint with** to make (someone) familiar with
WORD ORIGIN Latin *accognoscere* to know well

acquaintance ❶ *n* **1** a person whom one knows slightly **2** slight knowledge of a person or subject **3** **make the acquaintance of** to come into social contact with **4** the people one knows: *an actress of my acquaintance*

acquainted *adj* **1** on terms of familiarity but not intimacy **2** **acquainted with** familiar with: *she became acquainted with the classics of Chinese literature*

acquiesce (ak-wee-ess) *vb* **-escing, -esced** to agree to what someone wants **acquiescence** *n* **acquiescent** *adj*
WORD ORIGIN Latin *acquiescere*

acquire ❶ *vb* **-quiring, -quired** to get or develop (something such as an object, trait, or ability) **acquirement** *n*
WORD ORIGIN Latin *acquirere*

acquired taste *n* **1** a liking for something at first considered unpleasant **2** the thing liked

acquisition ❶ *n* **1** something acquired, often to add to a collection **2** the act of acquiring something

acquisitive *adj* eager to gain material possessions **acquisitively** *adv* **acquisitiveness** *n*

acquit ❶ *vb* **-quitting, -quitted** **1** to pronounce someone not guilty: *he's been acquitted of negligence* **2** to behave in a particular way: *she acquitted herself well in the meeting* **acquittal** *n*
WORD ORIGIN Old French *aquiter*

acre *n* **1** a unit of area equal to 4840 square yards (4046.86 square metres) **2** **acres** *informal* a large amount: *acres of skin*
WORD ORIGIN Old English *æcer*

acreage (ake-er-rij) *n* land area in acres

acrid (ak-rid) *adj* **1** unpleasantly strong-smelling **2** sharp in speech or manner **acridity** *n* **acridly** *adv*
WORD ORIGIN Latin *acer* sharp, sour

acrimony *n* bitterness and resentment felt about something **acrimonious** *adj*
WORD ORIGIN Latin *acrimonia*

acrobat *n* an entertainer who performs gymnastic feats requiring skill, agility, and balance **acrobatic**

THESAURUS

(*informal*), barrie (*Scot slang*), belting (*Brit slang*), pearler (*Austral slang*)

ache *vb* **1 = hurt**, suffer, burn, pain, smart, sting, pound, throb, be tender, twinge, be sore ▷ *n* **3 = pain**, discomfort, suffering, hurt, smart, smarting, cramp, throb, throbbing, irritation, tenderness, pounding, spasm, pang, twinge, soreness, throe (*rare*)

achieve *vb* **= accomplish**, reach, fulfil, finish, complete, gain, perform, earn, do, get, win, carry out, realize, obtain, conclude, acquire, execute, bring about, attain, consummate, procure, bring off (*informal*), effectuate, put the tin lid on

achievement *n* **1 = accomplishment**, effort, feat, deed, stroke, triumph, coup, exploit, act, attainment, feather in your cap

acid *adj* **5 = sour**, sharp, tart, pungent, biting, acidic, acerbic, acrid, acetic, vinegary, acidulous, acidulated, vinegarish, acerb **OPPOSITE:** sweet **6 = sharp**, cutting, biting, severe, bitter, harsh, stinging, scathing, acrimonious, barbed, pungent, hurtful, sarcastic, sardonic, caustic, vitriolic, acerbic, trenchant, mordant, mordacious **OPPOSITE:** kindly

acknowledge *vb* **1 = admit**, own up, allow, accept, reveal, grant, declare, recognize, yield, concede, confess, disclose, affirm, profess, divulge, accede, acquiesce, 'fess up (*US slang*) **OPPOSITE:** deny **2 = greet**, address, notice, recognize, salute, nod to, accost, tip your hat to **OPPOSITE:** snub **3 = reply to**, answer, notice, recognize, respond to, come back to, react to, write back to, retort to **OPPOSITE:** ignore

acquaintance *n* **1 = associate**, contact, ally, colleague, comrade, confrère **OPPOSITE:** intimate **2 = relationship**, association, exchange, connection, intimacy, fellowship, familiarity, companionship, social contact, cognizance, conversance, conversancy **OPPOSITE:** unfamiliarity

acquire *vb* **= get**, win, buy, receive, land, score (*slang*), gain, achieve, earn, pick up, bag, secure, collect, gather, realize, obtain, attain, amass, procure, come into possession of **OPPOSITE:** lose

acquisition *n* **1 = purchase**, buy, investment, property, gain, prize, asset, possession **2 = acquiring**, gaining, achievement, procurement, attainment, acquirement, obtainment

acquit *vb* **1 = clear**, free, release, deliver, excuse, relieve, discharge, liberate, vindicate, exonerate, absolve, exculpate **OPPOSITE:** find guilty

DICTIONARY

a

adj **acrobatically** *adv*
WORD ORIGIN Greek *akrobatēs* one who walks on tiptoe

acrobatics *pl n* the skills or feats of an acrobat

acronym *n* a word made from the initial letters of other words, for example UNESCO for the *United Nations Educational, Scientific, and Cultural Organization*
WORD ORIGIN Greek *akros* outermost + *onoma* name

acrophobia *n* abnormal fear of being at a great height
WORD ORIGIN Greek *akron* summit + *phobos* fear

acropolis (a-**crop**-pol-liss) *n* the citadel of an ancient Greek city
WORD ORIGIN Greek *akros* highest + *polis* city

across *prep* **1** from one side to the other side of **2** on or at the other side of ▷ *adv* **3** from one side to the other **4** on or to the other side
WORD ORIGIN Old French *a croix* crosswise

across-the-board *adj* affecting everyone in a particular group or place equally: *across-the-board tax cuts*

acrostic *n* a number of lines of writing, such as a poem, in which the first or last letters form a word or proverb
WORD ORIGIN Greek *akros* outermost + *stikhos* line of verse

acrylic *adj* **1** made of acrylic ▷ *n* **2** a man-made fibre used for clothes and blankets **3** a kind of paint made from acrylic acid
WORD ORIGIN Latin *acer* sharp + *olere* to smell

acrylic acid *n chem* a strong-smelling colourless corrosive liquid

acrylic resin *n chem* any of a group of polymers of acrylic acid, used as synthetic rubbers, in paints, and as plastics

act ❶ *n* **1** something done **2** a formal decision reached or law passed by a law-making body: *an act of parliament* **3** a major division of a play or opera **4** a short performance, such as a sketch or dance **5** a pretended attitude: *she appeared calm but it was just an act* **6 get in on the act** *informal* to become involved in something in order to share the benefit **7 get one's act together** *informal* to organize oneself ▷ *vb* **8** to do something **9** to perform (a part or role) in a play, film, or broadcast **10** to present (a play) on stage **11 act for** to be a substitute for: *Mr Lewis was acting for the head of the department* **12 act as** to serve the function of: *she is acting as my bodyguard* **13** to behave: *she acts as though she really hates you* **14** to behave in an unnatural way ▸ See also **act up**
WORD ORIGIN Latin *actum* a thing done

ACT Australian Capital Territory

acting ❶ *n* **1** the art of an actor ▷ *adj* **2** temporarily performing the duties of: *the acting president has declared a state of emergency*

actinide series *n chem* a series of 15 radioactive elements with increasing atomic numbers from actinium to lawrencium

actinium *n chem* a radioactive element of the actinide series, occurring as a decay product of uranium. Symbol: Ac
WORD ORIGIN Greek *aktis* ray

action ❶ *n* **1** doing something for a particular purpose **2** something done on a particular occasion **3** a lawsuit **4** movement during some physical activity **5** the operating mechanism in a gun or machine **6** the way in which something operates or works **7** *slang* the main activity in a place **8** the events that form the plot of a story or play **9** activity, force, or energy **10** a minor battle **11 actions** behaviour **12 out of action** not functioning

actionable *adj law* giving grounds for legal action

action painting *n* an art form in which paint is thrown, smeared, dripped, or spattered on the canvas

action replay *n* the rerunning of a small section of a television tape, for example of a sporting event

action stations *pl n* the positions taken up by individuals in preparation for battle or for some other activity

activate ❶ *vb* **-vating, -vated 1** to make something active **2** *physics* to make something radioactive **3** *chem* to increase the rate of a reaction **activation** *n*

active ❶ *adj* **1** busy and energetic **2** energetically involved in or working hard for: *active in the peace movement* **3** happening now and energetically: *the plan is under active discussion* **4** functioning or causing a reaction: *the active ingredient is held within the capsule* **5** (of a volcano) erupting periodically **6** *grammar* denoting a form of a verb used to indicate that the subject is performing the action, for example *kicked* in *The boy kicked the football* ▷ *n* **7** *grammar* the active form of a verb **actively** *adv*

active list *n mil* a list of officers available for full duty

active service *n* military duty in an operational area

activist ❶ *n* a person who works energetically to achieve political or social goals **activism** *n*

activity ❶ *n* **1** the state of being active **2** lively movement **3** *pl* **-ties** any specific action or pursuit: *he was engaged in political activities abroad*

act of God *n law* a sudden occurrence caused by natural forces, such as a flood

Acton[1] *n* a district of the London borough of Ealing

THESAURUS

act *n* **1 = deed**, action, step, performance, operation, doing, move, blow, achievement, stroke, undertaking, exploit, execution, feat, accomplishment, exertion **2 = law**, bill, measure, resolution, decree, statute, ordinance, enactment, edict **4 = performance**, show, turn, production, routine, presentation, gig *(informal)*, sketch **5 = pretence**, show, front, performance, display, attitude, pose, stance, fake, posture, façade, sham, veneer, counterfeit, feigning, affectation, dissimulation ▷ *vb* **8 = do something**, perform, move, function, go about, conduct yourself, undertake something **9 = perform**, mimic, mime

acting *n* **1 = performance**, playing, performing, theatre, dramatics, portraying, enacting, portrayal, impersonation, characterization, stagecraft ▷ *adj* **2 = temporary**, substitute, intervening, interim, provisional, surrogate, stopgap, pro tem

action *n* **1 = deed**, move, act, performance, blow, exercise, achievement, stroke, undertaking, exploit, feat, accomplishment, exertion **2 = measure**, act, step, operation, manoeuvre **3 = lawsuit**, case, cause, trial, suit, argument, proceeding, dispute, contest, prosecution, litigation **9 = energy**, activity, spirit, force, vitality, vigour, liveliness, vim **10 = battle**, war, fight, fighting, conflict, clash, contest, encounter, combat, engagement, hostilities, warfare, fray, skirmish, sortie, affray

activate *vb* **1 = start**, move, trigger (off), stimulate, turn on, set off, initiate, switch on, propel, rouse, prod, get going, mobilize, kick-start *(informal)*, set in motion, impel, galvanize, set going, actuate
OPPOSITE: stop

active *adj* **1a = busy**, involved, occupied, engaged, tiring, lively, energetic, bustling, restless, on the move, strenuous, tireless, on the go *(informal)* **OPPOSITE:** sluggish
1b = energetic, strong, spirited, quick, vital, alert, dynamic, lively, vigorous, potent, animated, vibrant, forceful, nimble, diligent, industrious, sprightly, vivacious, on the go *(informal)*, alive and kicking, spry, full of beans *(informal)*, bright-

DICTIONARY

a

Acton² *n* 1 **John Emerich Edward Dalberg,** 1st Baron. 1834–1902, English historian: a proponent of Christian liberal ethics and adviser of Gladstone 2 his grandfather, Sir **John Francis Edward** 1736–1811, European naval commander and statesman: admiral of Tuscany (1774–79) and Naples (1779 onwards) and chief minister of Naples (1779–1806)

actor ❶ *or fem* **actress** *n* a person who acts in a play, film, or broadcast

actual *adj* existing in reality or as a matter of fact
WORD ORIGIN Latin *actus* act

actuality *n, pl* **-ties** reality

actually ❶ *adv* as an actual fact; really

actuary *n, pl* **-aries** a person qualified to calculate commercial risks and probabilities involving uncertain future events, esp. in such contexts as life assurance **actuarial** *adj*
WORD ORIGIN Latin *actuarius* one who keeps accounts

actuate *vb* **-ating, -ated** 1 to start up a mechanical device 2 to motivate someone
WORD ORIGIN Medieval Latin *actuare*

act up *vb informal* to behave in a troublesome way

acuity (ak-kew-it-ee) *n* keenness of vision or thought
WORD ORIGIN Latin *acutus* acute

acumen (ak-yew-men) *n* the ability to make good decisions
WORD ORIGIN Latin: sharpness

acupuncture *n* a medical treatment involving the insertion of needles at various parts of the body to stimulate the nerve impulses **acupuncturist** *n*
WORD ORIGIN Latin *acus* needle + PUNCTURE

acute ❶ *adj* 1 severe or intense: *acute staff shortages* 2 penetrating in perception or insight 3 sensitive or keen: *it was amazing how acute your hearing got in the bush* 4 (of a disease) sudden and severe 5 *maths* (of an angle) of less than 90° 6 (of a hospital or bed) intended to accommodate short-term patients ▷ *n* 7 an acute accent **acutely** *adv* **acuteness** *n*
WORD ORIGIN Latin *acutus*

acute accent *n* the mark (´), used in some languages to indicate that the vowel over which it is placed is pronounced in a certain way

ad *n informal* an advertisement

AD (indicating years numbered from the supposed year of the birth of Christ) in the year of the Lord
WORD ORIGIN Latin *anno Domini*

ad- *prefix* 1 to or towards: *adverb* 2 near or next to: *adrenal*
WORD ORIGIN Latin

Ada *n* a high-level computer programming language, used esp. for military systems
WORD ORIGIN after *Ada*, Countess of Lovelace, pioneer in computer programming

adage (ad-ij) *n* a traditional saying that is generally accepted as being true
WORD ORIGIN Latin *adagium*

adagietto *music adv* 1 slowly, but more quickly than adagio ▷ *n, pl* **-tos** 2 a movement or piece to be performed fairly slowly

adagio (ad-dahj-yo) *music adv* 1 slowly ▷ *n, pl* **-gios** 2 a movement or piece to be performed slowly
WORD ORIGIN Italian

Adam *n* 1 *bible* the first man created by God 2 **not know someone from Adam** to not know someone at all

adamant ❶ *adj* unshakable in determination or purpose **adamantly** *adv*
WORD ORIGIN Greek *adamas* unconquerable

Adami *n* **Edward Fenech** born 1934, Maltese politician, president of Malta from 2004

Adamkus *n* **Valdas** born 1926, Lithuanian politician, president of Lithuania from 2004

Adamov *n* **Arthur** 1908–70, French dramatist, born in Russia: one of the foremost exponents of the Theatre of the Absurd. His plays include *Le Professeur Taranne* (1953), *Le Ping-Pong* (1955), and *Le Printemps '71* (1960)

Adam's apple *n* the projecting lump of thyroid cartilage at the front of a person's neck

adapt ❶ *vb* 1 to adjust (something or oneself) to different conditions 2 to change something to suit a new purpose **adaptable** *adj* **adaptability** *n*
WORD ORIGIN Latin *adaptare*

adaptation ❶ *n* 1 something that is produced by adapting something else: *a TV adaptation of a Victorian novel* 2 the act of adapting

adaptor *or* **adapter** *n* 1 a device used to connect several electrical appliances to a single socket 2 any device for connecting two parts of different sizes or types

ADC aide-de-camp

add ❶ *vb* 1 to combine (numbers or quantities) so as to make a larger number or quantity 2 to join something to something else so as to increase its size, effect, or scope: *these new rules will add an extra burden on already overworked officials* 3 to say or write something further 4 **add in** to include ▸ See also **add up**
WORD ORIGIN Latin *addere*

Addams *n* **Jane** 1860–1935, US social reformer, feminist, and pacifist, who founded Hull House, a social settlement in Chicago: Nobel peace prize 1931

addendum *n, pl* **-da** something added on, esp. an appendix to a book or magazine

adder *n* a small poisonous snake with a black zigzag pattern along the back
WORD ORIGIN Old English *nǣdre*

THESAURUS

eyed and bushy-tailed *(informal)*
OPPOSITE: inactive

activist *n* = **militant**, partisan, organizer, warrior

activity *n* 1 = **action**, work, life, labour, movement, energy, exercise, spirit, enterprise, motion, bustle, animation, vigour, hustle, exertion, hurly-burly, liveliness, activeness
OPPOSITE: inaction
3 = **pursuit**, act, project, scheme, task, pleasure, interest, enterprise, undertaking, occupation, hobby, deed, endeavour, pastime, avocation

actor *or* **actress** *n* = **performer**, player, artiste, leading man *or* lady, Thespian, luvvie *(informal)*, trouper, thesp *(informal)*, play-actor, dramatic artist, tragedian *or* tragedienne

actually *adv* = **really**, in fact, indeed, essentially, truly, literally, genuinely, in reality, in truth, in actuality, in point of fact, veritably, as a matter of fact

acute *adj* 2 = **perceptive**, sharp, keen, smart, sensitive, clever, subtle, piercing, penetrating, discriminating, discerning, ingenious, astute, intuitive, canny, incisive, insightful, observant, perspicacious OPPOSITE: slow
4 = **serious**, dangerous, critical, alarming, severe, grave, sudden

adamant *adj* = **determined**, firm, fixed, stiff, rigid, set, relentless, stubborn, uncompromising, insistent, resolute, inflexible, unrelenting, inexorable, unyielding, intransigent, immovable, unbending, obdurate, unshakable
OPPOSITE: flexible

adapt *vb* 1 = **adjust**, change, match, alter, modify, accommodate, comply, conform, reconcile, harmonize, familiarize, habituate, acclimatize
2 = **convert**, change, prepare, fit, fashion, make, shape, suit, qualify, transform, alter, modify, tailor, remodel, tweak *(informal)*, metamorphose, customize

adaptation *n* 1 = **conversion**, change, shift, variation, adjustment, transformation, modification, alteration, remodelling, reworking, refitting 2 = **acclimatization**, naturalization, habituation, familiarization, accustomedness

add *vb* 1 = **count up**, total, reckon, sum up, compute, add up, tot up
OPPOSITE: take away

DICTIONARY

a

addict ❶ *n* **1** a person who is unable to stop taking narcotic drugs **2** *informal* a person who is devoted to something: *he's a telly addict* **addictive** *adj*
WORD ORIGIN Latin *addictus* given over

addicted ❶ *adj* **1** dependent on a narcotic drug **2** *informal* devoted to something: *I'm a news freak and addicted to BBC Breakfast News* **addiction** *n*

addition ❶ *n* **1** the act of adding **2** a person or thing that is added **3** a mathematical operation in which the total of two or more numbers or quantities is calculated **4 in addition (to)** besides; as well (as) **additional** *adj* **additionally** *adv*

additive *n* any substance added to something, such as food, to improve it or prevent deterioration

addled *adj* **1** confused or unable to think clearly **2** (of eggs) rotten
WORD ORIGIN Old English *adela* filth

add-on *n* a feature that can be added to a standard model to give increased benefits

address ❶ *n* **1** the place at which someone lives **2** the conventional form by which the location of a building is described **3** a formal speech **4** *computers* a number giving the location of a piece of stored information ▷*vb* **5** to mark (a letter or parcel) with an address **6** to speak to **7** to direct one's attention to (a problem or an issue) **8 address oneself to a** to speak or write to **b** to apply oneself to: *we have got to address ourselves properly to this problem*
WORD ORIGIN Latin *ad-* to + *directus* direct

addressee *n* a person to whom a letter or parcel is addressed

adduce *vb* **-ducing, -duced** to mention something as evidence
WORD ORIGIN Latin *adducere* to lead to

add up *vb* **1** to calculate the total of (two or more numbers or quantities) **2** *informal* to make sense: *there's something about it that doesn't add up* **3 add up to** to amount to

adenoidal *adj* having a nasal voice or impaired breathing because of enlarged adenoids

adenoids (ad-in-oidz) *pl n* a mass of tissue at the back of the throat
WORD ORIGIN Greek *adenoeidēs* glandular

adept ❶ *adj* **1** proficient in something requiring skill ▷*n* **2** a person skilled in something **adeptness** *n*
WORD ORIGIN Latin *adipisci* to attain

adequate ❶ *adj* just enough in amount or just good enough in quality **adequacy** *n* **adequately** *adv*
WORD ORIGIN Latin *ad-* to + *aequus* equal

à deux (ah **duh**) *adj, adv* of or for two people
WORD ORIGIN French

ADHD *med* attention deficit hyperactivity disorder

adhere *vb* **-hering, -hered 1** to stick to **2** to act according to (a rule or agreement) **3** to be a loyal supporter of (something)
WORD ORIGIN Latin *adhaerere*

adherent *n* **1** a supporter or follower ▷*adj* **2** sticking or attached **adherence** *n*

adhesion *n* **1** the quality or condition of sticking together **2** *pathol* the joining together of two structures or parts of the body that are normally separate, for example after surgery

adhesive *n* **1** a substance used for sticking things together ▷*adj* **2** able or designed to stick to things

ad hoc *adj, adv* for a particular purpose only
WORD ORIGIN Latin: to this

Adichie *n* **Chimamanda Ngozi**, born 1977, Nigerian novelist; her novels include *Purple Hibiscus* (2003) and *Half of a Yellow Sun* (2006), which won the 2007 Orange Prize for Fiction

Adie *n* **Kathryn,** known as Kate. born 1945, British television journalist, noted esp. for her frontline reporting of revolutions, wars, etc.

adieu (a-dew) *interj, n, pl* **adieux** *or* **adieus** (a-dewz) goodbye
WORD ORIGIN French

ad infinitum *adv* endlessly: *we would not be able to sustain the currency ad infinitum*
WORD ORIGIN Latin

adipose *adj* of or containing fat; fatty: *adipose tissue*
WORD ORIGIN Latin *adeps* fat

adj. adjective

adjacent ❶ *adj* **1** near or next: *the schools were adjacent but there were separate doors* **2** *geom* (of a side of a right-angled triangle) lying between a specified angle and the right angle
WORD ORIGIN Latin *ad-* near + *jacere* to lie

adjective *n* a word that adds information about a noun or pronoun **adjectival** *adj*
WORD ORIGIN Latin *nomen adjectivum* attributive noun

adjoin ❶ *vb* to be next to and joined

THESAURUS

addict *n* **1 = junkie** *(informal)*, abuser, user *(informal)*, druggie *(informal)*, freak *(informal)*, fiend *(informal)*, mainliner *(slang)*, smackhead *(slang)*, space cadet *(slang)*, pill-popper *(informal)*, head *(slang)*, pothead *(slang)*, dope-fiend *(slang)*, cokehead *(slang)*, acidhead *(slang)*, hashhead *(slang)* **2** *(informal)* **= fan**, lover, nut *(slang)*, follower, enthusiast, freak *(informal)*, admirer, buff *(informal)*, junkie *(informal)*, devotee, fiend *(informal)*, adherent, rooter *(US)*, zealot, groupie *(slang)*, aficionado

addicted *adj* **1 = hooked**, dependent

addition *n* **1 = inclusion**, adding, increasing, extension, attachment, adjoining, insertion, incorporation, annexation, accession, affixing, augmentation **OPPOSITE:** removal **2 = extra**, supplement, complement, adjunct, increase, gain, bonus, extension, accessory, additive, appendix, increment, appendage, addendum **3 = counting up**, totalling, reckoning, summing up, adding up, computation, totting up, summation **OPPOSITE:** subtraction **4 in addition to = as well as**, along with, on top of, besides, to boot, additionally, over and above, to say nothing of, into the bargain

address 1 = home, house, lodging, pad *(slang)*, residence, dwelling, abode, domicile **2 = location**, place, point, position, situation, site, spot, venue, whereabouts, locus, locale **3 = speech**, talk, lecture, discourse, sermon, dissertation, harangue, homily, oration, spiel *(informal)*, disquisition ▷*vb* **6 = speak to**, talk to, greet, hail, salute, invoke, communicate with, accost, approach, converse with, apostrophize, korero *(NZ)*

adept *adj* **1 = skilful**, able, skilled, expert, masterly, practised, accomplished, versed, masterful, proficient, adroit, dexterous **OPPOSITE:** unskilled ▷*n* **2 = expert**, master, genius, buff *(informal)*, whizz *(informal)*, hotshot *(informal)*, rocket scientist *(informal, chiefly US)*, dab hand *(Brit informal)*, maven *(US)*

adequate *adj* **a = passable**, acceptable, middling, average, fair, ordinary, moderate, satisfactory, competent, mediocre, so-so *(informal)*, tolerable, up to scratch *(informal)*, presentable, unexceptional **OPPOSITE:** inadequate **b = sufficient**, enough, capable, suitable, requisite **OPPOSITE:** insufficient

adjacent *adj* **1 = adjoining**, neighbouring, nearby, abutting **OPPOSITE:** far away

adjoin *vb* **= connect with** *or* **to**, join, neighbour (on), link with, attach to, combine with, couple with, communicate with, touch on, border on, annex, approximate, unite with, verge on, impinge on, append, affix to, interconnect with

adjourn *vb* **2 = postpone**, delay, suspend, interrupt, put off, stay, defer, recess, discontinue, put on the back burner *(informal)*, prorogue, take a rain check on *(US & Canad informal)* **OPPOSITE:** continue

onto **adjoining** *adj*

adjourn ❶ *vb* **1** to close a court at the end of a session **2** to postpone or be postponed temporarily **3** *informal* to go elsewhere: *can we adjourn to the dining room?* **adjournment** *n*
WORD ORIGIN Old French *ajourner* to defer to an arranged day

adjudge *vb* **-judging, -judged** to declare someone to be something specified: *my wife was adjudged to be the guilty party*

adjudicate *vb* **-cating, -cated 1** to give a formal decision on a dispute **2** to serve as a judge, for example in a competition **adjudication** *n* **adjudicator** *n*
WORD ORIGIN Latin *adjudicare*

adjunct *n* **1** something added that is not essential **2** a person who is subordinate to another
WORD ORIGIN Latin *adjunctus* adjoined

adjure *vb* **-juring, -jured 1** to command someone to do something **2** to appeal earnestly to someone **adjuration** *n*
WORD ORIGIN Latin *adjurare*

adjust ❶ *vb* **1** to adapt to a new environment **2** to alter slightly, so as to be accurate or suitable **3** *insurance* to determine the amount payable in settlement of a claim **adjustable** *adj* **adjuster** *n*
WORD ORIGIN Old French *adjuster*

adjustment ❶ *n* **1** a slight alteration **2** the act of adjusting

adjutant (aj-oo-tant) *n* an officer in an army who acts as administrative assistant to a superior
WORD ORIGIN Latin *adjutare* to aid

ad-lib *vb* **-libbing, -libbed 1** to improvise a speech or piece of music without preparation ▷ *adj* **2** improvised: *ad-lib studio chat* ▷ *n* **3** an improvised remark ▷ *adv* **ad lib 4** spontaneously or freely
WORD ORIGIN short for Latin *ad libitum*, literally: according to pleasure

Adm. *Brit* Admiral

adman *n, pl* **-men** *informal* a man who works in advertising

admin *n informal* administration

administer ❶ *vb* **1** to manage (an organization or estate) **2** to organize and put into practice: *anyone can learn to administer the test procedure* **3** to give medicine to someone **4** to supervise the taking of (an oath)
WORD ORIGIN Latin *administrare*

administrate *vb* **-trating, -trated** to manage an organization

administration ❶ *n* **1** management of the affairs of an organization **2** the people who administer an organization **3** a government: *the first non-communist administration in the country's history* **4** the act of administering something, such as medicine or an oath **administrative** *adj*

administrator ❶ *n* a person who administers an organization or estate

admirable ❶ (ad-mer-a-bl) *adj* deserving or inspiring admiration: *the boldness of the undertaking is admirable* **admirably** *adv*

admiral *n* **1** Also called: **admiral of the fleet** a naval officer of the highest rank **2** any of various brightly coloured butterflies
WORD ORIGIN Arabic *amīr-al* commander of

Admiralty *n Brit* the former government department in charge of the Royal Navy

admire ❶ *vb* **-miring, -mired** to respect and approve of (a person or thing) **admiration** *n* **admirer** *n* **admiring** *adj* **admiringly** *adv*
WORD ORIGIN Latin *admirari* to wonder at

admissible *adj law* allowed to be brought as evidence in court

admission ❶ *n* **1** permission or the right to enter **2** permission to join an organization **3** the price charged for entrance **4** a confession: *she was, by her own admission, not educated*

admit ❶ *vb* **-mitting, -mitted 1** to confess or acknowledge (a crime or mistake) **2** to concede (the truth of something) **3** to allow (someone) to enter **4** to take (someone) in to a hospital for treatment: *he was admitted for tests* **5 admit to** to allow someone to participate in something **6 admit of** to allow for: *these rules admit of no violation*
WORD ORIGIN Latin *admittere*

admittance *n* **1** the right to enter **2** the act of entering a place

adjust *vb* **1 = adapt**, change, settle, convert, alter, accommodate, dispose, get used, accustom, conform, reconcile, harmonize, acclimatize, familiarize yourself, attune **2 = modify**, arrange, fix, tune (up), alter, adapt, remodel, tweak (*informal*), customize

adjustment *n* **1 = alteration**, setting, change, ordering, fixing, arrangement, tuning, repair, conversion, modifying, adaptation, modification, remodelling, redress, refinement, rectification **2 = acclimatization**, settling in, orientation, familiarization, change, regulation, settlement, amendment, reconciliation, adaptation, accustoming, revision, modification, naturalization, acculturation, harmonization, habituation, acclimation, inurement

administer *vb* **1 = manage**, run, control, rule, direct, handle, conduct, command, govern, oversee, supervise, preside over, be in charge of, superintend **2 = execute**, do, give, provide, apply, perform, carry out, impose, realize, implement, enforce, render, discharge, enact, dispense, mete out, bring off

administration *n* **1 = management**, government, running, control, performance, handling, direction, conduct, application, command, provision, distribution, governing, administering, execution, overseeing, supervision, manipulation, governance, dispensation, superintendence **2 = directors**, board, executive(s), bosses (*informal*), management, employers, directorate **3 = government**, authority, executive, leadership, ministry, regime, governing body

administrator *n* **= manager**, head, official, director, officer, executive, minister, boss (*informal*), agent, governor, controller, supervisor, bureaucrat, superintendent, gaffer (*informal, chiefly Brit*), organizer, mandarin, functionary, overseer, baas (*S African*)

admirable *adj* **= praiseworthy**, good, great, fine, capital, noted, choice, champion, prime, select, wonderful, excellent, brilliant, rare, cracking (*Brit informal*), outstanding, valuable, superb, distinguished, superior, sterling, worthy, first-class, notable, sovereign, dope (*slang*), world-class, exquisite, exemplary, first-rate, superlative, commendable, top-notch (*informal*), brill (*informal*), laudable, meritorious, estimable, tiptop, A1 *or* A-one (*informal*), bitchin' (*US slang*), chillin' (*US slang*), booshit (*Austral slang*), exo (*Austral slang*), sik (*Austral slang*), ka pai (*NZ*), rad (*informal*), phat (*slang*), schmick (*Austral informal*), beaut (*informal*), barrie (*Scot slang*), belting (*Brit slang*), pearler (*Austral slang*)
OPPOSITE: deplorable

admire *vb* **= respect**, value, prize, honour, praise, appreciate, esteem, approve of, revere, venerate, take your hat off to, have a good *or* high opinion of, think highly of
OPPOSITE: despise

admission *n* **1, 2 = admittance**, access, entry, introduction, entrance, acceptance, initiation, entrée, ingress **4 = confession**, admitting, profession, declaration, revelation, concession, allowance, disclosure, acknowledgement, affirmation, unburdening, avowal, divulgence, unbosoming

admit *vb* **1 = confess**, own up, confide, profess, own up, come clean (*informal*), avow, come out of the

DICTIONARY

a

admittedly *adv* it must be agreed: *my research is admittedly incomplete*
admixture *n* **1** a mixture **2** an ingredient
admonish *vb* to reprimand sternly **admonition** *n* **admonitory** *adj*
WORD ORIGIN Latin *admonere*
ad nauseam (ad naw-zee-am) *adv* to a boring or sickening extent: *she went on and on ad nauseam about her divorce*
WORD ORIGIN Latin: to (the point of) nausea
ado *n* fuss: *without further ado*
WORD ORIGIN Middle English *at do* a to-do
adobe (ad-oh-bee) *n* **1** a sun-dried brick **2** the claylike material from which such bricks are made **3** a building made of such bricks
WORD ORIGIN Spanish
adolescence ❶ *n* the period between puberty and adulthood
WORD ORIGIN Latin *adolescere* to grow up
adolescent ❶ *adj* **1** of or relating to adolescence **2** *informal* (of behaviour) immature ▷ *n* **3** an adolescent person
Adonis *n* a handsome young man
WORD ORIGIN name of a handsome youth in Greek myth
adopt ❶ *vb* **1** *law* to take someone else's child as one's own **2** to choose (a plan or method) **3** to choose (a country or name) to be one's own **adoptee** *n* **adoption** *n*
WORD ORIGIN Latin *adoptare*
adoptive *adj* **1** acquired or related by adoption: *an adoptive father* **2** of or relating to adoption
adorable *adj* very attractive; lovable
adore ❶ *vb* **adoring, adored 1** to love intensely or deeply **2** *informal* to like very much: *I adore being in the country* **3** to worship a god with religious rites **adoration** *n* **adoring** *adj* **adoringly** *adv*
WORD ORIGIN Latin *adorare*
adorn ❶ *vb* to decorate; increase the beauty of **adornment** *n*
WORD ORIGIN Latin *adornare*
Adorno *n* **Theodor Wiesengrund** 1903–69, German philosopher, sociologist, and music critic. His writings include *The Philosophy of the New Music* (1949) and *Negative Dialectics* (1966)
ADP automatic data processing
adrenal (ad-reen-al) *adj anat* **1** on or near the kidneys **2** of or relating to the adrenal glands
WORD ORIGIN Latin *ad-* near + *renes* kidneys
adrenal glands *pl n anat* two endocrine glands covering the upper surface of the kidneys
adrenalin *or* **adrenaline** *n biochem* a hormone secreted by the adrenal gland in response to stress. It increases heart rate, pulse rate, and blood pressure
Adrian *n* **Edgar Douglas,** Baron Adrian. 1889–1977, English physiologist, noted particularly for his research into the function of neurons: shared with Sherrington the Nobel prize for physiology and medicine 1932
adrift ❶ *adj, adv* **1** drifting **2** without a clear purpose **3** *informal* off course, wrong: *it was obvious that something had gone adrift*
adroit *adj* quick and skilful in how one behaves or thinks **adroitly** *adv* **adroitness** *n*
WORD ORIGIN French *à droit* rightly
adsorb *vb* (of a gas or vapour) to condense and form a thin film on a surface **adsorbent** *adj* **adsorption** *n*
WORD ORIGIN Latin *ad-* to + *sorbere* to drink in
ADT Atlantic Daylight Time
adulation *n* uncritical admiration
WORD ORIGIN Latin *adulari* to flatter
adult ❶ *n* **1** a mature fully grown person, animal, or plant ▷ *adj* **2** having reached maturity; fully developed **3** suitable for or typical of adult people: *she had very adult features* **4** sexually explicit: *adult films* **adulthood** *n*
WORD ORIGIN Latin *adultus* grown up
adulterate *vb* **-ating, -ated** to spoil something by adding inferior material **adulteration** *n*
WORD ORIGIN Latin *adulterare*
adulterer *or fem* **adulteress** *n* a person who has committed adultery
adultery *n, pl* **-teries** sexual unfaithfulness of a husband or wife **adulterous** *adj*
WORD ORIGIN Latin *adulterium*
adv. adverb
advance ❶ *vb* **-vancing, -vanced 1** to go or bring forward **2** to make progress: *this student has advanced in reading and writing* **3** to further a cause: *an association founded to advance the interests of ex-soldiers* **4 advance on** to move towards someone in a threatening manner **5** to present an idea for consideration **6** to lend a sum of money ▷ *n* **7** a forward

THESAURUS

closet, sing *(slang, chiefly US)*, cough *(slang)*, spill your guts *(slang)*, 'fess up *(US slang)* **2 = allow**, agree, accept, reveal, grant, declare, acknowledge, recognize, concede, disclose, affirm, divulge **OPPOSITE:** deny **3 = let in**, allow, receive, accept, introduce, take in, initiate, give access to, allow to enter **OPPOSITE:** keep out
adolescence *n* **= teens**, youth, minority, boyhood, girlhood, juvenescence
adolescent *adj* **1 = young**, growing, junior, teenage, juvenile, youthful, childish, immature, boyish, undeveloped, girlish, puerile, in the springtime of life **2** *(informal)* **= immature**, young, teen *(informal)*, juvenile, youthful, teenage ▷ *n* **3 = teenager**, girl, boy, kid *(informal)*, youth, lad, minor, young man, youngster, young woman, juvenile, young person, lass, young adult
adopt *vb* **1** *(law)* **= take in**, raise, nurse, mother, rear, foster, bring up, take care of **OPPOSITE:** abandon
adore *vb* **1 = love**, honour, admire, worship, esteem, cherish, bow to, revere, dote on, idolize **OPPOSITE:** hate
adorn *vb* **= decorate**, enhance, deck, trim, grace, array, enrich, garnish, ornament, embellish, emblazon, festoon, bedeck, beautify, engarland
adrift *adj* **1 = drifting**, afloat, cast off, unmoored, aweigh, unanchored **2 = aimless**, goalless, directionless, purposeless ▷ *adv* **3** *(informal)* **= wrong**, astray, off course, amiss, off target, wide of the mark
adult *n* **1 = grown-up**, mature person, person of mature age, grown *or* grown-up person, man *or* woman ▷ *adj* **2 = fully grown**, mature, grown-up, of age, ripe, fully fledged, fully developed, full grown **4 = pornographic**, blue, dirty, offensive, sexy, erotic, porn *(informal)*, obscene, taboo, filthy, indecent, sensual, hard-core, lewd, carnal, porno *(informal)*, X-rated *(informal)*, salacious, prurient, smutty
advance *vb* **1, 2 = progress**, proceed, go ahead, move up, come forward, go forward, press on, gain ground, make inroads, make headway, make your way, cover ground, make strides, move onward **OPPOSITE:** retreat **5 = suggest**, offer, present, propose, allege, cite, advocate, submit, prescribe, put forward, proffer, adduce, offer as a suggestion **OPPOSITE:** withhold **6 = lend**, loan, accommodate someone with, supply on credit **OPPOSITE:** withhold payment ▷ *n* **8 = improvement**, development, gain, growth, breakthrough, advancement, step, headway, inroads, betterment, furtherance, forward movement, amelioration, onward movement **10 = down payment**, credit, fee, deposit, retainer, prepayment, loan **12 in advance = beforehand**, earlier, ahead, previously, pre-need, in the lead, in the forefront *adj* **14 = prior**, early, previous, beforehand
advanced *adj* **1 = sophisticated**, foremost, modern, revolutionary, up-to-date, higher, leading, recent,

DICTIONARY

a

movement **8** improvement or progress: *the greatest advance in modern medicine* **9** a loan of money **10** a payment made before it is legally due **11** an increase in price: *any advance on fifty pounds?* **12 in advance** beforehand: *you have to pay in advance* **13 in advance of** ahead of in time or development ▹ *adj* **14** done or happening before an event: *advance warning* ▸ See also **advances**
WORD ORIGIN Latin *abante* from before

advanced ❶ *adj* **1** at a late stage in development **2** not elementary: *he was taking the advanced class in economics*

Advanced level *n Brit* ▸ a formal name for **A level**

advancement ❶ *n* promotion in rank or status

advances *pl n* approaches made to a person with the hope of starting a romantic or sexual relationship

advantage ❶ *n* **1** a more favourable position or state **2** benefit or profit: *they could make this work to their advantage* **3** *tennis* the point scored after deuce **4 take advantage of a** to use a person unfairly **b** to use an opportunity **5 to advantage** to good effect: *her hair was shaped to display to advantage her superb neck*
WORD ORIGIN Latin *abante* from before

advantaged *adj* in a superior social or financial position

advantageous *adj* likely to bring benefits **advantageously** *adv*

advection *n physics* the transferring of heat in a horizontal stream of gas
WORD ORIGIN Latin *ad-* to + *vehere* to carry

advent *n* an arrival: *the advent of the personal computer*
WORD ORIGIN Latin *ad-* to + *venire* to come

Advent *n* the season that includes the four Sundays before Christmas

Adventist *n* a member of a Christian group that believes in the imminent return of Christ

adventitious *adj* added or appearing accidentally
WORD ORIGIN Latin *adventicius* coming from outside

adventure ❶ *n* **1** a risky undertaking, the ending of which is uncertain: *our African adventure* **2** exciting or unexpected events
WORD ORIGIN Latin *advenire* to happen to (someone), arrive

adventure playground *n Brit, Austral & NZ* a playground for children that contains building materials and other equipment to build with or climb on

adventurer *or fem* **adventuress** *n* **1** a person who seeks money or power by unscrupulous means **2** a person who seeks adventure

adventurism *n* recklessness in politics or finance

adventurous ❶ *adj* daring or enterprising

adverb *n* a word that modifies a sentence, verb, adverb, or adjective, for example *easily, very,* and *happily* in *They could easily envy the very happily married couple* **adverbial** *adj*
WORD ORIGIN Latin *adverbium,* literally: added word

adversary ❶ (ad-verse-er-ree) *n, pl* **-saries** an opponent in a fight, disagreement, or sporting contest
WORD ORIGIN Latin *adversus* against

adverse ❶ *adj* **1** unfavourable to one's interests: *adverse effects* **2** antagonistic or hostile **adversely** *adv*
WORD ORIGIN Latin *ad-* towards + *vertere* to turn

adversity *n, pl* **-ties** very difficult or hard circumstances

advert ❶ *n informal* an advertisement

advertise ❶ *vb* **-tising, -tised 1** to present or praise (goods or a service) to the public, in order to encourage sales **2** to make (a vacancy, an event, or an article for sale) publicly known **advertiser** *n* **advertising** *n*
WORD ORIGIN Latin *advertere* to turn one's attention to

advertisement ❶ *n* any public announcement designed to sell goods or publicize an event

advice ❶ *n* **1** recommendation as to an appropriate choice of action **2** formal notification of facts
WORD ORIGIN Latin *ad* to + *visum* view

advisable *adj* sensible and likely to achieve the desired result **advisability** *n*

advise ❶ *vb* **-vising, -vised 1** to offer advice to **2** to inform or notify **adviser** *or* **advisor** *n*
WORD ORIGIN Latin *ad-* to + *videre* to see

advised *adj* thought-out: *ill-advised*

advisedly (ad-vize-id-lee) *adv* deliberately; after careful consideration: *I use the word advisedly*

advisory ❶ *adj* **1** able to offer advice

THESAURUS

prime, forward, ahead, supreme, extreme, principal, progressive, paramount, state-of-the-art, avant-garde, precocious, pre-eminent, up-to-the-minute, ahead of the times **OPPOSITE:** backward

advancement *n* **= promotion**, rise, gain, growth, advance, progress, improvement, betterment, preferment, amelioration

advantage *n* **1 = lead**, control, edge, sway, dominance, superiority, upper hand, precedence, primacy, pre-eminence **2 = benefit**, use, start, help, service, aid, profit, favour, asset, assistance, blessing, utility, boon, ace in the hole, ace up your sleeve **OPPOSITE:** disadvantage

adventure *n* **1 = venture**, experience, chance, risk, incident, enterprise, speculation, undertaking, exploit, fling, hazard, occurrence, contingency, caper, escapade

adventurous *adj* **= daring**, dangerous, enterprising, bold, risky, rash, have-a-go *(informal)*, hazardous, reckless, audacious, intrepid, foolhardy, daredevil, headstrong, venturesome, adventuresome, temerarious *(rare)* **OPPOSITE:** cautious

adversary *n* **= opponent**, rival, opposer, enemy, competitor, foe, contestant, antagonist **OPPOSITE:** ally

adverse *adj* **1a = harmful**, damaging, conflicting, dangerous, opposite, negative, destructive, detrimental, hurtful, antagonistic, injurious, inimical, inopportune, disadvantageous, unpropitious, inexpedient **OPPOSITE:** beneficial **1b = unfavourable**, bad, threatening, hostile, unfortunate, unlucky, ominous, unfriendly, untimely, unsuited, ill-suited, inopportune, disadvantageous, unseasonable **2 = negative**, opposing, reluctant, hostile, contrary, dissenting, unwilling, unfriendly, unsympathetic, ill-disposed

advert *n (informal)* **= advertisement**, bill, notice, display, commercial, ad *(informal)*, announcement, promotion, publicity, poster, plug *(informal)*, puff, circular, placard, blurb

advertise *vb* **1,2 = publicize**, promote, plug *(informal)*, announce, publish, push *(informal)*, display, declare, broadcast, advise, inform, praise, proclaim, puff, hype, notify, tout, flaunt, crack up *(informal)*, promulgate, make known, apprise, beat the drum *(informal)*, blazon, bring to public notice

advertisement *n* **= advert** *(informal)*, bill, notice, display, commercial, ad *(informal)*, announcement, promotion, publicity, poster, plug *(informal)*, puff, circular, placard, blurb

advice *n* **1 = guidance**, help, opinion, direction, suggestion, instruction, counsel, counselling, recommendation, injunction, admonition

advise *vb* **1 = recommend**, suggest, urge, counsel, advocate, caution, prescribe, commend, admonish, enjoin **2 = notify**, tell, report, announce, warn, declare, inform, acquaint, make known, apprise, let (someone) know

advisory *adj* **1 = advising**, helping,

DICTIONARY

a

▷ *n, pl* **-ries** **2** a statement giving advice or a warning **3** a person or organization that gives advice: *the Prime Minister's media advisory*

advocaat *n* a liqueur with a raw egg base
WORD ORIGIN Dutch

advocacy *n* active support of a cause or course of action

advocate ❶ *vb* **-cating, -cated** **1** to recommend a course of action publicly ▷ *n* **2** a person who upholds or defends a cause or course of action **3** a person who speaks on behalf of another in a court of law **4** *Scots law* a barrister
WORD ORIGIN Latin *advocare* to call, summon

adware *n computers* **1** software that collects information about a user's browsing patterns in order to display relevant advertisements **2** software that is produced with advertisements embedded within it

adze *or US* **adz** *n* a tool with a blade at right angles to the handle, used for shaping timber
WORD ORIGIN Old English *adesa*

AEA Atomic Energy Authority

AEC *US* Atomic Energy Commission

AEEU (in Britain) Amalgamated Engineering and Electrical Union

aegis (ee-jiss) *n* **under the aegis of** with the sponsorship or protection of
WORD ORIGIN Greek *aigis* shield of Zeus

Ælfric *n* called *Grammaticus.* ?955–?1020, English abbot, writer, and grammarian

Aeneas Silvius *or* **Aeneas Sylvius** *n* ▸ the literary name of **Pius II**

aeolian harp (ee-oh-lee-an) *n* a musical instrument that produces sounds when the wind passes over its strings
WORD ORIGIN after *Aeolus*, god of winds in Greek myth

aeon *or US* **eon** (ee-on) *n* **1** an immeasurably long period of time **2** the longest division of geological time
WORD ORIGIN Greek *aiōn*

aerate *vb* **-ating, -ated** to put gas into a liquid, for example when making a fizzy drink **aeration** *n*

aerial *n* **1** the metal pole or wire on a television or radio which transmits or receives signals ▷ *adj* **2** in, from, or operating in the air **3** extending high into the air **4** of or relating to aircraft
WORD ORIGIN Greek *aēr* air

aerial top dressing *n NZ* spreading of fertilizer from an aeroplane onto remote areas

aero-, aeri- *or* **aer-** *combining form* **1** relating to aircraft **2** relating to air, atmosphere, or gas
WORD ORIGIN Greek *aēr* air

aerobatics *n* spectacular manoeuvres, such as loops or rolls, performed by aircraft
WORD ORIGIN AERO- + (ACRO)BATICS

aerobe *n biol* an organism that requires oxygen to survive
WORD ORIGIN Greek *aēr* air + *bios* life

aerobic *adj* designed for or relating to aerobics: *aerobic exercise*

aerobics *n* exercises to increase the amount of oxygen in the blood and strengthen the heart and lungs

aerodrome *n* a small airport

aerodynamics *n* the study of how air flows around moving objects
aerodynamic *adj* **aerodynamicist** *n*

aero engine *n* an engine for an aircraft

aerofoil *n* a part of an aircraft, such as the wing, designed to give lift in flight

aerogram *n* an air-mail letter on a single sheet of light paper that seals to form an envelope

aeronautics *n* the study or practice of flight through the air
aeronautical *adj*

aeroplane *or US & Canad* **airplane** *n* a heavier-than-air powered flying vehicle with fixed wings
WORD ORIGIN AERO- + Greek *planos* wandering

aerosol *n* a small metal pressurized can from which a substance can be dispensed in a fine spray
WORD ORIGIN AERO- + SOL(UTION)

aerospace *n* **1** the earth's atmosphere and space beyond ▷ *adj* **2** of rockets or space vehicles: *the aerospace industry*

Aeschines *n* ?389–?314 BC, Athenian orator; the main political opponent of Demosthenes

aesthete *or US* **esthete** (eess-theet) *n* a person who has or who pretends to have a highly developed appreciation of beauty

aesthetic *or US* **esthetic** (iss-thet-ik) *adj* **1** relating to the appreciation of art and beauty ▷ *n* **2** a principle or set of principles relating to the appreciation of art and beauty
aesthetically *or US* **esthetically** *adv*
aestheticism *or US* **estheticism** *n*
WORD ORIGIN Greek *aisthanomai* to perceive, feel

aesthetics *or US* **esthetics** *n* **1** the branch of philosophy concerned with the study of the concepts of beauty and taste **2** the study of the rules and principles of art

Æthelbert *n* ▸ a variant spelling of **Ethelbert**

Æthelwulf *n* ▸ a variant spelling of **Ethelwulf**

aether *n* ▸ same as **ether** (senses 2, 3)

aetiology (ee-tee-ol-a-jee) *n* ▸ same as **etiology**

a.f. audio frequency

afar *n* **from afar** from or at a great distance

affable *adj* showing warmth and friendliness **affability** *n* **affably** *adv*
WORD ORIGIN Latin *affabilis*

affair ❶ *n* **1** an event or happening: *the Irangate affair* **2** a sexual relationship outside marriage **3** a thing to be done or attended to: *my wife's career is her own affair* **4** something previously specified: *lunch was a subdued affair*
WORD ORIGIN Old French *à faire* to do

affairs *pl n* **1** personal or business interests **2** matters of public interest: *foreign affairs*

affect[1] ❶ *vb* **1** to influence (someone or something): *the very difficult conditions continued to affect our performance* **2** (of pain or disease) to attack: *the virus can spread to affect the heart muscle* **3** to move someone emotionally: *the experience has affected him deeply*
WORD ORIGIN Latin *afficere*

affect[2] ❶ *vb* **1** to put on a show of: *he affects a certain disinterest* **2** to wear or use by preference: *he likes to be called Captain John and affects a nautical cap*
WORD ORIGIN Latin *affectare* to strive after

THESAURUS

recommending, counselling, consultative

advocate *vb* **1 = recommend**, support, champion, encourage, propose, favour, defend, promote, urge, advise, justify, endorse, campaign for, prescribe, speak for, uphold, press for, argue for, commend, plead for, espouse, countenance, hold a brief for *(informal)* **OPPOSITE:** oppose ▷ *n* **2 = supporter**, spokesman, champion, defender, speaker, pleader, campaigner, promoter, counsellor, backer, proponent, apostle, apologist, upholder, proposer **3 = lawyer**, attorney, solicitor, counsel **4** *(Scots law)* = barrister

affair *n* **1, 3 = matter**, thing, business, question, issue, happening, concern, event, subject, project, activity, incident, proceeding, circumstance, episode, topic, undertaking, transaction, occurrence **2 = relationship**, romance, intrigue, fling, liaison, flirtation, amour, dalliance

affect[1] *vb* **1 = influence**, involve, concern, impact, transform, alter, modify, change, manipulate, act on, sway, prevail over, bear upon, impinge upon **3 = emotionally move**, touch, upset, overcome, stir, disturb, perturb, impress on, tug at your heartstrings *(often facetious)*

affect[2] *vb* **1 = put on**, assume, adopt, pretend, imitate, simulate, contrive, aspire to, sham, counterfeit, feign

DICTIONARY

affectation *n* an attitude or manner put on to impress others
affected Ⓣ *adj* **1** behaving or speaking in a manner put on to impress others **2** pretended: *an affected indifference*
affecting *adj* arousing feelings of pity; moving
affection Ⓣ *n* **1** fondness or tenderness for a person or thing **2 affections** feelings of love; emotions: *I was angry with her for playing with their affections*
affectionate Ⓣ *adj* having or displaying tenderness, affection, or warmth **affectionately** *adv*
affectless *adj* **1** showing no emotion or concern for others **2** not causing any emotion: *an affectless novel*
affianced (af-**fie**-anst) *adj old-fashioned* engaged to be married
WORD ORIGIN Medieval Latin *affidare* to trust (oneself) to
affidavit (af-fid-**dave**-it) *n law* a written statement made under oath
WORD ORIGIN Medieval Latin, literally: he declares on oath
affiliate Ⓣ *vb* **-ating, -ated 1** (of a group) to link up with a larger group ▷ *n* **2** a person or organization that is affiliated with another **affiliation** *n*
WORD ORIGIN Medieval Latin *affiliatus* adopted as a son
affinity Ⓣ *n, pl* **-ties 1** a feeling of closeness to and understanding of a person **2** a close similarity in appearance, structure, or quality **3** a chemical attraction
WORD ORIGIN Latin *affinis* bordering on, related
affirm Ⓣ *vb* **1** to declare to be true **2** to state clearly one's support for (an idea or belief) **affirmation** *n*
WORD ORIGIN Latin *ad-* to + *firmare* to make firm
affirmative Ⓣ *adj* **1** indicating agreement: *an affirmative answer* ▷ *n* **2** a word or phrase indicating agreement, such as *yes*
affix *vb* **1** to attach or fasten ▷ *n* **2** a word or syllable added to a word to produce a derived or inflected form, such as *-ment* in *establishment*
WORD ORIGIN Medieval Latin *affixare*
afflict Ⓣ *vb* to cause someone suffering or unhappiness
WORD ORIGIN Latin *affligere* to knock against
affliction *n* **1** something that causes physical or mental suffering **2** a condition of great distress or suffering
affluent Ⓣ *adj* having plenty of money **affluence** *n*
WORD ORIGIN Latin *ad-* to + *fluere* to flow
affluent society *n* a society in which the material benefits of prosperity are widely available
afford Ⓣ *vb* **1 can afford** to be able to do or spare something without risking financial difficulties or undesirable consequences: *she can't afford to be choosy* **2** to give or supply: *afford me an opportunity to judge for myself* **affordable** *adj* **affordability** *n*
WORD ORIGIN Old English *geforthian* to further, promote
afforest *vb* to plant trees on **afforestation** *n*
WORD ORIGIN Medieval Latin *afforestare*
affray *n Brit, Austral & NZ* a noisy fight in a public place
WORD ORIGIN Vulgar Latin *exfridare* (unattested) to break the peace
affront *n* **1** a deliberate insult ▷ *vb* **2** to hurt someone's pride or dignity
WORD ORIGIN Old French *afronter* to strike in the face
afghan *n NZ* a type of biscuit
Afghan *adj* **1** of Afghanistan ▷ *n* **2** a person from Afghanistan **3** the language of Afghanistan
Afghan hound *n* a large slim dog with long silky hair
Afghani *n* **Jamal ad-Din al-** 1839–97, Iranian Muslim religious and political reformer; a proponent of Muslim unity, he resisted European interference in Muslim countries
aficionado (af-fish-yo-**nah**-do) *n, pl* **-dos** an enthusiastic fan of a sport or interest
WORD ORIGIN Spanish
afield *adv* **far afield** far away: *they used to travel as far afield as Hungary*
aflame *adv, adj* **1** in flames **2** deeply aroused: *his face was aflame with self-contempt and embarrassment*
afloat *adj* **1** floating **2** free of debt: *his goal is to keep the company afloat* **3** aboard ship ▷ *adv* **4** floating **5** free of debt **6** aboard ship; at sea
afoot *adj, adv* happening; in operation: *I had no suspicion of what was afoot*
afore *adv, prep, conj old-fashioned or dialect* before
aforementioned *adj* mentioned before
aforesaid *adj* referred to previously
aforethought *adj* premeditated: *malice aforethought*
a fortiori (eh for-tee-or-rye) *adv* for similar but more convincing reasons
WORD ORIGIN Latin
afraid Ⓣ *adj* **1** feeling fear or apprehension **2** regretful: *I'm afraid I lost my temper*
WORD ORIGIN Middle English *affraied*
afresh *adv* once more
African *adj* **1** of Africa ▷ *n* **2** a person from Africa
Africana *pl n* objects of cultural or historical interest from Africa
African-American *n* **1** an American

THESAURUS

affected *adj* **1, 2 = pretended**, artificial, contrived, put-on, assumed, mannered, studied, precious, stiff, simulated, mincing, sham, unnatural, pompous, pretentious, counterfeit, feigned, spurious, conceited, insincere, camp *(informal)*, la-di-da *(informal)*, arty-farty *(informal)*, phoney *or* phony *(informal)* **OPPOSITE:** genuine
affection *n* **1 = fondness**, liking, feeling, love, care, desire, passion, warmth, attachment, goodwill, devotion, kindness, inclination, tenderness, propensity, friendliness, amity, aroha (NZ)
affectionate *adj* **= fond**, loving, kind, caring, warm, friendly, attached, devoted, tender, doting, warm-hearted **OPPOSITE:** cool
affiliate *vb* **1 = associate**, unite, join, link, ally, combine, connect, incorporate, annex, confederate, amalgamate, band together
affinity *n* **1 = attraction**, liking, leaning, sympathy, inclination, rapport, fondness, partiality, aroha (NZ) **OPPOSITE:** hostility **2 = similarity**, relationship, relation, connection, alliance, correspondence, analogy, resemblance, closeness, likeness, compatibility, kinship **OPPOSITE:** difference
affirm *vb* **1 = declare**, state, maintain, swear, assert, testify, pronounce, certify, attest, avow, aver, asseverate, avouch **OPPOSITE:** deny **2 = confirm**, prove, sanction, endorse, ratify, verify, validate, bear out, substantiate, corroborate, authenticate **OPPOSITE:** refute
affirmative *adj* **1 = agreeing**, confirming, positive, approving, consenting, favourable, concurring, assenting, corroborative **OPPOSITE:** negative
afflict *vb* **= torment**, trouble, pain, hurt, wound, burden, distress, rack, try, plague, grieve, harass, ail, oppress, beset, smite
affluent *adj* **= wealthy**, rich, prosperous, loaded *(slang)*, well-off, opulent, well-heeled *(informal)*, well-to-do, moneyed, minted *(Brit slang)* **OPPOSITE:** poor
afford *vb* **2 = give**, offer, provide, produce, supply, grant, yield, render, furnish, bestow, impart
afraid *adj* **1 = scared**, frightened, nervous, anxious, terrified, shaken, alarmed, startled, suspicious, intimidated, fearful, cowardly, timid, apprehensive, petrified, panicky, panic-stricken, timorous, faint-hearted **OPPOSITE:** unafraid **2 = sorry**, apologetic, regretful, sad, distressed, unhappy **OPPOSITE:** pleased

DICTIONARY

a

of African descent ▹ *adj* **2** of African-Americans, their history, or their culture
Africander *n* a breed of humpbacked cattle originally from southern Africa
WORD ORIGIN Afrikaans *Afrikander*
African time *n S African slang* unpunctuality
African violet *n* a flowering house plant with pink or purple flowers and hairy leaves
Afrikaans *n* one of the official languages of South Africa, descended from Dutch
WORD ORIGIN Dutch
Afrikaner *n* a White South African whose native language is Afrikaans
Afro *n, pl* **-ros** a frizzy bushy hairstyle
Afro- *combining form* indicating Africa or African: *Afro-Caribbean*
Afro-American *n, adj* ▸ same as **African-American**
aft *adv, adj* at or towards the rear of a ship or aircraft
WORD ORIGIN shortened from ABAFT
after ⓣ *prep* **1** following in time or place **2** in pursuit of: *he was after my mother's jewellery* **3** concerning: *he asked after Laura* **4** considering: *you seem all right after what happened last night* **5** next in excellence or importance to **6** in imitation of; in the manner of **7** in accordance with: *a man after his own heart* **8** with the same name as: *the street is named after the designer of the church* **9** *US* past (the hour of): *fifteen after twelve* **10 after all a** in spite of everything: *I was, after all, a suspect* **b** in spite of expectations or efforts **11 after you** please go before me ▹ *adv* **12** at a later time; afterwards ▹ *conj* **13** at a time later than the time when: *she arrived after the reading had begun* ▹ *adj* **14** *naut* further aft: *the after cabin*
WORD ORIGIN Old English *æfter*
afterbirth *n* the placenta and fetal membranes expelled from the mother's womb after childbirth
aftercare *n* **1** the help and support given to a person discharged from a hospital or prison **2** the regular care required to keep something in good condition
afterdamp *n* a poisonous gas formed after the explosion of firedamp in a coal mine
aftereffect *n* any result occurring some time after its cause
afterglow *n* **1** the glow left after the source of a light has disappeared, for example after sunset **2** a pleasant feeling remaining after an enjoyable experience
afterlife *n* life after death
aftermath ⓣ *n* effects or results of an event considered collectively: *the aftermath of the weekend violence*
WORD ORIGIN *after* + Old English *mæth* a mowing
afternoon *n* the period between noon and evening
afterpains *pl n* pains caused by contraction of a woman's womb after childbirth
afters *n informal* the sweet course of a meal
aftersales *n* any customer service that follows the sale of a product
after-sales *adj*
aftershave *n* a scented lotion applied to a man's face after shaving
aftershock *n* one of a series of minor tremors occurring after the main shock of an earthquake
aftertaste *n* a taste that lingers on after eating or drinking
afterthought *n* **1** something thought of after the opportunity to use it has passed **2** an addition to something already completed
afterwards *or* **afterward** *adv* later
WORD ORIGIN Old English *æfterweard*
Ag *chem* silver
WORD ORIGIN Latin *argentum*
again ⓣ *adv* **1** another or a second time: *I want to look at that atlas again* **2** once more in a previously experienced state or condition: *he pictured her again as she used to be* **3** in addition to the original amount: *twice as much again* **4** on the other hand **5** moreover or furthermore: *she is beautiful and, again, intelligent* **6 again and again** continually or repeatedly
WORD ORIGIN Old English *ongegn* opposite to
against ⓣ *prep* **1** standing or leaning beside: *he leaned against a tree* **2** opposed to or in disagreement with **3** in contrast to: *his complexion was a sickly white against the black stubble of his beard* **4** coming in contact with: *rain rattled against the window* **5** having an unfavourable effect on: *the system works against you when you don't have money* **6** as a protection from: *a safeguard against bacteria* **7** in exchange for or in return for: *the dollar has gained very slightly against the yen* **8 as against** as opposed to; as compared with
WORD ORIGIN Middle English *ageines*
agape *adj* **1** (of the mouth) wide open **2** (of a person) very surprised
agar (ayg-ar) *or* **agar-agar** *n* a jelly-like substance obtained from seaweed and used as a thickener in food
WORD ORIGIN Malay
agaric *n* any fungus with gills on the underside of the cap, such as a mushroom
WORD ORIGIN Greek *agarikon*
Agassi *n* **Andre** born 1970, US tennis player: won the Wimbledon men's singles in 1992 and the US Open in 1994 and 1999
Agassiz *n* **Jean Louis Rodolphe** 1807–73, Swiss natural historian and geologist, settled in the US after 1846
agate (ag-git) *n* a hard semiprecious form of quartz with striped colouring
WORD ORIGIN Greek *akhatēs*
Agate *n* **James** (**Evershed**) 1877–1947, British theatre critic; drama critic for *The Sunday Times* (1923–47) and author of a nine-volume diary *Ego* (1935–49)
agave (a-gave-vee) *n* a tropical American plant with tall flower stalks and thick leaves
WORD ORIGIN Greek *agauos* illustrious
age ⓣ *n* **1** the length of time that a person or thing has existed **2** a period or state of human life **3** the latter part of human life **4** a period of history marked by some feature **5 ages** *informal* a long time **6 come of age** to become legally responsible for one's actions (usually at 18 years) ▹ *vb* **ageing** *or* **aging, aged 7** to become old: *skin type changes as one ages* **8** to appear or cause to appear older: *the years had not aged her in any way*
WORD ORIGIN Latin *aetas*
aged ⓣ *adj* **1** (ay-jid) advanced in years; old **2** (rhymes with **raged**) being at the age of: *a girl aged thirteen is missing*
Agee *n* **James** 1909–55, US novelist, poet, and film critic. His works include the autobiographical novel *A Death in the Family* (1957)
ageing *or* **aging** *n* **1** the fact or process of growing old ▹ *adj* **2** becoming or appearing older
ageism *or* **agism** *n* discrimination against people on the grounds of age
ageist *or* **agist** *n*
ageless *adj* **1** apparently never growing old **2** seeming to have existed for ever; eternal: *an ageless profession*

THESAURUS

after *prep* **1 = at the end of**, following, subsequent to **OPPOSITE:** before ▹ *adv* **12 = following**, later, next, succeeding, afterwards, subsequently, thereafter
aftermath *n* **= effects**, end, results, wake, consequences, outcome, sequel, end result, upshot, aftereffects
again *adv* **1, 2 = once more**, another time, anew, afresh **5 = also**, in addition, moreover, besides, furthermore
against *prep* **1, 4 = beside**, on, up against, in contact with, abutting, close up to **2 = opposed to**, anti (*informal*), opposing, counter, contra (*informal*), hostile to, in opposition to, averse to, opposite to, not in accord with
age *n* **1 = years**, days, generation,

DICTIONARY

agency ❶ *n, pl* **-cies 1** an organization providing a specific service: *an advertising agency* **2** the business or functions of an agent **3** action or power by which something happens: *the intervention of a human agency in the sequence of events*
WORD ORIGIN Latin *agere* to do

agenda ❶ *n* **1** a schedule or list of items to be attended to, for example at a meeting **2** *US & Canad* an appointment diary with room for storing addresses, telephone numbers, etc.
WORD ORIGIN Latin: things to be done

agent ❶ *n* **1** a person who arranges business for other people, esp. for actors or singers **2** a spy **3** a substance which causes change in other substances: *an emulsifying agent* **4** someone or something which causes an effect: *the agent of change*

agent noun *n* a noun representing a person or thing performing the action of a verb: *performer, suspender*

agent provocateur (azh-on prov-vok-at-**tur**) *n, pl* **agents provocateurs** (azh-on prov-vok-at-**tur**) a person employed by the authorities to tempt people to commit illegal acts and so be discredited or punished
WORD ORIGIN French

age-old *adj* very old; ancient

agglomerate *vb* **-ating, -ated 1** to form or be formed into a mass ▷*n* **2** a volcanic rock consisting of fused angular fragments of rock
WORD ORIGIN Latin *agglomerare*

agglomeration *n* a confused mass or cluster

agglutinate *vb* **-nating, -nated** to stick as if with glue **agglutination** *n*
WORD ORIGIN Latin *agglutinare*

aggrandize *or* **-dise** *vb* **-dizing, -dized** *or* **-dising, -dised** to make greater in size, power, or rank **aggrandizement** *or* **-disement** *n*
WORD ORIGIN Old French *aggrandir*

aggravate ❶ *vb* **-vating, -vated 1** to make (a disease, situation or problem) worse **2** *informal* to annoy **aggravating** *adj* **aggravation** *n*
WORD ORIGIN Latin *aggravare* to make heavier

aggravated *adj law* (of a criminal offence) made more serious by its circumstances

aggregate ❶ *n* **1** an amount or total formed from separate units **2** *geol* a rock, such as granite, consisting of a mixture of minerals **3** the sand and stone mixed with cement and water to make concrete ▷*adj* **4** formed of separate units collected into a whole ▷*vb* **-gating, -gated 5** to combine or be combined into a whole **6** to amount to (a particular number) **aggregation** *n*
WORD ORIGIN Latin *aggregare* to add to a flock or herd

aggression ❶ *n* **1** violent and hostile behaviour **2** an unprovoked attack **aggressor** *n*
WORD ORIGIN Latin *aggredi* to attack

aggressive ❶ *adj* **1** full of anger or hostility **2** forceful or determined: *an aggressive salesman* **aggressively** *adv* **aggressiveness** *n*

aggrieved *adj* upset and angry
WORD ORIGIN Latin *aggravare* to aggravate

aggro *n Brit, Austral & NZ slang* aggressive behaviour
WORD ORIGIN from *aggravation*

aghast *adj* overcome with amazement or horror
WORD ORIGIN Old English *gæstan* to frighten

agile *adj* **1** quick in movement; nimble **2** mentally quick or acute **agility** *n*
WORD ORIGIN Latin *agilis*

agin *prep dialect* against or opposed to: *he gave the usual line of talk agin the government*
WORD ORIGIN obsolete *again* against

agitate ❶ *vb* **-tating, -tated 1** to excite, disturb, or trouble **2** to shake or stir (a liquid) **3** to attempt to stir up public opinion for or against something **agitated** *adj* **agitatedly** *adv* **agitation** *n* **agitator** *n*
WORD ORIGIN Latin *agitare*

agitprop *n* political agitation and propaganda
WORD ORIGIN Russian *Agitpropbyuro*

THESAURUS

lifetime, stage of life, length of life, length of existence **3 = old age**, experience, maturity, completion, seniority, fullness, majority, maturation, senility, decline, advancing years, declining years, senescence, full growth, matureness **OPPOSITE:** youth **4 = time**, day(s), period, generation, era, epoch ▷*vb* **7 = grow old**, decline, weather, fade, deteriorate, wither **8 = mature**, season, condition, soften, mellow, ripen

aged *adj* **1 = old**, getting on, grey, ancient, antique, elderly, past it *(informal)*, age-old, antiquated, hoary, superannuated, senescent, cobwebby **OPPOSITE:** young

agency *n* **1 = business**, company, office, firm, department, organization, enterprise, establishment, bureau **3 = medium**, work, means, force, power, action, operation, activity, influence, vehicle, instrument, intervention, mechanism, efficiency, mediation, auspices, intercession, instrumentality

agenda *n* **1 = programme**, list, plan, schedule, diary, calendar, timetable

agent *n* **1 = representative**, deputy, substitute, advocate, rep *(informal)*, broker, delegate, factor, negotiator, envoy, trustee, proxy, surrogate, go-between, emissary **3 = force**, means, power, cause, instrument **4 = author**, officer, worker, actor, vehicle, instrument, operator, performer, operative, catalyst, executor, doer, perpetuator

aggravate *vb* **1 = make worse**, exaggerate, intensify, worsen, heighten, exacerbate, magnify, inflame, increase, add insult to injury, fan the flames of **OPPOSITE:** improve **2** *(informal)* **= annoy**, bother, provoke, needle *(informal)*, irritate, tease, hassle *(informal)*, gall, exasperate, nettle, pester, vex, irk, get under your skin *(informal)*, get on your nerves *(informal)*, nark *(Brit, Austral & NZ slang)*, get up your nose *(informal)*, be on your back *(slang)*, rub (someone) up the wrong way *(informal)*, get in your hair *(informal)*, get on your wick *(Brit slang)*, hack you off *(informal)* **OPPOSITE:** please

aggregate *n* **1 = total**, body, whole, amount, collection, mass, sum, combination, pile, mixture, bulk, lump, heap, accumulation, assemblage, agglomeration ▷*adj* **4 = collective**, added, mixed, combined, collected, corporate, assembled, accumulated, composite, cumulative ▷*vb* **5 = combine**, mix, collect, assemble, heap, accumulate, pile, amass

aggression *n* **1 = hostility**, malice, antagonism, antipathy, aggressiveness, ill will, belligerence, destructiveness, malevolence, pugnacity **2 = attack**, campaign, injury, assault, offence, raid, invasion, offensive, onslaught, foray, encroachment

aggressive *adj* **1 = hostile**, offensive, destructive, belligerent, unkind, unfriendly, malevolent, contrary, antagonistic, pugnacious, bellicose, quarrelsome, aggers *(Austral slang)*, biffo *(Austral slang)*, inimical, rancorous, ill-disposed **OPPOSITE:** friendly **2 = forceful**, powerful, convincing, effective, enterprising, dynamic, bold, militant, pushing, vigorous, energetic, persuasive, assertive, zealous, pushy *(informal)*, in-your-face *(slang)* **OPPOSITE:** submissive

agitate *vb* **1 = upset**, worry, trouble, disturb, excite, alarm, stimulate, distract, rouse, ruffle, inflame, incite, unnerve, disconcert, disquiet, fluster, perturb, faze, work someone up, give someone grief *(Brit & S African)* **OPPOSITE:** calm

DICTIONARY

a

aglitter *adj* sparkling or glittering
aglow *adj* glowing
aglu *or* **agloo** *n Canad* a breathing hole made in ice by a seal
WORD ORIGIN Inuit
AGM annual general meeting
Agnes *n* **Saint** ?292–?304 AD, Christian child martyr under Diocletian. Feast day: Jan 21
Agnesi *n* **Maria Gaetana** 1718–99, Italian mathematician and philosopher, noted for her work on differential calculus ▸ See **witch of Agnesi**
Agnew *n* **Spiro Theodore** 1918–96, US Republican politician; vice president (1969–73)
Agnon *n* **Shmuel Yosef,** real name Samuel Josef Czaczkes. 1888–1970, Israeli novelist, born in Austria-Hungary. His works, which treat contemporary Jewish themes, include *The Day Before Yesterday* (1945). Nobel prize for literature 1966
agnostic *n* **1** a person who believes that it is impossible to know whether God exists **2** a person who claims that the answer to some specific question cannot be known with certainty ▹*adj* **3** of or relating to agnostics **agnosticism** *n*
WORD ORIGIN A- + *gnostic* having knowledge
ago *adv* in the past: *fifty years ago*
WORD ORIGIN Old English *āgān* to pass away
agog *adj* eager or curious: *Marcia would be agog to hear his news*
WORD ORIGIN Old French *en gogues* in merriments
agonize *or* **-nise** *vb* **-nizing, -nized** *or* **-nising, -nised 1** to worry greatly **2** to suffer agony **agonizing** *or* **-nising** *adj* **agonizingly** *or* **-nisingly** *adv*
agony ❶ *n, pl* **-nies** acute physical or mental pain
WORD ORIGIN Greek *agōnia* struggle
agony aunt *n* a person who replies to readers' letters in an agony column
agony column *n* a newspaper or magazine feature offering advice on readers' personal problems
agoraphobia *n* a pathological fear of being in public places **agoraphobic** *adj, n*
WORD ORIGIN Greek *agora* marketplace + *phobos* fear
Agostini *n* **Giacomo** born 1944, Italian racing motorcyclist: world champion (500 cc. class) 1966–72, 1975; (350 cc. class) 1968–74
Agostino di Duccio *n* 1415–81, Italian sculptor, noted for his carved marble panels in the interior of the Tempio Malatestiano at Rimini
AGR advanced gas-cooled reactor
agrarian *adj* of or relating to land or agriculture **agrarianism** *n*
WORD ORIGIN Latin *ager* field
agree ❶ *vb* **agreeing, agreed 1** to be of the same opinion **2** to give assent; consent **3** to be consistent **4 agree on** to reach a joint decision about: *the ministers agreed on a strategy* **5 agree with** to be agreeable or suitable to (one's health or appearance): *marriage and motherhood must agree with you* **6** to concede: *the unions have agreed that the results of appraisal are relevant* **7** *grammar* to be the same in number, gender, and case as a connected word
WORD ORIGIN Old French *a gre* at will
agreeable *adj* **1** pleasant and enjoyable **2** prepared to consent: *I cannot say that she was agreeable to the project but she was resigned* **agreeably** *adv*
agreement ❶ *n* **1** the act or state of agreeing **2** a legally enforceable contract
agribusiness *n* **1** the use of intensive methods to increase profits in agriculture **2** all of the businesses that process, distribute, and support farm products
WORD ORIGIN *agri(culture) + business*
Agricola *n* **Gnaeus Julius** 40–93 AD, Roman general; governor of Britain who advanced Roman rule north to the Firth of Forth
agriculture ❶ *n* the rearing of crops and livestock; farming **agricultural** *adj* **agriculturalist** *n*
WORD ORIGIN Latin *ager* field + *cultura* cultivation
agrimony *n* a plant with small yellow flowers and bitter-tasting bristly fruits
WORD ORIGIN Greek *argemōnē* poppy
Agrippa *n* **Marcus Vipsanius** 63–12 BC, Roman general: chief adviser and later son-in-law of Augustus
Agrippina *n* **1** called *the Elder. c.* 14 BC–33 AD, Roman matron: granddaughter of Augustus, wife of Germanicus, mother of Caligula and Agrippina the Younger **2** called *the Younger.* 15–59 AD, mother of Nero, who put her to death after he became emperor
agrochemical *n* a chemical used in agriculture
agrodolce (ag-gro-**dole**-chay) *n* an Italian sweet-and-sour sauce
WORD ORIGIN Italian
agronomy (ag-**ron**-om-mee) *n* the science of land cultivation, soil management, and crop production **agronomist** *n*
WORD ORIGIN Greek *agros* field + *nemein* to manage
aground *adv* onto the bottom of shallow water: *they felt a jolt as the ship ran aground*
ague (aig-yew) *n* **1** *old-fashioned* malarial fever with shivering **2** a fit of shivering
WORD ORIGIN Old French *(fievre) ague* acute fever
ah *interj* an exclamation expressing pleasure, pain, sympathy, etc.
aha *interj* an exclamation expressing triumph, surprise, etc.
ahead ❶ *adv* **1** at or in the front; before **2** forwards: *go straight ahead* **3 get ahead** to achieve success: *I was young and hungry to get ahead* ▹*adj* **4** in a leading position: *he is ahead in the polls*
ahem *interj* a clearing of the throat, used to attract attention or express doubt
Ahern *n* **Bertie** born 1951, Irish politician; leader of the Fianna Fáil party from 1994; prime minister of the Republic of Ireland from 1997
ahi *n* ▸ another name for **yellowfin tuna**
WORD ORIGIN Hawaiian
ahoy *interj naut* a shout made to call a ship or to attract attention

THESAURUS

2 = stir, beat, mix, shake, disturb, toss, rouse, churn
agony *n* **= suffering**, pain, distress, misery, torture, discomfort, torment, hardship, woe, anguish, pangs, affliction, throes
agree *vb* **1 = concur**, engage, be as one, sympathize, assent, see eye to eye, be of the same opinion, be of the same mind, be down with *(informal)*
OPPOSITE: disagree
3 = correspond, match, accord, answer, fit, suit, square, coincide, tally, conform, chime, harmonize
5 agree with someone = suit, get on, be good for, befit
agreement *n* **1 = concurrence**, harmony, compliance, union, agreeing, concession, consent, unison, assent, concord, acquiescence
OPPOSITE: disagreement
2 = treaty, contract, bond, arrangement, alliance, deal *(informal)*, understanding, settlement, bargain, pact, compact, covenant, entente
agriculture *n* **= farming**, culture, cultivation, husbandry, tillage, agronomy, agronomics
ahead *adv* **1, 2 = in front**, on, forwards, in advance, onwards, towards the front, frontwards
aid *n* **1 = help**, backing, support, benefit, favour, relief, promotion, assistance, encouragement, helping hand, succour
OPPOSITE: hindrance
▹*vb* **3 = help**, second, support, serve, sustain, assist, relieve, avail, subsidize, abet, succour, be of service to, lend a hand to, give a leg up to *(informal)* **OPPOSITE:** hinder
aide *n* **= assistant**, supporter, deputy, attendant, helper, henchman,

AI 1 artificial insemination 2 artificial intelligence

aid ❶ *n* 1 money, equipment, or services provided for people in need; assistance 2 a person or device that helps or assists ▷*vb* 3 to help financially or in other ways
WORD ORIGIN Latin *adjutare* to help

Aid *or* **-aid** *n combining form* denoting a charitable organization that raises money for a particular cause: *Band Aid*

AID formerly, artificial insemination by donor

Aidan *n* **Saint** died 651 AD, Irish missionary in Northumbria, who founded the monastery at Lindisfarne (635). Feast day: Aug 31

aide ❶ *n* an assistant: *a senior aide to the Prime Minister*

aide-de-camp (aid-de-**kom**) *n, pl* **aides-de-camp** (aid-de-**kom**) a military officer serving as personal assistant to a senior
WORD ORIGIN French: camp assistant

AIDS acquired immunodeficiency syndrome: a viral disease that destroys the body's ability to fight infection

AIH artificial insemination by husband

Aiken *n* 1 **Conrad** (**Potter**) 1889–1973, US poet, short-story writer, and critic. His works include *Collected Poems* (1953) and the novel *Blue Voyage* (1927) 2 **Howard Hathaway** 1900–73, US mathematician; pioneered the construction of electronic computers

ail *vb literary* 1 to trouble or afflict 2 to feel unwell
WORD ORIGIN Old English *eglan*

aileron (**ale**-er-on) *n* a hinged flap on the back of an aircraft wing which controls rolling
WORD ORIGIN French *aile* wing

ailing ❶ *adj* unwell or unsuccessful over a long period: *an ailing company*

ailment ❶ *n* a slight illness

aim ❶ *vb* 1 to point (a weapon or missile) or direct (a blow or remark) at a particular person or object 2 to propose or intend: *they aim to provide full and equal rights to all groups* ▷*n* 3 the action of directing something at an object 4 intention or purpose 5 **take aim** to point a weapon or missile at a person or object
WORD ORIGIN Latin *aestimare* to estimate

aimless *adj* having no purpose or direction **aimlessly** *adv*

ain't *not standard* am not, is not, are not, have not, *or* has not: *it ain't fair*

air ❶ *n* 1 the mixture of gases that forms the earth's atmosphere. It consists chiefly of nitrogen, oxygen, argon, and carbon dioxide 2 the space above and around the earth; sky ▸Related adjective: **aerial** 3 a distinctive quality, appearance, or manner: *I thought he had an air of elegance and celebrity about him* 4 a simple tune 5 transportation in aircraft: *I went off to Italy by air and train* 6 **in the air** in circulation; current: *a sense of expectation is in the air* 7 **into thin air** leaving no trace behind 8 **on the air** in the act of broadcasting on radio or television 9 **up in the air** uncertain ▷*vb* 10 to make known publicly: *these issues will be aired at a ministerial meeting* 11 to expose to air to dry or ventilate 12 (of a television or radio programme) to be broadcast ▸See also **airs**
WORD ORIGIN Greek *aēr*

airbag *n* a safety device in a car, consisting of a bag that inflates automatically in an accident to protect the driver or passenger

air base *n* a centre from which military aircraft operate

airborne ❶ *adj* 1 carried by air 2 (of aircraft) flying; in the air

air brake *n* a brake in heavy vehicles that is operated by compressed air

airbrush *n* 1 an atomizer which sprays paint by means of compressed air ▷*vb* 2 to paint using an airbrush 3 to improve the image of (a person or thing) by hiding defects beneath a bland exterior

air chief marshal *n* a very senior officer in an air force

air commodore *n* a senior officer in an air force

air conditioning *n* a system for controlling the temperature and humidity of the air in a building **air-conditioned** *adj* **air conditioner** *n*

aircraft *n, pl* **-craft** any machine capable of flying, such as a glider or aeroplane

aircraft carrier *n* a warship with a long flat deck for the launching and landing of aircraft

aircraftman *n, pl* **-men** a serviceman of the most junior rank in an air force **aircraftwoman** *fem n*

air cushion *n* 1 an inflatable cushion 2 the pocket of air that supports a hovercraft

Airedale *n* a large terrier with rough tan-coloured hair and a black patch covering most of the back

airfield *n* a place where aircraft can land and take off

air force *n* the branch of a nation's armed services that is responsible for air warfare

air gun *n* a gun fired by means of compressed air

airhead *n slang* a person who is stupid or incapable of serious thought

air hostess *n chiefly Brit* a female flight attendant on an airline

airily *adv* in a light-hearted and casual manner

airing ❶ *n* 1 exposure to air or warmth for drying or ventilation 2 exposure to public debate: *both these notions got an airing during the campaign*

airing cupboard *n* a heated cupboard in which laundry is aired and kept dry

airless *adj* lacking fresh air; stuffy

air letter *n* ▸same as **aerogram**

airlift *n* 1 the transportation by air of troops or cargo when other routes are blocked ▷*vb* 2 to transport by an airlift

airline *n* an organization that provides scheduled flights for passengers or cargo

airliner *n* a large passenger aircraft

airlock *n* 1 a bubble of air blocking the flow of liquid in a pipe 2 an airtight chamber between places that do not have the same air pressure, such as in a spacecraft or submarine

THESAURUS

right-hand man, adjutant, second, helpmate, coadjutor *(rare)*

ailing *adj* **a = weak,** failing, poor, flawed, unstable, feeble, unsatisfactory, deficient, unsound **b = ill,** suffering, poorly, diseased, sick, weak, crook *(Austral & NZ informal)*, feeble, invalid, debilitated, sickly, unwell, infirm, off colour, under the weather *(informal)*, indisposed

ailment *n* **= illness,** disease, complaint, disorder, sickness, affliction, malady, infirmity, lurgy *(informal)*

aim *vb* **1 = point,** level, train, direct, sight, take aim (at) ▷*n* **4 = intention,** end, point, plan, course, mark, goal, design, target, wish, scheme, purpose, direction, desire, object, objective, ambition, intent, aspiration, Holy Grail *(informal)*

air *n* **1, 2 = atmosphere,** sky, heavens, aerosphere **3 = manner,** feeling, effect, style, quality, character, bearing, appearance, look, aspect, atmosphere, tone, mood, impression, flavour, aura, ambience, demeanour, vibe *(slang)* **4 = tune,** song, theme, melody, strain, lay, aria ▷*vb* **10 = publicize,** tell, reveal, exhibit, communicate, voice, express, display, declare, expose, disclose, proclaim, utter, circulate, make public, divulge, disseminate, ventilate, make known, give vent to, take the wraps off

airborne *adj* **1 = floating,** wind-borne **2 = flying,** floating, soaring, in the air, hovering, gliding, in flight, on the wing, wind-borne, volitant

airing *n* **1 = ventilation,** drying, freshening, aeration **2 = exposure,** display, expression, publicity, vent, utterance, dissemination

DICTIONARY

a

airmail *n* **1** the system of sending mail by aircraft **2** mail sent by aircraft
airman *or fem* **airwoman** *n, pl* **-men** *or* **-women** a person serving in an air force
air marshal *n* **1** a senior Royal Air Force officer of equivalent rank to a vice admiral in the Royal Navy **2** a Royal New Zealand Air Force officer of the highest rank when chief of defence forces
Air Miles *pl n Brit* points awarded on buying flight tickets and certain other products which can be used to pay for other flights
airplane ❶ *n US & Canad* an aeroplane
airplay *n* the broadcast performances of a record on radio
air pocket *n* a small descending air current that causes an aircraft to lose height suddenly
airport *n* a landing and taking-off area for civil aircraft, with facilities for aircraft maintenance and passenger arrival and departure
air pump *n* a device for pumping air into or out of something
air rage *n* aggressive behaviour by an airline passenger that endangers the safety of the crew and other passengers
air raid *n* an attack by enemy aircraft in which bombs are dropped
air rifle *n* a rifle fired by means of compressed air
airs ❶ *pl n* manners put on to impress people: *we're poor and we never put on airs*
airship *n* a lighter-than-air self-propelled aircraft
airsick *adj* nauseated from travelling in an aircraft
airside *n* the part of an airport nearest the aircraft
airspace *n* the atmosphere above a particular country, regarded as its territory
airspeed *n* the speed of an aircraft relative to the air in which it moves
airstrip *n* a cleared area for the landing and taking-off of aircraft
air terminal *n* a building in a city from which air passengers are transported to an airport
airtight *adj* **1** sealed so that air cannot enter **2** having no weak points: *your reasoning is airtight and your evidence sound*
airtime *n* the time allocated to a particular programme, topic, or type of material on radio or television
air vice-marshal *n* a senior officer in an air force
airwaves *pl n informal* radio waves used in radio and television broadcasting
airway *n* an air route used regularly by aircraft
airworthy *adj* (of an aircraft) safe to fly **airworthiness** *n*
airy *adj* **airier, airiest** **1** spacious and well ventilated **2** light-hearted and casual **3** having little basis in reality; fanciful: *airy assurances*
Airy *n* Sir **George Biddell** 1801–92, British astronomer, noted for his estimate of the earth's density from gravity measurements in mines; astronomer royal (1835–81)
Aisha *or* **Ayesha** *n* ?613–678 AD, the favourite wife of Mohammed; daughter of Abu Bekr
aisle ❶ (rhymes with **mile**) *n* a passageway separating seating areas in a church, theatre, or cinema, or separating rows of shelves in a supermarket
WORD ORIGIN Latin *ala* wing
aitchbone *n* a cut of beef from the rump bone
WORD ORIGIN Middle English *nache-bone*
Aitken *n* **1 Robert Grant** 1864–1951, US astronomer who discovered over three thousand double stars **2 William Maxwell** ▸ See **Beaverbrook**
ajar *adj, adv* (of a door) slightly open
WORD ORIGIN Old English *cierran* to turn
AK Alaska
AK-47 *n trademark* ▸ same as **Kalashnikov**
Akhmatova *n* **Anna** pseudonym of *Anna Gorenko*. 1889–1966, Russian poet: noted for her concise and intensely personal lyrics
akimbo *adv* (**with**) **arms akimbo** with hands on hips and elbows turned outwards
WORD ORIGIN Middle English *in kenebowe* in keen (ie sharp) bow
akin *adj* **akin to** similar or very close to: *the technique is akin to impressionist painting*
Al *chem* aluminium
AL Alabama
à la *prep* in the manner or style of: *laced with Gothic allusion à la David Lynch*
WORD ORIGIN French
alabaster *n* a kind of white stone used for making statues and vases
WORD ORIGIN Greek *alabastros*
à la carte *adj, adv* (of a menu) having dishes individually priced
WORD ORIGIN French
alacrity *n* speed or eagerness: *I accepted the invitation with alacrity*
WORD ORIGIN Latin *alacer* lively
Alagna *n* **Roberto** born 1963, Italian opera singer, born in France; a lyric tenor, he is married to the soprano Angela Gheorghiu
Alain-Fournier *n* real name *Henri-Alban Fournier*. 1886–1914, French novelist; author of *Le Grand Meaulnes* (1913; translated as *The Lost Domain*, 1959)
à la mode *adj* fashionable
WORD ORIGIN French
Alanbrooke *n* **Alan Francis Brooke**, 1st Viscount. 1883–1963, British field marshal; chief of Imperial General Staff (1941–46)
Alarcón *n* **Pedro Antonio de** 1833–91, Spanish novelist and short-story writer, noted for his humorous sketches of rural life, esp. in *The Three-Cornered Hat* (1874)
Alaric *n* ?370–410 AD, king of the Visigoths, who served under the Roman emperor Theodosius I but later invaded Greece and Italy, capturing Rome in 410
alarm ❶ *n* **1** fear aroused by awareness of danger **2** a noise warning of danger: *there had been no time to put on life jackets or to sound the alarm* **3** a device that transmits a warning **4** ▸ short for **alarm clock** ▹ *vb* **5** to fill with fear **6** to fit or activate a burglar alarm on (a house, car, etc.) **alarming** *adj*
WORD ORIGIN Old Italian *all'arme* to arms
alarm clock *n* a clock that sounds at a set time to wake a person up
alarmist *n* **1** a person who alarms others needlessly ▹ *adj* **2** causing needless alarm
alas *adv* **1** unfortunately or regrettably: *the answer, alas, is that they cannot get any for the moment* ▹ *interj* **2** *old-fashioned* an exclamation of grief or alarm
WORD ORIGIN Old French *ha las!*
alb *n* a long white linen robe worn by a Christian priest
WORD ORIGIN Latin *albus* white
Alba *n* **Duke of Alba** ▸ See **Alva**
albacore *n* a tuna found in warm seas which is valued as a food fish
WORD ORIGIN Arabic *al-bakrah*
Alban *n* **Saint** 3rd century AD, the first English martyr. He was beheaded by the Romans on the site on which St Alban's Abbey now stands, for admitting his conversion to Christianity. Feast day: June 17
Albanian *adj* **1** of Albania ▹ *n* **2** a person from Albania **3** the language of Albania
albatross *n* **1** a large sea bird with

THESAURUS

airplane *n* **= plane**, aircraft, jet, aeroplane, airliner, kite *(Brit slang)*, flying machine
airs *pl n* **= affectation**, arrogance, pretensions, pomposity, swank *(informal)*, hauteur, haughtiness, superciliousness, affectedness
aisle *n* **= passageway**, path, lane, passage, corridor, alley, gangway
alarm *n* **1 = fear**, horror, panic, anxiety, distress, terror, dread, dismay, fright, unease, apprehension, nervousness, consternation, trepidation, uneasiness **OPPOSITE:** calmness

DICTIONARY

very long wings **2** *golf* a score of three strokes under par for a hole
WORD ORIGIN Portuguese *alcatraz* pelican

Albee *n* **Edward** born 1928, US dramatist. His plays include *Who's Afraid of Virginia Woolf?* (1962), *Seascape* (1975), *Marriage Play* (1986), *Three Tall Women* (1990), and *Goat* (2004)

albeit *conj* even though: *these effects occur, albeit to a lesser degree*
WORD ORIGIN Middle English *al be it* although it be (that)

Albéniz *n* **Isaac** 1860–1909, Spanish composer; noted for piano pieces inspired by folk music, such as the suite *Iberia*

Albers *n* **Josef** 1888–1976, US painter, designer, and poet, born in Germany. His works include a series of abstract paintings entitled *Homage to the Square*

Alberti *n* **Leon Battista** 1404–72, Italian Renaissance architect, painter, writer, and musician; among his architectural designs are the façades of Sta. Maria Novella at Florence and S. Francesco at Rimini

Albert I *n* **1** *c.* 1255–1308, king of Germany (1298–1308) **2** 1875–1934, king of the Belgians (1909–34) **3** called *Albert the Bear. c.* 1100–70. German military leader: first margrave of Brandenburg

Albert II *n* full name *Albert Felix Humbert Theodore Christian Eugene Marie.* born 1934, king of Belgium from 1993

Albertus Magnus *n* **Saint** original name *Albert, Count von Böllstadt.* ?1193–1280, German scholastic philosopher; teacher of Thomas Aquinas and commentator on Aristotle. Feast day: Nov 15

albino *n, pl* **-nos** a person or animal with white or almost white hair and skin and pinkish eyes **albinism** *n*
WORD ORIGIN Latin *albus* white

Albinoni *n* **Tomaso** 1671–1750, Italian composer and violinist. He wrote concertos and over 50 operas

Albinus *n* ▸ another name for **Alcuin**

Albion *n* *poetic* Britain or England
WORD ORIGIN Latin

Alboin *n* died 573 AD, king of the Lombards (565–73); conqueror of N Italy

album *n* **1** a book with blank pages, for keeping photographs or stamps in **2** a long-playing record
WORD ORIGIN Latin: blank tablet

albumen *n* **1** egg white **2** *biochem* ▸ same as **albumin**
WORD ORIGIN Latin *albus* white

albumin *or* **albumen** *n* *biochem* a water-soluble protein found in blood plasma, egg white, milk, and muscle

Albuquerque[1] *n* a city in central New Mexico, on the Rio Grande. Pop: 471 856 (2003 est)

Albuquerque[2] *n* **Afonso de** 1453–1515, Portuguese navigator who established Portuguese colonies in the East by conquering Goa, Ceylon, Malacca, and Ormuz

Alcaeus *n* 7th century BC, Greek lyric poet who wrote hymns, love songs, and political odes

alchemy *n* a medieval form of chemistry concerned with trying to change base metals into gold and to find an elixir to prolong life indefinitely **alchemist** *n*
WORD ORIGIN Arabic *al* the + *kīmiyā'* transmutation

Alcman *n* 7th century BC, Greek lyric poet

Alcock *n* Sir **John William** 1892–1919, English aviator who with A.W. Brown made the first nonstop flight across the Atlantic (1919)

alcohol *n* **1** a colourless flammable liquid present in intoxicating drinks **2** intoxicating drinks generally
WORD ORIGIN Arabic *al-kuhl* powdered antimony

alcohol-free *adj* **1** (of beer or wine) containing only a trace of alcohol **2** (of a period of time) during which no alcohol is taken: *an alcohol-free evening*

alcoholic ❶ *n* **1** a person who is addicted to alcohol ▹ *adj* **2** of or relating to alcohol

alcoholism *n* a condition in which dependence on alcohol harms a person's health and everyday life

alcopop *n* *informal* an alcoholic drink that tastes like a soft drink
WORD ORIGIN ALCO(HOL) + POP[1] (sense 9)

alcove *n* a recess in the wall of a room
WORD ORIGIN Arabic *al-qubbah* the vault

Alcuin *or* **Albinus** *n* 735–804 AD, English scholar and theologian; friend and adviser of Charlemagne

aldehyde *n* *chem* any organic compound containing the group –CHO, derived from alcohol by oxidation
WORD ORIGIN New Latin *al(cohol) dehyd(rogenatum)* dehydrogenated alcohol

alder *n* a tree with toothed leaves and conelike fruits, often found in damp places
WORD ORIGIN Old English *alor*

alderman *n, pl* **-men** **1** (formerly, in England and Wales) a senior member of a local council, elected by other councillors **2** (in the US, Canada & Australia) a member of the governing body of a city
WORD ORIGIN Old English *ealdor* chief + *mann* man

Aldington *n* **Richard** 1892–1962, English poet, novelist, and biographer. His novels include *Death of a Hero* (1929) and *The Colonel's Daughter* (1931), which reflect postwar disillusion following World War I

Aldiss *n* **Brian W(ilson)** born 1925, British novelist, best known for his science fiction. His works include *Non-Stop* (1958), *Enemies of the System* (1978), *The Helliconia Trilogy* (1983–86), *Forgotten Life* (1988), and *The Detached Retina* (1995)

Aldrin *n* **Edwin Eugene Jr.**, known as *Buzz.* born 1930, US astronaut; the second man to set foot on the moon on July 20, 1969, during the Apollo 11 flight

Aldus Manutius *n* 1450–1515, Italian printer, noted for his fine editions of the classics. He introduced italic type

ale *n* **1** a beer fermented in an open vessel using yeasts that rise to the top of the brew **2** (formerly) an alcoholic drink that is unflavoured by hops **3** *Brit* ▸ another word for **beer**
WORD ORIGIN Old English *alu, ealu*

alehouse *n* *old-fashioned* a public house

Aleichem *n* **Sholom,** real name *Solomon Rabinowitz.* 1859–1916, US Jewish writer, born in Russia. His works include *Tevye the Milkman*, which was adapted for the stage musical *Fiddler on the Roof*

Aleixandre *n* **Vicente** 1898–1984, Spanish poet, whose collections include *La destrucción o el amor* (1935; Destruction or Love): Nobel prize for literature 1977

Alekhine *n* **Alexander** 1892–1946, Russian-born chess player who lived in France; world champion (1927–35, 1937–46)

Alemán *n* **Mateo** 1547–?1614, Spanish novelist, author of the picaresque novel *Guzmán de Alfarache* (1599)

Alembert *n* ▸ See **d'Alembert**

alembic *n* **1** an obsolete type of container used for distillation **2** anything that distils or purifies things
WORD ORIGIN Arabic *al-anbīq* the still

THESAURUS

2, 3 = danger signal, warning, bell, alert, siren, alarm bell, hooter, distress signal, tocsin ▹ *vb* **5 = frighten**, shock, scare, panic, distress, terrify, startle, rattle, dismay, daunt, unnerve, terrorize, put the wind up *(informal)*, give (someone) a turn *(informal)*, make (someone's) hair stand on end **OPPOSITE:** calm

alcoholic *n* **1 = drunkard**, drinker, drunk, boozer *(informal)*, toper, soak *(slang)*, lush *(slang)*, sponge *(informal)*, carouser, sot, tippler, wino *(informal)*, inebriate, dipsomaniac, hard drinker, tosspot *(informal)*, alky

DICTIONARY

a

alert ❶ *adj* **1** watchful and attentive **2 alert to** aware of ▷ *n* **3** a warning or the period during which a warning remains in effect **4 on the alert** watchful ▷ *vb* **5** to warn of danger **6** to make aware of a fact **alertness** *n*
WORD ORIGIN Italian *all'erta* on the watch

A level *n* **1** *Brit* the advanced level of a subject taken for the General Certificate of Education **2** a pass in a subject at A level

Alexander *n* **Harold** (**Rupert Leofric George**), Earl Alexander of Tunis. 1891–1969, British field marshal in World War II, who organized the retreat from Dunkirk and commanded in North Africa (1943) and Sicily and Italy (1944–45); governor general of Canada (1946–52); British minister of defence (1952–54)

Alexander I *n* **1** *c.* 1080–1124, king of Scotland (1107–24), son of Malcolm III **2** 1777–1825, tsar of Russia (1801–25), who helped defeat Napoleon and formed the Holy Alliance (1815)

Alexander III *n* **1** 1241–86, king of Scotland (1249–86), son of Alexander II **2** original name *Orlando Bandinelli*. died 1181, pope (1159–81), who excommunicated Barbarossa **3** 1845–94, tsar of Russia (1881–94), son of Alexander II

Alexander technique *n* a technique for improving posture by becoming more aware of it
WORD ORIGIN after Frederick Matthias *Alexander*, Australian actor

Alexandra *n* **1** 1844–1925, queen consort of Edward VII of Great Britain and Ireland **2** 1872–1918, the wife of Nicholas II of Russia; her misrule while Nicholas was supreme commander of the Russian forces during World War I precipitated the Russian Revolution

Alexis Mikhailovich *n* 1629–76, tsar of Russia (1645–76); father of Peter the Great

Alexius I Comnenus *n* 1048–1118, ruler of the Byzantine Empire (1081–1118)

alfalfa *n* a plant widely used for feeding farm animals
WORD ORIGIN Arabic *al-fasfasah*

al-Farabi *n* **Mohammed ibn Tarkhan** died 950, Muslim philosopher, physician, and mathematician, of central Asian origin

al Fayed *n* **Mohamed** born 1933, Egyptian-born businessman; owner of the Harrods department store from 1985 and of the Ritz Hotel, Paris, from 1979: his son Dodi Fayed (1956–97) died in the same Paris car crash as Diana, Princess of Wales

Alfieri *n* Count **Vittorio** 1749–1803, Italian dramatist and poet, noted for his classical tragedies and political satires

Alfonso VI *n* died 1109, king of Léon (1065–1109) and of Castile (1072–1109). He appointed his vassal, the Spanish hero El Cid, ruler of Valencia

Alfonso XIII *n* 1886–1941, king of Spain (1886–1931), who was forced to abdicate on the establishment of the republic in 1931

alfresco *adj, adv* in the open air
WORD ORIGIN Italian: in the cool

Alfvén *n* **Hannes Olaf Gösta** 1908–95, Swedish physicist, noted for his research on magnetohydrodynamics; shared the Nobel prize for physics in 1970

algae (al-jee) *pl n, sing* **alga** (al-ga) plants which grow in water or moist ground, and which have no true stems, roots, or leaves
WORD ORIGIN Latin *alga* seaweed

algebra *n* a branch of mathematics in which symbols are used to represent numbers **algebraic** *adj*
WORD ORIGIN Arabic *al-jabr* the reunion of broken parts

Alger *n* **Horatio** 1834–99, US author of adventure stories for boys, including *Ragged Dick* (1867)

ALGOL *n* an early computer programming language designed for mathematical and scientific purposes
WORD ORIGIN *alg(orithmic) o(riented) l(anguage)*

Algonquin *or* **Algonkin** *n* **1** a member of a North American Indian people formerly living along the St Lawrence and Ottawa Rivers in Canada **2** the language of this people

algorism *n* the Arabic or decimal system of counting
WORD ORIGIN from *al-Khuwārizmi*, 9th-century Persian mathematician

algorithm *n* a logical arithmetical or computational procedure for solving problems
WORD ORIGIN changed from ALGORISM

Algren *n* **Nelson** 1909–81, US novelist. His novels, mostly set in Chicago, include *Never Come Morning* (1942) and *The Man with the Golden Arm* (1949)

alias *adv* **1** also known as: *Iris florentina, alias orris root* ▷ *n, pl* **-ases 2** a false name
WORD ORIGIN Latin: otherwise

alibi *n, pl* **-bis 1** *law* a plea of being somewhere else when a crime was committed **2** *informal* an excuse ▷ *vb* **-biing, -bied 3** to provide someone with an alibi
WORD ORIGIN Latin: elsewhere

Alice band *n* a band worn across the head to hold the hair back from the face

alien ❶ *adj* **1** foreign **2** from another world **3 alien to** repugnant or opposed to: *these methods are alien to the world of politics* ▷ *n* **4** a person who is a citizen of a country other than the one in which he or she lives **5** a being from another world **6** a person who does not seem to fit in with his or her environment
WORD ORIGIN Latin *alienus*

alienable *adj law* able to be transferred to another owner

alienate ❶ *vb* **-ating, -ated 1** to cause a friend to become unfriendly or hostile **2** *law* to transfer the ownership of property to another person **alienation** *n*

alight[1] ❶ *vb* **alighting, alighted** *or* **alit 1** to step out of a vehicle or off a horse: *we alighted on Vladivostok station* **2** to land: *we saw thirty goldfinches*

THESAURUS

(slang), alko *or* alco *(Austral slang)* ▷ *adj* **2 = intoxicating**, hard, strong, stiff, brewed, fermented, distilled, vinous, inebriating, spirituous, inebriant

alert *adj* **1 = attentive**, careful, awake, wary, vigilant, perceptive, watchful, ready, on the lookout, circumspect, observant, on guard, wide-awake, on your toes, on the watch, keeping a weather eye on, heedful
OPPOSITE: careless
▷ *vb* **5 = warn**, signal, alarm, forewarn **6 = inform**, notify, tip off
OPPOSITE: lull

alien *adj* **1 = foreign**, outside, strange, imported, overseas, unknown, exotic, unfamiliar, not native, not naturalized
▷ *n* **4 = foreigner**, incomer, immigrant, stranger, outsider, newcomer, asylum seeker, outlander
OPPOSITE: citizen

alienate *vb* **1 = antagonize**, anger, annoy, offend, irritate, hassle *(informal)*, gall, repel, estrange, lose the affection of, disaffect, hack off *(informal)*

alight[1] *vb* **1 = get off**, descend, get down, disembark, dismount **2 = land**, light, settle, come down, descend, perch, touch down, come to rest **OPPOSITE:** take off

alight[2] *adj* **2 = lit up**, bright, brilliant, shining, illuminated, fiery

align *vb* **2 = line up**, even, order, range, sequence, regulate, straighten, coordinate, even up, make parallel, arrange in line

alike *adj* **1 = similar**, close, the same, equal, equivalent, uniform, parallel, resembling, identical, corresponding, akin, duplicate, analogous, homogeneous, of a piece, cut from the same cloth, like two peas in a pod **OPPOSITE:** different
▷ *adv* **2 = similarly**, identically, equally, uniformly, correspondingly, analogously **OPPOSITE:** differently

DICTIONARY

a

alighting on the ledge
WORD ORIGIN Old English *ālīhtan*

alight² ❶ *adj, adv* **1** on fire **2** illuminated: *the lamp on the desk was alight*

align ❶ (a-line) *vb* **1** to bring (a person or group) into agreement with the policy of another **2** to place (two objects) in a particular position in relation to each other **alignment** *n*
WORD ORIGIN Old French *à ligne* into line

alike ❶ *adj* **1** similar: *they were thought to be very alike* ▷ *adv* **2** in the same way: *they even dressed alike* **3** considered together: *players and spectators alike*
WORD ORIGIN Old English *gelīc*

alimentary *adj* of or relating to nutrition

alimentary canal *n* the tubular passage in the body through which food is passed and digested

alimony *n law* an allowance paid under a court order by one spouse to another after separation
WORD ORIGIN Latin *alimonia* sustenance

A-line *adj* (of a skirt) slightly flared

Ali Pasha *n* known as *the Lion of Janina.* 1741–1822, Turkish pasha and ruler of Albania (1787–1820), who was deposed and assassinated after intriguing against Turkey

aliphatic *adj chem* (of an organic compound) having an open chain structure
WORD ORIGIN Greek *aleiphar* oil

aliquant *adj maths* denoting or belonging to a number that is not an exact divisor of a given number
WORD ORIGIN Latin *aliquantus* somewhat

aliquot *adj maths* denoting or belonging to an exact divisor of a number
WORD ORIGIN Latin: several

A list *n* **1** the most socially desirable category ▷ *adj* **A-list 2** of the most socially desirable category: *an A-list event*

alive ❶ *adj* **1** living; having life **2** in existence: *he said that he would keep the company alive, no matter what* **3** lively **4 alive to** aware of **5 alive with** swarming with: *the rocky shoreline was alive with birds*
WORD ORIGIN Old English *on līfe* in life

alkali (alk-a-lie) *n chem* a substance that combines with acid and neutralizes it to form a salt
WORD ORIGIN Arabic *al-qili* the ashes (of saltwort)

alkaline *adj chem* having the properties of or containing an alkali **alkalinity** *n*

alkaloid *n chem* any of a group of organic compounds containing nitrogen. Many are poisonous and some are used as drugs

alkane *n chem* any saturated hydrocarbon with the general formula CnH_2n+2

alkene *n chem* any unsaturated hydrocarbon with the general formula CnH_2n

all ❶ *det* **1** the whole quantity or number (of): *all the banks agree; we're all to blame* **2** every one of a class: *almost all animals sneeze* ▷ *adj* **3** the greatest possible: *in all seriousness* **4** any whatever: *I'm leaving out all question of motive for the time being* **5 all along** since the beginning **6 all but** nearly **7 all in all** everything considered **8 all over a** finished **b** everywhere in or on: *we send them all over the world* **c** *informal* typically: *that's him all over* **9 all the** so much (more or less) than otherwise: *the need for new drugs is all the more important* **10 at all** used for emphasis: *my throat's no better at all* **11 be all for** *informal* to be strongly in favour of **12 for all** in spite of: *for all his cynicism, he's at heart a closet idealist* **13 in all** altogether: *there were five in all* ▷ *adv* **14** (in scores of games) each: *the score was two all* ▷ *n* **15 give one's all** to make the greatest possible effort
WORD ORIGIN Old English *eall*

Allah *n* the name of God in Islam

allay *vb* to reduce (fear, doubt, or anger)
WORD ORIGIN Old English *ālecgan* to put down

all clear *n* a signal indicating that danger is over

allegation ❶ *n* an unproved assertion or accusation

allege ❶ *vb* **-leging, -leged** to state without proof
WORD ORIGIN Latin *allegare* to dispatch on a mission

alleged ❶ *adj* stated but not proved: *the spot where the alleged crime took place* **allegedly** (al-lej-id-lee) *adv*

allegiance ❶ *n* loyalty or dedication to a person, cause, or belief
WORD ORIGIN Old French *lige* liege

allegory *n, pl* **-ries** a story, poem, or picture with an underlying meaning as well as the literal one **allegorical** *adj* **allegorize** *or* **-rise** *vb*
WORD ORIGIN Greek *allēgorein* to speak figuratively

allegretto *music adv* **1** fairly quickly or briskly ▷ *n, pl* **-tos 2** a piece or passage to be performed fairly quickly or briskly
WORD ORIGIN Italian

Allegri *n* **Gregorio** 1582–1652, Italian composer and singer. His compositions include a *Miserere* for nine voices

allegro *music adv* **1** in a brisk lively manner ▷ *n, pl* **-gros 2** a piece or passage to be performed in a brisk lively manner
WORD ORIGIN Italian

allele (al-leel) *n* any of two or more genes that are responsible for alternative characteristics, such as smooth or wrinkled seeds in peas

alleluia *interj* praise the Lord!
WORD ORIGIN Hebrew *halleluyah*

Allenby *n* **Edmund Henry Hynman,** 1st Viscount. 1861–1936, British field marshal who captured Palestine and Syria from the Turks in 1918; high commissioner in Egypt (1919–25)

allergen (al-ler-jen) *n* a substance capable of causing an allergic reaction **allergenic** *adj*

allergic ❶ *adj* **1** having or caused by an allergy **2 allergic to** *informal* having a strong dislike of: *father and son*

THESAURUS

alive *adj* **1 = living,** breathing, animate, having life, subsisting, existing, functioning, alive and kicking, in the land of the living (*informal*) **OPPOSITE:** dead
2 = in existence, existing, functioning, active, operative, in force, on-going, prevalent, existent, extant **OPPOSITE:** inoperative
3 = lively, spirited, active, vital, alert, eager, quick, awake, vigorous, cheerful, energetic, animated, brisk, agile, perky, chirpy (*informal*), sprightly, vivacious, full of life, spry, full of beans (*informal*), zestful **OPPOSITE:** dull

all *det* **1 = the whole amount,** everything, the whole, the total, the sum, the total amount, the aggregate, the totality, the sum total, the entirety, the entire amount, the complete amount
2 = every, each, every single, every one of, each and every ▷ *adj*
3 = complete, greatest, full, total, perfect, entire, utter

allegation *n* **= claim,** charge, statement, profession, declaration, plea, accusation, assertion, affirmation, deposition, avowal, asseveration, averment

allege *vb* **= claim,** hold, charge, challenge, state, maintain, advance, declare, assert, uphold, put forward, affirm, profess, depose, avow, aver, asseverate **OPPOSITE:** deny

alleged *adj* **= claimed,** supposed, declared, assumed, so-called, apparent, rumoured, stated, described, asserted, designated, presumed, affirmed, professed, reputed, hypothetical, putative, presupposed, averred, unproved

allegiance *n* **= loyalty,** duty, obligation, devotion, fidelity, homage, obedience, adherence, constancy, faithfulness, troth (*archaic*), fealty **OPPOSITE:** disloyalty

allergic *adj* **1 = sensitive,** affected, susceptible, sensitized, hypersensitive

DICTIONARY

a

seemed to have been allergic to each other from the start

allergy ❶ *n, pl* **-gies** **1** extreme sensitivity to a substance such as a food or pollen, which causes the body to react to any contact with it **2** *informal* a strong dislike for something
WORD ORIGIN Greek *allos* other + *ergon* activity

alleviate ❶ *vb* **-ating, -ated** to lessen (pain or suffering) **alleviation** *n*
WORD ORIGIN Latin *levis* light

alley ❶ *n* **1** a narrow passage between or behind buildings **2 a** a building containing lanes for tenpin bowling **b** a long narrow wooden lane down which the ball is rolled in tenpin bowling **3** a path in a garden, often lined with trees
WORD ORIGIN Old French *alee*

alleyway *n* a narrow passage with buildings or walls on both sides

all found *adv* (of charges for accommodation) including meals, heating, and other living expenses

Allhallows *n* ▸ same as **All Saints' Day**

alliance ❶ *n* **1** the state of being allied **2** a formal relationship between two or more countries or political parties to work together **3** the countries or parties involved
WORD ORIGIN Old French *alier* to ally

allied ❶ *adj* **1** united by a common aim or common characteristics: *the allied areas of telepathy and clairvoyance* **2 Allied** relating to the countries that fought against Germany and Japan in the Second World War: *the Allied bombing of German cities*

alligator *n* a large reptile of the southern US, similar to the crocodile but with a shorter broader snout
WORD ORIGIN Spanish *el lagarto* the lizard

all in *adj* **1** *informal* exhausted **2** (of wrestling) with no style forbidden ▹ *adv* **3** with all expenses included

Allingham *n* **Margery** 1904–66, British author of detective stories, featuring Albert Campion. Her works include *Tiger in the Smoke* (1952) and *The Mind Readers* (1965)

alliteration *n* the use of the same sound at the start of words occurring together, as in *round the rugged rock the ragged rascal ran* **alliterative** *adj*
WORD ORIGIN Latin *litera* letter

allocate ❶ *vb* **-cating, -cated** to assign to someone or for a particular purpose **allocation** *n*
WORD ORIGIN Latin *locus* a place

allopathy (al-**lop**-ath-ee) *n med* an orthodox method of treating disease, by using drugs that produce an effect opposite to the effect of the disease being treated, as contrasted with homeopathy **allopathic** *adj*
WORD ORIGIN Greek *allos* other + *pathos* suffering

allot *vb* **-lotting, -lotted** to assign as a share or for a particular purpose
WORD ORIGIN Old French *lot* portion

allotment *n* **1** *Brit* a small piece of land rented by a person to grow vegetables on **2** a portion allotted **3** distribution

allotrope *n chem* any of two or more physical forms in which an element can exist

allotropy *n chem* the existence of an element in two or more physical forms **allotropic** *adj*
WORD ORIGIN Greek *allos* other + *tropos* manner

all-out *adj informal* using one's maximum powers: *an all-out attack on inflation*

allow ❶ *vb* **1** to permit someone to do something **2** to set aside: *I allowed plenty of time* **3** to acknowledge (a point or claim) **4 allow for** to take into account **allowable** *adj*
WORD ORIGIN Late Latin *allaudare* to extol

allowance ❶ *n* **1** an amount of money given at regular intervals **2** (in Britain) an amount of a person's income that is not subject to income tax **3 make allowances for a** to treat or judge someone less severely because he or she has special problems **b** to take into account in one's plans

alloy *n* **1** a mixture of two or more metals ▹ *vb* **2** to mix metals in order to obtain a substance with a desired property
WORD ORIGIN Latin *alligare* to bind

all-purpose *adj* useful for many purposes

all right ❶ *adj* **1** acceptable or satisfactory: *is everything all right?* **2** unharmed; safe: *I'm going to check if he's all right* ▹ *interj* **3** an expression of approval or agreement ▹ *adv* **4** satisfactorily **5** safely **6** without doubt: *it was him all right*

all-round *adj* **1** having many skills; versatile: *an all-round player* **2** of broad scope; comprehensive: *we cannot do without up-to-date and all-round training*

all-rounder *n* a person with many skills and abilities

All Saints' Day *n* a Christian festival celebrated on November 1 to honour all the saints

All Souls' Day *n RC church* a day of prayer (November 2) for the dead in purgatory

allspice *n* a spice used in cooking, which comes from the berries of a tropical American tree

Allston *n* **Washington** 1779–1843, US painter and author, regarded as the earliest US Romantic painter. His paintings include *Elijah in the Desert* (1818) and *Moonlit Landscape* (1819)

all-time *adj informal* unsurpassed at a particular time: *one of boxing's all-time greats*

allude *vb* **-luding, -luded** ▪ **allude to** to refer indirectly to
WORD ORIGIN Latin *alludere*

allure *n* attractiveness or appeal
WORD ORIGIN Old French *alurer* to lure

alluring *adj* extremely attractive

allusion *n* an indirect reference

alluvial *adj* **1** of or relating to

THESAURUS

allergy *n* **1 = sensitivity**, reaction, susceptibility, antipathy, hypersensitivity, sensitiveness

alleviate *vb* **= ease**, reduce, relieve, moderate, smooth, dull, diminish, soften, check, blunt, soothe, subdue, lessen, lighten, quell, allay, mitigate, abate, slacken, assuage, quench, mollify, slake, palliate

alley *n* **1 = passage**, walk, lane, pathway, alleyway, passageway, backstreet

alliance *n* **2 = union**, league, association, agreement, marriage, connection, combination, coalition, treaty, partnership, federation, pact, compact, confederation, affinity, affiliation, confederacy, concordat **OPPOSITE:** division

allied *adj* **1a = united**, joined, linked, related, married, joint, combined, bound, integrated, unified, affiliated, leagued, confederate, amalgamated, cooperating, in league, hand in glove *(informal)*, in cahoots *(US informal)* **1b = connected**, joined, linked, tied, related, associated, syndicated, affiliated, kindred

allocate *vb* **= assign**, grant, distribute, designate, set aside, earmark, give out, consign, allow, budget, allot, mete, share out, apportion, appropriate

allow *vb* **1a = permit**, approve, enable, sanction, endure, license, brook, endorse, warrant, tolerate, put up with *(informal)*, authorize, stand, suffer, bear **OPPOSITE:** prohibit **1b = let**, permit, sanction, authorize, license, tolerate, consent to, countenance, concede to, assent to, give leave to, give the green light for, give a blank cheque to **OPPOSITE:** forbid **2 = give**, provide, grant, spare, devote, assign, allocate, set aside, deduct, earmark, remit, allot **3 = acknowledge**, accept, admit, grant, recognize, yield, concede, confess, acquiesce **4 allow for something = take into account**, consider, plan for, accommodate, provide for, arrange for, foresee, make provision for, make allowances for, make concessions for, keep in mind, set

DICTIONARY

a

alluvium ▷*n* **2** ▶same as **alluvium**
alluvium *n, pl* **-via** a fertile soil consisting of mud, silt, and sand deposited by flowing water
WORD ORIGIN Latin
ally ❶ *n, pl* **-lies 1** a country, person, or group with an agreement to support another ▷*vb* **-lies, -lying, -lied 2 ally oneself with** to agree to support another country, person, or group
WORD ORIGIN Latin *ligare* to bind
al-Maliki *n* **Nouri** born 1957, Iraqi politician, prime minister of Iraq from 2006
alma mater *n* the school, college, or university that one attended
WORD ORIGIN Latin: bountiful mother
almanac *n* a yearly calendar with detailed information on matters like anniversaries and phases of the moon
WORD ORIGIN Late Greek *almenikhiaka*
Alma-Tadema *n* Sir **Lawrence** 1836–1912, Dutch-English painter of studies of Greek and Roman life
almighty *adj* **1** having power over everything **2** *informal* very great: *there was an almighty bang* ▷*n* **3 the Almighty** God
Almodóvar *n* **Pedro** born 1949, Spanish film director. His provocative black comedies include *Women on the Verge of a Nervous Breakdown* (1988), *The Flower of My Secret* (1995), *Talk to Her* (2002), and *Volver* (2006)
almond *n* an edible oval nut with a yellowish-brown shell, which grows on a small tree
WORD ORIGIN Greek *amugdalē*
almoner *n Brit* a former name for a hospital social worker
WORD ORIGIN Old French *almosne* alms
almost ❶ *adv* very nearly
alms (**ahmz**) *pl n old-fashioned* donations of money or goods to the poor
WORD ORIGIN Greek *eleēmosunē* pity
almshouse *n Brit* (formerly) a house, financed by charity, which offered accommodation to the poor
aloe *n* **1** a plant with fleshy spiny leaves **2 aloes** a bitter drug made from aloe leaves
WORD ORIGIN Greek
aloe vera *n* a plant producing a juice which is used to treat skin and hair
aloft *adv* **1** in the air **2** *naut* in the rigging of a ship
WORD ORIGIN Old Norse *ā lopt*
alone ❶ *adj* **1** without anyone or anything else ▷*adv* **2** without anyone or anything else **3 leave someone** *or* **something alone** to refrain from annoying someone or interfering with something **4 let alone** not to mention: *it looked inconceivable that he could run again, let alone be elected*
WORD ORIGIN Old English *al one* all (entirely) one
along *prep* **1** over part or all of the length of: *we were going along the railway tracks* ▷*adv* **2** moving forward: *they were roaring along at 40mph* **3** in company with another or others: *let them go along for the ride* **4 along with** together with: *I'm including the good days along with the bad*
WORD ORIGIN Old English *andlang*
alongside *prep* **1** close beside ▷*adv* **2** near the side of something
aloof *adj* distant or haughty in manner
WORD ORIGIN obsolete *a loof* to windward
alopecia (al-loh-**pee**-sha) *n* loss of hair, usually due to illness
WORD ORIGIN Greek *alōpekia* mange in foxes
aloud ❶ *adv* in an audible voice
Aloysius *n* **Saint** full name *Aloysius Luigi Gonzaga*. 1568–91, Italian Jesuit who died nursing plague victims; the patron saint of youth. Feast day: June 21
alp *n* **1** a high mountain **2 the Alps** a high mountain range in S central Europe
WORD ORIGIN Latin *Alpes*
alpaca *n* **1** a South American mammal related to the llama, with dark shaggy hair **2** wool or cloth made from this hair
WORD ORIGIN South American Indian *allpaca*
alpenstock *n* a strong stick with an iron tip used by hikers and mountain climbers
WORD ORIGIN German
alpha *n* **1** the first letter in the Greek alphabet (Α, α) **2** *Brit* the highest grade in an examination or for a piece of academic work **3 alpha and omega** the first and last
alphabet *n* a set of letters in fixed conventional order, used in a writing system
WORD ORIGIN *alpha* + *beta*, the first two letters of the Greek alphabet
alphabetical *adj* in the conventional order of the letters of an alphabet
alphabetically *adv*
alphabetize *or* **-ise** *vb* **-izing, -ized** *or* **-ising, -ised** to put in alphabetical order **alphabetization** *or* **-isation** *n*
alphanumeric *adj* consisting of alphabetical and numerical symbols
alpha particle *n physics* a positively charged particle, emitted during some radioactive transformations
alpha ray *n physics* a stream of alpha particles
alpine *adj* **1** of high mountains **2 Alpine** of the Alps ▷*n* **3** a plant grown on or native to mountains
alpinist *n* a mountain climber
already ❶ *adv* **1** before the present time **2** before an implied or expected time
alright *adj, interj, adv not standard* ▶same as **all right**
Alsatian *n* a large wolflike dog
also ❶ *adv* in addition; too
WORD ORIGIN Old English *alswā*
also-ran *n* a loser in a race, competition, or election

THESAURUS

something aside for, take into consideration
allowance *n* **1 = pocket money**, grant, fee, payment, consideration, ration, handout, remittance
all right *adj* **1 = satisfactory**, O.K. *or* okay *(informal)*, average, fair, sufficient, standard, acceptable, good enough, adequate, so-so *(informal)*, up to scratch *(informal)*, passable, up to standard, up to the mark, unobjectionable
OPPOSITE: unsatisfactory
2 = well, O.K. *or* okay *(informal)*, strong, whole, sound, fit, safe, healthy, hale, unharmed, out of the woods, uninjured, unimpaired, up to par **OPPOSITE:** ill
ally *n* **1 = partner**, friend, colleague, associate, mate, accessory, comrade, helper, collaborator, accomplice, confederate, co-worker, bedfellow, cobber *(Austral & NZ old-fashioned, informal)*, coadjutor, abettor, E hoa (NZ) **OPPOSITE:** opponent
almost *adv* **= nearly**, about, approaching, close to, virtually, practically, roughly, all but, just about, not quite, on the brink of, not far from, approximately, well-nigh, as good as
alone *adj* **1a = solitary**, isolated, sole, separate, apart, abandoned, detached, by yourself, unattended, unaccompanied, out on a limb, unescorted, on your tod *(slang)*
OPPOSITE: accompanied
1b = lonely, abandoned, deserted, isolated, solitary, estranged, desolate, forsaken, forlorn, destitute, lonesome *(chiefly US & Canad)*, friendless ▷*adv* **2a = solely**, only, individually, singly, exclusively, uniquely **2b = by yourself**, independently, unaided, unaccompanied, without help, on your own, unassisted, without assistance, under your own steam
OPPOSITE: with help
aloud *adv* **= out loud**, clearly, plainly, distinctly, audibly, intelligibly
already *adv* **1, 2 = before now**, before, previously, at present, by now, by then, even now, by this time, just now, by that time, heretofore, as of now
also *adv* **= and**, too, further, plus,

DICTIONARY

a

Alta. Alberta
altar *n* **1** the table used for Communion in Christian churches **2** a raised structure on which sacrifices are offered and religious rites performed
WORD ORIGIN Latin *altus* high
altarpiece *n* a painting or a decorated screen set above and behind the altar in a Christian church
Altdorfer *n* **Albrecht** ?1480–?1538, German painter and engraver: one of the earliest landscape painters
alter ❶ *vb* to make or become different; change
WORD ORIGIN Latin *alter* other
alteration *n* a change or modification
altercation *n* a noisy argument
WORD ORIGIN Latin *altercari* to quarrel
alter ego *n* **1** a hidden side to one's personality **2** a very close friend
WORD ORIGIN Latin: other self
alternate ❶ *vb* **-nating, -nated 1** to occur by turns **2** to interchange regularly or in succession ▹ *adj* **3** occurring by turns **4** every second (one) of a series: *alternate days* **5** being a second choice **alternately** *adv* **alternation** *n*
WORD ORIGIN Latin *alternare*
alternate angles *pl n geom* two angles at opposite ends and on opposite sides of a line intersecting two other lines
alternating current *n* an electric current that reverses direction at frequent regular intervals
alternative ❶ *n* **1** a possibility of choice between two or more things **2** either or any of such choices ▹ *adj* **3** presenting a choice between two or more possibilities **4** of a lifestyle etc. that is less conventional or materialistic than is usual **alternatively** *adv*
alternative energy *n* a form of energy obtained from natural resources like waves and wind
alternative medicine *n* the treatment of disease by unconventional methods like homeopathy, and involving attention to the patient's emotional wellbeing
alternator *n* an electrical machine that generates an alternating current
although ❶ *conj* in spite of the fact that
Althusser *n* **Louis** 1918–90, French Marxist philosopher, author of *For Marx* (1965) and *Reading Capital* (1965): committed to a mental hospital (1981) after killing his wife
altimeter (al-tim-it-er) *n* an instrument that measures altitude
WORD ORIGIN Latin *altus* high + -METER
altitude *n* height, esp. above sea level
WORD ORIGIN Latin *altus* high, deep
Altman *n* **Robert** US film director, 1925–2006; his films include *M*A*S*H* (1970), *Nashville* (1975), *Short Cuts* (1994), and *Gosford Park* (2001)
alto *n, pl* **-tos 1** ▸ short for **contralto 2** the highest adult male voice **3** a singer with an alto voice **4** a musical instrument, for instance a saxophone, that is the second or third highest in its family ▹ *adj* **5** denoting such an instrument, singer, or voice: *an alto flute*
WORD ORIGIN Italian: high
altogether ❶ *adv* **1** completely: *an altogether different message* **2** on the whole: *this is not altogether a bad thing* **3** in total: *altogether, 25 aircraft took part* ▹ *n* **4 in the altogether** *informal* naked
alt.rock *n* a genre of rock music regarded by fans as being outside the mainstream
altruism *n* unselfish concern for the welfare of others **altruist** *n* **altruistic** *adj*
WORD ORIGIN Italian *altrui* others
alum *n chem* a double sulphate of aluminium and potassium, used in manufacturing and in medicine
WORD ORIGIN Latin *alumen*
aluminium *or US & Canad* **aluminum** *n chem* a light malleable silvery-white metallic element that does not rust. Symbol: Al
aluminize *or* **-ise** *vb* **-nizing, -nized** *or* **-nising, -nised** to cover with aluminium
alumnus (al-lumm-nuss) *or fem* **alumna** (al-lumm-na) *n, pl* **-ni** (-nie) *or* **-nae** (-nee) *chiefly US & Canad* a graduate of a school or college
WORD ORIGIN Latin: nursling, pupil
Alva *or* **Alba** *n* **Duke of,** title of *Fernando Alvarez de Toledo.* 1508–82, Spanish general and statesman who suppressed the Protestant revolt in the Netherlands (1567–72) and conquered Portugal (1580)
Alvarez *n* **Luis Walter** 1911–88, US physicist. He made (with Felix Bloch) the first measurement of the neutron's magnetic moment (1939). Nobel prize for physics 1968
alveolus (al-vee-ol-luss) *n, pl* **-li** (-lie) any small pit, cavity, or saclike dilation, such as a honeycomb cell, a tooth socket, or the tiny air sacs in the lungs
WORD ORIGIN Latin: a little hollow
always ❶ *adv* **1** without exception: *she was always at the top of her form in school work* **2** continually: *you're always shouting or whining* **3** in any case: *they're all adults, they can always say no*
WORD ORIGIN Old English *ealne weg* all the way
Alwyn *n* **William** 1905–85, British composer. His works include the oratorio *The Marriage of Heaven and Hell* (1936) and the *Suite of Scottish Dances* (1946)
alyssum *n* a garden plant with clusters of small white flowers
WORD ORIGIN Greek *alussos* curing rabies
Alzheimer's disease (alts-hime-erz) *n* a disorder of the brain resulting in a progressive decline in intellectual and physical abilities and eventual dementia
WORD ORIGIN after A. *Alzheimer,* German physician

THESAURUS

along with, in addition, as well, moreover, besides, furthermore, what's more, on top of that, to boot, additionally, into the bargain, as well as
alter *vb* **a = modify**, change, reform, shift, vary, transform, adjust, adapt, revise, amend, diversify, remodel, tweak *(informal)*, recast, reshape, metamorphose, transmute **b = change**, turn, vary, transform, adjust, adapt, metamorphose
alternate *vb* **1 = interchange**, change, alter, fluctuate, intersperse, take turns, oscillate, chop and change, follow one another, follow in turn **2 = intersperse**, interchange, exchange, swap, stagger, rotate ▹ *adj* **3 = alternating**, interchanging, every other, rotating, every second, sequential
alternative *n* **1, 2 = substitute**, choice, other, option, preference, recourse
although *conj* **= though**, while, even if, even though, whilst, albeit, despite the fact that, notwithstanding, even supposing, tho' *(US poetic)*
altogether *adv* **1a = absolutely**, quite, completely, totally, perfectly, fully, thoroughly, wholly, utterly, downright, one hundred per cent *(informal)*, undisputedly, lock, stock and barrel **1b = completely**, all, fully, entirely, comprehensively, thoroughly, wholly, every inch, one hundred per cent *(informal)*, in every respect **OPPOSITE:** partially **2 = on the whole**, generally, mostly, in general, collectively, all things considered, on average, for the most part, all in all, on balance, in toto *(Latin)*, as a whole **3 = in total**, in all, all told, taken together, in sum, everything included, in toto *(Latin)*
always *adv* **1 = habitually**, regularly, every time, inevitably, consistently, invariably, aye *(Scot)*, perpetually, without exception, customarily, unfailingly, on every occasion, day in, day out **OPPOSITE:** seldom **2 = continually**, constantly, all the time, forever, repeatedly, aye *(Scot)*, endlessly, persistently, eternally,

DICTIONARY

a

am *vb* (*with "I" as subject*) ▸ a form of the present tense of **be**
WORD ORIGIN Old English *eam*

Am *chem* americium

AM 1 amplitude modulation **2** (in Britain) Member of the National Assembly for Wales

Am. America(n)

a.m. before noon
WORD ORIGIN Latin *ante meridiem*

amah *n* (in the East, formerly) a nurse or maidservant
WORD ORIGIN Portuguese *ama*

amakwerekwere *n S African informal, derogatory* a term used by Black people to refer to foreign Africans
WORD ORIGIN from Xhosa *ama*, a plural prefix, + *kwerekwere* imitative of unintelligible sound

amalgam *n* **1** a blend or combination **2** an alloy of mercury with another metal: *dental amalgam*
WORD ORIGIN Medieval Latin *amalgama*

amalgamate *vb* **-ating, -mated 1** to combine or unite **2** to alloy (a metal) with mercury **amalgamation** *n*

amandla (a-mand-la) *n S African* a political slogan calling for power to the Black population
WORD ORIGIN Nguni (language group of southern Africa): power

amanuensis (am-man-yew-**en**-siss) *n, pl* **-ses** (-seez) a person who copies manuscripts or takes dictation
WORD ORIGIN Latin *servus a manu* slave at hand

Amanullah Khan *n* 1892–1960, emir (1919–26) and king (1926–29) of Afghanistan; he obtained Afghan independence from Britain (1919)

amaranth *n* **1** *poetic* an imaginary flower that never fades **2** a lily-like plant with small green, red, or purple flowers
WORD ORIGIN Greek *a-* not + *marainein* to fade

amaretti *pl n* Italian almond biscuits
WORD ORIGIN Italian *amaro* bitter

amaryllis *n* a lily-like plant with large red or white flowers and a long stalk
WORD ORIGIN *Amaryllis*, Greek name for a shepherdess

amass ❶ *vb* to accumulate or collect: *the desire to amass wealth*
WORD ORIGIN Latin *ad-* to + *massa* mass

amateur ❶ *n* **1** a person who engages in a sport or other activity as a pastime rather than as a profession **2** a person unskilled in a subject or activity ▹ *adj* **3** doing something out of interest, not for money **4** amateurish **amateurism** *n*
WORD ORIGIN Latin *amator* lover

amateurish *adj* lacking skill

amatory *adj* of or relating to romantic or sexual love
WORD ORIGIN Latin *amare* to love

amaut *or* **amowt** *n Canad* a hood on an Inuit woman's parka for carrying a child

amaze ❶ *vb* **amazing, amazed** to fill with surprise; astonish **amazement** *n* **amazing** *adj* **amazingly** *adv*
WORD ORIGIN Old English *āmasian*

Amazon *n* **1** a strong and powerful woman **2** *Greek myth* one of a race of women warriors of Scythia **Amazonian** *adj*
WORD ORIGIN Greek

Ambartsumian *n* **Viktor A**(**mazaspovich**) 1908–96, Armenian astrophysicist, renowned for his description of radio sources as explosions in the core of galaxies

ambassador ❶ *n* **1** a diplomat of the highest rank, sent to another country as permanent representative of his or her own country **2** a representative or messenger: *he saw himself as an ambassador for the game* **ambassadorial** *adj*
WORD ORIGIN Old Provençal *ambaisador*

amber *n* **1** a yellow translucent fossilized resin, used in jewellery ▹ *adj* **2** brownish-yellow
WORD ORIGIN Arabic *'anbar* ambergris

ambergris (am-ber-greece) *n* a waxy substance secreted by the sperm whale, which is used in making perfumes
WORD ORIGIN Old French *ambre gris* grey amber

ambidextrous *adj* able to use both hands with equal ease
WORD ORIGIN Latin *ambi-* both + *dexter* right hand

ambience *or* **ambiance** *n* the atmosphere of a place

ambient *adj* **1** surrounding: *low ambient temperatures* **2** creating a relaxing atmosphere: *ambient music*
WORD ORIGIN Latin *ambi-* round + *ire* to go

ambiguity ❶ *n, pl* **-ties 1** the possibility of interpreting an expression in more than one way **2** an ambiguous situation or expression: *the ambiguities of feminine identity*

ambiguous ❶ *adj* having more than one possible interpretation **ambiguously** *adv*
WORD ORIGIN Latin *ambigere* to go around

ambit *n* limits or boundary
WORD ORIGIN Latin *ambire* to go round

ambition ❶ *n* **1** strong desire for success **2** something so desired; a goal
WORD ORIGIN Latin *ambitio* a going round (of candidates)

ambitious ❶ *adj* **1** having a strong desire for success **2** requiring great effort or ability: *ambitious plans*

ambivalence (am-**biv**-a-lenss) *n* the state of feeling two conflicting emotions at the same time **ambivalent** *adj*

amble *vb* **-bling, -bled 1** to walk at a leisurely pace ▹ *n* **2** a leisurely walk or pace
WORD ORIGIN Latin *ambulare* to walk

Ambler *n* **Eric** 1909–1998, English novelist. His thrillers include *The Mask of Dimitrios* (1939), *Journey into Fear* (1940), *A Kind of Anger* (1964), and

THESAURUS

perpetually, incessantly, interminably, unceasingly, everlastingly, in perpetuum (*Latin*)

amass *vb* **= collect**, gather, assemble, compile, accumulate, aggregate, pile up, garner, hoard, scrape together, rake up, heap up

amateur *n* **1 = nonprofessional**, outsider, layman, dilettante, layperson, non-specialist, dabbler

amaze *vb* **= astonish**, surprise, shock, stun, alarm, stagger, startle, bewilder, astound, daze, confound, stupefy, flabbergast, bowl someone over (*informal*), boggle someone's mind, dumbfound

ambassador *n* **1 = representative**, minister, agent, deputy, diplomat, envoy, consul, attaché, emissary, legate, plenipotentiary

ambiguity *n* **1 = vagueness**, doubt, puzzle, uncertainty, obscurity, enigma, equivocation, inconclusiveness, indefiniteness, dubiety, dubiousness, tergiversation, indeterminateness, equivocality, doubtfulness, equivocacy

ambiguous *adj* **= unclear**, puzzling, uncertain, obscure, vague, doubtful, dubious, enigmatic, indefinite, inconclusive, cryptic, indeterminate, equivocal, Delphic, oracular, enigmatical, clear as mud (*informal*)
OPPOSITE: clear

ambition *n* **1 = enterprise**, longing, drive, fire, spirit, desire, passion, enthusiasm, warmth, striving, initiative, aspiration, yearning, devotion, zeal, verve, zest, fervour, eagerness, gusto, hankering, get-up-and-go (*informal*), ardour, keenness, avidity, fervency **2 = goal**, end, hope, design, dream, target, aim, wish, purpose, desire, intention, objective, intent, aspiration, Holy Grail (*informal*)

ambitious *adj* **1 = enterprising**, spirited, keen, active, daring, eager, intent, enthusiastic, hopeful, striving, vigorous, aspiring, energetic, adventurous, avid, zealous, intrepid, resourceful, purposeful, desirous
OPPOSITE: unambitious

DICTIONARY

a

Doctor Frigo (1974)

ambrosia *n* **1** something delightful to taste or smell **2** *classical myth* the food of the gods
WORD ORIGIN Greek: immortality

ambulance *n* a motor vehicle designed to carry sick or injured people
WORD ORIGIN Latin *ambulare* to walk

ambulatory *adj* **1** of or relating to walking **2** able to walk ▷*n, pl* **-ries 3** a place for walking in, such as a cloister

ambush ❶ *n* **1** the act of waiting in a concealed position to make a surprise attack **2** an attack from such a position ▷*vb* **3** to attack suddenly from a concealed position
WORD ORIGIN Old French *embuschier* to position in ambush

ameliorate (am-**meal**-yor-rate) *vb* **-rating, -rated** to make (something) better **amelioration** *n*
WORD ORIGIN Latin *melior* better

amen *interj* so be it: used at the end of a prayer
WORD ORIGIN Hebrew: certainly

amenable (a-**mean**-a-bl) *adj* likely or willing to cooperate
WORD ORIGIN Latin *minare* to drive (cattle)

amend ❶ *vb* to make small changes to something such as a piece of writing or a contract, in order to improve it: *he has amended the basic design*
WORD ORIGIN Old French *amender*

amendment ❶ *n* an improvement or correction

amends *pl n* **make amends for** to compensate for some injury or insult

amenity ❶ *n, pl* **-ties** a useful or enjoyable feature: *all kinds of amenities including horse riding and golf*
WORD ORIGIN Latin *amoenus* agreeable

amenorrhoea *or esp. US* **amenorrhea** (aim-men-or-**ree**-a) *n* abnormal absence of menstruation
WORD ORIGIN Greek *a-* not + *mēn* month + *rhein* to flow

Amen-Ra *n* an Egyptian god with a ram's head

American *adj* **1** of the United States of America or the American continent ▷*n* **2** a person from the United States of America or the American continent

American football *n* a game similar to rugby, played by two teams of eleven players

American Indian *n* **1** a member of any of the original peoples of America ▷*adj* **2** of any of these peoples

Americanism *n* an expression or custom that is characteristic of the people of the United States

Americanize *or* **-ise** *vb* **-izing, -ized** *or* **-ising, -ised** to make American in outlook or form

americium *n chem* a white metallic element artificially produced from plutonium. Symbol: Am
WORD ORIGIN from *America* (where it was first produced)

amethyst (**am**-myth-ist) *n* **1** a purple or violet variety of quartz used as a gemstone ▷*adj* **2** purple or violet
WORD ORIGIN Greek *amethustos* not drunken

Amex (**aah**-mex) **1** *trademark* American Express **2** American Stock Exchange

Amharic *n* the official language of Ethiopia

Amherst *n* **Jeffrey,** 1st Baron Amherst. 1717–97, British general who defeated the French in Canada (1758–60): governor general of British North America (1761–63)

amiable *adj* having a pleasant nature; friendly **amiability** *n* **amiably** *adv*
WORD ORIGIN Latin *amicus* friend

amicable *adj* characterized by friendliness: *ideally the parting should be amicable* **amicability** *n* **amicably** *adv*
WORD ORIGIN Latin *amicus* friend

amid ❶ *or* **amidst** *prep* in the middle of; among
WORD ORIGIN Old English *on middan* in the middle

amide *n chem* **1** any organic compound containing the group $-CONH_2$ **2** an inorganic compound having the general formula $M(NH_2)_x$, where M is a metal atom
WORD ORIGIN from *ammonia*

amidships *adv naut* at, near, or towards the centre of a ship

amine (**am**-**mean**) *n chem* an organic base formed by replacing one or more of the hydrogen atoms of ammonia by organic groups
WORD ORIGIN from *ammonium*

amino acid (am-**mean**-oh) *n chem* any of a group of organic compounds containing the **amino** group, $-NH_2$, and one or more carboxyl groups, $-COOH$, esp. one that is a component of protein

amir (am-**meer**) *n* ▸ same as **emir**
WORD ORIGIN Arabic

amiss *adv* **1** wrongly or badly: *anxious not to tread amiss* **2** **take something amiss** to be offended by something ▷*adj* **3** wrong or faulty
WORD ORIGIN Middle English *a mis,* from *mis* wrong

amity *n formal* friendship
WORD ORIGIN from Latin *amicus* friend

ammeter *n* an instrument for measuring an electric current in amperes
WORD ORIGIN *am(pere)* + -METER

ammo *n informal* ammunition

ammonia *n* **1** a colourless strong-smelling gas containing hydrogen and nitrogen **2** a solution of this in water
WORD ORIGIN ultimately from a substance found near the shrine of the Roman-Egyptian god Jupiter *Ammon*

ammonite *n* the fossilized spiral shell of an extinct sea creature
WORD ORIGIN Medieval Latin *cornu Ammonis* horn of Ammon

ammonium *adj chem* of or containing the chemical group NH_4- or the ion NH_4^+

ammunition ❶ *n* **1** bullets, bombs, and shells that can be fired from or as a weapon **2** facts that can be used in an argument
WORD ORIGIN Latin *munitio* fortification

amnesia *n* a partial or total loss of memory **amnesiac** *adj, n*
WORD ORIGIN Greek: forgetfulness

amnesty ❶ *n, pl* **-ties 1** a general pardon for offences against a government **2** a period during which a law is suspended, to allow people to confess to crime or give up weapons without fear of prosecution
WORD ORIGIN Greek *a-* not + *mnasthai* to remember

THESAURUS

ambush *n* **2 = trap**, snare, attack, lure, waylaying, ambuscade ▷*vb* **3 = trap**, attack, surprise, deceive, dupe, ensnare, waylay, ambuscade, bushwhack *(US)*

amend *vb* **= change**, improve, reform, fix, correct, repair, edit, alter, enhance, update, revise, modify, remedy, rewrite, mend, rectify, tweak *(informal)*, ameliorate, redraw

amendment *n* **a = addition**, change, adjustment, attachment, adaptation, revision, modification, alteration, remodelling, reformation, clarification, adjunct, addendum **b = change**, improvement, repair, edit, remedy, correction, revision, modification, alteration, mending, enhancement, reform, betterment, rectification, amelioration, emendation

amenity *n* **= facility**, service, advantage, comfort, convenience

amid *or* **amidst** *prep* **a = during**, among, at a time of, in an atmosphere of **b = in the middle of**, among, surrounded by, amongst, in the midst of, in the thick of

ammunition *n* **1 = munitions**, rounds, shot, shells, powder, explosives, cartridges, armaments, materiel, shot and shell

amnesty *n* **1 = general pardon**, mercy, pardoning, immunity, forgiveness, reprieve, oblivion, remission, clemency, dispensation, absolution, condonation

among *or* **amongst** *prep* **1 = in the**

amniocentesis *n, pl* **-ses** removal of amniotic fluid from the womb of a pregnant woman in order to detect possible abnormalities in the fetus **WORD ORIGIN** *amnion* + Greek *kentēsis* a pricking
amnion *n, pl* **-nia** the innermost of two membranes enclosing an embryo **amniotic** *adj* **WORD ORIGIN** Greek: a little lamb
amniotic fluid *n* the fluid surrounding the fetus in the womb
amoeba *or US* **ameba** (am-mee-ba) *n, pl* **-bae** (-bee) *or* **-bas** a microscopic single-cell creature that is able to change its shape **WORD ORIGIN** Greek *ameibein* to change
amok *or* **amuck** *adv* **run amok** to run about in a violent frenzy **WORD ORIGIN** Malay *amoq* furious assault
among ❶ *or* **amongst** *prep* **1** in the midst of: *she decided to dwell among the Greeks* **2** in the group, class, or number of: *he is among the top trainers* **3** to each of: *the stakes should be divided among the players* **4** with one another within a group: *sort it out among yourselves* **WORD ORIGIN** Old English *amang*
amoral (aim-mor-ral) *adj* without moral standards or principles **amorality** *n*
amorous *adj* feeling, displaying, or relating to sexual love or desire **WORD ORIGIN** Latin *amor* love
amorphous *adj* **1** lacking a definite shape **2** of no recognizable character or type **WORD ORIGIN** Greek *a-* not + *morphē* shape
amortize *or* **-tise** *vb* **-tizing, -tized** *or* **-tising, -tised** *finance* to pay off (a debt) gradually by periodic transfers to a sinking fund **WORD ORIGIN** Latin *ad* to + *mors* death
amount ❶ *n* **1** extent or quantity ▹ *vb* **2 amount to** to be equal or add up to **WORD ORIGIN** Old French *amonter* to go up
amour *n* a secret love affair **WORD ORIGIN** Latin *amor* love
amour-propre (am-moor-prop-ra) *n* self-esteem
amp *n* **1** an ampere **2** *informal* an amplifier
amperage *n* the strength of an electric current measured in amperes
ampere (am-pair) *n* the basic unit of electric current **WORD ORIGIN** after A. M. *Ampère*, French physicist & mathematician
ampersand *n* the character &, meaning *and* **WORD ORIGIN** shortened from *and per se and*, that is, the symbol & by itself (represents) *and*
amphetamine (am-fet-am-mean) *n* a drug used as a stimulant **WORD ORIGIN** shortened from chemical name
amphibian *n* **1** an animal, such as a newt, frog, or toad, that lives on land but breeds in water **2** a vehicle that can travel on both water and land
amphibious *adj* **1** living or operating both on land and in or on water **2** relating to a military attack launched from the sea against a shore **WORD ORIGIN** Greek *amphibios* having a double life
amphitheatre *or US* **amphitheater** *n* a circular or oval building without a roof, in which tiers of seats rise from a central open arena **WORD ORIGIN** Greek *amphitheatron*
amphora (am-for-ra) *n, pl* **-phorae** (-for-ree) an ancient Greek or Roman jar with two handles and a narrow neck **WORD ORIGIN** Greek *amphi-* on both sides + *phoreus* bearer
ample ❶ *adj* **1** more than sufficient: *there is already ample evidence* **2** large: *ample helpings of stewed pomegranates and pears* **WORD ORIGIN** Latin *amplus*
amplifier *n* an electronic device used to increase the strength of a current or sound signal
amplify *vb* **-fies, -fying, -fied** **1** *electronics* to increase the strength of (a current or sound signal) **2** to explain in more detail **3** to increase the size, extent, or effect of **amplification** *n* **WORD ORIGIN** Latin *amplificare*
amplitude *n* **1** greatness of extent **2** *physics* the maximum displacement from the zero or mean position of a wave or oscillation **WORD ORIGIN** Latin *amplus* spacious
amplitude modulation *n electronics* a method of transmitting information using radio waves in which the amplitude of the carrier wave is varied in accordance with the amplitude of the input signal
amply ❶ *adv* fully or generously: *she was amply rewarded for it*
ampoule *or US* **ampule** *n med* a small glass container in which liquids for injection are sealed **WORD ORIGIN** French
ampulla *n, pl* **-pullae** **1** *anat* the dilated end part of certain tubes in the body **2** *Christianity* a container for the wine and water, or the oil, used in church **WORD ORIGIN** Latin
amputate *vb* **-tating, -tated** to cut off (a limb or part of a limb) for medical reasons **amputation** *n* **WORD ORIGIN** Latin *am-* around + *putare* to prune
amputee *n* a person who has had a limb amputated
amuck *adv* ▸ same as **amok**
amulet *n* a trinket or jewel worn as a protection against evil **WORD ORIGIN** Latin *amuletum*
amuse ❶ *vb* **amusing, amused** **1** to cause to laugh or smile **2** to entertain or keep interested **amusing** *adj* **amusingly** *adv* **WORD ORIGIN** Old French *amuser* to cause to be idle
amusement ❶ *n* **1** the state of being amused **2** something that amuses or entertains someone
amusement arcade *n* a large room with coin-operated electronic games and fruit machines
amusement park *n* a large open-air entertainment area with rides and stalls
amylase *n* an enzyme present in saliva that helps to change starch into sugar
an *adj* (*indefinite article*) ▸ same as **a**: used before an initial vowel sound: *an old man; an hour* **WORD ORIGIN** Old English *ān* one
an- *prefix* ▸ see **a-**

THESAURUS

midst of, with, together with, in the middle of, amid, surrounded by, amidst, in the thick of **2 = in the group of**, one of, part of, included in, in the company of, in the class of, in the number of **3 = between**, to
amount *n* **1 = quantity**, lot, measure, size, supply, mass, volume, capacity, extent, bulk, number, magnitude, expanse
ample *adj* **1 = plenty of**, great, rich, liberal, broad, generous, lavish, spacious, abounding, abundant, plentiful, expansive, copious, roomy, unrestricted, voluminous, capacious, profuse, commodious, plenteous **OPPOSITE:** insufficient **2 = large**, great, big, full, wide, broad, extensive, generous, abundant, voluminous, bountiful
amply *adv* **= fully**, well, greatly, completely, richly, liberally, thoroughly, substantially, lavishly, extensively, generously, abundantly, profusely, copiously, plentifully, unstintingly, bountifully, without stinting, plenteously, capaciously **OPPOSITE:** insufficiently
amuse *vb* **1 = entertain**, please, delight, charm, cheer, tickle, gratify, beguile, enliven, regale, gladden **OPPOSITE:** bore **2 = occupy**, interest, involve, engage, entertain, absorb, divert, engross
amusement *n* **1 = enjoyment**, delight, entertainment, cheer, laughter, mirth, hilarity, merriment, gladdening, beguilement, regalement **OPPOSITE:** boredom

DICTIONARY

a

Anabaptist *n* **1** a member of a 16th-century Protestant movement that believed in adult baptism ▹*adj* **2** of this movement
WORD ORIGIN Late Greek *anabaptizein* to baptize again

anabolic steroid *n* a synthetic steroid hormone used to stimulate muscle and bone growth

anabolism *n biol* a metabolic process in which body tissues are synthesized from food
WORD ORIGIN Greek *anabolē* a rising up

anachronism (an-**nak**-kron-iz-zum) *n* **1** the representation of something in a historical context in which it could not have occurred or existed **2** a person or thing that seems to belong to another time **anachronistic** *adj*
WORD ORIGIN Greek *ana* against + *khronos* time

anaconda *n* a large S American snake which squeezes its prey to death
WORD ORIGIN probably from Sinhalese *henakandayā* whip snake

Anacreon *n* ?572–?488 BC, Greek lyric poet, noted for his short songs celebrating love and wine

anaemia *or US* **anemia** (an-**neem**-ee-a) *n* a deficiency of red blood cells or their haemoglobin content, resulting in paleness and lack of energy
WORD ORIGIN Greek *an* without + *haima* blood

anaemic *or US* **anemic** *adj* **1** having anaemia **2** pale and sickly-looking **3** lacking vitality

anaerobe *n biol* an organism that does not require oxygen **anaerobic** *adj*
WORD ORIGIN Greek *an* not + *aēr* air + *bios* life

anaesthesia *or US* **anesthesia** (an-niss-**theez**-ee-a) *n* loss of bodily feeling caused by disease or accident or by drugs such as ether: called **general anaesthesia** when consciousness is lost and **local anaesthesia** when only a specific area of the body is involved
WORD ORIGIN Greek

anaesthetic ❶ *or US* **anesthetic** (an-niss-**thet**-ik) *n* **1** a substance that causes anaesthesia ▹*adj* **2** causing anaesthesia

anaesthetist (an-**neess**-thet-ist) *n Brit* a doctor who administers anaesthetics

anaesthetize, anaesthetise *or US* **anesthetize** *vb* **-tizing, -tized** *or* **-tising, -tised** to cause to feel no pain by administering an anaesthetic

Anaglypta *n trademark* a thick embossed wallpaper, designed to be painted

anagram *n* a word or phrase made by rearranging the letters of another word or phrase
WORD ORIGIN Greek *anagrammatizein* to transpose letters

anal (**ain**-al) *adj* of or relating to the anus
WORD ORIGIN New Latin *analis*

analgesia *n* the absence of pain
WORD ORIGIN Greek

analgesic (an-nal-**jeez**-ik) *n* **1** a drug that relieves pain ▹*adj* **2** pain-relieving: *an analgesic balm*

analog *n US & computers* ▸same as **analogue**

analogize *or* **-gise** *vb* **-gizing, -gized** *or* **-gising, -gised 1** to use analogy in argument **2** to reveal analogy between (one thing and another)

analogous *adj* similar in some respects
WORD ORIGIN Greek *analogos* proportionate

analogue *or US* **analog** *n* **1** a physical object or quantity used to measure or represent another quantity **2** something that is analogous to something else ▹*adj* **3** displaying information by means of a dial: *analogue speedometers*

analogy ❶ *n, pl* **-gies 1** a similarity, usually in a limited number of features **2** a comparison made to show such a similarity **analogical** *adj*
WORD ORIGIN Greek *analogia*

anal-retentive *adj* (of a person) excessively fussy and concerned with order and minute details

analyse ❶ *or US* **-lyze** (**an**-nal-lize) *vb* **-lysing, -lysed** *or* **-lyzing, -lyzed 1** to examine (something) in detail in order to discover its meaning or essential features **2** to break (something) down into its components **3** to psychoanalyse (someone)

analysis ❶ (an-**nal**-liss-iss) *n, pl* **-ses** (-seez) **1** the separation of a whole into its parts for study or interpretation **2** a statement of the results of this **3** ▸short for **psychoanalysis**
WORD ORIGIN Greek *analusis* a dissolving

analyst *n* **1** a person who is skilled in analysis **2** a psychoanalyst

analytical *or* **analytic** *adj* relating to or using analysis **analytically** *adv*

Ananda *n* 5th century BC, the first cousin, favourite disciple, and personal attendant of the Buddha

anaphylactic shock *n* a severe, sometimes fatal, reaction to a substance to which a person has an extreme sensitivity, often involving respiratory difficulty and circulation failure
WORD ORIGIN Greek *ana* again + *phulaxis* guarding

anarchism *n* a doctrine advocating the abolition of government and its replacement by a social system based on voluntary cooperation

anarchist *n* **1** a person who advocates anarchism **2** a person who causes disorder or upheaval **anarchistic** *adj*

anarchy ❶ (**an**-ark-ee) *n* **1** general lawlessness and disorder **2** the absence of government **anarchic** *adj*
WORD ORIGIN Greek *an* without + *arkh-* leader

Anastasia *n* **Grand Duchess** 1901–?18, daughter of Tsar Nicholas II, believed to have been executed by the Bolsheviks in 1918, although several women subsequently claimed to be her

anastigmat *n* a lens corrected for astigmatism **anastigmatic** *adj*

anathema (an-**nath**-im-a) *n* a detested person or thing: *the very colour was anathema to him*
WORD ORIGIN Greek: something accursed

anathematize *or* **-tise** *vb* **-tizing, -tized** *or* **-tising, -tised** to curse: *he anathematized the world in general*

anatomist *n* an expert in anatomy

anatomy ❶ *n, pl* **-mies 1** the science of the physical structure of animals and plants **2** the structure of an animal or plant **3** *informal* a person's body: *the male anatomy* **4** a detailed analysis: *an anatomy of the massacre* **anatomical** *adj*
WORD ORIGIN Greek *ana* up + *temnein* to cut

Anaxagoras *n* ?500–428 BC, Greek philosopher who maintained that all things were composed of minute particles arranged by an

THESAURUS

2 = pastime, game, sport, joke, entertainment, hobby, recreation, distraction, diversion, lark, prank

anaesthetic *n* **1 = painkiller**, narcotic, sedative, opiate, anodyne, analgesic, soporific, stupefacient, stupefactive ▹*adj* **2 = pain-killing**, dulling, numbing, narcotic, sedative, opiate, deadening, anodyne, analgesic, soporific, sleep-inducing, stupefacient, stupefactive

analogy *n* **1 = similarity**, relation, parallel, correspondence, resemblance, correlation, likeness, equivalence, homology, similitude **2 = comparison**

analyse *vb* **1 = examine**, test, study, research, judge, estimate, survey, investigate, interpret, evaluate, inspect, work over **2 = break down**, consider, study, separate, divide, resolve, dissolve, dissect, think through, assay, anatomize

analysis *n* **1 = examination**, test, division, inquiry, investigation, resolution, interpretation, breakdown, scanning, separation,

DICTIONARY

a

eternal intelligence
Anaximander *n* 611–547 BC, Greek philosopher, astronomer, and mathematician who believed the first principle of the world to be the Infinite
Anaximenes *n* 6th century BC, Greek philosopher who believed air to be the primary substance
ANC African National Congress: South African political movement instrumental in bringing an end to apartheid
ancestor ❶ *n* **1** a person in former times from whom one is descended **2** a forerunner: *the immediate ancestor of rock and roll is rhythm and blues*
WORD ORIGIN Latin *antecedere* to go before
ancestral *adj* of or inherited from ancestors
ancestry *n, pl* **-tries** **1** family descent: *of Japanese ancestry* **2** origin or roots: *a vehicle whose ancestry dated back to the 1950s*
anchor *n* **1** a hooked device attached to a boat by a cable and dropped overboard to fasten the boat to the sea bottom **2** a source of stability or security: *a spiritual anchor* **3** **anchors** *slang* the brakes of a motor vehicle: *he rammed on the anchors* ▹*vb* **4** to use an anchor to hold (a boat) in one place **5** to fasten securely: *we anchored his wheelchair to a rock*
WORD ORIGIN Greek *ankura*
anchorage *n* a place where boats can be anchored
anchor ice *n Canad* ice that forms at the bottom of a lake or river
anchorite *n* a person who chooses to live in isolation for religious reasons
WORD ORIGIN Greek *anakhōrein* to retire
anchorman *or* **anchorwoman** *n* **1** a broadcaster in a central studio, who links up and presents items from outside camera units and reporters in other studios **2** the last person to compete in a relay team
anchovy (an-chov-ee) *n, pl* **-vies** a small marine food fish with a salty taste
WORD ORIGIN Spanish *anchova*
ancien régime (on-syan ray-**zheem**) *n* **1** the political and social system of France before the 1789 Revolution **2** a former system
WORD ORIGIN French: old regime
ancient ❶ *adj* **1** dating from very long ago **2** very old **3** of the far past, esp. before the collapse of the Western Roman Empire (476 AD) ▹*n* **4** **ancients** people who lived very long ago, such as the Romans and Greeks
WORD ORIGIN Latin *ante* before
ancillary *adj* **1** supporting the main work of an organization: *hospital ancillary workers* **2** used as an extra or supplement: *I had a small ancillary sleeping tent*
WORD ORIGIN Latin *ancilla* female servant
and ❶ *conj* **1** in addition to: *plants and birds* **2** as a consequence: *she fell downstairs and broke her neck* **3** afterwards: *she excused herself and left* **4** used for emphasis or to indicate repetition or continuity: *they called again and again* **5** used to express a contrast between instances of something: *there are jobs and jobs* **6** *informal* used in place of *to* in infinitives after verbs such as *try, go,* and *come*: *come and see us again*
WORD ORIGIN Old English
andante (an-**dan**-tay) *music adv* **1** moderately slowly ▹*n* **2** a passage or piece to be performed moderately slowly
WORD ORIGIN Italian *andare* to walk
andantino (an-dan-**tee**-no) *music adv* **1** slightly faster than andante ▹*n, pl* **-nos** **2** a passage or piece to be performed in this way
Andersen Nexø *n* ▸See **Nexø**
Anderson[1] *n* a river in N Canada, in the Northwest Territories, rising in lakes north of Great Bear Lake and flowing west and north to the Beaufort Sea. Length: about 580 km (360 miles)
Anderson[2] *n* **1** **Carl David** 1905–91, US physicist, who discovered the positron in cosmic rays (1932): Nobel prize for physics 1936 **2** **Elizabeth Garrett** 1836–1917, English physician and feminist: a campaigner for the admission of women to the professions **3** **John** 1893–1962, Australian philosopher, born in Scotland, whose theories are expounded in *Studies in Empirical Philosophy* (1962) **4** Dame **Judith,** real name *Frances Margaret Anderson.* 1898–1992, Australian stage and film actress **5** **Lindsay** (**Gordon**) 1923–94, British film and theatre director: his films include *This Sporting Life* (1963), *If* (1968), *O Lucky Man!* (1973), and *The Whales of August* (1987) **6** **Marian** 1902–93, US contralto, the first Black permanent member of the Metropolitan Opera Company, New York **7** **Philip Warren** born 1923, US physicist, noted for his work on solid-state physics. Nobel prize for physics 1977 **8** **Sherwood** 1874–1941, US novelist and short-story writer, best known for *Winesburg Ohio* (1919), a collection of short stories illustrating small-town life
Anderssen *n* **Adolf** 1818–79, German chess player: noted for the incisiveness of his combination play
andiron *n* either of a pair of metal stands for supporting logs in a fireplace
WORD ORIGIN Old French *andier*
and/or *conj not standard* either one or the other or both
Andrássy *n* Count **Gyula** 1823–90, Hungarian statesman; the first prime minister of Hungary under the Dual Monarchy of Austria-Hungary (1867)
André *n* **John** 1751–80, British major who was hanged as a spy for conspiring with Benedict Arnold during the War of American Independence
Andrea del Sarto *n* ▸See **Sarto**
Andretti *n* **Mario** born 1940, US racing driver: world champion (1978)
Andrewes *n* **Lancelot** 1555–1626, English bishop and theologian
Andrews *n* **Thomas** 1813–85, Irish physical chemist, noted for his work on the liquefaction of gases
Andrić *n* **Ivo** 1892–1975, Serbian novelist; author of *The Bridge on the Drina* (1945): Nobel prize for literature 1961
androgen *n* any of the steroids that promote the development of male sexual organs and certain male sexual characteristics
WORD ORIGIN Greek *anēr* man + *-gen* (suffix) producing
androgynous *adj* having both male and female characteristics
WORD ORIGIN Greek *anēr* man + *gunē* woman
android *n* a robot resembling a human being
WORD ORIGIN Late Greek *androeidēs* manlike
andrology (an-**drol**-la-jee) *n* the branch of medicine concerned with

THESAURUS

evaluation, scrutiny, sifting, anatomy, dissolution, dissection, assay, perusal, anatomization
anarchy *n* **1 = lawlessness**, revolution, riot, disorder, confusion, chaos, rebellion, misrule, disorganization, misgovernment **OPPOSITE:** order
anatomy *n* **2 = structure**, build, make-up, frame, framework, composition **4 = examination**, study, division, inquiry, investigation, analysis, dissection
ancestor *n* **1 = forefather**, predecessor, precursor, forerunner, forebear, antecedent, progenitor, tupuna *or* tipuna (NZ)
OPPOSITE: descendant
ancient *adj* **1 = classical**, old, former, past, bygone, primordial, primeval, olden **2 = very old**, early, aged, antique, obsolete, archaic, age-old, bygone, antiquated, hoary, olden, superannuated, antediluvian, timeworn, old as the hills
and *conj* **1 = also**, including, along with, together with, in addition to, as well as

DICTIONARY

a

diseases and conditions specific to men **andrologist** *n*
WORD ORIGIN Greek *anēr* man + -LOGY

anecdote ❶ *n* a short amusing account of an incident **anecdotal** *adj*
WORD ORIGIN Greek *anekdotos* not published

anemia *n US* anaemia

anemometer *n* an instrument for recording wind speed

anemone (an-nem-on-ee) *n* a flowering plant with white, purple, or red flowers
WORD ORIGIN Greek: windflower

aneroid barometer *n* a device for measuring air pressure, consisting of a partially evacuated chamber, in which variations in pressure cause a pointer on the lid to move
WORD ORIGIN Greek *a* not + *nēros* wet

anesthesia *n US* anaesthesia

aneurysm *or* **aneurism** (an-new-riz-zum) *n med* a permanent swelling of a blood vessel
WORD ORIGIN Greek *aneurunein* to dilate

anew *adv* **1** once more **2** in a different way

Anfinsen *n* **Christian Boehmer** 1916–95, US biochemist, noted for his research on the structure of enzymes. Nobel prize for chemistry 1972

angel ❶ *n* **1** a spiritual being believed to be an attendant or messenger of God **2** a conventional representation of an angel as a human being with wings **3** *informal* a person who is kind, pure, or beautiful **4** *informal* an investor in a theatrical production
WORD ORIGIN Greek *angelos* messenger

angel cake *or esp. US* **angel food cake** *n* a very light sponge cake

angelfish *n, pl* **-fish** *or* **-fishes** a South American aquarium fish with large fins

angelic *adj* **1** very kind, pure, or beautiful **2** of or relating to angels **angelically** *adv*

angelica (an-jell-ik-a) *n* a plant whose candied stalks are used in cookery
WORD ORIGIN Medieval Latin *(herba) angelica* angelic herb

Angell *n* Sir **Norman,** real name *Ralph Norman Angell Lane.* 1874–1967, English writer, pacifist, and economist, noted for his work on the economic futility of war, *The Great Illusion* (1910): Nobel peace prize 1933

Angelou *n* **Maya,** real name *Marguerite Johnson.* born 1928, US Black novelist, poet, and dramatist. Her works include the autobiographical novel I *Know Why the Caged Bird Sings* (1970) and its sequels

Angelus (an-jell-uss) *n RC church* **1** prayers recited in the morning, at midday, and in the evening **2** the bell signalling the times of these prayers
WORD ORIGIN Latin *Angelus domini nuntiavit Mariae* the angel of the Lord brought tidings to Mary

anger ❶ *n* **1** a feeling of extreme annoyance or displeasure ▷*vb* **2** to make (someone) angry
WORD ORIGIN Old Norse *angr* grief

angina (an-jine-a) *or* **angina pectoris** (peck-tor-riss) *n* a sudden intense pain in the chest caused by a momentary lack of adequate blood supply to the heart muscle
WORD ORIGIN Greek *ankhonē* a strangling

angle[1] ❶ *n* **1** the space between or shape formed by two straight lines or surfaces that meet **2** the divergence between two such lines or surfaces, measured in degrees **3** a recess or corner **4** point of view ▷*vb* **-gling, -gled 5** to move in or place at an angle **6** to write (an article) from a particular point of view
WORD ORIGIN Latin *angulus* corner

angle[2] *vb* **-gling, -gled 1** to fish with a hook and line **2 angle for** to try to get by hinting: *he's just angling for sympathy*
WORD ORIGIN Old English *angul* fish-hook

angler *n* a person who fishes with a hook and line

Angles *pl n* a race from N Germany who settled in E and N England in the 5th and 6th centuries AD
WORD ORIGIN Latin *Anglus* a person from Angul, Germany

Anglican *adj* **1** of or relating to the Church of England ▷*n* **2** a member of the Anglican Church
Anglicanism *n*
WORD ORIGIN Latin *Anglicus* English, of the Angles

Anglicism *n* an expression or custom that is peculiar to the English

anglicize *or* **-cise** *vb* **-cizing, -cized** *or* **-cising, -cised** to make or become English in outlook or form

angling *n* the art or sport of fishing with a hook and line

Anglo *n, pl* **-glos 1** *US* a White inhabitant of the US who is not of Latin extraction **2** *Canad* an English-speaking Canadian

Anglo- *combining form* English or British: *the history of Anglo-German relations*
WORD ORIGIN Medieval Latin *Anglii* the English

Anglo-French *adj* **1** of England and France **2** of the Anglo-French language ▷*n* **3** the Norman-French language of medieval England

Anglo-Indian *adj* **1** of England and India **2** denoting or relating to Anglo-Indians ▷*n* **3** a person of mixed British and Indian descent **4** an English person who has lived for a long time in India

Anglo-Norman *adj* **1** of or relating to the Norman conquerors of England or their language ▷*n* **2** a Norman inhabitant of England after 1066 **3** the Anglo-French language

Anglophile *n* a person who admires England or the English

Anglo-Saxon *n* **1** a member of any of the West Germanic tribes that settled in Britain from the 5th century AD **2** any White person whose native language is English **3** ▸same as **Old English 4** *informal* plain, blunt, and often rude English

THESAURUS

anecdote *n* **= story**, tale, sketch, short story, yarn, reminiscence, urban myth, urban legend

angel *n* **1, 2 = divine messenger**, spirit, cherub, archangel, seraph, spiritual being, guardian spirit **3** *(informal)* **= dear**, ideal, beauty, saint, treasure, darling, dream, jewel, gem, paragon

anger *n* **1 = rage**, passion, outrage, temper, fury, resentment, irritation, wrath, indignation, annoyance, agitation, ire, antagonism, displeasure, exasperation, irritability, spleen, pique, ill temper, vehemence, vexation, high dudgeon, ill humour, choler
OPPOSITE: calmness
▷*vb* **2 = enrage**, provoke, outrage, annoy, offend, excite, irritate, infuriate, hassle *(informal)*, aggravate *(informal)*, incense, fret, gall, madden, exasperate, nettle, vex, affront, displease, rile, pique, get on someone's nerves *(informal)*, antagonize, get someone's back up, put someone's back up, nark *(Brit, Austral & NZ slang)*, make someone's blood boil, get in someone's hair *(informal)*, get someone's dander up *(informal)* **OPPOSITE:** soothe

angle[1] *n* **1, 2 = gradient**, bank, slope, incline, inclination **3 = intersection**, point, edge, corner, knee, bend, elbow, crook, crotch, nook, cusp **4 = point of view**, position, approach, direction, aspect, perspective, outlook, viewpoint, slant, standpoint, take *(informal)*, side

angry *adj* **1 = furious**, cross, heated, mad *(informal)*, raging, provoked, outraged, annoyed, passionate, irritated, raving, hacked (off) *(US slang)*, choked, infuriated, hot, incensed, enraged, ranting, exasperated, irritable, resentful, nettled, snappy, indignant, irate, tumultuous, displeased, uptight *(informal)*, riled, up in arms, incandescent, ill-tempered, irascible, antagonized, waspish, piqued, hot under the collar

DICTIONARY

▷ *adj* **5** of the Anglo-Saxons or the Old English language **6** of the White Protestant culture of Britain and the US

angora *n* **1** a variety of goat, cat, or rabbit with long silky hair **2** the hair of the angora goat or rabbit **3** cloth made from this hair
WORD ORIGIN *Angora*, former name of Ankara, in Turkey

Angostura Bitters *pl n trademark* a bitter tonic, used as a flavouring in alcoholic drinks
WORD ORIGIN from *Angostura* in Venezuela

angry ❶ *adj* **-grier, -griest 1** feeling or expressing annoyance or rage **2** severely inflamed: *he had angry welts on his forehead* **3** dark and stormy: *angry waves* **angrily** *adv*

angst ❶ *n* a feeling of anxiety
WORD ORIGIN German

angstrom *n* a unit of length equal to 10^{-10} metre, used to measure wavelengths
WORD ORIGIN after Anders J. *Ångström*, Swedish physicist

anguish ❶ *n* great mental pain
WORD ORIGIN Latin *angustus* narrow

anguished *adj* feeling or showing great mental pain: *anguished cries*

angular *adj* **1** lean and bony: *his angular face* **2** having an angle or angles **3** measured by an angle: *angular momentum* **angularity** *n*

anhydride *n chem* a substance that combines with water to form an acid

anhydrous *adj chem* containing no water
WORD ORIGIN Greek *an* without + *hudōr* water

anil *n* a West Indian shrub which is a source of indigo
WORD ORIGIN Arabic *an-nīl*, the indigo

aniline *n chem* a colourless oily poisonous liquid, obtained from coal tar and used for making dyes, plastics, and explosives

animal ❶ *n* **1** *zool* any living being that is capable of voluntary movement and possesses specialized sense organs **2** any living being other than a human being **3** any living being with four legs **4** a cruel or coarse person **5** *facetious* a person or thing: *there's no such animal* ▷ *adj* **6** of or from animals **7** of or relating to physical needs or desires
WORD ORIGIN Latin *animalis* (adjective) living, breathing

animalcule *n* a microscopic animal

animal husbandry *n* the science of breeding, rearing, and caring for farm animals

animalism *n* **1** preoccupation with physical matters; sensuality **2** the doctrine that human beings lack a spiritual nature

animality *n* **1** the animal instincts of human beings **2** the state of being an animal

animalize *or* **-ise** *vb* **-izing, -ized** *or* **-ising, -ised** to make (a person) brutal or sensual

animal magnetism *n* the quality of being sexually attractive

animal rights *pl n* the rights of animals to be protected from human abuse

animal spirits *pl n* outgoing and boisterous enthusiasm
WORD ORIGIN from a vital force once supposed to be dispatched by the brain to all points of the body

animate ❶ *vb* **-mating, -mated 1** to give life to **2** to make lively **3** to produce (a story) as an animated cartoon ▷ *adj* **4** having life
WORD ORIGIN Latin *anima* breath, spirit

animated ❶ *adj* **1** interesting and lively **2** (of a cartoon) made by using animation **animatedly** *adv*

animated cartoon *n* a film produced by photographing a series of gradually changing drawings, which give the illusion of movement when the series is projected rapidly

animation ❶ *n* **1** the techniques used in the production of animated cartoons **2** liveliness and enthusiasm: *there's an animation in her that is new*

animator *n* a person who makes animated cartoons

animism *n* the belief that natural objects possess souls **animist** *n, adj* **animistic** *adj*
WORD ORIGIN Latin *anima* breath, spirit

animosity *n, pl* **-ties** a powerful dislike or hostility
WORD ORIGIN see ANIMUS

animus *n* intense dislike; hatred
WORD ORIGIN Latin: mind, spirit

anion (an-eye-on) *n* an ion with negative charge **anionic** *adj*
WORD ORIGIN Greek *ana-* up + *ienai* to go

anise (an-niss) *n* a Mediterranean plant with liquorice-flavoured seeds
WORD ORIGIN Greek *anison*

aniseed *n* the liquorice-flavoured seeds of the anise plant, used for flavouring

ankh *n* a T-shaped cross with a loop on the top, which symbolized eternal life in ancient Egypt
WORD ORIGIN Egyptian *'nh* life, soul

ankle *n* **1** the joint connecting the leg and the foot **2** the part of the leg just above the foot
WORD ORIGIN Old Norse

anklet *n* an ornamental chain worn round the ankle

ankylosis (ang-kill-**loh**-siss) *n* abnormal immobility of a joint, caused by a fibrous growth within the joint
WORD ORIGIN Greek *ankuloun* to crook

An Lu Shan *n* 703–57 AD, Chinese military governor. He declared himself emperor (756) and seized the capital Chang An; murdered by a eunuch slave

anna *n* a former Indian coin worth one sixteenth of a rupee
WORD ORIGIN Hindi *ānā*

annals *pl n* **1** yearly records of events **2** regular reports of the work of a society or other organization **annalist** *n*
WORD ORIGIN Latin *(libri) annales* yearly (books)

THESAURUS

(informal), on the warpath, hopping mad *(informal)*, foaming at the mouth, choleric, splenetic, wrathful, at daggers drawn, in high dudgeon, as black as thunder, ireful, tooshie *(Austral slang)*, off the air *(Austral slang)*, aerated **OPPOSITE:** calm

angst *n* = **anxiety**, worry, distress, torment, unease, apprehension, agitation, malaise, perturbation, vexation, fretfulness, disquietude, inquietude **OPPOSITE:** peace of mind

anguish *n* = **suffering**, pain, torture, distress, grief, misery, agony, torment, sorrow, woe, heartache, heartbreak, pang, throe

animal *n* **1, 2, 3** = **creature**, beast, brute **4** = **brute**, devil, monster, savage, beast, bastard *(informal, offensive)*, villain, barbarian, swine *(informal)*, wild man ▷ *adj* **7** = **physical**, gross, fleshly, bodily, sensual, carnal, brutish, bestial, animalistic

animate *vb* **2** = **enliven**, encourage, excite, urge, inspire, stir, spark, move, fire, spur, stimulate, revive, activate, rouse, prod, quicken, incite, instigate, kick-start *(informal)*, impel, energize, kindle, embolden, liven up, breathe life into, invigorate, gladden, gee up, vitalize, vivify, inspirit **OPPOSITE:** inhibit
▸ *adj* **4** = **living**, live, moving, alive, breathing, alive and kicking

animated *adj* **1** = **lively**, spirited, quick, excited, active, vital, dynamic, enthusiastic, passionate, vivid, vigorous, energetic, vibrant, brisk, buoyant, ardent, airy, fervent, zealous, elated, ebullient, sparky, sprightly, vivacious, gay, alive and kicking, full of beans *(informal)*, zestful **OPPOSITE:** listless

animation *n* **2** = **liveliness**, life, action, activity, energy, spirit, passion, enthusiasm, excitement, pep, sparkle, vitality, vigour, zeal, verve, zest, fervour, high spirits, dynamism, buoyancy, elation, exhilaration, gaiety, ardour, vibrancy, brio, zing *(informal)*,

DICTIONARY

a

Annan *n* **Kofi** born 1938, Ghanaian international civil servant; secretary-general of the United Nations (1997–2007): Nobel peace prize 2001 with the UN

anneal *vb* to toughen (glass or metal) by heat treatment
WORD ORIGIN Old English *onǣlan*

annelid *n* a worm with a segmented body, such as the earthworm
WORD ORIGIN Latin *anulus* ring

Anne of Austria *n* 1601–66, wife of Louis XIII of France and daughter of Philip III of Spain: regent of France (1643–61) for her son Louis XIV

Anne of Bohemia *n* 1366–94, queen consort of Richard II of England

Anne of Cleves *n* 1515–57, the fourth wife of Henry VIII of England: their marriage (1540) was annulled after six months

Anne of Denmark *n* 1574–1619, wife (from 1589) of James I of England and VI of Scotland

annex *vb* **1** to seize (territory) by conquest or occupation **2** to take without permission **3** to join or add (something) to something larger **annexation** *n*
WORD ORIGIN Latin *annectere* to attach to

annexe *or esp. US* **annex** *n* **1** an extension to a main building **2** a building used as an addition to a main one nearby

Annigoni *n* **Pietro** 1910–88, Italian painter; noted esp. for his portraits of President Kennedy (1961) and Queen Elizabeth II (1955 and 1970)

annihilate *vb* **-lating, -lated 1** to destroy (a place or a group of people) completely **2** *informal* to defeat totally in an argument or a contest **annihilation** *n*
WORD ORIGIN Latin *nihil* nothing

anniversary *n, pl* **-ries 1** the date on which an event, such as a wedding, occurred in some previous year **2** the celebration of this
WORD ORIGIN Latin *annus* year + *vertere* to turn

anno Domini *adv* in the year of our Lord

annotate *vb* **-tating, -tated** to add critical or explanatory notes to a written work **annotation** *n*
WORD ORIGIN Latin *nota* mark

announce ⊕ *vb* **-nouncing, -nounced 1** to make known publicly **2** to proclaim **3** to declare the arrival of (a person) **4** to be a sign of: *snowdrops announced the arrival of spring* **announcement** *n*
WORD ORIGIN Latin *annuntiare*

announcer *n* a person who introduces programmes on radio or television

annoy ⊕ *vb* **1** to irritate or displease **2** to harass sexually **annoyance** *n* **annoying** *adj*
WORD ORIGIN Latin *in odio (esse)* (to be) hated

annual ⊕ *adj* **1** occurring or done once a year: *the union's annual conference* **2** lasting for a year: *the annual subscription* ▷ *n* **3** a plant that completes its life cycle in one year **4** a book published once every year **annually** *adv*
WORD ORIGIN Latin *annus* year

annualize *or* **-ise** *vb* **-izing, -ized** *or* **-ising, -ised** to calculate (a rate) for or as if for a year

annuity *n, pl* **-ties** a fixed sum payable at specified intervals over a period
WORD ORIGIN Latin *annuus* annual

annul *vb* **-nulling, -nulled** to declare (a contract or marriage) invalid
WORD ORIGIN Latin *nullus* not any

annular (an-new-lar) *adj* ring-shaped
WORD ORIGIN Latin *anulus* ring

annular eclipse *n* an eclipse of the sun in which a ring of sunlight can be seen surrounding the shadow of the moon

annulate (an-new-lit) *adj* having, composed of, or marked with rings
WORD ORIGIN Latin *anulus* ring

annulment *n* the formal declaration that a contract or marriage is invalid

Annunciation *n* **1 the Annunciation** the announcement by the angel Gabriel to the Virgin Mary of her conception of Christ **2** the festival commemorating this, on March 25 (Lady Day)
WORD ORIGIN Latin *annuntiare* to announce

anode *n electronics* the positive electrode in an electrolytic cell or in an electronic valve
WORD ORIGIN Greek *anodos* a way up

anodize *or* **-dise** *vb* **-dizing, -dized** *or* **-dising, -dised** *chem* to coat (a metal) with a protective oxide film by electrolysis

anodyne *n* **1** something that relieves pain or distress ▷ *adj* **2** neutral **3** capable of relieving pain or distress
WORD ORIGIN Greek *an-* without + *odunē* pain

anoint *vb* to smear with oil as a sign of consecration
WORD ORIGIN Latin *inunguere*

anointing of the sick *n RC church* a sacrament in which a person who is dying is anointed by a priest

anomalous *adj* different from the normal or usual order or type
WORD ORIGIN Greek *an-* not + *homalos* even

anomaly ⊕ (an-nom-a-lee) *n, pl* **-lies** something that deviates from the normal; an irregularity

anomie *or* **anomy** (an-oh-mee) *n sociol* lack of social or moral standards
WORD ORIGIN Greek *a-* without + *nomos* law

anon *adv old-fashioned or informal* soon: *you shall see him anon*
WORD ORIGIN Old English *on āne* in one, that is, immediately

anon. anonymous

anonymize *or* **-ise** *vb* **-izing, -ized** *or* **-ising, -ised** to organize in a way that preserves anonymity: *anonymized AIDS screening*

anonymous ⊕ *adj* **1** by someone whose name is unknown or withheld: *an anonymous letter* **2** having no known name: *an anonymous writer* **3** lacking distinguishing characteristics: *an anonymous little town* **4 Anonymous** of an organization that helps applicants who remain anonymous: *Alcoholics Anonymous* **anonymity** *n*
WORD ORIGIN Greek *an-* without + *onoma* name

anorak *n* **1** a waterproof hip-length jacket with a hood **2** *Brit informal* a socially inept person with a hobby considered to be boring
WORD ORIGIN Greenland Inuktitut *ánorâq*

anorexia *or* **anorexia nervosa** *n* a psychological disorder characterized by fear of becoming fat and refusal to eat **anorexic** *adj, n*
WORD ORIGIN Greek *an-* without + *orexis* appetite

another *adj* **1** one more: *they don't have the right to demand another chance* **2** different: *you'll have to find another excuse* ▷ *pron* **3** one more: *help yourself to*

THESAURUS

vivacity, ebullience, briskness, airiness, sprightliness, pizzazz *or* pizazz *(informal)*

announce *vb* **1, 2 = make known**, tell, report, reveal, publish, declare, advertise, broadcast, disclose, intimate, proclaim, trumpet, make public, publicize, divulge, promulgate, propound, shout from the rooftops *(informal)*
OPPOSITE: keep secret

annoy *vb* **1 = irritate**, trouble, bore, anger, harry, bother, disturb, provoke, get *(informal)*, bug *(informal)*, needle *(informal)*, plague, tease, harass, hassle *(informal)*, aggravate *(informal)*, badger, gall, madden, ruffle, exasperate, nettle, molest, pester, vex, displease, irk, bedevil, rile, peeve, get under your skin *(informal)*, get on your nerves *(informal)*, nark *(Brit, Austral & NZ slang)*, get up your nose *(informal)*, give someone grief *(Brit & S African)*, make your blood boil, rub someone up the wrong way *(informal)*, get your goat *(slang)*, get in your hair *(informal)*, get on your wick *(Brit slang)*, get your dander up *(informal)*, get your back up, incommode, put your back up,

DICTIONARY

a

another **4** a different one: *one way or another*
WORD ORIGIN originally *an other*
Anouilh *n* **Jean** 1910–87, French dramatist, noted for his reinterpretations of Greek myths: his works include *Eurydice* (1942), *Antigone* (1944), and *Becket* (1959)
Ansermet *n* **Ernest** 1883–1969, Swiss orchestral conductor; principal conductor of Diaghilev's Ballet Russe
answer ❶ *vb* **1** to reply or respond (to) by word or act **2** to be responsible (to a person) **3** to reply correctly to (a question) **4** to respond or react: *a dog that answers to the name of Pugg* **5** to meet the requirements of **6** to give a defence of (a charge) ▷ *n* **7** a reply to a question, request, letter, or article **8** a solution to a problem **9** a reaction or response
WORD ORIGIN Old English *andswaru*
answerable *adj* **answerable for** *or* **to** responsible for or accountable to
answer back *vb* to reply rudely (to)
answering machine *n* a device for answering a telephone automatically and recording messages
ant *n* a small often wingless insect, living in highly organized colonies
WORD ORIGIN Old English *ǣmette*
antacid *chem n* **1** a substance used to treat acidity in the stomach ▷ *adj* **2** having the properties of this substance
antagonism *n* openly expressed hostility
antagonist *n* an opponent or adversary **antagonistic** *adj*
antagonize *or* **-nise** *vb* **-nizing, -nized** *or* **-nising, -nised** to arouse hostility in: *it was not prudent to antagonize a hired killer*
WORD ORIGIN Greek *anti-* against + *agōn* contest
antalkali (ant-alk-a-lie) *n chem* a substance that neutralizes alkalis
Antarctic *n* **1 the Antarctic** the area around the South Pole ▷ *adj* **2** of this region
WORD ORIGIN Greek *antarktikos*
Antarctic Circle *n* the imaginary circle around the earth at latitude 66° 32′ S
ante *n* **1** the stake put up before the deal in poker by the players **2** *informal* a sum of money representing a person's share **3 up the ante** *informal* to increase the costs or risks involved in an action ▷ *vb* **-teing, -ted** *or* **-teed 4** to place (one's stake) in poker **5 ante up** *informal* to pay
WORD ORIGIN Latin: before
ante- *prefix* before in time or position: *antediluvian; antechamber*
WORD ORIGIN Latin
anteater *n* a mammal with a long snout used for eating termites
antecedent *n* **1** an event or circumstance that happens or exists before another **2** *grammar* a word or phrase to which a relative pronoun, such as *who*, refers **3 antecedents** a person's ancestors and past history ▷ *adj* **4** preceding in time or order
WORD ORIGIN Latin *antecedere* to go before
antechamber *n* an anteroom
antedate *vb* **-dating, -dated 1** to be or occur at an earlier date than **2** to give (something) a date that is earlier than the actual date
antediluvian *adj* **1** belonging to the ages before the biblical Flood **2** old-fashioned
WORD ORIGIN Latin *ante-* before + *diluvium* flood
antelope *n, pl* **-lopes** *or* **-lope** any of a group of graceful deerlike mammals of Africa and Asia, which have long legs and horns
WORD ORIGIN Late Greek *antholops* a legendary beast
antenatal *adj* before birth; during pregnancy: *an antenatal clinic*
antenna *n* **1** *pl* **-nae** one of a pair of mobile feelers on the heads of insects, lobsters, and certain other creatures **2** *pl* **-nas** an aerial: TV *antennas*
WORD ORIGIN Latin: sail yard
antepenultimate *adj* **1** third from last ▷ *n* **2** anything that is third from last
ante-post *adj Brit* (of a bet) placed before the runners in a race are confirmed
anterior *adj* **1** at or towards the front **2** earlier
WORD ORIGIN Latin
anteroom *n* a small room leading into a larger room, often used as a waiting room
Antheil *n* **George** 1900–59, US composer. His best known work is the controversial *Le Ballet Méchanique* (1924) for motor horns, bells, and aeroplane propellers
anthem ❶ *n* **1** a song of loyalty or devotion: *a national anthem* **2** a piece of music for a choir, usually set to words from the Bible
WORD ORIGIN Late Latin *antiphona* antiphon
anther *n bot* the part of the stamen of a flower which contains the pollen
WORD ORIGIN Greek *anthos* flower
ant hill *n* a mound of soil built by ants around the entrance to their nest
anthology ❶ *n, pl* **-gies** a collection of poems or other literary pieces by various authors **anthologist** *n*
WORD ORIGIN Greek *anthos* flower + *legein* to collect
Anthony *n* **Saint** ?251–?356 AD, Egyptian hermit, commonly regarded as the founder of Christian monasticism. Feast day: Jan 17
Anthony of Padua *n* **Saint** 1195–1231, Franciscan friar, who preached in France and Italy. Feast day: June 13
anthracite *n* a hard coal that burns slowly with little smoke or flame but intense heat
WORD ORIGIN Greek *anthrax* coal
anthrax *n* a dangerous infectious disease of cattle and sheep, which can be passed to humans
WORD ORIGIN Greek: carbuncle
anthropocentric *adj* regarding the human being as the most important factor in the universe
WORD ORIGIN Greek *anthrōpos* human being + Latin *centrum* centre
anthropoid *adj* **1** resembling a human being ▷ *n* **2** an ape, such as the chimpanzee, that resembles a human being
anthropology *n* the study of human origins, institutions, and beliefs **anthropological** *adj* **anthropologist** *n*
WORD ORIGIN Greek *anthrōpos* human being + *logos* word
anthropomorphism *n* the attribution of human form or personality to a god, animal, or object **anthropomorphic** *adj*
anthropomorphous *adj* shaped like a human being
WORD ORIGIN Greek *anthrōpos*

THESAURUS

hack you off *(informal)*
OPPOSITE: soothe
annual *adj* **1 = once a year**, yearly **2 = yearlong**, yearly
anomaly *n* **= irregularity**, departure, exception, abnormality, rarity, inconsistency, deviation, eccentricity, oddity, aberration, peculiarity, incongruity
anonymous *adj* **1 = unsigned**, uncredited, unattributed, unattested
OPPOSITE: signed
2 = unnamed, unknown, unidentified, nameless, unacknowledged, incognito, unauthenticated, innominate
OPPOSITE: identified
answer *vb* **1 = reply**, explain, respond, resolve, acknowledge, react, return, retort, rejoin, refute **OPPOSITE:** ask ▷ *n* **7, 9 = reply**, response, reaction, resolution, explanation, plea, comeback, retort, report, return, defence, acknowledgement, riposte, counterattack, refutation, rejoinder
OPPOSITE: question
8 = solution, resolution, explanation
anthem *n* **1, 2 = song of praise**, carol, chant, hymn, psalm, paean, chorale, canticle
anthology *n* **= collection**, choice, selection, treasury, digest, compilation, garland, compendium,

DICTIONARY

human being + *morphē* form

anti *informal adj* **1** opposed to a party, policy, or attitude ▷*n* **2** an opponent of a party, policy, or attitude

anti- *prefix* **1** against or opposed to: *antiwar* **2** opposite to: *anticlimax* **3** counteracting or neutralizing: *antifreeze*
WORD ORIGIN Greek

anti-aircraft *adj* for defence against aircraft attack

antiballistic missile *n* a missile designed to destroy a ballistic missile in flight

antibiotic *n* **1** a chemical substance capable of destroying bacteria ▷*adj* **2** of or relating to antibiotics

antibody *n, pl* **-bodies** a protein produced in the blood which destroys bacteria

Antichrist *n* **1** *new testament* the chief enemy of Christ **2** an enemy of Christ or Christianity

anticipate ❶ *vb* **-pating, -pated 1** to foresee and act in advance of: *he anticipated some probing questions* **2** to look forward to **3** to make use of (something, such as one's salary) before receiving it **4** to mention (part of a story) before its proper time **anticipatory** *adj*
WORD ORIGIN Latin *ante-* before + *capere* to take

anticipation ❶ *n* the act of anticipating; expectation, premonition, or foresight: *smiling in happy anticipation*

anticlerical *adj* opposed to the power and influence of the clergy in politics

anticlimax *n* a disappointing conclusion to a series of events **anticlimactic** *adj*

anticline *n geol* a fold of rock raised up into a broad arch so that the strata slope down on both sides

anticlockwise *adv, adj* in the opposite direction to the rotation of the hands of a clock

anticoagulant (an-tee-koh-ag-yew-lant) *n* a substance that prevents the clotting of blood

antics ❶ *pl n* absurd acts or postures
WORD ORIGIN Italian *antico* something grotesque (from fantastic carvings found in ruins of ancient Rome)

anticyclone *n meteorol* an area of moving air of high pressure in which the winds rotate outwards

antidepressant *n* **1** a drug used to treat depression ▷*adj* **2** of or relating to such a drug

antidote *n* **1** *med* a substance that counteracts a poison **2** anything that counteracts a harmful condition: *exercise may be a good antidote to insomnia*
WORD ORIGIN Greek *anti-* against + *didonai* to give

antifreeze *n* a liquid added to water to lower its freezing point, used in the radiator of a motor vehicle to prevent freezing

antigen (an-tee-jen) *n* a substance, usually a toxin, that causes the body to produce antibodies
WORD ORIGIN *anti(body)* + *-gen* (suffix) producing

Antigonus I *n* known as *Cyclops.* 382–301 BC, Macedonian general under Alexander the Great; king of Macedon (306–301)

antihero *n, pl* **-roes** a central character in a novel, play, or film, who lacks the traditional heroic virtues

antihistamine *n* a drug that neutralizes the effects of histamine, used in the treatment of allergies

antiknock *n* a substance added to motor fuel to reduce knocking in the engine caused by too rapid combustion

antilogarithm *n maths* a number corresponding to a given logarithm

antimacassar *n* a cloth put over the back of a chair to prevent it getting dirty
WORD ORIGIN *anti-* + *Macassar (oil)*

antimatter *n physics* a hypothetical form of matter composed of antiparticles

antimony (an-tim-mon-ee) *n chem* a silvery-white metallic element that is added to alloys to increase their strength. Symbol: Sb
WORD ORIGIN Medieval Latin *antimonium*

antinomy (an-tin-nom-ee) *n, pl* **-mies** contradiction between two laws or principles that are reasonable in themselves
WORD ORIGIN Greek *anti-* against + *nomos* law

antinovel *n* a type of prose fiction in which conventional elements of the novel are rejected

antinuclear *adj* opposed to nuclear weapons or nuclear power

Antiochus III *n* known as *Antiochus the Great.* 242–187 BC, king of Syria (223–187), who greatly extended the Seleucid empire but was forced (190) to surrender most of Asia Minor to the Romans

Antiochus IV *n* ?215–164 BC, Seleucid king of Syria (175–164), who attacked the Jews and provoked the revolt of the Maccabees

antioxidant *n chem* a substance that slows down the process of oxidation

antiparticle *n nuclear physics* an elementary particle that has the same mass as its corresponding particle, but opposite charge and opposite magnetism

antipasto *n, pl* **-tos** an appetizer in an Italian meal
WORD ORIGIN Italian: before food

Antipater *n* ?398–319 BC, Macedonian general under Alexander the Great: regent of Macedon (334–323)

antipathy (an-tip-a-thee) *n* a feeling of strong dislike or hostility **antipathetic** *adj*
WORD ORIGIN Greek *anti-* against + *patheia* feeling

antipersonnel *adj* (of weapons or bombs) designed to be used against people rather than equipment

antiperspirant *n* a substance applied to the skin to reduce or prevent perspiration

antiphon *n* a hymn sung in alternate parts by two groups of singers
WORD ORIGIN Greek *anti-* against + *phōnē* sound

antipodes (an-tip-pod-deez) *pl n* **1** any two places that are situated diametrically opposite one another on the earth's surface **2 the Antipodes** Australia and New Zealand **antipodean** *adj*
WORD ORIGIN Greek plural of *antipous* having the feet opposite

antipope *n* a pope set up in opposition to the one chosen by church laws

antipyretic *adj* **1** reducing fever ▷*n* **2** a drug that reduces fever

antiquarian *adj* **1** collecting or dealing with antiquities or rare books ▷*n* **2** an antiquary

antiquary *n, pl* **-quaries** a person who collects, deals in, or studies antiques or ancient works of art

antiquated *adj* obsolete or old-fashioned
WORD ORIGIN Latin *antiquus* ancient

THESAURUS

miscellany, analects

anticipate *vb* **1 = expect**, predict, forecast, prepare for, look for, hope for, envisage, foresee, bank on, apprehend, foretell, think likely, count upon **2 = await**, look forward to, count the hours until

anticipation *n* **= expectancy**, hope, expectation, apprehension, foresight, premonition, preconception, foretaste, prescience, forethought, presentiment

antics *pl n* **= clowning**, tricks, stunts, mischief, larks, capers, pranks, frolics, escapades, foolishness, silliness, playfulness, skylarking, horseplay, buffoonery, tomfoolery, monkey tricks

antique *n* **1 = period piece**, relic, bygone, heirloom, collector's item, museum piece, object of virtu ▷*adj* **2 = vintage**, classic, antiquarian, olden

anxiety *n* **1 = uneasiness**, concern, care, worry, doubt, tension, alarm, distress, suspicion, angst, unease, apprehension, misgiving, suspense,

DICTIONARY

a

antique ❶ *n* **1** a decorative object or piece of furniture, of an earlier period, that is valued for its beauty, workmanship, and age ▷*adj* **2** made in an earlier period **3** *informal* old-fashioned
WORD ORIGIN Latin *antiquus* ancient
antiquity *n, pl* **-ties 1** great age **2** the far distant past **3 antiquities** objects dating from ancient times
antiracism *n* the policy of challenging racism or promoting racial tolerance **antiracist** *n, adj*
antirrhinum *n* a two-lipped flower of various colours, such as the snapdragon
WORD ORIGIN Greek *anti-* like, imitating + *rhis* nose
antiscorbutic *adj* preventing or curing scurvy
anti-Semitic *adj* discriminating against Jews **anti-Semite** *n* **anti-Semitism** *n*
antiseptic *adj* **1** preventing infection by killing germs ▷*n* **2** an antiseptic substance
antiserum *n* blood serum containing antibodies used to treat or provide immunity to a disease
antishake *adj* (of photographic equipment) reducing the blurring caused by movement of the person taking a photograph
antisocial *adj* **1** avoiding the company of other people **2** (of behaviour) annoying or harmful to other people
antisocial behaviour order *n* a civil order made against a troublesome individual which restricts his or her activities or movements
antistatic *adj* reducing the effects of static electricity
Antisthenes *n* ?445–365 BC, Greek philosopher, founder of the Cynic school, who taught that the only good was virtue, won by self-control and independence from worldly needs
antitank *adj* (of weapons) designed to destroy military tanks
antithesis (an-tith-iss-iss) *n, pl* **-ses** (-seez) **1** the exact opposite **2** *rhetoric* the placing together of contrasting ideas or words to produce an effect of balance, such as *where gods command, mere mortals must obey* **antithetical** *adj*
WORD ORIGIN Greek *anti-* against + *tithenai* to place
antitoxin *n* an antibody that acts against a toxin **antitoxic** *adj*
antitrades *pl n* winds blowing in the opposite direction from and above the trade winds
antitrust *adj US, Austral & S African* (of laws) opposing business monopolies
antivirus *adj* **1** relating to software designed to protect computer files from viruses ▷*n* **2** such a piece of software
antler *n* one of a pair of branched horns on the heads of male deer
WORD ORIGIN Old French *antoillier*
Antonello da Messina *n* ?1430–?79, Italian painter, born in Sicily. His paintings include *St Jerome in His Study* and *Portrait of a Man*
Antonescu *n* **Ion** 1882–1946, Romanian general and statesman; appointed prime minister (1940) by King Carol II. He was executed for war crimes
Antoninus Pius *n* 86–161 AD, emperor of Rome (138–161); adopted son and successor of Hadrian
Antonioni *n* **Michelangelo** 1912–2007, Italian film director; his films include *L'Avventura* (1959), *La Notte* (1961), *Blow-Up* (1966), *Zabriskie Point* (1970), *Beyond the Clouds* (1995), and *Just To Be Together* (2002)
antonym *n* a word that means the opposite of another
WORD ORIGIN Greek *anti-* opposite + *onoma* name
antrum *n, pl* **-tra** *anat* a natural cavity, esp. in a bone
WORD ORIGIN Latin: cave
Anubis *n* an Egyptian god with a jackal's head
anus (ain-uss) *n* the opening at the end of the alimentary canal, through which faeces are discharged
WORD ORIGIN Latin
anvil *n* a heavy iron block on which metals are hammered into particular shapes
WORD ORIGIN Old English *anfealt*
anxiety ❶ *n, pl* **-ties 1** a state of uneasiness about what may happen **2** eagerness: *she was uneasy with his mixture of diffidence and anxiety to please*
anxious ❶ *adj* **1** worried and tense **2** causing anxiety: *he was anxious about the enormity of the task ahead* **3** intensely desiring: *both sides were anxious for a deal* **anxiously** *adv*
WORD ORIGIN Latin *anxius*
any *det* **1** one, some, or several, no matter how much or what kind: *the jar opener fits over the top of any bottle or jar; have you left me any?* **2** even the smallest amount or even one: *we can't answer any questions; don't give her any* **3** whatever or whichever: *police may board any bus or train* **4** an indefinite or unlimited amount or number: *he would sign cheques for any amount of money* ▷*adv* **5** to even the smallest extent: *the outcome wouldn't have been any different*
WORD ORIGIN Old English *ǣnig*
anybody *pron* ▸same as **anyone**
anyhow *adv* ▸same as **anyway**
anyone *pron* **1** any person: *is anyone there?* **2** a person of any importance: *is he anyone?*
anything *pron* **1** any object, event, or action whatever: *they'll do anything to please you* ▷*adv* **2** in any way: *it is not a computer nor anything like a computer* **3 anything but** not at all: *the result is anything but simple*
anyway *adv* **1** at any rate; nevertheless **2** in any manner **3** carelessly
anywhere *adv* **1** in, at, or to any place **2 get anywhere** to be successful: *we will not get anywhere by being negative*
anzac *n NZ* a type of biscuit
Anzac *n* (in the First World War) a soldier serving with the Australian and New Zealand Army Corps
Anzac Day April 25, a public holiday in Australia and New Zealand commemorating the Anzac landing at Gallipoli in 1915
AOB (on the agenda for a meeting) any other business
aorta (eh-or-ta) *n* the main artery of the body, which carries oxygen-rich blood from the heart
WORD ORIGIN Greek *aortē* something lifted
Aouita *n* **Saïd** born 1960, Moroccan middle-distance runner: set new world records for the 1500 metres (1987–93), 2000 metres (1987–95), and 5000 metres (1987–94)
apace *adv literary* quickly: *repairs to the grid continued apace*
Apache *n, pl* **Apaches** *or* **Apache** a member of a Native American people of the southwestern US and N Mexico
WORD ORIGIN Mexican Spanish
apart ❶ *adj, adv* **1** to or in pieces: *he took a couple of cars apart and rebuilt them* **2** separate in time, place, or position: *my father and myself stood slightly apart from them* **3** individual or distinct: *a*

THESAURUS

nervousness, disquiet, trepidation, foreboding, restlessness, solicitude, perturbation, watchfulness, fretfulness, disquietude, apprehensiveness, dubiety
OPPOSITE: confidence
anxious *adj* **1, 2 = uneasy**, concerned, worried, troubled, upset, careful, wired *(slang)*, nervous, disturbed, distressed, uncomfortable, tense, fearful, unsettled, restless, neurotic, agitated, taut, disquieted, apprehensive, edgy, watchful, jittery *(informal)*, perturbed, on edge, ill at ease, twitchy *(informal)*, solicitous, overwrought, fretful, on tenterhooks, in suspense, hot and bothered, unquiet *(chiefly literary)*, like a fish out of water, antsy *(informal)*, angsty, on pins and needles, discomposed **OPPOSITE:** confident
3 = eager, keen, intent, yearning, impatient, itching, ardent, avid, expectant, desirous
OPPOSITE: reluctant
apart *adv* **1 = to pieces**, to bits, asunder, into parts **2a = away from**

DICTIONARY

a

nation apart **4** not being taken into account: *early timing difficulties apart, they encountered few problems* **5 apart from** other than: *apart from searching the house there is little more we can do*
WORD ORIGIN Old French *a part* at (the) side

apartheid *n* (formerly) the official government policy of racial segregation in South Africa
WORD ORIGIN Afrikaans *apart* + *-heid* -hood

apartment ❶ *n* **1** any room in a building, usually one of several forming a suite, used as living accommodation **2** *chiefly US & Canad* Also called (Brit): **flat** a set of rooms forming a home within a building usually incorporating other similar homes
WORD ORIGIN French *appartement*

apathy ❶ *n* lack of interest or enthusiasm **apathetic** *adj*
WORD ORIGIN Greek *a-* without + *pathos* feeling

ape *n* **1** an animal, such as a chimpanzee or gorilla, which is closely related to human beings and the monkeys, and which has no tail **2** a stupid, clumsy, or ugly man ▷ *vb* **aping, aped 3** to imitate **apelike** *adj*
WORD ORIGIN Old English *apa*

Apelles *n* 4th century BC, Greek painter of mythological subjects, none of whose work survives, his fame resting on the testimony of Pliny and other writers

apeman *n, pl* **-men** an extinct primate thought to have been the forerunner of true humans

aperient (ap-peer-ee-ent) *med adj* **1** having a mild laxative effect ▷ *n* **2** a mild laxative
WORD ORIGIN Latin *aperire* to open

aperitif (ap-per-rit-teef) *n* an alcoholic drink taken before a meal
WORD ORIGIN French

aperture *n* **1** a hole or opening **2** an opening in a camera or telescope that controls the amount of light entering it
WORD ORIGIN Latin *aperire* to open

apex *n* the highest point
WORD ORIGIN Latin: point

APEX Advance Purchase Excursion: a reduced fare for journeys booked a specified period in advance

aphasia *n* a disorder of the central nervous system that affects the ability to use and understand words
WORD ORIGIN Greek *a-* not + *phanai* to speak

aphelion (ap-heel-lee-on) *n, pl* **-lia** (-lee-a) *astron* the point in the orbit of a planet or comet when it is farthest from the sun
WORD ORIGIN Greek *apo-* from + *hēlios* sun

aphid (eh-fid) *or* **aphis** (eh-fiss) *n, pl* **aphids** *or* **aphides** (eh-fid-deez) a small insect which feeds by sucking the juices from plants
WORD ORIGIN New Latin

aphorism *n* a short clever saying expressing a general truth
WORD ORIGIN Greek *aphorizein* to define

aphrodisiac (af-roh-diz-zee-ak) *n* **1** a substance that arouses sexual desire ▷ *adj* **2** arousing sexual desire
WORD ORIGIN Greek *aphrodisios* belonging to *Aphrodite*, goddess of love

Aphrodite *n Greek myth* the goddess of love

apiary (ape-yar-ee) *n, pl* **-aries** a place where bees are kept **apiarist** *n*
WORD ORIGIN Latin *apis* bee

apical (ape-ik-kl) *adj* of, at, or being an apex

apiculture *n* the breeding and care of bees **apiculturist** *n*
WORD ORIGIN Latin *apis* bee + CULTURE

apiece ❶ *adv* each: *they had another cocktail apiece and then went down to dinner*

apish (ape-ish) *adj* **1** stupid or foolish **2** resembling an ape

aplomb (ap-plom) *n* calm self-possession
WORD ORIGIN French: uprightness

apocalypse *n* **1** the end of the world **2** an event of great destructive violence **apocalyptic** *adj*
WORD ORIGIN Greek *apo-* away + *kaluptein* to hide

Apocalypse *n* **the Apocalypse** *bible* the Book of Revelation, the last book of the New Testament

Apocrypha (ap-pok-rif-fa) *pl n* **the Apocrypha** the 14 books included as an appendix to the Old Testament, which are not accepted as part of the Hebrew scriptures
WORD ORIGIN Late Latin *apocrypha (scripta)* hidden (writings), from Greek *apokruptein* to hide away

apocryphal *adj* of questionable authenticity: *the paranoid and clearly apocryphal story*

apogee (ap-oh-jee) *n* **1** *astron* the point in its orbit around the earth when the moon or a satellite is farthest from the earth **2** the highest point: *the concept found its apogee in Renaissance Italy*
WORD ORIGIN Greek *apogaios* away from the earth

apolitical *adj* not concerned with political matters

Apollinaire *n* **Guillaume**, real name *Wilhelm Apollinaris de Kostrowitzki.* 1880–1918, French poet, novelist, and dramatist, regarded as a precursor of surrealism; author of *Alcoöls* (1913) and *Calligrammes* (1918)

Apollo *n classical myth* the god of the sun, music, and medicine

Apollonius of Perga *n* ?261–?190 BC, Greek mathematician, remembered for his treatise on conic sections

Apollonius of Rhodes *n* 3rd century BC, Greek epic poet and head of the Library of Alexandria. His principal work is the four-volume *Argonautica*

apologetic *adj* showing or expressing regret **apologetically** *adv*

apologetics *n* the branch of theology concerned with the reasoned defence of Christianity

apologia *n* a formal written defence of a cause

apologist *n* a person who offers a formal defence of a cause

apologize ❶ *or* **-gise** *vb* **-gizing, -gized** *or* **-gising, -gised** to say that one is sorry for some wrongdoing

apology ❶ *n, pl* **-gies 1** an expression of regret for some wrongdoing **2** ▸ same as **apologia 3 an apology for** a poor example of: *an apology for a man*
WORD ORIGIN Greek *apologia* a verbal defence, speech

apophthegm (ap-poth-em) *n* a short clever saying expressing a general truth

THESAURUS

each other, distant from each other
2b = aside, away, alone, independently, separately, singly, excluded, isolated, cut off, to one side, to yourself, by itself, aloof, to itself, by yourself, out on a limb
5 apart from = except for, excepting, other than, excluding, besides, not including, aside from, but, save, bar, not counting

apartment *n* **1 = rooms**, quarters, chambers, accommodation, living quarters **2** *(chiefly US & Canad)* **= flat**, room, suite, compartment, penthouse, duplex *(US & Canad)*, crib, bachelor apartment *(Canad)*

apathy *n* **= lack of interest**, indifference, inertia, coolness, passivity, coldness, stoicism, nonchalance, torpor, phlegm, sluggishness, listlessness, unconcern, insensibility, unresponsiveness, impassivity, passiveness, impassibility, unfeelingness, emotionlessness, uninterestedness **OPPOSITE:** interest

apiece *adv* **= each**, individually, separately, for each, to each, respectively, from each, severally
OPPOSITE: all together

apologize *vb* **= say sorry**, express regret, ask forgiveness, make an apology, beg pardon, say you are sorry

apology *n* **1 = regret**, explanation, excuse, confession, extenuation
3 apology for something *or* **someone = mockery of**, excuse for, imitation of, caricature of, travesty of, poor

DICTIONARY

a

WORD ORIGIN Greek *apophthengesthai* to speak frankly
apoplectic *adj* **1** of apoplexy **2** *informal* furious
apoplexy *n med* a stroke
WORD ORIGIN Greek *apoplēssein* to cripple by a stroke
apostasy (ap-**poss**-stass-ee) *n, pl* **-sies** abandonment of one's religious faith, political party, or cause
WORD ORIGIN Greek *apostasis* desertion
apostate *n* **1** a person who has abandoned his or her religion, political party, or cause ▷ *adj* **2** guilty of apostasy
a posteriori (**eh** poss-steer-ee-**or**-rye) *adj logic* involving reasoning from effect to cause
WORD ORIGIN Latin: from the latter
apostle *n* **1** one of the twelve disciples chosen by Christ to preach his gospel **2** an ardent supporter of a cause or movement
WORD ORIGIN Greek *apostolos* a messenger
apostolic (ap-poss-**stoll**-ik) *adj* **1** of or relating to the Apostles or their teachings **2** of or relating to the pope
Apostolic See *n* the see of the pope, at Rome
apostrophe[1] (ap-**poss**-trof-fee) *n* the punctuation mark (') used to indicate the omission of a letter or letters, such as *he's* for *he has* or *he is*, and to form the possessive, as in *John's father*
WORD ORIGIN Greek *apostrephein* to turn away
apostrophe[2] *n rhetoric* a digression from a speech to address an imaginary or absent person or thing
WORD ORIGIN Greek: a turning away
apostrophize *or* **-phise** *vb* **-phizing, -phized** *or* **-phising, -phised** *rhetoric* to address an apostrophe to
apothecary *n, pl* **-caries** *old-fashioned* a chemist
WORD ORIGIN Late Latin *apothecarius* warehouseman
apotheosis (ap-poth-ee-**oh**-siss) *n, pl* **-ses** (-seez) **1** a perfect example: *it was the apotheosis of elitism* **2** elevation to the rank of a god
WORD ORIGIN Greek
appal ❶ *or US* **appall** *vb* **-palling, -palled** to fill with horror; terrify
WORD ORIGIN Old French *appalir* to turn pale
appalling ❶ *adj* **1** causing dismay, horror, or revulsion **2** very bad
appallingly *adv*
apparatus ❶ *n* **1** a collection of equipment used for a particular purpose **2** any complicated device, system, or organization: *the whole apparatus of law enforcement*
WORD ORIGIN Latin
apparel (ap-**par**-rel) *n old-fashioned* clothing
WORD ORIGIN Latin *parare* to prepare
apparent ❶ *adj* **1** readily seen or understood; obvious **2** seeming as opposed to real: *he frowned in apparent bewilderment* **apparently** *adv*
WORD ORIGIN Latin *apparere* to appear
apparition *n* a ghost or ghostlike figure
WORD ORIGIN Latin *apparere* to appear
appeal ❶ *vb* **1** to make an earnest request **2 appeal to** to attract, please, or interest **3** *law* to apply to a higher court to review (a case or issue decided by a lower court) **4** to resort to a higher authority to change a decision **5** to call on in support of an earnest request: *he appealed for volunteers to help in relief work* **6** *cricket* to request the umpire to declare a batsman out ▷ *n* **7** an earnest request for money or help **8** the power to attract, please, or interest people **9** *law* a request for a review of a lower court's decision by a higher court **10** an application to a higher authority to change a decision that has been made **11** *cricket* a request to the umpire to declare the batsman out
WORD ORIGIN Latin *appellare* to entreat
appealing ❶ *adj* attractive or pleasing
appear ❶ *vb* **1** to come into sight **2** to seem: *it appears that no one survived the crash* **3** to come into existence: *a rash and small sores appeared around the shoulder and neck* **4** to perform: *she hadn't appeared in a film for almost fifty years* **5** to be present in court before a magistrate or judge: *two men have appeared in court in London charged with conspiracy* **6** to be published or become available: *both books appeared in 1934*
WORD ORIGIN Latin *apparere*
appearance ❶ *n* **1** a sudden or unexpected arrival of someone or

THESAURUS

substitute for
appal *vb* = **horrify**, shock, alarm, frighten, scare, terrify, outrage, disgust, dishearten, revolt, intimidate, dismay, daunt, sicken, astound, harrow, unnerve, petrify, scandalize, make your hair stand on end *(informal)*
appalling *adj* **1** = **horrifying**, shocking, terrible, alarming, frightening, scaring, awful, terrifying, horrible, grim, dreadful, intimidating, dismaying, horrific, fearful, daunting, dire, astounding, ghastly, hideous, shameful, harrowing, vile, unnerving, petrifying, horrid, unspeakable, frightful, nightmarish, abominable, disheartening, godawful *(slang)*, hellacious *(US slang)*
OPPOSITE: reassuring
2 = **awful**, terrible, tremendous, distressing, horrible, dreadful, horrendous, ghastly, godawful *(slang)*
apparatus *n* **1** = **equipment**, machine, tackle, gear, means, materials, device, tools, implements, mechanism, outfit, machinery, appliance, utensils, contraption *(informal)* **2** = **organization**, system, network, structure, bureaucracy, hierarchy, setup *(informal)*, chain of command
apparent *adj* **1** = **obvious**, marked, clear, plain, visible, bold, patent, evident, distinct, open, understandable, manifest, noticeable, blatant, conspicuous, overt, unmistakable, palpable, undeniable, discernible, salient, self-evident, indisputable, much in evidence, undisguised, unconcealed, indubitable, staring you in the face *(informal)*, plain as the nose on your face **OPPOSITE:** unclear
2 = **seeming**, supposed, alleged, outward, exterior, superficial, ostensible, specious
OPPOSITE: actual
appeal *vb* **1, 5** = **plead**, call, ask, apply, refer, request, sue, lobby, pray, beg, petition, solicit, implore, beseech, entreat, importune, adjure, supplicate **OPPOSITE:** refuse
▷ *n* **2 appeal to someone** = **attract**, interest, draw, please, invite, engage, charm, fascinate, tempt, lure, entice, enchant, captivate, allure, bewitch **7** = **plea**, call, application, request, prayer, petition, overture, invocation, solicitation, entreaty, supplication, suit, cry from the heart, adjuration
OPPOSITE: refusal
8 = **attraction**, charm, fascination, charisma, beauty, attractiveness, allure, magnetism, enchantment, seductiveness, interestingness, engagingness, pleasingness
OPPOSITE: repulsiveness
appealing *adj* = **attractive**, inviting, engaging, charming, winning, desirable, endearing, alluring, winsome, prepossessing
OPPOSITE: repellent
appear *vb* **1** = **come into view**, emerge, occur, attend, surface, come out, turn out, arise, turn up, be present, loom, show *(informal)*, issue, develop, arrive, show up *(informal)*, come to light, crop up *(informal)*, materialize, come forth, come into sight, show your face **OPPOSITE:** disappear
2 = **look (like** *or* **as if)**, seem, occur, look to be, come across as, strike you as
appearance *n* **1, 2** = **arrival**,

DICTIONARY

a

something at a place **2** the introduction or invention of something: *the appearance of credit cards* **3** an act or instance of appearing: *it will be his fiftieth appearance for his country* **4** the way a person or thing looks: *I spotted a man of extraordinary appearance* **5 keep up appearances** to maintain the public impression of wellbeing or normality **6 put in an appearance** to attend an event briefly **7 to all appearances** apparently: *to all appearances they seemed enthralled by what he was saying*

appease ⓘ *vb* **-peasing, -peased 1** to pacify (someone) by yielding to his or her demands **2** to satisfy or relieve (a feeling) **appeasement** *n*
WORD ORIGIN Old French *apaisier*

Appel *n* **Karel** 1921–2006, Dutch abstract expressionist painter

appellant *law n* **1** a person who appeals to a higher court to review the decision of a lower court ▸ *adj* **2** ▸ same as **appellate**

appellate (ap-pell-it) *adj law* **1** of appeals **2** (of a tribunal) having the power to review appeals

appellation *n formal* a name or title

append *vb formal* to add as a supplement: *a series of notes appended to his translation of the poems*
WORD ORIGIN Latin *pendere* to hang

appendage *n* a secondary part attached to a main part

appendicectomy *or esp. US, Canad & Austral* **appendectomy** *n, pl* **-mies** surgical removal of the appendix
WORD ORIGIN *appendix* + Greek *tomē* a cutting

appendicitis *n* inflammation of the appendix, causing abdominal pain

appendix ⓘ (ap-pen-dix) *n, pl* **-dices** (-diss-seez) *or* **-dixes 1** separate additional material at the end of a book **2** *anat* a short thin tube, closed at one end and attached to the large intestine at the other end
WORD ORIGIN Latin

appertain *vb* **appertain to** to belong to, relate to, or be connected with
WORD ORIGIN Latin *ad-* to + *pertinere* to pertain

appetence *or* **appetency** *n, pl* **-tences** *or* **-tencies** a craving or desire
WORD ORIGIN Latin *appetentia*

appetite ⓘ *n* **1** a desire for food or drink **2** a liking or willingness: *he had an insatiable appetite for publicity*
WORD ORIGIN Latin *appetere* to desire ardently

appetizer *or* **-iser** *n* a small amount of food or drink taken at the start of a meal to stimulate the appetite

appetizing *or* **-ising** *adj* stimulating the appetite; looking or smelling delicious

applaud ⓘ *vb* **1** to show approval of by clapping one's hands **2** to express approval of: *we applaud her determination and ambition*
WORD ORIGIN Latin *applaudere*

applause ⓘ *n* appreciation shown by clapping one's hands

apple *n* **1** a round firm fruit with red, yellow, or green skin and crisp whitish flesh, that grows on trees **2 apple of one's eye** a person that one loves very much
WORD ORIGIN Old English *æppel*

apple-pie bed *n* a bed made with the sheets folded so as to prevent the person from entering it

apple-pie order *n* **in apple-pie order** *informal* very tidy

applet *n computers* a computing program that runs within a page on the World Wide Web
WORD ORIGIN *app(lication program)* + *-let* small or lesser

appliance ⓘ *n* a machine or device that has a specific function

applicable ⓘ *adj* appropriate or relevant

applicant ⓘ *n* a person who applies for something, such as a job or grant

application ⓘ *n* **1** a formal request, for example for a job **2** the act of applying something to a particular use: *you can make practical application of this knowledge to everyday living* **3** concentrated effort: *success would depend on their talent and application* **4** the act of putting something, such as a lotion or paint, onto a surface

applicator *n* a device for applying cosmetics, medication, or some other substance

applied *adj* put to practical use: *applied mathematics*

appliqué (ap-plee-kay) *n* a kind of

THESAURUS

appearing, presence, turning up, introduction, showing up *(informal)*, emergence, advent **4 = look**, face, form, air, figure, image, looks, bearing, aspect, manner, expression, demeanour, mien *(literary)*

appease *vb* **1 = pacify**, satisfy, calm, soothe, quiet, placate, mollify, conciliate **OPPOSITE:** anger **2 = ease**, satisfy, calm, relieve, diminish, compose, quiet, blunt, soothe, subdue, lessen, alleviate, lull, quell, allay, mitigate, assuage, quench, tranquillize

appendix *n* **1 = supplement**, add-on, postscript, adjunct, appendage, addendum, addition, codicil

appetite *n* **1 = hunger 2 = desire**, liking, longing, demand, taste, passion, stomach, hunger, willingness, relish, craving, yearning, inclination, zeal, zest, propensity, hankering, proclivity, appetence, appetency
OPPOSITE: distaste

applaud *vb* **1 = clap**, encourage, praise, cheer, hail, acclaim, laud, give (someone) a big hand
OPPOSITE: boo
2 = praise, celebrate, approve, acclaim, compliment, salute, commend, extol, crack up *(informal)*, big up *(slang)*, eulogize
OPPOSITE: criticize

applause *n* **= ovation**, praise, cheering, cheers, approval, acclaim, clapping, accolade, big hand, commendation, hand-clapping, approbation, acclamation, eulogizing, plaudit

appliance *n* **= device**, machine, tool, instrument, implement, mechanism, apparatus, gadget, waldo

applicable *adj* **= appropriate**, fitting, fit, suited, useful, suitable, relevant, to the point, apt, pertinent, befitting, apposite, apropos, germane, to the purpose
OPPOSITE: inappropriate

applicant *n* **= candidate**, entrant, claimant, suitor, petitioner, aspirant, inquirer, job-seeker, suppliant, postulant

application *n* **1 = request**, claim, demand, appeal, suit, inquiry, plea, petition, requisition, solicitation **3 = effort**, work, study, industry, labour, trouble, attention, struggle, pains, commitment, hard work, endeavour, dedication, toil, diligence, perseverance, travail *(literary)*, attentiveness, assiduity, blood, sweat, and tears *(informal)*

apply *vb* **1 = request**, seek, appeal, put in, petition, inquire, solicit, claim, sue, requisition, make application **2 = use**, exercise, carry out, employ, engage, implement, practise, execute, assign, administer, exert, enact, utilize, bring to bear, put to use, bring into play **3 = put on**, work in, cover with, lay on, paint on, anoint, spread on, rub in, smear on, shampoo in, bring into contact with **4 = be relevant**, concern, relate, refer, be fitting, be appropriate, be significant, fit, suit, pertain, be applicable, bear upon, appertain **5 apply yourself = work hard**, concentrate, study, pay attention, try, commit yourself, buckle down *(informal)*, be assiduous, devote yourself, be diligent, dedicate yourself, make an effort, address yourself, be industrious, persevere

appoint *vb* **1 = assign**, name, choose, commission, select, elect, install, delegate, nominate **OPPOSITE:** fire **2 = decide**, set, choose, establish, determine, settle, fix, arrange, specify, assign, designate, allot
OPPOSITE: cancel

appointment *n* **1 = meeting**, interview, date, session, arrangement, consultation,

decoration in which one material is cut out and sewn or fixed onto another
WORD ORIGIN French: applied

apply ❶ *vb* **-plies, -plying, -plied 1** to make a formal request for something, such as a job or a loan **2** to put to practical use: *he applied his calligrapher's skill* **3** to put onto a surface: *the hand lotion should be applied whenever possible throughout the day* **4** to be relevant or appropriate: *he had been involved in research applied to flying wing aircraft* **5 apply oneself** to concentrate one's efforts or faculties
WORD ORIGIN Latin *applicare* to attach to

appoint ❶ *vb* **1** to assign officially to a job or position **2** to fix or decide (a time or place for an event) **3** to equip or furnish: *it was a beautifully appointed room with rows and rows of books*
appointee *n*
WORD ORIGIN Old French *apointer* to put into a good state

appointment ❶ *n* **1** an arrangement to meet a person **2** the act of placing someone in a job or position **3** the person appointed **4** the job or position to which a person is appointed **5 appointments** fixtures or fittings

apportion *vb* to divide out in shares

apposite *adj* suitable or appropriate: *an apposite saying*
WORD ORIGIN Latin *ad-* near + *ponere* to put

apposition *n* a grammatical construction in which a noun or group of words is placed after another to modify its meaning, for example *my friend the mayor*

appraisal ❶ *n* an assessment of the worth or quality of a person or thing

appraise *vb* **-praising, -praised** to assess the worth, value, or quality of
WORD ORIGIN Old French *aprisier*

appreciable *adj* enough to be noticed; significant **appreciably** *adv*

appreciate ❶ *vb* **-ating, -ated 1** to value highly: *we appreciate his music but can't afford £400 a seat* **2** to be aware of and understand: *I can fully appreciate how desperate you must feel* **3** to feel grateful for: *we do appreciate all you do for us* **4** to increase in value
WORD ORIGIN Latin *pretium* price

appreciation ❶ *n* **1** gratitude **2** awareness and understanding of a problem or difficulty **3** sensitive recognition of good qualities, as in art **4** an increase in value

appreciative *adj* feeling or expressing appreciation
appreciatively *adv*

apprehend *vb* **1** to arrest and take into custody **2** to grasp (something) mentally; understand
WORD ORIGIN Latin *apprehendere* to lay hold of

apprehension ❶ *n* **1** anxiety or dread **2** the act of arresting **3** understanding

apprehensive *adj* fearful or anxious about the future

apprentice ❶ *n* **1** someone who works for a skilled person for a fixed period in order to learn his or her trade ▷ *vb* **-ticing, -ticed 2** to take or place as an apprentice **apprenticeship** *n*
WORD ORIGIN Old French *aprendre* to learn

apprise *or* **-prize** *vb* **-prising, -prised** *or* **-prizing, -prized** to make aware: *I needed to apprise the students of the dangers that may be involved*
WORD ORIGIN French *apprendre* to teach; learn

appro *n* **on appro** *informal* on approval

approach ❶ *vb* **1** to come close or closer to **2** to make a proposal or suggestion to **3** to begin to deal with (a matter) ▷ *n* **4** the act of coming close or closer **5** a proposal or suggestion made to a person **6** the way or means of reaching a place; access **7** a way of dealing with a matter **8** an approximation **9** the course followed by an aircraft preparing for landing
approachable *adj*
WORD ORIGIN Latin *ad-* to + *prope* near

approach road *n NZ & S African* a smaller road leading into a major road

approbation *n* approval

appropriate ❶ *adj* **1** right or suitable ▷ *vb* **-ating, -ated 2** to take for one's own use without permission **3** to put (money) aside for a particular

engagement, fixture, rendezvous, tryst *(archaic)*, assignation **2 = selection**, naming, election, choosing, choice, commissioning, delegation, nomination, installation, assignment, allotment, designation **4 = job**, office, position, post, situation, place, station, employment, assignment, berth *(informal)*

appraisal *n* **= assessment**, opinion, estimate, judgment, evaluation, estimation, sizing up *(informal)*, recce *(slang)*

appreciate *vb* **1 = enjoy**, like, value, regard, respect, prize, admire, treasure, esteem, relish, cherish, savour, rate highly **OPPOSITE:** scorn **2 = be aware of**, know, understand, estimate, realize, acknowledge, recognize, perceive, comprehend, take account of, be sensitive to, be conscious of, sympathize with, be alive to, be cognizant of **OPPOSITE:** be unaware of **3 = be grateful for**, be obliged for, be thankful for, give thanks for, be indebted for, be in debt for, be appreciative of **OPPOSITE:** be ungrateful for **4 = increase**, rise, grow, gain, improve, mount, enhance, soar, inflate **OPPOSITE:** fall

appreciation *n* **1 = gratitude**, thanks, recognition, obligation, acknowledgment, indebtedness, thankfulness, gratefulness **OPPOSITE:** ingratitude **2 = awareness**, understanding, regard, knowledge, recognition, perception, sympathy, consciousness, sensitivity, realization, comprehension, familiarity, mindfulness, cognizance **OPPOSITE:** ignorance **3 = admiration**, liking, respect, assessment, esteem, relish, valuation, enjoyment, appraisal, estimation, responsiveness **4 = increase**, rise, gain, growth, inflation, improvement, escalation, enhancement **OPPOSITE:** fall

apprehension *n* **1 = anxiety**, concern, fear, worry, doubt, alarm, suspicion, dread, unease, mistrust, misgiving, disquiet, premonition, trepidation, foreboding, uneasiness, pins and needles, apprehensiveness **OPPOSITE:** confidence **2 = arrest**, catching, capture, taking, seizure **OPPOSITE:** release **3 = awareness**, understanding, knowledge, intelligence, ken, perception, grasp, comprehension **OPPOSITE:** incomprehension

apprentice *n* **1 = trainee**, student, pupil, novice, beginner, learner, neophyte, tyro, probationer **OPPOSITE:** master

approach *vb* **1 = move towards**, come to, reach, near, advance, catch up, meet, come close, gain on, converge on, come near, push forward, draw near, creep up on **2 = make a proposal to**, speak to, apply to, appeal to, proposition, solicit, sound out, make overtures to, make advances to, broach the matter with **3 = set about**, tackle, undertake, embark on, get down to, launch into, begin work on, commence on, make a start on, enter upon ▷ *n* **4 = advance**, coming, nearing, appearance, arrival, advent, drawing near **5 = proposal**, offer, appeal, advance, application, invitation, proposition, overture **6 = access**, way, drive, road, passage, entrance, avenue, passageway **7 = way**, means, course, style, attitude, method, technique, manner, procedure, mode, modus operandi

appropriate *adj* **1 = suitable**, right, fitting, fit, suited, correct, belonging, relevant, proper, to the point, in keeping, apt, applicable,

DICTIONARY

a

purpose **appropriately** *adv*
WORD ORIGIN Latin *ad-* to + *proprius* one's own

appropriation *n* **1** the act of putting money aside for a particular purpose **2** money put aside for a particular purpose

approval ⊕ *n* **1** consent **2** a favourable opinion **3 on approval** (of articles for sale) with an option to be returned without payment if unsatisfactory: *each volume in the collection will be sent to you on approval*

approve ⊕ *vb* **-proving, -proved** **1 approve of** to consider fair, good, or right **2** to authorize or agree to
WORD ORIGIN Latin *approbare*

approx. approximate or approximately

approximate *adj* **1** almost but not quite exact ▷ *vb* **-mating, -mated** **2 approximate to a** to come close to **b** to be almost the same as **approximately** *adv* **approximation** *n*
WORD ORIGIN Latin *ad-* to + *proximus* nearest

appurtenances *pl n* minor or additional features or possessions
WORD ORIGIN Old French *apartenance* secondary thing

APR annual percentage rate

Apr. April

après-ski (ap-ray-**skee**) *n* social activities after a day's skiing

apricot *n* **1** a yellowish-orange juicy fruit which resembles a small peach ▷ *adj* **2** yellowish-orange
WORD ORIGIN Latin *praecox* early-ripening

April *n* the fourth month of the year
WORD ORIGIN Latin *Aprilis*

April fool *n* a victim of a practical joke played on the April 1 (**April Fools' Day** *or* **All Fools' Day**)

a priori (eh pry-or-rye) *adj logic* involving reasoning from cause to effect
WORD ORIGIN Latin: from the previous

apron *n* **1** a garment worn over the front of the body to protect one's clothes **2** a hard-surfaced area at an airport or hangar for manoeuvring and loading aircraft **3** the part of a stage extending in front of the curtain **4 tied to someone's apron strings** dependent on or dominated by someone
WORD ORIGIN Old French *naperon* little cloth

apropos (ap-prop-**poh**) *adj* **1** appropriate ▷ *adv* **2** by the way; incidentally **3 apropos of** with regard to
WORD ORIGIN French *à propos* to the purpose

apse *n* an arched or domed recess at the east end of a church
WORD ORIGIN Greek *apsis* a fitting together

apsis (ap-siss) *n, pl* **apsides** (ap-sid-deez) *astron* either of two points lying at the extremities of the elliptical orbit of a planet or satellite
WORD ORIGIN see APSE

apt ⊕ *adj* **1** having a specified tendency: *they are apt to bend the rules* **2** suitable or appropriate **3** quick to learn: *she was turning out to be a more apt pupil than he had expected* **aptly** *adv* **aptness** *n*
WORD ORIGIN Latin *aptus* fitting

APT *Brit* Advanced Passenger Train

apteryx *n* ▸ same as **kiwi** (sense 1)
WORD ORIGIN Greek *a-* without + *pteron* wing

aptitude *n* natural tendency or ability

Apuleius *n* **Lucius** 2nd century AD, Roman writer, noted for his romance *The Golden Ass*

aqua *adj* ▸ short for **aquamarine**
WORD ORIGIN Latin: water

aqua fortis *n obsolete* nitric acid
WORD ORIGIN Latin: strong water

aqualung *n* an apparatus for breathing underwater, consisting of a mouthpiece attached to air cylinders

aquamarine *n* **1** a clear greenish-blue gemstone ▷ *adj* **2** greenish-blue
WORD ORIGIN Latin *aqua marina* sea water

aquaplane *n* **1** a board on which a person stands to be towed by a motorboat for sport ▷ *vb* **-planing, -planed 2** to ride on an aquaplane **3** (of a motor vehicle) to skim uncontrollably on a thin film of water

aqua regia (ak-wa **reej**-ya) *n* a mixture of nitric acid and hydrochloric acid
WORD ORIGIN New Latin: royal water; referring to its use in dissolving gold, the royal metal

aquarium *n, pl* **aquariums** *or* **aquaria** **1** a tank in which fish and other underwater creatures are kept **2** a building containing such tanks
WORD ORIGIN Latin *aquarius* relating to water

Aquarius *n astrol* the eleventh sign of the zodiac: the Water Carrier
WORD ORIGIN Latin

aquatic *adj* **1** growing or living in water **2** *sport* performed in or on water ▷ *n* **3** an aquatic animal or plant **4 aquatics** water sports
WORD ORIGIN Latin *aqua* water

aquatint *n* a print like a watercolour, produced by etching copper with acid
WORD ORIGIN Italian *acqua tinta* dyed water

aqua vitae (ak-wa **vee**-tie) *n old-fashioned* brandy
WORD ORIGIN Medieval Latin: water of life

aqueduct *n* a structure, often a bridge, that carries water across a

THESAURUS

pertinent, befitting, well-suited, well-timed, apposite, apropos, opportune, becoming, seemly, felicitous, germane, to the purpose, appurtenant, congruous
OPPOSITE: unsuitable
▷ *vb* **2a = seize**, take, claim, assume, take over, acquire, confiscate, annex, usurp, impound, pre-empt, commandeer, take possession of, expropriate, arrogate
OPPOSITE: relinquish
2b = steal, take, nick *(slang, chiefly Brit)*, pocket, pinch *(informal)*, pirate, poach, swipe *(slang)*, lift *(informal)*, heist *(US slang)*, embezzle, blag *(slang)*, pilfer, misappropriate, snitch *(slang)*, purloin, filch, plagiarize, thieve, peculate **3 = allocate**, allow, budget, devote, assign, designate, set aside, earmark, allot, share out, apportion **OPPOSITE:** withhold

approval *n* **1, 2 = consent**, agreement, sanction, licence, blessing, permission, recommendation, concession, confirmation, mandate, endorsement, leave, compliance, the go-ahead *(informal)*, countenance, ratification, the green light, assent, authorization, validation, acquiescence, imprimatur, concurrence, O.K. *or* okay *(informal)*, endorsation *(Canad)*

approve *vb* **1 approve of something** *or* **someone = favour**, like, support, respect, praise, appreciate, agree with, admire, endorse, esteem, acclaim, applaud, commend, be pleased with, have a good opinion of, regard highly, think highly of
2 = agree to, second, allow, pass, accept, confirm, recommend, permit, sanction, advocate, bless, endorse, uphold, mandate, authorize, ratify, go along with, subscribe to, consent to, buy into *(informal)*, validate, countenance, rubber stamp, accede to, give the go-ahead to *(informal)*, give the green light to, assent to, concur in, O.K. *or* okay *(informal)* **OPPOSITE:** veto

apt *adj* **1 = inclined**, likely, ready, disposed, prone, liable, given, predisposed, of a mind
2 = appropriate, timely, right, seemly, fitting, fit, related, correct, belonging, suitable, relevant, proper, to the point, applicable, pertinent, befitting, apposite, apropos, opportune, germane, to the purpose
OPPOSITE: inappropriate
3 = gifted, skilled, expert, quick, bright, talented, sharp, capable, smart, prompt, clever, intelligent, accomplished, ingenious, skilful, astute, adroit, teachable

valley or river
WORD ORIGIN Latin *aqua* water + *ducere* to convey
aqueous *adj* **1** of, like, or containing water **2** produced by the action of water
WORD ORIGIN Latin *aqua* water
aqueous humour *n physiol* the watery fluid in the eyeball, between the cornea and the lens
aquifer *n* a deposit of rock, such as sandstone, containing water that can be used to supply wells
WORD ORIGIN Latin *aqua* water + *ferre* to carry
aquiline *adj* **1** (of a nose) curved like an eagle's beak **2** of or like an eagle
WORD ORIGIN Latin *aquila* eagle
Aquino *n* **Corazón,** known as *Cory*. 1933–2009, Philippine stateswoman: president (1986–92)
Ar *chem* argon
AR Arkansas
Arab *n* **1** a member of a Semitic people originally from Arabia ▷ *adj* **2** of the Arabs
WORD ORIGIN Arabic *'Arab*
arabesque (ar-ab-**besk**) *n* **1** a ballet position in which one leg is raised behind and the arms are extended **2** *arts* an elaborate design of intertwined leaves, flowers, and scrolls **3** an ornate piece of music
WORD ORIGIN Italian *arabesco* in the Arabic style
Arabian *adj* **1** of Arabia or the Arabs ▷ *n* **2** ▸ same as **Arab**
Arabic *n* **1** the language of the Arabs ▷ *adj* **2** of this language, the Arabs, or Arabia
Arabic numerals *pl n* the symbols 1, 2, 3, 4, 5, 6, 7, 8, 9, 0, used to represent numbers
arable *adj* (of land) suitable for growing crops on
WORD ORIGIN Latin *arare* to plough
arachnid (ar-**rak**-nid) *n* an eight-legged insect-like creature, such as a spider, scorpion, or tick
WORD ORIGIN Greek *arakhnē* spider
Aragon[1] *n* an autonomous region of NE Spain: independent kingdom from the 11th century until 1479, when it was united with Castile to form modern Spain. Pop: 1 059 600 (2003 est). Area: 47 609 sq km (18 382 sq miles)
Aragon[2] *n* **Louis** (lwi) 1897–1982, French poet, essayist, and novelist; an early surrealist, later a committed Communist. His works include the verse collections *Le Crève-Coeur* (1941) and *Les Yeux d'Elsa* (1942) and the series of novels *Le Monde réel* (1933–51)
arak *n* ▸ same as **arrack**
Aramaic *n* an ancient Semitic language spoken in parts of Syria and the Lebanon
Aran *adj* (of knitwear) knitted in a complicated pattern traditional to the Aran Islands off the west coast of Ireland
Arany *n* **János** 1817–82, Hungarian epic poet, ballad writer, and scholar
Arber *n* **Werner** born 1929, Swiss microbiologist, noted for his work on restriction enzymes. Nobel prize for physiology or medicine 1978
arbiter *n* **1** a person empowered to judge in a dispute **2** a person with influential opinions about something: *the customer must be the ultimate arbiter of quality*
arbitrary ❶ *adj* **1** not done according to any plan or for any particular reason **2** without consideration for the wishes of others: *the arbitrary power of the king* **arbitrarily** *adv*
arbitrate *vb* **-trating, -trated** to settle (a dispute) by arbitration **arbitrator** *n*
WORD ORIGIN Latin *arbitrari* to give judgment
arbitration ❶ *n* the hearing and settlement of a dispute by an impartial referee chosen by both sides
arbor[1] *n US* ▸ same as **arbour**
arbor[2] *n* a revolving shaft or axle in a machine
WORD ORIGIN Latin: tree
arboreal (ahr-**bore**-ee-al) *adj* **1** of or resembling a tree **2** living in or among trees
arboretum (ahr-bore-**ee**-tum) *n, pl* **-ta** (-ta) a botanical garden where rare trees or shrubs are cultivated
WORD ORIGIN Latin *arbor* tree
arboriculture *n* the cultivation of trees or shrubs
WORD ORIGIN Latin *arbor* tree + CULTURE
arbor vitae (ahr-bore **vee**-tie) *n* an evergreen tree
WORD ORIGIN New Latin: tree of life
arbour *or US* **arbor** *n* a shelter in a garden shaded by trees or climbing plants
WORD ORIGIN Latin *herba* grass
Arbus *n* **Diane,** original name *Diane Nemerov*. 1923–71, US photographer, noted esp. for her portraits of vagrants, dwarfs, transvestites, etc.
Arbuthnot *n* **John** 1667–1735, Scottish physician and satirist: author of *The History of John Bull* (1712) and, with others, of the *Memoirs of Martinus Scriblerus* (1741)
arbutus (ar-**byew**-tuss) *n* an evergreen shrub with berries like strawberries
WORD ORIGIN Latin
arc ❶ *n* **1** something curved in shape **2** *maths* a section of a circle or other curve **3** *electronics* a stream of very bright light that forms when an electric current flows across a small gap between two electrodes ▷ *vb* **4** to form an arc
WORD ORIGIN Latin *arcus* bow, arch
ARC AIDS-related complex: relatively mild symptoms suffered in the early stages of infection with the AIDS virus
arcade ❶ *n* **1** a covered passageway lined with shops **2** a set of arches and their supporting columns
WORD ORIGIN Latin *arcus* bow, arch
Arcadian *literary adj* **1** rural, in an idealized way ▷ *n* **2** a person who leads a quiet simple country life
WORD ORIGIN *Arcadia*, rural district of Ancient Greece
arcane *adj* very mysterious
WORD ORIGIN Latin *arcanus* secret
arch[1] ❶ *n* **1** a curved structure that spans an opening or supports a bridge or roof **2** something curved **3** the curved lower part of the foot ▷ *vb* **4** to form an arch
WORD ORIGIN Latin *arcus* bow, arc
arch[2] ❶ *adj* **1** knowing or superior **2** coyly playful: *he gave an arch smile to indicate his pride* **archly** *adv*
WORD ORIGIN independent use of ARCH-
arch- *or* **archi-** *combining form* chief or principal: *archbishop; archenemy*
WORD ORIGIN Greek *arkhein* to rule
archaeobotany *n* the study of plant remains found at archaeological sites **archaeobotanist** *n*
archaeology *or* **archeology** *n* the study of ancient cultures by the scientific analysis of physical remains **archaeological** *or* **archeological** *adj* **archaeologist** *or* **archeologist** *n*
WORD ORIGIN Greek *arkhaiologia* study of what is ancient
archaeopteryx *n* an extinct primitive bird with teeth, a long tail, and well-developed wings

THESAURUS

OPPOSITE: slow
arbitrary *adj* **1 = random,** chance, optional, subjective, unreasonable, inconsistent, erratic, discretionary, personal, fanciful, wilful, whimsical, capricious
OPPOSITE: logical
arbitration *n* **= decision,** settlement, judgment, determination, adjudication, arbitrament
arc *n* **1 = curve,** bend, bow, arch, crescent, half-moon
arcade *n* **1 = mall, 2 = gallery,** cloister, portico, colonnade, covered walk, peristyle
arch[1] *n* **1 = archway,** curve, dome, span, vault **2 = curve,** bend, bow, crook, arc, hunch, sweep, hump, curvature, semicircle ▷ *vb* **4 = curve,** bridge, bend, bow, span, arc
arch[2] *adj* **2 = playful,** joking, teasing, humorous, sly, mischievous, saucy, tongue-in-cheek, jesting, jokey, pert, good-natured, roguish,

DICTIONARY

a

WORD ORIGIN Greek *arkhaios* ancient + *pterux* winged creature

archaeozoology *n* the study of animal remains found at archaeological sites **archaeozoologist** *n*

archaic (ark-**kay**-ik) *adj* **1** of a much earlier period **2** out of date or old-fashioned **3** (of a word or phrase) no longer in everyday use **archaically** *adv*

WORD ORIGIN Greek *arkhē* beginning

archaism (**ark**-kay-iz-zum) *n* an archaic word or style **archaistic** *adj*

archangel (**ark**-ain-jell) *n* an angel of the highest rank

archbishop *n* a bishop of the highest rank

archbishopric *n* the rank, office, or diocese of an archbishop

archdeacon *n* a church official ranking just below a bishop **archdeaconry** *n*

archdiocese *n* the diocese of an archbishop

archduchess *n* **1** a woman who holds the rank of archduke **2** the wife or widow of an archduke

archduchy *n, pl* **-duchies** the territory ruled by an archduke or archduchess

archduke *n* a duke of high rank, esp. one from Austria

archenemy *n, pl* **-mies** a chief enemy

archeology *n* ▸ same as **archaeology**

archer *n* a person who shoots with a bow and arrow

WORD ORIGIN Latin *arcus* bow

Archer[1] *n* **the Archer** the constellation Sagittarius, the ninth sign of the zodiac

Archer[2] *n* **1 Frederick Scott** 1813–57, British inventor and sculptor. He developed (1851) the wet collodion photographic process, enabling multiple copies of pictures to be made **2 Jeffrey** (**Howard**), Baron Archer of Weston-Super-Mare. born 1940, British novelist and Conservative politician. He was an MP from 1969 until 1974. His novels include *Kane and Abel* (1979), *Honour Among Thieves* (1993), and *The Fourth Estate* (1996): in 2000 he was imprisoned for perjury and attempting to pervert the course of justice **3 William** 1856–1924, Scottish critic and dramatist: made the first English translations of Ibsen

archery *n* the art or sport of shooting with a bow and arrow

archetype (**ark**-ee-type) *n* **1** a perfect or typical specimen **2** an original model; prototype **archetypal** *adj*

WORD ORIGIN Greek *arkhetupos* first-moulded

archidiaconal (ark-ee-die-**ak**-on-al) *adj* of an archdeacon or his office

archiepiscopal (ark-ee-ip-**piss**-kop-al) *adj* of an archbishop or his office

Archilochus *n* 7th century BC, Greek poet of Paros, notable for using his own experience as subject matter

Archimedes' principle (ark-ee-**mee**-deez) *n physics* the principle that the apparent loss in weight of an object immersed in a fluid is equal to the weight of the displaced fluid

WORD ORIGIN after *Archimedes*, Greek mathematician & physicist

archipelago (ark-ee-**pel**-a-go) *n, pl* **-gos 1** a group of islands **2** a sea full of small islands

WORD ORIGIN Greek *arkhi-* chief + *pelagos* sea

Archipenko *n* **Aleksandr Porfiryevich** 1887–1964, Russian sculptor and painter, in the US after 1923, whose work is characterized by economy of form

architect ❶ *n* **1** a person qualified to design and supervise the construction of buildings **2** any planner or creator: *you will be the architect of your own future*

WORD ORIGIN Greek *arkhi-* chief + *tektōn* workman

architecture ❶ *n* **1** the style in which a building is designed and built: *Gothic architecture* **2** the science of designing and constructing buildings **3** the structure or design of anything: *computer architecture* **architectural** *adj*

architrave (**ark**-ee-trave) *n archit* **1** a beam that rests on top of columns **2** a moulding around a doorway or window opening

WORD ORIGIN Italian, from *arch-* + *trave* beam

archive ❶ (**ark**-ive) *n* **1** a place where records or documents are kept **2 archives** a collection of records or documents **3** *computers* data put on tape or disk for long-term storage ▹ *vb* **4** to store in an archive

archivist (**ark**-iv-ist) *n* a person in charge of archives

archway *n* a passageway under an arch

Arcimboldo *n* **Giuseppe** 1527–93, Italian painter, best remembered for painting grotesque figures composed of fruit, vegetables, and meat

arctic ❶ *adj informal* very cold; freezing

Arctic ❶ *n* **1 the Arctic** the area around the North Pole ▹ *adj* **2** of this region

WORD ORIGIN Greek *arktikos* northern, literally: pertaining to (the constellation of) the Bear

Arctic Circle *n* the imaginary circle around the earth at latitude 66° 32′ N

arctic hare *n* a large hare of the Canadian Arctic whose fur turns white in winter

Arctic Monkeys *pl n* British rock group (formed 2002): comprising Alex Turner (born 1986; vocals, guitar), Jamie Cook (born 1985; guitar), Matt Helders (born 1986; drums, vocals) and Nick O'Malley (born 1985; bass guitar); the first major band to achieve widespread success through internet exposure

arctic willow *n* a low-growing shrub of the Canadian Arctic

arc welding *n* a technique in which metal is welded by heat generated by an electric arc

Arden[1] *n* **Forest of Arden** a region of N Warwickshire, part of a former forest: scene of Shakespeare's *As You Like It*

Arden[2] *n* **John** born 1930, British dramatist and novelist. His plays include *Serjeant Musgrave's Dance* (1959) and *The Workhouse Donkey* (1963); novels include *Silence Among the Weapons* (1982): he often works in collaboration with his wife Margaretta D'Arcy

ardent ❶ *adj* **1** passionate **2** intensely enthusiastic **ardently** *adv*

WORD ORIGIN Latin *ardere* to burn

ardour *or US* **ardor** *n* **1** emotional warmth; passion **2** intense enthusiasm

WORD ORIGIN Latin *ardere* to burn

arduous *adj* difficult to accomplish; strenuous

WORD ORIGIN Latin *arduus* steep, difficult

are[1] *vb* ▸ the plural form of the present tense of **be**: used as the singular form with *you*

WORD ORIGIN Old English *aron*

are[2] *n* a unit of measure equal to one hundred square metres

WORD ORIGIN Latin *area* piece of ground

area ❶ *n* **1** a section, part, or region **2** a part having a specified function: *reception area* **3** the size of a two-

THESAURUS

frolicsome, waggish

architect *n* **1 = designer**, planner, draughtsman, master builder

architecture *n* **1 = construction**, design, style **2 = design**, planning, building, construction, architectonics **3 = structure**, design, shape, make-up, construction, framework, layout, anatomy

archive *n* **1 = record office**, museum, registry, repository ▹ *pl n* **2 = records**, papers, accounts, rolls, documents, files, registers, deeds, chronicles, annals

arctic *adj (informal)* **= freezing**, cold, frozen, icy, chilly, frosty, glacial, frigid, gelid, frost-bound, cold as ice

Arctic *adj* **2 = polar**, far-northern, hyperborean

ardent *adj* **1 = passionate**, warm, spirited, intense, flaming, fierce,

DICTIONARY

dimensional surface **4** a subject field: *the area of literature* **5** a sunken area giving access to a basement **6** any flat, curved, or irregular expanse of a surface **7** range or scope
WORD ORIGIN Latin: level ground, threshing floor

area school *n NZ* a school in a rural area that includes primary and post-primary classes

arena ⊕ *n* **1** a seated enclosure where sports events take place **2** the area of an ancient Roman amphitheatre where gladiators fought **3** a sphere of intense activity: *the political arena*
WORD ORIGIN Latin *harena* sand

Arendt *n* **Hannah** 1906–75, US political philosopher, born in Germany. Her publications include *The Origins of Totalitarianism* (1951) and *Eichmann in Jerusalem* (1961)

aren't are not

areola *n, pl* **-lae** *or* **-las** a small circular area, such as the coloured ring around the human nipple
WORD ORIGIN Latin

Ares *n Greek myth* the god of war

arête *n* a sharp ridge separating valleys
WORD ORIGIN French: fishbone

Aretino *n* **Pietro** 1492–1556, Italian satirist, poet, and dramatist, noted for his satirical attacks on leading political figures

Argentine *or* **Argentinian** *adj* **1** of Argentina ▷*n* **2** a person from Argentina

Argerich *n* **Martha** born 1941, Argentinian concert pianist

argon *n chem* an unreactive odourless element of the rare gas series, forming almost 1 per cent of the atmosphere. Symbol: Ar
WORD ORIGIN Greek *argos* inactive

argosy *n, pl* **-sies** *old-fashioned or poetic* a large merchant ship, or a fleet of such ships
WORD ORIGIN Italian *Ragusea (nave)* (ship) of Ragusa, a former name for Dubrovnik

argot (ahr-go) *n* slang or jargon peculiar to a particular group
WORD ORIGIN French

argue ⊕ *vb* **-guing, -gued** **1** to try to prove by presenting reasons **2** to debate **3** to quarrel **4** to persuade: *we argued her out of going* **5** to suggest: *her looks argue despair* **arguable** *adj* **arguably** *adv*
WORD ORIGIN Latin *arguere* to make clear, accuse

argument ⊕ *n* **1** a quarrel **2** a discussion **3** a point presented to support or oppose a proposition

argumentation *n* the process of reasoning methodically

argumentative *adj* likely to argue

argy-bargy *or* **argie-bargie** *n, pl* **-bargies** *Brit informal* a squabbling argument
WORD ORIGIN Scots

aria (ah-ree-a) *n* an elaborate song for solo voice in an opera or choral work
WORD ORIGIN Italian

Arias Sánchez *n* **Oscar** born 1940, Costa Rican statesman; president (1986–90) and from 2006; Nobel peace prize 1987

arid *adj* **1** having little or no rain **2** uninteresting **aridity** *n*
WORD ORIGIN Latin *aridus*

Aries *n astrol* the first sign of the zodiac: the Ram
WORD ORIGIN Latin

aright *adv* correctly or properly

Ariosto *n* **Ludovico** 1474–1533, Italian poet, famous for his romantic epic *Orlando Furioso* (1516)

arise ⊕ *vb* **arising, arose, arisen** **1** to come into being: *the opportunity for action did not arise* **2** to come into notice: *people can seek answers to their problems as and when they arise* **3** **arise from** to happen as a result of **4** *old-fashioned* to get or stand up
WORD ORIGIN Old English *ārīsan*

Aristarchus of Samos *n* 3rd century BC, Greek astronomer who anticipated Copernicus in advancing the theory that the earth revolves around the sun

Aristarchus of Samothrace *n* ?220–?150 BC, Greek scholar: librarian at Alexandria, noted for his edition of Homer

Aristides *n* known as *Aristides the Just.* ?530–?468 BC, Athenian general and statesman, who played a prominent part in the Greek victories over the Persians at Marathon (490), Salamis (480), and Plataea (479)

Aristippus *n* ?435–?356 BC, Greek philosopher, who believed pleasure to be the highest good and founded the Cyrenaic school

aristocracy *n, pl* **-cies** **1** a class of people of high social rank **2** government by this class **3** a group of people considered to be outstanding in a particular sphere of activity
WORD ORIGIN Greek *aristos* best + *kratein* to rule

aristocrat *n* a member of the aristocracy

aristocratic ⊕ *adj* **1** of the aristocracy **2** grand or elegant

Aristotelian (ar-riss-tot-eel-ee-an) *adj* of Aristotle, 4th-century BC Greek philosopher, or his philosophy

arithmetic *n* **1** the branch of mathematics concerned with numerical calculations, such as addition, subtraction, multiplication, and division **2** calculations involving numerical operations **3** knowledge of or skill in arithmetic: *even simple arithmetic was*

THESAURUS

fiery, hot, fervent, impassioned, ablaze, lusty, vehement, amorous, hot-blooded, warm-blooded, fervid
OPPOSITE: cold
2 = enthusiastic, keen, eager, avid, zealous, keen as mustard
OPPOSITE: indifferent

area *n* **1 = region**, land, quarter, division, sector, district, stretch, territory, zone, plot, province, patch, neighbourhood, sphere, turf *(US slang)*, realm, domain, tract, locality, neck of the woods *(informal)* **1, 2 = part**, section, sector, portion **4 = realm**, part, department, field, province, arena, sphere, domain

arena *n* **1 = ring**, ground, stage, field, theatre, bowl, pitch, stadium, enclosure, park *(US & Canad)*, coliseum, amphitheatre **3 = scene**, world, area, stage, field, theatre, sector, territory, province, forum, scope, sphere, realm, domain

argue *vb* **1 = claim**, question, reason, challenge, insist, maintain, hold, allege, plead, assert, contend, uphold, profess, remonstrate, expostulate **2 = discuss**, debate, dispute, thrash out, exchange views on, controvert **3 = quarrel**, fight, row, clash, dispute, disagree, feud, squabble, spar, wrangle, bicker, have an argument, cross swords, be at sixes and sevens, fight like cat and dog, go at it hammer and tongs, bandy words, altercate

argument *n* **1 = quarrel**, fight, row, clash, dispute, controversy, disagreement, misunderstanding, feud, barney *(informal)*, squabble, wrangle, bickering, difference of opinion, tiff, altercation
OPPOSITE: agreement
2 = debate, questioning, claim, row, discussion, dispute, controversy, pleading, plea, contention, assertion, polemic, altercation, remonstrance, expostulation, remonstration **3 = reason**, case, reasoning, ground(s), defence, excuse, logic, justification, rationale, polemic, dialectic, line of reasoning, argumentation

arise *vb* **1, 2 = happen**, start, begin, follow, issue, result, appear, develop, emerge, occur, spring, set in, stem, originate, ensue, come about, commence, come to light, emanate, crop up *(informal)*, come into being, materialize **4a** *(old-fashioned)* **= get to your feet**, get up, rise, stand up, spring up, leap up **4b** *(old-fashioned)* **= get up**, wake up, awaken, get out of bed

aristocratic *adj* **1 = upper-class**, lordly, titled, gentle *(archaic)*, elite, gentlemanly, noble, patrician, blue-blooded, well-born, highborn
OPPOSITE: common

DICTIONARY

a

beyond him ▷ *adj also* **arithmetical 4** of or using arithmetic **arithmetically** *adv* **arithmetician** *n*
WORD ORIGIN Greek *arithmos* number

arithmetic mean *n* the average value of a set of terms, expressed as their sum divided by their number: *the arithmetic mean of 3, 4, and 8 is 5*

arithmetic progression *n* a sequence, each term of which differs from the preceding term by a constant amount, such as 3, 6, 9, 12

ark *n bible* the boat built by Noah, which survived the Flood
WORD ORIGIN Latin *arca* box, chest

Ark *n judaism* **1** Also called: **Holy Ark** the cupboard in a synagogue in which the Torah scrolls are kept **2** Also called: **Ark of the Covenant** a chest containing the laws of the Jewish religion, regarded as the most sacred symbol of God's presence among the Hebrew people

Arkwright *n* Sir **Richard** 1732–92, English cotton manufacturer: inventor of the spinning frame (1769) which produced cotton thread strong enough to be used as a warp

arm¹ ⓣ *n* **1** (in humans, apes, and monkeys) either of the upper limbs from the shoulder to the wrist **2** the sleeve of a garment **3** the side of a chair on which one's arm can rest **4** a subdivision or section of an organization: *the London-based arm of a Swiss bank* **5** something resembling an arm in appearance or function: *the arm of a record player* **6** power or authority: *the long arm of the law* **7 arm in arm** with arms linked **8 at arm's length** at a distance **9 with open arms** with warmth and hospitality
WORD ORIGIN Old English

arm² *vb* **1** to supply with weapons **2** to prepare (an explosive device) for use **3** to provide (a person or thing) with something that strengthens, or protects: *you will be armed with all the information you will ever need* ▸ See also **arms** > **armed** *adj*
WORD ORIGIN Latin *arma* arms, equipment

armada *n* **1** a large number of ships **2 the Armada** the great fleet sent by Spain against England in 1588
WORD ORIGIN Medieval Latin *armata* fleet, armed forces

armadillo *n, pl* **-los** a small S American burrowing mammal covered in strong bony plates
WORD ORIGIN Spanish *armado* armed (man)

Armageddon *n* **1** *new testament* the final battle between good and evil at the end of the world **2** a catastrophic and extremely destructive conflict
WORD ORIGIN Hebrew *har megiddōn*, mountain district of *Megiddo* (in N Palestine)

armament *n* **1 armaments** the weapon equipment of a military vehicle, ship, or aircraft **2** preparation for war
WORD ORIGIN Latin *armamenta* equipment

Armani *n* **Giorgio** born 1936, Italian fashion designer, noted for his restrained classical style

armature *n* **1** a revolving structure in an electric motor or generator, wound with the coils that carry the current **2** *sculpture* a framework to support the clay or other material used in modelling
WORD ORIGIN Latin *armatura* armour, equipment

armchair *n* **1** an upholstered chair with side supports for the arms ▷ *adj* **2** taking no active part: *we are, on the whole, a nation of armchair athletes*

armed forces *pl n* all the military forces of a nation or nations

armful *n* as much as can be held in the arms: *armfuls of lovely flowers*

armhole *n* the opening in a piece of clothing through which the arm passes

armistice (arm-miss-stiss) *n* an agreement between opposing armies to stop fighting
WORD ORIGIN Latin *arma* arms + *sistere* to stop

Armistice Day *n* the anniversary of the signing of the armistice that ended the First World War, on November 11, 1918

Armitage *n* **Simon** (**Robert**) born 1963, British poet and writer, whose collections include *Zoom!* (1989), *Killing Time* (1999), and *Universal Home Doctor* (2002)

armlet *n* a band or bracelet worn around the arm

armorial *adj* of or relating to heraldry or heraldic arms

armour ⓣ *or US* **armor** *n* **1** metal clothing worn by medieval warriors for protection in battle **2** *mil* armoured fighting vehicles in general **3** the protective metal plates on a tank or warship **4** protective covering, such as the shell of certain animals **5** a quality or attitude that gives protection ▷ *vb* **6** to equip or cover with armour
WORD ORIGIN Latin *armātūra* armour, equipment

armoured ⓣ *or US* **armored** *adj* **1** having a protective covering **2** consisting of armoured vehicles: *an armoured brigade*

armourer *or US* **armorer** *n* **1** a person who makes or mends arms and armour **2** a person in charge of small arms in a military unit

armour plate *n* a tough heavy steel for protecting warships and vehicles **armour-plated** *adj*

armoury *or US* **armory** *n, pl* **-mouries** *or* **-mories 1** a secure storage place for weapons **2** military supplies **3** resources on which to draw: *modern medicine has a large armoury of drugs for the treatment of mental illness*

armpit *n* **1** the hollow beneath the arm where it joins the shoulder **2** *slang* an extremely unpleasant place: *the armpit of the Mediterranean*

armrest *n* the part of a chair or sofa that supports the arm

arms *pl n* **1** weapons collectively **2** military exploits: *prowess in arms* **3** the heraldic symbols of a family or state **4 take up arms** to prepare to fight **5 under arms** armed and prepared for war **6 up in arms** prepared to protest strongly

army ⓣ *n, pl* **-mies 1** the military land forces of a nation **2** a large number of people or animals
WORD ORIGIN Medieval Latin *armata* armed forces

Arnaud *n* **Yvonne** 1892–1958, French actress, who was well-known on the London stage and in British films. A theatre in Guildford is named after her

Arne *n* **Thomas** (**Augustine**) 1710–78, English composer, noted for his setting of Shakespearean songs and for his song *Rule Britannia*

Arnim *n* **Achim von** 1781–1831, German romantic poet. He published, with Clemens Brentano, the collection of folk songs, *Des Knaben Wunderhorn* (1805–08)

Arnold¹ *n* a town in N central England, in S Nottinghamshire. Pop: 37 402 (2001)

Arnold² *n* **1** Sir **Malcolm** 1921–2006, English composer, esp. of orchestral works in a traditional idiom **2 Matthew** 1822–88, English poet, essayist, and literary critic, noted particularly for his poems *Sohrab and Rustum* (1853) and *Dover Beach* (1867), and for his *Essays in Criticism* (1865) and *Culture and Anarchy* (1869) **3** his father,

THESAURUS

arm¹ *n* **1 = upper limb**, limb, appendage

armour *n* **1, 3, 4 = protection**, covering, shield, sheathing, armour plate, chain mail, protective covering

armoured *adj* **1 = protected**, mailed, reinforced, toughened, bulletproof, armour-plated, steel-plated, ironclad, bombproof

army *n* **1 = soldiers**, military, troops, armed force, legions, infantry, military force, land forces, land force, soldiery **2 = vast number**, host, gang, mob, flock, array, legion, swarm, sea, pack, horde, multitude, throng

aroma *n* **1 = scent**, smell, perfume,

DICTIONARY

Thomas 1795–1842, English historian and educationalist, headmaster of Rugby School, noted for his reforms in public-school education

aroha *n NZ* love, compassion, or affection
WORD ORIGIN Māori

aroma ❶ *n* **1** a distinctive pleasant smell **2** a subtle pervasive quality or atmosphere
WORD ORIGIN Greek: spice

aromatherapy *n* the use of fragrant essential oils as a treatment in alternative medicine, often to relieve tension

aromatic *adj* **1** having a distinctive pleasant smell **2** *chem* (of an organic compound) having an unsaturated ring of atoms, usually six carbon atoms ▷*n* **3** something, such as a plant or drug, that gives off a fragrant smell

arose *vb* ▸ the past tense of **arise**

around ❶ *prep* **1** situated at various points in: *cameramen were positioned around the auditorium* **2** from place to place in: *he had spent twenty-five minutes driving around Amsterdam* **3** somewhere in or near **4** approximately in: *around 1980* ▷*adv* **5** in all directions from a point of reference: *there wasn't a house for miles around* **6** in the vicinity, esp. restlessly but idly: *I couldn't hang around too long* **7** in no particular place or direction: *a few tropical fish tanks dotted around* **8** *informal* present in some unknown or unspecified place **9** *informal* available: *cancer drugs have been around for years* **10 have been around** *informal* to have gained considerable experience of a worldly or social nature

arouse ❶ *vb* **arousing, aroused 1** to produce (a reaction, emotion, or response) **2** to awaken from sleep **arousal** *n*

Arp *n* **Jean** *or* **Hans** 1887–1966, Alsatian sculptor, painter, and poet, cofounder of the Dada movement in Zürich, noted particularly for his abstract organic sculptures based on natural forms

Arpád *n* died 907 AD, Magyar chieftain who conquered Hungary in the late 9th century

arpeggio (arp-**pej**-ee-oh) *n, pl* **-gios** a chord whose notes are played or sung in rapid succession
WORD ORIGIN Italian

arquebus (**ark**-wee-bus) *n* a portable long-barrelled gun dating from the 15th century
WORD ORIGIN Middle Dutch *hakebusse* hook gun

arrack *or* **arak** *n* a coarse alcoholic drink distilled in Eastern countries from grain or rice
WORD ORIGIN Arabic *'araq* sweat, sweet juice

arraign (ar-**rain**) *vb* **1** to bring (a prisoner) before a court to answer a charge **2** to accuse **arraignment** *n*
WORD ORIGIN Old French *araisnier* to accuse

arrange ❶ *vb* **-ranging, -ranged 1** to plan in advance: *my parents had arranged a surprise party* **2** to arrive at an agreement: *they had arranged to go to the cinema* **3** to put into a proper or systematic order **4** to adapt (a musical composition) for performance in a certain way
WORD ORIGIN Old French *a-* to + *rangier* to put in a row, range

arrangement ❶ *n* **1** a preparation or plan made for an event: *travel arrangements* **2** an agreement or a plan to do something **3** a thing composed of various ordered parts: *a flower arrangement* **4** the form in which things are arranged **5** an adaptation of a piece of music for performance in a different way

arrant *adj* utter or downright: *that's the most arrant nonsense I've ever heard*
WORD ORIGIN Middle English variant of *errant* (wandering, vagabond)

arras *n* a tapestry wall-hanging
WORD ORIGIN *Arras*, a town in N France

Arrau *n* **Claudio** 1903–91, Chilean pianist

array ❶ *n* **1** an impressive display or collection **2** an orderly arrangement, such as of troops in battle order **3** *computers* a data structure in which elements may be located by index numbers **4** *poetic* rich clothing ▷*vb* **5** to arrange in order **6** to dress in rich clothing
WORD ORIGIN Old French *arayer* to arrange

arrears *pl n* **1** money owed **2 in arrears** late in paying a debt
WORD ORIGIN Latin *ad* to + *retro* backwards

arrest ❶ *vb* **1** to take (a person) into custody **2** to slow or stop the development of **3** to catch and hold (one's attention) ▷*n* **4** the act of taking a person into custody **5 under arrest** being held in custody

THESAURUS

fragrance, bouquet, savour, odour, redolence

around *prep* **1 = surrounding**, about, enclosing, encompassing, framing, encircling, on all sides of, on every side of, environing
4 = approximately, about, nearly, close to, roughly, just about, in the region of, circa (*of a date*), in the vicinity of, not far off, in the neighbourhood of ▷*adv* **5, 7 = everywhere**, about, throughout, all over, here and there, on all sides, in all directions, to and fro

arouse *vb* **1 = stimulate**, encourage, inspire, prompt, spark, spur, foster, provoke, rouse, stir up, inflame, incite, instigate, whip up, summon up, whet, kindle, foment, call forth **OPPOSITE:** quell
2 = awaken, wake up, rouse, waken

arrange *vb* **1 = plan**, agree, prepare, determine, schedule, organize, construct, devise, contrive, fix up, jack up (*NZ informal*) **3 = put in order**, group, form, order, sort, class, position, range, file, rank, line up, organize, set out, sequence, exhibit, sort out (*informal*), array, classify, tidy, marshal, align, categorize, systematize, jack up (*NZ informal*) **OPPOSITE:** disorganize
4 = adapt, score, orchestrate, harmonize, instrument

arrangement *n* **1 = plan**, planning, provision, preparation
2 = agreement, contract, settlement, appointment, compromise, deal (*informal*), pact, compact, covenant
3, 4 = display, grouping, system, order, ordering, design, ranging, structure, rank, organization, exhibition, line-up, presentation, array, marshalling, classification, disposition, alignment, setup (*informal*) **5 = adaptation**, score, version, interpretation, instrumentation, orchestration, harmonization

array *n* **1, 2 = arrangement**, show, order, supply, display, collection, exhibition, line-up, mixture, parade, formation, presentation, spectacle, marshalling, muster, disposition
4 (*poetic*) **= clothing**, dress, clothes, threads (*slang*), garments, apparel, attire, garb, finery, regalia, raiment (*archaic, poetic*), schmutter (*slang*) ▷*vb* **5 = arrange**, show, group, order, present, range, display, line up, sequence, parade, exhibit, unveil, dispose, draw up, marshal, lay out, muster, align, form up, place in order, set in line (*military*) **6 = dress**, supply, clothe, wrap, deck, outfit, decorate, equip, robe, get ready, adorn, apparel (*archaic*), festoon, attire, fit out, garb, bedeck, caparison, accoutre

arrest *vb* **1 = capture**, catch, lift (*slang*), nick (*slang, chiefly Brit*), seize, run in (*slang*), nail (*informal*), bust (*informal*), collar (*informal*), take, detain, pinch (*informal*), nab (*informal*), apprehend, take prisoner, take into custody, lay hold of **OPPOSITE:** release
2 = stop, end, hold, limit, check, block, slow, delay, halt, stall, stay, interrupt, suppress, restrain, hamper, inhibit, hinder, obstruct, retard, impede **OPPOSITE:** speed up
3 = fascinate, hold, involve, catch, occupy, engage, grip, absorb, entrance, intrigue, rivet, enthral,

DICTIONARY

a

by the police **6** the slowing or stopping of something: *a cardiac arrest*
WORD ORIGIN Latin *ad* at, to + *restare* to stand firm, stop

arresting ❶ *adj* attracting attention; striking

Arrhenius *n* **Svante August** 1859–1927, Swedish chemist and physicist, noted for his work on the theory of electrolytic dissociation: Nobel prize for chemistry 1903

arrival ❶ *n* **1** the act of arriving **2** a person or thing that has just arrived **3** *informal* a recently born baby

arrive ❶ *vb* **-riving, -rived 1** to reach a place or destination **2 arrive at** to come to (a conclusion, idea, or decision) **3** to occur: *the crisis he predicted then has now arrived* **4** *informal* to be born **5** *informal* to attain success
WORD ORIGIN Latin *ad* to + *ripa* river bank

arrivederci (ar-reeve-a-der-chee) *interj* goodbye
WORD ORIGIN Italian

arrogant ❶ *adj* having an exaggerated opinion of one's own importance or ability **arrogance** *n* **arrogantly** *adv*
WORD ORIGIN Latin *arrogare* to claim as one's own

arrogate *vb* **-gating, -gated** to claim or seize without justification **arrogation** *n*
WORD ORIGIN Latin *arrogare*

arrow ❶ *n* **1** a long slender pointed weapon, with feathers at one end, that is shot from a bow **2** an arrow-shaped sign or symbol used to show the direction to a place
WORD ORIGIN Old English *arwe*

arrowhead *n* the pointed tip of an arrow

arrowroot *n* an easily digestible starch obtained from the root of a West Indian plant

Arroyo *n* **Gloria Macapagal** born 1948, Filipino stateswoman; president of the Philippines from 2001; vice-president (1998–2001)

arse *or US & Canad* **ass** *n taboo* the buttocks or anus
WORD ORIGIN Old English *ærs*

arsehole *or US & Canad* **asshole** *n taboo* **1** the anus **2** a stupid or annoying person

arsenal ❶ *n* **1** a building in which arms and ammunition are made or stored **2** a store of anything regarded as weapons: *this new weapon in the medical arsenal*
WORD ORIGIN Arabic *dār* house + *sinā'ah* manufacture

arsenic *n* **1** a toxic metalloid element. Symbol: As **2** a nontechnical name for **arsenic trioxide**, a highly poisonous compound used as a rat poison and insecticide ▷ *adj also* **arsenical 3** of or containing arsenic
WORD ORIGIN Syriac *zarnīg*

arson *n* the crime of intentionally setting fire to property **arsonist** *n*
WORD ORIGIN Latin *ardere* to burn

art ❶ *n* **1** the creation of works of beauty or other special significance **2** works of art collectively **3** human creativity as distinguished from nature **4** skill: *she was still new to the art of bargaining* **5** any branch of the visual arts, esp. painting **6 get something down to a fine art** to become proficient at something through practice ▸ See also **arts**
WORD ORIGIN Latin *ars* craftsmanship

Artaud *n* **Antonin** 1896–1948, French stage director and dramatist, whose concept of the theatre of cruelty is expounded in *Manifeste du théâtre de la cruauté* (1932) and *Le Théâtre et son double* (1938)

Artaxerxes I *n* died 425 BC, king of Persia (465–425): son of Xerxes I

Artaxerxes II *n* died ?358 BC, king of Persia (?404–?358). He defeated his brother Cyrus the Younger at Cunaxa (401)

Art Deco (art **deck**-oh) *n* a style of design, at its height in the 1930s, characterized by geometrical shapes
WORD ORIGIN French *art décoratif*

artefact *or* **artifact** *n* something made by human beings, such as a tool or a work of art
WORD ORIGIN Latin *ars* skill + *facere* to make

Artemis *n Greek myth* the goddess of hunting

arterial *adj* **1** of or affecting an artery **2** being a major route: *an arterial road*

arteriosclerosis (art-ear-ee-oh-skler-oh-siss) *n* thickening and loss of elasticity of the walls of the arteries. Nontechnical name: **hardening of the arteries**

artery *n, pl* **-teries 1** any of the tubes that carry oxygenated blood from the heart to various parts of the body **2** a major road or means of communication
WORD ORIGIN Latin *arteria*

artesian well (art-teez-yan) *n* a well receiving water from a higher altitude, so the water is forced to flow upwards
WORD ORIGIN from Old French *Arteis* Artois (in N France) where such wells were common

Artex *n trademark, Brit* a type of coating for walls and ceilings that gives a textured finish

art form *n* a recognized mode or medium of artistic expression

artful *adj* **1** cunning **2** skilful in achieving a desired end **artfully** *adv*

arthritis *n* inflammation of a joint or joints, causing pain and stiffness **arthritic** *adj, n*
WORD ORIGIN Greek *arthron* joint

arthropod *n* a creature, such as an insect or a spider, which has jointed legs and a hard case on its body
WORD ORIGIN Greek *arthron* joint + *pous* foot

artic *n Brit informal* an articulated lorry

artichoke *n* **1** Also called: **globe artichoke** the flower head of a thistle-like plant, cooked as a vegetable **2** ▸ same as **Jerusalem artichoke**
WORD ORIGIN Arabic *al-kharshūf*

THESAURUS

mesmerize, engross, spellbind ▷ *n* **4 = capture**, bust (*informal*), detention, seizure, apprehension **OPPOSITE:** release **6 = stoppage**, halt, suppression, obstruction, inhibition, blockage, hindrance **OPPOSITE:** acceleration

arresting *adj* **= striking**, surprising, engaging, dramatic, stunning, impressive, extraordinary, outstanding, remarkable, noticeable, conspicuous, salient, jaw-dropping **OPPOSITE:** unremarkable

arrival *n* **1 = appearance**, coming, arriving, entrance, advent, materialization **2 = newcomer**, arriver, incomer, visitor, caller, entrant, comer, visitant

arrive *vb* **1 = come**, appear, enter, turn up, show up (*informal*), materialize, draw near **OPPOSITE:** depart **3 = occur**, happen, take place, ensue, transpire, fall, befall **5** (*informal*) **= succeed**, make it (*informal*), triumph, do well, thrive, flourish, be successful, make good, prosper, cut it (*informal*), reach the top, become famous, make the grade (*informal*), get to the top, crack it (*informal*), hit the jackpot (*informal*), turn out well, make your mark (*informal*), achieve recognition, do all right for yourself (*informal*)

arrogant *adj* **= conceited**, lordly, assuming, proud, swaggering, pompous, pretentious, stuck up (*informal*), cocky, contemptuous, blustering, imperious, overbearing, haughty, scornful, puffed up, egotistical, disdainful, self-important, presumptuous, high-handed, insolent, supercilious, high and mighty (*informal*), overweening, immodest, swollen-headed, bigheaded (*informal*), uppish (*Brit informal*) **OPPOSITE:** modest

arrow *n* **1 = dart**, flight, reed (*archaic*), bolt, shaft (*archaic*), quarrel **2 = pointer**, indicator, marker

arsenal *n* **1 = armoury**, storehouse, ammunition dump, arms depot, ordnance depot **2 = store**, stock, supply, magazine, stockpile

DICTIONARY

a

article ❶ *n* **1** a written composition in a magazine or newspaper **2** an item or object **3** a clause in a written document **4** *grammar* any of the words *a, an,* or *the*
WORD ORIGIN Latin *articulus* small joint

articled *adj* bound by a written contract, such as one that governs a period of training: *an articled clerk*

articular *adj* of or relating to joints
WORD ORIGIN Latin *articulus* small joint

articulate ❶ *adj* **1** able to express oneself fluently and coherently **2** distinct, clear, or definite: *his amiable and articulate campaign attracted support* **3** *zool* possessing joints ▹ *vb* **-lating, -lated 4** to speak clearly and distinctly **5** to express coherently in words **articulately** *adv*
WORD ORIGIN Latin *articulare* to divide into joints

articulated lorry *n* a large lorry in two separate sections connected by a pivoted bar

articulation *n* **1** the expressing of an idea in words **2** the process of articulating a speech sound or the sound so produced **3** a being jointed together **4** *zool* a joint between bones or arthropod segments

artifact *n* ▸ same as **artefact**

artifice *n* **1** a clever trick **2** skill or cleverness
WORD ORIGIN Latin *ars* skill + *facere* to make

artificer (art-tiff-iss-er) *n* a skilled craftsman

artificial ❶ *adj* **1** man-made; not occurring naturally **2** made in imitation of a natural product: *artificial flavourings* **3** not sincere **artificiality** *n* **artificially** *adv*
WORD ORIGIN Latin *artificialis* belonging to art

artificial insemination *n* introduction of semen into the womb by means other than sexual intercourse

artificial intelligence *n* the branch of computer science aiming to produce machines which can imitate intelligent human behaviour

artificial respiration *n* any method of restarting a person's breathing after it has stopped

Artigas *n* **José Gervasio** 1764–1850, the national hero of Uruguay. He fought for Uruguayan independence from Argentina, but was driven into exile in 1820

artillery ❶ *n* **1** large-calibre guns **2** military units specializing in the use of such guns
WORD ORIGIN Old French *artillier* to equip with weapons

artisan *n* a skilled workman; craftsman **artisanal** *adj*
WORD ORIGIN French

artist *n* **1** a person who produces works of art such as paintings or sculpture **2** a person who is skilled at something **3** ▸ same as **artiste** > **artistic** *adj* **artistically** *adv*

artiste *n* a professional entertainer such as a singer or dancer

artistry *n* **1** artistic ability **2** great skill

artless *adj* **1** free from deceit or cunning: *artless generosity* **2** natural or unpretentious **artlessly** *adv*

Art Nouveau (ahr noo-**voh**) *n* a style of art and architecture of the 1890s, characterized by sinuous outlines and stylized natural forms
WORD ORIGIN French: new art

arts *pl n* **1 the arts** the nonscientific branches of knowledge **2** ▸ see **fine art 3** cunning schemes

artwork *n* all the photographs and illustrations in a publication

arty *adj* **artier, artiest** *informal* having an affected interest in art **artiness** *n*

arum lily *n* a plant with a white funnel-shaped leaf surrounding a yellow spike of flowers

Aryan (air-ree-an) *n* **1** (in Nazi ideology) a non-Jewish person of the Nordic type **2** a person supposedly descended from the Indo-Europeans ▹ *adj* **3** of Aryans
WORD ORIGIN Sanskrit *ārya* of noble birth

as ❶ *conj* **1** while or when: *he arrived just as the band finished the song* **2** in the way that: *they had talked and laughed as only the best of friends can* **3** that which; what: *George did as he was asked* **4** (of) which fact or event (referring to the previous statement): *to become wise, as we all know, is not easy* **5 as it were** in a way; in a manner of speaking: *he was, as it were, on probation* **6** since; seeing that **7** for instance ▹ *adv, conj* **8** used to indicate amount or extent in comparisons: *he was as fat as his mum and dad* ▹ *prep* **9** in the role of; being: *my task, as his physician, is to do the best that I can* **10 as for** *or* **to** with reference to **11 as if** *or* **though** as it would be if: *she felt as if she had been run over by a bulldozer* **12 as (it) is** in the existing state of affairs
WORD ORIGIN Old English *alswā* likewise

As *chem* arsenic

ASA 1 (in Britain) Amateur Swimming Association **2** (in Britain) Advertising Standards Authority

asafoetida *n* a strong-smelling plant resin used as a spice in Eastern cookery
WORD ORIGIN Medieval Latin *asa* gum + Latin *foetidus* evil-smelling

a.s.a.p. as soon as possible

asbestos *n* a fibrous mineral which does not burn, formerly widely used as a heat-resistant material
WORD ORIGIN Greek: inextinguishable

asbestosis *n* inflammation of the lungs resulting from inhalation of asbestos fibre

ASBO *Brit* antisocial behaviour order

ascend *vb* **1** to go or move up **2** to slope upwards **3 ascend the throne** to become king or queen
WORD ORIGIN Latin *ascendere*

ascendancy *or* **ascendance** *n* the condition of being dominant: *when*

THESAURUS

art *n* **1, 5 = artwork**, style of art, fine art, creativity **4 = skill**, knowledge, method, facility, craft, profession, expertise, competence, accomplishment, mastery, knack, ingenuity, finesse, aptitude, artistry, artifice *(archaic)*, virtuosity, dexterity, cleverness, adroitness

article *n* **1 = feature**, story, paper, piece, item, creation, essay, composition, discourse, treatise **2 = thing**, piece, unit, item, object, device, tool, implement, commodity, gadget, utensil **3 = clause**, point, part, heading, head, matter, detail, piece, particular, division, section, item, passage, portion, paragraph, proviso

articulate *adj* **1, 2 = expressive**, clear, effective, vocal, meaningful, understandable, coherent, persuasive, fluent, eloquent, lucid, comprehensible, communicative, intelligible **OPPOSITE:** incoherent ▹ *vb* **4 = pronounce**, say, talk, speak, voice, utter, enunciate, vocalize, enounce **5 = express**, say, tell, state, word, speak, declare, phrase, communicate, assert, pronounce, utter, couch, put across, enunciate, put into words, verbalize, asseverate

artificial *adj* **1, 2a = synthetic**, manufactured, plastic, man-made, non-natural **1, 2b = fake**, mock, imitation, bogus, simulated, phoney *or* phony *(informal)*, sham, pseudo *(informal)*, fabricated, counterfeit, spurious, ersatz, specious **OPPOSITE:** authentic **3 = insincere**, forced, affected, assumed, phoney *or* phony *(informal)*, put on, false, pretended, hollow, contrived, unnatural, feigned, spurious, meretricious **OPPOSITE:** genuine

artillery *n* **1 = big guns**, battery, cannon, ordnance, gunnery, cannonry

as *conj* **1 = when**, while, just as, at the time that, during the time that **2 = in the way that**, like, in the manner that **6 = since**, because, seeing that, considering that, on account of the fact that ▹ *prep* **9 = in**

DICTIONARY

a

hardliners were in the ascendancy last winter

ascendant or **ascendent** adj 1 dominant or influential ▷n 2 astrol the sign of the zodiac that is rising on the eastern horizon at a particular moment 3 **in the ascendant** increasing in power or influence

ascension n the act of ascending

Ascension Day n Christianity the 40th day after Easter, when the Ascension of Christ into Heaven is celebrated

ascent n 1 the act of ascending 2 an upward slope

ascertain vb to find out definitely **ascertainment** n
WORD ORIGIN Old French *acertener* to make certain

ascetic (ass-set-tik) n 1 a person who abstains from worldly comforts and pleasures ▷adj 2 rigidly abstinent and self-denying
WORD ORIGIN Greek *askētikos*

Asch n **Sholem** 1880–1957, US writer, born in Poland, who wrote in Yiddish. His works include biblical novels

Ascham n **Roger** ?1515–68, English humanist writer and classical scholar: tutor to Queen Elizabeth I

ASCII (ass-kee) n a code for transmitting data between computers
WORD ORIGIN *A(merican) S(tandard) C(ode for) I(nformation) I(nterchange)*

ascorbic acid (ass-**core**-bik) n a vitamin that occurs in citrus fruits, tomatoes, and green vegetables, and which prevents and cures scurvy. Also called: **vitamin C**
WORD ORIGIN A- + SCORBUTIC

ascribe vb **-cribing, -cribed** 1 to attribute, as to a particular origin: *headaches which may be ascribed to stress* 2 to consider that (a particular quality) is possessed by something or someone: *specific human qualities are ascribed to each of the four elements* **ascription** n
WORD ORIGIN Latin *ad* in addition + *scribere* to write

aseptic (eh-sep-tik) adj free from harmful bacteria

asexual (eh-sex-yew-al) adj 1 having no apparent sex or sex organs 2 (of reproduction) not involving sexual activity **asexually** adv

ash[1] n 1 the powdery substance formed when something is burnt 2 fine particles of lava thrown out by an erupting volcano
WORD ORIGIN Old English *æsce*

ash[2] n a tree with grey bark and winged seeds
WORD ORIGIN Old English *æsc*

ashamed ❶ adj 1 overcome with shame or remorse 2 unwilling through fear of humiliation or shame: *she'd be ashamed to admit to jealousy*
WORD ORIGIN Old English *āscamod*

ash can n US a dustbin

Ashcroft n Dame **Peggy** 1907–91, English stage and film actress

Ashdown n **Paddy,** Baron. real name *Jeremy John Durham Ashdown*. born 1941, British politician; leader of the Liberal Democrats (formerly the Social and Liberal Democrats) (1988–99); UN high representative in Bosnia-Herzegovina from 2002

Ashe n **Arthur** (**Robert**) 1943–93, US tennis player: US champion 1968; Wimbledon champion 1975

ashen adj pale with shock

ashes pl n 1 remains after burning 2 the remains of a human body after cremation

Ashes pl n **the Ashes** a cricket trophy competed for by England and Australia since 1882
WORD ORIGIN from a mock obituary of English cricket after a great Australian victory

Ashkenazy n **Vladimir** born 1937, Soviet-born Icelandic pianist and conductor

ashlar or **ashler** n 1 a square block of cut stone for use in building 2 a thin dressed stone used to face a wall
WORD ORIGIN Old French *aisselier* crossbeam

Ashley n 1 **Jack,** Baron. born 1922, British Labour politician and campaigner for deaf and disabled people 2 **Laura** 1925–85, British designer, who built up a successful chain of retail stores selling dresses and fabrics based on traditional English patterns

ashore ❶ adv towards or on land

ashram n a religious retreat where a Hindu holy man lives
WORD ORIGIN Sanskrit *ā´srama*

Ashton n Sir **Frederick** 1906–88, British ballet dancer and choreographer. His ballets include *Façade* (1931), to music by Walton, *La Fille mal gardée* (1960), *The Dream* (1964), and *A Month in the Country* (1976)

ashtray n a dish for tobacco ash and cigarette ends

Ashurbanipal or **Assurbanipal** n died ?626 BC, king of Assyria (?668–?626): son of Esarhaddon. He built the magnificent palace and library at Nineveh. Greek name: **Sardanapalus**

Ash Wednesday n the first day of Lent, named from the Christian custom of sprinkling ashes on penitents' heads

ashy adj **ashier, ashiest** 1 pale greyish 2 covered with ash

Asian adj 1 of Asia 2 Brit of the Indian subcontinent ▷n 3 a person from Asia 4 Brit a person from the Indian subcontinent or a descendant of one

Asian pear n an apple-shaped pear with crisp juicy flesh

Asiatic adj Asian

aside ❶ adv 1 to one side 2 out of other people's hearing: *her mother took her aside for a serious talk* 3 out of mind: *she pushed aside her fears of being beaten or killed* 4 into reserve: *a certain amount must also be put aside for defence and government* ▷n 5 a remark not meant to be heard by everyone present 6 a remark that is not connected with the subject being discussed

asinine (ass-in-nine) adj 1 obstinate or stupid 2 of or like an ass
WORD ORIGIN Latin *asinus* ass

ask ❶ vb 1 to say or write (something) in a form that requires an answer: *I asked him his name; 'do you think we'll have trouble landing?' he asked* 2 to make a request or demand: *the chairman asked for a show of hands* 3 to invite 4 to inquire about: *I pretended to be lost and asked for directions* 5 to expect: *is that too much to ask?*
WORD ORIGIN Old English *āscian*

ask after vb to make polite inquiries about the health of: *he asked after you*

askance (ass-**kanss**) adv **look askance at** a to look at with an oblique glance b to regard with suspicion
WORD ORIGIN origin unknown

askew adv, adj towards one side; crooked

Askey n **Arthur** 1900–82, British comedian

ask for vb 1 to seek to speak to 2 to request 3 informal to behave in a manner that is regarded as inviting (something): *you were asking for trouble there*

THESAURUS

the role of, being, under the name of, in the character of

ashamed adj 1 = **embarrassed**, sorry, guilty, upset, distressed, shy, humbled, humiliated, blushing, self-conscious, red-faced, chagrined, flustered, mortified, sheepish, bashful, prudish, crestfallen, discomfited, remorseful, abashed, shamefaced, conscience-stricken, discountenanced OPPOSITE: proud 2 = **reluctant**, afraid, embarrassed, scared, unwilling, loath, disinclined

ashore adv = **on land**, on the beach, on the shore, aground, to the shore, on dry land, shorewards, landwards

aside adv 1, 2, 3 = **to one side**, away, alone, separately, apart, alongside, beside, out of the way, on one side, to the side, in isolation, in reserve, out of mind ▷n 5 = **interpolation**, remark, parenthesis, digression, interposition, confidential remark

ask vb 1 = **inquire**, question, quiz, query, interrogate OPPOSITE: answer 3 = **invite**, bid, summon

asleep adj 1 = **sleeping**, napping,

DICTIONARY

asking price *n* the price suggested by a seller
aslant *adv* **1** at a slant ▹*prep* **2** slanting across
asleep ❶ *adj* **1** in or into a state of sleep **2** (of limbs) numb **3** *informal* not listening or paying attention
ASLEF (in Britain) Associated Society of Locomotive Engineers and Firemen
asp *n* a small viper of S Europe
WORD ORIGIN Greek *aspis*
asparagus *n* the young shoots of a plant of the lily family, which can be cooked and eaten
WORD ORIGIN Greek *asparagos*
aspartame *n* an artificial sweetener
Aspasia *n* 5th century BC, Greek courtesan; mistress of Pericles
aspect ❶ *n* **1** a distinct feature or element in a problem or situation **2** a position facing a particular direction: *the room's east-facing aspect* **3** appearance or look: *a room with a somewhat gloomy aspect*
WORD ORIGIN Latin *ad-* to, at + *specere* to look
aspen *n* a poplar tree whose leaves quiver in the wind
WORD ORIGIN Old English *æspe*
asperity (ass-per-rit-ee) *n, pl* **-ties** roughness or sharpness of temper
WORD ORIGIN Latin *asper* rough
aspersion *n* **cast aspersions on** to make disparaging or malicious remarks about
WORD ORIGIN Latin *aspergere* to sprinkle
asphalt *n* **1** a black tarlike substance used in road-surfacing and roofing materials ▹*vb* **2** to cover with asphalt
WORD ORIGIN Greek *asphaltos*, probably from *a-* not + *sphallein* to cause to fall; referring to its use as a binding agent
asphodel *n* a plant with clusters of yellow or white flowers
asphyxia (ass-fix-ee-a) *n* unconsciousness or death caused by lack of oxygen
WORD ORIGIN Greek *a-* without + *sphuxis* pulse
asphyxiate *vb* **-ating, -ated** to smother or suffocate **asphyxiation** *n*
aspic *n* a savoury jelly based on meat or fish stock, used as a mould for meat or vegetables
WORD ORIGIN French
aspidistra *n* a house plant with long tapered evergreen leaves
WORD ORIGIN Greek *aspis* shield
aspirant *n* a person who aspires, such as to a powerful position
aspirate *phonetics vb* **-rating, -rated** **1** to pronounce (a word or syllable) with an initial *h* ▹*n* **2** the sound represented in English and several other languages as *h*
aspiration ❶ *n* **1** a strong desire or aim **2** *phonetics* the pronunciation of an aspirated consonant **aspirational** *adj*
aspirator *n* a device for removing fluids from a body cavity by suction
aspire *vb* **-piring, -pired** to yearn for something or hope to do or be something: *it struck him as bizarre that somebody could aspire to be a dental technician* **aspiring** *adj*
WORD ORIGIN Latin *aspirare* to breathe upon
aspirin *n, pl* **-rin** *or* **-rins** **1** a drug used to relieve pain and fever **2** a tablet of aspirin
WORD ORIGIN German
ass[1] ❶ *n* **1** a mammal resembling the horse but with longer ears **2** a foolish person
WORD ORIGIN Old English *assa*
ass[2] *n US & Canad taboo* ▸same as **arse**
WORD ORIGIN Old English *ærs*
Assad *n* **1 Hafiz al** 1928–2000, Syrian statesman and general; president of Syria (1971–2000) **2** his son, **Bashar al** born 1965, Syrian statesman; president of Syria from 2000
assagai *n* ▸same as **assegai**
assail *vb* **1** to attack violently **2** to criticize strongly **3** to disturb: *he was assailed by a dizzy sensation* **assailant** *n*
WORD ORIGIN Latin *assilire* to leap on
assassin ❶ *n* a murderer of a prominent person
WORD ORIGIN Arabic *hashshāshīn*, plural of *hashshāsh* one who eats hashish
assassinate ❶ *vb* **-nating, -nated** to murder (a prominent person) **assassination** *n*
assault ❶ *n* **1** a violent attack, either physical or verbal ▹*vb* **2** to attack violently
WORD ORIGIN Old French *asaut*
assault and battery *n criminal law* a threat of attack to another person followed by actual attack
assault course *n* an obstacle course designed to give soldiers practice in negotiating hazards
assay *vb* **1** to analyse (a substance, such as gold) to find out how pure it is ▹*n* **2** an analysis of the purity of an ore or precious metal
WORD ORIGIN Old French *assai*
assegai *or* **assagai** *n, pl* **-gais** a sharp light spear used in southern Africa
WORD ORIGIN Arabic *az zaghayah*
assemblage *n* **1** a collection or group of things **2** the act of assembling
assemble ❶ *vb* **-bling, -bled** **1** to collect or gather together **2** to put

THESAURUS

dormant, crashed out *(slang)*, dozing, slumbering, snoozing *(informal)*, fast asleep, sound asleep, out for the count, dead to the world *(informal)*, in a deep sleep
aspect *n* **1 = feature**, point, side, factor, angle, characteristic, facet **2 = position**, view, situation, scene, bearing, direction, prospect, exposure, point of view, outlook **3 = appearance**, look, air, condition, quality, bearing, attitude, cast, manner, expression, countenance, demeanour, mien *(literary)*
aspiration *n* **1 = aim**, longing, end, plan, hope, goal, design, dream, wish, desire, object, intention, objective, ambition, craving, endeavour, yearning, eagerness, Holy Grail *(informal)*, hankering
ass[1] *n* **1 = donkey**, moke *(slang)*, jennet **2 = fool**, dope *(informal)*, jerk *(slang, chiefly US & Canad)*, idiot, plank *(Brit slang)*, berk *(Brit slang)*, wally *(slang)*, prat *(slang)*, charlie *(Brit informal)*, plonker *(slang)*, coot, geek *(slang)*, twit *(informal, chiefly Brit)*, bonehead *(slang)*, dunce, oaf, simpleton, airhead *(slang)*, jackass, dipstick *(Brit slang)*, gonzo *(slang)*, schmuck *(US slang)*, dork *(slang)*, nitwit *(informal)*, dolt, blockhead, ninny, divvy *(Brit slang)*, pillock *(Brit slang)*, halfwit, nincompoop, dweeb *(US slang)*, putz *(US slang)*, fathead *(informal)*, weenie *(US informal)*, eejit *(Scot & Irish)*, dumb-ass *(slang)*, numpty *(Scot informal)*, doofus *(slang, chiefly US)*, daftie *(informal)*, nerd *or* nurd *(slang)*, numbskull *or* numskull, twerp *or* twirp *(informal)*, dorba *or* dorb *(Austral slang)*, bogan *(Austral slang)*
assassin *n* **= murderer**, killer, slayer, liquidator, executioner, hit man *(slang)*, eliminator *(slang)*, hatchet man *(slang)*
assassinate *vb* **= murder**, kill, eliminate *(slang)*, take out *(slang)*, terminate, hit *(slang)*, slay, blow away *(slang, chiefly US)*, liquidate
assault *n* **1 = attack**, campaign, strike, rush, storm, storming, raid, invasion, charge, offensive, onset, onslaught, foray, incursion, act of aggression, inroad
OPPOSITE: defence
▹*vb* **2 = strike**, attack, beat, knock, punch, belt *(informal)*, bang, batter, clip *(informal)*, slap, bash *(informal)*, deck *(slang)*, sock *(slang)*, chin *(slang)*, smack, thump, set about, lay one on *(slang)*, clout *(informal)*, cuff, flog, whack, lob, beset, clobber *(slang)*, smite *(archaic)*, wallop *(informal)*, swat, fall upon, set upon, lay into *(informal)*, tonk *(slang)*, lambast(e), belabour, beat *or* knock seven bells out of *(informal)*
assemble *vb* **1a = gather**, meet, collect, rally, flock, accumulate, come together, muster, convene, congregate, foregather
OPPOSITE: scatter
1b = bring together, collect, gather, rally, summon, accumulate, round

DICTIONARY

together the parts of (a machine) **WORD ORIGIN** Old French *assembler*

assembler *n* **1** a person or thing that assembles **2** a computer program that converts a set of low-level symbolic data into machine language

assembly ❶ *n, pl* **-blies** **1** a number of people gathered together for a meeting **2** the act of assembling

assembly line *n* a sequence of machines and workers in a factory assembling a product

assemblyman *n, pl* **-men** a member of a legislative assembly

assent *n* **1** agreement, consent ▹*vb* **2** to agree
WORD ORIGIN Latin *assentiri*

assert ❶ *vb* **1** to state or declare **2** to insist upon (one's rights, etc.) **3 assert oneself** to speak and act forcefully
WORD ORIGIN Latin *asserere* to join to oneself

assertion ❶ *n* **1** a positive statement, usually made without evidence **2** the act of asserting

assertive ❶ *adj* confident and direct in dealing with others **assertively** *adv* **assertiveness** *n*

assess ❶ *vb* **1** to judge the worth or importance of **2** to estimate the value of (income or property) for taxation purposes **assessment** *n*
WORD ORIGIN Latin *assidere* to sit beside

assessor *n* **1** a person who values property for taxation or insurance purposes **2** a person with technical expertise called in to advise a court **3** a person who evaluates the merits of something

asset ❶ *n* **1** a thing or person that is valuable or useful **2** any property owned by a person or company
WORD ORIGIN Latin *ad-* to + *satis* enough

asset-stripping *n commerce* the practice of taking over a failing company at a low price and then selling the assets piecemeal **asset-stripper** *n*

asseverate *vb* **-ating, -ated** *formal* to declare solemnly **asseveration** *n*
WORD ORIGIN Latin *asseverare* to do (something) earnestly

assiduous *adj* **1** hard-working **2** done with care **assiduity** *n* **assiduously** *adv*
WORD ORIGIN Latin *assidere* to sit beside

assign ❶ *vb* **1** to select (someone) for a post or task **2** to give a task or duty (to someone) **3** to attribute to a specified cause **4** to set apart (a place or time) for a particular function or event: *to assign a day for the meeting* **5** *law* to transfer (one's right, interest, or title to property) to someone else
WORD ORIGIN Latin *assignare*

assignation (ass-sig-nay-shun) *n* a secret arrangement to meet, esp. one between lovers
WORD ORIGIN Latin *assignatio* a marking out

assignment ❶ *n* **1** something that has been assigned, such as a task **2** the act of assigning **3** *law* the transfer to another person of a right, interest, or title to property

assimilate *vb* **-lating, -lated** **1** to learn (information) and understand it thoroughly **2** to adjust or become adjusted: *they became assimilated to German culture* **3** to absorb (food) **assimilable** *adj* **assimilation** *n*
WORD ORIGIN Latin *ad-* to + *similis* like

assist ❶ *vb* **1** to give help or support ▹*n* **2** *sport* a pass by a player which enables another player to score a goal
WORD ORIGIN Latin *assistere* to stand by

assistance ❶ *n* help or support

assistant ❶ *n* **1** a helper or subordinate **2** ▸same as **shop assistant** ▹*adj* **3** junior or deputy: *assistant manager*

assistant referee *n soccer* ▸the official name for **linesman** (sense 1)

assizes *pl n Brit* (formerly in England and Wales) the sessions of the principal court in each county
WORD ORIGIN Latin *assidere* to sit beside

assoc. association

THESAURUS

up, marshal, come together, muster, convene, amass, congregate, call together, foregather, convoke **2 = put together**, make, join, set up, manufacture, build up, connect, construct, erect, piece together, fabricate, fit together **OPPOSITE:** take apart

assembly *n* **1 = gathering**, group, meeting, body, council, conference, crowd, congress, audience, collection, mass, diet, rally, convention, flock, company, house, congregation, accumulation, multitude, throng, synod, hui *(NZ)*, assemblage, conclave, aggregation, convocation, jamaat, runanga *(NZ)* **2 = putting together**, joining, setting up, manufacture, construction, building up, connecting, erection, piecing together, fabrication, fitting together

assert *vb* **1 = state**, argue, maintain, declare, allege, swear, pronounce, contend, affirm, profess, attest, predicate, postulate, avow, aver, asseverate, avouch *(archaic)* **OPPOSITE:** deny **2 = insist upon**, stress, defend, uphold, put forward, vindicate, press, stand up for **OPPOSITE:** retract **3 assert yourself = be forceful**, put your foot down *(informal)*, put yourself forward, make your presence felt, exert your influence

assertion *n* **1 = statement**, claim, allegation, profession, declaration, contention, affirmation, pronouncement, avowal, attestation, predication, asseveration **2 = insistence**, defence, stressing, maintenance, vindication

assertive *adj* **= confident**, firm, demanding, decided, forward, can-do *(informal)*, positive, aggressive, decisive, forceful, emphatic, insistent, feisty *(informal, chiefly US & Canad)*, pushy *(informal)*, in-your-face *(Brit slang)*, dogmatic, strong-willed, domineering, overbearing, self-assured **OPPOSITE:** meek

assess *vb* **1 = judge**, determine, estimate, fix, analyse, evaluate, rate, value, check out, compute, gauge, weigh up, appraise, size up *(informal)*, eye up **2 = evaluate**, rate, tax, value, demand, estimate, fix, impose, levy

asset *n* **1 = benefit**, help, service, aid, advantage, strength, resource, attraction, blessing, boon, good point, strong point, ace in the hole, feather in your cap, ace up your sleeve **OPPOSITE:** disadvantage

assign *vb* **1 = select for**, post, commission, elect, appoint, delegate, nominate, name, designate, choose for, stipulate for **2 = give**, set, grant, allocate, give out, consign, allot, apportion **3 = attribute**, credit, put down, set down, ascribe, accredit

assignment *n* **1 = task**, work, job, charge, position, post, commission, exercise, responsibility, duty, mission, appointment, undertaking, occupation, chore

assist *vb* **1 = help**, back, support, further, benefit, aid, encourage, work with, work for, relieve, collaborate with, cooperate with, abet, expedite, succour, lend a hand to, lend a helping hand to, give a leg up to *(informal)*

assistance *n* **= help**, backing, service, support, benefit, aid, relief, boost, promotion, cooperation, encouragement, collaboration, reinforcement, helping hand, sustenance, succour, furtherance, abetment **OPPOSITE:** hindrance

assistant *n* **1 = helper**, partner, ally, colleague, associate, supporter, deputy, subsidiary, aide, aider, second, accessory, attendant, backer, protagonist, collaborator, accomplice, confederate, auxiliary, henchman, right-hand man, adjutant, helpmate, coadjutor *(rare)*,

DICTIONARY

associate ❶ *vb* **-ating, -ated 1** to connect in the mind **2** to mix socially: *addicts are driven to associate with criminals* **3 be associated** *or* **associate oneself with** to be involved with (a group) because of shared views: *she had long been associated with the far right* ▷ *n* **4** a partner in business **5** a companion or friend ▷ *adj* **6** having partial rights or subordinate status: *an associate member* **7** joined with in business: *an associate director*
WORD ORIGIN Latin *ad-* to + *sociare* to join
association ❶ *n* **1** a group of people with a common interest **2** the act of associating or the state of being associated **3** friendship: *their association still had to remain a secret* **4** a mental connection of ideas or feelings: *the place contained associations for her*
association football *n* ▸ same as **soccer**
associative *adj maths* (of an operation such as multiplication or addition) producing the same answer regardless of the way the elements are grouped, for example $(2 \times 3) \times 4 = 2 \times (3 \times 4)$
assonance *n* the rhyming of vowel sounds but not consonants, as in *time* and *light*
WORD ORIGIN Latin *assonare* to sound
assorted ❶ *adj* **1** consisting of various kinds mixed together **2** matched: *an ill-assorted childless couple*
WORD ORIGIN Old French *assorter*
assortment *n* a collection of various things or sorts
asst assistant
assuage (ass-wage) *vb* **-suaging, -suaged** to relieve (grief, pain, or thirst)
WORD ORIGIN Latin *suavis* pleasant
assume ❶ *vb* **-suming, -sumed 1** to take to be true without proof **2** to undertake or take on: *every general staff officer was able to assume control of the army* **3** to make a pretence of: *the man had assumed a debonair attitude* **4** to take on: *her eyes assumed a scared haunted look*
WORD ORIGIN Latin *ad-* to + *sumere* to take up
assumed name *n* a false name used by someone to disguise his or her identity
assuming *conj* if it is assumed or taken for granted: *assuming the first two phases were successful, the third phase would follow*
assumption ❶ *n* **1** something that is taken for granted **2** the act of assuming power or possession
WORD ORIGIN Latin *assumptio* a taking up
Assumption *n Christianity* the taking up of the Virgin Mary into heaven when her earthly life was ended
assurance ❶ *n* **1** a statement or assertion intended to inspire confidence **2** feeling of confidence; certainty **3** insurance that provides for events that are certain to happen, such as death
Assurbanipal *n* ▸ a variant spelling of **Ashurbanipal**
assure ❶ *vb* **-suring, -sured 1** to promise or guarantee **2** to convince: *they assured me that they had not seen the document* **3** to make (something) certain **4** *chiefly Brit* to insure against loss of life
WORD ORIGIN Latin *ad-* to + *securus* secure
assured ❶ *adj* **1** confident or self-assured **2** certain to happen **3** *chiefly Brit* insured **assuredly** (a-sure-id-lee) *adv*
Assyrian *n* an inhabitant of ancient Assyria, a kingdom of Mesopotamia
AST Atlantic Standard Time

THESAURUS

abettor, cooperator
associate *vb* **1 = connect**, couple, league, link, mix, relate, pair, ally, identify, unite, join, combine, attach, affiliate, fasten, correlate, confederate, yoke, affix, lump together, cohere, mention in the same breath, conjoin, think of together **OPPOSITE:** separate
2 = socialize, mix, hang *(informal, chiefly US)*, accompany, hang out *(informal)*, run around *(informal)*, mingle, be friends, befriend, consort, hang about, hobnob, fraternize
OPPOSITE: avoid
▷ *n* **4, 5 = partner**, friend, ally, colleague, mate *(informal)*, companion, comrade, affiliate, collaborator, confederate, co-worker, workmate, main man *(slang, chiefly US)*, cobber *(Austral & NZ old-fashioned, informal)*, confrère, compeer, E hoa *(NZ)*
association *n* **1 = group**, company, club, order, union, class, society, league, band, set, troop, pack, camp, collection, gathering, organization, circle, corporation, alliance, coalition, partnership, federation, bunch, formation, faction, cluster, syndicate, congregation, batch, confederation, cooperative, fraternity, affiliation, posse *(slang)*, clique, confederacy, assemblage
2 = connection, union, joining, linking, tie, mixing, relation, bond, pairing, combination, mixture, blend, identification, correlation, linkage, yoking, juxtaposition, lumping together, concomitance
assorted *adj* **1 = various**, different, mixed, varied, diverse, diversified, miscellaneous, sundry, motley, variegated, manifold, heterogeneous
OPPOSITE: similar
assume *vb* **1 = presume**, think, believe, expect, accept, suppose, imagine, suspect, guess *(informal, chiefly US & Canad)*, take it, fancy, take for granted, infer, conjecture, postulate, surmise, presuppose
OPPOSITE: know
2 = take on, begin, accept, manage, bear, handle, shoulder, take over, don, acquire, put on, take up, embrace, undertake, set about, attend to, take responsibility for, embark upon, enter upon
3 = simulate, affect, adopt, put on, imitate, mimic, sham, counterfeit, feign, impersonate
assumption *n* **1 = presumption**, theory, opinion, belief, guess, expectation, fancy, suspicion, premise, acceptance, hypothesis, anticipation, inference, conjecture, surmise, supposition, presupposition, premise, postulation
2a = taking on, managing, handling, shouldering, putting on, taking up, takeover, acquisition **2b = seizure**, taking, takeover, acquisition, appropriation, wresting, confiscation, commandeering, expropriation, pre-empting, usurpation, arrogation
assurance *n* **1 = promise**, statement, guarantee, commitment, pledge, profession, vow, declaration, assertion, oath, affirmation, protestation, word, word of honour
OPPOSITE: lie
2 = confidence, conviction, courage, certainty, self-confidence, poise, assertiveness, security, faith, coolness, nerve, aplomb, boldness, self-reliance, firmness, self-assurance, certitude, sureness, self-possession, positiveness, assuredness **OPPOSITE:** self-doubt
assure *vb* **1 = promise to**, pledge to, vow to, guarantee to, swear to, attest to, confirm to, certify to, affirm to, give your word to, declare confidently to **2 = convince**, encourage, persuade, satisfy, comfort, prove to, reassure, soothe, hearten, embolden, win someone over, bring someone round **3 = make certain**, ensure, confirm, guarantee, secure, make sure, complete, seal, clinch
assured *adj* **1 = confident**, certain, positive, bold, poised, assertive, complacent, fearless, audacious, pushy *(informal)*, brazen, self-confident, self-assured, self-possessed, overconfident, dauntless, sure of yourself **OPPOSITE:** self-conscious
2 = certain, sure, ensured, confirmed, settled, guaranteed, fixed, secure, sealed, clinched, made certain, sound, in the bag *(slang)*,

DICTIONARY

astatine *n chem* a radioactive element occurring naturally in minute amounts or artificially produced by bombarding bismuth with alpha particles. Symbol: At
WORD ORIGIN Greek *astatos* unstable

Astbury *n* **John** 1688–1743, English potter; earliest of the great Staffordshire potters

aster *n* a plant with white, blue, purple, or pink daisy-like flowers
WORD ORIGIN Greek: star

asterisk *n* **1** a star-shaped character (*) used in printing or writing to indicate a footnote etc. ▷*vb* **2** to mark with an asterisk
WORD ORIGIN Greek *asteriskos* a small star

astern *adv, adj naut* **1** at or towards the stern of a ship **2** backwards **3** behind a vessel

asteroid *n* any of the small planets that orbit the sun between Mars and Jupiter
WORD ORIGIN Greek *asteroeidēs* starlike

asthma (ass-ma) *n* an illness causing difficulty in breathing **asthmatic** *adj, n*
WORD ORIGIN Greek

astigmatic *adj* relating to or affected with astigmatism
WORD ORIGIN Greek *a-* without + *stigma* spot, focus

astigmatism (eh-stig-mat-tiz-zum) *n* a defect of a lens, esp. of the eye, causing it not to focus properly

astir *adj* **1** out of bed **2** in motion

Aston *n* **Francis William** 1877–1945, English physicist and chemist, who developed the first mass spectrograph, using it to investigate the isotopic structures of elements: Nobel prize for chemistry 1922

astonish ❶ *vb* to surprise greatly **astonishing** *adj* **astonishment** *n*
WORD ORIGIN Latin *ex-* out + *tonare* to thunder

astound *vb* to overwhelm with amazement **astounding** *adj*
WORD ORIGIN Old French *estoner*

astraddle *prep* astride

astrakhan *n* **1** a fur made of the dark curly fleece of lambs from Astrakhan in Russia **2** a cloth resembling this

astral *adj* **1** relating to or resembling the stars **2** of the spirit world
WORD ORIGIN Greek *astron* star

astray *adj, adv* out of the right or expected way
WORD ORIGIN Old French *estraier* to stray

astride *adj* **1** with a leg on either side **2** with legs far apart ▷*prep* **3** with a leg on either side of

astringent *adj* **1** causing contraction of body tissue **2** checking the flow of blood from a cut **3** severe or harsh ▷*n* **4** an astringent drug or lotion **astringency** *n*
WORD ORIGIN Latin *astringens* drawing together

astro- *combining form* indicating a star or stars: *astrology*
WORD ORIGIN Greek

astrolabe *n* an instrument formerly used to measure the altitude of stars and planets
WORD ORIGIN Greek *astron* star + *lambanein* to take

astrology *n* the study of the alleged influence of the stars, planets, sun, and moon on human affairs **astrologer** *or* **astrologist** *n* **astrological** *adj*
WORD ORIGIN Greek *astron* star + *logos* word, account

astronaut *n* a person trained for travelling in space
WORD ORIGIN Greek *astron* star + *nautēs* sailor

astronautics *n* the science and technology of space flight **astronautical** *adj*

astronomical *or* **astronomic** *adj* **1** enormously large **2** of astronomy **astronomically** *adv*

astronomical unit *n* a unit of distance equal to the average distance between the earth and the sun (1.495×10^{11}m)

astronomy *n* the scientific study of heavenly bodies **astronomer** *n*
WORD ORIGIN Greek *astron* star + *nomos* law

astrophysics *n* the study of the physical and chemical properties of celestial bodies **astrophysical** *adj* **astrophysicist** *n*

Astroturf *n trademark* a brand of artificial grass
WORD ORIGIN from the *Astro(dome)*, sports stadium where it was first used + *turf*

Asturias[1] *n* a region and former kingdom of NW Spain, consisting of a coastal plain and the Cantabrian Mountains: a Christian stronghold against the Moors (8th to 13th centuries); rich mineral resources

Asturias[2] *n* **Miguel Ángel** 1899–1974, Guatemalan novelist and poet. His novels include *El Señor Presidente* (1946). Nobel prize for literature 1967

astute ❶ *adj* quick to notice or understand **astutely** *adv* **astuteness** *n*
WORD ORIGIN Latin *astutus*

asunder *adv, adj literary* into parts or pieces; apart

asylum ❶ *n* **1** refuge granted to a political refugee from a foreign country **2** (formerly) a mental hospital
WORD ORIGIN Greek *asulon*

asymmetric bars (ass-sim-met-rik, ay-sim-met-rik) *pl n gymnastics* a pair of bars parallel to each other but at different heights, used for various exercises

asymmetry *n* lack of symmetry **asymmetric** *or* **asymmetrical** *adj*

asymptote (ass-im-tote) *n* a straight line that is closely approached but never met by a curve **asymptotic** *adj*
WORD ORIGIN Greek *asumptōtos* not falling together

at *prep* **1** indicating location or position: *she had planted a vegetable garden at the back* **2** towards; in the direction of: *she was staring at the wall behind him* **3** indicating position in time: *we arrived at 12.30* **4** engaged in: *the innocent laughter of children at play* **5** during the passing of: *she works at night as a nurse's aide* **6** for; in exchange for: *crude oil is selling at its lowest price since September* **7** indicating the object of an emotion: *I'm angry at you because you were rude to me*
WORD ORIGIN Old English *æt*

At *chem* astatine

at. **1** atmosphere **2** atomic

Atahualpa *or* **Atabalipa** *n* ?1500–33, the last Inca emperor of Peru (1525–33), who was put to death by the Spanish under Pizarro

atavism (at-a-viz-zum) *n* **1** the recurrence of primitive characteristics that were present in distant ancestors but not in more

THESAURUS

dependable, beyond doubt, irrefutable, unquestionable, indubitable, nailed-on *(slang)* **OPPOSITE:** doubtful

astonish *vb* **= amaze**, surprise, stun, stagger, bewilder, astound, daze, confound, stupefy, boggle the mind, dumbfound, flabbergast *(informal)*

astute *adj* **= intelligent**, politic, bright, sharp, keen, calculating, clever, subtle, penetrating, knowing, shrewd, cunning, discerning, sly, on the ball *(informal)*, canny, perceptive, wily, crafty, artful, insightful, foxy, adroit, sagacious **OPPOSITE:** stupid

asylum *n* **1 = refuge**, security, haven, safety, protection, preserve, shelter, retreat, harbour, sanctuary **2 = mental hospital**, hospital, institution, psychiatric hospital, madhouse *(informal)*, funny farm *(facetious)*, loony bin *(slang)*, nuthouse *(slang)*, rubber room *(US slang)*, laughing academy *(US slang)*

athlete *n* **1 = sportsperson**, player, runner, competitor, contender, sportsman, contestant, gymnast, games player, sportswoman

athletic *adj* **1 = fit**, strong, powerful, healthy, active, trim, strapping, robust, vigorous, energetic, muscular, two-fisted, sturdy, husky *(informal)*, lusty, herculean, sinewy, brawny, able-bodied, well-proportioned **OPPOSITE:** feeble

athletics *pl n (Austral & Brit)* **= sports**,

DICTIONARY

a

recent ones **2** reversion to a former type **atavistic** *adj*
WORD ORIGIN Latin *atavus* great-grandfather's grandfather, ancestor

ataxia *n pathol* lack of muscular coordination **ataxic** *adj*
WORD ORIGIN Greek

ate *vb* ▸ the past tense of **eat**

atelier (at-tell-yay) *n* an artist's studio

Atget *n* **(Jean) Eugène Auguste** 1856–1927, French photographer, noted for his pictures of Parisian life

atheism (aith-ee-iz-zum) *n* the belief that there is no God **atheist** *n*
WORD ORIGIN Greek *a-* without + *theos* god

Athelstan *n* ?895–939 AD, king of Wessex and Mercia (924–939), who extended his kingdom to include most of England

Athena *or* **Athene** *n Greek myth* the goddess of wisdom

atherosclerosis *n, pl* **-ses** a disease in which deposits of fat cause the walls of the arteries to thicken **atherosclerotic** *adj*
WORD ORIGIN Greek *athērōma* tumour + SCLEROSIS

Atherton *n* **Mike**, full name *Michael Andrew Atherton*. born 1968, English cricketer: played for Lancashire (1987–2001) and England (1989–2001); captain of England (1993–1998)

athlete ❶ *n* **1** a person trained to compete in sports or exercises **2** *chiefly Brit* a competitor in track-and-field events
WORD ORIGIN Greek *athlos* a contest

athlete's foot *n* a fungal infection of the skin of the foot

athletic ❶ *adj* **1** physically fit or strong **2** of or for an athlete or athletics **athletically** *adv* **athleticism** *n*

athletics ❶ *pl n Austral & Brit* track-and-field events

at-home *n Austral & Brit* a social gathering in a person's home

athwart *prep* **1** across ▹ *adv* **2** transversely; from one side to another

atigi *n* a type of parka worn by the Inuit in Canada

Atkinson *n* Sir **Harry Albert** 1831–92, New Zealand statesman, born in England: prime minister of New Zealand (1876–77; 1883–84; 1887–91)

Atlantic *adj* of the Atlantic Ocean, the world's second largest ocean, bounded by the Arctic, the Antarctic, America, and Europe and Africa
WORD ORIGIN Greek *(pelagos) Atlantikos* (the sea) of Atlas (so called because it lay beyond the Atlas Mountains)

Atlanticism *n* belief in close economic and military cooperation between Europe and the United States **Atlanticist** *n*

Atlantis *n* (in ancient legend) a continent said to have sunk beneath the Atlantic west of Gibraltar

atlas *n* a book of maps
WORD ORIGIN because *Atlas*, a Titan in Greek mythology, was shown supporting the heavens in 16th-century books of maps

atmosphere ❶ *n* **1** the mass of gases surrounding the earth or any other heavenly body **2** the air in a particular place **3** a pervasive feeling or mood: *the atmosphere was tense* **4** a unit of pressure equal to the normal pressure of the air at sea level **atmospheric** *adj* **atmospherically** *adv*
WORD ORIGIN Greek *atmos* vapour + *sphaira* sphere

atmospherics *pl n* radio interference caused by electrical disturbance in the atmosphere

atoll *n* a circular coral reef surrounding a lagoon
WORD ORIGIN *atollon*, native name in the Maldive Islands

atom ❶ *n* **1 a** the smallest unit of matter which can take part in a chemical reaction **b** this entity as a source of nuclear energy **2** a very small amount
WORD ORIGIN Greek *atomos* that cannot be divided

atom bomb *n* ▸ same as **atomic bomb**

atomic *adj* **1** of or using atomic bombs or atomic energy **2** of atoms **atomically** *adv*

atomic bomb *or* **atom bomb** *n* a type of bomb in which the energy is provided by nuclear fission

atomic energy *n* ▸ same as **nuclear energy**

atomic mass unit *n* a unit of mass that is equal to one twelfth of the mass of an atom of carbon-12

atomic number *n* the number of protons in the nucleus of an atom of an element

atomic theory *n* any theory in which matter is regarded as consisting of atoms

atomic weight *n* the ratio of the average mass per atom of an element to one twelfth of the mass of an atom of carbon-12

atomize *or* **-ise** *vb* **-izing, -ized** *or* **-ising, -ised 1** to separate into free atoms **2** to reduce to fine particles or spray **3** to destroy by nuclear weapons

atomizer *or* **-iser** *n* a device for reducing a liquid to a fine spray

atonal (eh-tone-al) *adj* (of music) not written in an established key **atonality** *n*

atone *vb* **atoning, atoned** to make amends (for a sin, crime, or wrongdoing)

atonement *n* **1** something done to make amends for wrongdoing **2** *Christian theol* the reconciliation of humankind with God through the sacrificial death of Christ
WORD ORIGIN Middle English *at onement* in harmony

atop *prep* on top of

atrium *n, pl* **atria 1** *anat* the upper chamber of each half of the heart **2** a central hall that extends through several storeys in a modern building **3** the open main court of an ancient Roman house **atrial** *adj*
WORD ORIGIN Latin

atrocious *adj* **1** extremely cruel or wicked **2** horrifying or shocking **3** *informal* very bad **atrociously** *adv*
WORD ORIGIN Latin *atrox* dreadful

atrocity ❶ *n* **1** behaviour that is wicked or cruel **2** *pl* **-ties** an act of extreme cruelty

atrophy (at-trof-fee) *n, pl* **-phies 1** a wasting away of a physical organ or part **2** a failure to grow ▹ *vb* **-phies, -phying, -phied 3** to waste away
WORD ORIGIN Greek *atrophos* ill-fed

atropine *n* a poisonous alkaloid obtained from deadly nightshade
WORD ORIGIN New Latin *atropa* deadly nightshade

attach ❶ *vb* **1** to join, fasten, or connect **2** to attribute or ascribe: *he*

THESAURUS

games, races, exercises, contests, sporting events, gymnastics, track and field events, games of strength

atmosphere *n* **1 = air**, sky, heavens, aerosphere **3 = feeling**, feel, air, quality, character, environment, spirit, surroundings, tone, mood, climate, flavour, aura, ambience, vibes *(slang)*

atom *n* **2 = particle**, bit, spot, trace, scrap, molecule, grain, dot, fragment, fraction, shred, crumb, mite, jot, speck, morsel, mote, whit, tittle, iota, scintilla *(rare)*

atrocity *n* **1 = cruelty**, wrong, horror, brutality, wrongdoing, enormity, savagery, ruthlessness, wickedness, inhumanity, infamy, transgression, barbarity, viciousness, villainy, baseness, monstrousness, heinousness, nefariousness, shockingness, atrociousness, fiendishness, barbarousness, grievousness, villainousness **2 = act of cruelty**, wrong, crime, horror, offence, evil, outrage, cruelty, brutality, obscenity, wrongdoing, enormity, monstrosity, transgression, abomination, barbarity, villainy

attach *vb* **1 = affix**, stick, secure, bind, unite, add, join, couple, link, tie, fix, connect, lash, glue, adhere, fasten, annex, truss, yoke, append, make fast, cohere, subjoin, bootstrap to
OPPOSITE: detach

DICTIONARY

a

attaches particular importance to the proposed sale **3 attach oneself** *or* **be attached to** to become associated with or join
WORD ORIGIN Old French *atachier*

attaché (at-**tash**-shay) *n* a specialist attached to a diplomatic mission
WORD ORIGIN French

attaché case *n* a flat rectangular briefcase for carrying papers

attached ⓘ *adj* **1** married, engaged, or in an exclusive sexual relationship **2 attached to** fond of

attachment ⓘ *n* **1** affection or regard for **2** an accessory that can be fitted to a device to change what it can do

attack ⓘ *vb* **1** to launch a physical assault (against) **2** to criticize vehemently **3** to set about (a job or problem) with vigour **4** to affect adversely: *BSE attacks the animal's brain* **5** to take the initiative in a game or sport ▷*n* **6** the act of attacking **7** any sudden appearance of a disease or symptoms: *a bad attack of mumps*
attacker *n*
WORD ORIGIN Old Italian *attaccare*

attain ⓘ *vb* **1** to manage to do or get (something): *the country attained economic growth* **2** to reach
attainable *adj*
WORD ORIGIN Latin *attingere*

attainment *n* an achievement or the act of achieving something

attar *n* a perfume made from damask roses
WORD ORIGIN Persian *'atir* perfumed

attempt ⓘ *vb* **1** to make an effort (to do or achieve something); try ▷*n* **2** an endeavour to achieve something; effort **3 attempt on someone's life** an attack on someone with the intention to kill
WORD ORIGIN Latin *attemptare*

attend ⓘ *vb* **1** to be present at (an event) **2** to go regularly to a school, college, etc. **3** to look after: *the actors lounged in their canvas chairs, attended by sycophants* **4** to pay attention **5 attend to** to apply oneself to: *I've a few things I must attend to*
WORD ORIGIN Latin *attendere* to stretch towards

attendance ⓘ *n* **1** the act of attending **2** the number of people present **3** regularity in attending

attendant ⓘ *n* **1** a person who assists, guides, or provides a service ▷*adj* **2** associated: *nuclear power and its attendant dangers* **3** being in attendance

attendee *n* a person who is present at a specified event

attention ⓘ *n* **1** concentrated direction of the mind **2** consideration, notice, or observation **3** detailed care or treatment **4** the alert position in military drill **5 attentions** acts of courtesy: *the attentions of men seemed to embarrass her*

attentive *adj* **1** paying close attention **2** considerately helpful: *at society parties he is attentive to his wife*
attentively *adv* **attentiveness** *n*

attenuated *adj* **1** weakened **2** thin and extended **attenuation** *n*
WORD ORIGIN Latin *attenuare* to weaken

attest *vb* **1** to affirm or prove the truth of **2** to bear witness to (an act or event) **attestation** *n*
WORD ORIGIN Latin *testari* to bear witness

attested *adj Brit* (of cattle) certified to be free from a disease, such as tuberculosis

attic ⓘ *n* a space or room within the roof of a house
WORD ORIGIN from the *Attic* style of architecture

attire *n* clothes, esp. fine or formal ones
WORD ORIGIN Old French *atirier* to put in order

attired *adj* dressed in a specified way

attitude ⓘ *n* **1** the way a person thinks and behaves **2** a position of the body **3** *informal* a hostile manner **4** the orientation of an aircraft or spacecraft in relation to some plane or direction
WORD ORIGIN Latin *aptus* apt

attitudinize *or* **-nise** *vb* **-nizing, -nized** *or* **-nising, -nised** to adopt a pose or opinion for effect

attorney *n* **1** a person legally appointed to act for another **2** *US* a lawyer
WORD ORIGIN Old French *atourner* to direct to

attorney general *n, pl* **attorneys general** *or* **attorney generals** a chief law officer of some governments

attract ⓘ *vb* **1** to arouse the interest or admiration of **2** (of a magnet) to draw (something) closer by exerting a force on it
WORD ORIGIN Latin *attrahere* to draw towards

THESAURUS

2 = ascribe, connect, attribute, assign, place, associate, lay on, accredit, invest with, impute, reattribute

attached *adj* **1 = spoken for**, married, partnered, engaged, accompanied **2 attached to = fond of**, devoted to, affectionate towards, full of regard for

attachment *n* **1 = fondness**, liking, feeling, love, relationship, regard, bond, friendship, attraction, loyalty, affection, devotion, fidelity, affinity, tenderness, reverence, predilection, possessiveness, partiality, aroha (*NZ*) **OPPOSITE:** aversion
2 = accessory, fitting, extra, addition, component, extension, supplement, fixture, auxiliary, adaptor *or* adapter, supplementary part, add-on, adjunct, appendage, accoutrement, appurtenance

attack *vb* **1a = assault**, strike (at), mug, set about, ambush, assail, tear into, fall upon, set upon, lay into (*informal*) **OPPOSITE:** defend
1b = invade, occupy, raid, infringe, charge, rush, storm, encroach
2 = criticize, blame, abuse, blast, pan (*informal*), condemn, knock (*informal*), slam (*slang*), put down, slate (*informal*), have a go (at) (*informal*), censure, malign, berate, disparage, revile, vilify, tear into (*informal*), slag off (*Brit slang*), diss (*slang, chiefly US*), find fault with, impugn, go for the jugular, lambast(e), pick holes in, excoriate, bite someone's head off, snap someone's head off, pick to pieces ▷*n* **6a = assault**, charge, campaign, strike, rush, raid, invasion, offensive, aggression, blitz, onset, onslaught, foray, incursion, inroad **OPPOSITE:** defence
6b = criticism, panning (*informal*), slating (*informal*), censure, disapproval, slagging (*slang*), abuse, knocking (*informal*), bad press, vilification, denigration, calumny, character assassination, disparagement, impugnment
7 = bout, fit, access, spell, stroke, seizure, spasm, convulsion, paroxysm

attain *vb* **1 = obtain**, get, win, reach, effect, land, score (*slang*), complete, gain, achieve, earn, secure, realize, acquire, fulfil, accomplish, grasp, reap, procure **2 = reach**, achieve, realize, acquire, arrive at, accomplish

attempt *vb* **1 = try**, seek, aim, struggle, tackle, take on, experiment, venture, undertake, essay, strive, endeavour, have a go at (*informal*), make an effort, make an attempt, have a crack at, have a shot at (*informal*), try your hand at, do your best to, jump through hoops (*informal*), have a stab at (*informal*), take the bit between your teeth ▷*n* **2 = try**, go (*informal*), shot (*informal*), effort, trial, bid, experiment, crack (*informal*), venture, undertaking, essay, stab (*informal*), endeavour

attend *vb* **1 = be present**, go to, visit, be at, be there, be here, frequent, haunt, appear at, turn up at, patronize, show up at (*informal*), show yourself, put in an appearance at, present yourself at **OPPOSITE:** be absent
4 = pay attention, listen, follow, hear, mark, mind, watch, note, regard, notice, observe, look on, heed, take to heart, pay heed, hearken (*archaic*) **OPPOSITE:** ignore

attraction ❶ *n* **1** the act or quality of attracting **2** an interesting or desirable feature: *the Scottishness of Scott is an attraction, but by no means his only merit* **3** an object or place that people visit for interest: *this carefully preserved tourist attraction* **4** (of a magnet) a force by which one object attracts another

attractive ❶ *adj* appealing to the senses or mind **attractively** *adv* **attractiveness** *n*

attribute ❶ *vb* **-uting, -uted** **1 attribute to** to regard as belonging to or produced by: *a play attributed to William Shakespeare* ▷ *n* **2** a quality or feature representative of a person or thing **attributable** *adj* **attribution** *n*
WORD ORIGIN Latin *attribuere* to associate with

attributive *adj grammar* (of an adjective) coming before the noun modified

attrition *n* constant wearing down to weaken or destroy: *a war of attrition*
WORD ORIGIN Latin *atterere* to weaken

attune *vb* **-tuning, -tuned** to adjust or accustom (a person or thing)

ATV all-terrain vehicle: a vehicle with wheels designed to travel on rough ground

atypical (eh-tip-ik-kl) *adj* not typical **atypically** *adv*

Au *chem* gold
WORD ORIGIN Latin *aurum*

Auber *n* **Daniel François Esprit** 1782–1871, French composer, who was prominent in development of opéra comique. His works include 48 operas

aubergine (oh-bur-zheen) *n Brit* the dark purple fruit of a tropical plant, cooked and eaten as a vegetable
WORD ORIGIN French, from Arabic *al-bādindjān*

Aubrey *n* **John** 1626–97, English antiquary and author, noted for his vivid biographies of his contemporaries, *Brief Lives* (edited 1898)

aubrietia (aw-bree-sha) *n* a trailing purple-flowered rock plant
WORD ORIGIN after Claude *Aubriet*, painter of flowers and animals

auburn *adj* (of hair) reddish-brown
WORD ORIGIN (originally meaning: blond) Latin *albus* white

auction *n* **1** a public sale at which articles are sold to the highest bidder ▷ *vb* **2** to sell by auction
WORD ORIGIN Latin *auctio* an increasing

auctioneer *n* a person who conducts an auction

audacious *adj* **1** recklessly bold or daring **2** impudent or presumptuous **audacity** *n*
WORD ORIGIN Latin *audax* bold

audible *adj* loud enough to be heard **audibility** *n* **audibly** *adv*
WORD ORIGIN Latin *audire* to hear

audience ❶ *n* **1** a group of spectators or listeners at a concert or play **2** the people reached by a book, film, or radio or television programme **3** a formal interview
WORD ORIGIN Latin *audire* to hear

audio *adj* **1** of or relating to sound or hearing **2** of or for the transmission or reproduction of sound
WORD ORIGIN Latin *audire* to hear

audio book *n* a reading of a book recorded on tape

audio frequency *n* a frequency in the range 20 hertz to 20 000 hertz, audible to the human ear

audiometer (aw-dee-om-it-er) *n* an instrument for testing hearing

audiotypist *n* a typist trained to type from a dictating machine **audiotyping** *n*

audiovisual *adj* involving both hearing and sight: *audiovisual teaching aids*

audit *n* **1** an official inspection of business accounts, conducted by an independent qualified accountant **2** any thoroughgoing assessment or review: *an audit of their lifestyle* ▷ *vb* **auditing, audited** **3** to examine (business accounts) officially
WORD ORIGIN Latin *audire* to hear

audition *n* **1** a test of a performer's or musician's ability for a particular role or job ▷ *vb* **2** to test or be tested in an audition
WORD ORIGIN Latin *audire* to hear

auditor *n* a person qualified to audit accounts
WORD ORIGIN Latin *auditor* a hearer

auditorium *n, pl* **-toriums** *or* **-toria** **1** the area of a concert hall or theatre in which the audience sits **2** *US & Canad* a building for public meetings
WORD ORIGIN Latin

auditory *adj* of or relating to hearing
WORD ORIGIN Latin *audire* to hear

Auer *n* **Karl** (karl), Baron von Welsbach. 1858–1929, Austrian

attendance *n* **1 = presence**, being there, attending, appearance **2 = turnout**, audience, gate, congregation, house, crowd, throng, number present

attendant *n* **1 = assistant**, guide, guard, servant, companion, aide, escort, follower, steward, waiter, usher, warden, helper, auxiliary, custodian, page, menial, concierge, underling, lackey, chaperon, flunky ▷ *adj* **2 = accompanying**, related, associated, accessory, consequent, resultant, concomitant

attention *n* **1 = thinking**, thought, mind, notice, consideration, concentration, observation, scrutiny, heed, deliberation, contemplation, thoughtfulness, attentiveness, intentness, heedfulness **2 = awareness**, regard, notice, recognition, consideration, observation, consciousness **OPPOSITE:** inattention **3 = care**, support, concern, treatment, looking after, succour, ministration

attic *n* **= loft**, garret, roof space

attitude *n* **1 = opinion**, thinking, feeling, thought, view, position, approach, belief, mood, perspective, point of view, stance, outlook, viewpoint, slant, frame of mind **2 = position**, bearing, pose, stance, carriage, posture

attract *vb* **1 = allure**, interest, draw, invite, persuade, engage, charm, appeal to, fascinate, win over, tempt, lure (*informal*), induce, incline, seduce, entice, enchant, endear, lead on, coax, captivate, beguile, cajole, bewitch, decoy, inveigle, pull, catch (someone's) eye **OPPOSITE:** repel **2 = pull**, draw, magnetize

attraction *n* **1, 2 = appeal**, interest, draw, pull (*informal*), come-on (*informal*), charm, incentive, invitation, lure, bait, temptation, fascination, attractiveness, allure, inducement, magnetism, enchantment, endearment, enticement, captivation, temptingness, pleasingness **4 = pull**, draw, magnetism

attractive *adj* **a = seductive**, charming, tempting, interesting, pleasing, pretty, fair, beautiful, inviting, engaging, likable *or* likeable, lovely, winning, sexy (*informal*), pleasant, handsome, fetching, good-looking, glamorous, gorgeous, magnetic, cute, irresistible, enticing, provocative, captivating, beguiling, alluring, bonny, winsome, comely, prepossessing, hot (*informal*), fit (*Brit informal*) **OPPOSITE:** unattractive **b = appealing**, pleasing, inviting, fascinating, tempting, enticing, agreeable, irresistible **OPPOSITE:** unappealing

attribute *vb* **1 = ascribe**, apply, credit, blame, refer, trace, assign, charge, allocate, put down, set down, allot, impute ▷ *n* **2 = quality**, point, mark, sign, note, feature, property, character, element, aspect, symbol, characteristic, indication, distinction, virtue, trait, hallmark, facet, quirk, peculiarity, idiosyncrasy

audience *n* **1 = spectators**, company, house, crowd, gathering, gallery, assembly, viewers, listeners, patrons, congregation, turnout, onlookers, throng, assemblage **3 = interview**, meeting, hearing, exchange, reception, consultation

DICTIONARY

a

chemist who discovered the cerium-iron alloy used for flints in cigarette lighters and invented the incandescent gas mantle

Auerbach *n* **Frank (Helmuth)** born 1931, British painter, born in Germany, noted esp. for his use of impasto

au fait (oh fay) *adj* **1** (usually foll. by *with*) fully informed (about) **2** expert
WORD ORIGIN French: to the point

auf Wiedersehen (owf vee-der-zay-en) *interj* goodbye
WORD ORIGIN German

Aug. August

Augean (aw-jee-an) *adj* extremely dirty or corrupt
WORD ORIGIN from *Augeas,* in Greek mythology, king whose filthy stables Hercules cleaned in one day

auger *n* a pointed tool for boring holes
WORD ORIGIN Old English *nafugār* nave (ie hub of a wheel) spear

aught *pron old-fashioned or literary* anything whatever: *for aught I know*
WORD ORIGIN Old English *āwiht*

augment *vb* to make or become greater in number or strength **augmentation** *n*
WORD ORIGIN Latin *augere* to increase

augmented reality *n* an artificial environment created through the combination of real-world and computer-generated data

au gratin (oh grat-tan) *adj* cooked with a topping of breadcrumbs and sometimes cheese
WORD ORIGIN French

augur *vb* to be a good or bad sign of future events: *a double fault on the opening point did not augur well*
WORD ORIGIN Latin: diviner of omens

augury *n* **1** the foretelling of the future **2** *pl* **-ries** an omen

august *adj* dignified and imposing
WORD ORIGIN Latin *augustus*

August *n* the eighth month of the year
WORD ORIGIN Latin, after the emperor *Augustus*

Augustan *adj* **1** of the Roman emperor Augustus Caesar or the poets writing during his reign **2** of any literary period noted for refinement and classicism

auk *n* a northern sea bird with a heavy body, short wings, and black-and-white plumage
WORD ORIGIN Old Norse *ālka*

auld lang syne *n* times past
WORD ORIGIN Scots, literally: old long since

aunt *n* **1** a sister of one's father or mother **2** the wife of one's uncle **3** a child's term of address for a female friend of the parents
WORD ORIGIN Latin *amita* a father's sister

auntie *or* **aunty** *n, pl* **-ies** *informal* an aunt

Aunt Sally *n, pl* **-lies** **1** a figure used in fairgrounds as a target **2** any target for insults or criticism

au pair *n* a young foreign woman who does housework in return for board and lodging
WORD ORIGIN French

aura ⊕ *n, pl* **auras** *or* **aurae** **1** a distinctive air or quality associated with a person or thing **2** any invisible emanation
WORD ORIGIN Greek: breeze

aural *adj* of or using the ears or hearing **aurally** *adv*
WORD ORIGIN Latin *auris* ear

Aurangzeb *or* **Aurungzeb** *n* 1618–1707, Mogul emperor of Hindustan (1658–1707), whose reign marked both the height of Mogul prosperity and the decline of its power through the revolts of the Marathas

aureate *adj literary* **1** covered with gold **2** (of a style of writing or speaking) excessively elaborate
WORD ORIGIN Latin *aurum* gold

Aurelian *n* Latin name *Lucius Domitius Aurelianus.* ?212–275 AD, Roman emperor (270–275), who conquered Palmyra (273) and restored political unity to the Roman Empire

aureole *or* **aureola** *n* **1** a ring of light surrounding the head of a figure represented as holy; halo **2** the sun's corona, visible as a faint halo during eclipses
WORD ORIGIN Latin *aurum* gold

au revoir (oh riv-**vwahr**) *interj* goodbye
WORD ORIGIN French

auric *adj* of or containing gold in the trivalent state
WORD ORIGIN Latin *aurum* gold

Auric *n* **Georges** 1899–1983, French composer; one of *les Six.* His works include ballet and film music

auricle *n* **1** the upper chamber of the heart **2** the outer part of the ear **auricular** *adj*
WORD ORIGIN Latin *auris* ear

auricula *n, pl* **-lae** *or* **-las** an alpine primrose with leaves shaped like a bear's ear
WORD ORIGIN Latin *auris* ear

auriferous *adj* containing gold
WORD ORIGIN Latin *aurum* gold + *ferre* to bear

Auriol *n* **Vincent** 1884–1966, French statesman; president of the Fourth Republic (1947–54)

aurochs *n, pl* **-rochs** a recently extinct European wild ox
WORD ORIGIN German

aurora *n, pl* **-ras** *or* **-rae** **1** an atmospheric phenomenon of bands of light sometimes seen in the polar regions **2** *poetic* the dawn
WORD ORIGIN Latin: dawn

aurora australis *n* the aurora seen around the South Pole
WORD ORIGIN New Latin: southern aurora

aurora borealis *n* the aurora seen around the North Pole
WORD ORIGIN New Latin: northern aurora

auscultation *n* the listening to of the internal sounds of the body, usually with a stethoscope, to help with medical diagnosis
WORD ORIGIN Latin *auscultare* to listen attentively

Ausonius *n* **Decimus Magnus** ?310–?395 AD, Latin poet, born in Gaul

auspices (aw-spiss-siz) *pl n* **under the auspices of** with the support and approval of
WORD ORIGIN Latin *auspicium* augury from birds

auspicious *adj* showing the signs of future success

Aussie *n, adj informal* Australian

THESAURUS

aura *n* **1 = air**, feeling, feel, quality, atmosphere, tone, suggestion, mood, scent, aroma, odour, ambience, vibes *(slang)*, vibrations *(slang)*, emanation

austerity *n* **1a = plainness**, economy, simplicity, severity, starkness, spareness, Spartanism
1b = asceticism, economy, rigidity, abstinence, self-discipline, chastity, sobriety, continence, puritanism, solemnity, self-denial, strictness, abstemiousness, chasteness, exactingness, Spartanism

authentic *adj* **1 = real**, true, original, actual, pure, genuine, valid, faithful, undisputed, veritable, lawful, on the level *(informal)*, bona fide, dinkum *(Austral & NZ informal)*, pukka, the real McCoy, true-to-life **OPPOSITE:** fake
2 = accurate, true, certain, reliable, legitimate, authoritative, factual, truthful, dependable, trustworthy, veracious **OPPOSITE:** fictitious

author *n* **1 = writer**, composer, novelist, hack, creator, columnist, scribbler, scribe, essayist, wordsmith, penpusher, littérateur, man *or* woman of letters **2 = creator**, father, parent, mother, maker, producer, framer, designer, founder, architect, planner, inventor, mover, originator, prime mover, doer, initiator, begetter, fabricator

authoritarian *adj* **1 = strict**, severe, absolute, harsh, rigid, autocratic, dictatorial, dogmatic, imperious, domineering, unyielding, tyrannical, disciplinarian, despotic, doctrinaire **OPPOSITE:** lenient
▷ *n* **2 = disciplinarian**, dictator, tyrant, despot, autocrat, absolutist

authoritative *adj* **1 = reliable**, learned,

DICTIONARY

a

austere *adj* **1** stern or severe: *his austere and serious attitude to events* **2** self-disciplined or ascetic: *an extraordinarily austere and puritanical organization* **3** severely simple or plain: *the austere backdrop of grey*
WORD ORIGIN Greek *austēros* astringent

austerity ❶ *n, pl* **-ties 1** the state of being austere **2** reduced availability of luxuries and consumer goods

Austin[1] *n* a city in central Texas, on the Colorado River: state capital since 1845. Pop: 672 011 (2003 est)

Austin[2] *n* **1 Herbert,** 1st Baron. 1866–1941, British automobile engineer, who founded the Austin Motor Company **2 John** 1790–1859, British jurist, whose book *The Province of Jurisprudence Determined* (1832) greatly influenced legal theory and the English legal system **3 J(ohn) L(angshaw).** 1911–60, English philosopher, whose lectures *Sense and Sensibilia* and *How to do Things with Words* were published posthumously in 1962

Austin[3] *adj, n* ▸ another word for **Augustinian**
WORD ORIGIN C14: shortened form of AUGUSTINE

austral *adj* of or from the south
WORD ORIGIN Latin *auster* the south wind

Austral. 1 Australasia **2** Australia(n)

Australasian *adj* of Australia, New Zealand, and neighbouring islands

Australia Day *n* public holiday in Australia on January 26

Australian *adj* **1** of Australia ▹*n* **2** a person from Australia

Austrian *adj* **1** of Austria ▹*n* **2** a person from Austria

autarchy (aw-tar-kee) *n, pl* **-chies** absolute power or autocracy
WORD ORIGIN Greek *autarkhia*

autarky (aw-tar-kee) *n, pl* **-kies** a policy of economic self-sufficiency
WORD ORIGIN Greek *autarkeia*

authentic ❶ *adj* **1** of undisputed origin or authorship; genuine **2** reliable or accurate **3** *music* using period instruments, scores, and playing techniques **authentically** *adv* **authenticity** *n*
WORD ORIGIN Greek *authentikos*

authenticate *vb* **-cating, -cated** to establish as genuine **authentication** *n*

author ❶ *n* **1** a person who writes a book, article, or other written work **2** an originator or creator
WORD ORIGIN Latin *auctor*

authoritarian ❶ *adj* **1** insisting on strict obedience to authority ▹*n* **2** a person who insists on strict obedience to authority **authoritarianism** *n*

authoritative ❶ *adj* **1** recognized as being reliable: *the authoritative book on Shakespeare* **2** possessing authority; official **authoritatively** *adv*

authority ❶ *n, pl* **-ties 1** the power to command, control, or judge others **2** a person or group with this power: *a third escapee turned himself in to the authorities* **3** a decision-making organization or government department: *the local authority* **4** an expert in a particular field **5** official permission: *he had no authority to negotiate* **6** a position that has the power to command, control, or judge others: *people in authority* **7 on good authority** from reliable evidence **8** confidence resulting from expertise
WORD ORIGIN Latin *auctor* author

authorize ❶ *or* **-ise** *vb* **-izing, -ized** *or* **-ising, -ised 1** to give authority to **2** to give official permission for **authorization** *or* **-isation** *n*

Authorized Version *n* **the Authorized Version** an English translation of the Bible published in 1611

authorship *n* **1** the origin or originator of a written work or plan **2** the profession of writing

autism *n psychiatry* abnormal self-absorption, usually affecting children, characterized by lack of response to people and limited ability to communicate **autistic** *adj*
WORD ORIGIN Greek *autos* self

auto *n, pl* **-tos** *US & Canad informal* ▸ short for **automobile**

auto- *or sometimes before a vowel* **aut-** *combining form* **1** self; of or by the same one: *autobiography* **2** self-propelling: *automobile*
WORD ORIGIN Greek *autos* self

autobahn *n* a motorway in German-speaking countries
WORD ORIGIN German, from *Auto* car + *Bahn* road

autobiography *n, pl* **-phies** an account of a person's life written by that person **autobiographer** *n* **autobiographical** *adj*

autoclave *n* an apparatus for sterilizing objects by steam under pressure
WORD ORIGIN AUTO- + Latin *clavis* key

autocracy *n, pl* **-cies** government by an individual with unrestricted authority

autocrat *n* **1** a ruler with absolute authority **2** a dictatorial person **autocratic** *adj* **autocratically** *adv*
WORD ORIGIN AUTO- + Greek *kratos* power

autocross *n* a sport in which cars race over a circuit of rough grass

Autocue *n trademark* an electronic television prompting device displaying a speaker's script, unseen by the audience

auto-da-fé (aw-toe-da-fay) *n, pl* **autos-da-fé 1** *history* the ceremonial passing of sentence on heretics by the Spanish Inquisition **2** the burning to death of heretics
WORD ORIGIN Portuguese, literally: act of the faith

autofocus *n* a camera system in which the lens is focused automatically

autogiro *or* **autogyro** *n, pl* **-ros** a self-propelled aircraft resembling a helicopter but with an unpowered rotor

autograph *n* **1** a handwritten signature of a famous person ▹*vb* **2** to write one's signature on or in
WORD ORIGIN AUTO- + Greek *graphein* to write

automat *n US* a vending machine

automate *vb* **-mating, -mated** to make (a manufacturing process) automatic

automatic ❶ *adj* **1** (of a device or

THESAURUS

sound, true, accurate, valid, scholarly, faithful, authentic, definitive, factual, truthful, veritable, dependable, trustworthy
OPPOSITE: unreliable
2 = commanding, lordly, masterly, imposing, dominating, confident, decisive, imperative, assertive, autocratic, dictatorial, dogmatic, imperious, self-assured, peremptory
OPPOSITE: timid

authority *n* **1 = prerogative**, right, influence, might, force, power, control, charge, rule, government, weight, strength, direction, command, licence, privilege, warrant, say-so, sway, domination, jurisdiction, supremacy, dominion, ascendancy, mana (NZ) **2, 3 = powers that be**, government, police, officials, the state, management, administration, the system, the Establishment, Big Brother *(informal)*, officialdom **4 = expert**, specialist, professional, master, ace *(informal)*, scholar, guru, buff *(informal)*, wizard, whizz *(informal)*, virtuoso, connoisseur, arbiter, hotshot *(informal)*, fundi *(S African)* **6 = command**, power, control, rule, management, direction, grasp, sway, domination, mastery, dominion

authorize *vb* **1 = empower**, commission, enable, entitle, mandate, accredit, give authority to **2 = permit**, allow, suffer, grant, confirm, agree to, approve, sanction, endure, license, endorse, warrant, tolerate, ratify, consent to, countenance, accredit, vouch for, give leave, give the green light for, give a blank cheque to, give authority for **OPPOSITE:** forbid

automatic *adj* **1, 2 = mechanical**, robot, automated, mechanized,

DICTIONARY

a

mechanism) able to activate or regulate itself **2** (of a process) performed by automatic equipment **3** done without conscious thought **4** (of a firearm) utilizing some of the force of each explosion to reload and fire continuously **5** occurring as a necessary consequence: *the certificate itself carries no automatic legal benefits* ▷ *n* **6** an automatic firearm **7** a motor vehicle with automatic transmission **automatically** *adv*
WORD ORIGIN Greek *automatos* acting independently

automatic pilot *n* **1** a device that automatically maintains an aircraft on a preset course **2 on automatic pilot** repeating an action or process without thought

automatic transmission *n* a transmission system in a motor vehicle in which the gears change automatically

automation *n* the use of automatic, often electronic, methods to control industrial processes

automaton *n, pl* **-tons** *or* **-ta 1** a mechanical device operating under its own power **2** a person who acts mechanically
WORD ORIGIN Greek *automatos* spontaneous

automobile *n US & Canad* a motorcar

automotive *adj* **1** relating to motor vehicles **2** self-propelling

autonomous ❶ *adj* **1** having self-government **2** independent of others
WORD ORIGIN AUTO- + Greek *nomos* law

autonomy ❶ *n, pl* **-mies 1** the right or state of self-government **2** freedom to determine one's own actions and behaviour
WORD ORIGIN Greek *autonomia*

autopilot *n* an automatic pilot

autopsy *n, pl* **-sies** examination of a corpse to determine the cause of death
WORD ORIGIN Greek *autopsia* seeing with one's own eyes

autoroute *n* a motorway in French-speaking countries
WORD ORIGIN French, from *auto* car + *route* road

autostrada *n* a motorway in Italian-speaking countries
WORD ORIGIN Italian, from *auto* car + *strada* road

autosuggestion *n* a process in which a person unconsciously supplies the means of influencing his or her own behaviour or beliefs

autumn *n* **1** the season of the year between summer and winter **2** a period of late maturity followed by a decline **autumnal** *adj*
WORD ORIGIN Latin *autumnus*

aux. auxiliary

auxiliaries *pl n* foreign troops serving another nation

auxiliary *adj* **1** secondary or supplementary **2** supporting ▷ *n, pl* **-ries 3** a person or thing that supports or supplements
WORD ORIGIN Latin *auxilium* help

auxiliary verb *n* a verb used to indicate the tense, voice, or mood of another verb, such as *will* in *I will go*

AV (of the Bible) Authorized Version

av. 1 average **2** avoirdupois

avail *vb* **1** to be of use, advantage, or assistance (to) **2 avail oneself of** to make use of ▷ *n* **3** use or advantage: *to no avail*
WORD ORIGIN Latin *valere* to be strong

available ❶ *adj* **1** obtainable or accessible **2** able to be contacted and willing to talk: *a spokesman insisted she was not available for comment* **availability** *n* **availably** *adv*

avalanche ❶ *n* **1** a fall of large masses of snow and ice down a mountain **2** a sudden or overwhelming quantity of anything
WORD ORIGIN French

avant- (av-ong) *prefix* belonging to the avant-garde of a field: *avant-jazz*

avant-garde ❶ (av-ong-gard) *n* **1** those artists, writers, or musicians, whose techniques and ideas are in advance of those generally accepted ▷ *adj* **2** using ideas or techniques in advance of those generally accepted
WORD ORIGIN French: vanguard

avarice (av-a-riss) *n* extreme greed for wealth **avaricious** *adj*
WORD ORIGIN Latin *avere* to crave

avast *interj naut* stop! cease!
WORD ORIGIN probably Dutch *hou'vast* hold fast

avatar *n* **1** *hinduism* the appearance of a god in human or animal form **2** *computers* graphical representation of a person in a virtual environment, such as an online role-playing game
WORD ORIGIN Sanskrit *avatāra* a going down

Ave (ah-vay) *or* **Ave Maria** (ma-ree-a) *n* ▸ same as **Hail Mary**
WORD ORIGIN Latin: hail, Mary!

Ave. avenue

avenge *vb* **avenging, avenged** to inflict a punishment in retaliation for (harm done) or on behalf of (the person harmed) **avenger** *n*
WORD ORIGIN Latin *vindicare*

avenue ❶ *n* **1** a wide street **2** a road bordered by two rows of trees **3** a line of approach: *the United States was exhausting every avenue to achieve a diplomatic solution*
WORD ORIGIN French, from *avenir* to come to

aver (av-vur) *vb* **averring, averred** to state to be true **averment** *n*
WORD ORIGIN Latin *verus* true

average ❶ *n* **1** the typical or normal amount or quality **2** the result obtained by adding the numbers or quantities in a set and dividing the total by the number of members in the set **3 on average** usually or typically ▷ *adj* **4** usual or typical **5** calculated as an average **6** mediocre or inferior ▷ *vb* **-aging, -aged 7** to calculate or estimate the average of **8** to amount to or be on average

THESAURUS

push-button, self-regulating, self-propelling, self-activating, self-moving, self-acting, hands-off
OPPOSITE: done by hand
3 = involuntary, natural, unconscious, mechanical, spontaneous, reflex, instinctive, instinctual, unwilled
OPPOSITE: conscious

autonomous *adj* **1, 2 = self-ruling**, free, independent, sovereign, self-sufficient, self-governing, self-determining

autonomy *n* **1, 2 = independence**, freedom, sovereignty, self-determination, self-government, self-rule, self-sufficiency, home rule, rangatiratanga (NZ)
OPPOSITE: dependency

available *adj* **1 = accessible**, ready, to hand, convenient, handy, vacant, on hand, at hand, free, applicable, to be had, achievable, obtainable, on tap (*informal*), attainable, at your fingertips, at your disposal, ready for use **OPPOSITE:** in use

avalanche *n* **1 = snow-slide**, landslide, landslip, snow-slip **2 = large amount**, barrage, torrent, deluge, inundation

avant-garde *adj* **2 = progressive**, pioneering, way-out (*informal*), experimental, innovative, unconventional, far-out (*slang*), ground-breaking, innovatory
OPPOSITE: conservative

avenue *n* **1 = street**, way, course, drive, road, pass, approach, channel, access, entry, route, path, passage, entrance, alley, pathway, boulevard, driveway, thoroughfare

average *n* **1, 2 = standard**, normal, usual, par, mode, mean, rule, medium, norm, run of the mill, midpoint **3 on average = usually**, generally, normally, typically, for the most part, as a rule ▷ *adj* **4 = usual**, common, standard, general, normal, regular, ordinary, typical, commonplace, unexceptional
OPPOSITE: unusual
5 = mean, middle, medium, intermediate, median
OPPOSITE: minimum
▷ *vb* **8 = make on average**, be on average, even out to, do on average, balance out to

WORD ORIGIN Middle English *averay* loss arising from damage to ships, ultimately from Arabic *awār* damage

averse *adj* opposed: *he's not averse to publicity, of the right kind*
WORD ORIGIN Latin *avertere* to turn from

aversion *n* **1** extreme dislike or disinclination **2** a person or thing that arouses this

avert ❶ *vb* **1** to turn away: *he had to avert his eyes* **2** to ward off: *a final attempt to avert war*
WORD ORIGIN Latin *avertere* to turn from

Avesta *n* a collection of sacred writings of Zoroastrianism

avian (aiv-ee-an) *adj* of or like a bird: *the treatment of avian diseases*
WORD ORIGIN Latin *avis* bird

avian flu *n* ▸ another name for **bird flu**
WORD ORIGIN Latin *avis* bird

aviary *n, pl* **aviaries** a large enclosure in which birds are kept
WORD ORIGIN Latin *avis* bird

aviation *n* the art or science of flying aircraft
WORD ORIGIN Latin *avis* bird

aviator *n old-fashioned* the pilot of an aircraft **aviatrix** *fem n*

avid *adj* **1** very keen or enthusiastic: *he is an avid football fan* **2** eager: *avid for economic development* **avidity** *n* **avidly** *adv*
WORD ORIGIN Latin *avere* to long for

avocado *n, pl* **-dos** a pear-shaped tropical fruit with a leathery green skin and greenish-yellow flesh
WORD ORIGIN Spanish *aguacate*

avocation *n* **1** *Brit, Austral & NZ, old-fashioned* a person's regular job **2** *formal* a hobby
WORD ORIGIN Latin *avocare* to distract

avocet *n* a long-legged shore bird with a long slender upward-curving bill
WORD ORIGIN Italian *avocetta*

avoid ❶ *vb* **1** to refrain from doing **2** to prevent from happening **3** to keep out of the way of **avoidable** *adj* **avoidably** *adv* **avoidance** *n*
WORD ORIGIN Old French *esvuidier*

avoirdupois *or* **avoirdupois weight** (av-er-de-**poise**) *n* a system of weights based on the pound, which contains 16 ounces
WORD ORIGIN Old French *aver de peis* goods of weight

Avon[1] *n* **1** a former county of SW England, created in 1974 from areas of N Somerset and S Gloucestershire: replaced in 1996 by the unitary authorities of Bath and North East Somerset (Somerset), North Somerset (Somerset), South Gloucestershire (Gloucestershire), and Bristol **2** a river in central England, rising in Northamptonshire and flowing southwest through Stratford-on-Avon to the River Severn at Tewkesbury. Length: 154 km (96 miles) **3** a river in SW England, rising in Gloucestershire and flowing south and west through Bristol to the Severn estuary at **Avonmouth**. Length: 120 km (75 miles) **4** a river in S England, rising in Wiltshire and flowing south to the English Channel. Length: about 96 km (60 miles)

Avon[2] *n* **Earl of** ▸ title of (Anthony) **Eden**

avow *vb* **1** to state or affirm **2** to admit openly **avowal** *n* **avowed** *adj* **avowedly** (a-vow-id-lee) *adv*
WORD ORIGIN Latin *advocare* to call upon

avuncular *adj* (of a man) friendly, helpful, and caring towards someone younger
WORD ORIGIN Latin *avunculus* (maternal) uncle

await ❶ *vb* **1** to wait for **2** to be in store for

awake ❶ *adj* **1** not sleeping **2** alert or aware: *awake to the danger* ▹ *vb* **awaking, awoke** *or* **awaked, awoken** *or* **awaked 3** to emerge or rouse from sleep **4** to become or cause to become alert
WORD ORIGIN Old English *awacan*

awaken *vb* **1** to awake **2** to cause to be aware of: *anxieties awakened by reunification*

awakening *n* the start of a feeling or awareness in someone: *a picture of an emotional awakening*

award ❶ *vb* **1** to give (something) for merit **2** *law* to declare to be entitled, such as by decision of a court ▹ *n* **3** something awarded, such as a prize **4** *law* the decision of an arbitrator or court
WORD ORIGIN Old French *eswarder* to decide after investigation

aware ❶ *adj* **1 aware of** knowing about: *he's at least aware of the problem* **2** informed: *they are becoming more politically aware every day* **awareness** *n*
WORD ORIGIN Old English *gewær*

awash *adv, adj* washed over by water

away ❶ *adv* **1** from a particular place: *I saw them walk away and felt absolutely desolated* **2** in or to another, a usual, or a proper place: *he decided to put the car away in the garage* **3** at a distance: *keep away from the windows* **4** out of existence: *the pillars rotted away* **5** indicating motion or distance from a normal or proper place: *the child shook her head and looked away* **6** continuously: *he continued to scribble away* ▹ *adj* **7** not present: *he had been away from home for years* **8** distant: *the castle was farther away than he had thought* **9** *sport* played on an opponent's ground
WORD ORIGIN Old English *on weg* on way

awayday *n* a day trip taken for pleasure
WORD ORIGIN from *awayday ticket* a

THESAURUS

avert *vb* **1 = turn away**, turn, turn aside **2 = ward off**, avoid, prevent, frustrate, fend off, preclude, stave off, forestall

avoid *vb* **1 = refrain from**, bypass, dodge, eschew, escape, duck (out of) *(informal)*, fight shy of, shirk from **2 = prevent**, stop, frustrate, hamper, foil, inhibit, head off, avert, thwart, intercept, hinder, obstruct, impede, ward off, stave off, forestall, defend against **3 = keep away from**, dodge, shun, evade, steer clear of, sidestep, circumvent, bypass, slip through the net, body-swerve *(Scot)*, give a wide berth to

await *vb* **1 = wait for**, expect, look for, look forward to, anticipate, stay for **2 = be in store for**, wait for, be ready for, lie in wait for, be in readiness for

awake *adj* **1 = not sleeping**, sleepless, wide-awake, aware, waking, conscious, aroused, awakened, restless, restive, wakeful, bright-eyed and bushy-tailed
OPPOSITE: asleep
2 = alert, aware, on the lookout, alive, attentive, on the alert, observant, watchful, on guard, on your toes, heedful, vigilant ▹ *vb* **3 = wake up**, come to, wake, stir, awaken, rouse **4 = alert**, excite, stimulate, provoke, revive, arouse, activate, awaken, fan, animate, stir up, incite, kick-start *(informal)*, enliven, kindle, breathe life into, call forth, vivify

award *vb* **1 = present with**, give, grant, gift, distribute, render, assign, decree, hand out, confer, endow, bestow, allot, apportion, adjudge **2** *(law)* **= grant**, give, render, assign, decree, accord, confer, adjudge ▹ *n* **3 = prize**, gift, trophy, decoration, grant, bonsela *(S African)*, koha *(NZ)*

aware *adj* **2 = informed**, enlightened, knowledgeable, learned, expert, versed, up to date, in the picture, in the know *(informal)*, erudite, well-read, au fait *(French)*, in the loop, well-briefed, au courant *(French)*, clued-up *(informal)*
OPPOSITE: ignorant

away *adv* **1 = off**, elsewhere, abroad, hence, from here **3 = at a distance**, far, apart, remote, isolated **6 = continuously**, repeatedly, relentlessly, incessantly, interminably, unremittingly, uninterruptedly ▹ *adj* **7 = absent**, out, gone, elsewhere, abroad, not there, not here, not present, on vacation, not at home

DICTIONARY

a

special-rate day return by train

awe n **1** wonder and respect mixed with dread ▷ vb **awing, awed 2** to inspire with reverence or dread
WORD ORIGIN Old Norse *agi*

aweigh *adj naut* (of an anchor) no longer hooked into the bottom

awesome *adj* **1** inspiring or displaying awe **2** *slang* excellent or outstanding

awestruck *adj* overcome or filled with awe

awful *adj* **1** very bad or unpleasant **2** *informal* considerable or great: *that's an awful lot of money, isn't it?* **3** *obsolete* inspiring reverence or dread ▷ *adv* **4** *not standard* very: *I'm working awful hard on my lines*

awfully *adv* **1** in an unpleasant way **2** *informal* very: *we were both awfully busy*

awhile *adv* for a brief period

awkward *adj* **1** clumsy or ungainly **2** embarrassed: *he was awkward and nervous around girls* **3** difficult to deal with: *the lawyer was in an awkward situation* **4** difficult to use or handle: *it was small but heavy enough to make it awkward to carry* **5** embarrassing: *there were several moments of awkward silence*
awkwardly *adv* **awkwardness** *n*
WORD ORIGIN Old Norse *öfugr* turned the wrong way round

awl *n* a pointed hand tool for piercing wood, leather, etc.
WORD ORIGIN Old English *ǣl*

awn *n* any of the bristles growing from the flowering parts of certain grasses and cereals
WORD ORIGIN Old English *agen* ear of grain

awning *n* a canvas roof supported by a frame to give protection against the weather
WORD ORIGIN origin unknown

awoke *vb* ▸ a past tense and (now rare or dialectal) past participle of **awake**

awoken *vb* ▸ a past participle of **awake**

AWOL (eh-woll) *adj mil* absent without leave but without intending to desert

awry (a-**rye**) *adv, adj* **1** with a twist to one side; askew: *my neck was really awry after the journey* **2** amiss or faulty: *if a gear gets stuck, the whole system goes awry*
WORD ORIGIN Middle English *on wry*

axe or *US* **ax** *n, pl* **axes 1** a hand tool with one side of its head sharpened to a cutting edge, used for felling trees and splitting timber **2 an axe to grind** a favourite topic one wishes to promote **3** *informal* a severe cut in spending or in the number of staff employed ▷ *vb* **axing, axed 4** *informal* to dismiss (employees), restrict (expenditure), or terminate (a project)
WORD ORIGIN Old English *æx*

Axelrod *n* **Julius** 1912–2004, US neuropharmacologist, renowned for his work on catecholamines. Nobel prize for physiology or medicine (with von Euler and Bernard Katz) 1970

axes[1] *n* ▸ the plural of **axis**

axes[2] *n* ▸ the plural of **axe**

axial *adj* **1** forming or of an axis **2** in, on, or along an axis **axially** *adv*

axil *n* the angle where the stalk of a leaf joins a stem
WORD ORIGIN Latin *axilla* armpit

axiom *n* **1** a generally accepted principle **2** a self-evident statement
WORD ORIGIN Greek *axios* worthy

axiomatic *adj* **1** containing axioms **2** self-evident or obvious
axiomatically *adv*

axis (ax-iss) *n, pl* **axes** (ax-eez) **1** a real or imaginary line about which a body can rotate or about which an object or geometrical construction is symmetrical **2** one of two or three reference lines used in coordinate geometry to locate a point in a plane or in space
WORD ORIGIN Latin

axle *n* a shaft on which a wheel or pair of wheels revolves
WORD ORIGIN Old Norse *öxull*

axolotl *n* an aquatic salamander of N America
WORD ORIGIN Mexican Indian: water doll

ayah *n* (in parts of the former British Empire) a native maidservant or nursemaid
WORD ORIGIN Hindi *āyā*

ayatollah *n* one of a class of Islamic religious leaders in Iran
WORD ORIGIN Arabic *aya* sign + *allah* God

aye or **ay** *interj* **1** *Brit, Austral & NZ* yes ▷ *n* **2** an affirmative vote or voter
WORD ORIGIN probably from *I*, expressing assent

Ayesha *n* ▸ a variant spelling of **Aisha**

Aykroyd *n* **Dan** born 1952, Canadian film actor and screenwriter, best known for the television show *Saturday Night Live* (1975–80) and the films *The Blues Brothers* (1980), *Ghostbusters* (1984), and *Driving Miss Daisy* (1989)

Aylward *n* **Gladys** 1903–70, English missionary in China

Aymé *n* **Marcel** 1902–67, French

THESAURUS

awe *n* **1 = wonder**, fear, respect, reverence, horror, terror, dread, admiration, amazement, astonishment, veneration
OPPOSITE: contempt
▷ *vb* **2 = impress**, amaze, stun, frighten, terrify, cow, astonish, horrify, intimidate, daunt

awesome *adj* **1 = awe-inspiring**, striking, shocking, imposing, terrible, amazing, stunning, wonderful, alarming, impressive, frightening, awful, overwhelming, terrifying, magnificent, astonishing, horrible, dreadful, formidable, horrifying, intimidating, fearful, daunting, breathtaking, majestic, solemn, fearsome, wondrous *(archaic, literary)*, redoubtable, jaw-dropping, stupefying

awfully *adv* **1 = badly**, woefully, dreadfully, inadequately, disgracefully, wretchedly, unforgivably, shoddily, reprehensibly, disreputably
2 *(informal)* **= very**, extremely, terribly, exceptionally, quite, very much, seriously *(informal)*, greatly, immensely, exceedingly, excessively, dreadfully

awkward *adj* **1 = clumsy**, stiff, rude, blundering, coarse, bungling, lumbering, inept, unskilled, bumbling, unwieldy, ponderous, ungainly, gauche, gawky, uncouth, unrefined, artless, inelegant, uncoordinated, graceless, cack-handed *(informal)*, unpolished, clownish, oafish, inexpert, maladroit, ill-bred, all thumbs, ungraceful, skill-less, unskilful, butterfingered *(informal)*, unhandy, ham-fisted or ham-handed *(informal)*, unco *(Austral slang)*
OPPOSITE: graceful
4 = inconvenient, difficult, troublesome, cumbersome, unwieldy, unmanageable, clunky *(informal)*, unhandy
OPPOSITE: convenient
5 = embarrassing, difficult, compromising, sensitive, embarrassed, painful, distressing, delicate, uncomfortable, tricky, trying, humiliating, unpleasant, sticky *(informal)*, troublesome, perplexing, disconcerting, inconvenient, thorny, untimely, ill at ease, discomfiting, ticklish, inopportune, toe-curling *(slang)*, barro *(Austral slang)*, cringeworthy *(Brit informal)* **OPPOSITE:** comfortable

axe *n* **1 = hatchet**, chopper, tomahawk, cleaver, adze ▷ *vb* **4a** *(informal)* **= abandon**, end, pull, eliminate, cancel, scrap, wind up, turn off *(informal)*, relegate, cut back, terminate, dispense with, discontinue, pull the plug on
4b *(informal)* **= dismiss**, fire *(informal)*, sack *(informal)*, remove, get rid of, discharge, throw out, oust, give (someone) their marching orders, give the boot to *(slang)*, give the bullet to *(Brit slang)*, give the push to, kennet *(Austral slang)*, jeff *(Austral slang)*

axis *n* **1 = pivot**, shaft, axle, spindle, centre line

writer: noted for his light and witty narratives

Ayrshire *n* one of a breed of brown-and-white dairy cattle
WORD ORIGIN *Ayrshire*, district of Scotland

Ayub Khan *n* **Mohammed** 1907–74, Pakistani field marshal; president of Pakistan (1958–69)

AZ Arizona

azalea (az-zale-ya) *n* a garden shrub grown for its showy flowers
WORD ORIGIN Greek *azaleos* dry

Azaña *n* **Manuel** 1880–1940, Spanish statesman; president of the Spanish Republic (1936–39) until overthrown by Franco

Azikiwe *n* **Nnamdi** 1904–96, Nigerian statesman; first president of Nigeria (1963–66)

azimuth *n* **1** the arc of the sky between the zenith and the horizon **2** *surveying* the horizontal angle of a bearing measured clockwise from the north
WORD ORIGIN Arabic *as-samt* the path

Azorín *n* real name *José Martínez Ruiz*. 1874–1967, Spanish writer: noted for his stories of the Spanish countryside

Aztec *n* **1** a member of a Mexican Indian race who established a great empire, overthrown by the Spanish in the early 16th century **2** the language of the Aztecs ▷ *adj* **3** of the Aztecs or their language
WORD ORIGIN *Aztlan*, their traditional place of origin, literally: near the cranes

azure *n* **1** the deep blue colour of a clear blue sky **2** *poetic* a clear blue sky ▷ *adj* **3** deep blue
WORD ORIGIN Arabic *lāzaward* lapis lazuli

Bb

DICTIONARY

b *or* **B** *n, pl* **b's, B's** *or* **Bs 1** the second letter of the English alphabet **2 from A to B** ▸ see **a** (sense 2)
b *cricket* **a** bowled **b** bye
B 1 *music* the seventh note of the scale of C major **2** the second in a series, class, or rank **3** *chem* boron **4** *chess* bishop
b. born
Ba *chem* barium
BA 1 Bachelor of Arts **2** British Airways
baa *vb* **baaing, baaed 1** (of a sheep) to make a characteristic bleating sound ▹*n* **2** the cry made by a sheep
Baal Shem Tov *or* **Baal Shem Tob** *n* original name *Israel ben Eliezer* ?1700–60, Jewish religious leader, teacher, and healer in Poland: founder of modern Hasidism
baas ❶ *n S African* a boss
WORD ORIGIN Afrikaans
baaskap *n* (in South Africa) control by Whites of non-Whites
WORD ORIGIN Afrikaans
babaco *n* a greenish-yellow egg-shaped fruit
Babar *n* a variant spelling of **Baber**
babble *vb* **-bling, -bled 1** to talk in a quick, foolish, or muddled way **2** to make meaningless sounds: *children first gurgle and babble at random* **3** to disclose secrets carelessly **4** *literary* (of streams) to make a low murmuring sound ▹*n* **5** muddled or foolish speech **6** a murmuring sound **babbler** *n* **babbling** *n*
WORD ORIGIN probably imitative
babe *n* **1** a baby **2 babe in arms** *informal* a naive or inexperienced person **3** *slang* a girl, esp. an attractive one
babel (babe-el) *n* **1** a confusion of noises or voices **2** a scene of noise and confusion
WORD ORIGIN from the confusion of languages on the tower of *Babel* (Genesis 11:1–10)
Babel[1] *n* **1** *Old Testament* **a** Also called: **Tower of Babel** a tower presumptuously intended to reach from earth to heaven, the building of which was frustrated when Jehovah confused the language of the builders (Genesis 11:1–9) **b** the city, probably Babylon, in which this tower was supposedly built **2** (*often not capital*) **a** a confusion of noises or voices **b** a scene of noise and confusion
WORD ORIGIN from Hebrew *Bābhēl*, from Akkadian *Bāb-ilu*, literally: gate of God
Babel[2] *n* **Issak Emmanuilovich** 1894–1941, Russian short-story writer, whose works include *Stories from Odessa* (1924) and *Red Cavalry* (1926)
Baber, Babar, *or* **Babur** *n* original name *Zahir ud-Din Mohammed* 1483–1530, founder of the Mogul Empire: conquered India in 1526
Babeuf *n* **François Noël** 1760–97, French political agitator: plotted unsuccessfully to destroy the Directory and establish a communistic system
babiche *n Canad* thongs or lacings of rawhide
Babinet *n* **Jacques** 1794–1872, French physicist, noted for his work on the diffraction of light
Babington *n* **Anthony** 1561–86, English conspirator, executed for organizing an unsuccessful plot (1586) to assassinate Elizabeth I and place Mary, Queen of Scots, on the English throne
baboon *n* a medium-sized monkey with a long face, large teeth, and a fairly long tail
WORD ORIGIN Middle English *babewyn* gargoyle
Babur *n* a variant spelling of **Baber**
baby ❶ *n, pl* **-bies 1** a newborn child **2** the youngest or smallest of a family or group **3** a recently born animal **4** an immature person **5** *slang* a sweetheart **6** a project of personal concern **7 be left holding the baby** to be left with a responsibility ▹*adj* **8** comparatively small of its type: *baby carrots* ▹*vb* **-bies, -bying, -bied 9** to treat like a baby **babyhood** *n* **babyish** *adj*
WORD ORIGIN probably childish reduplication
baby bonus *n Canad informal* Family Allowance
baby-sit *vb* **-sitting, -sat** to act or work as a baby-sitter **baby-sitting** *n, adj*
baby-sitter *n* a person who takes care of a child while the parents are out
baccalaureate (back-a-**law**-ree-it) *n* the university degree of Bachelor of Arts
WORD ORIGIN Medieval Latin *baccalarius* bachelor
baccarat (**back**-a-rah) *n* a card game in which two or more punters gamble against the banker
WORD ORIGIN French *baccara*
bacchanalian (back-a-**nail**-ee-an) *adj literary* (of a party) unrestrained and involving a great deal of drinking and sometimes sexual activity
WORD ORIGIN from *Bacchus*, Greek & Roman god of wine
Bacchus *n classical myth* the god of wine; Dionysus
baccy *n Brit informal* tobacco
bach (batch) *NZ n* **1** a small holiday cottage ▹*vb* **2** to look after oneself when one's spouse is away
Bacharach *n* **Burt** born 1928, US composer of popular songs, usually with lyricist Hal David
bachelor *n* **1** an unmarried man **2** a person who holds a first degree from a university or college **bachelorhood** *n*
WORD ORIGIN Old French *bacheler* youth, squire
Bachelor of Arts *n* a person with a first degree from a university or college, usually in the arts
bacillary *adj* of or caused by bacilli
bacillus (bass-**ill**-luss) *n, pl* **-li** (-lie) a rod-shaped bacterium, esp. one causing disease
WORD ORIGIN Latin *baculum* walking stick
back ❶ *n* **1** the rear part of the human body, from the neck to the pelvis **2** the spinal column **3** the part or side of an object opposite the front **4** the part of anything less often seen or used **5** *ball games* a defensive player or position **6 at the back of one's mind** not in one's conscious thoughts **7 behind someone's back** secretly or deceitfully **8 put** *or* **get someone's back up** to annoy someone **9 turn one's back on someone** to refuse to help someone ▹*vb* **10** to move or cause to move backwards **11** to provide money for (a person or enterprise) **12** to bet on the success of: *to back a horse* **13** to provide (a pop singer) with a musical accompaniment **14** (foll. by *on* or *onto*)

THESAURUS

baas *n* = **master**, bo (*informal*), chief, ruler, commander, head, overlord, overseer
baby *n* **1** = **child**, infant, babe, wean (*Scot*), little one, bairn (*Scot & Northern English*), suckling, newborn child, babe in arms, sprog (*slang*), neonate, rug rat (*US & Canad informal*), ankle biter (*Austral slang*), tacker (*Austral slang*) ▹ *adj* **8** = **small**, little, minute, tiny, mini, wee, miniature, dwarf, diminutive, petite, midget, teeny (*informal*), pocket-sized, undersized, teeny-weeny (*informal*), Lilliputian, teensy-weensy (*informal*), pygmy *or* pigmy
back *n* **2** = **spine**, backbone, vertebrae, spinal column, vertebral column **3** = **rear**, other side, back end, rear side **OPPOSITE:** front **4** = **reverse**, rear, other side, wrong side, underside, flip side, verso ▹ *adj* **16** = **rear OPPOSITE:** front ▹ *vb* **11** = **subsidize**, help, support,

DICTIONARY

to have the back facing (towards): *his garden backs onto a school* **15** (of the wind) to change direction anticlockwise ▷ *adj* **16** situated behind: *back garden* **17** owing from an earlier date: *back rent* **18** remote: *a back road* ▷ *adv* **19** at, to, or towards the rear **20** to or towards the original starting point or condition: *I went back home* **21** in reply or retaliation: *to hit someone back* **22** in concealment or reserve: *to keep something back* **23 back and forth** to and fro **24 back to front a** in reverse **b** in disorder ▸ See also **back down, back off**, etc.
WORD ORIGIN Old English *bæc*

backbencher *n* a Member of Parliament who does not hold office in the government or opposition

backbite *vb* **-biting, -bit; -bitten** *or* **-bit** to talk spitefully about an absent person **backbiter** *n*

back boiler *n Brit* a tank at the back of a fireplace for heating water

backbone ⓣ *n* **1** the spinal column **2** strength of character **3** *computers* a central section that connects segments of a network

back-breaking *adj* (of work) exhausting

backburn *Austral & NZ vb* **1** to clear (an area of bush) by creating a fire that burns in the opposite direction from the wind **2** to prevent a bush fire from spreading by clearing an area of land in front of it ▷ *n* **3** the act or result of backburning

back catalogue *n* a musician's previous recordings, as opposed to their current recordings

backchat *n informal* impudent replies

backcloth *n* a painted curtain at the back of a stage set. Also called: **backdrop**

backcomb *vb* to comb (the hair) towards the roots to give more bulk to a hairstyle

back country *n Austral & NZ* land far away from settled areas

backdate *vb* **-dating, -dated** to make (a document) effective from a date earlier than its completion

back door *n* a means of entry to a job or position that is secret or obtained through influence

back down *vb* to withdraw an earlier claim

backer ⓣ *n* a person who gives financial or other support

backfire ⓣ *vb* **-firing, -fired 1** (of a plan or scheme) to fail to have the desired effect **2** (of an internal-combustion engine) to make a loud noise as a result of an explosion of unburnt gases in the exhaust system

backgammon *n* a game for two people played on a board with pieces moved according to throws of the dice
WORD ORIGIN *back* + obsolete *gammon* game

background ⓣ *n* **1** the events or circumstances that help to explain something **2** a person's social class, education, or experience **3** the part of a scene furthest from the viewer **4** an inconspicuous position: *in the background* **5** the space behind the chief figures or objects in a picture

backhand *n* **1** *tennis, etc.* a stroke made from across the body with the back of the hand facing the direction of the stroke **2** the side on which backhand strokes are made

backhanded *adj* **1** (of a blow or shot) performed with the arm moving from across the body **2** ambiguous or implying criticism: *a backhanded compliment*

backhander *n* **1** *slang* a bribe **2** a backhanded stroke or blow

backing ⓣ *n* **1** support **2** something that forms or strengthens the back of something **3** musical accompaniment for a pop singer

backing dog *n NZ* a dog that moves a flock of sheep by jumping on their backs

backlash ⓣ *n* **1** a sudden and adverse reaction **2** a recoil between interacting badly fitting parts in machinery

backlog *n* an accumulation of things to be dealt with

backlot *n* an area outside a film or television studio used for outdoor filming

back number *n* **1** an old issue of a newspaper or magazine **2** *informal* a person or thing considered to be old-fashioned

back off *vb* **1** to retreat **2** to abandon (an intention or objective)

back office *n* **1** the administrative staff of a financial institution or other business ▷ *adj* **2** of or relating to such staff: *back-office operations*

back out *vb* (often foll. by *of*) to withdraw from (an agreement)

backpack *n* **1** a rucksack ▷ *vb* **2** to go hiking or travelling with a backpack **backpacker** *n*

back passage *n* the rectum

back-pedal *vb* **-pedalling, -pedalled** *or US* **-pedaling, -pedaled** to retract or modify a previous opinion or statement

back room *n* **1** a place where secret research or planning is done ▷ *adj* **back-room 2** of or relating to secret research or planning: *back-room boys*

back seat *n informal* a less important or responsible position: *lyricism took a back seat to drama*

back-seat driver *n informal* a person who offers unwanted advice

backside *n informal* the buttocks

backslide *vb* **-sliding, -slid** to relapse into former bad habits or vices **backslider** *n*

backspace *vb* **-spacing, -spaced** to move a typewriter carriage or computer cursor backwards

backspin *n sport* a backward spin given to a ball to reduce its speed at impact

backstabbing *n* treacherous actions or remarks that are likely to cause harm to a person **backstabber** *n* **backstab** *vb*

backstage *adv* **1** behind the stage in a theatre ▷ *adj* **2** situated backstage

backstairs *or* **backstair** *adj* underhand: *backstairs gossip*

backstreet *n* **1** a street in a town far from the main roads ▷ *adj* **2** denoting secret or illegal activities: *a backstreet abortion*

backstroke *n swimming* a stroke performed on the back, using backward circular strokes of each arm

THESAURUS

finance, sponsor, assist, underwrite

backbone *n* **1 = spinal column**, spine, vertebrae, vertebral column **2 = strength of character**, will, character, bottle *(Brit slang)*, resolution, resolve, nerve, daring, courage, determination, guts, pluck, stamina, grit, bravery, fortitude, toughness, tenacity, willpower, mettle, boldness, firmness, spunk *(informal)*, fearlessness, steadfastness, moral fibre, hardihood, dauntlessness

backer *n* **a = supporter**, second, ally, angel *(informal)*, patron, promoter, subscriber, underwriter, helper, benefactor **b = advocate**, supporter, patron, sponsor, promoter, protagonist

backfire *vb* **1 = fail**, founder, flop *(informal)*, rebound, fall through, fall flat, boomerang, miscarry, misfire, go belly-up *(slang)*, turn out badly, meet with disaster

background *n* **1 = circumstances**, history, conditions, situation, atmosphere, environment, framework, ambience, milieu, frame of reference **2a = upbringing**, history, culture, environment, tradition, circumstances, breeding, milieu **2b = experience**, grounding, education, preparation, qualifications, credentials

backing *n* **1a = support**, seconding, championing, promotion, sanction, approval, blessing, encouragement, endorsement, patronage, accompaniment, advocacy, moral support, espousal **1b = assistance**, support, help, funds, aid, grant, subsidy, sponsorship, patronage

backlash *n* **1 = reaction**, response, resistance, resentment, retaliation, repercussion, counterblast,

DICTIONARY

b

backtrack *vb* **1** to go back along the same route one has just travelled **2** to retract or reverse one's opinion or policy

back up *vb* **1** to support **2** *computers* to make a copy of (a data file), esp. as a security copy **3** (of traffic) to become jammed behind an obstruction ▹*n* **backup 4** support or reinforcement **5** a reserve or substitute ▹*adj* **backup 6** able to be substituted: *a backup copy*

backward ⓣ *adj* **1** directed towards the rear **2** retarded in physical, material, or intellectual development **3** reluctant or bashful ▹*adv* **4** ▸same as **backwards** > **backwardness** *n*

backwards ⓣ *or* **backward** *adv* **1** towards the rear **2** with the back foremost **3** in the reverse of the usual direction **4** into a worse state: *the Gothic novel's been going backwards since Radcliffe* **5 bend over backwards** *informal* to make a special effort to please someone

backwash *n* **1** water washed backwards by the motion of oars or a ship **2** an unpleasant aftereffect of an event or situation

backwater *n* **1** an isolated or backward place or condition **2** a body of stagnant water connected to a river

backwoods *pl n* **1** any remote sparsely populated place **2** partially cleared, sparsely populated forests **backwoodsman** *n*

back yard *n* **1** a yard at the back of a house, etc. **2 in one's own back yard a** close at hand **b** involving or implicating one

bacon *n* **1** meat from the back and sides of a pig, dried, salted, and often smoked **2 bring home the bacon** *informal* **a** to achieve success **b** to provide material support
WORD ORIGIN Old French

bacteria ⓣ *pl n, sing* **-rium** a large group of microorganisms, many of which cause disease **bacterial** *adj*
WORD ORIGIN Greek *baktron* rod

bacteriology *n* the study of bacteria **bacteriologist** *n*

Bactrian camel *n* a two-humped camel
WORD ORIGIN *Bactria*, ancient country of Asia

bad ⓣ *adj* **worse, worst 1** not good; of poor quality **2** lacking skill or talent: *I'm so bad at that sort of thing* **3** harmful: *smoking is bad for you* **4** evil or immoral **5** naughty or mischievous **6** rotten or decayed: *a bad egg* **7** severe: *a bad headache* **8** incorrect or faulty: *bad grammar* **9** sorry or upset: *I feel bad about saying no* **10** unfavourable or distressing: *bad news* **11** offensive or unpleasant: *bad language* **12** not valid: *a bad cheque* **13** not recoverable: *a bad debt* **14 badder, baddest** *slang* good; excellent **15 not bad** *or* **not so bad** *informal* fairly good **16 too bad** *informal* (often used dismissively) regrettable ▹*n* **17** unfortunate or unpleasant events: *you've got to take the good with the bad* ▹*adv* **18** *not standard* badly: *to want something bad* **badness** *n*
WORD ORIGIN Middle English

bad blood *n* a feeling of intense hatred or hostility between people

bade *or* **bad** *vb* ▸a past tense of **bid**

Bader *n* Sir **Douglas** 1910–82, British fighter pilot. Despite losing both legs after a flying accident (1931), he became a national hero as a pilot in World War II

badge ⓣ *n* **1** a distinguishing emblem or mark worn to show membership or achievement **2** any revealing feature or mark
WORD ORIGIN Old French *bage*

badger ⓣ *n* **1** a stocky burrowing mammal with a black and white striped head ▹*vb* **2** to pester or harass
WORD ORIGIN probably from *badge*

badinage (bad-in-nahzh) *n* playful and witty conversation
WORD ORIGIN French

badly ⓣ *adv* **worse, worst 1** poorly; inadequately **2** unfavourably: *our plan worked out badly* **3** severely: *badly damaged* **4** very much: *he badly needed to improve his image* **5 badly off** poor

badminton *n* a game played with rackets and a shuttlecock which is hit back and forth across a high net
WORD ORIGIN *Badminton* House, Glos

Badoglio *n* **Pietro** 1871–1956, Italian marshal; premier (1943–44) following Mussolini's downfall: arranged an armistice with the Allies (1943)

Baeck *n* **Leo** 1873–1956, German Jewish theologian: a leader of the German Jews during the Nazi period. His major work is *The Essence of Judaism* (1905)

Baeyer *n* **Johann Friedrich Wilhelm Adolf von** 1835–1917, German chemist, noted for the synthesis of indigo: Nobel prize for chemistry 1905

Baez *n* **Joan** born 1941, US rock and folk singer and songwriter, noted for the pure quality of her voice and for her committed pacifist and protest songs

BAF British Athletics Federation

Bafana bafana (bah-fan-na) *pl n* *S African* the South African national soccer team
WORD ORIGIN from Nguni (language group of southern Africa) *bafana* the boys

THESAURUS

counteraction, retroaction

backward *adj* **2a = underdeveloped**, undeveloped **2b = slow**, behind, stupid, retarded, deficient, underdeveloped, subnormal, half-witted, behindhand, slow-witted, intellectually handicapped *(Austral)*

backwards *or* **backward** *adv* **1, 2 = towards the rear**, behind you, in reverse, rearwards

bacteria *pl n* **= microorganisms**, viruses, bugs *(slang)*, germs, microbes, pathogens, bacilli

bad *adj* **1 = inferior**, poor, inadequate, pathetic, faulty, duff *(Brit informal)*, unsatisfactory, mediocre, defective, second-class, deficient, imperfect, second-rate, shoddy, low-grade, erroneous, substandard, low-rent *(informal, chiefly US)*, two-bit *(US & Canad slang)*, crappy *(slang)*, end-of-the-pier *(Brit informal)*, poxy *(slang)*, dime-a-dozen *(informal)*, bush-league *(Austral & NZ informal)*, tinhorn *(US slang)*, half-pie *(NZ informal)*, bodger *or* bodgie *(Austral slang)*, strictly for the birds *(informal)* **OPPOSITE:** satisfactory **2 = incompetent**, poor, useless, incapable, unfit, inexpert **3 = harmful**, damaging, dangerous, disastrous, destructive, unhealthy, detrimental, hurtful, ruinous, deleterious, injurious, disadvantageous **OPPOSITE:** beneficial **4 = wicked**, criminal, evil, corrupt, worthless, base, vile, immoral, delinquent, sinful, depraved, debased, amoral, egregious, villainous, unprincipled, iniquitous, nefarious, dissolute, maleficent **OPPOSITE:** virtuous **5 = naughty**, defiant, perverse, wayward, mischievous, wicked, unruly, impish, undisciplined, roguish, disobedient **OPPOSITE:** well-behaved **6 = rotten**, off, rank, sour, rancid, mouldy, fetid, putrid, festy *(Austral slang)* **10 = unfavourable**, troubling, distressing, unfortunate, grim, discouraging, unpleasant, gloomy, adverse

badge *n* **1 = image**, brand, stamp, identification, crest, emblem, insignia **2 = mark**, sign, token

badger *vb* **2 = pester**, worry, harry, bother, bug *(informal)*, bully, plague, hound, get at, harass, nag, hassle *(informal)*, chivvy, importune, bend someone's ear *(informal)*, be on someone's back *(slang)*

badly *adv* **1 = poorly**, incorrectly, carelessly, inadequately, erroneously, imperfectly, ineptly, shoddily, defectively, faultily **OPPOSITE:** well **2 = unfavourably**, unsuccessfully **3 = severely**, greatly, deeply, seriously, gravely, desperately, sorely, dangerously, intensely, painfully, acutely, exceedingly

DICTIONARY

baffle ❶ *vb* **-fling, -fled** 1 to perplex ▷*n* 2 a mechanical device to limit or regulate the flow of fluid, light, or sound **bafflement** *n* **baffling** *adj*
WORD ORIGIN origin unknown

bag ❶ *n* 1 a flexible container with an opening at one end 2 the contents of such a container 3 a piece of luggage 4 a handbag. 5 a loose fold of skin under the eyes 6 any sac in the body of an animal 7 *offensive slang* an ugly or bad-tempered woman: *an old bag* 8 the amount of game taken by a hunter 9 **in the bag** *slang* assured of succeeding ▷*vb* **bagging, bagged** 10 to put into a bag 11 to bulge or cause to bulge 12 to capture or kill, as in hunting 13 *informal* to succeed in securing: *he bagged the best chair* ▸See also **bags**
WORD ORIGIN probably Old Norse *baggi*

bagatelle *n* 1 something of little value 2 a board game in which balls are struck into holes 3 a short piece of music
WORD ORIGIN French

Bagehot *n* **Walter** 1826–77, English economist and journalist: editor of *The Economist*; author of *The English Constitution* (1867) *Physics and Politics* (1872), and *Lombard Street* (1873)

bagel (bay-gl) *n* a hard ring-shaped bread roll
WORD ORIGIN Yiddish *beygel*

baggage ❶ *n* 1 suitcases packed for a journey 2 an army's portable equipment 3 *informal* previous knowledge or experience that may have an influence in new circumstances: *cultural baggage*
WORD ORIGIN Old French *bagage*

baggy ❶ *adj* **-gier, -giest** (of clothes) hanging loosely **bagginess** *n*

bag lady *n* a homeless woman who carries around all her possessions in shopping bags

Bagnold *n* **Enid** (**Algerine**) 1889–1981, British novelist and playwright; her works include the novel *National Velvet* (1935) and the play *The Chalk Garden* (1955)

bagpipes *pl n* a musical wind instrument in which sounds are produced in reed pipes by air from an inflated bag

bags *pl n* 1 *informal* a lot ▷*interj* 2 Also: **bags I** *children's slang Brit & NZ* an indication of the desire to do, be, or have something

bah *interj* an expression of contempt or disgust

Baha'ullah *n* title of *Mirza Hosein Ali*. 1817–92, Persian religious leader: originally a Shiite Muslim, later a disciple of the Bab: founder of the Baha'í Faith

bail[1] ❶ *law n* 1 a sum of money deposited with the court as security for a person's reappearance in court 2 the person giving such security 3 **jump bail** to fail to reappear in court after bail has been paid 4 **stand** *or* **go bail** to act as surety for someone ▷*vb* 5 (foll. by *out*) to obtain the release of (a person) from custody by depositing money with the court
WORD ORIGIN Old French: custody

bail[2] *or* **bale** *vb* **bail out** to remove water from (a boat) ▸See also **bail out**
WORD ORIGIN Old French *baille* bucket

bail[3] *n* 1 *cricket* either of two small wooden bars across the tops of the stumps 2 a partition between stalls in a stable or barn 3 *Austral & NZ* a framework in a cow shed used to secure the head of a cow during milking 4 a movable bar on a typewriter that holds the paper against the roller
WORD ORIGIN Old French *baile* stake

bailey *n* the outermost wall or court of a castle
WORD ORIGIN Old French *baille* enclosed court

Bailey *n* 1 **David** born 1938, English photographer 2 **Nathan** *or* **Nathaniel** died 1742, English lexicographer: compiler of *An Universal Etymological English Dictionary* (1721–27)

Bailey bridge *n* a temporary bridge that can be rapidly assembled
WORD ORIGIN after Sir Donald Coleman *Bailey*, its designer

bailiff *n* 1 *Brit* a sheriff's officer who serves writs and summonses 2 the agent of a landlord or landowner
WORD ORIGIN Old French *baillif*

bailiwick *n* 1 *law* the area over which a bailiff has power 2 a person's special field of interest
WORD ORIGIN *bailie* magistrate + obsolete *wick* district

Baillie *n* Dame **Isobel** 1895–1983, British soprano

bail out ❶ *or* **bale out** *vb* 1 *informal* to help (a person or organization) out of a predicament 2 to make an emergency parachute jump from an aircraft

bail up *vb* 1 *Austral & NZ informal* to confine (a cow) or (of a cow) to be confined by the head in a bail ▸See **bail**[3]. 2 *Austral history* (of a bushranger) to hold under guard in order to rob 3 *Austral* to submit to robbery without offering resistance 4 *Austral informal* to accost or detain, esp. in conversation; buttonhole

Bainbridge *n* **Beryl** 1934–2010, British novelist and playwright. Novels include *The Dressmaker* (1973), *Injury Time* (1977), *Master Georgie* (1998), and *According to Queeney* (2001)

bain-marie (ban-mar-ee) *n, pl* **bains-marie** a container for holding hot water, in which sauces and other dishes are gently cooked or kept warm
WORD ORIGIN French: bath of Mary

bairn *n Scot & N English* a child
WORD ORIGIN Old English *bearn*

Bairnsfather *n* **Bruce** 1888–1959, British cartoonist, born in India: best known for his cartoons of the war in the trenches during World War I

bait ❶ *n* 1 something edible fixed to a hook or in a trap to attract fish or animals 2 an enticement ▷*vb* 3 to put a piece of food on or in (a hook or trap) 4 to persecute or tease 5 to set dogs upon (a bear or badger)
WORD ORIGIN Old Norse *beita* to hunt

baize *n* a feltlike woollen fabric, usually green, which is used for the tops of billiard and card tables
WORD ORIGIN Old French *bai* reddish-brown

THESAURUS

baffle *vb* **1 = puzzle**, beat *(slang)*, amaze, confuse, stump, bewilder, astound, elude, confound, perplex, disconcert, mystify, flummox, boggle the mind of, dumbfound
OPPOSITE: explain

bag *n* **1 = sack**, container, poke *(Scot)*, sac, receptacle ▷*vb* **12 = catch**, get, kill, shoot, capture, acquire, trap **13 = get**, take, land, score *(slang)*, gain, pick up, capture, acquire, get hold of, come by, procure, make sure of, win possession of

baggage *n* **1 = luggage**, things, cases, bags, equipment, gear, trunks, suitcases, belongings, paraphernalia, accoutrements, impedimenta

baggy *adj* **= loose**, hanging, slack, loosened, bulging, not fitting, sagging, sloppy, floppy, billowing, roomy, slackened, ill-fitting, droopy, oversize, not tight OPPOSITE: tight

bail[1] *n* **1** *(law)* **= security**, bond, guarantee, pledge, warranty, surety, guaranty

bail out *vb* **1 = save**, help, free, release, aid, deliver, recover, rescue, get out, relieve, liberate, salvage, set free, save the life of, extricate, save (someone's) bacon *(Brit informal)*

bait *n* **2 = lure**, attraction, incentive, carrot *(informal)*, temptation, bribe, magnet, snare, inducement, decoy, carrot and stick, enticement, allurement ▷*vb* **4 = tease**, provoke, annoy, irritate, guy *(informal)*, bother, needle *(informal)*, plague *(informal)*, mock, rag, rib *(informal)*, wind up *(Brit slang)*, hound, torment, harass, ridicule, taunt, hassle *(informal)*, aggravate *(informal)*, badger, gall, persecute, pester, goad, irk, bedevil, take the mickey out of *(informal)*, chaff, gibe, get on the nerves of

DICTIONARY

b

bake *vb* **baking, baked 1** to cook by dry heat in an oven **2** to cook bread, pastry, or cakes **3** to make or become hardened by heat **4** *informal* to be extremely hot
WORD ORIGIN Old English *bacan*

bakeapple *n* cloudberry

baked beans *pl n* haricot beans, baked and tinned in tomato sauce

Bakelite (bake-a-lite) *n trademark* any of a class of resins used as electric insulators and for making plastics
WORD ORIGIN after L. H. *Baekeland*, inventor

baker *n* a person who makes or sells bread, cakes, etc.

Baker *n* **1** Sir **Benjamin** 1840–1907, British engineer who, with Sir John Fowler, designed and constructed much of the London underground railway, the Forth Railway Bridge, and the first Aswan Dam **2 Chet**, full name *Chesney H. Baker*. 1929–88, US jazz trumpeter and singer **3** Dame **Janet** born 1933, British mezzo-soprano **4** Sir **Samuel White** 1821–93, British explorer: discovered Lake Albert (1864)

baker's dozen *n* thirteen

bakery *n, pl* **-eries** a place where bread, cakes, etc. are made or sold

Bakewell *n* **Robert** 1725–95, English agriculturist; radically improved livestock breeding, esp. of cattle and sheep

baking powder *n* a powdered mixture that contains sodium bicarbonate and cream of tartar: used in baking as a raising agent

bakkie ❶ (buck-ee) *n S African* a small truck with an enclosed cab and an open goods area at the back
WORD ORIGIN Afrikaans *bak* container

baksheesh *n* (in some Eastern countries) money given as a tip or present
WORD ORIGIN Persian *bakhshīsh*

Bakst *n* **Leon Nikolayevich** 1866–1924, Russian painter and stage designer, noted particularly for his richly coloured sets for Diaghilev's *Ballet Russe* (1909–21)

Bakunin *n* **Mikhail** 1814–76, Russian anarchist and writer: a prominent member of the First International, expelled from it after conflicts with Marx

Balaclava *or* **Balaclava helmet** *n* a close-fitting woollen hood that covers the ears and neck
WORD ORIGIN after *Balaklava*, in the Crimea

Balaguer *n* **Joaquin** 1907–2002, Dominican statesman; president of the Dominican Republic (1960–62, 1966–78, 1986–96)

Balakirev *n* **Mily Alexeyevich** 1837–1910, Russian composer, whose works include two symphonic poems, two symphonies, and many arrangements of Russian folk songs

balalaika *n* a Russian musical instrument with a triangular body and three strings
WORD ORIGIN Russian

balance ❶ *n* **1** stability of mind or body: *lose one's balance* **2** a state of being in balance **3** harmony in the parts of a whole **4** the power to influence or control: *the balance of power* **5** something that remains: *the balance of what you owe* **6** *accounting* **a** the matching of debit and credit totals in an account **b** a difference between such totals **7** a weighing device **8 in the balance** in an undecided condition **9 on balance** after weighing up all the factors ▷ *vb* **-ancing, -anced 10** to weigh in or as if in a balance **11** to be or come into equilibrium **12** to bring into or hold in equilibrium **13** to compare the relative weight or importance of **14** to arrange so as to create a state of harmony **15** *accounting* to compare or equalize the credit and debit totals of (an account)
WORD ORIGIN Latin *bilanx* having two scales

balance of payments *n* the difference in value between a nation's total payments to foreign countries and its total receipts from foreign countries

balance of power *n* the equal distribution of military and economic power among countries

balance of trade *n* the difference in value between exports and imports of goods

balance sheet *n* a statement that shows the financial position of a business

Balbo *n* **Italo** 1896–1940, Italian Fascist politician and airman: minister of aviation (1929–33)

Balcon *n* Sir **Michael** 1896–1977, British film producer; his films made at Ealing Studios include the comedies *Kind Hearts and Coronets* (1949) and *The Lavender Hill Mob* (1951)

balcony ❶ *n, pl* **-nies 1** a platform projecting from a building with a balustrade along its outer edge, often with access from a door **2** an upper tier of seats in a theatre or cinema
WORD ORIGIN Italian *balcone*

bald ❶ *adj* **1** having no hair or fur, esp. of a man having no hair on the scalp **2** lacking natural covering **3** plain or blunt: *the bald facts* **4** (of a tyre) having a worn tread **baldly** *adv* **baldness** *n*
WORD ORIGIN Middle English *ballede*

balderdash *n* stupid or illogical talk
WORD ORIGIN origin unknown

balding *adj* becoming bald

Baldwin I *n* 1058–1118, crusader and first king of Jerusalem (1100–18), who captured Acre (1104), Beirut (1109), and Sidon (1110)

bale[1] *n* **1** a large bundle of hay or goods bound by ropes or wires for storage or transportation ▷ *vb* **baling, baled 2** to make (hay) or put (goods) into a bale or bales
WORD ORIGIN Old High German *balla* ball

bale[2] *vb* **baling, baled** ▸ same as **bail**[2]

baleen *n* whalebone
WORD ORIGIN Latin *balaena* whale

baleen whale *n* ▸ same as **whalebone whale**

baleful *adj* harmful, menacing, or vindictive **balefully** *adv*

Balenciaga *n* **Cristobal** 1895–1972, Spanish couturier

bale out *vb* ▸ same as **bail out**

Baliol *or* **Balliol** *n* **1 Edward** ?1283–1364, king of Scotland (1332, 1333–56) **2** his father, **John** 1249–1315, king of Scotland (1292–96): defeated and imprisoned by Edward I of England (1296)

balk *or* **baulk** *vb* **1** to stop short: *the horse balked at the jump* **2** to recoil: *France balked at the parliament having a veto* **3** to thwart, check, or foil: *he was balked in his plans*

THESAURUS

(informal), nark *(Brit, Austral & NZ slang)*, be on the back of *(slang)*, get in the hair of *(informal)*, get *or* take a rise out of, hack you off *(informal)*

bakkie *n (S African)* = **truck**, pick-up, van, lorry, pick-up truck

balance *n* **1a = equilibrium**, stability, steadiness, evenness, equipoise, counterpoise **OPPOSITE:** instability **1b = composure**, stability, restraint, self-control, poise, self-discipline, coolness, calmness, equanimity, self-restraint, steadiness, self-possession, self-mastery, strength of mind *or* will **2 = stability**, equanimity, constancy, steadiness **5, 6b = remainder**, rest, difference, surplus, residue ▷ *vb* **10, 13 = weigh**, consider, compare, estimate, contrast, assess, evaluate, set against, juxtapose **12 = stabilize**, level, steady **OPPOSITE:** overbalance **15** *(accounting)* **= calculate**, rate, judge, total, determine, estimate, settle, count, square, reckon, work out, compute, gauge, tally

balcony *n* **1 = terrace**, veranda **2 = upper circle**, gods, gallery

bald *adj* **1 = hairless**, bare, shorn, clean-shaven, tonsured, depilated, glabrous *(biology)*, baldheaded, baldpated **3 = plain**, direct, simple, straight, frank, severe, bare, straightforward, blunt, rude, outright, downright, forthright,

DICTIONARY

WORD ORIGIN Old English *balca* ridge

Balkan *adj* of any of the countries of the Balkan Peninsula in SE Europe, between the Adriatic and Aegean Seas

ball[1] ❶ *n* **1** a spherical or nearly spherical mass: *a ball of wool* **2** a round or roundish object used in various games **3** a single delivery of the ball in a game **4** any more or less rounded part of the body: *the ball of the foot* **5 have the ball at one's feet** to have the chance of doing something **6 on the ball** *informal* alert; informed **7 play ball** *informal* to cooperate **8 set** *or* **keep the ball rolling** to initiate or maintain the progress of an action, discussion, or project ▹ *vb* **9** to form into a ball ▸ See also **balls, balls-up**
WORD ORIGIN Old Norse *böllr*

ball[2] *n* **1** a lavish or formal social function for dancing **2 have a ball** *informal* to have a very enjoyable time
WORD ORIGIN Late Latin *ballare* to dance

ballad *n* **1** a narrative song or poem often with a chorus that is repeated **2** a slow sentimental song
WORD ORIGIN Old Provençal *balada* song accompanying a dance

ballade *n* **1** *prosody* a verse form consisting of three stanzas and an envoy, all ending with the same line **2** *music* a romantic instrumental composition

Ballance *n* **John** 1839–93, New Zealand statesman, born in Northern Ireland: prime minister of New Zealand (1891–93)

ball-and-socket joint *n anat* a joint in which a rounded head fits into a rounded cavity, allowing a wide range of movement

Ballantyne *n* **R(obert) M(ichael)** 1825–94, British author, noted for such adventure stories as *The Coral Island* (1857)

Ballard *n* **J(ames) G(raham)** 1930–2009, British novelist, born in China; his books include *Crash* (1973), *The Unlimited Dream Company* (1979), *Empire of the Sun* (1984), *Cocaine Nights* (1996), and *Super-Cannes* (2000)

ballast *n* **1** a substance, such as sand, used to stabilize a ship when it is not carrying cargo **2** crushed rock used for the foundation of a road or railway track ▹ *vb* **3** to give stability or weight to
WORD ORIGIN probably Low German

ball bearing *n* **1** an arrangement of steel balls placed between moving parts of a machine in order to reduce friction **2** a metal ball used in such an arrangement

ball boy *or fem* **ball girl** *n* (in tennis) a person who retrieves balls that go out of play

ball cock *n* a device consisting of a floating ball and valve for regulating the flow of liquid into a tank or cistern

ballerina *n* a female ballet dancer
WORD ORIGIN Italian

Ballesteros *n* **Severiano** born 1957, Spanish professional golfer: won the British Open Championship (1979; 1984; 1988)

ballet *n* **1** a classical style of expressive dancing based on precise conventional steps **2** a theatrical representation of a story performed by ballet dancers **balletic** *adj*
WORD ORIGIN Italian *balletto* a little dance

ball game *n* **1** a game played with a ball **2** *US & Canad* a game of baseball **3** *informal* a state of affairs: *a whole new ball game*

Balliol *n* See **Baliol**

ballistic missile *n* a launched weapon which is guided automatically in flight but falls freely at its target

ballistics *n* the study of the flight of projectiles, often in relation to firearms **ballistic** *adj*
WORD ORIGIN Greek *ballein* to throw

ballocks *pl n, interj* ▸ same as **bollocks**

balloon ❶ *n* **1** an inflatable rubber bag used as a plaything or party decoration **2** a large bag inflated with a lighter-than-air gas, designed to rise and float in the atmosphere with a basket for carrying passengers **3** an outline containing the words or thoughts of a character in a cartoon ▹ *vb* **4** to fly in a balloon **5** to swell or increase rapidly in size: *the cost of health care has ballooned* **balloonist** *n*
WORD ORIGIN Italian dialect *ballone* ball

ballot ❶ *n* **1** the practice of selecting a representative or course of action by voting **2** the number of votes cast in an election **3** the actual vote or paper indicating a person's choice ▹ *vb* **-loting, -loted 4** to vote or ask for a vote from: *we balloted the members on this issue* **5** to vote for or decide on something by ballot
WORD ORIGIN Italian *ballotta* a little ball

ballot box *n* a box into which voting papers are dropped on completion

ballot paper *n* a paper used for voting

ballpark *n* **1** *US & Canad* a stadium used for baseball games **2** *informal* approximate range: *in the right ballpark*

ballpoint *or* **ballpoint pen** *n* a pen which has a small ball bearing as a writing point

ballroom *n* a large hall for dancing

ballroom dancing *n* social dancing in couples to music in conventional rhythms, such as the waltz

balls *pl n taboo slang* **1** the testicles **2** nonsense **3** courage and determination **ballsy** *adj*

balls-up *taboo slang n* **1** something botched or muddled ▹ *vb* **balls up 2** to muddle or botch

bally *adj, adv Brit, old-fashioned slang* extreme or extremely: *a bally nuisance; he's too bally charming for his own good*

ballyhoo *n informal* unnecessary or exaggerated fuss
WORD ORIGIN origin unknown

balm *n* **1** an aromatic substance obtained from certain tropical trees and used for healing and soothing **2** something comforting or soothing: *her calmness was like a balm to my troubled mind* **3** an aromatic herb, lemon balm
WORD ORIGIN Latin *balsamum* balsam

Balmain *n* **Pierre Alexandre** 1914–82, French couturier

Balmer *n* **Johann Jakob** 1825–98, Swiss mathematician; discovered (1885) a formula giving the wavelengths of a series of lines in the hydrogen spectrum (the **Balmer series**)

balmy *adj* **balmier, balmiest 1** (of weather) mild and pleasant **2** ▸ same as **barmy**

baloney *or* **boloney** *n informal* nonsense
WORD ORIGIN *Bologna* (sausage)

balsa (**bawl**-sa) *n* **1** a tree of tropical America which yields light wood **2** Also: **balsawood** the light wood of this tree, used for making rafts, models, etc.
WORD ORIGIN Spanish: raft

balsam *n* **1** an aromatic resin obtained from various trees and shrubs and used in medicines and perfumes **2** any plant yielding balsam **3** a flowering plant, such as busy lizzie
WORD ORIGIN Greek *balsamon*

Balthus *n* real name *Balthasar Klossowski de Rola*. 1908–2001, French painter of Polish descent, noted esp. for his paintings of adolescent girls

balti (**boll**-ti, **bahl**-ti) *n* a spicy Indian dish served in a metal dish
WORD ORIGIN probably from the *Baltistan* region of Pakistan

Baltic (**bawl**-tik) *adj* of the Baltic Sea in N Europe or the states bordering it

THESAURUS

unadorned, unvarnished, straight from the shoulder

ball[1] *n* **1 = sphere**, drop, globe, pellet, orb, globule, spheroid

balloon *vb* **5 = expand**, rise, increase, extend, swell, blow up, enlarge, inflate, bulge, billow, dilate, be inflated, puff out, become larger, distend, bloat, grow rapidly

ballot *n* **1 = vote**, election, voting, poll, polling, referendum, show of hands

b

DICTIONARY

b

Baltimore[1] *n* a port in N Maryland, on Chesapeake Bay. Pop: Pop: 628 670 (2003 est)

Baltimore[2] *n* **1 David** born 1938, US molecular biologist: shared the Nobel prize for physiology or medicine (1975) for his discovery of reverse transcriptase **2 Lord** ▸ See **Calvert** (sense 1)

baluster *n* a set of posts supporting a rail
WORD ORIGIN French *balustre*

balustrade *n* an ornamental rail supported by a set of posts
WORD ORIGIN French

bamboo *n* a tall treelike tropical grass with hollow stems which are used to make canes, furniture, etc.
WORD ORIGIN probably from Malay *bambu*

bamboozle *vb* **-zling, -zled** *informal* **1** to cheat; mislead **2** to confuse **bamboozlement** *n*
WORD ORIGIN origin unknown

ban ⓣ *vb* **banning, banned 1** to prohibit or forbid officially ▹ *n* **2** an official prohibition
WORD ORIGIN Old English *bannan* to proclaim

banal (ban-**nahl**) *adj* lacking originality **banality** *n*
WORD ORIGIN Old French: common to all

banana *n* a crescent-shaped fruit that grows on a tropical or subtropical treelike plant
WORD ORIGIN Spanish or Portuguese, of African origin

banana republic *n informal* a small politically unstable country whose economy is dominated by foreign interests

band[1] ⓣ *n* **1** a group of musicians playing together, esp. on brass or percussion instruments **2** a group of people having a common purpose: *a band of revolutionaries* ▹ *vb* **3** (foll. by *together*) to unite
WORD ORIGIN French *bande*

band[2] ⓣ *n* **1** a strip of some material, used to hold objects together: *a rubber band* **2** a strip of fabric used as an ornament or to reinforce clothing **3** a stripe of contrasting colour or texture **4** a driving belt in machinery **5** *physics* a range of frequencies or wavelengths between two limits ▹ *vb* **6** to fasten or mark with a band
WORD ORIGIN Old French *bende*

bandage ⓣ *n* **1** a piece of material used to dress a wound or wrap an injured limb ▹ *vb* **-aging, -aged 2** to cover or wrap with a bandage
WORD ORIGIN French *bande* strip

bandanna *or* **bandana** *n* a large brightly-coloured handkerchief or neckerchief
WORD ORIGIN Hindi *bāndhnū* tie-dyeing

Bandaranaike *n* **1 Chandrika** ▸ See **Kumaratunge 2 Sirimavo** 1916–2000, prime minister of Sri Lanka, formerly Ceylon (1960–65; 1970–77; 1994–2000); the world's first woman prime minister **3** her husband, **Solomon** 1899–1959, prime minister of Ceylon (1956–59); assassinated

B & B bed and breakfast

bandbox *n* a lightweight usually cylindrical box for hats

bandeau (ban-doe) *n, pl* **-deaux** (-doze) a narrow ribbon worn round the head
WORD ORIGIN French

banderole *n* **1** a narrow flag usually with forked ends **2** a ribbon-like scroll bearing an inscription
WORD ORIGIN Old French

bandicoot *n* **1** an Australian marsupial with a long pointed muzzle and a long tail **2 bandicoot rat** any of three burrowing rats of S and SE Asia
WORD ORIGIN Telugu (language of SE India) *pandikokku*

bandit ⓣ *n* a robber, esp. a member of an armed gang **banditry** *n*
WORD ORIGIN Italian *bandito*

bandmaster *n* the conductor of a band

bandolier *n* a shoulder belt with small pockets for cartridges
WORD ORIGIN Old French *bandouliere*

band saw *n* a power-operated saw consisting of an endless toothed metal band running over two wheels

bandsman *n, pl* **-men** a player in a musical band

bandstand *n* a roofed outdoor platform for a band

bandwagon *n* **jump** *or* **climb on the bandwagon** to join a popular party or movement that seems assured of success

bandwidth *n* the range of frequencies used for transmitting electronic information

bandy *adj* **-dier, -diest 1** Also: **bandy-legged** having legs curved outwards at the knees **2** (of legs) curved outwards at the knees ▹ *vb* **-dies, -dying, -died 3** to exchange (words), sometimes in a heated manner **4 bandy about** to use (a name, term, etc.) frequently
WORD ORIGIN probably from Old French *bander* to hit back and forth

bane *n* a person or thing that causes misery or distress: *the bane of my life* **baneful** *adj*
WORD ORIGIN Old English *bana*

bang ⓣ *n* **1** a short loud explosive noise, such as the report of a gun **2** a hard blow or loud knock **3** *taboo slang* an act of sexual intercourse **4 with a bang** successfully: *the party went with a bang* ▹ *vb* **5** to hit or knock, esp. with a loud noise **6** to close (a door) noisily **7** to make or cause to make a loud noise, as of an explosion **8** *taboo slang* to have sexual intercourse with ▹ *adv* **9** with a sudden impact: *the car drove bang into a lamppost* **10** precisely: *bang in the middle*
WORD ORIGIN Old Norse *bang, banga* hammer

banger *n* **1** *Austral & Brit informal* an old decrepit car **2** *slang* a sausage **3** a firework that explodes loudly

Bangladeshi *adj* **1** of Bangladesh ▹ *n* **2** a person from Bangladesh

bangle *n* a bracelet worn round the

THESAURUS

ban *vb* **1a = prohibit**, black, bar, block, restrict, veto, forbid, boycott, suppress, outlaw, banish, disallow, proscribe, debar, blackball, interdict **OPPOSITE:** permit
1b = bar, prohibit, exclude, forbid, disqualify, preclude, debar, declare ineligible ▹ *n* **2 = prohibition**, block, restriction, veto, boycott, embargo, injunction, censorship, taboo, suppression, stoppage, disqualification, interdiction, interdict, proscription, disallowance, rahui (*NZ*), restraining order (*US*) (*law*) **OPPOSITE:** permission

band[1] *n* **1 = ensemble**, group, orchestra, combo **2 = gang**, company, group, set, party, team, lot, club, body, association, crowd, troop, pack, camp, squad, crew (*informal*), assembly, mob, horde, troupe, posse (*informal*), clique, coterie, bevy

band[2] *n* **2 = headband**, tie, strip, ribbon, fillet

bandage *n* **1 = dressing**, plaster, compress, gauze ▹ *vb* **2 = dress**, cover, bind, swathe

bandit *n* **= robber**, gunman, crook, outlaw, pirate, raider, gangster, plunderer, mugger (*informal*), hijacker, looter, highwayman, racketeer, desperado, marauder, brigand, freebooter, footpad

bang *n* **1 = explosion**, report, shot, pop, clash, crack, blast, burst, boom, slam, discharge, thump, clap, thud, clang, peal, detonation **2 = blow**, hit, box, knock, stroke, punch, belt (*informal*), rap, bump, bash (*informal*), sock (*slang*), smack, thump, buffet, clout (*informal*), cuff, clump (*slang*), whack, wallop (*informal*), slosh (*Brit slang*), tonk (*informal*), clomp (*slang*) ▹ *vb* **5** (*often with* **on**) **= hit**, pound, beat, strike, crash, knock, belt (*informal*), hammer, slam, rap, bump, bash (*informal*), thump, clatter, pummel, tonk (*informal*), beat *or* knock seven bells out of (*informal*)
7 = resound, beat, crash, burst, boom, echo, drum, explode, thunder, thump, throb, thud, clang ▹ *adv* **10 = exactly**, just, straight, square, squarely, precisely, slap, smack,

DICTIONARY

arm or sometimes round the ankle
WORD ORIGIN Hindi *bangrī*

banian *n* ▸ same as **banyan**

banish ❶ *vb* **1** to send into exile **2** to drive away: *it's the only way to banish weeds from the garden* **banishment** *n*
WORD ORIGIN Old French *banir*

banisters *or* **bannisters** *pl n* the railing and supporting balusters on a staircase
WORD ORIGIN altered from BALUSTER

banjo *n, pl* **-jos** *or* **-joes** a stringed musical instrument with a long neck and a circular drumlike body **banjoist** *n*
WORD ORIGIN US pronunciation of earlier *bandore*

bank[1] ❶ *n* **1** an institution offering services, such as the safekeeping and lending of money at interest **2** the building used by such an institution **3** the funds held by a banker or dealer in some gambling games **4** any supply, store, or reserve: *a data bank* ▹ *vb* **5** to deposit (cash or a cheque) in a bank **6** to transact business with a bank ▸ See also **bank on**
WORD ORIGIN probably from Italian *banca* bench, moneychanger's table

bank[2] ❶ *n* **1** a long raised mass, esp. of earth **2** a slope, as of a hill **3** the sloping side and ground on either side of a river ▹ *vb* **4** to form into a bank or mound **5** to cover (a fire) with ashes and fuel so that it will burn slowly **6** (of an aircraft) to tip to one side in turning
WORD ORIGIN Scandinavian

bank[3] ❶ *n* **1** an arrangement of similar objects in a row or in tiers ▹ *vb* **2** to arrange in a bank
WORD ORIGIN Old French *banc* bench

bankable *adj* likely to ensure financial success: *a bankable star* **bankability** *n*

bank account *n* an arrangement whereby a customer deposits money at a bank and may withdraw it when it is needed

bank card *n* any plastic card issued by a bank, such as a cash card or a cheque card

banker[1] *n* **1** a person who owns or manages a bank **2** the keeper of the bank in various gambling games

banker[2] *n Austral & NZ informal* a stream almost overflowing its banks: *the creek was running a banker*

banker's order *n* ▸ same as **standing order** (sense 1)

Bankhead *n* **Tallulah** (**Brockman**) 1902–68, US stage and film actress; her successes included the plays *The Little Foxes* (1939) and *The Skin of Our Teeth* (1942)

bank holiday *n* (in Britain) a public holiday when banks are closed by law

banking *n* the business engaged in by a bank

banknote *n* a piece of paper money issued by a central bank

bank on *vb* to rely on

bankrupt ❶ *n* **1** a person, declared by a court to be unable to pay his or her debts, whose property is sold and the proceeds distributed among the creditors **2** a person no longer having a particular quality: *a spiritual bankrupt* ▹ *adj* **3** declared insolvent **4** financially ruined **5** no longer having a particular quality: *morally bankrupt* ▹ *vb* **6** to make bankrupt **bankruptcy** *n*
WORD ORIGIN Old Italian *banca* BANK[1] + *rotta* broken

banksia *n* an Australian evergreen tree or shrub

banner ❶ *n* **1** a long strip of material displaying a slogan, advertisement, etc. **2** a placard carried in a demonstration **3** Also called: **banner headline** a large headline in a newspaper extending across the page **4** an advertisement, often animated, that extends across the width of a web page
WORD ORIGIN Old French *baniere*

bannock *n Scot* a round flat cake made from oatmeal or barley
WORD ORIGIN Old English *bannuc*

banns *pl n* the public announcement of an intended marriage
WORD ORIGIN plural of obsolete *bann* proclamation

banquet ❶ *n* **1** an elaborate formal dinner often followed by speeches ▹ *vb* **-queting, -queted 2** to hold or take part in a banquet
WORD ORIGIN Italian *banco* a table

banshee *n* (in Irish folklore) a female spirit whose wailing warns of a coming death
WORD ORIGIN Irish Gaelic *bean sídhe* woman of the fairy mound

bantam *n* **1** a small breed of domestic fowl **2** a small but aggressive person
WORD ORIGIN after *Bantam*, village in Java, said to be the original home of this fowl

bantamweight *n* a professional boxer weighing up to 118 lb (53.5 kg) or an amateur weighing up to 119 lb (54 kg)

banter *vb* **1** to tease jokingly ▹ *n* **2** teasing or joking conversation
WORD ORIGIN origin unknown

Banting *n* Sir **Frederick Grant** 1891–1941, Canadian physiologist: discovered the insulin treatment for diabetes with Best and Macleod (1922) and shared the Nobel prize for physiology or medicine with Macleod (1923)

Bantock *n* Sir **Granville** 1868–1946, British composer. His works include the *Hebridean Symphony* (1915), five ballets, and three operas

Bantu *n* **1** a group of languages of Africa **2** *pl* **-tu** *or* **-tus** *offensive* a Black speaker of a Bantu language ▹ *adj* **3** of the Bantu languages or the peoples who speak them
WORD ORIGIN Bantu *Ba-ntu* people

Bantustan *n offensive* formerly, an area in South Africa reserved for occupation by a Black African people. Official name: **homeland**
WORD ORIGIN *Bantu* + Hindi *-stan* country of

Banville *n* **Théodore de** 1823–91, French poet, who anticipated the Parnassian school in his perfection of form and command of rhythm

banyan *or* **banian** *n* an Indian tree whose branches grow down into the soil forming additional trunks
WORD ORIGIN Hindi *baniyā*

baobab (bay-oh-bab) *n* an African tree with a massive grey trunk, short angular branches, and large pulpy fruit
WORD ORIGIN probably from a

THESAURUS

plumb (*informal*)

banish *vb* **1 = expel**, transport, exile, outlaw, deport, drive away, expatriate, excommunicate
OPPOSITE: admit
2 = get rid of, remove, eliminate, eradicate, shake off, dislodge, see the back of

bank[1] *n* **1 = financial institution**, repository, depository **4 = store**, fund, stock, source, supply, reserve, pool, reservoir, accumulation, stockpile, hoard, storehouse ▹ *vb* **5 = deposit**, keep, save

bank[2] *n* **2 = mound**, banking, rise, hill, mass, pile, heap, ridge, dune, embankment, knoll, hillock, kopje *or* koppie (*S African*) **3 = side**, edge, margin, shore, brink, lakeside, waterside ▹ *vb* **6 = tilt**, tip, pitch, heel, slope, incline, slant, cant, camber

bank[3] *n* **1 = row**, group, line, train, range, series, file, rank, arrangement, sequence, succession, array, tier

bankrupt *adj* **3, 4 = insolvent**, broke (*informal*), spent, ruined, wiped out (*informal*), impoverished, beggared, in the red, on the rocks, destitute, gone bust (*informal*), in receivership, gone to the wall, in the hands of the receivers, on your uppers, in queer street (*informal*)
OPPOSITE: solvent

banner *n* **1 = flag**, standard, colours, jack, pennant, ensign, streamer, pennon **2 = placard**

banquet *n* **1 = feast**, spread (*informal*), dinner, meal, entertainment, revel, blowout (*slang*), repast, slap-up meal (*Brit informal*), hakari (*NZ*)

DICTIONARY

native African word

bap *n Brit* a large soft bread roll
WORD ORIGIN origin unknown

baptism *n* a Christian religious rite in which a person is immersed in or sprinkled with water as a sign of being cleansed from sin and accepted as a member of the Church **baptismal** *adj*

baptism of fire *n* **1** any introductory ordeal **2** a soldier's first experience of battle

Baptist *n* **1** a member of a Protestant denomination that believes in the necessity of adult baptism by immersion **2 the Baptist** John the Baptist ▷*adj* **3** of the Baptist Church

baptize *or* **-tise** *vb* **-tizing, -tized** *or* **-tising, -tised 1** *Christianity* to immerse (a person) in water or sprinkle water on (him or her) as part of the rite of baptism **2** to give a name to
WORD ORIGIN Greek *baptein* to bathe, dip

bar[1] ❶ *n* **1** a rigid usually straight length of metal, wood, etc. used as a barrier or structural part **2** a solid usually rectangular block of any material: *a bar of soap* **3** anything that obstructs or prevents: *a bar to women's mobility* **4** a counter or room where alcoholic drinks are served **5** a narrow band or stripe, as of colour or light **6** a heating element in an electric fire **7** ▸see **Bar 8** the place in a court of law where the accused stands during trial **9** *music* a group of beats that is repeated with a consistent rhythm throughout a piece of music **10** *football, etc.* ▸same as **crossbar 11** *heraldry* a narrow horizontal line across a shield **12 behind bars** in prison ▷*vb* **barring, barred 13** to secure with a bar: *to bar the door* **14** to obstruct: *the fallen tree barred the road* **15** to exclude: *he was barred from membership of the club* **16** to mark with a bar or bars ▷*prep* **17** except for
WORD ORIGIN Old French *barre*

bar[2] *n* a unit of pressure equal to 10^5 newtons per square metre
WORD ORIGIN Greek *baros* weight

Bar *n* **1 the Bar** barristers collectively **2 be called to the Bar** *Brit* to become a barrister

barachois *n* (in the Atlantic Provinces of Canada) a shallow lagoon formed by a sand bar

Barak *n* **Ehud** born 1942, Israeli Labour politician, prime minister (1999–2001)

Bárány *n* **Robert** 1876–1936, Austrian physician; devised the **Bárány test**, which detects diseases of the semicircular canals of the inner ear: Nobel prize for physiology or medicine 1914

barb *n* **1** a cutting remark **2** a point facing in the opposite direction to the main point of a fish-hook, harpoon, etc. **3** a beardlike growth, hair, or projection ▷*vb* **4** to provide with a barb or barbs **barbed** *adj*
WORD ORIGIN Latin *barba* beard

barbarian ❶ *n* **1** a member of a primitive or uncivilized people **2** a coarse or vicious person ▷*adj* **3** uncivilized or brutal

barbaric *adj* primitive or brutal

barbarism *n* **1** a brutal, coarse, or ignorant act **2** the condition of being backward, coarse, or ignorant **3** a substandard word or expression

barbarity *n, pl* **-ties 1** the state of being barbaric or barbarous **2** a vicious act

Barbarossa *n* **1** the nickname of the Holy Roman Emperor **Frederick I** ▸See **Frederick Barbarossa 2** real name *Khair ed-Din*. *c*. 1465–1546, Turkish pirate and admiral: conquered Tunis for the Ottomans (1534)

barbarous *adj* **1** uncivilized: *a barbarous and uninhabitable jungle* **2** brutal or cruel: *the barbarous tortures inflicted on them*
WORD ORIGIN Greek *barbaros* barbarian, non-Greek

barbecue *n* **1** a grill on which food is cooked over hot charcoal, usually out of doors **2** food cooked over hot charcoal, usually out of doors **3** a party or picnic at which barbecued food is served ▷*vb* **-cuing, -cued 4** to cook on a grill, usually over charcoal
WORD ORIGIN American Spanish *barbacoa* frame made of sticks

barbed wire *n* strong wire with sharp points protruding at close intervals

barbel *n* **1** a long thin growth that hangs from the jaws of certain fishes, such as the carp **2** a freshwater fish with such a growth
WORD ORIGIN Latin *barba* beard

barbell *n* a long metal rod to which heavy discs are attached at each end for weightlifting

barber *n* a person whose business is cutting men's hair and shaving beards
WORD ORIGIN Latin *barba* beard

Barber *n* **Samuel** 1910–81, US composer: his works include an *Adagio for Strings*, adapted from the second movement of his string quartet No. 1 (1936) and the opera *Vanessa* (1958)

Barbera *n* **Joseph** ▸See **Hanna**

barberry *n, pl* **-ries** a shrub with orange or red berries
WORD ORIGIN Arabic *barbāris*

barbican *n* a walled defence to protect a gate or drawbridge of a fortification
WORD ORIGIN Old French *barbacane*

Barbirolli *n* Sir **John** 1899–1970, English conductor of the Hallé Orchestra (1943–68)

barbiturate *n* a derivative of barbituric acid used in medicine as a sedative

barbituric acid *n* a crystalline solid used in the preparation of barbiturate drugs
WORD ORIGIN German *Barbitursäure*

Barbour *n trademark, Brit* a waterproof waxed jacket

Barbour *n* **John** *c*. 1320–95, Scottish poet: author of *The Bruce* (1376), a patriotic epic poem

Barbusse *n* **Henri** 1873–1935, French novelist and poet. His novels include *L'Enfer* (1908) and *Le Feu* (1916), reflecting the horror of World War I

barcarole *or* **barcarolle** *n* **1** a Venetian boat song **2** an instrumental composition resembling this
WORD ORIGIN French

bar chart *or* **graph** *n* a diagram consisting of vertical or horizontal bars whose lengths are proportional to amounts or quantities

Barclay *n* **Alexander** *c*. 1475–1552, English poet. His works include *The Ship of Fools* (1509) and *Eclogues* (*c*. 1513–14)

Barclay de Tolly *n* Prince **Mikhail** 1761–1818, Russian field marshal: commander in chief against Napoleon in 1812

THESAURUS

bar[1] *n* **1 = rod**, staff, stick, stake, rail, pole, paling, shaft, baton, mace, batten, palisade, crosspiece **3 = obstacle**, block, barrier, hurdle, hitch, barricade, snag, deterrent, obstruction, stumbling block, impediment, hindrance, interdict
OPPOSITE: aid
4 = public house, pub *(informal, chiefly Brit)*, counter, inn, local *(Brit informal)*, lounge, saloon, tavern, canteen, watering hole *(facetious, slang)*, boozer *(Brit, Austral & NZ informal)*, beer parlour *(Canad)*, roadhouse, hostelry *(archaic, facetious)*, alehouse *(archaic)*, taproom ▷*vb* **13 = lock**, block, secure, chain, attach, anchor, bolt, blockade, barricade, fortify, fasten, latch, obstruct, make firm, make fast **14 = block**, restrict, hold up, restrain, hamper, thwart, hinder, obstruct, impede, shut off **15 = exclude**, ban, forbid, prohibit, keep out of, disallow, shut out of, ostracize, debar, blackball, interdict, black
OPPOSITE: admit

barbarian *n* **2 = lout**, hooligan, illiterate, vandal, yahoo, bigot, philistine, ned *(Scot slang)*, hoon *(Austral & NZ)*, cougan *(Austral slang)*, scozza *(Austral slang)*, bogan *(Austral slang)*, ruffian, ignoramus, boor, lowbrow, vulgarian

DICTIONARY

bar code *n* an arrangement of numbers and parallel lines on a package, which can be electronically scanned at a checkout to give the price of the goods

bard *n* **1** *archaic or literary* a poet **2 a** (formerly) an ancient Celtic poet **b** a poet who wins a verse competition at a Welsh eisteddfod **3 the Bard** William Shakespeare, English playwright and poet
WORD ORIGIN Scottish Gaelic

bare ❶ *adj* **1** unclothed: used esp. of a part of the body **2** without the natural, conventional, or usual covering: *bare trees* **3** lacking appropriate furnishings, etc.: *a bare room* **4** simple: *the bare facts* **5** just sufficient: *the bare minimum* ▷ *vb* **baring, bared 6** to uncover
bareness *n*
WORD ORIGIN Old English *bær*

bareback *adj, adv* (of horse-riding) without a saddle

bare-faced *or* **barefaced** *adj* obvious or shameless: *a bare-faced lie*

barefoot *or* **barefooted** *adj, adv* with the feet uncovered

bareheaded *adj, adv* with the head uncovered

bare-knuckle *adj* **1** without boxing gloves **2** aggressive and without reservations

barely ❶ *adv* **1** only just: *barely enough* **2** scantily: *barely furnished*

Barenboim *n* **Daniel** born 1942, Israeli concert pianist and conductor, born in Argentina

bargain ❶ *n* **1** an agreement establishing what each party will give, receive, or perform in a transaction **2** something acquired or received in such an agreement **3** something bought or offered at a low price **4 drive a hard bargain** to forcefully pursue one's own profit in a transaction **5 into the bargain** besides ▷ *vb* **6** to negotiate the terms of an agreement or transaction
WORD ORIGIN Old French *bargaigne*

bargain for *vb* to anticipate

bargain on *vb* to rely or depend on

barge ❶ *n* **1** a flat-bottomed boat, used for transporting freight, esp. on canals **2** a boat, often decorated, used in pageants, etc. ▷ *vb* **barging, barged** *informal* **3** (foll. by *into*) to bump into **4** to push one's way violently **5** (foll. by *into* or *in*) to interrupt rudely: *he barged into our conversation*
WORD ORIGIN Medieval Latin *barga*

bargee *n Brit* a person in charge of a barge

bargepole *n* **1** a long pole used to propel a barge **2 not touch with a bargepole** *informal* to refuse to have anything to do with

bariatric *adj* of or relating to the treatment of obesity: *bariatric surgery*
WORD ORIGIN Greek *baros* weight + *iatrikos* of healing

Baring *n* **Evelyn**, 1st Earl of Cromer. 1841–1917, English administrator. As consul general in Egypt with plenipotentiary powers, he controlled the Egyptian government from 1883 to 1907

barista (bar-ee-sta) *n* a person who makes and sells coffee in a coffee bar

baritone *n* **1** the second lowest adult male voice **2** a singer with such a voice
WORD ORIGIN Greek *barus* low + *tonos* tone

barium (bare-ee-um) *n chem* a soft silvery-white metallic chemical element. Symbol: Ba
WORD ORIGIN Greek *barus* heavy

barium meal *n* a preparation of barium sulphate, which is opaque to X-rays, used in X-ray examination of the alimentary canal

bark[1] ❶ *n* **1** the loud harsh cry of a dog or certain other animals ▷ *vb* **2** (of a dog or other animal) to make its typical cry **3** to shout in an angry tone: *he barked an order* **4 bark up the wrong tree** *informal* to misdirect one's attention or efforts
WORD ORIGIN Old English *beorcan*

bark[2] ❶ *n* **1** an outer protective layer of dead corklike cells on the trunks of trees ▷ *vb* **2** to scrape or rub off (skin), as in an injury **3** to remove the bark from (a tree)
WORD ORIGIN Old Norse *börkr*

barker *n* a person at a fairground who loudly addresses passers-by to attract customers

Barker *n* **1 George (Granville)** 1913–91, British poet: author of *Calamiterror* (1937) and *The True Confession of George Barker* (1950) **2 Howard** born 1946, British playwright: his plays include *Claw* (1975), *The Castle* (1985), *A Hard Heart* (1992), and *13 Objects* (2003) **3 Ronnie**, full name *Ronald William George Barker*. 1929–2005, British comedian: known esp. for his partnership with Ronnie Corbett (born 1930) in the TV series *The Two Ronnies* (1971–85)

Barkhausen *n* **Heinrich Georg** 1881–1956, German physicist; discovered that ferromagnetic material in an increasing magnetic field becomes magnetized in discrete jumps (the **Barkhausen effect**)

barking *slang chiefly Brit adj* **1** mad or crazy ▷ *adv* **2** extremely: *barking mad*

Barkla *n* **Charles Glover** 1877–1944, British physicist, noted for his work on X-rays: Nobel prize for physics 1917

Bar Kochba, Bar Kokhba, *or* **Bar Kosba** *n* **Simeon** died 135 AD, Jewish leader who led an unsuccessful revolt against the Romans in Palestine

barley *n* **1** a tall grasslike plant with dense bristly flower spikes, widely cultivated for grain **2** the grain of this grass used in making beer and whisky and for soups
WORD ORIGIN Old English *bere*

barleycorn *n* a grain of barley, or barley itself

barley sugar *n* a brittle clear amber-coloured sweet

barley water *n* a drink made from an infusion of barley

barm *n* the yeasty froth on fermenting malt liquors
WORD ORIGIN Old English *bearm*

barmaid *n* a woman who serves in a pub

barman *n, pl* **-men** a man who serves in a pub

bar mitzvah *judaism n* **1** a ceremony marking the 13th birthday of a boy

THESAURUS

bare *adj* **1 = naked**, nude, stripped, exposed, uncovered, shorn, undressed, divested, denuded, in the raw *(informal)*, disrobed, unclothed, buck naked *(slang)*, unclad, scuddy *(slang)*, without a stitch on *(informal)*, in the bare scud *(slang)*, naked as the day you were born *(informal)*
OPPOSITE: dressed
3 = simple, basic, severe, spare, stark, austere, spartan, unadorned, unfussy, unvarnished, unembellished, unornamented, unpatterned, bare-bones
OPPOSITE: adorned
4 = plain, hard, simple, cold, basic, essential, obvious, sheer, patent, evident, stark, manifest, bald, literal, overt, unembellished

barely *adv* **1 = only just**, just, hardly, scarcely, at a push, almost not
OPPOSITE: completely

bargain *n* **1 = agreement**, deal *(informal)*, understanding, promise, contract, negotiation, arrangement, settlement, treaty, pledge, convention, transaction, engagement, pact, compact, covenant, stipulation **3 = good buy**, discount purchase, good deal, good value, steal *(informal)*, snip *(informal)*, giveaway, cheap purchase ▷ *vb* **6 = negotiate**, deal, contract, mediate, covenant, stipulate, arbitrate, transact, cut a deal

barge *n* **1 = canal boat**, lighter, narrow boat, scow, flatboat

bark[1] *n* **1 = yap**, bay, howl, snarl, growl, yelp, woof ▷ *vb* **2 = yap**, bay, howl, snarl, growl, yelp, woof

bark[2] *n* **1 = covering**, casing, cover, skin, protection, layer, crust, housing, cortex *(anatomy) (botany)*, rind, husk

b

DICTIONARY

and his assumption of religious obligations ▷ *adj* **2** (of a Jewish boy) having undergone this ceremony
WORD ORIGIN Hebrew: son of the law

barmy *adj* **-mier, -miest** *slang* insane
WORD ORIGIN originally, full of BARM, frothing, excited

barn *n* a large farm outbuilding, chiefly for storing grain, but also for livestock
WORD ORIGIN Old English *bere* barley + *ærn* room

barnacle *n* a marine shellfish that lives attached to rocks, ship bottoms, etc. **barnacled** *adj*
WORD ORIGIN Old French *bernac*

barnacle goose *n* a goose with a black-and-white head and body
WORD ORIGIN it was formerly believed that the goose developed from a shellfish

Barnave *n* **Antoine Pierre** 1761–93, French revolutionary. A prominent member of the National Assembly, he was executed for his royalist sympathies

barn dance *n* **1** *US & Canad* a party with square-dancing **2** *Brit* a progressive round country dance

Barnes *n* **1 Djuna** 1892–1982, US novelist, noted for *Nightwood* (1936) **2 William** 1801–86, British poet, best known for *Poems of Rural Life in the Dorset Dialect* (1879)

barney *n informal* a noisy fight or argument
WORD ORIGIN origin unknown

barn owl *n* an owl with a pale brown-and-white plumage and a heart-shaped face

barnstorm *vb* **1** *chiefly US & Canad* to tour rural districts making speeches in a political campaign **2** to tour rural districts putting on shows **barnstorming** *n, adj*

barnyard *n* a yard adjoining a barn

Barocchio *n* **Giacomo** ▸ See **Vignola**

barograph *n meteorol* a barometer that automatically keeps a record of changes in atmospheric pressure
WORD ORIGIN Greek *baros* weight + *graphein* to write

Baroja *n* **Pio** 1872–1956, Spanish Basque novelist, who wrote nearly 100 novels, including a series of twenty-two under the general title *Memorias de un Hombre de Acción* (1944–49)

barometer *n* an instrument for measuring atmospheric pressure, used to determine weather or altitude changes **barometric** *adj*
WORD ORIGIN Greek *baros* weight + *metron* measure

baron *n* **1** a member of the lowest rank of nobility in the British Isles **2** a powerful businessman or financier: *a press baron* **baronial** *adj*
WORD ORIGIN Old French

Baron-Cohen *n* **Sacha** born 1970, British television and film comedian, best known for his creation of the characters Ali G and Borat

baroness *n* **1** a woman holding the rank of baron **2** the wife or widow of a baron

baronet *n* a commoner who holds the lowest hereditary British title **baronetcy** *n*

barony *n, pl* **-nies** the domain or rank of a baron

baroque (bar-**rock**) *n* **1** a highly ornate style of architecture and art, popular in Europe from the late 16th to the early 18th century **2** a highly ornamented 17th-century style of music ▷ *adj* **3** ornate in style
WORD ORIGIN French from Portuguese *barroco* imperfectly shaped pearl

Barozzi *n* See (Giacomo Barozzi da) **Vignola**

barque (**bark**) *n* **1** a sailing ship, esp. one with three masts **2** *poetic* any boat
WORD ORIGIN Old Provençal *barca*

barrack[1] *vb* to house (soldiers) in barracks

barrack[2] *vb* **1** *Brit, Austral & NZ informal* to criticize loudly or shout against (a team or speaker) **2** *Austral & NZ* (foll. by *for*) to shout encouragement for (a team)
WORD ORIGIN Irish: to boast

barracks ● *pl n* **1** a building or group of buildings used to accommodate military personnel **2** a large and bleak building
WORD ORIGIN French *baraque*

barracuda (bar-rack-**kew**-da) *n, pl* **-da** *or* **-das** a tropical fish which feeds on other fishes
WORD ORIGIN American Spanish

barrage ● (**bar**-rahzh) *n* **1** a continuous delivery of questions, complaints, etc. **2** *mil* the continuous firing of artillery over a wide area **3** a construction built across a river to control the water level
WORD ORIGIN French *barrer* to obstruct

barrage balloon *n* a balloon tethered by cables, often with net suspended from it, used to deter low-flying air attack

barramundi *n* an edible Australian fish

Barras *n* **Paul François Jean Nicolas**, Vicomte de Barras. 1755–1829, French revolutionary: member of the Directory (1795–99)

Barrault *n* **Jean-Louis** 1910–94, French actor and director, noted particularly as a mime

barre (**bar**) *n* a rail at hip height used for ballet practice
WORD ORIGIN French

barrel *n* **1** a cylindrical container usually with rounded sides and flat ends, and held together by metal hoops **2** a unit of capacity of varying amount in different industries **3** the tube through which the bullet of a firearm is fired **4 over a barrel** *informal* powerless ▷ *vb* **-relling, -relled** *or US* **-reling, -reled 5** to put into a barrel or barrels
WORD ORIGIN Old French *baril*

barrel organ *n* a musical instrument played by turning a handle

barren ● *adj* **1** incapable of producing offspring **2** unable to support the growth of crops, fruit, etc.: *barren land* **3** unprofitable or unsuccessful: *Real Madrid have had a barren two seasons* **4** dull **barrenness** *n*
WORD ORIGIN Old French *brahain*

Barrès *n* **Maurice** 1862–1923, French novelist, essayist, and politician: a fervent nationalist and individualist

barricade ● *n* **1** a barrier, esp. one erected hastily for defence ▷ *vb* **-cading, -caded 2** to erect a barricade across (an entrance)
WORD ORIGIN Old French *barrique* a barrel

barrier ● *n* **1** anything that blocks a way or separates, such as a gate **2** anything that prevents progress: *a barrier of distrust* **3** anything that separates or hinders union: *a language barrier*
WORD ORIGIN Old French *barre* bar

barrier cream *n* a cream used to protect the skin

barrier reef *n* a long narrow ridge of coral, separated from the shore by deep water

barring *prep* unless something occurs; except for

THESAURUS

barracks *pl n* **1 = camp**, quarters, garrison, encampment, billet, cantonment, casern

barrage *n* **1 = torrent**, attack, mass, storm, assault, burst, stream, hail, outburst, rain, spate, onslaught, deluge, plethora, profusion **2 = bombardment**, attack, bombing, assault, shelling, battery, volley, blitz, salvo, strafe, fusillade, cannonade, curtain of fire

barren *adj* **1 = infertile**, sterile, childless, unproductive, nonproductive, infecund, unprolific

barricade *n* **1 = barrier**, wall, railing, fence, blockade, obstruction, rampart, fortification, bulwark, palisade, stockade ▷ *vb* **2 = bar**, block, defend, secure, lock, bolt, blockade, fortify, fasten, latch, obstruct

barrier *n* **1 = barricade**, wall, bar, block, railing, fence, pale, boundary, obstacle, ditch, blockade, obstruction, rampart, bulwark,

Barrington *n* **Jonah** born 1940, British squash player; winner of the Open Championship 1966–67, 1969–72

barrister *n* a lawyer who is qualified to plead in the higher courts
WORD ORIGIN from BAR[1]

Barros *n* **João de** 1496–1570, Portuguese historian: noted for his history of the Portuguese in the East Indies, *Décadas da Ásia* (1552–1615)

barrow[1] *n* **1** ▸ same as **wheelbarrow** **2** a handcart used by street traders
WORD ORIGIN Old English *bearwe*

barrow[2] *n* a heap of earth placed over a prehistoric tomb
WORD ORIGIN Old English *beorg*

barrow boy *n Brit* a man who sells goods from a barrow

Barry[1] *n* a port in SE Wales, in Vale of Glamorgan county borough on the Bristol Channel. Pop: 50 661 (2001)

Barry[2] *n* **1** Sir **Charles** 1795–1860, English architect: designer of the Houses of Parliament in London
2 Comtesse du ▸ See **du Barry**
3 John, real name *John Barry Prendergast*. born 1933, British composer of film scores, including several for films in the James Bond series

Barrymore *n* a US family of actors, esp. **Ethel** (1879–1959), **John** (1882–1942), and **Lionel** (1878–1954)

Bart. Baronet

Bart *n* **Lionel** 1930–99, British composer and playwright. His musicals include *Oliver* (1960)

barter *vb* **1** to trade goods or services in exchange for other goods or services, rather than for money ▹ *n* **2** trade by the exchange of goods
WORD ORIGIN Old French *barater* to cheat

Barth *n* **1 Heinrich** 1821–65, German explorer: author of *Travels and Discoveries in North and Central Africa* (1857–58) **2 John (Simmons)** born 1930, US novelist; his novels include *The Sot-Weed Factor* (1960), *Giles Goat-Boy* (1966), and *Once Upon a Time* (1994) **3 Karl** 1886–1968, Swiss Protestant theologian. He stressed man's dependence on divine grace in such works as *Commentary on Romans* (1919)

Bartholdi *n* **Frédéric August** 1834–1904, French sculptor and architect, who designed (1884) the Statue of Liberty

Bartoli *n* **Cecilia** born 1966, Italian mezzo-soprano, noted for her performances in Mozart and Rossini operas

Bartolommeo *n* **Fra** original name *Baccio della Porta*. 1472–1517, Italian painter of the Florentine school, noted for his austere religious works

baryon (bar-ree-on) *n* an elementary particle that has a mass greater than or equal to that of the proton
WORD ORIGIN Greek *barus* heavy

baryta (bar-rite-a) *n* a compound of barium, such as barium oxide
WORD ORIGIN Greek *barus* heavy

barytes (bar-rite-eez) *n* a colourless or white mineral: a source of barium
WORD ORIGIN Greek *barus* heavy

basal *adj* **1** at, of, or constituting a base **2** fundamental

basal metabolic rate *n* the amount of energy consumed by an animal's body at rest

basalt (bass-awlt) *n* a dark volcanic rock **basaltic** *adj*
WORD ORIGIN Greek *basanitēs* touchstone

bascule *n* a drawbridge that operates by a counterbalanced weight
WORD ORIGIN French: seesaw

base[1] ⓣ *n* **1** the bottom or supporting part of anything **2** the fundamental principle or part: *agriculture was the economic base of the city's growth* **3** a centre of operations, organization, or supply **4** a starting point: *the new discovery became the base for further research* **5** the main ingredient of a mixture: *to use rice as a base in cookery* **6** *chem* a compound that combines with an acid to form a salt **7** the lower side or face of a geometric construction **8** *maths* the number of units in a counting system that is equivalent to one in the next higher counting place: *10 is the base of the decimal system* **9** a starting or finishing point in any of various games ▹ *vb* **basing, based** **10** (foll. by *on* or *upon*) to use as a basis for **11** (foll. by *at* or *in*) to station, post, or place
WORD ORIGIN Latin *basis* pedestal

base[2] ⓣ *adj* **1** dishonourable or immoral: *base motives* **2** of inferior quality or value: *a base coin* **3** debased; counterfeit: *base currency*
WORD ORIGIN Late Latin *bassus* of low height

baseball *n* **1** a team game in which the object is to score runs by batting the ball and running round all four bases **2** the ball used in this game

baseless *adj* not based on fact

baseline *n* **1** a value or starting point on an imaginary scale with which other things are compared **2** a line at each end of a tennis court that marks the limit of play

baseliner *n tennis* a player who plays most of his or her shots from the back of court

basement *n* a partly or wholly underground storey of a building

base metal *n* a common metal such as copper or lead, that is not a precious metal

base rate *n* **1** the rate of interest used by a bank as a basis for its lending rates **2** the rate at which the Bank of England lends to other financial organizations, which effectively controls interest rates throughout the UK

bases[1] *n* ▸ the plural of **basis**

bases[2] *n* ▸ the plural of **base**[1]

Basescu *n* **Traian** born 1951, Romanian politician, president of Romania from 2007

bash ⓣ *informal vb* **1** to strike violently or crushingly **2** (foll. by *into*) to crash into ▹ *n* **3** a heavy blow **4 have a bash** *informal* to make an attempt
WORD ORIGIN origin unknown

bashful *adj* shy or modest **bashfully** *adv*
WORD ORIGIN *bash*, short for ABASH

-bashing *combining form informal or slang* **a** indicating a malicious attack on members of a group: *union-bashing* **b** indicating an activity undertaken energetically: *bible-bashing* **-basher** *n combining form*

Bashkirtseff *or* **Bashkirtsev** *n* **Marie**, original name *Marya Konstantinovna Bashkirtseva*. 1858–84, Russian painter and diarist who wrote in French, noted esp. for her *Journal* (1887)

Basho *n* full name **Matsuo Basho**, originally *Matsuo Munefusa*. 1644–94, Japanese poet and travel writer, noted esp. for his haiku

basic ⓣ *adj* **1** of or forming a base or basis **2** elementary or simple: *a few basic facts* **3** excluding additions or

THESAURUS

palisade, stockade

base[1] *n* **1 = bottom**, floor, lowest part, deepest part OPPOSITE: top **2 = foundation**, institution, organization, establishment, starting point **3 = centre**, post, station, camp, settlement, headquarters ▹ *vb* **10 = ground**, found, build, rest, establish, depend, root, construct, derive, hinge **11 = place**, set, post, station, establish, fix, locate, install, garrison

base[2] *adj* **1 = dishonourable**, evil, corrupt, infamous, disgraceful, vulgar, shameful, vile, immoral, scandalous, wicked, sordid, abject, despicable, depraved, ignominious, disreputable, contemptible, villainous, ignoble, discreditable, scungy *(Austral & NZ)* OPPOSITE: honourable

bash *vb* **1 = hit**, break, beat, strike, knock, smash, punch, belt *(informal)*, crush, deck *(slang)*, batter, slap, sock *(slang)*, chin *(slang)*, smack, thump, clout *(informal)*, whack *(informal)*, biff *(slang)*, clobber *(slang)*, wallop *(informal)*, slosh *(Brit slang)*, tonk *(informal)*, lay one on *(slang)*, beat *or* knock seven bells out of *(informal)*

basic *adj* **1a = fundamental**, main, key, essential, primary, vital, principal,

DICTIONARY

b

extras: *basic pay* **4** *chem* of or containing a base ▷*n* **5 basics** fundamental principles, facts, etc. **basically** *adv*

BASIC *n* a computer programming language that uses common English terms
WORD ORIGIN *b(eginner's) a(ll-purpose) s(ymbolic) i(nstruction) c(ode)*

basic slag *n* a slag produced in steel-making, containing calcium phosphate

Basie *n* **William**, known as *Count Basie*. 1904–84, US jazz pianist, bandleader, and composer: associated particularly with the polished phrasing and style of big-band jazz

basil *n* an aromatic herb used for seasoning food
WORD ORIGIN Greek *basilikos* royal

Basil *n* **Saint**, called *the Great*, ?329–379 AD, Greek patriarch: an opponent of Arianism and one of the founders of monasticism. Feast day: Jan 2, June 14, or Jan 1

Basil I *n* known as *the Macedonian*. died 886 AD, Byzantine emperor (876–86): founder of the Macedonian dynasty

basilica *n* **1** a Roman building, used for public administration, which is rectangular with two aisles and a rounded end **2** a Christian church of similar design
WORD ORIGIN Greek *basilikē oikia* the king's house

basilisk *n* (in classical legend) a serpent that could kill by its breath or glance
WORD ORIGIN Greek *basiliskos* royal child

basin *n* **1** a round wide container open at the top **2** the amount a basin will hold **3** a washbasin or sink **4** any partially enclosed area of water where ships or boats may be moored **5** the catchment area of a particular river **6** a depression in the earth's surface
WORD ORIGIN Old French *bacin*

basis ❶ *n, pl* **bases 1** something that underlies, supports, or is essential to an idea, belief, etc. **2** a principle on which something depends
WORD ORIGIN Greek: step

bask ❶ *vb* (foll. by *in*) **1** to lie in or be exposed (to pleasant warmth or sunshine) **2** to enjoy (approval or favourable conditions)
WORD ORIGIN Old Norse *bathask* to bathe

basket *n* **1** a container made of interwoven strips of wood or cane **2** the amount a basket will hold **3** *basketball* **a** the high horizontal hoop through which a player must throw the ball to score points **b** a point scored in this way
WORD ORIGIN Middle English

basketball *n* a team game in which points are scored by throwing the ball through a high horizontal hoop

basket weave *n* a weave of yarns, resembling that of a basket

basketwork *n* ▸same as **wickerwork**

basking shark *n* a very large plankton-eating shark, which often floats at the sea surface

basmati rice *n* a variety of long-grain rice with slender aromatic grains, used for savoury dishes
WORD ORIGIN Hindi: aromatic

Basov *n* **Nikolai Gennediyevich** 1922–2001, Russian physicist: shared the Nobel prize for physics (1964) for his pioneering work on the maser

basque *n* a tight-fitting bodice for women
WORD ORIGIN origin unknown

Basque *n* **1** a member of a people living in the W Pyrenees in France and Spain **2** the language of the Basques ▷*adj* **3** of the Basques
WORD ORIGIN Latin *Vasco*

bas-relief *n* sculpture in which the figures project slightly from the background
WORD ORIGIN Italian *basso rilievo*

bass[1] ❶ (base) *n* **1** the lowest adult male voice **2** a singer with such a voice **3** *informal* ▸same as **bass guitar** or **double bass** ▷*adj* **4** of the lowest range of musical notes: *the system is engineered to give good bass sound from very small speakers* **5** denoting a musical instrument that is lowest or second lowest in pitch in its family: *bass trombone* **6** of or relating to a bass guitar or double bass: *the band is unusual in that it has two bass players* **7** of or written for a singer with the lowest adult male voice: *the bass soloist in next week's performance of Handel's 'Messiah'*
WORD ORIGIN Middle English *bas*

bass[2] (rhymes with **gas**) *n* **1** various Australian freshwater and sea fish **2** a European spiny-finned freshwater fish
WORD ORIGIN Middle English

bass clef (base) *n* the clef that establishes F a fifth below middle C on the fourth line of the staff

bass drum (base) *n* a large drum of low pitch

basset hound *n* a smooth-haired dog with short legs and long ears
WORD ORIGIN French *bas* low

bass guitar (base) *n* an electric guitar with the same pitch and tuning as a double bass

bassinet *n* a wickerwork or wooden cradle or pram, usually hooded
WORD ORIGIN French: little basin

basso *n, pl* **-sos** *or* **-si** a singer with a bass voice
WORD ORIGIN Late Latin *bassus* low

bassoon *n* a woodwind instrument that produces a range of low sounds **bassoonist** *n*
WORD ORIGIN Italian *basso* deep

bastard *n* **1** *informal, offensive* an obnoxious or despicable person **2** *archaic or offensive* a person born of parents not married to each other **3** *informal* something extremely difficult or unpleasant ▷*adj* **4** *archaic or offensive* illegitimate by birth **5** counterfeit; spurious **bastardy** *n*
WORD ORIGIN Old French *bastart*

bastardize *or* **-ise** *vb* **-izing, -ized** *or* **-ising, -ised 1** to debase **2** to declare illegitimate

baste[1] *vb* **basting, basted** to sew with loose temporary stitches
WORD ORIGIN Old French *bastir* to build

baste[2] *vb* **basting, basted** to moisten (meat) during cooking with hot fat
WORD ORIGIN origin unknown

baste[3] *vb* **basting, basted** to thrash
WORD ORIGIN origin unknown

bastinado *n, pl* **-does 1** a punishment or torture by beating on the soles of the feet with a stick ▷*vb* **-doing, -doed 2** to beat (a person) in this way
WORD ORIGIN Spanish *baston* stick

bastion *n* **1** a projecting part of a fortification **2** a thing or person regarded as defending a principle or way of life: *a bastion of anti-communism*
WORD ORIGIN French *bastille* fortress

bat[1] *n* **1** any of various types of club used to hit the ball in certain sports

THESAURUS

constitutional, cardinal, inherent, elementary, indispensable, innate, intrinsic, elemental, immanent
1b = vital, needed, important, key, necessary, essential, primary, crucial, fundamental, elementary, indispensable, requisite
1c = essential, central, key, vital, fundamental, underlying, indispensable **OPPOSITE:** secondary
1d = main, key, essential, primary
2 = plain, simple, classic, severe, straightforward, Spartan, uncluttered, unadorned, unfussy, bog-standard *(informal)*, unembellished, bare-bones ▷*pl n*
5 = essentials, facts, principles, fundamentals, practicalities, requisites, nuts and bolts *(informal)*, hard facts, nitty-gritty *(informal)*, rudiments, brass tacks *(informal)*, necessaries

basis *n* **1, 2 = foundation**, support, base, ground, footing, theory, bottom, principle, premise, groundwork, principal element, chief ingredient

bask *vb* **1 = lie**, relax, lounge, sprawl, loaf, lie about, swim in, sunbathe, recline, loll, laze, outspan *(S African)*, warm yourself, toast yourself

bass[1] *adj* **4, 5, 7 = deep**, low, resonant, sonorous, low-pitched, deep-toned

DICTIONARY

2 *cricket* a batsman **3 off one's own bat a** of one's own accord **b** by one's own unaided efforts ▹ *vb* **batting, batted 4** to strike with or as if with a bat **5** *cricket, etc.* to take a turn at batting
WORD ORIGIN Old English *batt* club
bat² *n* **1** a nocturnal mouselike flying animal with leathery wings **2 blind as a bat** having extremely poor eyesight
WORD ORIGIN Scandinavian
bat³ *vb* **batting, batted 1** to flutter (one's eyelids) **2 not bat an eyelid** *informal* to show no surprise
WORD ORIGIN probably from obsolete *bate* flutter, beat
batch ❶ *n* **1** a group of similar objects or people dispatched or dealt with at the same time **2** the bread, cakes, etc. produced at one baking ▹ *vb* **3** to group (items) for efficient processing
WORD ORIGIN Middle English *bache*
batch processing *n* a system by which the computer programs of several users are submitted as a single batch
bated *adj* **with bated breath** in suspense or fear
Bates *n* **1** Sir **Alan** (**Arthur**) 1934–2003, British film and stage actor. His films include *A Kind of Loving* (1962), *Women in Love* (1969), *The Go-Between* (1971), and *The Cherry Orchard* (1999) **2 H**(**erbert**) **E**(**rnest**) 1905–74, English writer of short stories and novels, which include *The Darling Buds of May* (1958), *A Moment in Time* (1964), and *The Triple Echo* (1970)
bath ❶ *n* **1** a large container in which to wash the body **2** the act of washing in such a container **3** the amount of water in a bath **4 baths** a public swimming pool **5 a** a liquid in which something is immersed as part of a chemical process, such as developing photographs **b** the vessel containing such a liquid ▹ *vb* **6** *Brit* to wash in a bath
WORD ORIGIN Old English *bæth*
Bath chair *n* a wheelchair for invalids
bath cube *n* a cube of soluble scented material for use in a bath
bathe ❶ *vb* **bathing, bathed 1** to swim in open water for pleasure **2** to apply liquid to (the skin or a wound) in order to cleanse or soothe **3** *chiefly US & Canad* to wash in a bath **4** to spread over: *bathed in moonlight* ▹ *n* **5** *Brit* a swim in open water **bather** *n*
WORD ORIGIN Old English *bathian*
bathos (bay-thoss) *n* a sudden ludicrous descent from exalted to ordinary matters in speech or writing **bathetic** *adj*
WORD ORIGIN Greek: depth
bathrobe *n* **1** a loose-fitting garment for wear before or after a bath or swimming **2** *US & Canad* a dressing gown
bathroom *n* **1** a room with a bath or shower, washbasin, and toilet **2** *US & Canad* a toilet
bathyscaph *or* **bathyscaphe** *n* a deep-sea diving vessel for observation
WORD ORIGIN Greek *bathus* deep + *skaphē* light boat
bathysphere *n* a strong steel deep-sea diving sphere, lowered by cable
WORD ORIGIN Greek *bathus* deep + *sphere*
batik (bat-teek) *n* **a** a process of printing fabric in which areas not to be dyed are covered by wax **b** fabric printed in this way
WORD ORIGIN Javanese: painted
Batista *n* **Fulgencio**, full name *Batista y Zaldívar*. 1901–73, Cuban military leader and dictator: president of Cuba (1940–44, 1952–59); overthrown by Fidel Castro
batman *n, pl* **-men** an officer's servant in the armed forces
WORD ORIGIN Old French *bat* packsaddle
Batman¹ *n* a character in an American comic strip and several films who secretly assumes a batlike costume in order to fight crime
Batman² *n* **John** 1801–39, a pioneer who selected the site of the city of Melbourne
baton ❶ *n* **1** a thin stick used by the conductor of an orchestra or choir **2** *athletics* a short bar transferred from one runner to another in a relay race **3** a police officer's truncheon **4** a short stick or something shaped like one
WORD ORIGIN French
baton round *n* ▸ same as **plastic bullet**
bats *adj informal* mad or eccentric
batsman *n, pl* **-men** *cricket, etc.* a person who bats or specializes in batting
battalion *n* a military unit comprised of three or more companies
WORD ORIGIN French *bataillon*
batten¹ *n* **1** a strip of wood used to strengthen something or make it secure **2** a strip of wood used for holding a tarpaulin in place over a hatch on a ship ▹ *vb* **3** to strengthen or fasten with battens
WORD ORIGIN French *bâton* stick
batten² *vb* (foll. by *on*) to thrive at the expense of (someone else)
WORD ORIGIN probably from Old Norse *batna* to improve
Batten *n* **Jean** 1909–82, New Zealand aviator: the first woman to fly single-handed from Australia to Britain (1935)
batter¹ ❶ *vb* **1** to hit repeatedly **2** to damage or injure, as by blows, heavy wear, etc. **3** to subject (someone, usually a close relative) to repeated physical violence **battered** *adj* **batterer** *n* **battering** *n*
WORD ORIGIN Middle English *bateren*
batter² *n* a mixture of flour, eggs, and milk, used in cooking
WORD ORIGIN Middle English *bater*
batter³ *n baseball, etc.* a player who bats
battering ram *n* (esp. formerly) a large beam used to break down fortifications
battery *n, pl* **-teries 1** two or more primary cells connected to provide a source of electric current **2** a number of similar things occurring together: *a battery of questions* **3** *criminal law* unlawful beating or wounding of a person **4** *chiefly Brit* a series of cages for intensive rearing of poultry **5** a fortified structure on which artillery is mounted ▹ *adj* **6** kept in a series of cages for intensive rearing: *battery hens*
WORD ORIGIN Latin *battuere* to beat
battle ❶ *n* **1** a fight between large armed forces **2** conflict or struggle ▹ *vb* **-tling, -tled 3** to fight in or as if in military combat: *shop stewards*

THESAURUS

batch *n* **1 = group**, set, lot, crowd, pack, collection, quantity, bunch, accumulation, assortment, consignment, assemblage, aggregation
bath *n* **2 = wash**, cleaning, washing, soaping, shower, soak, cleansing, scrub, scrubbing, bathe, shampoo, sponging, douse, douche, ablution ▹ *vb* **6** *(Brit)* **= clean**, wash, soap, shower, soak, cleanse, scrub, bathe, tub, sponge, rinse, douse, scrub down, lave *(archaic)*
bathe *vb* **1 = swim 2 = cleanse**, clean, wash, soak, rinse **3** *(chiefly US & Canad)* **= wash**, clean, bath, soap, shower, soak, cleanse, scrub, tub, sponge, rinse, scrub down, lave *(archaic)* **4 = cover**, flood, steep, engulf, immerse, overrun, suffuse, wash over
baton *n* **4 = stick**, club, staff, stake, pole, rod, crook, cane, mace, wand, truncheon, sceptre, mere *(NZ)*, patu *(NZ)*
batter¹ *vb* **1 = beat**, hit, strike, knock, assault, smash, punch, belt *(informal)*, deck *(slang)*, bang, bash *(informal)*, lash, thrash, pound, lick *(informal)*, buffet, flog, maul, pelt, clobber *(slang)*, smite, wallop *(informal)*, pummel, tonk *(informal)*, cudgel, thwack, lambast(e), belabour, dash against, beat the living daylights out of, lay one on *(slang)*, drub, beat *or* knock seven bells out of *(informal)*
battle *n* **1 = fight**, war, attack, action, struggle, conflict, clash, set-to *(informal)*, encounter, combat, scrap

DICTIONARY

battling to improve conditions at work **4** to struggle: *she battled through the crowd*
WORD ORIGIN Latin *battuere* to beat

b

Battle[1] *n* a town in SE England, in East Sussex: site of the Battle of Hastings (1066); medieval abbey. Pop: 5190 (2001)

Battle[2] *n* **Kathleen** born 1948, US opera singer: a coloratura soprano, she made her professional debut in 1972 and sang with New York City's Metropolitan Opera (1977–94)

battle-axe *n* **1** a domineering woman **2** (formerly) a large broad-headed axe

battle cruiser *n* a high-speed warship with lighter armour than a battleship, but of the same size

battle cry *n* **1** a slogan used to rally the supporters of a campaign, movement, etc. **2** a shout uttered by soldiers going into battle

battledore *n* **1** Also called: **battledore and shuttlecock** an ancient racket game **2** a light racket used in this game
WORD ORIGIN Middle English *batyldoure*

battledress *n* the ordinary uniform of a soldier

battlefield ❶ *or* **battleground** *n* the place where a battle is fought

battlement *n* a wall with gaps, originally for firing through
WORD ORIGIN Old French *bataille* battle

battle royal *n* **1** a fight involving many combatants **2** a long violent argument

battleship *n* a large heavily armoured warship

batty ❶ *adj* **-tier, -tiest** *slang* **1** crazy **2** eccentric: *a batty OAP*
WORD ORIGIN from BAT[2]

bauble *n* a trinket of little value
WORD ORIGIN Old French *baubel* plaything

baud *n computers* a unit used to measure the speed of transmission of electronic data
WORD ORIGIN after J. M. E. *Baudot*, inventor

Baudouin I *n* 1930–93, king of Belgium (1951–93)

Baudrillard *n* **Jean** 1929–2007, French sociologist and theorist of postmodernism; his books include *Seduction* (1979), *America* (1986), and *The Spirit of Terrorism* (2002)

bauera *n* small evergreen Australian shrub

Bauhaus (bow-house) *adj* of a school of architecture and applied arts in Germany in the 1920s and 30s characterized by a functionalist approach to design
WORD ORIGIN German: building house

baulk *vb, n* ▸ same as **balk**

Baum *n* **L(yman) Frank** 1856–1919, US novelist, author of *The Wonderful Wizard of Oz* (1900) and its sequels

Baumgarten *n* **Alexander Gottlieb** 1714–62, German philosopher, noted for his pioneering work on aesthetics, a term that he originated

bauxite *n* a claylike substance that is the chief source of aluminium
WORD ORIGIN *(Les) Baux* in southern France, where originally found

bawdy *adj* **bawdier, bawdiest** (of language, writing, etc.) containing humorous references to sex **bawdily** *adv* **bawdiness** *n*
WORD ORIGIN Old French *baud* merry

bawdyhouse *n archaic* a brothel

bawl *vb* **1** to cry noisily **2** to shout loudly ▹ *n* **3** a loud shout or cry **bawling** *n*
WORD ORIGIN imitative

Bax *n* Sir **Arnold** (**Edward Trevor**) 1883–1953, English composer of romantic works, often based on Celtic legends, including the tone poem *Tintagel* (1917)

Baxter *n* **1 James** (**Keir**) 1926–72, New Zealand lyric poet. His works include *The Fallen House* (1953) and *In Fires of No Return* (1958) **2 Richard** 1615–91, English Puritan divine and devotional writer: prominent in church affairs during the Restoration

bay[1] ❶ *n* a stretch of shoreline that curves inwards
WORD ORIGIN Old French *baie*

bay[2] ❶ *n* **1** a recess in a wall **2** an area set aside for a particular purpose: *a sick bay; a loading bay* **3** ▸ same as **bay window 4** an area off a road in which vehicles may park or unload **5** a compartment in an aircraft: *the bomb bay*
WORD ORIGIN Old French *baee* gap

bay[3] ❶ *n* **1** a deep howl of a hound or wolf **2 at bay a** forced to turn and face attackers: *the stag at bay* **b** at a safe distance: *to keep his mind blank and his despair at bay* ▹ *vb* **3** to howl in deep prolonged tones
WORD ORIGIN Old French *abaiier* to bark

bay[4] *n* **1** a Mediterranean laurel tree with glossy aromatic leaves **2 bays** a wreath of bay leaves
WORD ORIGIN Latin *baca* berry

bay[5] *adj* **1** reddish-brown ▹ *n* **2** a reddish-brown horse
WORD ORIGIN Latin *badius*

Bayard[1] *n* a legendary horse that figures prominently in medieval romance

Bayard[2] *n* **Chevalier de**, original name *Pierre de Terrail* ?1473–1524, French soldier, known as *le chevalier sans peur et sans reproche* (the fearless and irreproachable knight)

Baybars I *n* 1223–77, sultan of Egypt and Syria (1260–77), of the Mameluke dynasty

THESAURUS

(informal), biffo *(Austral slang)*, engagement, warfare, fray, duel, skirmish, head-to-head, tussle, scuffle, fracas, scrimmage, sparring match, bagarre *(French)*, melee *or* mêlée, boilover *(Austral)*
OPPOSITE: peace
2a = conflict, campaign, struggle, debate, clash, dispute, contest, controversy, disagreement, crusade, strife, head-to-head, agitation
2b = campaign, drive, movement, push, struggle ▹ *vb* **3 = wrestle**, war, fight, argue, dispute, contest, combat, contend, feud, grapple, agitate, clamour, scuffle, lock horns
4 = struggle, work, labour, strain, strive, go for it *(informal)*, toil, make every effort, go all out *(informal)*, bend over backwards *(informal)*, go for broke *(slang)*, bust a gut *(informal)*, give it your best shot *(informal)*, break your neck *(informal)*, exert yourself, make an all-out effort *(informal)*, work like a Trojan, knock yourself out *(informal)*, do your damnedest *(informal)*, give it your all *(informal)*, rupture yourself *(informal)*

battlefield *n* **= battleground**, front, field, combat zone, field of battle

batty *adj (slang)* **1, 2 = crazy**, odd, mad, eccentric, bats *(slang)*, nuts *(slang)*, barking *(slang)*, peculiar, daft *(informal)*, crackers *(Brit slang)*, queer *(informal)*, insane, lunatic, loony *(slang)*, barmy *(slang)*, off-the-wall *(slang)*, touched, nutty *(slang)*, potty *(Brit informal)*, oddball *(informal)*, off the rails, cracked *(slang)*, bonkers *(slang, chiefly Brit)*, cranky *(US, Canad & Irish informal)*, dotty *(slang, chiefly Brit)*, loopy *(informal)*, crackpot *(informal)*, out to lunch *(informal)*, barking mad *(slang)*, out of your mind, outré, gonzo *(slang)*, screwy *(informal)*, doolally *(slang)*, off your trolley *(slang)*, off the air *(Austral slang)*, round the twist *(Brit slang)*, up the pole *(informal)*, off your rocker *(slang)*, not the full shilling *(informal)*, as daft as a brush *(informal, chiefly Brit)*, wacko *or* whacko *(slang)*, porangi *(NZ)*, daggy *(Austral & NZ informal)*

bay[1] *n* **= inlet**, sound, gulf, entrance, creek, cove, fjord, arm (of the sea), bight, ingress, natural harbour, sea loch *(Scot)*, firth *or* frith *(Scot)*

bay[2] *n* **1 = recess**, opening, corner, niche, compartment, nook, alcove, embrasure

bay[3] *n* **1 = cry**, bell, roar *(of a hound)*, quest, bark, lament, howl, wail, growl, bellow, clamour, yelp
▹ *vb* **3 = howl**, cry, roar *(of a hound)*, bark, lament, cry out, wail, growl, bellow, quest, bell, clamour, yelp

DICTIONARY

bayberry *n, pl* **-ries** a tropical American tree that yields an oil used in making bay rum. Also: **bay**

Bayezid II *n* ?1447–1512, sultan of Turkey; he greatly extended Turkish dominions in Greece and the Balkans

Bayle *n* **Pierre** 1647–1706, French philosopher and critic, noted for his *Dictionnaire historique et critique* (1697), which profoundly influenced Voltaire and the French Encyclopedists

bay leaf *n* the dried leaf of a laurel, used for flavouring in cooking

Baylis *n* **1 Lillian Mary** 1874–1937, British theatre manager: founded the Old Vic (1912) and the Sadler's Wells company for opera and ballet (1931) **2 Trevor** (**Graham**) born 1937, British inventor of the clockwork radio (1992)

bayonet *n* **1** a blade that can be attached to the end of a rifle and used as a weapon ▷ *vb* **-neting, -neted** *or* **-netting, -netted 2** to stab or kill with a bayonet
WORD ORIGIN *Bayonne*, a port in France, where it originated

bay rum *n* an aromatic liquid, used in medicines and cosmetics, which was originally obtained by distilling bayberry leaves with rum

bay window *n* a window projecting from a wall

bazaar ❶ *n* **1** a sale, esp. one in aid of charity **2** (esp. in the Orient) a market area, esp. a street of small stalls
WORD ORIGIN Persian *bāzār*

bazooka *n* a portable rocket launcher that fires a projectile capable of piercing armour
WORD ORIGIN after a pipe instrument devised by an American comedian

BB *Brit* Boys' Brigade

B2B business-to-business; denoting trade between commercial organizations rather than between businesses and private customers

BBC British Broadcasting Corporation

BBQ barbecue

BC 1 (indicating years numbered back from the supposed year of the birth of Christ) before Christ **2** British Columbia

BCE (used, esp. by non-Christians, in numbering years BC) before Common Era

BCG *trademark* Bacillus Calmette-Guérin (antituberculosis vaccine)

BD Bachelor of Divinity

BDS Bachelor of Dental Surgery

be ❶ *vb, present sing 1st person* **am;** *2nd person* **are;** *3rd person* **is.** *present pl* **are.** *past sing 1st person* **was;** *2nd person* **were;** *3rd person* **was.** *past pl* **were.** *present participle* **being.** *past participle* **been. 1** to exist; live: *I think, therefore I am* **2** to pay a visit; go: *have you been to Spain?* **3** to take place: *my birthday was last Thursday* **4** used as a linking verb between the subject of a sentence and its complement: *John is a musician; honey is sweet; the dance is on Saturday* **5** forms the progressive present tense: *the man is running* **6** forms the passive voice of all transitive verbs: *a good film is being shown on television tomorrow* **7** expresses intention, expectation, or obligation: *the president is to arrive at 9.30*
WORD ORIGIN Old English *bēon*

Be *chem* beryllium

BE Bachelor of Engineering

be- *prefix forming verbs mainly from nouns* **1** to surround or cover: *befog* **2** to affect completely: *bedazzle* **3** to consider as or cause to be: *befriend* **4** to provide or cover with: *bejewel* **5** (*from verbs*) at, for, against, on, or over: *bewail*
WORD ORIGIN Old English *be-, bi-* by

beach ❶ *n* **1** an area of sand or pebbles sloping down to the sea or a lake ▷ *vb* **2** to run or haul (a boat) onto a beach
WORD ORIGIN origin unknown

beachcomber *n* a person who searches shore debris for anything of worth

beachhead *n mil* an area of shore captured by an attacking army, on which troops and equipment are landed

beacon ❶ *n* **1** a signal fire or light on a hill or tower, used formerly as a warning of invasion **2** a lighthouse **3** a radio or other signal marking a flight course in air navigation **4** ▸ same as **Belisha beacon**
WORD ORIGIN Old English *beacen* sign

Beaconsfield[1] *n* a town in SE England, in Buckinghamshire. Pop: 12 292 (2001)

Beaconsfield[2] *n* **1st Earl of** ▸ title of (Benjamin) **Disraeli**

bead ❶ *n* **1** a small pierced piece of glass, wood, or plastic that may be strung with others to form a necklace, rosary, etc. **2** a small drop of moisture **3** a small metal knob acting as the sight of a firearm ▷ *vb* **4** to decorate with beads **beaded** *adj*
WORD ORIGIN Old English *bed* prayer

beading *n* a narrow rounded strip of moulding used for edging furniture

beadle *n* **1** *Brit* (formerly) a minor parish official who acted as an usher **2** *Scot* a church official who attends the minister
WORD ORIGIN Old English *bydel*

Beadle *n* **George Wells** 1903–89, US biologist, who shared the Nobel prize for physiology or medicine in 1958 for his work in genetics

beady *adj* **beadier, beadiest** small, round, and glittering: *beady eyes*

beagle *n* a small hound with a smooth coat, short legs, and drooping ears
WORD ORIGIN origin unknown

Beaglehole *n* **John** 1901–71, New Zealand historian and author. His works include *Exploration of the Pacific* (1934) and *The Journals of James Cook* (1955)

beak[1] *n* **1** the projecting horny jaws of a bird **2** *slang* a person's nose **beaky** *adj*
WORD ORIGIN Latin *beccus*

beak[2] *n Brit, Austral & NZ slang* a judge, magistrate, or headmaster
WORD ORIGIN originally thieves' jargon

beaker *n* **1** a tall drinking cup **2** a lipped glass container used in laboratories
WORD ORIGIN Old Norse *bikarr*

Beale *n* **Dorothea** 1831–1906, British schoolmistress, a champion of women's education and suffrage. As principal of Cheltenham Ladies' College (1858–1906) she introduced important reforms

beam ❶ *n* **1** a broad smile **2** a ray of light **3** a narrow flow of electromagnetic radiation or particles: *an electron beam* **4** a long thick piece of wood, metal, etc. used in building **5** the central shaft of a plough to which all the main parts are attached **6** the breadth of a ship at its widest part **7 off (the) beam** *informal* mistaken or irrelevant ▷ *vb* **8** to smile broadly **9** to send out or radiate **10** to divert or aim (a radio signal, light, etc.) in a certain direction: *the concert was*

THESAURUS

bazaar *n* **1 = fair**, fête, gala, festival, garden party, bring-and-buy **2 = market**, exchange, fair, marketplace, mart

be *vb* **1 = be alive**, live, exist, survive, breathe, last, be present, continue, endure, be living, be extant, happen

beach *n* **1 = shore**, coast, sands, margin, strand, seaside, shingle, lakeside, water's edge, lido, foreshore, seashore, plage, littoral, sea (*chiefly US*)

beacon *n* **1 = signal**, sign, rocket, beam, flare, bonfire, smoke signal, signal fire **2 = lighthouse**, pharos, watchtower

bead *n* **2 = drop**, tear, bubble, pearl, dot, drip, blob, droplet, globule, driblet

beam *n* **1 = smile**, grin **2 = ray**, bar, flash, stream, glow, radiation, streak, emission, shaft, gleam, glint, glimmer **4 = rafter**, support, timber, spar, plank, girder, joist ▷ *vb* **8 = smile**, grin **9 = radiate**, flash, shine, glow, glitter, glare, gleam, emit light, give off light **10 = transmit**, show, air,

DICTIONARY

beamed live from Geneva
WORD ORIGIN Old English
beam-ends *pl n* **on one's beam-ends** out of money
bean *n* **1** the seed or pod of various climbing plants, eaten as a vegetable **2** any of various beanlike seeds, such as coffee **3 full of beans** *informal* full of energy and vitality **4 not have a bean** *slang* to be without money
WORD ORIGIN Old English *bēan*
beanbag *n* **1** a small cloth bag filled with dried beans and thrown in games **2** a very large cushion filled with polystyrene granules and used as a seat
bean curd *n* ▸ same as **tofu**
beanfeast *n* *Brit informal* any festive or merry occasion
beanie *n* *Brit, Austral & NZ* close-fitting woollen hat
beano *n, pl* **beanos** *Brit, old-fashioned slang* a celebration or party
beanpole *n* *slang* a tall thin person
beansprout *n* a small edible shoot grown from a bean seed, often used in Chinese dishes
bear[1] ❶ *vb* **bearing, bore, borne 1** to support or hold up **2** to bring: *to bear gifts* **3** to accept the responsibility of: *to bear a heavier burden of taxation* **4** to give birth to **5** to produce by natural growth: *to bear fruit* **6** to tolerate or endure **7** to stand up to; sustain: *his story does not bear scrutiny* **8** to hold in the mind: *to bear a grudge* **9** to show or be marked with: *he still bears the scars* **10** to have, be, or stand in (relation or comparison): *her account bears no relation to the facts* **11** to move in a specified direction: *bear left* **12 bring to bear** to bring into effect ▸ See also **bear down on, bear on,** etc.
WORD ORIGIN Old English *beran*
bear[2] *n, pl* **bears** *or* **bear 1** a large heavily-built mammal with a long shaggy coat **2** a bearlike animal, such as the koala **3** an ill-mannered person **4** *stock exchange* a person who sells shares in anticipation of falling prices to make a profit on repurchase **5 like a bear with a sore head** *informal* bad-tempered, irritable
WORD ORIGIN Old English *bera*
bearable *adj* endurable; tolerable
bear-baiting *n* *history* an entertainment in which dogs attacked a chained bear
beard *n* **1** the hair growing on the lower parts of a man's face **2** any similar growth in animals ▹*vb* **3** to oppose boldly: *I bearded my formidable employer in her den* **bearded** *adj*
WORD ORIGIN Old English
bear down on *vb* **1** to press down on **2** to approach (someone) in a determined manner
Beardsley *n* **Aubrey** (**Vincent**) 1872–98, English illustrator: noted for his stylized black-and-white illustrations, esp. those for Oscar Wilde's *Salome* and Pope's *Rape of the Lock*
bearer ❶ *n* **1** a person or thing that carries, presents, or upholds something **2** a person who presents a note or bill for payment
bear hug *n* a rough tight embrace
bearing ❶ *n* **1** (foll. by *on* or *upon*) relevance to: *it has no bearing on this problem* **2** a part of a machine supporting another part, and usually reducing friction **3** the act of producing fruit or young **4** a person's general social conduct **5** the angular direction of a point measured from a known position **6** the position, as of a ship, fixed with reference to two or more known points **7 bearings** a sense of one's relative position: *I lost my bearings in the dark* **8** *heraldry* a device on a heraldic shield
bear on *vb* to be relevant to
bear out ❶ *vb* to show to be truthful: *the witness will bear me out*
bearskin *n* **1** the pelt of a bear **2** a tall fur helmet worn by certain British Army regiments
bear up *vb* to cope with hardships: *they are bearing up well under the pressure*
bear with *vb* to be patient with
beast ❶ *n* **1** a large wild animal **2** a brutal or uncivilized person **3** savage nature or characteristics: *the beast in man*
WORD ORIGIN Latin *bestia*
beastly ❶ *adj* *informal* **-lier, -liest** unpleasant; disagreeable
beat ❶ *vb* **beating, beat; beaten** *or* **beat 1** to strike with a series of violent blows **2** to move (wings) up and down **3** to throb rhythmically **4** *cookery* to stir or whisk vigorously **5** to shape (metal) by repeated blows **6** *music* to indicate (time) by one's hand or a baton **7** to produce (a sound) by striking a drum **8** to overcome or defeat: *he was determined to beat his illness* **9** to form (a path or track) by repeated use **10** to arrive, achieve, or finish before (someone or something): *she beat her team mate fair and square* **11** (foll. by *back, down* or *off* etc.) to drive, push, or thrust **12** to scour (woodlands or undergrowth) to rouse game for shooting **13** *slang* to puzzle or baffle: *it beats me* ▹*n* **14** a stroke or blow **15** the sound made by

THESAURUS

broadcast, cable, send out, relay, televise, radio, emit, put on the air
bear[1] *vb* **1 = support**, shoulder, sustain, endure, uphold, withstand, bear up under **OPPOSITE:** give up **2 = carry**, take, move, bring, lift, transfer, conduct, transport, haul, transmit, convey, relay, tote (*informal*), hump (*Brit slang*), lug **OPPOSITE:** put down **4 = give birth to**, produce, deliver, breed, bring forth, beget **5 = produce**, develop, generate, yield, bring forth **6a = suffer**, feel, experience, go through, sustain, stomach, endure, undergo, admit, brook, hack (*slang*), abide, put up with (*informal*) **6b = bring yourself to**, allow, accept, permit, endure, tolerate, hack (*informal*), countenance **8 = exhibit**, hold, maintain, entertain, harbour, cherish **9 = display**, have, show, hold, carry, possess, exhibit
bearer *n* **1a = agent**, carrier, courier, herald, envoy, messenger, conveyor, emissary, harbinger **1b = carrier**, runner, servant, porter
bearing *n* **1** (*usually with* **on** *or* **upon**) **= relevance**, relation, application, connection, import, reference, significance, pertinence, appurtenance **OPPOSITE:** irrelevance **4 = manner**, attitude, conduct, appearance, aspect, presence, behaviour, tone, carriage, posture, demeanour, deportment, mien (*literary*), air, comportment ▹*pl n* **7 = way**, course, position, situation, track, aim, direction, location, orientation, whereabouts
bear out *vb* **= support**, prove, confirm, justify, endorse, uphold, vindicate, validate, substantiate, corroborate, legitimize
beast *n* **1 = animal**, creature, brute **2 = brute**, monster, savage, barbarian, fiend, swine, ogre, ghoul, sadist
beastly *adj* (*informal*) **= unpleasant**, mean, terrible, awful, nasty, foul, rotten, horrid, disagreeable, irksome **OPPOSITE:** pleasant
beat *vb* **1a = batter**, break, hit, strike, knock, punch, belt (*informal*), whip, deck (*slang*), bruise, bash (*informal*), sock (*slang*), lash, chin (*slang*), pound, smack, thrash, cane, thump, lick (*informal*), buffet, clout (*informal*), flog, whack (*informal*), maul, clobber (*slang*), wallop (*informal*), tonk (*informal*), cudgel, thwack (*informal*), lambast(e), lay one on (*slang*), drub, beat *or* knock seven bells out of (*informal*) **1b = pound**, strike, hammer, batter, thrash, pelt **2 = flap**, thrash, flutter, agitate, wag, swish **3 = throb**, pulse, tick, thump, tremble, pound, quake, quiver, vibrate, pulsate, palpitate **7 = hit**, strike, bang **8 = defeat**, outdo, trounce, overcome, stuff (*slang*), master, tank (*slang*), crush, overwhelm, conquer, lick (*informal*), undo, subdue, excel, surpass, overpower, outstrip, clobber (*slang*), vanquish, outrun, subjugate, run rings around (*informal*), wipe the floor with (*informal*), knock spots off

DICTIONARY

a stroke or blow **16** a regular throb **17** an assigned route, as of a policeman **18** the basic rhythmic unit in a piece of music **19** pop or rock music characterized by a heavy rhythmic beat ▹ *adj* **20** *slang* totally exhausted ▸ See also **beat down, beat up** > **beating** *n*
WORD ORIGIN Old English *bēatan*

beatbox *n* **1** a drum machine ▹ *vb* **2** to simulate percussion instruments with the voice, esp. in hip-hop music **beatboxing** *n*

beat down *vb* **1** (of the sun) to shine intensely **2** *informal* to force or persuade (a seller) to accept a lower price

beater *n* **1** a device used for beating: *a carpet beater* **2** a person who rouses wild game

beatific *adj literary* **1** displaying great happiness **2** having a divine aura
WORD ORIGIN Latin *beatus*

beatify (bee-at-if-fie) *vb* **-fies, -fying, -fied** **1** *RC church* to declare (a deceased person) to be among the blessed in heaven: the first step towards canonization **2** to make extremely happy **beatification** *n*

beatitude *n* supreme blessedness or happiness
WORD ORIGIN Latin *beatitudo*

Beatitude *n Christianity* any of the blessings on the poor, meek, etc. in the Sermon on the Mount

Beat movement *n* a group of US writers who emerged in the 1950s, noted for their rejection of the social and political systems of the West and their espousal of alternative lifestyles

beatnik *n* a young person in the late 1950s who rebelled against conventional attitudes and styles of dress
WORD ORIGIN BEAT (noun) + -NIK

Beaton *n* Sir **Cecil** (**Walter Hardy**) 1904–80, British photographer, noted esp. for his society portraits

Beatrix *n* full name *Beatrix Wilhelmina Armgard*. born 1938, queen of the Netherlands from 1980

Beatty *n* **1 David,** 1st Earl Beatty. 1871–1936, British admiral of the fleet in World War I **2 Warren,** full name *Henry Warren Beatty*. Born 1937, US film actor and director: his films include *Bonnie and Clyde* (1967), *Heaven Can Wait* (1978), *Reds* (1981, also directed), *Bugsy* (1991), and *Bulworth* (1998, also wrote and directed)

beat up ❶ *informal vb* **1** to inflict severe physical damage on (someone) by striking or kicking repeatedly ▹ *n* **2** *Austral & NZ* a small matter deliberately exaggerated ▹ *adj* **beat-up** **3** dilapidated

beau (boh) *n, pl* **beaux** *or* **beaus** (bohz) **1** *chiefly US* a boyfriend **2** a man who is greatly concerned with his appearance
WORD ORIGIN French

Beaufort *n* **1 Henry** ?1374–1447, English cardinal, half-brother of Henry IV; chancellor (1403–04, 1413–17, 1424–26) **2** Lady **Margaret,** Countess of Richmond and Derby. ?1443–1509, mother of Henry VII. She helped to found two Cambridge colleges and was a patron of Caxton

Beaufort scale *n meteorol* a scale for measuring wind speeds, ranging from 0 (calm) to 12 (hurricane)
WORD ORIGIN after Sir Francis *Beaufort*, who devised it

Beauharnais *n* **1 Alexandre,** Vicomte de. 1760–94, French general, who served in the War of American Independence and the French Revolutionary wars; first husband of Empress Joséphine: guillotined **2** his son, **Eugène de** 1781–1824, viceroy of Italy (1805–14) for his stepfather Napoleon I **3** (**Eugénie**) **Hortense de** 1783–1837, queen of Holland (1806–10) as wife of Louis Bonaparte; daughter of Alexandre Beauharnais and sister of Eugène: mother of Napoleon III **4 Joséphine de**, previous name of the Empress Josephine ▸ See **Josephine**

Beaujolais *n* a red or white wine from southern Burgundy in France

Beaumarchais *n* **Pierre Augustin Caron de** 1732–99, French dramatist, noted for his comedies *The Barber of Seville* (1775) and *The Marriage of Figaro* (1784)

Beaumont[1] *n* a city in SE Texas. Pop: 112 434 (2003 est)

Beaumont[2] *n* **Francis** 1584–1616, English dramatist, who collaborated with John Fletcher on plays including *The Knight of the Burning Pestle* (1607) and *The Maid's Tragedy* (1611)

beauteous *adj poetic* beautiful

beautician *n* a person who works in a beauty salon

beautiful ❶ *adj* **1** being very attractive to look at **2** highly enjoyable; very pleasant **beautifully** *adv*

beautify *vb* **-fies, -fying, -fied** to make beautiful **beautification** *n*

beauty ❶ *n, pl* **-ties** **1** the combination of all the qualities of a person or thing that delight the senses and mind **2** a very attractive woman **3** *informal* an outstanding example of its kind **4** *informal* an advantageous feature: *the beauty of this job is the short hours*
WORD ORIGIN Latin *bellus* handsome

beauty queen *n* a woman who has been judged the most beautiful in a contest

beauty salon *or* **parlour** *n* an establishment that provides services such as hairdressing, facial treatment, and massage

beauty spot *n* **1** a place of outstanding beauty **2** a small dark-coloured spot formerly worn on a lady's face as decoration

beaver *n* **1** a large amphibious rodent with soft brown fur, a broad flat tail, and webbed hind feet **2** its fur **3** a tall hat made of this fur ▹ *vb* **4 beaver away** to work very hard and steadily
WORD ORIGIN Old English *beofor*

Bebel *n* **August** 1840–1913, German socialist leader: one of the founders of the Social Democratic Party (1869)

bebop *n* ▸ same as **bop**
WORD ORIGIN imitative of the rhythm

becalmed *adj* (of a sailing ship) motionless through lack of wind

THESAURUS

(informal), make mincemeat of *(informal)*, pip at the post, outplay, blow out of the water *(slang)*, put in the shade *(informal)*, bring to their knees ▹ *n* **16 = throb**, pounding, pulse, thumping, vibration, pulsating, palpitation, pulsation **17 = route**, way, course, rounds, path, circuit

beat up *vb (informal)* **= assault**, attack, batter, thrash, set about, do over *(Brit, Austral & NZ slang)*, work over *(slang)*, clobber *(slang)*, assail, set upon, lay into *(informal)*, put the boot in *(slang)*, lambast(e), duff up *(Brit slang)*, beat the living daylights out of *(informal)*, knock about *or* around, fill in *(Brit slang)*, beat *or* knock seven bells out of *(informal)*

beautiful *adj* **1 = attractive**, pretty, lovely, stunning *(informal)*, charming, tempting, pleasant, handsome, fetching, good-looking, gorgeous, fine, pleasing, fair, magnetic, delightful, cute, exquisite, enticing, seductive, graceful, captivating, appealing, radiant, alluring, drop-dead *(slang)*, ravishing, bonny, winsome, comely, prepossessing, hot *(informal)*, fit *(Brit informal)*
OPPOSITE: ugly

beauty *n* **1 = attractiveness**, charm, grace, bloom, glamour, fairness, elegance, symmetry *(formal, literary)*, allure, loveliness, handsomeness, pulchritude, comeliness, exquisiteness, seemliness
OPPOSITE: ugliness
2 = good-looker, looker *(informal, chiefly US)*, lovely *(slang)*, sensation, dazzler, belle, goddess, Venus, peach *(informal)*, cracker *(slang)*, wow *(slang, chiefly US)*, dolly *(slang)*, knockout *(informal)*, heart-throb, stunner *(informal)*, charmer, smasher *(informal)*, humdinger *(slang)*, glamour puss, beaut *(Austral & NZ slang)*

b

DICTIONARY

became *vb* ▸ the past tense of **become**

because ❶ *conj* **1** on account of the fact that: *because it's so cold we'll go home* **2 because of** on account of: *I lost my job because of her*
WORD ORIGIN Middle English *bi cause*

Beccaria *n* **Cesare Bonesana**, Marchese de. 1738–94, Italian legal theorist and political economist; author of the influential treatise *Crimes and Punishments* (1764), which attacked corruption, torture, and capital punishment

bechamel sauce (bay-sham-ell) *n* a thick white sauce flavoured with onion and seasonings
WORD ORIGIN after the Marquis of *Béchamel*, its inventor

Bechet *n* **Sidney (Joseph)** 1897–1959, US jazz soprano saxophonist and clarinettist

Bechstein *n* **Karl** 1826–1900, German piano maker; founder (1853) of the Bechstein company of piano manufacturers in Berlin

beck[1] *n* **at someone's beck and call** having to be constantly available to do as someone asks
WORD ORIGIN Middle English *becnen* to beckon

beck[2] *n* (in N England) a stream
WORD ORIGIN Old English *becc*

Beckenbauer *n* **Franz** born 1945, German footballer: team captain when West Germany won the World Cup (1974): manager of West Germany (1984–90), coaching the team to success in the 1990 World Cup

Becker *n* **Boris** born 1967, German tennis player: Wimbledon champion 1985, 1986, and 1989: the youngest man ever to win Wimbledon

Beckford *n* **William** 1759–1844, English writer and dilettante; author of the oriental romance *Vathek* (1787)

Beckmann *n* **1 Ernst Otto** 1853–1923, German chemist: devised the Beckmann thermometer, used for measuring small temperature changes in liquids **2 Max** 1884–1950, German expressionist painter

beckon ❶ *vb* **1** to summon with a gesture **2** to lure: *fame beckoned*
WORD ORIGIN Old English *bīecnan*

become ❶ *vb* **-coming, -came, -come** **1** to come to be: *he became Prime Minister last year* **2** (foll. by *of*) to happen to: *what became of him?* **3** to suit: *that dress becomes you*
WORD ORIGIN Old English *becuman* happen

becoming ❶ *adj* suitable or appropriate: *his conduct was not becoming to the rank of officer*

becquerel (beck-a-rell) *n* the SI unit of activity of a radioactive source
WORD ORIGIN after A. H. *Becquerel*, physicist

bed ❶ *n* **1** a piece of furniture on which to sleep **2** a plot of ground in which plants are grown **3** the bottom of a river, lake, or sea **4** any underlying structure or part **5** a layer of rock **6 get out of bed on the wrong side** *informal* to begin the day in a bad mood **7 go to bed with** to have sexual intercourse with ▹ *vb* **bedding, bedded 8** (foll. by *down*) to go to or put into a place to sleep or rest **9** to have sexual intercourse with **10** to place firmly into position: *the poles were bedded in concrete* **11** *geol* to form or be arranged in a distinct layer **12** to plant in a bed of soil
WORD ORIGIN Old English *bedd*

BEd Bachelor of Education

bed and breakfast *n chiefly Brit* overnight accommodation and breakfast

bedaub *vb* to smear over with something sticky or dirty

bedbug *n* a small blood-sucking wingless insect that infests dirty houses

bedclothes *pl n* coverings for a bed

bedding *n* **1** bedclothes, sometimes with a mattress **2** litter, such as straw, for animals **3** the distinct layered deposits of rocks

Beddoes *n* **Thomas Lovell** 1803–49, British poet, noted for his macabre imagery, esp. in *Death's Jest-Book* (1850)

bedeck *vb* to cover with decorations

bedevil (bid-dev-ill) *vb* **-illing, -illed** *or US* **-iling, -iled 1** to harass or torment **2** to throw into confusion
bedevilment *n*

bedfellow *n* **1** a temporary associate **2** a person with whom one shares a bed

Bedford[1] *n* **1** a town in SE central England, in Bedfordshire, on the River Ouse; administrative centre of Bedford unitary authority. Pop: 82 488 (2001) **2** a unitary authority of SE central England. Pop: 154 900 (2007 est). Area: 480 sq km (185 sq miles) **3** ▸ short for **Bedfordshire**

Bedford[2] *n* **1 David** born 1937, British composer, influenced by rock music **2 Duke of**, title of *John of Lancaster*. 1389–1435, son of Henry IV of England: protector of England and regent of France (1422–35)

bedlam *n* a noisy confused situation
WORD ORIGIN from Hospital of St Mary of *Bethlehem*, a former mental hospital in London

bed linen *n* sheets and pillowcases for a bed

Bedouin *n* **1** *pl* **-ins** *or* **-in** a nomadic Arab tribesman of the deserts of Arabia, Jordan, and Syria **2** a wanderer
WORD ORIGIN Arabic *badw* desert

bedpan *n* a shallow container used as a toilet by people who are not well enough to leave bed

bedraggled *adj* with hair or clothing that is untidy, wet, or dirty

bedridden *adj* unable to leave bed because of illness

bedrock *n* **1** the solid rock beneath the surface soil **2** basic principles or facts

bedroom *n* **1** a room used for sleeping ▹ *adj* **2** containing references to sex: *a bedroom comedy*

Beds Bedfordshire

bedside *n* **1** the area beside a bed ▹ *adj* **2** placed at or near the side of the bed: *the bedside table*

bedsit *or* **bedsitter** *n* a furnished sitting room with a bed

bedsore *n* an ulcer on the skin, caused by a lengthy period of lying in bed due to illness

bedspread *n* a top cover on a bed

bedstead *n* the framework of a bed

bedstraw *n* a plant with small white or yellow flowers

bed-wetting *n* involuntarily urinating in bed

bee[1] *n* **1** a four-winged insect that collects nectar and pollen to make honey and wax **2 have a bee in one's bonnet** to be obsessed with an idea
WORD ORIGIN Old English *bīo*

bee[2] *n* a social gathering to carry out a

THESAURUS

because *conj* **1 = since**, as, in that **2 because of = as a result of**, on account of, by reason of, thanks to, owing to

beckon *vb* **1 = gesture**, sign, wave, indicate, signal, nod, motion, summon, gesticulate

become *vb* **1 = come to be**, develop into, be transformed into, grow into, change into, evolve into, alter to, mature into, metamorphose into, ripen into **3 = suit**, fit, enhance, flatter, ornament, embellish, grace, harmonize with, set off

becoming *adj* **= appropriate**, right, seemly, fitting, fit, correct, suitable, decent, proper, worthy, in keeping, compatible, befitting, decorous, comme il faut *(French)*, congruous, meet *(archaic)*
OPPOSITE: inappropriate

bed *n* **1 = bedstead**, couch, berth, cot, pallet, divan **2 = plot**, area, row, strip, patch, ground, land, garden, border **4 = base**, footing, basis, bottom, foundation, underpinning, groundwork, bedrock, substructure, substratum

beer parlour *n (Canad)* **= tavern**, inn, bar, pub *(informal, chiefly Brit)*, public house, watering hole *(facetious, slang)*, boozer *(Brit, Austral & NZ informal)*, beverage room *(Canad)*, hostelry,

communal task: *quilting bee*
WORD ORIGIN probably from Old English *bēn* boon
Beeb *n* **the Beeb** *Brit informal* the BBC
beech *n* **1** a tree with smooth greyish bark **2** the hard wood of this tree **3** ▸ see **copper beech**
WORD ORIGIN Old English *bēce*
Beecher *n* **Henry Ward** 1813–87, US clergyman: a leader in the movement for the abolition of slavery
beechnut *n* the small brown triangular edible nut of the beech tree
beef *n* **1** the flesh of a cow, bull, or ox **2** *slang* a complaint ▹*vb* **3** *slang* to complain ▸ See also **beef up**
WORD ORIGIN Old French *boef*, from Latin *bos* ox
beefburger *n* a flat fried or grilled cake of minced beef; hamburger
beefcake *n slang* musclemen as displayed in photographs
beefeater *n* a yeoman warder of the Tower of London
beef tea *n* a drink made by boiling pieces of lean beef
beef tomato *or* **beefsteak tomato** *n* a type of large fleshy tomato
beef up *vb informal* to strengthen
beefy *adj* **beefier, beefiest 1** *informal* muscular **2** like beef **beefiness** *n*
beehive *n* a structure in which bees are housed
beekeeper *n* a person who keeps bees for their honey **beekeeping** *n*
beeline *n* **make a beeline for** to speedily take the most direct route to
Beelzebub (bee-ell-zib-bub) *n* Satan or any devil
WORD ORIGIN Hebrew *bá'al zebūb*, literally: lord of flies
been *vb* ▸ the past participle of **be**
beep *n* **1** a high-pitched sound, like that of a car horn ▹*vb* **2** to make or cause to make such a noise
WORD ORIGIN imitative
beer *n* **1** an alcoholic drink brewed from malt, sugar, hops, and water **2** a glass, can, or bottle containing this drink
WORD ORIGIN Old English *beor*
beer and skittles *n informal* enjoyment or pleasure
Beerbohm *n* Sir (**Henry**) **Max**(**imilian**) 1872–1956, English critic, wit, and caricaturist, whose works include *Zuleika Dobson* (1911), a satire on Oxford undergraduates
beer parlour ❶ *n Canad* a licensed place in which beer is sold and drunk
beery *adj* **beerier, beeriest** smelling or tasting of beer
beeswax *n* **1** a wax produced by honeybees for making honeycombs **2** this wax after refining, used in polishes, etc.
beet *n* a plant with an edible root and leaves, such as the sugar beet and beetroot
WORD ORIGIN Old English *bēte*
beetle[1] *n* **1** an insect with a hard wing-case closed over its back for protection ▹*vb* **-tling, -tled 2** (foll. by *along* or *off* etc.) *informal* to scuttle or scurry
WORD ORIGIN Old English *bitela*
beetle[2] *vb* **-tling, -tled** to overhang; jut: *the eaves of the roof beetled out over the windows* **beetling** *adj*
WORD ORIGIN origin unknown
beetle-browed *adj* having bushy or overhanging eyebrows
beetroot *n* a variety of the beet plant with a dark red root that may be eaten as a vegetable, in salads, or pickled
beet sugar *n* the sucrose obtained from sugar beet
befall *vb* **-falling, -fell, -fallen** *archaic or literary* to happen to
WORD ORIGIN Old English *befeallan*
befit *vb* **-fitting, -fitted** to be appropriate to or suitable for **befitting** *adj*
before ❶ *conj* **1** earlier than the time when **2** rather than: *she'll resign before she agrees to it* ▹*prep* **3** preceding in space or time; in front of; ahead of: *they stood before the altar* **4** in the presence of: *to be brought before a judge* **5** in preference to: *to put friendship before money* ▹*adv* **6** previously **7** in front
WORD ORIGIN Old English *beforan*
beforehand ❶ *adj, adv* early; in advance
befriend *vb* to become a friend to
befuddled *adj* stupefied or confused, as through alcoholic drink
beg ❶ *vb* **begging, begged 1** to ask for money or food in the street **2** to ask formally, humbly, or earnestly: *I beg forgiveness; I beg to differ* **3 beg the question** to put forward an argument that assumes the very point it is supposed to establish, or that depends on some other questionable assumption **4 go begging** to be unwanted or unused
WORD ORIGIN probably from Old English *bedecian*
began *vb* ▸ the past tense of **begin**
beget *vb* **-getting, -got** *or* **-gat; -gotten** *or* **-got** *old-fashioned* **1** to cause or create: *repetition begets boredom* **2** to father
WORD ORIGIN Old English *begietan*
beggar ❶ *n* **1** a person who lives by begging **2** *chiefly Brit* a fellow: *lucky beggar!* ▹*vb* **3 beggar description** to be impossible to describe **beggarly** *adj*
begin ❶ *vb* **-ginning, -gan, -gun 1** to start (something) **2** to bring or come into being **3** to start to say or speak **4** to have the least capacity to do something: *it doesn't even begin to address the problem* **beginner** *n*
WORD ORIGIN Old English *beginnan*
beginner's luck *n* exceptional luck supposed to attend a beginner
beginning ❶ *n* **1** a start **2 beginnings** an early part or stage **3** the place where or time when something starts **4** an origin; source
begone *interj* go away!
begonia *n* a tropical plant with

alehouse *(archaic)*, taproom
before *prep* **3a = earlier than**, ahead of, prior to, in advance of
OPPOSITE: after
3b = in front of, ahead of, in advance of, to the fore of **3c = ahead of**, in front of, in advance of **4 = in the presence of**, in front of ▹*adv* **6 = previously**, earlier, sooner, in advance, formerly **OPPOSITE:** after
beforehand *adv* **= in advance**, before, earlier, already, sooner, ahead, previously, in anticipation, before now, ahead of time
beg *vb* **1 = scrounge**, bum *(informal)*, blag *(slang)*, touch (someone) for *(slang)*, mooch *(slang)*, cadge, forage for, hunt around (for), sponge on (someone) for, freeload *(slang)*, seek charity, call for alms, solicit charity
OPPOSITE: give
2 = implore, plead with, beseech, desire, request, pray, petition, conjure, crave, solicit, entreat, importune, supplicate, go on bended knee to
beggar *n* **1 = tramp**, bankrupt, bum *(informal)*, derelict, drifter, down-and-out, pauper, vagrant, hobo *(chiefly US)*, vagabond, bag lady *(chiefly US)*, dosser *(Brit slang)*, derro *(Austral slang)*, starveling
begin *vb* **1a = start**, commence, proceed **OPPOSITE:** stop
1b = commence, start, initiate, embark on, set about, instigate, inaugurate, institute, make a beginning, set on foot **2 = come into existence**, start, appear, emerge, spring, be born, arise, dawn, be developed, be created, originate, commence, be invented, become available, crop up *(informal)*, come into being **3 = start talking**, start, initiate, commence, begin business, get *or* start the ball rolling
beginning *n* **1 = start**, opening, break *(informal)*, chance, source, opportunity, birth, origin, introduction, outset, starting point, onset, overture, initiation, inauguration, inception, commencement, opening move
OPPOSITE: end
3 = outset, start, opening, birth, onset, prelude, preface, commencement, kickoff *(informal)*

DICTIONARY

ornamental leaves and waxy flowers **WORD ORIGIN** after Michel *Bégon*, patron of science

b

begot *vb* ▸ a past tense and past participle of **beget**

begotten *vb* ▸ a past participle of **beget**

begrudge *vb* **-grudging, -grudged** **1** to envy (someone) the possession of something **2** to give or allow unwillingly: *he begrudged her an apology*

beguile (big-gile) *vb* **-guiling, -guiled** to charm (someone) into doing something he or she would not normally do

beguiling *adj* charming, often in a deceptive way

beguine (big-geen) *n* **1** a dance of South American origin **2** music for this dance **WORD ORIGIN** French *béguin* flirtation

begum (bay-gum) *n* (in certain Muslim countries) a woman of high rank **WORD ORIGIN** Turkish *begim*

begun *vb* ▸ the past participle of **begin**

behalf *n* **on** *or US & Canad* **in behalf of** in the interest of or for the benefit of **WORD ORIGIN** Old English *be* by + *halfe* side

Behan *n* **Brendan** 1923–64, Irish writer, noted esp. for his plays *The Quare Fellow* (1954) and *The Hostage* (1958) and for an account of his detention as a member of the Irish Republican Army, *Borstal Boy* (1958)

behave ❶ *vb* **-having, -haved** **1** to act or function in a particular way **2** to conduct oneself in a particular way: *the baby behaved very well* **3** to conduct oneself properly **WORD ORIGIN** Middle English

behaviour ❶ *or US* **behavior** *n* **1** manner of behaving **2** *psychol* the response of an organism to a stimulus **behavioural** *or US* **behavioral** *adj*

behavioural science *n* the scientific study of the behaviour of organisms

behaviourism *or US* **behaviorism** *n* a school of psychology that regards objective observation of the behaviour of organisms as the only valid subject for study **behaviourist** *or US* **behaviorist** *adj, n*

behead *vb* to remove the head from **WORD ORIGIN** Old English *beheāfdian*

beheld *vb* ▸ the past of **behold**

behemoth (bee-hee-moth) *n* a huge person or thing **WORD ORIGIN** Hebrew *bĕhēmāh* beast, name given to a huge beast in the Bible (Job 40:15)

behest *n* an order or earnest request: *I came at her behest* **WORD ORIGIN** Old English *behǣs*

behind ❶ *prep* **1** in or to a position further back than **2** in the past in relation to: *I want to leave the past behind me* **3** late according to: *running behind schedule* **4** concerning the circumstances surrounding: *the reasons behind his departure* **5** supporting: *I'm right behind you in your application* ▹ *adv* **6** in or to a position further back **7** remaining after someone's departure: *she left her books behind* **8** in arrears: *to fall behind with payments* ▹ *adj* **9** in a position further back ▹ *n* **10** *informal* the buttocks **WORD ORIGIN** Old English *behindan*

behindhand *adj, adv* **1** in arrears **2** backward **3** late

Behn *n* **Aphra** 1640–89, English dramatist and novelist, best known for her play *The Rover* (1678) and her novel *Oroonoko* (1688)

behold *vb* **-holding, -held** *archaic or literary* to look (at); observe **beholder** *n* **WORD ORIGIN** Old English *bihealdan*

beholden *adj* indebted; obliged: *I am beholden to you*

behove *vb* **-hoving, -hoved** *archaic* to be necessary or fitting for: *it behoves me to warn you* **WORD ORIGIN** Old English *behōfian*

Behrens *n* **Peter** 1868–1940, German architect

Behring *n* **1 Emil (Adolf) von** 1854–1917, German bacteriologist, who discovered diphtheria and tetanus antitoxins: Nobel prize for physiology or medicine 1901 **2** ▸ a variant spelling of **Bering**

Beiderbecke *n* **Leon Bismarcke**, known as *Bix*. 1903–31, US jazz cornettist, composer, and pianist

beige *adj* pale creamy-brown **WORD ORIGIN** Old French

being ❶ *n* **1** the state or fact of existing **2** essential nature; self **3** something that exists or is thought to exist: *a being from outer space* **4** a human being

Béjart, *n* **Maurice** born 1927, French dancer and choreographer. His choreography is characterized by a combination of classic and modern dance and acrobatics

bejewelled *or US* **bejeweled** *adj* decorated with jewels

Békésy *n* **Georg von** 1899–1972, US physicist, born in Hungary; noted for his work on the mechanism of hearing: Nobel prize for physiology or medicine 1961

bel *n* a unit for comparing two power levels or measuring the intensity of a sound, equal to 10 decibels **WORD ORIGIN** after A. G. *Bell*, scientist

belabour *or US* **belabor** *vb* to attack verbally or physically

belated *adj* late or too late: *belated greetings* **belatedly** *adv*

belay *vb* **-laying, -layed** **1** *naut* to secure a line to a pin or cleat **2** *naut* to stop **3** *mountaineering* to secure (a climber) by fixing a rope round a rock or piton **WORD ORIGIN** Old English *belecgan*

belch *vb* **1** to expel wind from the stomach noisily through the mouth **2** to expel or be expelled forcefully: *smoke belching from factory chimneys* ▹ *n* **3** an act of belching **WORD ORIGIN** Old English *bialcan*

beleaguered ❶ *adj* **1** struggling against difficulties or criticism: *the country's beleaguered health system* **2** besieged by an enemy: *a ship bringing food to the beleaguered capital of Monrovia* **WORD ORIGIN** BE- + obsolete *leaguer* a siege

belfry *n, pl* **-fries** **1** the part of a tower or steeple in which bells are hung **2** a tower or steeple

THESAURUS

behave *vb* **2 = act**, react, conduct yourself, acquit yourself, comport yourself **3** *(often reflexive)* **= be well-behaved**, be good, be polite, mind your manners, keep your nose clean, act correctly, act politely, conduct yourself properly **OPPOSITE:** misbehave

behaviour *n* **1 = conduct**, ways, actions, bearing, attitude, manner, manners, carriage, demeanour, deportment, mien *(literary)*, comportment

behind *prep* **1a = at the rear of**, at the back of, at the heels of **1b = after**, following **3 = later than**, after **4 = causing**, responsible for, the cause of, initiating, at the bottom of, to blame for, instigating **5 = supporting**, for, backing, on the side of, in agreement with ▹ *adv* **6 = after**, next, following, afterwards, subsequently, in the wake (of) **OPPOSITE:** in advance of **8 = overdue**, in debt, in arrears, behindhand ▹ *n* **10** *(informal)* **= bottom**, seat, bum *(Brit slang)*, butt *(US & Canad informal)*, buns *(US slang)*, buttocks, rump, posterior, tail *(informal)*, derrière *(euphemistic)*, tush *(US slang)*, jacksy *(Brit slang)*

being *n* **1 = life**, living, reality, animation, actuality **OPPOSITE:** nonexistence **2 = soul**, spirit, presence, substance, creature, essence, organism, entity **3, 4 = individual**, thing, body, animal, creature, human being, beast, mortal, living thing

beleaguered *adj* **1 = harassed**, troubled, plagued, tormented, hassled *(informal)*, aggravated *(informal)*, badgered, persecuted, pestered, vexed, put upon **2 = besieged**, surrounded, blockaded, encompassed, beset, encircled, assailed, hemmed in, hedged in, environed

DICTIONARY

WORD ORIGIN Germanic
Belgian *adj* **1** of Belgium ▷*n* **2** a person from Belgium
belgium sausage *n* NZ large smooth bland sausage
Belial (bee-lee-al) *n* the devil or Satan
WORD ORIGIN Hebrew *bəlīyya'al* worthless
belie *vb* **-lying, -lied 1** to show to be untrue: *the facts belied the theory* **2** to misrepresent: *the score belied the closeness of the match* **3** to fail to justify: *the promises were soon belied*
WORD ORIGIN Old English *belēogan*
belief ❶ *n* **1** trust or confidence: *belief in the free market* **2** opinion; conviction: *it's my firm belief* **3** a principle, etc. accepted as true, often without proof **4** religious faith
believe ❶ *vb* **-lieving, -lieved 1** to accept as true or real: *I believe God exists* **2** to think, assume, or suppose: *I believe you know my father* **3** to accept the statement or opinion of (a person) as true **4** to have religious faith **5 believe in** to be convinced of the truth or existence of: *I don't believe in ghosts* **believable** *adj* **believer** *n*
WORD ORIGIN Old English *beliefan*
Belisarius *n* ?505–565 AD, Byzantine general under Justinian I. He recovered North Africa from the Vandals and Italy from the Ostrogoths and led forces against the Persians
Belisha beacon (bill-lee-sha) *n Brit* a flashing orange globe mounted on a striped post, indicating a pedestrian crossing
WORD ORIGIN after L. Hore-*Belisha*, politician
belittle *vb* **-tling, -tled** to treat (something or someone) as having little value or importance
bell *n* **1** a hollow, usually metal, cup-shaped instrument that emits a ringing sound when struck **2** the sound made by such an instrument **3** an electrical device that rings or buzzes as a signal **4** something shaped like a bell **5** *Brit slang* a telephone call **6 ring a bell** to sound familiar; recall something previously experienced
WORD ORIGIN Old English *belle*
belladonna *n* **1** a drug obtained from deadly nightshade **2** ▸same as **deadly nightshade**
WORD ORIGIN Italian, literally: beautiful lady; supposed to refer to its use as a cosmetic
Bellamy *n* **David (James)** born 1933, British botanist, writer, and broadcaster
Bellarmine *n* **Saint Robert** 1542–1621, Italian Jesuit theologian and cardinal; an important influence during the Counter-Reformation
Bellay *n* **Joachim du** 1522–60, French poet, a member of the Pléiade
bell-bottoms *pl n* trousers that flare from the knee **bell-bottomed** *adj*
belle *n* a beautiful woman, esp. the most attractive woman at a function: *the belle of the ball*
WORD ORIGIN French
belles-lettres (bell-let-tra) *n* literary works, particularly essays and poetry
WORD ORIGIN French
bellicose *adj* warlike; aggressive
WORD ORIGIN Latin *bellum* war
belligerence *n* the act or quality of being belligerent or warlike
belligerent *adj* **1** marked by readiness to fight **2** relating to or engaged in a war ▷*n* **3** a person or country engaged in war
WORD ORIGIN Latin *bellum* war + *gerere* to wage
bell jar *n* a bell-shaped glass cover used to protect flower arrangements or cover apparatus to confine gases in experiments
Belloc *n* **Hilaire** 1870–1953, British poet, essayist, and historian, born in France, noted particularly for his verse for children in *The Bad Child's Book of Beasts* (1896) and *Cautionary Tales* (1907)
bellow ❶ *vb* **1** to make a loud deep cry like that of a bull **2** to shout in anger ▷*n* **3** the characteristic noise of a bull **4** a loud deep roar
WORD ORIGIN probably from Old English *bylgan*
Bellow *n* **Saul** 1915–2005, US novelist, born in Canada. His works include *Dangling Man* (1944), *The Adventures of Angie March* (1954), *Herzog* (1964), *Humboldt's Gift* (1975), *The Dean's December* (1981), and *Ravelstein* (2000): Nobel prize for literature 1976
bellows *n* **1** a device consisting of an air chamber with flexible sides that is used to create and direct a stream of air **2** a flexible corrugated part, such as that connecting the lens system of some cameras to the body
WORD ORIGIN plural of Old English *belig* belly
bell pull *n* a handle or cord pulled to operate a bell
bell push *n* a button pressed to operate an electric bell
bell-ringer *n* a person who rings church bells or musical handbells **bell-ringing** *n*
bells and whistles *pl n* attractive but nonessential additional features
WORD ORIGIN from the bells and whistles which used to decorate fairground organs
belly ❶ *n, pl* **-lies 1** the part of the body of a vertebrate containing the intestines and other organs **2** the stomach **3** the front, lower, or inner part of something **4 go belly up** *informal* to die, fail, or end ▷*vb* **-lies, -lying, -lied 5** to swell out; bulge
WORD ORIGIN Old English *belig*
bellyache *n* **1** *informal* a pain in the abdomen ▷*vb* **-aching, -ached 2** *slang* to complain repeatedly
bellybutton *n informal* the navel
belly dance *n* **1** a sensuous dance performed by women, with undulating movements of the abdomen ▷*vb* **belly-dance, -dancing, -danced 2** to dance thus **belly dancer** *n*
belly flop *n* **1** a dive into water in which the body lands horizontally ▷*vb* **belly-flop, -flopping, -flopped 2** to perform a belly flop
bellyful *n* **1** *slang* more than one can tolerate **2** as much as one wants or can eat
belly laugh *n* a loud deep hearty laugh
Belmondo *n* **Jean-Paul** born 1933, French film actor
belong ❶ *vb* **1** (foll. by *to*) to be the property of **2** (foll. by *to*) to be bound to (a person, organization, etc.) by ties of affection, association, membership, etc.: *the nations concerned belonged to NATO* **3** (foll. by *to*, *under* or *with* etc.) to be classified with: *it*

THESAURUS

belief *n* **1 = trust**, confidence, conviction, reliance
OPPOSITE: disbelief
2 = opinion, feeling, idea, view, theory, impression, assessment, notion, judgment, point of view, sentiment, persuasion, presumption
3 = faith, principles, doctrine, ideology, creed, dogma, tenet, credence, credo
believe *vb* **1, 3 = accept**, hold, buy (*slang*), trust, credit, depend on, rely on, swallow (*informal*), count on, buy into (*slang*), have faith in, swear by, be certain of, be convinced of, place confidence in, presume true, take as gospel, take on (*US*)
OPPOSITE: disbelieve
2 = think, consider, judge, suppose, maintain, estimate, imagine, assume, gather, guess (*informal, chiefly US & Canad*), reckon, conclude, deem, speculate, presume, conjecture, postulate, surmise
bellow *vb* **2 = shout**, call, cry (out), scream, roar, yell, howl, shriek, clamour, bawl, holler (*informal*) ▷*n* **4 = shout**, call, cry, scream, roar, yell, howl, shriek, bell, clamour, bawl
belly *n* **1, 2 = stomach**, insides (*informal*), gut, abdomen, tummy, paunch, vitals, breadbasket (*slang*), potbelly, corporation (*informal*), puku (*NZ*)
belong *vb* **4 = go with**, fit into, be part of, relate to, attach to, be connected with, pertain to, have as a proper place
belonging *n* **= fellowship**,

DICTIONARY

belongs to a different class of comets **4** (foll. by *to*) to be a part of: *this lid belongs to that tin* **5** to have a proper or usual place **6** *informal* to be acceptable, esp. socially
WORD ORIGIN Middle English *belongen*

belonging ❶ *n* a secure relationship: *they have a strong sense of belonging*

belongings ❶ *pl n* the things that a person owns or has with him or her

beloved ❶ *adj* **1** dearly loved ▷*n* **2** a person who is dearly loved

below ❶ *prep* **1** at or to a position lower than; under **2** less than **3** unworthy of; beneath ▷*adv* **4** at or to a lower position **5** at a later place in something written **6** *archaic* on earth or in hell
WORD ORIGIN Middle English *bilooghe*

belt ❶ *n* **1** a band of leather or cloth worn around the waist **2** an area where a specific thing is found; zone: *a belt of high pressure* **3** ▸ same as **seat belt** **4** a band of flexible material between rotating shafts or pulleys to transfer motion or transmit goods: *a fan belt; a conveyer belt* **5** *informal* a sharp blow **6** **below the belt** *informal* unscrupulous or cowardly **7** **tighten one's belt** to reduce expenditure **8** **under one's belt** as part of one's experience: *he had a string of successes under his belt* ▷*vb* **9** to fasten with or as if with a belt **10** to hit with a belt **11** *slang* to give (someone) a sharp blow **12** (foll. by *along*) *slang* to move very fast
WORD ORIGIN Old English

belter *n slang* an outstanding person or event: *a belter of a match*

belt out *vb informal* to sing (a song) loudly

belt up *vb* **1** *slang* to stop talking **2** to fasten with a belt

beluga (bill-loo-ga) *n* a large white sturgeon of the Black and Caspian Seas, from which caviar and isinglass are obtained
WORD ORIGIN Russian *byeluga*

belvedere *n* a building designed and situated to look out on pleasant scenery
WORD ORIGIN Italian: beautiful sight

Belyi *or* **Bely** *n* **Andrei**, real name *Boris Nikolayevich Bugaev*. 1880–1934, Russian poet, novelist, and critic: a leading exponent of symbolism. His novels include *Petersburg* (1913)

BEM British Empire Medal

Bembo[1] *n* **Pietro** 1470–1547, Italian scholar, poet, and cardinal (1539). His treatise *Prose della volgar lingua* (1525) helped to establish a standard form of literary Italian

Bembo[2] *n* a style of type
WORD ORIGIN after Pietro *Bembo*

bemoan *vb* to lament: *he's always bemoaning his fate*

bemused ❶ *adj* puzzled or confused

ben *n Scot, Irish* a mountain peak: *Ben Lomond*
WORD ORIGIN Gaelic *beinn*

Benacerraf *n* **Baruj** born 1920, US immunologist: shared the Nobel prize for physiology or medicine (1980) for his work on histocompatibility antigens

Benavente y Martínez *n* **Jacinto** 1866–1954, Spanish dramatist and critic, who wrote over 150 plays. Nobel prize for literature 1922

Benbow *n* **John** 1653–1702, English admiral, noted esp. for his heroic death during the War of the Spanish Succession

bench ❶ *n* **1** a long seat for more than one person **2** **the bench** **a** a judge or magistrate sitting in court **b** judges or magistrates collectively **3** a long and strong worktable
WORD ORIGIN Old English *benc*

benchmark ❶ *n* **1** a mark on a fixed object, used as a reference point in surveying **2** a criterion by which to measure something: *the speech was a benchmark of his commitment*

bench press *n* an exercise in which a person pushes a barbell upwards while lying flat on a bench

bend[1] ❶ *vb* **bending, bent** **1** to form a curve **2** to turn from a particular direction: *the road bends right* **3** (often foll. by *down* etc.) to incline the body **4** to submit: *to bend before public opinion* **5** to turn or direct (one's eyes, steps, or attention) **6** **bend someone's ear** *informal* to complain (to someone) for a long time **7** **bend the rules** *informal* to ignore or change rules to suit oneself ▷*n* **8** a curved part **9** the act of bending **10** **round the bend** *Brit slang* mad **bendy** *adj*
WORD ORIGIN Old English *bendan*

bend[2] *n heraldry* a diagonal line across a shield
WORD ORIGIN Old English: a band, strip

Benda *n* **Julien** 1867–1956, French philosopher and novelist, who defended reason and intellect and attacked the influence of Bergson: author of *La Trahison des clercs* (1927)

bender *n informal* **1** a drinking bout **2** a shelter made from plastic sheeting and woven branches

bends *pl n* **the bends** *informal* decompression sickness

bend sinister *n heraldry* a diagonal line across a shield, indicating a bastard line

beneath ❶ *prep* **1** below; under **2** too trivial for: *beneath his dignity* ▷*adv* **3** below; underneath
WORD ORIGIN Old English *beneothan*

Benedictine *n* **1** a monk or nun of the Christian order of Saint Benedict **2** a liqueur first made by Benedictine monks ▷*adj* **3** of Saint Benedict or his order

benediction *n* **1** a prayer for divine blessing **2** a Roman Catholic service in which the congregation is blessed with the sacrament **benedictory** *adj*
WORD ORIGIN Latin *benedictio*

Benedict XV *n* original name *Giacomo della Chiesa*. 1854–1922, pope (1914–22); noted for his repeated attempts to end World War I and for his organization of war relief

benefaction *n* **1** the act of doing

THESAURUS

relationship, association, loyalty, acceptance, attachment, inclusion, affinity, rapport, affiliation, kinship

belongings *pl n* **= possessions**, goods, things, effects, property, stuff, gear, paraphernalia, personal property, accoutrements, chattels, goods and chattels

beloved *adj* **1 = dear**, loved, valued, prized, dearest, sweet, admired, treasured, precious, darling, worshipped, adored, cherished, revered

below *prep* **1 = under**, underneath, lower than **2 = less than**, lower than ▷*adv* **4 = lower**, down, under, beneath, underneath

belt *n* **1 = waistband**, band, sash, girdle, girth, cummerbund, cincture **2** (*geography*) **= zone**, area, region, section, sector, district, stretch, strip, layer, patch, portion, tract **4 = conveyor belt**, band, loop, fan belt, drive belt

bemused *adj* **= puzzled**, stunned, confused, stumped, baffled, at sea, bewildered, muddled, preoccupied, dazed, perplexed, mystified, engrossed, clueless, stupefied, nonplussed, absent-minded, flummoxed, half-drunk, fuddled

bench *n* **1 = seat**, stall, pew **2a, 2b the bench = court**, judge, judges, magistrate, magistrates, tribunal, judiciary, courtroom **3 = worktable**, stand, table, counter, slab, trestle table, workbench

benchmark *n* **2 = reference point**, gauge, yardstick, measure, level, example, standard, model, reference, par, criterion, norm, touchstone

bend[1] *vb* **1 = twist**, turn, wind, lean, hook, bow, curve, arch, incline, arc, deflect, warp, buckle, coil, flex, stoop, veer, swerve, diverge, contort, inflect, incurvate ▷*n* **8 = curve**, turn, corner, hook, twist, angle, bow, loop, arc, zigzag, camber

beneath *prep* **1 = under**, below, underneath, lower than
OPPOSITE: over
2 = unworthy of, unfitting for, unsuitable for, inappropriate for, unbefitting ▷*adv* **3 = underneath**,

DICTIONARY

good, particularly donating to charity **2** the donation or help given **WORD ORIGIN** Latin *bene* well + *facere* to do

benefactor *n* a person who supports a person or institution by giving money **benefactress** *fem n*

benefice *n Christianity* a Church office that provides its holder with an income
WORD ORIGIN Latin *beneficium* benefit

beneficent (bin-eff-iss-ent) *adj* charitable; generous **beneficence** *n*
WORD ORIGIN Latin *beneficus*

beneficial ❶ *adj* helpful or advantageous
WORD ORIGIN Latin *beneficium* kindness

beneficiary ❶ *n, pl* **-ciaries 1** a person who gains or benefits **2** *law* a person entitled to receive funds or property under a trust, will, etc.

benefit ❶ *n* **1** something that improves or promotes **2** advantage or sake: *I'm doing this for your benefit* **3** a payment made by an institution or government to a person who is ill, unemployed, etc. **4** a theatrical performance or sports event to raise money for a charity ▹*vb* **-fiting, -fited** *or US* **-fitting, -fitted 5** to do or receive good; profit
WORD ORIGIN Latin *bene facere* to do well

benefit society *n US* ▸same as **friendly society**

Beneš *n* **Eduard** 1884–1948, Czech statesman; president of Czechoslovakia (1935–38; 1946–48) and of its government in exile (1939–45)

Benét *n* **Stephen Vincent** 1898–1943, US poet and novelist, best known for his poem on the American Civil War *John Brown's Body* (1928)

benevolence *n* **1** inclination to do good **2** an act of kindness **benevolent** *adj*

Bengali *n* **1** a member of a people living chiefly in Bangladesh and West Bengal **2** the language of this people ▹*adj* **3** of Bengal or the Bengalis

Ben-Gurion *n* **David**, original name *David Gruen*. 1886–1973, Israeli socialist statesman, born in Poland; first prime minister of Israel (1948–53, 1955–63)

benighted *adj* lacking cultural, moral, or intellectual enlightenment

benign ❶ (bin-nine) *adj* **1** showing kindliness **2** favourable: *a stroke of benign fate* **3** *pathol* (of a tumour, etc.) able to be controlled **benignly** *adv*
WORD ORIGIN Latin *benignus*

benignant *adj* **1** kind or gracious **2** ▸same as **benign** (senses 2, 3) ›**benignancy** *n*

benignity (bin-nig-nit-tee) *n, pl* **-ties** kindliness

Benjamin[1] *n* **1** *Old Testament* **a** the youngest and best-loved son of Jacob and Rachel (Genesis 35:16–18; 42:4) **b** the tribe descended from this patriarch **c** the territory of this tribe, northwest of the Dead Sea **2** *archaic* a youngest and favourite son

Benjamin[2] *n* **1 Arthur** 1893–1960, Australian composer. In addition to *Jamaican Rumba* (1938), he wrote five operas and a harmonica concerto (1953) **2 Walter** 1892–1940, German critic and cultural theorist

Benny *n* **Jack**, real name *Benjamin Kubelsky*. 1894–1974, US comedian

Benoît de Sainte-Maure *n* 12th-century French trouvère: author of the *Roman de Troie*, which contains the episode of Troilus and Cressida

Benson *n* **E(dward) F(rederic)** 1867–1940, British writer, noted esp. for a series of comic novels featuring the characters Mapp and Lucia

bent ❶ *adj* **1** not straight; curved **2** *slang* **a** dishonest; corrupt: *bent officials* **b** *Austral & Brit offensive slang* homosexual **3 bent on** determined to pursue (a course of action) ▹*n* **4** personal inclination or aptitude: *he had a strong practical bent in his nature*

Benthamism *n* the utilitarian philosophy of Jeremy Bentham, which holds that the ultimate goal of society should be to promote the greatest happiness of the greatest number **Benthamite** *n, adj*

Bentinck *n* Lord **William Cavendish** 1774–1839, British statesman, governor general of Bengal (1828–35)

bento *or* **bento box** *n* a thin box, made of plastic or lacquered wood, divided into compartments, which contain small separate dishes comprising a Japanese meal, esp. lunch
WORD ORIGIN Japanese *bento* box lunch

Benton *n* **Thomas Hart** 1889–1975, US painter of rural life; a leader of the American Regionalist painters in the 1930s

bentwood *n* **1** wood bent in moulds, used mainly for furniture ▹*adj* **2** made from such wood: *a bentwood chair*

benumb *vb* **1** to make numb or powerless **2** to stupefy (the mind, senses, will, etc.): *the work benumbed their minds and crushed their spirits*

Benz *n* **Karl** (**Friedrich**) 1844–1929, German engineer; designed and built the first car to be driven by an internal-combustion engine (1885)

benzene *n* a flammable poisonous liquid used as a solvent, insecticide, etc.
WORD ORIGIN from *benzoin*, a fragrant resin from certain Asiatic trees

benzine *n* a volatile liquid obtained from coal tar and used as a solvent

Ben-Zvi *n* **Itzhak** 1884–1963, Israeli statesman; president (1952–63)

bequeath ❶ *vb* **1** *law* to dispose of (property) as in a will **2** to hand down: *the author bequeaths no solutions*
WORD ORIGIN Old English *becwethan*

bequest *n* **1** the act of gifting money or property in a will **2** money or

THESAURUS

below, in a lower place ▸*related prefix:* sub-

beneficial *adj* **= favourable**, useful, valuable, helpful, profitable, benign, wholesome, advantageous, expedient, salutary, healthful, serviceable, salubrious, gainful **OPPOSITE:** harmful

beneficiary *n* **1 = recipient**, receiver, payee, assignee, legatee **2 = heir**, inheritor

benefit *n* **1 = good**, use, help, profit, gain, favour, utility, boon, mileage *(informal)*, avail **OPPOSITE:** harm **2 = advantage**, interest, aid, gain, favour, assistance, betterment ▹*vb* **5a = profit from**, make the most of, gain from, do well out of, reap benefits from, turn to your advantage **5b = help**, serve, aid, profit, improve, advance, advantage, enhance, assist, avail **OPPOSITE:** harm

benign *adj* **1 = benevolent**, kind, kindly, warm, liberal, friendly, generous, obliging, sympathetic, favourable, compassionate, gracious, amiable, genial, affable, complaisant **OPPOSITE:** unkind **3** *(medical)* **= harmless**, innocent, superficial, innocuous, curable, inoffensive, not dangerous, remediable **OPPOSITE:** malignant

bent *adj* **1 = misshapen**, twisted, angled, bowed, curved, arched, crooked, crippled, distorted, warped, deformed, tortuous, disfigured, out of shape **OPPOSITE:** straight ▹*n* **3 bent on = intent on**, set on, fixed on, predisposed to, resolved on, insistent on **4 = inclination**, ability, taste, facility, talent, leaning, tendency, preference, faculty, forte, flair, knack, penchant, bag *(slang)*, propensity, aptitude, predisposition, predilection, proclivity, turn of mind

bequeath *vb* **1 = leave**, will, give, grant, commit, transmit, hand down, endow, bestow, entrust, leave to by will **2 = give**, offer, accord, grant, afford, contribute, yield, lend, pass on, transmit, confer, bestow, impart

property that has been gifted in a will

Béranger *n* **Pierre Jean de** 1780–1857, French lyric and satirical poet

berate *vb* **-rating, -rated** to scold harshly

Berber *n* **1** a member of a Muslim people of N Africa **2** the language of this people ▹*adj* **3** of the Berbers

berberis *n* a shrub with red berries
WORD ORIGIN Medieval Latin

berceuse (bare-suhz) *n* **1** a lullaby **2** an instrumental piece suggestive of this
WORD ORIGIN French

Berdyayev *n* **Nikolai Aleksandrovich** 1874–1948, Russian philosopher. Although he was a Marxist, his Christian views led him to criticize Soviet communism and he was forced into exile (1922)

bereaved *adj* having recently lost a close relative or friend through death **bereavement** *n*
WORD ORIGIN Old English *bereafian* to deprive

bereft *adj* (foll. by *of*) deprived: *a government bereft of ideas*

Berenson *n* **Bernard** 1865–1959, US art historian, born in Lithuania: an authority on art of the Italian Renaissance

Beresford *n* **Bruce** born 1940, Australian film director. His films include *The Adventures of Barry McKenzie* (1972), *Breaker Morant* (1980), *Driving Miss Daisy* (1989) and *Evelyn* (2002)

beret (ber-ray) *n* a round flat close-fitting brimless cap
WORD ORIGIN French

berg[1] *n* ▸short for **iceberg**

berg[2] *n S African* a mountain

Berg *n* **1 Alban** (**Maria Johannes**) 1885–1935, Austrian composer: a pupil of Schoenberg. His works include the operas *Wozzeck* (1921) and *Lulu* (1935), a violin concerto (1935), chamber works, and songs **2 Paul** born 1926, US molecular biologist, the first to identify transfer RNA (1956). Nobel prize for chemistry 1980

bergamot *n* **1** a small Asian tree with sour pear-shaped fruit **2 essence of bergamot** a fragrant essential oil from the fruit rind of this plant, used in perfumery
WORD ORIGIN French *bergamote*

Bergius *n* **Friedrich** (**Karl Rudolph**) 1884–1949, German chemist, who invented a process for producing oil by high-pressure hydrogenation of coal: Nobel prize for chemistry 1931

Bergström *n* **Sune** 1916–2004, Swedish biochemist; shared the Nobel prize for medicine and physiology (1982) for work on prostaglandin

Beria *n* **Lavrenti Pavlovich** 1899–1953, Soviet chief of secret police; killed by his associates shortly after Stalin's death

beri-beri *n* a disease caused by a dietary deficiency of thiamine (vitamin B_1)
WORD ORIGIN Sinhalese

Bering *or* **Behring** *n* **Vitus** 1681–1741, Danish navigator, who explored the N Pacific for the Russians and discovered Bering Island and the Bering Strait

Berio *n* **Luciano** 1925–2003, Italian composer, living in the US, noted esp. for works that exploit instrumental and vocal timbre and technique

Beriosova *n* **Svetlana** 1932–98, British ballet dancer, born in Lithuania

berk *or* **burk** *n Brit, Austral & NZ slang* a stupid person; fool
WORD ORIGIN *Berkshire Hunt*, rhyming slang for *cunt*

berkelium *n chem* an artificial radioactive element. Symbol: Bk
WORD ORIGIN after *Berkeley*, California, where it was discovered

Berks Berkshire

Berlichingen *n* **Götz von**, called *the Iron Hand*. 1480–1562, German warrior knight, who robbed merchants and kidnapped nobles for ransom

Berlin[1] *n* the capital of Germany (1871–1945 and from 1990), formerly divided (1945–90) into the eastern sector, capital of East Germany, and the western sector, which formed an exclave in East German territory closely affiliated with West Germany: a wall dividing the sectors was built in 1961 by the East German authorities to stop the flow of refugees from east to west; demolition of the wall began in 1989 and the city was formally reunited in 1990: formerly (1618–1871) the capital of Brandenburg and Prussia. Pop: 3 388 477 (2003 est)

Berlin[2] *n* **1 Irving** original name *Israel Baline*, 1888–1989, US composer and writer of lyrics, born in Russia. His musical comedies include *Annie Get Your Gun* (1946); his most popular song is *White Christmas* **2 Sir Isaiah** 1909–97, British philosopher, born in Latvia, historian, and diplomat. His books include *Historical Inevitability* (1954) and *The Magus of the North* (1993)

berm *n NZ* narrow grass strip between the road and the footpath in a residential area

Bermuda shorts *pl n* shorts that come down to the knees
WORD ORIGIN after *Bermudas*, islands in NW Atlantic

Bernadette of Lourdes *n* **Saint** original name *Marie Bernarde Soubirous*. 1844–79, French peasant girl born in Lourdes, whose visions of the Virgin Mary led to the establishment of Lourdes as a centre of pilgrimage, esp. for the sick or crippled. Feast day: Feb 18

Bernadotte *n* **1 Folke**, Count. 1895–1948, Swedish diplomat, noted for his work with the Red Cross during World War II and as United Nations mediator in Palestine (1948). He was assassinated by Jewish terrorists **2 Jean Baptiste Jules** 1764–1844, French marshal under Napoleon; king of Norway and Sweden (1818–44) as Charles XIV

Bernanos *n* **Georges** 1888–1948, French novelist and Roman Catholic pamphleteer, best known for *The Diary of a Country Priest* (1936)

Bernhardt *n* **Sarah** original name *Rosine Bernard*. 1844–1923, French actress, regarded as one of the greatest tragic actresses of all time

Bernini *n* **Gian Lorenzo** 1598–1680, Italian painter, architect, and sculptor: the greatest exponent of the Italian baroque

Bernoulli *or* **Bernouilli** *n* **1 Daniel**, son of Jean Bernoulli. 1700–82, Swiss mathematician and physicist, who developed an early form of the kinetic theory of gases and stated the principle of conservation of energy in fluid dynamics **2 Jacques** *or* **Jakob** 1654–1705, Swiss mathematician, noted for his work on calculus and the theory of probability **3** his brother, **Jean** *or* **Johann** 1667–1748, Swiss mathematician who developed the calculus of variations

Bernoulli principle *n physics* the principle that the pressure in a moving fluid becomes less as the speed rises
WORD ORIGIN after Daniel *Bernoulli*

Bernstein *n* **Leonard** 1918–90, US conductor and composer, whose works include *The Age of Anxiety* (1949), the score of the musical *West Side Story* (1957), and *Mass* (1971)

berry *n, pl* **-ries** a small round fruit that grows on bushes or trees and is often edible
WORD ORIGIN Old English *berie*

Berry *n* **1 Chuck**, full name *Charles Edward Berry*. born 1926, US rock-and-roll guitarist, singer, and songwriter. His frequently covered songs include "Maybellene" (1955), "Roll Over Beethoven" (1956), "Johnny B. Goode" (1958), "Memphis, Tennessee" (1959), and "Promised Land" (1964) **2 Jean de France**, Duc de. 1340–1416, French prince, son of King John II; coregent (1380–88) for Charles VI and a famous patron of the arts

Berryman *n* **John** 1914–72, US poet and critic, author of *Homage to Mistress Bradstreet* (1956) and *Dream Songs* (1964–68)

berserk *adj* **go berserk** to become violent or destructive
WORD ORIGIN Icelandic *björn* bear + *serkr* shirt

DICTIONARY

berth ⓘ *n* **1** a bunk in a ship or train **2** *naut* a place assigned to a ship at a mooring **3** *naut* sufficient room for a ship to manoeuvre **4 give a wide berth to** to keep clear of ▹*vb* **5** *naut* to dock (a.ship) **6** to provide with a sleeping place **7** *naut* to pick up a mooring in an anchorage
WORD ORIGIN probably from BEAR[1]

Bertolucci *n* **Bernardo** born 1940, Italian film director: his films include *The Spider's Stratagem* (1970), *The Conformist* (1970), *1900* (1976), *The Last Emperor* (1987), *The Sheltering Sky* (1990), and *The Dreamers* (2003)

Berwick *n* **James Fitzjames**, Duke of Berwick. 1670–1734, marshal of France and illegitimate son of James II of England. He led French forces during the War of the Spanish Succession (1701–14)

beryl *n* a transparent hard mineral, used as a source of beryllium and as a gemstone
WORD ORIGIN Greek *bērullos*

beryllium *n* a toxic silvery-white metallic element. Symbol: Be
WORD ORIGIN Greek *bērullos*

Berzelius *n* Baron **Jöns Jakob** 1779–1848, Swedish chemist, who invented the present system of chemical symbols and formulas, discovered several elements, and determined the atomic and molecular weight of many substances

Besant *n* **Annie**, *née* **Wood** 1847–1933, British theosophist, writer, and political reformer in England and India

beseech *vb* **-seeching, -sought** *or* **-seeched** to ask earnestly; beg
WORD ORIGIN Middle English; see BE-, SEEK

beset *vb* **-setting, -set 1** to trouble or harass constantly **2** to surround or attack from all sides

beside ⓘ *prep* **1** next to; at, by, or to the side of **2** as compared with **3** away from: *beside the point* **4 beside oneself** overwhelmed; overwrought: *beside oneself with grief* ▹*adv* **5** at, by, to, or along the side of something or someone
WORD ORIGIN Old English *be sīdan*

besides ⓘ *adv* **1** in addition ▹*prep* **2** apart from; even considering ▹*conj* **3** anyway; moreover

besiege ⓘ *vb* **-sieging, -sieged 1** to surround with military forces to bring about surrender **2** to hem in **3** to overwhelm, as with requests

besmirch *vb* to tarnish (someone's name or reputation)

besom *n* a broom made of a bundle of twigs tied to a handle
WORD ORIGIN Old English *besma*

besotted *adj* **1** having an irrational passion for a person or thing **2** stupefied with alcohol

besought *vb* ▸ a past of **beseech**

bespatter *vb* **1** to splash with dirty water **2** to dishonour or slander

bespeak *vb* **-speaking, -spoke; -spoken** *or* **-spoke 1** to indicate or suggest: *imitation bespeaks admiration* **2** to engage or ask for in advance: *she was bespoke to a family in the town*

bespectacled *adj* wearing spectacles

bespoke *adj chiefly Brit* **1** (esp. of a suit) made to the customer's specifications **2** making or selling such suits: *a bespoke tailor*

Bessel *n* **Friedrich Wilhelm** 1784–1846, German astronomer and mathematician. He made the first authenticated measurement of a star's distance (1841) and systematized a series of mathematical functions used in physics

best ⓘ *adj* **1** ▸ the superlative of **good 2** most excellent of a particular group, category, etc. **3** most suitable, desirable, etc. ▹*adv* **4** ▸ the superlative of **well 5** in a manner surpassing all others; most attractively, etc. ▹*n* **6 the best** the most outstanding or excellent person, thing, or group in a category **7** the utmost effort: *I did my best* **8** a person's finest clothes **9 at best a** in the most favourable interpretation **b** under the most favourable conditions **10 for the best a** for an ultimately good outcome **b** with good intentions **11 get the best of** to defeat or outwit **12 make the best of** to cope as well as possible with ▹*vb* **13** to defeat
WORD ORIGIN Old English *betst*

bestial *adj* **1** brutal or savage **2** of or relating to a beast
WORD ORIGIN Latin *bestia* beast

bestiality *n, pl* **-ties 1** brutal behaviour, character, or action **2** sexual activity between a person and an animal

bestiary *n, pl* **-aries** a medieval collection of descriptions of animals

bestir *vb* **-stirring, -stirred** to cause (oneself) to become active

best man *n* the male attendant of the bridegroom at a wedding

bestow ⓘ *vb* to present (a gift) or confer (an honour) **bestowal** *n*

bestrew *vb* **-strewing, -strewed; -strewn** *or* **-strewed** to scatter or lie scattered over (a surface)

bestride *vb* **-striding, -strode** to have or put a leg on either side of

bestseller *n* a book or other product that has sold in great numbers
bestselling *adj*

bet ⓘ *n* **1** the act of staking a sum of money or other stake on the outcome of an event **2** the stake risked **3** a course of action: *your best bet is to go by train* **4** *informal* an opinion: *my bet is that you've been up to no good* ▹*vb* **betting, bet** *or* **betted 5** to make or place a bet with (someone) **6** to stake (money, etc.) in a bet **7** *informal* to predict (a certain outcome): *I bet she doesn't turn up* **8 you bet** *informal* of course
WORD ORIGIN probably short for *abet*

THESAURUS

berth *n* **1 = bunk**, bed, cot (*nautical*), hammock, billet **2** (*nautical*) **= anchorage**, haven, slip, port, harbour, dock, pier, wharf, quay ▹*vb* **5** (*nautical*) **= anchor**, land, dock, moor, tie up, drop anchor

beside *prep* **1 = next to**, near, close to, neighbouring, alongside, overlooking, next door to, adjacent to, at the side of, abreast of, cheek by jowl with **4 beside yourself = distraught**, desperate, mad, distressed, frantic, frenzied, hysterical, insane, crazed, demented, unbalanced, uncontrolled, deranged, berserk, delirious, unhinged, very anxious, overwrought, apoplectic, out of your mind, at the end of your tether

besides *adv* **1 = also**, too, further, otherwise, in addition, as well, moreover, furthermore, what's more, into the bargain ▹*prep* **2 = apart from**, barring, excepting, other than, excluding, as well (as), in addition to, over and above

besiege *vb* **1, 2 = surround**, confine, enclose, blockade, encompass, beset, encircle, close in on, hem in, shut in, lay siege to, hedge in, environ, beleaguer, invest (*rare*) **3 = harass**, worry, trouble, harry, bother, disturb, plague, hound, hassle (*informal*), badger, pester, importune, bend someone's ear (*informal*), give someone grief (*Brit & S African*), beleaguer

best *adj* **2 = finest**, leading, chief, supreme, principal, first, foremost, superlative, pre-eminent, unsurpassed, most accomplished, most skilful, most excellent ▹*adv* **5 = most highly**, most fully, most deeply ▹*n* **6 the best = the finest**, the pick, the choice, the flower, the cream, the elite, the crème de la crème

bestow *vb* **= present**, give, accord, award, grant, commit, hand out, lavish, confer, endow, entrust, impart, allot, honour with, apportion **OPPOSITE:** obtain

bet *n* **1 = gamble**, risk, stake, venture, pledge, speculation, hazard, flutter (*informal*), ante, punt, wager, long shot ▹*vb* **6 = gamble**, chance, stake, venture, hazard, speculate, punt (*chiefly Brit*), wager, put money, risk money, pledge money, put your shirt on

DICTIONARY

b

beta *n* **1** the second letter in the Greek alphabet (Β, β) **2** the second in a group or series
beta-blocker *n* a drug that decreases the activity of the heart: used in the treatment of high blood pressure and angina pectoris
beta-carotene *n biochem* the most important form of the plant pigment carotene, which occurs in milk, vegetables, and other foods and, when eaten by man and animals, is converted in the body to vitamin A
betake *vb* **-taking, -took, -taken** ▪ **betake oneself** *formal* to go or move: *he betook himself to the public house*
beta particle *n* a high-speed electron or positron emitted by a nucleus during radioactive decay or nuclear fission
betatron *n* a type of particle accelerator for producing high-energy beams of electrons
betel (bee-tl) *n* an Asian climbing plant, the leaves and nuts of which can be chewed
WORD ORIGIN Malayalam (language of SW India) *vettila*
bête noire (bet **nwahr**) *n, pl* **bêtes noires** a person or thing that one particularly dislikes or dreads
WORD ORIGIN French, literally: black beast
Bethe *n* **Hans Albrecht** 1906–2005, US physicist, born in Germany; noted for his research on astrophysics and nuclear physics: Nobel prize for physics 1967
Bethmann Hollweg *n* **Theobald von** 1856–1921, chancellor of Germany (1909–17)
betide *vb* **-tiding, -tided** to happen or happen to: *woe betide us if we're not ready on time*
WORD ORIGIN BE- + obsolete *tide* to happen
betoken *vb* to indicate; signify
betray ❶ *vb* **1** to hand over or expose (one's nation, friend, etc.) treacherously to an enemy **2** to disclose (a secret or confidence) treacherously **3** to reveal unintentionally: *his singing voice betrays his origins* **betrayal** *n* **betrayer** *n*
WORD ORIGIN Latin *tradere* to hand over
betroth *vb archaic* to promise to marry or to give in marriage **betrothal** *n*
WORD ORIGIN Middle English *betreuthen*
betrothed *old-fashioned adj* **1** engaged to be married ▹*n* **2** the person to whom one is engaged
better ❶ *adj* **1** ▸the comparative of **good** **2** more excellent than others **3** more suitable, attractive, etc. **4** improved or fully recovered in health **5** **the better part of** a large part of ▹*adv* **6** ▸the comparative of **well** **7** in a more excellent manner **8** in or to a greater degree **9** **better off** in more favourable circumstances, esp. financially **10** **had better** would be sensible, etc. to: *I had better be off* ▹*n* **11** **the better** something that is the more excellent, useful, etc. of two such things **12** **betters** people who are one's superiors, esp. in social standing **13** **get the better of** to defeat or outwit ▹*vb* **14** to improve upon
WORD ORIGIN Old English *betera*
better half *n humorous* one's spouse
betterment *n* improvement
better-off *adj* reasonably wealthy: *Catalonia aims to attract better-off tourists*
Betti *n* **Ugo** 1892–1953, Italian writer, noted esp.for his plays, including *La Padrona* (1927), *Corruzione al palazzo di giustizia* (1949), and *La Regina e gli insorte* (1951)
betting shop *n* (in Britain) a licensed bookmaker's premises not on a racecourse
between ❶ *prep* **1** at a point intermediate to two other points in space, time, etc. **2** in combination; together: *between them, they saved enough money to buy a car* **3** confined to: *between you and me* **4** indicating a linking relation or comparison **5** indicating alternatives, strictly only two alternatives ▹*adv also* **in between** **6** between one specified thing and another
WORD ORIGIN Old English *betwēonum*
betwixt *prep, adv* **1** *archaic* between **2** **betwixt and between** in an intermediate or indecisive position
Beuys *n* **Joseph** 1921–86, German artist, a celebrated figure of the avant-garde, noted esp. for his sculptures made of felt and animal fat
bevel *n* **1** a slanting edge ▹*vb* **-elling, -elled** *or US* **-eling, -eled** **2** to be inclined; slope **3** to cut a bevel on (a piece of timber, etc.)
WORD ORIGIN Old French *baer* to gape
bevel gear *n* a toothed gear meshed with another at an angle to it
beverage ❶ *n* any drink other than water
WORD ORIGIN Old French *bevrage*
beverage room *n Canad* ▸same as **beer parlour**
Beveridge *n* **William Henry**, 1st Baron Beveridge. 1879–1963, British economist, whose *Report on Social Insurance and Allied Services* (1942) formed the basis of social-security legislation in Britain
bevvy *n, pl* **-vies** *dialect* **1** an alcoholic drink **2** a session of drinking
WORD ORIGIN probably from Old French *bevee*, *buvee* drinking
bevy *n, pl* **bevies** a flock; a group
WORD ORIGIN origin unknown
bewail *vb* to express great sorrow over; lament
beware ❶ *vb* **-waring, -wared** (often foll. by *of*) to be wary (of); be on one's guard (against)
WORD ORIGIN *be* (imperative) + obsolete *war* wary
Bewick *n* **Thomas** 1753–1828, English wood engraver; his best-known works are *Chillingham Bull* (1789), a large woodcut, *Aesop's Fables* (1818), and his *History of British Birds* (1797–1804)
bewilder ❶ *vb* to confuse utterly; puzzle **bewildering** *adj* **bewilderment** *n*
WORD ORIGIN BE- + obsolete *wilder* to lose one's way
bewitch *vb* **1** to attract and fascinate **2** to cast a spell over **bewitching** *adj*
WORD ORIGIN Middle English *bewicchen*

THESAURUS

betray *vb* **1 = be disloyal to**, break with, grass on *(Brit slang)*, dob in *(Austral slang)*, double-cross *(informal)*, stab in the back, be unfaithful to, sell down the river *(informal)*, grass up *(slang)*, shop *(slang, chiefly Brit)*, put the finger on *(informal)*, inform on *or* against **2,3 = give away**, tell, show, reveal, expose, disclose, uncover, manifest, divulge, blurt out, unmask, lay bare, tell on, let slip, evince
better *adj* **2,3 = superior**, finer, worthier, higher-quality, surpassing, preferable, more appropriate, more useful, more valuable, more suitable, more desirable, streets ahead, more fitting, more expert
OPPOSITE: inferior
4 = well, stronger, improving, progressing, recovering, healthier, cured, mending, fitter, fully recovered, on the mend *(informal)*, more healthy, less ill ▹*adv* **7 = in a more excellent manner**, more effectively, more attractively, more advantageously, more competently, in a superior way **OPPOSITE:** worse
8 = to a greater degree, more completely, more thoroughly
OPPOSITE: worse
between *prep* **1 = amidst**, among, mid, in the middle of, betwixt
beverage *n* **= drink**, liquid, liquor, refreshment, draught, bevvy *(dialect)*, libation *(facetious)*, thirst quencher, potable, potation
beware *vb* **= be careful**, look out, watch out, be wary, be cautious, take heed, guard against something
bewilder *vb* **= confound**, surprise, stun, confuse, puzzle, baffle, mix up, daze, perplex, mystify, stupefy, befuddle, flummox, bemuse, dumbfound, nonplus, flabbergast *(informal)*

DICTIONARY

bey *n* **1** (in modern Turkey) a title of address, corresponding to *Mr* **2** (in the Ottoman Empire) a title given to provincial governors
WORD ORIGIN Turkish: lord

beyond ❶ *prep* **1** at or to a point on the other side of: *beyond those hills* **2** outside the limits or scope of ▹*adv* **3** at or to the other or far side of something **4** outside the limits of something ▹*n* **5 the beyond** the unknown, esp. life after death
WORD ORIGIN Old English *begeondan*

Beza *n* See **de Bèze**

bezel *n* **1** the sloping edge of a cutting tool **2** the slanting face of a cut gem **3** a groove holding a gem, watch crystal, etc.
WORD ORIGIN French *biseau*

bezique *n* a card game for two or more players
WORD ORIGIN French *bésigue*

B/F *or* **b/f** *book-keeping* brought forward

BFPO British Forces Post Office

Bh *chem* bohrium

Bhagavad-Gita (bug-a-vad-geet-a) *n* a sacred Hindu text composed about 200 BC
WORD ORIGIN Sanskrit: song of the Blessed One

bhaji *n, pl* **bhaji** *or* **bhajis** an Indian savoury made of chopped vegetables mixed in a spiced batter and deep-fried
WORD ORIGIN Hindi

bhang *n* a preparation of Indian hemp used as a narcotic and intoxicant
WORD ORIGIN Hindi

bhangra *n* a type of traditional Punjabi folk music combined with elements of Western pop music
WORD ORIGIN Hindi

Bhaskar *n* **Sanjeev** born 1964, British actor and writer of Asian origin, known for the TV comedy series *Goodness Gracious Me* (1998) and *The Kumars at No. 42* (2001–06)

bhp brake horsepower

Bi *chem* bismuth

bi- *combining form* **1** having two: *bifocal* **2** occurring or lasting for two: *biennial* **3** on both sides, directions, etc.: *bilateral* **4** occurring twice during: *biweekly* **5** *chem* **a** denoting a compound containing two identical cyclical hydrocarbon systems: *biphenyl* **b** indicating an acid salt of a dibasic acid: *sodium bicarbonate*
WORD ORIGIN Latin *bis* twice

Bialik *n* **Hayyim Nahman** *or* **Chaim Nachman** 1873–1934, Russian Jewish poet and writer. His long poems *The Talmud Student* (1894) and *In the City of Slaughter* (1903) established him as the major Hebrew poet of modern times

biannual *adj* occurring twice a year **biannually** *adv*

bias ❶ *n* **1** mental tendency, esp. prejudice **2** a diagonal cut across the weave of a fabric **3** *bowls* a bulge or weight inside one side of a bowl that causes it to roll in a curve ▹*vb* **-asing, -ased** *or* **-assing, -assed 4** to cause to have a bias; prejudice **biased** *or* **biassed** *adj*
WORD ORIGIN Old French *biais*

bias binding *n* a strip of material used for binding hems

biaxial *adj* (esp. of a crystal) having two axes

bib *n* **1** a piece of cloth or plastic worn to protect a very young child's clothes while eating **2** the upper front part of some aprons, dungarees, etc.
WORD ORIGIN Middle English *bibben* to drink

bibcock *n* a tap with a nozzle bent downwards

bibelot (bib-loh) *n* an attractive or curious trinket
WORD ORIGIN Old French *beubelet*

bibl. **1** bibliographical **2** bibliography

Bible *n* **1 the Bible** the sacred writings of the Christian religion, comprising the Old and New Testaments **2 bible** a book regarded as authoritative: *this guide has long been regarded as the hill walkers' bible* **biblical** *adj*
WORD ORIGIN Greek *biblion* book

Bible Belt *n* those states of the S US where Protestant fundamentalism is dominant

bibliography *n, pl* **-phies 1** a list of books on a subject or by a particular author **2** a list of sources used in a book, etc. **3** the study of the history, etc. of literary material **bibliographer** *n*
WORD ORIGIN Greek *biblion* book + *graphein* to write

bibliophile *n* a person who collects or is fond of books
WORD ORIGIN Greek *biblion* book + *philos* loving

bibulous *adj literary* addicted to alcohol
WORD ORIGIN Latin *bibere* to drink

bicameral *adj* (of a legislature) consisting of two chambers
WORD ORIGIN BI- + Latin *camera* chamber

bicarb *n* ▸ short for **bicarbonate of soda**

bicarbonate *n* a salt of carbonic acid

bicarbonate of soda *n* sodium bicarbonate used as medicine or a raising agent in baking

bicentenary *or US* **bicentennial** *adj* **1** marking a 200th anniversary ▹*n, pl* **-naries 2** a 200th anniversary

biceps *n, pl* **-ceps** *anat* a muscle with two origins, esp. the muscle that flexes the forearm
WORD ORIGIN BI- + Latin *caput* head

bicker *vb* to argue over petty matters; squabble
WORD ORIGIN origin unknown

bicolour, bicoloured *or US* **bicolor, bicolored** *adj* two-coloured

bicuspid *adj* **1** having two points ▹*n* **2** a bicuspid tooth

bicycle *n* **1** a vehicle with a metal frame and two wheels, one behind the other, pedalled by the rider ▹*vb* **-cling, -cled 2** to ride a bicycle
WORD ORIGIN BI- + Greek *kuklos* wheel

bid ❶ *vb* **bidding; bad, bade** *or* **bid; bidden** *or* **bid 1** to offer (an amount) in an attempt to buy something **2** to say (a greeting): *to bid farewell* **3** to order: *do as you are bid!* **4** *bridge, etc.* to declare how many tricks one expects to make ▹*n* **5 a** an offer of a specified amount **b** the price offered **6 a** the quoting by a seller of a price **b** the price quoted **7** an attempt, esp. to attain power **8** *bridge, etc.* the number of tricks a player undertakes to make **bidder** *n*
WORD ORIGIN Old English *biddan*

Bidault *n* **Georges** 1899–1983, French statesman; prime minister (1946, 1949–50). His opposition to Algerian independence led him to support the OAS: he was charged with treason (1963) and fled abroad

THESAURUS

beyond *prep* **1 = on the other side of**, outwith *(Scot)* **2a = past**, outwith *(Scot)* **2b = exceeding**, surpassing, superior to, out of reach of **2c = outside**, over, above, outwith *(Scot)*

bias *n* **1 = prejudice**, leaning, bent, tendency, inclination, penchant, intolerance, bigotry, propensity, favouritism, predisposition, nepotism, unfairness, predilection, proclivity, partiality, narrow-mindedness, proneness, one-sidedness **OPPOSITE:** impartiality ▹*vb* **4 = influence**, colour, weight, prejudice, distort, sway, warp, slant, predispose

bid *vb* **1 = make an offer**, offer, propose, submit, tender, proffer **2 = wish**, say, call, tell, greet **3 = tell**, call, ask, order, charge, require, direct, desire, invite, command, summon, instruct, solicit, enjoin ▹*n* **5a = offer**, price, attempt, amount, advance, proposal, sum, tender, proposition, submission **7 = attempt**, try, effort, venture, undertaking, go *(informal)*, shot *(informal)*, stab *(informal)*, crack *(informal)*, endeavour

bidding *n* **1 = order**, call, charge, demand, request, command, instruction, invitation, canon, beck, injunction, summons, behest, beck and call

DICTIONARY

biddable *adj* obedient
bidding ❶ *n* **1** an order or command: *she had done his bidding* **2** an invitation; summons: *he knew to knock and wait for bidding before he entered* **3** the bids in an auction, card game, etc.
Biddle *n* **John** 1615–62, English theologian; founder of Unitarianism in England
biddy *n, pl* **-dies** *informal* a woman, esp. an old gossipy one
WORD ORIGIN pet form of *Bridget*
biddy-bid, biddy-biddy *n, pl* **-bids, -biddies** NZ a low-growing plant with hooked burrs
bide *vb* **biding, bided** *or* **bode, bided** **1** *archaic or dialect* to remain **2** **bide one's time** to wait patiently for an opportunity
WORD ORIGIN Old English *bīdan*
bidet (bee-day) *n* a small low basin for washing the genital area
WORD ORIGIN French: small horse
biennial *adj* **1** occurring every two years ▷*n* **2** a plant that completes its life cycle in two years
bier *n* a stand on which a corpse or a coffin rests before burial
WORD ORIGIN Old English *bǣr*
Bierce *n* **Ambrose** (**Gwinett**) 1842–?1914, US journalist and author of humorous sketches, horror stories, and tales of the supernatural: he disappeared during a mission in Mexico (1913)
biff *slang n* **1** a blow with the fist ▷*vb* **2** to give (someone) such a blow
WORD ORIGIN probably imitative
bifid *adj* divided into two by a cleft in the middle
WORD ORIGIN BI- + Latin *findere* to split
bifocal *adj* having two different focuses, esp. (of a lens) permitting near and distant vision
bifocals *pl n* a pair of spectacles with bifocal lenses
bifurcate *vb* **-cating, -cated** **1** to fork into two branches ▷*adj* **2** forked into two branches **bifurcation** *n*
WORD ORIGIN BI- + Latin *furca* fork
big ❶ *adj* **bigger, biggest** **1** of great or considerable size, weight, number, or capacity **2** having great significance; important **3** important through having power, wealth, etc. **4 a** elder: *my big brother* **b** grown-up **5** generous: *that's very big of you* **6** extravagant; boastful: *big talk* **7** **too big for one's boots** conceited; unduly self-confident **8** in an advanced stage of pregnancy: *big with child* **9** **in a big way** in a very grand or enthusiastic way ▷*adv informal* **10** boastfully; pretentiously: *he talks big* **11** on a grand scale: *think big*
WORD ORIGIN origin unknown
bigamy *n* the crime of marrying a person while still legally married to someone else **bigamist** *n* **bigamous** *adj*
WORD ORIGIN BI- + Greek *gamos* marriage
big-bang theory *n* a cosmological theory that suggests that the universe was created as the result of a massive explosion
Big Brother *n* a person or organization that exercises total dictatorial control
WORD ORIGIN from the novel *Nineteen Eighty-Four* by George Orwell
big business *n* large commercial organizations collectively
big end *n* the larger end of a connecting rod in an internal-combustion engine
big game *n* large animals that are hunted or fished for sport
bighead *n informal* a conceited person **big-headed** *adj*
bight *n* **1** a long curved shoreline **2** the slack part or a loop in a rope
WORD ORIGIN Old English *byht*
big name *informal n* **1** a famous person ▷*adj* **big-name** **2** famous
bigot *n* a person who is intolerant, esp. regarding religion, politics, or race **bigoted** *adj* **bigotry** *n*
WORD ORIGIN Old French
big shot *n informal* an important person
Big Smoke *n* **the Big Smoke** *informal* a big city, esp. London
big stick *n informal* force or the threat of force
big time *n* **the big time** *informal* the highest level of a profession, esp. entertainment **big-timer** *n*
big top *n informal* the main tent of a circus
bigwig *n informal* an important person
bijou (bee-zhoo) *n, pl* **-joux** (-zhooz) **1** something small and delicately worked ▷*adj* **2** small but tasteful: *a bijou residence*
WORD ORIGIN French: a jewel
bike *n informal* a bicycle or motorcycle
biker *n* a person who rides a motorcycle
biker jacket *n* a short, close-fitting leather jacket often worn by motorcyclists
Bikila *n* **Abebe** 1932–73, Ethiopian long-distance runner: winner of the Marathon at the Olympic Games in Rome (1960) and Tokyo (1964)
bikini *n* a woman's brief two-piece swimming costume
WORD ORIGIN after *Bikini* atoll, from a comparison between the devastating effect of the atom-bomb test and the effect caused by women wearing bikinis
bilateral *adj* affecting or undertaken by two parties; mutual
bilberry *n, pl* **-ries** a blue or blackish edible berry that grows on a shrub
WORD ORIGIN probably Scandinavian
bilby *n, pl* **-bies** an Australian marsupial with long pointed ears and grey fur
bile *n* **1** a greenish fluid secreted by the liver to aid digestion of fats **2** irritability or peevishness
WORD ORIGIN Latin *bilis*
bilge *n* **1** *informal* nonsense **2** *naut* the bottom of a ship's hull **3** the dirty water that collects in a ship's bilge
WORD ORIGIN probably variant of *bulge*
bilharzia (bill-**hart**-see-a) *n* a disease caused by infestation of the body with blood flukes
WORD ORIGIN after T. *Bilharz*, who discovered the blood fluke
biliary *adj* of bile, the ducts that convey bile, or the gall bladder
bilingual *adj* **1** able to speak two languages **2** expressed in two languages **bilingualism** *n*
bilious *adj* **1** nauseous; sick: *a bilious attack* **2** *informal* bad-tempered; irritable: *the regime's most persistent and bilious critic* **3** (of a colour) harsh and offensive
WORD ORIGIN Latin *biliosus* full of bile
bilk *vb* to cheat or deceive, esp. to avoid making payment to **bilker** *n*
WORD ORIGIN perhaps variant of *balk*
bill[1] ❶ *n* **1** a statement of money owed for goods or services supplied **2** a draft of a proposed new law

THESAURUS

big *adj* **1 = large**, great, huge, giant, massive, vast, enormous, considerable, substantial, extensive, immense, spacious, gigantic, monumental, mammoth, bulky, burly, colossal, stellar *(informal)*, prodigious, hulking, ponderous, voluminous, elephantine, ginormous *(informal)*, humongous *or* humungous *(US slang)*, sizable *or* sizeable, supersize **OPPOSITE:** small **2 = important**, serious, significant, grave, urgent, paramount, big-time *(informal)*, far-reaching, momentous, major league *(informal)*, weighty **OPPOSITE:** unimportant **3 = powerful**, important, prime, principal, prominent, dominant, influential, paramount, eminent, puissant, skookum *(Canad)* **4a, 4b = grown-up**, adult, grown, mature, elder, full-grown **OPPOSITE:** young **5 = generous**, good, princely, noble, heroic, gracious, benevolent, disinterested, altruistic, unselfish, magnanimous, big-hearted
bill[1] *n* **1 = charges**, rate, costs, score, account, damage *(informal)*, statement, reckoning, expense, tally, invoice, note of charge **2 = act of**

presented to a law-making body **3** a printed notice or advertisement **4** *US & Canad* a piece of paper money; note **5** any list of items, events, etc. such as a theatre programme ▷ *vb* **6** to send or present an account for payment to (a person) **7** to advertise by posters **8** to schedule as a future programme: *next week they will discuss what are billed as new ideas for economic reform* **9** **fit** *or* **fill the bill** *informal* to be suitable or adequate
WORD ORIGIN Late Latin *bulla* document

bill² ❶ *n* **1** the projecting jaws of a bird; beak ▷ *vb* **2** **bill and coo** (of lovers) to kiss and whisper amorously
WORD ORIGIN Old English *bile*

billabong *n Austral* a pool in the bed of a stream with an interrupted water flow
WORD ORIGIN Aboriginal

billboard *n* a hoarding

billet¹ *vb* **-leting, -leted** **1** to assign a lodging to (a soldier) ▷ *n* **2** accommodation, esp. for a soldier, in civilian lodgings **3** *Austral & NZ* a person who is billeted
WORD ORIGIN Old French *billette*, from *bulle* a document

billet² *n* **1** a chunk of wood, esp. for fuel **2** a small bar of iron or steel
WORD ORIGIN Old French *billette* a little log

billet-doux (bill-ee-doo) *n, pl* **billets-doux** (bill-ee-dooz) *old-fashioned or jocular* a love letter
WORD ORIGIN French: a sweet letter

billhook *n* a tool with a hooked blade, used for chopping, etc.

billiards *n* a game in which a long cue is used to propel balls on a table
WORD ORIGIN Old French *billard* curved stick

billion *n, pl* **-lions** *or* **-lion** **1** one thousand million: 1 000 000 000 or 10^9 **2** (in Britain, originally) one million million: 1 000 000 000 000 or 10^{12} **3** *(often pl) informal* an extremely large but unspecified number: *billions of dollars*
billionth *adj, n*
WORD ORIGIN French

billionaire *n* a person who has money or property worth at least a billion pounds, dollars, etc.

bill of exchange *n* a document instructing a third party to pay a stated sum at a designated date or on demand

bill of fare *n* a menu

bill of health *n* **1** a certificate that confirms the health of a ship's company **2** **clean bill of health** *informal* **a** a good report of one's physical condition **b** a favourable account of a person's or a company's financial position

bill of lading *n* a document containing full particulars of goods shipped

billow *n* **1** a large sea wave **2** a swelling or surging mass, as of smoke or sound ▷ *vb* **3** to rise up or swell out **billowing** *adj, n* **billowy** *adj*
WORD ORIGIN Old Norse *bylgja*

billy *or* **billycan** *n, pl* **-lies** *or* **-lycans** a metal can or pot for boiling water etc. over a campfire
WORD ORIGIN Scots *billypot*

billy goat *n* a male goat

biltong *n S African* strips of meat dried and cured in the sun
WORD ORIGIN Afrikaans

bimbo *n, pl* **-bos** *slang* an attractive but empty-headed young woman
WORD ORIGIN Italian: little child

bimetallic *adj* consisting of two metals

bimetallism *n* the use of two metals, esp. gold and silver, in fixed relative values as the standard of value and currency **bimetallist** *n*

bin *n* **1** a container for rubbish, etc. **2** a large container for storing something in bulk, such as coal, grain, or bottled wine ▷ *vb* **binning, binned** **3** to put in a rubbish bin: *I bin my junk mail without reading it*
WORD ORIGIN Old English *binne* basket

binary (bine-a-ree) *adj* **1** composed of two parts **2** *maths, computers* of or expressed in a system with two as its base **3** *chem* containing atoms of two different elements ▷ *n, pl* **-ries** **4** something composed of two parts
WORD ORIGIN Late Latin *binarius*

binary star *n* a system of two stars revolving around a common centre of gravity

Binchy *n* **Maeve** born 1940, Irish novelist and journalist; her bestselling novels include *Circle of Friends* (1990) and *Quentins* (2002)

bind ❶ *vb* **binding, bound** **1** to make secure, such as with a rope **2** to unite with emotional ties or commitment **3** to place (someone) under legal or moral obligation **4** to place under certain constraints: *bound by the rules* **5** to stick together or cause to stick: *egg binds fat and flour* **6** to enclose and fasten (the pages of a book) between covers **7** to provide (a garment) with an edging **8** (foll. by *up*) to bandage ▷ *n* **9** *informal* a difficult or annoying situation
WORD ORIGIN Old English *bindan*

binder *n* **1** a firm cover for holding loose sheets of paper together **2** a person who binds books **3** something used to fasten or tie, such as rope or twine **4** *obsolete* a machine for cutting and binding grain into sheaves

bindery *n, pl* **-eries** a place in which books are bound

binding ❶ *n* **1** anything that binds or fastens **2** the covering of a book ▷ *adj* **3** imposing an obligation or duty

bind over *vb* to place (a person) under a legal obligation, esp. to keep the peace

bindweed *n* a plant that twines around a support

binge ❶ *n informal* **1** a bout of excessive eating or drinking **2** excessive indulgence in anything
WORD ORIGIN probably dialect: to soak

binge drinking *n* the practice of drinking excessive amounts of alcohol regularly

bingo *n* a gambling game in which numbers called out are covered by players on their individual cards. The first to cover a given arrangement is the winner
WORD ORIGIN origin unknown

binnacle *n* a housing for a ship's compass
WORD ORIGIN Late Latin *habitaculum* dwelling-place

THESAURUS

parliament, measure, proposal, piece of legislation, projected law **3 = advertisement**, notice, poster, leaflet, bulletin, circular, handout, placard, handbill, playbill **5 = list**, listing, programme, card, schedule, agenda, catalogue, inventory, roster, syllabus ▷ *vb* **6 = charge**, debit, invoice, send a statement to, send an invoice to **7 = advertise**, post, announce, push *(informal)*, declare, promote, plug *(informal)*, proclaim, tout, flaunt, publicize, crack up *(informal)*, give advance notice of

bill² *n* **1 = beak**, nib, neb *(archaic, dialect)*, mandible

bind *vb* **1 = tie**, unite, join, stick, secure, attach, wrap, rope, knot, strap, lash, glue, tie up, hitch, paste, fasten, truss, make fast
OPPOSITE: untie
3 = oblige, make, force, require, engage, compel, prescribe, constrain, necessitate, impel, obligate ▷ *n* **9** *(informal)* **= nuisance**, inconvenience, hassle *(informal)*, drag *(informal)*, spot *(informal)*, difficulty, bore, dilemma, pest, hot water *(informal)*, uphill *(S African)*, predicament, annoyance, quandary, pain in the neck *(informal)*, pain in the backside *(informal)*, pain in the butt *(informal)*

binding *adj* **3 = compulsory**, necessary, mandatory, imperative, obligatory, conclusive, irrevocable, unalterable, indissoluble
OPPOSITE: optional

binge *n* **1** *(informal)* **= bout**, session, spell, fling, feast, stint, spree, orgy, bender *(informal)*, jag *(slang)*, beano *(Brit slang)*, blind *(slang)*

DICTIONARY

b

Binnig *n* **Gerd** (**Karl**) born 1947, German physicist: shared the Nobel prize for physics (1986) for work on the superconductivity of semiconductors and development of the scanning tunnelling microscope

binocular *adj* involving or intended for both eyes: *binocular vision*
WORD ORIGIN BI- + Latin *oculus* eye

binoculars *pl n* an optical instrument for use with both eyes, consisting of two small telescopes joined together

binomial *n* **1** a mathematical expression consisting of two terms, such as $3x + 2y$ ▹ *adj* **2** referring to two names or terms
WORD ORIGIN BI- + Latin *nomen* name

binomial theorem *n* a general mathematical formula that expresses any power of a binomial without multiplying out, as in $(a+b)^2=a^2+2ab+b^2$

Binyon *n* (**Robert**) **Laurence** 1869–1943, British poet and art historian, best known for his elegiac war poems "For the Fallen" (1914) and "The Burning of the Leaves" (1944)

bio- *combining form* **1** indicating life or living organisms: *biogenesis* **2** indicating a human life or career: *biography*
WORD ORIGIN Greek *bios* life

bioastronautics *n* the study of the effects of space flight on living organisms

biochemistry *n* the study of the chemical compounds, reactions, etc. occurring in living organisms **biochemical** *adj* **biochemist** *n*

biocide *n* a substance used to destroy living things
WORD ORIGIN BIO- + Latin *caedere* to kill

biocoenosis *or US* **biocenosis** (bye-oh-see-**no**-siss) *n* the relationships between animals and plants subsisting together
WORD ORIGIN BIO- + Greek *koinōsis* sharing

biodegradable *adj* (of sewage and packaging) capable of being decomposed by natural means **biodegradability** *n*

biodiesel *n* a biofuel intended for use in diesel engines

biodiversity *n* the existence of a wide variety of plant and animal species in their natural environments

bioengineering *n* the design and manufacture of aids, such as artificial limbs, to help people with disabilities

biofuel *n* fuel derived from renewable biological resources

biogas *n* gaseous fuel produced by the fermentation of organic waste

biogenesis *n* the principle that a living organism must originate from a similar parent organism

biogenic (bye-oh-**jen**-ik) *adj* originating from a living organism

biography ❶ *n, pl* **-phies 1** an account of a person's life by another person **2** such accounts collectively **biographer** *n* **biographical** *adj*
WORD ORIGIN BIO- + Greek *graphein* to write

biol. 1 biological **2** biology

biological *adj* **1** of or relating to biology **2** (of a detergent) containing enzymes that remove natural stains, such as blood or grass **biologically** *adv*

biological clock *n* an inherent timing mechanism that controls the rhythmic repetition of processes in living organisms, such as sleeping

biological control *n* the control of destructive organisms, esp. insects, by nonchemical means, such as introducing a natural predator of the pest

biological warfare *n* the use of living organisms or their toxic products to induce death or incapacity in humans

biology *n* the study of living organisms **biologist** *n*

biomass *n* the total number of living organisms in a given area

biomechanics *n* the study of the mechanics of the movement of living organisms

biomedicine *n* **1** the medical and biological study of the effects of unusual environmental stress **2** the study of herbal remedies

biometric *adj* relating to the analysis of biological data using mathematical and statistical methods, especially for purposes of identification: *biometric passport*

biometry *or* **biometrics** *n* the analysis of biological data using mathematical and statistical methods, especially for purposes of identification

bionic *adj* **1** of or relating to bionics **2** (in science fiction) having physical functions augmented by electronic equipment
WORD ORIGIN BIO- + *(electro)nic*

bionics *n* **1** the study of biological functions in order to develop electronic equipment that operates similarly **2** the replacement of limbs or body parts by artificial electronically powered parts

biophysics *n* the physics of biological processes and the application of methods used in physics to biology **biophysical** *adj* **biophysicist** *n*

biopic (**bye**-oh-pick) *n informal* a film based on the life of a famous person
WORD ORIGIN *bio(graphical)* + *pic(ture)*

biopsy *n, pl* **-sies** examination of tissue from a living body to determine the cause or extent of a disease
WORD ORIGIN BIO- + Greek *opsis* sight

biorhythm *n* a complex recurring pattern of physiological states, believed to affect physical, emotional, and mental states

bioscope *n* **1** a kind of early film projector **2** *S African* a cinema

biosphere *n* the part of the earth's surface and atmosphere inhabited by living things

biosynthesis *n* the formation of complex compounds by living organisms **biosynthetic** *adj*

biotech *n* ▸ short for **biotechnology**

biotechnology *n* the use of microorganisms, such as cells or bacteria, in industry and technology

bioterrorism *n* the use of viruses, bacteria, etc. by terrorists **bioterrorist** *n*

biotin *n* a vitamin of the B complex, abundant in egg yolk and liver
WORD ORIGIN Greek *biotē* life

bipartisan *adj* consisting of or supported by two political parties

bipartite *adj* **1** consisting of or having two parts **2** affecting or made by two parties: *a bipartite agreement*

biped (**bye**-ped) *n* **1** any animal with two feet ▹ *adj also* **bipedal 2** having two feet
WORD ORIGIN BI- + Latin *pes* foot

biplane *n* an aeroplane with two sets of wings, one above the other

bipolar *adj* **1** having two poles **2** having two extremes **bipolarity** *n*

birch *n* **1** a tree with thin peeling bark and hard close-grained wood **2 the birch** a bundle of birch twigs or a birch rod used, esp. formerly, for flogging offenders ▹ *vb* **3** to flog with the birch
WORD ORIGIN Old English *bierce*

bird ❶ *n* **1** a two-legged creature with feathers and wings, which lays eggs and can usually fly ▸ Related adjective: **avian 2** *slang chiefly Brit* a girl or young woman **3** *informal* a person: *he's a rare bird* **4 a bird in the hand** something definite or certain **5 birds of a feather** people with the same ideas or interests **6 kill two birds with one stone** to accomplish two things with one action
WORD ORIGIN Old English *bridd*

bird flu *n* a form of influenza occurring in poultry caused by a virus capable of spreading to humans

THESAURUS

biography *n* **1 = life story**, life, record, account, profile, memoir, CV, life history, curriculum vitae

bird *n* **1 = feathered friend**, fowl, songbird ▸ *related adjectives:* avian ▸ *name of male:* cock ▸ *name of female:* hen ▸ *name of young:* chick, fledgeling, fledgling, nestling ▸ *collective nouns:* flock, flight ▸ *name of home:* nest

DICTIONARY

birdie *n* **1** *informal* a bird **2** *golf* a score of one stroke under par for a hole
birdlime *n* a sticky substance smeared on twigs to catch small birds
bird of paradise *n* a songbird of New Guinea, the male of which has brilliantly coloured plumage
bird of prey *n* a bird, such as a hawk or owl, that hunts other animals for food
birdseed *n* a mixture of various kinds of seeds for feeding cage birds
bird's-eye view *n* **1** a view seen from above **2** a general or overall impression of something
bird-watcher *n* a person who studies wild birds in their natural surroundings
Birendra Bir Bikram Shah Dev *n* 1945–2001, king of Nepal (1972–2001): he, his queen, and six other members of the royal family were shot dead by his son, Crown Prince Dipendra, who then committed suicide
biretta *n* *RC church* a stiff square clerical cap
WORD ORIGIN Italian *berretta*
Birgitta *n* **Saint Birgitta** ▸ See **Bridget** (sense 2)
Birkbeck *n* **George** 1776–1841, British educationalist, who helped to establish vocational training for working men: founder and first president of the London Mechanics Institute (1824), which later became Birkbeck College
Birkenhead[1] *n* a port in NW England, in Wirral unitary authority, Merseyside: former shipbuilding centre. Pop: 83729 (2001)
Birkenhead[2] *n* **Frederick Edwin Smith**, 1st Earl of, known as *F. E. Smith*. 1872–1930, British Conservative statesman, lawyer, and orator
Biro *n, pl* **-ros** *trademark* a kind of ballpoint pen
birth ⊤ *n* **1** the process of bearing young; childbirth **2** the act of being born **3** the beginning of something; origin **4** ancestry: *of noble birth* **5** **give birth to** **a** to bear (offspring) **b** to produce or originate (an idea, plan, etc.)
WORD ORIGIN Old Norse *byrth*
birth certificate *n* an official form stating the time and place of a person's birth
birth control *n* limitation of child-bearing by means of contraception
birthday *n* **1** an anniversary of the day of one's birth **2** the day on which a person was born
birthmark *n* a blemish on the skin formed before birth
birth mother *n* the woman who gives birth to a child, regardless of whether she is the genetic mother or subsequently brings up the child
birthplace *n* the place where someone was born or where something originated
birth rate *n* the ratio of live births to population, usually expressed per 1000 population per year
birthright *n* privileges or possessions that a person has or is believed to be entitled to as soon as he or she is born
Birtwistle *n* Sir **Harrison** born 1934, English composer, whose works include the operas *Punch and Judy* (1967), *The Mask of Orpheus* (1984), *Gawain* (1991), and *Exody* (1998)
biscuit *n* **1** a small flat dry sweet or plain cake **2** porcelain that has been fired but not glazed ▹ *adj* **3** pale brown or yellowish-grey
WORD ORIGIN Old French *(pain) bescuit* twice-cooked (bread)
bisect *vb* **1** *maths* to divide into two equal parts **2** to cut or split into two **bisection** *n*
WORD ORIGIN BI- + Latin *secare* to cut
bisexual *adj* **1** sexually attracted to both men and women **2** showing characteristics of both sexes ▹ *n* **3** a bisexual person **bisexuality** *n*
bishop *n* **1** a clergyman having spiritual and administrative powers over a diocese **2** a chessman capable of moving diagonally
WORD ORIGIN Greek *episkopos* overseer
Bishop *n* **Elizabeth** 1911–79, US poet, who lived in Brazil. Her poetry reflects her travelling experience, esp. in the tropics
bishopric *n* the see, diocese, or office of a bishop
bismuth *n* *chem* a brittle pinkish-white metallic element. Some compounds are used in alloys and in medicine. Symbol: Bi
WORD ORIGIN German *Wismut*
bison *n, pl* **-son** an animal of the cattle family with a massive head, shaggy forequarters, and a humped back
WORD ORIGIN Germanic
bisque[1] *n* a thick rich soup made from shellfish
WORD ORIGIN French
bisque[2] *adj* **1** pink-to-yellowish-tan ▹ *n* **2** *ceramics* ▸ same as **biscuit** (sense 2)
WORD ORIGIN shortened from *biscuit*
bistable *adj* (of an electronic system) having two stable states
bistro *n, pl* **-tros** a small restaurant
WORD ORIGIN French
bit[1] ⊤ *n* **1** a small piece, portion, or quantity **2** a short time or distance **3** **a bit** rather; somewhat: *a bit stupid* **4** **a bit of** rather: *a bit of a fool* **5** **bit by bit** gradually **6** **do one's bit** to make one's expected contribution
WORD ORIGIN Old English *bite* action of biting
bit[2] ⊤ *n* **1** a metal mouthpiece on a bridle for controlling a horse **2** a cutting or drilling tool, part, or head in a brace, drill, etc.
WORD ORIGIN Old English *bita*
bit[3] *vb* ▸ the past tense of **bite**
bit[4] *n* *maths, computers* **1** a single digit of binary notation, represented either by 0 or by 1 **2** the smallest unit of information, indicating the presence or absence of a single feature
WORD ORIGIN *b(inary + dig)it*
bitch *n* **1** a female dog, fox, or wolf **2** *slang, offensive* a malicious or spiteful woman **3** *informal* a difficult situation or problem ▹ *vb* **4** *informal* to complain; grumble
WORD ORIGIN Old English *bicce*
bitchy *adj* **bitchier, bitchiest** *informal* spiteful or malicious **bitchiness** *n*
bite ⊤ *vb* **biting, bit, bitten** **1** to grip, cut off, or tear with the teeth or jaws **2** (of animals or insects) to injure by puncturing (the skin) with the teeth or fangs **3** (of corrosive material) to eat away or into **4** to smart or cause to smart; sting **5** *angling* (of a fish) to take the bait or lure **6** to take firm hold of or act effectively upon: *turn the screw till it bites the wood* **7** *slang* to annoy or worry: *what's biting her?* ▹ *n* **8** the act of biting **9** a thing or amount bitten off **10** a wound or sting inflicted by biting **11** *angling* an attempt by a fish to take the bait or lure **12** a snack **13** a stinging or smarting sensation **biter** *n*
WORD ORIGIN Old English *bītan*
biting ⊤ *adj* **1** piercing; keen: *a biting wind* **2** sarcastic; incisive

THESAURUS

birth *n* **1 = childbirth**, delivery, nativity, parturition **OPPOSITE:** death **4 = ancestry**, line, race, stock, blood, background, breeding, strain, descent, pedigree, extraction, lineage, forebears, parentage, genealogy, derivation ▸ *related adjective:* natal
bit[1] *n* **1a = slice**, segment, fragment, crumb, mouthful, small piece, morsel **1b = piece**, scrap, small piece **1c = jot**, whit, tittle, iota
bit[2] *n* **1 = curb**, check, brake, restraint, snaffle
bite *vb* **1, 2 = nip**, cut, tear, wound, grip, snap, crush, rend, pierce, champ, pinch, chew, crunch, clamp, nibble, gnaw, masticate ▹ *n* **10 = wound**, sting, pinch, nip, prick **12 = snack**, food, piece, taste, refreshment, mouthful, morsel, titbit, light meal
biting *adj* **1 = piercing**, cutting, cold, sharp, freezing, frozen, bitter, raw, chill, harsh, penetrating, arctic, nipping, icy, blighting, chilly, wintry, gelid, cold as ice

DICTIONARY

b

bitmap *n computers* a picture created by colour or shading on a visual display unit
bit part *n* a very small acting role with few lines to speak
bitstream *n computers* a sequence of digital data transmitted electronically
bitten *vb* ▸ the past participle of **bite**
bitter ❶ *adj* **1** having an unpalatable harsh taste, as the peel of an orange **2** showing or caused by hostility or resentment **3** difficult to accept: *a bitter blow* **4** sarcastic: *bitter words* **5** bitingly cold: *a bitter night* ▹ *n* **6** *Brit* beer with a slightly bitter taste
bitterly *adv* **bitterness** *n*
WORD ORIGIN Old English *biter*
bittern *n* a large wading marsh bird with a booming call
WORD ORIGIN Old French *butor*
bitters *pl n* bitter-tasting spirits flavoured with plant extracts
bittersweet *adj* **1** tasting of or being a mixture of bitterness and sweetness **2** pleasant but tinged with sadness
bitty *adj* **-tier, -tiest** lacking unity; disjointed **bittiness** *n*
bitumen *n* a sticky or solid substance that occurs naturally in asphalt and tar and is used in road surfacing
bituminous *adj*
WORD ORIGIN Latin
bituminous coal *n* a soft black coal that burns with a smoky yellow flame
bivalve *n* **1** a sea creature, such as an oyster or mussel, that has a shell consisting of two hinged valves and breathes through gills ▹ *adj* **2** of these molluscs
bivouac *n* **1** a temporary camp, as used by soldiers or mountaineers ▹ *vb* **-acking, -acked 2** to make a temporary camp
WORD ORIGIN French
biz *n informal* business
bizarre ❶ *adj* odd or unusual, esp. in an interesting or amusing way
WORD ORIGIN Italian *bizzarro* capricious
Bjørnson *n* **Bjørnstjerne** 1832–1910, Norwegian poet, dramatist, novelist, theatre director, and newspaper editor; mainly remembered for social dramas, such as *The Bankrupt* (1875): Nobel prize for literature 1903
Bk *chem* berkelium
BL 1 *chiefly Brit* Bachelor of Law **2** Bachelor of Letters **3** Barrister-at-Law
blab *vb* **blabbing, blabbed** to divulge (secrets) indiscreetly
WORD ORIGIN Germanic
blabber *n* **1** a person who blabs ▹ *vb* **2** to talk without thinking
WORD ORIGIN Middle English *blabberen*
black ❶ *adj* **1** having no hue, owing to the absorption of all or almost all light; of the colour of coal **2** without light **3** without hope; gloomy: *the future looked black* **4** dirty or soiled **5** angry or resentful: *black looks* **6** unpleasant in a cynical or macabre manner: *black comedy* **7** (of coffee or tea) without milk or cream **8** wicked or harmful: *a black lie* ▹ *n* **9** the darkest colour; the colour of coal **10** a dye or pigment producing this colour **11** black clothing, worn esp. in mourning: *she was in black, as though in mourning* **12** complete darkness: *the black of the night* **13 in the black** in credit or without debt ▹ *vb* **14** ▸ same as **blacken 15** to polish (shoes or boots) with blacking **16** *Brit, Austral & NZ* (of trade unionists) to organize a boycott of (specified goods, work, etc.) ▸ See also **blackout** > **blackness** *n* **blackish** *adj*
WORD ORIGIN Old English *blæc*
Black[1] *n* **1** a member of a human population having dark pigmentation of the skin ▹ *adj* **2** of or relating to a Black person or Black people: *a Black neighbourhood*
Black[2] *n* **1** Sir **James** (**Whyte**) born 1924, British biochemist. He discovered beta-blockers and drugs for peptic ulcers: Nobel prize for physiology or medicine 1988 **2 Joseph** 1728–99, Scottish physician and chemist, noted for his pioneering work on carbon dioxide and heat
black-and-blue *adj* (of the skin) bruised, as from a beating
black-and-white *n* **1** a photograph, film, etc. in black, white, and shades of grey, rather than in colour **2 in black and white a** in print or writing **b** in extremes: *he always sees things in black and white*
black-backed gull *n* a large common black-and-white European gull
blackball[1] *vb* **1** to vote against **2** to exclude (someone) from a group, etc.
WORD ORIGIN from *black ball*, used formerly to veto
blackball[2] *n NZ* hard boiled sweet with black-and-white stripes
black bear *n* **1** a bear inhabiting forests of North America **2** a bear of central and E Asia
Blackbeard *n* nickname of (Edward) **Teach** ▸ See **Teach**
black belt *n judo, karate, etc.* **a** a black belt that signifies that the wearer has reached a high standard in martial art **b** a person entitled to wear this
blackberry *n, pl* **-ries** a small blackish edible fruit that grows on a woody bush with thorny stems. Also called: **bramble**
BlackBerry *n trademark* a hand-held device for sending and receiving e-mail
blackbird *n* a common European thrush, the male of which has black plumage and a yellow bill
blackboard *n* a hard or rigid surface made of a smooth usually dark substance, used for writing or drawing on with chalk, esp. in teaching
black box *n informal* a flight recorder
blackcap *n* a brownish-grey warbler, the male of which has a black crown
blackcock *n* the male of the black grouse
Black Country *n* **the Black Country** the formerly heavily industrialized West Midlands of England
blackcurrant *n* a very small blackish edible fruit that grows in bunches on a bush
blackdamp *n* air that is low in oxygen content and high in carbon dioxide as a result of an explosion in a mine
Black Death *n* **the Black Death** a form of bubonic plague in Europe and Asia during the 14th century
black economy *n Brit, Austral & NZ* that portion of the income of a nation that remains illegally undeclared

THESAURUS

2 = sarcastic, cutting, sharp, severe, stinging, withering, scathing, acrimonious, incisive, virulent, caustic, vitriolic, trenchant, mordant, mordacious
bitter *adj* **1 = sour**, biting, sharp, acid, harsh, unpleasant, tart, astringent, acrid, unsweetened, vinegary, acidulated, acerb **OPPOSITE:** sweet **2 = resentful**, hurt, wounded, angry, offended, sour, put out, sore, choked, crabbed, acrimonious, aggrieved, sullen, miffed *(informal)*, embittered, begrudging, peeved *(informal)*, piqued, rancorous **OPPOSITE:** happy **5 = freezing**, biting, severe, intense, raw, fierce, chill, stinging, penetrating, arctic, icy, polar, Siberian, glacial, wintry **OPPOSITE:** mild
bizarre *adj* **= strange**, odd, unusual, extraordinary, fantastic, curious, weird, way-out *(informal)*, peculiar, eccentric, abnormal, ludicrous, queer *(informal)*, irregular, rum *(Brit slang)*, uncommon, singular, grotesque, perplexing, uncanny, mystifying, off-the-wall *(slang)*, outlandish, comical, oddball *(informal)*, off the rails, zany, unaccountable, off-beat, left-field *(informal)*, freakish, wacko *(slang)*, outré, cockamamie *(slang, chiefly US)*, daggy *(Austral & NZ informal)* **OPPOSITE:** normal
black *adj* **1 = dark**, raven, ebony, sable, jet, dusky, pitch-black, inky, swarthy, stygian, coal-black, pitchy, murky **OPPOSITE:** light

DICTIONARY

blacken *vb* **1** to make or become black or dirty **2** to damage (someone's reputation); discredit: *they planned to blacken my father's name*

Blackett *n* **Patrick Maynard Stuart**, Baron. 1897–1974, English physicist, noted for his work on cosmic radiation and his discovery of the positron. Nobel prize for physics 1948

black eye *n* bruising round the eye

Black Friar *n* a Dominican friar

blackguard (blag-gard) *n* an unprincipled contemptible person **WORD ORIGIN** originally, lowest group at court

blackhead *n* **1** a black-tipped plug of fatty matter clogging a pore of the skin **2** a bird with black plumage on the head

black hole *n astron* a hypothetical region of space resulting from the collapse of a star and surrounded by a gravitational field from which neither matter nor radiation can escape

black ice *n* a thin transparent layer of new ice on a road

blacking *n* any preparation for giving a black finish to shoes, metals, etc.

blackjack[1] *n* pontoon or a similar card game **WORD ORIGIN** *black* + *jack* (the knave)

blackjack[2] *n chiefly US & Canad* a truncheon of leather-covered lead with a flexible shaft **WORD ORIGIN** *black* + *jack* (implement)

black lead *n* ▸ same as **graphite**

blackleg *n Brit* **1** a person who continues to work or does another's job during a strike ▹ *vb* **-legging, -legged 2** to refuse to join a strike

blacklist *n* **1** a list of people or organizations considered untrustworthy or disloyal ▹ *vb* **2** to put (someone) on a blacklist

black magic *n* magic used for evil purposes

blackmail ❶ *n* **1** the act of attempting to obtain money by threatening to reveal shameful information **2** the use of unfair pressure in an attempt to influence someone ▹ *vb* **3** to obtain or attempt to obtain money by intimidation **4** to attempt to influence (a person) by unfair pressure **blackmailer** *n* **WORD ORIGIN** *black* + Old English *māl* terms

Black Maria (mar-**rye**-a) *n* a police van for transporting prisoners

black mark *n* a discredit noted against someone

black market *n* a place or a system for buying or selling goods or currencies illegally, esp. in violation of controls or rationing **black marketeer** *n*

black mass *n* a blasphemous travesty of the Christian Mass, used in black magic

Blackmore *n* **R**(**ichard**) **D**(**oddridge**) 1825–1900, English novelist; author of *Lorna Doone* (1869)

blackout *n* **1** (in wartime) the putting out or hiding of all lights as a precaution against a night air attack **2** a momentary loss of consciousness, vision, or memory **3** a temporary electrical power failure **4** the prevention of information broadcasts: *a news blackout* ▹ *vb* **black out 5** to put out (lights) **6** to lose vision, consciousness, or memory temporarily **7** to stop (news, a television programme, etc.) from being broadcast

black pepper *n* a dark-coloured hot seasoning made from the dried berries and husks of the pepper plant

Black Power *n* a movement of Black people to obtain equality with Whites

Black Prince *n* **the Black Prince** ▸ See **Edward** (sense 1)

black pudding *n Brit* a black sausage made from pig's blood, suet, etc.

Black Rod *n* (in Britain) the chief usher of the House of Lords and of the Order of the Garter

black sheep *n* a person who is regarded as a disgrace or failure by his or her family or peer group

Blackshirt *n* a member of the Italian Fascist party before and during the Second World War

blacksmith *n* a person who works iron with a furnace, anvil, and hammer

black spot *n* **1** a place on a road where accidents frequently occur **2** an area where a particular situation is exceptionally bad: *an unemployment black spot*

Blackstone *n* Sir **William** 1723–80, English jurist noted particularly for his *Commentaries on the Laws of England* (1765–69), which had a profound influence on jurisprudence in the US

blackthorn *n* a thorny shrub with black twigs, white flowers, and small sour plumlike fruits

black tie *n* **1** a black bow tie worn with a dinner jacket ▸ *adj* **black-tie 2** denoting an occasion when a dinner jacket should be worn

Black Watch *n* **the Black Watch** the 3rd Battalion, Royal Regiment of Scotland in the British Army

black widow *n* an American spider, the female of which is highly venomous and commonly eats its mate

Blackwood[1] *n bridge* a conventional bidding sequence of four and five no-trumps, which are requests to the partner to show aces and kings respectively **WORD ORIGIN** after Easeley F. *Blackwood*, its American inventor

Blackwood[2] *n* **Algernon** (**Henry**) 1869–1951, British novelist and short-story writer; noted for his supernatural tales

bladder *n* **1** *anat* a membranous sac, usually containing liquid, esp. the urinary bladder **2** a hollow bag made of leather, etc. which becomes round when filled with air or liquid **3** a hollow saclike part in certain plants, such as seaweed **bladdery** *adj* **WORD ORIGIN** Old English *blǣdre*

blade *n* **1** the part of a sharp weapon, tool, or knife, that forms the cutting edge **2** the thin flattish part of a propeller, oar, or fan **3** the flattened part of a leaf, sepal, or petal **4** the long narrow leaf of a grass or related plant **WORD ORIGIN** Old English *blæd*

blag *vb* **blagging, blagged** *Brit slang* **1** to obtain by wheedling or cadging **2** to steal or rob **WORD ORIGIN** origin unknown

blain *n* a blister, blotch, or sore on the skin **WORD ORIGIN** Old English *blegen*

Blakey *n* **Art**, full name *Arthur Blakey*. (1919–90), US Black jazz drummer and leader of the Jazz Messengers band

blame ❶ *vb* **blaming, blamed 1** to consider (someone) responsible for: *I blame her for the failure* **2** (foll. by *on*) to put responsibility for (something)

THESAURUS

3 = gloomy, sad, depressing, distressing, horrible, grim, bleak, hopeless, dismal, ominous, sombre, morbid, mournful, morose, lugubrious, joyless, funereal, doleful, cheerless **OPPOSITE:** happy **5 = angry**, cross, furious, hostile, sour, menacing, moody, resentful, glowering, sulky, baleful, louring *or* lowering **OPPOSITE:** happy **8 = wicked**, bad, evil, corrupt, vicious, immoral, depraved, debased, amoral, villainous, unprincipled, nefarious, dissolute, iniquitous, irreligious, impious, unrighteous **OPPOSITE:** good

blackmail *n* **1, 2 = threat**, intimidation, ransom, compulsion, protection *(informal)*, coercion, extortion, pay-off *(informal)*, shakedown, hush money *(slang)*, exaction ▹ *vb* **3, 4 = threaten**, force, squeeze, compel, exact, intimidate, wring, coerce, milk, wrest, dragoon, extort, bleed *(informal)*, press-gang, hold to ransom

blame *vb* **1 = hold responsible**, accuse, denounce, indict, impeach, incriminate, impute, recriminate, point a *or* the finger at

b

DICTIONARY

on (someone): *she blames the failure on me* **3 be to blame** to be at fault ▷*n* **4** responsibility for something that is wrong: *they must take the blame for the failure* **5** an expression of condemnation: *analysts lay the blame on party activists* **blamable** *or* **blameable** *adj* **blameless** *adj*
WORD ORIGIN Late Latin *blasphemare* to blaspheme

blameworthy *adj* deserving blame **blameworthiness** *n*

Blanc[1] *n* **1 Mont Blanc** ▶ See **Mont Blanc 2 Cape Blanc** a headland in N Tunisia: the northernmost point of Africa **3 Cape Blanc** *or* **Cape Blanco** a peninsula in Mauritania, on the Atlantic coast

Blanc[2] *n* **(Jean Joseph Charles) Louis** 1811–82, French socialist and historian: author of *L'Organisation du travail* (1840), in which he advocated the establishment of cooperative workshops subsidized by the state

blanch *vb* **1** to whiten **2** to become pale, as with sickness or fear **3** to prepare (meat or vegetables) by plunging them in boiling water **4** to cause (celery, chicory, etc.) to grow white from lack of light
WORD ORIGIN Old French *blanc* white

Blanche of Castile *n* ?1188–1252, queen consort (1223–26) of Louis VIII of France, born in Spain. The mother of Louis IX, she acted as regent during his minority (1226–36) and his absence on a crusade (1248–52)

Blanchett *n* **Cate**, full name *Catherine Elise Blanchett*. born 1969, Australian actress; her films include *Elizabeth* (1998), the *Lord of the Rings* trilogy (2001–03), and *Notes on a Scandal* (2006)

blancmange (blam-**monzh**) *n* a jelly-like dessert of milk, stiffened usually with cornflour
WORD ORIGIN Old French *blanc manger* white food

Blanco *n* **Serge** born 1958, French Rugby Union footballer

bland *adj* **1** dull and uninteresting: *the bland predictability of the film* **2** (of food, drink etc.) flavourless **3** smooth in manner: *he looked at his visitor with a bland smile* **blandly** *adv*
WORD ORIGIN Latin *blandus* flattering

blandish *vb* to persuade by mild flattery; coax
WORD ORIGIN Latin *blandiri*

blandishments *pl n* flattery intended to coax or cajole

blank *adj* **1** (of a writing surface) not written on **2** (of a form, etc.) with spaces left for details to be filled in **3** without ornament or break: *a blank wall* **4** empty or void: *a blank space* **5** showing no interest or expression: *a blank look* **6** lacking ideas or inspiration: *his mind went blank* ▷*n* **7** an empty space **8** an empty space for writing in **9** the condition of not understanding: *my mind went a complete blank* **10** a mark, often a dash, in place of a word **11** ▶ same as **blank cartridge 12 draw a blank** to get no results from something ▷*vb* **13** (foll. by *out*) to cross out, blot, or obscure **14 blank something out** to refuse to think about; to clear from one's mind **15** *slang* to ignore: *the crowd blanked her for the first four numbers* **blankly** *adv*
WORD ORIGIN Old French *blanc* white

blank cartridge *n* a cartridge containing powder but no bullet

blank cheque *n* **1** a signed cheque on which the amount payable has not been specified **2** complete freedom of action

blanket *n* **1** a large piece of thick cloth for use as a bed covering **2** a concealing cover, as of smoke, leaves, or snow ▷*adj* **3** applying to or covering a wide group or variety of people, conditions, situations, etc.: *a blanket ban on all supporters travelling to away matches* ▷*vb* **-keting, -keted 4** to cover as if with a blanket **5** to cover a wide area; give blanket coverage to
WORD ORIGIN Old French *blancquete*

blanket stitch *n* a strong reinforcing stitch for the edges of blankets

blank verse *n* unrhymed verse

Blanqui *n* **Louis Auguste** 1805–81, French revolutionary, who organized secret socialist societies and preached violent insurrection; he spent over 30 years in prison

blare *vb* **blaring, blared 1** to sound loudly and harshly **2** to proclaim loudly: *the newspaper headlines blared the news* ▷*n* **3** a loud harsh noise
WORD ORIGIN Middle Dutch *bleren*

blarney *n* flattering talk
WORD ORIGIN after the *Blarney* Stone in SW Ireland, said to endow whoever kisses it with skill in flattery

Blasco Ibáñez *n* **Vicente** 1867–1928, Spanish novelist, whose books include *Blood and Sand* (1909) and *The Four Horsemen of the Apocalypse* (1916)

blasé (**blah**-zay) *adj* indifferent or bored, esp. through familiarity
WORD ORIGIN French

blaspheme *vb* **-pheming, -phemed 1** to speak disrespectfully of (God or sacred things) **2** to utter curses **blasphemer** *n*
WORD ORIGIN Greek *blasphēmos* evil-speaking

blasphemy *n, pl* **-mies** behaviour or language that shows disrespect for God or sacred things **blasphemous** *adj*

blast *n* **1** an explosion, such as that caused by dynamite **2** the charge used in a single explosion **3** a sudden strong gust of wind or air **4** a sudden loud sound, such as that made by a trumpet **5** a violent verbal outburst, esp. critical **6** *slang* a very enjoyable or thrilling experience: *the party was a blast* **7 at full blast** at maximum speed, volume, etc. ▷*interj* **8** *slang* an exclamation of annoyance ▷*vb* **9** to blow up (a rock, tunnel, etc.) with explosives **10** to make or cause to make a loud harsh noise **11** to criticize severely
WORD ORIGIN Old English *blǣst*

blasted *adj, adv slang* extreme or extremely: *a blasted idiot*

THESAURUS

OPPOSITE: absolve
2 = attribute to, credit to, assign to, put down to, impute to ▷*n* **4 = responsibility**, liability, rap *(slang)*, accountability, onus, culpability, answerability
OPPOSITE: praise

bland *adj* **1 = dull**, boring, weak, plain, flat, commonplace, tedious, vanilla *(informal)*, dreary, tiresome, monotonous, run-of-the-mill, uninspiring, humdrum, unimaginative, uninteresting, insipid, unexciting, ho-hum *(informal)*, vapid, unstimulating, undistinctive **OPPOSITE:** exciting **2 = tasteless**, weak, watered-down, insipid, flavourless, thin, unstimulating, undistinctive

blank *adj* **1, 2, 3, 4 = unmarked**, white, clear, clean, empty, plain, bare, void, spotless, unfilled, uncompleted
OPPOSITE: marked
5 = expressionless, empty, dull, vague, hollow, vacant, lifeless, deadpan, straight-faced, vacuous, impassive, inscrutable, inane, wooden, poker-faced *(informal)*
OPPOSITE: expressive
▷*n* **7, 8 = empty space**, space, gap **9 = void**, vacuum, vacancy, emptiness, nothingness, vacuity, tabula rasa

blanket *n* **1 = cover**, rug, coverlet, afghan **2 = covering**, cover, bed, sheet, coating, coat, layer, film, carpet, cloak, mantle, thickness ▷*vb* **4 = coat**, cover, hide, surround, cloud, mask, conceal, obscure, eclipse, cloak

blast *n* **1 = explosion**, crash, burst, discharge, blow-up, eruption, detonation **3 = gust**, rush, storm, breeze, puff, gale, flurry, tempest, squall, strong breeze **4 = blare**, blow, scream, trumpet, wail, resound, clamour, hoot, toot, honk, clang, peal ▷*vb* **9 = blow up**, bomb, destroy, burst, ruin, break up, explode, shatter, demolish, rupture, dynamite, put paid to, blow sky-high

DICTIONARY

blast furnace *n* a furnace for smelting using a blast of preheated air
blastoff *n* **1** the launching of a rocket under its own power ▷ *vb* **blast off 2** (of a rocket) to be launched
blatant ❶ (blay-tant) *adj* **1** glaringly obvious: *a blatant lie* **2** offensively noticeable: *their blatant disregard for my feelings* **blatantly** *adv*
WORD ORIGIN coined by Edmund Spenser, poet
blather *vb, n* ▸ same as **blether**
Blavatsky *n* **Elena Petrovna**, called *Madame Blavatsky*. 1831–91, Russian theosophist; author of *Isis Unveiled* (1877)
blaze[1] ❶ *n* **1** a strong fire or flame **2** a very bright light or glare **3** an outburst (of passion, patriotism, etc.) ▷ *vb* **blazing, blazed 4** to burn fiercely **5** to shine brightly **6** to become stirred, as with anger or excitement **7 blaze away** to shoot continuously ▸ See also **blazes**
WORD ORIGIN Old English *blæse*
blaze[2] *n* **1** a mark, usually indicating a path, made on a tree **2** a light-coloured marking on the face of an animal ▷ *vb* **blazing, blazed 3** to mark (a tree, path, etc.) with a blaze **4 blaze a trail** to explore new territories, areas of knowledge, etc.
WORD ORIGIN probably from Middle Low German *bles* white marking
blaze[3] *vb* **blazing, blazed** ■ **blaze something abroad** to make something widely known
WORD ORIGIN Middle Dutch *blāsen*
blazer *n* a fairly lightweight jacket, often in the colours of a sports club, school, etc.
blazes *pl n slang, euphemistic* hell
blazon *vb* **1** to proclaim publicly: *the newspaper photographs were blazoned on the front pages* **2** *heraldry* to describe or colour (heraldic arms) conventionally ▷ *n* **3** *heraldry* a coat of arms
WORD ORIGIN Old French *blason* coat of arms
bleach ❶ *vb* **1** to make or become white or colourless by exposure to sunlight, or by the action of chemical agents ▷ *n* **2** a bleaching agent
WORD ORIGIN Old English *blǣcan*
bleaching powder *n* a white powder consisting of chlorinated calcium hydroxide
bleak ❶ *adj* **1** exposed and barren **2** cold and raw **3** offering little hope; dismal: *a bleak future* **bleakly** *adv* **bleakness** *n*
WORD ORIGIN Old English *blāc* pale
bleary *adj* **blearier, bleariest 1** with eyes dimmed, by tears or tiredness: *a few bleary hacks* **2** indistinct or unclear **blearily** *adv*
bleary-eyed *or* **blear-eyed** *adj* with eyes blurred, such as with old age or after waking
Bleasdale *n* **Alan** born 1946, British playwright, best known for his television series *The Boys From the Blackstuff* (1983) and GBH (1991)
bleat *vb* **1** (of a sheep, goat, or calf) to utter its plaintive cry **2** to whine ▷ *n* **3** the characteristic cry of sheep, goats, and calves **4** a weak complaint or whine
WORD ORIGIN Old English *blǣtan*
bleed ❶ *vb* **bleeding, bled 1** to lose or emit blood **2** to remove or draw blood from (a person or animal) **3** (of plants) to exude (sap or resin), esp. from a cut **4** *informal* to obtain money, etc. from (someone), esp. by extortion **5** to draw liquid or gas from (a container or enclosed system) **6 my heart bleeds for you** I am sorry for you: often used ironically
WORD ORIGIN Old English *blēdan*
bleeding *adj, adv Brit slang* extreme or extremely: *a bleeding fool*
bleep *n* **1** a short high-pitched signal made by an electrical device **2** ▸ same as **bleeper** ▷ *vb* **3** to make a bleeping signal **4** to call (someone) by means of a bleeper
WORD ORIGIN imitative
bleeper *n* a small portable radio receiver that makes a bleeping signal
blemish *n* **1** a defect; flaw; stain ▷ *vb* **2** to spoil or tarnish
WORD ORIGIN Old French *blemir* to make pale
blench *vb* to shy away, as in fear
WORD ORIGIN Old English *blencan* to deceive
blend ❶ *vb* **1** to mix or mingle (components) **2** to mix (different varieties of tea, whisky, etc.) **3** to look good together; harmonize **4** (esp. of colours) to shade gradually into each other ▷ *n* **5** a mixture produced by blending
WORD ORIGIN Old English *blandan*
blende *n* a mineral consisting mainly of zinc sulphide: the chief source of zinc
blender *n* an electrical kitchen appliance for pureeing vegetables etc.
blenny *n, pl* **-nies** a small fish of coastal waters with a tapering scaleless body and long fins
WORD ORIGIN Greek *blennos* slime
bless ❶ *vb* **blessing, blessed** *or* **blest 1** to make holy by means of a religious rite **2** to give honour or glory to (a person or thing) as holy **3** to call upon God to protect **4** to worship or adore (God) **5 be blessed with** to be endowed with: *she is blessed with immense energy* **6 bless me!** an exclamation of surprise **7 bless you!** said to a person who has just sneezed
WORD ORIGIN Old English *blǣdsian* to sprinkle with sacrificial blood

THESAURUS

blatant *adj* **1 = obvious**, open, clear, plain, naked, sheer, patent, evident, pronounced, straightforward, outright, glaring, manifest, bald, transparent, noticeable, conspicuous, overt, unmistakable, flaunting, palpable, undeniable, brazen, flagrant, indisputable, ostentatious, unmitigated, cut-and-dried *(informal)*, undisguised, obtrusive, unsubtle, unconcealed
OPPOSITE: subtle
blaze[1] *n* **1 = inferno**, fire, flames, bonfire, combustion, conflagration **2 = flash**, glow, glitter, flare, glare, gleam, brilliance, radiance ▷ *vb* **4 = burn**, glow, flare, flicker, be on fire, go up in flames, be ablaze, fire, flash, flame **5 = shine**, flash, beam, glow, flare, glare, gleam, shimmer, radiate
bleach *vb* **1 = lighten**, wash out, blanch, peroxide, whiten, blench, etiolate
bleak *adj* **1 = exposed**, open, empty, raw, bare, stark, barren, desolate, gaunt, windswept, weather-beaten, unsheltered **OPPOSITE:** sheltered **2 = stormy**, cold, severe, bitter, rough, harsh, chilly, windy, tempestuous, intemperate **3 = dismal**, black, dark, depressing, grim, discouraging, gloomy, hopeless, dreary, sombre, unpromising, disheartening, joyless, cheerless, comfortless
OPPOSITE: cheerful
bleed *vb* **1 = lose blood**, flow, weep, trickle, gush, exude, spurt, shed blood **4** *(informal)* **= extort**, milk, squeeze, drain, exhaust, fleece
blend *vb* **1a = mix**, join, combine, compound, incorporate, merge, put together, fuse, unite, mingle, alloy, synthesize, amalgamate, interweave, coalesce, intermingle, meld, intermix, commingle, commix **1b = combine**, mix, link, integrate, merge, put together, fuse, unite, synthesize, marry, amalgamate **3 = go well**, match, fit, suit, go with, correspond, complement, coordinate, tone in, harmonize, cohere ▷ *n* **5 = mixture**, cross, mix, combination, compound, brew, composite, union, fusion, synthesis, alloy, medley, concoction, amalgam, amalgamation, meld, mélange *(French)*, conglomeration, admixture
bless *vb* **1, 3 = sanctify**, dedicate, ordain, exalt, anoint, consecrate, hallow, invoke happiness on
OPPOSITE: curse

b

DICTIONARY

blessed ❶ *adj* **1** made holy **2** *RC church* (of a person) beatified by the pope **3** bringing great happiness or good fortune: *he was blessed with good looks* **4** *euphemistic* damned: *I'm blessed if I know*

blessing ❶ *n* **1** the act of invoking divine protection or aid **2** approval; good wishes **3** a happy event

blest *vb* ▸ a past of **bless**

blether *Scot vb* **1** to speak foolishly at length ▹*n* **2** foolish talk **3** a person who blethers
WORD ORIGIN Old Norse *blathr* nonsense

blew *vb* ▸ the past tense of **blow**

blight ❶ *n* **1** a person or thing that spoils or prevents growth **2** any plant disease characterized by withering and shrivelling without rotting **3** a fungus or insect that causes blight in plants **4** an ugly urban district ▹*vb* **5** to cause to suffer a blight **6** to frustrate or disappoint: *blighted love* **7** to destroy: *the event blighted her life*
WORD ORIGIN origin unknown

blighter *n Brit, Austral & NZ informal* a despicable or irritating person or thing

Blighty *n Brit, Austral & NZ slang* **1** (used especially by troops serving abroad) Britain; home **2** *pl* **Blighties** (esp. in the First World War) a wound that causes the recipient to be sent home to Britain
WORD ORIGIN Hindi *bilāyatī* foreign land

blimey *interj Brit & NZ slang* an exclamation of surprise or annoyance
WORD ORIGIN short for *gorblimey* God blind me

blimp[1] *n* **1** a small nonrigid airship **2** *films* a soundproof cover fixed over a camera during shooting
WORD ORIGIN probably from *(type) B-limp*

blimp[2] *n chiefly Brit* a person who is stupidly complacent and reactionary. Also called: **Colonel Blimp**
WORD ORIGIN a cartoon character

blind ❶ *adj* **1** unable to see **2** unable or unwilling to understand: *she is blind to his faults* **3** not determined by reason: *blind hatred* **4** acting or performed without control or preparation **5** done without being able to see, relying on instruments for information **6** hidden from sight: *a blind corner* **7** closed at one end: *a blind alley* **8** completely lacking awareness or consciousness: *a blind stupor* **9** having no openings: *a blind wall* ▹*adv* **10** without being able to see ahead or using only instruments: *flying blind* **11** without adequate information: *we bought the house blind* **12 blind drunk** *informal* very drunk ▹*vb* **13** to deprive of sight permanently or temporarily **14** to deprive of good sense, reason, or judgment **15** to darken; conceal **16** to overwhelm by showing detailed knowledge: *he tried to blind us with science* ▹*n* **17** a shade for a window **18** any obstruction or hindrance to sight, light, or air **19** a person, action, or thing that serves to deceive or conceal the truth **blinding** *adj* **blindly** *adv* **blindness** *n*
WORD ORIGIN Old English

blind alley *n* **1** an alley open at one end only **2** *informal* a situation in which no further progress can be made

blind date *n informal* a prearranged social meeting between two people who have not met before

blindfold *vb* **1** to prevent (a person or animal) from seeing by covering the eyes ▹*n* **2** a piece of cloth used to cover the eyes ▹*adj, adv* **3** having the eyes covered with a cloth
WORD ORIGIN Old English *blindfellian* to strike blind

blind man's buff *n* a game in which a blindfolded person tries to catch and identify the other players
WORD ORIGIN obsolete *buff* a blow

blind spot *n* **1** a small oval-shaped area of the retina which is unable to see **2** a place where vision is obscured **3** a subject about which a person is ignorant or prejudiced

blindworm *n* ▸ same as **slowworm**

bling *adj slang* **1** flashy, ostentatious, glitzy, etc. ▹*n* **2** ostentatious jewellery

blink ❶ *vb* **1** to close and immediately reopen (the eyes), usually involuntarily **2** to shine intermittently or unsteadily ▹*n* **3** the act or an instance of blinking **4** a glance; glimpse **5 on the blink** *slang* not working properly
WORD ORIGIN variant of BLENCH

blinker *vb* **1** to provide (a horse) with blinkers **2** to obscure or be obscured with or as with blinkers

blinkered *adj* **1** considering only a narrow point of view **2** (of a horse) wearing blinkers

blinkers *pl n Austral & Brit* leather side pieces attached to a horse's bridle to prevent sideways vision

blinking *adj, adv informal* extreme or extremely: *a blinking idiot*

blip *n* **1** a repetitive sound, such as the kind produced by an electronic device **2** the spot of light on a radar screen indicating the position of an object **3** a temporary irregularity in the performance of something
WORD ORIGIN imitative

bliss ❶ *n* **1** perfect happiness; serene joy **2** the joy of heaven **blissful** *adj* **blissfully** *adv*
WORD ORIGIN Old English *blīths*

Bliss *n* Sir **Arthur** 1891–1975, British composer; Master of the Queen's Musick (1953–75). His works include the *Colour Symphony* (1922), film and ballet music, and a cello concerto (1970)

B list *n* **1** a category slightly below the

THESAURUS

blessed *adj* **1 = holy**, sacred, divine, adored, revered, hallowed, sanctified, beatified

blessing *n* **1 = benediction**, grace, dedication, thanksgiving, invocation, commendation, consecration, benison **OPPOSITE:** curse
2 = approval, backing, support, agreement, regard, favour, sanction, go-ahead *(informal)*, permission, leave, consent, mandate, endorsement, green light, ratification, assent, authorization, good wishes, acquiescence, approbation, concurrence, O.K. *or* okay *(informal)* **OPPOSITE:** disapproval

blight *n* **1 = curse**, suffering, evil, depression, corruption, distress, pollution, misery, plague, hardship, woe, misfortune, contamination, adversity, scourge, affliction, bane, wretchedness **OPPOSITE:** blessing
2, 3 = disease, plague, pest, fungus, contamination, mildew, contagion, infestation, pestilence, canker, cancer ▹*vb* **5, 6 = frustrate**, destroy, ruin, crush, mar, dash, wreck, spoil, crool *or* cruel *(Austral slang)*, scar, undo, mess up, annihilate, nullify, put a damper on

blind *adj* **1 = sightless**, unsighted, unseeing, eyeless, visionless, stone-blind **OPPOSITE:** sighted
2 *(usually followed by* **to***)* **= unaware of**, unconscious of, deaf to, ignorant of, indifferent to, insensitive to, oblivious of, unconcerned about, inconsiderate of, neglectful of, heedless of, insensible of, unmindful of, disregardful of **OPPOSITE:** aware
3 = unquestioning, prejudiced, wholesale, indiscriminate, uncritical, unreasoning, undiscriminating

blink *vb* **1 = flutter**, wink, bat **2 = flash**, flicker, sparkle, wink, shimmer, twinkle, glimmer, scintillate **5 on the blink** *(slang)* **= not working (properly)**, faulty, defective, playing up, out of action, malfunctioning, out of order, on the fritz *(US slang)*

bliss *n* **1 = joy**, ecstasy, euphoria, rapture, nirvana, felicity, gladness, blissfulness, delight, pleasure, heaven, satisfaction, happiness, paradise **OPPOSITE:** misery
2 = beatitude, ecstasy, exaltation, blessedness, felicity, holy joy

DICTIONARY

most socially desirable. ▷ *adj* **B-list** 2 of the category slightly below the most socially desirable: *B-list celebrities*

blister ❶ *n* 1 a small bubble on the skin filled with a watery fluid 2 a swelling containing air or liquid, such as on a painted surface ▷ *vb* 3 to have or cause to have blisters 4 to attack verbally with great scorn **blistering** *adj*
WORD ORIGIN Old French *blestre*

blithe *adj* 1 heedless; casual and indifferent 2 very happy or cheerful **blithely** *adv*
WORD ORIGIN Old English *blīthe*

blithering *adj informal* stupid; foolish: *you blithering idiot*
WORD ORIGIN variant of *blethering*

BLitt Bachelor of Letters
WORD ORIGIN Latin *Baccalaureus Litterarum*

blitz ❶ *n* 1 a violent and sustained attack by enemy aircraft 2 any intensive attack or concerted effort ▷ *vb* 3 to attack suddenly and intensively
WORD ORIGIN see BLITZKRIEG

Blitz *n* **the Blitz** the systematic bombing of Britain in 1940–41 by the German Air Force

blitzkrieg *n* a swift intensive military attack designed to defeat the opposition quickly
WORD ORIGIN German: lightning war

Blixen *n* **Karen** ▸ See **Dinesen**

blizzard *n* a blinding storm of wind and snow
WORD ORIGIN origin unknown

bloat *vb* 1 to cause to swell, as with a liquid or air 2 to cause to be puffed up, as with conceit 3 to cure (fish, esp. herring) by half drying in smoke **bloated** *adj*
WORD ORIGIN Old Norse *blautr* soaked

bloater *n Brit* a herring that has been salted in brine, smoked, and cured

blob *n* 1 a soft mass or drop 2 a spot of colour, ink, etc. 3 an indistinct or shapeless form or object
WORD ORIGIN imitative

bloc ❶ *n* a group of people or countries combined by a common interest
WORD ORIGIN French

Bloch *n* 1 **Ernest** 1880–1959, US composer, born in Switzerland, who found inspiration in Jewish liturgical and folk music: his works include the symphonies *Israel* (1916) and *America* (1926) 2 **Felix** 1905–83, US physicist, born in Switzerland: Nobel prize for physics (1952) for his work on the magnetic moments of atomic particles 3 **Konrad Emil** 1912–2000, US biochemist, born in Germany: shared the Nobel prize for physiology or medicine in 1964 for his work on fatty-acid metabolism 4 **Marc** 1886–1944, French historian and Resistance fighter; author of *Feudal Society* (1935) and *Strange Defeat* (1940), an essay on the fall of France: killed by the Nazis

block ❶ *n* 1 a large solid piece of wood, stone, etc. 2 such a piece on which particular tasks may be done, as chopping, cutting, etc. 3 a large building of offices, flats, etc. 4 a group of buildings in a city bounded by intersecting streets on each side 5 an obstruction or hindrance: *a writer with a block* 6 one of a set of wooden or plastic cubes used as a child's toy 7 *slang* a person's head 8 a piece of wood, metal, etc. engraved for printing 9 a casing housing one or more freely rotating pulleys ▸ See also **block and tackle** 10 a quantity considered as a single unit ▷ *vb* 11 to obstruct or impede by introducing an obstacle: *lorry drivers had blocked the routes to Paris* 12 to impede, retard, or prevent (an action or procedure) 13 to stamp (a title or design) on (a book cover, etc.) 14 *cricket* to play (a ball) defensively ▸ See also **block out** > **blockage** *n*
WORD ORIGIN Dutch *blok*

blockade ❶ *n* 1 *mil* the closing off of a port or region to prevent the passage of goods ▷ *vb* **-ading, -aded** 2 to impose a blockade on

block and tackle *n* a hoisting device in which a rope or chain is passed around a pair of blocks containing one or more pulleys

blockboard *n* a type of plywood consisting of strips of wood sandwiched between layers of veneer

blockbuster *n informal* 1 a film, novel, etc. that has been or is expected to be highly successful 2 a large bomb used to demolish extensive areas

blockhead *n* a stupid person **blockheaded** *adj*

blockie *n Austral* an owner of a small property, esp. a farm

block letter *n* a plain capital letter. Also called: **block capital**

block out *vb* 1 to plan or describe (something) in a general fashion 2 to prevent the entry or consideration of (something)

blog *n informal* a journal written on-line and accessible to users of the internet. Full name: **weblog** > **blogger** *n* **blogging** *n*

blogosphere *n informal* a collective term for the weblogs on the internet

Blok *n* **Aleksandr Aleksandrovich** 1880–1921, Russian poet whose poems, which include *Verses about the Beautiful Lady* (1901–2) and *Rasput'ya* (1902–4), contain a mixture of symbolism, romanticism, tragedy, and irony

bloke ❶ *n Brit, Austral & NZ informal* a man **blokeish** *or* **blokey** *adj*
WORD ORIGIN Shelta

blonde ❶ *or masc* **blond** *adj* 1 (of hair) fair 2 (of a person) having fair hair and a light complexion ▷ *n* 3 a person having light-coloured hair and skin **blondeness** *or masc* **blondness** *n*
WORD ORIGIN Old French

Blondin *n* **Charles**, real name *Jean-François Gravelet*. 1824–97, French acrobat and tightrope walker; best known for walking a tightrope across Niagara Falls (1859)

blood ❶ *n* 1 a reddish fluid in vertebrates that is pumped by the heart through the arteries and veins ▸ Related adjective: **haemal** 2 bloodshed, esp. when resulting in murder: *they were responsible for the spilling of blood throughout the country* 3 lifeblood 4 relationship through being of the same family, race, or kind; kinship 5 **the blood** royal or noble descent: *a prince of the blood* 6 **flesh and blood** a near kindred or kinship, esp. that between a parent and child b human nature: *it's more than flesh and blood can stand* 7 **in one's blood** as a natural or inherited characteristic or talent 8 newcomers viewed as an invigorating force: *new blood* 9 **in cold blood** showing no passion;

THESAURUS

blister *n* 1 = **sore**, boil, swelling, cyst, pimple, wen, blain, carbuncle, pustule, bleb, furuncle *(pathology)*

blitz *n* 1 = **attack**, strike, assault, raid, offensive, onslaught, bombardment, bombing campaign, blitzkrieg

bloc *n* = **group**, union, league, ring, alliance, coalition, axis, combine

block *n* 1 = **piece**, bar, square, mass, cake, brick, lump, chunk, cube, hunk, nugget, ingot 5 = **obstruction**, bar, barrier, obstacle, impediment, hindrance ▷ *vb* 11a = **obstruct**, close, stop, cut off, plug, choke, clog, shut off, stop up, bung up *(informal)*
OPPOSITE: clear
11b = **obscure**, bar, cut off, interrupt, obstruct, get in the way of, shut off

blockade *n* 1 = **stoppage**, block, barrier, restriction, obstacle, barricade, obstruction, impediment, hindrance, encirclement

bloke *n (informal)* = **man**, person, individual, customer *(informal)*, character *(informal)*, guy *(informal)*, fellow, punter *(informal)*, chap, boy, bod *(informal)*

blonde *or* **blond** *adj* 1 = **fair**, light, light-coloured, flaxen 2 = **fair-haired**, golden-haired, tow-headed

blood *n* 1 = **lifeblood**, gore, vital fluid 4 = **family**, relations, birth, descent, extraction, ancestry, lineage,

DICTIONARY

ruthlessly **10 make one's blood boil** to cause to be angry or indignant **11 make one's blood run cold** to fill with horror ▹ *vb* **12** *hunting* to cause (young hounds) to taste the blood of a freshly killed quarry **13** to initiate (a person) to war or hunting
WORD ORIGIN Old English *blōd*

Blood *n* **Thomas**, known as *Colonel Blood*. ?1618–80, Irish adventurer, who tried to steal the Crown Jewels (1671)

blood-and-thunder *adj* denoting melodramatic behaviour

blood bank *n* a place where blood is stored until required for transfusion

blood bath *n* a massacre

blood brother *n* a man or boy who has sworn to treat another as his brother, often in a ceremony in which their blood is mingled

blood count *n* determination of the number of red and white blood corpuscles in a specific sample of blood

blood-curdling *or* **bloodcurdling** *adj* terrifying

blood donor *n* a person who gives blood to be used for transfusion

blood group *n* any one of the various groups into which human blood is classified

blood heat *n* the normal temperature of the human body, 98.4°F or 37°C

bloodhound *n* a large hound, formerly used in tracking and police work

bloodless *adj* **1** without blood: *bloodless surgery* **2** conducted without violence: *a bloodless coup* **3** anaemic-looking; pale **4** lacking vitality; lifeless: *the bloodless ambience of supermarkets*

blood-letting *n* **1** bloodshed, esp. in a feud **2** the former medical practice of removing blood

bloodlust *n* a desire for violence and carnage

blood money *n* **1** money obtained by ruthlessly sacrificing others **2** money paid to a hired murderer **3** compensation paid to the relatives of a murdered person

blood orange *n* a variety of orange, the pulp of which is dark red when ripe

blood poisoning *n* ▸ same as **septicaemia**

blood pressure *n* the pressure exerted by the blood on the inner walls of the blood vessels

blood relation *or* **relative** *n* a person related by birth

bloodshed ❶ *n* slaughter; killing

bloodshot *adj* (of an eye) inflamed

blood sport *n* any sport involving the killing of an animal

bloodstained *adj* discoloured with blood

bloodstock *n* thoroughbred horses

bloodstream *n* the flow of blood through the vessels of a living body

bloodsucker *n* **1** an animal that sucks blood, esp. a leech **2** *informal* a person who preys upon another person, esp. by extorting money

bloodthirsty *adj* **-thirstier, -thirstiest** taking pleasure in bloodshed or violence

blood vessel *n* a tube through which blood travels in the body

bloody ❶ *adj* **bloodier, bloodiest 1** covered with blood **2** marked by much killing and bloodshed: *a bloody war* **3** cruel or murderous: *a bloody tyrant* ▹ *adj, adv* **4** *slang* extreme or extremely: *a bloody fool; a bloody good idea* ▹ *vb* **bloodies, bloodying, bloodied 5** to stain with blood

Bloody Caesar *n* a drink consisting of vodka, juice made from clams and tomatoes, Worcester sauce and Tabasco

Bloody Mary *n* a drink consisting of tomato juice and vodka

bloody-minded *adj Brit & NZ informal* deliberately obstructive and unhelpful

bloom ❶ *n* **1** a blossom on a flowering plant **2** the state or period when flowers open **3** a healthy or flourishing condition; prime **4** a youthful or healthy glow **5** a fine whitish coating on the surface of fruits or leaves ▹ *vb* **6** (of flowers) to open **7** to bear flowers **8** to flourish or grow **9** to be in a healthy, glowing condition
WORD ORIGIN Germanic

bloomer *n Brit informal* a stupid mistake; blunder
WORD ORIGIN from BLOOMING

bloomers *pl n* **1** *informal* women's baggy knickers **2** (formerly) loose trousers gathered at the knee worn by women
WORD ORIGIN after Mrs A. *Bloomer*, social reformer

Bloomfield *n* **Leonard** 1887–1949, US linguist, influential for his strictly scientific and descriptive approach to comparative linguistics; author of *Language* (1933)

blooming *adv, adj Brit informal* extreme or extremely: *blooming painful*
WORD ORIGIN euphemistic for *bloody*

blossom ❶ *n* **1** the flower or flowers of a plant, esp. producing edible fruit **2** the period of flowering ▹ *vb* **3** (of plants) to flower **4** to come to a promising stage
WORD ORIGIN Old English *blōstm*

blot *n* **1** a stain or spot, esp. of ink **2** something that spoils **3** a stain on one's character ▹ *vb* **blotting, blotted 4** to stain or spot **5** to cause a blemish in or on: *he blotted his copybook by missing a penalty* **6** to soak up (excess ink, etc.) by using blotting paper **7 blot out a** to darken or hide completely: *the mist blotted out the sea* **b** to block from one's mind: *to blot out the memories*
WORD ORIGIN Germanic

blotch *n* **1** an irregular spot or discoloration ▹ *vb* **2** to become or cause to become marked by such discoloration **blotchy** *adj*
WORD ORIGIN probably from *botch*, influenced by *blot*

blotter *n* a sheet of blotting paper

blotting paper *n* a soft absorbent paper, used for soaking up surplus ink

blotto *adj Brit, Austral & NZ slang* extremely drunk
WORD ORIGIN from *blot* (verb)

blouse *n* **1** a woman's shirtlike garment **2** a waist-length belted jacket worn by soldiers ▹ *vb* **blousing, bloused 3** to hang or cause to hang in full loose folds
WORD ORIGIN French

blouson (blew-zon) *n* a short loose jacket with a tight-fitting waist
WORD ORIGIN French

blow[1] ❶ *vb* **blowing, blew, blown 1** (of a current of air, the wind, etc.) to be or cause to be in motion **2** to move or be carried by or as if by wind **3** to expel (air, etc.) through the mouth or nose **4** to breathe hard; pant **5** to inflate with air or the breath **6** (of wind, etc.) to make a roaring sound **7** to cause (a musical instrument) to sound by forcing air into it **8** (often foll. by *up, down* or *in* etc.) to explode,

THESAURUS

kinship, kindred

bloodshed *n* **= killing**, murder, massacre, slaughter, slaying, carnage, butchery, blood-letting, blood bath

bloody *adj* **1 = bloodstained**, raw, bleeding, blood-soaked, blood-spattered **3 = cruel**, fierce, savage, brutal, vicious, ferocious, cut-throat, warlike, barbarous, sanguinary

bloom *n* **1 = flower**, bud, blossom **3 = prime**, flower, beauty, height, peak, flourishing, maturity, perfection, best days, heyday, zenith, full flowering **4 = glow**, flush, blush, freshness, lustre, radiance, rosiness **OPPOSITE:** pallor ▹ *vb* **6 = flower**, blossom, open, bud **OPPOSITE:** wither **8 = succeed**, flourish, thrive, prosper, fare well **OPPOSITE:** fail

blossom *n* **1 = flower**, bloom, bud, efflorescence, floret ▹ *vb* **3 = flower**, bloom, bud **4 = succeed**, progress, thrive, flourish, prosper

blow[1] *vb* **2a = move**, carry, drive, bear, sweep, fling, whisk, buffet, whirl, waft **2b = be carried**, hover, flutter, flit, flitter **3 = exhale**, breathe, pant, puff, breathe out, expel air **7 = play**,

DICTIONARY

break, or disintegrate completely **9** *electronics* (of a fuse or valve) to burn out because of excessive current **10** to shape (glass, etc.) by forcing air or gas through the material when molten **11** *slang* to spend (money) freely **12** *slang* to use (an opportunity) ineffectively **13** *slang* to expose or betray (a secret) **14** *past participle* **blowed** *informal* ▸ same as **damn 15 blow hot and cold** *informal* to keep changing one's attitude towards someone or something **16 blow one's top** *informal* to lose one's temper ▹*n* **17** the act or an instance of blowing **18** the sound produced by blowing **19** a blast of air or wind **20** *Brit slang* cannabis ▸ See also **blow away, blow out**, etc.
WORD ORIGIN Old English *blāwan*

blow² ❶ *n* **1** a powerful or heavy stroke with the fist, a weapon, etc. **2** a sudden setback: *the scheme was dealt a blow by the introduction of martial law* **3** an attacking action: *a blow for freedom* **4 come to blows a** to fight **b** to result in a fight
WORD ORIGIN probably Germanic

blow away *vb slang* **1** to kill by shooting **2** to defeat utterly

blow-by-blow *adj* explained in great detail: *a blow-by-blow account*

blow-dry *vb* **-dries, -drying, -dried 1** to style (the hair) while drying it with a hand-held hair dryer ▹*n* **2** this method of styling hair

blower *n* **1** a mechanical device, such as a fan, that blows **2** *informal* a telephone

blowfly *n, pl* **-flies** a fly that lays its eggs in meat

blowhole *n* **1** the nostril of a whale **2** a hole in ice through which seals, etc. breathe **3** a vent for air or gas **4** *geol* a hole in a cliff top leading to a sea cave

blowie *n Austral informal* a bluebottle

blown *vb* ▸ a past participle of **blow**

blow out *vb* **1** (of a flame) to extinguish or be extinguished **2** (of a tyre) to puncture suddenly **3** (of an oil or gas well) to lose oil or gas in an uncontrolled manner ▹*n* **blowout 4** a sudden burst in a tyre **5** the uncontrolled escape of oil or gas from a well **6** *slang* a large filling meal

blow over *vb* **1** to be forgotten **2** to cease or be finished: *the crisis blew over*

blowpipe *n* **1** a long tube from which poisoned darts, etc. are shot by blowing **2** a tube for blowing air into a flame to intensify its heat **3** an iron pipe used to blow glass into shape

blowsy *adj* **blowsier, blowsiest 1** (of a woman) slovenly or sluttish **2** (of a woman) ruddy in complexion
WORD ORIGIN dialect *blowze* beggar girl

blowtorch *or* **blowlamp** *n* a small burner that produces a very hot flame, used to remove old paint, soften metal, etc.

blow up *vb* **1** to explode or cause to explode **2** to inflate with air **3** to increase the importance of (something): *an affair blown up out of all proportions* **4** *informal* to lose one's temper **5** *informal* to reprimand (someone) **6** *informal* to enlarge (a photograph) **7** to come into existence with sudden force: *a crisis had blown up* ▹*n* **blow-up 8** *informal* an enlarged photograph

blowy *adj* **blowier, blowiest** windy

blubber *n* **1** the fatty tissue of aquatic mammals such as the whale **2** *informal* flabby body fat ▹*vb* **3** to sob without restraint
WORD ORIGIN probably imitative

bludge ❶ *Austral & NZ informal vb* **bludging, bludged 1** (foll. by *on*) to scrounge from **2** to evade work ▹*n* **3** a very easy task

bludgeon *n* **1** a stout heavy club, typically thicker at one end ▹*vb* **2** to hit as if with a bludgeon **3** to force; bully; coerce
WORD ORIGIN origin unknown

blue ❶ *n* **1** the colour of a clear unclouded sky **2** anything blue, such as blue clothing or blue paint: *she is clothed in blue* **3** a sportsman who represents or has represented Oxford or Cambridge University **4** *Brit informal* a Tory **5** *Austral & NZ slang* an argument or fight **6** Also: **bluey** *Austral & NZ slang* a court summons **7** *Austral & NZ informal* a mistake **8 out of the blue** unexpectedly ▹*adj* **bluer, bluest 9** of the colour blue; of the colour of a clear unclouded sky **10** (of the flesh) having a purple tinge from cold **11** depressed or unhappy **12** pornographic: *blue movies* ▹*vb* **blueing** *or* **bluing, blued 13** to make or become blue or bluer **14** *old-fashioned, informal* to spend extravagantly or wastefully: *I consoled myself by blueing my royalty cheque* ▸ See also **blues** > **blueness** *n*
WORD ORIGIN Old French *bleu*

blue baby *n* a baby born with a bluish tinge to the skin because of lack of oxygen in the blood

bluebell *n* a woodland plant with blue bell-shaped flowers

blueberry *n, pl* **-ries** a very small blackish edible fruit that grows on a North American shrub

bluebird *n* a North American songbird with a blue plumage

blue blood *n* royal or aristocratic descent

bluebook *n* **1** (in Britain) a government publication, usually the report of a commission **2** (in Canada) an annual statement of government accounts

bluebottle *n* **1** a large fly with a dark-blue body; blowfly **2** *Austral & NZ informal* a Portuguese man-of-war

blue cheese *n* cheese containing a blue mould, such as Stilton or Danish blue

blue chip *n* **1** *finance* a stock considered reliable ▹*adj* **blue-chip 2** denoting something considered to be a valuable asset

blue-collar *adj* denoting manual industrial workers

blue-eyed boy *n informal* a favourite

blue funk *n slang* a state of great terror

blue heeler *n Austral & NZ informal* a dog that controls cattle by biting their heels

bluenose *n* **1** *US slang* a puritanical or prudish person **2** Also: **bluenoser** (*sometimes cap*) *Canad informal* a native or inhabitant of Nova Scotia

blue pencil *n* **1** deletion or alteration of the contents of a book or other work ▹*vb* **blue-pencil, -cilling, -cilled** *or US* **-ciling, -ciled 2** to alter or delete parts of (a book, film, etc.)

blue peter *n* a signal flag of blue with a white square at the centre, displayed by a vessel about to leave port

blueprint ❶ *n* **1** an original description of a plan or idea that explains how it is expected to work

THESAURUS

sound, pipe, trumpet, blare, toot

blow² *n* **1 = knock**, stroke, punch, belt (*informal*), bang, rap, bash (*informal*), sock (*slang*), smack, thump, buffet, clout (*informal*), whack (*informal*), wallop (*informal*), slosh (*Brit slang*), tonk (*informal*), clump (*slang*), clomp (*slang*) **2 = setback**, shock, upset, disaster, reverse, disappointment, catastrophe, misfortune, jolt, bombshell, calamity, affliction, whammy (*informal, chiefly US*), choker (*informal*), sucker punch, bummer (*slang*), bolt from the blue, comedown (*informal*)

bludge *vb* **2** (*Austral & NZ informal*) **= slack**, skive (*Brit informal*), idle, shirk, gold-brick (*US slang*), bob off (*Brit slang*), scrimshank (*Brit military slang*)

blue *adj* **11 = depressed**, low, sad, unhappy, fed up, gloomy, dismal, melancholy, glum, dejected, despondent, downcast, down in the dumps (*informal*), down in the mouth, low-spirited, down-hearted
OPPOSITE: happy
12 = smutty, dirty, naughty, obscene, indecent, vulgar, lewd, risqué, X-rated (*informal*), bawdy, page-three, near the knuckle (*informal*)
OPPOSITE: respectable

blueprint *n* **1 = scheme**, plan, design,

b

DICTIONARY

2 a photographic print of plans, technical drawings, etc. consisting of white lines on a blue background

blue ribbon *n* **1** a badge awarded as the first prize in a competition **2** (in Britain) a badge of blue silk worn by members of the Order of the Garter

blues ● *pl n* **the blues 1** a feeling of depression or deep unhappiness **2** a type of folk song originating among Black Americans

blue-screen *adj* relating to a film technique in which actors are filmed against a blue screen so that special effects can be added later

blue-sky *adj* of research done for theoretical reasons rather than for practical application

bluestocking *n usually disparaging* a scholarly or intellectual woman
WORD ORIGIN from the blue worsted stockings worn by members of an 18th-century literary society

bluetit *n* a small European bird with a blue crown, wings, and tail and yellow underparts

bluetongue *n* an Australian lizard with a blue tongue

Bluetooth *n* a short-range radio technology that allows wireless communication between computers, mobile phones, etc.

blue whale *n* a very large bluish-grey whale: the largest mammal

bluff[1] ● *vb* **1** to pretend to be confident in order to influence (someone) ▹*n* **2** deliberate deception to create the impression of a strong position **3 call someone's bluff** to challenge someone to give proof of his or her claims
WORD ORIGIN Dutch *bluffen* to boast

bluff[2] ● *n* **1** a steep promontory, bank, or cliff **2** *Canad* a clump of trees on the prairie; copse ▹*adj* **3** good-naturedly frank and hearty
WORD ORIGIN probably from Middle Dutch *blaf* broad

bluish *or* **blueish** *adj* slightly blue

Blum *n* **Léon** 1872–1950, French socialist statesman; premier of France (1936–37; 1938; 1946–47)

Blumberg *n* **Baruch Samuel** born 1925, US physician, noted for work on antigens: shared the Nobel prize for physiology or medicine 1976

Blunden *n* **Edmund** (**Charles**) 1896–1974, British poet and scholar, noted esp. for *Undertones of War* (1928), a memoir of World War I in verse and prose

blunder ● *n* **1** a stupid or clumsy mistake ▹*vb* **2** to make stupid or clumsy mistakes **3** to act clumsily; stumble **blundering** *n, adj*
WORD ORIGIN Scandinavian

blunderbuss *n* an obsolete gun with wide barrel and flared muzzle
WORD ORIGIN Dutch *donderbus* thunder gun

Blunkett *n* **David** born 1947, British Labour politician; secretary of state for education and employment (1997–2001); home secretary (2001–04); secretary of state for work and pensions (2005)

blunt ● *adj* **1** (esp. of a knife) lacking sharpness **2** not having a sharp edge or point: *a blunt instrument* **3** (of people, manner of speaking, etc.) straightforward and uncomplicated ▹*vb* **4** to make less sharp **5** to diminish the sensitivity or perception of: *prison life has blunted his mind* **bluntly** *adv*
WORD ORIGIN Scandinavian

Blunt *n* **1 Anthony** 1907–83, British art historian and Soviet spy **2 Wilfred Scawen** 1840–1922, British poet, traveller, and anti-imperialist

blur ● *vb* **blurring, blurred 1** to make or become vague or less distinct **2** to smear or smudge **3** to make (the judgment, memory, or perception) less clear; dim ▹*n* **4** something vague, hazy, or indistinct **5** a smear or smudge **blurred** *adj* **blurry** *adj*
WORD ORIGIN perhaps variant of *blear*

blurb *n* a promotional description, such as on the jackets of books
WORD ORIGIN coined by G. Burgess, humorist and illustrator

blurt *vb* (foll. by *out*) to utter suddenly and involuntarily
WORD ORIGIN probably imitative

blush ● *vb* **1** to become suddenly red in the face, esp. from embarrassment or shame ▹*n* **2** a sudden reddening of the face, esp. from embarrassment or shame **3** a rosy glow **4** ▸same as **rosé**
WORD ORIGIN Old English *blȳscan*

blusher *n* a cosmetic applied to the cheeks to give a rosy colour

bluster *vb* **1** to speak loudly or in a bullying way **2** (of the wind) to be gusty ▹*n* **3** empty threats or protests **blustery** *adj*
WORD ORIGIN probably from Middle Low German *blüsteren* to blow violently

Blyth[1] *n* a port in N England, in SE Northumberland, on the North Sea. Pop: 35 691 (2001)

Blyth[2] *n* Sir **Chay** born 1940, British yachtsman. He sailed round the world alone (1970–71) and won many races

BM 1 Bachelor of Medicine **2** British Museum

BMA British Medical Association

THESAURUS

system, idea, programme, proposal, strategy, pattern, suggestion, procedure, plot, draft, outline, sketch, proposition, prototype, layout, pilot scheme **2 = plan**, scheme, project, pattern, draft, outline, sketch, layout

blues *pl n* **1 = depression**, gloom, melancholy, unhappiness, despondency, the hump (*Brit informal*), dejection, moodiness, low spirits, the dumps (*informal*), doldrums, gloominess, glumness

bluff[1] *vb* **1 = deceive**, lie, trick, fool, pretend, cheat, con, fake, mislead, sham, dupe, feign, delude, humbug, bamboozle (*informal*), hoodwink, double-cross (*informal*), pull the wool over someone's eyes ▹*n* **2 = deception**, show, lie, fraud, fake, sham, pretence, deceit, bravado, bluster, humbug, subterfuge, feint, mere show

bluff[2] *n* **1 = precipice**, bank, peak, cliff, ridge, crag, escarpment, promontory, scarp ▹*adj* **3 = hearty**, open, frank, blunt, sincere, outspoken, honest, downright, cordial, genial, affable, ebullient, jovial, plain-spoken, good-natured, unreserved, back-slapping **OPPOSITE:** tactful

blunder *n* **1 = mistake**, slip, fault, error, boob (*Brit slang*), oversight, gaffe, slip-up (*informal*), indiscretion, impropriety, howler (*informal*), bloomer (*Brit informal*), clanger (*informal*), faux pas, boo-boo (*informal*), gaucherie, barry *or* Barry Crocker (*Austral slang*) **OPPOSITE:** correctness ▹*vb* **2 = make a mistake**, blow it (*slang*), err, slip up (*informal*), cock up (*Brit slang*), miscalculate, foul up, drop a clanger (*informal*), put your foot in it (*informal*), drop a brick (*Brit informal*), screw up (*informal*) **OPPOSITE:** be correct **3 = stumble**, fall, reel, stagger, flounder, lurch, lose your balance

blunt *adj* **1, 2 = dull**, rounded, dulled, edgeless, unsharpened **OPPOSITE:** sharp **3 = frank**, forthright, straightforward, explicit, rude, outspoken, bluff, downright, upfront (*informal*), trenchant, brusque, plain-spoken, tactless, impolite, discourteous, unpolished, uncivil, straight from the shoulder **OPPOSITE:** tactful

blur *vb* **1a = become indistinct**, soften, become vague, become hazy, become fuzzy **1b = obscure**, make indistinct, mask, soften, muddy, obfuscate, make vague, befog, make hazy ▹*n* **4 = haze**, confusion, fog, obscurity, dimness, cloudiness, blear, blurredness, indistinctness

blush *vb* **1 = turn red**, colour, burn, flame, glow, flush, crimson, redden, go red (as a beetroot), turn scarlet **OPPOSITE:** turn pale ▹*n* **3 = reddening**, colour, glow, flush, pink tinge, rosiness, ruddiness, rosy tint

DICTIONARY

BMI *n* body mass index: an index used to indicate whether or not a person is a healthy weight for his or her height
B-movie *n* a film originally made as a supporting film, now considered a genre in its own right
BMR basal metabolic rate
BMus Bachelor of Music
BMX *n* **1** bicycle motocross: stunt riding over an obstacle course on a bicycle **2** a bicycle designed for bicycle motocross
BO 1 *informal* body odour **2** box office
boa *n* **1** a large nonvenomous snake of Central and South America that kills its prey by constriction **2** a woman's long thin scarf of feathers or fur
WORD ORIGIN Latin
boab (boh-ab) *n Austral informal* ▸short for **baobab**
Boabdil *n* original name *Abu-Abdullah*, called El Chico, ruled as *Mohammed XI*. died ?1538, last Moorish king of Granada (1482–83; 1486–92)
boa constrictor *n* a very large snake of tropical America and the West Indies that kills its prey by constriction
boar *n* **1** an uncastrated male pig **2** a wild pig
WORD ORIGIN Old English *bār*
board ● *n* **1** a long wide flat piece of sawn timber **2** a smaller flat piece of rigid material for a specific purpose: *ironing board* **3 a** a group of people who officially administer a company, trust, etc. **b** any other official group, such as examiners or interviewers **4** a person's meals, provided regularly for money **5** stiff cardboard or similar material, used for the outside covers of a book **6** a flat thin rectangular sheet of composite material, such as chipboard **7** *naut* the side of a ship **8** a portable surface for indoor games such as chess or backgammon **9 go by the board** *informal* to be in disuse, neglected, or lost **10 on board** on or in a ship, aeroplane, etc. ▹*vb* **11** to go aboard (a train or other vehicle) **12** to attack (a ship) by forcing one's way aboard **13** (foll. by *up* or *in* etc.) to cover with boards **14** to receive meals and lodging in return for money **15 board out** to arrange for (someone, esp. a child) to receive food and lodging away from home **16** (in ice hockey and box lacrosse) to bodycheck an opponent against the boards ▸See also **boards**
WORD ORIGIN Old English *bord*
boarder *n Brit* a pupil who lives at school during term time
boarding *n* **1** the act of embarking on an aircraft, train, ship, etc. **2** a structure of boards **3** timber boards collectively **4** (in ice hockey and box lacrosse) an act of bodychecking an opponent against the boards
boarding house *n* a private house that provides accommodation and meals for paying guests
boarding school *n* a school providing living accommodation for pupils
boardroom *n* a room where the board of directors of a company meets
boards *pl n* **1** a wooden wall forming the enclosure in which ice hockey or box lacrosse is played **2 the boards** the stage
Boas *n* **Franz** 1858–1942, US anthropologist, born in Germany. He made major contributions to cultural and linguistic anthropology in studies of North American Indians, including *The Mind of Primitive Man* (1911; 1938)
boast ● *vb* **1** to speak in excessively proud terms of one's possessions, talents, etc. **2** to possess (something to be proud of): *a team which boasts five current world record holders* ▹*n* **3** a bragging statement **4** something that is bragged about: *this proved to be a false boast*
WORD ORIGIN origin unknown
boastful *adj* tending to boast
boat *n* **1** a small vessel propelled by oars, paddle, sails, or motor **2** *informal* a ship **3** ▸see **gravy boat, sauce boat 4 in the same boat** sharing the same problems **5 miss the boat** to lose an opportunity **6 rock the boat** *informal* to cause a disturbance in the existing situation ▹*vb* **7** to travel or go in a boat, esp. as recreation
WORD ORIGIN Old English *bāt*
boater *n* a stiff straw hat with a straight brim and flat crown
boathouse *n* a shelter by the edge of a river, lake, etc. for housing boats
boating *n* rowing, sailing, or cruising in boats as a form of recreation
boatman *n, pl* **-men** a man who works on, hires out, or repairs boats
boatswain (boh-sn) *n naut* ▸same as **bosun**
boat train *n* a train scheduled to take passengers to or from a particular ship
bob[1] ● *vb* **bobbing, bobbed 1** to move or cause to move up and down repeatedly, such as while floating in water **2** to move or cause to move with a short abrupt movement, esp. of the head **3 bob up** to appear or emerge suddenly ▹*n* **4** a short abrupt movement, as of the head
WORD ORIGIN origin unknown
bob[2] *n* **1** a hairstyle in which the hair is cut short evenly all round the head **2** a dangling weight on a pendulum or plumb line ▹*vb* **bobbing, bobbed 3** to cut (the hair) in a bob
WORD ORIGIN Middle English *bobbe* bunch of flowers
bob[3] *n, pl* **bob** *Brit, Austral & NZ informal* (formerly) a shilling: *two bob*
WORD ORIGIN origin unknown
bobbejaan *n S African* **1** a baboon **2** a large black spider **3** a monkey wrench
WORD ORIGIN Afrikaans
bobbin *n* a reel on which thread or yarn is wound
WORD ORIGIN Old French *bobine*
bobble *n* **1** a tufted ball, usually woollen, that is used for decoration ▹*vb* **-bling, -bled 2** (of a ball) to bounce erratically because of an uneven playing surface
WORD ORIGIN from BOB[1]
bobby *n, pl* **-bies** *Brit informal* a British policeman
WORD ORIGIN after *Robert Peel*, who set up the Metropolitan Police Force
bobby pin *n US, Canad, Austral & NZ* a metal hairpin
bobotie (ba-boot-ee) *n S African* a traditional Cape dish of curried minced meat
WORD ORIGIN probably from Malay
bobsleigh *n* **1** a sledge for racing down a steeply banked ice-covered run ▹*vb* **2** to ride on a bobsleigh
bobtail *n* **1** a docked tail **2** an animal with such a tail ▹*adj also* **bobtailed 3** having the tail cut short
Boccherini *n* **Luigi** 1743–1805, Italian composer and cellist
Boccioni *n* **Umberto** 1882–1916, Italian painter and sculptor: principal theorist of the futurist movement
bocconcini (bok-on-chee-nee) *pl n* small bite-sized pieces of mozzarella cheese
WORD ORIGIN Italian
Boche (bosh) *n offensive slang* a German, esp. a German soldier
WORD ORIGIN French
bod *n informal* **1** a person: *he's a queer bod* **2** ▸short for **body** (sense 1)
WORD ORIGIN short for *body*

THESAURUS

board *n* **1 = plank**, panel, timber, slat, piece of timber **3b = council**, directors, committee, congress, ministry, advisers, panel, assembly, chamber, trustees, governing body, synod, directorate, quango, advisory group, conclave **4 = meals**, provisions, victuals, daily meals ▹*vb* **11 = get on**, enter, mount, embark, entrain, embus, enplane **OPPOSITE:** get off
boast *vb* **1 = brag**, crow, vaunt, bluster, talk big *(slang)*, blow your own trumpet, show off, be proud of, flaunt, congratulate yourself on, flatter yourself, pride yourself on, skite *(Austral & NZ informal)* **OPPOSITE:** cover up **2 = possess**, offer, present, exhibit
bob[1] *vb* **1 = bounce**, duck, leap, hop, weave, skip, jerk, wobble, quiver, oscillate, waggle

DICTIONARY

b

bode[1] *vb* **boding, boded** to be an omen of (good or ill); portend
WORD ORIGIN Old English *bodian*
bode[2] *vb* ▸ a past tense of **bide**
bodega *n* a shop in a Spanish-speaking country that sells wine
WORD ORIGIN Spanish
bodge *vb* **bodging, bodged** *Brit, Austral & NZ informal* to make a mess of; botch
bodice *n* **1** the upper part of a woman's dress, from the shoulder to the waist **2** a tight-fitting corset worn laced over a blouse, or (formerly) as a woman's undergarment
WORD ORIGIN originally Scots *bodies*, plural of *body*
bodily ⊕ *adj* **1** relating to the human body ▹ *adv* **2** by taking hold of the body: *he threw him bodily from the platform* **3** in person; in the flesh
bodkin *n* a blunt large-eyed needle
WORD ORIGIN origin unknown
body ⊕ *n, pl* **bodies** **1** the entire physical structure of an animal or human ▸ Related adjective: **corporal** **2** the trunk or torso **3** a corpse **4** a group regarded as a single entity: *a local voluntary body* **5** the main part of anything: *the body of a car* **6** a separate mass of water or land **7** the flesh as opposed to the spirit **8** fullness in the appearance of the hair **9** the characteristic full quality of certain wines **10** *informal* a person: *all the important bodies from the council were present* **11** a woman's one-piece undergarment **12** **keep body and soul together** to manage to survive
WORD ORIGIN Old English *bodig*
bodyboard *n* a small polystyrene surfboard **bodyboarder** *n*
body building *n* regular exercising designed to enlarge the muscles
bodycheck *ice hockey, etc.* *n* **1** obstruction of another player ▹ *vb* **2** to deliver a bodycheck to (an opponent)
bodyguard *n* a person or group of people employed to protect someone
body language *n* the communication of one's thoughts or feelings by the position or movements of one's body rather than by words
body politic *n* **the body politic** the people of a nation or the nation itself considered as a political entity
body search *n* **1** a search by police, customs officials, etc. that involves examination of a prisoner's or suspect's bodily orifices ▹ *vb* **body-search** **2** to search (a prisoner or suspect) in this manner
body shop *n* a repair yard for vehicle bodywork
body snatcher *n* (formerly) a person who robbed graves and sold the corpses for dissection
body stocking *n* **1** a one-piece undergarment for women, covering the torso **2** a tightly-fitting garment covering the whole of the body, worn esp. for dancing or exercising
body warmer *n* a sleeveless quilted jerkin, worn as an outer garment
bodywork *n* the external shell of a motor vehicle
Boer *n* a descendant of any of the Dutch or Huguenot colonists who settled in South Africa
WORD ORIGIN Dutch
boere- *combining form S African* rustic or country-style
WORD ORIGIN from Afrikaans *boer* a farmer
boeremeisie (boor-a-may-see) *n* *S African* a country girl of Afrikaans stock
boereseun (boor-a-see-oon) *n* *S African* a country boy of Afrikaans stock
boerewors (boor-a-vorss) *n S African* a traditional home-made farmer's sausage
Boethius *n* **Anicius Manlius Severinus** ?480–?524 AD, Roman philosopher and statesman, noted particularly for his work *De Consolatione Philosophiae*. He was accused of treason and executed by Theodoric
boffin *n informal, old-fashioned* a scientist or expert
WORD ORIGIN origin unknown
bog ⊕ *n* **1** a wet spongy area of land **2** *slang* a toilet **boggy** *adj* **bogginess** *n*
WORD ORIGIN Gaelic *bogach* swamp
Bogarde *n* Sir **Dirk**, real name *Derek Jules Gaspard Ulric Niven van den Bogaerde*. 1920–99, British film actor and writer: his films include *The Servant* (1963) and *Death in Venice* (1970). His writings include the autobiographical *A Postillion Struck by Lightning* (1977) and the novel *A Period of Adjustment* (1994)
bog down *vb* **bogging, bogged** to impede physically or mentally
bogey ⊕ *or* **bogy** *n* **1** an evil or mischievous spirit **2** something that worries or annoys **3** *golf* a score of one stroke over par on a hole **4** *slang* a piece of dried mucus from the nose
WORD ORIGIN probably obsolete *bug* an evil spirit
bogeyman *n, pl* **-men** a frightening person, real or imaginary, used as a threat, esp. to children
boggle *vb* **-gling, -gled** **1** to be surprised, confused, or alarmed: *the mind boggles at the idea* **2** to hesitate or be evasive when confronted with a problem
WORD ORIGIN probably Scots
bogie *or* **bogy** *n* an assembly of wheels forming a pivoted support at either end of a railway coach
WORD ORIGIN origin unknown
bogle (boh-gul) *n* a rhythmic dance performed to ragga music
WORD ORIGIN origin unknown
bog-standard *adj Brit & Irish slang* completely ordinary; run-of-the-mill
bogus ⊕ (boh-guss) *adj* not genuine
WORD ORIGIN origin unknown
bogy *n, pl* **-gies** ▸ same as **bogey** or **bogie**
bohemian *n* **1** a person, esp. an artist or writer, who lives an unconventional life ▹ *adj* **2** unconventional in appearance, behaviour, etc. **bohemianism** *n*
Bohemond I *n* ?1056–?1111, prince of Antioch (1099–1111); a leader of the first crusade, he helped to capture Antioch (1098)
Böhm *n* **Karl** (karl) 1894–1981, Austrian orchestral conductor
Böhme, Boehme, *or* **Böhm** *n* **Jakob** 1575–1624, German mystic
bohrium *n chem* an element artificially produced in minute quantities. Symbol: Bh
WORD ORIGIN after N. *Bohr*, physicist
Boiardo *n* **Matteo Maria**, conte de Scandiano 1434–94, Italian poet; author of the historical epic *Orlando Innamorato* (1487)
boil[1] ⊕ *vb* **1** to change or cause to change from a liquid to a vapour so rapidly that bubbles of vapour are formed in the liquid **2** to reach or cause to reach boiling point **3** to

THESAURUS

bodily *adj* **1 = physical**, material, actual, substantial, fleshly, tangible, corporal, carnal, corporeal
body *n* **1 = physique**, build, form, figure, shape, make-up, frame, constitution **2 = torso**, trunk **3 = corpse**, dead body, remains, stiff *(slang)*, relics, carcass, cadaver **4 = organization**, company, group, society, league, association, band, congress, institution, corporation, federation, outfit *(informal)*, syndicate, bloc, confederation **5 = main part**, matter, material, mass, substance, bulk, essence **6 = expanse**, mass, sweep
bog *n* **1 = marsh**, moss *(Scot & Northern English dialect)*, swamp, slough, wetlands, fen, mire, quagmire, morass, marshland, peat bog, pakihi (NZ), muskeg *(Canad)*
bogey *n* **2 = bugbear**, bête noire, horror, nightmare, bugaboo
bogus *adj* **= fake**, false, artificial, forged, dummy, imitation, sham, fraudulent, pseudo *(informal)*, counterfeit, spurious, ersatz, phoney *or* phony *(informal)*, assumed
OPPOSITE: genuine
boil[1] *vb* **4 = simmer**, bubble, foam,

DICTIONARY

cook or be cooked by the process of boiling **4** to bubble and be agitated like something boiling: *the sea was boiling* **5** to be extremely angry ▷*n* **6** the state or action of boiling ▸See also **boil away, boil down, boil over**
WORD ORIGIN Latin *bullire* to bubble
boil² ❶ *n* a red painful swelling with a hard pus-filled core caused by infection of the skin
WORD ORIGIN Old English *b̄yle*
boil away *vb* to cause (liquid) to evaporate completely by boiling or (of liquid) to evaporate completely
boil down *vb* **1** to reduce or be reduced in quantity by boiling **2 boil down to** to be the essential element in
Boileau *n* **Nicolas** full name *Nicolas Boileau-Despréaux*. 1636–1711, French poet and critic; author of satires, epistles, and *L'Art poétique* (1674), in which he laid down the basic principles of French classical literature
boiler *n* **1** a closed vessel in which water is heated to provide steam to drive machinery **2** a domestic device to provide hot water, esp. for central heating
boilermaker *n* a person who works with metal in heavy industry
boiler suit *n Brit* a one-piece overall
boiling point *n* **1** the temperature at which a liquid boils **2** *informal* the condition of being angered or highly excited
boil over *vb* **1** to overflow or cause to overflow while boiling **2** to burst out in anger or excitement
boisterous *adj* **1** noisy and lively; unruly **2** (of the sea, etc.) turbulent or stormy
WORD ORIGIN Middle English *boistuous*
Boito *n* **Arrigo** 1842–1918, Italian operatic composer and librettist, whose works include the opera *Mefistofele* (1868) and the librettos for Verdi's *Otello* and *Falstaff*
Bokassa I *n* original name *Jean Bedel Bokassa*. 1921–96, president of the Central African Republic (1972–76); emperor of the renamed Central African Empire from 1976 until overthrown in 1979
bold ❶ *adj* **1** courageous, confident, and fearless **2** immodest or impudent: *she gave him a bold look* **3** *Irish* (of a child) naughty; badly behaved **4** standing out distinctly; conspicuous: *a figure carved in bold relief*
boldly *adv* **boldness** *n*
WORD ORIGIN Old English *beald*
Bolden *n* **Buddy**, real name *Charles Bolden*. 1868–1931, US Black jazz cornet player; a pioneer of the New Orleans style
Boldrewood *n* **Rolf**, real name *Thomas Alexander Browne*. 1826–1915, Australian writer, born in the UK, noted for his novels of the Australian outback, esp. *Robbery Under Arms* (1882–3)
bole *n* the trunk of a tree
WORD ORIGIN Old Norse *bolr*
bolero *n, pl* **-ros** **1** a Spanish dance, usually in triple time **2** music for this dance **3** a short open jacket not reaching the waist
WORD ORIGIN Spanish
Bolingbroke *n* **1** the surname of Henry IV of England ▸See **Henry IV** **2 Henry St John**, 1st Viscount Bolingbroke. 1678–1751, English politician; fled to France in 1714 and acted as secretary of state to the Old Pretender; returned to England in 1723. His writings include *A Dissertation on Parties* (1733–34) and *Idea of a Patriot King* (1738)
boll *n* the rounded seed capsule of flax, cotton, etc.
WORD ORIGIN Dutch *bolle*
Böll *n* **Heinrich (Theodor)** 1917–85, German novelist and short-story writer; his novels include *Group Portrait with Lady* (1971): Nobel prize for literature 1972
bollard *n* **1** *Austral & Brit* a small post marking a kerb or traffic island or barring cars from entering **2** a strong wooden or metal post on a wharf, quay, etc. used for securing mooring lines
WORD ORIGIN perhaps from *bole*
bollocks *or* **ballocks** *taboo slang pl n* **1** the testicles ▷*n* **2** nonsense; rubbish ▷*interj* **3** an exclamation of annoyance, disbelief, etc.
WORD ORIGIN Old English *beallucas*
Bologna¹ *n* a city in N Italy, at the foot of the Apennines: became a free city in the Middle Ages; university (1088). Pop: 371 217 (2001). Ancient name: **Bononia**
Bologna² *n* **Giovanni da Bologna** ▸See **Giambologna**
Bolshevik *n* **1** (formerly) a Russian Communist **2** any Communist **3** *informal, offensive* any political radical, esp. a revolutionary
Bolshevism *n* **Bolshevist** *adj, n*
WORD ORIGIN Russian *Bol'shevik* majority
bolshie *or* **bolshy** *Brit & NZ informal adj* **1** difficult to manage; rebellious **2** politically radical or left-wing ▷*n, pl* **-shies** **3** any political radical
WORD ORIGIN from BOLSHEVIK
bolster ❶ *vb* **1** to support or strengthen: *the government were unwilling to bolster sterling* ▷*n* **2** a long narrow pillow **3** any pad or support
WORD ORIGIN Old English
bolt¹ ❶ *n* **1** a bar that can be slid into a socket to lock a door, gate, etc. **2** a metal rod or pin that has a head and a screw thread to take a nut **3** a flash (of lightning) **4** a sudden movement, esp. in order to escape **5** an arrow, esp. for a crossbow **6 a bolt from the blue** a sudden, unexpected, and usually unwelcome event **7 shoot one's bolt** to exhaust one's efforts ▷*vb* **8** to run away suddenly **9** to secure or lock with or as if with a bolt **10** to attach firmly one thing to another by means of a nut and bolt **11** to eat hurriedly: *bolting your food may lead to indigestion* **12** (of a horse) to run away without control **13** (of vegetables) to produce flowers and seeds too soon ▷*adv* **14 bolt upright** stiff and rigid
WORD ORIGIN Old English: arrow
bolt² *or* **boult** *vb* **1** to pass (flour, a powder, etc.) through a sieve **2** to examine and separate
WORD ORIGIN Old French *bulter*
Bolt *n* **1 Robert (Oxton)** 1924–95, British playwright. His plays include *A Man for All Seasons* (1960) and he also wrote a number of screenplays **2 Usain** born 1986, Jamaican athlete: winner of the 100 metres and the 200 metres in the 2008 Olympic Games, setting world records at both distances
bolt hole *n* a place of escape
Boltzmann *n* **Ludwig** 1844–1906, Austrian physicist. He established the principle of the equipartition of energy and developed the kinetic theory of gases with J. C. Maxwell
bomb ❶ *n* **1** a hollow projectile containing explosive, incendiary, or

THESAURUS

churn, seethe, fizz, froth, effervesce
boil² *n* **= pustule**, gathering, swelling, blister, blain, carbuncle, furuncle *(pathology)*
bold *adj* **1 = fearless**, enterprising, brave, daring, heroic, adventurous, courageous, gritty, gallant, gutsy *(slang)*, audacious, intrepid, valiant, plucky, undaunted, unafraid, unflinching, dauntless, lion-hearted, valorous **OPPOSITE:** timid
2 = impudent, forward, fresh *(informal)*, confident, rude, cheeky, brash, feisty *(informal, chiefly US & Canad)*, saucy, pushy *(informal)*, brazen, in-your-face *(Brit slang)*, shameless, sassy *(US informal)*, unabashed, pert, insolent, barefaced, spirited, forceful **OPPOSITE:** shy
bolster *vb* **1 = support**, help, aid, maintain, boost, strengthen, assist, prop, reinforce, hold up, cushion, brace, shore up, augment, buttress, buoy up, give a leg up to *(informal)*
bolt¹ *n* **1 = bar**, catch, lock, latch, fastener, sliding bar **2 = pin**, rod, peg, rivet ▷*vb* **9 = lock**, close, bar, secure, fasten, latch **11 = gobble**, stuff, wolf, cram, gorge, devour, gulp, guzzle, swallow whole
bomb *n* **1 = explosive**, charge, mine, shell, missile, device, rocket, grenade, torpedo, bombshell,

DICTIONARY

other destructive substance **2** an object in which an explosive device has been planted: *a car bomb* **3** *chiefly Brit slang* a large sum of money: *it cost a bomb* **4** *slang* a disastrous failure: *the new play was a total bomb* **5 like a bomb** *informal* with great speed or success **6 the bomb** a hydrogen or an atom bomb considered as the ultimate destructive weapon ▷ *vb* **7** to attack with a bomb or bombs; drop bombs (on) **8** (foll. by *along*) *informal* to move or drive very quickly **9** *slang* to fail disastrously ▸ See also **bomb out** > **bombing** *n*
WORD ORIGIN Greek *bombos* booming noise

bombard ⓣ *vb* **1** to attack with concentrated artillery fire or bombs **2** to attack persistently **3** to attack verbally, esp. with questions **4** *physics* to direct high-energy particles or photons against (atoms, nuclei, etc.) **bombardment** *n*
WORD ORIGIN Old French *bombarde* stone-throwing cannon

bombardier *n* **1** *Brit* a noncommissioned rank in the Royal Artillery **2** *US* the member of a bomber aircrew responsible for releasing the bombs

Bombardier *n Canad trademark* a snow tractor, usually having caterpillar tracks at the rear and skis at the front

bombast *n* pompous and flowery language **bombastic** *adj*
WORD ORIGIN Medieval Latin *bombax* cotton

Bombay duck *n* a fish that is eaten dried with curry dishes as a savoury
WORD ORIGIN through association with *Bombay* (now Mumbai), port in India

bombazine *n* a twill fabric, usually of silk and worsted, formerly worn dyed black for mourning
WORD ORIGIN Latin *bombyx* silk

bomber *n* **1** a military aircraft designed to carry out bombing missions **2** a person who plants bombs

Bomberg *n* **David** 1890–1957, British painter, noted esp.for his landscapes

bomb out *vb informal* fail disastrously

bombshell *n* a shocking or unwelcome surprise

bona fide (bone-a **fide**-ee) *adj* **1** genuine: *a bona fide manuscript* **2** undertaken in good faith: *a bona fide agreement*
WORD ORIGIN Latin

bonanza *n* **1** sudden and unexpected luck or wealth **2** *US & Canad* a mine or vein rich in ore
WORD ORIGIN Spanish: calm sea, hence, good luck

Bonaparte *n* **1** See **Napoleon I** **2 Jérôme**, brother of Napoleon I. 1784–1860, king of Westphalia (1807–13) **3 Joseph**, brother of Napoleon I. 1768–1844, king of Naples (1806–08) and of Spain (1808–13) **4 Louis**, brother of Napoleon I. 1778–1846, king of Holland (1806–10) **5 Lucien**, brother of Napoleon I. 1775–1840, prince of Canino

Bonar Law *n* See **Law** (sense 1)

Bonaventura *or* **Bonaventure** *n* **Saint**, called *the Seraphic Doctor*. 1221–74, Italian Franciscan monk, mystic, theologian, and philosopher; author of a *Life of St Francis* and *Journey of the Soul to God* Feast day: July 14

bonbon *n* a sweet
WORD ORIGIN French

bond ⓣ *n* **1** something that binds, fastens, or holds together **2** something that brings or holds people together; tie: *a bond of friendship* **3 bonds** something that restrains or imprisons **4** a written or spoken agreement, esp. a promise: *a marriage bond* **5** *chem* a means by which atoms are combined in a molecule **6** *finance* a certificate of debt issued in order to raise funds **7** *S African* the conditional pledging of property, esp. a house, as security for the repayment of a loan **8** *law* a written acknowledgment of an obligation to pay a sum or to perform a contract **9 in bond** *commerce* securely stored until duty is paid ▷ *vb* **10** to hold or be held together; bind **11** to form a friendship **12** to put or hold (goods) in bond
WORD ORIGIN Old Norse *band*

Bond *n* **Edward** born 1934, British dramatist: his plays, including *Saved* (1965), *Lear* (1971), *Restoration* (1981), and *In the Company of Men* (1990), are noted for their violent imagery and socialist commitment

bondage *n* **1** a sexual practice in which one partner is tied or chained up **2** slavery **3** subjection to some influence or duty

bonded *adj* **1** *finance* consisting of, secured by, or operating under a bond or bonds **2** *commerce* in bond

Bondi *n* Sir **Hermann** 1919–2005, British mathematician and cosmologist, born in Austria; joint originator (with Sir Fred Hoyle and Thomas Gold) of the steady-state theory of the universe

bond paper *n* superior quality writing paper

Bonds *n* **Barry** (**Lamar**) born 1964, US baseball player: holder of records for most home runs in a season (73) and a career (762)

bondservant *n* a serf or slave

bone *n* **1** any of the various structures that make up the skeleton in most vertebrates **2** the porous rigid tissue of which these parts are made **3** something consisting of bone or a bonelike substance **4 bones** the human skeleton **5** a thin strip of plastic, etc. used to stiffen corsets and brassieres **6 close to** *or* **near the bone** risqué or indecent **7 have a bone to pick** to have grounds for a quarrel **8 make no bones about a** to be direct and candid about **b** to have no scruples about **9 the bare bones** the essentials ▷ *vb* **boning, boned** **10** to remove the bones from (meat for cooking, etc.) **11** to stiffen (a corset, etc.) by inserting bones ▸ See also **bone up on** > **boneless** *adj*
WORD ORIGIN Old English *bān*

bone china *n* a type of fine porcelain containing powdered bone

bone-dry *adj informal* completely dry

bone-idle *adj* extremely lazy

bone meal *n* dried and ground animal bones, used as a fertilizer or in stock feeds

boneshaker *n slang* a decrepit or rickety vehicle

bone up on *vb informal* to study intensively

bonfire *n* a large outdoor fire
WORD ORIGIN Middle English *bone-fire*, from the use of bones as fuel

bongo *n, pl* **-gos** *or* **-goes** a small bucket-shaped drum, usually one of a pair, played by beating with the fingers
WORD ORIGIN American Spanish

Bongo *n* **Omar** original name *Albert Bernard Bongo*. born 1935, Gabonese statesman; president of Gabon from 1967

Bonheur *n* **Rosa** (roza) 1822–99, French painter of animals

bonhomie (bon-om-**mee**) *n* exuberant friendliness
WORD ORIGIN French

Boniface *n* **Saint** original name *Wynfrith*. ?680–?755 AD, Anglo-Saxon missionary: archbishop of Mainz (746–755). Feast day: June 5

THESAURUS

projectile ▷ *vb* **7 = blow up**, attack, destroy, assault, shell, blast, blitz, bombard, torpedo, open fire on, strafe, fire upon, blow sky-high

bombard *vb* **1 = bomb**, shell, blast, blitz, open fire, strafe, fire upon **2 = attack**, assault, batter, barrage, besiege, beset, assail

bond *n* **1 = fastening**, band, tie, binding, chain, cord, shackle, fetter, manacle **2 = tie**, union, coupling, link, association, relation, connection, alliance, attachment, affinity, affiliation **4 = agreement**, word, promise, contract, guarantee, pledge, obligation, compact, covenant ▷ *vb* **10 = fix**, hold, bind, connect, glue, gum, fuse, stick, paste, fasten **11 = form friendships**, connect

DICTIONARY

Boniface VIII *n* original name *Benedict Caetano*. ?1234–1303, pope (1294–1303)
Bonington *n* **1** Sir **Chris**(**tian John Storey**) born 1934, British mountaineer and writer; led 1970 Annapurna I and 1975 Everest expeditions; reached Everest summit in 1985 **2 Richard Parkes** 1801–28, British painter of landscapes and historical scenes
bonito (ba-nee-toh) *n, pl* **-os 1** a small tunny-like marine food fish **2** a related fish, whose flesh is dried and flaked and used in Japanese cookery
bonk *vb informal* **1** to have sexual intercourse **2** to hit **bonking** *n*
WORD ORIGIN probably imitative
bonkers *adj Brit, Austral & NZ slang* mad; crazy
WORD ORIGIN origin unknown
bon mot (bon moh) *n, pl* **bons mots** a clever and fitting remark
WORD ORIGIN French, literally: good word
Bonnard *n* **Pierre** 1867–1947, French painter and lithographer, noted for the effects of light and colour in his landscapes and sunlit interiors
bonnet *n* **1** the hinged metal cover over a motor vehicle's engine **2** any of various hats tied with ribbons under the chin **3** (in Scotland) a soft cloth cap
WORD ORIGIN Old French *bonet*
bonny *adj* **-nier, -niest 1** *Scot & N English dialect* beautiful: *a bonny lass* **2** good or fine
WORD ORIGIN Latin *bonus*
Bonporti *n* **Francesco Antonio** 1672–1749, Italian composer and violinist, noted esp.for his *Invenzioni* (1712), a series of short instrumental suites
bonsai *n, pl* **-sai** an ornamental tree or shrub grown in a small shallow pot in order to stunt its growth
WORD ORIGIN Japanese *bon* bowl + *sai* to plant
bonsela (bon-sell-a) *n S African informal* a small gift of money
WORD ORIGIN Zulu *ibanselo* gift
Bontempelli *n* **Massimo** 1878–1960, Italian dramatist, poet, novelist, and critic. His works include the play *Nostra Dea* (1925) and the novel *The Faithful Lover* (1953)
bonus ❶ *n* something given, paid, or received above what is due or expected
WORD ORIGIN Latin: good
bon voyage *interj* a phrase used to wish a traveller a pleasant journey
WORD ORIGIN French
bony *adj* **bonier, boniest 1** resembling or consisting of bone **2** thin **3** having many bones
Bonynge *n* **Richard** born 1930, Australian conductor, esp.of opera; married to the soprano Joan Sutherland
boo *interj* **1** a shout uttered to express dissatisfaction or contempt **2** an exclamation uttered to startle someone ▹ *vb* **booing, booed 3** to shout 'boo' at (someone or something) as an expression of disapproval
boob *slang n* **1** *Brit, Austral & NZ* an embarrassing mistake; blunder **2** a female breast **3** *Austral slang* a prison ▹ *vb* **4** *Brit, Austral & NZ* to make a blunder
WORD ORIGIN from *booby*
boobook (boo-book) *n* a small spotted Australian brown owl
booby *n, pl* **-bies 1** *old-fashioned* an ignorant or foolish person **2** a tropical marine bird related to the gannet
WORD ORIGIN Latin *balbus* stammering
booby prize *n* a mock prize given to the person with the lowest score in a competition
booby trap *n* **1** a hidden explosive device primed so as to be set off by an unsuspecting victim **2** a trap for an unsuspecting person, esp. one intended as a practical joke
boodle *n slang* money or valuables, esp. when stolen, counterfeit, or used as a bribe
WORD ORIGIN Dutch *boedel* possessions
boogie *vb* **-gieing, -gied** *slang* to dance to fast pop music
WORD ORIGIN origin unknown
boogie board *n* ▸ another name for **bodyboard**
boogie-woogie *n* a style of piano jazz using blues harmonies
WORD ORIGIN perhaps imitative
boohai *n NZ informal* **1** a very remote area **2 up the boohai** very mistaken or astray
WORD ORIGIN from the remote township of *Puhoi*
boohoo *vb* **-hooing, -hooed 1** to sob or pretend to sob noisily ▹ *n, pl* **-hoos 2** distressed or pretended sobbing
book ❶ *n* **1** a number of printed pages bound together along one edge and protected by covers **2** a written work or composition, such as a novel **3** a number of sheets of paper bound together: *an account book* **4 books** a record of the transactions of a business or society **5** the libretto of an opera or musical **6** a major division of a written composition, such as of a long novel or of the Bible **7** a number of tickets, stamps, etc. fastened together along one edge **8** a record of betting transactions **9 a closed book** a subject that is beyond comprehension: *art remains a closed book to him* **10 bring to book** to reprimand or require (someone) to give an explanation of his or her conduct **11 by the book** according to the rules **12 in someone's good** *or* **bad books** regarded by someone with favour (*or* disfavour) **13 throw the book at someone a** to charge someone with every relevant offence **b** to inflict the most severe punishment on someone ▹ *vb* **14** to reserve (a place, passage, etc.) or engage the services of (someone) in advance **15** (of a police officer) to take the name and address of (a person) for an alleged offence with a view to prosecution **16** (of a football referee) to take the name of (a player) who has broken the rules seriously ▸ See also **book in**
WORD ORIGIN Old English *bōc*
bookcase *n* a piece of furniture containing shelves for books
book club *n* a club that sells books at low prices to members, usually by mail order
book end *n* one of a pair of supports for holding a row of books upright
bookie *n informal* ▸ short for **bookmaker**
book in ❶ *vb chiefly Brit & NZ* to register one's arrival at a hotel
booking *n* **1** *Brit, Austral & NZ* a reservation, as of a table or seat **2** *theatre* an engagement of a performer
bookish *adj* **1** fond of reading; studious **2** forming opinions through reading rather than experience
book-keeping *n* the skill or occupation of systematically recording business transactions **book-keeper** *n*
booklet ❶ *n* a thin book with paper covers
bookmaker *n* a person who as an occupation accepts bets, esp. on horse racing **bookmaking** *n*
bookmark *n* **1** a strip of some

THESAURUS

bonus *n* **a = extra**, benefit, commission, prize, gift, reward, premium, dividend, hand-out, perk (*Brit informal*), bounty, gratuity, honorarium **b = advantage**, benefit, gain, extra, plus, asset, perk (*Brit informal*), icing on the cake
book *n* **1, 2 = work**, title, volume, publication, manual, paperback, textbook, tract, hardback, tome **3 = notebook**, album, journal, diary, pad, record book, Filofax®, notepad, exercise book, jotter, memorandum book ▹ *vb* **14 = reserve**, schedule, engage, line up, organize, charter, arrange for, procure, make reservations
book in *vb* **= register**, enter, enrol
booklet *n* **= brochure**, leaflet, hand-out, pamphlet, folder, mailshot, handbill

DICTIONARY

b

material put between the pages of a book to mark a place **2** *computers* an identifier put on a website that enables the user to return to it quickly and easily ▷ *vb* **3** *computers* to identify and store a website so that one can return to it quickly and easily

bookstall *n* a stall or stand where periodicals, newspapers, or books are sold

bookworm *n* **1** a person devoted to reading **2** a small insect that feeds on the binding paste of books

Boolean algebra (boo-lee-an) *n* a system of symbolic logic devised to codify nonmathematical logical operations: used in computers **WORD ORIGIN** after George *Boole*, mathematician

boom¹ ● *vb* **1** to make a loud deep echoing sound **2** to prosper vigorously and rapidly: *business boomed* ▷ *n* **3** a loud deep echoing sound **4** a period of high economic growth **WORD ORIGIN** imitative

boom² *n* **1** *naut* a spar to which the foot of a sail is fastened to control its position **2** a pole carrying an overhead microphone and projected over a film or television set **3** a barrier across a waterway **WORD ORIGIN** Dutch: tree

boomer *n Austral* a large male kangaroo

boomerang *n* **1** a curved wooden missile of Australian Aborigines which can be made to return to the thrower **2** an action or statement that recoils on its originator ▷ *vb* **3** (of a plan) to recoil unexpectedly, harming its originator **WORD ORIGIN** Aboriginal

boomslang *n* a large greenish venomous tree-living snake of southern Africa **WORD ORIGIN** Afrikaans

boon¹ ● *n* something extremely useful, helpful, or beneficial **WORD ORIGIN** Old Norse *bōn* request

boon² *adj* close or intimate: *boon companion* **WORD ORIGIN** Latin *bonus* good

Boone *n* **Daniel** 1734–1820, American pioneer, explorer, and guide, esp.in Kentucky

boongary (boong-gar-ree) *n* a tree kangaroo of NE Queensland, Australia

boor *n* an ill-mannered, clumsy, or insensitive person **boorish** *adj* **WORD ORIGIN** Old English *gebūr* dweller, farmer

boost ● *n* **1** encouragement or help: *a boost to morale* **2** an upward thrust or push **3** an increase or rise ▷ *vb* **4** to encourage or improve: *to boost morale* **5** to cause to rise; increase: *we significantly boosted our market share* **6** to advertise on a big scale **WORD ORIGIN** origin unknown

booster *n* **1** a supplementary injection of a vaccine given to ensure that the first injection will remain effective **2** a radio-frequency amplifier to strengthen signals **3** the first stage of a multistage rocket

boot¹ ● *n* **1** an outer covering for the foot that extends above the ankle **2** an enclosed compartment of a car for holding luggage **3** *informal* a kick: *he gave the door a boot* **4 lick someone's boots** to behave flatteringly towards someone **5 put the boot in** *slang* **a** to kick a person when already down **b** to finish something off with unnecessary brutality **6 the boot** *slang* dismissal from employment ▷ *vb* **7** to kick **8** to start up (a computer) **9 boot out** *informal* **a** to eject forcibly **b** to dismiss from employment **WORD ORIGIN** Middle English *bote*

boot² *n* **to boot** as well; in addition **WORD ORIGIN** Old English *bōt* compensation

boot camp *n* a centre for juvenile offenders, with strict discipline and hard physical exercise

bootee *n* a soft boot for a baby, esp. a knitted one

booth *n, pl* **booths 1** a small partially enclosed cubicle **2** a stall, esp. a temporary one at a fair or market **WORD ORIGIN** Scandinavian

Boothroyd *n* **Betty** Baroness. born 1929, British politician; speaker of the House of Commons (1992–2000)

bootleg *vb* **-legging, -legged 1** to make, carry, or sell (illicit goods, esp. alcohol) ▷ *adj* **2** produced, distributed, or sold illicitly **bootlegger** *n* **WORD ORIGIN** smugglers carried bottles of liquor concealed in their boots

bootless *adj* of little or no use; vain; fruitless **WORD ORIGIN** Old English *bōtlēas*

bootlicker *n informal* one who seeks favour by grovelling to someone in authority

booty¹ *n, pl* **-ties** any valuable article or articles obtained as plunder **WORD ORIGIN** Old French *butin*

booty² *n slang* the buttocks, esp. those of an attractive female **WORD ORIGIN** from *butt* the buttocks

booze *informal n* **1** alcoholic drink ▷ *vb* **boozing, boozed 2** to drink alcohol, esp. in excess **boozy** *adj* **WORD ORIGIN** Middle Dutch *būsen*

boozer *n informal* **1** a person who is fond of drinking **2** *Brit, Austral & NZ* a bar or pub

booze-up *n Brit, Austral & NZ slang* a drinking spree

bop *n* **1** a form of jazz with complex rhythms and harmonies ▷ *vb* **bopping, bopped 2** *informal* to dance to pop music **bopper** *n* **WORD ORIGIN** from BEBOP

bora *n Austral* an Aboriginal ceremony **WORD ORIGIN** from a native Australian language

boracic *adj* ▶ same as **boric**

borage *n* a Mediterranean plant with star-shaped blue flowers **WORD ORIGIN** Arabic *abū 'āraq* literally: father of sweat

borax *n* a white mineral in crystalline form used in making glass, soap, etc. **WORD ORIGIN** Persian *būrah*

Bordeaux *n* a red or white wine produced around Bordeaux in SW France

border ● *n* **1** the dividing line between political or geographic regions **2** a band or margin around or along the edge of something **3** a design around the edge of something **4** a narrow strip of ground planted with flowers or shrubs: *a herbaceous border* ▷ *vb* **5** to provide with a border **6 a** to be adjacent to; lie along the boundary of **b** to be nearly the same as; verge on: *a story that borders on the unbelievable* **WORD ORIGIN** Old French *bort* side of a ship

Border¹ *n* **the Border 1** (*often plural*) the

THESAURUS

boom¹ *vb* **1 = bang**, roll, crash, blast, echo, drum, explode, roar, thunder, rumble, resound, reverberate, peal **2 = increase**, flourish, grow, develop, succeed, expand, strengthen, do well, swell, thrive, intensify, prosper, burgeon, spurt **OPPOSITE:** fall ▷ *n* **3 = bang**, report, shot, crash, clash, blast, burst, explosion, roar, thunder, rumble, clap, peal, detonation **4 = expansion**, increase, development, growth, advance, jump, boost, improvement, spurt, upsurge, upturn, upswing **OPPOSITE:** decline

boon¹ *n* **= benefit**, advantage, blessing, godsend, gift

boost *n* **1 = encouragement**, help **3 = rise**, increase, advance, jump, addition, improvement, expansion, upsurge, upturn, increment, upswing, upward turn **OPPOSITE:** fall ▷ *vb* **5 = increase**, develop, raise, expand, add to, build up, heighten, enlarge, inflate, magnify, amplify, augment, jack up **OPPOSITE:** decrease

boot¹ *vb* **7 = kick**, punt, put the boot in(to) (*slang*), drop-kick

border *n* **1 = frontier**, line, marches, limit, bounds, boundary, perimeter, borderline, borderland **2, 3 = edge**, lip, margin, skirt, verge, rim, hem, brim, flange ▷ *vb* **5 = edge**, bound,

DICTIONARY

area straddling the border between England and Scotland **2** the area straddling the border between Northern Ireland and the Republic of Ireland **3** the region in S South Africa around East London

Border² *n* **Allan** (**Robert**) born 1955, Australian cricketer; captain of Australia (1985–94)

borderland *n* **1** land located on or near a boundary **2** an indeterminate state or condition

borderline *n* **1** a dividing line **2** an indeterminate position between two conditions: *the borderline between love and friendship* ▹*adj* **3** on the edge of one category and verging on another: *a borderline failure*

Borders *pl n* **the Borders** the area straddling the border between England and Scotland

Bordet *n* **Jules** (**Jean Baptiste Vincent**) 1870–1961, Belgian bacteriologist and immunologist, who discovered complement. Nobel prize for physiology or medicine 1919

bore¹ ⓘ *vb* **boring, bored 1** to produce (a hole) with a drill, etc. **2** to produce (a tunnel, mine shaft, etc.) by drilling ▹*n* **3** a hole or tunnel in the ground drilled in search of minerals, oil, etc. **4 a** the hollow of a gun barrel **b** the diameter of this hollow; calibre
WORD ORIGIN Old English *borian*

bore² ⓘ *vb* **boring, bored 1** to tire or make weary by being dull, repetitious, or uninteresting ▹*n* **2** a dull or repetitious person, activity, or state **bored** *adj* **boring** *adj*
WORD ORIGIN origin unknown

bore³ *n* a high wave moving up a narrow estuary, caused by the tide
WORD ORIGIN Old Norse *bāra*

bore⁴ *vb* ▸the past tense of **bear¹**

boreal forest (bore-ee-al) *n* the forest of northern latitudes, esp. in Scandinavia, Canada, and Siberia, consisting mainly of spruce and pine
WORD ORIGIN Latin *boreas* the north wind

boredom ⓘ *n* the state of being bored

boree (baw-ree) *n Austral* ▸same as **myall**

Borglum *n* (**John**) **Gutzon** 1867–1941, US sculptor, noted for his monumental busts of US presidents carved in the mountainside of Mount Rushmore

boric *adj* of or containing boron

boric acid *n* a white soluble crystalline solid used as a mild antiseptic

Boris I *n* known as *Boris of Bulgaria*. died 907 AD, khan of Bulgaria. His reign saw the conversion of Bulgaria to Christianity and the birth of a national literature

Borlaug *n* **Norman** (**Ernest**) 1914–2009, US agronomist, who bred new strains of high-yielding cereal crops for use in developing countries. Nobel peace prize 1970

Bormann *n* **Martin** 1900–45, German Nazi politician; Hitler's adviser and private secretary (1942–45): committed suicide

born *vb* **1** ▸a past participle of **bear¹** (sense 4) **2 not have been born yesterday** not to be gullible or foolish ▹*adj* **3** possessing certain qualities from birth: *a born musician* **4** being in a particular social status at birth: *ignobly born*

Born *n* **Max** 1882–1970, British nuclear physicist, born in Germany, noted for his fundamental contribution to quantum mechanics: Nobel prize for physics 1954

born-again *adj* **1** having experienced conversion, esp. to evangelical Christianity **2** showing the enthusiasm of someone newly converted to any cause: *a born-again romantic* ▹*n* **3** a person with fervent enthusiasm for a newfound cause

borne *vb* ▸a past participle of **bear¹**

Borodin *n* **Aleksandr Porfirevich** 1834–87, Russian composer, whose works include the unfinished opera *Prince Igor*, symphonies, songs, and chamber music

boron *n chem* a hard almost colourless crystalline metalloid element that is used in hardening steel. Symbol: B
WORD ORIGIN *bor(ax) + (carb)on*

boronia *n* an Australian aromatic flowering shrub

Borotra *n* **Jean** (**Robert**) 1898–1994, French tennis player: secretary general of physical education under the Vichy government (1940)

borough *n* **1** a town, esp. (in Britain) one that forms the constituency of an MP or that was originally incorporated by royal charter **2** any of the constituent divisions of Greater London or New York City
WORD ORIGIN Old English *burg*

Borromini *n* **Francesco**, original name *Francesco Castelli*. 1599–1667, Italian baroque architect, working in Rome: his buildings include the churches of San Carlo (1641) and Sant' Ivo (1660)

borrow ⓘ *vb* **1** to obtain (something, such as money) on the understanding that it will be returned to the lender **2** to adopt (ideas, words, etc.) from another source **borrower** *n* **borrowing** *n*
WORD ORIGIN Old English *borgian*

Borrow *n* **George** (**Henry**) 1803–81, English traveller and writer. His best-known works are the semiautobiographical novels of Gypsy life and language, *Lavengro* (1851) and its sequel *The Romany Rye* (1857)

borscht *or* **borsch** *n* a Russian soup based on beetroot
WORD ORIGIN Russian *borshch*

borstal *n* (formerly, in Britain) a prison for offenders aged 15 to 21
WORD ORIGIN after *Borstal*, village in Kent where the first institution was founded

borzoi *n* a tall dog with a narrow head and a long coat
WORD ORIGIN Russian: swift

bosh *n Brit, Austral & NZ informal* meaningless talk or opinions; nonsense
WORD ORIGIN Turkish *boş* empty

Bosnian *adj* **1** from Bosnia ▹*n* **2** a person from Bosnia

bosom *n* **1** the chest or breast of a person, esp. the female breasts **2** a protective centre or part: *the bosom of the family* **3** the breast considered as the seat of emotions ▹*adj* **4** very dear: *a bosom friend*
WORD ORIGIN Old English *bōsm*

boss¹ ⓘ *informal n* **1** a person in charge of or employing others ▹*vb* **2** to employ, supervise, or be in charge of **3 boss around** *or* **about** to be domineering or overbearing towards
WORD ORIGIN Dutch *baas* master

boss² *n* a raised knob or stud, esp. an ornamental one on a vault, shield, etc.
WORD ORIGIN Old French *boce*

THESAURUS

decorate, trim, fringe, rim, hem

bore¹ *vb* **1, 2 = drill**, mine, sink, tunnel, pierce, penetrate, burrow, puncture, perforate, gouge out

bore² *vb* **1 = tire**, exhaust, annoy, fatigue, weary, wear out, jade, wear down, be tedious, pall on, send to sleep **OPPOSITE:** excite
▹*n* **2 = nuisance**, pain *(informal)*, drag *(informal)*, headache *(informal)*, yawn *(informal)*, anorak *(informal)*, pain in the neck *(informal)*, dullard, dull person, tiresome person, wearisome talker

boredom *n* **= tedium**, apathy, doldrums, weariness, monotony, dullness, sameness, ennui, flatness, world-weariness, tediousness, irksomeness **OPPOSITE:** excitement

borrow *vb* **1 = take on loan**, touch (someone) for *(slang)*, scrounge *(informal)*, blag *(slang)*, mooch *(slang)*, cadge, use temporarily, take and return **OPPOSITE:** lend
2 = steal, take, use, copy, adopt, appropriate, acquire, pinch *(informal)*, pirate, poach, pilfer, filch, plagiarize

boss¹ *n* **1 = manager**, head, leader, director, chief, executive, owner, master, governor *(informal)*, employer, administrator, supervisor, superintendent, gaffer *(informal, chiefly Brit)*, foreman, overseer,

DICTIONARY

bossa nova *n* **1** a dance similar to the samba, originating in Brazil **2** music for this dance
WORD ORIGIN Portuguese

Bossuet *n* **Jacques Bénigne** 1627–1704, French bishop: noted for his funeral orations

bossy *adj* **bossier, bossiest** *informal* domineering, overbearing, or authoritarian **bossiness** *n*

bosun *or* **boatswain** (boh-sn) *n* an officer who is responsible for the maintenance of a ship and its equipment

bot. **1** botanical **2** botany

botany *n, pl* **-nies** the study of plants, including their classification, structure, etc. **botanical** *or* **botanic** *adj* **botanist** *n*
WORD ORIGIN Greek *botanē* plant

botch *vb* **1** to spoil through clumsiness or ineptitude **2** to repair badly or clumsily ▹ *n also* **botch-up** **3** a badly done piece of work or repair
WORD ORIGIN origin unknown

both *adj* **1** two considered together: *both parents were killed during the war* ▹ *pron* **2** two considered together: *both are to blame* ▹ *conj* **3** not just one but also the other of two (people or things): *both Darren and Keith enjoyed the match*
WORD ORIGIN Old Norse *bāthir*

Botham *n* Sir **Ian** (**Terence**) born 1955, English cricketer: played for Somerset (1973–86); Worcestershire (1987–91), and Durham (1991–93); captained England (1980–81)

Bothe *n* **Walther** (**Wilhelm Georg Franz**) 1891–1957, German physicist, who developed new methods of detecting subatomic particles. He shared the Nobel prize for physics 1954

bother **T** *vb* **1** to take the time or trouble: *don't bother to come with me* **2** to give annoyance, pain, or trouble to **3** to trouble (a person) by repeatedly disturbing; pester ▹ *n* **4** a state of worry, trouble, or confusion **5** a person or thing that causes fuss, trouble, or annoyance **6** *informal* a disturbance or fight: *a spot of bother* ▹ *interj* **7** *Brit, Austral & NZ* an exclamation of slight annoyance
WORD ORIGIN origin unknown

bothersome *adj* causing bother

Bothwell *n* **Earl of**, title of *James Hepburn*. 1535–78, Scottish nobleman; third husband of Mary Queen of Scots. He is generally considered to have instigated the murder of Darnley (1567)

bothy *n, pl* **bothies** *chiefly Scot* **1** a hut used for temporary shelter **2** (formerly) a farm worker's quarters
WORD ORIGIN perhaps from *booth*

Botox *n trademark* **1** a preparation of botulinum toxin used to treat muscle spasm and to remove wrinkles ▹ *vb* **2** to apply Botox to (a person or a part of the body)
WORD ORIGIN from BOT(ULINUM) (T)OX(IN)

bottle *n* **1** a container, often of glass and usually cylindrical with a narrow neck, for holding liquids **2** the amount such a container will hold **3** *Brit slang* courage; nerve: *you don't have the bottle* **4 the bottle** *informal* drinking of alcohol, esp. to excess ▹ *vb* **-tling, -tled** **5** to put or place in a bottle or bottles ▸ See also **bottle up**
WORD ORIGIN Late Latin *buttis* cask

bottle bank *n* a large container into which members of the public can throw glass bottles and jars for recycling

bottle-feed *vb* **-feeding, -fed** to feed (a baby) with milk from a bottle

bottle-green *adj* dark green

bottleneck *n* **1** a narrow stretch of road or a junction at which traffic is or may be held up **2** something that holds up progress

bottlenose dolphin *n* a grey or greenish dolphin with a bottle-shaped snout

bottle party *n* a party to which guests bring drink

bottler *n Austral & NZ, old-fashioned informal* an exceptional person or thing

bottle shop **T** *n Austral & NZ* a shop licensed to sell alcohol for drinking elsewhere

bottle store **T** *n S African* a shop licensed to sell alcohol for drinking elsewhere

bottle tree *n* an Australian tree with a bottle-shaped swollen trunk

bottle up *vb* to restrain (powerful emotion)

bottom **T** *n* **1** the lowest, deepest, or farthest removed part of a thing: *the bottom of a hill* **2** the least important or successful position: *the bottom of a class* **3** the ground underneath a sea, lake, or river **4** the underneath part of a thing **5** the buttocks **6 at bottom** in reality; basically **7 be at the bottom of** to be the ultimate cause of **8 get to the bottom of** to discover the real truth about ▹ *adj* **9** lowest or last
WORD ORIGIN Old English *botm*

bottomless *adj* **1** unlimited; inexhaustible: *bottomless resources* **2** very deep: *bottomless valleys*

bottom line *n* **1** the conclusion or main point of a process, discussion, etc. **2** the last line of a financial statement that shows the net profit or loss of a company or organization

bottom out *vb* to reach the lowest point and level out: *consumer spending has bottomed out*

botulism *n* severe food poisoning resulting from the toxin **botulin,** produced in imperfectly preserved food
WORD ORIGIN Latin *botulus* sausage

Botvinnik *n* **Mikhail Moiseivich** 1911–95, Soviet chess player; world champion (1948–57, 1958–60, 1961–63)

Boucher *n* **François** 1703–70, French rococo artist, noted for his delicate ornamental paintings of pastoral scenes and mythological subjects

Boucicault *n* **Dion** real name *Dionysius Lardner Boursiquot* 1822–90, Irish

THESAURUS

kingpin, big cheese *(old-fashioned, slang)*, baas *(S African)*, numero uno *(informal)*, Mister Big *(slang, chiefly US)*, sherang *(Austral & NZ)* ▹ *vb* **3 boss someone around** *(informal)* **= order around**, dominate, bully, intimidate, oppress, dictate to, terrorize, put upon, push around *(slang)*, browbeat, ride roughshod over, tyrannize, rule with an iron hand

bother *vb* **1, 2 = trouble**, concern, worry, upset, alarm, disturb, distress, annoy, dismay, gall, disconcert, vex, perturb, faze, put *or* get someone's back up **3 = pester**, plague, irritate, put out, harass, nag, hassle *(informal)*, inconvenience, molest, breathe down someone's neck, get on your nerves *(informal)*, nark *(Brit, Austral & NZ slang)*, bend someone's ear *(informal)*, give someone grief *(Brit & S African)*, get on your wick *(Brit slang)*
OPPOSITE: help
▹ *n* **4,5 = trouble**, problem, worry, difficulty, strain, grief *(Brit & S African)*, fuss, pest, irritation, hassle *(informal)*, nuisance, flurry, uphill *(S African)*, inconvenience, annoyance, aggravation, vexation
OPPOSITE: help

bottle shop *n (Austral & NZ)* **= off-licence** *(Brit)*, liquor store *(US & Canad)*, bottle store *(S African)*, package store *(US & Canad)*, offie *or* offy *(Brit informal)*

bottle store *n (S African)* **= off-licence** *(Brit)*, liquor store *(US & Canad)*, bottle shop *(Austral & NZ)*, package store *(US & Canad)*, offie *or* offy *(Brit informal)*

bottom *n* **1 = lowest part**, base, foot, bed, floor, basis, foundation, depths, support, pedestal, deepest part
OPPOSITE: top
4 = underside, sole, underneath, lower side **5 = buttocks**, behind *(informal)*, rear, butt *(US & Canad informal)*, bum *(Brit slang)*, buns *(US slang)*, backside, rump, seat, tail *(informal)*, rear end, posterior, derrière *(euphemistic)*, tush *(US slang)*, fundament, jacksy *(Brit slang)* ▹ *adj* **9 = lowest**, last, base, ground, basement, undermost
OPPOSITE: higher

DICTIONARY

dramatist and actor. His plays include *London Assurance* (1841), *The Octoroon* (1859), and *The Shaughran* (1874)

bouclé *n* a curled or looped yarn or fabric giving a thick knobbly effect
WORD ORIGIN French: curly

Boudin *n* **Eugène** 1824–98, French painter: one of the first French landscape painters to paint in the open air; a forerunner of impressionism

boudoir (boo-dwahr) *n* a woman's bedroom or private sitting room
WORD ORIGIN French, literally: room for sulking in

bouffant (boof-fong) *adj* (of a hairstyle) having extra height and width through backcombing
WORD ORIGIN French *bouffer* to puff up

Bougainville[1] *n* an island in the W Pacific, in Papua New Guinea: the largest of the Solomon Islands: unilaterally declared independence in 1990; occupied by government troops in 1992, and granted autonomy in 2001. Chief town: Kieta. Area: 10 049 sq km (3880 sq miles)

Bougainville[2] *n* **Louis Antoine de** 1729–1811, French navigator

bougainvillea *n* a tropical climbing plant with flowers surrounded by showy red or purple bracts
WORD ORIGIN after L. A. de *Bougainville*

bough *n* any of the main branches of a tree
WORD ORIGIN Old English *bōg* arm, twig

bought *vb* ▸ the past of **buy**

bouillon (boo-yon) *n* a thin clear broth or stock
WORD ORIGIN French *bouillir* to boil

Boulanger *n* **1 Georges** 1837–91, French general and minister of war (1886–87). Accused of attempting a coup d'état, he fled to Belgium, where he committed suicide **2 Nadia (Juliette)** 1887–1979, French teacher of musical composition: her pupils included Elliott Carter, Aaron Copland, Darius Milhaud, and Virgil Thomson. She is noted also for her work in reviving the works of Monteverdi

boulder *n* a smooth rounded mass of rock shaped by erosion
WORD ORIGIN Scandinavian

boulder clay *n* an unstratified glacial deposit of fine clay, boulders, and pebbles

boules (bool) *n* a game, popular in France, in which metal bowls are thrown to land as close as possible to a target ball
WORD ORIGIN French: balls

boulevard *n* a wide usually tree-lined road in a city
WORD ORIGIN Middle Dutch *bolwerc* bulwark; because originally often built on the ruins of an old rampart

boult *vb* ▸ same as **bolt**[2]

Boult *n* Sir **Adrian (Cedric)** 1889–1983, English conductor

Boulton *n* **Matthew** 1728–1809, British engineer and manufacturer, who financed Watt's steam engine and applied it to various industrial purposes

Boumédienne *n* **Houari** 1927–78, Algerian statesman and soldier: president of Algeria (1965–78) after overthrowing Ben Bella in a coup

bounce *vb* **bouncing, bounced 1** (of a ball, etc.) to rebound from an impact **2** to cause (a ball, etc.) to hit a solid surface and spring back **3** to move or cause to move suddenly; spring: *I bounced down the stairs* **4** *slang* (of a bank) to send (a cheque) back or (of a cheque) to be sent back unredeemed because of lack of funds in the account ▷ *n* **5** the action of rebounding from an impact **6** a leap or jump **7** springiness **8** *informal* vitality; vigour **bouncy** *adj*
WORD ORIGIN probably imitative

bounce back *vb* to recover one's health, good spirits, confidence, etc. easily

bouncer *n* **1** *slang* a person employed at a club, disco, etc. to prevent unwanted people from entering and to eject drunks or troublemakers **2** *cricket* a ball bowled so that it bounces high on pitching

bouncing *adj* vigorous and robust: *a bouncing baby*

Bouncy Castle *n trademark* a very large inflatable model, usually of a castle, on which children may bounce at fairs, etc.

bound[1] *vb* **1** ▸ the past of **bind** ▷ *adj* **2** tied as if with a rope **3** restricted or confined: *housebound* **4** certain: *it's bound to happen* **5** compelled or obliged: *they agreed to be bound by the board's recommendations* **6** (of a book) secured within a cover or binding **7 bound up with** closely or inextricably linked with

bound[2] *vb* **1** to move forwards by leaps or jumps **2** to bounce; spring away from an impact ▷ *n* **3** a jump upwards or forwards **4** a bounce, as of a ball
WORD ORIGIN Old French *bondir*

bound[3] *vb* **1** to place restrictions on; limit: *bounded by tradition* **2** to form a boundary of ▷ *n* **3** ▸ see **bounds**
> **boundless** *adj*
WORD ORIGIN Old French *bonde*

bound[4] *adj* going or intending to go towards: *homeward bound*
WORD ORIGIN Old Norse *buinn*, past participle of *būa* prepare

boundary *n, pl* **-ries 1** something that indicates the farthest limit, such as of an area **2** *cricket* **a** the marked limit of the playing area **b** a stroke that hits the ball beyond this limit, scoring four or six runs

bounden *adj old-fashioned* morally obligatory: *bounden duty*

bounder *n old-fashioned Brit slang* a morally reprehensible person; cad

bounds *pl n* **1** a limit; boundary: *their jealousy knows no bounds* **2** something that restricts or controls, esp. the standards of a society: *within the bounds of good taste*

bountiful *or* **bounteous** *adj literary* **1** plentiful; ample: *a bountiful harvest* **2** giving freely; generous

bounty *n, pl* **-ties 1** *literary* generosity; liberality **2** something provided in generous amounts: *nature's bounty* **3** a reward or premium by a government
WORD ORIGIN Latin *bonus* good

bouquet *n* **1** a bunch of flowers,

THESAURUS

bounce *vb* **1 = rebound**, return, thump, recoil, ricochet, spring back, resile **3 = bound**, spring, jump, leap, skip, caper, prance, gambol, jounce ▷ *n* **7 = springiness**, give, spring, bound, rebound, resilience, elasticity, recoil **8** *(informal)* **= life**, go *(informal)*, energy, pep, sparkle, zip *(informal)*, vitality, animation, vigour, exuberance, dynamism, brio, vivacity, liveliness, vim *(slang)*, lustiness, vivaciousness

bound[1] *adj* **2 = tied**, fixed, secured, attached, lashed, tied up, fastened, trussed, pinioned, made fast **4 = certain**, sure, fated, doomed, destined **5 = compelled**, obliged, forced, committed, pledged, constrained, obligated, beholden, duty-bound

bound[2] *vb* **1, 2 = leap**, bob, spring, jump, bounce, skip, vault, pounce ▷ *n* **3 = leap**, bob, spring, jump, bounce, hurdle, skip, vault, pounce, caper, prance, lope, frisk, gambol

bound[3] *vb* **1 = limit**, fix, define, restrict, confine, restrain, circumscribe, demarcate, delimit **2 = surround**, confine, enclose, terminate, encircle, circumscribe, hem in, demarcate, delimit

boundary *n* **1a = frontier**, edge, border, march, barrier, margin, brink **1b = edges**, limits, bounds, pale, confines, fringes, verges, precinct, extremities

bounds *pl n* **1 = boundary**, line, limit, edge, border, march, margin, pale, confine, fringe, verge, rim, perimeter, periphery

bouquet *n* **1 = bunch of flowers**, spray, garland, wreath, posy, buttonhole, corsage, nosegay, boutonniere **2 = aroma**, smell, scent, perfume, fragrance, savour, odour, redolence

DICTIONARY

esp. a large carefully arranged one **2** the aroma of wine
WORD ORIGIN French: thicket

bouquet garni *n, pl* **bouquets garnis** a bunch of herbs tied together and used for flavouring soups, stews, or stocks
WORD ORIGIN French

bourbon (bur-bn) *n* a whiskey distilled, chiefly in the US, from maize
WORD ORIGIN after *Bourbon* county, Kentucky, where it was first made

bourgeois (boor-zhwah) *often disparaging adj* **1** characteristic of or comprising the middle class **2** conservative or materialistic in outlook **3** (in Marxist thought) dominated by capitalism ▹*n, pl* **-geois 4** a member of the middle class, esp. one regarded as being conservative and materialistic
WORD ORIGIN Old French *borjois* citizen

Bourgeois *n* **Léon Victor Auguste** 1851–1925, French statesman; first chairman of the League of Nations: Nobel peace prize 1920

bourgeoisie (boor-zhwah-zee) *n* **the bourgeoisie 1** the middle classes **2** (in Marxist thought) the capitalist ruling class

Bourguiba *n* **Habib ben Ali** 1903–2000, Tunisian statesman: president of Tunisia (1957–87); a moderate and an advocate of gradual social change. He was deposed in a coup and kept under house arrest for the rest of his life

bourn *n chiefly S Brit* a stream
WORD ORIGIN Old French *bodne* limit

bourrée (boor-ray) *n* **1** a traditional French dance in fast duple time **2** music for this dance
WORD ORIGIN French

Bourse (boorss) *n* a stock exchange, esp. of Paris
WORD ORIGIN French: purse

bout *n* **1 a** a period of time spent doing something, such as drinking **b** a period of illness: *a bad bout of flu* **2** a boxing, wrestling or fencing match
WORD ORIGIN obsolete *bought* turn

boutique *n* a small shop, esp. one that sells fashionable clothes
WORD ORIGIN French

bouzouki *n* a Greek long-necked stringed musical instrument related to the mandolin
WORD ORIGIN Modern Greek

Bovet *n* **Daniel** 1907–92, Italian pharmacologist, born in Switzerland, noted for his pioneering work on antihistamine drugs. Nobel prize for physiology or medicine 1957

bovine *adj* **1** of or relating to cattle **2** dull, sluggish, or ugly
WORD ORIGIN Latin *bos* ox

bow[1] (rhymes with **cow**) *vb* **1** to lower (one's head) or bend (one's knee or body) as a sign of respect, greeting, agreement, or shame **2** to comply or accept: *bow to the inevitable* **3 bow and scrape** to behave in a slavish manner ▹*n* **4** a lowering or bending of the head or body as a mark of respect, etc. **5 take a bow** to acknowledge applause ▸See also **bow out**
WORD ORIGIN Old English *būgan*

bow[2] (rhymes with **know**) *n* **1** a decorative knot usually having two loops and two loose ends **2** a long stick across which are stretched strands of horsehair, used for playing a violin, viola, cello, etc. **3** a weapon for shooting arrows, consisting of an arch of flexible wood, plastic, etc. bent by a string fastened at each end **4** something that is curved, bent, or arched ▹*vb* **5** to form or cause to form a curve or curves
WORD ORIGIN Old English *boga* arch, bow

bow[3] (rhymes with **cow**) *n* **1** *chiefly naut* the front end or part of a vessel **2** *rowing* the oarsman at the bow
WORD ORIGIN probably Low German *boog*

Bow *n* **Clara**, known as the *It Girl.* 1905–65, US film actress, noted for her vivacity and sex appeal

bowdlerize *or* **-ise** *vb* **-izing, -ized** *or* **-ising, -ised** to remove passages or words regarded as indecent from (a play, novel, etc.) **bowdlerization** *or* **-isation** *n*
WORD ORIGIN after Thomas *Bowdler*, editor who expurgated Shakespeare

bowel *n* **1** an intestine, esp. the large intestine in man **2 bowels** entrails **3 bowels** the innermost part: *the bowels of the earth*
WORD ORIGIN Latin *botellus* a little sausage

Bowen *n* **Elizabeth** (**Dorothea Cole**) 1899–1973, British novelist and short-story writer, born in Ireland. Her novels include *The Death of the Heart* (1938) and *The Heat of the Day* (1949)

bower *n* a shady leafy shelter in a wood or garden
WORD ORIGIN Old English *būr* dwelling

bowerbird *n* a brightly coloured songbird of Australia and New Guinea

bowie knife *n* a stout hunting knife
WORD ORIGIN after Jim *Bowie*, Texan adventurer

bowl[1] *n* **1** a round container open at the top, used for holding liquid or serving food **2** the amount a bowl will hold **3** the hollow part of an object, esp. of a spoon or tobacco pipe
WORD ORIGIN Old English *bolla*

bowl[2] *n* **a** a wooden ball used in the game of bowls **b** a large heavy ball with holes for gripping used in the game of bowling ▹*vb* **2** to roll smoothly or cause to roll smoothly along the ground **3** *cricket* **a** to send (a ball) from one's hand towards the batsman **b** Also: **bowl out** to dismiss (a batsman) by delivering a ball that breaks his wicket **4** to play bowls **5 bowl along** to move easily and rapidly, as in a car ▸See also **bowl over, bowls**
WORD ORIGIN French *boule*

bow-legged *adj* having legs that curve outwards at the knees

bowler[1] *n* **1** a person who bowls in cricket **2** a player at the game of bowls

bowler[2] *n* a stiff felt hat with a rounded crown and narrow curved brim
WORD ORIGIN after John *Bowler*, hatter

Bowles *n* **Paul** 1910–99, US novelist, short-story writer, and composer, living in Tangiers. His novels include *The Sheltering Sky* (1949) and *The Spider's House* (1955)

bowline *n naut* **1** a line used to keep the sail taut against the wind **2** a knot used for securing a loop that will not slip at the end of a piece of rope
WORD ORIGIN probably from Middle Low German *bōlīne*

bowling *n* **1** a game in which a heavy ball is rolled down a long narrow alley at a group of wooden pins **2** *cricket* the act of delivering the ball to the batsman

THESAURUS

bourgeois *adj* **1, 2 = middle-class**, traditional, conventional, materialistic, hidebound, Pooterish

bout *n* **1a = period**, time, term, fit, session, stretch, spell, turn, patch, interval, stint **2 = fight**, match, battle, competition, struggle, contest, set-to, encounter, engagement, head-to-head, boxing match

bow[1] *vb* **1 = bend**, bob, nod, incline, stoop, droop, genuflect, make obeisance ▹*n* **4 = bending**, bob, nod, inclination, salaam, obeisance, kowtow, genuflection

bow[3] *n* **1** *(nautical)* **= prow**, head, stem, fore, beak

bowel *n* **2 = guts**, insides *(informal)*, intestines, innards *(informal)*, entrails, viscera, vitals **3 = depths**, hold, middle, inside, deep, interior, core, belly, midst, remotest part, deepest part, furthest part, innermost part

bowl[1] *n* **1 = basin**, plate, dish, vessel

bowl[2] *vb* **3a = throw**, hurl, launch, cast, pitch, toss, fling, chuck *(informal)*, lob *(informal)*

bowl over *vb* **1** *informal* to surprise (a person) greatly, in a pleasant way **2** to knock down

bowls *n* a game played on a very smooth area of grass in which opponents roll biased wooden bowls as near a small bowl (the jack) as possible

bow out *vb* to retire or withdraw gracefully

bowsprit *n naut* a spar projecting from the bow of a sailing ship
WORD ORIGIN Middle Low German *bōch* BOW[3] + *sprēt* pole

bowstring *n* the string of an archer's bow

bow tie *n* a man's tie in the form of a bow

bow window *n* a curved bay window

bow-wow *n* **1** ▸ a child's word for **dog** **2** an imitation of the bark of a dog

box[1] ⓣ *n* **1** a container with a firm base and sides and sometimes a removable or hinged lid **2** the contents of such a container **3** a separate compartment for a small group of people, as in a theatre **4** a compartment for a horse in a stable or a vehicle **5** a section of printed matter on a page, enclosed by lines or a border **6** a central agency to which mail is addressed and from which it is collected or redistributed: *a post-office box* **7** ▸ same as **penalty box** **8** **the box** *Brit informal* television ▹ *vb* **9** to put into a box ▸ See also **box in** > **boxlike** *adj*
WORD ORIGIN Greek *puxos* BOX[3]

box[2] ⓣ *vb* **1** to fight (an opponent) in a boxing match **2** to engage in boxing **3** to hit (esp. a person's ears) with the fist ▹ *n* **4** a punch with the fist, esp. on the ear
WORD ORIGIN origin unknown

box[3] *n* a slow-growing evergreen tree or shrub with small shiny leaves
WORD ORIGIN Greek *puxos*

boxer ⓣ *n* **1** a person who boxes **2** a medium-sized dog with smooth hair and a short nose

boxer shorts *or* **boxers** *pl n* men's underpants shaped like shorts but with a front opening

box girder *n* a girder that is hollow and square or rectangular in shape

box in *vb* to prevent from moving freely; confine

boxing *n* the act, art, or profession of fighting with the fists

Boxing Day *n* the first day after Christmas (in Britain, traditionally and strictly, the first weekday), observed as a holiday
WORD ORIGIN from the former custom of giving Christmas boxes to tradesmen on this day

box jellyfish *n* a highly venomous jellyfish with a cuboid body that lives in Australian tropical waters

box junction *n* (in Britain) a road junction marked with yellow crisscross lines which vehicles may only enter when their exit is clear

box lacrosse *n Canad* lacrosse played indoors

box number *n* a number used as an address for mail, esp. one used by a newspaper for replies to an advertisement

box office *n* **1** an office at a theatre, cinema, etc. where tickets are sold **2** the public appeal of an actor or production ▹ *adj* **box-office** **3** relating to the sales at the box office: *a box-office success*

box pleat *n* a flat double pleat made by folding under the fabric on either side of it

boxroom *n* a small room in which boxes, cases, etc. may be stored

box spring *n* a coiled spring contained in a boxlike frame, used for mattresses, chairs, etc.

boxwood *n* the hard yellow wood of the box tree, used to make tool handles, etc. ▸ See **box**[3]

boy ⓣ *n* **1** a male child **2** a man regarded as immature or inexperienced **3** *S African, offensive* a Black male servant **boyhood** *n* **boyish** *adj*
WORD ORIGIN origin unknown

Boyce *n* **William** ?1710–79, English composer, noted esp.for his church music and symphonies

boycott ⓣ *vb* **1** to refuse to deal with (an organization or country) as a protest against its actions or policy ▹ *n* **2** an instance or the use of boycotting
WORD ORIGIN after Captain *Boycott*, Irish land agent, a victim of such practices for refusing to reduce rents

Boycott *n* **Geoff(rey)** born 1940, English cricketer: captained Yorkshire (1970–78); played for England (1964–74, 1977–82)

Boyd *n* **1 Arthur** 1920–99, Australian painter and sculptor, noted for his large ceramic sculptures and his series of engravings **2 Martin (A'Beckett)** 1893–1972, Australian novelist, author of *Lucinda Brayford* (1946) and of the Langton tetralogy *The Cardboard Crown* (1952), *A Difficult Young Man* (1955), *Outbreak of Love* (1957), and *When Blackbirds Sing* (1962) **3 Michael** born 1955, British theatre director; artistic director of the Royal Shakespeare Company from 2003

Boyd Orr *n* **John**, 1st Baron Boyd Orr of Brechin Mearns. 1880–1971, Scottish biologist; director general of the United Nations Food and Agriculture Organization: Nobel peace prize 1949

Boyer *n* **Charles**, known as *the Great Lover*. 1899–1978, French film actor

boyfriend ⓣ *n* a male friend with whom a person is romantically or sexually involved

Boyle's law *n* the principle that the pressure of a gas varies inversely with its volume at constant temperature
WORD ORIGIN after Robert *Boyle*, scientist

boy scout *n* ▸ see **Scout**

BP **1** blood pressure **2** British Pharmacopoeia

bpi bits per inch (used of a computer tape)

Bq *physics* becquerel

Br *chem* bromine

Br. **1** Breton **2** Britain **3** British

bra *n* a woman's undergarment for covering and supporting the breasts
WORD ORIGIN from *brassiere*

braaivleis (brye-flayss) *S African n* **1** a grill on which food is cooked over hot charcoal, usually outdoors **2** an outdoor party at which food like this is served ▹ *vb* **3** to cook (food) on in this way. Also: **braai**
WORD ORIGIN Afrikaans

Brabham *n* Sir **John Arthur**, known as *Jack*. born 1926, Australian motor-racing driver: world champion 1959, 1960, and 1966

brace ⓣ *n* **1** something that steadies, binds, or holds up another thing **2** a beam or prop, used to stiffen a framework **3** a hand tool for drilling holes **4** a pair, esp. of game birds **5** either of a pair of characters, { }, used for connecting lines of printing or writing **6** ▸ see **braces** ▹ *vb*

THESAURUS

box[1] *n* **1 = container**, case, chest, trunk, pack, package, carton, casket, receptacle, ark *(dialect)*, portmanteau, coffret, kist *(Scot & Northern English dialect)* ▹ *vb* **9 = pack**, package, wrap, encase, bundle up

box[2] *vb* **2 = fight**, spar, exchange blows

boxer *n* **1 = fighter**, pugilist, prizefighter, sparrer

boy *n* **1 = lad**, kid *(informal)*, youth, fellow, youngster, chap *(informal)*, schoolboy, junior, laddie *(Scot)*, stripling

boycott *vb* **1 = embargo**, reject, snub, refrain from, spurn, blacklist, black, cold-shoulder, ostracize, blackball
OPPOSITE: support

boyfriend *n* **= sweetheart**, man, lover, young man, steady, beloved, valentine, admirer, suitor, beau, date, swain, toy boy, truelove, leman *(archaic)*, inamorato

brace *n* **1 = support**, stay, prop, bracer, bolster, bracket, reinforcement, strut, truss, buttress, stanchion ▹ *vb* **7 = steady**, support, balance, secure, stabilize **8 = support**, strengthen, steady, prop, reinforce, hold up, tighten, shove, bolster, fortify, buttress, shove up

DICTIONARY

bracing, braced 7 to steady or prepare (oneself) before an impact **8** to provide, strengthen, or fit with a brace
WORD ORIGIN Latin *bracchia* arms

brace and bit *n* a hand tool for boring holes, consisting of a cranked handle into which a drilling bit is inserted

bracelet *n* an ornamental chain or band worn around the arm or wrist
WORD ORIGIN Latin *bracchium* arm

bracelets *pl n slang* handcuffs

braces *pl n* **1** *Brit & NZ* a pair of straps worn over the shoulders for holding up the trousers **2** an appliance of metal bands and wires for correcting unevenness of teeth

brachiopod (brake-ee-oh-pod) *n* an invertebrate sea animal with a shell consisting of two valves
WORD ORIGIN Greek *brakhiōn* arm + *pous* foot

brachium (brake-ee-um) *n, pl* **brachia** (brake-ee-a) *anat* the arm, esp. the upper part
WORD ORIGIN Latin *bracchium* arm

bracing ❶ *adj* refreshing: *the bracing climate*

bracken *n* **1** a fern with large fronds **2** a clump of these ferns
WORD ORIGIN Scandinavian

bracket *n* **1** a pair of characters, [ ], ( ), or { }, used to enclose a section of writing or printing **2** a group or category falling within certain defined limits: *the lower income bracket* **3** an L-shaped or other support fixed to a wall to hold a shelf, etc. ▹ *vb* **-eting, -eted 4** to put (written or printed matter) in brackets **5** to group or class together
WORD ORIGIN Latin *braca* breeches

brackish *adj* (of water) slightly salty
WORD ORIGIN Middle Dutch *brac*

bract *n* a leaf, usually small and scaly, growing at the base of a flower
WORD ORIGIN Latin *bractea* thin metal plate

brad *n* a small tapered nail with a small head
WORD ORIGIN Old English *brord* point

Bradbury *n* **1** Sir **Malcolm** (**Stanley**) 1932–2000, British novelist and critic. His novels include *The History Man* (1975), *Rates of Exchange* (1983), *Cuts* (1988), and *Doctor Criminale* (1992) **2 Ray** born 1920, US science-fiction writer. His novels include *Fahrenheit 451* (1953), *Death is a Lonely Business* (1986), and *A Graveyard for Lunatics* (1990)

Bradlaugh *n* **Charles** 1833–91, British radical and freethinker: barred from taking his seat in parliament (1880–86) for refusing to take the parliamentary oath

Bradley *n* **1 A**(**ndrew**) **C**(**ecil**) 1851–1935, English critic; author of *Shakespearian Tragedy* (1904) **2 F**(**rancis**) **H**(**erbert**) 1846–1924, English idealist philosopher and metaphysical thinker; author of *Ethical Studies* (1876), *Principles of Logic* (1883), and *Appearance and Reality* (1893) **3 Henry** 1845–1923, English lexicographer; one of the editors of the *Oxford English Dictionary* **4 James** 1693–1762, English astronomer, who discovered the aberration of light and the nutation of the earth's axis

Bradstreet *n* **Anne** (**Dudley**) ?1612–72, US poet, born in England: regarded as the first significant US poet

brae *n Scot* a hill or slope
WORD ORIGIN Middle English *bra*

brag *vb* **bragging, bragged 1** to speak arrogantly and boastfully ▹ *n* **2** boastful talk or behaviour **3** a card game similar to poker
WORD ORIGIN origin unknown

braggart *n* a person who boasts loudly or exaggeratedly

Brahma *n* **1** a Hindu god, the Creator **2** ▸ same as **Brahman** (sense 2)

Brahman *n, pl* **-mans 1** Also: **Brahmin** a member of the highest or priestly caste in the Hindu caste system **2** *hinduism* the ultimate and impersonal divine reality of the universe **Brahmanic** *adj*
WORD ORIGIN Sanskrit: prayer

braid *vb* **1** to interweave (hair, thread, etc.) **2** to decorate with an ornamental trim or border ▹ *n* **3** a length of hair that has been braided **4** narrow ornamental tape of woven silk, wool, etc. **braiding** *n*
WORD ORIGIN Old English *bregdan*

Braille *n* a system of writing for the blind consisting of raised dots interpreted by touch
WORD ORIGIN after Louis *Braille*, its inventor

brain ❶ *n* **1** the soft mass of nervous tissue within the skull of vertebrates that controls and coordinates the nervous system **2** (*often pl*) *informal* intellectual ability: *he's got brains* **3** *informal* an intelligent person **4 on the brain** *informal* constantly in mind: *I had that song on the brain* **5 the brains** *informal* a person who plans and organizes something: *the brains behind the bid* ▹ *vb* **6** *slang* to hit (someone) hard on the head
WORD ORIGIN Old English *brægen*

brainchild *n informal* an idea or plan produced by creative thought

braindead *adj* **1** having suffered brain death **2** *informal* stupid

brain death *n* complete stoppage of breathing due to irreparable brain damage

brain drain *n informal* the emigration of scientists, technologists, academics, etc.

Braine *n* **John** (**Gerard**) 1922–86, English novelist, whose works include *Room at the Top* (1957) and *Life at the Top* (1962)

brainfood *n* any foodstuff containing nutrients thought to promote brain function

brainless *adj* stupid or foolish

brainstorm *n* **1** *informal* a sudden mental aberration **2** a sudden and violent attack of insanity **3** *informal* ▸ same as **brainwave**

brainstorming *n* a thorough discussion to solve problems or create ideas

brains trust *n* a group of knowledgeable people who discuss topics in public or on radio or television

brain-teaser *n informal* a difficult problem

brainwash *vb* to cause (a person) to alter his or her beliefs, by methods based on isolation, sleeplessness, etc. **brainwashing** *n*

brainwave *n informal* a sudden idea or inspiration

brain wave *n* a fluctuation of electrical potential in the brain

brainy *adj* **brainier, brainiest** *informal* clever; intelligent

braise *vb* **braising, braised** to cook (food) slowly in a closed pan with a small amount of liquid
WORD ORIGIN Old French *brese* live coals

brak¹ (bruck) *n S African* a crossbred dog; mongrel
WORD ORIGIN Dutch

brak² (bruck) *adj S African* (of water) slightly salty; brackish
WORD ORIGIN Afrikaans

brake¹ ❶ *n* **1** a device for slowing or stopping a vehicle **2** something that slows down or stops progress: *he put a brake on my enthusiasm* ▹ *vb* **braking, braked 3** to slow down or cause to slow down, by or as if by using a brake
WORD ORIGIN Middle Dutch *braeke*

brake² *n Brit* an area of dense undergrowth; thicket
WORD ORIGIN Old English *bracu*

brake horsepower *n* the rate at

THESAURUS

bracing *adj* **= refreshing**, fresh, cool, stimulating, reviving, lively, crisp, vigorous, rousing, brisk, uplifting, exhilarating, fortifying, chilly, rejuvenating, invigorating, energizing, healthful, restorative, tonic, rejuvenative **OPPOSITE:** tiring

brain *pl n* **2 = intelligence**, mind, reason, understanding, sense, capacity, smarts (*slang, chiefly US*), wit, intellect, savvy (*slang*), nous (*Brit slang*), suss (*slang*), shrewdness, sagacity

brake¹ *n* **2 = control**, check, curb, restraint, constraint, rein ▹ *vb*

DICTIONARY

which an engine does work, measured by the resistance of an applied brake
brake light *n* a red light at the rear of a motor vehicle that lights up when the brakes are applied
brake shoe *n* a curved metal casting that acts as a brake on a wheel
Bramante *n* **Donato** ?1444–1514, Italian architect and artist of the High Renaissance. He modelled his designs for domed centrally planned churches on classical Roman architecture
bramble *n* **1** a prickly plant or shrub such as the blackberry **2** *Scot, N English & NZ* a blackberry **brambly** *adj*
WORD ORIGIN Old English *brǣmbel*
bran *n* husks of cereal grain separated from the flour
WORD ORIGIN Old French
Branagh *n* **Kenneth** born 1961, British actor and director, born in Northern Ireland. He founded the Renaissance Theatre Company in 1986. His films include *Henry V* (1989), *Mary Shelley's Frankenstein* (1994), *Hamlet* (1997), and *Harry Potter and the Chamber of Secrets* (2002)
branch ⊙ *n* **1** a secondary woody stem extending from the trunk or main branch of a tree **2** one of a number of shops, offices, or groups that belongs to a central organization: *he was transferred to their Japanese branch* **3** a subdivision or subsidiary section of something larger or more complex: *branches of learning* ▷ *vb* **4** to divide, then develop in different directions **branchlike** *adj*
WORD ORIGIN Late Latin *branca* paw
branch off *vb* to diverge from the main way, road, topic, etc.
branch out *vb* to expand or extend one's interests
Brancusi *n* **Constantin** 1876–1957, Romanian sculptor, noted for his streamlined abstractions of animal forms
brand ⊙ *n* **1** a particular product or a characteristic that identifies a particular producer **2** a trade name or trademark **3** a particular kind or variety **4** an identifying mark made, usually by burning, on the skin of animals as a proof of ownership **5** an iron used for branding animals **6** a mark of disgrace **7** *archaic or poetic* a flaming torch ▷ *vb* **8** to label, burn, or mark with or as if with a brand **9** to label (someone): *he was branded a war criminal*
WORD ORIGIN Old English: fire
Brand *n* **Russell** born 1975, English comedian and television presenter
brandish *vb* to wave (a weapon, etc.) in a triumphant or threatening way
WORD ORIGIN Old French *brandir*
brand-new *adj* absolutely new
Brandt *n* **1 Bill**, full name *William Brandt*. 1905–83, British photographer. His photographic books include *The English at Home* (1936) and *Perspectives of Nudes* (1961) **2 Georg** 1694–1768, Swedish chemist, who isolated cobalt (1742) and exposed fraudulent alchemists **3 Willy** 1913–92, German statesman; socialist chancellor of West Germany (1969–74); chairman of the Social Democratic party (1964–87). His policy of détente and reconciliation with E Europe brought him international acclaim. Nobel peace prize 1971
brandy *n, pl* **-dies** an alcoholic spirit distilled from wine
WORD ORIGIN Dutch *brandewijn*
brandy snap *n* a crisp sweet biscuit, rolled into a cylinder
Branting *n* **Karl Hjalmar** 1860–1925, Swedish politician; prime minister (1920; 1921–23; 1924–25). He founded Sweden's welfare state and shared the Nobel peace prize 1921
brash ⊙ *adj* **1** tastelessly or offensively loud, or showy: *brash modernization* **2** impudent or bold: *I thought it was very brash of her to ask me* **brashness** *n*
WORD ORIGIN origin unknown
brass *n* **1** an alloy of copper and zinc **2** an object, ornament, or utensil made of brass **3 a** the large family of wind instruments including the trumpet, trombone, etc. made of brass **b** instruments of this family forming a section in an orchestra **4** ▸ same as **top brass 5** *N English dialect* money **6** *Brit* an engraved brass memorial tablet in a church **7** *informal* bold self-confidence; nerve
WORD ORIGIN Old English *bræs*
Brassaï *n* real name *Gyula Halész*. 1899–1984, French photographer, artist, and writer, born in Hungary: noted for his photographs of Paris by night
brass band *n* a group of musicians playing brass and percussion instruments
brasserie *n* a bar or restaurant serving drinks and cheap meals
WORD ORIGIN French *brasser* to stir
brass hat *n Brit informal* a top-ranking official, esp. a military officer
brassica *n* any plant of the cabbage and turnip family
WORD ORIGIN Latin: cabbage
brassiere *n* ▸ same as **bra**
WORD ORIGIN French
brass rubbing *n* an impression of an engraved brass tablet made by rubbing a paper placed over it with heelball or chalk
brass tacks *pl n* **get down to brass tacks** *informal* to discuss the realities of a situation
brassy *adj* **brassier, brassiest** **1** brazen or flashy **2** like brass, esp. in colour **3** (of sound) harsh and strident
brat *n* a child, esp. one who is unruly
WORD ORIGIN origin unknown
Brattain *n* **Walter Houser** 1902–87, US physicist, who shared the Nobel prize for physics (1956) with W. B. Shockley and John Bardeen for their invention of the transistor
bravado *n* an outward display of self-confidence
WORD ORIGIN Spanish *bravada*
brave ⊙ *adj* **1** having or displaying courage, resolution, or daring **2** fine; splendid: *a brave sight* ▷ *n* **3** a warrior of a Native American tribe of N America ▷ *vb* **braving, braved 4** to confront with resolution or courage: *she braved the 21 miles of Lake Tahoe* **bravery** *n*
WORD ORIGIN Italian *bravo*
bravo *interj* **1** well done! ▷ *n* **2** *pl* **-vos** a cry of 'bravo' **3** *pl* **-voes** *or* **-vos** a hired killer or assassin
WORD ORIGIN Italian
bravura *n* **1** a display of boldness or daring **2** *music* brilliance of execution
WORD ORIGIN Italian
brawl ⊙ *n* **1** a loud disagreement or fight ▷ *vb* **2** to quarrel or fight noisily
WORD ORIGIN probably from Dutch *brallen* to boast
brawn *n* **1** strong well-developed

THESAURUS

3 = slow, decelerate, reduce speed
branch *n* **1 = bough**, shoot, arm, spray, limb, sprig, offshoot, prong, ramification **2 = office**, department, unit, wing, chapter, bureau, local office **3 = division**, part, section, subdivision, subsection
brand *n* **2 = trademark** ▷ *vb* **8 = mark**, burn, label, stamp, scar **9 = stigmatize**, mark, label, expose, denounce, disgrace, discredit, censure, pillory, defame
brash *adj* **2 = bold**, forward, rude, arrogant, cocky, pushy *(informal)*, brazen, presumptuous, impertinent, insolent, impudent, bumptious, cocksure, overconfident, hubristic, full of yourself **OPPOSITE:** timid
brave *adj* **1 = courageous**, daring, bold, heroic, adventurous, gritty, fearless, resolute, gallant, gutsy *(slang)*, audacious, intrepid, valiant, plucky, undaunted, unafraid, unflinching, dauntless, lion-hearted, valorous **OPPOSITE:** timid ▷ *vb* **4 = confront**, face, suffer, challenge, bear, tackle, dare, endure, defy, withstand, stand up to **OPPOSITE:** give in to
brawl *n* **1 = fight**, battle, row *(informal)*, clash, disorder, scrap *(informal)*, fray, squabble, wrangle, skirmish, scuffle, punch-up *(Brit informal)*, free-for-all

DICTIONARY

b

muscles **2** physical strength **3** *Brit & NZ* a seasoned jellied loaf made from the head of a pig **brawny** *adj*
WORD ORIGIN Old French *braon* meat

bray *vb* **1** (of a donkey) to utter its characteristic loud harsh sound **2** to utter something with a loud harsh sound ▷ *n* **3** the loud harsh sound uttered by a donkey **4** a similar loud sound
WORD ORIGIN Old French *braire*

braze *vb* **brazing, brazed** to join (two metal surfaces) by fusing brass between them
WORD ORIGIN Old French: to burn

brazen *adj* **1** shameless and bold **2** made of or resembling brass **3** having a ringing metallic sound ▷ *vb* **4 brazen it out** to face and overcome a difficult or embarrassing situation boldly or shamelessly **brazenly** *adv*

brazier[1] (bray-zee-er) *n* a portable metal container for burning charcoal or coal
WORD ORIGIN French *braise* live coals

brazier[2] *n* a worker in brass

brazil *n* **1** the red wood of various tropical trees of America **2** ▸ same as **brazil nut**
WORD ORIGIN Old Spanish *brasa* glowing coals; referring to the redness of the wood

Brazilian *adj* **1** of Brazil ▷ *n* **2** a person from Brazil

brazil nut *n* a large three-sided nut of a tropical American tree

breach ⓣ *n* **1** a breaking of a promise, obligation, etc. **2** any serious disagreement or separation **3** a crack, break, or gap ▷ *vb* **4** to break (a promise, law, etc.) **5** to break through or make an opening or hole in
WORD ORIGIN Old English *bræc*

breach of promise *n law* (formerly) failure to carry out one's promise to marry

breach of the peace *n law* an offence against public order causing an unnecessary disturbance of the peace

bread ⓣ *n* **1** a food made from a dough of flour or meal mixed with water or milk, usually raised with yeast and then baked **2** necessary food **3** *slang* money ▷ *vb* **4** to cover (food) with breadcrumbs before cooking
WORD ORIGIN Old English *brēad*

bread and butter *n informal* a means of support; livelihood

breadboard *n* **1** a wooden board on which bread is sliced **2** an experimental arrangement of electronic circuits

breadfruit *n, pl* **-fruits** *or* **-fruit** a tree of the Pacific Islands, whose edible round fruit has a texture like bread when baked

breadline *n* **on the breadline** impoverished; living at subsistence level

breadth ⓣ *n* **1** the extent or measurement of something from side to side **2** openness and lack of restriction, esp. of viewpoint or interest; liberality
WORD ORIGIN Old English *brād* broad

breadwinner *n* a person supporting a family with his or her earnings

break ⓣ *vb* **breaking, broke, broken** **1** to separate or become separated into two or more pieces **2** to damage or become damaged so as not to work **3** to burst or cut the surface of (skin) **4** to fracture (a bone) in (a limb, etc.) **5** to fail to observe (an agreement, promise, or law): *they broke their promise* **6** to reveal or be revealed: *she broke the news gently* **7** (foll. by *with*) to separate oneself from **8** to stop for a rest: *to break a journey* **9** to bring or come to an end: *the winter weather broke at last* **10** to weaken or overwhelm or be weakened or overwhelmed, as in spirit: *he felt his life was broken by his illness* **11** to cut through or penetrate: *silence broken by shouts* **12** to improve on or surpass: *she broke three world records* **13** (often foll. by *in*) to accustom (a horse) to the bridle and saddle, to being ridden, etc. **14** (foll. by *of*) to cause (a person) to give up (a habit): *this cure will break you of smoking* **15** to weaken the impact or force of: *this net will break his fall* **16** to decipher: *to break a code* **17** to lose the order of: *to break ranks* **18** to reduce to poverty or the state of bankruptcy **19** to come into being: *light broke over the mountains* **20** (foll. by *into*) **a** to burst into (song, laughter, etc.) **b** to change to (a faster pace) **21** to open with explosives: *to break a safe* **22 a** (of waves) to strike violently against **b** (of waves) to collapse into foam or surf **23** *snooker* to scatter the balls at the start of a game **24** *boxing, wrestling* (of two fighters) to separate from a clinch **25** (of the male voice) to undergo a change in register, quality, and range at puberty **26** to interrupt the flow of current in (an electrical circuit) **27 break camp** to pack up and leave a camp **28 break even** to make neither a profit nor a loss **29 break the mould** to make a change that breaks an established habit or pattern ▷ *n* **30** the act or result of breaking; fracture **31** a brief rest **32** a sudden rush, esp. to escape: *they made a sudden break for freedom* **33** any sudden interruption in a continuous action **34** *Brit & NZ* a short period between classes at school **35** a (short) holiday **36** *informal* a fortunate opportunity, esp. to prove oneself **37** *informal* a piece of good or bad luck **38** *billiards, snooker* a series of successful shots during one turn **39** *snooker* the opening shot that scatters the placed balls **40** a discontinuity in an electrical circuit **41 break of day** the dawn ▸ See also **breakaway, break down**, etc. **breakable** *adj*
WORD ORIGIN Old English *brecan*

breakage *n* **1** the act or result of breaking **2** compensation or

THESAURUS

(*informal*), fracas, altercation, rumpus, broil, tumult, affray (*law*), shindig (*informal*), donnybrook, ruckus (*informal*), scrimmage, shindy (*informal*), biffo (*Austral slang*), bagarre (*French*), melee *or* mêlée ▷ *vb* **2 = fight**, battle, scrap (*informal*), wrestle, wrangle, tussle, scuffle, go at it hammer and tongs, fight like Kilkenny cats, altercate

breach *n* **1 = nonobservance**, abuse, violation, infringement, trespass, disobedience, transgression, contravention, infraction, noncompliance
OPPOSITE: compliance
3 = opening, crack, break, hole, split, gap, rent, rift, rupture, aperture, chasm, cleft, fissure

bread *n* **2 = food**, provisions, fare, necessities, subsistence, kai (*NZ informal*), nourishment, sustenance, victuals, nutriment, viands, aliment **3** (*slang*) **= money**, funds, cash, finance, necessary (*informal*), silver, tin (*slang*), brass (*Northern English dialect*), dough (*slang*), dosh (*Brit & Austral slang*), needful (*informal*), shekels (*informal*), dibs (*slang*), ackers (*slang*), spondulicks (*slang*), rhino (*Brit slang*)

breadth *n* **1 = extent**, area, reach, range, measure, size, scale, spread, sweep, scope, magnitude, compass, expanse, vastness, amplitude, comprehensiveness, extensiveness

break *vb* **1 = shatter**, separate, destroy, split, divide, crack, snap, smash, crush, fragment, demolish, sever, trash (*slang*), disintegrate, splinter, smash to smithereens, shiver
OPPOSITE: repair
3 = burst, tear, split **4 = fracture**, crack, smash **5 = disobey**, breach, defy, violate, disregard, flout, infringe, contravene, transgress, go counter to, infract (*law*)
OPPOSITE: obey
6a = be revealed, come out, be reported, be published, be announced, be made public, be proclaimed, be let out, be imparted, be divulged, come out in the wash
6b = reveal, tell, announce, declare, disclose, proclaim, divulge, make known **9 = stop**, cut, check, suspend, interrupt, cut short, discontinue

allowance for goods damaged while in use, transit, etc.

breakaway *n* **1** loss or withdrawal of a group of members from an association, club, etc. **2** *Austral* a stampede of cattle, esp. at the smell of water ▹ *adj* **3** dissenting: *a breakaway faction* ▹ *vb* **break away 4** to leave hastily or escape **5** to withdraw or quit

break dance *n* **1** an acrobatic dance style associated with hip-hop music, originating in the 1980s ▹ *vb* **break-dance, -dancing, -danced 2** to perform a break dance **break dancing** *n*

break down ⓘ *vb* **1** to cease to function; become ineffective **2** to give way to strong emotion or tears **3** to crush or destroy **4** to have a nervous breakdown **5** to separate into component parts: *with exercise the body breaks down fat to use as fuel* **6** to separate or cause to separate into simpler chemical elements; decompose **7** to analyse or be subjected to analysis ▹ *n* **breakdown 8** an act or instance of breaking down; collapse **9** ▸ same as **nervous breakdown 10** an analysis of something into its parts

breaker *n* **1** a large sea wave with a white crest or one that breaks into foam on the shore **2** a citizens' band radio operator

breakfast *n* **1** the first meal of the day ▹ *vb* **2** to eat breakfast
WORD ORIGIN BREAK + FAST[2]

break in ⓘ *vb* **1** to enter a building, illegally, esp. by force **2** to interrupt **3** to accustom (a person or animal) to normal duties or practice **4** to use or wear (new shoes or new equipment) until comfortable or running smoothly ▹ *n* **break-in 5** the act of illegally entering a building, esp. by thieves

breaking point *n* the point at which something or someone gives way under strain

breakneck *adj* (of speed or pace) excessively fast and dangerous

break off *vb* **1** to sever or detach **2** to end (a relationship or association) **3** to stop abruptly

break out *vb* **1** to begin or arise suddenly: *fighting broke out between the two factions* **2** to make an escape, esp. from prison **3 break out in** to erupt in (a rash or spots) ▹ *n* **break-out 4** an escape, esp. from prison

break through ⓘ *vb* **1** to penetrate **2** to achieve success after lengthy efforts ▹ *n* **breakthrough 3** a significant development or discovery

break up *vb* **1** to separate or cause to separate **2** to put an end to (a relationship) or (of a relationship) to come to an end **3** to dissolve or cause to dissolve: *the meeting broke up at noon* **4** *Brit* (of a school) to close for the holidays ▹ *n* **break-up 5** a separation or disintegration

breakwater *n* a massive wall built out into the sea to protect a shore or harbour from the force of waves

bream *n, pl* **bream 1** a freshwater fish covered with silvery scales **2** a food fish of European seas **3** a food fish of Australasian seas
WORD ORIGIN Old French *bresme*

Bream *n* **Julian** (**Alexander**) born 1933, English guitarist and lutenist

breast ⓘ *n* **1** either of the two soft fleshy milk-secreting glands on a woman's chest **2** the front part of the body from the neck to the abdomen; chest **3** the corresponding part in certain other mammals **4** the source of human emotions **5** the part of a garment that covers the breast **6 make a clean breast of something** to divulge truths about oneself ▹ *vb literary* **7** to reach the summit of: *breasting the mountain top* **8** to confront boldly; face: *breast the storm*
WORD ORIGIN Old English *brēost*

breastbone *n* ▸ same as **sternum**

breast-feed *vb* **-feeding, -fed** to feed (a baby) with milk from the breast; suckle

breastplate *n* a piece of armour covering the chest

breaststroke *n* a swimming stroke in which the arms are extended in front of the head and swept back on either side

breastwork *n fortifications* a temporary defensive work, usually breast-high

breath ⓘ *n* **1** the taking in and letting out of air during breathing **2** a single instance of this **3** the air taken in or let out during breathing **4** the vapour, heat, or odour of air breathed out **5** a slight gust of air **6** a short pause or rest **7** a suggestion or slight evidence; suspicion: *trembling at the least breath of scandal* **8** a whisper or soft sound **9 catch one's breath a** to rest until breathing is normal **b** to stop breathing momentarily from excitement, fear, etc. **10 out of breath** gasping for air after exertion **11 save one's breath** to avoid useless talk **12 take someone's breath away** to overwhelm someone with surprise, etc. **13 under one's breath** in a quiet voice or whisper
WORD ORIGIN Old English *brǣth*

breathable *adj* **1** (of air) fit to be breathed **2** (of material) allowing air to pass through so that perspiration can evaporate

Breathalyser *or* **-lyzer** *n Brit trademark* a device for estimating the amount of alcohol in the breath **breathalyse** *or* **-lyze** *vb*
WORD ORIGIN *breath + (an)alyser*

breathe ⓘ *vb* **breathing, breathed 1** to take in oxygen and give out carbon dioxide; respire **2** to exist; be alive **3** to rest to regain breath or composure **4** (esp. of air) to blow lightly **5** to exhale or emit: *the dragon breathed fire* **6** to impart; instil: *a change that breathed new life into Polish industry* **7** to speak softly; whisper **8 breathe again** *or* **freely** *or* **easily** to feel relief **9 breathe one's last** to die

breather *n informal* a short pause for rest

breathing *n* **1** the passage of air into and out of the lungs to supply the body with oxygen **2** the sound this makes

breathing space *n* a short period during which a difficult situation temporarily becomes less severe: *the cut in interest rates creates a breathing space for struggling businesses*

breathless ⓘ *adj* **1** out of breath; gasping, etc. **2** holding one's breath or having it taken away by excitement, etc. **3** (esp. of the

10 = weaken, undermine, cow, tame, subdue, demoralize, dispirit **12 = beat**, top, better, exceed, go beyond, excel, surpass, outstrip, outdo, cap *(informal)* ▹ *n* **30 = fracture**, opening, tear, hole, split, crack, gap, rent, breach, rift, rupture, gash, cleft, fissure **35 = holiday**, leave, vacation, time off, recess, awayday, schoolie *(Austral)*, accumulated day off *or* ADO *(Austral)* **36** *(informal)* **= stroke of luck**, chance, opportunity, advantage, fortune, opening

breakdown *n* **8 = collapse**, crackup *(informal)*

break-in *n* **5 = burglary**, robbery, breaking and entering, home invasion *(Austral & NZ)*

breakthrough *n* **3 = development**, advance, progress, improvement, discovery, find, finding, invention, step forward, leap forwards, turn of events, quantum leap

breast *n* **1 = bosom**, boob *(slang)*, tit *(slang)*, booby *(slang)*

breath *n* **2 = inhalation**, breathing, pant, gasp, gulp, wheeze, exhalation, respiration

breathe *vb* **1 = inhale and exhale**, pant, gasp, puff, gulp, wheeze, respire, draw in breath

breathless *adj* **1 = out of breath**, winded, exhausted, panting, gasping, choking, gulping, wheezing, out of whack *(informal)*, short-winded **2 = excited**, anxious, curious, eager, enthusiastic, impatient, agog, on tenterhooks, in suspense

DICTIONARY

atmosphere) motionless and stifling **breathlessness** *n*

breathtaking ❶ *adj* causing awe or excitement

breath test *n* a chemical test of a driver's breath to determine the amount of alcohol consumed

bred *vb* ▸ the past of **breed**

bredie (**breed**-ee) *n S African* a meat and vegetable stew
WORD ORIGIN Portuguese *bredo* ragout

breech *n* **1** the buttocks **2** the part of a firearm behind the barrel
WORD ORIGIN Old English *brēc*, plural of *brōc* leg covering

breech delivery *n* birth of a baby with the feet or buttocks appearing first

breeches *pl n* trousers extending to the knee or just below, worn for riding, etc.

breeches buoy *n* a pulley device with a life buoy and pair of breeches attached, which is used as a means of transference between ships or rescue from the sea

breed ❶ *vb* **breeding, bred 1** to produce new or improved strains of (domestic animals and plants) **2** to produce or cause to produce by mating **3** to bear (offspring) **4** to bring up; raise: *she was city bred* **5** to produce or be produced: *the agreement bred confidence between the two* ▷ *n* **6** a group of animals, esp. domestic animals, within a species, that have certain clearly defined characteristics **7** a kind, sort, or group: *he was a gentleman, a breed not greatly admired* **8** a lineage or race **breeder** *n*
WORD ORIGIN Old English *brēdan*

breeder reactor *n* a nuclear reactor that produces more fissionable material than it uses

breeding ❶ *n* **1** the process of producing plants or animals by controlled methods of reproduction **2** the process of bearing offspring **3** the result of good upbringing or training

breeze[1] ❶ *n* **1** a gentle or light wind **2** *informal* an easy task ▷ *vb* **breezing, breezed 3** to move quickly or casually: *he breezed into the room*
WORD ORIGIN probably from Old Spanish *briza*

breeze[2] *n* ashes of coal, coke, or charcoal
WORD ORIGIN French *braise* live coals

breeze block *n* a light building brick made from the ashes of coal, coke, etc. bonded together by cement

breezy *adj* **breezier, breeziest 1** fresh; windy **2** casual or carefree

Brel *n* **Jacques** 1929–78, Belgian-born composer and singer, based in Paris. His songs include "Ne me quitte pas" ("If You Go Away")

Brendel *n* **Alfred** born 1931, Austrian pianist and poet

Bren gun *n* an air-cooled gas-operated light machine gun
WORD ORIGIN after *Br(no)*, Czech Republic, and *En(field)*, England, where it was made

Brennan *n* **Christopher John** 1870–1932, Australian poet and classical scholar, disciple of Mallarmé and exponent of French symbolism in Australian verse

brent *or esp. US* **brant** *n* a small goose with dark grey plumage and a short neck

Brentano *n* **Clemens** (**Maria**) 1778–1842, German romantic poet and compiler of fairy stories and folk songs esp.(with Achim von Arnim) the collection *Des Knaben Wunderhorn* (1805–08)

Brenton *n* **Howard** born 1942, British dramatist, author of such controversial plays as *The Churchill Play* (1974), *The Romans in Britain* (1980), (with David Hare) *Pravda* (1985), and several topical satires with Tariq Ali

Bresson *n* **Robert** 1901–99, French film director: his films include *Le Journal d'un curé de campagne* (1950), *Une Femme douce* (1969), and *L'Argent* (1983)

brethren *pl n archaic* ▸ a plural of **brother**

Breton[1] *adj* **1** of, relating to, or characteristic of Brittany, its people, or their language ▷ *n* **2** a native or inhabitant of Brittany, esp. one who speaks the Breton language **3** the indigenous language of Brittany, belonging to the Brythonic subgroup of the Celtic family of languages

Breton[2] *n* **André** 1896–1966, French poet and art critic: founder and chief theorist of surrealism, publishing the first surrealist manifesto in 1924

Breuer *n* **1 Josef** 1842–1925, Austrian physician: treated the mentally ill by hypnosis **2 Marcel Lajos** 1902–81, US architect and furniture designer, born in Hungary. He developed bent plywood and tubular metal furniture and designed the UNESCO building in Paris (1953–58)

breve *n* an accent (˘), placed over a vowel to indicate that it is short or is pronounced in a specified way
WORD ORIGIN Latin *brevis* short

breviary *n, pl* **-ries** *RC church* a book of psalms, hymns, prayers, etc. to be recited daily
WORD ORIGIN Latin *brevis* short

brevity *n* **1** a short duration; brief time **2** lack of verbosity
WORD ORIGIN Latin *brevitas*

brew ❶ *vb* **1** to make (beer, ale, etc.) from malt and other ingredients by steeping, boiling, and fermentation **2** to prepare (a drink, such as tea) by infusing **3** to devise or plan: *to brew a plot* **4** to be in the process of being brewed **5** to be about to happen or forming: *a rebellion was brewing* ▷ *n* **6** a beverage produced by brewing, esp. tea or beer **7** an instance of brewing: *last year's brew* **brewer** *n*
WORD ORIGIN Old English *brēowan*

brewery *n, pl* **-eries** a place where beer, ale, etc. is brewed

Brewster *n* Sir **David** 1781–1868, Scottish physicist, noted for his studies of the polarization of light

Brian *n* **Havergal** 1876–1972, English composer, who wrote 32 symphonies, including the large-scale *Gothic Symphony* (1919–27)

Brian Boru *n* ?941–1014, king of Ireland (1002–14): killed during the defeat of the Danes at the battle of Clontarf

Briand *n* **Aristide** (aristid) 1862–1932, French socialist statesman: prime minister of France 11 times. He was responsible for the separation of Church and State (1905) and he advocated a United States of Europe. Nobel peace prize 1926

briar[1] *or* **brier** *n* **1** a shrub of S Europe, with a hard woody root (briarroot)

THESAURUS

breathtaking *adj* **= amazing**, striking, exciting, brilliant, dramatic, stunning *(informal)*, impressive, thrilling, overwhelming, magnificent, astonishing, sensational, eye-popping *(informal)*, awesome, wondrous *(archaic, literary)*, awe-inspiring, jaw-dropping, heart-stirring

breed *vb* **1 = rear**, tend, keep, raise, maintain, farm, look after, care for, bring up, nurture, nourish **2, 3 = reproduce**, multiply, propagate, procreate, produce offspring, bear young, bring forth young, generate offspring, beget offspring, develop **5 = produce**, cause, create, occasion, generate, bring about, arouse, originate, give rise to, stir up ▷ *n* **6 = variety**, race, stock, type, species, strain, pedigree **7 = kind**, sort, type, variety, brand, stamp

breeding *n* **3 = refinement**, style, culture, taste, manners, polish, grace, courtesy, elegance, sophistication, delicacy, cultivation, politeness, civility, gentility, graciousness, urbanity, politesse

breeze[1] *n* **1 = light wind**, air, whiff, draught, gust, waft, zephyr, breath of wind, current of air, puff of air, capful of wind ▷ *vb* **3 = sweep**, move briskly, pass, trip, sail, hurry, sally, glide, flit

brew *vb* **1 = make**, ferment, prepare by fermentation **2 = boil**, make, soak, steep, stew, infuse *(tea)* **5 = start**, develop, gather, foment

2 a tobacco pipe made from this root
WORD ORIGIN French *bruyère*
briar[2] *n* ▸ same as **brier**[1]
bribe ❶ *vb* **bribing, bribed 1** to promise, offer, or give something, often illegally, to (a person) to receive services or gain influence ▷ *n* **2** a reward, such as money or favour, given or offered for this purpose **bribery** *n*
WORD ORIGIN Old French *briber* to beg
bric-a-brac *n* miscellaneous small ornamental objects
WORD ORIGIN French
Brice *n* **Fanny**, real name *Fannie Borach*. 1891–1951, US actress and singer. The film *Funny Girl* was based on her life
brick *n* **1** a rectangular block of baked or dried clay, used in building construction **2** the material used to make such blocks **3** any rectangular block: *a brick of ice cream* **4** bricks collectively **5** *informal* a reliable, trustworthy, or helpful person **6 drop a brick** *Brit & NZ informal* to make a tactless or indiscreet remark ▷ *vb* **7** (foll. by *in*, *up* or *over*) to construct, line, pave, fill, or wall up with bricks: *they bricked up access to the historic pillar*
WORD ORIGIN Middle Dutch *bricke*
brickbat *n* **1** blunt criticism **2** a piece of brick used as a weapon
WORD ORIGIN BRICK + BAT[1]
bricklayer *n* a person who builds with bricks
brick-red *adj* reddish-brown
bridal *adj* of a bride or a wedding
WORD ORIGIN Old English *brȳdealu* bride ale
bride *n* a woman who has just been or is about to be married
WORD ORIGIN Old English *brȳd*
bridegroom *n* a man who has just been or is about to be married
WORD ORIGIN Old English *brȳdguma*
bridesmaid *n* a girl or young woman who attends a bride at her wedding
bridge[1] ❶ *n* **1** a structure that provides a way over a railway, river, etc. **2** a platform from which a ship is piloted and navigated **3** the hard ridge at the upper part of the nose **4** a dental plate containing artificial teeth that is secured to natural teeth **5** a piece of wood supporting the strings of a violin, guitar, etc. ▷ *vb* **bridging, bridged 6** to build or provide a bridge over (something) **7** to connect or reduce the distance between: *talks aimed at bridging the gap between the two sides*
WORD ORIGIN Old English *brycg*
bridge[2] *n* a card game for four players, based on whist, in which the trump suit is decided by bidding between the players
WORD ORIGIN origin unknown
Bridge *n* **Frank** 1879–1941, English composer, esp.of chamber music. He taught Benjamin Britten
bridgehead *n mil* a fortified or defensive position at the end of a bridge nearest to the enemy
Bridges *n* **Robert** (**Seymour**) 1844–1930, English poet: poet laureate (1913–30)
Bridget *n* **Saint Bridget 1** Also: **Bride, Brigid** 453–523 AD, Irish abbess; a patron saint of Ireland. Feast day: Feb 1 **2** Also: **Birgitta** ?1303-73, Swedish nun and visionary; patron saint of Sweden. Feast day: July 23
bridgework *n* a partial denture attached to the surrounding teeth
bridging loan *n* a loan made to cover the period between two transactions, such as the buying of another house before the sale of the first is completed
Bridgman *n* **Percy Williams** 1882–1961, US physicist: Nobel prize for physics (1946) for his work on high-pressure physics and thermodynamics
Bridie *n* **James**, real name *Osborne Henry Mavor*. 1888–1951, Scottish physician and dramatist, who founded the Glasgow Citizens' Theatre. His plays include *The Anatomist* (1930)
bridle *n* **1** headgear for controlling a horse, consisting of straps and a bit and reins **2** something that curbs or restrains ▷ *vb* **-dling, -dled 3** to show anger or indignation: *he bridled at the shortness of her tone* **4** to put a bridle on (a horse) **5** to restrain; curb
WORD ORIGIN Old English *brigdels*
bridle path *n* a path suitable for riding or leading horses
Brie (bree) *n* a soft creamy white cheese
WORD ORIGIN *Brie*, region in N France
brief ❶ *adj* **1** short in duration **2** short in length or extent; scanty: *a brief bikini* **3** terse or concise ▷ *n* **4** a condensed statement or written synopsis **5** *law* a document containing all the facts and points of law of a case by which a solicitor instructs a barrister to represent a client **6** *RC church* a papal letter that is less formal than a bull **7** Also called: **briefing** instructions **8 hold a brief for** to argue for; champion **9 in brief** in short; to sum up ▷ *vb* **10** to prepare or instruct (someone) by giving a summary of relevant facts **11** *English law* **a** to instruct (a barrister) by brief **b** to retain (a barrister) as counsel **briefly** *adv*
WORD ORIGIN Latin *brevis*
briefcase *n* a flat portable case for carrying papers, books, etc.
briefs *pl n* men's or women's underpants without legs
brier[1] *or* **briar** *n* any of various thorny shrubs or other plants, such as the sweetbrier
WORD ORIGIN Old English *brēr, brǣr*
brier[2] *n* ▸ same as **briar**[1]
brig[1] *n naut* a two-masted square-rigged ship
WORD ORIGIN from BRIGANTINE
brig[2] *n Scot & N English* a bridge
Brig. Brigadier
brigade ❶ *n* **1** a military formation smaller than a division and usually commanded by a brigadier **2** a group of people organized for a certain task: *a rescue brigade*
WORD ORIGIN Old French
brigadier *n* a senior officer in an army, usually commanding a brigade
brigalow *n Austral* a type of acacia tree
WORD ORIGIN from a native Australian language
brigand *n* a bandit, esp. a member of a gang operating in mountainous areas
WORD ORIGIN Old French
brigantine *n* a two-masted sailing ship

THESAURUS

bribe *vb* **1 = buy off**, reward, pay off (*informal*), lure, corrupt, get at, square, suborn, grease the palm *or* hand of (*slang*), influence by gifts, oil the palm of (*informal*) ▷ *n* **2 = inducement**, incentive, pay-off (*informal*), graft (*informal*), sweetener (*slang*), kickback (*US*), sop, backhander (*slang*), enticement, hush money (*slang*), payola (*informal*), allurement, corrupting gift, reward for treachery
bridge[1] *n* **1 = arch**, span, viaduct, flyover, overpass, fixed link (*Canad*) ▷ *vb* **6 = span**, cross, go over, cross over, traverse, reach across, extend across, arch over **7 = reconcile**, unite, resolve **OPPOSITE:** divide
brief *adj* **1 = short**, fast, quick, temporary, fleeting, swift, short-lived, little, hasty, momentary, ephemeral, quickie (*informal*), transitory **OPPOSITE:** long ▷ *n* **4 = summary**, résumé, outline, sketch, abstract, summing-up, digest, epitome, rundown, synopsis, précis, recapitulation, abridgment ▷ *vb* **10 = inform**, prime, prepare, advise, fill in (*informal*), instruct, clue in (*informal*), gen up (*Brit informal*), put in the picture (*informal*), give a rundown, keep (someone) posted, give the gen (*Brit informal*)
brigade *n* **1 = corps**, company, force, unit, division, troop, squad, crew, team, outfit, regiment, contingent, squadron, detachment **2 = group**, party, body, band, camp, squad, organization, crew, bunch (*informal*)

b

DICTIONARY

WORD ORIGIN Old Italian *brigantino* pirate ship

Briggs *n* **Henry** 1561–1631, English mathematician: introduced common logarithms

Brighouse[1] *n* a town in N England, in Calderdale unitary authority, West Yorkshire: machine tools, textiles, engineering. Pop: 32 360 (2001)

Brighouse[2] *n* **Harold** 1882–1958, British novelist and dramatist, best known for his play *Hobson's Choice* (1915)

bright Ⓣ *adj* **1** emitting or reflecting much light; shining **2** (of colours) intense or vivid **3** full of promise: *a bright future* **4** lively or cheerful **5** quick-witted or clever ▷ *adv* **6** brightly: *the light burned bright in his office* **brightly** *adv* **brightness** *n*
WORD ORIGIN Old English *beorht*

Bright *n* **John** 1811–89, British liberal statesman, economist, and advocate of free trade: with Richard Cobden he led the Anti-Corn-Law League (1838–46)

brighten Ⓣ *vb* **1** to make or become bright or brighter **2** to make or become cheerful

Brigid *n* **Saint Brigid** ▸ See **Bridget** (sense 1)

brill *n, pl* **brill** *or* **brills** a European flatfish similar to the turbot
WORD ORIGIN probably Cornish *brȳthel* mackerel

Brillat-Savarin *n* **Anthelme** 1755–1826, French lawyer and gourmet; author of *Physiologie du Goût* (1825)

brilliance Ⓣ *or* **brilliancy** *n* **1** great brightness **2** excellence in physical or mental ability **3** splendour

brilliant Ⓣ *adj* **1** shining with light; sparkling **2** (of a colour) vivid **3** splendid; magnificent: *a brilliant show* **4** of outstanding intelligence or intellect ▷ *n* **5** a diamond cut with many facets to increase its sparkle
WORD ORIGIN French *brillant* shining

brilliantine *n* a perfumed oil used to make the hair smooth and shiny
WORD ORIGIN French

brim Ⓣ *n* **1** the upper rim of a cup, bowl, etc. **2** a projecting edge of a hat ▷ *vb* **brimming, brimmed 3** to be full to the brim: *he saw the tears that brimmed in her eyes* **brimless** *adj*
WORD ORIGIN Middle High German *brem*

brimful *adj* (foll. by *of*) completely filled with

brimstone *n obsolete* sulphur
WORD ORIGIN Old English *brynstān*

brindled *adj* brown or grey streaked with a darker colour: *a brindled dog*
WORD ORIGIN Middle English *brended*

Brindley *n* **James** 1716–72, British canal builder, who constructed (1759–61) the Bridgewater Canal, the first in England

brine *n* **1** a strong solution of salt and water, used for pickling **2** *literary* the sea or its water
WORD ORIGIN Old English *brīne*

bring Ⓣ *vb* **bringing, brought 1** to carry, convey, or take (something or someone) to a designated place or person **2** to cause to happen: *responsibility brings maturity* **3** to cause to come to mind: *it brought back memories* **4** to cause to be in a certain state, position, etc.: *the punch brought him to his knees* **5** to make (oneself): *she couldn't bring herself to do it* **6** to sell for: *the painting brought a large sum* **7** *law* **a** to institute (proceedings, charges, etc.) **b** to put (evidence, etc.) before a tribunal ▸ See also **bring about, bring down,** etc.
WORD ORIGIN Old English *bringan*

bring about Ⓣ *vb* to cause to happen: *a late harvest brought about by bad weather*

bring-and-buy sale *n Brit & NZ* an informal sale, often for charity, to which people bring items for sale and buy those that others have brought

bring down *vb* to cause to fall

bring forth *vb* to give birth to

bring forward *vb* **1** to move (a meeting or event) to an earlier date or time **2** to present or introduce (a subject) for discussion **3** *book-keeping* to transfer (a sum) to the top of the next page or column

bring in *vb* **1** to yield (income, profit, or cash) **2** to introduce (a legislative bill, etc.) **3** to return (a verdict)

bring off Ⓣ *vb* to succeed in achieving (something difficult)

bring out *vb* **1** to produce, publish, or have (a book) published **2** to expose, reveal, or cause to be seen: *he brought out the best in me* **3** (foll. by *in*) to cause (a person) to become covered with (a rash, spots, etc.)

bring over *vb* to cause (a person) to change allegiances

bring round *vb* **1** to restore (a person) to consciousness after a faint **2** to convince (another person) of an opinion or point of view

bring to *vb* to restore (a person) to consciousness: *the smelling salts brought her to*

bring up Ⓣ *vb* **1** to care for and train (a child); rear **2** to raise (a subject) for discussion; mention **3** to vomit (food)

brinjal *n S African & Indian* the aubergine, cooked and eaten as a vegetable
WORD ORIGIN Portuguese *berinjela*

brink Ⓣ *n* **1** the edge or border of a steep place **2** the land at the edge of

THESAURUS

bright *adj* **1 = shining**, flashing, beaming, glowing, blazing, sparkling, glittering, dazzling, illuminated, gleaming, shimmering, twinkling, radiant, luminous, glistening, resplendent, scintillating, lustrous, lambent, effulgent **2 = vivid**, rich, brilliant, intense, glowing, colourful, highly-coloured **5 = clever**, brilliant, smart, sensible, cunning, ingenious, inventive, canny

brighten *vb* **1 = light up**, shine, glow, gleam, clear up, lighten, enliven **OPPOSITE:** dim

brilliance *or* **brilliancy** *n* **1 = brightness**, blaze, intensity, sparkle, glitter, dazzle, gleam, sheen, lustre, radiance, luminosity, vividness, resplendence, effulgence, refulgence **OPPOSITE:** darkness **2 = cleverness**, talent, wisdom, distinction, genius, excellence, greatness, aptitude, inventiveness, acuity, giftedness, braininess **OPPOSITE:** stupidity **3 = splendour**, glamour, grandeur, magnificence, éclat, gorgeousness, illustriousness, pizzazz *or* pizazz (*informal*), gilt

brilliant *adj* **1 = bright**, shining, intense, sparkling, glittering, dazzling, vivid, radiant, luminous, ablaze, resplendent, scintillating, lustrous, coruscating, refulgent, lambent **OPPOSITE:** dark **3 = splendid**, grand, famous, celebrated, rare, supreme, outstanding, remarkable, superb, magnificent, sterling, glorious, exceptional, notable, renowned, heroic, admirable, eminent, sublime, illustrious **4 = intelligent**, sharp, intellectual, alert, clever, quick, acute, profound, rational, penetrating, discerning, inventive, astute, brainy, perspicacious, quick-witted **OPPOSITE:** stupid

brim *n* **1 = rim**, edge, border, lip, margin, verge, brink, flange ▷ *vb* **3 = be full**, spill, well over, run over, overflow, spill over, brim over

bring *vb* **1a = fetch**, take, carry, bear, transfer, deliver, transport, import, convey **1b = take**, guide, conduct, accompany, escort, usher **2, 4 = cause**, produce, create, effect, occasion, result in, contribute to, inflict, wreak, engender

bring about *vb* **= cause**, produce, create, effect, manage, achieve, occasion, realize, generate, accomplish, give rise to, make happen, effectuate, bring to pass

bring off *vb* **= accomplish**, achieve, perform, carry out, succeed, execute, discharge, pull off, carry off, bring to pass

bring up *vb* **= rear**, raise, support, train, develop, teach, nurse, breed, foster, educate, care for, nurture

brink *n* **1, 2 = edge**, point, limit,

DICTIONARY

a body of water **3 on the brink of** very near, on the point of: *on the brink of disaster*
WORD ORIGIN Middle Dutch *brinc*
brinkmanship *n* the practice of pressing a dangerous situation to the limit of safety in order to win an advantage
briny *adj* **brinier, briniest 1** of or like brine; salty ▹*n* **2 the briny** *informal* the sea
brio *n* liveliness; vigour
WORD ORIGIN Italian
briquette *n* a small brick made of compressed coal dust, used for fuel
WORD ORIGIN French
brisk ❶ *adj* **1** lively and quick; vigorous: *brisk trade* **2** invigorating or sharp: *brisk weather* **3** practical and businesslike: *his manner was brisk* **briskly** *adv*
WORD ORIGIN probably variant of BRUSQUE
brisket *n* beef from the breast of a cow
WORD ORIGIN probably Scandinavian
brisling *n* ▸same as **sprat**
WORD ORIGIN Norwegian
Brissot *n* **Jacques-Pierre** 1754–93, French journalist and revolutionary; leader of the Girondists: executed by the Jacobins
bristle ❶ *n* **1** any short stiff hair, such as on a pig's back **2** something resembling these hairs: *toothbrush bristle* ▹*vb* **-tling, -tled 3** to stand up or cause to stand up like bristles **4** to show anger or indignation: *she bristled at the suggestion* **5** to be thickly covered or set: *the hedges bristled with blossom* **bristly** *adj*
WORD ORIGIN Old English *byrst*
Bristow *n* **Eric** born 1957, British darts player
Brit *n informal* a British person
Brit. 1 Britain **2** British
Britannia *n* a female warrior carrying a trident and wearing a helmet, personifying Great Britain
Britannia metal *n* an alloy of tin with antimony and copper
Britannic *adj* of Britain; British: *Her Britannic Majesty*
britches *pl n* ▸same as **breeches**
British *adj* **1** of Britain or the British Commonwealth **2** denoting the English language as spoken and written in Britain ▹*pl n* **3 the British** the people of Britain
British Summer Time *n* a time set one hour ahead of Greenwich Mean Time: used in Britain from the end of March to the end of October, providing an extra hour of daylight in the evening. Abbrev: **BST**
Briton *n* **1** a native or inhabitant of Britain **2** *history* any of the early Celtic inhabitants of S Britain
WORD ORIGIN of Celtic origin
brittle ❶ *adj* **1** easily cracked or broken; fragile **2** curt or irritable: *a brittle reply* **3** hard or sharp in quality: *a brittle laugh* **brittly** *adv*
WORD ORIGIN Old English *brēotan* to break
broach *vb* **1** to initiate or introduce (a topic) for discussion **2** to tap or pierce (a container) to draw off (a liquid) **3** to open in order to begin to use ▹*n* **4** a spit for roasting meat
WORD ORIGIN Latin *brochus* projecting
broad ❶ *adj* **1** having great breadth or width **2** of vast extent: *broad plains* **3** not detailed; general **4** clear and open: *broad daylight* **5** obvious: *broad hints* **6** tolerant: *a broad view* **7** extensive: *broad support* **8** vulgar or coarse **9** strongly marked: *he spoke broad Australian English* ▹*n* **10** *slang chiefly US & Canad* a woman **11 the Broads** in East Anglia, a group of shallow lakes connected by a network of rivers **broadly** *adv*
WORD ORIGIN Old English *brād*
B-road *n* a secondary road in Britain
broadband *n* a telecommunications technique that uses a wide range of frequencies to allow messages to be sent simultaneously
broad bean *n* the large edible flattened seed of a Eurasian bean plant
broadcast ❶ *n* **1** a transmission or programme on radio or television ▹*vb* **-casting, -cast** *or* **-casted 2** to transmit (announcements or programmes) on radio or television **3** to take part in a radio or television programme **4** to make widely known throughout an area: *to broadcast news* **5** to scatter (seed, etc.) **broadcaster** *n* **broadcasting** *n*
broaden ❶ *vb* to make or become broad or broader; widen
broad gauge *n* a railway track with a greater distance between the lines than the standard gauge of 56½ inches
broad-leaved *adj* denoting trees other than conifers; having broad rather than needle-shaped leaves
broadloom *adj* of or designating carpets woven on a wide loom
broad-minded *adj* **1** tolerant of opposing viewpoints; liberal **2** not easily shocked
broadsheet *n* a newspaper in a large format
broadside *n* **1** a strong or abusive verbal or written attack **2** *naval* the simultaneous firing of all the guns on one side of a ship **3** *naut* the entire side of a ship ▹*adv* **4** with a broader side facing an object
broadsword *n* a broad-bladed sword used for cutting rather than stabbing
brocade *n* **1** a rich fabric woven with a raised design ▹*vb* **-cading, -caded 2** to weave with such a design
WORD ORIGIN Spanish *brocado*
broccoli *n* a variety of cabbage with greenish flower heads
WORD ORIGIN Italian
brochette (brosh-ett) *n* a skewer used for holding pieces of meat or vegetables while grilling
WORD ORIGIN Old French *brochete*

THESAURUS

border, lip, margin, boundary, skirt, frontier, fringe, verge, threshold, rim, brim
brisk *adj* **1 = quick**, lively, energetic, active, vigorous, animated, bustling, speedy, nimble, agile, sprightly, vivacious, spry **OPPOSITE:** slow **3 = short**, sharp, brief, blunt, rude, tart, abrupt, no-nonsense, terse, gruff, pithy, brusque, offhand, monosyllabic, ungracious, uncivil, snappish
bristle *n* **1 = hair**, spine, thorn, whisker, barb, stubble, prickle ▹*vb* **3 = stand up**, rise, prickle, stand on end, horripilate **4 = be angry**, rage, seethe, flare up, bridle, see red, be infuriated, spit *(informal)*, go ballistic *(slang, chiefly US)*, be maddened, wig out *(slang)*, get your dander up *(slang)*
brittle *adj* **1 = fragile**, delicate, crisp, crumbling, frail, crumbly, breakable, shivery, friable, frangible, shatterable **OPPOSITE:** tough
broad *adj* **1 = wide**, large, ample, generous, expansive **2 = large**, huge, comfortable, vast, extensive, ample, spacious, expansive, roomy, voluminous, capacious, uncrowded, commodious, beamy *(of a ship)*, sizable *or* sizeable **OPPOSITE:** narrow **3 = general**, loose, vague, approximate, indefinite, ill-defined, inexact, nonspecific, unspecific, undetailed **7 = full**, general, comprehensive, complete, wide, global, catholic, sweeping, extensive, wide-ranging, umbrella, thorough, unlimited, inclusive, far-reaching, exhaustive, all-inclusive, all-embracing, overarching, encyclopedic
broadcast *n* **1 = transmission**, show, programme, telecast, podcast ▹*vb* **2 = transmit**, show, send, air, radio, cable, beam, send out, relay, televise, disseminate, put on the air, podcast, open-line *(Canad)* **4 = make public**, report, announce, publish, spread, advertise, proclaim, circulate, disseminate, promulgate, shout from the rooftops *(informal)*
broaden *vb* **= expand**, increase, develop, spread, extend, stretch, open up, swell, supplement, widen, enlarge, augment **OPPOSITE:** restrict

b

DICTIONARY

brochure ❶ *n* a pamphlet or booklet, esp. one containing introductory information or advertising
WORD ORIGIN French

broderie anglaise *n* open embroidery on white cotton, fine linen, etc.
WORD ORIGIN French: English embroidery

Brodsky *n* **Joseph**, original name *Iosif Aleksandrovich Brodsky*. 1940–96, US poet, born in the Soviet Union. His collections include *The End of a Beautiful Era* (1977). Nobel prize for literature 1987

broekies ❶ (brook-eez) *pl n S African informal* underpants
WORD ORIGIN Afrikaans

brogue[1] *n* a sturdy walking shoe, often with ornamental perforations
WORD ORIGIN Irish Gaelic *bróg*

brogue[2] *n* a broad gentle-sounding dialectal accent, esp. that used by the Irish in speaking English
WORD ORIGIN origin unknown

broil *vb* ▸ same as **grill** (sense 1)
WORD ORIGIN Old French *bruillir*

broiler *n* a young tender chicken suitable for roasting

broke ❶ *vb* **1** ▸ the past tense of **break** ▹ *adj* **2** *informal* having no money

broken ❶ *vb* **1** ▸ the past participle of **break** ▹ *adj* **2** fractured, smashed, or splintered **3** interrupted; disturbed: *broken sleep* **4** not functioning **5** (of a promise or contract) violated; infringed **6** (of the speech of a foreigner) imperfectly spoken: *broken English* **7** Also: **broken-in** made tame by training **8** exhausted or weakened, as through ill-health or misfortune

broken chord *n* ▸ same as **arpeggio**

broken-down *adj* **1** worn out, as by age or long use; dilapidated **2** not in working order

brokenhearted *adj* overwhelmed by grief or disappointment

broken home *n* a family which does not live together because the parents are separated or divorced

broker ❶ *n* **1** an agent who buys or sells goods, securities, etc.: *insurance broker* **2** a person who deals in second-hand goods
WORD ORIGIN Anglo-French *brocour* broacher

brokerage *n* commission charged by a broker

broker-dealer *n* ▸ same as **stockbroker**

brolga *n* a large grey Australian crane with a trumpeting call. Also called: **native companion**

brolly *n, pl* **-lies** *Brit, Austral & NZ informal* an umbrella

bromide *n* **1** *chem* any compound of bromine with another element or radical **2** a dose of sodium or potassium bromide given as a sedative **3** a boring, meaningless, or obvious remark

bromide paper *n* a type of photographic paper coated with an emulsion of silver bromide

bromine *n chem* a dark red liquid chemical element that gives off a pungent vapour. Symbol: Br
WORD ORIGIN Greek *brōmos* bad smell

bronchial *adj* of or relating to both of the bronchi or the smaller tubes into which they divide

bronchiole *n* any of the smallest bronchial tubes

bronchitis *n* inflammation of the bronchial tubes, causing coughing and difficulty in breathing

bronchus (bronk-uss) *n, pl* **bronchi** (bronk-eye) either of the two main branches of the windpipe
WORD ORIGIN Greek *bronkhos*

bronco *n, pl* **-cos** (in the US and Canada) a wild or partially tamed horse
WORD ORIGIN Mexican Spanish

brontosaurus *n* a very large plant-eating four-footed dinosaur that had a long neck and long tail
WORD ORIGIN Greek *brontē* thunder + *sauros* lizard

bronze ❶ *n* **1** an alloy of copper and smaller proportions of tin **2** a statue, medal, or other object made of bronze ▹ *adj* **3** made of or resembling bronze **4** yellowish-brown ▹ *vb* **bronzing, bronzed 5** (esp. of the skin) to make or become brown; tan
WORD ORIGIN Italian *bronzo*

Bronze Age *n* a phase of human culture, lasting in Britain from about 2000 to 500 BC during which weapons and tools were made of bronze

bronze medal *n* a medal awarded as third prize

Bronzino *n* **Il**, real name *Agnolo di Cosimo*. 1503–72, Florentine mannerist painter

brooch *n* an ornament with a hinged pin and catch, worn fastened to clothing
WORD ORIGIN Old French *broche*

brood ❶ *n* **1** a number of young animals, esp. birds, produced at one hatching **2** all the children in a family: often used jokingly ▹ *vb* **3** (of a bird) to sit on or hatch eggs **4** to think long and unhappily about something: *he brooded on his failure to avert the confrontation* **brooding** *n, adj*
WORD ORIGIN Old English *brōd*

broody *adj* **broodier, broodiest 1** moody; introspective **2** (of poultry) wishing to sit on or hatch eggs **3** *informal* (of a woman) wishing to have a baby

brook[1] ❶ *n* a natural freshwater stream
WORD ORIGIN Old English *brōc*

brook[2] *vb* to bear; tolerate: *she would brook no opposition*
WORD ORIGIN Old English *brūcan*

Brook *n* **Peter** (**Paul Stephen**) born 1925, British stage and film director, noted esp.for his experimental work in the theatre

Brooke *n* **1 Alan Francis** ▸ See **Alanbrooke 2** Sir **James** 1803–68, British soldier; first rajah of Sarawak (1841–63) **3 Rupert** (**Chawner**) 1887–1915, British lyric poet, noted for his idealistic war poetry, which

THESAURUS

brochure *n* **= booklet**, advertisement, leaflet, hand-out, circular, pamphlet, folder, mailshot, handbill

broekies *pl n* (*S African informal*) **= underpants**, pants, briefs, drawers, knickers, panties, boxer shorts, Y-fronts®, underdaks (*Austral slang*)

broke *adj* **2** (*informal*) **= penniless**, short, ruined, bust (*informal*), bankrupt, impoverished, in the red, cleaned out (*slang*), insolvent, down and out, skint (*Brit slang*), strapped for cash (*informal*), dirt-poor (*informal*), flat broke (*informal*), penurious, on your uppers, stony-broke (*Brit slang*), in queer street (*informal*), without two pennies to rub together (*informal*), without a penny to your name **OPPOSITE:** rich

broken *adj* **2 = smashed**, destroyed, burst, shattered, fragmented, fractured, demolished, severed, ruptured, rent, separated, shivered **3 = interrupted**, disturbed, incomplete, erratic, disconnected, intermittent, fragmentary, spasmodic, discontinuous **4 = defective**, not working, ruined, imperfect, out of order, not functioning, on the blink (*slang*), on its last legs, kaput (*informal*) **6 = imperfect**, halting, hesitating, stammering, disjointed

broker *n* **1, 2 = dealer**, marketer, agent, trader, supplier, merchant, entrepreneur, negotiator, chandler, mediator, intermediary, wholesaler, middleman, factor, purveyor, go-between, tradesman, merchandiser

bronze *adj* **4 = reddish-brown**, copper, tan, rust, chestnut, brownish, copper-coloured, yellowish-brown, reddish-tan, metallic brownsee:

brood *n* **1 = offspring**, young, issue, breed, infants, clutch, hatch, litter, chicks, progeny **2 = children**, family, offspring, progeny, nearest and dearest, flesh and blood, ainga (*NZ*) ▹ *vb* **4 = think**, obsess, muse, ponder, fret, meditate, agonize, mull over, mope, ruminate, eat your heart out, dwell upon, repine

brook[1] *n* **= stream**, burn (*Scot & Northern English*), rivulet, gill (*dialect*), beck, watercourse, rill, streamlet, runnel (*literary*)

made him a national hero
Brookner *n* **Anita** born 1928, British writer and art historian. Her novels include *Hotel du Lac* (1984), which won the Booker Prize, *Brief Lives* (1990), and *The Next Big Thing* (2002)
Brooks *n* **1 Geraldine** born 1955, Australian writer. Her novels include *March* (2005), which won the Pulitzer prize **2 Mel**, real name *Melvyn Kaminsky*. born 1926, US comedy writer, actor, and film director. His films include *The Producers* (1968), *Blazing Saddles* (1974), *High Anxiety* (1977), and *Dracula: Dead and Loving It* (1996) **3 (Troyal) Garth** born 1962, US country singer and songwriter; his bestselling records include *Ropin' the Wind* (1991) and *Scarecrow* (2001)
broom *n* **1** a type of long-handled sweeping brush **2** a yellow-flowered shrub **3 a new broom** a newly appointed official, etc. eager to make radical changes
WORD ORIGIN Old English *brōm*
broomstick *n* the long handle of a broom
Broonzy *n* **William Lee Conley**, called *Big Bill*. 1893–1958, US blues singer and guitarist
bros. *or* **Bros.** brothers
broth *n* a soup made by boiling meat, vegetables, etc. in water
WORD ORIGIN Old English
brothel *n* a house where men pay to have sexual intercourse with prostitutes
WORD ORIGIN short for *brothel-house*, from Middle English *brothel* useless person
brother **T** *n* **1** a man or boy with the same parents as another person ▸ Related adjective: **fraternal** **2** a man belonging to the same group, trade union, etc. as another or others; fellow member **3** comrade; friend **4** *Christianity* a member of a male religious order
WORD ORIGIN Old English *brōthor*
brotherhood *n* **1** fellowship **2** an association, such as a trade union **3** the state of being a brother
brother-in-law *n, pl* **brothers-in-law** **1** the brother of one's wife or husband **2** the husband of one's sister
brotherly **T** *adj* of or like a brother, esp. in showing loyalty and affection
brougham (brew-am) *n* a horse-drawn closed carriage with a raised open driver's seat in front
WORD ORIGIN after Lord *Brougham*
brought *vb* ▸ the past of **bring**
brouhaha *n* loud confused noise
WORD ORIGIN French
brow *n* **1** the part of the face from the eyes to the hairline; forehead **2** ▸ same as **eyebrow** **3** the jutting top of a hill
WORD ORIGIN Old English *brū*
browbeat *vb* **-beating, -beat, -beaten** to frighten (someone) with threats
brown **T** *adj* **1** of the colour of wood or the earth **2** (of bread) made from wheatmeal or wholemeal flour **3** deeply tanned ▹ *n* **4** the colour of wood or the earth **5** anything brown, such as brown paint or brown clothing: *clad in brown* ▹ *vb* **6** to make or become brown or browner, for example as a result of cooking **brownish** *adj*
WORD ORIGIN Old English *brūn*
brown bear *n* a large ferocious brownish bear of N America, Europe and Asia
brown coal *n* ▸ same as **lignite**
Browne *n* **1 Coral (Edith)** 1913–91, Australian actress: married to Vincent Price **2 Hablot Knight** ▸ See **Phiz** **3** Sir **Thomas** 1605–82, English physician and author, noted for his magniloquent prose style. His works include *Religio Medici* (1642) and *Hydriotaphia or Urn Burial* (1658)
browned-off *adj informal chiefly Brit* thoroughly bored and depressed
brownfield *adj* relating to an urban area which has previously been built on: *brownfield sites*
Brownian motion *n physics* the random movement of particles in a fluid, caused by continuous bombardment from molecules of the fluid
WORD ORIGIN after Robert *Brown*, physicist
brownie *n* **1** (in folklore) an elf said to do helpful work, esp. household chores, at night **2** a small square nutty chocolate cake
Brownie Guide *or* **Brownie** *n* a member of the junior branch of the Guides
Brownie point *n* a notional mark to one's credit for being seen to do the right thing
browning *n Brit* a substance used to darken gravies
brown paper *n* a kind of coarse unbleached paper used for wrapping
brown rice *n* unpolished rice, in which the grains retain the outer yellowish-brown layer (bran)
Brown Shirt *n* **1** (in Nazi Germany) a storm trooper **2** a member of any fascist party or group
brown trout *n* a common brownish trout
browse **T** *vb* **browsing, browsed** **1** to look through (a book or articles for sale) in a casual leisurely manner **2** *computers* to read hypertext, esp. on the World Wide Web **3** (of deer, goats, etc.) to feed upon vegetation by continual nibbling ▹ *n* **4** an instance of browsing
WORD ORIGIN French *broust* bud
browser *n computers* a software package that enables a user to read hypertext, esp. on the World Wide Web
Broz *n* **Josip**. original name of Marshal Tito ▸ See **Tito**
Brubeck *n* **Dave** born 1920, US modern jazz pianist and composer; formed his own quartet in 1951
brucellosis *n* an infectious disease of cattle, goats, and pigs, caused by bacteria and transmittable to humans
WORD ORIGIN after Sir David *Bruce*, bacteriologist
Bruch *n* **Max** 1838–1920, German composer, noted chiefly for his three violin concertos
Bruckner *n* **Anton** 1824–96, Austrian composer and organist in the Romantic tradition. His works include nine symphonies, four masses, and a Te Deum
Brudenell *n* **James Thomas**, the 7th Earl of Cardigan ▸ See **Cardigan**
bruise **T** *vb* **bruising, bruised** **1** to injure (body tissue) without breaking the skin, usually with discoloration, or (of body tissue) to be injured in this way **2** to hurt (someone's feelings) **3** to damage (fruit) ▹ *n* **4** a bodily injury without a break in the skin, usually with discoloration
WORD ORIGIN Old English *brȳsan*
bruiser *n informal* a strong tough person, esp. a boxer or a bully
brumby *n, pl* **-bies** *Austral* **1** a wild horse **2** an unruly person
WORD ORIGIN origin unknown
Brummell *n* **George Bryan**, called *Beau Brummell*. 1778–1840, English

THESAURUS

brother *n* **1 = male sibling** **4 = monk**, cleric, friar, monastic, religious, regular ▸ *related adjective:* fraternal
brotherly *adj* **= fraternal**, friendly, neighbourly, sympathetic, affectionate, benevolent, kind, amicable, altruistic, philanthropic
brown *adj* **1 = brunette**, dark, bay, coffee, chocolate, brick, toasted, ginger, rust, chestnut, hazel, dun, auburn, tawny, umber, donkey brown, fuscous **3 = tanned**, browned, bronze, bronzed, tan, dusky, sunburnt ▹ *vb* **6 = fry**, cook, grill, sear, sauté
browse *vb* **1 = skim**, scan, glance at, survey, look through, look round, dip into, leaf through, peruse, flip through, examine cursorily **3 = graze**, eat, feed, crop, pasture, nibble
bruise *vb* **1 = hurt**, injure, mark, blacken **3 = damage**, mark, mar, blemish, discolour ▹ *n* **4 = discoloration**, mark, injury, trauma *(pathology)*, blemish, black mark, contusion, black-and-blue

DICTIONARY

dandy: leader of fashion in the Regency period

brunch *n* a meal eaten late in the morning, combining breakfast with lunch
WORD ORIGIN BR(EAKFAST) + (L)UNCH

Brunelleschi *n* **Filippo** 1377–1446, Italian architect, whose works in Florence include the dome of the cathedral, the Pazzi chapel of Santa Croce, and the church of San Lorenzo

brunette *n* a girl or woman with dark brown hair
WORD ORIGIN French

Brüning *n* **Heinrich.** 1885–1970, German statesman; chancellor (1930–32). He was forced to resign in 1932, making way for the Nazis

Bruno *n* **1 Franklin Roy**, known as *Frank.* born 1961, British heavyweight boxer **2 Giordano** 1548–1600, Italian philosopher, who developed a pantheistic monistic philosophy: he was burnt at the stake for heresy

brunt *n* the main force or shock of a blow, attack, etc.: *the town bore the brunt of the earthquake*

bruschetta (broo-**sket**-ta) *n* an Italian open sandwich of toasted bread topped with olive oil and tomatoes, olives, etc.
WORD ORIGIN Italian

brush¹ ⊙ *n* **1** a device made of bristles, hairs, wires, etc. set into a firm back or handle: used to apply paint, groom the hair, etc. **2** the act of brushing **3** a brief encounter, esp. an unfriendly one **4** the bushy tail of a fox **5** an electric conductor, esp. one made of carbon, that conveys current between stationary and rotating parts of a generator, motor, etc. ▷ *vb* **6** to clean, scrub, or paint with a brush **7** to apply or remove with a brush or brushing movement **8** to touch lightly and briefly ▸ See also **brush aside, brush off, brush up**
WORD ORIGIN Old French *broisse*

brush² ⊙ *n* a thick growth of shrubs and small trees; scrub
WORD ORIGIN Old French *broce*

brush aside *or* **away** *vb* to dismiss (a suggestion or an idea) without consideration; disregard

brushed *adj textiles* treated with a brushing process to raise the nap and give a softer and warmer finish: *brushed nylon*

brush off ⊙ *slang vb* **1** to dismiss and ignore (a person), esp. curtly ▷ *n* **brushoff 2 give someone the brushoff** to reject someone

brush turkey *n* a bird of New Guinea and Australia resembling the domestic fowl, with black plumage

brush up ⊙ *vb* **1** (often foll. by *on*) to refresh one's knowledge or memory of (a subject) ▷ *n* **brush-up 2** *Brit* the act of tidying one's appearance: *have a wash and brush-up*

brushwood *n* **1** cut or broken-off tree branches, twigs, etc. **2** ▸ same as **brush²**

brushwork *n* a characteristic manner of applying paint with a brush: *Rembrandt's brushwork*

brusque *adj* blunt or curt in manner or speech **brusquely** *adv* **brusqueness** *n*
WORD ORIGIN Italian *brusco* sour

Brussels sprout *n* a vegetable like a tiny cabbage

brut (broot) *adj* (of champagne or sparkling wine) very dry

brutal ⊙ *adj* **1** cruel; vicious; savage **2** harsh or severe **3** extremely honest or frank in speech or manner **brutality** *n* **brutally** *adv*

brutalism *n* an austere architectural style of the 1950s on, characterized by the use of exposed concrete and angular shapes

brutalize *or* **-ise** *vb* **-izing, -ized** *or* **-ising, -ised 1** to make or become brutal **2** to treat (someone) brutally **brutalization** *or* **-isation** *n*

brute *n* **1** a brutal person **2** any animal except man; beast ▷ *adj* **3** wholly instinctive or physical, like that of an animal: *cricket is not a game of brute force* **4** without reason or intelligence **5** coarse and grossly sensual
WORD ORIGIN Latin *brutus* irrational

brutish *adj* **1** of or resembling a brute; animal **2** coarse; cruel; stupid

Bruton *n* **John Gerard** born 1947, Irish politician: leader of the Fine Gael party (1990–2001); prime minister of the Republic of Ireland (1994–97)

Bryant *n* **David** born 1931, British bowler; many times world champion

bryony *n, pl* **-nies** a herbaceous climbing plant with greenish flowers and red or black berries
WORD ORIGIN Greek *bruōnia*

Brythonic (brith-on-ik) *n* **1** the S group of Celtic languages, consisting of Welsh, Cornish, and Breton ▷ *adj* **2** of this group of languages
WORD ORIGIN Welsh *Brython* Celt

BS **1** Bachelor of Surgery **2** British Standard(s)

BSc Bachelor of Science

BSE bovine spongiform encephalopathy: a fatal virus disease of cattle

BSI British Standards Institution

B-side *n* the less important side of a gramophone record

BSL British Sign Language

BST British Summer Time

Bt Baronet

BT British Telecom

btu *or* **BThU** British thermal unit

bubble ⊙ *n* **1** a small globule of air or a gas in a liquid or a solid **2** a thin film of liquid forming a ball around air or a gas: *a soap bubble* **3** a dome, esp. a transparent glass or plastic one **4** an unreliable scheme or enterprise ▷ *vb* **-bling, -bled 5** to form bubbles **6** to move or flow with a gurgling sound **7 bubble over** to express an emotion freely: *she was bubbling over with excitement*
WORD ORIGIN probably Scandinavian

bubble and squeak *n Brit, Austral & NZ* a dish of boiled cabbage and potatoes fried together

bubble bath *n* **1** a substance used to scent, soften, and foam in bath water **2** a bath with such a substance

bubble car *n Brit* a small car of the 1950s with a transparent bubble-shaped top

bubble gum *n* a type of chewing gum that can be blown into large bubbles

bubble wrap *n* a type of polythene wrapping containing many small air pockets, used to protect breakable goods

bubbly ⊙ *adj* **-blier, -bliest 1** lively;

THESAURUS

mark

brush¹ *n* **1 = broom**, sweeper, besom **3 = encounter**, meeting, confrontation, rendezvous ▷ *vb* **6 = clean**, wash, polish, buff **8 = touch**, come into contact with, sweep, kiss, stroke, glance, flick, scrape, graze, caress

brush² *n* **= shrubs**, bushes, scrub, underwood, undergrowth, thicket, copse, brushwood

brush off *vb (slang)* **1 = ignore**, cut, reject, dismiss, slight, blank *(slang)*, put down, snub, disregard, scorn, disdain, spurn, rebuff, repudiate, disown, cold-shoulder, kiss off *(slang, chiefly US & Canad)*, send to Coventry

brush up *or* **brush up on** *vb* **1 = revise**, study, go over, cram, polish up, read up on, relearn, bone up on *(informal)*, refresh your memory

brutal *adj* **1 = cruel**, harsh, savage, grim, vicious, ruthless, ferocious, callous, sadistic, heartless, atrocious, inhuman, merciless, cold-blooded, inhumane, brutish, bloodthirsty, remorseless, barbarous, pitiless, uncivilized, hard-hearted
OPPOSITE: kind
2 = harsh, tough, severe, rough, rude, indifferent, insensitive, callous, merciless, unconcerned, uncaring, gruff, bearish, tactless, unfeeling, impolite, uncivil, unmannerly
OPPOSITE: sensitive

bubble *n* **1 = air ball**, drop, bead, blister, blob, droplet, globule, vesicle ▷ *vb* **5 = foam**, fizz, froth, churn, agitate, percolate, effervesce **6 = gurgle**, splash, murmur, trickle, ripple, babble, trill, burble, lap, purl, plash

DICTIONARY

animated; excited **2** full of or resembling bubbles ▹*n* **3** *informal* champagne

Buber *n* **Martin** 1878–1965, Jewish theologian, existentialist philosopher, and scholar of Hasidism, born in Austria, whose works include *I and Thou* (1923), *Between Man and Man* (1946), and *Eclipse of God* (1952)

bubo (byew-boh) *n, pl* **-boes** *pathol* inflammation and swelling of a lymph node, esp. in the armpit or groin **bubonic** (bew-bonn-ik) *adj*
WORD ORIGIN Greek *boubōn* groin

bubonic plague *n* an acute infectious disease characterized by the formation of buboes

buccaneer *n* a pirate, esp. in the Caribbean in the 17th and 18th centuries
WORD ORIGIN French *boucanier*

Buchner *n* **Eduard** 1860–1917, German chemist who demonstrated that alcoholic fermentation is due to enzymes in the yeast: Nobel prize for chemistry 1907

Büchner *n* **Georg** 1813–37, German dramatist; regarded as a forerunner of the Expressionists: author of *Danton's Death* (1835) and *Woyzeck* (1837)

buck[1] *n* **1** the male of the goat, hare, kangaroo, rabbit, and reindeer **2** *archaic* a spirited young man **3** the act of bucking ▹*vb* **4** (of a horse or other animal) to jump vertically, with legs stiff and back arched **5** (of a horse, etc.) to throw (its rider) by bucking **6** *informal* to resist or oppose obstinately: *bucking the system* ▸See also **buck up**
WORD ORIGIN Old English *bucca* he-goat

buck[2] *n US, Canad, Austral & NZ informal* a dollar
WORD ORIGIN origin unknown

buck[3] *n* **pass the buck** *informal* to shift blame or responsibility onto another
WORD ORIGIN probably from *buckhorn knife*, placed before a player in poker to indicate that he was the next dealer

Buck *n* **Pearl S(ydenstricker)** 1892–1973, US novelist, noted particularly for her novel of Chinese life *The Good Earth* (1931): Nobel prize for literature 1938

bucket *n* **1** an open-topped cylindrical container with a handle **2** the amount a bucket will hold **3** a bucket-like part of a machine, such as the scoop on a mechanical shovel **4** **kick the bucket** *slang* to die ▹*vb* **-eting, -eted** **5** (often foll. by *down*) (of rain) to fall very heavily
WORD ORIGIN Old English *būc*

bucket shop *n* **1** *chiefly Brit* a travel agency specializing in cheap airline tickets **2** an unregistered firm of stockbrokers that engages in fraudulent speculation

Buckingham[1] *n* a town in S central England, in Buckinghamshire; university (1975). Pop: 12 512 (2001)

Buckingham[2] *n* **1** **George Villiers, 1st Duke of** 1592–1628, English courtier and statesman; favourite of James I and Charles I: his arrogance, military incompetence, and greed increased the tensions between the King and Parliament that eventually led to the Civil War **2** his son, **George Villiers, 2nd Duke of** 1628–87, English courtier and writer; chief minister of Charles II and member of the Cabal (1667–73)

Buckland *n* **William** 1784–1856, English geologist; he became a proponent of the idea of catastrophic ice ages

buckle ❶ *n* **1** a clasp for fastening together two loose ends, esp. of a belt or strap ▹*vb* **-ling, -led** **2** to fasten or be fastened with a buckle **3** to bend or cause to bend out of shape, esp. as a result of pressure or heat
WORD ORIGIN Latin *buccula* cheek strap

buckle down *vb informal* to apply oneself with determination

buckler *n* a small round shield worn on the forearm
WORD ORIGIN Old French *bocler*

Bucks Buckinghamshire

buckshee *adj Brit slang* without charge; free
WORD ORIGIN from BAKSHEESH

buckshot *n* large lead pellets used for hunting game

buckskin *n* **1** a strong greyish-yellow suede leather, originally made from deerskin **2** **buckskins** trousers made of buckskin

buckteeth *pl n* projecting upper front teeth **buck-toothed** *adj*

buckthorn *n* a thorny shrub whose berries were formerly used as a purgative

buck up *vb informal* **1** to make or become more cheerful or confident **2** to make haste

buckwheat *n* **1** a type of small black seed used as animal fodder and in making flour **2** the flour obtained from such seeds
WORD ORIGIN Middle Dutch *boecweite*

bucolic (byew-koll-ik) *adj* **1** of the countryside or country life; rustic **2** of or relating to shepherds; pastoral ▹*n* **3** a pastoral poem
WORD ORIGIN Greek *boukolos* cowherd

bud ❶ *n* **1** a swelling on the stem of a plant that develops into a flower or leaf **2** a partially opened flower: *rosebud* **3** any small budlike outgrowth: *taste buds* **4** **nip something in the bud** to put an end to something in its initial stages ▹*vb* **budding, budded** **5** (of plants and some animals) to produce buds **6** *horticulture* to graft (a bud) from one plant onto another
WORD ORIGIN Middle English *budde*

Buddhism *n* a religion founded by the Buddha that teaches that all suffering can be brought to an end by overcoming greed, hatred, and delusion **Buddhist** *n, adj*

budding ❶ *adj* beginning to develop or grow: *a budding actor*

buddleia *n* a shrub which has long spikes of purple flowers
WORD ORIGIN after A. *Buddle*, botanist

buddy *n, pl* **-dies** **1** *chiefly US & Canad informal* a friend **2** a volunteer who helps and supports a person suffering from AIDS ▹*vb* **-dies, -dying, -died** **3** to act as a buddy to (a person suffering from AIDS)
WORD ORIGIN probably variant of BROTHER

budge ❶ *vb* **budging, budged** **1** to move slightly: *he refuses to budge off that chair* **2** to change or cause to change opinions: *nothing would budge him from this idea*
WORD ORIGIN Old French *bouger*

Budge *n* **Don(ald)** 1915–2000, US tennis player, the first man to win the Grand Slam of singles championships (Australia, France, Wimbledon, and the US) in one year (1938)

budgerigar *n* a small cage bird bred in many different-coloured varieties
WORD ORIGIN Aboriginal

budget ❶ *n* **1** a plan of expected income and expenditure over a specified period **2** the total amount of money allocated for a specific

THESAURUS

bubbly *adj* **1 = lively**, happy, excited, animated, merry, bouncy, elated, sparky, alive and kicking, full of beans *(informal)* **2 = frothy**, sparkling, fizzy, effervescent, carbonated, foamy, sudsy, lathery

buckle *n* **1 = fastener**, catch, clip, clasp, hasp ▹*vb* **2 = fasten**, close, secure, hook, clasp **3a = distort**, bend, warp, crumple, contort **3b = collapse**, bend, twist, fold, give way, subside, cave in, crumple

bud *n* **1 = shoot**, branch, sprout, twig, sprig, offshoot, scion

budding *adj* **= developing**, beginning, growing, promising, potential, burgeoning, fledgling, embryonic

budge *vb* **1a = move**, roll, slide, stir, give way, change position **1b = dislodge**, move, push, roll, remove, transfer, shift, slide, stir, propel

budget *n* **2 = allowance**, means, funds, income, finances, resources,

DICTIONARY

purpose during a specified period ▹ *adj* **3** inexpensive: *a budget hotel* ▹ *vb* **-eting, -eted 4** to enter or provide for in a budget **5** to plan the expenditure of (money or time) **budgetary** *adj*
WORD ORIGIN Latin *bulga* leather pouch

Budget *n* **the Budget** an annual estimate of British government expenditures and revenues and the financial plans for the following financial year

budget deficit *n* the amount by which government spending exceeds income from taxation, etc.

budgie *n informal* ▸ same as **budgerigar**

buff[1] ⓣ *n* **1** a soft thick flexible undyed leather **2** a cloth or pad of material used for polishing **3 in the buff** *informal* completely naked ▹ *adj* **4** dull yellowish-brown **5** *informal* in a condition of high physical fitness and body tone ▹ *vb* **6** to clean or polish (a metal, floor, shoes, etc.) with a buff
WORD ORIGIN Late Latin *bufalus* buffalo

buff[2] ⓣ *n informal* an expert on or devotee of a given subject: *an opera buff*
WORD ORIGIN from the buff-coloured uniforms worn by volunteer firemen in New York City

buffalo *n, pl* **-loes** *or* **-lo 1** a type of cattle with upward-curving horns **2** ▸ same as **water buffalo 3** *US & Canad* a bison
WORD ORIGIN Greek *bous* ox

Buffalo Bill *n* nickname of *William Frederick Cody*. 1846–1917, US showman who toured Europe and the US with his famous *Wild West Show*

buffer[1] ⓣ *n* **1** one of a pair of spring-loaded steel pads at the ends of railway vehicles and railway tracks that reduces shock on impact **2** a person or thing that lessens shock or protects from damaging impact, circumstances, etc. **3** *chem* **a** a substance added to a solution to resist changes in its acidity or alkalinity **b** Also called: **buffer solution** a solution containing such a substance **4** *computers* a device for temporarily storing data ▹ *vb* **5** to cushion; provide a buffer for
WORD ORIGIN from BUFFET[2]

buffer[2] *n Brit informal* a stupid or bumbling person, esp. a man: *an old buffer*
WORD ORIGIN origin unknown

buffer state *n* a small and usually neutral state between two rival powers

buffet[1] ⓣ (boof-fay, buff-ay) *n* **1** a counter where light refreshments are served **2** a meal at which guests help themselves from a number of dishes
WORD ORIGIN French

buffet[2] (buff-it) *vb* **-feting, -feted 1** to knock against or about; batter: *the ship was buffeted by strong winds* **2** to hit, esp. with the fist ▹ *n* **3** a blow, esp. with a hand
WORD ORIGIN Old French *buffeter*

Buffet *n* **Bernard** 1928–99, French painter and engraver. His works are characterized by sombre tones and thin angular forms

buffet car (boof-fay) *n Brit* a railway coach where light refreshments are served

Buffett *n* **Warren** (**Edward**) born 1930, US financier and philanthropist

Buffon *n* **Georges Louis Leclerc, Comte de** 1707–88, French encyclopedist of natural history; principal author of *Histoire naturelle* (36 vols., 1749–89), containing the *Époques de la nature* (1777), which foreshadowed later theories of evolution

buffoon *n* a person who amuses others by silly behaviour **buffoonery** *n*
WORD ORIGIN Latin *bufo* toad

bug ⓣ *n* **1** any of various insects having piercing and sucking mouthparts **2** *chiefly US & Canad* any insect **3** *informal* a minor illness caused by a germ or virus **4** *informal* a small error, esp. in a computer or computer program **5** *informal* an obsessive idea or hobby **6** *informal* a concealed microphone used for recording conversations in spying **7** *Austral* a flattish edible shellfish ▹ *vb* **bugging, bugged** *informal* **8** to irritate or upset (someone) **9** to conceal a microphone in (a room or telephone)
WORD ORIGIN origin unknown

Bugatti *n* **Ettore** (**Arco Isidoro**) 1881–1947, Italian car manufacturer; founder of the Bugatti car factory at Molsheim (1909)

bugbear *n* a thing that causes obsessive anxiety
WORD ORIGIN obsolete *bug* an evil spirit + BEAR[2]

bugger *n* **1** *taboo slang* a person or thing considered to be unpleasant or difficult **2** *slang* a humorous or affectionate term for someone: *a friendly little bugger* **3** a person who practises buggery ▹ *vb* **4** *slang* to tire; weary **5** to practise buggery with ▹ *interj* **6** *taboo slang* an exclamation of annoyance or disappointment
WORD ORIGIN Medieval Latin *Bulgarus* Bulgarian heretic

bugger about *or* **around** *vb slang* **1** to fool about and waste time **2** to create difficulties for: *they really buggered me about when I tried to get my money back*

bugger off *vb taboo slang* to go away; depart

bugger up *vb slang* to spoil or ruin (something)

buggery *n Brit, Austral & NZ* anal intercourse

buggy *n, pl* **-gies 1** a light horse-drawn carriage having two or four wheels **2** a lightweight folding pram for babies or young children
WORD ORIGIN origin unknown

bugle *music n* **1** a brass instrument used chiefly for military calls ▹ *vb* **-gling, -gled 2** to play or sound (on) a bugle **bugler** *n*
WORD ORIGIN short for *bugle horn* ox horn, from Latin *buculus* bullock

build ⓣ *vb* **building, built 1** to make or construct by joining parts or materials: *more than 100 bypasses have been built in the past decade* **2** to establish and develop: *it took ten years to build the business* **3** to make in a particular way or for a particular purpose: *she's built for speed, not stamina* **4** (often foll. by *up*) to increase in

THESAURUS

allocation ▹ *vb* **5 = plan**, estimate, allocate, cost, ration, apportion, cost out

buff[1] *adj* **4 = fawn**, cream, tan, beige, yellowish, ecru, straw-coloured, sand-coloured, yellowish-brown, biscuit-coloured, camel-coloured, oatmeal-coloured ▹ *vb* **6 = polish**, clean, smooth, brush, shine, rub, wax, brighten, burnishsee:

buff[2] *n (informal)* **= expert**, fan, addict, enthusiast, freak *(informal)*, admirer, whizz *(informal)*, devotee, connoisseur, fiend *(informal)*, grandmaster, hotshot *(informal)*, aficionado, wonk *(informal)*, maven *(US)*, fundi *(S African)*

buffer[1] *n* **2 = safeguard**, screen, shield, cushion, intermediary, bulwark

buffet[1] *n* **1 = snack bar**, café, cafeteria, brasserie, salad bar, refreshment counter **2 = smorgasbord**, counter, cold table

bug *n* **3** *(informal)* **= illness**, disease, complaint, virus, infection, disorder, disability, sickness, ailment, malaise, affliction, malady, lurgy *(informal)* ▹ *vb* **8** *(informal)* **= annoy**, bother, disturb, needle *(informal)*, plague, irritate, harass, hassle *(informal)*, aggravate *(informal)*, badger, gall, nettle, pester, vex, irk, get under your skin *(informal)*, get on your nerves *(informal)*, nark *(Brit, Austral & NZ slang)*, get up your nose *(informal)*, be on your back *(slang)*, get in your hair *(informal)*, get on your wick *(Brit slang)*, hack you off *(informal)* **9 = tap**, eavesdrop, listen in on, wiretap

build *vb* **1 = construct**, make, raise, put up, assemble, erect, fabricate, form **OPPOSITE:** demolish

intensity ▹*n* **5** physical form, figure, or proportions: *he has an athletic build* **WORD ORIGIN** Old English *byldan*

builder *n* a person who constructs houses and other buildings

building ⊕ *n* **1** a structure, such as a house, with a roof and walls **2** the business of building houses, etc.

building society *n* a cooperative banking enterprise where money can be invested and mortgage loans made available

build up ⊕ *vb* **1** to construct (something) gradually, systematically, and in stages **2** to increase by degrees: *he steadily built up a power base* **3** to prepare for or gradually approach a climax ▹*n* **build-up 4** a progressive increase in number or size: *the build-up of industry* **5** a gradual approach to a climax **6** extravagant publicity or praise, esp. as a campaign

built *vb* ▸the past of **build**

built-in *adj* **1** included as an essential part: *a built-in cupboard* **2** essential: *a built-in instinct*

built-up *adj* **1** having many buildings: *a built-up area* **2** increased by the addition of parts: *built-up heels*

Bukharin *n* **Nikolai Ivanovich** 1888–1938, Soviet Bolshevik leader: executed in one of Stalin's purges

bulb *n* **1** ▸same as **light bulb 2** the onion-shaped base of the stem of some plants, which sends down roots **3** a plant, such as a daffodil, which grows from a bulb **4** any bulb-shaped thing **bulbous** *adj* **WORD ORIGIN** Greek *bolbos* onion

Bulgakov *n* **Mikhail Afanaseyev** 1891–1940, Soviet novelist, dramatist, and short-story writer; his novels include *The Master and Margerita* (1966–67)

Bulganin *n* **Nikolai Aleksandrovich** 1895–1975, Soviet statesman and military leader; chairman of the council of ministers (1955–58)

Bulgarian *adj* **1** of Bulgaria ▹*n* **2** a person from Bulgaria **3** the language of Bulgaria

bulge ⊕ *n* **1** a swelling or an outward curve on a normally flat surface **2** a sudden increase in number, esp. of population ▹*vb* **bulging, bulged 3** to swell outwards **bulging** *adj* **WORD ORIGIN** Latin *bulga* bag

bulimia *n* a disorder characterized by compulsive overeating followed by vomiting **bulimic** *adj, n* **WORD ORIGIN** Greek *bous* ox + *limos* hunger

bulk ⊕ *n* **1** volume or size, esp. when great **2** the main part: *he spends the bulk of his time abroad* **3** a large body, esp. of a person **4** the part of food which passes unabsorbed through the digestive system **5 in bulk** in large quantities: *how frequently do you buy food in bulk for your family?* ▹*vb* **6 bulk large** to be or seem important or prominent **WORD ORIGIN** Old Norse *bulki* cargo

bulk buying *n* the purchase of goods in large amounts, often at reduced prices

bulkhead *n* any upright partition in a ship or aeroplane **WORD ORIGIN** probably from Old Norse *bálkr* partition + HEAD

bulky *adj* **bulkier, bulkiest** very large and massive, esp. so as to be unwieldy **bulkiness** *n*

bull[1] *n* **1** a male of domestic cattle, esp. one that is sexually mature **2** the male of various other animals including the elephant and whale **3** a very large, strong, or aggressive person **4** *stock Exchange* a speculator who buys in anticipation of rising prices in order to make a profit on resale **5** *chiefly Brit* ▸same as **bull's-eye** (senses 1, 2) **6 like a bull in a china shop** clumsy **7 take the bull by the horns** to face and tackle a difficulty without shirking **WORD ORIGIN** Old English *bula*

bull[2] *n* a ludicrously self-contradictory or nonsensical statement **WORD ORIGIN** origin unknown

bull[3] *n* a formal document issued by the pope **WORD ORIGIN** Latin *bulla* round object

bull bars *pl n* a large protective metal grille on the front of some vehicles, esp. four-wheel-drive vehicles

bulldog *n* a thickset dog with a broad head and a muscular body

bulldog clip *n* a clip for holding papers together, consisting of two metal clamps and a spring

bulldoze *vb* **-dozing, -dozed 1** to move, demolish, or flatten with a bulldozer **2** *informal* to coerce (someone) into doing something by intimidation **WORD ORIGIN** origin unknown

bulldozer *n* a powerful tractor fitted with caterpillar tracks and a blade at the front, used for moving earth

bullet ⊕ *n* a small metallic missile used as the projectile of a gun or rifle **WORD ORIGIN** French *boulette* little ball

bulletin ⊕ *n* **1** a broadcast summary of the news **2** an official statement on a matter of public interest **3** a periodical published by an organization for its members **WORD ORIGIN** Italian *bulla* papal edict

bulletin board *n* **1** *US* ▸same as **notice board 2** *computers* a type of data-exchange system by which messages can be sent and read

bullfight *n* a public show, popular in Spain, in which a matador baits and usually kills a bull in an arena **bullfighter** *n* **bullfighting** *n*

bullfinch *n* a common European songbird with a black head and, in the male, a pinkish breast

bullfrog *n* any of various large frogs having a loud deep croak

bullion *n* gold or silver in the form of bars and ingots **WORD ORIGIN** Anglo-French: mint

bull-necked *adj* having a short thick neck

bullock *n* a gelded bull; steer **WORD ORIGIN** Old English *bulluc*

bullring *n* an arena for staging bullfights

bull's-eye *n* **1** the small central disc of a target or a dartboard **2** a shot hitting this **3** *informal* something that exactly achieves its aim **4** a peppermint-flavoured boiled sweet **5** a small circular window **6** a thick disc of glass set into a ship's deck, etc. to admit light **7** the glass boss at the centre of a sheet of blown glass **8 a** a convex lens used as a condenser **b** a lamp or lantern containing such a lens

bullshit *taboo slang n* **1** exaggerated or foolish talk; nonsense ▹*vb* **-shitting, -shitted 2** to talk bullshit to: *don't bullshit me*

bull terrier *n* a terrier with a muscular body and a short smooth coat

THESAURUS

▹*n* **5 = physique**, form, body, figure, shape, structure, frame

building *n* **1 = structure**, house, construction, dwelling, erection, edifice, domicile, pile

build-up *n* **4 = increase**, development, growth, expansion, accumulation, enlargement, escalation, upsurge, intensification, augmentation

bulge *n* **1 = lump**, swelling, bump, projection, hump, protuberance, protrusion **OPPOSITE:** hollow **2 = increase**, rise, boost, surge, intensification ▹*vb* **3 = swell out**, project, expand, swell, stand out, stick out, protrude, puff out, distend, bag

bulk *n* **1 = size**, volume, dimensions, magnitude, substance, vastness, amplitude, immensity, bigness, largeness, massiveness **2 = majority**, mass, most, body, quantity, best part, major part, lion's share, better part, generality, preponderance, main part, plurality, nearly all, greater number

bullet *n* **= projectile**, ball, shot, missile, slug, pellet

bulletin *n* **1, 2 = report**, account, statement, message, communication, announcement, dispatch, communiqué, notification,

DICTIONARY

bully ⊕ *n, pl* **-lies 1** a person who hurts, persecutes, or intimidates weaker people ▹ *vb* **-lies, -lying, -lied 2** to hurt, intimidate, or persecute (a weaker or smaller person) ▹ *interj* **3 bully for you** *or* **him, etc.** *informal* well done! bravo!: now usually used sarcastically
WORD ORIGIN originally, sweetheart, fine fellow, swaggering coward, probably from Middle Dutch *boele* lover

bully beef *n* canned corned beef
WORD ORIGIN French *bœuf bouilli* boiled beef

bully-off *hockey n* **1** the method of restarting play in which two opposing players stand with the ball between them and strike their sticks together three times before trying to hit the ball ▹ *vb* **bully off 2** to restart play with a bully-off
WORD ORIGIN origin unknown

Bülow *n* Prince **Bernhard von** 1849–1929, chancellor of Germany (1900–09)

bulrush *n* **1** a tall reedlike marsh plant with brown spiky flowers **2** *bible* ▸ same as **papyrus** (sense 1)
WORD ORIGIN Middle English *bulrish*

Bultmann *n* **Rudolf Karl** 1884–1976, German theologian, noted for his demythologizing approach to the New Testament

bulwark *n* **1** a wall or similar structure used as a fortification; rampart **2** a person or thing acting as a defence
WORD ORIGIN Middle High German *bolwerk*

Bulwer-Lytton *n* ▸ See **Lytton**

bum[1] *n Brit, Austral & NZ slang* the buttocks or anus
WORD ORIGIN origin unknown

bum[2] *informal n* **1** a disreputable loafer or idler **2** a tramp; hobo ▹ *vb* **bumming, bummed 3** to get by begging; cadge: *to bum a lift* **4 bum around** to spend time to no good purpose; loaf ▹ *adj* **5** of poor quality; useless: *he hit a bum note*
WORD ORIGIN probably from German *bummeln* to loaf

bumbag *n* a small bag worn on a belt around the waist

bumble *vb* **-bling, -bled 1** to speak or do in a clumsy, muddled, or inefficient way **2** to move in a clumsy or unsteady way **bumbling** *adj, n*
WORD ORIGIN origin unknown

bumblebee *n* a large hairy bee
WORD ORIGIN obsolete *bumble* to buzz

Bumbry *n* **Grace** born 1937, US soprano and mezzo-soprano

bumf *or* **bumph** *n Brit, Austral & NZ* **1** *informal* official documents or forms **2** *slang* toilet paper
WORD ORIGIN short for *bumfodder*

bump ⊕ *vb* **1** to knock or strike (someone or something) with a jolt **2** to travel or proceed in jerks and jolts **3** to hurt by knocking ▹ *n* **4** an impact; knock; jolt; collision **5** a dull thud from an impact or collision **6** a lump on the body caused by a blow **7** a raised uneven part, such as on a road surface ▸ See also **bump into, bump off, bump up** > **bumpy** *adj*
WORD ORIGIN probably imitative

bumper[1] *n* a horizontal bar attached to the front and rear of a vehicle to protect against damage from impact

bumper[2] ⊕ *n* **1** a glass or tankard, filled to the brim, esp. as a toast **2** an unusually large or fine example of something ▹ *adj* **3** unusually large, fine, or abundant: *a bumper crop*
WORD ORIGIN probably obsolete *bump* to bulge

bumph *n* ▸ same as **bumf**

bump into *vb informal* to meet (someone) by chance

bumpkin *n* an awkward simple rustic person: *a country bumpkin*
WORD ORIGIN probably from Dutch

bump off *vb slang* to murder (someone)

bumptious *adj* offensively self-assertive or conceited
WORD ORIGIN probably *bump* + *fractious*

bump up *vb informal* to increase (prices) by a large amount

bun *n* **1** a small sweetened bread roll, often containing currants or spices **2** a small round cake **3** a hairstyle in which long hair is gathered into a bun shape at the back of the head
WORD ORIGIN origin unknown

bunch ⊕ *n* **1** a number of things growing, fastened, or grouped together: *a bunch of grapes; a bunch of keys* **2** a collection; group: *a bunch of queries* **3** a group or company: *a bunch of cowards* ▹ *vb* **4** to group or be grouped into a bunch
WORD ORIGIN origin unknown

Bunche *n* **Ralph Johnson** 1904–71, US diplomat and United Nations official: awarded the Nobel peace prize in 1950 for his work as UN mediator in Palestine (1948–49); UN undersecretary (1954–71)

bundle ⊕ *n* **1** a number of things or a quantity of material gathered or loosely bound together: *a bundle of sticks* **2** something wrapped or tied for carrying; package **3** *biol* a collection of strands of specialized tissue such as nerve fibres **4** *bot* a strand of conducting tissue within plants ▹ *vb* **-dling, -dled 5** (foll. by *out, off* or *into* etc.) to cause (someone) to go, esp. roughly or unceremoniously: *she bundled them unceremoniously out into the garden* **6** to push or throw (something), esp. in a quick untidy way: *the soiled items were bundled into a black plastic bag*
WORD ORIGIN probably from Middle Dutch *bundel*

bundle up *vb* to make (something) into a bundle or bundles

bundu *n S African & Zimbabwean slang* a largely uninhabited wild region far from towns
WORD ORIGIN from a Bantu language

bun fight *n Brit, Austral & NZ slang* a tea party

bung *n* **1** a stopper, esp. of cork or rubber, used to close something such as a cask or flask **2** ▸ same as **bunghole** ▹ *vb* **3** (foll. by *up*) *informal* to close or seal (something) with or as if with a bung **4** *Brit, Austral & NZ slang* to throw (something) somewhere in a careless manner; sling
WORD ORIGIN Middle Dutch *bonghe*

bungalow *n* a one-storey house
WORD ORIGIN Hindi *banglā* (house) of Bengali type

bungee jumping *or* **bungy jumping** *n* a sport in which a person jumps from a high bridge, tower, etc. to

THESAURUS

news flash

bully *n* **1 = persecutor**, tough, oppressor, tormentor, bully boy, browbeater, coercer, ruffian, intimidator ▹ *vb* **2 = persecute**, intimidate, torment, hound, oppress, pick on, victimize, terrorize, push around *(slang)*, ill-treat, ride roughshod over, maltreat, tyrannize, overbear

bump *vb* **2 = jerk**, shake, bounce, rattle, jar, jog, lurch, jolt, jostle, jounce ▹ *n* **4 = knock**, hit, blow, shock, impact, rap, collision, thump **6 = lump**, swelling, bulge, hump, node, nodule, protuberance, contusion

bumper[2] *adj* **3 = exceptional**, excellent, exo *(Austral slang)*, massive, unusual, mega *(slang)*, jumbo *(informal)*, abundant, whacking *(informal, chiefly Brit)*, spanking *(informal)*, whopping *(informal)*, bountiful

bunch *n* **1a = bouquet**, spray, sheaf **1b = cluster**, clump **3 = group**, band, crowd, party, team, troop, gathering, crew *(informal)*, gang, knot, mob, flock, swarm, multitude, posse *(informal)*, bevy
4 bunch together *or* **up = group**, crowd, mass, collect, assemble, cluster, flock, herd, huddle, congregate

bundle *n* **1 = bunch**, group, collection, mass, pile, quantity, stack, heap, rick, batch, accumulation, assortment ▹ *vb* **5 = push**, thrust, shove, throw, rush, hurry, hasten,

which he or she is connected by a rubber rope
WORD ORIGIN from *bungie*, slang word for India rubber

bunghole *n* a hole in a cask or barrel through which liquid can be drained

bungle ❶ *vb* **-gling, -gled** 1 to spoil (an operation) through clumsiness or incompetence; botch ▷ *n* 2 a clumsy or unsuccessful performance; blunder **bungler** *n* **bungling** *adj, n*
WORD ORIGIN origin unknown

Bunin *n* **Ivan Alekseyevich** 1870–1953, Russian novelist and poet; author of *The Gentleman from San Francisco* (1922)

bunion *n* an inflamed swelling of the first joint of the big toe
WORD ORIGIN origin unknown

bunk[1] *n* 1 a narrow shelflike bed fixed along a wall, esp. in a caravan or ship 2 ▸ same as **bunk bed**
WORD ORIGIN probably from *bunker*

bunk[2] *n informal* ▸ same as **bunkum**

bunk[3] *n* **do a bunk** 1 *Brit, Austral & NZ slang* to make a hurried and secret departure 2 *Brit, NZ & S African* be absent without permission
WORD ORIGIN origin unknown

bunk bed *n* one of a pair of beds constructed one above the other to save space

bunker *n* 1 an obstacle on a golf course, usually a sand-filled hollow bordered by a ridge 2 an underground shelter 3 a large storage container for coal etc.
WORD ORIGIN Scots *bonkar*

bunkum *n* empty talk; nonsense
WORD ORIGIN after *Buncombe*, North Carolina, alluded to in an inane speech by its Congressional representative

bunny *n, pl* **-nies** ▸ a child's word for **rabbit**
WORD ORIGIN Scottish Gaelic *bun* rabbit's tail

bunny girl *n* a night-club hostess whose costume includes a rabbit-like tail and ears

Bunsen burner *n* a gas burner consisting of a metal tube with an adjustable air valve at the base
WORD ORIGIN after R. W. *Bunsen*, chemist

bunting[1] *n* decorative flags, pennants, and streamers
WORD ORIGIN origin unknown

bunting[2] *n* a songbird with a short stout bill
WORD ORIGIN origin unknown

Bunting *n* **Basil** 1900–85, British poet, author of *Briggflatts* (1966)

Buñuel *n* **Luis** 1900–83, Spanish film director. He collaborated with Salvador Dali on the first surrealist films, *Un Chien andalou* (1929) and *L'Age d'or* (1930). His later films include *Viridiana* (1961), *Belle de jour* (1966), and *The Discreet Charm of the Bourgeoisie* (1972)

bunya *n* a tall dome-shaped Australian coniferous tree

bunyip *n Austral* a legendary monster said to live in swamps and lakes
WORD ORIGIN from a native Australian language

Buonaparte *n* the Italian spelling of **Bonaparte**

buoy ❶ *n* 1 a brightly coloured floating object anchored to the sea bed for marking moorings, navigable channels, or obstructions in the water ▷ *vb* 2 (foll. by *up*) to prevent from sinking: *the life belt buoyed him up* 3 to raise the spirits of; hearten: *exports are on the increase, buoyed by a weak dollar* 4 *naut* to mark (a channel or obstruction) with a buoy or buoys
WORD ORIGIN probably Germanic

buoyant ❶ *adj* 1 able to float in or rise to the surface of a liquid 2 (of a liquid or gas) able to keep a body afloat 3 thriving: *a buoyant economy* 4 cheerful or resilient **buoyancy** *n*

bur *or* **burr** *n* 1 a seed case or flower head with hooks or prickles 2 any plant that produces burs
WORD ORIGIN probably from Old Norse

Burbage *n* 1 **James** ?1530–97, English actor and theatre manager, who built (1576) the first theatre in England 2 his son, **Richard** ?1567–1619, English actor, associated with Shakespeare

burble *vb* **-bling, -bled** 1 to make or utter with a bubbling sound; gurgle 2 to talk quickly and excitedly
WORD ORIGIN probably imitative

burbot *n, pl* **-bots** *or* **-bot** a freshwater fish of the cod family that has barbels around its mouth
WORD ORIGIN Old French *bourbotte*

Burckhardt *n* **Jacob Christoph** 1818–97, Swiss art and cultural historian; author of *The Civilisation of the Renaissance in Italy* (1860)

burden[1] ❶ *n* 1 something that is carried; load 2 something that is difficult to bear ▸ Related adjective: **onerous** *vb* 3 to put or impose a burden on; load 4 to weigh down; oppress **burdensome** *adj*
WORD ORIGIN Old English *byrthen*

burden[2] *n* 1 a line of words recurring at the end of each verse of a song 2 the theme of a speech, book, etc.
WORD ORIGIN Old French *bourdon* droning sound

burdock *n* a weed with large heart-shaped leaves, and burlike fruits
WORD ORIGIN BUR + DOCK[4]

bureau ❶ (byew-roe) *n, pl* **-reaus** *or* **-reaux** (-rose) 1 an office or agency, esp. one providing services for the public 2 *US* a government department 3 *chiefly Brit* a writing desk with pigeonholes and drawers against which the writing surface can be closed when not in use 4 *US* a chest of drawers
WORD ORIGIN French

bureaucracy ❶ *n, pl* **-cies** 1 a rigid system of administration based upon organization into bureaus, division of labour, a hierarchy of authority, etc. 2 government by such a system 3 government officials collectively 4 any administration in which action is impeded by unnecessary official procedures

bureaucrat ❶ *n* 1 an official in a bureaucracy 2 an official who adheres rigidly to bureaucracy **bureaucratic** *adj*

bureau de change *n* a place where

THESAURUS

jostle, hustle

bungle *vb* **1 = mess up**, blow *(slang)*, ruin, spoil, blunder, fudge, screw up *(informal)*, botch, cock up *(Brit slang)*, miscalculate, make a mess of, mismanage, muff, foul up, make a nonsense of *(informal)*, bodge *(informal)*, make a pig's ear of *(informal)*, flub *(US slang)*, crool or cruel *(Austral slang)*, louse up *(slang)*
OPPOSITE: accomplish

buoy *n* **1 = float**, guide, signal, marker, beacon

buoyant *adj* **1 = floating**, light, floatable **4 = cheerful**, happy, bright, lively, sunny, animated, upbeat *(informal)*, joyful, carefree, bouncy, breezy, genial, jaunty, chirpy *(informal)*, sparky, vivacious, debonair, blithe, full of beans *(informal)*, peppy *(informal)*, light-hearted
OPPOSITE: gloomy

burden[1] *n* **1 = load**, weight, cargo, freight, bale, consignment, encumbrance **2 = trouble**, care, worry, trial, weight, responsibility, stress, strain, anxiety, sorrow, grievance, affliction, onus, albatross, millstone, encumbrance ▷ *vb* **3, 4 = weigh down**, worry, load, tax, strain, bother, overwhelm, handicap, oppress, inconvenience, overload, saddle with, encumber, trammel, incommode

bureau *n* **1a = agency 1b = office**, department, section, branch, station, unit, division, subdivision **3 = desk**, writing desk

bureaucracy *n* **1, 2, 3 = government**, officials, authorities, administration, ministry, the system, civil service, directorate, officialdom, corridors of power **4 = red tape**, regulations, officialdom, officialese, bumbledom

bureaucrat *n* **1 = official**, minister, officer, administrator, civil servant, public servant, functionary,

DICTIONARY

foreign currencies can be exchanged
WORD ORIGIN French

burette *or US* **buret** *n* a graduated glass tube with a stopcock on one end for dispensing known volumes of fluids
WORD ORIGIN Old French *buire* ewer

burgeon *vb* to develop or grow rapidly; flourish
WORD ORIGIN Old French *burjon*

burger *n informal* ▸ same as **hamburger**

Bürger *n* **Gottfried August** 1747–94, German lyric poet, noted particularly for his ballad *Lenore* (1773)

Burgess *n* **1 Anthony**, real name *John Burgess Wilson*. 1917–93, English novelist and critic: his novels include *A Clockwork Orange* (1962), *Tremor of Intent* (1966), *Earthly Powers* (1980), and *Any Old Iron* (1989) **2 Guy** 1911–63, British spy, who fled to the Soviet Union (with Donald Maclean) in 1951

burgh *n* (in Scotland until 1975) a town with a degree of self-government
WORD ORIGIN Scots form of *borough*

burgher *n archaic* a citizen, esp. one from the Continent
WORD ORIGIN German *Bürger* or Dutch *burger*

Burghley *or* **Burleigh** *n* **William Cecil**, 1st Baron Burghley. 1520–98, English statesman: chief adviser to Elizabeth I; secretary of state (1558–72) and Lord High Treasurer (1572–98)

burglar ❶ *n* a person who illegally enters a property to commit a crime
WORD ORIGIN Medieval Latin *burglator*

burglary ❶ *n, pl* **-ries** the crime of entering a building as a trespasser to commit theft or another offence

burgle *vb* **-gling, -gled** to break into (a house, shop, etc.)

burgomaster *n* the chief magistrate of a town in Austria, Belgium, Germany, or the Netherlands
WORD ORIGIN Dutch *burgemeester*

Burgoyne *n* **John** 1722–92, British general in the War of American Independence who was forced to surrender at Saratoga (1777)

Burgundy *n* **1** a red or white wine produced in the Burgundy region, around Dijon in France ▹ *adj* **2 burgundy** dark purplish-red

burial ❶ *n* the burying of a dead body

burin (byoor-in) *n* a steel chisel used for engraving metal, wood, or marble
WORD ORIGIN French

burk *n Brit slang* ▸ same as **berk**

burka *n* ▸ another spelling of **burqa**

burl *or* **birl** *n informal* **1** *Scot, Austral, & NZ* an attempt; try: *give it a burl* **2** *Austral & NZ* a ride in a car
WORD ORIGIN from Scots *birl* to spin or turn

Burleigh *n* a variant spelling of **Burghley**

burlesque *n* **1** an artistic work, esp. literary or dramatic, satirizing a subject by caricaturing it **2** *US & Canad theatre* a bawdy comedy show of the late 19th and early 20th centuries ▹ *adj* **3** of or characteristic of a burlesque
WORD ORIGIN Italian *burla* a jest

burly *adj* **-lier, -liest** large and thick of build; sturdy
WORD ORIGIN Germanic

burn[1] ❶ *vb* **burning, burnt** *or* **burned** **1** to be or set on fire **2** to destroy or be destroyed by fire **3** to damage, injure, or mark by heat: *he burnt his hand* **4** to die or put to death by fire **5** to be or feel hot: *my forehead is burning* **6** to smart or cause to smart: *brandy burns your throat* **7** to feel strong emotion, esp. anger or passion **8** to use for the purposes of light, heat, or power: *to burn coal* **9** to form by or as if by fire: *to burn a hole* **10** to char or become charred: *the toast is burning* **11** to record data on (a compact disc) **12 burn one's bridges** *or* **boats** to commit oneself to a particular course of action with no possibility of turning back **13 burn one's fingers** to suffer from having meddled or interfered ▹ *n* **14** an injury caused by exposure to heat, electrical, chemical, or radioactive agents **15** a mark caused by burning ▸ See also **burn out**
WORD ORIGIN Old English *beornan*

burn[2] *n Scot & N English* a small stream
WORD ORIGIN Old English *burna*

Burne-Jones *n* Sir **Edward** 1833–98, English Pre-Raphaelite painter and designer of stained-glass windows and tapestries

burner *n* the part of a stove or lamp that produces flame or heat

Burnet *n* **1 Gilbert** 1643–1715, Scottish bishop and historian, who played a prominent role in the Glorious Revolution (1688–89); author of *The History of My Own Times* (2 vols: 1724 and 1734) **2** Sir (**Frank**) **Macfarlane** 1899–1985, Australian physician and virologist, who shared a Nobel prize for physiology or medicine in 1960 with P. B. Medawar for their work in immunology **3 Thomas**. 1635–1715, English theologian who tried to reconcile science and religion in his *Sacred theory of the Earth* (1680–89)

Burnett *n* **Frances Hodgson** 1849–1924, US novelist, born in England; author of *Little Lord Fauntleroy* (1886) and *The Secret Garden* (1911)

Burney *n* **1 Charles** 1726–1814, English composer and music historian, whose books include *A General History of Music* (1776–89) **2** his daughter, **Frances** known as *Fanny*; married name *Madame D'Arblay*. 1752–1840, English novelist and diarist: author of *Evelina* (1778). Her *Diaries and Letters* (1768–1840) are of historical interest

burning ❶ *adj* intense; passionate **2** urgent; crucial: *a burning problem*

burning glass *n* a convex lens for concentrating the sun's rays to produce fire

burnish *vb* to make or become shiny or smooth by friction; polish
WORD ORIGIN Old French *brunir* to make brown

burnous *n* a long circular cloak with a hood, worn esp. by Arabs
WORD ORIGIN Arabic *burnus*

burn out *vb* **1** to become or cause to become inoperative as a result of heat or friction: *the clutch burnt out* ▹ *n* **burnout 2** total exhaustion and inability to work effectively as a result of excessive demands or overwork

burnt *vb* **1** ▸ a past of **burn**[1] ▹ *adj* **2** affected by or as if by burning; charred

burp *n* **1** *informal* a belch ▹ *vb* **2** *informal* to belch **3** to cause (a baby) to belch
WORD ORIGIN imitative

burqa *or* **burka** *n* a long enveloping garment worn by Muslim women in public, covering all but the wearer's eyes
WORD ORIGIN from Arabic

burr *n* **1** the soft trilling sound given to the letter (r) in some English dialects **2** a whirring or humming sound **3** a rough edge left on metal or paper after cutting **4** a small hand-operated drill

THESAURUS

apparatchik, office-holder, mandarin

burglar *n* = **housebreaker**, thief, robber, pilferer, filcher, cat burglar, sneak thief, picklock

burglary *n* = **breaking and entering**, housebreaking, break-in, home invasion (*Austral & NZ*)

burial *n* = **funeral**, interment, burying, obsequies, entombment, inhumation, exequies, sepulture

burn[1] *vb* **1** = **be on fire**, blaze, be ablaze, smoke, flame, glow, flare, flicker, go up in flames **2** = **set on fire**, light, ignite, kindle, incinerate, reduce to ashes **7a** = **be passionate**, blaze, be excited, be aroused, be inflamed **7b** = **seethe**, fume, be angry, simmer, smoulder **10** = **scorch**, toast, sear, char, singe, brand

burning *adj* **1** = **intense**, passionate, earnest, eager, frantic, frenzied, ardent, fervent, impassioned, zealous, vehement, all-consuming, fervid **OPPOSITE:** mild **2** = **crucial**, important, pressing, significant, essential, vital, critical,

DICTIONARY

WORD ORIGIN origin unknown
Burr *n* **Aaron** 1756–1836, US vice-president (1800–04), who fled after killing a political rival in a duel and plotted to create an independent empire in the western US; acquitted (1807) of treason
Burra *n* **Edward (John)** 1905–76, British painter, noted esp.for his depiction of squalid and grotesque subjects
burrawang *n* an Australian plant with fern-like flowers and an edible nut
Burrell *n* **Paul** born 1958, British butler and confidant to Diana, Princess of Wales. After her death he was charged with but (2003) acquitted of stealing from her estate. His book, *A Royal Duty* (2003), revealed intimate details of her life
burrow ❶ *n* **1** a hole dug in the ground by a rabbit or other small animal ▷ *vb* **2** to dig (a tunnel or hole) in, through, or under ground **3** to move through a place by or as if by digging **4** to delve deeply: *he burrowed into his coat pocket* **5** to live in or as if in a burrow
WORD ORIGIN probably variant of *borough*
bursar *n* a treasurer of a school, college, or university
WORD ORIGIN Medieval Latin *bursarius* keeper of the purse
bursary *n, pl* **-ries** **1** a scholarship or grant awarded esp. in Scottish and New Zealand schools and universities **2** *NZ* a state examination for senior pupils at secondary school
burst ❶ *vb* **bursting, burst** **1** to break or cause to break open or apart suddenly and noisily; explode **2** to come or go suddenly and forcibly: *he burst into the room* **3** to be full to the point of breaking open: *bursting at the seams* **4** (foll. by *into*) to give vent to (something) suddenly or loudly: *she burst into song* ▷ *n* **5** an instance of breaking open suddenly; explosion **6** a break; breach: *there was a burst in the pipe* **7** a sudden increase of effort; spurt: *a burst of speed* **8** a sudden and violent occurrence or outbreak: *a burst of applause*
WORD ORIGIN Old English *berstan*
burton *n* **go for a burton** *Brit & NZ slang* **a** to be broken, useless, or lost **b** to die
WORD ORIGIN origin unknown
bury ❶ *vb* **buries, burying, buried** **1** to place (a corpse) in a grave **2** to place (something) in the earth and cover it with soil **3** to cover (something) from sight; hide **4** to occupy (oneself) with deep concentration: *he buried himself in his work* **5** to dismiss (a feeling) from the mind: *they decided to bury any hard feelings*
WORD ORIGIN Old English *byrgan*
bus *n* **1** a large motor vehicle designed to carry passengers between stopping places along a regular route **2** *informal* a car or aircraft that is old and shaky **3** *electronics, computers* an electrical conductor used to make a common connection between several circuits ▷ *vb* **bussing, bussed** *or* **busing, bused** **4** to travel or transport by bus **5** *chiefly US & Canad* to transport (children) by bus from one area to another in order to create racially integrated schools
WORD ORIGIN short for OMNIBUS
busby *n, pl* **-bies** a tall fur helmet worn by certain British soldiers
WORD ORIGIN origin unknown
Busby *n* Sir **Matthew**, known as *Matt*. 1909–94, British footballer. He managed Manchester United (1946–69)
bush[1] ❶ *n* **1** a dense woody plant, smaller than a tree, with many branches; shrub **2** a dense cluster of such shrubs; thicket **3** something resembling a bush, esp. in density: *a bush of hair* **4** **the bush** an uncultivated area covered with trees or shrubs in Australia, Africa, New Zealand, and Canada **5** *Canad* an area on a farm on which timber is grown and cut **6** **beat about the bush** to avoid the point at issue
WORD ORIGIN Germanic
bush[2] *n* **1** a thin metal sleeve or tubular lining serving as a bearing ▷ *vb* **2** to fit a bush to (a casing or bearing)
WORD ORIGIN Middle Dutch *busse* box
bushbaby *n, pl* **-babies** a small agile tree-living mammal with large eyes and a long tail
bushed *adj informal* extremely tired; exhausted
bushel *n Brit* an obsolete unit of dry or liquid measure equal to 8 gallons (36.4 litres)
WORD ORIGIN Old French *boissel*
bush jacket *n* a casual jacket with four patch pockets and a belt
bush line *n Canad* an airline operating in the bush country of Canada's northern regions
bush lot *n Canad* ▸ same as **bush**[1] (sense 5)
bushman *n, pl* **-men** *Austral & NZ* a person who lives or travels in the bush
Bushman *n, pl* **-men** a member of a hunting and gathering people of southern Africa
WORD ORIGIN Afrikaans *boschjesman*
bush pilot *n Canad* a pilot who operates a plane in the bush country
bush sickness *n NZ* a disease of animals caused by mineral deficiency in old bush country
bush-sick *adj*
bush telegraph *n* a means of spreading rumour or gossip
bush tucker *n Austral* **a** any wild animal, insect, plant etc. traditionally used as food by Australian Aborigines **b** a style of cooking using these ingredients
bushveld *n S African* bushy countryside
WORD ORIGIN Afrikaans
bushwalking *n Austral* the leisure activity of walking in the bush
bushwalker *n*
bushy *adj* **bushier, bushiest** **1** (of hair) thick and shaggy **2** covered or overgrown with bushes
business ❶ *n* **1** the purchase and sale of goods and services **2** a commercial or industrial establishment **3** a trade or profession **4** commercial activity: *the two countries should do business with each other* **5** proper or rightful concern or responsibility: *mind your own business* **6** an affair; matter: *it's a dreadful business* **7** serious work or activity: *get down to business* **8** a difficult or complicated matter: *it's a*

THESAURUS

acute, compelling, urgent
burrow *n* **1 = hole**, shelter, tunnel, den, lair, retreat ▷ *vb* **2 = dig**, tunnel, excavate **4 = delve**, search, dig, probe, ferret, rummage, forage, fossick *(Austral & NZ)*
burst *vb* **1 = explode**, blow up, break, split, crack, shatter, fragment, shiver, disintegrate, puncture, rupture, rend asunder **2a = rush**, run, break, break out, erupt, spout, gush forth **2b = barge**, charge, rush, shove ▷ *n* **5 = explosion**, crack, blast, blasting, bang, discharge **7 = rush**, surge, fit, outbreak, outburst, spate, gush, torrent, eruption, spurt, outpouring
bury *vb* **1 = inter**, lay to rest, entomb, sepulchre, consign to the grave, inearth, inhume, inurn
OPPOSITE: dig up
3 = hide, cover, conceal, stash *(informal)*, secrete, cache, stow away
OPPOSITE: uncover
5 = forget, draw a veil over, think no more of, put in the past, not give another thought to
bush[1] *n* **1, 2 = shrub**, plant, hedge, thicket, shrubbery **4 the bush = the wilds**, brush, scrub, woodland, backwoods, back country *(US)*, scrubland, backlands *(US)*
business *n* **1, 4 = trade**, selling, trading, industry, manufacturing, commerce, dealings, merchandising **2 = establishment**, company, firm, concern, organization, corporation, venture, enterprise **3 = profession**, work, calling, job, line, trade, career,

DICTIONARY

b

business trying to see him **9 mean business** to be in earnest
WORD ORIGIN Old English *bisignis* care, attentiveness
businesslike *adj* efficient and methodical
businessman ❶ *or fem* **businesswoman** *n, pl* **-men** *or* **-women** a person engaged in commercial or industrial business, usually an owner or executive
business park *n* an area specially designated to accommodate business offices, light industry, etc.
business rate *n* a tax levied on businesses, based on the value of their premises
business school *n* an institution that offers courses to managers in aspects of business, such as marketing, finance, and law
busker *n* a person who entertains for money in streets or stations **busk** *vb*
WORD ORIGIN perhaps from Spanish *buscar* to look for
busman's holiday *n informal* a holiday spent doing the same as one does at work
Buss *n* **Frances Mary** 1827–94, British educationalist; a pioneer of secondary education for girls, who campaigned for women's admission to university
Bussell *n* **Darcey (Andrea)** born 1969, British ballet dancer, principal ballerina with the Royal Ballet (1989–2006)
bust¹ ❶ *n* **1** a woman's bosom **2** a sculpture of the head, shoulders, and upper chest of a person
WORD ORIGIN Italian *busto* a sculpture
bust² ❶ *informal vb* **busting, busted** *or* **bust 1** to burst or break **2** (of the police) to raid or search (a place) or arrest (someone) **3** *US & Canad* to demote in military rank ▹ *adj* **4** broken **5 go bust** to become bankrupt
WORD ORIGIN from *burst*
bustard *n* a bird with a long strong legs, a heavy body, a long neck, and speckled plumage
bustle¹ ❶ *vb* **-tling, -tled 1** (often foll. by *about*) to hurry with a great show of energy or activity ▹ *n* **2** energetic and noisy activity **bustling** *adj*
WORD ORIGIN probably obsolete *buskle* to prepare
bustle² *n* a cushion or framework worn by women in the late 19th century at the back in order to expand the skirt
WORD ORIGIN origin unknown
bust-up *informal n* **1** a serious quarrel, esp. one ending a relationship **2** *Brit, Austral & NZ* a disturbance or brawl ▹ *vb* **bust up 3** to quarrel and part **4** to disrupt (a meeting), esp. violently
busy ❶ *adj* **busier, busiest 1** actively or fully engaged; occupied **2** crowded with or characterized by activity **3** (of a telephone line) in use; engaged ▹ *vb* **busies, busying, busied 4** to make or keep (someone, esp. oneself) busy; occupy **busily** *adv*
WORD ORIGIN Old English *bisig*
busybody *n, pl* **-bodies** a meddlesome, prying, or officious person
but ❶ *conj* **1** contrary to expectation: *he cut his hand but didn't cry* **2** in contrast; on the contrary: *I like seafood but my husband doesn't* **3** other than: *we can't do anything but wait* **4** without it happening: *we never go out but it rains* ▹ *prep* **5** except: *they saved all but one* **6 but for** were it not for: *but for you, we couldn't have managed* ▹ *adv* **7** only: *I can but try; he was but a child* ▹ *n* **8** an objection: *ifs and buts*
WORD ORIGIN Old English *būtan* without, except
but and ben *n Scot* a two-roomed cottage consisting of an outer room (**but**) and an inner room (**ben**)
WORD ORIGIN Old English *būtan* outside + *binnan* inside
butane (**byew**-tane) *n* a colourless gas used in the manufacture of rubber and fuels
WORD ORIGIN from *butyl*
butch *adj slang* (of a woman or man) markedly or aggressively masculine
WORD ORIGIN from *butcher*
butcher ❶ *n* **1** a person who sells meat **2** a person who kills animals for meat **3** a brutal murderer ▹ *vb* **4** to kill and prepare (animals) for meat **5** to kill (people) at random or brutally **6** to make a mess of; botch
WORD ORIGIN Old French *bouchier*
butcherbird *n* an Australian magpie that impales its prey on thorns
butchery *n, pl* **-eries 1** senseless slaughter **2** the business of a butcher
Bute¹ *n* an island off the coast of SW Scotland, in Argyll and Bute council area: situated in the Firth of Clyde, separated from the Cowal peninsula by the **Kyles of Bute**. Chief town: Rothesay. Pop: 7228 (2001). Area: 121 sq km (47 sq miles)
Bute² *n* **John Stuart**, 3rd Earl of Bute. 1713–92, British Tory statesman; prime minister (1762–63)
Butenandt *n* **Adolf Frederick Johann** 1903–95, German organic chemist. He shared the Nobel prize for chemistry (1939) for his pioneering work on sex hormones
Buthelezi *n* **Mangosouthu Gatsha**, known as *Chief Buthelezi*. born 1928, Zulu leader, chief minister of the KwaZulu territory of South Africa from 1970 until its abolition in 1994; founder of the Inkatha movement and advocate of Zulu autonomy; minister of home affairs (1994–2004)
butler *n* the head manservant of a household, in charge of the wines, table, etc.
WORD ORIGIN Old French *bouteille* bottle
Butler *n* **1 Joseph** 1692–1752, English bishop and theologian, author of *Analogy of Religion* (1736) **2 Josephine (Elizabeth)** 1828–1906, British social reformer, noted esp.for her campaigns against state regulation of prostitution **3 Reg**, full name *Reginald Cotterell Butler*. 1913–81, British metal sculptor; his works include *The Unknown Political Prisoner* (1953) **4 R(ichard) A(usten)**, Baron Butler of Saffron Walden, known as *Rab Butler*. 1902–82, British Conservative politician: Chancellor of the

THESAURUS

function, employment, craft, occupation, pursuit, vocation, métier **5 = concern**, affair **6 = matter**, issue, subject, point, problem, question, responsibility, task, duty, function, topic, assignment
businessman *n* **= executive**, director, manager, merchant, capitalist, administrator, entrepreneur, tycoon, industrialist, financier, tradesman, homme d'affaires *(French)*
bust¹ *n* **1 = bosom**, breasts, chest, front
bust² *vb* **1 = break**, smash, split, burst, shatter, fracture, rupture, break into fragments **2 = arrest**, catch, lift *(slang)*, raid, cop *(slang)*, nail *(informal)*, collar *(informal)*, nab *(informal)*, feel your collar *(slang)*
5 go bust = go bankrupt, fail, break, be ruined, become insolvent
bustle¹ *vb* **1 = hurry**, tear, rush, dash, scramble, fuss, flutter, beetle, hasten, scuttle, scurry, scamper
OPPOSITE: idle
▹ *n* **2 = activity**, to-do, stir, excitement, hurry, fuss, flurry, haste, agitation, commotion, ado, tumult, hurly-burly, pother
OPPOSITE: inactivity
busy *adj* **1 = active**, brisk, diligent, industrious, assiduous, rushed off your feet **OPPOSITE:** idle
2 = hectic, full, active, tiring, exacting, energetic, strenuous, on the go *(informal)* ▹ *vb* **4 busy yourself = occupy yourself**, be engrossed, immerse yourself, involve yourself, amuse yourself, absorb yourself, employ yourself, engage yourself, keep busy *or* occupied
but *conj* **2 = however**, still, yet, nevertheless ▹ *prep* **5 = except (for)**, save, bar, barring, excepting, excluding, with the exception of ▹ *adv* **7 = only**, just, simply, merely
butcher *n* **3 = murderer**, killer, slaughterer, slayer, destroyer,

Exchequer (1951–55); Home Secretary (1957–62); Foreign Secretary (1963–64) **5 Samuel** 1612–80, English poet and satirist; author of *Hudibras* (1663–78) **6 Samuel** 1835–1902, British novelist, noted for his satirical work *Erewhon* (1872) and his autobiographical novel *The Way of All Flesh* (1903)

butt[1] ❶ *n* **1** the thicker or blunt end of something, such as the stock of a rifle **2** the unused end of a cigarette or cigar; stub **3** *chiefly US & Canad slang* the buttocks
WORD ORIGIN Middle English

butt[2] ❶ *n* **1** a person or thing that is the target of ridicule or teasing **2** *shooting, archery* **a** a mound of earth behind the target **b butts** the target range
WORD ORIGIN Old French *but*

butt[3] ❶ *vb* **1** to strike (something or someone) with the head or horns **2** (foll. by *in* or *into*) to intrude, esp. into a conversation; interfere ▷*n* **3** a blow with the head or horns
WORD ORIGIN Old French *boter*

butt[4] ❶ *n* a large cask for collecting or storing liquids
WORD ORIGIN Late Latin *buttis* cask

Butt *n* Dame **Clara** 1872–1936, English contralto

butte (**byewt**) *n US & Canad* an isolated steep flat-topped hill
WORD ORIGIN Old French *bute* mound behind a target

butter *n* **1** an edible fatty yellow solid made from cream by churning **2** any substance with a butter-like consistency, such as peanut butter ▷*vb* **3** to put butter on or in (something) ▸See also **butter up** > **buttery** *adj*
WORD ORIGIN Greek *bous* cow + *turos* cheese

butter bean *n* a large pale flat edible bean

buttercup *n* a small bright yellow flower

Butterfield *n* **William** 1814–1900, British architect of the Gothic Revival; his buildings include Keble College, Oxford (1870) and All Saints, Margaret Street, London (1849–59)

butterfingers *n informal* a person who drops things by mistake or fails to catch things

butterflies *pl n informal* a nervous feeling in the stomach

butterfly *n, pl* **-flies 1** an insect with a slender body and brightly coloured wings **2** a swimming stroke in which the arms are plunged forward together in large circular movements **3** a person who never settles with one interest or occupation for long
WORD ORIGIN Old English *buttorflēoge*

butterfly nut *n* ▸same as **wing nut**

buttermilk *n* the sourish liquid remaining after the butter has been separated from milk

butterscotch *n* a hard brittle toffee made with butter, brown sugar, etc.

butter up *vb* to flatter

Butterworth *n* **1 George** 1885–1916, British composer, noted for his interest in folk song and his settings of Housman's poems **2 Nick** born 1946, English writer and illustrator of children's books, many of which feature Percy, the animal-loving park keeper

buttery *n, pl* **-teries** *Brit* (in some universities) a room in which food and drink are sold to students
WORD ORIGIN Latin *butta* cask

buttock *n* **1** either of the two large fleshy masses that form the human rump **2** the corresponding part in some mammals
WORD ORIGIN perhaps from Old English *buttuc* round slope

button *n* **1** a disc or knob of plastic, wood, etc. attached to a garment, which fastens two surfaces together by passing through a buttonhole **2** a small disc that operates a door bell or machine when pressed **3** a small round object, such as a sweet or badge **4 not worth a button** *Brit* of no value; useless ▷*vb* **5** to fasten (a garment) with a button or buttons
WORD ORIGIN Old French *boton*

buttonhole *n* **1** a slit in a garment through which a button is passed to fasten two surfaces together **2** a flower worn pinned to the lapel or in the buttonhole ▷*vb* **-holing, -holed 3** to detain (a person) in conversation

button mushroom *n* an unripe mushroom

button up *vb* **1** to fasten (a garment) with a button or buttons **2** *informal* to conclude (business) satisfactorily: *we've got it all buttoned up*

buttress *n* **1** a construction, usually of brick or stone, built to support a wall **2** any support or prop ▷*vb* **3** to support (a wall) with a buttress **4** to support or sustain: *his observations are buttressed by the most recent scholarly research*

WORD ORIGIN Old French *bouter* to thrust

butty *n, pl* **-ties** *chiefly N English dialect* a sandwich: *a jam butty*
WORD ORIGIN from *buttered (bread)*

butyl (**byew**-tile) *adj* of or containing any of four isomeric forms of the group C_4H_9–: *butyl rubber*
WORD ORIGIN Latin *butyrum* butter

buxom *adj* (of a woman) healthily plump, attractive, and full-bosomed
WORD ORIGIN Middle English *buhsum* compliant

Buxtehude *n* **Dietrich** 1637–1707, Danish composer and organist, resident in Germany from 1668, who influenced Bach and Handel

buy ❶ *vb* **buying, bought 1** to acquire (something) by paying a sum of money for it; purchase **2** to be capable of purchasing: *money can't buy love* **3** to acquire by any exchange or sacrifice: *the rise in interest rates was just to buy time until the weekend* **4** to bribe (someone) **5** *slang* to accept (something) as true **6** (foll. by *into*) to purchase shares of (a company) ▷*n* **7** a purchase: *a good buy.* ▸See also **buy in, buy into**, etc.
WORD ORIGIN Old English *bycgan*

buyer *n* **1** a person who buys; customer **2** a person employed to buy merchandise for a shop or factory

buy in *vb* to purchase (goods) in large quantities

buy into *vb* to agree with (an argument or theory)

buy off *vb* to pay (someone) to drop a charge or end opposition

buy-out *n* **1** the purchase of a company, often by its former employees ▷*vb* **buy out 2** to purchase the ownership of a company or property from (someone)

buy up *vb* **1** to purchase all that is available of (something) **2** to purchase a controlling interest in (a company)

buzz *n* **1** a rapidly vibrating humming sound, such as of a bee **2** a low sound, such as of many voices in conversation **3** *informal* a telephone call **4** *informal* a sense of excitement ▷*vb* **5** to make a vibrating sound like that of a prolonged *z* **6** (of a place) to be filled with an air of excitement: *the city buzzed with the news* **7** to summon (someone) with a buzzer **8** *informal* to fly an aircraft very low over (people, buildings, or another

THESAURUS

liquidator, executioner, cut-throat, exterminator ▷*vb* **4 = slaughter**, prepare, carve, cut up, dress, cut, clean, joint **5 = kill**, slaughter, massacre, destroy, cut down, assassinate, slay, liquidate, exterminate, put to the sword

butt[1] *n* **1 = end**, handle, shaft, stock, shank, hilt, haft **2 = stub**, end, base, foot, tip, tail, leftover, fag end *(informal)*

butt[2] *n* **1 = target**, victim, object, point, mark, subject, dupe, laughing stock, Aunt Sally

butt[3] *vb* **1 = knock**, push, bump, punch, buck, thrust, ram, shove, poke, buffet, prod, jab, bunt

butt[4] *n* **= cask**, drum, barrel, cylinder

buy *vb* **1 = purchase**, get, score *(slang)*, secure, pay for, obtain, acquire, invest in, shop for, procure

DICTIONARY

aircraft) **9** **buzz about** *or* **around** to move around quickly and busily
WORD ORIGIN imitative

b

buzzard *n* a bird of prey with broad wings and tail and a soaring flight
WORD ORIGIN Latin *buteo* hawk

buzzer *n* an electronic device that produces a buzzing sound as a signal

buzzkill *or* **buzzkiller** *n informal* someone or something that stops people from enjoying themselves

buzz off *vb Austral & Brit informal* to go away; depart

buzz word *n informal* a word, originally from a particular jargon, which becomes a popular vogue word

by ❶ *prep* **1** used to indicate the performer of the action of a passive verb: *seeds eaten by the birds* **2** used to indicate the person responsible for a creative work: *three songs by Britten* **3** via; through: *enter by the back door* **4** used to indicate a means used: *he frightened her by hiding behind the door* **5** beside; next to; near: *a tree by the stream* **6** passing the position of; past: *I drove by the place she works* **7** not later than; before: *return the books by Tuesday* **8** used to indicate extent: *it is hotter by five degrees* **9** multiplied by: *four by three equals twelve* **10** during the passing of: *by night* **11** placed between measurements of the various dimensions of something: *a plank fourteen inches by seven* ▷ *adv* **12** near: *the house is close by* **13** away; aside: *he put some money by each week* **14** passing a point near something; past: *he drove by* ▷ *n, pl* **byes** **15** ▸ same as **bye¹**
WORD ORIGIN Old English *bī*

Byam Shaw *n* **Glen Alexander** 1904–81, British actor and theatre director; director of the Shakespeare Memorial Theatre (1953–59)

by and by *adv* presently or eventually

by and large *adv* in general; on the whole

Byatt *n* **Dame A(ntonia) S(usan)** born 1936, British novelist; her books include *The Virgin in the Garden* (1978), *Possession* (1990), and *A Whistling Woman* (2002)

bye¹ *n* **1** *sport* status of a player or team who wins a preliminary round by virtue of having no opponent **2** *cricket* a run scored off a ball not struck by the batsman **3** **by the bye** incidentally; by the way
WORD ORIGIN variant of *by*

bye² *or* **bye-bye** *interj informal* goodbye

by-election *or* **bye-election** *n* an election held during the life of a parliament to fill a vacant seat

bygone *adj* past; former: *a bygone age*

bygones *pl n* **let bygones be bygones** to agree to forget past quarrels

bylaw *or* **bye-law** *n* a rule made by a local authority
WORD ORIGIN probably Scandinavian

by-line *n* **1** a line under the title of an article in a newspaper or magazine giving the author's name **2** ▸ same as **touchline**

Byng *n* **1** **George**, Viscount Torrington 1663–1733, British admiral: defeated fleet of James Edward Stuart, the Old Pretender, off Scotland (1708); defeated Spanish fleet off Messina (1717) **2** his son **John** 1704–57, English admiral: executed after failing to relieve Minorca **3** **Julian Hedworth George**, 1st Viscount Byng of Vimy. 1862–1935, British general in World War I; governor general of Canada (1921–26)

BYO, BYOG *n Austral & NZ* an unlicensed restaurant at which diners may bring their own alcoholic drink
WORD ORIGIN *bring your own (grog)*

bypass ❶ *n* **1** a main road built to avoid a city **2** a secondary pipe, channel, or appliance through which the flow of a substance, such as gas or electricity, is redirected **3** a surgical operation in which the blood flow is redirected away from a diseased or blocked part of the heart ▷ *vb* **4** to go around or avoid (a city, obstruction, problem, etc.) **5** to proceed without reference to (regulations or a superior); get round; avoid

by-play *n* secondary action in a play, carried on apart while the main action proceeds

by-product *n* **1** a secondary or incidental product of a manufacturing process **2** a side effect

Byrd *n* **1** **Richard Evelyn** 1888–1957, US rear admiral, aviator, and polar explorer **2** **William** 1543–1623, English composer and organist, noted for his madrigals, masses, and music for virginals

Byrds *pl n* **the** US folk-rock and country-rock group (1964–73), noted for their vocal harmonies and 12-string guitar sound. Their albums include *Mr. Tambourine Man* (1965), *Younger Than Yesterday* (1967), and *Sweetheart of the Rodeo* (1968)

byre *n Brit* a shelter for cows
WORD ORIGIN Old English *bȳre*

byroad *n* a secondary or side road

bystander *n* a person present but not involved; onlooker; spectator

byte *n computers* a group of bits processed as one unit of data
WORD ORIGIN origin unknown

byway *n* a secondary or side road, esp. in the country

byword *n* **1** a person or thing regarded as a perfect example of something: *their name is a byword for quality* **2** a common saying; proverb

Byzantine *adj* **1** of Byzantium, an ancient Greek city on the Bosphorus **2** of the Byzantine Empire, the continuation of the Roman Empire in the East **3** of the style of architecture developed in the Byzantine Empire, with massive domes, rounded arches, and mosaics **4** (of attitudes, methods, etc.) inflexible or complicated ▷ *n* **5** an inhabitant of Byzantium

THESAURUS

OPPOSITE: sell
▷ *n* **7** = **purchase**, deal, bargain, acquisition, steal *(informal)*, snip *(informal)*, giveaway

by *prep* **1, 2** = **through**, under the aegis of, through the agency of **3** = **via**, over, by way of **5, 6** = **near**, past, along, close to, closest to, neighbouring, next to, beside, nearest to, adjoining, adjacent to ▷ *adv* **12** = **nearby**, close, handy, at hand, within reach

bypass *vb* **4** = **get round**, avoid, evade, circumvent, outmanoeuvre, body-swerve *(Scot)* **5** = **go round**, skirt, circumvent, depart from, deviate from, pass round, detour round **OPPOSITE:** cross

Cc

DICTIONARY

C

c **1** centi- **2** *cricket* caught **3** cubic **4** the speed of light in free space

C **1** *music* the first note of a major scale containing no sharps or flats (**C major**) **2** *chem* carbon **3** Celsius **4** centigrade **5** century: C20 **6** coulomb **7** the Roman numeral for 100 **8** a high-level computer programming language

c. (used preceding a date) about: *c. 1800*
WORD ORIGIN Latin *circa*

Ca *chem* calcium

CA **1** California **2** Central America **3** Chartered Accountant

ca. (used preceding a date) about: *ca. 1930*
WORD ORIGIN Latin *circa*

cab *n* **1** a taxi **2** the enclosed driver's compartment of a lorry, bus, or train
WORD ORIGIN from *cabriolet*

cabal (kab-**bal**) *n* **1** a small group of political plotters **2** a secret plot or conspiracy
WORD ORIGIN French *cabale*

Caballé *n* **Montserrat** born 1933, Spanish operatic soprano

cabaret (**kab**-a-ray) *n* **1** a floor show of dancing and singing at a nightclub or restaurant **2** a place providing such entertainment
WORD ORIGIN French: tavern

cabbage *n* **1** a vegetable with a large head of green or reddish-purple leaves **2** *informal* a person who is unable to move or think, as a result of brain damage: *he can only exist as a cabbage who must be cared for by his relatives*
WORD ORIGIN Norman French *caboche* head

cabbage tree *n* NZ a palm-like tree with a bare trunk and spiky leaves

cabbage white *n* a large white butterfly whose larvae feed on cabbage leaves

cabbie *or* **cabby** *n, pl* **-bies** *informal* a taxi driver

caber *n Scot* a heavy section of trimmed tree trunk tossed in competition at Highland games
WORD ORIGIN Gaelic *cabar* pole

Cabernet Sauvignon (**kab**-er-nay so-veen-yon) *n* a dry red wine produced in the Bordeaux region of France and elsewhere
WORD ORIGIN French

cabin *n* **1** a room used as living quarters in a ship or boat **2** a small simple dwelling: *a log cabin* **3** the enclosed part of an aircraft in which the passengers or crew sit
WORD ORIGIN Late Latin *capanna* hut

cabin boy *n* a boy who waits on the officers and passengers of a ship

cabin cruiser *n* a motorboat with a cabin

cabinet *n* a piece of furniture containing shelves, cupboards, or drawers for storage or display: *a filing cabinet; a cocktail cabinet*
WORD ORIGIN Old French *cabine* cabin

Cabinet *n* a committee of senior government ministers or advisers to a president

cabinet-maker *n* a person who makes fine furniture **cabinet-making** *n*

cabin fever *n Canad* acute depression resulting from being isolated or sharing cramped quarters

cable *n* **1** a strong thick rope of twisted hemp or wire **2** a bundle of wires covered with plastic or rubber that conducts electricity **3** a telegram sent abroad by submarine cable or telephone line **4** Also called: **cable stitch** a knitted design which resembles a twisted rope ▷ *vb* **-bling, -bled** **5** to send (someone) a message by cable
WORD ORIGIN Late Latin *capulum* halter

cable car *n* a vehicle that is pulled up a steep slope by a moving cable

cablegram *n* ▶ a more formal name for **cable** (sense 3)

cable television *n* a television service in which the subscriber's television is connected to a central receiver by cable

caboodle *n* **the whole caboodle** *informal* the whole lot
WORD ORIGIN origin unknown

caboose *n* **1** *US & Canad* a railway car at the rear of a train, used as quarters for the crew **2** *Canad* a mobile building used as a cookhouse or bunkhouse for a work crew
WORD ORIGIN Dutch *cabūse*

Cabral *n* **Pedro Álvarez** ?1460–?1526, Portuguese navigator: discovered and took possession of Brazil for Portugal in 1500

cabriolet (kab-ree-oh-**lay**) *n* a small two-wheeled horse-drawn carriage with a folding hood
WORD ORIGIN French: a little skip; referring to the lightness of movement

cacao (kak-**kah**-oh) *n* a tropical American tree with seed pods (**cacao beans**) from which cocoa and chocolate are prepared
WORD ORIGIN Mexican Indian *cacauatl* cacao beans

cachalot *n* the sperm whale
WORD ORIGIN Portuguese *cachalote*

cache (**kash**) *n* a hidden store of weapons, provisions, or treasure
WORD ORIGIN French *cacher* to hide

cachet (**kash**-shay) *n* prestige or distinction: *a Mercedes carries a certain cachet*
WORD ORIGIN French

cachou *n* a lozenge eaten to sweeten the breath
WORD ORIGIN Malay *kāchu*

cack-handed *adj informal* clumsy: *I open cans in a very cack-handed way*
WORD ORIGIN dialect *cack* excrement

cackle *vb* **-ling, -led** **1** to laugh shrilly **2** (of a hen) to squawk with shrill broken notes ▷ *n* **3** the sound of cackling **cackling** *adj*
WORD ORIGIN probably imitative

cacophony (kak-**koff**-on-ee) *n* harsh discordant sound: *a cacophony of barking* **cacophonous** *adj*
WORD ORIGIN Greek *kakos* bad + *phōnē* sound

cactus *n, pl* **-tuses** *or* **-ti** a thick fleshy desert plant with spines but no leaves
WORD ORIGIN Greek *kaktos* type of thistle

cad *n old-fashioned, informal* a man who behaves dishonourably **caddish** *adj*
WORD ORIGIN from *caddie*

cadaver (kad-**dav**-ver) *n med* a corpse
WORD ORIGIN Latin

cadaverous *adj* pale, thin, and haggard

Cadbury *n* **George** 1839–1922, British Quaker industrialist and philanthropist. He established, with his brother **Richard Cadbury** (1835–99), the chocolate-making company Cadbury Brothers and the garden village Bournville, near Birmingham, for their workers

caddie *n* **1** a person who carries a golfer's clubs ▷ *vb* **-dying, -died** **2** to act as a caddie
WORD ORIGIN from *cadet*

THESAURUS

cab *n* **1 = taxi,** minicab, taxicab, hackney, hackney carriage

cabin *n* **1 = room,** berth, quarters, compartment, deckhouse **2 = hut,** shed, cottage, lodge, cot *(archaic)*, shack, chalet, shanty, hovel, bothy, whare (NZ)

cabinet *n* **= cupboard,** case, locker, dresser, closet, press, chiffonier

Cabinet *n* **= council,** committee, administration, ministry, assembly, board

cad *n (old-fashioned, informal)* **= scoundrel** *(slang)*, rat *(informal)*, bounder *(Brit old-fashioned, slang)*, cur, knave, rotter *(slang, chiefly Brit)*, heel, scumbag *(slang)*, churl, dastard *(archaic)*, wrong 'un *(Austral slang)*

DICTIONARY

caddis fly *n* an insect whose larva (the **caddis worm**) lives underwater in a protective case of silk, sand, and stones

caddy[1] *n, pl* **-dies** *chiefly Brit* a small container for tea
WORD ORIGIN Malay *kati*

caddy[2] *n, pl* **-dies,** *vb* **-dies, -dying, -died** ▸ same as **caddie**

Cade *n* **Jack** died 1450, English leader of the Kentish rebellion against the misgovernment of Henry VI (1450)

cadence (kade-enss) *n* **1** the rise and fall in the pitch of the voice **2** the close of a musical phrase
WORD ORIGIN Latin *cadere* to fall

cadenza *n* a complex solo passage in a piece of music
WORD ORIGIN Italian

cadet *n* a young person training for the armed forces or the police
WORD ORIGIN French

cadge *vb* **cadging, cadged** *informal* to get (something) from someone by taking advantage of his or her generosity **cadger** *n*
WORD ORIGIN origin unknown

cadi *n* a judge in a Muslim community
WORD ORIGIN Arabic *qādī* judge

cadmium *n chem* bluish-white metallic element found in zinc ores and used in electroplating and alloys. Symbol: Cd
WORD ORIGIN Latin *cadmia* zinc ore

cadre (kah-der) *n* a small group of people selected and trained to form the core of a political organization or military unit
WORD ORIGIN Latin *quadrum* square

Cadwalader *n* 7th century AD, legendary king of the Britons, probably a confusion of several historical figures

caecum *or US* **cecum** (seek-um) *n, pl* **-ca** (-ka) the pouch at the beginning of the large intestine
WORD ORIGIN short for Latin *intestinum caecum* blind intestine

Cædmon *n* 7th century AD, Anglo-Saxon poet and monk, the earliest English poet whose name survives

Caenozoic *adj* ▸ same as **Cenozoic**

Caerphilly *n* a creamy white mild-flavoured cheese

Caesar (seez-ar) *n* **1** a Roman emperor **2** any emperor or dictator
WORD ORIGIN after Gaius Julius *Caesar,* Roman general & statesman
3 ▸ short for **Caesar salad**

Caesarean, Caesarian *or US* **Cesarean** (siz-zair-ee-an) *n* ▸ short for **Caesarean section**

Caesarean section *n* surgical incision into the womb in order to deliver a baby
WORD ORIGIN from the belief that Julius Caesar was delivered in this way

Caesar salad *n* a salad of lettuce, cheese, and croutons with a dressing of olive oil, garlic, and lemon juice
WORD ORIGIN after *Caesar* Cardini, its inventor

caesium *or US* **cesium** *n chem* a silvery-white metallic element used in photocells. Symbol: Cs
WORD ORIGIN Latin *caesius* bluish-grey

caesura (siz-your-ra) *n, pl* **-ras** *or* **-rae** (-ree) a pause in a line of verse
WORD ORIGIN Latin: a cutting

Caetano *n* **Marcello** 1906–80, prime minister of Portugal from 1968 until he was replaced by an army coup in 1974

café ❶ *n* **1** a small or inexpensive restaurant that serves drinks and snacks or light meals **2** *S African* a corner shop
WORD ORIGIN French

cafeteria *n* a self-service restaurant
WORD ORIGIN American Spanish: coffee shop

caff *n slang* a café

caffeine *n* a stimulant found in tea, coffee, and cocoa
WORD ORIGIN German *Kaffee* coffee

caftan *n* ▸ same as **kaftan**

cage ❶ *n* **1** an enclosure made of bars or wires, for keeping birds or animals in **2** the enclosed platform of a lift in a mine ▹ *vb* **caging, caged 3** to confine in a cage **caged** *adj*
WORD ORIGIN Latin *cavea* enclosure

cagey *adj* **cagier, cagiest** *informal* reluctant to go into details; wary: *he is cagey about what he paid for the business* **cagily** *adv*
WORD ORIGIN origin unknown

Cagliari[1] *n* a port in Italy, the capital of Sardinia, on the S coast. Pop: 164 249 (2001)

Cagliari[2] *n* **Paolo** ▸ original name of (Paolo) **Veronese**

Cagliostro *n* Count **Alessandro di,** original name *Giuseppe Balsamo.* 1743–95, Italian adventurer and magician, who was imprisoned for life by the Inquisition for his association with freemasonry

Cagney *n* **James** 1899–1986, US film actor, esp. in gangster roles; his films include *The Public Enemy* (1931), *Angels with Dirty Faces* (1938), *The Roaring Twenties* (1939), and *Yankee Doodle Dandy* (1942) for which he won an Oscar

cagoule (kag-gool) *n Brit* a lightweight hooded waterproof jacket
WORD ORIGIN French

cahoots *pl n* **in cahoots** *informal* conspiring together: *the loan sharks were in cahoots with the home-improvement companies*
WORD ORIGIN origin unknown

caiman *n, pl* **-mans** ▸ same as **cayman**

Caine *n* Sir **Michael** real name *Maurice Micklewhite.* born 1933, British film actor. His films include *The Ipcress File* (1965), *Get Carter* (1971), *Educating Rita* (1983), *Hannah and Her Sisters* (1986), and *The Cider House Rules* (1999)

cairn *n* a mound of stones erected as a memorial or marker
WORD ORIGIN Gaelic *carn*

cairngorm *n* a smoky yellow or brown quartz gemstone
WORD ORIGIN *Cairn Gorm* (blue cairn), mountain in Scotland

caisson (kayss-on) *n* a watertight chamber used to carry out construction work under water
WORD ORIGIN French

Caius *n* same as **Gaius**

Cajal *n* **Santiago Ramon y** 1852–1934, Spanish histologist, a pioneer of modern neurophysiology: shared the Nobel prize for medicine 1906

cajole *vb* **-joling, -joled** to persuade by flattery; coax: *he allowed himself to be cajoled into staying on* **cajolery** *n*
WORD ORIGIN French *cajoler*

Cajun *n* **1** a native of Louisiana descended from 18th-century Acadian immigrants **2** the dialect of French spoken by such people **3** the music of this ethnic group ▹ *adj* **4** denoting or relating to such people, their language, or their music
WORD ORIGIN from ACADIAN

cake ❶ *n* **1** a sweet food baked from a mixture of flour, sugar, eggs, etc. **2** a flat compact mass of something: *a cake of soap* **3 have one's cake and eat it** to enjoy both of two incompatible alternatives **4 piece of cake** *informal* something that is easy to do **5 sell like hot cakes** *informal* to be sold very quickly: *commercial novels sell like hot cakes* ▹ *vb* **caking, caked 6** to form into a hardened mass or crust: *there was blood caked an inch thick on the walls*
WORD ORIGIN Old Norse *kaka*

cal. calorie (small)

Cal. 1 Calorie (large) **2** California

calabash *n* **1** a large round gourd that grows on a tropical American tree **2** a bowl made from the dried hollow shell of a calabash
WORD ORIGIN obsolete French *calabasse*

calabrese (kal-lab-bray-zee) *n* a kind of green sprouting broccoli
WORD ORIGIN Italian: from Calabria (region of SW Italy)

THESAURUS

café *n* **1 = snack bar,** restaurant, cafeteria, coffee shop, brasserie, coffee bar, tearoom, lunchroom, eatery *or* eaterie

cage *n* **1 = enclosure,** pen, coop, hutch, pound, corral *(US)*

cake *n* **2 = block,** bar, slab, lump, cube, loaf, mass

DICTIONARY

calamari *n* squid cooked for eating, esp. cut into rings and fried in batter **WORD ORIGIN** from Italian, plural of *calamaro* squid
calamine *n* a pink powder consisting chiefly of zinc oxide, used to make soothing skin lotions and ointments **WORD ORIGIN** Medieval Latin *calamina*
calamitous *adj* resulting in or from disaster: *the country's calamitous economic decline*
calamity *n, pl* **-ties** a disaster or misfortune **WORD ORIGIN** Latin *calamitas*
Calamity Jane *n* real name **Martha Canary** ?1852–1903 US frontierswoman, noted for her skill at shooting and riding
calcareous (kal-**care**-ee-uss) *adj* of or containing calcium carbonate **WORD ORIGIN** Latin *calx* lime
calciferol *n* a substance found in fish oils and used in the treatment of rickets. Also called: **vitamin D$_2$** **WORD ORIGIN** *calcif(erous + ergost)erol*, a substance in plants that is a source of vitamin D
calciferous *adj* producing salts of calcium, esp. calcium carbonate
calcify *vb* **-fies, -fying, -fied** to harden by the depositing of calcium salts **calcification** *n* **WORD ORIGIN** Latin *calx* lime
calcine *vb* **-cining, -cined** to oxidize (a substance) by heating **calcination** *n* **WORD ORIGIN** Medieval Latin *calcinare* to heat
calcite *n* a colourless or white form of calcium carbonate
calcium *n chem* a soft silvery-white metallic element found in bones, teeth, limestone, and chalk. Symbol: Ca **WORD ORIGIN** Latin *calx* lime
calcium carbonate *n* a white crystalline salt found in limestone, chalk, and pearl, used to make cement
calcium hydroxide *n* a white crystalline alkali used to make mortar and soften water
calcium oxide *n* ▸ same as **quicklime**
calculable *adj* able to be computed or estimated
calculate *vb* **-lating, -lated 1** to solve or find out by a mathematical procedure or by reasoning **2** to aim to have a particular effect: *this ad campaign is calculated to offend* **WORD ORIGIN** Latin *calculare*, from *calculus* pebble used as a counter
calculated ❶ *adj* **1** undertaken after considering the likelihood of success: *a calculated gamble* **2** carefully planned: *a calculated and callous murder*
calculating ❶ *adj* selfishly scheming
calculation ❶ *n* **1** the act or result of calculating **2** selfish scheming: *there was an element of calculation in her insistence on arriving after dark*
calculator *n* a small electronic device for doing mathematical calculations
calculus *n* **1** the branch of mathematics dealing with infinitesimal changes to a variable number or quantity **2** *pl* **-li** *pathol* ▸ same as **stone** (sense 7) **WORD ORIGIN** Latin: pebble
Calder *n* **Alexander** 1898–1976, US sculptor, who originated mobiles and stabiles (moving or static abstract sculptures, generally suspended from wire)
Calderón de la Barca *n* **Pedro** 1600–81, Spanish dramatist, whose best-known work is *La Vida es Sueño*. He also wrote *autos sacramentales*, outdoor plays for the feast of Corpus Christi, 76 of which survive
Caldwell *n* **Erskine** 1903–87, US novelist whose works include *Tobacco Road* (1933)
Caledonian *adj* Scottish **WORD ORIGIN** from *Caledonia*, the Roman name for Scotland
calendar *n* **1** a chart showing a year divided up into months, weeks, and days **2** a system for determining the beginning, length, and divisions of years: *the Jewish calendar* **3** a schedule of events or appointments: *concerts were an important part of the social calendar of the Venetian nobility* **WORD ORIGIN** Latin *kalendae* the calends
calender *n* **1** a machine in which paper or cloth is smoothed by passing it between rollers ▹*vb* **2** to smooth in such a machine **WORD ORIGIN** French *calandre*
calends *or* **kalends** *pl n* (in the ancient Roman calendar) the first day of each month **WORD ORIGIN** Latin *kalendae*
calendula *n* a plant with orange-and-yellow rayed flowers **WORD ORIGIN** Medieval Latin
calf[1] *n, pl* **calves 1** a young cow, bull, elephant, whale, or seal **2** ▸ same as **calfskin** **WORD ORIGIN** Old English *cealf*
calf[2] *n, pl* **calves** the back of the leg between the ankle and the knee **WORD ORIGIN** Old Norse *kālfi*
calf love *n* adolescent infatuation
calfskin *n* fine leather made from the skin of a calf
calibrate *vb* **-brating, -brated** to mark the scale or check the accuracy of (a measuring instrument) **calibration** *n*
calibre ❶ *or US* **caliber** (**kal**-lib-ber) *n* **1** a person's ability or worth: *a poet of Wordsworth's calibre* **2** the diameter of the bore of a gun or of a shell or bullet **WORD ORIGIN** Arabic *qālib* shoemaker's last, mould
calico *n* a white or unbleached cotton fabric **WORD ORIGIN** *Calicut*, town in India
californium *n chem* a radioactive metallic element produced artificially. Symbol: Cf **WORD ORIGIN** after the University of *California*, where it was discovered
caliper *n US* ▸ same as **calliper**
caliph *n islam* the title of the successors of Mohammed as rulers of the Islamic world **WORD ORIGIN** Arabic *khalīfa* successor
caliphate *n* the office, jurisdiction, or reign of a caliph
calisthenics *n* ▸ same as **callisthenics**
call ❶ *vb* **1** to name: *a town called Eyemouth* **2** to describe (someone or something) as being: *they called him a Hitler* **3** to speak loudly so as to attract attention **4** to telephone: *he left a message for Lynch to call him* **5** to summon: *a doctor must be called immediately* **6** to pay someone a visit: *the social worker called and she didn't answer the door* **7** to arrange: *the meeting was called for the lunch hour* **8 call someone's bluff** ▸ see **bluff**[1] (sense 3) ▹*n* **9** a cry or shout **10** the cry made by a bird or animal **11** a communication by telephone **12** a short visit: *I paid a call on an old friend* **13** a summons or invitation: *the police and fire brigade continued to respond to calls* **14** need, demand, or desire: *a call for economic sanctions* **15** allure or fascination: *the call of the open road*

THESAURUS

calculated *adj* **1, 2 = deliberate**, planned, considered, studied, intended, intentional, designed, aimed, purposeful, premeditated **OPPOSITE:** unplanned
calculating *adj* **= scheming**, designing, sharp, shrewd, cunning, contriving, sly, canny, devious, manipulative, crafty, Machiavellian **OPPOSITE:** direct
calculation *n* **1 = computation**, working out, reckoning, figuring, estimate, forecast, judgment, estimation, result, answer **2 = planning**, intention, deliberation, foresight, contrivance, forethought, circumspection, premeditation
calibre *or (US)* **caliber** *n* **1 = worth**, quality, ability, talent, gifts, capacity, merit, distinction, faculty, endowment, stature **2 = diameter**, bore, gauge, measure
call *vb* **1 = name**, entitle, dub, designate, term, style, label, describe as, christen, denominate **3 = cry**, announce, shout, scream, proclaim, yell, cry out, whoop **OPPOSITE:** whisper **4 = phone**, contact, telephone, ring (up) *(informal, chiefly Brit)*, give

DICTIONARY

C

16 on call available when summoned: *there's a doctor on call in town* ▸ See also **call for, call in,** etc.
caller *n*
WORD ORIGIN Old English *ceallian*

call box *n* a soundproof enclosure for a public telephone

call centre *n Brit, Austral & NZ* an office where staff carry out an organization's telephone transactions

call for *vb* **1** to require: *appendicitis calls for removal of the appendix* **2** to come and fetch

call girl *n* a prostitute with whom appointments are made by telephone

Callicrates *n* 5th century BC, Greek architect: with Ictinus, designed the Parthenon

calligraphy *n* beautiful handwriting
calligrapher *n* **calligraphic** *adj*
WORD ORIGIN Greek *kallos* beauty + -GRAPHY

Callimachus *n* **1** late 5th century BC, Greek sculptor, reputed to have invented the Corinthian capital **2** ?305–?240 BC, Greek poet of the Alexandrian School; author of hymns and epigrams

call in *vb* **1** to summon to one's assistance: *she called in a contractor to make the necessary repairs* **2** to pay a brief visit **3** to demand payment of (a loan): *if the share price continues to drop, some banks may call in their loans*

calling ❶ *n* **1** a strong urge to follow a particular profession or occupation, esp. a caring one **2** a profession or occupation, esp. a caring one

Calliope *n Greek myth* the Muse of epic poetry

calliper *or US* **caliper** *n* **1** a metal splint for supporting the leg **2** a measuring instrument consisting of two steel legs hinged together
WORD ORIGIN variant of *calibre*

callisthenics *or* **calisthenics** *n* light exercises designed to promote general fitness **callisthenic** *or* **calisthenic** *adj*
WORD ORIGIN Greek *kalli-* beautiful + *sthenos* strength

call off *vb* **1** to cancel or abandon: *the strike has now been called off* **2** to order (a dog or a person) to stop attacking someone

call on *or* **upon** *vb* to make an appeal or request to: *church leaders called on political leaders to resume the discussions*

callous *adj* showing no concern for other people's feelings **callously** *adv* **callousness** *n*
WORD ORIGIN Latin *callosus*

calloused *adj* covered in calluses

call out *vb* **1** to shout loudly **2** to summon to one's assistance: *the army and air force have been called out to help drop food packets* **3** to order (workers) to strike

callow *adj* young and inexperienced: *a callow youth*
WORD ORIGIN Old English *calu*

Callow *n* **Simon** born 1949, British actor and theatre director

call up *vb* **1** to summon for active military service **2** to cause one to remember ▹ *n* **call-up 3** a general order to report for military service

callus *n, pl* **-luses** an area of hard or thickened skin on the hand or foot
WORD ORIGIN Latin *callum* hardened skin

calm ❶ *adj* **1** not showing or not feeling agitation or excitement **2** not ruffled by the wind: *a flat calm sea* **3** (of weather) windless ▹ *n* **4** a peaceful state ▹ *vb* **5** (often foll. by *down*) to make or become calm
calmly *adv* **calmness** *n*
WORD ORIGIN Late Latin *cauma* heat, hence a rest during the heat of the day

Calor Gas *n trademark, Brit* butane gas liquefied under pressure in portable containers for domestic use

caloric (kal-**or**-ik) *adj* of heat or calories

calorie *n* **1** a unit of measure for the energy value of food **2** Also: **small calorie** the quantity of heat required to raise the temperature of 1 gram of water by 1°C
WORD ORIGIN Latin *calor* heat

Calorie *n* **1** Also: **large calorie** a unit of heat, equal to one thousand calories **2** the amount of a food capable of producing one calorie of energy

calorific *adj* of calories or heat

calumniate *vb* **-ating, -ated** to make false or malicious statements about (someone)

calumny *n, pl* **-nies** a false or malicious statement; slander
WORD ORIGIN Latin *calumnia* slander

Calvary *n Christianity* the place just outside the walls of Jerusalem where Jesus Christ was crucified
WORD ORIGIN Latin *calvaria* skull

calve *vb* **calving, calved** to give birth to a calf

Calvert *n* **1** Sir **George,** 1st Baron Baltimore. ?1580–1632, English statesman; founder of the colony of Maryland **2** his son, **Leonard** 1606–47, English statesman; first colonial governor of Maryland (1634–47)

calves *n* ▸ the plural of **calf**

Calvinism *n* the theological system of Calvin, the 16th-century French theologian, stressing predestination and salvation solely by God's grace
Calvinist *n, adj* **Calvinistic** *adj*

Calvino *n* **Italo** 1923–85, Italian novelist and short-story writer. His works include *Our Ancestors* (1960) and *Invisible Cities* (1972)

calypso *n, pl* **-sos** a West Indian song with improvised topical lyrics
WORD ORIGIN probably from *Calypso,* sea nymph in Greek mythology

calyx (**kale**-ix) *n, pl* **calyxes** *or* **calyces** (**kal**-iss-seez) the outer leaves that protect the developing bud of a flower
WORD ORIGIN Latin: shell, husk

Calzaghe *n* **Joe** born 1972, Welsh boxer: world middleweight champion from 1997

calzone (kal-**zone**-ee) *n* a folded pizza filled with cheese, tomatoes, etc.

cam *n* a part of an engine that converts a circular motion into a to-and-fro motion
WORD ORIGIN Dutch *kam* comb

camaraderie *n* familiarity and trust between friends
WORD ORIGIN French

camber *n* a slight upward curve to the centre of a road surface
WORD ORIGIN Latin *camurus* curved

Cambodian *adj* **1** of Cambodia ▹ *n* **2** a person from Cambodia

Cambrian *adj geol* of the period of geological time about 600 million years ago

cambric *n* a fine white linen fabric
WORD ORIGIN Flemish *Kamerijk* Cambrai

THESAURUS

(someone) a bell *(Brit slang)* ▹ *n* **9 = cry**, shout, scream, yell, whoop **OPPOSITE:** whisper **12 = visit 13 = request**, order, demand, appeal, notice, command, announcement, invitation, plea, summons, supplication **14 = need**, cause, reason, grounds, occasion, excuse, justification, claim **15 = attraction**, draw, pull *(informal)*, appeal, lure, attractiveness, allure, magnetism

calling *n* **2 = profession**, work, business, line, trade, career, mission, employment, province, occupation, pursuit, vocation, walk of life, life's work, métier

calm *adj* **1 = cool**, relaxed, composed, sedate, undisturbed, collected, unmoved, dispassionate, unfazed *(informal)*, impassive, unflappable *(informal)*, unruffled, unemotional, self-possessed, imperturbable, equable, keeping your cool, unexcited, unexcitable, as cool as a cucumber, chilled *(informal)* **OPPOSITE:** excited **2, 3 = still**, quiet, smooth, peaceful, mild, serene, tranquil, placid, halcyon, balmy, restful, windless, pacific **OPPOSITE:** rough ▹ *n* **4a = peacefulness**, peace, serenity, calmness **4b = stillness**, peace, quiet, hush, serenity, tranquillity, repose, calmness, peacefulness ▹ *vb* **5a = soothe**, settle,

DICTIONARY

Cambs Cambridgeshire

Cambyses *n* died ?522 BC, king of Persia (529–522 BC), who conquered Egypt (525); son of Cyrus the Great

camcorder *n* a combined portable video camera and recorder

Camden[1] *n* a borough of N Greater London. Pop: 210 700 (2003 est). Area: 21 sq km (8 sq miles)

Camden[2] *n* **William** 1551–1623, English antiquary and historian; author of *Britannia* (1586)

came *vb* ▸ the past tense of **come**

camel *n* either of two humped mammals, the dromedary and Bactrian camel, that can survive long periods without food or water in desert regions
WORD ORIGIN Greek *kamēlos*

camellia (kam-**meal**-ya) *n* an ornamental shrub with glossy leaves and white, pink, or red flowers
WORD ORIGIN after G. J. *Kamel*, Jesuit missionary

camel's hair *or* **camelhair** *n* soft cloth, usually tan in colour, which is made from camel's hair and is used to make coats

Camembert (**kam**-mem-bare) *n* a soft creamy cheese
WORD ORIGIN *Camembert*, village in Normandy

cameo *n, pl* **cameos** **1** a brooch or ring with a profile head carved in relief **2** a small but important part in a film or play played by a well-known actor or actress
WORD ORIGIN Italian *cammeo*

camera *n* **1** a piece of equipment used for taking photographs or pictures for television or cinema **2 in camera** in private
WORD ORIGIN Greek *kamara* vault

cameraman *n, pl* **-men** a man who operates a camera for television or cinema

camera obscura *n* a darkened room with an opening through which images of outside objects are projected onto a flat surface
WORD ORIGIN New Latin

camera phone *n* a mobile phone incorporating a camera

Cameron *n* **1 David** (**William Donald**) born 1966, British politician; leader of the Conservative party from 2005; prime minister from 2010 **2** (**Mark**) **James** (**Walter**) 1911–85, British journalist, author, and broadcaster. His books include *Witness in Vietnam* (1966) and *Point of Departure* (1967). **3 James** born 1954, Canadian film director and screenwriter; his films include *The Terminator* (1984), *Aliens* (1986) and *Titanic* (1997) **4 Julia Margaret** 1815–79, British photographer, born in India, renowned for her portrait photographs

camiknickers *pl n Brit* a woman's undergarment consisting of knickers attached to a camisole top

camisole *n* a woman's bodice-like garment with shoulder straps
WORD ORIGIN French

Camoëns *or Portuguese* **Camões** *n* **Luis Vaz de** 1524–80, Portuguese epic poet; author of *The Lusiads* (1572)

camomile *or* **chamomile** (**kam**-mo-mile) *n* a sweet-smelling plant used to make herbal tea
WORD ORIGIN Greek *khamaimēlon* earth-apple (referring to the scent of the flowers)

camouflage ❶ (**kam**-moo-flahzh) *n* **1** the use of natural surroundings or artificial aids to conceal or disguise something ▹ *vb* **-flaging, -flaged** **2** to conceal by camouflage
WORD ORIGIN French

camp[1] ❶ *n* **1** a place where people stay in tents **2** a collection of huts and other buildings used as temporary lodgings for military troops or for prisoners of war **3** a group that supports a particular doctrine: *the socialist camp* ▹ *vb* **4** to stay in a camp **camper** *n* **camping** *n*
WORD ORIGIN Latin *campus* field

camp[2] ❶ *informal adj* **1** effeminate or homosexual **2** consciously artificial, vulgar, or affected ▹ *vb* **3 camp it up** to behave in a camp manner
WORD ORIGIN origin unknown

Camp *n* **Walter** (**Chauncey**) 1859–1925, US sportsman and administrator; he introduced new rules to American football, which distinguished it from rugby

campaign ❶ *n* **1** a series of coordinated activities designed to achieve a goal **2** *mil* a number of operations aimed at achieving a single objective ▹ *vb* **3** to take part in a campaign: *he paid tribute to all those who'd campaigned for his release* **campaigner** *n*
WORD ORIGIN Latin *campus* field

Campanella *n* **Tommaso** 1568–1639, Italian philosopher and Dominican friar. During his imprisonment by the Spaniards (1599–1626) he wrote his celebrated utopian fantasy, *La città del sole*

campanile (camp-an-**neel**-lee) *n* a bell tower, usually one not attached to another building
WORD ORIGIN Italian

campanology *n* the art of ringing bells **campanologist** *n*
WORD ORIGIN Late Latin *campana* bell

campanula *n* a plant with blue or white bell-shaped flowers
WORD ORIGIN New Latin: a little bell

camp bed *n* a lightweight folding bed

Campbell *n* **1** Sir **Colin,** Baron Clyde. 1792–1863, British field marshal who relieved Lucknow for the second time (1857) and commanded in Oudh, suppressing the Indian Mutiny **2 Donald** 1921–67, English water speed record-holder **3** Sir **Malcolm,** father of Donald Campbell. 1885–1948, English racing driver and land speed record-holder **4** Mrs **Patrick,** original name *Beatrice Stella Tanner.* 1865–1940, English actress **5 Roy** 1901–57, South African poet. His poetry is often satirical and includes *The Flaming Terrapin* (1924) **6 Thomas** 1777–1844, Scottish poet and critic, noted particularly for his war poems *Hohenlinden* and *Ye Mariners of England*

Campese *n* **David** born 1962, Australian rugby union player

camp follower *n* **1** a person who supports a particular group or organization without being a member of it **2** a civilian who unofficially provides services to military personnel

camphor *n* a sweet-smelling crystalline substance obtained from the wood of the **camphor tree**, which is used medicinally and in mothballs
WORD ORIGIN Arabic *kāfūr*

camphorated *adj* impregnated with camphor

Campin *n* **Robert** 1379–1444, Flemish painter, noted esp. for his altarpieces: usually identified with the so-called Master of Flémalle

campion *n* a red, pink, or white European wild flower
WORD ORIGIN origin unknown

Campion *n* **1 Saint Edmund** 1540–81, English Jesuit martyr. He joined the Jesuits in 1573 and returned to England (1580) as a missionary. He was charged with treason and hanged **2 Jane** born 1954, New

THESAURUS

quiet, relax, appease, still, allay, assuage, quieten **OPPOSITE:** excite **5b = placate**, hush, pacify, mollify **OPPOSITE:** aggravate

camouflage *n* **1 = protective colouring**, mimicry, false appearance, deceptive markings ▹ *vb* **2 = disguise**, cover, screen, hide, mask, conceal, obscure, veil, cloak, obfuscate **OPPOSITE:** reveal

camp[1] *n* **1 = camp site**, tents, encampment, camping ground **2 = bivouac**, cantonment (*military*)

camp[2] *adj* **1 = effeminate**, campy (*informal*), camped up (*informal*), poncy (*slang*) **2 = affected**, mannered, artificial, posturing, ostentatious, campy (*informal*), camped up (*informal*)

campaign *n* **1 = drive**, appeal, movement, push (*informal*), offensive, crusade **2 = operation**, drive, attack, movement, push, offensive, expedition, crusade, jihad

DICTIONARY

Zealand film director and screenwriter: her films include *An Angel at My Table* (1990), *The Piano* (1993), *Holy Smoke* (1999), and *In the Cut* (2003) **3 Thomas** 1567–1620, English poet and musician, noted particularly for his songs for the lute

C

camp oven *n Austral & NZ* a heavy metal pot or box with a lid, used for baking over an open fire

camp site *n* a place where people can stay in tents

campus *n, pl* **-puses** the grounds and buildings of a university or college
WORD ORIGIN Latin: field

camshaft *n* a part of an engine consisting of a rod to which cams are attached

Camus *n* **Albert** 1913–60, French novelist, dramatist, and essayist, noted for his pessimistic portrayal of man's condition of isolation in an absurd world: author of the novels *L'Étranger* (1942) and *La Peste* (1947), the plays *Le Malentendu* (1945) and *Caligula* (1946), and the essays *Le Mythe de Sisyphe* (1942) and *L'Homme révolté* (1951): Nobel prize for literature 1957

can[1] *vb, past* **could 1** be able to: *make sure he can breathe easily* **2** be allowed to: *you can swim in the large pool*
WORD ORIGIN Old English *cunnan*

can[2] *n* **1** a metal container, usually sealed, for food or liquids ▷*vb* **canning, canned 2** to put (something) into a can
WORD ORIGIN Old English *canne*

Can. 1 Canada **2** Canadian

Canada Day *n* (in Canada) July 1, a public holiday marking the anniversary of the day in 1867 when Canada became a dominion

Canada goose *n* a greyish-brown North American goose with a black neck and head

Canada jay *n* a grey jay of northern N America, notorious for stealing

Canadian *adj* **1** of Canada ▷*n* **2** a person from Canada

Canadiana *pl n* objects relating to Canadian history and culture

Canadian football *n* a game like American football played on a grass field between teams of 12 players

Canadianism *n* **1** the Canadian national character or spirit **2** a linguistic feature peculiar to Canada or Canadians

Canadianize *or* **-ise** *vb* **-izing, -ized** *or* **-ising, -ised** to make Canadian

Canadian Shield *n* the wide area of Precambrian rock extending over most of central and E Canada: rich in minerals

Canadien *or fem* **Canadienne** (kan-ad-ee-en) *n* a French Canadian
WORD ORIGIN French: Canadian

canaille (kan-nye) *n* the masses or rabble
WORD ORIGIN French, from Italian *canaglia* pack of dogs

canal ❶ *n* **1** an artificial waterway constructed for navigation or irrigation **2** a passage or duct in a person's body: *the alimentary canal*
WORD ORIGIN Latin *canna* reed

Canaletto *n* original name *Giovanni Antonio Canale*. 1697–1768, Italian painter and etc her, noted particularly for his highly detailed paintings of cities, esp. Venice, which are marked by strong contrasts of light and shade

canalize *or* **-lise** *vb* **-lizing, -lized** *or* **-lising, -lised 1** to give direction to (a feeling or activity) **2** to convert into a canal **canalization** *or* **-lisation** *n*

canapé (kan-nap-pay) *n* a small piece of bread or toast spread with a savoury topping
WORD ORIGIN French: sofa

canard *n* a false report
WORD ORIGIN French: a duck

canary *n, pl* **-naries** a small yellow songbird often kept as a pet

canasta *n* a card game like rummy, played with two packs of cards
WORD ORIGIN Spanish: basket (because two packs, or a basketful, of cards are required)

cancan *n* a lively high-kicking dance performed by a female group
WORD ORIGIN French

cancel ❶ *vb* **-celling, -celled** *or US* **-celing, -celed 1** to stop (something that has been arranged) from taking place **2** to mark (a cheque or stamp) with an official stamp to prevent further use **3 cancel out** to make ineffective by having the opposite effect: *economic vulnerability cancels out any possible political gain* **cancellation** *n*
WORD ORIGIN Late Latin *cancellare* to strike out, make like a lattice

cancer ❶ *n* **1** a serious disease resulting from a malignant growth or tumour, caused by abnormal and uncontrolled cell division **2** a malignant growth or tumour **3** an evil influence that spreads dangerously: *their country would remain a cancer of instability* **cancerous** *adj*
WORD ORIGIN Latin: crab, creeping tumour

Cancer *n* **1** *astrol* the fourth sign of the zodiac; the Crab **2 tropic of Cancer** ▸see **tropic** (sense 1)
WORD ORIGIN Latin

candela (kan-dee-la) *n* the SI unit of luminous intensity (the amount of light a source gives off in a given direction)
WORD ORIGIN Latin: candle

Candela *n* **Felix** 1910–97, Mexican architect, noted for his naturalistic modern style and thin prestressed concrete roofs

candelabrum *or* **candelabra** *n, pl* **-bra, -brums** *or* **-bras** a large branched holder for candles or overhead lights
WORD ORIGIN Latin *candela* candle

candid *adj* honest and straightforward in speech or behaviour **candidly** *adv*
WORD ORIGIN Latin *candere* to be white

candidate ❶ *n* **1** a person seeking a job or position **2** a person taking an examination **3** a person or thing regarded as suitable or likely for a particular fate or position: *someone who smokes, drinks, or eats too much is a candidate for heart disease* **candidacy** *or* **candidature** *n*
WORD ORIGIN Latin *candidatus* clothed in white

candied *adj* coated with or cooked in sugar: *candied peel*

candle *n* **1** a stick or block of wax or tallow surrounding a wick, which is burned to produce light **2 burn the candle at both ends** to exhaust oneself by doing too much
WORD ORIGIN Latin *candela*

candlelight *n* the light from a candle or candles **candlelit** *adj*

Candlemas *n Christianity* February 2, the Feast of the Purification of the Virgin Mary

candlepower *n* the luminous intensity of a source of light: now expressed in candelas

candlestick *or* **candleholder** *n* a holder for a candle

candlewick *n* cotton with a tufted pattern, used to make bedspreads and dressing gowns

Candolle *n* **Augustin Pyrame de** 1778–1841, Swiss botanist; his *Théorie élémentaire de la botanique* (1813) introduced a new system of plant classification

candour *or US* **candor** *n* honesty and straightforwardness of speech or behaviour
WORD ORIGIN Latin *candor*

candy *n, pl* **-dies** *chiefly US & Canad*

THESAURUS

canal *n* **1 = waterway**, channel, passage, conduit, duct, watercourse

cancel *vb* **1 = call off**, drop, abandon, forget about
3 cancel something out = counterbalance, offset, make up for, compensate for, redeem, neutralize, nullify, obviate, balance out

cancer *n* **2 = growth**, tumour, carcinoma *(pathology)*, malignancy **3 = evil**, corruption, rot, sickness, blight, pestilence, canker

candidate *n* **1 = contender**, competitor, applicant, nominee, entrant, claimant, contestant, suitor, aspirant, possibility, runner

DICTIONARY

a sweet or sweets
WORD ORIGIN Arabic *qand* cane sugar
candyfloss *n Brit* a light fluffy mass of spun sugar, held on a stick
candy-striped *adj* having narrow coloured stripes on a white background
candytuft *n* a garden plant with clusters of white, pink, or purple flowers
cane *n* **1** the long flexible stems of the bamboo or any similar plant **2** strips of such stems, woven to make wickerwork **3** a bamboo stem tied to a garden plant to support it **4** a flexible rod used to beat someone **5** a slender walking stick ▷ *vb* **caning, caned 6** to beat with a cane
WORD ORIGIN Greek *kanna*
cane sugar *n* the sugar that is obtained from sugar cane
cane toad *n* a large toad used to control insects and other pests of sugar cane plantations
Canetti *n* **Elias** 1905–94, British novelist and writer, born in Bulgaria, who usually wrote in German. His works include the novel *Auto da Fé* (1935). Nobel prize for literature 1981
canine (kay-nine) *adj* **1** of or like a dog ▷ *n* **2** a sharp-pointed tooth between the incisors and the molars
WORD ORIGIN Latin *canis* dog
canister *n* a metal container for dry food
WORD ORIGIN Latin *canistrum* basket woven from reeds
canker *n* **1** an ulceration or ulcerous disease **2** something evil that spreads and corrupts
WORD ORIGIN Latin *cancer* cancerous sore
cannabis ❶ *n* a drug obtained from the dried leaves and flowers of the hemp plant
WORD ORIGIN Greek *kannabis*
canned *adj* **1** preserved in a can **2** *informal* recorded in advance: *canned carols*
cannelloni *or* **canneloni** *pl n* tubular pieces of pasta filled with meat or cheese
WORD ORIGIN Italian
cannery *n, pl* **-neries** a place where foods are canned
cannibal *n* **1** a person who eats human flesh **2** an animal that eats the flesh of other animals of its kind
cannibalism *n*
WORD ORIGIN Spanish *Canibales* natives of Cuba and Haiti
cannibalize *or* **-ise** *vb* **-izing, -ized** *or* **-ising, -ised** to use parts from (one machine or vehicle) to repair another
canning *n* the process of sealing food in cans to preserve it
cannon ❶ *n, pl* **-nons** *or* **-non 1** a large gun consisting of a metal tube mounted on a carriage, formerly used in battles **2** an automatic aircraft gun **3** *billiards* a shot in which the cue ball strikes two balls successively ▷ *vb* **4 cannon into** to collide with
WORD ORIGIN Italian *canna* tube
cannonade *n* continuous heavy gunfire
cannonball *n* a heavy metal ball fired from a cannon
cannon fodder *n* men regarded as expendable in war
cannot *vb* can not
canny *adj* **-nier, -niest** shrewd or cautious **cannily** *adv*
WORD ORIGIN from *can* (in the sense: to know how)
canoe *n* a light narrow open boat, propelled by one or more paddles
canoeist *n*
WORD ORIGIN Carib
canoeing *n* the sport of rowing or racing in a canoe
canon¹ *n* a priest serving in a cathedral
WORD ORIGIN Late Latin *canonicus* person living under a rule
canon² ❶ *n* **1** *Christianity* a Church decree regulating morals or religious practices **2** a general rule or standard: *the Marx-Engels canon* **3** a list of the works of an author that are accepted as authentic: *the Yeats canon* **4** a piece of music in which a melody in one part is taken up in one or more other parts successively
WORD ORIGIN Greek *kanōn* rule
canonical *adj* **1** conforming with canon law **2** included in a canon of writings
canonical hour *n RC church* one of the seven prayer times appointed for each day
canonicals *pl n* the official clothes worn by clergy when taking services
canonize *or* **-ise** *vb* **-izing, -ized** *or* **-ising, -ised** *RC church* to declare (a dead person) to be a saint
canonization *or* **-isation** *n*
canon law *n* the body of laws of a Christian Church
canoodle *vb* **-dling, -dled** *slang* to kiss and cuddle
WORD ORIGIN origin unknown
canopied *adj* covered with a canopy: *canopied niches*
canopy ❶ *n, pl* **-pies 1** an ornamental awning above a bed or throne **2** a rooflike covering over an altar, niche, or door **3** any large or wide covering: *the thick forest canopy* **4** the part of a parachute that opens out **5** the transparent hood of an aircraft cockpit
WORD ORIGIN Greek *kōnōpeion* bed with a mosquito net
Canova *n* **Antonio** 1757–1822, Italian neoclassical sculptor
cant¹ *n* **1** insincere talk concerning religion or morals **2** specialized vocabulary of a particular group, such as thieves or lawyers ▷ *vb* **3** to use cant: *canting hypocrites*
WORD ORIGIN probably from Latin *cantare* to sing
cant² *n* **1** a tilted position ▷ *vb* **2** to tilt or overturn: *the engine was canted to one side*
WORD ORIGIN perhaps from Latin *canthus* iron hoop round a wheel
can't *vb* can not
cantabile (kan-tah-bill-lay) *adv music* flowing and melodious
WORD ORIGIN Italian
cantaloupe *or* **cantaloup** *n Brit* a kind of melon with sweet-tasting orange flesh
WORD ORIGIN *Cantaluppi*, near Rome, where first cultivated in Europe
cantankerous *adj* quarrelsome or bad-tempered
WORD ORIGIN origin unknown
cantata (kan-tah-ta) *n* a musical setting of a text, consisting of arias, duets, and choruses
WORD ORIGIN Italian
canteen *n* **1** a restaurant attached to a workplace or school **2** a box containing a set of cutlery
WORD ORIGIN Italian *cantina* wine cellar
Canteloube *n* **(Marie) Joseph** 1879–1957, French composer, best known for his *Chants d'Auvergne* (1923–30)
canter *n* **1** a gait of horses that is faster than a trot but slower than a gallop ▷ *vb* **2** (of a horse) to move at a canter
WORD ORIGIN short for *Canterbury trot*, the pace at which pilgrims rode to Canterbury
canticle *n* a short hymn with words from the Bible
WORD ORIGIN Latin *canticulum*
cantilever *n* a beam or girder fixed at one end only
WORD ORIGIN origin unknown

THESAURUS

cannabis *n* **= marijuana**, pot *(slang)*, dope *(slang)*, hash *(slang)*, blow *(slang)*, smoke *(informal)*, stuff *(slang)*, leaf *(slang)*, tea *(US slang)*, grass *(slang)*, chronic *(US slang)*, weed *(slang)*, hemp, gage *(US obsolete, slang)*, hashish, mary jane *(US slang)*, ganja, bhang, kif, sinsemilla, dagga *(S African)*, charas
cannon *n* **1 = gun**, big gun, artillery piece, field gun, mortar
canon² *n* **2 = rule**, standard, principle, regulation, formula, criterion, dictate, statute, yardstick, precept **3 = list**, index, catalogue, syllabus, roll
canopy *n* **1, 2 = awning**, covering, shade, shelter, sunshade

DICTIONARY

cantilever bridge *n* a bridge made of two cantilevers which meet in the middle

canto (kan-toe) *n, pl* **-tos** a main division of a long poem
WORD ORIGIN Italian: song

canton *n* a political division of a country, such as Switzerland
WORD ORIGIN Old French: corner

Cantonese *adj* **1** of Canton, a port in SE China ▹*n* **2** *pl* **-nese** a person from Canton **3** the Chinese dialect of Canton

cantonment (kan-toon-ment) *n* a permanent military camp in British India
WORD ORIGIN Old French *canton* corner

cantor *n judaism* a man employed to lead synagogue services
WORD ORIGIN Latin: singer

Canuck *n, adj US & Canad informal* Canadian
WORD ORIGIN origin unknown

canvas *n* **1** a heavy cloth of cotton, hemp, or jute, used to make tents and sails and for painting on in oils **2** an oil painting done on canvas **3 under canvas** in a tent: *sleeping under canvas*
WORD ORIGIN Latin *cannabis* hemp

canvass *vb* **1** to try to persuade (people) to vote for a particular candidate or party in an election **2** to find out the opinions of (people) by conducting a survey ▹*n* **3** the activity of canvassing **canvasser** *n* **canvassing** *n*
WORD ORIGIN probably from obsolete sense of *canvas* (to toss someone in a canvas sheet, hence, to criticize)

canyon *n* a deep narrow steep-sided valley
WORD ORIGIN Spanish *cañon*

canyoning *n* the sport of travelling down a river situated in a canyon by a variety of means including scrambling, swimming, and abseiling

caoutchouc (cow-chook) *n* ▸same as **rubber**[1] (sense 1)
WORD ORIGIN from S American Indian

cap **T** *n* **1** a soft close-fitting covering for the head **2** *sport* a cap given to someone selected for a national team **3** a small flat lid: *petrol cap* **4** a small amount of explosive enclosed in paper and used in a toy gun **5** a contraceptive device placed over the mouth of the womb **6** an upper financial limit **7 cap in hand** humbly ▹*vb* **capping, capped 8** to cover or top with something: *a thick cover of snow capped the cars* **9** *sport* to select (a player) for a national team: *Australia's most capped player* **10** to impose an upper level on (a tax): *charge capping* **11** *informal* to outdo or excel: *capping anecdote with anecdote*
WORD ORIGIN Late Latin *cappa* hood

CAP (in the EU) Common Agricultural Policy

cap. capital

Capa *n* **Robert,** real name *André Friedmann.* 1913–54, Hungarian photographer, who established his reputation as a photojournalist during the Spanish Civil War

capability **T** *n, pl* **-ties** the ability or skill to do something

Capablanca *n* **José Raúl**, called *Capa* or *the Chess Machine* 1888–1942, Cuban chess player; world champion 1921–27

capable **T** *adj* **1** having the ability or skill to do something: *a side capable of winning the championship* **2** competent and efficient: *capable high achievers* **capably** *adv*
WORD ORIGIN Latin *capere* to take

capacious *adj* having a large capacity or area
WORD ORIGIN Latin *capere* to take

capacitance *n physics* **1** the ability of a capacitor to store electrical charge **2** a measure of this

capacitor *n physics* a device for storing a charge of electricity

capacity **T** *n, pl* **-ties 1** the ability to contain, absorb, or hold something **2** the maximum amount something can contain or absorb: *filled to capacity* **3** the ability to do something: *his capacity to elicit great loyalty* **4** a position or function: *acting in an official capacity* **5** the maximum output of which an industry or factory is capable: *the refinery had a capacity of three hundred thousand barrels a day* **6** *physics* ▸same as **capacitance** ▹*adj* **7** of the maximum amount or number possible: *a capacity crowd*
WORD ORIGIN Latin *capere* to take

caparisoned (kap-par-riss-sond) *adj* (esp. of a horse) magnificently decorated or dressed
WORD ORIGIN Old Spanish *caparazón* saddlecloth

cape[1] *n* a short sleeveless cloak
WORD ORIGIN Late Latin *cappa*

cape[2] **T** *n* a large piece of land that juts out into the sea
WORD ORIGIN Latin *caput* head

Cape *n* **the Cape 1** the Cape of Good Hope **2** the SW region of South Africa's Cape Province

Capello *n* **Fabio** born 1946. Italian football player and coach; manager of clubs including Real Madrid and AC Milan as well as the Italian national team (1972–76); appointed manager of the England national team 2007

caper *n* **1** a high-spirited escapade ▹*vb* **2** to skip about light-heartedly
WORD ORIGIN probably from CAPRIOLE

capercaillie *or* **capercailzie** (kap-per-kale-yee) *n* a large black European woodland grouse
WORD ORIGIN Scottish Gaelic *capull coille* horse of the woods

capers *pl n* the pickled flower buds of a Mediterranean shrub, used in making sauces
WORD ORIGIN Greek *kapparis* caper plant

capillarity *n physics* a phenomenon caused by surface tension that results in the surface of a liquid rising or falling in contact with a solid

capillary (kap-pill-a-ree) *n, pl* **-laries 1** *anat* one of the very fine blood vessels linking the arteries and the veins ▹*adj* **2** (of a tube) having a fine bore **3** *anat* of the capillaries
WORD ORIGIN Latin *capillus* hair

capital[1] **T** *n* **1** the chief city of a country, where the government meets **2** the total wealth owned or used in business by an individual or group **3** wealth used to produce more wealth by investment **4 make capital out of** to gain advantage from: *to make political capital out of the*

THESAURUS

cap *vb* **8 = top**, cover, crown **11** *(informal)* **= beat**, top, better, exceed, eclipse, lick *(informal)*, surpass, transcend, outstrip, outdo, run rings around *(informal)*, put in the shade, overtop

capability *n* **= ability**, means, power, potential, facility, capacity, qualification(s), faculty, competence, proficiency, wherewithal, potentiality **OPPOSITE:** inability

capable *adj* **1 = able**, fitted, suited, adapted, adequate **OPPOSITE:** incapable **2 = accomplished**, experienced, masterly, qualified, talented, gifted, efficient, clever, intelligent, competent, apt, skilful, adept, proficient **OPPOSITE:** incompetent

capacity *n* **1 = size**, room, range, space, volume, extent, dimensions, scope, magnitude, compass, amplitude **3 = ability**, power, strength, facility, gift, intelligence, efficiency, genius, faculty, capability, forte, readiness, aptitude, aptness, competence *or* competency **4 = function**, position, role, post, appointment, province, sphere, service, office

cape[2] *n* **= headland**, point, head, peninsula, ness *(archaic)*, promontory

capital[1] *n* **2, 3 = money**, funds, stock, investment(s), property, cash, finance, finances, financing, resources, assets, wealth, principal, means, wherewithal ▹*adj* **8** *(old-fashioned)* **= first-rate**, fine, excellent, superb, sterling, splendid, world-class

DICTIONARY

hostage situation **5** a capital letter ▷ *adj* **6** *law* involving or punishable by death: *a capital offence* **7** denoting the large letter used as the initial letter in a sentence, personal name, or place name **8** *Brit, Austral & NZ, old-fashioned* excellent or first-rate: *a capital dinner*
WORD ORIGIN Latin *caput* head

capital² *n* the top part of a column or pillar
WORD ORIGIN Old French *capitel*, from Latin *caput* head

capital gain *n* profit from the sale of an asset

capital goods *pl n econ* goods that are themselves utilized in the production of other goods

capitalism ● *n* an economic system based on the private ownership of industry

capitalist *adj* **1** based on or supporting capitalism: *capitalist countries* ▷ *n* **2** a supporter of capitalism **3** a person who owns a business **capitalistic** *adj*

capitalize *or* **-ise** *vb* **-izing, -ized** *or* **-ising, -ised 1 capitalize on** to take advantage of: *to capitalize on the available opportunities* **2** to write or print (words) in capital letters **3** to convert (debt or earnings) into capital stock **capitalization** *or* **-isation** *n*

capital levy *n* a tax on capital or property as contrasted with a tax on income

capitally *adv old-fashioned* in an excellent manner; admirably

capital punishment *n* the punishment of death for committing a serious crime

capital stock *n* **1** the value of the total shares that a company can issue **2** the total capital existing in an economy at a particular time

capitation *n* a tax of a fixed amount per person
WORD ORIGIN Latin *caput* head

capitulate *vb* **-lating, -lated** to surrender under agreed conditions **capitulation** *n*
WORD ORIGIN Medieval Latin *capitulare* to draw up under headings

capo *n, pl* **-pos** a device fitted across the strings of a guitar or similar instrument so as to raise the pitch
WORD ORIGIN Italian *capo tasto* head stop

capoeira (kap-poo-eer-uh) *n* a combination of martial art and dance, which originated among African slaves in 19th-century Brazil
WORD ORIGIN from Portuguese

capon (kay-pon) *n* a castrated cock fowl fattened for eating
WORD ORIGIN Latin *capo*

caponata (kap-uh-nah-tuh) *n* a dish of fried seasoned aubergine and other vegetables, served as an appetizer
WORD ORIGIN Italian

Capote *n* **Truman** 1924–84, US writer; his novels include *Other Voices, Other Rooms* (1948) and *In Cold Blood* (1964), based on an actual multiple murder

Capp *n* **Al,** full name *Alfred Caplin*. 1909–79, US cartoonist, famous for his comic strip *Li'l Abner*

cappuccino (kap-poo-cheen-oh) *n, pl* **-nos** coffee with steamed milk, usually sprinkled with powdered chocolate
WORD ORIGIN Italian

Capra *n* **Frank** 1896–1992, US film director born in Italy. His films include *It Happened One Night* (1934), *It's a Wonderful Life* (1946), and several propaganda films during World War II

caprice (kap-reess) *n* **1** a sudden change of attitude or behaviour **2** a tendency to have such changes
WORD ORIGIN Italian *capriccio* a shiver, caprice

capricious *adj* having a tendency to sudden unpredictable changes of attitude or behaviour **capriciously** *adv*

Capricorn *n* **1** *astrol* the tenth sign of the zodiac; the Goat **2 tropic of Capricorn** ▸ see **tropic** (sense 1)
WORD ORIGIN Latin *caper* goat + *cornu* horn

capriole *n* **1** an upward but not forward leap made by a horse ▷ *vb* **-oling, -oled 2** to perform a capriole
WORD ORIGIN Latin *capreolus*, *caper* goat

caps. capital letters

capsicum *n* a kind of pepper used as a vegetable or ground to produce a spice
WORD ORIGIN Latin *capsa* box

capsize *vb* **-sizing, -sized** (of a boat) to overturn accidentally
WORD ORIGIN origin unknown

capstan *n* a vertical rotating cylinder round which a ship's rope or cable is wound
WORD ORIGIN Old Provençal *cabestan*

capstone *n* ▸ same as **copestone** (sense 2)

capsule ● *n* **1** a soluble gelatine case containing a dose of medicine **2** *bot* a plant's seed case that opens when ripe **3** *anat* a membrane or sac surrounding an organ or part **4** ▸ see **space capsule** ▷ *adj* **5** very concise: *capsule courses*
WORD ORIGIN Latin *capsa* box

capsulize *or* **-ise** *vb* **-izing, -ized** *or* **-ising, -ised 1** to state (information) in a highly condensed form **2** to enclose in a capsule

Capt. Captain

captain ● *n* **1** the person in charge of a ship, boat, or civil aircraft **2** a middle-ranking naval officer **3** a junior officer in the army **4** the leader of a team or group ▷ *vb* **5** to be captain of **captaincy** *n*
WORD ORIGIN Latin *caput* head

caption *n* **1** a title, brief explanation, or comment accompanying a picture ▷ *vb* **2** to provide with a caption
WORD ORIGIN Latin *captio* a seizing

captious *adj* tending to make trivial criticisms
WORD ORIGIN Latin *captio* a seizing

captivate ● *vb* **-vating, -vated** to attract and hold the attention of; enchant **captivating** *adj*
WORD ORIGIN Latin *captivus* captive

captive ● *n* **1** a person who is kept in confinement ▷ *adj* **2** kept in confinement **3** (of an audience) unable to leave
WORD ORIGIN Latin *captivus*

captivity ● *n* the state of being kept in confinement

captor *n* a person who captures a person or animal

capture ● *vb* **-turing, -tured 1** to take by force **2** to succeed in representing (something elusive) in words, pictures, or music: *today's newspapers capture the mood of the nation* **3** *physics* (of an atomic nucleus) to acquire (an additional particle) ▷ *n* **4** the act of capturing or the state

THESAURUS

capitalism *n* **= private enterprise,** free enterprise, private ownership, laissez faire *or* laisser faire

capsule *n* **1 = pill,** tablet, lozenge, bolus **2** *(botany)* **= pod,** case, shell, vessel, sheath, receptacle, seed case

captain *n* **1 = commander,** officer, skipper, (senior) pilot **4 = leader,** boss, master, skipper, chieftain, head, number one *(informal)*, chief

captivate *vb* **= charm,** attract, fascinate, absorb, entrance, dazzle, seduce, enchant, enthral, beguile, allure, bewitch, ravish, enslave, mesmerize, ensnare, hypnotize, enrapture, sweep off your feet, enamour, infatuate **OPPOSITE:** repel

captive *n* **1 = prisoner,** hostage, convict, prisoner of war, detainee, internee ▷ *adj* **2 = confined,** caged, imprisoned, locked up, enslaved, incarcerated, ensnared, subjugated, penned, restricted

captivity *n* **= confinement,** custody, detention, imprisonment, incarceration, internment, durance *(archaic)*, restraint

capture *vb* **1 = catch,** arrest, take, bag, secure, seize, nail *(informal)*, collar *(informal)*, nab *(informal)*, apprehend, lift *(slang)*, take prisoner, take into custody, feel your collar *(slang)* **OPPOSITE:** release ▷ *n* **4 = arrest,** catching, trapping, imprisonment, seizure, apprehension, taking, taking captive

DICTIONARY

of being captured
WORD ORIGIN Latin *capere* to take
Capuana *n* **Luigi** 1839–1915, Italian realist novelist, dramatist, and critic. His works include the novel *Giacinta* (1879) and the play *Malia* (1895)
capuchin (kap-yew-chin) *n* a S American monkey with a cowl of thick hair on the top of its head
WORD ORIGIN Italian *cappuccio* hood
Capuchin *n* **1** a friar belonging to a branch of the Franciscan Order founded in 1525 ▷ *adj* **2** of this order
WORD ORIGIN Italian *cappuccio* hood
capybara *n* the largest living rodent, found in S America
car ➊ *n* **1** a motorized road vehicle designed to carry a small number of people **2** the passenger compartment of a cable car, airship, lift, or balloon **3** *US & Canad* a railway carriage
WORD ORIGIN Latin *carra*, *carrum* two-wheeled wagon
caracal *n* a lynx with reddish fur, which inhabits deserts of N Africa and S Asia
WORD ORIGIN Turkish *kara kūlāk* black ear
Caracalla *n* real name *Marcus Aurelius Antoninus*, original name *Bassianus*. 188–217 AD, Roman emperor (211–17): ruled with cruelty and extravagance; assassinated
Caractacus *n* same as **Caratacus**
carafe (kar-raff) *n* a wide-mouthed bottle for water or wine
WORD ORIGIN Arabic *gharrāfah* vessel
carambola *n* a yellow edible star-shaped fruit that grows on a Brazilian tree
WORD ORIGIN Spanish
caramel *n* **1** a chewy sweet made from sugar and milk **2** burnt sugar, used for colouring and flavouring food
WORD ORIGIN French
caramelize *or* **-ise** *vb* **-izing, -ized** *or* **-ising, -ised** to turn into caramel
carapace *n* the thick hard upper shell of tortoises and crustaceans
WORD ORIGIN Spanish *carapacho*
carat *n* **1** a unit of weight of precious stones, equal to 0.20 grams **2** a measure of the purity of gold in an alloy, expressed as the number of parts of gold in 24 parts of the alloy
WORD ORIGIN Arabic *qīrāt* weight of four grains
Caratacus, Caractacus, *or* **Caradoc** *n* died ?54 AD, British chieftain: led an unsuccessful resistance against the Romans (43–50)
caravan *n* **1** a large enclosed vehicle designed to be pulled by a car or horse and equipped to be lived in **2** (in some Eastern countries) a company of traders or other travellers journeying together
WORD ORIGIN Persian *kārwān*
caravanning *n* travelling or holidaying in a caravan
caravanserai *n* (in some Eastern countries, esp. formerly) a large inn enclosing a courtyard, providing accommodation for caravans
WORD ORIGIN Persian *kārwānsarāī* caravan inn
caraway *n* a Eurasian plant with seeds that are used as a spice in cooking
WORD ORIGIN Arabic *karawyā*
carb *n informal* ▸ short for **carbohydrate**
carbide *n chem* a compound of carbon with a metal
carbine *n* a type of light rifle
WORD ORIGIN French *carabine*
carbohydrate *n* any of a large group of energy-producing compounds, including sugars and starches, that contain carbon, hydrogen, and oxygen
carbolic acid *n* a disinfectant derived from coal tar
carbon *n* **1** a nonmetallic element occurring in three forms, charcoal, graphite, and diamond, and present in all organic compounds. Symbol: C **2** ▸ short for **carbon paper** or **carbon copy**
WORD ORIGIN Latin *carbo* charcoal
carbonaceous *adj* of, resembling, or containing carbon
carbonate *n* a salt or ester of carbonic acid
carbonated *adj* (of a drink) containing carbon dioxide; fizzy
carbon black *n* powdered carbon produced by partial burning of natural gas or petroleum, used in pigments and ink
carbon capture *n* the removal and storage of carbon dioxide emissions from power plants and factories, instead of releasing it into the atmosphere
carbon copy *n* **1** a duplicate obtained by using carbon paper **2** *informal* a person or thing that is identical or very similar to another
carbon dating *n* a technique for finding the age of organic materials, such as wood, based on their content of radioactive carbon
carbon dioxide *n* a colourless odourless incombustible gas formed during breathing, and used in fire extinguishers and in making fizzy drinks
carbon footprint *n* a measure of the amount of carbon dioxide released into the atmosphere through a single endeavour or through the activities of a person, company, etc. over a given period
carbonic *adj* containing carbon
carbonic acid *n* a weak acid formed when carbon dioxide combines with water
carboniferous *adj* yielding coal or carbon
Carboniferous *adj geol* of the period of geological time about 330 million years ago, during which coal seams were formed
carbonize *or* **-ise** *vb* **-izing, -ized** *or* **-ising, -ised** **1** to turn into carbon as a result of partial burning **2** to coat (a substance) with carbon
carbonization *or* **-isation** *n*
carbon monoxide *n* a colourless odourless poisonous gas formed by the incomplete burning of carbon compounds; part of the gases that come from a vehicle's exhaust
carbon-neutral *adj* not affecting the overall volume of carbon dioxide in the atmosphere
carbon offset *n* a compensatory measure made by an individual or company for carbon emissions, such as tree planting
carbon paper *n* a thin sheet of paper coated on one side with a dark waxy pigment, containing carbon, used to make a duplicate of something as it is typed or written
carbon tax *n* a tax on the emissions caused by the burning of coal, gas, and oil, aimed at reducing the production of greenhouse gases
carbon tetrachloride *n* a colourless nonflammable liquid used as a solvent, cleaning fluid, and insecticide
car boot sale *n* a sale of goods from car boots in a site hired for the occasion
Carborundum *n trademark* an abrasive material consisting of silicon carbide
carboxyl group *or* **radical** *n chem* the chemical group –COOH: the functional group in organic acids
carboy *n* a large bottle protected by a basket or box
WORD ORIGIN Persian *qarāba*
carbuncle *n* a large painful swelling under the skin like a boil
WORD ORIGIN Latin *carbo* coal
carburettor *or US & Canad* **carburetor** *n* a device in an internal-combustion engine that mixes petrol with air and regulates the intake of the mixture into the engine
carcass *or* **carcase** *n* **1** the dead body of an animal **2** *informal* a person's body: *ask that person to move his carcass*
WORD ORIGIN Old French *carcasse*

THESAURUS

car *n* **1 = vehicle**, motor, wheels (*informal*), auto (*US*), automobile, jalopy (*informal*), motorcar, machine **3** (*US & Canad*) **= (railway) carriage**, coach, cable car, dining car, sleeping car, buffet car, van

DICTIONARY

carcinogen *n* a substance that produces cancer **carcinogenic** *adj*
WORD ORIGIN Greek *karkinos* cancer

carcinoma *n, pl* **-mas** *or* **-mata** a malignant tumour
WORD ORIGIN Greek *karkinos* cancer

card[1] *n* **1** a piece of stiff paper or thin cardboard used for identification, reference, proof of membership, or sending greetings or messages: *a Christmas card* **2** one of a set of small pieces of cardboard, marked with figures or symbols, used for playing games or for fortune-telling **3** a small rectangle of stiff plastic with identifying numbers for use as a credit card, cheque card, or charge card **4** *old-fashioned informal* a witty or eccentric person ▸ See also **cards**
WORD ORIGIN Greek *khartēs* leaf of papyrus

card[2] *n* **1** a machine or tool for combing fibres of cotton or wool to disentangle them before spinning ▹ *vb* **2** to process with such a machine or tool
WORD ORIGIN Latin *carduus* thistle

cardamom *n* a spice that is obtained from the seeds of a tropical plant
WORD ORIGIN Greek *kardamon* cress + *amōmon* an Indian spice

cardboard *n* a thin stiff board made from paper pulp

card-carrying *adj* being an official member of an organization: *a card-carrying Conservative*

Cardenal *n* **Ernesto** born 1925, Nicaraguan poet, revolutionary, and Roman Catholic priest; an influential figure in the Sandinista movement

Cárdenas *n* **Lázaro** 1895–1970, Mexican statesman and general; president of Mexico (1934–40)

cardholder *n* a person who owns a credit or debit card

cardiac *adj* of or relating to the heart
WORD ORIGIN Greek *kardia* heart

cardigan *n* a knitted jacket
WORD ORIGIN after 7th Earl of *Cardigan*

Cardin *n* **Pierre** born 1922, French couturier, noted esp. for his collections for men

cardinal ❶ *n* **1** any of the high-ranking clergymen of the Roman Catholic Church who elect the pope and act as his chief counsellors ▹ *adj* **2** fundamentally important; principal
WORD ORIGIN Latin *cardo* hinge

cardinal number *n* a number denoting quantity but not order in a group, for example one, two, or three

cardinal points *pl n* the four main points of the compass: north, south, east, and west

cardinal virtues *pl n* the most important moral qualities, traditionally justice, prudence, temperance, and fortitude

card index *n* an index in which each item is separately listed on systematically arranged cards

cardiogram *n* an electrocardiogram ▸ See **electrocardiograph**

cardiograph *n* an electrocardiograph **cardiographer** *n* **cardiography** *n*

cardiology *n* the branch of medicine dealing with the heart and its diseases **cardiologist** *n*

cardiothoracic *adj* of or relating to the heart or the chest

cardiovascular *adj* of or relating to the heart and the blood vessels

Cardoso *n* **Fernando Henrique** born 1931, Brazilian statesman; president (1995–2002)

cards *n* **1** any game played with cards, or card games generally **2 lay one's cards on the table** to declare one's intentions openly **3 on the cards** likely to take place: *a military coup was on the cards* **4 play one's cards right** to handle a situation cleverly

cardsharp *or* **cardsharper** *n* a professional card player who cheats

Carducci *n* **Giosuè** 1835–1907, Italian poet: Nobel prize for literature 1906

Cardus *n* Sir **Neville** 1889–1975, British music critic and cricket writer

card vote *n Brit & NZ* a vote by delegates in which each delegate's vote counts as a vote by all his or her constituents

care ❶ *vb* **caring, cared 1** to be worried or concerned: *he does not care what people think about him* **2** to like (to do something): *anybody care to go out?* **3 care for a** to look after or provide for: *it is still largely women who care for dependent family members* **b** to like or be fond of: *he did not care for his concentration to be disturbed; I don't suppose you could ever care for me seriously* **4 I couldn't care less** I am completely indifferent ▹ *n* **5** careful or serious attention; caution: *treat all raw meat with extreme care to avoid food poisoning* **6** protection or charge: *the children are now in the care of a state orphanage* **7** trouble or worry: *his mind turned towards money cares* **8 care of** (written on envelopes) at the address of **9 in** *or* **into care** *Brit & NZ* (of a child) made the legal responsibility of a local authority or the state by order of a court **10 take care** to be careful **11 take care of** to look after: *women have to take greater care of themselves during pregnancy*
WORD ORIGIN Old English *cearian*

careen *vb* to tilt over to one side
WORD ORIGIN Latin *carina* keel

career ❶ *n* **1** the series of jobs in a profession or occupation that a person has through his or her life: *a career in child psychology* **2** the part of a person's life spent in a particular occupation or type of work: *a school career punctuated with exams* ▹ *vb* **3** to rush in an uncontrolled way ▹ *adj* **4** having chosen to dedicate his or her life to a particular occupation: *a career soldier*
WORD ORIGIN Latin *carrus* two-wheeled wagon

careerist *n* a person who seeks to advance his or her career by any means possible **careerism** *n*

carefree *adj* without worry or responsibility

careful ❶ *adj* **1** cautious in attitude or action **2** very exact and thorough **carefully** *adv* **carefulness** *n*

careless ❶ *adj* **1** done or acting with insufficient attention **2** unconcerned in attitude or action

THESAURUS

cardinal *adj* **2 = principal**, first, highest, greatest, leading, important, chief, main, prime, central, key, essential, primary, fundamental, paramount, foremost, pre-eminent **OPPOSITE:** secondary

care *vb* **1 = be concerned**, mind, bother, be interested, be bothered, give a damn, concern yourself ▹ *n* **3b care for something** *or* **someone = like**, enjoy, take to, relish, be fond of, be keen on, be partial to **5 = caution**, attention, regard, pains, consideration, heed, prudence, vigilance, forethought, circumspection, watchfulness, meticulousness, carefulness **OPPOSITE:** carelessness **6 = custody**, keeping, control, charge, management, protection, supervision, guardianship, safekeeping, ministration **7 = worry**, concern, pressure, trouble, responsibility, stress, burden, anxiety, hardship, woe, disquiet, affliction, tribulation, perplexity, vexation **OPPOSITE:** pleasure

career *n* **1 = occupation**, calling, employment, pursuit, vocation, livelihood, life's work ▹ *vb* **3 = rush**, race, speed, tear, dash, barrel (along) *(informal, chiefly US & Canad)*, bolt, hurtle, burn rubber *(informal)*

careful *adj* **1 = cautious**, painstaking, scrupulous, fastidious, circumspect, punctilious, chary, heedful, thoughtful, discreet **OPPOSITE:** careless **2 = thorough**, full, particular, accurate, precise, intensive, in-depth, meticulous, conscientious, attentive, exhaustive, painstaking, scrupulous, assiduous **OPPOSITE:** casual

careless *adj* **1a = slapdash**, irresponsible, sloppy *(informal)*, cavalier, offhand, neglectful, slipshod, lackadaisical, inattentive

DICTIONARY

carelessly *adv* **carelessness** *n*

carer *n* a person who looks after someone who is ill or old, often a relative: *the group offers support for the carers of those with dementia*

C

caress *n* **1** a gentle affectionate touch or embrace ▹ *vb* **2** to touch gently and affectionately
WORD ORIGIN Latin *carus* dear

caret (kar-ret) *n* a symbol (‸) indicating a place in written or printed matter where something is to be inserted
WORD ORIGIN Latin: there is missing

caretaker ⊕ *n* **1** a person employed to look after a place or thing ▹ *adj* **2** performing the duties of an office temporarily: *a caretaker administration*

Carew *n* **Thomas** ?1595–?1639, English Cavalier poet

careworn *adj* showing signs of stress or worry

Carey *n* **1 George** (**Leonard**) born 1935, Archbishop of Canterbury (1991–2002) **2 Peter** born 1943, Australian novelist and writer; his novels include *Illywhacker* (1985), *Oscar and Lucinda* (1988), and *True History of the Kelly Gang* (2001) **3 William** 1761–1834, British orientalist and pioneer Baptist missionary in India

cargo ⊕ *n, pl* **-goes** *or esp. US* **-gos** goods carried by a ship, aircraft, or other vehicle
WORD ORIGIN Spanish *cargar* to load

cargo pants *or* **trousers** *pl n* loose trousers with a large external pocket on the side of each leg

Carib *n* **1** *pl* **-ibs** *or* **-ib** a member of a group of Native American peoples of NE South America and the S West Indies **2** any of the languages of these peoples
WORD ORIGIN Spanish *Caribe*

Caribbean *adj* of the Caribbean Sea, bounded by Central America, South America, and the West Indies, or the surrounding countries and islands

caribou *n, pl* **-bou** *or* **-bous** a large North American reindeer
WORD ORIGIN from a Native American language

caricature ⊕ *n* **1** a drawing or description of a person which exaggerates characteristic features for comic effect **2** a description or explanation of something that is so exaggerated or over-simplified that it is difficult to take seriously: *the classic caricature of the henpecked husband* ▹ *vb* **-turing, -tured 3** to make a caricature of
WORD ORIGIN Italian *caricatura* a distortion

caries (care-reez) *n* tooth decay
WORD ORIGIN Latin: decay

carillon (kar-rill-yon) *n* **1** a set of bells hung in a tower and played either from a keyboard or mechanically **2** a tune played on such bells
WORD ORIGIN French

caring *adj* **1** feeling or showing care and compassion for other people **2** of or relating to professional social or medical care: *the caring professions*

carjack *vb* to attack (a driver in a car) in order to rob the driver or to steal the car for another crime
WORD ORIGIN CAR + (HI)JACK

cark *vb* **cark it** *Austral & NZ slang* to die

Carling *n* **Will**(**iam**) born 1965, British Rugby Union footballer; captain of England (1988–96)

Carlos *n* **Don** full name *Carlos María Isidro de Borbón*. 1788–1855, second son of Charles IV: pretender to the Spanish throne and leader of the Carlists

Carlota *n* original name *Marie Charlotte Amélie Augustine Victoire Clémentine Léopoldine*. 1840–1927, wife of Maximilian; empress of Mexico (1864–67)

Carl XVI Gustaf *n* born 1946, king of Sweden from 1973

Carmelite *n* **1** a Christian friar or nun belonging to the order of Our Lady of Carmel ▹ *adj* **2** of this order
WORD ORIGIN after Mount *Carmel*, in Palestine, where the order was founded

Carmichael *n* **Hoaglund Howard**, known as *Hoagy*. 1899–1981, US pianist, singer, and composer of such standards as "Star Dust" (1929)

carminative *adj* **1** able to relieve flatulence ▹ *n* **2** a carminative drug
WORD ORIGIN Latin *carminare* to card wool, comb out

carmine *adj* vivid red
WORD ORIGIN Arabic *qirmiz* kermes

carnage ⊕ *n* extensive slaughter of people
WORD ORIGIN Latin *caro* flesh

carnal *adj* of a sexual or sensual nature: *carnal knowledge* **carnality** *n*
WORD ORIGIN Latin *caro* flesh

Carnap *n* **Rudolf** 1891–1970, US logical positivist philosopher, born in Germany: attempted to construct a formal language for the empirical sciences that would eliminate ambiguity

carnation *n* a cultivated plant with clove-scented white, pink, or red flowers
WORD ORIGIN Latin *caro* flesh

Carné *n* **Marcel** 1906–96, French film director. His films include *Le Jour se lève* (1939), *Les Portes de la nuit* (1946), and *La Bible* (1976)

carnelian *n* a reddish-yellow variety of chalcedony, used as a gemstone
WORD ORIGIN Old French *corneline*

carnet (kar-nay) *n* a customs licence permitting motorists to take their cars across certain frontiers
WORD ORIGIN French: notebook

carnival ⊕ *n* **1** a festive period with processions, music, and dancing in the street **2** a travelling funfair
WORD ORIGIN Old Italian *carnelevare* a removing of meat (referring to the Lenten fast)

carnivore (car-niv-vore) *n* **1** a meat-eating animal **2** *informal* an aggressively ambitious person
carnivorous (car-niv-or-uss) *adj*
WORD ORIGIN Latin *caro* flesh + *vorare* to consume

Carnot *n* **1 Lazare** (**Nicolas Marguerite**), known as *the Organizer of Victory*. 1753–1823, French military engineer and administrator: organized the French Revolutionary army (1793–95) **2 Nicolas Léonard Sadi** 1796–1832, French physicist, whose work formed the basis for the second law of thermodynamics, enunciated in 1850; author of *Réflexions sur la puissance motrice du feu* (1824)

Caro *n* **1** Sir **Antony** born 1924, British sculptor, best known for his abstract steel sculptures **2 Joseph** (**ben Ephraim**) 1488–1575, Jewish legal scholar and mystic, born in Spain; compiler of the *Shulhan Arukh* (1564–65), the most authoritative Jewish legal code

carob *n* the pod of a Mediterranean tree, used as a chocolate substitute
WORD ORIGIN Arabic *al kharrūbah*

THESAURUS

OPPOSITE: careful
1b = negligent, hasty, unconcerned, cursory, perfunctory, thoughtless, indiscreet, unthinking, forgetful, absent-minded, inconsiderate, heedless, remiss, incautious, unmindful **OPPOSITE:** careful
2 = nonchalant, casual, offhand, artless, unstudied **OPPOSITE:** careful

caretaker *n* **1 = warden**, keeper, porter, superintendent, curator, custodian, watchman, janitor, concierge

cargo *n* **= load**, goods, contents, shipment, freight, merchandise, baggage, ware, consignment, tonnage, lading

caricature *n* **1, 2 = parody**, cartoon, distortion, satire, send-up (*Brit informal*), travesty, takeoff (*informal*), lampoon, burlesque, mimicry, farce ▹ *vb* **3 = parody**, take off (*informal*), mock, distort, ridicule, mimic, send up (*Brit informal*), lampoon, burlesque, satirize

carnage *n* **= slaughter**, murder, massacre, holocaust, havoc, bloodshed, shambles, mass murder, butchery, blood bath

carnival *n* **1 = festival**, fair, fête, celebration, gala, jubilee, jamboree, Mardi Gras, revelry, merrymaking, fiesta, holiday

DICTIONARY

carol ❶ *n* **1** a joyful religious song sung at Christmas ▷ *vb* **-olling, -olled** *or US* **-oling, -oled 2** to sing carols **3** to sing joyfully
WORD ORIGIN Old French

Carol II *n* 1893–1953, king of Romania (1930–40), who was deposed by the Iron Guard

Caroline of Ansbach *n* 1683–1737, wife of George II of Great Britain

Caroline of Brunswick *n* 1768–1821, wife of George IV of the United Kingdom: tried for adultery (1820)

carotene *n biochem* any of four orange-red hydrocarbons, found in many plants, converted to vitamin A in the liver
WORD ORIGIN from Latin *carota* carrot

carotid (kar-rot-id) *n* **1** either of the two arteries that supply blood to the head and neck ▷ *adj* **2** of either of these arteries
WORD ORIGIN Greek *karoun* to stupefy; so named because pressure on them produced unconsciousness

carousal *n* a merry drinking party

carouse *vb* **-rousing, -roused** to have a merry drinking party: *carousing with friends*
WORD ORIGIN German *(trinken) gar aus* (to drink) right out

carousel (kar-roo-sell) *n* **1** a revolving conveyor for luggage at an airport or for slides for a projector **2** *US & Canad* a merry-go-round
WORD ORIGIN Italian *carosello*

carp[1] *n, pl* **carp** *or* **carps** a large freshwater food fish
WORD ORIGIN Old French *carpe*

carp[2] ❶ *vb* to complain or find fault
carping *adj, n*
WORD ORIGIN Old Norse *karpa* to boast

carpaccio (kar-patch-ee-oh) *n* an Italian dish of thin slices of raw meat or fish
WORD ORIGIN Italian

Carpaccio *n* **Vittore** ?1460–?1525, Italian painter of the Venetian school

carpal *n* a wrist bone
WORD ORIGIN Greek *karpos* wrist

car park *n* an area or building reserved for parking cars

carpel *n* the female reproductive organ of a flowering plant
WORD ORIGIN Greek *karpos* fruit

carpenter ❶ *n* a person who makes or repairs wooden structures
WORD ORIGIN Latin *carpentarius* wagon-maker

Carpenter *n* **John Alden** 1876–1951, US composer, who used jazz rhythms in orchestral music: his works include the ballet *Skyscrapers* (1926) and the orchestral suite *Adventures in a Perambulator* (1915)

Carpentier *n* **Georges**, known as *Gorgeous Georges*. 1894–1975, French boxer: world light-heavyweight champion (1920–22)

carpentry *n* the skill or work of a carpenter

carpet *n* **1** a heavy fabric for covering floors **2** a covering like a carpet: *a carpet of leaves* **3 on the carpet** *informal* being or about to be reprimanded **4 sweep something under the carpet** to conceal or keep silent about something that one does not want to be discovered ▷ *vb* **-peting, -peted 5** to cover with a carpet or a covering like a carpet
WORD ORIGIN Latin *carpere* to pluck, card

carpetbag *n* a travelling bag made of carpeting

carpetbagger *n* **1** a politician who seeks office in a place where he or she has no connections **2** *Brit* a person who makes a short-term investment in a mutual savings or life-assurance organization in order to benefit from free shares issued following the organization's conversion to a public limited company

carpeting *n* carpet material or carpets in general

carpet snake *n* a large nonvenomous Australian snake with a carpet-like pattern on its back

car phone *n* a telephone that operates by cellular radio for use in a car

carport *n* a shelter for a car, consisting of a roof supported by posts

carpus *n, pl* **-pi** the set of eight bones of the human wrist
WORD ORIGIN Greek *karpos*

Carracci *n* a family of Italian painters, born in Bologna: **Agostino** (1557–1602); his brother, **Annibale** (1560–1609), noted for his frescoes, esp. in the Palazzo Farnese, Rome; and their cousin, **Ludovico** (1555–1619). They were influential in reviving the classical tradition of the Renaissance and founded a teaching academy (1582) in Bologna

carrageen *n* an edible red seaweed of North America and N Europe
WORD ORIGIN *Carragheen*, near Waterford, Ireland

Carrel *n* **Alexis** 1873–1944, French surgeon and biologist, active in the US (1905–39): developed a method of suturing blood vessels, making the transplantation of arteries and organs possible: Nobel prize for physiology or medicine 1912

Carreras *n* **José** born 1947, Spanish tenor

Carrey *n* **Jim** born 1962, Canadian-born Hollywood actor noted for his comedy roles; films include *Ace Ventura, Pet Detective* (1994), *Liar Liar* (1997), *The Truman Show* (1998), and *The Majestic* (2001)

carriage ❶ *n* **1** *Brit, Austral & NZ* one of the sections of a train for passengers **2** the way a person holds and moves his or her head and body **3** a four-wheeled horse-drawn passenger vehicle **4** the moving part of a machine, such as a typewriter, that supports and shifts another part **5** the charge made for conveying goods
WORD ORIGIN Old French *cariage*

carriage clock *n* a style of portable clock, originally used by travellers

carriageway *n* **1** *Brit* the part of a road along which traffic passes in one direction: *the westbound carriageway of the M4* **2** *NZ* the part of a road used by vehicles

carrier *n* **1** a person, vehicle, or organization that carries something: *armoured personnel carriers* **2** a person or animal that, without suffering from a disease, is capable of transmitting it to others **3** ▸ short for **aircraft carrier**

carrier bag *n Brit* a large plastic or paper bag for carrying shopping

carrier pigeon *n* a homing pigeon used for carrying messages

Carrington *n* **1 Dora,** known as *Carrington*. 1893–1932, British painter, engraver, and letter writer; a member of the Bloomsbury Group **2 Peter (Alexander Rupert),** 6th Baron. born 1919, British Conservative politician: secretary of state for defence (1970–74); foreign secretary (1979–82); secretary general of NATO (1984–88)

carrion *n* dead and rotting flesh
WORD ORIGIN Latin *caro* flesh

carrion crow *n* a scavenging European crow with a completely black plumage and bill

carrot *n* **1** a long tapering orange root vegetable **2** something offered as an incentive
WORD ORIGIN Greek *karōton*

carroty *adj* (of hair) reddish-orange

carry ❶ *vb* **-ries, -rying, -ried 1** to take from one place to another **2** to have

THESAURUS

carol *n* **1 = song**, noel, hymn, Christmas song, canticle

carp[2] *vb* **= find fault**, complain, beef *(slang)*, criticize, nag, censure, reproach, quibble, cavil, pick holes, kvetch *(US slang)*, nit-pick *(informal)*
OPPOSITE: praise

carpenter *n* **= joiner**, cabinet-maker, woodworker

carriage *n* **2 = bearing**, posture, gait, deportment, air **3 = vehicle**, coach, trap, gig, cab, wagon, hackney, conveyance

carry *vb* **1 = convey**, take, move, bring, bear, lift, transfer, conduct,

DICTIONARY

with one habitually, for example in one's pocket or handbag: *to carry a donor card* **3** to transmit or be transmitted: *to carry disease* **4** to have as a factor or result: *the charge of desertion carries a maximum penalty of twenty years* **5** to be pregnant with: *women carrying Down's Syndrome babies* **6** to hold (one's head or body) in a specified manner: *she always wears a sari and carries herself like an Indian* **7** to secure the adoption of (a bill or motion): *the resolution was carried by fewer than twenty votes* **8** (of a newspaper or television or radio station) to include in the contents: *several papers carried front-page pictures of the Russian president* **9** *maths* to transfer (a number) from one column of figures to the next **10** to travel a certain distance or reach a specified point: *his faint voice carried no farther than the front few rows* **11** **carry the can** *informal* to take all the blame for something ▸ See also **carry away, carry forward**, etc.
WORD ORIGIN Latin *carrum* transport wagon

carry away *vb* **be** *or* **get carried away** to be engrossed in or fascinated by something to the point of losing self-control: *he could be carried away by his own rhetoric*

carrycot *n* a light portable bed for a baby, with handles and a hood, which usually also serves as the body of a pram

carry forward *vb* to transfer (an amount) to the next column, page, or accounting period

carry off *vb* **1** to lift and take (someone or something) away: *the German striker was carried off after snapping an Achilles tendon* **2** to win: *who will carry off this year's honours is unclear* **3** to handle (a situation) successfully: *he had the presence and social ability to carry off the job* **4** to cause to die: *the circulatory disorder which carried off other members of his family*

carry on 🅣 *vb* **1** to continue: *we'll carry on exactly where we left off* **2** to do, run, or take part in: *the vast trade carried on in the city* **3** *informal* to cause a fuss: *I don't want to carry on and make a big scene* ▹ *n* **carry-on 4** *informal chiefly Brit* a fuss

carry out 🅣 *vb* **1** to follow (an order or instruction) **2** to accomplish (a task): *to carry out repairs*

carry over *vb* to extend from one period or situation into another: *major debts carried over from last year*

carry through *vb* to bring to completion: *these are difficult policies to carry through*

carsick *adj* nauseated from riding in a car

Carson *n* **1 Christopher,** known as *Kit Carson*. 1809–68, US frontiersman, trapper, scout, and Indian agent **2 Edward Henry,** Baron. 1854–1935, Anglo-Irish politician and lawyer; led northern Irish resistance to the British government's plan for home rule for Ireland **3 Rachel** (**Louise**) 1907–64, US marine biologist and science writer; author of *Silent Spring* (1962) **4 Willie,** full name *William Hunter Fisher Carson*. born 1942, Scottish jockey; retired in 1997

cart *n* **1** an open horse-drawn vehicle, usually with two wheels, used to carry goods or passengers **2** any small vehicle that is pulled or pushed by hand ▹ *vb* **3** to carry, usually with some effort: *men carted bricks and tiles and wooden boards* ▸ See also **cart off**
WORD ORIGIN Old Norse *kartr*

Carte *n* See **D'Oyly Carte**

carte blanche *n* complete authority: *she's got carte blanche to redecorate*
WORD ORIGIN French: blank paper

cartel *n* an association of competing firms formed in order to fix prices
WORD ORIGIN German *Kartell*

Carteret *n* **John,** 1st Earl Granville. 1690–1763, British statesman, diplomat, and orator who led the opposition to Walpole (1730–42), after whose fall he became a leading minister as secretary of state (1742–44)

Cartesian *adj* of René Descartes, 17th-century French philosopher and mathematician, or his works
WORD ORIGIN *Cartesius*, Latin form of Descartes

Cartesian coordinates *pl n* a set of numbers that determine the location of a point in a plane or in space by its distance from two fixed intersecting lines

carthorse *n* a large heavily built horse kept for pulling carts or for farm work

Carthusian *n* **1** a Christian monk or nun belonging to a strict monastic order founded in 1084 ▹ *adj* **2** of this order
WORD ORIGIN Latin *Carthusia* Chartreuse, near Grenoble

Cartier *n* **Jacques** 1491–1557, French navigator and explorer in Canada, who discovered the St Lawrence River (1535)

Cartier-Bresson *n* **Henri** 1908–2004, French photographer

cartilage (kar-till-ij) *n* a strong flexible tissue forming part of the skeleton **cartilaginous** *adj*
WORD ORIGIN Latin *cartilago*

Cartland *n* Dame **Barbara** (**Hamilton**) 1901–2000, British novelist, noted for her prolific output of popular romantic fiction

cart off *vb* to take (someone) somewhere forcefully: *we had been carted off to the security police building*

cartography *n* the art of making maps or charts **cartographer** *n* **cartographic** *adj*
WORD ORIGIN French *carte* map, chart

carton 🅣 *n* **1** a cardboard box or container **2** a container of waxed paper in which drinks are sold
WORD ORIGIN Italian *carta* card

cartoon 🅣 *n* **1** a humorous or satirical drawing in a newspaper or magazine **2** ▸ same as **comic strip** **3** ▸ same as **animated cartoon** ▹ **cartoonist** *n*
WORD ORIGIN Italian *cartone* pasteboard

cartouche *n* **1** an ornamental tablet or panel in the form of a scroll **2** (in ancient Egypt) an oblong or oval figure containing royal or divine names
WORD ORIGIN French: scroll, cartridge

cartridge *n* **1** a metal casing containing an explosive charge and bullet for a gun **2** the part of the pick-up of a record player that converts the movements of the stylus into electrical signals **3** a sealed container of film or tape, or ink for a special kind of pen
WORD ORIGIN from French *cartouche*

cartridge belt *n* a belt with loops or pockets for holding cartridges

cartridge clip *n* a metallic container holding cartridges for an automatic gun

cartridge paper *n* a type of heavy rough drawing paper

cartwheel *n* **1** a sideways somersault supported by the hands with legs outstretched **2** the large spoked wheel of a cart

Cartwright *n* **1 Edmund** 1743–1823, British clergyman, who invented the power loom **2** Dame **Silvia** (née *Poulter*). born 1943, New Zealand lawyer. She became a High Court judge in 1993; governor general of

THESAURUS

transport, haul, transmit, fetch, relay, cart, tote (*informal*), hump (*Brit slang*), lug **3 = transmit**, transfer, spread, pass on

carry-on *n* **4** (*informal, chiefly Brit*) **= fuss**, disturbance, racket, fracas, commotion, rumpus, tumult, hubbub, shindy (*informal*)

carry out *vb* **1, 2 = perform**, effect, achieve, realize, implement, fulfil, accomplish, execute, discharge, consummate, carry through

carton *n* **1 = box**, case, pack, package, container

cartoon *n* **1 = drawing**, parody, satire, caricature, comic strip, takeoff (*informal*), lampoon, sketch **3 = animation**, animated film,

DICTIONARY

New Zealand (2001–06)
Caruso *n* **Enrico** 1873–1921, an outstanding Italian operatic tenor; one of the first to make gramophone records
carve ❶ *vb* **carving, carved 1** to cut in order to form something: *carving wood* **2** to form (something) by cutting: *the statue which was carved by Michelangelo* **3** to slice (cooked meat) ▸ See also **carve out, carve up** > **carver** *n*
WORD ORIGIN Old English *ceorfan*
carve out *vb informal* to make or create: *to carve out a political career*
Carver *n* **George Washington** ?1864–1943, US agricultural chemist and botanist
carvery *n, pl* **-veries** a restaurant where customers pay a set price for unrestricted helpings of carved meat and other food
carve up *vb* **1** to divide or share out: *in 1795, Poland was carved up between three empires* ▹ *n* **carve-up 2** the division or sharing out of something: *a territorial carve-up*
carving *n* a figure or design produced by carving stone or wood
carving knife *n* a long-bladed knife for carving cooked meat
carwash *n* a place fitted with equipment for automatically washing cars
Cary *n* **(Arthur) Joyce (Lunel)** 1888–1957, British novelist; author of *Mister Johnson* (1939), *A House of Children* (1941), and *The Horse's Mouth* (1944)
caryatid (kar-ree-at-id) *n* a supporting column in the shape of a female figure
WORD ORIGIN Greek *Karuatides* priestesses of Artemis at *Karuai* (Caryae), in Laconia
Casals *n* **Pablo** 1876–1973, Spanish cellist and composer, noted for his interpretation of J. S. Bach's cello suites
Casanova *n* a promiscuous man
WORD ORIGIN after Giovanni *Casanova*, Italian adventurer
Casaubon *n* **Isaac** 1559–1614, French Protestant theologian and classical scholar
casbah *n* the citadel of a North African city
WORD ORIGIN Arabic *kasba* citadel
cascade ❶ *n* **1** a waterfall or series of waterfalls over rocks **2** something flowing or falling like a waterfall: *a cascade of luxuriant hair* ▹ *vb* **-cading, -caded 3** to flow or fall in a cascade: *rays of sunshine cascaded down*
WORD ORIGIN Italian *cascare* to fall
cascading style sheet *n computers* a file recording style details, such as fonts, colours, etc. that ensures style is consistent over all the pages of a website
cascara *n* the bark of a N American shrub, used as a laxative
WORD ORIGIN Spanish: bark
case[1] ❶ *n* **1** a single instance or example of something: *cases of teenage pregnancies* **2** a matter for discussion: *the case before the Ethics Committee* **3** a specific condition or state of affairs: *a sudden-death play-off in the case of a draw* **4** a set of arguments supporting an action or cause: *I put my case before them* **5** a person or problem dealt with by a doctor, social worker, or solicitor **6 a** an action or lawsuit: *a rape case* **b** the evidence offered in court to support a claim: *he will try to show that the case against his client is largely circumstantial* **7** *grammar* a form of a noun, pronoun, or adjective showing its relation to other words in the sentence: *the accusative case* **8** *informal* an amusingly eccentric person **9 in any case** no matter what **10 in case** so as to allow for the possibility that: *the President has ordered a medical team to stand by in case hostages are released* **11 in case of** in the event of: *in case of a future conflict*
WORD ORIGIN Old English *casus* (grammatical) case, associated with Old French *cas* a happening; both from Latin *cadere* to fall
case[2] ❶ *n* **1** a container, such as a box or chest **2** a suitcase **3** a protective outer covering ▹ *vb* **casing, cased 4** *slang* to inspect carefully (a place one plans to rob)
WORD ORIGIN Latin *capsa* box
case-hardened *adj* having been made callous by experience: *a case-hardened senior policewoman*
case history *n* a record of a person's background or medical history
casein *n* a protein found in milk, which forms the basis of cheese
WORD ORIGIN Latin *caseus* cheese
case law *n* law established by following judicial decisions made in earlier cases
caseload *n* the number of cases that someone like a doctor or social worker deals with at any one time
casement *n* a window that is hinged on one side
WORD ORIGIN probably from Old French *encassement* frame
Casement *n* Sir **Roger (David)** 1864–1916, British diplomat and Irish nationalist: hanged by the British for treason in attempting to gain German support for Irish independence
case study *n* an analysis of a group or person in order to make generalizations about a larger group or society as a whole
casework *n* social work based on close study of the personal histories and circumstances of individuals and families **caseworker** *n*
cash ❶ *n* **1** banknotes and coins, rather than cheques **2** *informal* money: *strapped for cash* ▹ *adj* **3** of, for, or paid in cash: *cash hand-outs* ▹ *vb* **4** to obtain or pay banknotes or coins for (a cheque or postal order) ▸ See also **cash in on**
WORD ORIGIN Old Italian *cassa* money box
Cash *n* **Johnny** 1932–2003, US country-and-western singer, guitarist, and songwriter. His recordings include the hits "I Walk the Line" (1956), "Ring of Fire" (1963), "A Boy named Sue" (1969), and the *American Recordings* series of albums (1994–2003)
cash-and-carry *adj* operating on a basis of cash payment for goods that are taken away by the purchaser: *the cash-and-carry wholesalers*
cashback *n* **1** a discount offered in return for immediate payment **2** a service by which a customer in a shop can draw out cash on a debit card
cash-book *n book-keeping* a journal in which all money transactions are recorded

C

THESAURUS

animated cartoon
carve *vb* **1 = sculpt**, form, cut, chip, sculpture, whittle, chisel, hew, fashion **2 = etch**, engrave, inscribe, fashion, slash
cascade *n* **1 = waterfall**, falls, torrent, flood, shower, fountain, avalanche, deluge, downpour, outpouring, cataract ▹ *vb* **3 = flow**, fall, flood, pour, plunge, surge, spill, tumble, descend, overflow, gush, teem, pitch
case[1] *n* **1 = instance**, example, occasion, specimen, occurrence **2, 3 = situation**, event, circumstance(s), state, position, condition, context, dilemma, plight, contingency, predicament **6a** *(Law)* **= lawsuit**, process, trial, suit, proceedings, dispute, cause, action
case[2] *n* **1a = cabinet**, box, chest, holder **1b = container**, compact, capsule, carton, cartridge, canister, casket, receptacle **1c = crate**, box **2 = suitcase**, bag, grip, trunk, holdall, portmanteau, valise **3 = covering**, casing, cover, shell, wrapping, jacket, envelope, capsule, folder, sheath, wrapper, integument
cash *n* **1, 2 = money**, change, funds, notes, ready *(informal)*, the necessary *(informal)*, resources, currency, silver, bread *(slang)*, coin, tin *(slang)*, brass *(Northern English dialect)*, dough *(slang)*, rhino *(Brit slang)*, banknotes, bullion, dosh *(Brit & Austral slang)*, wherewithal, coinage, needful *(informal)*, specie, shekels *(informal)*, dibs *(slang)*, ready money, ackers *(slang)*, spondulicks *(slang)*

DICTIONARY

cash card *n* a card issued by a bank or building society which can be inserted into a cash dispenser in order to obtain money
cash crop *n* a crop produced for sale rather than for subsistence
cash desk *n* a counter or till in a shop where purchases are paid for
cash discount *n* a discount granted to a purchaser who pays within a specified period
cash dispenser *n* a computerized device outside a bank which supplies cash when a special card is inserted and the user's code number keyed in
cashew *n* an edible kidney-shaped nut
WORD ORIGIN S American Indian *acajū*
cash flow *n* the movement of money into and out of a business
cashier[1] *n* a person responsible for handling cash in a bank, shop, or other business
WORD ORIGIN French *casse* money chest
cashier[2] *vb* to dismiss with dishonour from the armed forces
WORD ORIGIN Latin *quassare* to QUASH
cash in on *vb informal* to gain profit or advantage from: *trying to cash in on the dispute*
cashmere *n* a very fine soft wool obtained from goats
WORD ORIGIN from *Kashmir*, in SW central Asia
cash on delivery *n* a system involving cash payment to the carrier on delivery of merchandise. Abbrev: **COD**
cash register *n* a till that has a mechanism for displaying and adding the prices of the goods sold
Casimir III *n* known as *the Great*. 1310–70, king of Poland (1333–70)
Casimir IV *n* 1427–92, grand duke of Lithuania (1440–92) and king of Poland (1447–92)
casing *n* a protective case or covering
casino *n, pl* **-nos** a public building or room where gambling games are played
WORD ORIGIN Italian
cask *n* **1** a strong barrel used to hold alcoholic drink **2** *Austral* a cubic carton containing wine, with a tap for dispensing
WORD ORIGIN Spanish *casco* helmet
casket *n* **1** a small box for valuables **2** US a coffin
WORD ORIGIN probably from Old French *cassette* little box
Cassandra *n* someone whose prophecies of doom are unheeded
WORD ORIGIN Trojan prophetess in Greek mythology
Cassatt *n* **Mary** 1845–1926, US impressionist painter, who lived in France
cassava *n* a starch obtained from the root of a tropical American plant, used to make tapioca
WORD ORIGIN West Indian *caçábi*
casserole *n* **1** a covered dish in which food is cooked slowly, usually in an oven, and served **2** a dish cooked and served in this way: *beef casserole* ▷ *vb* **-roling, -roled 3** to cook in a casserole
WORD ORIGIN French
cassette *n* a plastic case containing a reel of film or magnetic tape
WORD ORIGIN French: little box
cassia *n* **1** a tropical plant whose pods yield a mild laxative **2 cassia bark** a cinnamon-like spice obtained from the bark of a tropical Asian tree
WORD ORIGIN Greek *kasia*
Cassiodorus *n* **Flavius Magnus Aurelius** ?490–?585 AD, Roman statesman, writer, and monk; author of *Variae*, a collection of official documents written for the Ostrogoths
Cassirer *n* **Ernst** 1874–1945, German neo-Kantian philosopher. *The Philosophy of Symbolic Forms* (1923–29) analyses the symbols that underlie all manifestations, including myths and language, of human culture
Cassius Longinus *n* **Gaius** died 42 BC, Roman general: led the conspiracy against Julius Caesar (44); defeated at Philippi by Antony (42)
Cassivelaunus *n* 1st century BC, British chieftain, king of the Catuvellauni tribe, who organized resistance to Caesar's invasion of Britain (54 BC)
cassock *n* an ankle-length garment, usually black, worn by some Christian priests
WORD ORIGIN Italian *casacca* a long coat
Casson *n* Sir **Hugh** (**Maxwell**) 1910–99, British architect; president of the Royal Academy of Arts (1976–84)
cassowary *n, pl* **-waries** a large flightless bird of Australia and New Guinea
WORD ORIGIN Malay *kĕsuari*
cast ❶ *n* **1** the actors in a play collectively **2 a** an object made of material that has been shaped, while molten, by a mould **b** the mould used to shape such an object **3** *surgery* a rigid casing made of plaster of Paris for immobilizing broken bones while they heal **4** a sort, kind, or style: *people of an academic cast of mind* **5** a slight squint in the eye ▷ *vb* **casting, cast 6** to select (an actor) to play a part in a play or film **7** to give or deposit (a vote) **8** to express (doubts or aspersions) **9** to cause to appear: *a shadow cast by the grandstand; the gloom cast by the recession* **10 a** to shape (molten material) by pouring it into a mould **b** to make (an object) by such a process **11** to throw (a fishing line) into the water **12** to throw with force: *cast into a bonfire* **13** to direct (a glance): *he cast his eye over the horse-chestnut trees* **14** to roll or throw (a dice) **15 cast aside** to abandon or reject: *cast aside by her lover* **16 cast a spell a** to perform magic **b** to have an irresistible influence ▸ See also **cast around, cast back**, etc.
WORD ORIGIN Old Norse *kasta*
castanets *pl n* a musical instrument, used by Spanish dancers, consisting of curved pieces of hollow wood, held between the fingers and thumb and clicked together
WORD ORIGIN Spanish *castañeta*, from *castaña* chestnut
cast around *or* **about** *vb* to make a mental or visual search: *he cast around for a job*
castaway *n* a person who has been shipwrecked
cast back *vb* to turn (the mind) to the past
cast down *vb* to make (a person) feel discouraged or dejected
caste ❶ *n* **1** any of the four major hereditary classes into which Hindu society is divided **2** social rank
WORD ORIGIN Latin *castus* pure, not polluted
castellated *adj* having turrets and battlements, like a castle
WORD ORIGIN Medieval Latin *castellare* to fortify as a castle
caster *n* ▸ same as **castor**
caster sugar *n* finely ground white sugar
castigate *vb* **-gating, -gated** to find fault with or reprimand (a person) harshly **castigation** *n*
WORD ORIGIN Latin *castigare* to correct
Castiglione *n* Count **Baldassare** 1478–1529, Italian diplomat and writer, noted particularly for his

THESAURUS

cast *n* **1 = actors**, company, players, characters, troupe, dramatis personae **4 = type**, turn, sort, kind, style, stamp ▷ *vb* **6 = choose**, name, pick, select, appoint, assign, allot **9 = give out**, spread, deposit, shed, distribute, scatter, emit, radiate, bestow, diffuse **10a, 10b = mould**, set, found, form, model, shape **12, 14 = throw**, project, launch, pitch, shed, shy, toss, thrust, hurl, fling, chuck (*informal*), sling, lob, impel, drive, drop **13 = bestow**, give, level, accord, direct, confer
caste *n* **1, 2 = class**, order, race, station, rank, status, stratum, social order, lineage

DICTIONARY

dialogue on ideal courtly life, *Il Libro del Cortegiano* (The Courtier) (1528)
casting *n* an object that has been cast in metal from a mould
casting vote *n* the deciding vote used by the chairperson of a meeting when an equal number of votes are cast on each side
cast iron *n* **1** iron containing so much carbon that it is brittle and must be cast into shape rather than wrought ▹*adj* **cast-iron 2** made of cast iron **3** definite or unchallengeable: *cast-iron guarantees*
castle ❶ *n* **1** a large fortified building or set of buildings, often built as a residence for a ruler or nobleman in medieval Europe **2** ▸same as **rook²**
WORD ORIGIN Latin: castellum
castle in the air *or* **in Spain** *n* a hope or desire unlikely to be realized
Castlereagh¹ *n* a district of E Northern Ireland, in Co Down. Pop: 66 076 (2003 est). Area.: 85 sq km (33 sq miles)
Castlereagh² *n* **Viscount** title of *Robert Stewart, Marquis of Londonderry*. 1769–1822, British statesman: as foreign secretary (1812–22) led the Grand Alliance against Napoleon and attended the Congress of Vienna (1815)
Castner *n* **Hamilton Young** 1858–98, US chemist, who devised the **Castner process** for extracting sodium from sodium hydroxide
cast-off *adj* **1** discarded because no longer wanted or needed: *cast-off clothing* ▹*n* **2** a person or thing that has been discarded because no longer wanted or needed ▹*vb* **cast off 3** to discard (something no longer wanted or needed) **4** to untie a ship from a dock **5** to knot and remove (a row of stitches, esp. the final row) from the needle in knitting
cast on *vb* to make (a row of stitches) on the needle in knitting
castor *n* a small swivelling wheel fixed to a piece of furniture to enable it to be moved easily in any direction
castor oil *n* an oil obtained from the seeds of an Indian plant, used as a lubricant and purgative
castrate *vb* **-trating, -trated 1** to remove the testicles of **2** to deprive of vigour or masculinity
castration *n*
WORD ORIGIN Latin *castrare*
castrato *n, pl* **-ti** *or* **-tos** (in 17th- and 18th-century opera) a male singer whose testicles were removed before puberty, allowing the retention of a soprano or alto voice
WORD ORIGIN Italian
casual ❶ *adj* **1** being or seeming careless or nonchalant: *he was casual about security* **2** occasional or irregular: *casual workers* **3** shallow or superficial: *casual relationships* **4** for informal wear: *a casual jacket* **5** happening by chance or without planning: *a casual comment* ▹*n* **6** an occasional worker **casually** *adv*
WORD ORIGIN Latin *casus* event, chance
casuals *pl n* **1** informal clothing **2** *Brit* young men wearing expensive casual clothes who go to football matches in order to start fights
casualty ❶ *n, pl* **-ties 1** a person who is killed or injured in an accident or war **2** the hospital department where victims of accidents are given emergency treatment **3** a person or thing that has suffered as the result of a particular event or circumstance: *583 job losses with significant casualties among public-sector employees*
casuarina (kass-yew-a-**reen**-a) *n* an Australian tree with jointed green branches
WORD ORIGIN from Malay *kĕsuari*, referring to the resemblance of the branches to the feathers of the cassowary
casuistry *n* reasoning that is misleading or oversubtle **casuist** *n*
WORD ORIGIN Latin *casus* case
cat ❶ *n* **1** a small domesticated mammal with thick soft fur and whiskers **2** a wild animal related to the cat, such as the lynx, lion, or tiger ▸Related adjective: **feline 3 let the cat out of the bag** to disclose a secret **4 raining cats and dogs** raining very heavily **5 set the cat among the pigeons** to stir up trouble **catlike** *adj*
WORD ORIGIN Latin *cattus*
catabolism *n biol* a metabolic process in which complex molecules are broken down into simple ones with the release of energy **catabolic** *adj*
WORD ORIGIN Greek *kata-* down + *ballein* to throw
cataclysm (kat-a-kliz-zum) *n* **1** a violent upheaval of a social, political, or military nature: *the cataclysm of the Second World War* **2** a disaster such as an earthquake or a flood
cataclysmic *adj*
WORD ORIGIN Greek *katakluzein* to flood
catacombs (kat-a-koomz) *pl n* an underground burial place consisting of tunnels with side recesses for tombs
WORD ORIGIN Late Latin *catacumbas* cemetery near Rome
catafalque (kat-a-falk) *n* a raised platform on which a body lies in state before or during a funeral
WORD ORIGIN Italian *catafalco*
Catalan *adj* **1** of Catalonia ▹*n* **2** a language of Catalonia in NE Spain **3** a person from Catalonia
catalepsy *n* a trancelike state in which the body is rigid
cataleptic *adj*
WORD ORIGIN Greek *katalēpsis* a seizing
catalogue ❶ *or US* **catalog** *n* **1** a book containing details of items for sale **2** a list of all the books of a library **3** a list of events, qualities, or things considered as a group: *a catalogue of killings* ▹*vb* **-loguing, -logued** *or* **-loging, -loged 4** to enter (an item) in a catalogue **5** to list a series of (events, qualities, or things): *the report catalogues two decades of human-rights violations* **cataloguer** *n*
WORD ORIGIN Greek *katalegein* to list
catalpa *n* a tree of N America and Asia with bell-shaped whitish flowers
WORD ORIGIN Carolina Creek (a Native American language) *kutuhlpa* winged head
catalyse *or US* **-lyze** *vb* **-lysing, -lysed** *or* **-lyzing, -lyzed** to influence (a chemical reaction) by catalysis
catalysis *n* acceleration of a chemical reaction by the action of a catalyst
catalytic *adj*
WORD ORIGIN Greek *kataluein* to dissolve
catalyst *n* **1** a substance that speeds up a chemical reaction without itself undergoing any permanent chemical change **2** a person or thing that causes an important change to take place: *a catalyst for peace*
catalytic converter *n* a device which uses catalysts to reduce the quantity of poisonous substances emitted by the exhaust of a motor vehicle
catalytic cracker *n* a unit in an oil

THESAURUS

castle *n* **1 = fortress**, keep, palace, tower, peel, chateau, stronghold, citadel, fastness
casual *adj* **1 = careless**, relaxed, informal, indifferent, unconcerned, apathetic, blasé, offhand, nonchalant, insouciant, lackadaisical **OPPOSITE:** serious **4 = informal**, leisure, sporty, non-dressy **OPPOSITE:** formal **5 = chance**, unexpected, random, accidental, incidental, unforeseen, unintentional, fortuitous *(informal)*, serendipitous, unpremeditated **OPPOSITE:** planned
casualty *n* **1 = fatality**, death, loss, wounded **3 = victim**, sufferer
cat *n* **1 = feline**, pussy *(informal)*, moggy *(slang)*, puss *(informal)*, ballarat *(Austral informal)*, tabby ▸*related adjective:* feline ▸*name of male:* tom ▸*name of female:* queen ▸*name of young:* kitten
catalogue *or (US)* **catalog** *n* **1, 2 = list**, record, schedule, index, register, directory, inventory, gazetteer ▹*vb* **4 = list**, file, index, register, classify, inventory, tabulate, alphabetize

DICTIONARY

refinery in which mineral oils are converted into fuels by a catalytic process

catamaran *n* a boat with twin parallel hulls
WORD ORIGIN Tamil *kattumaram* tied timber

C

catamite *n* a boy kept as a homosexual partner
WORD ORIGIN Latin *Catamitus,* variant of *Ganymedes* Ganymede, cupbearer to the gods in Greek mythology

catapult *n* **1** a Y-shaped device with a loop of elastic fastened to the ends of the prongs, used by children for firing stones **2** a device used to launch aircraft from a warship ▹*vb* **3** to shoot forwards or upwards violently: *traffic catapulted forward with a roar* **4** to cause (someone) suddenly to be in a particular situation: *catapulted to stardom*
WORD ORIGIN Greek *kata-* down + *pallein* to hurl

cataract *n* **1** *pathol* **a** a condition in which the lens of the eye becomes partially or totally opaque **b** the opaque area **2** a large waterfall
WORD ORIGIN Greek *katarassein* to dash down

catarrh (**kat**-tar) *n* excessive mucus in the nose and throat, often experienced during or following a cold **catarrhal** *adj*
WORD ORIGIN Greek *katarrhein* to flow down

catastrophe ❶ (kat-**ass**-trof-fee) *n* a great and sudden disaster or misfortune **catastrophic** *adj*
WORD ORIGIN Greek *katastrephein* to overturn

catatonia *n* a form of schizophrenia in which the sufferer experiences stupor, with outbreaks of excitement **catatonic** *adj*
WORD ORIGIN Greek *kata-* down + *tonos* tension

cat burglar *n* a burglar who enters buildings by climbing through upper windows

catcall *n* a shrill whistle or cry of disapproval or derision

catch ❶ *vb* **catching, caught 1** to seize and hold **2** to capture (a person or a fish or animal) **3** to surprise in an act: *two boys were caught stealing* **4** to reach (a bus, train, or plane) in time to board it **5** to see or hear: *you'll have to be quick if you want to catch her DJ-ing* **6** to be infected with (an illness) **7** to entangle or become entangled **8** to attract (someone's attention, imagination, or interest) **9** to comprehend or make out: *you have to work hard to catch his tone and meaning* **10** to reproduce (a quality) accurately in a work of art **11** (of a fire) to start burning **12** *cricket* to dismiss (a batsman) by catching a ball struck by him before it touches the ground **13 catch at a** to attempt to grasp **b** to take advantage of (an opportunity) **14 catch it** *informal* to be punished ▹*n* **15** a device such as a hook, for fastening a door, window, or box **16** the total number of fish caught **17** *informal* a concealed or unforeseen drawback **18** an emotional break in the voice **19** *informal* a person considered worth having as a husband or wife **20** *cricket* the act of catching a ball struck by a batsman before it touches the ground, resulting in him being out ▸See also **catch on, catch out, catch up**
WORD ORIGIN Latin *capere* to seize

catchcry *n, pl* **-cries** *Austral* a well-known, frequently used phrase, esp. one associated with a particular group

catching ❶ *adj* infectious

catchment *n* **1** a structure in which water is collected **2** all the people served by a school or hospital in a particular catchment area

catchment area *n* **1** the area of land draining into a river, basin, or reservoir **2** the area served by a particular school or hospital

catch on *vb informal* **1** to become popular or fashionable **2** to understand: *I was slow to catch on to what she was trying to tell me*

catch out *vb informal chiefly Brit* to trap (someone) in an error or a lie

catchpenny *adj Brit* designed to have instant appeal without regard for quality

catch phrase *n* a well-known phrase or slogan associated with a particular entertainer or other celebrity

catch-22 *n* a situation in which a person is frustrated by a set of circumstances that prevent any attempt to escape from them
WORD ORIGIN from the title of a novel by J Heller

catch up *vb* **1 be caught up in** to be unwillingly or accidentally involved in: *hundreds of civilians have been caught up in the clashes* **2 catch up on** *or* **with** to bring (something) up to date: *he had a lot of paperwork to catch up on* **3 catch up with** to reach or pass (someone or something): *she ran to catch up with him*

catchword *n* a well-known and frequently used phrase or slogan

catchy *adj* **catchier, catchiest** (of a tune) pleasant and easily remembered

catechism (**kat**-tik-kiz-zum) *n* instruction on the doctrine of a Christian Church by a series of questions and answers
WORD ORIGIN Greek *katēkhizein* to catechize

catechize *or* **-echise** *vb* **-echizing, -echized** *or* **-echising, -echised 1** to instruct in Christianity using a catechism **2** to question (someone) thoroughly **catechist** *n*
WORD ORIGIN Greek *katēkhizein*

categorical *or* **categoric** *adj* absolutely clear and certain: *he was categorical in his denial* **categorically** *adv*

categorize *or* **-rise** *vb* **-rizing, -rized** *or* **-rising, -rised** to put in a category **categorization** *or* **-risation** *n*

category ❶ *n, pl* **-ries** a class or group of things or people with some quality or qualities in common
WORD ORIGIN Greek *katēgoria* assertion

cater *vb* **1** to provide what is needed or wanted: *operating theatres that can cater for open-heart surgery* **2** to provide food or services: *chef is pleased to cater for vegetarians and vegans*
WORD ORIGIN Anglo-Norman *acater* to buy

THESAURUS

catastrophe *n* **= disaster**, tragedy, calamity, meltdown *(informal)*, cataclysm, trouble, trial, blow, failure, reverse, misfortune, devastation, adversity, mishap, affliction, whammy *(informal, chiefly US)*, bummer *(slang)*, mischance, fiasco

catch *vb* **1a = seize**, get, grab, snatch **1b = grab**, take, grip, seize, grasp, clutch, lay hold of **OPPOSITE:** release **2a = capture**, arrest, trap, seize, nail *(informal)*, nab *(informal)*, snare, lift *(slang)*, apprehend, ensnare, entrap, feel your collar *(slang)* **OPPOSITE:** free **2b = trap**, capture, snare, entangle, ensnare, entrap **3 = discover**, surprise, find out, expose, detect, catch in the act, take unawares **6 = contract**, get, develop, suffer from, incur, succumb to, go down with **OPPOSITE:** escape ▹*n* **15 = fastener**, hook, clip, bolt, latch, clasp, hasp, hook and eye, snib *(Scot)*, sneck *(dialect, chiefly Scot & Northern English)* **17** *(informal)* **= drawback**, trick, trap, disadvantage, hitch, snag, stumbling block, fly in the ointment **OPPOSITE:** advantage

catching *adj* **= infectious**, contagious, transferable, communicable, infective, transmittable **OPPOSITE:** non-infectious

category *n* **= class**, grouping, heading, head, order, sort, list, department, type, division, section, rank, grade, classification, genre

cattle *pl n* **= cows**, stock, beasts, livestock, bovines ▸*related adjective:* bovine ▸*collective nouns:* drove, herd

caterer *n* a person whose job is to provide food for social events such as parties and weddings

catering *n* the supplying of food for a social event

caterpillar *n* **1** the wormlike larva of a butterfly or moth **2** *trademark* Also: **caterpillar track** an endless track, driven by cogged wheels, used to propel a heavy vehicle such as a bulldozer
WORD ORIGIN probably from Old French *catepelose* hairy cat

caterwaul *vb* **1** to make a yowling noise like a cat ▷ *n* **2** such a noise
WORD ORIGIN imitative

Catesby *n* **Robert** 1573–1605, English conspirator, leader of the Gunpowder Plot (1605): killed while resisting arrest

catfish *n, pl* **-fish** *or* **-fishes** a freshwater fish with whisker-like barbels around the mouth

catgut *n* a strong cord made from dried animals' intestines, used to string musical instruments and sports rackets

catharsis (kath-**thar**-siss) *n* **1** the relief of strong suppressed emotions, for example through drama or psychoanalysis **2** evacuation of the bowels, esp. with the use of a laxative
WORD ORIGIN Greek *kathairein* to purge, purify

cathartic *adj* **1** causing catharsis ▷ *n* **2** a drug that causes catharsis

Cathay *n* a literary or archaic name for China
WORD ORIGIN Medieval Latin *Cataya*

cathedral *n* the principal church of a diocese
WORD ORIGIN Greek *kathedra* seat

Cather *n* **Willa (Sibert)** 1873–1947, US novelist, whose works include *O Pioneers!* (1913) and *My Ántonia* (1918)

Catherine de' Medici *or* **Catherine de Médicis** *n* 1519–89, queen of Henry II of France; mother of Francis II, Charles IX, and Henry III of France; regent of France (1560–74). She was largely responsible for the massacre of Protestants on Saint Bartholomew's Day (1572)

Catherine I *n* ?1684–1727, second wife of Peter the Great, whom she succeeded as empress of Russia (1725–27)

Catherine of Aragon *n* 1485–1536, first wife of Henry VIII of England and mother of Mary I. The annulment of Henry's marriage to her (1533) against papal authority marked an initial stage in the English Reformation

Catherine of Braganza *n* 1638–1705, wife of Charles II of England, daughter of John IV of Portugal

Catherine of Siena *n* **Saint** 1347–80, Italian mystic and ascetic; patron saint of the Dominican order. Feast day: April 29

Catherine wheel *n* a firework that rotates, producing sparks and coloured flame
WORD ORIGIN after St *Catherine* of Alexandria, martyred on a spiked wheel

catheter (**kath**-it-er) *n* a slender flexible tube inserted into a body cavity to drain fluid
WORD ORIGIN Greek *kathienai* to insert

cathode *n* *electronics* the negative electrode in an electrolytic cell or in an electronic valve or tube
WORD ORIGIN Greek *kathodos* a descent

cathode rays *pl n* a stream of electrons emitted from the surface of a cathode in a valve

cathode-ray tube *n* a valve in which a beam of electrons is focused onto a fluorescent screen to produce a visible image, used in television receivers and visual display units

catholic *adj* (of tastes or interests) covering a wide range
WORD ORIGIN Greek *katholikos* universal

Catholic *Christianity adj* **1** of the Roman Catholic Church ▷ *n* **2** a member of the Roman Catholic Church **Catholicism** *n*

Catiline *n* Latin name *Lucius Sergius Catilina* ?108–62 BC, Roman politician: organized an unsuccessful conspiracy against Cicero (63–62) **Catilinarian** *adj*

cation (**kat**-eye-on) *n* a positively charged ion
WORD ORIGIN Greek *kata-* down + *ienai* to go

catkin *n* a drooping flower spike found on trees such as the birch, hazel, and willow
WORD ORIGIN obsolete Dutch *katteken* kitten

catmint *n* a Eurasian plant with scented leaves that attract cats. Also: **catnip**

catnap *n* **1** a short sleep or doze ▷ *vb* **-napping, -napped 2** to sleep or doze for a short time or intermittently

cat-o'-nine-tails *n, pl* **-tails** a rope whip with nine knotted thongs, formerly used to inflict floggings as a punishment

cat's cradle *n* a game played by making patterns with a loop of string between the fingers

catseyes *pl n trademark, Brit, Austral & NZ* glass reflectors set into the road at intervals to indicate traffic lanes by reflecting light from vehicles' headlights

cat's paw *n* a person used by someone else to do unpleasant things for him or her
WORD ORIGIN from the tale of a monkey who used a cat's paw to draw chestnuts out of a fire

cattle ❶ *pl n* domesticated cows and bulls ▸ Related adjective: **bovine**
WORD ORIGIN Old French *chatel* chattel

cattle-cake *n* concentrated food for cattle in the form of cakelike blocks

cattle-grid *or NZ* **cattle-stop** *n* a grid covering a hole dug in a road to prevent livestock crossing while allowing vehicles to pass unhindered

catty *adj* **-tier, -tiest** *informal* spiteful: *her remarks were amusing and only slightly catty* **cattiness** *n*

Catullus *n* **Gaius Valerius** ?84–?54 BC, Roman lyric poet, noted particularly for his love poems **Catullan** *adj*

catwalk *n* **1** a narrow pathway over the stage of a theatre or along a bridge **2** a narrow platform where models display clothes in a fashion show

Caucasian *or* **Caucasoid** *adj* **1** of the predominantly light-skinned racial group of humankind ▷ *n* **2** a member of this group

Cauchy *n* **Augustin Louis**, Baron Cauchy. 1789–1857, French mathematician, noted for his work on the theory of functions and the wave theory of light

caucus *n, pl* **-cuses 1** a local committee or faction of a political party **2** a political meeting to decide future plans **3** NZ a formal meeting of all MPs of one party
WORD ORIGIN probably of Native American origin

caudal *adj zool* at or near the tail or back part of an animal's body
WORD ORIGIN Latin *cauda* tail

caught *vb* ▸ the past of **catch**

caul *n anat* a membrane sometimes covering a child's head at birth
WORD ORIGIN Old French *calotte* close-fitting cap

cauldron *or* **caldron** *n* a large pot used for boiling
WORD ORIGIN Latin *caldarium* hot bath

Caulfield *n* **Patrick (Joseph)** 1936–2005, British painter and printmaker

cauliflower *n* a vegetable with a large head of white flower buds surrounded by green leaves
WORD ORIGIN Italian *caoli fiori* cabbage flowers

cauliflower ear *n* permanent swelling and distortion of the ear, caused by repeated blows usually received in boxing

caulk *vb* to fill in (cracks) with paste or some other material
WORD ORIGIN Latin *calcare* to trample

causal *adj* of or being a cause: *a causal connection* **causally** *adv*

causation *or* **causality** *n* **1** the production of an effect by a cause **2** the relationship of cause and effect

causative *adj* producing an effect: *bright lights seem to be a causative factor in some migraines*

C

C

DICTIONARY

cause ⓣ *n* **1** something that produces a particular effect **2** grounds for action; justification: *there is cause for concern* **3** an aim or principle which an individual or group is interested in and supports: *the Socialist cause* ▷ *vb* **causing, caused 4** to be the cause of **causeless** *adj*
WORD ORIGIN Latin *causa*

cause célèbre (kawz sill-leb-ra) *n, pl* **causes célèbres** (kawz sill-leb-ras) a controversial legal case, issue, or person
WORD ORIGIN French

causeway *n* a raised path or road across water or marshland
WORD ORIGIN Middle English *cauciwey* paved way

caustic *adj* **1** capable of burning or corroding by chemical action: *caustic soda* **2** bitter and sarcastic: *caustic critics* ▷ *n* **3** *chem* a caustic substance **caustically** *adv*
WORD ORIGIN Greek *kaiein* to burn

caustic soda *n* ▸ same as **sodium hydroxide**

cauterize *or* **-ise** *vb* **-izing, -ized** *or* **-ising, -ised** to burn (a wound) with heat or a caustic agent to prevent infection **cauterization** *or* **-isation** *n*
WORD ORIGIN Greek *kaiein* to burn

caution ⓣ *n* **1** care or prudence, esp. in the face of danger **2** warning: *a word of caution* **3** *law chiefly Brit* a formal warning given to a person suspected of an offence ▷ *vb* **4** to warn or advise: *he cautioned against an abrupt turnaround* **cautionary** *adj*
WORD ORIGIN Latin *cautio*

cautious ⓣ *adj* showing or having caution **cautiously** *adv*

Cavaco Silva *n* **Aníbal** born 1939, Portuguese statesman; prime minister (1985–95); president from 2006

Cavafy *n* **Constantine** Greek name *Kavafis*. 1863–1933, Greek poet of Alexandria in Egypt

cavalcade *n* a procession of people on horseback or in cars
WORD ORIGIN Italian *cavalcare* to ride on horseback

Cavalcanti *n* **Guido** ?1255–1300, Italian poet, noted for his love poems

cavalier *adj* **1** showing haughty disregard; offhand ▷ *n* **2** *old-fashioned* a gallant or courtly gentleman
WORD ORIGIN Late Latin *caballarius* rider

Cavalier *n* a supporter of Charles I during the English Civil War

Cavallini *n* **Pietro** ?1250–?1330, Italian fresco painter and mosaicist. His works include the mosaics of the *Life of the Virgin* in Santa Maria, Trastevere, Rome

cavalry ⓣ *n* the part of an army originally mounted on horseback, but now often using fast armoured vehicles **cavalryman** *n*
WORD ORIGIN Italian *cavaliere* horseman

cave ⓣ *n* a hollow in the side of a hill or cliff, or underground
WORD ORIGIN Latin *cavus* hollow

caveat (kav-vee-at) *n* **1** *law* a formal notice requesting the court not to take a certain action without warning the person lodging the caveat **2** a caution
WORD ORIGIN Latin: let him beware

cave in *vb* **1** to collapse inwards **2** *informal* to yield completely under pressure: *the government caved in to the revolutionaries' demands* ▷ *n* **cave-in 3** the sudden collapse of a roof or piece of ground

Cavell *n* **Edith Louisa** 1865–1915, English nurse: executed by the Germans in World War I for helping Allied prisoners to escape

caveman *n, pl* **-men 1** a prehistoric cave dweller **2** *informal* a man who is primitive or brutal in behaviour

Cavendish *n* **Henry** 1731–1810, British physicist and chemist: recognized hydrogen, determined the composition of water, and calculated the density of the earth by an experiment named after him

cavern *n* a large cave
WORD ORIGIN Latin *cavus* hollow

cavernous *adj* like a cavern in vastness, depth, or hollowness: *the cavernous building*

caviar *or* **caviare** *n* the salted roe of the sturgeon, regarded as a delicacy and usually served as an appetizer
WORD ORIGIN Turkish *havyār*

cavil *vb* **-illing, -illed** *or US* **-iling, -iled 1** to raise annoying petty objections ▷ *n* **2** a petty objection
WORD ORIGIN Latin *cavillari* to jeer

caving *n* the sport of climbing in and exploring caves **caver** *n*

cavity ⓣ *n, pl* **-ties 1** a hollow space **2** *dentistry* a decayed area on a tooth
WORD ORIGIN Latin *cavus* hollow

cavort *vb* to skip about; caper

Cavour *n* Conte **Camillo Benso di** 1810–61, Italian statesman and premier of Piedmont-Sardinia (1852–59; 1860–61): a leader of the movement for the unification of Italy

caw *n* **1** the cry of a crow, rook, or raven ▷ *vb* **2** to make this cry
WORD ORIGIN imitative

Cawdrey *n* **Robert** 16th–17th-century English schoolmaster and lexicographer: compiled the first English dictionary (*A Table Alphabeticall*) in 1604

Cawley *n* **Evonne** (née *Goolagong*) born 1951, Australian tennis player: Wimbledon champion 1971 and 1980; Australian champion 1974–76

cay *n* a small low island or bank of sand and coral fragments
WORD ORIGIN Spanish *cayo*

cayenne pepper *or* **cayenne** *n* a very hot red spice made from the dried seeds of capsicums
WORD ORIGIN S American Indian *quiynha*

Cayley *n* **1 Arthur** 1821–93, British mathematician, who invented matrices **2** Sir **George** 1773–1857, British engineer and pioneer of aerial navigation. He constructed the first man-carrying glider (1853) and invented the caterpillar tractor

cayman *or* **caiman** *n, pl* **-mans** a tropical American reptile similar to an alligator
WORD ORIGIN Carib

caz *adj slang* ▸ short for **casual**

CB 1 Citizens' Band **2** Commander of the Order of the Bath

CBC Canadian Broadcasting Corporation

CBE Commander of the Order of the British Empire (a Brit. title)

CBI Confederation of British Industry

cc *or* **c.c. 1** carbon copy **2** cubic centimetre

CC 1 County Council **2** Cricket Club

CCS cascading style sheet

THESAURUS

cause *n* **1 = origin**, source, agency, spring, agent, maker, producer, root, beginning, creator, genesis, originator, prime mover, mainspring **OPPOSITE:** result **2 = reason**, call, need, grounds, basis, incentive, motive, motivation, justification, inducement **3 = aim**, movement, purpose, principle, object, ideal, enterprise, end ▷ *vb* **4 = produce**, begin, create, effect, lead to, occasion, result in, generate, provoke, compel, motivate, induce, bring about, give rise to, precipitate, incite, engender **OPPOSITE:** prevent

caution *n* **1 = care**, discretion, heed, prudence, vigilance, alertness, forethought, circumspection, watchfulness, belt and braces, carefulness, heedfulness **OPPOSITE:** carelessness **3 = reprimand**, warning, injunction, admonition ▷ *vb* **4 = warn**, urge, advise, alert, tip off, forewarn, put you on your guard

cautious *adj* **= careful**, guarded, alert, wary, discreet, tentative, prudent, vigilant, watchful, judicious, circumspect, cagey (*informal*), on your toes, chary, belt-and-braces, keeping a weather eye on **OPPOSITE:** careless

cavalry *n* **= horsemen**, horse, mounted troops **OPPOSITE:** infantrymen

cave *n* **= hollow**, cavern, grotto, den, cavity

cavity *n* **1 = hollow**, hole, gap, pit, dent, crater

DICTIONARY

CCTV closed-circuit television
cd candela
Cd *chem* cadmium
CD compact disc
CDI compact disc interactive: a system for storing a mix of software, data, audio, and compressed video for interactive use under processor control
C.diff *or* **C.difficile** Clostridium difficile
Cdn. Canadian
CD player *n* a device for playing compact discs
Cdr Commander
CD-R compact disk recordable
CD-ROM compact disc read-only memory: a compact disc used with a computer system as a read-only optical disc
CD-RW compact disk read-write
CDT Central Daylight Time
CD-video *n* a compact-disc player that, when connected to a television and a hi-fi, produces high-quality stereo sound and synchronized pictures from a compact disc
Ce *chem* cerium
cease ⓣ *vb* **ceasing, ceased 1** to bring or come to an end ▷*n* **2 without cease** without stopping
WORD ORIGIN Latin *cessare*
ceasefire *n* a temporary period of truce
ceaseless *adj* without stopping **ceaselessly** *adv*
Ceauşescu *n* **Nicolae** 1918–89, Romanian statesman; chairman of the state council (1967–89) and president of Romania (1974–89): deposed and executed
Cecil *n* **1** Lord **David** 1902–86, English literary critic and biographer **2 Robert** ▸ See (3rd Marquess of) **Salisbury 3 William** ▸ See (William Cecil) **Burghley**
Cecilia *n* **Saint** died ?230 AD, Roman martyr; patron saint of music. Feast day: Nov 22
cedar *n* **1** a coniferous tree with needle-like evergreen leaves and barrel-shaped cones **2** the sweet-smelling wood of this tree
WORD ORIGIN Greek *kedros*
cede *vb* **ceding, ceded** to transfer or surrender (territory or legal rights)
WORD ORIGIN Latin *cedere* to yield
cedilla *n* a character (,) placed underneath a *c*, esp. in French or Portuguese, indicating that it is to be pronounced (s), not (k)
WORD ORIGIN Spanish: little *z*
Ceefax *n trademark* (in Britain) the BBC teletext service
ceilidh (kay-lee) *n* an informal social gathering in Scotland or Ireland with folk music and country dancing
WORD ORIGIN Gaelic
ceiling *n* **1** the inner upper surface of a room **2** an upper limit set on something such as a payment or salary **3** the upper altitude to which an aircraft can climb
WORD ORIGIN origin unknown
Cela *n* **Camilo José** 1916–2002, Spanish novelist and essayist. His works include *The Family of Pascual Duarte* (1942), *La Colmena* (1951), and *La Cruz de San Andres* (1994). Nobel prize for literature 1989
Celan *n* **Paul,** real name *Paul Antschel*. 1920–70, Romanian Jewish poet, writing in German, whose work reflects the experience of Nazi persecution
celandine *n* a wild plant with yellow flowers
WORD ORIGIN Greek *khelidōn* swallow; the plant's season was believed to parallel the migration of swallows
celebrant *n* a person who performs or takes part in a religious ceremony
celebrate ⓣ *vb* **-brating, -brated 1** hold festivities: *let's celebrate!* **2** to hold festivities to mark (a happy event, birthday, or anniversary) **3** to perform (a solemn or religious ceremony) **4** to praise publicly: *the novel is justly celebrated as a masterpiece* **celebration** *n* **celebratory** *adj*
WORD ORIGIN Latin *celeber* numerous, renowned
celebrated ⓣ *adj* well known: *the celebrated musician*
celebrity ⓣ *n, pl* **-ties 1** a famous person **2** the state of being famous
celeriac (sill-ler-ree-ak) *n* a variety of celery with a large turnip-like root
celerity (sill-ler-rit-tee) *n formal* swiftness
WORD ORIGIN Latin *celeritas*
celery *n* a vegetable with long green crisp edible stalks
WORD ORIGIN Greek *selinon* parsley
celesta *n* an instrument like a small piano in which key-operated hammers strike metal plates
WORD ORIGIN French *céleste* heavenly
celestial *adj* **1** heavenly or divine: *celestial music* **2** of or relating to the sky or space: *celestial objects such as pulsars and quasars*
WORD ORIGIN Latin *caelum* heaven
celestial equator *n* an imaginary circle lying on the celestial sphere in a plane perpendicular to the earth's axis
celestial sphere *n* an imaginary sphere of infinitely large radius enclosing the universe
celibate *adj* **1** unmarried or abstaining from sex, esp. because of a religious vow of chastity ▷*n* **2** a celibate person **celibacy** *n*
WORD ORIGIN Latin *caelebs* unmarried
Céline *n* **Louis-Ferdinand,** real name *Louis-Ferdinand Destouches*. 1894–1961, French novelist and physician; became famous with his controversial first novel *Journey to the End of the Night* (1932)
cell ⓣ *n* **1** *biol* the smallest unit of an organism that is able to function independently **2** a small simple room in a prison, convent, or monastery **3** any small compartment, such as a cell of a honeycomb **4** a small group operating as the core of a larger organization: *Communist cells* **5** a device that produces electrical energy by chemical action **6** *US & Canad* a cellular telephone
WORD ORIGIN Latin *cella* room, storeroom
cellar *n* **1** an underground room, usually used for storage **2** a place where wine is stored **3** a stock of bottled wines
WORD ORIGIN Latin *cellarium* food store

THESAURUS

cease *vb* **1a = stop**, end, finish, be over, come to an end, peter out, die away **OPPOSITE:** start **1b = discontinue**, end, stop, fail, finish, give up, conclude, suspend, halt, terminate, break off, refrain, leave off, give over *(informal)*, bring to an end, desist, belay *(nautical)* **OPPOSITE:** begin
celebrate *vb* **1a = rejoice**, party, enjoy yourself, carouse, live it up *(informal)*, whoop it up *(informal)*, make merry, paint the town red *(informal)*, go on a spree, put the flags out, roister, kill the fatted calf **1b = commemorate**, honour, observe, toast, drink to, keep **3 = perform**, observe, preside over, officiate at, solemnize
celebrated *adj* **= renowned**, popular, famous, outstanding, distinguished, well-known, prominent, glorious, acclaimed, notable, eminent, revered, famed, illustrious, pre-eminent, lionized **OPPOSITE:** unknown
celebrity *n* **1 = personality**, name, star, superstar, big name, dignitary, luminary, bigwig *(informal)*, celeb *(informal)*, face *(informal)*, big shot *(informal)*, personage, megastar *(informal)*, V.I.P. **OPPOSITE:** nobody **2 = fame**, reputation, honour, glory, popularity, distinction, prestige, prominence, stardom, renown, pre-eminence, repute, éclat, notability **OPPOSITE:** obscurity
cell *n* **2 = room**, chamber, lock-up, compartment, cavity, cubicle, dungeon, stall **4 = unit**, group, section, core, nucleus, caucus, coterie

C

DICTIONARY

cellarage *n* **1** the area of a cellar **2** a charge for storing goods in a cellar

Cellini *n* **Benvenuto** 1500–71, Italian sculptor, goldsmith, and engraver, noted also for his autobiography

cello (**chell**-oh) *n, pl* **-los** a large low-pitched musical instrument of the violin family, held between the knees and played with a bow
cellist *n*
WORD ORIGIN short for *violoncello*

Cellophane *n trademark* a thin transparent material made from cellulose that is used as a protective wrapping, esp. for food
WORD ORIGIN *cellulose* + Greek *phainein* to shine, appear

cellular *adj* **1** of, consisting of, or resembling a cell or cells: *cellular changes* **2** woven with an open texture: *cellular blankets* **3** designed for or using cellular radio: *cellular phones*

cellular radio *n* radio communication, used esp. in car phones, based on a network of transmitters each serving a small area known as a cell

cellulite *n* fat deposits under the skin alleged to resist dieting

celluloid *n* **1** a kind of plastic made from cellulose nitrate and camphor, used to make toys and, formerly, photographic film **2** the cinema or films generally: *a Shakespeare play committed to celluloid*

cellulose *n* the main constituent of plant cell walls, used in making paper, rayon, and plastics

cellulose acetate *n* a nonflammable material used to make film, lacquers, and artificial fibres

cellulose nitrate *n* a compound used in plastics, lacquers, and explosives

Celsius *adj* denoting a measurement on the Celsius scale
WORD ORIGIN after Anders *Celsius*, astronomer who invented it

Celsius scale *n* a scale of temperature in which 0° represents the melting point of ice and 100° represents the boiling point of water

Celt (kelt) *n* **1** a person from Scotland, Ireland, Wales, Cornwall, or Brittany **2** a member of a people who inhabited Britain, Gaul, and Spain in pre-Roman times
WORD ORIGIN Latin *Celtae* the Celts

Celtic (**kel**-tik, **sel**-tik) *n* **1** a group of languages that includes Gaelic, Welsh, and Breton ▹ *adj* **2** of the Celts or the Celtic languages

cement **T** *n* **1 a** a fine grey powder made of limestone and clay, mixed with water and sand to make mortar or concrete **b** mortar or concrete **2** something that unites, binds, or joins things or people: *bone cement; the cement of fear and hatred of the Left* **3** *dentistry* a material used for filling teeth ▹ *vb* **4** to join, bind, or cover with cement **5** to make (a relationship) stronger: *this would cement a firm alliance between the army and rebels*
WORD ORIGIN Latin *caementum* stone from the quarry

cemetery **T** *n, pl* **-teries** a place where dead people are buried: *a military cemetery*
WORD ORIGIN Greek *koimētērion* room for sleeping

cenotaph *n* a monument honouring soldiers who died in a war
WORD ORIGIN Greek *kenos* empty + *taphos* tomb

Cenozoic *or* **Caenozoic** (see-no-**zoh**-ik) *adj geol* of the most recent geological era, beginning 65 million years ago, characterized by the development and increase of the mammals
WORD ORIGIN Greek *kainos* recent + *zōion* animal

censer *n* a container for burning incense

censor **T** *n* **1** a person authorized to examine films, letters, or publications, in order to ban or cut anything considered obscene or objectionable ▹ *vb* **2** to ban or cut portions of (a film, letter, or publication)
WORD ORIGIN Latin *censere* to consider

censorious *adj* harshly critical

censorship *n* the practice or policy of censoring films, letters, or publications

censure **T** *n* **1** severe disapproval ▹ *vb* **-suring, -sured 2** to criticize (someone or something) severely
WORD ORIGIN Latin *censere* to assess

census *n, pl* **-suses** an official periodic count of a population including such information as sex, age, and occupation
WORD ORIGIN Latin *censere* to assess

cent *n* a monetary unit worth one hundredth of the main unit of currency in many countries
WORD ORIGIN Latin *centum* hundred

cent. **1** central **2** century

centaur *n Greek myth* a creature with the head, arms, and torso of a man, and the lower body and legs of a horse
WORD ORIGIN Greek *kentauros*

centavo *n, pl* **-vos** a monetary unit worth one hundredth of the main unit of currency in Portugal and many Latin American countries
WORD ORIGIN Spanish: one hundredth part

centenarian *n* a person who is at least 100 years old

centenary (sen-**teen**-a-ree) *n, pl* **-naries** *chiefly Brit* a 100th anniversary or the celebration of one. US equivalent: **centennial**
WORD ORIGIN Latin *centum* hundred

center *n, vb US* ▸ same as **centre**

centesimal *n* **1** one hundredth ▹ *adj* **2** of or divided into hundredths
WORD ORIGIN Latin *centum* hundred

centi- *prefix* **1** denoting one hundredth: *centimetre* **2** a hundred: *centipede*
WORD ORIGIN Latin *centum* hundred

centigrade *adj* ▸ same as **Celsius**

centigram *or* **centigramme** *n* one hundredth of a gram

centilitre *or US* **centiliter** *n* a measure of volume equivalent to one hundredth of a litre

centime (**son**-teem) *n* a monetary unit worth one hundredth of the main unit of currency in a number of countries
WORD ORIGIN Latin *centum* hundred

centimetre *or US* **centimeter** *n* a unit of length equal to one hundredth of a metre

centipede *n* a small wormlike creature with many legs

central **T** *adj* **1** of, at, or forming the centre of something: *eastern and central parts of the country* **2** main or principal: *a central issue* **centrally** *adv*
centrality *n*

central bank *n* a national bank that

THESAURUS

cement *n* **1a, 1b = mortar**, plaster, paste **2 = sealant**, glue, gum, adhesive, binder ▹ *vb* **4 = stick**, join, bond, attach, seal, glue, plaster, gum, weld, solder

cemetery *n* **= graveyard**, churchyard, burial ground, necropolis, God's acre

censor *vb* **2 = expurgate**, cut, blue-pencil, bowdlerize

censure *n* **1 = disapproval**, criticism, blame, condemnation, rebuke, reprimand, reproach, dressing down *(informal)*, stick *(slang)*, stricture, reproof, castigation, obloquy, remonstrance
OPPOSITE: approval
▹ *vb* **2 = criticize**, blame, abuse, condemn, carpet *(informal)*, denounce, put down, slate *(informal, chiefly US)*, rebuke, reprimand, reproach, scold, berate, castigate, chide, tear into *(informal)*, diss *(slang, chiefly US)*, blast, read the riot act, reprove, upbraid, slap on the wrist, lambast(e), bawl out *(informal)*, excoriate, rap over the knuckles, chew out *(US & Canad informal)*, tear (someone) off a strip *(Brit informal)*, give (someone) a rocket *(Brit & NZ informal)*, reprehend
OPPOSITE: applaud

central *adj* **1 = inner**, middle, mid, interior **OPPOSITE:** outer **2 = main**, chief, key, essential, primary, principal, fundamental, focal **OPPOSITE:** minor

DICTIONARY

acts as the government's banker, controls credit, and issues currency

Central European Time *n* the standard time adopted by Western European countries one hour ahead of Greenwich Mean Time, corresponding to British Summer Time. Abbrev: **CET**

central government *n* the government of a whole country, as opposed to the smaller organizations that govern counties, towns, and districts

central heating *n* a system for heating a building by means of radiators or air vents connected to a central source of heat **centrally heated** *adj*

centralism *n* the principle of bringing a country or an organization under central control **centralist** *adj*

centralize *or* **-ise** *vb* **-izing, -ized** *or* **-ising, -ised** to bring (a country or an organization) under central control **centralization** *or* **-isation** *n*

central locking *n* a system by which all the doors of a motor vehicle are locked automatically when the driver's door is locked manually

central nervous system *n* the part of the nervous system of vertebrates that consists of the brain and spinal cord

central processing unit *n* the part of a computer that performs logical and arithmetical operations on the data

central reservation *n* *Brit & NZ* the strip that separates the two sides of a motorway or dual carriageway

centre ❶ *or US* **center** *n* **1** the middle point or part of something **2** a place where a specified activity takes place: *a shopping centre* **3** a person or thing that is a focus of interest: *the centre of a long-running dispute* **4** a place of activity or influence: *the parliament building was the centre of resistance* **5** a political party or group that favours moderation **6** *sport* a player who plays in the middle of the field rather than on a wing ▷ *vb* **-tring, -tred** *or US* **-tering, -tered 7** to put in the centre of something **8 centre on** to have as a centre or main theme: *the summit is expected to centre on expanding the role of the UN*
WORD ORIGIN Greek *kentron* needle, sharp point

centreboard *or US* **centerboard** *n* a supplementary keel for a sailing boat or dinghy

centrefold *or US* **centerfold** *n* a large coloured illustration, often a photograph of a naked or scantily dressed young woman, folded to form the centre pages of a magazine

centre forward *n* *sport* the middle player in the forward line of a team

centre half *or* **centre back** *n* *soccer* a defender who plays in the middle of the defence

centre of gravity *n* the point in an object around which its mass is evenly distributed

centre pass *n* *hockey* a push or hit made in any direction to start the game

centrepiece *or US* **centerpiece** *n* **1** the most important item of a group of things: *she was the centrepiece of this conference* **2** an ornament for the centre of a table

centrifugal (sent-**riff**-few-gl) *adj* **1** moving or tending to move away from a centre **2** of or operated by centrifugal force: *centrifugal extractors*
WORD ORIGIN Greek *kentron* centre + Latin *fugere* to flee

centrifugal force *n* a force that acts outwards on any body that rotates or moves along a curved path

centrifuge *n* a machine that separates substances by the action of centrifugal force

centripetal (sent-**rip**-it-al) *adj* moving or tending to move towards a centre
WORD ORIGIN Greek *kentron* centre + Latin *petere* to seek

centripetal force *n* a force that acts inwards on any body that rotates or moves along a curved path

centrist *n* a person who holds moderate political views

centurion *n* (in ancient Rome) the officer in command of a century
WORD ORIGIN Latin *centurio*

century *n, pl* **-ries 1** a period of 100 years **2** a score of 100 runs in cricket **3** (in ancient Rome) a unit of foot soldiers, originally consisting of 100 men
WORD ORIGIN Latin *centuria*

CEO chief executive officer

cephalopod (**seff**-a-loh-pod) *n* a sea mollusc with a head and tentacles, such as the octopus
WORD ORIGIN Greek *kephalē* head + *pous* foot

ceramic *n* **1** a hard brittle material made by heating clay to a very high temperature **2** an object made of this material ▷ *adj* **3** made of ceramic: *ceramic tiles*
WORD ORIGIN Greek *keramos* potter's clay

ceramics *n* the art of producing ceramic objects **ceramicist** *or* **ceramist** *n*

Cerberus (**sir**-ber-uss) *n* *Greek myth* a three-headed dog who guarded the entrance to Hades

cere *n* a soft waxy swelling, containing the nostrils, at the base of the upper beak of a parrot
WORD ORIGIN Latin *cera* wax

cereal *n* **1** any grass that produces an edible grain, such as oat, wheat, or rice **2** the grain produced by such a plant **3** a breakfast food made from this grain, usually eaten mixed with milk
WORD ORIGIN Latin *cerealis* concerning agriculture

cerebellum (serr-rib-**bell**-lum) *n, pl* **-lums** *or* **-la** (-la) the back part of the brain, which controls balance and muscular coordination
WORD ORIGIN Latin

cerebral (**serr**-rib-ral) *adj* **1** of the brain: *a cerebral haemorrhage* **2** involving intelligence rather than emotions or instinct: *the cerebral joys of the literary world*

cerebral palsy *n* a condition in which the limbs and muscles are permanently weak, caused by damage to the brain

cerebrate (**serr**-rib-rate) *vb* **-brating, -brated** *usually facetious* to use the mind; think **cerebration** *n*

cerebrospinal *adj* of the brain and spinal cord: *a sample of cerebrospinal fluid*

cerebrovascular (serr-rib-roh-**vass**-kew-lar) *adj* of the blood vessels and blood supply of the brain

cerebrum (**serr**-rib-rum) *n, pl* **-brums** *or* **-bra** (-bra) the main part of the human brain, associated with thought, emotion, and personality
WORD ORIGIN Latin: the brain

ceremonial ❶ *adj* **1** of ceremony or ritual ▷ *n* **2** a system of formal rites; ritual **ceremonially** *adv*

ceremonious *adj* excessively polite or formal **ceremoniously** *adv*

ceremony ❶ *n, pl* **-nies 1** a formal act or ritual performed for a special occasion: *a wedding ceremony* **2** formally polite behaviour **3 stand on ceremony** to insist on or act with excessive formality
WORD ORIGIN Latin *caerimonia* what is sacred

Cerenkov *n* ▸ See **Cherenkov**

THESAURUS

centre *n* **1 = middle**, heart, focus, core, nucleus, hub, pivot, kernel, crux, bull's-eye, midpoint
OPPOSITE: edge
▷ *vb* **8 centre on something** *or* **someone = focus**, concentrate, cluster, revolve, converge

ceremonial *adj* **1 = formal**, public, official, ritual, stately, solemn, liturgical, courtly, ritualistic
OPPOSITE: informal
▷ *n* **2 = ritual**, ceremony, rite, formality, solemnity

ceremony *n* **1 = ritual**, service, rite, observance, commemoration, solemnities **2 = formality**, ceremonial, propriety, decorum, formal courtesy

C

C

DICTIONARY

Ceres *n* the Roman goddess of agriculture

cerise (ser-reess) *adj* cherry-red
WORD ORIGIN French: cherry

cerium *n chem* a steel-grey metallic element found only in combination with other elements. Symbol: Ce
WORD ORIGIN from *Ceres* (an asteroid)

CERN Conseil Européen pour la Recherche Nucléaire: a European organization for research in high-energy particle physics

Cernuda *n* **Luis** 1902–63, Spanish poet. His major work is the autobiographical *Reality and Desire* (1936–64)

cert *n* **a dead cert** *informal* something that is certain to happen or to be successful

cert. certificate

certain ❶ *adj* **1** positive and confident about something: *he was certain they would agree* **2** definitely known: *it is by no means certain the tomb still exists* **3** sure or bound: *the cuts are certain to go ahead* **4** some but not much: *a certain amount* **5** particular: *certain aspects* **6** named but not known: *a running commentary by a certain Mr Fox* **7 for certain** without doubt
WORD ORIGIN Latin *certus* sure

certainly ❶ *adv* without doubt: *he will certainly be back*

certainty ❶ *n* **1** the condition of being certain **2** *pl* **-ties** something established as inevitable

certifiable *adj* considered to be legally insane

certificate ❶ *n* an official document stating the details of something such as birth, death, or completion of an academic course
WORD ORIGIN Old French *certifier* to certify

certified *adj* **1** holding or guaranteed by a certificate: *a certified acupuncturist* **2** declared legally insane

certify ❶ *vb* **-fies, -fying, -fied 1** to confirm or attest to **2** to guarantee (that certain required standards have been met) **3** to declare legally insane **certification** *n*
WORD ORIGIN Latin *certus* certain + *facere* to make

certitude *n formal* confidence or certainty

cervical smear *n med* a smear taken from the neck (cervix) of the womb for detection of cancer

cervix *n, pl* **cervixes** *or* **cervices 1** the lower part of the womb that extends into the vagina **2** *anat* the neck **cervical** *adj*
WORD ORIGIN Latin

cesium *n US* ▸ same as **caesium**

cessation *n* an ending or pause: *a cessation of hostilities*
WORD ORIGIN Latin *cessare* to be idle

cession *n* the act of ceding territory or legal rights
WORD ORIGIN Latin *cedere* to yield

cesspool *or* **cesspit** *n* a covered tank or pit for collecting and storing sewage or waste water
WORD ORIGIN Old French *souspirail* air vent

CET Central European Time

cetacean (sit-tay-shun) *n* a sea creature such as a whale or dolphin, which belongs to a family of fish-shaped mammals and breathes through a blowhole
WORD ORIGIN Greek *kētos* whale

cetane (see-tane) *n* a colourless liquid hydrocarbon, used as a solvent
WORD ORIGIN Latin *cetus* whale

cetane number *n* a measure of the quality of a diesel fuel expressed as the percentage of cetane in it

Cetshwayo *or* **Cetewayo** *n* ?1826–84, king of the Zulus (1873–79): defeated the British at Isandhlwana (1879) but was overwhelmed by them at Ulundi (1879); captured, he stated his case in London, and was reinstated as ruler of part of Zululand (1883)

cf compare
WORD ORIGIN Latin *confer*

Cf *chem* californium

CF Canadian Forces

CFB Canadian Forces Base

CFC chlorofluorocarbon

CFL Canadian Football League

CFS chronic fatigue syndrome

cg centigram

CGI computer-generated image(s)

cgs units *pl n* a metric system of units based on the centimetre, gram, and second: for scientific and technical purposes, replaced by SI units

CH Companion of Honour (a Brit. title)

ch. 1 chapter **2** church

Chablis (**shab**-lee) *n* a dry white wine made around Chablis, France

Chabrier *n* (**Alexis**) **Emmanuel** 1841–94, French composer; noted esp. for the orchestral rhapsody *España* (1883)

Chabrol *n* **Claude** born 1930, French film director, whose films, such as *Le Beau Serge* (1958), *Les Biches* (1968), *Le Boucher* (1969), *Au coeur du mensonge* (1999), and *La Fleur du mal* (2003) explore themes of jealousy, guilt, and murder

cha-cha *or* **cha-cha-cha** *n* **1** a modern ballroom dance from Latin America **2** music for this dance
WORD ORIGIN American (Cuban) Spanish

chaconne *n* a musical form consisting of a set of variations on a repeated melodic bass line

chad *n* the small pieces removed during the punching of holes in punch cards, printer paper, etc.

Chadwick *n* **1** Sir **Edwin** 1800–90, British social reformer, known for his *Report on the Sanitary Condition of the Labouring Population of Great Britain* (1842) **2** Sir **James** 1891–1974, British physicist: discovered the neutron (1932): Nobel prize for physics 1935 **3 Lynn** (**Russell**) 1914–2003, British sculptor in metal

chafe *vb* **chafing, chafed 1** to make sore or worn by rubbing **2** to be annoyed or impatient: *the lower castes are chafing against 20 years of servitude*
WORD ORIGIN Old French *chaufer* to warm

chafer *n* a large slow-moving beetle
WORD ORIGIN Old English *ceafor*

chaff[1] *n* **1** grain husks separated from the seeds during threshing **2** something of little worth; rubbish: *you had to be a very perceptive listener to sort the wheat from the chaff of his discourse*
WORD ORIGIN Old English *ceaf*

chaff[2] *vb* to tease good-naturedly
WORD ORIGIN probably slang variant of *chafe*

chaffinch *n* a small European

THESAURUS

certain *adj* **1 = sure**, convinced, positive, confident, satisfied, assured, free from doubt
OPPOSITE: unsure
2a = known, true, positive, plain, ascertained, unmistakable, conclusive, undoubted, unequivocal, undeniable, irrefutable, unquestionable, incontrovertible, indubitable, nailed-on *(slang)*
OPPOSITE: doubtful
2b = fixed, decided, established, settled, definite **OPPOSITE:** indefinite
3a = bound, sure, fated, destined
OPPOSITE: unlikely
3b = inevitable, unavoidable, inescapable, inexorable, ineluctable

certainly *adv* **= definitely**, surely, truly, absolutely, undoubtedly, positively, decidedly, without doubt, unquestionably, undeniably, without question, unequivocally, indisputably, assuredly, indubitably, doubtlessly, come hell or high water, irrefutably

certainty *n* **1 = confidence**, trust, faith, conviction, assurance, certitude, sureness, positiveness
OPPOSITE: doubt
2a = inevitability
OPPOSITE: uncertainty
2b = fact, truth, reality, sure thing *(informal)*, surety, banker

certificate *n* **= document**, licence, warrant, voucher, diploma, testimonial, authorization, credential(s)

certify *vb* **1, 2 = confirm**, show, declare, guarantee, witness, assure, endorse, testify, notify, verify, ascertain, validate, attest, corroborate, avow, authenticate, vouch for, aver

DICTIONARY

songbird with black-and-white wings and, in the male, a reddish body and blue-grey head
WORD ORIGIN Old English *ceaf* CHAFF[1] + *finc* finch
chafing dish *n* a dish with a heating apparatus beneath it, for cooking or keeping food warm at the table
Chagall *n* **Marc** 1887–1985, French painter and illustrator, born in Russia, noted for his richly coloured pictures of men, animals, and objects in fantastic combinations and often suspended in space: his work includes 12 stained glass windows for a synagogue in Jerusalem (1961) and the decorations for the ceiling of the Paris Opera House (1964)
chagrin (**shag**-grin) *n* a feeling of annoyance and disappointment
WORD ORIGIN French
chagrined *adj* annoyed and disappointed
chain ❶ *n* **1** a flexible length of metal links, used for fastening, binding, or connecting, or in jewellery **2 chains** anything that restricts or restrains someone: *bound by the chains of duty* **3** a series of connected facts or events **4** a number of establishments, such as hotels or shops, that have the same owner or management **5** *chem* a number of atoms or groups bonded together so that the resulting molecule, ion, or radical resembles a chain **6** a row of mountains or islands ▷ *vb* **7** to restrict, fasten or bind with or as if with a chain: *the demonstrators chained themselves to railings*
WORD ORIGIN Latin *catena*
Chain *n* Sir **Ernst Boris** 1906–79, British biochemist, born in Germany: purified and adapted penicillin for clinical use; with Fleming and Florey shared the Nobel prize for physiology or medicine 1945
chain gang *n US* a group of convicted prisoners chained together
chain letter *n* a letter, often with a request for or promise of money, that is sent to many people who are asked to send copies to other people
chain mail *n* ▸ same as **mail²**
chain reaction *n* **1** a series of events, each of which causes the next **2** a chemical or nuclear reaction in which the product of one step triggers the following step
chain saw *n* a motor-driven saw in which the cutting teeth form links in a continuous chain
chain-smoke *vb* **-smoking, -smoked** to smoke continuously, lighting one cigarette from the preceding one
chain smoker *n*
chair *n* **1** a seat with a back and four legs, for one person to sit on **2** an official position of authority or the person holding it: *the chair of the Security Council* **3** a professorship **4 in the chair** presiding over a meeting **5 the chair** *informal* the electric chair ▷ *vb* **6** to preside over (a meeting)
WORD ORIGIN Greek *kathedra*
chairlift *n* a series of chairs suspended from a moving cable for carrying people up a slope
chairman *or* (*fem*) **chairwoman** ❶ *n, pl* **-men** a person who is in charge of a company's board of directors or a meeting **chairmanship** *n*
chaise (**shaze**) *n* a light horse-drawn carriage with two wheels
WORD ORIGIN French
chaise longue (**long**) *n, pl* **chaise longues** *or* **chaises longues** a couch with a back and a single armrest
WORD ORIGIN French
chalcedony (kal-**sed**-don-ee) *n, pl* **-nies** a form of quartz composed of very fine crystals, often greyish or blue in colour
WORD ORIGIN Greek *khalkēdōn* a precious stone
chalet *n* **1** a type of Swiss wooden house with a steeply sloping roof **2** a similar house used as a ski lodge or holiday home
WORD ORIGIN French
Chaliapin *n* **Fyodor Ivanovich** 1873–1938, Russian operatic bass singer
chalice (**chal**-liss) *n* **1** *poetic* a drinking cup or goblet **2** *Christianity* a gold or silver goblet containing the wine at communion
WORD ORIGIN Latin *calix* cup
chalk *n* **1** a soft white rock consisting of calcium carbonate **2** a piece of chalk, either white or coloured, used for writing and drawing on blackboards **3 as different as chalk and cheese** *informal* totally different **4 not by a long chalk** *informal* by no means: *you haven't finished by a long chalk* ▷ *vb* **5** to draw or mark with chalk
chalky *adj*
WORD ORIGIN Latin *calx* limestone
chalk up *vb informal* **1** to score or register: *the home side chalked up a 9-1 victory* **2** to charge or credit (money) to an account
challenge ❶ *n* **1** a demanding or stimulating situation **2** a call to engage in a contest, fight, or argument **3** a questioning of a statement or fact **4** a demand by a sentry for identification or a password **5** *law* a formal objection to a juror ▷ *vb* **-lenging, -lenged 6** to invite or call (someone) to take part in a contest, fight, or argument **7** to call (a decision or action) into question **8** to order (a person) to stop and be identified **9** *law* to make formal objection to (a juror)
challenger *n* **challenging** *adj*
WORD ORIGIN Latin *calumnia* calumny
challenged *adj* disabled as specified: *physically challenged; mentally challenged*
chalybeate (kal-**lib**-bee-it) *adj* containing or impregnated with iron salts: *a natural chalybeate spring rises at the edge of the lake*
WORD ORIGIN Greek *khalups* iron
chamber ❶ *n* **1** a meeting hall, usually one used for a legislative or judicial assembly **2** a room equipped for a particular purpose: *a decompression chamber* **3** a legislative or judicial assembly: *the Senate, the upper chamber of Canada's parliament* **4** *old-fashioned or poetic* a room in a house, esp. a bedroom **5** a compartment or cavity: *the heart chambers* **6** a compartment for a cartridge or shell in a gun ▸ See also **chambers**
WORD ORIGIN Greek *kamara* vault
chamberlain *n history* an officer who managed the household of a king or nobleman
WORD ORIGIN Old French *chamberlayn*
chambermaid *n* a woman employed to clean bedrooms in a hotel
chamber music *n* classical music to be performed by a small group of musicians
Chamber of Commerce *n* an organization of local business people to promote, regulate, and protect their interests
chamber pot *n* a bowl for urine, formerly used in bedrooms
chambers *pl n* **1** a judge's room for hearing private cases not taken in open court **2** (in England) the set of rooms used as offices by a barrister

THESAURUS

chain *n* **1 = tether**, coupling, link, bond, shackle, fetter, manacle **3 = series**, set, train, string, sequence, succession, progression, concatenation ▷ *vb* **7 = bind**, confine, restrain, handcuff, shackle, tether, fetter, manacle
chairman *or* **chairwoman** *n* **a = director**, president, chief, executive, chairperson **b = master of ceremonies**, spokesman, chair, speaker, MC, chairperson
challenge *n* **1 = test**, trial, opposition, confrontation, defiance, ultimatum, face-off (*slang*) **2 = dare**, provocation, summons to contest, wero (*NZ*) ▷ *vb* **6 = dare**, invite, provoke, defy, summon, call out, throw down the gauntlet **7 = dispute**, question, tackle, confront, defy, object to, disagree with, take issue with, impugn, throw down (*US slang*)
chamber *n* **1 = hall**, room **2, 4 = room**, bedroom, apartment, enclosure, cubicle **3 = council**, assembly, legislature, legislative body **5 = compartment**, hollow, cavity

DICTIONARY

C

chameleon (kam-**meal**-yon) *n* a small lizard with long legs that is able to change colour to blend in with its surroundings
WORD ORIGIN Greek *khamai* on the ground + *leōn* lion

chamfer (**cham**-fer) *n* **1** a bevelled surface at an edge or corner ▷ *vb* **2** to cut a chamfer on or in
WORD ORIGIN Old French *chant* edge + *fraindre* to break

chamois *n, pl* **-ois 1** (**sham**-wah) a small mountain antelope of Europe and SW Asia **2** (**sham**-ee) a soft suede leather made from the skin of this animal or from sheep or goats **3** (**sham**-ee). Also: **chamois leather, shammy, chammy** a piece of such leather or similar material, used for cleaning and polishing
WORD ORIGIN Old French

chamomile (**kam**-mo-mile) *n* ▸ same as **camomile**

champ[1] *vb* **1** to chew noisily **2 champ at the bit** *informal* to be restless or impatient to do something
WORD ORIGIN probably imitative

champ[2] *n informal* ▸ short for **champion** (sense 1)

champagne *n* **1** a white sparkling wine produced around Reims and Épernay, France ▷ *adj* **2** denoting a luxurious lifestyle: *a champagne capitalist*
WORD ORIGIN *Champagne*, region of France

Champaigne *n* **Philippe de** 1602–74, French painter, born in Brussels: noted particularly for his portraits and historical and religious scenes

champers (**sham**-perz) *n slang* champagne

champion ⊙ *n* **1** a person, plant, or animal that has defeated all others in a competition: *the Olympic 100 metres champion* **2** someone who defends a person or cause: *a champion of the downtrodden* ▷ *vb* **3** to support: *he unceasingly championed equal rights and opportunities* ▷ *adj* **4** *N English dialect* excellent **championship** *n*
WORD ORIGIN Latin *campus* field

Champollion *n* **Jean François** 1790–1832, French Egyptologist, who deciphered the hieroglyphics on the Rosetta stone

chance ⊙ *n* **1** the extent to which something is likely to happen; probability **2** an opportunity or occasion to do something: *a chance to escape rural poverty* **3** a risk or gamble: *the government is not in the mood to take any more chances* **4** the unknown and unpredictable element that causes something to happen in one way rather than another: *in buddhism there is no such thing as chance or coincidence* **5 by chance** without planning: *by chance she met an old school friend* **6 on the off chance** acting on the slight possibility: *he had called on the agents on the off chance that he might learn something of value* ▷ *vb* **chancing, chanced 7** to risk or hazard: *a few picnickers chanced the perilous footpath* **8** to do something without planning to: *I chanced to look down* **9 chance on** *or* **upon** to discover by accident: *I chanced upon a copy of this book*
WORD ORIGIN Latin *cadere* to occur

chancel *n* the part of a church containing the altar and choir
WORD ORIGIN Latin *cancelli* lattice

chancellery *or* **chancellory** *n, pl* **-leries** *or* **-lories 1** *Austral & Brit* the residence or office of a chancellor **2** *US* the office of an embassy or consulate
WORD ORIGIN Anglo-French *chancellerie*

chancellor *n* **1** the head of government in several European countries **2** *US* the president of a university **3** *Brit, Austral & Canad* the honorary head of a university **chancellorship** *n*
WORD ORIGIN Late Latin *cancellarius* porter

Chancellor of the Exchequer *n Brit* the cabinet minister responsible for finance

Chancery *n* (in England) the Lord Chancellor's court, a division of the High Court of Justice
WORD ORIGIN shortened from CHANCELLERY

chancre (**shang**-ker) *n pathol* a painless ulcer that develops as a primary symptom of syphilis
WORD ORIGIN French

chancy *adj* **chancier, chanciest** *informal* uncertain or risky

chandelier (shan-dill-**eer**) *n* an ornamental hanging light with branches and holders for several candles or bulbs
WORD ORIGIN French

chandler *n* a dealer in a specified trade or merchandise: *a ship's chandler* **chandlery** *n*
WORD ORIGIN Old French *chandelier* dealer in candles

Chandler *n* **Raymond (Thornton)** 1888–1959, US thriller writer: created Philip Marlowe, one of the first detective heroes in fiction

Chandragupta *n* Greek name *Sandracottos.* died ?297 BC, ruler of N India, who founded the Maurya dynasty (325) and defeated Seleucus (?305)

change ⊙ *n* **1** the fact of becoming different **2** variety or novelty: *they wanted to print some good news for a change* **3** a different set, esp. of clothes **4** money exchanged for its equivalent in a larger denomination or in a different currency **5** the balance of money when the amount paid is larger than the amount due **6** coins of a small denomination ▷ *vb* **-ging, -ged 7** to make or become different **8** to replace with or exchange for another: *the Swedish Communist Party changed its name to the Left Party* **9** to give and receive (something) in return: *slaves and masters changed places* **10** to give or receive (money) in exchange for its equivalent sum in a smaller denomination or different currency **11** to put on other clothes **12** to get off one bus, train or airliner and on to another: *there's no direct train, so you'll need to change at York* ▸ See also **change down, changeover, change up** > **changeless** *adj*
WORD ORIGIN Latin *cambire* to exchange, barter

changeable *adj* changing often **changeability** *n*

change down *vb* to select a lower gear when driving

changeling *n* a child believed to have been exchanged by fairies for the parents' real child

change of life *n* the menopause

changeover *n* **1** a complete change from one system, attitude, or

THESAURUS

champion *n* **1 = winner**, hero, victor, conqueror, title holder, warrior **2 = defender**, guardian, patron, backer, protector, upholder, vindicator ▷ *vb* **3 = support**, back, defend, promote, advocate, fight for, uphold, espouse, stick up for *(informal)*

chance *n* **1 = probability**, odds, possibility, prospect, liability, likelihood **OPPOSITE:** certainty **2 = opportunity**, opening, occasion, time, scope, window **3 = risk**, speculation, gamble, hazard **4 = accident**, fortune, luck, fate, destiny, coincidence, misfortune, providence **OPPOSITE:** design ▷ *vb* **7 = risk**, try, stake, venture, gamble, hazard, wager

change *n* **1 = alteration**, innovation, transformation, modification, mutation, metamorphosis, permutation, transmutation, difference, revolution, transition **2 = variety**, break *(informal)*, departure, variation, novelty, diversion, whole new ball game *(informal)* **OPPOSITE:** monotony **3 = exchange**, trade, conversion, swap, substitution, interchange ▷ *vb* **7a = alter**, reform, transform, adjust, moderate, revise, modify, remodel, reorganize, restyle, convert **OPPOSITE:** keep **7b = shift**, vary, transform, alter, modify, diversify, fluctuate, mutate, metamorphose, transmute **OPPOSITE:** stay **8, 9 = exchange**, trade, replace, substitute, swap, interchange

DICTIONARY

product to another ▷ *vb* **change over** **2** to swap places or activities: *the train crews changed over at the frontier*

change up *vb* to select a higher gear when driving

channel ❶ *n* **1** a band of radio frequencies assigned for the broadcasting of a radio or television signal **2** a path for an electrical signal or computer data **3** a means of access or communication: *reports coming through diplomatic channels* **4** a broad strait connecting two areas of sea **5** the bed or course of a river, stream, or canal **6** a navigable course through an area of water **7** a groove ▷ *vb* **-nelling, -nelled** *or US* **-neling, -neled** **8** to direct or convey through a channel or channels: *tunnels that channel the pilgrims into the area; to channel funds abroad*
WORD ORIGIN Latin *canalis* pipe, conduit

Channel *n* **the Channel** the English Channel

channel-hop *vb* **-hopping, -hopped** to change television channels repeatedly using a remote control device

chant ❶ *vb* **1** to repeat (a slogan) over and over **2** to sing or recite (a psalm) ▷ *n* **3** a rhythmic or repetitious slogan repeated over and over, usually by more than one person **4** a religious song with a short simple melody in which several words or syllables are sung on one note
WORD ORIGIN Latin *canere* to sing

chanter *n* the pipe on a set of bagpipes on which the melody is played

chanticleer *n* a name for a cock, used in fables
WORD ORIGIN Old French *chanter cler* to sing clearly

chanty *n, pl* **-ties** ▸ same as **shanty²**

Chanukah *or* **Hanukkah** (hah-na-ka) *n* an eight-day Jewish festival, held in December, commemorating the rededication of the temple by Judas Maccabaeus
WORD ORIGIN Hebrew

chaos ❶ *n* complete disorder or confusion **chaotic** *adj* **chaotically** *adv*
WORD ORIGIN Greek *khaos*

chap ❶ *n informal* a man or boy
WORD ORIGIN from Old English *cēapman* pedlar

chapati *or* **chapatti** *n* (in Indian cookery) a kind of flat thin unleavened bread
WORD ORIGIN Hindi

chapel *n* **1** a place of worship with its own altar, in a church or cathedral **2** a similar place of worship in a large house or institution **3** (in England and Wales) a Nonconformist place of worship **4** (in Scotland) a Roman Catholic church **5** the members of a trade union in a newspaper office, printing house, or publishing firm
WORD ORIGIN Latin *cappa* cloak: originally the sanctuary where the cloak of St Martin was kept

chaperone (shap-per-rone) *n* **1** an older person who accompanies and supervises a young person or young people on social occasions ▷ *vb* **-oning, -oned** **2** to act as a chaperone to
WORD ORIGIN Old French *chape* hood

chaplain *n* a clergyman attached to a chapel, military body, or institution **chaplaincy** *n*
WORD ORIGIN Late Latin *cappella* chapel

chaplet *n* a garland worn on the head
WORD ORIGIN Old French *chapelet*

chapman *n, pl* **-men** *old-fashioned* a travelling pedlar
WORD ORIGIN Old English *cēapman*

Chapman *n* **George** 1559–1634, English dramatist and poet, noted for his translation of Homer

chapped *adj* (of the skin) raw and cracked, through exposure to cold
WORD ORIGIN probably Germanic

Chappell *n* **Greg(ory Stephen)** born 1948, Australian cricketer: first Australian to score over 7000 test runs

chappie *n informal* a man or boy

chaps *pl n* leather leggings without a seat, worn by cowboys
WORD ORIGIN shortened from Spanish *chaparejos*

chapter ❶ *n* **1** a division of a book **2** a period in a life or history: *the latest chapter in the long and complex tale of British brewing* **3** a sequence of events: *a chapter of accidents* **4** a branch of some societies or clubs **5** a group of the canons of a cathedral **6** **chapter and verse** exact authority for an action or statement
WORD ORIGIN Latin *caput* head

char¹ *vb* **charring, charred** to blacken by partial burning
WORD ORIGIN short for *charcoal*

char² *Brit informal n* **1** ▸ short for **charwoman** ▷ *vb* **charring, charred** **2** to clean other people's houses as a job
WORD ORIGIN Old English *cerr* turn of work

char³ *n Brit old-fashioned slang* tea
WORD ORIGIN Chinese *ch'a*

char⁴ *n, pl* **char** *or* **chars** a troutlike fish of cold lakes and northern seas
WORD ORIGIN origin unknown

charabanc (shar-rab-bang) *n Brit, old-fashioned* a coach for sightseeing
WORD ORIGIN French: wagon with seats

character ❶ *n* **1** the combination of qualities distinguishing an individual person, group of people, or place: *the unique charm and character of this historic town* **2** a distinguishing quality or characteristic: *bodily movements of a deliberate character* **3** reputation, esp. good reputation: *a man of my Dad's character and standing in the community* **4** an attractively unusual or interesting quality: *the little town was full of life and character* **5** a person represented in a play, film, or story **6** an unusual or amusing person: *quite a character* **7** *informal* a person: *a flamboyant character* **8** a single letter, numeral, or symbol used in writing or printing **9** **in** *or* **out of character** typical *or* not typical of the apparent character of a person **characterless** *adj*
WORD ORIGIN Greek *kharaktēr* engraver's tool

character assassination *n* an attempt to destroy someone's good reputation by slander or deliberate misrepresentation of his or her views: *he described the accusation as 'an appalling piece of character assassination'*

C

THESAURUS

channel *n* **3 = means**, way, course, approach, medium, route, path, avenue **4, 5, 6 = strait**, sound, route, passage, canal, waterway, main **7 = duct**, chamber, artery, groove, gutter, furrow, conduit ▷ *vb* **8 = direct**, guide, conduct, transmit, convey

chant *n* **4 = song**, carol, chorus, melody, psalm ▷ *vb* **2 = sing**, chorus, recite, intone, carol

chaos *n* **= disorder**, confusion, mayhem, anarchy, lawlessness, pandemonium, entropy, bedlam, tumult, disorganization
OPPOSITE: orderliness

chap *n (informal)* **= fellow**, man, person, individual, type, sort, customer *(informal)*, character, guy *(informal)*, bloke *(Brit informal)*, cove *(slang)*, dude *(US & Canad informal)*, boykie *(S African informal)*

chapter *n* **1 = section**, part, stage, division, episode, topic, segment, instalment **2 = period**, time, stage, phase

character *n* **1 = personality**, nature, make-up, cast, constitution, bent, attributes, temper, temperament, complexion, disposition, individuality, marked traits **2 = nature**, kind, quality, constitution, calibre **3 = reputation**, honour, integrity, good name, rectitude **5 = role**, part, persona **6 = eccentric**, card *(informal)*, original, nut *(slang)*, flake *(slang, chiefly US)*, oddity, oddball *(informal)*, odd bod *(informal)*, queer fish *(Brit informal)*, wacko *or* whacko *(informal)* **8 = symbol**, mark, sign, letter, figure, type, device, logo, emblem, rune, cipher, hieroglyph

DICTIONARY

C

characteristic ❶ *n* **1** a distinguishing feature or quality **2** *maths* the integral part of a logarithm: *the characteristic of 2.4771 is 2* ▷ *adj* **3** typical or representative of someone or something: *the prime minister fought with characteristic passion*
characteristically *adv*

characterization *or* **-isation** *n* **1** the description or portrayal of a person by an actor or writer: *a novel full of rich characterization and complex plotting* **2** the act or an instance of characterizing

characterize ❶ *or* **-ise** *vb* **-izing, -ized** *or* **-ising, -ised** **1** to be a characteristic of: *the violence that characterized the demonstrations* **2** to describe: *we have made what I would characterize as outstanding progress*

charade (shar-**rahd**) *n* an absurd pretence
WORD ORIGIN French

charades *n* a game in which one team acts out each syllable of a word or phrase, which the other team has to guess

charcoal *n* **1** a black form of carbon made by partially burning wood or other organic matter **2** a stick of this used for drawing **3** a drawing done in charcoal ▷ *adj* **4** Also: **charcoal-grey** very dark grey
WORD ORIGIN origin unknown

Charcot *n* **Jean Martin** 1825–93, French neurologist, noted for his attempt using hypnotism to find an organic cause for hysteria, which influenced Freud

Chardin *n* **Jean-Baptiste Siméon** 1699–1779, French still-life and genre painter, noted for his subtle use of scumbled colour

Chardonnay (**shar**-don-nay) *n* a white wine produced in the Burgundy region of France and elsewhere
WORD ORIGIN French

Chardonnet *n* (**Louis Marie**) **Hilaire Bernigaud**, Comte de. 1839–1924, French chemist and industrialist who produced rayon, the first artificial fibre

Chargaff *n* **Erwin** 1905–2002, US biochemist, born in Austria, noted esp. for his work on DNA

charge ❶ *vb* **charging, charged** **1** to ask (an amount of money) as a price **2** to enter a debit against a person's account for (a purchase) **3** to accuse (someone) formally of a crime in a court of law **4** to make a rush at or sudden attack upon **5** to fill (a glass) **6** to cause (an accumulator or capacitor) to take and store electricity **7** to fill or saturate with liquid or gas: *old mine workings charged with foul gas* **8** to fill with a feeling or mood: *the emotionally charged atmosphere* **9** *formal* to command or assign: *the president has charged his foreign minister with trying to open talks* ▷ *n* **10** a price charged for something; cost **11** a formal accusation of a crime in a court of law **12** an onrush or attack **13** custody or guardianship: *in the charge of the police* **14** a person or thing committed to someone's care: *a nanny reported the cruel father of one of her charges to social workers* **15** **a** a cartridge or shell **b** the explosive required to fire a gun **16** *physics* **a** the attribute of matter responsible for all electrical phenomena, existing in two forms, positive and negative **b** the total amount of electricity stored in a capacitor or an accumulator **17** **in charge of** in control of and responsible for: *in charge of defence and foreign affairs*
WORD ORIGIN Old French *chargier* to load

chargeable *adj* **1** liable to be taxed or charged **2** liable to result in a legal charge

charge card *n* a card issued by a chain store, shop, or organization, that enables customers to obtain goods and services for which they pay later

chargé d'affaires (**shar**-zhay daf-**fair**) *n, pl* **chargés d'affaires** (**shar**-zhay daf-**fair**) **1** the temporary head of a diplomatic mission in the absence of the ambassador or minister **2** the head of a small or unimportant diplomatic mission
WORD ORIGIN French

charge hand *n* a workman ranked just below a foreman

charge nurse *n* a nurse in charge of a hospital ward

charger *n* **1** a device for charging a battery **2** (in the Middle Ages) a warhorse

char-grilled *adj* (of food) grilled over charcoal

chariot *n* a two-wheeled horse-drawn vehicle used in ancient times for wars and races
WORD ORIGIN Old French *char* car

charioteer *n* a chariot driver

charisma ❶ (kar-**rizz**-ma) *n* the quality or power of an individual to attract, influence, or inspire people
charismatic (kar-rizz-**mat**-ik) *adj*
WORD ORIGIN Greek *kharis* grace, favour

charismatic movement *n Christianity* a group that believes in divine gifts such as instantaneous healing and uttering unintelligible sounds while in a religious ecstasy

charitable ❶ *adj* **1** kind or lenient in one's attitude towards others **2** of or for charity: *a charitable organization*
charitably *adv*

charity ❶ *n* **1** *pl* **-ties** an organization set up to provide help to those in need **2** the giving of help, such as money or food, to those in need **3** help given to those in need; alms **4** a kindly attitude towards people
WORD ORIGIN Latin *caritas* affection

charlady *n, pl* **-ladies** *Brit* ▸ same as **charwoman**

charlatan (**shar**-lat-tan) *n* a person

THESAURUS

characteristic *n* **1 = feature**, mark, quality, property, attribute, faculty, trait, quirk, peculiarity, idiosyncrasy ▷ *adj* **3 = typical**, special, individual, specific, representative, distinguishing, distinctive, peculiar, singular, idiosyncratic, symptomatic
OPPOSITE: rare

characterize *vb* **1 = distinguish**, mark, identify, brand, inform, stamp, typify

charge *vb* **3 = accuse**, indict, impeach, incriminate, arraign
OPPOSITE: acquit
4 = attack, assault, assail
OPPOSITE: retreat
7, 8 = fill, load, instil, suffuse, lade ▷ *n* **10 = price**, rate, cost, amount, payment, expense, toll, expenditure, outlay, damage (*informal*)
11 = accusation, allegation, indictment, imputation
OPPOSITE: acquittal
12 = attack, rush, assault, onset, onslaught, stampede, sortie
OPPOSITE: retreat
13 = care, trust, responsibility, custody, safekeeping **14a = duty**, office, concern, responsibility, remit **14b = ward**, pupil, protégé, dependant

charisma *n* **= charm**, appeal, personality, attraction, lure, allure, magnetism, force of personality, mojo (*US slang*)

charitable *adj* **1 = kind**, understanding, forgiving, sympathetic, favourable, tolerant, indulgent, lenient, considerate, magnanimous, broad-minded
OPPOSITE: unkind
2 = benevolent, liberal, generous, lavish, philanthropic, bountiful, beneficent **OPPOSITE:** mean

charity *n* **1 = charitable organization**, fund, movement, trust, endowment **2, 3 = donations**, help, relief, gift, contributions, assistance, hand-out, philanthropy, alms-giving, benefaction, largesse *or* largess, koha (NZ)
OPPOSITE: meanness
4 = kindness, love, pity, humanity, affection, goodness, goodwill, compassion, generosity, indulgence, bounty, altruism, benevolence, fellow feeling, bountifulness, tenderheartedness, aroha (NZ)
OPPOSITE: ill will

DICTIONARY

who claims expertise that he or she does not have
WORD ORIGIN Italian *ciarlare* to chatter

Charles Albert *n* 1798–1849, king of Sardinia-Piedmont (1831–49) during the Risorgimento: abdicated after the failure of his revolt against Austria

Charles III *n* **1** known as *Charles the Fat*. 839–888 AD, Holy Roman Emperor (881–887) and, as Charles II, king of France (884–887). He briefly reunited the empire of Charlemagne **2** 1716–88, king of Spain (1759–88), who curbed the power of the Church and tried to modernize his country

Charles IV *n* **1** known as *Charles the Fair*. 1294–1328, king of France (1322–28): brother of Isabella of France, with whom he intrigued against her husband, Edward II of England **2** 1316–78, king of Bohemia (1346–78) and Holy Roman Emperor (1355–78) **3** 1748–1819, king of Spain (1788–1808), whose reign saw the domination of Spain by Napoleonic France: abdicated **4** title as king of Hungary of Charles I ▸ See **Charles I** (sense 5)

Charles IX *n* 1550–74, king of France (1560–74), son of Catherine de' Medici and Henry II: his reign was marked by war between Huguenots and Catholics

Charles' law *n physics* the principle that the volume of a gas varies in proportion to its temperature at constant pressure
WORD ORIGIN after Jacques *Charles*, physicist

charleston *n* a lively dance of the 1920s
WORD ORIGIN after *Charleston*, South Carolina

Charles V *n* **1** known as *Charles the Wise*. 1337–80, king of France (1364–80) during the Hundred Years' War **2** 1500–58, Holy Roman Emperor (1519–56), king of Burgundy and the Netherlands (1506–55), and, as Charles I, king of Spain (1516–56): his reign saw the empire threatened by Francis I of France, the Turks, and the spread of Protestantism; abdicated

Charles VI *n* **1** known as *Charles the Mad* or *Charles the Well-Beloved*. 1368–1422, king of France (1380–1422): defeated by Henry V of England at Agincourt (1415), he was forced by the Treaty of Troyes (1420) to recognize Henry as his successor **2** 1685–1740, Holy Roman Emperor (1711–40). His claim to the Spanish throne (1700) led to the War of the Spanish Succession

Charles VII *n* **1** 1403–61, king of France (1422–61), son of Charles VI. He was excluded from the French throne by the Treaty of Troyes, but following Joan of Arc's victory over the English at Orléans (1429), was crowned **2** 1697–1745, Holy Roman Emperor (1742–45) during the War of the Austrian Succession

Charles X *n* **1** title of *Charles Gustavus*. 1622–60, king of Sweden, who warred with Poland and Denmark in an attempt to create a unified Baltic state **2** 1757–1836, king of France (1824–30): his attempt to restore absolutism led to his enforced exile

Charles XI *n* 1655–97, king of Sweden (1660–97), who established an absolute monarchy and defeated Denmark (1678)

Charles XIV *n* the title as king of Sweden and Norway of Jean Baptiste Jules Bernadotte ▸ See **Bernadotte**

charlie *n Brit old-fashioned informal* a fool

charlock *n* a weed with hairy leaves and yellow flowers
WORD ORIGIN Old English *cerlic*

charlotte *n* a dessert made with fruit and bread or cake crumbs: *apple charlotte*
WORD ORIGIN French

charm ❶ *n* **1** the quality of attracting, fascinating, or delighting people **2** a trinket worn on a bracelet **3** a small object worn for supposed magical powers **4** a magic spell ▹*vb* **5** to attract, fascinate, or delight **6** to influence or obtain by personal charm: *you can easily be charmed into changing your mind* **7** to protect as if by magic: *a charmed life* **charmer** *n* **charmless** *adj*
WORD ORIGIN Latin *carmen* song

charming ❶ *adj* delightful or attractive **charmingly** *adv*

charm offensive *n* a concentrated attempt to gain favour by being helpful and obliging

charnel house *n* (formerly) a building or vault for the bones of the dead
WORD ORIGIN Latin *carnalis* fleshly

Charnley *n* Sir **John** 1911–82, British surgeon noted for his invention of an artificial hip joint and his development of hip-replacement surgery

charollais (**sharr**-ol-lay) *n* a breed of large white beef cattle
WORD ORIGIN Monts du *Charollais*, E France

Charpentier *n* **1 Gustave** 1860–1956, French composer, whose best-known work is the opera *Louise* (1900) **2 Marc-Antoine** ?1645–1704, French composer, best known for his sacred music, particularly the *Te Deum*

chart ❶ *n* **1** a graph, table, or sheet of information in the form of a diagram **2** a map of the sea or the stars **3 the charts** *informal* the weekly lists of the bestselling pop records or the most popular videos ▹*vb* **4** to plot the course of **5** to make a chart of **6** to appear in the pop charts
WORD ORIGIN Greek *khartēs* papyrus

charter ❶ *n* **1** a formal document granting or demanding certain rights or liberties: *a children's charter* **2** the fundamental principles of an organization: *the UN Charter* **3** the hire or lease of transportation for private use ▹*vb* **4** to lease or hire by charter **5** to grant a charter to
WORD ORIGIN Latin *charta* leaf of papyrus

chartered accountant *n* an accountant who has passed the examinations of the Institute of Chartered Accountants

Charteris *n* **Leslie,** original name *Leslie Charles Bowyer Yin*. 1907–93, British novelist, born in Singapore: created the character Simon Templar, known as The Saint, the central character in many adventure novels

Chartism *n English history* a movement (1838–48) for social and political reforms, demand for which was presented to Parliament in charters **Chartist** *n, adj*

THESAURUS

charm *n* **1 = attraction**, appeal, fascination, allure, magnetism, desirability, allurement **OPPOSITE:** repulsiveness **2 = trinket 3 = talisman**, amulet, lucky piece, good-luck piece, fetish **4 = spell**, magic, enchantment, sorcery, makutu (NZ) ▹*vb* **5 = attract**, win, please, delight, fascinate, absorb, entrance, win over, enchant, captivate, beguile, allure, bewitch, ravish, mesmerize, enrapture, enamour **OPPOSITE:** repel **6 = persuade**, seduce, coax, beguile, cajole, sweet-talk *(informal)*

charming *adj* **= attractive**, pleasing, appealing, engaging, lovely, winning, pleasant, fetching, delightful, cute, irresistible, seductive, captivating, eye-catching, bewitching, delectable, winsome, likable *or* likeable **OPPOSITE:** unpleasant

chart *n* **1 = table**, diagram, blueprint, graph, tabulation, plan, map ▹*vb* **4 = monitor**, follow, record, note, document, register, trace, outline, log, graph, tabulate **5 = plot**, map out, delineate, sketch, draft, graph, tabulate

charter *n* **1 = document**, right, contract, bond, permit, licence, concession, privilege, franchise, deed, prerogative, indenture **2 = constitution**, laws, rules, code ▹*vb* **4 = hire**, commission, employ, rent, lease **5 = authorize**, permit, sanction, entitle, license, empower, give authority

DICTIONARY

chartreuse (shar-truhz) *n* a green or yellow liqueur made from herbs
WORD ORIGIN after *La Grande Chartreuse*, monastery near Grenoble, where the liqueur is produced

charwoman *n, pl* **-women** *Brit* a woman whose job is to clean other people's houses

chary (chair-ee) *adj* **charier, chariest** wary or careful: *chary of interfering*
WORD ORIGIN Old English *cearig*

Charybdis (kar-rib-diss) *n* **1** a ship-devouring monster in classical mythology, identified with a whirlpool off the coast of Sicily **2 between Scylla and Charybdis** ▸ see **Scylla**

chase[1] *vb* **chasing, chased 1** to pursue (a person or animal) persistently or quickly **2** to force (a person or animal) to leave a place **3** *informal* to court (someone) in an unsubtle manner **4** *informal* to rush or run: *chasing around the world* **5** *informal* to pursue (something or someone) energetically in order to obtain results or information ▹*n* **6** the act or an instance of chasing a person or animal
WORD ORIGIN Latin *capere* to take

chase[2] *vb* **chasing, chased** to engrave or emboss (metal)
WORD ORIGIN Old French *enchasser*

chaser *n* a drink drunk after another of a different kind, for example beer after whisky

chasm (kaz-zum) *n* **1** a very deep crack in the ground **2** a wide difference in interests or feelings: *a deep chasm separating science from politics*
WORD ORIGIN Greek *khasma*

chassis (shass-ee) *n, pl* **chassis** (shass-eez) the steel frame, wheels, and mechanical parts of a vehicle
WORD ORIGIN French

chaste *adj* **1** abstaining from sex outside marriage or from all sexual intercourse **2** (of conduct or speech) pure, decent, or modest: *a chaste kiss on the forehead* **3** simple in style: *chaste furniture* **chastely** *adv* **chastity** *n*
WORD ORIGIN Latin *castus* pure

chasten (chase-en) *vb* to subdue (someone) by criticism
WORD ORIGIN Latin *castigare*

chastise *vb* **-tising, -tised 1** to scold severely **2** *old-fashioned* to punish by beating **chastisement** *n*
WORD ORIGIN Middle English *chastisen*

chasuble (chazz-yew-bl) *n Christianity* a long sleeveless robe worn by a priest when celebrating Mass
WORD ORIGIN Late Latin *casubla* garment with a hood

chat *n* **1** an informal conversation ▹*vb* **chatting, chatted 2** to have an informal conversation ▸ See also **chat up**
WORD ORIGIN short for *chatter*

chateau (shat-toe) *n, pl* **-teaux** (-toe) *or* **-teaus** a French country house or castle
WORD ORIGIN French

chatelaine (shat-tell-lane) *n* (formerly) the mistress of a large house or castle
WORD ORIGIN French

Chatham[1] *n* **1** a town in SE England, in N Kent on the River Medway: formerly royal naval dockyard. Pop: 73 468 (2001) **2** a town in SE Canada, in SE Ontario on the Thames River. Pop: 44156 (2001)

Chatham[2] *n* **1st Earl of** title of the elder (William) Pitt ▸ See **Pitt** (sense 1)

chatline *n* a telephone service enabling callers to join in general conversation with each other

chatroom *n* a site on the internet where users have group discussions by electronic mail

chat show *n* a television or radio show in which guests are interviewed informally

chattels *pl n old-fashioned* possessions
WORD ORIGIN Old French *chatel* personal property

chatter *vb* **1** to speak quickly and continuously about unimportant things **2** (of birds or monkeys) to make rapid repetitive high-pitched noises **3** (of the teeth) to click together rapidly through cold or fear ▹*n* **4** idle talk or gossip **5** the high-pitched repetitive noise made by a bird or monkey
WORD ORIGIN imitative

chatterbox *n informal* a person who talks a great deal, usually about unimportant things

chattering classes *n* **the chattering classes** *informal, often derogatory* the members of the educated sections of society who enjoy discussion of political, social, and cultural issues

Chatterton *n* **Thomas** 1752–70, British poet; author of spurious medieval verse and prose: he committed suicide at the age of 17

chatty *adj* **-tier, -tiest 1** (of a person) fond of friendly, informal conversation; talkative **2** (of a letter) informal and friendly; gossipy

chat up *vb Austral & Brit informal* to talk flirtatiously to (someone) with a view to starting a romantic or sexual relationship

chauffeur *n* **1** a person employed to drive a car for someone ▹*vb* **2** to act as driver for (someone) **chauffeuse** *fem n*
WORD ORIGIN French: stoker

chauvinism (show-vin-iz-zum) *n* an irrational belief that one's own country, race, group, or sex is superior: *male chauvinism* **chauvinist** *n, adj* **chauvinistic** *adj*
WORD ORIGIN after Nicolas *Chauvin*, French soldier under Napoleon

chav *n Brit slang, derogatory* a young working-class person who dresses in casual sports clothes

Chavannes *n* ▸ See **Puvis de Chavannes**

cheap *adj* **1** costing relatively little; inexpensive **2** of poor quality; shoddy: *planks of cheap, splintery pine* **3** not valued highly; not worth much: *promises are cheap* **4** *informal* mean or despicable: *a cheap jibe* ▹*n* **5 on the cheap** *Brit informal* at a low cost ▹*adv* **6** at a low cost **cheaply** *adv* **cheapness** *n*
WORD ORIGIN Old English *ceap* barter, price

cheapen *vb* **1** to lower the reputation of; degrade **2** to reduce the price of

cheap-jack *n informal* a person who sells cheap and shoddy goods

THESAURUS

chase[1] *vb* **1 = pursue**, follow, track, hunt, run after, course **2 = drive away**, drive, expel, hound, send away, send packing, put to flight **4** *(informal)* **= rush**, run, race, shoot, fly, speed, dash, sprint, bolt, dart, hotfoot ▹*n* **6 = pursuit**, race, hunt, hunting

chat *n* **1 = talk**, tête-à-tête, conversation, gossip, heart-to-heart, natter, blather, schmooze *(slang)*, blether *(Scot)*, chinwag *(Brit inform.* confab *(informal)*, craic *(Irish informa.* korero *(NZ)* ▹*vb* **2 = talk**, gossip, jaw *(slang)*, natter, blather, schmooze *(slang)*, blether *(Scot)*, shoot the breeze *(US slang)*, chew the rag *or* fat *(slang)*

chatter *vb* **1 = prattle**, chat, rabbit on *(Brit informal)*, babble, gab *(informal)*, natter, tattle, jabber, blather, schmooze *(slang)*, blether *(Scot)*, run off at the mouth *(US slang)*, prate, gossip ▹*n* **4 = prattle**, chat, rabbit *(Brit informal)*, gossip, babble, twaddle, gab *(informal)*, natter, tattle, jabber, blather, blether *(Scot)*

cheap *adj* **1 = inexpensive**, sale, economy, reduced, keen, reasonable, bargain, low-priced, low-cost, cut-price, economical, cheapo *(informal)* **OPPOSITE:** expensive **2 = inferior**, poor, worthless, second-rate, shoddy, tawdry, tatty, trashy, substandard, low-rent *(informal, chiefly US)*, two-bit *(US & Canad slang)*, crappy *(slang)*, two a penny, rubbishy, dime-a-dozen *(informal)*, tinhorn *(US slang)*, bodger *or* bodgie *(Austral slang)* **OPPOSITE:** good **4** *(informal)* **= despicable**, mean, low, base, vulgar, sordid, contemptible, scurvy, scungy *(Austral & NZ)* **OPPOSITE:** decent

cheapskate *n informal* a miserly person

cheat ❶ *vb* **1** to defraud: *he cheated her out of millions* **2** to act dishonestly in order to gain some advantage or profit **3 cheat on** *informal* to be unfaithful to (one's spouse or lover) ▷*n* **4** a person who cheats **5** a fraud or deception
WORD ORIGIN short for *escheat*

check ❶ *vb* **1** to examine, investigate, or make an inquiry into **2** to slow the growth or progress of **3** to stop abruptly **4** to correspond or agree: *that all checks with our data here* ▷*n* **5** a test to ensure accuracy or progress **6** a means to ensure against fraud or error **7** a break in progress; stoppage **8** *US* ▸same as **cheque** **9** *chiefly US & Canad* the bill in a restaurant **10** a pattern of squares or crossed lines **11** a single square in such a pattern **12** *chess* the state or position of a king under direct attack **13 in check** under control or restraint ▷*interj* **14** *chiefly US & Canad* an expression of agreement ▸See also **check in, check out**, etc.
WORD ORIGIN Old French *eschec* a check at chess

checked *adj* having a pattern of squares

checker *n US & Canad* **1** ▸same as **chequer** **2** ▸same as **draughtsman** (sense 3)

checkered *adj US & Canad* ▸same as **chequered**

checkers *n US & Canad* ▸same as **draughts**

check in *vb* **1 a** to register one's arrival at a hotel or airport **b** to register the arrival of (guests or passengers) at a hotel or airport ▷*n* **check-in** **2 a** the formal registration of arrival at a hotel or airport **b** the place where one registers one's arrival at a hotel or airport

check list *n* a list to be referred to for identification or verification

checkmate *n* **1** *chess* the winning position in which an opponent's king is under attack and unable to escape **2** utter defeat ▷*vb* **-mating, -mated** **3** *chess* to place the king of (one's opponent) in checkmate **4** to thwart or defeat
WORD ORIGIN Arabic *shāh māt* the king is dead

check out *vb* **1** to pay the bill and leave a hotel **2** to investigate, examine, or look at: *he asked if he could check out the old man's theory; start the evening off by checking out one of the in bars in the city* ▷*n* **checkout** **3** a counter in a supermarket, where customers pay

checkpoint *n* a place where vehicles or travellers are stopped for identification or inspection

checkup *n* a thorough examination to see if a person or thing is in good condition

check up on *vb* to investigate the background of

Cheddar *n* a firm orange or yellowy-white cheese
WORD ORIGIN *Cheddar*, village in Somerset, where it was originally made

cheek ❶ *n* **1** either side of the face below the eye **2** *informal* impudence, boldness, or lack of respect **3** *informal* a buttock **4 cheek by jowl** close together **5 turn the other cheek** to refuse to retaliate ▷*vb* **6** *Brit, Austral & NZ informal* to speak or behave disrespectfully to someone
WORD ORIGIN Old English *ceace*

cheekbone *n* the bone at the top of the cheek, just below the eye

cheeky ❶ *adj* **cheekier, cheekiest** disrespectful; impudent **cheekily** *adv* **cheekiness** *n*

cheep *n* **1** the short weak high-pitched cry of a young bird ▷*vb* **2** to utter a cheep
WORD ORIGIN imitative

cheer ❶ *vb* **1** to applaud or encourage with shouts **2 cheer up** to make or become happy or hopeful; comfort or be comforted ▷*n* **3** a shout of applause or encouragement **4** a feeling of cheerfulness: *the news brought little cheer*
WORD ORIGIN Middle English (in the sense: face, welcoming aspect), from Greek *kara* head

cheerful ❶ *adj* **1** having a happy disposition **2** pleasantly bright: *a cheerful colour* **3** ungrudging: *a cheerful giver* **cheerfully** *adv* **cheerfulness** *n*

cheerio *interj* **1** *informal* a farewell greeting ▷*n* **2** *Austral & NZ* a small red cocktail sausage

cheerleader *n* a person who leads a crowd in cheers, usually at sports events

cheerless *adj* dreary or gloomy

cheers *interj informal chiefly Brit* **1** a drinking toast **2** a farewell greeting **3** an expression of gratitude

cheery *adj* **cheerier, cheeriest** cheerful **cheerily** *adv*

cheese[1] *n* **1** a food made from coagulated milk curd **2** a block of this
WORD ORIGIN Latin *caseus*

cheese[2] *n* **big cheese** *slang* an important person
WORD ORIGIN perhaps from Hindi *chiz* thing

cheeseburger *n* a hamburger with a slice of cheese melted on top of it

cheesecake *n* **1** a dessert with a biscuit-crumb base covered with a sweet cream-cheese mixture and sometimes with a fruit topping

cheat *vb* **1 = deceive**, skin *(slang)*, trick, fool, take in *(informal)*, con *(informal)*, stiff *(slang)*, sting *(informal)*, mislead, rip off *(slang)*, fleece, hoax, defraud, dupe, beguile, gull *(archaic)*, do *(informal)*, swindle, stitch up *(slang)*, victimize, bamboozle *(informal)*, hoodwink, double-cross *(informal)*, diddle *(informal)*, take for a ride *(informal)*, bilk, pull a fast one on *(informal)*, screw *(informal)*, finagle *(informal)*, scam *(slang)* ▷*n* **4 = deceiver**, sharper, cheater, shark, charlatan, trickster, con man *(informal)*, impostor, fraudster, double-crosser *(informal)*, swindler, grifter *(slang, chiefly US & Canad)*, rorter *(Austral slang)*, chiseller *(informal)*, rogue trader

check *vb* **1 = examine**, test, study, look at, research, note, confirm, investigate, monitor, probe, tick, vet, inspect, look over, verify, work over, scrutinize, make sure of, inquire into, take a dekko at *(Brit slang)* **OPPOSITE:** overlook **2 = stop**, control, limit, arrest, delay, halt, curb, bar, restrain, inhibit, rein, thwart, hinder, repress, obstruct, retard, impede, bridle, stem the flow of, nip in the bud, put a spoke in someone's wheel **OPPOSITE:** further ▷*n* **5 = examination**, test, research, investigation, inspection, scrutiny, once-over *(informal)* **6 = control**, limitation, restraint, constraint, rein, obstacle, curb, obstruction, stoppage, inhibition, impediment, hindrance, damper

cheek *n* **2** *(informal)* **= impudence**, face *(informal)*, front, nerve, sauce *(informal)*, gall *(informal)*, disrespect, audacity, neck *(informal)*, lip *(slang)*, temerity, chutzpah *(US & Canad informal)*, insolence, impertinence, effrontery, brass neck *(Brit informal)*, brazenness, sassiness *(US informal)*

cheeky *adj* **= impudent**, rude, forward, fresh *(informal)*, insulting, saucy, audacious, sassy *(US informal)*, pert, disrespectful, impertinent, insolent, lippy *(US & Canad slang)* **OPPOSITE:** respectful

cheer *vb* **1 = applaud**, hail, acclaim, clap, hurrah **OPPOSITE:** boo **2a cheer someone up = comfort**, encourage, brighten, hearten, enliven, gladden, gee up, jolly along *(informal)* **2b cheer up = take heart**, rally, perk up, buck up *(informal)* ▷*n* **3 = applause**, ovation

cheerful *adj* **1 = happy**, bright, contented, glad, optimistic, bucked *(informal)*, enthusiastic, sparkling, gay, sunny, jolly, animated, merry, upbeat *(informal)*, buoyant, hearty, cheery, joyful, jovial, genial, jaunty, chirpy *(informal)*, sprightly, blithe, light-hearted **OPPOSITE:** sad **2 = pleasant**, bright, sunny, gay, enlivening **OPPOSITE:** gloomy

DICTIONARY

2 *slang* magazine photographs of naked or scantily dressed women
cheesecloth *n* a light, loosely woven cotton cloth
cheesed off *adj Brit, Austral & NZ slang* bored, disgusted, or angry
WORD ORIGIN origin unknown
cheeseparing *adj* 1 mean or miserly ▷ *n* 2 meanness or miserliness
cheesy *adj* **cheesier, cheesiest** 1 like cheese 2 *informal* (of a smile) broad but possibly insincere 3 *informal* in poor taste: *a cheesy game show*
cheetah *n* a large fast-running wild cat of Africa and SW Asia, which has a light brown coat with black spots
WORD ORIGIN Hindi *cītā*
Cheever *n* **John** 1912–82, US novelist and short-story writer. His novels include *The Wapshot Chronicle* (1957) and *Bullet Park* (1969)
chef *n* a cook, usually the head cook, in a restaurant or hotel
WORD ORIGIN French
chef-d'oeuvre (shay-**durv**) *n, pl* **chefs-d'oeuvre** (shay-**durv**) a masterpiece
WORD ORIGIN French
Chelsea Pensioner *n* an inhabitant of the Chelsea Royal Hospital in SW London, a home for old and infirm soldiers
chem. 1 chemical 2 chemist 3 chemistry
chemical ⊕ *n* 1 any substance used in or resulting from a reaction involving changes to atoms or molecules ▷ *adj* 2 of or used in chemistry 3 of, made from, or using chemicals: *a chemical additive found in many foods* **chemically** *adv*
chemical engineering *n* the applications of chemistry in industrial processes **chemical engineer** *n*
chemical warfare *n* warfare using weapons such as gases and poisons
chemin de fer (shem-**man** de **fair**) *n* a gambling game, a variation of baccarat
WORD ORIGIN French: railway, referring to the fast tempo of the game
chemise (shem-**meez**) *n* a woman's old-fashioned loose-fitting slip or dress
WORD ORIGIN Late Latin *camisa*
chemist ⊕ *n* 1 *Brit, Austral & NZ* a shop selling medicines and cosmetics 2 *Brit, Austral & NZ* a qualified dispenser of prescribed medicines 3 a specialist in chemistry
WORD ORIGIN Medieval Latin *alchimista* alchemist
chemistry *n* the branch of science concerned with the composition, properties, and reactions of substances
chemotherapy *n* the treatment of disease, often cancer, by means of chemicals
Cheney *n* **Richard B**(**ruce**), known as *Dick.* born 1941, US Republican politician; vice-president from 2001
Chénier *n* 1 **André** (**Marie de**) 1762–94, French poet; his work was influenced by the ancient Greek elegiac poets. He was guillotined during the French Revolution 2 his brother, **Marie-Joseph** (**Blaise de**) 1764–1811, French dramatist and politician. He wrote patriotic songs and historical plays, such as *Charles IX* (1789)
chenille (shen-**neel**) *n* 1 a thick soft tufty yarn 2 a fabric made of this
WORD ORIGIN French
Chephren *n* ▸ See **Khafre**
cheque *or US* **check** *n* a written order to someone's bank to pay money from his or her account to the person to whom the cheque is made out
WORD ORIGIN from *check* (in the sense: means of verification)
cheque book *n* a book of detachable blank cheques issued by a bank
cheque card *n Brit* a plastic card issued by a bank guaranteeing payment of a customer's cheques
chequer *or US* **checker** *n* a piece used in Chinese chequers ▸ See also **chequers**
WORD ORIGIN Middle English: chessboard
chequered *or US* **checkered** *adj* 1 marked by varied fortunes: *a chequered career* 2 marked with alternating squares of colour
chequers *or US* **checkers** *n* the game of draughts
Cherenkov *or* **Cerenkov** *n* **Pavel Alekseyevich** 1904–90, Soviet physicist: noted for work on the effects produced by high-energy particles: shared Nobel prize for physics 1958
cherish ⊕ *vb* 1 to cling to (an idea or feeling): *cherished notions* 2 to care for
WORD ORIGIN Latin *carus* dear
Chernenko *n* **Konstantin** (**Ustinovich**) 1911–85, Soviet statesman; general secretary of the Soviet Communist Party (1984–85)
Cherokee *n* 1 a member of a Native American people, formerly of the Appalachian mountains, now living chiefly in Oklahoma 2 the language of this people
cheroot (sher-**root**) *n* a cigar with both ends cut off squarely
WORD ORIGIN Tamil *curuttu* curl, roll
cherry *n, pl* **-ries** 1 a small round soft fruit with red or blackish skin and a hard stone 2 the tree on which this fruit grows ▷ *adj* 3 deep red: *cherry lips*
WORD ORIGIN Greek *kerasios*
cherry tomato *n* a miniature tomato, slightly bigger than a cherry
cherub *n, pl* **cherubs** *or (for sense 1)* **cherubim** 1 *Christianity* an angel, often represented as a winged child 2 an innocent or sweet child **cherubic** (chair-**roo**-bik) *adj*
WORD ORIGIN Hebrew *kĕrūbh*
Cherubini *n* (**Maria**) **Luigi** (**Carlo Zenobio Salvatore**) 1760–1842, Italian composer, noted particularly for his church music and his operas
chervil *n* an aniseed-flavoured herb
WORD ORIGIN Old English *cerfelle*
Cherwell *n* **1st Viscount** title of *Frederick Alexander Lindemann.* 1886–1957, British physicist, born in Germany, noted for his research on heat capacity, aeronautics, and atomic physics. He was scientific adviser to Winston Churchill during World War II
Cheshire cheese *n* a mild white or pale orange cheese with a crumbly texture
chess *n* a game of skill for two players using a chessboard on which chessmen are moved, with the object of checkmating the opponent's king
WORD ORIGIN Old French *esches*, plural of *eschec* check
chessboard *n* a square board divided into 64 squares of two alternating colours, for playing chess
chessman *n, pl* **-men** a piece used in chess
WORD ORIGIN Middle English *chessemeyne* chess company
chest ⊕ *n* 1 the front of the body, from the neck to the waist 2 **get something off one's chest** *informal* to unburden oneself of worries or secrets by talking about them 3 a heavy box for storage or shipping: *a tea chest*
WORD ORIGIN Greek *kistē* box
chesterfield *n* 1 a large couch with high padded sides and back 2 *Canad* any sofa or couch
WORD ORIGIN after a 19th-century Earl of *Chesterfield*
Chesterfield[1] *n* an industrial town in N central England, in Derbyshire: famous 14th-century church with twisted spire. Pop: 70 260 (2001)

THESAURUS

chemical *n* 1 = **compound**, drug, substance, synthetic substance, potion
chemist *n* 2 = **pharmacist**, apothecary *(obsolete)*, pharmacologist, dispenser
cherish *vb* 1 = **cling to**, prize, treasure, hold dear, cleave to
OPPOSITE: despise
2 = **care for**, love, support, comfort, look after, shelter, treasure, nurture, cosset, hold dear OPPOSITE: neglect
chest *n* 1 = **breast**, front 3 = **box**, case, trunk, crate, coffer, ark *(dialect)*, casket, strongbox ▸ *related adjective:* pectoral

DICTIONARY

Chesterfield² *n* **Philip Dormer Stanhope,** 4th Earl of Chesterfield. 1694–1773, English statesman and writer, noted for his elegance, suavity, and wit; author of *Letters to His Son* (1774)

Chesterton *n* **G(ilbert) K(eith)** 1874–1936, English essayist, novelist, poet, and critic

chestnut *n* **1** a reddish-brown edible nut **2** the tree that this nut grows on **3** a horse of a reddish-brown colour **4** *informal* an old or stale joke ▹*adj* **5** dark reddish-brown: *chestnut hair*
WORD ORIGIN Greek *kastanea*

chest of drawers *n* a piece of furniture consisting of a set of drawers in a frame

chesty *adj* **chestier, chestiest** *Brit informal* suffering from or symptomatic of chest disease: *chesty colds* **chestiness** *n*

cheval glass (shev-**val**) *n* a full-length mirror mounted so as to swivel within a frame
WORD ORIGIN French *cheval* support (literally: horse)

chevalier (shev-a-**leer**) *n* **1** a member of the French Legion of Honour **2** a chivalrous man
WORD ORIGIN Medieval Latin *caballarius* horseman

Chevalier *n* **1 Albert** 1861–1923, British music hall entertainer, remembered for his cockney songs **2 Maurice** 1888–1972, French singer and film actor

Cheviot *n* a large British sheep with a heavy medium-length fleece
WORD ORIGIN *Cheviot* Hills on borders of England & Scotland

chevron (**shev**-ron) *n* a V-shaped pattern, such as those worn on the sleeve of a military uniform to indicate rank
WORD ORIGIN Old French

chew ⊕ *vb* **1** to work the jaws and teeth in order to grind (food) ▹*n* **2** the act of chewing **3** something that is chewed, such as a sweet or a piece of tobacco
WORD ORIGIN Old English *ceowan*

chewing gum *n* a flavoured gum which is chewed but not swallowed

chew over *vb* to consider carefully

chewy *adj* **chewier, chewiest** of a consistency requiring a lot of chewing

chez (shay) *prep* at the home of
WORD ORIGIN French

Chiang Ch'ing *n* a variant transliteration of the Chinese name for **Jiang Qing**

Chiang Ching-kuo *or* **Jiang Jing Guo** *n* 1910–88, Chinese statesman; the son of Chiang Kai-shek. He was prime minister of Taiwan (1971–78); president (1978–88)

chianti (kee-**ant**-ee) *n* a dry red wine produced in Tuscany, Italy

chiaroscuro (kee-ah-roh-**skew**-roh) *n, pl* **-ros** the distribution of light and shade in a picture
WORD ORIGIN Italian *chiaro* clear + *oscuro* obscure

chic ⊕ (**sheek**) *adj* **1** stylish or elegant ▹*n* **2** stylishness or elegance
WORD ORIGIN French

chicane (shik-**kane**) *n* an obstacle placed on a motor-racing circuit to slow the cars down
WORD ORIGIN French *chicaner* to quibble

chicanery *n* trickery or deception

Chichester¹ *n* a city in S England, administrative centre of West Sussex: Roman ruins; 11th-century cathedral; Festival Theatre. Pop: 27 477 (2001)

Chichester² *n* Sir **Francis** 1901–72, British yachtsman, who sailed alone round the world in *Gipsy Moth IV* (1966–67)

chick *n* **1** a baby bird, esp. a domestic fowl **2** *slang* a young woman
WORD ORIGIN short for *chicken*

chicken *n* **1** a domestic fowl bred for its flesh or eggs **2** the flesh of this bird used for food **3** *slang* a coward ▹*adj* **4** *slang* cowardly
WORD ORIGIN Old English *ciecen*

chicken feed *n slang* a trifling amount of money

chicken-hearted *adj* easily frightened; cowardly

chicken out *vb informal* to fail to do something through cowardice

chickenpox *n* an infectious viral disease, usually affecting children, which produces an itchy rash

chicken wire *n* wire netting

chickpea *n* an edible hard yellow pealike seed
WORD ORIGIN Latin *cicer*

chickweed *n* a common garden weed with small white flowers

chicory *n* **1** a plant grown for its leaves, which are used in salads, and for its roots **2** the root of this plant, roasted, dried, and used as a coffee substitute
WORD ORIGIN Greek *kikhōrion*

chide *vb* **chiding, chided** *old-fashioned* to rebuke or scold
WORD ORIGIN Old English *cīdan*

chief ⊕ *n* **1** the head of a group or body of people **2** the head of a tribe ▹*adj* **3** most important: *the chief suspects* **4** highest in rank: *the Chief Constable*
WORD ORIGIN Latin *caput* head

chiefly ⊕ *adv* **1** especially or essentially **2** mainly or mostly

chief petty officer *n* a senior noncommissioned officer in a navy

chieftain *n* the leader of a tribe or clan
WORD ORIGIN Late Latin *capitaneus* commander

chief technician *n* a noncommissioned officer in the Royal Air Force

Ch'ien-lung *n* a variant transliteration of the Chinese name for **Qian Long**

chiffchaff *n* a European warbler with a yellowish-brown plumage
WORD ORIGIN imitative

chiffon (**shif**-fon) *n* a fine see-through fabric of silk or nylon
WORD ORIGIN French *chiffe* rag

chiffonier *or* **chiffonnier** (shiff-on-**near**) *n* **1** a tall elegant chest of drawers **2** a wide low open-fronted cabinet
WORD ORIGIN French

chignon (**sheen**-yon) *n* a roll or knot of long hair pinned up at the back of the head
WORD ORIGIN French

chigoe (**chig**-go) *n* a tropical flea that burrows into the skin. Also: **chigger**
WORD ORIGIN Carib *chigo*

chihuahua (chee-**wah**-wah) *n* a tiny short-haired dog, originally from Mexico
WORD ORIGIN after *Chihuahua*, state in Mexico

chilblain *n* an inflammation of the fingers or toes, caused by exposure to cold
WORD ORIGIN CHILL (noun) + BLAIN

child ⊕ *n, pl* **children 1** a young human being; boy or girl **2** a son or daughter ▸ Related adjective: **filial**

THESAURUS

chew *vb* **1 = munch**, bite, grind, champ, crunch, gnaw, chomp, masticate

chic *adj* **1 = stylish**, smart, elegant, fashionable, trendy *(Brit informal)*, up-to-date, modish, à la mode, voguish *(informal)*, schmick *(Austral informal)* **OPPOSITE:** unfashionable

chief *n* **1, 3 = head**, leader, director, manager, lord, boss *(informal)*, captain, master, governor, commander, principal, superior, ruler, superintendent, chieftain, ringleader, baas *(S African)*, ariki *(NZ)*, sherang *(Austral & NZ)*
OPPOSITE: subordinate

chiefly *adv* **1 = especially**, essentially, principally, primarily, above all **2 = mainly**, largely, usually, mostly, in general, on the whole, predominantly, in the main

child *n* **1 = youngster**, baby, kid *(informal)*, minor, infant, babe, juvenile, toddler, tot, wean *(Scot)*, little one, brat, bairn *(Scot)*, suckling, nipper *(informal)*, chit, babe in arms, sprog *(slang)*, munchkin *(informal, chiefly US)*, rug rat *(slang)*, nursling, littlie *(Austral informal)*, ankle-biter *(Austral & US slang)*, tacker *(Austral slang)* **2 = offspring**, issue, descendant, progeny ▸ *related adjective:* filial ▸ *related prefix:* paedo-

DICTIONARY

3 a childish or immature person **4** the product of an influence or environment: *a child of the Army* **5 with child** *old-fashioned* pregnant **childless** *adj* **childlessness** *n*
WORD ORIGIN Old English *cild*

childbearing *n* **1** the process of giving birth to a child ▷*adj* **2 of childbearing age** of an age when women are able to give birth to children

child benefit *n Brit* a regular government payment to parents of children up to a certain age

childbirth *n* the act of giving birth to a child ▸Related adjective: **natal**

Childers *n* (**Robert**) **Erskine** 1870–1922, Irish politician, executed by the Irish Free State for his IRA activities: author of the spy story *The Riddle of the Sands* (1903)

childhood *n* the time or condition of being a child

childish *adj* **1** immature or silly: *childish fighting over who did what* **2** of or like a child: *childish illnesses*

childlike *adj* like a child, for example in being innocent or trustful

child minder *n* a person who looks after children whose parents are working

children *n* ▸the plural of **child**

child's play *n informal* something that is easy to do

chill *n* **1** a feverish cold **2** a moderate coldness **3** a feeling of coldness resulting from a cold or damp environment or from sudden fear ▷*vb* **4** to make (something) cool or cold: *chilled white wine* **5** to cause (someone) to feel cold or frightened **6** *informal* to calm oneself ▷*adj* **7** unpleasantly cold: *chill winds* **chilling** *adj* **chillingly** *adv*
WORD ORIGIN Old English *ciele*

chilled *or* **chilled-out** *adj informal* relaxed or easy-going in character or behaviour

chiller *n* **1** ▸short for **spine-chiller** **2** a cooling or refrigerating device

chilli *or* **chili** *n* **1** *pl* **chillies** *or* **chilies** the small red or green hot-tasting pod of a type of capsicum, used in cookery, often in powdered form **2** ▸short for **chilli con carne**
WORD ORIGIN Mexican Indian

chilli con carne *n* a highly seasoned Mexican dish of meat, onions, beans, and chilli powder
WORD ORIGIN Spanish: chilli with meat

chill out *informal vb* **1** to relax, esp. after energetic dancing at a rave ▷*adj* **chill-out 2** suitable for relaxation after energetic dancing: *a chill-out area*

chilly *adj* **-lier, -liest 1** causing or feeling moderately cold **2** without warmth; unfriendly: *a chilly reception*

chilly bin *n NZ informal* a portable insulated container for packing food and drink in ice

Chiltern Hundreds *pl n* (in Britain) a nominal office that an MP applies for in order to resign his seat

chime *n* **1** the musical ringing sound made by a bell or clock ▷*vb* **chiming, chimed 2** (of a bell) to make a clear musical ringing sound **3** (of a clock) to indicate (the time) by chiming
WORD ORIGIN Latin *cymbalum* cymbal

chime in *vb* to say something just after someone else has spoken

chimera (kime-**meer**-a) *n* **1** a wild and unrealistic dream or idea **2** *Greek myth* a fire-breathing monster with the head of a lion, body of a goat, and tail of a serpent
WORD ORIGIN Greek *khimaira* she-goat

chimerical *adj* wildly fanciful or imaginary

chime with *vb* to agree or be consistent with

chimney *n* a hollow vertical structure that carries smoke or steam away from a fire or engine
WORD ORIGIN Greek *kaminos* oven

chimney breast *n* the walls surrounding the base of a chimney or fireplace

chimneypot *n* a short pipe on the top of a chimney

chimney stack *n* the part of a chimney sticking up above a roof

chimney sweep *n* a person who cleans soot from chimneys

chimp *n informal* ▸short for **chimpanzee**

chimpanzee *n* an intelligent small black ape of central W Africa
WORD ORIGIN African dialect

chin *n* the front part of the face below the mouth
WORD ORIGIN Old English *cinn*

china[1] *n* **1** ceramic ware of a type originally from China **2** dishes or ornamental objects made of china
WORD ORIGIN Persian *chīnī*

china[2] *n Brit & S African informal* a friend or companion
WORD ORIGIN from cockney rhyming slang *china plate* mate

china clay *n* ▸same as **kaolin**

Chinaman *n, pl* **-men** *old-fashioned or offensive* a man from China

Chinatown *n* a section of a town or city outside China with a mainly Chinese population

chinchilla *n* **1** a small S American rodent bred in captivity for its soft silvery-grey fur **2** the fur of this animal
WORD ORIGIN Spanish

chine *n* **1** a cut of meat including part of the backbone ▷*vb* **chining, chined 2** to cut (meat) along the backbone
WORD ORIGIN Old French *eschine*

Chinese *adj* **1** of China ▷*n* **2** *pl* **-nese** a person from China or a descendant of one **3** any of the languages of China

Chinese chequers *n* a game played with marbles or pegs on a six-pointed star-shaped board

Chinese lantern *n* a collapsible lantern made of thin paper

Chinese leaves *pl n* the edible leaves of a Chinese cabbage

Chinese puzzle *n* a complicated puzzle or problem

chink[1] *n* a small narrow opening: *a chink of light*
WORD ORIGIN Old English *cine* crack

chink[2] *vb* **1** to make a light ringing sound ▷*n* **2** a light ringing sound
WORD ORIGIN imitative

chinless wonder *n Brit informal* a person, usually upper-class, lacking strength of character

chinoiserie (sheen-**wahz**-a-ree) *n* **1** a style of decorative art based on imitations of Chinese motifs **2** objects in this style
WORD ORIGIN French *chinois* Chinese

Chinook *n* **1** *pl* **-nook** *or* **-nooks** a member of a Native American people

THESAURUS

childbirth *n* **= child-bearing**, labour, delivery, lying-in, confinement, parturition

childhood *n* **= youth**, minority, infancy, schooldays, immaturity, boyhood *or* girlhood

childish *adj* **1 = immature**, silly, juvenile, foolish, trifling, frivolous, infantile, puerile OPPOSITE: mature **2 = youthful**, young, boyish *or* girlish

chill *n* **2 = coldness**, bite, nip, sharpness, coolness, rawness, crispness, frigidity **3 = shiver**, frisson, goose pimples, goose flesh ▷*vb* **4 = cool**, refrigerate, freeze ▷*adj* **7 = chilly**, biting, sharp, freezing, raw, bleak, wintry, frigid, parky (*Brit informal*)

chilly *adj* **1 = cool**, fresh, sharp, crisp, penetrating, brisk, breezy, draughty, nippy, parky (*Brit informal*), blowy OPPOSITE: warm **2 = unfriendly**, hostile, unsympathetic, frigid, unresponsive, unwelcoming, cold as ice OPPOSITE: friendly

china[1] *n* **1, 2 = pottery**, ceramics, ware, porcelain, crockery, tableware, service

china[2] *n* (*Brit & S African informal*) **= friend**, pal, mate (*informal*), buddy (*informal*), companion, best friend, intimate, cock (*Brit informal*), close friend, comrade, chum (*informal*), crony, main man (*slang, chiefly US*), soul mate, homeboy (*slang, chiefly US*), cobber (*Austral & NZ old-fashioned, informal*), bosom friend, boon companion, E hoa (*NZ*)

DICTIONARY

of the Pacific coast of N America **2** the language of this people

Chinook salmon *n* a Pacific salmon valued as a food fish

chinos (**chee**-nohz) *pl n* trousers made of a kind of hard-wearing cotton
WORD ORIGIN *chino*, the cloth; origin unknown

chintz *n* a printed patterned cotton fabric with a glazed finish, used for curtains and chair coverings
WORD ORIGIN Hindi *chīnt*

chintzy *adj* **chintzier, chintziest 1** of or covered with chintz **2** (of a room or house) decorated in an excessively fussy or twee way

chinwag *n Brit, Austral & NZ informal* a chat

chip ❶ *n* **1** a thin strip of potato fried in deep fat **2** *US, Canad, Austral & NZ* a potato crisp **3** *electronics* a tiny wafer of semiconductor material, such as silicon, processed to form an integrated circuit **4** a counter used to represent money in gambling games **5** a small piece removed by chopping, cutting, or breaking **6** a mark left where a small piece has been broken off something **7 chip off the old block** *informal* a person who resembles one of his or her parents in personality **8 have a chip on one's shoulder** *informal* to be resentful or bear a grudge **9 when the chips are down** *informal* at a time of crisis ▷*vb* **chipping, chipped 10** to break small pieces from
WORD ORIGIN Old English *cipp*

chip and PIN *n* a system for authorizing credit- or debit-card payment requiring the purchaser to enter a personal identification number

chipboard *n* thin rigid board made of compressed wood particles

chip in *vb informal* **1** to contribute to a common fund **2** to interrupt with a remark

chipmunk *n* a squirrel-like striped burrowing rodent of North America and Asia
WORD ORIGIN from a Native American language

chipolata *n chiefly Brit* a small sausage
WORD ORIGIN Italian *cipolla* onion

Chippendale *adj* (of furniture) by or in the style of Thomas Chippendale, with Chinese and Gothic motifs, curved legs, and massive carving

chipset *n* a highly integrated circuit on the motherboard of a computer that controls many of its data transfer functions

Chirac *n* **Jacques** (**René**) born 1932, French Gaullist politician: president of France (1995–2007); prime minister (1974–76 and 1986–88); mayor of Paris (1977–95)

Chirico *n* **Giorgio de** 1888–1978, Italian artist born in Greece: profoundly influenced the surrealist movement

chiropody (kir-**rop**-pod-ee) *n* the treatment of minor foot complaints like corns **chiropodist** *n*

chiropractic (kire-oh-**prak**-tik) *n* a system of treating bodily disorders by manipulation of the spine **chiropractor** *n*
WORD ORIGIN Greek *kheir* hand + *praktikos* practical

chirp *vb* **1** (of some birds and insects) to make a short high-pitched sound **2** *Brit, Austral & NZ* to speak in a lively fashion ▷*n* **3** a chirping sound
WORD ORIGIN imitative

chirpy *adj* **chirpier, chirpiest** *informal* lively and cheerful **chirpiness** *n*

chirrup *vb* **1** (of some birds) to chirp repeatedly ▷*n* **2** a chirruping sound
WORD ORIGIN variant of *chirp*

chisel *n* **1** a metal tool with a sharp end for shaping wood or stone ▷*vb* **-elling, -elled** *or US* **-eling, -eled 2** to carve or form with a chisel
WORD ORIGIN Latin *caesus* cut

chiselled *or US* **chiseled** *adj* finely or sharply formed: *chiselled angular features*

chit[1] *n* a short official note, such as a memorandum, requisition, or receipt. Also: **chitty**
WORD ORIGIN Hindi *cittha* note

chit[2] *n Brit, Austral & NZ, old-fashioned* a pert or impudent girl
WORD ORIGIN Middle English: young animal, kitten

chitchat *n* chat or gossip

chitin (**kite**-in) *n* the tough substance forming the outer layer of the bodies of arthropods
WORD ORIGIN Greek *khitōn* tunic

chitterlings *pl n* the intestines of a pig or other animal prepared as food
WORD ORIGIN origin unknown

chivalrous *adj* gallant or courteous **chivalrously** *adv*

chivalry *n* **1** courteous behaviour, esp. by men towards women **2** the medieval system and principles of knighthood **chivalric** *adj*
WORD ORIGIN Old French *chevalier* knight

chives *pl n* the long slender hollow leaves of a small Eurasian plant, used in cooking for their onion-like flavour
WORD ORIGIN Latin *caepa* onion

chivvy *vb* **-vies, -vying, -vied** *Brit* to harass or nag
WORD ORIGIN probably from *Chevy Chase*, a Scottish ballad

chloral hydrate *n* a colourless crystalline solid used as a sedative

chlorate *n chem* any salt containing the ion ClO_3^-

chloride *n chem* **1** any compound of chlorine and another element and radical **2** any salt or ester of hydrochloric acid

chlorinate *vb* **-ating, -ated 1** to disinfect (water) with chlorine **2** *chem* to combine or treat (a substance) with chlorine: *chlorinated hydrocarbons* **chlorination** *n*

chlorine *n* a poisonous strong-smelling greenish-yellow gaseous element, used in water purification and as a disinfectant, and, combined with sodium, to make common salt. Symbol: Cl

chloro- *combining form* green
WORD ORIGIN Greek *khlōros*

chlorofluorocarbon *n chem* any of various gaseous compounds of carbon, hydrogen, chlorine, and fluorine, used as refrigerants and aerosol propellants, some of which break down the ozone in the atmosphere

chloroform *n* a sweet-smelling liquid, used as a solvent and cleansing agent, and formerly as an anaesthetic
WORD ORIGIN CHLORO- + *formyl*: see FORMIC ACID

chlorophyll *or US* **chlorophyl** *n* the green colouring matter of plants, which enables them to convert sunlight into energy
WORD ORIGIN CHLORO- + Greek *phullon* leaf

chloroplast *n biol* one of the parts of a plant cell that contains chlorophyll
WORD ORIGIN CHLORO- + Greek *plastos* formed

chock *n* **1** a block or wedge of wood used to prevent the sliding or rolling of a heavy object ▷*vb* **2** to fit with or secure by a chock
WORD ORIGIN origin unknown

chock-a-block *adj* filled to capacity

chock-full *adj* completely full

chocolate *n* **1** a food made from roasted ground cacao seeds, usually sweetened and flavoured **2** a sweet or drink made from this ▷*adj* **3** deep brown **chocolaty** *adj*
WORD ORIGIN Aztec *xocolatl*

choice ❶ *n* **1** the act of choosing or selecting **2** the opportunity or power

C

THESAURUS

chip *n* **4 = counter**, disc, token **5 = fragment**, scrap, shaving, flake, paring, wafer, sliver, shard **6 = scratch**, nick, flaw, notch, dent ▷*vb* **10 = nick**, damage, gash

choice *n* **1, 2, 3 = selection**, preference, election, pick **4 = option**, say, alternative **5 = range**, variety, selection, assortment ▷*adj* **6 = best**, bad *(slang)*, special, prime, nice, prize, select, excellent, elect, crucial *(slang)*, exclusive, elite, superior, exquisite, def *(slang)*, booshit *(Austral slang)*, exo *(Austral slang)*, sik *(Austral slang)*, hand-picked, dainty, rad *(informal)*, phat *(slang)*, schmick *(Austral informal)*

DICTIONARY

of choosing: *parental choice* **3** a person or thing chosen or that may be chosen: *the president's choice as the new head of the CIA* **4** an alternative action or possibility: *they had no choice but to accept* **5** a range from which to select: *a choice of weapons* ▷ *adj* **6** of high quality: *choice government jobs* **7** carefully chosen: *a few choice words* **8** vulgar: *choice language*
WORD ORIGIN Old French *choisir* to choose

choir *n* **1** an organized group of singers, usually for singing in church **2** the part of a church, in front of the altar, occupied by the choir
WORD ORIGIN Latin *chorus*

choirboy *n* a boy who sings in a church choir

Choiseul[1] *n* an island in the SW Pacific Ocean, in the Solomon Islands: hilly and densely forested. Area: 3885 sq km (1500 sq miles)

Choiseul[2] *n* **Étienne François**, Duc de. 1719–85, French statesman; foreign minister (1758–70)

choke ⓣ *vb* **choking, choked 1** to hinder or stop the breathing of (a person or animal) by strangling or smothering **2** to have trouble in breathing, swallowing, or speaking **3** to block or clog up: *the old narrow streets become choked to a standstill* **4** to hinder the growth of: *weeds would outgrow and choke the rice crop* ▷ *n* **5** a device in a vehicle's engine that enriches the petrol-air mixture by reducing the air supply
WORD ORIGIN Old English *ācēocian*

choke back *vb* to suppress (tears or anger)

choked *adj informal* disappointed or angry: *I still feel choked about him leaving*

choker *n* a tight-fitting necklace

choke up *vb* **1** to block completely **2 choked up** *informal* overcome with emotion

choko *n, pl* **-kos** *Austral & NZ* the pear-shaped fruit of a tropical American vine, eaten as a vegetable
WORD ORIGIN Brazilian Indian

choler (kol-ler) *n archaic* anger or bad temper
WORD ORIGIN Greek *kholē* bile

cholera (kol-ler-a) *n* a serious infectious disease causing severe diarrhoea and stomach cramps, caught from contaminated water or food
WORD ORIGIN Greek *kholē* bile

choleric *adj* bad-tempered

cholesterol (kol-lest-er-oll) *n* a fatty alcohol found in all animal fats, tissues, and fluids, an excess of which is thought to contribute to heart and artery disease
WORD ORIGIN Greek *kholē* bile + *stereos* solid

chomp *vb* to chew (food) noisily

chook *n informal chiefly Austral & NZ* a hen or chicken

choose ⓣ *vb* **choosing, chose, chosen 1** to select (a person, thing, or course of action) from a number of alternatives **2** to like or please: *when she did choose to reveal her secret, the group were initially hushed* **3** to consider it desirable or proper: *I don't choose to read that sort of book*
WORD ORIGIN Old English *ceosan*

choosy *adj* **choosier, choosiest** *informal* fussy; hard to please

chop[1] ⓣ *vb* **chopping, chopped 1** (often foll. by *down* or *off*) to cut (something) with a blow from an axe or other sharp tool **2** to cut into pieces **3** *boxing, karate* to hit (an opponent) with a short sharp blow **4** *Brit, Austral & NZ informal* to dispense with or reduce **5** *sport* to hit (a ball) sharply downwards ▷ *n* **6** a cutting blow **7** a slice of mutton, lamb, or pork, usually including a rib **8** *sport* a sharp downward blow or stroke **9 the chop** *slang* dismissal from employment
WORD ORIGIN variant of *chap*: see CHAPPED

chop[2] *vb* **chopping, chopped 1 chop and change** to change one's mind repeatedly **2 chop logic** to use excessively subtle or involved argument
WORD ORIGIN Old English *ceapian* to barter

chop chop *adv pidgin English* quickly

chopper *n* **1** *informal* a helicopter **2** *chiefly Brit* a small hand axe **3** a butcher's cleaver **4** a type of bicycle or motorcycle with very high handlebars **5** *NZ* a child's bicycle

choppy *adj* **-pier, -piest** (of the sea) fairly rough **choppiness** *n*

chops *pl n Brit, Austral & NZ informal* **1** the jaws or cheeks **2 lick one's chops** to anticipate something with pleasure
WORD ORIGIN origin unknown

chopsticks *pl n* a pair of thin sticks of ivory, wood, or plastic, used for eating Chinese or other East Asian food
WORD ORIGIN pidgin English, from Chinese

chop suey *n* a Chinese-style dish of chopped meat, bean sprouts, and other vegetables in a sauce
WORD ORIGIN Chinese *tsap sui* odds and ends

choral *adj* of or for a choir

chorale (kor-rahl) *n* **1** a slow stately hymn tune **2** *chiefly US* a choir or chorus
WORD ORIGIN German *Choralgesang* choral song

chord[1] *n* **1** *maths* a straight line connecting two points on a curve **2** *anat* ▶ same as **cord 3 strike** *or* **touch a chord** to bring about an emotional response, usually of sympathy
WORD ORIGIN Greek *khordē* string

chord[2] *n* the simultaneous sounding of three or more musical notes
WORD ORIGIN short for *accord*

chordate *n* any animal that has a long fibrous rod just above the gut to support the body, such as the vertebrates

chore ⓣ *n* **1** a small routine task **2** an unpleasant task
WORD ORIGIN Old English *cerr* a turn of work

chorea (kor-ree-a) *n* a disorder of the nervous system characterized by uncontrollable brief jerky movements
WORD ORIGIN Greek *khoreia* dance

choreograph *vb* to compose the steps and dances for (a piece of music or ballet)

choreography *n* **1** the composition of steps and movements for ballet and other dancing **2** the steps and movements of a ballet or dance **choreographer** *n* **choreographic** *adj*
WORD ORIGIN Greek *khoreia* dance + -GRAPHY

chorister *n* a singer in a church choir

chortle *vb* **-tling, -tled 1** to chuckle with amusement ▷ *n* **2** an amused chuckle
WORD ORIGIN coined by Lewis Carroll

chorus ⓣ *n, pl* **-ruses 1** a large choir **2** a piece of music to be sung by a large choir **3** a part of a song repeated after each verse **4** something expressed by many people at once: *a chorus of boos* **5** the noise made by a group of birds or small animals: *the dawn chorus* **6** a group of singers or dancers who perform together in a show **7** (in ancient Greece) a group of actors who commented on the action of a play **8** (in Elizabethan drama) the

THESAURUS

choke *vb* **1 = strangle**, throttle, asphyxiate **2 = suffocate**, stifle, smother, overpower, asphyxiate **3, 4 = block**, dam, clog, obstruct, bung, constrict, occlude, congest, close, stop, bar

choose *vb* **1 = pick**, take, prefer, select, elect, adopt, opt for, designate, single out, espouse, settle on, fix on, cherry-pick, settle upon, predestine **OPPOSITE:** reject **2, 3 = wish**, want, desire, see fit

chop[1] *vb* **1 = cut**, fell, axe, slash, hack, sever, shear, cleave, hew, lop, truncate

chore *n* **1, 2 = task**, job, duty, burden, hassle *(informal)*, fag *(informal)*, errand, no picnic

DICTIONARY

actor who spoke the prologue and epilogue **9 in chorus** in unison ▷ *vb* **10** to sing or say together
WORD ORIGIN Greek *khoros*
chorus girl *n* a young woman who dances or sings in the chorus of a show or film
chose *vb* ▸ the past tense of **choose**
chosen *vb* **1** ▸ the past participle of **choose** ▷ *adj* **2** selected for some special quality: *the chosen one*
Chou En-lai *or* **Zhou En Lai** *n* 1898–1976, Chinese Communist statesman; foreign minister of the People's Republic of China (1949–58) and premier (1949–76)
chough (chuff) *n* a large black bird of the crow family
WORD ORIGIN origin unknown
choux pastry (shoo) *n* a very light pastry made with eggs
WORD ORIGIN French *pâte choux* cabbage dough
chow *n* **1** a thick-coated dog with a curled tail, originally from China **2** *informal* food
WORD ORIGIN pidgin English
chowder *n* a thick soup containing clams or fish
WORD ORIGIN French *chaudière* kettle
chow mein *n* a Chinese-American dish consisting of chopped meat or vegetables fried with noodles
WORD ORIGIN from Chinese
Chrétien de Troyes *n* 12th century, French poet, who wrote the five Arthurian romances *Erec; Cligès; Lancelot, le chevalier de la charette; Yvain, le chevalier au lion;* and *Perceval, le conte del Graal* (?1155–?1190), the first courtly romances
chrism *n* consecrated oil used for anointing in some churches
WORD ORIGIN Greek *khriein* to anoint
Christ *n* **1** Jesus of Nazareth (Jesus Christ), regarded by Christians as the Messiah of Old Testament prophecies **2** the Messiah of Old Testament prophecies **3** an image or picture of Christ ▷ *interj* **4** *taboo slang* an oath expressing annoyance or surprise
WORD ORIGIN Greek *khristos* anointed one
christen Ⓣ *vb* **1** ▸ same as **baptize** **2** to give a name to (a person or thing) **3** *informal* to use for the first time **christening** *n*
WORD ORIGIN Old English *cristnian*
Christendom *n* all Christian people or countries
Christian *n* **1** a person who believes in and follows Jesus Christ **2** *informal* a person who displays the virtues of kindness and mercy encouraged in the teachings of Jesus Christ ▷ *adj* **3** of Jesus Christ, Christians, or Christianity **4** kind or good
Christian[1] *n* **1 a** a person who believes in and follows Jesus Christ **b** a member of a Christian Church or denomination **2** *informal* a person who possesses Christian virtues, esp. practical ones ▷ *adj* **3** of, relating to, or derived from Jesus Christ, his teachings, example, or his followers **4** (*sometimes not capital*) exhibiting kindness or goodness **Christianly** *adj, adv*
Christian[2] *n* **Charlie** 1919–42, US jazz guitarist
Christian Era *n* the period beginning with the year of Christ's birth
Christianity *n* **1** the religion based on the life and teachings of Christ **2** Christian beliefs or practices **3** ▸ same as **Christendom**
Christian IV *n* 1577–1648, king of Denmark and Norway (1588–1648): defeated in the Thirty Years' War (1629) and by Sweden (1645)
Christianize *or* **-ise** *vb* **-izing, -ized** *or* **-ising, -ised** **1** to convert to Christianity **2** to fill with Christian principles, spirit, or outlook **Christianization** *or* **-isation** *n*
Christian name *n* a personal name formally given to Christians at baptism: loosely used to mean a person's first name
Christian Science *n* the religious system founded by Mary Baker Eddy (1866), which emphasizes spiritual regeneration and healing through prayer **Christian Scientist** *n*
Christian X *n* 1890–1947, king of Denmark (1912–47) and Iceland (1918–44)
Christina *n* 1626–89, queen of Sweden (1632–54), daughter of Gustavus Adolphus, noted particularly for her patronage of literature
Christine de Pisan *n* ?1364–?1430, French poet and prose writer, born in Venice. Her works include ballads, rondeaux, lays, and a biography of Charles V of France
Christmas Ⓣ *n* **1 a** *Christianity* a festival commemorating the birth of Christ, held by most Churches to have occurred on December 25 **b** Also: **Christmas Day** December 25, as a day of secular celebrations when gifts and greetings are exchanged ▷ *adj* **2** connected with or taking place at the time of year when this festival is celebrated: *the Christmas holidays* **Christmassy** *adj*
WORD ORIGIN Old English *Crīstes mæsse* Mass of Christ
Christmas box *n* a tip or present given at Christmas, esp. to postmen or tradesmen
Christmas Eve *n* the evening or the whole day before Christmas Day
Christmas pudding *n* *Austral & Brit* a rich steamed pudding containing suet, dried fruit, and spices
Christmas rose *n* an evergreen plant with white or pink winter-blooming flowers
Christmas tree *n* an evergreen tree or an imitation of one, decorated as part of Christmas celebrations
Christo *n* full name **Christo Jaracheff** born 1935, US artist, born in Bulgaria; best known for works in which he wraps buildings, monuments, or natural features in canvas or plastic
Christoff *n* **Boris** 1919–93, Bulgarian bass-baritone, noted esp. for his performance in the title role of Mussorgsky's *Boris Godunov*
Christophe *n* **Henri** 1767–1820, Haitian revolutionary leader; king of Haiti (1811–20)
Christopher *n* **Saint** 3rd century AD, Christian martyr; patron saint of travellers
chromate *n* *chem* any salt or ester of chromic acid
chromatic *adj* **1** of or in colour or colours **2** *music* **a** involving the sharpening or flattening of notes or the use of such notes **b** of the chromatic scale **chromatically** *adv*
WORD ORIGIN Greek *khrōma* colour
chromatics *n* the science of colour
chromatic scale *n* a twelve-note scale including all the semitones of the octave
chromatin *n* *biochem* the part of the nucleus of a cell that forms the chromosomes and can easily be dyed
WORD ORIGIN from *chrome*
chromatography *n* the technique of separating and analysing the components of a mixture of liquids or gases by slowly passing it through an adsorbing material
WORD ORIGIN Greek *khrōma* colour + -GRAPHY
chrome *n* **1** ▸ same as **chromium** **2** anything plated with chromium ▷ *vb* **chroming, chromed** **3** to plate with chromium
WORD ORIGIN Greek *khrōma* colour
chromite *n* a brownish-black mineral which is the only commercial source of chromium
chromium *n* *chem* a hard grey metallic element, used in steel alloys and electroplating to increase hardness and corrosion resistance. Symbol: Cr
WORD ORIGIN from *chrome*

THESAURUS

chorus *n* **1, 6 = choir**, singers, ensemble, vocalists, choristers **2, 3 = refrain**, response, strain, burden **9 in chorus = in unison**, as one, all together, in concert, in harmony, in accord, with one voice
christen *vb* **2a = baptize**, name **2b = name**, call, term, style, title, dub, designate
Christmas *n* **1a = the festive season**, Noël, Xmas (*informal*), Yule (*archaic*), Yuletide (*archaic*)

DICTIONARY

chromosome *n* any of the microscopic rod-shaped structures that appear in a cell nucleus during cell division, consisting of units (genes) that are responsible for the transmission of hereditary characteristics
WORD ORIGIN Greek *khrōma* colour + *sōma* body

chromosphere *n* a gaseous layer of the sun's atmosphere extending from the photosphere to the corona

chronic *adj* **1** (of a disease) developing slowly or lasting for a long time **2** (of a bad habit or bad behaviour) having continued for a long time; habitual: *chronic drug addiction* **3** very serious or severe: *chronic food shortages* **4** *Brit, Austral & NZ informal* very bad: *the play was chronic* **chronically** *adv*
WORD ORIGIN Greek *khronos* time

chronic fatigue syndrome *n* a condition characterized by painful muscles and general weakness sometimes persisting long after a viral illness

chronicle ⓣ *n* **1** a record of events in chronological order ▹*vb* **-cling, -cled** **2** to record in or as if in a chronicle **chronicler** *n*
WORD ORIGIN Greek *khronika* annals

chronological *adj* **1** (of a sequence of events) arranged in order of occurrence **2** relating to chronology **chronologically** *adv*

chronology *n, pl* **-gies 1** the arrangement of dates or events in order of occurrence **2** the determining of the proper sequence of past events **3** a table of events arranged in order of occurrence **chronologist** *n*
WORD ORIGIN Greek *khronos* time + -LOGY

chronometer *n* a timepiece designed to be accurate in all conditions
WORD ORIGIN Greek *khronos* time + -METER

chrysalis (kriss-a-liss) *n* an insect in the stage between larva and adult, when it is in a cocoon
WORD ORIGIN Greek *khrusos* gold

chrysanthemum *n* a garden plant with large round flowers made up of many petals
WORD ORIGIN Greek *khrusos* gold + *anthemon* flower

Chrysostom *n* Saint **John** ?345–407 AD, Greek patriarch; archbishop of Constantinople (398–404). Feast day: Sept 13 or Nov 13

Chuang-tzu *n* a variant transliteration of the Chinese name for **Zhuangzi**

chub *n, pl* **chub** *or* **chubs** a common freshwater game fish of the carp family with a dark greenish body
WORD ORIGIN origin unknown

chubby *adj* **-bier, -biest** plump and round **chubbiness** *n*
WORD ORIGIN perhaps from *chub*

Ch'ü Ch'iu-pai *n* a variant transliteration of the Chinese name for **Qu Qiu Bai**

chuck¹ ⓣ *vb* **1** *informal* to throw carelessly **2** *informal* (sometimes foll. by *in* or *up*) to give up; reject: *he chucked in his job* **3** to pat (someone) affectionately under the chin **4** *Austral & NZ informal* to vomit ▹*n* **5** a throw or toss **6** a pat under the chin ▸See also **chuck off, chuck out**
WORD ORIGIN origin unknown

chuck² *n* **1** Also: **chuck steak** a cut of beef from the neck to the shoulder blade **2** a device that holds a workpiece in a lathe or a tool in a drill
WORD ORIGIN variant of *chock*

chuck³ *n W Canad* **1** a large body of water **2** Also: **saltchuck** the sea
WORD ORIGIN Chinook

chuckle ⓣ *vb* **-ling, -led 1** to laugh softly or to oneself ▹*n* **2** a partly suppressed laugh
WORD ORIGIN probably from *chuck* cluck

chuck off *vb* (often foll. by *at*) *Austral & NZ informal* to abuse or make fun of

chuck out *vb informal* to throw out

chuddies *pl n Indian informal* underpants

chuff *vb* to move while making a puffing sound, as a steam engine
WORD ORIGIN imitative

chuffed *adj informal* pleased or delighted: *I suppose you're feeling pretty chuffed*
WORD ORIGIN origin unknown

chug *n* **1** a short dull sound like the noise of an engine ▹*vb* **chugging, chugged 2** (esp. of an engine) to operate or move with this sound: *lorries chug past*
WORD ORIGIN imitative

chukka *or* **chukker** *n polo* a period of continuous play, usually 7½ minutes
WORD ORIGIN Hindi *cakkar*

chum ⓣ *n* **1** *informal* a close friend ▹*vb* **chumming, chummed 2 chum up with** to form a close friendship with
WORD ORIGIN probably from *chamber fellow*

chummy *adj* **-mier, -miest** *informal* friendly **chummily** *adv* **chumminess** *n*

chump *n* **1** *informal* a stupid person **2** a thick piece of meat **3** a thick block of wood **4 off one's chump** *Brit slang* crazy
WORD ORIGIN origin unknown

chunk ⓣ *n* **1** a thick solid piece of something **2** a considerable amount
WORD ORIGIN variant of CHUCK²

chunky *adj* **chunkier, chunkiest 1** thick and short **2** containing thick pieces **3** *chiefly Brit* (of clothes, esp. knitwear) made of thick bulky material **chunkiness** *n*

church *n* **1** a building for public Christian worship **2** religious services held in a church **3** a particular Christian denomination **4** Christians collectively **5** the clergy as distinguished from the laity **6 Church** institutional religion as a political or social force: *conflict between Church and State*
WORD ORIGIN Greek *kuriakon (dōma)* the Lord's (house)

Church *n* **Charlotte** born 1986, Welsh soprano, who made her name with the album *Voice of an Angel* (1998) when she was 12

churchgoer *n* a person who attends church regularly

Churchill¹ *n* **1** a river in E Canada, rising in SE Labrador and flowing north and southeast over Churchill Falls, then east to the Atlantic. Length: about 1000 km (600 miles). Former name: **Hamilton River 2** a river in central Canada, rising in NW Saskatchewan and flowing east through several lakes to Hudson Bay. Length: about 1600 km (1000 miles)

Churchill² *n* **1 Caryl** born 1938, British playwright; her plays include *Cloud Nine* (1978), *Top Girls* (1982), *Serious Money* (1987), and *Far Away* (2000) **2 Charles** 1731–64, British poet, noted for his polemical satires. His works include *The Rosciad* (1761) and *The Prophecy of Famine* (1763) **3 John** ▸See (1st Duke of) **Marlborough 4** Lord **Randolph** 1849–95, British Conservative politician: secretary of state for India (1885–86) and chancellor of the Exchequer and leader of the House of Commons (1886) **5** his son, Sir **Winston (Leonard Spencer)** 1874–1965, British

THESAURUS

chronicle *n* **1 = record**, story, history, account, register, journal, diary, narrative, annals, blog *(informal)* ▹*vb* **2 = record**, tell, report, enter, relate, register, recount, set down, narrate, put on record

chuck¹ *vb* **1** *(informal)* **= throw**, cast, pitch, shy, toss, hurl, fling, sling, heave **2** *(informal)* **= give up** *or* **over**, leave, stop, abandon, cease, resign from, pack in, jack in **4** *(slang)* **= vomit**, throw up *(informal)*, spew, heave *(slang)*, puke *(slang)*, barf *(US slang)*, chunder *(slang, chiefly Austral)*, upchuck *(US slang)*, do a technicolour yawn, toss your cookies *(US slang)*

chuckle *vb* **1 = laugh**, giggle, snigger, chortle, titter ▹*n* **2 = laugh**, giggle, snigger, chortle, titter

chum *n* **1** *(informal)* **= friend**, mate *(informal)*, pal *(informal)*, companion, cock *(Brit informal)*, comrade, crony, main man *(slang, chiefly US)*, cobber *(Austral & NZ old-fashioned,*

DICTIONARY

Conservative statesman, orator, and writer, noted for his leadership during World War II. He held various posts under both Conservative and Liberal governments, including 1st Lord of the Admiralty (1911–15), before becoming prime minister (1940–45; 1951–55). His writings include *The World Crisis* (1923–29), *Marlborough* (1933–38), *The Second World War* (1948–54), and *History of the English-Speaking Peoples* (1956–58): Nobel prize for literature 1953

churchman *n, pl* **-men** a clergyman

Church of England *n* the reformed established state Church in England, with the sovereign as its temporal head

Church of Scotland *n* the established Presbyterian church in Scotland

churchwarden *n* **1** *Church of England, Episcopal Church* a lay assistant of a parish priest **2** an old-fashioned long-stemmed tobacco pipe made of clay

churchyard *n* the grounds round a church, used as a graveyard

churl *n* **1** a surly ill-bred person **2** *archaic* a farm labourer
WORD ORIGIN Old English *ceorl*

churlish *adj* surly and rude

churn ⊕ *n* **1** a machine in which cream is shaken to make butter **2** a large container for milk ▷*vb* **3** to stir (milk or cream) vigorously in order to make butter **4** to move about violently: *a hot tub of churning water*
WORD ORIGIN Old English *ciern*

churn out *vb informal* to produce (something) rapidly and in large numbers

chute[1] (**shoot**) *n* a steep sloping channel or passage down which things may be dropped
WORD ORIGIN Old French *cheoite* fallen

chute[2] *n informal* ▸short for **parachute**

Chu Teh *or* **Zhu De** *n* 1886–1976, Chinese military leader and politician; he became commander in chief of the Red Army (1931) and was chairman of the Standing Committee of the National People's Congress of the People's Republic of China (1959–76)

chutney *n* a pickle of Indian origin, made from fruit, vinegar, spices, and sugar: *mango chutney*
WORD ORIGIN Hindi *catni*

chutzpah (**hhoots**-pa) *n informal* unashamed self-confidence; impudence
WORD ORIGIN Yiddish

Chu Xi *or* **Chu Hsi** *n* 1130–1200, Chinese philosopher, known for his neo-Confucian commentaries, the *Ssu shu* or *Four Books*

chyle *n* a milky fluid formed in the small intestine during digestion
WORD ORIGIN Greek *khulos* juice

chyme *n* the thick fluid mass of partially digested food that leaves the stomach
WORD ORIGIN Greek *khumos* juice

chypre (**sheep**-ra) *n* a perfume made from sandalwood
WORD ORIGIN French: Cyprus

Ci curie

CI Channel Islands

CIA Central Intelligence Agency; a US bureau responsible for espionage and intelligence activities

ciabatta (cha-**bat**-ta) *n* a type of bread made with olive oil
WORD ORIGIN Italian: slipper

Ciano *n* **Galeazzo,** full name *Conte Galeazzo Ciano di Cortellazzo*. 1903–44, Italian fascist politician; minister of foreign affairs (1936–43) and son-in-law of Mussolini, whose supporters shot him

Cibber *n* **Colley** 1671–1757, English actor and dramatist; poet laureate (1730–57)

cicada (sik-**kah**-da) *n* a large broad insect, found in hot countries, that makes a high-pitched drone
WORD ORIGIN Latin

cicatrix (**sik**-a-trix) *n, pl* **cicatrices** (sik-a-**trice**-eez) the tissue that forms in a wound during healing; scar
WORD ORIGIN Latin: scar

cicerone (siss-a-**rone**-ee) *n, pl* **-nes** *or* **-ni** *literary* a person who guides and informs sightseers
WORD ORIGIN after *Cicero*, Roman orator

CID (in Britain) Criminal Investigation Department; the detective division of a police force

cider *n* an alcoholic drink made from fermented apple juice
WORD ORIGIN Hebrew *shēkhār* strong drink

cigar *n* a tube-like roll of cured tobacco leaves for smoking
WORD ORIGIN Spanish *cigarro*

cigarette *n* a thin roll of shredded tobacco in thin paper, for smoking
WORD ORIGIN French: a little cigar

cilantro (sil-**lan**-tro) *n chiefly US & Canad* a European plant, cultivated for its aromatic seeds and leaves, used in flavouring foods. Also called: **coriander**
WORD ORIGIN Spanish

cilium *n, pl* **cilia** *biol* **1** any of the short threads projecting from a cell or organism, whose rhythmic beating causes movement **2** an eyelash **ciliary** *adj*
WORD ORIGIN Latin

Çiller *n* **Tansu** born 1945, Turkish politician; prime minister (1993–96)

Cimabue *n* **Giovanni** ?1240–?1302, Italian painter of the Florentine school, who anticipated the movement, led by Giotto, away from the Byzantine tradition in art towards a greater naturalism

Cimarosa *n* **Domenico** 1749–1801, Italian composer, chiefly remembered for his opera buffa *The Secret Marriage* (1792)

Cimon *n* died 449 BC, Athenian military and naval commander: defeated the Persians at Eurymedon (?466)

C in C *mil* Commander in Chief

cinch (**sinch**) *n* **1** *informal* an easy task **2** *slang* a certainty
WORD ORIGIN Spanish *cincha* saddle girth

cinchona (sing-**kone**-a) *n* **1** a South American tree or shrub with medicinal bark **2** its dried bark which yields quinine **3** a drug made from cinchona bark
WORD ORIGIN after the Countess of *Chinchón*

Cincinnatus *n* **Lucius Quinctius** ?519–438 BC, Roman general and statesman, regarded as a model of simple virtue; dictator of Rome during two crises (458; 439), retiring to his farm after each one

cincture *n literary* something, such as a belt or girdle, that goes around another thing
WORD ORIGIN Latin *cingere* to gird

cinder *n* **1** a piece of material that will not burn, left after burning coal or wood **2** **cinders** ashes
WORD ORIGIN Old English *sinder*

Cinderella *n* a poor, neglected, or unsuccessful person or thing
WORD ORIGIN after *Cinderella*, the heroine of a fairy tale

cine camera *n* a camera for taking moving pictures

cinema ⊕ *n* **1** a place designed for showing films **2** **the cinema** **a** the art or business of making films **b** films collectively **cinematic** *adj*
WORD ORIGIN shortened from *cinematograph*

cinematograph *n chiefly Brit* a combined camera, printer, and projector **cinematographer** *n* **cinematographic** *adj*
WORD ORIGIN Greek *kinēma* motion + -GRAPH

THESAURUS

informal), E hoa *(NZ)*

chunk *n* **1 = piece**, block, mass, portion, lump, slab, hunk, nugget, wad, dollop *(informal)*, wodge *(Brit informal)*

churn *vb* **3 = stir up**, beat, disturb, swirl, agitate **4 = swirl**, boil, toss, foam, seethe, froth

cinema *n* **1 = pictures**, movies, picture-house, flicks *(slang)* **2a, 2b = films**, pictures, movies, the big screen *(informal)*, motion pictures, the silver screen

DICTIONARY

cinematography *n* the technique of making films: *he won an Oscar for his stunning cinematography*

cineraria *n* a garden plant with daisy-like flowers
WORD ORIGIN Latin *cinis* ashes

cinerarium *n, pl* **-raria** a place for keeping the ashes of the dead after cremation **cinerary** *adj*
WORD ORIGIN Latin *cinerarius* relating to ashes

Cinna *n* **Lucius Cornelius** died 84 BC, Roman patrician; an opponent of Sulla

cinnabar *n* **1** a heavy red mineral containing mercury **2** a large red-and-black European moth
WORD ORIGIN Greek *kinnabari*

cinnamon *n* the spice obtained from the aromatic bark of a tropical Asian tree
WORD ORIGIN Hebrew *qinnamown*

cinquefoil *n* **1** a plant with five-lobed compound leaves **2** an ornamental carving in the form of five arcs arranged in a circle
WORD ORIGIN Latin *quinquefolium* plant with five leaves

Cinque Ports *pl n* an association of ports on the SE coast of England, with certain ancient duties and privileges

cipher *or* **cypher** (**sife**-er) *n* **1** a method of secret writing using substitution of letters according to a key **2** a secret message **3** the key to a secret message **4** a person or thing of no importance **5** *obsolete* the numeral zero ▷*vb* **6** to put (a message) into secret writing
WORD ORIGIN Arabic *sifr* zero

circa (**sir**-ka) *prep* (used with a date) approximately; about: *circa 1788*
WORD ORIGIN Latin

circadian *adj* of biological processes that occur regularly at 24-hour intervals
WORD ORIGIN Latin *circa* about + *dies* day

circle ❶ *n* **1** a curved line surrounding a central point, every point of the line being the same distance from the centre **2** the figure enclosed by such a curve **3** something formed or arranged in the shape of a circle: *they ran round in little circles* **4** a group of people sharing an interest, activity, or upbringing: *his judgment is well respected in diplomatic circles* **5** *theatre* the section of seats above the main level of the auditorium **6** a process or chain of events or parts that forms a connected whole; cycle **7 come full circle** to arrive back at one's starting point ▷*vb* **-cling, -cled 8** to move in a circle (around) **9** to enclose in a circle
WORD ORIGIN Latin *circus*

circlet *n* a small circle or ring, esp. a circular ornament worn on the head
WORD ORIGIN Old French *cerclet* little circle

circuit ❶ *n* **1** a complete route or course, esp. one that is circular or that lies around an object **2** a complete path through which an electric current can flow **3 a** a periodical journey around an area, as made by judges or salesmen **b** the places visited on such a journey **4** a motor-racing track **5** *sport* a series of tournaments in which the same players regularly take part: *the professional golf circuit* **6** a number of theatres or cinemas under one management
WORD ORIGIN Latin *circum* around + *ire* to go

circuit breaker *n* a device that stops the flow of current in an electrical circuit if there is a fault

circuitous (sir-**kew**-it-uss) *adj* indirect and lengthy: *a circuitous route*

circuitry (**sir**-kit-tree) *n* **1** the design of an electrical circuit **2** the system of circuits used in an electronic device

circular ❶ *adj* **1** of or in the shape of a circle **2** travelling in a circle **3** (of an argument) not valid because a statement is used to prove the conclusion and the conclusion to prove the statement **4** (of letters or announcements) intended for general distribution ▷*n* **5** a letter or advertisement sent to a large number of people at the same time **circularity** *n*

circularize *or* **-ise** *vb* **-izing, -ized** *or* **-ising, -ised** to distribute circulars to

circular saw *n* a power-driven saw in which a circular disc with a toothed edge is rotated at high speed

circulate ❶ *vb* **-lating, -lated 1** to send, go, or pass from place to place or person to person: *rumours were circulating that he was about to resign* **2** to move through a circuit or system, returning to the starting point: *regular exercise keeps the blood circulating around the body* **3** to move around the guests at a party, talking to different people: *it wasn't like her not to circulate among all the guests* **circulatory** *adj*
WORD ORIGIN Latin *circulari*

circulation ❶ *n* **1** the flow of blood from the heart through the arteries, and then back through the veins to the heart, where the cycle is renewed **2** the number of copies of a newspaper or magazine that are sold **3** the distribution of newspapers or magazines **4** sending or moving around: *the circulation of air* **5 in circulation a** (of currency) being used by the public **b** (of people) active in a social or business context

circum- *prefix* around; on all sides: *circumlocution*
WORD ORIGIN Latin

circumcise *vb* **-cising, -cised 1** to remove the foreskin of (a male) **2** to cut or remove the clitoris of (a female) **3** to perform such an operation as a religious rite on (someone) **circumcision** *n*
WORD ORIGIN Latin CIRCUM- + *caedere* to cut

circumference *n* **1** the boundary of a specific area or figure, esp. of a circle **2** the distance round this **circumferential** *adj*
WORD ORIGIN Latin CIRCUM- + *ferre* to bear

circumflex *n* a mark (ˆ) placed over a vowel to show that it is pronounced in a particular way, for instance as a long vowel in French
WORD ORIGIN Latin CIRCUM- + *flectere* to bend

circumlocution *n* **1** an indirect way of saying something **2** an indirect expression **circumlocutory** *adj*

circumnavigate *vb* **-gating, -gated** to sail, fly, or walk right around **circumnavigation** *n*

circumscribe *vb* **-scribing, -scribed 1** *formal* to limit or restrict within certain boundaries: *the President's powers are circumscribed by the Constitution* **2** *geom* to draw a geometric figure around (another figure) so that the two are in contact but do not intersect **circumscription** *n*
WORD ORIGIN Latin CIRCUM- + *scribere* to write

circumspect *adj* cautious and careful

THESAURUS

circle *n* **1, 2, 3 = ring**, round, band, disc, loop, hoop, cordon, perimeter, halo **4 = group**, company, set, school, club, order, class, society, crowd, assembly, fellowship, fraternity, clique, coterie ▷*vb* **8 = wheel**, spiral, revolve, rotate, whirl, pivot **9 = go round**, ring, surround, belt, curve, enclose, encompass, compass, envelop, encircle, circumscribe, hem in, gird, circumnavigate, enwreath

circuit *n* **1 = lap**, round, tour, revolution, orbit, perambulation **3a, 3b = course**, round, tour, track, route, journey **4 = racetrack**, course, track, racecourse

circular *adj* **1 = round**, ring-shaped, discoid **2 = circuitous**, cyclical, orbital ▷*n* **5 = advertisement**, notice, ad (*informal*), announcement, advert (*Brit informal*), press release

circulate *vb* **1 = spread**, issue, publish, broadcast, distribute, diffuse, publicize, propagate, disseminate, promulgate, make known **2 = flow**, revolve, rotate, radiate

circulation *n* **1 = bloodstream**, blood flow **2 = distribution**, currency, readership **3 = spread**, distribution, transmission, dissemination

DICTIONARY

not to take risks **circumspection** *n* **circumspectly** *adv*
WORD ORIGIN Latin CIRCUM- + *specere* to look
circumstance ❶ *n* **1** an occurrence or condition that accompanies or influences a person or event **2** unplanned events and situations which cannot be controlled: *a victim of circumstance* **3 pomp and circumstance** formal display or ceremony **4 under** *or* **in no circumstances** in no case; never **5 under the circumstances** because of conditions
WORD ORIGIN Latin CIRCUM- + *stare* to stand
circumstantial *adj* **1** (of evidence) strongly suggesting something but not proving it **2** fully detailed
circumstantiate *vb* **-ating, -ated** to prove by giving details
circumvent *vb formal* **1** to avoid or get round (a rule, restriction, etc.) **2** to outwit (a person) **circumvention** *n*
WORD ORIGIN Latin CIRCUM- + *venire* to come
circus *n, pl* **-cuses 1** a travelling company of entertainers such as acrobats, clowns, trapeze artists, and trained animals **2** a public performance given by such a company **3** *Brit* an open place in a town where several streets meet **4** *informal* a hectic or well-published situation: *her second marriage turned into a media circus* **5** (in ancient Rome) an open-air stadium for chariot races or public games **6** a travelling group of professional sportsmen: *the Formula One circus*
WORD ORIGIN Greek *kirkos* ring
cirque (**sirk**) *n* a steep-sided semicircular hollow found in mountainous areas
cirrhosis (sir-**roh**-siss) *n* a chronic progressive disease of the liver, often caused by drinking too much alcohol
WORD ORIGIN Greek *kirrhos* orange-coloured
cirrocumulus (sirr-oh-**kew**-myew-luss) *n, pl* **-li** (-lie) a high cloud of ice crystals grouped into small separate globular masses
cirrostratus (sirr-oh-**strah**-tuss) *n, pl* **-ti** (-tie) a uniform layer of cloud above about 6000 metres
cirrus *n, pl* **-ri 1** a thin wispy cloud found at high altitudes **2** a plant tendril **3** a slender tentacle in certain sea creatures
WORD ORIGIN Latin: curl
CIS Commonwealth of Independent States
cisalpine *adj* on this (the southern) side of the Alps, as viewed from Rome
cisco *n, pl* **-coes** *or* **-cos** a whitefish, esp. the lake herring of cold deep lakes of North America
WORD ORIGIN from a Native American language
cissy *n, pl* **-sies,** *adj* ▸ same as **sissy**
Cistercian *n* **1** a Christian monk or nun belonging to an especially strict Benedictine order ▹ *adj* **2** of or relating to this order
WORD ORIGIN *Cîteaux,* original home of the order
cistern *n* **1** a water tank, esp. one which holds water for flushing a toilet **2** an underground reservoir
WORD ORIGIN Latin *cista* box
citadel *n* a fortress in a city
WORD ORIGIN Latin *civitas*
citation *n* **1** an official commendation or award, esp. for bravery **2** the quoting of a book or author **3** a quotation
cite ❶ *vb* **citing, cited 1** to quote or refer to (a passage, book, or author) **2** to bring forward as proof **3** to summon to appear before a court of law **4** to mention or commend (someone) for outstanding bravery **5** to enumerate: *the president cited the wonders of the American family*
WORD ORIGIN Old French *citer* to summon
citified *adj often disparaging* having the customs, manners, or dress of city people
citizen ❶ *n* **1** a native or naturalized member of a state or nation **2** an inhabitant of a city or town
citizenry *n* citizens collectively
Citizens' Band *n* a range of radio frequencies for use by the public for private communication
citizenship *n* the condition or status of a citizen, with its rights and duties
citrate *n* any salt or ester of citric acid
citric *adj* of or derived from citrus fruits or citric acid
citric acid *n* a weak acid found especially in citrus fruits and used as a flavouring (**E330**)
citron *n* **1** a lemon-like fruit of a small Asian tree **2** the candied rind of this fruit, for decorating foods
WORD ORIGIN Latin *citrus* citrus tree
citronella *n* **1** a tropical Asian grass with lemon-scented leaves **2** the aromatic oil obtained from this grass
citrus fruit *n* juicy, sharp-tasting fruit such as oranges, lemons, or limes
WORD ORIGIN Latin *citrus* citrus tree
city ❶ *n, pl* **cities 1** any large town **2** (in Britain) a town that has received this title from the Crown **3** the people of a city collectively **4** (in the US and Canada) a large town with its own government established by charter from the state or provincial government
WORD ORIGIN Latin *civis* citizen
City *n* **the City** *Brit* **1** the area in central London in which the United Kingdom's major financial business is transacted **2** the various financial institutions in this area
city editor *n* **1** *Brit* (on a newspaper) the editor in charge of business news **2** *US & Canad* (on a newspaper) the editor in charge of local news
city-state *n ancient history* a state consisting of a sovereign city and its dependencies
civet (**siv**-vit) *n* **1** a spotted catlike mammal of Africa and S Asia **2** the musky fluid produced by this animal, used in perfumes
WORD ORIGIN Arabic *zabād* civet perfume
civic ❶ *adj* of a city or citizens **civically** *adv*
civic centre *n Brit & NZ* a complex of public buildings, including recreational facilities and offices of local government
civics *n* the study of the rights and responsibilities of citizenship
civil ❶ *adj* **1** of or occurring within the state or between citizens: *civil unrest* **2** of or relating to the citizen as an individual: *civil rights* **3** not part of the military, legal or religious structures of a country: *civil aviation* **4** polite or courteous: *he seemed very civil and listened politely* **civilly** *adv*
WORD ORIGIN Latin *civis* citizen
civil defence *n* the organizing of civilians to deal with enemy attacks and natural disasters

THESAURUS

4 = flow, circling, motion, rotation
circumstance *n* **1a** *(usually plural)* **= condition,** situation, scenario, contingency, state of affairs, lie of the land **1b** *(usually plural)* **= detail,** fact, event, particular, respect, factor **2 = chance,** the times, accident, fortune, luck, fate, destiny, misfortune, providence
cite *vb* **1, 2 = quote,** name, evidence, advance, mention, extract, specify, allude to, enumerate, adduce
citizen *n* **1, 2 = inhabitant,** resident, dweller, ratepayer, denizen, subject, freeman, burgher, townsman
▸ *related adjective:* civil
city *n* **1 = town,** metropolis, municipality, conurbation, megalopolis
civic *adj* **= public,** community, borough, municipal, communal, local
civil *adj* **1 = civic,** home, political, domestic, interior, municipal
OPPOSITE: state
4 = polite, obliging, accommodating, civilized, courteous, considerate, affable, courtly, well-bred, complaisant, well-mannered
OPPOSITE: rude

DICTIONARY

civil disobedience *n* a nonviolent protest, such as a refusal to obey laws or pay taxes

civil engineer *n* a person qualified to design and construct public works, such as roads or bridges **civil engineering** *n*

civilian *n* **1** a person who is not a member of the armed forces or police ▹*adj* **2** not relating to the armed forces or police: *civilian clothes*

civility *n, pl* **-ties 1** polite or courteous behaviour **2 civilities** polite words or actions

civilization ⊙ *or* **-lisation** *n* **1** the total culture and way of life of a particular people, nation, region, or period **2** a human society that has a complex cultural, political, and legal organization **3** the races collectively who have achieved such a state **4** cities or populated areas, as contrasted with sparsely inhabited areas **5** intellectual, cultural, and moral refinement

civilize ⊙ *or* **-lise** *vb* **-lizing, -lized** *or* **-lising, -lised 1** to bring out of barbarism into a state of civilization **2** to refine, educate, or enlighten **civilized** *or* **-lised** *adj*

civil law *n* **1** the law of a state, relating to private and civilian affairs **2** a system of law based on that of ancient Rome

civil liberties *pl n* a person's rights to freedom of speech and action

civil list *n* (in Britain) the annual amount given by Parliament to the royal household and the royal family

civil marriage *n law* a marriage performed by an official other than a clergyman

civil rights *pl n* the personal rights of the individual citizen to have equal treatment and equal opportunities

civil servant *n* a member of the civil service

civil service *n* the service responsible for the public administration of the government of a country

civil war *n* war between people of the same country

civvies *pl n Brit, Austral & NZ slang* civilian clothes as opposed to uniform

civvy street *n slang* civilian life

CJD Creutzfeldt-Jakob disease: a fatal virus disease that affects the central nervous system

cl centilitre

Cl *chem* chlorine

clack *n* **1** the sound made by two hard objects striking each other ▹*vb* **2** to make this sound
WORD ORIGIN imitative

clad *vb* ▸a past of **clothe**

cladding *n* **1** the material used to cover the outside of a building **2** a protective metal coating attached to another metal
WORD ORIGIN special use of CLAD

cladistics *n* a method of grouping animals by measurable likenesses
WORD ORIGIN Greek *klados* branch

claim ⊙ *vb* **1** to assert as a fact: *he had claimed to be too ill to return* **2** to demand as a right or as one's property: *you can claim housing benefit to help pay your rent* **3** to call for or need: *this problem claims our attention* **4** to cause the death of: *violence which has claimed at least fifty lives* **5** to succeed in obtaining; win: *she claimed her fifth European tour victory with a closing round of 64* ▹*n* **6** an assertion of something as true or real **7** an assertion of a right; a demand for something as due **8** a right or just title to something: *a claim to fame* **9** anything that is claimed, such as a piece of land staked out by a miner **10 a** a demand for payment in connection with an insurance policy **b** the sum of money demanded **claimant** *n*
WORD ORIGIN Latin *clamare* to shout

Clair *n* **René**, real name *René Chomette*. 1898–1981, French film director; noted for his comedies including *An Italian Straw Hat* (1928) and pioneering sound films such as *Sous les toits de Paris* (1930); later films include *Les Belles de nuit* (1952)

clairvoyance *n* the alleged power of perceiving things beyond the natural range of the senses
WORD ORIGIN French: clear-seeing

clairvoyant *n* **1** a person claiming to have the power to foretell future events ▹*adj* **2** of or possessing clairvoyance

clam *n* an edible shellfish with a hinged shell ▸See also **clam up**
WORD ORIGIN earlier *clamshell* shell that clamps

clamber *vb* **1** to climb awkwardly, using hands and feet ▹*n* **2** a climb performed in this manner
WORD ORIGIN probably variant of *climb*

clammy *adj* **-mier, -miest** unpleasantly moist and sticky **clammily** *adv* **clamminess** *n*
WORD ORIGIN Old English *clǣman* to smear

clamour ⊙ *or US* **clamor** *n* **1** a loud protest **2** a loud and persistent noise or outcry ▹*vb* **3 clamour for** to demand noisily **4** to make a loud noise or outcry **clamorous** *adj*
WORD ORIGIN Latin *clamare* to cry out

clamp¹ ⊙ *n* **1** a mechanical device with movable jaws for holding things together tightly **2** ▸see **wheel clamp** ▹*vb* **3** to fix or fasten with a clamp **4** to immobilize (a car) by means of a wheel clamp
WORD ORIGIN Dutch or Low German *klamp*

clamp² *n* a mound of a harvested root crop, covered with straw and earth to protect it from winter weather
WORD ORIGIN Middle Dutch *klamp* heap

clamp down *vb* **1 clamp down on a** to become stricter about **b** to suppress (something regarded as undesirable) ▹*n* **clampdown 2** a sudden restriction placed on an activity

clam up *vb* **clamming, clammed** *informal* to keep or become silent

clan ⊙ *n* **1** a group of families with a common surname and a common ancestor, esp. among Scottish Highlanders **2** an extended family related by ancestry or marriage: *America's leading political clan, the Kennedys* **3** a group of people with common characteristics, aims, or interests **clansman** *n*
WORD ORIGIN Scottish Gaelic *clann*

Clancy *n* **Tom** born 1947, US novelist; his thrillers, many of which have been filmed, include *The Hunt for Red October* (1984), *Clear and Present Danger* (1989), *Debt of Honour* (1994) and *Red Rabbit* (2002)

clandestine *adj formal* secret and concealed: *a base for clandestine activities* **clandestinely** *adv*
WORD ORIGIN Latin *clam* secretly

clang *vb* **1** to make a loud ringing noise, as metal does when it is struck ▹*n* **2** a ringing metallic noise
WORD ORIGIN Latin *clangere*

clanger *n* **drop a clanger** *informal* to

THESAURUS

civilization *n* **2 = society**, people, community, nation, polity **5 = culture**, development, education, progress, enlightenment, sophistication, advancement, cultivation, refinement

civilize *vb* **1, 2 = cultivate**, improve, polish, educate, refine, tame, enlighten, humanize, sophisticate

claim *vb* **1 = assert**, insist, maintain, allege, uphold, profess, hold **3 = demand**, call for, ask for, insist on ▹*n* **6 = assertion**, statement, allegation, declaration, contention, pretension, affirmation, protestation **7 = demand**, application, request, petition, call **8 = right**, title, entitlement

clamour *n* **2 = noise**, shouting, racket, outcry, din, uproar, agitation, blare, commotion, babel, hubbub, brouhaha, hullabaloo, shout

clamp¹ *n* **1 = vice**, press, grip, bracket, fastener ▹*vb* **3 = fasten**, fix, secure, clinch, brace, make fast

clan *n* **1, 2 = family**, house, group, order, race, society, band, tribe, sept, fraternity, brotherhood, sodality, ainga *(NZ)*, ngai *or* ngati *(NZ)* **3 = group**, set, crowd, circle, crew

DICTIONARY

make a very noticeable mistake
clangour *or US* **clangor** *n* a loud continuous clanging sound **clangorous** *adj*
WORD ORIGIN Latin *clangor*
clank *n* **1** an abrupt harsh metallic sound ▷*vb* **2** to make such a sound
WORD ORIGIN imitative
clannish *adj* (of a group) tending to exclude outsiders: *the villagers can be very clannish*
clap[1] ⊙ *vb* **clapping, clapped 1** to applaud by striking the palms of one's hands sharply together **2** to place or put quickly or forcibly: *in former times he would have been clapped in irons or shot* **3** to strike (a person) lightly with an open hand as in greeting **4** to make a sharp abrupt sound like two objects being struck together **5 clap eyes on** *informal* to catch sight of ▷*n* **6** the act or sound of clapping **7** a sharp abrupt sound, esp. of thunder **8** a light blow
WORD ORIGIN Old English *clæppan*
clap[2] *n slang* gonorrhoea
WORD ORIGIN Old French *clapier* brothel
clapped out *adj informal* worn out; dilapidated
clapper *n* **1** a small piece of metal hanging inside a bell, which causes it to sound when struck against the side **2 like the clappers** *Brit informal* extremely quickly: *he left, pedalling like the clappers*
clapperboard *n* a pair of hinged boards clapped together during film shooting to help in synchronizing sound and picture
Clapton *n* **Eric** born 1945, British rock guitarist, noted for his virtuoso style, his work with the Yardbirds (1963–65), Cream (1966–68), and, with Derek and the Dominos, the album *Layla* (1970); later solo work includes *Unplugged* (1992)
claptrap *n informal* foolish or pretentious talk: *pseudo-intellectual claptrap*
claque *n formal* **1** a group of people hired to applaud **2** a group of fawning admirers
WORD ORIGIN French *claquer* to clap
Clare[1] *n* a county of W Republic of Ireland, in Munster between Galway Bay and the Shannon estuary. County town: Ennis. Pop: 103 277 (2002). Area: 3188 sq km (1231 sq miles)
Clare[2] *n* **1 Anthony** (**Ward**) 1942–2007, Irish psychiatrist and broadcaster; presenter of the radio series *In the Psychiatrist's Chair* from 1982 **2 John** 1793–1864, English poet, noted for his descriptions of country life, particularly in *The Shepherd's Calendar* (1827) and *The Rural Muse* (1835). He was confined in a lunatic asylum from 1837
Clare of Assisi *n* **Saint** 1194–1253, Italian nun; founder of the Franciscan Order of Poor Clares. Feast day: Aug 11
claret (klar-rit) *n* **1** a dry red wine, esp. one from Bordeaux ▷*adj* **2** purplish-red
WORD ORIGIN Latin *clarus* clear
clarify ⊙ *vb* **-fies, -fying, -fied 1** to make or become clear or easy to understand **2** to make or become free of impurities, esp. by heating: *clarified butter* **clarification** *n*
WORD ORIGIN Latin *clarus* clear + *facere* to make
clarinet *n* a keyed woodwind instrument with a single reed **clarinettist** *n*
WORD ORIGIN French *clarinette*
clarion *n* **1** an obsolete high-pitched trumpet **2** its sound
WORD ORIGIN Latin *clarus* clear
clarion call *n* strong encouragement to do something
clarity ⊙ *n* clearness
WORD ORIGIN Latin *claritas*
Clarke *n* **1** Sir **Arthur C**(**harles**) 1917–2008, British science-fiction writer, who helped to develop the first communications satellites. He scripted the film *2001, A Space Odyssey* (1968) **2 Austin** 1896–1974, Irish poet and verse dramatist. His volumes include *The Vengeance of Fionn* (1917), *Night and Morning* (1938), and *Ancient Lights* (1955) **3 Jeremiah** ?1673-1707, English composer and organist, best known for his *Trumpet Voluntary*, formerly attributed to Purcell **4 Kenneth Harry** born 1940, British Conservative politician: secretary of state for health (1988-1990); secretary of state for education (1990-1992); home secretary (1992-93); chancellor of the exchequer (1993-97) **5 Marcus** (**Andrew Hislop**) 1846–81, Australian novelist born in England, noted for his novel *For the Term of His Natural Life*, published in serial form (1870–72); other works include *Twixt Shadow and Shine* (1875)
Clarkson *n* **Thomas** 1760–1846, British campaigner for the abolition of slavery
clash ⊙ *vb* **1** to come into conflict **2** to be incompatible **3** (of dates or events) to coincide **4** (of colours or styles) to look ugly or incompatible together: *patterned fabrics which combine seemingly clashing shades to great effect* **5** to make a loud harsh sound, esp. by striking together ▷*n* **6** a collision or conflict **7** a loud harsh noise
WORD ORIGIN imitative
clasp ⊙ *n* **1** a fastening, such as a catch or hook, for holding things together **2** a firm grasp or embrace ▷*vb* **3** to grasp or embrace tightly **4** to fasten together with a clasp
WORD ORIGIN origin unknown
clasp knife *n* a large knife with blades which fold into the handle
class ⊙ *n* **1** a group of people sharing a similar social and economic position **2** the system of dividing society into such groups **3** a group of people or things sharing a common characteristic **4 a** a group of pupils or students who are taught together **b** a meeting of a group of students for tuition **5** a standard of quality or attainment: *second class* **6** *informal* excellence or elegance, esp. in dress, design, or behaviour: *a full-bodied red wine with real class* **7** *biol* one of the groups into which a phylum is divided, containing one or more orders **8 in a class of its own** *or* **in a class by oneself** without an equal for

THESAURUS

(*informal*), gang, faction, coterie, schism, cabal
clap[1] *vb* **1 = applaud**, cheer, acclaim, give (someone) a big hand
OPPOSITE: boo
clarify *vb* **1 = explain**, resolve, interpret, illuminate, clear up, simplify, make plain, elucidate, explicate, clear the air about, throw *or* shed light on
clarity *n* **= clearness**, precision, simplicity, transparency, lucidity, explicitness, intelligibility, obviousness, straightforwardness, comprehensibility
OPPOSITE: obscurity
clash *vb* **1 = conflict**, grapple, wrangle, lock horns, cross swords, war, feud, quarrel **2 = disagree**, conflict, vary, counter, differ, depart, contradict, diverge, deviate, run counter to, be dissimilar, be discordant **4 = not go**, jar, not match, be discordant **5 = crash**, bang, rattle, jar, clatter, jangle, clang, clank ▷*n* **6a = conflict**, fight, brush, confrontation, collision, showdown (*informal*), boilover (*Austral*) **6b = disagreement**, difference, division, argument, dispute, dissent, difference of opinion
clasp *n* **1 = fastening**, catch, grip, hook, snap, pin, clip, buckle, brooch, fastener, hasp, press stud **2 = grasp**, hold, grip, embrace, hug ▷*vb* **3 = grasp**, hold, press, grip, seize, squeeze, embrace, clutch, hug, enfold
class *n* **3, 7a = group**, grouping, set, order, league, division, rank, caste, status, sphere **3, 7b = type**, set, sort, kind, collection, species, grade, category, stamp, genre, classification, denomination, genus ▷*vb* **10 = classify**, group, rate, rank, brand, label, grade, designate, categorize, codify

C

DICTIONARY

ability, talent, etc. ▹*adj* **9** *informal* excellent, skilful, or stylish: *a class act* ▹*vb* **10** to place in a class
WORD ORIGIN Latin *classis* class, rank

class-conscious *adj* aware of belonging to a particular social rank

classic *adj* **1** serving as a standard or model of its kind; typical: *it is a classic symptom of iron deficiency* **2** of lasting interest or significance because of excellence: *the classic work on Central America* **3** characterized by simplicity and purity of form: *a classic suit* ▹*n* **4** an author, artist, or work of art of the highest excellence **5** a creation or work considered as definitive
WORD ORIGIN Latin *classicus* of the first rank

classical *adj* **1** of or in a restrained conservative style: *it had been built in the 18th century in a severely classical style* **2** *music* **a** in a style or from a period marked by stability of form, intellectualism, and restraint **b** denoting serious art or music in general **3** of or influenced by ancient Greek and Roman culture **4** of the form of a language historically used for formal and literary purposes: *classical Chinese* **5** (of an education) based on the humanities and the study of Latin and Greek **classically** *adv*

classic car *n chiefly Brit* a car that is more than 25 years old

classicism *n* **1** an artistic style based on Greek and Roman models, showing emotional restraint and regularity of form **2** knowledge of the culture of ancient Greece and Rome **classicist** *n*

classics *pl n* **1** the study of ancient Greek and Roman literature and culture **2 the classics a** those works of literature regarded as great or lasting **b** the ancient Greek and Latin languages

classification *n* **1** placing things systematically in categories **2** a division or category in a classifying system **classificatory** *adj*
WORD ORIGIN French

classified *adj* **1** arranged according to some system of classification **2** *government* (of information) not available to people outside a restricted group, esp. for reasons of national security

classify *vb* **-fies, -fying, -fied 1** to arrange or order by classes **2** *government* to declare (information) to be officially secret **classifiable** *adj*

classless *adj* **1** not belonging to a class **2** distinguished by the absence of economic or social distinctions: *a classless society*

classmate *n* a friend or contemporary in the same class of a school

classroom *n* a room in a school where lessons take place

classy *adj* **classier, classiest** *informal* stylish and sophisticated **classiness** *n*

clatter *vb* **1** to make a rattling noise, as when hard objects hit each other ▹*n* **2** a rattling sound or noise
WORD ORIGIN Old English *clatrung* clattering

Claude *n* **Albert** 1898–1983, US cell biologist, born in Belgium: shared the Nobel prize for physiology or medicine (1974) for work on microsomes and mitochondria

Claudel *n* **Paul** (**Louis Charles Marie**) 1868–1955, French dramatist, poet, and diplomat, whose works testify to his commitment to the Roman Catholic faith. His plays include *L'Annonce faite à Marie* (1912) and *Le Soulier de satin* (1919–24)

Claude Lorrain *n* real name *Claude Gelée*. 1600–82, French painter, esp. of idealized landscapes, noted for his subtle depiction of light

Claudius *n* full name *Tiberius Claudius Drusus Nero Germanicus*. 10 BC–54 AD, Roman emperor (41–54); invaded Britain (43); poisoned by his fourth wife, Agrippina

Claudius II *n* full name *Marcus Aurelius Claudius*, called *Gothicus*. 214–270 AD, Roman emperor (268–270)

clause *n* **1** a section of a legal document such as a will or contract **2** *grammar* a group of words, consisting of a subject and a predicate including a finite verb, that does not necessarily constitute a sentence **clausal** *adj*
WORD ORIGIN Latin *clausula* conclusion

Clausewitz *n* **Karl von** 1780–1831, Prussian general, noted for his works on military strategy, esp. *Vom Kriege* (1833)

Clausius *n* **Rudolf Julius** 1822–88, German physicist and mathematician. He enunciated the second law of thermodynamics (1850) and developed the kinetic theory of gases

claustrophobia *n* an abnormal fear of being in a confined space **claustrophobic** *adj*
WORD ORIGIN Latin *claustrum* cloister + -PHOBIA

clavichord *n* an early keyboard instrument with a very soft tone
WORD ORIGIN Latin *clavis* key + *chorda* string

clavicle *n* either of the two bones connecting the shoulder blades with the upper part of the breastbone; the collarbone
WORD ORIGIN Latin *clavis* key

claw *n* **1** a curved pointed nail on the foot of birds, some reptiles, and certain mammals **2** a similar part in some invertebrates, such as a crab's pincer ▹*vb* **3** to scrape, tear, or dig with claws or nails: *she clawed his face with her fingernails* **4** to achieve (something) only after overcoming great difficulties: *he clawed his way to power and wealth; settlers attempting to claw a living from the desert*
WORD ORIGIN Old English *clawu*

claw back *vb* **1** to get back (something) with difficulty **2** to recover (a part of a grant or allowance) in the form of a tax or financial penalty

clay *n* **1** a very fine-grained earth, soft when moist and hardening when baked, used to make bricks and pottery **2** earth or mud **3** *poetic* the material of the human body **clayey, clayish** *or* **claylike** *adj*
WORD ORIGIN Old English *clǣg*

Clay *n* **1 Cassius** ▸ See **Muhammad Ali** **2 Henry** 1777–1852, US statesman and orator; secretary of state (1825–29)

claymore *n* a large two-edged broadsword used formerly by

THESAURUS

classic *adj* **1 = typical**, standard, model, regular, usual, ideal, characteristic, definitive, archetypal, exemplary, quintessential, time-honoured, paradigmatic, dinki-di *(Austral informal)* **2a = masterly**, best, finest, master, world-class, consummate, first-rate **OPPOSITE:** second-rate **2b = lasting**, enduring, abiding, immortal, undying, ageless, deathless ▹*n* **4, 5 = standard**, masterpiece, prototype, paradigm, exemplar, masterwork, model

classification *n* **1 = categorization**, grading, cataloguing, taxonomy, codification, sorting, analysis, arrangement, profiling **2 = class**, grouping, heading, head, order, sort, list, department, type, division, section, rank, grade

classify *vb* **1 = categorize**, sort, file, rank, arrange, grade, catalogue, codify, pigeonhole, tabulate, systematize

classy *adj (informal)* **= high-class**, select, exclusive, superior, elegant, stylish, posh *(informal, chiefly Brit)*, swish *(informal, chiefly Brit)*, up-market, urbane, swanky *(informal)*, top-drawer, ritzy *(slang)*, high-toned, schmick *(Austral informal)*

clause *n* **1 = section**, condition, article, item, chapter, rider, provision, passage, point, part, heading, paragraph, specification, proviso, stipulation

claw *n* **1 = nail**, talon **2 = pincer**, nipper ▹*vb* **3 = scratch**, tear, dig, rip, scrape, graze, maul, scrabble, mangle, mangulate *(Austral slang)*, lacerate

DICTIONARY

Scottish Highlanders
WORD ORIGIN Gaelic *claidheamh mōr* great sword
clay pigeon *n* a disc of baked clay hurled into the air from a machine as a target for shooting
Clayton's *adj Austral & NZ informal* acting as an imitation or substitute: *this latest ploy is simply a Clayton's resignation*
WORD ORIGIN from the trademark of a non-alcoholic drink marketed as 'the drink you have when you're not having a drink'
CLC Canadian Labour Congress
clean ❶ *adj* **1** free from dirt or impurities: *clean water* **2** habitually hygienic and neat **3** morally sound: *clean living* **4** without objectionable language or obscenity: *good clean fun* **5** without anything in it or on it: *a clean sheet of paper* **6** causing little contamination or pollution: *rape seed oil may provide a clean alternative to petrol* **7** recently washed; fresh **8** thorough or complete: *a clean break with the past* **9** skilful and done without fumbling; dexterous: *a clean catch* **10** *sport* played fairly and without fouls **11** free from dishonesty or corruption: *clean government* **12** simple and streamlined in design: *the clean lines and colourful simplicity of these ceramics* **13** (esp. of a driving licence) showing or having no record of offences **14** *slang* **a** innocent **b** not carrying illegal drugs, weapons, etc. ▷ *vb* **15** to make or become free of dirt: *he wanted to help me clean the room* ▷ *adv* **16** in a clean way **17** *not standard* completely: *she clean forgot to face the camera* **18 come clean** *informal* to make a revelation or confession ▷ *n* **19** the act or an instance of cleaning: *the fridge could do with a clean* ▸ See also **clean up**
WORD ORIGIN Old English *clǣne*
clean-cut *adj* **1** clearly outlined **2** wholesome in appearance
cleaner *n* **1** a person, device, or substance that removes dirt **2** a shop or firm that provides a dry-cleaning service **3 take someone to the cleaners** *informal* to rob or defraud someone
cleanly (kleen-lee) *adv* **1** easily or smoothly **2** in a fair manner ▷ *adj* (klen-lee), **-lier, -liest 3** habitually clean or neat **cleanliness** *n*
cleanse ❶ *vb* **cleansing, cleansed 1** to remove dirt from **2** to remove evil or guilt from **cleanser** *n*
clean-shaven *adj* (of men) having the facial hair shaved off
clean sheet *n sport* an instance of conceding no goals or points in a match
clean-tech *informal adj* **1** using clean technology ▷ *n* **2** ▸ same as **clean technology**
clean technology *n* techniques that minimize the damage caused to the environment as a result of manufacturing processes
Cleanthes *n* ?300–?232 BC, Greek philosopher: succeeded Zeno as head of the Stoic school
clean up *vb* **1** to make (something) free from dirt **2** to make tidy or presentable **3** to rid (a place) of undesirable people or conditions **4** *informal* to make a great profit ▷ *n* **cleanup 5** the process of cleaning up
clear ❶ *adj* **1** free from doubt or confusion: *clear evidence of police thuggery* **2** certain in the mind; sure: *I am still not clear about what they can and cannot do* **3** easy to see or hear; distinct **4** perceptive, alert: *clear thinking* **5** evident or obvious: *it is not clear how he died* **6** transparent: *clear glass doors* **7** free from darkness or obscurity; bright **8** (of sounds or the voice) not harsh or hoarse **9** even and pure in tone or colour **10** free of obstruction; open: *a clear path runs under the trees* **11** (of weather) free from dullness or clouds **12** without blemish or defect: *a clear skin* **13** free of suspicion, guilt, or blame: *a clear conscience* **14** (of money) without deduction; net **15** free from debt or obligation **16** without qualification or limitation; complete: *a clear lead* ▷ *adv* **17** in a clear or distinct manner **18** completely **19 clear of** out of the way of: *once we were clear of the harbour we headed east* ▷ *n* **20 in the clear** free of suspicion, guilt, or blame ▷ *vb* **21** to free from doubt or confusion **22** to rid of objects or obstructions **23** to make or form (a path) by removing obstructions **24** to move or pass by or over without contact: *he cleared the fence easily* **25** to make or become free from darkness or obscurity **26** to rid (one's throat) of phlegm **27 a** (of the weather) to become free from dullness, fog, or rain **b** (of mist or fog) to disappear **28** (of a cheque) to pass through one's bank and be charged against one's account **29** to free from impurity or blemish **30** to obtain or give (clearance) **31** to prove (someone) innocent of a crime or mistake **32** to permit (someone) to see or handle classified information **33** to make or gain (money) as profit **34** to discharge or settle (a debt) **35 clear the air** to sort out a misunderstanding ▸ See also **clear away, clear off**, etc. **clearly** *adv*
WORD ORIGIN Latin *clarus*
clearance *n* **1** the act of clearing: *slum clearance* **2** permission for a vehicle or passengers to proceed **3** official permission to have access to secret

THESAURUS

clean *adj* **1, 6 = hygienic**, natural, fresh, sterile, pure, purified, antiseptic, sterilized, unadulterated, uncontaminated, unpolluted, decontaminated
OPPOSITE: contaminated
3, 4, 11 = moral, good, pure, decent, innocent, respectable, upright, honourable, impeccable, exemplary, virtuous, chaste, undefiled
OPPOSITE: immoral
7 = spotless, fresh, washed, immaculate, laundered, impeccable, flawless, sanitary, faultless, squeaky-clean, hygienic, unblemished, unsullied, unstained, unsoiled, unspotted **OPPOSITE:** dirty
8 = complete, final, whole, total, perfect, entire, decisive, thorough, conclusive, unimpaired ▷ *vb*
15 = cleanse, wash, bath, sweep, dust, wipe, vacuum, scrub, sponge, rinse, mop, launder, scour, purify, do up, swab, disinfect, deodorize, sanitize, deep clean **OPPOSITE:** dirty
cleanse *vb* **1 = clean**, wash, scrub, rinse, scour **2 = absolve**, clear, purge, purify
clear *adj* **1, 5 = obvious**, plain, apparent, bold, patent, evident, distinct, pronounced, definite, manifest, blatant, conspicuous, unmistakable, express, palpable, unequivocal, recognizable, unambiguous, unquestionable, cut-and-dried *(informal)*, incontrovertible
OPPOSITE: ambiguous
2 = certain, sure, convinced, positive, satisfied, resolved, explicit, definite, decided **OPPOSITE:** confused
3 = distinct, audible, perceptible
OPPOSITE: indistinct
4 = comprehensible, explicit, articulate, understandable, coherent, lucid, user-friendly, intelligible **OPPOSITE:** confused
6 = transparent, see-through, translucent, crystalline, glassy, limpid, pellucid **OPPOSITE:** opaque
7, 11 = bright, fine, fair, shining, sunny, luminous, halcyon, cloudless, undimmed, light, unclouded
OPPOSITE: cloudy
10 = unobstructed, open, free, empty, unhindered, unimpeded, unhampered **OPPOSITE:** blocked
12, 13 = untroubled, clean, pure, innocent, stainless, immaculate, unblemished, untarnished, guiltless, sinless, undefiled ▷ *vb*
22, 23 = unblock, unclog, free, loosen, extricate, disengage, open, disentangle **24 = pass over**, jump, leap, vault, miss
25, 27a, 27b = brighten, break up, lighten **29 = remove**, clean, wipe, cleanse, tidy (up), sweep away
31 = absolve, acquit, vindicate, exonerate **OPPOSITE:** blame

DICTIONARY

C

information or areas **4** space between two parts in motion

clearance sale *n* a sale in which a shop sells off unwanted goods at reduced prices

clear away *vb* to remove (dishes, etc.) from the table after a meal

clear-cut Ⓣ *adj* **1** easy to distinguish or understand: *there is no clear-cut distinction between safe and unsafe areas of the city* **2** clearly outlined

clearing *n* an area with few or no trees or shrubs in wooded or overgrown land

clearing bank *n* (in Britain) any bank that makes use of the central clearing house in London

clearing house *n* **1** *banking* an institution where cheques and other commercial papers drawn on member banks are cancelled against each other so that only net balances are payable **2** a central agency for the collection and distribution of information or materials

clear off *vb informal* to go away: often used as a command

clear out *vb* **1** to remove and sort the contents of (a room or container) **2** *informal* to go away: often used as a command ▹*n* **clear-out 3** an act of clearing someone or something out

clear up *vb* **1** to put (a place or thing that is disordered) in order **2** to explain or solve (a mystery or misunderstanding) **3** (of an illness) to become better **4** (of the weather) to become brighter

clearway *n Austral & Brit* a stretch of road on which motorists may stop only in an emergency

cleat *n* **1** a wedge-shaped block attached to a structure to act as a support **2** a piece of wood or iron with two projecting ends round which ropes are fastened
WORD ORIGIN Germanic

cleavage *n* **1** the space between a woman's breasts, as revealed by a low-cut dress **2** a division or split **3** (of crystals) the act of splitting or the tendency to split along definite planes so as to make smooth surfaces

cleave¹ *vb* **cleaving; cleft, cleaved** *or* **clove; cleft, cleaved** *or* **cloven 1** to split apart: *cleave the stone along the fissures* **2** to make by or as if by cutting: *a two-lane highway that cleaved its way through the northern extremities of the Everglades*
WORD ORIGIN Old English *clēofan*

cleave² *vb* **cleaving, cleaved** to cling or stick: *a farmhouse cleaved to the hill*
WORD ORIGIN Old English *cleofian*

cleaver *n* a heavy knife with a square blade, used for chopping meat

cleavers *n* a plant with small white flowers and sticky fruits
WORD ORIGIN Old English *clīfe*

Cleese *n* **John** (**Marwood**) born 1939, British comedy writer and actor, noted for the TV series *Monty Python's Flying Circus* (1969–74) and *Fawlty Towers* (1975, 1978). His films include *A Fish Called Wanda* (1988) and *Fierce Creatures* (1997)

clef *n music* a symbol placed at the beginning of each stave indicating the pitch of the music written after it
WORD ORIGIN French

cleft *n* **1** a narrow opening in a rock **2** an indentation or split ▹*adj* **3 in a cleft stick** in a very difficult position ▹*vb* **4** ▸a past of **cleave¹**

cleft palate *n* a congenital crack in the mid line of the hard palate

Cleisthenes *n* 6th century BC, Athenian statesman: democratized the political structure of Athens

Cleland *n* **John** 1709–89, British writer, best known for his bawdy novel *Fanny Hill* (1748–49)

clematis *n* a climbing plant grown for its large colourful flowers
WORD ORIGIN Greek *klēma* vine twig

Clemenceau *n* **Georges Eugène Benjamin** 1841–1929, French statesman; prime minister of France (1906–09; 1917–20); negotiated the Treaty of Versailles (1919)

clemency *n* mercy

Clemens *n* **Samuel Langhorne** ▸See **Twain**

clement *adj* **1** (of the weather) mild **2** merciful
WORD ORIGIN Latin *clemens* mild

Clement I *n* **Saint,** called *Clement of Rome*. pope (?88–?97 AD). Feast day: Nov 23

clementine *n* a citrus fruit resembling a tangerine
WORD ORIGIN French

Clement of Alexandria *n* **Saint** original name *Titus Flavius Clemens*. ?150–?215 AD, Greek Christian theologian: head of the catechetical school at Alexandria; teacher of Origen. Feast day: Dec 5

Clement V *n* original name *Bertrand de Got*. ?1264–1314, pope (1305–14): removed the papal seat from Rome to Avignon in France (1309)

Clement VII *n* original name *Giulio de' Medici*. 1478–1534, pope (1523–34): refused to authorize the annulment of the marriage of Henry VIII of England to Catherine of Aragon (1533)

clench *vb* **1** to close or squeeze together (the teeth or a fist) tightly **2** to grasp or grip firmly ▹*n* **3** a firm grasp or grip
WORD ORIGIN Old English *beclencan*

Clendinnen *n* **Inga** born 1934. Australian historian and writer. Her books include *Reading the Holocaust* (1998) and *Tiger's Eye – a Memoir* (2000)

Cleon *n* died 422 BC, Athenian demagogue and military leader

clerestory (**clear**-store-ee) *n, pl* **-ries** a row of windows in the upper part of the wall of the nave of a church above the roof of the aisle **clerestoried** *adj*
WORD ORIGIN *clear + storey*

clergy Ⓣ *n, pl* **-gies** priests and ministers as a group
WORD ORIGIN see CLERK

clergyman *n, pl* **-men** a member of the clergy

cleric *n* a member of the clergy

clerical *adj* **1** of clerks or office work: *a clerical job* **2** of or associated with the clergy: *a Lebanese clerical leader*

clerical collar *n* a stiff white collar with no opening at the front, worn by the clergy in certain Churches

clerihew *n* a form of comic or satiric verse, consisting of two couplets and containing the name of a well-known person
WORD ORIGIN after E. *Clerihew* Bentley, who invented it

clerk *n* **1** an employee in an office, bank, or court who keeps records, files, and accounts **2** *US & Canad* a hotel receptionist **3** *archaic* a scholar ▹*vb* **4** to work as a clerk **clerkship** *n*
WORD ORIGIN Greek *klērikos* cleric, from *klēros* heritage

clerk of works *n* an employee who oversees building work

clever Ⓣ *adj* **1** displaying sharp intelligence or mental alertness **2** skilful with one's hands **3** smart in a superficial way **4** *Brit informal* sly or cunning **cleverly** *adv* **cleverness** *n*
WORD ORIGIN Middle English *cliver*

clianthus *n* a plant of Australia and New Zealand with clusters of ornamental scarlet flowers

THESAURUS

clear-cut *adj* **1 = straightforward**, specific, plain, precise, black-and-white, explicit, definite, unequivocal, unambiguous, cut-and-dried *(informal)*

clergy *n* **= priesthood**, ministry, clerics, clergymen, churchmen, the cloth, holy orders, ecclesiastics

clever *adj* **1 = intelligent**, quick, bright, talented, gifted, keen, capable, smart, sensible, rational, witty, apt, discerning, knowledgeable, astute, brainy *(informal)*, quick-witted, sagacious, knowing, deep, expert
OPPOSITE: stupid
2 = skilful, able, talented, gifted, capable, inventive, adroit, dexterous
OPPOSITE: inept
4 = shrewd, bright, cunning, ingenious, inventive, astute, resourceful, canny
OPPOSITE: unimaginative

cliché *n* **= platitude**, stereotype,

WORD ORIGIN probably from Greek *kleos* glory + *anthos* flower

cliché (klee-shay) ❶ *n* an expression or idea that is no longer effective because of overuse **clichéd** *or* **cliché'd** *adj*
WORD ORIGIN French

click *n* **1** a short light often metallic sound ▷*vb* **2** to make a clicking sound: *cameras clicked and whirred* **3** Also: **click on** *computers* to press and release (a button on a mouse) or select (a particular function) by pressing and releasing a button on a mouse **4** *informal* to become suddenly clear: *it wasn't until I saw the photograph that everything clicked into place* **5** *slang* (of two people) to get on well together: *I met him at a dinner party and we clicked straight away* **6** *slang* to be a great success: *the film cost so much that if it hadn't clicked at the box office we'd have been totally wiped out*
WORD ORIGIN imitative

client ❶ *n* **1** someone who uses the services of a professional person or organization **2** a customer **3** *computers* a program or work station that requests data from a server
WORD ORIGIN Latin *cliens* retainer

clientele (klee-on-**tell**) *n* customers or clients collectively

cliff ❶ *n* a steep rock face, esp. along the seashore
WORD ORIGIN Old English *clif*

cliffhanger *n* a film, game, etc. which is exciting and full of suspense because its outcome is uncertain **cliffhanging** *adj*

climacteric *n* **1** ▸ same as **menopause** **2** the period in the life of a man corresponding to the menopause, during which sexual drive and fertility diminish
WORD ORIGIN Greek *klimakter* rung of a ladder

climate ❶ *n* **1** the typical weather conditions of an area **2** an area with a particular kind of climate **3** a prevailing trend: *the current economic climate* **climatic** *adj* **climatically** *adv*
WORD ORIGIN Greek *klima* inclination, region

climax ❶ *n* **1** the most intense or highest point of an experience or of a series of events: *a striking climax to the year's efforts to promote tourism* **2** a decisive moment in a dramatic or other work: *the film has a climax set atop a gale-swept lighthouse* **3** an orgasm ▷*vb* **4** *not standard* to reach or bring to a climax **climactic** *adj*
WORD ORIGIN Greek *klimax* ladder

climb ❶ *vb* **1** to go up or ascend (stairs, a mountain, etc.) **2** to move or go with difficulty: *she climbed through a window* **3** to rise to a higher point or intensity: *I grew increasingly delirious as my temperature climbed* **4** to increase in value or amount: *the number could eventually climb to half-a-million* **5** to ascend in social position: *he climbed the ranks of the organization* **6** (of plants) to grow upwards by twining, using tendrils or suckers **7** to incline or slope upwards: *the road climbed up through the foothills* **8** **climb into** *informal* to put on or get into: *I climbed into the van* ▷*n* **9** the act or an instance of climbing **10** a place or thing to be climbed, esp. a route in mountaineering **climbable** *adj* **climber** *n* **climbing** *n, adj*
WORD ORIGIN Old English *climban*

climb down *vb* **1** to retreat (from an opinion or position) ▷*n* **climb-down** **2** a retreat from an opinion or position

clime *n poetic* a region or its climate

clinch ❶ *vb* **1** to settle (an argument or agreement) decisively **2** to secure (a nail) by bending the protruding point over **3** to engage in a clinch, as in boxing or wrestling ▷*n* **4** the act of clinching **5** *boxing, wrestling* a movement in which one or both competitors hold on to the other to avoid punches or regain wind **6** *slang* a lovers' embrace
WORD ORIGIN variant of *clench*

clincher *n informal* something decisive, such as fact, argument, or point scored

Cline *n* **Patsy**, original name *Virginia Patterson Hensley*. 1932–63, US country singer; her bestselling records include "Walking After Midnight", "I Fall to Pieces", and "Leavin' On Your Mind"

cling ❶ *vb* **clinging, clung** **1** (often foll. by *to*) to hold fast or stick closely (to something) **2** to be emotionally overdependent on **3** to continue to do or believe in: *he clings to the belief that people are capable of change* **clinging** *or* **clingy** *adj*
WORD ORIGIN Old English *clingan*

clingfilm *n Brit* a thin polythene material used for wrapping food

clinic *n* **1** a place in which outpatients are given medical treatment or advice **2** a similar place staffed by specialist physicians or surgeons: *I have an antenatal clinic on Friday afternoon* **3** *Brit & NZ* a private hospital or nursing home **4** the teaching of medicine to students at the bedside
WORD ORIGIN Greek *klinē* bed

clinical ❶ *adj* **1** of or relating to the observation and treatment of patients directly: *clinical trials of a new drug* **2** of or relating to a clinic **3** logical and unemotional: *they have a somewhat clinical attitude to their children's upbringing* **4** (of a room or buildings) plain, simple, and usually unattractive **clinically** *adv*

clinical thermometer *n* a thermometer for measuring the temperature of the body

clink[1] *vb* **1** to make a light sharp metallic sound ▷*n* **2** such a sound
WORD ORIGIN perhaps from Middle Dutch *klinken*

clink[2] *n slang* prison
WORD ORIGIN after *Clink*, a former prison in London

clinker *n* the fused coal left over in a fire or furnace
WORD ORIGIN Dutch *klinker* a type of brick

clinker-built *adj* (of a boat or ship) with a hull made from overlapping planks
WORD ORIGIN obsolete *clinker* a nailing together, probably from *clinch*

Clio *n Greek myth* the Muse of history

clip[1] ❶ *vb* **clipping, clipped** **1** to cut or trim with scissors or shears **2** to remove a short section from (a film or newspaper) **3** *Austral & Brit* to punch a hole in (something, esp. a ticket) **4** *informal* to strike with a sharp, often slanting, blow **5** to shorten (a word) **6** *slang* to obtain (money) by cheating ▷*n* **7** the act of clipping **8** a short extract from a film **9** something that has been clipped **10** *informal* a sharp, often

THESAURUS

commonplace, banality, truism, bromide, old saw, hackneyed phrase, chestnut *(informal)*

client *n* **1, 2 = customer**, consumer, buyer, patron, shopper, habitué, patient

cliff *n* **= rock face**, overhang, crag, precipice, escarpment, face, scar, bluff

climate *n* **1, 2 = weather**, country, region, temperature, clime

climax *n* **1 = culmination**, head, top, summit, height, highlight, peak, pay-off *(informal)*, crest, high point, zenith, apogee, high spot *(informal)*, acme, ne plus ultra *(Latin)*

climb *vb* **1 = ascend**, scale, mount, go up, clamber, shin up **2 = clamber**, descend, scramble, dismount **3 = rise**, go up, soar, ascend, fly up

clinch *vb* **1a = secure**, close, confirm, conclude, seal, verify, sew up *(informal)*, set the seal on **1b = settle**, decide, determine, tip the balance

cling *vb* **1a = clutch**, grip, embrace, grasp, hug, hold on to, clasp **1b = stick to**, attach to, adhere to, fasten to, twine round

clinical *adj* **3 = unemotional**, cold, scientific, objective, detached, analytic, impersonal, antiseptic, disinterested, dispassionate, emotionless

clip[1] *vb* **1 = trim**, cut, crop, dock, prune, shorten, shear, cut short, snip, pare **4** *(informal)* **= smack**, strike, box,

DICTIONARY

slanting, blow: *a clip on the ear* **11** *informal* speed: *proceeding at a smart clip* **12** *Austral & NZ* the total quantity of wool shorn, as in one place or season
WORD ORIGIN Old Norse *klippa* to cut

C

clip² ❶ *n* **1** a device for attaching or holding things together **2** an article of jewellery that can be clipped onto a dress or hat **3** ▸ short for **paperclip** or **cartridge clip** ▹ *vb* **clipping, clipped 4** to attach or hold together with a clip
WORD ORIGIN Old English *clyppan* to embrace

clipboard *n* a portable writing board with a clip at the top for holding paper

clip joint *n slang* a nightclub in which customers are overcharged

clipped *adj* (of speech) abrupt, clearly pronounced, and using as few words as possible

clipper *n* a fast commercial sailing ship

clippers *pl n* a tool used for clipping and cutting

clippie *n Brit old-fashioned informal* a bus conductress

clipping *n* something cut out, esp. an article from a newspaper

clique (kleek) *n* a small exclusive group of friends or associates **cliquey, cliquy** *or* **cliquish** *adj*
WORD ORIGIN French

Clisthenes *n* ▸ a variant spelling of **Cleisthenes**

clit *n taboo Slang* ▸ short for **clitoris**

clitoris (klit-or-riss) *n* a small sexually sensitive organ at the front of the vulva **clitoral** *adj*
WORD ORIGIN Greek *kleitoris*

Clive *n* **Robert,** Baron Clive of Plassey. 1725–74, British general and statesman, whose victory at Plassey (1757) strengthened British control in India

Cllr councillor

cloaca (kloh-ake-a) *n, pl* **-cae** a cavity in most animals, except higher mammals, into which the alimentary canal and the genital and urinary ducts open
WORD ORIGIN Latin: sewer

cloak ❶ *n* **1** a loose sleeveless outer garment, fastened at the throat and falling straight from the shoulders **2** something that covers or conceals ▹ *vb* **3** to hide or disguise **4** to cover with or as if with a cloak
WORD ORIGIN Medieval Latin *clocca* cloak, bell

cloak-and-dagger *adj* of or involving mystery and secrecy

cloakroom *n* **1** a room in which coats may be left temporarily **2** *Brit, euphemistic* a toilet

clobber¹ *vb informal* **1** to batter **2** to defeat utterly **3** to criticize severely
WORD ORIGIN origin unknown

clobber² *n Brit, Austral & NZ informal* personal belongings, such as clothes
WORD ORIGIN origin unknown

cloche (klosh) *n* **1** *Brit, Austral & NZ* a small glass or plastic cover for protecting young plants **2** a woman's close-fitting hat
WORD ORIGIN French: bell

clock¹ *n* **1** a device for showing the time, either through pointers that revolve over a numbered dial, or through a display of figures **2** a device with a dial for recording or measuring **3** the downy head of a dandelion that has gone to seed **4** ▸ short for **time clock 5** *informal* ▸ same as **speedometer** or **mileometer 6** *Brit slang* the face **7 round the clock** all day and all night ▹ *vb* **8** to record (time) with a stopwatch, esp. in the calculation of speed **9** *Brit, Austral & NZ slang* to strike, esp. on the face or head **10** *informal* to turn back the mileometer on (a car) illegally so that its mileage appears less **11** *Brit slang* to see or notice
WORD ORIGIN Medieval Latin *clocca* bell

clock² *n* an ornamental design on the side of a sock
WORD ORIGIN origin unknown

clock in *or* **on** *vb* to register one's arrival at work on an automatic time recorder

clock out *or* **off** *vb* to register one's departure from work on an automatic time recorder

clock up *vb* to record or reach (a total): *he has now clocked up over 500 games for the club*

clockwise *adv, adj* in the direction in which the hands of a clock rotate

clockwork *n* **1** a mechanism similar to that of a spring-driven clock, as in a wind-up toy **2 like clockwork** with complete regularity and precision

clod *n* **1** a lump of earth or clay **2** *Brit, Austral & NZ* a dull or stupid person **cloddish** *adj*
WORD ORIGIN Old English

clodhopper *n informal* **1** a clumsy person **2 clodhoppers** large heavy shoes

clog ❶ *vb* **clogging, clogged 1** to obstruct or become obstructed with thick or sticky matter **2** to encumber **3** to stick in a mass ▹ *n* **4** a wooden or wooden-soled shoe
WORD ORIGIN origin unknown

cloisonné (klwah-zon-nay) *n* a design made by filling in a wire outline with coloured enamel
WORD ORIGIN French

cloister *n* **1** a covered pillared walkway within a religious building **2** a place of religious seclusion, such as a monastery ▹ *vb* **3** to confine or seclude in or as if in a monastery
WORD ORIGIN Medieval Latin *claustrum* monastic cell, from Latin *claudere* to close

cloistered *adj* sheltered or protected

clomp *n, vb* ▸ same as **clump** (senses 2, 3)

clone *n* **1** a group of organisms or cells of the same genetic constitution that have been reproduced asexually from a single plant or animal **2** *informal* a person who closely resembles another **3** *slang* a mobile phone that has been given the electronic identity of an existing mobile phone, so that calls made on it are charged to that owner ▹ *vb* **cloning, cloned 4** to produce as a clone **5** *informal* to produce near copies of (a person) **6** *slang* to give (a mobile phone) the electronic identity of an existing mobile phone so that calls made on it are charged to that owner **cloning** *n*
WORD ORIGIN Greek *klōn* twig, shoot

clonk *vb* **1** to make a loud dull thud **2** *informal* to hit ▹ *n* **3** a loud thud
WORD ORIGIN imitative

Clooney *n* **George** born 1961, US film actor; he starred in the television series ER (1994–99) and the films *The Perfect Storm* (2000), and *Ocean's Eleven* (2001), *Confessions of a Dangerous Mind* (2002, also directed), and *Syriana* (2005, also directed)

close¹ ❶ *vb* **closing, closed 1** to shut: *he lay back and closed his eyes* **2** to bar, obstruct, or fill up (an entrance, a hole, etc.): *the blockades had closed major roads, railways and border crossings* **3** to cease or cause to cease giving service: *both stores closed at 9 p.m.; the Shipping Company closed its offices in Bangkok* **4** to end; terminate: *'Never,' she said, so firmly that it closed the subject* **5** (of

THESAURUS

knock, punch, belt (*informal*), thump, clout (*informal*), cuff, whack, wallop (*informal*), skelp (*dialect*) ▹ *n* **10** (*informal*) **= smack**, strike, box, knock, punch, belt (*informal*), thump, clout (*informal*), cuff, whack, wallop (*informal*), skelp (*dialect*)

clip² *vb* **4 = attach**, fix, secure, connect, pin, staple, fasten, affix, hold

cloak *n* **1 = cape**, coat, wrap, mantle **2 = covering**, layer, blanket, shroud ▹ *vb* **3 = hide**, cover, screen, mask, disguise, conceal, obscure, veil, camouflage **4 = cover**, coat, wrap, blanket, shroud, envelop

clog *vb* **1 = obstruct**, block, jam, hamper, hinder, impede, bung, stop up, dam up, occlude, congest

close¹ *vb* **1 = shut**, lock, push to, fasten, secure **OPPOSITE:** open **2 = block up**, bar, seal, shut up **OPPOSITE:** open **3 = shut down**, finish, cease,

agreements or deals) to complete or be completed successfully **6** to come closer (to): *he was still in second place but closing fast on the leader* **7** to take hold: *his small fingers closed around the coin* **8** *stock Exchange* to have a value at the end of a day's trading, as specified: *the pound closed four-and-a-half cents higher* **9** to join the ends or edges of something: *to close a circuit* ▷*n* **10** the act of closing **11** the end or conclusion: *the close of play* **12** (rhymes with **dose**) *Brit* a courtyard or quadrangle enclosed by buildings **13** *Scot* the entry from the street to a tenement building ▸See also **close down, close in,** etc.
WORD ORIGIN Latin *claudere*

close² ⓣ *adj* **1** near in space or time **2** intimate: *we were such close friends in those days* **3** near in relationship: *the dead man seems to have had no close relatives* **4** careful, strict, or searching: *their research will not stand up to close scrutiny* **5** having the parts near together: *a close formation* **6** near to the surface; short: *an NCO's haircut, cropped close on top, shaved clean at sides and back* **7** almost equal: *a close game* **8** not deviating or varying greatly from something: *a close resemblance* **9** confined or enclosed **10** oppressive, heavy, or airless: *damp, close weather* **11** strictly guarded: *he had been placed in close arrest* **12** secretive or reticent **13** miserly; not generous **14** restricted as to public admission or membership ▷*adv* **15** closely; tightly **16** near or in proximity
closely *adv* **closeness** *n*
WORD ORIGIN Old French *clos*

closed ⓣ *adj* **1** blocked against entry **2** only admitting a selected group of people; exclusive: *he had a fairly closed circle of friends* **3** not open to question or debate **4** *maths* **a** (of a curve or surface) completely enclosing an area or volume **b** (of a set) made up of members on which a specific operation, such as addition, gives as its result another existing member of the set

closed circuit *n* a complete electrical circuit through which current can flow

closed-circuit television *n* a television system used within a limited area such as a building

close down *vb* **1** to stop operating or working: *the factory closed down many years ago* ▷*n* **close-down 2** *Brit & NZ radio, television* the end of a period of broadcasting

closed shop *n Brit, Austral & NZ* (formerly) a place of work in which all workers had to belong to a particular trade union

close harmony *n* a type of singing in which all parts except the bass lie close together

close in *vb* **1** (of days) to become shorter with the approach of winter **2 close in on** to advance on so as to encircle or surround

close quarters *pl n* **at close quarters a** engaged in hand-to-hand combat **b** very near together

close season *n* **1** the period of the year when it is illegal to kill certain game or fish **2** *sport* the period of the year when there is no domestic competition

close shave *n informal* a narrow escape

closet *n* **1** *US & Austral* a small cupboard **2** a small private room **3** ▸short for **water closet** ▷*adj* **4** private or secret: *a closet homosexual* ▷*vb* **-eting, -eted 5** to shut away in private, esp. in order to talk: *he was closeted with the President*
WORD ORIGIN Old French *clos* enclosure

close-up *n* **1** a photograph or film or television shot taken at close range **2** a detailed or intimate view or examination ▷*vb* **close up 3** to shut entirely: *every other shop front seemed to be closed up* **4** to draw together: *the ranks closed up and marched on* **5** (of wounds) to heal completely

close with *vb* to engage in battle with (an enemy)

Clostridium difficile *n* a bacterium of the human intestine which is a common cause of colitis in hospital patients. Often shortened to: **C.diff, C.difficile**

closure *n* **1** the act of closing or the state of being closed **2** something that closes or shuts **3** a procedure by which a debate may be stopped and an immediate vote taken **4** *chiefly US* **a** a resolution of a significant event or relationship in a person's life **b** the sense of contentment experienced after such a resolution

clot *n* **1** a soft thick lump formed from liquid **2** *informal* a stupid person ▷*vb* **clotting, clotted 3** to form soft thick lumps
WORD ORIGIN Old English *clott*

cloth ⓣ *n, pl* **cloths 1** a fabric formed by weaving, felting, or knitting fibres **2** a piece of such fabric used for a particular purpose **3 the cloth** the clergy
WORD ORIGIN Old English *clāth*

clothe ⓣ *vb* **clothing, clothed** *or* **clad 1** to put clothes on **2** to provide with clothes **3** to cover or envelop (something) so as to change its appearance: *a small valley clothed in thick woodland*
WORD ORIGIN Old English *clāthian*

clothes ⓣ *pl n* **1** articles of dress **2** *chiefly Brit* ▸short for **bedclothes**
WORD ORIGIN Old English *clāthas*, plural of *clāth* cloth

clotheshorse *n* **1** a frame on which to hang laundry for drying or airing

C

THESAURUS

discontinue **3, 4 = wind up**, finish, axe *(informal)*, shut down, terminate, discontinue, mothball **4 = end**, finish, complete, conclude, wind up, culminate, terminate
OPPOSITE: begin
5 = clinch, confirm, secure, conclude, seal, verify, sew up *(informal)*, set the seal on **7 = come together**, join, connect
OPPOSITE: separate
▷*n* **11 = end**, ending, finish, conclusion, completion, finale, culmination, denouement

close² *adj* **1 = near**, neighbouring, nearby, handy, adjacent, adjoining, hard by, just round the corner, within striking distance *(informal)*, cheek by jowl, proximate, within spitting distance *(informal)*, within sniffing distance, a hop, skip and a jump away **OPPOSITE:** far
1, 16 = imminent, near, approaching, impending, at hand, upcoming, nigh, just round the corner
OPPOSITE: far away
2 = intimate, loving, friendly, familiar, thick *(informal)*, attached, devoted, confidential, inseparable, dear **OPPOSITE:** distant
4 = careful, detailed, searching, concentrated, keen, intense, minute, alert, intent, thorough, rigorous, attentive, painstaking, assiduous
7 = even, level, neck and neck, fifty-fifty *(informal)*, evenly matched, equally balanced **8 = noticeable**, marked, strong, distinct, pronounced **9, 10 = stifling**, confined, oppressive, stale, suffocating, stuffy, humid, sweltering, airless, muggy, unventilated, heavy, thick
OPPOSITE: airy

closed *adj* **1 = shut**, locked, sealed, fastened **OPPOSITE:** open
2 = exclusive, select, restricted
3 = finished, over, ended, decided, settled, concluded, resolved, terminated

cloth *n* **1 = fabric**, material, textiles, dry goods, stuff

clothe *vb* **1, 2 = dress**, outfit, rig, array, robe, drape, get ready, swathe, apparel, attire, fit out, garb, doll up *(slang)*, accoutre, cover, deck
OPPOSITE: undress

clothes *pl n* **1 = clothing**, wear, dress, gear *(informal)*, habits, get-up *(informal)*, outfit, costume, threads *(slang)*, wardrobe, ensemble, garments, duds *(informal)*, apparel, clobber *(Brit slang)*, attire, garb, togs *(informal)*, vestments, glad rags *(informal)*, raiment *(archaic, poetic)*, rigout *(informal)*

C

DICTIONARY

2 a person who is extremely concerned with his or her appearance
clothesline *n* a piece of rope from which clean washing is hung to dry
clothes peg *n* a small wooden or plastic clip for attaching washing to a clothesline
clothier *n* a person who makes or sells clothes or cloth
clothing ● *n* **1** garments collectively **2** something that covers or clothes
Clotilda *n* ?475–?545 AD, wife of Clovis I of the Franks, whom she converted (496) to Christianity
clotted cream *n Brit* a thick cream made from scalded milk
cloud ● *n* **1** a mass of water or ice particles visible in the sky **2** a floating mass of smoke, dust, etc. **3** a large number of insects or other small animals in flight **4** something that darkens, threatens, or carries gloom **5 in the clouds** not in contact with reality **6 on cloud nine** *informal* elated; very happy **7 under a cloud a** under reproach or suspicion **b** in a state of gloom or bad temper ▷ *vb* **8** to make or become more difficult to see through: *my glasses kept clouding up; mud clouded the water* **9** to confuse or impair: *his judgment was no longer clouded by alcohol* **10** to make or become gloomy or depressed: *insanity clouded the last years of his life* ▸ See also **cloud over** > **cloudless** *adj*
WORD ORIGIN Old English *clūd* rock, hill
cloudburst *n* a heavy fall of rain
cloud chamber *n physics* an apparatus for detecting high-energy particles by observing their tracks through a chamber containing a supersaturated vapour
cloud-cuckoo-land *n* a place of fantasy or impractical ideas
cloud over *vb* **1** (of the sky or weather) to become cloudy: *it was clouding over and we thought it would rain* **2** (of a person's face or eyes) to suddenly look gloomy or depressed: *Grace's face clouded over and she turned away*
cloudy *adj* **cloudier, cloudiest** **1** covered with cloud or clouds **2** (of liquids) opaque or muddy **3** confused or unclear **cloudily** *adv* **cloudiness** *n*
Clouet *n* **François**, ?1515–72, and his father, **Jean**, ?1485–?1540, French portrait painters
Clough *n* **1 Arthur Hugh** 1819–61, British poet, author of *Amours de Voyage* (1858) and *Dipsychus* (1865) **2 Brian** 1935–2004, English footballer and manager
clout ● *n* **1** *informal* a fairly hard blow **2** power or influence ▷ *vb* **3** *informal* to hit hard
WORD ORIGIN Old English *clūt* piece of cloth
clove[1] *n* a dried closed flower bud of a tropical tree, used as a spice
WORD ORIGIN Latin *clavus* nail
clove[2] *n* a segment of a bulb of garlic
WORD ORIGIN Old English *clufu* bulb
clove[3] *vb* ▸ a past tense of **cleave**[1]
clove hitch *n* a knot used to fasten a rope to a spar or a larger rope
cloven *vb* **1** ▸ a past participle of **cleave**[1] ▷ *adj* **2** split or divided
cloven hoof *or* **foot** *n* the divided hoof of a pig, goat, cow, or deer
clover *n* **1** a plant with three-lobed leaves and dense flower heads **2 in clover** *informal* in ease or luxury
WORD ORIGIN Old English *clāfre*
Clovis I *n* German name *Chlodwig*. ?466–511 AD, king of the Franks (481–511), who extended the Merovingian kingdom to include most of Gaul and SW Germany
clown ● *n* **1** a comic entertainer, usually bizarrely dressed and made up, appearing in the circus **2** an amusing person **3** a clumsy rude person ▷ *vb* **4** to behave foolishly **5** to perform as a clown **clownish** *adj*
WORD ORIGIN origin unknown
cloying *adj* so sweet or pleasurable that it ultimately becomes sickly: *cloying sentimentality* **cloyingly** *adv*
WORD ORIGIN Middle English *cloy* originally to nail, hence, to obstruct
club ● *n* **1** a group or association of people with common aims or interests **2** the building used by such a group **3** a stout stick used as a weapon **4** a stick or bat used to strike the ball in various sports, esp. golf **5** an establishment or regular event at which people dance to records; disco: *a new weekly club with resident DJ* **6** a building in which members go to meet, dine, read, etc. **7** *chiefly Brit* an organization, esp. in a shop, set up as a means of saving **8** a playing card marked with one or more black trefoil symbols **9** ▸ short for **Indian club** ▷ *vb* **clubbing, clubbed 10** to beat with a club **11 club together** to combine resources or efforts for a common purpose
WORD ORIGIN Old Norse *klubba*
club class *n* **1** a class of air travel which is less luxurious than first class but more luxurious than economy class ▷ *adj* **club-class 2** of this class of air travel
club foot *n* a congenital deformity of the foot
clubhouse *n* the premises of a sports or other club, esp. a golf club
club root *n* a fungal disease of cabbages and related plants, in which the roots become thickened and distorted
cluck *n* **1** the low clicking noise made by a hen ▷ *vb* **2** (of a hen) to make a clicking sound **3** to express (a feeling) by making a similar sound: *the landlady was clucking feverishly behind them*
WORD ORIGIN imitative
clue ● *n* **1** something that helps to solve a problem or unravel a mystery **2 not have a clue a** to be completely baffled **b** to be ignorant or incompetent ▷ *adj* **3 clued-up** shrewd and well-informed
WORD ORIGIN variant of *clew* ball of thread
clueless *adj slang* helpless or stupid
clump ● *n* **1** a small group of things or people together **2** a dull heavy tread ▷ *vb* **3** to walk or tread heavily **4** to form into clumps **clumpy** *adj*
WORD ORIGIN Old English *clympe*
clumsy ● *adj* **-sier, -siest 1** lacking in

THESAURUS

clothing *n* **1 = clothes**, wear, dress, gear (*informal*), habits, get-up (*informal*), outfit, costume, threads (*slang*), wardrobe, ensemble, garments, duds (*informal*), apparel, clobber (*Brit slang*), attire, garb, togs (*informal*), vestments, glad rags (*informal*), raiment (*archaic, poetic*), rigout (*informal*)
cloud *n* **1 = mist**, fog, haze, obscurity, vapour, nebula, murk, darkness, gloom ▷ *vb* **8 = darken**, dim, be overshadowed, be overcast **9 = confuse**, obscure, distort, impair, muddle, disorient
clout *n* **1 = thump**, blow, crack, punch, slap, sock (*slang*), cuff, wallop (*informal*), skelp (*dialect*) **2 = influence**, power, standing, authority, pull, weight, bottom, prestige, mana (*NZ*) ▷ *vb* **3 = hit**, strike, punch, deck (*slang*), slap, sock (*slang*), chin (*slang*), smack, thump, cuff, clobber (*slang*), wallop (*informal*), box, wham, lay one on (*slang*), skelp (*dialect*)
clown *n* **1 = comedian**, fool, harlequin, jester, buffoon, pierrot, dolt **2 = joker**, comic, prankster ▷ *vb* **4** (*usually with* **around**) **= play the fool**, mess about, jest, act the fool, act the goat, play the goat
club *n* **1 = association**, company, group, union, society, circle, lodge, guild, fraternity, set, order, sodality **3 = stick**, bat, bludgeon, truncheon, cosh (*Brit*), cudgel ▷ *vb* **10 = beat**, strike, hammer, batter, bash, clout (*informal*), bludgeon, clobber (*slang*), pummel, cosh (*Brit*), beat *or* knock seven bells out of (*informal*)
clue *n* **1 = indication**, lead, sign, evidence, tip, suggestion, trace, hint, suspicion, pointer, tip-off, inkling, intimation
clump *n* **1 = cluster**, group, bunch, bundle, shock ▷ *vb* **3 = stomp**, stamp, stump, thump, lumber, tramp, plod, thud, clomp

skill or physical coordination: *an extraordinarily clumsy player* **2** badly made or done **3** said or done without thought or tact: *I took the clumsy hint and left* **clumsily** *adv* **clumsiness** *n*
WORD ORIGIN Middle English *clumse* to benumb

clung *vb* ▸ the past of **cling**

clunk *n* **1** a dull metallic sound ▹ *vb* **2** to make such a sound
WORD ORIGIN imitative

cluster ❶ *n* **1** a number of things growing, fastened, or occurring close together **2** a number of people or things grouped together ▹ *vb* **3** to gather or be gathered in clusters
WORD ORIGIN Old English *clyster*

clutch¹ ❶ *vb* **1** to seize with or as if with hands or claws **2** to grasp or hold firmly **3 clutch at** to attempt to get hold or possession of ▹ *n* **4** a device that enables two revolving shafts to be joined or disconnected, esp. one that transmits the drive from the engine to the gearbox in a vehicle **5** the pedal which operates the clutch in a car **6** a firm grasp **7 clutches a** hands or claws in the act of clutching: *his free kick escaped the clutches of the rival goalkeeper* **b** power or control: *rescued from the clutches of the Gestapo*
WORD ORIGIN Old English *clyccan*

clutch² *n* **1** a set of eggs laid at the same time **2** a group, bunch, or cluster: *a clutch of gloomy economic reports*
WORD ORIGIN Old Norse *klekja* to hatch

clutch bag *n* a handbag without handles

clutter ❶ *vb* **1** to scatter objects about (a place) in an untidy manner ▹ *n* **2** an untidy heap or mass of objects **3** a state of untidiness
WORD ORIGIN Middle English *clotter*

Clydesdale *n* a heavy powerful carthorse, originally from Scotland

cm centimetre

Cm *chem* curium

Cmdr Commander

CND Campaign for Nuclear Disarmament

CNS *biol* central nervous system

Co *chem* cobalt

CO **1** Colorado **2** Commanding Officer

Co.¹ *or* **co.** **1** Company **2 and co.** *informal* and the rest of them: *Harold and co.*

Co.² County

co- *prefix* **1** together; joint or jointly: *coproduction* **2** indicating partnership or equality: *co-star; copilot* **3** to the same or a similar degree: *coextend* **4** (in mathematics and astronomy) of the complement of an angle: *cosecant*
WORD ORIGIN Latin; see COM-

c/o **1** care of **2** *book-keeping* carried over

coach ❶ *n* **1** a large comfortable single-decker bus used for sightseeing or long-distance travel **2** a railway carriage **3** a large four-wheeled enclosed carriage, usually horse-drawn **4** a trainer or instructor: *the coach of the Mexican national team* **5** a tutor who prepares students for examinations ▹ *vb* **6** to train or teach **coaching** *n*
WORD ORIGIN from *Kocs*, village in Hungary where horse-drawn coaches were first made

coachman *n, pl* **-men** the driver of a horse-drawn coach or carriage

coachwork *n* the body of a car

coagulate (koh-**ag**-yew-late) *vb* **-lating, -lated** to change from a liquid into a soft semisolid mass; clot **coagulant** *n* **coagulation** *n*
WORD ORIGIN Latin *coagulare*

coal *n* **1** a compact black or dark brown rock consisting largely of carbon formed from partially decomposed vegetation: a fuel and a source of coke, coal gas, and coal tar **2** one or more lumps of coal **3 coals to Newcastle** something supplied to a place where it is already plentiful
WORD ORIGIN Old English *col*

coalesce (koh-a-**less**) *vb* **-lescing, -lesced** to unite or come together in one body or mass **coalescence** *n* **coalescent** *adj*
WORD ORIGIN Latin *co-* together + *alescere* to increase

coalface *n* the exposed seam of coal in a mine

coalfield *n* an area rich in deposits of coal

coal gas *n* a mixture of gases produced by the distillation of bituminous coal and used for heating and lighting

coalition ❶ (koh-a-**lish**-un) *n* a temporary alliance, esp. between political parties
WORD ORIGIN Latin *coalescere* to coalesce

coal scuttle *n* a container for holding coal for a domestic fire

coal tar *n* a black tar, produced by the distillation of bituminous coal, used for making drugs and chemical products

coal tit *n* a small songbird with a black head with a white patch on the nape

coaming *n* a raised frame round a ship's hatchway for keeping out water
WORD ORIGIN origin unknown

coarse ❶ *adj* **1** rough in texture or structure **2** unrefined or indecent: *coarse humour* **3** of inferior quality **coarsely** *adv* **coarseness** *n*
WORD ORIGIN origin unknown

coarse fish *n Brit* a freshwater fish that is not of the salmon family **coarse fishing** *n*

coarsen *vb* to make or become coarse

coast ❶ *n* **1** the place where the land meets the sea **2 the coast is clear** *informal* the obstacles or dangers are gone ▹ *vb* **3** to move by momentum or force of gravity, without the use of power **4** to proceed without great effort: *they coasted to a 31-9 win in the pairs* **coastal** *adj*
WORD ORIGIN Latin *costa* side, rib

coaster *n* **1** a small mat placed under a bottle or glass to protect a table **2** *Brit* a small ship used for coastal trade

coastguard *n* **1** an organization which aids shipping, saves lives at sea, and prevents smuggling **2** a member of this

THESAURUS

clumsy *adj* **1 = awkward**, blundering, bungling, lumbering, inept, bumbling, ponderous, ungainly, gauche, accident-prone, gawky, heavy, uncoordinated, cack-handed *(informal)*, inexpert, maladroit, ham-handed *(informal)*, like a bull in a china shop, klutzy *(US & Canad slang)*, unskilful, butterfingered *(informal)*, ham-fisted *(informal)*, unco *(Austral slang)*
OPPOSITE: skilful

cluster *n* **1, 2 = gathering**, group, collection, bunch, knot, clump, assemblage ▹ *vb* **3 = gather**, group, collect, bunch, assemble, flock, huddle

clutch¹ *vb* **1 = seize**, catch, grab, grasp, snatch **2 = hold**, grip, embrace, grasp, cling to, clasp ▹ *pl n* **7a, 7b = power**, hands, control, grip, possession, grasp, custody, sway, keeping, claws

clutter *vb* **1 = litter**, scatter, strew, mess up **OPPOSITE:** tidy
▹ *n* **3 = untidiness**, mess, disorder, confusion, litter, muddle, disarray, jumble, hotchpotch **OPPOSITE:** order

coach *n* **1, 3 = bus**, charabanc
4, 5 = instructor, teacher, trainer, tutor, handler ▹ *vb* **6 = instruct**, train, prepare, exercise, drill, tutor, cram

coalition *n* **= alliance**, union, league, association, combination, merger, integration, compact, conjunction, bloc, confederation, fusion, affiliation, amalgam, amalgamation, confederacy

coarse *adj* **1 = rough**, crude, unfinished, homespun, impure, unrefined, rough-hewn, unprocessed, unpolished, coarse-grained, unpurified
OPPOSITE: smooth
2 = vulgar, offensive, rude, indecent, improper, raunchy *(slang)*, earthy, foul-mouthed, bawdy, impure, smutty, impolite, ribald, immodest, indelicate

coast *n* **1 = shore**, border, beach, strand, seaside, coastline, seaboard

DICTIONARY

coastline *n* the outline of a coast
coat ❶ *n* **1** an outer garment with sleeves, covering the body from the shoulders to below the waist **2** the hair, wool, or fur of an animal **3** any layer that covers a surface ▹*vb* **4** to cover with a layer
WORD ORIGIN Old French *cote*
coat hanger *n* a curved piece of wood, wire, or plastic, fitted with a hook and used to hang up clothes
coating *n* a layer or film spread over a surface: *a thick coating of breadcrumbs*
coat of arms *n* the heraldic emblem of a family or organization
coat of mail *n history* a protective garment made of linked metal rings or plates
coax ❶ *vb* **1** to persuade (someone) gently **2** to obtain (something) by persistent coaxing **3** to work on (something) carefully and patiently so as to make it function as desired: *I watched him coax the last few drops of beer out of his glass*
WORD ORIGIN obsolete *cokes* a fool
coaxial (koh-ax-ee-al) *adj* **1** *electronics* (of a cable) transmitting by means of two concentric conductors separated by an insulator **2** having a common axis
cob *n* **1** a male swan **2** a thickset type of horse **3** the stalk of an ear of maize **4** *Austral & Brit* a round loaf of bread **5** *Brit* a hazel tree or hazelnut
WORD ORIGIN origin unknown
cobalt *n chem* a brittle hard silvery-white metallic element used in alloys. Symbol: Co
WORD ORIGIN Middle High German *kobolt* goblin; from the miners' belief that goblins placed it in the silver ore
cobber ❶ *n Austral or old-fashioned NZ informal* a friend
WORD ORIGIN dialect *cob* to take a liking to someone
Cobbett *n* **William** 1763–1835, English journalist and social reformer; founded *The Political Register* (1802); author of *Rural Rides* (1830)
cobble *n* a cobblestone
cobbled *adj* (of a street or road) paved with cobblestones
cobbler *n* a person who makes or mends shoes
WORD ORIGIN origin unknown
cobblers *pl n Brit, Austral & NZ slang* nonsense
WORD ORIGIN rhyming slang *cobblers' awls* balls
cobblestone *n* a rounded stone used for paving
WORD ORIGIN from *cob*
cobble together *vb* **-bling, -bled** to put together clumsily: *a coalition cobbled together from parties with widely differing aims*
Cobden *n* **Richard** 1804–65, British economist and statesman: with John Bright a leader of the successful campaign to abolish the Corn Laws (1846)
Cobham *n* **Lord Cobham** title of Sir John Oldcastle ▸ See **Oldcastle**
cobia (koh-bee-a) *n* a large dark-striped game fish of tropical and subtropical seas
COBOL *n* a high-level computer programming language designed for general commercial use
WORD ORIGIN *co(mmon) b(usiness) o(riented) l(anguage)*
cobra *n* a highly venomous hooded snake of tropical Africa and Asia
WORD ORIGIN Latin *colubra* snake
cobweb *n* **1** a web spun by certain spiders **2** a single thread of such a web **cobwebbed** *adj* **cobwebby** *adj*
WORD ORIGIN Old English *(ātor)coppe* spider
cobwebs *pl n* mustiness, confusion, or obscurity: *her election dusted away the cobwebs that normally surround the presidency*
coca *n* the dried leaves of a S American shrub which contain cocaine
WORD ORIGIN S American Indian *kúka*
Coca-Cola *n trademark* a carbonated soft drink
cocaine *n* an addictive drug derived from coca leaves, used as a narcotic and local anaesthetic
coccyx (kok-six) *n, pl* **coccyges** (kok-**sije**-eez) *anat* a small triangular bone at the base of the spine in human beings and some apes **coccygeal** *adj*
WORD ORIGIN Greek *kokkux* cuckoo, from its likeness to a cuckoo's beak
cochineal *n* a scarlet dye obtained from a Mexican insect, used for colouring food
WORD ORIGIN Greek *kokkos* kermes berry
Cochise *n* died 1874, Apache Indian chief
cochlea (kok-lee-a) *n, pl* **-leae** (-lee-ee) *anat* the spiral tube in the internal ear, which converts sound vibrations into nerve impulses **cochlear** *adj*
WORD ORIGIN Greek *kokhlias* snail
cock *n* **1** a male bird, esp. of domestic fowl **2** a stopcock **3** *taboo slang* a penis **4** the hammer of a gun **5** *Brit informal* friend: used as a term of address ▹*vb* **6** to draw back the hammer of (a gun) so that it is ready to fire **7** to lift and turn (part of the body) in a particular direction ▸ See also **cockup**
WORD ORIGIN Old English *cocc*
cockabully *n* a small fresh-water fish of New Zealand
WORD ORIGIN Māori *kokopu*
cockade *n* a feather or rosette worn on the hat as a badge
WORD ORIGIN French *coq* cock
cock-a-hoop *adj Brit, Austral & NZ* in very high spirits
WORD ORIGIN origin unknown
cock-a-leekie *n* a Scottish soup of chicken boiled with leeks
cock-and-bull story *n informal* an obviously improbable story, esp. one used as an excuse
cockatiel *n* a crested Australian parrot with a greyish-brown and yellow plumage
cockatoo *n, pl* **-toos** a light-coloured crested parrot of Australia and the East Indies
WORD ORIGIN Malay *kakatua*
cockatrice *n* a legendary monster that could kill with a glance
WORD ORIGIN Late Latin *calcatrix* trampler
cockchafer *n* a large flying beetle
WORD ORIGIN COCK + *chafer* beetle
Cockcroft *n* Sir **John Douglas** 1897–1967, English nuclear physicist. With E. T. S. Walton, he produced the first artificial transmutation of an atomic nucleus (1932) and shared the Nobel prize for physics 1951
cocked hat *n* **1** a hat with three corners and a turned-up brim **2** **knock into a cocked hat** *slang* to outdo or defeat
cockerel *n* a young domestic cock, less than a year old
Cockerell *n* Sir **Christopher Sydney** 1910–99, British engineer, who invented the hovercraft
cocker spaniel *n* a small spaniel
WORD ORIGIN from *cocking* hunting woodcocks
cockeyed *adj informal* **1** crooked or askew **2** foolish or absurd **3** cross-eyed
cockfight *n* a fight between two gamecocks fitted with sharp metal spurs
cockie, cocky *n, pl* **-kies** *Austral & NZ informal* a cockatoo
cockle *n* **1** an edible bivalve shellfish **2** its shell **3** **warm the cockles of one's heart** to make one feel happy
WORD ORIGIN Greek *konkhule* mussel
cockleshell *n* **1** the rounded shell of

THESAURUS

coat *n* **2 = fur**, hair, skin, hide, wool, fleece, pelt **3 = layer**, covering, coating, overlay ▹*vb* **4 = cover**, spread, plaster, smear
coax *vb* **1 = persuade**, cajole, talk into, wheedle, sweet-talk *(informal)*, prevail upon, inveigle, soft-soap *(informal)*, twist (someone's) arm, flatter, entice, beguile, allure
OPPOSITE: bully
cobber *n (Austral & NZ old-fashioned, informal)* **= friend**, pal, mate *(informal)*, buddy *(informal)*, china *(Brit & S African informal)*, best friend, intimate, cock *(Brit informal)*, close friend, comrade,

the cockle **2** a small light boat

cockney *n* **1** a native of London, esp. of its East End **2** the urban dialect of London or its East End ▷ *adj* **3** characteristic of cockneys or their dialect
WORD ORIGIN Middle English *cokeney* cock's egg, later applied contemptuously to townsmen

cockpit *n* **1** the compartment in an aircraft for the pilot and crew **2** the driver's compartment in a racing car **3** *naut* a space in a small vessel containing the wheel and tiller **4** the site of many battles or conflicts: *the south of the country is a cockpit of conflicting interests* **5** an enclosure used for cockfights

cockroach *n* a beetle-like insect which is a household pest
WORD ORIGIN Spanish *cucaracha*

cockscomb *n* ▸same as **coxcomb**

cocksure *adj* overconfident or arrogant
WORD ORIGIN origin unknown

cocktail ❶ *n* **1** a mixed alcoholic drink **2** an appetizer of seafood or mixed fruits **3** any combination of diverse elements: *Central America was a cocktail of death, poverty, and destruction*
WORD ORIGIN origin unknown

cockup *Austral & Brit slang n* **1** something done badly ▷ *vb* **cock up** **2** to ruin or spoil

cocky *adj* **cockier, cockiest** excessively proud of oneself **cockily** *adv* **cockiness** *n*

coco *n, pl* **-cos** the coconut palm
WORD ORIGIN Portuguese: grimace

cocoa *or* **cacao** *n* **1** a powder made by roasting and grinding cocoa beans **2** a hot or cold drink made from cocoa powder
WORD ORIGIN from CACAO

cocoa bean *n* a cacao seed

cocoa butter *n* a fatty solid obtained from cocoa beans and used for confectionery and toiletries

coconut *n* **1** the fruit of a type of palm tree (**coconut palm**), which has a thick fibrous oval husk and a thin hard shell enclosing edible white flesh. The hollow centre is filled with a milky fluid (**coconut milk**) **2** the flesh of the coconut

coconut matting *n* coarse matting made from the husk of the coconut

cocoon *n* **1** a silky protective covering produced by a silkworm or other insect larva, in which the pupa develops **2** a protective covering ▷ *vb* **3** to wrap in or protect as if in a cocoon
WORD ORIGIN Provençal *coucoun* eggshell

cocotte *n* a small fireproof dish in which individual portions of food are cooked and served
WORD ORIGIN French

Cocteau *n* **Jean** 1889–1963, French dramatist, novelist, poet, critic, designer, and film director. His works include the novel *Les Enfants terribles* (1929) and the play *La Machine infernale* (1934)

cod[1] *n, pl* **cod** *or* **cods** a large food fish
WORD ORIGIN probably Germanic

cod[2] *adj Brit slang* having the character of an imitation or parody: *the chorus were dressed in exuberant cod-medieval costumes*
WORD ORIGIN origin unknown

COD cash (in the US, collect) on delivery

coda (**kode**-a) *n music* the final part of a musical movement or work
WORD ORIGIN Italian: tail

coddle *vb* **-dling, -dled** **1** to pamper or overprotect **2** to cook (eggs) in water just below boiling point
WORD ORIGIN origin unknown

code ❶ *n* **1** a system of letters, symbols, or prearranged signals, by which information can be communicated secretly or briefly **2** a set of principles or rules: *a code of practice* **3** a system of letters or digits used for identification purposes: *area code; tax code* ▷ *vb* **coding, coded** **4** to translate or arrange into a code
WORD ORIGIN Latin *codex* book, wooden block

codeine (**kode**-een) *n* a drug made mainly from morphine, used as a painkiller and sedative
WORD ORIGIN Greek *kōdeia* head of a poppy

codex (**koh**-dex) *n, pl* **-dices** (-diss-seez) a volume of manuscripts of an ancient text
WORD ORIGIN Latin: wooden block, book

codfish *n, pl* **-fish** *or* **-fishes** a cod

codger *n Brit, Austral & NZ informal* an old man
WORD ORIGIN probably variant of *cadger*

codicil (**cod**-iss-ill) *n law* an addition to a will
WORD ORIGIN from CODEX

codify (**kode**-if-fie) *vb* **-fies, -fying, -fied** to organize or collect together (rules or procedures) systematically **codification** *n*

codling *n* a young cod

cod-liver oil *n* an oil extracted from fish, rich in vitamins A and D

codpiece *n history* a bag covering the male genitals, attached to breeches
WORD ORIGIN obsolete *cod* scrotum

codswallop *n Brit, Austral & NZ slang* nonsense
WORD ORIGIN origin unknown

Cody *n* **William Frederick** ▸the real name of **Buffalo Bill**

Coe *n* **Sebastian**, Baron. born 1956, English middle-distance runner and Conservative politician: winner of the 1500 metres in the 1980 and 1984 Olympic Games; holds 1000 m record; held records at 800 m, 1500 m, and a mile: member of parliament (1992–97)

coeducation *n* the education of boys and girls together **coeducational** *adj*

coefficient *n* **1** *maths* a number or constant placed before and multiplying another quantity: *the coefficient of the term 3xyz is 3* **2** *physics* a number or constant used to calculate the behaviour of a given substance under specified conditions

coelacanth (**seel**-a-kanth) *n* a primitive marine fish, thought to be extinct until a living specimen was discovered in 1938
WORD ORIGIN Greek *koilos* hollow + *akanthos* spine

coelenterate (seel-**lent**-a-rate) *n* any invertebrate that has a saclike body with a single opening, such as a jellyfish or coral
WORD ORIGIN Greek *koilos* hollow + *enteron* intestine

coeliac *or US* **celiac** *n* a person who suffers from coeliac disease ▷ *adj* of or related to the abdomen
WORD ORIGIN Greek *koilia* belly

coeliac disease (**seel**-ee-ak) *n* a disease which makes the digestion of food difficult
WORD ORIGIN Greek *koilia* belly

Coen *n* **Jan Pieterszoon** 1587–1629, Dutch colonial administrator; governor general of the Dutch East Indies (1618–23, 1627–29)

coenobite (**seen**-oh-bite) *n* a member of a religious order in a monastic community
WORD ORIGIN Greek *koinos* common + *bios* life

coequal *adj, n* equal

coerce (koh-**urss**) *vb* **-ercing, -erced** to compel or force **coercion** *n*
WORD ORIGIN Latin *co-* together + *arcere* to enclose

coercive *adj* using force or authority to make a person do something against his or her will

Coeur *n* **Jacques** ?1395–1456, French merchant; councillor and court banker to Charles VII of France

coeval (koh-**eev**-al) *adj* **1** contemporary **2** *n* a contemporary **coevally** *adv*

THESAURUS

chum (*informal*), crony, alter ego, main man (*slang, chiefly US*), soul mate, homeboy (*slang, chiefly US*), bosom friend, boon companion, E hoa (*NZ*)

cocktail *n* **3 = mixture**, combination, compound, blend, concoction, mix, amalgamation, admixture

code *n* **1 = cipher**, cryptograph **2 = principles**, rules, manners, custom, convention, ethics, maxim, etiquette, system, kawa (*NZ*), tikanga (*NZ*)

DICTIONARY

C

WORD ORIGIN Latin *co-* together + *aevum* age
coexist *vb* **1** to exist together at the same time or in the same place **2** to exist together in peace despite differences **coexistence** *n* **coexistent** *adj*
coextensive *adj* covering the same area, either literally or figuratively: *the concepts of 'the nation' and 'the people' are not coextensive*
C of E Church of England
coffee *n* **1** a drink made from the roasted and ground seeds of a tall tropical shrub **2** Also called: **coffee beans** the beanlike seeds of this shrub **3** the shrub yielding these seeds ▷ *adj* **4** medium-brown
WORD ORIGIN Turkish *kahve*, from Arabic *qahwah* coffee, wine
coffee bar *n* a café; snack bar
coffee house *n* a place where coffee is served, esp. one that was a fashionable meeting place in 18th-century London
coffee mill *n* a machine for grinding roasted coffee beans
coffee table *n* a small low table
coffee-table book *n* a large expensive illustrated book
coffer *n* **1** a chest for storing valuables **2 coffers** a store of money **3** an ornamental sunken panel in a ceiling or dome
WORD ORIGIN Greek *kophinos* basket
cofferdam *n* a watertight enclosure pumped dry to enable construction work or ship repairs to be done
coffered *adj* (of a ceiling or dome) decorated with ornamental sunken panels
coffin *n* a box in which a corpse is buried or cremated
WORD ORIGIN Latin *cophinus* basket
cog *n* **1** one of the teeth on the rim of a gearwheel **2** a gearwheel, esp. a small one **3** an unimportant person in a large organization or process
WORD ORIGIN Scandinavian
cogent (koh-jent) *adj* forcefully convincing **cogency** *n*
WORD ORIGIN Latin *co-* together + *agere* to drive
cogitate (koj-it-tate) *vb* **-tating, -tated** to think deeply about (something) **cogitation** *n* **cogitative** *adj*
WORD ORIGIN Latin *cogitare*
cognac (kon-yak) *n* high-quality French brandy
cognate *adj* **1** derived from a common original form: *cognate languages* **2** related to or descended from a common ancestor ▷ *n* **3** a cognate word or language **4** a relative **cognation** *n*
WORD ORIGIN Latin *co-* same + *gnatus* born
cognition *n formal* **1** the processes of getting knowledge, including perception, intuition and reasoning **2** the results of such a process **cognitive** *adj*
WORD ORIGIN Latin *cognoscere* to learn
cognizance *or* **cognisance** *n formal* **1** knowledge or understanding **2 take cognizance of** to take notice of **3** the range or scope of knowledge or understanding **cognizant** *or* **cognisant** *adj*
WORD ORIGIN Latin *cognoscere* to learn
cognomen (kog-noh-men) *n, pl* **-nomens** *or* **-nomina** (-nom-min-a) *formal* **1** a nickname **2** a surname **3** an ancient Roman's third name or nickname
WORD ORIGIN Latin: additional name
cognoscenti (kon-yo-shen-tee) *pl n, sing* **-te** (-tee) connoisseurs
WORD ORIGIN obsolete Italian
cogwheel *n* ▸ same as **gearwheel**
cohabit *vb* to live together as husband and wife without being married **cohabitation** *n*
WORD ORIGIN Latin *co-* together + *habitare* to live
cohabitee *n* a person who lives with, and has a sexual and romantic relationship with, someone to whom he or she is not married
cohere *vb* **-hering, -hered 1** to hold or stick firmly together **2** to be logically connected or consistent
WORD ORIGIN Latin *co-* together + *haerere* to cling
coherent ❶ *adj* **1** logical and consistent **2** capable of intelligible speech **3** cohering or sticking together **4** *physics* (of two or more waves) having the same frequency and a constant fixed phase difference **coherence** *n*
cohesion *n* **1** sticking together **2** *physics* the force that holds together the atoms or molecules in a solid or liquid **cohesive** *adj*
cohort *n* **1** a band of associates **2** a tenth part of an ancient Roman Legion
WORD ORIGIN Latin *cohors* yard, company of soldiers
coif *n* **1** a close-fitting cap worn in the Middle Ages **2** a hairstyle ▷ *vb* **coiffing, coiffed 3** to arrange (the hair)
WORD ORIGIN Late Latin *cofea* helmet, cap
coiffeur *n* a hairdresser **coiffeuse** *fem n*
WORD ORIGIN French
coiffure *n* a hairstyle
WORD ORIGIN French
coil[1] ❶ *vb* **1** to wind or be wound into loops **2** to move in a winding course ▷ *n* **3** something wound in a connected series of loops **4** a single loop of such a series **5** a contraceptive device in the shape of a coil, inserted in the womb **6** an electrical conductor wound into a spiral, to provide inductance
WORD ORIGIN Old French *coillir* to collect together
coil[2] *n* **mortal coil** the troubles of the world
WORD ORIGIN coined by William Shakespeare
coin ❶ *n* **1** a metal disc used as money **2** metal currency collectively ▷ *vb* **3** to invent (a new word or phrase) **4** to make or stamp (coins) **5 coin it in** *or* **coin money** *informal* to make money rapidly
WORD ORIGIN Latin *cuneus* wedge
coinage *n* **1** coins collectively **2** the currency of a country **3** a newly invented word or phrase **4** the act of coining
coincide ❶ *vb* **-ciding, -cided 1** to happen at the same time **2** to agree or correspond exactly: *what she had said coincided exactly with his own thinking* **3** to occupy the same place in space
WORD ORIGIN Latin *co-* together + *incidere* to occur
coincidence ❶ *n* **1** a chance occurrence of simultaneous or apparently connected events **2** a coinciding
coincident *adj* **1** having the same position in space or time **2 coincident with** in exact agreement with
coincidental *adj* resulting from coincidence; not intentional **coincidentally** *adv*
coir *n* coconut fibre, used in making rope and matting
WORD ORIGIN Malayalam (a language of SW India) *kāyar* rope

THESAURUS

coherent *adj* **1 = consistent**, reasoned, organized, rational, logical, meaningful, systematic, orderly
OPPOSITE: inconsistent
2 = articulate, lucid, comprehensible, intelligible
OPPOSITE: unintelligible
coil[1] *vb* **1 = wind**, twist, curl, loop, spiral, twine **2 = curl**, wind, twist, snake, loop, entwine, twine, wreathe, convolute
coin *n* **2 = money**, change, cash, silver, copper, dosh (*Brit & Austral slang*), specie, kembla (*Austral slang*) ▷ *vb* **3 = invent**, create, make up, frame, forge, conceive, originate, formulate, fabricate, think up
coincide *vb* **1 = occur simultaneously**, coexist, synchronize, be concurrent **2 = agree**, match, accord, square, correspond, tally, concur, harmonize
OPPOSITE: disagree
coincidence *n* **1 = chance**, accident, luck, fluke, eventuality, stroke of

DICTIONARY

coitus (koh-it-uss) *or* **coition** (koh-ish-un) *n* sexual intercourse **coital** *adj*
WORD ORIGIN Latin *coire* to meet
coke[1] *n* **1** a solid fuel left after gas has been distilled from coal ▹*vb* **coking, coked 2** to become or convert into coke
WORD ORIGIN probably dialect *colk* core
coke[2] *n slang* cocaine
Coke *n trademark* ▸ short for **Coca-Cola**
Coke[1] *n trademark* ▸ short for **Coca-Cola**
Coke[2] *n* **1** Sir **Edward** 1552–1634, English jurist, noted for his defence of the common law against encroachment from the Crown: the Petition of Right (1628) was largely his work **2 Thomas William,** 1st Earl of Leicester, known as *Coke of Holkham*. 1752–1842, English agriculturist: pioneered agricultural improvement and considerably improved productivity at his Holkham estate in Norfolk
col *n* the lowest point of a ridge connecting two mountain peaks
WORD ORIGIN French: neck
Col. Colonel
cola *n* **1** a soft drink flavoured with an extract from the nuts of a tropical tree **2** the W African tree whose nuts contain this extract
WORD ORIGIN probably variant of W African *kolo* nut
colander *n* a bowl with a perforated bottom for straining or rinsing foods
WORD ORIGIN Latin *colum* sieve
Colbert *n* **1 Claudette**, real name *Claudette Lily Chauchoin*. 1905–96, French-born Hollywood actress, noted for her sophisticated comedy roles; her films include *It Happened One Night* (1934) and *The Palm Beach Story* (1942) **2 Jean Baptiste** 1619–83, French statesman; chief minister to Louis XIV: reformed the taille and pursued a mercantilist policy, creating a powerful navy and merchant fleet and building roads and canals
cold ❶ *adj* **1** low in temperature: *the cold March wind; cans of cold beer* **2** not hot enough: *eat your food before it gets cold!* **3** lacking in affection or enthusiasm **4** not affected by emotion: *the cold truth* **5** dead **6** (of a trail or scent in hunting) faint **7** (of a colour) giving the impression of coldness **8** *slang* unconscious **9** *informal* (of a seeker) far from the object of a search **10** denoting the contacting of potential customers without previously approaching them to establish their interest: *cold mailing* **11 cold comfort** little or no comfort **12 have** *or* **get cold feet** to be or become fearful or reluctant **13 in cold blood** deliberately and without mercy **14 leave someone cold** *informal* to fail to excite or impress someone **15 throw cold water on** *informal* to discourage ▹*n* **16** the absence of heat **17** a viral infection of the nose and throat characterized by catarrh and sneezing **18** the sensation caused by loss or lack of heat **19 (out) in the cold** *informal* neglected or ignored ▹*adv* **20** *informal* unrehearsed or unprepared: *he played his part cold* **coldly** *adv* **coldness** *n*
WORD ORIGIN Old English *ceald*
cold-blooded *adj* **1** callous or cruel **2** *zool* (of all animals except birds and mammals) having a body temperature that varies according to the temperature of the surroundings
cold chisel *n* a toughened steel chisel
cold cream *n* a creamy preparation used for softening and cleansing the skin
cold frame *n* an unheated wooden frame with a glass top, used to protect young plants
cold front *n meteorol* the boundary line between a warm air mass and the cold air pushing it from beneath and behind
cold-hearted *adj* lacking in feeling or warmth **cold-heartedness** *n*
cold shoulder *informal n* **1 give someone the cold shoulder** to snub someone ▹*vb* **cold-shoulder 2** to treat with indifference
cold snap *n* a short period of cold and frosty weather
cold sore *n* a cluster of blisters near the lips, caused by a virus
cold storage *n* **1** the storage of things in a refrigerated place **2** *informal* a state of temporary disuse: *the idea has been in cold storage ever since*
cold sweat *n informal* coldness and sweating as a bodily reaction to fear or nervousness
cold turkey *n slang* a method of curing drug addiction by the sudden withdrawal of all doses
cold war *n* a state of political hostility between two countries without actual warfare
cole *n* any of various plants such as the cabbage and rape
WORD ORIGIN Latin *caulis* cabbage
Cole *n* **Nat 'King'**, real name *Nathaniel Adams Cole*. 1917–65, US popular singer and jazz pianist
Coleman *n* **Ornette** born 1930, US avant-garde jazz alto saxophonist and multi-instrumentalist
Colenso *n* **John William** 1814–83, British churchman; Anglican bishop of Natal from 1853: charged with heresy for questioning the accuracy of the Pentateuch
Coleridge-Taylor *n* **Samuel** 1875–1912, British composer, best known for his trilogy of oratorios *Song of Hiawatha* (1898–1900)
coleslaw *n* a salad dish of shredded raw cabbage in a dressing
WORD ORIGIN Dutch *koolsalade* cabbage salad
Colet *n* **John** ?1467–1519, English humanist and theologian; founder of St Paul's School, London (1509)
Colette *n* full name *Sidonie Gabrielle Claudine Colette*. 1873–1954, French novelist; her works include *Chéri* (1920), *Gigi* (1944), and the series of *Claudine* books
coley *n Brit* an edible fish with white or grey flesh
WORD ORIGIN perhaps from *coalfish*
colic *n* severe pains in the stomach and bowels **colicky** *adj*
WORD ORIGIN Greek *kolon* COLON[2]
Coligny *or* **Coligni** *n* **Gaspard de**, Seigneur de Châtillon. 1519–72, French Huguenot leader
colitis (koh-lie-tiss) *n* inflammation of the colon, usually causing diarrhoea and lower abdominal pain
collaborate ❶ *vb* **-rating, -rated 1** to work with another or others on a joint project **2** to cooperate with an enemy invader **collaboration** *n* **collaborative** *adj* **collaborator** *n*
WORD ORIGIN Latin *com-* together + *laborare* to work
collage (kol-lahzh) *n* **1** an art form in which various materials or objects are glued onto a surface to make a picture **2** a picture made in this way **3** a work, such as a piece of music, created by combining unrelated styles **collagist** *n*
WORD ORIGIN French
collagen *n* a protein found in cartilage and bone that yields gelatine when boiled
WORD ORIGIN Greek *kolla* glue

THESAURUS

luck, happy accident, fortuity
cold *adj* **1 = chilly**, biting, freezing, bitter, raw, chill, harsh, bleak, arctic, icy, frosty, wintry, frigid, inclement, parky *(Brit informal)*, cool
OPPOSITE: hot
3a = distant, reserved, indifferent, aloof, glacial, cold-blooded, apathetic, frigid, unresponsive, unfeeling, passionless, undemonstrative, standoffish
OPPOSITE: emotional
3b = unfriendly, indifferent, stony, lukewarm, glacial, unmoved, unsympathetic, apathetic, frigid, inhospitable, unresponsive
OPPOSITE: friendly
▹*n* **16 = coldness**, chill, frigidity, chilliness, frostiness, iciness
collaborate *vb* **1 = work together**, team up, join forces, cooperate, play ball *(informal)*, participate
2 = conspire, cooperate, collude, fraternize

DICTIONARY

collapse ❶ *vb* **-lapsing, -lapsed 1** to fall down or cave in suddenly **2** to fail completely: *a package holiday company which collapsed last year* **3** to fall down from lack of strength, exhaustion, or illness: *he collapsed with an asthma attack* **4** to sit down and rest because of tiredness or lack of energy: *she collapsed in front of the telly when she got home* **5** to fold compactly, esp. for storage ▷*n* **6** the act of falling down or falling to pieces **7** a sudden failure or breakdown
WORD ORIGIN Latin *collabi* to fall in ruins

collapsible *adj* able to be folded up for storage

collar ❶ *n* **1** the part of a garment round the neck **2** a band of leather, rope, or metal placed around an animal's neck **3** *biol* a ringlike marking around the neck of a bird or animal **4** a cut of meat, esp. bacon, from the neck of an animal **5** a ring or band around a pipe, rod, or shaft ▷*vb Brit, Austral & NZ informal* **6** to seize; arrest **7** to catch in order to speak to **8** to take for oneself
WORD ORIGIN Latin *collum* neck

collarbone *n* ▸same as **clavicle**

collate *vb* **-lating, -lated 1** to examine and compare carefully **2** to gather together and put in order **collator** *n*
WORD ORIGIN Latin *com-* together + *latus* brought

collateral *n* **1** security pledged for the repayment of a loan **2** a person, animal, or plant descended from the same ancestor as another but through a different line ▷*adj* **3** descended from a common ancestor but through different lines **4** additional but subordinate: *a spokeswoman said that there was no collateral information to dispute the assurances the government had been given* **5** situated or running side by side: *collateral ridges of mountains*
WORD ORIGIN Latin *com-* together + *lateralis* of the side

collateral damage *n mil* unintentional civilian casualties or damage to civilian property caused by military action: *to minimize collateral damage maximum precision in bombing is required*

collation *n* **1** the act or result of collating **2** *formal* a light meal

colleague ❶ *n* a fellow worker, esp. in a profession
WORD ORIGIN Latin *collega*

collect[1] ❶ *vb* **1** to gather together or be gathered together **2** to gather (objects, such as stamps) as a hobby or for study **3** to go to a place to fetch (a person or thing) **4** to receive payments of (taxes, dues, or contributions) **5** to regain control of (oneself or one's emotions)
WORD ORIGIN Latin *com-* together + *legere* to gather

collect[2] *n Christianity* a short prayer said during certain church services
WORD ORIGIN Medieval Latin *oratio ad collectam* prayer at the assembly

collected ❶ *adj* **1** calm and self-controlled **2** brought together into one book or set of books: *the collected works of Dickens*

collection ❶ *n* **1** things collected or accumulated **2** a group of people **3** the act or process of collecting **4** a selection of clothes usually presented by a particular designer **5** a sum of money collected, as in church **6** a regular removal of letters from a postbox

collective ❶ *adj* **1** done by or characteristic of individuals acting as a group: *the army's collective wisdom regarding peacekeeping* ▷*n* **2** a group of people working together on an enterprise and sharing the benefits from it **collectively** *adv*

collective bargaining *n* negotiation between a trade union and an employer on the wages and working conditions of the employees

collective noun *n* a noun that is singular in form but that refers to a group of people or things, as *crowd* or *army*

collectivism *n* the theory that the state should own all means of production **collectivist** *adj*

collectivize *or* **-vise** *vb* **-vizing, -vized** *or* **-vising, -vised** to organize according to the theory of collectivism **collectivization** *or* **-visation** *n*

collector *n* **1** a person who collects objects as a hobby **2** a person employed to collect debts, rents, or tickets

collector's item *n* an object highly valued by collectors for its beauty or rarity

colleen *n Irish* a girl
WORD ORIGIN Irish Gaelic *cailín*

college *n* **1** an institution of higher or further education that is not a university **2** a self-governing section of certain universities **3** *Brit & NZ* a name given to some secondary schools **4** an organized body of people with specific rights and duties: *the president is elected by an electoral college* **5** a body organized within a particular profession, concerned with regulating standards **6** the staff and students of a college
WORD ORIGIN Latin *collega* colleague

collegian *n* a member of a college

collegiate *adj* **1** of a college or college students **2** (of a university) composed of various colleges

Collette *n* **Toni**, full name *Antonia Collette*. born 1972, Australian film actress. Her films include *Muriel's Wedding* (1994), *The Sixth Sense* (1999) and *Little Miss Sunshine* (2006)

collide ❶ *vb* **-liding, -lided 1** to crash together violently **2** to conflict or disagree
WORD ORIGIN Latin *com-* together + *laedere* to strike

collie *n* a silky-haired dog used for herding sheep and cattle
WORD ORIGIN Scots, probably from earlier *colie* black

collier *n chiefly Brit* **1** a coal miner **2** a ship designed to carry coal

colliery *n, pl* **-lieries** *chiefly Brit* a coal mine and its buildings

Collins *n* **1 Michael** 1890–1922, Irish republican revolutionary: a leader of Sinn Féin; member of the Irish delegation that negotiated the treaty

THESAURUS

collapse *vb* **1 = fall down**, fall, give way, subside, cave in, crumple, fall apart at the seams **2 = fail**, fold, founder, break down, fall through, come to nothing, go belly-up *(informal)* ▷*n* **6 = falling down**, ruin, falling apart, cave-in, disintegration, subsidence **7 = failure**, slump, breakdown, flop, downfall

collar *vb* **6** *(informal)* **= seize**, catch, arrest, appropriate, grab, capture, nail *(informal)*, nab *(informal)*, apprehend, lay hands on

colleague *n* **= fellow worker**, partner, ally, associate, assistant, team-mate, companion, comrade, helper, collaborator, confederate, auxiliary, workmate, confrère

collect[1] *vb* **1 = assemble**, meet, rally, cluster, come together, convene, converge, congregate, flock together
OPPOSITE: disperse
1, 2 = gather, save, assemble, heap, accumulate, aggregate, amass, stockpile, hoard **OPPOSITE:** scatter

collected *adj* **1 = calm**, together *(slang)*, cool, confident, composed, poised, serene, sedate, self-controlled, unfazed *(informal)*, unperturbed, unruffled, self-possessed, keeping your cool, unperturbable, as cool as a cucumber, chilled *(informal)*
OPPOSITE: nervous

collection *n* **1a = accumulation**, set, store, mass, pile, heap, stockpile, hoard, congeries **1b = compilation**, accumulation, anthology **2 = group**, company, crowd, gathering, assembly, cluster, congregation, assortment, assemblage
3 = gathering, acquisition, accumulation **5a = contribution**, donation, alms **5b = offering**, offertory

collective *adj* **1 = joint**, united, shared, common, combined, corporate, concerted, unified, cooperative
OPPOSITE: individual

DICTIONARY

with Great Britain (1921) that established the Irish Free State **2** (**William**) **Wilkie** 1824–89, British author, noted particularly for his suspense novel *The Moonstone* (1868) **3 William** 1721–59, British poet, noted for his odes; regarded as a precursor of romanticism

collision ❶ *n* **1** a violent crash between moving objects **2** the conflict of opposed ideas or wishes
WORD ORIGIN Latin *collidere* to collide

collision course *n* **1** a trajectory of movement likely to result in a collision **2** a course of action likely to result in a serious disagreement or confrontation: *the union is on an inevitable collision course with the government*

collocate *vb* **-cating, -cated** (of words) to occur together regularly **collocation** *n*

colloid *n* a mixture of particles of one substance suspended in a different substance **colloidal** *adj*
WORD ORIGIN Greek *kolla* glue

collop *n* a small slice of meat
WORD ORIGIN Scandinavian

colloquial *adj* suitable for informal speech or writing **colloquially** *adv*

colloquialism *n* **1** a colloquial word or phrase **2** the use of colloquial words and phrases

colloquium *n, pl* **-quiums** *or* **-quia** an academic conference or seminar
WORD ORIGIN Latin; see COLLOQUY

colloquy *n, pl* **-quies** *formal* a conversation or conference **colloquist** *n*
WORD ORIGIN Latin *com-* together + *loqui* to speak

collude *vb* **-luding, -luded** to cooperate secretly or dishonestly with someone
WORD ORIGIN Latin *colludere* to conspire

collusion *n* secret or illegal agreement or cooperation **collusive** *adj*

collywobbles *pl n slang* **1** an intense feeling of nervousness **2** an upset stomach
WORD ORIGIN probably from *colic* + *wobble*

cologne *n* a perfumed toilet water
WORD ORIGIN *Cologne*, Germany, where it was first manufactured

colon[1] *n, pl* **-lons** the punctuation mark (:) used before an explanation or an example, a list, or an extended quotation
WORD ORIGIN Greek *kōlon* limb, clause

colon[2] *n, pl* **-lons** *or* **-la** the part of the large intestine connected to the rectum **colonic** *adj*
WORD ORIGIN Greek *kolon* large intestine

colonel *n* a senior commissioned officer in the army or air force **colonelcy** *n*
WORD ORIGIN Old Italian *colonnello* column of soldiers

colonial *adj* **1** of or inhabiting a colony or colonies **2** of a style of architecture popular in North America in the 17th and 18th centuries: *a colonial mansion* **3** *Austral* of a style of architecture popular during Australia's colonial period ▹*n* **4** an inhabitant of a colony

colonial goose *n NZ, old-fashioned* stuffed roast mutton

colonialism *n* the policy of acquiring and maintaining colonies, esp. for exploitation **colonialist** *n, adj*

colonist *n* a settler in or inhabitant of a colony

colonize *or* **-nise** *vb* **-nizing, -nized** *or* **-nising, -nised 1** to establish a colony in (an area) **2** to settle in (an area) as colonists **colonization** *or* **-nisation** *n*

colonnade *n* a row of evenly spaced columns, usually supporting a roof **colonnaded** *adj*
WORD ORIGIN French *colonne* column

colony ❶ *n, pl* **-nies 1** a group of people who settle in a new country but remain under the rule of their homeland **2** the territory occupied by such a settlement **3** a group of people with the same nationality or interests, forming a community in a particular place: *an artists' colony* **4** *zool* a group of the same type of animal or plant living or growing together **5** *bacteriol* a group of microorganisms when grown on a culture medium
WORD ORIGIN Latin *colere* to cultivate, inhabit

colophon *n* a publisher's symbol on a book
WORD ORIGIN Greek *kolophōn* a finishing stroke

color *n, vb US* ▸same as **colour**

Colorado beetle *n* a black-and-yellow beetle that is a serious pest of potatoes
WORD ORIGIN *Colorado*, state of central US

coloration *or* **colouration** *n* arrangement of colours: *a red coloration of the eyes*

coloratura *n music* **1** a part for a solo singer which has much complicated ornamentation of the basic melody **2** a soprano who specializes in such music
WORD ORIGIN obsolete Italian, literally: colouring

colossal *adj* **1** very large in size: *the turbulent rivers and colossal mountains of New Zealand* **2** very serious or significant: *a colossal legal blunder*

colossus *n, pl* **-si** *or* **-suses 1** a very large statue **2** a huge or important person or thing
WORD ORIGIN Greek *kolossos*

colostomy *n, pl* **-mies** an operation to form an opening from the colon onto the surface of the body, for emptying the bowel
WORD ORIGIN COLON[2] + Greek *stoma* mouth

colour ❶ *or US* **color** *n* **1** a property of things that results from the particular wavelengths of light which they reflect or give out, producing a sensation in the eye **2** a colour, such as a red or green, that possesses hue, as opposed to black, white, or grey **3** a substance, such as a dye, that gives colour **4** the skin complexion of a person **5** the use of all the colours in painting, drawing, or photography **6** the distinctive tone of a musical sound **7** details which give vividness or authenticity: *I walked the streets and absorbed the local colour* **8** semblance or pretext: *under colour of* ▹*vb* **9** to apply colour to (something) **10** to influence or distort: *anger coloured her judgment* **11** to become red in the face, esp. when embarrassed or annoyed **12** to give a convincing appearance to: *he coloured his account of what had happened* ▸See also **colours**
WORD ORIGIN Latin *color*

colour bar *n* racial discrimination by whites against non-whites

colour-blind *adj* **1** unable to distinguish between certain colours, esp. red and green **2** not discriminating on grounds of skin colour: *colour-blind policies* **colour blindness** *n*

coloured *or US* **colored** *adj* having a colour or colours other than black or white: *coloured glass bottles; a peach-coloured outfit with matching hat*

Coloured *or US* **Colored** *n* **1** *offensive* a person who is not White **2** in South Africa, a person of racially mixed parentage or descent ▹*adj* **3** *S African*

THESAURUS

collide *vb* **1 = crash**, clash, meet head-on, come into collision **2 = conflict**, clash, be incompatible, be at variance

collision *n* **1 = crash**, impact, accident, smash, bump, pile-up *(informal)*, prang *(informal)* **2 = conflict**, opposition, clash, clashing, encounter, disagreement, incompatibility

colony *n* **2 = settlement**, territory, province, possession, dependency, outpost, dominion, satellite state, community

colour *or (US)* **color** *n* **2 = hue**, tone, shade, tint, tinge, tincture, colourway **3 = paint**, stain, dye, tint, pigment, tincture, coloration, colourwash, colorant ▹*vb* **11 = blush**, flush, crimson, redden, go crimson, burn, go as red as a beetroot

DICTIONARY

of mixed White and non-White parentage

colourful ❶ *or US* **colorful** *adj* **1** with bright or richly varied colours **2** vivid or distinctive in character

colouring *or US* **coloring** *n* **1** the application of colour **2** something added to give colour **3** appearance with regard to shade and colour **4** the colour of a person's complexion

colourless *or US* **colorless** *adj* **1** without colour: *a colourless gas* **2** dull and uninteresting: *a colourless personality* **3** grey or pallid in tone or hue: *a watery sun hung low in the colourless sky*

colours *or US* **colors** *pl n* **1** the flag of a country, regiment, or ship **2** *Brit sport* a badge or other symbol showing membership of a team, esp. at a school or college **3** **nail one's colours to the mast** to commit oneself publicly to a course of action **4** **show one's true colours** to display one's true nature or character

colour sergeant *n* a sergeant who carries the regimental, battalion, or national colours

colour supplement *n Brit* an illustrated magazine accompanying a newspaper

colt *n* **1** a young male horse or pony **2** *sport* a young and inexperienced player
WORD ORIGIN Old English: young ass

Coltrane *n* **John** (**William**) 1926–67, US jazz tenor and soprano saxophonist and composer

coltsfoot *n, pl* **-foots** a weed with yellow flowers and heart-shaped leaves

Colum *n* **Padraic** 1881–1972, Irish lyric poet, resident in the US (1914–72)

Columba[1] *n, Latin genitive* **Columbae** as in *Alpha Columbae.* a small constellation in the S hemisphere south of Orion
WORD ORIGIN Latin, literally: dove

Columba[2] *n* **Saint** ?521–597 AD, Irish missionary: founded the monastery at Iona (563) from which the Picts were converted to Christianity. Feast day: June 9

columbine *n* a plant that has brightly coloured flowers with five spurred petals
WORD ORIGIN Medieval Latin *columbina herba* dovelike plant

column ❶ *n* **1** an upright pillar usually having a cylindrical shaft, a base, and a capital **2** a form or structure in the shape of a column: *a column of smoke* **3** a vertical division of a newspaper page **4** a regular feature in a paper: *a cookery column* **5** a vertical arrangement of numbers **6** *mil* a narrow formation in which individuals or units follow one behind the other **columnar** *adj*
WORD ORIGIN Latin *columna*

columnist *n* a journalist who writes a regular feature in a newspaper

com- *or* **con-** *prefix* used with a main word to mean together; with; jointly: *commingle*
WORD ORIGIN Latin, from *cum* with

coma ❶ *n* a state of unconsciousness from which a person cannot be aroused, caused by injury, disease, or drugs
WORD ORIGIN Greek *kōma* heavy sleep

Comanche (kom-**man**-chee) *n, pl* **-ches** *or* **-che** a member of a N American Indian people, formerly living in the plains to the east of the Rockies, now chiefly in Oklahoma

Comaneci *n* **Nadia** born 1961, Romanian gymnast; gold medal winner in the 1976 Olympic Games: defected to the US in 1989

comatose *adj* **1** in a coma **2** sound asleep

comb ❶ *n* **1** a toothed instrument for disentangling or arranging hair **2** a tool or machine that cleans and straightens wool or cotton **3** a fleshy serrated crest on the head of a domestic fowl **4** a honeycomb ▷ *vb* **5** to use a comb on **6** to search with great care: *police combed the streets for the missing girl*
WORD ORIGIN Old English *camb*

combat ❶ *n* **1** a fight or struggle ▷ *vb* **-bating, -bated 2** to fight: *a coordinated approach to combating the growing drugs problem* **combative** *adj*
WORD ORIGIN Latin *com-* with + *battuere* to beat

combatant *n* **1** a person taking part in a combat ▷ *adj* **2** engaged in or ready for combat

combat trousers *or* **combats** *pl n* loose casual trousers with large pockets on the sides of the legs

combe *n* ▸ same as **coomb**

comber *n* a long curling wave

combination ❶ *n* **1** the act of combining or state of being combined **2** people or things combined **3** the set of numbers or letters that opens a combination lock **4** a motorcycle with a sidecar **5** *maths* an arrangement of the members of a set into specified groups without regard to order in the group

combination lock *n* a lock that can only be opened when a set of dials is turned to show a specific sequence of numbers or letters

combinations *pl n Brit* a one-piece undergarment with long sleeves and legs

combine ❶ *vb* **-bining, -bined 1** to join together **2** to form a chemical compound ▷ *n* **3** an association of people or firms for a common purpose **4** ▸ short for **combine harvester**
WORD ORIGIN Latin *com-* together + *bini* two by two

combine harvester *n* a machine used to reap and thresh grain in one process

combings *pl n* the loose hair or fibres removed by combing, esp. from animals

combining form *n* a part of a word that occurs only as part of a compound word, such as *anthropo-* in *anthropology*

combo *n, pl* **-bos** a small group of jazz musicians

combustible *adj* capable of igniting and burning easily

combustion *n* **1** the process of

THESAURUS

colourful *adj* **1 = bright**, rich, brilliant, intense, vivid, vibrant, psychedelic, motley, variegated, jazzy *(informal)*, multicoloured, Day-glo®, kaleidoscopic **OPPOSITE:** drab **2 = interesting**, rich, unusual, stimulating, graphic, lively, distinctive, vivid, picturesque, characterful **OPPOSITE:** boring

column *n* **1 = pillar**, support, post, shaft, upright, obelisk **6 = line**, train, row, file, rank, string, queue, procession, cavalcade

coma *n* **= unconsciousness**, trance, oblivion, lethargy, stupor, torpor, insensibility

comb *vb* **5 = untangle**, arrange, groom, dress **6 = search**, hunt through, sweep, rake, sift, scour, rummage, ransack, forage, fossick *(Austral & NZ)*, go through with a fine-tooth comb

combat *n* **1 = fight**, war, action, battle, conflict, engagement, warfare, skirmish **OPPOSITE:** peace ▷ *vb* **2 = fight**, battle against, oppose, contest, engage, cope with, resist, defy, withstand, struggle against, contend with, do battle with, strive against **OPPOSITE:** support

combination *n* **1 = association**, union, alliance, coalition, merger, federation, consortium, unification, syndicate, confederation, cartel, confederacy, cabal **2 = mixture**, mix, compound, blend, composite, amalgam, amalgamation, meld, coalescence

combine *vb* **1a = join together**, link, connect, integrate, merge, fuse, amalgamate, meld **1b = unite**, associate, team up, unify, get together, collaborate, join forces, cooperate, join together, pool resources **OPPOSITE:** split up **2 = amalgamate**, marry, mix, bond, bind, compound, blend, incorporate, integrate, merge, put

DICTIONARY

burning **2** a chemical reaction in which a substance combines with oxygen to produce heat and light **WORD ORIGIN** Latin *comburere* to burn up

come ❶ *vb* **coming, came, come 1** to move towards a place considered near to the speaker or hearer: *come and see me as soon as you can* **2** to arrive or reach: *turn left and continue until you come to a cattle-grid; he came to Britain in the 1920s* **3** to occur: *Christmas comes but once a year* **4** to happen as a result: *no good will come of this* **5** to occur to the mind: *the truth suddenly came to me* **6** to reach a specified point, state, or situation: *a dull brown dress that came down to my ankles; he'd come to a decision* **7** to be produced: *it also comes in other colours* **8 come from** to be or have been a resident or native (of): *my mother comes from Greenock* **9** to become: *it was like a dream come true* **10** *slang* to have an orgasm **11** *Brit & NZ informal* to play the part of: *don't come the innocent with me* **12** (*subjunctive use*) when a specified time arrives: *come next August* **13 as ... as they come** the most characteristic example of a type: *he's an arrogant swine and as devious as they come* **14 come again?** *informal* what did you say? **15 come to light** to be revealed ▷ *interj* **16** an exclamation expressing annoyance or impatience: *come now!* ▸ See also **come about, come across,** etc. **WORD ORIGIN** Old English *cuman*

come about *vb* to happen

come across ❶ *vb* **1** to meet or find by accident **2** to communicate the intended meaning or impression **3 come across as** to give a certain impression

come at *vb* to attack: *he came at me with an axe*

comeback ❶ *n informal* **1** a return to a former position or status **2** a response or retaliation ▷ *vb* **come back 3** to return, esp. to the memory **4** to become fashionable again

come between *vb* to cause the estrangement or separation of (two people)

come by *vb* to find or obtain, esp. accidentally: *Graham filled him in on how he came by the envelope*

Comecon (kom-meek-on) *n* (formerly) an economic league of Soviet-oriented Communist nations **WORD ORIGIN** *Co(uncil for) M(utual) Econ(omic Aid)*

comedian ❶ *or fem* **comedienne** *n* **1** an entertainer who tells jokes **2** a person who performs in comedy

comedown *n* **1** a decline in status or prosperity **2** *informal* a disappointment ▷ *vb* **come down 3** (of prices) to become lower **4** to reach a decision: *a 1989 court ruling came down in favour of three councils who wanted Sunday trading banned* **5** to be handed down by tradition or inheritance **6 come down with** to begin to suffer from (illness) **7 come down on** to reprimand sharply **8 come down to** to amount to: *at the end the case came down to the one simple issue* **9 come down in the world** to lose status or prosperity

comedy ❶ *n, pl* **-dies 1** a humorous film, play, or broadcast **2** such works as a genre **3** the humorous aspect of life or of events **4** (in classical literature) a play which ends happily **WORD ORIGIN** Greek *kōmos* village festival + *aeidein* to sing

come forward *vb* **1** to offer one's services **2** to present oneself

come-hither *adj informal* flirtatious and seductive: *a come-hither look*

come in *vb* **1** to prove to be: *it came in useful* **2** to become fashionable or seasonable **3** to finish a race (in a certain position) **4** to be received: *reports of more deaths came in today* **5** (of money) to be received as income **6** to be involved in a situation: *where do I come in?* **7 come in for** to be the object of: *she came in for a lot of criticism*

come into *vb* **1** to enter **2** to inherit

comely *adj* **-lier, -liest** *old-fashioned* good-looking **comeliness** *n* **WORD ORIGIN** Old English *cymlic* beautiful

Comenius *n* **John Amos,** Czech name *Jan Amos Komensky.* 1592–1670, Czech educational reformer

come of *vb* to result from: *nothing came of it*

come off *vb* **1** to emerge from a situation in a certain position: *the people who have come off worst are the poor* **2** *informal* to take place **3** *informal* to have the intended effect: *it was a gamble that didn't come off*

come-on *n* **1** *informal* a lure or enticement ▷ *vb* **come on 2** (of power or water) to start running or functioning **3** to make progress: *my plants are coming on nicely* **4** to begin: *I think I've got a cold coming on* **5** to make an entrance on stage **6** to make a certain impression: *he comes on like a hard man* **7 come on to** *informal* to make sexual advances to

come out *vb* **1** to be made public or revealed: *it was only then that the truth came out* **2** to be published or put on sale: *their latest album which came out last month* **3** Also: **come out of the closet** to reveal something formerly concealed, esp. that one is a homosexual **4** *chiefly Brit* to go on strike **5** to declare oneself: *the report has come out in favour of maintaining child benefit* **6** to end up or turn out: *this wine consistently came out top in our tastings; the figures came out exactly right* **7 come out in** to become covered with (a rash or spots) **8 come out with** to say or disclose: *she came out with a remark that left me speechless* **9** to enter society formally

come over *vb* **1** to influence or affect: *I don't know what's come over me* **2** to communicate the intended meaning or impression **3** to give a certain impression **4** to change sides or opinions **5** *informal* to feel a particular sensation: *it makes him come over slightly queasy*

come round *vb* **1** to recover consciousness **2** to change one's opinion

comestibles *pl n* food **WORD ORIGIN** Latin *comedere* to eat up

comet *n* a heavenly body that travels round the sun, leaving a long bright trail behind it **WORD ORIGIN** Greek *komētēs* long-haired

come through *vb* to survive or endure (an illness or difficult situation) successfully

come to *vb* **1** to regain consciousness **2** to amount to (a total figure)

come up *vb* **1** to be mentioned or arise: *we hope that the difficulties that have arisen in the past will not keep coming up* **2** to be about to happen: *the club has important games coming up* **3 come up against** to come into conflict with **4 come up in the world** to rise in status **5 come up to** to meet a

THESAURUS

together, fuse, synthesize **OPPOSITE:** separate

come *vb* **1 = approach**, near, advance, move towards, draw near **2, 6 = reach**, extend **3, 4 = happen**, fall, occur, take place, come about, come to pass **7 = be available**, be made, be offered, be produced, be on offer

come across *vb* **1a = meet**, encounter, run into, bump into *(informal)* **1b = find**, discover, notice, unearth, stumble upon, hit upon, chance upon, happen upon, light upon **2 = arrive**, move, appear, enter, turn up *(informal)*, show up *(informal)*, materialize **3 = seem**, look, seem to be, appear to be, give the impression of being

comeback *n* **1** *(informal)* **= return**, revival, rebound, resurgence, rally, recovery, triumph **2 = response**, reply, retort, retaliation, riposte, rejoinder

comedian *n* **1, 2 = comic**, laugh *(informal)*, wit, clown, funny man, humorist, wag, joker, jester, dag *(NZ informal)*, card *(informal)*

comedy *n* **2 = humour**, fun, joking, farce, jesting, slapstick, wisecracking, hilarity, witticisms, facetiousness, chaffing **OPPOSITE:** seriousness

DICTIONARY

standard **6** **come up with** to produce or propose: *he has a knack for coming up with great ideas*
come upon *vb* to meet or encounter unexpectedly
comeuppance *n informal* deserved punishment
WORD ORIGIN from *come up* (in the sense: to appear before a court)
comfit *n* a sugar-coated sweet
WORD ORIGIN Latin *confectum* something prepared
comfort *n* **1** a state of physical ease or well-being **2** relief from suffering or grief **3** a person or thing that brings ease **4** **comforts** things that make life easier or more pleasant: *the comforts of home* ▷ *vb* **5** to soothe or console **6** to bring physical ease to **comforting** *adj*
WORD ORIGIN Latin *con-* (intensive) + *fortis* strong
comfortable *adj* **1** giving comfort; relaxing **2** free from trouble or pain **3** *informal* well-off financially **4** not afraid or embarrassed: *he was not comfortable expressing sympathy* **comfortably** *adv*
comforter *n* **1** a person or thing that comforts **2** *Brit* a baby's dummy **3** *Brit* a woollen scarf
comfrey *n* a tall plant with bell-shaped blue, purple, or white flowers
WORD ORIGIN Latin *conferva* water plant
comfy *adj* **-fier, -fiest** *informal* comfortable
comic *adj* **1** humorous; funny **2** of or relating to comedy ▷ *n* **3** a comedian **4** a magazine containing comic strips
WORD ORIGIN Greek *kōmikos*
comical *adj* causing amusement, often because of being ludicrous or ridiculous: *an enthusiasm comical to behold* **comically** *adv*
comic opera *n* an opera with speech and singing that tells an amusing story
comic strip *n* a sequence of drawings in a newspaper or magazine, telling a humorous story or an adventure
Comines *or* **Commines** *n* **Philippe de** ?1447–?1511, French diplomat and historian, noted for his *Mémoires* (1489–98)
coming *adj* **1** (of time or events) approaching or next: *in the coming weeks* **2** likely to be important in the future: *he was regarded as a coming man at the Foreign Office* **3** **have it coming to one** *informal* to deserve what one is about to suffer ▷ *n* **4** arrival or approach
comity *n, pl* **-ties** *formal* friendly politeness, esp. between different countries
WORD ORIGIN Latin *comis* affable
comma *n* the punctuation mark (,) indicating a slight pause and used where there is a list of items or to separate the parts of a sentence
WORD ORIGIN Greek *komma* clause
command *vb* **1** to order or compel **2** to have authority over **3** to deserve and get: *a public figure who commands almost universal respect* **4** to look down over: *the house commands a magnificent view of the sea and the islands* ▷ *n* **5** an authoritative instruction that something must be done **6** the authority to command **7** knowledge; control: *a fluent command of French* **8** a military or naval unit with a specific function **9** *computers* a part of a program consisting of a coded instruction to the computer to perform a specified function
WORD ORIGIN Latin *com-* (intensive) + *mandare* to order
commandant *n* an officer in charge of a place or group of people
commandeer *vb* **1** to seize for military use **2** to take as if by right: *he commandeered the one waiting taxi outside the station*
WORD ORIGIN Afrikaans *kommandeer*
commander *n* **1** an officer in command of a military group or operation **2** a middle-ranking naval officer **3** a high-ranking member of some orders of knights
commander-in-chief *n, pl* **commanders-in-chief** the supreme commander of a nation's armed forces
commanding *adj* **1** being in charge: *the commanding officer* **2** in a position or situation where success looks certain: *a commanding lead* **3** having the air of authority: *a commanding voice* **4** having a wide view
commandment *n* a divine command, esp. one of the Ten Commandments in the Old Testament
commando *n, pl* **-dos** *or* **-does** **a** a military unit trained to make swift raids in enemy territory **b** a member of such a unit
WORD ORIGIN Dutch *commando* command
commedia dell'arte (kom-**made**-ee-a dell-**art**-tay) *n* a form of improvised comedy popular in Italy in the 16th century, with stock characters and a stereotyped plot
WORD ORIGIN Italian
commemorate *vb* **-rating, -rated** to honour or keep alive the memory of: *a series of events to commemorate the end of the Second World War* **commemoration** *n* **commemorative** *adj*
WORD ORIGIN Latin *com-* (intensive) + *memorare* to remind
commence *vb* **-mencing, -menced** to begin
WORD ORIGIN Latin *com-* (intensive) + *initiare* to begin
commencement *n* **1** the beginning;

THESAURUS

comfort *n* **1 = ease**, luxury, wellbeing, opulence **2 = consolation**, cheer, encouragement, succour, help, support, aid, relief, ease, compensation, alleviation OPPOSITE: annoyance ▷ *vb* **5, 6 = console**, encourage, ease, cheer, strengthen, relieve, reassure, soothe, hearten, solace, assuage, gladden, commiserate with OPPOSITE: distress
comfortable *adj* **1 = pleasant**, homely, easy, relaxing, delightful, enjoyable, cosy, agreeable, restful OPPOSITE: unpleasant **2 = at ease**, happy, at home, contented, relaxed, serene OPPOSITE: uncomfortable **3** *(informal)* **= well-off**, prosperous, affluent, well-to-do, comfortably-off, in clover *(informal)*
comic *adj* **1 = funny**, amusing, witty, humorous, farcical, comical, light, joking, droll, facetious, jocular, waggish OPPOSITE: sad ▷ *n* **3 = comedian**, funny man, humorist, wit, clown, wag, jester, dag *(NZ informal)*, buffoon
coming *adj* **1 = approaching**, next, future, near, due, forthcoming, imminent, in store, impending, at hand, upcoming, on the cards, in the wind, nigh, just round the corner ▷ *n* **4 = arrival**, approach, advent, accession
command *vb* **1 = order**, tell, charge, demand, require, direct, bid, compel, enjoin OPPOSITE: beg **2 = have authority over**, lead, head, control, rule, manage, handle, dominate, govern, administer, supervise, be in charge of, reign over OPPOSITE: be subordinate to ▷ *n* **5 = order**, demand, direction, instruction, requirement, decree, bidding, mandate, canon, directive, injunction, fiat, ultimatum, commandment, edict, behest, precept **6 = management**, power, control, charge, authority, direction, supervision **7 = domination**, control, rule, grasp, sway, mastery, dominion, upper hand, power, government
commander *n* **1 = leader**, director, chief, officer, boss, head, captain, baas *(S African)*, ruler, commander-in-chief, commanding officer, C in C, C.O., sherang *(Austral & NZ)*
commanding *adj* **2 = dominant**, controlling, dominating, superior, decisive, advantageous
commemorate *vb* **= celebrate**, remember, honour, recognize, salute, pay tribute to, immortalize, memorialize OPPOSITE: ignore
commence *vb* **a = embark on**, start,

DICTIONARY

start **2** *US & Canad* a graduation ceremony

commend ❶ *vb* **1** to praise in a formal manner: *the judge commended her bravery* **2** to recommend: *he commended the scheme warmly* **3** to entrust: *I commend my child to your care* **commendable** *adj* **commendation** *n*
WORD ORIGIN Latin *com-* (intensive) + *mandare* to entrust

commensurable *adj* **1** measurable by the same standards **2** *maths* **a** having a common factor **b** having units of the same dimensions and being related by whole numbers **commensurability** *n*

commensurate *adj* **1** corresponding in degree, size, or value **2** commensurable
WORD ORIGIN Latin *com-* same + *mensurare* to measure

comment ❶ *n* **1** a remark, criticism, or observation **2** a situation or event that expresses some feeling: *a sad comment on the nature of many relationships* **3** talk or gossip **4** a note explaining or criticizing a passage in a text **5 no comment** I decline to say anything about the matter ▷*vb* **6** to remark or express an opinion
WORD ORIGIN Latin *commentum* invention

commentariat *n* the journalists and broadcasters who analyse and comment on current affairs
WORD ORIGIN from COMMENTATOR + PROLETARIAT

commentary ❶ *n, pl* **-taries 1** a spoken accompaniment to an event, broadcast, or film **2** a series of explanatory notes on a subject

commentate *vb* **-tating, -tated** to act as a commentator

commentator ❶ *n* **1** a person who provides a spoken commentary for a broadcast, esp. of a sporting event **2** an expert who reports on and analyses a particular subject

commerce *n* **1** the buying and selling of goods and services **2** *literary* social relations
WORD ORIGIN Latin *commercium*

commercial ❶ *adj* **1** of or engaged in commerce: *commercial exploitation of sport* **2** sponsored or paid for by an advertiser: *commercial radio* **3** having profit as the main aim: *this is a more commercial, accessible album than its predecessor* ▷*n* **4** a radio or television advertisement

commercialism *n* **1** the principles and practices of commerce **2** exclusive or inappropriate emphasis on profit

commercialize *or* **-ise** *vb* **-izing, -ized** *or* **-ising, -ised 1** to make commercial **2** to exploit for profit, esp. at the expense of quality **commercialization** *or* **-isation** *n*

commercial traveller *n* a travelling salesman

commie *n, pl* **-mies,** *adj informal & offensive* Communist

Commines *n* a variant spelling of (Philippe de) **Comines**

commingle *vb* **-gling, -gled** to mix or be mixed

commis (kom-iss, kom-ee) *adj Brit* (of a waiter or chef) apprentice: *the commis chef*
WORD ORIGIN French

commiserate *vb* **-ating, -ated** (usually foll. by *with*) to express sympathy or pity (for) **commiseration** *n*
WORD ORIGIN Latin *com-* together + *miserari* to bewail

commissar *n* formerly, an official responsible for political education in Communist countries

commissariat *n* a military department in charge of food supplies
WORD ORIGIN Medieval Latin *commissarius* commissary

commissary *n, pl* **-saries 1** *US* a shop supplying food or equipment, as in a military camp **2** a representative or deputy
WORD ORIGIN Medieval Latin *commissarius* official in charge

commission ❶ *n* **1** an order for a piece of work, esp. a work of art or a piece of writing **2** a duty given to a person or group to perform **3** the fee or percentage paid to a salesperson for each sale made **4** a group of people appointed to perform certain duties: *a new parliamentary commission on defence* **5** the act of committing a sin or crime **6** *mil* the rank or authority officially given to an officer **7** authority to perform certain duties **8 in** *or* **out of commission** in *or* not in working order ▷*vb* **9** to place an order for: *a report commissioned by the United Nations; a new work commissioned by the BBC Symphony Orchestra* **10** *mil* to give a commission to **11** to prepare (a ship) for active service **12** to grant authority to
WORD ORIGIN Latin *committere* to commit

commissionaire *n chiefly Brit* a uniformed doorman at a hotel, theatre, or cinema
WORD ORIGIN French

commissioned officer *n* a military officer holding a rank by a commission

commissioner *n* **1** an appointed official in a government department or other organization **2** a member of a commission

commit ❶ *vb* **-mitting, -mitted 1** to perform (a crime or error) **2** to hand over or allocate: *a marked reluctance to commit new money to business* **3** to pledge to a cause or a course of action **4** to send (someone) to prison or hospital **5 commit to memory** to memorize **6 commit to paper** to write down
WORD ORIGIN Latin *committere* to join

commitment ❶ *n* **1** dedication to a cause or principle **2** an obligation, responsibility, or promise that restricts freedom of action **3** the act of committing or state of being committed

committal *n* the official consignment of a person to a prison or mental hospital

committed *adj* having pledged oneself to a particular belief or

THESAURUS

open, begin, initiate, originate, instigate, inaugurate, enter upon **OPPOSITE:** stop
b = start, open, begin, go ahead **OPPOSITE:** end

commend *vb* **1 = praise**, acclaim, applaud, compliment, extol, approve, big up *(slang)*, eulogize, speak highly of **OPPOSITE:** criticize **2 = recommend**, suggest, approve, advocate, endorse, vouch for, put in a good word for

comment *n* **1 = remark**, statement, observation **4 = note**, criticism, explanation, illustration, commentary, exposition, annotation, elucidation ▷*vb* **6 = remark**, say, note, mention, point out, observe, utter, opine, interpose

commentary *n* **1, 2 = narration**, report, review, explanation, description, voice-over

commentator *n* **1 = reporter**, special correspondent, sportscaster, commenter **2 = critic**, interpreter, annotator

commercial *adj* **1 = mercantile**, business, trade, trading, sales **3 = materialistic**, mercenary, profit-making, venal, monetary, exploited, pecuniary

commission *n* **2 = duty**, authority, trust, charge, task, function, mission, employment, appointment, warrant, mandate, errand **3 = fee**, cut, compensation, percentage, allowance, royalties, brokerage, rake-off *(slang)* **4 = committee**, board, representatives, commissioners, delegation, deputation, body of commissioners ▷*vb* **9 = appoint**, order, contract, select, engage, delegate, nominate, authorize, empower, depute

commit *vb* **1, 2 = do**, perform, carry out, execute, enact, perpetrate

commitment *n* **1 = dedication**, loyalty, devotion, adherence **OPPOSITE:** indecisiveness **2 = responsibility**, tie, duty, obligation, liability, engagement

DICTIONARY

course of action: *a committed pacifist*

committee *n* a group of people appointed to perform a specified service or function
WORD ORIGIN Middle English *committen* to entrust

C

commode *n* **1** a chair with a hinged flap concealing a chamber pot **2** a chest of drawers
WORD ORIGIN French

commodious *adj* with plenty of space
WORD ORIGIN Latin *commodus* convenient

commodity *n, pl* **-ties** something that can be bought or sold
WORD ORIGIN Latin *commoditas* suitability

commodore *n* **1** *Brit* a senior commissioned officer in the navy **2** the president of a yacht club
WORD ORIGIN probably from Dutch *commandeur*

Commodus *n* **Lucius Aelius Aurelius**, son of Marcus Aurelius. 161–192 AD, Roman emperor (180–192), noted for his tyrannical reign

common ⊕ *adj* **1** frequently encountered: *a fairly common plant; this disease is most common in kittens and young cats* **2** widespread among people in general: *common practice* **3** belonging to two or more people: *we share common interests* **4** belonging to the whole community: *common property* **5** low-class, vulgar, or coarse **6** *maths* belonging to two or more: *the lowest common denominator* **7** not belonging to the upper classes: *the common people* **8** **common or garden** *informal* ordinary ▹*n* **9** a piece of open land belonging to all the members of a community **10** **in common** shared, in joint use ▸ See also **Commons**
> **commonly** *adv*
WORD ORIGIN Latin *communis* general

commonality *n, pl* **-ties 1** the sharing of common attributes **2** the ordinary people

commonalty *n, pl* **-ties 1** the ordinary people **2** the members of an incorporated society

common cold *n* ▸ same as **cold** (sense 17)

commoner *n* a person who does not belong to the nobility

common fraction *n* ▸ same as **simple fraction**

common law *n* **1** law based on judges' decisions and custom, as distinct from written laws ▹*adj* **common-law 2** (of a relationship) regarded as a marriage through being long-standing

Common Market *n* ▸ a former name for **European Union**

commonplace ⊕ *adj* **1** so common or frequent as not to be worth commenting on: *foreign holidays have now become commonplace* **2** dull or unoriginal: *a commonplace observation* ▹*n* **3** a cliché **4** an ordinary thing
WORD ORIGIN translation of Latin *locus communis* argument of wide application

common room *n chiefly Brit & Austral* a sitting room for students or staff in schools or colleges

commons *pl n* **1** *Brit* shared food or rations **2** **short commons** reduced rations

Commons *n* **the Commons** ▸ same as **House of Commons**

common sense ⊕ *n* **1** good practical understanding ▹*adj* **common-sense 2** inspired by or displaying this

common time *n music* a time signature with four crotchet beats to the bar; four-four time: *a dance in common time*

commonwealth *n* the people of a state or nation viewed politically

Commonwealth *n* **the Commonwealth a** Official name: **the Commonwealth of Nations** an association of sovereign states that are or at some time have been ruled by Britain **b** the official title of the federated states of Australia

commotion *n* noisy disturbance
WORD ORIGIN Latin *com-* (intensive) + *movere* to move

communal ⊕ *adj* **1** belonging to or used by a community as a whole **2** of a commune **communally** *adv*

communautaire (kom-**myune**-aw-ter) *adj* supporting the principles of the European Union
WORD ORIGIN French: community

commune[1] ⊕ *n* **1** a group of people living together and sharing possessions and responsibilities **2** the smallest district of local government in Belgium, France, Italy, and Switzerland
WORD ORIGIN Latin *communia* things held in common

commune[2] *vb* **-muning, -muned** ▪ **commune with a** to experience strong emotion for: *communing with nature* **b** to talk intimately with
WORD ORIGIN Old French *comuner* to hold in common

communicable *adj* **1** capable of being communicated **2** (of a disease) capable of being passed on easily

communicant *n Christianity* a person who receives Communion

communicate ⊕ *vb* **-cating, -cated 1** to exchange (thoughts) or make known (information or feelings) by speech, writing, or other means **2** (usually foll. by *to*) to transmit (to): *the reaction of the rapturous audience communicated itself to the performers* **3** to have a sympathetic mutual understanding **4** *Christianity* to receive Communion **communicator** *n* **communicative** *adj*
WORD ORIGIN Latin *communicare* to share

communicating *adj* making or having a direct connection from one room to another: *the suite is made up of three communicating rooms; the communicating door*

communication ⊕ *n* **1** the exchange

THESAURUS

common *adj* **1 = usual**, standard, daily, regular, ordinary, familiar, plain, conventional, routine, frequent, everyday, customary, commonplace, vanilla *(slang)*, habitual, run-of-the-mill, humdrum, stock, workaday, bog-standard *(Brit & Irish slang)*, a dime a dozen **OPPOSITE:** rare **2 = popular**, general, accepted, standard, routine, widespread, universal, prevailing, prevalent **3 = shared**, collective **4 = collective**, public, community, social, communal **OPPOSITE:** personal **5 = vulgar**, low, inferior, coarse, plebeian **OPPOSITE:** refined **7 = ordinary**, average, simple, typical, undistinguished, dinki-di *(Austral informal)* **OPPOSITE:** important

commonplace *adj* **1, 2 = everyday**, common, ordinary, widespread, pedestrian, customary, mundane, vanilla *(slang)*, banal, run-of-the-mill, humdrum, dime-a-dozen *(informal)* **OPPOSITE:** rare ▹*n* **3 = cliché**, platitude, banality, truism

common sense *n* **1 = good sense**, sound judgment, level-headedness, practicality, prudence, nous *(Brit slang)*, soundness, reasonableness, gumption *(Brit informal)*, horse sense, native intelligence, mother wit, smarts *(slang, chiefly US)*, wit

communal *adj* **1 = public**, shared, general, joint, collective, communistic **OPPOSITE:** private

commune[1] *n* **1 = community**, collective, cooperative, kibbutz

communicate *vb* **1a = contact**, talk, speak, phone, correspond, make contact, be in touch, ring up *(informal, chiefly Brit)*, be in contact, get in contact, e-mail, text **1b = make known**, report, announce, reveal, publish, declare, spread, disclose, pass on, proclaim, transmit, convey, impart, divulge, disseminate **OPPOSITE:** keep secret **2 = pass on**, transfer, spread, transmit

communication *n* **1a = contact**, conversation, correspondence, intercourse, link, relations, connection **1b = passing on**, spread, circulation, transmission, disclosure, imparting, dissemination, conveyance **2 = message**, news, report, word, information, statement, intelligence, announcement,

DICTIONARY

of information, ideas, or feelings **2** something communicated, such as a message **3 communications** means of travelling or sending messages

communication cord *n Brit* a chain in a train which may be pulled by a passenger to stop the train in an emergency

communion *n* **1** a sharing of thoughts, emotions, or beliefs **2 communion with** strong feelings for: *private communion with nature* **3** a religious group with shared beliefs and practices: *the Anglican communion*
WORD ORIGIN Latin *communis* common

Communion *n Christianity* **1** a ritual commemorating Christ's Last Supper by the consecration of bread and wine **2** the consecrated bread and wine. Also called: **Holy Communion**

communiqué (kom-**mune**-ik-kay) *n* an official announcement
WORD ORIGIN French

communism ❶ *n* the belief that private ownership should be abolished and all work and property should be shared by the community **communist** *n, adj*
WORD ORIGIN French *communisme*

Communism *n* **1** a political movement based upon the writings of Karl Marx that advocates communism **2** the political and social system established in countries with a ruling Communist Party **Communist** *n, adj*

community ❶ *n, pl* **-ties 1** all the people living in one district **2** a group of people with shared origins or interests: *the local Jewish community* **3** a group of countries with certain interests in common **4** the public; society **5** a group of interdependent plants and animals inhabiting the same region
WORD ORIGIN Latin *communis* common

community centre *n* a building used by a community for social gatherings or activities

community charge *n* ▸in Britain, the formal name for **poll tax**

community college *n US & Canad* a nonresidential college offering two-year courses of study

community service *n* organized unpaid work intended for the good of the community: often used as a punishment for minor criminals

commutative *adj maths* giving the same result irrespective of the order of the numbers or symbols

commutator *n* a device used to change alternating electric current into direct current

commute *vb* **-muting, -muted 1** to travel some distance regularly between one's home and one's place of work **2** *law* to reduce (a sentence) to one less severe **3** to substitute **4** to pay (an annuity or pension) at one time, instead of in instalments ▹*n* **5** a journey made by commuting **commutable** *adj* **commutation** *n*
WORD ORIGIN Latin *com-* mutually + *mutare* to change

commuter ❶ *n* a person who regularly travels a considerable distance to work

compact[1] ❶ *adj* **1** closely packed together **2** neatly fitted into a restricted space **3** concise; brief ▹*vb* **4** to pack closely together ▹*n* **5** a small flat case containing a mirror and face powder **compactly** *adv* **compactness** *n*
WORD ORIGIN Latin *com-* together + *pangere* to fasten

compact[2] ❶ *n* a contract or agreement
WORD ORIGIN Latin *com-* together + *pacisci* to contract

compact disc *n* a small digital audio disc on which the sound is read by an optical laser system

companion ❶ *n* **1** a person who associates with or accompanies someone: *a travelling companion* **2** a woman paid to live or travel with another woman **3** a guidebook or handbook **4** one of a pair **companionship** *n*
WORD ORIGIN Late Latin *companio* one who eats bread with another

companionable *adj* friendly and pleasant to be with **companionably** *adv*

companionway *n* a ladder from one deck to another in a ship

company ❶ *n, pl* **-nies 1** a business organization **2** a group of actors **3** a small unit of troops **4** the officers and crew of a ship **5** the fact of being with someone: *I enjoy her company* **6** a number of people gathered together **7** a guest or guests **8** a person's associates **9 keep someone company** to accompany someone **10 part company** to disagree or separate
WORD ORIGIN see COMPANION

company sergeant-major *n mil* the senior noncommissioned officer in a company

comparable ❶ *adj* **1** worthy of comparison **2** able to be compared (with) **comparability** *n*

comparative ❶ *adj* **1** relative: *despite the importance of his discoveries, he died in comparative poverty* **2** involving comparison: *comparative religion* **3** *grammar* the form of an adjective or adverb that indicates that the quality denoted is possessed to a greater extent. In English the comparative is marked by the suffix *-er* or the word *more* ▹*n* **4** the comparative form of an adjective or adverb **comparatively** *adv*

compare ❶ *vb* **-paring, -pared 1** to examine in order to observe

THESAURUS

disclosure, dispatch, e-mail, text

communism *n (usually cap.)* **= socialism**, Marxism, Stalinism, collectivism, Bolshevism, Marxism-Leninism, state socialism, Maoism, Trotskyism, Eurocommunism, Titoism

community *n* **1, 4 = society**, people, public, association, population, residents, commonwealth, general public, populace, body politic, state, company

commuter *n* **= daily traveller**, passenger, suburbanite

compact[1] *adj* **1 = closely packed**, firm, solid, thick, dense, compressed, condensed, impenetrable, impermeable, pressed together
OPPOSITE: loose
3 = concise, brief, to the point, succinct, terse, laconic, pithy, epigrammatic, pointed
OPPOSITE: lengthy

compact[2] *n* **= agreement**, deal, understanding, contract, bond, arrangement, alliance, treaty, bargain, pact, covenant, entente, concordat

companion *n* **1 = friend**, partner, ally, colleague, associate, mate *(informal)*, gossip *(archaic)*, buddy *(informal)*, comrade, accomplice, crony, confederate, consort, main man *(slang, chiefly US)*, homeboy *(slang, chiefly US)*, cobber *(Austral & NZ old-fashioned, informal)* **2 = assistant**, aide, escort, attendant

company *n* **1 = business**, firm, association, corporation, partnership, establishment, syndicate, house, concern **2, 6 = group**, troupe, set, community, league, band, crowd, camp, collection, gathering, circle, crew, assembly, convention, ensemble, throng, coterie, bevy, assemblage, party, body **3 = troop**, unit, squad, team **5 = companionship**, society, presence, fellowship **7 = guests**, party, visitors, callers

comparable *adj* **1 = similar**, related, alike, corresponding, akin, analogous, of a piece, cognate, cut from the same cloth **2 = equal**, equivalent, on a par, tantamount, a match, proportionate, commensurate, as good
OPPOSITE: unequal

comparative *adj* **1 = relative**, qualified, by comparison, approximate

compare *vb* **1 = contrast**, balance, weigh, set against, collate, juxtapose

DICTIONARY

resemblances or differences: *the survey compared the health of three groups of children* **2 compare to** to declare to be like: *one ambulance driver compared the carnage to an air crash* **3** (usually foll. by *with*) to resemble: *his storytelling compares with the likes of Le Carré* **4** to bear a specified relation when examined: *this full-flavoured white wine compares favourably with more expensive French wines* **5 compare notes** to exchange opinions ▷*n* **6 beyond compare** without equal
WORD ORIGIN Latin *com-* together + *par* equal

comparison ⊕ *n* **1** a comparing or being compared **2** likeness or similarity: *there is no comparison at all between her and Catherine* **3** *grammar* the positive, comparative, and superlative forms of an adjective or adverb **4 in comparison to** *or* **with** compared to **5 bear** *or* **stand comparison with** to be able to be compared with (something else), esp. favourably: *his half-dozen best novels can stand comparison with anyone's*

compartment ⊕ *n* **1** one of the sections into which a railway is sometimes divided **2** a separate section: *filing the information away in some compartment of his mind* **3** a small storage space: *the ice-making compartment of the fridge*
WORD ORIGIN French *compartiment*

compartmentalize *or* **-ise** *vb* **-izing, -ized** *or* **-ising, -ised** to put into categories or sections

compass ⊕ *n* **1** an instrument for finding direction, with a magnetized needle which points to magnetic north **2** limits or range: *within the compass of a normal sized book such a comprehensive survey is not possible* **3 compasses** an instrument used for drawing circles or measuring distances, that consists of two arms, joined at one end
WORD ORIGIN Latin *com-* together + *passus* step

compassion ⊕ *n* a feeling of distress and pity for the suffering or misfortune of another
WORD ORIGIN Latin *com-* with + *pati* to suffer

compassionate ⊕ *adj* showing or having compassion
compassionately *adv*

compassionate leave *n* leave from work granted on the grounds of family illness or bereavement

compatible ⊕ *adj* **1** able to exist together harmoniously
2 consistent: *his evidence is fully compatible with the other data* **3** (of pieces of equipment) capable of being used together **compatibility** *n*
WORD ORIGIN Late Latin *compati* to suffer with

compatriot *n* a fellow countryman or countrywoman
WORD ORIGIN French *compatriote*

compel ⊕ *vb* **-pelling, -pelled 1** to force (to be or do something) **2** to obtain by force: *his performance compelled attention*
WORD ORIGIN Latin *com-* together + *pellere* to drive

compelling ⊕ *adj* **1** arousing strong interest: *a compelling new novel*
2 convincing: *compelling evidence*

compendious *adj* brief but comprehensive

compendium *n, pl* **-diums** *or* **-dia 1** *Brit* a selection of different table games in one container **2** a concise but comprehensive summary
WORD ORIGIN Latin: a saving, literally: something weighed

compensate ⊕ *vb* **-sating, -sated 1** to make amends to (someone), esp. for loss or injury **2** to cancel out the effects of (something): *the car's nifty handling fails to compensate for its many flaws* **3** to serve as compensation for (injury or loss) **compensatory** *adj*
WORD ORIGIN Latin *compensare*

compensation ⊕ *n* **1** payment made as reparation for loss or injury **2** the act of making amends for something

compere *Brit, Austral & NZ n* **1** a person who introduces a stage, radio, or television show ▷*vb* **-pering, -pered 2** to be the compere of
WORD ORIGIN French: godfather

compete ⊕ *vb* **-peting, -peted 1** to take part in (a contest or competition) **2** to strive (to achieve something or to be successful): *able to compete on the international market*
WORD ORIGIN Latin *com-* together + *petere* to seek

competence ⊕ *or* **competency** *n* **1** the ability to do something well or effectively **2** a sufficient income to live on **3** the state of being legally competent or qualified

competent ⊕ *adj* **1** having sufficient skill or knowledge: *he was a very competent engineer* **2** suitable or sufficient for the purpose: *it was a competent performance, but hardly a remarkable one* **3** having valid legal authority: *lawful detention after conviction by a competent court*
WORD ORIGIN Latin *competens*

THESAURUS

2 compare to something = liken to, parallel, identify with, equate to, correlate to, mention in the same breath as

comparison *n* **1 = contrast**, distinction, differentiation, juxtaposition, collation
2 = similarity, analogy, resemblance, correlation, likeness, comparability

compartment *n* **1 = section**, carriage, berth **3 = bay**, chamber, booth, locker, niche, cubicle, alcove, pigeonhole, cubbyhole, cell

compass *n* **2 = range**, field, area, reach, scope, sphere, limit, stretch, bound, extent, zone, boundary, realm

compassion *n* **= sympathy**, understanding, charity, pity, humanity, mercy, heart, quarter, sorrow, kindness, tenderness, condolence, clemency, commiseration, fellow feeling, soft-heartedness, tender-heartedness, aroha (*NZ*)
OPPOSITE: indifference

compassionate *adj* **= sympathetic**, kindly, understanding, tender, pitying, humanitarian, charitable, humane, indulgent, benevolent, lenient, merciful, kind-hearted, tender-hearted **OPPOSITE:** uncaring

compatible *adj* **1 = like-minded**, harmonious, in harmony, in accord, of one mind, of the same mind, en rapport (*French*)
OPPOSITE: incompatible
2 = consistent, in keeping, consonant, congenial, congruent, reconcilable, congruous, accordant, agreeable **OPPOSITE:** inappropriate

compel *vb* **1 = force**, make, urge, enforce, railroad (*informal*), drive, oblige, constrain, hustle (*slang*), necessitate, coerce, bulldoze (*informal*), impel, dragoon

compelling *adj* **1 = fascinating**, gripping, irresistible, enchanting, enthralling, hypnotic, spellbinding, mesmeric **OPPOSITE:** boring
2 = convincing, telling, powerful, forceful, conclusive, weighty, cogent, irrefutable

compensate *vb* **1 = recompense**, repay, refund, reimburse, indemnify, make restitution, requite, remunerate, satisfy, make good
2 = balance, cancel (out), offset, make up for, redress, counteract, neutralize, counterbalance **3 = make amends for**, make up for, atone for, pay for, do penance for, cancel out, make reparation for, make redress for

compensation *n* **1 = reparation**, damages, payment, recompense, indemnification, offset, remuneration, indemnity, restitution, reimbursement, requital
2 = recompense, amends, reparation, restitution, atonement

compete *vb* **1 = take part**, participate, be in the running, be a competitor, be a contestant, play **2 = contend**, fight, rival, vie, challenge, struggle, contest, strive, pit yourself against

competence *n* **1, 3 = ability**, skill, talent, capacity, expertise, proficiency, competency, capability
OPPOSITE: incompetence

competent *adj* **1 = able**, skilled, capable, clever, endowed, proficient

DICTIONARY

competition ❶ *n* **1** the act of competing; rivalry: *competition for places was keen* **2** an event in which people compete **3** the opposition offered by competitors **4** people against whom one competes

competitive ❶ *adj* **1** involving rivalry: *the increasingly competitive computer industry* **2** characterized by an urge to compete: *her naturally competitive spirit* **3** of good enough value to be successful against commercial rivals: *we offer worldwide flights at competitive prices* **competitiveness** *n*

competitor ❶ *n* a person, team, or firm that competes

compile ❶ *vb* **-piling, -piled 1** to collect and arrange (information) from various sources **2** *computers* to convert (commands for a computer) from the language used by the person using it into machine code suitable for the computer, using a compiler **compilation** *n*
WORD ORIGIN Latin *com-* together + *pilare* to thrust down, pack

compiler *n* **1** a person who compiles information **2** a computer program that converts a high-level programming language into the machine language used by a computer

complacency ❶ *n* extreme self-satisfaction **complacent** *adj* **complacently** *adv*

complain ❶ *vb* **1** to express resentment or displeasure **2 complain of** to state that one is suffering from a pain or illness: *he complained of breathing trouble and chest pains* **3** to make a formal protest: *he complained to the police about his rowdy neighbours*
WORD ORIGIN Latin *com-* (intensive) + *plangere* to bewail

complainant *n law* a plaintiff

complaint ❶ *n* **1** the act of complaining **2** a reason for complaining **3** a mild illness **4** a formal protest

complaisant (kom-**play**-zant) *adj* willing to please or oblige **complaisance** *n*
WORD ORIGIN Latin *complacere* to please greatly

complement ❶ *n* **1** a person or thing that completes something **2** a complete amount or number: *a full complement of staff nurses and care assistants* **3** the officers and crew needed to man a ship **4** *grammar* a word or words added to the verb to complete the meaning of the predicate in a sentence, as *a fool* in *He is a fool* or *that he would come* in *I hoped that he would come* **5** *maths* the angle that when added to a specified angle produces a right angle ▷ *vb* **6** to complete or form a complement to
WORD ORIGIN Latin *com-* (intensive) + *plere* to fill

complementary ❶ *adj* **1** forming a complete or balanced whole **2** forming a complement

complementary medicine *n* ▸ same as **alternative medicine**

complete ❶ *adj* **1** thorough; absolute: *it was a complete shambles* **2** perfect in quality or kind: *he is the complete modern footballer* **3** finished **4** having all the necessary parts **5 complete with** having as an extra feature or part: *a mansion complete with swimming pool* ▷ *vb* **-pleting, -pleted 6** to finish **7** to make whole or perfect **completely** *adv* **completion** *n*
WORD ORIGIN Latin *complere* to fill up

complex ❶ *adj* **1** made up of interconnected parts **2** intricate or complicated **3** *maths* of or involving complex numbers ▷ *n* **4** a whole made up of related parts: *a leisure complex including a gymnasium, squash courts, and a 20-metre swimming pool* **5** *psychoanal* a group of unconscious feelings that influences a person's behaviour **6** *informal* an obsession or phobia: *I have never had a complex about my height*
WORD ORIGIN Latin *com-* together + *plectere* to braid

complex fraction *n maths* a fraction in which the numerator or denominator or both contain fractions

complexion ❶ *n* **1** the colour and general appearance of the skin of a person's face **2** character or nature:

THESAURUS

OPPOSITE: incompetent
3 = fit, qualified, equal, appropriate, suitable, sufficient, adequate **OPPOSITE:** unqualified

competition *n* **1 = rivalry**, opposition, struggle, contest, contention, strife, one-upmanship *(informal)* **2 = contest**, event, championship, tournament, head-to-head **3, 4 = opposition**, field, rivals, challengers

competitive *adj* **1 = cut-throat**, aggressive, fierce, ruthless, relentless, antagonistic, dog-eat-dog **2 = ambitious**, pushing, opposing, aggressive, two-fisted, vying, contentious, combative

competitor *n* **a = rival**, competition, opposition, adversary, antagonist **b = contestant**, participant, contender, challenger, entrant, player, opponent

compile *vb* **1 = put together**, collect, gather, organize, accumulate, marshal, garner, amass, cull, anthologize

complacency *n* **= smugness**, satisfaction, gratification, contentment, self-congratulation, self-satisfaction

complain *vb* **1 = find fault**, moan, grumble, whinge *(informal)*, beef *(slang)*, carp, fuss, bitch *(slang)*, groan, grieve, lament, whine, growl, deplore, grouse, gripe *(informal)*, bemoan, bleat, put the boot in *(slang)*, bewail, kick up a fuss *(informal)*, grouch *(informal)*, bellyache *(slang)*, kvetch *(US slang)*, nit-pick *(informal)*

complaint *n* **1, 2 = grumble**, criticism, beef *(slang)*, moan, bitch *(slang)*, lament, grievance, wail, dissatisfaction, annoyance, grouse, gripe *(informal)*, grouch *(informal)*, plaint, fault-finding **3 = disorder**, problem, trouble, disease, upset, illness, sickness, ailment, affliction, malady, indisposition **4 = protest**, accusation, objection, grievance, remonstrance, charge

complement *n* **1 = accompaniment**, companion, accessory, completion, finishing touch, rounding-off, adjunct, supplement **2 = total**, capacity, quota, aggregate, contingent, entirety ▷ *vb* **6 = enhance**, complete, improve, boost, crown, add to, set off, heighten, augment, round off

complementary *adj* **1, 2 = matching**, companion, corresponding, compatible, reciprocal, interrelating, interdependent, harmonizing **OPPOSITE:** incompatible

complete *adj* **1, 2 = total**, perfect, absolute, utter, outright, thorough, consummate, out-and-out, unmitigated, dyed-in-the-wool, thoroughgoing, deep-dyed *(usually derogatory)* **3 = finished**, done, ended, completed, achieved, concluded, fulfilled, accomplished **OPPOSITE:** unfinished **4a = entire**, full, whole, intact, unbroken, faultless, undivided, unimpaired **OPPOSITE:** incomplete **4b = unabridged**, full, entire ▷ *vb* **6 = finish**, conclude, fulfil, accomplish, do, end, close, achieve, perform, settle, realize, execute, discharge, wrap up *(informal)*, terminate, finalize **OPPOSITE:** start **7 = perfect**, accomplish, finish off, round off, crown, cap **OPPOSITE:** spoil

complex *adj* **1 = compound**, compounded, multiple, composite, manifold, heterogeneous, multifarious **2 = complicated**, difficult, involved, mixed, elaborate, tangled, mingled, intricate, tortuous, convoluted, knotty, labyrinthine, circuitous **OPPOSITE:** simple ▷ *n* **4 = structure**, system, scheme, network, organization, aggregate, composite, synthesis **6** *(informal)* **= obsession**, preoccupation, phobia, fixation, fixed idea, idée fixe *(French)*

complexion *n* **1 = skin**, colour,

C

DICTIONARY

the political complexion of the government **WORD ORIGIN** Latin *complexio* a combination

complexity ❶ *n, pl* **-ties 1** the state or quality of being intricate or complex **2** something complicated

C

complex number *n* any number of the form *a* + b*i*, where *a* and *b* are real numbers and i = √–1

compliance *n* **1** complying **2** a tendency to do what others want **compliant** *adj*

complicate ❶ *vb* **-cating, -cated** to make or become complex or difficult to deal with
WORD ORIGIN Latin *complicare* to fold together

complicated ❶ *adj* difficult to understand or deal with

complication ❶ *n* **1** something which makes a situation more difficult to deal with: *an added complication is the growing concern for the environment* **2** a medical condition arising as a consequence of another

complicity *n, pl* **-ties** the fact of being an accomplice in a crime

compliment ❶ *n* **1** an expression of praise **2 compliments** formal greetings ▷*vb* **3** to express admiration for
WORD ORIGIN Italian *complimento*

complimentary ❶ *adj* **1** expressing praise **2** free of charge: *a complimentary drink*

comply ❶ *vb* **-plies, -plying, -plied** to act in accordance (with a rule, order, or request)
WORD ORIGIN Spanish *cumplir* to complete

component ❶ *n* **1** a constituent part or feature of a whole **2** *maths* one of a set of two or more vectors whose resultant is a given vector ▷*adj* **3** forming or functioning as a part or feature: *over 60 component parts*
WORD ORIGIN Latin *componere* to put together

comport *vb formal* **1 comport oneself** to behave in a specified way **2 comport with** to suit or be appropriate to **comportment** *n*
WORD ORIGIN Latin *comportare* to collect

compose ❶ *vb* **-posing, -posed 1** to put together or make up **2** to be the component elements of **3** to create (a musical or literary work) **4** to calm (oneself) **5** to arrange artistically **6** *printing* to set up (type)
WORD ORIGIN Latin *componere* to put in place

composed ❶ *adj* (of people) in control of their feelings

composer *n* a person who writes music

composite *adj* **1** made up of separate parts **2** (of a plant) with flower heads made up of many small flowers, such as the dandelion **3** *maths* capable of being factorized: *a composite function* ▷*n* **4** something composed of separate parts **5** a composite plant
WORD ORIGIN Latin *compositus* well arranged

Composite *adj* of a style of classical architecture which combines elements of the Ionic and Corinthian styles

composite school *n Canad* a secondary school which offers both academic courses and vocational training

composition ❶ *n* **1** the act of putting together or composing **2** something composed **3** the things or parts which make up a whole **4** a work of music, art, or literature **5** the harmonious arrangement of the parts of a work of art **6** a written exercise; an essay **7** *printing* the act or technique of setting up type

compositor *n* a person who arranges type for printing

compos mentis *adj* sane
WORD ORIGIN Latin

compost *n* **1** a mixture of decaying plants and manure, used as a fertilizer **2** soil mixed with fertilizer, used for growing plants ▷*vb* **3** to make (vegetable matter) into compost
WORD ORIGIN Latin *compositus* put together

composure *n* the state of being calm or unworried

compote *n* fruit stewed with sugar or in a syrup
WORD ORIGIN French

compound[1] ❶ *n* **1** *chem* a substance that contains atoms of two or more chemical elements held together by chemical bonds **2** any combination

THESAURUS

colouring, hue, skin tone, pigmentation **2 = nature**, character, make-up, cast, stamp, disposition

complexity *n* **1, 2 = complication**, involvement, intricacy, entanglement, convolution

complicate *vb* **= make difficult**, confuse, muddle, embroil, entangle, make intricate, involve **OPPOSITE:** simplify

complicated *adj* **a = involved**, difficult, puzzling, troublesome, problematic, perplexing **OPPOSITE:** simple
b = complex, involved, elaborate, intricate, Byzantine **OPPOSITE:** understandable
c *(of an attitude)* **= convoluted**, labyrinthine

complication *n* **1 = problem**, difficulty, obstacle, drawback, snag, uphill *(S African)*, stumbling block, aggravation

compliment *n* **1 = praise**, honour, tribute, courtesy, admiration, bouquet, flattery, eulogy **OPPOSITE:** criticism
▷*pl n* **2 = greetings**, regards, respects, good wishes, salutation **OPPOSITE:** insult
▷*vb* **3 = praise**, flatter, salute, congratulate, pay tribute to, commend, laud, extol, crack up *(informal)*, pat on the back, sing the praises of, wax lyrical about, big up *(slang, chiefly Caribbean)*, speak highly of **OPPOSITE:** criticize

complimentary *adj* **1 = flattering**, approving, appreciative, congratulatory, eulogistic, commendatory **OPPOSITE:** critical
2 = free, donated, courtesy, honorary, free of charge, on the house, gratuitous, gratis

comply *vb* **= obey**, follow, respect, agree to, satisfy, observe, fulfil, submit to, conform to, adhere to, abide by, consent to, yield to, defer to, accede to, act in accordance with, perform, acquiesce with **OPPOSITE:** defy

component *n* **1 = part**, piece, unit, item, element, ingredient, constituent ▷*adj* **3 = constituent**, composing, inherent, intrinsic

compose *vb* **1 = arrange**, make up, construct, put together, order, organize **2 = put together**, make up, constitute, comprise, make, build, form, fashion, construct, compound **OPPOSITE:** destroy
3 = create, write, produce, imagine, frame, invent, devise, contrive
4 compose yourself = calm yourself, be still, control yourself, settle yourself, collect yourself, pull yourself together

composed *adj* **= calm**, together *(slang)*, cool, collected, relaxed, confident, poised, at ease, laid-back *(informal)*, serene, tranquil, sedate, self-controlled, level-headed, unfazed *(informal)*, unflappable, unruffled, self-possessed, imperturbable, unworried, keeping your cool, as cool as a cucumber, chilled *(informal)*, grounded **OPPOSITE:** agitated

composition *n* **1 = production**, creation, making, fashioning, formation, putting together, invention, compilation, formulation **3 = design**, form, structure, make-up, organization, arrangement, constitution, formation, layout, configuration **4 = creation**, work, piece, production, opus, masterpiece, chef-d'oeuvre *(French)* **6 = essay**, writing, study, exercise, treatise, literary work

compound[1] *n* **2 = combination**, mixture, blend, composite, conglomerate, fusion, synthesis, alloy, medley, amalgam, meld,

DICTIONARY

of two or more parts, features, or qualities **3** a word formed from two existing words or combining forms ▹ *vb* **4** to combine so as to create a compound **5** to make by combining parts or features: *the film's score is compounded from surging strings, a heavenly chorus and jazzy saxophones* **6** to intensify by an added element: *the problems of undertaking relief work are compounded by continuing civil war* **7** *law* to agree not to prosecute in return for payment: *to compound a crime* ▹ *adj* **8** composed of two or more parts or elements **9** *music* with a time in which the number of beats per bar is a multiple of three: *such tunes are usually in a form of compound time, for example six-four* **compoundable** *adj*
WORD ORIGIN Latin *componere* to put in order

compound² *n* a fenced enclosure containing buildings, such as a camp for prisoners of war
WORD ORIGIN Malay *kampong* village

compound fracture *n* a fracture in which the broken bone pierces the skin

compound interest *n* interest paid on a sum and its accumulated interest

comprehend ❶ *vb* **1** to understand **2** to include **comprehensible** *adj*
WORD ORIGIN Latin *comprehendere*

comprehension ❶ *n* **1** understanding **2** inclusion

comprehensive ❶ *adj* **1** of broad scope or content **2** (of car insurance) providing protection against most risks, including third-party liability, fire, theft, and damage **3** *Brit* of the comprehensive school system ▹ *n* **4** *Brit* a comprehensive school

comprehensive school *n Brit* a secondary school for children of all abilities

compress ❶ *vb* **1** to squeeze together **2** to condense ▹ *n* **3** a cloth or pad applied firmly to some part of the body to cool inflammation or relieve pain
WORD ORIGIN Latin *comprimere*

compression *n* **1** the act of compressing **2** the reduction in volume and increase in pressure of the fuel mixture in an internal-combustion engine before ignition

compressor *n* a device that compresses a gas

comprise ❶ *vb* **-prising, -prised 1** to be made up of: *the group comprised six French diplomats, five Italians and three Bulgarians* **2** to form or make up: *women comprised 57 per cent of all employees, but less than 10 per cent of managers*
WORD ORIGIN French *compris* included

compromise ❶ (**kom**-prom-mize) *n* **1** settlement of a dispute by concessions on each side: *everyone pleaded for compromise; the compromise was only reached after hours of hard bargaining* **2** the terms of such a settlement **3** something midway between different things ▹ *vb* **-mising, -mised 4** to settle (a dispute) by making concessions **5** to put (oneself or another person) in a dishonourable position ▹ *adj* **6** being, or having the nature or, a compromise: *a compromise solution* **compromising** *adj*
WORD ORIGIN Latin *compromittere* to promise at the same time

Compton *n* **1 Arthur Holly** 1892–1962, US physicist, noted for his research on X-rays, gamma rays, and nuclear energy: Nobel prize for physics 1927 **2 Denis** 1918–97, English cricketer, who played for Middlesex and England (1937–57); broke two records in 1947 scoring 3816 runs and 18 centuries in one season

Compton-Burnett *n* Dame **Ivy** 1884–1969, English novelist. Her novels include *Men and Wives* (1931) and *Mother and Son* (1955)

comptroller *n* a financial controller

compulsion *n* **1** an irresistible urge to perform some action **2** compelling or being compelled
WORD ORIGIN Latin *compellere* to compel

compulsive ❶ *adj* **1** resulting from or acting from a compulsion **2** irresistible or absorbing **compulsively** *adv*

compulsory ❶ *adj* required by regulations or laws

compulsory purchase *n* the enforced purchase of a property by a local authority or government department

compunction *n* a feeling of guilt or regret
WORD ORIGIN Latin *compungere* to sting

computation *n* a calculation involving numbers or quantities **computational** *adj*

compute ❶ *vb* **-puting, -puted** to calculate (an answer or result), often by using a computer
WORD ORIGIN Latin *computare*

computer *n* an electronic device that processes data according to a set of instructions

computer game *n* a game played on a home computer by manipulating a joystick or keys in response to the graphics on the screen

THESAURUS

composition **OPPOSITE:** element
▹ *adj* **8 = complex**, multiple, composite, conglomerate, intricate, not simple **OPPOSITE:** simple
▹ *vb* **4 = combine**, unite, mix, blend, fuse, mingle, synthesize, concoct, amalgamate, coalesce, intermingle, meld **OPPOSITE:** divide
6 = intensify, add to, complicate, worsen, heighten, exacerbate, aggravate, magnify, augment, add insult to injury **OPPOSITE:** lessen

comprehend *vb* **1 = understand**, see, take in, perceive, grasp, conceive, make out, discern, assimilate, see the light, fathom, apprehend, get the hang of *(informal)*, get the picture, know **OPPOSITE:** misunderstand

comprehension *n* **1 = understanding**, grasp, conception, realization, sense, knowledge, intelligence, judgment, perception, discernment
OPPOSITE: incomprehension

comprehensive *adj* **1 = broad**, full, complete, wide, catholic, sweeping, extensive, blanket, umbrella, thorough, inclusive, exhaustive, all-inclusive, all-embracing, overarching, encyclopedic
OPPOSITE: limited

compress *vb* **1 = squeeze**, crush, squash, constrict, press, crowd, wedge, cram **2 = condense**, contract, concentrate, compact, shorten, summarize, abbreviate

comprise *vb* **1 = be composed of**, include, contain, consist of, take in, embrace, encompass, comprehend
2 = make up, form, constitute, compose

compromise *n* **1 = give-and-take**, agreement, settlement, accommodation, concession, adjustment, trade-off, middle ground, half measures
OPPOSITE: disagreement
▹ *vb* **4 = meet halfway**, concede, make concessions, give and take, strike a balance, strike a happy medium, go fifty-fifty *(informal)*
OPPOSITE: disagree
5 = undermine, expose, embarrass, weaken, prejudice, endanger, discredit, implicate, jeopardize, dishonour, imperil
OPPOSITE: support

compulsive *adj* **1 = obsessive**, confirmed, chronic, persistent, addictive, uncontrollable, incurable, inveterate, incorrigible
2a = fascinating, gripping, absorbing, compelling, captivating, enthralling, hypnotic, engrossing, spellbinding **2b = irresistible**, overwhelming, compelling, urgent, neurotic, besetting, uncontrollable, driving

compulsory *adj* **= obligatory**, forced, required, binding, mandatory, imperative, requisite, de rigueur *(French)* **OPPOSITE:** voluntary

compute *vb* **= calculate**, rate, figure, total, measure, estimate, count, reckon, sum, figure out, add up, tally, enumerate

DICTIONARY

computerize *or* **-ise** *vb* **-izing, -ized** *or* **-ising, -ised 1** to equip with a computer **2** to control or perform (operations) by means of a computer **computerization** *or* **-isation** *n*

C

computing *n* **1** the activity of using computers and writing programs for them **2** the study of computers and their application

comrade ⓣ *n* **1** a fellow member of a union or a socialist political party **2** a companion **comradely** *adj* **comradeship** *n*
WORD ORIGIN French *camarade*

con¹ ⓣ *informal n* **1** ▸same as **confidence trick** ▹*vb* **conning, conned 2** to swindle or defraud

con² *n* ▸see **pros and cons**
WORD ORIGIN Latin *contra* against

con³ *n slang* a convict

Con *politics* Conservative

con- *prefix* ▸see **com-**

concatenation *n formal* a series of linked events
WORD ORIGIN Latin *com-* together + *catena* chain

concave *adj* curving inwards like the inside surface of a ball **concavity** *n*
WORD ORIGIN Latin *concavus* arched

conceal ⓣ *vb* **1** to cover and hide **2** to keep secret **concealment** *n*
WORD ORIGIN Latin *com-* (intensive) + *celare* to hide

concede ⓣ *vb* **-ceding, -ceded 1** to admit (something) as true or correct **2** to give up or grant (something, such as a right) **3** to acknowledge defeat in (a contest or argument)
WORD ORIGIN Latin *concedere*

conceit *n* **1** an excessively high opinion of oneself **2** *literary* a far-fetched or clever comparison
WORD ORIGIN see CONCEIVE

conceited *adj* having an excessively high opinion of oneself **conceitedness** *n*

conceivable *adj* capable of being understood, believed, or imagined **conceivably** *adv*

conceive ⓣ *vb* **-ceiving, -ceived 1** to imagine or think **2** to consider in a certain way: *we must do what we conceive to be right* **3** to form in the mind **4** to become pregnant
WORD ORIGIN Latin *concipere* to take in

concentrate ⓣ *vb* **-trating, -trated 1** to focus all one's attention, thoughts, or efforts on something: *she tried hard to concentrate, but her mind kept flashing back to the previous night* **2** to bring or come together in large numbers or amounts in one place: *a flawed system that concentrates power in the hands of the few* **3** to make (a liquid) stronger by removing water from it ▹*n* **4** a concentrated substance **concentrated** *adj*
WORD ORIGIN Latin *com-* same + *centrum* centre

concentration ⓣ *n* **1** intense mental application **2** the act of concentrating **3** something that is concentrated **4** the amount or proportion of a substance in a mixture or solution

concentration camp *n* a prison camp for civilian prisoners, as in Nazi Germany

concentric *adj* having the same centre: *concentric circles*
WORD ORIGIN Latin *com-* same + *centrum* centre

concept ⓣ *n* an abstract or general idea: *one of the basic concepts of quantum theory*
WORD ORIGIN Latin *concipere* to conceive

conception ⓣ *n* **1** a notion, idea, or plan **2** the fertilization of an egg by a sperm in the Fallopian tube followed by implantation in the womb **3** origin or beginning: *the gap between the conception of an invention and its production*
WORD ORIGIN Latin *concipere* to conceive

conceptual *adj* of or based on concepts

conceptualize *or* **-ise** *vb* **-izing, -ized** *or* **-ising, -ised** to form a concept or idea of **conceptualization** *or* **-isation** *n*

concern ⓣ *n* **1** anxiety or worry: *the current concern over teenage pregnancies* **2** something that is of interest or importance to a person **3** regard or interest: *a scrupulous concern for client confidentiality* **4** a business or firm ▹*vb* **5** to worry or make anxious **6** to involve or interest: *he had converted the building into flats without concerning himself with the niceties of planning permission* **7** to be relevant or important to
WORD ORIGIN Latin *com-* together + *cernere* to sift

concerned ⓣ *adj* **1** interested or involved: *I have spoken to the person concerned and he has no recollection of*

THESAURUS

comrade *n* **2 = companion**, friend, partner, ally, colleague, associate, fellow, mate *(informal)*, pal *(informal)*, buddy *(informal)*, compatriot, crony, confederate, co-worker, main man *(slang, chiefly US)*, homeboy *(slang, chiefly US)*, cobber *(Austral & NZ old-fashioned, informal)*, compeer

con¹ *vb* **2 = swindle**, trick, cheat, rip off *(slang)*, kid *(informal)*, skin *(slang)*, stiff *(slang)*, mislead, deceive, hoax, defraud, dupe, gull *(archaic)*, rook *(slang)*, humbug, bamboozle *(informal)*, hoodwink, double-cross *(informal)*, diddle *(informal)*, take for a ride *(informal)*, inveigle, do the dirty on *(Brit informal)*, bilk, sell a pup, pull a fast one on *(informal)*, scam *(slang)*

conceal *vb* **1 = hide**, bury, stash *(informal)*, secrete, cover, screen, disguise, obscure, camouflage
OPPOSITE: reveal
2 = keep secret, hide, disguise, mask, suppress, veil, dissemble, draw a veil over, keep dark, keep under your hat
OPPOSITE: show

concede *vb* **1 = admit**, allow, accept, acknowledge, own, grant, confess
OPPOSITE: deny
2 = give up, yield, hand over, surrender, relinquish, cede
OPPOSITE: conquer

conceive *vb* **1, 2 = imagine**, envisage, comprehend, visualize, think, believe, suppose, fancy, appreciate, grasp, apprehend **3 = think up**, form, produce, create, develop, design, project, purpose, devise, formulate, contrive **4 = become pregnant**, get pregnant, become impregnated

concentrate *vb* **1 = focus your attention**, focus, pay attention, be engrossed, apply yourself
OPPOSITE: pay no attention
2a = focus, centre, converge, bring to bear **2b = gather**, collect, cluster, accumulate, congregate
OPPOSITE: scatter

concentration *n* **1 = attention**, application, absorption, single-mindedness, intentness
OPPOSITE: inattention
2 = focusing, centring, consolidation, convergence, bringing to bear, intensification, centralization
3 = convergence, collection, mass, cluster, accumulation, aggregation
OPPOSITE: scattering

concept *n* **= idea**, view, image, theory, impression, notion, conception, hypothesis, abstraction, conceptualization

conception *n* **1 = idea**, plan, design, image, concept, notion **2 = impregnation**, insemination, fertilization, germination

concern *n* **1a = anxiety**, fear, worry, distress, unease, apprehension, misgiving, disquiet **1b = worry**, care, anxiety **2a = affair**, issue, matter, consideration **2b = business**, job, charge, matter, department, field, affair, responsibility, task, mission, pigeon *(informal)* **3a = care**, interest, regard, consideration, solicitude, attentiveness **3b = importance**, interest, bearing, relevance **4 = company**, house, business, firm, organization, corporation, enterprise, establishment ▹*vb* **5 = worry**, trouble, bother, disturb, distress, disquiet, perturb, make uneasy, make anxious **6 = be about**, cover, deal with, go into, relate to, have to do with **7 = be relevant to**, involve, affect, regard, apply to, bear on, have something to do with,

DICTIONARY

saying such a thing **2** worried or anxious: *we are increasingly concerned for her safety*
concerning ❶ *prep* about; regarding
concert *n* **1** a performance of music by players or singers in front of an audience **2 in concert a** working together **b** (of musicians or singers) performing live
WORD ORIGIN Latin *com-* together + *certare* strive
concerted *adj* decided or planned by mutual agreement: *a concerted effort*
concertina *n* **1** a small musical instrument similar to an accordion ▷ *vb* **-naing, -naed 2** to collapse or fold up like a concertina
WORD ORIGIN from *concert*
concerto (kon-**chair**-toe) *n, pl* **-tos** *or* **-ti** (-tee) a large-scale composition for an orchestra and one or more soloists
WORD ORIGIN Italian
concert pitch *n* the internationally agreed pitch to which concert instruments are tuned for performance
concession ❶ *n* **1** any grant of rights, land, or property by a government, local authority, or company **2** a reduction in price for a certain category of person: *fare concessions for senior citizens* **3** the act of yielding or conceding **4** something conceded **5** *Canad* **a** a land subdivision in a township survey **b** ▸ same as **concession road** > **concessionary** *adj*
WORD ORIGIN Latin *concedere* to concede
concessionaire *n* someone who holds a concession
concession road *n Canad* one of a series of roads separating concessions in a township
conch *n, pl* **conchs** *or* **conches 1** a marine mollusc with a large brightly coloured spiral shell **2** its shell
WORD ORIGIN Greek *konkhē* shellfish
concierge (kon-see-**airzh**) *n* (esp. in France) a caretaker in a block of flats
WORD ORIGIN French
conciliate *vb* **-ating, -ated** to try to end a disagreement with or pacify (someone) **conciliator** *n*
WORD ORIGIN Latin *conciliare* to bring together
conciliation *n* **1** the act of conciliating **2** a method of helping the parties in a dispute to reach agreement, esp. divorcing or separating couples to part amicably
conciliatory *adj* intended to end a disagreement
concise *adj* brief and to the point **concisely** *adv* **conciseness** *or* **concision** *n*
WORD ORIGIN Latin *concidere* to cut short
conclave *n* **1** a secret meeting **2** *RC church* a private meeting of cardinals to elect a new pope
WORD ORIGIN Latin *clavis* key
conclude ❶ *vb* **-cluding, -cluded 1** to decide by reasoning: *the investigation concluded that key data for the paper were faked* **2** to come or bring to an end: *the festival concludes on December 19th* **3** to arrange or settle finally: *officials have refused to comment on the failure to conclude an agreement*
WORD ORIGIN Latin *concludere*
conclusion ❶ *n* **1** a final decision, opinion, or judgment based on reasoning: *the obvious conclusion is that something is being covered up* **2** end or ending **3** outcome or result: *if you take that strategy to its logical conclusion you end up with communism* **4 in conclusion** finally **5 jump to conclusions** to come to a conclusion too quickly, without sufficient thought or evidence
conclusive *adj* putting an end to doubt: *there is no conclusive proof of this* **conclusively** *adv*
concoct *vb* **1** to make by combining different ingredients **2** to invent or make up (a story or plan) **concoction** *n*
WORD ORIGIN Latin *coquere* to cook
concomitant *adj* **1** existing or along with (something else): *the concomitant health gains* ▷ *n* **2** something that is concomitant
WORD ORIGIN Latin *com-* with + *comes* companion
concord *n* **1** agreement or harmony **2** peaceful relations between nations **3** *music* a harmonious combination of musical notes **concordant** *adj*
WORD ORIGIN Latin *com-* same + *cor* heart
concordance *n* **1** a state of harmony or agreement **2** an alphabetical list of words in a literary work, with the context and often the meaning
concordat *n formal* a treaty or agreement, such as one between the Vatican and another state
WORD ORIGIN Latin *concordatum* something agreed
concourse *n* **1** a large open space in a public place, where people can meet: *a crowded concourse at Heathrow Airport* **2** a crowd
WORD ORIGIN Latin *concurrere* to run together
concrete ❶ *n* **1** a building material made of cement, sand, stone and water that hardens to a stonelike mass ▷ *vb* **-creting, -creted 2** to cover with concrete ▷ *adj* **3** made of concrete **4** specific as opposed to general **5** relating to things that can be perceived by the senses, as opposed to abstractions
WORD ORIGIN Latin *concrescere* to grow together
concretion *n* **1** a solidified mass **2** the act of solidifying
concubine (kon-kew-bine) *n* **1** *old-fashioned* a woman living with a man as his wife, but not married to him **2** a secondary wife in polygamous societies **concubinage** *n*
WORD ORIGIN Latin *concumbere* to lie together
concupiscence (kon-**kew**-piss-enss) *n formal* strong sexual desire **concupiscent** *adj*
WORD ORIGIN Latin *concupiscere* to covet

THESAURUS

pertain to, interest, touch
concerned *adj* **1 = involved**, interested, active, mixed up, implicated, privy to **2 = worried**, troubled, upset, bothered, disturbed, anxious, distressed, uneasy
OPPOSITE: indifferent
concerning *prep* **= regarding**, about, re, touching, respecting, relating to, on the subject of, as to, with reference to, in the matter of, apropos of, as regards
concession *n* **1 = privilege**, right, permit, licence, franchise, entitlement, indulgence, prerogative **2 = reduction**, saving, grant, discount, allowance **3 = surrender**, yielding, conceding, renunciation, relinquishment **4 = compromise**, agreement, settlement, accommodation, adjustment, trade-off, give-and-take, half measures
conclude *vb* **1 = decide**, judge, establish, suppose, determine, assume, gather, reckon *(informal)*, work out, infer, deduce, surmise **2a = come to an end**, end, close, finish, wind up, draw to a close
OPPOSITE: begin
2b = bring to an end, end, close, finish, complete, wind up, terminate, round off
OPPOSITE: begin
3 = accomplish, effect, settle, bring about, fix, carry out, resolve, clinch, pull off, bring off *(informal)*
conclusion *n* **1 = decision**, agreement, opinion, settlement, resolution, conviction, verdict, judgment, deduction, inference **2 = end**, ending, close, finish, completion, finale, termination, bitter end, result **3 = outcome**, result, upshot, consequence, sequel, culmination, end result, issue
concrete *adj* **4 = specific**, precise, explicit, definite, clear-cut, unequivocal, unambiguous
OPPOSITE: vague
5 = real, material, actual, substantial, sensible, tangible, factual **OPPOSITE:** abstract

DICTIONARY

C

concur *vb* **-curring, -curred** to agree; be in accord
WORD ORIGIN Latin *concurrere* to run together

concurrence *n* **1** agreement **2** simultaneous occurrence

concurrent *adj* **1** taking place at the same time or place **2** meeting at, approaching, or having a common point: *concurrent lines* **3** in agreement **concurrently** *adv*

concuss *vb* to injure (the brain) by a fall or blow
WORD ORIGIN Latin *concutere* to disturb greatly

concussion *n* **1** a brain injury caused by a blow or fall, usually resulting in loss of consciousness **2** violent shaking

Condé *n* **Prince de**, title of *Louis II de Bourbon, Duc d'Enghien*, called *the Great Condé*. 1621–86, French general, who led Louis XIV's armies against the Fronde (1649) but joined the Fronde in a new revolt (1650–52). He later fought for both France and Spain

condemn ⓣ *vb* **1** to express strong disapproval of **2** to pronounce sentence on in a court of law **3** to force into a particular state: *a system that condemns most of our youngsters to failure* **4** to judge or declare (something) unfit for use **5** to indicate the guilt of: *everything the man had said condemned him, morally if not technically* **condemnation** *n* **condemnatory** *adj*
WORD ORIGIN Latin *condemnare*

condensation *n* **1** anything that has condensed from a vapour, esp. on a window **2** the act of condensing, or the state of being condensed

condense *vb* **-densing, -densed 1** to express in fewer words **2** to increase the density of; concentrate **3** to change from a gas to a liquid or solid
WORD ORIGIN Latin *condensare*

condensed milk *n* milk thickened by evaporation, with sugar added

condenser *n* **1** an apparatus for reducing gases to their liquid or solid form by the removal of heat **2** ▸ same as **capacitor 3** a lens that concentrates light

condescend *vb* **1** to behave patronizingly towards (one's supposed inferiors) **2** to do something as if it were beneath one's dignity **condescending** *adj* **condescension** *n*
WORD ORIGIN Church Latin *condescendere*

Condillac *n* **Étienne Bonnot de** 1715–80, French philosopher. He developed Locke's view that all knowledge derives from the senses in his *Traité des sensations* (1754)

condiment *n* any seasoning for food, such as salt, pepper, or sauces
WORD ORIGIN Latin *condire* to pickle

condition ⓣ *n* **1** a particular state of being: *the human condition; the van is in very poor condition* **2 conditions** circumstances: *worsening weather conditions; the government pledged to improve living and working conditions* **3** a necessary requirement for something else to happen: *food is a necessary condition for survival* **4** a restriction or a qualification **5** a term of an agreement: *the conditions of the lease are set out* **6** state of physical fitness, esp. good health: *she is in a serious condition in hospital; out of condition* **7** an ailment: *a heart condition* **8 on condition that** provided that ▹ *vb* **9** to accustom or alter the reaction of (a person or animal) to a particular stimulus or situation **10** to treat with a conditioner **11** to make fit or healthy **12** to influence or determine the form that something takes: *he argued that the failure of Latin American industry was conditioned by international economic structures* **conditioning** *n, adj*
WORD ORIGIN Latin *con-* together + *dicere* to say

conditional ⓣ *adj* **1** depending on other factors **2** *grammar* expressing a condition on which something else depends, for example 'If he comes' is a conditional clause in the sentence 'If he comes I shall go'

conditioner *n* a thick liquid used when washing to make hair or clothes feel softer

condo *n, pl* **-dos** *US & Canad informal* a condominium building or apartment

condolence *n* sympathy expressed for someone in grief or pain **condole** *vb*
WORD ORIGIN Latin *com-* together + *dolere* to grieve

condom *n* a rubber sheath worn on the penis or in the vagina during sexual intercourse to prevent conception or infection
WORD ORIGIN origin unknown

condominium *n, pl* **-ums 1** *Austral, US & Canad* **a** an apartment building in which each apartment is individually owned **b** an apartment in such a building **2** joint rule of a state by two or more other states
WORD ORIGIN Latin *com-* together + *dominium* ownership

condone ⓣ *vb* **-doning, -doned** to overlook or forgive (an offence or wrongdoing)
WORD ORIGIN Latin *com-* (intensive) + *donare* to donate

condor *n* a very large rare S American vulture
WORD ORIGIN S American Indian *kuntur*

Condorcet *n* **Marie Jean Antoine Nicolas de Caritat,** Marquis de. 1743–94, French philosopher and politician. His works include *Sketch for a Historical Picture of the Progress of the Human Mind* (1795)

conducive *adj* (often foll. by *to*) likely to lead to or produce (a result)
WORD ORIGIN Latin *com-* together + *ducere* to lead

conduct ⓣ *n* **1** behaviour **2** the management or handling of an activity or business ▹ *vb* **3** to carry out: *the police are conducting an investigation into the affair* **4 conduct oneself** to behave (oneself) **5** to control (an orchestra or choir) by the movements of the hands or a baton **6** to accompany and guide (people or a party): *a conducted tour* **7** to transmit (heat or electricity)

THESAURUS

condemn *vb* **1 = denounce**, damn, criticize, disapprove, censure, reprove, upbraid, excoriate, reprehend, blame **OPPOSITE:** approve **2 = sentence**, convict, damn, doom, pass sentence on **OPPOSITE:** acquit

condition *n* **1a = state**, order, shape, nick (*Brit informal*), trim **1b = situation**, state, position, status, circumstances, plight, status quo (*Latin*), case, predicament **3, 4, 5 = requirement**, terms, rider, provision, restriction, qualification, limitation, modification, requisite, prerequisite, proviso, stipulation, rule, demand **6 = health**, shape, fitness, trim, form, kilter, state of health, fettle, order **7 = ailment**, problem, complaint, weakness, malady, infirmity ▹ *pl n* **2 = circumstances**, situation, environment, surroundings, way of life, milieu ▹ *vb* **9 = train**, teach, educate, adapt, accustom, inure, habituate

conditional *adj* **1 = dependent**, limited, qualified, contingent, provisional, with reservations **OPPOSITE:** unconditional

condone *vb* **= overlook**, excuse, forgive, pardon, disregard, turn a blind eye to, wink at, look the other way, make allowance for, let pass **OPPOSITE:** condemn

conduct *n* **1 = behaviour**, ways, bearing, attitude, manners, carriage, demeanour, deportment, mien (*literary*), comportment **2 = management**, running, control, handling, administration, direction, leadership, organization, guidance, supervision ▹ *vb* **3 = carry out**, run, control, manage, direct, handle, organize, govern, regulate, administer, supervise, preside over **4 conduct yourself = behave yourself**, act, carry yourself, acquit yourself, deport yourself, comport yourself **6 = accompany**, lead, escort, guide, attend, steer, convey, usher, pilot

DICTIONARY

WORD ORIGIN Latin *com-* together + *ducere* to lead

conductance *n* the ability of a specified body to conduct electricity

conduction *n* the transmission of heat or electricity

conductivity *n* the property of transmitting heat, electricity, or sound

conductor *n* **1** a person who conducts an orchestra or choir **2** an official on a bus who collects fares **3** *US, Canad & NZ* a railway official in charge of a train **4** something that conducts electricity or heat **conductress** *fem n*

conduit (kon-dew-it) *n* **1** a route or system for transferring things from one place to another: *a conduit for smuggling cocaine into the United States* **2** a channel or tube for carrying a fluid or electrical cables **3** a means of access or communication
WORD ORIGIN Latin *conducere* to lead

cone *n* **1** a geometric solid consisting of a circular or oval base, tapering to a point **2** a cone-shaped wafer shell used to contain ice cream **3** the scaly fruit of a conifer tree **4** *Brit, Austral & NZ* a plastic cone used as a temporary traffic marker on roads **5** a type of cell in the retina, sensitive to colour and bright light
WORD ORIGIN Greek *kōnus* pine cone, geometrical cone

coney *n* ▸ same as **cony**

confab *n informal* a conversation

confabulation *n formal* a conversation
WORD ORIGIN Latin *confabulari* to talk together

confection *n* **1** any sweet food, such as a cake or a sweet **2** *old-fashioned* an elaborate piece of clothing
WORD ORIGIN Latin *confectio* a preparing

confectioner *n* a person who makes or sells confectionery

confectionery *n, pl* **-eries 1** sweets and chocolates collectively: *a drop in confectionery sales* **2** the art or business of a confectioner

confederacy *n, pl* **-cies** a union of states or people joined for a common purpose **confederal** *adj*
WORD ORIGIN Late Latin *confoederatio* agreement

confederate *n* **1** a state or individual that is part of a confederacy **2** an accomplice or conspirator ▹ *adj* **3** united; allied ▹ *vb* **-ating, -ated 4** to unite in a confederacy
WORD ORIGIN Late Latin *confoederare* to unite by a league

Confederate *adj* of or supporting those American states which withdrew from the USA in 1860–61, leading to the American Civil War

confederation *n* **1** a union or alliance of states or groups **2** confederating or being confederated **3** a federation

confer ❶ *vb* **-ferring, -ferred 1** to discuss together **2** to grant or give: *the power conferred by wealth* **conferment** *n* **conferrable** *adj*
WORD ORIGIN Latin *com-* together + *ferre* to bring

conference ❶ *n* a meeting for formal consultation or discussion
WORD ORIGIN Medieval Latin *conferentia*

confess ❶ *vb* **1** to admit (a fault or crime) **2** to admit to be true, esp. reluctantly **3** *Christianity* to declare (one's sins) to God or to a priest, so as to obtain forgiveness
WORD ORIGIN Latin *confiteri* to admit

confession ❶ *n* **1** something confessed **2** an admission of one's faults, sins, or crimes **3 confession of faith** a formal public statement of religious beliefs

confessional *n* **1** *Christianity* a small room or enclosed stall in a church where a priest hears confessions ▹ *adj* **2** of or suited to a confession

confessor *n* **1** *Christianity* a priest who hears confessions and gives spiritual advice **2** *history* a person who demonstrates his Christian religious faith by the holiness of his life: *Edward the Confessor*

confetti *n* small pieces of coloured paper thrown at weddings
WORD ORIGIN Italian

confidant ❶ *or fem* **confidante** *n* a person to whom private matters are confided
WORD ORIGIN French *confident*

confide *vb* **-fiding, -fided 1 confide in** to tell (something) in confidence to **2** *formal* to entrust into another's keeping
WORD ORIGIN Latin *confidere*

confidence ❶ *n* **1** trust in a person or thing **2** belief in one's own abilities **3** trust or a trustful relationship: *she won first the confidence, then the admiration, of her bosses* **4** something confided, such as a secret **5 in confidence** as a secret

confidence trick *n* a swindle in which the swindler gains the victim's trust in order to cheat him or her

confident ❶ *adj* **1** having or showing certainty: *we are now confident that this technique works* **2** sure of oneself **confidently** *adv*
WORD ORIGIN Latin *confidere* to have complete trust in

confidential ❶ *adj* **1** spoken or given in confidence **2** entrusted with another's secret affairs: *a confidential secretary* **3** suggestive of intimacy: *a halting, confidential manner* **confidentiality** *n* **confidentially** *adv*

confiding *adj* trusting: *a close and confiding relationship* **confidingly** *adv*

configuration *n* **1** the arrangement of the parts of something **2** the form or outline of such an arrangement
WORD ORIGIN Late Latin *configurare* to model on something

confine ❶ *vb* **-fining, -fined 1** to keep within bounds **2** to restrict the free movement of: *a nasty dose of flu which confined her to bed for days* ▹ *n* **3 confines** boundaries or limits
WORD ORIGIN Latin *finis* boundary

confinement *n* **1** being confined **2** the period of childbirth

THESAURUS

confer *vb* **1 = discuss**, talk, consult, deliberate, discourse, converse, parley **2 = grant**, give, present, accord, award, hand out, bestow, vouchsafe

conference *n* **= meeting**, congress, discussion, convention, forum, consultation, seminar, symposium, hui *(NZ)*, convocation, colloquium

confess *vb* **1 = admit**, acknowledge, disclose, confide, own up, come clean *(informal)*, divulge, blurt out, come out of the closet, make a clean breast of, get (something) off your chest *(informal)*, spill your guts *(slang)*, 'fess up *(US)*, sing *(slang, chiefly US)* **OPPOSITE:** cover up **2 = declare**, own up, allow, prove, reveal, grant, confirm, concede, assert, manifest, affirm, profess, attest, evince, aver

confession *n* **1, 2 = admission**, revelation, disclosure, acknowledgment, avowal, divulgence, exposure, unbosoming

confidant *or* **confidante** *n* **= close friend**, familiar, intimate, crony, alter ego, bosom friend

confidence *n* **1 = trust**, belief, faith, dependence, reliance, credence **OPPOSITE:** distrust **2 = self-assurance**, courage, assurance, aplomb, boldness, self-reliance, self-possession, nerve **OPPOSITE:** shyness **5 in confidence = in secrecy**, privately, confidentially, between you and me (and the gatepost), (just) between ourselves

confident *adj* **1 = certain**, sure, convinced, positive, secure, satisfied, counting on **OPPOSITE:** unsure **2 = self-assured**, positive, assured, bold, self-confident, self-reliant, self-possessed, sure of yourself, can-do *(informal)* **OPPOSITE:** insecure

confidential *adj* **1 = secret**, private, intimate, classified, privy, off the record, hush-hush *(informal)* **3 = secretive**, low, soft, hushed

confine *vb* **1 = imprison**, enclose, shut up, intern, incarcerate, circumscribe, hem in, immure, keep, cage **2 = restrict**, limit ▹ *pl n* **3 = limits**, bounds, boundaries, compass,

DICTIONARY

confirm ❶ *vb* **1** to prove to be true or valid **2** to reaffirm (something), so as to make (it) more definite: *she confirmed that she is about to resign as leader of the council* **3** to strengthen: *this cruise confirmed my first impressions of the boat's performance* **4** to formally make valid **5** to administer the rite of confirmation to
WORD ORIGIN Latin *confirmare*

confirmation ❶ *n* **1** the act of confirming **2** something that confirms **3** a rite in several Christian churches that admits a baptized person to full church membership

confirmed ❶ *adj* long-established in a habit or condition: *a confirmed bachelor*

confiscate ❶ *vb* **-cating, -cated** to seize (property) by authority **confiscation** *n*
WORD ORIGIN Latin *confiscare* to seize for the public treasury

conflagration *n* a large destructive fire
WORD ORIGIN Latin *com-* (intensive) + *flagrare* to burn

conflate *vb* **-flating, -flated** to combine or blend into a whole **conflation** *n*
WORD ORIGIN Latin *conflare* to blow together

conflict ❶ *n* **1** opposition between ideas or interests **2** a struggle or battle ▷*vb* **3** to be incompatible **conflicting** *adj*
WORD ORIGIN Latin *confligere* to combat

confluence *n* **1** a place where rivers flow into one another **2** a gathering **confluent** *adj*
WORD ORIGIN Latin *confluere* to flow together

conform ❶ *vb* **1** to comply with accepted standards, rules, or customs **2** (usually foll. by *with*) to be like or in accordance with: *people tend to absorb ideas that conform with their existing beliefs, and reject those that do not*
WORD ORIGIN Latin *confirmare* to strengthen

conformation *n* **1** the general shape of an object **2** the arrangement of the parts of an object

conformist *adj* **1 a** (of a person) behaving or thinking like most other people rather than in an original or unconventional way: *a shy and conformist type of boy* **b** (of an organization or society) expecting everyone to behave in the same way: *the school was a dull, conformist place for staff and students alike* ▷*n* **2** a person who behaves or thinks like most other people rather than in an original or unconventional way

conformity *n, pl* **-ities 1** compliance in actions or behaviour with certain accepted rules, customs, or standards **2** likeness

confound ❶ *vb* **1** to astound or bewilder **2** to fail to distinguish between **3 confound it!** damn it!
WORD ORIGIN Latin *confundere* to mingle, pour together

confounded *adj* **1** *informal* damned: *what a confounded nuisance!* **2** bewildered; confused: *her silent, utterly confounded daughter*

confrere (kon-frair) *n* a colleague: *their Gallic confreres*
WORD ORIGIN Medieval Latin *confrater*

confront ❶ *vb* **1** (of a problem or task) to present itself to **2** to meet face to face in hostility or defiance **3** to present (someone) with something, esp. in order to accuse or criticize: *she finally confronted him with her suspicions*
WORD ORIGIN Latin *com-* together + *frons* forehead

confrontation ❶ *n* a serious argument or fight

Confucianism *n* the teachings of Confucius (551–479 BC), the ancient Chinese philosopher, which emphasize moral order **Confucian** *n, adj* **Confucianist** *n*

confuse ❶ *vb* **-fusing, -fused 1** to fail to distinguish between one thing and another **2** to perplex or disconcert **3** to make unclear: *he confused his talk with irrelevant detail* **4** to throw into disorder **confusing** *adj* **confusingly** *adv*
WORD ORIGIN Latin *confundere* to pour together

confused ❶ *adj* **1** lacking a clear understanding of something **2** disordered and difficult to understand or make sense of: *a confused dream*

confusion ❶ *n* **1** mistaking one person or thing for another **2** bewilderment **3** lack of clarity **4** disorder

THESAURUS

precincts, circumference, edge, pale

confirm *vb* **1 = prove**, support, establish, back up, verify, validate, bear out, substantiate, corroborate, authenticate **3 = strengthen**, establish, settle, fix, secure, assure, reinforce, clinch, verify, fortify **4 = ratify**, establish, approve, sanction, endorse, authorize, certify, validate, authenticate

confirmation *n* **1 = affirmation**, approval, acceptance, endorsement, ratification, assent, agreement **OPPOSITE:** disapproval **2 = proof**, evidence, testimony, verification, ratification, validation, corroboration, authentication, substantiation **OPPOSITE:** repudiation

confirmed *adj* **= long-established**, seasoned, rooted, chronic, hardened, habitual, ingrained, inveterate, inured, dyed-in-the-wool

confiscate *vb* **= seize**, appropriate, impound, commandeer, sequester, expropriate **OPPOSITE:** give back

conflict *n* **1 = dispute**, difference, opposition, hostility, disagreement, friction, strife, fighting, antagonism, variance, discord, bad blood, dissension, divided loyalties **OPPOSITE:** agreement **2a = struggle**, battle, clash, strife **2b = battle**, war, fight, clash, contest, set-to (*informal*), encounter, combat, engagement, warfare, collision, contention, strife, head-to-head, fracas, boilover (*Austral*) **OPPOSITE:** peace ▷*vb* **3 = be incompatible**, clash, differ, disagree, contend, strive, collide, be at variance **OPPOSITE:** agree

conform *vb* **1 = fit in**, follow, yield, adjust, adapt, comply, obey, fall in, toe the line, follow the crowd, run with the pack, follow convention **2** (*with* **with**) **= fulfil**, meet, match, suit, satisfy, agree with, obey, abide by, accord with, square with, correspond with, tally with, harmonize with

confound *vb* **1 = bewilder**, baffle, amaze, confuse, astonish, startle, mix up, astound, perplex, surprise, mystify, flummox, boggle the mind, be all Greek to (*informal*), dumbfound, nonplus, flabbergast (*informal*)

confront *vb* **1 = trouble**, face, afflict, perplex, perturb, bedevil **2, 3 = challenge**, face, oppose, tackle, encounter, defy, call out, stand up to, come face to face with, accost, face off (*slang*) **OPPOSITE:** evade

confrontation *n* **= conflict**, fight, crisis, contest, set-to (*informal*), encounter, showdown (*informal*), head-to-head, face-off (*slang*), boilover (*Austral*)

confuse *vb* **1 = mix up with**, take for, mistake for, muddle with **2 = bewilder**, puzzle, baffle, perplex, mystify, fluster, faze, flummox, bemuse, be all Greek to (*informal*), nonplus **3 = obscure**, cloud, complicate, muddle, darken, make more difficult, muddy the waters

confused *adj* **1 = bewildered**, puzzled, baffled, at sea, muddled, dazed, perplexed, at a loss, taken aback, disorientated, muzzy (*US informal*), nonplussed, flummoxed, at sixes and sevens, thrown off balance, discombobulated (*informal, chiefly US & Canad*), not with it (*informal*), not knowing if you are coming or going **OPPOSITE:** enlightened **2 = disorderly**, disordered, chaotic, mixed up, jumbled, untidy, out of order, in disarray, topsy-turvy,

DICTIONARY

confute *vb* **-futing, -futed** to prove to be wrong **confutation** *n*
WORD ORIGIN Latin *confutare* to check, silence
conga *n* **1** a Latin American dance performed by a number of people in single file **2** a large single-headed drum played with the hands ▷ *vb* **-gaing, -gaed 3** to dance the conga
WORD ORIGIN from American Spanish
congeal *vb* to change from a liquid to a semisolid state
WORD ORIGIN Latin *com-* together + *gelare* to freeze
congenial *adj* **1** friendly, pleasant, or agreeable: *he found the Botanic Gardens a most congenial place for strolling* **2** having a similar disposition or tastes **congeniality** *n*
WORD ORIGIN *con-* (same) + *genial*
congenital *adj* (of an abnormal condition) existing at birth but not inherited: *congenital heart disease* **congenitally** *adv*
WORD ORIGIN Latin *con-* together + *genitus* born
conger *n* a large sea eel
WORD ORIGIN Greek *gongros*
congested *adj* **1** crowded to excess **2** clogged or blocked **congestion** *n*
WORD ORIGIN Latin *congerere* to pile up
conglomerate *n* **1** a large corporation made up of many different companies **2** a thing composed of several different elements **3** a type of rock consisting of rounded pebbles or fragments held together by silica or clay ▷ *vb* **-ating, -ated 4** to form into a mass ▷ *adj* **5** made up of several different elements **6** (of rock) consisting of rounded pebbles or fragments held together by silica or clay **conglomeration** *n*
WORD ORIGIN Latin *conglomerare* to roll up
congratulate ❶ *vb* **-lating, -lated 1** to express one's pleasure to (a person) at his or her success or good fortune **2 congratulate oneself** to consider oneself clever or fortunate (as a result of): *she congratulated herself on her own business acumen* **congratulatory** *adj*
WORD ORIGIN Latin *congratulari*
congratulations ❶ *pl n, interj* expressions of pleasure or joy on another's success or good fortune
congregate *vb* **-gating, -gated** to collect together in or as a crowd
WORD ORIGIN Latin *congregare* to collect into a flock
congregation ❶ *n* a group of worshippers **congregational** *adj*
Congregationalism *n* a system of Protestant church government in which each church is self-governing **Congregationalist** *adj, n*
congress ❶ *n* a formal meeting of representatives for discussion **congressional** *adj*
WORD ORIGIN Latin *com-* together + *gradi* to walk
Congress *n* the federal legislature of the US, consisting of the House of Representatives and the Senate **Congressional** *adj* **Congressman** *n* **Congresswoman** *fem n*
Congreve *n* **William** 1670–1729, English dramatist, a major exponent of Restoration comedy; author of *Love for Love* (1695) and *The Way of the World* (1700)
congruent *adj* **1** agreeing or corresponding **2** *geom* identical in shape and size: *congruent triangles* **congruence** *n*
WORD ORIGIN Latin *congruere* to agree
congruous *adj formal* **1** appropriate or in keeping: *an elegant, though not altogether congruous, wing was added to the house in 1735* **2** corresponding or agreeing: *this finding is congruous with Adam's 1982 study* **congruity** *n*
WORD ORIGIN Latin *congruere* to agree
conical *adj* in the shape of a cone
conic section *n* a figure, either a circle, ellipse, parabola, or hyperbola, formed by the intersection of a plane and a cone
conifer *n* a tree or shrub bearing cones and evergreen leaves, such as the fir or larch **coniferous** *adj*
WORD ORIGIN Latin *conus* cone + *ferre* to bear
conjecture *n* **1** the formation of conclusions from incomplete evidence **2** a guess ▷ *vb* **-turing, -tured 3** to form (an opinion or conclusion) from incomplete evidence **conjectural** *adj*
WORD ORIGIN Latin *conjicere* to throw together
conjoin *vb* to join or become joined
conjoined twins *pl n* ▸ the technical name for **Siamese twins**
conjugal (kon-jew-gal) *adj* of marriage: *conjugal rights*
WORD ORIGIN Latin *conjunx* wife or husband
conjugate *vb* (kon-jew-gate), **-gating, -gated 1** *grammar* to give the inflections of (a verb) **2** (of a verb) to undergo inflection according to a specific set of rules **3** *formal* to combine: *a country in which conjugatin Marxism with Christianity has actually been tried* ▷ *n* (**kon-jew-git**) **4** *formal* something formed by conjugation: *haemoglobin is a conjugate of a protein with an iron-containing pigment*
WORD ORIGIN Latin *com-* together + *jugare* to connect
conjugation *n* **1** *grammar* **a** inflection of a verb for person, number, tense, voice and mood **b** the complete set of the inflections of a given verb **2** a joining
conjunction *n* **1** joining together **2** simultaneous occurrence of events **3** a word or group of words that connects words, phrases, or clauses; for example *and*, *if*, and *but* **4** *astron* the apparent nearness of two heavenly bodies to each other **conjunctional** *adj*
conjunctiva *n, pl* **-vas** *or* **-vae** the delicate mucous membrane that covers the eyeball and inner eyelid **conjunctival** *adj*
WORD ORIGIN New Latin *membrana conjunctiva* the conjunctive membrane
conjunctive *adj* **1** joining or joined **2** used as a conjunction: *a conjunctive adverb* ▷ *n* **3** a word or words used as a conjunction
WORD ORIGIN Latin *conjungere* to join
conjunctivitis *n* inflammation of the conjunctiva
conjuncture *n* a combination of events, esp. one that leads to a crisis
conjure ❶ *vb* **-juring, -jured 1** to make (something) appear, as if by magic **2** to perform tricks that appear to be magic **3** to summon (a spirit or demon) by magic **4** *formal or literary* to appeal earnestly to: *I conjure you by all which you profess: answer me!* **conjuring** *n*
WORD ORIGIN Latin *conjurare* to swear together

C

THESAURUS

disorganized, higgledy-piggledy (*informal*), at sixes and sevens, disarranged, disarrayed
OPPOSITE: tidy
confusion *n* **2 = bewilderment**, doubt, uncertainty, puzzlement, perplexity, mystification, bafflement, perturbation
OPPOSITE: enlightenment
4 = disorder, chaos, turmoil, upheaval, muddle, bustle, shambles, disarray, commotion, disorganization, disarrangement
OPPOSITE: order
congratulate *vb* **1 = compliment**, pat on the back, wish joy to
congratulations *pl n* **= good wishes**, greetings, compliments, best wishes, pat on the back, felicitations ▷ *interj* **= good wishes**, greetings, compliments, best wishes, felicitations
congregation *n* **= parishioners**, host, brethren, crowd, assembly, parish, flock, fellowship, multitude, throng, laity, flock
congress *n* **= meeting**, council, conference, diet, assembly, convention, conclave, legislative assembly, convocation, hui (NZ), runanga (NZ)
conjure *vb* **1a = produce**, generate, bring about, give rise to, make,

DICTIONARY

conjure up ⓘ *vb* **1** to create an image in the mind: *the name Versailles conjures up a past of sumptuous grandeur* **2** to produce as if from nowhere: *he conjured up a fabulous opening goal*
conjuror *or* **conjurer** *n* a person who performs magic tricks for people's entertainment
conk *Brit, Austral & NZ slang n* **1** the head or nose ▹*vb* **2** to strike (someone) on the head or nose
WORD ORIGIN probably changed from *conch*
conker *n* ▸same as **horse chestnut** (sense 2)
conkers *n Brit* a game in which a player swings a horse chestnut (conker), threaded onto a string, against that of another player to try to break it
WORD ORIGIN dialect *conker* snail shell, originally used in the game
conk out *vb informal* **1** (of a machine or car) to break down **2** to become tired or fall asleep suddenly
WORD ORIGIN origin unknown
con man *n informal* a person who swindles someone by means of a confidence trick
Conn *n* 2nd century AD, king of Leinster and high king of Ireland
connect ⓘ *vb* **1** to link or be linked: *high blood pressure is closely connected to heart disease* **2** to put into telephone communication with **3** (of two public vehicles) to have the arrival of one timed to occur just before the departure of the other, for the convenience of passengers **4** to associate in the mind: *he had always connected sex with violence and attacks rather than loving and concern* **5** to relate by birth or marriage: *she was distantly connected with the Wedgwood family*
connective *adj*
WORD ORIGIN Latin *connectere* to bind together
connection ⓘ *or* **connexion** *n* **1** a relationship or association **2** a link or bond **3** a link between two components in an electric circuit **4 a** an opportunity to transfer from one public vehicle to another **b** the vehicle scheduled to provide such an opportunity **5** an influential acquaintance **6** a relative **7** logical sequence in thought or expression **8** a telephone link **9** *slang* a supplier of illegal drugs, such as heroin **10 in connection with** with reference to: *a number of people have been arrested in connection with the explosion*
connective tissue *n* body tissue that supports organs, fills the spaces between them, and forms tendons and ligaments
Connell *n* **Desmond** born 1926, Irish cardinal; Archbishop of Dublin and primate of Ireland (1988–2004)
Connery *n* Sir **Sean,** real name *Thomas Connery.* born 1929, Scottish film actor, who played James Bond in such films as *Goldfinger* (1964). His later films include *The Name of the Rose* (1986), *Indiana Jones and the Last Crusade* (1989), and *Finding Forrester* (2000)
conning tower *n* the raised observation tower containing the periscope on a submarine
WORD ORIGIN *con* to steer a ship
connivance *n* encouragement or permission of wrongdoing
connive *vb* **-niving, -nived 1 connive at** to allow or encourage (wrongdoing) by ignoring it **2** to conspire
WORD ORIGIN Latin *connivere* to blink, hence, leave uncensured
connoisseur (kon-noss-**sir**) *n* a person with special knowledge of the arts, food, or drink
WORD ORIGIN French
Connolly *n* **1 Billy** born 1942, Scottish comedian **2 Cyril** (**Vernon**) 1903–74, British critic and writer, founder and editor of *Horizon* (1939–50): his books include *Enemies of Promise* (1938) **3 James** 1868–1916, Irish labour leader: executed by the British for his part in the Easter Rising (1916)
Connors *n* **Jimmy** born 1952, US tennis player: Wimbledon champion 1974 and 1982; US champion 1974, 1976, 1978, 1982, and 1983
connotation *n* an additional meaning or association implied by a word: *the German term carries a connotation of elitism* **connote** *vb*
WORD ORIGIN Latin *con-* + together *notare* to mark, note
connubial (kon-**new**-bee-al) *adj formal* of marriage: *connubial bliss*
WORD ORIGIN Latin *conubium* marriage
conquer ⓘ *vb* **1** to defeat (an opponent or opponents) **2** to overcome (a difficulty or feeling) **3** to gain possession of (a place) by force or war **conquering** *adj* **conqueror** *n*
WORD ORIGIN Latin *conquirere* to search for
conquest ⓘ *n* **1** the act of conquering **2** a person or thing that has been conquered **3** a person whose affections have been won
conquistador *n, pl* **-dors** *or* **-dores** one of the Spanish conquerors of Mexico and Peru in the 16th century
WORD ORIGIN Spanish: conqueror
Cons. Conservative
consanguineous *adj formal* related by birth **consanguinity** *n*
WORD ORIGIN Latin *con-* with + *sanguis* blood
conscience ⓘ *n* **1** the sense of right and wrong that governs a person's thoughts and actions **2** a feeling of guilt: *he showed no hint of conscience over the suffering he had inflicted* **3 in (all) conscience** in fairness **4 on one's conscience** causing feelings of guilt
WORD ORIGIN Latin *conscire* to know
conscience-stricken *adj* feeling guilty because of having done something wrong
conscientious *adj* **1** painstaking or thorough in one's work **2** governed by conscience **conscientiously** *adv* **conscientiousness** *n*
conscientious objector *n* a person who refuses to serve in the armed forces on moral or religious grounds
conscious ⓘ *adj* **1** alert and awake **2** aware of one's surroundings and of oneself **3** aware (of something):

THESAURUS

create, effect, produce as if by magic
conjure up *vb* **1 = bring to mind**, recall, evoke, recreate, recollect **2 = produce as if by magic**
connect *vb* **1 = link**, join, couple, attach, fasten, affix, unite
OPPOSITE: separate
1, 4 = associate, unite, join, couple, league, link, mix, relate, pair, ally, identify, combine, affiliate, correlate, confederate, lump together, mention in the same breath, think of together
connection *n* **1 = association**, relationship, link, relation, bond, correspondence, relevance, tie-in, correlation, interrelation **2 = link**, coupling, junction, fastening, tie **5, 6 = contact**, friend, relation, ally, associate, relative, acquaintance, kin, kindred, kinsman, kith
conquer *vb* **1 = defeat**, overcome, overthrow, beat, stuff *(slang)*, master, tank *(slang)*, triumph, crush, humble, lick *(informal)*, undo, subdue, rout, overpower, quell, get the better of, clobber *(slang)*, vanquish, subjugate, prevail over, checkmate, run rings around *(informal)*, wipe the floor with *(informal)*, make mincemeat of *(informal)*, put in their place, blow out of the water *(slang)*, bring to their knees **OPPOSITE:** lose to
2 = overcome, beat, defeat, master, rise above, overpower, get the better of, surmount, best **3 = seize**, obtain, acquire, occupy, overrun, annex, win
conquest *n* **1a = takeover**, coup, acquisition, invasion, occupation, appropriation, annexation, subjugation, subjection **1b = defeat**, victory, triumph, overthrow, pasting *(slang)*, rout, mastery, vanquishment
conscience *n* **1 = principles**, scruples, moral sense, sense of right and wrong, still small voice **2 = guilt**, shame, regret, remorse, contrition, self-reproach, self-condemnation
conscious *adj* **1, 2 = awake**, wide-awake, sentient, alive

DICTIONARY

he was conscious of a need to urinate **4** deliberate or intentional: *a conscious attempt* **5** of the part of the mind that is aware of a person's self, surroundings, and thoughts, and that to a certain extent determines choices of action ▷*n* **6** the conscious part of the mind **consciously** *adv* **consciousness** *n*
WORD ORIGIN Latin *com-* with + *scire* to know

conscript *n* **1** a person who is enrolled for compulsory military service ▷*vb* **2** to enrol (someone) for compulsory military service
WORD ORIGIN Latin *conscriptus* enrolled

conscription *n* compulsory military service

consecrate *vb* **-crating, -crated 1** to make or declare sacred or for religious use **2** to devote or dedicate (something) to a specific purpose **3** *Christianity* to sanctify (bread and wine) to be received as the body and blood of Christ **consecration** *n*
WORD ORIGIN Latin *consecrare*

consecutive ⊕ *adj* following in order without interruption: *three consecutive nights of rioting* **consecutively** *adv*
WORD ORIGIN Latin *consequi* to pursue

consensus ⊕ *n* general or widespread agreement
WORD ORIGIN Latin *consentire* to agree

consent ⊕ *n* **1** agreement, permission, or approval **2 age of consent** the age at which sexual intercourse is permitted by law ▷*vb* **3** to permit or agree (to) **consenting** *adj*
WORD ORIGIN Latin *consentire* to agree

consequence ⊕ *n* **1** a logical result or effect **2** significance or importance: *we said little of consequence to each other; a woman of little consequence* **3 in consequence** as a result **4 take the consequences** to accept whatever results from one's action

consequent *adj* **1** following as an effect **2** following as a logical conclusion
WORD ORIGIN Latin *consequens* following closely

consequential *adj* **1** important or significant **2** following as a result

consequently ⊕ *adv* as a result; therefore

conservancy *n* environmental conservation

conservation ⊕ *n* **1** protection and careful management of the environment and natural resources **2** protection from change, loss, or injury **3** *physics* the principle that the quantity of a specified aspect of a system, such as momentum or charge, remains constant **conservationist** *n*

conservative ⊕ *adj* **1** favouring the preservation of established customs and values, and opposing change **2** moderate or cautious: *a conservative estimate* **3** conventional in style: *people in this area are conservative in their tastes* ▷*n* **4** a conservative person **conservatism** *n*

Conservative ⊕ *adj* **1** of or supporting the Conservative Party, the major right-wing political party in Britain, which believes in private enterprise and capitalism **2** of or supporting a similar right-wing party in other countries ▷*n* **3** a supporter or member of the Conservative Party

conservatoire (kon-serv-a-twahr) *n* a school of music
WORD ORIGIN French

conservatory *n, pl* **-tories 1** a greenhouse attached to a house **2** a conservatoire

conserve ⊕ *vb* **-serving, -served 1** to protect from harm, decay, or loss **2** to preserve (fruit or other food) with sugar ▷*n* **3** fruit preserved by cooking in sugar
WORD ORIGIN Latin *conservare* to keep safe

consider ⊕ *vb* **1** to be of the opinion that **2** to think carefully about (a problem or decision) **3** to bear in mind: *Corsica is well worth considering for those seeking a peaceful holiday in beautiful surroundings* **4** to have regard for or care about: *you must try to consider other people's feelings more* **5** to discuss (something) in order to make a decision **6** to look at: *he considered her and she forced herself to sit calmly under his gaze*
WORD ORIGIN Latin *considerare* to inspect closely

considerable ⊕ *adj* **1** large enough to reckon with: *a considerable number of people* **2** a lot of: *he was in considerable pain* **considerably** *adv*

considerate *adj* thoughtful towards other people

C

THESAURUS

OPPOSITE: asleep
3 (*often with* **of**) = **aware of**, wise to (*slang*), alert to, responsive to, cognizant of, sensible of, clued-up on (*informal*), percipient of
OPPOSITE: unaware
4 = **deliberate**, knowing, reasoning, studied, responsible, calculated, rational, reflective, self-conscious, intentional, wilful, premeditated
OPPOSITE: unintentional

consecutive *adj* = **successive**, running, following, succeeding, in turn, uninterrupted, chronological, sequential, in sequence, seriatim

consensus *n* = **agreement**, general agreement, unanimity, common consent, unity, harmony, assent, concord, concurrence, kotahitanga (*NZ*)

consent *n* **1** = **agreement**, sanction, approval, go-ahead (*informal*), permission, compliance, green light, assent, acquiescence, concurrence, O.K. *or* okay (*informal*)
OPPOSITE: refusal
▷ *vb* **3** = **agree**, approve, yield, permit, comply, concur, assent, accede, acquiesce, play ball (*informal*)
OPPOSITE: refuse

consequence *n* **1** = **result**, effect, outcome, repercussion, end, issue, event, sequel, end result, upshot **2** = **importance**, interest, concern, moment, value, account, note, weight, import, significance, portent

consequently *adv* = **as a result**, thus, therefore, necessarily, hence, subsequently, accordingly, for that reason, thence, ergo

conservation *n* **1** = **preservation**, saving, protection, maintenance, custody, safeguarding, upkeep, guardianship, safekeeping **2** = **economy**, saving, thrift, husbandry, careful management, thriftiness

conservative *adj* **1, 3** = **traditional**, guarded, quiet, conventional, moderate, cautious, sober, reactionary, die-hard, middle-of-the-road, hidebound
OPPOSITE: radical
▷ *n* **4** = **traditionalist**, moderate, reactionary, die-hard, middle-of-the-roader, stick-in-the-mud (*informal*) **OPPOSITE:** radical

Conservative *adj* **1, 2** = **Tory**, Republican (*US*), right-wing ▷ *n* **3** = **Tory**, Republican (*US*), right-winger

conserve *vb* **1a** = **save**, husband, take care of, hoard, store up, go easy on, use sparingly **OPPOSITE:** waste
1b = **protect**, keep, save, preserve

consider *vb* **1** = **think**, see, believe, rate, judge, suppose, deem, view as, look upon, regard as, hold to be, adjudge **2** = **think about**, study, reflect on, examine, weigh, contemplate, deliberate, muse, ponder, revolve, meditate, work over, mull over, eye up, ruminate, chew over, cogitate, turn over in your mind **3, 4** = **bear in mind**, remember, regard, respect, think about, care for, take into account, reckon with, take into consideration, make allowance for, keep in view

considerable *adj* **1** = **large**, goodly, much, great, marked, comfortable, substantial, reasonable, tidy, lavish, ample, noticeable, abundant, plentiful, tolerable, appreciable, sizable *or* sizeable

DICTIONARY

C

consideration ◐ *n* **1** careful thought **2** a fact to be taken into account when making a decision **3** thoughtfulness for other people **4** payment for a service **5 take into consideration** to bear in mind **6 under consideration** being currently discussed

considered *adj* **1** presented or thought out with care: *a considered opinion* **2** thought of in a specified way: *highly considered*

considering ◐ *conj, prep* **1** taking (a specified fact) into account: *considering the mileage the car had done, it was lasting well* ▷ *adv* **2** *informal* taking into account the circumstances: *it's not bad considering*

consign *vb* **1** to give into the care or charge of **2** to put irrevocably: *those events have been consigned to history* **3** to put (in a specified place or situation): *only a few months ago such demands would have consigned the student leaders to prisons and labour camps* **4** to address or deliver (goods): *a cargo of oil drilling equipment consigned to Saudi Arabia* **consignee** *n* **consignor** *n*
WORD ORIGIN Latin *consignare* to put one's seal to, sign

consignment *n* **1** a shipment of goods **2** the act or an instance of consigning: *the goods are sent to Hong Kong for onward consignment to customers in the area*

consist ◐ *vb* **1 consist of** to be made up of: *a match consists of seven games* **2 consist in** to have as its main or only part: *his madness, if he is mad, consists in believing that he is a sundial*
WORD ORIGIN Latin *consistere* to stand firm

consistency ◐ *n, pl* **-encies 1** degree of thickness or smoothness **2** being consistent

consistent ◐ *adj* **1** holding to the same principles **2** in agreement **consistently** *adv*

consolation ◐ *n* **1** a person or thing that is a comfort in a time of sadness or distress **2** a consoling or being consoled

consolation prize *n* something given to console the loser of a game

console[1] ◐ *vb* **-soling, -soled** to comfort (someone) in sadness or distress **consolable** *adj*
WORD ORIGIN Latin *consolari*

console[2] *n* **1** a panel of controls for electronic equipment **2** a cabinet for a television or audio equipment **3** an ornamental bracket used to support a wall fixture **4** the desklike case of an organ, containing the pedals, stops, and keys
WORD ORIGIN Old French *consolateur* one that provides support

consolidate ◐ *vb* **-dating, -dated 1** to make or become stronger or more stable **2** to combine into a whole **consolidation** *n* **consolidator** *n*
WORD ORIGIN Latin *consolidare* to make firm

consommé (kon-som-may) *n* a thin clear meat soup
WORD ORIGIN French

consonance *n formal* agreement or harmony

consonant *n* **1 a** a speech sound made by partially or completely blocking the breath streams, for example *b* or *f* **b** a letter representing this ▷ *adj* **2 consonant with** in keeping or agreement with: *an individualistic style of religion, more consonant with liberal society* **3** harmonious: *this highly-dissonant chord is followed by a more consonant one*
WORD ORIGIN Latin *consonare* to sound at the same time

consort *vb* **1 consort with** to keep company with ▷ *n* **2** a husband or wife of a reigning monarch **3** a small group of voices or instruments
WORD ORIGIN Latin *consors* partner

consortium *n, pl* **-tia** an association of business firms
WORD ORIGIN Latin: partnership

conspectus *n formal* a survey or summary
WORD ORIGIN Latin: a viewing

conspicuous ◐ *adj* **1** clearly visible **2** noteworthy or striking: *conspicuous bravery* **conspicuously** *adv*
WORD ORIGIN Latin *conspicuus*

conspiracy ◐ *n, pl* **-cies 1** a secret plan to carry out an illegal or harmful act **2** the act of making such plans

conspire ◐ *vb* **-spiring, -spired 1** to plan a crime together in secret **2** to act together as if by design: *the weather and the recession conspired to hit wine production and sales* **conspirator** *n* **conspiratorial** *adj*
WORD ORIGIN Latin *conspirare* to plot together

constable *n* a police officer of the lowest rank
WORD ORIGIN Late Latin *comes stabuli* officer in charge of the stable

constabulary *n, pl* **-laries** *chiefly Brit* the police force of an area

constant ◐ *adj* **1** continuous: *she has endured constant criticism, mockery and humiliation* **2** unchanging: *the average speed of the winds remained constant over this period* **3** faithful ▷ *n* **4** *maths, physics* a quantity or number which

THESAURUS

OPPOSITE: small

consideration *n* **1 = thought**, study, review, attention, regard, analysis, examination, reflection, scrutiny, deliberation, contemplation, perusal, cogitation **2 = factor**, point, issue, concern, element, aspect, determinant **3 = thoughtfulness**, concern, respect, kindness, friendliness, tact, solicitude, kindliness, considerateness **4 = payment**, fee, reward, remuneration, recompense, perquisite, tip

considering *prep* **1 = taking into account**, in the light of, bearing in mind, in view of, keeping in mind, taking into consideration

consist *vb* **1 consist of something = be made up of**, include, contain, incorporate, amount to, comprise, be composed of **2 consist in something = lie in**, involve, reside in, be expressed by, subsist in, be found *or* contained in

consistency *n* **1 = texture**, density, thickness, firmness, viscosity, compactness **2 = agreement**, harmony, correspondence, accordance, regularity, coherence, compatibility, uniformity, constancy, steadiness, steadfastness, evenness, congruity

consistent *adj* **1a = steady**, even, regular, stable, constant, persistent, dependable, unchanging, true to type, undeviating **OPPOSITE:** erratic **1b = coherent**, logical, compatible, harmonious, consonant, all of a piece **OPPOSITE:** contradictory **2 = compatible**, agreeing, in keeping, harmonious, in harmony, consonant, in accord, congruent, congruous, accordant **OPPOSITE:** incompatible

consolation *n* **1, 2 = comfort**, help, support, relief, ease, cheer, encouragement, solace, succour, alleviation, assuagement

console[1] *vb* **= comfort**, cheer, relieve, soothe, support, encourage, calm, solace, assuage, succour, express sympathy for **OPPOSITE:** distress

consolidate *vb* **1 = strengthen**, secure, reinforce, cement, fortify, stabilize **2 = combine**, unite, join, marry, merge, unify, amalgamate, federate, conjoin

conspicuous *adj* **1 = obvious**, clear, apparent, visible, patent, evident, manifest, noticeable, blatant, discernible, salient, perceptible, easily seen **OPPOSITE:** inconspicuous

conspiracy *n* **1, 2 = plot**, scheme, intrigue, collusion, confederacy, cabal, frame-up *(slang)*, machination, league, golden circle

conspire *vb* **1 = plot**, scheme, intrigue, devise, manoeuvre, contrive, machinate, plan, hatch treason **2 = work together**, combine, contribute, cooperate, concur, tend, conduce

constant *adj* **1 = continuous**, sustained, endless, persistent, eternal, relentless, perpetual, continual, never-ending, habitual, uninterrupted, interminable, unrelenting, incessant, everlasting,

remains invariable: *the velocity of light is a constant* **5** something that is unchanging **constancy** *n* **constantly** *adv*
WORD ORIGIN Latin *constare* to be steadfast

Constant *n* **Benjamin**, real name *Henri Benjamin Constant de Rebecque.* 1767–1830, French writer and politician: author of the psychological novel *Adolphe* (1816)

Constantine II *n* official title *Constantine XIII.* born 1940, king of Greece (1964–73): went into exile when the army seized power in 1967. He was officially deposed in 1973 and Greece became a republic

Constantine VII *n* known as *Porphyrogenitus.* 905–59 AD, Byzantine emperor (913–59) and scholar: his writings are an important source for Byzantine history

Constantine XI *n* 1404–53, last Byzantine emperor (1448–53): killed when Constantinople was captured by the Turks

constellation *n* **1** a group of stars which form a pattern and are given a name **2** a group of people or things: *the constellation of favourable circumstances*
WORD ORIGIN Latin *com-* together + *stella* star

consternation *n* a feeling of anxiety or dismay

constipated *adj* unable to empty one's bowels
WORD ORIGIN Latin *constipare* to press closely together

constipation *n* a condition in which emptying one's bowels is difficult

constituency *n, pl* **-cies 1** the area represented by a Member of Parliament **2** the voters in such an area

constituent ❶ *n* **1** a person living in an MP's constituency **2** a component part ▷ *adj* **3** forming part of a whole: *the constituent parts of the universe* **4** having the power to make or change a constitution of a state: *a constituent assembly*
WORD ORIGIN Latin *constituere* to constitute

constitute ❶ *vb* **-tuting, -tuted 1** to form or make up: *the amazing range of crags that constitute the Eglwyseg Mountains* **2** to set up (an institution) formally
WORD ORIGIN Latin *com-* (intensive) + *statuere* to place

constitution ❶ *n* **1** the principles on which a state is governed **2 the Constitution** (in certain countries) the statute embodying such principles **3** a person's state of health **4** the make-up or structure of something: *changes in the very constitution of society*

constitutional ❶ *adj* **1** of a constitution **2** authorized by or in accordance with the Constitution of a nation: *constitutional monarchy* **3** inherent in the nature of a person or thing: *a constitutional sensitivity to cold* ▷ *n* **4** a regular walk taken for the good of one's health **constitutionally** *adv*

constitutive *adj* **1** forming a part of something **2** with the power to appoint or establish

constrain ❶ *vb* **1** to compel or force: *he felt constrained to apologize* **2** to limit, restrict, or inhibit: *the mobility of workers is constrained by the serious housing shortage*
WORD ORIGIN Latin *constringere* to bind together

constrained *adj* embarrassed or unnatural: *his constrained expression*

constraint ❶ *n* **1** something that limits a person's freedom of action **2** repression of natural feelings **3** a forced unnatural manner

constrict *vb* **1** to make smaller or narrower by squeezing **2** to limit or restrict **constrictive** *adj*
WORD ORIGIN Latin *constringere* to tie up together

constriction *n* **1** a feeling of tightness in some part of the body, such as the chest **2** a narrowing **3** something that constricts

constrictor *n* **1** a snake that coils around and squeezes its prey to kill it **2** a muscle that contracts an opening

construct ❶ *vb* **1** to build or put together **2** *geom* to draw (a figure) to specified requirements **3** to compose (an argument or sentence) ▷ *n* **4** a complex idea resulting from the combination of simpler ideas **5** something formulated or built systematically **constructor** *n*
WORD ORIGIN Latin *construere* to build

construction ❶ *n* **1** the act of constructing or manner in which a thing is constructed **2** something that has been constructed **3** the business or work of building houses or other structures **4** *formal* an interpretation: *the financial markets will put the worst possible construction on any piece of news which might affect them* **5** *grammar* the way in which words are arranged in a sentence, clause, or phrase **constructional** *adj*

constructive ❶ *adj* **1** useful and helpful: *constructive criticism* **2** *law* deduced by inference; not openly expressed **constructively** *adv*

construe *vb* **-struing, -strued 1** to interpret the meaning of (something): *her indifference was construed as rudeness* **2** to analyse the grammatical structure of (a sentence) **3** to combine (words) grammatically **4** *old-fashioned* to translate literally
WORD ORIGIN Latin *construere* to build

consul *n* **1** an official representing a state in a foreign country **2** one of the two chief magistrates in ancient Rome **consular** *adj* **consulship** *n*
WORD ORIGIN Latin

consulate *n* **1** the workplace and official home of a consul **2** the position or period of office of a consul

C

THESAURUS

ceaseless, unremitting, nonstop **OPPOSITE:** occasional
2 = unchanging, even, fixed, regular, permanent, stable, steady, uniform, continual, unbroken, immutable, immovable, invariable, unalterable, unvarying, firm **OPPOSITE:** changing
3 = faithful, true, devoted, loyal, stalwart, staunch, dependable, trustworthy, trusty, steadfast, unfailing, tried-and-true
OPPOSITE: undependable

constituent *n* **1 = voter**, elector, member of the electorate
2 = component, element, ingredient, part, unit, factor, principle ▷ *adj*
3 = component, basic, essential, integral, elemental

constitute *vb* **1 = make up**, make, form, compose, comprise

constitution *n* **3 = state of health**, build, body, make-up, frame, physique, physical condition
4 = structure, form, nature, make-up, organization, establishment, formation, composition, character, temper, temperament, disposition

constitutional *adj* **1, 2 = legitimate**, official, legal, chartered, statutory, vested

constrain *vb* **1 = force**, pressure, urge, bind, compel, oblige, necessitate, coerce, impel, pressurize, drive
2 = restrict, confine, curb, restrain, rein, constrict, hem in, straiten, check, chain

constraint *n* **1 = restriction**, limitation, curb, rein, deterrent, hindrance, damper, check

construct *vb* **1 = build**, make, form, create, design, raise, establish, set up, fashion, shape, engineer, frame, manufacture, put up, assemble, put together, erect, fabricate
OPPOSITE: demolish
3 = create, make, form, set up, organize, compose, put together, formulate

construction *n* **1 = building**, assembly, creation, formation, composition, erection, fabrication **4** *(formal)* **= interpretation**, meaning, reading, sense, explanation, rendering, take *(informal, chiefly US)*, inference

constructive *adj* **1 = helpful**, positive, useful, practical, valuable, productive **OPPOSITE:** unproductive

C

DICTIONARY

consult ❶ *vb* **1** to ask advice from or discuss matters with (someone): *he never consults his wife about what he's about to do* **2** to refer to for information: *he consulted his watch*
WORD ORIGIN Latin *consultare*

consultant ❶ *n* **1** a specialist doctor with a senior position in a hospital **2** a specialist who gives expert professional advice **consultancy** *n*

consultation ❶ *n* **1** the act of consulting **2** a meeting for discussion or the seeking of advice **consultative** *adj*

consulting *adj* acting as an adviser on professional matters: *consulting engineers*

consulting room *n* a room in which a doctor sees patients

consume ❶ *vb* **-suming, -sumed** **1** to eat or drink **2** to use up **3** to destroy: *the ship blew up and was consumed by flames* **4** to obsess: *he was consumed with jealousy over the ending of their affair* **consumable** *adj* **consuming** *adj*
WORD ORIGIN Latin *com-* (intensive) + *sumere* to take up

consumer ❶ *n* a person who buys goods or uses services

consumer durables *pl n* manufactured products that have a relatively long life, such as cars or televisions

consumer goods *pl n* goods bought for personal needs rather than those required for the production of other goods or services

consumerism *n* **1** the belief that a high level of consumer spending is desirable and beneficial to the economy: *the obsessive consumerism of the 80s* **2** protection of the rights of consumers

consummate *vb* (**kon**-sum-mate), **-mating, -mated** **1** to make (a marriage) legal by sexual intercourse **2** to complete or fulfil ▹ *adj* (kon-**sum**-mit) **3** supremely skilled: *a consummate craftsman* **4** complete or extreme: *consummate skill; consummate ignorance* **consummation** *n*
WORD ORIGIN Latin *consummare* to complete

consumption ❶ *n* **1** the quantity of something consumed or used: *for such a powerful car, fuel consumption is modest* **2** the act of eating or drinking something: *this meat is unfit for human consumption* **3** *econ* purchase of goods and services for personal use **4** *old-fashioned* tuberculosis of the lungs

consumptive *adj* **1** wasteful or destructive **2** of tuberculosis of the lungs ▹ *n* **3** a person with tuberculosis of the lungs

cont. continued

contact ❶ *n* **1** the state or act of communication: *the airport lost contact with the plane shortly before the crash* **2** the state or act of touching: *rugby is a game of hard physical contact* **3** an acquaintance who might be useful in business **4** a connection between two electrical conductors in a circuit **5** a person who has been exposed to a contagious disease ▹ *vb* **6** to come or be in communication or touch with
WORD ORIGIN Latin *contingere* to touch on all sides

contact lens *n* a small lens placed on the eyeball to correct defective vision

contagion *n* **1** the passing on of disease by contact **2** a contagious disease **3** a corrupting influence that tends to spread
WORD ORIGIN Latin *contagio* infection

contagious *adj* **1** (of a disease) capable of being passed on by contact **2** (of a person) capable of passing on a transmissible disease **3** spreading from person to person: *contagious enthusiasm*

contain ❶ *vb* **1** to hold or be capable of holding: *the bag contained a selection of men's clothing* **2** to have as one of its ingredients or constituents: *tea and coffee both contain appreciable amounts of caffeine* **3** to consist of: *the book contains 13 very different and largely separate chapters* **4** to check or restrain (feelings or behaviour) **5** to prevent from spreading or going beyond fixed limits: *the blockade was too weak to contain the French fleet* **containable** *adj*
WORD ORIGIN Latin *continere*

container ❶ *n* **1** an object used to hold or store things in **2** a large standard-sized box for transporting cargo by lorry or ship

containerize *or* **-ise** *vb* **-izing, -ized** *or* **-ising, -ised** **1** to pack (cargo) in large standard-sized containers **2** to fit (a port, ship, or lorry) to carry goods in standard-sized containers
containerization *or* **-isation** *n*

containment *n* the prevention of the spread of something harmful

contaminate ❶ *vb* **-nating, -nated** **1** to make impure; pollute **2** to make radioactive **contaminant** *n* **contamination** *n*
WORD ORIGIN Latin *contaminare* to defile

contemn *vb formal* to regard with contempt
WORD ORIGIN Latin *contemnere*

contemplate ❶ *vb* **-plating, -plated** **1** to think deeply about **2** to consider as a possibility **3** to look at thoughtfully **4** to meditate **contemplation** *n*
WORD ORIGIN Latin *contemplare*

THESAURUS

consult *vb* **1a = ask**, refer to, turn to, interrogate, take counsel, ask advice of, pick (someone's) brains, question **1b = confer**, talk, debate, deliberate, commune, compare notes, consider **2 = refer to**, check in, look in

consultant *n* **2 = specialist**, adviser, counsellor, authority

consultation *n* **1 = discussion**, talk, council, conference, dialogue **2 = meeting**, interview, session, appointment, examination, deliberation, hearing

consume *vb* **1 = eat**, swallow, devour, put away, gobble (up), eat up, guzzle, polish off (*informal*) **2 = use up**, use, spend, waste, employ, absorb, drain, exhaust, deplete, squander, utilize, dissipate, expend, eat up, fritter away **3 = destroy**, devastate, demolish, ravage, annihilate, lay waste **4** (*often passive*) **= obsess**, dominate, absorb, preoccupy, devour, eat up, monopolize, engross

consumer *n* **= buyer**, customer, user, shopper, purchaser

consumption *n* **1 = using up**, use, loss, waste, drain, consuming, expenditure, exhaustion, depletion, utilization, dissipation **4** (*old-fashioned*) **= tuberculosis**, atrophy, T.B., emaciation

contact *n* **1 = communication**, link, association, connection, correspondence, intercourse **2 = touch**, contiguity **3 = connection**, colleague, associate, liaison, acquaintance, confederate ▹ *vb* **6 = get** *or* **be in touch with**, call, reach, approach, phone, ring (up) (*informal, chiefly Brit*), write to, speak to, communicate with, get hold of, touch base with (*US & Canad informal*), e-mail, text

contain *vb* **1 = hold**, incorporate, accommodate, enclose, have capacity for **2, 3 = include**, consist of, embrace, comprise, embody, comprehend **4, 5 = restrain**, control, hold in, curb, suppress, hold back, stifle, repress, keep a tight rein on

container *n* **1 = holder**, vessel, repository, receptacle

contaminate *vb* **1 = pollute**, infect, stain, corrupt, taint, sully, defile, adulterate, befoul, soil
OPPOSITE: purify

contemplate *vb* **1 = think about**, consider, ponder, mull over, reflect upon, ruminate (upon), meditate on, brood over, muse over, deliberate over, revolve *or* turn over in your mind **2 = consider**, plan, think of, propose, intend, envisage, foresee, have in view *or* in mind **3 = look at**, examine, observe, check out (*informal*), inspect, gaze at, behold, eye up, view, study, regard, survey, stare at, scrutinize, eye

contemporary *adj* **1, 3 = modern**, latest, recent, current, with it (*informal*), trendy (*Brit informal*),

DICTIONARY

contemplative *adj* 1 of or given to contemplation ▷ *n* 2 a person dedicated to religious contemplation
contemporaneous *adj* happening at the same time **contemporaneity** *n*
contemporary ● *adj* 1 existing or occurring at the present time 2 living or occurring in the same period 3 modern in style or fashion 4 of approximately the same age ▷ *n, pl* **-raries** 5 a person or thing living at the same time or of approximately the same age as another
WORD ORIGIN Latin *com-* together + *temporarius* relating to time
contempt ● *n* 1 scorn 2 **hold in contempt** to scorn or despise 3 deliberate disrespect for the authority of a court of law: *contempt of court*
WORD ORIGIN Latin *contemnere* to scorn
contemptible *adj* deserving to be despised or hated: *a contemptible lack of courage*
contemptuous *adj* showing or feeling strong dislike or disrespect **contemptuously** *adv*
contend ● *vb* 1 **contend with** to deal with 2 to assert 3 to compete or fight 4 to argue earnestly **contender** *n*
WORD ORIGIN Latin *contendere* to strive
content[1] ● *n* 1 **contents** everything inside a container 2 **contents** a list of chapters at the front of a book 3 the meaning or substance of a piece of writing, often as distinguished from its style or form 4 the amount of a substance contained in a mixture: *the water vapour content of the atmosphere*
WORD ORIGIN Latin *contentus* contained
content[2] ● *adj* 1 satisfied with things as they are 2 willing to accept a situation or a proposed course of action ▷ *vb* 3 to satisfy (oneself or another person) ▷ *n* 4 peace of mind **contentment** *n*
WORD ORIGIN Latin *contentus* contented, having restrained desires
contented ● *adj* satisfied with one's situation or life **contentedly** *adv* **contentedness** *n*
contention *n* 1 disagreement or dispute 2 a point asserted in argument 3 **bone of contention** a point of dispute
WORD ORIGIN Latin *contentio*
contentious ● *adj* 1 causing disagreement 2 tending to quarrel **contentiousness** *n*
contest ● *n* 1 a game or match in which people or teams compete 2 a struggle for power or control ▷ *vb* 3 to dispute: *he has said he will not contest the verdict* 4 to take part in (a contest or struggle for power): *all parties which meet the legal requirements will be allowed to contest the election* **contestable** *adj*
WORD ORIGIN Latin *contestari* to introduce a lawsuit
contestant ● *n* a person who takes part in a contest
context ● *n* 1 the circumstances relevant to an event or fact 2 the words before and after a word or passage in a piece of writing that contribute to its meaning: *taken out of context, lines like these sound ridiculous, but, as part of a scrupulously written play, they are just right* **contextual** *adj*
WORD ORIGIN Latin *com-* together + *texere* to weave
contiguous *adj formal* very near or touching
WORD ORIGIN Latin *contiguus*
continent[1] *n* one of the earth's large landmasses (Asia, Australia, Africa, Europe, North and South America, and Antarctica) **continental** *adj*
WORD ORIGIN Latin *terra continens* continuous land
continent[2] *adj* 1 able to control one's bladder and bowels 2 sexually restrained **continence** *n*
WORD ORIGIN Latin *continere* to contain, retain
Continent *n* **the Continent** the mainland of Europe as distinct from the British Isles **Continental** *adj*
continental breakfast *n* a light breakfast of coffee and rolls
continental climate *n* a climate with hot summers, cold winters, and little rainfall, typical of the interior of a continent
continental drift *n geol* the theory that the earth's continents drift gradually over the surface of the planet, due to currents in its mantle
continental quilt *n Brit* a large quilt used as a bed cover in place of the top sheet and blankets
continental shelf *n* the gently sloping shallow sea bed surrounding a continent
contingency ● *n, pl* **-cies** 1 an unknown or unforeseen future event or condition 2 something dependent on a possible future event
contingent *n* 1 a group of people with a common interest, that represents a larger group: *a contingent of European scientists* 2 a military group that is part of a larger force: *the force includes a contingent of the Foreign Legion* ▷ *adj* 3 (foll. by *on* or *upon*) dependent on (something uncertain) 4 happening by chance
WORD ORIGIN Latin *contingere* to touch, befall
continual ● *adj* 1 occurring without interruption 2 recurring frequently **continually** *adv*

THESAURUS

up-to-date, present-day, in fashion, up-to-the-minute, à la mode, newfangled, happening *(informal)*, present, ultramodern OPPOSITE: old-fashioned
2, 4 = coexisting, concurrent, contemporaneous, synchronous, coexistent ▷ *n* **5 = peer**, fellow, equal
contempt *n* **1 = scorn**, disdain, mockery, derision, disrespect, disregard OPPOSITE: respect
contend *vb* **2 = argue**, hold, maintain, allege, assert, affirm, avow, aver **3 = compete**, fight, struggle, clash, contest, strive, vie, grapple, jostle, skirmish
content[1] *n* **3 = subject matter**, ideas, matter, material, theme, text, substance, essence, gist **4 = amount**, measure, size, load, volume, capacity ▷ *pl n* **1 = constituents**, elements, load, ingredients
content[2] *adj* **1 = satisfied**, happy, pleased, contented, comfortable, fulfilled, at ease, gratified, agreeable, willing to accept ▷ *n* **4 = satisfaction**, peace, ease, pleasure, comfort, peace of mind, gratification, contentment
contented *adj* **= satisfied**, happy, pleased, content, comfortable, glad, cheerful, at ease, thankful, gratified, serene, at peace
OPPOSITE: discontented
contentious *adj* **2 = argumentative**, wrangling, perverse, bickering, combative, pugnacious, quarrelsome, litigious, querulous, cavilling, disputatious, factious, captious
contest *n* **1 = competition**, game, match, trial, tournament, head-to-head **2 = struggle**, fight, battle, debate, conflict, dispute, encounter, controversy, combat, discord ▷ *vb* **3 = oppose**, question, challenge, argue, debate, dispute, object to, litigate, call in *or* into question **4 = compete in**, take part in, fight in, go in for, contend for, vie in
contestant *n* **= competitor**, candidate, participant, contender, entrant, player, aspirant
context *n* **1 = circumstances**, times, conditions, situation, ambience **2 = frame of reference**, background, framework, relation, connection
contingency *n* **1, 2 = possibility**, happening, chance, event, incident, accident, emergency, uncertainty, eventuality, juncture
continual *adj* **1 = constant**, endless, continuous, eternal, perpetual, uninterrupted, interminable, incessant, everlasting, unremitting, unceasing OPPOSITE: erratic **2 = frequent**, regular, repeated, repetitive, recurrent, oft-repeated
OPPOSITE: occasional

DICTIONARY

WORD ORIGIN Latin *continuus* uninterrupted

continuance *n* **1** the act of continuing **2** duration

continuation ❶ *n* **1** the act of continuing **2** a part or thing added, such as a sequel **3** a renewal of an interrupted action or process

continue ❶ *vb* **-tinuing, -tinued 1** to remain or cause to remain in a particular condition or place **2** to carry on (doing something): *we continued kissing; heavy fighting continued until Thursday afternoon* **3** to resume after an interruption: *we'll continue after lunch* **4** to go on to a further place: *the road continues on up the hill*
WORD ORIGIN Latin *continuare* to join together

continuity ❶ *n, pl* **-ties 1** a smooth development or sequence **2** the arrangement of scenes in a film so that they follow each other logically and without breaks

continuo *n, pl* **-tinuos** *music* a continuous bass accompaniment played usually on a keyboard instrument
WORD ORIGIN Italian

continuous ❶ *adj* **1** without end: *a continuous process* **2** not having any breaks or gaps in it: *a continuous line of boats; continuous rain* **continuously** *adv*
WORD ORIGIN Latin *continuus*

continuum *n, pl* **-tinua** *or* **-tinuums** a continuous series or whole, no part of which is noticeably different from the parts immediately next to it, although the ends or extremes of it are very different from each other: *the continuum from minor misbehaviour to major crime*
WORD ORIGIN Latin

contort *vb* to twist or bend out of shape **contortion** *n*
WORD ORIGIN Latin *contortus* intricate

contortionist *n* a performer who contorts his or her body to entertain others

contour *n* **1** an outline **2** ▸ same as **contour line** ▹ *vb* **3** to shape so as to form or follow the contour of something
WORD ORIGIN Italian *contornare* to sketch

contour line *n* a line on a map or chart joining points of equal height or depth

contra- *prefix* **1** against or contrasting: *contraceptive* **2** (in music) lower in pitch: *contrabass*
WORD ORIGIN Latin *contra* against

contraband *n* **1** smuggled goods ▹ *adj* **2** (of goods) smuggled
WORD ORIGIN Spanish *contrabanda*

contraception *n* the deliberate use of artificial or natural means to prevent pregnancy
WORD ORIGIN CONTRA- + CONCEPTION

contraceptive *n* **1** a device, such as a condom, that is used to prevent pregnancy ▹ *adj* **2** providing or relating to contraception: *the contraceptive pill*

contract ❶ *n* **1** a formal agreement between two or more parties **2** a document setting out a formal agreement ▹ *vb* **3** to make a formal agreement with (a person or company) to do or deliver (something) **4** to enter into (a relationship or marriage) formally: *she had contracted an alliance with a wealthy man* **5** to make or become smaller, narrower, or shorter **6** to become affected by (an illness) **7** to draw (muscles) together or (of muscles) to be drawn together **8** to shorten (a word or phrase) by omitting letters or syllables, usually indicated in writing by an apostrophe **contractible** *adj*
WORD ORIGIN Latin *contractus* agreement

contract bridge *n* the most common variety of bridge, in which only tricks bid and won count towards the game

contraction ❶ *n* **1** a contracting or being contracted **2** a shortening of a word or group of words, often marked by an apostrophe, for example *I've come* for *I have come* **3 contractions** *med* temporary shortening and tensing of the uterus during pregnancy and labour

contractor *n* a person or firm that supplies materials or labour for other companies

contract out *vb Brit* to agree not to take part in a scheme

contractual *adj* of or in the nature of a contract

contradict ❶ *vb* **1** to declare the opposite of (a statement) to be true **2** (of a fact or statement) to suggest that (another fact or statement) is wrong **contradiction** *n*
WORD ORIGIN Latin *contra-* against + *dicere* to speak

contradictory ❶ *adj* (of facts or statements) inconsistent

contradistinction *n* a distinction made by contrasting different qualities **contradistinctive** *adj*

contraflow *n* a flow of road traffic going alongside but in an opposite direction to the usual flow

contralto *n, pl* **-tos** *or* **-ti 1** the lowest female voice **2** a singer with such a voice
WORD ORIGIN Italian

contraption *n informal* a strange-looking device or gadget
WORD ORIGIN origin unknown

contrapuntal *adj music* of or in counterpoint

THESAURUS

continuation *n* **1 = continuing**, lasting, carrying on, maintenance, keeping up, endurance, perpetuation, prolongation
2 = addition, extension, supplement, sequel, resumption, postscript

continue *vb* **1 = remain**, last, stay, rest, survive, carry on, live on, endure, stay on, persist, abide **OPPOSITE:** quit
2 = keep on, go on, maintain, pursue, sustain, carry on, stick to, keep up, prolong, persist in, keep at, persevere, stick at, press on with **OPPOSITE:** stop
3 = resume, return to, take up again, proceed, carry on, recommence, pick up where you left off **OPPOSITE:** stop
4 = go on, advance, progress, proceed, carry on, keep going, crack on *(informal)*

continuity *n* **1 = cohesion**, flow, connection, sequence, succession, progression, wholeness, interrelationship

continuous *adj* **2 = constant**, continued, extended, prolonged, unbroken, uninterrupted, unceasing **OPPOSITE:** occasional

contract *n* **1 = agreement**, deal *(informal)*, commission, commitment, arrangement, understanding, settlement, treaty, bargain, convention, engagement, pact, compact, covenant, bond, stipulation, concordat ▹ *vb* **3 = agree**, arrange, negotiate, engage, pledge, bargain, undertake, come to terms, shake hands, covenant, make a deal, commit yourself, enter into an agreement **OPPOSITE:** refuse
5a = constrict, confine, tighten, shorten, wither, compress, condense, shrivel **5b = lessen**, reduce, shrink, diminish, decrease, dwindle **OPPOSITE:** increase
6 = catch, get, develop, acquire, incur, be infected with, go down with, be afflicted with **OPPOSITE:** avoid
7 = tighten, narrow, knit, purse, shorten, pucker **OPPOSITE:** stretch

contraction *n* **1 = tightening**, narrowing, tensing, shortening, drawing in, constricting, shrinkage
2 = abbreviation, reduction, shortening, compression, diminution, constriction, elision

contradict *vb* **1 = negate**, deny, oppose, counter, contravene, rebut, impugn, controvert **OPPOSITE:** confirm
2 = dispute, deny, challenge, belie, fly in the face of, make a nonsense of, be at variance with

contradictory *adj* **= inconsistent**, conflicting, opposed, opposite, contrary, incompatible, paradoxical, irreconcilable, antithetical, discrepant

DICTIONARY

WORD ORIGIN Italian *contrappunto* counterpoint
contrariwise *adv* **1** from a contrasting point of view **2** in the opposite way
contrary ❶ *n, pl* **-ries 1 on** *or* **to the contrary** in opposition to what has just been said or implied ▷ *adj* **2** opposed; completely different: *a contrary view, based on equally good information* **3** perverse; obstinate **4** (of the wind) unfavourable ▷ *adv* **contrary to 5** in opposition or contrast to: *contrary to popular belief* **6** in conflict with: *contrary to nature*
contrariness *n*
WORD ORIGIN Latin *contrarius* opposite
contrast ❶ *n* **1** a difference which is clearly seen when two things are compared **2** a person or thing showing differences when compared with another **3** the degree of difference between the colours in a photograph or television picture ▷ *vb* **4** to compare or be compared in order to show the differences between (things): *he contrasts that society with contemporary America* **5 contrast with** to be very different from: *her speed of reaction contrasted with her husband's vagueness* **contrasting** *adj*
WORD ORIGIN Latin *contra-* against + *stare* to stand
contravene *vb* **-vening, -vened** *formal* to break (a rule or law)
contravention *n*
WORD ORIGIN Latin *contra-* against + *venire* to come
contretemps (kon-tra-tahn) *n, pl* **-temps** an embarrassing minor disagreement
WORD ORIGIN French
contribute ❶ *vb* **-uting, -uted** (often foll. by *to*) **1** to give (support or money) for a common purpose or fund **2** to supply (ideas or opinions) **3 contribute to** to be partly responsible (for): *his own unconvincing play contributed to his defeat* **4** to write (an article) for a publication
contribution *n* **contributory** *adj*
contributor *n*
WORD ORIGIN Latin *contribuere* to collect
contrite *adj* full of guilt or regret
contritely *adv* **contrition** *n*
WORD ORIGIN Latin *contritus* worn out
contrivance *n* **1** an ingenious device **2** an elaborate or deceitful plan **3** the act or power of contriving
contrive ❶ *vb* **-triving, -trived 1** to make happen: *he had already contrived the murder of King Alexander* **2** to devise or construct ingeniously: *he contrived a plausible reason to fly back to London; he contrived a hook from a bent nail*
WORD ORIGIN Old French *controver*
control ❶ *n* **1** power to direct something: *the province is mostly under guerrilla control* **2** a curb or check: *import controls* **3 controls** instruments used to operate a machine **4** a standard of comparison used in an experiment **5** an experiment used to verify another by having all aspects identical except for the one that is being tested ▷ *vb* **-trolling, -trolled 6** to have power over: *the gland which controls the body's metabolic rate* **7** to limit or restrain: *he could not control his jealousy* **8** to regulate or operate (a machine) **9** to restrict the authorized supply of (certain drugs)
controllable *adj*
WORD ORIGIN Old French *conteroller* to regulate
controller *n* **1** a person who is in charge **2** a person in charge of the financial aspects of a business
control tower *n* a tall building at an airport from which air traffic is controlled
controversy ❶ *n, pl* **-sies** argument or debate concerning a matter about which there is strong disagreement
controversial *adj*
WORD ORIGIN Latin *contra-* against + *vertere* to turn
contumacy (kon-tume-mass-ee) *n, pl* **-cies** *literary* obstinate disobedience
contumacious (kon-tume-may-shuss) *adj*
WORD ORIGIN Latin *contumax* obstinate
contumely (kon-tume-mill-ee) *n, pl* **-lies** *literary* **1** scornful or insulting treatment **2** a humiliating insult
WORD ORIGIN Latin *contumelia*
contusion *n formal* a bruise
contuse *vb*
WORD ORIGIN Latin *contusus* bruised
conundrum *n* **1** a puzzling question or problem **2** a riddle whose answer contains a pun
WORD ORIGIN origin unknown
conurbation *n* a large heavily populated urban area formed by the growth and merging of towns
WORD ORIGIN Latin *con-* together + *urbs* city
convalesce *vb* **-lescing, -lesced** to recover health after an illness or operation
WORD ORIGIN Latin *com-* (intensive) + *valescere* to grow strong
convalescence *n* **1** gradual return to health after illness or an operation **2** the period during which such recovery occurs **convalescent** *n, adj*
convection *n* the transmission of heat caused by movement of molecules from cool regions to warmer regions of lower density
WORD ORIGIN Latin *convehere* to bring together
convector *n* a heating device which gives out hot air
convene ❶ *vb* **-vening, -vened** to gather or summon for a formal meeting

C

THESAURUS

contrary *adj* **2 = opposite**, different, opposed, clashing, counter, reverse, differing, adverse, contradictory, inconsistent, diametrically opposed, antithetical **OPPOSITE:** in agreement
3 = perverse, difficult, awkward, wayward, intractable, wilful, obstinate, cussed (*informal*), stroppy (*Brit slang*), cantankerous, disobliging, unaccommodating, thrawn (*Scot & Northern English dialect*) **OPPOSITE:** cooperative
contrast *n* **1 = difference**, opposition, comparison, distinction, foil, disparity, differentiation, divergence, dissimilarity, contrariety ▷ *vb* **4 = differentiate**, compare, oppose, distinguish, set in opposition
contribute *vb* **1 = give**, provide, supply, donate, furnish, subscribe, chip in (*informal*), bestow
3 contribute to something = be partly responsible for, lead to, be instrumental in, be conducive to, conduce to, help
contrive *vb* **1, 2 = devise**, plan, fabricate, create, design, scheme, engineer, frame, manufacture, plot, construct, invent, improvise, concoct, wangle (*informal*)
control *n* **1 = power**, government, rule, authority, management, direction, command, discipline, guidance, supervision, jurisdiction, supremacy, mastery, superintendence, charge
2 = restraint, check, regulation, brake, limitation, curb ▷ *pl n* **3 = instruments**, dash, dials, console, dashboard, control panel ▷ *vb* **6 = have power over**, lead, rule, manage, boss (*informal*), direct, handle, conduct, dominate, command, pilot, govern, steer, administer, oversee, supervise, manipulate, call the shots, call the tune, reign over, keep a tight rein on, have charge of, superintend, have (someone) in your pocket, keep on a string **7a = limit**, restrict, curb, delimit **7b = restrain**, limit, check, contain, master, curb, hold back, subdue, repress, constrain, bridle, rein in
controversy *n* **= argument**, debate, row, discussion, dispute, contention, quarrel, squabble, strife, wrangle, wrangling, polemic, altercation, dissension
convene *vb* **a = call**, gather, assemble, summon, bring together, muster, convoke **b = meet**, gather, rally, assemble, come together, muster, congregate

DICTIONARY

WORD ORIGIN Latin *convenire* to assemble

convener *or* **convenor** *n* a person who calls or chairs a meeting: *the shop stewards' convener at the factory* **convenership** *or* **convenorship** *n*

C

convenience ❶ *n* **1** the quality of being suitable or convenient **2 at your convenience** at a time suitable to you **3** an object that is useful: *a house with every modern convenience* **4** *euphemistic chiefly Brit* a public toilet

convenience food *n* food that needs little preparation and can be used at any time

convenient ❶ *adj* **1** suitable or opportune **2** easy to use **3** nearby
WORD ORIGIN Latin *convenire* to be in accord with

convent *n* **1** a building where nuns live **2** a school in which the teachers are nuns **3** a community of nuns
WORD ORIGIN Latin *conventus* meeting

conventicle *n Brit & US history* a secret or unauthorized religious meeting
WORD ORIGIN Latin *conventiculum*

convention ❶ *n* **1** the established view of what is thought to be proper behaviour **2** an accepted rule or method: *a convention used by printers* **3** a formal agreement or contract between people and nations **4** a large formal assembly of a group with common interests
WORD ORIGIN Latin *conventio* an assembling

conventional ❶ *adj* **1** following the accepted customs and lacking originality **2** established by accepted usage or general agreement **3** (of weapons or warfare) not nuclear **conventionally** *adv*

conventionality *n, pl* **-ties 1** the quality of being conventional **2** something conventional

conventionalize *or* **-ise** *vb* **-izing, -ized** *or* **-ising, -ised** to make conventional

converge ❶ *vb* **-verging, -verged 1** to move towards or meet at the same point **2** (of opinions or effects) to move towards a shared conclusion or result **convergence** *n* **convergent** *adj*
WORD ORIGIN Latin *com-* together + *vergere* to incline

conversant *adj* **conversant with** having knowledge or experience of
WORD ORIGIN Latin *conversari* to keep company with

conversation ❶ *n* informal talk between two or more people

conversational *adj* **1** of or used in conversation: *conversational French* **2** resembling informal spoken language: *the author's easy, conversational style*

conversationalist *n* a person with a specified ability at conversation: *a brilliant conversationalist*

conversation piece *n* something, such as an unusual object, that provokes conversation

converse[1] *vb* **-versing, -versed** to have a conversation
WORD ORIGIN Latin *conversari* to keep company with

converse[2] *adj* **1** reversed or opposite ▷*n* **2** a statement or idea that is the opposite of another **conversely** *adv*
WORD ORIGIN Latin *conversus* turned around

conversion ❶ *n* **1** a change or adaptation **2** *maths* a calculation in which a weight, volume, or distance is worked out in a different system of measurement: *the conversion from Fahrenheit to Celsius* **3** a change to another belief or religion **4** *rugby* a score made after a try by kicking the ball over the crossbar from a place kick
WORD ORIGIN Latin *conversio* a turning around

convert ❶ *vb* **1** to change or adapt **2** to cause (someone) to change in opinion or belief **3** to change (a measurement) from one system of units to another **4** to change (money) into a different currency **5** *rugby* to make a conversion after (a try) ▷*n* **6** a person who has been converted to another belief or religion **converter** *or* **convertor** *n*
WORD ORIGIN Latin *convertere* to turn around, alter

convertible *adj* **1** capable of being converted **2** *finance* (of a currency) freely exchangeable into other currencies ▷*n* **3** a car with a folding or removable roof

convex *adj* curving outwards like the outside surface of a ball **convexity** *n*
WORD ORIGIN Latin *convexus* vaulted, rounded

convey ❶ *vb* **1** to communicate (information) **2** to carry or transport from one place to another **3** (of a channel or path) to transfer or transmit **4** *law* to transfer (the title to property) **conveyable** *adj* **conveyor** *n*
WORD ORIGIN Old French *conveier*

conveyance *n* **1** *old-fashioned* a vehicle **2** *law* **a** a transfer of the legal title to property **b** the document effecting such a transfer **3** the act of conveying: *the conveyance of cycles on peak hour trains* **conveyancer** *n*

conveyancing *n* the branch of law dealing with the transfer of

THESAURUS

convenience *n* **1a = suitability**, fitness, appropriateness, opportuneness **1b = usefulness**, utility, serviceability, handiness
OPPOSITE: uselessness
1c = accessibility, availability, nearness, handiness **3 = appliance**, facility, comfort, amenity, labour-saving device, help

convenient *adj* **1a = suitable**, fitting, fit, handy, satisfactory
1b = appropriate, timely, suited, suitable, beneficial, well-timed, opportune, seasonable, helpful
2 = useful, practical, handy, serviceable, labour-saving
OPPOSITE: useless
3 = nearby, available, accessible, handy, at hand, within reach, close at hand, just round the corner
OPPOSITE: inaccessible

convention *n* **1, 2 = custom**, practice, tradition, code, usage, protocol, formality, etiquette, propriety, kawa (NZ), tikanga (NZ), rule
3 = agreement, contract, treaty, bargain, pact, compact, protocol, stipulation, concordat **4 = assembly**, meeting, council, conference, congress, convocation, hui (NZ), runanga (NZ)

conventional *adj* **1 = unoriginal**, routine, stereotyped, pedestrian, commonplace, banal, prosaic, run-of-the-mill, hackneyed, vanilla (*slang*) **OPPOSITE:** unconventional
1, 2 = traditional, accepted, prevailing, orthodox, customary, prevalent, hidebound, wonted
2 = ordinary, standard, normal, regular, usual, vanilla (*slang*), habitual, bog-standard (*Brit & Irish slang*), common

converge *vb* **1, 2 = come together**, meet, join, combine, gather, merge, coincide, mingle, intersect

conversation *n* **= talk**, exchange, discussion, dialogue, tête-à-tête, conference, communication, chat, gossip, intercourse, discourse, communion, converse, powwow, colloquy, chinwag (*Brit informal*), confabulation, confab (*informal*), craic (*Irish informal*), korero (NZ) ▸ *related adjective:* colloquial

conversion *n* **1a = change**, transformation, metamorphosis, transfiguration, transmutation, transmogrification (*humorous*)
1b = adaptation, reconstruction, modification, alteration, remodelling, reorganization

convert *vb* **1a = change**, turn, transform, alter, metamorphose, transpose, transmute, transmogrify (*humorous*) **1b = adapt**, modify, remodel, reorganize, customize, restyle **2 = reform**, save, convince, proselytize, bring to God ▷*n* **6 = neophyte**, disciple, proselyte, catechumen

convey *vb* **1 = communicate**, impart, reveal, relate, disclose, make known, tell **2 = carry**, transport, move, bring, support, bear, conduct, transmit, fetch

ownership of property
conveyor belt *n* an endless moving belt driven by rollers and used to transport objects, esp. in a factory
convict ❶ *vb* **1** to declare (someone) guilty of an offence ▷ *n* **2** a person serving a prison sentence
WORD ORIGIN Latin *convictus* convicted
conviction ❶ *n* **1** a firmly held belief or opinion **2** an instance of being found guilty of a crime: *he had several convictions for petty theft* **3** a convincing or being convinced **4 carry conviction** to be convincing
convince ❶ *vb* **-vincing, -vinced** to persuade by argument or evidence **convinced** *adj* **convincible** *adj* **convincing** *adj*
WORD ORIGIN Latin *convincere* to demonstrate incontrovertibly
convivial *adj* sociable or lively: *a convivial atmosphere; convivial company* **conviviality** *n*
WORD ORIGIN Late Latin *convivialis*
convocation *n formal* a large formal meeting
convoke *vb* **-voking, -voked** *formal* to call together
WORD ORIGIN Latin *convocare*
convoluted *adj* **1** coiled or twisted **2** (of an argument or sentence) complex and difficult to understand
convolution *n* **1** a coil or twist **2** an intricate or confused matter or condition **3** a convex fold in the surface of the brain
convolvulus *n, pl* **-luses** *or* **-li** a twining plant with funnel-shaped flowers and triangular leaves
WORD ORIGIN Latin: bindweed
convoy *n* a group of vehicles or ships travelling together
WORD ORIGIN Old French *convoier* to convey
convulse *vb* **-vulsing, -vulsed 1** to shake or agitate violently **2** (of muscles) to undergo violent spasms **3** *informal* to be overcome (with laughter or rage) **4** to disrupt the normal running of: *student riots have convulsed India* **convulsive** *adj*
WORD ORIGIN Latin *con-* together + *vellere* to pluck, pull
convulsion *n* **1** a violent muscular spasm **2** a violent upheaval **3 convulsions** *informal* uncontrollable laughter: *I was in convulsions*
cony *or* **coney** *n, pl* **-nies** *or* **-neys** *Brit* **1** a rabbit **2** rabbit fur
WORD ORIGIN Latin *cuniculus* rabbit
Conybeare *n* **William Daniel** 1787–1857, British geologist. He summarized all that was known about rocks at the time in *Outlines of the Geology of England and Wales* (1822)
coo *vb* **cooing, cooed 1** (of a dove or pigeon) to make a soft murmuring sound **2 bill and coo** to murmur softly or lovingly ▷ *n* **3** a cooing sound ▷ *interj* **4** *Brit slang* an exclamation of surprise or amazement **cooing** *adj, n*
WORD ORIGIN imitative
cooee *interj* **1** *Brit, Austral & NZ* a call used to attract attention **2** *Austral & NZ* **within cooee** within calling distance: *the school was within cooee of our house*
WORD ORIGIN Aboriginal
cook *vb* **1** to prepare (food) by heating or (of food) to be prepared in this way **2** *slang* to alter or falsify (figures or accounts): *she had cooked the books* ▷ *n* **3** a person who prepares food for eating ▸ See also **cook up**
WORD ORIGIN Latin *coquere*
cook-chill *n* a method of food preparation used by caterers, in which cooked dishes are chilled rapidly and reheated as required
Cooke *n* **Norman**, real name *Quentin Cooke*, also known as *Fatboy Slim*. born 1963, British disc jockey, pop musician, and record producer; hit records include *You've Come a Long Way, Baby* (1998) and "Praise You" (2001)
cooker *n* **1** *chiefly Brit* an apparatus for cooking heated by gas or electricity **2** *Brit* an apple suitable for cooking but not for eating raw
cookery *n* the art or practice of cooking ▸ Related adjective: **culinary**
cookery book *or* **cookbook** *n* a book containing recipes for cooking
cookie *n, pl* **cookies 1** *US & Canad* a biscuit **2 that's the way the cookie crumbles** *informal* that is how things inevitably are **3** *informal* a person: *a real tough cookie*
WORD ORIGIN Dutch *koekje* little cake
Cookson *n* Dame **Catherine** 1906–98, British novelist, known for her popular novels set in northeast England
cook up *vb informal* to invent (a story or scheme)
cool ❶ *adj* **1** moderately cold: *it should be served cool, even chilled* **2** comfortably free of heat: *it was one of the few cool days that summer* **3** calm and unemotional: *a cool head* **4** indifferent or unfriendly: *the idea met with a cool response* **5** calmly impudent **6** *informal* (of a large sum of money) without exaggeration: *a cool million* **7** *informal* sophisticated or elegant **8** (of a colour) having violet, blue, or green predominating **9** *informal* marvellous ▷ *vb* **10** to make or become cooler **11** to calm down ▷ *n* **12** coolness: *in the cool of the evening* **13** *slang* calmness; composure: *he lost his cool and wantonly kicked the ball away* **coolly** *adv* **coolness** *n*
WORD ORIGIN Old English *cōl*
coolant *n* a fluid used to cool machinery while it is working
cool drink *n S African* a soft drink
cooler *n* a container for making or keeping things cool
coolibah *n* an Australian eucalypt that grows beside rivers
WORD ORIGIN Aboriginal
coolie *n old-fashioned, offensive* an unskilled Oriental labourer
WORD ORIGIN Hindi *kuli*
cooling tower *n* a tall hollow structure in a factory or power station, inside which hot water cools as it trickles down
Coomaraswamy *n* **Ananda** (**Kentish**) 1877–1947, Ceylonese art historian and interpreter of Indian culture to the West
coomb *or* **coombe** *n* a short valley or deep hollow

C

THESAURUS

convict *vb* **1 = find guilty**, sentence, condemn, imprison, pronounce guilty ▷ *n* **2 = prisoner**, criminal, con *(slang)*, lag *(slang)*, villain, felon, jailbird, malefactor
conviction *n* **1, 4 = belief**, view, opinion, principle, faith, persuasion, creed, tenet, kaupapa (NZ)
3 = certainty, confidence, assurance, fervour, firmness, earnestness, certitude
convince *vb* **a = assure**, persuade, satisfy, prove to, reassure
b = persuade, induce, coax, talk into, prevail upon, inveigle, twist (someone's) arm, bring round to the idea of
cool *adj* **1 = cold**, chilled, chilling, refreshing, chilly, nippy
OPPOSITE: warm
3 = calm, together *(slang)*, collected, relaxed, composed, laid-back *(informal)*, serene, sedate, self-controlled, placid, level-headed, dispassionate, unfazed *(informal)*, unruffled, unemotional, self-possessed, imperturbable, unexcited, chilled *(informal)*
OPPOSITE: agitated
4a = unfriendly, reserved, distant, indifferent, aloof, lukewarm, unconcerned, uninterested, frigid, unresponsive, offhand, unenthusiastic, uncommunicative, unwelcoming, standoffish
OPPOSITE: friendly
4b = unenthusiastic, indifferent, lukewarm, uninterested, apathetic, unresponsive, unwelcoming ▷ *vb*
10a = lose heat, cool off
OPPOSITE: warm (up)
10b = make cool, freeze, chill, refrigerate, cool off **OPPOSITE:** warm (up)
▷ *n* **12 = coldness**, chill, coolness
13 *(slang)* **= calmness**, control, temper, composure, self-control, poise, self-discipline, self-possession

DICTIONARY

C

WORD ORIGIN Old English *cumb*

coon *n* **1** *informal* ▸short for **raccoon** **2** *offensive slang* a Negro or Australian Aborigine **3** *S African, offensive* a person of mixed race

coop[1] *n* **1** a cage or pen for poultry or small animals ▹*vb* **2 coop up** to confine in a restricted place
WORD ORIGIN Latin *cupa* basket, cask

coop[2] *or* **co-op** (koh-op) *n Brit, Austral & NZ* a cooperative society or a shop run by a cooperative society

cooper *n* a person who makes or repairs barrels or casks
WORD ORIGIN see coop[1]

Cooper *n* **1 Anthony Ashley** ▸See (Earl of) **Shaftesbury** **2 Cary (Lynn)** born 1940, British psychologist, noted for his studies of behaviour at work and the causes and treatment of stress **3 Gary,** real name *Frank James Cooper.* 1901–61, US film actor; his many films include *Sergeant York* (1941) and *High Noon* (1952), for both of which he won Oscars **4** Sir **Henry** born 1934, British boxer; European heavyweight champion (1964; 1968–71) **5 James Fenimore** 1789–1851, US novelist, noted for his stories of American Indians, esp. *The Last of the Mohicans* (1826) **6 Leon Neil** born 1930, US physicist, noted for his work on the theory of superconductivity. He shared the Nobel prize for physics 1972 **7 Samuel** 1609–72, English miniaturist

cooperate ❶ *or* **co-operate** *vb* **1** to work or act together **2** to assist or be willing to assist **cooperation** *or* **co-operation** *n*
WORD ORIGIN Latin *co-* with + *operari* to work

cooperative ❶ *or* **co-operative** *adj* **1** willing to cooperate **2** (of an enterprise or farm) owned and managed collectively ▹*n* **3** a cooperative organization

cooperative society *n* a commercial enterprise owned and run by customers or workers, in which the profits are shared among the members

coopt *or* **co-opt** (koh-opt) *vb* to add (someone) to a group by the agreement of the existing members
WORD ORIGIN Latin *cooptare* to choose, elect

coordinate *or* **co-ordinate** *vb* **-nating, -nated 1** to bring together and cause to work together efficiently ▹*n* **2** *maths* any of a set of numbers defining the location of a point with reference to a system of axes ▹*adj* **3** of or involving coordination **4** of or involving the use of coordinates: *coordinate geometry* **coordination** *or* **co-ordination** *n* **coordinator** *or* **co-ordinator** *n*
WORD ORIGIN Latin *co-* together + *ordinatio* arranging

coordinates *or* **co-ordinates** *pl n* clothes designed to be worn together

coot *n* **1** a small black water bird **2** *Brit, Austral & NZ* a foolish person
WORD ORIGIN probably Low German

cop *slang n* **1** a policeman **2 not much cop** of little value or worth ▹*vb* **copping, copped 3** to take or seize **4 cop it** to get into trouble or be punished: *he copped it after he was spotted driving a car without a seat belt* ▸See also **cop out**
WORD ORIGIN perhaps from Old French *caper* to seize

copal *n* a resin used in varnishes

copartner *n* a partner or associate **copartnership** *n*

cope[1] ❶ *vb* **coping, coped 1** to deal successfully (with): *well-nourished people cope better with stress* **2** to tolerate or endure: *the ability to cope with his pain*
WORD ORIGIN Old French *coper* to strike, cut

cope[2] *n* a large ceremonial cloak worn by some Christian priests
WORD ORIGIN Late Latin *cappa* hooded cloak

cope[3] *vb* **coping, coped** to provide (a wall) with a coping
WORD ORIGIN probably from French *couper* to cut

copeck *n* ▸same as **kopeck**

Copernican (kop-per-nik-an) *adj* of the theory that the earth and the planets rotate round the sun
WORD ORIGIN after *Copernicus,* astronomer

copestone *n* **1** Also called: **coping stone** a stone used to form a coping **2** the stone at the top of a building or wall

copier *n* a person or machine that copies

copilot *n* the second pilot of an aircraft

coping *n* a layer of rounded or sloping bricks on the top of a wall

coping saw *n* a handsaw with a U-shaped frame, used for cutting curves in wood

copious (kope-ee-uss) *adj* existing or produced in large quantities **copiously** *adv*
WORD ORIGIN Latin *copiosus*

Copland *n* **Aaron** 1900–90, US composer of orchestral and chamber music, ballets, and film music

Copley *n* **John Singleton** 1738–1815, US painter

cop out *slang vb* **1** to avoid taking responsibility or committing oneself ▹*n* **cop-out 2** a way or an instance of avoiding responsibility or commitment
WORD ORIGIN probably from COP

copper[1] *n* **1** a soft reddish metallic element, used in such alloys as brass and bronze. Symbol: Cu **2** *informal* any copper or bronze coin **3** *chiefly Brit* a large metal container used to boil water ▹*adj* **4** reddish-brown
WORD ORIGIN Latin *Cyprium aes* Cyprian metal, from Greek *Kupris* Cyprus

copper[2] *n Brit slang* a policeman
WORD ORIGIN from COP (verb)

copper beech *n* a European beech with reddish leaves

copper-bottomed *adj* financially reliable
WORD ORIGIN from the practice of coating the bottom of ships with copper to prevent the timbers rotting

copperhead *n* a poisonous snake with a reddish-brown head

copperplate *n* **1** an elegant handwriting style **2** a polished copper plate engraved for printing **3** a print taken from such a plate

copper sulphate *n* a blue crystalline copper salt used in electroplating and in plant sprays

coppice *n* a small group of trees or bushes growing close together
WORD ORIGIN Old French *copeiz*

Coppola *n* **Francis Ford** born 1939, US film director. His films include *The Godfather* (1972), *Apocalypse Now* (1979), *Tucker* (1988), and *The Rainmaker* (1999)

copra *n* the dried oil-yielding kernel of the coconut
WORD ORIGIN Malayalam (a language of SW India) *koppara* coconut

copse *n* ▸same as **coppice**
WORD ORIGIN from COPPICE

Copt *n* **1** a member of the Coptic Church, a part of the Christian Church which was founded in Egypt **2** an Egyptian descended from the ancient Egyptians
WORD ORIGIN Coptic *kyptios* Egyptian

Coptic *n* **1** the language of the Copts, descended from Ancient Egyptian

THESAURUS

cooperate *vb* **1 = work together,** collaborate, coordinate, join forces, conspire, concur, pull together, pool resources, combine your efforts
OPPOSITE: conflict

cooperative *adj* **1 = helpful,** obliging, accommodating, supportive, responsive, onside *(informal)* **2 = shared,** united, joint, combined, concerted, collective, unified, coordinated, collaborative

cope[1] *vb* **1, 2a cope with something = deal with,** handle, struggle with, grapple with, wrestle with, contend with, tangle with, tussle with, weather **1, 2b = manage,** get by *(informal)*, struggle through, rise to the occasion, survive, carry on, make out *(informal)*, make the grade, hold your own

copy *n* **1 = reproduction,** duplicate,

DICTIONARY

and surviving only in the Coptic Church ▷ *adj* **2** of the Copts or the Coptic Church

copula *n, pl* **-las** *or* **-lae** a verb, such as *be*, that is used to link the subject with the complement of a sentence, as in *he became king*
WORD ORIGIN Latin: bond

copulate *vb* **-lating, -lated** to have sexual intercourse **copulation** *n*
WORD ORIGIN Latin *copulare* to join together

copy ❶ *n, pl* **copies 1** a thing made to look exactly like another **2** a single specimen of a book, magazine, or record of which there are many others exactly the same: *my copy of 'Death on the Nile'* **3** written material for printing **4** the text of an advertisement **5** *journalism informal* suitable material for an article: *disasters are always good copy* ▷ *vb* **copies, copying, copied 6** to make a copy (of) **7** to act or try to be like another
WORD ORIGIN Latin *copia* abundance

copybook *n* **1** a book of specimens of handwriting for imitation **2 blot one's copybook** *informal* to spoil one's reputation by a mistake or indiscretion ▷ *adj* **3** done exactly according to the rules **4** trite or unoriginal

copycat *n informal* a person who imitates or copies someone

copyist *n* **1** a person who makes written copies **2** an imitator: *although the songs are derivative, it is unfair to dismiss the band as mere copyists*

copyright *n* **1** the exclusive legal right to reproduce and control an original literary, musical, or artistic work ▷ *vb* **2** to take out a copyright on ▷ *adj* **3** protected by copyright

copy typist *n* a typist who types from written or typed drafts rather than dictation

copywriter *n* a person employed to write advertising copy

coquette *n* a woman who flirts **coquetry** *n* **coquettish** *adj*
WORD ORIGIN French

coracle *n* a small round boat made of wicker covered with skins
WORD ORIGIN Welsh *corwgl*

coral *n* **1** the stony substance formed by the skeletons of marine animals called polyps, often forming an island or reef **2** any of the polyps whose skeletons form coral ▷ *adj* **3** orange-pink
WORD ORIGIN Greek *korallion*

cor anglais *n, pl* **cors anglais** *music* an alto woodwind instrument of the oboe family
WORD ORIGIN French: English horn

corbel *n archit* a stone or timber support sticking out of a wall
WORD ORIGIN Old French: a little raven

corbie *n Scot* a raven or crow
WORD ORIGIN Latin *corvus*

cord ❶ *n* **1** string or thin rope made of twisted strands **2** *anat* a structure in the body resembling a rope: *the vocal cords* **3** a ribbed fabric like corduroy **4** *US, Canad, Austral & NZ* an electrical flex **5** a unit for measuring cut wood, equal to 128 cubic feet ▷ *adj* **6** (of fabric) ribbed ▶ See also **cords**
WORD ORIGIN Greek *khordē*

cordate *adj* heart-shaped

Corday *n* **Charlotte**, full name *Marie Anne Charlotte Corday d'Armont*. 1768–93, French Girondist revolutionary, who assassinated Marat

corded *adj* **1** tied or fastened with cord **2** (of a fabric) ribbed: *white corded silk* **3** (of muscles) standing out like cords

cordial *adj* **1** warm and friendly: *a cordial atmosphere* **2** heartfelt or sincere: *I developed a cordial dislike for the place* ▷ *n* **3** a drink with a fruit base: *lime cordial* **cordially** *adv*
WORD ORIGIN Latin *cor* heart

cordiality *n* warmth of feeling

cordite *n* a smokeless explosive used in guns and bombs
WORD ORIGIN from *cord*, because of its stringy appearance

cordless *adj* (of an electrical appliance such as a kettle or telephone) powered by an internal battery or kept in a holder which is connected to the mains, so that there is no cable connecting the appliance itself to the electrical mains

cordon ❶ *n* **1** a chain of police, soldiers, or vehicles guarding an area **2** an ornamental braid or ribbon **3** *horticulture* a fruit tree trained to grow as a single stem bearing fruit ▷ *vb* **4 cordon off** to put or form a cordon round
WORD ORIGIN Old French: a little cord

cordon bleu (**bluh**) *adj* (of cookery or cooks) of the highest standard: *a cordon bleu chef*
WORD ORIGIN French: blue ribbon

cordon sanitaire *n* **1** a line of buffer states shielding a country **2** a guarded line isolating an infected area
WORD ORIGIN French, literally: sanitary line

cords *pl n* trousers made of corduroy

corduroy *n* a heavy cotton fabric with a velvety ribbed surface
WORD ORIGIN origin unknown

corduroys *pl n* trousers made of corduroy

core ❶ *n* **1** the central part of certain fleshy fruits, containing the seeds **2** the central or essential part of something: *the historic core of the city* **3** a piece of magnetic soft iron inside an electromagnet or transformer **4** *geol* the central part of the earth **5** a cylindrical sample of rock or soil, obtained by the use of a hollow drill **6** *physics* the region of a nuclear reactor containing the fissionable material **7** *computers* the main internal memory of a computer ▷ *vb* **coring, cored 8** to remove the core from (fruit)
WORD ORIGIN origin unknown

corella *n* a white Australian cockatoo

Corelli *n* **1 Arcangelo** 1653–1713, Italian violinist and composer of sonatas and concerti grossi **2 Marie**, real name *Mary Mackay*. 1854–1924, British novelist. Her melodramatic works include *The Sorrows of Satan* (1895) and *The Murder of Delicia* (1896)

co-respondent *n* a person with whom someone being sued for divorce is claimed to have committed adultery

corgi *n* a short-legged sturdy dog
WORD ORIGIN Welsh *cor* dwarf + *ci* dog

Cori *n* **Carl Ferdinand** 1896–1984, US biochemist, born in Bohemia; shared a Nobel prize for physiology or medicine (1947) with his wife **Gerty Theresa Radnitz Cori** (1896–1957) and Bernardo Houssay, for elucidating the stages of glycolysis

coriander *n* a European plant, cultivated for its aromatic seeds and leaves, used in flavouring foods
WORD ORIGIN Greek *koriannon*

Corinthian *adj* **1** of Corinth, a port in S Greece **2** of a style of classical architecture characterized by a bell-shaped capital with carved leaf-shaped ornaments ▷ *n* **3** a person from Corinth

Coriolanus *n* **Gaius Marcius** 5th century BC, a legendary Roman general, who allegedly led an army against Rome but was dissuaded

THESAURUS

photocopy, carbon copy, image, print, fax, representation, fake, replica, imitation, forgery, counterfeit, Xerox®, transcription, likeness, replication, facsimile, Photostat® **OPPOSITE:** original
▷ *vb* **6 = reproduce**, replicate, duplicate, photocopy, transcribe, counterfeit, Xerox®, Photostat® **OPPOSITE:** create
7 = imitate, act like, emulate, behave like, follow, repeat, mirror, echo, parrot, ape, mimic, simulate, follow suit, follow the example of

cord *n* **1 = rope**, line, string, twine

cordon *n* **1 = chain**, line, ring, barrier, picket line
4 cordon something off = surround, isolate, close off, fence off, separate, enclose, picket, encircle

core *n* **2 = heart**, essence, nucleus, kernel, crux, gist, nub, pith

DICTIONARY

from conquering it by his mother and wife

cork *n* **1** the thick light porous outer bark of a Mediterranean oak **2** a piece of cork used as a stopper **3** *bot* the outer bark of a woody plant ▷ *vb* **4** to stop up (a bottle) with a cork
WORD ORIGIN probably from Arabic *qurq*

corkage *n* a charge made at a restaurant for serving wine bought elsewhere

corked *adj* (of wine) spoiled through being stored in a bottle with a decayed cork

corker *n* *old-fashioned slang* a splendid or outstanding person or thing

corkscrew *n* **1** a device for pulling corks from bottles, usually consisting of a pointed metal spiral attached to a handle ▷ *adj* **2** like a corkscrew in shape ▷ *vb* **3** to move in a spiral or zigzag course

corm *n* the scaly bulblike underground stem of certain plants
WORD ORIGIN Greek *kormos* tree trunk

cormorant *n* a large dark-coloured long-necked sea bird
WORD ORIGIN Old French *corp* raven + *-mareng* of the sea

corn[1] *n* **1** a cereal plant such as wheat, oats, or barley **2** the grain of such plants **3** *US, Canad, Austral & NZ* maize **4** *slang* something unoriginal or oversentimental
WORD ORIGIN Old English

corn[2] *n* a painful hardening of the skin around a central point in the foot, caused by pressure
WORD ORIGIN Latin *cornu* horn

corn circle *n* ▸ same as **crop circle**

corncob *n* the core of an ear of maize, to which the kernels are attached

corncrake *n* a brown bird with a harsh grating cry

cornea (**korn**-ee-a) *n* the transparent membrane covering the eyeball **corneal** *adj*
WORD ORIGIN Latin *cornu* horn

corned beef *n* cooked beef preserved in salt

cornelian *n* ▸ same as **carnelian**

corner ⓘ *n* **1** the place or angle formed by the meeting of two converging lines or surfaces **2** the space within the angle formed, as in a room **3** the place where two streets meet **4** a sharp bend in a road **5** a remote place: *far-flung corners of the world* **6** any secluded or private place **7** *sport* a free kick or shot taken from the corner of the field **8 cut corners** to take the shortest or easiest way at the expense of high standards **9 turn the corner** to pass the critical point of an illness or a difficult time ▷ *adj* **10** on or in a corner: *a corner seat* ▷ *vb* **11** to force (a person or animal) into a difficult or inescapable position **12** (of a vehicle or its driver) to turn a corner **13** to obtain a monopoly of
WORD ORIGIN Latin *cornu* point, horn

corner shop *n* a small general shop serving a neighbourhood

cornerstone *n* **1** an indispensable part or basis: *the food we eat is one of the cornerstones of good health* **2** a stone at the corner of a wall

cornet *n* **1** a brass instrument of the trumpet family **2** *Brit* a cone-shaped ice-cream wafer **cornetist** *n*
WORD ORIGIN Latin *cornu* horn

corn exchange *n* a building where corn is bought and sold

cornflakes *pl n* a breakfast cereal made from toasted maize

cornflour *n* **1** a fine maize flour, used for thickening sauces **2** *NZ* fine wheat flour

cornflower *n* a small plant with blue flowers

Cornforth *n* Sir **John Warcup** born 1917, Australian chemist, who shared the 1975 Nobel prize for chemistry with Vladimir Prelog for their work on stereochemistry

cornice (**korn**-iss) *n* **1** a decorative moulding round the top of a wall or building **2** *archit* the projecting mouldings at the top of a column
WORD ORIGIN Old French

Cornish *adj* **1** of Cornwall ▷ *n* **2** a Celtic language of Cornwall, extinct by 1800 ▷ *pl n* **3 the Cornish** the people of Cornwall

Cornish pasty *n* a pastry case with a filling of meat and vegetables

cornucopia (korn-yew-**kope**-ee-a) *n* **1** a great abundance: *a cornucopia of rewards* **2** a symbol of plenty, consisting of a horn overflowing with fruit and flowers
WORD ORIGIN Latin *cornu copiae* horn of plenty

Cornwallis *n* **Charles**, 1st Marquis Cornwallis. 1738–1805, British general in the War of American Independence: commanded forces defeated at Yorktown (1781): defeated Tipu Sahib (1791): governor general of Bengal (1786–93, 1805): negotiated the Treaty of Amiens (1801)

Cornwell *n* **Patricia D** (**aniels**) born 1956, US crime novelist; her novels, many of which feature the pathologist Dr Kay Scarpetta, include *Postmortem* (1990), *The Last Precinct* (2000), and *Isle of Dogs* (2002)

corny *adj* **cornier, corniest** *slang* unoriginal or oversentimental

corolla *n* the petals of a flower collectively
WORD ORIGIN Latin: garland

corollary (kor-**oll**-a-ree) *n, pl* **-laries** **1** a proposition that follows directly from another that has been proved **2** a natural consequence
WORD ORIGIN Latin *corollarium* money paid for a garland

corona (kor-**rone**-a) *n, pl* **-nas** *or* **-nae** (-nee) **1** a circle of light around a luminous body, usually the moon **2** the outermost part of the sun's atmosphere, visible as a faint halo during a total eclipse **3** a long cigar with blunt ends **4** *bot* a crownlike part of some flowers on top of the seed or on the inner side of the corolla **5** *physics* an electrical glow appearing around the surface of a charged conductor
WORD ORIGIN Latin: crown

coronary (**kor**-ron-a-ree) *adj* **1** *anat* of the arteries that supply blood to the heart ▷ *n, pl* **-naries** **2** a coronary thrombosis
WORD ORIGIN Latin *coronarius* belonging to a wreath or crown

coronary thrombosis *n* a condition where the blood flow to the heart is blocked by a clot in a coronary artery

coronation *n* the ceremony of crowning a monarch
WORD ORIGIN Latin *coronare* to crown

coronavirus *n* a type of airborne virus accounting for 10–30% of all colds
WORD ORIGIN from its corona-like appearance under an electron microscope

coroner *n* a public official responsible for the investigation of violent, sudden, or suspicious deaths
WORD ORIGIN Anglo-French *corouner*

coronet *n* **1** a small crown worn by princes or peers **2** a band of jewels worn as a headdress
WORD ORIGIN Old French *coronete*

Corot *n* **Jean Baptiste Camille** 1796–1875, French landscape and portrait painter

corpora *pl n* ▸ the plural of **corpus**

corporal[1] *n* a noncommissioned officer in an army
WORD ORIGIN Old French *caporal*, from Latin *caput* head

corporal[2] *adj* of the body
WORD ORIGIN Latin *corpus* body

corporal punishment *n* physical punishment, such as caning

THESAURUS

corner *n* **1 = angle**, joint, crook **4 = bend**, curve **6 = space**, hole, niche, recess, cavity, hideaway, nook, cranny, hide-out, hidey-hole (*informal*) ▷ *vb* **11 = trap**, catch, run to earth, bring to bay **13** (*a market*) **= monopolize**, take over, dominate, control, hog (*slang*), engross, exercise *or* have a monopoly of

corporation *n* **1 = business**, company, concern, firm, society, association, organization, enterprise, establishment, corporate body **2 = town council**, council, municipal authorities, civic authorities

corporate *adj* 1 relating to business corporations: *corporate finance* 2 shared by a group 3 forming a corporation; incorporated
WORD ORIGIN Latin *corpus* body
corporation ❶ *n* 1 a large business or company 2 a city or town council 3 *informal* a large paunch **corporative** *adj*
corporatism *n* organization of a state on the lines of a business enterprise, with substantial government management of the economy
corporeal (kore-**pore**-ee-al) *adj* of the physical world rather than the spiritual
WORD ORIGIN Latin *corpus* body
corps ❶ (kore) *n, pl* **corps** 1 a military unit with a specific function: *medical corps* 2 an organized body of people: *the diplomatic corps*
WORD ORIGIN French
corps de ballet *n* the members of a ballet company
WORD ORIGIN French
corpse ❶ *n* a dead body, esp. of a human being
WORD ORIGIN Latin *corpus*
corpulent *adj* fat or plump **corpulence** *n*
WORD ORIGIN Latin *corpulentus*
corpus *n, pl* **-pora** a collection of writings, such as one by a single author or on a specific topic: *the corpus of Marxist theory*
WORD ORIGIN Latin: body
corpuscle *n* a red blood cell (see **erythrocyte**) or white blood cell (see **leucocyte**) **corpuscular** *adj*
WORD ORIGIN Latin *corpusculum* a little body
corral *US & Canad* *n* 1 an enclosure for cattle or horses ▷ *vb* **-ralling, -ralled** 2 to put in a corral
WORD ORIGIN Spanish
corrasion *n geol* erosion of rocks caused by fragments transported over them by water, wind, or ice
WORD ORIGIN Latin *corradere* to scrape together
correct ❶ *adj* 1 free from error; true: *the correct answer* 2 in conformity with accepted standards: *in most cultures there is a strong sense of correct sexual conduct* ▷ *vb* 3 to make free from or put right errors 4 to indicate the errors in (something) 5 to rebuke or punish in order to improve: *I stand corrected* 6 to make conform to a standard **correctly** *adv* **correctness** *n*
WORD ORIGIN Latin *corrigere* to make straight
correction ❶ *n* 1 an act or instance of correcting 2 an alteration correcting something: *corrections to the second proofs* 3 a reproof or punishment **correctional** *adj*
corrective *adj* intended to put right something that is wrong: *corrective action*
Correggio *n* **Antonio Allegri da** 1494–1534, Italian painter, noted for his striking use of perspective and foreshortening
correlate *vb* **-lating, -lated** 1 to place or be placed in a mutual relationship: *water consumption is closely correlated to the number of people living in a house* ▷ *n* 2 either of two things mutually related **correlation** *n*
correlative *adj* 1 having a mutual relationship 2 *grammar* (of words, usually conjunctions) corresponding to each other and occurring regularly together, for example *neither* and *nor*
correspond ❶ *vb* 1 to be consistent or compatible (with) 2 to be similar (to) 3 to communicate (with) by letter **corresponding** *adj* **correspondingly** *adv*
WORD ORIGIN Latin *com-* together + *respondere* to respond
correspondence ❶ *n* 1 communication by letters 2 the letters exchanged in this way 3 relationship or similarity
correspondence course *n* a course of study conducted by post
correspondent ❶ *n* 1 a person who communicates by letter 2 a person employed by a newspaper or news service to report on a special subject or from a foreign country
corridor ❶ *n* 1 a passage in a building or a train 2 a strip of land or airspace that provides access through the territory of a foreign country 3 **corridors of power** the higher levels of government or the Civil Service
WORD ORIGIN Old Italian *corridore*, literally: place for running
corrie *n* (in Scotland) a circular hollow on the side of a hill
WORD ORIGIN Gaelic *coire* cauldron
corrigendum (kor-rij-**end**-um) *n, pl* **-da** (-da) 1 an error to be corrected 2 a slip of paper inserted into a book after printing, listing corrections
WORD ORIGIN Latin: that which is to be corrected
corroborate *vb* **-rating, -rated** to support (a fact or opinion) by giving proof **corroboration** *n* **corroborative** *adj*
WORD ORIGIN Latin *com-* (intensive) + *roborare* to make strong
corroboree *n Austral* 1 an Aboriginal gathering or dance of festive or warlike character 2 *informal* any noisy gathering
WORD ORIGIN Aboriginal
corrode *vb* **-roding, -roded** 1 to eat away or be eaten away by chemical action or rusting 2 to destroy gradually: *rumours corroding the public's affection for the royal family*
WORD ORIGIN Latin *corrodere* to gnaw to pieces
corrosion *n* 1 the process by which something, esp. a metal, is corroded 2 the result of corrosion **corrosive** *adj*
corrugate *vb* **-gating, -gated** to fold into alternate grooves and ridges **corrugation** *n*
WORD ORIGIN Latin *corrugare*
corrugated iron *n* a thin sheet of iron or steel, formed with alternating ridges and troughs
corrupt ❶ *adj* 1 open to or involving bribery or other dishonest practices: *corrupt practices* 2 morally depraved

THESAURUS

corps *n* **1, 2 = team**, unit, regiment, detachment, company, body, band, division, troop, squad, crew, contingent, squadron
corpse *n* **= body**, remains, carcass, cadaver, stiff *(slang)*
correct *adj* **1 = accurate**, right, true, exact, precise, flawless, faultless, on the right lines, O.K. *or* okay *(informal)* **OPPOSITE:** inaccurate **2a = right**, standard, regular, appropriate, acceptable, strict, proper, precise **2b = proper**, seemly, standard, fitting, diplomatic, kosher *(informal)* **OPPOSITE:** inappropriate ▷ *vb* **3 = rectify**, remedy, redress, right, improve, reform, cure, adjust, regulate, amend, set the record straight, emend **OPPOSITE:** spoil **5 = rebuke**, discipline, reprimand, chide, admonish, chastise, chasten, reprove, punish **OPPOSITE:** praise
correction *n* **1, 2 = rectification**, improvement, amendment, adjustment, modification, alteration, emendation **3 = punishment**, discipline, reformation, admonition, chastisement, reproof, castigation
correspond *vb* **1 = be consistent**, match, agree, accord, fit, square, coincide, complement, be related, tally, conform, correlate, dovetail, harmonize **OPPOSITE:** differ **3 = communicate**, write, keep in touch, exchange letters, e-mail, text
correspondence *n* **1 = communication**, writing, contact **2 = letters**, post, mail **3 = relation**, match, agreement, fitness, comparison, harmony, coincidence, similarity, analogy, correlation, conformity, comparability, concurrence, congruity
correspondent *n* **1 = letter writer**, pen friend *or* pen pal **2 = reporter**, journalist, contributor, special correspondent, journo *(slang)*, hack
corridor *n* **1 = passage**, alley, aisle, hallway, passageway
corrupt *adj* **1 = dishonest**, bent *(slang)*, crooked *(informal)*, rotten, shady *(informal)*, fraudulent, unscrupulous, unethical, venal, unprincipled

DICTIONARY

3 (of a text or data) made unreliable by errors or alterations ▷ *vb* **4** to make corrupt **corruptive** *adj*
WORD ORIGIN Latin *corruptus* spoiled

corruptible *adj* capable of being corrupted

C

corruption ❶ *n* **1** dishonesty and illegal behaviour **2** the act of corrupting morally or sexually **3** the process of rotting or decaying **4** an unintentional or unauthorized alteration in a text or data **5** an altered form of a word

corsage (kore-**sahzh**) *n* a small bouquet worn on the bodice of a dress
WORD ORIGIN Old French *cors* body

corsair *n* **1** a pirate **2** a pirate ship **3** a privateer
WORD ORIGIN Old French *corsaire*

corse *n archaic* a corpse

corselet *n* **1** a woman's one-piece undergarment, combining corset and bra **2** a piece of armour to cover the trunk
WORD ORIGIN Old French *cors* bodice

corset *n* **1** a close-fitting undergarment worn by women to shape the torso **2** a similar garment worn by either sex to support and protect the back **corsetry** *n*
WORD ORIGIN Old French: a little bodice

cortege (kore-**tayzh**) *n* a funeral procession
WORD ORIGIN Italian *corteggio*

cortex (kore-tex) *n, pl* **-tices** (-tiss-seez) *anat* the outer layer of the brain or some other internal organ **cortical** *adj*
WORD ORIGIN Latin: bark, outer layer

cortisone *n* a steroid hormone used in treating rheumatoid arthritis, allergies, and skin diseases
WORD ORIGIN *corticosterone*, a hormone

Cortot *n* **Alfred** 1877–1962, French pianist, born in Switzerland

corundum *n* a hard mineral used as an abrasive, and of which the ruby and white sapphire are precious forms
WORD ORIGIN Tamil *kuruntam*

coruscate *vb* **-cating, -cated** *formal* to emit flashes of light; sparkle **coruscating** *adj* **coruscation** *n*
WORD ORIGIN Latin *coruscare* to flash

corvette *n* a lightly armed escort warship
WORD ORIGIN perhaps from Middle Dutch *corf*

corymb *n bot* a flat-topped flower cluster with the stems growing progressively shorter towards the centre
WORD ORIGIN Greek *korumbos* cluster

cos[1] *or* **cos lettuce** *n* a lettuce with a long slender head and crisp leaves
WORD ORIGIN after *Kos*, the Aegean island of its origin

cos[2] cosine

cosec (**koh**-sek) cosecant

cosecant (koh-**seek**-ant) *n* (in trigonometry) the ratio of the length of the hypotenuse to that of the opposite side in a right-angled triangle

Cosgrave *n* **1 Liam** born 1920, Irish statesman; prime minister of the Republic of Ireland (1973–77) **2** his father, **W**(**illiam**) **T**(**homas**) 1880–1965, Irish statesman; first prime minister (president of the executive council) of the Irish Free State (1922–32)

cosh *chiefly Brit n* **1** a heavy blunt weapon, often made of hard rubber ▷ *vb* **2** to hit on the head with a cosh
WORD ORIGIN Romany *kosh*

cosignatory *n, pl* **-ries** a person or country that signs a document jointly with others

cosine (**koh**-sine) *n* (in trigonometry) the ratio of the length of the adjacent side to that of the hypotenuse in a right-angled triangle
WORD ORIGIN see CO-, SINE

cosmetic ❶ *n* **1** anything applied to the face or body in order to improve the appearance ▷ *adj* **2** done or used to improve the appearance of the face or body **3** improving in appearance only: *glossy brochures are part of a cosmetic exercise*
WORD ORIGIN Greek *kosmētikos*, from *kosmein* to arrange

cosmetic surgery *n* surgery performed to improve the appearance, rather than for medical reasons

cosmic ❶ *adj* **1** of or relating to the whole universe: *the cosmic order* **2** occurring in or coming from outer space: *cosmic dust*

cosmogony *n, pl* **-nies** the study of the origin of the universe
WORD ORIGIN Greek *kosmos* world + *gonos* creation

cosmology *n* the study of the origin and nature of the universe **cosmological** *adj* **cosmologist** *n*
WORD ORIGIN Greek *kosmos* world + -LOGY

cosmonaut *n* the Russian name for an astronaut
WORD ORIGIN Russian *kosmonavt*, from Greek *kosmos* universe + *nautēs* sailor

cosmopolitan ❶ *adj* **1** composed of people or elements from many different countries or cultures **2** having lived and travelled in many countries **3** sophisticated and cultured ▷ *n* **4** a cosmopolitan person **cosmopolitanism** *n*
WORD ORIGIN Greek *kosmos* world + *politēs* citizen

cosmos *n* the universe considered as an ordered system
WORD ORIGIN Greek *kosmos* order

Cossack *n* **1** a member of a S Russian people, famous as horsemen and dancers ▷ *adj* **2** of the Cossacks: *a Cossack dance*
WORD ORIGIN Russian *kazak* vagabond

cosset *vb* **-seting, -seted** to pamper or pet
WORD ORIGIN origin unknown

cost ❶ *n* **1** the amount of money, time, or energy required to obtain or produce something **2** suffering or sacrifice: *these were crucial truths which rugby never grasped, to its cost* **3** the amount paid for a commodity by its seller: *to sell at cost* **4 costs** *law* the expenses of a lawsuit **5 at all costs** regardless of any cost or effort involved **6 at the cost of** at the expense of losing: *they eventually triumphed, but at the cost of many lives* ▷ *vb* **costing, cost 7** to be obtained or obtainable in exchange for: *calls cost 36p a minute cheap rate, 48p at other times* **8** to involve the loss or sacrifice of: *a fall which almost cost him his life*

THESAURUS

OPPOSITE: honest
2 = depraved, abandoned, vicious, degenerate, debased, demoralized, profligate, dishonoured, defiled, dissolute **3 = distorted**, doctored, altered, falsified ▷ *vb* **4 = deprave**, pervert, subvert, debase, demoralize, debauch **OPPOSITE:** reform

corruption *n* **1 = dishonesty**, fraud, fiddling *(informal)*, graft *(informal)*, bribery, extortion, profiteering, breach of trust, venality, shady dealings *(informal)*, shadiness **2 = depravity**, vice, evil, degradation, perversion, decadence, impurity, wickedness, degeneration, immorality, iniquity, profligacy, viciousness, sinfulness, turpitude, baseness **4 = distortion**, doctoring, falsification

cosmetic *adj* **3 = superficial**, surface, touching-up, nonessential

cosmic *adj* **1 = universal**, general, omnipresent, all-embracing, overarching **2 = extraterrestrial**, stellar

cosmopolitan *adj* **3 = sophisticated**, worldly, cultured, refined, cultivated, urbane, well-travelled, worldly-wise
OPPOSITE: unsophisticated

cost *n* **1 = price**, worth, expense, rate, charge, figure, damage *(informal)*, amount, payment, expenditure, outlay **2 = loss**, suffering, damage, injury, penalty, hurt, expense, harm, sacrifice, deprivation, detriment ▷ *vb* **7 = sell at**, come to, set (someone) back *(informal)*, be priced at,

9 costing, costed to estimate the cost of producing something
WORD ORIGIN Latin *constare* to stand at, cost

cost accounting *n* the recording and controlling of all the costs involved in running a business **cost accountant** *n*

costal *adj* of the ribs

cost-effective *adj* providing adequate financial return in relation to outlay

Costello *n* **Elvis,** real name *Declan McManus*. born 1954, British rock singer and songwriter. His recordings include *This Year's Model* (1978), "Oliver's Army" (1979), *Spike, Brutal Youth* (1994), and *When I Was Cruel* (2003)

costermonger *n Brit* a person who sells fruit and vegetables from a barrow in the street
WORD ORIGIN *costard* a kind of apple + *monger* trader

costive *adj old-fashioned* having or causing constipation
WORD ORIGIN Old French *costivé*

costly ❶ *adj* **-lier, -liest 1** expensive **2** involving great loss or sacrifice: *a bitter and costly war* **costliness** *n*

Costner *n* **Kevin** born 1955, US film actor: his films include *Robin Hood: Prince of Thieves* (1990), *Dances with Wolves* (1990; also directed), *JFK* (1991), *Waterworld* (1995), and *Open Range* (2003)

cost of living *n* the average cost of the basic necessities of life, such as food, housing, and clothing

costume ❶ *n* **1** a style of dressing, including all the clothes and accessories, typical of a particular country or period **2** the clothes worn by an actor or performer: *a jester's costume* **3** ▸ short for **swimming costume** ▹ *vb* **-tuming, -tumed 4** to provide with a costume: *she was costumed by many of the great Hollywood designers* **costumed** *adj*
WORD ORIGIN Italian: dress, custom

costume jewellery *n* inexpensive but attractive jewellery

costumier *n* a maker or supplier of theatrical or fancy dress costumes

cosy ❶ *or US* **cozy** *adj* **-sier, -siest** *or US* **-zier, -ziest 1** warm and snug **2** intimate and friendly: *a cosy chat* ▹ *n, pl* **-sies** *or US* **-zies 3** a cover for keeping things warm: *a tea cosy* **cosiness** *or US* **coziness** *n*
WORD ORIGIN Scots

cot¹ *n* **1** a bed with high sides for a baby or very young child **2** a small portable bed
WORD ORIGIN Hindi *khāt* bedstead

cot² *n* **1** *literary or archaic* a small cottage **2** a cote
WORD ORIGIN Old English

cot³ cotangent

cotangent *n* (in trigonometry) the ratio of the length of the adjacent side to that of the opposite side in a right-angled triangle

cot death *n* the unexplained sudden death of a baby while asleep

cote *or* **cot** *n* a small shelter for birds or animals
WORD ORIGIN Old English

coterie (kote-er-ee) *n* a small exclusive group of friends or people with common interests
WORD ORIGIN French

Cotman *n* **John Sell** 1782–1842, English landscape watercolourist and etcher

cotoneaster (kot-tone-ee-**ass**-ter) *n* a garden shrub with red berries

cottage ❶ *n* a small simple house, usually in the country **cottager** *n*
WORD ORIGIN from COT²

cottage cheese *n* a mild soft white cheese made from skimmed milk curds

cottage industry *n* a craft industry in which employees work at home

cottage pie *n* a dish of minced meat topped with mashed potato

cottaging *n Brit, Austral & NZ slang* homosexual activity between men in a public lavatory
WORD ORIGIN from *cottage* (in the sense: a public lavatory)

cotter¹ *n machinery* a bolt or wedge that is used to secure parts of machinery
WORD ORIGIN Middle English *cotterel*

cotter² *n Scot & history* a farm labourer occupying a cottage and land rent-free
WORD ORIGIN see COT²

cotter pin *n machinery* a split pin used to hold parts together and fastened by having the ends spread apart after it is inserted

cotton *n* **1** the soft white downy fibre surrounding the seeds of a plant grown in warm climates, used to make cloth and thread **2** cloth or thread made from cotton fibres **cottony** *adj*
WORD ORIGIN Arabic *qutn*

Cotton *n* **Henry** 1907–87, British golfer: three times winner of the British Open

cotton bud *n* a small stick with cotton wool tips used for cleaning the ears, applying make-up, etc.

cotton on *vb informal* to understand or realize the meaning (of): *it has taken the world 20 years to cotton on to this idea*

cotton wool *n* absorbent fluffy cotton, used for surgical dressings and to apply creams to the skin

cotyledon (kot-ill-ee-don) *n* the first leaf produced by a plant embryo
WORD ORIGIN Greek *kotulē* cup

couch *n* **1** a piece of upholstered furniture for seating more than one person **2** a bed on which patients of a doctor or a psychoanalyst lie during examination or treatment ▹ *vb* **3** to express in a particular style of language: *a proclamation couched in splendidly archaic phraseology* **4** *archaic* (of an animal) to crouch, as when preparing to leap
WORD ORIGIN Old French *coucher* to lay down

couchette (koo-**shett**) *n* a bed converted from seats on a train or ship
WORD ORIGIN French

couch grass *n* a grassy weed which spreads quickly

couch potato *n slang* a physically lazy person, esp. one who spends most of the day in front of the television

Coué *n* **Émile** 1857–1926, French psychologist and pharmacist: advocated psychotherapy by autosuggestion ▸ **Couéism** *n*

cougan *n Austral slang* a drunk and rowdy person

cougar (koo-gar) *n* ▸ same as **puma**
WORD ORIGIN from S American Indian

cough ❶ *vb* **1** to expel air abruptly and noisily from the lungs **2** (of an engine or other machine) to make a sound similar to this ▹ *n* **3** an act or sound of coughing **4** an illness which causes frequent coughing
WORD ORIGIN Old English *cohhetten*

cough up *vb* **1** *informal* to give up (money or information) **2** to bring up into the mouth by coughing: *to cough up blood*

could *vb* **1** used to make the past tense of **can¹** **2** used to make the subjunctive mood of **can¹**, esp. in polite requests or conditional sentences: *could I have a word with you,*

THESAURUS

command a price of **8 = lose**, deprive of, cheat of

costly *adj* **1 = expensive**, dear, stiff, excessive, steep *(informal)*, highly-priced, exorbitant, extortionate
OPPOSITE: inexpensive
2 = damaging, disastrous, harmful, catastrophic, loss-making, ruinous, deleterious

costume *n* **1, 2 = outfit**, dress, clothing, get-up *(informal)*, uniform, ensemble, robes, livery, apparel, attire, garb, national dress

cosy *adj* **1 = snug**, warm, secure, comfortable, sheltered, comfy *(informal)*, tucked up, cuddled up, snuggled down **2 = intimate**, friendly, informal

cottage *n* **= cabin**, lodge, hut, shack, chalet, but-and-ben *(Scot)*, cot, whare *(NZ)*

cough *vb* **1 = clear your throat**, bark, hawk, hack, hem ▹ *n* **3 = frog** *or* **tickle in your throat**, bark, hack

DICTIONARY

C

please? **3** used to indicate the suggestion of a course of action: *we could make a fortune from selling players, but that would not be in the long-term interests of the club* **4** used to indicate a possibility: *it could simply be a spelling mistake*
WORD ORIGIN Old English *cūthe*

couldn't could not

coulis (koo-lee) *n* a thin purée of vegetables or fruit, usually served as a sauce surrounding a dish: *rum truffle cake with raspberry coulis*
WORD ORIGIN French: purée

coulomb (koo-lom) *n* the SI unit of electric charge
WORD ORIGIN after C. A. de *Coulomb*, physicist

coulter (kole-ter) *n* a vertical blade on a plough in front of the ploughshare
WORD ORIGIN Latin *culter* ploughshare, knife

council ❶ *n* **1** a group meeting for discussion or consultation **2** a legislative or advisory body: *the United Nations Security Council* **3** *Brit* the local governing authority of a town or county **4** *Austral* the local governing authority of a district or shire ▷ *adj* **5** of or provided by a local council: *a council house*
WORD ORIGIN Latin *concilium* assembly

councillor *or US* **councilor** *n* a member of a council

council tax *n* (in Britain) a tax based on the relative value of property levied to fund local council services

counsel ❶ *n* **1** advice or guidance **2** discussion or consultation: *when it was over they took counsel of their consciences* **3** a barrister or group of barristers who conduct cases in court and advise on legal matters ▷ *vb* **-selling, -selled** *or US* **-seling, -seled** **4** to give advice or guidance to **5** to recommend or urge
counselling *or US* **counseling** *n*
WORD ORIGIN Latin *consilium* deliberating body

counsellor *or US* **counselor** *n* **1** an adviser **2** *US* a lawyer who conducts cases in court

count¹ ❶ *vb* **1** to say numbers in ascending order up to and including: *count from one to ten* **2** to add up or check (each thing in a group) in order to find the total: *he counted the money he had left* **3** to be important: *it's the thought that counts* **4** to consider: *he can count himself lucky* **5** to take into account or include: *the time he'd spent in prison on remand counted towards his sentence* **6 not counting** excluding **7** *music* to keep time by counting beats ▷ *n* **8** the act of counting **9** the number reached by counting: *a high pollen count* **10** *law* one of a number of charges **11 keep** *or* **lose count** to keep or fail to keep an accurate record of items or events **12 out for the count** unconscious ▸ See also **count against, countdown**, etc.
countable *adj*
WORD ORIGIN Latin *computare* to calculate

count² *n* a middle-ranking European nobleman
WORD ORIGIN Latin *comes* associate

count against *vb* to have an effect or influence that makes something more unlikely: *his age counts against him getting promotion*

countdown *n* the act of counting backwards to zero to time exactly an operation such as the launching of a rocket

countenance *n* **1** *literary* the face or facial expression ▷ *vb* **-nancing, -nanced** **2** to support or tolerate
WORD ORIGIN Latin *continentia* restraint, control

counter¹ *n* **1** a long flat surface in a bank or shop, on which business is transacted **2** a small flat disc used in board games **3** a disc or token used as an imitation coin **4 under the counter** (of the sale of goods) illegal
WORD ORIGIN Latin *computare* to compute

counter² *n* an apparatus for counting things

counter³ ❶ *vb* **1** to say or do (something) in retaliation or response **2** to oppose or act against **3** to return the attack of (an opponent) ▷ *adv* **4** in an opposite or opposing direction or manner **5 run counter to** to be in direct contrast with ▷ *adj* **6** opposing or opposite ▷ *n* **7** something that is contrary or opposite to something else **8** an opposing action **9** a return attack, such as a blow in boxing
WORD ORIGIN Latin *contra* against

counter- *prefix* **1** against or opposite: *counterattack* **2** complementary or corresponding: *counterpart*
WORD ORIGIN Latin *contra*

counteract *vb* to act against or neutralize **counteraction** *n* **counteractive** *adj*

counterattack *n* **1** an attack in response to an attack ▷ *vb* **2** to make a counterattack (against)

counterbalance *n* **1** a weight or influence that balances or neutralizes another ▷ *vb* **-ancing, -anced** **2** to act as a counterbalance to

counterbid *n* a bid made in response to a bid from another party, offering more favourable terms to the seller

counterblast *n* an aggressive response to a verbal attack

counterclockwise *adv, adj US & Canad* ▸ same as **anticlockwise**

counterespionage *n* activities to counteract enemy espionage

counterfeit *adj* **1** made in imitation of something genuine with the intent to deceive or defraud: *counterfeit currency* **2** pretended: *counterfeit friendship* ▷ *n* **3** an imitation designed to deceive or defraud ▷ *vb* **4** to make a fraudulent imitation of **5** to feign: *surprise is an easy emotion to counterfeit*
WORD ORIGIN Old French *contrefait*

counterfoil *n Brit* the part of a cheque or receipt kept as a record

counterintelligence *n* activities designed to frustrate enemy espionage

countermand *vb* to cancel (a previous order)
WORD ORIGIN Old French *contremander*

countermeasure *n* action taken to counteract some other action

counterpane *n* a bed covering
WORD ORIGIN Medieval Latin *culcita puncta* quilted mattress

counterpart ❶ *n* **1** a person or thing

THESAURUS

council *n* **1 = committee**, governing body, board, panel, quango, jamaat **2 = governing body**, house, parliament, congress, cabinet, ministry, diet, panel, assembly, chamber, convention, synod, conclave, convocation, conference, runanga (*NZ*)

counsel *n* **1 = advice**, information, warning, direction, suggestion, recommendation, caution, guidance, admonition **3 = legal adviser**, lawyer, attorney, solicitor, advocate, barrister ▷ *vb* **5 = advise**, recommend, advocate, prescribe, warn, urge, caution, instruct, exhort, admonish

count¹ *vb* **2** (*often with* **up**) **= add (up)**, total, reckon (up), tot up, score, check, estimate, calculate, compute, tally, number, enumerate, cast up **3 = matter**, be important, cut any ice (*informal*), carry weight, tell, rate, weigh, signify, enter into consideration **4 = consider**, judge, regard, deem, think of, rate, esteem, look upon, impute **5 = include**, number among, take into account or consideration

counter³ *vb* **1 = retaliate**, return, answer, reply, respond, come back, retort, hit back, rejoin, strike back
OPPOSITE: yield
2 = oppose, meet, block, resist, offset, parry, deflect, repel, rebuff, fend off, counteract, ward off, stave off, repulse, obviate, hold at bay ▷ *adv* **4 = opposite to**, against, versus, conversely, in defiance of, at variance with, contrarily, contrariwise
OPPOSITE: in accordance with

counterpart *n* **1 = opposite number**,

DICTIONARY

complementary to or corresponding to another **2** a duplicate of a legal document

counterpoint *n* **1** the harmonious combining of two or more parts or melodies **2** a melody or part combined in this way ▷ *vb* **3** to set in contrast
WORD ORIGIN Old French *contrepoint* an accompaniment set against the notes of a melody

counterpoise *vb* **-poising, -poised** to oppose with something of equal weight or effect: *counterpoising humour and horror*

counterproductive *adj* having an effect opposite to the one intended

countersign *vb* **1** to sign (a document already signed by another) as confirmation ▷ *n* **2** the signature so written

countersink *vb* **-sinking, -sank, -sunk** to drive (a screw) into a shaped hole so that its head is below the surface

countertenor *n* **1** an adult male voice with an alto range **2** a singer with such a voice

counterterrorism *n* activities intended to prevent terrorist acts or to eradicate terrorist groups **counterterrorist** *adj*

countess *n* **1** a woman holding the rank of count or earl **2** the wife or widow of a count or earl

countless ❶ *adj* too many to count

count noun *n* a noun that may be preceded by an indefinite article and can be used in the plural, such as *telephone* or *thing*

count on ❶ *vb* to rely or depend on

count out *vb* **1** *informal* to exclude **2** to declare (a boxer) defeated when he has not risen from the floor within ten seconds

countrified *adj* having an appearance or manner associated with the countryside rather than a town

country ❶ *n, pl* **-tries 1** an area distinguished by its people, culture, language, or government **2** the territory of a nation or state **3** the people of a nation or state **4** the part of the land that is away from cities or industrial areas **5** a person's native land **6** ▸ same as **country and western 7 across country** not keeping to roads **8 go to the country** *Brit & NZ* to dissolve Parliament and hold a general election
WORD ORIGIN Medieval Latin *contrata (terra)* (land) lying opposite

country and western *or* **country music** *n* popular music based on American White folk music

country club *n* a club in the country, which has sporting and social facilities

country dance *n* a type of British folk dance performed in rows or circles

countryman *n, pl* **-men 1** a person from one's own country **2** *Brit, Austral & NZ* a person who lives in the country **countrywoman** *fem n*

countryside ❶ *n* land away from the cities

county ❶ *n, pl* **-ties 1** (in some countries) a division of a country ▷ *adj* **2** *Brit informal* upper-class
WORD ORIGIN Old French *conté* land belonging to a count

coup ❶ (koo) *n* **1** a brilliant and successful action **2** a coup d'état
WORD ORIGIN French

coup de grâce (koo de **grahss**) *n, pl* **coups de grâce** (koo de **grahss**) a final or decisive action
WORD ORIGIN French

coup d'état (koo day-**tah**) *n, pl* **coups d'état** (kooz day-**tah**) a sudden violent or illegal overthrow of a government
WORD ORIGIN French

coupé (koo-pay) *n* a sports car with two doors and a sloping fixed roof
WORD ORIGIN French *carrosse coupé* cut-off carriage

Couperin *n* **François** 1668–1733, French composer, noted for his harpsichord suites and organ music

Coupland *n* **Douglas** born 1961, Canadian novelist and journalist; novels include *Generation X* (1991), *Girlfriend in a Coma* (1998), and *City of Glass* (2000)

couple ❶ *n* **1** two people who are married or romantically involved **2** two partners in a dance or game **3 a couple of a** a pair of: *a couple of guys* **b** *informal* a few: *a couple of weeks* ▷ *pron* **4 a couple a** two **b** *informal* a few: *give him a couple* ▷ *vb* **-pling, -pled 5** to connect or link: *an ingrained sense of shame, coupled with a fear of ridicule* **6** *literary* to have sexual intercourse
WORD ORIGIN Latin *copula* a bond

couplet *n* two successive lines of verse, usually rhyming and of the same metre

coupling *n* a device for connecting things, such as railway cars or trucks

coupon ❶ *n* **1** a piece of paper entitling the holder to a discount or free gift **2** a detachable slip that can be used as a commercial order form **3** *Brit* a football pools entry form
WORD ORIGIN Old French *colpon* piece cut off

courage ❶ *n* **1** the ability to face danger or pain without fear **2 the courage of one's convictions** the confidence to act according to one's beliefs
WORD ORIGIN Latin *cor* heart

courageous ❶ *adj* showing courage **courageously** *adv*

Courbet *n* **Gustave** 1819–77, French painter, a leader of the realist movement; noted for his depiction of contemporary life

courgette *n* a type of small vegetable marrow
WORD ORIGIN French

courier ❶ *n* **1** a person who looks after and guides travellers **2** a person paid to deliver urgent messages
WORD ORIGIN Latin *currere* to run

THESAURUS

equal, twin, equivalent, peer, match, fellow, mate

countless *adj* = **innumerable**, legion, infinite, myriad, untold, limitless, incalculable, immeasurable, numberless, uncounted, multitudinous, endless, measureless **OPPOSITE:** limited

count on *or* **upon something** *or* **someone** *vb* = **depend on**, trust, rely on, bank on, take for granted, lean on, reckon on, take on trust, believe in, pin your faith on

country *n* **1** = **nation**, state, land, commonwealth, kingdom, realm, sovereign state, people **3** = **people**, community, nation, society, citizens, voters, inhabitants, grass roots, [illegible] populace, citizenry, public [illegible]**de**, rural areas, provinces, outdoors, sticks (*informal*), farmland, outback (*Austral & NZ*), the middle of nowhere, green belt, wide open spaces (*informal*), backwoods, back country (*US*), the back of beyond, bush (*NZ & S African*), backlands (*US*), boondocks (*US slang*) **OPPOSITE:** town

countryside *n* = **country**, rural areas, outdoors, farmland, outback (*Austral & NZ*), green belt, wide open spaces (*informal*), sticks (*informal*)

county *n* **1** = **province**, district, shire

coup *n* **1** = **masterstroke**, feat, stunt, action, stroke, exploit, manoeuvre, deed, accomplishment, tour de force (*French*), stratagem, stroke of genius

couple *n* **2** = **pair**, two, brace, span (*of horses or oxen*), duo, twain (*archaic*), twosome

coupon *n* **1, 2** = **slip**, ticket, certificate, token, voucher, card, detachable portion

courage *n* **1** = **bravery**, nerve, fortitude, boldness, balls (*taboo, slang*), bottle (*Brit slang*), resolution, daring, guts (*informal*), pluck, grit, heroism, mettle, firmness, gallantry, valour, spunk (*informal*), fearlessness, intrepidity **OPPOSITE:** cowardice

courageous *adj* = **brave**, daring, bold, plucky, hardy, heroic, gritty, stalwart, fearless, resolute, gallant, audacious, intrepid, valiant, indomitable, dauntless, ballsy (*taboo, slang*), lion-hearted, valorous, stouthearted **OPPOSITE:** cowardly

courier *n* **1** = **guide**, representative, escort, conductor, chaperon, cicerone, dragoman **2** = **messenger**,

DICTIONARY

Cournand *n* **André (Frederic)** 1895–1988, US physician, born in France: shared the 1956 Nobel prize for physiology or medicine for his work on heart catheterization

Courrèges *n* **André** born 1923, French couturier: helped to launch unisex fashion in the mid-1960s

course Ⓣ *n* **1** a complete series of lessons or lectures: *a training course* **2** a sequence of medical treatment prescribed for a period of time: *a course of antibiotics* **3** an onward movement in time or space: *during the course of his career he worked with many leading actors* **4** a route or direction taken: *the ships were blown off course by a gale* **5** the path or channel along which a river moves **6** an area on which a sport is played or a race is held: *a golf course* **7** any of the successive parts of a meal **8** a continuous, usually horizontal layer of building material, such as bricks or tiles, at one level in a building **9** a mode of conduct or action: *the safest course of action was to do nothing* **10** the natural development of a sequence of events: *allow the fever to run its course* **11** a period of time: *over the course of the last two years* **12 as a matter of course** as a natural or normal consequence or event **13 in the course of** in the process of **14 in due course** at the natural or appropriate time **15 of course a** (*adv*) as expected; naturally **b** (*interj*) certainly; definitely ▷*vb* **coursing, coursed 16** (of a liquid) to run swiftly **17** to hunt with hounds that follow the quarry by sight and not scent

WORD ORIGIN Latin *cursus* a running

coursebook *n* a book that is used as part of an educational course

courser¹ *n* **1** a person who courses hounds **2** a hound trained for coursing

courser² *n literary* a swift horse; steed

WORD ORIGIN Old French *coursier*

coursework *n* work done by a student and assessed as part of an educational course

coursing *n* hunting with hounds trained to hunt game by sight

court Ⓣ *n* **1** *law* **a** a judicial body which hears and makes decisions on legal cases **b** the room or building in which such a body meets **2** a marked area used for playing a racket game **3** an area of ground wholly or partly surrounded by walls or buildings **4** a name given to some short street, blocks of flats, or large country houses as a part of their address: *Carlton Court* **5** the residence or retinue of a sovereign **6** any formal assembly held by a sovereign **7 go to court** to take legal action **8 hold court** to preside over a group of admirers **9 out of court** without a trial or legal case **10 pay court to** to give flattering attention to ▷*vb* **11** to attempt to gain the love of **12** to pay attention to (someone) in order to gain favour **13** to try to obtain (something): *he has not courted controversy, but he has certainly attracted it* **14** to make oneself open or vulnerable to: *courting disaster*

WORD ORIGIN Latin *cohors* cohort

Court *n* **Margaret** (née *Smith*) born 1942, Australian tennis player: Australian champion 1960–66, 1969–71, and 1973; US champion 1962, 1965, 1969–70, and 1973; Wimbledon champion 1963, 1965, and 1970

court card *n* (in a pack of playing cards) a king, queen, or jack

WORD ORIGIN earlier *coat-card*, from the decorative coats worn by the figures depicted

courteous *adj* polite and considerate in manner **courteously** *adv* **courteousness** *n*

WORD ORIGIN Middle English *corteis* with courtly manners

courtesan (kore-tiz-**zan**) *n history* a mistress or high-class prostitute

WORD ORIGIN Old French *courtisane*

courtesy Ⓣ *n, pl* **-sies 1** politeness; good manners **2** a courteous act or remark **3 by courtesy of** with the consent of

WORD ORIGIN Old French *corteis* courteous

courthouse *n* a public building in which courts of law are held

courtier *n* an attendant at a royal court

courtly *adj* **-lier, -liest 1** ceremoniously polite **2** of or suitable for a royal court **courtliness** *n*

court martial *n, pl* **court martials** *or* **courts martial 1** the trial of a member of the armed forces charged with breaking military law ▷*vb* **court-martial, -tialling, -tialled** *or US* **-tialing, -tialed 2** to try by court martial

courtship *n* the courting of an intended spouse or mate

court shoe *n* a low-cut shoe for women, without laces or straps

courtyard Ⓣ *n* an open area of ground surrounded by walls or buildings

couscous (**kooss**-kooss) *n* **1** a type of semolina used in North African cookery **2** a spicy North African dish, consisting of steamed semolina served with a stew

WORD ORIGIN Arabic *kouskous*

cousin *n* the child of one's aunt or uncle. Also called: **first cousin**

WORD ORIGIN Latin *consobrinus*

Cousin *n* **Victor** 1792–1867, French philosopher and educational reformer

couture (koo-**toor**) *n* **1** high-fashion designing and dressmaking ▷*adj* **2** relating to high fashion design and dress-making: *couture clothes*

WORD ORIGIN French: sewing

couturier *n* a person who designs fashion clothes for women

WORD ORIGIN French

covalency *or US* **covalence** *n chem* **1** the ability to form a bond in which two atoms share a pair of electrons **2** the number of covalent bonds which a particular atom can make with others **covalent** *adj*

cove¹ Ⓣ *n* a small bay or inlet

WORD ORIGIN Old English *cofa*

cove² *n old-fashioned, slang* a fellow; chap

WORD ORIGIN probably from Romany *kova*

THESAURUS

runner, carrier, bearer, herald, envoy, emissary

course *n* **1 = classes**, course of study, programme, schedule, lectures, curriculum, studies **3 = progression**, order, unfolding, development, movement, advance, progress, flow, sequence, succession, continuity, advancement, furtherance, march **4, 5 = route**, way, line, road, track, channel, direction, path, passage, trail, orbit, tack, trajectory **6 = racecourse**, race, circuit, cinder track, lap **9 = procedure**, plan, policy, programme, method, conduct, behaviour, manner, mode, regimen **11 = period**, time, duration, term, passing, sweep, passage, lapse ▷*vb* **15a, 15b of course = naturally**, certainly, obviously, definitely, undoubtedly, needless to say, without a doubt, indubitably **16 = run**, flow, stream, gush, race, speed, surge, dash, tumble, scud, move apace **17 = hunt**, follow, chase, pursue

court *n* **1a, 1b = law court**, bar, bench, tribunal, court of justice, seat of judgment **5a = palace**, hall, castle, manor **5b = royal household**, train, suite, attendants, entourage, retinue, cortege ▷*vb* **11 = woo**, go (out) with, go steady with (*informal*), date, chase, pursue, take out, make love to, run after, walk out with, keep company with, pay court to, set your cap at, pay your addresses to, step out with (*informal*) **12 = cultivate**, seek, flatter, solicit, pander to, curry favour with, fawn upon **13 = invite**, seek, attract, prompt, provoke, bring about, incite

courtesy *n* **1 = politeness**, grace, good manners, civility, gallantry, good breeding, graciousness, affability, urbanity, courtliness **2 = favour**, consideration, generosity, kindness, indulgence, benevolence

courtyard *n* **= yard**, square, piazza, quadrangle, area, plaza, enclosure, cloister, quad (*informal*), peri[illegible]

cove¹ *n* **= bay**, sound, [illegible]

DICTIONARY

coven (kuv-ven) *n* a meeting of witches
WORD ORIGIN Latin *convenire* to come together

covenant ⓣ (kuv-ven-ant) *n* **1** *chiefly Brit* a formal agreement to make an annual payment to charity **2** *law* a formal sealed agreement **3** *bible* God's promise to the Israelites and their commitment to worship him alone ▷*vb* **4** to agree by a legal covenant **covenanter** *n*
WORD ORIGIN Latin *convenire* to come together, agree

Covenanter *n Scots history* a person upholding either of two 17th-century covenants to establish and defend Presbyterianism

Coventry *n* **send someone to Coventry** to punish someone by refusing to speak to him or her
WORD ORIGIN after *Coventry*, England

cover ⓣ *vb* **1** to place something over so as to protect or conceal **2** to put a garment on; clothe **3** to extend over or lie thickly on the surface of: *the ground was covered with dry leaves* **4** (sometimes foll. by *up*) to screen or conceal; hide from view **5** to travel over **6** to protect (an individual or group) by taking up a position from which fire may be returned if those being protected are fired upon **7** to keep a gun aimed at **8 a** to insure against loss or risk **b** to provide for (loss or risk) by insurance **9** to include or deal with: *the course covers accounting, economics, statistics, law and computer applications* **10** to act as reporter or photographer on (a news event) for a newspaper or magazine **11** (of a sum of money) to be enough to pay for (something) **12** *music* to record a cover version of **13** *sport* to guard or obstruct (an opponent, team-mate, or area) **14 cover for** to deputize for (a person) **15** (foll. by *for* or *up for*) to provide an alibi (for): *can my men count on your friends at City Hall to cover for us?* ▷*n* **16** anything which covers **17** a blanket or bedspread **18** the outside of a book or magazine **19** a pretext or disguise: *he claimed UN resolutions were being used as a cover for planned American aggression* **20** an envelope or other postal wrapping: *under plain cover* **21** an individual table setting **22** insurance **23** a cover version **24 the covers** *cricket* the area roughly at right angles to the pitch on the off side and about halfway to the boundary **25 break cover** to come out from a shelter or hiding place **26 take cover** to make for a place of safety or shelter **27 under cover** protected or in secret ▸See also **cover-up** >**covering** *adj, n*
WORD ORIGIN Latin *cooperire* to cover completely

coverage *n journalism* the amount of reporting given to a subject or event

cover charge *n* a fixed service charge added to the bill in a restaurant

Coverdale *n* **Miles** 1488–1568, the first translator of the complete Bible into English (1535)

cover girl *n* an attractive woman whose picture appears on the cover of a magazine

covering letter *n* an accompanying letter sent as an explanation

coverlet *n* ▸same as **bedspread**

cover note *n Austral & Brit* a temporary certificate from an insurance company giving proof of a current policy

covert *adj* **1** concealed or secret ▷*n* **2** a thicket or woodland providing shelter for game **3** *ornithol* any of the small feathers on the wings and tail of a bird that surround the bases of the larger feathers **covertly** *adv*
WORD ORIGIN Old French: covered

cover-up *n* **1** concealment or attempted concealment of a mistake or crime ▷*vb* **cover up 2** to cover completely **3** to attempt to conceal (a mistake or crime)

cover version *n* a version by a different artist of a previously recorded musical item

covet ⓣ *vb* **-eting, -eted** to long to possess (something belonging to another person)
WORD ORIGIN Latin *cupiditas* cupidity

covetous *adj* jealously longing to possess something **covetously** *adv* **covetousness** *n*

covey (kuv-vee) *n* **1** a small flock of grouse or partridge **2** a small group of people
WORD ORIGIN Old French *cover* to sit on, hatch

Covilhã *n* **Pero da** ?1460–?1526, Portuguese explorer, who established relations between Portugal and Ethiopia

cow[1] *n* **1** the mature female of cattle **2** the mature female of various other mammals, such as the elephant or whale **3** *not in technical use* any domestic species of cattle **4** *informal, offensive* a disagreeable woman
WORD ORIGIN Old English *cū*

cow[2] *vb* to frighten or subdue with threats
WORD ORIGIN Old Norse *kūga* to oppress

coward ⓣ *n* a person who is easily frightened and avoids dangerous or difficult situations **cowardly** *adj*
WORD ORIGIN Latin *cauda* tail

cowardice *n* lack of courage

cowbell *n* a bell hung around a cow's neck

cowboy ⓣ *n* **1** (in the US and Canada) a ranch worker who herds and tends cattle, usually on horseback **2** a conventional character of Wild West folklore or films **3** *Brit, Austral, NZ informal* an irresponsible or unscrupulous worker or businessman **cowgirl** *fem n*

cowcatcher *n US & Canad* a fender on the front of a locomotive to clear the track of animals or other obstructions

cow cocky *n Austral & NZ* a one-man dairy farmer

Cowdrey *n* (**Michael**) **Colin**, Baron. 1932–2000, English cricketer. He played for Kent and in 114 Test matches (captaining England 27 times)

THESAURUS

bayou, firth *or* frith *(Scot)*, anchorage

covenant *n* **2 = promise**, contract, agreement, commitment, arrangement, treaty, pledge, bargain, convention, pact, compact, concordat, trust

cover *vb* **1, 4 = conceal**, cover up, screen, hide, shade, curtain, mask, disguise, obscure, hood, veil, cloak, shroud, camouflage, enshroud **OPPOSITE:** reveal
2 = clothe, invest, dress, wrap, envelop **OPPOSITE:** uncover
3a = overlay, blanket, eclipse, mantle, canopy, overspread, layer
3b = coat, cake, plaster, smear, envelop, spread, encase, daub, overspread **5 = travel over**, cross, traverse, pass through *or* over, range **6 = protect**, guard, defend, shelter, shield, watch over **9 = consider**, deal with, examine, investigate, detail, describe, survey, refer to, tell of, recount **10 = report on**, write about, commentate on, give an account of, relate, tell of, narrate, write up **11 = pay for**, fund, provide for, offset, be enough for ▷*n* **16 = covering**, case, top, cap, coating, envelope, lid, canopy, sheath, wrapper, awning **17 = bedclothes**, bedding, sheet, blanket, quilt, duvet, eiderdown **18 = jacket**, case, binding, wrapper **19 = disguise**, front, screen, mask, cover-up, veil, cloak, façade, pretence, pretext, window-dressing, smoke screen **22 = insurance**, payment, protection, compensation, indemnity, reimbursement

covet *vb* **= long for**, desire, fancy *(informal)*, envy, crave, aspire to, yearn for, thirst for, begrudge, hanker after, lust after, set your heart on, have your eye on, would give your eyeteeth for

coward *n* **= wimp**, chicken *(slang)*, scaredy-cat *(informal)*, sneak, pussy *(slang, chiefly US)*, yellow-belly *(slang)*

cowboy *n* **1, 2 = cowhand**, drover, herder, rancher, stockman, cattleman, herdsman, gaucho, buckaroo *(US)*, ranchero *(US)*, cowpuncher *(US informal)*, broncobuster *(US)*, wrangler *(US)*

DICTIONARY

Cowell *n* **Simon** born 1959, British manager of pop groups and TV personality, best known as an outspoken judge on the TV talent contests *Pop Idol* and *The X Factor*

cower *vb* to cringe or shrink in fear
WORD ORIGIN Middle Low German *kūren* to lie in wait

cowl *n* **1** a loose hood **2** a monk's hooded robe **3** a cover fitted to a chimney to increase ventilation and prevent draughts **cowled** *adj*
WORD ORIGIN Latin *cucullus* hood

Cowley *n* **Abraham** 1618–67, English poet and essayist, who introduced the Pindaric ode to English literature

cowlick *n* a tuft of hair over the forehead

cowling *n* a streamlined detachable metal covering around an engine

co-worker *n* a fellow worker: *these habits can drive your boss and co-workers crazy*

cow parsley *n* a hedgerow plant with umbrella-shaped clusters of white flowers

cowpat *n* a pool of cow dung

Cowper *n* **William** 1731–1800, English poet, noted for his nature poetry, such as in *The Task* (1785), and his hymns

cowpox *n* a contagious disease of cows, the virus of which is used to make smallpox vaccine

cowrie *n, pl* **-ries** the glossy brightly-marked shell of a marine mollusc
WORD ORIGIN Hindi *kaurī*

cowslip *n* a European wild plant with yellow flowers
WORD ORIGIN Old English *cūslyppe*, from *cū* cow + *slyppe* slime, dung

cox *n* **1** a coxswain ▷*vb* **2** to act as coxswain of (a boat)

Cox *n* **David** 1783–1859, English landscape painter

coxcomb *or* **cockscomb** *n* **1** the comb of a domestic cock **2** *informal* a conceited dandy

coxswain (kok-sn) *n* the person who steers a lifeboat or rowing boat
WORD ORIGIN *cock* a ship's boat + SWAIN

coy *adj* **1** affectedly shy and modest **2** unwilling to give information **coyly** *adv* **coyness** *n*
WORD ORIGIN Latin *quietus* quiet

coyote (koy-ote-ee) *n, pl* **-otes** *or* **-ote** a small wolf of the deserts and prairies of North America
WORD ORIGIN Mexican Indian *coyotl*

Coypel *n* **Antoine** 1661–1722, French baroque painter, noted esp. for his large biblical compositions

coypu *n, pl* **-pus** *or* **-pu** a beaver-like amphibious rodent, bred for its fur
WORD ORIGIN From a Native American language, *kóypu*

cozen *vb literary* to cheat or trick **cozenage** *n*
WORD ORIGIN originally a cant term

Cpl Corporal

CPU *computers* central processing unit

Cr *chem* chromium

crab *n* **1** an edible shellfish with five pairs of legs, the first pair modified into pincers **2** ▸short for **crab louse** **3** **catch a crab** *rowing* to make a stroke in which the oar misses the water or digs too deeply, causing the rower to fall backwards
WORD ORIGIN Old English *crabba*

crab apple *n* a kind of small sour apple

Crabbe *n* **George** 1754–1832, English narrative poet, noted for his depiction of impoverished rural life in *The Village* (1783) and *The Borough* (1810)

crabbed *adj* **1** (of handwriting) cramped and hard to read **2** bad-tempered
WORD ORIGIN probably from *crab*, because of its sideways movement & *crab apple*, because of its sourness

crabby *adj* **-bier, -biest** bad-tempered

crab louse *n* a parasitic louse living in the pubic area of humans

crack ⓣ *vb* **1** to break or split without complete separation of the parts **2** to break with a sudden sharp sound **3** to make or cause to make a sudden sharp sound: *the coachman cracked his whip* **4** (of the voice) to become harsh or change pitch suddenly **5** *informal* to fail or break down: *he had cracked under the strain of losing his job* **6** to yield or cease to resist: *he had cracked under torture* **7** to hit with a forceful or resounding blow **8** to break into or force open: *it'll take me longer if I have to crack the safe myself* **9** to solve or decipher (a code or problem) **10** *informal* to tell (a joke) **11** to break (a molecule) into smaller molecules or radicals by heat or catalysis as in the distillation of petroleum **12** to open (a bottle) for drinking **13** **crack it** *informal* to achieve something ▷*n* **14** a sudden sharp noise **15** a break or fracture without complete separation of the two parts **16** a narrow opening or fissure **17** *informal* a sharp blow **18** **crack of dawn** daybreak **19** a broken or cracked tone of voice **20** *informal* an attempt **21** *informal* a gibe or joke **22** *slang* a highly addictive form of cocaine **23** *chiefly Irish informal* fun; informal entertainment **24** **a fair crack of the whip** *informal* a fair chance or opportunity ▷*adj* **25** *slang* first-class or excellent: *crack troops* ▸See also **crack down, crack up**
WORD ORIGIN Old English *cracian*

crackbrained *adj* idiotic or crazy: *a crackbrained scheme*

crack down ⓣ *vb* **1** **crack down on** to take severe measures against ▷*n* **crackdown** **2** severe or repressive measures

cracked ⓣ *adj* **1** damaged by cracking **2** harsh-sounding **3** *informal* crazy

cracked wheat *n* whole wheat cracked between rollers so that it will cook more quickly

cracker *n* **1** a thin crisp unsweetened biscuit **2** a decorated cardboard tube, pulled apart with a bang, containing a paper hat and a joke or a toy **3** a small explosive firework **4** *slang* an excellent or notable thing or person

crackers *adj Brit & NZ slang* insane

cracking *adj* **1** **get cracking** *informal* to start doing something immediately **2** **a cracking pace** *informal* a high speed ▷*adv, adj* **3** *Brit informal* first-class: *five cracking good saves* ▷*n* **4** the oil-refining process in which heavy oils are broken down into smaller molecules by heat or catalysis

crackle *vb* **-ling, -led** **1** to make small sharp popping noises ▷*n* **2** a crackling sound **crackly** *adj*

crackling *n* **1** a series of small sharp popping noises **2** the crisp browned skin of roast pork

crackpot *informal n* **1** an eccentric person ▷*adj* **2** eccentric: *crackpot philosophies*

crack up *vb* **1** *informal* to have a physical or mental breakdown **2** to begin to break into pieces: *there are*

THESAURUS

crack *vb* **1a = break**, split, burst, snap, fracture, splinter, craze, rive **1b = cleave**, break **2 = snap**, ring, crash, burst, explode, crackle, pop, detonate **5, 6 = break down**, collapse, yield, give in, give way, succumb, lose control, be overcome, go to pieces **7** *(informal)* **= hit**, clip *(informal)*, slap, smack, thump, buffet, clout *(informal)*, cuff, whack, wallop *(informal)*, chop **9 = solve**, work out, resolve, interpret, clarify, clear up, fathom, decipher, suss (out) *(slang)*, get to the bottom of, disentangle, elucidate, get the answer to ▷*n* **14 = snap**, pop, crash, burst, explosion, clap, report **15, 16a = break**, chink, gap, breach, fracture, rift, cleft, crevice, fissure, cranny, interstice **15, 16b = split**, break, chip, breach, fracture, rupture, cleft **17** *(informal)* **= blow**, slap, smack, thump, buffet, clout *(informal)*, cuff, whack, wallop *(informal)*, clip *(informal)* **21** *(informal)* **= joke**, dig, insult, gag *(informal)*, quip, jibe, wisecrack, witticism, funny remark, smart-alecky remark ▷*adj* **25** *(slang)* **= first-class**, choice, excellent, ace, elite, superior, world-class, first-rate, hand-picked

crackdown *n* **2 = clampdown**, crushing, repression, suppression

cracked *adj* **1 = broken**, damaged,

DICTIONARY

worrying reports of buildings cracking up as the earth dries out and foundations move
3 not all it is cracked up to be *informal* not as good as people have claimed it to be ▷*n* **crackup**
4 *informal* a physical or mental breakdown

-cracy *n combining form* indicating a type of government or rule: *plutocracy; mobocracy.* ▸See also **-crat**
WORD ORIGIN Greek *kratos* power

cradle ❶ *n* **1** a baby's bed on rockers **2** a place where something originates: *the cradle of civilization* **3** a supporting framework or structure **4** a platform or trolley in which workmen are suspended on the side of a building or ship ▷*vb* **-dling, -dled 5** to hold gently as if in a cradle
WORD ORIGIN Old English *cradol*

cradle-snatcher *n informal* a person who marries or has a sexual relationship with someone much younger than himself or herself

craft ❶ *n* **1** an occupation requiring skill or manual dexterity **2** skill or ability **3** cunning or guile **4** *pl* **craft** a boat, ship, aircraft, or spacecraft ▷*vb* **5** to make skilfully
WORD ORIGIN Old English *cræft* skill, strength

craftsman ❶ *or fem* **craftswoman** *n, pl* **-men** *or* **-women 1** a skilled worker **2** a skilled artist **craftsmanship** *n*

crafty *adj* **-tier, -tiest** skilled in deception **craftily** *adv* **craftiness** *n*

crag *n* a steep rugged rock or peak **craggy** *adj*
WORD ORIGIN Celtic

craic *n* ▸an Irish spelling of **crack** (sense 23)

Craig *n* **Edward Gordon** 1872–1966, English theatrical designer, actor, and director. His nonrealistic scenic design greatly influenced theatre in Europe and the US

Craigie *n* Sir **William A(lexander)** 1867–1957, Scottish lexicographer; joint editor of the *Oxford English Dictionary* (1901–33), and of *A Dictionary of American English on Historical Principles* (1938–44)

crake *n zool* a bird of the rail family, such as the corncrake
WORD ORIGIN Old Norse *krāka* crow or *krākr* raven

cram ❶ *vb* **cramming, crammed 1** to force (more people or things) into (a place) than it can hold **2** to eat or feed to excess **3** *chiefly Brit* to study hard just before an examination
WORD ORIGIN Old English *crammian*

Cram *n* **Steve** born 1960, English middle-distance runner: European 1500 m champion (1981, 1986); world 1500 m champion (1983)

crammer *n* a person or school that prepares pupils for an examination

cramp[1] ❶ *n* **1** a sudden painful contraction of a muscle **2** temporary stiffness of a muscle group from overexertion: *writer's cramp* **3** severe stomach pain **4** a clamp for holding masonry or timber together ▷*vb* **5** to affect with a cramp
WORD ORIGIN Old French *crampe*

cramp[2] ❶ *vb* **1** to confine or restrict **2 cramp someone's style** *informal* to prevent someone from impressing another person or from behaving naturally: *shyness will cramp their style*
WORD ORIGIN Middle Dutch *crampe* hook

cramped ❶ *adj* **1** closed in **2** (of handwriting) small and irregular

crampon *n* a spiked iron plate strapped to a boot for climbing on ice
WORD ORIGIN French

Cranach *n* **Lucas**, known as *the Elder*, real name *Lucas Müller*. 1472–1553, German painter, etc.her, and designer of woodcuts

cranberry *n, pl* **-ries** a sour edible red berry
WORD ORIGIN Low German *kraanbere* crane berry

crane *n* **1** a machine for lifting and moving heavy objects, usually by suspending them from a movable projecting arm **2** a large wading bird with a long neck and legs ▷*vb* **craning, craned 3** to stretch out (the neck) in order to see something
WORD ORIGIN Old English *cran*

Crane *n* **1 (Harold) Hart** 1899–1932, US poet; author of *The Bridge* (1930) **2 Stephen** 1871–1900, US novelist and short-story writer, noted particularly for his novel *The Red Badge of Courage* (1895) **3 Walter** 1845–1915, British painter, illustrator of children's books, and designer of textiles and wallpaper

crane fly *n* a fly with long legs, slender wings, and a narrow body

cranesbill *n* a plant with pink or purple flowers

cranial *adj* of or relating to the skull

craniology *n* the scientific study of the human skull
WORD ORIGIN Greek *kranion* skull + -LOGY

cranium *n, pl* **-niums** *or* **-nia** *anat* **1** the skull **2** the part of the skull that encloses the brain
WORD ORIGIN Greek *kranion*

crank *n* **1** a device for transmitting or converting motion, consisting of an arm projecting at right angles from a shaft **2** a handle incorporating a crank, used to start an engine or motor **3** *informal* an eccentric or odd person ▷*vb* **4** to turn with a crank **5** to start (an engine) with a crank
WORD ORIGIN Old English *cranc*

crankcase *n* the metal case that encloses the crankshaft in an internal-combustion engine

Cranko *n* **John** 1927–73, British choreographer, born in South Africa: director of the Stuttgart Ballet (1961–73)

crankpin *n* a short cylindrical pin in a crankshaft, to which the connecting rod is attached

crankshaft *n* a shaft with one or more cranks, to which the connecting rods are attached

cranky *adj* **crankier, crankiest** *informal* **1** eccentric **2** bad-tempered **crankiness** *n*

cranny *n, pl* **-nies** a narrow opening
WORD ORIGIN Old French *cran*

crap[1] *slang n* **1** nonsense **2** junk **3** *taboo* faeces ▷*vb* **crapping, crapped 4** *taboo* to defecate **crappy** *adj*
WORD ORIGIN Middle English *crappe* chaff

crap[2] *n* ▸same as **craps**

crape *n* ▸same as **crepe**

craps *n* **1** a gambling game played with two dice **2 shoot craps** to play this game

THESAURUS

split, chipped, flawed, faulty, crazed, defective, imperfect, fissured

cradle *n* **1 = crib**, cot, Moses basket, bassinet **2 = birthplace**, beginning, source, spring, origin, fount, fountainhead, wellspring ▷*vb* **5 = hold**, support, rock, nurse, nestle

craft *n* **1 = occupation**, work, calling, business, line, trade, employment, pursuit, vocation, handiwork, handicraft **2 = skill**, art, ability, technique, know-how (*informal*), expertise, knack, aptitude, artistry, dexterity, workmanship **4 = vessel**, boat, ship, plane, aircraft, spacecraft, barque

craftsman *n* **1 = skilled worker**, artisan, master, maker, wright, technician, artificer, smith

cram *vb* **1a = stuff**, force, jam, ram, shove, compress, compact **1b = pack**, fill, stuff **1c = squeeze**, press, crowd, pack, crush, pack in, fill to overflowing, overfill, overcrowd **3 = study**, revise, swot, bone up (*informal*), grind, swot up, mug up (*slang*)

cramp[1] *n* **1 = spasm**, pain, ache, contraction, pang, stiffness, stitch, convulsion, twinge, crick, shooting pain

cramp[2] *vb* **1 = restrict**, hamper, inhibit, hinder, check, handicap, confine, hamstring, constrain, obstruct, impede, shackle, circumscribe, encumber

cramped *adj* **1 = restricted**, confined, overcrowded, crowded, packed, narrow, squeezed, uncomfortable, awkward, closed in, congested, circumscribed, jammed in, hemmed in **OPPOSITE:** spacious

DICTIONARY

WORD ORIGIN probably from *crabs* lowest throw at dice

crapulent *or* **crapulous** *adj literary* given to or resulting from excessive eating or drinking **crapulence** *n*

WORD ORIGIN Latin *crapula* drunkenness

crash ❶ *n* **1** a collision involving a vehicle or vehicles **2** a sudden descent of an aircraft as a result of which it crashes **3** a sudden loud noise **4** a breaking and falling to pieces **5** the sudden collapse of a business or stock exchange ▷ *vb* **6** to cause (a vehicle or aircraft) to collide with another vehicle, the ground, or some other object or (of vehicles or aircraft) to be involved in a collision **7** to make or cause to make a loud smashing noise **8** to drop with force and break into pieces with a loud noise **9** to break or smash into pieces with a loud noise **10** (of a business or stock exchange) to collapse or fail suddenly **11** to move violently or noisily **12** (of a computer system or program) to fail suddenly because of a malfunction **13** *Austral & Brit informal* to gate-crash ▷ *adj* **14** requiring or using great effort in order to achieve results quickly: *a crash course*

WORD ORIGIN probably Middle English *crasen* to smash + *dasshen* to strike

Crashaw *n* **Richard** 1613–49, English religious poet, noted esp. for the *Steps to the Temple* (1646)

crash barrier *n* a safety barrier along the centre of a motorway, around a racetrack, or at the side of a dangerous road

crash dive *n* **1** a sudden steep emergency dive by a submarine ▷ *vb* **crash-dive, -diving, -dived 2** to perform a crash dive

crash helmet *n* a helmet worn by motorcyclists to protect the head in case of a crash

crashing *adj informal* extreme: *a crashing bore*

crash-land *vb* (of an aircraft) to land in an emergency, causing damage **crash-landing** *n*

crash out *vb informal* **1** to go to sleep or become unconscious **2** to be eliminated from a competition in a way that brings disgrace or embarrassment

crash team *n* a medial team with special equipment who can arrive quickly to treat a patient having a heart attack

crass *adj* stupid and insensitive: *the enquiry is crass and naive* **crassly** *adv* **crassness** *n*

WORD ORIGIN Latin *crassus* thick

Crassus *n* **Marcus Licinius** ?115–53 BC, Roman general; member of the first triumvirate with Caesar and Pompey

-crat *n combining form* indicating a supporter or member of a particular form of government: *autocrat; democrat* **-cratic** *or* **-critical** *adj combining form*

WORD ORIGIN Greek *-kratēs*

crate ❶ *n* **1** a large container made of wooden slats, used for packing goods **2** *slang* an old car or aeroplane ▷ *vb* **crating, crated 3** to put in a crate **crateful** *n*

WORD ORIGIN Latin *cratis* wickerwork

crater ❶ *n* **1** the bowl-shaped opening in a volcano or a geyser **2** a cavity made by the impact of a meteorite or an explosion **3** a roughly circular cavity on the surface of the moon and some planets ▷ *vb* **4** to make or form craters in (a surface, such as the ground) **cratered** *adj*

WORD ORIGIN Greek *kratēr* mixing bowl

cravat *n* a scarf worn round the neck instead of a tie

WORD ORIGIN French *cravate*

crave ❶ *vb* **craving, craved 1** to desire intensely: *a vulnerable, unhappy girl who craved affection* **2** *formal* to beg or plead for: *may I crave your lordship's indulgence?* **craving** *n*

WORD ORIGIN Old English *crafian*

craven *adj* **1** cowardly ▷ *n* **2** a coward

WORD ORIGIN Middle English *cravant*

craw *n* **1** the crop of a bird **2** the stomach of an animal **3 stick in one's craw** *informal* to be difficult for one to agree with or accept

WORD ORIGIN Middle English

crawfish *n, pl* **-fish** *or* **-fishes** ▸ same as **crayfish**

Crawford *n* **1 Joan**, real name *Lucille le Sueur*. 1908–77, US film actress, who portrayed ambitious women in such films as *Mildred Pierce* (1945) **2 Michael**, real name *Michael Dumbell Smith*. born 1942, British actor

crawl ❶ *vb* **1** to move on one's hands and knees **2** (of insects, worms or snakes) to creep slowly **3** to move very slowly **4** to act in a servile manner **5** to be or feel as if covered with crawling creatures: *the kind of smile that made your hair stand on end and your flesh crawl* ▷ *n* **6** a slow creeping pace or motion **7** *swimming* a stroke in which the feet are kicked like paddles while each arm in turn reaches forward and pulls back through the water

WORD ORIGIN probably from Old Norse *krafla*

Craxi *n* **Bettino** 1934–2000, Italian socialist statesman; prime minister (1983–87)

crayfish *or esp. US* **crawfish** *n, pl* **-fish** *or* **-fishes** an edible shellfish like a lobster

WORD ORIGIN Old French *crevice* crab

crayon *n* **1** a small stick or pencil of coloured wax or clay ▷ *vb* **2** to draw or colour with a crayon

WORD ORIGIN Latin *creta* chalk

craze ❶ *n* **1** a short-lived fashion or enthusiasm ▷ *vb* **crazing, crazed 2** to make mad **3** *ceramics, metallurgy* to develop or cause to develop fine cracks: *you must prevent the drill crazing the glazed surface of the tile*

WORD ORIGIN probably from Old Norse

crazed ❶ *adj* **1** wild and uncontrolled in behaviour **2** (of porcelain) having fine cracks

crazy ❶ *adj* **-zier, -ziest** *informal* **1** ridiculous **2 crazy about**

THESAURUS

crash *n* **1, 2 = collision**, accident, smash, wreck, prang *(informal)*, bump, pile-up *(informal)*, smash-up **3 = smash**, clash, boom, smashing, bang, thunder, thump, racket, din, clatter, clattering, thud, clang **5 = collapse**, failure, depression, ruin, bankruptcy, downfall ▷ *vb* **8 = plunge**, hurtle, precipitate yourself **10 = collapse**, fail, go under, be ruined, go bust *(informal)*, fold up, go broke *(informal)*, go to the wall, go belly up *(informal)*, smash, fold **11 = fall**, pitch, plunge, sprawl, topple, lurch, hurtle, come a cropper *(informal)*, overbalance, fall headlong

crate *n* **1 = container**, case, box, packing case, tea chest

crater *n* **1, 2 = hollow**, hole, depression, dip, cavity, shell hole

crave *vb* **1 = long for**, yearn for, hanker after, be dying for, want, need, require, desire, fancy *(informal)*, hope for, cry out for *(informal)*, thirst for, pine for, lust after, pant for, sigh for, set your heart on, hunger after, eat your heart out over, would give your eyeteeth for **2** *(informal)* **= beg**, ask for, seek, petition, pray for, plead for, solicit, implore, beseech, entreat, supplicate

crawl *vb* **1, 2, 3 = creep**, slither, go on all fours, move on hands and knees, inch, drag, wriggle, writhe, move at a snail's pace, worm your way, advance slowly, pull *or* drag yourself along **OPPOSITE:** run **4 = grovel**, creep, cringe, humble yourself, abase yourself

craze *n* **1 = fad**, thing, fashion, trend, passion, rage, enthusiasm, mode, vogue, novelty, preoccupation, mania, infatuation, the latest thing *(informal)*

crazed *adj* **1 = mad**, crazy, raving, insane, lunatic, demented, unbalanced, deranged, berserk, unhinged, berko *(Austral slang)*, off the air *(Austral slang)*, porangi *(NZ)*

crazy *adj* **1** *(informal)* **= ridiculous**, wild, absurd, inappropriate, foolish,

extremely fond of: *he was crazy about me* **3** extremely annoyed or upset **4** insane **crazily** *adv* **craziness** *n*

crazy paving *n Brit, Austral & NZ* a form of paving on a path, made of irregular slabs of stone

creak *vb* **1** to make or move with a harsh squeaking sound ▷*n* **2** a harsh squeaking sound **creaky** *adj* **creakiness** *n*
WORD ORIGIN imitative

cream ● *n* **1** the fatty part of milk, which rises to the top **2** a cosmetic or medication that resembles cream in consistency **3** any of various foods resembling or containing cream **4** the best part of something **5 cream sherry** a full-bodied sweet sherry ▷*adj* **6** yellowish-white ▷*vb* **7** to beat (foodstuffs) to a light creamy consistency **8** to remove the cream from (milk) **9** to prepare or cook (foodstuffs) with cream or milk **10 cream off** to take away the best part of **creamy** *adj*
WORD ORIGIN Late Latin *cramum*

cream cheese *n* a type of very rich soft white cheese

creamer *n chiefly Brit* a powdered milk substitute for coffee

creamery *n, pl* **-eries** a place where dairy products are made or sold

cream of tartar *n* a purified form of the tartar produced in wine-making, an ingredient in baking powder

crease ● *n* **1** a line made by folding or pressing **2** a wrinkle or furrow, esp. on the face **3** *cricket* any of four lines near each wicket marking positions for the bowler or batsman ▷*vb* **creasing, creased 4** to make or become wrinkled or furrowed **creasy** *adj*
WORD ORIGIN Middle English *crēst*

create ● *vb* **-ating, -ated 1** to cause to come into existence **2** to be the cause of **3** to appoint to a new rank or position **4** *Brit slang* to make an angry fuss
WORD ORIGIN Latin *creare*

creation ● *n* **1** a creating or being created **2** something brought into existence or created

Creation *n Christianity* **1** God's act of bringing the universe into being **2** the universe as thus brought into being by God

creationism *n* the doctrine that ascribes the origins of all things to God's acts of creation rather than to evolution **creationist** *n, adj*

creative ● *adj* **1** having the ability to create **2** imaginative or inventive ▷*n* **3** a creative person, esp. one who devises advertising campaigns **creativity** *n*

creator ● *n* a person who creates

Creator *n* **the Creator** God

creature ● *n* **1** an animal, bird, or fish **2** a person **3** a person or thing controlled by another

crèche *n* **1** a day nursery for very young children **2** a supervised play area provided for young children for short periods
WORD ORIGIN French

cred *n slang* ▸short for **credibility**

credence (**kreed**-enss) *n* belief in the truth or accuracy of a statement: *the question is, how much credence to give to their accounts?*
WORD ORIGIN Latin *credere* to believe

credentials ● *pl n* **1** something that entitles a person to credit or confidence **2** a document giving evidence of the bearer's identity or qualifications

credibility gap *n* the difference between claims or statements made and the true facts

credible ● *adj* **1** capable of being believed; convincing: *there is no credible evidence* **2** trustworthy or reliable: *the latest claim is the only one to involve a credible witness* **credibility** *n*
WORD ORIGIN Latin *credere* to believe

credit ● *n* **1 a** the system of allowing

ludicrous, irresponsible, unrealistic, unwise, senseless, preposterous, potty (*Brit informal*), short-sighted, unworkable, foolhardy, idiotic, nonsensical, half-baked (*informal*), inane, fatuous, ill-conceived, quixotic, imprudent, impracticable, cockeyed (*informal*), cockamamie (*slang, chiefly US*), porangi (*NZ*)
OPPOSITE: sensible
4 = insane, mad, unbalanced, deranged, touched, cracked (*slang*), mental (*slang*), nuts (*slang*), barking (*slang*), daft (*informal*), batty (*slang*), crazed, lunatic, demented, cuckoo (*informal*), barmy (*slang*), off-the-wall (*slang*), off the air (*Austral slang*), nutty (*slang*), potty (*Brit informal*), berserk, delirious, bonkers (*slang, chiefly Brit*), idiotic, unhinged, loopy (*informal*), crackpot (*informal*), out to lunch (*informal*), round the bend (*slang*), barking mad (*slang*), out of your mind, maniacal, not all there (*informal*), doolally (*slang*), off your head (*slang*), off your trolley (*slang*), round the twist (*Brit slang*), up the pole (*informal*), of unsound mind, not right in the head, off your rocker (*slang*), not the full shilling (*informal*), a bit lacking upstairs (*informal*), as daft as a brush (*informal, chiefly Brit*), mad as a hatter, mad as a March hare, nutty as a fruitcake (*slang*), porangi (*NZ*) **OPPOSITE:** sane

cream *n* **2 = lotion**, ointment, oil, essence, cosmetic, paste, emulsion, salve, liniment, unguent **4 = best**, elite, prime, pick, flower, the crème de la crème ▷*adj* **6 = off-white**, ivory, yellowish-white*see:*

crease *n* **1 = fold**, ruck, line, tuck, ridge, groove, pucker, corrugation **2 = wrinkle**, line, crow's-foot ▷*vb* **4a = crumple**, rumple, pucker, crinkle, fold, ridge, double up, crimp, ruck up, corrugate **4b = wrinkle**, crumple, screw up

create *vb* **1 = make**, form, produce, develop, design, generate, invent, coin, compose, devise, initiate, hatch, originate, formulate, give birth to, spawn, dream up (*informal*), concoct, beget, give life to, bring into being *or* existence **OPPOSITE:** destroy **2 = cause**, lead to, occasion, bring about **3 = appoint**, make, found, establish, set up, invest, install, constitute

creation *n* **1a = making**, generation, formation, conception, genesis **1b = setting up**, development, production, institution, foundation, constitution, establishment, formation, laying down, inception, origination **2a = universe**, world, life, nature, cosmos, natural world, living world, all living things **2b = invention**, production, concept, achievement, brainchild (*informal*), concoction, handiwork, pièce de résistance (*French*), magnum opus, chef-d'oeuvre (*French*)

creative *adj* **2 = imaginative**, gifted, artistic, inventive, original, inspired, clever, productive, fertile, ingenious, visionary

creator *n* **= maker**, father, author, framer, designer, architect, inventor, originator, initiator, begetter

creature *n* **1 = living thing**, being, animal, beast, brute, critter (*US dialect*), quadruped, dumb animal, lower animal **2 = person**, man, woman, individual, character, fellow, soul, human being, mortal, body

credentials *pl n* **1 = qualifications**, ability, skill, capacity, fitness, attribute, capability, endowment(s), accomplishment, eligibility, aptitude, suitability **2 = certification**, document, reference(s), papers, title, card, licence, recommendation, passport, warrant, voucher, deed, testament, diploma, testimonial, authorization, missive, letters of credence, attestation, letter of recommendation *or* introduction

credible *adj* **1 = believable**, possible, likely, reasonable, probable, plausible, conceivable, imaginable, tenable, verisimilar
OPPOSITE: unbelievable
2 = reliable, honest, dependable, trustworthy, sincere, trusty
OPPOSITE: unreliable

credit *n* **6 = praise**, honour, recognition, glory, thanks, approval, fame, tribute, merit, acclaim,

DICTIONARY

customers to receive goods or services before payment **b** the time allowed for paying for such goods or services **2** reputation for trustworthiness in paying debts **3 a** the positive balance in a person's bank account **b** the sum of money that a bank makes available to a client in excess of any deposit **4** a sum of money or equivalent purchasing power, available for a person's use **5** *accounting* **a** acknowledgment of a sum of money by entry on the right-hand side of an account **b** an entry or total of entries on this side **6** praise or approval, as for an achievement or quality: *you must give him credit for his perseverance* **7** a person or thing who is a source of praise or approval: *he is a credit to his family* **8** influence or reputation based on the good opinion of others: *he acquired credit within the community* **9** belief or confidence in someone or something: *this theory is now gaining credit among the scientific community* **10** *education* **a** distinction awarded to an examination candidate obtaining good marks **b** certification that a section of an examination syllabus has been satisfactorily completed **11 on credit** with payment to be made at a future date ▹*vb* **-iting, -ited 12** *accounting* **a** to enter (an item) as a credit in an account **b** to acknowledge (a payer) by making such an entry **13 credit with** to attribute to: *credit us with some intelligence* **14** to believe ▸See also **credits**
WORD ORIGIN Latin *credere* to believe

creditable *adj* deserving praise or honour **creditably** *adv*

credit account *n Brit* a credit system in which shops allow customers to obtain goods and services before payment

credit card *n* a card issued by banks or shops, allowing the holder to buy on credit

credit crunch *n* a period during which there is a sudden reduction in the availability of credit from banks, mortgage lenders, etc.

creditor *n* a person or company to whom money is owed

credit rating *n* an evaluation of the ability of a person or business to repay money lent

credits *pl n* a list of people responsible for the production of a film, programme, or record

creditworthy *adj* (of a person or a business) regarded as deserving credit on the basis of earning power and previous record of debt repayment **creditworthiness** *n*

credo *n, pl* **-dos** a creed

credulity *n* willingness to believe something on little evidence

credulous *adj* **1** too willing to believe: *he has convinced only a few credulous American intellectuals* **2** arising from or showing credulity: *credulous optimism*
WORD ORIGIN Latin *credere* to believe

creed ❶ *n* **1** a system of beliefs or principles **2** a formal statement of the essential parts of Christian belief
WORD ORIGIN Latin *credo* I believe

Creed *n* **Frederick** 1871–1957, Canadian inventor, resident in Scotland from 1897, noted for his invention of the teleprinter, first used in 1912

creek ❶ *n* **1** a narrow inlet or bay **2** *US, Canad, Austral & NZ* a small stream or tributary **3 up the creek** *slang* in a difficult position
WORD ORIGIN Old Norse *kriki* nook

creel *n* a wickerwork basket used by fishermen
WORD ORIGIN Scots

creep ❶ *vb* **creeping, crept 1** to move quietly and cautiously **2** to crawl with the body near to or touching the ground **3** to have the sensation of something crawling over the skin, from fear or disgust: *she makes my flesh creep* **4** (of plants) to grow along the ground or over rocks ▹*n* **5** a creeping movement **6** *slang* an obnoxious or servile person
WORD ORIGIN Old English *crēopan*

creeper *n* **1** a plant, such as ivy, that grows by creeping **2** *US & Canad* ▸same as **tree creeper**

creeps ❶ *pl n* **give someone the creeps** *informal* to give someone a feeling of fear or disgust

creepy *adj* **creepier, creepiest** *informal* causing a feeling of fear or disgust **creepiness** *n*

creepy-crawly *n, pl* **-crawlies** *Brit informal* a small crawling creature

cremate *vb* **-mating, -mated** to burn (a corpse) to ash **cremation** *n*
WORD ORIGIN Latin *cremare*

crematorium *n, pl* **-riums** *or* **-ria** a building where corpses are cremated

crème de la crème *n* the very best: *the crème de la crème of cities*
WORD ORIGIN French

crème de menthe *n* a liqueur flavoured with peppermint
WORD ORIGIN French

crenellated *or US* **crenelated** *adj* having battlements **crenellation** *or US* **crenelation** *n*
WORD ORIGIN Late Latin *crena* a notch

creole *n* **1** a language developed from a mixture of different languages which has become the main language of a place ▹*adj* **2** of or relating to a creole
WORD ORIGIN Spanish

Creole *n* **1** (in the West Indies and Latin America) a native-born person of mixed European and African descent **2** (in the Gulf States of the US) a native-born person of French descent **3** the French creole spoken in the Gulf States ▹*adj* **4** of or relating to any of these peoples: *Creole cooking*

creosote *n* **1** a thick dark liquid made from coal tar and used for preserving wood **2** a colourless liquid made from wood tar and used as an antiseptic ▹*vb* **-soting, -soted 3** to treat with creosote
WORD ORIGIN Greek *kreas* flesh + *sōtēr* preserver

crepe (**krayp**) *n* **1** a thin light fabric with a crinkled texture **2** a very thin pancake, often folded around a filling **3** a type of rubber with a wrinkled surface, used for the soles of shoes
WORD ORIGIN French

crepe paper *n* paper with a crinkled texture, used for decorations

crept *vb* ▸the past of **creep**

crepuscular *adj* **1** of or like twilight **2** (of animals) active at twilight
WORD ORIGIN Latin *crepusculum* dusk

Cres. Crescent

crescendo (krish-end-oh) *n, pl* **-dos 1** a gradual increase in loudness **2** a musical passage that gradually gets louder ▹*adv* **3** gradually getting louder
WORD ORIGIN Italian

THESAURUS

acknowledgment, kudos, commendation, Brownie points **7 = source of satisfaction** *or* **pride**, asset, honour, feather in your cap **8 = prestige**, reputation, standing, position, character, influence, regard, status, esteem, clout *(informal)*, good name, estimation, repute **9 = belief**, trust, confidence, faith, reliance, credence ▹*vb* **13 credit someone with something = attribute to**, assign to, ascribe to, accredit to, impute to, chalk up to *(informal)* **14 = believe**, rely on, have faith in, trust, buy *(slang)*, accept, depend on, swallow *(informal)*, fall for, bank on

creed *n* **1 = belief**, principles, profession *(of faith)*, doctrine, canon, persuasion, dogma, tenet, credo, catechism, articles of faith

creek *n* **1 = inlet**, bay, cove, bight, firth *or* frith *(Scot)* **2** *(US, Canad, Austral & NZ)* **= stream**, brook, tributary, bayou, rivulet, watercourse, streamlet, runnel

creep *vb* **1 = sneak**, steal, tiptoe, slink, skulk, approach unnoticed ▹*n* **6** *(slang)* **= bootlicker** *(informal)*, sneak, sycophant, crawler *(slang)*, toady

creeps *pl n* **give someone the creeps** *(informal)* **= disgust**, frighten, scare, repel, repulse, make your hair stand on end, make you squirm

crescent ❶ *n* **1** the curved shape of the moon when in its first or last quarter **2** *chiefly Brit & NZ* a crescent-shaped street ▹*adj* **3** crescent-shaped
WORD ORIGIN Latin *crescere* to grow

cress *n* a plant with strong-tasting leaves, used in salads and as a garnish
WORD ORIGIN Old English *cressa*

Cressent *n* **Charles** 1685–1768, French cabinetmaker, noted esp. for his marquetry using coloured woods

crest ❶ *n* **1** the top of a mountain, hill, or wave **2** a tuft or growth of feathers or skin on the top of a bird's or animal's head **3** a heraldic design or figure used on a coat of arms and elsewhere **4** an ornamental plume or emblem on top of a helmet ▹*vb* **5** to come or rise to a high point **6** to lie at the top of **7** to reach the top of (a hill or wave) **crested** *adj*
WORD ORIGIN Latin *crista*

crestfallen *adj* disappointed or disheartened

Cretaceous *adj geol* of the period of geological time about 135 million years ago, at the end of which the dinosaurs died out
WORD ORIGIN Latin *creta* chalk

cretin *n* **1** *informal* a very stupid person **2** *no longer in technical use* a person who is mentally handicapped and physically deformed because of a thyroid deficiency **cretinism** *n* **cretinous** *adj*
WORD ORIGIN French from Latin *Christianus* Christian, alluding to the humanity of such people despite their handicaps

cretonne *n* a heavy printed cotton or linen fabric, used in furnishings
WORD ORIGIN French

crevasse *n* a deep open crack in a glacier
WORD ORIGIN French

crevice *n* a narrow crack or gap in rock
WORD ORIGIN Latin *crepare* to crack

crew¹ ❶ *n* **1** the people who man a ship or aircraft **2** a group of people working together: *a film crew* **3** *informal* any group of people ▹*vb* **4** to serve as a crew member on a ship or boat
WORD ORIGIN Middle English *crue* reinforcement, from Latin *crescere* to increase

crew² *vb archaic* ▸a past of **crow²**

crew cut *n* a closely cut haircut for men

crewel *n* a loosely twisted worsted yarn, used in embroidery
crewelwork *n*
WORD ORIGIN origin unknown

crew neck *n* a plain round neckline
crew-neck *or* **crew-necked** *adj*

crib *n* **1** a piece of writing stolen from elsewhere **2** a translation or list of answers used by students, often dishonestly **3** a baby's cradle **4** a rack or manger for fodder **5** a model of the manger scene at Bethlehem **6** ▸short for **cribbage** **7** NZ a small holiday house ▹*vb* **cribbing, cribbed** **8** to copy (someone's work) dishonestly **9** to confine in a small space
WORD ORIGIN Old English *cribb*

cribbage *n* a card game for two to four players, who each try to win a set number of points before the others
WORD ORIGIN origin unknown

crib-wall *n* NZ a retaining wall built against an earth bank

Crichton *n* **1 James** 1560–82, Scottish scholar and writer, called *the Admirable Crichton* because of his talents **2 (John) Michael** 1942–2008, US novelist, screenwriter, and film director; his thrillers, many of which have been filmed, include *The Andromeda Strain* (1969), *Jurassic Park* (1990), and *Disclosure* (1994)

crick *informal n* **1** a painful muscle spasm or cramp in the neck or back ▹*vb* **2** to cause a crick in
WORD ORIGIN origin unknown

cricket¹ *n* **1** a game played by two teams of eleven players using a ball, bats, and wickets **2** **not cricket** *informal* not fair play **cricketer** *n*
WORD ORIGIN Old French *criquet* wicket

cricket² *n* a jumping insect like a grasshopper, which produces a chirping sound by rubbing together its forewings
WORD ORIGIN Old French *criquer* to creak, imitative

cried *vb* ▸the past of **cry**

crier *n* an official who makes public announcements

crime ❶ *n* **1** an act prohibited and punished by law **2** unlawful acts collectively **3** *informal* a disgraceful act: *to be a woman writing music is neither a crime against nature nor a freakish rarity*
WORD ORIGIN Latin *crimen*

criminal ❶ *n* **1** a person guilty of a crime ▹*adj* **2** of or relating to crime or its punishment **3** *informal* senseless or disgraceful **criminally** *adv* **criminality** *n*

criminalize *or* **-ise** *vb* **-izing, -ized** *or* **-ising, -ised** **1** to make (an action or activity) criminal **2** to treat (a person) as a criminal

criminology *n* the scientific study of crime **criminologist** *n*
WORD ORIGIN Latin *crimen* crime + -LOGY

crimp *vb* **1** to fold or press into ridges **2** to curl (hair) tightly with curling tongs **3** *chiefly US informal* to restrict or hinder: *a slowdown in the US economy could crimp some big Swedish concerns' profits* ▹*n* **4** the act or result of crimping
WORD ORIGIN Old English *crympan*

Crimplene *n trademark* a crease-resistant synthetic fabric

crimson *adj* deep purplish-red
WORD ORIGIN Arabic *qirmizi* kermes (dried bodies of insects used to make a red dye)

cringe *vb* **cringing, cringed** **1** to shrink or flinch in fear: *he cringed and shrank against the wall* **2** to behave in a submissive or timid way: *women who cringe before abusive husbands* **3** *informal* to be very embarrassed: *I cringe every time I see that old photo of me* ▹*n* **4** the act of cringing
WORD ORIGIN Old English *cringan* to yield in battle

crinkle *vb* **-kling, -kled** **1** to become slightly creased or folded ▹*n* **2** a crease or fold **crinkly** *adj*
WORD ORIGIN Old English *crincan* to bend

THESAURUS

crescent *n* **1 = meniscus**, sickle, new moon, half-moon, old moon, sickle-shape

crest *n* **1 = top**, summit, peak, ridge, highest point, pinnacle, apex, head, crown, height **2 = tuft**, crown, comb, plume, mane, tassel, topknot, cockscomb **3 = emblem**, badge, symbol, insignia, charge, bearings, device

crew¹ *n* **1 = (ship's) company**, hands, (ship's) complement **2 = team**, company, party, squad, gang, corps, working party, posse **3** *(informal)* **= crowd**, set, lot, bunch *(informal)*, band, troop, pack, camp, gang, mob, herd, swarm, company, horde, posse *(informal)*, assemblage

crime *n* **1 = offence**, job *(informal)*, wrong, fault, outrage, atrocity, violation, trespass, felony, misdemeanour, misdeed, transgression, unlawful act **2 = lawbreaking**, corruption, delinquency, illegality, wrong, vice, sin, guilt, misconduct, wrongdoing, wickedness, iniquity, villainy, unrighteousness, malefaction

criminal *n* **1 = lawbreaker**, convict, con *(slang)*, offender, crook *(informal)*, lag *(slang)*, villain, culprit, sinner, delinquent, felon, con man *(informal)*, rorter *(Austral slang)*, jailbird, malefactor, evildoer, transgressor, skelm *(S African)*, rogue trader, perp *(US & Canad informal)* ▹*adj* **2 = unlawful**, illicit, lawless, wrong, illegal, corrupt, crooked *(informal)*, vicious, immoral, wicked, culpable, under-the-table, villainous, nefarious, iniquitous, indictable, felonious, bent *(slang)* **OPPOSITE:** lawful **3** *(informal)* **= disgraceful**, ridiculous, foolish, senseless, scandalous, preposterous, deplorable

DICTIONARY

crinoline *n* a petticoat stiffened with hoops to make the skirt stand out
WORD ORIGIN Latin *crinis* hair + *lino* flax

Crippen *n* **Hawley Harvey,** known as *Doctor Crippen*. 1862–1910, US doctor living in England: executed for poisoning his wife; the first criminal to be apprehended by the use of radiotelegraphy

cripple ❶ *n offensive* **1** a person who is lame or disabled **2** a person with a mental or social problem: *an emotional cripple* ▷ *vb* **-pling, -pled 3** to make a cripple of **4** to damage (something) **crippled** *adj* **crippling** *adj*
WORD ORIGIN Old English *crypel*

Cripps *n* Sir (**Richard**) **Stafford** 1889–1952, British Labour statesman; Chancellor of the Exchequer (1947–50)

crisis ❶ *n, pl* **-ses 1** a crucial stage or turning point in the course of anything **2** a time of extreme trouble or danger
WORD ORIGIN Greek *krisis* decision

crisp ❶ *adj* **1** fresh and firm: *a crisp green salad* **2** dry and brittle: *bake until crisp and golden brown* **3** clean and neat: *crisp white cotton* **4** (of weather) cold but invigorating: *a crisp autumn day* **5** clear and sharp: *the telescope is designed to provide the first crisp images of distant galaxies* **6** lively or brisk: *the service is crisp and efficient* ▷ *n* **7** *Brit* a very thin slice of potato fried till crunchy ▷ *vb* **8** to make or become crisp **crisply** *adv* **crispness** *n*
WORD ORIGIN Latin *crispus* curled

crispbread *n* a thin dry biscuit made of wheat or rye

Crispi *n* **Francesco** 1819–1901, Italian statesman; premier (1887–91; 1893–96)

Crispin *n* **Saint,** 3rd century AD, legendary Roman Christian martyr, with his brother **Crispinian**: they are the patron saints of shoemakers. Feast day: Oct 25

crispy *adj* **crispier, crispiest** hard and crunchy **crispiness** *n*

crisscross *vb* **1** to move in or mark with a crosswise pattern ▷ *adj* **2** (of lines) crossing one another in different directions

criterion ❶ *n, pl* **-ria** *or* **-rions** a standard by which something can be judged or decided
WORD ORIGIN Greek *kritērion*

critic ❶ *n* **1** a professional judge of art, music, or literature **2** a person who finds fault and criticizes
WORD ORIGIN Greek *kritēs* judge

critical ❶ *adj* **1** very important or dangerous: *this was a critical moment in her career* **2** so seriously ill or injured as to be in danger of dying: *he is in a critical condition in hospital* **3** fault-finding or disparaging: *the article is highly critical of the government* **4** examining and judging analytically and without bias: *he submitted the plans to critical examination* **5** of a critic or criticism **6** *physics* denoting a constant value at which the properties of a system undergo an abrupt change: *the critical temperature above which the material loses its superconductivity* **7** (of a nuclear power station or reactor) having reached a state in which a nuclear chain reaction becomes self-sustaining **critically** *adv*

criticism ❶ *n* **1** fault-finding or censure **2** an analysis of a work of art or literature **3** the occupation of a critic **4** a work that sets out to analyse

criticize ❶ *or* **-cise** *vb* **-cizing, -cized** *or* **-cising, -cised 1** to find fault with **2** to analyse (something)

critique *n* **1** a critical essay or commentary **2** the act or art of criticizing
WORD ORIGIN French

croak *vb* **1** (of a frog or crow) to make a low hoarse cry **2** to utter or speak with a croak **3** *slang* to die ▷ *n* **4** a low hoarse sound **croaky** *adj*
WORD ORIGIN Old English *crācettan*

Croatian (kroh-ay-shun) *adj* **1** of Croatia ▷ *n* **2** a person from Croatia **3** the dialect of Serbo-Croat spoken in Croatia

Croce *n* **Benedetto** 1866–1952, Italian philosopher, critic, and statesman: an opponent of Fascism, he helped re-establish liberalism in postwar Italy

crochet (kroh-shay) *vb* **-cheting, -cheted 1** to make (a piece of needlework) by looping and intertwining thread with a hooked needle ▷ *n* **2** work made by crocheting
WORD ORIGIN French: small hook

crock[1] *n* an earthenware pot or jar
WORD ORIGIN Old English *crocc* pot

crock[2] *n* **old crock** *Brit, Austral & NZ slang* a person or thing that is old or broken-down
WORD ORIGIN Scots

crockery *n* china dishes or earthenware vessels collectively

crocodile *n* **1** a large amphibious tropical reptile **2** *Brit, Austral & NZ informal* a line of people, esp. schoolchildren, walking two by two
WORD ORIGIN Greek *krokodeilos* lizard

crocodile tears *pl n* an insincere show of grief
WORD ORIGIN from the belief that crocodiles wept over their prey to lure further victims

crocus *n, pl* **-cuses** a plant with white,

THESAURUS

cripple *vb* **3 = disable**, paralyse, lame, debilitate, mutilate, maim, incapacitate, enfeeble, weaken, hamstring **4 = damage**, destroy, ruin, bring to a standstill, halt, spoil, cramp, impair, put paid to, vitiate, put out of action **OPPOSITE:** help

crisis *n* **1 = critical point**, climax, point of no return, height, confrontation, crunch *(informal)*, turning point, culmination, crux, moment of truth, climacteric, tipping point **2 = emergency**, plight, catastrophe, predicament, pass, trouble, disaster, mess, dilemma, strait, deep water, meltdown *(informal)*, extremity, quandary, dire straits, exigency, critical situation

crisp *adj* **1, 2 = firm**, crunchy, crispy, crumbly, fresh, brittle, unwilted **OPPOSITE:** soft **3 = clean**, smart, trim, neat, tidy, orderly, spruce, snappy, clean-cut, well-groomed, well-pressed **4 = bracing**, fresh, refreshing, brisk, invigorating **OPPOSITE:** warm

criterion *n* **= standard**, test, rule, measure, principle, proof, par, norm, canon, gauge, yardstick, touchstone, bench mark

critic *n* **1 = judge**, authority, expert, analyst, commentator, pundit, reviewer, connoisseur, arbiter, expositor **2 = fault-finder**, attacker, detractor, knocker *(informal)*

critical *adj* **1 = crucial**, decisive, momentous, deciding, pressing, serious, vital, psychological, urgent, all-important, pivotal, high-priority, now or never **OPPOSITE:** unimportant **2 = grave**, serious, dangerous, acute, risky, hairy *(slang)*, precarious, perilous **OPPOSITE:** safe **3 = disparaging**, disapproving, scathing, derogatory, nit-picking *(informal)*, censorious, cavilling, fault-finding, captious, carping, niggling, nit-picky *(informal)* **OPPOSITE:** complimentary **4 = analytical**, penetrating, discriminating, discerning, diagnostic, perceptive, judicious, accurate, precise **OPPOSITE:** undiscriminating

criticism *n* **1 = fault-finding**, censure, disapproval, disparagement, stick *(slang)*, knocking *(informal)*, panning *(informal)*, slamming *(slang)*, slating *(informal)*, flak *(informal)*, slagging *(slang)*, strictures, bad press, denigration, brickbats *(informal)*, character assassination, critical remarks, animadversion **2 = analysis**, review, notice, assessment, judgment, commentary, evaluation, appreciation, appraisal, critique, elucidation

criticize *vb* **1 = find fault with**, censure, disapprove of, knock *(informal)*, blast, pan *(informal)*, condemn, slam *(slang)*, carp, put

DICTIONARY

yellow, or purple flowers in spring
WORD ORIGIN Greek *krokos* saffron

croft *n* a small farm worked by one family in Scotland **crofter** *n* **crofting** *adj, n*
WORD ORIGIN Old English

croissant (**krwah**-son) *n* a flaky crescent-shaped bread roll
WORD ORIGIN French

Crome *n* **John,** known as *Old Crome.* 1768–1821, English landscape painter and etcher

cromlech *n Brit* **1** a circle of prehistoric standing stones **2** *no longer in technical use* a dolmen
WORD ORIGIN Welsh

Crompton *n* **1 Richmal**, full name *Richmal Crompton Lamburn*. 1890–1969, British children's author, best known for her *Just William* stories **2 Samuel** 1753–1827, British inventor of the spinning mule (1779)

crone *n* a witchlike old woman
WORD ORIGIN Old French *carogne* carrion

Cronin *n* **1 A(rchibald) J(oseph)** 1896–1981, British novelist and physician. His works include *Hatter's Castle* (1931), *The Judas Tree* (1961), and *Dr Finlay's Casebook*, a TV series based on his medical experiences **2 James Watson** born 1931, US physicist; shared the Nobel prize for physics (1980) for his work on parity conservation in weak interactions

Cronje *n* **Hansie**, full name *Wessel Johannes Cronje* (1969–2002); South African cricketer. He captained South Africa (1994–2000); banned for life from cricket for match-fixing in 2001

crony *n, pl* **-nies** a close friend
WORD ORIGIN Greek *khronios* long-lasting

crook ❶ *n* **1** *informal* a dishonest person **2** a bent or curved place or thing: *she held the puppy in the crook of her arm* **3** a bishop's or shepherd's staff with a hooked end ▷ *adj* **4** *Austral & NZ informal* **a** ill **b** of poor quality **c** unpleasant; bad **5 go (off) crook** *Austral & NZ informal* to lose one's temper **6 go crook at** *or* **on** *Austral & NZ informal* to rebuke or upbraid ▷ *vb* **7** to bend or curve
WORD ORIGIN Old Norse *krokr* hook

crooked ❶ *adj* **1** bent or twisted **2** set at an angle **3** *informal* dishonest or illegal **crookedly** *adv* **crookedness** *n*

croon *vb* to sing, hum, or speak in a soft low tone **crooner** *n*
WORD ORIGIN Middle Dutch *crōnen* to groan

crop ❶ *n* **1** a cultivated plant, such as a cereal, vegetable, or fruit plant **2** the season's total yield of farm produce **3** any group of things appearing at one time: *a remarkable crop of new Scottish plays* **4** the handle of a whip **5** ▸ short for **riding crop** **6** a pouchlike part of the gullet of a bird, in which food is stored or prepared for digestion **7** a short cropped hairstyle ▷ *vb* **cropping, cropped** **8** to cut (something) very short **9** to produce or harvest as a crop **10** (of animals) to feed on (grass) **11** to clip part of (the ear or ears) of (an animal), esp. for identification ▸ See also **crop up**
WORD ORIGIN Old English *cropp*

crop circle *n* a pattern made up of ring shapes formed by the unexplained flattening of cereals growing in a field

cropper *n* **come a cropper** *informal* **a** to fail completely **b** to fall heavily

crop top *n* a short T-shirt or vest that reveals the wearer's midriff

crop up ❶ *vb informal* to occur or appear unexpectedly

croquet (**kroh**-kay) *n* a game played on a lawn in which balls are hit through hoops
WORD ORIGIN French

croquette (kroh-**kett**) *n* a fried cake of mashed potato, meat, or fish
WORD ORIGIN French

crosier *n* ▸ same as **crozier**

Crosland *n* **Anthony** 1918–77, British Labour politician and socialist theorist, author of *The Future of Socialism* (1957)

cross ❶ *vb* **1** to move or go across (something): *she crossed the street to the gallery* **2** to meet and pass: *further south, the way is crossed by Brewer Street* **3** *Brit & NZ* to draw two parallel lines across (a cheque) and so make it payable only into a bank account **4** to mark with a cross or crosses **5** to cancel or delete with a cross or with lines: *she crossed out the first three words* **6** to place across or crosswise: *he sat down and crossed his legs* **7** to make the sign of the cross upon as a blessing **8** to annoy or anger someone by challenging or opposing their wishes and plans **9** to interbreed or cross-fertilize **10** *football* to pass (the ball) from a wing to the middle of the field **11** (of each of two letters in the post) to be sent before the other is received **12** (of telephone lines) to interfere with each other so that several callers are connected together at one time **13 cross one's fingers** to fold one finger across another in the hope of bringing good luck **14 cross one's heart** to promise by making the sign of a cross over one's heart **15 cross one's mind** to occur to one briefly or suddenly ▷ *n* **16** a structure, symbol, or mark consisting of two intersecting lines

C

THESAURUS

down, slate (*informal*), have a go (at) (*informal*), disparage, tear into (*informal*), diss (*slang, chiefly US*), nag at, lambast(e), pick holes in, pick to pieces, give (someone *or* something) a bad press, pass strictures upon, nit-pick (*informal*) **OPPOSITE:** praise

crook *n* **1** (*informal*) **= criminal**, rogue, cheat, thief, shark, lag (*slang*), villain, robber, racketeer, fraudster, swindler, knave (*archaic*), grifter (*slang, chiefly US & Canad*), chiseller (*informal*), skelm (*S African*) ▷ *adj* **5 go (off) crook** (*Austral & NZ informal*) **= lose your temper**, be furious, rage, go mad, lose it (*informal*), seethe, crack up (*informal*), see red (*informal*), lose the plot (*informal*), go ballistic (*slang, chiefly US*), blow a fuse (*slang, chiefly US*), fly off the handle (*informal*), be incandescent, go off the deep end (*informal*), throw a fit (*informal*), wig out (*slang*), go up the wall (*slang*), blow your top, lose your rag (*slang*), be beside yourself, flip your lid (*slang*)

crooked *adj* **1 = bent**, twisted, bowed, curved, irregular, warped, deviating, out of shape, misshapen **OPPOSITE:** straight **2 = at an angle**, angled, tilted, to one side, uneven, slanted, slanting, squint, awry, lopsided, askew, asymmetric, off-centre, skewwhiff (*Brit informal*), unsymmetrical **3** (*informal*) **= dishonest**, criminal, illegal, corrupt, dubious, questionable, unlawful, shady (*informal*), fraudulent, unscrupulous, under-the-table, bent (*slang*), shifty, deceitful, underhand, unprincipled, dishonourable, nefarious, knavish **OPPOSITE:** honest

crop *n* **2 = yield**, produce, gathering, fruits, harvest, vintage, reaping, season's growth ▷ *vb* **8 = cut**, reduce, trim, clip, dock, prune, shorten, shear, snip, pare, lop **10 = graze**, eat, browse, feed on, nibble

crop up *vb* (*informal*) **= happen**, appear, emerge, occur, arise, turn up, spring up

cross *vb* **1a = go across**, pass over, traverse, cut across, move across, travel across **1b = span**, bridge, ford, go across, extend over **2 = intersect**, meet, intertwine, crisscross **8 = oppose**, interfere with, hinder, obstruct, deny, block, resist, frustrate, foil, thwart, impede **9 = interbreed**, mix, blend, cross-pollinate, crossbreed, hybridize, cross-fertilize, intercross ▷ *n* **18 = crucifix** **24 = mixture**, combination, blend, amalgam, amalgamation **25 = trouble**, worry, trial, load, burden, grief, misery, woe, misfortune, affliction, tribulation ▷ *adj* **27 = angry**, impatient, irritable, annoyed, put out, hacked (off) (*informal*), crusty, snappy, grumpy, vexed, sullen, surly,

DICTIONARY

17 an upright post with a bar across it, used in ancient times as a means of execution **18** a representation of the Cross on which Jesus Christ was executed as an emblem of Christianity **19** a symbol (×) used as a signature or error mark **20 the sign of the cross** a sign made with the hand by some Christians to represent the Cross **21** a medal or monument in the shape of a cross **22** the place in a town or village where a cross has been set up **23** *biol* **a** the process of crossing; hybridization **b** a hybrid **24** a mixture of two things **25** a hindrance or misfortune: *we've all got our own cross to bear* **26** *football* a pass of the ball from a wing to the middle of the field ▷*adj* **27** angry **28** lying or placed across: *a cross beam* **crossly** *adv* **crossness** *n*
WORD ORIGIN Latin *crux*

Cross *n* **the Cross** **a** the cross on which Jesus Christ was crucified **b** Christianity

cross- *combining form* **1** indicating action from one individual or group to another: *cross-cultural; cross-refer* **2** indicating movement or position across something: *crosscurrent; crosstalk* **3** indicating a crosslike figure or intersection: *crossbones*

Cross[1] *n* **the Cross** **1** the cross on which Jesus Christ was crucified **2** the Crucifixion of Jesus

Cross[2] *n* **Richard Assheton**, 1st Viscount. 1823–1914, British Conservative statesman, home secretary (1874–80); noted for reforms affecting housing, public health, and the employment of women and children in factories

crossbar *n* **1** a horizontal beam across a pair of goalposts **2** the horizontal bar on a man's bicycle

cross-bench *n* *Brit* a seat in Parliament for a member belonging to neither the government nor the opposition **cross-bencher** *n*

crossbill *n* a finch that has a bill with crossed tips

crossbow *n* a weapon consisting of a bow fixed across a wooden stock, which releases an arrow when the trigger is pulled

crossbreed *vb* **-breeding, -bred** **1** to produce (a hybrid animal or plant) by crossing two different species ▷*n* **2** a hybrid animal or plant

crosscheck *vb* **1** to check the accuracy of (something) by using a different method ▷*n* **2** a crosschecking

cross-country *adj, adv* **1** by way of open country or fields ▷*n* **2** a long race held over open ground

crosscut *vb* **-cutting, -cut** **1** to cut across ▷*adj* **2** cut across ▷*n* **3** a transverse cut or course

cross-examine *vb* **-examining, -examined** **1** *law* to question (a witness for the opposing side) in order to check his or her testimony **2** to question closely or relentlessly **cross-examination** *n* **cross-examiner** *n*

cross-eyed *adj* with one or both eyes turning inwards towards the nose

cross-fertilize *or* **-lise** *vb* **-lizing, -lized** *or* **-lising, -lised** to fertilize (an animal or plant) by fusion of male and female reproductive cells from different individuals of the same species **cross-fertilization** *or* **-lisation** *n*

crossfire *n* **1** *mil* gunfire crossing another line of fire **2** a lively exchange of ideas or opinions

crosshatch *vb* *drawing* to shade with two or more sets of parallel lines that cross one another

crossing *n* **1** a place where a street, railway, or river may be crossed **2** the place where one thing crosses another **3** a journey across water

cross-legged *adj* sitting with the legs bent and the knees pointing outwards

Crossman *n* **Richard** (**Howard Stafford**) 1907–74, British Labour politician. His diaries, published posthumously as the *Crossman Papers* (1975), revealed details of cabinet discussions

crosspatch *n* *informal* a bad-tempered person
WORD ORIGIN *cross* + obsolete *patch* fool

cross-ply *adj* (of a tyre) having the fabric cords in the outer casing running diagonally to stiffen the sidewalls

cross-purposes *pl n* **at cross-purposes** misunderstanding each other in a discussion

cross-question *vb* to cross-examine

cross-refer *vb* **-referring, -referred** to refer from one part of something to another

cross-reference *n* **1** a reference within a text to another part of the text ▷*vb* **-referencing, -referenced** **2** to cross-refer

crossroad *n* *US & Canad* **1** a road that crosses another road **2** a road that connects one main road to another

crossroads *n* **1** the point at which roads cross one another **2 at the crossroads** at the point at which an important choice has to be made

cross section *n* **1** *maths* a surface formed by cutting across a solid, usually at right angles to its longest axis **2** a random sample regarded as representative: *a cross section of society* **cross-sectional** *adj*

cross-stitch *n* an embroidery stitch made from two crossing stitches

crosstalk *n* **1** *Brit* rapid or witty talk **2** unwanted signals transferred between communication channels

crosswalk *n* *US & Canad* a place marked where pedestrians may cross a road

crosswise *or* **crossways** *adj* **1** across **2** in the shape of a cross ▷*adv* **3** across: *slice the celery crosswise* **4** in the shape of a cross

crossword puzzle *or* **crossword** *n* a puzzle in which vertically and horizontally crossing words suggested by clues are written into a grid of squares

crotch *n* **1** the forked part of the human body between the legs **2** the corresponding part of a pair of trousers or pants **3** any forked part formed by the joining of two things: *the crotch of the tree* **crotched** *adj*
WORD ORIGIN probably variant of CRUTCH

crotchet *n* *music* a note having the time value of a quarter of a semibreve
WORD ORIGIN Old French *crochet* little hook

crotchety *adj* *informal* bad-tempered

crouch ❶ *vb* **1** to bend low with the legs and body pulled close together ▷*n* **2** this position
WORD ORIGIN Old French *crochir* to become bent like a hook

croup[1] (**kroop**) *n* a throat disease of children, with a hoarse cough and laboured breathing
WORD ORIGIN Middle English: to cry hoarsely, probably imitative

croup[2] (**kroop**) *n* the hindquarters of a horse
WORD ORIGIN Old French *croupe*

croupier (**kroop-ee-ay**) *n* a person who collects bets and pays out winnings at a gambling table
WORD ORIGIN French

crouton *n* a small piece of fried or toasted bread served in soup
WORD ORIGIN French

crow[1] *n* **1** a large black bird with a harsh call **2 as the crow flies** in

THESAURUS

fractious, petulant, disagreeable, short, churlish, peeved (*informal*), ill-tempered, irascible, cantankerous, tetchy, ratty (*Brit & NZ informal*), tooshie (*Austral slang*), testy, fretful, waspish, in a bad mood, grouchy (*informal*), querulous, shirty (*slang, chiefly Brit*), peevish, splenetic, crotchety (*informal*), snappish, ill-humoured, captious, pettish, out of humour, hoha (*NZ*)
OPPOSITE: good-humoured

crouch *vb* **1 = bend down**, kneel, squat, stoop, bow, duck, hunch

crow *vb* **2 = gloat**, triumph, boast, swagger, brag, vaunt, bluster, exult, blow your own trumpet

crowd *n* **1 = multitude**, mass,

DICTIONARY

a straight line
WORD ORIGIN Old English *crāwa*
crow² vb **1** *past* **crowed** *or* **crew** (of a cock) to utter a shrill squawking sound **2** to boast about one's superiority **3** (of a baby) to utter cries of pleasure ▷ *n* **4** a crowing sound
WORD ORIGIN Old English *crāwan*
crowbar *n* a heavy iron bar used as a lever
crowd *n* **1** a large number of things or people gathered together **2** a particular group of people: *we got to know a French crowd from Lyons* **3 the crowd** the masses ▷ *vb* **4** to gather together in large numbers **5** to press together into a confined space **6** to fill or occupy fully **7** *informal* to make (someone) uncomfortable by coming too close **crowded** *adj*
WORD ORIGIN Old English *crūdan*
crowd-pleaser *n* a person or thing that appeals to a large proportion of an audience **crowd-pleasing** *adj*
Crowe *n* **Russell** born 1964, Australian film actor, born in New Zealand. His films include *LA Confidential* (1997), *Gladiator* (2000), for which he won an Oscar, *A Beautiful Mind* (2001), and *Master and Commander* (2003)
crown *n* **1** a monarch's ornamental headdress, usually made of gold and jewels **2** a wreath for the head, given as an honour **3** the highest or central point of something arched or curved: *the crown of the head* **4 a** the enamel-covered part of a tooth projecting beyond the gum **b** a substitute crown, usually of gold or porcelain, fitted over a decayed or broken tooth **5** a former British coin worth 25 pence **6** the outstanding quality or achievement: *the last piece is the crown of the evening* ▷ *vb* **7** to put a crown on the head of (someone) to proclaim him or her monarch **8** to put on the top of **9** to reward **10** to form the topmost part of **11** to put the finishing touch to (a series of events): *he crowned a superb display with three goals* **12** to attach a crown to (a tooth) **13** *Brit, Austral & NZ slang* to hit over the head **14** *draughts* to promote (a draught) to a king by placing another draught on top of it
WORD ORIGIN Greek *korōnē*
Crown *n* **the Crown** the power or institution of the monarchy
crown colony *n* a British colony controlled by the Crown
crown court *n* a local criminal court in England and Wales
Crown Derby *n* a type of fine porcelain made at Derby
crown jewels *pl n* the jewellery used by a sovereign on ceremonial occasions
crown-of-thorns *n* a starfish with a spiny outer covering that feeds on living coral
crown prince *n* the male heir to a sovereign throne **crown princess** *n*
crow's feet *pl n* wrinkles at the outer corners of the eye
crow's nest *n* a lookout platform fixed at the top of a ship's mast
crozier *or* **crosier** *n* a hooked staff carried by bishops as a symbol of office
WORD ORIGIN Old French *crossier* staff-bearer
crucial *adj* **1** of exceptional importance **2** *Brit slang* very good **crucially** *adv*
WORD ORIGIN Latin *crux* cross
cruciate *adj* shaped or arranged like a cross **cruciately** *adv*
WORD ORIGIN Latin *crux* cross
cruciate ligament *n anat* either of a pair of ligaments that cross each other in the knee
crucible *n* a pot in which metals or other substances are melted
WORD ORIGIN Medieval Latin *crucibulum* night lamp
crucifix *n* a model cross with a figure of Christ upon it
WORD ORIGIN Church Latin *crucifixus* the crucified Christ
crucifixion *n* a method of execution by fastening to a cross, normally by the hands and feet
Crucifixion *n* **1 the Crucifixion** the crucifying of Christ **2** a representation of this
cruciform *adj* shaped like a cross
crucify *vb* **-fies, -fying, -fied 1** to put to death by crucifixion **2** to treat cruelly **3** *slang* to defeat or ridicule totally
WORD ORIGIN Latin *crux* cross + *figere* to fasten
crud *n slang* a sticky or encrusted substance **cruddy** *adj*
WORD ORIGIN earlier form of CURD
crude *adj* **1** rough and simple: *crude farm implements* **2** tasteless or vulgar **3** in a natural or unrefined state ▷ *n* **4** ▸ short for **crude oil** > **crudely** *adv* **crudity** *or* **crudeness** *n*
WORD ORIGIN Latin *crudus* bloody, raw
Cruden *n* **Alexander** 1701–70, Scottish bookseller and compiler of a well-known biblical concordance (1737)
crude oil *n* unrefined petroleum
crudités (crew-dit-tay) *pl n* a selection of raw vegetables often served with a variety of dips before a meal
WORD ORIGIN French *crudité* rawness
cruel *adj* **1** deliberately causing pain without pity **2** causing pain or suffering **cruelly** *adv* **cruelty** *n*
WORD ORIGIN Latin *crudelis*
cruet *n* **1** a small container for pepper, salt, etc. at table **2** a set of such containers on a stand
WORD ORIGIN Old French *crue* flask
Cruft *n* **Charles** 1852–1938, British dog breeder, who organized the first (1886) of the annual dog shows known as Cruft's
Cruikshank *n* **George** 1792–1878, English illustrator and caricaturist

THESAURUS

assembly, throng, company, press, army, host, pack, mob, flock, herd, swarm, horde, rabble, concourse, bevy **2 = group**, set, lot, circle, gang, bunch *(informal)*, clique ▷ *vb* **4 = flock**, press, push, mass, collect, gather, stream, surge, cluster, muster, huddle, swarm, throng, congregate, foregather **5 = squeeze**, pack, pile, bundle, cram **6 = congest**, pack, cram
crown *n* **1 = coronet**, tiara, diadem, circlet, coronal *(poetic)*, chaplet **2 = laurel wreath**, trophy, distinction, prize, honour, garland, laurels, wreath, kudos **3 = high point**, head, top, tip, summit, crest, pinnacle, apex ▷ *vb* **7 = install**, invest, honour, dignify, ordain, inaugurate **8, 10 = top**, cap, be on top of, surmount **11 = cap**, finish, complete, perfect, fulfil, consummate, round off, put the finishing touch to, put the tin lid on, be the climax *or* culmination of **13** *(slang)* **= strike**, belt *(informal)*, bash, hit over the head, box, punch, cuff, biff *(slang)*, wallop
crucial *adj* **1a** *(informal)* **= vital**, important, pressing, essential, urgent, momentous, high-priority **1b = critical**, central, key, psychological, decisive, pivotal, now or never
crude *adj* **1a = rough**, undeveloped, basic, outline, unfinished, makeshift, sketchy, unformed **1b = simple**, rudimentary, basic, primitive, coarse, clumsy, rough-and-ready, rough-hewn **2 = vulgar**, dirty, rude, obscene, coarse, indecent, crass, tasteless, lewd, X-rated *(informal)*, boorish, smutty, uncouth, gross **OPPOSITE:** tasteful **3 = unrefined**, natural, raw, unprocessed, unpolished, unprepared **OPPOSITE:** processed
cruel *adj* **1 = brutal**, ruthless, callous, sadistic, inhumane, hard, fell *(archaic)*, severe, harsh, savage, grim, vicious, relentless, murderous, monstrous, unnatural, unkind, heartless, atrocious, inhuman, merciless, cold-blooded, malevolent, hellish, depraved, spiteful, brutish, bloodthirsty, remorseless, barbarous, pitiless, unfeeling, hard-hearted, stony-hearted **OPPOSITE:** kind **2 = bitter**, severe, painful, ruthless, traumatic, grievous, unrelenting, merciless, pitiless

DICTIONARY

C

cruise ❶ *n* **1** a sail taken for pleasure, stopping at various places ▹*vb* **cruising, cruised 2** to sail about from place to place for pleasure **3** (of a vehicle, aircraft, or ship) to travel at a moderate and efficient speed **4** to proceed steadily or easily: *they cruised into the final of the qualifying competition*
WORD ORIGIN Dutch *kruisen* to cross

cruise missile *n* a low-flying subsonic missile that is guided throughout its flight

cruiser *n* **1** a large fast warship armed with medium-calibre weapons **2** Also called: **cabin cruiser** a motorboat with a cabin

cruiserweight *n* a professional boxer weighing up to 195 pounds (88.5 kg)

crumb ❶ *n* **1** a small fragment of bread or other dry food **2** a small bit or scrap: *a crumb of comfort*
WORD ORIGIN Old English *cruma*

crumble ❶ *vb* **-bling, -bled 1** to break into crumbs or fragments **2** to fall apart or decay ▹*n* **3** a baked pudding consisting of stewed fruit with a crumbly topping: *rhubarb crumble* **crumbly** *adj* **crumbliness** *n*

crumby *adj* **crumbier, crumbiest 1** full of crumbs **2** ▸same as **crummy**

crummy *adj* **-mier, -miest** *slang* **1** of very bad quality: *a crummy hotel* **2** unwell: *I felt really crummy*
WORD ORIGIN variant spelling of *crumby*

crumpet *n* **1** a light soft yeast cake, eaten buttered **2** *chiefly Brit slang* sexually attractive women collectively
WORD ORIGIN origin unknown

crumple ❶ *vb* **-pling, -pled 1** to crush or become crushed into untidy wrinkles or creases **2** to collapse in an untidy heap: *her father lay crumpled on the floor* ▹*n* **3** an untidy crease or wrinkle **crumply** *adj*
WORD ORIGIN obsolete *crump* to bend

crunch ❶ *vb* **1** to bite or chew with a noisy crushing sound **2** to make a crisp or brittle sound ▹*n* **3** a crunching sound **4 the crunch** *informal* the critical moment or situation **crunchy** *adj* **crunchiness** *n*
WORD ORIGIN imitative

crupper *n* **1** a strap that passes from the back of a saddle under a horse's tail **2** the horse's rump
WORD ORIGIN Old French *crupiere*

crusade ❶ *n* **1** any of the medieval military expeditions undertaken by European Christians to recapture the Holy Land from the Muslims **2** a vigorous campaign in favour of a cause ▹*vb* **-sading, -saded 3** to take part in a crusade **crusader** *n*
WORD ORIGIN Latin *crux* cross

cruse *n* a small earthenware container for liquids
WORD ORIGIN Old English *crūse*

crush ❶ *vb* **1** to press or squeeze so as to injure, break, or put out of shape **2** to break or grind into small pieces **3** to control or subdue by force **4** to extract (liquid) by pressing: *crush a clove of garlic* **5** to defeat or humiliate utterly **6** to crowd together ▹*n* **7** a dense crowd **8** the act of crushing **9** *informal* an infatuation: *I had a teenage crush on my French teacher* **10** a drink made by crushing fruit: *orange crush*
WORD ORIGIN Old French *croissir*

crush barrier *n* a barrier put up to separate sections of large crowds and prevent crushing

crust ❶ *n* **1** the hard outer part of bread **2** the baked shell of a pie or tart **3** any hard outer layer: *a thin crust of snow* **4** the solid outer shell of the earth ▹*vb* **5** to cover with or form a crust
WORD ORIGIN Latin *crusta* hard surface, rind

crustacean *n* **1** an animal with a hard outer shell and several pairs of legs, which usually lives in water, such as a crab or lobster ▹*adj* **2** of crustaceans
WORD ORIGIN Latin *crusta* shell

crusty *adj* **crustier, crustiest 1** having a crust **2** rude or irritable **crustiness** *n*

crutch *n* **1** a long staff with a rest for the armpit, used by a lame person to support the weight of the body **2** something that supports **3** *Brit* ▸same as **crotch** (sense 1)
WORD ORIGIN Old English *crycc*

crutchings *pl n Austral & NZ* the wool clipped from a sheep's hindquarters

crux *n, pl* **cruxes** *or* **cruces** a crucial or decisive point
WORD ORIGIN Latin: cross

cry ❶ *vb* **cries, crying, cried 1** to shed tears **2** to make a loud vocal sound, usually to express pain or fear or to appeal for help **3** to utter loudly or shout **4** (of an animal or bird) to utter loud characteristic sounds **5 cry for** to appeal urgently for ▹*n, pl* **cries 6** a fit of weeping **7** the act or sound of crying **8** the characteristic utterance of an animal or bird **9** an urgent appeal: *a cry for help* **10** a public demand: *a cry for more law and order on the streets* **11 a far cry from** something very different from **12 in full cry a** in eager pursuit **b** in the middle of talking or doing something ▸See also **cry off**
WORD ORIGIN Old French *crier*

crying *adj* **a crying shame** something that demands immediate attention

cry off ❶ *vb informal* to withdraw from an arrangement

cryogenics *n* the branch of physics concerned with very low temperatures and their effects **cryogenic** *adj*
WORD ORIGIN Greek *kruos* cold + *-genēs* born

THESAURUS

cruise *n* **1 = sail**, voyage, boat trip, sea trip ▹*vb* **2 = sail**, coast, voyage **3 = travel along**, coast, drift, keep a steady pace

crumb *n* **1 = bit**, grain, particle, fragment, shred, speck, sliver, morsel **2 = morsel**, scrap, atom, shred, mite, snippet, sliver, soupçon *(French)*

crumble *vb* **1 = crush**, fragment, crumb, pulverize, pound, grind, powder, granulate **2a = disintegrate**, collapse, break up, deteriorate, decay, fall apart, perish, degenerate, decompose, tumble down, moulder, go to pieces **2b = collapse**, break down, deteriorate, decay, fall apart, degenerate, go to pieces, go to rack and ruin

crumple *vb* **1a = crush**, squash, screw up, scrumple **1b = crease**, wrinkle, rumple, ruffle, pucker **2 = collapse**, sink, go down, fall

crunch *vb* **1 = chomp**, champ, munch, masticate, chew noisily, grind **4 the crunch** *(informal)* **= critical point**, test, crisis, emergency, crux, moment of truth, hour of decision

crusade *n* **1 = holy war**, jihad **2 = campaign**, drive, movement, cause, push ▹*vb* **3 = campaign**, fight, push, struggle, lobby, agitate, work

crush *vb* **1 = crease**, wrinkle, crumple, rumple, scrumple, ruffle **1, 2 = squash**, pound, break, smash, squeeze, crumble, crunch, mash, compress, press, crumple, pulverize **3 = overcome**, overwhelm, put down, subdue, overpower, quash, quell, extinguish, stamp out, vanquish, conquer **5 = demoralize**, depress, devastate, discourage, humble, put down *(slang)*, humiliate, squash, flatten, deflate, mortify, psych out *(informal)*, dishearten, dispirit, deject ▹*n* **7 = crowd**, mob, horde, throng, press, pack, mass, jam, herd, huddle, swarm, multitude, rabble

crust *n* **3 = layer**, covering, coating, incrustation, film, outside, skin, surface, shell, coat, caking, scab, concretion

cry *vb* **1 = weep**, sob, bawl, shed tears, keen, greet *(Scot archaic)*, wail, whine, whimper, whinge *(informal)*, blubber, snivel, yowl, howl your eyes out **OPPOSITE:** laugh **2, 3 = shout**, call, scream, roar, hail, yell, howl, call out, exclaim, shriek, bellow, whoop, screech, bawl, holler *(informal)*, ejaculate, sing out, halloo, vociferate **OPPOSITE:** whisper ▹*n* **6a = weep**, greet *(Scot archaic)*, sob, howl, bawl, blubber, snivel **6b = weeping**, sobbing, blubbering, snivelling **7 = shout**, call, scream,

DICTIONARY

crypt *n* a vault or underground chamber, such as one beneath a church, used as a burial place
WORD ORIGIN Greek *kruptē*

cryptic *adj* having a hidden or secret meaning; puzzling: *no-one knew what he meant by that cryptic remark*
cryptically *adv*
WORD ORIGIN Greek *kruptos* concealed

cryptogam *n bot* a plant that reproduces by spores not seeds
WORD ORIGIN Greek *kruptos* hidden + *gamos* marriage

cryptography *n* the art of writing in and deciphering codes
cryptographer *n* **cryptographic** *adj*
WORD ORIGIN Greek *kruptos* hidden + -GRAPHY

crystal *n* **1** a solid with a regular internal structure and symmetrical arrangement of faces **2** a single grain of a crystalline substance **3** a very clear and brilliant glass **4** something made of crystal **5** crystal glass articles collectively **6** *electronics* a crystalline element used in certain electronic devices, such as a detector or oscillator ▷*adj* **7** bright and clear: *the crystal waters of the pool*
WORD ORIGIN Greek *krustallos* ice, crystal

crystal ball *n* the glass globe used in crystal gazing

crystal gazing *n* **1** the act of staring into a crystal ball supposedly in order to see future events **2** the act of trying to foresee or predict **crystal gazer** *n*

crystalline *adj* **1** of or like crystal or crystals **2** clear

crystallize, crystalize *or* **-ise** *vb* **-izing, -ized** *or* **-ising, -ised 1** to make or become definite **2** to form into crystals **3** to preserve (fruit) in sugar
crystallization, crystalization *or* **-isation** *n*

crystallography *n* the science of crystal structure

crystalloid *n* a substance that in solution can pass through a membrane

crystal meth *n informal* crystal methamphetamine, a concentrated and highly potent form of methamphetamine with dangerous side effects

Cs *chem* caesium

CSA (in Britain) Child Support Agency

CSE (formerly, in Britain) Certificate of Secondary Education: an examination the first grade pass of which was an equivalent to a GCE O level

CS gas *n* a gas causing tears and painful breathing, used to control civil disturbances
WORD ORIGIN initials of its US inventors, Ben Carson and Roger Staughton

CST Central Standard Time

CT Connecticut

CT scanner *n* an X-ray machine that can produce cross-sectional images of the soft tissues
WORD ORIGIN *c(omputerized) t(omography) scanner*

CTV Canadian Television (Network Limited)

Cu *chem* copper
WORD ORIGIN Late Latin *cuprum*

cu. cubic

cub *n* **1** the young of certain mammals, such as the lion or bear **2** a young or inexperienced person ▷*vb* **cubbing, cubbed 3** to give birth to (cubs)
WORD ORIGIN origin unknown

Cub *n* ▸ short for **Cub Scout**

Cuban *adj* **1** from Cuba ▷*n* **2** a person from Cuba

cubbyhole *n* a small enclosed space or room
WORD ORIGIN dialect *cub* cattle pen

cube *n* **1** an object with six equal square faces **2** the product obtained by multiplying a number by itself twice: *the cube of 2 is 8* ▷*vb* **cubing, cubed 3** to find the cube of (a number) **4** to cut into cubes
WORD ORIGIN Greek *kubos*

cube root *n* the number or quantity whose cube is a given number or quantity: *2 is the cube root of 8*

cubic *adj* **1 a** having three dimensions **b** having the same volume as a cube with length, width, and depth each measuring the given unit: *a cubic metre* **2** having the shape of a cube **3** *maths* involving the cubes of numbers

cubicle *n* an enclosed part of a large room, screened for privacy
WORD ORIGIN Latin *cubiculum*

cubic measure *n* a system of units for the measurement of volumes

cubism *n* a style of art, begun in the early 20th century, in which objects are represented by geometrical shapes **cubist** *adj, n*

cubit *n* an ancient measure of length based on the length of the forearm
WORD ORIGIN Latin *cubitum* elbow, cubit

cuboid *adj* **1** shaped like a cube ▷*n* **2** *maths* a geometric solid whose six faces are rectangles

Cub Scout *or* **Cub** *n* a member of a junior branch of the Scout Association

cuckold *literary or old-fashioned n* **1** a man whose wife has been unfaithful to him ▷*vb* **2** to make a cuckold of
WORD ORIGIN Middle English *cukeweld*

cuckoo *n, pl* **cuckoos 1** a migratory bird with a characteristic two-note call, noted for laying its eggs in the nests of other birds ▷*adj* **2** *informal* insane or foolish
WORD ORIGIN Old French *cucu*, imitative

cuckoopint *n* a plant with arrow-shaped leaves, purple flowers, and red berries

cuckoo spit *n* a white frothy mass produced on plants by the larvae of some insects

cucumber *n* **1** a long fruit with thin green rind and crisp white flesh, used in salads **2 as cool as a cucumber** calm and self-possessed
WORD ORIGIN Latin *cucumis*

cud *n* **1** partially digested food which a ruminant brings back into its mouth to chew again **2 chew the cud** to think deeply
WORD ORIGIN Old English *cudu*

cuddle ❶ *vb* **-dling, -dled 1** to hug or embrace fondly **2 cuddle up** to lie close and snug ▷*n* **3** a fond hug
cuddly *adj*
WORD ORIGIN origin unknown

cudgel *n* a short thick stick used as a weapon
WORD ORIGIN Old English *cycgel*

Cudlipp *n* **Hugh,** Baron 1913–98, British newspaper editor, a pioneer of tabloid journalism: editorial director of the *Daily Mirror* (1952–63)

Cudworth *n* **Ralph** 1617–88, English philosopher and theologian. His works include *True Intellectual System of the Universe* (1678) and *A Treatise concerning Eternal and Immutable Morality* (1731)

cue[1] ❶ *n* **1** a signal to an actor or musician to begin speaking or playing **2** a signal or reminder **3 on cue** at the right moment ▷*vb* **cueing, cued 4** to give a cue to
WORD ORIGIN perhaps from the letter *q*, used in an actor's script to represent Latin *quando* when

cue[2] *n* **1** a long tapering stick used to hit the balls in billiards, snooker, or pool ▷*vb* **cueing, cued 2** to hit (a ball) with a cue
WORD ORIGIN variant of QUEUE

cuff[1] *n* **1** the end of a sleeve **2** *US, Canad, Austral & NZ* a turn-up on trousers **3 off the cuff** *informal* impromptu: *he delivers many speeches off the cuff*

THESAURUS

roar, yell, howl, shriek, bellow, whoop, screech, hoot, ejaculation, bawl, holler *(informal)*, exclamation, squawk, yelp, yoo-hoo

cry off *vb (informal)* **= back out,** withdraw, quit, cop out *(slang)*, beg off, excuse yourself

cuddle *vb* **1a = hug,** embrace, clasp, fondle, cosset **1b = pet,** hug, canoodle *(slang)*, bill and coo **2 cuddle up = snuggle,** nestle

cue[1] *n* **2 = signal,** sign, nod, hint,

C

DICTIONARY

WORD ORIGIN Middle English *cuffe* glove

cuff² *Brit, Austral & NZ vb* **1** to strike with an open hand ▷*n* **2** a blow with an open hand

WORD ORIGIN origin unknown

C

cuff link *n* one of a pair of decorative fastenings for shirt cuffs

cuisine (quiz-zeen) *n* **1** a style of cooking: *Italian cuisine* **2** the range of food served in a restaurant

WORD ORIGIN French

Culbertson *n* **Ely** 1891–1955, US authority on contract bridge

cul-de-sac *n, pl* **culs-de-sac** *or* **cul-de-sacs** a road with one end blocked off

WORD ORIGIN French: bottom of the bag

culinary *adj* of the kitchen or cookery

WORD ORIGIN Latin *culina* kitchen

cull *vb* **1** to choose or gather **2** to remove or kill (the inferior or surplus) animals from a herd ▷*n* **3** the act of culling

WORD ORIGIN Latin *colligere* to gather together

Cullen *n* **William Douglas**, Baron. born 1935, Scottish judge who conducted public inquiries into the Piper Alpha disaster (1990), the Dunblane school shootings (1996), and the Ladbroke Grove rail disaster (1999)

culminate ❶ *vb* **-nating, -nated** to reach the highest point or climax: *the parade culminated in a memorial service*

culmination *n*

WORD ORIGIN Latin *culmen* top

culottes *pl n* women's flared trousers cut to look like a skirt

WORD ORIGIN French

culpable *adj* deserving blame

culpability *n*

WORD ORIGIN Latin *culpa* fault

Culpeper *n* **Nicholas** 1616–54, English herbalist and astrologer; his unauthorized translation (1649) of the College of Physicians' *Pharmacopoeia* and his *Herbal* (1653) popularized herbalism

culprit ❶ *n* the person guilty of an offence or misdeed

WORD ORIGIN Anglo-French *culpable* guilty + *prit* ready

cult ❶ *n* **1** a specific system of religious worship **2** a sect devoted to the beliefs of a cult **3** devoted attachment to a person, idea, or activity **4** a popular fashion: *the bungee-jumping cult* ▷*adj* **5** very popular among a limited group of people: *a cult TV series*

WORD ORIGIN Latin *cultus* cultivation, refinement

cultish *adj* intended to appeal to a small group of fashionable people

cultivate ❶ *vb* **-vating, -vated** **1** to prepare (land) to grow crops **2** to grow (plants) **3** to develop or improve (something) by giving special attention to it: *he tried to cultivate a reputation for fairness* **4** to try to develop a friendship with (a person)

WORD ORIGIN Latin *colere* to till

cultivated *adj* well-educated: *a civilized and cultivated man*

cultivation *n* **1** the act of cultivating **2** culture or refinement

cultivator *n* a farm implement used to break up soil and remove weeds

culture ❶ *n* **1** the ideas, customs, and art of a particular society **2** a particular civilization at a particular period **3** a developed understanding of the arts **4** development or improvement by special attention or training: *physical culture* **5** the cultivation and rearing of plants or animals **6** a growth of bacteria for study ▷*vb* **-turing, -tured** **7** to grow (bacteria) in a special medium

cultural *adj*

WORD ORIGIN Latin *colere* to till

cultured ❶ *adj* **1** showing good taste or manners **2** artificially grown or synthesized

cultured pearl *n* a pearl artificially grown in an oyster shell

culture shock *n sociol* the feelings of isolation and anxiety experienced by a person on first coming into contact with a culture very different from his or her own

culvert *n* a drain or pipe that crosses under a road or railway

WORD ORIGIN origin unknown

cum *prep* with: *a small living-cum-dining room*

WORD ORIGIN Latin

Cumberland¹ *n* (until 1974) a county of NW England, now part of Cumbria

Cumberland² *n* **1 Richard** 1631–1718, English theologian and moral philosopher; bishop of Peterborough (1691–1718) **2 William Augustus** Duke of Cumberland, known as *Butcher Cumberland*. 1721–65, English soldier, younger son of George II, noted for his defeat of Charles Edward Stuart at Culloden (1746) and his subsequent ruthless destruction of Jacobite rebels

cumbersome *or* **cumbrous** *adj* **1** awkward because of size or shape **2** difficult because of complexity: *the cumbersome appeals procedure*

cumin *or* **cummin** *n* **1** the spicy-smelling seeds of a Mediterranean herb, used in cooking **2** the plant from which these seeds are obtained

WORD ORIGIN Greek *kuminon*

cummerbund *n* a wide sash worn round the waist, esp. with a dinner jacket

WORD ORIGIN Hindi *kamarband*, from Persian *kamar* loins + *band* band

Cummings *n* **Edward Estlin** (preferred typographical representation of name **e. e. cummings**). 1894–1962, US poet

cumquat *n* ▸same as **kumquat**

cumulative (kew-myew-la-tiv) *adj* growing in amount, strength, or effect by small steps: *the cumulative effect of twelve years of war*

cumulus (kew-myew-luss) *n, pl* **-li** (-lie) a thick or billowing white or dark grey cloud

WORD ORIGIN Latin: mass

Cunard *n* **Sir Samuel** (1787–1865). Canadian shipping magnate, founder of the Cunard line

cuneiform (kew-nif-form) *n* **1** an ancient system of writing using wedge-shaped characters ▷*adj* **2** written in cuneiform

WORD ORIGIN Latin *cuneus* wedge

cunjevoi *n Austral* **1** a plant of tropical Asia and Australia with small flowers, cultivated for its edible rhizome **2** a sea squirt

cunnilingus *n* the kissing and licking

THESAURUS

prompt, reminder, suggestion

culminate *vb* **= end up**, end, close, finish, conclude, wind up, climax, terminate, come to a head, come to a climax, rise to a crescendo

culprit *n* **= offender**, criminal, villain, sinner, delinquent, felon, person responsible, guilty party, wrongdoer, miscreant, evildoer, transgressor, perp *(US & Canad informal)*

cult *n* **1, 2 = sect**, following, body, faction, party, school, church, faith, religion, denomination, clique, hauhau *(NZ)* **3 = obsession**, worship, admiration, devotion, reverence, veneration, idolization **4 = craze**, fashion, trend, fad

cultivate *vb* **1, 2 = farm**, work, plant, tend, till, harvest, plough, bring under cultivation **3 = develop**, establish, acquire, foster, devote yourself to, pursue **4 = court**, associate with, seek out, run after, consort with, butter up, dance attendance upon, seek someone's company *or* friendship, take trouble *or* pains with

culture *n* **1 = lifestyle**, habit, way of life, mores **2 = civilization**, society, customs, way of life **3 = refinement**, education, breeding, polish, enlightenment, accomplishment, sophistication, good taste, erudition, gentility, urbanity

cultured *adj* **1 = refined**, advanced, polished, intellectual, educated, sophisticated, accomplished, scholarly, enlightened, knowledgeable, well-informed, genteel, urbane, erudite, highbrow, well-bred, well-read

OPPOSITE: uneducated

DICTIONARY

of a woman's genitals by her sexual partner
WORD ORIGIN Latin *cunnus* vulva + *lingere* to lick
cunning ❶ *adj* **1** clever at deceiving **2** made with skill ▹ *n* **3** cleverness at deceiving **4** skill or ingenuity
WORD ORIGIN Old English *cunnende*
Cunningham *n* **Merce** 1919–2009. US dancer and choreographer. His experimental ballets include *Suit for Five* (1956) and *Travelogue* (1977)
Cunninghame Graham *n* **R(obert) B(ontine)** 1852–1936, Scottish traveller, writer, and politician, noted for his essays and short stories: first president (1928) of the Scottish Nationalist Party
Cunobelinus *n* also called *Cymbeline*. died ?42 AD, British ruler of the Catuvellauni tribe (?10–?42); founder of Colchester (?10)
cunt *n taboo* **1** the female genitals **2** *offensive slang* a stupid or obnoxious person
WORD ORIGIN Middle English
cup ❶ *n* **1** a small bowl-shaped drinking container with a handle **2** the contents of a cup **3** something shaped like a cup: *a bra with padded cups* **4** a cup-shaped trophy awarded as a prize **5** a sporting contest in which a cup is awarded to the winner **6** a mixed drink with fruit juice or wine as a base: *claret cup* **7** one's lot in life: *his cup of bitterness was full to overflowing* **8** **someone's cup of tea** *informal* someone's chosen or preferred thing ▹ *vb* **cupping, cupped 9** to form (the hands) into the shape of a cup **10** to hold in cupped hands
WORD ORIGIN Old English *cuppe*
cupboard ❶ *n* a piece of furniture or a recess with a door, for storage
cupboard love *n* a show of love put on in order to gain something
Cup Final *n* **1** the annual final of the FA or Scottish Cup soccer competition **2** the final of any cup competition
Cupid *n* **1** the Roman god of love, represented as a winged boy with a bow and arrow **2** a picture or statue of Cupid
WORD ORIGIN Latin *cupido* desire
cupidity (kew-**pid**-it-ee) *n formal* strong desire for wealth or possessions
WORD ORIGIN Latin *cupere* to long for
cupola (**kew**-pol-la) *n* **1** a domed roof or ceiling **2** a small dome on the top of a roof **3** an armoured revolving gun turret on a warship
WORD ORIGIN Latin *cupa* tub
cupreous (**kew**-pree-uss) *adj* of or containing copper
WORD ORIGIN Latin *cuprum* copper
cupric (**kew**-prick) *adj* of or containing copper in the divalent state
cupronickel (kew-proh-**nik**-el) *n* a copper alloy containing up to 40 per cent nickel
cup tie *n Brit sport* an eliminating match between two teams in a cup competition
cur *n* **1** a vicious mongrel dog **2** a contemptible person
WORD ORIGIN Middle English *kurdogge*
curable *adj* capable of being cured **curability** *n*
curaçao (**kew**-rah-so) *n* an orange-flavoured liqueur
curacy (**kew**-rah-see) *n, pl* **-cies** the work or position of a curate
curare (kew-**rah**-ree) *n* a poisonous resin obtained from a South American tree, used as a muscle relaxant in medicine
WORD ORIGIN Carib *kurari*
curate *n* a clergyman who assists a vicar or parish priest
WORD ORIGIN Medieval Latin *cura* spiritual oversight
curative *adj* **1** able to cure ▹ *n* **2** something able to cure
curator *n* the person in charge of a museum or art gallery **curatorial** *adj* **curatorship** *n*
WORD ORIGIN Latin: one who cares
curb ❶ *n* **1** something that restrains or holds back **2** a horse's bit with an attached chain or strap, used to check the horse **3** a raised edge that strengthens or encloses ▹ *vb* **4** to control or restrain ▸ See also **kerb**
WORD ORIGIN Latin *curvus* curved
curcumin *n* a yellow pigment, present in turmeric, that is an antioxidant and has anti-inflammatory properties
curd *n* **1** coagulated milk, used in making cheese or as a food **2** any similar substance: *bean curd*
WORD ORIGIN origin unknown
curd cheese *n* a mild smooth white cheese made from skimmed milk curds
curdle *vb* **-dling, -dled 1** to turn into curd; coagulate **2** **make someone's blood curdle** to fill someone with horror
cure ❶ *vb* **curing, cured 1** to get rid of (an ailment or problem) **2** to restore (someone) to health **3** to preserve (meat or fish) by salting or smoking **4** to preserve (leather or tobacco) by drying **5** to vulcanize (rubber) ▹ *n* **6** a restoration to health **7** medical treatment that restores health **8** a means of restoring health or improving a situation **9** a curacy
WORD ORIGIN Latin *cura* care
cure-all *n* something supposed to cure all ailments or problems
curette *or* **curet** *n* **1** a surgical instrument for scraping tissue from body cavities ▹ *vb* **-retting, -retted 2** to scrape with a curette **curettage** *n*
WORD ORIGIN French
curfew *n* **1** a law which states that people must stay inside their houses after a specific time at night **2** the time set as a deadline by such a law **3** *history* the ringing of a bell at a fixed time, as a signal for putting out fires and lights
WORD ORIGIN Old French *cuevrefeu* cover the fire
Curia *n, pl* **-riae** the court and government of the Roman Catholic Church **curial** *adj*
WORD ORIGIN Latin
curie *n* the standard unit of radioactivity
WORD ORIGIN after Pierre *Curie*, French physicist
curio (**kew**-ree-oh) *n, pl* **-rios** a rare or unusual thing valued as a collector's item
WORD ORIGIN from *curiosity*
curiosity ❶ *n, pl* **-ties 1** eagerness to know or find out **2** a rare or unusual thing
curious ❶ *adj* **1** eager to learn or know **2** eager to find out private details **3** unusual or peculiar **curiously** *adv*
WORD ORIGIN Latin *curiosus* taking

THESAURUS

cunning *adj* **1 = crafty**, sly, devious, artful, sharp, subtle, tricky, shrewd, astute, canny, wily, Machiavellian, shifty, foxy, guileful **OPPOSITE:** frank **2a = ingenious**, subtle, imaginative, shrewd, sly, astute, devious, artful, Machiavellian **2b = skilful**, clever, deft, adroit, dexterous **OPPOSITE:** clumsy ▹ *n* **3 = craftiness**, guile, trickery, shrewdness, deviousness, artfulness, slyness, wiliness **OPPOSITE:** candour **4 = skill**, art, ability, craft, subtlety, ingenuity, finesse, artifice, dexterity, cleverness, deftness, astuteness, adroitness **OPPOSITE:** clumsiness
cup *n* **1 = mug**, goblet, chalice, teacup, beaker, demitasse, bowl **4 = trophy**
cupboard *n* **= cabinet**, closet, locker, press
curb *n* **1 = restraint**, control, check, brake, limitation, rein, deterrent, bridle ▹ *vb* **4 = restrain**, control, check, contain, restrict, moderate, suppress, inhibit, subdue, hinder, repress, constrain, retard, impede, stem the flow of, keep a tight rein on
cure *vb* **1 = make better**, correct, heal, relieve, remedy, mend, rehabilitate, help, ease **2 = restore to health**, restore, heal **3, 4 = preserve**, smoke, dry, salt, pickle, kipper ▹ *n* **7, 8 = remedy**, treatment, medicine, healing, antidote, corrective, panacea, restorative, nostrum
curiosity *n* **1 = inquisitiveness**,

DICTIONARY

pains over something

curium (kew-ree-um) *n chem* a silvery-white metallic radioactive element artificially produced from plutonium. Symbol: Cm
WORD ORIGIN after Pierre & Marie *Curie*, French physicists

curl ❶ *vb* **1** to twist (hair) or (of hair) to grow in coils or ringlets **2** to twist into a spiral or curve **3** to play the game of curling **4 curl one's lip** to show contempt by raising a corner of the lip ▹*n* **5** a coil of hair **6** a curved or spiral shape ▸See also **curl up** > **curly** *adj*
WORD ORIGIN probably from Middle Dutch *crullen*

curler *n* **1** a pin or small tube for curling hair **2** a person who plays curling

curlew *n* a large wading bird with a long downward-curving bill
WORD ORIGIN Old French *corlieu*

curlicue *n* an intricate ornamental curl or twist
WORD ORIGIN *curly* + CUE²

curling *n* a game played on ice, in which heavy stones with handles are slid towards a target circle

curl up *vb* **1** to lie or sit with legs drawn up **2** to be embarrassed or horrified

curmudgeon *n* a bad-tempered or mean person **curmudgeonly** *adj*
WORD ORIGIN origin unknown

Curnow *n* (**Thomas**) **Allen** (**Monro**) 1911–2001, New Zealand poet and anthologist

currajong *n* ▸same as **kurrajong**

currant *n* **1** a small dried seedless raisin **2** a small round acid berry, such as the redcurrant
WORD ORIGIN earlier *rayson of Corannte* raisin of Corinth

currawong *n* an Australian songbird
WORD ORIGIN Aboriginal

currency ❶ *n, pl* **-cies 1** the system of money or the actual coins and banknotes in use in a particular country **2** general acceptance or use: *ideas that had gained currency during the early 1960s*
WORD ORIGIN Latin *currere* to run, flow

current ❶ *adj* **1** of the immediate present: *current affairs; the current economic climate* **2** most recent or up-to-date: *the current edition* **3** commonly accepted: *current thinking on this issue* **4** circulating and valid at present: *current coins* ▹*n* **5** a flow of water or air in a particular direction **6** *physics* a flow or rate of flow of electric charge through a conductor **7** a general trend or drift: *two opposing currents of thought* **currently** *adv*
WORD ORIGIN Latin *currere* to run, flow

current account *n* a bank account from which money may be drawn at any time using a chequebook or computerized card

curriculum *n, pl* **-la** *or* **-lums 1** all the courses of study offered by a school or college **2** a course of study in one subject at a school or college: *the history curriculum* **curricular** *adj*
WORD ORIGIN Latin: course

curriculum vitae (vee-tie) *n, pl* **curricula vitae** an outline of someone's educational and professional history, prepared for job applications
WORD ORIGIN Latin: the course of one's life

curry¹ *n, pl* **-ries 1** a dish of Indian origin consisting of meat or vegetables in a hot spicy sauce **2** curry seasoning or sauce **3 curry powder** a mixture of spices for making curry ▹*vb* **-ries, -rying, -ried 4** to prepare (food) with curry powder
WORD ORIGIN Tamil *kari* sauce, relish

curry² *vb* **-ries, -rying, -ried 1** to groom (a horse) **2** to dress (leather) after it has been tanned **3 curry favour** to ingratiate oneself with an important person
WORD ORIGIN Old French *correer* to make ready

Curry *n* **John** (**Anthony**) 1949–94, British ice skater: won the figure-skating gold medal in the 1976 Olympic Games

currycomb *n* a ridged comb used for grooming horses

curse ❶ *vb* **cursing, cursed 1** to swear or swear at (someone) **2** to call on supernatural powers to bring harm to (someone or something) ▹*n* **3** a profane or obscene expression, usually of anger **4** an appeal to a supernatural power for harm to come to a person **5** harm resulting from a curse **6** something that causes great trouble or harm **7 the curse** *informal* menstruation or a menstrual period
WORD ORIGIN Old English *cursian*

cursed ❶ *adj* **1** under a curse: *he is now sick after being cursed by the witch doctor* **2 cursed with** having (something unfortunate or unwanted): *their new-born son had been cursed with a genetic defect*

cursive *adj* **1** of handwriting or print in which letters are joined in a flowing style ▹*n* **2** a cursive letter or printing type
WORD ORIGIN Medieval Latin *cursivus* running

cursor *n* **1** a movable point of light that shows a specific position on a

THESAURUS

interest, prying, snooping *(informal)*, nosiness *(informal)*, infomania **2 = oddity**, wonder, sight, phenomenon, spectacle, freak, marvel, novelty, rarity

curious *adj* **1, 2 = inquisitive**, interested, questioning, searching, inquiring, peering, puzzled, peeping, meddling, prying, snoopy *(informal)*, nosy *(informal)*
OPPOSITE: uninterested
3 = strange, unusual, bizarre, odd, novel, wonderful, rare, unique, extraordinary, puzzling, unexpected, exotic, mysterious, marvellous, peculiar, queer *(informal)*, rum *(Brit slang)*, singular, unconventional, quaint, unorthodox
OPPOSITE: ordinary

curl *vb* **1 = crimp**, wave, perm, frizz **2a = twirl**, turn, bend, twist, curve, loop, spiral, coil, meander, writhe, corkscrew, wreathe **2b = wind**, entwine, twine ▹*n* **5 = ringlet**, lock **6 = twist**, spiral, coil, kink, whorl, curlicue

currency *n* **1 = money**, coinage, legal tender, medium of exchange, bills, notes, coins **2 = acceptance**, exposure, popularity, circulation, vogue, prevalence

current *adj* **1, 2 = present**, fashionable, ongoing, up-to-date, in, now *(informal)*, happening *(informal)*, contemporary, in the news, sexy *(informal)*, trendy *(Brit informal)*, topical, present-day, in fashion, in vogue, up-to-the-minute
OPPOSITE: out-of-date
3 = prevalent, general, common, accepted, popular, widespread, in the air, prevailing, circulating, going around, customary, rife, in circulation ▹*n* **5a = flow**, course, undertow, jet, stream, tide, progression, river, tideway **5b = draught**, flow, breeze, puff **7 = mood**, feeling, spirit, atmosphere, trend, tendency, drift, inclination, vibe *(slang)*, undercurrent

curse *vb* **1a = swear**, cuss *(informal)*, blaspheme, use bad language, turn the air blue *(informal)*, be foul-mouthed, take the Lord's name in vain **1b = abuse**, damn, scold, swear at, revile, vilify, fulminate, execrate, vituperate, imprecate ▹*n* **3 = oath**, obscenity, blasphemy, expletive, profanity, imprecation, swearword **4 = malediction**, jinx, anathema, hoodoo *(informal)*, evil eye, excommunication, imprecation, execration **6 = affliction**, evil, plague, scourge, cross, trouble, disaster, burden, ordeal, torment, hardship, misfortune, calamity, tribulation, bane, vexation

cursed *adj* **1 = under a curse**, damned, doomed, jinxed, bedevilled, fey *(Scot)*, star-crossed, accursed, ill-fated

curtail *vb* **1, 2 = reduce**, cut, diminish,

DICTIONARY

visual display unit **2** the sliding part of a slide rule or other measuring instrument

cursory *adj* hasty and usually superficial **cursorily** *adv*
WORD ORIGIN Late Latin *cursorius* of running

curt *adj* so blunt and brief as to be rude **curtly** *adv* **curtness** *n*
WORD ORIGIN Latin *curtus* cut short

curtail ❶ *vb* **1** to cut short: *the opening round was curtailed by heavy rain* **2** to restrict: *a plan to curtail drinks advertising* **curtailment** *n*
WORD ORIGIN obsolete *curtal* to dock

curtain ❶ *n* **1** a piece of material hung at an opening or window to shut out light or to provide privacy **2** a hanging cloth that conceals all or part of a theatre stage from the audience **3** the end of a scene or a performance in the theatre, marked by the fall or closing of the curtain **4** the rise or opening of the curtain at the start of a performance **5** something forming a barrier or screen: *a curtain of rain* ▷ *vb* **6** to shut off or conceal with a curtain **7** to provide with curtains
WORD ORIGIN Late Latin *cortina*

curtain call *n theatre* a return to the stage by performers to receive applause

curtain-raiser *n* **1** *theatre* a short play performed before the main play **2** a minor event happening before a major one

curtains *pl n informal* death or ruin; the end

curtsy *or* **curtsey** *n, pl* **-sies** *or* **-seys** **1** a woman's formal gesture of respect made by bending the knees and bowing the head ▷ *vb* **-sies, -sying, -sied** *or* **-seys, -seying, -seyed** **2** to make a curtsy
WORD ORIGIN variant of *courtesy*

curvaceous *adj informal* having a curved shapely body

curvature *n* the state or degree of being curved

curve ❶ *n* **1** a continuously bending line with no straight parts **2** something that curves or is curved **3** curvature **4** *maths* a system of points whose coordinates satisfy a given equation **5** a line representing data on a graph ▷ *vb* **curving, curved** **6** to form into or move in a curve **curvy** *adj*
WORD ORIGIN Latin *curvare* to bend

curvet *n* **1** a horse's low leap with all four feet off the ground ▷ *vb* **-vetting, -vetted** *or* **-veting, -veted** **2** to make such a leap
WORD ORIGIN Latin *curvare* to bend

curvilinear *adj* consisting of or bounded by a curved line

Curzon *n* **1** Sir **Clifford** 1907–82, English pianist **2 George Nathaniel**, 1st Marquis Curzon of Kedleston. 1859–1925, British Conservative statesman; viceroy of India (1898–1905)

Cusack *n* **Cyril (James)** 1910–93, Irish actor

cuscus *n, pl* **-cuses** a large nocturnal possum of N Australia and New Guinea
WORD ORIGIN probably from a native word in New Guinea

Cushing *n* **Harvey Williams** 1869–1939, US neurosurgeon: identified a pituitary tumour as a cause of the disease named after him

cushion ❶ *n* **1** a bag filled with a soft material, used to make a seat more comfortable **2** something that provides comfort or absorbs shock **3** the resilient felt-covered rim of a billiard table ▷ *vb* **4** to protect from injury or shock **5** to lessen the effects of **6** to provide with cushions **cushiony** *adj*
WORD ORIGIN Latin *culcita* mattress

cushy *adj* **cushier, cushiest** *informal* easy: *a cushy job*
WORD ORIGIN Hindi *khush* pleasant

cusp *n* **1** a small point on the grinding or chewing surface of a tooth **2** a point where two curves meet **3** *astrol* any division between houses or signs of the zodiac **4** *astron* either of the points of a crescent moon
WORD ORIGIN Latin *cuspis* pointed end

cuss *informal n* **1** a curse or oath **2** an annoying person ▷ *vb* **3** to swear or swear at

cussed (**kuss**-id) *adj informal* **1** obstinate: *the older she got the more cussed she became* **2** ▸ same as **cursed** > **cussedness** *n*

custard *n* **1** a sauce made of milk and sugar thickened with cornflour **2** a baked sweetened mixture of eggs and milk
WORD ORIGIN Middle English *crustade* kind of pie

custodian *n* the person in charge of a public building **custodianship** *n*

custody ❶ *n, pl* **-dies** **1** the act of keeping safe **2** imprisonment prior to being tried **custodial** *adj*
WORD ORIGIN Latin *custos* guard, defender

custom ❶ *n* **1** a long-established activity, action, or festivity: *the custom of serving port after dinner* **2** the long-established habits or traditions of a society **3** a usual practice or habit: *she held his hand more tightly than was her custom in public* **4** regular use of a shop or business ▷ *adj* **5** made to the specifications of an individual customer: *a custom car; custom-tailored suits* ▸ See also **customs**
WORD ORIGIN Latin *consuetudo*

customary ❶ *adj* **1** usual **2** established by custom **customarily** *adv* **customariness** *n*

custom-built *or* **-made** *adj* made according to the specifications of an individual customer

customer ❶ *n* **1** a person who buys goods or services **2** *informal* a person with whom one has to deal: *a tricky customer*

custom house *n* a government office where customs are collected

customize *or* **-ise** *vb* **-izing, -ized** *or* **-ising, -ised** to make (something) according to a customer's individual requirements

customs ❶ *n* **1** duty charged on imports or exports **2** the government department responsible for collecting this **3** the area at a port, airport, or border where baggage and freight are examined for dutiable goods

cut ❶ *vb* **cutting, cut** **1** to open up or

THESAURUS

decrease, dock, cut back, shorten, lessen, cut short, pare down, retrench

curtain *n* **1 = hanging**, drape (*chiefly US*), portière

curve *n* **1 = bend**, turn, loop, arc, curvature, camber ▷ *vb* **6 = bend**, turn, wind, twist, bow, arch, snake, arc, coil, swerve

cushion *n* **1 = pillow**, pad, bolster, headrest, beanbag, scatter cushion, hassock ▷ *vb* **4 = protect**, support, bolster, cradle, buttress **5 = soften**, dampen, muffle, mitigate, deaden, suppress, stifle

custody *n* **1 = care**, charge, protection, supervision, preservation, auspices, aegis, tutelage, guardianship, safekeeping, keeping, trusteeship, custodianship **2 = imprisonment**, detention, confinement, incarceration

custom *n* **1, 2 = tradition**, practice, convention, ritual, form, policy, rule, style, fashion, usage, formality, etiquette, observance, praxis, unwritten law, kaupapa (*NZ*) **3 = habit**, way, practice, manner, procedure, routine, mode, wont **4 = customers**, business, trade, patronage

customary *adj* **1 = usual**, general, common, accepted, established, traditional, normal, ordinary, familiar, acknowledged, conventional, routine, everyday
OPPOSITE: unusual
2 = accustomed, regular, usual, habitual, wonted

customer *n* **1 = client**, consumer, regular (*informal*), buyer, patron, shopper, purchaser, habitué

customs *pl n* **1 = import charges**, tax, duty, toll, tariff

cut *vb* **1, 2a = slit**, saw, score, nick,

DICTIONARY

penetrate (a person or thing) with a sharp instrument **2** (of a sharp instrument) to penetrate or open up (a person or thing) **3** to divide or be divided with or as if with a sharp instrument **4** to trim **5** to abridge or shorten **6** to reduce or restrict: *cut your intake of fried foods* **7** to form or shape by cutting **8** to reap or mow **9** *sport* to hit (the ball) so that it spins and swerves **10** to hurt the feelings of (a person): *her rudeness cut me to the core* **11** *informal* to pretend not to recognize **12** *informal* to absent oneself from without permission: *he found the course boring, and was soon cutting classes* **13** to stop (doing something): *cut the nonsense* **14** to dilute or adulterate: *heroin cut with talcum powder* **15** to make a sharp or sudden change in direction: *the path cuts to the right just after you pass the quarry* **16** to grow (teeth) through the gums **17** *films* **a** to call a halt to a shooting sequence **b cut to** to move quickly to (another scene) **18** *films* to edit (film) **19** to switch off (a light or engine) **20** to make (a commercial recording): *he cut his first solo album in 1971* **21** *cards* **a** to divide (the pack) at random into two parts after shuffling **b** to pick cards from a spread pack to decide the dealer or who plays first **22 cut a dash** to make a stylish impression **23 cut a person dead** *informal* to ignore a person completely **24 cut and run** *informal* to escape quickly from a difficult situation **25 cut both ways a** to have both good and bad effects **b** to serve both sides of an argument **26 cut it fine** *informal* to allow little margin of time or space **27 cut no ice** *informal* to fail to make an impression **28 cut one's teeth on** *informal* to get experience from ▹*n* **29** the act of cutting **30** a stroke or incision made by cutting **31** a piece cut off **32** a channel or path cut or hollowed out **33** a reduction: *a pay cut* **34** a deletion in a text, film, or play **35** *informal* a portion or share **36** the style in which hair or a garment is cut **37** a direct route; short cut **38** *sport* a stroke which makes the ball spin and swerve **39** *films* an immediate transition from one shot to the next **40** *Brit* a canal **41 a cut above** *informal* superior to; better than ▹*adj* **42** made or shaped by cutting **43** reduced by cutting: *the shop has hundreds of suits, all at cut prices* **44** adulterated or diluted **45 cut and dried** *informal* settled in advance ▸See also **cut across, cutback**, etc.
WORD ORIGIN probably from Old Norse

cut across *vb* **1** to go against (ordinary restrictions or expectations): *this dilemma has cut across class divisions* **2** to cross or traverse

cutaneous (kew-**tane**-ee-uss) *adj* of the skin
WORD ORIGIN Latin *cutis* skin

cutaway *adj* (of a drawing or model) having part of the outside omitted to reveal the inside

cutback ❶ *n* **1** a decrease or reduction ▹*vb* **cut back 2** to shorten by cutting **3** (often foll. by *on*) to make a reduction: *we may cut back on other expenditure*

cut down *vb* **1** to fell **2** (often foll. by *on*) to make a reduction: *cut down on the amount of salt you eat* **3** to kill **4 cut someone down to size** to cause someone to feel less important or to be less conceited

cute ❶ *adj* **1** appealing or attractive **2** *informal* clever or shrewd **cuteness** *n*
WORD ORIGIN from ACUTE

cut glass *n* **1** glass with patterns cut into the surface ▹*adj* **cut-glass 2** upper-class; refined: *Victoria with her cut-glass accent*

Cuthbert *n* **Saint** ?635–87 AD, English monk; bishop of Lindisfarne. Feast day: March 20

cuticle (**kew**-tik-kl) *n* **1** hardened skin round the base of a fingernail or toenail **2** ▸same as **epidermis**
WORD ORIGIN Latin *cuticula* skin

cut in *vb* **1** to interrupt **2** to move in front of another vehicle, leaving too little space

cutlass *n* a curved one-edged sword formerly used by sailors
WORD ORIGIN French *coutelas*

cutler *n* a person who makes or sells cutlery
WORD ORIGIN Latin *culter* knife

cutlery *n* knives, forks, and spoons, used for eating

cutlet *n* **1** a small piece of meat taken from the neck or ribs **2** a flat croquette of chopped meat or fish
WORD ORIGIN Old French *costelette* a little rib

cut off *vb* **1** to remove or separate by cutting **2** to stop the supply of **3** to interrupt (a person who is speaking), esp. during a telephone conversation **4** to bring to an end **5** to disinherit: *cut off without a penny* **6** to intercept so as to prevent retreat or escape ▹*n* **cutoff 7** the point at which something is cut off; limit **8** *chiefly US* a short cut **9** a device to stop the flow of a fluid in a pipe

cut out *vb* **1** to shape by cutting **2** to delete or remove **3** *informal* to stop doing (something) **4** (of an engine) to cease to operate suddenly **5** (of an electrical device) to switch off, usually automatically **6 be cut out for** to be suited or equipped for: *you're not cut out for this job* **7 have one's work cut out** to have as much work as one can manage ▹*n* **cutout 8** a device that automatically switches off a circuit or engine as a safety device **9** something that has been cut out from something else

cut-price *or esp. US* **cut-rate** *adj* **1** at a reduced price **2** offering goods or services at prices below the standard price

cutter *n* **1** a person or tool that cuts **2** a small fast boat

cut-throat *adj* **1** fierce or ruthless in competition: *the cut-throat world of international finance* **2** (of a card game) played by three people: *cut-throat poker* ▹*n* **3** a murderer **4** *Brit & NZ* a razor with a long blade that folds into its handle

cutting ❶ *n* **1** an article cut from a newspaper or magazine **2** a piece

THESAURUS

slice, slash, pierce, hack, penetrate, notch **1, 2b = slash**, nick, wound, lance, gash, lacerate, incise **3a = chop**, split, divide, slice, segment, dissect, cleave, part **3b = carve**, slice **3c = sever**, cut in two, sunder **4 = trim**, shave, hack, snip **4, 8 = clip**, mow, trim, dock, prune, snip, pare, lop **5 = abridge**, edit, shorten, curtail, condense, abbreviate, précis **OPPOSITE:** extend **6 = reduce**, lower, slim (down), diminish, slash, decrease, cut back, rationalize, ease up on, downsize, kennet (*Austral slang*), jeff (*Austral slang*) **OPPOSITE:** increase **7 = shape**, carve, engrave, chisel, form, score, fashion, chip, sculpture, whittle, sculpt, inscribe, hew **10 = hurt**, wound, upset, sting, grieve, pain, hurt someone's feelings **11** (*informal*) **= ignore**, avoid, slight, blank (*slang*), snub, spurn, freeze (someone) out (*informal*), cold-shoulder, turn your back on, send to Coventry, look straight through (someone) **OPPOSITE:** greet **15 = cross**, interrupt, intersect, bisect ▹*n* **30a = incision**, nick, rent, stroke, rip, slash, groove, slit, snip **30b = gash**, nick, wound, slash, graze, laceration **33 = reduction**, fall, lowering, slash, decrease, cutback, diminution **35** (*informal*) **= share**, piece, slice, percentage, portion, kickback (*chiefly US*), rake-off (*slang*) **36 = style**, look, form, fashion, shape, mode, configuration

cutback *n* **1 = reduction**, cut, retrenchment, economy, decrease, lessening

cute *adj* **1 = appealing**, sweet, attractive, engaging, charming, delightful, lovable, winsome, winning, cutesy (*informal, chiefly US*)

cutting *adj* **5 = hurtful**, wounding, severe, acid, bitter, malicious, scathing, acrimonious, barbed,

DICTIONARY

cut from a plant for rooting or grafting **3** a passage cut through high ground for a road or railway **4** the editing process of a film ▷ *adj* **5** (of a remark) likely to hurt the feelings **6** keen; piercing: *a cutting wind* **7** designed for cutting: *the hatchet's blade is largely stone, but its cutting edge is made of copper*

cutting edge *n* the leading position in any field; forefront: *the cutting edge of space technology*

cuttlefish *n, pl* **-fish** *or* **-fishes** a flat squidlike mollusc which squirts an inky fluid when in danger
WORD ORIGIN Old English *cudele*

cut up *vb* **1** to cut into pieces **2** *informal* (of a driver) to overtake or pull in front of (another driver) in a dangerous manner **3 be cut up** *informal* to be very upset **4 cut up rough** *Brit informal* to become angry or violent

Cuvier *n* **Georges (Jean-Leopold-Nicolas-Frédéric)**, Baron. 1769–1832, French zoologist and statesman; founder of the sciences of comparative anatomy and palaeontology

Cuyp *or* **Kuyp** *n* **Aelbert** 1620–91, Dutch painter of landscapes and animals

CV curriculum vitae

cwm (koom) *n* (in Wales) a valley
WORD ORIGIN Welsh

cwt hundredweight

cyanic acid *n* a colourless poisonous volatile liquid acid

cyanide *n* any of a number of highly poisonous substances containing a carbon-nitrogen group of atoms

cyanogen *n* a poisonous colourless flammable gas
WORD ORIGIN Greek *kuanos* dark blue

cyanosis *n pathol* a blue discoloration of the skin, caused by a deficiency of oxygen in the blood
WORD ORIGIN Greek *kuanos* dark blue

cyber- *combining form* indicating computers: *cyberspace*
WORD ORIGIN from CYBERNETICS

cybercafé *n* a café equipped with computer terminals which customers can use to access the internet
WORD ORIGIN CYBER- + CAFÉ

cybernetics *n* the branch of science in which electronic and mechanical systems are studied and compared to biological systems **cybernetic** *adj*
WORD ORIGIN Greek *kubernētēs* steersman

cyberspace *n* the hypothetical environment which contains all the data stored in computers
WORD ORIGIN CYBER- + SPACE

cybersquatting *n* the practice of registering an internet domain name that is likely to be wanted by another person or organization in the hope that it can be sold to them for a profit **cybersquatter** *n*

cyclamen (sik-la-men) *n* a plant with white, pink, or red flowers, with turned-back petals
WORD ORIGIN Greek *kuklaminos*

cycle ❶ *vb* **-cling, -cled 1** to ride a bicycle **2** to occur in cycles ▷ *n* **3** *Brit, Austral & NZ* a bicycle **4** *US* a motorcycle **5** a complete series of recurring events **6** the time taken or needed for one such series **7** a single complete movement in an electrical, electronic, or mechanical process **8** a set of plays, songs, or poems about a figure or event **cycling** *n*
WORD ORIGIN Greek *kuklos*

cyclical *or* **cyclic** *adj* **1** occurring in cycles **2** *chem* (of an organic compound) containing a closed ring of atoms

cyclist *n* a person who rides a bicycle

cyclo- *or before a vowel* **cycl-** *combining form* **1** indicating a circle or ring: *cyclotron* **2** *chem* denoting a cyclical compound: *cyclopropane*
WORD ORIGIN Greek *kuklos* cycle

cyclometer (sike-**lom**-it-er) *n* a device that records the number of revolutions made by a wheel and the distance travelled

cyclone *n* **1** a body of moving air below normal atmospheric pressure, which often brings rain **2** a violent tropical storm **cyclonic** *adj*
WORD ORIGIN Greek *kuklōn* a turning around

cyclopedia *or* **cyclopaedia** *n* ▸ same as **encyclopedia**

Cyclops *n, pl* **Cyclopes** *or* **Cyclopses** *classical myth* one of a race of giants having a single eye in the middle of the forehead
WORD ORIGIN Greek *Kuklōps* round eye

cyclotron *n* an apparatus, used in atomic research, which accelerates charged particles by means of a strong vertical magnetic field

cyder *n* ▸ same as **cider**

cygnet *n* a young swan
WORD ORIGIN Latin *cygnus* swan

cylinder *n* **1** a solid or hollow body with circular equal ends and straight parallel sides **2** a container or other object shaped like a cylinder **3** the chamber in an internal-combustion engine within which the piston moves **4** the rotating mechanism of a revolver, containing cartridge chambers **cylindrical** *adj*
WORD ORIGIN Greek *kulindein* to roll

cymbal *n* a percussion instrument consisting of a round brass plate which is struck against another or hit with a stick **cymbalist** *n*
WORD ORIGIN Greek *kumbē* something hollow

Cymbeline *n* ▸ See **Cunobelinus**

cyme *n bot* a flower cluster which has a single flower on the end of each stem and of which the central flower blooms first **cymose** *adj*
WORD ORIGIN Greek *kuma* anything swollen

Cymric (kim-rik) *adj* **1** of Wales ▷ *n* **2** the Celtic language of Wales

Cynewulf, Kynewulf, *or* **Cynwulf** *n* ?8th century AD, Anglo-Saxon poet; author of *Juliana, The Ascension, Elene,* and *The Fates of the Apostles*

cynic ❶ (**sin**-ik) *n* a person who believes that people always act selfishly
WORD ORIGIN Greek *kuōn* dog

Cynic *n* a member of an ancient Greek philosophical school that had contempt for worldly things **Cynicism** *n*

cynical ❶ *adj* **1** believing that people always act selfishly **2** sarcastic or sneering **cynically** *adv*

cynicism ❶ *n* the attitude or beliefs of a cynic

cynosure (**sin**-oh-zyure) *n literary* a centre of interest or attention
WORD ORIGIN Greek *Kunosoura* dog's tail (name of the constellation of Ursa Minor)

cypher (**sife**-er) *n, vb* ▸ same as **cipher**

cypress *n* **1** an evergreen tree with dark green leaves **2** the wood of this tree
WORD ORIGIN Greek *kuparissos*

Cyprian[1] *adj* **1** of or relating to Cyprus **2** of or resembling the ancient orgiastic worship of Aphrodite on Cyprus ▷ *n* **3** (*often not capital*) *obsolete* a licentious person, esp. a prostitute or dancer ▷ *n, adj* **4** ▸ another word for **Cypriot**

Cyprian[2] *n* **Saint** ?200–258 AD, bishop of Carthage and martyr. Feast day: Sept 26 or 16

Cypriot *adj* **1** of Cyprus ▷ *n* **2** a person from Cyprus **3** the dialect of Greek

THESAURUS

sarcastic, sardonic, caustic, vitriolic, trenchant, pointed **OPPOSITE:** kind

cycle *n* **5, 7 = series of events**, round (*of years*), circle, revolution, rotation

cynic *n* **= sceptic**, doubter, pessimist, misanthrope, misanthropist, scoffer

cynical *adj* **1 = unbelieving**, sceptical, disillusioned, pessimistic, disbelieving, mistrustful **OPPOSITE:** optimistic **2 = sceptical**, mocking, ironic, sneering, pessimistic, scoffing, contemptuous, sarcastic, sardonic, scornful, distrustful, derisive, misanthropic **OPPOSITE:** trusting

cynicism *n* **a = scepticism**, pessimism, sarcasm, misanthropy, sardonicism **b = disbelief**, doubt, scepticism, mistrust

spoken in Cyprus

Cyrillic *adj* of the Slavic alphabet devised supposedly by Saint Cyril, now used primarily for Russian and Bulgarian

Cyril of Alexandria *n* **Saint** ?375–444 AD, Christian theologian and patriarch of Alexandria. Feast day: June 27 or June 9

Cyrus *n* **1** known as *Cyrus the Great* or *Cyrus the Elder.* died ?529 BC, king of Persia and founder of the Persian empire **2** called *the Younger.* died 401 BC, Persian satrap of Lydia: revolted against his brother Artaxerxes II, but was killed at the battle of Cunaxa ▸ See also **anabasis, katabasis**

cyst (sist) *n* **1** *pathol* an abnormal membranous sac containing fluid or diseased matter **2** *anat* any normal sac in the body

WORD ORIGIN Greek *kustis* pouch, bag

cystic fibrosis *n* a congenital disease, usually affecting young children, which causes breathing disorders and malfunctioning of the pancreas

cystitis (siss-tite-iss) *n* inflammation of the bladder, causing a desire to urinate frequently, accompanied by a burning sensation

-cyte *n combining form* indicating a cell: *leucocyte*

WORD ORIGIN Greek *kutos* vessel

cytology (site-ol-a-jee) *n* the study of plant and animal cells **cytological** *adj* **cytologically** *adv* **cytologist** *n*

cytoplasm *n* the protoplasm of a cell excluding the nucleus **cytoplasmic** *adj*

czar (zahr) *n* ▸ same as **tsar**

Czech *adj* **1** of the Czech Republic ▹ *n* **2** a person from the Czech Republic **3** the language of the Czech Republic

Czechoslovak *or* **Czechoslovakian** *adj* **1** of the former Czechoslovakia ▹ *n* **2** a person from the former Czechoslovakia

Czerny *n* **Karl** 1791–1857, Austrian pianist, composer, and teacher, noted for his studies

Dd

DICTIONARY

d 1 *physics* density 2 deci-

D 1 *music* the second note of the scale of C major 2 *chem* deuterium 3 the Roman numeral for 500

d. 1 *Brit & NZ* (before decimalization) penny *or* pennies
WORD ORIGIN Latin *denarius* 2 died 3 daughter

dab[1] ❶ *vb* **dabbing, dabbed** 1 to pat lightly and quickly 2 to apply with short tapping strokes: *dabbing antiseptic on cuts* ▹ *n* 3 a small amount of something soft or moist 4 a light stroke or tap 5 **dabs** *slang chiefly Brit* fingerprints
WORD ORIGIN imitative

dab[2] *n* a small European flatfish covered with rough toothed scales
WORD ORIGIN Anglo-French *dabbe*

dabble *vb* **-bling, -bled** 1 to be involved in an activity in a superficial way: *she dabbles in right-wing politics* 2 to splash (one's toes or fingers) in water **dabbler** *n*
WORD ORIGIN probably from Dutch *dabbelen*

dab hand *n informal* a person who is particularly skilled at something: *a dab hand with a needle and thread*
WORD ORIGIN origin unknown

dace *n, pl* **dace** *or* **daces** a European freshwater fish of the carp family
WORD ORIGIN Old French *dars* dart

dachshund *n* a small dog with short legs and a long body
WORD ORIGIN German *Dachs* badger + *Hund* dog

dactyl *n prosody* a metrical foot of three syllables, one long followed by two short **dactylic** *adj*
WORD ORIGIN Greek *daktulos* finger, comparing the finger's three joints to the three syllables

dad *or* **daddy** *n informal* father
WORD ORIGIN from child's *da da*

Dada *or* **Dadaism** *n* an art movement of the early 20th century that systematically used arbitrary and absurd concepts **Dadaist** *n, adj*
WORD ORIGIN French: hobbyhorse

Dadd *n* **Richard** 1817–86, British painter of mythological and fairy scenes. He was committed to an asylum for patricide

daddy-longlegs *n informal* 1 *Brit* crane fly 2 a small web-spinning spider with long legs

dado (day-doe) *n, pl* **-does** *or* **-dos** 1 the lower part of an interior wall, often separated by a rail, that is decorated differently from the upper part 2 *archit* the part of a pedestal between the base and the cornice
WORD ORIGIN Italian: die, die-shaped pedestal

daemon (deem-on) *n* ▸ same as **demon**

daffodil *n* 1 a spring plant with yellow trumpet-shaped flowers ▹ *adj* 2 brilliant yellow
WORD ORIGIN variant of Latin *asphodelus* asphodel

daft ❶ *adj informal chiefly Brit* 1 foolish or crazy 2 **daft about** very enthusiastic about: *he's daft about football*
WORD ORIGIN Old English *gedæfte* gentle, foolish

Dafydd ap Gruffudd *n* died 1283, Welsh leader. Claiming the title Prince of Wales (1282), he led an unsuccessful revolt against Edward I: executed

Dafydd ap Gwilym *n* ?1320–?1380, Welsh poet

dag ❶ *NZ n* 1 the dried dung on a sheep's rear 2 *informal* an amusing person ▹ *pl n* 3 **rattle one's dags** *informal* hurry up ▹ *vb* 4 to remove the dags from a sheep
WORD ORIGIN origin unknown

dagga ❶ (duhh-a) *n S African* a local name for marijuana
WORD ORIGIN probably from Khoi (language of southern Africa) *daxa*

dagger *n* 1 a short knifelike weapon with a double-edged pointed blade 2 a character (†) used to indicate a cross-reference 3 **at daggers drawn** in a state of open hostility 4 **look daggers** to glare with hostility
WORD ORIGIN origin unknown

daggy ❶ *adj Austral & NZ informal* 1 untidy; dishevelled 2 eccentric

daguerreotype (dag-gair-oh-type) *n* a type of early photograph produced on chemically treated silver
WORD ORIGIN after L. *Daguerre*, its inventor

Dahl *n* **Roald** 1916–90, British writer with Norwegian parents, noted for his short stories and such children's books as *Charlie and the Chocolate Factory* (1964)

dahlia (day-lya) *n* a garden plant with showy flowers
WORD ORIGIN after Anders *Dahl*, botanist

Dáil Éireann (doil air-in) *or* **Dáil** *n* (in the Republic of Ireland) the lower chamber of parliament
WORD ORIGIN Irish *dáil* assembly + *Éireann* of Eire

daily ❶ *adj* 1 occurring every day or every weekday: *there have been daily airdrops of food, blankets, and water* 2 of or relating to a single day or to one day at a time: *her home help comes in on a daily basis; exercise has become part of our daily lives* ▹ *adv* 3 every day ▹ *n, pl* **-lies** 4 *Austral & Brit* a daily newspaper 5 *Brit informal* a woman employed to clean someone's house
WORD ORIGIN Old English *dæglīc*

Daimler *n* **Gottlieb** (**Wilhelm**) 1834–1900, German engineer and car manufacturer, who collaborated with Nikolaus Otto in inventing the first internal-combustion engine (1876)

dainty *adj* **-tier, -tiest** 1 delicate, pretty, or elegant: *dainty little pink shoes* ▹ *n, pl* **-ties** 2 *Brit* a small choice cake or sweet **daintily** *adv*
WORD ORIGIN Old French *deintié*

THESAURUS

dab[1] *vb* **1 = pat**, touch, tap, wipe, blot, swab **2 = apply**, daub, stipple ▹ *n* **3 = spot**, bit, drop, pat, fleck, smudge, speck, dollop *(informal)*, smidgen *or* smidgin *(informal, chiefly US & Canad)* **4 = touch**, stroke, flick, smudge

daft *adj* **1a = stupid**, simple, crazy, silly, absurd, foolish, giddy, goofy, idiotic, inane, loopy *(informal)*, witless, crackpot *(informal)*, out to lunch *(informal)*, dopey *(informal)*, scatty *(Brit informal)*, asinine, gonzo *(slang)*, doolally *(slang)*, off your head *(informal)*, off your trolley *(slang)*, up the pole *(informal)*, dumb-ass *(slang)*, wacko *or* whacko *(slang)*, off the air *(Austral slang)*

dag *n* 2 *(NZ informal)* **= joker**, comic, wag, wit, comedian, clown, kidder *(informal)*, jester, humorist, prankster **3 rattle your dags** *(NZ informal)* **= hurry up**, get a move on, step on it *(informal)*, get your skates on *(informal)*, make haste

dagga *n* **= cannabis**, marijuana, pot *(slang)*, dope *(slang)*, hash *(slang)*, black *(slang)*, blow *(slang)*, smoke *(informal)*, stuff *(slang)*, leaf *(slang)*, tea *(US slang)*, grass *(slang)*, chronic *(US slang)*, weed *(slang)*, hemp, gage *(US obsolete, slang)*, hashish, mary jane *(US slang)*, ganja, bhang, kif, wacky baccy *(slang)*, sinsemilla, charas

daggy *adj* **1 = untidy**, unkempt, dishevelled, tousled, disordered, messy, ruffled, scruffy, rumpled, bedraggled, ratty *(informal)*, straggly, windblown, disarranged, mussed up *(informal)* **2 = eccentric**, odd, strange, bizarre, weird, peculiar, abnormal, queer *(informal)*, irregular, uncommon, quirky, singular, unconventional, idiosyncratic, off-the-wall *(slang)*, outlandish, whimsical, rum *(Brit slang)*, capricious, anomalous, freakish, aberrant, wacko *(slang)*, outré

daily *adj* **1 = everyday**, regular, circadian *(biology)*, diurnal, quotidian ▹ *adv* **3 = every day**, day by day, day after day, once a day, per diem

DICTIONARY

daiquiri (dak-eer-ee) *n, pl* **-ris** an iced drink containing rum, lime juice, and sugar
WORD ORIGIN after *Daiquiri*, town in Cuba

dairy *n, pl* **dairies 1** a company or shop that sells milk and milk products **2** a place where milk and cream are stored or made into butter and cheese **3** food containing milk or milk products: *I can't eat dairy* **4** *NZ* small shop selling groceries and milk often outside normal trading hours ▷ *adj* **5** of milk or milk products: *dairy produce*
WORD ORIGIN Old English *dǣge* servant girl

dairy cattle *n* cows reared mainly for their milk

dairy farm *n* a farm where cows are kept mainly for their milk

dairymaid *n Brit, Austral & NZ* (formerly) a woman employed to milk cows

dairyman *n Brit, Austral & S African* a man employed to look after cows

dais (day-iss) *n* a raised platform in a hall or meeting place used by a speaker
WORD ORIGIN Old French *deis*

daisy *n, pl* **-sies** a small low-growing flower with a yellow centre and pinkish-white petals
WORD ORIGIN Old English *dægesēge* day's eye

daisy chain *n* a string of daisies joined together by their stems to make a necklace

daisywheel *n* a flat disc in a word processor with radiating spokes for printing characters

dal[1] *n* ▸ same as **dhal**

dal[2] decalitre(s)

Daladier *n* **Édouard** 1884–1970, French radical socialist statesman; premier of France (1933; 1934; 1938–40) and signatory of the Munich Pact (1938)

Dalai Lama *n* the chief lama and (until 1959) ruler of Tibet

dale *n* an open valley
WORD ORIGIN Old English *dæl*

Dale *n* Sir **Henry Hallet** 1875–1968, English physiologist: shared a Nobel prize for physiology or medicine in 1936 with Otto Loewi for their work on the chemical transmission of nerve impulses

d'Alembert *n* **Jean Le Rond** 1717–83, French mathematician, physicist, and rationalist philosopher, noted for his contribution to Newtonian physics in *Traité de dynamique* (1743) and for his collaboration with Diderot in editing the *Encyclopédie*

Dalén *n* **Nils Gustaf** 1869–1937, Swedish engineer, inventor of an automatic light-controlled valve known as 'Solventil'. Nobel prize for physics 1912

Dalglish *n* **Kenny,** born 1951, Scottish footballer: a striker, he played for Celtic (1968–77) and for Liverpool (1977–89): manager of Liverpool (1985–91), of Blackburn Rovers (1991–95), and of Newcastle United (1997–98): Scotland's most-capped footballer

Dalhousie *n* **1 9th Earl of,** title of *George Ramsay.* 1770–1838, British general; governor of the British colonies in Canada (1819–28) **2** his son, **1st Marquis and 10th Earl of,** title of *James Andrew Broun Ramsay.* 1812–60, British statesman: governor general of India (1848–56)

Dallapiccola *n* **Luigi** 1904–75, Italian composer of twelve-tone music. His works include the opera *Il Prigioniero* (1944–48) and the ballet *Marsia* (1948)

dalliance *n old-fashioned* flirtation

dally *vb* **-lies, -lying, -lied 1** *old-fashioned* to waste time or dawdle **2 dally with** to deal frivolously with: *to dally with someone's affections*
WORD ORIGIN Anglo-French *dalier* to gossip

Dalmatian *n* a large dog with a smooth white coat and black spots

dam[1] ❶ *n* **1** a barrier built across a river to create a lake **2** a lake created by such a barrier ▷ *vb* **damming, dammed 3** to block up (a river) by a dam
WORD ORIGIN probably from Middle Low German

dam[2] *n* the female parent of an animal such as a sheep or horse
WORD ORIGIN variant of *dame*

dam[3] decametre(s)

Dam *n* **(Carl Peter) Henrik** 1895–1976, Danish biochemist who discovered vitamin K (1934): Nobel prize for physiology or medicine 1943

damage ❶ *vb* **-aging, -aged 1** to harm or injure ▷ *n* **2** injury or harm caused to a person or thing **3** *informal* cost: *what's the damage?* **damaging** *adj*
WORD ORIGIN Latin *damnum* injury, loss

damages ❶ *pl n law* money awarded as compensation for injury or loss

damask *n* a heavy fabric with a pattern woven into it, used for tablecloths, curtains, etc.
WORD ORIGIN *Damascus*, where fabric originally made

dame *n slang* a woman
WORD ORIGIN Latin *domina* lady

Dame ❶ *n* (in Britain) the title of a woman who has been awarded the Order of the British Empire or another order of chivalry

Damien *n* **Joseph**, known as *Father Damien.* 1840–89, Belgian Roman Catholic missionary to the leper colony at Molokai, Hawaii

damn ❶ *interj* **1** *slang* an exclamation of annoyance ▷ *adv* **2** *slang Also* **damned** extremely ▷ *adj* **3** *slang Also* **damned** extreme: *a damn good idea* ▷ *vb* **4** to condemn as bad or worthless **5** to curse **6** (of God) to condemn to hell or eternal punishment **7** to prove (someone) guilty **8 damn with faint praise** to praise so unenthusiastically that the effect is condemnation ▷ *n* **9 not give a damn** *informal* not care **damning** *adj*
WORD ORIGIN Latin *damnum* loss, injury

damnable *adj* very unpleasant or annoying **damnably** *adv*

damnation *interj* **1** an exclamation of anger ▷ *n* **2** *theol* eternal punishment

damned *adj* **1** condemned to hell ▷ *adv, adj slang* **2** extreme or extremely: *a damned good try* **3** used to indicate amazement or refusal: *I'm damned if I'll do it!*

damnedest *n* **do one's damnedest** *informal* to do one's best: *I'm doing my damnedest to make myself clear*

Damon *n* **Matt** born 1970, US film actor and screenwriter. His films include *Good Will Hunting* (1997, which he co-wrote), *Saving Private Ryan* (1998), *The Talented Mr Ripley* (1999) and the 'Bourne' series (2002–07)

damp ❶ *adj* **1** slightly wet ▷ *n* **2** slight

THESAURUS

dam[1] *n* **1 = barrier**, wall, barrage, obstruction, embankment, hindrance ▷ *vb* **3 = block up**, block, hold in, restrict, check, confine, choke, hold back, barricade, obstruct

damage *vb* **1 = spoil**, hurt, injure, smash, harm, ruin, crush, devastate, mar, wreck, shatter, weaken, gut, demolish, undo, trash *(slang)*, total *(slang)*, impair, ravage, mutilate, annihilate, incapacitate, raze, deface, play (merry) hell with *(informal)* **OPPOSITE:** fix ▷ *n* **2 = destruction**, harm, loss, injury, suffering, hurt, ruin, crushing, wrecking, shattering, devastation, detriment, mutilation, impairment, annihilation, ruination **OPPOSITE:** improvement **3** *(informal)* **= cost**, price, charge, rate, bill, figure, amount, total, payment, expense, outlay

damages *pl n (law)* **= compensation**, fine, payment, satisfaction, amends, reparation, indemnity, restitution, reimbursement, atonement, recompense, indemnification, meed *(archaic)*, requital

Dame *n* **= lady**, baroness, dowager, grande dame *(French)*, noblewoman, peeress

damn *vb* **4 = criticize**, condemn, blast, pan *(informal)*, slam *(slang)*, denounce, put down, slate *(informal)*, censure, castigate, tear into *(informal)*, diss *(slang, chiefly US)*, inveigh against,

DICTIONARY

wetness; moisture ▷ *vb* **3** to make slightly wet **4 damp down a** to reduce the intensity of (someone's emotions or reactions): *they attempted to damp down protests* **b** to reduce the flow of air to (a fire) to make it burn more slowly **damply** *adv* **dampness** *n*
WORD ORIGIN Middle Low German: steam

dampcourse *or* **damp-proof course** *n* a layer of waterproof material built into the base of a wall to prevent moisture rising

dampen ❶ *vb* **1** to reduce the intensity of **2** to make damp

damper *n* **1 put a damper on** to produce a depressing or inhibiting effect on **2** a movable plate to regulate the draught in a stove or furnace **3** the pad in a piano or harpsichord that deadens the vibration of each string as its key is released **4** *chiefly Austral & NZ* any of various unleavened loaves and scones, typically cooked on an open fire

Dampier *n* **William** 1652–1715, English navigator, pirate, and writer: sailed around the world twice

damsel *n archaic or poetic* a young woman
WORD ORIGIN Old French *damoisele*

damson *n* a small blue-black edible plumlike fruit that grows on a tree
WORD ORIGIN Latin *prunum damascenum* Damascus plum

dan *n judo, karate* **1** any of the 10 black-belt grades of proficiency **2** a competitor entitled to dan grading
WORD ORIGIN Japanese

Dana *n* **James Dwight** 1813–95, American geologist; noted for his work *The System of Mineralogy* (1837)

Danby *n* **1** Also: **1st Duke of Leeds 1st Earl of**, title of *Thomas Osborne*. 1631–1712, English politician; Lord Treasurer (1673–78): regarded as the founder of the Tory party **2 Francis**. 1793–1861, Irish painter of romantic landscapes and historical subjects

dance ❶ *vb* **dancing, danced 1** to move the feet and body rhythmically in time to music **2** to perform (a particular dance): *to dance a tango* **3** to skip or leap **4** to move in a rhythmic way: *their reflection danced in the black waters* **5 dance attendance on someone** to carry out someone's slightest wish in an overeager manner ▷ *n* **6** a social meeting arranged for dancing **7** a series of rhythmic steps and movements in time to music **8** a piece of music in the rhythm of a particular dance **dancer** *n* **dancing** *n, adj*
WORD ORIGIN Old French *dancier*

dancehall *n* a style of dance-oriented reggae

D and C *n med* dilatation of the cervix and curettage of the uterus: a minor operation to clear the womb or remove tissue for diagnosis

dandelion *n* a wild plant with yellow rayed flowers and deeply notched leaves
WORD ORIGIN Old French *dent de lion* tooth of a lion, referring to its leaves

dander *n* **get one's dander up** *Brit, Austral & NZ slang* to become angry
WORD ORIGIN from *dandruff*

dandified *adj* dressed like or resembling a dandy

dandle *vb* **-dling, -dled** to move (a young child) up and down on one's knee
WORD ORIGIN origin unknown

Dandolo *n* **Enrico** *c.* 1108–1205, Venetian statesman; doge (1192–1205). During the fourth Crusade he won Greek colonies for Venice

dandruff *n* loose scales of dry dead skin shed from the scalp
WORD ORIGIN origin unknown

dandy *n, pl* **-dies 1** a man who is greatly concerned with the elegance of his appearance ▷ *adj* **-dier, -diest 2** *informal* very good or fine
WORD ORIGIN origin unknown

dandy-brush *n* a stiff brush used for grooming a horse

Dane *n* a person from Denmark

danger ❶ *n* **1** the possibility that someone may be injured or killed **2** someone or something that may cause injury or harm **3** a likelihood that something unpleasant will happen: *the danger of flooding*
WORD ORIGIN Middle English *daunger* power, hence power to inflict injury

danger money *n* extra money paid to compensate for the risks involved in dangerous work

dangerous ❶ *adj* likely or able to cause injury or harm **dangerously** *adv*

dangle ❶ *vb* **-gling, -gled 1** to hang loosely **2** to display (something attractive) as an enticement
WORD ORIGIN probably imitative

Daniel[1] *n* **1** *Old Testament* **a** a youth who was taken into the household of Nebuchadnezzar, received guidance and apocalyptic visions from God, and was given divine protection when thrown into the lions' den **b** the book that recounts these experiences and visions (in full **The Book of the Prophet Daniel**) **2** (often preceded by *a*) a wise upright person
WORD ORIGIN sense 2: referring to Daniel in the Apocryphal *Book of Susanna*

Daniel[2] *n* **1 Paul (Wilson).** born 1958, British conductor; musical director of the English National Opera 1997–2003 **2 Samuel.** ?1562–1619, English poet and writer: author of the sonnet sequence *Delia* (1592)

Danish *adj* **1** of Denmark ▷ *n* **2** the language of Denmark

Danish blue *n* a white cheese with blue veins and a strong flavour

Danish pastry *n* a rich puff pastry filled with apple, almond paste, etc. and topped with icing

dank *adj* (esp. of cellars or caves) unpleasantly damp and chilly
WORD ORIGIN probably from Old Norse

Dankworth *n* Sir **John (Philip William)** 1927–2010, British jazz composer, bandleader, and saxophonist: married to Cleo Laine

D'Annunzio *n* **Gabriele** 1863–1938, Italian poet, dramatist, novelist, national hero, and Fascist. His works include the poems in *Alcione* (1904) and the drama *La Figlia di Iorio* (1904)

Danton *n* **Georges Jacques** 1759–94, French revolutionary leader: a

THESAURUS

lambast(e), excoriate, denunciate
OPPOSITE: praise

damp *adj* **1 = moist**, wet, dripping, soggy, humid, sodden, dank, sopping, clammy, dewy, muggy, drizzly, vaporous **OPPOSITE:** dry ▷ *n* **2 = moisture**, liquid, humidity, drizzle, dew, dampness, wetness, dankness, clamminess, mugginess **OPPOSITE:** dryness ▷ *vb* **3 = moisten**, wet, soak, dampen, lick, moisturize, humidify **4a damp something down = curb**, reduce, check, cool, moderate, dash, chill, dull, diminish, discourage, restrain, inhibit, stifle, allay, deaden, pour cold water on

dampen *vb* **1 = reduce**, check, moderate, dash, dull, restrain, deter, stifle, lessen, smother, muffle, deaden **2 = moisten**, wet, spray, make damp, bedew, besprinkle

dance *vb* **1 = prance**, rock, trip, swing, spin, hop, skip, sway, whirl, caper, jig, frolic, cavort, gambol, bob up and down, cut a rug (*informal*) **3 = caper**, trip, spring, jump, bound, leap, bounce, hop, skip, romp, frolic, cavort, gambol ▷ *n* **6 = ball**, social, hop (*informal*), disco, knees-up (*Brit informal*), discotheque, dancing party, B and S (*Austral informal*)

danger *n* **1 = jeopardy**, vulnerability, insecurity, precariousness, endangerment **2 = hazard**, risk, threat, menace, peril, pitfall

dangerous *adj* **= perilous**, threatening, risky, hazardous, exposed, alarming, vulnerable, nasty, ugly, menacing, insecure, hairy (*slang*), unsafe, precarious, treacherous, breakneck, parlous (*archaic*), fraught with danger, chancy (*informal*), unchancy (*Scot*)
OPPOSITE: safe

d

DICTIONARY

founder member of the Committee of Public Safety (1793) and minister of justice (1792–94). He was overthrown by Robespierre and guillotined

Da Ponte *n* **Lorenzo**, real name *Emmanuele Conegliano* 1749–1838, Italian writer; Mozart's librettist for *The Marriage of Figaro* (1786), *Don Giovanni* (1787), and *Cosi fan tutte* (1790)

dapper *adj* (of a man) neat in appearance and slight in build
WORD ORIGIN Middle Dutch

dappled *adj* **1** marked with spots of a different colour; mottled **2** covered in patches of light and shadow
WORD ORIGIN origin unknown

dapple-grey *n* a horse with a grey coat and darker coloured spots

Darby *n* **Abraham** 1677–1717, British iron manufacturer: built the first coke-fired blast furnace (1709)

Darby and Joan *n chiefly Brit* a happily married elderly couple
WORD ORIGIN couple in 18th-century ballad

Darcy *n* **(James) Les(lie)** 1895–1917, Australian boxer and folk hero, who lost only five professional fights and was never knocked out, considered a martyr after his death from septicaemia during a tour of the United States

dare *vb* **daring, dared 1** to be courageous enough to try (to do something) **2** to challenge (someone) to do something risky **3 I dare say a** it is quite possible **b** probably ▹ *n* **4** a challenge to do something risky
WORD ORIGIN Old English *durran*

daredevil *n* **1** a recklessly bold person ▹ *adj* **2** recklessly bold or daring

daring *adj* **1** willing to do things that may be dangerous ▹ *n* **2** the courage to do things that may be dangerous **daringly** *adv*

Dario *n* **Rubén**, real name *Félix Rubén Garcia Sarmiento.* 1867–1916, Nicaraguan poet whose poetry includes *Prosas Profanas* (1896)

Darius III *n* died 330 BC, last Achaemenid king of Persia (336–330), who was defeated by Alexander the Great

dark *adj* **1** having little or no light **2** (of a colour) reflecting little light: *dark brown* **3** (of hair or skin) brown or black **4** (of thoughts or ideas) gloomy or sad **5** sinister or evil: *a dark deed* **6** sullen or angry: *a dark scowl* **7** secret or mysterious: *keep it dark* ▹ *n* **8** absence of light; darkness **9** night or nightfall **10 in the dark** in ignorance **darkly** *adv* **darkness** *n*
WORD ORIGIN Old English *deorc*

dark age *n* a period of ignorance or barbarism

Dark Ages *pl n* the period of European history between 500 and 1000 AD

darken *vb* **1** to make or become dark or darker **2** to make gloomy, angry, or sad

dark horse *n* a person who reveals little about himself or herself, esp. someone who has unexpected talents

darkroom *n* a darkened room in which photographs are developed

Darlan *n* **Jean Louis Xavier François** 1881–1942, French admiral and member of the Vichy government. He cooperated with the Allies after their invasion of North Africa; assassinated

darling *n* **1** a person very much loved: used as a term of address **2** a favourite: *the darling of the gossip columns* ▹ *adj* **3** beloved **4** pleasing: *a darling film*
WORD ORIGIN Old English *dēorling*

darn[1] *vb* **1** to mend a hole in (a knitted garment) with a series of interwoven stitches ▹ *n* **2** a patch of darned work on a garment
WORD ORIGIN origin unknown

darn[2] *interj, adj, adv, vb, n euphemistic* ▸ same as **damn**

darnel *n* a weed that grows in grain fields
WORD ORIGIN origin unknown

Darnley *n* **Lord** title of *Henry Stuart* (or *Stewart*). 1545–67, Scottish nobleman; second husband of Mary, Queen of Scots and father of James I of England. After murdering his wife's secretary, Rizzio (1566), he was himself assassinated (1567)

dart *n* **1** a small narrow pointed missile that is thrown or shot, as in the game of darts **2** a sudden quick movement **3** a tapered tuck made in dressmaking ▹ *vb* **4** to move or throw swiftly and suddenly **darting** *adj*
WORD ORIGIN Germanic

dartboard *n* a circular board used as the target in the game of darts

darts *n* a game in which darts are thrown at a dartboard

Darwinism *or* **Darwinian theory** *n* the theory of the origin of animal and plant species by evolution **Darwinian** *adj, n* **Darwinist** *n, adj*
WORD ORIGIN after Charles *Darwin*, English naturalist

dash *vb* **1** to move hastily; rush **2** to hurl; crash: *deep-sea rollers dashing spray over jagged rocks* **3** to frustrate: *prospects for peace have been dashed* ▹ *n* **4** a sudden quick movement **5** a small amount: *a dash of milk* **6** a mixture of style and courage: *the commander's dash did not impress him* **7** the punctuation mark (—), used to

THESAURUS

dangle *vb* **1 = hang**, swing, trail, sway, flap, hang down, depend **2 = offer**, flourish, brandish, flaunt, tempt someone with, lure someone with, entice someone with, tantalize someone with

dare *vb* **1 = risk doing**, venture, presume, make bold *(archaic)*, hazard doing, brave doing **2 = challenge**, provoke, defy, taunt, goad, throw down the gauntlet

daring *adj* **1 = brave**, bold, adventurous, rash, have-a-go *(informal)*, reckless, fearless, audacious, intrepid, impulsive, valiant, plucky, game *(informal)*, daredevil, venturesome, (as) game as Ned Kelly *(Austral slang)*
OPPOSITE: timid
▹ *n* **2 = bravery**, nerve *(informal)*, courage, face *(informal)*, spirit, bottle *(Brit slang)*, guts *(informal)*, pluck, grit, audacity, boldness, temerity, derring-do *(archaic)*, spunk *(informal)*, fearlessness, rashness, intrepidity
OPPOSITE: timidity

dark *adj* **1 = dim**, murky, shady, shadowy, grey, cloudy, dingy, overcast, dusky, unlit, pitch-black, indistinct, poorly lit, sunless, tenebrous, darksome *(literary)*, pitchy, unilluminated **3 = black**, brunette, ebony, dark-skinned, sable, dusky, swarthy **OPPOSITE:** fair
4 = gloomy, sad, grim, miserable, low, bleak, moody, dismal, pessimistic, melancholy, sombre, morbid, glum, mournful, morose, joyless, doleful, cheerless
OPPOSITE: cheerful
5 = evil, foul, horrible, sinister, infamous, vile, satanic, wicked, atrocious, sinful, hellish, infernal, nefarious, damnable **7 = secret**, deep, hidden, mysterious, concealed, obscure, mystic, enigmatic, puzzling, occult, arcane, cryptic, abstruse, recondite, Delphic ▹ *n* **8 = darkness**, shadows, gloom, dusk, obscurity, murk, dimness, semi-darkness, murkiness **9 = night**, twilight, evening, evo *(Austral slang)*, dusk, night-time, nightfall

darken *vb* **1a = cloud**, shadow, shade, obscure, eclipse, dim, deepen, overshadow, blacken, becloud
OPPOSITE: brighten
1b = make dark, shade, blacken, make darker, deepen

darling *n* **1 = beloved**, love, dear, dearest, angel, treasure, precious, loved one, sweetheart, sweetie, truelove, dear one ▹ *adj* **3 = beloved**, dear, dearest, sweet, treasured, precious, adored, cherished, revered

dart *vb* **4 = dash**, run, race, shoot, fly, speed, spring, tear, rush, bound, flash, hurry, sprint, bolt, hasten, whizz, haste, flit, scoot

dash *vb* **1 = rush**, run, race, shoot, fly, career, speed, spring, tear, bound, hurry, barrel (along) *(informal, chiefly*

DICTIONARY

indicate a change of subject **8** the symbol (–), used in combination with the symbol *dot* (.) in Morse code ▸ See also **dash off**
WORD ORIGIN Middle English *daschen, dassen*
dashboard *n* the instrument panel in a car, boat, or aircraft
dasher *n Canad* one of the boards surrounding an ice-hockey rink
dashing ❶ *adj* stylish and attractive: *a splendidly dashing character*
dash off *vb* to write down or finish off hastily
dassie *n S African* a hyrax, esp. a rock hyrax
WORD ORIGIN Afrikaans
dastardly *adj old-fashioned* mean and cowardly
WORD ORIGIN Middle English *dastard* dullard
dasyure (dass-ee-your) *n* a small marsupial of Australia, New Guinea, and adjacent islands
DAT digital audio tape
dat. dative
data ❶ *n* **1** a series of observations, measurements, or facts; information **2** *computers* the numbers, digits, characters, and symbols operated on by a computer
WORD ORIGIN Latin: (things) given
database *n* **1** a store of information in a form that can be easily handled by a computer **2** a large store of information: *a database of knowledge*
data capture *n* a process for converting information into a form that can be handled by a computer
data processing *n* a sequence of operations performed on data, esp. by a computer, in order to extract or interpret information
date[1] ❶ *n* **1** a specified day of the month **2** the particular day or year when an event happened **3 a** an appointment, esp. with a person to whom one is romantically or sexually attached **b** the person with whom the appointment is made **4 to date** up to now ▹ *vb* **dating, dated 5** to mark (a letter or cheque) with the date **6** to assign a date of occurrence or creation to **7** to reveal the age of: *that dress dates her* **8** to make or become old-fashioned: *it's the freshest look this year but may date quickly* **9** *informal chiefly US & Canad* to be a boyfriend or girlfriend of **10 date from** *or* **date back to** to have originated at (a specified time)
WORD ORIGIN Latin *dare* to give, as in *epistula data Romae* letter handed over at Rome
date[2] *n* the dark-brown, sweet tasting fruit of the date palm
WORD ORIGIN Greek *daktulos* finger
dated ❶ *adj* unfashionable; outmoded
dateless *adj* likely to remain fashionable or interesting regardless of age
dateline *n journalism* information placed at the top of an article stating the time and place the article was written
Date Line *n* ▸ short for **International Date Line**
date palm *n* a tall palm grown in tropical regions for its fruit
date rape *n* the act of a man raping a woman or pressuring her into having sex while they are on a date together
dative *n grammar* the grammatical case in certain languages that expresses the indirect object
WORD ORIGIN Latin *dativus*
datum *n, pl* **-ta** a single piece of information usually in the form of a fact or statistic
WORD ORIGIN Latin: something given
daub *vb* **1** to smear (paint or mud) quickly or carelessly over a surface **2** to paint (a picture) clumsily or badly ▹ *n* **3** a crude or badly done painting: *a typical child's daub*
WORD ORIGIN Old French *dauber* to paint
Daubigny *n* **Charles François** 1817–78, French landscape painter associated with the Barbizon School
Daudet *n* **Alphonse** 1840–97, French novelist, short-story writer, and dramatist: noted particularly for his humorous sketches of Provençal life, as in *Lettres de mon moulin* (1866)
daughter *n* **1** a female child **2** a girl or woman who comes from a certain place or is connected with a certain thing: *a daughter of the church* ▹ *adj* **3** *biol* denoting a cell, chromosome, etc. produced by the division of one of its own kind **4** *physics* (of a nuclide) formed from another nuclide by radioactive decay
daughterly *adj*
WORD ORIGIN Old English *dohtor*
daughter-in-law *n, pl* **daughters-in-law** the wife of one's son
Daumier *n* **Honoré** 1808–79, French painter and lithographer, noted particularly for his political and social caricatures
daunting ❶ *adj* intimidating or worrying: *this project grows more daunting every day*
WORD ORIGIN Latin *domitare* to tame
dauntless *adj* fearless; not discouraged
dauphin (daw-fin) *n* formerly, the eldest son of the king of France
WORD ORIGIN Old French: originally a family name
Davenant *n* Sir **William** 1606–68, English dramatist and poet: poet laureate (1638–68). His plays include *Love and Honour* (1634)
davenport *n* **1** *chiefly Brit* a writing desk with drawers at the side **2** *Austral, US & Canad* a large sofa
WORD ORIGIN sense 1 supposedly after Captain *Davenport*, who commissioned the first ones
David I *n* 1084–1153, king of Scotland (1124–53) who supported his niece Matilda's claim to the English throne and unsuccessfully invaded England on her behalf
David II *n* 1324–71, king of Scotland (1329–71): he was forced into exile in France (1334–41) by Edward de Baliol;

d

THESAURUS

US & Canad), sprint, bolt, dart, hasten, scurry, haste, stampede, burn rubber (*informal*), make haste, hotfoot **OPPOSITE:** dawdle
2a = throw, cast, pitch, slam, toss, hurl, fling, chuck (*informal*), propel, project, sling, lob (*informal*)
2b = crash, break, smash, shatter, shiver, splinter ▹ *n* **4 = rush**, run, race, sprint, bolt, dart, spurt, sortie
5 = drop, little, bit, shot (*informal*), touch, spot, suggestion, trace, hint, pinch, sprinkling, tot, trickle, nip, tinge, soupçon (*French*) **OPPOSITE:** lot
6 = style, spirit, flair, flourish, vigour, verve, panache, élan, brio, vivacity
dashing *adj* (*old-fashioned*) **= stylish**, smart, elegant, dazzling, flamboyant, sporty, swish (*informal, chiefly Brit*), urbane, jaunty, dapper, showy
data *n* **1 = details**, facts, figures, materials, documents, intelligence, statistics, gen (*Brit informal*), dope (*informal*), info (*informal*) **2** (*computing*) **= information**, input
date[1] *n* **2 = time**, stage, period
3a = appointment, meeting, arrangement, commitment, engagement, rendezvous, tryst, assignation **3b = partner**, escort, friend, steady (*informal*), plus-one (*informal*) ▹ *vb* **6 = put a date on**, determine the date of, assign a date to, fix the period of **8 = become dated**, become old-fashioned, obsolesce
10 date from *or* **date back to** (*a time or date*) **= come from**, belong to, originate in, exist from, bear a date of
dated *adj* **= old-fashioned**, outdated, out of date, obsolete, archaic, unfashionable, antiquated, outmoded, passé, out, old hat, untrendy (*Brit informal*), démodé (*French*), out of the ark (*informal*) **OPPOSITE:** modern
daunting *adj* **= intimidating**, alarming, frightening, discouraging, awesome, unnerving, disconcerting, demoralizing, off-putting (*Brit informal*), disheartening **OPPOSITE:** reassuring

DICTIONARY

captured following the battle of Neville's Cross (1346), and imprisoned by the English (1346–57)

Davies *n* **1** Sir **John** 1569–1626, English poet, author of *Orchestra or a Poem of Dancing* (1596) and the philosophical poem *Nosce Teipsum* (1599) **2** Sir **Peter Maxwell** born 1934, British composer whose works include the operas *Taverner* (1967), *The Martyrdom of St Magnus* (1977), and *Resurrection* (1988), six symphonies, and the ten Strathclyde Concertos; appointed Master of the Queen's Music in 2004 **3** (**William**) **Robertson** 1913–95, Canadian novelist and dramatist. His novels include *Leaven of Malice* (1954), *Fifth Business* (1970), *The Rebel Angels* (1981), *What's Bred in the Bone* (1985), and *The Cunning Man* (1994) **4 W**(**illiam**) **H**(**enry**) 1871–1940, Welsh poet, noted also for his *Autobiography of a Super-tramp* (1908)

Davisson *n* **Clinton Joseph** 1881–1958, US physicist, noted for his discovery of electron diffraction; shared the Nobel prize for physics in 1937

davit (dav-vit) *n* a crane, usually one of a pair, on the side of a ship for lowering or hoisting a lifeboat
WORD ORIGIN Anglo-French *daviot*, from *Davi* David

Davy Jones's locker *n* the ocean's bottom, regarded as the grave of those lost or buried at sea
WORD ORIGIN origin unknown

Davy lamp *n* ▸ same as **safety lamp**
WORD ORIGIN after Sir Humphrey *Davy*, chemist

dawdle *vb* **-dling, -dled** to walk slowly or lag behind
WORD ORIGIN origin unknown

Dawes *n* **Charles Gates** 1865–1951, US financier, diplomat, and statesman, who devised the Dawes Plan for German reparations payments after World War I; vice president of the US (1925–29); Nobel peace prize 1925

Dawkins *n* **Richard** born 1941, British zoologist, noted for such works as *The Selfish Gene* (1976), *The Blind Watchmaker* (1986), *River Out of Eden* (1995), and *The God Delusion* (2006)

dawn ❶ *n* **1** daybreak **2** the beginning of something ▹ *vb* **3** to begin to grow light after the night **4** to begin to develop or appear **5 dawn on** *or* **upon** to become apparent (to someone)
WORD ORIGIN Old English *dagian* to dawn

dawn chorus *n* the singing of birds at dawn

day ❶ *n* **1** the period of 24 hours from one midnight to the next **2** the period of light between sunrise and sunset **3** the part of a day occupied with regular activity, esp. work **4** a period or point in time: *in days gone by; in Shakespeare's day* **5** a day of special observance: *Christmas Day* **6** a time of success or recognition: *his day will come* **7 all in a day's work** part of one's normal activity **8 at the end of the day** in the final reckoning **9 call it a day** to stop work or other activity **10 day in, day out** every day without changing **11 that'll be the day a** that is most unlikely to happen **b** I look forward to that ▸ Related adjective: **diurnal**
WORD ORIGIN Old English *dæg*

Day *n* Sir **Robin** 1923–2000, British radio and television journalist, noted esp. for his political interviews

Dayan *n* **Moshe** 1915–81, Israeli soldier and statesman; minister of defence (1967; 1969–74) and foreign minister (1977–79)

daybreak *n* the time in the morning when light first appears

day centre *n* a place that provides care where elderly or handicapped people can spend the day

daydream *n* **1** a pleasant fantasy indulged in while awake ▹ *vb* **2** to indulge in idle fantasy **daydreamer** *n*

Day-Glo *adj* (of a colour) luminous in daylight: *Day-Glo pink*
WORD ORIGIN from a trade name for a brand of fluorescent paint

Day-Lewis *or* **Day Lewis** *n* **C**(**ecil**) 1904–72, British poet, critic, and (under the pen name *Nicholas Blake*) author of detective stories; poet laureate (1968–72)

daylight ❶ *n* **1** light from the sun **2** daytime **3** daybreak **4 see daylight** to realize that the end of a difficult task is approaching ▸ See also **daylights**

daylight robbery *n informal* blatant overcharging

daylights *pl n informal* **1 beat the living daylights out of someone** to beat someone soundly **2 scare the living daylights out of someone** to frighten someone greatly

daylight-saving time *n* time set one hour ahead of the local standard time, to provide extra daylight in the evening in summer

Day of Atonement *n* ▸ same as **Yom Kippur**

day release *n Brit* a system whereby workers go to college one day a week for vocational training

day return *n* a reduced fare for a train or bus journey travelling both ways in one day

day room *n* a communal living room in a hospital or similar institution

daytime *n* the time from sunrise to sunset

day-to-day *adj* routine; everyday

daze ❶ *vb* **dazing, dazed 1** to cause to be in a state of confusion or shock ▹ *n* **2** a state of confusion or shock: *in a daze* **dazed** *adj*
WORD ORIGIN Old Norse *dasa*

dazzle ❶ *vb* **-zling, -zled 1** to impress greatly: *she was dazzled by his wit* **2** to blind for a short time by sudden excessive light: *he passed two cars and they dazzled him with their headlights* ▹ *n* **3** bright light that dazzles **dazzling** *adj* **dazzlingly** *adv*
WORD ORIGIN from *daze*

dB *or* **db** decibel(s)

Db *chem* dubnium

DBE Dame (Commander of the Order) of the British Empire

DC 1 direct current **2** District of Columbia

DCC digital compact cassette: a magnetic tape cassette on which sound can be recorded digitally

DD Doctor of Divinity

D-day *n* the day selected for the start of some operation
WORD ORIGIN after *D(ay)-day*, the day of the Allied invasion of Europe on June 6, 1944

DDS *or* **DDSc** Doctor of Dental Surgery *or* Science

DDT *n* dichlorodiphenyltrichloroethane; an insecticide, now banned in many countries

DE Delaware

de- *prefix* **1** indicating removal: *dethrone* **2** indicating reversal: *declassify* **3** indicating departure from: *decamp*
WORD ORIGIN Latin

deacon *n Christianity* **1** (in episcopal churches) an ordained minister

THESAURUS

dawn *n* **1 = daybreak**, morning, sunrise, dawning, daylight, aurora *(poetic)*, crack of dawn, sunup, cockcrow, dayspring *(poetic)* **2 = beginning**, start, birth, rise, origin, dawning, unfolding, emergence, outset, onset, advent, genesis, inception ▹ *vb* **3 = grow light**, break, brighten, lighten **4 = begin**, start, open, rise, develop, emerge, unfold, originate **5 dawn on** *or* **upon someone = hit**, strike, occur to, register *(informal)*, become apparent, come to mind, cross your mind, come into your head, flash across your mind

day *n* **1 = twenty-four hours**, working day **2 = daytime**, daylight, daylight hours **4 = time**, age, era, prime, period, generation, heyday, epoch

daylight *n* **1 = sunlight**, sunshine, light of day

daze *vb* **1 = stun**, shock, paralyse, numb, stupefy, benumb ▹ *n* **2 = shock**, confusion, distraction, trance, bewilderment, stupor, trancelike state

dazzle *vb* **1 = impress**, amaze, fascinate, overwhelm, astonish, awe, overpower, bowl over *(informal)*,

ranking immediately below a priest 2 (in some Protestant churches) a lay official who assists the minister
WORD ORIGIN Greek *diakonos* servant
deactivate *vb* **-vating, -vated** to make (a bomb or other explosive device) harmless
dead ❶ *adj* 1 no longer alive 2 no longer in use or finished: *a dead language; a dead match* 3 unresponsive 4 (of a limb) numb 5 complete or absolute: *there was dead silence* 6 *informal* very tired 7 (of a place) lacking activity 8 *electronics* a drained of electric charge b not connected to a source of electric charge 9 *sport* (of a ball) out of play 10 **dead from the neck up** *informal* stupid 11 **dead to the world** *informal* fast asleep ▹ *n* 12 a period during which coldness or darkness is most intense: *the dead of winter* ▹ *adv* 13 *informal* extremely: *dead easy* 14 suddenly and abruptly: *stop dead* 15 **dead on** exactly right
WORD ORIGIN Old English *dēad*
deadbeat *n informal* a lazy or socially undesirable person
dead beat *adj informal* exhausted
dead duck *n slang* something that is doomed to failure
deaden *vb* to make (something) less intense: *drugs deaden the pain; heavy curtains deadened the echo*
deadening *adj*
dead end *n* 1 a cul-de-sac 2 a situation in which further progress is impossible: *efforts to free the hostages had reached a dead end*
deadhead *n US & Canad* 1 *informal* a person who does not pay on a bus, at a game, etc. 2 *informal* a commercial vehicle travelling empty 3 *slang* a dull person 4 *US & Canad* a totally or partially submerged log floating in a lake
dead heat *n* a tie for first place between two or more participants in a race or contest
dead letter *n* 1 a letter that cannot be delivered or returned due to lack of information 2 a law or rule that is no longer enforced
deadline ❶ *n* a time or date by which a job or task must be completed
deadlock ❶ *n* a point in a dispute at which no agreement can be reached
deadlocked *adj* having reached a deadlock
dead loss *n informal* a useless person or thing
deadly ❶ *adj* **-lier, -liest** 1 likely to cause death: *deadly poison* 2 *informal* extremely boring ▹ *adv, adj* 3 like or suggestive of death: *deadly pale* ▹ *adv* 4 extremely: *she was being deadly serious*
deadly nightshade *n* a poisonous plant with purple bell-shaped flowers and black berries
dead man's handle *or* **pedal** *n* a safety device which only allows equipment to operate when a handle or pedal is being pressed
dead march *n* solemn funeral music played to accompany a procession
dead-nettle *n* a plant with leaves like nettles but without stinging hairs
deadpan *adj* 1 deliberately emotionless ▹ *adv* 2 in a deliberately emotionless manner
dead reckoning *n* a method of establishing one's position using the distance and direction travelled
dead set *adv* firmly decided: *he is dead set on leaving*
dead soldier *or* **marine** *n informal* an empty beer or spirit bottle
dead weight *n* 1 a heavy weight or load 2 the difference between the loaded and the unloaded weights of a ship
dead wood *n informal* people or things that are no longer useful
deaf ❶ *adj* 1 unable to hear 2 **deaf to** refusing to listen or take notice of
deafness *n*
WORD ORIGIN Old English *dēaf*
deaf-and-dumb *adj offensive* unable to hear or speak
deafblind *adj* unable to hear or see
deafen *vb* to make deaf, esp. momentarily by a loud noise
deafening *adj*
deaf-mute *n* a person who is unable to hear or speak
Deak *n* **Ferenc** 1803–76, Hungarian statesman: minister of justice following the 1848 Hungarian uprising. The Austro-Hungarian dual monarchy was largely his creation
deal¹ ❶ *n* 1 an agreement or transaction 2 a particular type of treatment received: *a fair deal* 3 a large amount: *the land alone is worth a good deal* 4 *cards* a player's turn to distribute the cards 5 **big deal** *slang* an important matter: often used sarcastically ▹ *vb* **dealing, dealt** (**delt**) 6 to inflict (a blow) on 7 *slang* to sell any illegal drug 8 **deal in** to engage in commercially 9 **deal out** to apportion or distribute ▸ See also **deal with**
WORD ORIGIN Old English *dǣlan*
deal² *n* 1 a plank of softwood timber 2 the sawn wood of various coniferous trees
WORD ORIGIN Middle Low German *dele* plank
dealer ❶ *n* 1 a person or organization whose business involves buying and selling things 2 *slang* a person who sells illegal drugs 3 *cards* the person who distributes the cards
dealings *pl n* business relations with a person or organization
dealt *vb* ▸ the past of **deal¹**
deal with ❶ *vb* 1 to take action on: *he was not competent to deal with the legal aspects* 2 to be concerned with: *I do not*

THESAURUS

overawe, hypnotize, stupefy, take your breath away, strike dumb
2 = **blind**, confuse, daze, bedazzle
dead *adj* 1 = **deceased**, gone, departed, late, perished, extinct, defunct, passed away, pushing up (the) daisies **OPPOSITE:** alive
4 = **numb**, frozen, paralysed, insensitive, inert, deadened, immobilized, unfeeling, torpid, insensible, benumbed 5 *(of a centre, silence, or a stop)* = **total**, complete, perfect, entire, absolute, utter, outright, thorough, downright, unqualified 6 *(informal)* = **exhausted**, tired, worn out, spent, wasted, done in *(informal)*, all in *(slang)*, drained, wiped out *(informal)*, sapped, knackered *(slang)*, prostrated, clapped out *(Brit, Austral & NZ informal)*, tired out, ready to drop, dog-tired *(informal)*, zonked *(slang)*, dead tired, dead beat *(informal)*, shagged out *(Brit slang)*, worn to a frazzle *(informal)*, on your last legs *(informal)*, creamcrackered *(Brit slang)* ▹ *n*
12 = **middle**, heart, depth, thick, midst
deadline *n* = **time limit**, cutoff point, target date *or* time, limit
deadlock *n* = **impasse**, stalemate, standstill, halt, cessation, gridlock, standoff, full stop
deadly *adj* 1 = **lethal**, fatal, deathly, dangerous, devastating, destructive, mortal, murderous, poisonous, malignant, virulent, pernicious, noxious, venomous, baleful, death-dealing, baneful 2 *(informal)* = **boring**, dull, tedious, flat, monotonous, uninteresting, mind-numbing, unexciting, ho-hum *(informal)*, wearisome, as dry as dust
deaf *adj* 1 = **hard of hearing**, without hearing, stone deaf
deal¹ *n* 1 *(informal)* = **agreement**, understanding, contract, business, negotiation, arrangement, bargain, transaction, pact
3 = **amount**, quantity, measure, degree, mass, volume, share, portion, bulk ▹ *vb*
8 **deal in something** = **sell**, trade in, stock, traffic in, buy and sell
9 **deal something out** = **distribute**, give, administer, share, divide, assign, allocate, dispense, bestow, allot, mete out, dole out, apportion
dealer *n* 1 = **trader**, marketer, merchant, supplier, wholesaler, purveyor, tradesman, merchandiser
deal with *vb* 2 = **be concerned with**, involve, concern, touch, regard, apply to, bear on, pertain to, be relevant to, treat of

DICTIONARY

wish to deal with specifics **3** to do business with

dean *n* **1** the chief administrative official of a college or university faculty **2** *chiefly Church of England* the chief administrator of a cathedral or collegiate church
WORD ORIGIN Late Latin *decanus* one set over ten people

d

Dean[1] *n* **Forest of Dean** a forest in W England, in Gloucestershire, between the Rivers Severn and Wye: formerly a royal hunting ground

Dean[2] *n* **1 Christopher** See **Torvill and Dean** **2 James** (**Byron**) 1931–55, US film actor, who became a cult figure; his films include *East of Eden* and *Rebel Without a Cause* (both 1955). He died in a car crash

deanery *n, pl* **-eries 1** a place where a dean lives **2** the parishes presided over by a rural dean

dear ⓣ *n* **1** (often used in direct address) someone regarded with affection ▷ *adj* **2** beloved; precious **3 a** highly priced **b** charging high prices **4** a form of address used at the beginning of a letter before the name of the recipient: *Dear Mr Anderson* **5 dear to** important or close to ▷ *interj* **6** an exclamation of surprise or dismay: *oh dear, I've broken it* ▷ *adv* **7** dearly: *her errors have cost her dear* **dearly** *adv*
WORD ORIGIN Old English *dēore*

dearth (dirth) *n* an inadequate amount; scarcity
WORD ORIGIN Middle English *derthe*

death ⓣ *n* **1** the permanent end of life in a person or animal **2** an instance of this: *his sudden death* **3** ending or destruction **4 at death's door** likely to die soon **5 catch one's death (of cold)** *informal* to contract a severe cold **6 like death warmed up** *informal* looking or feeling very ill or very tired **7 put to death** to execute **8 to death a** until dead **b** very much: *I had probably scared him to death*
WORD ORIGIN Old English *dēath*

deathbed *n* the bed in which a person dies or is about to die

deathblow *n* a thing or event that destroys hope

death certificate *n* a document signed by a doctor certifying the death of a person and stating the cause of death if known

death duty *n* ▸ (in Britain) the former name for **inheritance tax**

death knell *n* something that heralds death or destruction

deathless *adj* everlasting because of fine qualities: *highbrow, deathless, and often endless prose*

deathly ⓣ *adj* **1** resembling death: *a deathly pallor* **2** deadly

death mask *n* a cast taken from the face of a person who has recently died

death rate *n* the ratio of deaths in an area or group to the population of that area or group

death row *n US* part of a prison where convicts awaiting execution are imprisoned

death's-head *n* a human skull or a picture of one used to represent death or danger

death trap *n* a place or vehicle considered very unsafe

death warrant *n* **1** the official authorization for carrying out a sentence of death **2 sign one's (own) death warrant** to cause one's own destruction

deathwatch beetle *n* a beetle that bores into wood and produces a tapping sound

deb *n informal* a debutante

debacle ⓣ (day-**bah**-kl) *n* something that ends in a disastrous failure, esp. because it has not been properly planned
WORD ORIGIN French

debar *vb* **-barring, -barred** to prevent (someone) from doing something

debase *vb* **-basing, -based** to lower in quality, character, or value **debasement** *n*
WORD ORIGIN see DE-, BASE[2]

debatable *adj* not absolutely certain: *her motives are highly debatable*

debate ⓣ *n* **1** a discussion **2** a formal discussion, as in a parliament, in which opposing arguments are put forward ▷ *vb* **-bating, -bated 3** to discuss (something) formally **4** to consider (possible courses of action)
WORD ORIGIN Old French *debatre*

debauch (dib-**bawch**) *vb* to make someone bad or corrupt, esp. sexually
WORD ORIGIN Old French *desbaucher* to corrupt

debauched *adj* immoral; sexually corrupt

debauchery *n* excessive drunkenness or sexual activity

debenture *n* a long-term bond, bearing fixed interest and usually unsecured, issued by a company or governmental agency **debentured** *adj*
WORD ORIGIN Latin *debentur mihi* there are owed to me

debenture stock *n* shares issued by a company, guaranteeing a fixed return at regular intervals

de Bèze *n* **Théodore**.1519–1605, French Calvinist theologian and scholar, who lived in Switzerland. He succeeded Calvin as leader of the Swiss Protestants

debilitate *vb* **-tating, -tated** to make gradually weaker **debilitation** *n* **debilitating** *adj*
WORD ORIGIN Latin *debilis* weak

debility *n, pl* **-ties** a state of weakness, esp. caused by illness

debit *n* **1** the money, or a record of the money, withdrawn from a person's bank account **2** *accounting* **a** acknowledgment of a sum owing by entry on the left side of an account **b** an entry or the total of entries on this side ▷ *vb* **-iting, -ited 3** to charge (an account) with a debt: *they had debited our account* **4** *accounting* to record (an item) as a debit in an account
WORD ORIGIN Latin *debitum* debt

debit card *n* a card issued by a bank or building society enabling customers to pay for goods by inserting it into a computer-controlled device at the place of sale, which is connected through the telephone network to the bank or building society

debonair *or* **debonnaire** *adj* (of a man) confident, charming, and well-dressed
WORD ORIGIN Old French

debouch *vb* **1** (esp. of troops) to move

THESAURUS

dear *n* **1 = darling**, love, dearest, sweet, angel, treasure, precious, beloved, loved one, sweetheart, truelove ▷ *adj* **2 = beloved**, close, valued, favourite, respected, prized, dearest, sweet, treasured, precious, darling, intimate, esteemed, cherished, revered **OPPOSITE:** hated **3a, 3b = expensive**, costly, high-priced, excessive, pricey (*informal*), at a premium, overpriced, exorbitant **OPPOSITE:** cheap

death *n* **1, 2 = dying**, demise, bereavement, end, passing, release, loss, departure, curtains (*informal*), cessation, expiration, decease, quietus **OPPOSITE:** birth **3 = destruction**, ending, finish, ruin, wiping out, undoing, extinction, elimination, downfall, extermination, annihilation, obliteration, ruination **OPPOSITE:** beginning

deathly *adj* **1 = deathlike**, white, pale, ghastly, wan, gaunt, haggard, bloodless, pallid, ashen, sallow, cadaverous, ashy, like death warmed up (*informal*)

debacle *n* **= disaster**, catastrophe, fiasco

debate *n* **1 = discussion**, talk, argument, dispute, analysis, conversation, consideration, controversy, dialogue, contention, deliberation, polemic, altercation, disputation ▷ *vb* **3 = discuss**, question, talk about, argue about, dispute, examine, contest, deliberate, contend, wrangle, thrash out, controvert **4 = consider**, reflect, think about, weigh, contemplate, deliberate, ponder, revolve, mull

DICTIONARY

into a more open space **2** (of a river, glacier, etc.) to flow into a larger area or body **debouchment** *n*
WORD ORIGIN Old French *dé-* from + *bouche* mouth

debrief *vb* to interrogate (a soldier, diplomat, astronaut, etc.) on the completion of a mission **debriefing** *n*

debris ● (deb-ree) *n* **1** fragments of something destroyed; rubble **2** a mass of loose stones and earth
WORD ORIGIN French

de Broglie *n* **1** Prince **Louis Victor**. 1892–1987, French physicist, noted for his research in quantum mechanics and his development of wave mechanics: Nobel prize for physics 1929 **2** his brother, **Maurice**, Duc de Broglie. 1875–1960, French physicist, noted for his research into X-ray spectra

Debs *n* **Eugene Victor** 1855–1926, US labour leader; five times Socialist presidential candidate (1900–20)

debt ● *n* **1** a sum of money owed **2 bad debt** a debt that is unlikely to be paid **3 in debt** owing money **4 in someone's debt** grateful to someone for his or her help: *I couldn't have managed without you – I'm in your debt*
WORD ORIGIN Latin *debitum*

debt of honour *n* a debt that is morally but not legally binding

debtor ● *n* a person who owes money

debug *vb* **-bugging, -bugged** *informal* **1** to locate and remove defects in (a computer program) **2** to remove concealed microphones from (a room or telephone)

debunk *vb informal* to expose the falseness of: *many commonly held myths are debunked by the book* **debunker** *n*
WORD ORIGIN DE- + BUNK[2]

debut ● (day-byoo) *n* the first public appearance of a performer
WORD ORIGIN French

debutante (day-byoo-tont) *n* a young upper-class woman who is formally presented to society
WORD ORIGIN French

Debye *n* **Peter Joseph Wilhelm** 1884–1966, Dutch chemist and physicist, working in the US: Nobel prize for chemistry (1936) for his work on dipole moments

Dec. December

decade *n* a period of ten years
WORD ORIGIN Greek *deka* ten

decadence (deck-a-denss) *n* a decline in morality or culture **decadent** *adj*
WORD ORIGIN Medieval Latin *decadentia* a falling away

decaf (dee-kaf) *informal n* **1** decaffeinated coffee ▷ *adj* **2** decaffeinated

decaffeinated (dee-kaf-fin-ate-id) *adj* with the caffeine removed: *decaffeinated tea*

decagon *n geom* a figure with ten sides **decagonal** *adj*
WORD ORIGIN Greek *deka* ten + *gōnia* angle

decahedron (deck-a-heed-ron) *n* a solid figure with ten plane faces **decahedral** *adj*
WORD ORIGIN Greek *deka* ten + *hedra* base

decalitre *or US* **decaliter** *n* a measure of volume equivalent to 10 litres

Decalogue *n* ▸ same as **Ten Commandments**
WORD ORIGIN Greek *deka* ten + *logos* word

decametre *or US* **decameter** *n* a unit of length equal to ten metres

decamp *vb* to leave secretly or suddenly

decant *vb* **1** to pour (a liquid, esp. wine) from one container to another **2** *chiefly Brit* to rehouse (people) while their homes are being renovated
WORD ORIGIN Medieval Latin *de-* from + *canthus* spout, rim

decanter *n* a stoppered bottle into which a drink is poured for serving

decapitate *vb* **-tating, -tated** to behead **decapitation** *n*
WORD ORIGIN Latin *de-* from + *caput* head

decapod *n* **1** a creature, such as a crab, with five pairs of walking limbs **2** a creature, such as a squid, with eight short tentacles and two longer ones
WORD ORIGIN Greek *deka* ten + *pous* foot

decarbonize *or* **-ise** *vb* **-izing, -ized** *or* **-ising, -ised** to remove carbon from (an internal-combustion engine) **decarbonization** *or* **-isation** *n*

decathlon *n* an athletic contest in which each athlete competes in ten different events **decathlete** *n*
WORD ORIGIN Greek *deka* ten + *athlon* contest

Decatur *n* **Stephen** 1779–1820, US naval officer, noted for his raid on Tripoli harbour (1804) and his role in the War of 1812

decay ● *vb* **1** to decline gradually in health, prosperity, or quality **2** to rot or cause to rot **3** *physics* (of an atomic nucleus) to undergo radioactive disintegration ▷ *n* **4** the process of something rotting: *too much sugar can cause tooth decay* **5** the state brought about by this process **6** *physics* disintegration of a nucleus, occurring spontaneously or as a result of electron capture
WORD ORIGIN Latin *de-* from + *cadere* to fall

decease *n formal* death
WORD ORIGIN Latin *decedere* to depart

deceased ● *adj formal* **1** dead ▷ *n* **2** a dead person: *the deceased*

deceit *n* behaviour intended to deceive

deceitful *adj* full of deceit

deceive ● *vb* **-ceiving, -ceived** **1** to mislead by lying **2 deceive oneself** to refuse to acknowledge something one knows to be true **3** to be unfaithful to (one's sexual partner)
WORD ORIGIN Latin *decipere* to ensnare, cheat

decelerate *vb* **-ating, -ated** to slow down **deceleration** *n*
WORD ORIGIN DE- + (AC)CELERATE

December *n* the twelfth month of the year
WORD ORIGIN Latin: the tenth month (the Roman year originally began with March)

decencies *pl n* generally accepted standards of good behaviour

decency ● *n* conformity to the

THESAURUS

over, ruminate, give thought to, cogitate, meditate upon

debris *n* **1 = remains**, bits, pieces, waste, ruins, wreck, rubbish, fragments, litter, rubble, wreckage, brash, detritus, dross

debt *n* **1 = debit**, bill, score, due, duty, commitment, obligation, liability, arrears **3 in debt = owing**, liable, accountable, in the red *(informal)*, in arrears, beholden, in hock *(informal, chiefly US)*

debtor *n* **= borrower**, mortgagor

debut *n* **= entrance**, beginning, launch, launching, introduction, first appearance, inauguration

decay *vb* **1 = decline**, sink, break down, diminish, dissolve, crumble, deteriorate, fall off, dwindle, lessen, wane, disintegrate, degenerate
OPPOSITE: grow
2 = rot, break down, disintegrate, spoil, crumble, deteriorate, perish, degenerate, fester, decompose, mortify, moulder, go bad, putrefy ▷ *n* **4 = rot**, rotting, deterioration, corruption, mould, blight, perishing, disintegration, corrosion, decomposition, gangrene, mortification, canker, caries, putrefaction, putrescence, cariosity, putridity

deceased *adj* **1 = dead**, late, departed, lost, gone, expired, defunct, lifeless, pushing up daisies *(informal)*

deceive *vb* **1 = take in**, trick, fool *(informal)*, cheat, con *(informal)*, kid *(informal)*, stiff *(slang)*, sting *(informal)*, mislead, betray, lead (someone) on *(informal)*, hoax, dupe, beguile, delude, swindle, outwit, ensnare, bamboozle *(informal)*, hoodwink, entrap, double-cross *(informal)*, take for a ride *(informal)*, pull a fast one on *(slang)*, cozen, scam *(slang)*, pull the wool over (someone's) eyes

decency *n* **= propriety**, correctness, decorum, fitness, good form,

DICTIONARY

prevailing standards of what is right

decennial *adj* **1** lasting for ten years **2** occurring every ten years

decent *adj* **1** conforming to an acceptable standard or quality: *a decent living wage; he's made a few decent films* **2** polite or respectable: *he's a decent man* **3** fitting or proper: *that's the decent thing to do* **4** conforming to conventions of sexual behaviour **5** *informal* kind; generous: *she was pretty decent to me* **decently** *adv*
WORD ORIGIN Latin *decens* suitable

decentralize *or* **-ise** *vb* **-izing, -ized** *or* **-ising, -ised** to reorganize into smaller local units **decentralization** *or* **-isation** *n*

deception *n* **1** the act of deceiving someone or the state of being deceived **2** something that deceives; trick

deceptive *adj* likely or designed to deceive **deceptively** *adv* **deceptiveness** *n*

deci- *combining form* denoting one tenth: *decimetre*
WORD ORIGIN Latin *decimus* tenth

decibel *n* a unit for comparing two power levels or measuring the intensity of a sound
WORD ORIGIN DECI- + BEL

decide *vb* **-ciding, -cided 1** to reach a decision: *we must decide on suitable action; he decided to stay on* **2** to cause to reach a decision **3** to settle (a question): *possible profits decided the issue* **4** to influence the outcome of (a contest) decisively: *the goal that decided the match came just before half-time*
WORD ORIGIN Latin *decidere* to cut off

decided *adj* **1** definite or noticeable: *a decided improvement* **2** strong and definite: *he has decided views on the matter* **decidedly** *adv*

deciduous *adj* **1** (of a tree) shedding all leaves annually **2** (of antlers or teeth) being shed at the end of a period of growth
WORD ORIGIN Latin *deciduus* falling off

decilitre *or US* **deciliter** *n* a measure of volume equivalent to one tenth of a litre

decimal *n* **1** a fraction written in the form of a dot followed by one or more numbers, for example $.2 = 2/10$ ▷ *adj* **2** relating to or using powers of ten **3** expressed as a decimal
WORD ORIGIN Latin *decima* a tenth

decimal currency *n* a system of currency in which the units are parts or powers of ten

decimalize *or* **-ise** *vb* **-izing, -ized** *or* **-ising, -ised** to change (a system or number) to the decimal system **decimalization** *or* **-isation** *n*

decimal point *n* the dot between the unit and the fraction of a number in the decimal system

decimal system *n* a number system with a base of ten, in which numbers are expressed by combinations of the digits 0 to 9

decimate *vb* **-mating, -mated** to destroy or kill a large proportion of **decimation** *n*
WORD ORIGIN Latin *decimare*

decimetre *or US* **decimeter** *n* a unit of length equal to one tenth of a metre

decipher *vb* **1** to make out the meaning of (something obscure or illegible) **2** to convert from code into plain text **decipherable** *adj*

decision *n* **1** a choice or judgment made about something **2** the act of making up one's mind **3** the ability to make quick and definite decisions
WORD ORIGIN Latin *decisio* a cutting off

decisive *adj* **1** having great influence on the result of something: *the decisive goal was scored in the closing minutes* **2** having the ability to make quick decisions **decisively** *adv* **decisiveness** *n*

deck *n* **1** an area of a ship that forms a floor, at any level **2** a similar area in a bus **3** ▸ same as **tape deck 4** *US & Austral* a pack of playing cards **5 clear the decks** *informal* to prepare for action, as by removing obstacles ▷ *vb* **6** *slang* to knock (a person) to the ground
WORD ORIGIN Middle Dutch *dec* a covering

deck chair *n* a folding chair with a wooden frame and a canvas seat

Decker *n* a variant spelling of (Thomas) **Dekker**

decking *n* a wooden deck or platform, esp. one in a garden for deck chairs, etc.

deckle edge *n* a rough edge on paper, often left as ornamentation **deckle-edged** *adj*
WORD ORIGIN the *deckle* is the frame that holds the pulp in paper making

deck out *vb* to make more attractive by decorating: *the village was decked out in the blue-and-white flags*

declaim *vb* **1** to speak loudly and dramatically **2 declaim against** to protest against loudly and publicly **declamation** *n* **declamatory** *adj*
WORD ORIGIN Latin *declamare*

declaration *n* **1** a firm, emphatic statement **2** an official announcement or statement **declaratory** *adj*

declare *vb* **-claring, -clared 1** to state firmly and forcefully **2** to

THESAURUS

respectability, etiquette, appropriateness, seemliness

decent *adj* **1 = satisfactory**, average, fair, all right, reasonable, suitable, sufficient, acceptable, good enough, adequate, competent, ample, tolerable, up to scratch, passable, up to standard, up to the mark **OPPOSITE:** unsatisfactory
2, 4 = respectable, nice, pure, proper, modest, polite, chaste, presentable, decorous **3 = proper**, becoming, seemly, fitting, fit, appropriate, suitable, respectable, befitting, decorous, comme il faut *(French)* **OPPOSITE:** improper
5 *(informal)* **= good**, kind, friendly, neighbourly, generous, helpful, obliging, accommodating, sympathetic, comradely, benign, gracious, benevolent, courteous, amiable, amicable, sociable, genial, peaceable, companionable, well-disposed

deception *n* **1 = trickery**, fraud, deceit, hypocrisy, cunning, treachery, guile, duplicity, insincerity, legerdemain, dissimulation, craftiness, fraudulence, deceitfulness, deceptiveness **OPPOSITE:** honesty
2 = trick, lie, fraud, cheat, bluff, sham, snare, hoax, decoy, ruse, artifice, subterfuge, canard, feint, stratagem, porky *(Brit slang)*, pork pie *(Brit slang)*, wile, hokum *(slang, chiefly US & Canad)*, leg-pull *(Brit informal)*, imposture, snow job *(slang, chiefly US & Canad)*, fastie *(Austral slang)*

decide *vb* **1 = make a decision**, make up your mind, reach *or* come to a decision, end, choose, determine, purpose, elect, conclude, commit yourself, come to a conclusion **OPPOSITE:** hesitate
3, 4 = settle, determine, conclude, resolve

decision *n* **1 = judgment**, finding, ruling, order, result, sentence, settlement, resolution, conclusion, outcome, verdict, decree, arbitration
3 = decisiveness, purpose, resolution, resolve, determination, firmness, forcefulness, purposefulness, resoluteness, strength of mind *or* will

decisive *adj* **1 = crucial**, significant, critical, final, positive, absolute, influential, definite, definitive, momentous, conclusive, fateful **OPPOSITE:** uncertain
2 = resolute, decided, firm, determined, forceful, uncompromising, incisive, trenchant, strong-minded **OPPOSITE:** indecisive

declaration *n* **1 = affirmation**, profession, assertion, revelation, disclosure, acknowledgment, protestation, avowal, averment
2a = announcement, proclamation, decree, notice, manifesto, notification, edict, pronouncement, promulgation, pronunciamento
2b = statement, testimony,

DICTIONARY

announce publicly or officially: *a state of emergency has been declared* **3** to state officially that (someone or something) is as specified: *he was declared fit to play* **4** to acknowledge (dutiable goods or income) for tax purposes **5** *cards* to decide (the trump suit) by making the winning bid **6** *cricket* to bring an innings to an end before the last batsman is out **7 declare for** *or* **against** to state one's support or opposition for something **WORD ORIGIN** Latin *declarare* to make clear

declassify *vb* **-fies, -fying, -fied** to state officially that (information or a document) is no longer secret **declassification** *n*

declension *n grammar* changes in the form of nouns, pronouns, or adjectives to show case, number, and gender **WORD ORIGIN** Latin *declinatio* a bending aside, hence variation

declination *n* **1** *astron* the angular distance of a star or planet north or south from the celestial equator **2** the angle made by a compass needle with the direction of the geographical north pole

decline ⊙ *vb* **-clining, -clined 1** to become smaller, weaker, or less important **2** to politely refuse to accept or do (something) **3** *grammar* to list the inflections of (a noun, pronoun, or adjective) ▷*n* **4** a gradual weakening or loss **WORD ORIGIN** Latin *declinare* to bend away

declivity *n, pl* **-ties** a downward slope **declivitous** *adj* **WORD ORIGIN** Latin *declivitas*

declutch *vb* to disengage the clutch of a motor vehicle

decoct *vb* to extract the essence from (a substance) by boiling **decoction** *n* **WORD ORIGIN** Latin *decoquere* to boil down

decode *vb* **-coding, -coded** to convert from code into ordinary language **decoder** *n*

decoke *vb* **-coking, -coked** ▸same as **decarbonize**

décolletage (day-kol-**tahzh**) *n* a low-cut dress or neckline **WORD ORIGIN** French

décolleté (day-**kol**-tay) *adj* **1** (of a woman's garment) low-cut ▷*n* **2** a low-cut neckline **WORD ORIGIN** French

decommission *vb* to dismantle or remove from service (a nuclear reactor, weapon, ship, etc. which is no longer required)

decompose *vb* **-posing, -posed 1** to rot **2** to break up or separate into constituent parts **decomposition** *n*

decompress *vb* **1** to free from pressure **2** to return (a diver) to normal atmospheric pressure **decompression** *n*

decompression sickness *n* a disorder characterized by severe pain and difficulty in breathing caused by a sudden and sustained change in atmospheric pressure

decongestant *n* a drug that relieves nasal congestion

decontaminate *vb* **-nating, -nated** to make (a place or object) safe by removing poisons, radioactivity, etc. **decontamination** *n*

decor ⊙ (**day**-core) *n* a style or scheme of interior decoration and furnishings in a room or house **WORD ORIGIN** French

decorate ⊙ *vb* **-rating, -rated 1** to make more attractive by adding some ornament or colour **2** to paint or wallpaper **3** to confer a mark of distinction, esp. a medal, upon **decorative** *adj* **decorator** *n* **WORD ORIGIN** Latin *decorare*

Decorated style *or* **architecture** *n* a 14th-century style of English architecture characterized by the ogee arch, geometrical tracery, and floral decoration

decoration ⊙ *n* **1** an addition that makes something more attractive or ornate **2** the way in which a room or building is decorated **3** something, esp. a medal, conferred as a mark of honour

decorous (**deck**-or-uss) *adj* polite, calm, and sensible in behaviour **decorously** *adv* **decorousness** *n* **WORD ORIGIN** Latin *decorus*

decorum (dik-**core**-um) *n* polite and socially correct behaviour

decoy *n* **1** a person or thing used to lure someone into danger **2** an image of a bird or animal, used to lure game into a trap or within shooting range ▷*vb* **3** to lure into danger by means of a decoy **WORD ORIGIN** probably from Dutch *de kooi* the cage

decrease ⊙ *vb* **-creasing, -creased 1** to make or become less in size, strength, or quantity ▷*n* **2** a lessening; reduction **3** the amount by which something has been diminished **decreasing** *adj* **decreasingly** *adv* **WORD ORIGIN** Latin *decrescere* to grow less

decree ⊙ *n* **1** a law made by someone in authority **2** a judgment of a court

THESAURUS

deposition, attestation

declare *vb* **1a = state**, claim, announce, voice, express, maintain, confirm, assert, proclaim, pronounce, utter, notify, affirm, profess, avow, aver, asseverate **1b = testify**, state, witness, swear, assert, affirm, certify, attest, bear witness, vouch, give testimony, asseverate **2 = make known**, tell, reveal, show, broadcast, confess, communicate, disclose, convey, manifest, make public

decline *vb* **1a = fall**, fail, drop, contract, lower, sink, flag, fade, shrink, diminish, decrease, slow down, fall off, dwindle, lessen, wane, ebb, slacken **OPPOSITE:** rise **1b = deteriorate**, fade, weaken, pine, decay, worsen, lapse, languish, degenerate, droop **OPPOSITE:** improve **2 = refuse**, reject, turn down, avoid, deny, spurn, abstain, forgo, send your regrets, say 'no' **OPPOSITE:** accept ▷*n* **4a = depression**, recession, slump, falling off, downturn, dwindling, lessening, diminution, abatement **OPPOSITE:** rise **4b = deterioration**, fall, failing, slump, weakening, decay, worsening, descent, downturn, disintegration, degeneration, atrophy, decrepitude, retrogression, enfeeblement **OPPOSITE:** improvement

decor *or* **décor** *n* **= decoration**, colour scheme, ornamentation, furnishing style

decorate *vb* **1 = adorn**, deck, trim, embroider, garnish, ornament, embellish, festoon, bedeck, beautify, grace, engarland **2 = do up**, paper, paint, wallpaper, renovate (*informal*), furbish **3 = pin a medal on**, cite, confer an honour on *or* upon

decoration *n* **1a = ornament**, trimmings, garnish, frill, scroll, spangle, festoon, trinket, bauble, flounce, arabesque, curlicue, furbelow, falderal, cartouch(e) **1b = adornment**, trimming, garnishing, enhancement, elaboration, embellishment, ornamentation, beautification **3 = medal**, award, order, star, colours, ribbon, badge, emblem, garter

decrease *vb* **1a = drop**, decline, lessen, contract, lower, ease, shrink, diminish, fall off, dwindle, wane, subside, abate, peter out, slacken **1b = reduce**, cut, lower, contract, depress, moderate, weaken, diminish, turn down, slow down, cut down, shorten, dilute, impair, lessen, curtail, wind down, abate, tone down, truncate, abridge, downsize **OPPOSITE:** increase ▷*n* **2 = lessening**, decline, reduction, loss, falling off, downturn, dwindling, contraction, ebb, cutback, subsidence, curtailment, shrinkage, diminution, abatement **OPPOSITE:** growth

decree *n* **1 = law**, order, ruling, act, demand, command, regulation, mandate, canon, statute, covenant,

DICTIONARY

▷ *vb* **decreeing, decreed 3** to order by decree
WORD ORIGIN Latin *decretum* ordinance
decree absolute *n* the final decree in divorce proceedings, which leaves the parties free to remarry
decree nisi *n* a provisional decree in divorce proceedings, which will later be made absolute unless cause is shown why it should not
WORD ORIGIN Latin *nisi* unless
decrepit *adj* weakened or worn out by age or long use **decrepitude** *n*
WORD ORIGIN Latin *crepare* to creak
decretal *n* *RC church* a papal decree
WORD ORIGIN Late Latin *decretalis*
decry *vb* **-cries, -crying, -cried** to express open disapproval of
WORD ORIGIN Old French *descrier*
decrypt *vb* **1** to decode (a message) with or without previous knowledge of its key **2** to make intelligible (a television or other signal) that has been deliberately distorted for transmission ▸ See also **encrypt** > **decryption** *n*
WORD ORIGIN DE- + (EN)CRYPT
Dedekind *n* **(Julius Wilhelm) Richard** 1831–1916, German mathematician, who devised a way (the **Dedekind cut**) of according irrational and rational numbers the same status
dedicate ⓣ *vb* **-cating, -cated 1** to devote (oneself or one's time) wholly to a special purpose or cause **2** to inscribe or address (a book, piece of music, etc.) to someone as a token of affection or respect **3** to play (a record) on radio for someone as a greeting **4** to set apart for sacred uses
WORD ORIGIN Latin *dedicare* to announce
dedicated ⓣ *adj* **1** devoted to a particular purpose or cause **2** *computers* designed to fulfil one function
dedication ⓣ *n* **1** wholehearted devotion **2** an inscription in a book dedicating it to a person
deduce *vb* **-ducing, -duced** to reach (a conclusion) by reasoning from evidence; work out **deducible** *adj*
WORD ORIGIN Latin *de-* away + *ducere* to lead
deduct ⓣ *vb* to subtract (a number, quantity, or part)
WORD ORIGIN Latin *deducere* to deduce
deductible *adj* **1** capable of being deducted **2** *US* tax-deductible
deduction ⓣ *n* **1** the act or process of subtracting **2** something that is deducted **3** *logic* **a** a process of reasoning by which a conclusion necessarily follows from a set of general premises **b** a conclusion reached by this process
deductive *adj*
de Duve *n* **Christian** born 1917, Belgian biochemist, who discovered lysosomes: shared the Nobel prize (1974) for his work in cell biology
Dee[1] *n* **1** a river in N Wales and NW England, rising in S Gwynedd and flowing east and north to the Irish Sea. Length: about 112 km (70 miles) **2** a river in NE Scotland, rising in the Cairngorms and flowing east to the North Sea. Length: about 140 km (87 miles) **3** a river in S Scotland, flowing south to the Solway Firth. Length: about 80 km (50 miles)
Dee[2] *n* **John** 1527–1608, English mathematician, astrologer, and magician: best known for his preface (1570) to the first edition of Euclid in English
deed ⓣ *n* **1** something that is done **2** a notable achievement **3** action as opposed to words **4** *law* a legal document, esp. one concerning the ownership of property
WORD ORIGIN Old English *dēd*
deed box *n* a strong box in which deeds and other documents are kept
deed poll *n* *law* a deed made by one party only, esp. to change one's name
deejay *n* *informal* a disc jockey
WORD ORIGIN from the initials DJ
deem *vb* to judge or consider: *common sense is deemed to be a virtue*
WORD ORIGIN Old English *dēman*
deep ⓣ *adj* **1** extending or situated far down from a surface: *a deep ditch* **2** extending or situated far inwards, backwards, or sideways **3** of a specified dimension downwards, inwards, or backwards: *six metres deep* **4** coming from or penetrating to a great depth **5** difficult to understand **6** of great intensity: *deep doubts* **7 deep in** totally absorbed in: *deep in conversation* **8** (of a colour) intense or dark **9** low in pitch: *a deep laugh* **10 go off the deep end** *informal* to lose one's temper **11 in deep water** *informal* in a tricky position or in trouble ▷ *n* **12** any deep place on land or under water **13 the deep a** *poetic* the ocean **b** *cricket* the area of the field relatively far from the pitch **14** the most profound, intense, or central part: *the deep of winter* ▷ *adv* **15** late: *deep into the night* **16** profoundly or intensely: *deep down I was afraid it was all my fault* **deeply** *adv*
WORD ORIGIN Old English *dēop*
deepen ⓣ *vb* to make or become deeper or more intense
deep-freeze *n* **1** ▸ same as **freezer** ▷ *vb* **-freezing, -froze, -frozen 2** to freeze or keep in a deep-freeze

THESAURUS

ordinance, proclamation, enactment, edict, dictum, precept **2 = judgment**, finding, order, result, ruling, decision, award, conclusion, verdict, arbitration ▷ *vb* **3 = order**, rule, command, decide, demand, establish, determine, proclaim, dictate, prescribe, pronounce, lay down, enact, ordain
dedicate *vb* **1 = devote**, give, apply, commit, concern, occupy, pledge, surrender, give over to **2 = offer**, address, assign, inscribe
dedicated *adj* **1 = committed**, devoted, sworn, enthusiastic, single-minded, zealous, purposeful, given over to, wholehearted **OPPOSITE:** indifferent
dedication *n* **1 = commitment**, loyalty, devotion, allegiance, adherence, single-mindedness, faithfulness, wholeheartedness, devotedness **OPPOSITE:** indifference **2 = inscription**, message, address
deduct *vb* **= subtract**, remove, take off, withdraw, take out, take from, take away, reduce by, knock off *(informal)*, decrease by **OPPOSITE:** add
deduction *n* **1 = subtraction**, reduction, allowance, concession **2 = discount**, reduction, cut, concession, allowance, decrease, rebate, diminution **3a = reasoning**, thinking, thought, reason, analysis, logic, cogitation, ratiocination **3b = conclusion**, finding, verdict, judgment, assumption, inference, corollary
deed *n* **1, 2 = action**, act, performance, achievement, exploit, feat **4** *(law)* **= document**, title, contract, title deed, indenture
deep *adj* **1 = big**, wide, broad, profound, yawning, cavernous, bottomless, unfathomable, fathomless, abyssal **OPPOSITE:** shallow **5 = secret**, hidden, unknown, mysterious, concealed, obscure, abstract, veiled, esoteric, mystifying, impenetrable, arcane, abstruse, recondite **6 = intense**, great, serious *(informal)*, acute, extreme, grave, profound, heartfelt, unqualified, abject, deeply felt, heartrending **OPPOSITE:** superficial **8 = dark**, strong, rich, warm, intense, vivid **OPPOSITE:** light **9 = low**, booming, bass, full, mellow, resonant, sonorous, mellifluous, dulcet, low-pitched, full-toned **OPPOSITE:** high ▷ *n* **13a the deep** *(poetic)* **= the ocean**, the sea, the waves, the main, the drink *(informal)*, the high seas, the briny *(informal)*
deepen *vb* **a = intensify**, increase, grow, strengthen, reinforce, escalate, magnify, augment **b = dig out**, excavate, scoop out, hollow out, scrape out
de facto *adv* **1 = in fact**, really, actually, in effect, in reality ▷ *adj*

DICTIONARY

deep-fry *vb* **-fries, -frying, -fried** to cook in hot oil deep enough to completely cover the food
deep-laid *adj* (of a plan) carefully worked out and kept secret
deep-rooted *or* **deep-seated** *adj* (of ideas, beliefs, etc.) firmly fixed or held
deep-vein thrombosis *n* a blood clot in one of the major veins, usually in the legs or pelvis
deer *n, pl* **deer** *or* **deers** a large hoofed mammal
WORD ORIGIN Old English *dēor* beast
deerstalker *n* a cloth hat with peaks at the front and back and earflaps
de-escalate *vb* to reduce the intensity of (a problem or situation) **de-escalation** *n*
def *adj* **deffer, deffest** *slang* very good
WORD ORIGIN perhaps from *definitive*
deface *vb* **-facing, -faced** to deliberately spoil the surface or appearance of **defacement** *n*
de facto ❶ *adv* **1** in fact ▷ *adj* **2** existing in fact, whether legally recognized or not
WORD ORIGIN Latin
defalcate *vb* **-cating, -cated** *law* to make wrong use of funds entrusted to one **defalcation** *n*
WORD ORIGIN Medieval Latin *defalcare* to cut off
defame *vb* **-faming, -famed** to attack the good reputation of **defamation** *n* **defamatory** (dif-fam-a-tree) *adj*
WORD ORIGIN Latin *diffamare* to spread by unfavourable report
default ❶ *n* **1** a failure to do something, esp. to meet a financial obligation or to appear in court **2** *computers* an instruction to a computer to select a particular option unless the user specifies otherwise **3 by default** happening because something else has not happened: *they gained a colony by default because no other European power wanted it* **4 in default of** in the absence of ▷ *vb* **5** to fail to fulfil an obligation, esp. to make payment when due **defaulter** *n*
WORD ORIGIN Old French *defaillir* to fail
defeat ❶ *vb* **1** to win a victory over **2** to thwart or frustrate: *this accident has defeated all his hopes of winning* ▷ *n* **3** the act of defeating or state of being defeated
WORD ORIGIN Old French *desfaire* to undo, ruin
defeatism *n* a ready acceptance or expectation of defeat **defeatist** *n, adj*
defecate *vb* **-cating, -cated** to discharge waste from the body through the anus **defecation** *n*
WORD ORIGIN Latin *defaecare*
defect ❶ *n* **1** an imperfection or blemish ▷ *vb* **2** to desert one's country or cause to join the opposing forces **defection** *n* **defector** *n*
WORD ORIGIN Latin *deficere* to forsake, fail
defective *adj* imperfect or faulty: *defective hearing*
defence ❶ *or US* **defense** *n* **1** resistance against attack **2** something that provides such resistance **3** an argument or piece of writing in support of something that has been criticized or questioned **4** a country's military resources **5** *law* a defendant's denial of the truth of a charge **6** *law* the defendant and his or her legal advisers collectively **7** *sport* the players in a team whose function is to prevent the opposing team from scoring **8 defences** fortifications **defenceless** *or US* **defenseless** *adj*
WORD ORIGIN Latin *defendere* to defend
defend ❶ *vb* **1** to protect from harm or danger **2** to support in the face of criticism: *I spoke up to defend her* **3** to represent (a defendant) in court **4** to protect (a title or championship) against a challenge **defender** *n*
WORD ORIGIN Latin *defendere* to ward off
defendant ❶ *n* a person accused of a crime
defensible *adj* capable of being defended because believed to be right **defensibility** *n*
defensive ❶ *adj* **1** intended for defence **2** guarding against criticism or exposure of one's failings: *he can be highly defensive and wary* ▷ *n* **3 on the defensive** in a position of defence, as in being ready to reject criticism **defensively** *adv*
defer[1] ❶ *vb* **-ferring, -ferred** to delay until a future time; postpone: *payment was deferred indefinitely* **deferment** *or* **deferral** *n*
WORD ORIGIN Old French *differer* to be different, postpone
defer[2] *vb* **-ferring, -ferred** ▪ **defer to** to comply with the wishes (of)
WORD ORIGIN Latin *deferre* to bear down
deference *n* polite and respectful behaviour
deferential *adj* showing respect **deferentially** *adv*
defiance ❶ *n* open resistance to authority or opposition **defiant** *adj*
defibrillator *n med* an apparatus for

THESAURUS

2 = actual, real, existing
default *n* **1a = failure**, want, lack, fault, absence, neglect, defect, deficiency, lapse, omission, dereliction **1b = nonpayment**, evasion ▷ *vb* **5 = fail to pay**, dodge, evade, rat *(informal)*, neglect, levant *(Brit)*, welch *or* welsh *(slang)*
defeat *vb* **1 = beat**, crush, overwhelm, conquer, stuff *(slang)*, master, worst, tank *(slang)*, overthrow, lick *(informal)*, undo, subdue, rout, overpower, quell, trounce, clobber *(slang)*, vanquish, repulse, subjugate, run rings around *(informal)*, wipe the floor with *(informal)*, make mincemeat of *(informal)*, pip at the post, outplay, blow out of the water *(slang)*
OPPOSITE: surrender
2 = frustrate, foil, thwart, ruin, baffle, confound, balk, get the better of, forestall, stymie ▷ *n* **3a = conquest**, beating, overthrow, pasting *(slang)*, rout, debacle, trouncing, repulse, vanquishment
OPPOSITE: victory
3b = frustration, failure, reverse, disappointment, setback, thwarting
defect *n* **1 = deficiency**, want, failing, lack, mistake, fault, error, absence, weakness, flaw, shortcoming, inadequacy, imperfection, frailty, foible ▷ *vb* **2 = desert**, rebel, quit, revolt, change sides, apostatize, tergiversate
defence *or (US)* **defense** *n* **1, 2 = protection**, cover, security, guard, shelter, refuge, resistance, safeguard, immunity **3 = argument**, explanation, excuse, plea, apology, justification, vindication, rationalization, apologia, exoneration, exculpation, extenuation **4 = armaments**, weapons **5 = plea** *(law)*, case, claim, pleading, declaration, testimony, denial, alibi, vindication, rebuttal ▷ *pl n* **8 = shield**, barricade, fortification, bastion, buttress, rampart, bulwark, fastness, fortified pa (NZ)
defend *vb* **1 = protect**, cover, guard, screen, secure, preserve, look after, shelter, shield, harbour, safeguard, fortify, ward off, watch over, stick up for *(informal)*, keep safe, give sanctuary **2 = support**, champion, justify, maintain, sustain, plead for, endorse, assert, stand by, uphold, vindicate, stand up for, espouse, speak up for, stick up for *(informal)*
defendant *n* **= accused**, respondent, appellant, litigant, prisoner at the bar
defensive *adj* **1 = protective**, defending, opposing, safeguarding, watchful, on the defensive, on guard **2 = oversensitive**, uptight *(informal)*
defer[1] *vb* **= postpone**, delay, put off, suspend, shelve, set aside, adjourn, hold over, procrastinate, put on ice *(informal)*, put on the back burner *(informal)*, protract, take a rain check on *(US & Canad informal)*, prorogue
defiance *n* **= resistance**, challenge, opposition, confrontation, contempt, disregard, provocation, disobedience, insolence,

DICTIONARY

stopping fibrillation of the heart by application of an electric current

deficiency ❶ *n, pl* **-cies 1** the state of being deficient **2** a lack or shortage

deficiency disease *n* any condition, such as scurvy, caused by a lack of vitamins or other essential substances

deficient *adj* **1** lacking something essential **2** inadequate in quantity or quality
WORD ORIGIN Latin *deficere* to fall short

deficit ❶ *n* the amount by which a sum is lower than that expected or required
WORD ORIGIN Latin: there is lacking

defile[1] *vb* **-filing, -filed 1** to make foul or dirty **2** to make unfit for ceremonial use **defilement** *n*
WORD ORIGIN Old French *defouler* to trample underfoot, abuse

defile[2] *n* a narrow pass or gorge: *the sandy defile of Wadi Rum*
WORD ORIGIN French *défiler* to file off

define ❶ *vb* **-fining, -fined 1** to describe the nature of **2** to state precisely the meaning of **3** to show clearly the outline of: *the picture was sharp and cleanly defined* **4** to fix with precision; specify: *define one's duties* **definable** *adj*
WORD ORIGIN Latin *definire* to set bounds to

definite ❶ *adj* **1** firm, clear, and precise: *I have very definite views on this subject* **2** having precise limits or boundaries **3** known for certain: *it's definite that they have won* **definitely** *adv*
WORD ORIGIN Latin *definitus* limited, distinct

definite article *n grammar* the word 'the'

definition ❶ *n* **1** a statement of the meaning of a word or phrase **2** a description of the essential qualities of something **3** the quality of being clear and distinct **4** sharpness of outline

definitive ❶ *adj* **1** final and unable to be questioned or altered: *a definitive verdict* **2** most complete, or the best of its kind: *the book was hailed as the definitive Dickens biography* **definitively** *adv*

deflate *vb* **-flating, -flated 1** to collapse or cause to collapse through the release of gas **2** to take away the self-esteem or conceit from **3** to cause deflation of (an economy)
WORD ORIGIN DE- + (IN)FLATE

deflation *n* **1** *econ* a reduction in economic activity resulting in lower levels of output and investment **2** a feeling of sadness following excitement **deflationary** *adj*

deflect ❶ *vb* to turn or cause to turn aside from a course **deflection** *n* **deflector** *n*
WORD ORIGIN Latin *deflectere*

deflower *vb literary* to deprive (a woman) of her virginity

defoliate *vb* **-ating, -ated** to deprive (a plant) of its leaves **defoliant** *n* **defoliation** *n*
WORD ORIGIN Latin *de-* from + *folium* leaf

De Forest *n* **Lee** 1873–1961, US inventor of telegraphic, telephonic, and radio equipment: patented the first triode valve (1907)

deforestation *n* the cutting down or destruction of forests

deform *vb* to put (something) out of shape or spoil its appearance
WORD ORIGIN Latin *de-* from + *forma* shape beauty

deformed *adj* disfigured or misshapen

deformity *n, pl* **-ties 1** *pathol* a distortion of an organ or part **2** the state of being deformed

defraud *vb* to cheat out of money, property, or a right to do something

defray *vb* to provide money to cover costs or expenses **defrayal** *n*
WORD ORIGIN Old French *deffroier* to pay expenses

defrock *vb* to deprive (a priest) of ecclesiastical status

defrost *vb* **1** to make or become free of frost or ice **2** to thaw (frozen food) by removing from a deep-freeze

deft *adj* quick and skilful in movement; dexterous **deftly** *adv* **deftness** *n*
WORD ORIGIN Middle English variant of *daft* (in the sense: gentle)

defunct *adj* no longer existing or working properly
WORD ORIGIN Latin *defungi* to discharge (one's obligations), die

defuse *or US sometimes* **defuze** *vb* **-fusing, -fused** *or* **-fuzing, -fuzed 1** to remove the fuse of (an explosive device) **2** to reduce the tension in (a difficult situation): *I said it in a bid to defuse the situation*

defy ❶ *vb* **-fies, -fying, -fied 1** to resist openly and boldly **2** to elude in a baffling way: *his actions defy explanation* **3** *formal* to challenge (someone to do something)
WORD ORIGIN Old French *desfier*

Degas *n* **Hilaire Germain Edgar** 1834–1917, French impressionist painter and sculptor, noted for his brilliant draughtsmanship and ability to convey movement, esp. in his studies of horse racing and ballet dancers

De Gasperi *n* **Alcide** 1881–1954, Italian statesman; prime minister (1945–53). An antifascist, he led the Christian Democratic party during World War II from the Vatican City

degenerate ❶ *adj* **1** having deteriorated to a lower mental, moral, or physical level ▷*n* **2** a degenerate person ▷*vb* **-ating, -ated 3** to become degenerate **degeneracy** *n*
WORD ORIGIN Latin *degener*

THESAURUS

insubordination, rebelliousness, recalcitrance, contumacy
OPPOSITE: obedience

deficiency *n* **1 = failing**, fault, weakness, defect, flaw, drawback, shortcoming, imperfection, frailty, demerit **2 = lack**, want, deficit, absence, shortage, deprivation, inadequacy, scarcity, dearth, privation, insufficiency, scantiness
OPPOSITE: sufficiency

deficit *n* **= shortfall**, shortage, deficiency, loss, default, arrears

define *vb* **1 = describe**, interpret, characterize, explain, spell out, expound **3 = mark out**, outline, limit, bound, delineate, circumscribe, demarcate, delimit **4 = establish**, detail, determine, specify, designate

definite *adj* **1a = specific**, exact, precise, clear, particular, express, determined, fixed, black-and-white, explicit, clear-cut, cut-and-dried (*informal*), clearly defined
OPPOSITE: vague
1b = clear, explicit, black-and-white, clear-cut, unequivocal, unambiguous, guaranteed, cut-and-dried (*informal*) **1c = noticeable**, marked, clear, decided, striking, noted, particular, obvious, dramatic, considerable, remarkable, apparent, evident, distinct, notable, manifest, conspicuous **3 = certain**, decided, sure, settled, convinced, positive, confident, assured
OPPOSITE: uncertain

definition *n* **1 = description**, interpretation, explanation, clarification, exposition, explication, elucidation, statement of meaning **3, 4 = sharpness**, focus, clarity, contrast, precision, distinctness

definitive *adj* **1 = final**, convincing, absolute, clinching, decisive, definite, conclusive, irrefutable **2 = authoritative**, greatest, ultimate, reliable, most significant, exhaustive, superlative, mother of all (*informal*)

deflect *vb* **= turn aside**, turn, bend, twist, sidetrack

defy *vb* **1 = resist**, oppose, confront, face, brave, beard, disregard, stand up to, spurn, flout, disobey, hold out against, put up a fight (against), hurl defiance at, contemn

degenerate *adj* **1 = depraved**, base, corrupt, fallen, low, perverted, degraded, degenerated, immoral, decadent, debased, debauched, dissolute, pervy (*slang*)

DICTIONARY

departing from its kind, ignoble
degeneration *n* **1** the process of degenerating **2** *biol* the loss of specialization or function by organisms
degenerative *adj* (of a disease or condition) getting steadily worse
degrade ❶ *vb* **-grading, -graded** **1** to reduce to dishonour or disgrace **2** to reduce in status or quality **3** *chem* to decompose into atoms or smaller molecules **degradation** *n* **degrading** *adj*
WORD ORIGIN Latin *de-* from + *gradus* rank, degree
degree ❶ *n* **1** a stage in a scale of relative amount or intensity: *this task involved a greater degree of responsibility* **2** an academic award given by a university or college on successful completion of a course **3** *grammar* any of the forms of an adjective used to indicate relative amount or intensity **4** a unit of temperature. Symbol: ° **5** a measure of angle equal to one three-hundred-and-sixtieth of the circumference of a circle. Symbol: ° **6** a unit of latitude or longitude. Symbol: ° **7** **by degrees** little by little; gradually
WORD ORIGIN Latin *de-* down + *gradus* step
de Havilland *n* Sir **Geoffrey** 1882–1965, British aircraft designer. He produced many military aircraft and the first jet airliners
dehisce *vb* **-hiscing, -hisced** (of the seed capsules of some plants) to burst open spontaneously **dehiscence** *n* **dehiscent** *adj*
WORD ORIGIN Latin *dehiscere* to split open
dehumanize *or* **-ise** *vb* **-izing, -ized** *or* **-ising, -ised** **1** to deprive of the qualities thought of as being best in human beings, such as kindness **2** to make (an activity) mechanical or routine **dehumanization** *or* **-isation** *n*
dehydrate *vb* **-drating, -drated** **1** to remove water from (food) in order to preserve it **2** **be dehydrated** (of a person) to become weak or ill through losing too much water from the body **dehydration** *n*
de-ice *vb* **de-icing, de-iced** to free of ice **de-icer** *n*
deify (day-if-fie) *vb* **-fies, -fying, -fied** to treat or worship (someone or something) as a god **deification** *n*
WORD ORIGIN Latin *deus* god + *facere* to make
Deighton *n* **Len** born 1929, British thriller writer. His books include *The Ipcress File* (1962), *Bomber* (1970), and the trilogy *Berlin Game, Mexico Set*, and *London Match* (1983–85)
deign (dane) *vb* to do something that one considers beneath one's dignity: *she did not deign to reply*
WORD ORIGIN Latin *dignari* to consider worthy
deindustrialization *or* **-sation** *n* a decline in the importance of a country's manufacturing industry
deism (dee-iz-zum) *n* belief in the existence of God based only on natural reason, without reference to revelation **deist** *n, adj* **deistic** *adj*
deity (dee-it-ee) *n, pl* **-ties** **1** a god or goddess **2** the state of being divine
WORD ORIGIN Latin *deus* god
Deity *n* **the Deity** God
déjà vu (day-zhah **voo**) *n* a feeling of having experienced before something that is happening at the present moment
WORD ORIGIN French: already seen
dejected *adj* in low spirits; downhearted **dejectedly** *adv* **dejection** *n*
WORD ORIGIN Latin *deicere* to cast down
de jure *adv* according to law
WORD ORIGIN Latin
deke *Canad slang vb* **deking, deked** **1** (in ice hockey or box lacrosse) to draw (a defending player) out of position by faking a shot or movement ▷ *n* **2** such a shot or movement
WORD ORIGIN from *decoy*
Dekker *or* **Decker** *n* **Thomas** ?1572–?1632, English dramatist and pamphleteer, noted particularly for his comedy *The Shoemaker's Holiday* (1600) and his satirical pamphlet *The Gull's Hornbook* (1609)
dekko *n Brit, Austral & NZ slang* **have a dekko** have a look
WORD ORIGIN Hindi *dekhnā* to see
de Kooning *n* **Willem** 1904–97, US abstract expressionist painter, born in Holland
de la Beche *n* **Henry** 1796–1855, English geologist. His work led to the founding of the Geological Survey (1835)
Delacroix *n* **(Ferdinand Victor) Eugène** 1798–1863, French romantic painter whose use of colour and free composition influenced impressionism. His paintings of historical and contemporary scenes include *The Massacre at Chios* (1824)
de la Mare *n* **Walter (John)** 1873–1956, English poet and novelist, noted esp. for his evocative verse for children. His works include the volumes of poetry *The Listeners and Other Poems* (1912) and *Peacock Pie* (1913) and the novel *Memoirs of a Midget* (1921)
Delaroche *n* **(Hippolyte) Paul** 1797–1859, French painter of portraits and sentimental historical scenes, such as *The Children of Edward IV in the Tower* (1830)
Delaunay *n* **Robert** 1885–1941, French painter, whose abstract use of colour characterized Orphism, an attempt to introduce more colour into austere forms of Cubism
De La Warr *n* **Baron,** title of *Thomas West*, known as *Lord Delaware.* 1577–1618, English administrator in America; first governor of Virginia (1610)
delay ❶ *vb* **1** to put (something) off to a later time **2** to slow up or cause to be late **3** **a** to hesitate in doing something **b** to deliberately take longer than necessary to do something ▷ *n* **4** the act of delaying **5** a period of inactivity or waiting before something happens or continues
WORD ORIGIN Old French *des-* off + *laier* to leave
Delbrück *n* **Max** 1906–81, US molecular biologist, born in Germany. Noted for his work on bacteriophages, he shared the Nobel prize for physiology or medicine in 1969
delectable *adj* delightful or very attractive
WORD ORIGIN Latin *delectare* to delight
delectation *n formal* great pleasure and enjoyment
Deledda *n* **Grazia** 1875–1936, Italian novelist, noted for works, such as *La Madre* (1920), on peasant life in Sardinia: Nobel prize for literature 1926
delegate ❶ *n* **1** a person chosen to represent others at a conference or meeting ▷ *vb* **-gating, -gated** **2** to entrust (duties or powers) to another person **3** to appoint as a representative

d

THESAURUS

▷ *vb* **3 = decline**, slip, sink, decrease, deteriorate, worsen, rot, decay, lapse, fall off, regress, go to pot, retrogress
degrade *vb* **1 = demean**, disgrace, humiliate, injure, shame, corrupt, humble, discredit, pervert, debase, dishonour, cheapen
OPPOSITE: ennoble
degree *n* **1 = amount**, measure, rate, stage, extent, grade, proportion, gradation
delay *vb* **1 = put off**, suspend, postpone, stall, shelve, prolong, defer, hold over, temporize, put on the back burner *(informal)*, protract, take a rain check on *(US & Canad informal)* **2 = hold up**, detain, hold back, stop, arrest, halt, hinder, obstruct, retard, impede, bog down, set back, slow up OPPOSITE: speed (up)
▷ *n* **5 = hold-up**, wait, check, setback, interruption, obstruction, stoppage, impediment, hindrance
delegate *n* **1 = representative**, agent, deputy, ambassador, commissioner, envoy, proxy, depute *(Scot)*, legate,

DICTIONARY

WORD ORIGIN Latin *delegare* to send on a mission

delegation ❶ *n* **1** a group chosen to represent others **2** the act of delegating

de Lesseps *n* Vicomte **Ferdinand Marie** 1805–94, French diplomat: directed the construction of the Suez Canal (1859–69) and the unsuccessful first attempt to build the Panama Canal (1881–89)

delete ❶ *vb* **-leting, -leted** to remove or cross out (something printed or written) **deletion** *n*
WORD ORIGIN Latin *delere*

deleterious (del-lit-eer-ee-uss) *adj formal* harmful or injurious
WORD ORIGIN Greek *dēlētērios*

Delft *n* tin-glazed earthenware which originated in Delft in the Netherlands, typically with blue decoration on a white ground. Also: **delftware**

deliberate ❶ *adj* **1** carefully thought out in advance; intentional **2** careful and unhurried: *a deliberate gait* ▷ *vb* **-ating, -ated 3** to consider (something) deeply; think over **deliberately** *adv* **deliberative** *adj*
WORD ORIGIN Latin *deliberare* to consider well

deliberation ❶ *n* **1** careful consideration **2** calmness and absence of hurry **3 deliberations** formal discussions

Delibes *n* (**Clément Philibert**) **Léo** 1836–91, French composer, noted particularly for his ballets *Coppélia* (1870) and *Sylvia* (1876), and the opera *Lakmé* (1883)

delicacy ❶ *n, pl* **-cies 1** fine or subtle quality, construction, etc.: *delicacy of craftsmanship* **2** fragile or graceful beauty **3** something that is considered particularly nice to eat **4** frail health **5** refinement of feeling, manner, or appreciation: *the delicacy of the orchestra's playing* **6** need for careful or tactful treatment

delicate ❶ *adj* **1** fine or subtle in quality or workmanship **2** having a fragile beauty **3** (of colour, smell, or taste) pleasantly subtle **4** easily damaged; fragile **5** precise or sensitive in action: *the delicate digestive system* **6** requiring tact: *a delicate matter* **7** showing consideration for the feelings of other people **delicately** *adv*
WORD ORIGIN Latin *delicatus* affording pleasure

delicatessen *n* a shop selling unusual or imported foods, often already cooked or prepared
WORD ORIGIN German *Delikatessen* delicacies

delicious ❶ *adj* **1** very appealing to taste or smell **2** extremely enjoyable **deliciously** *adv*
WORD ORIGIN Latin *deliciae* delights

delight ❶ *n* **1** extreme pleasure **2** something or someone that causes this ▷ *vb* **3** to please greatly **4 delight in** to take great pleasure in **delightful** *adj* **delightfully** *adv*
WORD ORIGIN Latin *delectare* to please

delighted *adj* greatly pleased

delimit *vb* **-iting, -ited** to mark or lay down the limits of **delimitation** *n*

delineate (dill-lin-ee-ate) *vb* **-ating, -ated 1** to show by drawing **2** to describe in words **delineation** *n*
WORD ORIGIN Latin *delineare* to sketch out

delinquent *n* **1** someone, esp. a young person, who breaks the law ▷ *adj* **2** repeatedly breaking the law **delinquency** *n*
WORD ORIGIN Latin *delinquens* offending

deliquesce *vb* **-quescing, -quesced** (esp. of certain salts) to dissolve in water absorbed from the air **deliquescence** *n* **deliquescent** *adj*
WORD ORIGIN Latin *deliquescere* to melt away

delirious *adj* **1** suffering from delirium **2** wildly excited and happy **deliriously** *adv*

delirium *n* **1** a state of excitement and mental confusion, often with hallucinations **2** violent excitement
WORD ORIGIN Latin: madness

delirium tremens (trem-enz) *n* a severe condition characterized by delirium and trembling, caused by chronic alcoholism
WORD ORIGIN New Latin: trembling delirium

Delius *n* **Frederick** 1862–1934, English

THESAURUS

spokesman *or* spokeswoman ▷ *vb* **2 = entrust**, transfer, hand over, give, pass on, assign, relegate, consign, devolve **3 = appoint**, commission, select, contract, engage, nominate, designate, mandate, authorize, empower, accredit, depute

delegation *n* **1 = deputation**, envoys, contingent, commission, embassy, legation **2 = commissioning**, relegation, assignment, devolution, committal, deputizing, entrustment

delete *vb* **= remove**, cancel, cut out, erase, edit, excise, strike out, obliterate, efface, blot out, cross out, expunge, dele, rub out, edit out, blue-pencil

deliberate *adj* **1 = intentional**, meant, planned, considered, studied, designed, intended, conscious, calculated, thoughtful, wilful, purposeful, premeditated, prearranged, done on purpose **OPPOSITE:** accidental **2 = careful**, measured, slow, cautious, wary, thoughtful, prudent, circumspect, methodical, unhurried, heedful **OPPOSITE:** hurried ▷ *vb* **3 = consider**, think, ponder, discuss, debate, reflect, consult, weigh, meditate, mull over, ruminate, cogitate

deliberation *n* **1 = consideration**, thought, reflection, study, speculation, calculation, meditation, forethought, circumspection, cogitation **3** *(usually plural)* **= discussion**, talk, conference, exchange, debate, analysis, conversation, dialogue, consultation, seminar, symposium, colloquy, confabulation

delicacy *n* **1 = fragility**, frailty, brittleness, flimsiness, frailness, frangibility **2 = daintiness**, charm, grace, elegance, neatness, prettiness, slenderness, exquisiteness **3 = treat**, luxury, goody, savoury, dainty, morsel, titbit, choice item, juicy bit, bonne bouche *(French)* **5a = sensitivity**, understanding, consideration, judgment, perception, diplomacy, discretion, skill, finesse, tact, thoughtfulness, savoir-faire, adroitness, sensitiveness **5b = lightness**, accuracy, precision, elegance, sensibility, purity, subtlety, refinement, finesse, nicety, fineness, exquisiteness **6 = difficulty**, sensitivity, stickiness *(informal)*, precariousness, critical nature, touchiness, ticklishness

delicate *adj* **1 = fine**, detailed, elegant, exquisite, graceful **3 = subtle**, fine, nice, soft, delicious, faint, refined, muted, subdued, pastel, understated, dainty **OPPOSITE:** bright **4 = fragile**, weak, frail, brittle, tender, flimsy, dainty, breakable, frangible **7 = diplomatic**, sensitive, careful, subtle, thoughtful, discreet, prudent, considerate, judicious, tactful **OPPOSITE:** insensitive

delicious *adj* **1 = delectable**, tasty, luscious, choice, savoury, palatable, dainty, mouthwatering, yummy *(slang)*, scrumptious *(informal)*, appetizing, toothsome, ambrosial, lekker *(S African slang)*, nectareous, yummo *(Austral slang)* **OPPOSITE:** unpleasant

delight *n* **1 = pleasure**, joy, satisfaction, comfort, happiness, ecstasy, enjoyment, bliss, felicity, glee, gratification, rapture, gladness **OPPOSITE:** displeasure ▷ *vb* **3 = please**, satisfy, content, thrill, charm, cheer, amuse, divert, enchant, rejoice, gratify, ravish, gladden, give pleasure to, tickle pink *(informal)* **OPPOSITE:** displease **4 delight in** *or* **take a delight in something** *or* **someone = like**, love, enjoy, appreciate, relish, indulge in,

DICTIONARY

composer, who drew inspiration from folk tunes and the sounds of nature. His works include the opera *A Village Romeo and Juliet* (1901), *A Mass of Life* (1905), and the orchestral variations *Brigg Fair* (1907)

deliver ❶ *vb* **1** to carry (goods or mail) to a destination **2** to hand over: *the tenants were asked to deliver up their keys* **3** to aid in the birth of (offspring) **4** to present (a lecture or speech) **5** to release or rescue (from captivity or danger) **6** to strike (a blow) suddenly **7** *informal* Also: **deliver the goods** to produce something promised **deliverance** *n*
WORD ORIGIN Latin *de-* from + *liberare* to free

delivery ❶ *n, pl* **-eries 1 a** the act of delivering goods or mail **b** something that is delivered **2** the act of giving birth to a baby **3** manner or style in public speaking: *her delivery was clear and humorous* **4** *cricket* the act or manner of bowling a ball **5** *S African* a semi-official slogan for the provision of services to previously disadvantaged communities

dell *n chiefly Brit* a small wooded hollow
WORD ORIGIN Old English

Deller *n* **Alfred** (**George**) 1912–79, British countertenor

Del Mar *n* **Norman** 1919–94, British conductor, associated esp. with 20th-century British music

Delorme *or* **de l'Orme** *n* **Philibert** ?1510–70, French Renaissance architect of the Tuileries, Paris

de los Angeles *n* **Victoria** 1923–2005, Spanish soprano

delouse *vb* **-lousing, -loused** to rid (a person or animal) of lice

Delphic *adj* obscure or ambiguous, like the ancient Greek oracle at Delphi

delphinium *n, pl* **-iums** *or* **-ia** a large garden plant with spikes of blue flowers
WORD ORIGIN Greek *delphis* dolphin

del Sarto *n* See **Sarto**

delta *n* **1** the fourth letter in the Greek alphabet (Δ, δ) **2** the flat area at the mouth of some rivers where the main stream splits up into several branches

delude *vb* **-luding, -luded** to make someone believe something that is not true
WORD ORIGIN Latin *deludere*

deluge (del-lyooj) *n* **1** a great flood of water **2** torrential rain **3** an overwhelming number ▷ *vb* **-uging, -uged 4** to flood **5** to overwhelm
WORD ORIGIN Latin *diluere* to wash away

Deluge *n* **the Deluge** ▸ same as the **Flood**

delusion ❶ *n* **1** a mistaken idea or belief **2** the state of being deluded **delusive** *adj* **delusory** *adj*

de luxe *adj* rich or sumptuous; superior in quality: *a de luxe hotel*
WORD ORIGIN French

Delvaux *n* **Paul** 1897–1994, Belgian surrealist painter: his works portray dreamlike figures in mysterious settings

delve *vb* **delving, delved 1** to research deeply or intensively (for information) **2** *old-fashioned* to dig
WORD ORIGIN Old English *delfan*

demagnetize *or* **-ise** *vb* **-izing, -ized** *or* **-ising, -ised** to remove magnetic properties **demagnetization** *or* **-isation** *n*

demagogue *or US sometimes* **demagog** *n* a political agitator who attempts to win support by appealing to the prejudice and passions of the mob **demagogic** *adj* **demagogy** *n*
WORD ORIGIN Greek *dēmagōgos* people's leader

demand ❶ *vb* **1** to request forcefully **2** to require as just, urgent, etc.: *the situation demands intervention* **3** to claim as a right ▷ *n* **4** a forceful request **5** something that requires special effort or sacrifice: *demands upon one's time* **6** *econ* willingness and ability to purchase goods and services **7 in demand** sought after; popular **8 on demand** as soon as requested: *the funds will be available on demand*
WORD ORIGIN Latin *demandare* to commit to

demanding ❶ *adj* requiring a lot of skill, time, or effort: *a demanding relationship*

demarcation *n* the act of establishing limits or boundaries, esp. between the work performed by members of different trade unions
WORD ORIGIN Spanish *demarcar* to appoint the boundaries of

demean *vb* **1** to undermine the status or dignity of (someone or something) **2 demean oneself** to do something unworthy of one's status or character: *there is no doubt that he will lose face with the boss by having to demean himself in this way*
WORD ORIGIN DE- + MEAN[2]

demeanour *or US* **demeanor** *n* the way a person behaves
WORD ORIGIN Old French *de-* (intensive) + *mener* to lead

demented *adj* mad; insane **dementedly** *adv*
WORD ORIGIN Late Latin *dementare* to drive mad

dementia (dim-men-sha) *n* a state of serious mental deterioration
WORD ORIGIN Latin: madness

demerara sugar *n* brown crystallized cane sugar from the West Indies
WORD ORIGIN after *Demerara*, a region of Guyana

demerit *n* **1** a fault or disadvantage **2** *US & Canad* a mark given against a student for failure or misconduct

demesne (dim-mane) *n* **1** land surrounding a house or manor **2** *property law* the possession of one's own property or land **3** a region or district; domain
WORD ORIGIN Old French *demeine*

Demeter *n Greek myth* the goddess of agriculture

demi- *combining form* **1** half: *demirelief* **2** of less than full size, status, or rank: *demigod*
WORD ORIGIN Latin *dimidius* half

demigod *n* **1 a** a being who is part mortal, part god **b** a lesser deity **2** a godlike person

demijohn *n* a large bottle with a short narrow neck, often encased in wickerwork
WORD ORIGIN probably from French *dame-jeanne*

THESAURUS

savour, revel in, take pleasure in, glory in, luxuriate in

deliver *vb* **1 = bring**, carry, bear, transport, distribute, convey, cart **2** (*sometimes with* **over** *or* **up**) **= hand over**, present, commit, give up, yield, surrender, turn over, relinquish, make over **4 = give**, read, present, announce, publish, declare, proclaim, pronounce, utter, give forth **5 = release**, free, save, rescue, loose, discharge, liberate, acquit, redeem, ransom, emancipate **6 = strike**, give, deal, launch, throw, direct, aim, administer, inflict

delivery *n* **1a = handing over**, transfer, distribution, transmission, dispatch, consignment, conveyance, transmittal **1b = consignment**, goods, shipment, batch **2 = childbirth**, labour, confinement, parturition **3 = speech**, speaking, expression, pronunciation, utterance, articulation, intonation, diction, elocution, enunciation, vocalization

delusion *n* **1 = misconception**, mistaken idea, misapprehension, fancy, illusion, deception, hallucination, fallacy, self-deception, false impression, phantasm, misbelief

demand *vb* **1 = request**, ask (for), order, expect, claim, seek, call for, insist on, exact, appeal for, solicit **2 = require**, take, want, need, involve, call for, entail, necessitate, cry out for **OPPOSITE:** provide ▷ *n* **4 = request**, order, charge, bidding **6 = need**, want, call, market, claim, requirement, necessity

demanding *adj* **= difficult**, trying, hard, taxing, wearing, challenging, tough, exhausting, exacting, exigent **OPPOSITE:** easy

DICTIONARY

demilitarize *or* **-rise** *vb* **-rizing, -rized** *or* **-rising, -rised** to remove all military forces from (an area): *demilitarized zone* **demilitarization** *or* **-risation** *n*

demimonde *n* **1** (esp. in the 19th century) a class of women considered to be outside respectable society because of promiscuity **2** any group considered not wholly respectable
WORD ORIGIN French: half-world

Demirel *n* **Süleyman** born 1924, Turkish statesman; prime minister (1965–71; 1975–77; 1977–78; 1979–80; 1991–93) and president (1993–2000)

demise ❶ *n* **1** the eventual failure of something originally successful **2** *euphemistic, formal* death **3** *property law* a transfer of an estate by lease ▷ *vb* **-mising, -mised 4** *property law* to transfer for a limited period; lease
WORD ORIGIN Old French *demis* dismissed

demi-sec *adj* (of wines) medium-sweet

demisemiquaver *n music* a note with the time value of one thirty-second of a semibreve

demist *vb* to make or become free of condensation **demister** *n*

demo *n, pl* **-os** *informal* **1** ▸ short for **demonstration** (sense 1) **2** a demonstration record or tape

demob *vb* **-mobbing, -mobbed** *Brit, Austral & NZ informal* to demobilize

demobilize *or* **-lise** *vb* **-lizing, -lized** *or* **-lising, -lised** to release from the armed forces **demobilization** *or* **-lisation** *n*

democracy ❶ *n, pl* **-cies 1** a system of government or organization in which the citizens or members choose leaders or make other important decisions by voting **2** a country in which the citizens choose their government by voting
WORD ORIGIN Greek *dēmokratia*

democrat *n* a person who believes in democracy

Democrat ❶ *n US politics* a member or supporter of the Democratic Party, the more liberal of the two main political parties in the US **Democratic** *adj*

democratic ❶ *adj* of or relating to a country, organization, or system in which leaders are chosen or decisions are made by voting **democratically** *adv*

demodulation *n electronics* the process by which an output wave or signal is obtained having the characteristics of the original modulating wave or signal

demography *n* the study of population statistics, such as births and deaths **demographic** *adj*
WORD ORIGIN Greek *dēmos* the populace + -GRAPHY

de Molina *n* **Tirso** Pen name of *Gabriel Téllez*. ?1571–1648, Spanish dramatist; author of the first dramatic treatment of the Don Juan legend *El Burlador de Sevilla* (1630)

demolish ❶ *vb* **1** to tear down or break up (buildings) **2** to put an end to; destroy: *I demolished her argument in seconds* **3** *facetious* to eat up: *he demolished the whole cake* **demolisher** *n* **demolition** *n*
WORD ORIGIN Latin *demoliri* to throw down

demon ❶ *n* **1** an evil spirit **2** a person, obsession, etc. thought of as evil or persistently tormenting **3** a person extremely skilful in or devoted to a given activity: *a demon at cricket* **demonic** *adj*
WORD ORIGIN Greek *daimōn* spirit, fate

demonetize *or* **-tise** *vb* **-tizing, -tized** *or* **-tising, -tised** to withdraw from use as currency **demonetization** *or* **-tisation** *n*

demoniac *or* **demoniacal** *adj* **1** appearing to be possessed by a devil **2** suggesting inner possession or inspiration: *the demoniac fire of genius* **3** frantic or frenzied: *demoniac activity* **demoniacally** *adv*

demonize *or* **-ise** *vb* **-izing, -ized** *or* **-ising, -ised 1** to make into a demon **2** to describe as evil or guilty: *America is demonized by many in France*

demonolatry *n* the worship of demons
WORD ORIGIN *demon* + Greek *latreia* worship

demonology *n* the study of demons or demonic beliefs
WORD ORIGIN *demon* + -LOGY

demonstrable *adj* able to be proved **demonstrably** *adv*

demonstrate ❶ *vb* **-strating, -strated 1** to show or prove by reasoning or evidence **2** to display and explain the workings of (a machine, product, etc.) **3** to reveal the existence of: *the adult literacy campaign demonstrated the scale of educational deprivation* **4** to show support or opposition by public parades or rallies
WORD ORIGIN Latin *demonstrare* to point out

demonstration ❶ *n* **1** a march or public meeting to demonstrate opposition to something or support for something **2** an explanation, display, or experiment showing how something works **3** proof or evidence leading to proof

demonstrative *adj* **1** tending to show one's feelings freely and openly **2** *grammar* denoting a word used to point out the person or thing referred to, such as *this* and *those* **3 demonstrative of** giving proof of **demonstratively** *adv*

demonstrator *n* **1** a person who demonstrates how a device or machine works **2** a person who takes part in a public demonstration

demoralize *or* **-ise** *vb* **-izing, -ized** *or* **-ising, -ised** to deprive (someone) of confidence or enthusiasm: *she had been demoralized and had just given up* **demoralization** *or* **-isation** *n*

demote *vb* **-moting, -moted** to lower in rank or position **demotion** *n*
WORD ORIGIN DE- + (PRO)MOTE

demotic *adj* of or relating to the common people
WORD ORIGIN Greek *dēmotikos*

Dempsey *n* **Jack** real name *William Harrison Dempsey*. 1895–1983, US boxer; world heavyweight champion (1919–26)

demur *vb* **-murring, -murred 1** to show reluctance; object ▷ *n*

THESAURUS

demise *n* **1 = failure**, end, fall, defeat, collapse, ruin, breakdown, overthrow, downfall, dissolution, termination **2** *(euphemistic)* **= death**, end, dying, passing, departure, expiration, decease

democracy *n* **1 = self-government**, republic, commonwealth, representative government, government by the people

Democrat *n* **= left-winger**

democratic *adj* **= self-governing**, popular, republican, representative, autonomous, populist, egalitarian

demolish *vb* **1 = knock down**, level, destroy, ruin, overthrow, dismantle, flatten, trash *(slang)*, total *(slang)*, tear down, bulldoze, raze, pulverize
OPPOSITE: build
2 = destroy, wreck, overturn, overthrow, undo, blow out of the water *(slang)*

demon *n* **1 = evil spirit**, devil, fiend, goblin, ghoul, malignant spirit, atua (NZ), wairua (NZ) **3 = wizard**, master, ace *(informal)*, addict, fanatic, fiend

demonstrate *vb* **1 = show**, evidence, express, display, indicate, exhibit, manifest, make clear *or* plain, flag up **1, 3 = prove**, show, establish, indicate, make clear, manifest, evidence, testify to, evince, show clearly, flag up **2 = describe**, show, explain, teach, illustrate **4 = march**, protest, rally, object, parade, picket, say no to, remonstrate, take up the cudgels, express disapproval, hikoi (NZ)

demonstration *n* **1 = march**, protest, rally, sit-in, parade, procession, demo *(informal)*, picket, mass lobby, hikoi *(NZ)* **2 = display**, show, performance, explanation, description, presentation, demo *(informal)*, exposition **3 = indication**, proof, testimony, confirmation, affirmation, validation, substantiation, attestation

DICTIONARY

2 without demur without objecting
WORD ORIGIN Latin *demorari* to linger
demure *adj* quiet, reserved, and rather shy **demurely** *adv* **demureness** *n*
WORD ORIGIN perhaps from Old French *demorer* to delay, linger
demutualize *or* **-ise** *vb* **-izing, -ized** *or* **-ising, -ised** (of a mutual savings or life-assurance organization) to convert to a public limited company **demutualization** *or* **-isation** *n*
demystify *vb* **-fies, -fying, -fied** to remove the mystery from: *he attempted to demystify the contemporary jargon of psychology* **demystification** *n*
den *n* **1** the home of a wild animal; lair **2** *chiefly US* a small secluded room in a home, often used for a hobby **3** a place where people indulge in criminal or immoral activities: *a den of iniquity*
WORD ORIGIN Old English *denn*
denarius (din-**air**-ee-uss) *n, pl* **-narii** (-**nair**-ee-eye) a silver coin of ancient Rome, often called a penny in translation
WORD ORIGIN Latin
denary (**dean**-a-ree) *adj* calculated by tens; decimal
WORD ORIGIN Latin *denarius*
denationalize *or* **-ise** *vb* **-izing, -ized** *or* **-ising, -ised** to transfer (an industry or a service) from public to private ownership **denationalization** *or* **-isation** *n*
denature *vb* **-turing, -tured 1** to change the nature of **2** to make (alcohol) unfit to drink by adding another substance
Dench *n* Dame **Judi** (**Olivia**) born 1934, British actress and theatre director
dendrology *n* the study of trees
WORD ORIGIN Greek *dendron* tree + -LOGY
dene *or* **dean** *n* *chiefly Brit* a narrow wooded valley
Deneuve *n* **Catherine**, original name *Catherine Dorléac*. born 1943, French film actress: her films include *Les Parapluies de Cherbourg* (1964), *Belle de Jour* (1967), *Indochine* (1992), and *Dancing in the Dark* (2000)
dengue (**deng**-gee) *n* a viral disease transmitted by mosquitoes, characterized by headache, fever, pains in the joints, and a rash
WORD ORIGIN probably of African origin
denial *n* **1** a statement that something is not true **2** a rejection of a request **3** *psychol* a process by which painful thoughts are not permitted into the consciousness
denier (**den**-yer) *n* a unit of weight used to measure the fineness of silk and man-made fibres
WORD ORIGIN Old French: coin
denigrate *vb* **-grating, -grated** to criticize (someone or something) unfairly **denigration** *n* **denigrator** *n*
WORD ORIGIN Latin *denigrare* to make very black
denim *n* **1** a hard-wearing cotton fabric used for jeans, skirts, etc. **2 denims** jeans made of denim
WORD ORIGIN French *(serge) de Nîmes* (serge) of Nîmes, in S France
Denis *n* **1 Maurice** 1870–1943, French painter and writer on art. One of the leading Nabis, he defined a picture as "essentially a flat surface covered with colours assembled in a certain order" **2 Saint Denis** *or* **Saint Denys** 3rd century AD, first bishop of Paris; patron saint of France. Feast day: Oct 9
denizen *n* **1** a person, animal, or plant that lives or grows in a particular place **2** an animal or plant established in a place to which it is not native
WORD ORIGIN Old French *denzein*
Denning *n* Baron **Alfred Thompson** 1899–1999, English judge; Master of the Rolls 1962–82
Dennis *n* **C**(**larence**) **J**(**ames**) 1876–1938, the poet of the Australian larrikin, esp. in *The Songs of a Sentimental Bloke* (1915) and *The Moods of Ginger Mick* (1916)
denominate *vb* **-nating, -nated** to give a specific name to; designate
WORD ORIGIN Latin *denominare*
denomination *n* **1** a group which has slightly different beliefs from other groups within the same faith **2** a unit in a system of weights, values, or measures: *coins of small denomination have been withdrawn* **3** a name given to a class or group; classification **denominational** *adj*
denominator *n* the number below the line in a fraction, as 8 in ⅞
denote *vb* **-noting, -noted 1** to be a sign or indication of: *these contracts denote movement on the widest possible scale* **2** (of a word or phrase) to have as a literal or obvious meaning **denotation** *n*
WORD ORIGIN Latin *denotare* to mark
denouement (day-**noo**-mon) *n* the final outcome or solution in a play or other work
WORD ORIGIN French
denounce *vb* **-nouncing, -nounced 1** to condemn openly or vehemently **2** to give information against
WORD ORIGIN Latin *denuntiare* to make an official proclamation, threaten
dense *adj* **1** thickly crowded or closely packed **2** difficult to see through: *dense clouds of smoke* **3** *informal* stupid or dull **4** (of a film, book, etc.) difficult to follow or understand: *the content should be neither too dense nor too abstract* **densely** *adv*
WORD ORIGIN Latin *densus* thick
density *n, pl* **-ties 1** the degree to which something is filled or occupied: *an average population density* **2** *physics* a measure of the compactness of a substance, expressed as its mass per unit volume **3** a measure of a physical quantity per unit of length, area, or volume
dent *n* **1** a hollow in the surface of something ▷ *vb* **2** to make a dent in
WORD ORIGIN variant of *dint*
dental *adj* of or relating to the teeth or dentistry
WORD ORIGIN Latin *dens* tooth
dental floss *n* a waxed thread used to remove particles of food from between the teeth
dental surgeon *n* ▸ same as **dentist**
dentate *adj* having teeth or toothlike notches

THESAURUS

den *n* **1 = lair**, hole, shelter, cave, haunt, cavern, hide-out **2** *(chiefly US)* **= study**, retreat, sanctuary, hideaway, cloister, sanctum, cubbyhole, snuggery
denial *n* **1 = negation**, dismissal, contradiction, dissent, disclaimer, retraction, repudiation, disavowal, adjuration **OPPOSITE:** admission **2 = refusal**, veto, rejection, prohibition, rebuff, repulse
denomination *n* **1 = religious group**, belief, sect, persuasion, creed, school, hauhau (NZ) **2 = unit**, value, [illegible], grade
[illegible] *vb* **1 = condemn**, attack, censure, decry, castigate, revile, vilify, proscribe, stigmatize, impugn, excoriate, declaim against **2 = report**, dob in *(Austral slang)*
dense *adj* **1 = thick**, close, heavy, solid, substantial, compact, compressed, condensed, impenetrable, close-knit, thickset **OPPOSITE:** thin **2 = heavy**, thick, substantial, opaque, impenetrable **3 = stupid** *(informal)*, slow, thick, dull, dumb *(informal)*, crass, dozy *(Brit informal)*, dozy *(Brit informal)*, stolid, dopey *(informal)*, moronic, obtuse, brainless, blockheaded, braindead *(informal)*, dumb-ass *(informal)*, dead from the neck up *(informal)*, thickheaded, blockish, dim-witted *(informal)*, slow-witted, thick-witted **OPPOSITE:** bright
density *n* **1 = tightness**, closeness, thickness, compactness, impenetrability, denseness, crowdedness **2 = mass**, body, bulk, consistency, solidity
dent *n* **1 = hollow**, chip, indentation, depression, impression, pit, dip, crater, ding *(Austral & NZ obsolete, informal)*, dimple, concavity ▷ *vb* **2 = make a dent in**, press in, gouge, depress, hollow, imprint, push in, dint, make concave

DICTIONARY

WORD ORIGIN Latin *dentatus*

dentifrice (den-tif-riss) *n* paste or powder for cleaning the teeth
WORD ORIGIN Latin *dens* tooth + *fricare* to rub

dentine (den-teen) *n* the hard dense tissue that forms the bulk of a tooth
WORD ORIGIN Latin *dens* tooth

dentist *n* a person qualified to practise dentistry
WORD ORIGIN French *dentiste*

dentistry *n* the branch of medicine concerned with the teeth and gums

dentition *n* the typical arrangement, type, and number of teeth in a species
WORD ORIGIN Latin *dentitio* a teething

denture *n* (*often pl*) a partial or full set of artificial teeth
WORD ORIGIN French *dent* tooth

denude *vb* **-nuding, -nuded 1** to make bare; strip: *the atrocious weather denuded the trees* **2** *geol* to expose (rock) by the erosion of the layers above **denudation** *n*

denumerable *adj maths* countable

denunciation *n* open condemnation; denouncing
WORD ORIGIN Latin *denuntiare* to proclaim

deny ❶ *vb* **-nies, -nying, -nied 1** to declare (a statement) to be untrue **2** to refuse to give or allow: *we have been denied permission* **3** to refuse to acknowledge: *the baron denied his wicked son*
WORD ORIGIN Latin *denegare*

deodar *n* a Himalayan cedar with drooping branches
WORD ORIGIN Hindi

deodorant *n* a substance applied to the body to prevent or disguise the odour of perspiration

deodorize *or* **-ise** *vb* **-izing, -ized** *or* **-ising, -ised** to remove or disguise the odour of **deodorization** *or* **-isation** *n*

deoxyribonucleic acid *n* ▸ same as **DNA**

Depardieu *n* **Gérard** born 1948, French film actor. His films include *Jean de Florette* (1986), *Cyrano de Bergerac* (1990), *Green Card* (1991), *The Man in the Iron Mask* (1997), and *Tais-toi* (2003)

depart ❶ *vb* **1** to leave **2** to differ or deviate: *to depart from the original concept*
WORD ORIGIN Old French *departir*

departed *adj euphemistic* dead

department ❶ *n* **1** a specialized division of a large business organization, hospital, university, etc. **2** a major subdivision of the administration of a government **3** an administrative division in several countries, such as France **4** *informal* a specialized sphere of activity: *wine-making is my wife's department* **departmental** *adj*
WORD ORIGIN French *département*

department store *n* a large shop divided into departments selling many kinds of goods

departure ❶ *n* **1** the act of departing **2** a divergence from previous custom, rule, etc. **3** a course of action or venture: *the album represents a new departure for them*

depend ❶ *vb* **depend on a** to put trust (in); rely (on) **b** to be influenced or determined (by): *the answer depends on four main issues* **c** to rely (on) for income or support
WORD ORIGIN Latin *dependere* to hang from

dependable *adj* reliable and trustworthy **dependability** *n* **dependably** *adv*

dependant *n* a person who depends on another for financial support

dependence *n* **1** the state of relying on something in order to be able to survive or operate properly **2** reliance or trust: *they had a bond between them of mutual dependence and trust*

dependency *n, pl* **-cies 1** a territory subject to a state on which it does not border **2** *psychol* overreliance on another person or on a drug

dependent ❶ *adj* **1** depending on a person or thing for aid or support **2 dependent on** *or* **upon** influenced or conditioned by

depict ❶ *vb* **1** to represent by drawing, painting, etc. **2** to describe in words **depiction** *n*
WORD ORIGIN Latin *depingere*

depilatory (dip-pill-a-tree) *adj* **1** able or serving to remove hair ▸ *n, pl* **-ries 2** a chemical used to remove hair
WORD ORIGIN Latin *depilare* to pull out the hair

deplete ❶ *vb* **-pleting, -pleted 1** to use up (supplies or money) **2** to reduce in number **depletion** *n*
WORD ORIGIN Latin *deplere* to empty out

deplorable *adj* very bad or unpleasant **deplorably** *adv*

deplore ❶ *vb* **-ploring, -plored** to express or feel strong disapproval of
WORD ORIGIN Latin *deplorare* to weep bitterly

deploy ❶ *vb* to organize (troops or resources) into a position ready for immediate and effective action **deployment** *n*
WORD ORIGIN Latin *displicare* to unfold

deponent *n law* a person who makes a statement on oath
WORD ORIGIN Latin *deponens* putting down

depopulate *vb* **-lating, -lated** to cause to be reduced in population **depopulation** *n*

deport ❶ *vb* **1** to remove forcibly from

THESAURUS

deny *vb* **1 = contradict**, oppose, counter, disagree with, rebuff, negate, rebut, refute, gainsay (*archaic, literary*) **OPPOSITE:** admit **2 = refuse**, decline, forbid, reject, rule out, veto, turn down, prohibit, withhold, preclude, disallow, negate, begrudge, interdict **OPPOSITE:** permit **3 = renounce**, reject, discard, revoke, retract, repudiate, renege, disown, rebut, disavow, recant, disclaim, abjure, abnegate, refuse to acknowledge *or* recognize

depart *vb* **1 = leave**, go, withdraw, retire, disappear, quit, retreat, exit, go away, vanish, absent (yourself), start out, migrate, set forth, take (your) leave, decamp, hook it (*slang*), slope off, pack your bags (*informal*), make tracks, rack off (*Austral & NZ slang*) **OPPOSITE:** arrive **2 = deviate**, vary, differ, stray, veer, swerve, diverge, digress, turn aside

department *n* **1, 2 = section**, office, unit, station, division, branch, bureau, subdivision

departure *n* **1 = leaving**, going, retirement, withdrawal, exit, going away, removal, exodus, leave-taking **OPPOSITE:** arrival **2 = shift**, change, difference, variation, innovation, novelty, veering, deviation, branching out, divergence, digression

depend on *vb* **a = count on**, turn to, trust in, bank on, lean on, rely upon, confide in, build upon, calculate on, reckon on **b = be determined by**, be based on, be subject to, hang on, rest on, revolve around, hinge on, be subordinate to, be contingent on

dependent *or* (*sometimes US*) **dependant** *adj* **1 = reliant**, vulnerable, helpless, powerless, weak, defenceless **OPPOSITE:** independent **2 = determined by**, depending on, subject to, influenced by, relative to, liable to, conditional on, contingent on

depict *vb* **1 = illustrate**, portray, picture, paint, outline, draw, sketch, render, reproduce, sculpt, delineate, limn **2 = describe**, present, represent, detail, outline, sketch, characterize

deplete *vb* **1 = use up**, reduce, drain, exhaust, consume, empty, decrease, evacuate, lessen, impoverish, expend **OPPOSITE:** increase

deplore *vb* **= disapprove of**, condemn, object to, denounce, censure, abhor, deprecate, take a dim view of, excoriate

deploy *vb* (*troops or military resources*) **= use**, station, set up, position, arrange, set out, dispose, utilize, spread out, distribute

DICTIONARY

a country **2 deport oneself** to behave in a specified manner
WORD ORIGIN Latin *deportare* to carry away, banish
deportation *n* the act of expelling someone from a country
deportee *n* a person deported or awaiting deportation
deportment *n* the way in which a person moves and stands: *she had the manners and deportment of a great lady*
WORD ORIGIN Old French *deporter* to conduct (oneself)
depose ❶ *vb* **-posing, -posed 1** to remove from an office or position of power **2** *law* to testify on oath
WORD ORIGIN Latin *deponere* to put aside
deposit ❶ *vb* **-iting, -ited 1** to put down **2** to entrust (money or valuables) for safekeeping **3** to place (money) in a bank account or other savings account **4** to lay down naturally: *the river deposits silt* ▷ *n* **5** a sum of money placed in a bank account or other savings account **6** money given in part payment for goods or services **7** an amount of a substance left on a surface as a result of a chemical or geological process
WORD ORIGIN Latin *depositus* put down
deposit account *n Brit* a bank account that earns interest
depositary *n, pl* **-taries** a person or group to whom something is entrusted for safety
deposition *n* **1** *law* the sworn statement of a witness used in court in his or her absence **2** the act of deposing **3** the act of depositing **4** something deposited
WORD ORIGIN Late Latin *depositio* a laying down, testimony
depositor *n* a person who places or has money on deposit in a bank or similar organization: *panic-stricken depositors*
depository *n, pl* **-ries 1** a store where furniture, valuables, etc. can be kept for safety **2** ▸ same as **depositary**
depot ❶ (dep-oh) *n* **1** a place where goods and vehicles are kept when not in use **2** *US, Canad & NZ* a bus or railway station
WORD ORIGIN French
Depp *n* **Johnny**, full name *John Christopher*, born 1963, US actor; his films include *Edward Scissorhands* (1990), *Sleepy Hollow* (1999), and the *Pirates of the Caribbean* series (2003–11)
depraved *adj* morally bad; corrupt
WORD ORIGIN Latin *depravare* to distort, corrupt
depravity *n, pl* **-ties** moral corruption
deprecate *vb* **-cating, -cated** to express disapproval of **deprecation** *n* **deprecatory** *adj*
WORD ORIGIN Latin *deprecari* to avert, ward off
depreciate *vb* **-ating, -ated 1** to decline in value or price **2** to deride or criticize **depreciatory** *adj*
WORD ORIGIN Latin *de-* down + *pretium* price
depreciation ❶ *n* **1** *accounting* the reduction in value of a fixed asset through use, obsolescence, etc. **2** a decrease in the exchange value of a currency **3** the act or an instance of belittling
depredation *n* plundering; pillage
WORD ORIGIN Latin *depraedare* to pillage
depress ❶ *vb* **1** to make sad and gloomy **2** to lower (prices) **3** to push down **depressing** *adj* **depressingly** *adv*
WORD ORIGIN Old French *depresser*
depressant *adj* **1** *med* able to reduce nervous or functional activity; sedative ▷ *n* **2** a depressant drug
depressed ❶ *adj* **1** low in spirits; downcast **2** suffering from economic hardship, such as unemployment: *the current depressed conditions* **3** pressed down or flattened
depression ❶ *n* **1** a mental state in which a person has feelings of gloom and inadequacy **2** an economic condition in which there is substantial unemployment, low output and investment; slump **3** *meteorol* a mass of air below normal atmospheric pressure, which often causes rain **4** a sunken place
Depression *n* **the Depression** the worldwide economic depression of the early 1930s
depressive *adj* causing sadness and lack of energy
Depretis *n* **Agostino** 1813–87, Italian statesman; prime minister (1876–78; 1878–79; 1881–87). His policy led to the Triple Alliance (1882) between Italy, Austria-Hungary, and Germany
deprive *vb* **-priving, -prived** ▪ **deprive of** to prevent from having or enjoying **deprivation** *n*
WORD ORIGIN Latin *de-* from + *privare* to deprive of
deprived ❶ *adj* lacking adequate living conditions, education, etc.: *deprived ghettos*
dept department
depth ❶ *n* **1** the distance downwards, backwards, or inwards **2** intensity of emotion or feeling **3** the quality of having a high degree of knowledge, insight, and understanding **4** intensity of colour **5** lowness of

THESAURUS

deport *vb* **1 = expel**, exile, throw out, oust, banish, expatriate, extradite, evict, send packing, show you the door
depose *vb* **1 = oust**, dismiss, displace, degrade, downgrade, cashier, demote, dethrone, remove from office
deposit *vb* **1 = put**, place, lay, drop, settle **2, 3 = store**, keep, put, bank, save, lodge, entrust, consign, hoard, stash *(informal)*, lock away, put in storage ▷ *n* **6 = down payment**, security, stake, pledge, warranty, instalment, retainer, part payment **7 = accumulation**, growth, mass, build-up, layer
depot *n* **1 = arsenal**, warehouse, storehouse, repository, depository, dump **2** *(US & Canad)* **= bus station**, station, garage, terminus
depreciation *n* **2 = devaluation**, fall, drop, depression, slump, deflation
depress *vb* **1 = sadden**, upset, distress, chill, discourage, grieve, daunt, oppress, desolate, weigh down, cast down, bring tears to your eyes, make sad, dishearten, dispirit, make your heart bleed, aggrieve, deject, make despondent, cast a gloom upon, harsh someone's mellow or buzz
OPPOSITE: cheer
2 = devalue, depreciate, cheapen, devaluate **3 = press down**, push, squeeze, lower, flatten, compress, push down, bear down on
depressed *adj* **1 = sad**, down, low, blue, unhappy, discouraged, fed up, moody, gloomy, pessimistic, melancholy, sombre, glum, mournful, dejected, despondent, dispirited, downcast, morose, disconsolate, crestfallen, doleful, downhearted, heavy-hearted, down in the dumps *(informal)*, cheerless, woebegone, down in the mouth *(informal)*, low-spirited **2 = poverty-stricken**, poor, deprived, distressed, disadvantaged, rundown, impoverished, needy, destitute, down at heel **3 = sunken**, hollow, recessed, set back, indented, concave
depression *n* **1 = despair**, misery, sadness, dumps *(informal)*, the blues, melancholy, unhappiness, hopelessness, despondency, the hump *(Brit informal)*, bleakness, melancholia, dejection, wretchedness, low spirits, gloominess, dolefulness, cheerlessness, downheartedness **2 = recession**, slump, economic decline, credit crunch, stagnation, inactivity, hard *or* bad times **4 = hollow**, pit, dip, bowl, valley, sink, impression, dent, sag, cavity, excavation, indentation, dimple, concavity
deprived *adj* **= poor**, disadvantaged, needy, in need, lacking, bereft, destitute, in want, denuded, down at heel, necessitous
OPPOSITE: prosperous
depth *n* **1 = deepness**, drop, measure, extent, profundity, profoundness

d

DICTIONARY

pitch **6 depths a** a remote inaccessible region: *the depths of the forest* **b** the most severe part: *the depths of depression* **c** a low moral state **7 out of one's depth a** in water deeper than one is tall **b** beyond the range of one's competence or understanding
WORD ORIGIN Middle English *dep* deep

depth charge *n* a bomb used to attack submarines that explodes at a preset depth of water

deputation *n* a body of people appointed to represent others

depute *vb* **-puting, -puted** to appoint (someone) to act on one's behalf
WORD ORIGIN Late Latin *deputare* to assign, allot

deputize *or* **-tise** *vb* **-tizing, -tized** *or* **-tising, -tised** (usually foll. by *for*) to act as deputy

deputy ❶ *n, pl* **-ties** a person appointed to act on behalf of another
WORD ORIGIN Old French *deputer* to appoint

De Quincey *n* **Thomas** 1785–1859, English critic and essayist, noted particularly for his *Confessions of an English Opium Eater* (1821)

derail *vb* to cause (a train or tram) to go off the rails **derailment** *n*

derailleur (dee-**rail**-yer) *n* a type of gear-change mechanism for bicycles

deranged *adj* **1** mad, or behaving in a wild and uncontrolled way **2** in a state of disorder **derangement** *n*
WORD ORIGIN from Old French *desrengier* to disorder, disturb

derby *n, pl* **-bies** *US & Canad* a bowler hat

Derby *n, pl* **-bies 1 the Derby** an annual horse race for three-year-olds, run at Epsom Downs, Surrey **2 local derby** a sporting event between teams from the same area
WORD ORIGIN after the Earl of *Derby*, who founded the race in 1780

deregulate *vb* **-lating, -lated** to remove regulations or controls from **deregulation** *n*

derelict ❶ *adj* **1** abandoned or unused and falling into ruins ▷ *n* **2** a social outcast or vagrant
WORD ORIGIN Latin *derelinquere* to abandon

dereliction *n* **1** the state of being abandoned **2 dereliction of duty** wilful neglect of one's duty

derestrict *vb Brit, Austral & NZ* to make (a road) free from speed limits **derestriction** *n*

deride *vb* **-riding, -rided** to speak of or treat with contempt or ridicule **derision** *n*
WORD ORIGIN Latin *deridere* to laugh to scorn

de rigueur (de rig-**gur**) *adj* required by fashion
WORD ORIGIN French, literally: of strictness

derisive *adj* mocking or scornful **derisively** *adv*

derisory *adj* too small or inadequate to be considered seriously: *the shareholders have dismissed the offer as derisory*

derivation *n* the origin or descent of something, such as a word

derivative *adj* **1** based on other sources; not original ▷ *n* **2** a word, idea, etc. that is derived from another **3** *maths* the rate of change of one quantity with respect to another

derive *vb* **-riving, -rived** to draw or be drawn (from) in source or origin
WORD ORIGIN Old French *deriver* to spring from

dermatitis *n* inflammation of the skin
WORD ORIGIN Greek *derma* skin

dermatology *n* the branch of medicine concerned with the skin **dermatologist** *n*
WORD ORIGIN Greek *derma* skin + -LOGY

Dermot MacMurrough *n* ?1110–71, king of Leinster, who, by enlisting the support of the English to win back his kingdom, was responsible for the English conquest of Ireland

derogate *vb* **-gating, -gated** ▪ **derogate from** to cause to seem inferior; detract from **derogation** *n*
WORD ORIGIN Latin *derogare* to diminish

derogatory (dir-**rog**-a-tree) *adj* expressing or showing a low opinion of someone or something

derrick *n* **1** a simple crane that has lifting tackle slung from a boom **2** the framework erected over an oil well to enable drill tubes to be raised and lowered
WORD ORIGIN after *Derrick*, famous hangman

derring-do *n archaic or literary* a daring spirit or deed
WORD ORIGIN Middle English *durring don* daring to do

derv *n Brit* diesel oil, when used for road transport
WORD ORIGIN *d(iesel) e(ngine) r(oad) v(ehicle)*

dervish *n* a member of a Muslim religious order noted for a frenzied, ecstatic, whirling dance
WORD ORIGIN Persian *darvīsh* mendicant monk

Desai *n* **1 Morarji (Ranchhodji)** 1896–1995, Indian statesman, noted for his asceticism. He founded the Janata party in opposition to Indira Gandhi, whom he defeated in the 1977 election; prime minister of India (1977–79) **2 Kiran**, born 1971, Indian writer; her novel *The Inheritance of Loss* (2006) won the Man Booker Prize

desalination *n* the process of removing salt, esp. from sea water

descale *vb* to remove the hard coating which sometimes forms inside kettles, pipes, etc.

descant *n* **1** a tune played or sung above a basic melody ▷ *adj* **2** of the highest member in a family of musical instruments: *a descant clarinet*
WORD ORIGIN Latin *dis-* apart + *cantus* song

descend ❶ *vb* **1** to move down (a slope, staircase, etc.) **2** to move or fall to a lower level, pitch, etc. **3 be descended from** to be connected by a blood relationship to **4 descend on** to visit unexpectedly **5 descend to** to stoop to (unworthy behaviour)
WORD ORIGIN Latin *descendere*

descendant *n* a person or animal descended from an individual, race, or species

descendent *adj* descending

descent ❶ *n* **1** the act of descending **2** a downward slope **3** a path or way leading downwards **4** derivation from an ancestor; family origin **5** a decline or degeneration

Deschamps *n* **1 Émile**, full name *Émile Deschamps de Saint-Armand*. 1791–1871, French poet, dramatist, and

THESAURUS

3 = insight, intelligence, wisdom, penetration, profundity, acuity, discernment, perspicacity, sagacity, astuteness, profoundness, perspicuity **OPPOSITE:** superficiality

deputy *n* **= substitute**, representative, ambassador, agent, commissioner, delegate, lieutenant, proxy, surrogate, second-in-command, nuncio, legate, vicegerent, number two

derelict *adj* **1 = abandoned**, deserted, ruined, neglected, discarded, forsaken, dilapidated ▷ *n* **2 = tramp**, bum (*informal*), outcast, drifter, down-and-out, vagrant, hobo (*chiefly US*), vagabond, bag lady, dosser (*Brit slang*), derro (*Austral slang*)

descend *vb* **1 = go down**, come down, walk down, move down, climb down **2a = fall**, drop, sink, go down, plunge, dive, tumble, plummet, subside, move down **OPPOSITE:** rise **2b = slope**, dip, incline, slant, gravitate **3 be descended from = originate from**, derive from, spring from, proceed from, issue from

descent *n* **1 = fall**, drop, plunge, coming down, swoop **2, 3 = slope**, drop, dip, incline, slant, declination, declivity **4 = origin**, extraction, ancestry, lineage, family tree, parentage, heredity, genealogy, derivation **5 = decline**, deterioration, degradation, decadence,

librettist: a leading figure in the French romantic movement **2 Eustache.** ?1346–?1406, French poet, noted for his *Miroir de mariage*, a satirical attack on women

describe ❶ *vb* **-scribing, -scribed 1** to give an account of (something or someone) in words **2** to trace the outline of (a circle, etc.)
WORD ORIGIN Latin *describere* to copy off, write out

description ❶ *n* **1** a statement or account that describes someone or something **2** the act of describing **3** sort, kind, or variety: *antiques of every description*

descriptive *adj* describing something: *it was a very descriptive account of the play* **descriptively** *adv*

descry *vb* **-scries, -scrying, -scried 1** to catch sight of **2** to discover by looking carefully
WORD ORIGIN Old French *descrier* to proclaim

desecrate *vb* **-crating, -crated** to violate the sacred character of (an object or place) **desecration** *n*
WORD ORIGIN DE- + (CON)SECRATE

desegregate *vb* **-gating, -gated** to end racial segregation in (a school or other public institution) **desegregation** *n*

deselect *vb* **1** *computers* to cancel (a highlighted selection of data) on a computer screen **2** *Brit politics* (of a constituency organization) to refuse to select (an MP) for re-election **deselection** *n*

desensitize *or* **-tise** *vb* **-tizing, -tized** *or* **-tising, -tised** to make insensitive or less sensitive: *the patient was desensitized to the allergen; to desensitize photographic film*

desert[1] ❶ *n* a region that has little or no vegetation because of low rainfall
WORD ORIGIN Church Latin *desertum*

desert[2] ❶ *vb* **1** to abandon (a person or place) without intending to return **2** *chiefly mil* to leave (a post or duty) with no intention of returning **deserted** *adj* **deserter** *n* **desertion** *n*
WORD ORIGIN Latin *deserere*

desertification *n* a process by which fertile land turns into desert

desert island *n* a small uninhabited island in the tropics

deserts *pl n* **get one's just deserts** get the punishment one deserves
WORD ORIGIN Old French *deserte* something deserved

deserve ❶ *vb* **-serving, -served** to be entitled to or worthy of
WORD ORIGIN Latin *deservire* to serve devotedly

deserved ❶ *adj* rightfully earned **deservedly** (diz-**zerv**-id-lee) *adv*

deserving ❶ *adj* worthy of a reward, help, or praise

deshabille (day-zab-**beel**) *or* **dishabille** *n* the state of being partly dressed
WORD ORIGIN French *déshabillé*

desi *Indian English adj* **1** indigenous or local ▷ *n* **2** *informal* a person considered to be of South Asian origin
WORD ORIGIN Hindi

de Sica *n* **Vittorio** 1902–74, Italian film actor and director. His films, in the neorealist tradition, include *Shoeshine* (1946) and *Bicycle Thieves* (1948)

desiccate ❶ *vb* **-cating, -cated** to remove most of the water from; dry **desiccated** *adj* **desiccation** *n*
WORD ORIGIN Latin *desiccare* to dry up

design ❶ *vb* **1** to work out the structure or form of (something), by making a sketch or plans **2** to plan and make (something) artistically **3** to intend (something) for a specific purpose: *the move is designed to reduce travelling costs* ▷ *n* **4** a sketch, plan, or preliminary drawing **5** the arrangement or features of an artistic or decorative work: *he built it to his own design* **6** a finished artistic or decorative creation **7** the art of designing **8** an intention; purpose **9 have designs on** to plot to gain possession of
WORD ORIGIN Latin *designare* to mark out, describe

designate ❶ (**dez**-zig-nate) *vb* **-nating, -nated 1** to give a name to or describe as: *vessels sunk during battle are designated as war graves* **2** to select (someone) for an office or duty; appoint ▷ *adj* **3** appointed, but not yet in office: *a Prime Minister designate*
WORD ORIGIN Latin *designatus* marked out

designated driver *n* a person who volunteers not to drink alcohol at a social event, in order to drive people who have been drinking

designation *n* **1** something that designates, such as a name **2** the act of designating

designedly (dee-**zine**-id-lee) *adv* by intention

designer ❶ *n* **1** a person who draws up original sketches or plans from which things are made ▷ *adj* **2** designed by a well-known fashion designer: *a wardrobe full of designer clothes* **3** having an appearance of fashionable trendiness: *designer stubble*

designing *adj* cunning and scheming

d

THESAURUS

degeneration, debasement

describe *vb* **1a = relate**, tell, report, present, detail, explain, express, illustrate, specify, chronicle, recount, recite, impart, narrate, set forth, give an account of **1b = portray**, depict, characterize, define, sketch **2 = trace**, draw, outline, mark out, delineate

description *n* **1 = account**, report, explanation, representation, sketch, narrative, portrayal, depiction, narration, characterization, delineation **2 = calling**, naming, branding, labelling, dubbing, designation **3 = kind**, sort, type, order, class, variety, brand, species, breed, category, kidney, genre, genus, ilk

desert[1] *n* **= wilderness**, waste, wilds, wasteland

desert[2] *vb* **1a = abandon**, leave, give up, quit *(informal)*, withdraw from, move out of, relinquish, renounce, vacate, forsake, go away from, leave empty, relinquish possession of **1b = leave**, abandon, strand, betray, maroon, walk out on *(informal)*, forsake, jilt, run out on *(informal)*, throw over, leave stranded, leave high and dry, leave (someone) in the lurch **OPPOSITE:** take care of **2 = abscond**, defect, decamp, go over the hill *(military)* *(slang)*

deserve *vb* **= merit**, warrant, be entitled to, have a right to, win, rate, earn, justify, be worthy of, have a claim to

deserved *adj* **= well-earned**, just, right, meet *(archaic)*, fitting, due, fair, earned, appropriate, justified, suitable, merited, proper, warranted, rightful, justifiable, condign

deserving *adj* **= worthy**, righteous, commendable, laudable, praiseworthy, meritorious, estimable **OPPOSITE:** undeserving

desiccate *vb* **= dry**, drain, evaporate, dehydrate, parch, exsiccate

design *vb* **1 = plan**, describe, draw, draft, trace, outline, invent, devise, sketch, formulate, contrive, think out, delineate **2 = create**, make, plan, project, fashion, scheme, propose, invent, devise, tailor, draw up, conceive, originate, contrive, fabricate, think up **3 = intend**, mean, plan, aim, purpose ▷ *n* **4 = plan**, drawing, model, scheme, draft, outline, sketch, blueprint, delineation **5 = pattern**, form, figure, style, shape, organization, arrangement, construction, motif, configuration **8 = intention**, end, point, aim, goal, target, purpose, object, objective, intent

designate *vb* **1 = name**, call, term, style, label, entitle, dub, nominate, christen **2 = appoint**, name, choose, commission, select, elect, delegate, nominate, assign, depute

designer *n* **1a = couturier**, stylist **1b = producer**, architect, deviser, creator, planner, inventor, artificer, originator

DICTIONARY

desirable ❶ *adj* **1** worth having or doing: *a desirable lifestyle* **2** arousing sexual desire **desirability** *n* **desirably** *adv*

desire ❶ *vb* **-siring, -sired 1** to want very much **2** *formal* to request: *we desire your company at the wedding of our daughter* ▷ *n* **3** a wish or longing **4** sexual appetite **5** a person or thing that is desired
WORD ORIGIN Latin *desiderare*

desirous *adj* (usually foll. by *of*) having a desire for: *deeply desirous of regaining the leadership*

desist *vb* to stop doing: *please desist from talking*
WORD ORIGIN Latin *desistere*

desk *n* **1** a piece of furniture with a writing surface and usually drawers **2** a service counter in a public building, such as a hotel **3** the section of a newspaper or television station responsible for a particular subject: *the picture desk*
WORD ORIGIN Medieval Latin *desca* table

deskill *vb* **1** to mechanize or computerize (a job) thereby reducing the skill required to do it **2** to deprive (employees) of the opportunity to use their skills **deskilling** *n*

desktop *n* **1** the main screen display on a personal computer ▷ *adj* **2** (esp. of a computer system) for use at a desk

desktop publishing *n* a computer system which combines text and graphics and presents them in a professional-looking printed format

Desmond *n* **15th Earl of,** title of *Gerald Fitzgerald*. died 1583, Anglo-Irish nobleman, who led a Catholic rebellion (1579) against English domination of Ireland

Desmoulins *n* **(Lucie Simplice) Camille (Benoît)** 1760–94, French revolutionary leader, pamphleteer, and orator

desolate *adj* **1** uninhabited and bleak **2** made uninhabitable; devastated **3** without friends, hope, or encouragement **4** gloomy or dismal; depressing ▷ *vb* **-lating, -lated 5** to deprive of inhabitants **6** to make barren; devastate **7** to make wretched or forlorn **desolately** *adv* **desolateness** *n*
WORD ORIGIN Latin *desolare* to leave alone

desolation *n* **1** ruin or devastation **2** solitary misery; wretchedness

De Soto *n* **Hernando** ?1500–42, Spanish explorer, who discovered the Mississippi River (1541). Also: **Fernando De Soto**

despair ❶ *n* **1** total loss of hope ▷ *vb* **2** to lose or give up hope: *we must not despair of finding a peaceful solution*
WORD ORIGIN Old French *despoir* hopelessness

despatch *vb, n* ▸ same as **dispatch**

Despenser *n* **Hugh le,** Earl of Winchester. 1262–1326, English statesman, a favourite of Edward II. Together with his son **Hugh,** *the Younger* (?1290–1326), he was executed by the king's enemies

desperado *n, pl* **-does** *or* **-dos** a reckless person ready to commit any violent illegal act
WORD ORIGIN probably pseudo-Spanish

desperate ❶ *adj* **1** willing to do anything to improve one's situation **2** (of an action) undertaken as a last resort **3** very grave: *in desperate agony* **4** having a great need or desire: *I was desperate for a child* **desperately** *adv*
WORD ORIGIN Latin *desperare* to have no hope

desperation ❶ *n* **1** desperate recklessness **2** the state of being desperate

despicable *adj* deserving contempt **despicably** *adv*

despise ❶ *vb* **-pising, -pised** to look down on with contempt
WORD ORIGIN Latin *despicere* to look down

despite ❶ *prep* in spite of
WORD ORIGIN Old French *despit*

despoil *vb formal* to plunder **despoliation** *n*
WORD ORIGIN Latin *despoliare*

despondent *adj* dejected or depressed **despondency** *n* **despondently** *adv*
WORD ORIGIN Latin *despondere* to lose heart

despot *n* any person in power who acts tyrannically **despotic** *adj* **despotically** *adv*
WORD ORIGIN Greek *despotēs* lord, master

despotism *n* **1** absolute or tyrannical government **2** tyrannical behaviour

des Prés *or* **Desprez** *n* **Josquin** ?1450–1521, Flemish Renaissance composer of masses, motets, and chansons

Dessalines *n* **Jean Jacques** ?1758–1806, emperor of Haiti (1804–06) after driving out the French; assassinated

dessert *n* the sweet course served at the end of a meal
WORD ORIGIN French

dessertspoon *n* a spoon between a tablespoon and a teaspoon in size

destination ❶ *n* the place to which someone or something is going

destined ❶ (dess-tinnd) *adj* **1** certain to be or do something: *the school is destined to close this summer* **2** heading towards a specific destination: *some of the oil was destined for Eastern Europe*

THESAURUS

desirable *adj* **1a = advantageous**, useful, valuable, helpful, profitable, of service, convenient, worthwhile, beneficial, preferable, advisable
OPPOSITE: disadvantageous
1b = popular OPPOSITE: unpopular
2 = attractive, appealing, beautiful, winning, interesting, pleasing, pretty, fair, inviting, engaging, lovely, charming, fascinating, sexy *(informal)*, handsome, fetching, good-looking, eligible, glamorous, gorgeous, magnetic, cute, enticing, seductive, captivating, alluring, adorable, bonny, winsome, comely, prepossessing
OPPOSITE: unattractive

desire *vb* **1 = want**, long for, crave, fancy, hope for, ache for, covet, aspire to, wish for, yearn for, thirst for, hanker after, set your heart on, desiderate ▷ *n* **3 = wish**, want, longing, need, hope, urge, yen *(informal)*, hunger, appetite, aspiration, ache, craving, yearning, inclination, thirst, hankering **4 = lust**, passion, libido, appetite, lechery, carnality, lasciviousness, concupiscence, randiness *(informal, chiefly Brit)*, lustfulness

despair *n* **1 = despondency**, depression, misery, gloom, desperation, anguish, melancholy, hopelessness, dejection, wretchedness, disheartenment ▷ *vb* **2 = lose hope**, give up, lose heart, be despondent, be dejected

desperate *adj* **2 = last-ditch**, dangerous, daring, determined, wild, violent, furious, risky, frantic, rash, hazardous, precipitate, hasty, audacious, madcap, foolhardy, headstrong, impetuous, death-defying **3 = grave**, great, pressing, serious, critical, acute, severe, extreme, urgent, dire, drastic, very grave

desperation *n* **1 = recklessness**, madness, defiance, frenzy, impetuosity, rashness, foolhardiness, heedlessness **2 = misery**, worry, trouble, pain, anxiety, torture, despair, agony, sorrow, distraction, anguish, unhappiness, heartache, hopelessness, despondency

despise *vb* **= look down on**, loathe, scorn, disdain, spurn, undervalue, deride, detest, revile, abhor, have a down on *(informal)*, contemn
OPPOSITE: admire

despite *prep* **= in spite of**, in the face of, regardless of, even with, notwithstanding, in defiance of, in the teeth of, undeterred by, in contempt of

destination *n* **= stop**, station, haven, harbour, resting-place, terminus, journey's end, landing-place

destined *adj* **1 = fated**, meant, intended, designed, certain, bound, doomed, ordained, predestined, foreordained

DICTIONARY

WORD ORIGIN Latin *destinare* to appoint
destiny ⓘ *n, pl* **-nies** **1** the future destined for a person or thing **2** the predetermined course of events **3** the power that predetermines the course of events
WORD ORIGIN Old French *destinee*
destitute *adj* lacking the means to live; totally impoverished
destitution *n*
WORD ORIGIN Latin *destituere* to leave alone
de-stress *vb* to become or cause to become less stressed or anxious
destroy ⓘ *vb* **1** to ruin; demolish **2** to put an end to **3** to kill (an animal) **4** to crush or defeat
WORD ORIGIN Latin *destruere* to pull down
destroyer *n* **1** a small heavily armed warship **2** a person or thing that destroys
destructible *adj* capable of being destroyed
destruction ⓘ *n* **1** the act of destroying something or state of being destroyed **2** a cause of ruin
WORD ORIGIN Latin *destructio* a pulling down
destructive ⓘ *adj* **1** causing or capable of causing harm, damage, or injury **2** intended to discredit, esp. without positive suggestions or help: *destructive speeches against the platform* **destructively** *adv*
desuetude (diss-**syoo**-it-tude) *n formal* the condition of not being in use
WORD ORIGIN Latin *desuescere* to lay aside a habit
desultory (**dez**-zl-tree) *adj* **1** passing or jumping from one thing to another; disconnected: *desultory conversation* **2** occurring in a random way: *a desultory thought* **desultorily** *adv*
WORD ORIGIN Latin *de-* from + *salire* to jump
detach ⓘ *vb* **1** to disengage and separate **2** *mil* to send (a regiment, officer, etc.) on a special assignment **detachable** *adj*
WORD ORIGIN Old French *destachier*
detached ⓘ *adj* **1** *Brit, Austral & S African* separate or standing apart: *a detached farmhouse* **2** showing no emotional involvement: *she continued to watch him in her grave and detached manner*
detachment ⓘ *n* **1** the state of not being personally involved in something **2** *mil* a small group of soldiers separated from the main group
detail ⓘ *n* **1** an item that is considered separately **2** an item considered to be unimportant: *a mere detail* **3** treatment of individual parts: *the census provides a considerable amount of detail* **4** a small section of a work of art often enlarged to make the smaller features more distinct **5** *chiefly mil* **a** personnel assigned a specific duty **b** the duty **6** **in detail** including all the important particulars ▷ *vb* **7** to list fully **8** *chiefly mil* to select (personnel) for a specific duty
WORD ORIGIN Old French *detailler* to cut in pieces
detailed ⓘ *adj* having many details
detain ⓘ *vb* **1** to delay (someone) **2** to force (someone) to stay: *the police detained him for questioning* **detainee** *n* **detainment** *n*
WORD ORIGIN Latin *detinere*
detect ⓘ *vb* **1** to perceive or notice: *to detect a note of sarcasm* **2** to discover the existence or presence of: *to detect alcohol in the blood* **detectable** *adj* **detector** *n*
WORD ORIGIN Latin *detegere* to uncover
detection *n* **1** the act of noticing, discovering, or sensing something **2** the act or process of extracting information
detective ⓘ *n* **a** a police officer who investigates crimes **b** ▸ same as **private detective**
detente (**day**-**tont**) *n* the easing of tension between nations
WORD ORIGIN French
detention ⓘ *n* **1** imprisonment, esp. of a suspect awaiting trial **2** a form of punishment in which a pupil is detained after school
detention centre *n* a place where young people may be detained for

THESAURUS

destiny *n* **1 = fate**, fortune, lot, portion, doom, nemesis, divine decree **3 = fortune**, chance, karma, providence, kismet, predestination, divine will
destroy *vb* **1 = ruin**, smash, crush, waste, devastate, break down, wreck, shatter, gut, wipe out, dispatch, dismantle, demolish, trash *(slang)*, total *(slang)*, ravage, slay, eradicate, torpedo, extinguish, desolate, annihilate, put paid to, raze, blow to bits, extirpate, blow sky-high **3 = slaughter**, kill, exterminate
destruction *n* **1a = ruin**, havoc, wreckage, crushing, wrecking, shattering, undoing, demolition, devastation, annihilation, ruination **1b = massacre**, overwhelming, slaughter, overthrow, extinction, end, downfall, liquidation, obliteration, extermination, eradication
destructive *adj* **1 = devastating**, fatal, deadly, lethal, harmful, damaging, catastrophic, detrimental, hurtful, pernicious, noxious, ruinous, calamitous, cataclysmic, baleful, deleterious, injurious, baneful, maleficent
detach *vb* **1a = separate**, free, remove, divide, isolate, cut off, sever, loosen, segregate, disconnect, tear off, disengage, disentangle, unfasten, disunite, uncouple, unhitch, disjoin, unbridle **OPPOSITE:** attach **1b = free**, remove, separate, isolate, cut off, segregate, disengage
detached *adj* **1 = separate**, free, severed, disconnected, loosened, discrete, unconnected, undivided, disjoined **2 = objective**, neutral, impartial, reserved, aloof, impersonal, disinterested, unbiased, dispassionate, uncommitted, uninvolved, unprejudiced **OPPOSITE:** subjective
detachment *n* **1 = indifference**, fairness, neutrality, objectivity, impartiality, coolness, remoteness, nonchalance, aloofness, unconcern, disinterestedness, nonpartisanship **2** *(military)* **= unit**, party, force, body, detail, squad, patrol, task force
detail *n* **1 = point**, fact, feature, particular, respect, factor, count, item, instance, element, aspect, specific, component, facet, technicality **2 = fine point**, part, particular, nicety, minutiae, triviality **5a** *(military)* **= party**, force, body, duty, squad, assignment, fatigue, detachment ▷ *vb* **7 = list**, describe, relate, catalogue, portray, specify, depict, recount, rehearse, recite, narrate, delineate, enumerate, itemize, tabulate, particularize
detailed *adj* **= comprehensive**, full, complete, minute, particular, specific, extensive, exact, thorough, meticulous, exhaustive, all-embracing, itemized, encyclopedic, blow-by-blow, particularized **OPPOSITE:** brief
detain *vb* **1 = delay**, keep, stop, hold up, hamper, hinder, retard, impede, keep back, slow up *or* down **2 = hold**, arrest, confine, restrain, imprison, intern, take prisoner, take into custody, hold in custody
detect *vb* **1 = notice**, see, spot, catch, note, identify, observe, remark, recognize, distinguish, perceive, scent, discern, ascertain, descry **2 = discover**, find, reveal, catch, expose, disclose, uncover, track down, unmask
detective *n* **= investigator**, cop *(slang)*, copper *(slang)*, dick *(slang, chiefly US)*, constable, tec *(slang)*, private eye, sleuth *(informal)*, private investigator, gumshoe *(US slang)*, bizzy *(slang)*, C.I.D. man
detention *n* **1 = imprisonment**, custody, restraint, keeping in, quarantine, confinement, porridge *(slang)*, incarceration **OPPOSITE:** release

d

DICTIONARY

short periods of time by order of a court

deter ❶ *vb* **-terring, -terred** to discourage or prevent (someone) from doing something by instilling fear or doubt in them
WORD ORIGIN Latin *deterrere*

detergent *n* **1** a chemical substance used for washing clothes, dishes, etc. ▹*adj* **2** having cleansing power
WORD ORIGIN Latin *detergens* wiping off

deteriorate ❶ *vb* **-rating, -rated** to become worse **deterioration** *n*
WORD ORIGIN Latin *deterior* worse

determinant *adj* **1** serving to determine or affect ▹*n* **2** a factor that controls or influences what will happen **3** *maths* a square array of elements that represents the sum of certain products of these elements

determinate *adj* definitely limited or fixed

determination ❶ *n* **1** the condition of being determined; resoluteness **2** the act of making a decision

determine ❶ *vb* **-mining, -mined 1** to settle (an argument or a question) conclusively **2** to find out the facts about (something): *the tests determined it was in fact cancer* **3** to fix in scope, extent, etc.: *to determine the degree of the problem* **4** to make a decision
WORD ORIGIN Latin *determinare* to set boundaries to

determined ❶ *adj* firmly decided **determinedly** *adv*

determiner *n grammar* a word, such as a number, article, or personal pronoun, that determines the meaning of a noun phrase

determinism *n* the theory that human choice is not free, but is decided by past events **determinist** *n, adj*

deterrent ❶ *n* **1** something that deters **2** a weapon or set of weapons held by one country to deter another country attacking ▹*adj* **3** tending to deter **deterrence** *n*
WORD ORIGIN Latin *deterrens* hindering

detest *vb* to dislike intensely **detestable** *adj*
WORD ORIGIN Latin *detestari*

detestation *n* intense hatred

dethrone *vb* **-throning, -throned** to remove from a throne or deprive of any high position **dethronement** *n*

detonate *vb* **-nating, -nated** to make (an explosive device) explode or (of an explosive device) to explode **detonation** *n*
WORD ORIGIN Latin *detonare* to thunder down

detonator *n* a small amount of explosive or a device used to set off an explosion

detour *n* a deviation from a direct route or course of action
WORD ORIGIN French

detoxify *vb* **-fies, -fying, -fied** to remove poison from **detoxification** *n*

detract *vb* **detract from** to make (something) seem less good, valuable, or impressive: *I wouldn't want to detract from your triumph* **detractor** *n* **detraction** *n*
WORD ORIGIN Latin *detrahere* to pull away, disparage

detriment *n* disadvantage or damage **detrimental** *adj* **detrimentally** *adv*
WORD ORIGIN Latin *detrimentum* a rubbing off

detritus (dit-**trite**-uss) *n* **1** a loose mass of stones and silt worn away from rocks **2** debris **detrital** *adj*
WORD ORIGIN Latin: a rubbing away

de trop (de **troh**) *adj* unwanted or unwelcome: *I know when I'm de trop, so I'll leave you two together*
WORD ORIGIN French

detumescence *n* the subsidence of a swelling
WORD ORIGIN Latin *detumescere* to cease swelling

deuce (**dyewss**) *n* **1** *tennis* a tied score that requires one player to gain two successive points to win the game **2** a playing card or dice with two spots
WORD ORIGIN Latin *duo* two

deus ex machina *n* an unlikely development introduced into a play or film to resolve the plot

deuterium *n* a stable isotope of hydrogen. Symbol: D or ^{2}H
WORD ORIGIN Greek *deuteros* second

deuterium oxide *n* ▸same as **heavy water**

Deutsch *n* **Otto Erich** 1883–1967, Austrian music historian and art critic, noted for his catalogue of Schubert's works (1951)

Deutschmark (**doytch**-mark) *or* **Deutsche Mark** (**doytch**-a) *n* a former monetary unit of Germany
WORD ORIGIN German: German mark

deutzia (**dyewt**-see-a) *n* a shrub with clusters of pink or white flowers

de Valois *n* Dame **Ninette** original name *Edris Stannus*. 1898–2001, British ballet dancer and choreographer, born in Ireland: a founder of the Vic-Wells Ballet Company (1931), which under her direction became the Royal Ballet (1956)

devalue *vb* **-valuing, -valued 1** to reduce the exchange value of (a currency) **2** to reduce the value of (something or someone) **devaluation** *n*

devastate ❶ *vb* **-tating, -tated** to damage (a place) severely or destroy it **devastation** *n*
WORD ORIGIN Latin *devastare*

devastated *adj* shocked and extremely upset **devastating** *adj* **devastatingly** *adv*

develop ❶ *vb* **1** to grow or bring to a later, more elaborate, or more advanced stage **2** to come or bring into existence: *the country has developed a consumer society* **3** to make or become gradually clearer or more widely known **4** to follow as a result of something: *Cubism developed from attempts to give painting a more intellectual*

THESAURUS

deter *vb* **a = discourage**, inhibit, put off, frighten, intimidate, daunt, hinder, dissuade, talk out of **b = prevent**, stop, check, curb, damp, restrain, prohibit, hinder, debar

deteriorate *vb* **= decline**, worsen, degenerate, slump, degrade, depreciate, go downhill, go to the dogs *(informal)*, go to pot
OPPOSITE: improve

determination *n* **1 = resolution**, purpose, resolve, drive, energy, conviction, courage, dedication, backbone, fortitude, persistence, tenacity, perseverance, willpower, boldness, firmness, staying power, stubbornness, constancy, single-mindedness, earnestness, obstinacy, steadfastness, doggedness, relentlessness, resoluteness, indomitability, staunchness
OPPOSITE: indecision

determine *vb* **1a = affect**, control, decide, rule, condition, direct, influence, shape, govern, regulate, ordain **1b = decide on**, choose, establish, purpose, fix, elect, resolve **2, 3 = settle**, learn, establish, discover, check, find out, work out, detect, certify, verify, ascertain **4 = decide**, purpose, conclude, resolve, make up your mind

determined *adj* **= resolute**, firm, dogged, fixed, constant, bold, intent, persistent, relentless, stalwart, persevering, single-minded, purposeful, tenacious, undaunted, strong-willed, steadfast, unwavering, immovable, unflinching, strong-minded

deterrent *n* **1 = discouragement**, obstacle, curb, restraint, impediment, check, hindrance, disincentive, defensive measures, determent **OPPOSITE:** incentive

devastate *vb* **= destroy**, waste, ruin, sack, wreck, spoil, demolish, trash *(slang)*, level, total *(slang)*, ravage, plunder, desolate, pillage, raze, lay waste, despoil

develop *vb* **1 = grow**, advance, progress, mature, evolve, flourish, blossom, ripen **2a = establish**, set up, promote, generate, undertake, initiate, embark on, cultivate, instigate, inaugurate, set in motion **2b = form**, start, begin, contract,

DICTIONARY

concept of form **5** to contract (an illness) **6** to improve the value or change the use of (land) **7** to exploit the natural resources of (a country or region) **8** *photog* to treat (a photographic plate or film) to produce a visible image
WORD ORIGIN Old French *desveloper* to unwrap

developer *n* **1** a person who develops property **2** *photog* a chemical used to develop photographs or films

developing country *n* a poor or nonindustrial country that is seeking to develop its resources by industrialization

development ⊙ *n* **1** the process of growing or developing **2** the product of developing **3** an event or incident that changes a situation **4** an area of land that has been developed **developmental** *adj*

development area *n* (in Britain) an area which has experienced economic depression and which is given government assistance to establish new industry

deviant ⊙ *adj* **1** deviating from what is considered acceptable behaviour ▷*n* **2** a person whose behaviour deviates from what is considered to be acceptable **deviance** *n*

deviate *vb* **-ating, -ated 1** to differ from others in belief or thought **2** to depart from one's usual or previous behaviour **deviation** *n*
WORD ORIGIN Late Latin *deviare* to turn aside from the direct road

device ⊙ *n* **1** a machine or tool used for a particular purpose **2** *euphemistic* a bomb **3** a scheme or plan **4** a design or emblem **5 leave someone to his** *or* **her own devices** to leave someone alone to do as he or she wishes
WORD ORIGIN Old French *devis* contrivance + *devise* intention

devil ⊙ *n* **1** *theol* **the Devil** the chief spirit of evil and enemy of God **2** any evil spirit **3** a person regarded as wicked **4** a person: *lucky devil* **5** a person regarded as daring: *be a devil!* **6** *informal* something difficult or annoying **7 between the devil and the deep blue sea** between equally undesirable alternatives **8 give the devil his due** to acknowledge the talent or success of an unpleasant person **9 talk of the devil!** used when an absent person who has been the subject of conversation arrives unexpectedly **10 the devil** used as an exclamation to show surprise or annoyance: *what the devil is she doing here?* ▷*vb* **-illing, -illed** *or US* **-iling, -iled 11** to prepare (food) by coating with a highly flavoured spiced mixture **12** *chiefly Brit* to do routine literary work for a lawyer or author
WORD ORIGIN Greek *diabolos* enemy, accuser

devilish *adj* **1** of or like a devil; fiendish ▷*adv, adj* **2** *informal* extreme or extremely: *devilish good food* **devilishly** *adv*

devil-may-care *adj* happy-go-lucky; reckless

devilment *n* mischievous conduct

devilry *n* **1** reckless fun or mischief **2** wickedness

devil's advocate *n* a person who takes an opposing or unpopular point of view for the sake of argument

Devine *n* **George** (**Alexander Cassady**) 1910–65, British stage director and actor: founded (1956) the English Stage Company in London's Royal Court Theatre

devious *adj* **1** insincere and dishonest **2** (of a route or course of action) indirect **deviously** *adv*
WORD ORIGIN Latin *devius* lying to one side of the road

devise ⊙ *vb* **-vising, -vised** to work out (something) in one's mind
WORD ORIGIN Old French *deviser* to divide

devoid ⊙ *adj* **devoid of** completely lacking in a particular quality: *she was a woman totally devoid of humour*
WORD ORIGIN Old French *devoider* to remove

devolution *n* a transfer of authority from a central government to regional governments **devolutionist** *n, adj*
WORD ORIGIN Medieval Latin *devolutio* a rolling down

devolve *vb* **-volving, -volved** to pass or cause to pass to a successor or substitute, as duties or power
WORD ORIGIN Latin *devolvere* to roll down

Devon *n* a breed of large red cattle originally from Devon

Devonian *adj* **1** *geol* of the period of geological time about 405 million years ago **2** of or relating to Devon

Devonshire *n* **8th Duke of,** title of *Spencer Compton Cavendish*. 1833–1908, British politician, also known (1858–91) as Lord Hartington. He led the Liberal Party (1874–80) and left it to found the Liberal Unionist Party (1886)

devote ⊙ *vb* **-voting, -voted** to apply or dedicate (one's time, money, or effort) to a particular purpose
WORD ORIGIN Latin *devovere* to vow

devoted ⊙ *adj* feeling or demonstrating loyalty or devotion:

THESAURUS

establish, pick up, breed, acquire, generate, foster, originate **3 = expand**, extend, work out, elaborate, unfold, enlarge, broaden, amplify, augment, dilate upon

development *n* **1a = growth**, increase, growing, advance, progress, spread, expansion, extension, evolution, widening, maturing, unfolding, unravelling, advancement, progression, thickening, enlargement **1b = establishment**, forming, generation, institution, invention, initiation, inauguration, instigation, origination **3 = event**, change, happening, issue, result, situation, incident, circumstance, improvement, outcome, phenomenon, evolution, unfolding, occurrence, upshot, turn of events, evolvement

deviant *adj* **1 = perverted**, sick *(informal)*, twisted, bent *(slang)*, abnormal, queer *(informal, derogatory)*, warped, perverse, wayward, kinky *(slang)*, devious, deviate, freaky *(slang)*, aberrant, pervy *(slang)*, sicko *(informal)* **OPPOSITE:** normal ▷*n* **2 = pervert**, freak, queer *(informal, derogatory)*, misfit, sicko *(informal)*, odd type

device *n* **1 = gadget**, machine, tool, instrument, implement, invention, appliance, apparatus, gimmick, utensil, contraption, contrivance, waldo, gizmo *or* gismo *(slang, chiefly US & Canad)* **3 = ploy**, scheme, strategy, plan, design, project, shift, trick, manoeuvre, stunt, dodge, expedient, ruse, artifice, gambit, stratagem, wile

devil *n* **1 the Devil = Satan**, Lucifer, Prince of Darkness, Old One, Deuce, Old Gentleman *(informal)*, Lord of the Flies, Old Harry *(informal)*, Mephistopheles, Evil One, Beelzebub, Old Nick *(informal)*, Mephisto, Belial, Clootie *(Scot)*, deil *(Scot)*, Apollyon, Old Scratch *(informal)*, Foul Fiend, Wicked One, archfiend, Old Hornie *(informal)*, Abbadon **2 = evil spirit**, demon, fiend, ghoul, hellhound, atua *(NZ)*, wairua *(NZ)* **3 = brute**, monster, savage, beast, villain, rogue, barbarian, fiend, terror, swine, ogre **4 = person**, individual, soul, creature, thing, human being, beggar

devise *vb* **= work out**, plan, form, design, imagine, frame, arrange, plot, construct, invent, conceive, formulate, contrive, dream up, concoct, think up

devoid *adj* *(with* **of)** **= lacking in**, without, free from, wanting in, sans *(archaic)*, bereft of, empty of, deficient in, denuded of, barren of

devote *vb* **= dedicate**, give, commit, apply, reserve, pledge, surrender, assign, allot, give over, consecrate, set apart

devoted *adj* **= dedicated**, loving, committed, concerned, caring, true,

DICTIONARY

he was clearly devoted to his family **devotedly** *adv*

devotee ❶ (dev-vote-tee) *n* **1** a person fanatically enthusiastic about a subject or activity **2** a zealous follower of a religion

devotion ❶ *n* **1** strong attachment to or affection for someone or something **2** religious zeal; piety **3 devotions** religious observance or prayers **devotional** *adj*

devour ❶ *vb* **1** to eat up greedily **2** to engulf and destroy **3** to read avidly **devouring** *adj* **WORD ORIGIN** Latin *devorare* to gulp down

devout ❶ *adj* **1** deeply religious **2** sincere; heartfelt: *a devout confession* **devoutly** *adv* **WORD ORIGIN** Latin *devotus* faithful

Devoy *n* Dame **Susan** (**Elizabeth Anne**) born 1964, New Zealand squash player; winner of the World Open Championship 1985, 1987, 1990, and 1992

De Vries *n* **Hugo** 1848–1935, Dutch botanist, who rediscovered Mendel's laws and developed the mutation theory of evolution

dew *n* drops of water that form on the ground or on a cool surface at night from vapour in the air **dewy** *adj* **WORD ORIGIN** Old English *dēaw*

dewberry *n, pl* **-berries** a type of bramble with blue-black fruits

dewclaw *n* a nonfunctional claw on a dog's leg

de Wet *n* **Christian Rudolf** 1854–1922, Afrikaner military commander and politician, who led the Orange Free State army in the second Boer War (1899–1902). He was imprisoned for treason (1914) after organizing an Afrikaner nationalist rebellion

Dewey *n* **John** 1859–1952, US pragmatist philosopher and educator: an exponent of progressivism in education, he formulated an instrumentalist theory of learning through experience. His works include *The School and Society* (1899), *Democracy and Education* (1916), and *Logic: the Theory of Inquiry* (1938)

Dewey Decimal System *n* a system of library book classification with ten main subject classes **WORD ORIGIN** after Melvil *Dewey*, educator

de Wint *n* **Peter** 1784–1849, English landscape painter

de Witt *n* **Johan** 1625–72, Dutch statesman; chief minister of the United Provinces of the Netherlands (1653–72)

dewlap *n* a loose fold of skin hanging under the throat in cattle, dogs, etc. **WORD ORIGIN** Middle English *dew* + *lap* hanging flap

dew-worm *n US & Canad* a large earthworm used as fishing bait

dewy-eyed *adj* innocent and inexperienced

dexter *adj* of or on the right side of a shield, etc. from the bearer's point of view **WORD ORIGIN** Latin

Dexter *n* **John** 1925–90, British actor and theatre director

dexterity *n* **1** skill in using one's hands **2** mental quickness **WORD ORIGIN** Latin *dexteritas* aptness, readiness

dexterous *adj* possessing or done with dexterity **dexterously** *adv*

dextrin *or* **dextrine** *n* a sticky substance obtained from starch: used as a thickening agent in food **WORD ORIGIN** French *dextrine*

dextrose *n* a glucose occurring in fruit, honey, and in the blood of animals

DFC (in Britain) Distinguished Flying Cross

dg decigram

DH *Brit* Department of Health

dhal *or* **dal** *n* **1** the nutritious pealike seed of a tropical shrub **2** a curry made from lentils or other pulses **WORD ORIGIN** Hindi *dāl*

dharma *n* **1** *hinduism* moral law or behaviour **2** *buddhism* ideal truth **WORD ORIGIN** Sanskrit

dhoti *n, pl* **-tis** a long loincloth worn by men in India **WORD ORIGIN** Hindi

DI *Brit* Donor Insemination: a method of making a woman pregnant by transferring sperm from a man other than her husband or regular partner using artificial means

di- *prefix* **1** twice; two; double: *dicotyledon* **2** containing two specified atoms or groups of atoms: *carbon dioxide* **WORD ORIGIN** Greek

diabetes (die-a-beet-eez) *n* a medical condition in which the body is unable to control the level of sugar in the blood **WORD ORIGIN** Greek: a passing through

diabetic *n* **1** a person who has diabetes ▷ *adj* **2** of or having diabetes **3** suitable for people suffering from diabetes: *diabetic chocolate*

diabolic *adj* of the Devil; satanic **WORD ORIGIN** Greek *diabolos* devil

diabolical *adj informal* **1** unpleasant or annoying: *the weather was diabolical* **2** extreme: *diabolical cheek* **3** ▸ same as **diabolic** > **diabolically** *adv*

diabolism *n* **a** witchcraft or sorcery **b** worship of devils **diabolist** *n*

diaconate *n* the position or period of office of a deacon **diaconal** *adj* **WORD ORIGIN** Late Latin *diaconatus*

diacritic *n* a sign placed above or below a character or letter to indicate phonetic value or stress **WORD ORIGIN** Greek *diakritikos* serving to distinguish

diadem *n old-fashioned* a small jewelled crown or headband, usually worn by royalty: *a gold diadem* **WORD ORIGIN** Greek: royal headdress

diaeresis *or esp. US* **dieresis** (die-air-iss-iss) *n, pl* **-ses** (-seez) the mark (¨) placed over the second of two adjacent vowels to indicate that it is to be pronounced separately, as in naïve **WORD ORIGIN** Greek: a division

diagnose ❶ *vb* **-nosing, -nosed** to determine by diagnosis

diagnosis ❶ (die-ag-no-siss) *n, pl* **-ses** (-seez) the discovery and identification of diseases from the examination of symptoms **diagnostic** *adj* **WORD ORIGIN** Greek: a distinguishing

diagonal *adj* **1** *maths* connecting any two vertices in a polygon that are not adjacent **2** slanting ▷ *n* **3** a diagonal line, plane, or pattern **diagonally** *adv*

THESAURUS

constant, loyal, faithful, fond, ardent, staunch, devout, steadfast **OPPOSITE:** disloyal

devotee *n* **1 = enthusiast**, fan, supporter, follower, addict, admirer, buff (*informal*), fanatic, adherent, aficionado

devotion *n* **1a = love**, passion, affection, intensity, attachment, zeal, fondness, fervour, adoration, ardour, earnestness **1b = dedication**, commitment, loyalty, allegiance, fidelity, adherence, constancy, faithfulness **OPPOSITE:** indifference **2 = worship**, reverence, spirituality, holiness, piety, sanctity, adoration, godliness, religiousness, devoutness **OPPOSITE:** irreverence ▷ *pl n* **3 = prayers**, religious observance, church service, divine office

devour *vb* **1 = eat**, consume, swallow, bolt, dispatch, cram, stuff, wolf, gorge, gulp, gobble, guzzle, polish off (*informal*), pig out on (*slang*) **3 = enjoy**, go through, absorb, appreciate, take in, relish, drink in, delight in, revel in, be preoccupied with, feast on, be engrossed by, read compulsively *or* voraciously

devout *adj* **1 = religious**, godly, pious, pure, holy, orthodox, saintly, reverent, prayerful **OPPOSITE:** irreverent

diagnose *vb* **= identify**, determine, recognize, distinguish, interpret, pronounce, pinpoint

diagnosis *n* **= identification**, discovery, recognition, detection

DICTIONARY

WORD ORIGIN Greek *dia-* through + *gōnia* angle

diagram n a sketch or plan showing the form or workings of something **diagrammatic** *adj*
WORD ORIGIN Greek *diagraphein* to mark out

dial *n* **1** the face of a clock or watch, marked with divisions representing units of time **2** the graduated disc on a measuring instrument **3** the control on a radio or television set used to change the station **4** a numbered disc on the front of some telephones ▷*vb* **dialling, dialled** *or* US **dialing, dialed 5** to try to establish a telephone connection with (someone) by operating the dial or buttons on a telephone
WORD ORIGIN Latin *dies* day

dialect *n* a form of a language spoken in a particular geographical area **dialectal** *adj*
WORD ORIGIN Greek *dialektos* speech, dialect

dialectic *n* **1** logical debate by question and answer to resolve differences between two views **2** the art of logical argument **dialectical** *adj*
WORD ORIGIN Greek *dialektikē (tekhnē)* (the art) of argument

dialling tone *or US, Canad, Austral & NZ* **dial tone** *n* a continuous sound heard on picking up a telephone receiver, indicating that a number can be dialled

dialogue *or US sometimes* **dialog** *n* **1** conversation between two people **2** a conversation in a literary or dramatic work **3** a discussion between representatives of two nations or groups
WORD ORIGIN Greek *dia-* between + *legein* to speak

dialysis (die-**al**-iss-iss) *n, pl* **-ses** (-seez) **1** *med* the filtering of blood through a semipermeable membrane to remove waste products **2** the separation of the particles in a solution by filtering through a semipermeable membrane **dialyser** *or* **-lyzer** *n* **dialytic** *adj*
WORD ORIGIN Greek *dialuein* to tear apart, dissolve

diamagnetism *n* the phenomenon exhibited by substances that are repelled by both poles of a magnet

diamanté (die-a-**man**-tee) *adj* decorated with glittering bits of material, such as sequins
WORD ORIGIN French

diameter *n* **a** a straight line through the centre of a circle or sphere **b** the length of such a line
WORD ORIGIN Greek *dia-* through + *metron* measure

diametric *or* **diametrical** *adj* **1** of or relating to a diameter **2** completely opposed: *the diametric opposition of the two camps* **diametrically** *adv*

diamond *n* **1** a usually colourless exceptionally hard precious stone of crystallized carbon **2** *geom* a figure with four sides of equal length forming two acute and two obtuse angles **3** a playing card marked with one or more red diamond-shaped symbols **4** *baseball* the playing field ▷*adj* **5** (of an anniversary) the sixtieth: *diamond wedding*
WORD ORIGIN Latin *adamas* the hardest iron or steel, diamond

Diana *n* the Roman goddess of hunting

diapason (die-a-**pay**-zon) *n music* **1** either of two stops found throughout the range of a pipe organ **2** the range of an instrument or voice
WORD ORIGIN Greek *dia pasōn* through all (the notes)

diaper *n US & Canad* a nappy
WORD ORIGIN Medieval Greek *diaspros* pure white

diaphanous (die-**af**-fan-uss) *adj* (of fabrics) fine and translucent
WORD ORIGIN Greek *diaphanēs* transparent

diaphoretic *n* **1** a drug that causes perspiration or sweat ▷*adj* **2** relating to or causing perspiration or sweat

diaphragm (**die**-a-fram) *n* **1** *anat* the muscular partition that separates the abdominal cavity and chest cavity **2** ▸same as **cap** (sense 5) **3** a device to control the amount of light entering an optical instrument **4** a thin vibrating disc which converts sound to electricity or vice versa, as in a microphone or loudspeaker
WORD ORIGIN Greek *dia-* across + *phragma* fence

diapositive *n* a positive transparency; slide

diarist *n* a person who writes a diary that is subsequently published

diarrhoea *or esp. US* **diarrhea** (die-a-**ree**-a) *n* frequent discharge of abnormally liquid faeces
WORD ORIGIN Greek *dia-* through + *rhein* to flow

diary *n, pl* **-ries 1** a book containing a record of daily events, appointments, or observations **2** a written record of daily events, appointments, or observations
WORD ORIGIN Latin *dies* day

Dias *or* **Diaz** *n* **Bartholomeu** ?1450–1500, Portuguese navigator who discovered the sea route from Europe to the East via the Cape of Good Hope (1488)

Diaspora (die-**ass**-spore-a) *n* **1** the dispersion of the Jews after the Babylonian conquest of Palestine **2** a dispersion of people originally belonging to one nation
WORD ORIGIN Greek: a scattering

diastase (**die**-ass-stayss) *n* an enzyme that converts starch into sugar **diastasic** *adj*
WORD ORIGIN Greek *diastasis* a separation

diastole (die-**ass**-stoh-lee) *n* dilation of the chambers of the heart **diastolic** *adj*

diatom *n* a microscopic unicellular alga
WORD ORIGIN Greek *diatomos* cut in two

diatomic *adj* containing two atoms

diatonic *adj* of or relating to any scale of five tones and two semitones produced by playing the white keys of a keyboard instrument
WORD ORIGIN Greek *diatonos* extending

diatribe *n* a bitter critical attack
WORD ORIGIN Greek *dia-* through + *tribein* to rub

Diaz *n* **1** a variant spelling of **Dias 2 Cameron.** born 1972, US film actress; films include *The Mask* (1994), *There's Something About Mary* (1998), and *Gangs of New York* (2003) **3 (José de la Cruz) Porfirio.** 1830–1915, Mexican general and statesman; president of Mexico (1877–80; 1884–1911)

Díaz de Vivar *n* **Rodrigo** the original name of El Cid ▸See **Cid**

dibble *n* a small hand tool used to make holes in the ground for bulbs, seeds, or roots
WORD ORIGIN origin unknown

DiCaprio *n* **Leonardo** born 1974, US film actor; his films include *Romeo and Juliet* (1996), *Titanic* (1997), *Gangs of New York* (2003), and *The Departed* (2006)

dice *n, pl* **dice 1** a small cube, each of whose sides has a different number of spots (1 to 6), used in games of chance ▷*vb* **dicing, diced 2** to cut (food) into small cubes **3 dice with death** to take a risk
WORD ORIGIN originally plural of DIE[2]

dicey *adj* **dicier, diciest** *informal* dangerous or tricky

dichotomy (die-**kot**-a-mee) *n, pl* **-mies** division into two opposed

THESAURUS

diagram *n* **= plan**, figure, drawing, chart, outline, representation, sketch, layout, graph

dialogue *n* **1 = conversation**, discussion, communication, discourse, converse, colloquy, confabulation, duologue, interlocution **3 = discussion**, conference, exchange, debate, confabulation

diary *n* **1 = journal**, chronicle, day-to-day account, blog *(informal)* **2 = engagement book**, Filofax®, appointment book

DICTIONARY

groups or parts **dichotomous** *adj*
WORD ORIGIN Greek *dicha* in two + *temnein* to cut
dichromatic *adj* having two colours
WORD ORIGIN Greek *di-* double + *khrōma* colour
dick *n slang* **1** *taboo* a penis **2 clever dick** an opinionated person
WORD ORIGIN *Dick* familiar form of *Richard*
dickens *n* **the dickens** *informal* used as an exclamation to show surprise, confusion, or annoyance: *what the dickens do you think you're doing?*
WORD ORIGIN from the name *Dickens*
Dickensian *adj* **1** of Charles Dickens (1812–70), British novelist **2** denoting poverty, distress, and exploitation, as depicted in the novels of Dickens
Dickinson *n* **Emily** 1830–86, US poet, noted for her short mostly unrhymed mystical lyrics
dicky[1] *n, pl* **dickies** a false shirt front
WORD ORIGIN from *Dick*, name
dicky[2] *adj* **dickier, dickiest** *Brit & NZ informal* shaky or weak: *a dicky heart*
WORD ORIGIN origin unknown
dicky-bird *n* a child's word for a bird
dicky-bow *n Brit* a bow tie
dicotyledon (die-kot-ill-**leed**-on) *n* a flowering plant with two seed leaves
dictate ⓘ *vb* **-tating, -tated 1** to say (words) aloud for another person to transcribe **2** to seek to impose one's will on others ▷ *n* **3** an authoritative command **4** a guiding principle: *the dictates of reason*
WORD ORIGIN Latin *dictare* to say repeatedly
dictation *n* **1** the act of dictating words to be taken down in writing **2** the words dictated
dictator ⓘ *n* **1** a ruler who has complete power **2** a person who behaves in a tyrannical manner **dictatorship** *n*
dictatorial *adj* **1** of or pertaining to a dictator **2** tyrannical; overbearing **dictatorially** *adv*
diction *n* the manner of pronouncing words and sounds
WORD ORIGIN Latin *dicere* to speak
dictionary ⓘ *n, pl* **-aries 1 a** a book that consists of an alphabetical list of words with their meanings **b** a similar book giving equivalent words in two languages **2** a reference book listing terms and giving information about a particular subject
WORD ORIGIN Late Latin *dictio* word
dictum *n, pl* **-tums** *or* **-ta 1** a formal statement; pronouncement **2** a popular saying or maxim
WORD ORIGIN Latin
did *vb* ▸ the past tense of **do**[1]
didactic *adj* intended to teach or instruct people: *an Impressionist work can be as didactic in its way as a sermon* **didactically** *adv* **didacticism** *n*
WORD ORIGIN Greek *didaktikos* skilled in teaching
diddle *vb* **-dling, -dled** *informal* to swindle **diddler** *n*
WORD ORIGIN Jeremy *Diddler*, a scrounger in a 19th-century play
Diderot *n* **Denis** 1713–84, French philosopher, noted particularly for his direction (1745–72) of the great French *Encyclopédie*
didgeridoo *n* an Australian Aboriginal deep-toned wind instrument
WORD ORIGIN imitative
didn't did not
die[1] ⓘ *vb* **dying, died 1** (of a person, animal, or plant) to cease all biological activity permanently **2** (of something inanimate) to cease to exist **3** to lose strength, power, or energy by degrees **4** to stop working: *the engine died* **5 be dying** to be eager (for something or to do something) **6 be dying of** *informal* to be nearly overcome with (laughter, boredom, etc.) **7 die hard** to change or disappear only slowly: *old loyalties die hard* **8 to die for** *informal* highly desirable: *a salary to die for* ▸ See also **die down, die out**
WORD ORIGIN Old English *dīegan*
die[2] *n* **1** a shaped block used to cut or form metal **2** a casting mould **3** ▸ same as **dice** (sense 1) **4 the die is cast** an irrevocable decision has been taken
WORD ORIGIN Latin *dare* to give, play
die down *vb* **1** to lose strength or power by degrees **2** to become calm: *the storm has died down now*
die-hard *or* **diehard** *n* a person who resists change
dieldrin *n* a highly toxic crystalline insecticide
dielectric *n* **1** a substance of very low electrical conductivity; insulator ▷ *adj* **2** having the properties of a dielectric
WORD ORIGIN Greek *dia-* through + ELECTRIC
die out *or* **off** *vb* to become extinct or disappear after a gradual decline
dieresis (die-**air**-iss-iss) *n, pl* **-ses** (-seez) ▸ same as **diaeresis**
diesel *n* **1** ▸ same as **diesel engine 2** a vehicle driven by a diesel engine **3** *informal* diesel oil
WORD ORIGIN after R. *Diesel*, engineer
diesel-electric *n* a locomotive with a diesel engine driving an electric generator
diesel engine *n* an internal-combustion engine in which oil is ignited by compression
diesel oil *or* **fuel** *n* a fuel obtained from petroleum distillation, used in diesel engines
diet[1] ⓘ *n* **1** the food that a person or animal regularly eats **2** a specific allowance or selection of food, to control weight or for health reasons: *a high-fibre diet* ▷ *vb* **3** to follow a special diet so as to lose weight ▷ *adj* **4** suitable for eating with a weight-reduction diet: *diet soft drinks* **dietary** *adj* **dieter** *n*
WORD ORIGIN Greek *diaita* mode of living
diet[2] ⓘ *n* a legislative assembly in some countries
WORD ORIGIN Medieval Latin *dieta* public meeting
dietary fibre *n* the roughage in fruits and vegetables that aids digestion
dietetic *adj* prepared for special dietary requirements
dietetics *n* the study of diet, nutrition, and the preparation of food

THESAURUS

dictate *vb* **1 = speak**, say, utter, read out ▷ *n* **3 = command**, order, decree, word, demand, direction, requirement, bidding, mandate, injunction, statute, fiat, ultimatum, ordinance, edict, behest **4 = principle**, law, rule, standard, code, criterion, ethic, canon, maxim, dictum, precept, axiom, moral law
dictator *n* **1, 2 = absolute ruler**, tyrant, despot, oppressor, autocrat, absolutist, martinet
dictionary *n* **1a, 1b, 2 = wordbook**, vocabulary, glossary, encyclopedia, lexicon, concordance
die[1] *vb* **1 = pass away**, depart, expire, perish, buy it *(US slang)*, check out *(US slang)*, kick it *(slang)*, croak *(slang)*, give up the ghost, go belly-up *(slang)*, snuff it *(slang)*, peg out *(informal)*, kick the bucket *(slang)*, buy the farm *(US slang)*, peg it *(informal)*, decease, cark it *(Austral & NZ slang)*, pop your clogs *(informal)*, breathe your last, hop the twig *(slang)* **OPPOSITE:** live **3 = dwindle**, end, decline, pass, disappear, sink, fade, weaken, diminish, vanish, decrease, decay, lapse, wither, wilt, lessen, wane, subside, ebb, die down, die out, abate, peter out, die away, grow less **OPPOSITE:** increase **4 = stop**, fail, halt, break down, run down, stop working, peter out, fizzle out, lose power, seize up, conk out *(informal)*, go kaput *(informal)*, go phut, fade out *or* away
diet[1] *n* **1 = food**, provisions, fare, rations, subsistence, kai *(NZ informal)*, nourishment, sustenance, victuals, commons, edibles, comestibles, nutriment, viands, aliment **2 = fast**, regime, abstinence, regimen, dietary regime
diet[2] *n (often cap.)* **= council**, meeting, parliament, sitting, congress, chamber, convention, legislature, legislative assembly

DICTIONARY

dietician *n* a person qualified to advise people about healthy eating

Dietrich *n* **Marlene**, real name *Maria Magdalene von Losch*. 1901–92, US film actress and cabaret singer, born in Germany

differ ⓘ *vb* **1** to be dissimilar in quality, nature, or degree **2** to disagree
WORD ORIGIN Latin *differre* to scatter, be different

difference ⓘ *n* **1** the state or quality of being unlike **2** a disagreement or argument **3** the result of the subtraction of one number or quantity from another **4 make a difference** to have an effect **5 split the difference a** to compromise **b** to divide a remainder equally

different ⓘ *adj* **1** partly or completely unlike **2** new or unusual **3** not identical or the same; other: *he wears a different tie every day* **differently** *adv*

differential *adj* **1** of, relating to, or using a difference **2** *maths* involving differentials ▷*n* **3** a factor that differentiates between two comparable things **4** *maths* a minute difference between values in a scale **5** *chiefly Brit* the difference between rates of pay for different types of labour, esp. within a company or industry

differential calculus *n* the branch of mathematics concerned with derivatives and differentials

differential gear *n* the gear in the driving axle of a road vehicle that permits one driving wheel to rotate faster than the other when cornering

differentiate ⓘ *vb* **-ating, -ated 1** to perceive or show the difference (between) **2** to make (one thing) distinct from other such things **3** *maths* to determine the derivative of a function or variable
differentiation *n*

difficult ⓘ *adj* **1** not easy to do, understand, or solve **2** not easily pleased or satisfied: *a difficult patient* **3** full of hardships or trials: *he had recently had a difficult time with his job as a self-employed builder*

difficulty ⓘ *n, pl* **-ties 1** the state or quality of being difficult **2** a task or problem that is hard to deal with **3** a troublesome or embarrassing situation: *in financial difficulties* **4** an objection or obstacle: *you're just making difficulties* **5** lack of ease; awkwardness: *he could run only with difficulty*
WORD ORIGIN Latin *difficultas*

diffident *adj* lacking self-confidence; shy **diffidence** *n* **diffidently** *adv*
WORD ORIGIN Latin *dis-* not + *fidere* to trust

diffract *vb* to cause to undergo diffraction **diffractive** *adj*

diffraction *n* **1** *physics* a deviation in the direction of a wave at the edge of an obstacle in its path **2** the formation of light and dark fringes by the passage of light through a small aperture
WORD ORIGIN Latin *diffringere* to shatter

diffuse *vb* **-fusing, -fused 1** to spread over a wide area **2** *physics* to cause to undergo diffusion ▷*adj* **3** spread out over a wide area **4** lacking conciseness **diffusible** *adj* **diffuser** *n*
WORD ORIGIN Latin *diffusus* spread abroad

diffusion *n* **1** the act of diffusing or the fact of being diffused; dispersion **2** *physics* the random thermal motion of atoms and molecules in gases, liquids, and some solids **3** *physics* the transmission or reflection of light, in which the radiation is scattered in many directions

dig ⓘ *vb* **digging, dug 1** to cut into, break up, and turn over or remove (earth), esp. with a spade **2** to excavate (a hole or tunnel) by digging, usually with an implement or (of animals) with claws **3** to obtain by digging: *dig out potatoes* **4** to find by effort or searching: *he dug out a mini cassette from his pocket* **5** *informal* to like or understand **6** (foll. by *in* or *into*) to thrust or jab ▷*n* **7** the act of digging **8** an archaeological excavation **9** a thrust or poke **10** a cutting remark ▸See also **dig in**
WORD ORIGIN Middle English *diggen*

digest ⓘ *vb* **1** to subject (food) to a process of digestion **2** to absorb mentally ▷*n* **3** a shortened version of a book, report, or article
digestible *adj*

d

THESAURUS

differ *vb* **2 = disagree**, clash, dispute, dissent **OPPOSITE:** agree

difference *n* **1 = dissimilarity**, contrast, variation, change, variety, exception, distinction, diversity, alteration, discrepancy, disparity, deviation, differentiation, peculiarity, divergence, singularity, particularity, distinctness, unlikeness **OPPOSITE:** similarity **2 = disagreement**, conflict, argument, row, clash, dispute, set-to (*informal*), controversy, contention, quarrel, strife, wrangle, tiff, contretemps, discordance, contrariety **OPPOSITE:** agreement **3 = remainder**, rest, balance, remains, excess

different *adj* **1 = dissimilar**, opposed, contrasting, changed, clashing, unlike, altered, diverse, at odds, inconsistent, disparate, deviating, divergent, at variance, discrepant, streets apart **2 = unusual**, unique, special, strange, rare, extraordinary, bizarre, distinctive, something else, peculiar, uncommon, singular, unconventional, out of the ordinary, left-field (*informal*), atypical

differentiate *vb* **1 = distinguish**, separate, discriminate, contrast, discern, mark off, make a distinction, tell apart, set off *or* apart **2 = make different**, separate, distinguish, characterize, single out, segregate, individualize, mark off, set apart, set off

difficult *adj* **1a = hard**, tough, taxing, demanding, challenging, painful, exacting, formidable, uphill, strenuous, problematic, arduous, onerous, laborious, burdensome, wearisome, no picnic (*informal*), toilsome, like getting blood out of a stone **OPPOSITE:** easy **1b = problematical**, involved, complex, complicated, delicate, obscure, abstract, baffling, intricate, perplexing, thorny, knotty, abstruse, ticklish, enigmatical **OPPOSITE:** simple **2 = troublesome**, trying, awkward, demanding, rigid, stubborn, perverse, fussy, tiresome, intractable, fastidious, fractious, unyielding, obstinate, intransigent, unmanageable, unbending, uncooperative, hard to please, refractory, obstreperous, pig-headed, bull-headed, unaccommodating, unamenable **OPPOSITE:** cooperative

difficulty *n* **2, 4 = problem**, trouble, obstacle, hurdle, dilemma, hazard, complication, hassle (*informal*), snag, uphill (*S African*), predicament, pitfall, stumbling block, impediment, hindrance, tribulation, quandary, can of worms (*informal*), point at issue, disputed point **5 = hardship**, labour, pain, strain, awkwardness, painfulness, strenuousness, arduousness, laboriousness

dig *vb* **1 = turn over**, till, break up, hoe **2a = hollow out**, mine, pierce, quarry, excavate, gouge, scoop out **2b = delve**, tunnel, burrow, grub **6 = poke**, drive, push, stick, punch, stab, thrust, shove, prod, jab ▷*n* **9 = poke**, thrust, butt, nudge, prod, jab, punch **10 = cutting remark**, crack (*slang*), insult, taunt, sneer, jeer, quip, barb, wisecrack (*informal*), gibe

digest *vb* **1 = ingest**, absorb, incorporate, dissolve, assimilate **2 = take in**, master, absorb, grasp, drink in, soak up, devour, assimilate ▷*n* **3 = summary**, résumé, abstract, epitome, condensation, compendium, synopsis, précis, abridgment

DICTIONARY

WORD ORIGIN Latin *digerere* to divide

digestion *n* **1** the process of breaking down food into easily absorbed substances **2** the body's system for doing this

digestive *adj* relating to digestion

digger *n* a machine used for excavation

dig in *vb* **1** to mix (compost or fertilizer) into the soil by digging **2** *informal* to begin to eat vigorously **3** *informal* (of soldiers) to dig a trench and prepare for an enemy attack **4 dig one's heels in** *informal* to refuse to move or be persuaded

digit (dij-it) *n* **1** a finger or toe **2** any numeral from 0 to 9
WORD ORIGIN Latin *digitus* toe, finger

digital *adj* **1** displaying information as numbers rather than with a dial **2** representing data as a series of numerical values **3** of or possessing digits **digitally** *adv*

digital audio tape *n* magnetic tape on which sound is recorded digitally, giving high-fidelity reproduction

digital clock *or* **watch** *n* a clock or watch in which the time is indicated by digits rather than by hands on a dial

digital computer *n* a computer in which the input consists of numbers, letters, and other characters that are represented internally in binary notation

digitalis *n* a drug made from foxglove leaves: used as a heart stimulant
WORD ORIGIN Latin: relating to a finger (from the shape of the foxglove flowers)

digital recording *n* a sound recording process that converts audio or analogue signals into a series of pulses

digital switchover *n* the process of changing the method of transmitting television from analogue to digital format

digital television *n* television in which the picture information is transmitted in digital form and decoded at the television receiver

digitate *adj* **1** (of leaves) having leaflets in the form of a spread hand **2** (of animals) having digits

digitize *or* **-ise** *vb* **-izing, -ized** *or* **-ising, -ised** to transcribe (data) into a digital form for processing by a computer **digitizer** *or* **-iser** *n*

dignified *adj* calm, impressive, and worthy of respect

dignify *vb* **-fies, -fying, -fied 1** to add distinction to: *the meeting was dignified by the minister* **2** to add a semblance of dignity to by the use of a pretentious name or title: *she dignifies every plant with its Latin name*
WORD ORIGIN Latin *dignus* worthy + *facere* to make

dignitary *n, pl* **-taries** a person of high official position or rank

dignity ❶ *n, pl* **-ties 1** serious, calm, and controlled behaviour or manner **2** the quality of being worthy of honour **3** sense of self-importance: *he considered the job beneath his dignity*
WORD ORIGIN Latin *dignus* worthy

digraph *n* two letters used to represent a single sound, such as *gh* in *tough*

digress *vb* to depart from the main subject in speech or writing **digression** *n*
WORD ORIGIN Latin *digressus* turned aside

digs *pl n Brit, Austral & S African informal* lodgings
WORD ORIGIN from *diggings*, perhaps referring to where one digs or works

dihedral *adj* having or formed by two intersecting planes

dilapidated *adj* (of a building) having fallen into ruin **dilapidation** *n*
WORD ORIGIN Latin *dilapidare* to waste

dilate *vb* **-lating, -lated** to make or become wider or larger: *her eyes dilated in the dark* **dilation** *or* **dilatation** *n*
WORD ORIGIN Latin *dilatare* to spread out

dilatory (dill-a-tree) *adj* tending or intended to waste time **dilatorily** *adv* **dilatoriness** *n*
WORD ORIGIN Late Latin *dilatorius*

dildo *n, pl* **-dos** an object used as a substitute for an erect penis
WORD ORIGIN origin unknown

dilemma ❶ *n* a situation offering a choice between two equally undesirable alternatives
WORD ORIGIN Greek *di-* double + *lēmma* proposition

dilettante (dill-it-tan-tee) *n, pl* **-tantes** *or* **-tanti** a person whose interest in a subject is superficial rather than serious **dilettantism** *n*
WORD ORIGIN Italian

diligent *adj* **1** careful and persevering in carrying out tasks or duties **2** carried out with care and perseverance: *a diligent approach to work* **diligence** *n* **diligently** *adv*
WORD ORIGIN Latin *diligere* to value

dill *n* a sweet-smelling herb used for flavouring
WORD ORIGIN Old English *dile*

dilly-dally *vb* **-lies, -lying, -lied** *Brit, Austral & NZ informal* to dawdle or waste time
WORD ORIGIN reduplication of *dally*

dilute ❶ *vb* **-luting, -luted 1** to make (a liquid) less concentrated by adding water or another liquid **2** to make (someone's power, idea, or role) weaker or less effective: *socialists used their majority in parliament to dilute legislation crucial to developing a market economy* ▷ *adj* **3** *chem* (of a solution) having a low concentration **dilution** *n*
WORD ORIGIN Latin *diluere*

diluvian *or* **diluvial** *adj* of a flood, esp. the great Flood described in the Old Testament
WORD ORIGIN Latin *diluere* to wash away

dim ❶ *adj* **dimmer, dimmest 1** badly lit **2** not clearly seen; faint: *a dim figure in the doorway* **3** not seeing clearly: *eyes dim with tears* **4** *informal* mentally dull **5** not clear in the mind; obscure: *a dim awareness* **6** lacking in brightness or lustre: *a dim colour* **7 take a dim view of** to disapprove of ▷ *vb* **dimming, dimmed 8** to become or cause to become dim **9** to cause to seem less bright **10** *US & Canad* ▸ same as **dip** (sense 4) > **dimly** *adv* **dimness** *n*
WORD ORIGIN Old English *dimm*

DiMaggio *n* **Joe** 1914–99, US baseball player

Dimbleby *n* **Richard** 1913–65, British broadcaster

dime *n* a coin of the US and Canada

THESAURUS

dignity *n* **1 = decorum**, breeding, gravity, majesty, grandeur, respectability, nobility, propriety, solemnity, gentility, courtliness, loftiness, stateliness **3 = self-importance**, pride, self-esteem, self-respect, self-regard, self-possession, amour-propre *(French)*

dilemma *n* **= predicament**, problem, difficulty, spot *(informal)*, fix *(informal)*, mess, puzzle, jam *(informal)*, embarrassment, plight, strait, pickle *(informal)*, how-do-you-do *(informal)*, quandary, perplexity, tight corner *or* spot

dilute *vb* **1 = water down**, thin (out), weaken, adulterate, make thinner, cut *(informal)* **OPPOSITE:** condense **2 = reduce**, weaken, diminish, temper, decrease, lessen, diffuse, mitigate, attenuate **OPPOSITE:** intensify

dim *adj* **1 = poorly lit**, dark, gloomy, murky, shady, shadowy, dusky, crepuscular, darkish, tenebrous, unilluminated, caliginous *(archaic)* **2 = unclear**, obscured, faint, blurred, fuzzy, shadowy, hazy, indistinguishable, bleary, undefined, out of focus, ill-defined, indistinct, indiscernible **OPPOSITE:** distinct **4** *(informal)* **= stupid**, slow, thick, dull, dense, dumb *(informal)*, daft *(informal)*, dozy *(Brit informal)*, obtuse, unintelligent, asinine, slow on the uptake *(informal)*, braindead *(informal)*, doltish **OPPOSITE:** bright **6 = cloudy**, grey, gloomy, dismal, overcast, leaden **OPPOSITE:** bright ▷ *vb* **8a = grow** *or* **become faint**, fade,

worth ten cents
WORD ORIGIN Latin *decem* ten
dimension ❶ *n* **1** an aspect or factor: *the attack brought a whole new dimension to the bombing campaign* **2 dimensions** scope or extent **3** (*often pl*) a measurement of the size of something in a particular direction **dimensional** *adj*
WORD ORIGIN Latin *dimensio* an extent
dimer *n chem* a molecule made up of two identical molecules bonded together
diminish ❶ *vb* **1** to make or become smaller, fewer, or less **2** *music* to decrease (a minor interval) by a semitone **3** to reduce in authority or status
WORD ORIGIN Latin *deminuere* to make smaller + archaic *minish* to lessen
diminuendo *music n, pl* **-dos 1 a** a gradual decrease in loudness **b** a passage which gradually decreases in loudness ▷*adv* **2** gradually decreasing in loudness
WORD ORIGIN Italian
diminution *n* reduction in size, volume, intensity, or importance
WORD ORIGIN Latin *deminutio*
diminutive *adj* **1** very small; tiny **2** *grammar* **a** denoting an affix added to a word to convey the meaning *small* or *unimportant* or to express affection, as for example, the suffix *-ette* in French **b** denoting a word formed by the addition of a diminutive affix ▷*n* **3** *grammar* a diminutive word or affix **diminutiveness** *n*
dimmer *n* **1** a device for dimming an electric light **2** *US* **a** a dipped headlight on a road vehicle **b** a parking light on a car
dimple *n* **1** a small natural dent on the cheeks or chin ▷*vb* **-pling, -pled 2** to produce dimples by smiling
WORD ORIGIN Middle English *dympull*
dimwit *n informal* a stupid person **dim-witted** *adj*
din ❶ *n* **1** a loud unpleasant confused noise ▷*vb* **dinning, dinned 2 din something into someone** to instil something into someone by constant repetition
WORD ORIGIN Old English *dynn*
dinar (dee-nahr) *n* a monetary unit of various Balkan, Middle Eastern, and North African countries
WORD ORIGIN Latin *denarius* a Roman coin
d'Indy *n* (**Paul Marie Theodore**) **Vincent** 1851–1931, French composer. His works include operas, chamber music, and the *Symphony on a French Mountaineer's Song* (1866)
dine ❶ *vb* **dining, dined 1** to eat dinner **2 dine on** *or* **off** to make one's meal of: *the guests dined on roast beef*
WORD ORIGIN Old French *disner*
diner *n* **1** a person eating a meal in a restaurant **2** *chiefly US & Canad* a small cheap restaurant **3** ▸short for **dining car**
Dinesen *n* **Isak**, pen name of *Baroness Karen Blixen*. 1885–1962, Danish author of short stories in Danish and English, including *Seven Gothic Tales* (1934) and *Winter's Tales* (1942). Her life story was told in the film *Out of Africa* (1986)
dinette *n* an alcove or small area for use as a dining room
ding *n Austral dated & NZ informal* a small dent in a vehicle
Dingaan *n* died 1840, Zulu chief (1828–40), who fought the Boer colonists in Natal
ding-dong *n* **1** the sound of a bell **2** a violent exchange of blows or words
WORD ORIGIN imitative
dinges (ding-uss) *n S African informal* a jocular word for something whose name is unknown or forgotten; thingumabob
WORD ORIGIN Dutch *ding* thing
dinghy (ding-ee, ding-gee) *n, pl* **-ghies** a small boat, powered by sail, oars, or outboard motor
WORD ORIGIN Hindi or Bengali *dingi*
dingle *n* a small wooded hollow or valley
WORD ORIGIN origin unknown
dingo *n, pl* **-goes** an Australian native wild dog
WORD ORIGIN Aboriginal
dingy (din-jee) *adj* **-gier, -giest 1** *Brit, Austral & NZ* dull, neglected, and drab: *he waited in this dingy little outer office* **2** shabby and discoloured: *she was wearing dingy white overalls* **dinginess** *n*
WORD ORIGIN origin unknown
dining car *n* a railway coach in which meals are served
dining room *n* a room where meals are eaten
dinkum ❶ *adj Austral & NZ informal* genuine or right: *a fair dinkum offer*
WORD ORIGIN English dialect: work
dinky *adj* **dinkier, dinkiest** *chiefly Brit informal* small and neat; dainty
WORD ORIGIN dialect *dink* neat
dinky-di *adj Austral informal* typical
WORD ORIGIN variant of DINKUM
dinner ❶ *n* **1** the main meal of the day, eaten either in the evening or at midday **2** a formal social occasion at which an evening meal is served
WORD ORIGIN Old French *disner* to dine
dinner jacket *n* a man's semiformal black evening jacket without tails
dinner service *n* a set of matching dishes suitable for serving a meal
dinosaur *n* any of a large order of extinct prehistoric reptiles many of which were gigantic
WORD ORIGIN Greek *deinos* fearful + *sauros* lizard
dint *n* **by dint of** by means of: *by dint of their own efforts*
WORD ORIGIN Old English *dynt* a blow
D'Inzeo *n* **Piero**, born 1923, and his brother **Raimondo**, born 1925, Italian showjumping riders
Dio Cassius *n* ?155–?230 AD, Roman historian. His *History of Rome* covers the period of Rome's transition from Republic to Empire
diocesan *adj* of or relating to a diocese
diocese (die-a-siss) *n* the district over which a bishop has control
WORD ORIGIN Greek *dioikēsis* administration
Dio Chrysostom *n* 2nd century AD, Greek orator and philosopher
Diocletian *n* full name *Gaius Aurelius Valerius Diocletianus*. 245–313 AD, Roman emperor (284–305), who divided the empire into four administrative units (293) and instigated the last severe persecution of the Christians (303)
diode *n* **1** a semiconductor device for converting alternating current to direct current **2** an electronic valve with two electrodes between which a current can flow only in one direction
WORD ORIGIN Greek *di-* double + *hodos* a way, road
Diodorus Siculus *n* 1st century BC, Greek historian, noted for his history of the world in 40 books, of

d

THESAURUS

dull, grow *or* become dim
8b = darken, dull, cloud over **9 = turn down**, lower, fade, dull, bedim
dimension *n* **1 = aspect**, side, feature, angle, facet **2 = extent**, size, magnitude, importance, scope, greatness, amplitude, largeness
diminish *vb* **1a = decrease**, decline, lessen, contract, weaken, shrink, dwindle, wane, recede, subside, ebb, taper, die out, fade away, abate, peter out **OPPOSITE:** grow
1b = reduce, cut, decrease, lessen, contract, lower, weaken, curtail, abate, retrench **OPPOSITE:** increase
din *n* **1 = noise**, row, racket, crash, clash, shout, outcry, clamour, clatter, uproar, commotion, pandemonium, babel, hubbub, hullabaloo, clangour **OPPOSITE:** silence
dine *vb* **1 = eat**, lunch, feast, sup, chow down (*slang*)
dinkum *adj* (*Austral & NZ informal*) **= genuine**, honest, natural, frank, sincere, candid, upfront (*informal*), artless, guileless
dinner *n* **1 = meal**, main meal, spread (*informal*), repast, blowout (*slang*), collation, refection **2 = banquet**, feast, blowout (*slang*), repast,

DICTIONARY

which 15 are extant

dioecious (die-**eesh**-uss) *adj* (of plants) having the male and female reproductive organs on separate plants
WORD ORIGIN Greek *di-* twice + *oikia* house

Diogenes *n* ?412–?323 BC, Greek Cynic philosopher, who rejected social conventions and advocated self-sufficiency and simplicity of life

Dion *n* **Céline** born 1968, Canadian singer. Her worldwide hit singles include 'My Heart Will Go On' (1998)

Dionysian (die-on-**niz**-zee-an) *adj* wild or orgiastic
WORD ORIGIN from *Dionysus*, Greek god of wine

Dionysius *n* called *the Elder* ?430–367 BC, tyrant of Syracuse (405–367), noted for his successful campaigns against Carthage and S Italy

Dionysius Exiguus *n* died ?556 AD, Scythian monk and scholar, who is believed to have introduced the current method of reckoning dates on the basis of the Christian era

Dionysius of Halicarnassus *n* died ?7 BC, Greek historian and rhetorician; author of a history of Rome

Dionysius the Areopagite *n* 1st century AD, Greek Christian, thought to have been the first Bishop of Athens: long considered the author of influential theological works actually written *c.* 500 ▸ See **Pseudo-Dionysius**

Dionysus *n Greek myth* the god of wine

Diophantus *n* 3rd century AD, Greek mathematician, noted for his treatise on the theory of numbers, *Arithmetica*

dioptre *or US* **diopter** (die-**op**-ter) *n* a unit for measuring the refractive power of a lens
WORD ORIGIN Greek *dia-* through + *opsesthai* to see

Dior *n* **Christian** 1905–57, French couturier, noted for his New Look of narrow waist with a long full skirt (1947); he also created the waistless sack dress

diorama *n* **1** a miniature three-dimensional scene, in which models of figures are seen against a background **2** a picture made up of illuminated translucent curtains, viewed through an aperture
WORD ORIGIN Greek *dia-* through + *horama* view

dioxide *n* an oxide containing two oxygen atoms per molecule

dip ❶ *vb* **dipping, dipped 1** to plunge or be plunged quickly or briefly into a liquid **2** to put one's hands into something, esp. to obtain an object: *she dipped into her handbag looking for change* **3** to slope downwards **4** to switch (car headlights) from the main to the lower beam **5** to undergo a slight decline, esp. temporarily: *sales dipped in November* **6** to immerse (farm animals) briefly in a chemical to rid them of insects **7** to lower or be lowered briefly: *she dipped her knee in a curtsy* ▹*n* **8** the act of dipping **9** a brief swim **10** a liquid chemical in which farm animals are dipped **11** a depression, esp. in a landscape **12** a momentary sinking down **13** a creamy mixture into which pieces of food are dipped before being eaten ▸ See also **dip into**
WORD ORIGIN Old English *dyppan*

Dip Ed (in Britain) Diploma in Education

diphtheria (dif-**theer**-ree-a) *n* a contagious disease producing fever and difficulty in breathing and swallowing
WORD ORIGIN Greek *diphthera* leather; from the membrane that forms in the throat

diphthong *n* a vowel sound, occupying a single syllable, in which the speaker's tongue moves continuously from one position to another, as in the pronunciation of *a* in *late*
WORD ORIGIN Greek *di-* double + *phthongos* sound

dip into *vb* **1** to draw upon: *he dipped into his savings* **2** to read passages at random from (a book or journal)

diploid *adj biol* denoting a cell or organism with pairs of homologous chromosomes
WORD ORIGIN Greek *di-* double + *-ploos* -fold

diploma *n* a document conferring a qualification or recording successful completion of a course of study
WORD ORIGIN Latin: official document, literally: letter folded double

diplomacy ❶ *n* **1** the conduct of the relations between nations by peaceful means **2** skill in the management of international relations **3** tact or skill in dealing with people

diplomat ❶ *n* an official, such as an ambassador, engaged in diplomacy

diplomatic ❶ *adj* **1** of or relating to diplomacy **2** skilled in negotiating between nations **3** tactful in dealing with people **diplomatically** *adv*
WORD ORIGIN French *diplomatique* concerning the documents of diplomacy; see DIPLOMA

diplomatic immunity *n* the freedom from legal action and exemption from taxation which diplomats have in the country where they are working

dipole *n* **1** two equal but opposite electric charges or magnetic poles separated by a small distance **2** a molecule that has two such charges or poles **dipolar** *adj*

dipper *n* **1** a ladle used for dipping **2** a songbird that inhabits fast-flowing streams

diprotodont (die-**pro**-toe-dont) *n* a marsupial with fewer than three upper incisor teeth on each side of the jaw

dipsomania *n* a compulsive desire to drink alcoholic beverages
dipsomaniac *n, adj*
WORD ORIGIN Greek *dipsa* thirst + *mania* madness

dipstick *n* a rod with notches on it dipped into a container to indicate the fluid level

dip switch *n* a device for dipping headlights on a vehicle

dipterous *adj* having two wings or winglike parts
WORD ORIGIN Greek *dipteros* two-winged

diptych (**dip**-tik) *n* a painting on two hinged panels
WORD ORIGIN Greek *di-* double + *ptuchē* a panel

dire ❶ *adj* disastrous, urgent, or terrible: *he was now in dire financial straits*
WORD ORIGIN Latin *dirus* ominous

direct ❶ *adj* **1** shortest; straight: *a*

THESAURUS

beanfeast (*Brit informal*), carousal, hakari (*NZ*)

dip *vb* **1, 6 = plunge**, immerse, bathe, duck, rinse, douse, dunk, souse **3 = slope**, drop (down), descend, fall, decline, pitch, sink, incline, drop away **7 = drop (down)**, set, fall, lower, disappear, sink, fade, slump, descend, tilt, subside, sag, droop ▹*n* **8 = plunge**, ducking, soaking, drenching, immersion, douche, submersion **11 = hollow**, hole, depression, pit, basin, dent, trough, indentation, concavity **12 = nod**, drop, lowering, slump, sag

diplomacy *n* **1 = statesmanship**, statecraft, international negotiation **3 = tact**, skill, sensitivity, craft, discretion, subtlety, delicacy, finesse, savoir-faire, artfulness
OPPOSITE: tactlessness

diplomat *n* **= official**, ambassador, envoy, statesman, consul, attaché, emissary, chargé d'affaires

diplomatic *adj* **1 = consular**, official, foreign-office, ambassadorial, foreign-politic **3 = tactful**, politic, sensitive, subtle, delicate, polite, discreet, prudent, adept, considerate, judicious, treating with kid gloves
OPPOSITE: tactless

dire *adj* **= desperate**, pressing, critical, terrible, crucial, alarming, extreme, awful, appalling, urgent, cruel, horrible, disastrous, grim, dreadful, gloomy, fearful, dismal, drastic,

direct route **2** without intervening people: *they secretly arranged direct links to their commanders* **3** honest; frank: *he was polite but very direct* **4** diametric: *the direct opposite* **5** in an unbroken line of descent: *a direct descendant* ▹ *adv* **6** directly; straight ▹ *vb* **7** to conduct or control the affairs of **8** to give orders with authority to (a person or group) **9** to tell (someone) the way to a place **10** to address (a letter, parcel, etc.) **11** to address (a look or remark) at someone: *the look she directed at him was one of unconcealed hatred* **12 a** to provide guidance to (actors, cameramen, etc.) in (a play or film) **b** to supervise the making or staging of (a film or play)
directness *n*
WORD ORIGIN Latin *dirigere* to guide

direct access *n* a method of reading data from a computer file without reading through the file from the beginning

direct current *n* an electric current that flows in one direction only

direct debit *n* an order given to a bank or other financial institution by an account holder to pay an amount of money from the account to a specified person or company at regular intervals

direction ❶ *n* **1** the course or line along which a person or thing moves, points, or lies **2** management or guidance: *the campaign was successful under his direction* **3** the work of a stage or film director

directional *adj* **1** of or showing direction **2** *electronics* (of an aerial) transmitting or receiving radio waves more effectively in some directions than in others

directions ❶ *pl n* instructions for doing something or for reaching a place

directive ❶ *n* an instruction; order

directly ❶ *adv* **1** in a direct manner **2** at once; without delay **3** immediately or very soon: *I'll do that directly* ▹ *conj* **4** as soon as: *we left directly the money arrived*

direct object *n grammar* a noun, pronoun, or noun phrase denoting the person or thing receiving the direct action of a verb. For example, *a book* in *They bought Anne a book*

director ❶ *n* **1** a person or thing that directs or controls **2** a member of the governing board of a business, trust, etc. **3** the person responsible for the artistic and technical aspects of the making of a film or television programme **directorial** *adj*
directorship *n*

directorate *n* **1** a board of directors **2** the position of director

director-general *n, pl* **directors-general** a person in overall charge of certain large organizations

directory *n, pl* **-ries** **1** a book listing names, addresses, and telephone numbers of individuals or business companies **2** *computers* an area of a disk containing the names and locations of the files it currently holds

direct speech *n* the reporting of what someone has said by quoting the exact words

direct tax *n* a tax paid by the person or organization on which it is levied

dirge *n* **1** a chant of lamentation for the dead **2** any mournful song
WORD ORIGIN Latin *dirige* direct (imperative), opening word of antiphon used in the office of the dead

Dirichlet *n* **Peter Gustav Lejeune** 1805–59, German mathematician, noted for his work on number theory and calculus

dirigible (dir-rij-jib-bl) *adj* **1** able to be steered ▹ *n* **2** ▹ same as **airship**
WORD ORIGIN Latin *dirigere* to direct

dirk *n* a dagger, formerly worn by Scottish Highlanders
WORD ORIGIN Scots *durk*

dirndl *n* **1** a woman's dress with a full gathered skirt and fitted bodice **2** a gathered skirt of this kind
WORD ORIGIN from German

dirt ❶ *n* **1** any unclean substance, such as mud; filth **2** loose earth; soil **3** packed earth, cinders, etc. used to make a racetrack **4** obscene speech or writing **5** *informal* harmful gossip
WORD ORIGIN Old Norse *drit* excrement

dirt-cheap *adj, adv* at an extremely low price

dirt-poor *adj chiefly US* extremely poor

dirt track *n* a racetrack made of packed earth or cinders

dirty ❶ *adj* **dirtier, dirtiest** **1** covered or marked with dirt; filthy **2** causing one to become grimy: *a dirty job* **3** (of a colour) not clear and bright **4** unfair, dishonest, or unkind: *dirty tricks* **5 a** obscene: *dirty*

THESAURUS

catastrophic, ominous, horrid, woeful, ruinous, calamitous, cataclysmic, portentous, godawful *(slang)*, exigent

direct *adj* **1a = quickest**, shortest **1b = straight**, through
OPPOSITE: circuitous
2 = first-hand, personal, immediate
OPPOSITE: indirect
3 = straightforward, open, straight, frank, blunt, sincere, outspoken, honest, matter-of-fact, downright, candid, forthright, truthful, upfront *(informal)*, man-to-man, plain-spoken
OPPOSITE: indirect
▹ *adv* **6 = non-stop**, straight ▹ *vb* **7 = control**, run, manage, lead, rule, guide, handle, conduct, advise, govern, regulate, administer, oversee, supervise, dispose, preside over, mastermind, call the shots, call the tune, superintend **8 = order**, command, instruct, charge, demand, require, bid, enjoin, adjure **9 = guide**, show, lead, point the way, point in the direction of **10 = address**, send, mail, route, label, superscribe **11 = aim**, point, turn, level, train, focus, fix, cast

direction *n* **1 = way**, course, line, road, track, bearing, route, path **2 = management**, government, control, charge, administration, leadership, command, guidance, supervision, governance, oversight, superintendence

directions *pl n* **= instructions**, rules, information, plan, briefing, regulations, recommendations, indication, guidelines, guidance

directive *n* **= order**, ruling, regulation, charge, notice, command, instruction, dictate, decree, mandate, canon, injunction, imperative, fiat, ordinance, edict

directly *adv* **1a = straight**, unswervingly, without deviation, by the shortest route, in a beeline **1b = honestly**, openly, frankly, plainly, face-to-face, overtly, point-blank, unequivocally, truthfully, candidly, unreservedly, straightforwardly, straight from the shoulder *(informal)*, without prevarication **2 = at once**, presently, soon, quickly, as soon as possible, in a second, straightaway, forthwith, posthaste **3 = immediately**, promptly, instantly, right away, straightaway, speedily, instantaneously, pronto *(informal)*, pdq *(slang)*

director *n* **1, 2 = controller**, head, leader, manager, chief, executive, chairman, boss *(informal)*, producer, governor, principal, administrator, supervisor, organizer, baas *(S African)*, helmer, sherang *(Austral & NZ)*

dirt *n* **1 = filth**, muck, grime, dust, mud, stain, crap *(taboo, slang)*, tarnish, smudge, mire, impurity, slob *(Irish)*, crud *(slang)*, kak *(S African taboo, slang)*, grot *(slang)* **2 = soil**, ground, earth, clay, turf, clod, loam, loam

dirty *adj* **1 = filthy**, soiled, grubby, nasty, foul, muddy, polluted, messy, sullied, grimy, unclean, mucky, grotty *(slang)*, grungy *(slang, chiefly US & Canad)*, scuzzy *(slang, chiefly US)*, begrimed, festy *(Austral slang)*
OPPOSITE: clean
4 = dishonest, illegal, unfair, cheating, corrupt, crooked, deceiving, fraudulent, treacherous, deceptive, unscrupulous, crafty, deceitful, double-dealing,

DICTIONARY

jokes **b** sexually clandestine: *a dirty weekend* **6** revealing dislike or anger: *a dirty look* **7** (of weather) rainy or stormy **8 dirty work** unpleasant or illicit activity ▹*n* **9 do the dirty on** *informal* to behave meanly towards ▹*vb* **dirties, dirtying, dirtied 10** to make dirty; soil **dirtiness** *n*

d

dirty bomb *n informal* a bomb made from nuclear waste combined with conventional explosives that is capable of spreading radioactive material over a wide area

dis *vb* **disses, dissing, dissed** *slang chiefly US* ▸same as **diss**

dis- *prefix* **1** indicating reversal: *disconnect* **2** indicating negation or lack: *dissimilar; disgrace* **3** indicating removal or release: *disembowel*

disability ⊤ *n, pl* **-ties 1** a severe physical or mental illness that restricts the way a person lives his or her life **2** something that disables someone

disable ⊤ *vb* **-abling, -abled** to make ineffective, unfit, or incapable **disablement** *n*

disabled ⊤ *adj* lacking one or more physical powers, such as the ability to walk or to coordinate one's movements

disabuse *vb* **-abusing, -abused** to rid (someone) of a mistaken idea: *Arnold felt unable to disabuse her of her prejudices*

disaccharide (die-sack-a-ride) *n* a sugar, such as sucrose, whose molecules consist of two linked monosaccharides

disadvantage ⊤ *n* **1** an unfavourable or harmful circumstance **2 at a disadvantage** in a less favourable position than other people: *he continued to insist that he was at a disadvantage at the hearings* **disadvantageous** *adj*

disadvantaged *adj* socially or economically deprived

disaffected *adj* having lost loyalty to or affection for someone or something; alienated: *three million disaffected voters* **disaffection** *n*

disagree ⊤ *vb* **-greeing, -greed 1** to have differing opinions or argue about (something) **2** to fail to correspond; conflict **3** to cause physical discomfort to: *curry disagrees with me*

disagreeable *adj* **1** (of an incident or situation) unpleasant **2** (of a person) bad-tempered or disobliging **disagreeably** *adv*

disagreement ⊤ *n* **1** refusal or failure to agree **2** a difference between results, totals, etc. which shows that they cannot all be true **3** an argument

disallow *vb* to reject as untrue or invalid; cancel

disappear ⊤ *vb* **1** to cease to be visible; vanish **2** to go away or become lost, esp. without explanation **3** to cease to exist: *the pain has disappeared* **disappearance** *n*

disappoint ⊤ *vb* **1** to fail to meet the expectations or hopes of; let down **2** to prevent the fulfilment of (a plan, etc.); frustrate **disappointed** *adj* **disappointing** *adj*
WORD ORIGIN Old French *desapointier*

disappointment ⊤ *n* **1** the feeling of being disappointed **2** a person or thing that disappoints

disapprobation *n* disapproval

disapprove ⊤ *vb* **-proving, -proved** to consider wrong or bad **disapproval** *n* **disapproving** *adj*

disarm ⊤ *vb* **1** to deprive of weapons **2** to win the confidence or affection of **3** (of a country) to decrease the size and capability of one's armed forces

disarmament ⊤ *n* the reduction of fighting capability by a country

disarming ⊤ *adj* removing hostility or suspicion **disarmingly** *adv*

disarrange *vb* **-ranging, -ranged** to throw into disorder **disarrangement** *n*

disarray ⊤ *n* **1** confusion and lack of discipline **2** extreme untidiness ▹*vb* **3** to throw into confusion

disassociate *vb* **-ating, -ated** ▸same

THESAURUS

unsporting, knavish *(archaic)*
OPPOSITE: honest
5a = obscene, rude, coarse, indecent, blue, offensive, gross, filthy, vulgar, pornographic, sleazy, suggestive, lewd, risqué, X-rated *(informal)*, bawdy, salacious, smutty, off-colour, unwholesome, page-three
OPPOSITE: decent
▹*vb* **10 = soil**, foul, stain, spoil, smear, muddy, pollute, blacken, mess up, smudge, sully, defile, smirch, begrime **OPPOSITE:** clean

disability *n* **1 = handicap**, affliction, disorder, defect, impairment, disablement, infirmity

disable *vb* **= handicap**, weaken, cripple, damage, hamstring, paralyse, impair, debilitate, incapacitate, prostrate, unman, immobilize, put out of action, enfeeble, render inoperative, render *hors de combat*

disabled *adj* **= differently abled**, physically challenged, handicapped, challenged, weakened, crippled, paralysed, lame, mutilated, maimed, incapacitated, infirm, bedridden
OPPOSITE: able-bodied

disadvantage *n* **1a = drawback**, trouble, burden, weakness, handicap, liability, minus *(informal)*, flaw, hardship, nuisance, snag, inconvenience, downside, impediment, hindrance, privation, weak point, fly in the ointment *(informal)* **OPPOSITE:** advantage
1b = harm, loss, damage, injury, hurt, prejudice, detriment, disservice
OPPOSITE: benefit

disagree *vb* **1 = differ (in opinion)**, argue, debate, clash, dispute, contest, fall out *(informal)*, contend, dissent, quarrel, wrangle, bicker, take issue with, have words *(informal)*, cross swords, be at sixes and sevens **OPPOSITE:** agree
3 = make ill, upset, sicken, trouble, hurt, bother, distress, discomfort, nauseate, be injurious

disagreement *n* **3 = argument**, row, difference, division, debate, conflict, clash, dispute, falling out, misunderstanding, dissent, quarrel, squabble, strife, wrangle, discord, tiff, altercation **OPPOSITE:** agreement

disappear *vb* **1 = vanish**, recede, drop out of sight, vanish off the face of the earth, evanesce, be lost to view *or* sight **OPPOSITE:** appear
3 = cease, end, fade, vanish, dissolve, expire, evaporate, perish, die out, pass away, cease to exist, melt away, leave no trace, cease to be known

disappoint *vb* **1 = let down**, dismay, fail, dash, disillusion, sadden, vex, chagrin, dishearten, disenchant, dissatisfy, disgruntle

disappointment *n* **1 = regret**, distress, discontent, dissatisfaction, disillusionment, displeasure, chagrin, disenchantment, dejection, despondency, discouragement, mortification, unfulfilment
2 = letdown, blow, disaster, failure, setback, fiasco, misfortune, calamity, whammy *(informal, chiefly US)*, choker *(informal)*, washout *(informal)*

disapprove *vb* **= condemn**, object to, dislike, censure, deplore, deprecate, frown on, take exception to, take a dim view of, find unacceptable, have a down on *(informal)*, discountenance, look down your nose at *(informal)*, raise an *or* your eyebrow
OPPOSITE: approve

disarm *vb* **1, 3 = demilitarize**, disband, demobilize, deactivate **2 = win over**, persuade

disarmament *n* **= arms reduction**, demobilization, arms limitation, demilitarization, de-escalation

disarming *adj* **= charming**, winning, irresistible, persuasive, likable *or* likeable

disarray *n* **1 = confusion**, upset, disorder, indiscipline, disunity, disharmony, disorganization, unruliness, discomposure, disorderliness **OPPOSITE:** order
2 = untidiness, state, mess, chaos, tangle, mix-up, muddle, clutter, shambles, jumble, hotchpotch, hodgepodge *(US)*, dishevelment,

as **dissociate** > **disassociation** *n*
disaster ❶ *n* **1** an accident that causes great distress or destruction **2** something, such as a project, that fails or has been ruined **disastrous** *adj* **disastrously** *adv*
WORD ORIGIN Italian *disastro*
disavow *vb* to deny connection with or responsibility for (something) **disavowal** *n*
disband *vb* to stop or cause to stop functioning as a unit or group **disbandment** *n*
disbar *vb* **-barring, -barred** to deprive (a barrister) of the right to practise
disbelieve *vb* **-lieving, -lieved 1** to reject (a person or statement) as being untruthful **2 disbelieve in** to have no faith or belief in: *to disbelieve in the supernatural* **disbelief** *n*
disburse *vb* **-bursing, -bursed** to pay out **disbursement** *n*
WORD ORIGIN Old French *desborser*
disc *n* **1** a flat circular object **2** a gramophone record **3** *anat* a circular flat structure in the body, esp. between the vertebrae **4** *computers* ▸ same as **disk**
WORD ORIGIN Latin *discus* discus
discard ❶ *vb* to get rid of (something or someone) as useless or undesirable
WORD ORIGIN DIS- + *card* (the playing card)
disc brake *n* a brake in which two pads rub against a flat disc
discern *vb* to see or be aware of (something) clearly **discernible** *adj*
WORD ORIGIN Latin *discernere* to divide
discerning *adj* having or showing good judgment **discernment** *n*
discharge ❶ *vb* **-charging, -charged 1** to release or allow to go **2** to dismiss (someone) from duty or employment **3** to fire (a gun) **4** to cause to pour forth: *the scar was red and swollen and began to discharge pus* **5** to remove (the cargo) from a boat, etc.; unload **6** to meet the demands of (a duty or responsibility) **7** to relieve oneself of (a debt) **8** *physics* to take or supply electrical current from (a cell or battery) ▹ *n* **9** something that is discharged **10** dismissal or release from an office, job, etc. **11** a pouring out of a fluid; emission **12** *physics* a conduction of electricity through a gas
disciple ❶ (diss-**sipe**-pl) *n* **1** a follower of the doctrines of a teacher **2** one of the personal followers of Christ during his earthly life
WORD ORIGIN Latin *discipulus* pupil
disciplinarian *n* a person who practises strict discipline
disciplinary *adj* of or imposing discipline; corrective
discipline ❶ *n* **1** the practice of imposing strict rules of behaviour on other people **2** the ability to behave and work in a controlled manner **3** a particular area of academic study ▹ *vb* **-plining, -plined 4** to improve or attempt to improve the behaviour of (oneself or someone else) by training or rules **5** to punish
WORD ORIGIN Latin *disciplina* teaching
disciplined *adj* able to behave and work in a controlled way
disc jockey *n* a person who announces and plays recorded pop records on a radio programme or at a disco
disclaim *vb* **1** to deny (responsibility for or knowledge of something) **2** to give up (any claim to)
disclaimer *n* a statement denying responsibility for or knowledge of something
disclose ❶ *vb* **-closing, -closed 1** to make (information) known **2** to allow to be seen: *she agreed to disclose the contents of the box* **disclosure** *n*
disco *n, pl* **-cos 1** a nightclub for dancing to amplified pop records **2** an occasion at which people dance to amplified pop records **3** mobile equipment for providing music for a disco
WORD ORIGIN from DISCOTHEQUE
discography *n, pl* **-phies** a classified list of gramophone records
discolour *or US* **discolor** *vb* to change in colour; to fade or stain **discoloration** *n*
discomfit *vb* **-fiting, -fited** to make uneasy or confused **discomfiture** *n*
WORD ORIGIN Old French *desconfire* to destroy
discomfort ❶ *n* **1** a mild pain **2** a feeling of worry or embarrassment **3 discomforts** conditions that cause

pig's breakfast *(informal)*
OPPOSITE: tidiness
disaster *n* **1 = catastrophe**, trouble, blow, accident, stroke, reverse, tragedy, ruin, misfortune, adversity, calamity, mishap, whammy *(informal, chiefly US)*, misadventure, car crash *(informal)*, train wreck *(informal)*, cataclysm, act of God, bummer *(slang)*, ruination, mischance **2 = failure**, mess, flop *(informal)*, catastrophe, rout, debacle, cock-up *(Brit slang)*, washout *(informal)*
discard *vb* **= get rid of**, drop, remove, throw away *or* out, reject, abandon, dump *(informal)*, shed, scrap, axe *(informal)*, ditch *(slang)*, junk *(informal)*, chuck *(informal)*, dispose of, relinquish, dispense with, jettison, repudiate, cast aside **OPPOSITE:** keep
discharge *vb* **1 = release**, free, clear, liberate, pardon, let go, acquit, allow to go, set free, exonerate, absolve **2 = dismiss**, sack *(informal)*, fire *(informal)*, remove, expel, discard, oust, eject, cashier, give (someone) the boot *(slang)*, give (someone) the sack *(informal)*, kennet *(Austral slang)*, jeff *(Austral slang)* **3 = fire**, shoot, set off, explode, let off, detonate, let loose *(informal)* **4 = pour forth**, release, empty, leak, emit, dispense, void, gush, ooze, exude, give off, excrete, disembogue **6 = carry out**, perform, fulfil, accomplish, do, effect, realize, observe, implement, execute, carry through **7 = pay**, meet, clear, settle, square (up), honour, satisfy, relieve, liquidate ▹ *n* **10a = release**, liberation, clearance, pardon, acquittal, remittance, exoneration **10b = dismissal**, notice, removal, the boot *(slang)*, expulsion, the sack *(informal)*, the push *(slang)*, marching orders *(informal)*, ejection, demobilization, kiss-off *(slang, chiefly US & Canad)*, the bum's rush *(slang)*, the (old) heave-ho *(informal)*, the order of the boot *(slang)*, congé, your books *or* cards *(informal)* **11 = emission**, flow, ooze, secretion, excretion, pus, seepage, suppuration
disciple *n* **1 = follower**, student, supporter, pupil, convert, believer, partisan, devotee, apostle, adherent, proselyte, votary, catechumen
OPPOSITE: teacher
2 = apostle
discipline *n* **1 = control**, rule, authority, direction, regulation, supervision, orderliness, strictness **2 = self-control**, control, restraint, self-discipline, coolness, cool, willpower, calmness, self-restraint, orderliness, self-mastery, strength of mind *or* will **3 = field of study**, area, subject, theme, topic, course, curriculum, speciality, subject matter, branch of knowledge, field of inquiry *or* reference ▹ *vb* **4 = train**, control, govern, check, educate, regulate, instruct, restrain **5 = punish**, correct, reprimand, castigate, chastise, chasten, penalize, bring to book, reprove
disclose *vb* **1 = make known**, tell, reveal, publish, relate, broadcast, leak, confess, communicate, unveil, utter, make public, impart, divulge, out *(informal)*, let slip, spill the beans about *(informal)*, blow wide open *(slang)*, get off your chest *(informal)*, spill your guts about *(slang)*
OPPOSITE: keep secret
2 = show, reveal, expose, discover, exhibit, unveil, uncover, lay bare, bring to light, take the wraps off
OPPOSITE: hide
discomfort *n* **1 = pain**, suffering, hurt, smarting, ache, throbbing, irritation, tenderness, pang, malaise, twinge, soreness
OPPOSITE: comfort

DICTIONARY

physical uncomfortableness: *the physical discomforts of pregnancy*

discommode *vb* **-moding, -moded** to cause inconvenience **discommodious** *adj*
WORD ORIGIN DIS- + obsolete *commode* to suit

discompose *vb* **-posing, -posed** to disturb or upset someone **discomposure** *n*

disconcert *vb* to disturb the confidence or self-possession of; upset, embarrass, or take aback **disconcerting** *adj*

disconnect *vb* **1** to undo or break the connection between (two things) **2** to stop the supply of (gas or electricity to a building) ▷ *n* **3** a lack of connection: disconnection: *a disconnect between political discourse and the public* **disconnection** *n*

disconnected *adj* (of speech or ideas) not logically connected

disconsolate *adj* sad beyond comfort **disconsolately** *adv*
WORD ORIGIN Medieval Latin *disconsolatus*

discontent ❶ *n* lack of contentment, as with one's condition or lot in life **discontented** *adj* **discontentedly** *adv*

discontinue *vb* **-uing, -ued** to come or bring to an end; stop

discontinuous *adj* characterized by interruptions; intermittent **discontinuity** *n*

discord *n* **1** lack of agreement or harmony between people **2** harsh confused sounds **3** a combination of musical notes that lacks harmony
WORD ORIGIN Latin *discors* at variance

discordant *adj* **1** at variance; disagreeing **2** harsh in sound; inharmonious **discordance** *n*

discotheque *n* ▸ same as **disco**
WORD ORIGIN French

discount ❶ *vb* **1** to leave (something) out of account as being unreliable, prejudiced, or irrelevant **2** to deduct (an amount or percentage) from the price of something ▷ *n* **3** a deduction from the full amount of a price **4 at a discount** below the regular price

discountenance *vb* **-nancing, -nanced** to make (someone) ashamed or confused

discourage ❶ *vb* **-aging, -aged 1** to deprive of the will or enthusiasm to persist in something **2** to oppose by expressing disapproval **discouragement** *n* **discouraging** *adj*

discourse ❶ *n* **1** conversation **2** a formal treatment of a subject in speech or writing ▷ *vb* **-coursing, -coursed 3** to speak or write (about) at length
WORD ORIGIN Medieval Latin *discursus* argument

discourteous *adj* showing bad manners; rude **discourteously** *adv* **discourtesy** *n*

discover ❶ *vb* **1** to be the first to find or find out about **2** to learn about for the first time **3** to find after study or search **discoverer** *n*

discovery ❶ *n, pl* **-eries 1** the act of discovering **2** a person, place, or thing that has been discovered

discredit ❶ *vb* **-iting, -ited 1** to damage the reputation of (someone) **2** to cause (an idea) to be disbelieved or distrusted ▷ *n* **3** something that causes disgrace **discreditable** *adj*

discreet ❶ *adj* **1** careful to avoid embarrassment when dealing with secret or private matters **2** unobtrusive: *there was a discreet entrance down a side alley* **discreetly** *adv*
WORD ORIGIN Old French *discret*

discrepancy ❶ *n, pl* **-cies** a conflict or variation between facts, figures, or claims **discrepant** *adj*
WORD ORIGIN Latin *discrepare* to differ in sound

discrete *adj* separate or distinct **discreteness** *n*
WORD ORIGIN Latin *discretus* separated

discretion ❶ (diss-**kresh**-on) *n* **1** the quality of behaving so as to avoid social embarrassment or distress **2** freedom or authority to make judgments and to act as one sees fit: *at his discretion* **discretionary** *adj*

discriminate ❶ *vb* **-nating, -nated 1** to make a distinction against or in favour of a particular person or group **2** to recognize or understand

THESAURUS

2 = uneasiness, worry, anxiety, doubt, alarm, distress, suspicion, apprehension, misgiving, nervousness, disquiet, agitation, qualms, trepidation, perturbation, apprehensiveness, dubiety, inquietude **OPPOSITE:** reassurance

discontent *n* **= dissatisfaction**, unhappiness, displeasure, regret, envy, restlessness, uneasiness, vexation, discontentment, fretfulness

discount *vb* **1 = disregard**, reject, ignore, overlook, discard, set aside, dispel, pass over, repudiate, disbelieve, brush off *(slang)*, lay aside, pooh-pooh ▷ *n* **3 = deduction**, cut, reduction, concession, allowance, rebate, cut price

discourage *vb* **1 = dishearten**, daunt, deter, crush, put off, depress, cow, dash, intimidate, dismay, unnerve, unman, overawe, demoralize, cast down, put a damper on, psych out *(informal)*, dispirit, deject **OPPOSITE:** hearten **2 = put off**, deter, prevent, dissuade, talk out of, discountenance **OPPOSITE:** encourage

discourse *n* **1 = conversation**, talk, discussion, speech, communication, chat, dialogue, converse **2 = speech**, talk, address, essay, lecture, sermon, treatise, dissertation, homily, oration, disquisition, whaikorero (NZ)

discover *vb* **2 = find out**, see, learn, reveal, spot, determine, notice, realize, recognize, perceive, detect, disclose, uncover, discern, ascertain, suss (out) *(slang)*, get wise to *(informal)* **3 = find**, come across, uncover, unearth, turn up, dig up, come upon, bring to light, light upon

discovery *n* **1 = finding out**, news, announcement, revelation, disclosure, realization **2 = invention**, launch, institution, introduction, pioneering, innovation, initiation, inauguration, induction, coinage, origination

discredit *vb* **1 = disgrace**, blame, shame, smear, stain, humiliate, degrade, taint, slur, detract from, disparage, vilify, slander, sully, dishonour, stigmatize, defame, bring into disrepute, bring shame upon **OPPOSITE:** honour **2 = dispute**, question, challenge, deny, reject, discount, distrust, mistrust, repudiate, cast doubt on *or* upon, disbelieve, pooh-pooh ▷ *n* **3 = disgrace**, scandal, shame, disrepute, smear, stigma, censure, slur, ignominy, dishonour, imputation, odium, ill-repute, aspersion **OPPOSITE:** honour

discreet *adj* **1 = tactful**, diplomatic, politic, reserved, guarded, careful, sensible, cautious, wary, discerning, prudent, considerate, judicious, circumspect, sagacious **OPPOSITE:** tactless

discrepancy *n* **= disagreement**, difference, variation, conflict, contradiction, inconsistency, disparity, variance, divergence, dissonance, incongruity, dissimilarity, discordance, contrariety

discretion *n* **1 = tact**, care, consideration, judgment, caution, diplomacy, good sense, prudence, acumen, wariness, discernment, circumspection, sagacity, carefulness, judiciousness, heedfulness **OPPOSITE:** tactlessness **2 = choice**, will, wish, liking, mind, option, pleasure, preference, inclination, disposition, predilection, volition

discriminate *vb* **2 = differentiate**, distinguish, discern, separate, assess, evaluate, tell the difference, draw a distinction

discrimination *n* **1 = prejudice**, bias, injustice, intolerance, bigotry, favouritism, unfairness, inequity **2 = discernment**, taste, judgment,

DICTIONARY

a difference: *to discriminate between right and wrong* **discriminating** *adj*
WORD ORIGIN Latin *discriminare* to divide

discrimination ❶ *n* **1** unfair treatment of a person, racial group, or minority **2** subtle appreciation in matters of taste **3** the ability to see fine distinctions

discriminatory *adj* based on prejudice

discursive *adj* passing from one topic to another
WORD ORIGIN Latin *discursus* a running to and fro

discus *n field sports* a disc-shaped object with a heavy middle, thrown by athletes
WORD ORIGIN Greek *diskos*

discuss ❶ *vb* **1** to consider (something) by talking it over **2** to treat (a subject) in speech or writing **discussion** *n*
WORD ORIGIN Latin *discutere* to dash to pieces

disdain ❶ *n* **1** a feeling of superiority and dislike; contempt ▷ *vb* **2** to refuse or reject with disdain: *he disdained domestic conventions* **disdainful** *adj* **disdainfully** *adv*
WORD ORIGIN Old French *desdeign*

disease ❶ *n* an unhealthy condition in a person, animal, or plant which is caused by bacteria or infection **diseased** *adj*
WORD ORIGIN Old French *desaise*

diseconomy *n econ* a disadvantage, such as higher costs, resulting from the scale on which a business operates

disembark *vb* to land or cause to land from a ship, aircraft, or other vehicle **disembarkation** *n*

disembodied *adj* **1** lacking a body **2** seeming not to be attached to or come from anyone **disembodiment** *n*

disembowel *vb* **-elling, -elled** *or US* **-eling, -eled** to remove the entrails of **disembowelment** *n*

disempower *vb* to deprive (a person) of power or authority **disempowerment** *n*

disenchanted *adj* disappointed and disillusioned (with something) **disenchantment** *n*

disenfranchise *vb* **-chising, -chised** to deprive (someone) of the right to vote or of other rights of citizenship

disengage *vb* **-gaging, -gaged** **1** to release from a connection **2** *mil* to withdraw from close action **disengagement** *n*

disentangle *vb* **-gling, -gled** **1** to release from entanglement or confusion **2** to unravel or work out **disentanglement** *n*

disequilibrium *n* a loss or absence of stability or balance

disestablish *vb* to deprive (a church or religion) of established status **disestablishment** *n*

disfavour *or US* **disfavor** *n* **1** disapproval or dislike **2** the state of being disapproved of or disliked

disfigure *vb* **-uring, -ured** to spoil the appearance or shape of **disfigurement** *n*

disfranchise *vb* **-chising, -chised** ▸ same as **disenfranchise**

disgorge *vb* **-gorging, -gorged** **1** to vomit **2** to discharge (contents)

disgrace ❶ *n* **1** a condition of shame, loss of reputation, or dishonour **2** a shameful person or thing **3** exclusion from confidence or trust: *he was sent home in disgrace* ▷ *vb* **-gracing, -graced** **4** to bring shame upon (oneself or others) **disgraceful** *adj* **disgracefully** *adv*

disgruntled ❶ *adj* sulky or discontented: *the disgruntled home supporters* **disgruntlement** *n*
WORD ORIGIN DIS- + obsolete *gruntle* to complain

disguise ❶ *vb* **-guising, -guised** **1** to change the appearance or manner in order to conceal the identity of (someone or something) **2** to misrepresent (something) in order to obscure its actual nature or meaning ▷ *n* **3** a mask, costume, or manner that disguises **4** the state of being disguised **disguised** *adj*
WORD ORIGIN Old French *desguisier*

disgust ❶ *n* **1** a great loathing or distaste ▷ *vb* **2** to sicken or fill with loathing **disgusted** *adj* **disgusting** *adj*
WORD ORIGIN Old French *desgouster* to sicken

dish ❶ *n* **1** a container used for holding or serving food, esp. an open shallow container **2** the food in a dish **3** a particular kind of food **4** ▸ short for **dish aerial** **5** *informal* an attractive person ▸ See also **dish out, dish up**
WORD ORIGIN Old English *disc*

dishabille (diss-a-**beel**) *n* ▸ same as **deshabille**

dish aerial *n* a large disc-shaped aerial with a concave reflector, used to receive signals in radar, radio telescopes, and satellite broadcasting

disharmony *n* lack of agreement or harmony **disharmonious** *adj*

dishcloth *n* a cloth for washing dishes

dishearten *vb* to weaken or destroy the hope, courage, or enthusiasm of **disheartened** *adj* **disheartening** *adj*

dishevelled *or US* **disheveled** *adj* (of a person's hair, clothes, or general appearance) disordered and untidy
WORD ORIGIN Old French *deschevelé*

dishonest ❶ *adj* not honest or fair **dishonestly** *adv* **dishonesty** *n*

d

THESAURUS

perception, insight, penetration, subtlety, refinement, acumen, keenness, sagacity, acuteness, clearness

discuss *vb* **1 = talk about**, consider, debate, review, go into, examine, argue about, thrash out, ventilate, reason about, exchange views on, deliberate about, weigh up the pros and cons of, converse about, confer about

disdain *n* **1 = contempt**, dislike, scorn, arrogance, indifference, sneering, derision, hauteur, snobbishness, contumely, haughtiness, superciliousness ▷ *vb* **2 = scorn**, reject, despise, slight, disregard, spurn, undervalue, deride, look down on, belittle, sneer at, pooh-pooh, contemn, look down your nose at *(informal)*, misprize

disease *n* **= illness**, condition, complaint, upset, infection, disorder, sickness, ailment, affliction, malady, infirmity, indisposition, lurgy *(informal)*

disgrace *n* **1 = shame**, contempt, discredit, degradation, disrepute, ignominy, dishonour, infamy, opprobrium, odium, disfavour, obloquy, disesteem
OPPOSITE: honour
2 = scandal, stain, stigma, blot, blemish ▷ *vb* **4 = shame**, stain, humiliate, discredit, degrade, taint, sully, dishonour, stigmatize, defame, abase, bring shame upon
OPPOSITE: honour

disgruntled *adj* **= discontented**, dissatisfied, annoyed, irritated, put out, hacked (off) *(US slang)*, grumpy, vexed, sullen, displeased, petulant, sulky, peeved, malcontent, testy, peevish, huffy, cheesed off *(Brit slang)*, hoha *(NZ)*

disguise *vb* **1 = hide**, cover, conceal, screen, mask, suppress, withhold, veil, cloak, shroud, camouflage, keep secret, hush up, draw a veil over, keep dark, keep under your hat ▷ *n* **3 = costume**, get-up *(informal)*, mask, camouflage, false appearance

disgust *vb* **2 = sicken**, outrage, offend, revolt, put off, repel, nauseate, gross out *(US slang)*, turn your stomach, fill with loathing, cause aversion
OPPOSITE: delight

dish *n* **2, 3 = food**, fare, recipe

dishonest *adj* **= deceitful**, corrupt, crooked *(informal)*, designing, lying, bent *(slang)*, false, unfair, cheating, deceiving, shady *(informal)*, fraudulent, treacherous, deceptive, unscrupulous, crafty, swindling, disreputable, untrustworthy, double-dealing, unprincipled, mendacious, perfidious, untruthful, guileful, knavish *(archaic)*
OPPOSITE: honest

DICTIONARY

dishonour *or US* **dishonor** *vb* **1** to treat with disrespect **2** to refuse to pay (a cheque) ▷ *n* **3** a lack of honour or respect **4** a state of shame or disgrace **5** something that causes a loss of honour **dishonourable** *adj* **dishonourably** *adv*
dish out *vb* **1** *informal* to distribute **2 dish it out** to inflict punishment
dish up *vb* to serve (food)
dishwasher *n* a machine for washing and drying dishes, cutlery, etc.
dishwater *n* **1** water in which dishes have been washed **2 like dishwater** (of tea) very weak
dishy *adj* **dishier, dishiest** *informal* good-looking
disillusion *vb* **1** to destroy the illusions or false ideas of (someone) ▷ *n also* **disillusionment 2** the state of being disillusioned
disillusioned *adj* disappointed at finding out reality does not match one's ideals
disincentive *n* something that discourages someone from behaving or acting in a particular way
disinclined *adj* unwilling or reluctant **disinclination** *n*
disinfect *vb* to rid of harmful germs by cleaning with a chemical substance **disinfection** *n*
disinfectant *n* a substance that destroys harmful germs
disinformation *n* false information intended to mislead
disingenuous *adj* dishonest and insincere **disingenuously** *adv*
disinherit *vb* **-iting, -ited** *law* to deprive (an heir) of inheritance **disinheritance** *n*
disintegrate ⓘ *vb* **-grating, -grated 1** to lose cohesion; break up: *the business disintegrated* **2** (of an object) to break into fragments; shatter **3** *physics* **a** to undergo nuclear fission or include nuclear fission in **b** ▸ same as **decay** (sense 3) ▷ **disintegration** *n*
disinter *vb* **-terring, -terred 1** to dig up **2** to bring to light; expose
disinterested *adj* **1** free from bias; objective **2** *not standard* feeling or showing a lack of interest; uninterested **disinterest** *n*
disjointed *adj* having no coherence; disconnected: *a disjointed conversation*
disjunctive *adj* serving to disconnect or separate
disk *n* **1** *chiefly US & Canad* ▸ same as **disc 2** *computers* a storage device, consisting of a stack of plates coated with a magnetic layer, which rotates rapidly as a single unit
WORD ORIGIN see DISC
disk drive *n computers* the controller and mechanism for reading and writing data on computer disks
dislike ⓘ *vb* **-liking, -liked 1** to consider unpleasant or disagreeable ▷ *n* **2** a feeling of not liking something or someone
dislocate *vb* **-cating, -cated 1** to displace (a bone or joint) from its normal position **2** to disrupt or shift out of place **dislocation** *n*
dislodge *vb* **-lodging, -lodged** to remove (something) from a previously fixed position
disloyal *adj* not loyal; deserting one's allegiance or duty **disloyalty** *n*
dismal ⓘ *adj* **1** gloomy and depressing **2** *informal* of poor quality **dismally** *adv*
WORD ORIGIN Medieval Latin *dies mali* unlucky days
dismantle ⓘ *vb* **-tling, -tled 1** to take apart piece by piece **2** to cause (an organization or political system) to stop functioning by gradually reducing its power or purpose
WORD ORIGIN Old French *desmanteler*
dismay ⓘ *vb* **1** to fill with alarm or depression ▷ *n* **2** a feeling of alarm or depression
WORD ORIGIN Old French *des-* (intensive) + *esmayer* to frighten
dismember *vb* **1** to remove the limbs of **2** to cut to pieces **dismemberment** *n*
dismiss ⓘ *vb* **1** to remove (an employee) from a job **2** to allow (someone) to leave **3** to put out of one's mind; no longer think about **4** (of a judge) to state that (a case) will not be brought to trial **5** *cricket* to bowl out (a side) for a particular number of runs **dismissal** *n* **dismissive** *adj*
WORD ORIGIN Latin *dis-* from + *mittere* to send
dismount *vb* to get off a horse or bicycle
disobedient *adj* refusing to obey **disobedience** *n*
disobey ⓘ *vb* to neglect or refuse to obey (a person or an order)
disobliging *adj* unwilling to help
disorder ⓘ *n* **1** a state of untidiness and disorganization **2** public

THESAURUS

disintegrate *vb* **2 = break up**, crumble, fall apart, separate, shatter, splinter, break apart, fall to pieces, go to pieces, disunite
dislike *vb* **1 = hate**, object to, loathe, despise, shun, scorn, disapprove of, detest, abhor, recoil from, take a dim view of, be repelled by, be averse to, disfavour, have an aversion to, abominate, have a down on (*informal*), disrelish, have no taste *or* stomach for, not be able to bear *or* abide *or* stand **OPPOSITE:** like
▷ *n* **2 = hatred**, disgust, hostility, loathing, disapproval, distaste, animosity, aversion, antagonism, displeasure, antipathy, enmity, animus, disinclination, repugnance, odium, detestation, disapprobation **OPPOSITE:** liking
dismal *adj* **1a = sad**, gloomy, melancholy, black, dark, depressing, discouraging, bleak, dreary, sombre, forlorn, despondent, lugubrious, sorrowful, wretched, funereal, cheerless, dolorous **OPPOSITE:** happy **1b = gloomy**, depressing, dull, dreary, lugubrious, cheerless **OPPOSITE:** cheerful **2 = bad**, awful, dreadful, rotten (*informal*), terrible, poor, dire, duff (*Brit informal*), abysmal, frightful, godawful (*slang*)
dismantle *vb* **1 = take apart**, strip, demolish, raze, disassemble, unrig, take to pieces *or* bits
dismay *vb* **1a = alarm**, frighten, scare, panic, distress, terrify, appal, startle, horrify, paralyse, unnerve, put the wind up (someone) (*informal*), give (someone) a turn (*informal*), affright, fill with consternation **1b = disappoint**, upset, sadden, dash, discourage, put off, daunt, disillusion, let down, vex, chagrin, dishearten, dispirit, disenchant, disgruntle ▷ *n* **2a = alarm**, fear, horror, panic, anxiety, distress, terror, dread, fright, unease, apprehension, nervousness, agitation, consternation, trepidation, uneasiness **2b = disappointment**, upset, distress, frustration, dissatisfaction, disillusionment, chagrin, disenchantment, discouragement, mortification
dismiss *vb* **1 = sack**, fire (*informal*), remove (*informal*), axe (*informal*), discharge, oust, lay off, kick out (*informal*), cashier, send packing (*informal*), give (someone) notice, kiss off (*slang, chiefly US & Canad*), give (someone) their marching orders, give (someone) the push (*informal*), give (someone) the elbow, give (someone) the boot (*slang*), give (someone) the bullet (*Brit slang*), kennet (*Austral slang*), jeff (*Austral slang*) **2 = let go**, free, release, discharge, dissolve, liberate, disperse, disband, send away **3a = reject**, disregard, spurn, repudiate, pooh-pooh **3b = banish**, drop, dispel, shelve, discard, set aside, eradicate, cast out, lay aside, put out of your mind
disobey *vb* **a = defy**, ignore, rebel, resist, disregard, refuse to obey, dig your heels in (*informal*), go counter to **b = infringe**, defy, refuse to obey, flout, violate, contravene, overstep, transgress, go counter to
disorder *n* **1 = untidiness**, mess, confusion, chaos, muddle, state, clutter, shambles, disarray, jumble, irregularity, disorganization,

violence or rioting **3** an illness **disordered** *adj*

disorderly ❶ *adj* **1** untidy and disorganized **2** uncontrolled; unruly **3** *law* violating public peace

disorganize *or* **-ise** *vb* **-izing, -ized** *or* **-ising, -ised** to disrupt the arrangement or system of **disorganization** *or* **-isation** *n*

disorientate *or* **disorient** *vb* **-tating, -tated** *or* **-enting, -ented** to cause (someone) to lose his or her bearings **disorientation** *n*

disown *vb* to deny any connection with (someone)

disparage *vb* **-aging, -aged** to speak contemptuously of **disparagement** *n* **disparaging** *adj*
WORD ORIGIN Old French *desparagier*

disparate *adj* utterly different in kind **disparity** *n*
WORD ORIGIN Latin *disparare* to divide

dispassionate *adj* not influenced by emotion; objective **dispassionately** *adv*

dispatch ❶ *or* **despatch** *vb* **1** to send off to a destination or to perform a task **2** to carry out (a duty or task) promptly **3** to murder ▹ *n* **4** an official communication or report, sent in haste **5** a report sent to a newspaper by a correspondent **6** murder **7** **with dispatch** quickly
WORD ORIGIN Italian *dispacciare*

dispatch rider *n Brit, Austral & NZ* a motorcyclist who carries dispatches

dispel ❶ *vb* **-pelling, -pelled** to disperse or drive away
WORD ORIGIN Latin *dispellere*

dispensable *adj* not essential; expendable

dispensary *n, pl* **-ries** a place where medicine is prepared and given out

dispensation *n* **1** the act of distributing or dispensing **2** *chiefly RC church* permission to dispense with an obligation of church law **3** any exemption from an obligation **4** the ordering of life and events by God

dispense ❶ *vb* **-pensing, -pensed** **1** to distribute in portions **2** to prepare and distribute (medicine) **3** to administer (the law, etc.) **4** **dispense with** to do away with or manage without **dispenser** *n*
WORD ORIGIN Latin *dispendere* to weigh out

dispensing optician *n* ▸ see **optician** (sense 2)

disperse ❶ *vb* **-persing, -persed** **1** to scatter over a wide area **2** to leave or cause to leave a gathering: *police dispersed rioters* **3** to separate (light) into its different wavelengths **4** to separate (particles) throughout a solid, liquid, or gas **dispersal** *or* **dispersion** *n*
WORD ORIGIN Latin *dispergere* to scatter widely

dispirit *vb* to make downhearted **dispirited** *adj* **dispiriting** *adj*

displace ❶ *vb* **-placing, -placed** **1** to move (something) from its usual place **2** to remove (someone) from a post or position of authority

displaced person *n* a person forced from his or her home or country, esp. by war or revolution

displacement *n* **1** the act of displacing **2** *physics* the weight or volume of liquid displaced by an object submerged or floating in it **3** *maths* the distance measured in a particular direction from a reference point. Symbol: *s*

display ❶ *vb* **1** to show **2** to reveal or make evident: *to display anger* ▹ *n* **3** the act of exhibiting or displaying **4** something displayed **5** an exhibition **6** *electronics* a device capable of representing information visually, as on a screen **7** *zool* a pattern of behaviour by which an animal attracts attention while courting, defending its territory, etc.
WORD ORIGIN Anglo-French *despleier* to unfold

displease *vb* **-pleasing, -pleased** to annoy or offend (someone) **displeasure** *n*

disport *vb* **disport oneself** to indulge oneself in pleasure
WORD ORIGIN Anglo-French *desporter*

disposable ❶ *adj* **1** designed for disposal after use: *disposable cigarette lighters* **2** available for use if needed: *disposable capital*

d

THESAURUS

hotchpotch, derangement, hodgepodge (*US*), pig's breakfast (*informal*), disorderliness **2 = disturbance**, fight, riot, turmoil, unrest, quarrel, upheaval, brawl, clamour, uproar, turbulence, fracas, commotion, rumpus, tumult, hubbub, shindig (*informal*), hullabaloo, scrimmage, unruliness, shindy (*informal*), bagarre (*French*), biffo (*Austral slang*) **3 = illness**, disease, complaint, condition, sickness, ailment, affliction, malady, infirmity, indisposition

disorderly *adj* **1 = untidy**, confused, chaotic, messy, irregular, jumbled, indiscriminate, shambolic (*informal*), disorganized, higgledy-piggledy (*informal*), unsystematic **OPPOSITE:** tidy **2 = unruly**, disruptive, rowdy, turbulent, unlawful, stormy, rebellious, boisterous, tumultuous, lawless, riotous, unmanageable, ungovernable, refractory, obstreperous, indisciplined

dispatch *or* **despatch** *vb* **1 = send**, transmit, forward, express, communicate, consign, remit **2 = carry out**, perform, fulfil, effect, finish, achieve, settle, dismiss, conclude, accomplish, execute, discharge, dispose of, expedite, make short work of (*informal*) **3 = kill**, murder, destroy, do in (*slang*), eliminate (*slang*), take out (*slang*), execute, butcher, slaughter, assassinate, slay, finish off, put an end to, do away with, blow away (*slang, chiefly US*), liquidate, annihilate, exterminate, take (someone's) life, bump off (*slang*) ▹ *n* **4, 5 = message**, news, report, story, letter, account, piece, item, document, communication, instruction, bulletin, communiqué, missive

dispel *vb* **= drive away**, dismiss, eliminate, resolve, scatter, expel, disperse, banish, rout, allay, dissipate, chase away

dispense *vb* **1 = distribute**, assign, allocate, allot, mete out, dole out, share out, apportion, deal out, disburse **2 = prepare**, measure, supply, mix **3 = administer**, direct, operate, carry out, implement, undertake, enforce, execute, apply, discharge

disperse *vb* **1 = scatter**, spread, distribute, circulate, strew, diffuse, dissipate, disseminate, throw about **2 = break up**, separate, dismiss, disappear, send off, vanish, scatter, dissolve, rout, dispel, disband, part company, demobilize, go (their) separate ways **OPPOSITE:** gather **4 = dissolve**, disappear, vanish, evaporate, break up, dissipate, melt away, evanesce

displace *vb* **1 = move**, shift, disturb, budge, misplace, disarrange, derange

display *vb* **1 = show**, present, exhibit, unveil, open to view, take the wraps off, put on view **OPPOSITE:** conceal **1, 2a = expose**, show, reveal, bare, exhibit, uncover, lay bare, expose to view **1, 2b = demonstrate**, show, reveal, register, expose, disclose, betray, manifest, divulge, make known, evidence, evince ▹ *n* **3 = proof**, exhibition, demonstration, evidence, expression, exposure, illustration, revelation, testimony, confirmation, manifestation, affirmation, substantiation **4 = show**, exhibition, demonstration, parade, spectacle, pageant, pageantry **5 = exhibition**, show, demonstration, presentation, showing, array, expo (*informal*), exposition

disposable *adj* **1 = throwaway**, paper, nonreturnable **2 = available**, expendable, free for use, consumable, spendable, at your service

DICTIONARY

disposal ❶ *n* **1** the act or means of getting rid of something **2 at one's disposal** available for use

dispose ❶ *vb* **-posing, -posed** **1 dispose of** **a** to throw away **b** to give, sell, or transfer to another **c** to deal with or settle: *I disposed of that problem right away* **d** to kill **2** to arrange or place in a particular way: *around them are disposed the moulded masks of witch doctors*
WORD ORIGIN Latin *disponere* to set in different places

disposed *adj* **1** willing or eager (to do something): *few would feel disposed to fault his judgment* **2** having an inclination as specified (towards someone or something): *my people aren't too well disposed towards defectors*

disposition ❶ *n* **1** a person's usual temperament **2** a tendency or habit **3** arrangement; layout

dispossess *vb* to deprive (someone) of (a possession) **dispossessed** *adj* **dispossession** *n*

disproportion *n* lack of proportion or equality

disproportionate *adj* out of proportion **disproportionately** *adv*

disprove *vb* **-proving, -proved** to show (an assertion or claim) to be incorrect

dispute ❶ *n* **1** a disagreement between workers and their employer **2** an argument between two or more people **3 beyond dispute** unable to be questioned or denied: *it's beyond dispute that tensions already existed between them* ▷*vb* **-puting, -puted** **4** to argue or quarrel about (something) **5** to doubt the validity of **6** to fight over possession of **disputation** *n* **disputatious** *adj*
WORD ORIGIN Latin *disputare* to discuss

disqualify ❶ *vb* **-fies, -fying, -fied** **1** to officially ban (someone) from doing something: *he was disqualified from driving for ten years* **2** to make ineligible, as for entry to an examination **disqualification** *n*

disquiet *n* **1** a feeling of anxiety or uneasiness ▷*vb* **2** to make (someone) anxious **disquieting** *adj* **disquietude** *n*

disquisition *n* a formal written or oral examination of a subject

disregard ❶ *vb* **1** to give little or no attention to; ignore ▷*n* **2** lack of attention or respect

disrepair *n* the condition of being worn out or in poor working order

disreputable *adj* having or causing a bad reputation **disreputably** *adv*

disrepute *n* a loss or lack of good reputation

disrespect *n* contempt or lack of respect **disrespectful** *adj*

disrobe *vb* **-robing, -robed** *literary* to undress

disrupt ❶ *vb* to interrupt the progress of **disruption** *n* **disruptive** *adj*
WORD ORIGIN Latin *disruptus* burst asunder

diss *vb slang chiefly US* to treat (a person) with contempt
WORD ORIGIN from DISRESPECT

dissatisfied ❶ *adj* displeased or discontented **dissatisfaction** *n*

dissect *vb* **1** to cut open (a corpse) to examine it **2** to examine critically and minutely: *the above conclusion causes one to dissect that policy more closely* **dissection** *n*
WORD ORIGIN Latin *dissecare*

dissemble *vb* **-bling, -bled** to conceal one's real motives or emotions by pretence **dissembler** *n*
WORD ORIGIN Latin *dissimulare*

disseminate *vb* **-nating, -nated** to spread (information, ideas, etc.) widely **dissemination** *n*
WORD ORIGIN Latin *disseminare*

dissension *n* disagreement and argument
WORD ORIGIN Latin *dissentire* to dissent

dissent ❶ *vb* **1** to disagree **2** *Christianity* to reject the doctrines of an established church ▷*n* **3** a disagreement **4** *Christianity* separation from an established church **dissenter** *n* **dissenting** *adj*
WORD ORIGIN Latin *dissentire* to disagree

Dissenter *n Christianity chiefly Brit* a Protestant who refuses to conform to the established church

dissentient *adj* dissenting from the opinion of the majority

dissertation *n* **1** a written thesis, usually required for a higher degree **2** a long formal speech
WORD ORIGIN Latin *dissertare* to debate

disservice *n* a harmful action

dissident ❶ *n* **1** a person who disagrees with a government or a powerful organization ▷*adj* **2** disagreeing or dissenting **dissidence** *n*
WORD ORIGIN Latin *dissidere* to be remote from

dissimilar *adj* not alike; different **dissimilarity** *n*

dissimulate *vb* **-lating, -lated** to conceal one's real feelings by pretence **dissimulation** *n*

dissipate *vb* **-pating, -pated** **1** to

THESAURUS

disposal *n* **1 = throwing away**, dumping *(informal)*, scrapping, removal, discarding, clearance, jettisoning, ejection, riddance, relinquishment
2 at your disposal = available, ready, to hand, accessible, convenient, handy, on hand, at hand, obtainable, on tap, expendable, at your fingertips, at your service, free for use, ready for use, consumable, spendable

dispose *vb* **1d dispose of someone = kill**, murder, destroy, do in *(slang)*, take out *(slang)*, execute, slaughter, dispatch, assassinate, slay, do away with, knock off *(slang)*, liquidate, neutralize, exterminate, take (someone's) life, bump off *(slang)*, wipe (someone) from the face of the earth *(informal)* **2 = arrange**, put, place, group, set, order, stand, range, settle, fix, rank, distribute, array

disposition *n* **1 = character**, nature, spirit, make-up, constitution, temper, temperament **2 = tendency**, inclination, propensity, habit, leaning, bent, bias, readiness, predisposition, proclivity, proneness **3 = arrangement**, grouping, ordering, organization, distribution, disposal, placement

dispute *n* **1 = disagreement**, conflict, argument, falling out, dissent, friction, strife, discord, altercation **2 = argument**, row, clash, controversy, disturbance, contention, feud, quarrel, brawl, squabble, wrangle, difference of opinion, tiff, dissension, shindig *(informal)*, shindy *(informal)*, bagarre *(French)* ▷*vb* **5 = contest**, question, challenge, deny, doubt, oppose, object to, contradict, rebut, impugn, controvert, call in *or* into question

disqualify *vb* **1 = ban**, rule out, prohibit, preclude, debar, declare ineligible, disentitle

disregard *vb* **1 = ignore**, discount, take no notice of, overlook, neglect, pass over, turn a blind eye to, disobey, laugh off, make light of, pay no attention to, pay no heed to, leave out of account, brush aside *or* away **OPPOSITE:** pay attention to ▷*n* **2 = ignoring**, neglect, contempt, indifference, negligence, disdain, disrespect, heedlessness

disrupt *vb* **= interrupt**, stop, upset, hold up, interfere with, unsettle, obstruct, cut short, intrude on, break up *or* into

dissatisfied *adj* **= discontented**, frustrated, unhappy, disappointed, fed up, disgruntled, not satisfied, unfulfilled, displeased, unsatisfied, ungratified **OPPOSITE:** satisfied

dissent *n* **3 = disagreement**, opposition, protest, resistance, refusal, objection, discord, demur, dissension, dissidence, nonconformity, remonstrance **OPPOSITE:** assent

dissident *n* **1 = protester**, rebel, dissenter, demonstrator, agitator, recusant, protest marcher ▷*adj* **2 = dissenting**, disagreeing, nonconformist, heterodox,

DICTIONARY

waste or squander **2** to scatter or break up
WORD ORIGIN Latin *dissipare* to disperse

dissipated *adj* showing signs of overindulgence in alcohol or other physical pleasures

dissipation *n* **1** the process of dissipating **2** unrestrained indulgence in physical pleasures

dissociate *vb* **-ating, -ated** **1 dissociate oneself from** to deny or break an association with (a person or organization) **2** to regard or treat as separate **dissociation** *n*

dissoluble *adj* ▸ same as **soluble** > **dissolubility** *n*
WORD ORIGIN Latin *dissolubilis*

dissolute *adj* leading an immoral life
WORD ORIGIN Latin *dissolutus* loose

dissolution *n* **1** the act of officially breaking up an organization or institution **2** the act of officially ending a formal agreement, such as a marriage **3** the formal ending of a meeting or assembly, such as a Parliament

dissolve ❶ *vb* **-solving, -solved** **1** to become or cause to become liquid; melt **2** to officially break up (an organization or institution) **3** to formally end: *the campaign started as soon as Parliament was dissolved last month* **4** to collapse emotionally: *she dissolved in loud tears* **5** *films, television* to fade out one scene and replace with another to make two scenes merge imperceptibly
WORD ORIGIN Latin *dissolvere* to make loose

dissonance *n* a lack of agreement or harmony between things: *this dissonance of colours* **dissonant** *adj*

dissuade *vb* **-suading, -suaded** to deter (someone) by persuasion from doing something or believing in something **dissuasion** *n*
WORD ORIGIN Latin *dissuadere*

dissyllable *or* **disyllable** *n* a word of two syllables **dissyllabic** *or* **disyllabic** *adj*

distaff *n* the rod on which flax is wound for spinning
WORD ORIGIN Old English *distæf*

distaff side *n* the female side of a family

distance ❶ *n* **1** the space between two points or places **2** the state of being apart **3** a distant place **4** remoteness in manner **5 the distance** the most distant part of the visible scene **6 go the distance a** *boxing* to complete a bout without being knocked out **b** to complete an assigned task or responsibility **7 keep one's distance** to maintain a reserved attitude to another person ▹ *vb* **-tancing, -tanced 8 distance oneself from** *or* **be distanced from** to separate oneself or be separated mentally from

distance learning *n* a teaching system involving video and written material for studying at home

distant ❶ *adj* **1** far-off; remote **2** far apart **3** separated by a specified distance: *five kilometres distant* **4** apart in relationship: *a distant cousin* **5** going to a faraway place **6** remote in manner; aloof **7** abstracted: *a distant look entered her eyes* **distantly** *adv*
WORD ORIGIN Latin *dis-* apart + *stare* to stand

distaste *n* a dislike of something offensive

distasteful *adj* unpleasant or offensive **distastefulness** *n*

Di Stéfano *n* **Alfredo** born 1926, Argentinian-born football player, who played for Argentina, Colombia, Spain, and Real Madrid

distemper[1] *n* a highly contagious viral disease that can affect young dogs
WORD ORIGIN Latin *dis-* apart + *temperare* to regulate

distemper[2] *n* **1** paint mixed with water, glue, etc. which is used for painting walls ▹ *vb* **2** to paint with distemper
WORD ORIGIN Latin *dis-* (intensive) + *temperare* to mingle

distend *vb* to expand by pressure from within; swell **distensible** *adj* **distension** *n*
WORD ORIGIN Latin *distendere*

distich (diss-stick) *n* *prosody* a unit of two verse lines
WORD ORIGIN Greek *di-* two + *stikhos* row, line

distil *or US* **distill** *vb* **-tilling, -tilled** **1** to subject to or obtain by distillation **2** to give off (a substance) in drops **3** to extract the essence of
WORD ORIGIN Latin *de-* down + *stillare* to drip

distillation *n* **1** the process of evaporating a liquid and condensing its vapour **2** Also: **distillate** a concentrated essence

distiller *n* a person or company that makes spirits

distillery *n, pl* **-eries** a place where alcoholic drinks are made by distillation

distinct ❶ *adj* **1** not the same; different: *these two areas produce wines with distinct characteristics* **2** clearly seen, heard, or recognized: *it is not possible to draw a distinct line between the two categories; there's a distinct smell of burning* **3** clear and definite: *there is a distinct possibility of rain* **4** obvious: *a distinct improvement* **distinctly** *adv*
WORD ORIGIN Latin *distinctus*

distinction ❶ *n* **1** the act of distinguishing or differentiating **2** a distinguishing feature **3** the state of being different or distinguishable **4** special honour, recognition, or fame **5** excellence of character **6** a symbol of honour or rank

THESAURUS

schismatic, dissentient

dissolve *vb* **1 = melt**, soften, thaw, flux, liquefy, deliquesce **2, 3 = end**, dismiss, suspend, axe *(informal)*, break up, wind up, overthrow, terminate, discontinue, dismantle, disband, disunite

distance *n* **1 = space**, length, extent, range, stretch, gap, interval, separation, span, width
4 = aloofness, reserve, detachment, restraint, indifference, stiffness, coolness, coldness, remoteness, frigidity, uninvolvement, standoffishness

distant *adj* **1 = far-off**, far, remote, removed, abroad, out-of-the-way, far-flung, faraway, outlying, afar
OPPOSITE: close
6 = reserved, cold, withdrawn, cool, formal, remote, stiff, restrained, detached, indifferent, aloof, unfriendly, reticent, haughty, unapproachable, standoffish
OPPOSITE: friendly
7 = faraway, blank, abstracted, vague, absorbed, distracted, unaware, musing, vacant, preoccupied, bemused, oblivious, dreamy, daydreaming, absent-minded, inattentive

distinct *adj* **1 = different**, individual, separate, disconnected, discrete, dissimilar, unconnected, unattached
OPPOSITE: similar
2 = striking, sharp, dramatic, stunning *(informal)*, outstanding, bold, noticeable, well-defined **3, 4 = definite**, marked, clear, decided, obvious, sharp, plain, apparent, patent, evident, black-and-white, manifest, noticeable, conspicuous, clear-cut, unmistakable, palpable, recognizable, unambiguous, observable, perceptible, appreciable
OPPOSITE: vague

distinction *n* **2 = feature**, quality, characteristic, name, mark, individuality, peculiarity, singularity, distinctiveness, particularity **3 = difference**, contrast, variation, differential, discrepancy, disparity, deviation, differentiation, fine line, distinctness, dissimilarity **4 = merit**, credit, honour, integrity, excellence, righteousness, rectitude, uprightness **5 = excellence**, note, quality, worth, account, rank, reputation, importance, consequence, fame, celebrity, merit, superiority, prominence, greatness, eminence, renown, repute

DICTIONARY

distinctive ❶ *adj* easily recognizable; characteristic **distinctively** *adv* **distinctiveness** *n*

distingué (diss-**tang**-gay) *adj* distinguished or noble
WORD ORIGIN French

distinguish ❶ *vb* **1** to make, show, or recognize a difference: *I have tried to distinguish between fact and theory* **2** to be a distinctive feature of: *what distinguishes the good teenage reader from the less competent one?* **3** to make out by hearing, seeing, or tasting: *she listened but could distinguish nothing except the urgency of their discussion* **4** **distinguish oneself** to make oneself noteworthy **distinguishable** *adj* **distinguishing** *adj*
WORD ORIGIN Latin *distinguere* to separate

distinguished ❶ *adj* **1** dignified in appearance or behaviour **2** highly respected: *a distinguished historian*

distort ❶ *vb* **1** to alter or misrepresent (facts) **2** to twist out of shape; deform **3** *electronics* to reproduce or amplify (a signal) inaccurately **distorted** *adj* **distortion** *n*
WORD ORIGIN Latin *distorquere* to turn different ways

distract ❶ *vb* **1** to draw (a person or his or her attention) away from something **2** to amuse or entertain
WORD ORIGIN Latin *distrahere* to pull in different directions

distracted ❶ *adj* unable to concentrate because one's mind is on other things

distraction ❶ *n* **1** something that diverts the attention **2** something that serves as an entertainment **3** mental turmoil

distrain *vb law* to seize (personal property) to enforce payment of a debt **distraint** *n*
WORD ORIGIN Latin *di-* apart + *stringere* to draw tight

distrait (diss-**tray**) *adj* absent-minded or abstracted
WORD ORIGIN French

distraught ❶ (diss-**trawt**) *adj* upset or agitated
WORD ORIGIN obsolete *distract*

distress ❶ *n* **1** extreme unhappiness or worry **2** great physical pain **3** financial trouble **4** **in distress** in dire need of help ▷ *vb* **5** to upset badly **distressing** *adj* **distressingly** *adv*
WORD ORIGIN Latin *districtus* divided in mind

distressed ❶ *adj* **1** much troubled; upset **2** in great physical pain **3** in financial difficulties **4** (of furniture or fabric) having signs of ageing artificially applied

distributary *n, pl* **-taries** one of several outlet streams draining a river, esp. on a delta

distribute ❶ *vb* **-uting, -uted 1** to hand out or deliver (leaflets, mail, etc.) **2** to share (something) among the members of a particular group
WORD ORIGIN Latin *distribuere*

distribution ❶ *n* **1** the delivering of leaflets, mail, etc. to individual people or organizations **2** the sharing out of something among a particular group **3** the arrangement or spread of anything over an area, space, or period of time: *the unequal distribution of wealth* **4** *commerce* the process of satisfying the demand for goods and services

distributive *adj* **1** of or relating to distribution **2** *maths* of the rule that the same result is produced when multiplication is performed on a set of numbers as when performed on the members of the set individually

distributor *n* **1** a wholesaler who distributes goods to retailers in a specific area **2** the device in a petrol engine that sends the electric current to the sparking plugs

district ❶ *n* **1** an area of land regarded as an administrative or geographical unit **2** an area which has recognizable or special features: *an upper-class residential district*
WORD ORIGIN Medieval Latin *districtus* area of jurisdiction

district court judge *n Austral & NZ* a judge presiding over a lower court

district nurse *n* (in Britain) a nurse who attends to patients in their homes within a particular district

distrust ❶ *vb* **1** to regard as untrustworthy ▷ *n* **2** a feeling of

THESAURUS

distinctive *adj* **= characteristic**, special, individual, specific, unique, typical, extraordinary, distinguishing, peculiar, singular, idiosyncratic **OPPOSITE:** ordinary

distinguish *vb* **1 = differentiate**, determine, separate, discriminate, decide, judge, discern, ascertain, tell the difference, make a distinction, tell apart, tell between **2 = characterize**, mark, separate, single out, individualize, set apart **3 = make out**, recognize, perceive, know, see, tell, pick out, discern

distinguished *adj* **2 = eminent**, great, important, noted, famous, celebrated, well-known, prominent, esteemed, acclaimed, notable, renowned, prestigious, elevated, big-time *(informal)*, famed, conspicuous, illustrious, major league *(informal)* **OPPOSITE:** unknown

distort *vb* **1 = misrepresent**, twist, bias, disguise, pervert, slant, colour, misinterpret, falsify, garble **2 = deform**, bend, twist, warp, buckle, mangle, mangulate *(Austral slang)*, disfigure, contort, gnarl, misshape, malform

distract *vb* **1 = divert**, sidetrack, draw away, turn aside, lead astray, draw *or* lead away from **2 = amuse**, occupy, entertain, beguile, engross

distracted *adj* **= agitated**, troubled, confused, puzzled, at sea, bewildered, bemused, confounded, perplexed, flustered, in a flap *(informal)*

distraction *n* **1 = disturbance**, interference, diversion, interruption **2 = entertainment**, recreation, amusement, diversion, pastime, divertissement, beguilement

distraught *adj* **= frantic**, wild, desperate, mad, anxious, distressed, raving, distracted, hysterical, worked-up, agitated, crazed, overwrought, out of your mind, at the end of your tether, wrought-up, beside yourself

distress *n* **1, 2 = suffering**, pain, worry, anxiety, torture, grief, misery, agony, sadness, discomfort, torment, sorrow, woe, anguish, heartache, affliction, desolation, wretchedness **3 = need**, suffering, trouble, trial, difficulties, poverty, misery, hard times, hardship, straits, misfortune, adversity, calamity, affliction, privation, destitution, ill-fortune, ill-luck, indigence ▷ *vb* **5 = upset**, worry, trouble, pain, wound, bother, disturb, dismay, grieve, torment, harass, afflict, harrow, agitate, sadden, perplex, disconcert, agonize, fluster, perturb, faze, throw (someone) off balance

distressed *adj* **1 = upset**, worried, troubled, anxious, distracted, tormented, distraught, afflicted, agitated, saddened, wretched **3 = poverty-stricken**, poor, impoverished, needy, destitute, indigent, down at heel, straitened, penurious

distribute *vb* **1a = hand out**, dispense, give out, dish out *(informal)*, disseminate, deal out, disburse, pass round **1b = circulate**, deliver, convey **2 = share**, give, deal, divide, assign, administer, allocate, dispose, dispense, allot, mete out, dole out, apportion, measure out

distribution *n* **1 = delivery**, mailing, transport, transportation, handling **2 = sharing**, division, assignment, rationing, allocation, partition, allotment, dispensation, apportionment **3 = spread**, organization, arrangement, location, placement, disposition

district *n* **1, 2 = area**, community, region, sector, quarter, ward, parish, neighbourhood, vicinity, locality, locale, neck of the woods *(informal)*

distrust *vb* **1 = suspect**, doubt, discredit, be wary of, wonder about, mistrust, disbelieve, be suspicious of, be sceptical of, misbelieve

DICTIONARY

suspicion or doubt **distrustful** *adj*
disturb ❶ *vb* **1** to intrude on; interrupt **2** to upset or worry **3** to disarrange; muddle **4** to inconvenience **disturbing** *adj* **disturbingly** *adv*
WORD ORIGIN Latin *disturbare*
disturbance ❶ *n* **1** an interruption or intrusion **2** an unruly outburst in public
disturbed ❶ *adj psychiatry* emotionally upset, troubled, or maladjusted
disunite *vb* **-niting, -nited** to cause disagreement among **disunion** *n* **disunity** *n*
disuse *n* the state of being neglected or no longer used; neglect
disused *adj* no longer used
disyllable *n* ▸ same as **dissyllable**
ditch ❶ *n* **1** a narrow channel dug in the earth for drainage or irrigation ▷ *vb* **2** *slang* to abandon or discard: *she ditched her boyfriend last month*
WORD ORIGIN Old English *dīc*
dither *vb* **1** *chiefly Brit & NZ* to be uncertain or indecisive ▷ *n* **2** *chiefly Brit* a state of indecision or agitation **ditherer** *n* **dithery** *adj*
WORD ORIGIN Middle English *didder*
dithyramb *n* (in ancient Greece) a passionate choral hymn in honour of Dionysus **dithyrambic** *adj*
WORD ORIGIN Greek *dithurambos*
ditto *n, pl* **-tos** **1** the above; the same: used in lists to avoid repetition, and represented by the mark (,,) placed under the thing repeated ▷ *adv* **2** in the same way
WORD ORIGIN Italian (dialect) *detto* said
ditty *n, pl* **-ties** a short simple song or poem
WORD ORIGIN Latin *dictare* to say repeatedly
ditzy *or* **ditsy** *adj* **ditzier, ditziest** *or* **ditsier, ditsiest** *slang* silly and scatterbrained
WORD ORIGIN perhaps from DOTTY + DIZZY
diuretic (die-yoor-**et**-ik) *n* a drug that increases the flow of urine
WORD ORIGIN Greek *dia-* through + *ourein* to urinate
diurnal (die-**urn**-al) *adj* **1** happening during the day or daily **2** (of animals) active during the day
WORD ORIGIN Latin *diurnus*
diva *n, pl* **-vas** *or* **-ve** a distinguished female singer; prima donna
WORD ORIGIN Latin: a goddess
divalent *adj chem* having two valencies or a valency of two **divalency** *n*
divan *n* **a** a low bed with a thick base under the mattress **b** a couch with no back or arms
WORD ORIGIN Turkish *dīvān*
dive ❶ *vb* **diving, dived** *or US* **dove, dived** **1** to plunge headfirst into water **2** (of a submarine or diver) to submerge under water **3** (of a bird or aircraft) to fly in a steep nose-down descending path **4** to move quickly in a specified direction: *he dived for the door* **5** **dive in** *or* **into** **a** to put (one's hand) quickly or forcefully (into) **b** to start doing (something) enthusiastically ▷ *n* **6** a headlong plunge into water **7** the act of diving **8** a steep nose-down descent of a bird or aircraft **9** *slang* a disreputable bar or club
WORD ORIGIN Old English *dӯfan*
dive bomber *n* a military aircraft designed to release bombs on a target during a dive **dive-bomb** *vb*
diver *n* **1** a person who works or explores underwater **2** a person who dives for sport **3** a large diving bird of northern oceans with a straight pointed bill and webbed feet
diverge *vb* **-verging, -verged** **1** to separate and go in different directions **2** to be at variance; differ: *the two books diverge in setting and in style* **3** to deviate (from a prescribed course) **divergence** *n* **divergent** *adj*
WORD ORIGIN Latin *dis-* apart + *vergere* to turn
diverse ❶ *adj* **1** having variety; assorted **2** different in kind
WORD ORIGIN Latin *diversus* turned in different directions
diversify ❶ *vb* **-fies, -fying, -fied** **1** to create different forms of; vary **2** (of an enterprise) to vary (products or operations) in order to expand or reduce the risk of loss **diversification** *n*
WORD ORIGIN Latin *diversus* different + *facere* to make
diversion ❶ *n* **1** *chiefly Brit* an official detour used by traffic when a main route is closed **2** something that distracts someone's attention or concentration **3** the act of diverting from a specified course **4** a pleasant or amusing pastime or activity **diversionary** *adj*
diversity ❶ *n* **1** the quality of being different or varied **2** a point of difference
divert ❶ *vb* **1** to change the course or direction of (traffic) **2** to distract the

d

THESAURUS

OPPOSITE: trust
▷ *n* **2 = suspicion**, question, doubt, disbelief, scepticism, mistrust, misgiving, qualm, wariness, lack of faith, dubiety OPPOSITE: trust
disturb *vb* **1, 4 = interrupt**, trouble, bother, startle, plague, disrupt, put out, interfere with, rouse, hassle, inconvenience, pester, intrude on, butt in on **2 = upset**, concern, worry, trouble, shake, excite, alarm, confuse, distress, distract, dismay, unsettle, agitate, ruffle, confound, unnerve, vex, fluster, perturb, derange, discompose OPPOSITE: calm **3 = muddle**, disorder, mix up, mess up, disorganize, jumble up, disarrange, muss *(US & Canad)*
disturbance *n* **1 = upset**, bother, disorder, confusion, distraction, intrusion, interruption, annoyance, agitation, hindrance, perturbation, derangement **2 = disorder**, bother *(informal)*, turmoil, riot, upheaval, fray, brawl, uproar, agitation, fracas, commotion, rumpus, tumult, hubbub, shindig *(informal)*, ruction *(informal)*, ruckus *(informal)*, shindy *(informal)*
disturbed *adj* **a** *(psychiatry)* **= unbalanced**, troubled, disordered, unstable, neurotic, upset, deranged, unsound, maladjusted OPPOSITE: balanced **b = worried**, concerned, troubled, upset, bothered, nervous, anxious, uneasy OPPOSITE: calm
ditch *n* **1 = channel**, drain, trench, dyke, furrow, gully, moat, watercourse ▷ *vb* **2a** *(slang)* **= get rid of**, dump *(informal)*, scrap, discard, dispose of, dispense with, jettison, throw out *or* overboard **2b** *(slang)* **= leave**, drop, abandon, dump *(informal)*, axe *(informal)*, get rid of, bin *(informal)*, chuck *(informal)*, forsake, jilt
dive *vb* **1 = plunge**, drop, jump, pitch, leap, duck, dip, descend, plummet **2 = go underwater**, submerge **3 = nose-dive**, fall, plunge, crash, pitch, swoop, plummet ▷ *n* **6 = plunge**, spring, jump, leap, dash, header *(informal)*, swoop, lunge, nose dive
diverse *adj* **1 = various**, mixed, varied, diversified, assorted, miscellaneous, several, sundry, motley, manifold, heterogeneous, of every description **2 = different**, contrasting, unlike, varying, differing, separate, distinct, disparate, discrete, dissimilar, divergent, discrepant
diversify *vb* **1 = vary**, change, expand, transform, alter, spread out, branch out
diversion *n* **1** *(chiefly Brit)* **= detour**, deviation, circuitous route, roundabout way, indirect course **2 = distraction**, deviation, deflection, digression **3** *(chiefly Brit)* **= deviation**, departure, straying, divergence, digression **4 = pastime**, play, game, sport, delight, pleasure, entertainment, hobby, relaxation, recreation, enjoyment, distraction, amusement, gratification, divertissement, beguilement
diversity *n* **1 = difference**, diversification, variety, divergence, multiplicity, heterogeneity, variegation, diverseness
divert *vb* **1 = redirect**, switch, avert, deflect, deviate, sidetrack, turn aside

DICTIONARY

attention of **3** to entertain or amuse
WORD ORIGIN Latin *divertere* to turn aside

diverticulitis *n* inflammation of pouches in the wall of the colon, causing lower abdominal pain
WORD ORIGIN Latin *deverticulum* path, track

divertimento *n, pl* **-ti** a piece of entertaining music in several movements
WORD ORIGIN Italian

divest *vb* **1** to strip (of clothes) **2** to deprive of a role, function, or quality: *the chairman felt duty-bound to stay with the company after it was divested of all its aviation interests*
WORD ORIGIN earlier *devest*

divide ❶ *vb* **-viding, -vided 1** to separate into parts **2** to share or be shared out in parts **3** to disagree or cause to disagree: *experts are divided over the plan* **4** to keep apart or be a boundary between **5** to categorize or classify **6** to calculate how many times one number can be contained in another ▹*n* **7** a division or split **8** *chiefly US & Canad* an area of high ground separating drainage basins
WORD ORIGIN Latin *dividere* to force apart

dividend ❶ *n* **1** a portion of a company's profits paid to its shareholders **2** an extra benefit: *Saudi progressives saw a dividend to the crisis* **3** *maths* a number to be divided by another number
WORD ORIGIN Latin *dividendum* what is to be divided

divider *n* a screen placed so as to divide a room into separate areas

dividers *pl n* compasses with two pointed arms, used for measuring or dividing lines

divination *n* the art of discovering future events as though by supernatural powers

divine ❶ *adj* **1** of God or a god **2** godlike **3** *informal* splendid or perfect ▹*n* **4** a priest who is learned in theology ▹*vb* **-vining, -vined 5** to discover (something) by intuition or guessing **divinely** *adv* **diviner** *n*
WORD ORIGIN Latin *divus* a god

diving bell *n* a diving apparatus with an open bottom, supplied with compressed air from above

diving board *n* a platform from which swimmers may dive

diving suit *n* a waterproof suit used for diving with a detachable helmet and an air supply

divining rod *n* a forked twig said to move when held over ground in which water or metal is to be found

divinity *n, pl* **-ties 1** the study of religion **2** a god or goddess **3** the state of being divine

divisible *adj* capable of being divided **divisibility** *n*

division ❶ *n* **1** the separation of something into two or more distinct parts **2** the act of dividing or sharing out **3** one of the parts into which something is divided **4** the mathematical operation of dividing **5** a difference of opinion **6** a part of an organization that has been made into a unit for administrative or other reasons **7** a formal vote in Parliament **8** one of the groups of teams that make up a football or other sports league **9** *army* a major formation containing the necessary arms to sustain independent combat **10** *biol* one of the major groups into which the plant kingdom is divided, corresponding to a phylum **divisional** *adj*
WORD ORIGIN Latin *dividere* to divide

division sign *n* the symbol ÷, placed between two numbers to indicate that the first number should be divided by the second, as in 12 ÷ 6 = 2

divisive (div-vice-iv) *adj* tending to cause disagreement: *he played an important role in defusing potentially divisive issues*

divisor *n* a number to be divided into another number

divorce ❶ *n* **1** the legal ending of a marriage **2** a separation, esp. one that is permanent ▹*vb* **-vorcing, -vorced 3** to separate or be separated by divorce **4** to remove or separate
WORD ORIGIN Latin *divertere* to separate

divorcee *or masc* **divorcé** *n* a person who is divorced

divot *n* a small piece of turf

divulge *vb* **-vulging, -vulged** to make known: *I am not permitted to divulge his name* **divulgence** *n*
WORD ORIGIN Latin *divulgare*

divvy[1] *vb* **-vies, -vying, -vied ▪ divvy up** *informal* to divide and share

divvy[2] *n, pl* **-vies** *Brit dialect* a stupid person

Diwali (duh-wah-lee) *n* an annual Hindu festival honouring Lakshmi, the goddess of wealth

Dixie *n* the southern states of the US. Also called: **Dixieland**
WORD ORIGIN origin unknown

Dixon *n* **Willie**, full name *William James Dixon*. 1915–92, US blues musician, songwriter, and record producer, whose songs have been recorded by many other artists

DIY *or* **d.i.y.** *Brit, Austral & NZ* do-it-yourself

dizzy ❶ *adj* **-zier, -ziest 1** feeling giddy **2** unable to think clearly; confused **3** tending to cause giddiness or confusion ▹*vb* **-zies, -zying, -zied 4** to cause to feel giddy or confused **dizzily** *adv* **dizziness** *n*
WORD ORIGIN Old English *dysig* silly

DJ *or* **dj 1** disc jockey **2** *Brit* dinner jacket

Djilas *n* **Milovan** 1911–95, Yugoslav

THESAURUS

2 = distract, shift, deflect, detract, sidetrack, lead astray, draw *or* lead away from **3 = entertain**, delight, amuse, please, charm, gratify, beguile, regale

divide *vb* **1 = separate**, part, split, cut (up), sever, shear, segregate, cleave, subdivide, bisect, sunder **OPPOSITE:** join **2 = share**, distribute, allocate, portion, dispense, allot, mete, dole out, apportion, deal out, measure out, divvy (up) *(informal)* **3 = split**, break up, alienate, embroil, come between, disunite, estrange, sow dissension, cause to disagree, set at variance *or* odds, set *or* pit against one another

dividend *n* **1 = bonus**, share, cut *(informal)*, gain, extra, plus, portion, divvy *(informal)*

divine *adj* **1 = heavenly**, spiritual, holy, immortal, supernatural, celestial, angelic, superhuman, godlike, cherubic, seraphic, supernal *(literary)*, paradisaical **3** *(informal)* **= wonderful**, perfect, beautiful, excellent, lovely, stunning *(informal)*, glorious, marvellous, splendid, gorgeous, delightful, exquisite, radiant, superlative, ravishing ▹*vb* **5 = guess**, understand, suppose, suspect, perceive, discern, infer, deduce, apprehend, conjecture, surmise, foretell, intuit, prognosticate

division *n* **1 = separation**, dividing, splitting up, detaching, partition, cutting up, bisection **2 = sharing**, distribution, assignment, rationing, allocation, allotment, apportionment **3 = part**, bit, piece, section, sector, class, category, segment, portion, fraction, compartment **5 = disagreement**, split, breach, feud, rift, rupture, abyss, chasm, variance, discord, difference of opinion, estrangement, disunion **OPPOSITE:** unity **6 = department**, group, head, sector, branch, subdivision

divorce *n* **1 = separation**, split, break-up, parting, split-up, rift, dissolution, severance, estrangement, annulment, decree nisi, disunion ▹*vb* **3 = split up**, separate, part company, annul your marriage, dissolve your marriage

dizzy *adj* **1 = giddy**, faint, light-headed, swimming, reeling, staggering, shaky, wobbly, off balance, unsteady, vertiginous, woozy *(informal)*, weak at the knees **2 = confused**, dazzled, at sea, bewildered, muddled, bemused, dazed, disorientated, befuddled,

politician and writer; vice president (1953–54): imprisoned (1956–61, 1962–66) for his criticism of the communist system

djinni *or* **djinny** *n, pl* **djinn** ▸ same as **jinni**

dl decilitre(s)

DLitt *or* **DLit** **1** Doctor of Letters **2** Doctor of Literature
WORD ORIGIN Latin *Doctor Litterarum*

DLL *computers* dynamic link library: a set of programs that can be activated and then discarded by other programs

dm decimetre(s)

DM Deutschmark

DMus Doctor of Music

DNA deoxyribonucleic acid, the main constituent of the chromosomes of all organisms

DNA fingerprinting *or* **DNA profiling** *n* ▸ same as **genetic fingerprinting**

D-notice *n Austral & Brit* an official notice sent to newspapers prohibiting the publication of certain security information
WORD ORIGIN from their administrative classification letter

do[1] *vb* **does, doing, did, done** **1** to perform or complete (a deed or action): *we do a fair amount of entertaining* **2** to be adequate: *it's not what I wanted but it will have to do* **3** to provide: *this hotel only does bed and breakfast* **4** to make tidy or elegant: *he watched her do her hair* **5** to improve: *that style does nothing for you* **6** to find an answer to (a problem or puzzle) **7** to conduct oneself: *do as you want* **8** to cause or produce: *herbal teas have active ingredients that can do good* **9** to give or grant: *do me a favour* **10** to work at as a course of study or a job **11** to mimic **12** to achieve a particular speed, amount, or rate: *this computer system can do 40 different cross checks; this car can do sixty miles to the gallon* **13** **a** used to form questions: *do you like it?* **b** used to intensify positive statements and commands: *tensions do exist* **c** used to form negative statements or commands: *do not talk while I'm talking!* **d** used to replace an earlier verb: *he drinks much more than I do* **14** *informal* to visit (a place) as a tourist: *we plan to do the States this year* **15** *slang* to serve (a period of time) as a prison sentence **16** *informal* to cheat or rob: *I was done out of ten pounds* **17** *slang* **a** to arrest **b** to convict of a crime: *he was done for 3 years for housebreaking* **18** *slang chiefly Brit* to assault **19** *slang* to take or use (drugs) **20** **make do** to manage with whatever is available ▷ *n, pl* **dos** *or* **do's** **21** *informal chiefly Brit & NZ* a party or other social event **22** **do's and don'ts** *informal* rules ▸ See also **do away with, do by**, etc.
WORD ORIGIN Old English *dōn*

do[2] *n, pl* **dos** *music* ▸ same as **doh**

do away with *vb* to get rid of (someone or something)

Dobbyn *n* **Dave** born 1957, New Zealand singer and songwriter; member of Th'Dudes (1976–80) with whom he had the hit singles "Be Mine Tonight" (1979) and "Bliss" (1979); founder of DD Smash (1981–85) with whom he released the album *Cool Bananas* (1982); solo albums include: *Loyal* (1986) and *Footrot Flats: The Dog's Tale* (1986)

Dobell *n* Sir **William** 1899–1970, Australian portrait and landscape painter. Awarded the Archibald prize (1943) for his famous painting of *Joshua Smith* which resulted in a heated clash between the conservatives and the moderns and led to a lawsuit. His other works include *The Cypriot* (1940), *The Billy Boy* (1943), and *Portrait of a strapper* (1941)

Doberman pinscher *or* **Doberman** *n* a large dog with a glossy black-and-tan coat
WORD ORIGIN after L. *Dobermann*, dog breeder

dob in *vb* **dobbing, dobbed** *Austral & NZ informal* **1** to inform against **2** to contribute to a fund

do by *vb* to treat in the manner specified: *he felt badly done by*

Dobzhansky *n* **Theodosius** 1900–75, US biologist, born in Russia, noted for work on evolution and genetic variation

doc *n informal* ▸ same as **doctor**

DOC (in New Zealand) Department of Conservation

Docherty *n* **Pete** born 1979, English rock musician and songwriter; member of The Libertines (1997–2004) and Babyshambles (from 2005)

docile *adj* (of a person or animal) easily controlled **docilely** *adv* **docility** *n*
WORD ORIGIN Latin *docilis* easily taught

dock[1] *n* **1** an enclosed area of water where ships are loaded, unloaded, or repaired **2** a wharf or pier ▷ *vb* **3** to moor or be moored at a dock **4** to link (two spacecraft) or (of two spacecraft) to be linked together in space
WORD ORIGIN Middle Dutch *docke*

dock[2] *vb* **1** to deduct (an amount) from (a person's wages) **2** to remove part of (an animal's tail) by cutting through the bone
WORD ORIGIN Middle English *dok*

dock[3] *n* an enclosed space in a court of law where the accused person sits or stands
WORD ORIGIN Flemish *dok* sty

dock[4] *n* a weed with broad leaves
WORD ORIGIN Old English *docce*

docker *n Brit* a person employed to load and unload ships

docket *n* **1** *chiefly Brit* a label on a package or other delivery, stating contents, delivery instructions, etc. ▷ *vb* **-eting, -eted** **2** to fix a docket to (a package or other delivery)
WORD ORIGIN origin unknown

dockyard *n* a place where ships are built or repaired

Doc Martens *pl n trademark* a brand of lace-up boots with thick lightweight resistant soles

doctor *n* **1** a person licensed to practise medicine **2** a person who has been awarded a doctorate **3** *chiefly US & Canad* a person licensed to practise dentistry or veterinary medicine ▷ *vb* **4** to change in order to deceive: *she confessed to having doctored the figures* **5** to poison or drug (food or drink) **6** to castrate (an

THESAURUS

light-headed, punch-drunk, fuddled

do[1] *vb* **1 = perform**, work, achieve, carry out, produce, effect, complete, conclude, undertake, accomplish, execute, discharge, pull off, transact **2 = be adequate**, be enough, be sufficient, answer, serve, suit, content, satisfy, suffice, be of use, pass muster, cut the mustard, fill the bill *(informal)*, meet requirements **6 = solve**, work out, resolve, figure out, decode, decipher, puzzle out ▷ *n* **21** *(informal, chiefly Brit & NZ)* **= party**, gathering, function, social, event, affair, at-home, occasion, celebration, reception, bash *(informal)*, rave *(Brit slang)*, get-together *(informal)*, festivity, knees-up *(Brit informal)*, beano *(Brit slang)*, social gathering, shindig *(informal)*, soirée, rave-up *(Brit slang)*, hooley *or* hoolie *(chiefly Irish & NZ)*

do away with **= get rid of**, remove, eliminate, axe *(informal)*, abolish, junk *(informal)*, pull, chuck *(informal)*, discard, put an end to, dispense with, discontinue, put paid to, pull the plug on

dock[1] *n* **1, 2 = port**, haven, harbour, pier, wharf, quay, waterfront, anchorage ▷ *vb* **3 = moor**, land, anchor, put in, tie up, berth, drop anchor **4** *(of a spacecraft)* **= link up**, unite, join, couple, rendezvous, hook up

dock[2] *vb* **1 = deduct**, subtract **2 = cut off**, crop, clip, shorten, curtail, cut short

doctor *n* **1 = physician**, medic *(informal)*, general practitioner, medical practitioner, G.P. ▷ *vb* **4 = change**, alter, interfere with, disguise, pervert, fudge, tamper with, tinker with, misrepresent, falsify, meddle with, mess about with **5 = add to**, spike, cut, mix something with something, dilute, water down, adulterate

DICTIONARY

animal) **doctoral** *adj*
WORD ORIGIN Latin: teacher
doctorate *n* the highest academic degree in any field of knowledge
doctrinaire *adj* stubbornly insistent on the application of a theory without regard to practicality
doctrine ● (**dock**-trin) *n* **1** a body of teachings of a religious, political, or philosophical group **2** a principle or body of principles that is taught or advocated **doctrinal** *adj*
WORD ORIGIN Latin *doctrina* teaching
docudrama *n* a film or television programme based on true events, presented in a dramatized form
document ● *n* **1** a piece of paper that provides an official record of something ▷ *vb* **2** to record or report (something) in detail **3** to support (a claim) with evidence
WORD ORIGIN Latin *documentum* a lesson
documentary *n, pl* **-ries 1** a film or television programme presenting the facts about a particular subject ▷ *adj* **2** of or based on documents: *vital documentary evidence has been found*
documentation *n* documents supplied as proof or evidence of something
docu-soap *n* a television documentary series presenting the lives of the people filmed as entertainment
Dodd *n* **C**(**harles**) **H**(**arold**) 1884–1973, British New Testament scholar. His works include *The Parables of the Kingdom* (1935)
dodder *vb* to move unsteadily
dodderer *n* **doddery** *adj*
WORD ORIGIN variant of earlier *dadder*
doddle *n Brit, Austral & NZ informal* something easily accomplished: *the test turned out to be a doddle*
WORD ORIGIN origin unknown
dodecagon (doe-**deck**-a-gon) *n* a polygon with twelve sides
WORD ORIGIN Greek *dōdeka* twelve + *gōnia* angle
dodecahedron (doe-deck-a-**heed**-ron) *n* a solid figure with twelve plane faces
dodge ● *vb* **dodging, dodged 1** to avoid being hit, caught, or seen by moving suddenly **2** to evade by cleverness or trickery: *the Government will not be able to dodge the issue* ▷ *n* **3** a cunning and deceitful trick
WORD ORIGIN origin unknown
Dodgem *n trademark* a small electric car driven and bumped against similar cars in a rink at a funfair
dodger *n* a person who evades a duty or obligation
Dodgson *n* **Charles Lutwidge** the real name of Lewis Carroll ▸ See **Carroll**
dodgy ● *adj* **dodgier, dodgiest** *Brit, Austral, & NZ informal* **1** dangerous, risky, or unreliable: *he's in a very dodgy political position* **2** untrustworthy: *they considered him a very dodgy character*
dodo *n, pl* **dodos** *or* **dodoes 1** a large extinct bird that could not fly **2 as dead as a dodo** no longer existing
WORD ORIGIN Portuguese *duodo* stupid
do down *vb* to belittle or humiliate: *the moderate constructionist does not wish to do science down*
doe *n, pl* **does** *or* **doe** the female of the deer, hare, or rabbit
WORD ORIGIN Old English *dā*
DOE (in Britain) Department of the Environment
doek (rhymes with **book**) *n S African informal* a square of cloth worn on the head by women
WORD ORIGIN Afrikaans
Doenitz *n* a variant spelling of **Dönitz**
doer *n* an active or energetic person
does *vb* ▸ third person singular of the present tense of **do**[1]
doff *vb* to take off or lift (one's hat) in salutation
WORD ORIGIN Old English *dōn of*
do for *vb informal* **1** to cause the ruin, death, or defeat of: *I'm done for if this error comes to light* **2** to do housework for **3 do well for oneself** to thrive or succeed
dog ● *n* **1** a domesticated canine mammal occurring in many different breeds **2** any other member of the dog family, such as the dingo or coyote ▸ Related adjective: **canine 3** the male of animals of the dog family **4** *informal* a person: *you lucky dog!* **5** *US & Canad informal* something unsatisfactory or inferior **6 a dog's life** a wretched existence **7 dog eat dog** ruthless competition **8 like a dog's dinner** dressed smartly and ostentatiously ▷ *vb* **dogging, dogged 9** to follow (someone) closely **10** to trouble: *dogged by ill health* ▸ See also **dogs**
WORD ORIGIN Old English *docga*
dog box *n Austral & NZ informal* ▸ same as **doghouse**
dogcart *n* a light horse-drawn two-wheeled cart
dog collar *n* **1** a collar for a dog **2** *informal* a clerical collar
dog days *pl n Brit, Austral & NZ* the hottest period of the summer
WORD ORIGIN in ancient times reckoned from the heliacal rising of the Dog Star
doge (doje) *n* (formerly) the chief magistrate of Venice or Genoa
WORD ORIGIN Latin *dux* leader
dog-eared *adj* **1** (of a book) having pages folded down at the corner **2** shabby or worn
dog-end *n Brit, Austral & NZ informal* a cigarette end
dogfight *n* **1** close-quarters combat between fighter aircraft **2** any rough fight
dogfish *n, pl* **-fish** *or* **-fishes** a small shark
dogged ● (**dog**-gid) *adj* obstinately determined **doggedly** *adv* **doggedness** *n*
doggerel *n* poorly written, usually comic, verse
WORD ORIGIN Middle English *dogerel* worthless
doggo *adv* **lie doggo** *informal* to hide and keep quiet
WORD ORIGIN probably from *dog*
doggy *or* **doggie** *n, pl* **-gies 1** ▸ a child's word for a **dog** ▷ *adj* **-gier,**

THESAURUS

doctrine *n* **1, 2 = teaching**, principle, belief, opinion, article, concept, conviction, canon, creed, dogma, tenet, precept, article of faith, kaupapa *(NZ)*
document *n* **1 = paper**, form, certificate, report, record, testimonial, authorization, legal form ▷ *vb* **2, 3 = support**, back up, certify, verify, detail, instance, validate, substantiate, corroborate, authenticate, give weight to, particularize
dodge *vb* **1 = duck**, dart, swerve, sidestep, shoot, shift, turn aside, body-swerve *(Scot)* **2a = evade**, avoid, escape, get away from, elude, body-swerve *(Scot)*, slip through the net of **2b = avoid**, hedge, parry, get out of, evade, shirk ▷ *n* **3 = trick**, scheme, ploy, trap, device, fraud, con *(slang)*, manoeuvre, deception, scam *(slang)*, gimmick, hoax, wheeze *(Brit slang)*, deceit, ruse, artifice, subterfuge, canard, feint, stratagem, contrivance, machination, fastie *(Austral slang)*
dodgy *adj* **1** *(Brit, Austral & NZ informal)* **= risky**, difficult, tricky, dangerous, delicate, uncertain, problematic(al), unreliable, dicky *(Brit informal)*, dicey *(informal, chiefly Brit)*, ticklish, chancy *(informal)*, shonky *(Austral & NZ informal)*
dog *n* **1 = hound**, canine, bitch, puppy, pup, mongrel, tyke, mutt *(slang)*, pooch *(slang)*, cur, man's best friend, kuri *or* goorie *(NZ)*, brak *(S African)* ▸ *related adjective:* canine ▸ *name of female:* bitch ▸ *name of young:* pup, puppy ▷ *vb* **9 = pursue**, follow, track, chase, shadow, harry, tail *(informal)*, trail, hound, stalk, go after, give chase to **10 = plague**, follow, trouble, haunt, hound, torment, afflict
dogged *adj* **= determined**, steady, persistent, stubborn, firm, staunch, persevering, resolute, single-minded, tenacious, steadfast, unyielding, obstinate, indefatigable, immovable, stiff-necked,

DICTIONARY

-giest 2 of or like a dog 3 fond of dogs: *I suppose dogs are all right but doggy folk can be real bores*
doggy bag *n* a bag in which leftovers from a meal may be taken away, supposedly for the diner's dog
doghouse *n* 1 *US & Canad* a kennel 2 **in the doghouse** *informal* in disfavour
dogie, dogy *or* **dogey** (dohg-ee) *n, pl* **-gies** *or* **-geys** *US & Canad* a motherless calf
WORD ORIGIN from *dough-guts,* because they were fed on flour-and-water paste
dog in the manger *n* a person who prevents others from using something he has no use for
dogleg *n* a sharp bend
dogma *n* a doctrine or system of doctrines proclaimed by authority as true
WORD ORIGIN Greek: opinion
dogmatic *adj* habitually stating one's opinions in a forceful or arrogant manner **dogmatically** *adv* **dogmatism** *n*
do-gooder *n informal* a well-intentioned but naive or impractical person
dog paddle *n* a swimming stroke in which the hands are paddled in imitation of a swimming dog. Also called: **doggy paddle**
dogs *pl n* 1 **the dogs** *Austral & Brit informal* greyhound racing 2 **go to the dogs** *informal* to go to ruin physically or morally 3 **let sleeping dogs lie** to leave things undisturbed
dogsbody *n, pl* **-bodies** *informal* a person who carries out boring or unimportant tasks for others
dog-tired *adj informal* exhausted
dogwatch *n* either of two watches aboard ship, from four to six pm or from six to eight pm
doh *or* **do** *n music* (in tonic sol-fa) the first note of any ascending major scale
Dohnányi *n* **Ernö** or **Ernst von** 1877–1960, Hungarian pianist and composer whose works include *Variations on a Nursery Theme* (1913) for piano and orchestra
doily *or* **doyley** *n, pl* **-lies** *or* **-leys** a decorative lacelike paper mat laid on a plate
WORD ORIGIN after *Doily,* a London draper
do in *vb slang* 1 to kill 2 to exhaust
doings *pl n* 1 deeds or actions: *her brother's doings upset her terribly* ▷ *n* 2 *informal* anything of which the name is not known or is left unsaid: *do you have the doings to open this?*
Doisy *n* **Edward Adelbert** 1893–1986, US biochemist. He discovered (1939) the nature of vitamin K and shared a Nobel prize for medicine with Carl Dam (1943)
do-it-yourself *n* the practice of constructing and repairing things oneself
Dolby *n trademark* a system used in tape recorders which reduces noise level on recorded or broadcast sound
doldrums *n* **the doldrums** 1 **a** a feeling of depression **b** a state of inactivity 2 a belt of sea along the equator noted for absence of winds
WORD ORIGIN probably from Old English *dol* dull
dole ❶ *n* 1 **the dole** *Brit, Austral & NZ informal* money received from the state while unemployed 2 **on the dole** *Brit, Austral & NZ informal* receiving benefit while unemployed ▷ *vb* **doling, doled** 3 **dole out** to distribute in small quantities
WORD ORIGIN Old English *dāl* share
dole bludger *n Austral & NZ informal* a person who chooses to live off unemployment benefit
doleful *adj* dreary or mournful **dolefully** *adv* **dolefulness** *n*
WORD ORIGIN from Latin *dolere* to lament
Dolin *n* Sir **Anton**, real name *Sydney Healey-Kay*. 1904–83, British ballet dancer and choreographer: with Alicia Markova he founded (1949) the London Festival Ballet
D'Oliviera *n* **Basil** (**Lewis**) born 1931, South African cricketer, who played for Worcestershire and England
doll *n* 1 a small model of a human being, used as a toy 2 *slang* a pretty girl or young woman
WORD ORIGIN probably from *Doll,* pet name for *Dorothy*
dollar *n* the standard monetary unit of various countries
WORD ORIGIN Low German *daler*
Dollfuss *n* **Engelbert** 1892–1934, Austrian statesman, chancellor (1932–34), who was assassinated by Austrian Nazis
dollop *n informal* an amount of food served in a lump: *he shook the bottle and added a large dollop of ketchup*
WORD ORIGIN origin unknown
doll up *vb slang* **get dolled up** to dress (oneself) in a stylish or showy manner
dolly *n, pl* **-lies** 1 ▸ a child's word for a **doll** (sense 1) 2 *films, television* a wheeled support on which a camera may be mounted 3 Also called: **dolly bird** *slang chiefly Brit* an attractive and fashionable girl
dolman sleeve *n* a sleeve that is very wide at the armhole and tapers to a tight wrist
WORD ORIGIN Turkish *dolaman* a winding round
dolmen *n* a prehistoric monument consisting of a horizontal stone supported by vertical stones, thought to be a tomb
WORD ORIGIN French
Dolmetsch *n* **Arnold** 1858–1940, British musician, born in France. He contributed greatly to the revival of interest in early music and instruments
dolomite *n* a mineral consisting of calcium magnesium carbonate
WORD ORIGIN after Déodat de *Dolomieu,* mineralogist
dolphin *n* a sea mammal of the whale family, with a long pointed snout
WORD ORIGIN Greek *delphis*
dolphinarium *n* an aquarium for dolphins, esp. one in which they give public displays
dolt *n* a stupid person **doltish** *adj*
WORD ORIGIN probably related to Old English *dol* stupid
Domagk *n* **Gerhard** 1895–1964, German biochemist: Nobel prize for medicine (1939) for isolating sulphanilamide for treating bacterial infections
domain *n* 1 a particular area of activity or interest 2 land under one ruler or government 3 *computers* a group of computers that have the same suffix in their names on the internet, specifying the country, type of institution, etc. where they are located 4 *NZ* a public park
WORD ORIGIN French *domaine*
dome *n* 1 a rounded roof built on a circular base 2 something shaped like this
WORD ORIGIN Latin *domus* house
domed *adj* shaped like a dome
Domenichino *n* full name **Domenico Zampieri** 1581–1641, Italian Baroque painter, noted for his frescoes and the altarpiece *Last Communion of St Jerome* (1614)
Domenico Veneziano *n* died 1461, Italian painter, noted for the St Lucy Altarpiece
domestic ❶ *adj* 1 of one's own country or a specific country: *the domestic economy was generally better* 2 of the home or family 3 enjoying

d

THESAURUS

unshakable, unflagging, pertinacious **OPPOSITE:** irresolute
dole *n* 3 **dole something out** = **give out**, share, deal out, distribute, divide, assign, administer, allocate, hand out, dispense, allot, mete, apportion
domestic *adj* 1 = **home**, internal, native, indigenous, not foreign 2 = **household**, home, family, private, domiciliary 3 = **home-loving**, homely, housewifely, stay-at-home, domesticated 5 = **domesticated**, trained, tame, house, pet, house-trained ▷ *n* 6 = **servant**, help, maid, woman (*informal*), daily, char (*informal*), charwoman, daily help

DICTIONARY

home or family life: *she was never a very domestic sort of person* **4** intended for use in the home: *the kitchen was equipped with all the latest domestic appliances* **5** (of an animal) bred or kept as a pet or for the supply of food ▷*n* **6** a household servant
domestically *adv*
WORD ORIGIN Latin *domesticus* belonging to the house

domesticate *vb* **-cating, -cated 1** to bring or keep (wild animals or plants) under control or cultivation **2** to accustom (someone) to home life **domestication** *n*

domesticity *n, pl* **-ties 1** home life **2** devotion to home life

domestic science *n* the study of cooking, needlework, and other household skills

Domett *n* **Alfred** 1811–87, New Zealand poet, colonial administrator, and statesman, born in England: prime minister of New Zealand (1862–63)

domicile (**dom**-miss-ile) *n* **1** *formal* a person's regular dwelling place **2** *law* the country in which a person has his or her permanent legal residence **domiciliary** *adj*
WORD ORIGIN Latin *domus* house

domiciled *adj* living in a particular place: *the holding company was domiciled in Bermuda*

dominant ❶ *adj* **1** having control, authority, or influence: *a dominant leader* **2** main or chief: *coal is still, worldwide, the dominant fuel* **3** *genetics* (in a pair of genes) designating the gene that produces a particular character in an organism
dominance *n*

dominate ❶ *vb* **-nating, -nated 1** to control or govern **2** to tower above (surroundings): *the building had been designed to dominate the city skyscape* **3** to predominate in **dominating** *adj*
domination *n*
WORD ORIGIN Latin *dominari* to be lord over

dominee (**doom**-in-nee) *n S African* a minister of the Dutch Reformed Church
WORD ORIGIN Dutch, from Latin *dominus* master

domineering *adj* acting arrogantly or tyrannically
WORD ORIGIN Dutch *domineren*

Domingo *n* **Placido** born 1941, Spanish operatic tenor

Dominican *n* **1** a friar or nun of the Christian order founded by Saint Dominic ▷*adj* **2** of the Dominican order

dominion *n* **1** control or authority **2** the land governed by one ruler or government **3** (formerly) a self-governing division of the British Empire
WORD ORIGIN Latin *dominium* ownership

domino¹ *n, pl* **-noes** a small rectangular block marked with dots, used in dominoes
WORD ORIGIN Italian, perhaps from *domino!* master!, said by the winner

domino² *n, pl* **-noes** *or* **-nos** a large hooded cloak worn with an eye mask at a masquerade
WORD ORIGIN Latin *dominus* lord, master

Domino *n* **Fats** real name *Antoine Domino* born 1928, US rhythm-and-blues and rock-and-roll pianist, singer, and songwriter. His singles include "Ain't that a Shame" (1955) and "Blueberry Hill" (1956)

dominoes *n* a game in which dominoes with matching halves are laid together

Domitian *n* full name *Titus Flavius Domitianus*. 51–96 AD, Roman emperor (81–96): instigated a reign of terror (93); assassinated

don¹ ❶ *vb* **donning, donned** to put on (clothing)
WORD ORIGIN Middle English

don² *n* **1** *Brit* a member of the teaching staff at a university or college **2** a Spanish gentleman or nobleman **3** (in the Mafia) the head of a family
WORD ORIGIN Latin *dominus* lord

Donald *n* ?1031–1100, king of Scotland (1093–94; 1094–97)

donate ❶ *vb* **-nating, -nated** to give (something) to a charity or other organization

donation ❶ *n* **1** the act of donating **2** a contribution to a charity or other organization
WORD ORIGIN Latin *donum* gift

Donatus *n* **1 Auelius**. 4th century AD, Latin grammarian, who taught Saint Jerome; his textbook *Ars Grammatica* was used throughout the Middle Ages **2** 4th century AD, bishop of Carthage; leader of the Donatists, a heretical Christian sect originating in N Africa in 311 AD

donder *S African slang vb* **1** to beat (someone) up ▷*n* **2** a wretch; swine
WORD ORIGIN Dutch *donderen* to swear, bully

done *vb* **1** ▸the past participle of **do¹** ▷*interj* **2** an expression of agreement: *£60 seems reasonable, done!* ▷*adj* **3** (of a task) completed **4** (of food) cooked enough **5** used up: *the milk is done* **6** *Brit, Austral & NZ* socially acceptable: *the done thing* **7** *informal* cheated or tricked **8 done in** *or* **up** *informal* exhausted

doner kebab *n* a dish of grilled minced lamb, served in a split slice of unleavened bread
WORD ORIGIN Turkish *döner* rotating

dongle *n computers* **1** a plug-in device that allows a computer user to access the internet via mobile broadband **2** an electronic device that accompanies software to prevent the unauthorized copying of programs

Dönitz *or* **Doenitz** *n* **Karl** (karl) 1891–1980, German admiral; commander in chief of the German navy (1943–45); as head of state after Hitler's death he surrendered to the Allies (May 7, 1945)

Donizetti *n* **Gaetano** 1797–1848, Italian operatic composer: his works include *Lucia di Lammermoor* (1835), *La Fille du régiment* (1840), and *Don Pasquale* (1843)

donjon *n* the heavily fortified central tower of a castle
WORD ORIGIN archaic variant of *dungeon*

Don Juan *n* a successful seducer of women
WORD ORIGIN after the legendary Spanish philanderer

donkey *n* **1** a long-eared member of the horse family **2** a person who is considered to be stupid or stubborn
WORD ORIGIN origin unknown

donkey jacket *n Brit, Austral & NZ* a man's thick hip-length jacket with a waterproof panel across the shoulders

donkey's years *pl n informal* a long time

donkey-work *n* uninteresting groundwork

Donleavy *n* **J**(ames) **P**(atrick) born 1926, Irish-American novelist. His books include *The Ginger Man* (1956),

THESAURUS

dominant *adj* **1 = controlling**, leading, ruling, commanding, supreme, governing, superior, presiding, authoritative, ascendant **2 = main**, chief, primary, outstanding, principal, prominent, influential, prevailing, paramount, prevalent, predominant, pre-eminent **OPPOSITE:** minor

dominate *vb* **1 = control**, lead, rule, direct, master, govern, monopolize, tyrannize, have the upper hand over, lead by the nose *(informal)*, overbear, have the whip hand over, domineer, keep under your thumb **2 = tower above**, overlook, survey, stand over, loom over, stand head and shoulders above, bestride

don¹ *vb* **= put on**, get into, dress in, pull on, change into, get dressed in, clothe yourself in, slip on *or* into

donate *vb* **= give**, present, contribute, grant, commit, gift, hand out, subscribe, endow, chip in *(informal)*, bestow, entrust, impart, bequeath, make a gift of

donation *n* **2 = contribution**, gift, subscription, offering, present, grant, hand-out, boon, alms, stipend, gratuity, benefaction, largesse *or* largess, koha (NZ)

DICTIONARY

The Onion Eaters (1971), *Are You Listening Rabbi Löw?* (1987), and *The Lady Who Liked Clean Rest Rooms* (1995)

Donnelly *n* **Declan** born 1975, British television presenter, who appears with Antony McPartlin as Ant and Dec

donnish *adj* resembling a university don; pedantic or fussy

donor ❶ *n* **1** *med* a person who gives blood or organs for use in the treatment of another person **2** a person who makes a donation
WORD ORIGIN Latin *donare* to give

donor card *n* a card carried by someone to show that the body parts specified may be used for transplants after the person's death

Don Quixote (don kee-hoe-tee) *n* an impractical idealist
WORD ORIGIN after the hero of Miguel de Cervantes' novel *Don Quixote de la Mancha*

don't do not

doodle *vb* **-dling, -dled 1** to scribble or draw aimlessly ▹*n* **2** a shape or picture drawn aimlessly
WORD ORIGIN originally, a foolish person

Doohan *n* **Michael K** (**Mick**) born 1965, Australian racing motorcyclist; 500 cc world champion 1994–98

Doolittle *n* **Hilda** known as H.D. 1886–1961, US imagist poet and novelist, living in Europe

doom ❶ *n* **1** death or a terrible fate ▹*vb* **2** to destine or condemn to death or a terrible fate
WORD ORIGIN Old English *dōm*

doomsday *or* **domesday** *n* **1** the day on which the Last Judgment will occur **2** any dreaded day
WORD ORIGIN Old English *dōmes dæg* Judgment Day

doona *n Austral* a large quilt used as a bed cover in place of the top sheet and blankets

door ❶ *n* **1** a hinged or sliding panel for closing the entrance to a building, room, or cupboard **2** a doorway or entrance **3** a means of access or escape: *the door to happiness* **4 lay something at someone's door** to blame someone for something **5 out of doors** in the open air
WORD ORIGIN Old English *duru*

doorjamb *n* one of the two vertical posts that form the sides of a door frame. Also called: **doorpost**

doorman *n, pl* **-men** a man employed to be on duty at the main entrance of a large building

doormat *n* **1** a mat, placed at an entrance, for wiping dirt from shoes **2** *informal* a person who offers little resistance to being treated badly

Doors *pl n* **the** US rock group (1965–73), originally comprising Jim Morrison, Ray Manzarek (born 1935), Robby Krieger (born 1946), and John Densmore (born 1945) ▸ See also **Morrison** (sense 2)

doorstep *n* **1** a step in front of a door **2** *informal* a thick slice of bread

doorstop *n* a heavy object or one fixed to the floor, which prevents a door from closing or from striking a wall

door-to-door *adj* **1** (of selling) from one house to the next **2** (of a journey) direct

doorway *n* an opening into a building or room

doosra (dooz-ruh) *n cricket* a delivery bowled by an off-spinner that turns the opposite way from an off-break
WORD ORIGIN Urdu, Hindi

dop *n S African informal* a tot or small drink, usually alcoholic
WORD ORIGIN Afrikaans

dope ❶ *n* **1** *slang* an illegal drug, such as cannabis **2** a drug administered to a person or animal to affect performance in a race or other sporting competition **3** *informal* a slow-witted person **4** confidential information **5** a thick liquid, such as a lubricant ▹*vb* **doping, doped 6** to administer a drug to
WORD ORIGIN Dutch *doop* sauce

dopey *or* **dopy** *adj* **dopier, dopiest 1** *informal* half-asleep, as when under the influence of a drug **2** *slang* silly

doppelgänger (dop-pl-geng-er) *n legend* a ghostly duplicate of a living person
WORD ORIGIN German *Doppelgänger* double-goer

Doppler effect *n* a change in the apparent frequency of a sound or light wave as a result of relative motion between the observer and the source
WORD ORIGIN after C. J. *Doppler*, physicist

Doráti *n* **Antal** 1906–88, US conductor and composer

dorba *n Austral informal* a stupid, inept, or clumsy person

Doré *n* (**Paul**) **Gustave** 1832–83, French illustrator, whose style tended towards the grotesque. He illustrated the Bible, Dante's *Inferno*, Cervantes' *Don Quixote*, and works by Rabelais

Dorgon *n* 1612–50, Manchurian prince, who ruled China as regent (1643–50) and helped to establish the Ching dynasty

Doric *adj* **1** of a style of classical architecture characterized by a heavy fluted column and a simple capital ▹*n* **2** a rustic dialect, esp. a Scots one
WORD ORIGIN *Doris*, in ancient Greece

dormant *adj* **1** temporarily quiet, inactive, or not being used **2** *biol* alive but in a resting condition
dormancy *n*
WORD ORIGIN Latin *dormire* to sleep

dormer *or* **dormer window** *n* a window that is built upright in a sloping roof
WORD ORIGIN Latin *dormitorium* dormitory

dormitory *n, pl* **-ries 1** a large room, esp. at a school, containing several beds **2** a building, esp. at a college, providing living accommodation ▹*adj* **3** *Austral & Brit* denoting an area from which most of the residents commute to work: *the swelling suburban dormitory areas*
WORD ORIGIN Latin *dormitorium*, from *dormire* to sleep

Dormobile *n trademark* a vanlike vehicle specially equipped for living in while travelling

dormouse *n, pl* **-mice** a small rodent resembling a mouse with a furry tail
WORD ORIGIN origin unknown

dorp ❶ *n S African* a small town or village
WORD ORIGIN Dutch

dorsal *adj anat, zool* of or on the back
WORD ORIGIN Latin *dorsum* back

dory *n, pl* **-ries** a spiny-finned food fish. Also called: **John Dory**
WORD ORIGIN French *dorée* gilded

DOS *computers* disk operating system

THESAURUS

donor *n* **2 = giver**, contributor, benefactor, philanthropist, grantor *(law)*, donator, almsgiver
OPPOSITE: recipient

doom *n* **1 = destruction**, ruin, catastrophe, death, downfall ▹*vb* **2 = condemn**, sentence, consign, foreordain, destine, predestine, preordain

door *n* **2 = opening**, entry, entrance, exit, doorway, ingress, egress

dope *n* **1** *(slang)* **= drugs**, narcotics, opiates, dadah *(Austral slang)* **3** *(informal)* **= idiot**, fool, jerk *(slang, chiefly US & Canad)*, plank *(Brit slang)*, charlie *(Brit informal)*, berk *(Brit slang)*, wally *(slang)*, prat *(slang)*, plonker *(slang)*, coot, geek *(slang)*, twit *(informal, chiefly Brit)*, dunce, oaf, simpleton, dimwit *(informal)*, dipstick *(Brit slang)*, gonzo *(slang)*, schmuck *(US slang)*, dork *(slang)*, nitwit *(informal)*, dolt, blockhead, divvy *(Brit slang)*, pillock *(Brit slang)*, dweeb *(US slang)*, putz *(US slang)*, fathead *(informal)*, eejit *(Scot & Irish)*, dumb-ass *(slang)*, numpty *(Scot informal)*, lamebrain *(informal)*, nerd *or* nurd *(slang)*, numbskull *or* numskull, dorba *or* dorb *(Austral slang)*, bogan *(Austral slang)* ▹*vb* **6 = drug**, doctor, knock out, inject, sedate, stupefy, anaesthetize, narcotize

dorp *n* *(S African)* **= town**, village, settlement, municipality, kainga *or* kaika *(NZ)*

DICTIONARY

d

dose ❶ *n* **1** a specific quantity of a medicine taken at one time **2** *informal* something unpleasant to experience: *a dose of the cold* **3** the total energy of radiation absorbed **4** *slang* a sexually transmitted infection ▷ *vb* **dosing, dosed 5** to administer a quantity of medicine to (someone) **dosage** *n*
WORD ORIGIN Greek *dosis* a giving

dosh *n slang* money

dosing strip *n* (in New Zealand) an area for treating dogs suspected of having hydatid disease

Dos Passos *n* **John** (**Roderigo**) 1896–1970, US novelist of the Lost Generation; author of *Three Soldiers* (1921), *Manhattan Transfer* (1925), and the trilogy *USA* (1930–36)

doss *slang vb* **1 doss down** to sleep on a makeshift bed **2** to pass time aimlessly: *I doss around a lot* ▷ *n* **3** a task requiring little effort
WORD ORIGIN origin unknown

dosshouse *n slang* a cheap lodging house for homeless people

dossier (doss-ee-ay) *n* a collection of papers about a subject or person
WORD ORIGIN French

dot ❶ *n* **1** a small round mark **2** the small round mark used to represent the short sound in Morse code **3 on the dot** at exactly the arranged time ▷ *vb* **dotting, dotted 4** to mark with a dot **5** to scatter or intersperse: *there are numerous churches dotted around Rome* **6 dot one's i's and cross one's t's** *informal* to pay meticulous attention to detail
WORD ORIGIN Old English *dott* head of a boil

dotage *n* feebleness of mind as a result of old age
WORD ORIGIN Middle English *doten* to dote

dotard *n* a person who is feeble-minded through old age

dotcom *or* **dot.com** *n* a company that conducts most of its business on the internet
WORD ORIGIN from *.com*, the domain name suffix of businesses trading on the internet

dote *vb* **doting, doted** ■ **dote on** *or* **upon** to love (someone or something) to an excessive degree **doting** *adj*
WORD ORIGIN Middle English *doten*

dotterel *n* a shore bird with reddish-brown underparts and white bands around the head and neck
WORD ORIGIN Middle English *dotrelle*

dottle *n* the tobacco left in a pipe after smoking
WORD ORIGIN obsolete *dot* lump

dotty *adj* **-tier, -tiest** *slang* slightly crazy **dottiness** *n*
WORD ORIGIN from *dot*

Dou, Dow, *or* **Douw** *n* **Gerard** 1613–75, Dutch portrait and genre painter

double ❶ *adj* **1** as much again in size, strength, number, etc.: *a double scotch* **2** composed of two equal or similar parts **3** designed for two users: *a double bed* **4** folded in half: *the blanket had been folded double* **5** stooping: *she was bent double over the flower bed* **6** ambiguous: *a double meaning* **7** false, deceitful, or hypocritical: *double standards* **8** *music* (of an instrument) sounding an octave lower: *a double bass* ▷ *adv* **9** twice over: *that's double the amount requested* ▷ *n* **10** twice the size, strength, number, etc. **11** a double measure of spirits **12** a person who closely resembles another person **13** a bet on two horses in different races in which any winnings from the first race are placed on the horse in the later race **14 at** *or* **on the double** quickly or immediately ▷ *vb* **-bling, -bled 15** to make or become twice as much **16** to bend or fold so that one part covers another **17** to play two parts or serve two roles **18** to turn sharply **19** *bridge* to make a call that will double certain scoring points if the preceding bid becomes the contract **20 double for** to act as substitute ▸ See also **double back, doubles, double up** > **doubler** *n*
WORD ORIGIN Latin *duplus* twofold

double agent *n* a spy employed by two enemy countries at the same time

double back *vb* to go back in the opposite direction: *I doubled back searching for the track*

double-barrelled *or US* **-barreled** *adj* **1** (of a gun) having two barrels **2** *Brit* (of a surname) having hyphenated parts

double bass *n* a stringed instrument, the largest and lowest member of the violin family

double-breasted *adj* (of a garment) having overlapping fronts

double-check *vb* to make certain by checking again

double chin *n* a fold of fat under the chin

double cream *n Austral & Brit* thick cream with a high fat content

double-cross *vb* **1** to cheat or betray ▷ *n* **2** an instance of double-crossing

double-dealing *n* treacherous or deceitful behaviour

double-decker *n* **1** *chiefly Brit* a bus with two passenger decks one on top of the other ▷ *adj* **2** *informal* having two layers: *a double-decker sandwich*

double-double *n* **1** *chiefly US & Canad basketball* the feat of scoring 10 or more in each of two classes of quantifiable positive action (such as points, assists, rebounds, etc.) **2** *Canad* a cup of coffee served with two helpings of cream and sugar

double Dutch *n informal* speech or writing that is difficult to understand: *it was double Dutch to me*

double-edged *adj* **1** (of a remark) malicious in intent though apparently complimentary **2** (of a knife) having a cutting edge on either side of the blade

double entendre (**doob**-bl on-**tond**-ra) *n* a word or phrase with two interpretations, esp. with one meaning that is rude
WORD ORIGIN obsolete French

double entry *n* a book-keeping system in which a transaction is entered as a debit in one account and as a credit in another

double glazing *n* a window consisting of two layers of glass separated by a space, fitted to reduce heat loss

double Gloucester (**glost**-er) *n* a smooth orange-red cheese with a mild flavour

double-jointed *adj* (of a person) having unusually flexible joints

double knitting *n* a medium thickness of knitting wool

double negative *n* a grammatical construction, considered incorrect, in which two negatives are used where one is needed, for example *I wouldn't never have believed it*

double-park *vb* to park (a vehicle) alongside another vehicle, causing an obstruction

double pneumonia *n* pneumonia affecting both lungs

double-quick *adj* **1** very quick ▷ *adv*

THESAURUS

dose *n* **1** *(medical)* = **measure**, amount, allowance, portion, prescription, ration, draught, dosage, potion

dot *n* **1** = **spot**, point, mark, circle, atom, dab, mite, fleck, jot, speck, full stop, speckle, mote, iota **3 on the dot** = **on time**, promptly, precisely, exactly *(informal)*, to the minute, on the button *(informal)*, punctually ▷ *vb* **5** = **spot**, stud, fleck, speckle

double *adj* **2** = **matching**, coupled, doubled, paired, twin, duplicate, in pairs, binate *(botany)* **6** = **dual**, enigmatic, cryptic, twofold, Delphic, enigmatical ▷ *n* **12** = **twin**, lookalike, spitting image, copy, fellow, mate, counterpart, clone, replica, ringer *(slang)*, impersonator *(informal)*, dead ringer *(slang)*, Doppelgänger, duplicate ▷ *n* **14 at** *or* **on the double** = **at once**, now, immediately, directly, quickly, promptly, right now, straight away, right away, briskly, without delay, pronto *(informal)*, at full speed, in double-quick time, this instant, this very minute, pdq *(slang)*, posthaste, tout de suite *(French)* ▷ *vb* **15** = **multiply by two**, duplicate, increase twofold, repeat, enlarge, magnify **16** = **fold up** *or* **over**

2 in a very quick manner
doubles *n* a game between two pairs of players
double standard *n* a set of principles that allows greater freedom to one person or group than to another
doublet (dub-lit) *n history* a man's close-fitting jacket, with or without sleeves
WORD ORIGIN Old French
double take *n* a delayed reaction by a person to a remark or situation: *she did a double take when he said he was leaving*
double talk *n* deceptive or ambiguous talk
doublethink *n* the acceptance of conflicting facts or principles at the same time
double time *n* **1** *Brit, Austral & NZ* a doubled wage rate sometimes paid for overtime work **2** *music* two beats per bar
double up *vb* **1** to bend or cause to bend in two: *she was doubled up with stomach cramps* **2** to share with other people: *we only took two cars, so we had to double up*
double whammy *n informal* a devastating setback made up of two elements
doubloon *n* a former Spanish gold coin
WORD ORIGIN Spanish *doblón*
doubly *adv* **1** to or in a greater degree, quantity, or measure: *I have to be doubly careful* **2** in two ways: *the defence debate was doubly complicated*
doubt ❶ *n* **1** uncertainty about the truth, facts, or existence of something **2** an unresolved difficulty or point **3** **give someone the benefit of the doubt** accept that someone is speaking the truth **4** **no doubt** almost certainly ▹ *vb* **5** to be inclined to disbelieve: *I doubt that we are late* **6** to distrust or be suspicious of: *he doubted their motives* **doubter** *n*
WORD ORIGIN Latin *dubitare* to hesitate
doubtful ❶ *adj* **1** unlikely or improbable: *it's doubtful that I will marry again* **2** unsure or uncertain: *I was doubtful about some of his ideas* **doubtfully** *adv* **doubtfulness** *n*
doubtless ❶ *adv* probably or almost certainly: *somebody will know and doubtless somebody will ring us*
douche (doosh) *n* **1** a stream of water directed onto or into the body for cleansing or medical purposes **2** an instrument for applying a douche ▹ *vb* **douching, douched** **3** to cleanse or treat by means of a douche
WORD ORIGIN French
dough *n* **1** a thick mixture of flour and water or milk, used for making bread, pastry, or biscuits **2** *slang* money
WORD ORIGIN Old English *dāg*
doughnut *n* a small cake of sweetened dough cooked in hot fat
doughty (dowt-ee) *adj* **-tier, -tiest** *old-fashioned* brave and determined
WORD ORIGIN Old English *dohtig*
Doughty *n* **Charles Montagu** 1843–1926, English writer and traveller; author of *Travels in Arabia Deserta* (1888)
Douglas[1] *n* a town and resort on the Isle of Man, capital of the island, on the E coast. Pop: 25 347 (2001)
Douglas[2] *n* **1** **C(lifford) H(ugh)** 1879–1952, British economist, who originated the theory of social credit **2** **Gavin** ?1474–1522, Scottish poet, the first British translator of the *Aeneid* **3** **Keith** (**Castellain**) 1920–44, British poet, noted for his poems of World War II: killed in action **4** **Michael K(irk)** born 1944, US film actor; his films include *Romancing the Stone* (1984), *Wall Street* (1987), *Basic Instinct* (1992), and *Wonder Boys* (2000) **5** (**George**) **Norman** 1868–1952, British writer, esp. of books on southern Italy such as *South Wind* (1917) **6** **Tommy,** full name *Thomas Clement Douglas* (1904–86). Canadian statesman: premier of Saskatchewan 1944–61
do up *vb* **1** to wrap and make into a bundle: *he did up the parcel* **2** to fasten: *to do up one's blouse* **3** to renovate or redecorate
dour (doo-er, dow-er) *adj* sullen and unfriendly **dourness** *n*
WORD ORIGIN probably from Latin *durus* hard
douse *or* **dowse** (rhymes with mouse) *vb* **dousing, doused** *or* **dowsing, dowsed** **1** to drench with water or other liquid **2** to put out (a light)
WORD ORIGIN origin unknown
dove *n* **1** a bird with a heavy body, small head, and short legs **2** *politics* a person opposed to war
WORD ORIGIN Old English *dūfe*
dovecote *or* **dovecot** *n* a box, shelter, or part of a house built for doves or pigeons to live in
dove-grey *adj* greyish-brown
dovetail *n* **1** Also called: **dovetail joint** a wedge-shaped joint used to fit two pieces of wood tightly together ▹ *vb* **2** to fit together closely or neatly: *her resignation dovetails well with the new structure*
Dovzhenko *n* **Aleksandr Petrovitch** 1894–1956, Soviet film director. His films include *Zemlya* (1930) and *Ivan* (1932)
Dow *n* See **Dou**
dowager *n* a woman possessing property or a title obtained from her dead husband
WORD ORIGIN Old French *douagiere*
Dowding *n* Baron **Hugh Caswall Tremenheere,** nicknamed *Stuffy.* 1882–1970, British air chief marshal. As commander in chief of Fighter Command (1936–40), he contributed greatly to the British victory in the Battle of Britain (1940)
dowdy *adj* **-dier, -diest** wearing dull and unfashionable clothes **dowdily** *adv* **dowdiness** *n*
WORD ORIGIN Middle English *dowd* slut
dowel *n* a wooden or metal peg that fits into two corresponding holes to join larger pieces of wood or metal together
WORD ORIGIN Middle Low German *dövel* plug
Dowell *n* **Anthony** born 1943, British ballet dancer. He became director of the Royal Ballet in 1986
dower *n* **1** the life interest in a part of her husband's estate allotted to a widow by law **2** *archaic* a dowry
WORD ORIGIN Latin *dos* gift
dower house *n* a house for the use of a widow, often on her deceased husband's estate
do with *vb* **1** **could do with** need or would benefit from: *I could do with*

THESAURUS

doubt *n* **1a = uncertainty,** confusion, hesitation, dilemma, scepticism, misgiving, suspense, indecision, bewilderment, lack of confidence, hesitancy, perplexity, vacillation, lack of conviction, irresolution, dubiety **OPPOSITE:** certainty
1b = suspicion, scepticism, distrust, fear, apprehension, mistrust, misgivings, disquiet, qualms, incredulity, lack of faith **OPPOSITE:** belief
▹ *vb* **6 = disbelieve,** question, suspect, query, distrust, mistrust, lack confidence in, misgive **OPPOSITE:** believe
doubtful *adj* **1 = unlikely,** unclear, dubious, unsettled, dodgy (*Brit, Austral & NZ informal*), questionable, ambiguous, improbable, indefinite, unconfirmed, inconclusive, debatable, indeterminate, iffy (*informal*), equivocal, inexact **OPPOSITE:** certain
2 = unsure, uncertain, hesitant, suspicious, hesitating, sceptical, unsettled, tentative, wavering, unresolved, perplexed, undecided, unconvinced, vacillating, leery (*slang*), distrustful, in two minds (*informal*), irresolute **OPPOSITE:** certain
doubtless *adv* **= probably,** presumably, most likely
do without something *or* **someone = manage without,** give up, dispense with, forgo, kick (*informal*), sacrifice, abstain from, get along without

DICTIONARY

some royal treatment **2 have to do with** to be associated with: *his illness has a lot to do with his failing the exam* **3 to do with** concerning; related to: *this book has to do with the occult*

do without ❶ *vb* to manage without

Dowland *n* **John** ?1563–1626, English lutenist and composer of songs and lute music

down[1] ❶ *prep* **1** from a higher to a lower position in or on **2** at a lower or further level or position on, in, or along: *I wandered down the corridor* ▷ *adv* **3** at or to a lower level or position: *he bent down* **4** indicating lowering or destruction: *to bring down an aircraft* **5** indicating intensity or completion: *calm down and mind your manners* **6** immediately: *cash down* **7** on paper: *she copied it down* **8** away from a more important place: *he came down from head office* **9** reduced to a state of lack: *he was down to his last pound* **10** lacking a specified amount: *down several pounds* **11** lower in price **12** from an earlier to a later time: *the ring was handed down from my grandmother* **13** to a finer state: *to grind down* **14** *sport* being a specified number of points or goals behind an opponent **15** (of a person) being inactive, owing to illness: *down with the cold* ▷ *adj* **16** depressed or unhappy: *he seems very down today* ▷ *vb* **17** *informal* to eat or drink quickly **18** to fell (someone or something) ▷ *n* **19 have a down on** *informal* to feel hostile towards: *you seem to have a down on the family tonight*
WORD ORIGIN Old English *dūne* from the hill

down[2] *n* soft fine feathers **downy** *adj*
WORD ORIGIN Old Norse *dūnn*

down-and-out *n* **1** a person who is homeless and destitute ▷ *adj* **2** without any means of support; destitute

downbeat *adj informal* **1** depressed or gloomy: *she was in one of her downbeat moods* **2** casual and restrained: *the chairman's statement was decidedly downbeat* ▷ *n* **3** *music* the first beat of a bar

downcast *adj* **1** sad and dejected **2** (of the eyes) directed downwards

downer *n slang* **1** a barbiturate, tranquillizer, or narcotic **2 on a downer** in a state of depression

downfall ❶ *n* **1** a sudden loss of position or reputation **2** the cause of this

downgrade ❶ *vb* **-grading, -graded** to reduce in importance or value

downhearted *adj* sad and discouraged

downhill *adj* **1** going or sloping down ▷ *adv* **2** towards the bottom of a hill **3 go downhill** *informal* to deteriorate

Downing Street *n* the British prime minister or the British government
WORD ORIGIN after the street in London which contains the official residence of the prime minister and the chancellor of the exchequer

download *vb* **1** to transfer (data) from the memory of one computer to that of another ▷ *n* **2** a file transferred in this way

down-market *adj* cheap, popular, and of poor quality

down payment *n* the deposit paid on an item purchased on hire-purchase, mortgage, etc.: *an initial down payment is usually required*

downpour *n* a heavy continuous fall of rain

downright ❶ *adv* **1** extremely: *it's just downright cruel* ▷ *adj* **2** absolute; utter: *Crozier is a downright thief*

down-river *adj, adv* nearer the mouth of a river

downs *pl n* an area of low grassy hills, esp. in S England

downshifting *n* the practice of simplifying one's lifestyle and becoming less materialistic

downside *n* the disadvantageous aspect of a situation: *the downside of capitalism*

downsize *vb* **1** to reduce the number of people employed by (a company) **2** to reduce the size of or produce a smaller version of (something)

Down's syndrome *or esp. US, Canad & Austral* **Down syndrome** *n pathol* a genetic disorder characterized by mental impairment and physical abnormalities, including a flattish face and a vertical fold of skin at the inner edge of the eye
WORD ORIGIN after John *Langdon-Down*, physician

downstairs *adv* **1** down the stairs; to or on a lower floor ▷ *n* **2** a lower or ground floor

downstream *adv, adj* in or towards the lower part of a stream; with the current

downtime *n commerce* time during which a computer or other machine is not working

down-to-earth ❶ *adj* sensible or practical

downtown *chiefly US, Canad, & NZ n* **1** the central or lower part of a city, esp. the main commercial area ▷ *adv* **2** towards, to, or into this area

downtrodden *adj* oppressed and lacking the will to resist

downturn *n* a drop in the success of an economy or a business

down under *informal n* **1** Australia or New Zealand ▷ *adv* **2** in or to Australia or New Zealand

downward ❶ *adj* **1** descending from a higher to a lower level, condition, or position ▷ *adv* **2** ▸ same as **downwards** > **downwardly** *adv*

downwards *or* **downward** *adv* **1** from a higher to a lower level, condition, or position **2** from an earlier time or source to a later one

downwind *adv, adj* in the same direction towards which the wind is blowing; with the wind from behind

dowry *n, pl* **-ries** the property brought by a woman to her husband at marriage
WORD ORIGIN Latin *dos*

dowse (rhymes with **cows**) *vb* **dowsing, dowsed** to search for underground water or minerals using a divining rod **dowser** *n*
WORD ORIGIN origin unknown

Dowson *n* **Ernest** (**Christopher**) 1867–1900, English Decadent poet noted for his lyric *Cynara*

doxology *n, pl* **-gies** a hymn or verse of praise to God
WORD ORIGIN Greek *doxologos* uttering praise

doyen (doy-en) *n* the senior member of a group, profession, or society **doyenne** (doy-en) *fem n*
WORD ORIGIN French

D'Oyly Carte *n* **Richard** 1844–1901, British impresario noted for his productions of the operettas of Gilbert and Sullivan

doze *vb* **dozing, dozed** **1** to sleep lightly or for a short period **2 doze off** to fall into a light sleep ▷ *n* **3** a short sleep
WORD ORIGIN probably from

THESAURUS

down[1] *adj* **16 = depressed**, low, sad, blue, unhappy, discouraged, miserable, fed up, dismal, pessimistic, melancholy, glum, dejected, despondent, dispirited, downcast, morose, disheartened, crestfallen, downhearted, down in the dumps *(informal)*, sick as a parrot *(informal)*, low-spirited ▷ *vb* **17** *(informal)* **= swallow**, drink (down), drain, gulp (down), put away *(informal)*, toss off

downfall *n* **1 = ruin**, fall, destruction, collapse, breakdown, disgrace, overthrow, descent, undoing, comeuppance *(slang)*, comedown

downgrade *vb* **= demote**, degrade, take down a peg *(informal)*, lower or reduce in rank OPPOSITE: promote

downright *adj* **2 = complete**, absolute, utter, total, positive, clear, plain, simple, explicit, outright, blatant, unequivocal, unqualified, out-and-out, categorical, undisguised, thoroughgoing, arrant, deep-dyed *(usually derogatory)*

down-to-earth *adj* **= sensible**, practical, realistic, common-sense, matter-of-fact, sane, no-nonsense, hard-headed, unsentimental, plain-spoken, grounded

downward *adj* **1 = descending**, declining, heading down, earthward

DICTIONARY

Old Norse *dūs* lull
dozen *adj, n* twelve **dozenth** *adj*
WORD ORIGIN Latin *duodecim*
dozy *adj* **dozier, doziest 1** feeling sleepy **2** *Brit informal* stupid and slow-witted
DP displaced person
DPB (in New Zealand) Domestic Purposes Benefit
dpi *computers* dots per inch
DPP (in Britain) Director of Public Prosecutions
Dr 1 Doctor **2** Drive
drab *adj* **drabber, drabbest 1** dull and dreary **2** light olive-brown **drabness** *n*
WORD ORIGIN Old French *drap* cloth
Drabble *n* **Margaret** born 1939, British novelist and editor. Her novels include *The Needle's Eye* (1972), *The Radiant Way* (1987), and *The Seven Sisters* (2002). She edited the 1985 edition of the *Oxford Companion to Literature*
drachm (**dram**) *n Brit* a unit of liquid measure equal to one eighth of a fluid ounce (3.55 ml)
WORD ORIGIN variant of DRAM
drachma *n, pl* **-mas** *or* **-mae** a former monetary unit of Greece
WORD ORIGIN Greek *drakhmē* a handful
Draco[1] *n, Latin genitive* **Draconis** a faint extensive constellation twisting around the N celestial pole and lying between Ursa Major and Cepheus
WORD ORIGIN from Latin, from Greek *drakōn* DRAGON
Draco[2] *n* 7th century BC, Athenian statesman and lawmaker, whose code of laws (621) prescribed death for almost every offence
draconian *adj* severe or harsh: *draconian measures were taken by the government*
WORD ORIGIN after DRACO
draft ❶ *n* **1** a preliminary outline of a letter, book, or speech **2** a written order for payment of money by a bank **3** *US & Austral* selection for compulsory military service ▷ *vb* **4** to write a preliminary outline of a letter, book, or speech **5** to send (personnel) from one place to another to carry out a specific job **6** *chiefly US* to select for compulsory military service ▷ *n, vb* **7** *US* ▸ same as **draught**
WORD ORIGIN variant of DRAUGHT
drag ❶ *vb* **dragging, dragged 1** to pull with force along the ground **2** to trail on the ground **3** to persuade (someone) to go somewhere: *he didn't want to come so I had to drag him along* **4** to move (oneself) slowly and with difficulty: *I had to drag myself out of bed this morning* **5** to linger behind: *she dragged along behind her mother* **6** to search (a river) with a dragnet or hook **7** to draw (on a cigarette) **8** *computers* to move (a graphics image) from one place to another on the screen by manipulating a mouse with its button held down **9 drag away** *or* **from** to force (oneself) to come away from something interesting: *I was completely spellbound and couldn't drag myself away from the film* **10 drag on** *or* **out** to last or be prolonged tediously: *winter dragged on* **11 drag one's feet** *informal* to act with deliberate slowness ▷ *n* **12** a person or thing that slows up progress **13** *informal* a tedious or boring thing: *it was a drag having to walk two miles to the station every day* **14** *informal* a draw on a cigarette **15** an implement, such as a dragnet, used for dragging **16** *aeronautics* the resistance to the motion of a body passing through air **17 in drag** (of a man) wearing women's clothes, usually as a form of entertainment ▸ See also **drag up**
WORD ORIGIN Old English *dragan* to draw
draggle *vb* **-gling, -gled** to make or become wet or dirty by trailing on the ground
WORD ORIGIN Middle English
dragnet *n* a net used to scour the bottom of a pond or river when searching for something
dragoman *n, pl* **-mans** *or* **-men** (in some Middle Eastern countries) a professional interpreter or guide
WORD ORIGIN Arabic *targumān*
dragon *n* **1** a mythical monster that resembles a large fire-breathing lizard **2** *informal* a fierce woman **3 chase the dragon** *slang* to smoke opium or heroin
WORD ORIGIN Greek *drakōn*
dragonfly *n, pl* **-flies** a brightly coloured insect with a long slender body and two pairs of wings
dragoon *n* **1** a heavily armed cavalryman ▷ *vb* **2** to coerce or force: *we were dragooned into participating*
WORD ORIGIN French *dragon*
drag race *n* a race in which specially built or modified cars or motorcycles are timed over a measured course **drag racing** *n*
drag up *vb informal* to revive (an unpleasant fact or story)
drain ❶ *n* **1** a pipe that carries off water or sewage **2** a cause of a continuous reduction in energy or resources: *the expansion will be a drain on resources* **3** a metal grid on a road or pavement through which rainwater flows **4 down the drain** wasted ▷ *vb* **5** to draw off or remove (liquid) from **6** to flow (away) or filter (off) **7** to dry or be emptied as a result of liquid running off or flowing away **8** to drink the entire contents of (a glass or cup) **9** to make constant demands on (energy or resources); exhaust **10** (of a river) to carry off the surface water from (an area)
WORD ORIGIN Old English *drēahnian*
drainage *n* **1** a system of pipes, drains, or ditches used to drain water or other liquids **2** the process or a method of draining
draining board *n* a grooved surface at the side of a sink, used for draining washed dishes
drainpipe *n* a pipe for carrying off rainwater or sewage
drake *n* the male of a duck
WORD ORIGIN origin unknown
dram *n* **1** a small amount of spirits, such as whisky **2** a unit of weight equal to one sixteenth of an ounce (avoirdupois)
WORD ORIGIN Greek *drakhmē*; see DRACHMA
drama ❶ *n* **1** a serious play for theatre, television, or radio **2** plays in general, as a form of literature **3** the art of writing, producing, or acting in a play **4** a situation that is exciting or highly emotional
WORD ORIGIN Greek: something performed

THESAURUS

draft *n* **1 = outline**, plan, sketch, version, rough, abstract, delineation, preliminary form **2 = money order**, bill (of exchange), cheque, postal order ▷ *vb* **4 = outline**, write, plan, produce, create, design, draw, frame, compose, devise, sketch, draw up, formulate, contrive, delineate
drag *vb* **1 = pull**, draw, haul, trail, tow, tug, jerk, yank, hale, lug ▷ *n* **13** *(informal)* **= nuisance**, pain *(informal)*, bore, bother, pest, hassle *(informal)*, inconvenience, annoyance, pain in the neck, pain in the backside *(informal)*, pain in the butt *(informal)*
drain *n* **1 = sewer**, channel, pipe, sink, outlet, ditch, trench, conduit, duct, culvert, watercourse **2 = reduction**, strain, drag, expenditure, exhaustion, sapping, depletion ▷ *vb* **5 = remove**, draw, empty, withdraw, milk, tap, pump, bleed, evacuate **6 = flow out**, leak, discharge, trickle, ooze, seep, exude, well out, effuse **7 = empty 8 = drink up**, swallow, finish, put away *(informal)*, quaff, gulp down **9a = exhaust**, tire, wear out, strain, weaken, fatigue, weary, debilitate, prostrate, tax, tire out, enfeeble, enervate **9b = consume**, waste, exhaust, empty, deplete, use up, sap, dissipate, swallow up
drama *n* **1 = play**, show, stage show, stage play, dramatization, theatrical piece **2, 3 = theatre**, acting, dramatic art, stagecraft, dramaturgy, Thespian art **4 = excitement**, crisis, dramatics, spectacle, turmoil, histrionics, theatrics *see:* **dramatist**

DICTIONARY

dramatic ❶ *adj* **1** of or relating to drama **2** like a drama in suddenness or effectiveness: *the government's plan has had a dramatic effect on employment in television* **3** acting or performed in a flamboyant way: *he spread his hands in a dramatic gesture of helplessness* **dramatically** *adv*

dramatics *n* **1** the art of acting or producing plays ▷ *pl n* **2** exaggerated, theatrical behaviour

dramatis personae (drah-mat-tiss per-soh-nigh) *pl n* the characters in a play
WORD ORIGIN New Latin

dramatist ❶ *n* a playwright: *Austria's greatest living dramatist*

dramatize *or* **-tise** *vb* **-tizing, -tized** *or* **-tising, -tised 1** to rewrite (a book or story) in a form suitable for performing on stage **2** to express (something) in a dramatic or exaggerated way: *he dramatizes his illness* **dramatization** *or* **-tisation** *n*

drank *vb* ▸ the past tense of **drink**

drape ❶ *vb* **draping, draped 1** to cover with material or fabric **2** to hang or arrange in folds **3** to place casually: *he draped his arm across the back of the seat* ▸ See also **drapes**
WORD ORIGIN Old French *draper*

draper *n Brit* a person who sells fabrics and sewing materials

Draper *n* **1 Henry** 1837–82, US astronomer, who contributed to stellar classification and spectroscopy **2** his father, **John William** 1811–82, US chemist and historian, born in England, made the first photograph of the moon

drapery *n, pl* **-peries 1** fabric or clothing arranged and draped **2** fabrics and cloth collectively

drapes *pl n Austral, NZ, US & Canad* material hung at an opening or window to shut out light or to provide privacy

drastic ❶ *adj* strong and severe: *the police are taking drastic measures against car thieves* **drastically** *adv*
WORD ORIGIN Greek *drastikos*

drat *interj slang* an exclamation of annoyance
WORD ORIGIN probably alteration of *God rot*

draught ❶ *or US* **draft** *n* **1** a current of cold air, usually one coming into a room or vehicle **2** a portion of liquid to be drunk, esp. a dose of medicine **3** a gulp or swallow: *she took a deep draught then a sip* **4 on draught** (of beer) drawn from a cask **5** one of the flat discs used in the game of draughts. US and Canad. equivalent: **checker 6 feel the draught** to be short of money ▷ *adj* **7** (of an animal) used for pulling heavy loads: *horses are specialized draught animals*
WORD ORIGIN probably Old Norse *drahtr*

draught beer *n* beer stored in a cask

draughtboard *n* a square board divided into 64 squares, used for playing draughts

draughts *n* a game for two players using a draughtboard and 12 draughtsmen each
WORD ORIGIN plural of *draught* (in obsolete sense: a chess move)

draughtsman *or US* **draftsman** *n, pl* **-men 1** a person employed to prepare detailed scale drawings of equipment, machinery, or buildings **2** a person skilled in drawing **3** US and Canad. equivalent: **checker** *Brit* a flat disc used in the game of draughts **draughtsmanship** *n*

draughty *or US* **drafty** *adj* **draughtier, draughtiest** *or US* **draftier, draftiest** exposed to draughts of air **draughtily** *adv* **draughtiness** *n*

draw ❶ *vb* **drawing, drew, drawn 1** to sketch (a picture, pattern, or diagram) with a pen or pencil **2** to cause (a person or thing) to move closer or further away from a place by pulling **3** to bring, take, or pull (something) out of a container: *he drew a gun and laid it on the table* **4** to take (something) from a particular source: *the inhabitants drew water from the well two miles away* **5** to move in a specified direction: *he drew alongside me* **6** to attract: *she drew enthusiastic audiences from all over the country* **7** to formulate or decide: *he drew similar conclusions* **8** to cause to flow: *the barman nodded and drew two pints* **9** to choose or be given by lottery: *Brazil have drawn Spain in the semi-final of the Cup* **10** (of two teams or contestants) to finish a game with an equal number of points **11** *archery* to bend (a bow) by pulling the string **12** to cause (pus) to discharge from an abscess or wound ▷ *n* **13** a raffle or lottery **14** *informal* a person, place, show, or event that attracts a large audience **15** a contest or game ending in a tie ▸ See also **drawback, draw in**, etc.
WORD ORIGIN Old English *dragan*

drawback ❶ *n* **1** a disadvantage or hindrance ▷ *vb* **draw back 2** to move backwards: *the girl drew back as though in pain* **3** to turn aside from an undertaking: *the prime minister drew back from his original intention*

drawbridge *n* a bridge that may be raised to prevent access or to enable vessels to pass

drawer *n* **1** a sliding box-shaped part of a piece of furniture used for storage **2** a person or thing that draws

drawers *pl n old-fashioned* an undergarment worn on the lower part of the body

draw in *vb* **1** (of a train) to arrive at a station **2 the nights are drawing in** the hours of daylight are becoming shorter

drawing ❶ *n* **1** a picture or plan made by means of lines on a surface **2** the art of making drawings

drawing pin *n Brit & NZ* a short tack with a broad smooth head used for fastening papers to a drawing board or other surface

drawing room *n* a room where visitors are received and entertained

drawl *vb* **1** to speak slowly with long vowel sounds ▷ *n* **2** the way of speech of someone who drawls **drawling** *adj*

THESAURUS

dramatic *adj* **1 = theatrical**, Thespian, dramaturgical, dramaturgic **2a = exciting**, emotional, thrilling, tense, startling, sensational, breathtaking, electrifying, melodramatic, climactic, high-octane *(informal)*, shock-horror *(facetious)*, suspenseful **2b = powerful**, striking, stunning *(informal)*, impressive, effective, vivid, jaw-dropping **OPPOSITE:** ordinary **3 = expressive**

dramatist *n* **= playwright**, screenwriter, scriptwriter, dramaturge

drape *vb* **1 = cover**, wrap, fold, array, adorn, swathe

drastic *adj* **= extreme**, strong, radical, desperate, severe, harsh, dire, forceful

draught *or (US)* **draft** *n* **1 = breeze**, current, movement, flow, puff, influx, gust, current of air **3 = drink**

draw *vb* **1 = sketch**, design, outline, trace, portray, paint, depict, mark out, map out, delineate **2 = pull**, drag, haul, tow, tug **4, 12 = extract**, take, remove, drain **6 = entice**, bring in **7 = deduce**, make, get, take, derive, infer ▷ *n* **14** *(informal)* **= appeal**, interest, pull *(informal)*, charm, attraction, lure, temptation, fascination, attractiveness, allure, magnetism, enchantment, enticement, captivation, temptingness **15 = tie**, deadlock, stalemate, impasse, dead heat

drawback *n* **1 = disadvantage**, trouble, difficulty, fault, handicap, obstacle, defect, deficiency, flaw, hitch, nuisance, snag, downside, stumbling block, impediment, detriment, imperfection, hindrance, fly in the ointment *(informal)* **OPPOSITE:** advantage

drawing *n* **1 = picture**, illustration, representation, cartoon, sketch, portrayal, depiction, study, outline, delineation

drawn *adj* **2 = tense**, worn, strained,

DICTIONARY

WORD ORIGIN probably frequentative of *draw*

drawn ❶ *vb* **1** ▸ the past participle of **draw** ▹ *adj* **2** haggard, tired, or tense in appearance

draw off *vb* to cause (a liquid) to flow from something

draw on *vb* **1** to make use of from a source or fund: *they are able to draw on a repertoire of around 400 songs* **2** (of a period of time) to come near or pass by: *summer draws on; time draws on*

draw out *vb* **1** (of a train) to leave a station **2** to encourage (someone) to talk freely: *therapy groups will continue to draw her out* **3** **draw out of** to find out (information) from

drawstring *n* a cord run through a hem around an opening, so that when it is pulled tighter, the opening closes

draw up *vb* **1** to prepare and write out: *the signatories drew up a draft agreement* **2** (of a vehicle) to come to a halt

dray *n* a low cart used for carrying heavy loads
WORD ORIGIN Old English *dræge* dragnet

Drayton *n* **Michael** 1563–1631, English poet. His work includes odes and pastorals, and *Poly-Olbion* (1613–22), on the topography of England

dread ❶ *vb* **1** to anticipate with apprehension or terror ▹ *n* **2** great fear
WORD ORIGIN Old English *ondrǣdan*

dreadful ❶ *adj* **1** extremely disagreeable or shocking **2** extreme: *there were dreadful delays* **dreadfully** *adv*

dreadlocks *pl n* hair worn in the Rastafarian style of tightly curled strands

dreadnought *n* **1** a type of battleship with heavy guns **2** a heavy overcoat

dream ❶ *n* **1** an imagined series of events experienced in the mind while asleep **2** a daydream: *the dream of success turning into a nightmare* **3** a goal or aim: *Unity has been their constant dream* **4** a wonderful person or thing: *her house is a dream* ▹ *vb* **dreaming, dreamed** *or* **dreamt** **5** to experience (a dream) **6** to indulge in daydreams **7** to be unrealistic: *you're dreaming if you think we can win* **8** **dream of** to consider the possibility of: *she would not dream of taking his advice* **9** **dream of** *or* **about** to have an image of or fantasy about: *they often dream about what life will be like for them on the outside* ▹ *adj* **10** beautiful or pleasing: *a dream kitchen* **dreamer** *n*
WORD ORIGIN Old English *drēam* song

dream team *n informal* a group of people regarded as having the perfect combination of talents

dream ticket *n* a combination of two people, esp. candidates in an election, that is considered to be ideal

dream up *vb* to formulate in the imagination: *a character dreamed up by a scriptwriter*

dreamy *adj* **dreamier, dreamiest** **1** vague or impractical: *she was wild-eyed and dreamy* **2** relaxing or gentle: *I felt this dreamy contentment* **3** *informal* wonderful or impressive: *he drives a dreamy Jaguar* **dreamily** *adv* **dreaminess** *n*

dreary ❶ *adj* **drearier, dreariest** dull or uninteresting: *there are long streets of dreary red houses spreading everywhere* **drearily** *adv* **dreariness** *n*
WORD ORIGIN Old English *drēorig* gory

dredge[1] *n* **1** a machine used to scoop or suck up silt or mud from a river bed or harbour ▹ *vb* **dredging, dredged** **2** to remove silt or mud from (a river bed or harbour) by means of a dredge **3** to search for (a submerged object) with or as if with a dredge **dredger** *n*
WORD ORIGIN origin unknown

dredge[2] *vb* **dredging, dredged** to sprinkle (food) with a substance, such as flour **dredger** *n*
WORD ORIGIN Old French *dragie*

dredge up *vb informal* to remember (something obscure or half-forgotten): *I didn't retain you to dredge up unfortunate incidents from my past*

dregs *pl n* **1** solid particles that settle at the bottom of some liquids **2** **the dregs** the worst or most despised elements: *the dregs of colonial society*
WORD ORIGIN Old Norse *dregg*

Dreiser *n* **Theodore** (**Herman Albert**) 1871–1945, US novelist; his works include *Sister Carrie* (1900) and *An American Tragedy* (1925)

drench ❶ *vb* **1** to make completely wet **2** to give medicine to (an animal) **drenching** *n, adj*
WORD ORIGIN Old English *drencan* to cause to drink

Dresden *or* **Dresden china** *n* delicate and decorative porcelain made near Dresden, Germany

dress ❶ *n* **1** a one-piece garment worn by a woman or girl, with a skirt and bodice and sometimes sleeves **2** complete style of clothing: *contemporary dress* ▹ *adj* **3** suitable for a formal occasion: *he was wearing a dress shirt* ▹ *vb* **4** to put clothes on **5** to put on formal clothes **6** to apply protective covering to (a wound) **7** to cover (a salad) with dressing **8** to prepare (meat, poultry, or fish) for selling or cooking by cleaning or gutting **9** to put a finish on (the surface of stone, metal, or other building material) ▸ See also **dress up**
WORD ORIGIN Old French *drecier* to arrange

dressage (**dress**-ahzh) *n* **a** the method of training horses to perform manoeuvres as a display of obedience **b** the manoeuvres performed
WORD ORIGIN French

dress circle *n* the first gallery in a theatre

dress code *n* a set of rules regarding the style of dress acceptable in an office, restaurant, etc.

THESAURUS

stressed, tired, pinched, fatigued, harassed, fraught, sapped, harrowed, haggard

dread *vb* **1 = fear**, shrink from, cringe at the thought of, quail from, shudder to think about, have cold feet about *(informal)*, anticipate with horror, tremble to think about ▹ *n* **2 = fear**, alarm, horror, terror, dismay, fright, apprehension, consternation, trepidation, apprehensiveness, affright

dreadful *adj* **1a = terrible**, shocking, awful, alarming, distressing, appalling, tragic, horrible, formidable, fearful, dire, horrendous, hideous, monstrous, from hell *(informal)*, grievous, atrocious, frightful, godawful *(slang)*, hellacious *(US slang)* **1b = awful**, terrible, horrendous, frightful **2 = serious**, terrible, awful, appalling, horrendous, monstrous, unspeakable, abysmal

dream *n* **1 = vision**, illusion, delusion, hallucination, reverie **2 = daydream** **3 = ambition**, wish, fantasy, desire, Holy Grail *(informal)*, pipe dream **4 = delight**, pleasure, joy, beauty, treasure, gem, marvel, pearler *(Austral slang)*, beaut *(Austral & NZ slang)* ▹ *vb* **5 = have dreams**, hallucinate **6 = daydream**, stargaze, build castles in the air *or* in Spain **9 dream of something** *or* **someone = daydream about**, fantasize about

dreary *adj* **= dull**, boring, tedious, routine, drab, tiresome, lifeless, monotonous, humdrum, colourless, uneventful, uninteresting, mind-numbing, ho-hum *(informal)*, wearisome, as dry as dust **OPPOSITE:** exciting

drench *vb* **1 = soak**, flood, wet, duck, drown, steep, swamp, saturate, inundate, souse, imbrue

dress *n* **1 = frock**, gown, garment, robe **2 = clothing**, clothes, gear *(informal)*, costume, threads *(slang)*, garments, apparel, attire, garb, togs, raiment *(archaic, poetic)*, vestment, schmutter *(slang)*, habiliment ▹ *vb* **4a = put on clothes**, don clothes, slip on *or* into something **OPPOSITE:** undress **4b = clothe** **6 = bandage**, treat, plaster, bind up

DICTIONARY

dresser[1] *n* **1** a piece of furniture with shelves and cupboards, used for storing or displaying dishes **2** *US* a chest of drawers
WORD ORIGIN Old French *drecier* to arrange

dresser[2] *n* **1** a person who dresses in a specified way: *Lars was a meticulous, elegant dresser* **2** *theatre* a person employed to assist performers with their costumes

dressing *n* **1** a sauce for food: *salad dressing* **2** *US & Canad* ▸same as **stuffing** (sense 1) **3** a covering for a wound **4** manure or fertilizer spread on land **5** a gluey material used for stiffening paper, textiles, etc.

dressing-down *n informal* a severe reprimand

dressing gown *n* a loose-fitting garment worn over one's pyjamas or nightdress

dressing room *n* a room used for changing clothes and applying make-up, esp. a backstage room in a theatre

dressing table *n* a piece of bedroom furniture with a mirror and a set of drawers

dressmaker *n* a person who makes clothes for women **dressmaking** *n*

dress rehearsal *n* **1** the last rehearsal of a play, opera, or show using costumes, lighting, and other effects **2** any full-scale practice: *astronauts are in the midst of a two day dress rehearsal of their launch countdown*

dress shirt *n* a man's evening shirt, worn as part of formal evening dress

dress suit *n* a man's evening suit

dress up *vb* **1** to put on glamorous or stylish clothes **2** to put fancy dress on: *the guests dressed up like cowboys* **3** to disguise (something) to make it more attractive or acceptable: *the offer was simply an old one dressed up in new terms*

dressy *adj* **dressier, dressiest 1** (of clothes or occasions) elegant **2** (of people) dressing stylishly
dressiness *n*

drew *vb* ▸the past tense of **draw**

drey *or* **dray** *n Austral & Brit* a squirrel's nest
WORD ORIGIN origin unknown

Dreyfus *n* **Alfred** 1859–1935, French army officer, a Jew whose false imprisonment for treason (1894) raised issues of anti-semitism and militarism that dominated French politics until his release (1906)

dribble ⊕ *vb* **-bling, -bled 1** to flow or allow to flow in a thin stream or drops **2** to allow saliva to trickle from the mouth **3** (in soccer, hockey, etc.) to propel (the ball) by kicking or tapping in quick succession ▹*n* **4** a small quantity of liquid falling in drops or flowing in a thin stream **5** a small supply: *there's only a dribble of milk left* **6** an act or instance of dribbling
dribbler *n*
WORD ORIGIN obsolete *drib*, variant of *drip*

dribs and drabs *pl n informal* small occasional amounts

dried *vb* ▸the past of **dry**

drier[1] *adj* ▸a comparative of **dry**

drier[2] *n* ▸same as **dryer**[1]

Driesch *n* **Hans Adolf Eduard** 1867–1941, German zoologist and embryologist

driest *adj* ▸a superlative of **dry**

drift ⊕ *vb* **1** to be carried along by currents of air or water **2** to move aimlessly from one place or activity to another **3** to wander away from a fixed course or point **4** (of snow) to pile up in heaps ▹*n* **5** something piled up by the wind or current, as a snowdrift **6** a general movement or development: *there has been a drift away from family control* **7** the main point of an argument or speech: *I was beginning to get his drift* **8** the extent to which a vessel or aircraft is driven off course by winds, etc. **9** a current of water created by the wind
WORD ORIGIN Old Norse

drifter *n* **1** a person who moves aimlessly from place to place **2** a boat used for drift-net fishing

drift net *n* a fishing net that is allowed to drift with the tide

driftwood *n* wood floating on or washed ashore by the sea

drill[1] ⊕ *n* **1** a machine or tool for boring holes **2** *mil* training in procedures or movements, as for parades **3** strict and often repetitious training **4** *informal* correct procedure: *he knows the drill as well as anybody* ▹*vb* **5** to bore a hole in (something) with or as if with a drill **6** to instruct or be instructed in military procedures or movements **7** to teach by rigorous exercises or training
WORD ORIGIN Middle Dutch *drillen*

drill[2] *n* **1** a machine for planting seeds in rows **2** a furrow in which seeds are sown **3** a row of seeds planted by means of a drill ▹*vb* **4** to plant (seeds) by means of a drill
WORD ORIGIN origin unknown

drill[3] *n* a hard-wearing cotton cloth, used for uniforms
WORD ORIGIN German *Drillich*

drill[4] *n* a W African monkey, related to the mandrill
WORD ORIGIN from a West African word

drilling platform *n* an offshore structure that supports a drilling rig

drilling rig *n* the complete machinery, equipment, and structures needed to drill an offshore oil well

drily *or* **dryly** *adv* in a dry manner

drink ⊕ *vb* **drinking, drank, drunk 1** to swallow (a liquid) **2** to consume alcohol, esp. to excess **3** to bring (oneself) into a specified condition by consuming alcohol: *he drank himself senseless every night* **4 drink someone's health** to wish someone health or happiness with a toast **5 drink in** to pay close attention to: *I drank in what the speaker said* **6 drink to** to drink a toast to: *I drank to their engagement* ▹*n* **7** liquid suitable for drinking **8** a portion of liquid for drinking **9** alcohol, or the habit of drinking too much of it **drinkable** *adj*
drinker *n*
WORD ORIGIN Old English *drincan*

drink-driving *adj* of or relating to driving a car after drinking alcohol: *a drink-driving offence*

Drinkwater *n* **John** 1882–1937, English dramatist, poet, and critic; author of chronicle plays such as *Abraham Lincoln* (1918) and *Mary Stuart* (1921)

THESAURUS

dribble *vb* **1 = run**, drip, trickle, drop, leak, ooze, seep, fall in drops **2 = drool**, drivel, slaver, slobber, drip saliva

drift *vb* **1 = float**, go (aimlessly), bob, coast, slip, sail, slide, glide, meander, waft, be carried along, move gently **2 = wander**, stroll, stray, roam, meander, rove, range, straggle, traipse *(informal)*, stravaig *(Scot & Northern English dialect)*, peregrinate **3 = stray**, wander, roam, meander, digress, get sidetracked, go off at a tangent, get off the point **4 = pile up**, gather, accumulate, amass, bank up ▹*n* **5 = pile**, bank, mass, heap, mound, accumulation **7 = meaning**, point, gist, aim, direction, object, import, intention, implication, tendency, significance, thrust, tenor, purport

drill[1] *n* **1 = bit**, borer, gimlet, rotary tool, boring tool **2, 3 = training**, exercise, discipline, instruction, preparation, repetition **4** *(informal)* **= practice** ▹*vb* **5 = bore**, pierce, penetrate, sink in, puncture, perforate **6, 7 = train**, coach, teach, exercise, discipline, practise, instruct, rehearse

drink *vb* **1 = swallow**, drain, sip, suck, gulp, sup, swig *(informal)*, swill, guzzle, imbibe, quaff, partake of, toss off **2 = booze** *(informal)*, tipple, tope, hit the bottle *(informal)*, bevvy *(dialect)*, bend the elbow *(informal)*, go on a binge *or* bender *(informal)* ▹*n* **7 = beverage**, refreshment, potion, liquid, thirst quencher **8 = glass**, cup, swallow, sip, draught, gulp, swig *(informal)*, taste, tipple, snifter *(informal)*, noggin **9 = alcohol**, booze *(informal)*, liquor, spirits, the bottle *(informal)*, Dutch courage, hooch *or* hootch *(informal, chiefly US & Canad)*

DICTIONARY

drip ❶ *vb* **dripping, dripped** 1 to fall or let fall in drops ▹*n* 2 a drop of liquid 3 the falling of drops of liquid 4 the sound made by falling drops 5 *informal* a weak or foolish person 6 *med* a device that administers a liquid drop by drop into a vein
WORD ORIGIN Old English *dryppan*

drip-dry *adj* 1 (of clothes or fabrics) designed to dry without creases if hung up when wet ▹*vb* **-dries, -drying, -dried** 2 to dry or become dry thus

drip-feed *vb* **-feeding, -fed** 1 to feed (someone) a liquid drop by drop, usually through a vein ▹*n* **drip feed** 2 ▸ same as **drip** (sense 6)

dripping *n* the fat that comes from meat while it is being roasted

drive ❶ *vb* **driving, drove, driven** 1 to guide the movement of (a vehicle) 2 to transport or be transported in a vehicle 3 to goad into a specified state: *the black despair that finally drove her to suicide* 4 to push or propel: *he drove the nail into the wall with a hammer* 5 *sport* to hit (a ball) very hard and straight 6 *golf* to strike (the ball) with a driver 7 to chase (game) from cover 8 **drive home** to make (a point) clearly understood by emphasis ▹*n* 9 a journey in a driven vehicle 10 a road for vehicles, esp. a private road leading to a house 11 a special effort made by a group of people for a particular purpose: *a charity drive* 12 energy, ambition, or initiative 13 *psychol* a motive or interest: *sex drive* 14 a sustained and powerful military offensive 15 the means by which power is transmitted in a machine 16 *sport* a hard straight shot or stroke
WORD ORIGIN Old English *drīfan*

drive at *vb informal* to intend or mean: *he had no idea what she was driving at*

drive-by *n informal* an incident in which a person is shot at by a person in a moving vehicle

drive-in *n* 1 a cinema, restaurant, etc. offering a service where people remain in their cars while using the service provided ▹*adj* 2 denoting a cinema, etc. of this kind

drivel *n* 1 foolish talk ▹*vb* **-elling, -elled** *or US* **-eling, -eled** 2 to speak foolishly 3 to allow (saliva) to flow from the mouth
WORD ORIGIN Old English *dreflian* to slaver

driven *vb* ▸ the past participle of **drive**

driver *n* 1 a person who drives a vehicle 2 *golf* a long-shafted club with a large head and steep face, used for tee shots

driver's licence *n Canad & Austral* an official document authorizing a person to drive a motor vehicle. Also called (in Britain and certain other countries): **driving licence**

drive-thru *n* 1 a takeaway restaurant, bank, etc. designed so that customers can use it without leaving their cars ▹*adj* 2 denoting a restaurant etc. of this kind

drive-time *n* 1 the time of day when many people are driving to or from work, considered as a broadcasting slot ▹*adj* 2 of this time of day: *the daily drive-time show*

driveway *n* a path for vehicles connecting a building to a public road

driving licence *n* an official document authorizing a person to drive a motor vehicle

drizzle *n* 1 very light rain ▹*vb* **-zling, -zled** 2 to rain lightly **drizzly** *adj*
WORD ORIGIN Old English *drēosan* to fall

Drnovsek *n* **Ivan** born 1950, Slovenian politician, president of Slovenia from 2002

Drobny *n* **Jaroslav** 1921–2001, British tennis and ice-hockey player, born in Czechoslovakia: Wimbledon champion 1954: a member of the Czech ice-hockey team in the 1948 Olympic Games

droll *adj* quaintly amusing **drollery** *n* **drolly** *adv*
WORD ORIGIN French *drôle* scamp

dromedary (**drom**-mid-er-ee) *n, pl* **-daries** a camel with a single hump
WORD ORIGIN Greek *dromas* running

drone¹ *n* 1 a male honeybee 2 a person who lives off the work of others
WORD ORIGIN Old English *drān*

drone² *vb* **droning, droned** 1 to make a monotonous low dull sound 2 **drone on** to talk in a monotonous tone without stopping ▹*n* 3 a monotonous low dull sound 4 a single-reed pipe in a set of bagpipes
WORD ORIGIN related to DRONE¹

drongo *n* a tropical songbird with a glossy black plumage, a forked tail, and a stout bill

drool *vb* 1 **drool over** to show excessive enthusiasm for or pleasure in 2 ▸ same as **drivel** (senses 2, 3)
WORD ORIGIN probably alteration of DRIVEL

droop *vb* 1 to sag, as from weakness or lack of support 2 to be overcome by weariness: *her eyelids drooped as if she were falling asleep* **drooping** *adj*
WORD ORIGIN Old Norse *drūpa*

droopy *adj* hanging or sagging downwards: *a droopy moustache*

drop ❶ *vb* **dropping, dropped** 1 to fall or allow (something) to fall vertically 2 to decrease in amount, strength, or value 3 to fall to the ground, as from exhaustion 4 to sink to a lower position, as on a scale 5 to mention casually: *he dropped a hint* 6 to set down (passengers or goods): *can you drop me at the hotel?* 7 *informal* to send: *drop me a letter* 8 to discontinue: *can we drop the subject?* 9 *informal* to be no longer friendly with: *I dropped him when I discovered his political views* 10 to leave out in speaking: *he has a tendency to drop his h's* 11 (of animals) to give birth to (offspring) 12 *sport* to omit (a player) from a team 13 to lose (a game or point) 14 **drop back** to progress more slowly than other people going in the same direction 15 **drop in** *or* **by** *informal* to pay someone a casual visit ▹*n* 16 a small quantity of liquid forming a round shape 17 a small quantity of liquid 18 a small round sweet: *a lemon drop* 19 a decrease in amount, strength, or value 20 the vertical distance that anything may fall 21 the act of unloading troops or supplies by parachute ▸ See also **drop off, dropout, drops**
WORD ORIGIN Old English *dropian*

THESAURUS

drip *vb* 1 = **drop**, splash, sprinkle, trickle, dribble, exude, drizzle, plop ▹*n* 2 = **drop**, bead, trickle, dribble, droplet, globule, pearl, driblet 5 *(informal)* = **weakling**, wet *(Brit informal)*, weed *(informal)*, softie *(informal)*, mummy's boy *(informal)*, namby-pamby, ninny, milksop

drive *vb* 1 = **operate**, manage, direct, guide, handle, steer 2 = **go (by car)**, ride (by car), motor, travel by car 3 = **force**, press, prompt, spur, compel, motivate, oblige, railroad *(informal)*, prod, constrain, prick, coerce, goad, impel, dragoon, actuate 4a = **push**, propel 4b = **thrust**, push, sink, dig, hammer, plunge, stab, ram 7 = **herd**, urge, impel ▹*n* 9 = **run**, ride, trip, journey, spin *(informal)*, hurl *(Scot)*, outing, excursion, jaunt 11 = **campaign**, push *(informal)*, crusade, action, effort, appeal, advance, surge 12 = **initiative**, push *(informal)*, energy, enterprise, ambition, pep, motivation, zip *(informal)*, vigour, get-up-and-go *(informal)*

drop *vb* 1 = **plunge**, fall, dive, tumble, descend, plummet 2 = **fall**, lower, decline, diminish 3 = **sink**, fall, descend, droop 4 *(often with* **away**) = **decline**, fall, sink 8 = **quit**, give up, abandon, cease, axe *(informal)*, kick *(informal)*, terminate, relinquish, remit, discontinue, forsake ▹*n* 16 = **droplet**, bead, globule, bubble, pearl, drip, driblet 17 = **dash**, shot *(informal)*, spot, taste, trace, pinch, sip, tot, trickle, nip, dab, mouthful 19 = **decrease**, fall, cut, lowering, decline, reduction, slump, fall-off, downturn, deterioration, cutback, diminution, decrement 20 = **fall**, plunge, descent, abyss, chasm, precipice

DICTIONARY

drop curtain *n theatre* a curtain that can be raised and lowered onto the stage

droplet *n* a very small drop of liquid

drop off *vb* **1** to set down (passengers or goods) **2** *informal* to fall asleep **3** to decrease or decline: *sales dropped off during our period of transition*

dropout ⊙ *n* **1** a person who rejects conventional society **2** a student who does not complete a course of study ▷ *vb* **drop out 3** to abandon or withdraw (from an institution or group)

dropper *n* a small tube with a rubber part at one end for drawing up and dispensing drops of liquid

droppings *pl n* the dung of certain animals, such as rabbits or birds

drops *pl n* any liquid medication applied by means of a dropper

drop scone *n* a flat spongy cake made by dropping a spoonful of batter on a hot griddle

dropsy *n* an illness in which watery fluid collects in the body **dropsical** *adj*
WORD ORIGIN Middle English *ydropesie*, from Greek *hudōr* water

drosky *or* **droshky** *n, pl* **-kies** an open four-wheeled carriage, formerly used in Russia
WORD ORIGIN Russian *drozhki*

dross ⊙ *n* **1** the scum formed on the surfaces of molten metals **2** anything of inferior quality: *we can't publish this dross*
WORD ORIGIN Old English *drōs* dregs

drought ⊙ (rhymes with **out**) *n* a prolonged period of time during which no rain falls
WORD ORIGIN Old English *drūgoth*

drove[1] *vb* ▸ the past tense of **drive**

drove[2] ⊙ *n* **1** a herd of livestock being driven together **2** a moving crowd of people
WORD ORIGIN Old English *drāf* herd

drover *n* a person who drives sheep or cattle

drown ⊙ *vb* **1** to die or kill by immersion in liquid **2** to drench thoroughly **3** to make (a sound) impossible to hear by making a loud noise
WORD ORIGIN probably from Old English *druncnian*

drowse *vb* **drowsing, drowsed** to be sleepy, dull, or sluggish
WORD ORIGIN probably from Old English *drūsian* to sink

drowsy *adj* **drowsier, drowsiest 1** feeling sleepy **2** peaceful and quiet: *row upon row of windows looked out over drowsy parkland* **drowsily** *adv* **drowsiness** *n*

drubbing *n* an utter defeat, as in a contest: *the Communists received a drubbing*
WORD ORIGIN probably from Arabic *dáraba* to beat

drudge *n* **1** a person who works hard at an uninteresting task ▷ *vb* **drudging, drudged 2** to work at such tasks
WORD ORIGIN origin unknown

drudgery *n* uninteresting work that must be done

drug ⊙ *n* **1** any substance used in the treatment, prevention, or diagnosis of disease **2** a chemical substance, such as a narcotic, taken for the effects it produces ▷ *vb* **drugging, drugged 3** to administer a drug to (a person or animal) in order to induce sleepiness or unconsciousness **4** to mix a drug with (food or drink): *who drugged my wine?*
WORD ORIGIN Old French *drogue*

drug addict *n* a person who is dependent on narcotic drugs

druggist *n US & Canad* a pharmacist

drugstore *n US & Canad* a pharmacy where a wide variety of goods are available

Druid *n* a member of an ancient order of Celtic priests **Druidic** *or* **Druidical** *adj*
WORD ORIGIN Latin *druides*

drum ⊙ *n* **1** a percussion instrument sounded by striking a skin stretched across the opening of a hollow cylinder **2** the sound produced by a drum **3** an object shaped like a drum: *an oil drum* **4** ▸ same as **eardrum** ▷ *vb* **drumming, drummed 5** to play (music) on a drum **6** to tap rhythmically or regularly: *he drummed his fingers on the desk* **7** to fix in someone's mind by constant repetition: *my father always drummed into us how privileged we were* ▸ See also **drum up** > **drummer** *n*
WORD ORIGIN Middle Dutch *tromme*

drumbeat *n* the sound made by beating a drum

drumhead *n* the part of a drum that is struck

drum machine *n* a synthesizer programmed to reproduce the sound of percussion instruments

drum major *n* the noncommissioned officer in the army who is in command of the drums and the band when paraded together

drum majorette *n* a girl who marches at the head of a procession, twirling a baton

Drummond of Hawthornden *n* **William** 1585–1649, Scottish poet, historian, and royalist pamphleteer

drumstick *n* **1** a stick used for playing a drum **2** the lower joint of the leg of a cooked fowl

drum up *vb* to obtain (support or business) by making requests or canvassing

drunk ⊙ *vb* **1** ▸ the past participle of **drink** ▷ *adj* **2** intoxicated with alcohol to the extent of losing control over normal functions **3** overwhelmed by strong influence or emotion: *he was half drunk with satisfaction at his victory over the intruder* ▷ *n* **4** a person who is drunk or drinks habitually to excess
WORD ORIGIN Old English *druncen*, past participle of *drincan* to drink

THESAURUS

drop out *vb* **3 = leave**, stop, give up, withdraw, quit, pull out, back out, renege, throw in the towel, cop out *(slang)*, fall by the wayside

dross *n* **2 = nonsense**, garbage *(chiefly US)*, drivel, twaddle, pants *(slang)*, rot, crap *(slang)*, trash, hot air *(informal)*, tosh *(slang, chiefly Brit)*, pap, bilge *(informal)*, tripe *(informal)*, gibberish, guff *(slang)*, havers *(Scot)*, moonshine, claptrap *(informal)*, hogwash, hokum *(slang, chiefly US & Canad)*, codswallop *(Brit slang)*, piffle *(informal)*, poppycock *(informal)*, balderdash, bosh *(informal)*, wack *(US slang)*, eyewash *(informal)*, stuff and nonsense, flapdoodle *(slang)*, tommyrot, horsefeathers *(US slang)*, bunkum *or* buncombe *(chiefly US)*, bizzo *(Austral slang)*, bull's wool *(Austral & NZ slang)*

drought *n* **= water shortage**, dryness, dry weather, dry spell, aridity, drouth *(Scot)*, parchedness
OPPOSITE: flood

drove[2] *n* **1, 2** *(often plural)* **= herd**, company, crowds, collection, gathering, mob, flocks, swarm, horde, multitude, throng

drown *vb* **1 = go down**, go under **2 = drench**, flood, soak, steep, swamp, saturate, engulf, submerge, immerse, inundate, deluge **3** *(often with* **out***)* **= overwhelm**, overcome, wipe out, overpower, obliterate, swallow up

drug *n* **1 = medication**, medicine, remedy, physic, medicament **2 = dope** *(slang)*, narcotic *(slang)*, stimulant, opiate, dadah *(Austral slang)* ▷ *vb* **3 = knock out**, dope *(slang)*, numb, deaden, stupefy, anaesthetize

drum *vb* **5, 6 = pound**, beat, tap, rap, lash, thrash, tattoo, throb, pulsate, reverberate

drunk *adj* **2 = intoxicated**, loaded *(slang, chiefly US & Canad)*, tight *(informal)*, canned *(slang)*, flying *(slang)*, bombed *(slang)*, stoned *(slang)*, wasted *(slang)*, smashed *(slang)*, steaming *(slang)*, wrecked *(slang)*, soaked *(informal)*, out of it *(slang)*, plastered *(slang)*, drunken, blitzed *(slang)*, lit up *(slang)*, merry *(Brit informal)*, stewed *(slang)*, pickled *(informal)*, bladdered *(slang)*, under the influence *(informal)*, sloshed *(slang)*, tipsy, maudlin, well-oiled *(slang)*, legless *(informal)*, paralytic *(informal)*, tired and emotional *(euphemistic)*, steamboats *(Scot slang)*, tiddly *(slang,*

DICTIONARY

drunkard *n* a person who is frequently or habitually drunk
drunken *adj* **1** intoxicated with alcohol **2** habitually drunk **3** caused by or relating to alcoholic intoxication: *a drunken argument* **drunkenly** *adv* **drunkenness** *n*
drupe *n* a fleshy fruit with a stone, such as the peach or cherry
WORD ORIGIN Greek *druppa* olive
dry ❶ *adj* **drier, driest** *or* **dryer, dryest** **1** lacking moisture **2** having little or no rainfall **3** having the water drained away or evaporated: *a dry gully for the most part of the year* **4** not providing milk: *a dry cow* **5** (of the eyes) free from tears **6** *Brit, Austral & NZ informal* thirsty **7** eaten without butter or jam: *a dry cracker* **8** (of wine) not sweet **9** dull and uninteresting: *a dry subject* **10** (of humour) subtle and sarcastic **11** prohibiting the sale of alcoholic liquor: *a dry district* ▷ *vb* **dries, drying, dried 12** to make or become dry **13** to preserve (food) by removing the moisture ▸ See also **dry out, dry up** > **dryness** *n*
WORD ORIGIN Old English *drȳge*
dryad *n, pl* **dryads** *or* **dryades** (dry-ad-deez) *Greek myth* a wood nymph
WORD ORIGIN Greek *druas*
dry battery *n* an electric battery composed of dry cells
dry cell *n* an electric cell in which the electrolyte is in the form of a paste to prevent it from spilling
dry-clean *vb* to clean (clothes, etc.) with a solvent other than water **dry-cleaner** *n* **dry-cleaning** *n*
dry dock *n* a dock that can be pumped dry to permit work on a ship's bottom
dryer[1] *n* any device that removes moisture by heating or by hot air
dryer[2] *adj* ▸ same as **drier**[1]
dry ice *n* solid carbon dioxide used as a refrigerant
dryly *adv* ▸ same as **drily**
dry out *vb* **1** to make or become dry **2** to undergo or cause to undergo treatment for alcoholism or drug addiction
dry rot *n* **1** crumbling and drying of timber, caused by certain fungi **2** a fungus causing this decay
dry run *n informal* a rehearsal
Drysdale[1] *n* Sir **George Russell** 1912–81, Australian painter, esp. of landscapes
Drysdale[2] *n* a New Zealand breed of sheep with hair growing among its wool: bred for its coat which is used in making carpets
dry stock *n* NZ cattle raised for meat
dry-stone *adj* (of a wall) made without mortar
dry up *vb* **1** to make or become dry **2** to dry (dishes, cutlery, etc.) with a tea towel after they have been washed **3** (of a resource) to come to an end **4** *informal* to stop speaking: *she suddenly dried up in the middle of her speech*
DSC *Brit mil* Distinguished Service Cross
DSO *Brit mil* Distinguished Service Order
DSS *Brit* Department of Social Security
DSW (in New Zealand) Department of Social Welfare
DTP *computers* desktop publishing
DT's *informal* delirium tremens
dual ❶ *adj* having two parts, functions, or aspects: *dual controls; dual nationality* **duality** *n*
WORD ORIGIN Latin *duo* two
dual carriageway *n Brit, Austral & NZ* a road with a central strip of grass or concrete to separate traffic travelling in opposite directions
dub[1] *vb* **dubbing, dubbed** to give (a person or place) a name or nickname: *he is dubbed a racist despite his strong denials*
WORD ORIGIN Old English *dubbian*
dub[2] *vb* **dubbing, dubbed 1** to provide (a film) with a new soundtrack in a different language **2** to provide (a film or tape) with a soundtrack ▷ *n* **3** *music* a style of reggae record production involving exaggeration of instrumental parts, echo, etc.
WORD ORIGIN shortened from DOUBLE
du Barry *n* **Comtesse**, original name *Marie Jeanne Bécu*. ?1743–93, mistress of Louis XV, guillotined in the French Revolution
dubbin *n* a kind of thick grease applied to leather to soften it and make it waterproof
WORD ORIGIN *dub* to dress leather
Dubček *n* **Alexander** 1921–92, Czechoslovak statesman. His reforms as first secretary of the Czechoslovak Communist Party prompted the Russian invasion of 1968
du Bellay *n* See **Bellay**
dubious ❶ (dew-bee-uss) *adj* **1** not entirely honest, safe, or reliable: *this allegation was at best dubious and at worst an outright fabrication* **2** unsure or undecided: *she felt dubious about the entire proposition* **3** of doubtful quality or worth: *she had the dubious honour of being taken for his mother* **dubiety** (dew-by-it-ee) *n* **dubiously** *adv*
WORD ORIGIN Latin *dubius* wavering
dubnium *n chem* an element produced in minute quantities by bombarding plutonium with high-energy neon ions. Symbol: Db
WORD ORIGIN after *Dubna* in Russia, where it was first reported
Dubois *n* **W(illiam) E(dward) B(urghardt)** 1868–1963, US Black sociologist, writer, and political activist; a founder of the National Association for the Advancement of Colored People (NAACP)
Dubuffet *n* **Jean** 1901–85, French painter, inspired by graffiti and the untrained art of children and psychotics
ducal (duke-al) *adj* of a duke
ducat (duck-it) *n* a former European gold or silver coin
WORD ORIGIN Old Italian *ducato*
Duccio di Buoninsegna *n* ?1255–?1318, Italian painter; founder of the Sienese school
Duchamp *n* **Marcel** 1887–1968, US painter and sculptor, born in France; noted as a leading exponent of Dada. His best-known work is *Nude Descending a Staircase* (1912)
duchess *n* **1** a woman who holds the rank of duke **2** the wife or widow of a duke
WORD ORIGIN Old French *duchesse*
duchy *n, pl* **duchies** the area of land owned or ruled by a duke or duchess
WORD ORIGIN Old French *duche*

THESAURUS

chiefly Brit), zonked (*slang*), blotto (*slang*), fuddled, inebriated, out to it (*Austral & NZ slang*), sottish, tanked up (*slang*), bacchic, half seas over (*informal*), bevvied (*dialect*), babalas (*S African*), fu' (*Scot*), pie-eyed (*slang*) ▷ *n* **4 = drunkard**, alcoholic, lush (*slang*), boozer (*informal*), toper, sot, soak (*slang*), wino (*informal*), inebriate, alko *or* alco (*Austral slang*)
dry *adj* **2 = dehydrated**, dried-up, arid, torrid, parched, desiccated, waterless, juiceless, sapless, moistureless OPPOSITE: wet **6 = thirsty**, parched **9 = dull**, boring, tedious, commonplace, dreary, tiresome, monotonous, run-of-the-mill, humdrum, unimaginative, uninteresting, mind-numbing, ho-hum (*informal*)
OPPOSITE: interesting
10 = sarcastic, cutting, sharp, keen, cynical, low-key, sly, sardonic, deadpan, droll, ironical, quietly humorous ▷ *vb* **12 = drain**, make dry **13** (*often with* **out**) **= dehydrate**, make dry, desiccate, sear, parch, dehumidify OPPOSITE: wet
dual *adj* **= twofold**, double, twin, matched, coupled, paired, duplicate, binary, duplex
dubious *adj* **1, 3 = suspect**, suspicious, crooked, dodgy (*Brit, Austral & NZ informal*), questionable, unreliable, shady (*informal*), unscrupulous, fishy (*informal*), disreputable, untrustworthy, undependable
OPPOSITE: trustworthy
2 = unsure, uncertain, suspicious, hesitating, doubtful, sceptical, tentative, wavering, hesitant, undecided, unconvinced, iffy

DICTIONARY

duck[1] *n, pl* **ducks** *or* **duck** **1** a water bird with short legs, webbed feet, and a broad blunt bill **2** the flesh of this bird used for food **3** the female of such a bird **4** *cricket* a score of nothing **5** **like water off a duck's back** without effect: *I reprimanded him but it was like water off a duck's back*
WORD ORIGIN Old English *dūce*

d

duck[2] ❶ *vb* **1** to move (the head or body) quickly downwards, to escape being seen or avoid a blow **2** to plunge suddenly under water **3** *informal* to dodge (a duty or responsibility)
WORD ORIGIN Middle English

duck-billed platypus *n* ▸ see **platypus**

duckling *n* a young duck

ducks and drakes *n* **1** a game in which a flat stone is bounced across the surface of water **2** **play ducks and drakes with** *informal* to use recklessly: *he has played ducks and drakes with his life*

duct *n* **1** a tube, pipe, or channel through which liquid or gas is sent **2** a tube in the body through which liquid such as tears or bile can pass
WORD ORIGIN Latin *ducere* to lead

ductile *adj* (of a metal) able to be shaped into sheets or drawn out into threads **ductility** *n*
WORD ORIGIN Latin *ductilis*

dud *informal n* **1** an ineffectual person or thing: *they had the foresight to pick on someone who was not a total dud* ▹ *adj* **2** bad or useless: *a dud cheque*
WORD ORIGIN origin unknown

dude *n informal* **1** *US & Canad* a man: *he was a black dude in his late twenties* **2** *chiefly US & Canad old-fashioned* a dandy **3** *Western US & Canad* a city dweller who spends his or her holiday on a ranch
WORD ORIGIN origin unknown

dudgeon *n* **in high dudgeon** angry or resentful: *the scientist departed in high dudgeon*
WORD ORIGIN origin unknown

due ❶ *adj* **1** expected to happen, be done, or arrive at a particular time: *he is due to return on Thursday* **2** immediately payable: *the balance is now due* **3** owed as a debt: *they finally agreed to pay her the money she was due* **4** fitting or proper: *he was found guilty of driving without due care and attention* **5** **due to** happening or existing as a direct result of someone or something else: *the cause of death was chronic kidney failure due to diabetes* ▹ *n* **6** something that is owed or required **7** **give someone his** *or* **her due** to acknowledge someone's good points: *I'll give him his due, he's resourceful* ▹ *adv* **8** directly or exactly: *due west*
WORD ORIGIN Latin *debere* to owe

duel ❶ *n* **1** a formal fight between two people using guns, swords, or other weapons to settle a quarrel ▹ *vb* **duelling, duelled** *or US* **dueling, dueled** **2** to fight in a duel **duellist** *n*
WORD ORIGIN Latin *duellum,* poetical variant of *bellum* war

duenna *n* (esp. in Spain) an elderly woman acting as chaperone to girls
WORD ORIGIN Spanish *dueña*

dues ❶ *pl n* membership fees paid to a club or organization: *union dues*

duet *n* a piece of music sung or played by two people **duettist** *n*
WORD ORIGIN Latin *duo* two

duff ❶ *adj* **1** *chiefly Brit informal* broken or useless: *my car had a duff clutch* ▹ *vb* **2** *golf informal* to bungle (a shot) **3** **duff up** *Brit slang* to beat (someone) severely
WORD ORIGIN probably from *duffer*

duffel *or* **duffle** *n* ▸ same as **duffel coat**
WORD ORIGIN after *Duffel,* Belgian town

duffel bag *n* a cylinder-shaped canvas bag fastened with a drawstring

duffel coat *n* a wool coat usually with a hood and fastened with toggles

duffer *n informal* a dull or incompetent person
WORD ORIGIN origin unknown

Duffy *n* **Carol Ann** born 1955, British poet and writer; appointed poet laureate 2009; her collections include *Standing Female Nude* (1985), *The World's Wife* (1999), and *Rapture* (2005)

Du Fu *or* **Tu Fu** *n* 712–770 AD, Chinese poet of the Tang dynasty

Dufy *n* **Raoul** 1877–1953, French painter and designer whose style is characterized by swift calligraphic draughtsmanship and bright colouring

dug[1] *vb* ▸ the past of **dig**

dug[2] *n* a teat or udder of a female animal
WORD ORIGIN Scandinavian

du Gard *n* See **Martin du Gard**

dugite (**doo**-gyte) *n* a medium-sized Australian venomous snake

dugong *n* a whalelike mammal found in tropical waters
WORD ORIGIN Malay *duyong*

dugout *n* **1** a canoe made by hollowing out a log **2** *Brit* (at a sports ground) the covered bench where managers and substitutes sit **3** *mil* a covered shelter dug in the ground to provide protection

Du Guesclin *n* **Bertrand** ?1320–80, French military leader; as constable of France (1370–80), he helped to drive the English from France

Duhamel *n* **Georges** 1884–1966, French novelist, poet, and dramatist; author of *La Chronique des Pasquier* (1933–45)

duiker *or* **duyker** (**dike**-er) *n, pl* **-kers** *or* **-ker** a small African antelope
WORD ORIGIN Dutch: diver

Duisenberg *n* **Willem Frederik,** known as *Wim.* 1935–2005, Dutch economist; president of the European Central Bank (1998–2003)

du jour (doo **zhoor**) *adj informal* currently fashionable
WORD ORIGIN French, literally: of the day

Dukas *n* **Paul** 1865–1935, French composer best known for the orchestral scherzo *The Sorcerer's Apprentice* (1897)

duke *n* **1** a nobleman of the highest rank **2** the prince or ruler of a small principality or duchy **dukedom** *n*
WORD ORIGIN Latin *dux* leader

Dulbecco *n* **Renato** born 1914, US physician and molecular biologist, born in Italy: shared the Nobel prize for physiology or medicine (1975) for cancer research

dulcet (**dull**-sit) *adj* (of a sound) soothing or pleasant: *she smiled and, in dulcet tones, told me I would be next*
WORD ORIGIN Latin *dulcis* sweet

dulcimer *n* a tuned percussion instrument consisting of a set of strings stretched over a sounding board and struck with hammers
WORD ORIGIN Old French *doulcemer*

dull ❶ *adj* **1** not interesting: *the finished article would make dull reading* **2** slow to learn or understand **3** (of an ache)

THESAURUS

(informal), leery *(slang),* distrustful, in two minds *(informal)* **OPPOSITE:** sure

duck[2] *vb* **1 = bob,** drop, lower, bend, bow, dodge, crouch, stoop **2 = dunk,** wet, plunge, dip, submerge, immerse, douse, souse **3** *(informal)* **= dodge,** avoid, escape, evade, elude, sidestep, circumvent, shirk, body-swerve *(Scot)*

due *adj* **1 = expected,** scheduled, expected to arrive **2, 3 = payable,** outstanding, owed, owing, unpaid, in arrears **4 = fitting,** deserved, appropriate, just, right, becoming, fit, justified, suitable, merited, proper, obligatory, rightful, requisite, well-earned, bounden ▹ *n* **6 = right(s),** privilege, deserts, merits, prerogative, comeuppance *(informal)* ▹ *adv* **8 = directly,** dead, straight, exactly, undeviatingly

duel *n* **1 = single combat,** affair of honour ▹ *vb* **2 = fight,** struggle, clash, compete, contest, contend, vie with, lock horns

dues *pl n* **= membership fee,** charges, fee, contribution, levy

duff *adj* **1** *(Brit, Austral & NZ informal)* **= bad,** poor, useless, pathetic, inferior, worthless, unsatisfactory, defective, deficient, imperfect, substandard, low-rent *(informal, chiefly US),* poxy *(slang),* pants *(informal),* bodger or bodgie *(Austral slang)*

dull *adj* **1 = boring,** tedious, dreary,

DICTIONARY

not intense: *I have a dull ache in the middle of my back* **4** (of weather) not bright or clear **5** not lively or energetic: *she appeared, looking dull and apathetic* **6** (of colour) lacking brilliance **7** (of the blade of a knife) not sharp **8** (of a sound) not loud or clear: *his head fell back to the carpet with a dull thud* ▹*vb* **9** to make or become dull **dullness** *n* **dully** *adv*
WORD ORIGIN Old English *dol*

dullard *n old-fashioned* a dull or stupid person

Dulles *n* **John Foster** 1888–1959, US statesman and lawyer; secretary of state (1953–59)

dulse *n* a seaweed with large red edible fronds
WORD ORIGIN Irish *duilesc* seaweed

duly ❶ *adv* **1** in a proper manner: *my permit was duly stamped* **2** at the proper time: *the photographer duly arrived*

Du Maurier *n* **1** Dame **Daphne** 1907–89, English novelist; author of *Rebecca* (1938) and *My Cousin Rachel* (1951) **2** her grandfather, **George Louis Palmella Busson** 1834–96, British novelist and illustrator; author of *Trilby* (1894) **3** his son, Sir **Gerald** (**Hubert Edward**) 1873–1934, British actor-manager: father of Daphne Du Maurier

dumb ❶ *adj* **1** lacking the power to speak **2** lacking the power of human speech: *the event was denounced as cruelty to dumb animals* **3** temporarily unable to speak: *I was struck dumb when I heard the news* **4** done or performed without speech: *I looked at her in dumb puzzlement* **5** *informal* stupid or slow to understand ▸See also **dumb down** > **dumbly** *adv*
WORD ORIGIN Old English

dumbbell *n* **1** a short bar with a heavy ball or disc at either end, used for physical exercise **2** *slang chiefly US & Canad* a stupid person

dumb down *vb* to make (something) less intellectually demanding or sophisticated: *a move to dumb down its news coverage*

dumbfounded *adj* speechless with amazement: *she sat open-mouthed and dumbfounded*
WORD ORIGIN *dumb* + (*con*)*found*

dumb show *n* meaningful gestures without speech

dumbstruck *adj* temporarily speechless through shock or surprise

dumbwaiter *n* **1** a lift for carrying food, etc. from one floor of a building to another **2** *Brit* **a** a stand placed near a dining table to hold food **b** a revolving circular tray placed on a table to hold food

dumdum *or* **dumdum bullet** *n* a soft-nosed bullet that expands on impact and causes large and serious wounds
WORD ORIGIN after *Dum-Dum*, town near Calcutta where originally made

dummy ❶ *n, pl* **-mies** **1** a large model that looks like a human being, used for displaying clothes in a shop, as a target, etc. **2** a copy of an object, often lacking some essential feature of the original **3** *slang* a stupid person **4** *bridge* **a** the hand exposed on the table by the declarer's partner and played by the declarer **b** the declarer's partner **5** a rubber teat for babies to suck ▹*adj* **6** imitation or substitute: *you can train them with dummy bombs and live ammunition*
WORD ORIGIN from *dumb*

dummy run *n* a practice or test carried out to test if any problems remain: *we'll do a dummy run on the file to see if the program works*

Du Mont *n* **Allen Balcom** 1901–65, US inventor and electronics manufacturer. He developed the cathode-ray tube used in television sets and oscilloscopes

dump ❶ *vb* **1** to drop or let fall in a careless manner: *he dumped the books on the bed* **2** *informal* to abandon (someone or something) without proper care: *the unwanted babies were dumped in orphanages* **3** to dispose of (nuclear waste) **4** *commerce* to sell (goods) in bulk and at low prices, usually in another country, in order to keep prices high in the home market **5** *computers* to record (the contents of the memory) on a storage device at a series of points during a computer run ▹*n* **6** a place where rubbish is left **7** *informal* a dirty, unattractive place: *you're hardly in this dump out of choice* **8** *mil* a place where weapons or supplies are stored
WORD ORIGIN probably from Old Norse

dumpling *n* **1** a small ball of dough cooked and served with stew **2** a round pastry case filled with fruit: *an apple dumpling*
WORD ORIGIN obsolete *dump* lump

dumps *pl n* **down in the dumps** *informal* feeling depressed and miserable
WORD ORIGIN probably from Middle Dutch *domp* haze

dumpy *adj* **dumpier, dumpiest** short and plump
WORD ORIGIN perhaps related to DUMPLING

dun[1] *vb* **dunning, dunned** **1** to press (a debtor) for payment ▹*n* **2** a demand for payment
WORD ORIGIN origin unknown

dun[2] *adj* brownish-grey
WORD ORIGIN Old English *dunn*

Dunant *n* **Jean Henri** 1828–1910, Swiss humanitarian, founder of the International Red Cross (1864): shared the Nobel peace prize 1901

d

THESAURUS

flat, dry, plain, commonplace, tiresome, monotonous, prosaic, run-of-the-mill, humdrum, unimaginative, dozy, uninteresting, mind-numbing, ho-hum (*informal*), vapid, as dry as dust
OPPOSITE: exciting
4 = cloudy, dim, gloomy, dismal, overcast, leaden, turbid
OPPOSITE: bright
5 = lifeless, dead, heavy, slow, indifferent, sluggish, insensitive, apathetic, listless, unresponsive, passionless, insensible
OPPOSITE: lively
7 = blunt, dulled, blunted, not keen, not sharp, edgeless, unsharpened
OPPOSITE: sharp

duly *adv* **1 = properly**, fittingly, correctly, appropriately, accordingly, suitably, deservedly, rightfully, decorously, befittingly **2 = on time**, promptly, in good time, punctually, at the proper time

dumb *adj* **1 = unable to speak**, mute
OPPOSITE: articulate
3, 4 = silent, mute, speechless, inarticulate, tongue-tied, wordless, voiceless, soundless, at a loss for words, mum **5** (*informal*) **= stupid**, thick, dull, foolish, dense, dozy (*Brit informal*), dim, obtuse, unintelligent, asinine, braindead (*informal*), dim-witted (*informal*)
OPPOSITE: clever

dummy *n* **1 = model**, figure, mannequin, form, manikin, lay figure **2 = imitation**, copy, duplicate, sham, counterfeit, replica **3** (*slang*) **= fool**, jerk (*slang, chiefly US & Canad*), idiot, plank (*Brit slang*), charlie (*Brit informal*), berk (*Brit slang*), wally (*slang*), prat (*slang*), plonker (*slang*), coot, geek (*slang*), dunce, oaf, simpleton, dullard, dimwit (*informal*), dipstick (*Brit slang*), gonzo (*slang*), schmuck (*US slang*), dork (*slang*), nitwit (*informal*), dolt, blockhead, divvy (*Brit slang*), pillock (*Brit slang*), dweeb (*US slang*), fathead (*informal*), weenie (*US informal*), eejit (*Scot & Irish*), dumb-ass (*slang*), numpty (*Scot informal*), doofus (*slang, chiefly US*), lamebrain (*informal*), nerd *or* nurd (*slang*), numbskull *or* numskull, dorba *or* dorb (*Austral slang*), bogan (*Austral slang*) ▹*adj* **6 = imitation**, false, fake, artificial, mock, bogus, simulated, sham, phoney *or* phony (*informal*)

dump *vb* **1 = drop**, deposit, throw down, let fall, fling down **2 = get rid of**, tip, discharge, dispose of, unload, jettison, empty out, coup (*Scot*), throw away *or* out ▹*n* **6 = rubbish tip**, tip, junkyard, rubbish heap, refuse heap **7** (*informal*) **= pigsty**, hole (*informal*), joint (*slang*), slum, shack, shanty, hovel

d

DICTIONARY

Dunbar[1] *n* a port and resort in SE Scotland, in East Lothian: scene of Cromwell's defeat of the Scots (1650). Pop: 6354 (2001)

Dunbar[2] *n* **William** ?1460–?1520, Scottish poet, noted for his satirical, allegorical, and elegiac works

Duncan *n* **Isadora** 1878–1927, US dancer and choreographer, who influenced modern ballet by introducing greater freedom of movement

Duncan I *n* died 1040, king of Scotland (1034–40); killed by Macbeth

Duncan Smith *n* **(George) Iain** born 1954, British politician; leader of the Conservative Party (2001–03)

dunce *n Brit, Austral & NZ* a person who is stupid or slow to learn
WORD ORIGIN *Dunses*, term of ridicule applied to the followers of John *Duns Scotus*, scholastic theologian

Dundee[1] *n* **1** a port in E Scotland, in City of Dundee council area, on the Firth of Tay: centre of the former British jute industry; university (1967). Pop: 154 674 (2001) **2 City of Dundee** a council area in E Scotland. Pop: 143 090 (2003 est). Area: 65 sq km (25 sq miles)

Dundee[2] *n* **1st Viscount**, title of *John Graham of Claverhouse*. ?1649–89, Scottish Jacobite leader, who died from his wounds after winning the battle of Killiecrankie

dunderhead *n Brit, Austral & NZ* a slow-witted person
WORD ORIGIN probably from Dutch *donder* thunder + HEAD

dune *n* a mound or ridge of drifted sand
WORD ORIGIN Middle Dutch

dung *n* the faeces from large animals
WORD ORIGIN Old English: prison

dungarees *pl n* trousers with a bib attached
WORD ORIGIN *Dungrī*, district of Bombay, where the fabric used originated

dungeon *n* a prison cell, often underground
WORD ORIGIN Old French *donjon*

dunghill *n* a heap of dung

dunk *vb* **1** to dip (a biscuit or piece of bread) in a drink or soup before eating it **2** to put (something) in liquid: *dunk the garment in the dye for 15 minutes* **3** *basketball* to drop (the ball) through the hoop after having leapt high enough to have the hands above the rim ▷ *n* **4** *basketball* a scoring shot in which a player drops the ball through the hoop after having leapt high enough to have the hands above the rim
WORD ORIGIN Old High German *dunkōn*

dunlin *n* a small sandpiper, of northern and arctic regions, with a brown back and a black breast
WORD ORIGIN from DUN[2]

Dunlop *n* **John Boyd** 1840–1921, Scottish veterinary surgeon, who devised the first successful pneumatic tyre, which was manufactured by the company named after him

dunnock *n* ▸ same as **hedge sparrow**
WORD ORIGIN from DUN[2]

dunny ⓣ *n, pl* **-nies** *Austral or old-fashioned NZ informal* a toilet
WORD ORIGIN of obscure origin

Dunois *n* **Jean**, Comte de Dunois, known as *the Bastard of Orléans*. ?1403–68, French military commander, who defended Orléans against the English until the siege was raised by Joan of Arc (1429)

Dunsany *n* **18th Baron**, title of *Edward John Moreton Drax Plunkett*. 1878–1957, Irish dramatist and short-story writer

Dunstable[1] *n* an industrial town in SE central England, in Bedfordshire. Pop: 50 775 (2001)

Dunstable[2] *n* **John** died 1453, English composer, esp. of motets and mass settings, noted for his innovations in harmony and rhythm

Dunstan *n* **Saint** ?909–988 AD, English prelate and statesman; archbishop of Canterbury (959–988). He revived monasticism in England on Benedictine lines and promoted education. Feast day: May 19

duo *n, pl* **duos** **1** two singers or musicians who sing or play music together as a pair **2** *informal* two people who have something in common or do something together: *when they're together they make an impressive duo*
WORD ORIGIN Latin: two

duodecimal *adj* relating to twelve or twelfths
WORD ORIGIN Latin *duodecim* twelve

duodenum (dew-oh-**deen**-um) *n* the first part of the small intestine, just below the stomach **duodenal** *adj*
WORD ORIGIN Medieval Latin *intestinum duodenum digitorum* intestine of twelve fingers' length

duologue *or US sometimes* **duolog** *n* a part or all of a play in which the speaking roles are limited to two actors
WORD ORIGIN DUO + (MONO)LOGUE

DUP (in Northern Ireland) Democratic Unionist Party

Duparc *n* **Henri**, full name *Marie Eugène Henri Fouques Duparc*. 1848–1933, French composer of songs noted for their sad brooding quality

dupe *vb* **duping, duped** **1** to deceive or cheat: *you duped me into doing exactly what you wanted* ▷ *n* **2** a person who is easily deceived
WORD ORIGIN French

duple *adj* **1** ▸ same as **double** **2** *music* having two beats in a bar
WORD ORIGIN Latin *duplus* double

Dupleix *n* Marquis **Joseph François** 1697–1763, French governor general in India (1742–54). His plan to establish a French empire in India was frustrated by Clive

Duplessis-Mornay *n* a variant of (Philippe de) **Mornay**

duplex *n* **1** *US & Canad* **a** an apartment on two floors **b** *US & Austral* a semidetached house ▷ *adj* **2** having two parts
WORD ORIGIN Latin: twofold

duplicate ⓣ *adj* **1** copied exactly from an original: *he had a duplicate key to the front door* ▷ *n* **2** an exact copy **3 in duplicate** in two exact copies: *submit the draft in duplicate, please* ▷ *vb* **-cating, -cated** **4** to make an exact copy of **5** to do again (something that has already been done) **duplication** *n* **duplicator** *n*
WORD ORIGIN Latin *duplicare* to double

duplicity *n* deceitful behaviour: *he is a man of duplicity, who turns things to his advantage*
WORD ORIGIN Old French *duplicite*

du Pré *n* **Jacqueline** 1945–87, English cellist. Multiple sclerosis ended her performing career (1973) after which she became a cello teacher

Dupré *n* **Marcel** 1886–1971, French organist and composer, noted as an improviser

durable ⓣ *adj* strong and long-lasting: *the car's body was made of a light but durable plastic* **durability** *n*
WORD ORIGIN Latin *durare* to last

THESAURUS

dunny *n (Austral & NZ old-fashioned, informal)* **= toilet**, lavatory, bathroom, loo *(Brit informal)*, W.C., bog *(slang)*, Gents *or* Ladies, can *(US & Canad slang)*, john *(slang, chiefly US & Canad)*, head(s) *(nautical) (slang)*, throne *(informal)*, closet, privy, cloakroom *(Brit)*, urinal, latrine, washroom, powder room, crapper *(taboo, slang)*, water closet, khazi *(slang)*, pissoir *(French)*, little boy's room *or* little girl's room *(informal)*, (public) convenience, bogger *(Austral slang)*, brasco *(Austral slang)*

duplicate *adj* **1 = identical**, matched, matching, twin, corresponding, twofold ▷ *n* **2a = copy**, facsimile **2b = photocopy**, copy, reproduction, replica, Xerox®, carbon copy, Photostat® ▷ *vb* **4 = copy**, photocopy, Xerox®, Photostat® **5 = repeat**, reproduce, echo, copy, clone, replicate

durable *adj* **= hard-wearing**, strong, tough, sound, substantial, reliable, resistant, sturdy, long-lasting
OPPOSITE: fragile

DICTIONARY

durable goods *pl n* goods that do not require frequent replacement. Also called: **durables**
Durán *n* **Roberto** born 1951, Panamanian boxer
Durante *n* **Jimmy**, known as *Schnozzle*. 1893–1980, US comedian
Duras *n* **Marguerite**, real name *Marguerite Donnadieu*. 1914–96, French novelist born in Giadinh, Indochina (now in Vietnam). Her works include *The Sea Wall* (1950), *Practicalities* (1990), *Écrire* (1993), and the script for the film *Hiroshima mon amour* (1960)
duration ❶ *n* the length of time that something lasts
WORD ORIGIN Latin *durare* to last
durbar *n* **a** (formerly) the court of a native ruler or a governor in India **b** a reception at such a court
WORD ORIGIN Hindi *darbār*
duress *n* physical or moral pressure used to force someone to do something: *confessions obtained under duress*
WORD ORIGIN Latin *durus* hard
during *prep* throughout or within the limit of (a period of time)
WORD ORIGIN Latin *durare* to last
Durkan *n* **(John) Mark** born 1960, Northern Irish politician; leader of the Social Democratic and Labour Party (SDLP) from 2001
Durkheim *n* **Émile** 1858–1917, French sociologist, whose pioneering works include *De la Division du travail social* (1893)
Durrell *n* **1 Gerald (Malcolm)** 1925–95, British zoologist and writer: his books include *The Bafut Beagles* (1954), *My Family and Other Animals* (1956), and *The Aye-aye and I* (1992) **2** his brother, **Lawrence (George)** 1912–90, British poet and novelist; author of *The Alexandria Quartet* of novels, consisting of *Justine* (1957), *Balthazar* (1958), *Mountolive* (1958), and *Clea* (1960). Later works include *The Avignon Quintet* of novels (1974–85)
Dürrenmatt *n* **Friedrich** 1921–90, Swiss dramatist and writer of detective stories, noted for his grotesque and paradoxical treatment of the modern world: author of *The Visit* (1956) and *The Physicists* (1962)
Duruflé *n* **Maurice** 1902–86, French composer and organist, best known for his *Requiem* (1947)
Duse *n* **Eleonora** 1858–1924, Italian actress, noted as a tragedienne
dusk ❶ *n* the time just before nightfall when it is almost dark
WORD ORIGIN Old English *dox*
dusky *adj* **duskier, duskiest 1** dark in colour: *her gold earings gleamed against her dusky cheeks* **2** dim or shadowy: *the dusky room was crowded with absurd objects*
duskily *adv* **duskiness** *n*
dust ❶ *n* **1** small dry particles of earth, sand, or dirt **2 bite the dust a** to stop functioning: *my television has finally bitten the dust* **b** to fall down dead **3 shake the dust off one's feet** to depart angrily **4 throw dust in someone's eyes** to confuse or mislead someone ▷ *vb* **5** to remove dust from (furniture) by wiping **6** to sprinkle (something) with a powdery substance: *serve dusted with brown sugar and cinnamon*
WORD ORIGIN Old English *dūst*
dustbin *n* a large, usually cylindrical, container for household rubbish
dust bowl *n* a dry area in which the surface soil is exposed to wind erosion
dustcart *n chiefly Brit & NZ* a lorry for collecting household rubbish
dust cover *n* **1** ▸ same as **dustsheet 2** ▸ same as **dust jacket**
duster *n* a cloth used for dusting
dust jacket *or* **cover** *n* a removable paper cover used to protect a book
dustman *n, pl* **-men** *Brit* a man whose job is to collect household rubbish
dust mite *n* one of two varieties of mites that feed on shed human skin cells and whose excrement is a household allergen
dustpan *n* a short-handled shovel into which dust is swept from floors
dustsheet *n* a large cloth cover used to protect furniture from dust
dust-up *n informal* a fight or argument
dusty ❶ *adj* **dustier, dustiest 1** covered with dust **2** (of a colour) tinged with grey
Dutch *adj* **1** of the Netherlands ▷ *n* **2** the language of the Netherlands ▷ *pl n* **3 the Dutch** the people of the Netherlands ▷ *adv* **4 go Dutch** *informal* to go on an outing where each person pays his or her own expenses
Dutch auction *n* an auction in which the price is lowered by stages until a buyer is found
Dutch barn *n Brit* a farm building with a steel frame and a curved roof
Dutch courage *n* false courage gained from drinking alcohol
Dutch elm disease *n* a fungal disease of elm trees
Dutchman *or fem* **Dutchwoman** *n, pl* **-men** *or* **-women** a person from the Netherlands
Dutch oven *n* **1** an iron or earthenware container with a lid, used for stews, etc. **2** a metal box, open in front, for cooking in front of an open fire
Dutch treat *n informal* an outing where each person pays his or her own expenses
Dutch uncle *n informal* a person who criticizes or scolds frankly and severely
duteous *adj formal or archaic* dutiful or obedient
dutiable *adj* (of goods) requiring payment of duty
dutiful *adj* doing what is expected: *she is a responsible and dutiful mother*
dutifully *adv*
Dutton *n* **Clarence Edward** 1841–1912, American geologist who first developed the theory of isostasy
duty ❶ *n, pl* **-ties 1** the work performed as part of one's job: *it is his duty to supervise the memorial services* **2** a obligation to fulfil one's responsibilities: *it's my duty as a doctor to keep it confidential* **3** a government tax on imports **4 on** *or* **off duty** at (or not at) work
WORD ORIGIN Anglo-French *dueté*
duty-bound *adj* morally obliged to do something: *we are duty-bound to take whatever measures are necessary*
duty-free *adj, adv* with exemption from customs or excise duties
duty-free shop *n* a shop, esp. at an airport, that sells duty-free goods
Duvalier *n* **1 François** known as *Papa Doc*. 1907–71, president of Haiti (1957–71) **2** his son, **Jean-Claude** known as *Baby Doc*. born 1951, Haitian statesman; president of Haiti 1971–86; deposed and exiled
duvet (doo-vay) *n* ▸ same as **continental quilt**
WORD ORIGIN French
Du Vigneaud *n* **Vincent** 1901–78, US biochemist: Nobel prize for chemistry (1955) for his synthesis of the hormones oxytocin and vasopressin
DVD Digital Versatile *or* Video Disk: a type of compact disc that can store large amounts of video and audio information
DVLA *Brit* Driver and Vehicle Licensing Agency
DVT deep-vein thrombosis
dwaal *n S African* a state of absent-

THESAURUS

duration *n* **= length**, time, period, term, stretch, extent, spell, span, time frame, timeline
dusk *n* **= twilight**, evening, evo *(Austral slang)*, nightfall, sunset, dark, sundown, eventide, gloaming *(Scot poetic)* OPPOSITE: dawn
dust *n* **1a = grime**, grit, powder, powdery dirt **1b = particles**, fine fragments ▷ *vb* **6 = sprinkle**, cover, powder, spread, spray, scatter, sift, dredge
dusty *adj* **1 = dirty**, grubby, unclean, unswept, undusted
duty *n* **1, 2 = responsibility**, job, task, work, calling, business, service, office, charge, role, function, mission, province, obligation, assignment, pigeon *(informal)*, onus **3 = tax**, customs, toll, levy, tariff, excise, due, impost

DICTIONARY

mindedness; a daze
WORD ORIGIN Afrikaans

dwang *n NZ & S African* a short piece of wood inserted in a timber-framed wall

dwarf ❶ *vb* **1** to cause (someone or something) to seem small by being much larger ▹ *adj* **2** (of an animal or plant) much below the average size for the species: *a dwarf evergreen shrub* ▹ *n, pl* **dwarfs** *or* **dwarves 3** a person who is smaller than average size **4** (in folklore) a small ugly manlike creature, often possessing magical powers
WORD ORIGIN Old English *dweorg*

dwell ❶ *vb* **dwelling, dwelt** *or* **dwelled** *formal, literary* to live as a permanent resident **dweller** *n*
WORD ORIGIN Old English *dwellan* to seduce, get lost

dwelling ❶ *n formal, literary* a place of residence

dwell on *or* **upon** *vb* to think, speak, or write at length about (something)

dwindle ❶ *vb* **-dling, -dled** to grow less in size, strength, or number
WORD ORIGIN Old English *dwīnan*

Dy *chem* dysprosium

dye ❶ *n* **1** a colouring substance **2** the colour produced by dyeing ▹ *vb* **dyeing, dyed 3** to colour (hair or fabric) by applying a dye **dyer** *n*
WORD ORIGIN Old English *dēag*

dyed-in-the-wool *adj* having strong and unchanging attitudes or opinions: *he's a dyed-in-the-wool communist*

dying ❶ *vb* **1** ▸ the present participle of **die**[1] ▹ *adj* **2** occurring at the moment of death: *in accordance with his dying wish* **3** (of a person or animal) very ill and likely to die soon **4** becoming less important or less current: *coal mining is a dying industry*

dyke[1] *or esp. US* **dike** *n* **1** a wall built to prevent flooding **2** a ditch **3** *Scot* a dry-stone wall
WORD ORIGIN Old English *dic* ditch

dyke[2] *or* **dike** *n slang* a lesbian
WORD ORIGIN origin unknown

Dyke *n* **Greg**(**ory**) born 1947, British television executive; director-general of the BBC (2000–04)

dynamic ❶ *adj* **1** (of a person) full of energy, ambition, or new ideas **2** relating to a force of society, history, or the mind that produces a change: *the government needs a more dynamic policy towards the poor* **3** *physics* relating to energy or forces that produce motion **dynamically** *adv*
WORD ORIGIN Greek *dunamis* power

dynamics *n* **1** the branch of mechanics concerned with the forces that change or produce the motions of bodies ▹ *pl n* **2** those forces that produce change in any field or system **3** *music* the various degrees of loudness called for in a performance

dynamism *n* great energy or enthusiasm

dynamite *n* **1** an explosive made of nitroglycerine **2** *informal* a dangerous or exciting person or thing: *she's still dynamite* ▹ *vb* **-miting, -mited 3** to mine or blow (something) up with dynamite
WORD ORIGIN Greek *dunamis* power

dynamo *n, pl* **-mos** a device for converting mechanical energy into electricity
WORD ORIGIN short for *dynamoelectric machine*

dynamoelectric *adj* of the conversion of mechanical energy into electricity or vice versa

dynamometer (dine-a-**mom**-it-er) *n* an instrument for measuring mechanical power or force

dynast *n* a hereditary ruler
WORD ORIGIN Greek *dunasthai* to be powerful

dynasty ❶ *n, pl* **-ties 1** a series of rulers of a country from the same family **2** a period of time during which a country is ruled by the same family **dynastic** *adj*
WORD ORIGIN Greek *dunastēs* dynast

dysentery *n* infection of the intestine which causes severe diarrhoea
WORD ORIGIN Greek *dusentera* bad bowels

dysfunction *n* **1** *med* any disturbance or abnormality in the function of an organ or part **2** (esp. of a family) failure to show the characteristics or fulfil the purposes accepted as normal or beneficial **dysfunctional** *adj*

dyslexia *n* a developmental disorder that causes learning difficulty with reading, writing, and numeracy **dyslexic** *adj, n*
WORD ORIGIN Greek *dus-* not + *lexis* word

dysmenorrhoea *or esp. US* **dysmenorrhea** *n* painful or difficult menstruation
WORD ORIGIN Greek *dus-* bad + *rhoia* a flowing

Dyson *n* Sir **James** born 1947, British businessman and industrial designer; inventor of the bagless vacuum cleaner (1979–93)

dyspepsia *n* indigestion **dyspeptic** *adj, n*
WORD ORIGIN Greek *dus-* bad + *pepsis* digestion

dysprosium *n chem* a metallic element of the lanthanide series. Symbol: Dy
WORD ORIGIN Greek *dusprositos* difficult to get near

dystrophy (**diss**-trof-fee) *n* ▸ see **muscular dystrophy**
WORD ORIGIN Greek *dus-* not + *trophē* food

THESAURUS

4 on duty = at work, busy, engaged, on active service

dwarf *vb* **1 = tower above** *or* **over**, dominate, overlook, stand over, loom over, stand head and shoulders above ▹ *adj* **2 = miniature**, small, baby, tiny, pocket, dwarfed, diminutive, petite, bonsai, pint-sized, undersized, teeny-weeny, Lilliputian, teensy-weensy *n* **4 = gnome**, midget, Lilliputian, Tom Thumb, munchkin *(informal, chiefly US)*, homunculus, manikin, hop-o'-my-thumb, pygmy *or* pigmy

dwell *vb (formal, literary)* **= live**, stay, reside, rest, quarter, settle, lodge, abide, hang out *(informal)*, sojourn, establish yourself

dwelling *n (formal, literary)* **= home**, house, residence, abode, quarters, establishment, lodging, pad *(slang)*, habitation, domicile, dwelling house, whare *(NZ)*

dwindle *vb* **= lessen**, fall, decline, contract, sink, fade, weaken, shrink, diminish, decrease, decay, wither, wane, subside, ebb, die down, die out, abate, shrivel, peter out, die away, waste away, taper off, grow less **OPPOSITE:** increase

dye *n* **2 = colouring**, colour, pigment, stain, tint, tinge, colorant ▹ *vb* **3 = colour**, stain, tint, tinge, pigment, tincture

dying *adj* **2 = final**, last, parting, departing **3 = near death**, going, failing, fading, doomed, expiring, ebbing, near the end, moribund, fading fast, in extremis *(Latin)*, at death's door, not long for this world, on your deathbed, breathing your last **4 = failing**, declining, sinking, foundering, diminishing, decreasing, dwindling, subsiding

dynamic *adj* **1, 2 = energetic**, spirited, powerful, active, vital, driving, electric, go-ahead, lively, magnetic, vigorous, animated, high-powered, forceful, go-getting *(informal)*, tireless, indefatigable, high-octane *(informal)*, zippy *(informal)*, full of beans *(informal)* **OPPOSITE:** apathetic

dynasty *n* **1, 2 = empire**, house, rule, regime, sovereignty

Ee

DICTIONARY

e *maths* a number used as the base of natural logarithms. Approximate value: 2.718 282...

E **1** *music* the third note of the scale of C major **2** East(ern) **3** English **4** *physics* **a** energy **b** electromotive force **5** *slang* the drug ecstasy or an ecstasy tablet

e- *prefix* electronic: *e-mail; e-tailer*

E- *prefix* used with a number following it to indicate that something, such as a food additive, conforms to an EU standard

each Ⓣ *adj* **1** every one of two or more people or things considered individually: *each year* ▷ *pron* **2** every one of two or more people or things: *each had been given one room to design* ▷ *adv* **3** for, to, or from each person or thing: *twenty pounds each* **4** **each other** (of two or more people) each one to or at the other or others; one another: *they stared at each other*
WORD ORIGIN Old English *ǣlc*

Eadred *n* died 955 AD, king of England (946–55): regained Northumbria (954) from the Norwegian king Eric Bloodaxe

Eadwig *or* **Edwy** *n* died 959 AD, king of England (955–57)

eager Ⓣ *adj* very keen to have or do something **eagerly** *adv* **eagerness** *n*
WORD ORIGIN Latin *acer* sharp, keen

eagle *n* **1** a large bird of prey with broad wings and strong soaring flight **2** *golf* a score of two strokes under par for a hole
WORD ORIGIN Latin *aquila*

eagle-eyed *adj* having very sharp eyesight

eaglet *n* a young eagle

Eakins *n* **Thomas** 1844–1916, US painter of portraits and sporting life: a noted realist

ear¹ Ⓣ *n* **1** the part of the body with which a person or animal hears **2** the external, visible part of the ear **3** the ability to hear musical and other sounds and interpret them accurately: *a good ear for languages* **4** willingness to listen: *they are always willing to lend an ear* **5** **be all ears** to be prepared to listen attentively to something **6** **fall on deaf ears** to be ignored: *his words fell on deaf ears* **7** **in one ear and out the other** heard but quickly forgotten or ignored **8** **out on one's ear** *informal* dismissed suddenly and unpleasantly **9** **play by ear** to play without written music **10** **play it by ear** *informal* to make up one's plan of action as one goes along **11** **turn a deaf ear to** to be deliberately unresponsive to: *many countries have turned a deaf ear to their cries for help* **12** **up to one's ears in** *informal* deeply involved in
WORD ORIGIN Old English *ēare*

ear² *n* the part of a cereal plant, such as wheat or barley, that contains the seeds
WORD ORIGIN Old English *ēar*

earache *n* pain in the ear

earbash *vb Brit, Austral & NZ informal* to talk incessantly **earbashing** *n*

eardrum *n* the thin membrane separating the external ear from the middle ear

earful *n informal* a scolding or telling-off

earl *n* (in Britain) a nobleman ranking below a marquess and above a viscount **earldom** *n*
WORD ORIGIN Old English *eorl*

Earl Grey *n* a variety of China tea flavoured with oil of bergamot

ear lobe *n* the soft hanging lowest part of the human ear

early Ⓣ *adj* **-lier, -liest** **1** occurring or arriving before the correct or expected time **2** in the first part of a period of time: *early April* **3** near the beginning of the development or history of something: *early Britain was very primitive; early models of this car rust easily* ▷ *adv* **4** occurring or arriving before the correct or expected time **5** in the first part of a period of time **6** near the beginning of the development or history of something: *early in the war*
WORD ORIGIN Old English *ǣrlīce*

Early English *n* a style of architecture used in England in the 12th and 13th centuries, characterized by narrow pointed arches and ornamental intersecting stonework in windows

earmark Ⓣ *vb* **1** to set (something) aside for a specific purpose ▷ *n* **2** a feature that enables the nature of something to be identified: *it had all the earmarks of a disaster*

earn Ⓣ *vb* **1** to gain or be paid (money) in return for work **2** to acquire or deserve through one's behaviour or action: *you've earned a good night's sleep* **3** to make (money) as interest or profit: *her savings earned 8% interest* **earner** *n*
WORD ORIGIN Old English *earnian*

earnest¹ Ⓣ *adj* **1** serious and sincere, often excessively so ▷ *n* **2** **in earnest** with serious or sincere intentions **earnestly** *adv* **earnestness** *n*
WORD ORIGIN Old English *eornost*

earnest² *n Brit, Austral & NZ, old-fashioned* a part payment given in advance as a guarantee of the remainder, esp. to confirm a contract
WORD ORIGIN Old French *erres* pledges

earnings Ⓣ *pl n* money earned

earphone *n* a small device connected to a radio or tape recorder and worn over the ear, so that a person can

THESAURUS

each *adj* **1 = every**, every single ▷ *pron* **2 = every one**, all, each one, each and every one, one and all ▷ *adv* **3 = apiece**, individually, singly, for each, to each, respectively, per person, from each, per head, per capita

eager *adj* **a** *(often with* **to** *or* **for***)* **= anxious**, keen, raring, hungry, intent, yearning, impatient, itching, thirsty, zealous
OPPOSITE: unenthusiastic
b = keen, interested, earnest, intense, enthusiastic, passionate, ardent, avid *(informal)*, fervent, zealous, fervid, keen as mustard, bright-eyed and bushy-tailed *(informal)* **OPPOSITE:** uninterested

ear¹ *n* **3 = sensitivity**, taste, discrimination, appreciation, musical perception

early *adj* **1 = premature**, forward, advanced, untimely, unseasonable
OPPOSITE: belated
2 = first, opening, earliest, initial, introductory **3 = primitive**, first, earliest, young, original, undeveloped, primordial, primeval
OPPOSITE: developed
▷ *adv* **4a = in good time**, beforehand, ahead of schedule, in advance, with time to spare, betimes *(archaic)*
OPPOSITE: late
4b = too soon, before the usual time, prematurely, ahead of time
OPPOSITE: late

earmark *vb* **1 = set aside**, reserve, label, flag, tag, allocate, designate, mark out, keep back

earn *vb* **1 = be paid**, make, get, receive, draw, gain, net, collect, bring in, gross, procure, clear, get paid, take home **2 = deserve**, win, gain, attain, justify, merit, warrant, be entitled to, reap, be worthy of

earnest¹ *adj* **1a = serious**, keen, grave, intense, steady, dedicated, eager, enthusiastic, passionate, sincere, thoughtful, solemn, ardent, fervent, impassioned, zealous, staid, keen as mustard **OPPOSITE:** frivolous
1b = determined, firm, dogged, constant, urgent, intent, persistent, ardent, persevering, resolute, heartfelt, zealous, vehement, wholehearted **OPPOSITE:** half-hearted

earnings *pl n* **= income**, pay, wages, revenue, reward, proceeds, salary, receipts, return, remuneration,

DICTIONARY

listen to a broadcast or tape without anyone else hearing it

ear-piercing *adj* extremely loud or shrill

earplug *n* a piece of soft material placed in the ear to keep out noise or water

earring *n* a piece of jewellery worn in or hanging from the ear lobe

earshot *n* the range within which a sound can be heard: *out of earshot*

ear-splitting *adj* extremely loud or shrill

earth ❶ *n* **1** (*sometimes cap*) the planet that we live on, the third planet from the sun, the only one on which life is known to exist ▸ Related adjective: **terrestrial** **2** the part of the surface of this planet that is not water **3** the soil in which plants grow **4** the hole in which a fox lives **5** a wire in a piece of electrical equipment through which electricity can escape into the ground if a fault develops **6** **come down to earth** to return to reality from a daydream or fantasy **7** **on earth** used for emphasis: *what on earth happened?* ▹ *vb* **8** to fit (a piece of electrical equipment) with an earth **WORD ORIGIN** Old English *eorthe*

earthbound *adj* **1** unable to leave the surface of the earth **2** lacking in imagination

earthen *adj* made of earth or baked clay: *an earthen floor*

earthenware *n* dishes and other objects made of baked clay: *an earthenware flowerpot*

earthly ❶ *adj* **-lier, -liest** **1** of life on earth as opposed to any heavenly or spiritual state **2** *informal* conceivable or possible: *what earthly reason would they have for lying?*

earthquake *n* a series of vibrations at the earth's surface caused by movement of the earth's crust

earth science *n* any science, such as geology, concerned with the structure, age, etc. of the earth

earth-shattering *adj* very surprising or shocking: *an earth-shattering event*

earthwards *adv* towards the earth

earthwork *n* **1** excavation of earth, as in engineering construction **2** a fortification made of earth

earthworm *n* a common worm that burrows in the soil

earthy *adj* **earthier, earthiest** **1** open and direct in the treatment of sex, excretion, etc. **2** of or like earth: *earthy colours* **earthiness** *n*

earwig *n* a thin brown insect with pincers at the tip of its abdomen **WORD ORIGIN** Old English *ēarwicga*, from *ēare* ear + *wicga* beetle

ease ❶ *n* **1** lack of difficulty **2** freedom from discomfort or worry **3** rest, leisure, or relaxation **4** freedom from poverty: *a life of leisure and ease* **5** **at ease** **a** *mil* (of a soldier) standing in a relaxed position with the feet apart **b** in a relaxed attitude or frame of mind ▹ *vb* **easing, eased** **6** to make or become less difficult or severe: *the pain gradually eased* **7** to move into or out of a place or situation slowly and carefully **8** **ease off** *or* **up** to lessen or cause to lessen in severity, pressure, tension, or strain: *the rain eased off* **WORD ORIGIN** Old French *aise*

easel *n* a frame on legs, used for supporting an artist's canvas, a display, or a blackboard **WORD ORIGIN** Dutch *ezel* ass

easily ❶ *adv* **1** without difficulty **2** without doubt; by far: *easily the most senior Chinese leader to visit the West*

east *n* **1** one of the four cardinal points of the compass, at 90° clockwise from north **2** the direction along a line of latitude towards the sunrise **3** **the east** any area lying in or towards the east ▹ *adj* **4** situated in, moving towards, or facing the east **5** (esp. of the wind) from the east ▹ *adv* **6** in, to, or towards the east **WORD ORIGIN** Old English *ēast*

East *n* **1** **the East** **a** the southern and eastern parts of Asia **b** (esp. formerly) the countries in Eastern Europe and Asia which are or have been under Communist rule ▹ *adj* **2** of or denoting the eastern part of a country or region

eastbound *adj* going towards the east

Easter *n* **1** *Christianity* a festival commemorating the Resurrection of Christ ▹ *adj* **2** taking place at the time of the year when this festival is celebrated: *the Easter holidays* **WORD ORIGIN** Old English *ēastre*

Easter egg *n* a chocolate egg given at Easter

easterly *adj* **1** of or in the east ▹ *adv, adj* **2** towards the east **3** from the east: *an easterly breeze*

eastern *adj* **1** situated in or towards the east **2** facing or moving towards the east **3** (*sometimes cap*) of or characteristic of the east or East **easternmost** *adj*

Easterner *n* a person from the east of a country or region

eastern hemisphere *n* the half of the globe that contains Europe, Asia, Africa, and Australia

eastings *pl n* a series of numbers in a grid reference indicating the distance eastwards from a given meridian

Eastman *n* **George** 1854–1932, US manufacturer of photographic equipment: noted for the introduction of roll film and developments in colour photography

eastward *adj, adv also* **eastwards** **1** towards the east ▹ *n* **2** the eastward part or direction

easy ❶ *adj* **easier, easiest** **1** not difficult; simple: *the house is easy to keep clean* **2** free from pain, care, or anxiety: *an easy life* **3** tolerant and undemanding; easy-going **4** defenceless or readily fooled: *easy prey* **5** moderate and not involving any great effort: *an easy ride* **6** *informal* ready to fall in with any suggestion

THESAURUS

takings, stipend, take-home pay, emolument, gross pay, net pay

earth *n* **1 = world**, planet, globe, sphere, orb, earthly sphere, terrestrial sphere **2 = ground**, land, dry land, terra firma **3 = soil**, ground, land, dust, mould, clay, dirt, turf, sod, silt, topsoil, clod, loam

earthly *adj* **1 = worldly**, material, physical, secular, mortal, mundane, terrestrial, temporal, human, materialistic, profane, telluric, sublunary, non-spiritual, tellurian, terrene **OPPOSITE:** spiritual **2** (*informal*) **= possible**, likely, practical, feasible, conceivable, imaginable

ease *n* **1 = straightforwardness**, simplicity, readiness **2 = peace of mind**, peace, content, quiet, comfort, happiness, enjoyment, serenity, tranquillity, contentment, calmness, quietude **OPPOSITE:** agitation **3, 4 = comfort**, luxury, leisure, relaxation, prosperity, affluence, rest, repose, restfulness **OPPOSITE:** hardship ▹ *vb* **6a = relieve**, calm, moderate, soothe, lessen, alleviate, appease, lighten, lower, allay, relax, still, mitigate, assuage, pacify, mollify, tranquillize, palliate **OPPOSITE:** aggravate **7 = move carefully**, edge, guide, slip, inch, slide, creep, squeeze, steer, manoeuvre **8** (*often with* **off** *or* **up**) **= reduce**, moderate, weaken, diminish, decrease, slow down, dwindle, lessen, die down, abate, slacken, grow less, de-escalate

easily *adv* **1 = without difficulty**, smoothly, readily, comfortably, effortlessly, simply, with ease, straightforwardly, without trouble, standing on your head, with your eyes closed *or* shut

easy *adj* **1 = simple**, straightforward, no trouble, not difficult, effortless, painless, clear, light, uncomplicated, child's play (*informal*), plain sailing, undemanding, a pushover (*slang*), a piece of cake (*informal*), no bother, a bed of roses, easy-peasy (*slang*) **OPPOSITE:** hard **2a = untroubled**, contented, relaxed, satisfied, calm, peaceful, serene, tranquil, quiet, undisturbed,

made: *he wanted to do something and I was easy about it* **7** *informal* pleasant and not involving any great effort to enjoy: *easy on the eye* ▷*adv* **8 go easy on a** to avoid using too much of: *he'd tried to go easy on the engines* **b** to treat less severely than is deserved: *go easy on him, he's just a kid* **9 take it easy** to relax and avoid stress or undue hurry **easiness** *n*
WORD ORIGIN Old French *aisié*

easy chair *n* a comfortable upholstered armchair

easy-going *adj* relaxed in manner or attitude; very tolerant

eat ❶ *vb* **eating, ate, eaten 1** to take (food) into the mouth and swallow it **2** to have a meal: *sometimes we eat out of doors* **3** *informal* to make anxious or worried: *what's eating you?* **4 eat away** *or* **into** *or* **up** to destroy or use up partly or wholly: *inflation ate into the firm's profits* ▶ See also **eat out, eat up** > **eater** *n*
WORD ORIGIN Old English *etan*

eatable *adj* fit or suitable for eating

eating *n* **1** food in relation to its quality or taste: *these add up to lots of vitamins and minerals, and good eating* ▷*adj* **2** suitable for eating uncooked: *eating apples*

eat out *vb* to eat at a restaurant

eat up *vb* **1** to eat or consume entirely: *eat up these potatoes* **2** *informal* to affect severely: *I was eaten up by jealousy*

eau de Cologne (oh de kol-**lone**) *n* ▶ full form of **cologne**
WORD ORIGIN French: water of Cologne

eau de vie (oh de **vee**) *n* brandy or a similar alcoholic drink
WORD ORIGIN French: water of life

eaves *pl n* the edge of a sloping roof that overhangs the walls
WORD ORIGIN Old English *efes*

eavesdrop *vb* **-dropping, -dropped** to listen secretly to a private conversation **eavesdropper** *n*
WORD ORIGIN Old English *yfesdrype* water dripping from the eaves

eavestrough *n Canad* a gutter at the eaves of a building

ebb ❶ *vb* **1** (of the sea or the tide) to flow back from its highest point **2** to fall away or decline: *her anger ebbed away* ▷*n* **3** the flowing back of the tide from high to low water **4 at a low ebb** in a weak state: *her creativity was at a low ebb*
WORD ORIGIN Old English *ebba* ebb-tide

Ebbinghaus *n* **Hermann** 1850–1909, German experimental psychologist who undertook the first systematic and large-scale studies of memory and devised tests using nonsense syllables

Eberhard *n* **Johann August** 1739–1809, German philosopher and lexicographer, best known for his German dictionary (1795–1802)

Ebert *n* **Friedrich** 1871–1925, German Social Democratic statesman; first president of the German Republic (1919–25)

ebony *n* **1** a very hard dark-coloured wood used to make furniture etc. ▷*adj* **2** very deep black
WORD ORIGIN Greek *ebenos*

ebullient *adj* full of enthusiasm or excitement **ebullience** *n*
WORD ORIGIN Latin *ebullire* to bubble forth, be boisterous

EC 1 European Commission **2** European Community: a former name for the European Union

eccentric ❶ *adj* **1** unconventional or odd **2** (of circles) not having the same centre ▷*n* **3** a person who behaves unconventionally or oddly **eccentrically** *adv*
WORD ORIGIN Greek *ek-* away from + *kentron* centre

eccentricity *n* **1** unconventional or odd behaviour **2** *pl* **-ties** an unconventional or odd habit or act

Eccles[1] *n* a town in NW England, in Salford unitary authority, Greater Manchester. Pop: 36 610 (2001)

Eccles[2] *n* Sir **John Carew** 1903–97, Australian physiologist: shared the Nobel prize for physiology (1963) with A. L. Hodgkin and A. F. Huxley for their work on conduction of nervous impulses

ecclesiastic *n* **1** a member of the clergy ▷*adj* **2** of or relating to the Christian Church or its clergy
WORD ORIGIN Greek *ekklēsia* assembly

ecclesiastical *adj* of or relating to the Christian Church or its clergy

Ecclestone *n* **Bernard**, known as *Bernie*. born 1930, British businessman and sports administrator; head of Formula One motor racing from 1995

Ecevit *n* **Bülent** 1925–2006, Turkish politician and journalist: prime minister of Turkey (1974, 1977, 1978–79, 1998–2002)

ECG electrocardiogram

Echegaray y Eizaguirre *n* **José** 1832–1916, Spanish dramatist, statesman, and mathematician. His plays include *Madman or Saint* (1877); Nobel prize for literature 1904

echelon (**esh**-a-lon) *n* **1** a level of power or responsibility: *the upper echelons of society* **2** *mil* a formation in which units follow one another but are spaced out sideways to allow each a line of fire ahead
WORD ORIGIN French *échelon* rung of a ladder

echidna (ik-**kid**-na) *n, pl* **-nas, -nae** (-nee) an Australian spiny egg-laying mammal. Also called: **spiny anteater**

echinoderm (ik-**kine**-oh-durm) *n* a sea creature with a five-part symmetrical body, such as a starfish or sea urchin
WORD ORIGIN Greek *ekhinos* sea urchin + *derma* skin

echo ❶ *n, pl* **-oes 1 a** the reflection of sound by a solid object **b** a sound reflected by a solid object **2** a repetition or imitation of someone else's opinions **3** something that

unworried **2b = carefree**, comfortable, leisurely, trouble-free, untroubled, cushy *(informal)*
OPPOSITE: difficult
3 = tolerant, light, liberal, soft, flexible, mild, laid-back *(informal)*, indulgent, easy-going, lenient, permissive, unoppressive
OPPOSITE: strict

eat *vb* **1 = consume**, swallow, chew, scoff *(slang)*, devour, munch, tuck into *(informal)*, put away, gobble, polish off *(informal)*, wolf down **2 = have a meal**, lunch, breakfast, dine, snack, feed, graze *(informal)*, have lunch, have dinner, have breakfast, nosh *(slang)*, take food, have supper, break bread, chow down *(slang)*, take nourishment

ebb *vb* **1 = flow back**, go out, withdraw, sink, retreat, fall back, wane, recede, fall away **2 = decline**, drop, sink, flag, weaken, shrink, diminish, decrease, deteriorate, decay, dwindle, lessen, subside, degenerate, fall away, fade away, abate, peter out, slacken ▷*n* **3 = flowing back**, going out, withdrawal, retreat, wane, waning, regression, low water, low tide, ebb tide, outgoing tide, falling tide, receding tide

eccentric *adj* **1 = odd**, strange, bizarre, weird, peculiar, abnormal, queer *(informal)*, irregular, uncommon, quirky, singular, unconventional, idiosyncratic, off-the-wall *(slang)*, outlandish, whimsical, rum *(Brit slang)*, capricious, anomalous, freakish, aberrant, wacko *(slang)*, outré, daggy *(Austral & NZ informal)*
OPPOSITE: normal
▷*n* **3 = crank** *(informal)*, character *(informal)*, nut *(slang)*, freak *(informal)*, flake *(slang, chiefly US)*, oddity, oddball *(informal)*, loose cannon, nonconformist, wacko *(slang)*, case *(informal)*, screwball *(slang, chiefly US & Canad)*, card *(informal)*, odd fish *(informal)*, kook *(US & Canad informal)*, queer fish *(Brit informal)*, rum customer *(Brit slang)*, weirdo *or* weirdie *(informal)*

echo *n* **1a, 1b = reverberation**, ringing, repetition, answer, resonance, resounding **2 = copy**, reflection, clone, reproduction, imitation, duplicate, double, reiteration ▷*vb*

DICTIONARY

brings back memories: *an echo of the past* **4** the signal reflected back to a radar transmitter by an object ▷ *vb* **-oing, -oed 5** (of a sound) to be reflected off an object in such a way that it can be heard again **6** (of a place) to be filled with a sound and its echoes: *the church echoed with singing* **7** (of people) to repeat or imitate (what someone else has said): *his conclusion echoed that of Jung*
echoing *adj*
WORD ORIGIN Greek *ēkhō*

e

echo chamber *n* a room with walls that reflect sound, used to create an echo effect in recording and broadcasting

echolocation *n* the discovery of an object's position by measuring the time taken for an echo to return from it

echo sounder *n* a navigation device that determines depth by measuring the time taken for a pulse of sound to reach the sea bed and for the echo to return

Eck *n* **Johann**, original name *Johann Mayer.* 1486–1543, German Roman Catholic theologian; opponent of Luther and the Reformation

Eckert *n* **John Presper** 1919–95, US electronics engineer: built the first electronic computer with John W. Mauchly in 1946

Eckhart *n* **Johannes**, called *Meister Eckhart.* ?1260–?1327, German Dominican theologian, mystic, and preacher

éclair *n* a finger-shaped cake of choux pastry, filled with cream and coated with chocolate
WORD ORIGIN French: lightning (probably because it does not last long)

eclampsia *n pathol* a serious condition that can develop towards the end of a pregnancy, causing high blood pressure, swelling, and convulsions

eclectic *adj* **1** composed of elements selected from a wide range of styles, ideas, or sources: *the eclectic wine list includes bottles from all round the world* **2** selecting elements from a wide range of styles, ideas, or sources: *an eclectic approach that takes the best from all schools of psychology* ▷ *n* **3** a person who takes an eclectic approach
eclecticism *n*
WORD ORIGIN Greek *eklegein* to select

eclipse ⓘ *n* **1** the obscuring of one star or planet by another. A **solar eclipse** occurs when the moon passes between the sun and the earth; a **lunar eclipse** when the earth passes between the sun and the moon **2** a loss of importance, power, or fame: *communism eventually went into eclipse* ▷ *vb* **eclipsing, eclipsed 3** to overshadow or surpass **4** (of a star or planet) to hide (another planet or star) from view
WORD ORIGIN Greek *ekleipsis* a forsaking

ecliptic *n astron* the great circle on the celestial sphere representing the apparent annual path of the sun relative to the stars

eco- *combining form* denoting ecology or ecological: *ecotourism*

Eco *n* **Umberto** born 1932, Italian semiologist and writer. His novels include *The Name of the Rose* (1981) and *Foucault's Pendulum* (1988)

E.coli (ee-koal-eye) *n* a common bacterium often found in the intestines
WORD ORIGIN shortened from *Escherichia coli*, after Theodor *Escherich*, paediatrician

ecological *adj* **1** of or relating to ecology **2** tending or intended to benefit or protect the environment: *an ecological approach to agriculture*
ecologically *adv*

ecology *n* the study of the relationships between people, animals, and plants, and their environment **ecologist** *n*
WORD ORIGIN Greek *oikos* house

e-commerce *or* **ecommerce** *n* business transactions conducted on the internet

econ. economy

economic ⓘ *adj* **1** of or relating to an economy or economics **2** *Austral & Brit* capable of being produced or operated for profit **3** *informal* inexpensive or cheap

economical ⓘ *adj* **1** not requiring a lot of money to use: *low fuel consumption makes this car very economical* **2** (of a person) spending money carefully and sensibly **3** using no more time, effort, or resources than is necessary **4 economical with the truth** *euphemistic* deliberately withholding information
economically *adv*

economics *n* **1** the study of the production and consumption of goods and services and the commercial activities of a society ▷ *pl n* **2** financial aspects: *the economics of health care*

economist *n* a person who specializes in economics

economize *or* **-mise** *vb* **-mizing, -mized** *or* **-mising, -mised** to reduce expense or waste: *people are being advised to economize on fuel use*

economy ⓘ *n, pl* **-mies 1** the system by which the production, distribution, and consumption of goods and services is organized in a country or community: *the rural economy* **2** the ability of a country to generate wealth through business and industry: *unless the economy improves, more jobs will be lost* **3** careful use of money or resources to save expense, time, or energy **4** an instance of this: *we can make economies by reusing envelopes* ▷ *adj* **5** denoting a class of air travel that is cheaper than first-class **6** offering a larger quantity for a lower price: *an economy pack*
WORD ORIGIN Greek *oikos* house + *nemein* to manage

economy-class syndrome *n* a deep-vein thrombosis that has developed in the legs or pelvis of a person travelling for a long time in cramped conditions
WORD ORIGIN reference to the restricted legroom of cheaper seats on passenger aircraft

economy of scale *n econ* a fall in average costs resulting from an increase in the scale of production

ecosystem *n ecology* the system of relationships between animals and plants and their environment

ecotourism *n* tourism designed to contribute to the protection of the environment or at least minimize damage to it **ecotourist** *n*

ecru *adj* pale creamy-brown
WORD ORIGIN French

ecstasy ⓘ *n, pl* **-sies 1** a state of

THESAURUS

5, 6 = reverberate, repeat, resound, ring, resonate **7 = recall**, reflect, copy, mirror, resemble, reproduce, parrot, imitate, reiterate, ape

eclipse *n* **1 = obscuring**, covering, blocking, shading, dimming, extinction, darkening, blotting out, occultation ▷ *vb* **3 = surpass**, exceed, overshadow, excel, transcend, outdo, outclass, outshine, leave *or* put in the shade *(informal)*

economic *adj* **1 = financial**, business, trade, industrial, commercial, mercantile **2** *(Brit)* **= profitable**, successful, commercial, rewarding, productive, lucrative, worthwhile, viable, solvent, cost-effective, money-making, profit-making, remunerative **3** *(informal)* **= economical**, fair, cheap, reasonable, modest, low-priced, inexpensive

economical *adj* **2 = thrifty**, sparing, careful, prudent, provident, frugal, parsimonious, scrimping, economizing **OPPOSITE:** extravagant **3 = efficient**, sparing, cost-effective, money-saving, time-saving, work-saving, unwasteful **OPPOSITE:** wasteful

economy *n* **1 = financial system**, financial state **3 = thrift**, saving, restraint, prudence, providence, husbandry, retrenchment, frugality, parsimony, thriftiness, sparingness

ecstasy *n* **1 = rapture**, delight, joy,

DICTIONARY

extreme delight or joy **2** *slang* a strong drug that acts as a stimulant and can cause hallucinations **ecstatic** *adj* **ecstatically** *adv*
WORD ORIGIN Greek *ekstasis* displacement, trance

ECT electroconvulsive therapy: the treatment of depression and some other mental disorders by passing a current of electricity through the brain, producing a convulsion

ectomorph *n physiol* a person with a thin body build ▸ see also **endomorph, mesomorph** > **ectomorphic** *adj*
WORD ORIGIN Greek *ektos* outside + *morphē* shape

ectopic *adj med* (of an organ or other body part) congenitally displaced or abnormally positioned
WORD ORIGIN Greek *ektopos* out of position

ectoplasm *n* (in spiritualism) the substance that supposedly is emitted from the body of a medium during a trance
WORD ORIGIN Greek *ektos* outside + *plasma* something moulded

ecumenical *adj* **1** of or relating to the Christian Church throughout the world **2** tending to promote unity among Christian churches
WORD ORIGIN Greek *oikoumenikos* of the inhabited world

ecumenism *or* **ecumenicism** *n* the aim of unity among Christian churches throughout the world

eczema (ek-sim-a, ig-zeem-a) *n pathol* a condition in which the skin becomes inflamed and itchy
WORD ORIGIN Greek *ek-* out + *zein* to boil

ed. 1 edition **2** editor

Edam *n* a round yellow Dutch cheese with a red waxy covering
WORD ORIGIN after *Edam*, in Holland

Edberg *n* **Stefan** born 1966, Swedish tennis player: Wimbledon champion 1988, 1990

Eddery *n* **Patrick,** known as *Pat.* born 1952, Irish jockey

Eddington *n* Sir **Arthur Stanley** 1882–1944, English astronomer and physicist, noted for his research on the motion, internal constitution, and luminosity of stars and for his elucidation of the theory of relativity

eddo (ed-doh) *n, pl* **eddoes** ▸ same as **taro**

eddy *n, pl* **-dies 1** a circular movement of air, water, or smoke ▹ *vb* **-dies, -dying, -died 2** to move with a gentle circular motion; swirl gently
WORD ORIGIN probably from Old Norse

Edelman *n* **Gerald Maurice** born 1929, US biochemist: he shared the Nobel prize for physiology or medicine (1972) with Rodney Porter for determining the structure of antibodies

edelweiss (ade-el-vice) *n* a small white alpine flower
WORD ORIGIN German: noble white

edema (id-deem-a) *n, pl* **-mata** ▸ same as **oedema**

Eden *n* **1** Also called: **Garden of Eden** *bible* the garden in which Adam and Eve were placed at the Creation **2** a place of great delight or contentment
WORD ORIGIN Hebrew *'ēdhen* place of pleasure

edentate *n* **1** a mammal with few or no teeth, such as an armadillo or a sloth ▹ *adj* **2** denoting such a mammal
WORD ORIGIN Latin *edentatus* lacking teeth

Edgar *n* **1** 944–975 AD, king of Mercia and Northumbria (957–975) and of England (959–975) **2** ?1074–1107, king of Scotland (1097–1107), fourth son of Malcolm III. He overthrew his uncle Donald to gain the throne **3 David** born 1948, British dramatist, noted for political plays such as *Destiny* (1976), *Maydays* (1983), and *Albert Speer* (1999): he adapted (1980) *Nicholas Nickleby* and (1991) *Dr Jekyll and Mr Hyde* for the RSC

Edgar Atheling *n* ?1050–?1125, grandson of Edmund II; Anglo-Saxon pretender to the English throne in 1066

edge ❶ *n* **1** a border or line where something ends or begins: *the edge of the city* **2** a line along which two faces or surfaces of a solid meet **3** the sharp cutting side of a blade **4** keenness, sharpness, or urgency: *there was a nervous edge to his voice* **5 have the edge on** to have a slight advantage over **6 on edge** nervous and irritable **7 set someone's teeth on edge** to make someone acutely irritated ▹ *vb* **edging, edged 8** to make, form, or be an edge or border for: *a pillow edged with lace* **9** to move very gradually in a particular direction: *I edged through to the front of the crowd*
WORD ORIGIN Old English *ecg*

edgeways *or esp. US & Canad* **edgewise** *adv* **1** with the edge forwards or uppermost **2 get a word in edgeways** to interrupt a conversation in which someone else is talking continuously

Edgeworth *n* **Maria** 1767–1849, Anglo-Irish novelist: her works include *Castle Rackrent* (1800) and *The Absentee* (1812)

edging *n* anything placed along an edge for decoration

edgy *adj* **edgier, edgiest** nervous, irritable, or anxious **edginess** *n*

edible *adj* fit to be eaten; eatable **edibility** *n*
WORD ORIGIN Latin *edere* to eat

edict (ee-dikt) *n* a decree or order given by any authority
WORD ORIGIN Latin *edicere* to declare

edifice (ed-if-iss) *n* **1** a large or impressive building **2** an elaborate system of beliefs and institutions: *the crumbling edifice of Communist rule*
WORD ORIGIN Latin *aedificare* to build

edify (ed-if-fie) *vb* **-fies, -fying, -fied** to inform or instruct (someone) with a view to improving his or her morals or understanding **edification** *n* **edifying** *adj*
WORD ORIGIN Latin *aedificare* to build

Edinburgh[1] *n* **1** the capital of Scotland and seat of the Scottish Parliament (from 1999), in City of Edinburgh council area on the S side of the Firth of Forth: became the capital in the 15th century; castle; three universities (including University of Edinburgh, 1583); commercial and cultural centre, noted for its annual festival. Pop: 430 082 (2001) **2 City of** a council area in central Scotland, created from part of Lothian region in 1996. Pop: 448 370 (2003 est). Area: 262 sq km (101 sq miles)

Edinburgh[2] *n* **Duke of,** title of Prince *Philip Mountbatten.* born 1921, husband of Elizabeth II of Great Britain and Northern Ireland

edit ❶ *vb* **editing, edited 1** to prepare (text) for publication by checking and improving its accuracy or clarity **2** to be in charge of (a newspaper or magazine) **3** to prepare (a film, tape, etc.) by rearranging or selecting material **4 edit out** to remove (a section) from a text, film, etc.

THESAURUS

enthusiasm, frenzy, bliss, trance, euphoria, fervour, elation, rhapsody, exaltation, transport, ravishment
OPPOSITE: agony

edge *n* **1 = border**, side, line, limit, bound, lip, margin, outline, boundary, fringe, verge, brink, threshold, rim, brim, perimeter, contour, periphery, flange **4 = sharpness**, point, sting, urgency, bitterness, keenness, pungency, acuteness **6 on edge = tense**, excited, wired *(slang)*, nervous, eager, impatient, irritable, apprehensive, edgy, uptight *(informal)*, ill at ease, twitchy *(informal)*, tetchy, on tenterhooks, keyed up, antsy *(informal)*, adrenalized ▹ *vb* **8 = border**, shape, bind, trim, fringe, rim, hem, pipe **9 = inch**, ease, creep, worm, slink, steal, sidle, work, move slowly

edit *vb* **1 = revise**, check, improve, correct, polish, adapt, rewrite, censor, condense, annotate, rephrase, redraft, copy-edit, emend, prepare for publication, redact

DICTIONARY

edition ❶ *n* **1** a particular version of a book, newspaper, or magazine produced at one time: *the revised paperback edition* **2** a single television or radio programme which forms part of a series: *the first edition goes on the air in 30 minutes*

editor *n* **1** a person who edits **2** a person in overall charge of a newspaper or magazine **3** a person in charge of one section of a newspaper or magazine: *the Political Editor* **4** a person in overall control of a television or radio programme **editorship** *n*
WORD ORIGIN Latin *edere* to publish

editorial *n* **1** an article in a newspaper expressing the opinion of the editor or publishers ▹ *adj* **2** of editing or editors: *an editorial meeting* **3** relating to the contents and opinions of a magazine or newspaper: *the paper's editorial policy* **editorially** *adv*

Edmund *n* **Saint,** also called *Saint Edmund Rich*. 1175–1240, English churchman: archbishop of Canterbury (1234–40). Feast day: Nov 16

Edmund I *n* ?922–946 AD, king of England (940–946)

Edmund II *n* called *Edmund Ironside*. ?980–1016, king of England in 1016. His succession was contested by Canute and they divided the kingdom between them

EDP electronic data processing

EDT Eastern Daylight Time

educate ❶ *vb* **-cating, -cated 1** to teach (someone) over a long period of time so that he or she acquires knowledge and understanding of a range of subjects **2** to send (someone) to a particular educational establishment: *he was educated at mission schools* **3** to teach (someone) about a particular matter: *a campaign to educate people to the dangers of smoking* **educative** *adj*
WORD ORIGIN Latin *educare* to rear, educate

educated ❶ *adj* **1** having an education, esp. a good one **2** displaying culture, taste, and knowledge **3 educated guess** a guess that is based on experience

education ❶ *n* **1** the process of acquiring knowledge and understanding **2** knowledge and understanding acquired through study and training: *education is the key to a good job* **3** the process of teaching, esp. at a school, college, or university **4** the theory of teaching and learning **educational** *adj* **educationally** *adv* **educationalist** *or* **educationist** *n*

Edward[1] *n* **Lake Edward** a lake in central Africa, between Uganda and the Democratic Republic of Congo in the Great Rift Valley: empties through the Semliki River into Lake Albert. Area: about 2150 sq km (830 sq miles). Former official name: **Lake Amin**

Edward[2] *n* **1** known as *the Black Prince*. 1330–76, Prince of Wales, the son of Edward III of England. He won victories over the French at Crécy (1346) and Poitiers (1356) in the Hundred Years' War **2 Prince** born 1964, Earl of Wessex, third son of Elizabeth II of Great Britain and Northern Ireland. In 1999 he married Sophie Rhys-Jones (born 1965); their daughter Louise was born in 2003

Edwardian *adj* of or in the reign of King Edward VII of Great Britain and Ireland (1901–10)

Edwards *n* **1 Gareth** (**Owen**) born 1947, Welsh Rugby Union footballer: halfback for Wales (1967–78) and the British Lions (1968–74) **2 Jonathan** 1703–58, American Calvinist theologian and metaphysician; author of *The Freedom of the Will* (1754) **3 Jonathan** born 1966, British athlete: gold medallist in the Olympic triple jump (2000)

Edward the Elder *n* died 924 AD, king of England (899–924), son of Alfred the Great

Edward the Martyr *n* **Saint** ?963–978 AD, king of England (975–78), son of Edgar: murdered. Feast day: March 18

Edwin *n* ?585–633 AD, king of Northumbria (617–633) and overlord of all England except Kent

EEC European Economic Community: a former name for the European Union

EEG electroencephalogram

eel *n* a slimy snakelike fish
WORD ORIGIN Old English *ǣl*

e'er *adv poetic* ▸ short for **ever**

eerie ❶ *adj* **eerier, eeriest** strange and frightening **eerily** *adv*
WORD ORIGIN probably from Old English *earg* cowardly

efface *vb* **-facing, -faced 1** to obliterate or make dim: *nothing effaced the memory* **2** to rub out or erase **3 efface oneself** to make oneself inconspicuous **effacement** *n*
WORD ORIGIN French *effacer* to obliterate the face

effect ❶ *n* **1** a change or state of affairs caused by something or someone: *the gales have had a serious effect on the crops* **2** power to influence or produce a result: *the wine had little effect on him* **3** the condition of being operative: *a new law has come into effect* **4** the overall impression: *the whole effect is one of luxury* **5** basic meaning or purpose: *words to that effect* **6** an impression, usually a contrived one: *he paused for effect* **7** a physical phenomenon: *the greenhouse effect* **8 in effect** for all practical purposes: *in effect he has no choice* **9 take effect** to begin to produce results ▹ *vb* **10** to cause (something) to take place: *a peace treaty was effected*
WORD ORIGIN Latin *efficere* to accomplish

effective ❶ *adj* **1** producing a desired result: *an effective vaccine against HIV*

THESAURUS

edition *n* **1a = printing**, publication **1b = copy**, impression, number **1c = version**, volume, issue **2 = programme** *(TV, radio)*

educate *vb* **1 = teach**, school, train, coach, develop, improve, exercise, inform, discipline, rear, foster, mature, drill, tutor, instruct, cultivate, enlighten, civilize, edify, indoctrinate

educated *adj* **1 = taught**, schooled, coached, informed, tutored, instructed, nurtured, well-informed, well-read, well-taught
OPPOSITE: uneducated
2 = cultured, lettered, intellectual, learned, informed, experienced, polished, literary, sophisticated, refined, cultivated, enlightened, knowledgeable, civilized, tasteful, urbane, erudite, well-bred
OPPOSITE: uncultured

education *n* **1, 2 = learning**, schooling, culture, breeding, scholarship, civilization, cultivation, refinement **3 = teaching**, schooling, training, development, coaching, improvement, discipline, instruction, drilling, tutoring, nurture, tuition, enlightenment, erudition, indoctrination, edification

eerie *adj* **= uncanny**, strange, frightening, ghostly, weird, mysterious, scary *(informal)*, sinister, uneasy, fearful, awesome, unearthly, supernatural, unnatural, spooky *(informal)*, creepy *(informal)*, spectral, eldritch *(poetic)*, preternatural

effect *n* **1 = result**, consequence, conclusion, outcome, event, issue, aftermath, fruit, end result, upshot **2 = impression**, feeling, impact, influence **5 = purpose**, meaning, impression, sense, import, drift, intent, essence, thread, tenor, purport ▹ *vb* **10 = bring about**, make, cause, produce, create, complete, achieve, perform, carry out, fulfil, accomplish, execute, initiate, give rise to, consummate, actuate, effectuate

effective *adj* **1 = efficient**, successful, useful, active, capable, valuable, helpful, adequate, productive, operative, competent, serviceable, efficacious, effectual
OPPOSITE: ineffective
2 = in operation, official, current, legal, real, active, actual, in effect, valid, operative, in force, in

2 officially coming into operation: *the new rates become effective at the end of May* 3 impressive: *a highly effective speech* 4 in reality, although not officially or in theory: *he is in effective control of the company* **effectively** *adv* **effectiveness** *n*

effects ❶ *pl n* 1 personal belongings 2 lighting, sounds, etc. to accompany a stage, film, or broadcast production

effectual *adj* 1 producing the intended result 2 (of a document etc.) having legal force **effectually** *adv*

effeminate *adj* (of a man) displaying characteristics regarded as typical of a woman **effeminacy** *n*
WORD ORIGIN Latin *femina* woman

effervescent *adj* 1 (of a liquid) giving off bubbles of gas 2 (of a person) lively and enthusiastic **effervescence** *n*
WORD ORIGIN Latin *effervescere* to foam up

effete (if-feet) *adj* weak, powerless, and decadent
WORD ORIGIN Latin *effetus* exhausted by bearing young

efficacious *adj* producing the intended result **efficacy** *n*
WORD ORIGIN Latin *efficere* to achieve

efficient ❶ *adj* working or producing effectively without wasting effort, energy, or money **efficiency** *n* **efficiently** *adv*
WORD ORIGIN Latin *efficiens* effecting

effigy (ef-fij-ee) *n, pl* **-gies** 1 a statue or carving of someone, often as a memorial: *a 14th-century wooden effigy of a knight* 2 a crude representation of someone, used as a focus for contempt: *an effigy of the president was set on fire*
WORD ORIGIN Latin *effingere* to portray

efflorescence *n* 1 the blooming of flowers on a plant 2 a brief period of high-quality artistic activity
WORD ORIGIN Latin *efflorescere* to blossom

effluent *n* liquid discharged as waste, for instance from a factory or sewage works
WORD ORIGIN Latin *effluere* to flow out

effluvium *n, pl* **-via** an unpleasant smell, such as the smell of decaying matter
WORD ORIGIN Latin: a flowing out

efflux *n* 1 the process of flowing out 2 something that flows out

effort ❶ *n* 1 physical or mental energy needed to do something 2 a determined attempt to do something 3 achievement or creation: *his earliest literary efforts* **effortless** *adj* **effortlessly** *adv*
WORD ORIGIN Latin *fortis* strong

effrontery *n* insolence or boldness
WORD ORIGIN Late Latin *effrons* putting forth one's forehead

effusion *n* 1 an unrestrained verbal expression of emotions or ideas 2 a sudden pouring out: *small effusions of blood*
WORD ORIGIN Latin *effundere* to shed

effusive *adj* enthusiastically showing pleasure, gratitude, or approval **effusively** *adv* **effusiveness** *n*

EFL English as a Foreign Language

EFTA European Free Trade Association

EFTPOS electronic funds transfer at point of sale

e.g. for example
WORD ORIGIN Latin *exempli gratia*

egalitarian *adj* 1 expressing or supporting the idea that all people should be equal ▷ *n* 2 a person who believes that all people should be equal **egalitarianism** *n*
WORD ORIGIN French *égal* equal

Egas Moniz *n* **Antonio Caetanio de Abreu Freire** 1874–1955, Portuguese neurologist: shared the Nobel prize for physiology or medicine (1949) with Walter Hess for their development of prefrontal leucotomy

Egbert *n* ?775–839 AD, king of Wessex (802–839); first overlord of all England (829–830)

egg ❶ *n* 1 the oval or round object laid by the females of birds, reptiles, and other creatures, containing a developing embryo 2 a hen's egg used for food 3 a type of cell produced in the body of a female animal which can develop into a baby if fertilized by a male reproductive cell 4 **have egg on one's face** *informal* to have been made to look ridiculous 5 **put all one's eggs in one basket** to rely entirely on one action or decision, with no alternative in case of failure
WORD ORIGIN Old Norse

egg cup *n* a small cup for holding a boiled egg

egghead *n informal* an intellectual person

eggnog *n* a drink made of raw eggs, milk, sugar, spice, and brandy or rum
WORD ORIGIN *egg* + *nog* strong ale

egg on ❶ *vb* to encourage (someone) to do something foolish or daring
WORD ORIGIN Old English *eggian*

eggplant *n US, Canad, Austral & NZ* a dark purple tropical fruit, cooked and eaten as a vegetable

eggshell *n* 1 the hard porous outer layer of a bird's egg ▷ *adj* 2 (of paint) having a very slight sheen

Egmont[1] *n* **Mount Egmont** an extinct volcano in New Zealand, in W central North Island in the **Egmont National Park:** an almost perfect cone. Height: 2518 m (8261 ft). Official name: **Mount Taranaki**

Egmont[2] *n* **Lamoral**, Count of Egmont, Prince of Gavre. 1522–68, Flemish statesman and soldier. He attempted to secure limited reforms and religious tolerance in the Spanish government of the Netherlands, refused to join William the Silent's rebellion, but was nevertheless executed for treason by the Duke of Alva

ego *n, pl* **egos** 1 the part of a person's self that is able to recognize that person as being distinct from other people and things 2 a person's opinion of his or her own worth: *men with fragile egos*
WORD ORIGIN Latin: I

egocentric *adj* thinking only of one's own interests and feelings **egocentricity** *n*

Egoli (eh-goh-li) *n* an informal name for Johannesburg
WORD ORIGIN from Zulu *eGoli* place of gold

egomania *n* an obsessive concern with fulfilling one's own needs and desires, regardless of the effect on other people **egomaniac** *n*

THESAURUS

execution **OPPOSITE:** inoperative **3 = powerful**, strong, convincing, persuasive, telling, impressive, compelling, potent, forceful, striking, emphatic, weighty, forcible, cogent **OPPOSITE:** weak **4 = virtual**, essential, practical, implied, implicit, tacit, unacknowledged

effects *pl n* **1 = belongings**, goods, things, property, stuff, gear, furniture, possessions, trappings, paraphernalia, personal property, accoutrements, chattels, movables

efficient *adj* **a = effective**, successful, structured, productive, powerful, systematic, streamlined, cost-effective, methodical, well-organized, well-planned, labour-saving, effectual **OPPOSITE:** inefficient **b = competent**, able, professional, capable, organized, productive, skilful, adept, ready, proficient, businesslike, well-organized, workmanlike **OPPOSITE:** incompetent

effort *n* **1 = exertion**, work, labour, trouble, force, energy, struggle, stress, application, strain, striving, graft, toil, hard graft, travail *(literary)*, elbow grease *(facetious)*, blood, sweat, and tears *(informal)* **2 = attempt**, try, endeavour, shot *(informal)*, bid, essay, go *(informal)*, stab *(informal)*

egg *n* **3 = ovum**, gamete, germ cell

egg someone on = incite, push, encourage, urge, prompt, spur, provoke, prod, goad, exhort

DICTIONARY

egotism *or* **egoism** *n* concern only for one's own interests and feelings **egotist** *or* **egoist** *n* **egotistical, egoistical** *or* **egotistic, egoistic** *adj*

ego trip *n informal* something that a person does in order to boost his or her self-image

egregious (ig-**greej**-uss) *adj* shockingly bad: *egregious government waste*
WORD ORIGIN Latin *egregius* outstanding (literally: standing out from the herd)

e

egress (**ee**-gress) *n formal* **1** the act of going out **2** a way out or exit
WORD ORIGIN Latin *egredi* to come out

egret (**ee**-grit) *n* a wading bird like a heron, with long white feathery plumes
WORD ORIGIN Old French *aigrette*

Egyptian *adj* **1** of Egypt **2** of the ancient Egyptians ▷ *n* **3** a person from Egypt **4** a member of an ancient people who established an advanced civilization in Egypt **5** the language of the ancient Egyptians

Egyptology *n* the study of the culture of ancient Egypt **Egyptologist** *n*

eh *interj* **1** an exclamation used to ask for repetition or confirmation **2** *Canad & E Scot* a filler phrase used to make a pause in speaking, or add slight emphasis: *it's broken, eh, so I can't play for six weeks*

Ehrenburg *or* **Erenburg** *n* **Ilya Grigorievich** 1891–1967, Soviet novelist and journalist. His novel *The Thaw* (1954) was the first published in the Soviet Union to deal with repression under Stalin

Ehrlich *n* **Paul** 1854–1915, German bacteriologist, noted for his pioneering work in immunology and chemotherapy and for his discovery of a remedy for syphilis: Nobel prize for physiology or medicine 1908

Eichendorff *n* **Joseph**, Freiherr von. 1788–1857, German poet and novelist, regarded as one of the greatest German romantic lyricists

Eichler *n* **August Wilhelm** 1839–87, German botanist: devised the system on which modern plant classification is based

Eichmann *n* **Karl Adolf** 1902–62, Austrian Nazi official, who took a leading role in organizing the extermination of the European Jews. He escaped to Argentina after World War II, but was captured and executed in Israel as a war criminal

eider *or* **eider duck** *n* a large sea duck of the N hemisphere
WORD ORIGIN Old Norse *æthr*

eiderdown *n* a thick warm cover for a bed, filled with soft feathers, originally the breast feathers of the female eider duck

Eid-ul-Adha (**eed**-ool-**ah**-da) *n* an annual Muslim festival, marking the end of the pilgrimage to Mecca
WORD ORIGIN from Arabic *id ul adha* festival of sacrifice

Eid-ul-Fitr (**eed**-ool-**feet**-er) *n* an annual Muslim festival, marking the end of Ramadan
WORD ORIGIN from Arabic *id ul fitr* festival of fast-breaking

Eigen *n* **Manfred** born 1927, German physical chemist: shared the Nobel prize for chemistry (1967) for developing his relaxation technique for studying fast reactions

eight *n* **1** the cardinal number that is the sum of one and seven **2** a numeral, 8 or VIII, representing this number **3** something representing or consisting of eight units **4** *rowing* **a** a light narrow boat rowed by eight people **b** the crew of such a boat ▷ *adj* **5** amounting to eight: *eight apples* **eighth** *adj, n*
WORD ORIGIN Old English *eahta*

eighteen *n* **1** the cardinal number that is the sum of ten and eight **2** a numeral, 18 or XVIII, representing this number **3** something representing or consisting of 18 units ▷ *adj* **4** amounting to eighteen: *eighteen months* **eighteenth** *adj, n*

eightfold *adj* **1** having eight times as many or as much **2** composed of eight parts ▷ *adv* **3** by eight times as many or as much

eightsome reel *n* a lively Scottish country dance for eight people

eighty *n, pl* **eighties** **1** the cardinal number that is the product of ten and eight **2** a numeral, 80 or LXXX, representing this number **3** something representing or consisting of 80 units ▷ *adj* **4** amounting to eighty: *eighty miles* **eightieth** *adj, n*

Eijkman *n* **Christiaan** 1858–1930, Dutch physician, who discovered that beriberi is caused by nutritional deficiency: Nobel prize for physiology or medicine 1929

eina (**ay**-na) *interj S African* an exclamation of pain
WORD ORIGIN Khoi (language of southern Africa)

einsteinium *n chem* a radioactive metallic element artificially produced from plutonium. Symbol: Es
WORD ORIGIN after Albert *Einstein*, physicist

Einthoven *n* **Willem** 1860–1927, Dutch physiologist. A pioneer of electrocardiography, he was awarded the Nobel prize for physiology or medicine in 1924

Eire *n* Ireland or the Republic of Ireland
WORD ORIGIN Irish Gaelic

EIS Educational Institute of Scotland

Eisenstaedt *n* **Alfred** 1898–1995, US photographer, born in Germany

eisteddfod (ice-**sted**-fod) *n* a Welsh festival with competitions in music, poetry, drama, and art
WORD ORIGIN Welsh: session

either *adj, pron* **1** one or the other (of two): *we were offered either fish or beef* **2** both one and the other: *we sat at either end of a long settee* ▷ *conj* **3** used preceding two or more possibilities joined by *or*: *it must be stored either in the fridge or in a cool place* ▷ *adv* **4** likewise: *I don't eat meat and my husband doesn't either* **5** used to qualify or modify a previous statement: *he wasn't exactly ugly, but he wasn't an oil painting either*
WORD ORIGIN Old English *ǣgther*

ejaculate *vb* **-lating, -lated** **1** to discharge semen from the penis while having an orgasm **2** *literary* to say or shout suddenly **ejaculation** *n* **ejaculatory** *adj*
WORD ORIGIN Latin *ejaculari* to hurl out

eject ❶ *vb* **1** to push or send out forcefully **2** to compel (someone) to leave a place or position **3** to leave an aircraft rapidly in mid-flight, using an ejector seat **ejection** *n* **ejector** *n*
WORD ORIGIN Latin *ejicere*

ejector seat *or* **ejection seat** *n* a seat in a military aircraft that throws the pilot out in an emergency

eke out *vb* **eking, eked** **1** to make (a supply) last for a long time by using as little as possible **2** to manage to sustain (a living) despite having barely enough food or money
WORD ORIGIN obsolete *eke* to enlarge

Ekman *n* **Vagn Walfrid** 1874–1954 Swedish oceanographer: discoverer of the **Ekman Spiral** (a complex interaction on the surface of the sea between wind, rotation of the earth, and friction forces) and the **Ekman Layer** (the thin top layer of the sea that flows at 90° to the wind direction)

elaborate ❶ *adj* **1** very complex because of having many different parts: *elaborate equipment* **2** having a

THESAURUS

eject *vb* **2 = throw out**, remove, turn out, expel *(slang)*, exile, oust, banish, deport, drive out, evict, boot out *(informal)*, force to leave, chuck out *(informal)*, bounce, turf out *(informal)*, give the bum's rush *(slang)*, show someone the door, throw someone out on their ear *(informal)* **3 = bail out**, escape, get out

elaborate *adj* **1 = complicated**, detailed, studied, laboured, perfected, complex, careful, exact, precise, thorough, intricate, skilful, painstaking **2 = ornate**, detailed, involved, complex, fancy,

very complicated design: *elaborate embroidery* ▹ *vb* **-rating, -rated** **3 elaborate on** to describe in more detail: *he did not elaborate on his plans* **4** to develop (a plan or theory) in detail **elaborately** *adv* **elaboration** *n*
WORD ORIGIN Latin *elaborare* to take pains
Elagabalus *n* ▸ same as **Heliogabalus**
élan (ale-an) *n* style and liveliness
WORD ORIGIN French
eland (eel-and) *n* a large spiral-horned antelope of southern Africa
WORD ORIGIN Dutch: elk
elapse *vb* **elapsing, elapsed** (of time) to pass by
WORD ORIGIN Latin *elabi* to slip away
elastane *n* a synthetic fibre that is able to return to its original shape after being stretched
elastic ❶ *adj* **1** capable of returning to its original shape after stretching, compression, or other distortion **2** capable of being adapted to meet the demands of a particular situation: *an elastic interpretation of the law* **3** made of elastic ▹ *n* **4** tape, cord, or fabric containing flexible rubber **elastically** *adv* **elasticated** *adj* **elasticity** *n*
WORD ORIGIN Greek *elastikos* propellent
elastic band *n* a rubber band
elated *adj* extremely happy and excited **elatedly** *adv*
WORD ORIGIN Latin *elatus* carried away
elation *n* a feeling of great happiness and excitement
elbow *n* **1** the joint between the upper arm and the forearm **2** the part of a garment that covers the elbow ▹ *vb* **3** to push with one's elbow or elbows: *she elbowed him aside; he elbowed his way to the bar*
WORD ORIGIN Old English *elnboga*
elbow grease *n facetious* vigorous physical labour, esp. hard rubbing
elbow room *n* sufficient scope to move or to function
elder[1] ❶ *adj* **1** (of one of two people) born earlier ▹ *n* **2** an older person: *have some respect for your elders* **3** a senior member of a tribe, who has authority **4** (in certain Protestant Churches) a member of the church who has certain administrative, teaching, or preaching powers
WORD ORIGIN Old English *eldra*
elder[2] *n* a shrub or small tree with clusters of small white flowers and dark purple berries
WORD ORIGIN Old English *ellern*
Elder *n* **Mark Philip** born 1947, British conductor; musical director of the English National Opera (1979–93) and of the Hallé Orchestra from 2000
elderberry *n, pl* **-ries 1** the fruit of the elder **2** ▸ same as **elder**[2]
elderly *adj* **1** rather old ▹ *pl n* **2 the elderly** old people
elder statesman *n* a respected influential older person, esp. a politician
eldest *adj* (of a person, esp. a child) oldest
WORD ORIGIN Old English *eldesta*
Eldon *n* Earl of, title of **John Scott** 1751–1838, British statesman and jurist; Lord Chancellor (1801–06, 1807–27): an inflexible opponent of parliamentary reform, Catholic emancipation, and the abolition of slavery
El Dorado (el dor-**rah**-doe) *n* **1** a fabled city in South America, supposedly rich in treasure **2** Also: **eldorado** any place of great riches or fabulous opportunity
WORD ORIGIN Spanish: the golden (place)
eldritch *adj poetic Scot* unearthly or weird
WORD ORIGIN origin unknown
Eleanor of Aquitaine *n* ?1122–1204, queen of France (1137–52) by her marriage to Louis VII and queen of England (1154–89) by her marriage to Henry II; mother of the English kings Richard I and John
elect ❶ *vb* **1** to choose (someone) to fill a position by voting for him or her: *she was elected President in 1990* **2** to choose or decide: *those who elected to stay* ▹ *adj* **3** voted into office but not yet having taken over from the current office-bearer: *the President elect* ▹ *pl n* **4 the elect** any group of people specially chosen for some privilege **electable** *adj*
WORD ORIGIN Latin *eligere* to select
election ❶ *n* **1 a** a process whereby people vote for a person or party to fill a position: *last month's presidential election* **b** ▸ short for **general election** **2** the gaining of political power or taking up of a position in an organization as a result of being voted for: *he will be seeking election as the President of Romania*
electioneering *n* the act of taking an active part in a political campaign, for example by canvassing
elective *adj* **1** of or based on selection by vote: *an elective office* **2** not compulsory or necessary: *an elective hysterectomy*
elector *n* **1** someone who is eligible to vote in an election **2** (in the Holy Roman Empire) any of the German princes who were entitled to elect a new emperor: *the Elector of Hanover*
electoral *adj* of or relating to elections: *the electoral system* **electorally** *adv*
electoral register *n* the official list of all the people in an area who are eligible to vote in elections
electorate *n* **1** all the people in an area or country who have the right to vote in an election **2** the rank or territory of an elector of the Holy Roman Empire
electric ❶ *adj* **1** produced by, transmitting, or powered by electricity: *an electric fire* **2** very tense or exciting: *the atmosphere was electric* ▹ *n* **3 electrics** *Brit* an electric circuit or electric appliances
WORD ORIGIN Greek *ēlektron* amber (because friction causes amber to become electrically charged)
electrical *adj* of or relating to electricity **electrically** *adv*
electrical engineering *n* the branch of engineering concerned with practical applications of electricity and electronics **electrical engineer** *n*
electric blanket *n* a blanket fitted with an electric heating element, used to warm a bed
electric chair *n* (in the US) a chair for executing criminals by passing a strong electric current through them
electric eel *n* an eel-like South American freshwater fish, which

e

THESAURUS

complicated, decorated, extravagant, intricate, baroque, ornamented, fussy, embellished, showy, ostentatious, florid **OPPOSITE:** plain ▹ *vb* **3** *(usually with* **on** *or* **upon)** **= expand upon**, extend upon, enlarge on, amplify upon, embellish, flesh out, add detail to **OPPOSITE:** simplify **4 = develop**, improve, enhance, polish, complicate, decorate, refine, garnish, ornament, flesh out
elastic *adj* **1 = flexible**, yielding, supple, rubbery, pliable, plastic, springy, pliant, tensile, stretchy, ductile, stretchable **OPPOSITE:** rigid **2 = adaptable**, yielding, variable, flexible, accommodating, tolerant, adjustable, supple, complaisant **OPPOSITE:** inflexible
elder[1] *adj* **1 = older**, first, senior, first-born, earlier born ▹ *n* **2 = older person**, senior
elect *vb* **1 = vote for**, choose, pick, determine, select, appoint, opt for, designate, pick out, settle on, decide upon **2 = choose**, decide, prefer, select, opt
election *n* **1a = vote**, poll, ballot, determination, referendum, franchise, plebiscite, show of hands **2 = appointment**, choosing, picking, choice, selection
electric *adj* **1 = electric-powered**, powered, cordless, battery-operated, electrically-charged, mains-operated **2 = charged**, exciting, stirring, thrilling, stimulating, dynamic, tense, rousing, electrifying, adrenalized

DICTIONARY

can stun or kill its prey with a powerful electric shock
electric field *n physics* a region of space surrounding a charged particle within which another charged particle experiences a force
electric guitar *n* an electrically amplified guitar
electrician *n* a person trained to install and repair electrical equipment
electricity *n* **1** a form of energy associated with stationary or moving electrons, ions, or other charged particles **2** the supply of electricity to houses, factories, etc. for heating, lighting, etc.
electric shock *n* pain and muscular spasms caused by an electric current passing through the body
electrify *vb* **-fies, -fying, -fied 1** to adapt or equip (a system or device) to work by electricity: *the whole track has now been electrified* **2** to provide (an area) with electricity **3** to startle or excite intensely **electrification** *n*
electrifying *adj* very exciting and surprising
electro- *combining form* electric or electrically: *electroconvulsive*
WORD ORIGIN Greek *ēlektron* amber; see ELECTRIC
electrocardiograph *n* an instrument for making tracings (**electrocardiograms**) recording the electrical activity of the heart
electrocute *vb* **-cuting, -cuted** to kill or injure by an electric shock **electrocution** *n*
WORD ORIGIN ELECTRO- + (EXE)CUTE
electrode *n* a small piece of metal used to take an electric current to or from a power source, piece of equipment, or living body
electrodynamics *n* the branch of physics concerned with the interactions between electrical and mechanical forces
electroencephalograph (ill-lek-tro-en-**sef**-a-loh-graf) *n* an instrument for making tracings (**electroencephalograms**) recording the electrical activity of the brain
electrolysis (ill-lek-**troll**-iss-iss) *n* **1** the process of passing an electric current through a liquid in order to produce a chemical reaction in the liquid **2** the destruction of living tissue, such as hair roots, by an electric current
electrolyte *n* a solution or molten substance that conducts electricity **electrolytic** *adj*
electromagnet *n* a magnet consisting of a coil of wire wound round an iron core through which a current is passed
electromagnetic *adj* **1** of or operated by an electromagnet **2** of or relating to electromagnetism **electromagnetically** *adv*
electromagnetism *n* magnetism produced by an electric current
electromotive *adj physics* of or producing an electric current
electromotive force *n physics* **1** a source of energy that can cause current to flow in an electrical circuit **2** the rate at which energy is drawn from such a source when a unit of current flows through the circuit, measured in volts
electron *n physics* an elementary particle in all atoms that has a negative electrical charge
electronegative *adj physics* **1** having a negative electric charge **2** tending to gain or attract electrons
electronic *adj* **1** (of a device, circuit, or system) containing transistors, silicon chips, etc. which control the current passing through it **2** making use of electronic systems: *electronic surveillance devices* **electronically** *adv*
electronic mail *n* ▸ see **e-mail**
electronic publishing *n* the publication of information on discs, magnetic tape, etc. so that it can be accessed by computer
electronics *n* the technology concerned with the development, behaviour, and applications of devices and circuits, for example televisions and computers, which make use of electronic components such as transistors or silicon chips
electron microscope *n* a powerful microscope that uses electrons, rather than light, to produce a magnified image
electronvolt *n physics* a unit of energy equal to the work done on an electron accelerated through a potential difference of 1 volt
electroplate *vb* **-plating, -plated 1** to coat (an object) with metal by dipping it in a special liquid through which an electric current is passed ▹ *n* **2** electroplated articles collectively
electropositive *adj physics* **1** having a positive electric charge **2** tending to release electrons
electrostatics *n* the branch of physics concerned with static electricity **electrostatic** *adj*
elegant ❶ *adj* **1** attractive and graceful or stylish **2** cleverly simple and clear: *an elegant summary* **elegance** *n* **elegantly** *adv*
WORD ORIGIN Latin *elegans* tasteful
elegiac *adj literary* sad, mournful, or plaintive
elegy (**el**-lij-ee) *n, pl* **-gies** a mournful poem or song, esp. a lament for the dead
WORD ORIGIN Greek *elegos* lament
element ❶ *n* **1** one of the fundamental components making up a whole **2** *chem* any of the known substances that cannot be separated into simpler substances by chemical means **3** a distinguishable section of a social group: *liberal elements in Polish society* **4** a degree: *an element of truth* **5** a metal part in an electrical device, such as a kettle, that changes the electric current into heat **6** one of the four substances (earth, air, water, and fire) formerly believed to make up the universe **7** *maths* any of the members of a set **8 in one's element** in a situation in which one is happy and at ease: *she was in her element behind the wheel* **9 elements a** the basic principles of something **b** weather conditions, esp. wind, rain, and cold: *only 200 braved the elements*
WORD ORIGIN Latin *elementum*
elemental *adj* of or like basic and powerful natural forces or passions
elementary ❶ *adj* **1** simple, basic, and straightforward: *elementary precautions* **2** involving only the most basic principles of a subject: *elementary mathematics*
elementary particle *n physics* any of several entities, such as electrons, neutrons, or protons, that are less complex than atoms
elementary school *n* **1** *Brit* ▸ same as **primary school 2** *US & Canad* a state school for the first six to eight years of a child's education
elephant *n* **1** a very large four-legged animal that has a very long flexible

THESAURUS

elegant *adj* **1 = stylish**, fine, beautiful, sophisticated, delicate, artistic, handsome, fashionable, refined, cultivated, chic, luxurious, exquisite, nice, discerning, graceful, polished, sumptuous, genteel, choice, tasteful, urbane, courtly, modish, comely, à la mode, schmick *(Austral informal)*
OPPOSITE: inelegant

element *n* **1 = component**, part, feature, unit, section, factor, principle, aspect, foundation, ingredient, constituent, subdivision **3 = group**, faction, clique, set, party, circle **4 = trace**, suggestion, hint, dash, suspicion, tinge, smattering, soupçon **8 in your element = in a situation you enjoy**, in your natural environment, in familiar surroundings ▹ *pl n* **9b = weather conditions**, climate, the weather, wind and rain, atmospheric conditions, powers of nature, atmospheric forces

elementary *adj* **1 = simple**, clear, easy, plain, straightforward, rudimentary, uncomplicated, facile, undemanding, unexacting
OPPOSITE: complicated

DICTIONARY

nose called a trunk, large ears, and two ivory tusks, and lives in Africa or India **2 elephant in the room** an obvious truth deliberately ignored by all parties in a situation
WORD ORIGIN Greek *elephas*

elephantiasis (el-lee-fan-tie-a-siss) *n pathol* a skin disease, caused by parasitic worms, in which the affected parts of the body become extremely enlarged

elephantine *adj* like an elephant, esp. in being huge, clumsy, or ponderous

elevate ❶ *vb* **-vating, -vated 1** to raise in rank or status: *she had elevated flirting to an art form* **2** to lift to a higher place: *this action elevates the upper back*
WORD ORIGIN Latin *elevare*

elevated ❶ *adj* **1** higher than normal: *elevated cholesterol levels* **2** (of ideas or pursuits) on a high intellectual or moral level: *elevated discussions about postmodernism* **3** (of land or part of a building) higher than the surrounding area

elevation *n* **1** the act of elevating someone or something: *his elevation to the peerage* **2** height above sea level **3** a raised area **4** a scale drawing of one side of a building

elevator *n* **1** *Austral, US & Canad* a lift for carrying people **2** a mechanical hoist

eleven *n* **1** the cardinal number that is the sum of ten and one **2** a numeral, 11 or XI, representing this number **3** something representing or consisting of 11 units **4** a team of 11 players in football, cricket, etc. ▹ *adj* **5** amounting to eleven: *eleven years* **eleventh** *adj, n*
WORD ORIGIN Old English *endleofan*

eleven-plus *n* (in Britain, esp. formerly) an examination taken by children aged 10 or 11 that determines the type of secondary education they will be given

elevenses *pl n Brit, Austral, S Africa & NZ informal* a mid-morning snack

eleventh hour *n* **1** the latest possible time ▹ *adj* **eleventh-hour 2** done at the latest possible time: *an eleventh-hour rescue*

elf *n, pl* **elves** (in folklore) a small mischievous fairy
WORD ORIGIN Old English *ælf*

elfin *adj* **1** small and delicate: *her elfin features* **2** of or relating to elves

Eliade *n* **Mircea** 1907–86, Romanian scholar and writer, noted for his study of religious symbolism. His works include *Patterns of Comparative Religion* (1949)

elicit ❶ *vb* **1** to bring about (a response or reaction): *her remarks elicited a sharp retort* **2** to draw out (information) from someone: *a phone call elicited the fact that she had just awakened*
WORD ORIGIN Latin *elicere*

elide *vb* **eliding, elided** to omit (a syllable or vowel) from a spoken word
WORD ORIGIN Latin *elidere* to knock

eligible ❶ *adj* **1** meeting the requirements or qualifications needed: *he may be eligible for free legal services* **2** *old-fashioned* desirable as a spouse **eligibility** *n*
WORD ORIGIN Latin *eligere* to elect

eliminate ❶ *vb* **-nating, -nated 1** to get rid of (something or someone unwanted, unnecessary, or not meeting the requirements needed): *he can be eliminated from the list of suspects* **2** to remove (a competitor or team) from a contest, esp. following a defeat: *they were eliminated in the third round* **3** *slang* to murder in cold blood: *Stalin had thousands of his former comrades eliminated* **elimination** *n*
WORD ORIGIN Latin *eliminare* to turn out of the house

elision *n* omission of a syllable or vowel from a spoken word
WORD ORIGIN Latin *elidere* to elide

elite ❶ (ill-eet) *n* the most powerful, rich, or gifted members of a group or community
WORD ORIGIN French

elitism *n* **1** the belief that society should be governed by a small group of people who are superior to everyone else **2** pride in being part of an elite **elitist** *n, adj*

elixir (ill-ix-er) *n* **1** an imaginary substance that is supposed to be capable of prolonging life and changing base metals into gold **2** a liquid medicine mixed with syrup
WORD ORIGIN Arabic *al iksīr*

Elizabeth[1] *n* **1** a city in NE New Jersey, on Newark Bay. Pop: 123 215 (2003 est) **2** a town in SE South Australia, part of Adelaide. Pop: 26 428 (2006)

Elizabeth[2] *n* **1 Saint Elizabeth** *or* **Saint Elisabeth** *new testament* the wife of Zacharias, mother of John the Baptist, and kinswoman of the Virgin Mary. Feast day: Nov 5 or 8 **2** pen name *Carmen Sylva*. 1843–1916, queen of Romania (1881–1914) and author **3** Russian name *Yelizaveta Petrovna*. 1709–62, empress of Russia (1741–62); daughter of Peter the Great **4** title *the Queen Mother*; original name Lady *Elizabeth Bowes-Lyon*. 1900–2002, queen of Great Britain and Northern Ireland (1936–52) as the wife of George VI; mother of Elizabeth II

Elizabethan *adj* **1** of or in the reign of Queen Elizabeth I of England (1558–1603) **2** a person who lived during the reign of Queen Elizabeth I

Elizabeth of Hungary *n* **Saint** 1207–31, Hungarian princess who devoted herself to charity and asceticism. Feast day: Nov 17 and 19

elk *n* a very large deer of N Europe and Asia with broad flat antlers
WORD ORIGIN Old English *eolh*

Ellenborough *n* **Earl of**, title of Edward Law. 1780–1871, British colonial administrator: governor general of India (1742–44)

ellipse *n* an oval shape resembling a flattened circle

ellipsis (ill-lip-siss) *n, pl* **-ses** (-seez) **1** the omission of a word or words from a sentence **2** *printing* three dots (...) indicating an omission
WORD ORIGIN Greek *elleipein* to leave out

ellipsoid *n geom* a surface whose plane sections are ellipses or circles

elliptical *or* **elliptic** *adj* **1** oval-shaped **2** (of speech or writing) obscure or ambiguous

Ellis *n* **1 Alexander John** 1814–90, English philologist: made the first systematic survey of the phonology of British dialects **2 (Henry) Havelock** 1859–1939, English essayist: author of works on the psychology of sex

elm *n* **1** a tall tree with broad leaves **2** the hard heavy wood of this tree
WORD ORIGIN Old English

elocution *n* the art of speaking clearly in public **elocutionist** *n*
WORD ORIGIN Latin *e-* out + *loqui* to speak

elongate (eel-long-gate) *vb* **-gating,**

THESAURUS

elevate *vb* **1 = promote**, raise, advance, upgrade, exalt, kick upstairs *(informal)*, aggrandize, give advancement to **2 = raise**, lift, heighten, uplift, hoist, lift up, raise up, hike up, upraise

elevated *adj* **2 = high-minded**, high, fine, grand, noble, inflated, dignified, sublime, lofty, high-flown, pompous, exalted, bombastic **OPPOSITE:** humble **3 = raised**, high, lifted up, upraised

elicit *vb* **1 = bring about**, cause, derive, bring out, evoke, give rise to, draw out, bring forth, bring to light, call forth **2 = obtain**, extract, exact, evoke, wrest, draw out, extort, educe

eligible *adj* **1 = entitled**, fit, qualified, suited, suitable **OPPOSITE:** ineligible **2 = available**, free, single, unmarried, unattached

eliminate *vb* **1 = remove**, end, stop, withdraw, get rid of, abolish, cut out, dispose of, terminate, banish, eradicate, put an end to, do away with, dispense with, stamp out, exterminate, get shot of, wipe from the face of the earth

elite *n* **= aristocracy**, best, pick, elect, cream, upper class, nobility, gentry, high society, crème de la crème *(French)*, flower, nonpareil **OPPOSITE:** rabble

e

DICTIONARY

-gated to make or become longer **elongation** *n*
WORD ORIGIN Latin *e-* away + *longe* (adverb) far

elope *vb* **eloping, eloped** (of two people) to run away secretly to get married **elopement** *n*
WORD ORIGIN Anglo-French *aloper*

eloquence *n* the ability to speak or write in a skilful and convincing way

eloquent Ⓣ *adj* **1** (of speech or writing) fluent and persuasive **2** (of a person) able to speak in a fluent and persuasive manner **3** visibly or vividly expressive: *he raised an eloquent eyebrow* **eloquently** *adv*
WORD ORIGIN Latin *e-* out + *loqui* to speak

Els *n* **Ernie**, full name *Theodore Ernest Els*. born 1969; South African golfer: won the British Open Championship (2002) and the US Open Championship (1994, 1997)

else *adv* **1** in addition or more: *what else do you want to know?* **2** other or different: *it was unlike anything else that had happened* **3 or else a** if not, then: *tell us soon or else we shall go mad* **b** *informal* or something terrible will result: used as a threat: *do it our way or else*
WORD ORIGIN Old English *elles*

elsewhere Ⓣ *adv* in or to another place

ELT English Language Teaching

Elton *n* **1 Ben(jamin) (Charles)** born 1959, British comedian, scriptwriter, playwright, and novelist; his work includes the *Blackadder* series for television (1987–89), the play *Gasping* (1990), and the novel *High Society* (2002) **2 Charles Sutherland** 1900–91, British zoologist: initiated the study of animal ecology

Éluard *n* **Paul**, real name *Eugène-Émile-Paul Grindel*. 1895–1952, French surrealist poet, noted for his political and love poems

elucidate *vb* **-dating, -dated** to make (something obscure or difficult) clear **elucidation** *n*
WORD ORIGIN Late Latin *elucidare* to enlighten

elude Ⓣ *vb* **eluding, eluded 1** to avoid or escape from (someone or something) **2** to fail to be understood or remembered by: *the mysteries of commerce elude me*
WORD ORIGIN Latin *eludere* to deceive

elusive Ⓣ *adj* **1** difficult to find or catch **2** difficult to remember or describe **elusiveness** *n*

elver *n* a young eel
WORD ORIGIN variant of *eelfare* eel-journey

elves *n* ▸ the plural of **elf**

Elyot *n* Sir **Thomas** ?1490–1546, English scholar and diplomat; author of *The Boke named the Governour* (1531), a treatise in English on education

Elysium (ill-**liz**-zee-um) *n* **1** *Greek myth* the dwelling place of the blessed after death **2** a state or place of perfect bliss **Elysian** *adj*
WORD ORIGIN Greek *Ēlusion pedion* blessed fields

Elytis *n* **Odysseus**, real name *Odysseus Alepoudelis*. 1912–96, Greek poet, author of the long poems *Axion Est* (1959) and *Maria Nefeli* (1978): Nobel prize for literature 1979

emaciated (im-**mace**-ee-ate-id) *adj* extremely thin through illness or lack of food **emaciation** *n*
WORD ORIGIN Latin *macer* thin

e-mail *or* **email** (**ee**-mail) *n* **1** the transmission of messages from one computer terminal to another ▷ *vb* **2** to contact (a person) by e-mail **3** to send (a message) by e-mail

emanate Ⓣ (**em**-a-nate) *vb* **-nating, -nated** to come or seem to come from someone or something: *an aura of power emanated from him* **emanation** *n*
WORD ORIGIN Latin *emanare* to flow out

emancipate *vb* **-pating, -pated** to free from social, political, or legal restrictions **emancipation** *n*
WORD ORIGIN Latin *emancipare* to give independence (to a son)

emasculate *vb* **-lating, -lated** to deprive of power or strength **emasculation** *n*
WORD ORIGIN Latin *emasculare* to remove the testicles of

embalm *vb* to preserve (a corpse) by the use of chemicals and oils
WORD ORIGIN Old French *embaumer*

embankment *n* a man-made ridge of earth or stone that carries a road or railway or prevents a river or lake from overflowing

embargo Ⓣ *n, pl* **-goes 1** an order by a government or international body prohibiting trade with a country: *the world trade embargo against Iraq* ▷ *vb* **-going, -goed 2** to place an official prohibition on
WORD ORIGIN Spanish

embark Ⓣ *vb* **1** to go on board a ship or aircraft **2 embark on** to begin (a new project or venture) **embarkation** *n*
WORD ORIGIN Old Provençal *embarcar*

embarrass Ⓣ *vb* **1** to make (someone) feel shy, ashamed, or guilty about something **2** to cause political problems for (a government or party) **3** to cause to have financial difficulties **embarrassed** *adj* **embarrassing** *adj* **embarrassingly** *adv* **embarrassment** *n*
WORD ORIGIN Italian *imbarrare* to confine within bars

embassy *n, pl* **-sies 1** the residence or place of business of an ambassador **2** an ambassador and his or her assistants and staff
WORD ORIGIN Old Provençal *ambaisada*

embattled *adj* **1** (of a country) involved in fighting a war, esp. when surrounded by enemies **2** facing many problems and difficulties: *the embattled Mayor*

embed *vb* **-bedding, -bedded 1** to fix firmly in a surrounding solid mass: *the boy has shrapnel embedded in his spine* **2** to fix (an attitude or idea) in a society or in someone's mind: *corruption was deeply embedded in the ruling party*

THESAURUS

eloquent *adj* **1, 2 = silver-tongued**, moving, powerful, effective, stirring, articulate, persuasive, graceful, forceful, fluent, expressive, well-expressed **OPPOSITE:** inarticulate **3 = expressive**, telling, pointed, revealing, significant, pregnant, vivid, meaningful, indicative, suggestive

elsewhere *adv* **= in** *or* **to another place**, away, abroad, hence *(archaic)*, somewhere else, not here, in other places, in *or* to a different place

elude *vb* **1 = evade**, escape, lose, avoid, flee, duck *(informal)*, dodge, get away from, shake off, run away from, circumvent, outrun, body-swerve *(Scot)* **2 = escape**, baffle, frustrate, puzzle, stump, be beyond (someone), confound

elusive *adj* **1 = difficult to catch**, tricky, slippery, difficult to find, evasive, shifty **2 = indefinable**, puzzling, fleeting, subtle, baffling, indefinite, transient, intangible, indescribable, transitory, indistinct

emanate *vb (often with* **from***)* **= flow**, emerge, spring, proceed, arise, stem, derive, originate, issue, come forth

embargo *n* **1 = ban**, bar, block, barrier, restriction, boycott, restraint, check, prohibition, moratorium, stoppage, impediment, blockage, hindrance, interdiction, interdict, proscription, rahui *(NZ)* ▷ *vb* **2 = block**, stop, bar, ban, restrict, boycott, check, prohibit, impede, blacklist, proscribe, ostracize, debar, interdict

embark *vb* **1 = go aboard**, climb aboard, board ship, step aboard, go on board, take ship **OPPOSITE:** get off **2 embark on something = begin**, start, launch, enter, engage, take up, set out, undertake, initiate, set about, plunge into, commence, broach

embarrass *vb* **1 = shame**, distress, show up *(informal)*, humiliate, disconcert, chagrin, fluster, mortify, faze, discomfit, make uncomfortable, make awkward, discountenance, nonplus, abash, discompose, make ashamed, put out of countenance

DICTIONARY

embellish *vb* **1** to make (something) more attractive by adding decorations **2** to make (a story) more interesting by adding details which may not be true **embellishment** *n*
WORD ORIGIN Old French *embelir*

ember *n* a smouldering piece of coal or wood remaining after a fire has died
WORD ORIGIN Old English *ǣmyrge*

embezzle *vb* **-zling, -zled** to steal (money) that belongs to the company or organization that one works for **embezzlement** *n* **embezzler** *n*
WORD ORIGIN Anglo-French *embeseiller* to destroy

embittered *adj* feeling anger and despair as a result of misfortune: *embittered by poverty* **embitterment** *n*

emblazon (im-**blaze**-on) *vb* **1** to decorate with a coat of arms, slogan, etc.: *a jacket emblazoned with his band's name* **2** to proclaim or publicize: *I am not sure he would want his name emblazoned in my column*

emblem *n* an object or design chosen to symbolize an organization or idea **emblematic** *adj*
WORD ORIGIN Greek *emblēma* insertion

embody ❶ *vb* **-bodies, -bodying, -bodied** **1** to be an example of or express (an idea or other abstract concept) **2** to include as part of a whole: *the proposal has been embodied in a draft resolution* **embodiment** *n*

embolden *vb* to make bold

embolism *n pathol* the blocking of a blood vessel by a blood clot, air bubble, etc.

embolus *n, pl* **-li** *pathol* a blood clot, air bubble, or other stoppage that blocks a small blood vessel
WORD ORIGIN Greek *embolos* stopper

emboss *vb* to mould or carve a decoration on (a surface) so that it stands out from the surface
WORD ORIGIN Old French *embocer*

embrace ❶ *vb* **-bracing, -braced** **1** to clasp (someone) with one's arms as an expression of affection or a greeting **2** to accept eagerly: *he has embraced the Islamic faith* **3** to include or be made up of: *a church that embraces two cultures* ▷ *n* **4** an act of embracing
WORD ORIGIN Latin *im-* in + *bracchia* arms

embrasure *n* **1** an opening for a door or window which is wider on the inside of the wall than on the outside **2** an opening in a battlement or wall, for shooting through
WORD ORIGIN French

embrocation *n* a lotion rubbed into the skin to ease sore muscles
WORD ORIGIN Greek *brokhē* a moistening

embroider *vb* **1** to do decorative needlework on (a piece of cloth or a garment) **2** to add imaginary details to (a story) **embroiderer** *n*
WORD ORIGIN Old French *embroder*

embroidery *n* **1** decorative needlework, usually on cloth or canvas **2** the act of adding imaginary details to a story

embroil ❶ *vb* to involve (oneself or another person) in problems or difficulties **embroilment** *n*
WORD ORIGIN French *embrouiller*

embryo ❶ (**em**-bree-oh) *n, pl* **-bryos** **1** an unborn animal or human being in the early stages of development, in humans up to approximately the end of the second month of pregnancy **2** something in an early stage of development: *the embryo of a serious comic novel*
WORD ORIGIN Greek *embruon*

embryology *n* the scientific study of embryos

embryonic *adj* **1** of or relating to an embryo **2** in an early stage

emend *vb* to make corrections or improvements to (a text) **emendation** *n*
WORD ORIGIN Latin *e-* out + *mendum* a mistake

emerald *n* **1** a green transparent variety of beryl highly valued as a gem ▷ *adj* **2** bright green
WORD ORIGIN Greek *smaragdos*

Emerald Isle *n poetic* Ireland

emerge ❶ *vb* **emerging, emerged** **1** to come into view out of something: *two men emerged from the pub* **2** to come out of a particular state of mind or way of existence: *she emerged from the trance* **3** to come to the end of a particular event or situation: *no party emerged from the election with a clear majority* **4** to become apparent, esp. as the result of a discussion or investigation: *it emerged that he had been drinking* **5** to come into existence over a long period of time: *a new style of dance music emerged in the late 1980s* **emergence** *n* **emergent** *adj*
WORD ORIGIN Latin *emergere* to rise up from

emergency ❶ *n, pl* **-cies** **1** an unforeseen or sudden occurrence, esp. of danger demanding immediate action **2 state of emergency** a time of crisis, declared by a government, during which normal laws and civil rights can be suspended ▷ *adj* **3** for use in an emergency: *the emergency exit* **4** made necessary because of an emergency: *emergency surgery*

emeritus (im-**mer**-rit-uss) *adj* retired, but retaining one's title on an honorary basis: *a professor emeritus*
WORD ORIGIN Latin *merere* to deserve

emery *n* a hard greyish-black mineral used for smoothing and polishing
WORD ORIGIN Greek *smuris* powder for rubbing

emery board *n* a strip of cardboard coated with crushed emery, for filing one's fingernails

emetic (im-**met**-ik) *n* **1** a substance that causes vomiting ▷ *adj* **2** causing vomiting
WORD ORIGIN Greek *emetikos*

EMF electromotive force

emigrate ❶ *vb* **-grating, -grated** to leave one's native country to settle in another country **emigrant** *n, adj* **emigration** *n*
WORD ORIGIN Latin *emigrare*

e

THESAURUS

embody *vb* **1 = personify**, represent, express, realize, incorporate, stand for, manifest, exemplify, symbolize, typify, incarnate, actualize, reify, concretize **2** *(often with* **in***)* **= incorporate**, include, contain, combine, collect, concentrate, organize, take in, integrate, consolidate, bring together, encompass, comprehend, codify, systematize

embrace *vb* **1 = hug**, hold, cuddle, seize, squeeze, grasp, clasp, envelop, encircle, enfold, canoodle *(slang)*, take *or* hold in your arms **2 = accept**, support, receive, welcome, adopt, grab, take up, seize, make use of, espouse, take on board, welcome with open arms, avail yourself of, receive enthusiastically **3 = include**, involve, cover, deal with, contain, take in, incorporate, comprise, enclose, provide for, take into account, embody, encompass, comprehend, subsume ▷ *n* **4 = hug**, hold, cuddle, squeeze, clinch *(slang)*, clasp, canoodle *(slang)*

embroil *vb* **= involve**, complicate, mix up, implicate, entangle, mire, ensnare, encumber, enmesh

embryo *n* **1 = fetus**, unborn child, fertilized egg **2 = germ**, beginning, source, root, seed, nucleus, rudiment

emerge *vb* **1 = come out**, appear, come up, surface, rise, proceed, arise, turn up, spring up, emanate, materialize, issue, come into view, come forth, become visible, manifest yourself
OPPOSITE: withdraw
4 = become apparent, develop, come out, turn up, become known, come to light, crop up, transpire, materialize, become evident, come out in the wash

emergency *n* **1 = crisis**, danger, difficulty, accident, disaster, necessity, pinch, plight, scrape *(informal)*, strait, catastrophe, predicament, calamity, extremity, quandary, exigency, critical situation, urgent situation ▷ *adj* **3, 4 = urgent**, crisis, immediate

emigrate *vb* **= move abroad**, move, relocate, migrate, remove, resettle, leave your country

DICTIONARY

émigré (em-mig-gray) *n* someone who has left his or her native country for political reasons
WORD ORIGIN French

Emin *n* **Tracey** born 1963, British artist, noted for provocative multimedia works such as *Everyone I Have Ever Slept With* (1995) and *My Bed* (1999)

Eminem *n* real name *Marshall Mathers III.* born 1972, US White rap performer noted for his controversial lyrics; recordings include *The Slim Shady LP* (1999) and *The Eminem Show* (2002); he also starred in the film *8 Mile* (2002)

e

eminence *n* **1** the state of being well-known and well-respected **2** a piece of high ground

Eminence *n* **Your** *or* **His Eminence** a title used to address or refer to a cardinal

éminence grise (em-in-nonss **greez**) *n, pl* **éminences grises** a person who wields power and influence unofficially
WORD ORIGIN French, literally: grey eminence, originally applied to Père Joseph, secretary of Cardinal Richelieu

eminent ❶ *adj* well-known and well-respected
WORD ORIGIN Latin *eminere* to stand out

eminently *adv* extremely: *eminently sensible*

emir (em-**meer**) *n* an independent ruler in the Islamic world **emirate** *n*
WORD ORIGIN Arabic *'amīr* commander

emissary *n, pl* **-saries** an agent sent on a mission by a government or head of state
WORD ORIGIN Latin *emissarius*

emission ❶ *n* **1** the act of giving out heat, light, a smell, etc. **2** energy or a substance given out by something: *exhaust emissions from motor vehicles*

emit ❶ *vb* **emitting, emitted 1** to give or send forth (heat, light, a smell, etc.) **2** to produce (a sound)
WORD ORIGIN Latin *emittere* to send out

Emmental (em-men-tahl) *n* a hard Swiss cheese with holes in it
WORD ORIGIN after *Emmenthal*, valley in Switzerland

Emmet *n* **Robert** 1778–1803, Irish nationalist, executed for leading an uprising for Irish independence

emollient *adj* **1** (of skin cream or lotion) having a softening effect **2** helping to avoid confrontation; calming: *his emollient political style* ▹*n* **3** a cream or lotion that softens the skin
WORD ORIGIN Latin *emollire* to soften

emolument *n* fees or wages from employment
WORD ORIGIN Latin *emolumentum* benefit; originally fee paid to a miller

emote *vb* **emoting, emoted** to display exaggerated emotion, as if acting

emoticon (im-mote-ik-kon) *n computers* ▸same as **smiley** (sense 2)
WORD ORIGIN EMOT(ION) + ICON

emotion ❶ *n* **1** any strong feeling, such as joy or fear **2** the part of a person's character based on feelings rather than thought: *the conflict between emotion and logic*
WORD ORIGIN Latin *emovere* to disturb

emotional ❶ *adj* **1** of or relating to the emotions: *emotional abuse* **2** influenced by feelings rather than rational thinking: *he was too emotional to be a good doctor* **3** appealing to the emotions: *emotional appeals for public support* **4** showing one's feelings openly, esp. when upset: *he became very emotional and burst into tears*
emotionalism *n* **emotionally** *adv*

emotive *adj* tending or designed to arouse emotion

empathize *or* **-thise** *vb* **-thizing, -thized** *or* **-thising, -thised** (often foll. by *with*) to sense and understand someone else's feelings as if they were one's own

empathy *n* the ability to sense and understand someone else's feelings as if they were one's own
empathic *adj*
WORD ORIGIN Greek *empatheia* affection, passion

Empedocles *n* ?490–430 BC, Greek philosopher and scientist, who held that the world is composed of four elements, air, fire, earth, and water, which are governed by the opposing forces of love and discord

emperor *n* a man who rules an empire
WORD ORIGIN Latin *imperare* to command

emperor penguin *n* a very large Antarctic penguin with orange-yellow patches on its neck

emphasis ❶ *n, pl* **-ses 1** special importance or significance given to something, such as an object or idea **2** stress on a particular syllable, word, or phrase in speaking
WORD ORIGIN Greek

emphasize ❶ *or* **-sise** *vb* **-sizing, -sized** *or* **-sising, -sised** to give emphasis or prominence to: *to emphasize her loyalty*

emphatic ❶ *adj* **1** expressed, spoken, or done forcefully: *an emphatic denial of*

THESAURUS

eminent *adj* **= prominent**, high, great, important, noted, respected, grand, famous, celebrated, outstanding, distinguished, well-known, superior, esteemed, notable, renowned, prestigious, elevated, paramount, big-time *(informal)*, foremost, high-ranking, conspicuous, illustrious, major league *(informal)*, exalted, noteworthy, pre-eminent
OPPOSITE: unknown

emission *n* **1 = giving off** *or* **out**, release, shedding, leak, radiation, discharge, transmission, venting, issue, diffusion, utterance, ejaculation, outflow, issuance, ejection, exhalation, emanation, exudation

emit *vb* **1 = give off**, release, shed, leak, transmit, discharge, send out, throw out, vent, issue, give out, radiate, eject, pour out, diffuse, emanate, exude, exhale, breathe out, cast out, give vent to, send forth
OPPOSITE: absorb
2 = utter, produce, voice, give out, let out

emotion *n* **1 = feeling**, spirit, soul, passion, excitement, sensation, sentiment, agitation, fervour, ardour, vehemence, perturbation
2 = instinct, sentiment, sensibility, intuition, tenderness, gut feeling, soft-heartedness

emotional *adj* **1 = psychological**, private, personal, hidden, spiritual, inner **2, 4 = passionate**, enthusiastic, sentimental, fiery, feeling, susceptible, responsive, ardent, fervent, zealous, temperamental, excitable, demonstrative, hot-blooded, fervid, touchy-feely *(informal)*
OPPOSITE: dispassionate
3 = moving, touching, affecting, exciting, stirring, thrilling, sentimental, poignant, emotive, heart-rending, heart-warming, tear-jerking *(informal)*

emphasis *n* **1 = importance**, attention, weight, significance, stress, strength, priority, moment, intensity, insistence, prominence, underscoring, pre-eminence
2 = stress, accent, accentuation, force, weight

emphasize *vb* **a = highlight**, stress, insist, underline, draw attention to, flag up, dwell on, underscore, weight, play up, make a point of, give priority to, press home, give prominence to, prioritize
OPPOSITE: minimize
b = stress, accent, accentuate, lay stress on, put the accent on

emphatic *adj* **1 = significant**, marked, strong, striking, powerful, telling, storming *(informal)*, impressive, pronounced, decisive, resounding, momentous, conclusive
OPPOSITE: insignificant
2 = forceful, decided, certain, direct, earnest, positive, absolute, distinct, definite, vigorous, energetic, unmistakable, insistent,

DICTIONARY

the allegations **2** forceful and positive: *he was emphatic about his desire for peace talks* **emphatically** *adv*
WORD ORIGIN Greek *emphainein* to display

emphysema (em-fiss-see-ma) *n pathol* a condition in which the air sacs of the lungs are grossly enlarged, causing breathlessness
WORD ORIGIN Greek *emphusēma* a swelling up

empire ❶ *n* **1** a group of countries under the rule of a single person or sovereign state **2** a large industrial organization that is controlled by one person: *the heiress to a jewellery empire*
WORD ORIGIN Latin *imperare* to command

empire-builder *n informal* a person who seeks extra power by increasing the number of his or her staff **empire-building** *n, adj*

empirical ❶ *adj* derived from experiment, experience, and observation rather than from theory or logic: *there is no empirical data to support this claim* **empirically** *adv*
WORD ORIGIN Greek *empeirikos* practised

empiricism *n philosophy* the doctrine that all knowledge derives from experience **empiricist** *n*

emplacement *n* a prepared position for an artillery gun

employ ❶ *vb* **1** to hire (someone) to do work in return for money **2** to keep busy or occupy: *she was busily employed cutting the grass* **3** to use as a means: *you can employ various methods to cut your heating bills* ▷ *n* **4 in the employ of** doing regular paid work for: *he is in the employ of The Sunday Times* **employable** *adj*
WORD ORIGIN Old French *emploier*

employee ❶ *or US* **employe** *n* a person who is hired to work for someone in return for payment

employer ❶ *n* a person or company that employs workers

employment ❶ *n* **1** the act of employing or state of being employed **2** a person's work or occupation **3** the availability of jobs for the population of a town, country, etc.: *the party's commitment to full employment*

emporium *n, pl* **-riums** *or* **-ria** *old-fashioned* a large retail shop with a wide variety of merchandise
WORD ORIGIN Latin, from Greek *emporos* merchant

empower ❶ *vb* to give (someone) the power or authority to do something

empowerment *n* **1** the giving or delegation of power; authority **2** *S African* a semi-official slogan for the empowering of previously disadvantaged populations

empress *n* **1** a woman who rules an empire **2** the wife or widow of an emperor
WORD ORIGIN Latin *imperatrix*

Empson *n* Sir **William** 1906–84, English poet and critic; author of *Seven Types of Ambiguity* (1930)

empty ❶ *adj* **-tier, -tiest 1** containing nothing **2** without inhabitants; unoccupied **3** without purpose, substance, or value: *he contemplated yet another empty weekend* **4** insincere or trivial: *empty words* **5** *informal* drained of energy or emotion **6** *maths, logic* (of a set or class) containing no members ▷ *vb* **-ties, -tying, -tied 7** to make or become empty **8** to remove from something: *they emptied out the remains of the tin of paint* ▷ *n, pl* **-ties 9** an empty container, esp. a bottle **emptiness** *n*
WORD ORIGIN Old English *ǣmtig*

empty-handed *adj* having gained nothing: *the robbers ran off empty-handed*

empty-headed *adj* silly or incapable of serious thought

empyrean (em-pie-ree-an) *n poetic* the sky or the heavens
WORD ORIGIN Greek *empuros* fiery

EMS European Monetary System: the system enabling some EU members to coordinate their exchange rates

emu *n* a large Australian long-legged bird that cannot fly
WORD ORIGIN Portuguese *ema* ostrich

EMU 1 European Monetary Union **2** Economic and Monetary Union

emulate ❶ *vb* **-lating, -lated** to imitate (someone) in an attempt to do as well as or better than him or her **emulation** *n* **emulator** *n*
WORD ORIGIN Latin *aemulus* competing with

emulsifier *n* a substance that helps to combine two liquids, esp. a water-based liquid and an oil

emulsify *vb* **-fies, -fying, -fied** to make or form into an emulsion

emulsion *n* **1** a mixture of two liquids in which particles of one are suspended evenly throughout the other **2** *photog* a light-sensitive

e

THESAURUS

unequivocal, vehement, forcible, categorical **OPPOSITE:** hesitant

empire *n* **1 = kingdom**, territory, province, federation, commonwealth, realm, domain, imperium *(rare)* **2 = organization**, company, business, firm, concern, corporation, consortium, syndicate, multinational, conglomeration

empirical *adj* **= first-hand**, direct, observed, practical, actual, experimental, pragmatic, factual, experiential **OPPOSITE:** hypothetical

employ *vb* **1 = hire**, commission, appoint, take on, retain, engage, recruit, sign up, enlist, enrol, have on the payroll **2 = spend**, fill, occupy, involve, engage, take up, make use of, use up **3 = use**, apply, exercise, exert, make use of, utilize, ply, bring to bear, put to use, bring into play, avail yourself of

employee *or (US)* **employe** *n* **= worker**, labourer, workman, staff member, member of staff, hand, wage-earner, white-collar worker, blue-collar worker, hired hand, job-holder, member of the workforce

employer *n* **a = boss** *(informal)*, manager, head, leader, director, chief, executive, owner, owner, master, chief executive, governor *(informal)*, skipper, managing director, administrator, patron, supervisor, superintendent, gaffer *(informal, chiefly Brit)*, foreman, proprietor, manageress, overseer, kingpin, honcho *(informal)*, big cheese *(slang, old-fashioned)*, baas *(S African)*, numero uno *(informal)*, Mister Big *(slang, chiefly US)*, sherang *(Austral & NZ)* **b = company**, business, firm, organization, establishment, outfit *(informal)*

employment *n* **1 = taking on**, commissioning, appointing, hire, hiring, retaining, engaging, appointment, recruiting, engagement, recruitment, enlisting, enrolling, enlistment, enlrolment **2 = job**, work, business, position, trade, post, situation, employ, calling, profession, occupation, pursuit, vocation, métier

empower *vb* **a = authorize**, allow, commission, qualify, permit, sanction, entitle, delegate, license, warrant, give power to, give authority to, invest with power **b = enable**, equip, emancipate, give means to, enfranchise

empty *adj* **1, 2 = bare**, clear, abandoned, deserted, vacant, free, void, desolate, destitute, uninhabited, unoccupied, waste, unfurnished, untenanted, without contents **OPPOSITE:** full **3 = worthless**, meaningless, hollow, pointless, unsatisfactory, futile, unreal, senseless, frivolous, fruitless, aimless, inane, valueless, purposeless, otiose, bootless *(old-fashioned)* **OPPOSITE:** meaningful **4 = meaningless**, cheap, hollow, vain, idle, trivial, ineffective, futile, insubstantial, insincere ▷ *vb* **7a = clear**, drain, gut, void, unload, pour out, unpack, unburden, remove the contents of **OPPOSITE:** fill **7b = exhaust**, consume the contents of, void, deplete, use up **OPPOSITE:** replenish

emulate *vb* **= imitate**, follow, copy, mirror, echo, mimic, take after, follow in the footsteps of, follow the example of, take a leaf out of someone's book, model yourself on

DICTIONARY

coating for paper or film **3** a type of water-based paint
WORD ORIGIN Latin *emulgere* to milk out

enable ⊕ *vb* **-abling, -abled 1** to provide (someone) with the means or opportunity to do something **2** to make possible: *to enable the best possible chance of cure*

enabling act *n* a legislative act giving certain powers to a person or organization

enact ⊕ *vb* **1** to establish by law: *plans to enact a bill of rights* **2** to perform (a story or play) by acting **enactment** *n*

enamel *n* **1** a coloured glassy coating on the surface of articles made of metal, glass, or pottery **2** an enamel-like paint or varnish **3** the hard white substance that covers teeth ▷*vb* **-elling, -elled** *or US* **-eling, -eled 4** to decorate or cover with enamel
WORD ORIGIN Old French *esmail*

enamoured *or US* **enamored** *adj* **enamoured of a** in love with **b** very fond of and impressed by: *he is not enamoured of Moscow*
WORD ORIGIN Latin *amor* love

en bloc *adv* as a whole; all together
WORD ORIGIN French

enc. 1 enclosed **2** enclosure

encamp *vb formal* to set up a camp **encampment** *n*

encapsulate *vb* **-lating, -lated 1** to put in a concise form; summarize **2** to enclose in, or as if in, a capsule **encapsulation** *n*

encase *vb* **-casing, -cased** to enclose or cover completely: *her arms were encased in plaster* **encasement** *n*

encephalitis (en-sef-a-lite-iss) *n* inflammation of the brain **encephalitic** *adj*
WORD ORIGIN Greek *en-* in + *kephalē* head

encephalogram *n* an electroencephalogram
WORD ORIGIN Greek *en-* in + *kephalē* head + *gramma* drawing

enchant ⊕ *vb* **1** to delight and fascinate **2** to cast a spell on **enchanted** *adj* **enchantment** *n* **enchanter** *n* **enchantress** *fem n*
WORD ORIGIN Latin *incantare* to chant a spell

enchilada (en-chill-lah-da) *n* a Mexican dish consisting of a tortilla filled with meat, served with chilli sauce

encircle *vb* **-cling, -cled** to form a circle round **encirclement** *n*

Encke *n* **Johann Franz** 1791–1865, German astronomer, who discovered **Encke's Division** in the outer ring of Saturn

enclave *n* a part of a country entirely surrounded by foreign territory: *a Spanish enclave*
WORD ORIGIN Latin *in-* in + *clavis* key

enclose ⊕ *vb* **-closing, -closed 1** to surround completely: *the house enclosed a courtyard* **2** to include along with something else: *he enclosed a letter with the parcel*

enclosed *adj* kept separate from the normal everyday activities of the outside world: *an enclosed community of nuns*

enclosure *n* **1** an area of land enclosed by a fence, wall, or hedge **2** something, such as a cheque, enclosed with a letter

encode *vb* **-coding, -coded** to convert (a message) into code

encomium *n* a formal expression of praise
WORD ORIGIN Latin

encompass ⊕ *vb* **1** to enclose within a circle; surround **2** to include all of: *the programme encompasses the visual arts, music, literature, and drama*

encore *interj* **1** again: used by an audience to demand a short extra performance ▷*n* **2** an extra song or piece performed at a concert in response to enthusiastic demand from the audience
WORD ORIGIN French

encounter ⊕ *vb* **1** to meet (someone) unexpectedly **2** to be faced with: *he had rarely encountered such suffering* **3** to meet (an opponent or enemy) in a competition or battle ▷*n* **4** a casual or unexpected meeting **5** a game or battle: *a fierce encounter between the army and armed rebels*
WORD ORIGIN Latin *in-* in + *contra* against, opposite

encourage ⊕ *vb* **-aging, -aged 1** to give (someone) the confidence to do something **2** to stimulate (something or someone) by approval or help **encouragement** *n* **encouraging** *adj*
WORD ORIGIN French *encourager*

encroach *vb* to intrude gradually on someone's rights or on a piece of land **encroachment** *n*
WORD ORIGIN Old French *encrochier* to seize

encrust *vb* to cover (a surface) with a layer of something, such as jewels or ice **encrustation** *n*

encrypt *vb* **1** to put (a message or data) into a coded form **2** to distort (a television or other signal) so that it cannot be received without the use of specific equipment ▸See also **decrypt** > **encryption** *n*
WORD ORIGIN Greek *en-* in + *kruptos* hidden

encumber *vb* **1** to hinder or impede: *neither was greatly encumbered with social engagements* **2** to burden with a load or with debts
WORD ORIGIN Old French *en-* into + *combre* a barrier

encumbrance *n* something that impedes or is burdensome

encyclical (en-sik-lik-kl) *n* a letter sent by the pope to all Roman Catholic bishops
WORD ORIGIN Greek *kuklos* circle

THESAURUS

enable *vb* **1, 2 = allow**, permit, facilitate, empower, give someone the opportunity, give someone the means **OPPOSITE:** prevent

enact *vb* **1 = establish**, order, pass, command, approve, sanction, proclaim, decree, authorize, ratify, ordain, validate, legislate, make law **2 = perform**, play, act, present, stage, represent, put on, portray, depict, act out, play the part of, appear as *or* in, personate

enchant *vb* **1 = fascinate**, delight, charm, entrance, dazzle, captivate, enthral, beguile, bewitch, ravish, mesmerize, hypnotize, cast a spell on, enrapture, enamour, spellbind

enclose *or* **inclose** *vb* **1 = surround**, cover, circle, bound, wrap, fence, pound, pen, hedge, confine, close in, encompass, wall in, encircle, encase, fence in, impound, circumscribe, hem in, shut in, environ **2 = send with**, include, put in, insert

encompass *vb* **1 = surround**, circle, enclose, close in, envelop, encircle, fence in, ring, girdle, circumscribe, hem in, shut in, environ, enwreath **2 = include**, hold, involve, cover, admit, deal with, contain, take in, embrace, incorporate, comprise, embody, comprehend, subsume

encounter *vb* **1 = meet**, confront, come across, run into *(informal)*, bump into *(informal)*, run across, come upon, chance upon, meet by chance, happen on *or* upon **2 = experience**, meet, face, suffer, have, go through, sustain, endure, undergo, run into, live through ▷*n* **4 = meeting**, brush, confrontation, rendezvous, chance meeting **5 = battle**, fight, action, conflict, clash, dispute, contest, set to *(informal)*, run-in *(informal)*, combat, confrontation, engagement, collision, skirmish, head-to-head, face-off *(slang)*

encourage *vb* **1 = inspire**, comfort, rally, cheer, stimulate, reassure, animate, console, rouse, hearten, cheer up, embolden, buoy up, pep up, boost someone's morale, give hope to, buck up *(informal)*, gee up, lift the spirits of, give confidence to, inspirit **OPPOSITE:** discourage **2a = urge**, persuade, prompt, spur, coax, incite, egg on, abet **OPPOSITE:** dissuade **2b = promote**, back, help, support, increase, further, aid, forward, advance, favour, boost, strengthen, foster, advocate, stimulate,

DICTIONARY

encyclopedia *or* **encyclopaedia** *n* a book or set of books, often in alphabetical order, containing facts about many different subjects or about one particular subject
WORD ORIGIN Greek *enkuklios* general + *paideia* education
encyclopedic *or* **encyclopaedic** *adj* (of knowledge or information) very full and thorough; comprehensive
end ⓣ *n* **1** one of the two extreme points of something such as a road **2** the surface at one of the two extreme points of an object: *a pencil with a rubber at one end* **3** the extreme extent or limit of something: *the end of the runway* **4** the most distant place or time that can be imagined: *the ends of the earth* **5** the act or an instance of stopping doing something or stopping something from continuing: *I want to put an end to all the gossip* **6** the last part of something: *at the end of the story* **7** a remnant or fragment: *cigarette ends* **8** death or destruction **9** the purpose of an action: *he will only use you to achieve his own ends* **10** *sport* either of the two defended areas of a playing field **11 in the end** finally **12 make ends meet** to have just enough money to meet one's needs **13 no end** used for emphasis: *these moments give me no end of trouble* **14 on end** *informal* without pause or interruption: *for months on end* **15 the end** *slang* the worst; esp. beyond the limits of endurance ▷ *vb* **16** to bring or come to a finish **17 end it all** *informal* to commit suicide ▸ See also **end up**
WORD ORIGIN Old English *ende*
endanger ⓣ *vb* to put in danger
endangered *adj* (of a species of animal) in danger of becoming extinct
endear *vb* to cause to be liked: *his wit endeared him to a great many people*
endearing *adj*
endearment *n* an affectionate word or phrase
endeavour ⓣ *or US* **endeavor** *formal vb* **1** to try (to do something) ▷ *n* **2** an effort to do something
WORD ORIGIN Middle English *endeveren*
endemic *adj* present within a localized area or only found in a particular group of people: *he found 100 species of plant endemic to that ridge*
WORD ORIGIN Greek *en-* in + *dēmos* the people
Enders *n* **John Franklin** 1897–1985, US microbiologist: shared the Nobel prize for physiology or medicine (1954) with Frederick Robbins and Thomas Weller for their work on viruses
ending ⓣ *n* **1** the last part or conclusion of something: *the film has a happy ending* **2** the tip or end of something: *nerve endings*
endive *n* a plant with crisp curly leaves, used in salads
WORD ORIGIN Old French
endless ⓣ *adj* **1** having no end; eternal or infinite **2** continuing too long or continually recurring: *an endless stream of visitors* **endlessly** *adv*
endmost *adj* nearest the end
endocrine *adj* of or denoting a gland that secretes hormones directly into the blood stream, or a hormone secreted by such a gland
WORD ORIGIN Greek *endon* within + *krinein* to separate
endogenous (en-**dodge**-in-uss) *adj* *biol* developing or originating from within
endometrium (end-oh-**meet**-tree-um) *n* the mucous membrane lining the womb **endometrial** *adj*
WORD ORIGIN Greek *endon* within + *mētra* womb
endomorph *n* *physiol* a person with a fat and heavy body build ▸ See also **ectomorph, mesomorph** > **endomorphic** *adj*
WORD ORIGIN Greek *endon* within + *morphē* shape
endorphin *n* any of a group of chemicals found in the brain, which have an effect similar to morphine
endorsation *n* *Canad* approval or support
endorse ⓣ *vb* **-dorsing, -dorsed 1** to give approval or support to **2** to sign the back of (a cheque) to specify the payee **3** *chiefly Brit* to record a conviction on (a driving licence) **endorsement** *n*
WORD ORIGIN Old French *endosser* to put on the back
endoscope *n* *med* a long slender medical instrument used for examining the interior of hollow organs **endoscopy** *n*
endoskeleton *n* *zool* an internal skeleton, such as the bony skeleton of vertebrates
endothermic *adj* (of a chemical reaction) involving or requiring the absorption of heat
endow ⓣ *vb* **1** to provide with a source

THESAURUS

endorse, commend, succour
OPPOSITE: prevent
end *n* **1, 3 = extremity**, limit, edge, border, bound, extent, extreme, margin, boundary, terminus **2 = tip**, point, head, peak, extremity
5a = close, ending, finish, expiry, expiration **OPPOSITE:** beginning
5b = finish, close, stop, resolution, conclusion, closure, wind-up, completion, termination, cessation
6 = conclusion, ending, climax, completion, finale, culmination, denouement, consummation
OPPOSITE: start
7 = remnant, butt, bit, stub, scrap, fragment, stump, remainder, leftover, tail end, oddment, tag end
8 = death, dying, ruin, destruction, passing on, doom, demise, extinction, dissolution, passing away, extermination, annihilation, expiration, ruination **9 = purpose**, point, reason, goal, design, target, aim, object, mission, intention, objective, drift, intent, aspiration
▷ *vb* **16a = stop**, finish, complete, resolve, halt, cease, axe (*informal*), dissolve, wind up, terminate, call off, discontinue, put paid to, bring to an end, pull the plug on, call a halt to, nip in the bud, belay (*nautical*)
OPPOSITE: start
16b = finish, close, conclude, wind up, culminate, terminate, come to an end, draw to a close **OPPOSITE:** begin
endanger *vb* **= put at risk**, risk, threaten, compromise, hazard, jeopardize, imperil, put in danger, expose to danger **OPPOSITE:** save
endeavour *vb* **1 = try**, labour, attempt, aim, struggle, venture, undertake, essay, strive, aspire, have a go, go for it (*informal*), make an effort, have a shot (*informal*), have a crack (*informal*), take pains, bend over backwards (*informal*), do your best, go for broke (*slang*), bust a gut (*informal*), give it your best shot (*informal*), jump through hoops (*informal*), have a stab (*informal*), break your neck (*informal*), make an all-out effort (*informal*), knock yourself out (*informal*), do your damnedest (*informal*), give it your all (*informal*), rupture yourself (*informal*)
▷ *n* **2 = attempt**, try, shot (*informal*), effort, trial, go (*informal*), aim, bid, crack (*informal*), venture, enterprise, undertaking, essay, stab (*informal*)
ending *n* **1 = finish**, end, close, resolution, conclusion, summing up, wind-up, completion, finale, termination, culmination, cessation, denouement, last part, consummation **OPPOSITE:** start
endless *adj* **1 = eternal**, constant, infinite, perpetual, continual, immortal, unbroken, unlimited, uninterrupted, limitless, interminable, incessant, boundless, everlasting, unending, ceaseless, inexhaustible, undying, unceasing, unbounded, measureless, unfading
OPPOSITE: temporary
endorse *vb* **1 = approve**, back, support, champion, favour, promote, recommend, sanction, sustain, advocate, warrant, prescribe, uphold, authorize, ratify, affirm, approve of, subscribe to, espouse, vouch for, throw your weight behind
2 = sign, initial, countersign, sign on the back of, superscribe, undersign
endow *vb* **1 = finance**, fund, pay for,

DICTIONARY

of permanent income, esp. by leaving money in a will **2 endowed with** provided with or possessing (a quality or talent)
WORD ORIGIN Old French *endouer*

endowment ❶ *n* **1** the money given to an institution, such as a hospital **2** a natural talent or quality

endowment assurance *or* **insurance** *n* a kind of life insurance that pays a specified sum directly to the policyholder at a designated date or to his or her beneficiary should he or she die before this date

e

endpaper *n* either of two leaves at the front and back of a book pasted to the inside of the cover

end product *n* the final result of a process

end up *vb* **1** to arrive at a place by a roundabout route or without intending to: *the van somehow ended up in Bordeaux* **2** to arrive at a particular condition or situation without expecting to: *I thought I was going to hate it, but I ended up enjoying myself*

endurance ❶ *n* the ability to withstand prolonged hardship

endure ❶ *vb* **-during, -dured 1** to bear (hardship) patiently: *the children allegedly endured sexual abuse* **2** to tolerate or put up with: *I cannot endure your disloyalty any longer* **3** to last for a long time **endurable** *adj*
WORD ORIGIN Latin *indurare* to harden

enduring *adj* long-lasting

endways *or esp. US & Canad* **endwise** *adv* having the end forwards or upwards

enema (en-im-a) *n med* a quantity of fluid inserted into the rectum to empty the bowels, for example before an operation
WORD ORIGIN Greek: injection

enemy ❶ *n, pl* **-mies 1** a person who is hostile or opposed to a person, group, or idea **2** a hostile nation or people **3** something that harms or opposes something: *oil is an enemy of the environment* ▸ Related adjective: **inimical** *adj* **4** of or belonging to an enemy: *enemy troops*
WORD ORIGIN Latin *inimicus* hostile

energetic ❶ *adj* **1** having or showing energy and enthusiasm: *an energetic campaigner for democracy* **2** involving a lot of movement and physical effort: *energetic exercise* **energetically** *adv*

energize *or* **-ise** *vb* **-gizing, -gized** *or* **-gising, -gised** to stimulate or enliven

energy ❶ *n, pl* **-gies 1** capacity for intense activity; vigour **2** intensity or vitality of action or expression; forcefulness **3** *physics* the capacity to do work and overcome resistance **4** a source of power, such as electricity
WORD ORIGIN Greek *energeia* activity

energy drink *n* a soft drink designed to boost the drinker's energy levels

enervate *vb* **-vating, -vated** to deprive of strength or vitality **enervating** *adj* **enervation** *n*
WORD ORIGIN Latin *enervare* to remove the nerves from

Enesco *n* **Georges**, original name *George Enescu*. 1881–1955, Romanian violinist and composer

enfant terrible (on-fon ter-reeb-la) *n, pl* **enfants terribles** a talented but unconventional or indiscreet person
WORD ORIGIN French, literally: terrible child

enfeeble *vb* **-bling, -bled** to make (someone or something) weak

enfilade *mil n* **1** a burst of gunfire sweeping from end to end along a line of troops ▹ *vb* **-lading, -laded 2** to attack with an enfilade
WORD ORIGIN French *enfiler* to thread on string

enfold *vb* **1** to cover (something) by, or as if by, wrapping something round it: *darkness enfolded the city* **2** to embrace or hug

enforce ❶ *vb* **-forcing, -forced 1** to ensure that (a law or decision) is obeyed **2** to impose (obedience) by, or as if by, force **enforceable** *adj* **enforcement** *n*

enfranchise *vb* **-chising, -chised** to grant (a person or group of people) the right to vote **enfranchisement** *n*

Eng. 1 England **2** English

engage ❶ *vb* **-gaging, -gaged 1** Also: **be engaged** (usually foll. by *in*) to take part or participate: *he engaged in criminal and illegal acts; they were engaged in espionage* **2** to involve (a person or his or her attention) intensely: *there's nothing to engage the intellect in this film* **3** to employ (someone) to do something **4** to promise to do something **5** *mil* to begin a battle with **6** to bring (part of a machine or other mechanism) into operation, esp. by causing components to interlock **7 engage in conversation** to start a conversation with

THESAURUS

award, grant, invest in, confer, settle on, bestow, make over, bequeath, purvey, donate money to

endowed *adj* **2** *(usually with* **with***)* **= provided**, favoured, graced, blessed, supplied, furnished, enriched

endowment *n* **1 = provision**, fund, funding, award, income, grant, gift, contribution, revenue, subsidy, presentation, donation, legacy, hand-out, boon, bequest, stipend, bestowal, benefaction, largesse *or* largess, koha *(NZ)*

endurance *n* **= staying power**, strength, resolution, resignation, determination, patience, submission, stamina, fortitude, persistence, tenacity, perseverance, toleration, sufferance, doggedness, stickability *(informal)*, pertinacity

endure *vb* **1 = experience**, suffer, bear, weather, meet, go through, encounter, cope with, sustain, brave, undergo, withstand, live through, thole *(Scot)* **3 = last**, live, continue, remain, stay, hold, stand, go on, survive, live on, prevail, persist, abide, be durable, wear well

enemy *n* **1 = foe**, rival, opponent, the opposition, competitor, the other side, adversary, antagonist **OPPOSITE:** friend

energetic *adj* **1a = forceful**, strong, determined, powerful, storming *(informal)*, active, aggressive, dynamic, vigorous, potent, hard-hitting, high-powered, strenuous, punchy *(informal)*, forcible, high-octane *(informal)* **1b = lively**, spirited, active, dynamic, vigorous, animated, brisk, tireless, bouncy, indefatigable, alive and kicking, zippy *(informal)*, full of beans *(informal)*, bright-eyed and bushy-tailed *(informal)* **OPPOSITE:** lethargic **2 = strenuous**, hard, taxing, demanding, tough, exhausting, vigorous, arduous

energy *n* **1 = strength**, might, force, power, activity, intensity, stamina, exertion, forcefulness **2 = liveliness**, life, drive, fire, spirit, determination, pep, go *(informal)*, zip *(informal)*, vitality, animation, vigour, verve, zest, resilience, get-up-and-go *(informal)*, élan, brio, vivacity, vim *(slang)* **4 = power**

enforce *vb* **1 = carry out**, apply, implement, fulfil, execute, administer, put into effect, put into action, put into operation, put in force **2 = impose**, force, require, urge, insist on, compel, exact, oblige, constrain, coerce

engage *vb* **1 = participate in**, join in, take part in, undertake, practise, embark on, enter into, become involved in, set about, partake of **2a = captivate**, win, draw, catch, arrest, fix, attract, capture, charm, attach, fascinate, enchant, allure, enamour **2b = occupy**, involve, draw, busy, grip, absorb, tie up, preoccupy, immerse, engross **3 = employ**, commission, appoint, take on, hire, retain, recruit, enlist, enrol, put on the payroll **OPPOSITE:** dismiss **5** *(military)* **= begin battle with**, attack, take on, encounter, combat, fall on, battle with, meet, fight with, assail, face off *(slang)*, wage war on, join battle with, give battle to, come to close quarters with **6 = set going**, apply, trigger, activate, switch on, energize, bring into operation

engaged *adj* **1 = betrothed**, promised,

DICTIONARY

WORD ORIGIN Old French *en-* in + *gage* a pledge

engaged ❶ *adj* **1** having made a promise to get married **2** (of a telephone line or a toilet) already being used

engagement ❶ *n* **1** a business or social appointment **2** the period when a couple has agreed to get married but the wedding has not yet taken place **3** a limited period of employment, esp. in the performing arts **4** a battle

engagement ring *n* a ring worn by a woman engaged to be married

engaging ❶ *adj* pleasant and charming **engagingly** *adv*

engender *vb* to produce (a particular feeling, atmosphere, or situation)
WORD ORIGIN Latin *ingenerare*

engine ❶ *n* **1** any machine designed to convert energy into mechanical work, esp. one used to power a vehicle **2** a railway locomotive
WORD ORIGIN Latin *ingenium* nature, talent

engineer ❶ *n* **1** a person trained in any branch of engineering **2** a person who repairs and maintains mechanical or electrical devices **3** a soldier trained in engineering and construction work **4** an officer responsible for a ship's engines **5** *US & Canad* a train driver ▷*vb* **6** to cause or plan (an event or situation) in a clever or devious manner **7** to design or construct as a professional engineer

engineering *n* the profession of applying scientific principles to the design and construction of engines, cars, buildings, bridges, roads, and electrical machines

English *adj* **1** of England or the English language ▷*n* **2** the principal language of Britain, Ireland, Australia, New Zealand, the US, Canada, and several other countries ▷*pl n* **3 the English** the people of England

English breakfast *n* a breakfast including cooked food, such as bacon and eggs

Englishman *or fem* **Englishwoman** *n, pl* **-men** *or* **-women** a person from England

engorge *vb* **-gorging, -gorged** *pathol* to clog or become clogged with blood **engorgement** *n*

engrave *vb* **-graving, -graved 1** to carve or etch a design or inscription into (a surface) **2** to print (designs or characters) from a plate into which they have been cut or etched **3** to fix deeply or permanently in the mind **engraver** *n*
WORD ORIGIN *en-* in + obsolete *grave* to carve

engraving ❶ *n* **1** a printing surface that has been engraved **2** a print made from this

engross (en-**groce**) *vb* to occupy the attention of (someone) completely **engrossing** *adj*
WORD ORIGIN *en-* in + Latin *grossus* thick

engulf ❶ *vb* **1** to immerse, plunge, or swallow up: *engulfed by flames* **2** to overwhelm: *a terrible fear engulfed her*

enhance ❶ *vb* **-hancing, -hanced** to improve or increase in quality, value, or power: *grilling on the barbecue enhances the flavour* **enhancement** *n* **enhancer** *n*
WORD ORIGIN Old French *enhaucier*

enigma *n* something or someone that is mysterious or puzzling **enigmatic** *adj* **enigmatically** *adv*
WORD ORIGIN Creek *ainissesthai* to speak in riddles

enjoin *vb* **1** to order (someone) to do something **2** to impose (a particular kind of behaviour) on someone: *the sect enjoins poverty on its members* **3** *law* to prohibit (someone) from doing something by an injunction
WORD ORIGIN Old French *enjoindre*

enjoy ❶ *vb* **1** to receive pleasure from **2** to have or experience (something, esp. something good): *many fat people enjoy excellent health* **3 enjoy oneself** to have a good time **enjoyable** *adj* **enjoyably** *adv* **enjoyment** *n*
WORD ORIGIN Old French *enjoir*

enlarge ❶ *vb* **-larging, -larged 1** to make or grow larger **2 enlarge on** to speak or write about in greater detail **enlargement** *n* **enlarger** *n*

enlighten ❶ *vb* to give information or understanding to **enlightening** *adj*

enlightened ❶ *adj* **1** rational and having beneficial effects: *an enlightened approach to social welfare* **2** (of a person) tolerant and unprejudiced

e

THESAURUS

pledged, affianced, promised in marriage **OPPOSITE:** unattached **2 = in use**, busy, tied up, unavailable **OPPOSITE:** free

engagement *n* **1 = appointment**, meeting, interview, date, commitment, arrangement, rendezvous **2 = betrothal**, marriage contract, troth *(archaic)*, agreement to marry **4 = battle**, fight, conflict, action, struggle, clash, contest, encounter, combat, confrontation, skirmish, face-off *(slang)*

engaging *adj* **= charming**, interesting, pleasing, appealing, attractive, lovely, fascinating, entertaining, winning, pleasant, fetching *(informal)*, delightful, cute, enchanting, captivating, agreeable, lovable, winsome, cutesy *(informal, chiefly US)*, likable *or* likeable **OPPOSITE:** unpleasant

engine *n* **1 = machine**, motor, mechanism, generator, dynamo

engineer *n* **1 = designer**, producer, architect, developer, deviser, creator, planner, inventor, stylist, artificer, originator, couturier **2 = worker**, specialist, operator, practitioner, operative, driver, conductor, technician, handler, skilled employee ▷*vb* **6 = bring about**, plan, control, cause, effect, manage, set up *(informal)*, scheme, arrange, plot, manoeuvre, encompass, mastermind, orchestrate, contrive, concoct, wangle *(informal)*, finagle *(informal)* **7 = design**, plan, create, construct, devise, originate

engraving *n* **1, 2 = print**, block, impression, carving, etching, inscription, plate, woodcut, dry point

engulf *vb* **1 = immerse**, bury, flood (out), plunge, consume, drown, swamp, encompass, submerge, overrun, inundate, deluge, envelop, swallow up **2 = overwhelm**, overcome, crush, absorb, swamp, engross

enhance *vb* **= improve**, better, increase, raise, lift, boost, add to, strengthen, reinforce, swell, intensify, heighten, elevate, magnify, augment, exalt, embellish, ameliorate **OPPOSITE:** reduce

enjoy *vb* **1 = take pleasure in** *or* **from**, like, love, appreciate, relish, delight in, revel in, be pleased with, be fond of, be keen on, rejoice in, be entertained by, find pleasure in, find satisfaction in, take joy in **OPPOSITE:** hate **2 = have**, use, own, experience, possess, have the benefit of, reap the benefits of, have the use of, be blessed *or* favoured with

enlarge *vb* **1a = expand**, increase, extend, add to, build up, widen, intensify, blow up *(informal)*, heighten, broaden, inflate, lengthen, magnify, amplify, augment, make bigger, elongate, make larger **OPPOSITE:** reduce **1b = grow**, increase, extend, stretch, expand, swell, wax, multiply, inflate, lengthen, diffuse, elongate, dilate, become bigger, puff up, grow larger, grow bigger, become larger, distend, bloat **2 enlarge on something = expand on**, develop, add to, fill out, elaborate on, flesh out, expatiate on, give further details about

enlighten *vb* **= inform**, tell, teach, advise, counsel, educate, instruct, illuminate, make aware, edify, apprise, let know, cause to understand

enlightened *adj* **2 = informed**, aware, liberal, reasonable, educated, sophisticated, refined, cultivated, open-minded, knowledgeable, literate, broad-minded **OPPOSITE:** ignorant

DICTIONARY

enlightenment ⓣ *n* the act of enlightening or the state of being enlightened

enlist ⓣ *vb* **1** to enter the armed forces **2** to obtain (someone's help or support) **enlistment** *n*

enlisted *adj* (of a man or woman in the US Army or Navy) being below the rank of an officer

enliven *vb* to make lively, cheerful, or bright **enlivening** *adj*

en masse *adv* all together; as a group **WORD ORIGIN** French

enmeshed *adj* deeply involved: *enmeshed in turmoil*

enmity *n* a feeling of hostility or ill will **WORD ORIGIN** Latin *inimicus* hostile

Ennius *n* **Quintus** 239–169 BC, Roman epic poet and dramatist

ennoble *vb* **-bling, -bled 1** to make (someone) a member of the nobility **2** to make (someone or his or her life) noble or dignified: *poverty does not ennoble people*

ennui (on-**nwee**) *n literary* boredom and dissatisfaction resulting from lack of activity or excitement **WORD ORIGIN** French

enormity *n* **1** extreme wickedness **2** *pl* **-ties** an act of great wickedness **3** the vastness or extent of a problem or difficulty

enormous ⓣ *adj* unusually large in size, extent, or degree **enormously** *adv* **WORD ORIGIN** Latin *e-* out of, away from + *norma* rule, pattern

enough ⓣ *adj* **1** as much or as many as necessary **2 that's enough!** used to stop someone behaving in a particular way ▹ *pron* **3** an adequate amount or number: *I don't know enough about the subject to be able to speak about it* ▹ *adv* **4** as much as necessary **5** fairly or quite: *that's a common enough experience* **6** very: used to give emphasis to the preceding word: *funnily enough, I wasn't alarmed* **7** just adequately: *he sang well enough* **WORD ORIGIN** Old English *genōh*

en passant (on pass-**on**) *adv* in passing: *references made en passant* **WORD ORIGIN** French

enquire *vb* **-quiring, -quired** ▸ same as **inquire** > **enquiry** *n*

enrage ⓣ *vb* **-raging, -raged** to make extremely angry

enraptured *adj* filled with delight and fascination

enrich ⓣ *vb* **1** to improve or increase the quality or value of: *his poetry has vastly enriched the English language* **2** to improve in nutritional value, colour, or flavour: *a sauce enriched with beer* **3** to make wealthy or wealthier **enriched** *adj* **enrichment** *n*

Enright *n* **D**(**ennis**) **J**(**oseph**) 1920–2002, British poet, essayist, and editor

enrol ⓣ *or US* **enroll** *vb* **-rolling, -rolled** to become or cause to become a member **enrolment** *or US* **enrollment** *n*

en route ⓣ *adv* on or along the way **WORD ORIGIN** French

ensconce *vb* **-sconcing, -sconced** to settle firmly or comfortably **WORD ORIGIN** Middle English *en-* in + *sconce* fortification

ensemble ⓣ (on-**som**-bl) *n* **1** all the parts of something considered as a whole **2** the complete outfit of clothes a person is wearing **3** a group of musicians or actors performing together **4** *music* a passage in which all or most of the performers are playing or singing at once **WORD ORIGIN** French: together

enshrine *vb* **-shrining, -shrined** to contain and protect (an idea or right) in a society, legal system, etc.: *the university's independence is enshrined in its charter*

enshroud *vb* to cover or hide (an object) completely, as if by draping something over it: *fog enshrouded the forest*

ensign *n* **1** a flag flown by a ship to indicate its nationality **2** any flag or banner **3** (in the US Navy) a commissioned officer of the lowest rank **4** (formerly, in the British infantry) a commissioned officer of the lowest rank **WORD ORIGIN** Latin *insignia* badges

enslave *vb* **-slaving, -slaved** to make a slave of (someone) **enslavement** *n*

ensnare *vb* **-snaring, -snared 1** to trap or gain power over (someone) by dishonest or underhand means **2** to catch (an animal) in a snare

Ensor *n* **James** (**Sydney**) 1860–1949, Belgian expressionist painter, noted for his macabre subjects

ensue ⓣ *vb* **-suing, -sued 1** to happen next **2** to occur as a consequence: *if glaucoma is not treated, blindness can ensue* **ensuing** *adj* **WORD ORIGIN** Latin *in-* in + *sequi* to follow

en suite *adj, adv* (of a bathroom) connected to a bedroom and entered directly from it: *an en-suite bathroom; a room with a bathroom en suite* **WORD ORIGIN** French, literally: in sequence

ensure ⓣ *or esp. US* **insure** *vb* **-suring, -sured 1** to make certain: *we must ensure that similar accidents do not happen again* **2** to make safe or protect: *female athletes should take extra iron to ensure against anaemia*

THESAURUS

enlightenment *n* **= understanding**, information, learning, education, teaching, knowledge, instruction, awareness, wisdom, insight, literacy, sophistication, comprehension, cultivation, refinement, open-mindedness, edification, broad-mindedness

enlist *vb* **1 = join up**, join, enter (into), register, volunteer, sign up, enrol **2 = obtain**, get, gain, secure, engage, procure

enormous *adj* **= huge**, massive, vast, extensive, tremendous, gross, excessive, immense, titanic, jumbo *(informal)*, gigantic, monstrous, mammoth, colossal, mountainous, stellar *(informal)*, prodigious, gargantuan, elephantine, astronomic, ginormous *(informal)*, Brobdingnagian, humongous *or* humungous *(US slang)*, supersize **OPPOSITE:** tiny

enough *adj* **1 = sufficient**, adequate, ample, abundant, as much as you need, as much as is necessary ▹ *pron* **3 = sufficiency**, plenty, sufficient, abundance, adequacy, right amount, ample supply ▹ *adv* **4, 5 = sufficiently**, amply, fairly, moderately, reasonably, adequately, satisfactorily, abundantly, tolerably, passably

enrage *vb* **= anger**, provoke, irritate, infuriate, aggravate *(informal)*, incense, gall, madden, inflame, exasperate, incite, antagonize, make you angry, nark *(Brit, Austral & NZ slang)*, make your blood boil, get your back up, make you see red *(informal)*, put your back up **OPPOSITE:** calm

enrich *vb* **1 = enhance**, develop, improve, boost, supplement, refine, cultivate, heighten, endow, augment, ameliorate, aggrandize **3 = make rich**, make wealthy, make affluent, make prosperous, make well-off

enrol *or (US)* **enroll** *vb* **a = enlist**, register, be accepted, be admitted, join up, matriculate, put your name down for, sign up *or* on **b = recruit**, take on, engage, enlist

en route *adv* **= on** *or* **along the way**, travelling, on the road, in transit, on the journey

ensemble *n* **1 = collection**, set, body, whole, total, sum, combination, entity, aggregate, entirety, totality, assemblage, conglomeration **2 = outfit**, suit, get-up *(informal)*, costume **3 = group**, company, band, troupe, cast, orchestra, chorus, supporting cast

ensue *vb* **1, 2 = follow**, result, develop, succeed, proceed, arise, stem, derive, come after, issue, befall, flow, come next, come to pass *(archaic)*, supervene, be consequent on, turn out *or* up **OPPOSITE:** come first

ensure *vb* **1 = make certain**, guarantee, secure, make sure, confirm, warrant, certify **2 = protect**, defend, secure, safeguard, guard, make safe

DICTIONARY

ENT *med* ear, nose, and throat
entablature *n archit* the part of a classical building supported by the columns, consisting of an architrave, a frieze, and a cornice
WORD ORIGIN Italian *intavolatura* something put on a table, hence, something laid flat
entail ❶ *vb* **1** to bring about or impose inevitably: *few women enter marriage knowing what it really entails* **2** *Brit, Austral & NZ property law* to restrict the ability to inherit (a piece of property) to designated heirs
WORD ORIGIN Middle English *en-* in + *taille* limitation
entangle *vb* **-gling, -gled 1** to catch very firmly in something, such as a net or wire: *a fishing line had entangled his legs* **2** to involve in a complicated series of problems or difficulties: *he entangles himself in contradictions* **3** to involve in a troublesome relationship: *she kept getting entangled with unsuitable boyfriends*
entanglement *n*
entente (on-tont) *n* ▸ short for **entente cordiale**
WORD ORIGIN French: understanding
entente cordiale (cord-ee-**ahl**) *n* a friendly understanding between two or more countries
WORD ORIGIN French: cordial understanding
enter ❶ *vb* **1** to come or go into (a particular place): *he entered the room* **2** to join (a party or organization) **3** to become involved in or take part in: *1500 schools entered the competition* **4** to become suddenly present or noticeable in: *a note of anxiety entered his voice* **5** to record (an item) in a journal or list **6** *theatre* to come on stage: used as a stage direction: *enter Joseph* **7** to begin (a new process or period of time): *the occupation of the square has entered its eleventh day*
WORD ORIGIN Latin *intrare*
enteric (en-**ter**-ik) *adj* of the intestines
WORD ORIGIN Greek *enteron* intestine
enter into *vb* **1** to be an important factor in (a situation or plan): *money doesn't enter into it: it's a matter of principle* **2** to start to do or be involved in (a process or series of events): *the government will not enter into negotiations with terrorists*
enteritis (en-ter-**rite**-iss) *n* inflammation of the small intestine
enterprise ❶ *n* **1** a business firm **2** a project or undertaking, esp. one that requires boldness or effort **3** boldness and energy
WORD ORIGIN Old French *entreprendre* to undertake
enterprising ❶ *adj* full of boldness and initiative **enterprisingly** *adv*
entertain ❶ *vb* **1** to provide amusement for (a person or audience) **2** to show hospitality to (guests) **3** to consider (an idea or suggestion)
WORD ORIGIN Old French *entre-* mutually + *tenir* to hold
entertainer *n* a person who entertains, esp. professionally
entertaining *adj* **1** interesting, amusing, and enjoyable ▹*n* **2** the provision of hospitality to guests: *the smart kitchen is perfect for entertaining*
entertainment ❶ *n* **1** enjoyment and interest: *a match of top-quality entertainment and goals* **2** an act or show that entertains, or such acts and shows collectively
enthral *or US* **enthrall** (en-**thrawl**) *vb* **-thralling, -thralled** to hold the attention or interest of **enthralling** *adj* **enthralment** *or US* **enthrallment** *n*
enthrone *vb* **-throning, -throned 1** to place (a person) on a throne in a ceremony to mark the beginning of his or her new role as a monarch or bishop **2** to give an important or prominent position to (something): *the religious fundamentalism now enthroned in American life*
enthronement *n*
enthuse *vb* **-thusing, -thused** to feel or cause to feel enthusiasm
enthusiasm ❶ *n* ardent and lively interest or eagerness: *your enthusiasm for literature*
WORD ORIGIN Greek *enthousiazein* to be possessed by a god
enthusiast ❶ *n* a person who is very interested in and keen on something
enthusiastic *adj* **enthusiastically** *adv*
entice ❶ *vb* **-ticing, -ticed** to attract (someone) away from one place or activity to another **enticement** *n*
enticing *adj*
WORD ORIGIN Old French *enticier*
entire ❶ *adj* made up of or involving all of something, including every detail, part, or aspect **entirely** *adv*
WORD ORIGIN Latin *integer* whole

THESAURUS

entail *vb* **1 = involve**, require, cause, produce, demand, lead to, call for, occasion, need, impose, result in, bring about, give rise to, encompass, necessitate
enter *vb* **1 = come** *or* **go in** *or* **into**, arrive, set foot in somewhere, cross the threshold of somewhere, make an entrance **OPPOSITE:** exit **2 = join**, start work at, begin work at, sign up for, enrol in, become a member of, enlist in, commit yourself to **OPPOSITE:** leave **3a = participate in**, join (in), be involved in, get involved in, play a part in, partake in, associate yourself with, start to be in **3b = compete in**, contest, take part in, join in, fight, sign up for, go in for **5 = record**, note, register, log, list, write down, take down, inscribe, set down, put in writing **7 = begin**, start, take up, move into, set about, commence, set out on, embark upon
enterprise *n* **1 = firm**, company, business, concern, operation, organization, establishment, commercial undertaking **2 = venture**, operation, project, adventure, undertaking, programme, pursuit, endeavour **3 = initiative**, energy, spirit, resource, daring, enthusiasm, push *(informal)*, imagination, drive, pep, readiness, vigour, zeal, ingenuity, originality, eagerness, audacity, boldness, get-up-and-go *(informal)*, alertness, resourcefulness, gumption *(informal)*, adventurousness, imaginativeness
enterprising *adj* **= resourceful**, original, spirited, keen, active, daring, alert, eager, bold, enthusiastic, vigorous, imaginative, energetic, adventurous, ingenious, up-and-coming, audacious, zealous, intrepid, venturesome
entertain *vb* **1 = amuse**, interest, please, delight, occupy, charm, enthral, cheer, divert, recreate *(rare)*, regale, give pleasure to **2 = show hospitality to**, receive, accommodate, treat, put up, lodge, be host to, have company of, invite round, ask round, invite to a meal, ask for a meal **3 = consider**, support, maintain, imagine, think about, hold, foster, harbour, contemplate, conceive of, ponder, cherish, bear in mind, keep in mind, think over, muse over, give thought to, cogitate on, allow yourself to consider
entertainment *n* **1 = enjoyment**, fun, pleasure, leisure, satisfaction, relaxation, recreation, enjoyment, distraction, amusement, diversion **2 = pastime**, show, sport, performance, play, treat, presentation, leisure activity, beer and skittles
enthusiasm *n* **= keenness**, interest, passion, excitement, warmth, motivation, relish, devotion, zeal, zest, fervour, eagerness, ardour, vehemence, earnestness, zing *(informal)*, avidity
enthusiast *n* **= fan**, supporter, lover, follower, addict, freak *(informal)*, admirer, buff *(informal)*, fanatic, devotee, fiend *(informal)*, adherent, zealot, aficionado
entice *vb* **= lure**, attract, invite, persuade, draw, tempt, induce, seduce, lead on, coax, beguile, allure, cajole, decoy, wheedle, prevail on, inveigle, dangle a carrot in front of
entire *adj* **= whole**, full, complete, total

DICTIONARY

entirety *n, pl* **-ties** 1 all of a person or thing: *you must follow this diet for the entirety of your life* 2 **in its entirety** as a whole

entitle ⊕ *vb* **-tling, -tled** 1 to give (someone) the right to do or have something 2 to give a name or title to (a book or film) **entitlement** *n*

entity ⊕ *n, pl* **-ties** something that exists in its own right and not merely as part of a bigger thing
WORD ORIGIN Latin *esse* to be

e

entomb *vb* 1 to place (a corpse) in a tomb 2 to bury or trap: *a circulatory system entombed in fat* **entombment** *n*

entomology *n* the study of insects **entomological** *adj* **entomologist** *n*
WORD ORIGIN Greek *entomon* insect

entourage (on-toor-ahzh) *n* a group of people who assist or travel with an important or well-known person
WORD ORIGIN French *entourer* to surround

entozoon (en-toe-zoe-on) *n, pl* **-zoa** (-zoe-a) a parasite, such as a tapeworm, that lives inside another animal

entrails *pl n* 1 the internal organs of a person or animal; intestines 2 the innermost parts of anything
WORD ORIGIN Latin *interanea* intestines

entrance[1] ⊕ *n* 1 something, such as a door or gate, through which it is possible to enter a place 2 the act of coming into a place, esp. with reference to the way in which it is done: *she made a sudden startling entrance* 3 *theatre* the act of appearing on stage 4 the right to enter a place: *he refused her entrance because she was carrying her Scottie dog* 5 ability or permission to join or become involved with a group or organization: *entrance to the profession should be open to men and women alike* ▷ *adj* 6 necessary in order to enter something: *they have paid entrance fees for English-language courses*

entrance[2] ⊕ *vb* **-trancing, -tranced** to fill with delight **entrancement** *n* **entrancing** *adj*

entrant ⊕ *n* a person who enters a university, competition, etc.

entrap *vb* **-trapping, -trapped** 1 to trick (someone) into danger or difficulty 2 to catch in a trap **entrapment** *n*

entreat *vb* to ask (someone) earnestly to do something
WORD ORIGIN Old French *entraiter*

entreaty *n, pl* **-treaties** an earnest request or plea

entrecote (on-tra-coat) *n* a steak of beef cut from between the ribs
WORD ORIGIN French

entrée (on-tray) *n* 1 the right to enter a place 2 a dish served before a main course 3 *chiefly US* the main course
WORD ORIGIN French

entrench *vb* 1 to fix or establish firmly: *the habit had become entrenched* 2 *mil* to fortify (a position) by digging trenches around it **entrenchment** *n*

entrepreneur ⊕ *n* the owner of a business who attempts to make money by risk and initiative **entrepreneurial** *adj*
WORD ORIGIN French

entropy (en-trop-ee) *n* 1 *formal* lack of pattern or organization 2 *physics* a thermodynamic quantity that represents the amount of energy present in a system that cannot be converted into work because it is tied up in the atomic structure of the system
WORD ORIGIN Greek *entropē* a turning towards

entrust ⊕ *vb* 1 to give (someone) a duty or responsibility: *Miss Conway, who was entrusted with the child's education* 2 to put (something) into the care of someone: *he stole all the money we had entrusted to him*

entry ⊕ *n, pl* **-tries** 1 something, such as a door or gate, through which it is possible to enter a place 2 the act of coming in to a place, esp. with reference to the way in which it is done 3 the right to enter a place: *he was refused entry to Britain* 4 the act of joining an organization or group: *Britain's entry into the EU* 5 a brief note, article, or group of figures in a diary, book, or computer file 6 a quiz form, painting, etc. submitted in an attempt to win a competition 7 a person, horse, car, etc. entering a competition ▷ *adj* 8 necessary in order to enter something: *entry fee*

entwine *vb* **-twining, -twined** to twist together or round something else

E number *n* any of a series of numbers with the prefix E- indicating a specific food additive recognized by the EU

enumerate *vb* **-ating, -ated** 1 to name or list one by one 2 to count 3 *Canad* to compile the voting list for an area **enumeration** *n* **enumerator** *n*
WORD ORIGIN Latin *e-* out + *numerare* to count

enunciate *vb* **-ating, -ated** 1 to pronounce (words) clearly 2 to state precisely or formally **enunciation** *n*
WORD ORIGIN Latin *enuntiare* to declare

enuresis (en-yoo-reece-iss) *n* involuntary urination, esp. during sleep
WORD ORIGIN Greek *en-* in + *ouron* urine

envelop *vb* to cover, surround, or enclose **envelopment** *n*
WORD ORIGIN Old French *envoluper*

envelope ⊕ *n* 1 a flat covering of paper, that can be sealed, used to enclose a letter, etc. 2 any covering, wrapper, or enclosing structure: *an envelope of filo pastry* 3 *geom* a curve that is tangential to each one of a group of curves

THESAURUS

entitle *vb* 1 = **give the right to**, allow, enable, permit, sanction, license, qualify for, warrant, authorize, empower, enfranchise, make eligible 2 = **call**, name, title, term, style, label, dub, designate, characterize, christen, give the title of, denominate

entity *n* = **thing**, being, body, individual, object, presence, existence, substance, quantity, creature, organism

entrance[1] *n* 1 = **way in**, opening, door, approach, access, entry, gate, passage, avenue, doorway, portal, inlet, ingress, means of access **OPPOSITE:** exit
2, 3 = **appearance**, coming in, entry, arrival, introduction, ingress **OPPOSITE:** exit
4, 5 = **admission**, access, entry, entrée, admittance, permission to enter, ingress, right of entry

entrance[2] *vb* = **enchant**, delight, charm, absorb, fascinate, dazzle, captivate, transport, enthral, beguile, bewitch, ravish, gladden, enrapture, spellbind **OPPOSITE:** bore

entrant *n* = **competitor**, player, candidate, entry, participant, applicant, contender, contestant

entrepreneur *n* = **businessman** *or* **businesswoman**, tycoon, director, executive, contractor, industrialist, financier, speculator, magnate, impresario, business executive

entrust *or* **intrust** *vb* 1 = **give custody of**, trust, deliver, commit, delegate, hand over, turn over, confide, commend, consign 2 (*usually with* **with**) = **assign**, charge, trust, invest, authorize

entry *n* 1 = **way in**, opening, door, approach, access, gate, passage, entrance, avenue, doorway, portal, inlet, passageway, ingress, means of access 2 = **coming in**, entering, appearance, arrival, entrance **OPPOSITE:** exit
3 = **admission**, access, entrance, admittance, entrée, permission to enter, right of entry
4 = **introduction**, presentation, initiation, inauguration, induction, debut, investiture 5 = **record**, listing, account, note, minute, statement, item, registration, memo, memorandum, jotting

envelope *n* 2 = **wrapping**, casing, case, covering, cover, skin, shell, coating, jacket, sleeve, sheath, wrapper

environment *n* 1a = **surroundings**,

DICTIONARY

WORD ORIGIN French *envelopper* to wrap round

Enver Pasha *n* 1881–1922, Turkish soldier and leader of the Young Turks: minister of war (1914–18)

enviable *adj* so desirable or fortunate that it is likely to cause envy **enviably** *adv*

envious *adj* feeling, showing, or resulting from envy **enviously** *adv*

environment ⊙ (en-vire-on-ment) *n* **1** the surroundings in which a person, animal, or plant lives **2** *ecology* **the environment** the natural world of land, sea, air, plants, and animals: *nuclear waste must be prevented from leaking into the environment* **environmental** *adj*
WORD ORIGIN French *environs* surroundings

environmentalist ⊙ *n* a person concerned with the protection and preservation of the natural environment

environs *pl n* a surrounding area, esp. the outskirts of a city

envisage ⊙ *or US* **envision** *vb* **-aging, -aged** *or* **-ioning, -ioned** to believe to be possible or likely in the future: *the commission envisages a mix of government and private funding*
WORD ORIGIN French *en-* in + *visage* face

envoy ⊙ *n* **1** a messenger or representative **2** a diplomat ranking next below an ambassador
WORD ORIGIN French *envoyer* to send

envy ⊙ *n, pl* **-vies 1** a feeling of discontent aroused by someone else's possessions, achievements, or qualities **2** something that causes envy: *their standards are the envy of the world* ▷ *vb* **-vies, -vying, -vied 3** to wish that one had the possessions, achievements, or qualities of (someone else) **envyingly** *adv*
WORD ORIGIN Latin *invidia*

enzyme *n* any of a group of complex proteins, that act as catalysts in specific biochemical reactions **enzymatic** *adj*
WORD ORIGIN Greek *en-* in + *zumē* leaven

Eocene (ee-oh-seen) *adj* of the epoch of geological time about 55 million years ago
WORD ORIGIN Greek *ēōs* dawn + *kainos* new

Eolithic *adj* of the early period of the Stone Age, when crude stone tools were used

Eötvös *n* Baron **Roland von** 1848–1919, Hungarian physicist noted for his studies of gravity and surface tension

EP *n* an extended-play gramophone record, which is 7 inches in diameter and has a longer recording on each side than a single does

Epaminondas *n* ?418–362 BC, Greek Theban statesman and general: defeated the Spartans at Leuctra (371) and Mantinea (362) and restored power in Greece to Thebes

epaulette *n* a piece of ornamental material on the shoulder of a garment, esp. a military uniform
WORD ORIGIN French

épée (ep-pay) *n* a straight-bladed sword used in fencing

ephedrine (eff-fid-dreen) *n* an alkaloid used for the treatment of asthma and hay fever
WORD ORIGIN *Ephedra*, genus of plants which produce it

ephemera (if-fem-a-ra) *pl n* items designed to last only for a short time, such as programmes or posters

ephemeral *adj* lasting only for a short time
WORD ORIGIN Greek *hēmera* day

epic *n* **1** a long exciting book, poem, or film, usually telling of heroic deeds **2** a long narrative poem telling of the deeds of a legendary hero ▷ *adj* **3** very large or grand: *a professional feud of epic proportions*
WORD ORIGIN Greek *epos* word, song

epicene *adj* (esp. of a man) having characteristics or features that are not definitely male or female
WORD ORIGIN Greek *epikoinos* common to many

epicentre *or US* **epicenter** *n* the point on the earth's surface immediately above the origin of an earthquake
WORD ORIGIN Greek *epi* above + *kentron* point

Epictetus *n* ?50–?120 AD, Greek Stoic philosopher, who stressed self-renunciation and the brotherhood of man

epicure *n* a person who enjoys good food and drink **epicurism** *n*
WORD ORIGIN after *Epicurus*, Greek philosopher, who held that pleasure is the highest good

epicurean *adj* **1** devoted to sensual pleasures, esp. food and drink ▷ *n* **2** ▸ same as **epicure** ▸ **epicureanism** *n*

epidemic ⊙ *n* **1** a widespread occurrence of a disease **2** a rapid development or spread of something: *an epidemic of rape* ▷ *adj* **3** (esp. of a disease) affecting many people in an area: *stress has now reached epidemic proportions*
WORD ORIGIN Greek *epi* among + *dēmos* people

epidemiology (ep-pid-deem-ee-ol-a-jee) *n* the branch of medical science concerned with the occurrence and control of diseases in populations **epidemiologist** *n*

epidermis *n* the thin protective outer layer of the skin **epidermal** *adj*
WORD ORIGIN Greek *epi* upon + *derma* skin

epidural (ep-pid-dure-al) *adj* **1** on or over the outermost membrane covering the brain and spinal cord (**dura mater**) ▷ *n* **2 a** an injection of anaesthetic into the space outside the outermost membrane enveloping the spinal cord **b** anaesthesia produced by this method
WORD ORIGIN from *dura mater*

epiglottis *n* a thin flap of cartilage at the back of the mouth that covers the entrance to the larynx during swallowing
WORD ORIGIN Greek *epi* upon + *glōtta* tongue

epigram *n* **1** a witty remark **2** a short poem with a witty ending **epigrammatic** *adj*
WORD ORIGIN Greek *epi* upon + *graphein* to write

epigraph *n* **1** a quotation at the beginning of a book **2** an inscription on a monument or building
WORD ORIGIN Greek *epi* upon + *graphein* to write

epilepsy *n* a disorder of the central nervous system which causes periodic loss of consciousness and sometimes convulsions
WORD ORIGIN Greek *epi* upon + *lambanein* to take

epileptic *adj* **1** of or having epilepsy ▷ *n* **2** a person who has epilepsy

epilogue *n* a short concluding passage or speech at the end of a book or play
WORD ORIGIN Greek *epi* upon + *logos* word, speech

e

THESAURUS

setting, conditions, situation, medium, scene, circumstances, territory, background, atmosphere, context, habitat, domain, milieu, locale **1b** *(ecology)* **= habitat**, home, surroundings, territory, terrain, locality, natural home

environmentalist *n* **= conservationist**, ecologist, green, friend of the earth

envisage *vb* **= foresee**, see, expect, predict, anticipate, envision

envoy *n* **1 = messenger**, agent, deputy, representative, delegate, courier, intermediary, emissary **2 = ambassador**, minister, diplomat, emissary, legate, plenipotentiary

envy *n* **1 = covetousness**, spite, hatred, resentment, jealousy, bitterness, malice, ill will, malignity, resentfulness, enviousness *(informal)* ▷ *vb* **3a = be jealous (of)**, resent, begrudge, be envious (of) **3b = covet**, desire, crave, aspire to, yearn for, hanker after

epidemic *n* **1 = outbreak**, plague, growth, spread, scourge, contagion **2 = spate**, plague, outbreak, wave, rash, eruption, upsurge

e

DICTIONARY

epiphany (ip-piff-a-nee) *n, pl* **-nies** a moment of great or sudden revelation
WORD ORIGIN Greek *epiphaneia* an appearing

Epiphany *n, pl* **-nies** a Christian festival held on January 6 commemorating, in the Western church, the manifestation of Christ to the Magi and, in the Eastern church, the baptism of Christ

episcopacy (ip-piss-kop-a-see) *n* **1** government of a Church by bishops **2** *pl* **-cies** ▸ same as **episcopate**

episcopal (ip-piss-kop-al) *adj* of or relating to bishops
WORD ORIGIN Greek *episkopos* overseer

Episcopal Church *n* (in Scotland and the US) a self-governing branch of the Anglican Church

episcopalian *adj also* **episcopal** **1** practising or advocating Church government by bishops ▹*n* **2** an advocate of such Church government

Episcopalian (ip-piss-kop-pale-ee-an) *adj* **1** of or relating to the Episcopal Church ▹*n* **2** a member of this Church **Episcopalianism** *n*

episcopate (ip-piss-kop-it) *n* **1** the office, status, or term of office of a bishop **2** bishops collectively

episiotomy (ip-peez-ee-ot-tom-ee) *n, pl* **-tomies** an operation involving cutting into the area between the genitals and the anus sometimes performed during childbirth to make the birth easier

episode ❶ *n* **1** an event or series of events **2** any of the sections into which a novel or a television or radio serial is divided
WORD ORIGIN Greek *epi* in addition + *eisodios* coming in

episodic *adj* **1** resembling or relating to an episode **2** occurring at irregular and infrequent intervals

epistemology (ip-iss-stem-ol-a-jee) *n* the theory of knowledge, esp. the critical study of its validity, methods, and scope **epistemological** *adj* **epistemologist** *n*
WORD ORIGIN Greek *epistēmē* knowledge

epistle *n* **1** *formal or humorous* a letter **2** a literary work in letter form, esp. a poem
WORD ORIGIN Greek *epistolē*

Epistle *n new testament* any of the letters written by the apostles

epistolary *adj* **1** of or relating to letters **2** (of a novel) presented in the form of a series of letters

epitaph *n* **1** a commemorative inscription on a tombstone **2** a commemorative speech or written passage
WORD ORIGIN Greek *epi* upon + *taphos* tomb

epithelium *n, pl* **-lia** *anat* a cellular tissue covering the external and internal surfaces of the body **epithelial** *adj*
WORD ORIGIN Greek *epi* upon + *thēlē* nipple

epithet *n* a word or short phrase used to describe someone or something: *these tracks truly deserve that overworked epithet 'classic'*
WORD ORIGIN Greek *epitithenai* to add

epitome (ip-pit-a-mee) *n* **1** a person or thing that is a typical example of a characteristic or class: *the epitome of rural tranquillity* **2** a summary, esp. of a written work
WORD ORIGIN Greek *epitemnein* to abridge

epitomize *or* **-mise** *vb* **-mizing, -mized** *or* **-mising, -mised** to be or make a perfect or typical example of

EPNS electroplated nickel silver

epoch (ee-pok) *n* **1** a long period of time marked by some predominant characteristic: *the cold-war epoch* **2** the beginning of a new or distinctive period: *the invention of nuclear weapons marked an epoch in the history of warfare* **3** *geol* a unit of time within a period during which a series of rocks is formed **epochal** *adj*
WORD ORIGIN Greek *epokhē* cessation

epoch-making *adj* very important or significant

eponymous (ip-pon-im-uss) *adj* **1** (of a person) being the person after whom a literary work, film, etc. is named: *the eponymous heroine in the film of Jane Eyre* **2** (of a literary work, film, etc.) named after its central character or creator: *The Stooges' eponymous debut album*
WORD ORIGIN Greek *epōnumos* giving a significant name

EPOS electronic point of sale

epoxy *chem adj* **1** of or containing an oxygen atom joined to two different groups that are themselves joined to other groups **2** of or consisting of an epoxy resin ▹*n, pl* **epoxies** **3** an epoxy resin
WORD ORIGIN Greek *epi* upon + OXY(GEN)

epoxy resin *n* a tough resistant thermosetting synthetic resin, used in laminates and adhesives

EPROM *n computers* erasable programmable read-only memory: a storage device that can be reprogrammed to hold different data

Epsom salts *pl n* a medicinal preparation of hydrated magnesium sulphate, used to empty the bowels
WORD ORIGIN after *Epsom*, a town in England

Epstein *n* Sir **Jacob** 1880–1959, British sculptor, born in the US of Russo-Polish parents

equable (ek-wab-bl) *adj* **1** even-tempered and reasonable **2** (of a climate) not varying much throughout the year, and neither very hot nor very cold **equably** *adv*
WORD ORIGIN Latin *aequabilis*

equal ❶ *adj* **1** identical in size, quantity, degree, or intensity **2** having identical privileges, rights, or status **3** applying in the same way to all people or in all circumstances: *equal rights* **4** **equal to** having the necessary strength, ability, or means for: *she was equal to any test the corporation put to her* ▹*n* **5** a person or thing equal to another ▹*vb* **equalling, equalled** *or US* **equaling, equaled** **6** to be equal to; match **7** to make or do something equal to: *he has equalled his world record in the men's 100 metres* **equally** *adv*
WORD ORIGIN Latin *aequalis*

equality ❶ *n, pl* **-ties** the state of being equal

equalize *or* **-ise** *vb* **-izing, -ized** *or* **-ising, -ised** **1** to make equal or uniform **2** (in a sport) to reach the same score as one's opponent or opponents **equalization** *or* **-isation** *n* **equalizer** *or* **-iser** *n*

equal opportunity *n* the offering of employment or promotion equally to all, without discrimination as to sex, race, colour, etc.

equanimity *n* calmness of mind or temper; composure
WORD ORIGIN Latin *aequus* even + *animus* mind, spirit

THESAURUS

episode *n* **1 = event**, experience, happening, matter, affair, incident, circumstance, adventure, business, occurrence, escapade **2 = instalment**, part, act, scene, section, chapter, passage

equal *adj* **1** (*often with* **to** *or* **with**) **= identical**, the same, matched, matching, like, equivalent, uniform, alike, corresponding, tantamount, one and the same, proportionate, commensurate **OPPOSITE:** unequal **2, 3 = fair**, just, impartial, egalitarian, unbiased, even-handed, equable **OPPOSITE:** unfair ▹*n* **5 = match**, equivalent, fellow, twin, mate, peer, parallel, counterpart, compeer ▹*vb* **6 = be equal to**, match, reach, rival, come up to, be level with, be even with **7 = be as good as**, match, compare with, equate with, measure up to, be as great as

equality *n* **a = fairness**, equal opportunity, equal treatment, egalitarianism, fair treatment, justness **OPPOSITE:** inequality **b = sameness**, balance, identity, similarity, correspondence, parity, likeness, uniformity, equivalence,

DICTIONARY

equate ⓣ *vb* **equating, equated 1** to make or regard as equivalent **2** *maths* to form an equation from **equatable** *adj*
equation ⓣ *n* **1** a mathematical statement that two expressions are equal **2** a situation or problem in which a number of different factors need to be considered: *this plan leaves human nature out of the equation* **3** the act of equating **4** *chem* a representation of a chemical reaction using symbols of the elements
equator *n* an imaginary circle around the earth at an equal distance from the North Pole and the South Pole
WORD ORIGIN Medieval Latin *(circulus) aequator (diei et noctis)* (circle) that equalizes (the day and night)
equatorial *adj* of, like, or existing at or near the equator
equerry (ek-kwer-ee) *n, pl* **-ries** *Brit* an officer of the royal household who acts as a personal attendant to a member of the royal family
WORD ORIGIN Old French *escuirie* group of squires
equestrian *adj* **1** of or relating to horses and riding **2** on horseback: *an equestrian statue of the Queen* **equestrianism** *n*
WORD ORIGIN Latin *equus* horse
equidistant *adj* equally distant **equidistance** *n*
equilateral *adj* **1** having all sides of equal length ▷ *n* **2** a geometric figure having all sides of equal length
equilibrium ⓣ *n, pl* **-ria 1** a stable condition in which forces cancel one another **2** a state of mental and emotional balance; composure
WORD ORIGIN Latin *aequi-* equal + *libra* balance
equine *adj* of or like a horse
WORD ORIGIN Latin *equus* horse
equinoctial *adj* **1** relating to or occurring at an equinox ▷ *n* **2** a storm at or near an equinox
equinox *n* either of the two occasions when day and night are of equal length, around March 21 and September 23
WORD ORIGIN Latin *aequi-* equal + *nox* night
equip ⓣ *vb* **equipping, equipped 1** to provide with supplies, components, etc.: *the car comes equipped with a catalytic converter* **2** to provide with abilities, understanding, etc.: *stress is something we are all equipped to cope with*
WORD ORIGIN Old French *eschiper* to fit out (a ship)
equipment ⓣ *n* **1** a set of tools or devices used for a particular purpose: *communications equipment* **2** an act of equipping
equipoise *n* the state of being perfectly balanced; equilibrium
equitable ⓣ *adj* fair and reasonable **equitably** *adv*
equitation *n* the study of riding and horsemanship
WORD ORIGIN Latin *equitare* to ride
equities *pl n* ▸ same as **ordinary shares**
equity *n, pl* **-ties 1** the quality of being impartial; fairness **2** *law* a system of using principles of natural justice and fair conduct to reach a judgment when common law is inadequate or inappropriate **3** the difference in value between a person's debts and the value of the property on which they are secured: *negative equity*
WORD ORIGIN Latin *aequus* level, equal
Equity *n Brit, Austral, & NZ* the actors' trade union
equivalent ⓣ *n* **1** something that has the same use or function as something else: *Denmark's equivalent to Silicon Valley* ▷ *adj* **2** equal in value, quantity, significance, etc. **3** having the same or a similar effect or meaning **equivalence** *n*
WORD ORIGIN Latin *aequi-* equal + *valere* to be worth
equivocal *adj* **1** capable of varying interpretations; ambiguous **2** deliberately misleading or vague **3** of doubtful character or sincerity: *the party's commitment to genuine reform is equivocal* **equivocally** *adv*
WORD ORIGIN Latin *aequi-* equal + *vox* voice
equivocate *vb* **-cating, -cated** to use vague or ambiguous language in order to deceive someone or to avoid telling the truth **equivocation** *n* **equivocator** *n*
er *interj* a sound made when hesitating in speech
Er *chem* erbium
ER Queen Elizabeth
WORD ORIGIN Latin *Elizabeth Regina*
era ⓣ *n* **1** a period of time considered as distinctive; epoch **2** an extended period of time measured from a fixed point: *the Communist era* **3** *geol* a major division of time
WORD ORIGIN Latin *aera* counters, pieces of brass money
eradicate ⓣ *vb* **-cating, -cated** to destroy or get rid of completely: *measures to eradicate racism* **eradicable** *adj* **eradication** *n* **eradicator** *n*
WORD ORIGIN Latin *e-* out + *radix* root
erase ⓣ *vb* **erasing, erased 1** to destroy all traces of: *he could not erase the memory of his earlier defeat* **2** to rub or wipe out (something written) **3** to remove sound or information from (a magnetic tape or disk) **erasable** *adj*
WORD ORIGIN Latin *e-* out + *radere* to scrape
eraser *n* an object, such as a piece of rubber, for erasing something written
erasure *n* **1** an erasing **2** the place or mark where something has been erased
Erato *n Greek myth* the Muse of love poetry

e

THESAURUS

evenness, coequality, equatability
OPPOSITE: disparity
equate *vb* **1a = identify**, associate, connect, compare, relate, mention in the same breath, think of in connection with, think of together **1b = make equal**, match, balance, square, even up, equalize
equation *n* **3 = equating**, match, agreement, balancing, pairing, comparison, parallel, equality, correspondence, likeness, equivalence, equalization
equilibrium *n* **1 = stability**, balance, symmetry, steadiness, evenness, equipoise, counterpoise
equip *vb* **1 = supply**, provide, stock, dress, outfit, arm, rig, array, furnish, endow, attire, fit out, deck out, kit out, fit up, accoutre **2 = prepare**, qualify, educate, get ready, endow
equipment *n* **1 = apparatus**, stock, supplies, material, stuff, tackle, gear, tools, provisions, kit, rig, baggage, paraphernalia, accoutrements, appurtenances, equipage
equitable *adj* **= even-handed**, just, right, fair, due, reasonable, proper, honest, impartial, rightful, unbiased, dispassionate, proportionate, unprejudiced, nondiscriminatory
equivalent *n* **1 = equal**, counterpart, correspondent, twin, peer, parallel, match, opposite number ▷ *adj* **2, 3 = equal**, even, same, comparable, parallel, identical, alike, corresponding, correspondent, synonymous, of a kind, tantamount, interchangeable, of a piece with, commensurate, homologous
OPPOSITE: different
era *n* **1, 2 = age**, time, period, stage, date, generation, cycle, epoch, aeon, day *or* days
eradicate *vb* **= wipe out**, eliminate, remove, destroy, get rid of, abolish, erase, excise, extinguish, stamp out, obliterate, uproot, weed out, annihilate, put paid to, root out, efface, exterminate, expunge, extirpate, wipe from the face of the earth
erase *vb* **1 = delete**, cancel out, wipe out, remove, eradicate, excise, obliterate, efface, blot out, expunge **2 = rub out**, remove, wipe out, delete, scratch out

DICTIONARY

Eratosthenes *n* ?276–?194 BC, Greek mathematician and astronomer, who calculated the circumference of the earth by observing the angle of the sun's rays at different places

erbium *n chem* a soft silvery-white element of the lanthanide series of metals. Symbol: Er
WORD ORIGIN after *Ytterby*, Sweden

ere *conj, prep poetic* before
WORD ORIGIN Old English *ǣr*

e

erect ❶ *vb* **1** to build **2** to raise to an upright position **3** to found or form: *the caricature of socialism erected by Lenin* ▷ *adj* **4** upright in posture or position **5** *physiol* (of the penis, clitoris, or nipples) firm or rigid after swelling with blood, esp. as a result of sexual excitement **erection** *n*
WORD ORIGIN Latin *erigere* to set up

erectile *adj physiol* (of an organ, such as the penis) capable of becoming erect

eremite (air-rim-mite) *n* a Christian hermit
WORD ORIGIN Greek *erēmos* lonely

Erenburg *n* ▸ a variant spelling of (Ilya Grigorievich) **Ehrenburg**

ergo *conj* therefore
WORD ORIGIN Latin

ergonomic *adj* **1** designed to minimize effort and discomfort **2** of or relating to ergonomics

ergonomics *n* the study of the relationship between workers and their environment
WORD ORIGIN Greek *ergon* work + (ECO)NOMICS

ergot *n* **1** a disease of a cereal, such as rye, caused by a fungus **2** the dried fungus used in medicine
WORD ORIGIN French: spur (of a cock)

Erhard *n* **Ludwig** 1897–1977, German statesman: chief architect of the *Wirtschaftswunder* ("economic miracle") of West Germany's recovery after World War II; chancellor (1963–66)

Eric XIV *n* 1533–77, king of Sweden (1560–68). His attempts to dominate the Baltic led to war with Denmark (1563–70); deposed and imprisoned

Erigena *n* **John Scotus** ?800–?877 AD, Irish Neo-Platonist philosopher

Eriksson *n* **Sven-Goran** born 1948, Swedish football manager; head coach of the England team (2001–06)

Erin *n archaic or poetic* Ireland
WORD ORIGIN Irish Gaelic *Éirinn*

Erlanger *n* **Joseph** 1874–1965, US physiologist. He shared a Nobel prize for physiology or medicine (1944) with Gasser for their work on the electrical signs of nervous activity

Ermanaric *n* died ?375 AD, king of the Ostrogoths: ruled an extensive empire in eastern Europe, which was overrun by the Huns in the 370s

ermine *n, pl* **-mines** *or* **-mine** **1** the stoat in northern regions, where it has a white winter coat **2** the fur of this animal, used to trim state robes of judges, nobles, etc.
WORD ORIGIN Medieval Latin *Armenius (mus)* Armenian (mouse)

erne *or* **ern** *n* a fish-eating sea eagle
WORD ORIGIN Old English *earn*

Ernie *n* (in Britain) a machine that randomly selects winning numbers of Premium Bonds
WORD ORIGIN acronym of Electronic Random Number Indicator Equipment

Ernst *n* **Max** 1891–1976, German painter, resident in France and the US, a prominent exponent of Dada and surrealism: developed the technique of collage

erode ❶ *vb* **eroding, eroded** **1** to wear down or away **2** to deteriorate or cause to deteriorate
WORD ORIGIN Latin *e-* away + *rodere* to gnaw

erogenous (ir-roj-in-uss) *adj* sensitive to sexual stimulation: *an erogenous zone*
WORD ORIGIN Greek *erōs* love + *-genēs* born

erosion ❶ *n* **1** the wearing away of rocks or soil by the action of water, ice, or wind **2** a gradual lessening or reduction: *an erosion of national sovereignty* **erosive** *or* **erosional** *adj*

erotic ❶ *adj* of, concerning, or arousing sexual desire or giving sexual pleasure **erotically** *adv*
WORD ORIGIN Greek *erōs* love

erotica *pl n* explicitly sexual literature or art

eroticism *n* **1** erotic quality or nature **2** the use of sexually arousing symbolism in literature or art **3** sexual excitement or desire

err *vb* **1** to make a mistake **2** to sin
WORD ORIGIN Latin *errare*

errand *n* **1** a short trip to get or do something for someone **2** **run an errand** to make such a trip
WORD ORIGIN Old English *ǣrende*

errant *adj* **1** behaving in a way considered to be unacceptable: *an errant schoolboy* **2** *old-fashioned or literary* wandering in search of adventure: *a knight errant* **errantry** *n*
WORD ORIGIN Latin *iter* journey

erratic ❶ *adj* **1** irregular or unpredictable: *his increasingly erratic behaviour* ▷ *n* **2** *geol* a rock that has been transported by glacial action **erratically** *adv*
WORD ORIGIN Latin *errare* to wander

erratum *n, pl* **-ta** an error in writing or printing
WORD ORIGIN Latin

erroneous *adj* based on or containing an error or errors; incorrect **erroneously** *adv*

error ❶ *n* **1** a mistake, inaccuracy, or misjudgment **2** the act or state of being wrong or making a misjudgment: *the plane was shot down in error* **3** the amount by which the actual value of a quantity might differ from an estimate: *a 3% margin of error*
WORD ORIGIN Latin

ersatz (air-zats) *adj* made in imitation of something more expensive: *ersatz coffee*
WORD ORIGIN German *ersetzen* to substitute

Erse *n, adj* Irish Gaelic
WORD ORIGIN Lowland Scots *Erisch* Irish

Ershad *n* **Hussain Mohammed** born 1930, Bangladeshi soldier and statesman. He seized power in a coup in 1982, becoming president in 1983. He was deposed in 1990

THESAURUS

erect *vb* **1, 2 = build**, raise, set up, lift, pitch, mount, stand up, rear, construct, put up, assemble, put together, elevate **OPPOSITE:** demolish **3 = found**, establish, form, create, set up, institute, organize, put up, initiate ▷ *adj* **4 = upright**, raised, straight, standing, stiff, firm, rigid, vertical, elevated, perpendicular, pricked-up **OPPOSITE:** bent

erode *vb* **1a = disintegrate**, crumble, deteriorate, corrode, break up, grind down, waste away, wear down *or* away **1b = destroy**, consume, spoil, crumble, eat away, corrode, break up, grind down, abrade, wear down *or* away **2 = weaken**, destroy, undermine, diminish, impair, lessen, wear away

erosion *n* **1 = disintegration**, deterioration, corrosion, corrasion, wearing down *or* away, grinding down **2 = deterioration**, wearing, undermining, destruction, consumption, weakening, spoiling, attrition, eating away, abrasion, grinding down, wearing down *or* away

erotic *adj* **= sexual**, sexy *(informal)*, crude, explicit, rousing, sensual, seductive, vulgar, stimulating, steamy *(informal)*, suggestive, aphrodisiac, voluptuous, carnal, titillating, bawdy, lustful, sexually arousing, erogenous, amatory

erratic *adj* **1 = unpredictable**, variable, unstable, irregular, shifting, eccentric, abnormal, inconsistent, uneven, unreliable, wayward, capricious, desultory, changeable, aberrant, fitful, inconstant **OPPOSITE:** regular

error *n* **1 = mistake**, slip, fault, blunder, flaw, boob *(Brit slang)*, delusion, oversight, misconception, fallacy, inaccuracy, howler *(informal)*, bloomer *(Brit informal)*, boner *(slang)*, miscalculation, misapprehension, solecism, erratum, barry *or* Barry Crocker *(Austral slang)*

Erskine *n* **Thomas,** 1st Baron. 1750–1823, Scottish lawyer: noted as a defence advocate, esp. in cases involving civil liberties

erstwhile *adj* **1** former ▷*adv* **2** *archaic* formerly

Erté *n* real name *Romain de Tirtoff.* 1892–1990, French fashion illustrator and designer, born in Russia, noted for his extravagant costumes and tableaux for the Folies-Bergère in Paris

eruct *or* **eructate** *vb formal* to belch **eructation** *n*
WORD ORIGIN Latin *e-* out + *ructare* to belch

erudite (air-rude-ite) *adj* having or showing great academic knowledge **erudition** *n*
WORD ORIGIN Latin *erudire* to polish

erupt ⊕ *vb* **1** (of a volcano) to throw out molten lava, ash, and steam in a sudden and violent way **2** to burst forth suddenly and violently: *riots erupted across the country* **3** (of a group of people) to suddenly become angry and aggressive: *the meeting erupted in fury* **4** (of a blemish) to appear on the skin **eruptive** *adj* **eruption** *n*
WORD ORIGIN Latin *e-* out + *rumpere* to burst

erysipelas (air-riss-**sip**-ill-ass) *n* an acute disease of the skin, with fever and raised purplish patches
WORD ORIGIN Greek *erusi-* red + *-pelas* skin

erythrocyte (ir-**rith**-roe-site) *n* a red blood cell that transports oxygen through the body
WORD ORIGIN Greek *eruthros* red + *kutos* hollow vessel

Es *chem* einsteinium

escalate ⊕ *vb* **-lating, -lated** to increase or be increased in size, seriousness, or intensity **escalation** *n*
WORD ORIGIN from *escalator*

escalator *n* a moving staircase consisting of stair treads fixed to a conveyor belt
WORD ORIGIN Latin *scala* ladder

escalope (ess-kal-lop) *n* a thin slice of meat, usually veal
WORD ORIGIN Old French: shell

escapade *n* a mischievous act or adventure
WORD ORIGIN French

escape ⊕ *vb* **-caping, -caped 1** to get away or break free from (confinement) **2** to manage to avoid (something dangerous, unpleasant, or difficult) **3** (of gases, liquids, etc.) to leak gradually **4** to elude; be forgotten by: *those little round cakes whose name escapes me* ▷*n* **5** the act of escaping or state of having escaped **6** a way of avoiding something difficult, dangerous, or unpleasant: *his frequent illnesses provided an escape from intolerable stress* **7** a means of relaxation or relief: *he found temporary escape through the local cinema* **8** a leakage of gas or liquid
WORD ORIGIN Late Latin *e-* out + *cappa* cloak

escapee *n* a person who has escaped from prison

escapement *n* the mechanism in a clock or watch which connects the hands to the pendulum or balance

escape road *n* a small road leading off a steep hill, into which a car can be driven if the brakes fail

escape velocity *n* the minimum velocity necessary for a particle, space vehicle, etc. to escape from the gravitational field of the earth or other celestial body

escapism *n* an inclination to retreat from unpleasant reality, for example through fantasy **escapist** *n, adj*

escapologist *n* an entertainer who specializes in freeing himself or herself from chains, ropes, etc. **escapology** *n*

escarpment *n* the long continuous steep face of a ridge or mountain
WORD ORIGIN French *escarpement*

eschatology (ess-cat-**tol**-a-jee) *n* the branch of theology concerned with the end of the world **eschatological** *adj*
WORD ORIGIN Greek *eskhatos* last

escheat (iss-**cheat**) *law n* **1** formerly, the return of property to the state in the absence of legal heirs **2** the property so reverting ▷*vb* **3** to obtain (land) by escheat
WORD ORIGIN Old French *escheoir* to fall to the lot of

eschew (iss-**chew**) *vb* to avoid doing or being involved in (something disliked or harmful) **eschewal** *n*
WORD ORIGIN Old French *eschiver*

escort ⊕ *n* **1** people or vehicles accompanying another to protect or guard them **2** a person who accompanies someone of the opposite sex on a social occasion ▷*vb* **3** to act as an escort to
WORD ORIGIN French *escorte*

escritoire (ess-kree-**twahr**) *n* a writing desk with compartments and drawers
WORD ORIGIN Medieval Latin *scriptorium* writing room in a monastery

escudo (ess-kew-doe) *n, pl* **-dos** a former monetary unit of Portugal
WORD ORIGIN Spanish: shield

esculent *formal adj* **1** edible ▷*n* **2** any edible substance
WORD ORIGIN Latin *esculentus* good to eat

escutcheon *n* **1** a shield displaying a coat of arms **2 blot on one's escutcheon** a stain on one's honour
WORD ORIGIN Latin *scutum* shield

Esenin *or* **Yesenin** *n* **Sergey Aleksandrovich** 1895–1925, Soviet poet, author of *Confessions of a Hooligan* (1924): married to Isadora Duncan

Eskimo *n* **1** *pl* **-mos** *or* **-mo** a member of a group of peoples who live in N Canada, Greenland, Alaska, and E Siberia **2** the language of these peoples ▷*adj* **3** of the Eskimos
WORD ORIGIN Algonquian *esquimawes*

ESN *Brit* educationally subnormal; formerly used to designate a child who needs special schooling

esoteric (ee-so-ter-rik) *adj*

erupt *vb* **1 = explode**, blow up, flare up, emit lava **2a = gush**, burst out, be ejected, burst forth, pour forth, belch forth, spew forth *or* out **2b = start**, break out, begin, explode, flare up, burst out, boil over **4** *(medical)* **= break out**, appear, flare up

escalate *vb* **a = grow**, increase, extend, intensify, expand, surge, be increased, mount, heighten
OPPOSITE: decrease
b = increase, develop, extend, intensify, expand, build up, step up, heighten, enlarge, magnify, amplify
OPPOSITE: lessen

escape *vb* **1 = get away**, flee, take off, fly, bolt, skip, slip away, abscond, decamp, hook it *(slang)*, do a runner *(slang)*, do a bunk *(Brit slang)*, fly the coop *(US & Canad informal)*, make a break for it, slip through your fingers, skedaddle *(informal)*, take a powder *(US & Canad slang)*, make your getaway, take it on the lam *(US & Canad slang)*, break free *or* out, make *or* effect your escape, run away *or* off, do a Skase *(Austral informal)* **2 = avoid**, miss, evade, dodge, shun, elude, duck, steer clear of, circumvent, body-swerve *(Scot)* **3** *(usually with* **from**) **= leak out**, flow out, drain away, discharge, gush out, emanate, seep out, exude, spurt out, spill out, pour forth ▷*n* **5 = getaway**, break, flight, break-out, bolt, decampment **6 = avoidance**, evasion, circumvention, elusion **7 = relaxation**, relief, recreation, distraction, diversion, pastime **8 = leak**, emission, discharge, outpouring, gush, spurt, outflow, leakage, drain, seepage, issue, emanation, efflux, effluence, outpour

escort *n* **1 = guard**, protection, safeguard, bodyguard, company, train, convoy, entourage, retinue, cortege **2 = companion**, partner, attendant, guide, squire *(rare)*, protector, beau, chaperon ▷*vb* **3 = accompany**, lead, partner, conduct, guide, guard, shepherd, convoy, usher, squire, hold (someone's) hand, chaperon

DICTIONARY

understood by only a small number of people, esp. because they have special knowledge **esoterically** *adv*
WORD ORIGIN Greek *esōterō* inner
ESP extrasensory perception
esp. especially
espadrille (ess-pad-drill) *n* a light canvas shoe with a braided cord sole
WORD ORIGIN French
espalier (ess-pal-yer) *n* **1** a shrub or fruit tree trained to grow flat **2** the trellis on which such plants are grown
WORD ORIGIN French
esparto *or* **esparto grass** *n, pl* **-tos** any of various grasses of S Europe and N Africa, used to make ropes, mats, etc.
WORD ORIGIN Greek *spartos* a kind of rush
especial *adj formal* ▸ same as **special**
WORD ORIGIN Latin *specialis* individual
especially ⓣ *adv* **1** particularly: *people are dying, especially children and babies* **2** more than usually: *an especially virulent disease*
Esperanto *n* an international artificial language **esperantist** *n, adj*
WORD ORIGIN literally: the one who hopes, pseudonym of Dr L. L. Zamenhof, its Polish inventor
espionage ⓣ (ess-pyon-ahzh) *n* **1** the use of spies to obtain secret information, esp. by governments **2** the act of spying
WORD ORIGIN French *espionnage*
esplanade *n* a long open level stretch of ground, esp. beside the seashore or in front of a fortified place
WORD ORIGIN French
espousal *n* **1** adoption or support: *his espousal of the free market* **2** *old-fashioned* a marriage or engagement ceremony
espouse *vb* **-pousing, -poused** **1** to adopt or give support to (a cause, ideal, etc.) **2** *old-fashioned* (esp. of a man) to marry
WORD ORIGIN Latin *sponsare*
espresso *n, pl* **-sos** coffee made by forcing steam or boiling water through ground coffee
WORD ORIGIN Italian: pressed
esprit (ess-pree) *n* spirit, liveliness, or wit
WORD ORIGIN French
esprit de corps (de kore) *n* consciousness of and pride in belonging to a particular group
WORD ORIGIN French
espy *vb* **espies, espying, espied** to catch sight of
WORD ORIGIN Old French *espier*
Esq. esquire
esquire *n* **1** *chiefly Brit* a title of respect placed after a man's name and usually shortened to *Esq.*: *I Davies, Esquire* **2** (in medieval times) the attendant of a knight
WORD ORIGIN Late Latin *scutarius* shield bearer
essay ⓣ *n* **1** a short literary composition on a single subject **2** a short piece of writing on a subject done as an exercise by a student **3** an attempt ▹ *vb* **4** *formal* to attempt: *he essayed a faint smile*
WORD ORIGIN Old French *essai* an attempt
essayist *n* a person who writes essays
essence ⓣ *n* **1** the most important and distinctive feature of something, which determines its identity **2** a concentrated liquid used to flavour food **3** **in essence** essentially **4** **of the essence** vitally important
WORD ORIGIN Latin *esse* to be
essential ⓣ *adj* **1** vitally important; absolutely necessary: *it is essential to get this finished on time* **2** basic or fundamental: *she translated the essential points of the lecture into English* ▹ *n* **3** something fundamental or indispensable **essentially** *adv*
essential oil *n* any of various volatile oils in plants, which have the odour or flavour of the plant from which they are extracted
Essex[1] *n* **1** a county of SE England, on the North Sea and the Thames estuary; the geographical and ceremonial county includes Thurrock and Southend-on-Sea, which became independent unitary authorities in 1998. Administrative centre: Chelmsford. Pop (excluding unitary authorities): 1324100 (2003 est). Area (excluding unitary authorities): 3446 sq km (1310 sq miles) **2** an Anglo-Saxon kingdom that in the early 7th century AD comprised the modern county of Essex and much of Hertfordshire and Surrey. By the late 8th century, Essex had become a dependency of the kingdom of Mercia
Essex[2] *n* **2nd Earl of,** title of *Robert Devereux*. ?1566–1601, English soldier and favourite of Queen Elizabeth I; executed for treason
EST **1** Eastern Standard Time **2** electric-shock treatment
est. **1** established **2** estimate(d)
establish ⓣ *vb* **1** to create or set up (an organization, link, etc.): *the regime wants to establish better relations with neighbouring countries* **2** to make become firmly associated with a particular activity or reputation: *the play that established him as a major dramatist* **3** to prove: *a test to establish if your baby has any chromosomal disorder* **4** to cause (a principle) to be accepted: *our study establishes the case for further research*
WORD ORIGIN Latin *stabilis* firm, stable
Established Church *n* a church, such as the Church of England, that is recognized as the official church of a country
establishment ⓣ *n* **1** the act of establishing or state of being established **2** **a** a business organization or other institution **b** a place of business **3** the people employed by an organization
Establishment ⓣ *n* **the Establishment** a group of people

THESAURUS

especially *adv* **1 = notably**, largely, chiefly, mainly, mostly, principally, strikingly, conspicuously, outstandingly **2 = very**, specially, particularly, signally, extremely, remarkably, unusually, exceptionally, extraordinarily, markedly, supremely, uncommonly
espionage *n* **1, 2 = spying**, intelligence, surveillance, counter-intelligence, undercover work
essay *n* **1, 2 = composition**, study, paper, article, piece, assignment, discourse, tract, treatise, dissertation, disquisition ▹ *vb* **4** *(formal)* **= attempt**, try, test, take on, undertake, strive for, endeavour, have a go at, try out, have a shot at *(informal)*, have a crack at *(informal)*, have a bash at *(informal)*
essence *n* **1 = fundamental nature**, nature, being, life, meaning, heart, spirit, principle, soul, core, substance, significance, entity, bottom line, essential part, kernel, crux, lifeblood, pith, quintessence, basic characteristic, quiddity **2 = concentrate**, spirits, extract, elixir, tincture, distillate
essential *adj* **1 = vital**, important, needed, necessary, critical, crucial, key, indispensable, requisite, vitally important, must-have
OPPOSITE: unimportant
2 = fundamental, main, basic, radical, key, principal, constitutional, cardinal, inherent, elementary, innate, hard-wired, intrinsic, elemental, immanent
OPPOSITE: secondary
▹ *n* **3 = prerequisite**, principle, fundamental, necessity, must, basic, requisite, vital part, sine qua non *(Latin)*, rudiment, must-have
establish *vb* **1 = set up**, found, start, create, institute, organize, install, constitute, inaugurate **2 = secure**, form, base, ground, plant, settle, fix, root, implant, entrench, ensconce, put down roots **3 = prove**, show, confirm, demonstrate, ratify, certify, verify, validate, substantiate, corroborate, authenticate
establishment *n* **1 = creation**, founding, setting up, foundation, institution, organization, formation, installation, inauguration,

DICTIONARY

having authority within a society: usually seen as conservative

estate ❶ *n* **1** a large piece of landed property, esp. in the country **2** *Austral & Brit* a large area of land with houses or factories built on it: *an industrial estate* **3** *law* property or possessions, esp. of a deceased person **4** *history* any of the orders or classes making up a society
WORD ORIGIN Latin *status* condition

estate agent *n Austral & Brit* a person whose job is to help people buy and sell houses and other property

estate car *n Brit* a car which has a long body with a door at the back end and luggage space behind the rear seats

estate duty *n* ▸ a former name for **inheritance tax**

esteem ❶ *n* **1** admiration and respect ▹ *vb* **2** to have great respect or high regard for (someone) **3** *formal* to judge or consider: *I should esteem it a kindness* **esteemed** *adj*
WORD ORIGIN Latin *aestimare* to assess the worth of

ester *n chem* a compound produced by the reaction between an acid and an alcohol
WORD ORIGIN German

Esterházy *n* a noble Hungarian family that produced many soldiers, diplomats, and patrons of the arts. Prince **Miklós József Esterházy** (1714–90) rebuilt the family castle of Esterháza and employed Haydn as his musical director (1766–90)

Estienne *or* **Étienne** *n* a family of French printers, scholars, and dealers in books, including **Henri** ?1460–1520, who founded the printing business in Paris, his son **Robert**, 1503–59, and his grandson **Henri**, 1528–98

estimable *adj* worthy of respect

estimate ❶ *vb* **-mating, -mated 1** to form an approximate idea of (size, cost, etc.); calculate roughly **2** to form an opinion about; judge **3** to submit an approximate price for a job to a prospective client ▹ *n* **4** an approximate calculation **5** a statement of the likely charge for certain work **6** an opinion
estimator *n*
WORD ORIGIN Latin *aestimare* to assess the worth of

estimation *n* **1** a considered opinion; judgment: *overall, he went up in my estimation* **2** the act of estimating

Estonian *adj* **1** from Estonia ▹ *n* **2** a person from Estonia

estranged *adj* **1** no longer living with one's husband or wife: *his estranged wife* **2** having quarrelled and lost touch with one's family or friends: *I am estranged from my son*
estrangement *n*
WORD ORIGIN from Latin *extraneus* foreign

estuary ❶ *n, pl* **-aries** the widening channel of a river where it nears the sea **estuarine** *adj*
WORD ORIGIN Latin *aestus* tide

ET *Brit* Employment Training: a government scheme offering training in technology and business skills for unemployed people

ETA estimated time of arrival

e-tail (ee-tail) *n* retail conducted via the internet

et al. 1 and elsewhere
WORD ORIGIN Latin *et alibi*
2 and others
WORD ORIGIN Latin *et alii*

etc. et cetera

et cetera *or* **etcetera** (et set-ra) *adv* **1** and the rest; and others; or the like **2** and so forth
WORD ORIGIN Latin *et* and + *cetera* the other (things)

etceteras *pl n* miscellaneous extra things or people

etch ❶ *vb* **1** to wear away the surface of a metal, glass, etc. by the action of an acid **2** to cut a design or pattern into a printing plate with acid **3** to imprint vividly: *the scene is etched on my mind* **etcher** *n*
WORD ORIGIN Dutch *etsen*

etching ❶ *n* **1** the art or process of preparing or printing etched designs **2** a print made from an etched plate

eternal ❶ *adj* **1** without beginning or end; lasting for ever **2** unchanged by time: *eternal truths* **3** seemingly unceasing: *his eternal whingeing* **4** of or like God or a god: *the Eternal Buddha*
eternally *adv*
WORD ORIGIN Latin *aeternus*

eternal triangle *n* an emotional or sexual relationship in which there are conflicts between a man and two women or a woman and two men

eternity ❶ *n, pl* **-ties 1** endless or infinite time **2** a seemingly endless period of time: *it seemed an eternity before he could feel his heart beating again* **3** the timeless existence after death **4** the state of being eternal

eternity ring *n* a ring given as a token of lasting affection, esp. one set all around with stones to symbolize continuity

ethane *n* a flammable gaseous alkane obtained from natural gas and petroleum: used as a fuel
WORD ORIGIN from *ethyl*

THESAURUS

enactment **2a = organization**, company, business, firm, house, concern, operation, structure, institution, institute, corporation, enterprise, outfit *(informal)*, premises, setup *(informal)*

Establishment *n* **the Establishment = the authorities**, the system, the powers that be, the ruling class, the established order, institutionalized authority

estate *n* **1 = lands**, property, area, grounds, domain, manor, holdings, demesne, homestead *(US & Canad)* **2** *(chiefly Brit)* **= area**, centre, park, development, site, zone, plot **3** *(law)* **= property**, capital, assets, fortune, goods, effects, wealth, possessions, belongings

esteem *n* **1 = respect**, regard, honour, consideration, admiration, reverence, estimation, veneration ▹ *vb* **2 = respect**, admire, think highly of, like, love, value, prize, honour, treasure, cherish, revere, reverence, be fond of, venerate, regard highly, take off your hat to

estimate *vb* **1 = calculate roughly**, value, guess, judge, reckon, assess, evaluate, gauge, number, appraise **2 = think**, believe, consider, rate, judge, hold, rank, guess, reckon, assess, conjecture, surmise ▹ *n* **4 = approximate calculation**, guess, reckoning, assessment, judgment, evaluation, valuation, appraisal, educated guess, guesstimate *(informal)*, rough calculation, ballpark figure *(informal)*, approximate cost, approximate price, appraisement **6 = assessment**, opinion, belief, appraisal, evaluation, conjecture, appraisement, judgment, estimation, surmise

estuary *n* **= inlet**, mouth, creek, firth, fjord

etch *vb* **1 = corrode**, eat into, burn into **2, 3 = engrave**, cut, impress, stamp, carve, imprint, inscribe, furrow, incise, ingrain

etching *n* **1, 2 = print**, impression, carving, engraving, imprint, inscription

eternal *adj* **1, 2 = everlasting**, lasting, permanent, enduring, endless, perennial, perpetual, timeless, immortal, unending, unchanging, immutable, indestructible, undying, without end, unceasing, imperishable, deathless, sempiternal *(literary)* **OPPOSITE:** transitory **3 = interminable**, constant, endless, abiding, infinite, continual, immortal, never-ending, everlasting, ceaseless, unremitting, deathless **OPPOSITE:** occasional

eternity *n* **1, 4 = perpetuity**, immortality, infinity, timelessness, endlessness, infinitude, time without end **2 = ages**, years, an age, centuries, for ever *(informal)*, aeons, donkey's years *(informal)*, yonks *(informal)*, a month of Sundays *(informal)*, a long time *or* while, an age *or* eternity **3 = the afterlife**, heaven, paradise, the next world, the hereafter

DICTIONARY

ethanoic acid *n* ▸ same as **acetic acid**
ethanol *n* ▸ same as **alcohol** (sense 1)
Ethelbert *or* **Æthelbert** *n* **Saint** ?552–616 AD, king of Kent (560–616): converted to Christianity by St Augustine; issued the earliest known code of English laws. Feast day: Feb 24 or 25
Ethelwulf *or* **Æthelwulf** *n* died 858 AD, king of Wessex (839–858)
ethene *n* ▸ same as **ethylene**

e

ether *n* **1** a colourless sweet-smelling liquid used as a solvent and anaesthetic **2** the substance formerly believed to fill all space and to transmit electromagnetic waves **3** the upper regions of the atmosphere; clear sky. Also (for senses 2 and 3): **aether**
WORD ORIGIN Greek *aithein* to burn
ethereal (eth-eer-ee-al) *adj* **1** extremely delicate or refined **2** heavenly or spiritual **ethereally** *adv*
WORD ORIGIN Greek *aithēr* ether
Etherege *n* Sir **George** ?1635–?92, English Restoration dramatist; author of the comedies *The Comical Revenge* (1664), *She would if she could* (1668), and *The Man of Mode* (1676)
ethic *n* a moral principle or set of moral values held by an individual or group
WORD ORIGIN Greek *ēthos* custom
ethical ⓘ *adj* **1** of or based on a system of moral beliefs about right and wrong **2** in accordance with principles of professional conduct **3** of or relating to ethics **ethically** *adv*
ethics ⓘ *pl n* **1** a code of behaviour, esp. of a particular group, profession, or individual: *business ethics* **2** the moral fitness of a decision, course of action, etc. ▹*n* **3** the study of the moral value of human conduct
Ethiopian *adj* **1** of Ethiopia ▹*n* **2** a person from Ethiopia
ethnic ⓘ *or* **ethnical** *adj* **1** of or relating to a human group with racial, religious, and linguistic characteristics in common **2** characteristic of another culture, esp. a peasant one: *ethnic foodstuffs* **ethnically** *adv*
WORD ORIGIN Greek *ethnos* race
ethnic cleansing *n* the practice, by the dominant ethnic group in an area, of removing other ethnic groups by expulsion or extermination
ethnocentric *adj* of or relating to the belief that one's own nation, culture, or group is intrinsically superior **ethnocentricity** *n*
ethnology *n* the branch of anthropology that deals with races and peoples and their relations to one another **ethnological** *adj* **ethnologist** *n*
ethos (eeth-oss) *n* the distinctive spirit and attitudes of a people, culture, etc.
WORD ORIGIN Greek
ethyl (eth-ill) *adj* of, consisting of, or containing the monovalent group C_2H_5–
WORD ORIGIN from *ether*
ethyl alcohol *n* ▸ same as **alcohol** (sense 1)
ethylene *or* **ethene** *n* a colourless flammable gaseous alkene used to make polythene and other chemicals
Étienne *n* ▸ a variant spelling of **Estienne**
etiolate (ee-tee-oh-late) *vb* **-lating, -lated 1** *formal* to become or cause to become weak **2** *bot* to make a green plant paler through lack of sunlight **etiolation** *n*
WORD ORIGIN French *étioler* to make pale
etiology *n, pl* **-gies 1** the study of causation **2** the study of the cause of diseases **etiological** *adj*
WORD ORIGIN Greek *aitia* cause + -LOGY
etiquette *n* **1** the customs or rules of behaviour regarded as correct in social life **2** a conventional code of practice in certain professions
WORD ORIGIN French
étude (ay-tewd) *n music* a short composition for a solo instrument, esp. intended to be played as an exercise or to demonstrate virtuosity
WORD ORIGIN French: study
etymology *n, pl* **-gies 1** the study of the sources and development of words **2** an account of the source and development of a word **etymological** *adj* **etymologist** *n*
WORD ORIGIN Greek *etumon* basic meaning + -LOGY
Eu *chem* europium
EU European Union
eucalyptus *or* **eucalypt** *n, pl* **-lyptuses, -lyptus** *or* **-lypts** any of a mostly Australian genus of trees, widely cultivated for timber and gum, and for the medicinal oil in their leaves (**eucalyptus oil**)
WORD ORIGIN Greek *eu-* well + *kaluptos* covered
Eucharist (yew-kar-ist) *n* **1** the Christian sacrament commemorating Christ's Last Supper by the consecration of bread and wine **2** the consecrated elements of bread and wine **Eucharistic** *adj*
WORD ORIGIN Greek *eukharistos* thankful
Eucken *n* **Rudolph Christoph** 1846–1926, German idealist philosopher: Nobel prize for literature 1908
Euclidean *or* **Euclidian** (yew-klid-ee-an) *adj* denoting a system of geometry based on the rules of Euclid, 3rd-century BC Greek mathematician
Eudoxus of Cnidus *n* ?406–?355 BC, Greek astronomer and mathematician; believed to have calculated the length of the solar year
Eugène *n* **Prince,** title of *François Eugène de Savoie-Carignan.* 1663–1736, Austrian general, born in France: with Marlborough defeated the French at Blenheim (1704), Oudenaarde (1708), and Malplaquet (1709)
eugenics (yew-jen-iks) *n* the study of methods of improving the human race, esp. by selective breeding **eugenic** *adj* **eugenically** *adv* **eugenicist** *n*
WORD ORIGIN Greek *eugenēs* well-born
Eugénie *n* original name *Eugénia Maria de Montijo de Guzman, Comtesse de Téba.* 1826–1920, Empress of France (1853–71) as wife of Napoleon III
Euler-Chelpin *n* **Hans** (**Karl August**) **von** 1873–1964, Swedish biochemist, born in Germany: shared the Nobel prize for chemistry (1929) with Sir Arthur Harden for their work on enzymes: father of Ulf von Euler
eulogize *or* **-gise** *vb* **-gizing, -gized** *or* **-gising, -gised** to praise (a person or thing) highly in speech or writing **eulogistic** *adj*
eulogy *n, pl* **-gies 1** a speech or piece of writing praising a person or thing, esp. a person who has recently died **2** high praise
WORD ORIGIN Greek *eulogia* praise
eunuch *n* a man who has been castrated, esp. (formerly) a guard in a harem
WORD ORIGIN Greek *eunoukhos* bedchamber attendant
euphemism *n* an inoffensive word or phrase substituted for one considered offensive or upsetting, such as *departed* for *dead* **euphemistic** *adj* **euphemistically** *adv*
WORD ORIGIN Greek *eu-* well + *phēmē* speech

THESAURUS

ethical *adj* **1, 2 = right**, morally right, morally acceptable, good, just, fitting, fair, responsible, principled, correct, decent, proper, upright, honourable, honest, righteous, virtuous **OPPOSITE:** unethical
3 = moral, behavioural
ethics *pl n* **1 = moral code**, standards, principles, morals, conscience, morality, moral values, moral principles, moral philosophy, rules of conduct, moral beliefs, tikanga (NZ)
ethnic *or* **ethnical** *adj* **1, 2 = cultural**, national, traditional, native, folk, racial, genetic, indigenous

DICTIONARY

euphonious *adj* pleasing to the ear
euphonium *n* a brass musical instrument with four valves, resembling a small tuba
WORD ORIGIN *euph(ony + harm)onium*
euphony *n, pl* **-nies** a pleasing sound, esp. in speech
WORD ORIGIN Greek *eu-* well + *phōnē* voice
euphoria ⓘ *n* a feeling of great but often unjustified or exaggerated happiness **euphoric** *adj*
WORD ORIGIN Greek *eu-* well + *pherein* to bear
Eur. 1 Europe 2 European
Eurasian *adj* 1 of Europe and Asia 2 of mixed European and Asian descent ▷*n* 3 a person of mixed European and Asian descent
eureka (yew-**reek**-a) *interj* an exclamation of triumph on discovering or solving something
WORD ORIGIN Greek *heurēka* I have found (it)
euro *n, pl* **euros** the unit of the European Union's single currency
Euro- *combining form* Europe or European
Eurocentric *adj* chiefly concerned with Europe and European culture: *a Eurocentric view of British history*
Euroland *or* **Eurozone** *n* the geographical area containing the countries that have joined the European single currency
European *adj* 1 of Europe ▷*n* 2 a person from Europe 3 a person of European descent 4 an advocate of closer links between the countries of Europe, esp. those in the European Union **Europeanism** *n*
European Community *or* **European Economic Community** *n* ▸former names for **European Union**
European Union *n* an economic organization of W European states, which have some shared monetary, social, and political goals
Europhile (you-roh-file) *n* 1 a person who admires Europe or the European Union ▷*adj* 2 marked by admiration of Europe or the European Union
europium *n chem* a silvery-white element of the lanthanide series. Symbol: Eu
WORD ORIGIN after *Europe*
Euro-sceptic *n* 1 (in Britain) a person who is opposed to closer links with the European Union ▷*adj* 2 (in Britain) opposing closer links with the European Union: *three Euro-sceptic MPs*
Eurozone *n* ▸same as **Euroland**
Eusebio *n* **Silva Ferreira da** born 1942, Portuguese footballer
Eusebius *n* ?265–?340 AD, bishop of Caesarea: author of a history of the Christian Church to 324 A.D
Eustachian tube *n* a tube that connects the middle ear with the pharynx and equalizes the pressure between the two sides of the eardrum
WORD ORIGIN after Bartolomeo *Eustachio*, anatomist
Euterpe *n Greek myth* the Muse of lyric poetry
euthanasia ⓘ *n* the act of killing someone painlessly, esp. to relieve suffering from an incurable illness
WORD ORIGIN Greek: easy death
eV electronvolt
evacuate ⓘ *vb* **-ating, -ated** 1 to send away from a dangerous place to a safe place: *200 people were evacuated from their homes because of the floods* 2 to empty (a place) of people because it has become dangerous: *the entire street was evacuated until the fire was put out* 3 *physiol* to discharge waste from the body **evacuation** *n* **evacuee** *n*
WORD ORIGIN Latin *evacuare* to empty
evade ⓘ *vb* **evading, evaded** 1 to get away from or avoid (imprisonment, captors, etc.) 2 to get around, shirk, or dodge (the law, a duty, etc.) 3 to avoid answering (a question)
WORD ORIGIN Latin *evadere* to go forth
evaluate ⓘ *vb* **-ating, -ated** to find or judge the quality or value of something **evaluation** *n*
WORD ORIGIN French *évaluer*
evanesce *vb* **-nescing, -nesced** *formal* to fade gradually from sight
WORD ORIGIN Latin *evanescere*
evanescent *adj formal* quickly fading away; ephemeral or transitory **evanescence** *n*
evangelical *Christianity adj* 1 of or following from the Gospels 2 of certain Protestant sects which emphasize salvation through faith alone and a belief in the absolute authority of the Bible ▷*n* 3 a member of an evangelical sect 4 displaying missionary zeal in promoting something **evangelicalism** *n* **evangelically** *adv*
WORD ORIGIN Greek *evangelion* good news
evangelism *n* the practice of spreading the Christian gospel
evangelist *n* a preacher, sometimes itinerant **evangelistic** *adj*
Evangelist *n* any of the writers of the Gospels: Matthew, Mark, Luke, or John
evangelize *or* **-lise** *vb* **-lizing, -lized** *or* **-lising, -lised** to preach the Christian gospel (to) **evangelization** *or* **-lisation** *n*
Evans *n* 1 Sir **Arthur** (**John**) 1851–1941, British archaeologist, whose excavations of the palace of Knossos in Crete provided evidence for the existence of the Minoan civilization 2 Dame **Edith** (**Mary Booth**) 1888–1976, British actress 3 Sir **Geraint** (**Llewellyn**) 1922–92, Welsh operatic baritone 4 **Herbert McLean** 1882–1971, US anatomist and embryologist; discoverer of vitamin E (1922) 5 **Mary Ann** real name of (George) **Eliot** 6 **Oliver** 1755–1819, US engineer: invented the continuous production line and a high-pressure steam engine 7 **Walker** 1903–75, US photographer, noted esp.for his studies of rural poverty in the Great Depression
evaporate ⓘ *vb* **-rating, -rated** 1 to change from a liquid or solid to a vapour 2 to become less and less and finally disappear: *faith in the government evaporated rapidly after the election* **evaporable** *adj* **evaporation** *n*
WORD ORIGIN Latin *e-* out + *vapor* steam
evaporated milk *n* thick unsweetened tinned milk from which some of the water has been removed
evasion *n* 1 the act of evading something, esp. a duty or

e

THESAURUS

euphoria *n* = **elation**, joy, ecstasy, bliss, glee, rapture, high spirits, exhilaration, jubilation, intoxication, transport, exaltation, joyousness **OPPOSITE:** despondency
euthanasia *n* = **mercy killing**, assisted suicide
evacuate *vb* 1 = **remove**, clear, withdraw, expel, move out, send to a safe place 2 = **abandon**, leave, clear, desert, quit, depart (from), withdraw from, pull out of, move out of, relinquish, vacate, forsake, decamp from
evade *vb* 1, 2 = **avoid**, escape, dodge, get away from, shun, elude, eschew, steer clear of, sidestep, circumvent, duck, shirk, slip through the net of, escape the clutches of, body-swerve (*Scot*) **OPPOSITE:** face
3 = **avoid answering**, parry, circumvent, fend off, balk, cop out of (*slang*), fence, fudge, hedge, prevaricate, flannel (*Brit informal*), beat about the bush about, equivocate
evaluate *vb* = **assess**, rate, value, judge, estimate, rank, reckon, weigh, calculate, gauge, weigh up, appraise, size up (*informal*), assay
evaporate *vb* 1a = **disappear**, vaporize, dematerialize, evanesce, melt, vanish, dissolve, disperse, dry up, dispel, dissipate, fade away, melt away 1b = **dry up**, dry, dehydrate, vaporize, desiccate 2 = **fade away**, disappear, fade, melt, vanish, dissolve, disperse, dissipate, melt away

DICTIONARY

responsibility, by cunning or illegal means: *tax evasion* **2** cunning or deception used to dodge a question, duty, etc.

evasive *adj* **1** seeking to evade; not straightforward: *an evasive answer* **2** avoiding or seeking to avoid trouble or difficulties: *evasive action* **evasively** *adv*

Evatt *n* **Herbert Vere** 1894–1965, Australian jurist and Labor political leader, president of the General Assembly of the United Nations 1948–49

eve ● *n* **1** the evening or day before some special event **2** the period immediately before an event: *on the eve of the Second World War* **3** *poetic or old-fashioned* evening
WORD ORIGIN variant of EVEN²

Eve *n bible* the first woman, created by God from Adam's rib

Evelyn *n* **John** 1620–1706, English author, noted chiefly for his diary (1640–1706)

even¹ ● *adj* **1** level and regular; flat **2** on the same level: *make sure the surfaces are even with one another* **3** regular and unvarying: *an even pace* **4** equally balanced between two sides **5** equal in number, quantity, etc. **6** (of a number) divisible by two **7** denoting alternatives, events, etc. that have an equal probability: *they have a more than even chance of winning the next election* **8** having scored the same number of points **9 even money** *or* **evens** a bet in which the winnings are exactly the same as the amount staked **10 get even with** *informal* to exact revenge on; settle accounts with ▷*adv* **11** used to suggest that the content of a statement is unexpected or paradoxical: *it's chilly in Nova Scotia, even in August* **12** used to intensify a comparative adjective or adverb: *an even greater demand* **13** used to introduce a word that is stronger and more accurate than one already used: *a normal, even inevitable aspect of ageing* **14** used preceding a hypothesis to emphasize that whether or not the condition is fulfilled, the statement remains valid: *the remark didn't call for an answer even if he could have thought of one* **15 even so** in spite of any assertion to the contrary; nevertheless **16 even though** despite the fact that ▶See also **even out, even up** >**evenly** *adv* **evenness** *n*
WORD ORIGIN Old English *efen*

even² *n poetic or old-fashioned* **1** eve **2** evening
WORD ORIGIN Old English *ǣfen*

even-handed *adj* fair; impartial

evening ● *n* **1** the latter part of the day, esp. from late afternoon until nightfall ▷*adj* **2** of or in the evening: *the evening meal*
WORD ORIGIN Old English *ǣfnung*

evening class *n Brit, Austral & NZ* an educational class for adults, held during the evening

evening dress *n* clothes for a formal occasion during the evening

evening primrose *n* a plant with yellow flowers that open in the evening

evening star *n* a planet, usually Venus, seen shining brightly just after sunset

even out *vb* to make or become even, by the removal of bumps, inequalities, etc.

evensong *n Church of England* the daily evening service. Also called: **Evening Prayer**

event ● *n* **1** anything that takes place, esp. something important **2** a planned and organized occasion: *the wedding was one of the social events of the year* **3** any one contest in a sporting programme **4 in any event** *or* **at all events** whatever happens **5 in the event** when it came to the actual or final outcome: *in the event, neither of them turned up* **6 in the event of** if (such a thing) happens **7 in the event that** if it should happen that
WORD ORIGIN Latin *evenire* to happen

even-tempered *adj* calm and not easily angered

eventful *adj* full of exciting or important incidents

eventide *n archaic or poetic* evening

eventing *n Brit, Austral & NZ* riding competitions (esp. **three-day events**), usually involving cross-country riding, jumping, and dressage

eventual ● *adj* happening or being achieved at the end of a situation or process: *the Fascists' eventual victory in the Spanish Civil War* **eventually** *adv*

eventuality *n, pl* **-ties** a possible occurrence or result: *I was utterly unprepared for such an eventuality*

even up *vb* to make or become equal

ever ● *adv* **1** at any time: *it was the fourth fastest time ever* **2** always: *ever present* **3** used to give emphasis: *tell him to put to sea as soon as ever he can* **4 ever so** *or* **ever such** *informal chiefly Brit* used to give emphasis: *I'm ever so sorry*
WORD ORIGIN Old English *ǣfre*

evergreen *adj* **1** (of certain trees and shrubs) bearing foliage throughout the year ▷*n* **2** an evergreen tree or shrub

everlasting *adj* **1** never coming to an end; eternal **2** lasting so long or occurring so often as to become tedious **everlastingly** *adv*

Everly Brothers *pl n* **the** US pop singing duo comprising Don Everly (born 1937) and Phil Everly (born 1939), noted for their close harmonies

evermore *adv* all time to come

Evert *n* **Chris(tine)** born 1954, US tennis player: Wimbledon champion 1974, 1976, and 1981; US champion 1975–78, 1980, and 1982

every ● *adj* **1** each without exception: *they were winning every battle* **2** the greatest or best possible: *there is every reason to believe in the sincerity of their commitment* **3** each: *every 20 years* **4 every bit as** *informal* just as: *she's every bit as clever as you* **5 every other** each alternate: *every other month*
WORD ORIGIN Old English *ǣfre* ever + *ǣlc* each

everybody ● *pron* every person; everyone

everyday ● *adj* **1** commonplace or

THESAURUS

eve *n* **1 = night before**, day before, vigil **2 = brink**, point, edge, verge, threshold

even¹ *adj* **1, 2 = level**, straight, flat, plane, smooth, true, steady, uniform, parallel, flush, horizontal, plumb **OPPOSITE:** uneven
3 = regular, stable, constant, steady, smooth, uniform, unbroken, uninterrupted, unwavering, unvarying, metrical **OPPOSITE:** variable
4, 8 = equally matched, level, tied, drawn, on a par, neck and neck, fifty-fifty *(informal)*, equalized, all square, equally balanced **OPPOSITE:** ill-matched
5 = equal, like, the same, matching, similar, uniform, parallel, identical, comparable, commensurate, coequal **OPPOSITE:** unequal

evening *n* **1 = dusk** *(archaic)*, night, sunset, twilight, sundown, eve, vesper *(archaic)*, eventide *(archaic, poetic)*, gloaming *(Scot poetic)*, e'en *(archaic, poetic)*, close of day, crepuscule, even, evo *(Austral slang)*

event *n* **1, 2 = incident**, happening, experience, matter, affair, occasion, proceeding, fact, business, circumstance, episode, adventure, milestone, occurrence, escapade
3 = competition, game, tournament, contest, bout

eventual *adj* **= final**, later, resulting, future, overall, concluding, ultimate, prospective, ensuing, consequent

ever *adv* **1 = at any time**, at all, in any case, at any point, by any chance, on any occasion, at any period
2 = always, for ever, at all times, relentlessly, eternally, evermore, unceasingly, to the end of time, everlastingly, unendingly, aye *(Scot)*

every *adj* **1 = each**, each and every, every single

everybody *pron* **= everyone**, each one, the whole world, each person, every person, all and sundry, one and all

everyday *adj* **1, 3 = ordinary**, common,

DICTIONARY

usual **2** happening each day **3** suitable for or used on ordinary days

Everyman *n* the ordinary person; common man
WORD ORIGIN after the central figure in a medieval morality play

everyone ❶ *pron* every person; everybody

everything ❶ *pron* **1** the whole; all things: *everything had been carefully packed* **2** the thing that is most important: *work was everything to her*

everywhere ❶ *adv* to or in all parts or places

evict *vb* to expel (someone) legally from his or her home or land **eviction** *n*
WORD ORIGIN Latin *evincere* to vanquish utterly

evidence ❶ *n* **1** something which provides ground for belief or disbelief: *there is no evidence that depression is inherited* **2** *law* matter produced before a court of law in an attempt to prove or disprove a point in issue **3** **in evidence** on display; apparent ▷ *vb* **-dencing, -denced** **4** to show clearly; demonstrate: *you evidenced no talent for music*

evident ❶ *adj* easy to see or understand **evidently** *adv*
WORD ORIGIN Latin *videre* to see

evidential *adj* of, serving as, or based on evidence **evidentially** *adv*

evil ❶ *n* **1** a force or power that brings about wickedness and harm: *the battle between good and evil* **2** a wicked or morally wrong act or thing: *the evil of racism* ▷ *adj* **3** (of a person) deliberately causing great harm and misery; wicked: *an evil dictator* **4** (of an act, idea, etc.) causing great harm and misery; morally wrong: *what you did was deeply evil* **5** very unpleasant: *it was fascinating to see people vanish as if we had some very evil smell* **evilly** *adv*
WORD ORIGIN Old English *yfel*

evildoer *n* a person who does evil **evildoing** *n*

evil eye *n* **the evil eye** a look superstitiously supposed to have the power of inflicting harm

evince *vb* **evincing, evinced** *formal* to show or display (a quality or feeling) clearly: *a humility which he had never evinced in earlier days*
WORD ORIGIN Latin *evincere* to overcome

eviscerate *vb* **-ating, -ated** to remove the internal organs of; disembowel **evisceration** *n*
WORD ORIGIN Latin *e-* out + *viscera* entrails

evocation *n* the act of evoking **evocative** *adj*

evoke ❶ *vb* **evoking, evoked** **1** to call or summon up (a memory or feeling) from the past **2** to provoke or bring about: *his sacking evoked a huge public protest*
WORD ORIGIN Latin *evocare* to call forth

evolution ❶ *n* **1** *biol* a gradual change in the characteristics of a population of animals or plants over successive generations **2** a gradual development, esp. to a more complex form **evolutionary** *adj*
WORD ORIGIN Latin *evolutio* an unrolling

evolve ❶ *vb* **evolving, evolved** **1** to develop gradually **2** (of animal or plant species) to undergo evolution
WORD ORIGIN Latin *evolvere* to unfold

e-voting *n* the application of electronic technology to cast and count votes in an election

Ewart *n* **Gavin** (**Buchanan**) 1916–95, British poet, noted for his light satirical verse

ewe *n* a female sheep
WORD ORIGIN Old English *ēowu*

ewer *n* a large jug with a wide mouth
WORD ORIGIN Latin *aqua* water

ex[1] *prep finance* excluding or without: *ex dividend*
WORD ORIGIN Latin: out of, from

ex[2] *n, pl* **exes** *informal* one's former wife or husband

ex- *prefix* **1** out of, outside, or from: *exit* **2** former: *his glamorous ex-wife*
WORD ORIGIN Latin

exacerbate (ig-**zass**-er-bate) *vb* **-bating, -bated** to make (pain, emotion, or a situation) worse **exacerbation** *n*
WORD ORIGIN Latin *acerbus* bitter

exact ❶ *adj* **1** correct in every detail; strictly accurate **2** precise, as opposed to approximate **3** based on measurement and the formulation of laws: *forecasting floods is not an exact science* ▷ *vb* **4** to obtain or demand as a right, esp. through force or strength: *the rebels called for revenge to be exacted for the killings*

THESAURUS

usual, familiar, conventional, routine, dull, stock, accustomed, customary, commonplace, mundane, vanilla *(slang)*, banal, habitual, run-of-the-mill, unimaginative, workaday, unexceptional, bog-standard *(Brit & Irish slang)*, common or garden *(informal)*, dime-a-dozen *(informal)*, wonted **OPPOSITE:** unusual

everyone *pron* **= everybody**, each one, the whole world, each person, every person, all and sundry, one and all

everything *pron* **1 = all**, the whole, the total, the lot, the sum, the whole lot, the aggregate, the entirety, each thing, the whole caboodle *(informal)*, the whole kit and caboodle *(informal)*

everywhere *adv* **a = all over**, all around, the world over, high and low, in each place, in every nook and cranny, far and wide *or* near, to *or* in every place **b = all around**, all over, in each place, in every nook and cranny, ubiquitously, far and wide *or* near, to *or* in every place

evidence *n* **1 = proof**, grounds, data, demonstration, confirmation, verification, corroboration, authentication, substantiation **2** *(law)* **= testimony**, statement, witness, declaration, submission, affirmation, deposition, avowal, attestation, averment ▷ *vb* **4 = show**, prove, reveal, display, indicate, witness, demonstrate, exhibit, manifest, signify, denote, testify to, evince

evident *adj* **= obvious**, clear, plain, apparent, visible, patent, manifest, tangible, noticeable, blatant, conspicuous, unmistakable, palpable, salient, indisputable, perceptible, incontrovertible, incontestable, plain as the nose on your face **OPPOSITE:** hidden

evil *n* **1 = wickedness**, bad, wrong, vice, corruption, sin, wrongdoing, depravity, immorality, iniquity, badness, viciousness, villainy, sinfulness, turpitude, baseness, malignity, heinousness, maleficence **2 = act of cruelty**, crime, ill, horror, outrage, cruelty, brutality, misfortune, mischief, affliction, monstrosity, abomination, barbarity, villainy ▷ *adj* **3, 4 = wicked**, bad, wrong, corrupt, vicious, vile, malicious, base, immoral, malignant, sinful, unholy, malevolent, heinous, depraved, villainous, nefarious, iniquitous, reprobate, maleficent **4 = harmful**, painful, disastrous, destructive, dire, catastrophic, mischievous, detrimental, hurtful, woeful, pernicious, ruinous, sorrowful, deleterious, injurious, baneful *(archaic)* **5 = offensive**, nasty, foul, unpleasant, vile, noxious, disagreeable, putrid, pestilential, mephitic

evoke *vb* **2 = arouse**, cause, excite, stimulate, induce, awaken, give rise to, stir up, rekindle, summon up **OPPOSITE:** suppress

evolution *n* **1** *(biology)* **= rise**, development, adaptation, natural selection, Darwinism, survival of the fittest, evolvement **2 = development**, growth, advance, progress, working out, expansion, extension, unfolding, progression, enlargement, maturation, unrolling

evolve *vb* **1 = develop**, metamorphose, adapt yourself **2 = grow**, develop, advance, progress, mature

exact *adj* **1 = accurate**, very, correct, true, particular, right, express, specific, careful, precise, identical,

DICTIONARY

WORD ORIGIN Latin *exigere* to demand

exacting ❶ *adj* making rigorous or excessive demands

exaction *n formal* **1** the act of obtaining or demanding money as a right **2** a sum or payment exacted

exactitude *n* the quality of being exact; precision

exactly ❶ *adv* **1** with complete accuracy and precision: *I don't know exactly where they live* **2** in every respect: *he looks exactly like his father* ▷ *interj* **3** just so! precisely!

exaggerate ❶ *vb* **-ating, -ated 1** to regard or represent as greater than is true **2** to make greater or more noticeable **exaggerated** *adj* **exaggeratedly** *adv* **exaggeration** *n*
WORD ORIGIN Latin *exaggerare* to heap up

exalt *vb* **1** to praise highly **2** to raise to a higher rank **exalted** *adj* **exaltation** *n*
WORD ORIGIN Latin *exaltare* to raise

exam *n* ▸ short for **examination**

examination ❶ *n* **1** the act of examining **2** *education* exercises, questions, or tasks set to test a person's knowledge and skill **3** *med* physical inspection of a patient **4** *law* the formal questioning of a person on oath

examine ❶ *vb* **-ining, -ined 1** to inspect carefully or in detail; investigate **2** *education* to test a person's knowledge of a subject by written or oral questions **3** *med* to investigate a patient's state of health **4** *law* to formally question someone on oath **examinee** *n* **examiner** *n*
WORD ORIGIN Latin *examinare* to weigh

example ❶ *n* **1** a specimen that is typical of its group; sample: *a fine example of Georgian architecture* **2** a particular event, object, or person that demonstrates a point or supports an argument, theory, etc.: *Germany is a good example of how federalism works in practice* **3** a person, action, or thing that is worthy of imitation **4** a punishment or the person punished regarded as a warning to others **5 for example** as an illustration
WORD ORIGIN Latin *exemplum*

exasperate *vb* **-ating, -ated** to cause great irritation to **exasperated** *adj* **exasperating** *adj* **exasperation** *n*
WORD ORIGIN Latin *exasperare* to make rough

ex cathedra *adj, adv* **1** with the authority of one's official position **2** *RC church* (of doctrines of faith or morals) defined by the pope as infallibly true
WORD ORIGIN Latin: from the chair

excavate *vb* **-vating, -vated 1** to unearth (buried objects) methodically to discover information about the past **2** to make a hole in something by digging into it or hollowing it out: *one kind of shrimp excavates a hole for itself* **excavation** *n* **excavator** *n*
WORD ORIGIN Latin *excavare* to make hollow

exceed ❶ *vb* **1** to be greater in degree or quantity **2** to go beyond the limit of (a restriction)
WORD ORIGIN Latin *excedere* to go beyond

exceedingly *adv* very; extremely

excel ❶ *vb* **-celling, -celled 1** to be better than; surpass **2 excel in** *or* **at** to be outstandingly good at
WORD ORIGIN Latin *excellere* to rise up

excellence ❶ *n* the quality of being exceptionally good

Excellency *or* **Excellence** *n, pl* **-lencies** *or* **-lences Your** *or* **His** *or* **Her Excellency** a title used to address a high-ranking official, such as an ambassador

excellent ❶ *adj* exceptionally good; outstanding

THESAURUS

authentic, faithful, explicit, definite, orderly, literal, unequivocal, faultless, on the money (*US*), unerring, veracious
OPPOSITE: approximate
▷ *vb* **4a = demand**, claim, require, call for, force, impose, command, squeeze, extract, compel, wring, wrest, insist upon, extort **4b = inflict**, apply, impose, administer, mete out, deal out

exacting *adj* **a = demanding**, hard, taxing, difficult, tough, painstaking
OPPOSITE: easy
b = strict, severe, harsh, stern, rigid, rigorous, stringent, oppressive, imperious, unsparing

exactly *adv* **1 = accurately**, correctly, definitely, truly, precisely, strictly, literally, faithfully, explicitly, rigorously, unequivocally, scrupulously, truthfully, methodically, unerringly, faultlessly, veraciously **2 = precisely**, just, expressly, prompt (*informal*), specifically, bang on (*informal*), to the letter, on the button (*informal*)

exaggerate *vb* **1, 2 = overstate**, emphasize, enlarge, inflate, embroider, magnify, overdo, amplify, exalt, embellish, overestimate, overemphasize, pile it on about (*informal*), blow up out of all proportion, lay it on thick about (*informal*), lay it on with a trowel about (*informal*), make a production (out) of (*informal*), make a federal case of (*US informal*), hyperbolize

examination *n* **2 = exam**, test, research, paper, investigation, practical, assessment, quiz, evaluation, oral, appraisal, catechism **3** (*medical*) **= checkup**, analysis, going-over (*informal*), exploration, health check, check, medical, once-over (*informal*)

examine *vb* **1 = inspect**, test, consider, study, check, research, review, survey, investigate, explore, probe, analyse, scan, vet, check out, ponder, look over, look at, sift through, work over, pore over, appraise, scrutinize, peruse, take stock of, assay, recce (*slang*), look at carefully, go over *or* through **2** (*education*) **= test**, question, assess, quiz, evaluate, appraise, catechize **3** (*medical*) **= check**, analyse, check over **4** (*law*) **= question**, quiz, interrogate, cross-examine, grill (*informal*), give the third degree to (*informal*)

example *n* **1 = instance**, specimen, case, sample, illustration, case in point, particular case, particular instance, typical case, exemplification, representative case **2, 3 = illustration**, model, ideal, standard, norm, precedent, pattern, prototype, paradigm, archetype, paragon, exemplar **4 = warning**, lesson, caution, deterrent, admonition

exceed *vb* **1 = surpass**, better, pass, eclipse, beat, cap (*informal*), top, be over, be more than, overtake, go beyond, excel, transcend, be greater than, outstrip, outdo, outreach, be larger than, outshine, surmount, be superior to, outrun, run rings around (*informal*), outdistance, knock spots off (*informal*), put in the shade (*informal*) **2 = go over the limit of**, go beyond, overstep, go beyond the bounds of

excel *vb* **1 = be superior**, better, pass, eclipse, beat, top, cap (*informal*), exceed, go beyond, surpass, transcend, outdo, outshine, surmount, run rings around (*informal*), put in the shade (*informal*), outrival **2 excel in** *or* **at something = be good at**, be master of, predominate in, shine at, be proficient in, show talent in, be skilful at, have (something) down to a fine art, be talented at

excellence *n* **= high quality**, worth, merit, distinction, virtue, goodness, perfection, superiority, purity, greatness, supremacy, eminence, virtuosity, transcendence, pre-eminence, fineness

excellent *adj* **= outstanding**, good, great, fine, prime, capital, noted, choice, champion, cool (*informal*), select, brilliant, very good, cracking (*Brit informal*), crucial (*slang*), mean (*slang*), superb, distinguished,

DICTIONARY

except ❶ *prep* 1 Also: **except for** not including; apart from: *everyone except Jill laughed* 2 **except that** but for the fact that ▷ *vb* 3 to leave out or exclude
WORD ORIGIN Latin *excipere* to take out

excepting *prep* except

exception ❶ *n* 1 anything excluded from or not conforming to a general rule or classification 2 **take exception to** to make objections to

exceptionable *adj* open to objection

exceptional ❶ *adj* 1 forming an exception 2 having much more than average intelligence, ability, or skill **exceptionally** *adv*

excerpt ❶ *n* 1 a passage taken from a book, speech, etc.; extract ▷ *vb* 2 to take a passage from a book, speech, etc.
WORD ORIGIN Latin *excerptum* (something) picked out

excess ❶ *n* 1 the state or act of going beyond normal or permitted limits 2 an immoderate or abnormal amount 3 the amount, number, etc. by which one thing exceeds another 4 behaviour regarded as too extreme or immoral to be acceptable: *a life of sex, drugs, and drunken excess* 5 **excesses** acts or actions that are unacceptably cruel or immoral: *one of the bloodiest excesses of a dictatorial regime* 6 **in excess of** more than 7 **to excess** to an extreme or unhealthy extent: *he had started to drink to excess* ▷ *adj* 8 more than normal, necessary, or permitted: *excess fat* **excessive** *adj* **excessively** *adv*
WORD ORIGIN Latin *excedere* to go beyond

excess luggage *or* **baggage** *n* luggage that is more in weight or number of pieces than an airline, etc. will carry free

exchange ❶ *vb* **-changing, -changed** 1 (of two or more people, governments, etc.) to give each other (something similar) at the same time: *they nervously exchanged smiles* 2 to replace (one thing) with another, esp. to replace unsatisfactory goods: *could I exchange this for a larger size, please?* ▷ *n* 3 the act of exchanging 4 anything given or received as an equivalent or substitute for something else 5 an argument 6 Also called: **telephone exchange** a centre in which telephone lines are interconnected 7 a place where securities or commodities are traded, esp. by brokers or merchants 8 a transfer of sums of money of equivalent value, as between different currencies 9 the system by which commercial debts are settled, esp. by bills of exchange, without direct payment of money **exchangeable** *adj*
WORD ORIGIN Latin *cambire* to barter

exchange rate *n* the rate at which the currency unit of one country may be exchanged for that of another

Exchequer *n government* (in Britain and certain other countries) the accounting department of the Treasury
WORD ORIGIN Old French *eschequier* counting table

excise[1] *n* 1 a tax on goods, such as spirits, produced for the home market 2 *Brit* that section of the government service responsible for the collection of excise, now the Board of Customs and Excise
WORD ORIGIN Latin *assidere* to sit beside, assist in judging

excise[2] *vb* **-cising, -cised** 1 to delete a passage from a book 2 to remove an organ or part surgically **excision** *n*
WORD ORIGIN Latin *excidere* to cut down

exciseman *n, pl* **-men** *Brit* (formerly) a government agent who collected excise and prevented smuggling

excitable *adj* nervous and easily excited **excitability** *n*

excite ❶ *vb* **-citing, -cited** 1 to make (a person) feel so happy that he or she is unable to relax because he or she is looking forward eagerly to something: *he was excited at the long-awaited arrival of a son* 2 to cause or arouse (an emotion, response, etc.): *the idea strongly excited his interest* 3 to arouse sexually 4 *physiol* to cause a response in (an organ, tissue, or part) 5 *physics* to raise (an atom, molecule, etc.) to a higher energy level **excited** *adj* **excitedly** *adv*
WORD ORIGIN Latin *exciere* to stimulate

excitement ❶ *n* 1 the state of being excited 2 a person or thing that excites

e

THESAURUS

fantastic, magnificent, superior, sterling, worthy, first-class, marvellous, exceptional, terrific, splendid, notable, mega *(slang)*, topping *(Brit slang)*, sovereign, dope *(slang)*, world-class, exquisite, admirable, exemplary, wicked *(slang)*, first-rate, def *(slang)*, superlative, top-notch *(informal)*, brill *(informal)*, pre-eminent, meritorious, estimable, tiptop, bodacious *(slang, chiefly US)*, boffo *(slang)*, jim-dandy *(slang)*, A1 *or* A-one *(informal)*, bitchin' *(US slang)*, chillin' *(US slang)*, booshit *(Austral slang)*, exo *(Austral slang)*, sik *(Austral slang)*, rad *(informal)*, phat *(slang)*, schmick *(Austral informal)*, beaut *(informal)*, barrie *(Scot slang)*, belting *(Brit slang)*, pearler *(Austral slang)*
OPPOSITE: terrible

except *prep* 1 *(often with* **for**) = **apart from**, but for, saving, bar, barring, excepting, other than, excluding, omitting, with the exception of, aside from, save *(archaic)*, not counting, exclusive of ▷ *vb* 3 = **exclude**, rule out, leave out, omit, disregard, pass over

exception *n* 1 = **special case**, departure, freak, anomaly, inconsistency, deviation, quirk, oddity, peculiarity, irregularity

exceptional *adj* 1 = **unusual**, special, odd, strange, rare, extraordinary, unprecedented, peculiar, abnormal, irregular, uncommon, inconsistent, singular, deviant, anomalous, atypical, aberrant
OPPOSITE: ordinary
2 = **remarkable**, special, excellent, extraordinary, outstanding, superior, first-class, marvellous, notable, phenomenal, first-rate, prodigious, unsurpassed, one in a million, bodacious *(slang, chiefly US)*, unexcelled OPPOSITE: average

excerpt *n* 1 = **extract**, part, piece, section, selection, passage, portion, fragment, quotation, citation, pericope

excess *n* 2 = **surfeit**, surplus, overdose, overflow, overload, plethora, glut, overabundance, superabundance, superfluity OPPOSITE: shortage
4 = **overindulgence**, extravagance, profligacy, debauchery, dissipation, intemperance, indulgence, prodigality, extreme behaviour, immoral behaviour, dissoluteness, immoderation, exorbitance, unrestraint
OPPOSITE: moderation

exchange *vb* 1, 2 = **interchange**, change, trade, switch, swap, truck, barter, reciprocate, bandy, give to each other, give to one another ▷ *n* 3 = **interchange**, dealing, trade, switch, swap, traffic, trafficking, truck, swapping, substitution, barter, bartering, reciprocity, tit for tat, quid pro quo

excite *vb* 1 = **thrill**, inspire, stir, stimulate, provoke, awaken, animate, move, fire, rouse, exhilarate, agitate, quicken, inflame, enliven, galvanize, foment
2 = **arouse**, stimulate, provoke, evoke, rouse, stir up, fire, elicit, work up, incite, instigate, whet, kindle, waken 3 = **titillate**, thrill, stimulate, turn on *(slang)*, arouse, get going *(informal)*, electrify

excitement *n* 1 = **exhilaration**, action, activity, passion, heat, thrill, adventure, enthusiasm, fever, warmth, flurry, animation, furore, ferment, agitation, commotion, elation, ado, tumult, perturbation, discomposure

DICTIONARY

exciting ⊙ *adj* causing excitement; stirring; stimulating **excitingly** *adv*

exclaim ⊙ *vb* to cry out or speak suddenly or excitedly, as from surprise, delight, horror, etc.
WORD ORIGIN Latin *exclamare*

exclamation *n* **1** an abrupt or excited cry or utterance **2** the act of exclaiming **exclamatory** *adj*

exclamation mark *or US* **point** *n* the punctuation mark (!) used after exclamations and forceful commands

exclude ⊙ *vb* **-cluding, -cluded 1** to keep out; prevent from entering **2** to leave out of consideration
exclusion *n*
WORD ORIGIN Latin *excludere*

excluding *prep* excepting

exclusive ⊙ *adj* **1** excluding or incompatible with anything else: *these two theories are mutually exclusive* **2** not shared: *exclusive rights* **3** used or lived in by a privileged minority, esp. a fashionable clique: *an exclusive skiing resort* **4** not including the numbers, dates, etc. mentioned **5 exclusive of** except for; not taking account of **6 exclusive to** limited to; found only in ▷*n* **7** a story reported in only one newspaper **exclusively** *adv*
exclusivity *or* **exclusiveness** *n*

excommunicate *vb* **-cating, -cated** to expel (someone) from membership of a church and ban him or her from taking part in its services
excommunication *n*
WORD ORIGIN Late Latin *excommunicare* to exclude from the community

excoriate *vb* **-ating, -ated 1** *literary* to censure severely **2** to strip skin from a person or animal **excoriation** *n*
WORD ORIGIN Late Latin *excoriare* to strip, flay

excrement *n* waste matter discharged from the body; faeces
excremental *adj*
WORD ORIGIN Latin *excernere* to sift, excrete

excrescence *n* something that protrudes, esp. an outgrowth from a part of the body **excrescent** *adj*
WORD ORIGIN Latin *excrescere* to grow out

excreta (ik-**skree**-ta) *pl n* urine and faeces discharged from the body

excrete *vb* **-creting, -creted** to discharge waste matter, such as urine, sweat, or faeces, from the body **excretion** *n* **excretory** *adj*
WORD ORIGIN Latin *excernere* to discharge

excruciating *adj* **1** unbearably painful; agonizing **2** hard to bear: *never had an afternoon passed with such excruciating slowness* **excruciatingly** *adv*
WORD ORIGIN Latin *excruciare* to torture

exculpate *vb* **-pating, -pated** to free from blame or guilt
WORD ORIGIN Latin *ex* from + *culpa* fault

excursion ⊙ *n* a short outward and return journey, esp. for sightseeing, etc.; outing
WORD ORIGIN Latin *excurrere* to run out

excuse ⊙ *n* **1** an explanation offered to justify an action which has been criticized or as a reason for not fulfilling an obligation, etc. ▷*vb* **-cusing, -cused 2** to put forward a reason or justification for (an action, fault, or offending person) **3** to pardon (a person) or overlook (a fault) **4** to free (someone) from having to carry out a task, obligation, etc.: *a doctor's letter excusing him from games at school* **5** to allow to leave **6 be excused** *euphemistic* to go to the toilet **7 excuse me!** an expression used to catch someone's attention or to apologize for an interruption, disagreement, etc.
excusable *adj*
WORD ORIGIN Latin *ex* out + *causa* cause, accusation

ex-directory *adj Brit & NZ* not listed in a telephone directory by request

execrable (**eks**-sik-rab-bl) *adj* of very poor quality **execrably** *adv*
WORD ORIGIN see EXECRATE

execrate *vb* **-crating, -crated 1** to feel and express loathing and hatred of (someone or something) **2** to curse (a person or thing) **execration** *n*
WORD ORIGIN Latin *exsecrari* to curse

executable *adj computers* **1** (of a program) able to be run ▷*n* **2** a file containing a program that will run as soon as it is opened

execute ⊙ *vb* **-cuting, -cuted 1** to put a condemned person to death **2** to carry out or accomplish **3** to produce or create (a work of art) **4** *law* to render (a deed) effective, for example by signing it **5** to carry out the terms of (a contract, will, etc.) **executer** *n*
WORD ORIGIN Old French *executer*

execution ⊙ *n* **1** the act of executing **2** the carrying out or undergoing of a sentence of death **3** the manner in which something is performed; technique

executioner *n* a person whose job is to kill people who have been sentenced to death

executive ⊙ *n* **1** a person or group

THESAURUS

exciting *adj* **a = stimulating,** inspiring, dramatic, gripping, stirring, thrilling, moving, sensational, rousing, exhilarating, electrifying, intoxicating, rip-roaring *(informal)* **OPPOSITE:** boring
b = titillating, stimulating, sexy *(informal)*, arousing, erotic, provocative

exclaim *vb* **= cry out,** call, declare, cry, shout, proclaim, yell, utter, call out, ejaculate, vociferate

exclude *vb* **1 = keep out,** bar, ban, veto, refuse, forbid, boycott, embargo, prohibit, disallow, shut out, proscribe, black, refuse to admit, ostracize, debar, blackball, interdict, prevent from entering
OPPOSITE: let in
2a = omit, reject, eliminate, rule out, miss out, leave out, preclude, repudiate **OPPOSITE:** include
2b = eliminate, reject, ignore, rule out, except, leave out, set aside, omit, pass over, not count, repudiate, count out

exclusive *adj* **2 = entire,** full, whole, complete, total, absolute, undivided
3 = select, fashionable, stylish, private, limited, choice, narrow, closed, restricted, elegant, posh *(informal, chiefly Brit)*, chic, selfish, classy *(slang)*, restrictive, aristocratic, high-class, swish *(informal, chiefly Brit)*, up-market, snobbish, top-drawer, ritzy *(slang)*, high-toned, clannish, discriminative, cliquish
OPPOSITE: unrestricted

excursion *n* **= trip,** airing, tour, journey, outing, expedition, ramble, day trip, jaunt, pleasure trip

excuse *n* **1 = justification,** reason, explanation, defence, grounds, plea, apology, pretext, vindication, mitigation, mitigating circumstances, extenuation
OPPOSITE: accusation
▷*vb* **2 = justify,** explain, defend, vindicate, condone, mitigate, apologize for, make excuses for
OPPOSITE: blame
3 = forgive, pardon, overlook, tolerate, indulge, acquit, pass over, turn a blind eye to, exonerate, absolve, bear with, wink at, make allowances for, extenuate, exculpate
4 = free, relieve, liberate, exempt, release, spare, discharge, let off, absolve **OPPOSITE:** convict

execute *vb* **1 = put to death,** kill, shoot, hang, behead, decapitate, guillotine, electrocute **2 = perform,** do, carry out, accomplish **5 = carry out,** effect, finish, complete, achieve, realize, do, implement, fulfil, enforce, accomplish, render, discharge, administer, prosecute, enact, consummate, put into effect, bring off

execution *n* **1 = carrying out,** performance, operation, administration, achievement, effect, prosecution, rendering, discharge, enforcement, implementation, completion, accomplishment, realization, enactment, bringing off, consummation **2 = killing,** hanging, the death penalty, the rope, capital

responsible for the administration of a project or business **2** the branch of government responsible for carrying out laws, decrees, etc. ▷ *adj* **3** having the function of carrying plans, orders, laws, etc. into effect: *the executive producer* **4** of or for executives: *the executive car park* **5** *informal* very expensive or exclusive: *executive cars*

executor *n law* a person appointed by someone to ensure that the conditions set out in his or her will are carried out **executorial** *adj* **executrix** *fem n*

exegesis (eks-sij-**jee**-siss) *n, pl* **-ses** (-seez) explanation of a text, esp. of the Bible
WORD ORIGIN Greek *exēgeisthai* to interpret

exemplar *n* **1** a person or thing to be copied; model **2** a typical specimen; example
WORD ORIGIN Latin *exemplum* example

exemplary *adj* **1** so good as to be an example worthy of imitation **2** (of a punishment) extremely harsh, so as to discourage others from committing a similar crime

exemplify ❶ *vb* **-fies, -fying, -fied 1** to show by example **2** to serve as an example of **exemplification** *n*
WORD ORIGIN Latin *exemplum* example + *facere* to make

exempt ❶ *adj* **1** not subject to an obligation, tax, etc. ▷ *vb* **2** to release (someone) from an obligation, tax, etc. **exemption** *n*
WORD ORIGIN Latin *exemptus* removed

exequies (**eks**-sik-weez) *pl n, sing* **-quy** funeral rites
WORD ORIGIN Latin *exequiae*

exercise ❶ *n* **1** physical exertion, esp. for training or keeping fit **2** an activity planned to achieve a particular purpose: *the group's meeting was mainly an exercise in mutual reassurance* **3** a set of movements, tasks, etc. designed to improve or test one's ability or fitness **4** the use or practice of (a right, power, or authority) **5** *mil* a manoeuvre or simulated combat operation ▷ *vb* **-cising, -cised 6** to put into use; make use of: *we urge all governments involved to exercise restraint* **7** to take exercise or perform exercises **8** to practise using in order to develop or train: *to exercise one's voice* **9** to worry or vex: *Western governments have been exercised by the need to combat international terrorism* **10** *mil* to carry out simulated combat, manoeuvres, etc. **exerciser** *n*
WORD ORIGIN Latin *exercere* to drill

exert ❶ *vb* **1** to use influence, authority, etc. forcefully or effectively **2 exert oneself** to make a special effort
WORD ORIGIN Latin *exserere* to thrust out

exertion *n* **1** effort or exercise, esp. physical effort: *the sudden exertion of running for a bus* **2** the act or an instance of using one's influence, powers, or authority: *the exertion of parental authority*

exeunt (**eks**-see-unt) they go out: used as a stage direction
WORD ORIGIN Latin

exfoliate *vb* **-ating, -ated 1** to peel off in scales or layers **2** to remove dead cells from the skin by washing with a granular cosmetic preparation **exfoliation** *n*

ex-gratia (eks-**gray**-sha) *adj* given as a favour where no legal obligation exists: *an ex-gratia payment*
WORD ORIGIN New Latin: out of kindness

exhale *vb* **-haling, -haled 1** to expel breath or smoke from the lungs; breathe out **2** to give off or to be given off as gas, fumes, etc.: *the crater exhaled smoke* **exhalation** *n*
WORD ORIGIN Latin *exhalare*

exhaust ❶ *vb* **1** to tire out **2** to use up totally **3** to discuss a topic so thoroughly that no more remains to be said ▷ *n* **4** gases ejected from an engine as waste products **5** the parts of an engine through which waste gases pass **exhausted** *adj* **exhaustible** *adj*
WORD ORIGIN Latin *exhaurire* to draw out

exhaustion ❶ *n* **1** extreme tiredness **2** the act of exhausting or state of being exhausted

exhaustive *adj* very thorough; comprehensive **exhaustively** *adv*

exhibit ❶ *vb* **1** to display (a work of art) to the public **2** to show (a quality or feeling): *they exhibited extraordinary courage* ▷ *n* **3** an object exhibited to the public **4** *law* a document or object produced in court as evidence **exhibitor** *n*
WORD ORIGIN Latin *exhibere* to hold forth

THESAURUS

punishment, beheading, the electric chair, the guillotine, the noose, the scaffold, electrocution, decapitation, the firing squad, necktie party *(informal)*

executive *n* **1 = administrator**, official, director, manager, chairman, managing director, controller, chief executive officer, senior manager, chairwoman, chairperson **1, 2 = administration**, government, directors, management, leadership, hierarchy, directorate ▷ *adj* **3 = administrative**, controlling, directing, governing, regulating, decision-making, managerial

exemplify *vb* **1, 2 = show**, represent, display, demonstrate, instance, illustrate, exhibit, depict, manifest, evidence, embody, serve as an example of

exempt *adj* **1 = immune**, free, excepted, excused, released, spared, clear, discharged, liberated, not subject to, absolved, not liable to
OPPOSITE: liable
▷ *vb* **2 = grant immunity**, free, except, excuse, release, spare, relieve, discharge, liberate, let off, exonerate, absolve

exercise *n* **1 = exertion**, training, activity, action, work, labour, effort, movement, discipline, toil, physical activity **3 = task**, problem, lesson, assignment, work, schooling, practice, schoolwork **4 = use**, practice, application, operation, employment, discharge, implementation, enjoyment, accomplishment, fulfilment, exertion, utilization **5** *(military)* **= manoeuvre**, campaign, operation, movement, deployment ▷ *vb* **6 = put to use**, use, apply, employ, practise, exert, enjoy, wield, utilize, bring to bear, avail yourself of **7, 8 = train**, work out, practise, drill, keep fit, inure, do exercises

exert *vb* **1 = apply**, use, exercise, employ, wield, make use of, utilize, expend, bring to bear, put forth, bring into play **2 exert yourself = make an effort**, work, labour, struggle, strain, strive, endeavour, go for it *(informal)*, try hard, toil, bend over backwards *(informal)*, do your best, go for broke *(slang)*, bust a gut *(informal)*, spare no effort, make a great effort, give it your best shot *(informal)*, break your neck *(informal)*, apply yourself, put yourself out, make an all-out effort *(informal)*, get your finger out *(Brit informal)*, pull your finger out *(Brit informal)*, knock yourself out *(informal)*, do your damnedest *(informal)*, give it your all *(informal)*, rupture yourself *(informal)*

exhaust *vb* **1 = tire out**, tire, fatigue, drain, disable, weaken, cripple, weary, sap, wear out, debilitate, prostrate, enfeeble, make tired, enervate **2 = use up**, spend, finish, consume, waste, go through, run through, deplete, squander, dissipate, expend

exhaustion *n* **1 = tiredness**, fatigue, weariness, lassitude, feebleness, prostration, debilitation, enervation **2 = depletion**, emptying, consumption, using up

exhibit *vb* **1 = display**, show, present, set out, parade, unveil, flaunt, put on view **2 = show**, reveal, display, demonstrate, air, evidence, express, indicate, disclose, manifest, evince, make clear *or* plain

DICTIONARY

exhibition ● *n* **1** a public display of art, skills, etc. **2** the act of exhibiting or the state of being exhibited: *an exhibition of bad temper* **3 make an exhibition of oneself** to behave so foolishly that one attracts public attention

exhibitionism *n* **1** a compulsive desire to attract attention to oneself **2** a compulsive desire to expose one's genitals publicly **exhibitionist** *n*

e

exhilarate *vb* **-rating, -rated** to make (someone) feel lively and cheerful **exhilaration** *n*
WORD ORIGIN Latin *exhilarare*

exhilarating *adj* causing strong feelings of excitement and happiness

exhort *vb formal* to urge (someone) earnestly **exhortation** *n*
WORD ORIGIN Latin *exhortari*

exhume (ig-zyume) *vb* **-huming, -humed** *formal* to dig up something buried, esp. a corpse **exhumation** *n*
WORD ORIGIN Latin *ex* out + *humus* the ground

exigency *n, pl* **-gencies** *formal* **1** an urgent demand or need **2** an emergency **exigent** *adj*
WORD ORIGIN Latin *exigere* to require

exiguous *adj formal* scanty or meagre **exiguity** *n*
WORD ORIGIN Latin *exiguus*

exile ● *n* **1** a prolonged, usually enforced absence from one's country **2** a person banished or living away from his or her country ▷ *vb* **-iling, -iled 3** to expel (someone) from his or her country; banish
WORD ORIGIN Latin *exsilium*

exist ● *vb* **1** to have being or reality; be: *does God exist?* **2** to only just be able to keep oneself alive, esp. because of poverty or hunger **3** to be living; live **4** to be present under specified conditions or in a specified place **existing** *adj*
WORD ORIGIN Latin *exsistere* to step forth

existence ● *n* **1** the fact or state of being real, live, or actual **2** a way of life, esp. a poor or hungry one **3** everything that exists **existent** *adj*

existential *adj* **1** of or relating to existence, esp. human existence **2** of or relating to existentialism

existentialism *n* a philosophical movement stressing personal experience and responsibility of the individual, who is seen as a free agent **existentialist** *adj, n*

exit ● *n* **1** a way out **2** the act of going out **3** *theatre* the act of going offstage **4** *Austral & Brit* a point at which vehicles may leave or join a motorway ▷ *vb* **exiting, exited 5** to go away or out; depart **6** *theatre* to go offstage: used as a stage direction: *exit bleeding from the room*
WORD ORIGIN Latin *exire* to go out

exocrine *adj* of or denoting a gland, such as the sweat gland, that discharges its product through a duct
WORD ORIGIN Greek *exō* outside + *krinein* to separate

exodus ● (eks-so-duss) *n* the departure of a large number of people
WORD ORIGIN Greek *ex* out + *hodos* way

Exodus *n bible* the second book of the Old Testament, containing a description of the departure of the Israelites from Egypt

ex officio (eks off-**fish**-ee-oh) *adv, adj* by right of position or office
WORD ORIGIN Latin

exonerate *vb* **-ating, -ated** to clear (someone) of blame or a criminal charge **exoneration** *n*
WORD ORIGIN Latin *exonerare* to free from a burden

exorbitant *adj* (of prices, demands, etc.) excessively great or high: *an exorbitant rent* **exorbitantly** *adv*
WORD ORIGIN Latin *ex* out, away + *orbita* track

exorcize *or* **-cise** *vb* **-cizing, -cized** *or* **-cising, -cised** to expel (evil spirits) by prayers and religious rites **exorcism** *n* **exorcist** *n*
WORD ORIGIN Greek *ex* out + *horkos* oath

exoskeleton *n zool* the protective or supporting structure covering the outside of the body of many animals, for example insects or crabs

exothermic *adj* (of a chemical reaction) involving or leading to the giving off of heat

exotic ● *adj* **1** having a strange allure or beauty **2** originating in a foreign country; not native ▷ *n* **3** a non-native plant **exotically** *adv*
WORD ORIGIN Greek *exō* outside

exotica *pl n* exotic objects, esp. as a collection

expand ● *vb* **1** to make or become greater in extent, size, or scope **2** to spread out; unfold **3 expand on** to go into more detail about (a story or subject) **4** to become increasingly relaxed, friendly, and talkative **5** *maths* to express a function or expression as the sum or product of terms **expandable** *adj*
WORD ORIGIN Latin *expandere* to spread out

expanse *n* an uninterrupted wide area; stretch: *a large expanse of water*

expansible *adj* able to expand

THESAURUS

exhibition *n* **1 = show**, display, exhibit, showing, fair, representation, presentation, spectacle, showcase, expo *(informal)*, exposition **2 = display**, show, performance, demonstration, airing, revelation, manifestation

exile *n* **1 = banishment**, expulsion, deportation, eviction, separation, ostracism, proscription, expatriation **2 = expatriate**, refugee, outcast, émigré, deportee ▷ *vb* **3 = banish**, expel, throw out, deport, oust, drive out, eject, expatriate, proscribe, cast out, ostracize

exist *vb* **2 = survive**, stay alive, make ends meet, subsist, eke out a living, scrape by, scrimp and save, support yourself, keep your head above water, get along *or* by **3 = live**, be present, be living, last, survive, breathe, endure, be in existence, be, be extant, have breath **4 = occur**, happen, stand, remain, obtain, be present, prevail, abide

existence *n* **1 = reality**, being, life, survival, duration, endurance, continuation, subsistence, actuality, continuance **2 = life**, situation, way of life, life style

exit *n* **1 = way out**, door, gate, outlet, doorway, vent, gateway, escape route, passage out, egress **OPPOSITE:** entry **2 = departure**, withdrawal, retreat, farewell, going, retirement, goodbye, exodus, evacuation, decamping, leave-taking, adieu ▷ *vb* **5 = depart**, leave, go out, withdraw, retire, quit, retreat, go away, say goodbye, bid farewell, make tracks, take your leave, go offstage *(theatre)* **OPPOSITE:** enter

exodus *n* **= departure**, withdrawal, retreat, leaving, flight, retirement, exit, migration, evacuation

exotic *adj* **1 = unusual**, different, striking, strange, extraordinary, bizarre, fascinating, curious, mysterious, colourful, glamorous, peculiar, unfamiliar, outlandish **OPPOSITE:** ordinary **2 = foreign**, alien, tropical, external, extraneous, naturalized, extrinsic, not native

expand *vb* **1a = get bigger**, increase, grow, extend, swell, widen, blow up, wax, heighten, enlarge, multiply, inflate, thicken, fill out, lengthen, fatten, dilate, become bigger, puff up, become larger, distend **OPPOSITE:** contract **1b = make bigger**, increase, develop, extend, widen, blow up, heighten, enlarge, multiply, broaden, inflate, thicken, fill out, lengthen, magnify, amplify, augment, dilate, make larger, distend, bloat, protract **OPPOSITE:** reduce **2 = spread (out)**, open (out), stretch (out), unfold, unravel, diffuse, unfurl, unroll, outspread **3 expand on something = go into detail about**, embellish, elaborate on, develop, flesh out,

DICTIONARY

or be expanded
expansion ❶ *n* 1 the act of expanding 2 an increase or development, esp. in the activities of a company
expansionism *n* the practice of expanding the economy or territory of a country **expansionist** *n, adj*
expansive *adj* 1 wide or extensive 2 friendly, open, and talkative **expansiveness** *n*
expat *adj, n* ▸ short for **expatriate**
expatiate (iks-pay-shee-ate) *vb* **-ating, -ated** ■ **expatiate on** *formal* to speak or write at length on (a subject) **expatiation** *n*
WORD ORIGIN Latin *exspatiari* to digress
expatriate ❶ (eks-pat-ree-it) *adj* 1 living away from one's native country: *an expatriate American* 2 exiled ▷ *n* 3 a person living away from his or her native country 4 an exile **expatriation** *n*
WORD ORIGIN Latin *ex* out, away + *patria* native land
expect ❶ *vb* 1 to regard as likely 2 to look forward to or be waiting for 3 to require (something) as an obligation: *he expects an answer by January* 4 **be expecting** *informal* to be pregnant
WORD ORIGIN Latin *exspectare* to watch for
expectancy *n* 1 something expected, esp. on the basis of a norm: *a life expectancy of 78* 2 anticipation or expectation
expectant *adj* 1 expecting or hopeful 2 **a** pregnant **b** married to or living with a woman who is pregnant: *an expectant father* **expectantly** *adv*
expectation ❶ *n* 1 the state of expecting or of being expected 2 something looked forward to, whether feared or hoped for 3 belief that someone should behave in a particular way: *women with expectations of old-fashioned gallantry*
expectorant *med adj* 1 helping to bring up phlegm from the respiratory passages ▷ *n* 2 an expectorant medicine
expectorate *vb* **-rating, -rated** *formal* to cough up and spit out (phlegm from the respiratory passages) **expectoration** *n*
WORD ORIGIN Latin *expectorare* to drive from the breast, expel
expediency *or* **expedience** *n, pl* **-encies** *or* **-ences** 1 the use of methods that are advantageous rather than fair or just 2 appropriateness or suitability
expedient (iks-pee-dee-ent) *n* 1 something that achieves a particular purpose: *income controls were used only as a short-term expedient* ▷ *adj* 2 useful or advantageous in a given situation: *they only talk about human rights when it is politically expedient*
WORD ORIGIN Latin *expediens* setting free; see EXPEDITE
expedite *vb* **-diting, -dited** *formal* 1 to hasten the progress of 2 to do quickly
WORD ORIGIN Latin *expedire* to free the feet
expedition ❶ *n* 1 an organized journey or voyage, esp. for exploration 2 the people and equipment comprising an expedition 3 a pleasure trip or excursion: *an expedition to the seaside* **expeditionary** *adj*
WORD ORIGIN Latin *expedire* to prepare, expedite
expeditious *adj* done quickly and efficiently
expel ❶ *vb* **-pelling, -pelled** 1 to drive out with force 2 to dismiss from a school, club, etc. permanently
WORD ORIGIN Latin *expellere*
expend *vb formal* to spend or use up (time, energy, or money)
WORD ORIGIN Latin *expendere* to weigh out, pay
expendable *adj* 1 not worth preserving 2 able to be sacrificed to achieve an objective, esp. a military one
expenditure ❶ *n* 1 something expended, esp. money 2 the amount expended
expense ❶ *n* 1 a particular payment of money; expenditure 2 the amount of money needed to buy or do something; cost 3 **expenses** money spent in the performance of a job, etc. 4 something requiring money for its purchase or upkeep 5 **at the expense of** to the detriment of
WORD ORIGIN Latin *expensus* weighed out
expense account *n* 1 an arrangement by which an employee's expenses are refunded by his or her employer 2 a record of such expenses
expensive ❶ *adj* costing a great deal of money **expensiveness** *n*
experience ❶ *n* 1 direct personal participation or observation of something: *his experience of prison life* 2 a particular incident, feeling, etc. that a person has undergone 3 accumulated knowledge, esp. of practical matters ▷ *vb* **-encing, -enced** 4 to participate in or undergo 5 to be moved by; feel
WORD ORIGIN Latin *experiri* to prove
experienced ❶ *adj* skilful or knowledgeable as a result of having done something many times before
experiential *adj philosophy* relating to

THESAURUS

expound on, enlarge on, expatiate on, add detail to
expansion *n* 1 = **enlargement**, inflation, increase, growth, swelling, unfolding, expanse, unfurling, opening out, distension 2 = **increase**, development, growth, spread, diffusion, magnification, multiplication, amplification, augmentation
expatriate *adj* 1, 2 = **exiled**, refugee, banished, emigrant, émigré, expat ▷ *n* 3, 4 = **exile**, refugee, emigrant, émigré
expect *vb* 1 = **think**, believe, suppose, assume, trust, imagine, reckon, forecast, calculate, presume, foresee, conjecture, surmise, think likely 2 = **anticipate**, look forward to, predict, envisage, await, hope for, contemplate, bargain for, look ahead to 3 = **require**, demand, want, wish, look for, call for, ask for, hope for, insist on, count on, rely upon
expectation *n* 1 *(usually plural)* = **projection**, supposition, assumption, calculation, belief, forecast, assurance, likelihood, probability, presumption, conjecture, surmise, presupposition 2 = **anticipation**, hope, possibility, prospect, chance, fear, promise, looking forward, excitement, prediction, outlook, expectancy, apprehension, suspense
expedition *n* 1 = **journey**, exploration, mission, voyage, tour, enterprise, undertaking, quest, trek
expel *vb* 1 = **drive out**, discharge, throw out, force out, let out, eject, issue, dislodge, spew, belch, cast out 2a = **throw out**, exclude, ban, bar, dismiss, discharge, relegate, kick out *(informal)*, ask to leave, send packing, turf out *(informal)*, black, debar, drum out, blackball, give the bum's rush *(slang)*, show you the door, throw out on your ear *(informal)* OPPOSITE: let in 2b = **banish**, exile, oust, deport, expatriate, evict, force to leave, proscribe OPPOSITE: take in
expenditure *n* 1 = **spending**, payment, expense, outgoings, cost, charge, outlay, disbursement 2 = **consumption**, use, using, application, output
expense *n* 1, 2 = **cost**, charge, expenditure, payment, spending, output, toll, consumption, outlay, disbursement
expensive *adj* = **costly**, high-priced, lavish, extravagant, rich, dear, stiff, excessive, steep *(informal)*, pricey, overpriced, exorbitant OPPOSITE: cheap
experience *n* 1, 3 = **knowledge**, understanding, practice, skill, evidence, trial, contact, expertise, know-how *(informal)*, proof, involvement, exposure, observation, participation, familiarity, practical knowledge 2 = **event**, affair, incident, happening, test, trial, encounter, episode, adventure, ordeal, occurrence ▷ *vb*

DICTIONARY

or derived from experience
experiment ❶ *n* **1** a test or investigation to provide evidence for or against a theory: *a scientific experiment* **2** the trying out of a new idea or method ▷ *vb* **3** to carry out an experiment or experiments **experimentation** *n* **experimenter** *n*
WORD ORIGIN Latin *experiri* to test
experimental ❶ *adj* **1** relating to, based on, or having the nature of an experiment **2** trying out new ideas or methods **experimentally** *adv*
expert ❶ *n* **1** a person who has extensive skill or knowledge in a particular field ▷ *adj* **2** skilful or knowledgeable **3** of, involving, or done by an expert **expertly** *adv*
WORD ORIGIN Latin *expertus* known by experience
expertise ❶ (eks-per-**teez**) *n* special skill, knowledge, or judgment
WORD ORIGIN French
expiate *vb* **-ating, -ated** *formal* to make amends for (a sin or wrongdoing) **expiation** *n*
WORD ORIGIN Latin *expiare*
expiration *n* **1** the finish of something; expiry **2** the act, process, or sound of breathing out **expiratory** *adj*
expire ❶ *vb* **-piring, -pired 1** to finish or run out; come to an end **2** to breathe out air **3** to die
WORD ORIGIN Latin *exspirare* to breathe out
expiry *n, pl* **-ries** a coming to an end, esp. of the period of a contract
explain ❶ *vb* **1** to make something easily understandable, esp. by giving a clear and detailed account of it **2** to justify or attempt to justify oneself by giving reasons for one's actions **3 explain away** to offer excuses or reasons for (mistakes)
WORD ORIGIN Latin *explanare* to flatten, make clear
explanation ❶ *n* **1** the reason or reasons why a particular event or situation happened: *there is no reasonable explanation for her behaviour* **2** a detailed account or description: *a 90-minute explanation of his love of jazz*
explanatory *adj* serving or intended to serve as an explanation
expletive (iks-**plee**-tiv) *n* an exclamation or swearword expressing emotion rather than meaning
WORD ORIGIN Latin *explere* to fill up
explicable *adj* capable of being explained
explicate *vb* **-cating, -cated** *formal* to make clear; explain **explication** *n*
WORD ORIGIN Latin *explicare* to unfold
explicit ❶ *adj* **1** precisely and clearly expressed, leaving nothing to implication: *an explicit commitment to democracy* **2** leaving little to the imagination; graphically detailed: *the film contains some sexually explicit scenes* **3** (of a person) expressing something in a precise and clear way, so as to leave no doubt about what is meant **explicitly** *adv*
WORD ORIGIN Latin *explicitus* unfolded
explode ❶ *vb* **-ploding, -ploded 1** to burst with great violence; blow up **2** (of a gas) to undergo a sudden violent expansion as a result of a fast chemical or nuclear reaction **3** to react suddenly or violently with emotion **4** (esp. of a population) to increase rapidly **5** to show (a theory, etc.) to be baseless
WORD ORIGIN Latin *explodere* to drive off by clapping
exploit ❶ *vb* **1** to take advantage of a person or situation for one's own ends **2** to make the best use of ▷ *n* **3** a notable deed or feat **exploitation**

THESAURUS

4, 5 = undergo, have, know, feel, try, meet, face, suffer, taste, go through, observe, sample, encounter, sustain, perceive, endure, participate in, run into, live through, behold, come up against, apprehend, become familiar with
experienced *adj* **= knowledgeable**, trained, professional, skilled, tried, tested, seasoned, expert, master, qualified, familiar, capable, veteran, practised, accomplished, competent, skilful, adept, well-versed **OPPOSITE:** inexperienced
experiment *n* **1 = test**, trial, investigation, examination, venture, procedure, demonstration, observation, try-out, assay, trial run, scientific test, dummy run **2 = research**, investigation, analysis, observation, research and development, experimentation, trial and error ▷ *vb* **3 = test**, investigate, trial, research, try, examine, pilot, sample, verify, put to the test, assay
experimental *adj* **1 = test**, trial, pilot, preliminary, provisional, tentative, speculative, empirical, exploratory, trial-and-error, fact-finding, probationary **2 = innovative**, new, original, radical, creative, ingenious, avant-garde, inventive, ground-breaking
expert *n* **1 = specialist**, authority, professional, master, pro *(informal)*, ace *(informal)*, genius, guru, pundit, buff *(informal)*, wizard, adept, whizz *(informal)*, maestro, virtuoso, connoisseur, hotshot *(informal)*, past master, dab hand *(Brit informal)*, wonk *(informal)*, maven *(US)*, fundi *(S African)* **OPPOSITE:** amateur ▷ *adj* **2 = skilful**, trained, experienced, able, professional, skilled, master, masterly, qualified, talented, outstanding, clever, practised, accomplished, handy, competent, apt, adept, knowledgeable, virtuoso, deft, proficient, facile, adroit, dexterous **OPPOSITE:** unskilled
expertise *n* **= skill**, knowledge, know-how *(informal)*, facility, grip, craft, judgment, grasp, mastery, knack, proficiency, dexterity, cleverness, deftness, adroitness, aptness, expertness, knowing inside out, ableness, masterliness, skilfulness
expire *vb* **1 = become invalid**, end, finish, conclude, close, stop, run out, cease, lapse, terminate, come to an end, be no longer valid **3 = die**, decease, depart, buy it *(US slang)*, check out *(US slang)*, perish, kick it *(slang)*, croak *(slang)*, go belly-up *(slang)*, snuff it *(informal)*, peg out *(informal)*, kick the bucket *(informal)*, peg it *(informal)*, depart this life, meet your maker, cark it *(Austral & NZ slang)*, pop your clogs *(informal)*, pass away *or* on
explain *vb* **1 = make clear** *or* **plain**, describe, demonstrate, illustrate, teach, define, solve, resolve, interpret, disclose, unfold, clarify, clear up, simplify, expound, elucidate, put into words, throw light on, explicate *(formal)*, give the details of **2 = account for**, excuse, justify, give a reason for, give an explanation for
explanation *n* **1 = reason**, meaning, cause, sense, answer, account, excuse, motive, justification, vindication, mitigation, the why and wherefore **2 = description**, report, definition, demonstration, teaching, resolution, interpretation, illustration, clarification, exposition, simplification, explication, elucidation
explicit *adj* **1 = clear**, obvious, specific, direct, certain, express, plain, absolute, exact, precise, straightforward, definite, overt, unequivocal, unqualified, unambiguous, categorical **OPPOSITE:** vague **3 = frank**, direct, open, specific, positive, plain, patent, graphic, distinct, outspoken, upfront *(informal)*, unambiguous, unrestricted, unrestrained, uncensored, unreserved **OPPOSITE:** indirect
explode *vb* **1a = blow up**, erupt, burst, go off, shatter, shiver **1b = detonate**, set off, discharge, let off **3 = lose your temper**, rage, erupt, blow up *(informal)*, lose it *(informal)*, crack up *(informal)*, see red *(informal)*, lose the plot *(informal)*, become angry, have a fit *(informal)*, go ballistic *(slang, chiefly US)*, hit the roof *(informal)*, throw a

DICTIONARY

n **exploiter** *n*
WORD ORIGIN Old French: accomplishment

exploitative *adj* tending to take advantage of a person or situation for one's own ends

explore ● *vb* **-ploring, -plored 1** to examine or investigate, esp. systematically **2** to travel into an unfamiliar region, esp. for scientific purposes **exploration** *n* **exploratory** *or* **explorative** *adj* **explorer** *n*
WORD ORIGIN Latin *ex* out + *plorare* to cry aloud

explosion ● *n* **1** an exploding **2** a violent release of energy resulting from a rapid chemical or nuclear reaction **3** a sudden or violent outburst of activity, noise, emotion, etc. **4** a rapid increase

explosive ● *adj* **1** able or likely to explode **2** potentially violent: *an explosive situation* ▷*n* **3** a substance capable of exploding **explosiveness** *n*

expo *n, pl* **-pos** ▸short for **exposition** (sense 3)

exponent *n* **1** a person who advocates an idea, cause, etc.: *an exponent of free speech* **2** a person who is a skilful performer of some activity: *one of the greatest modern exponents of the blues* **3** *maths* a number placed as a superscript to another number indicating how many times the number is to be used as a factor
WORD ORIGIN Latin *exponere* to expound

exponential *adj* **1** *maths* of or involving numbers raised to an exponent **2** *informal* very rapid **exponentially** *adv*

export *n* **1** the sale of goods and services to a foreign country: *a ban on the export of arms* **2 exports** goods or services sold to a foreign country ▷*vb* **3** to sell goods or services or transport goods to a foreign country **exporter** *n*
WORD ORIGIN Latin *exportare* to carry away

expose ● *vb* **-posing, -posed 1** to uncover (something previously covered) **2** to reveal the truth about (someone or something), esp. when it is shocking or scandalous: *an MP whose private life was recently exposed in the press* **3** to leave (a person or thing) unprotected in a potentially harmful situation: *workers were exposed to relatively low doses of radiation* **4 expose someone to** to give someone an introduction to or experience of (something new) **5** *photog* to subject (a film) to light **6 expose oneself** to display one's sexual organs in public
WORD ORIGIN Latin *exponere* to set out

exposé (iks-**pose**-ay) *n* the bringing of a scandal, crime, etc. to public notice
WORD ORIGIN French

exposed *adj* **1** not concealed; displayed for viewing: *the exposed soles of his shoes* **2** without shelter from the elements **3** vulnerable: *the enemy attacked our army's exposed flank*

exposition *n* **1** a systematic explanation of a subject **2** the act of expounding or setting out a viewpoint **3** a large public exhibition **4** *music* the first statement of the themes of a movement
WORD ORIGIN Latin *exponere* to display

expository *adj* explanatory

ex post facto *adj* having retrospective effect
WORD ORIGIN Latin *ex* from + *post* afterwards + *factus* done

expostulate *vb* **-lating, -lated** ■ **expostulate with** to reason or argue with, esp. in order to dissuade or as a protest **expostulation** *n* **expostulatory** *adj*
WORD ORIGIN Latin *expostulare* to require

exposure ● *n* **1** the state of being exposed to, or lacking protection from, something: *the body cannot cope with sudden exposure to stress* **2** the revealing of the truth about someone or something, esp. when it is shocking or scandalous: *the exposure of a loophole in the tax laws* **3** the harmful effect on a person's body caused by lack of shelter from the weather, esp. the cold **4** appearance before the public, as on television **5** *photog* **a** the act of exposing a film to light **b** an area on a film that has been exposed **6** *photog* **a** the intensity of light falling on a film multiplied by the time for which it is exposed **b** a combination of lens aperture and shutter speed used in taking a photograph

exposure meter *n photog* an instrument for measuring the intensity of light so that suitable camera settings can be chosen

expound *vb* to explain a theory, belief, etc. in detail
WORD ORIGIN Latin *exponere* to set forth

express ● *vb* **1** to state (an idea or feeling) in words; utter: *two record labels have expressed an interest in signing the band* **2** to show (an idea or feeling): *his body and demeanour expressed distrust* **3** to indicate through a symbol or formula **4** to squeeze out (juice, etc.) **5 express oneself** to communicate one's thoughts or ideas ▷*adj* **6** explicitly stated **7** deliberate and specific: *she came with the express purpose of causing a row*

THESAURUS

tantrum, blow a fuse *(slang, chiefly US)*, go berserk *(slang)*, go mad *(slang)*, fly off the handle *(informal)*, go spare *(Brit slang)*, become enraged, go off the deep end *(informal)*, go up the wall *(slang)*, blow your top *(informal)*, go crook *(Austral & NZ slang)*, fly into a temper, flip your lid *(slang)*, do your nut *(Brit slang)* **4 = increase**, grow, develop, extend, advance, shoot up, soar, boost, expand, build up, swell, step up *(informal)*, escalate, multiply, proliferate, snowball, aggrandize **5 = disprove**, discredit, refute, belie, demolish, repudiate, put paid to, invalidate, debunk, prove impossible, prove wrong, give the lie to, blow out of the water *(slang)*

exploit *vb* **1 = take advantage of**, abuse, use, manipulate, milk, misuse, dump on *(slang, chiefly US)*, ill-treat, play on *or* upon **2 = make the best use of**, use, make use of, utilize, cash in on *(informal)*, capitalize on, put to use, make capital out of, use to advantage, use to good advantage, live off the backs of, turn to account, profit by *or* from ▷*n* **3 = feat**, act, achievement, enterprise, adventure, stunt, deed, accomplishment, attainment, escapade

explore *vb* **1 = investigate**, consider, research, survey, search, prospect, examine, probe, analyse, look into, inspect, work over, scrutinize, inquire into **2 = travel around**, tour, survey, scout, traverse, range over, recce *(slang)*, reconnoitre, case *(slang)*, have *or* take a look around

explosion *n* **1, 2 = blast**, crack, burst, bang, discharge, report, blowing up, outburst, clap, detonation **3a = outburst**, fit, storm, attack, surge, flare-up, eruption, paroxysm **3b = outbreak**, flare-up, eruption, upsurge **4 = increase**, rise, development, growth, boost, expansion, enlargement, escalation, upturn

explosive *adj* **1 = unstable**, dangerous, volatile, hazardous, unsafe, perilous, combustible, inflammable **2 = fiery**, violent, volatile, stormy, touchy, vehement, chippy *(informal)* ▷*n* **3 = bomb**, mine, shell, missile, rocket, grenade, charge, torpedo, incendiary

expose *vb* **1 = uncover**, show, reveal, display, exhibit, present, unveil, manifest, lay bare, take the wraps off, put on view **OPPOSITE:** hide **3 = make vulnerable**, subject, leave open, lay open

exposure *n* **3 = hypothermia**, frostbite, extreme cold, intense cold

express *vb* **1 = state**, communicate, convey, articulate, say, tell, put, word, speak, voice, declare, phrase, assert, pronounce, utter, couch, put across, enunciate, put into words, give voice to, verbalize, asseverate

DICTIONARY

8 of or for rapid transportation of people, mail, etc. ▷*n* **9** a fast train stopping at only a few stations **10** *chiefly US & Canad* a system for sending mail rapidly ▷*adv* **11** using a system for rapid transportation of people, mail, etc.: *please send this letter express: it's very urgent!* **expressible** *adj*
WORD ORIGIN Latin *exprimere* to force out

e

expression *n* **1** the transforming of ideas into words **2** a showing of emotion without words **3** communication of emotion through music, painting, etc. **4** a look on the face that indicates mood or emotion **5** a particular phrase used conventionally to express something **6** *maths* a variable, function, or some combination of these **expressionless** *adj*

expressionism *n* an early 20th-century artistic and literary movement which sought to express emotions rather than to represent the physical world **expressionist** *n, adj*

expression mark *n music* one of a set of symbols indicating how a piece or passage is to be performed

expressive *adj* **1** of or full of expression **2 expressive of** showing or suggesting: *looks expressive of hatred and revenge*

expressly *adv* **1** definitely **2** deliberately and specifically

expressway *n chiefly US* a motorway

expropriate *vb* **-ating, -ated** *formal* (of a government or other official body) to take (money or property) away from its owners **expropriation** *n* **expropriator** *n*
WORD ORIGIN Medieval Latin *expropriare* to deprive of possessions

expulsion *n* the act of expelling or the fact of being expelled **expulsive** *adj*
WORD ORIGIN Latin *expellere* to expel

expunge (iks-**sponge**) *vb* **-punging, -punged** *formal* to remove all traces of: *he had tried to expunge his failure from his mind*
WORD ORIGIN Latin *expungere* to blot out

expurgate (**eks**-per-gate) *vb* **-gating, -gated** to amend a piece of writing by removing sections thought to be offensive **expurgation** *n* **expurgator** *n*
WORD ORIGIN Latin *expurgare* to clean out

exquisite *adj* **1** extremely beautiful or attractive **2** showing unusual delicacy and craftsmanship **3** sensitive or discriminating: *exquisite manners* **4** intensely felt: *exquisite joy* **exquisitely** *adv*
WORD ORIGIN Latin *exquisitus* excellent

ex-serviceman *or fem* **ex-servicewoman** *n, pl* **-men** *or* **-women** a person who has served in the armed forces

extant *adj* still in existence; surviving
WORD ORIGIN Latin *exstans* standing out

extemporaneous *adj* spoken or performed without preparation **extemporaneously** *adv*

extempore (iks-**temp**-or-ee) *adj, adv* without planning or preparation
WORD ORIGIN Latin *ex tempore* instantaneously

extemporize *or* **-rise** *vb* **-rizing, -rized** *or* **-rising, -rised** to perform or speak without preparation **extemporization** *or* **-risation** *n* **extemporizer** *or* **-riser** *n*

extend *vb* **1** to make bigger or longer than before: *they extended the house by building a conservatory* **2** to reach to a certain distance or in a certain direction: *the suburbs extend for many miles* **3** to last for a certain time: *in Norway maternity leave extends to 52 weeks* **4** to broaden the meaning or scope of: *the law was extended to ban all guns* **5** to make something exist or be valid for longer than before: *her visa was extended for three months* **6** to present or offer: *a tradition of extending asylum to refugees* **7** to straighten or stretch out (part of the body): *she extended a hand in welcome* **8 extend oneself** to make use of all one's ability or strength, often because forced to: *she'll have to really extend herself if she wants to win* **extendable** *adj*
WORD ORIGIN Latin *extendere* to stretch out

extended family *n* a social unit in which parents, children, grandparents, and other relatives live as a family unit

extensible *adj* capable of being extended

extension *n* **1** a room or rooms added to an existing building **2** a development that includes or affects more people or things than before: *an extension of democracy within the EU* **3** an additional telephone connected to the same line as another **4** an extra period of time in which something continues to exist or be valid: *an extension of the contract for another 2 years* ▷*adj* **5** denoting something that can be extended or that extends another object: *an extension ladder* **6** of or relating to the provision of teaching

THESAURUS

2 = show, indicate, exhibit, demonstrate, reveal, disclose, intimate, convey, testify to, depict, designate, manifest, embody, signify, symbolize, denote, divulge, bespeak, make known, evince ▷*adj* **6 = explicit**, clear, direct, precise, pointed, certain, plain, accurate, exact, distinct, definite, outright, unambiguous, categorical **7 = specific**, exclusive, particular, sole, special, deliberate, singular, clear-cut, especial **8 = fast**, direct, quick, rapid, priority, prompt, swift, high-speed, speedy, quickie *(informal)*, nonstop, expeditious

expression *n* **1 = statement**, declaration, announcement, communication, mention, assertion, utterance, articulation, pronouncement, enunciation, verbalization, asseveration **2 = indication**, demonstration, exhibition, display, showing, show, sign, symbol, representation, token, manifestation, embodiment **4 = look**, countenance, face, air, appearance, aspect, mien *(literary)* **5 = phrase**, saying, word, wording, term, language, speech, remark, maxim, idiom, adage, choice of words, turn of phrase, phraseology, locution, set phrase

expressive *adj* **1 = vivid**, strong, striking, telling, moving, lively, sympathetic, energetic, poignant, emphatic, eloquent, forcible
OPPOSITE: impassive

expulsion *n* **a = ejection**, exclusion, dismissal, removal, exile, discharge, eviction, banishment, extrusion, proscription, expatriation, debarment, dislodgment **b = discharge**, emptying, emission, voiding, spewing, secretion, excretion, ejection, seepage, suppuration

exquisite *adj* **1 = beautiful**, elegant, graceful, pleasing, attractive, lovely, charming, comely
OPPOSITE: unattractive
2 = fine, beautiful, lovely, elegant, precious, delicate, dainty **4 = intense**, acute, severe, sharp, keen, extreme, piercing, poignant, excruciating

extend *vb* **1 = make longer**, prolong, lengthen, draw out, spin out, elongate, drag out, protract
OPPOSITE: shorten
1, 4 = widen, increase, develop, expand, spread, add to, enhance, supplement, enlarge, broaden, diversify, amplify, augment
OPPOSITE: reduce
2 = spread out, reach, stretch, continue, carry on **3 = last**, continue, go on, stretch, carry on **6 = offer**, give, hold out, present, grant, advance, yield, reach out, confer, stretch out, stick out, bestow, impart, proffer, put forth
OPPOSITE: withdraw
7 = stretch, stretch out, spread out, unfurl, straighten out, unroll

extension *n* **1 = annexe**, wing, addition, supplement, branch, appendix, add-on, adjunct,

DICTIONARY

and other facilities by a school or college to people who cannot attend full-time courses

extensive ❶ *adj* **1** covering a large area: *extensive moorland* **2** very great in effect: *the bomb caused extensive damage* **3** containing many details, ideas, or items on a particular subject: *an extensive collection of modern art* **extensively** *adv*

extensor *n* any muscle that stretches or extends an arm, leg, or other part of the body

extent ❶ *n* **1** the length, area, or size of something **2** the scale or seriousness of a situation or difficulty: *the extent of the damage* **3** the degree or amount to which something applies: *to a certain extent that's true*

extenuate *vb* **-ating, -ated** *formal* to make an offence or fault less blameworthy, by giving reasons that partly excuse it **extenuating** *adj* **extenuation** *n*
WORD ORIGIN Latin *extenuare* to make thin

exterior ❶ *n* **1** a part or surface that is on the outside **2** the outward appearance of a person: *Jim's grumpy exterior concealed a warm heart* **3** a film scene shot outside ▷ *adj* **4** of, situated on, or suitable for the outside **5** coming or acting from outside or abroad
WORD ORIGIN Latin comparative of *exterus* on the outside

exterior angle *n* an angle of a polygon contained between one side extended and the adjacent side

exterminate *vb* **-nating, -nated** to destroy a group or type of people, animals, or plants completely **extermination** *n* **exterminator** *n*
WORD ORIGIN Latin *exterminare* to drive away

external ❶ *adj* **1** of, situated on, or suitable for the outside: *there was damage to the house's external walls* **2** coming or acting from outside: *most ill health is caused by external influences* **3** of or involving foreign nations: *Hong Kong's external trade* **4** *anat* situated on or near the outside of the body: *the external ear* **5** brought into an organization to do a task which must be done impartially, esp. one involving testing or checking: *external examiners* **6** of or relating to someone taking a university course, but not attending a university: *an external degree* ▷ *n* **7 externals** obvious circumstances or aspects, esp. superficial ones: *despite the war, the externals of life in the city remain normal* **externality** *n* **externally** *adv*
WORD ORIGIN Latin *externus*

externalize *or* **-ise** *vb* **-izing, -ized** *or* **-ising, -ised** to express (thoughts or feelings) in words or actions **externalization** *or* **-isation** *n*

extinct ❶ *adj* **1** (of an animal or plant species) having died out **2** no longer in existence, esp. because of social changes: *shipbuilding is virtually extinct in Scotland* **3** (of a volcano) no longer liable to erupt
WORD ORIGIN Latin *exstinguere* to extinguish

extinction ❶ *n* **1** the dying out of a plant or animal species **2** the end of a particular way of life or type of activity

extinguish *vb* **1** to put out (a fire or light) **2** to remove or destroy entirely **extinguishable** *adj* **extinguisher** *n*
WORD ORIGIN Latin *exstinguere*

extirpate (eks-ter-pate) *vb* **-pating, -pated** to remove or destroy completely: *the Romans attempted to extirpate the Celtic religion* **extirpation** *n*
WORD ORIGIN Latin *exstirpare* to root out

extol *or US* **extoll** *vb* **-tolling, -tolled** to praise lavishly
WORD ORIGIN Latin *extollere* to elevate

extort *vb* to obtain money or favours by intimidation, violence, or the misuse of authority **extortion** *n*
WORD ORIGIN Latin *extorquere* to wrest away

extortionate *adj* (of prices, profits, etc.) much higher than is fair **extortionately** *adv*

extra ❶ *adj* **1** more than is usual, expected or needed; additional ▷ *n* **2** a person or thing that is additional **3** something for which an additional charge is made **4** *films* a person temporarily engaged, usually for crowd scenes **5** *cricket* a run not scored from the bat **6** an additional edition of a newspaper ▷ *adv* **7** unusually; exceptionally
WORD ORIGIN probably from *extraordinary*

extra- *prefix* outside or beyond an area or scope: *extracellular; extraterrestrial*
WORD ORIGIN Latin

extract ❶ *vb* **1** to pull out or uproot by force **2** to remove from a container **3** to derive (pleasure, information, etc.) from some source **4** *informal* to obtain (money, information, etc.) from someone who is not willing to provide it: *a confession extracted by force* **5** to obtain (a substance) from a material or the ground by mining,

THESAURUS

appendage, ell, addendum **2 = development**, expansion, widening, increase, stretching, broadening, continuation, enlargement, diversification, amplification, elongation, augmentation **4 = lengthening**, extra time, continuation, postponement, prolongation, additional period of time, protraction

extensive *adj* **1 = large**, considerable, substantial, spacious, wide, sweeping, broad, expansive, capacious, commodious **OPPOSITE:** confined **2 = great**, large, huge, extended, vast, widespread, comprehensive, universal, large-scale, far-reaching, prevalent, far-flung, all-inclusive, voluminous, humongous *or* humungous *(US slang)* **OPPOSITE:** limited **3 = comprehensive**, complete, thorough, lengthy, long, wide, wholesale, pervasive, protracted, all-inclusive **OPPOSITE:** restricted

extent *n* **1 = size**, area, range, length, reach, bounds, sweep, sphere, width, compass, breadth, ambit **2, 3 = magnitude**, amount, degree, scale, level, measure, stretch, quantity, bulk, duration, expanse, amplitude

exterior *n* **1 = outside**, face, surface, covering, finish, skin, appearance, aspect, shell, coating, façade, outside surface ▷ *adj* **4 = outer**, outside, external, surface, outward, superficial, outermost **OPPOSITE:** inner

external *adj* **1 = outer**, outside, surface, apparent, visible, outward, exterior, superficial, outermost **OPPOSITE:** internal **3 = foreign**, international, alien, exotic, exterior, extraneous, extrinsic **OPPOSITE:** domestic **5, 6 = outside**, visiting, independent, extramural **OPPOSITE:** inside

extinct *adj* **1 = dead**, lost, gone, vanished, defunct **OPPOSITE:** living

extinction *n* **1, 2 = dying out**, death, destruction, abolition, oblivion, extermination, annihilation, eradication, obliteration, excision, extirpation

extra *adj* **1a = additional**, more, new, other, added, further, fresh, accessory, supplementary, auxiliary, add-on, supplemental, ancillary **OPPOSITE:** vital **1b = surplus**, excess, reserve, spare, unnecessary, redundant, needless, unused, leftover, superfluous, extraneous, unneeded, inessential, supernumerary, supererogatory ▷ *n* **2 = addition**, bonus, supplement, accessory, complement, add-on, affix, adjunct, appendage, addendum, supernumerary, appurtenance **OPPOSITE:** necessity ▷ *adv* **7 = exceptionally**, very, specially, especially, particularly, extremely, remarkably, unusually, extraordinarily, uncommonly

extract *vb* **1 = pull out**, remove, take

DICTIONARY

distillation, digestion, etc.: *oil extracted from shale* **6** to copy out (an article, passage, etc.) from a publication ▷*n* **7** something extracted, such as a passage from a book, etc. **8** a preparation containing the concentrated essence of a substance **extractive** *adj* **extractor** *n*
WORD ORIGIN Latin *extrahere* to draw out

extraction *n* **1** the act or an instance of extracting **2** the removal of a tooth by a dentist: *few patients need an extraction* **3** the origin or ancestry of a person: *he is of German extraction*

extractor fan *n* a fan used to remove stale air from a room

extracurricular *adj* not part of the normal courses taken by students: *her free time is devoted to extracurricular duties*

extradite *vb* **-diting, -dited** to hand over an alleged offender to the country where the crime took place for trial: *an agreement to extradite him to Hong Kong* **extraditable** *adj* **extradition** *n*
WORD ORIGIN Latin *ex* away + *traditio* a handing over

extrajudicial *adj* **1** outside the ordinary course of legal proceedings: *extrajudicial evidence* **2** beyond the jurisdiction or authority of the court: *an extrajudicial opinion*

extramarital *adj* occurring between a married person and a person other than his or her spouse: *an extramarital affair*

extramural *adj* connected with but outside the normal courses of a university or college
WORD ORIGIN Latin *extra* beyond + *murus* wall

extraneous (iks-**train**-ee-uss) *adj* not essential or relevant to the situation or subject being considered
WORD ORIGIN Latin *extraneus* external

extraordinary ❶ *adj* **1** very unusual or surprising: *the extraordinary sight of my grandfather wearing a dress* **2** having some special or extreme quality: *an extraordinary first novel* **3** (of a meeting, ambassador, etc.) specially called or appointed to deal with one particular topic **extraordinarily** *adv*
WORD ORIGIN Latin *extraordinarius* beyond what is usual

extraordinary rendition *n* the process by which a country seizes a terrorist suspect and then transports him or her for interrogation to a country where due process of law is unlikely to be respected

extrapolate (iks-**trap**-a-late) *vb* **-lating, -lated 1** to infer something not known from the known facts, using logic and reason **2** *maths* to estimate the value of a function or measurement beyond the known values, by the extension of a curve **extrapolation** *n*
WORD ORIGIN EXTRA- + *-polate*, as in *interpolate*

extrasensory *adj* of or relating to extrasensory perception

extrasensory perception *n* the supposed ability to obtain information without the use of normal senses of sight, hearing, etc.

extravagant ❶ *adj* **1** spending more than is reasonable or affordable **2** costing more than is reasonable or affordable: *an extravagant gift* **3** going beyond usual or reasonable limits: *extravagant expectations* **4** (of behaviour or gestures) extreme, esp. in order to make a particular impression: *an extravagant display of affection* **5** very elaborate and impressive: *extravagant costumes* **extravagance** *n*
WORD ORIGIN Latin *extra* beyond + *vagari* to wander

extravaganza *n* **1** an elaborate and lavish entertainment **2** any fanciful display, literary composition, etc.
WORD ORIGIN Italian: extravagance

extravert *adj, n* ▸same as **extrovert**

extreme ❶ *adj* **1** of a high or the highest degree or intensity **2** exceptionally severe or unusual: *people can survive extreme conditions* **3** (of an opinion, political group, etc.) beyond the limits regarded as acceptable; fanatical **4** farthest or outermost ▷*n* **5** either of the two limits of a scale or range **6 go to extremes** to be unreasonable in speech or action **7 in the extreme** to the highest or further degree: *the effect was dramatic in the extreme* **extremely** *adv*
WORD ORIGIN Latin *extremus* outermost

extreme sport *n* any of various sports with a high risk of injury or death

extreme unction *n RC church* ▸a former name for **anointing of the sick**

extremist ❶ *n* **1** a person who favours or uses extreme or violent methods, esp. to bring about political change ▷*adj* **2** holding extreme opinions or using extreme methods **extremism** *n*

extremity *n, pl* **-ties 1** the farthest point **2** an unacceptable or extreme nature or degree: *the extremity of his views alienated other nationalists* **3** an extreme condition, such as misfortune **4 extremities** hands and feet

extricate *vb* **-cating, -cated** to free from a difficult or complicated situation or place **extricable** *adj* **extrication** *n*

THESAURUS

out, draw, uproot, pluck out, extirpate **2 = take out**, draw, pull, remove, withdraw, pull out, bring out **4 = elicit**, get, obtain, force, draw, gather, derive, exact, bring out, evoke, reap, wring, glean, coerce, wrest ▷*n* **7 = passage**, selection, excerpt, cutting, clipping, abstract, quotation, citation **8 = essence**, solution, concentrate, juice, distillation, decoction, distillate

extraordinary *adj* **1 = unusual**, surprising, odd, strange, unique, remarkable, bizarre, curious, weird, unprecedented, peculiar, unfamiliar, uncommon, unheard-of, unwonted **OPPOSITE:** ordinary **2 = remarkable**, special, wonderful, outstanding, rare, amazing, fantastic, astonishing, marvellous, eye-popping *(informal)*, exceptional, notable, serious *(informal)*, phenomenal, singular, wondrous *(archaic, literary)*, out of this world *(informal)*, extremely good **OPPOSITE:** unremarkable

extravagant *adj* **1 = wasteful**, excessive, lavish, prodigal, profligate, spendthrift, imprudent, improvident **OPPOSITE:** economical **3, 4 = excessive**, exaggerated, outrageous, wild, fantastic, absurd, foolish, over the top *(slang)*, unreasonable, preposterous, fanciful, unrestrained, inordinate, outré, immoderate, O.T.T. *(slang)* **OPPOSITE:** moderate

extreme *adj* **1 = great**, high, highest, greatest, worst, supreme, acute, severe, maximum, intense, ultimate, utmost, mother of all *(informal)*, uttermost **OPPOSITE:** mild **2 = severe**, radical, strict, harsh, stern, rigid, dire, drastic, uncompromising, unbending **3 = radical**, unusual, excessive, exceptional, exaggerated, outrageous, over the top *(slang)*, unreasonable, uncommon, unconventional, fanatical, zealous, out-and-out, inordinate, egregious, intemperate, immoderate, O.T.T. *(slang)* **OPPOSITE:** moderate **4 = farthest**, furthest, far, final, last, ultimate, remotest, terminal, utmost, far-off, faraway, outermost, most distant, uttermost **OPPOSITE:** nearest ▷*n* **5 = limit**, end, edge, opposite, pole, ultimate, boundary, antithesis, extremity, acme

extremist *n* **1 = radical**, activist, militant, enthusiast, fanatic, devotee, die-hard, bigot, zealot, energumen ▷*adj* **2 = extreme**, wild, mad, enthusiastic, passionate, frenzied, obsessive, fanatical, fervent, zealous, bigoted, rabid, immoderate, overenthusiastic

WORD ORIGIN Latin *extricare*

extrinsic *adj* 1 not an integral or essential part 2 originating or acting from outside **extrinsically** *adv*
WORD ORIGIN Latin *exter* outward + *secus* alongside

extroversion *n psychol* the directing of one's interests outwards, esp. towards making social contacts

extrovert *adj* 1 lively and outgoing 2 *psychol* concerned more with external reality than inner feelings ▷*n* 3 a person who has these characteristics **extroverted** *adj*
WORD ORIGIN *extro-* (variant of EXTRA-, contrasting with *intro-*) + Latin *vertere* to turn

extrude *vb* **-truding, -truded** 1 to squeeze or force out 2 to produce moulded sections of plastic, metal, etc. by forcing through a shaped die **extruded** *adj* **extrusion** *n*
WORD ORIGIN Latin *extrudere* to thrust out

exuberant *adj* 1 full of vigour and high spirits 2 (of vegetation) growing thickly; flourishing **exuberance** *n*
WORD ORIGIN Latin *exuberans* abounding

exude *vb* **-uding, -uded** 1 (of a liquid or smell) to seep or flow out slowly and steadily 2 to seem to have (a quality or feeling) to a great degree: *the Chancellor exuded confidence* **exudation** *n*
WORD ORIGIN Latin *exsudare*

exult *vb* to be joyful or jubilant **exultation** *n* **exultant** *adj*
WORD ORIGIN Latin *exsultare* to jump for joy

Eyck *n* ▸ See **van Eyck**

eye ❶ *n* 1 the organ of sight in humans and animals 2 the external part of an eye, often including the area around it 3 (*often pl*) the ability to see or record what is happening: *the eyes of an entire nation were upon us* 4 a look, glance, or gaze 5 attention or observation: *his new shirt caught my eye* 6 the ability to judge or appreciate something: *his shrewd eye for talent* 7 (*often pl*) opinion, judgment, or authority: *in the eyes of the law* 8 a dark spot on a potato from which new shoots can grow 9 a small hole, such as the one at the blunt end of a sewing needle 10 a small area of calm in the centre of a storm, hurricane, or tornado 11 **all eyes** *informal* acutely vigilant 12 **an eye for an eye** justice consisting of an equivalent action to the original wrong or harm 13 **have eyes for** to be interested in 14 **in one's mind's eye** imagined or remembered vividly 15 **in the public eye** exposed to public curiosity 16 **keep an eye on** to take care of 17 **keep an eye open** *or* **out for** to watch with special attention for 18 **keep one's eyes peeled** *or* **skinned** to watch vigilantly 19 **look someone in the eye** to look openly and without embarrassment at someone 20 **make eyes at someone** to look at someone in an obviously attracted manner 21 **more than meets the eye** hidden motives, meanings, or facts 22 **my eye!** *old-fashioned informal* nonsense! 23 **see eye to eye with** to agree with 24 **set** *or* **lay** *or* **clap eyes on** to see: *I never laid eyes on him again* 25 **turn a blind eye to** *or* **close one's eyes to** to pretend not to notice 26 **up to one's eyes in** extremely busy with 27 **with an eye to** with the intention of 28 **with one's eyes open** in full knowledge of all the facts ▷*vb* **eyeing** *or* **eying, eyed** 29 to look at carefully or warily ▸ See also **eye up** > **eyeless** *adj* **eyelike** *adj*
WORD ORIGIN Old English *ēage*

eyeball *n* 1 the entire ball-shaped part of the eye 2 **eyeball to eyeball** in close confrontation ▷*vb* 3 *slang* to stare at

eyebrow *n* 1 the bony ridge over each eye 2 the arch of hair on this ridge 3 **raise an eyebrow** to show doubt or disapproval

eye-catching *adj* very striking and tending to catch people's attention **eye-catcher** *n*

eye dog *n NZ* a dog trained to control sheep by staring at them

eyeful *n* 1 *slang* a good look at or view of something 2 *slang* an attractive sight, esp. a woman 3 an amount of liquid, dust, etc. that has got into someone's eye

eyeglass *n* a lens for aiding defective vision

eyelash *n* any of the short hairs that grow from the edge of the eyelids

eyelet *n* 1 a small hole for a lace or cord to be passed through 2 a small metal ring reinforcing such a hole

eyelevel *adj* level with a person's eyes: *an eyelevel oven*

eyelid *n* either of the two folds of skin that cover an eye when it is closed

eyeliner *n* a cosmetic used to outline the eyes

eye-opener *n informal* something startling or revealing

eyepiece *n* the lens in a microscope, telescope, etc. into which the person using it looks

eye shadow *n* a coloured cosmetic worn on the upper eyelids

eyesight *n* the ability to see: *poor eyesight*

eyesore *n* something very ugly

eyestrain *n* fatigue or irritation of the eyes, caused by tiredness or a failure to wear glasses

eyetooth *n, pl* **-teeth** 1 either of the two canine teeth in the upper jaw 2 **give one's eyeteeth for** to go to any lengths to achieve or obtain (something)

eye up *vb informal* to look at (someone) in a way that indicates sexual interest

eyewash *n* 1 a lotion for the eyes 2 *informal* nonsense; rubbish

eyewitness *n* a person present at an event who can describe what happened

Eyre[1] *n* **Lake Eyre** a shallow salt lake or salt flat in NE central South Australia, about 11 m (35 ft) below sea level, divided into two areas (North and South); it usually contains little or no water. Maximum area: 9600 sq km (3700 sq miles)
WORD ORIGIN C19: named after Edward John *Eyre*

Eyre[2] *n* 1 **Edward John** 1815–1901, British explorer and colonial administrator. He was governor of Jamaica (1864–66) until his authorization of 400 executions to suppress an uprising led to his recall 2 Sir **Richard** born 1943, British theatre director: director of the Royal National Theatre (1988–97)

eyrie *n* 1 the nest of an eagle, built in a high inaccessible place 2 any high isolated place
WORD ORIGIN Latin *area* open field, hence, nest

Eysenck *n* **Hans Jürgen** 1916–97, British psychologist, born in Germany, who developed a dimensional theory of personality that stressed the influence of heredity

THESAURUS

eye *n* **1, 2 = eyeball**, optic (*informal*), peeper (*slang*), orb (*poetic*), organ of vision, organ of sight **3** (*often plural*) **= eyesight**, sight, vision, observation, perception, ability to see, range of vision, power of seeing **5 = observance**, observation, supervision, surveillance, attention, notice, inspection, heed, vigil, watch, lookout, vigilance, alertness, watchfulness **6 = appreciation**, taste, recognition, judgment, discrimination, perception, discernment **10 = centre**, heart, middle, mid, core, nucleus ▷ *vb* **29 = look at**, view, study, watch, check, regard, survey, clock (*Brit slang*), observe, stare at, scan, contemplate, check out (*informal*), inspect, glance at, gaze at, behold (*archaic, literary*), eyeball (*slang*), scrutinize, peruse, get a load of (*informal*), take a dekko at (*Brit slang*), have *or* take a look at ▸ *related adjectives*: ocular, ophthalmic, optic

Ff

f[1] *physics* frequency
f[2], **f/** *or* **f:** f-number
F **1** *music* the fourth note of the scale of C major **2** Fahrenheit **3** farad(s) **4** *chem* fluorine **5** *physics* force **6** franc(s)
f. *or* **F.** **1** fathom(s) **2** female **3** *grammar* feminine **4** *pl* **ff.** following (page)
fa *n music* ▸ same as **fah**
FA (in Britain) Football Association
F.A.B. *interj Brit informal* an expression of agreement to, or acknowledgement of, a command
WORD ORIGIN from British television series, *Thunderbirds*
Fabian (fay-bee-an) *adj* **1** of the Fabian Society, which aims to establish socialism gradually and democratically ▹*n* **2** a member of the Fabian Society **Fabianism** *n*
WORD ORIGIN after *Fabius,* Roman general, who wore out Hannibal's strength while avoiding a pitched battle
fable ❶ *n* **1** a short story, often one with animals as characters, that illustrates a moral **2** an unlikely story which is usually untrue **3** a story about mythical characters or events
WORD ORIGIN Latin *fabula* story
fabled *adj* well-known from anecdotes and stories rather than experience: *the fabled Timbuktu*
Fablon *n trademark* a brand of adhesive-backed plastic used for covering surfaces
Fabre *n* **Jean Henri** 1823–1915, French entomologist; author of many works on insect life, remarkable for their vivid and minute observation, esp. *Souvenirs Entomologiques* (1879–1907). Nobel prize for literature 1910
fabric ❶ *n* **1** any cloth made from yarn or fibres by weaving or knitting **2** the structure that holds a system together: *the fabric of society* **3** the walls, floor, and roof of a building
WORD ORIGIN Latin *faber* craftsman
fabricate *vb* **-cating, -cated** **1** to invent a story or lie: *fabricated reports about the opposition* **2** to make or build **fabrication** *n*
WORD ORIGIN Latin *fabrica* workshop
Fabry *n* **Charles** 1867–1945, French physicist: discovered ozone in the upper atmosphere
fabulous ❶ *adj* **1** *informal* extremely good **2** almost unbelievable: *a city of fabulous wealth* **3** told of in fables and legends: *a fabulous horned creature* **fabulously** *adv*
WORD ORIGIN Latin *fabulosus* celebrated in fable
façade ❶ (fass-**sahd**) *n* **1** the front of a building **2** a front or deceptive outer appearance
WORD ORIGIN French
face ❶ *n* **1** the front of the head from the forehead to the lower jaw **2** **a** one's expression: *as his eyes met hers his face sobered* **b** a distorted expression to show disgust or defiance: *she was pulling a face at him* **3** the front or main side of an object, building, etc. **4** the surface of a clock or watch that has the numbers or hands on it **5** the functional side of an object, such as a tool or playing card **6** the exposed area of a mine from which coal or metal can be mined **7** *Brit slang* a well-known or important person **8** **in the face of** in spite of: *a determined character in the face of adversity* **9** **lose face** to lose one's credibility **10** **on the face of it** to all appearances **11** **put a good** *or* **brave face on** to maintain a cheerful appearance despite misfortune **12** **save face** to keep one's good reputation **13** **set one's face against** to oppose with determination **14** **to someone's face** directly and openly ▹*vb* **facing, faced** **15** to look towards **16** to be opposite **17** to be confronted by: *they were faced with the prospect of high inflation* **18** to provide with a surface of a different material ▸ See also **face up to**
WORD ORIGIN Latin *facies* form
face card *n* a playing card showing a king, queen, or jack
faceless *adj* without individual identity or character: *faceless government officials*
face-lift *n* **1** cosmetic surgery for tightening sagging skin and smoothing wrinkles on the face **2** an outward improvement designed to give a more modern appearance: *the stadium was given a face-lift*
facer *n Brit old-fashioned informal* a difficulty or problem
face-saving *adj* preventing damage to one's reputation **face-saver** *n*
facet *n* **1** an aspect of something, such as a personality **2** any of the surfaces of a cut gemstone
WORD ORIGIN French *facette* little face
facetious (fass-**see**-shuss) *adj* joking, or trying to be amusing, esp. at inappropriate times **facetiously** *adv*
WORD ORIGIN Old French *facetie* witticism
face up to ❶ *vb* to accept an unpleasant fact or reality
face value *n* apparent worth or meaning: *only a fool would take it at face value*
facia (fay-shee-a) *n, pl* **-ciae** (-shee-ee) ▸ same as **fascia**
facial *adj* **1** of the face ▹*n* **2** a beauty treatment for the face **facially** *adv*
facile (fass-ile) *adj* **1** (of a remark, argument, etc.) overly simple and showing lack of real thought

THESAURUS

fable *n* **1, 3 = legend**, myth, parable, allegory, story, tale, apologue **2 = fiction**, lie, fantasy, myth, romance, invention, yarn *(informal)*, fabrication, falsehood, fib, figment, untruth, fairy story *(informal)*, urban myth, white lie, tall story *(informal)*, urban legend **OPPOSITE:** fact
fabric *n* **1 = cloth**, material, stuff, textile, web **2 = framework**, structure, make-up, organization, frame, foundations, construction, constitution, infrastructure **3 = structure**, foundations, construction, framework, infrastructure
fabulous *adj* **1** *(informal)* **= wonderful**, excellent, brilliant, superb, spectacular, fantastic *(informal)*, marvellous, sensational *(informal)*, first-rate, brill *(informal)*, magic *(informal)*, out-of-this-world *(informal)* **OPPOSITE:** ordinary **2 = astounding**, amazing, extraordinary, remarkable, incredible, astonishing, eye-popping *(informal)*, legendary, immense, unbelievable, breathtaking, phenomenal, inconceivable **3 = legendary**, imaginary, mythical, fictitious, made-up, fantastic, invented, unreal, mythological, apocryphal
façade *n* **1 = front**, face, exterior, frontage **2 = show**, front, appearance, mask, exterior, guise, pretence, veneer, semblance
face *n* **1 = countenance**, features, kisser *(slang)*, profile, dial *(Brit slang)*, mug *(slang)*, visage, physiognomy, lineaments, phiz *or* phizog *(slang)* **2a = expression**, look, air, appearance, aspect, countenance **3 = side**, front, cover, outside, surface, aspect, exterior, right side, elevation, facet, vertical surface ▹*vb* **16 = look onto**, overlook, be opposite, look out on, front onto, give towards *or* onto **17 = confront**, meet, encounter, deal with, oppose, tackle, cope with, experience, brave, defy, come up against, be confronted by, face off *(slang)*
face up to *vb* **= accept**, deal with, tackle, acknowledge, cope with, confront, come to terms with, meet head-on, reconcile yourself to

DICTIONARY

2 easily performed or achieved: *a facile winner of his only race this year*
WORD ORIGIN Latin *facilis* easy

facilitate ❶ *vb* **-tating, -tated** to make easier the progress of: *the agreement helped facilitate trade between the countries* **facilitation** *n*

facility ❶ *n, pl* **-ties** 1 **facilities** the means or equipment needed for an activity: *leisure and shopping facilities* 2 the ability to do things easily and well 3 skill or ease: *grown human beings can forget with remarkable facility*
WORD ORIGIN Latin *facilis* easy

facing *n* 1 a piece of material used esp. to conceal the seam of a garment 2 **facings** contrasting collar and cuffs on a jacket 3 an outer layer of material applied to the surface of a wall

facsimile (fak-**sim**-ill-ee) *n* 1 an exact copy 2 ▸ same as **fax** (senses 1, 2)
WORD ORIGIN Latin *fac simile!* make something like it!

fact ❶ *n* 1 an event or thing known to have happened or existed 2 a truth that can be proved from experience or observation 3 a piece of information 4 **after** *or* **before the fact** *criminal law* after or before the commission of the offence 5 **as a matter of fact** *or* **in fact** in reality or actuality 6 **fact of life** an inescapable truth, esp. an unpleasant one ▸ See also **facts of life**
WORD ORIGIN Latin *factum* something done

faction[1] ❶ *n* 1 a small group of people within a larger body, but differing from it in certain aims and ideas 2 strife within a group **factional** *adj*
WORD ORIGIN Latin *factio* a making

faction[2] *n* a dramatized presentation of actual events
WORD ORIGIN blend of FACT + FICTION

factious *adj* inclined to quarrel and cause divisions: *a factious political party is unelectable*

factitious *adj* artificial rather than natural
WORD ORIGIN Latin *facticius*

factor ❶ *n* 1 an element that contributes to a result: *reliability was an important factor in the success of the car* 2 *maths* any whole number that will divide exactly into a given number, for example 2 and 3 are factors of 6 3 a quantity by which an amount is multiplied or divided to become that number of times bigger or smaller: *production increased by a factor of 3* 4 *med* any of several substances that participate in the clotting of blood: *factor VIII* 5 a level on a scale of measurement: *suntan oil with a factor of 5* 6 (in Scotland) the manager of an estate
WORD ORIGIN Latin: one who acts

factorial *maths n* 1 the product of all the whole numbers from one to a given whole number ▹ *adj* 2 of factorials or factors

factorize *or* **-rise** *vb* **-izing, -ized** *or* **-ising, -ised** *maths* to resolve a whole number into factors **factorization** *or* **-risation** *n*

factory ❶ *n, pl* **-ries** a building where goods are manufactured in large quantities
WORD ORIGIN Late Latin *factorium*, from *facere* to make

factory farm *n Brit, Austral & NZ* a farm in which animals are given foods that increase the amount of meat, eggs, or milk they yield

factory farming *n*

factory ship *n* a vessel that processes fish supplied by a fleet

factotum *n* a person employed to do all kinds of work
WORD ORIGIN Latin *fac!* do! + *totum* all

facts of life *pl n* the details of sexual behaviour and reproduction

factual ❶ *adj* concerning facts rather than opinions or theories: *a factual report* **factually** *adv*

faculty ❶ *n, pl* **-ties** 1 one of the powers of the mind or body, such as memory, sight, or hearing 2 any ability or power, either inborn or acquired: *his faculties of reasoning were considerable* 3 **a** a department within a university or college **b** its staff **c** *chiefly US & Canad* all the teaching staff of a university, school, or college
WORD ORIGIN Latin *facultas* capability

fad ❶ *n informal* 1 an intense but short-lived fashion: *the skateboard fad* 2 a personal whim **faddish** *adj*
WORD ORIGIN origin unknown

faddy *adj* **-dier, -diest** unreasonably fussy, particularly about food

fade ❶ *vb* **fading, faded** 1 to lose brightness, colour, or strength 2 **fade away** *or* **out** to vanish slowly
WORD ORIGIN Middle English *fade* dull

fade in *or* **out** *vb* (of vision or sound in a film or broadcast) to increase or decrease gradually

faeces *or esp. US* **feces** (**fee**-seez) *pl n* bodily waste matter discharged through the anus **faecal** *or esp. US* **fecal** (**fee**-kl) *adj*
WORD ORIGIN Latin: dregs

f

THESAURUS

facilitate *vb* = **further**, help, forward, promote, ease, speed up, pave the way for, make easy, expedite, oil the wheels of, smooth the path of, assist the progress of **OPPOSITE:** hinder

facility *n* 1 *(pl)* = **amenity**, means, aid, opportunity, advantage, resource, equipment, provision, convenience, appliance 2 = **ability**, skill, talent, gift, craft, efficiency, knack, fluency, proficiency, dexterity, quickness, adroitness, expertness, skilfulness 3 = **ease**, readiness, fluency, smoothness, effortlessness **OPPOSITE:** difficulty

fact *n* 1 = **event**, happening, act, performance, incident, deed, occurrence, fait accompli *(French)* 2 = **truth**, reality, gospel (truth), certainty, verity, actuality, naked truth **OPPOSITE:** fiction

faction[1] *n* 1 = **group**, set, party, division, section, camp, sector, minority, combination, coalition, gang, lobby, bloc, contingent, pressure group, caucus, junta, clique, coterie, schism, confederacy, splinter group, cabal, ginger group, public-interest group *(US & Canad)* 2 = **dissension**, division, conflict, rebellion, disagreement, friction, strife, turbulence, variance, discord, infighting, disunity, sedition, tumult, disharmony, divisiveness **OPPOSITE:** agreement

factor *n* 1 = **element**, thing, point, part, cause, influence, item, aspect, circumstance, characteristic, consideration, component, determinant

factory *n* = **works**, plant, mill, workshop, assembly line, shop floor, manufactory *(obsolete)*

factual *adj* = **true**, objective, authentic, unbiased, close, real, sure, correct, genuine, accurate, exact, precise, faithful, credible, matter-of-fact, literal, veritable, circumstantial, unadorned, dinkum *(Austral & NZ informal)*, true-to-life **OPPOSITE:** fictitious

faculty *n* 1 = **power**, reason, sense, intelligence, mental ability, physical ability 2 = **ability**, power, skill, facility, talent, gift, capacity, bent, capability, readiness, knack, propensity, aptitude, dexterity, cleverness, adroitness, turn **OPPOSITE:** failing 3a = **department**, school, discipline, profession, branch of learning 3b, 3c = **teaching staff**, staff, teachers, professors, lecturers *(chiefly US)*

fad *n* 1 = **craze**, fashion, trend, fancy, rage, mode, vogue, mania 2 = **whim**, affectation

fade *vb* 1a = **become pale**, dull, dim, bleach, wash out, blanch, discolour, blench, lose colour, lose lustre, decolour 1b = **grow dim**, dim, fade away, become less loud 1c *(with* **away** *or* **out**) = **dwindle**, disappear, vanish, melt away, fall, fail, decline, flag, dissolve, dim, disperse, wither, wilt, wane, perish, ebb, languish, die out, droop, shrivel, die away, waste away, vanish into thin air, become unimportant, evanesce, etiolate

DICTIONARY

Faeroese *or* **Faroese** (fair-oh-eez) *adj* **1** of the Faeroes, islands in the N Atlantic ▷ *n* **2** *pl* **-ese** a person from the Faeroes **3** the language of the Faeroes

faff about *vb Brit & S African informal* to dither or fuss
WORD ORIGIN origin unknown

fag[1] *n* **1** *informal* a boring or tiring task: *weeding was a fag* **2** *Brit* (esp. formerly) a young public school boy who performs menial chores for an older boy ▷ *vb* **fagging, fagged 3** *Brit* to do menial chores in a public school
WORD ORIGIN origin unknown

fag[2] *n slang* a cigarette
WORD ORIGIN origin unknown

fag[3] *n offensive slang, chiefly US & Canad* ▸ short for **faggot**[2]

fag end *n* **1** the last and worst part: *another dull game at the fag end of the football season* **2** *Brit & NZ informal* the stub of a cigarette

fagged *adj informal* exhausted by hard work. Also: **fagged out**

faggot[1] *or esp. US* **fagot** *n* **1** *Brit, Austral & NZ* a ball of chopped liver bound with herbs and bread **2** a bundle of sticks
WORD ORIGIN from Old French

faggot[2] *n offensive slang* a male homosexual
WORD ORIGIN special use of FAGGOT[1]

fah *n music* (in tonic sol-fa) the fourth note of any ascending major scale

Fahd ibn Abdul Aziz *n* 1923–2005, king of Saudi Arabia (1982–2005)

Fahrenheit (far-ren-hite) *adj* of or measured according to the scale of temperature in which 32° represents the melting point of ice and 212° the boiling point of water
WORD ORIGIN after Gabriel *Fahrenheit*, physicist

Faidherbe *n* **Louis Léon César** 1818–89, French soldier and governor of Senegal (1854–65); founder of Dakar

faïence (fie-ence) *n* tin-glazed earthenware
WORD ORIGIN *Faenza*, N Italy, where made

fail *vb* **1** to be unsuccessful in an attempt **2** to stop operating **3** to judge or be judged as being below the officially accepted standard required in a course or examination **4** to prove disappointing or useless to someone: *the government has failed the homeless* **5** to neglect or be unable to do something: *he failed to repair the car* **6** to go bankrupt ▷ *n* **7** a failure to attain the required standard **8 without fail a** regularly or without exception: *use this shampoo once a week without fail* **b** definitely: *they agreed to enforce the embargo without fail*
WORD ORIGIN Latin *fallere* to disappoint

failing *n* **1** a weak point ▷ *prep* **2 failing that** alternatively: *your doctor will normally be able to advise you or, failing that, one of the self-help agencies*

fail-safe *adj* **1** designed to return to a safe condition in the event of a failure or malfunction **2** safe from failure

failure *n* **1** the act or an instance of failing **2** someone or something that is unsuccessful: *he couldn't help but regard his own son as a failure* **3** the fact of something required or expected not being done or not happening: *his failure to appear at the meeting* **4** a halt in normal operation: *heart failure* **5** a decline or loss of something: *crop failure* **6** the fact of not reaching the required standard in an examination or test

fain *adv old-fashioned* gladly or willingly
WORD ORIGIN Old English *fægen*

faint *adj* **1** lacking clarity, brightness, or volume: *her voice was very faint* **2** feeling dizzy or weak **3** lacking conviction or force: *a faint attempt to smile* ▷ *vb* **4** to lose consciousness ▷ *n* **5** a sudden loss of consciousness **faintly** *adv*
WORD ORIGIN Old French *faindre* to be idle

faint-hearted *adj* lacking courage and confidence

fair[1] *adj* **1** reasonable and just: *a move towards fair trade* **2** in agreement with rules **3** light in colour: *her fair skin* **4** *old-fashioned* young and beautiful: *a fair maiden* **5** quite good: *a fair attempt at making a soufflé* **6** quite large: *they made a fair amount of money* **7** (of the tide or wind) favourable to the passage of a ship or plane **8** fine or cloudless **9 fair and square** in a

THESAURUS

fail *vb* **1 = be unsuccessful**, founder, fall flat, come to nothing, fall, miss, go down, break down, flop *(informal)*, be defeated, fall short, fall through, fall short of, fizzle out *(informal)*, come unstuck, run aground, miscarry, be in vain, misfire, fall by the wayside, go astray, come to grief, come a cropper *(informal)*, bite the dust, go up in smoke, go belly-up *(slang)*, come to naught, lay an egg *(slang, chiefly US & Canad)*, go by the board, not make the grade *(informal)*, go down like a lead balloon *(informal)*, turn out badly, fall flat on your face, meet with disaster, be found lacking *or* wanting **OPPOSITE:** succeed
2a = stop working, stop, die, give up, break down, cease, stall, cut out, malfunction, conk out *(informal)*, go on the blink *(informal)*, go phut
2b = give out, disappear, fade, dim, dwindle, wane, gutter, languish, peter out, die away, grow dim, sink
4 = disappoint, abandon, desert, neglect, omit, let down, forsake, turn your back on, be disloyal to, break your word, forget **6 = go bankrupt**, crash, collapse, fold *(informal)*, close down, go under, go bust *(informal)*, go out of business, be wound up, go broke *(informal)*, go to the wall, go into receivership, go into liquidation, become insolvent, smash
8a without fail = without exception, regularly, constantly, invariably, religiously, unfailingly, conscientiously, like clockwork, punctually, dependably

failing *n* **1 = shortcoming**, failure, fault, error, weakness, defect, deficiency, lapse, flaw, miscarriage, drawback, misfortune, blemish, imperfection, frailty, foible, blind spot **OPPOSITE:** strength

failure *n* **1 = lack of success**, defeat, collapse, abortion, wreck, frustration, breakdown, overthrow, miscarriage, fiasco, downfall
OPPOSITE: success
2 = loser, disappointment, no-good, flop *(informal)*, write-off, incompetent, no-hoper *(chiefly Austral)*, dud *(informal)*, clinker *(slang, chiefly US)*, black sheep, washout *(informal)*, clunker *(informal)*, dead duck *(slang)*, ne'er-do-well, nonstarter

faint *adj* **1a = dim**, low, light, soft, thin, faded, whispered, distant, dull, delicate, vague, unclear, muted, subdued, faltering, hushed, bleached, feeble, indefinite, muffled, hazy, ill-defined, indistinct
OPPOSITE: clear
1b = slight, weak, feeble, unenthusiastic, remote, slim, vague, slender **2 = dizzy**, giddy, light-headed, vertiginous, weak, exhausted, fatigued, faltering, wobbly, drooping, languid, lethargic, muzzy, woozy *(informal)*, weak at the knees, enervated
OPPOSITE: energetic
▷ *vb* **4 = pass out**, black out, lose consciousness, keel over *(informal)*, fail, go out, collapse, fade, weaken, languish, swoon *(literary)*, flake out *(informal)* ▷ *n* **5 = blackout**, collapse, coma, swoon *(literary)*, unconsciousness, syncope *(pathology)*

fair[1] *adj* **1, 2 = unbiased**, impartial, even-handed, unprejudiced, just, clean, square, equal, objective, reasonable, proper, legitimate, upright, honourable, honest, equitable, lawful, trustworthy, on the level *(informal)*, disinterested, dispassionate, above board, according to the rules
OPPOSITE: unfair

DICTIONARY

correct or just way ▷ *adv* **10** in a fair way **11** absolutely or squarely: *he was caught fair off his guard* **fairness** *n*
WORD ORIGIN Old English *fæger*

fair² ❶ *n* **1** a travelling entertainment with sideshows, rides, and amusements **2** an exhibition of goods produced by a particular industry to promote business: *the Frankfurt book fair*
WORD ORIGIN Latin *feriae* holidays

Fairbanks¹ *n* a city in central Alaska, at the terminus of the Alaska Highway. Pop: 30 970 (2003 est)

Fairbanks² *n* **1 Douglas (Elton)**, real name *Julius Ullman*. 1883–1939, US film actor and producer **2** his son, **Douglas, Jnr** 1909–2000, US film actor

fair copy *n* a neat copy, without mistakes or alterations, of a piece of writing

Fairfax *n* **Thomas,** 3rd Baron Fairfax. 1612–71, English general and statesman: commanded the Parliamentary army (1645–50), defeating Charles I at Naseby (1645). He was instrumental in restoring Charles II to the throne (1660)

fair game *n* a person regarded as a justifiable target for criticism or ridicule

fairground *n* an open space used for a fair

fairing *n* a metal structure fitted around parts of an aircraft, car, etc. to reduce drag
WORD ORIGIN *fair* to streamline

Fair Isle *n* an intricate multicoloured knitted pattern
WORD ORIGIN after one of the Shetland Islands where this type of pattern originated

fairly ❶ *adv* **1** to a moderate degree or extent: *in the Philippines labour is fairly cheap* **2** to a great degree or extent: *the folder fairly bulged with documents* **3** as deserved: *the pound was fairly valued against the Deutschmark*

fair play *n* a conventional standard of honourable behaviour

fair sex *n* **the fair sex** *old-fashioned* women collectively

fair trade *n* the practice of buying goods from producers in the developing world at a guaranteed price

fairway *n* **1** (on a golf course) the mown areas between tees and greens **2** *naut* a part of a river or sea on which ships may sail

fair-weather *adj* not reliable in difficult situations: *a fair-weather friend*

fairy ❶ *n, pl* **fairies 1** an imaginary supernatural being with magical powers **2** *offensive slang* a male homosexual
WORD ORIGIN Old French *faerie* fairyland, from *feie* fairy

fairy floss *n Austral* a light fluffy mass of spun sugar, held on a stick. Also called: **candy floss**

fairy godmother *n* a generous friend who appears unexpectedly and offers help in time of trouble

fairyland *n* **1** an imaginary place where fairies live **2** an enchanted or wonderful place

fairy lights *pl n* small coloured electric bulbs used as decoration, esp. on a Christmas tree

fairy penguin *n* a small penguin with a bluish head and back, found on the Australian coast

fairy ring *n* a ring of dark grass caused by fungi

fairy tale ❶ *or* **story** *n* **1** a story about fairies or magical events **2** a highly improbable account: *his report was little more than a fairy tale* ▷ *adj* **fairy-tale 3** of or like a fairy tale: *a fairy-tale wedding* **4** highly improbable: *a fairy-tale account of his achievements*

Faisal I *or* **Feisal I** *n* 1885–1933, king of Syria (1920) and first king of Iraq (1921–33): a leader of the Arab revolt against the Turks (1916–18)

Faisal Ibn Abdul Aziz *n* 1905–75, king of Saudi Arabia (1964–75)

Faisal II *or* **Feisal II** *n* 1935–58, last king of Iraq (1939–58)

fait accompli (fate ak-kom-plee) *n* something already done and beyond alteration: *they had to accept the invasion as a fait accompli*
WORD ORIGIN French

faith ❶ *n* **1** strong belief in something, esp. without proof **2** a specific system of religious beliefs **3** complete confidence or trust, such as in a person or remedy **4** allegiance to a person or cause **5 bad faith** dishonesty **6 good faith** honesty
WORD ORIGIN Latin *fides* trust, confidence

faithful ❶ *adj* **1** remaining true or loyal **2** maintaining sexual loyalty to one's lover or spouse **3** consistently reliable: *my old, but faithful, four-cylinder car* **4** accurate in detail: *a faithful translation of the book* ▷ *pl n* **the faithful 5 a** the believers in a religious faith **b** loyal followers **faithfully** *adv* **faithfulness** *n*

faith healing *n* treatment of a sick person through the power of religious faith **faith healer** *n*

faithless *adj* treacherous or disloyal

fajitas (fa-hee-taz) *pl n* a Mexican dish of soft tortillas wrapped around fried strips of meat or vegetables
WORD ORIGIN Mexican Spanish

fake ❶ *vb* **faking, faked 1** to cause something not genuine to appear real or more valuable by fraud **2** to pretend to have (an illness, emotion,

f

THESAURUS

3 = light, golden, blonde *or* blond, yellowish, fair-haired, light-coloured, flaxen-haired, towheaded, tow-haired **4** *(old-fashioned)* **= beautiful**, pretty, attractive, lovely, handsome, good-looking, bonny, comely, beauteous, well-favoured, fit *(Brit informal)* **OPPOSITE:** ugly
5, 6 = respectable, middling, average, reasonable, decent, acceptable, moderate, adequate, satisfactory, not bad, mediocre, so-so *(informal)*, tolerable, passable, O.K. *or* okay *(informal)*, all right **8 = fine**, clear, dry, bright, pleasant, sunny, favourable, clement, cloudless, unclouded, sunshiny

fair² *n* **1 = carnival**, fête, gala, bazaar **2 = exhibition**, show, market, festival, mart, expo *(informal)*, exposition

fairly *adv* **1 = moderately**, rather, quite, somewhat, reasonably, adequately, pretty well, tolerably, passably **2 = positively**, really, simply, absolutely, in a manner of speaking, veritably **3 = equitably**, objectively, legitimately, honestly, justly, lawfully, without prejudice, dispassionately, impartially, even-handedly, without bias

fairy *n* **1 = sprite**, elf, brownie, hob, pixie, puck, imp, leprechaun, peri, Robin Goodfellow

fairy tale *or* **fairy story** *n* **1 = folk tale**, romance, traditional story **2 = lie**, fantasy, fiction, invention, fabrication, untruth, porky *(Brit slang)*, pork pie *(Brit slang)*, urban myth, tall story, urban legend, cock-and-bull story *(informal)*

faith *n* **2 = religion**, church, belief, persuasion, creed, communion, denomination, dogma **OPPOSITE:** agnosticism
3 = confidence, trust, credit, conviction, assurance, dependence, reliance, credence **OPPOSITE:** distrust

faithful *adj* **1, 3 = loyal**, true, committed, constant, attached, devoted, dedicated, reliable, staunch, truthful, dependable, trusty, steadfast, unwavering, true-blue, immovable, unswerving **OPPOSITE:** disloyal
4 = accurate, just, close, true, strict, exact, precise

fake *vb* **1 = forge**, copy, reproduce, fabricate, counterfeit, falsify **2 = sham**, affect, assume, put on, pretend, simulate, feign, go through the motions of ▷ *n* **3a = forgery**, copy, fraud, reproduction, dummy, imitation, hoax, counterfeit **3b = charlatan**, deceiver, sham, quack, mountebank, phoney *or* phony *(informal)* ▷ *adj* **4 = artificial**, false, forged, counterfeit, affected, assumed, put-on, pretend *(informal)*,

DICTIONARY

etc.) ▹*n* **3** an object, person, or act that is not genuine ▹*adj* **4** not genuine: *fake fur*
WORD ORIGIN probably from Italian *facciare* to make or do

fakir (fay-keer) *n* **1** a Muslim religious ascetic who spurns worldly possessions **2** a Hindu holy man
WORD ORIGIN Arabic *faqīr* poor

falcon *n* a type of bird of prey that can be trained to hunt other birds and small animals
WORD ORIGIN Late Latin *falco* hawk

falconry *n* **1** the art of training falcons to hunt **2** the sport of hunting with falcons **falconer** *n*

Faldo *n* **Nick** born 1957, British golfer: winner of the British Open Championship (1987, 1990, 1992) and the US Masters (1989, 1990, 1996)

fall ❶ *vb* **falling, fell, fallen 1** to descend by the force of gravity from a higher to a lower place **2** to drop suddenly from an upright position **3** to collapse to the ground **4** to become less or lower in number or quality: *inflation fell by one percentage point* **5** to slope downwards **6** to be badly wounded or killed **7** to give in to attack: *in 1939 Barcelona fell to the Nationalists* **8** to lose power or status **9** to pass into a specified condition: *I fell asleep* **10** to adopt a downhearted expression: *his face fell and he pouted like a child* **11** (of night or darkness) to begin **12** to occur at a specified time: *Christmas falls on a Sunday* **13** to give in to temptation or sin **14 fall apart a** to break owing to long use or poor construction: *the chassis is falling apart* **b** to become disorganized and ineffective: *since you resigned, the office has fallen apart* **15 fall short** to prove inadequate **16 fall short of** to fail to reach (a standard) ▹*n* **17** an instance of falling **18** an amount of something, such as snow or soot, that has fallen **19** a decrease in value or number **20** a decline in status or importance: *the town's fall from prosperity* **21** a capture or overthrow: *the fall of Budapest in February 1945* **22** *wrestling* a scoring move, pinning both shoulders of one's opponent to the floor for a specified period **23** *chiefly US* autumn ▸See also **fall about, fall away, falls**, etc.
WORD ORIGIN Old English *feallan*

Fall *n* **the Fall** *theol* the state of mankind's innate sinfulness following Adam's sin of disobeying God

Falla *n* **Manuel de** 1876–1946, Spanish composer and pianist, composer of the opera *La Vida Breve* (1905), the ballet *The Three-Cornered Hat* (1919), guitar and piano music, and songs

fall about *vb* to laugh uncontrollably

fallacy *n, pl* **-cies 1** an incorrect or misleading notion based on inaccurate facts or faulty reasoning: *the fallacy underlying the government's industrial policy* **2** reasoning that is unsound **fallacious** *adj*
WORD ORIGIN Latin *fallere* to deceive

fall away *vb* **1** to slope down: *the ground fell away sharply to the south* **2** to decrease in size or intensity: *obstacles to all-party talks are falling away with amazing speed*

fall back *vb* **1** to retreat **2 fall back on** to have to choose (a less acceptable alternative): *they had to fall back on other lines of defence*

fall behind *vb* **1** to fail to keep up **2** to be in arrears, such as with a payment

fall down *vb* **1** to drop suddenly or collapse **2** to fail to meet requirements **3** (of an argument or idea) to fail at a specific point: *in one area only did the case fall down*

fallen *vb* **1** ▸the past participle of **fall** ▹*adj* **2** *old-fashioned* (of a woman) having had sex outside marriage **3** killed in battle

fall for *vb* **1** to become strongly attracted to (someone) **2** to be deceived by (a lie or trick)

fall guy *n informal* **1** the victim of a confidence trick **2** a person who is publicly blamed for something, though it may not be his or her fault

fallible *adj* **1** (of a person) liable to make mistakes **2** capable of error: *our all-too-fallible economic indicators* **fallibility** *n*
WORD ORIGIN Latin *fallere* to deceive

fall in *vb* **1** to collapse **2** to get into line or formation in a display, march, or procession **3 fall in with a** to meet and join **b** to agree with or support (a person or a suggestion)

falling star *n informal* a meteor

fall off *vb* **1** to drop unintentionally to the ground from (a bicycle, horse, etc.) **2** to decrease in size or intensity: *demand for beef began to fall off*

fall on *vb* **1** to attack (an enemy) **2** to meet with (something unpleasant): *his family had fallen on hard times* **3** to affect: *a horrified hush fell on the company* **4 fall on one's feet** to emerge unexpectedly well from a difficult situation

Fallopian tube *n* either of a pair of slender tubes through which eggs pass from the ovaries to the uterus in female mammals
WORD ORIGIN after Gabriello *Fallopio*, anatomist

fallout *n* **1** radioactive material in the atmosphere following a nuclear explosion **2** unpleasant circumstances following an event: *the political fallout of the riots* ▹*vb* **fall out 3** *informal* to disagree and quarrel: *I hope we don't fall out over this issue* **4** to leave a military formation

fallow[1] *adj* (of land) left unseeded after being ploughed to regain fertility for a future crop
WORD ORIGIN Old English *fealga*

fallow[2] *adj* light yellowish-brown
WORD ORIGIN Old English *fealu*

fallow deer *n* a deer that has a reddish coat with white spots in summer

falls *pl n* a waterfall

fall through *vb* to fail before completion: *his transfer deal fell through*

fall to *vb* **1** to become the responsibility of: *it fell to the Prime Minister to announce the plans* **2** to begin (some activity, such as eating, working, or fighting)

false ❶ *adj* **1** not in accordance with the truth or facts: *false allegations* **2** not real or genuine but intended to seem so: *false teeth* **3** misleading or deceptive: *their false promises* **4** forced or insincere: *false cheer* **5** based on

THESAURUS

mock, imitation, sham, pseudo *(informal)*, feigned, pinchbeck, phoney *or* phony *(informal)*
OPPOSITE: genuine

fall *vb* **1, 2, 3 = drop**, plunge, tumble, plummet, trip, settle, crash, collapse, pitch, sink, go down, come down, dive, stumble, descend, topple, subside, cascade, trip over, drop down, nose-dive, come a cropper *(informal)*, keel over, go head over heels **OPPOSITE:** rise
4 = decrease, drop, decline, go down, flag, slump, diminish, fall off, dwindle, lessen, subside, ebb, abate, depreciate, become lower
OPPOSITE: increase
6 = be killed, die, be lost, perish, be slain, be a casualty, meet your end
OPPOSITE: survive
7 = be overthrown, be taken, surrender, succumb, yield, submit, give way, capitulate, be conquered, give in *or* up, pass into enemy hands
OPPOSITE: triumph
12 = occur, happen, come about, chance, take place, fall out, befall, come to pass ▹*n* **17 = drop**, slip, plunge, dive, spill, tumble, descent, plummet, nose dive **19 = decrease**, drop, lowering, decline, reduction, slump, dip, falling off, dwindling, lessening, diminution, cut
21 = collapse, defeat, surrender, downfall, death, failure, ruin, resignation, destruction, overthrow, submission, capitulation

false *adj* **1 = incorrect**, wrong, mistaken, misleading, faulty, inaccurate, invalid, improper, unfounded, erroneous, inexact
OPPOSITE: correct
2 = artificial, forged, fake, mock, reproduction, synthetic, replica, imitation, bogus, simulated, sham,

DICTIONARY

mistaken ideas **falsely** *adv* **falseness** *n*
WORD ORIGIN Latin *falsus*

false alarm *n* a situation that appears to be dangerous but turns out not to be: *air-raid sirens sounded once but it turned out to be a false alarm*

falsehood *n* **1** the quality of being untrue **2** a lie

false pretences *pl n* **under false pretences** so as to mislead people about one's true intentions

false start *n athletics & swimming* an occasion when one competitor starts a race before the starter's signal has been given, which means that all competitors have to be recalled and the race restarted

falsetto *n, pl* **-tos** a voice pitch higher than one's normal range
WORD ORIGIN Italian

falsies *pl n informal* pads worn to exaggerate the size of a woman's breasts

falsify *vb* **-fies, -fying, -fied** to make a report or evidence false by alteration in order to deceive **falsification** *n*
WORD ORIGIN Latin *falsus* false + *facere* to make

falsity *n, pl* **-ties 1** the state of being false **2** a lie

falter ● *vb* **1** to be hesitant, weak, or unsure **2** (of a machine) to lose power or strength in an uneven way: *the engine began to falter and the plane lost height* **3** to speak nervously and without confidence **4** to stop moving smoothly and start moving unsteadily: *as he neared the house his steps faltered* **faltering** *adj*
WORD ORIGIN origin unknown

fame ● *n* the state of being widely known or recognized
WORD ORIGIN Latin *fama* report

famed *adj* extremely well-known: *a nation famed for its efficiency*

familial *adj formal* of or relating to the family

familiar ● *adj* **1** well-known **2** frequent or common: *it was a familiar argument* **3 familiar with** well acquainted with **4** friendly and informal **5** more intimate than is acceptable ▷ *n* **6** an animal or bird believed to share with a witch her supernatural powers **7** a friend **familiarly** *adv* **familiarity** *n*
WORD ORIGIN Latin *familia* family

familiarize *or* **-rise** *vb* **-rizing, -rized** *or* **-rising, -rised** to make (oneself or someone else) fully aware of a particular subject **familiarization** *or* **-risation** *n*

family ● *n, pl* **-lies 1** a social group consisting of parents and their offspring ▸ Related adjective: **familial 2** one's wife or husband and one's children **3** one's children **4** a group descended from a common ancestor **5** all the people living together in one household **6** any group of related objects or beings: *a family of chemicals* **7** *biol* one of the groups into which an order is divided, containing one or more genera: *the cat family* ▷ *adj* **8** of or suitable for a family or any of its members: *films for a family audience* **9 in the family way** *informal* pregnant
WORD ORIGIN Latin *familia*

Family Allowance *n* **1** ▸ in Britain, a former name for **child benefit 2** (in Canada) an allowance formerly paid by the Federal Government to the parents of dependent children

family assistance *n* (in New Zealand) a tax credit given to families on the basis of their income and family size

family doctor *n Brit, Austral & NZ informal* ▸ same as **general practitioner**

family man *n* **1** a man with a wife and children **2** a man who loves his family and spends a lot of time with them

family name *n* a surname, esp. when regarded as representing a family's good reputation

family planning *n* the control of the number of children in a family by the use of contraceptives

family tree *n* a chart showing the relationships between individuals in a family over many generations

famine ● *n* a severe shortage of food
WORD ORIGIN Latin *fames* hunger

famish *vb* **be famished** *or* **famishing** to be very hungry
WORD ORIGIN Latin *fames* hunger

famous ● *adj* known to or recognized by many people
WORD ORIGIN Latin *famosus*

famously *adv* **1** well-known: *her famously relaxed manner* **2** very well: *the two got on famously*

fan[1] ● *n* **1** any device for creating a current of air, esp. a rotating machine of blades attached to a central hub **2** a hand-held object, usually made of paper, which creates a draught of cool air when waved **3** something shaped like such a fan, such as the tail of certain birds ▷ *vb* **fanning, fanned 4** to create a draught of air in the direction of someone or something **5 fan out** to spread out in the shape of a fan: *the troops fanned out along the beach*
WORD ORIGIN Latin *vannus*

f

THESAURUS

pseudo *(informal)*, counterfeit, feigned, spurious, ersatz, pretended
OPPOSITE: real
3 = untrue, fraudulent, unreal, concocted, fictitious, trumped up, fallacious, untruthful, truthless
OPPOSITE: true

falter *vb* **1 = hesitate**, delay, waver, vacillate, break **OPPOSITE:** persevere
3 = stutter, pause, stumble, hesitate, stammer, speak haltingly

fame *n* **= prominence**, glory, celebrity, stardom, name, credit, reputation, honour, prestige, stature, eminence, renown, repute, public esteem, illustriousness **OPPOSITE:** obscurity

familiar *adj* **1, 2 = well-known**, household, everyday, recognized, common, stock, domestic, repeated, ordinary, conventional, routine, frequent, accustomed, customary, mundane, recognizable, common or garden *(informal)*
OPPOSITE: unfamiliar
4a = friendly, close, dear, intimate, confidential, amicable, chummy *(informal)*, buddy-buddy *(slang, chiefly US & Canad)*, palsy-walsy *(informal)*
OPPOSITE: formal
4b = relaxed, open, easy, friendly, free, near, comfortable, intimate, casual, informal, amicable, cordial, free-and-easy, unreserved, unconstrained, unceremonious, hail-fellow-well-met
5 = disrespectful, forward, bold, presuming, intrusive, presumptuous, impudent, overfamiliar, overfree

family *n* **1, 2 = relations**, people, children, issue, relatives, household, folk *(informal)*, offspring, descendants, brood, kin, nuclear family, progeny, kindred, next of kin, kinsmen, ménage, kith and kin, your nearest and dearest, kinsfolk, your own flesh and blood, ainga *(NZ)*, rellies *(Austral slang)*
3 = children, kids *(informal)*, offspring, little ones, munchkins *(informal, chiefly US)*, littlies *(Austral informal)*
4 = ancestors, forebears, parentage, forefathers, house, line, race, blood, birth, strain, tribe, sept, clan, descent, dynasty, pedigree, extraction, ancestry, lineage, genealogy, line of descent, stemma, stirps **6, 7 = species**, group, class, system, order, kind, network, genre, classification, subdivision, subclass

famine *n* **= hunger**, want, starvation, deprivation, scarcity, dearth, destitution

famous *adj* **= well-known**, celebrated, acclaimed, notable, noted, excellent, signal, honoured, remarkable, distinguished, prominent, glorious, legendary, renowned, eminent, conspicuous, illustrious, much-publicized, lionized, far-famed
OPPOSITE: unknown

fan[1] *n* **1 = blower**, ventilator, air conditioner, vane, punkah *(in India)*, blade, propeller ▷ *vb* **4 = blow**, cool, refresh, air-condition, ventilate, air-cool, winnow *(rare)*

DICTIONARY

fan[2] ⓣ *n* a person who admires or is enthusiastic about a pop star, actor, sport, or hobby: *he was a big fan of Woody Allen*
WORD ORIGIN from *fanatic*

fanatic ⓣ *n* **1** a person whose enthusiasm for something, esp. a political or religious cause, is extreme **2** *informal* a person devoted to a particular hobby or pastime ▹*adj also* **fanatical 3** excessively enthusiastic **fanatically** *adv* **fanaticism** *n*
WORD ORIGIN Latin *fanaticus* belonging to a temple, hence, inspired by a god, frenzied

fanbase *n* a body of admirers of a particular pop singer, sports team, etc.

fan belt *n* the belt that drives a cooling fan in a car engine

fancier *n* a person with a keen interest in the thing specified: *a pigeon fancier*

fanciful *adj* **1** not based on fact **2** made in a curious or imaginative way: *fanciful architecture* **3** guided by unrestrained imagination: *fanciful tales of fairy folk* **fancifully** *adv*

fan club *n* **1** an organized group of admirers of a particular pop singer or star **2 be a member of someone's fan club** *informal* to approve of someone strongly

fancy ⓣ *adj* **-cier, -ciest 1** special, unusual, and elaborate **2** (often used ironically) superior in quality **3** (of a price) higher than expected ▹*n, pl* **-cies 4** a sudden spontaneous idea **5** a sudden or irrational liking for a person or thing **6** *old-fashioned or literary* a person's imagination ▹*vb* **-cies, -cying, -cied 7** *Brit informal* to be physically attracted to (another person) **8** *informal* to have a wish for **9** to picture in the imagination **10** to think or suppose: *I fancy I am redundant here* **11 fancy oneself** to have a high opinion of oneself ▹*interj* **12** Also: **fancy that!** an exclamation of surprise **fancily** *adv*
WORD ORIGIN Middle English *fantsy*

fancy dress *n* clothing worn for a party at which people dress up to look like a particular animal or character

fancy-free *adj* free from commitments, esp. marriage

fancy goods *pl n* small decorative gifts

fancy man *n old-fashioned slang* a woman's lover

fancy woman *n old-fashioned slang* a man's lover

fancywork *n* ornamental needlework

fandango *n, pl* **-gos 1** a lively Spanish dance **2** music for this dance
WORD ORIGIN Spanish

fanfare *n* a short rousing tune played on brass instruments
WORD ORIGIN French

fang *n* **1** the long pointed tooth of a poisonous snake through which poison is injected **2** the canine tooth of a meat-eating mammal
WORD ORIGIN Old English: what is caught, prey

Fang Lizhi *n* born 1936, Chinese astrophysicist and human-rights campaigner, living in the US from 1990

Fa Ngum *n* 1316–74, founder and first king of Lan Xang (1354–73), a kingdom that included the present-day republic of Laos; abdicated

fanjet *n* ▸same as **turbofan**

fanlight *n* a semicircular window over a door or another window

fanny *n, pl* **-nies** *slang* **1** *Austral & Brit taboo* the female genitals **2** *chiefly US & Canad* the buttocks
WORD ORIGIN origin unknown

fantail *n* **1** a breed of domestic pigeon with a large tail like a fan **2** a fly-catching bird of Australia, New Zealand, and SE Asia with a broad fan-shaped tail

fantasia *n* **1** any musical work not composed in a strict form **2** a mixture of popular tunes arranged as a continuous whole
WORD ORIGIN Italian: fancy

fantasize *or* **-sise** *vb* **-sizing, -sized** *or* **-sising, -sised** to imagine pleasant but unlikely events

fantastic ⓣ *adj* **1** *informal* excellent **2** *informal* very large in degree or amount: *a fantastic amount of money* **3** strange or exotic in appearance: *fantastic costumes* **4** difficult to believe or unlikely to happen **fantastically** *adv*

fantasy ⓣ *n, pl* **-sies 1** a far-fetched idea **2** imagination unrestricted by reality **3** a daydream **4** fiction with a large fantasy content **5** *music* ▸same as **fantasia** ▹*adj* **6** of a competition in which a participant selects players for an imaginary, ideal team and points are awarded according to the actual performances of the chosen players: *fantasy football*
WORD ORIGIN Greek *phantazein* to make visible

Fantin-Latour *n* (**Ignace**) **Henri** (**Joseph Théodore**) 1836–1904, French painter, noted for his still lifes and portrait groups

fan vaulting *n archit* vaulting with ribs that radiate like those of a fan from the top part of a pillar

fanzine (fan-zeen) *n* a magazine produced by fans of a specific interest, football club, etc. for fellow fans

FAQ *n computers* frequently asked question *or* questions: a text file containing basic information on a particular subject

far ⓣ *adv* **farther, farthest** *or* **further,**

THESAURUS

fan[2] *n* **a = supporter**, lover, follower, enthusiast, admirer, groupie *(slang)*, rooter *(US)* **b = devotee**, addict, freak *(informal)*, buff *(informal)*, fiend *(informal)*, adherent, zealot, aficionado

fanatic *n* **1, 2 = extremist**, activist, militant, addict, enthusiast, buff *(informal)*, visionary, devotee, bigot, zealot, energumen

fancy *adj* **1 = elaborate**, decorated, decorative, extravagant, intricate, baroque, ornamented, ornamental, ornate, elegant, fanciful, embellished **OPPOSITE:** plain ▹*n* **4, 5 = whim**, thought, idea, desire, urge, notion, humour, impulse, inclination, caprice ▹*vb* **7** *(Brit informal)* **= be attracted to**, find attractive, desire, lust after, like, prefer, favour, take to, go for, be captivated by, have an eye for, have a thing about *(informal)*, have eyes for, take a liking to **8** *(informal)* **= wish for**, want, desire, would like, hope for, dream of, relish, long for, crave, be attracted to, yearn for, thirst for, hanker after, have a yen for **10 = suppose**, think, believe, imagine, guess *(informal, chiefly US & Canad)*, reckon, conceive, infer, conjecture, surmise, think likely, be inclined to think

fantastic *adj* **1** *(informal)* **= wonderful**, great, excellent, very good, mean *(slang)*, topping *(Brit slang)*, cracking *(Brit informal)*, crucial *(slang)*, smashing *(informal)*, superb, tremendous *(informal)*, magnificent, marvellous, terrific *(informal)*, sensational *(informal)*, mega *(slang)*, awesome *(slang)*, dope *(slang)*, world-class, first-rate, def *(slang)*, brill *(informal)*, out of this world *(informal)*, boffo *(slang)*, jim-dandy *(slang)*, bitchin' *(US slang)*, chillin' *(US slang)*, booshit *(Austral slang)*, exo *(Austral slang)*, sik *(Austral slang)*, rad *(informal)*, phat *(slang)*, schmick *(Austral informal)*, beaut *(informal)*, barrie *(Scot slang)*, belting *(Brit slang)*, pearler *(Austral slang)* **OPPOSITE:** ordinary
3 = strange, bizarre, weird, exotic, peculiar, imaginative, queer, grotesque, quaint, unreal, fanciful, outlandish, whimsical, freakish, chimerical, phantasmagorical
4 = implausible, unlikely, incredible, absurd, irrational, preposterous, capricious, cock-and-bull *(informal)*, cockamamie *(slang, chiefly US)*, mad

fantasy *n* **1, 3 = daydream**, dream, wish, fancy, delusion, reverie, flight of fancy, pipe dream
2 = imagination, fancy, invention, creativity, originality

furthest **1** at, to, or from a great distance **2** at or to a remote time: *as far back as 1984* **3** by a considerable degree: *far greater* **4** **as far as** **a** to the degree or extent that **b** to the distance or place of **c** *informal* with reference to **5** **by far** by a considerable margin **6** **far and away** by a very great margin: *far and away the ugliest building in the city* **7** **far and wide** in a great many places over a large area **8** **go far** **a** to be successful **b** to be sufficient or last long: *her wages didn't go far* **9** **go too far** to go beyond reasonable limits: *the press have gone too far this time* **10** **so far** **a** up to the present moment **b** up to a certain point, extent, or degree ▹*adj* **11** distant in space or time: *the far south* **12** extending a great distance **13** more distant: *over in the far corner* **14** **far from** by no means: *the battle is far from over*
WORD ORIGIN Old English *feorr*

farad *n physics* the SI unit of electric capacitance
WORD ORIGIN after Michael *Faraday*, physicist

faraway *adj* **1** very distant **2** dreamy or absent-minded: *a faraway look in his eyes*

farce ⓘ *n* **1** a humorous play involving characters in unlikely and ridiculous situations **2** the style of comedy of this kind **3** a ludicrous situation: *the game degenerated into farce* **farcical** *adj* **farcically** *adv*
WORD ORIGIN Latin *farcire* to stuff, interpolate passages (in plays)

fare ⓘ *n* **1** the amount charged or paid for a journey in a bus, train, or plane **2** a paying passenger **3** a range of food and drink: *marvellous picnic fare* ▹*vb* **faring, fared** **4** to get on (in a specified way): *he fared well in the exam*
WORD ORIGIN Old English *faran*

Far East *n* the countries of E Asia **Far Eastern** *adj*

fare stage *n* **1** a section of a bus journey for which a set charge is made **2** the bus stop marking the end of such a section

farewell ⓘ *interj* **1** *old-fashioned* goodbye ▹*n* **2** the act of saying goodbye and leaving ▹*vb* **3** NZ to say goodbye ▹*adj* **4** parting or closing: *the President's farewell speech*

far-fetched *adj* unlikely to be true

far-flung *adj* **1** distributed over a wide area **2** far distant or remote

Fargo *n* **William** 1818–81, US businessman: founded (1852) with Henry Wells the express mail service Wells, Fargo and Company

Farhi *n* **Nicole** born 1946, French fashion designer based in Britain: married to Sir David Hare

farinaceous *adj* containing starch or having a starchy texture
WORD ORIGIN Latin *far* coarse meal

farm ⓘ *n* **1** a tract of land, usually with a house and buildings, cultivated as a unit or used to rear livestock **2** a unit of land or water devoted to the growing or rearing of some particular type of fruit, animal, or fish: *a salmon farm; an ostrich farm* ▹*vb* **3** **a** to cultivate land **b** to rear animals or fish on a farm **4** to do agricultural work as a way of life **5** to collect and keep the profits from a tax district or business ▸ See also **farm out**
WORD ORIGIN Old French *ferme* rented land

farmed *adj* (of fish or game) reared on a farm rather than caught in the wild

farmer *n* a person who owns or manages a farm

Farmer *n* **John** ?1565–1605, English madrigal composer and organist

farmers' market *n* a market at which farm produce is sold directly to the public by the producer

farm hand *n* a person who is hired to work on a farm

farmhouse *n* a house attached to a farm

farming *n* the business or skill of agriculture

farmland *n* land that is used for or suitable for farming

farm out *vb* **1** to send (work) to be done by another person or firm **2** (of the state) to put a child into the care of a private individual

farmstead *n* a farm and its main buildings

farmyard *n* the small area of land enclosed by or around the farm buildings

Farnese *n* **1 Alesandro**. original name of Pope Paul III ▸ See also **Paul III** **2 Alessandro,** duke of Parma and Piacenza. 1545–92, Italian general, statesman, and diplomat in the service of Philip II of Spain. As governor of the Netherlands (1578–92), he successfully suppressed revolts against Spanish rule

far-off *adj* distant in space or time: *a far-off land*

Farouk I *or* **Faruk I** *n* 1920–65, last king of Egypt (1936–52). He was forced to abdicate (1952)

far-out *adj* **1** very unusual or strange: *the idea was so far-out it was ludicrous* **2** *informal* wonderful

Farquhar *n* **George** 1678–1707, Irish-born dramatist; author of comedies such as *The Recruiting Officer* (1706) and *The Beaux' Stratagem* (1707)

farrago (far-rah-go) *n, pl* **-gos** *or* **-goes** a hotchpotch or mixture, esp. a ridiculous or unbelievable one: *a farrago of patriotic nonsense*

far-reaching *adj* extensive in influence, effect, or range

Farrell *n* **1 Colin (James)** born 1976, Irish film actor; he appeared in the TV series *Ballykissangel* before starring in the films *Tigerland* (2000), *Minority Report* (2002), and *Alexander* (2004) **2 J(ames) G(ordon)** 1935–79, British novelist: author of *Troubles* (1970), *The Siege of Krishnapur* (1973), and *The Singapore Grip* (1978) **3 James T(homas)** 1904–79, US writer. His works include the trilogy *Young* (1932), *The Young Manhood of Studs Lonigan* (1934), and *Judgment Day* (1935)

farrier *n chiefly Brit* a person who shoes horses
WORD ORIGIN Latin *ferrarius* smith

farrow *n* **1** a litter of piglets ▹*vb* **2** (of a sow) to give birth to a litter
WORD ORIGIN Old English *fearh*

far-seeing *adj* having wise judgment

f

THESAURUS

far *adv* **1 = a long way**, miles, deep, a good way, afar, a great distance **3 = much**, greatly, very much, extremely, significantly, considerably, decidedly, markedly, incomparably ▹*adj* **11 = remote**, distant, far-flung, faraway, long, removed, out-of-the-way, far-removed, outlying, off the beaten track **OPPOSITE:** near

farce *n* **1, 2 = comedy**, satire, slapstick, burlesque, buffoonery, broad comedy **3 = mockery**, joke, nonsense, parody, shambles, sham, absurdity, malarkey, travesty, ridiculousness

fare *n* **1 = charge**, price, ticket price, transport cost, ticket money, passage money **3 = food**, meals, diet, provisions, board, commons, table, feed, menu, rations, tack *(informal)*, kai *(NZ informal)*, nourishment, sustenance, victuals, nosebag *(slang)*, nutriment, vittles *(obsolete, dialect)*, eatables ▹*vb* **4 = get on**, do, manage, make out, prosper, get along

farewell *interj* **1** *(old-fashioned)* **= goodbye**, bye *(informal)*, so long, see you, take care, good morning, bye-bye *(informal)*, good day, all the best, good night, good evening, good afternoon, see you later, ciao *(Italian)*, have a nice day (US), adieu *(French)*, au revoir *(French)*, be seeing you, auf Wiedersehen *(German)*, adios *(Spanish)*, mind how you go, haere ra (NZ) ▹*n* **2 = goodbye**, parting, departure, leave-taking, adieu, valediction, sendoff *(informal)*, adieux *or* adieus

farm *n* **1, 2 = smallholding**, holding, ranch *(chiefly US & Canad)*, farmstead, land, station *(Austral & NZ)*, acres, vineyard, plantation, croft *(Scot)*, grange, homestead, acreage ▹*vb* **3a, 3b, 4 = cultivate**, work, plant, operate, till the soil, grow crops on, bring under cultivation, keep animals on, practise husbandry

DICTIONARY

far-sighted *adj* **1** able to look forward and plan ahead **2** *US* long-sighted

fart *taboo n* **1** an emission of intestinal gas from the anus ▷ *vb* **2** to break wind
WORD ORIGIN Middle English *farten*

farther *adv* **1** to or at a greater distance in space or time **2** in addition ▷ *adj* **3** more distant or remote in space or time
WORD ORIGIN Middle English

farthermost *adj* most distant or remote

farthest *adv* **1** to or at the greatest distance in space or time ▷ *adj* **2** most distant or remote in space or time
WORD ORIGIN Middle English *ferthest*

farthing *n* a former British coin worth a quarter of an old penny
WORD ORIGIN Old English *fēorthing*

farthingale *n* a hoop worn under skirts in the Elizabethan period
WORD ORIGIN Old Spanish *verdugo* rod

Faruk I *n* ▸ a variant spelling of **Farouk I**

fasces (fass-eez) *pl n, sing* **-cis** (-siss) (in ancient Rome) a bundle of rods containing an axe with its blade pointing out; a symbol of a magistrate's power
WORD ORIGIN Latin

fascia *or* **facia** (fay-shee-a) *n, pl* **-ciae** (-shee-ee) **1** the flat surface above a shop window **2** *archit* a flat band or surface **3** *Brit* the outer panel which surrounds the instruments and dials of a motor vehicle
WORD ORIGIN Latin: band

fascinate ❶ *vb* **-nating, -nated** to attract and delight by arousing interest **fascinating** *adj* **fascinatingly** *adv* **fascination** *n*
WORD ORIGIN Latin *fascinum* a bewitching

Fascism (fash-iz-zum) *n* **1** the authoritarian and nationalistic political movement in Italy (1922–43) **2** any ideology or movement like this **Fascist** *n, adj*
WORD ORIGIN Italian *fascio* political group

fashion ❶ *n* **1** style in clothes, hairstyles, behaviour, etc. that is popular at a particular time **2** the way that something happens or is done: *conversing in a very animated fashion* **3** **after a fashion** in some way, but not very well: *he apologized, after a fashion, for his haste* ▷ *vb* **4** to form, make, or shape: *he had fashioned a crude musical instrument*
WORD ORIGIN Latin *facere* to make

fashionable ❶ *adj* **1** popular with a lot of people at a particular time **2** popular among well-off or famous people: *the fashionable Côte d'Azur* **fashionably** *adv*

Fassbinder *n* **Rainer Werner** 1946–82, West German film director. His films include *The Bitter Tears of Petra von Kant* (1972), *Fear Eats the Soul* (1974), and *The Marriage of Maria Braun* (1978)

fast[1] ❶ *adj* **1** acting or moving quickly **2** accomplished in or lasting a short time **3** adapted to or allowing for rapid movement: *the fast lane* **4** (of a clock or watch) indicating a time in advance of the correct time **5** given to a life of expensive and exciting activities: *the desire for a fast life* **6** firmly fixed, fastened, or shut **7** (of colours and dyes) not likely to fade **8** *photog* very sensitive and able to be used in low-light conditions **9** **fast friends** devoted and loyal friends **10** **pull a fast one** *informal* play an unscrupulous trick ▷ *adv* **11** quickly **12** **fast asleep** in a deep sleep **13** firmly and tightly: *stuck fast* **14** **play fast and loose** to behave in an insincere or unreliable manner
WORD ORIGIN Old English *fæst* strong, tight

fast[2] ❶ *vb* **1** to go without food for a period of time, esp. for religious reasons ▷ *n* **2** a period of fasting
WORD ORIGIN Old English *fæstan*

fast-breeder reactor *n* a nuclear reactor that produces more fissionable material (plutonium) than it consumes for the purposes of generating electricity

fasten ❶ *vb* **1** to make or become secure or joined **2** to close by fixing firmly in place or locking **3** **fasten on** **a** to direct one's attention in a concentrated way towards: *the mind needs such imagery to fasten on to* **b** to take a firm hold on **fastener** *n*
WORD ORIGIN Old English *fæstnian*

fastening *n* something that fastens something, such as a clasp or lock

fast food *n* food, such as hamburgers, that is prepared and served very quickly

fastidious *adj* **1** paying great attention to neatness, detail, and order: *a fastidious dresser* **2** excessively concerned with cleanliness **fastidiously** *adv* **fastidiousness** *n*
WORD ORIGIN Latin *fastidiosus* scornful

fast lane *n* **1** the outside lane on a motorway for overtaking or travelling fast **2** *informal* the quickest but most competitive route to success: *the hectic pace of life in the corporate fast lane*

fastness *n Brit & Austral, literary* a stronghold or safe place that is hard to get to

fast-track *adj* **1** taking the quickest but most competitive route to success or personal advancement: *a fast-track marketer's dream* ▷ *vb* **2** to speed up the progress of (a project or person)

THESAURUS

fascinate *vb* = **entrance**, delight, charm, absorb, intrigue, enchant, rivet, captivate, enthral, beguile, allure, bewitch, ravish, transfix, mesmerize, hypnotize, engross, enrapture, interest greatly, enamour, hold spellbound, spellbind, infatuate
OPPOSITE: bore

fashion *n* **1** = **style**, look, trend, rage, custom, convention, mode, vogue, usage, craze, fad, latest style, prevailing taste, latest **2** = **method**, way, style, approach, manner, mode ▷ *vb* **4** = **make**, shape, cast, construct, work, form, create, design, manufacture, forge, mould, contrive, fabricate

fashionable *adj* **1, 2** = **popular**, in fashion, trendy (*Brit informal*), cool (*slang*), in (*informal*), latest, happening (*informal*), current, modern, with it (*informal*), usual, smart, hip (*slang*), prevailing, stylish, chic, up-to-date, customary, genteel, in vogue, all the rage, up-to-the-minute, modish, à la mode, voguish (*informal*), trendsetting, all the go (*informal*), schmick (*Austral informal*), funky
OPPOSITE: unfashionable

fast[1] *adj* **1, 2** = **quick**, flying, winged, rapid, fleet, hurried, accelerated, swift, speedy, brisk, hasty, nimble, mercurial, sprightly, nippy (*Brit informal*) **OPPOSITE:** slow
5 = **dissipated**, wild, exciting, loose, extravagant, reckless, immoral, promiscuous, giddy, self-indulgent, wanton, profligate, impure, intemperate, dissolute, rakish, licentious, gadabout (*informal*)
6 = **fixed**, firm, sound, stuck, secure, tight, jammed, fortified, fastened, impregnable, immovable
OPPOSITE: unstable
9 = **close**, lasting, firm, permanent, constant, devoted, loyal, faithful, stalwart, staunch, steadfast, unwavering ▷ *adv* **11** = **quickly**, rapidly, swiftly, hastily, hurriedly, speedily, presto, apace, in haste, like a shot (*informal*), at full speed, hell for leather (*informal*), like lightning, hotfoot, like a flash, at a rate of knots, like the clappers (*Brit informal*), like a bat out of hell (*slang*), pdq (*slang*), like nobody's business (*informal*), posthaste, like greased lightning (*informal*), with all haste
OPPOSITE: slowly
13 = **securely**, firmly, tightly, fixedly

fast[2] *vb* **1** = **go hungry**, abstain, go without food, deny yourself, practise abstention, refrain from food *or* eating ▷ *n* **2** = **fasting**, diet, abstinence

fasten *vb* **1a** = **tie**, bind, lace, tie up **1b** = **fix**, join, link, connect, grip, attach, anchor, affix, make firm, make fast **2** = **secure**, close, lock,

DICTIONARY

fat ❶ *adj* **fatter, fattest 1** having more flesh on the body than is thought necessary or desirable; overweight **2** (of meat) containing a lot of fat **3** thick or wide: *his obligatory fat cigar* **4** profitable or productive: *fat years for the farmers are few and far between* **5 a fat chance** *slang* unlikely to happen **6 a fat lot of good** *slang* not at all good or useful ▷ *n* **7** extra or unwanted flesh on the body **8** a greasy or oily substance obtained from animals or plants and used in cooking **9 the fat is in the fire** an action has been taken from which disastrous consequences are expected **10 the fat of the land** the best that is obtainable **fatless** *adj* **fatness** *n*
WORD ORIGIN Old English *fætt* crammed

fatal ❶ *adj* **1** resulting in death: *a fatal accident* **2** resulting in unfortunate consequences: *Gorbachov's second fatal mistake* **fatally** *adv*
WORD ORIGIN Latin *fatum* fate

fatalism *n* the belief that all events are decided in advance by God or Fate so that human beings are powerless to alter their destiny **fatalist** *n* **fatalistic** *adj* **fatalistically** *adv*

fatality *n, pl* **-ties** a death caused by an accident or disaster

fate ❶ *n* **1** the ultimate force that supposedly predetermines the course of events **2** the inevitable fortune that happens to a person or thing **3** death or downfall: *Custer met his fate at Little Bighorn*
WORD ORIGIN Latin *fatum*

fated ❶ *adj* **1** certain to be or do something: *he was always fated to be a musician* **2** doomed to death or destruction

fateful *adj* having important, and usually disastrous, consequences **fatefully** *adv*

Fates *pl n classical myth* the goddesses who control human destiny

fathead *n informal* a stupid person **fatheaded** *adj*

father ❶ *n* **1** a male parent **2** a person who founds a line or family; forefather **3** a man who starts, creates, or invents something: *the father of democracy in Costa Rica* **4** a leader of an association or council: *the city fathers* ▷ *vb* **5** (of a man) to be the biological cause of the conception and birth of (a child) **fatherhood** *n*
WORD ORIGIN Old English *fæder*

Father ❶ *n* **1** God **2** a title used for Christian priests **3** any of the early writers on Christian doctrine

Father Christmas *n* ▸ same as **Santa Claus**

father-in-law *n, pl* **fathers-in-law** the father of one's wife or husband

fatherland *n* a person's native country

fatherly ❶ *adj* kind or protective, like a father

Father's Day *n* a day celebrated in honour of fathers

fathom *n* **1** a unit of length, used in navigation, equal to six feet (1.83 metres) ▷ *vb* **2** to understand by thinking carefully about: *I couldn't fathom his intentions* **fathomable** *adj*
WORD ORIGIN Old English *fæthm*

fathomless *adj* too deep or difficult to fathom

fatigue ❶ (fat-**eeg**) *n* **1** extreme physical or mental tiredness **2** the weakening of a material caused by repeated stress or movement **3** the duties of a soldier that are not military **4 fatigues** a soldier's clothing for nonmilitary or battlefield duties ▷ *vb* **-tiguing, -tigued 5** to make or become weary or exhausted
WORD ORIGIN Latin *fatigare* to tire

fat stock *n* livestock fattened and ready for market

fatten *vb* to grow or cause to grow fat or fatter **fattening** *adj*

fatty ❶ *adj* **-tier, -tiest 1** containing or derived from fat **2** greasy or oily ▷ *n, pl* **-ties 3** *informal* a fat person

fatty acid *n* any of a class of organic acids some of which, such as stearic acid, are found in animal or vegetable fats

fatuity *n, pl* **-ties 1** foolish thoughtlessness **2** a fatuous remark

fatuous *adj* foolish, inappropriate, and showing no thought **fatuously** *adv*
WORD ORIGIN Latin *fatuus*

faucet ❶ (**faw**-set) *n* **1** a tap fitted to a barrel **2** *US & Canad* a tap
WORD ORIGIN Old French *fausset*

fault ❶ *n* **1** responsibility for something wrong **2** a defect or failing: *they shut the production line to remedy a fault* **3** a weakness in a person's character **4** *geol* a fracture in the earth's crust with displacement of the rocks on either side **5** *tennis, squash, etc.* a serve that bounces outside the proper service court or fails to get over the net **6** (in showjumping) a penalty mark for failing to clear, or refusing, a fence **7 be at fault** to be to blame for something wrong **8 find fault with** to seek out minor imperfections in **9 to a fault** more than is usual or

f

THESAURUS

chain, seal, bolt, do up

fat *adj* **1 = overweight**, large, heavy, plump, gross, stout, obese, fleshy, beefy *(informal)*, tubby, portly, roly-poly, rotund, podgy, corpulent, elephantine, broad in the beam *(informal)*, solid **OPPOSITE:** thin **2 = fatty**, greasy, lipid, adipose, oleaginous, suety, oily **OPPOSITE:** lean ▷ *n* **7 = fatness**, flesh, bulk, obesity, cellulite, weight problem, flab, blubber, paunch, fatty tissue, adipose tissue, corpulence, beef *(informal)*

fatal *adj* **1 = lethal**, deadly, mortal, causing death, final, killing, terminal, destructive, malignant, incurable, pernicious **OPPOSITE:** harmless **2 = disastrous**, devastating, crippling, lethal, catastrophic, ruinous, calamitous, baleful, baneful **OPPOSITE:** minor

fate *n* **1 = destiny**, chance, fortune, luck, the stars, weird *(archaic)*, providence, nemesis, kismet, predestination, divine will **2 = fortune**, destiny, lot, portion, cup, horoscope

fated *adj* **1 = destined**, doomed, predestined, preordained, foreordained, pre-elected

father *n* **1 = daddy** *(informal)*, dad *(informal)*, male parent, patriarch, pop *(US informal)*, governor *(informal)*, old man *(Brit informal)*, pa *(informal)*, old boy *(informal)*, papa *(old-fashioned, informal)*, sire, pater, biological father, foster father, begetter, paterfamilias, birth father **2 = forefather**, predecessor, ancestor, forebear, progenitor, tupuna *or* tipuna *(NZ)* **3 = founder**, author, maker, architect, creator, inventor, originator, prime mover, initiator ▷ *vb* **5 = sire**, parent, conceive, bring to life, beget, procreate, bring into being, give life to, get

Father *n* **2 = priest**, minister, vicar, parson, pastor, cleric, churchman, padre *(informal)*, confessor, abbé, curé, man of God

fatherly *adj* **= paternal**, kind, kindly, tender, protective, supportive, benign, affectionate, indulgent, patriarchal, benevolent, forbearing

fatigue *n* **1 = tiredness**, lethargy, weariness, ennui, heaviness, debility, languor, listlessness, overtiredness **OPPOSITE:** freshness ▷ *vb* **5 = tire**, exhaust, weaken, weary, drain, fag (out) *(informal)*, whack *(Brit informal)*, wear out, jade, take it out of *(informal)*, poop *(informal)*, tire out, knacker *(slang)*, drain of energy, overtire **OPPOSITE:** refresh

fatty *adj* **1, 2 = greasy**, fat, creamy, oily, adipose, oleaginous, suety, rich

faucet *n* **2** *(US & Canad)* **= tap**, spout, spigot, stopcock, valve

fault *n* **1 = responsibility**, liability, guilt, accountability, culpability **2, 3 = failing**, lack, weakness, defect, deficiency, flaw, drawback, shortcoming, snag, blemish, imperfection, Achilles heel, weak point, infirmity, demerit **OPPOSITE:** strength

DICTIONARY

necessary: *generous to a fault* ▷ *vb* **10** to criticize or blame **11** *geol* to undergo or cause to undergo a fault **faultless** *adj* **faultlessly** *adv*
WORD ORIGIN Latin *fallere* to fail
fault-finding *n* continual criticism
faulty ❶ *adj* **faultier, faultiest** badly designed or not working properly: *a faulty toaster*
faun *n* (in Roman legend) a creature with the head and torso of a man and the legs, ears, and horns of a goat
WORD ORIGIN Latin *Faunus*, god of forests

f

fauna *n, pl* **-nas** *or* **-nae** all the animal life of a given place or time: *the fauna of the Arctic*
WORD ORIGIN Late Latin *Fauna*, a goddess of living things
faux pas (foe **pah**) *n, pl* **faux pas** (foe **pahz**) a socially embarrassing action or mistake
WORD ORIGIN French
favour ❶ *or US* **favor** *n* **1** an approving attitude: *the company looked with favour on his plan* **2** an act done out of goodwill or generosity **3** bias at the expense of others: *his fellow customs officers, showing no favour, demanded to see his luggage* **4** **in** *or* **out of favour** regarded with approval *or* disapproval **5** **in favour of** **a** approving **b** to the benefit of ▷ *vb* **6** to prefer **7** to show bias towards (someone) at the expense of others: *parents sometimes favour the youngest child in the family* **8** to support or agree with (something): *he favours the abolition of capital punishment* **favoured** *or US* **favored** *adj*
WORD ORIGIN Latin *favere* to protect
favourable ❶ *or US* **favorable** *adj* **1** advantageous, encouraging, or promising: *a favourable climate for business expansion* **2** giving consent or approval **favourably** *or US* **favorably** *adv*
favourite ❶ *or US* **favorite** *adj* **1** most liked ▷ *n* **2** a person or thing regarded with especial preference or liking **3** *sport* a competitor thought likely to win
WORD ORIGIN Latin *favere* to protect
favouritism *or US* **favoritism** *n* the practice of giving special treatment to a person or group: *favouritism in the allocation of government posts*
Fawcett *n* Dame **Millicent Garrett** 1847–1929, British suffragette
fawn[1] *n* **1** a young deer aged under one year ▷ *adj* **2** pale greyish-brown
WORD ORIGIN Latin *fetus* offspring
fawn[2] *vb* **fawn on** **1** to seek attention from (someone) by insincere flattery: *it makes me sick to see the way you fawn on that awful woman* **2** (of a dog) to try to please (someone) by a show of extreme friendliness **fawning** *adj*
WORD ORIGIN Old English *fægnian* to be glad
fax *n* **1** an electronic system for transmitting an exact copy of a document **2** a document sent by this system **3** Also called: **fax machine, facsimile machine** a machine which transmits and receives exact copies of documents ▷ *vb* **4** to send (a document) by this system
WORD ORIGIN short for *facsimile*
Fa Xian *or* **Fa-hsien** *n* original name *Sehi*. 5th century AD, Chinese Buddhist monk: his pilgrimage to India (399–414) began relations between China and India
fazed *adj* worried or disconcerted
WORD ORIGIN Old English *fēsian*
FBI (in the US) Federal Bureau of Investigation
FC (in Britain) Football Club
FD Defender of the Faith: the title of the British sovereign as head of the Church of England
WORD ORIGIN Latin *Fidei Defensor*
Fe *chem* iron
WORD ORIGIN Latin *ferrum*
fealty *n, pl* **-ties** (in feudal society) the loyalty sworn to a lord by his tenant or servant
WORD ORIGIN Latin *fidelitas* fidelity
fear ❶ *n* **1** a feeling of distress or alarm caused by danger or pain that is about to happen **2** something that causes fear **3** possibility or likelihood: *there is no fear of her agreeing to that* **4** **no fear** *informal* certainly not ▷ *vb* **5** to be afraid of (someone or something) **6** *formal* to be sorry: *I fear the children were not very good yesterday* **7** **fear for** to feel anxiety about something **fearless** *adj* **fearlessly** *adv*
WORD ORIGIN Old English *fǣr*

THESAURUS

8 find fault with something *or* **someone = criticize**, complain about, whinge about *(informal)*, whine about *(informal)*, quibble, diss *(slang, chiefly US)*, carp at, take to task, pick holes in, grouse about *(informal)*, haul over the coals *(informal)*, pull to pieces, nit-pick *(informal)*
9 to a fault = excessively, overly *(US)*, unduly, ridiculously, in the extreme, needlessly, out of all proportion, preposterously, overmuch, immoderately ▷ *vb*
10 = criticize, blame, complain, condemn, moan about, censure, hold (someone) responsible, hold (someone) accountable, find fault with, call to account, impugn, find lacking, hold (someone) to blame
faulty *adj* **= defective**, damaged, not working, malfunctioning, broken, bad, flawed, impaired, imperfect, blemished, out of order, on the blink
favour *or (US)* **favor** *n* **1 = approval**, grace, esteem, goodwill, kindness, friendliness, commendation, partiality, approbation, kind regard
OPPOSITE: disapproval
2 = good turn, service, benefit, courtesy, kindness, indulgence, boon, good deed, kind act, obligement *(Scot archaic)*
OPPOSITE: wrong
3 = favouritism, preference, bias, nepotism, preferential treatment, partisanship, jobs for the boys *(informal)*, partiality, one-sidedness
▷ *vb* **6 = prefer**, opt for, like better, incline towards, choose, pick, desire, select, elect, adopt, go for, fancy, single out, plump for, be partial to
OPPOSITE: object to
7 = indulge, reward, spoil, esteem, side with, pamper, befriend, be partial to, smile upon, pull strings for *(informal)*, have in your good books, treat with partiality, value
8 = support, like, back, choose, champion, encourage, approve, fancy, advocate, opt for, subscribe to, commend, stand up for, espouse, be in favour of, countenance, patronize
OPPOSITE: oppose
favourable *or (US)* **favorable** *adj*
1a = positive, kind, understanding, encouraging, welcoming, friendly, approving, praising, reassuring, enthusiastic, sympathetic, benign, commending, complimentary, agreeable, amicable, well-disposed, commendatory
OPPOSITE: disapproving
1b = advantageous, timely, good, promising, fit, encouraging, fair, appropriate, suitable, helpful, hopeful, convenient, beneficial, auspicious, opportune, propitious
OPPOSITE: disadvantageous
2 = affirmative, agreeing, confirming, positive, assenting, corroborative
favourite *or (US)* **favorite** *adj*
1 = preferred, favoured, best-loved, most-liked, special, choice, dearest, pet, esteemed, fave *(informal)* ▷ *n*
2 = darling, pet, preference, blue-eyed boy *(informal)*, pick, choice, dear, beloved, idol, fave *(informal)*, teacher's pet, the apple of your eye
fear *n* **1 = dread**, horror, panic, terror, dismay, awe, fright, tremors, qualms, consternation, alarm, trepidation, timidity, fearfulness, blue funk *(informal)*, apprehensiveness, cravenness
2 = bugbear, bête noire, horror, nightmare, anxiety, terror, dread, spectre, phobia, bogey, thing *(informal)* ▷ *vb* **5 = be afraid of**, dread, be scared of, be frightened of, shudder at, be fearful of, be apprehensive about, tremble at, be terrified by, have a horror of, take

fearful ⓣ *adj* 1 afraid and full of fear 2 frightening or causing fear: *the ship hit a fearful storm* 3 *informal* very bad: *they were making a fearful noise* **fearfully** *adv*

fearsome *adj* terrible or frightening

feasible ⓣ *adj* able to be done: *a manned journey to Mars is now feasible* **feasibility** *n* **feasibly** *adv*
WORD ORIGIN Anglo-French *faisable*

feast ⓣ *n* 1 a large and special meal for many people 2 something extremely pleasing: *a feast of colour* 3 an annual religious celebration ▹*vb* 4 to take part in a feast 5 to give a feast to 6 **feast on** to eat a large amount of: *down come hundreds of vultures to feast on the remains* 7 **feast one's eyes on** to look at (someone or something) with a great deal of attention and pleasure
WORD ORIGIN Latin *festus* joyful

Feast of Tabernacles *n* ▸same as **Sukkoth**

feat ⓣ *n* a remarkable, skilful, or daring action: *an extraordinary feat of engineering*
WORD ORIGIN Anglo-French *fait*

feather ⓣ *n* 1 any of the flat light structures that form the plumage of birds, each consisting of a shaft with soft thin hairs on either side 2 **feather in one's cap** a cause for pleasure at one's achievements ▹*vb* 3 to fit, cover, or supply with feathers 4 *rowing* to turn an oar parallel to the water between strokes, in order to lessen wind resistance 5 **feather one's nest** to collect possessions and money to make one's life comfortable, often dishonestly **feathered** *adj* **feathery** *adj*
WORD ORIGIN Old English *fether*

feather bed *n* 1 a mattress filled with feathers or down ▹*vb* **featherbed, -bedding, -bedded** 2 to pamper or spoil (someone)

featherbedding *n* the practice of working in a factory or office deliberately slowly and inefficiently so that more workers are employed than are necessary

featherbrain *n* an empty-headed or forgetful person **featherbrained** *adj*

featherweight *n* 1 a professional or an amateur boxer weighing up to 126 pounds (57 kg) 2 something very light or of little importance: *a political featherweight*

feature ⓣ *n* 1 **features** any one of the parts of the face, such as the nose, chin, or mouth 2 a prominent or distinctive part of something: *regular debates were a feature of our final year* 3 the main film in a cinema programme 4 an item appearing regularly in a newspaper or magazine 5 a prominent story in a newspaper ▹*vb* **-turing, -tured** 6 to have as a feature or make a feature of: *this cooker features a fan-assisted oven* 7 to give special prominence to: *the film features James Mason as Rommel* **featureless** *adj*
WORD ORIGIN Anglo-French *feture*

Feb. February

febrile (fee-brile) *adj formal* 1 very active and nervous: *increasingly febrile activity at the Stock Exchange* 2 of or relating to fever
WORD ORIGIN Latin *febris* fever

February *n, pl* **-aries** the second month of the year
WORD ORIGIN Latin *Februarius mensis* month of expiation

Fechner *n* **Gustav Theodor** 1801–87, German physicist, philosopher, and psychologist, noted particularly for his work on psychophysics, *Elemente der Psychophysik* (1860)

feckless *adj* irresponsible and lacking character and determination: *her feckless brother was always in debt*
WORD ORIGIN obsolete *feck* value, effect

fecund *adj literary* 1 fertile or capable of producing many offspring 2 intellectually productive or creative: *an extraordinarily fecund year even by Mozart's standards* **fecundity** *n*
WORD ORIGIN Latin *fecundus*

fed *vb* ▸the past of **feed**

federal *adj* 1 of a form of government in which power is divided between one central and several regional governments 2 of the central government of a federation 3 *Austral* of a style of house built around the time of Federation **federalism** *n* **federalist** *n, adj*
WORD ORIGIN Latin *foedus* league

Federal *adj* of or supporting the Union government during the American Civil War

Federal Government *n* the national government of a federated state, such as that of Canada located in Ottawa or of Australia in Canberra

federalize *or* **-ise** *vb* **-izing, -ized** *or* **-ising, -ised** 1 to unite in a federal union 2 to subject to federal control **federalization** *or* **-isation** *n*

federate *vb* **-ating, -ated** to unite in a federal union **federative** *adj*

federation ⓣ *n* 1 the union of several provinces, states, etc. 2 any alliance

f

fright at, have a phobia about, have qualms about, live in dread of, be in a blue funk about *(informal)*, have butterflies in your stomach about *(informal)*, shake in your shoes about **6 = regret**, feel, suspect, have a feeling, have a hunch, have a sneaking suspicion, have a funny feeling **7 fear for something** *or* **someone = worry about**, be concerned about, be anxious about, tremble for, be distressed about, feel concern for, be disquieted over

fearful *adj* **1a = scared**, afraid, alarmed, frightened, nervous, terrified, apprehensive, petrified, jittery *(informal)* OPPOSITE: unafraid **1b = timid**, afraid, frightened, scared, alarmed, wired *(slang)*, nervous, anxious, shrinking, tense, intimidated, uneasy, neurotic, hesitant, apprehensive, jittery *(informal)*, panicky, nervy *(Brit informal)*, diffident, jumpy, timorous, pusillanimous, faint-hearted OPPOSITE: brave **3** *(informal)* **= frightful**, shocking, terrible, awful, distressing, appalling, horrible, grim, dreadful, horrific, dire, horrendous, ghastly, hideous, monstrous, harrowing, gruesome, grievous, unspeakable, atrocious, hair-raising, hellacious *(US slang)*

feasible *adj* **= practicable**, possible, reasonable, viable, workable, achievable, attainable, realizable, likely OPPOSITE: impracticable

feast *n* **1 = banquet**, repast, spread *(informal)*, dinner, entertainment, barbecue, revel, junket, beano *(Brit slang)*, blowout *(slang)*, carouse, slap-up meal *(Brit informal)*, beanfeast *(Brit informal)*, jollification, carousal, festive board, treat, hakari *(NZ)* **3 = festival**, holiday, fête, celebration, holy day, red-letter day, religious festival, saint's day, -fest, gala day ▹*vb* **4 = eat your fill**, wine and dine, overindulge, eat to your heart's content, stuff yourself, consume, indulge, gorge, devour, pig out *(slang)*, stuff your face *(slang)*, fare sumptuously, gormandize

feat *n* **= accomplishment**, act, performance, achievement, enterprise, undertaking, exploit, deed, attainment, feather in your cap

feather *n* **1 = plume**

feature *n* **1** *(pl)* **= face**, countenance, physiognomy, lineaments **2a = aspect**, quality, characteristic, attribute, point, mark, property, factor, trait, hallmark, facet, peculiarity **2b = highlight**, draw, attraction, innovation, speciality, specialty, main item, crowd puller *(informal)*, special attraction, special **4, 5 = article**, report, story, piece, comment, item, column ▹*vb* **6 = spotlight**, present, promote, set off, emphasize, play up, accentuate, foreground, call attention to, give prominence to, give the full works *(slang)*

federation *n* **1, 2 = union**, league, association, alliance, combination, coalition, partnership, consortium, syndicate, confederation,

DICTIONARY

f

or association of organizations which have freely joined together for a common purpose: *a federation of twenty regional unions*

Federer *n* **Roger** born 1981, Swiss tennis player: won both the Wimbledon men's singles and the US Open each year 2004–07

fed up ⓣ *adj informal* annoyed or bored

fee ⓣ *n* **1** a charge paid to be allowed to do something: *many people resent the licence fee* **2** a payment asked by professional people for their services **3** *property law* an interest in land that can be inherited. The interest can be with unrestricted rights (**fee simple**) or restricted (**fee tail**)
WORD ORIGIN Old French *fie*

feeble ⓣ *adj* **1** lacking in physical or mental strength **2** not effective or convincing: *feeble excuses for Scotland's latest defeat* **feebly** *adv*
WORD ORIGIN Old French *feble*

feeble-minded *adj* unable to think or understand effectively

feed ⓣ *vb* **feeding, fed 1** to give food to (a person or an animal) **2** to give (something) as food: *people feeding bread to their cattle* **3** to eat food: *red squirrel feed in the pines* **4** to supply or prepare food for **5** to provide what is needed for the continued existence, operation, or growth of: *illustrations which will feed an older child's imagination; pools fed by waterfalls* ▷*n* **6** the act of feeding **7** food, esp. that given to animals or babies **8** *Brit, Austral & NZ informal* a meal
WORD ORIGIN Old English *fēdan*

feedback *n* **1** information in response to an inquiry or experiment: *considerable feedback from the customers* **2** the return of part of the output of an electronic circuit to its input **3** the return of part of the sound output of a loudspeaker to the microphone, so that a high-pitched whine is produced

feeder *n* **1** a device used to feed an animal, child, or sick person **2** an animal or a person who feeds: *these larvae are voracious feeders* **3** a road, rail, or air service that links outlying areas to the main network **4** a tributary or channel of a river

feel ⓣ *vb* **feeling, felt 1** to have a physical or emotional sensation of: *he felt a combination of shame and relief* **2** to become aware of or examine by touching **3** Also: **feel in one's bones** to sense by intuition **4** to believe or think: *I felt I got off pretty lightly* **5 feel for** to show compassion (towards) **6 feel like** to have an inclination (for something or doing something): *I feel like going to the cinema* **7 feel up to** to be fit enough for (something or doing something) ▷*n* **8** the act of feeling **9** an impression: *all this mixing and matching has a French feel to it* **10** the sense of touch **11** an instinctive ability: *a feel for art*
WORD ORIGIN Old English *fēlan*

feeler *n* **1** an organ on an insect's head that is sensitive to touch **2 put out feelers** to make informal suggestions or remarks designed to probe the reactions of others

feeling ⓣ *n* **1** an emotional reaction: *a feeling of discontent* **2 feelings** emotional sensitivity: *I don't want to hurt your feelings* **3** instinctive appreciation and understanding: *your feeling for language* **4** an intuitive understanding that cannot be explained: *I began to have a sinking feeling that I was not going to get rid of her* **5** opinion or view: *it was his feeling that the report was a misinterpretation of what had been said* **6** capacity for sympathy or affection: *moved by feeling for his fellow citizens* **7 a** the ability to experience physical sensations: *he has no feeling in his left arm* **b** the sensation so experienced **8** the impression or mood created by something: *a feeling of excitement in the air* **9 bad feeling** resentment or anger between people, for example after an argument or an injustice: *his refusal may have triggered bad feeling between the two men* **feelingly** *adv*

feet *n* **1** ▸the plural of **foot 2 be run** *or* **rushed off one's feet** to be very busy **3 feet of clay** a weakness that is not widely known **4 have** *or* **keep one's feet on the ground** to be practical and reliable **5 put one's feet up** to take a rest **6 stand on one's own feet** to be independent **7 sweep off one's feet** to fill with enthusiasm

feign (fane) *vb* to pretend to experience (a particular feeling): *he didn't have to feign surprise* **feigned** *adj*
WORD ORIGIN Old French *feindre*

Feininger *n* **Lyonel** 1871–1956, US artist, who worked at the Bauhaus, noted for his use of superimposed translucent planes of colour

feint[1] (faint) *n* **1** a misleading movement designed to distract an opponent, such as in boxing or fencing ▷*vb* **2** to make a feint
WORD ORIGIN Old French *feindre* to feign

feint[2] (faint) *n printing* paper that has pale lines across it for writing on
WORD ORIGIN variant of *faint*

Feisal I *n* a ▸variant spelling of **Faisal I**

THESAURUS

amalgamation, confederacy, entente, Bund *(German)*, copartnership, federacy

fed up *adj (informal)* **= cheesed off**, down, depressed, bored, tired, annoyed, hacked (off) *(US slang)*, weary, gloomy, blue, dismal, discontented, dissatisfied, glum, sick and tired *(informal)*, browned-off *(informal)*, down in the mouth *(informal)*, brassed off *(Brit slang)*, hoha *(NZ)*

fee *n* **1, 2 = charge**, pay, price, cost, bill, account, payment, wage, reward, hire, salary, compensation, toll, remuneration, recompense, emolument, honorarium, meed *(archaic)*

feeble *adj* **1 = weak**, failing, exhausted, weakened, delicate, faint, powerless, frail, debilitated, sickly, languid, puny, weedy *(informal)*, infirm, effete, enfeebled, doddering, enervated, etiolated, shilpit *(Scot)* **OPPOSITE:** strong **2a = inadequate**, weak, pathetic, insufficient, incompetent, ineffective, inefficient, lame, insignificant, ineffectual, indecisive **2b = unconvincing**, poor, thin, weak, slight, tame, pathetic, lame, flimsy, paltry, flat **OPPOSITE:** effective

feed *vb* **3a = graze**, eat, browse, pasture **3b = eat**, drink milk, take nourishment **4 = cater for**, provide for, nourish, provide with food, supply, sustain, nurture, cook for, wine and dine, victual, provision ▷*n* **7 = food**, fodder, forage, silage, provender, pasturage **8** *(Brit, Austral & NZ informal)* **= meal**, spread *(informal)*, dinner, lunch, tea, breakfast, feast, supper, tuck-in *(informal)*, nosh *(slang)*, repast, nosh-up *(Brit slang)*

feel *vb* **1a = experience**, suffer, bear, go through, endure, undergo, have a sensation of, have **1b = be aware of**, have a sensation of, be sensible of, enjoy **2 = touch**, handle, manipulate, run your hands over, finger, stroke, paw, maul, caress, fondle **3 = sense**, be aware, be convinced, have a feeling, have the impression, intuit, have a hunch, feel in your bones **4 = believe**, consider, judge, deem, think, hold, be of the opinion that ▷*n* **9 = impression**, feeling, air, sense, quality, atmosphere, mood, aura, ambience, vibes *(slang)*

feeling *n* **1 = emotion**, sentiment **4 = impression**, idea, sense, notion, suspicion, consciousness, hunch, apprehension, inkling, presentiment **5 = opinion**, view, attitude, belief, point of view, instinct, inclination **6a = ardour**, love, care, affection, warmth, tenderness, fondness, fervour **6b = sympathy**, understanding, concern, pity, appreciation, sensitivity, compassion, sorrow, sensibility, empathy, fellow feeling **7a = sense of touch**, sense, perception, sensation, feel, touch **7b = sensation**, sense, impression, awareness **8 = atmosphere**, mood, aura, ambience, feel, air, quality, vibes *(slang)*

DICTIONARY

Feisal II *n* a ▸variant spelling of **Faisal II**

feisty ⓘ (fie-stee) *adj* **feistier, feistiest** *informal* **1** showing courage or spirit **2** *US & Canad* frisky **3** *US & Canad* irritable
WORD ORIGIN from dialect *feist* small dog

feldspar *or* **felspar** *n* a hard mineral that is the main constituent of igneous rocks **feldspathic** *or* **felspathic** *adj*
WORD ORIGIN German *feldspath*

felicitations *pl n, interj* expressions of pleasure at someone's success or good fortune; congratulations

felicitous *adj* appropriate and well-chosen: *a felicitous combination of architectural styles*

felicity *n* **1** great happiness and pleasure **2** the quality of being pleasant or desirable: *small moments of architectural felicity amidst acres of monotony* **3** *pl* **-ties** an appropriate and well-chosen remark: *Nietzsche's verbal felicities are not lost in translation*
WORD ORIGIN Latin *felicitas* happiness

feline *adj* **1** of or belonging to the cat family **2** like a cat, esp. in stealth or grace ▹*n* **3** any member of the cat family **felinity** *n*
WORD ORIGIN Latin *feles* cat

fell[1] *vb* ▸the past tense of **fall**

fell[2] ⓘ *vb* **1** to cut down (a tree) **2** to knock down (a person), esp. in a fight
WORD ORIGIN Old English *fellan*

fell[3] *adj* **in one fell swoop** in one single action or on one single occasion: *they arrested all the hooligans in one fell swoop*
WORD ORIGIN Middle English *fel*

fell[4] *n Scot & N English* a mountain, hill, or moor
WORD ORIGIN Old Norse *fjall*

fell[5] *n* an animal's skin or hide with its hair
WORD ORIGIN Old High German *fel* skin

fellatio (fill-lay-shee-oh) *n* a sexual activity in which the penis is stimulated by the partner's mouth
WORD ORIGIN Latin *fellare* to suck

felloe *or* **felly** *n, pl* **-loes** *or* **-lies** a segment or the whole rim of a wooden wheel
WORD ORIGIN Old English *felge*

fellow ⓘ *n* **1** a man or boy **2** comrade or associate **3** a person in the same group or condition: *he earned the respect of his fellows at Dunkirk* **4** a member of the governing body at any of various universities or colleges **5** (in Britain) a postgraduate research student ▹*adj* **6** in the same group or condition: *a conversation with a fellow passenger*
WORD ORIGIN Old English *fēolaga*

Fellow *n* a senior member of an academic institution

fellow feeling *n* sympathy existing between people who have shared similar experiences

fellowship ⓘ *n* **1** the state of sharing mutual interests or activities **2** a society of people sharing mutual interests or activities **3** companionship or friendship **4** *education* a financed research post providing study facilities

fellow traveller *n history* a person who sympathized with the Communist Party but was not a member of it

felon *n criminal law* (formerly) a person who committed a serious crime
WORD ORIGIN Old French: villain

felony *n, pl* **-nies** *criminal law* (formerly) a serious crime, such as murder or arson **felonious** *adj*

felspar *n* ▸same as **feldspar**

felt[1] *vb* ▸the past of **feel**

felt[2] *n* a matted fabric of wool, made by working the fibres together under pressure
WORD ORIGIN Old English

felt-tip pen *n* a pen with a writing point made from pressed fibres

fem. **1** female **2** feminine

female *adj* **1** of the sex producing offspring **2** of or characteristic of a woman **3** (of reproductive organs such as the ovary and carpel) capable of producing reproductive cells (**gametes**) that are female **4** (of flowers) not having parts in which pollen is produced (**stamens**) **5** (of a mechanical component) having an opening into which a projecting male component can be fitted ▹*n* **6** a female person, animal, or plant
WORD ORIGIN Latin *femina* a woman

feminine ⓘ *adj* **1** possessing qualities considered typical of or appropriate to a woman **2** of women **3** *grammar* denoting a gender of nouns that includes some female animate things **femininity** *n*
WORD ORIGIN Latin *femina* a woman

feminism *n* a doctrine or movement that advocates equal rights for women **feminist** *n, adj*

femme fatale (**fam** fat-**tahl**) *n, pl* **femmes fatales** (**fam** fat-**tahlz**) an alluring or seductive woman who leads men into dangerous or difficult situations by her charm
WORD ORIGIN French

femto- *combining form* denoting 10^{-15}: *femtometer*
WORD ORIGIN Danish *femten* fifteen

femur (**fee**-mer) *n, pl* **femurs** *or* **femora** (**fee**-mer-ra) the thighbone **femoral** *adj*
WORD ORIGIN Latin: thigh

fen *n Brit* low-lying flat marshy land
WORD ORIGIN Old English *fenn*

fence ⓘ *n* **1** a barrier that encloses an area such as a garden or field, usually made of posts connected by wire rails or boards **2** an obstacle for a horse to jump in steeplechasing or showjumping **3** *slang* a dealer in stolen property **4** *machinery* a guard or guide, esp. in a circular saw or plane **5** **(sit) on the fence** (to be) unwilling to commit oneself ▹*vb* **fencing, fenced** **6** to construct a fence on or around (a piece of land) **7** **fence in** *or* **off** to close in *or* separate off with or as if with a fence **8** to fight using swords or foils **9** to argue cleverly but evasively: *they fenced for a while, weighing each other up*
WORD ORIGIN Middle English *fens*, from *defens* defence

fencing *n* **1** the sport of fighting with swords or foils **2** materials used for making fences

fend *vb* **1** **fend for oneself** to look after oneself; be independent **2** **fend off** to defend oneself against (verbal or physical attack)
WORD ORIGIN Middle English *fenden*

fender *n* **1** a low metal barrier that stops coals from falling out of a fireplace **2** a soft but solid object, such as a coil of rope, hung over the side of a vessel to prevent damage

THESAURUS

feisty *adj* **1** *(informal)* = **fiery**, spirited, bold, plucky, vivacious, (as) game as Ned Kelly *(Austral slang)*

fell[2] *vb* **1** = **cut down**, cut, level, demolish, flatten, knock down, hew, raze **2** = **knock down**, floor, flatten, strike down, prostrate, deck *(slang)*

fellow *n* **1** = **man**, boy, person, individual, customer *(informal)*, character, guy *(informal)*, bloke *(Brit informal)*, punter *(informal)*, chap *(informal)* **2** = **associate**, colleague, peer, co-worker, member, friend, partner, equal, companion, comrade, crony, compeer

fellowship *n* **1, 3** = **camaraderie**, intimacy, communion, familiarity, brotherhood, companionship, sociability, amity, kindliness, fraternization, companionability, intercourse **2** = **society**, club, league, association, organization, guild, fraternity, brotherhood, sisterhood, order, sodality

feminine *adj* **1** = **womanly**, pretty, soft, gentle, tender, modest, delicate, graceful, girlie, girlish, ladylike
OPPOSITE: masculine

fence *n* **1** = **barrier**, wall, defence, guard, railings, paling, shield, hedge, barricade, hedgerow, rampart, palisade, stockade, barbed wire ▹*vb* **7** *(with* **in** *or* **off***)* = **enclose**, surround, bound, hedge, pound, protect, separate, guard, defend, secure, pen, restrict, confine, fortify, encircle, coop, impound, circumscribe

DICTIONARY

when docking **3** *US & Canad* the wing of a car

Fénelon *n* **François de Salignac de La Mothe** 1651–1715, French theologian and writer; author of *Maximes des saints* (1697), a defence of quietism, and *Les aventures de Télémaque* (1699), which was construed as criticizing the government of Louis XIV

fenestration *n* the arrangement of windows in a building
WORD ORIGIN Latin *fenestra* window

feng shui (fung shway) *n* the Chinese art of deciding the best design or position of a grave, building, etc. in order to bring good luck
WORD ORIGIN Chinese *feng* wind + *shui* water

Fenian (feen-yan) *n* (formerly) a member of an Irish revolutionary organization founded to fight for an independent Ireland **Fenianism** *n*
WORD ORIGIN after *Fianna*, legendary band of Irish warriors

fenland *n Brit* an area of low-lying flat marshy land

fennel *n* a fragrant plant whose seeds, leaves, and root are used in cookery
WORD ORIGIN Old English *fenol*

Fenton *n* **James** (**Martin**) born 1949, British poet, journalist, and critic. His poetry includes the collections *A German Requiem* (1980) and *Out of Danger* (1993)

fenugreek *n* a Mediterranean plant grown for its heavily scented seeds
WORD ORIGIN Old English *fēnogrēcum*

feoff (feef) *n* ▸ same as **fief**
WORD ORIGIN Anglo-French

feral *adj* **1** (of animals and plants) existing in a wild state, esp. after being domestic or cultivated **2** savage
WORD ORIGIN Latin *ferus* savage

Ferdinand I *n* **1** known as *Ferdinand the Great*. ?1016–65, king of Castile (1035–65) and León (1037–65): achieved control of the Moorish kings of Saragossa, Seville, and Toledo **2** 1503–64, king of Hungary and Bohemia (1526–64); Holy Roman Emperor (1558–64), bringing years of religious warfare to an end **3** 1751–1825, king of the Two Sicilies (1816–25); king of Naples (1759–1806; 1815–25), as Ferdinand IV, being dispossessed by Napoleon (1806–15) **4** 1793–1875, king of Hungary (1830–48) and emperor of Austria (1835–48); abdicated after the Revolution of 1848 in favour of his nephew, Franz Josef I **5** 1861–1948, ruling prince of Bulgaria (1887–1908) and tsar from 1908 until his abdication in 1918 **6** 1865–1927, king of Romania (1914–27); sided with the Allies in World War I

Ferdinand II *n* 1578–1637, Holy Roman Emperor (1619–37); king of Bohemia (1617–19; 1620–37) and of Hungary (1617–37). His anti-Protestant policies led to the Thirty Years' War

Ferdinand III *n* 1608–57, Holy Roman Emperor (1637–57) and king of Hungary (1625–57); son of Ferdinand II

Ferdinand VII *n* 1784–1833, king of Spain (1808; 1814–33). He precipitated the Carlist Wars by excluding his brother Don Carlos as his successor

Ferguson *n* Sir **Alex**(**ander**) **Chapman** born 1941, Scottish footballer and manager; manager of Manchester United from 1986

Ferlinghetti *n* **Lawrence** born 1920, US poet of the Beat Generation. His poetry includes the collections *Pictures of the Gone World* (1955) and *When I Look at Pictures* (1990)

ferment *n* **1** excitement and unrest caused by change or uncertainty **2** any substance, such as yeast, that causes fermentation ▹ *vb* **3** to undergo or cause to undergo fermentation
WORD ORIGIN Latin *fermentum* yeast

fermentation *n* a chemical reaction in which an organic molecule splits into simpler substances, esp. the conversion of sugar to ethyl alcohol by yeast

fermium *n chem* an element artificially produced by neutron bombardment of plutonium. Symbol: Fm
WORD ORIGIN after Enrico *Fermi*, physicist

Fermor *n* Sir **Patrick** (**Michael**) **Leigh** born 1915, British traveller and author, noted esp. for the travel books *A Time of Gifts* (1977) and *Between the Woods and the Water* (1986)

fern *n* a flowerless plant with roots, stems, and long feathery leaves that reproduces by releasing spores **ferny** *adj*
WORD ORIGIN Old English *fearn*

Fernandel *n* real name *Fernand Joseph Désiré Contandin*. 1903–71, French comic film actor

ferocious ❶ *adj* savagely fierce or cruel **ferocity** *n*
WORD ORIGIN Latin *ferox*

Ferrar *n* **Nicholas** 1592–1637, English mystic. He founded (1625) an Anglican religious community at Little Gidding, Huntingdonshire

Ferrari *n* **Enzo** 1898–1988, Italian designer and manufacturer of racing cars

ferret *n* **1** a small yellowish-white animal related to the weasel and bred for hunting rats and rabbits ▹ *vb* **-reting, -reted 2** to hunt rabbits or rats with ferrets **3** to search around **4 ferret out a** to drive from hiding **b** to find by determined investigation: *she could ferret out little knowledge of his background*
WORD ORIGIN Latin *fur* thief

ferric *adj* of or containing iron in the trivalent state
WORD ORIGIN Latin *ferrum* iron

Ferrier *n* **Kathleen** 1912–53, British contralto; noted for her expressive voice

Ferris wheel *n* a large vertical fairground wheel with hanging seats for riding on
WORD ORIGIN after G. W. G. *Ferris*, American engineer

ferroconcrete *n* ▸ same as **reinforced concrete**

ferrous *adj* of or containing iron in the divalent state
WORD ORIGIN Latin *ferrum* iron

ferruginous (fur-**rooj**-in-uss) *adj* (of a mineral or rock) containing iron
WORD ORIGIN Latin *ferrum* iron

ferrule *n* a metal ring or cap placed over the end of a stick for added strength
WORD ORIGIN Latin *viria* bracelet

ferry ❶ *n, pl* **-ries 1** a boat for transporting passengers and vehicles across a body of water, esp. as a regular service **2** such a service ▹ *vb* **-ries, -rying, -ried 3** to transport or go by ferry **4** to transport (passengers or goods) on a regular basis **ferryman** *n*
WORD ORIGIN Old English *ferian* to carry

fertile ❶ *adj* **1** capable of producing offspring, crops, or vegetation **2** *biol* capable of growth and development: *fertile seeds* **3** highly productive: *a fertile imagination* **4** *physics* (of a substance) able to be transformed into fissile or fissionable material **fertility** *n*
WORD ORIGIN Latin *fertilis*

fertilize *or* **-lise** *vb* **-lizing, -lized** *or* **-lising, -lised 1** to provide (an animal

THESAURUS

ferocious *adj* **a = fierce**, violent, savage, ravening, predatory, feral, rapacious, wild **OPPOSITE:** gentle **b = cruel**, bitter, brutal, vicious, ruthless, relentless, barbaric, merciless, brutish, bloodthirsty, barbarous, pitiless, tigerish

ferry *n* **1 = ferry boat**, boat, ship, passenger boat, packet boat, packet ▹ *vb* **3, 4 = transport**, bring, carry, ship, take, run, shuttle, convey, chauffeur

fertile *adj* **1 = productive**, rich, flowering, lush, fat, yielding, prolific, abundant, plentiful, fruitful, teeming, luxuriant, generative, fecund, fruit-bearing, flowing with milk and honey, plenteous **OPPOSITE:** barren

fertilizer *or* **fertiliser** *n* **= compost**, muck, manure, dung, guano, marl,

DICTIONARY

or plant) with sperm or pollen to bring about fertilization **2** to supply (soil) with nutrients **fertilization** *or* **-lisation** *n*

fertilizer ❶ *or* **-liser** *n* any substance, such as manure, added to soil to increase its productivity

fervent *or* **fervid** *adj* intensely sincere and passionate **fervently** *adv*
WORD ORIGIN Latin *fervere* to boil

fervour *or US* **fervor** *n* great intensity of feeling or belief
WORD ORIGIN Latin *fervere* to boil

fescue *n* a pasture and lawn grass with stiff narrow leaves
WORD ORIGIN Old French *festu*

fest *n* an event at which the emphasis is on a particular activity: *fashion fest*
WORD ORIGIN German: festival

fester *vb* **1** to grow worse and increasingly hostile: *the bitterness which had been festering beneath the surface* **2** (of a wound) to form pus **3** to rot and decay: *rubbish festered in the heat*
WORD ORIGIN Old French *festre* suppurating sore

festival ❶ *n* **1** an organized series of special events and performances: *the Edinburgh Festival* **2** a day or period set aside for celebration
WORD ORIGIN Latin *festivus* joyful

festive ❶ *adj* of or like a celebration
WORD ORIGIN Latin *festivus* joyful

festivity *n, pl* **-ties 1** happy celebration: *a spirit of joy and festivity* **2 festivities** celebrations

festoon *vb* **1** to drape with decorations: *Christmas trees festooned with fairy lights* ▷ *n* **2** a decorative chain of flowers or ribbons suspended in loops
WORD ORIGIN Italian *festone* ornament for a feast

feta *n* a white Greek cheese made from sheep's or goat's milk
WORD ORIGIN Modern Greek

fetal alcohol syndrome *n* a condition in newborn babies caused by excessive alcohol intake by the mother during pregnancy: characterized by various defects including mental retardation

fetch[1] ❶ *vb* **1** to go after and bring back **2** to be sold for (a certain price): *Impressionist pictures fetch very high prices* **3** *informal* to give someone (a blow or slap) **4 fetch and carry** to perform menial tasks
WORD ORIGIN Old English *feccan*

fetch[2] *n* the ghost or apparition of a living person
WORD ORIGIN origin unknown

fetching ❶ *adj informal* attractive: *a fetching dress*

fetch up *vb* **1** *US & NZ informal* to arrive or end up **2** *slang* to vomit food

fete (fate) *n* **1** an event, usually outdoors, with stalls, competitions, etc. held to raise money for charity ▷ *vb* **feting, feted 2** to honour and entertain (someone) publicly: *the President was feted with an evening of music and dancing*
WORD ORIGIN French

fetid *or* **foetid** *adj* having a stale and unpleasant smell
WORD ORIGIN Latin *fetere* to stink

fetish *n* **1 a** a form of behaviour in which a person derives sexual satisfaction from handling an object **b** any object that is involved in such behaviour **2** any object, activity, etc. to which one is excessively devoted: *cleanliness is almost a fetish with her* **3** an object that is believed to have magical powers **fetishism** *n* **fetishist** *n*
WORD ORIGIN Portuguese *feitiço* sorcery

fetlock *n* **1** the back part of a horse's leg, just behind the hoof **2** the tuft of hair growing from this part
WORD ORIGIN Middle English *fetlak*

fetter *n* **1 fetters** checks or restraints: *free from the fetters of religion* **2** a chain fixed around a prisoner's ankle ▷ *vb* **3** to prevent from behaving freely and naturally: *fettered by bureaucracy* **4** to tie up in fetters
WORD ORIGIN Old English *fetor*

fettle *n* **in fine fettle** in good spirits or health
WORD ORIGIN Old English *fetel* belt

fetus *or* **foetus** (fee-tuss) *n, pl* **-tuses** the embryo of a mammal in the later stages of development **fetal** *or* **foetal** *adj*
WORD ORIGIN Latin: offspring

feu *n Scots Law* a right to the use of land in return for a fixed annual payment (**feu duty**)
WORD ORIGIN Old French

Feuchtwanger *n* **Lion** 1884–1958, German novelist and dramatist, lived in the US (1940–58): noted for his historical novels, including *Die hässliche Herzogin* (1923) and *Jud Süss* (1925)

feud ❶ *n* **1** long and bitter hostility between two families, clans, or individuals ▷ *vb* **2** to carry on a feud
WORD ORIGIN Old French *feide*

feudal *adj* of or characteristic of feudalism
WORD ORIGIN Medieval Latin *feudum* fief

feudalism *n* the legal and social system in medieval Europe, in which people were given land and protection by a lord in return for which they worked and fought for him. Also called: **feudal system**

Feuerbach *n* **Ludwig Andreas** 1804–72, German materialist philosopher: in *The Essence of Christianity* (1841), translated into English by George Eliot (1853), he maintained that God is merely an outward projection of man's inner self

fever ❶ *n* **1** an abnormally high body temperature, accompanied by a fast pulse rate, shivering, and nausea ▸ Related adjective: **febrile 2** any disease characterized by a high temperature **3** intense nervous excitement: *she waited in a fever of anxiety*
WORD ORIGIN Latin *febris*

feverish *or* **fevered** *adj* **1** suffering from fever **2** in a state of nervous excitement: *a feverish scramble to buy shares* **feverishly** *adv*

fever pitch *n* a state of intense excitement

few ❶ *adj* **1** hardly any: *few homes had telephones in Paris in the 1930s* **2 a few** a small number of: *a few days ago* **3 a good few** *informal* several **4 few and far between** scarce **5 quite a few** *informal* several
WORD ORIGIN Old English *fēawa*

f

THESAURUS

bone meal, dressing

festival *n* **1 = celebration**, fair, carnival, gala, treat, fête, entertainment, jubilee, fiesta, festivities, jamboree, -fest, field day **2 = holy day**, holiday, feast, commemoration, feast day, red-letter day, saint's day, fiesta, fête, anniversary

festive *adj* **= celebratory**, happy, holiday, carnival, jolly, merry, gala, hearty, jubilant, cheery, joyous, joyful, jovial, convivial, gleeful, back-slapping, Christmassy, mirthful, sportive, light-hearted, festal, gay **OPPOSITE:** mournful

fetch[1] *vb* **1 = bring**, pick up, collect, go and get, get, carry, deliver, conduct, transport, go for, obtain, escort, convey, retrieve **2 = sell for**, make, raise, earn, realize, go for, yield, bring in

fetching *adj (informal)* **= attractive**, sweet, charming, enchanting, fascinating, intriguing, cute, enticing, captivating, alluring, winsome

feud *n* **1 = hostility**, row, conflict, argument, faction, falling out, disagreement, rivalry, contention, quarrel, grudge, strife, bickering, vendetta, discord, enmity, broil, bad blood, estrangement, dissension ▷ *vb* **2 = quarrel**, row, clash, dispute, fall out, contend, brawl, war, squabble, duel, bicker, be at odds, be at daggers drawn

fever *n* **3 = excitement**, heat, passion, intensity, flush, turmoil, ecstasy, frenzy, ferment, agitation, fervour, restlessness, delirium

few *adj* **1 = not many**, one or two, hardly any, scarcely any, rare, thin, scattered, insufficient, scarce, scant, meagre, negligible, sporadic, sparse,

DICTIONARY

fey *adj* **1** vague and whimsically strange **2** having the ability to look into the future
WORD ORIGIN Old English *fæge* marked out for death

Feydeau *n* **Georges** 1862–1921, French dramatist, noted for his farces, esp. *La Dame de chez Maxim* (1899) and *Occupe-toi d'Amélie* (1908)

fez *n, pl* **fezzes** a round red brimless hat with a flat top and a tassel hanging from it. Formerly worn by men in Turkey and some Arab countries
WORD ORIGIN Turkish

f

ff. and the following (pages, lines, etc.)

fiancé *or fem* **fiancée** (fee-on-say) *n* a person who is engaged to be married
WORD ORIGIN Old French *fiancier* to promise, betroth

fiasco ❶ *n, pl* **-cos** *or* **-coes** an action or attempt that fails completely in a ridiculous or disorganized way: *the invasion of Cuba ended in a fiasco*
WORD ORIGIN Italian: flask; sense development obscure

fiat (fie-at) *n* **1** an official order issued without the consultation of those expected to obey it: *the junta ruled by fiat* **2** official permission
WORD ORIGIN Latin: let it be done

fib *n* **1** a trivial and harmless lie ▷ *vb* **fibbing, fibbed 2** to tell such a lie **fibber** *n*
WORD ORIGIN origin unknown

Fibiger *n* **Johannes Andreas Grib** 1867–1928, Danish physician: Nobel prize for physiology or medicine (1926) for his work in cancer research

fibre ❶ *or US* **fiber** *n* **1** a natural or synthetic thread that may be spun into yarn **2** a threadlike animal or plant tissue: *a simple network of nerve fibres* **3** a fibrous substance that helps the body digest food: *fruits, vegetables, grains, lentils, and beans are high in fibre* **4** strength of character: *moral fibre* **5** essential substance or nature: *my every fibre sang out in sudden relief* **fibrous** *adj*
WORD ORIGIN Latin *fibra* filament, entrails

fibreboard *n* a building material made of compressed wood

fibreglass *n* **1** material consisting of matted fine glass fibres, used as insulation **2** a light strong material made by bonding fibreglass with a synthetic resin, used for boats and car bodies

fibre optics *n* the transmission of information by light along very thin flexible fibres of glass **fibre optic** *adj*

fibril (fibe-rill) *n* a small fibre

fibrillation *n* uncontrollable twitching of muscle fibres, esp. those of the heart

fibrin *n* a white insoluble elastic protein formed when blood clots

fibrinogen (fib-rin-no-jen) *n biol* a soluble plasma protein involved in blood clotting

fibro *n Austral* a mixture of cement and asbestos fibre, used in sheets for building. Short for: **fibrocement**

fibroid (fibe-royd) *adj* **1** *anat* (of structures or tissues) containing or resembling fibres ▷ *n* **2** a harmless tumour composed of fibrous connective tissue

fibrosis (fibe-roh-siss) *n* the formation of an abnormal amount of fibrous tissue

fibrositis (fibe-roh-site-iss) *n* inflammation of fibrous tissue, esp. of the back muscles, causing pain and stiffness

fibula (fib-yew-la) *n, pl* **-lae** (-lee) *or* **-las** the outer and thinner of the two bones between the knee and ankle of the human leg **fibular** *adj*
WORD ORIGIN Latin: a clasp

fiche (feesh) *n* a sheet of film for storing publications in miniature form

Ficino *n* **Marsilio** 1433–99, Italian Neoplatonist philosopher: attempted to integrate Platonism with Christianity

fickle *adj* **1** changeable in purpose, affections, etc.: *notoriously fickle voters* **2** (of the weather) changing often and suddenly **fickleness** *n*
WORD ORIGIN Old English *ficol* deceitful

fiction ❶ *n* **1** literary works invented by the imagination, such as novels **2** an invented story or explanation: *the fiction that the Baltic states freely joined the USSR* **3** *law* something assumed to be true for the sake of convenience, though probably false **fictional** *adj*
WORD ORIGIN Latin *fictio* a fashioning

fictionalize *or* **-ise** *vb* **-izing, -ized** *or* **-ising, -ised** to make into fiction

fictitious *adj* **1** not genuine: *rumours of false accounting and fictitious loans had surrounded the bank for years* **2** of or in fiction

fiddle ❶ *n* **1** *informal or disparaging* the violin **2** a violin played as a folk instrument **3** *Brit & NZ informal* a dishonest action or scheme **4 on the fiddle** *informal* engaged in an illegal or fraudulent undertaking **5 fit as a fiddle** *informal* in very good health **6 play second fiddle** *informal* to undertake a role that is less important or powerful than someone else's ▷ *vb* **-dling, -dled 7** to play (a tune) on the fiddle **8** *informal* to do (something) by illegal or dishonest means **9** *informal* to falsify (accounts) **10 fiddle with** to move or touch (something) restlessly or nervously **11 fiddle about** *or* **around** *informal* to waste time
WORD ORIGIN Old English *fithele*

fiddle-faddle *interj old-fashioned* nonsense
WORD ORIGIN reduplication of *fiddle*

fiddler *n* **1** a person who plays the fiddle **2** a small burrowing crab **3** *informal* a person who dishonestly alters something or lies in order to get money

fiddlesticks *interj* an expression of annoyance or disagreement

fiddling ❶ *adj* small or unimportant

fiddly *adj* **-dlier, -dliest** small and awkward to do or handle

fidelity ❶ *n, pl* **-ties 1** faithfulness to one's spouse or lover **2** loyalty to a person, belief, or cause **3** accuracy in reporting detail: *an account of the invasion written with objectivity and fidelity* **4** *electronics* the degree to which an amplifier or radio accurately reproduces the input signal
WORD ORIGIN Latin *fides* faith

THESAURUS

infrequent, scanty, inconsiderable
OPPOSITE: many

fiasco *n* **= flop**, failure, disaster, ruin, mess *(informal)*, catastrophe, rout, debacle, cock-up *(Brit slang)*, washout *(informal)*

fibre *or (US)* **fiber** *n* **1, 2 = thread**, strand, filament, tendril, pile, texture, staple, wisp, fibril

fiction *n* **1 = tale**, story, novel, legend, myth, romance, fable, storytelling, narration, creative writing, work of imagination **2 = lie**, fancy, fantasy, invention, improvisation, fabrication, concoction, falsehood, untruth, porky *(Brit slang)*, pork pie *(Brit slang)*, urban myth, tall story, urban legend, cock and bull story *(informal)*, figment of the imagination

fiddle *n* **3** *(Brit & NZ informal)* **= fraud**, racket, scam *(slang)*, piece of sharp practice, fix, sting *(informal)*, graft *(informal)*, swindle, wangle *(informal)* ▷ *vb* **8, 9** *(informal)* **= cheat**, cook *(informal)*, fix, manoeuvre *(informal)*, graft *(informal)*, diddle *(informal)*, wangle *(informal)*, gerrymander, finagle *(informal)*

fiddling *adj* **= trivial**, small, petty, trifling, insignificant, unimportant, pettifogging, futile

fidelity *n* **1, 2 = loyalty**, faith, integrity, devotion, allegiance, constancy, faithfulness, dependability, trustworthiness, troth *(archaic)*, fealty, staunchness, devotedness, lealty *(archaic, Scot)*, true-heartedness
OPPOSITE: disloyalty
3 = accuracy, precision, correspondence, closeness, adherence, faithfulness, exactitude, exactness, scrupulousness, preciseness **OPPOSITE:** inaccuracy

fidget *vb* **-eting, -eted 1** to move about restlessly **2 fidget with** to make restless or uneasy movements with (something): *he broke off, fidgeting with the papers, unable to meet their gaze* ▹*n* **3** a person who fidgets **4 the fidgets** a state of restlessness: *these youngsters are very highly strung and tend to get the fidgets* **fidgety** *adj*
WORD ORIGIN earlier *fidge*

fiduciary (fid-**yewsh**-ya-ree) *law n* **1** a person bound to act for someone else's benefit, as a trustee ▹*adj* **2** of or relating to a trust or trustee
WORD ORIGIN Latin *fiducia* trust

fie *interj obsolete or facetious* an exclamation of disapproval
WORD ORIGIN Old French *fi*

fief (**feef**) *n* (in feudal Europe) land granted by a lord in return for military service
WORD ORIGIN Old French *fie*

fiefdom *n* **1** (in Feudal Europe) the property owned by a lord **2** an area over which a person has influence or authority

field ❶ *n* **1** an area of uncultivated grassland; meadow **2** a piece of cleared land used for pasture or growing crops **3** a marked off area on which sports or athletic competitions are held **4** an area that is rich in minerals or other natural resources: *an oil field* **5 a** all the competitors in a competition **b** the competitors in a competition excluding the favourite **6** a battlefield **7** *cricket* the fielders collectively **8** a wide expanse of land covered by some substance such as snow or lava **9** an area of human activity or knowledge: *the most distinguished physicist in the field of quantum physics* **10** a place away from the laboratory or classroom where practical work is done **11** the surface or background of something, such as a flag **12** *physics* In full: **field of force** the region surrounding a body, such as a magnet, within which it can exert a force on another similar body not in contact with it **13 play the field** *informal* to have many romantic relationships before getting married ▹*adj* **14** *mil* of equipment or personnel for operations in the field: *field guns* ▹*vb* **15** *sport* to catch or return (the ball) as a fielder **16** *sport* to send (a player or team) onto the field to play **17** *sport* (of a player or team) to act or take turn as a fielder or fielders **18** *informal* to deal successfully with (a question or remark)
WORD ORIGIN Old English *feld*

Field *n* **John** 1782–1837, Irish composer and pianist, lived in Russia from 1803: invented the nocturne

field day *n* **1** *informal* an opportunity or occasion for unrestrained action, esp. if previously denied or restricted: *the revelations gave the press a field day* **2** *mil* a day devoted to manoeuvres or exercises

fielder *n cricket, etc.* a member of the fielding side

field event *n* a competition, such as the discus, that takes place on a field as opposed to the track

fieldfare *n* a type of large thrush
WORD ORIGIN Old English *feldefare*

field glasses *pl n* binoculars

field hockey *n US & Canad* hockey played on a field, as distinguished from ice hockey

Fielding *n* **Henry** 1707–54, English novelist and dramatist, noted particularly for his picaresque novel *Tom Jones* (1749) and for *Joseph Andrews* (1742), which starts as a parody of Richardson's *Pamela*: also noted as an enlightened magistrate and a founder of the Bow Street runners (1749)

field marshal *n* an officer holding the highest rank in certain armies

fieldmouse *n, pl* **-mice** a nocturnal mouse that lives in woods and fields

field officer *n* an officer holding the rank of major, lieutenant colonel, or colonel

fieldsman *n, pl* **-men** *cricket* a fielder

field sports *pl n* sports carried on in the countryside, such as hunting or fishing

field trip *n* an expedition, esp. by students, to study something at first hand

fieldwork *n mil* a temporary structure used in defending a place or position

field work *n* an investigation made in the field as opposed to the classroom or laboratory **field worker** *n*

fiend (**feend**) *n* **1** an evil spirit **2** a cruel or wicked person **3** *informal* a person who is extremely interested in or fond of something: *a fitness fiend* **fiendish** *adj* **fiendishly** *adv*
WORD ORIGIN Old English *fēond*

Fiend *n* **the Fiend** the devil

Fiennes *n* **1 Ralph** (**Nathanial**) born 1962, British actor; his films include *Schindler's List* (1993), *The English Patient* (1997), *The End of the Affair* (2000), and *Spider* (2002) **2** Sir **Ranulph** (**Twistleton-Wykeham-**) born 1944, British explorer; led the first surface journey around the earth's polar axis (1979–82); unsupported crossing of Antarctica (1992–93)

fierce ❶ *adj* **1** very aggressive or angry: *a fierce dog* **2** intense or strong: *a fierce wind* **fiercely** *adv*
WORD ORIGIN Latin *ferus*

fiery ❶ (**fire**-ee) *adj* **fierier, fieriest 1** consisting of or like fire: *a fiery explosion* **2** displaying strong passion, esp. anger: *a fiery speech* **3** (of food) very spicy **fierily** *adv* **fieriness** *n*

fiesta *n* (esp. in Spain and Latin America) a religious festival or carnival
WORD ORIGIN Spanish

FIFA (**fee**-fa) International Association Football Federation
WORD ORIGIN French *Fédération Internationale de Football Association*

fife *n* a small high-pitched flute, often used in military bands
WORD ORIGIN Old High German *pfīfa*

Fife[1] *n* a council area and historical county of E central Scotland, bordering on the North Sea between the Firths of Tay and Forth: coastal lowlands in the north and east, with several ranges of hills; mainly agricultural. Administrative centre: Glenrothes. Pop: 352 040 (2003 est). Area: 1323 sq km (511 sq miles)

Fife[2] *n* **Duncan** ▸ See **Duncan Phyfe**

fifteen *n* **1** the cardinal number that is the sum of ten and five **2** a numeral, 15 or XV, representing this number **3** something representing or consisting of 15 units **4** a Rugby Union team ▹*adj* **5** amounting to fifteen: *fifteen trees* **fifteenth** *adj, n*

fifth *adj* **1** of or being number five in a series ▹*n* **2** one of five equal parts of

f

THESAURUS

field *n* **1, 2 = meadow**, land, green, lea *(poetic)*, pasture, mead *(archaic)*, greensward *(archaic, literary)* **5a = competitors**, competition, candidates, runners, applicants, entrants, contestants **9 = speciality**, line, area, department, environment, territory, discipline, province, pale, confines, sphere, domain, specialty, sphere of influence, purview, metier, sphere of activity, bailiwick, sphere of interest, sphere of study ▹*vb* **15** *(sport)* **= retrieve**, return, stop, catch, pick up **18** *(informal)* **= deal with**, answer, handle, respond to, reply to, deflect, turn aside

fierce *adj* **1 = ferocious**, wild, dangerous, cruel, savage, brutal, aggressive, menacing, vicious, fiery, murderous, uncontrollable, feral, untamed, barbarous, fell *(archaic)*, threatening, baleful, truculent, tigerish, aggers *(Austral slang)*, biffo *(Austral slang)* **OPPOSITE:** gentle **2a = intense**, strong, keen, passionate, relentless, cut-throat **2b = stormy**, strong, powerful, violent, intense, raging, furious, howling, uncontrollable, boisterous, tumultuous, tempestuous, blustery, inclement **OPPOSITE:** tranquil

fiery *adj* **1 = burning**, flaming, glowing, blazing, on fire, red-hot, ablaze, in flames, aflame, afire **2 = excitable**, violent, fierce, passionate, irritable, impetuous, irascible, peppery, hot-headed, choleric

DICTIONARY

something **3** *music* the interval between one note and the note three-and-a-half tones higher or lower than it **4** an additional high gear fitted to some vehicles, esp. certain sports cars

fifth column *n* any group that secretly helps the enemies of its own country or organization **fifth columnist** *n*

fifty *n, pl* **-ties** **1** the cardinal number that is the product of ten and five **2** a numeral, 50 or L, representing this number **3** something representing or consisting of 50 units ▹ *adj* **4** amounting to fifty: *fifty bodies* **fiftieth** *adj, n*

fifty-fifty *adj, adv informal* **1** in equal parts **2** just as likely to happen as not to happen: *a fifty-fifty chance of survival*

fig *n* **1** a soft sweet fruit full of tiny seeds, which grows on a tree **2 not care** *or* **give a fig** not to care at all: *he did not give a fig for his enemies*
WORD ORIGIN Latin *ficus* fig tree

fig. **1** figurative(ly) **2** figure

fight ⊕ *vb* **fighting, fought** **1** to struggle against (an enemy) in battle or physical combat **2** to struggle to overcome or destroy: *to fight drug trafficking* **3** to carry on (a battle or contest) **4** to make (one's way) somewhere with difficulty: *they fought their way upstream* **5 fight for** to uphold (a cause) by struggling: *fight for your rights* **6 fight it out** to struggle or compete until a decisive result is obtained **7 fight shy of** to avoid: *they fought shy of direct involvement in the conflict* ▹ *n* **8** a battle **9** a quarrel or contest **10** a boxing match **11 put up a fight** to offer resistance **fighting** *n*
WORD ORIGIN Old English *feohtan*

fighter ⊕ *n* **1** a professional boxer **2** a person who has determination **3** *mil* an armed aircraft for destroying other aircraft

fighting chance *n* a slight chance of success dependent on a struggle

fight off *vb* **1** to drive away (an attacker) **2** to struggle to avoid: *to fight off infection*

fig leaf *n* **1** a representation of a leaf of the fig tree used in sculpture to cover the genitals of nude figures **2** anything used to conceal something thought to be shameful: *the agreement was a fig leaf for Hitler's violation of the treaty*

figment *n* **a figment of one's imagination** something nonexistent and only imagined by someone
WORD ORIGIN Latin *fingere* to shape

figuration *n* ornamentation

figurative *adj* **1** (of language) abstract, imaginative, or symbolic; not literal **2** (of art) involving realistic representation of people and things **figuratively** *adv*

figure ⊕ *n* **1** a written symbol for a number **2** an amount expressed in numbers **3 figures** calculations with numbers **4** visible shape or form; outline **5** a slim bodily shape: *it's not good for your figure* **6** a well-known person: *a public figure* **7** a representation in painting or sculpture, esp. of the human body **8** an illustration or diagram in a text **9** a decorative pattern **10** a fixed set of movements in dancing or skating **11** *geom* any combination of points, lines, curves, or planes **12** *music* a characteristic short pattern of notes **13 figure of fun** a person who is often laughed at by other people ▹ *vb* **-uring, -ured** **14** to calculate (sums or amounts) **15** *US, Canad, Austral & NZ informal* to consider **16** to be included or play a part: *a house which figures in several of White's novels* **17** *informal* to be consistent with expectation: *Small-time crook, earns most of his cash as an informer. – That figures*
WORD ORIGIN Latin *figura* a shape

figured *adj* **1** decorated with a design: *a chair upholstered in figured velvet* **2** *music* ornamental

figurehead ⊕ *n* **1** a person who is formally the head of a movement or an organization, but has no real authority **2** a carved bust on the bow of some sailing vessels

figure of speech *n* an expression, such as a simile, in which words do not have their literal meaning

figure out ⊕ *vb informal* to work out, solve, or understand: *I can't figure him out*

figure skating *n* ice skating in which the skater traces outlines of selected patterns **figure skater** *n*

figurine *n* a small carved or moulded figure
WORD ORIGIN French

filament *n* **1** the thin wire inside a light bulb that emits light **2** *electronics* a high-resistance wire forming the cathode in some valves **3** a single strand of fibre **4** *bot* the stalk of a stamen **filamentary** *adj*
WORD ORIGIN Latin *filum* thread

filbert *n* the brown edible nuts of the hazel
WORD ORIGIN after St *Philbert*, because the nuts are ripe around his feast day, August 22

filch *vb* to steal in small amounts
WORD ORIGIN Middle English *filchen* to steal, attack

file[1] ⊕ *n* **1** a folder or box used to keep documents in order **2** the documents, etc. kept in this way **3** documents or information about a

THESAURUS

fight *vb* **1a = oppose**, campaign against, dispute, contest, resist, defy, contend, withstand, stand up to, take issue with, make a stand against **1b = battle**, assault, combat, war with, go to war, do battle, wage war, take up arms, bear arms against, engage in hostilities, carry on war, engage **3 = engage in**, conduct, wage, pursue, carry on ▹ *n* **8a = battle**, campaign, movement, struggle **8b = conflict**, war, action, clash, contest, encounter, brush, combat, engagement, hostilities, skirmish, passage of arms **9 = row**, argument, dispute, quarrel, squabble **10 = brawl**, set-to *(informal)*, riot, scrap *(informal)*, confrontation, rumble *(US & NZ slang)*, fray, duel, skirmish, head-to-head, tussle, scuffle, free-for-all *(informal)*, fracas, altercation, dogfight, joust, dissension, affray *(law)*, shindig *(informal)*, scrimmage, sparring match, exchange of blows, shindy *(informal)*, melee *or* mêlée, biffo *(Austral slang)*, boilover *(Austral)*

fighter *n* **1 = boxer**, wrestler, bruiser *(informal)*, pugilist, prize fighter

figure *n* **1 = digit**, character, symbol, number, numeral, cipher **5 = shape**, build, body, frame, proportions, chassis *(slang)*, torso, physique **6 = personage**, force, face *(informal)*, leader, person, individual, character, presence, somebody, personality, celebrity, worthy, notable, big name, dignitary, notability **8 = diagram**, drawing, picture, illustration, representation, sketch, emblem **9 = design**, shape, pattern, device, motif, depiction ▹ *vb* **14 = calculate**, work out, compute, tot up, add, total, count, reckon, sum, tally **16 = feature**, act, appear, contribute to, be included, be mentioned, play a part, be featured, have a place in, be conspicuous

figurehead *n* **1 = nominal head**, leader in name only, titular head, front man, name, token, dummy, puppet, mouthpiece, cipher, nonentity, straw man *(chiefly US)*, man of straw

figure out *vb (informal)* **= understand**, make out, fathom, make head or tail of *(informal)*, see, solve, resolve, comprehend, make sense of, decipher, think through, suss (out) *(slang)*

file[1] *n* **1 = folder**, case, portfolio, binder **2, 3 = dossier**, record, information, data, documents, case history, report, case **4 = line**, row, chain, string, column, queue, procession ▹ *vb* **7 = arrange**, order, classify, put in place, slot in *(informal)*, categorize, pigeonhole, put in order **8 = register**, record, enter, log, put on record **11 = march**, troop, parade, walk in line, walk behind one another

file[2] *vb* **2 = smooth**, shape, polish, rub, refine, scrape, rasp, burnish

DICTIONARY

specific subject or person: *the doctor handed him his file* **4** a line of people in marching formation, one behind another **5** *computers* an organized collection of related records **6 on file** recorded for reference, as in a file ▹ *vb* **filing, filed 7** to place (a document) in a file **8** to place (a legal document) on public or official record **9** to bring a lawsuit, esp. for divorce **10** to submit (a report or story) to a newspaper **11** to march or walk in a line
WORD ORIGIN Latin *filum* a thread

file² ❶ *n* **1** a hand tool consisting of a steel blade with small cutting teeth on its faces, used for shaping or smoothing ▹ *vb* **filing, filed 2** to shape or smooth (a surface) with a file
WORD ORIGIN Old English *fīl*

file sharing *n* the practice of sharing computer data or space on a network

filial *adj* of or suitable to a son or daughter: *filial duty*
WORD ORIGIN Latin *filius* son

filibuster *n* **1** the process of obstructing legislation by means of long speeches so that time runs out and a vote cannot be taken **2** a legislator who engages in such obstruction ▹ *vb* **3** to obstruct (legislation) with such delaying tactics
WORD ORIGIN probably from Dutch *vrijbuiter* pirate

filigree *n* **1** delicate ornamental work of gold or silver wire ▹ *adj* **2** made of filigree
WORD ORIGIN Latin *filum* thread + *granum* grain

filings *pl n* shavings or particles removed by a file: *iron filings*

Filipino (fill-lip-pee-no) *adj* **1** of the Philippines ▹ *n, pl* **-nos 2** Also (fem): **Filipina** a person from the Philippines

fill ❶ *vb* (often foll. by *up*) **1** to make or become full **2** to occupy the whole of: *their supporters filled the entire stand* **3** to plug (a gap or crevice) **4** to meet (a requirement or need) satisfactorily: *this book fills a major gap* **5** to cover (a page or blank space) with writing or drawing **6** to hold and perform the duties of (an office or position) **7** to appoint or elect an occupant to (an office or position) ▹ *n* **8 one's fill** sufficient for one's needs or wants ▸ See also **fill in, fill out, fill up**
WORD ORIGIN Old English *fyllan*

filler *n* **1** a paste used for filling in cracks or holes in a surface before painting **2** *journalism* an item to fill space between more important articles

fillet *n* **1** a piece of boneless meat or fish **2** a thin strip of ribbon or lace worn in the hair or around the neck **3** *archit* a narrow flat moulding ▹ *vb* **-leting, -leted 4** to cut or prepare (meat or fish) as a fillet
WORD ORIGIN Latin *filum* thread

fill in *vb* **1** to complete (a form) **2** to act as a substitute **3** to put material into (a hole) so as to make it level with a surface **4** *informal* to give (a person) fuller details

filling ❶ *n* **1** a substance or thing used to fill something: *a sandwich filling* **2** *dentistry* a substance that fills a gap or cavity of a tooth ▹ *adj* **3** (of food or a meal) substantial and satisfying

filling station *n chiefly Brit* a place where petrol and other supplies for motorists are sold

fillip *n* **1** something that adds stimulation or enjoyment **2** the action of holding a finger towards the palm with the thumb and suddenly releasing it with a snapping sound
WORD ORIGIN imitative

fill out *vb* **1** to fill in (a form or application) **2** to make or become plumper, thicker, or rounder **3** to make more substantial: *he filled out his speech with a few jokes*

fill up *vb* **1** to complete (a form or application) **2** to make or become full

filly *n, pl* **-lies** a young female horse
WORD ORIGIN Old Norse *fylja*

film ❶ *n* **1 a** a sequence of images projected onto a screen, creating the illusion of movement **b** a form of entertainment in such a sequence of images ▸ Related adjective: **cinematic 2** a thin flexible strip of cellulose coated with a photographic emulsion, used to make negatives and slides **3** a thin coating, covering, or layer: *a fine film of dust covered the floor* **4** a thin sheet of any material, as of plastic for packaging ▹ *vb* **5 a** to photograph with a movie or video camera **b** to make a film of (a screenplay or event) **6 film over** to cover or become covered with a thin layer ▹ *adj* **7** of or relating to films or the cinema
WORD ORIGIN Old English *filmen* membrane

filmic *adj* of or suggestive of films or the cinema **filmically** *adv*

film star *n* a popular film actor or actress

film strip *n* a strip of film composed of different images projected separately as slides

filmy *adj* **filmier, filmiest** very thin and almost transparent: *a shirt of filmy black chiffon* **filmily** *adv* **filminess** *n*

filo *or* **filo pastry** (feel-o) *n* a type of flaky Greek pastry in very thin sheets
WORD ORIGIN Modern Greek *phullon* leaf

Filofax *n trademark* a type of loose-leaf ring binder, used as a portable personal filing system

filter ❶ *n* **1** a substance, such as paper or sand, that allows fluid to pass but retains solid particles **2** any device containing such a substance, esp. a tip on the mouth end of a cigarette **3** any electronic or acoustic device that blocks signals of certain frequencies while allowing others to pass **4** any transparent disc of gelatine or glass used to reduce the intensity of given frequencies from the light leaving a lamp or entering a camera **5** *Brit* a traffic signal which permits vehicles to turn either left or right when the main signals are red ▹ *vb* **6** Also: **filter out** to remove or separate (particles) from (a liquid or gas) by a filter **7** Also: **filter through** to pass through a filter or something like a filter
WORD ORIGIN Medieval Latin *filtrum* piece of felt used as a filter

filter out *or* **through** *vb* to become known gradually: *the crowd broke up when the news filtered through*

filter paper *n* a porous paper used for filtering liquids

filter tip *n* **1** an attachment to the mouth end of a cigarette for trapping impurities **2** a cigarette with such an attachment **filter-tipped** *adj*

filth *n* **1** disgusting dirt and muck **2** offensive material or language **filthiness** *n* **filthy** *adj*
WORD ORIGIN Old English *fȳlth*

f

THESAURUS

fill *vb* **1a = top up**, fill up, make full, become full, brim over **1b = swell**, expand, inflate, become bloated, extend, balloon, fatten **1c = stock**, supply, store, pack, load, furnish, replenish **2 = pack**, crowd, squeeze, cram, throng **3 = plug**, close, stop, seal, cork, bung, block up, stop up **4 = fulfil**, hold, perform, carry out, occupy, take up, execute, discharge, officiate

filling *n* **1 = stuffing**, padding, filler, wadding, inside, insides, contents, innards *(informal)* ▹ *adj* **3 = satisfying**, heavy, square, substantial, ample

film *n* **1a = movie**, picture, flick *(slang)*, motion picture **1b = cinema**, the movies **3 = layer**, covering, cover, skin, coating, coat, dusting, tissue, membrane, scum, gauze, integument, pellicle ▹ *vb* **5a = photograph**, record, shoot, video, videotape, take **5b = adapt for the screen**, make into a film

filter *n* **1 = sieve**, mesh, gauze, strainer, membrane, riddle, sifter ▹ *vb* **6 = purify**, treat, strain, refine, riddle, sift, sieve, winnow, filtrate, screen **7 = trickle**, leach, seep, percolate, well, escape, leak, penetrate, ooze, dribble, exude

DICTIONARY

filtrate *n* **1** a liquid or gas that has been filtered ▷ *vb* **-trating, -trated** **2** to filter **filtration** *n*
WORD ORIGIN Medieval Latin *filtrare* to filter

fin *n* **1** any of the winglike projections from a fish's body enabling it to balance and swim **2** *Brit* a vertical surface to which the rudder is attached at the rear of an aeroplane **3** a swimmer's flipper **finned** *adj*
WORD ORIGIN Old English *finn*

fin. **1** finance **2** financial

finagle (fin-nay-gl) *vb* **-gling, -gled** *informal* to use or achieve by craftiness or trickery
WORD ORIGIN origin unknown

final *adj* **1** of or occurring at the end; last **2** having no possibility of further discussion, action, or change: *a final decision* ▷ *n* **3** a deciding contest between the winners of previous rounds in a competition ▶ See also **finals** > **finality** *n* **finally** *adv*
WORD ORIGIN Latin *finis* limit, boundary

finale (fin-**nah**-lee) *n* the concluding part of a dramatic performance or musical composition
WORD ORIGIN Italian

finalist *n* a contestant who has reached the last stage of a competition

finalize *or* **-ise** *vb* **-izing, -ized** *or* **-ising, -ised** to put into final form; settle: *plans have yet to be finalized* **finalization** *or* **-isation** *n*

finals *pl n* **1** the deciding part of a competition **2** *education, Brit & S African* the last examinations in an academic course

finance *vb* **-nancing, -nanced** **1** to provide or obtain funds for (a project or large purchase) ▷ *n* **2** the system of money, credit, and investment **3** management of money, loans, or credits: *the dangerous political arena of public-sector finance* **4** funds or the provision of funds **5** **finances** money resources: *the company's crumbling finances*
WORD ORIGIN Old French *finer* to end, settle by payment

financial *adj* **1** of or relating to finance, finances, or people who manage money **2** *Austral & NZ informal* having ready money **financially** *adv*

financial year *n* any annual accounting period

financier *n* a person who is engaged in large-scale financial operations

finch *n* a small songbird with a short strong beak
WORD ORIGIN Old English *finc*

find *vb* **finding, found** **1** to discover by chance **2** to discover by search or effort **3** to realize or become aware: *I have found that if you make the effort then people will be more willing to help you* **4** to consider (someone or something) to have a particular quality: *his business partner had found that odd* **5** to experience (a particular feeling): *she found comfort in his words* **6** *law* to pronounce (the defendant) guilty or not guilty **7** to reach (a target) **8** to provide, esp. with difficulty: *we'll find room for you too* **9** **find one's feet** to become capable or confident ▷ *n* **10** a person or thing that is found, esp. a valuable discovery: *the archaeological find of the century*
WORD ORIGIN Old English *findan*

finder *n* **1** a small telescope fitted to a larger one **2** a person or thing that finds **3** *photog* ▶ short for **viewfinder**

finding *n* the conclusion reached after an inquiry or investigation

find out *vb* **1** to learn something that one did not already know **2** **find someone out** to discover that someone has been dishonest or deceitful

fine[1] *adj* **1** very good **2** superior in skill: *a fine doctor* **3** (of weather) clear and dry **4** *informal* quite well: *I felt fine* **5** satisfactory: *as far as we can tell, everything is fine* **6** of delicate or careful workmanship: *fine porcelain* **7** subtle: *too fine a distinction* **8** very thin or slender: *fine soft hair* **9** very small: *fine print* **10** (of edges or blades) sharp **11** fancy, showy, or smart **12** good-looking **13** *ironic* disappointing or terrible: *a fine mess!* ▷ *adv* **14** *informal* very well: *that's what we've always done, and it suits us just fine* ▷ *vb* **fining, fined** **15** to make (something) finer or thinner **16** **fine down** to make (a theory or criticism) more precise or exact **finely** *adv*
WORD ORIGIN Latin *finis* end, boundary, as in *finis honorum* the highest degree of honour

fine[2] *n* **1** a payment imposed as a penalty ▷ *vb* **fining, fined** **2** to impose a fine on
WORD ORIGIN Old French *fin*

fine art *n* **1** art produced chiefly to appeal to the sense of beauty **2** any of the fields in which such art is produced, such as painting, sculpture, and engraving

fine-drawn *adj* **1** (of arguments or distinctions) subtle **2** (of wire) drawn out until very fine

finery *n* elaborate or showy decoration, esp. clothing and

THESAURUS

final *adj* **1 = last**, latest, end, closing, finishing, concluding, ultimate, terminal, last-minute, eventual, terminating **OPPOSITE:** first
2 = irrevocable, absolute, decisive, definitive, decided, finished, settled, definite, conclusive, irrefutable, incontrovertible, unalterable, determinate

finale *n* **= climax**, ending, close, conclusion, culmination, denouement, last part, epilogue, last act, crowning glory, finis
OPPOSITE: opening

finance *vb* **1 = fund**, back, support, pay for, guarantee, float, invest in, underwrite, endow, subsidize, bankroll *(US)*, set up in business, provide security for, provide money for ▷ *n* **2 = economics**, business, money, banking, accounts, investment, commerce, financial affairs, money management ▷ *pl n* **5 = resources**, money, funds, capital, cash, affairs, budgeting, assets, cash flow, financial affairs, money management, wherewithal, financial condition

financial *adj* **1 = economic**, business, money, budgeting, budgetary, commercial, monetary, fiscal, pecuniary

find *vb* **1, 2 = discover**, turn up, uncover, unearth, spot, expose, come up with, locate, detect, come across, track down, catch sight of, stumble upon, hit upon, espy, ferret out, chance upon, light upon, put your finger on, lay your hand on, run to ground, run to earth, descry
OPPOSITE: lose
3 = observe, learn, note, discover, notice, realize, remark, come up with, arrive at, perceive, detect, become aware, experience, ascertain ▷ *n* **10 = discovery**, catch, asset, bargain, acquisition, good buy

fine[1] *adj* **1 = excellent**, good, great, striking, choice, beautiful, masterly, select, rare, very good, supreme, impressive, outstanding, magnificent, superior, accomplished, sterling, first-class, divine, exceptional, splendid, world-class, exquisite, admirable, skilful, ornate, first-rate, showy
OPPOSITE: poor
2 = brilliant, quick, keen, alert, clever, intelligent, penetrating, astute
3 = sunny, clear, fair, dry, bright, pleasant, clement, balmy, cloudless
OPPOSITE: cloudy
5 = satisfactory, good, all right, suitable, acceptable, convenient, agreeable, hunky-dory *(informal)*, fair, O.K. *or* okay *(informal)* **6a = delicate**, light, thin, sheer, lightweight, flimsy, wispy, gossamer, diaphanous, gauzy, chiffony
OPPOSITE: coarse
6b = exquisite, delicate, fragile, dainty **8 = thin**, small, light, narrow, wispy **11 = stylish**, expensive, elegant, refined, tasteful, quality, schmick *(Austral informal)*

fine[2] *n* **1 = penalty**, damages, punishment, forfeit, financial penalty, amercement *(obsolete)* ▷ *vb*

DICTIONARY

jewellery: *the actress dressed up in her finery*
fines herbes (feenz **airb**) *pl n* finely chopped mixed herbs, used to flavour omelettes
WORD ORIGIN French
finespun *adj* **1** spun or drawn out to a fine thread **2** excessively subtle or concerned with minute detail: *a finespun theological debate*
finesse (fin-**ness**) *n* **1** elegant and delicate skill **2** subtlety and tact in handling difficult situations: *a lack of diplomatic finesse* **3** *bridge, whist* an attempt to win a trick when opponents hold a high card in the suit led by playing a lower card ▷ *vb* **-nessing, -nessed 4** to bring about with finesse **5** *bridge, whist* to play (a card) as a finesse
WORD ORIGIN Old French
fine-tooth comb *or* **fine-toothed comb** *n* **1** a comb with fine teeth set closely together **2 go over with a fine-tooth comb** to examine very thoroughly
fine-tune *vb* **-tuning, -tuned** to make fine adjustments to (something) so that it works really well
finger ❶ *n* **1** one of the four long jointed parts of the hand **2** the part of a glove made to cover a finger **3** something that resembles a finger in shape or function **4** a quantity of liquid in a glass as deep as a finger is wide **5 get** *or* **pull one's finger out** *Brit & NZ informal* to begin or speed up activity, esp. after initial delay **6 put one's finger on** to identify precisely **7 put the finger on** *informal* to inform on or identify, esp. for the police **8 twist around one's little finger** to have easy and complete influence over ▷ *vb* **9** to touch or manipulate with the fingers; handle **10** to use one's fingers in playing (a musical instrument) **11** *informal, chiefly US* to identify as a criminal or suspect
fingerless *adj*
WORD ORIGIN Old English
fingerboard *n* the long strip of hard wood on a violin, guitar, etc. upon which the strings are stopped by the fingers
finger bowl *n* a small bowl of water for rinsing the fingers at table during a meal, esp. at a formal dinner
fingering *n* **1** the technique of using one's fingers in playing a musical instrument **2** the numerals in a musical part indicating this
fingernail *n* a thin hard clear plate covering part of the upper surface of the end of each finger
fingerprint *n* **1** an impression of the pattern of ridges on the inner surface of the end of each finger and thumb ▷ *vb* **2** to take an inked impression of the fingerprints of (a person) **3** to take a sample of the DNA of (a person)
fingerstall *n* a protective covering for a finger
fingertip *n* **1** the end of a finger **2 have at one's fingertips** to know thoroughly
finicky *or* **finicking** *adj* **1** extremely fussy **2** overelaborate or ornate: *finicky designer patterns*
WORD ORIGIN earlier *finical*, from FINE[1]
finis *n* the end: used at the end of books
WORD ORIGIN Latin
finish ❶ *vb* **1** to bring to an end; conclude or stop **2** to be at or come to the end; use up **3** to bring to a desired or complete condition **4** to put a particular surface texture on (wood, cloth, or metal) **5 finish off a** to complete by doing the last part of: *he finished off his thesis last week* **b** to destroy or defeat completely: *he finished off Faldo at the 16th hole* **6 finish with** to end a relationship with (someone) ▷ *n* **7** the final stage or part; end **8** death or absolute defeat **9** the surface texture of wood, cloth, or metal **10** a thing or event that completes
WORD ORIGIN Latin *finire*
finishing school *n* a private school for girls that teaches social skills and polite behaviour
finite (**fine**-ite) *adj* **1** having limits in size, space, or time: *finite supplies of fossil fuels* **2** *maths, logic* having a countable number of elements **3** *grammar* denoting any form of a verb inflected for person, number, and tense
WORD ORIGIN Latin *finitus* limited
Finlay *n* **Carlos Juan** 1833–1915, Cuban physician: discovered that the mosquito was the vector of yellow fever
Finn *n* a person from Finland
Finn *n* **Neil** (**Mullane**) born 1958, New Zealand singer and songwriter; lead singer with the group Crowded House (from 1985) with whom he recorded the albums *Crowded House* (1986), *Woodface* (1991), and *Time on Earth* (2007). Solo albums include *Try Whistling This* (1998)
Finn[1] *n* **1** a native, inhabitant, or citizen of Finland **2** a speaker of a Finnic language, esp. one of the original inhabitants of Russia, who were pushed northwards during the Slav migrations **3** a type of dinghy, designed to be sailed by one person
WORD ORIGIN Old English *Finnas* (plural); related to Old Norse *Finnr* Finn, Latin *Fennī* the Finns, Greek *Phinnoi*
Finn[2] *n* known as *Finn MacCool*. (in Irish legend) chief of the Fianna, father of the heroic poet Ossian
finnan haddock *or* **haddie** *n* a smoked haddock
WORD ORIGIN *Findon*, town near Aberdeen
Finney *n* **1 Albert** born 1936, British stage and film actor **2 Tom** born 1922, English footballer: won 76 international caps as a winger
Finnish *adj* **1** of Finland ▷ *n* **2** the language of Finland
fino (**fee**-no) *n* a very dry sherry
WORD ORIGIN Spanish: fine
Finsen *n* **Niels Ryberg** 1860–1904, Danish physician; founder of phototherapy: Nobel prize for physiology or medicine 1903
Finzi *n* **Gerald** 1901–56, British composer. His works include the cantata *Dies Natalis* (1940)
fiord (fee-**ord**) *n* ▸ same as **fjord**
fipple flute *n* an end-blown flute with a plug (**fipple**) at the mouthpiece, such as the recorder or flageolet
fir *n* a pyramid-shaped tree with needle-like leaves and erect cones
WORD ORIGIN Old English *furh*
Firbank *n* (**Arthur Annesley**) **Ronald** 1886–1926, English novelist, whose works include *Valmouth* (1919), *The Flower beneath the Foot* (1923), and *Concerning the Eccentricities of Cardinal Pirelli* (1926)
Firdausi *or* **Firdusi** *n* pen name of *Abul Qasim Mansur* ?935–1020 AD, Persian epic poet; author of *Shah Nama* (*The Book of Kings*), a chronicle of the legends and history of Persia

THESAURUS

2 = penalize, charge, punish
finger *vb* **9 = touch**, feel, handle, play with, manipulate, paw *(informal)*, maul, toy with, fiddle with *(informal)*, meddle with, play about with
finish *vb* **1, 2a = stop**, close, complete, achieve, conclude, cease, accomplish, execute, discharge, culminate, wrap up *(informal)*, terminate, round off, bring to a close or conclusion **OPPOSITE:** start **1, 2b = end**, stop, conclude, wind up, terminate **2 = use up**, use, spend, empty, exhaust, expend **3 = get done**, complete, put the finishing touch(es) to, finalize, do, deal with, settle, conclude, fulfil, carry through, get out of the way, make short work of **4 = coat**, polish, stain, texture, wax, varnish, gild, veneer, lacquer, smooth off, face ▷ *n* **7 = end**, ending, close, closing, conclusion, run-in, winding up *(informal)*, wind-up, completion, finale, termination, culmination, cessation, last stage(s), denouement, finalization **OPPOSITE:** beginning **9 = surface**, appearance, polish, shine, grain, texture, glaze, veneer, lacquer, lustre, smoothness, patina

DICTIONARY

fire ⓘ *n* **1** the state of combustion producing heat, flames, and often smoke **2** *Brit* burning coal or wood, esp. in a hearth to heat a room **3** a destructive uncontrolled burning that destroys building, crops, etc. **4** an electric or gas device for heating a room **5** the act of shooting weapons **6** passion and enthusiasm: *her questions brought new fire to the debate* **7 catch fire** to start burning **8 on fire a** burning **b** ardent or eager **9 open fire** to start firing a gun, artillery, etc. **10 play with fire** to be involved in something risky **11 set fire to** *or* **set on fire a** to ignite **b** to arouse or excite **12 under fire** being attacked, such as by weapons or by harsh criticism ▹*vb* **firing, fired 13** to discharge (a firearm) **14** to detonate (an explosive device) **15** *informal* to dismiss from employment **16** to ask a lot of questions quickly in succession **17** *ceramics* to bake in a kiln to harden the clay **18** to kindle or be kindled **19** (of an internal-combustion engine) to produce an electrical spark which causes the fuel to burn and the engine to start **20** to provide with fuel **21** to arouse to strong emotion: *he fired his team mates with enthusiasm*
WORD ORIGIN Old English *fyr*

fire alarm *n* a device to give warning of fire

firearm *n* a weapon, such as a pistol, that fires bullets

fireball *n* **1** ball-shaped lightning **2** the hot ionized gas at the centre of a nuclear explosion **3** a large bright meteor **4** *slang* an energetic person

firebomb *n* a bomb that is designed to cause fires

firebrand *n* a person who arouses passionate political feelings, often causing trouble

firebreak *n* a strip of open land in a forest to stop the advance of a fire

firebrick *n* a heat-resistant brick, used for lining furnaces, flues, and fireplaces

fire brigade *n Austral & Brit* an organized body of firefighters

fire clay *n* a heat-resistant clay used in making firebricks and furnace linings

firecracker *n* a firework which produces a loud bang

firedamp *n Brit, Austral & NZ* an explosive mixture of hydrocarbons, chiefly methane, formed in coal mines

firedog *n* ▸ same as **andiron**

fire door *n* a door made of noncombustible material that prevents a fire spreading within a building

fire drill *n* a rehearsal of procedures for escape from a fire

fire-eater *n* **1** a performer who pretends to swallow flaming rods **2** a very quarrelsome person

fire engine *n* a vehicle that carries firefighters and firefighting equipment to a fire

fire escape *n* a metal staircase or ladder on the outside of a building for escape in the event of fire

fire-extinguisher *n* a portable device for spraying water, foam, or powder to extinguish a fire

firefighter *n* a person whose job is to put out fires and rescue people endangered by them **firefighting** *adj, n*

firefly *n, pl* **-flies** a beetle that glows in the dark

fireguard *n* a screen made of wire mesh put before an open fire to protect against sparks

fire hall *n Canad* a fire station

fire hydrant *n* an outlet from a water main in the street, from which firefighters can draw water in an emergency

fire irons *pl n* a shovel, poker, and tongs for tending a domestic fire

fireman *n, pl* **-men 1** a man whose job is to put out fires and rescue people endangered by them **2** (on steam trains) the man who stokes the fire

fireplace *n* an open recess at the base of a chimney for a fire; hearth

fireplug *n chiefly US & NZ* ▸ same as **fire hydrant**

fire power *n mil* the amount of fire that can be delivered by a unit or weapon

fire raiser *n Brit* a person who deliberately sets fire to property **fire raising** *n*

fire ship *n history* a ship loaded with explosives, set on fire and left to drift among an enemy's warships

fireside *n* the hearth

fire station *n* a building where firefighting vehicles and equipment are stationed

firetrap *n* a building that would burn easily or one without fire escapes

firewall *n computers* software that prevents unauthorized access to a computer network from the internet

firewater *n informal* any alcoholic spirit

firework *n* a device containing chemicals that is ignited to produce coloured sparks and sometimes bangs

fireworks ⓘ *pl n* **1** a show in which fireworks are let off **2** *informal* an outburst of temper **3** an exciting and impressive performance, speech, or piece of writing: *Dickens' verbal fireworks*

firing *n* **1** a discharge of a firearm **2** the process of baking ceramics in a kiln **3** something used as fuel

firing line *n* **1** *mil* the positions from which fire is delivered **2** the leading or most vulnerable position in an activity: *the manager is in the firing line after a string of bad results*

firing squad *n* a group of soldiers appointed to shoot a condemned criminal dead

firkin *n* **1** a small wooden barrel or similar container **2** *Brit* a unit of capacity equal to nine gallons
WORD ORIGIN Middle Dutch *vierde* fourth

firm[1] ⓘ *adj* **1** not soft or yielding to a touch or pressure **2** securely in position **3** definitely established: *a firm agreement* **4** having determination or strength: *if you are firm and consistent she will come to see things your way* ▹*adv* **5 stand firm** to

THESAURUS

fire *n* **3 = flames**, blaze, combustion, inferno, conflagration, holocaust **5 = bombardment**, shooting, firing, shelling, hail, volley, barrage, gunfire, sniping, flak, salvo, fusillade, cannonade **6 = passion**, force, light, energy, heat, spirit, enthusiasm, excitement, dash, intensity, sparkle, life, vitality, animation, vigour, zeal, splendour, verve, fervour, eagerness, dynamism, lustre, radiance, virtuosity, élan, ardour, brio, vivacity, impetuosity, burning passion, scintillation, fervency, pizzazz *or* pizazz *(informal)* ▹*vb* **13, 14a = let off**, shoot, launch, shell, loose, set off, discharge, hurl, eject, detonate, let loose *(informal)*, touch off **13, 14b = shoot**, explode, discharge, detonate, pull the trigger **15** *(informal)* **= dismiss**, sack *(informal)*, get rid of, discharge, lay off, make redundant, cashier, give notice, show the door, give the boot *(slang)*, kiss off *(slang, chiefly US & Canad)*, give the push, give the bullet *(Brit slang)*, give marching orders, give someone their cards, give the sack to *(informal)*, kennet *(Austral slang)*, jeff *(Austral slang)* **21 = inspire**, excite, stir, stimulate, motivate, irritate, arouse, awaken, animate, rouse, stir up, quicken, inflame, incite, electrify, enliven, spur on, galvanize, inspirit, impassion

fireworks *pl n* **1 = pyrotechnics**, illuminations, feux d'artifice **2** *(informal)* **= trouble**, row, storm, rage, temper, wax *(informal, chiefly Brit)*, uproar, hysterics, paroxysms, fit of rage

firm[1] *adj* **1 = hard**, solid, compact, dense, set, concentrated, stiff, compacted, rigid, compressed, inflexible, solidified, unyielding, congealed, inelastic, jelled, close-grained, jellified **OPPOSITE:** soft **2 = secure**, strong, fixed, secured,

refuse to give in ▹*vb* **6** to make or become firm: *to firm up flabby thighs*
firmly *adv* **firmness** *n*
WORD ORIGIN Latin *firmus*
firm² ❶ *n* **1** a business company **2** *Brit slang* a gang of criminals or football hooligans
WORD ORIGIN Spanish *firma* signature
firmament *n literary* the sky or the heavens
WORD ORIGIN Late Latin *firmamentum*
first ❶ *adj* **1** earliest in time or order **2** rated, graded, or ranked above all other levels: *the First Lord of the Admiralty* **3** denoting the lowest forward gear in a motor vehicle **4** *music* denoting the highest voice part in a chorus or one of the sections of an orchestra: *the first violin* ▹*n* **5** the person or thing coming before all others **6** the beginning or outset **7** *education, chiefly Brit* an honours degree of the highest class **8** the lowest forward gear in a motor vehicle ▹*adv* **9** before anything else: *I would advise you to try surgery first* **10** for the first time: *this story first came to public attention in January 1984*
WORD ORIGIN Old English *fyrest*
first aid *n* immediate medical assistance given in an emergency
first-born *adj* **1** eldest of the children in a family ▹*n* **2** the eldest child in a family
first class *n* **1** the class or grade of the best or highest value, rank, or quality ▹*adj* **first-class** **2** of the best or highest class or grade **3** excellent **4** denoting the most comfortable class of accommodation in a hotel, aircraft, or train **5** denoting mail that is handled faster than second-class mail ▹*adv* **first-class** **6** by first-class mail, transport, etc.
first-day cover *n philately* an envelope postmarked on the first day of the issue of its stamps
first-degree burn *n* a burn in which the skin surface is red and painful
first floor *n* **1** the storey of a building immediately above the one at ground level **2** *US* the storey at ground level
first-foot *Scot & NZ n* **1** the first person to enter a household in the New Year ▹*vb* **2** to visit (someone) as first-foot
first-footing *n*
first fruits *pl n* **1** the first results or profits of an undertaking **2** fruit that ripens first
first-hand *adj* **1** obtained directly from the original source ▹*adv* **2** directly from the original source **3 at first hand** directly
First Lady *n* (in the US) the wife of the president
firstly *adv* ▸same as **first** (sense 9)
first mate *n* an officer second in command to the captain of a merchant ship
First Minister *n* **1** the chief minister of the Scottish Parliament **2** the chief minister of the Northern Ireland Assembly
First Nation *n* one of the formally recognized Canadian aboriginal communities
first night *n* the first public performance of a play or other production
first offender *n* a person convicted of a criminal offence for the first time
first officer *n* ▸same as **first mate**
First Peoples *pl n Canad* a collective term for the Native Canadian peoples, the Inuit and the métis
first person *n* the form of a pronoun or verb used by the speaker to refer to himself or herself, or a group including himself or herself
first-person shooter *n* a computer game in which the player aims and shoots at targets, and the graphics displayed are seen from the viewpoint of the shooter
first-rate *adj* of the best quality; excellent
First Secretary *n* the chief minister of the National Assembly for Wales
firth *n* a narrow inlet of the sea, esp. in Scotland
WORD ORIGIN Old Norse *fjörthr* fjord
fiscal *adj* **1** of or relating to government finances, esp. tax revenues ▹*n* **2** ▸(in Scotland) same as **procurator fiscal**
WORD ORIGIN Latin *fiscalis* concerning the state treasury
Fischer *n* **1 Emil Hermann** 1852–1919, German chemist, noted particularly for his work on synthetic sugars and the purine group: Nobel prize for chemistry 1902 **2 Ernst Otto** 1918–94, German chemist: shared the Nobel prize for chemistry in 1973 with Geoffrey Wilkinson for his work on inorganic complexes **3 Hans** 1881–1945, German chemist, noted particularly for his work on chlorophyll, haemin, and the porphyrins: Nobel prize for chemistry 1930 **4 Robert James**, known as *Bobby*. 1943–2008, US chess player; world champion 1972–75
Fischer-Dieskau *n* **Dietrich** born 1925, German baritone, noted particularly for his interpretation of Schubert's song cycles
Fischer von Erlach *n* **Johann Bernhard** 1656–1723, Austrian architect: a leading exponent of the German baroque
fish ❶ *n, pl* **fish** *or* **fishes** **1** a cold-blooded animal with a backbone, gills, and usually fins and a skin covered in scales, that lives in water ▸Related adjective: **piscine** **2** the flesh of fish used as food **3 cold fish** a person who shows little emotion **4 drink like a fish** to drink alcohol to excess **5 have other fish to fry** to have other more important concerns **6 like a fish out of water** ill at ease in an unfamiliar situation ▹*vb* **7** to attempt to catch fish **8** to fish in (a particular area of water): *the first trawler to fish these waters* **9** to grope for and find with some difficulty: *he fished a cigarette from his pocket* **10 fish for** to seek (something) indirectly: *he was fishing for compliments*
WORD ORIGIN Old English *fisc*
fishcake *n* a fried flattened ball of flaked fish mixed with mashed potatoes
fisherman *n, pl* **-men** a person who fishes as a profession or for sport
fishery *n, pl* **-eries** **1 a** the industry of catching, processing, and selling fish **b** a place where this is carried on **2** a place where fish are reared
fish-eye lens *n photog* a lens with a highly curved front that covers almost 180°
fishfinger *n* an oblong piece of fish coated in breadcrumbs
fishing *n* the occupation of catching fish

THESAURUS

rooted, stable, steady, anchored, braced, robust, cemented, fast, sturdy, embedded, fastened, riveted, taut, stationary, motionless, immovable, unmoving, unshakeable, unfluctuating
OPPOSITE: unstable
3 = definite, hard, clear, confirmed, settled, fixed, hard-and-fast, cut-and-dried *(informal)*
4 = determined, true, settled, fixed, resolved, strict, definite, set on, adamant, stalwart, staunch, resolute, inflexible, steadfast, unyielding, unwavering, immovable, unflinching, unswerving, unbending, obdurate, unshakeable, unalterable, unshaken, unfaltering
OPPOSITE: wavering
firm² *n* **1 = company**, business, concern, association, organization, house, corporation, venture, enterprise, partnership, establishment, undertaking, outfit *(informal)*, consortium, conglomerate
first *adj* **1 = earliest**, initial, opening, introductory, original, maiden, primitive, primordial, primeval, pristine **2a = top**, best, winning, premier **2b = foremost**, highest, greatest, leading, head, ruling, chief, prime, supreme, principal, paramount, overriding, pre-eminent ▹*adv* **9 = to begin with**, firstly, initially, at the beginning, in the first place, beforehand, to start with, at the outset, before all else
fish *vb* **7 = angle**, net, cast, trawl

DICTIONARY

fishing rod *n* a long tapered flexible pole for use with a fishing line and, usually, a reel

fishmeal *n* ground dried fish used as feed for farm animals or as a fertilizer

fishmonger *n chiefly Brit* a seller of fish

fishnet *n* an open mesh fabric resembling netting, sometimes used for tights or stockings

fishplate *n* a flat piece of metal joining one rail or beam to the next, esp. on railway tracks

fishtail *n* a nozzle having a long narrow slot at the top, placed over a Bunsen burner to produce a thin fanlike flame

fishwife *n, pl* **-wives** a coarse or bad-tempered woman with a loud voice

fishy *adj* **fishier, fishiest** **1** of or suggestive of fish **2** *informal* suspicious or questionable: *something a bit fishy about his explanation* **fishily** *adv*

fissile *adj* **1** capable of undergoing nuclear fission **2** tending to split

fission *n* **1** the act or process of splitting into parts **2** *biol* a form of asexual reproduction involving a division into two or more equal parts **3** the splitting of atomic nuclei with the release of a large amount of energy **fissionable** *adj*
WORD ORIGIN Latin *fissio* a splitting

fissure (**fish**-er) *n* any long narrow cleft or crack, esp. in a rock
WORD ORIGIN Latin *fissus* split

fist *n* a hand with the fingers clenched into the palm
WORD ORIGIN Old English *fȳst*

fisticuffs *pl n* fighting with the fists
WORD ORIGIN probably from obsolete *fisty* with the fist + CUFF[2]

fistula (**fist**-yew-la) *n pathol* a long narrow ulcer
WORD ORIGIN Latin: tube, ulcer

fit[1] ❶ *vb* **fitting, fitted** **1** to be appropriate or suitable for **2** to be of the correct size or shape (for) **3** to adjust in order to make appropriate **4** to try clothes on and note any adjustments needed **5** to make competent or ready: *the experience helped to fit him for the task* **6** to correspond with the facts or circumstances: *this part doesn't fit the rest of his theory* ▷ *adj* **fitter, fittest** **7** appropriate **8** in good health **9** worthy or suitable: *houses fit for human habitation* ▷ *n* **10** the manner in which something fits: *the suit was an excellent fit* ▸ See also **fit in, fit out** > **fitly** *adv* **fitness** *n*
WORD ORIGIN probably from Middle Dutch *vitten*

fit[2] ❶ *n* **1** a sudden attack or convulsion, such as an epileptic seizure **2** a sudden short burst or spell: *fits of laughter; a fit of pique* **3** **in fits and starts** in spasmodic spells **4** **have a fit** *informal* to become very angry
WORD ORIGIN Old English *fitt* conflict

fitful *adj* occurring in irregular spells **fitfully** *adv*

fit in *vb* **1** to give a place or time to (someone or something) **2** to belong or conform, esp. after adjustment

fitment *n* **1** an accessory attached to a machine **2** *chiefly Brit* a detachable part of the furnishings of a room

fit out *vb* to equip: *he started to fit out a ship in secret*

fitted *adj* **1** designed for excellent fit: *a fitted suit* **2** (of a carpet) covering a floor completely **3** **a** (of furniture) built to fit a particular space **b** (of a kitchen, bathroom, etc.) having equipment and furniture built or selected to suit the measurements of the room **4** (of sheets) having ends that are elasticated to fit tightly over a mattress

fitter *n* **1** a person who is skilled in the installation and adjustment of machinery **2** a person who fits garments

fitting ❶ *adj* **1** appropriate or proper ▷ *n* **2** an accessory or part **3** the trying-on of clothes so that they can be adjusted to fit **4** **fittings** furnishings or accessories in a building **fittingly** *adv*

Fittipaldi *n* **Emerson** born 1946, Brazilian motor-racing driver: world champion in 1972 and 1974

Fitzpatrick *n* **Sean** born 1963, New Zealand Rugby Union footballer; captain of the All Blacks (1992–98)

Fitzsimmons *n* **Bob** 1862–1917, New Zealand boxer, born in England: world middleweight (1891–97), heavyweight (1897–99), and light-heavyweight (1903–05) champion

five *n* **1** the cardinal number that is the sum of one and four **2** a numeral, 5 or V, representing this number **3** something representing or consisting of five units ▷ *adj* **4** amounting to five: *five years* ▸ See also **fives**
WORD ORIGIN Old English *fīf*

five-eighth *n* **1** *Austral* (in rugby) a player positioned between the scrum-half and the inside-centre **2** *NZ* (in rugby) either of two players positioned between the halfback and the centre

fivefold *adj* **1** having five times as many or as much **2** composed of five parts ▷ *adv* **3** by five times as many or as much

fivepins *n* a bowling game played esp. in Canada

fiver *n Brit, Austral & NZ informal* a five-pound or five-dollar note

fives *n* a ball game similar to squash but played with bats or the hands

fix ❶ *vb* **1** to make or become firm, stable, or secure **2** to repair **3** to attach or place permanently: *fix the mirror to the wall* **4** to settle definitely or decide upon: *the meeting is fixed for the 12th* **5** to direct (the eyes etc.) steadily: *she fixed her eyes upon the jewels* **6** *informal* to unfairly influence the outcome of: *the fight was fixed by the promoter* **7** *informal* to put a stop to the

THESAURUS

fit[1] *vb* **1, 6 = suit**, meet, match, belong to, agree with, go with, conform to, correspond to, accord with, be appropriate to, concur with, tally with, dovetail with, be consonant with **3 = adapt**, fashion, shape, arrange, alter, adjust, modify, tweak (*informal*), customize **5 = equip**, provide, arm, prepare, outfit, accommodate, fit out, kit out, rig out, accoutre ▷ *adj* **7, 9 = appropriate**, qualified, suitable, competent, right, becoming, meet (*archaic*), seemly, trained, able, prepared, fitting, fitted, ready, skilled, correct, deserving, capable, adapted, proper, equipped, good enough, adequate, worthy, convenient, apt, well-suited, expedient, apposite
OPPOSITE: inappropriate
8 = healthy, strong, robust, sturdy, well, trim, strapping, hale, in good shape, in good condition, in good health, toned up, as right as rain, in good trim, able-bodied
OPPOSITE: unfit

fit[2] *n* **1 = seizure**, attack, bout, spasm, convulsion, paroxysm **2 = bout**, burst, outbreak, outburst, spell

fitting *adj* **1 = appropriate**, suitable, proper, apt, right, becoming, meet (*archaic*), seemly, correct, decent, desirable, apposite, decorous, comme il faut (*French*)
OPPOSITE: unsuitable
▷ *n* **2 = accessory**, part, piece, unit, connection, component, attachment

fix *vb* **2 = repair**, mend, service, sort, correct, restore, adjust, regulate, see to, overhaul, patch up, get working, put right, put to rights **3 = place**, join, stick, attach, set, position, couple, plant, link, establish, tie, settle, secure, bind, root, connect, locate, pin, install, anchor, glue, cement, implant, embed, fasten, make fast **4 = decide**, set, name, choose, limit, establish, determine, settle, appoint, arrange, define, conclude, resolve, arrive at, specify, agree on **5 = focus**, direct at, level at, fasten on, rivet on **6** (*informal*) **= rig**, set up (*informal*), influence, manipulate, bribe, manoeuvre, fiddle (*informal*), pull strings (*informal*) ▷ *n* **12** (*informal*) **= mess**, spot (*informal*), corner, hole (*slang*), difficulty, jam

DICTIONARY

activities of (someone): *the Party was determined to fix him* **8** *informal* to prepare: *let me fix you a drink* **9** *photog* to treat (a film, plate, or paper) with fixer to make the image permanent **10** to convert (atmospheric nitrogen) into nitrogen compounds **11** *slang* to inject a narcotic drug ▷ *n* **12** *informal* a difficult situation **13** the reckoning of a navigational position of a ship by radar, etc. **14** *slang* an injection of a narcotic ▸ See also **fix up**
WORD ORIGIN Latin *fixus* fixed

fixation *n* **1** an obsessive interest in something **2** *psychol* a strong attachment of a person to another person or an object in early life **3** *chem* the conversion of nitrogen in the air into a compound, esp. a fertilizer **fixated** *adj*

fixative *n* **1** a fluid sprayed over drawings to prevent smudging **2** a liquid used to hold objects, esp. dentures, in place **3** a substance added to a perfume to make it less volatile

fixed ❶ *adj* **1** attached or placed so as to be immovable **2** stable: *fixed rates* **3** unchanging and appearing artificial: *a fixed smile* **4** established as to relative position: *a fixed point* **5** always at the same time **6** (of ideas) firmly maintained **7** *informal* equipped or provided for, esp. with money or possessions **8** *informal* illegally arranged: *a fixed trial* **fixedly** (**fix**-id-lee) *adv*

fixed star *n* an extremely distant star that appears to be almost stationary

fixer *n* **1** *photog* a solution used to make an image permanent **2** *slang* a person who makes arrangements, esp. illegally

fixity *n, pl* **-ties** the state or quality of a person's gaze, attitude, or concentration not changing or weakening: *a remarkable fixity of purpose*

fixture *n* **1** an object firmly fixed in place, esp. a household appliance **2** something or someone regarded as fixed in a particular place or position: *the diplomatic wife seems a fixture of international politics* **3 a** a sports match **b** the date of it

fix up *vb* **1** to arrange **2 fix up with** to provide with: *can you fix me up with tickets?*

fizz ❶ *vb* **1** to make a hissing or bubbling sound **2** (of a drink) to produce bubbles of carbon dioxide ▷ *n* **3** a hissing or bubbling sound **4** releasing of small bubbles of gas by a liquid **5** any effervescent drink **fizzy** *adj* **fizziness** *n*
WORD ORIGIN imitative

fizzle *vb* **-zling, -zled 1** to make a hissing or bubbling sound **2 fizzle out** *informal* to fail or die out, esp. after a promising start
WORD ORIGIN probably from obsolete *fist* to break wind

fjord (fee-**ord**) *n* a long narrow inlet of the sea between high cliffs, esp. in Norway
WORD ORIGIN Norwegian, from Old Norse *fjörthr*

FL Florida

fl. fluid

flab *n* unsightly or unwanted fat on the body
WORD ORIGIN from *flabby*

flabbergasted *adj informal* completely astonished
WORD ORIGIN origin unknown

flabby *adj* **-bier, -biest 1** having flabby flesh **2** loose or limp **3** weak and lacking purpose: *flabby hesitant leaders* **flabbiness** *n*
WORD ORIGIN alteration of *flappy*, from *flap*

flaccid (**flak**-sid) *adj* soft and limp **flaccidity** *n*
WORD ORIGIN Latin *flaccidus*

flag[1] ❶ *n* **1** a piece of cloth often attached to a pole, used as an emblem or for signalling **2** a code inserted into a computer file to distinguish certain information ▷ *vb* **flagging, flagged 3** to mark with a tag or sticker **4** NZ to give up an activity **5 flag down** to signal (a vehicle) to stop **6 flag up** bring something to someone's attention
WORD ORIGIN origin unknown

flag[2] *n* ▸ same as **iris** (sense 2)
WORD ORIGIN origin unknown

flag[3] ❶ *vb* **flagging, flagged 1** to lose enthusiasm or energy **2** to become limp **flagging** *adj*
WORD ORIGIN origin unknown

flag[4] *n* ▸ short for **flagstone**

flag day *n Brit* a day on which money is collected by a charity and small stickers are given to contributors

flagellate *vb* (**flaj**-a-late), **-lating, -lated 1** to whip, esp. in religious penance or for sexual pleasure ▷ *adj* (**flaj**-a-lit) **2** possessing one or more flagella **3** like a whip **flagellation** *n*
WORD ORIGIN Latin *flagellare* to whip

flagellum (flaj-**jell**-lum) *n, pl* **-la** (-la) *or* **-lums 1** *biol* a long whiplike outgrowth that acts as an organ of movement **2** *bot* a long thin shoot or runner
WORD ORIGIN Latin: a little whip

flageolet (flaj-a-**let**) *n* a high-pitched musical instrument of the recorder family
WORD ORIGIN French

flag fall *n Austral* the minimum charge for hiring a taxi, to which the rate per kilometre is added

flagged *adj* paved with flagstones

flag of convenience *n* a foreign flag flown by a ship registered in that country to gain financial or legal advantage

flag of truce *n* a white flag indicating an invitation to an enemy to negotiate

flagon *n* **1** a large bottle of wine, cider, etc. **2** a narrow-necked jug for containing liquids
WORD ORIGIN Late Latin *flasco* flask

flagpole *or* **flagstaff** *n* a pole on which a flag is flown

flagrant (**flayg**-rant) *adj* openly outrageous: *flagrant violation of international law* **flagrancy** *n*
WORD ORIGIN Latin *flagrare* to blaze, burn

flagship *n* **1** a ship aboard which the commander of a fleet is quartered **2** the most important ship belonging to a shipping company **3** the most modern or impressive product or asset of an organization: *the company has opened its own flagship store*

Flagstad *n* **Kirsten** 1895–1962, Norwegian operatic soprano, noted particularly for her interpretations of Wagner

flagstone *n* a flat slab of hard stone for paving
WORD ORIGIN Old Norse *flaga* slab

flag up *vb* to bring (something) to someone's attention; point out

flag-waving *n informal* an emotional appeal to patriotic feeling

Flaherty *n* **Robert (Joseph)** 1884–1951, US film director, a pioneer of documentary film; his work

THESAURUS

(informal), dilemma, embarrassment, plight, hot water *(informal)*, pickle *(informal)*, uphill *(S African)*, predicament, difficult situation, quandary, tight spot, ticklish situation

fixed *adj* **1 = immovable**, set, established, secure, rooted, permanent, attached, anchored, rigid, made fast **OPPOSITE:** mobile **5 = agreed**, set, planned, decided, established, settled, arranged, resolved, specified, definite **6 = inflexible**, set, steady, resolute, unwavering, unflinching, unblinking, unbending, undeviating **OPPOSITE:** wavering

fizz *vb* **1 = sputter**, buzz, sparkle, hiss, crackle **2 = bubble**, froth, fizzle, effervesce, produce bubbles

flag[1] *n* **1 = banner**, standard, colours, jack, pennant, ensign, streamer, pennon, banderole, gonfalon ▷ *vb* **3 = mark**, identify, indicate, label, tab, pick out, note, docket **5 flag down = hail**, stop, signal, salute, wave down

flag[3] *vb* **1 = weaken**, fall, die, fail, decline, sink, fade, slump, pine, faint, weary, fall off, succumb, falter, wilt, wane, ebb, sag, languish, abate, droop, peter out, taper off, feel the pace, lose your strength

DICTIONARY

includes *Nanook of the North* (1922) and *Elephant Boy* (1935)

flail *n* **1** a tool formerly used for threshing grain by hand ▷*vb* **2** to wave about wildly: *arms flailing, they staggered about* **3** to beat with or as if with a flail
WORD ORIGIN Latin *flagellum* whip

flair ❶ *n* **1** natural ability **2** originality and stylishness
WORD ORIGIN French

flak *n* **1** anti-aircraft fire **2** severe criticism: *most of the flak was directed at the umpire*
WORD ORIGIN German *Fl(ieger) a(bwehr)k(anone)* aircraft defence gun

flake[1] ❶ *n* **1** a small thin piece chipped off an object or substance **2** a small piece: *flakes of snow* **3** *slang* an eccentric or unreliable person ▷*vb* **flaking, flaked 4** to peel or cause to peel off in flakes **5** to break into small thin pieces: *bake for 30 minutes, or until the fish is firm and flakes easily* **flaky** *adj*
WORD ORIGIN from Old Norse

flake[2] *n* (in Australia) the commercial name for the meat of the gummy shark

flake out *vb informal* to collapse or fall asleep from exhaustion

flak jacket *n* a reinforced sleeveless jacket for protection against gunfire or shrapnel

flambé (flahm-bay) *vb* **flambéeing, flambéed** to cook or serve (food) in flaming brandy
WORD ORIGIN French

flamboyant ❶ *adj* **1** behaving in a very noticeable, extravagant way: *a flamboyant jazz pianist* **2** very bright and showy **flamboyance** *n*
WORD ORIGIN French: flaming

flame ❶ *n* **1** a hot luminous body of burning gas coming in flickering streams from burning material **2 flames** the state of burning: *half the building was in flames* **3** intense passion: *the flame of love* **4** *informal* an abusive message sent by e-mail ▷*vb* **flaming, flamed 5** to burn brightly **6** to become red or fiery: *colour flamed in Sally's cheeks* **7** to become angry or excited **8** *informal* to send (someone) an abusive message by e-mail
WORD ORIGIN Latin *flamma*

flamenco *n, pl* **-cos 1** a rhythmic Spanish dance accompanied by a guitar and vocalist **2** music for this dance
WORD ORIGIN Spanish

flame-thrower *n* a weapon that ejects a stream or spray of burning fluid

flaming *adj* **1** burning with flames **2** glowing brightly **3** very angry and heated: *a flaming row* ▷*adj* **4** *informal* extreme; damned: *what the flaming hell do you think you're doing?* ▷*adv* **5** *informal* extremely; damned: *I was flaming mad about what happened*

flamingo *n, pl* **-gos** *or* **-goes** a large pink wading bird with a long neck and legs
WORD ORIGIN Portuguese *flamengo*

Flamininus *n* **Titus Quinctius** ?230–?174 BC, Roman general and statesman: defeated Macedonia (197) and proclaimed the independence of the Greek states (196)

Flaminius *n* **Gaius** died 217 BC, Roman statesman and general: built the Flaminian Way; defeated by Hannibal at Trasimene (217)

flammable *adj* easily set on fire; inflammable **flammability** *n*

Flamsteed *n* **John** 1646–1719, English astronomer: the first Astronomer Royal and first director of the Royal Observatory, Greenwich (1675). He increased the accuracy of existing stellar catalogues, greatly aiding navigation

flan *n* an open sweet or savoury tart
WORD ORIGIN French

flange *n* a projecting collar or rim on an object for strengthening it or for attaching it to another object
WORD ORIGIN origin unknown

flank ❶ *n* **1** the side of a man or animal between the ribs and the hip **2** a cut of beef from the flank **3** the side of a naval or military formation ▷*vb* **4** to be positioned at the side of (a person or thing)
WORD ORIGIN Old French *flanc*

flannel *n* **1** *Brit* a small piece of towelling cloth used to wash the face **2** a soft light woollen fabric used for clothing **3 flannels** trousers made of flannel **4** *Brit informal* evasive talk that avoids giving any commitment or direct answer ▷*vb* **-nelling, -nelled** *or US* **-neling, -neled 5** *Brit informal* to flatter or talk evasively
WORD ORIGIN Welsh *gwlân* wool

flannelette *n* a cotton imitation of flannel, used to make sheets and nightdresses

Flannery *n* **Tim**, full name *Timothy Fridtjof Flannery*. born 1956, Australian zoologist, palaeontologist and environmentalist. His books include *The Weather Makers* (2006)

flap ❶ *vb* **flapping, flapped 1** to move backwards and forwards or up and down, like a bird's wings in flight ▷*n* **2** the action of or noise made by flapping **3** a piece of material attached at one edge and usually used to cover an opening, such as on a pocket **4** a hinged section of an aircraft wing that is raised or lowered to control the aircraft's speed **5** *informal* a state of panic or agitation
WORD ORIGIN probably imitative

flapjack *n* **1** *Brit* a chewy biscuit made with rolled oats **2** *NZ* a small thick pancake

flapper *n* (in the 1920s) a lively young woman who dressed and behaved unconventionally

flare ❶ *vb* **flaring, flared 1** to burn with an unsteady or sudden bright flame **2** (of temper, violence, or trouble) to break out suddenly **3** to spread outwards from a narrow to a wider shape ▷*n* **4** an unsteady flame **5** a sudden burst of flame **6 a** a blaze of light used to illuminate, signal distress, alert, etc. **b** the device producing such a blaze **7 flares** trousers with legs that flare out at the bottom **flared** *adj*
WORD ORIGIN origin unknown

flare up *vb* **1** to burst suddenly into fire **2** *informal* to burst into anger

flash ❶ *n* **1** a sudden short blaze of intense light or flame **2** a sudden occurrence of a particular emotion or experience: *a flash of anger* **3** a very brief time: *in a flash he was inside and locked the door behind him* **4** a short unscheduled news announcement

THESAURUS

flair *n* **1 = ability**, feel, talent, gift, genius, faculty, accomplishment, mastery, knack, aptitude **2 = style**, taste, dash, chic, elegance, panache, discernment, stylishness

flake[1] *n* **1, 2 = chip**, scale, layer, peeling, shaving, disk, wafer, sliver, lamina, squama *(biology)*

flamboyant *adj* **1 = camp** *(informal)*, dashing, theatrical **2 = showy**, rich, elaborate, over the top *(informal)*, extravagant, baroque, ornate, ostentatious, rococo

flame *n* **1 = fire**, light, spark, glow, blaze, brightness, inferno ▷*vb* **5 = burn**, flash, shine, glow, blaze, flare, glare

flank *n* **1 = side**, quarter, hip, thigh, loin, haunch, ham **3 = wing**, side, sector, aspect

flap *vb* **1a = flutter**, wave, swing, swish, flail **1b = beat**, wave, thrash, flutter, agitate, wag, vibrate, shake, thresh ▷*n* **2 = flutter**, beating, waving, shaking, swinging, bang, banging, swish **5** *(informal)* **= panic**, state *(informal)*, agitation, commotion, sweat *(informal)*, stew *(informal)*, dither *(chiefly Brit)*, fluster, twitter *(informal)*, tizzy *(informal)*

flare *vb* **1 = blaze**, flame, dazzle, glare, flicker, flutter, waver, burn up **3 = widen**, spread, broaden, spread out, dilate, splay ▷*n* **4, 5 = flame**, burst, flash, blaze, dazzle, glare, flicker

flash *n* **1 = blaze**, ray, burst, spark, beam, sparkle, streak, flare, dazzle, shaft, glare, gleam, flicker, shimmer, twinkle, scintillation, coruscation ▷*adj* **8** *(informal)* **= ostentatious**, smart, glamorous, trendy, showy,

5 *Austral & Brit* an emblem on a uniform or vehicle to identify its military formation **6** *photog* ▸short for **flashlight 7 flash in the pan** a project, person, etc. that enjoys only short-lived success ▹*adj* **8** *informal* ostentatious or vulgar **9** brief and rapid: *a flash fire* ▹*vb* **10** to burst or cause to burst suddenly into flame **11** to shine with a bright light suddenly or repeatedly **12** to move very fast **13** to come rapidly (into the mind or vision) **14 a** to signal very fast: *a warning was flashed onto a computer screen in the cockpit* **b** to signal by use of a light, such as car headlights **15** *informal* to display in a boastful and extravagant way: *flashing banknotes around* **16** *informal* to show briefly **17** *Brit slang* to expose oneself indecently **flasher** *n*
WORD ORIGIN origin unknown

flashback *n* a scene in a book, play, or film that shows earlier events

flashbulb *n photog* a small light bulb that produces a bright flash of light

flash drive *n* a portable computer hard drive and data storage device

flash flood *n* a sudden short-lived flood

flashing *n* a weatherproof material used to cover the joins in a roof

flashlight *n* **1** *photog* the brief bright light emitted by a flashbulb **2** *chiefly US & Canad* a torch

flash point *n* **1** a critical time beyond which a situation will inevitably erupt into violence **2** the lowest temperature at which the vapour above a liquid can be ignited

flashy *adj* **flashier, flashiest** showy in a vulgar way: *a loud and flashy tie* **flashily** *adv* **flashiness** *n*

flask *n* **1** ▸same as **vacuum flask 2** a small flat container for alcoholic drink designed to be carried in a pocket **3** a bottle with a narrow neck, esp. used in a laboratory
WORD ORIGIN Medieval Latin *flasca, flasco*

flat[1] ❶ *adj* **flatter, flattest** **1** horizontal or level: *roofs are now flat instead of slanted* **2** even or smooth: *a flat surface* **3** lying stretched out at full length **4** (of a tyre) deflated **5** (of shoes) having an unraised heel **6** without qualification; total: *a flat rejection* **7** fixed: *a flat rate* **8** unexciting: *a picture curiously flat in tone* **9** without variation or emotion: *a flat voice* **10** (of drinks) no longer fizzy **11** (of a battery) fully discharged **12** (of paint) without gloss **13** *music* **a** denoting a note that has been lowered in pitch by one chromatic semitone: *B flat* **b** (of an instrument, voice, etc.) out of tune by being too low in pitch ▹*adv* **14** in or into a level or flat position: *the boat was knocked almost flat* **15** completely: *flat broke* **16** exactly: *in three months flat* **17** *music* **a** lower than a standard pitch **b** too low in pitch: *singing flat* **18 fall flat (on one's face)** to fail to achieve a desired effect **19 flat out** *informal* with maximum speed and effort ▹*n* **20** a flat object or part **21** low-lying land, esp. a marsh **22** a mud bank exposed at low tide **23** *music* **a** an accidental that lowers the pitch of a note by one semitone. Symbol: ♭ **b** a note affected by this accidental **24** *theatre* a wooden frame covered with painted canvas, used to form part of a stage setting **25** a punctured car tyre **26 the flat** *chiefly Brit* the season of flat racing **flatly** *adv*
WORD ORIGIN Old Norse *flatr*

flat[2] ❶ *n* **1** a set of rooms forming a home entirely on one floor of a building ▹*vb* **flatting, flatted** **2** *Austral & NZ* to share a flat **3 go flatting** *Austral & NZ* to leave home to share a flat
WORD ORIGIN Old English *flett* floor, hall, house

flatboat *n* a flat-bottomed boat for transporting goods on a canal

flatfish *n, pl* **-fish** *or* **-fishes** a sea fish, such as the sole, which has a flat body with both eyes on the uppermost side

flat-footed *adj* **1** having less than the usual degree of arching in the insteps of the feet **2** *informal* clumsy or insensitive

flathead *n* a common Australian flatfish

flatiron *n* (formerly) an iron for pressing clothes that was heated by being placed on a stove

flatlet *n Brit, Austral & S African* a small flat

flatmate *n* a person with whom one shares a flat

flat-pack *adj* (of furniture, etc.) supplied in pieces in a flat box for assembly by the buyer

flat racing *n* the racing of horses on racecourses without jumps

flatscreen *n* a slimline television set or computer monitor with a flat screen

flat spin *n* **1** an aircraft spin in which the longitudinal axis is more nearly horizontal than vertical **2** *informal* a state of confusion

flatten ❶ *vb* **1** to make or become flat or flatter **2** *informal* **a** to knock down or injure **b** to crush or subdue

flatter ❶ *vb* **1** to praise insincerely, esp. in order to win favour **2** to show to advantage: *she wore a simple green cotton dress which she knew flattered her* **3** to make (a person) appear more attractive than in reality: *a portrait that flattered him* **4** to cater to the vanity of (a person): *I was flattered by her praise* **5 flatter oneself** to believe, perhaps mistakenly, something good about oneself **flatterer** *n*
WORD ORIGIN Old French *flater* to lick, fawn upon

f

THESAURUS

cheap, bling *(slang)* ▹*vb* **10, 11 = blaze**, shine, beam, sparkle, glitter, flare, glare, gleam, light up, flicker, shimmer, twinkle, glint, glisten, scintillate, coruscate **12 = speed**, race, shoot, fly, tear, sweep, dash, barrel (along) *(informal, chiefly US & Canad)*, whistle, sprint, bolt, streak, dart, zoom, burn rubber *(informal)* **14a = show quickly**, display **15** *(informal)* **= show off**, display, exhibit, flourish, flaunt **16** *(informal)* **expose**, show quickly

flat[1] *adj* **1, 2 = even**, level, levelled, plane, smooth, uniform, horizontal, unbroken, planar **OPPOSITE:** uneven **4 = punctured**, collapsed, burst, blown out, deflated, empty **6 = absolute**, firm, direct, straight, positive, fixed, plain, final, explicit, definite, outright, unconditional, downright, unmistakable, unequivocal, unqualified, out-and-out, categorical, peremptory **8 = dull**, dead, empty, boring, depressing, pointless, tedious, stale, lacklustre, tiresome, lifeless, monotonous, uninteresting, insipid, unexciting, spiritless **OPPOSITE:** exciting **9 = monotonous**, boring, uniform, dull, tedious, droning, tiresome, unchanging, colourless, toneless, samey *(informal)*, uninflected, unvaried **11 = used up**, finished, empty, drained, expired ▹*adv* **15 = completely**, directly, absolutely, categorically, precisely, exactly, utterly, outright, point blank, unequivocally **19 flat out** *(informal)* **= at full speed**, all out, to the full, hell for leather *(informal)*, as hard as possible, at full tilt, at full gallop, posthaste, for all you are worth, under full steam

flat[2] *n* **1 = apartment**, rooms, quarters, digs, suite, penthouse, living quarters, duplex *(US & Canad)*, bachelor apartment *(Canad)*

flatten *vb* **1 = level**, roll, plaster, squash, compress, trample, iron out, even out, smooth off **2a** *(informal)* **= destroy**, level, ruin, demolish, knock down, pull down, tear down, throw down, bulldoze, raze, remove, kennet *(Austral slang)*, jeff *(Austral slang)*

flatter *vb* **1 = praise**, compliment, pander to, sweet-talk *(informal)*, court, humour, puff, flannel *(Brit informal)*, fawn, cajole, lay it on (thick) *(slang)*, wheedle, inveigle, soft-soap *(informal)*, butter up, blandish **2 = suit**, become, enhance,

DICTIONARY

flattery *n, pl* **-teries** excessive or insincere praise

flattie *n NZ & S African informal* flat tyre

flatulent *adj* suffering from or caused by too much gas in the stomach or intestines **flatulence** *n*
WORD ORIGIN Latin *flatus* blowing

flatworm *n* a worm, such as a tapeworm, with a flattened body

flaunt *vb* to display (oneself or one's possessions) arrogantly: *flaunting his new car*
WORD ORIGIN origin unknown

flautist (flaw-tist) *n* a flute player
WORD ORIGIN Italian *flautista*

flavour ❶ *or US* **flavor** *n* **1** taste perceived in food or liquid in the mouth **2** a distinctive quality or atmosphere: *Rome has its own particular flavour* ▹ *vb* **3** to give flavour to: *salmon flavoured with dill* **flavourless** *or US* **flavorless** *adj*
WORD ORIGIN Old French *flaour*

flavouring *or US* **flavoring** *n* a substance used to flavour food

flaw ❶ *n* **1** an imperfection or blemish **2** a mistake in something that makes it invalid: *a flaw in the system* **flawed** *adj* **flawless** *adj*
WORD ORIGIN probably from Old Norse *flaga* stone slab

flax *n* **1** a plant that has blue flowers and is cultivated for its seeds and the fibres of its stems **2** its fibres, made into linen fabrics **3** NZ a perennial plant producing a fibre that is used by Māoris for decorative work and weaving baskets
WORD ORIGIN Old English *fleax*

flaxen *adj* **1** of flax **2** (of hair) pale yellow

Flaxman *n* **John** 1755–1826, English neoclassical sculptor and draughtsman, noted particularly for his monuments and his engraved illustrations for the *Iliad*, the *Odyssey*, and works by Dante and Aeschylus

flay *vb* **1** to strip off the skin of, esp. by whipping **2** to criticize severely
WORD ORIGIN Old English *flēan*

flea *n* **1** a small wingless jumping insect feeding on the blood of mammals and birds **2 flea in one's ear** *informal* a sharp rebuke
WORD ORIGIN Old English *flēah*

fleabite *n* **1** the bite of a flea **2** a slight annoyance or discomfort

flea-bitten *adj* **1** bitten by or infested with fleas **2** *informal* shabby or decrepit: *a flea-bitten hotel*

flea market *n* an open-air market selling cheap second-hand goods

fleapit *n informal* a shabby cinema or theatre

fleck *n* **1** a small marking or streak **2** a small or tiny piece of something: *a fleck of grit* ▹ *vb* **3** to speckle: *a grey suit flecked with white*
WORD ORIGIN probably from Old Norse *flekkr* stain, spot

Flecker *n* **James Elroy** 1884–1915, English poet and dramatist; author of *Hassan* (1922)

fled *vb* ▸ the past of **flee**

fledged *adj* **1** (of young birds) able to fly **2** qualified and competent: *a fully fledged doctor*
WORD ORIGIN Old English *-flycge*, as in *unflycge* unfledged

fledgling *or* **fledgeling** *n* **1** a young bird that has grown feathers ▹ *adj* **2** new or inexperienced: *Poland's fledgling market economy*

flee ❶ *vb* **fleeing, fled 1** to run away from (a place, danger, etc.) **2** to run or move quickly
WORD ORIGIN Old English *flēon*

fleece *n* **1** the coat of wool that covers a sheep **2** the wool removed from a sheep at one shearing **3** sheepskin or a fabric with soft pile, used as a lining for coats, etc. **4** *Brit* a jacket or top made of this fabric **5** a warm outdoor jacket or top made from a polyester fabric with a brushed nap ▹ *vb* **fleecing, fleeced 6** to defraud or overcharge **7** ▸ same as **shear** (sense 1)
WORD ORIGIN Old English *flēos*

fleecy *adj* **1** of or resembling fleece ▹ *n, pl* **-ies 2** *NZ informal* a person who collects fleeces after shearing and prepares them for baling

fleet[1] ❶ *n* **1** a number of warships organized as a tactical unit **2** all the ships of a nation or company: *the British merchant fleet* **3** a number of vehicles under the same ownership
WORD ORIGIN Old English *flēot* ship, flowing water

fleet[2] *adj* rapid in movement
WORD ORIGIN probably from Old English *flēotan* to float

fleet chief petty officer *n* a noncommissioned officer in a navy

fleeting ❶ *adj* rapid and soon passing: *a fleeting moment* **fleetingly** *adv*

Fleet Street *n* **1** the street in London where many newspaper offices were formerly situated **2** British national newspapers collectively: *Fleet Street's obsession with the Royal Family*

Fleming *n* a person from Flanders or Flemish-speaking Belgium

Flemish *adj* **1** of Flanders, in Belgium ▹ *n* **2** one of the two official languages of Belgium ▹ *pl n* **3 the Flemish** people from Flanders or Flemish-speaking Belgium

flesh ❶ *n* **1** the soft part of the body of an animal or human, esp. muscular tissue ▸ Related adjective: **carnal** **2** *informal* excess weight; fat **3** the meat of animals as opposed to that of fish or, sometimes, fowl **4** the thick soft part of a fruit or vegetable **5 the flesh** sexuality or sensuality: *pleasures of the flesh* **6 flesh and blood** human beings or human nature: *it is almost more than flesh and blood can bear* **7 in the flesh** in person; actually present **8 one's own flesh and blood** one's own family **9 press the flesh** *informal* to shake hands with large numbers of people, esp. in political campaigning
WORD ORIGIN Old English *flǣsc*

flesh-coloured *adj* yellowish-pink

fleshly *adj* **-lier, -liest 1** relating to sexuality or sensuality: *the fleshly implications of their love* **2** worldly as opposed to spiritual

flesh out *vb* to expand on or give more details to: *further meetings will be needed to flesh out the agreement*

fleshpots *pl n* places, such as brothels

THESAURUS

set off, embellish, do something for, show to advantage

flavour *or* **flavor** *n* **1 = taste**, seasoning, flavouring, savour, extract, essence, relish, smack, aroma, odour, zest, tang, zing *(informal)*, piquancy, tastiness
OPPOSITE: blandness
2 = quality, feeling, feel, style, property, touch, character, aspect, tone, suggestion, stamp, essence, tinge, soupçon *(French)* ▹ *vb*
3 = season, spice, add flavour to, enrich, infuse, imbue, pep up, leaven, ginger up, lace

flaw *n* **1 = weakness**, failing, defect, weak spot, spot, fault, scar, blemish, imperfection, speck, disfigurement, chink in your armour

flee *vb* **1, 2 = run away**, leave, escape, bolt, fly, avoid, split *(slang)*, take off *(informal)*, get away, vanish, depart, run off, shun, make off, abscond, decamp, take flight, hook it *(slang)*, do a runner *(slang)*, scarper *(Brit slang)*, slope off, cut and run *(informal)*, make a run for it, beat a hasty retreat, turn tail, fly the coop *(US & Canad informal)*, make a quick exit, skedaddle *(informal)*, make yourself scarce *(informal)*, take a powder *(US & Canad slang)*, make your escape, make your getaway, take it on the lam *(US & Canad slang)*, take to your heels

fleet[1] *n* **1, 2 = navy**, vessels, task force, squadron, warships, flotilla, armada, naval force, sea power, argosy

fleeting *adj* **= momentary**, short, passing, flying, brief, temporary, short-lived, fugitive, transient, flitting, ephemeral, transitory, evanescent, fugacious, here today, gone tomorrow OPPOSITE: lasting

flesh *n* **1 = fat**, muscle, beef *(informal)*, tissue, body, brawn **2** *(informal)* **= fatness**, fat, adipose tissue, corpulence, weight **3 = meat**, food **8 your own flesh and blood = family**, blood, relations, relatives, kin, kindred, kith and kin, blood

DICTIONARY

and strip clubs, where sexual desires are catered to
WORD ORIGIN from the Biblical use as applied to Egypt (Exodus 16:3)
flesh wound *n* a wound affecting superficial tissues
fleshy *adj* **fleshier, fleshiest 1** plump **2** resembling flesh **3** *bot* (of some fruits) thick and pulpy **fleshiness** *n*
Fletcher *n* **John** 1579–1625, English Jacobean dramatist, noted for his romantic tragicomedies written in collaboration with Francis Beaumont, esp. *Philaster* (1610) and *The Maid's Tragedy* (1611)
fleur-de-lys *or* **fleur-de-lis** (flur-de-lee) *n, pl* **fleurs-de-lys** *or* **fleurs-de-lis** (flur-de-leez) a representation of a lily with three distinct petals
WORD ORIGIN Old French *flor de lis* lily flower
Fleury *n* **André Hercule de** 1653–1743, French cardinal and statesman: Louis XV's chief adviser and virtual ruler of France (1726–43)
flew *vb* ▸ the past tense of **fly**[1]
flews *pl n* the fleshy hanging upper lip of a bloodhound or similar dog
WORD ORIGIN origin unknown
flex *n* **1** *Austral & Brit* a flexible insulated electric cable: *a coiled kettle flex* ▷ *vb* **2** to bend **3** to bend and stretch (a muscle)
WORD ORIGIN Latin *flexus* bent, winding
flexible ❶ *adj* **1** able to be bent easily without breaking **2** adaptable to changing circumstances: *flexible working arrangements* **flexibility** *n* **flexibly** *adv*
flexitime *n* a system permitting flexibility of working hours at the beginning or end of the day, provided an agreed total is worked
flibbertigibbet *n old-fashioned* an irresponsible, silly, gossipy person
WORD ORIGIN origin unknown
flick ❶ *vb* **1** to touch or move with the finger or hand in a quick jerky movement **2** to move with a short sudden movement, often repeatedly: *the windscreen wipers flicked back and forth* **3 flick through** to look at (a book or magazine) quickly or idly ▷ *n* **4** a tap or quick stroke
WORD ORIGIN imitative
flicker ❶ *vb* **1** to give out an unsteady or irregular light **2** to move quickly to and fro ▷ *n* **3** an unsteady or brief light **4** a brief or faint indication of emotion: *a flicker of fear in his voice*
WORD ORIGIN Old English *flicorian*
flick knife *n* a knife with a retractable blade that springs out when a button is pressed
flicks *pl n slang, old-fashioned* the cinema
flier *n* ▸ same as **flyer**
flight[1] ❶ *n* **1** a journey by aircraft **2** the act or manner of flying **3** a group of flying birds or aircraft **4** an aircraft flying on a scheduled journey **5** a set of stairs between one landing and the next **6 flight of fancy** an idea that is imaginative but not practical **7** small plastic or feather fins at the rear of an arrow or dart which make it stable in flight
WORD ORIGIN Old English *flyht*
flight[2] ❶ *n* **1** the act of running away, esp. from danger **2 put to flight** to cause to run away **3 take (to) flight** to run away
WORD ORIGIN Old English *flyht* (unattested)
flight attendant *n* a person who attends to the needs of passengers on a commercial flight
flight deck *n* **1** the crew compartment in an airliner **2** the upper deck of an aircraft carrier from which aircraft take off
flightless *adj* (of certain birds and insects) unable to fly
flight lieutenant *n* a junior commissioned officer in an air force
flight recorder *n* an electronic device in an aircraft for storing information concerning its performance in flight. It is often used to determine the cause of a crash. Also called: **black box**
flight sergeant *n* a noncommissioned officer in an air force
flighty *adj* **flightier, flightiest** frivolous and not very reliable or serious **flightiness** *n*
flimsy *adj* **-sier, -siest 1** not strong or substantial **2** light and thin: *a flimsy gauze mask* **3** not very convincing: *flimsy evidence* **flimsily** *adv* **flimsiness** *n*
WORD ORIGIN origin unknown
flinch *vb* **1** to draw back suddenly from pain or something unpleasant **2 flinch from** to avoid: *I wouldn't flinch from saying that to his face*
WORD ORIGIN Old French *flenchir*
fling ❶ *vb* **flinging, flung 1** to throw with force **2** to move or go hurriedly or violently: *she flung her arms open wide* **3** to put or send without warning: *they used to fling me in jail* **4** to put (something) somewhere hurriedly or carelessly **5 fling oneself into** to apply oneself with enthusiasm to ▷ *n* **6** a short spell of self-indulgent enjoyment **7** a brief romantic or sexual relationship **8** a vigorous Scottish country dance: *a Highland fling*
WORD ORIGIN from Old Norse
flint *n* **1** a very hard stone that produces sparks when struck with steel **2** any piece of flint, esp. one used as a primitive tool **3** a small piece of an iron alloy, used in cigarette lighters **flinty** *adj*
WORD ORIGIN Old English
flintlock *n* an obsolete gun in which the powder was lit by a spark produced by a flint
Flintoff *n* **Andrew** born 1977, English cricketer; played for Lancashire and England (from 1998)
flip ❶ *vb* **flipping, flipped 1** to throw (something light or small) carelessly **2** to turn (something) over: *flip the fish on its back* **3** to turn (a device or machine) on or off by quickly pressing a switch **4** to throw (an object such as a coin) so that it turns in the air **5** to buy and sell an asset (often property) quickly for profit **6** (in Britain) to change the designation of an MP's primary and secondary residences in order to maximize a claim from public funds

f

THESAURUS

relations, kinsfolk, ainga (*NZ*), rellies (*Austral slang*)
flexible *adj* **1 = pliable**, plastic, yielding, elastic, supple, lithe, limber, springy, willowy, pliant, tensile, stretchy, whippy, lissom(e), ductile, bendable, mouldable
OPPOSITE: rigid
2 = adaptable, open, variable, adjustable, discretionary
OPPOSITE: inflexible
flick *vb* **1 = strike**, tap, jab, remove quickly, hit, touch, stroke, rap, flip, peck, whisk, dab, fillip **2 = jerk**, pull, tug, lurch, jolt **3 flick through something = browse**, glance at, skim, leaf through, flip through, thumb through, skip through
flicker *vb* **1 = twinkle**, flash, sparkle, flare, shimmer, gutter, glimmer **2 = flutter**, waver, quiver, vibrate ▷ *n* **3 = glimmer**, flash, spark, flare, gleam **4 = trace**, drop, breath, spark, atom, glimmer, vestige, iota
flight[1] *n* **1 = journey**, trip, voyage **2 = aviation**, flying, air transport, aeronautics, aerial navigation **3 = flock**, group, unit, cloud, formation, squadron, swarm, flying group
flight[2] *n* **1 = escape**, fleeing, departure, retreat, exit, running away, exodus, getaway, absconding
fling *vb* **1 = throw**, toss, hurl, chuck (*informal*), launch, cast, pitch, send, shy, jerk, propel, sling, precipitate, lob (*informal*), catapult, heave, let fly ▷ *n* **6 = binge**, good time, bash, bit of fun, party, rave (*Brit slang*), spree, indulgence (*informal*), beano (*Brit slang*), night on the town, rave-up (*Brit slang*), hooley or hoolie (*chiefly Irish & NZ*)
flip *vb* **1 = toss**, throw, cast, pitch, flick, fling, sling **2 = spin**, turn, overturn, turn over, roll over, twist **3 = flick**, switch, snap ▷ *n* **9 = toss**, throw, cast, pitch, spin, snap, twist, flick, jerk

DICTIONARY

7 flip through to look at (a book or magazine) idly **8** Also: **flip one's lid** *slang* to fly into an emotional outburst ▹ *n* **9** a snap or tap, usually with the fingers ▹ *adj* **10** *informal* flippant or pert
WORD ORIGIN probably imitative

flipchart *n* a large pad of paper mounted on a stand, used in giving lectures, etc.

flip-flop *n Brit & S African* a rubber-soled sandal attached to the foot by a thong between the big toe and the next toe
WORD ORIGIN reduplication of *flip*

f

flippant *adj* treating serious matters with inappropriate light-heartedness or lack of respect **flippancy** *n*
WORD ORIGIN probably from *flip*

flipper *n* **1** the flat broad limb of seals, whales, and other aquatic animals specialized for swimming **2** either of a pair of rubber paddle-like devices worn on the feet as an aid in swimming

flirt ⓘ *vb* **1** to behave as if sexually attracted to someone **2** (foll. by *with*) to consider lightly; toy with: *he had often flirted with the idea of emigrating* ▹ *n* **3** a person who flirts **flirtation** *n* **flirtatious** *adj*
WORD ORIGIN origin unknown

flit *vb* **flitting, flitted 1** to fly or move along rapidly and lightly **2** to pass quickly: *a shadow flitted across his face* **3** *Scot & N English dialect* to move house **4** *Brit informal* to leave hurriedly and stealthily in order to avoid debts ▹ *n* **5** the act of flitting **6 do a flit** *NZ informal* to abandon rented accommodation
WORD ORIGIN Old Norse *flytja* to carry

flitch *n* a side of pork salted and cured
WORD ORIGIN Old English *flicce*

flitter *vb rare* ▸ same as **flutter**

float ⓘ *vb* **1** to rest on the surface of a fluid without sinking **2** to move lightly or freely across a surface or through air or water **3** to move about aimlessly, esp. in the mind: *a pleasant image floated into his mind* **4 a** to launch (a commercial enterprise, etc.) **b** to offer for sale on the stock market **5** *finance* to allow (a currency) to fluctuate against other currencies ▹ *n* **6** an inflatable object that helps people learning to swim stay afloat **7** *angling* an indicator attached to a baited line that moves when a fish bites **8** a long rigid boatlike structure, of which there are usually two, attached to an aircraft instead of wheels so that it can land on and take off from water **9** a decorated lorry that is part of a procession **10** a small delivery vehicle: *a milk float* **11** *Austral & NZ* a vehicle for transporting horses **12** a sum of money used to cover small expenses or provide change **13** the hollow floating ball of a ball cock
WORD ORIGIN Old English *flotian*

floatation *n* ▸ same as **flotation**

floating ⓘ *adj* **1** (of a population) moving about; not settled **2** (of an organ or part) displaced or abnormally movable: *a floating kidney* **3** (of a voter) not committed to one party **4** *finance* **a** (of capital) available for current use **b** (of a currency) free to fluctuate against other currencies

floating rib *n* a lower rib not attached to the breastbone

floats *pl n theatre* footlights

flocculent *adj* like tufts of wool **flocculence** *n*
WORD ORIGIN Latin *floccus* tuft of wool

flock[1] ⓘ *n* **1** a group of animals of one kind, esp. sheep or birds **2** a large number of people **3** a congregation of Christians regarded as the responsibility of a member of the clergy ▹ *vb* **4** to gather together or move in large numbers
WORD ORIGIN Old English *flocc*

flock[2] *n* **1** waste from fabrics such as cotton or wool, used for stuffing mattresses ▹ *adj* **2** (of wallpaper) having a velvety raised pattern
WORD ORIGIN Latin *floccus* tuft of wool

floe *n* a sheet of floating ice
WORD ORIGIN probably from Norwegian *flo* slab, layer

flog ⓘ *vb* **flogging, flogged 1** to beat harshly, esp. with a whip or stick **2** (sometimes foll. by *off*) *informal* to sell **3** *Austral & NZ informal* to steal **4 flog a dead horse** *chiefly Brit* to waste one's energy **flogging** *n*
WORD ORIGIN probably from Latin *flagellare*

flood ⓘ *n* **1** an overflowing of water on an area that is normally dry **2** a large amount of water **3** the rising of the tide from low to high water ▸ Related adjectives: **diluvial, diluvian 4** a large amount: *a flood of letters* **5** *theatre* ▸ short for **floodlight** ▹ *vb* **6** to cover or become covered with water **7** to fill to overflowing **8** to put a large number of goods on sale on (a market) at the same time, often at a cheap price: *the US was flooded with cheap televisions* **9** to flow or surge: *the memories flooded back* **10** to supply excess petrol to (a petrol engine) so that it cannot work properly **11** to bleed profusely from the womb **flooding** *n*
WORD ORIGIN Old English *flōd*

Flood[1] *n* **the Flood** *Old Testament* the flood extending over all the earth from which Noah and his family and livestock were saved in the ark (Genesis 7–8); the Deluge

Flood[2] *n* **Henry** 1732–91, Anglo-Irish politician: leader of the parliamentary opposition to English rule

floodgate *n* **1** a gate used to control the flow of water **2 floodgates** controls against an outpouring of

THESAURUS

flirt *vb* **1 = chat up**, lead on *(informal)*, dally with, make advances at, make eyes at, coquet, philander, make sheep's eyes at **2** *(foll. by* **with***)* **= toy with**, consider, entertain, play with, dabble in, trifle with, give a thought to, expose yourself to ▹ *n* **3 = tease**, philanderer, coquette, heart-breaker, wanton, trifler

float *vb* **1 = be buoyant**, stay afloat, be *or* lie on the surface, rest on water, hang, hover, poise, displace water
OPPOSITE: sink
2 = glide, sail, drift, move gently, bob, coast, slide, be carried, slip along **4a, 4b = launch**, offer, sell, set up, promote, get going, push off
OPPOSITE: dissolve

floating *adj* **1 = free**, wandering, variable, fluctuating, unattached, migratory, movable, unfixed **3 = uncommitted**, wavering, undecided, indecisive, vacillating, sitting on the fence *(informal)*, unaffiliated, independent

flock[1] *n* **1 = herd**, group, flight, drove, colony, gaggle, skein **2 = crowd**, company, group, host, collection, mass, gathering, assembly, convoy, herd, congregation, horde, multitude, throng, bevy ▹ *vb* **4a = stream**, crowd, mass, swarm, throng **4b = gather**, group, crowd, mass, collect, assemble, herd, huddle, converge, throng, congregate, troop

flog *vb* **1 = beat**, whip, lash, thrash, whack, scourge, hit hard, trounce, castigate, chastise, flay, lambast(e), flagellate, punish severely, beat *or* knock seven bells out of *(informal)*

flood *n* **1 = deluge**, downpour, flash flood, inundation, tide, overflow, torrent, spate, freshet **2 = torrent**, flow, rush, stream, tide, abundance, multitude, glut, outpouring, profusion **4a = series**, stream, avalanche, barrage, spate, torrent **4b = outpouring**, rush, stream, surge, torrent ▹ *vb* **6a = immerse**, swamp, submerge, inundate, deluge, drown, cover with water **6b = engulf**, flow into, rush into, sweep into, overwhelm, surge into, swarm into, pour into, gush into **7 = pour over**, swamp, run over, overflow, inundate, brim over **8 = saturate**, fill, choke, swamp, glut, oversupply, overfill **9 = stream**, flow, rush, pour, surge

emotion: *it had opened the floodgates of her anxiety*

floodlight *n* **1** a lamp that casts a broad intense light, used in the theatre or to illuminate sports grounds or the exterior of buildings ▹ *vb* **-lighting, -lit 2** to illuminate by floodlight

flood plain *n geog* a flat area bordering a river, made of sediment deposited during flooding

floor ❶ *n* **1** the lower surface of a room **2** a storey of a building **3** a flat bottom surface: *the ocean floor* **4** that part of a legislative hall in which debate is conducted **5** a minimum limit: *a wages floor for low-paid employees* **6 have the floor** to have the right to speak in a debate or discussion ▹ *vb* **7** to knock to the ground **8** *informal* to disconcert or defeat
WORD ORIGIN Old English *flōr*

floorboard *n* one of the boards forming a floor

floored *adj* covered with a floor: *an attic floored with pine planks*

flooring *n* **1** the material used in making a floor: *pine flooring* **2** a floor

floor plan *n* a scale drawing of the arrangement of rooms on one floor of a building

floor show *n* a series of entertainments, such as singing and dancing, in a nightclub

floozy, floozie *or* **floosie** *n, pl* **-zies** *or* **-sies** *slang, old-fashioned* a woman considered to be disreputable or immoral
WORD ORIGIN origin unknown

flop ❶ *vb* **flopping, flopped 1** to bend, fall, or collapse loosely or carelessly **2** *informal* to fail: *his first big film flopped* **3** to fall or move with a sudden noise ▹ *n* **4** *informal* a complete failure **5** the act of flopping **floppy** *adj*
WORD ORIGIN variant of *flap*

floppy disk *n* a flexible magnetic disk that stores data in the memory of a digital computer

flora *n* all the plant life of a given place or time
WORD ORIGIN *Flora*, Roman goddess of flowers

floral ❶ *adj* decorated with or consisting of flowers or patterns of flowers

Florentine *adj* **1** of Florence, a city in central Italy ▹ *n* **2** a person from Florence

floret (flaw-ret) *n* a small flower forming part of a composite flower head
WORD ORIGIN Old French *florete*

floribunda *n* a type of rose whose flowers grow in large clusters
WORD ORIGIN New Latin *floribundus* flowering freely

florid *adj* **1** having a red or flushed complexion **2** very ornate and extravagant: *florid prose*
WORD ORIGIN Latin *floridus* blooming

florin *n* a former British, Australian and New Zealand coin, equivalent to ten pence or twenty cents
WORD ORIGIN Old Italian *fiorino* Florentine coin

Florio *n* **John** ?1553–?1625, English lexicographer, noted for his translation of Montaigne's *Essays* (1603)

florist *n* a person or shop selling flowers

floss *n* **1** fine silky fibres, such as those obtained from silkworm cocoons **2** ▸ see **dental floss** ▹ *vb* **3** to clean (between the teeth) with dental floss **flossy** *adj*
WORD ORIGIN probably from Old French *flosche* down

flotation *or* **floatation** *n* the launching or financing of a commercial enterprise by bond or share issues

flotilla *n* a small fleet or a fleet of small ships
WORD ORIGIN Spanish *flota* fleet

Flotow *n* **Friedrich von** 1812–83, German composer of operas, esp. *Martha* (1847)

flotsam *n* **1** floating wreckage from a ship **2 flotsam and jetsam a** odds and ends **b** *Brit* homeless or vagrant people
WORD ORIGIN Anglo-French *floteson*

flounce[1] *vb* **flouncing, flounced 1** to move or go with emphatic movements ▹ *n* **2** the act of flouncing
WORD ORIGIN Scandinavian

flounce[2] *n* an ornamental frill on a garment or tablecloth
WORD ORIGIN Old French *froncir* to wrinkle

flounder[1] ❶ *vb* **1** to struggle to move or stay upright, esp. in water or mud **2** to behave or speak in an awkward, confused way
WORD ORIGIN probably a blend of FOUNDER + BLUNDER

flounder[2] *n, pl* **-der** *or* **-ders** an edible flatfish
WORD ORIGIN Scandinavian

flour *n* **1** a powder prepared by grinding grain, esp. wheat ▹ *vb* **2** to sprinkle (food or utensils) with flour **floury** *adj*
WORD ORIGIN Middle English *flur* 'flower', i.e. best part

flourish ❶ *vb* **1** to be active, successful, or widespread; prosper **2** to be at the peak of development **3** to wave (something) dramatically ▹ *n* **4** a dramatic waving or sweeping movement: *he created a flourish with an imaginary wand* **5** an ornamental curly line in writing **6** a fancy or extravagant action or part of something: *he took his tie off with a flourish* **flourishing** *adj*
WORD ORIGIN Latin *florere* to flower

flout (rhymes with **out**) *vb* to deliberately disobey (a rule, law, etc.)
WORD ORIGIN probably from Middle English *flouten* to play the flute

flow ❶ *vb* **1** (of liquids) to move in a stream **2** (of blood, electricity, etc.) to circulate **3** to move steadily and

floor *n* **1 = ground 2 = storey**, level, stage, tier ▹ *vb* **7 = knock down**, fell, knock over, prostrate, deck *(slang)* **8** *(informal)* **= disconcert**, stump, baffle, confound, beat, throw *(informal)*, defeat, puzzle, conquer, overthrow, bewilder, perplex, bowl over *(informal)*, faze, discomfit, bring up short, dumbfound, nonplus

flop *vb* **1 = hang down**, hang, dangle, sag, droop, hang limply **2** *(informal)* **= fail**, close, bomb *(US & Canad slang)*, fold *(informal)*, founder, fall short, fall flat, come to nothing, come unstuck, misfire, go belly-up *(slang)*, go down like a lead balloon *(informal)*
OPPOSITE: succeed
3 = slump, fall, drop, collapse, sink, tumble, topple ▹ *n* **4** *(informal)* **= failure**, disaster, loser, fiasco, debacle, washout *(informal)*, cockup *(Brit slang)*, nonstarter
OPPOSITE: success

floral *adj* **= flowery**, flower-patterned

flounder[1] *vb* **1 = struggle**, toss, thrash, plunge, stumble, tumble, muddle, fumble, grope, wallow **2a = falter**, struggle, stall, slow down, run into trouble, come unstuck *(informal)*, be in difficulties, hit a bad patch **2b = dither**, struggle, blunder, be confused, falter, be in the dark, be out of your depth

flourish *vb* **1a = thrive**, increase, develop, advance, progress, boom, bloom, blossom, prosper, burgeon
OPPOSITE: fail
1b = succeed, do well, be successful, move ahead, get ahead, go places *(informal)*, go great guns *(slang)*, go up in the world **1c = grow**, thrive, develop, flower, succeed, get on, bloom, blossom, prosper, bear fruit, be vigorous, be in your prime **3 = wave**, brandish, sweep, swish, display, shake, swing, wield, flutter, wag, flaunt, vaunt, twirl ▹ *n* **4 = wave**, sweep, brandish, swish, shaking, swing, dash, brandishing, twirling, twirl, showy gesture **5 = curlicue**, sweep, decoration, swirl, plume, embellishment, ornamentation **6 = show**, display, parade, fanfare

flow *vb* **1, 2 = run**, course, rush, sweep, move, issue, pass, roll, flood, pour, slide, proceed, stream, run out, surge, spill, go along, circulate, swirl, glide, ripple, cascade, whirl, overflow, gush, inundate, deluge,

DICTIONARY

smoothly: *a golf club with rich-looking cars flowing into it* **4** to be produced effortlessly: *words flowed from him in a steady stream* **5** to hang freely: *her hair loose and flowing down her back* **6** to be abundant: *at the buffet lunch, wine flowed like water* **7** (of tide water) to rise ▷*n* **8** the act, rate, or manner of flowing: *the abundant flow of water through domestic sprinklers* **9** a continuous stream or discharge **10** the advancing of the tide
WORD ORIGIN Old English *flōwan*

flow chart *or* **sheet** *n* a diagram showing a sequence of operations in an industrial process, computer program, etc.

flower ❶ *n* **1** the part of a plant that is, usually, brightly coloured, and quickly fades, producing seeds **2** a plant grown for its colourful flowers ▸Related adjective: **floral** **3** the best or finest part: *in the flower of her youth* **4 in flower** with flowers open ▷*vb* **5** to produce flowers; bloom **6** to reach full growth or maturity: *liberty only flowers in times of peace*
WORD ORIGIN Latin *flos*

flowered *adj* decorated with flowers or a floral design

flowerpot *n* a pot in which plants are grown

flowery *adj* **1** decorated with flowers or floral patterns **2** (of language or style) containing elaborate literary expressions **floweriness** *n*

flown *vb* ▸the past participle of **fly**[1]

fl. oz. fluid ounce(s)

Flt Lt Flight Lieutenant

Flt Sgt Flight Sergeant

flu *n informal* ▸short for **influenza**

fluctuate ❶ *vb* **-ating, -ated** to change frequently and erratically: *share prices fluctuated wildly throughout the day* **fluctuation** *n*
WORD ORIGIN Latin *fluctus* a wave

flue *n* a passage or pipe in a chimney, used to carry off smoke, gas, or hot air
WORD ORIGIN origin unknown

fluent ❶ *adj* **1** able to speak or write with ease: *they spoke fluent English; fluent in French* **2** spoken or written with ease **fluency** *n* **fluently** *adv*
WORD ORIGIN Latin *fluere* to flow

fluff *n* **1** soft light particles, such as the down of cotton or wool **2** *informal* a mistake, esp. in speaking or reading lines ▷*vb* **3** to make or become soft and puffy **4** *informal* to make a mistake in performing **fluffy** *adj* **fluffiness** *n*
WORD ORIGIN probably from earlier *flue* downy matter

fluid ❶ *n* **1** a substance, such as a liquid or gas, that can flow and has no fixed shape ▷*adj* **2** capable of flowing and easily changing shape **3** constantly changing or apt to change **fluidity** *n*
WORD ORIGIN Latin *fluere* to flow

fluid ounce *n* **1** *Brit* a unit of liquid measure equal to one twentieth of an Imperial pint (28.4 ml) **2** *US* a unit of liquid measure equal to one sixteenth of a US pint (29.6 ml)

fluke[1] *n* an accidental stroke of luck **fluky** *adj*
WORD ORIGIN origin unknown

fluke[2] *n* **1** the flat triangular point of an anchor **2** either of the two lobes of the tail of a whale
WORD ORIGIN perhaps a special use of FLUKE[3] (in the sense: a flounder, flatfish)

fluke[3] *n* any parasitic flatworm, such as the liver fluke
WORD ORIGIN Old English *flōc*

flume *n* **1** a narrow sloping channel for water **2** an enclosed water slide at a swimming pool

flummery *n informal* silly or trivial talk
WORD ORIGIN Welsh *llymru*

flummox *vb* to puzzle or confuse
WORD ORIGIN origin unknown

flung *vb* ▸the past of **fling**

flunk *vb US, Canad, Austral, NZ & S African informal* to fail (an examination, course, etc.)
WORD ORIGIN origin unknown

flunky *or* **flunkey** *n, pl* **flunkies** *or* **flunkeys** **1** a manservant who wears ceremonial dress **2** a person who performs small unimportant tasks for a powerful or important person in the hope of being rewarded
WORD ORIGIN origin unknown

fluor (flew-or) *n* ▸same as **fluorspar**
WORD ORIGIN Latin: a flowing; so called from its use as a metallurgical flux

fluoresce *vb* **-rescing, -resced** to exhibit fluorescence
WORD ORIGIN back formation from FLUORESCENCE

fluorescence *n* **1** *physics* the emission of light from atoms or molecules that are bombarded by particles, such as electrons, or by radiation from a separate source **2** the radiation emitted as a result of fluorescence **fluorescent** *adj*
WORD ORIGIN from *fluor*

fluorescent lamp *n* a lamp in which ultraviolet radiation from an electrical gas discharge causes a thin layer of phosphor on a tube's inside surface to fluoresce

fluoridate *vb* **-dating, -dated** to add fluoride to (water) as protection against tooth decay **fluoridation** *n*

fluoride *n chem* any compound containing fluorine and another element or radical

fluorinate *vb* **-nating, -nated** to treat or combine with fluorine **fluorination** *n*

fluorine *n chem* a poisonous strong-smelling pale yellow gas that is the most reactive of all the elements. Symbol: F

fluoroscopy (floor-oss-kop-ee) *n* ▸same as **radioscopy**

fluorspar, fluor *or US & Canad* **fluorite** *n* a white or colourless mineral, consisting of calcium fluoride in crystalline form: the chief ore of fluorine

flurry ❶ *n, pl* **-ries** **1** a short rush of vigorous activity or movement **2** a light gust of wind or rain or fall of snow ▷*vb* **-ries, -rying, -ried** **3** to confuse or bewilder
WORD ORIGIN obsolete *flurr* to scatter

flush[1] ❶ *vb* **1** to blush or cause to blush **2** to send water quickly through (a pipe or a toilet) so as to clean it **3** to elate: *she was flushed with excitement* ▷*n*

THESAURUS

spurt, teem, spew, squirt, purl, well forth **3 = pour**, move, sweep, flood, stream, overflow **4 = issue**, follow, result, emerge, spring, pour, proceed, arise, derive, ensue, emanate ▷*n* **8 = stream**, current, movement, motion, course, issue, flood, drift, tide, spate, gush, flux, outpouring, outflow, undertow, tideway

flower *n* **1 = bloom**, blossom, efflorescence **3a = elite**, best, prime, finest, pick, choice, cream, height, crème de la crème *(French)*, choicest part **3b = height**, prime, peak, vigour, freshness, greatest *or* finest point ▷*vb* **5 = bloom**, open, mature, flourish, unfold, blossom, burgeon, effloresce **6 = blossom**, grow, develop, progress, mature, thrive, flourish, bloom, bud, prosper

fluctuate *vb* **= change**, swing, vary, alter, hesitate, alternate, waver, veer, rise and fall, go up and down, ebb and flow, seesaw

fluent *adj* **2 = effortless**, natural, articulate, well-versed, glib, facile, voluble, smooth-spoken

fluid *n* **1 = liquid**, solution, juice, liquor, sap ▷*adj* **2 = liquid**, running, flowing, watery, molten, melted, runny, liquefied, in solution, aqueous **OPPOSITE:** solid

flurry *n* **1 = commotion**, stir, bustle, flutter, to-do, excitement, hurry, fuss, disturbance, flap, whirl, furore, ferment, agitation, fluster, ado, tumult **2 = gust**, shower, gale, swirl, squall, storm

flush[1] *vb* **1 = blush**, colour, burn, flame, glow, crimson, redden, suffuse, turn red, go red, colour up, go as red as a beetroot **2 = cleanse**, wash out, swab, rinse out, flood, drench, syringe, swill, hose down, douche ▷*n* **4 = blush**, colour, glow, reddening, redness, rosiness

flush[2] *adj* **1 = level**, even, true, flat, square, plane **2** *(informal)* **= wealthy**,

DICTIONARY

4 a rosy colour, esp. in the cheeks **5** a sudden flow, such as of water **6** a feeling of elation: *in the flush of victory* **7** freshness: *in the first flush of youth*
flushed *adj*
WORD ORIGIN perhaps from FLUSH[3]
flush[2] ❶ *adj* **1** level with another surface **2** *informal* having plenty of money ▷*adv* **3** so as to be level
WORD ORIGIN probably from FLUSH[1] (in the sense: spring out)
flush[3] *vb* to drive out of a hiding place
WORD ORIGIN Middle English *flusshen*
flush[4] *n* (in poker and similar games) a hand containing only one suit
WORD ORIGIN Latin *fluxus* flux
fluster *vb* **1** to make or become nervous or upset ▷*n* **2** a nervous or upset state
WORD ORIGIN from Old Norse
flute *n* **1** a wind instrument consisting of a tube of wood or metal with holes in the side stopped either by the fingers or keys. The breath is directed across a mouth hole in the side **2** a tall narrow wineglass, used esp. for champagne ▷*vb* **fluting, fluted 3** to utter in a high-pitched tone **fluty** *adj*
WORD ORIGIN Old French *flahute*
fluted *adj* having decorated grooves
fluting *n* a design or decoration of flutes on a column
flutter ❶ *vb* **1** to wave rapidly **2** (of birds or butterflies) to flap the wings **3** to move with an irregular motion **4** *pathol* (of the heart) to beat abnormally rapidly **5** to move about restlessly ▷*n* **6** a quick flapping or vibrating motion **7** a state of nervous excitement or confusion **8** excited interest **9** *Brit informal* a modest bet **10** *pathol* an abnormally rapid beating of the heart **11** *electronics* a slow variation in pitch in a sound-reproducing system
WORD ORIGIN Old English *floterian* to float to and fro
fluvial (flew-vee-al) *adj* of or relating to a river
WORD ORIGIN Latin *fluvius* river
flux *n* **1** continuous change or instability **2** a flow or discharge **3** a substance mixed with a metal oxide to assist in fusion **4** *physics* **a** the rate of flow of particles, energy, or a fluid **b** the strength of a field in a given area: *magnetic flux*
WORD ORIGIN Latin *fluxus* a flow
fly[1] ❶ *vb* **flies, flying, flew, flown 1** to move through the air on wings or in an aircraft **2** to control the flight of (an aircraft) **3** to float, flutter, display, or be displayed in the air: *the Red Cross flag flew at each corner of the compound* **4** to transport or be transported through the air by aircraft, wind, etc. **5** to move very quickly or suddenly: *the front door flew open* **6** to pass quickly: *how time flies* **7** to escape from (an enemy or a place) **8 fly a kite** to release information or take a step in order to test public opinion **9 fly at** to attack (someone) **10 fly high** *informal* to have a high aim **11 let fly** *informal* to lose one's temper: *a young child letting fly at you in a sudden moment of temper* ▷*n, pl* **flies 12** Also: **flies** a closure that conceals a zip, buttons, or other fastening, as on trousers **13** a flap forming the entrance to a tent **14 flies** *theatre* the space above the stage, used for storing scenery
WORD ORIGIN Old English *flēogan*
fly[2] *n, pl* **flies 1** a small insect with two pairs of wings **2** any of various similar but unrelated insects, such as the dragonfly **3** *angling* a lure made from a fish-hook attached with feathers to resemble a fly **4 fly in the ointment** *informal* a slight flaw that detracts from value or enjoyment **5 fly on the wall** a person who watches others, while not being noticed himself or herself **6 there are no flies on him** *or* **her** *informal* he or she is no fool
WORD ORIGIN Old English *flēoge*
fly[3] *adj slang, chiefly Brit* sharp and cunning
WORD ORIGIN origin unknown
flyaway *adj* **1** (of hair) very fine and soft **2** frivolous or light-hearted: *a flyaway remark*
flyblown *adj* **1** covered with blowfly eggs **2** in a dirty and bad condition
fly-by-night *informal adj* **1** unreliable or untrustworthy, esp. in money matters ▷*n* **2** an untrustworthy person
flycatcher *n* a small insect-eating songbird
flyer *or* **flier** *n* **1** a small advertising leaflet **2** a person or thing that flies or moves very fast **3** *old-fashioned* an aircraft pilot
fly-fishing *n angling* fishing using artificial flies as lures
flying ❶ *n* **1** the act of piloting, navigating, or travelling in an aircraft ▷*adj* **2** hurried and brief: *a flying visit* **3** fast or built for speed: *Australia's flying fullback* **4** hanging, waving, or floating freely: *flags flying proudly*
flying boat *n* a seaplane in which the fuselage consists of a hull that provides buoyancy
flying buttress *n* an arch and vertical column that supports a wall from the outside
flying colours *pl n* conspicuous success; triumph: *they passed with flying colours*
flying fish *n* a fish of warm and tropical seas, with winglike fins used for gliding above the water
flying fox *n* **1** a large fruit bat of tropical Africa and Asia **2** *Austral & NZ* a platform suspended from an overhead cable, used for transporting people or materials
flying officer *n* a junior commissioned officer in an air force
flying saucer *n* an unidentified disc-shaped flying object alleged to come from outer space
flying squad *n* a small group of police or soldiers ready to move into action quickly
flying start *n* **1** any promising beginning: *a flying start to the new financial year* **2** a start to a race in which the competitor is already travelling at speed as he or she

THESAURUS

rich, rolling *(slang)*, well-off, in the money *(informal)*, in funds, well-heeled *(informal)*, replete, moneyed, well-supplied, minted *(Brit slang)*
flutter *vb* **1 = beat**, bat, flap, tremble, shiver, flicker, ripple, waver, fluctuate, agitate, ruffle, quiver, vibrate, palpitate **3, 5 = flit**, hover, flitter ▷*n* **6a = tremor**, tremble, shiver, shudder, palpitation **6b = vibration**, twitching, quiver, quivering **7 = agitation**, state *(informal)*, confusion, excitement, flap *(informal)*, tremble, flurry, dither *(chiefly Brit)*, commotion, fluster, tumult, perturbation, state of nervous excitement
fly[1] *vb* **1 = take wing**, soar, glide, take to the air, wing, mount, sail, hover, flutter, flit **2 = pilot**, control, operate, steer, manoeuvre, navigate, be at the controls, aviate **3a = flutter**, wave, float, flap **3b = display**, show, flourish, brandish **4 = airlift**, send by plane, take by plane, take in an aircraft **5 = rush**, race, shoot, career, speed, tear, dash, hurry, barrel (along) *(informal, chiefly US & Canad)*, sprint, bolt, dart, zoom, hare *(Brit informal)*, hasten, whizz *(informal)*, scoot, scamper, burn rubber *(informal)*, be off like a shot *(informal)* **6 = pass swiftly**, pass, glide, slip away, roll on, flit, elapse, run its course, go quickly **7 = leave**, disappear, get away, depart, run, escape, flee, take off, run from, shun, clear out *(informal)*, light out *(informal)*, abscond, decamp, take flight, do a runner *(slang)*, run for it, cut and run *(informal)*, fly the coop *(US & Canad informal)*, beat a retreat, make a quick exit, make a getaway, show a clean pair of heels, skedaddle *(informal)*, hightail *(informal, chiefly US)*, take a powder *(US & Canad slang)*, hasten away, make your escape, take it on the lam *(US & Canad slang)*, take to your heels
flying *adj* **2 = hurried**, brief, rushed, fleeting, short-lived, hasty, transitory, fugacious

DICTIONARY

passes the starting line
flyleaf *n, pl* **-leaves** the inner leaf of the endpaper of a book
flyover *n* an intersection of two roads at which one is carried over the other by a bridge
flypaper *n* paper with a sticky and poisonous coating, hung up to trap flies
fly-past *n* a ceremonial flight of aircraft over a given area
fly sheet *n* a piece of canvas drawn over the ridgepole of a tent to form an outer roof
fly spray *n* a liquid used to destroy flies, sprayed from an aerosol
flyweight *n* a professional or an amateur boxer weighing up to 112 pounds (51 kg)
flywheel *n* a heavy wheel that regulates the speed of a machine
Fm *chem* fermium
FM frequency modulation
f-number *n photog* the ratio of the effective diameter of a lens to its focal length
Fo *n* **Dario** born 1926, Italian playwright and actor. His plays include *The Accidental Death of an Anarchist* (1970), *Trumpets and Raspberries* (1984), and *The Tricks of the Trade* (1991): Nobel prize for literature 1997
foal *n* **1** the young of a horse or related animal ▹*vb* **2** to give birth to (a foal)
WORD ORIGIN Old English *fola*
foam ⊕ *n* **1** a mass of small bubbles of gas formed on the surface of a liquid **2** frothy saliva **3** a light spongelike solid used for insulation, packing, etc. ▹*vb* **4** to produce or cause to produce foam **5** **foam at the mouth** to be very angry **foamy** *adj*
WORD ORIGIN Old English *fām*
fob *n* **1** a chain by which a pocket watch is attached to a waistcoat **2** a small pocket in a man's waistcoat, for holding a watch
WORD ORIGIN Germanic
f.o.b. *or* **FOB** *commerce* free on board
fob off *vb* **fobbing, fobbed 1** to pretend to satisfy (a person) with lies or excuses **2** to sell or pass off (inferior goods) as valuable
WORD ORIGIN probably from German *foppen* to trick
focal *adj* **1** of or relating to a focus **2** situated at or measured from the focus
focal length *n* the distance from the focal point of a lens or mirror to the surface of the mirror or the centre of the lens
focal point *n* **1** the point where the rays of light from a lens or mirror meet **2** the centre of attention or interest: *a focal point for the new high-technology industries*
Foch *n* **Ferdinand** 1851–1929, marshal of France; commander in chief of Allied armies on the Western front in World War I (1918)
focus ⊕ (foe-kuss) *vb* **-cusing, -cused** *or* **-cussing, -cussed 1** to adjust one's eyes or an instrument on an object so that its image is clear **2** to concentrate ▹*n, pl* **-cuses** *or* **-ci** (-sigh, -kye, -kee) **3** a point of convergence of light or sound waves, or a point from which they appear to diverge **4** **in focus** (of an object or image being viewed) clear and sharp **5** **out of focus** (of an object or image being viewed) blurred and fuzzy **6** ▸same as **focal point** or **focal length 7** *optics* the state of an optical image when it is distinct or the state of an instrument producing this image **8** a point upon which attention or activity is concentrated: *the focus was on health and education* **9** *geom* a fixed reference point on the concave side of a conic section, used when defining its eccentricity
WORD ORIGIN Latin: hearth, fireplace
focus group *n* a group of people gathered by a market research company to discuss and assess a product or service
fodder *n* bulk feed for livestock, esp. hay or straw
WORD ORIGIN Old English *fōdor*
foe ⊕ *n formal or literary* an enemy
WORD ORIGIN Old English *fāh* hostile
FoE *or* **FOE** Friends of the Earth
foetid *adj* ▸same as **fetid**
foetus *n, pl* **-tuses** ▸same as **fetus**
fog ⊕ *n* **1** a mass of droplets of condensed water vapour suspended in the air, often greatly reducing visibility **2** *photog* a blurred area on a developed negative, print, or transparency ▹*vb* **fogging, fogged 3** to envelop or become enveloped with or as if with fog **foggy** *adj*
WORD ORIGIN probably from Old Norse
Fogarty *n* **Carl** (**George**) born 1965, British racing motorcyclist; Superbike world champion 1994, 1995, 1998, 1999
fog bank *n* a distinct mass of fog, esp. at sea
fogbound *adj* prevented from operating by fog
fogey *or* **fogy** *n, pl* **-geys** *or* **-gies** an extremely old-fashioned person: *a stick-in-the-mud old fogey* **fogeyish** *or* **fogyish** *adj*
WORD ORIGIN origin unknown
foghorn *n* a large horn sounded at intervals as a warning to ships in fog
foible *n* a slight peculiarity or minor weakness: *he was intolerant of other people's foibles*
WORD ORIGIN obsolete French form of *faible* feeble
foil[1] ⊕ *vb* to baffle or frustrate (a person or an attempt)
WORD ORIGIN Middle English *foilen* to trample
foil[2] ⊕ *n* **1** metal in the form of very thin sheets **2** a person or thing setting off another thing to advantage: *mint sauce is an excellent foil to lamb*
WORD ORIGIN Latin *folia* leaves
foil[3] *n* a light slender flexible sword tipped by a button, used in fencing
WORD ORIGIN origin unknown
foist *vb* **foist on** to force (someone) to have or experience (something): *the tough economic policies which have been foisted on the developing world*
WORD ORIGIN probably from obsolete Dutch *vuisten* to enclose in one's hand
Fokine *n* **Michel** 1880–1942, US choreographer, born in Russia, regarded as the creator of modern ballet. He worked with Diaghilev as director of the Ballet Russe (1909–15), producing works such as *Les Sylphides* and *Petrushka*
Fokker *n* **Anthony Herman Gerard** 1890–1939, Dutch designer and builder of aircraft, born in Java
fold[1] ⊕ *vb* **1** to bend double so that one part covers another **2** to bring together and intertwine (the arms or

THESAURUS

foam *n* **1 = froth**, spray, bubbles, lather, suds, spume, head ▹*vb* **4 = bubble**, boil, fizz, froth, lather, effervesce
focus *vb* **1 = fix**, train, direct, aim **2 = concentrate**, centre, spotlight, zero in on *(informal)*, meet, join, direct, aim, pinpoint, converge, rivet, bring to bear, zoom in ▹*n* **3 = centre**, focal point, central point, core, bull's eye, centre of attraction, centre of activity, cynosure
foe *n (formal or literary)* **= enemy**, rival, opponent, adversary, antagonist, foeman *(archaic)* **OPPOSITE:** friend
fog *n* **1 = mist**, gloom, haze, smog, murk, miasma, murkiness, peasouper *(informal)*
foil[1] *vb* **= thwart**, stop, check, defeat, disappoint, counter, frustrate, hamper, baffle, elude, balk, circumvent, outwit, nullify, checkmate, nip in the bud, put a spoke in (someone's) wheel *(Brit)*
foil[2] *n* **2 = complement**, setting, relief, contrast, background, antithesis
fold[1] *vb* **1 = bend**, double, gather, tuck, overlap, crease, pleat, intertwine, double over, turn under **6** *(informal)* **= go bankrupt**, close, fail, crash, collapse, founder, shut down, go under, be ruined, go bust *(informal)*, go to the wall, go belly-up

DICTIONARY

legs) **3 fold up** to enclose in a surrounding material **4** *literary* to clasp (a person) in one's arms **5** Also: **fold in** to mix (ingredients) by gently turning one over the other with a spoon **6** *informal* (of a business, organization, or project) to fail or go bankrupt ▷*n* **7** a piece or section that has been folded **8** a mark, crease, or hollow made by folding **9** a bend in stratified rocks that results from movements within the earth's crust
WORD ORIGIN Old English *fealdan*
fold² *n* **1** *Brit, Austral and S African* a small enclosure for sheep **2** a church or the members of it
WORD ORIGIN Old English *falod*
folder *n* a binder or file for holding loose papers
folding door *n* a door with two or more vertical hinged leaves that can be folded one against another
foliaceous *adj* **1** like a leaf **2** *geol* consisting of thin layers
WORD ORIGIN Latin *foliaceus*
foliage *n* **1** the green leaves of a plant **2** leaves together with the stems, twigs, and branches they are attached to, esp. when used for decoration
WORD ORIGIN Old French *fuellage*
foliation *n* **1** *bot* **a** the process of producing leaves **b** the state of being in leaf **2** a leaflike decoration
folio *n, pl* **-lios 1** a sheet of paper folded in half to make two leaves for a book **2** a book of the largest common size made up of such sheets **3 a** a leaf of paper numbered on the front side only **b** the page number of a book **4** NZ a collection of related material ▷*adj* **5** of or made in the largest book size, common esp. in early centuries of European printing: *the entire series is being reissued, several in the original folio format*
WORD ORIGIN Latin *in folio* in a leaf
folk ⓘ *pl n* **1** people in general, esp. those of a particular group or class: *ordinary folk* **2** Also: **folks** *informal* members of one's family; relatives ▷*n* **3** *informal* ▸short for **folk music** **4** a people or tribe ▷*adj* **5** originating from or traditional to the common people of a country: *folk art*
WORD ORIGIN Old English *folc*
folk dance *n* **1** a traditional country dance **2** music for such a dance
folk etymology *n* the gradual change in the form of a word through the influence of a more familiar word, as for example *crayfish* from its Middle English form *crevis*
folklore *n* the traditional beliefs of a people as expressed in stories and songs
folk music *n* **1** music that is passed on from generation to generation **2** a piece written in the style of this music
folk song *n* **1** a song handed down among the common people **2** a modern song like this **folk singer** *n*
folksy *adj* **-sier, -siest** simple and unpretentious, sometimes in an artificial way
follicle *n* any small sac or cavity in the body, esp. one from which a hair grows **follicular** *adj*
WORD ORIGIN Latin *folliculus* small bag
follow ⓘ *vb* **1** to go or come after **2** to accompany: *he followed Isabel everywhere* **3** to be a logical or natural consequence of **4** to keep to the course or track of **5** to act in accordance with: *follow the rules below and it will help you a great deal* **6** to accept the ideas or beliefs of **7** to understand (an explanation) **8** to have a keen interest in: *he's followed the singer's career for more than 25 years* **9** to choose to receive someone's updates on the Twitter website
▸See also **follow-on, follow through, follow up**
WORD ORIGIN Old English *folgian*
follower ⓘ *n* **1** a person who accepts the teachings of another: *a follower of Nietzsche* **2** a supporter, such as of a sport or team
following ⓘ *adj* **1** about to be mentioned **2** next in time **3** (of winds or currents) moving in the same direction as a vessel ▷*prep* **4** as a result of: *uncertainty following the collapse of communism* ▷*n* **5** a group of supporters or enthusiasts
follow-on *cricket* *n* **1** an immediate second innings forced on a team scoring a prescribed number of runs fewer than its opponents in the first innings ▷*vb* **follow on 2** to play a follow-on: *England had to follow on*
follow through *vb* **1** to continue an action or series of actions until finished **2** *sport* to continue a stroke, kick, etc. after striking the ball ▷*n* **follow-through 3** *sport* continuation of a kick, stroke, etc. after striking the ball: *Faldo's controlled follow-through*
follow up *vb* **1** to investigate (a person, evidence, etc.) closely **2** to continue (action) after a beginning, esp. to increase its effect ▷*n* **follow-up 3** something done to reinforce an initial action: *a routine follow-up to his operation*
folly ⓘ *n, pl* **-lies 1** the quality of being foolish **2** a foolish action, idea, etc. **3** an imitation castle, temple, etc. built as a decoration in a large garden or park
WORD ORIGIN Old French *folie* madness
foment (foam-ent) *vb* to encourage or stir up (trouble) **fomentation** *n*
WORD ORIGIN Latin *fomentum* a poultice

THESAURUS

(slang) ▷*n* **7, 8 = crease**, turn, gather, bend, layer, overlap, wrinkle, pleat, ruffle, furrow, knife-edge, double thickness, folded portion
folk *pl n* **1 = people**, persons, humans, individuals, men and women, human beings, humanity, inhabitants, mankind, mortals **2** *(usually plural, informal)* **= family**, parents, relations, relatives, tribe, clan, kin, kindred, ainga *(NZ)*, rellies *(Austral slang)*
follow *vb* **1a = pursue**, track, dog, hunt, chase, shadow, tail *(informal)*, trail, hound, stalk, run after
OPPOSITE: avoid
1b = come after, go after, come next
OPPOSITE: precede
2 = accompany, attend, escort, come after, go behind, tag along behind, bring up the rear, come behind, come *or* go with, tread on the heels of **3 = result**, issue, develop, spring, flow, proceed, arise, ensue, emanate, be consequent, supervene **5 = obey**, observe, comply with, adhere to, mind, watch, note, regard, stick to, heed, conform to, keep to, pay attention to, be guided by, toe the line, act according to, act in accordance with, give allegiance to
OPPOSITE: ignore
7 = understand, get, see, catch, realize, appreciate, take in, grasp, catch on *(informal)*, keep up with, comprehend, fathom, get the hang of *(informal)*, get the picture **8 = keep up with**, support, be interested in, cultivate, be devoted to, be a fan of, keep abreast of, be a devotee *or* supporter of
follower *n* **1, 2 = supporter**, fan, representative, convert, believer, admirer, backer, partisan, disciple, protagonist, devotee, worshipper, apostle, pupil, cohort *(chiefly US)*, adherent, henchman, groupie *(slang)*, habitué, votary
OPPOSITE: leader
following *adj* **1 = coming**, about to be mentioned **2 = next**, subsequent, successive, ensuing, coming, later, succeeding, specified, consequent, consequential ▷*n* **5 = supporters**, backing, public, support, train, fans, audience, circle, suite, patronage, clientele, entourage, coterie, retinue
folly *n* **1 = foolishness**, bêtise *(rare)*, nonsense, madness, stupidity, absurdity, indiscretion, lunacy, recklessness, silliness, idiocy, irrationality, imprudence, rashness, imbecility, fatuity, preposterousness, daftness *(informal)*, desipience
OPPOSITE: wisdom

DICTIONARY

fond ❶ *adj* **1 fond of** having a liking for **2** loving and affectionate: *his fond parents* **3** (of hopes or wishes) cherished but unlikely to be realized **fondly** *adv* **fondness** *n*
WORD ORIGIN Middle English *fonnen* to be foolish

Fonda *n* **1 Henry** 1905–82, US film actor. His many films include *Young Mr Lincoln* (1939), *The Grapes of Wrath* (1940), *Twelve Angry Men* (1957), and *On Golden Pond* (1981) for which he won an Oscar **2** his daughter **Jane** born 1937, US film actress. Her films include *Klute* (1971) for which she won an Oscar, *Julia* (1977), *The China Syndrome* (1979), *On Golden Pond* (1981), and *The Old Gringo* (1989) **3** her brother, **Peter** born 1939, US film actor, who made his name in *Easy Rider* (1969); later films include *Ulee's Gold* (1997)

fondant *n* (a sweet made from) a thick flavoured paste of sugar and water
WORD ORIGIN French

fondle *vb* **-dling, -dled** to touch or stroke tenderly
WORD ORIGIN obsolete *fond* to fondle

fondue *n* a Swiss dish, consisting of melted cheese into which small pieces of bread are dipped
WORD ORIGIN French: melted

font¹ *n* a large bowl in a church for baptismal water
WORD ORIGIN Latin *fons* fountain

font² *n printing* ▸ same as **fount²**

Fontane *n* **Theodor** 1819–98, German novelist and journalist; his novels include *Vor dem Sturm* (1878) and *Effi Briest* (1898)

fontanelle *or esp. US* **fontanel** *n anat* a soft membranous gap between the bones of a baby's skull
WORD ORIGIN Old French *fontanele* a little spring

Fontenelle *n* **Bernard le Bovier de** 1657–1757, French philosopher. His writings include *Digressions sur les anciens et les modernes* (1688) and *Éléments de la géométrie de l'infini* (1727)

food ❶ *n* any substance that can be taken into the body by a living organism and changed into energy and body tissue ▸ Related adjective: **gastronomy**
WORD ORIGIN Old English *fōda*

food chain *n ecology* a series of organisms in a community, each member of which feeds on another in the chain and is in turn eaten

food group *n* any of the categories into which different foods may be placed according to the type of nourishment they supply

foodie *n informal* a person with a keen interest in food and cookery

food poisoning *n* an acute illness caused by food that is contaminated by bacteria

food processor *n* a machine for chopping, mixing, or liquidizing food

foodstuff *n* any substance that can be used as food

fool¹ ❶ *n* **1** a person who lacks sense or judgment **2** a person who is made to appear ridiculous **3** (formerly) a professional jester living in a royal or noble household **4 play** *or* **act the fool** to deliberately act foolishly ▹ *vb* **5** to deceive (someone), esp. in order to make them look ridiculous **6 fool around** *or* **about with** *informal* to act or play with irresponsibly or aimlessly **7** to speak or act in a playful or jesting manner
WORD ORIGIN Latin *follis* bellows

fool² *n chiefly Brit* a dessert made from a puree of fruit with cream
WORD ORIGIN perhaps from FOOL¹

foolery *n* foolish behaviour

foolhardy *adj* **-hardier, -hardiest** recklessly adventurous **foolhardily** *adv* **foolhardiness** *n*
WORD ORIGIN Old French *fol* foolish + *hardi* bold

foolish ❶ *adj* very silly, unwise, or absurd **foolishly** *adv* **foolishness** *n*

foolproof *adj informal* **1** incapable of going wrong; infallible: *a foolproof identification system* **2** (of machines etc.) guaranteed to function as intended despite human misuse or error

foolscap *n chiefly Brit* a standard paper size, 34.3 × 43.2 cm
WORD ORIGIN from the watermark of a *fool's* (i.e. dunce's) *cap*, formerly used on it

fool's errand *n* a fruitless undertaking

fool's gold *n* a yellow-coloured mineral, such as pyrite, that is sometimes mistaken for gold

fool's paradise *n* a state of happiness based on false hopes or beliefs

foosball *n US & Canad* a game in which opponents on either side of a purpose-built table attempt to strike a ball into the other side's goal by moving horizontal bars with miniatures of footballers attached

foot *n, pl* **feet 1** the part of the leg below the ankle joint that is in contact with the ground during

THESAURUS

fond *adj* **2 = loving**, caring, warm, devoted, tender, adoring, affectionate, indulgent, doting, amorous **OPPOSITE:** indifferent **3 = unrealistic**, empty, naive, vain, foolish, deluded, indiscreet, credulous, overoptimistic, delusive, delusory, absurd **OPPOSITE:** sensible

food *n* **= nourishment**, cooking, provisions, fare, board, commons, table, eats *(slang)*, stores, feed, diet, meat, bread, menu, tuck *(informal)*, tucker *(Austral & NZ informal)*, rations, nutrition, cuisine, tack *(informal)*, refreshment, scoff *(slang)*, nibbles, grub *(slang)*, foodstuffs, subsistence, kai *(NZ informal)*, larder, chow *(informal)*, sustenance, nosh *(slang)*, daily bread, victuals, edibles, comestibles, provender, nosebag *(slang)*, pabulum *(rare)*, nutriment, vittles *(obsolete, dialect)*, viands, aliment, eatables *(slang)*, survival rations

fool¹ *n* **1 = simpleton**, idiot, mug *(Brit slang)*, berk *(Brit slang)*, charlie *(Brit informal)*, silly, goose *(informal)*, dope *(informal)*, jerk *(slang, chiefly US & Canad)*, dummy *(slang)*, ass *(US & Canad taboo slang)*, clot *(Brit informal)*, plank *(Brit slang)*, sap *(slang)*, wally *(slang)*, illiterate, prat *(slang)*, plonker *(slang)*, coot, moron, nit *(informal)*, git *(Brit slang)*, geek *(slang)*, twit *(informal, chiefly Brit)*, bonehead *(slang)*, chump *(informal)*, dunce, imbecile *(informal)*, loon, clod, cretin, oaf, bozo *(US slang)*, dullard, dimwit *(informal)*, ignoramus, dumbo *(slang)*, jackass, dipstick *(Brit slang)*, gonzo *(slang)*, schmuck *(US slang)*, dork *(slang)*, nitwit *(informal)*, dolt, blockhead, ninny, divvy *(Brit slang)*, bird-brain *(informal)*, pillock *(Brit slang)*, halfwit, nincompoop, dweeb *(US slang)*, putz *(US slang)*, fathead *(informal)*, weenie *(US informal)*, schlep *(US slang)*, eejit *(Scot & Irish)*, dumb-ass *(slang)*, pea-brain *(slang)*, dunderhead, numpty *(Scot informal)*, doofus *(slang, chiefly US)*, lamebrain *(informal)*, mooncalf, thickhead, clodpate *(archaic)*, nerd *or* nurd *(slang)*, numbskull *or* numskull, twerp *or* twirp *(informal)*, dorba *or* dorb *(Austral slang)*, bogan *(Austral slang)* **OPPOSITE:** genius
2 = dupe, butt, mug *(Brit slang)*, sucker *(slang)*, gull *(archaic)*, stooge *(slang)*, laughing stock, pushover *(informal)*, fall guy *(informal)*, chump *(informal)*, greenhorn *(informal)*, easy mark *(informal)* **3 = jester**, comic, clown, harlequin, motley, buffoon, pierrot, court jester, punchinello, joculator *or (fem.)* joculatrix, merry-andrew ▹ *vb* **5 = deceive**, cheat, mislead, delude, kid *(informal)*, trick, take in, con *(informal)*, stiff *(slang)*, have (someone) on, bluff, hoax, dupe, beguile, gull *(archaic)*, swindle, make a fool of, bamboozle, hoodwink, take for a ride *(informal)*, put one over on *(informal)*, play a trick on, pull a fast one on *(informal)*, scam *(slang)*

foolish *adj* **= unwise**, silly, absurd, rash, unreasonable, senseless, short-sighted, ill-advised, foolhardy, nonsensical, inane, indiscreet, ill-judged, ill-considered, imprudent, unintelligent, asinine,

standing and walking **2** the part of a garment covering a foot **3** a unit of length equal to 12 inches (0.3048 metre) **4** the bottom, base, or lower end of something: *at the foot of the hill; the foot of the page* **5** *old-fashioned* infantry **6** *prosody* a group of two or more syllables in which one syllable has the major stress, forming the basic unit of poetic rhythm **7 one foot in the grave** *informal* near to death **8 on foot** walking **9 put one's best foot forward** to try to do one's best **10 put one's foot down** *informal* to act firmly **11 put one's foot in it** *informal* to make an embarrassing and tactless mistake **12 under foot** on the ground ▹ *vb* **13 foot it** *informal* to travel on foot **14 foot the bill** to pay the entire cost of something ▸ See also **feet** > **footless** *adj*
WORD ORIGIN Old English *fōt*

Foot *n* **Michael** (**Mackintosh**) 1913–2010, British Labour politician and journalist; secretary of state for employment (1974–76); leader of the House of Commons (1976–79); leader of the Labour Party (1980–83)

footage *n* **1** a length of film **2** the sequences of filmed material: *footage of refugees leaving the city*

foot-and-mouth disease *n* a highly infectious viral disease of cattle, pigs, sheep, and goats, in which blisters form in the mouth and on the feet

football *n* **1** any of various games played with a ball in which two teams compete to kick, head, or propel the ball into each other's goal **2** the ball used in any of these games **footballer** *n*

football pools *pl n* ▸ same as **pools**

footbridge *n* a narrow bridge for the use of pedestrians

footfall *n* the sound of a footstep

foothills *pl n* relatively low hills at the foot of a mountain

foothold *n* **1** a secure position from which further progress may be made: *a firm foothold in Europe's telecommunications market* **2** a ledge or other place where a foot can be securely positioned, as during climbing

footing ❶ *n* **1** basis or foundation: *on a sound financial footing* **2** the relationship between two people or groups: *on an equal footing* **3** a secure grip by or for the feet

footle *vb* **-ling, -led** *chiefly Brit informal* to loiter aimlessly **footling** *adj*
WORD ORIGIN probably from French *foutre* to copulate with

footlights *pl n theatre* lights set in a row along the front of the stage floor

footloose *adj* free to go or do as one wishes

footman *n, pl* **-men** a male servant in uniform

footnote *n* a note printed at the bottom of a page

footpad *n old-fashioned* a highwayman, on foot rather than horseback

footpath ❶ *n* **1** a narrow path for walkers only **2** *Austral & NZ* a raised space alongside a road, for pedestrians

footplate *n chiefly Brit* a platform in the cab of a locomotive on which the crew stand to operate the controls

footprint *n* **1** an indentation or outline of the foot on a surface **2** the shape and size of the area something occupies: *enlarging the footprint of the building*

footsie *n informal* flirtation involving the touching together of feet

footsore *adj* having sore or tired feet, esp. from much walking

footstep ❶ *n* **1** a step in walking **2** the sound made by walking **3** a footmark **4 follow in someone's footsteps** to continue the example of another

footstool *n* a low stool used for supporting the feet of a seated person

footwear *n* anything worn to cover the feet

footwork *n* the way in which the feet are used, for example in sports or dancing: *nimble footwork*

fop *n* a man who is excessively concerned with fashion **foppery** *n* **foppish** *adj*
WORD ORIGIN perhaps from Middle English *foppe* fool

for *prep* **1** directed or belonging to: *a bottle of beer for himself* **2** to the advantage of: *he spelt it out for her* **3** in the direction of: *he headed for the door* **4** over a span of (time or distance): *she considered him coolly for a moment* **5** in favour of: *support for the war* **6** in order to get: *for a bit of company* **7** designed to meet the needs of: *the instructions are for right-handed players* **8** at a cost of: *two dishes for one* **9** in place of: *she had to substitute for her mother because they woke late* **10** because of: *dancing for joy* **11** regarding the usual characteristics of: *unusually warm for the time of year* **12** concerning: *our idea for the last scene* **13** as being: *do you take me for an idiot?* **14** at (a specified time): *multiparty elections are planned for next year* **15** to do or take part in: *two guests for dinner* **16** in the duty or task of: *that's for you to decide* **17** in relation to; as it affects: *it's too hard for me* **18** in order to preserve or retain: *fighting for survival* **19** as a direct equivalent to: *word for word* **20** in order to become or enter: *training for the priesthood* **21** in exchange for: *the cash was used to pay for food, shelter, and medical supplies* **22 for all** ▸ see **all** (sense 12) **23 for it** *Austral & Brit informal* liable for punishment or blame: *you'll be for it if you get caught* ▹ *conj* **24** *formal* because or seeing that: *implausibility cries aloud, and this is a pity, for much of the narrative is entertaining*
WORD ORIGIN Old English

forage (for-ridge) *vb* **-aging, -aged** **1** to search for food **2** to obtain by searching about: *she foraged for her shoes* ▹ *n* **3** food for horses or cattle, esp. hay or straw **4** the act of searching for food or provisions
WORD ORIGIN Old French *fourrage*

forage cap *n* a cap with a flat round crown and a visor, worn by soldiers when not in battle or on parade

foramen (for-ray-men) *n, pl* **-ramina** (-ram-in-a) *or* **-ramens** *anat* a natural hole, esp. one in a bone through which nerves pass
WORD ORIGIN Latin

forasmuch as *conj old-fashioned or legal* seeing that or since

foray ❶ *n* **1** a short raid or incursion **2** a first attempt or new undertaking: *his first foray into films*
WORD ORIGIN Middle English *forrayen* to pillage

forbade *or* **forbad** *vb* ▸ the past tense of **forbid**

forbear[1] *vb* **-bearing, -bore, -borne** to cease or refrain (from doing something) **forbearance** *n*
WORD ORIGIN Old English *forberan*

forbear[2] *n* ▸ same as **forebear**

forbid ❶ *vb* **-bidding, -bade** *or* **-bad, -bidden** *or* **-bid** to prohibit or refuse to allow
WORD ORIGIN Old English *forbēodan*

forbidding ❶ *adj* severe and

f

THESAURUS

injudicious, incautious
OPPOSITE: sensible

footing *n* **1 = basis**, foundation, foothold, base position, ground, settlement, establishment, installation, groundwork
2 = relationship, terms, position, basis, state, standing, condition, relations, rank, status, grade

footpath *n* **2** *(Austral & NZ)* **= pavement**, sidewalk *(US & Canad)*

footstep *n* **1, 2 = step**, tread, footfall

foray *n* **1 = raid**, sally, incursion, inroad, attack, assault, invasion, swoop, reconnaissance, sortie, irruption

forbid *vb* **= prohibit**, ban, disallow, proscribe, exclude, rule out, veto, outlaw, inhibit, hinder, preclude, make illegal, debar, interdict
OPPOSITE: permit

forbidding *adj* **= threatening**, severe, frightening, hostile, grim, menacing, sinister, daunting, ominous, unfriendly, foreboding, baleful, bodeful **OPPOSITE:** inviting

DICTIONARY

threatening in appearance or manner: *a very large and forbidding building*

forbore *vb* ▸ the past tense of **forbear[1]**

forborne *vb* ▸ the past participle of **forbear[1]**

force[1] *n* **1** strength or power: *the force of the impact had thrown him into the fireplace* **2** exertion or the use of exertion against a person or thing that resists: *they used force and repression against those who opposed their policies* **3** *physics* an influence that changes a body from a state of rest to one of motion or changes its rate of motion. Symbol: F **4 a** intellectual or moral influence: *the Superintendent acknowledged the force of the Chief Constable's argument* **b** a person or thing with such influence: *Hitler quickly became the decisive force behind German foreign policy* **5** drive or intensity: *he reacted with frightening speed and force* **6** a group of people organized for particular duties or tasks: *a UN peacekeeping force* **7 in force a** (of a law) having legal validity **b** in great strength or numbers ▹ *vb* **forcing, forced 8** to compel (a person, group, etc.) to do something through effort, superior strength, etc.: *forced into an arranged marriage* **9** to acquire or produce through effort, superior strength, etc.: *he forced a smile* **10** to propel or drive despite resistance **11** to break down or open (a lock, door, etc.) **12** to impose or inflict: *a series of opposition strikes forced the appointment of a coalition government* **13** to cause (plants or farm animals) to grow at an increased rate
WORD ORIGIN Latin *fortis* strong

force[2] *n* (in N England) a waterfall
WORD ORIGIN Old Norse *fors*

forced *adj* **1** done because of force: *forced labour* **2** false or unnatural: *forced jollity* **3** due to an emergency: *a forced landing*

force-feed *vb* **-feeding, -fed** to force (a person or animal) to swallow food

forceful *adj* **1** strong, emphatic, and confident: *a forceful speech* **2** effective **forcefully** *adv*

forcemeat *n* a mixture of chopped ingredients used for stuffing
WORD ORIGIN from *force* (see FARCE) + *meat*

forceps *n, pl* **-ceps** a surgical instrument in the form of a pair of pincers
WORD ORIGIN Latin *formus* hot + *capere* to seize

forcible *adj* **1** involving physical force **2** convincing or effective: *a strong shrewd mind and a steady forcible manner* **forcibly** *adv*

ford *n* **1** a shallow area in a river that can be crossed by car, on horseback, etc. ▹ *vb* **2** to cross (a river) over a shallow area **fordable** *adj*
WORD ORIGIN Old English

fore *adj* **1** at, in, or towards the front: *the fore foot* ▹ *n* **2** the front part **3 fore and aft** located at both ends of a vessel: *two double cabins fore and aft* **4 to the fore** to the front or prominent position ▹ *interj* **5** a golfer's shouted warning to a person in the path of a flying ball
WORD ORIGIN Old English

fore- *prefix* **1** before in time or rank: *foregoing* **2** at or near the front: *foreground*
WORD ORIGIN Old English

forearm[1] *n* the part of the arm from the elbow to the wrist

forearm[2] *vb* to prepare or arm beforehand

forebear *or* **forbear** *n* an ancestor

foreboding *n* a strong feeling that something bad is about to happen

forecast *vb* **-casting, -cast** *or* **-casted 1** to predict or calculate (weather, events, etc.), in advance ▹ *n* **2** a statement predicting the weather **3** a prediction **forecaster** *n*

forecastle, fo'c's'le *or* **fo'c'sle** (foke-sl) *n* the raised front part of a ship

foreclose *vb* **-closing, -closed** *law* to take possession of property bought with borrowed money because repayment has not been made: *the banks have been reluctant to foreclose on troubled borrowers* **foreclosure** *n*
WORD ORIGIN Old French *for-* out + *clore* to close

forecourt *n* a courtyard in front of a building, such as one in a filling station

forefather *n* an ancestor

forefinger *n* the finger next to the thumb. Also called: **index finger**

forefoot *n, pl* **-feet** either of the front feet of an animal

forefront *n* **1** the most active or prominent position: *at the forefront of medical research* **2** the very front

foregather *or* **forgather** *vb* to gather together or assemble

forego[1] *vb* **-going, -went, -gone** to precede in time, place, etc.
WORD ORIGIN Old English *foregān*

forego[2] *vb* **-going, -went, -gone** ▸ same as **forgo**

foregoing *adj* (esp. of writing or speech) going before; preceding

foregone conclusion *n* an inevitable result

foreground *n* **1** the part of a view, esp. in a picture, nearest the viewer **2** an important or prominent position

forehand *tennis, squash, etc. adj* **1** (of a stroke) made so that the racket is held with the wrist facing the direction of play ▹ *n* **2** a forehand stroke

forehead *n* the part of the face between the natural hairline and the eyes
WORD ORIGIN Old English *forhēafod*

foreign *adj* **1** of, located in, or coming from another country, area, or people **2** dealing or concerned with another country, area, or people: *the Foreign Minister* **3** not familiar; strange **4** in an abnormal place or position: *a foreign body in the food*
WORD ORIGIN Latin *foris* outside

THESAURUS

force[1] *n* **1 = power**, might, pressure, energy, stress, strength, impact, muscle, momentum, impulse, stimulus, vigour, potency, dynamism, life **OPPOSITE:** weakness **2 = compulsion**, pressure, violence, enforcement, constraint, oppression, coercion, duress, arm-twisting *(informal)* **5 = intensity**, vigour, vehemence, fierceness, drive, emphasis, persistence **6 = army**, unit, division, corps, company, body, host, troop, squad, patrol, regiment, battalion, legion, squadron, detachment ▹ *vb* **8 = compel**, make, drive, press, pressure, urge, overcome, oblige, railroad *(informal)*, constrain, necessitate, coerce, impel, strong-arm *(informal)*, dragoon, pressurize, press-gang, put the squeeze on *(informal)*, obligate, twist (someone's) arm, put the screws on *(informal)*, bring pressure to bear upon **10 = push**, thrust, propel **11 = break open**, blast, wrench, prise, wrest, use violence on

forced *adj* **1 = compulsory**, enforced, slave, unwilling, mandatory, obligatory, involuntary, conscripted **OPPOSITE:** voluntary **2 = false**, affected, strained, wooden, stiff, artificial, contrived, unnatural, insincere, laboured **OPPOSITE:** natural

forceful *adj* **1 = dynamic**, powerful, vigorous, potent, assertive **OPPOSITE:** weak **2 = powerful**, strong, convincing, effective, compelling, persuasive, weighty, pithy, cogent, telling

forecast *vb* **1 = predict**, anticipate, foresee, foretell, call, plan, estimate, calculate, divine, prophesy, augur, forewarn, prognosticate, vaticinate *(rare)* ▹ *n* **3 = prediction**, projection, anticipation, prognosis, planning, guess, outlook, prophecy, foresight, conjecture, forewarning, forethought

forefront *n* **1 = lead**, centre, front, fore, spearhead, prominence, vanguard, foreground, leading position, van

foreign *adj* **1 = alien**, overseas, exotic, unknown, outside, strange, imported, borrowed, remote, distant, external, unfamiliar, far off,

DICTIONARY

foreigner ❶ *n* **1** a person from a foreign country **2** an outsider
foreign minister *or* **secretary** *n* (in Britain) a cabinet minister who is responsible for a country's dealings with other countries
foreign office *n* (in Britain) the ministry of a country that is concerned with dealings with other states
foreknowledge *n* knowledge of something before it actually happens
foreleg *n* either of the front legs of an animal
forelock *n* a lock of hair growing or falling over the forehead
foreman *n, pl* **-men 1** a person who supervises other workmen **2** *law* the leader of a jury
Foreman *n* **George** born 1949, US boxer: WBA world heavyweight champion (1973–74); he regained the title in 1994 but refused to fight the WBA's top-ranked challenger and was stripped of the title in 1995; recognized as WBU champion until 1997
foremast *n* the mast nearest the bow of a ship
foremost ❶ *adj* **1** first in time, place, or importance: *Germany's foremost conductor* ▷ *adv* **2** first in time, place, or importance
WORD ORIGIN Old English *formest*, from *forma* first
forename *n* first name
forenoon *n* the daylight hours before noon
forensic (for-ren-sik) *adj* used in or connected with a court of law **forensically** *adv*
WORD ORIGIN Latin *forensis* public
forensic medicine *n* the application of medical knowledge for the purposes of the law, such as in determining the cause of death
foreordain *vb* to determine (events, etc.) in the future
forepaw *n* either of the front feet of a land mammal that does not have hooves
foreplay *n* sexual stimulation before intercourse
forerunner *n* **1** a person or thing that existed or happened before another and is similar in some way: *a forerunner of the surrealist painters* **2** a person or thing that is a sign of what will happen in the future
foresail *n* the main sail on the foremast of a ship
foresee ❶ *vb* **-seeing, -saw, -seen** to see or know beforehand **foreseeable** *adj*
foreshadow *vb* to show, indicate, or suggest in advance
foreshore *n* the part of the shore between high- and low-tide marks
foreshorten *vb* to see or draw (an object) from such an angle that it appears to be shorter than it really is
foresight *n* **1** the ability to anticipate and provide for future needs **2** the front sight on a firearm
foreskin *n anat* the fold of skin covering the tip of the penis
forest *n* **1** a large wooded area with a thick growth of trees and plants **2** a group of narrow or tall objects standing upright: *a forest of waving arms* **3** NZ an area planted with pines or other trees that are not native to the country **forested** *adj*
WORD ORIGIN Medieval Latin *forestis* unfenced woodland, from Latin *foris* outside
forestall *vb* to delay, stop, or guard against beforehand: *an action forestalling any further talks*
WORD ORIGIN Middle English *forestallen* to waylay
forestation *n* the planting of trees over a wide area
forester *n* a person skilled in forestry or in charge of a forest
Forester *n* **C**(**ecil**) **S**(**cott**) 1899–1966, English novelist; creator of Captain Horatio Hornblower in a series of novels on the Napoleonic Wars
forestry *n* the science or skill of growing and maintaining trees in a forest, esp. to obtain wood
foretaste *n* an early but limited experience of something to come
foretell *vb* **-telling, -told** *literary* to correctly predict (an event, a result, etc.) beforehand
forethought *n* thoughtful planning for future events: *a little forethought can avoid a lot of problems later*
foretoken *n* a sign of a future event
for ever ❶ *or* **forever** *adv* **1** without end **2** at all times **3** *informal* for a long time: *I could go on for ever about similar incidents*
forewarn *vb* to warn beforehand
foreword *n* an introductory statement to a book
forfeit ❶ (for-fit) *n* **1** something lost or given up as a penalty for a fault, mistake, etc. ▷ *vb* **2** to lose as a forfeit ▷ *adj* **3** lost as a forfeit **forfeiture** *n*
WORD ORIGIN Old French *forfet* offence
forgather *vb* ▸ same as **foregather**
forgave *vb* ▸ the past tense of **forgive**
forge[1] ❶ *n* **1** a place in which metal is worked by heating and hammering; smithy **2** a furnace used for heating metal ▷ *vb* **forging, forged 3** to shape (metal) by heating and hammering **4** to make a fraudulent imitation of (a signature, money, a painting, etc.) **5** to create (an alliance, relationship, etc.) **forger** *n*
WORD ORIGIN Old French *forgier* to construct
forge[2] *vb* **forging, forged 1** to move at a steady pace **2 forge ahead** to increase speed or progress; take the lead
WORD ORIGIN origin unknown
forgery *n, pl* **-geries 1** an illegal copy of a painting, banknote, antique, etc. **2** the crime of making a fraudulent imitation
forget ❶ *vb* **-getting, -got, -gotten 1** to fail to remember (someone or something once known) **2** to neglect, either by mistake or on purpose **3** to leave behind by mistake **4 forget oneself** to act in an uncharacteristically unrestrained or unacceptable manner: *behave yourself or I might forget myself and slap your wrists* **forgettable** *adj*
WORD ORIGIN Old English *forgietan*
forgetful *adj* **1** tending to forget **2 forgetful of** inattentive to or neglectful of: *Fiona, forgetful of the time, was still in bed* **forgetfully** *adv*

f

THESAURUS

outlandish, beyond your ken
OPPOSITE: native
foreigner *n* **1, 2 = alien**, incomer, immigrant, non-native, stranger, newcomer, settler, outlander
foremost *adj* **1 = leading**, best, first, highest, front, chief, prime, primary, supreme, initial, most important, principal, paramount, inaugural, pre-eminent, headmost
foresee *vb* **= predict**, forecast, anticipate, envisage, prophesy, foretell, forebode, vaticinate *(rare)*, divine
for ever *or* **forever** *adv* **1 = evermore**, always, ever, for good, for keeps, for all time, in perpetuity, for good and all *(informal)*, till the cows come home *(informal)*, world without end, till the end of time, till Doomsday
2 = constantly, always, all the time, continually, endlessly, persistently, eternally, perpetually, incessantly, interminably, unremittingly, everlastingly
forfeit *n* **1 = penalty**, fine, damages, forfeiture, loss, mulct, amercement *(obsolete)* ▷ *vb* **2 = relinquish**, lose, give up, surrender, renounce, be deprived of, say goodbye to, be stripped of
forge[1] *vb* **3 = create**, make, work, found, form, model, fashion, shape, cast, turn out, construct, devise, mould, contrive, fabricate, hammer out, beat into shape **4 = fake**, copy, reproduce, imitate, counterfeit, feign, falsify, coin **5 = form**, build, create, establish, set up, fashion, shape, frame, construct, invent, devise, mould, contrive, fabricate, hammer out, make, work
forget *vb* **2 = neglect**, overlook, omit, not remember, be remiss, fail to remember **3 = leave behind**, lose, lose sight of, mislay

DICTIONARY

forget-me-not *n* a low-growing plant with clusters of small blue flowers

forgive ❶ *vb* **-giving, -gave, -given** **1** to stop feeling anger and resentment towards (a person) or at (an action that has caused upset or harm) **2** to pardon (a mistake) **3** to free from (a debt)
WORD ORIGIN Old English *forgiefan*

forgiveness ❶ *n* the act of forgiving or the state of being forgiven

forgiving *adj* willing to forgive

forgo *or* **forego** *vb* **-going, -went, -gone** to give up or do without
WORD ORIGIN Old English *forgān*

forgot *vb* **1** ▸ the past tense of **forget** **2** *old-fashioned or dialect* ▸ a past participle of **forget**

forgotten *vb* ▸ a past participle of **forget**

fork ❶ *n* **1** a small tool with long thin prongs on the end of a handle, used for lifting food to the mouth **2** a larger similar-shaped gardening tool, used for lifting or digging **3 forks** the part of a bicycle that links the handlebars to the front wheel **4 a** (of a road, river, etc.) a division into two or more branches **b** the point where the division begins **c** such a branch ▹ *vb* **5** to pick up, dig, etc. with a fork **6** to be divided into two or more branches **7** to take one or other branch at a fork in a road, etc.
WORD ORIGIN Latin *furca*

forked ❶ *adj* **1** having a fork or forklike parts **2** zigzag: *forked lightning*

fork-lift truck *n* a vehicle with two moveable arms at the front that can be raised and lowered for transporting and unloading goods

fork out *vb slang* to pay, esp. with reluctance

forlorn *adj* **1** lonely, unhappy, and uncared-for **2** (of a place) having a deserted appearance **3** desperate and without any expectation of success: *a final, apparently forlorn attempt to save the war-torn country* **forlornly** *adv*
WORD ORIGIN Old English *forloren* lost

forlorn hope *n* **1** a hopeless enterprise **2** a faint hope
WORD ORIGIN changed (by folk etymology) from Dutch *verloren hoop* lost troop

form ❶ *n* **1** the shape or appearance of something **2** a visible person or animal **3** the particular mode in which a thing or person appears: *wood in the form of paper* **4** a type or kind: *abortion was widely used as a form of birth control* **5** physical or mental condition **6** a printed document, esp. one with spaces in which to fill details or answers **7** the previous record of a horse, athlete, etc. **8** *Brit slang* a criminal record **9** *education, chiefly Brit & NZ* a group of children who are taught together **10** manners and etiquette: *it is considered bad form not to wear a tie* **11** the structure and arrangement of a work of art or piece of writing as distinguished from its content **12** a bench **13** a hare's nest **14** any of the various ways in which a word may be spelt or inflected ▹ *vb* **15** to give shape to or take shape, esp. a particular shape **16** to come or bring into existence: *glaciers dammed the valley bottoms with debris behind which lakes have formed* **17** to make or construct or be made or constructed **18** to train or mould by instruction or example **19** to acquire or develop: *they've formed this impression; we formed a bond* **20** to be an element of: *they had formed part of a special murder unit*
WORD ORIGIN Latin *forma* shape, model

formal ❶ *adj* **1** of or following established conventions: *formal talks; a formal announcement* **2** characterized by conventional forms of ceremony and behaviour: *a small formal dinner party* **3** suitable for occasions organized according to conventional ceremony: *formal cocktail frocks* **4** methodical and organized: *a formal approach* **5** (of education and training) given officially at a school, college, etc.: *he had no formal training in maths* **6** symmetrical in form: *a formal garden* **7** relating to the form or structure of something as distinguished from its substance or content: *they addressed the formal elements of the structure of police work* **8** *philosophy* logically deductive rather than based on facts and observation **formally** *adv*
WORD ORIGIN Latin *formalis*

formaldehyde (for-**mal**-de-hide) *n* a colourless poisonous strong-smelling gas, used as formalin and in synthetic resins. Also: **methanal**
WORD ORIGIN *form(ic)* + *aldehyde*

formalin *n* a solution of formaldehyde in water, used as a disinfectant and as a preservative for biological specimens

formalism *n* concerned with outward appearances and structure at the expense of content **formalist** *n*

formality ❶ *n, pl* **-ties** **1** something done as a requirement of custom or good manners: *he dealt with the formalities regarding the cremation* **2** a necessary procedure without real effect: *trials were often a mere formality*

THESAURUS

forgive *vb* **1 = excuse**, pardon, bear no malice towards, not hold something against, understand, acquit, condone, remit, let off *(informal)*, turn a blind eye to, exonerate, absolve, bury the hatchet, let bygones be bygones, turn a deaf ear to, accept (someone's) apology
OPPOSITE: blame

forgiveness *n* **= pardon**, mercy, absolution, exoneration, overlooking, amnesty, acquittal, remission, condonation

fork *vb* **6, 7 = branch**, part, separate, split, divide, diverge, subdivide, branch off, go separate ways, bifurcate

forked *adj* **1 = branching**, split, branched, divided, pronged, tined, Y-shaped, bifurcate(d) **2 = zigzag**, angled

form *n* **1 = shape**, formation, configuration, construction, cut, model, fashion, structure, pattern, cast, appearance, stamp, mould **4 = type**, sort, kind, variety, way, system, order, class, style, practice, method, species, manner, stamp, description **5 = condition**, health, shape, nick *(informal)*, fitness, trim, good condition, good spirits, fettle **6 = document**, paper, sheet, questionnaire, application **9** *(education, chiefly Brit & NZ)* **= class**, year, set, rank, grade, stream **10 = procedure**, behaviour, manners, etiquette, use, rule, conduct, ceremony, custom, convention, ritual, done thing, usage, protocol, formality, wont, right practice, kawa *(NZ)*, tikanga *(NZ)* ▹ *vb* **15 = arrange**, combine, line up, organize, assemble, dispose, draw up **15, 16 = take shape**, grow, develop, materialize, rise, appear, settle, show up *(informal)*, accumulate, come into being, crystallize, become visible **16 = establish**, start, found, launch, set up, invent, devise, put together, bring about, contrive **17 = make**, produce, model, fashion, build, create, shape, manufacture, stamp, construct, assemble, forge, mould, fabricate **19 = develop**, pick up, acquire, cultivate, contract, get into *(informal)* **20 = constitute**, make up, compose, comprise, serve as, make

formal *adj* **1 = official**, express, explicit, authorized, set, legal, fixed, regular, approved, strict, endorsed, prescribed, rigid, certified, solemn, lawful, methodical, pro forma *(Latin)* **2a = ceremonial**, traditional, solemn, ritualistic, dressy **2b = conventional**, established, traditional

formality *n* **1, 2 = convention**, form, conventionality, matter of form, procedure, ceremony, custom, gesture, ritual, rite **3 = correctness**, seriousness, decorum, ceremoniousness, protocol, etiquette, politesse, p's and q's, punctilio

format *n* **1 = arrangement**, form, style, make-up, look, plan, design,

DICTIONARY

with the verdict decided beforehand **3** strict observance of ceremony

formalize *or* **-ise** *vb* **-izing, -ized** *or* **-ising, -ised 1** to make official or valid **2** to give a definite form to **formalization** *or* **-isation** *n*

Forman *n* **Miloš** born 1932, Czech film director working in the USA since 1968. His films include *One Flew over the Cuckoo's Nest* (1976), *Amadeus* (1985), and *The People vs Larry Flynt* (1996)

format Ⓣ *n* **1** the shape, size, and general appearance of a publication **2** style or arrangement, such as of a television programme: *a chat-show format* **3** *computers* the arrangement of data on disk or magnetic tape to comply with a computer's input device ▷*vb* **-matting, -matted 4** to arrange in a specified format
WORD ORIGIN Latin *formatus* formed

formation Ⓣ *n* **1** the act of having or taking form or existence **2** something that is formed **3** the manner in which something is arranged **4** an arrangement of people or things acting as a unit, such as a troop of soldiers **5** a series of rocks or clouds of a particular structure or shape

formative *adj* **1** of or relating to formation, development, or growth: *formative years at school* **2** shaping or moulding: *the formative influence on his life*

Formby *n* **George** Real name *George Booth*. 1904–61, British comedian. He made many musical films in the 1930s, accompanying his songs on the ukulele

former Ⓣ *adj* **1** belonging to or occurring in an earlier time: *a grotesque parody of a former greatness* **2** having been at a previous time: *the former prime minister* ▷*n* **3 the former** the first or first mentioned of two

formerly Ⓣ *adv* in the past

Formica *n trademark* a hard laminated plastic used esp. for heat-resistant surfaces

formic acid *n* an acid derived from ants
WORD ORIGIN Latin *formica* ant

formidable Ⓣ *adj* **1** frightening because very difficult to deal with or overcome: *the Finnish winter presents formidable problems to drivers* **2** extremely impressive: *a formidable Juventus squad* **formidably** *adv*
WORD ORIGIN Latin *formido* fear

formless *adj* without a definite shape or form

formula Ⓣ (**form**-yew-la) *n, pl* **-las** *or* **-lae** (-lee) **1** a group of letters, numbers, or other symbols which represents a mathematical or scientific rule **2** a plan or set of rules for doing or producing something: *a formula for peace in the Middle East* **3** an established form of words, as used in religious ceremonies, legal proceedings, etc. **4** a powder used to make a milky drink for babies **5** *motor racing* the category in which a car competes, judged according to engine size **formulaic** *adj*
WORD ORIGIN Latin *forma* form

formulary *n, pl* **-laries** a book of prescribed formulas

formulate Ⓣ *vb* **-lating, -lated 1** to express in a formula **2** to plan or describe precisely and clearly: *formulate a regional energy strategy* **formulation** *n*

fornicate *vb* **-cating, -cated** to have sexual intercourse without being married **fornicator** *n*
WORD ORIGIN Latin *fornix* vault, brothel situated therein

fornication *n* voluntary sexual intercourse outside marriage

Forrest *n* **John**, 1st Baron Forrest. 1847–1918, Australian statesman and explorer; first premier of Western Australia (1890–1901)

forsake *vb* **-saking, -sook, -saken 1** to withdraw support or friendship from **2** to give up (something valued or enjoyed)
WORD ORIGIN Old English *forsacan*

forsooth *adv old-fashioned* in truth or indeed
WORD ORIGIN Old English *forsōth*

Forster *n* **E**(**dward**) **M**(**organ**) 1879–1970, English novelist, short-story writer, and essayist. His best-known novels are *A Room with a View* (1908), *Howard's End* (1910), and *A Passage to India* (1924), in all of which he stresses the need for sincerity and sensitivity in human relationships and criticizes English middle-class values

forswear *vb* **-swearing, -swore, -sworn 1** to reject or renounce with determination **2** to testify falsely in a court of law
WORD ORIGIN Old English *forswearian*

Forsyth *n* **1 Bill** born 1947, Scottish writer and director. His films include *Gregory's Girl* (1981), *Local Hero* (1983), and *Gregory's Two Girls* (1999) **2 Frederick** born 1938, British thriller writer. His books include *The Day of the Jackal* (1970), *The Odessa File* (1972), and *The Fourth Protocol* (1984)

forsythia (for-**syth**-ee-a) *n* a shrub with yellow flowers which appear in spring before the leaves
WORD ORIGIN after William *Forsyth*, botanist

fort Ⓣ *n* **1** a fortified building or position **2 hold the fort** *informal* to keep things in operation during someone's absence
WORD ORIGIN Latin *fortis* strong

forte[1] Ⓣ (**for**-tay) *n* something at which a person excels: *cooking is his forte*
WORD ORIGIN Latin *fortis* strong

forte[2] *adv music* loudly
WORD ORIGIN Italian

forth Ⓣ *adv* **1** *formal or old-fashioned* forward, out, or away: *running back and forth across the street; Christopher Columbus set forth on his epic voyage of discovery* **2 and so forth** and so on
WORD ORIGIN Old English

forthcoming Ⓣ *adj* **1** about to appear or happen: *the forthcoming elections*

f

THESAURUS

type, appearance, construction, presentation, layout

formation *n* **1 = establishment**, founding, forming, setting up, starting, production, generation, organization, manufacture, constitution **3 = development**, shaping, constitution, evolution, moulding, composition, compilation, accumulation, genesis, crystallization **4, 5 = arrangement**, grouping, figure, design, structure, pattern, rank, organization, array, disposition, configuration

former *adj* **2 = previous**, one-time, erstwhile, ex-, late, earlier, prior, sometime, foregoing, antecedent, anterior, quondam, whilom *(archaic)*, ci-devant *(French)* **OPPOSITE:** current

formerly *adv* **= previously**, earlier, in the past, at one time, before, lately, once, already, heretofore, aforetime *(archaic)*

formidable *adj* **2 = impressive**, great, powerful, tremendous, mighty, terrific, awesome, invincible, indomitable, redoubtable, puissant

formula *n* **2 = method**, plan, policy, rule, principle, procedure, recipe, prescription, blueprint, precept, modus operandi, way

formulate *vb* **1 = express**, detail, frame, define, specify, articulate, set down, codify, put into words, systematize, particularize, give form to **2 = devise**, plan, develop, prepare, work out, invent, evolve, coin, forge, draw up, originate, map out

fort *n* **1 = fortress**, keep, station, camp, tower, castle, garrison, stronghold, citadel, fortification, redoubt, fastness, blockhouse, fortified pa (NZ) **2 hold the fort** *(informal)* **= take responsibility**, cover, stand in, carry on, take over the reins, maintain the status quo, deputize, keep things moving, keep things on an even keel

forte[1] *n* **= speciality**, strength, talent, strong point, métier, long suit *(informal)*, gift **OPPOSITE:** weak point

forth *adv* **1a** *(formal or old-fashioned)* **= forward**, out, away, ahead, onward, outward **1b = out**, into the open, out of concealment

forthcoming *adj* **1 = approaching**, coming, expected, future,

DICTIONARY

2 given or made available **3** (of a person) willing to give information
forthright *adj* direct and outspoken
forthwith *adv* at once
fortification *n* **1** the act of fortifying **2 fortifications** walls, mounds, etc. used to strengthen the defences of a place
fortified wine *n* wine mixed with a small amount of brandy or alcohol, such as port or sherry
fortify ❶ *vb* **-fies, -fying, -fied 1** to make (a place) defensible, such as by building walls **2** to strengthen physically, mentally, or morally: *the news fortified their resolve to succeed* **3** to increase the nutritious value of (a food), such as by adding vitamins
WORD ORIGIN Latin *fortis* strong + *facere* to make
fortissimo *adv music* very loudly
WORD ORIGIN Italian
fortitude ❶ *n* calm and patient courage in trouble or pain
WORD ORIGIN Latin *fortitudo* courage
fortnight *n* a period of 14 consecutive days
WORD ORIGIN Old English *fēowertīene niht* fourteen nights
fortnightly *chiefly Brit adj* **1** occurring or appearing once each fortnight ▷ *adv* **2** once a fortnight
FORTRAN *n* a high-level computer programming language designed for mathematical and scientific purposes
WORD ORIGIN *for(mula) tran(slation)*
fortress ❶ *n* a large fort or fortified town
WORD ORIGIN Latin *fortis* strong
fortuitous (for-**tyew**-it-uss) *adj* happening by chance, esp. by a lucky chance **fortuitously** *adv*
WORD ORIGIN Latin *fortuitus*
fortunate ❶ *adj* **1** having good luck **2** occurring by good luck
fortunately *adv*
fortune ❶ *n* **1** a very large sum of money **2** luck, esp. when favourable **3** *(often pl)* a person's destiny **4** a power regarded as being responsible for human affairs **5** wealth or material prosperity
WORD ORIGIN Latin *fors* chance
fortune-teller *n* a person who claims to predict events in other people's lives
forty *n, pl* **-ties 1** the cardinal number that is the product of ten and four **2** a numeral, 40 or XL, representing this number **3** something representing or consisting of 40 units ▷ *adj* **4** amounting to forty: *forty pages* **fortieth** *adj, n*
forty-ninth parallel *n Canad informal* the border with the USA, which is in part delineated by the parallel line of latitude at 49°N
forty winks *n informal* a short light sleep
forum *n* **1** a meeting or medium for the open discussion of subjects of public interest **2** (in ancient Roman cities) an open space serving as a marketplace and centre of public business **3** (in South Africa) a pressure group of leaders and representatives
WORD ORIGIN Latin
forward *adj* **1** directed or moving ahead **2** at, in, or near the front **3** overfamiliar or disrespectful **4** well developed or advanced **5** of or relating to the future or favouring change ▷ *n* **6** an attacking player in any of various sports, such as soccer ▷ *adv* **7** ▸ same as **forwards** ▷ *vb* **8** to send (a letter, etc.) on to an ultimate destination **9** to advance or promote: *the veneer of street credibility he had used to forward his career*
WORD ORIGIN Old English *foreweard*
forwards ❶ *or* **forward** *adv* **1** towards or at a place ahead or in advance, esp. in space but also in time **2** towards the front
Foscolo *n* **Ugo**, real name *Niccolò Foscolo*. 1778–1827, Italian poet and writer; his patriotic verse includes *Dei sepolcri* (1807)
fosse *or* **foss** *n* a ditch or moat, esp. one dug as a fortification
WORD ORIGIN Latin *fossa*
fossick ❶ *vb Austral & NZ* **1** to search for gold or precious stones in abandoned workings, rivers, etc. **2** to search for, through, or in something; to forage
WORD ORIGIN probably from English dialect *fussock* to bustle about
fossil *n* **1** remains of a plant or animal that existed in a past geological age, occurring in the form of mineralized bones, shells, etc. ▷ *adj* **2** of, like, or being a fossil
WORD ORIGIN Latin *fossilis* dug up
fossil fuel *n* fuel, such as coal or oil, formed from the decayed remains of prehistoric animals and plants
fossilize *or* **-ise** *vb* **-izing, -ized** *or* **-ising, -ised 1** to convert or be converted into a fossil **2** to become out-of-date or inflexible: *fossilized political attitudes*
foster ❶ *adj* **1** of or involved in the bringing up of a child not one's own: *foster care* ▷ *vb* **2** to bring up (a child not one's own) **3** to promote the growth or development of: *Catherine fostered knowledge and patronized the arts*
fostering *n*
WORD ORIGIN Old English *fōstrian* to feed
Foster *n* **1 Jodie** born 1962, US film actress and director: her films include *Taxi Driver* (1976), *The Accused* (1988), *The Silence of the Lambs* (1990), *Little Man Tate* (1991; also directed), *Nell* (1995), and *Panic Room* (2002) **2 Norman**, Baron. born 1935, British architect. His works include the Willis Faber building (1978) in Ipswich, Stansted Airport, Essex (1991), Chek Lap Kok Airport, Hong Kong (1998), the renovation of the Reichstag, Berlin (1999), and City Hall, London (2002) **3 Stephen Collins** 1826–64, US composer of songs such as *The Old Folks at Home* and *Oh Susanna*

THESAURUS

imminent, prospective, impending, upcoming **2 = available**, ready, accessible, at hand, in evidence, obtainable, on tap *(informal)* **3 = communicative**, open, free, informative, expansive, sociable, chatty, talkative, unreserved
fortify *vb* **1 = protect**, defend, secure, strengthen, reinforce, support, brace, garrison, shore up, augment, buttress, make stronger, embattle
fortitude *n* **= courage**, strength, resolution, determination, guts *(informal)*, patience, pluck, grit, endurance, bravery, backbone, perseverance, firmness, staying power, valour, fearlessness, strength of mind, intrepidity, hardihood, dauntlessness, stoutheartedness
fortress *n* **= castle**, fort, stronghold, citadel, redoubt, fastness, fortified pa *(NZ)*
fortunate *adj* **1 = lucky**, happy, favoured, bright, golden, rosy, on a roll, jammy *(Brit slang)*, in luck, having a charmed life, born with a silver spoon in your mouth **OPPOSITE:** unfortunate **2 = providential**, auspicious, fortuitous, felicitous, timely, promising, encouraging, helpful, profitable, convenient, favourable, advantageous, expedient, opportune, propitious
fortune *n* **2 = luck**, accident, fluke *(informal)*, stroke of luck, serendipity, hap *(archaic)*, twist of fate, run of luck **3** *(often pl)* **= destiny**, life, lot, experiences, history, condition, success, means, circumstances, expectation, adventures **4 = chance**, fate, destiny, providence, the stars, Lady Luck, kismet, fortuity **5 = wealth**, means, property, riches, resources, assets, pile *(informal)*, possessions, treasure, prosperity, mint, gold mine, wad *(US & Canad slang)*, affluence, opulence, tidy sum *(informal)* **OPPOSITE:** poverty
forwards *adv* **1 = forth**, on, ahead, onwards **OPPOSITE:** backward(s)
fossick *vb* **2** *(Austral & NZ)* **= search**, hunt, explore, ferret, check, forage, rummage
foster *vb* **2 = bring up**, mother, raise, nurse, look after, rear, care for, take care of, nurture **3 = develop**, support,

DICTIONARY

fought *vb* ▸ the past of **fight**

foul ❶ *adj* **1** offensive or loathsome: *a foul deed* **2** stinking or dirty **3** full of dirt or offensive matter **4** (of language) obscene or vulgar **5** unfair: *by fair or foul means* **6** (of weather) unpleasant **7** very bad-tempered and irritable: *he was in a foul mood* **8** *informal* disgustingly bad ▹ *n* **9** *sport* a violation of the rules ▹ *vb* **10** to make dirty or polluted **11** to make or become entangled **12** to make or become clogged **13** *sport* to commit a foul against (an opponent) ▹ *adv* **14 fall foul of** to come into conflict with **WORD ORIGIN** Old English *fūl*

foul-mouthed *adj* habitually using swearwords and bad language

foul play *n* **1** violent activity esp. murder **2** a violation of the rules in a game

foul up *vb* **1** *informal* to mismanage or bungle **2** to contaminate **3** to block or choke ▹ *n* **foul-up 4** a state of disorder resulting from mistakes or carelessness: *a foul-up by their computers*

found[1] *vb* ▸ the past of **find**

found[2] ❶ *vb* **1** to bring into being or establish (something, such as an institution) **2** to lay the foundation of **3 founded on** having a basis in: *a political system founded on fear* **founder** *n* **founding** *adj* **WORD ORIGIN** Latin *fundus* bottom

found[3] *vb* **1** to cast (metal or glass) by melting and pouring into a mould **2** to make (articles) in this way **founder** *n* **WORD ORIGIN** Latin *fundere* to melt

foundation ❶ *n* **1** the basic experience, idea, or attitude on which a way of life or belief is based: *respect for the law is the foundation of commercial society* **2** a construction below the ground that distributes the load of a building, wall, etc. **3** the base on which something stands **4** the act of founding **5** an endowment for the support of an institution, such as a college **6** an institution supported by an endowment **7** a cosmetic used as a base for make-up

foundation stone *n* a stone laid at a ceremony to mark the foundation of a new building

founder ❶ *vb* **1** to break down or fail: *his negotiations have foundered on economic grounds* **2** (of a ship) to sink **3** to sink into or become stuck in soft ground **4** (of a horse) to stumble or go lame **WORD ORIGIN** Old French *fondrer* to submerge

foundling *n chiefly Brit* an abandoned baby whose parents are not known **WORD ORIGIN** Middle English *foundeling*

foundry *n, pl* **-ries** a place where metal is melted and cast

fount[1] *n* **1** *poetic* a spring or fountain **2** a source or supply: *a fount of knowledge* **WORD ORIGIN** from *fountain*

fount[2] *n printing, chiefly Brit* a complete set of type of one style and size **WORD ORIGIN** Old French *fonte* a founding, casting

fountain ❶ *n* **1** an ornamental feature in a pool or lake consisting of a jet of water forced into the air by a pump **2** a jet or spray of water **3** a natural spring of water **4** a source or supply: *a fountain of many new ideas about the causes of cancer* **5** a cascade of sparks, lava, etc. **WORD ORIGIN** Latin *fons* spring

fountainhead *n* a principal or original source

fountain pen *n* a pen supplied with ink from a container inside it

Fouqué *n* **Friedrich Heinrich Karl**, Baron de la Motte. 1777–1843, German romantic writer; author of *Undine* (1811)

Fouquet *n* **1 Jean** ?1420–?80, French painter and miniaturist **2** Also: **Foucquet Nicolas**, *Marquis de Belle-Isle*. 1615–80, French statesman; superintendent of finance (1653–61) under Louis XIV. He was imprisoned for embezzlement, having been denounced by Colbert

Fouquier-Tinville *n* **Antoine Quentin** 1746–95, French revolutionary; as public prosecutor (1793–94) during the Reign of Terror, he sanctioned the guillotining of Desmoulins, Danton, and Robespierre

four *n* **1** the cardinal number that is the sum of one and three **2** a numeral, 4 or IV, representing this number **3** something representing or consisting of four units **4** *cricket* a score of four runs, obtained by hitting the ball so that it crosses the boundary after hitting the ground **5** *rowing* **a** a rowing boat propelled by four oarsmen **b** the crew of such a rowing boat ▹ *adj* **6** amounting to four: *four zones* **WORD ORIGIN** Old English *fēower*

four-by-four *n* a vehicle with four-wheel drive

fourfold *adj* **1** having four times as many or as much **2** composed of four parts ▹ *adv* **3** by four times as many or as much

four-in-hand *n* a carriage drawn by four horses and driven by one driver

four-letter word *n* any of several short English words referring to sex or excrement: regarded generally as offensive or obscene

Fournier *n* ▸ See **Alain-Fournier**

f

THESAURUS

further, encourage, feed, promote, stimulate, uphold, nurture, cultivate, foment **OPPOSITE:** suppress

foul *adj* **1 = offensive**, bad, base, wrong, evil, notorious, corrupt, vicious, infamous, disgraceful, shameful, vile, immoral, scandalous, wicked, sinful, despicable, heinous, hateful, abhorrent, egregious, abominable, dishonourable, nefarious, iniquitous, detestable **OPPOSITE:** admirable **2, 3 = dirty**, rank, offensive, nasty, disgusting, unpleasant, revolting, contaminated, rotten, polluted, stinking, filthy, tainted, grubby, repellent, squalid, repulsive, sullied, grimy, nauseating, loathsome, unclean, impure, grotty *(slang)*, fetid, grungy *(slang, chiefly US & Canad)*, putrid, malodorous, noisome, scuzzy *(slang, chiefly US)*, mephitic, olid, yucky *or* yukky *(slang)*, festy *(Austral slang)*, yucko *(Austral slang)* **OPPOSITE:** clean **4 = obscene**, crude, indecent, foul-mouthed, low, blue, dirty, gross, abusive, coarse, filthy, vulgar, lewd, profane, blasphemous, scurrilous, smutty, scatological **5 = unfair**, illegal, dirty, crooked, shady *(informal)*, fraudulent, unjust, dishonest, unscrupulous, underhand, inequitable, unsportsmanlike ▹ *vb* **10 = dirty**, soil, stain, contaminate, smear, pollute, taint, sully, defile, besmirch, smirch, begrime, besmear **OPPOSITE:** clean

found[2] *vb* **1, 2 = establish**, start, set up, begin, create, institute, organize, construct, constitute, originate, endow, inaugurate, bring into being

foundation *n* **1 = basis**, heart, root, mainstay, beginning, support, ground, rest, key, principle, fundamental, premise, starting point, principal element **2, 3 = substructure**, underpinning, groundwork, bedrock, base, footing, bottom **4 = setting up**, institution, instituting, organization, settlement, establishment, initiating, originating, starting, endowment, inauguration

founder *vb* **1 = fail**, collapse, break down, abort, fall through, be unsuccessful, come to nothing, come unstuck, miscarry, misfire, fall by the wayside, come to grief, bite the dust, go belly-up *(slang)*, go down like a lead balloon *(informal)* **2 = sink**, go down, be lost, submerge, capsize, go to the bottom

fountain *n* **1, 3 = font**, spring, reservoir, spout, fount, water feature, well **2 = jet**, stream, spray, gush **4 = source**, fount, wellspring, wellhead, beginning, rise, cause, origin, genesis, commencement, derivation, fountainhead

DICTIONARY

four-poster *n* a bed with posts at each corner supporting a canopy and curtains
fourscore *adj old-fashioned* eighty
foursome *n* **1** a group of four people **2** *golf* a game between two pairs of players
foursquare *adv* **1** squarely or firmly ▷ *adj* **2** solid and strong **3** forthright and uncompromising
four-stroke *adj* designating an internal-combustion engine in which the piston makes four strokes for every explosion
fourteen *n* **1** the cardinal number that is the sum of ten and four **2** a numeral, 14 or XIV, representing this number **3** something representing or consisting of 14 units ▷ *adj* **4** amounting to fourteen: *fourteen points* **fourteenth** *adj, n*
fourth *adj* **1** of or being number four in a series **2** denoting the highest forward gear in a motor vehicle ▷ *n* **3** the highest forward gear in a motor vehicle
fourth dimension *n* **1** the dimension of time, which in addition to three spatial dimensions specifies the position of a point or particle **2** the concept in science fiction of an extra dimension **fourth-dimensional** *adj*
fourth estate *n* the press
four-wheel drive *n* a system in a vehicle in which all four wheels are connected to the source of power
fowl ❶ *n* **1** a domesticated bird such as a hen **2** any other bird that is used as food or hunted as game **3** the meat of fowl **4** *old-fashioned* a bird ▷ *vb* **5** to hunt or snare wild birds
WORD ORIGIN Old English *fugol*
Fowler *n* **Henry Watson** 1858–1933, English lexicographer and grammarian; compiler of *Modern English Usage* (1926)
Fowles *n* **John** (**Martin**) 1926–2005, British novelist. His books include *The Collector* (1963), *The Magus* (1966), *The French Lieutenant's Woman* (1969), and *The Tree* (1991)
fox *n, pl* **foxes** *or* **fox** **1** a doglike wild animal with a pointed muzzle and a bushy tail **2** its reddish-brown or grey fur **3** a person who is cunning and sly ▷ *vb* **4** *informal* to confuse or puzzle
WORD ORIGIN Old English
Foxe *n* **John** 1516–87, English Protestant clergyman; author of *History of the Acts and Monuments of the Church* (1563), popularly known as the *Book of Martyrs*
foxglove *n* a tall plant with purple or white flowers
foxhole *n mil* a small pit dug to provide shelter against enemy fire
foxhound *n* a breed of short-haired terrier, originally kept for hunting foxes
fox-hunting *n* the activity of hunting foxes with hounds
foxtrot *n* **1** a ballroom dance with slow and quick steps **2** music for this ▷ *vb* **-trotting, -trotted** **3** to perform this dance
foxy *adj* **foxier, foxiest** **1** of or resembling a fox, esp. in craftiness **2** reddish-brown **foxily** *adv* **foxiness** *n*
foyer ❶ (foy-ay) *n* an entrance hall in a hotel, theatre, or cinema
WORD ORIGIN French: fireplace
fp forte-piano
FP **1** fire plug **2** freezing point
Fr[1] *Christianity* **a** Father **b** Frater
WORD ORIGIN Latin *brother*
Fr[2] *chem* francium
fr. **1** franc **2** from
fracas (frak-ah) *n* a noisy quarrel or fight
WORD ORIGIN French
fraction ❶ *n* **1** *maths* a numerical quantity that is not a whole number **2** any part or subdivision **3** a very small proportion or amount of something **4** *chem* a component of a mixture separated by distillation **fractional** *adj* **fractionally** *adv*
WORD ORIGIN Latin *fractus* broken
fractional distillation *or* **fractionation** *n chem* the process of separating the constituents of a liquid mixture by heating it and condensing the components separately according to their different boiling points
fractious *adj* (esp. of children) easily upset and angered, often due to tiredness
WORD ORIGIN obsolete *fraction* discord
fracture ❶ *n* **1** breaking, esp. the breaking or cracking of a bone ▷ *vb* **-turing, -tured** **2** to break **fractural** *adj*
WORD ORIGIN Latin *frangere* to break
fragile ❶ *adj* **1** able to be broken or damaged easily **2** in a weakened physical state: *you're looking a bit fragile this morning* **fragility** *n*
WORD ORIGIN Latin *fragilis*
fragment ❶ *n* **1** a piece broken off **2** an incomplete piece: *fragments of information* ▷ *vb* **3** to break into small pieces or different parts **fragmentation** *n*
WORD ORIGIN Latin *fragmentum*
fragmentary *adj* made up of small or unconnected pieces: *fragmentary evidence to support his theory*
Fragonard *n* **Jean-Honoré** 1732–1806, French artist, noted for richly coloured paintings typifying the frivolity of 18th- century French court life
fragrance ❶ *n* **1** a pleasant smell **2** a perfume or scent
fragrant ❶ *adj* having a pleasant smell
WORD ORIGIN Latin *fragrare* to emit a smell
frail ❶ *adj* **1** physically weak and delicate **2** easily damaged: *the frail aircraft* **3** easily tempted
WORD ORIGIN Old French *frele*
frailty *n* **1** physical or moral weakness **2** *pl* **-ties** an inadequacy or fault resulting from moral weakness
frame ❶ *n* **1** an open structure that gives shape and support to something, such as a building **2** an enclosing case or border into which something is fitted: *the window frame*

THESAURUS

fowl *n* **1, 3 = poultry**
foyer *n* **= entrance hall**, lobby, reception area, vestibule, anteroom, antechamber
fraction *n* **2 = percentage**, share, cut, division, section, proportion, slice, ratio, portion, quota, subdivision, moiety
fracture *n* **1a = break**, split, crack **1b = cleft**, opening, split, crack, gap, rent, breach, rift, rupture, crevice, fissure, schism ▷ *vb* **2a = break**, crack **2b = split**, separate, divide, rend, fragment, splinter, rupture
fragile *adj* **1a = unstable**, weak, vulnerable, delicate, uncertain, insecure, precarious, flimsy **1b = fine**, weak, delicate, frail, feeble, brittle, flimsy, dainty, easily broken, breakable, frangible **OPPOSITE:** durable **2 = unwell**, poorly, weak, delicate, crook (*Austral & NZ informal*), shaky, frail, feeble, sickly, unsteady, infirm
fragment *n* **1, 2 = piece**, part, bit, scrap, particle, portion, fraction, shiver, shred, remnant, speck, sliver, wisp, morsel, oddment, chip ▷ *vb* **3a = break**, split, shatter, crumble, shiver, disintegrate, splinter, come apart, break into pieces, come to pieces **OPPOSITE:** fuse **3b = break up**, divide, split up, disunite
fragrance *n* **1 = scent**, smell, perfume, bouquet, aroma, balm, sweet smell, sweet odour, redolence, fragrancy **OPPOSITE:** stink **2 = perfume**, scent, cologne, eau de toilette, eau de Cologne, toilet water, Cologne water
fragrant *adj* **= aromatic**, perfumed, balmy, redolent, sweet-smelling, sweet-scented, odorous, ambrosial, odoriferous **OPPOSITE:** stinking
frail *adj* **1 = feeble**, weak, puny, decrepit, infirm **OPPOSITE:** strong **2 = flimsy**, weak, vulnerable, delicate, fragile, brittle, unsound, wispy, insubstantial, breakable, frangible, slight
frame *n* **2 = casing**, framework, structure, shell, system, form, construction, fabric, skeleton,

f

DICTIONARY

3 the system around which something is built up: *caught up in the frame of the revolution* **4** the structure of the human body **5** one of a series of exposures on film used in making motion pictures **6** a television picture scanned by electron beams at a particular frequency **7** *snooker* **a** a single game in a match **b** a wooden triangle used to arrange the red balls in formation before the start of a game **8** ▸short for **cold frame** **9** *slang* a frame-up **10** **frame of mind** a state of mind: *in a complacent frame of mind* ▹*vb* **framing, framed** **11** to construct by fitting parts together **12** to create and develop (plans or a policy) **13** to construct (a statement) in a particular kind of language **14** to provide or enclose with a frame **15** *slang* to conspire to incriminate (someone) on a false charge
WORD ORIGIN Old English *framian* to avail

Frame *n* **Janet** 1924–2004, New Zealand writer: author of the novels *Owls Do Cry* (1957) and *Faces in the Water* (1961), the collection of verse *The Pocket* (1967), and volumes of autobiography including *An Angel at My Table* (1984), which was made into a film in 1990

frame of reference *n* **1** a set of standards that determines behaviour **2** any set of planes or curves, such as the three coordinate axes, used to locate a point in space

frame-up *n slang* a conspiracy to incriminate someone on a false charge

framework ❶ *n* **1** a particular set of beliefs, ideas, or rules referred to in order to solve a problem: *a moral framework* **2** a structure supporting something

franc *n* the standard monetary unit of Switzerland, various African countries, and formerly of France and Belgium
WORD ORIGIN Latin *Rex Francorum* King of the Franks, inscribed on 14th-century francs

France[1] *n* a republic in W Europe, between the English Channel, the Mediterranean, and the Atlantic: the largest country wholly in Europe; became a republic in 1793 after the French Revolution and an empire in 1804 under Napoleon; reverted to a monarchy (1815–48), followed by the Second Republic (1848–52), the Second Empire (1852–70), the Third Republic (1870–1940), and the Fourth and Fifth Republics (1946 and 1958); a member of the European Union. It is generally flat or undulating in the north and west and mountainous in the south and east. Official language: French. Religion: Roman Catholic majority. Currency: euro. Capital: Paris. Pop: 60 434 000 (2004 est). Area: (including Corsica) 551 600 sq km (212 973 sq miles). ▸Related adjectives: **French, Gallic**

France[2] *n* **Anatole**, real name *Anatole François Thibault*. 1844–1924, French novelist, short-story writer, and critic. His works include *Le Crime de Sylvestre Bonnard* (1881), *L'Île des Pingouins* (1908), and *La Révolte des anges* (1914): Nobel prize for literature 1921

Francesca *n* ▸See **Piero della Francesca**

franchise *n* **1** the right to vote, esp. for a member of parliament **2** any exemption, privilege, or right granted by a public authority **3** *commerce* authorization granted to a distributor to sell a company's goods ▹*vb* **-chising, -chised** **4** *commerce, chiefly US & Canad* to grant (a person, firm, etc.) a franchise
WORD ORIGIN Old French *franchir* to set free

Francis *n* **1** **Dick**, full name *Richard Stanley Francis*. born 1920, British thriller writer, formerly a champion jockey. His books include *Dead Cert* (1962), *The Edge* (1988), and *Come to Grief* (1995) **2** Sir **Philip** 1740–1818, British politician; probable author of the *Letters of Junius* (1769–72). He played an important part in the impeachment of Warren Hastings (1788–95)

Franciscan *n* **1** a member of a Christian religious order of friars or nuns founded by Saint Francis of Assisi ▹*adj* **2** of this order

Francis I *n* **1** 1494–1547, king of France (1515–47). His reign was dominated by his rivalry with Emperor Charles V for the control of Italy. He was a noted patron of the arts and learning **2** 1708–65, duke of Lorraine (1729–37), grand duke of Tuscany (1737–65), and Holy Roman Emperor (1745–65). His marriage (1736) to Maria Theresa led to the War of the Austrian Succession (1740–48) **3** ▸title as emperor of Austria of **Francis II**

Francis II *n* **1** 1544–60, king of France (1559–60); son of Henry II and Catherine de' Medici; first husband of Mary, Queen of Scots **2** 1768–1835, last Holy Roman Emperor (1792–1806) and, as Francis I, first emperor of Austria (1804–35). The Holy Roman Empire was dissolved (1806) following his defeat by Napoleon at Austerlitz

francium *n chem* an unstable radioactive element of the alkali-metal group. Symbol: Fr
WORD ORIGIN from *France*, because first found there

Franck *n* **1** **César** (**Auguste**) 1822–90, French composer, organist, and teacher, born in Belgium. His works, some of which make use of cyclic form, include a violin sonata, a string quartet, the *Symphony in D Minor* (1888), and much organ music **2** **James** 1882–1964, US physicist, born in Germany: shared a Nobel prize for physics with Gustav Hertz (1925) for work on the quantum theory, particularly the effects of bombarding atoms with electrons

Franco- *combining form* indicating France or French: *the Franco-Prussian war*
WORD ORIGIN Medieval Latin *Francus*

frangipani (fran-jee-**pah**-nee) *n* **1** an Australian evergreen tree with large yellow fragrant flowers **2** a tropical shrub with fragrant white or pink flowers

frank ❶ *adj* **1** honest and straightforward in speech or attitude ▹*vb* **2** to put a mark on (a letter), ensuring free carriage ▹*n* **3** an official mark stamped to a letter ensuring free delivery **frankly** *adv* **frankness** *n*
WORD ORIGIN Medieval Latin *francus* free

Frank *n* a member of the West Germanic peoples who in the late 4th century AD gradually conquered most of Gaul
WORD ORIGIN Old English *Franca*

Frankenstein *n* a creation or monster that brings disaster and is beyond the control of its creator. Also called: **Frankenstein's monster**
WORD ORIGIN after Baron

THESAURUS

chassis **4 = physique**, build, form, body, figure, skeleton, anatomy, carcass, morphology **10 frame of mind = mood**, state, spirit, attitude, humour, temper, outlook, disposition, mind-set, fettle ▹*vb* **12 = devise**, plan, form, shape, institute, draft, compose, sketch, forge, put together, conceive, hatch, draw up, formulate, contrive, map out, concoct, cook up, block out **14a = mount**, case, enclose **14b = surround**, ring, enclose, close in, encompass, envelop, encircle, fence in, hem in

framework *n* **1 = system**, plan, order, scheme, arrangement, fabric, schema, frame of reference, the bare bones **2 = structure**, body, frame, foundation, shell, fabric, skeleton

frank *adj* **1 = candid**, open, free, round, direct, plain, straightforward, blunt, outright, sincere, outspoken, honest, downright, truthful, forthright, upfront *(informal)*, unrestricted, plain-spoken, unreserved, artless, ingenuous, straight from the shoulder *(informal)*
OPPOSITE: secretive

DICTIONARY

Frankenstein, who created a monster from parts of corpses in the novel by Mary Shelley

frankfurter *n* a smoked sausage of pork or beef
WORD ORIGIN short for German *Frankfurter Wurst* sausage from Frankfurt

frankincense *n* an aromatic gum resin burnt as incense
WORD ORIGIN Old French *franc* free, pure + *encens* incense

Frankish *n* **1** the ancient West Germanic language of the Franks ▹*adj* **2** of the Franks or their language

frantic ● *adj* **1** distracted with fear, pain, joy, etc. **2** hurried and disorganized: *frantic activity* **frantically** *adv*
WORD ORIGIN Latin *phreneticus* mad

Franz Josef I *n* English name *Francis Joseph I.* 1830–1916, emperor of Austria (1848–1916) and king of Hungary (1867–1916)

frappé *adj* (esp. of drinks) chilled
WORD ORIGIN French

fraternal *adj* **1** of a brother; brotherly **2** designating twins that developed from two separate fertilized ova **fraternally** *adv*
WORD ORIGIN Latin *frater* brother

fraternity ● *n, pl* **-ties** **1** a body of people united in interests, aims, etc. **2** friendship between groups of people **3** *US & Canad* a society of male students

fraternize *or* **-nise** *vb* **-nizing, -nized** *or* **-nising, -nised** to associate on friendly terms: *fraternizing with the customers is off-limits* **fraternization** *or* **-nisation** *n*

fratricide *n* **1** the act of killing one's brother **2** a person who kills his or her brother **fratricidal** *adj*
WORD ORIGIN Latin *frater* brother + *caedere* to kill

Frau (rhymes with **how**) *n, pl* **Frauen** *or* **Fraus** a German form of address equivalent to *Mrs* or *Ms*
WORD ORIGIN German

fraud ● *n* **1** deliberate deception or cheating intended to gain an advantage **2** an act of such deception **3** *informal* a person who acts in a false or deceitful way
WORD ORIGIN Latin *fraus*

fraudster *n* a person who commits a fraud; swindler

fraudulent ● *adj* **1** acting with intent to deceive **2** proceeding from fraud **fraudulence** *n*
WORD ORIGIN Latin *fraudulentus*

fraught (frawt) *adj* **1** **fraught with** involving or filled with: *we expected the trip to be fraught with difficulties* **2** tense or anxious
WORD ORIGIN Middle Dutch *vrachten*

Fräulein (froy-line) *n, pl* **-lein** *or* **-leins** a German form of address equivalent to *Miss*
WORD ORIGIN German

Fraunhofer *n* **Joseph von** 1787–1826, German physicist and optician, who investigated spectra of the sun, planets, and fixed stars, and improved telescopes and other optical instruments

fray[1] *n* **1** *Brit, Austral & NZ* a noisy quarrel or brawl **2** **the fray** any challenging conflict: *at the height of the run-glut Warne entered the fray*
WORD ORIGIN short for *affray*

fray[2] ● *vb* **1** to wear away into loose threads, esp. at an edge **2** to make or become strained or irritated
WORD ORIGIN French *frayer* to rub

Frayn *n* **Michael** born 1933, British playwright, novelist, and translator; his plays include *The Two of Us* (1970), *Noises Off* (1982), *Copenhagen* (1998), and *Democracy* (2004); novels include *A Landing on the Sun* (1991) and *Spies* (2002)

Frazer *n* Sir **James George** 1854–1941, Scottish anthropologist; author of many works on primitive religion, and magic, esp. *The Golden Bough* (1890)

Frazier *n* **Joe** born 1944, US boxer: won the world heavyweight title in 1970 and was the first to beat Muhammad Ali professionally (1971)

frazil (fray-zil) *n* small pieces of ice that form in water moving turbulently enough to prevent the formation of a sheet of ice
WORD ORIGIN French *fraisil* cinders

frazzle *n informal* the state of being exhausted: *worn to a frazzle*
WORD ORIGIN probably from Middle English *faselen* to fray

freak ● *n* **1** a person, animal, or plant that is abnormal or deformed **2** an object, event, etc. that is abnormal: *a statistical freak* **3** *informal* a person whose appearance or behaviour is very unusual **4** *informal* a person who is very enthusiastic about something specified: *a health freak* ▹*adj* **5** abnormal or unusual: *a freak accident* **freakish** *adj* **freaky** *adj*
WORD ORIGIN origin unknown

freak out *vb informal* to be or cause to be in a heightened emotional state

freckle *n* **1** a small brownish spot on the skin ▹*vb* **-ling, -led** **2** to mark or become marked with freckles **freckled** *adj*
WORD ORIGIN Old Norse *freknur* freckles

Frederick Barbarossa *n* official title *Frederick I.* ?1123–90, Holy Roman Emperor (1155–90), king of Germany (1152–90). His attempt to assert imperial rights in Italy ended in his defeat at Legnano (1176) and the independence of the Lombard cities (1183)

Frederick Henry *n* 1584–1647, prince of Orange and count of Nassau; son of William (I) the Silent

Frederick I *n* **1** ▸ See **Frederick Barbarossa** **2** 1657–1713, first king of Prussia (1701–13); son of Frederick William

Frederick II *n* 1194–1250, Holy Roman Emperor (1220–50), king of Germany (1212–50), and king of Sicily (1198–1250)

THESAURUS

frantic *adj* **1 = frenzied**, wild, mad, raging, furious, raving, distracted, distraught, berserk, uptight *(informal)*, overwrought, at the end of your tether, beside yourself, at your wits' end, berko *(Austral slang)*
OPPOSITE: calm
2 = hectic, desperate, frenzied, fraught *(informal)*, frenetic

fraternity *n* **1 = circle**, company, set, order, clan, guild
2 = companionship, fellowship, brotherhood, kinship, camaraderie, comradeship **3** *(US & Canad)* **= brotherhood**, club, union, society, league, association, sodality

fraud *n* **1 = deception**, deceit, treachery, swindling, guile, trickery, duplicity, double-dealing, chicanery, sharp practice, imposture, fraudulence, spuriousness
OPPOSITE: honesty
2a = scam, craft, cheat, sting *(informal)*, deception *(slang)*, artifice, humbug, canard, stratagems, chicane **2b = hoax**, trick, cheat, con *(informal)*, deception, sham, spoof *(informal)*, prank, swindle, ruse, practical joke, joke, fast one *(informal)*, imposture, fastie *(Austral slang)* **3** *(informal)* **= impostor**, cheat, fake, bluffer, sham, hoax, hoaxer, forgery, counterfeit, pretender, charlatan, quack, fraudster, swindler, mountebank, grifter *(slang, chiefly US & Canad)*, double-dealer, phoney *or* phony *(informal)*

fraudulent *adj* **1, 2 = deceitful**, false, crooked *(informal)*, untrue, sham, treacherous, dishonest, deceptive, counterfeit, spurious, crafty, swindling, double-dealing, duplicitous, knavish, phoney *or* phony *(informal)*, criminal
OPPOSITE: genuine

fray[2] *vb* **1 = wear thin**, wear, rub, fret, wear out, chafe, wear away, become threadbare

freak *n* **2 = aberration**, eccentric, anomaly, abnormality, sport *(biology)*, monster, mutant, oddity, monstrosity, malformation, rara avis *(Latin)*, queer fish *(Brit informal)*, teratism **3** *(informal)* **= weirdo** *or* **weirdie** *(informal)*, eccentric, oddity, case *(informal)*, character *(informal)*, nut *(slang)*, flake *(slang, chiefly US)*,

Frederick III *n* **1** 1415–93, Holy Roman Emperor (1452–93) and, as Frederick IV, king of Germany (1440–93) **2** called *the Wise*. 1463–1525, elector of Saxony (1486–1525). He protected Martin Luther in Wartburg Castle after the Diet of Worms (1521)

Frederick IV *n* See **Frederick III** (sense 1)

Frederick IX *n* 1899–1972, king of Denmark (1947–72)

Frederick V *n* called *the Winter King*. 1596–1632, elector of the Palatinate (1610–23) and king of Bohemia (1619–20). He led the revolt of Bohemian Protestants at the beginning of the Thirty Years' War

Frederick William *n* called *the Great Elector*. 1620–88, elector of Brandenburg (1640–88)

Frederick William I *n* 1688–1740, king of Prussia (1713–40); son of Frederick I: reformed the Prussian army

Frederick William II *n* 1744–97, king of Prussia (1786–97)

Frederick William III *n* 1770–1840, king of Prussia (1797–1840)

Frederick William IV *n* 1795–1861, king of Prussia (1840–61). He submitted to the 1848 Revolution but refused the imperial crown offered by the Frankfurt Parliament (1849). In 1857 he became insane and his brother, William I, became regent (1858–61)

free ❶ *adj* **freer, freest 1** able to act at will; not under compulsion or restraint **2** not enslaved or confined **3** (of a country) independent **4** (of a translation) not exact or literal **5** provided without charge: *free school meals* **6** not occupied or in use; available: *is this seat free?* **7** (of a person) not busy **8** open or available to all **9** not fixed or joined; loose: *the free end* **10** without obstruction or blockage: *the free flow of capital* **11** *chem* chemically uncombined: *free nitrogen* **12 free and easy** casual or tolerant **13 free from** not subject to: *free from surveillance* **14 free with** using or giving (something) a lot: *he was free with his tongue* **15 make free with** to behave too familiarly towards ▹ *adv* **16** in a free manner **17** without charge or cost ▹ *vb* **freeing, freed 18** to release or liberate **19** to remove obstructions or impediments from **20** to make available or usable: *capital freed by the local authority* **21 free of** or **from** to relieve or rid of (obstacles, pain, etc.) **freely** *adv*
WORD ORIGIN Old English *frēo*

-free *adj combining form* free from: *duty-free; nuclear-free zones*

freebie *n slang* something provided without charge

freeboard *n* the space or distance between the deck of a vessel and the water line

freebooter *n* a pirate
WORD ORIGIN Dutch *vrijbuit* booty

freeborn *adj history* not born in slavery

Free Church *n chiefly Brit* any Protestant Church other than the Established Church

freecycle *n* **1** an informal network of citizens who promote recycling online by offering one another unwanted items free of charge ▹ *vb* **2** to recycle (an unwanted item) by offering it free of charge

freediving *n* the sport or activity of diving without the aid of breathing apparatus

freedman *n, pl* **-men** *history* a man freed from slavery

freedom ❶ *n* **1** the state of being free, esp. to enjoy political and civil liberties **2** exemption or immunity: *freedom from government control* **3** liberation, such as from slavery **4** the right or privilege of unrestricted access: *freedom of the skies* **5** self-government or independence **6** the power to order one's own actions **7** ease or frankness of manner

free enterprise *n* an economic system in which commercial organizations compete for profit with little state control

free fall *n* **1** the part of a parachute descent before the parachute opens **2** free descent of a body in which gravity is the only force acting on it

free-for-all *n informal* a disorganized brawl or argument involving all those present

free hand *n* **1** unrestricted freedom to act: *the president must be able to deal with foreign hostilities with a free hand* ▹ *adj, adv* **freehand 2** (done) by hand without the use of guiding instruments

freehold *property law n* **1** tenure of property for life without restrictions ▹ *adj* **2** of or held by freehold **freeholder** *n*

free house *n Brit* a public house not bound to sell only one brewer's products

free kick *n soccer* an unopposed kick of the ball awarded for a foul or infringement

freelance *n* **1** a self-employed person doing specific pieces of work for various employers ▹ *vb* **-lancing, -lanced 2** to work as a freelance ▹ *adj, adv* **3** of or as a freelance
WORD ORIGIN originally applied to a mercenary soldier

freeloader *n slang* a person who habitually depends on others for food, accommodation, etc.

free love *n old-fashioned* the practice of having sexual relationships outside marriage, often several relationships at the same time

freeman *n, pl* **-men** a person who has been given the freedom of a city as an honour in return for public service

Freeman *n* **Cathy,** full name *Catherine Astrid Salome Freeman*. born 1973,

f

THESAURUS

oddball *(informal)*, nonconformist, screwball *(slang, chiefly US & Canad)*, odd fish *(informal)*, kook *(US & Canad informal)*, queer fish *(Brit informal)* **4** *(informal)* **= enthusiast**, fan, nut *(slang)*, addict, buff *(informal)*, fanatic, devotee, fiend *(informal)*, aficionado ▹ *adj* **5 = abnormal**, chance, unusual, unexpected, exceptional, unpredictable, queer, erratic, unparalleled, unforeseen, fortuitous, unaccountable, atypical, aberrant, fluky *(informal)*, odd, bizarre

free *adj* **1a = allowed**, permitted, unrestricted, unimpeded, open, clear, able, loose, unattached, unregulated, disengaged, untrammelled, unobstructed, unhampered, unengaged **1b = independent**, unfettered, unrestrained, uncommitted, footloose, unconstrained, unengaged, not tied down **2 = at liberty**, loose, liberated, at large, off the hook *(slang)*, on the loose
OPPOSITE: confined
5 = complimentary, for free *(informal)*, for nothing, unpaid, for love, free of charge, on the house, without charge, gratuitous, at no cost, gratis, buckshee *(Brit slang)* **6 = available**, extra, empty, spare, vacant, unused, uninhabited, unoccupied, untaken ▹ *vb* **18a = clear**, deliver, disengage, cut loose, release, rescue, rid, relieve, exempt, undo, redeem, ransom, extricate, unburden, unshackle **18b = release**, liberate, let out, set free, deliver, loose, discharge, unleash, let go, untie, emancipate, unchain, turn loose, uncage, set at liberty, unfetter, disenthrall, unbridle, manumit
OPPOSITE: confine
19 = disentangle, extricate, disengage, detach, separate, loose, unfold, unravel, disconnect, untangle, untwist, unsnarl

freedom *n* **3 = liberty**, release, discharge, emancipation, deliverance, manumission
OPPOSITE: captivity
5 = independence, democracy, sovereignty, autonomy, self-determination, emancipation, self-government, home rule, autarchy, rangatiratanga *(NZ)* **6 = licence**, latitude, a free hand, free rein, play, power, range, opportunity, ability, facility, scope, flexibility, discretion, leeway, carte blanche, blank cheque, elbowroom
OPPOSITE: restriction

DICTIONARY

Australian sprinter; winner of the 200m and 400m in the 1994 Commonwealth Games and the 400m in the 2000 Olympic Games

free-market *adj* denoting an economic system which allows supply and demand to regulate prices and wages

Freemason *n* Also called: **Mason** a member of a widespread secret order whose members are pledged to help each other **Freemasonry** *n*

free-range *adj* kept or produced in natural conditions: *free-range eggs*

freesia *n* a plant with fragrant tubular flowers
WORD ORIGIN after F. H. T. *Freese*, physician

free space *n* a region that has no gravitational and electromagnetic fields

freestanding *adj* not attached to or supported by another object

freestyle *n* **1** a competition, such as in swimming, in which each participant may use a style of his or her choice **2** Also called: **all-in wrestling** a style of professional wrestling with no internationally agreed set of rules

freethinker *n* a person who forms his or her ideas independently of authority, esp. in matters of religion

free trade *n* international trade that is free of such government interference as protective tariffs and import quotas

free verse *n* unrhymed verse without a fixed rhythm

Freeview *n trademark* (in Britain) a free service providing digital terrestrial television

freeway ● *n US & Austral* a motorway

freewheel *vb* **1** to travel downhill on a bicycle without pedalling ▷ *n* **2** a device in the rear hub of a bicycle wheel that permits it to rotate freely while the pedals are stationary

freewheeling *adj* behaving in a relaxed spontaneous manner, without any long-term plans or commitments: *he had to change his freewheeling lifestyle after his son was born*

free will *n* **1** the ability to make a choice without outside coercion or pressure: *you walked in here of your own free will* **2** *philosophy* the belief that human behaviour is an expression of personal choice and is not determined by physical forces, Fate, or God

Free World *n* the non-Communist countries collectively

freeze ● *vb* **freezing, froze, frozen** **1** to change from a liquid to a solid by the reduction of temperature, such as water to ice **2** to preserve (food) by subjection to extreme cold **3** to cover or become covered with ice **4** to fix fast or become fixed (to something) because of frost **5** to feel or cause to feel the effects of extreme cold **6** to die of extreme cold **7** to become motionless through fear, shock, etc. **8** to cause (moving film) to stop at a particular frame **9** to fix (prices, incomes, etc.) at a particular level **10** to forbid by law the exchange or collection of (loans, assets, etc.) ▷ *n* **11** the act of freezing or state of being frozen **12** *meteorol* a spell of temperatures below freezing point **13** the fixing of incomes, prices, etc. by legislation
WORD ORIGIN Old English *frēosan*

freeze-dry *vb* **-dries, -drying, -dried** to preserve (food) by rapid freezing and drying in a vacuum

freeze out *vb* to prevent (someone) from being involved in an activity, conversation, etc. by being unfriendly or reserved

freezer *n* an insulated cabinet for cold-storage of perishable foods

freezing ● *adj informal* very cold

freezing point *n* the temperature below which a liquid turns into a solid

freezing works *n Austral & NZ* a slaughterhouse at which animals are slaughtered and carcasses frozen especially for export

Frege *n* **Gottlob** 1848–1925, German logician and philosopher, who laid the foundations of modern formal logic and semantics in his *Begriffsschrift* (1879)

freight ● (frate) *n* **1 a** commercial transport of goods **b** the cargo transported **c** the cost of this **2** *chiefly Brit* a ship's cargo or part of it ▷ *vb* **3** to transport (goods) by freight **4** to load with goods for transport
WORD ORIGIN Middle Dutch *vrecht*

freighter *n* a ship or aircraft designed for transporting cargo

French[1] ● *n* **1** the official language of France: also an official language of Switzerland, Belgium, Canada, and certain other countries. It is the native language of approximately 70 million people; also used for diplomacy. Historically, French is an Indo-European language belonging to the Romance group ▸ See also **Old French, Anglo-French** **2 the French** (*functioning as plural*) the natives, citizens, or inhabitants of France collectively **3** ▸ See **French vermouth** ▷ *adj* **4** relating to, denoting, or characteristic of France, the French, or their language ▸ Related prefixes: **Franco-, Gallo-** **5** (in Canada) of or relating to French Canadians
Frenchness *n*
WORD ORIGIN Old English *Frencisc* French, Frankish; see FRANK

French[2] *n* Sir **John Denton Pinkstone**, 1st Earl of Ypres. 1852–1925, British field marshal in World War I: commanded the British Expeditionary Force in France and Belgium (1914–15); Lord Lieutenant of Ireland (1918–21)

French beans *pl n* green beans, the pods of which are eaten

French bread *n* white bread in a long, thin, crusty loaf

French Canadian *n* a Canadian citizen whose native language is French

French chalk *n* a variety of talc used to mark cloth or remove grease stains

French dressing *n* a salad dressing made from oil and vinegar with seasonings

French fries *pl n chiefly US & Canad* potato chips

French horn *n music* a valved brass wind instrument with a coiled tube

Frenchify *vb* **-fies, -fying, -fied** *informal* to make or become French in appearance, etc.

French letter *n Brit & NZ slang* a condom

Frenchman *or fem* **Frenchwoman** *n, pl* **-men** *or* **-women** a person from France

French polish *n* a shellac varnish for wood, giving a high gloss

French seam *n* a seam in which the edges are enclosed

French windows *pl n* a window extending to floor level, used as a door

Freneau *n* **Philip** 1752–1832, US poet, journalist, and patriot; editor of the *National Gazette* (1791–93)

frenetic (frin-net-ik) *adj* wild,

THESAURUS

freeway *n* (*US & Austral*) **= motorway** (*Brit*), autobahn (*German*), autoroute (*French*), autostrada (*Italian*)

freeze *vb* **1, 3 = ice over** *or* **up**, harden, stiffen, solidify, congeal, become solid, glaciate **5 = chill**, benumb **9 = fix**, hold, limit, hold up, peg **10 = suspend**, stop, shelve, curb, cut short, discontinue

freezing *adj* **a = icy**, biting, bitter, raw, chill, chilled, penetrating, arctic, numbing, polar, Siberian, frosty, glacial, wintry, parky (*Brit informal*), cold as ice, frost-bound, cutting **b = frozen**, chilled, numb, chilly, very cold, shivery, benumbed, frozen to the marrow

freight *n* **1a = transportation**, traffic, delivery, carriage, shipment, haulage, conveyance, transport **1b, 2 = cargo**, goods, contents, load, lading, delivery, burden, haul, bulk, shipment, merchandise, bales, consignment, payload, tonnage

French[1] *adj* **4 = Gallic**

frenzy *n* **1 = fury**, transport, passion, rage, madness, turmoil, distraction,

DICTIONARY

excited, and uncontrolled
frenetically *adv*
WORD ORIGIN Greek *phrenitis* insanity

frenzy ❶ *n, pl* **-zies** 1 violent or wild and uncontrollable behaviour 2 excited or agitated activity: *a frenzy of speculation* **frenzied** *adj*
WORD ORIGIN Late Latin *phrenesis* madness, from Greek *phren* mind

Freon *n trademark* any of a group of gas or liquid chemical compounds of methane with chlorine and fluorine: used in propellants, aerosols, and solvents

frequency *n, pl* **-cies** 1 the number of times that an event occurs within a given period 2 the state of being frequent 3 *physics* the number of times a wave repeats itself in a given time

frequency distribution *n* statistical data arranged to show the frequency with which the possible values of a variable occur

frequency modulation *n* a method of transmitting information by varying the frequency of the carrier wave in accordance with the amplitude of the input signal

frequent ❶ *adj* 1 happening often 2 habitual ▷*vb* 3 to visit often: *a spa town frequented by the Prussian nobility*
frequently *adv*
WORD ORIGIN Latin *frequens* numerous

frequentative *grammar adj* 1 denoting a verb or an affix meaning repeated action ▷*n* 2 a frequentative verb or affix

fresco *n, pl* **-coes** *or* **-cos** 1 a method of wall-painting using watercolours on wet plaster 2 a painting done in this way
WORD ORIGIN Italian: fresh plaster

Frescobaldi *n* **Girolamo** 1583–1643, Italian organist and composer, noted esp. for his organ and harpsichord music

fresh ❶ *adj* 1 newly made, acquired, etc. 2 not thought of before; novel: *fresh ideas* 3 most recent: *fresh allegations* 4 further or additional: *a fresh supply* 5 (of food) not canned or frozen 6 (of water) not salty 7 bright and clear: *a fresh morning* 8 (of a wind) cold and fairly strong 9 not tired; alert 10 not worn or faded: *the fresh colours of spring* 11 having a healthy or ruddy appearance 12 having recently come (from somewhere): *cakes fresh from the oven* 13 youthful or inexperienced 14 *informal* overfamiliar or disrespectful ▷*adv* 15 recently: *a delicious fresh-baked cake*
freshly *adv* **freshness** *n*
WORD ORIGIN Old English *fersc*

freshen *vb* 1 to make or become fresh or fresher 2 (of the wind) to become stronger 3 **freshen up** to wash and tidy up one's appearance: *I'll go and freshen up*

fresher *or* **freshman** *n, pl* **-ers** *or* **-men** *Brit & US* a first-year student at college or university

freshet *n* 1 the sudden overflowing of a river 2 a stream of fresh water emptying into the sea

freshwater *adj* of or living in fresh water

Fresnel *n* **Augustin Jean** 1788–1827, French physicist: worked on the interference of light, contributing to the wave theory of light

fret[1] ❶ *vb* **fretting, fretted** 1 to worry: *he would fret about the smallest of problems* 2 to rub or wear away 3 to feel or give annoyance ▷*n* 4 a state of irritation or anxiety
WORD ORIGIN Old English *fretan* to eat

fret[2] *n* 1 a repetitive geometrical figure used for ornamentation ▷*vb* **fretting, fretted** 2 to ornament with fret or fretwork
WORD ORIGIN Old French *frete* interlaced design used on a shield

fret[3] *n* a small metal bar set across the fingerboard of a musical instrument, such as a guitar, as a guide to fingering
WORD ORIGIN origin unknown

fretful *adj* irritable or upset **fretfully** *adv*

fret saw *n* a fine-toothed saw with a long thin narrow blade, used for cutting designs in thin wood or metal

fretwork *n* decorative geometrical carving in wood

Freudian (froy-dee-an) *adj* of or relating to Sigmund Freud (1856–1939), Austrian psychiatrist, or his ideas **Freudianism** *n*

Freudian slip *n* a slip of the tongue that may reveal an unconscious wish

Freytag *n* **Gustav** 1816–95, German novelist and dramatist; author of the comedy *Die Journalisten* (1853) and *Soll und Haben* (1855), a novel about German commercial life

Fri. Friday

friable (fry-a-bl) *adj* easily broken up
friability *n*
WORD ORIGIN Latin *friare* to crumble

friar *n* a member of a male Roman Catholic religious order
WORD ORIGIN Latin *frater* brother

friar's balsam *n* a compound with a camphor-like smell, used as an inhalant to relieve bronchitis

friary *n, pl* **-aries** a house of friars

fricassee *n* stewed meat, esp. chicken or veal, served in a thick white sauce
WORD ORIGIN Old French

fricative *n* 1 a consonant produced by friction of breath through a partly closed mouth, such as (f) or (z) ▷*adj* 2 relating to or being a fricative
WORD ORIGIN Latin *fricare* to rub

friction ❶ *n* 1 a resistance encountered when one body moves relative to another body with which it is in contact 2 the act of rubbing one object against another 3 disagreement or conflict
frictional *adj*
WORD ORIGIN Latin *fricare* to rub

THESAURUS

seizure, hysteria, mania, insanity, agitation, aberration, lunacy, delirium, paroxysm, derangement
OPPOSITE: calm

frequent *adj* **1, 2 = common**, repeated, usual, familiar, constant, everyday, persistent, reiterated, recurring, customary, continual, recurrent, habitual, incessant
OPPOSITE: infrequent
▷*vb* **3 = visit**, attend, haunt, be found at, patronize, hang out at *(informal)*, visit often, go to regularly, be a regular customer of **OPPOSITE:** keep away

fresh *adj* **2, 3 = new**, original, novel, unusual, latest, different, recent, modern, up-to-date, this season's, unconventional, unorthodox, ground-breaking, left-field *(informal)*, new-fangled, modernistic
OPPOSITE: old
4 = additional, more, new, other, added, further, extra, renewed, supplementary, auxiliary
5 = natural, raw, crude, unsalted, unprocessed, uncured, unpreserved, undried, green **OPPOSITE:** preserved
8 = cool, cold, refreshing, brisk, chilly, nippy **9 = lively**, rested, bright, keen, vital, restored, alert, bouncing, revived, refreshed, vigorous, energetic, sprightly, invigorated, spry, chipper *(informal)*, full of beans *(informal)*, like a new man, full of vim and vigour *(informal)*, unwearied, bright-eyed and bushy-tailed *(informal)*
OPPOSITE: weary
14 *(informal)* **= cheeky** *(informal)*, bold, brazen, impertinent, forward, familiar, flip *(informal)*, saucy, audacious, sassy *(US informal)*, pert, disrespectful, presumptuous, insolent, impudent, smart-alecky *(informal)* **OPPOSITE:** well-mannered

fret[1] *vb* **1 = worry**, anguish, brood, agonize, obsess, lose sleep, upset yourself, distress yourself

friction *n* **1 = resistance**, rubbing, scraping, grating, irritation, erosion, fretting, attrition, rasping, chafing, abrasion, wearing away **2 = rubbing**, scraping, grating, fretting, rasping, chafing, abrasion **3 = conflict**, opposition, hostility, resentment, disagreement, rivalry, discontent, wrangling, bickering, animosity, antagonism, discord, bad feeling, bad blood, dissension,

DICTIONARY

Friday *n* the sixth day of the week
WORD ORIGIN Old English *Frīgedæg* day of Freya, Norse goddess
fridge *n* a cabinet for keeping food and drink cool. In full: **refrigerator**
fried *vb* ▸ the past of **fry¹**
Friedan *n* **Betty** 1921–2006, US feminist, founder and first president (1966–70) of the National Organization for Women. Her books include *The Feminine Mystique* (1963), *The Second Stage* (1982), and *The Fountain of Life* (1993)
Friedrich *n* **Caspar David** 1774–1840, German romantic landscape painter, noted for his skill in rendering changing effects of light
friend 🅣 *n* **1** a person known well to another and regarded with liking, affection, and loyalty **2** an ally in a fight or cause **3** a patron or supporter: *our cause has many influential friends throughout Europe* **4 make friends (with)** to become friendly (with) ▹ *vb* **5** to choose to be friends with someone on the social networking site Facebook **friendless** *adj* **friendship** *n*
WORD ORIGIN Old English *frēond*
Friend *n* a member of the Society of Friends; Quaker
friendly 🅣 *adj* **-lier, -liest 1** showing or expressing liking, goodwill, or trust **2** on the same side; not hostile **3** tending to help or support ▹ *n, pl* **-lies 4** *sport* a match played for its own sake and not as part of a competition **friendliness** *n*
-friendly *adj combining form* helpful, easy, or good for the person or thing specified: *a user-friendly computer system; the development of an environment-friendly weedkiller*
friendly society *n Brit* an association of people who pay regular dues in return for old-age pensions, sickness benefits, etc.
frier *n* a fryer
fries *pl n* ▸ short for **French fries**
Friese-Greene *n* **William** 1855–1921, British photographer. He invented (with Mortimer Evans) the first practicable motion-picture camera
Friesian (free-zhan) *n* any of several breeds of black-and-white dairy cattle
frieze (freeze) *n* **1** a sculptured or decorated band on a wall **2** *archit* the horizontal band between the architrave and cornice of a classical temple
WORD ORIGIN French *frise*
frigate (frig-it) *n* **1** a fast warship, smaller than a destroyer **2** a medium-sized warship of the 18th and 19th centuries
WORD ORIGIN French *frégate*
fright 🅣 *n* **1** sudden fear or alarm **2** a sudden alarming shock **3** *informal* a very strange or unattractive person or thing
WORD ORIGIN Old English *fryhto*
frighten 🅣 *vb* **1** to terrify or scare **2** to force (someone) to do something from fear **frightening** *adj*
frightful *adj* **1** very alarming or horrifying **2** annoying or disagreeable: *a frightful pair of socks* **3** *informal* extreme: *a frightful mess* **frightfully** *adv*
frigid (frij-id) *adj* **1** (esp. of a woman) lacking sexual responsiveness **2** very cold: *the frigid air* **3** formal or stiff in behaviour or temperament **frigidity** *n*
WORD ORIGIN Latin *frigidus* cold
frill *n* **1** a long narrow strip of fabric with many folds in it attached at one edge of something as a decoration **2** an unnecessary part of something added to make it more attractive or interesting: *no fuss, no frills, just a purity of sound and clarity of vision* **frilly** *or* **frilled** *adj*
WORD ORIGIN origin unknown
frilled lizard *n* a large tree-living Australian lizard with an erectile fold of skin around the neck
fringe 🅣 *n* **1** hair cut short and hanging over the forehead **2** an ornamental edge of hanging threads, tassels, etc. **3** an outer edge: *London's southern fringe* **4** the minor and less important parts of an activity or organization: *two agents on the fringes of espionage activity* **5** a small group of people within a larger body, but differing from it in certain aims and ideas: *the radical fringe of the Green Party* ▹ *adj* **6** (of theatre) unofficial or unconventional ▹ *vb* **fringing, fringed 7** to form a border for: *sandy paths fringing the water's edge* **8** to decorate with a fringe: *tinsel fringed the desk*
WORD ORIGIN Latin *fimbria* fringe, border
fringe benefit *n* a benefit given in addition to a regular salary or wage
fringed *adj* **1** (of clothes, curtains, etc.) decorated with a fringe **2 fringed with** *or* **by** bordered with or by: *a field fringed with trees*
Frink *n* Dame **Elisabeth** 1930–93, British sculptor
frippery *n, pl* **-peries 1** showy but useless ornamentation **2** unimportant or trivial matters
WORD ORIGIN Old French *frepe* frill, rag
Frisbee *n trademark* a light plastic disc thrown with a spinning motion for recreation
Frisch *n* **1 Karl von** 1886–1982, Austrian zoologist; studied animal behaviour, esp. of bees; shared the Nobel prize for physiology or medicine 1973 **2 Max** 1911–91,

THESAURUS

incompatibility, disharmony, dispute
friend *n* **1 = companion**, pal, mate *(informal)*, buddy *(informal)*, partner, china *(Brit & S African informal)*, familiar, best friend, intimate, close friend, comrade, chum *(informal)*, crony, alter ego, confidant, playmate, confidante, main man *(slang, chiefly US)*, soul mate, homeboy *(slang, chiefly US)*, cobber *(Austral & NZ)*, E hoa *(NZ old-fashioned, informal)*, bosom friend, boon companion, Achates
OPPOSITE: foe
2, 3 = supporter, ally, associate, sponsor, advocate, patron, backer, partisan, protagonist, benefactor, adherent, well-wisher
friendly *adj* **1a = amiable**, kind, kindly, welcoming, warm, neighbourly, thick *(informal)*, attached, pally *(informal)*, helpful, sympathetic, fond, outgoing, comradely, confiding, affectionate, receptive, benevolent, attentive, sociable, genial, affable, fraternal, good, close, on good terms, chummy *(informal)*, peaceable, companionable, clubby, well-disposed, buddy-buddy *(slang, chiefly US & Canad)*, palsy-walsy *(informal)*, matey *or* maty *(Brit informal)*, on visiting terms **1b = amicable**, warm, familiar, pleasant, intimate, informal, benign, conciliatory, cordial, congenial, convivial
OPPOSITE: unfriendly
fright *n* **1 = fear**, shock, alarm, horror, panic, terror, dread, dismay, quaking, apprehension, consternation, trepidation, cold sweat, fear and trembling, (blue) funk *(informal)* **OPPOSITE:** courage
2 = scare, start, turn, surprise, shock, jolt, the creeps *(informal)*, the shivers, the willies *(slang)*, the heebie-jeebies *(slang)*
frighten *vb* **1 = scare**, shock, alarm, terrify, cow, appal, startle, intimidate, dismay, daunt, unnerve, petrify, unman, terrorize, scare (someone) stiff, put the wind up (someone) *(informal)*, scare the living daylights out of (someone) *(informal)*, make your hair stand on end *(informal)*, get the wind up, make your blood run cold, throw into a panic, affright *(archaic)*, freeze your blood, make (someone) jump out of his skin *(informal)*, throw into a fright
OPPOSITE: reassure
fringe *n* **2 = border**, edging, edge, binding, trimming, hem, frill, tassel, flounce **3 = edge**, limits, border, margin, march, marches, outskirts, perimeter, periphery, borderline ▹ *adj* **6 = unofficial**, alternative, radical, innovative, avant-garde, unconventional, unorthodox

DICTIONARY

Swiss dramatist and novelist. His works are predominantly satirical and include the plays *Biedermann und die Brandstifter* (1953) and *Andorra* (1961), and the novel *Stiller* (1954) **3 Otto** 1904–79, British nuclear physicist, born in Austria, who contributed to the development of the first atomic bomb **4 Ragnar (Anton Kittil)** 1895–1973, Norwegian economist, who pioneered the study of econometrics and greatly influenced the management of the Norwegian economy from 1945: shared the first Nobel prize for economics (1969) with Jan Tinbergen

Frisian (free-zhan) *n* **1** a language spoken in the NW Netherlands **2** a speaker of this language ▹*adj* **3** of this language or its speakers
WORD ORIGIN Latin *Frisii* people of northern Germany

frisk *vb* **1** to leap, move about, or act in a playful manner **2** *informal* to search (someone) by feeling for concealed weapons, etc. ▹*n* **3** a playful movement **4** *informal* an instance of frisking a person
WORD ORIGIN Old French *frisque*

frisky *adj* **friskier, friskiest** lively, high-spirited, or playful **friskily** *adv*

frisson (freess-on) *n* a short sudden feeling of fear or excitement
WORD ORIGIN French

fritter *n* a piece of food, such as apple, that is dipped in batter and fried in deep fat
WORD ORIGIN Latin *frigere* to fry

fritter away *vb* to waste: *he did not fritter away his energy on trivialities*
WORD ORIGIN obsolete *fitter* to break into small pieces

frivolous *adj* **1** not serious or sensible in content, attitude, or behaviour **2** unworthy of serious or sensible treatment: *frivolous distractions* **frivolity** *n*
WORD ORIGIN Latin *frivolus*

frizz *vb* **1** (of hair) to form or cause (hair) to form tight curls ▹*n* **2** hair that has been frizzed **frizzy** *adj*
WORD ORIGIN French *friser* to curl

frizzle[1] *vb* **-zling, -zled** **1** to form (hair) into tight crisp curls ▹*n* **2** a tight curl
WORD ORIGIN probably related to Old English *frīs* curly

frizzle[2] *vb* **-zling, -zled** to cook or heat until crisp or shrivelled up
WORD ORIGIN probably blend of *fry* + *sizzle*

Frobisher *n* Sir **Martin** ?1535–94, English navigator and explorer: made three unsuccessful voyages in search of the Northwest Passage (1576; 1577; 1578), visiting Labrador and Baffin Island

frock *n old-fashioned* **1** a girl's or woman's dress **2** a loose garment, formerly worn by peasants
WORD ORIGIN Old French *froc*

frock coat *n* a man's skirted coat, as worn in the 19th century

Fröding *n* **Gustaf** 1860–1911, Swedish poet. His popular lyric verse includes the collections *Guitar and Concertina* (1891), *New Poems* (1894), and *Splashes and Rags* (1896)

frog[1] *n* **1** a smooth-skinned tailless amphibian with long back legs used for jumping **2 a frog in one's throat** phlegm on the vocal cords, hindering speech
WORD ORIGIN Old English *frogga*

frog[2] *n* a military style fastening on a coat consisting of a button and a loop **frogging** *n*
WORD ORIGIN origin unknown

frog[3] *n* horny material in the centre of the sole of a horse's foot
WORD ORIGIN origin unknown

frogman *n, pl* **-men** a swimmer equipped with a rubber suit, flippers, and breathing equipment for working underwater

frogmarch *n* **1** a method of carrying a resisting person in which each limb is held and the victim is face downwards ▹*vb* **2** to carry in a frogmarch or cause to move forward unwillingly

frogspawn *n* a jelly-like substance containing a frog's eggs

Froissart *n* **Jean** ?1333–?1400, French chronicler and poet, noted for his *Chronique*, a vivid history of Europe from 1325 to 1400

frolic *vb* **-icking, -icked** **1** to run and play in a lively way ▹*n* **2** lively and merry behaviour **3** a light-hearted occasion
WORD ORIGIN Dutch *vrolijk*

frolicsome *adj* merry and playful

from *prep* **1** indicating the original location, situation, etc.: *from America* **2** in a period of time starting at: *from 1950 to the current year* **3** indicating the distance between two things or places: *60 miles from the Iraqi border* **4** indicating a lower amount: *from 5 to 6* **5** showing the model of: *drawn from life* **6** used with a verbal noun to denote prohibition, etc.: *she was banned from smoking at meetings* **7** because of: *five hundred horses collapsed from exhaustion*
WORD ORIGIN Old English *fram*

fromage frais (from-ahzh fray) *n* a low-fat soft cheese with a smooth light texture
WORD ORIGIN French: fresh cheese

Fromm *n* **Erich** 1900–80, US psychologist and philosopher, born in Germany. His works include *The Art of Loving* (1956) and *To Have and To Be* (1976)

frond *n* **1** the compound leaf of a fern **2** the leaf of a palm
WORD ORIGIN Latin *frons*

front ❶ *n* **1** that part or side that is forward, or most often seen or used **2** a position or place directly before or ahead **3** the beginning, opening, or first part **4** the position of leadership **5** a promenade at a seaside resort **6** *mil* **a** the total area in which opposing armies face each other **b** the space in which a military unit is operating **7** *meteorol* the dividing line between two different air masses **8** an outward appearance: *he put on a bold front* **9** *informal* a business or other activity serving as a respectable cover for another, usually criminal, organization **10** Also called: **front man** a nominal leader of an organization **11** a particular field of activity: *on the economic front* **12** a group of people with a common goal: *the National Liberation Front* ▹*adj* **13** of, at, or in the front ▹*vb* **14** to face (onto) **15** to be a front of or for **16** to appear as a presenter in (a television show) **17** to be the leader of (a band) on stage
WORD ORIGIN Latin *frons* forehead, foremost part

frontage *n* **1** the facade of a building or the front of a plot of ground **2** the extent of the front of a shop, plot of land, etc.

frontal *adj* **1** of, at, or in the front **2** of or relating to the forehead
WORD ORIGIN Latin *frons* forehead

front bench *n* (in Britain) the leadership of either the Government or Opposition in the House of Commons or in various other legislative assemblies **front-bencher** *n*

Frontenac *or* **Frontenac et Palluau** *n* **Comte de** title of *Louis de Buade*. 1620–98, governor of New France (1672–82; 1689–98)

frontier ❶ *n* **1** the region of a country bordering on another or a line marking such a boundary **2** the edge of the settled area of a country

THESAURUS

front *n* **1a = foreground**, fore, forefront, nearest part **1b = exterior**, facing, face, façade, frontage, anterior, obverse, forepart **3 = head**, start, lead, beginning, top, fore, forefront **6a** *(mil)* **= front line**, trenches, vanguard, firing line, van **9** *(informal)* **= disguise**, cover, blind, mask, cover-up, cloak, façade, pretext ▹*adj* **13a = foremost**, at the front **OPPOSITE:** back **13b = leading**, first, lead, head, foremost, topmost, headmost ▹*vb* **14** *(often with* **onto***)* **= face onto**, overlook, look out on, have a view of, look over *or* onto

frontier *n* **1 = border**, limit, edge, bound, boundary, confines, verge,

DICTIONARY

3 frontiers the limit of knowledge in a particular field: *twenty years ago, laser spectroscopy was on the frontiers of chemical research*
WORD ORIGIN Old French *front* part which is opposite

frontispiece *n* an illustration facing the title page of a book
WORD ORIGIN Late Latin *frontispicium* facade

frontrunner *n informal* the leader or a favoured contestant in a race or election

frosh *n US & Canad informal* a freshman

f

frost ❶ *n* **1** a white deposit of ice particles **2** an atmospheric temperature of below freezing point, producing this deposit ▷*vb* **3** to cover with frost **4** to kill or damage (plants) with frost
WORD ORIGIN Old English

frostbite *n* destruction of tissues, esp. of the fingers, ears, toes, and nose, by freezing **frostbitten** *adj*

frosted *adj* (of glass) having the surface roughened so that it cannot be seen through clearly

frosting *n chiefly US & Canad* icing

frosty *adj* **frostier, frostiest** **1** characterized by frost: *the frosty air* **2** covered by frost **3** unfriendly or disapproving: *a frosty reception from the bank manager* **frostily** *adv* **frostiness** *n*

froth *n* **1** a mass of small bubbles of air or a gas in a liquid **2** a mixture of saliva and air bubbles formed at the lips in certain diseases, such as rabies **3** trivial but superficially attractive ideas or entertainment ▷*vb* **4** to produce or cause to produce froth **frothy** *adj*
WORD ORIGIN Old Norse *frotha*

Froude *n* **1 James Anthony** 1818–94, English historian; author of a controversial biography (1882–84) of Carlyle. **2** his brother **William** 1810–79, English civil engineer

frown ❶ *vb* **1** to wrinkle one's brows in worry, anger, or concentration **2 frown on** to disapprove of: *smoking at work is frowned on* ▷*n* **3** the act of frowning **4** a look of disapproval or displeasure
WORD ORIGIN Old French *froigner*

frowsty *adj* **frowstier, frowstiest** *Brit* stale or musty
WORD ORIGIN from *frowzy*

frowzy *or* **frowsy** *adj* **frowzier, frowziest** *or* **frowsier, frowsiest** **1** slovenly or unkempt in appearance **2** musty and stale
WORD ORIGIN origin unknown

froze *vb* ▸ the past tense of **freeze**

frozen ❶ *vb* **1** ▸ the past participle of **freeze** ▷*adj* **2** turned into or covered with ice **3** killed or stiffened by extreme cold **4** (of food) preserved by a freezing process **5 a** (of prices or wages) officially fixed at a certain level **b** (of business assets) not convertible into cash **6** motionless: *she was frozen in horror*

FRS (in Britain) Fellow of the Royal Society

fructify *vb* **-fies, -fying, -fied** to bear or cause to bear fruit
WORD ORIGIN Latin *fructus* fruit + *facere* to produce

fructose *n* a crystalline sugar occurring in honey and many fruits
WORD ORIGIN Latin *fructus* fruit

frugal (froo-gl) *adj* **1** economical in the use of money or resources; thrifty **2** meagre and inexpensive: *a frugal meal* **frugality** *n* **frugally** *adv*
WORD ORIGIN Latin *frugi* useful, temperate

fruit ❶ *n* **1** any fleshy part of a plant that supports the seeds and is edible, such as the strawberry **2** *bot* the ripened ovary of a flowering plant, containing one or more seeds **3** any plant product useful to man, including grain and vegetables **4 fruits** the results of an action or effort, esp. if pleasant: *they have enjoyed the fruits of a complete victory* ▷*vb* **5** to bear fruit
WORD ORIGIN Latin *fructus* enjoyment, fruit

fruiterer *n chiefly Brit & Austral* a person who sells fruit

fruit fly *n* **1** a small fly that feeds on and lays its eggs in plant tissues **2** a similar fly that feeds on plant sap, decaying fruit, etc. and is widely used in genetic experiments

fruitful *adj* **1** producing good and useful results: *a fruitful relationship* **2** bearing much fruit **fruitfully** *adv*

fruition (froo-ish-on) *n* **1** the fulfilment of something worked for or desired **2** the act or condition of bearing fruit
WORD ORIGIN Latin *frui* to enjoy

fruitless *adj* **1** producing nothing of value: *a fruitless debate* **2** without fruit **fruitlessly** *adv*

fruit machine *n Brit & NZ* a coin-operated gambling machine that pays out money when a particular combination of diagrams, usually of fruit, appears on a screen

fruit salad *or* **cocktail** *n* a dish consisting of pieces of different kinds of fruit

fruit sugar *n* ▸ same as **fructose**

fruity *adj* **fruitier, fruitiest** **1** of or like fruit **2** (of a voice) mellow or rich **3** *informal, chiefly Brit* referring humorously to things relating to sex **fruitiness** *n*

frump *n* a woman who dresses in a dull and old-fashioned way **frumpy** *or* **frumpish** *adj*
WORD ORIGIN Middle Dutch *verrompelen* to wrinkle

frustrate ❶ *vb* **-trating, -trated** **1** to upset or anger (a person) by presenting difficulties that cannot be overcome: *his lack of ambition frustrated me* **2** to hinder or prevent (the efforts, plans, or desires) of **frustrating** *adj* **frustration** *n*
WORD ORIGIN Latin *frustrare* to cheat

frustrated ❶ *adj* dissatisfied or unfulfilled

frustum *n, pl* **-tums** *or* **-ta** *geom* the part of a solid, such as a cone or pyramid, contained between the base and a plane parallel to the base that intersects the solid
WORD ORIGIN Latin: piece

fry[1] *vb* **fries, frying, fried** **1** to cook or be cooked in fat or oil, usually over direct heat ▷*n, pl* **fries** **2** Also: **fry-up** *informal* a dish of mixed fried food ▸ See also **fries** > **fryer** *or* **frier** *n*
WORD ORIGIN Latin *frigere*

fry[2] *pl n* **1** the young of various species of fish **2** ▸ see **small fry**
WORD ORIGIN Old French *freier* to spawn

Fry *n* **1 Christopher** 1907–2005, English dramatist; author of the verse dramas *A Phoenix Too Frequent* (1946), *The Lady's Not For Burning* (1948), and *Venus Observed* (1950) **2 Elizabeth** 1780–1845, English prison reformer and Quaker **3 Roger Eliot** 1866–1934, English art critic and painter who helped to introduce the postimpressionists to Britain. His books include *Vision and Design* (1920) and *Cézanne* (1927) **4 Stephen (John)** born 1957, British writer, actor, and

THESAURUS

perimeter, borderline, dividing line, borderland, marches

frost *n* **1, 2 = hoarfrost**, freeze, freeze-up, Jack Frost, rime

frown *vb* **1 = glare**, scowl, glower, make a face, look daggers, knit your brows, give a dirty look, lour *or* lower ▷*n* **4 = scowl**, glare, glower, dirty look

frozen *adj* **2 = icy**, hard, solid, frosted, arctic, ice-covered, icebound **3 = ice-cold**, freezing, numb, very cold, frigid, frozen stiff, chilled to the marrow **4 = chilled**, cold, iced, refrigerated, ice-cold

fruit *n* **4** *(pl)* **= result**, reward, outcome, end result, return, effect, benefit, profit, advantage, consequence

frustrate *vb* **2 = thwart**, stop, check, block, defeat, disappoint, counter, confront, spoil, foil, baffle, inhibit, hobble, balk, circumvent, forestall, neutralize, stymie, nullify, render null and void, crool *or* cruel *(Austral slang)* **OPPOSITE:** further

frustrated *adj* **= disappointed**, discouraged, infuriated, discontented, exasperated, resentful, embittered, irked, disheartened, carrying a chip on

DICTIONARY

comedian; his novels include *The Liar* (1991) and *The Stars' Tennis Balls* (2000)
frying pan *n* **1** a long-handled shallow pan used for frying **2 out of the frying pan into the fire** from a bad situation to a worse one
FSH *biol* follicle-stimulating hormone: a hormone secreted by the pituitary gland
f-stop *n photog* any of the lens aperture settings of a camera
ft. foot or feet
ftp file transfer protocol: a standard protocol for transferring files across a network, esp. the internet
Fuad I *n* original name *Ahmed Fuad Pasha*. 1868–1936, sultan of Egypt (1917–22) and king (1922–36)
Fuchs *n* **1 Klaus Emil** 1911–88, East German physicist. He was born in Germany, became a British citizen (1942), and was imprisoned (1950–59) for giving secret atomic research information to the Soviet Union **2** Sir **Vivian Ernest** 1908–99, English explorer and geologist: led the Commonwealth Trans-Antarctic Expedition (1955–58)
fuchsia (fyew-sha) *n* an ornamental shrub with hanging purple, red, or white flowers
WORD ORIGIN after Leonhard *Fuchs*, botanist
fuck *taboo vb* **1** to have sexual intercourse with (someone) ▷ *n* **2** an act of sexual intercourse **3** *slang* a partner in sexual intercourse **4 not give a fuck** not to care at all ▷ *interj* **5** *offensive* an expression of strong disgust or anger **fucking** *n, adj, adv*
WORD ORIGIN Germanic
fuck off *vb offensive taboo slang* to go away
fuck up *vb offensive taboo slang* to make a mess of (something)
fuddle *vb* **-dling, -dled 1** to cause to be confused or intoxicated ▷ *n* **2** a confused state **fuddled** *adj*
WORD ORIGIN origin unknown
fuddy-duddy *n, pl* **-dies** *informal* a person, esp. an elderly one, who is extremely conservative or dull
WORD ORIGIN origin unknown
fudge[1] *n* a soft sweet made from sugar, butter, and milk
WORD ORIGIN origin unknown
fudge[2] ❶ *vb* **fudging, fudged 1** to make (an issue or problem) less clear deliberately **2** to avoid making a firm statement or decision
WORD ORIGIN origin unknown
fuel *n* **1** any substance burned for heat or power, such as coal or petrol **2** the material that produces energy by fission in a nuclear reactor **3 add fuel to** to make (a difficult situation) worse ▷ *vb* **fuelling, fuelled** or *US* **fueling, fueled 4** to supply with or receive fuel **5** to intensify or make worse (a feeling or situation): *the move is bound to fuel speculation*
WORD ORIGIN Old French *feu* fire
fuel cell *n* a cell in which chemical energy is converted directly into electrical energy
Fuentes *n* **Carlos** born 1928, Mexican novelist and writer. His novels include *A Change of Skin* (1967), *Terra Nostra* (1975), and *Cristóbal Nonato* (1987)
fug *n chiefly Brit & NZ* a hot stale atmosphere **fuggy** *adj*
WORD ORIGIN origin unknown
Fugard *n* **Athol** born 1932, South African dramatist and theatre director. His plays include *The Blood-Knot* (1961), *Sizwe Bansi is Dead* (1972), *Statements after an Arrest under the Immorality Act* (1974), and *The Captain's Tiger* (1999)
fugitive ❶ (fyew-jit-iv) *n* **1** a person who flees, esp. from arrest or pursuit ▷ *adj* **2** fleeing **3** not permanent; fleeting
WORD ORIGIN Latin *fugere* to take flight
fugu *n* any of various marine pufferfish eaten in Japan once certain lethally poisonous parts have been removed
WORD ORIGIN Japanese
fugue (fyewg) *n* a musical form consisting of a theme repeated above or below the continuing first statement **fugal** *adj*
WORD ORIGIN French
Führer *n* a leader: the title used by Hitler as Nazi dictator
WORD ORIGIN German
-ful *suffix* **1** full of or characterized by: *painful; restful* **2** able or tending to: *useful* ▷ *suffix* **3** as much as will fill the thing specified: *mouthful*
fulcrum *n, pl* **-crums** or **-cra** the pivot about which a lever turns
WORD ORIGIN Latin: foot of a couch
fulfil ❶ or *US* **fulfill** *vb* **-filling, -filled 1** to bring about the achievement of (a desire or promise) **2** to carry out (a request or order) **3** to satisfy (demands or conditions) **4 fulfil oneself** to achieve one's potential **fulfilment** or *US* **fulfillment** *n*
WORD ORIGIN Old English *fulfyllan*
full[1] ❶ *adj* **1** holding as much or as many as possible **2** abundant in supply: *full of enthusiasm* **3** having consumed enough food or drink **4** (of the face or figure) rounded or plump **5** complete: *the full amount* **6** with all privileges or rights: *full membership* **7** *music* powerful or rich in volume and sound **8** (of a garment) containing a large amount of fabric **9 full of** engrossed with: *she had been full of her own plans lately* **10 full of oneself** full of pride or conceit **11 full up** filled to capacity ▷ *adv* **12** completely or entirely **13** directly or right: *she hit him full in the face* **14 full well** very or extremely well: *we knew full well that she was watching every move we made* ▷ *n* **15 in full** without omitting or shortening **16 to the full** thoroughly or fully **fullness** or *esp. US* **fulness** *n*
WORD ORIGIN Old English
full[2] *vb* to make (cloth) more compact during manufacture through shrinking and beating
WORD ORIGIN Old French *fouler*
fullback *n soccer, hockey, & rugby* a defensive player
full-blooded *adj* **1** vigorous or enthusiastic **2** (esp. of horses) having ancestors of a single race or breed
full-blown *adj* fully developed
full board *n* the daily provision by a hotel of bed, breakfast, and midday and evening meals
full-bodied *adj* having a full rich flavour or quality: *a full-bodied vintage port*
fuller's earth *n* a natural absorbent clay used for fulling cloth
full-frontal *adj informal* exposing the genitals to full view
full house *n* **1** a theatre filled to capacity **2** (in bingo) the set of numbers needed to win

f

THESAURUS

your shoulder *(informal)*
fudge[2] *vb* **1 = misrepresent**, fake, flannel *(Brit informal)*, falsify **2 = equivocate**, avoid, dodge, evade, hedge, stall
fugitive *n* **1 = runaway**, refugee, deserter, escapee, runagate *(archaic)*
fulfil or *(US)* **fulfill** *vb* **1 = achieve**, realize, satisfy, attain, consummate, bring to fruition, perfect **2 = carry out**, perform, execute, discharge, keep, effect, finish, complete, achieve, conclude, accomplish, bring to completion
OPPOSITE: neglect
3a = satisfy, please, content, cheer, refresh, gratify, make happy
3b = comply with, meet, fill, satisfy, observe, obey, conform to, answer
full[1] *adj* **1 = filled**, stocked, brimming, replete, complete, entire, loaded, sufficient, intact, gorged, saturated, bursting at the seams, brimful **3 = satiated**, satisfied, having had enough, replete, sated **4 = plump**, rounded, voluptuous, shapely, well-rounded, buxom, curvaceous **6 = comprehensive**, complete, thorough, exhaustive, all-inclusive, all-embracing, unabridged **7** *(music)* **= rich**, strong, deep, loud, distinct, resonant, sonorous, clear
OPPOSITE: thin
8 = voluminous, large, loose, baggy, billowing, puffy, capacious, loose-fitting, balloon-like **OPPOSITE:** tight

DICTIONARY

full-length *adj* 1 (of a mirror, portrait, etc.) showing the complete human figure 2 not abridged
full moon *n* the phase of the moon when it is visible as a fully illuminated disc
full-on *adj informal* complete; unrestrained: *full-on military intervention*
full-scale ❶ *adj* 1 (of a plan) of actual size 2 using all resources; all-out
full stop *n* the punctuation mark (.) used at the end of a sentence and after abbreviations. Also called (esp. US and Canad.): **period**
full-time *adj* 1 for all of the normal working week: *a full-time job* ▷ *adv* **full time** 2 on a full-time basis: *she worked full time until she was 72* ▷ *n* **full time** 3 *soccer, rugby & hockey* the end of the game
full toss *or* **pitch** *n cricket* a bowled ball that reaches the batsman without bouncing
fully ❶ *adv* 1 to the greatest degree or extent 2 amply or adequately 3 at least: *fully a hundred people*
fully-fashioned *adj* (of stockings or knitwear) shaped and seamed so as to fit closely
fulmar *n* a heavily-built Arctic sea bird with a short tail
WORD ORIGIN Scandinavian
fulminate *vb* **-nating, -nated** ▪ **fulminate against** to criticize or denounce angrily **fulmination** *n*
WORD ORIGIN Latin *fulmen* lightning that strikes
fulsome *adj* 1 exaggerated and elaborate, and often sounding insincere: *fulsome praise* 2 *not standard* extremely complimentary
Fulton *n* **Robert** 1765–1815, US engineer: designed the first successful steamboat (1807) and steam warship (1814)
fumble ❶ *vb* **-bling, -bled** 1 to use the hands clumsily or grope about blindly: *fumbling for a cigarette* 2 to say or do awkwardly ▷ *n* 3 the act of fumbling
WORD ORIGIN probably Scandinavian
fume ❶ *vb* **fuming, fumed** 1 to be overcome with anger or fury 2 to give off (fumes) or (of fumes) to be given off, esp. during a chemical reaction 3 to treat with fumes ▷ *n* 4 *(often pl)* pungent or toxic vapour, gas, or smoke: *exhaust fumes*
WORD ORIGIN Latin *fumus* smoke, vapour
fumigate (fyew-mig-gate) *vb* **-gating, -gated** to treat (something contaminated) with fumes **fumigation** *n*
WORD ORIGIN Latin *fumus* smoke + *agere* to drive
fun ❶ *n* 1 pleasant, enjoyable, and light-hearted activity or amusement 2 **for** *or* **in fun** for amusement or as a joke 3 **make fun of** *or* **poke fun at** to ridicule or tease ▷ *adj* 4 (of a person) amusing and likeable 5 (of a place or activity) amusing and enjoyable
WORD ORIGIN obsolete *fon* to make a fool of
function ❶ *n* 1 the intended role or purpose of a person or thing 2 an official or formal social gathering 3 a factor, the precise nature of which depends upon another thing in some way: *muscle breakdown is a function of vitamin E deficiency* 4 *maths* a quantity, the value of which depends on the varying value of another quantity 5 a sequence of operations that a computer or calculator performs when a specified key is pressed ▷ *vb* 6 to operate or work 7 **function as** to perform the action or role of (something or someone else)
WORD ORIGIN Latin *functio*
functional ❶ *adj* 1 of or performing a function 2 practical rather than decorative 3 in working order 4 *med* affecting a function of an organ without structural change **functionally** *adv*
functional food *n* a food containing additives which provide extra nutritional value. Also called: **nutraceutical**
functionalism *n* the theory that the form of a thing should be determined by its use **functionalist** *n, adj*
functionary *n, pl* **-aries** a person acting in an official capacity, such as for a government; official
fund ❶ *n* 1 a reserve of money set aside for a certain purpose 2 a supply or store of something ▷ *vb* 3 to provide money to 4 *finance* to convert (short-term debt) into long-term debt bearing fixed interest ▸ See also **funds** > **funder** *n*
WORD ORIGIN Latin *fundus* the bottom, piece of land
fundamental ❶ *adj* 1 essential or primary: *fundamental mathematical concepts* 2 basic: *a fundamental error* ▷ *n*

THESAURUS

full-scale *adj* 2 = **major**, extensive, wide-ranging, all-out, sweeping, comprehensive, proper, thorough, in-depth, exhaustive, all-encompassing, thoroughgoing, full-dress
fully *adv* 1a = **completely**, totally, perfectly, entirely, absolutely, altogether, thoroughly, intimately, wholly, positively, utterly, every inch, heart and soul, to the hilt, one hundred per cent, in all respects, from first to last, lock, stock and barrel 1b = **in all respects**, completely, totally, entirely, altogether, thoroughly, wholly
fumble *vb* 1 = **grope**, flounder, paw *(informal)*, scrabble, feel around
fume *vb* 1 = **rage**, boil, seethe, see red *(informal)*, storm, rave, rant, smoulder, crack up *(informal)*, go ballistic *(slang, chiefly US)*, champ at the bit *(informal)*, blow a fuse *(slang, chiefly US)*, fly off the handle *(informal)*, get hot under the collar *(informal)*, go off the deep end *(informal)*, wig out *(slang)*, go up the wall *(slang)*, get steamed up about *(slang)* ▷ *n* 4 *(often pl)* = **smoke**, gas, exhaust, pollution, haze, vapour, smog, miasma, exhalation, effluvium
fun *n* 1a = **amusement**, sport, treat, pleasure, entertainment, cheer, good time, recreation, enjoyment, romp, distraction, diversion, frolic, junketing, merriment, whoopee *(informal)*, high jinks, living it up, jollity, beer and skittles *(informal)*, merrymaking, jollification 1b = **enjoyment**, pleasure, joy, cheer, mirth, gaiety OPPOSITE: gloom 3 **make fun of something** *or* **someone** = **mock**, tease, ridicule, poke fun at, take off, rag, rib *(informal)*, laugh at, taunt, mimic, parody, deride, send up *(Brit informal)*, scoff at, sneer at, lampoon, make a fool of, pour scorn on, take the mickey out of *(Brit informal)*, satirize, pull someone's leg, hold up to ridicule, make a monkey of, make sport of, make the butt of, make game of ▷ *adj* 5 = **enjoyable**, entertaining, pleasant, amusing, lively, diverting, witty, convivial
function *n* 1 = **purpose**, business, job, concern, use, part, office, charge, role, post, operation, situation, activity, exercise, responsibility, task, duty, mission, employment, capacity, province, occupation, raison d'être *(French)* 2 = **reception**, party, affair, gathering, bash *(informal)*, lig *(Brit slang)*, social occasion, soiree, do *(informal)* ▷ *vb* 6 = **work**, run, operate, perform, be in business, be in running order, be in operation *or* action, go 7 *(with* **as**) = **act**, serve, operate, perform, behave, officiate, act the part of, do duty, have the role of, be in commission, be in operation *or* action, serve your turn
functional *adj* 2 = **practical**, utility, utilitarian, serviceable, hard-wearing, useful 3 = **working**, operative, operational, in working order, going, prepared, ready, viable, up and running, workable, usable
fund *n* 1 = **reserve**, stock, supply, store, collection, pool, foundation, endowment, tontine ▷ *vb* 3 = **finance**, back, support, pay for, promote, float, endow, subsidize,

DICTIONARY

3 fundamentals the most important and basic parts of a subject or activity **4** the lowest note of a harmonic series **fundamentally** *adv*

fundamentalism *n* **1** *Christianity* the view that the Bible is literally true **2** *islam* a movement favouring strict observance of Islamic law **fundamentalist** *n, adj*

fundamental particle *n physics* ▸ same as **elementary particle**

fundholding *n* the system in which general practitioners may choose to receive a fixed budget from which they pay for non-urgent hospital treatment and drug costs for patients

fundi ❶ (foon-dee) *n S African* an expert
WORD ORIGIN Nguni (language group of southern Africa) *umfindisi*

funding *n* **1** the provision of money for a project or organization **2** the amount of money provided

fundraiser *n* **1** a person involved in organizing fundraising activities **2** an event held to raise money for a cause

fundraising *n* **1** the activity involved in raising money for a cause ▹ *adj* **2** of, for, or relating to fundraising: *a fundraising disco*

funds ❶ *pl n* money that is readily available

funeral ❶ *n* **1** a ceremony at which a dead person is buried or cremated **2 it's your funeral** *informal* a mistake has been made and you alone will be responsible for its consequences ▹ *adj* **3** of or for a funeral **funerary** *adj*
WORD ORIGIN Latin *funus*

funeral director *n* an undertaker

funeral parlour *n* a place where the dead are prepared for burial or cremation

funereal (fyew-neer-ee-al) *adj* suggestive of a funeral; gloomy or sombre **funereally** *adv*

funfair *n Brit* an amusement park with machines to ride on and stalls

fungicide *n* a substance used to destroy fungi
WORD ORIGIN FUNGUS + Latin *caedere* to kill

fungoid *adj* resembling a fungus

fungous *adj* appearing suddenly and spreading quickly like a fungus

fungus *n, pl* **fungi** *or* **funguses** a plant without leaves, flowers, or roots, that reproduce by spores, including moulds, yeasts, and mushrooms **fungal** *adj*
WORD ORIGIN Latin

funicular (fyew-nik-yew-lar) *n* a railway up the side of a mountain, consisting of two cars at either end of a cable passing round a driving wheel at the summit. Also called: **funicular railway**
WORD ORIGIN Latin *funis* rope

funk[1] *old-fashioned Brit n* **1** a state of nervousness, fear, or depression **2** a coward ▹ *vb* **3** to avoid doing (something) through fear
WORD ORIGIN origin unknown

funk[2] *n* a type of Black dance music with a strong beat
WORD ORIGIN from *funky*

funky *adj* **-kier, -kiest** (of jazz or pop) having a strong beat
WORD ORIGIN from obsolete *funk* to smoke tobacco, perhaps referring to music that is smelly, i.e. earthy

funnel *n* **1** a tube with a wide mouth tapering to a small hole, used for pouring liquids into narrow openings **2** a chimney of a ship or steam train ▹ *vb* **-nelling, -nelled** *or US* **-neling, -neled 3** to move or cause to move through or as if through a funnel
WORD ORIGIN Old Provençal *fonilh*

funnel-web *n Austral* a large poisonous black spider that builds funnel-shaped webs

funny ❶ *adj* **-nier, -niest 1** causing amusement or laughter; humorous **2** peculiar or odd **3** *informal* faint or ill: *this smell is making me feel a bit funny* **4 funny business** *informal* suspicious or dubious behaviour **funnily** *adv* **funniness** *n*

funny bone *n* a sensitive area near the elbow where the nerve is close to the surface of the skin

fur *n* **1** the dense coat of fine silky hairs on many mammals **2** the skin of certain animals, with the hair left on **3** a garment made of fur **4 make the fur fly** to cause a scene or disturbance **5** *informal* a whitish coating on the tongue, caused by illness **6** *Brit* a deposit on the insides of water pipes or kettles, caused by hard water ▹ *vb* **furring, furred 7** Also: **fur up** to cover or become covered with a furlike deposit
WORD ORIGIN Old French *fuerre* sheath

furbelow *n old-fashioned* **1** a pleated or gathered piece of material used as a decoration on a woman's garment; ruffle **2 furbelows** showy ornamentation
WORD ORIGIN French dialect *farbella* a frill

furbish *vb formal* to brighten up or renovate
WORD ORIGIN Old French *fourbir* to polish

furcate *vb* **-cating, -cated 1** to divide into two parts ▹ *adj* **2** forked: *furcate branches* **furcation** *n*
WORD ORIGIN Latin *furca* a fork

Furies *pl n, sing* **Fury** *classical myth* the goddesses of vengeance, who pursued unpunished criminals

furious ❶ *adj* **1** extremely angry or annoyed **2** violent or unrestrained, such as in speed or energy: *fast and furious dance routines* **furiously** *adv*

f

THESAURUS

stake, capitalize, provide money for, put up the money for

fundamental *adj* **1 = central**, first, most important, prime, key, necessary, basic, essential, primary, vital, radical, principal, cardinal, integral, indispensable, intrinsic
OPPOSITE: incidental
2 = basic, essential, underlying, organic, profound, elementary, rudimentary

fundi *n (S African)* **= expert**, authority, specialist, professional, master, pro *(informal)*, ace *(informal)*, genius, guru, pundit, buff *(informal)*, maestro, virtuoso, boffin *(Brit informal)*, hotshot *(informal)*, past master, dab hand *(Brit informal)*, wonk *(informal)*, maven *(US)*

funds *pl n* **= money**, capital, cash, finance, means, savings, necessary *(informal)*, resources, assets, silver, bread *(slang)*, wealth, tin *(slang)*, brass *(Northern English dialect)*, dough *(slang)*, rhino *(Brit slang)*, the ready *(informal)*, dosh *(Brit & Austral slang)*, hard cash, the wherewithal, needful *(informal)*, shekels *(informal)*, dibs *(slang)*, ready money, ackers *(slang)*, spondulicks *(slang)*

funeral *n* **1 = burial**, committal, laying to rest, cremation, interment, obsequies, entombment, inhumation

funny *adj* **1a = humorous**, amusing, comical, entertaining, killing *(informal)*, rich, comic, silly, ridiculous, diverting, absurd, jolly, witty, hilarious, ludicrous, laughable, farcical, slapstick, riotous, droll, risible, facetious, jocular, side-splitting, waggish, jocose OPPOSITE: unfunny
1b = comic, comical, a scream, a card *(informal)*, a caution *(informal)*
2 = peculiar, odd, strange, unusual, remarkable, bizarre, puzzling, curious, weird, mysterious, suspicious, dubious, queer, rum *(Brit slang)*, quirky, perplexing **3** *(informal)* **= ill**, poorly *(informal)*, queasy, sick, odd, crook *(Austral & NZ informal)*, ailing, queer, unhealthy, seedy *(informal)*, unwell, out of sorts *(informal)*, off-colour *(informal)*, under the weather *(informal)*

furious *adj* **1 = angry**, mad, raging, boiling, fuming, choked, frantic, frenzied, infuriated, incensed, enraged, maddened, inflamed, very angry, cross, livid *(informal)*, up in arms, incandescent, on the warpath *(informal)*, foaming at the mouth, wrathful, in high dudgeon, wroth *(archaic)*, fit to be tied *(slang)*, beside yourself, tooshie *(Austral slang)*
OPPOSITE: pleased

DICTIONARY

furl *vb* to roll up (an umbrella, flag, or sail) neatly and securely
WORD ORIGIN Old French *ferm* tight + *lier* to bind

furlong *n* a unit of length equal to 220 yards (201.168 metres)
WORD ORIGIN Old English *furlang*, from *furh* furrow + *lang* long

furlough (fur-loh) *n* leave of absence from military or other duty
WORD ORIGIN Dutch *verlof*

furnace *n* **1** an enclosed chamber in which heat is produced to destroy refuse or smelt ores **2** *informal* a very hot place
WORD ORIGIN Latin *fornax*

furnish ⓘ *vb* **1** to provide (a house or room) with furniture, etc. **2** to supply or provide **furnished** *adj*
WORD ORIGIN Old French *fournir*

furnishings *pl n* furniture, carpets, and fittings with which a room or house is furnished

furniture ⓘ *n* the large movable articles, such as chairs and tables, that equip a room or house
WORD ORIGIN Old French *fournir* to equip

Furnivall *n* **Frederick James** 1825–1910, English philologist: founder of the Early English Text Society and one of the founders of the *Oxford English Dictionary*

furore ⓘ (fyew-**ror**-ee) *n* a very angry or excited reaction by people to something: *the furore over 'The Satanic Verses'*
WORD ORIGIN Latin *furor* frenzy

Furphy *n* **Joseph**, pen name *Tom Collins* 1843–1912, Australian author. His works include the classic Australian novel *Such is Life* (1903) and *The Buln-Buln and the Brolga* (1948)

furrier *n* a person who makes or sells fur garments
WORD ORIGIN Middle English *furour*

furrow *n* **1** a long narrow trench made in the ground by a plough **2** any long deep groove, esp. a deep wrinkle on the forehead ▹*vb* **3** to become wrinkled **4** to make furrows in (land)
WORD ORIGIN Old English *furh*

furry *adj* **-rier, -riest** like or covered with fur or something furlike

further ⓘ *adv* **1** in addition **2** to a greater degree or extent **3** to or at a more advanced point **4** to or at a greater distance in time or space ▹*adj* **5** additional **6** more distant or remote in time or space ▹*vb* **7** to assist the progress of (something) **furtherance** *n*
WORD ORIGIN Old English *furthor*

further education *n* (in Britain, Australia, and South Africa) formal education beyond school other than at university

furthermore ⓘ *adv* in addition

furthest ⓘ *adv* **1** to the greatest degree or extent **2** to or at the greatest distance in time or space; farthest ▹*adj* **3** most distant in time or space; farthest

furtive *adj* sly, cautious, and secretive **furtively** *adv*
WORD ORIGIN Latin *furtivus* stolen

Furtwängler *n* **Wilhelm** 1886–1954, German conductor, noted for his interpretations of Wagner

fury ⓘ *n, pl* **-ries 1** violent anger **2** uncontrolled violence: *the fury of the sea* **3** an outburst of violent anger **4** a person with a violent temper **5 like fury** *old-fashioned* with great energy, strength, or power
WORD ORIGIN Latin *furere* to be furious

Fury *n, pl* **-ries** ▸see **Furies**

furze *n* gorse **furzy** *adj*
WORD ORIGIN Old English *fyrs*

fuse[1] *or US* **fuze** *n* **1** a lead containing an explosive for detonating a bomb ▹*vb* **fusing, fused** *or US* **fuzing, fuzed 2** to equip with such a fuse
WORD ORIGIN Latin *fusus* spindle

fuse[2] *n* **1** a protective device for safeguarding electric circuits, containing a wire that melts and breaks the circuit when the current exceeds a certain value ▹*vb* **fusing, fused 2** *Brit* to fail or cause to fail as a result of a fuse blowing **3** to equip (a plug or circuit) with a fuse **4** to join or become combined: *the two ideas fused in his mind* **5** to unite or become united by melting **6** to become or cause to become liquid, esp. by the action of heat
WORD ORIGIN Latin *fusus* melted, cast

fuselage (fyew-zill-lahzh) *n* the main body of an aircraft
WORD ORIGIN French

Fuseli *n* **Henry** original name *Johann Heinrich Füssli*. 1741–1825, British painter, born in Switzerland. His paintings include *Nightmare* (1782)

fusible *adj* capable of being melted

fusilier (fyew-zill-**leer**) *n* (formerly) an infantryman armed with a light musket: a term still used in the names of certain British regiments
WORD ORIGIN French

fusillade (fyew-zill-**lade**) *n* **1** a rapid continual discharge of firearms **2** a sudden outburst of criticism, questions, etc.
WORD ORIGIN French *fusiller* to shoot

fusilli (foo-**zee**-li) *n* pasta in the form of short spirals
WORD ORIGIN Italian

fusion *n* **1** the act or process of melting together **2** something produced by fusing **3** a kind of popular music that is a blend of two or more styles, such as jazz and funk **4** something new created by a mixture of qualities, ideas, or things **5** ▸see **nuclear fusion** ▹*adj* **6** relating to a style of cooking that combines traditional Western techniques and ingredients with those used in Eastern cuisine
WORD ORIGIN Latin *fusio* a melting

fuss ⓘ *n* **1** needless activity and worry **2** complaint or objection: *it was silly to make a fuss over seating arrangements* **3** an exhibition of affection or admiration: *when I arrived my nephews*

THESAURUS

2 = violent, wild, intense, fierce, savage, turbulent, stormy, agitated, boisterous, tumultuous, vehement, unrestrained, tempestuous, impetuous, ungovernable

furnish *vb* **1 = decorate**, fit, fit out, appoint, provide, stock, supply, store, provision, outfit, equip, fit up, purvey **2 = supply**, give, offer, provide, present, reveal, grant, afford, hand out, endow, bestow

furniture *n* **= household goods**, furnishings, fittings, house fittings, goods, things *(informal)*, effects, equipment, appointments, possessions, appliances, chattels, movable property, movables

furore *n* **= commotion**, to-do, stir, excitement, fury, disturbance, flap *(informal)*, outburst, frenzy, outcry, uproar, brouhaha, hullabaloo

further *adv* **1 = in addition**, moreover, besides, furthermore, also, yet, on top of, what's more, to boot, additionally, over and above, as well as, into the bargain ▹*adj* **5 = additional**, more, new, other, extra, fresh, supplementary ▹*vb* **7 = promote**, help, develop, aid, forward, champion, push, encourage, speed, advance, work for, foster, contribute to, assist, plug *(informal)*, facilitate, pave the way for, hasten, patronize, expedite, succour, lend support to **OPPOSITE:** hinder

furthermore *adv* **= moreover**, further, in addition, besides, too, as well, not to mention, what's more, to boot, additionally, into the bargain

furthest *adj* **3 = most distant**, extreme, ultimate, remotest, outermost, uttermost, furthermost, outmost

fury *n* **1 = anger**, passion, rage, madness, frenzy, wrath, ire, red mist *(informal)*, impetuosity **OPPOSITE:** calmness
2 = violence, force, power, intensity, severity, turbulence, ferocity, savagery, vehemence, fierceness, tempestuousness **OPPOSITE:** peace

fuss *n* **1 = commotion**, to-do, worry, upset, bother, stir, confusion, excitement, hurry, flap *(informal)*, bustle, flutter, flurry, agitation, fidget, fluster, ado, hue and cry,

DICTIONARY

made a big fuss of me ▹*vb* **4** to worry unnecessarily **5** to be excessively concerned over trivial matters **6** to bother (a person) **7** **fuss over** to show great or excessive concern or affection for
WORD ORIGIN origin unknown

fusspot *n informal* a person who is difficult to please and complains often

fussy *adj* **fussier, fussiest 1** inclined to fuss **2** very particular about detail **3** overelaborate: *a fussy, overdecorated palace* **fussily** *adv*

fustian *n* **1** (formerly) a hard-wearing fabric of cotton mixed with flax or wool **2** pompous talk or writing
WORD ORIGIN Old French *fustaigne*

fusty *adj* **-tier, -tiest 1** smelling of damp or mould **2** old-fashioned **fustiness** *n*
WORD ORIGIN Middle English *fust* wine cask

futile ❶ (fyew-tile) *adj* **1** useless or having no chance of success **2** foolish and of no value: *her futile remarks began to annoy me* **futility** *n*
WORD ORIGIN Latin *futtilis* pouring out easily

futon (foo-tonn) *n* a Japanese padded quilt, laid on the floor as a bed

future ❶ *n* **1** the time yet to come **2** undetermined events that will occur in that time **3** the condition of a person or thing at a later date **4** prospects: *he had faith in its future* **5** *grammar* a tense of verbs used when the action specified has not yet taken place **6** **in future** from now on ▹*adj* **7** that is yet to come or be **8** of or expressing time yet to come **9** destined to become **10** *grammar* in or denoting the future as a tense of verbs ▸See also **futures**
WORD ORIGIN Latin *futurus* about to be

future perfect *grammar adj* **1** denoting a tense of verbs describing an action that will have been performed by a certain time ▹*n* **2** the future perfect tense

futures *pl n* commodities bought or sold at an agreed price for delivery at a specified future date

futurism *n* an early 20th-century artistic movement making use of the characteristics of the machine age **futurist** *n, adj*

futuristic *adj* **1** of design or technology that appears to belong to some future time **2** of futurism

futurity *n, pl* **-ties 1** future **2** a future event

futurology *n* the study or prediction of the future of mankind

fuzz[1] *n* a mass or covering of fine or curly hairs, fibres, etc.
WORD ORIGIN probably from Low German *fussig* loose

fuzz[2] *n Brit, Austral & NZ slang* the police or a policeman
WORD ORIGIN origin unknown

fuzzy ❶ *adj* **fuzzier, fuzziest 1** of, like, or covered with fuzz **2** unclear, blurred, or distorted: *some fuzzy pictures from a Russian radar probe* **3** (of hair) tightly curled **fuzzily** *adv* **fuzziness** *n*

fwd forward

FX *films informal* special effects
WORD ORIGIN a phonetic respelling of *effects*

THESAURUS

palaver, storm in a teacup (*Brit*), pother **2 = complaint**, row, protest, objection, trouble, display, argument, difficulty, upset, bother, unrest, hassle (*informal*), squabble, furore, altercation

futile *adj* **1 = useless**, vain, unsuccessful, pointless, empty, hollow, in vain, worthless, barren, sterile, fruitless, forlorn, unproductive, abortive, to no avail, ineffectual, unprofitable, valueless, unavailing, otiose, profitless, nugatory, without rhyme or reason, bootless **OPPOSITE:** useful

future *n* **1 = time to come**, hereafter, what lies ahead **4 = prospect**, expectation, outlook ▹*adj* **7, 9 = forthcoming**, to be, coming, later, expected, approaching, to come, succeeding, fated, ultimate, subsequent, destined, prospective, eventual, ensuing, impending, unborn, in the offing **OPPOSITE:** past

fuzzy *adj* **1 = frizzy**, fluffy, woolly, downy, flossy, down-covered, linty, napped **2 = indistinct**, faint, blurred, vague, distorted, unclear, shadowy, bleary, unfocused, out of focus, ill-defined **OPPOSITE:** distinct

f

Gg

g **1** gallon(s) **2** gram(s) **3** acceleration due to gravity

G **1** *music* the fifth note of the scale of C major **2** gravity **3** good **4** giga- **5** *slang* grand (a thousand pounds or dollars)

G8 Group of Eight

G20 Group of Twenty: an international organization established to promote global economic stability

Ga *chem* gallium

GA Georgia

gab *informal vb* **gabbing, gabbed** **1** to talk a lot, esp. about unimportant things ▷*n* **2** idle talk **3** **gift of the gab** the ability to talk easily and persuasively
WORD ORIGIN probably from Irish Gaelic *gob* mouth

gabardine *or* **gaberdine** *n* **1** a strong twill cloth used esp. for raincoats **2** a coat made of this cloth
WORD ORIGIN Old French *gauvardine* pilgrim's garment

gabble *vb* **-bling, -bled** **1** to speak rapidly and indistinctly: *the interviewee started to gabble furiously* ▷*n* **2** rapid and indistinct speech
WORD ORIGIN Middle Dutch *gabbelen*

gable *n* the triangular upper part of a wall between the sloping ends of a ridged roof **gabled** *adj*
WORD ORIGIN probably from Old Norse *gafl*

Gable *n* **(William) Clark** 1901–60, US film actor. His films include *It Happened One Night* (1934), *San Francisco* (1936), *Gone with the Wind* (1939), *Mogambo* (1953), and *The Misfits* (1960)

Gabor *n* **Dennis** 1900–79, British electrical engineer, born in Hungary. He invented holography: Nobel prize for physics 1971

Gabriel[1] *n bible* one of the archangels, the messenger of good news (Daniel 8:16–26; Luke 1:11–20, 26–38)

Gabriel[2] *n* **Jacques-Ange** 1698–1782, French architect: designed the Petit Trianon at Versailles

Gabrieli *or* **Gabrielli** *n* **1 Andrea** 1520–86, Italian organist and composer; chief organist of St Mark's, Venice **2** his nephew, **Giovanni** 1558–1612, Italian organist and composer

gad *vb* **gadding, gadded** (foll. by *about* or *around*) to go about in search of pleasure
WORD ORIGIN obsolete *gadling* companion

gadabout *n informal* a person who restlessly seeks amusement

gadfly *n, pl* **-flies** **1** a large fly that bites livestock **2** a constantly irritating person
WORD ORIGIN obsolete *gad* sting

gadget ❶ *n* a small mechanical device or appliance **gadgetry** *n*
WORD ORIGIN perhaps from French *gâchette* trigger

gado-gado *n* an Indonesian dish of cooked mixed vegetables and hard-boiled eggs served with a peanut sauce
WORD ORIGIN Bahasa Indonesia

gadoid (gay-doid) *adj* **1** of or belonging to the cod family of marine fishes ▷*n* **2** any gadoid fish
WORD ORIGIN New Latin *gadus* cod

gadolinium *n chem* a silvery-white metallic element of the rare-earth group. Symbol: Gd
WORD ORIGIN after Johan *Gadolin*, mineralogist

gadzooks *interj archaic* a mild oath
WORD ORIGIN perhaps from *God's hooks* the nails of the cross, from *Gad*, archaic euphemism for *God*

Gael (gayl) *n* a Gaelic-speaker of Scotland, Ireland, or the Isle of Man **Gaeldom** *n*
WORD ORIGIN Gaelic *Gaidheal*

Gaelic (gal-lik, gay-lik) *n* **1** any of the closely related Celtic languages of Scotland, Ireland, or the Isle of Man ▷*adj* **2** of the Celtic people of Scotland, Ireland, or the Isle of Man, or their language

gaff[1] *n* **1** *angling* a pole with a hook attached for landing large fish **2** *naut* a spar hoisted to support a fore-and-aft sail
WORD ORIGIN Provençal *gaf* boat hook

gaff[2] *n* **blow the gaff** *Brit slang* to give away a secret
WORD ORIGIN origin unknown

gaffe *n* something said or done that is socially upsetting or incorrect
WORD ORIGIN French

gaffer *n* **1** *informal, chiefly Brit* a boss or foreman **2** an old man: often used affectionately **3** *informal* the senior electrician on a television or film set
WORD ORIGIN from *godfather*

gag[1] ❶ *vb* **gagging, gagged** **1** to choke as if about to vomit or as if struggling for breath **2** to stop up (a person's mouth), usually with a piece of cloth, to prevent them from speaking or crying out **3** to deprive of free speech ▷*n* **4** something, usually a piece of cloth, stuffed into or tied across the mouth **5** any restraint on free speech **6** a device for keeping the jaws apart: *a dentist's gag*
WORD ORIGIN Middle English *gaggen*

gag[2] ❶ *informal n* **1** a joke, usually one told by a professional comedian ▷*vb* **gagging, gagged** **2** to tell jokes
WORD ORIGIN origin unknown

gaga (gah-gah) *adj informal* **1** confused and suffering some memory loss as a result of old age **2** foolishly doting: *she's gaga over him*
WORD ORIGIN French

gage[1] *n* (formerly) a glove or other object thrown down to indicate a challenge to fight
WORD ORIGIN Old French

gage[2] *n, vb* **gaging, gaged** *US* ▸same as **gauge**

Gage *n* **Thomas** 1721–87, British general and governor in America; commander in chief of British forces at Bunker Hill (1775)

gaggle *n* **1** *informal* a group of people gathered together **2** a flock of geese
WORD ORIGIN Germanic

gaiety *n, pl* **-ties** **1** a state of lively good spirits **2** festivity; merrymaking

gaily *adv* **1** in a lively manner; cheerfully **2** with bright colours

gain ❶ *vb* **1** to acquire (something desirable) **2** to increase, improve, or advance: *wholesale prices gained 5.6 percent* **3** to get to; reach: *gaining the top the hill* **4** (of a watch or clock) to become or be too fast **5** **gain on** to get nearer to or catch up on ▷*n* **6** something won or acquired; profit; advantage: *a clear gain would result* **7** an increase in size or amount **8** *electronics* the ratio of the output signal of an amplifier to the input

THESAURUS

gadget *n* = **device**, thing, appliance, machine, tool, implement, invention, instrument, novelty, apparatus, gimmick, utensil, contraption *(informal)*, gizmo *(slang, chiefly US & Canad)*, contrivance

gag[1] *vb* **1** = **retch**, choke, heave **3** = **suppress**, silence, subdue, muffle, curb, stifle, muzzle, quieten ▷*n* **4** = **muzzle**, tie, restraint

gag[2] *n* **1** *(informal)* = **joke**, crack *(slang)*, funny *(informal)*, quip, pun, jest, wisecrack *(informal)*, sally, witticism

gain *vb* **1a** = **acquire**, get, receive, achieve, earn, pick up, win, secure, collect, gather, obtain, build up, attain, glean, procure **1b** = **attain**, earn, get, achieve, win, reach, get to, secure, obtain, acquire, arrive at, procure **5** **gain on something** *or* **someone** = **get nearer to**, close in on, approach, catch up with, narrow the gap on ▷*n* **6** = **profit**, income, earnings, proceeds, winnings, return, produce, benefit, advantage, yield, dividend, acquisition,

DICTIONARY

signal, usually measured in decibels
WORD ORIGIN Old French *gaaignier*
gainful *adj* useful or profitable
gainfully *adv*
gainsay *vb* **-saying, -said** *archaic or literary* to deny or contradict
WORD ORIGIN Middle English *gainsaien*, from *gain-* against + *saien* to say
Gainsborough *n* **Thomas** 1727–88, English painter, noted particularly for his informal portraits and for his naturalistic landscapes
Gaiseric *n* ▸ same as **Genseric**
gait *n* **1** manner of walking **2** (of horses and dogs) the pattern of footsteps at a particular speed, such as a trot
WORD ORIGIN variant of *gate*
gaiters *pl n* cloth or leather coverings for the legs or ankles
WORD ORIGIN French *guêtre*
Gaitskell *n* **Hugh** (**Todd Naylor**) 1906–63, British politician; leader of the Labour Party (1955–63)
Gaius *or* **Caius** *n* **1** ?110–?180 AD, Roman jurist. His *Institutes* were later used as the basis for those of Justinian **2 Gaius Caesar** ▸ See **Caligula**
gal *n slang* a girl
gala ❶ (gah-la) *n* **1** a special social occasion, esp. a special performance **2** *chiefly Brit* a sporting occasion with competitions in several events: *next week's sports gala*
WORD ORIGIN Old French *galer* to make merry
galactic *adj* of the Galaxy or other galaxies
galaxy *n, pl* **-axies 1** a star system held together by gravitational attraction **2** a collection of brilliant people or things: *a galaxy of legal talent*
WORD ORIGIN Middle English (in the sense: the Milky Way); from Greek *gala* milk
Galaxy *n* **the Galaxy** the spiral galaxy that contains the solar system. Also called: **Milky Way**
Galba *n* **Servius Sulpicius** ?3 BC–69 AD, Roman emperor (68–69) after the assassination of Nero
Galbraith *n* **John Kenneth** 1908–2006, US economist and diplomat born in Canada; author of *The Affluent Society* (1958), *The New Industrial State* (1967), and *The Culture of Contentment* (1992)
Galbraithian *adj*
gale ❶ *n* **1** a strong wind, specifically one of force 8 on the Beaufort scale **2 gales** a loud outburst: *gales of laughter*
WORD ORIGIN origin unknown
galena *or* **galenite** *n* a soft bluish-grey mineral consisting of lead sulphide: the chief source of lead
WORD ORIGIN Latin: lead ore
Galerius *n* full name *Gaius Galerius Valerius Maximianus*. ?250–311 AD, Eastern Roman Emperor (305–311): noted for his persecution of Christians
Galia melon *n* a kind of melon with a raised network texture on the skin and sweet flesh
gall[1] (gawl) *n* **1** *informal* bold impudence: *she was stunned I had the gall to ask* **2** a feeling of great bitterness **3** *physiol, obsolete* ▸ same as **bile**
WORD ORIGIN Old Norse
gall[2] ❶ (gawl) *vb* **1** to annoy or irritate **2** to make the skin sore by rubbing ▷ *n* **3** something that causes annoyance **4** a sore on the skin caused by rubbing
WORD ORIGIN Germanic
gall[3] (gawl) *n* an abnormal outgrowth on a tree or plant caused by parasites
WORD ORIGIN Latin *galla*
gallant *adj* **1** persistent and courageous in the face of overwhelming odds: *a gallant fight* **2** (of a man) making a show of polite attentiveness to women **3** having a reputation for bravery: *Police Medal for gallant and meritorious services* ▷ *n* **4** *history* a young man who tried to impress women with his fashionable clothes or daring acts
gallantly *adv*
WORD ORIGIN Old French *galer* to make merry
gallantry *n* **1** showy, attentive treatment of women **2** great bravery in war or danger
gall bladder *n* a muscular sac, attached to the liver, that stores bile
galleon *n* a large three-masted sailing ship used from the 15th to the 18th centuries
WORD ORIGIN Spanish *galeón*
gallery *n, pl* **-leries 1** a room or building for displaying works of art **2** a balcony running along or around the inside wall of a church, hall, or other building **3** *theatre* **a** an upper floor that projects from the rear and contains the cheapest seats **b** the audience seated there **4** an underground passage in a mine or cave **5** a group of spectators, for instance at a golf match **6 play to the gallery** to try to gain approval by appealing to popular taste
WORD ORIGIN Old French *galerie*
galley *n* **1** the kitchen of a ship, boat, or aircraft **2** a ship propelled by oars or sails, used in ancient or medieval times
WORD ORIGIN Old French *galie*
galley slave *n* **1** a criminal or slave forced to row in a galley **2** *informal* a drudge
Gallic *adj* **1** French **2** of ancient Gaul or the Gauls
Gallicism *n* a word or idiom borrowed from French
gallinaceous *adj* of an order of birds, including poultry, pheasants, and grouse, that have a heavy rounded body
WORD ORIGIN Latin *gallina* hen
galling (gawl-ing) *adj* annoying or bitterly humiliating
gallium *n chem* a silvery metallic element used in high-temperature thermometers and low-melting alloys. Symbol: Ga
WORD ORIGIN Latin *gallus* cock, translation of French *coq* in the name of its discoverer, *Lecoq* de Boisbaudran
gallivant *vb* to go about in search of pleasure
WORD ORIGIN perhaps from *gallant*
gallon *n* **1** *Brit* a unit of liquid measure equal to 4.55 litres **2** *US* a unit of liquid measure equal to 3.79 litres
WORD ORIGIN Old Northern French *galon*
gallop ❶ *vb* **1** (of a horse) to run fast with a two-beat stride in which all four legs are off the ground at once **2** to ride (a horse) at a gallop **3** to move or progress rapidly ▷ *n* **4** the fast two-beat gait of horses **5** a galloping
WORD ORIGIN Old French *galoper*
Galloway *n* a breed of black cattle originally bred in Galloway
WORD ORIGIN after *Galloway*, district of SW Scotland
gallows *n, pl* **-lowses** *or* **-lows 1** a wooden structure consisting of two

g

THESAURUS

attainment, lucre, emolument
OPPOSITE: loss
gala *n* **1 = festival**, party, fête, celebration, carnival, festivity, pageant, jamboree
gale *n* **1 = storm**, hurricane, tornado, cyclone, whirlwind, blast, gust, typhoon, tempest, squall **2** *(pl)* **= outburst**, scream, roar, fit, storm, shout, burst, explosion, outbreak, howl, shriek, eruption, peal, paroxysm
gall[2] *vb* **1 = annoy**, provoke, irritate, aggravate *(informal)*, get *(informal)*, trouble, bother, disturb, plague, madden, ruffle, exasperate, nettle, vex, displease, irk, rile *(informal)*, peeve *(informal)*, get under your skin *(informal)*, get on your nerves *(informal)*, nark *(Brit, Austral & NZ slang)*, get up your nose *(informal)*, make your blood boil, rub up the wrong way, get on your wick *(Brit slang)*, get your back up, put your back up, hack you off *(informal)*
gallop *vb* **1 = run**, race, shoot, career, speed, bolt, stampede **3 = dash**, run, race, shoot, fly, career, speed, tear, rush, barrel (along) *(informal, chiefly US & Canad)*, sprint, dart, zoom

DICTIONARY

upright posts with a crossbeam, used for hanging criminals **2 the gallows** execution by hanging
WORD ORIGIN Old Norse *galgi*

gallstone *n* a small hard mass formed in the gall bladder or its ducts

Gallup *n* **George Horace** 1901–84, US statistician: devised the Gallup Poll; founded the American Institute of Public Opinion (1935) and its British counterpart (1936)

Gallup Poll *n* a sampling of the views of a representative cross section of the population, usually used to forecast voting
WORD ORIGIN after G. H. *Gallup*, statistician

g

galop *n* **1** a 19th-century dance in quick duple time **2** music for this dance
WORD ORIGIN French

galore *adj* in abundance: *there were bargains galore*
WORD ORIGIN Irish Gaelic *go leór* to sufficiency

galoshes *pl n Brit, Austral & NZ* a pair of waterproof overshoes
WORD ORIGIN Old French *galoche* wooden shoe

Galsworthy *n* **John** 1867–1933, English novelist and dramatist, noted for *The Forsyte Saga* (1906–28): Nobel prize for literature 1932

Galt *n* **John** 1779–1839, Scottish novelist, noted for his ironic humour, esp. in *Annals of the Parish* (1821), *The Provost* (1822), and *The Entail* (1823)

Galton *n* Sir **Francis** 1822–1911, English explorer and scientist, a cousin of Charles Darwin, noted for his researches in heredity, meteorology, and statistics. He founded the study of eugenics and the theory of anticyclones

galumph *vb Brit, Austral & NZ informal* to leap or move about clumsily or joyfully
WORD ORIGIN probably a blend of GALLOP + TRIUMPH

galvanic *adj* **1** of or producing an electric current by chemical means, such as in a battery **2** *informal* stimulating, startling, or energetic

galvanize *or* **-nise** *vb* **-nizing, -nized** *or* **-nising, -nised 1** to stimulate into action **2** to cover (metal) with a protective zinc coating **3** to stimulate by an electric current **galvanization** *or* **-nisation** *n*
WORD ORIGIN after Luigi *Galvani*, physiologist

galvanometer *n* a sensitive instrument for detecting or measuring small electric currents

Gambetta *n* **Léon** 1838–82, French statesman; prime minister (1881–82). He organized resistance during the Franco-Prussian War (1870–71) and was a founder of the Third Republic (1871)

gambit *n* **1** an opening remark or action intended to gain an advantage **2** *chess* an opening move in which a piece, usually a pawn, is sacrificed to gain an advantageous position
WORD ORIGIN Italian *gambetto* a tripping up

gamble ❶ *vb* **-bling, -bled 1** to play games of chance to win money or prizes **2** to risk or bet (something) on the outcome of an event or sport **3 gamble away** to lose by gambling **4 gamble on** to act with the expectation of: *she has gambled on proving everyone wrong* ▷ *n* **5** a risky act or venture **6** a bet or wager **gambler** *n* **gambling** *n*
WORD ORIGIN probably variant of GAME[1]

gamboge (gam-**boje**) *n* a gum resin obtained from a tropical Asian tree, used as a yellow pigment and as a purgative
WORD ORIGIN from *Cambodia*, where first found

gambol *vb* **-bolling, -bolled** *or US* **-boling, -boled 1** to jump about playfully; frolic ▷ *n* **2** playful jumping about; frolicking
WORD ORIGIN French *gambade*

game[1] ❶ *n* **1** an amusement for children **2** a competitive activity with rules **3** a single period of play in such an activity **4** (in some sports) the score needed to win **5** a single contest in a series; match **6** ▸ short for **computer game 7** style or ability in playing a game: *in the second set his overall game improved markedly* **8** an activity that seems to operate according to unwritten rules: *the political game of power* **9** an activity undertaken in a spirit of playfulness: *people who regard life as a game* **10** wild animals, birds, or fish, hunted for sport or food **11** the flesh of such animals, used as food **12** an object of pursuit: *fair game* **13** *informal* a trick or scheme: *what's his game?* **14 games** an event consisting of various sporting contests, usually in athletics: *Commonwealth Games* **15 give the game away** to reveal one's intentions or a secret **16 on the game** *slang* working as a prostitute **17 play the game** to behave fairly **18 the game is up** the scheme or trick has been found out and so cannot succeed ▷ *adj* **19** *informal* full of fighting spirit; plucky **20** *informal* prepared or willing: *I'm always game for a new sensation* ▷ *vb* **gaming, gamed 21** to play games of chance for money; gamble **gamely** *adv* **gameness** *n*
WORD ORIGIN Old English *gamen*

game[2] *adj Brit, Austral & NZ* lame: *he had a game leg*
WORD ORIGIN probably from Irish *cam* crooked

gamekeeper *n Brit* a person employed to take care of game on an estate

game plan *n* **1** *US & Canad* a strategy for playing a particular game **2** any plan or strategy

gamer *n* a person who plays computer games

games console *n* a small machine, linked to a television set, used for playing video games

gamesmanship *n informal* the art of winning by cunning practices without actually cheating

gamester *n* a gambler

gamete (gam-eet) *n* a cell that can fuse with another in reproduction **gametic** *or* **gametal** *adj*
WORD ORIGIN Greek *gametē* wife

gamey *or* **gamy** *adj* **gamier, gamiest** having the smell or flavour of game

gamin *n* a street urchin
WORD ORIGIN French

gamine (gam-een) *n* a slim and boyish girl or young woman
WORD ORIGIN French

gaming *n* gambling

gamma *n* the third letter in the Greek alphabet (Λ, λ)

THESAURUS

gamble *vb* **1, 2 = bet**, play, game, stake, speculate, back, punt, wager, put money on, have a flutter *(informal)*, try your luck, put your shirt on, lay *or* make a bet **2 = risk**, chance, stake, venture, hazard, wager **4 gamble on = take a chance**, back, speculate, take the plunge, stick your neck out *(informal)*, put your faith *or* trust in ▷ *n* **5 = risk**, chance, venture, lottery, speculation, uncertainty, leap in the dark **OPPOSITE:** certainty **6 = bet**, flutter *(informal)*, punt *(chiefly Brit)*, wager

game[1] *n* **1, 9 = amusement**, joke, entertainment, diversion, lark **3, 5 = match**, meeting, event, competition, tournament, clash, contest, round, head-to-head **10 = wild animals** *or* **birds**, prey, quarry **13** *(informal)* **= scheme**, plan, design, strategy, trick, plot, tactic, manoeuvre, dodge, ploy, scam, stratagem, fastie *(Austral slang)* ▷ *adj* **19** *(informal)* **= brave**, courageous, dogged, spirited, daring, bold, persistent, gritty, fearless, feisty *(informal, chiefly US & Canad)*, persevering, intrepid, valiant, plucky, unflinching, dauntless, (as) game as Ned Kelly *(Austral slang)* **OPPOSITE:** cowardly **20** *(informal)* **= willing**, prepared, ready, keen, eager, interested, inclined, disposed, up for it *(informal)*, desirous

DICTIONARY

gamma radiation *n* electromagnetic radiation of shorter wavelength and higher energy than X-rays

gamma rays *pl n* streams of gamma radiation

gammon *n* **1** cured or smoked ham **2** the hindquarter of a side of bacon **WORD ORIGIN** Old French *gambe* leg

gammy *adj* **-mier, -miest** *Brit & NZ slang* (of the leg) lame **WORD ORIGIN** dialect variant of GAME[2]

gamp *n Brit informal* an umbrella **WORD ORIGIN** after Mrs *Gamp* in Dickens' *Martin Chuzzlewit*

gamut *n* **1** entire range or scale: *a rich gamut of facial expressions* **2** *music* **a** a scale **b** the whole range of notes **WORD ORIGIN** Medieval Latin, from *gamma*, the lowest note of the hexachord as established by Guido d'Arezzo + *ut* (now, *doh*), the first of the notes of the scale *ut, re, mi, fa, sol, la, si*

gamy *adj* ▸ same as **gamey**

Gance *n* **Abel** 1889–1981, French film director, whose works include *J'accuse* (1919, 1937) and *Napoléon* (1927), which introduced the split-screen technique

gander *n* **1** a male goose **2** *informal* a quick look: *have a gander* **WORD ORIGIN** Old English *gandra, ganra*

gang[1] ❶ *n* **1** a group of people who go around together, often to commit crime **2** an organized group of workmen ▹ *vb* **3** to become or act as a gang ▸ See also **gang up on** **WORD ORIGIN** Old English: journey

gang[2] *vb Scot* to go or walk **WORD ORIGIN** Old English *gangan*

gangbang *n slang* sexual intercourse between one woman and several men one after the other, esp. against her will

gangland *n* the criminal underworld

gangling *or* **gangly** *adj* lanky and awkward in movement **WORD ORIGIN** see GANG[2]

ganglion *n, pl* **-glia** *or* **-glions** a collection of nerve cells outside the brain and spinal cord **ganglionic** *adj* **WORD ORIGIN** Greek: cystic tumour

gangplank *n naut* a portable bridge for boarding and leaving a ship

gangrene *n* decay of body tissue caused by the blood supply being interrupted by disease or injury **gangrenous** *adj* **WORD ORIGIN** Greek *gangraina* an eating sore

gangsta rap *n* a style of rap music originating from US Black street culture **WORD ORIGIN** phonetic rendering of GANGSTER

gangster ❶ *n* a member of an organized gang of criminals **gangsterism** *n*

gangue *n* valueless material in an ore **WORD ORIGIN** German *Gang* vein of metal, course

gang up on *or* **against** *vb informal* to combine in a group against

gangway *n* **1** *Brit* an aisle between rows of seats **2** ▸ same as **gangplank** **3** an opening in a ship's side to take a gangplank

gannet *n* **1** a heavily built white sea bird **2** *Brit slang* a greedy person **WORD ORIGIN** Old English *ganot*

ganoid *adj* **1** (of the scales of certain fishes) consisting of an inner bony layer covered with an enamel-like substance **2** (of a fish) having such scales ▹ *n* **3** a ganoid fish **WORD ORIGIN** Greek *ganos* brightness

gantry *n, pl* **-tries** a large metal framework used to support something, such as a travelling crane, or to position a rocket on its launch pad **WORD ORIGIN** Latin *cantherius* supporting frame, pack ass

gaol (jayl) *n, vb Austral & Brit* ▸ same as **jail** > **gaoler** *n*

Gao Xingjian *n* born 1940, Chinese dramatist, novelist, and dissident, living in France from 1987; his works include the play *Chezhan* (*Bus Stop*, 1983) and the novel *Lingshan* (*Soul Mountain*, 1989): Nobel prize for literature 2000

gap ❶ *n* **1** a break or opening in something **2** an interruption or interval **3** a difference in ideas or viewpoint: *the generation gap* **gappy** *adj* **WORD ORIGIN** Old Norse: chasm

gape ❶ *vb* **gaping, gaped** **1** to stare in wonder with the mouth open **2** to open the mouth wide, as in yawning **3** to be or become wide open: *a hole gaped in the roof* **gaping** *adj* **WORD ORIGIN** Old Norse *gapa*

gap year *n* a year's break between leaving school and starting further education

garage *n* **1** a building used to keep cars **2** a place where cars are repaired and petrol is sold ▹ *vb* **-aging, -aged** **3** to put or keep a car in a garage **WORD ORIGIN** French

garage sale *n* a sale of household items held at a person's home, usually in the garage

garb *n* **1** clothes, usually the distinctive dress of an occupation or group: *modern military garb* ▹ *vb* **2** to clothe **WORD ORIGIN** Old French *garbe* graceful contour

garbage *n* **1** *US, Austral & NZ* household waste **2** worthless rubbish or nonsense **WORD ORIGIN** probably from Anglo-French

garbled *adj* (of a story, message, etc.) jumbled and confused **WORD ORIGIN** Old Italian *garbellare* to strain, sift

García Márquez *n* **Gabriel** born 1928, Colombian novelist and short-story writer. His novels include *One Hundred Years of Solitude* (1967), *The Autumn of the Patriarch* (1977), *Love in the Time of Cholera* (1984), and *News of a Kidnapping* (1996). Nobel prize for literature 1982

garçon (garss-**on**) *n* a waiter **WORD ORIGIN** French

garda *n, pl* **gardaí** a member of the police force of the Republic of Ireland **WORD ORIGIN** Irish Gaelic: guard

garden *n* **1** an area of land usually next to a house, for growing flowers, fruit, or vegetables ▸ Related adjective: **horticultural** **2** Also: **gardens** a cultivated area of land open to the public: *Kensington Gardens* **3** **lead someone up the garden path** *informal* to mislead or deceive someone ▹ *vb* **4** to work in or take care of a garden **gardener** *n* **gardening** *n* **WORD ORIGIN** Old French *gardin*

garden centre *n* a place where plants and gardening tools and equipment are sold

garden city *n Brit* a planned town of limited size surrounded by countryside

gardenia (gar-**deen**-ya) *n* **1** a large fragrant waxy white flower **2** the evergreen shrub on which it grows **WORD ORIGIN** after Dr Alexander *Garden*, botanist

gardening leave *n chiefly Brit informal* a period during which an employee

THESAURUS

gang[1] *n* **1 = group**, crowd, pack, company, party, lot, band, crew (*informal*), bunch, mob, horde

gangster *n* **= hoodlum** (*chiefly US*), crook (*informal*), thug, bandit, heavy (*slang*), tough, hood (*US slang*), robber, gang member, mobster (*US slang*), racketeer, desperado, ruffian, brigand, wise guy (*US*), tsotsi (*S African*)

gap *n* **1 = opening**, space, hole, break, split, divide, crack, rent, breach, slot, vent, rift, aperture, cleft, chink, crevice, fissure, cranny, perforation, interstice **2 = interval**, pause, recess, interruption, respite, lull, interlude, breathing space, hiatus, intermission, lacuna, entr'acte **3 = difference**, gulf, contrast, disagreement, discrepancy, inconsistency, disparity, divergence

gape *vb* **1 = stare**, wonder, goggle, gawp (*Brit slang*), gawk **3 = open**, split, crack, yawn

g

DICTIONARY

who is about to leave a company continues to receive a salary but does not work

Gardiner *n* **1** Sir **John Eliot** born 1943, British conductor, noted for performances using period instruments; founded the Monteverdi Choir in 1965 and the Orchestre Révolutionnaire et Romantique in 1990 **2 Stephen** ?1483–1555, English bishop and statesman; lord chancellor (1553–55). He opposed Protestantism, supporting the anti-Reformation policies of Mary I

Gardner *n* **Ava** 1922–90, US film actress. Her films include *The Killers* (1946), *The Sun also Rises* (1957), and *The Night of the Iguana* (1964)

g

garfish *n* **1** a freshwater fish with a long body and very long toothed jaws **2** a sea fish with similar characteristics

gargantuan *adj* huge or enormous
WORD ORIGIN after *Gargantua,* a giant in Rabelais' *Gargantua and Pantagruel*

gargle *vb* **-gling, -gled 1** to rinse the mouth and throat with (a liquid) by slowly breathing out through the liquid ▹*n* **2** the liquid used for gargling **3** the act or sound of gargling
WORD ORIGIN Old French *gargouille* throat

gargoyle *n* (on ancient buildings) a waterspout below the roof, carved in the form of a grotesque face or figure
WORD ORIGIN Old French *gargouille* gargoyle, throat

garish *adj* crudely bright or colourful **garishly** *adv* **garishness** *n*
WORD ORIGIN obsolete *gaure* to stare

garland ❶ *n* **1** a wreath of flowers and leaves worn round the head or neck or hung up ▹*vb* **2** to decorate with a garland or garlands
WORD ORIGIN Old French *garlande*

garlic *n* the bulb of a plant of the onion family, with a strong taste and smell, made up of small segments which are used in cooking **garlicky** *adj*
WORD ORIGIN Old English *gārlēac*

garment ❶ *n* (*often pl*) an article of clothing
WORD ORIGIN Old French *garniment*

garner *vb* to collect or gather: *the financial rewards garnered by his book*
WORD ORIGIN Latin *granum* grain

Garner *n* **1 Erroll** 1921–77, US jazz pianist and composer **2 Helen** born 1942. Australian novelist and journalist. Her books include the novels *Monkey Grip* (1977), *The Idea of Perfection* (2002) and *The Children's Bach* (1984) and the nonfiction *The First Stone* (1995)

garnet *n* a red semiprecious gemstone
WORD ORIGIN Old French *grenat* red, from *pome grenate* pomegranate

Garnett *n* **1 Constance** 1862–1946, British translator of Russian novels **2** her son, **David** 1892–1981, British novelist and editor. His novels include *Lady Into Fox* (1922) and *Aspects of Love* (1955)

garnish ❶ *vb* **1** to decorate (food) with something to add to its appearance or flavour ▹*n* **2** a decoration for food
WORD ORIGIN Old French *garnir* to adorn, equip

garret *n* an attic in a house
WORD ORIGIN Old French *garite* watchtower

Garrett *n* **Lesley** born 1955, British soprano; principal soprano with the English National Opera from 1984

garrison ❶ *n* **1** soldiers who guard a base or fort **2** the place itself ▹*vb* **3** to station (soldiers) in (a fort or base)
WORD ORIGIN Old French *garir* to defend

garrotte *or* **garotte** *n* **1** a Spanish method of execution by strangling **2** a cord, wire, or iron collar, used to strangle someone ▹*vb* **-rotting, -rotted 3** to execute with a garrotte
WORD ORIGIN Spanish *garrote*

garrulous *adj* constantly chattering; talkative **garrulousness** *n*
WORD ORIGIN Latin *garrire* to chatter

garter *n* **1** a band, usually of elastic, worn round the leg to hold up a sock or stocking **2** *US & Canad* a suspender
WORD ORIGIN Old French *gartier*

Garter *n* **the Order of the Garter** the highest order of British knighthood

garter stitch *n* knitting in which all the rows are knitted in plain stitch

gas ❶ *n, pl* **gases** *or* **gasses 1** an airlike substance that is neither liquid nor solid at room temperature and atmospheric pressure **2** a fossil fuel in the form of a gas, used as a source of heat **3** an anaesthetic in the form of a gas **4** *mining* firedamp or the explosive mixture of firedamp and air **5** *US, Canad, Austral & NZ* petrol **6** a poisonous gas used in war **7** *informal* idle talk or boasting **8** *slang* an entertaining person or thing: *Monterey was a gas for musicians and fans alike* **9** *US informal* gas generated in the alimentary canal ▹*vb* **gases** *or* **gasses, gassing, gassed 10** to subject to gas fumes so as to make unconscious or to suffocate **11** *informal* to talk a lot; chatter
WORD ORIGIN coined from Greek *khaos* atmosphere

gasbag *n* *informal* a person who talks too much

gas chamber *n* an airtight room which is filled with poison gas to kill people

Gascoigne *n* **Paul,** known as *Gazza.* born 1967, English footballer

gaseous *adj* of or like a gas

gash *n* **1** a long deep cut ▹*vb* **2** to make a long deep cut in
WORD ORIGIN Old French *garser* to scratch, wound

gasholder *n* a large tank for storing gas before distributing it to users

gasify *vb* **-fies, -fying, -fied** to change into a gas **gasification** *n*

Gaskell *n* **Mrs** married name of *Elizabeth Cleghorn Stevenson.* 1810–65, English novelist. Her novels include *Mary Barton* (1848), an account of industrial life in Manchester, and *Cranford* (1853), a social study of a country village

gasket *n* a piece of paper, rubber, or metal sandwiched between the faces of a metal joint to provide a seal
WORD ORIGIN probably from French *garcette* rope's end

gaslight *n* **1** a lamp in which light is produced by burning gas **2** the light produced by such a lamp

gasman *n, pl* **-men** a man employed to read household gas meters and install or repair gas fittings, etc.

gas mask *n* a mask fitted with a chemical filter to protect the wearer from breathing in harmful gases

gas meter *n* a device for measuring and recording the amount of gas passed through it

gasoline *or* **gasolene** *n* *US & Canad* petrol

gasometer (gas-som-it-er) *n* ▸ same as **gasholder**

gasp ❶ *vb* **1** to draw in the breath

THESAURUS

garland *n* **1 = wreath,** band, bays, crown, honours, loop, laurels, festoon, coronet, coronal, chaplet ▹*vb* **2 = adorn,** crown, deck, festoon, wreathe

garment *n* (*often pl*) **= clothes,** wear, dress, clothing, gear (*slang*), habit, get-up (*informal*), uniform, outfit, costume, threads (*slang*), array, robes, duds (*informal*), apparel, clobber (*Brit slang*), attire, garb, togs, vestments, articles of clothing, raiment (*archaic*), rigout (*informal*), habiliment

garnish *vb* **1 = decorate,** adorn, ornament, embellish, deck, festoon, trim, bedeck **OPPOSITE:** strip ▹*n* **2 = decoration,** ornament, embellishment, adornment, ornamentation, trimming, trim

garrison *n* **1 = troops,** group, unit, section, command, armed force, detachment **2 = fort,** fortress, camp, base, post, station, stronghold, fortification, encampment, fortified pa (*NZ*) ▹*vb* **3 = station,** position, post, mount, install, assign, put on duty

gas *n* **1 = fumes,** vapour **5** (*US, Canad, Austral & NZ*) **= petrol,** gasoline

gasp *vb* **1 = pant,** blow, puff, choke,

sharply or with difficulty **2** to utter breathlessly ▷ *n* **3** a short convulsive intake of breath
WORD ORIGIN Old Norse *geispa* to yawn

Gasparovic *n* **Ivan** born 1941, Slovakian politician, president of Slovakia from 2004

gas ring *n* a circular metal pipe with several holes in it fed with gas for cooking

Gassendi *n* **Pierre** 1592–1655, French physicist and philosopher, who promoted an atomic theory of matter

Gasser *n* **Herbert Spencer** 1888–1963, US physiologist: shared a Nobel prize for physiology or medicine (1944) with Erlanger for work on electrical signs of nervous activity

gassy *adj* **-sier, -siest** filled with, containing, or like gas **gassiness** *n*

gastric *adj* of the stomach

gastric juice *n* a digestive fluid secreted by the stomach

gastric ulcer *n* an ulcer on the lining of the stomach

gastritis *n* inflammation of the lining of the stomach, causing vomiting or gastric ulcers

gastroenteritis *n* inflammation of the stomach and intestine, causing vomiting and diarrhoea

gastronomy *n* the art of good eating **gastronomic** *adj*
WORD ORIGIN Greek *gastēr* stomach + *nomos* law

gastropod *n* a mollusc, such as a snail or whelk, that has a single flat muscular foot, eyes on stalks, and usually a spiral shell
WORD ORIGIN Greek *gastēr* stomach + *-podos* -footed

gasworks *n* a factory in which coal gas is made

gate ❶ *n* **1** a movable barrier, usually hinged, for closing an opening in a wall or fence **2 a** the number of people admitted to a sporting event or entertainment **b** the total entrance money received from them **3** an exit at an airport by which passengers get to an aircraft **4** *electronics* a circuit with one or more input terminals and one output terminal, the output being determined by the combination of input signals **5** a slotted metal frame that controls the positions of the gear lever in a motor vehicle
WORD ORIGIN Old English *geat*

gateau (gat-toe) *n, pl* **-teaux** (-toes) a large rich layered cake
WORD ORIGIN French

gate-crash *vb informal* to gain entry to (a party) without invitation **gate-crasher** *n*

gatehouse *n* a building at or above a gateway

gate-leg table *or* **gate-legged table** *n* a table with leaves supported by hinged legs that can swing back to let the leaves hang from the frame

gateway *n* **1** an entrance that may be closed by a gate **2** a means of entry or access: *his only gateway to the outside world* **3** *computers* hardware and software that connect incompatible computer networks, allowing them to communicate

gather ❶ *vb* **1** to come or bring together **2** to increase gradually in (pace, speed, or momentum) **3** to prepare oneself for a task or challenge by collecting one's thoughts, strength, or courage **4** to learn from information given; conclude: *this is pretty important, I gather* **5** to draw (fabric) into small folds or tucks **6** to pick or harvest (crops) ▷ *n* **7 gathers** small folds or tucks in fabric
WORD ORIGIN Old English *gadrian*

gathering ❶ *n* a group of people, usually meeting for some particular purpose: *the Braemar Highland Gathering*

GATT General Agreement on Tariffs and Trade: a former name for the World Trade Organization

gauche (gohsh) *adj* socially awkward
WORD ORIGIN French

gaucho (gow-choh) *n, pl* **-chos** a cowboy of the South American pampas
WORD ORIGIN American Spanish

Gaudier-Brzeska *n* **Henri**, original name *Henri Gaudier*. 1891–1915, French vorticist sculptor

gaudy *adj* **gaudier, gaudiest** vulgarly bright or colourful **gaudily** *adv* **gaudiness** *n*
WORD ORIGIN from *gaud* trinket

gauge ❶ (gayj) *vb* **gauging, gauged** **1** to estimate or judge (people's feelings or reactions) **2** to measure using a gauge ▷ *n* **3** an instrument for measuring quantities: *a petrol gauge* **4** a scale or standard of measurement **5** a standard for estimating people's feelings or reactions: *a gauge of public opinion* **6** the diameter of the barrel of a gun **7** the distance between the rails of a railway track
WORD ORIGIN from Old French

Gaul *n* a native of ancient Gaul

Gaultier *n* **Jean-Paul** born 1952, French fashion designer

gaunt *adj* **1** bony and emaciated in appearance **2** (of a place) bleak or desolate: *the gaunt disused flour mill* **gauntness** *n*
WORD ORIGIN origin unknown

gauntlet¹ *n* **1** a long heavy protective glove **2** a medieval armoured glove **3 take up the gauntlet** to accept a challenge
WORD ORIGIN Old French *gantelet*

gauntlet² *n* **run the gauntlet** to be exposed to criticism or harsh treatment
WORD ORIGIN Swedish *gatlopp* passageway

gauss (rhymes with **mouse**) *n, pl* **gauss** the cgs unit of magnetic flux density
WORD ORIGIN after K. F. *Gauss*, mathematician

Gauteng *n* a province of N South Africa

Gautier *n* **Théophile** 1811–72, French poet, novelist, and critic. His early extravagant romanticism gave way to a preoccupation with poetic form and expression that anticipated the Parnassians

gauze *n* a transparent, loosely woven cloth, often used for surgical dressings **gauzy** *adj*
WORD ORIGIN French *gaze*

Gavaskar *n* **Sunil Manohar** born 1949, Indian cricketer. He captained India 1978–83 and 1984–85

gave *vb* ▸ the past tense of **give**

THESAURUS

gulp, fight for breath, catch your breath ▷ *n* **3 = pant**, puff, gulp, intake of breath, sharp intake of breath

gate *n* **1 = barrier**, opening, door, access, port *(Scot)*, entrance, exit, gateway, portal, egress

gather *vb* **1a = congregate**, assemble, get together, collect, group, meet, mass, rally, flock, come together, muster, convene, converge, rendezvous, foregather
OPPOSITE: scatter
1b = assemble, group, collect, round up, marshal, bring together, muster, convene, call together
OPPOSITE: disperse
2 = build up, rise, increase, grow, develop, expand, swell, intensify, wax, heighten, deepen, enlarge, thicken **4 = understand**, believe, hear, learn, assume, take it, conclude, presume, be informed, infer, deduce, surmise, be led to believe **5 = fold**, tuck, pleat, ruffle, pucker, shirr **6 = pick**, harvest, pluck, reap, garner, glean

gathering *n* **= assembly**, group, crowd, meeting, conference, company, party, congress, mass, rally, convention, knot, flock, get-together *(informal)*, congregation, muster, turnout, multitude, throng, hui *(NZ)*, concourse, assemblage, conclave, convocation, runanga *(NZ)*

gauge *vb* **1 = judge**, estimate, guess, assess, evaluate, rate, appraise, reckon, adjudge **2 = measure**, calculate, evaluate, value, size, determine, count, weigh, compute, ascertain, quantify ▷ *n* **3 = meter**, indicator, dial, measuring instrument

g

DICTIONARY

gavel (gav-vl) *n* a small hammer used by a judge, auctioneer, or chairman to call for order or attention
WORD ORIGIN origin unknown

gavotte *n* **1** an old formal dance in quadruple time **2** music for this dance
WORD ORIGIN French

gawk *vb* **1** to stare stupidly ▹*n* **2** a clumsy stupid person
WORD ORIGIN Old Danish *gaukr*

gawky *adj* **gawkier, gawkiest** clumsy and awkward

gawp *vb slang* to stare stupidly
gawper *n*
WORD ORIGIN Middle English *galpen*

gay ⓣ *adj* **1** homosexual **2** carefree and merry: *with gay abandon* **3** bright and cheerful: *smartly dressed in gay colours* ▹*n* **4** a homosexual, esp. a homosexual man: *solidarity amongst lesbians and gays*
WORD ORIGIN Old French *gai*

Gay *n* **John** 1685–1732, English poet and dramatist; author of *The Beggar's Opera* (1728)

gaydar *n informal* the supposed ability of a homosexual person to determine whether or not another person is homosexual

Gaye *n* **Marvin** 1939–84, US soul singer and songwriter; recordings include "I Heard It Through the Grapevine" (1969), *What's Going On* (1971), and "Sexual Healing" (1982): shot dead by his father

gayness *n* homosexuality

gaze ⓣ *vb* **gazing, gazed 1** to look long and steadily at someone or something ▹*n* **2** a long steady look
WORD ORIGIN Swedish dialect *gasa* to gape at

gazebo (gaz-zee-boh) *n, pl* **-bos** a summerhouse or pavilion with a good view
WORD ORIGIN perhaps a pseudo-Latin coinage based on *gaze*

gazelle *n* a small graceful fawn-coloured antelope of Africa and Asia
WORD ORIGIN Arabic *ghazāl*

gazette ⓣ *n* an official newspaper that gives lists of announcements, for instance in legal or military affairs
WORD ORIGIN French

gazetteer *n* a book or section of a book that lists and describes places

gazump *vb Austral & Brit informal* to raise the price of a house after agreeing a price verbally with an intending buyer
WORD ORIGIN origin unknown

gazunder *vb Brit informal* to reduce an offer on a house immediately before exchanging contracts, having earlier agreed a higher price with (the seller) **gazunderer** *n*

GB 1 Great Britain **2** Also: **Gb** gigabyte

GBH (in Britain and South Africa) grievous bodily harm

GC George Cross (a British award for bravery)

GCE 1 (formerly in Britain) General Certificate of Education **2** *informal* a pass in a GCE examination

GCSE 1 (in Britain) General Certificate of Secondary Education; an examination in specified subjects which replaced the GCE O level and CSE **2** *informal* a pass in a GCSE examination

Gd *chem* gadolinium

g'day *interj Austral & NZ informal* ▸ same as **good day**

GDP gross domestic product

Ge *chem* germanium

gear ⓣ *n* **1** a set of toothed wheels that engages with another or with a rack in order to change the speed or direction of transmitted motion **2** a mechanism for transmitting motion by gears **3** the setting of a gear to suit engine speed or direction: *a higher gear; reverse gear* **4** clothing or personal belongings **5** equipment for a particular task: *police in riot gear* **6 in** *or* **out of gear** with the gear mechanism engaged or disengaged ▹*vb* **7** to prepare or organize for something: *to gear for war* ▸ See also **gear up**
WORD ORIGIN Old Norse *gervi*

gearbox *n* the metal casing enclosing a set of gears in a motor vehicle

gearing *n* a system of gears designed to transmit motion

gear lever *or US & Canad* **gearshift** *n* a lever used to engage or change gears in a motor vehicle

gear up *vb* to prepare for an activity: *to gear up for a massive relief operation*

gearwheel *n* one of the toothed wheels in the gears of a motor vehicle

Geber *n* Latinized form of Jabir, assumed in honour of Jabir ibn Hayyan by a 14th-century alchemist, probably Spanish: he described the preparation of nitric and sulphuric acids

Gebrselassie *n* **Haile** born 1973, Ethiopian athlete; Olympic gold medallist in the 10 000 metres in 1996 and 2000

gecko *n, pl* **geckos** a small tropical lizard
WORD ORIGIN Malay *ge'kok*

gee *interj US & Canad informal* a mild exclamation of surprise, admiration, etc.. Also: **gee whizz**
WORD ORIGIN euphemism for *Jesus*

Gee *n* **Maurice** born 1931, New Zealand novelist

geebung (gee-bung) *n* **1** an Australian tree or shrub with an edible but tasteless fruit **2** the fruit of this tree

geek *n informal* a boring and unattractive person **geeky** *adj*
WORD ORIGIN perhaps from Scottish *geck* fool

geelbek (heel-bek) *n S African* an edible marine fish with yellow jaws
WORD ORIGIN Afrikaans *geel* yellow + *bek* mouth

geese *n* ▸ the plural of **goose**[1]

geezer *n Brit, Austral & NZ informal* a man
WORD ORIGIN probably dialect pronunciation of *guiser*, a mummer

Geiger counter (guy-ger) *or* **Geiger-Müller counter** *n* an instrument for detecting and measuring radiation
WORD ORIGIN after Hans *Geiger*, physicist

Geikie *n* Sir **Archibald** 1835–1924, Scottish geologist noted for his study of British volcanic rocks

geisha (gay-sha) *n* a professional female companion for men in Japan, trained in music, dancing, and conversation
WORD ORIGIN Japanese

gel (jell) *n* **1** a thick jelly-like substance, esp. one used to keep a hairstyle in shape ▹*vb* **gelling, gelled 2** to become a gel **3** ▸ same as

THESAURUS

gay *adj* **1 = homosexual**, camp *(informal)*, lesbian, pink *(informal)*, queer *(informal, derogatory)*, same-sex, sapphic, moffie *(S African slang)* **2 = cheerful**, happy, bright, glad, lively, sparkling, sunny, jolly, animated, merry, upbeat *(informal)*, buoyant, cheery, joyous, joyful, carefree, jaunty, chirpy *(informal)*, vivacious, jovial, gleeful, debonair, blithe, insouciant, full of beans *(informal)*, light-hearted **OPPOSITE:** sad **3 = colourful**, rich, bright, brilliant, vivid, flamboyant, flashy, gaudy, garish, showy **OPPOSITE:** drab ▹*n* **4 = homosexual**, lesbian, fairy *(slang)*, queer *(informal, derogatory)*, faggot *(slang, chiefly US & Canad)*, auntie *or* aunty *(Austral slang)*, lily *(Austral slang)* **OPPOSITE:** heterosexual

gaze *vb* **1 = stare**, look, view, watch, regard, contemplate, gape, eyeball *(slang)*, ogle, look fixedly ▹*n* **2 = stare**, look, fixed look

gazette *n* **= newspaper**, paper, journal, organ, periodical, news-sheet

gear *n* **1, 2 = mechanism**, works, action, gearing, machinery, cogs, cogwheels, gearwheels **4 = clothing**, wear, dress, clothes, habit, outfit, costume, threads *(slang)*, array, garments, apparel, attire, garb, togs, rigout **5 = equipment**, supplies, tackle, tools, instruments, outfit, rigging, rig, accessories, apparatus, trappings, paraphernalia, accoutrements, appurtenances,

DICTIONARY

jell 4 to apply gel to (one's hair)
WORD ORIGIN from *gelatine*
gelatine (jell-a-teen) *or* **gelatin** *n* a clear water-soluble protein made by boiling animal hides and bones, used in cooking, photography, etc.
WORD ORIGIN Latin *gelare* to freeze
gelatinous (jill-**at**-in-uss) *adj* with a thick, semi-liquid consistency
geld *vb* **gelding, gelded** *or* **gelt** to castrate (a horse or other animal)
WORD ORIGIN Old Norse *gelda*
gelding *n* a castrated male horse
WORD ORIGIN Old Norse *geldingr*
Geldof *n* **Bob** Full name *Robert Frederick Zenon Geldof.* born 1954, Irish rock singer and philanthropist: formerly lead vocalist with the Boomtown Rats (1977–86): organizer of the Band Aid charity for famine relief in Africa. He received an honorary knighthood in 1986
Gelée *n* **Claude** ▸the original name of **Claude Lorrain**
gelignite *n* a type of dynamite used for blasting
WORD ORIGIN GELATINE + Latin *ignis* fire
Gell-Mann *n* **Murray** born 1929, US physicist, noted for his research on the interaction and classification of elementary particles: Nobel prize for physics in 1969
gem ⓣ *n* **1** a precious stone used for decoration ▸Related adjective: **lapidary 2** a person or thing regarded as precious or special: *a perfect gem of a hotel*
WORD ORIGIN Latin *gemma* bud, precious stone
gemfish *n* an Australian food fish with a delicate flavour
Gemini *n astrol* the third sign of the zodiac; the Twins
WORD ORIGIN Latin
gemsbok (**hemss**-bok) *n S African* ▸same as **oryx**
WORD ORIGIN Afrikaans
gemstone *n* a precious or semiprecious stone, esp. one which has been cut and polished
gen *n Brit, Austral & NZ informal* information: *I want to get as much gen as I can about the American market* ▸See also **gen up on**
WORD ORIGIN from *gen(eral information)*
Gen. General
gendarme (**zhahn**-darm) *n* a member of the French police force
WORD ORIGIN French
gender *n* **1** the state of being male, female, or neuter **2** the classification of nouns in certain languages as masculine, feminine, or neuter
WORD ORIGIN Latin *genus* kind
gene (jean) *n* a unit composed of DNA forming part of a chromosome, by which inherited characteristics are transmitted from parent to offspring
WORD ORIGIN German *Gen*
genealogy (jean-ee-**al**-a-jee) *n* **1** the direct descent of an individual or group from an ancestor **2** *pl* **-gies** a chart showing the descent of an individual or group **genealogical** *adj* **genealogist** *n*
WORD ORIGIN Greek *genea* race
genera (**jen**-er-a) *n* ▸a plural of **genus**
general ⓣ *adj* **1** common or widespread: *general goodwill* **2** of, affecting, or including all or most of the members of a group **3** not specialized or specializing: *a general hospital* **4** including various or miscellaneous items: *general knowledge* **5** not definite; vague: *the examples used will give a general idea* **6** highest in authority or rank: *the club's general manager* ▹*n* **7** a very senior military officer **8 in general** generally; mostly or usually
WORD ORIGIN Latin *generalis*
general anaesthetic *n* a substance that causes general anaesthesia ▸See **anaesthesia**
general election *n* an election in which representatives are chosen in all constituencies of a state
generalissimo *n, pl* **-mos** a supreme commander of combined armed forces
WORD ORIGIN Italian
generality *n* **1** *pl* **-ties** a general principle or observation: *speaking in generalities* **2** *old-fashioned* the majority: *the generality of mankind*
generalization *or* **-isation** *n* a principle or statement based on specific instances but applied generally: *the argument sinks to generalizations and name-calling*
generalize *or* **-ise** *vb* **-izing, -ized** *or* **-ising, -ised 1** to form general principles or conclusions from specific instances **2** to speak in generalities **3** to make widely used or known: *generalized violence*
generally ⓣ *adv* **1** usually; as a rule: *these protests have generally been peaceful* **2** commonly or widely: *it's generally agreed he has performed well* **3** not specifically; broadly: *what are your thoughts generally about the war?*
general practitioner *n* a doctor who does not specialize but has a general medical practice in which he or she treats all illnesses
general-purpose *adj* having a variety of uses: *general-purpose cooking oil*
general staff *n* officers who assist commanders in the planning and execution of military operations
general strike *n* a strike by all or most of the workers of a country
generate ⓣ *vb* **-ating, -ated** to produce or create
WORD ORIGIN Latin *generare* to beget
generation ⓣ *n* **1** all the people of approximately the same age: *the younger generation* **2** a successive stage in descent of people or animals: *passed on from generation to generation* **3** the average time between two generations of a species, about 35 years for humans: *an alliance which has lasted a generation* **4** a specified stage of development: *the next generation of fighter aircraft* **5** production, esp. of electricity or heat
generation gap *n* the difference in outlook and the lack of understanding between people of different generations
generation X *n* people born between the mid-1960s and mid-1970s who are highly educated and underemployed
WORD ORIGIN from the novel *Generation X: Tales for an Accelerated Culture* by Douglas Coupland
generative *adj* capable of producing or originating something
generator *n* a device for converting mechanical energy into electrical energy

g

THESAURUS

equipage ▹*vb* **7 = equip**, fit, suit, adjust, adapt, rig, tailor
gem *n* **1 = precious stone**, jewel, stone, semiprecious stone **2 = treasure**, pick, prize, jewel, flower, pearl, masterpiece, paragon, humdinger *(slang)*, taonga *(NZ)*
general *adj* **1, 4 = widespread**, accepted, popular, public, common, broad, extensive, universal, prevailing, prevalent **OPPOSITE:** individual **2 = universal**, overall, widespread, collective, across-the-board, all-inclusive **OPPOSITE:** exceptional **5 = vague**, broad, loose, blanket, sweeping, unclear, inaccurate, approximate, woolly, indefinite, hazy, imprecise, ill-defined, inexact, unspecific, undetailed **OPPOSITE:** specific
generally *adv* **1 = usually**, commonly, typically, regularly, normally, on average, on the whole, for the most part, almost always, in most cases, by and large, ordinarily, as a rule, habitually, conventionally, customarily **OPPOSITE:** occasionally **2 = commonly**, widely, publicly, universally, extensively, popularly, conventionally, customarily **OPPOSITE:** individually
generate *vb* **= produce**, create, make, form, cause, initiate, bring about, originate, give rise to, engender, whip up **OPPOSITE:** end
generation *n* **1 = age group**, peer group **2, 3 = age**, period, era, time, days, lifetime, span, epoch

DICTIONARY

generic ❶ (jin-ner-ik) *adj* of a whole class, or group, or genus **generically** *adv*
WORD ORIGIN Latin *genus* kind, race

generous ❶ *adj* **1** ready to give freely; unselfish **2** free from pettiness in character and mind **3** large or plentiful: *a generous donation* **generously** *adv* **generosity** *n*
WORD ORIGIN Latin *generosus* nobly born

genesis ❶ (jen-iss-iss) *n, pl* **-ses** (-seez) the beginning or origin of anything
WORD ORIGIN Greek

Genesis *n bible* the first book of the Old Testament, containing a description of the creation the world

Genet *n* **Jean** 1910–86, French dramatist and novelist; his novels include *Notre-Dame des Fleurs* (1944) and his plays *Les Bonnes* (1947) and *Le Balcon* (1956)

gene therapy *n genetics* the replacement or alteration of defective genes in order to prevent the occurrence of inherited diseases

genetic (jin-net-tik) *adj* of genetics, genes, or the origin of something **genetically** *adv*
WORD ORIGIN from *genesis*

genetically modified *adj* (of an organism) having DNA which has been altered for the purpose of improvement or correction of defects

genetic code *n biochem* the order in which the four nucleic acid bases of DNA are arranged in the molecule for transmitting genetic information to the cells

genetic engineering *n* alteration of the genetic structure of an organism in order to produce more desirable traits

genetic fingerprinting *n* the use of a person's unique pattern of DNA, which can be obtained from blood, saliva, or tissue, as a means of identification **genetic fingerprint** *n*

genetics *n* the study of heredity and variation in organisms **geneticist** *n*

Geneviève *n* **Saint** ?422–?512 AD, French nun; patron saint of Paris. Feast day: Jan 3

genial (jean-ee-al) *adj* cheerful, easy-going, and friendly **geniality** *n* **genially** *adv*
WORD ORIGIN Latin *genius* guardian deity

genie (jean-ee) *n* (in fairy tales) a servant who appears by magic and fulfils a person's wishes
WORD ORIGIN Arabic *jinni* demon

Genie *n Canad* an award given by the Academy of Canadian Cinema and Television in recognition of Canadian cinematic achievements

genital *adj* of the sexual organs or reproduction
WORD ORIGIN Latin *genitalis* concerning birth

genitals *or* **genitalia** (jen-it-ail-ya) *pl n* the external sexual organs

genitive *n grammar* a grammatical case in some languages used to indicate a relation of ownership or association
WORD ORIGIN Latin *genetivus* relating to birth

genius ❶ (jean-yuss) *n, pl* **-uses** **1** a person with exceptional ability in a particular subject or activity **2** such ability **3** a person considered as exerting influence of a certain sort: *the evil genius behind the drug-smuggling empire*
WORD ORIGIN Latin

genocide (jen-no-side) *n* the deliberate killing of a people or nation **genocidal** *adj*
WORD ORIGIN Greek *genos* race + Latin *caedere* to kill

genome *n* **1** the full complement of genetic material within an organism **2** all the genes comprising a haploid set of chromosomes
WORD ORIGIN from GENE + CHROMOSOME

genomics *n* the branch of molecular genetics concerned with the study of genomes

genotoxic *adj* harmful to genetic material

genre ❶ (zhahn-ra) *n* **1** a kind or type of literary, musical, or artistic work: *the mystery and supernatural genres* **2** a kind of painting depicting incidents from everyday life
WORD ORIGIN French

Genseric *or* **Gaiseric** *n* ?390–477 AD, king of the Vandals (428–77). He seized Roman lands, esp. extensive parts of N Africa, and sacked Rome (455)

gent *n Brit, Austral & NZ informal* ▸ short for **gentleman**

genteel *adj* **1** overly concerned with being polite **2** respectable, polite, and well-bred **genteelly** *adv*
WORD ORIGIN French *gentil* well-born

gentian (jen-shun) *n* a mountain plant with blue or purple flowers
WORD ORIGIN Latin *gentiana*

gentian violet *n* a violet-coloured solution used as an antiseptic and in the treatment of burns

Gentile[1] *n* **1** a person who is not a Jew ▹ *adj* **2** not Jewish
WORD ORIGIN Latin *gentilis* belonging to the same tribe

Gentile[2] *n* **Giovanni** 1875–1944, Italian Idealist philosopher and Fascist politician: minister of education (1922–24)

Gentile da Fabriano *n* original name *Niccolo di Giovanni di Massio*. ?1370–1427, Italian painter. His works, in the International Gothic style, include the *Adoration of the Magi* (1423)

gentility *n, pl* **-ties** **1** noble birth or ancestry **2** respectability and good manners
WORD ORIGIN Old French *gentilite*

gentle ❶ *adj* **1** kind and calm in character **2** temperate or moderate: *gentle autumn rain* **3** soft; not sharp or harsh: *gentle curves* **gentleness** *n* **gently** *adv*
WORD ORIGIN Latin *gentilis* belonging to the same family

gentlefolk *pl n old-fashioned* people regarded as being of good breeding

THESAURUS

generic *adj* **= collective**, general, common, wide, sweeping, comprehensive, universal, blanket, inclusive, all-encompassing **OPPOSITE:** specific

generous *adj* **1 = liberal**, lavish, free, charitable, free-handed, hospitable, prodigal, bountiful, open-handed, unstinting, beneficent, princely, bounteous, munificent, ungrudging **OPPOSITE:** mean
2 = magnanimous, kind, noble, benevolent, good, big, high-minded, unselfish, big-hearted, ungrudging
3 = plentiful, lavish, ample, abundant, full, rich, liberal, overflowing, copious, bountiful, unstinting, profuse, bounteous (*literary*), plenteous **OPPOSITE:** meagre

genesis *n* **= beginning**, source, root, origin, start, generation, birth, creation, dawn, formation, outset, starting point, engendering, inception, commencement, propagation **OPPOSITE:** end

genius *n* **1 = master**, expert, mastermind, brain (*informal*), buff (*informal*), intellect (*informal*), adept, maestro, virtuoso, whiz (*informal*), hotshot (*informal*), rocket scientist (*informal, chiefly US*), wonk (*informal*), brainbox, maven (*US*), master-hand, fundi (*S African*) **OPPOSITE:** dunce
2 = brilliance, ability, talent, capacity, gift, bent, faculty, excellence, endowment, flair, inclination, knack, propensity, aptitude, cleverness, creative power

genre *n* **1 = type**, group, school, form, order, sort, kind, class, style, character, fashion, brand, species, category, stamp, classification, genus, subdivision

gentle *adj* **1 = kind**, loving, kindly, peaceful, soft, quiet, pacific, tender, mild, benign, humane, compassionate, amiable, meek, lenient, placid, merciful, kind-hearted, sweet-tempered, tender-hearted **OPPOSITE:** unkind
2 = moderate, low, light, easy, soft, calm, slight, mild, soothing, clement, temperate, balmy **OPPOSITE:** violent

DICTIONARY

gentleman *n, pl* **-men** 1 a cultured, courteous, and well-bred man 2 a man who comes from a family of high social position 3 a polite name for a man **gentlemanly** *adj*

gentrification *n* a process by which the character of a traditionally working-class area is made fashionable by middle-class people **gentrify** *vb*

gentry *n Brit old-fashioned* people just below the nobility in social rank
WORD ORIGIN Old French *genterie*

gents *n Austral & Brit informal* a men's public toilet

genuflect *vb* to bend the knee as a sign of reverence or deference, esp. in church **genuflection** *n*
WORD ORIGIN Latin *genu* knee + *flectere* to bend

genuine ❶ *adj* 1 real and exactly what it appears to be: *a genuine antique* 2 sincerely felt: *genuine concern* 3 (of a person) honest and without pretence **genuinely** *adv* **genuineness** *n*
WORD ORIGIN Latin *genuinus* inborn

gen up on *vb* **genning, genned** *Austral & Brit informal* to become, or make someone else, fully informed about

genus (**jean**-uss) *n, pl* **genera** *or* **genuses** 1 *biol* one of the groups into which a family is divided, containing one or more species 2 a class or group
WORD ORIGIN Latin: race

geocentric *adj* 1 having the earth as a centre 2 measured as from the centre of the earth

geodesic *adj* 1 relating to the geometry of curved surfaces ▷*n* 2 the shortest line between two points on a curved surface

geodesy *n* the study of the shape and size of the earth
WORD ORIGIN Greek *gē* earth + *daiein* to divide

Geoffrey of Monmouth *n* ?1100–54, Welsh bishop and chronicler; author of *Historia Regum Britanniae*, the chief source of Arthurian legends

geography *n* 1 the study of the earth's surface, including physical features, climate, and population 2 the physical features of a region **geographer** *n* **geographical** *or* **geographic** *adj* **geographically** *adv*
WORD ORIGIN Greek *gē* earth + -GRAPHY

geology *n* 1 the study of the origin, structure, and composition of the earth 2 the geological features of an area **geologist** *n* **geological** *adj* **geologically** *adv*
WORD ORIGIN Greek *gē* earth + -LOGY

geometric *or* **geometrical** *adj* 1 of geometry 2 consisting of shapes used in geometry, such as circles, triangles, and straight lines: *geometric design* **geometrically** *adv*

geometric progression *n* a sequence of numbers, each of which differs from the succeeding one by a constant ratio, for example 1, 2, 4, 8

geometry *n* the branch of mathematics concerned with points, lines, curves, and surfaces **geometrician** *n*
WORD ORIGIN Greek *geōmetrein* to measure the land

geophysics *n* the study of the earth's physical properties and the physical forces which affect it **geophysical** *adj* **geophysicist** *n*

Geordie *Brit n* 1 a person from Tyneside 2 the Tyneside dialect ▷*adj* 3 of Tyneside: *a Geordie accent*

George[1] *n* 1 **David Lloyd** ▸See **Lloyd George** 2 Sir **Edward** (**Alan John**), known as *Eddie*. born 1938, British economist, governor of the Bank of England (1993–2003) 3 **Henry** 1839–97, US economist: advocated a single tax on land values, esp. in *Progress and Poverty* (1879) 4 **Saint** died ?303 AD, Christian martyr, the patron saint of England; the hero of a legend in which he slew a dragon. Feast day: April 23 5 **Stefan** (**Anton**) 1868–1933, German poet and aesthete. Influenced by the French Symbolists, esp. Mallarmé and later by Nietzsche, he sought for an idealized purity of form in his verse. He refused Nazi honours and went into exile in 1933

George[2] *n Brit informal* the automatic pilot in an aircraft
WORD ORIGIN C20: originally a slang name for an airman

George Cross *n* a British award for bravery, usually awarded to civilians

georgette (jor-**jet**) *n* a thin crepe dress material
WORD ORIGIN after Mme *Georgette*, a French dressmaker

Georgian *adj* 1 of or in the reigns of any of the kings of Great Britain and Ireland called George 2 denoting a style of architecture or furniture prevalent in Britain in the 18th century: *an elegant Georgian terrace in Edinburgh*

geospatial *adj* of or relating to the relative position of things on the earth's surface

geostationary *adj* (of a satellite) orbiting so as to remain over the same point on the earth's surface

geotechnical *adj* relating to the application of technology to engineering problems caused by geological factors

geothermal *adj* of or using the heat in the earth's interior

geranium *n* a cultivated plant with scarlet, pink, or white flowers
WORD ORIGIN Latin: cranesbill

Gérard *n* **François** (**Pascal Simon**), Baron. 1770–1837, French painter, court painter to Napoleon I and Louis XVIII

gerbil (**jur**-bill) *n* a small rodent with long back legs, often kept as a pet
WORD ORIGIN French *gerbille*

Gergiev *n* **Valery Abesalovich** born 1953, Russian conductor; musical director of the Kirov (now the Mariinsky) Opera from 1988

geriatric *adj* 1 of geriatrics or old people ▷*n* 2 an old person, esp. as a patient

geriatrics *n* the branch of medicine concerned with illnesses affecting old people

Géricault *n* (**Jean Louis André**) **Théodore** 1791–1824, French romantic painter, noted for his skill in capturing movement, esp. of horses

germ ❶ *n* 1 a tiny living thing, esp. one that causes disease: *a diphtheria germ* 2 the beginning from which something may develop: *the germ of a book*
WORD ORIGIN Latin *germen* sprout, seed

German *adj* 1 of Germany ▷*n* 2 a person from Germany 3 the official language of Germany, Austria, and parts of Switzerland

germane *adj* relevant: *the studies provided some evidence germane to these questions*
WORD ORIGIN Latin *germanus* of the same race

Germanic *n* 1 the ancient language from which English, German, and the Scandinavian languages developed ▷*adj* 2 of this ancient language or the languages that developed from it 3 characteristic of German people or things: *Germanic-looking individuals*

THESAURUS

3 = **slow**, easy, slight, deliberate, moderate, gradual, imperceptible

genuine *adj* 1 = **authentic**, real, original, actual, sound, true, pure, sterling, valid, legitimate, honest, veritable, bona fide, dinkum *(Austral & NZ informal)*, the real McCoy
OPPOSITE: counterfeit
2 = **heartfelt**, sincere, honest, earnest, real, true, frank, unaffected, wholehearted, unadulterated, unalloyed, unfeigned
OPPOSITE: affected
3 = **sincere**, straightforward, honest, natural, frank, candid, upfront *(informal)*, dinkum *(Austral & NZ informal)*, artless, guileless
OPPOSITE: hypocritical

germ *n* 1 = **microbe**, virus, bug *(informal)*, bacterium, bacillus, microorganism 2 = **beginning**, root, seed, origin, spark, bud, embryo, rudiment

DICTIONARY

Germanicus Caesar *n* 15 BC–19 AD, Roman general; nephew of the emperor Tiberius; waged decisive campaigns against the Germans (14–16)

germanium *n chem* a brittle grey metalloid element that is a semiconductor and is used in transistors. Symbol: Ge
WORD ORIGIN after *Germany*

German measles *n* ▸ same as **rubella**

German shepherd dog *n* ▸ same as **Alsatian**

germ cell *n* a sexual reproductive cell

germicide *n* a substance used to destroy germs
WORD ORIGIN *germ* + Latin *caedere* to kill

g

germinal *adj* **1** of or in the earliest stage of development: *the germinal phases of the case* **2** of germ cells

germinate *vb* **-nating, -nated** to grow or cause to grow **germination** *n*
WORD ORIGIN Latin *germinare* to sprout

germ warfare *n* the military use of disease-spreading bacteria against an enemy

gerontology *n* the scientific study of ageing and the problems of old people **gerontologist** *n*
WORD ORIGIN Greek *gerōn* old man + -LOGY

gerrymandering *n* the practice of dividing the constituencies of a voting area so as to give one party an unfair advantage
WORD ORIGIN from Elbridge *Gerry*, US politician + *(sala)mander*, from the salamander-like outline of a reshaped electoral district

gerund (jer-rund) *n* a noun formed from a verb, ending in *-ing*, denoting an action or state, for example *running*
WORD ORIGIN Latin *gerundum* something to be carried on

Gervais *n* **Ricky** born 1962, British comedian and actor, best known for his starring role in the TV series *The Office* (2001–02), which he also co-wrote and co-directed

gesso (jess-oh) *n* plaster used for painting or in sculpture
WORD ORIGIN Italian: chalk

Gestapo *n* the secret state police of Nazi Germany
WORD ORIGIN German *Ge(heime) Sta(ats)po(lizei)* secret state police

gestation *n* **1** the process of carrying and developing babies in the womb during pregnancy, or the time during which this process takes place **2** the process of developing a plan or idea in the mind
WORD ORIGIN Latin *gestare* to bear

gesticulate *vb* **-lating, -lated** to make expressive movements with the hands and arms, usually while talking **gesticulation** *n*
WORD ORIGIN Latin *gesticulari*

gesture ❶ *n* **1** a movement of the hands, head, or body to express or emphasize an idea or emotion **2** something said or done to indicate intention, or as a formality: *a gesture of goodwill* ▹ *vb* **-turing, -tured** **3** to make expressive movements with the hands and arms
WORD ORIGIN Latin *gestus*

Gesualdo *n* **Carlo**, Prince of Venosa. ?1560–1613, Italian composer, esp. of madrigals

get ❶ *vb* **getting, got** **1** to come into possession of **2** to bring or fetch **3** to catch (an illness) **4** to become: *they get frustrated and angry* **5** to cause to be done or to happen: *he got a wart removed; to get steamed up* **6** to hear or understand: *did you get that joke?* **7** to reach (a place or point): *we could not get to the airport in time* **8** to catch (a bus or train) **9** to persuade: *she was trying to get him to give secrets away* **10** *informal* to annoy: *you know what really gets me?* **11** *informal* to baffle: *now you've got me* **12** *informal* to hit: *a bit of grenade got me on the left hip* **13** *informal* to be revenged on **14** *informal* to start: *we got talking about it; it got me thinking* ▹ *n* **15** *Brit slang* ▸ same as **git** ▸ See also **get about, get across**, etc.
WORD ORIGIN Old English *gietan*

get about *or* **around** *vb* **1** to be socially active **2** (of news or a rumour) to circulate

get across ❶ *vb* to make (something) understood

get at *vb* **1** to gain access to: *to get at the information on these disks* **2** to imply or mean: *it is hard to see quite what he is getting at* **3** to annoy or criticize persistently: *people who know they're being got at*

get away *vb* **1** to escape or leave **2** **get away with** to do (something wrong) without being caught or punished ▹ *interj* **3** an exclamation of disbelief ▹ *n* **getaway** **4** the act of escaping, usually by criminals ▹ *adj* **getaway** **5** used to escape: *the getaway car was abandoned*

get back *vb* **1** to have (something) returned to one **2** to return to a former state or activity: *get back to normal* **3** **get back at** to retaliate against **4** **get one's own back** *informal* to get one's revenge

get by ❶ *vb informal* to manage in spite of difficulties: *he saw for himself what people did to get by*

get in *vb* **1** to arrive **2** to be elected **3** **get in on** to join in (an activity)

get off *vb* **1** to leave (a bus, train, etc.) **2** to escape the consequences of or punishment for an action: *the real culprits have got off scot-free* **3** **get off with** *Austral & Brit informal* to begin a romantic or sexual relationship with

get on *vb* **1** to enter (a bus, train, etc.) **2** to have a friendly relationship: *he had a flair for getting on with people* **3** to grow old: *he was getting on in years* **4** (of time) to elapse: *the time was getting on* **5** to make progress: *how are the children getting on?* **6** **get on with** to continue to do: *you can get on with whatever you were doing before* **7** **getting on for** approaching (a time, age, or amount): *getting on for half a century ago*

get out *vb* **1** to leave or escape **2** to become known **3** to gain something of significance or value: *that's all I got out of it* **4** **get out of** to avoid: *to get out of doing the dishes*

get over *vb* **1** to recover from (an illness or unhappy experience) **2** to overcome (a problem) **3** **get over with** to bring (something necessary but unpleasant) to an end: *better to get it over with*

get round *vb* **1** to overcome (a problem or difficulty) **2** (of news or a rumour) to circulate **3** *informal* to

THESAURUS

gesture *n* **1 = sign**, action, signal, motion, indication, gesticulation ▹ *vb* **3 = signal**, sign, wave, indicate, motion, beckon, gesticulate

get *vb* **1 = obtain**, receive, gain, acquire, win, land, score *(slang)*, achieve, net, pick up, bag, secure, attain, reap, get hold of, come by, glean, procure, get your hands on, come into possession of **2 = fetch**, bring, collect **3 = catch**, develop, contract, succumb to, fall victim to, go down with, come down with, become infected with, be afflicted with, be smitten by **4 = become**, grow, turn, wax, come to be **6 = understand**, follow, catch, see, notice, realize, appreciate, be aware of, take in, perceive, grasp, comprehend, fathom, apprehend, suss (out) *(slang)*, get the hang of *(informal)*, get your head round **9 = persuade**, convince, win over, induce, influence, sway, entice, coax, incite, impel, talk into, wheedle, prevail upon **10** *(informal)* **= annoy**, upset, anger, bother, disturb, trouble, bug *(informal)*, irritate, aggravate *(informal)*, gall, madden, exasperate, nettle, vex, irk, rile, pique, get on your nerves *(informal)*, nark *(Brit, Austral & NZ slang)*, get up your nose *(informal)*, give someone grief *(Brit & S African)*, make your blood boil, get your goat *(slang)*, get on your wick *(Brit slang)*, get your back up, hack you off *(informal)*

get across *vb* **= communicate**, publish, spread, pass on, transmit, convey, impart, get (something) through, disseminate, bring home,

gain the indulgence of (someone) by praise or flattery: *a child who learned to get round everybody and have her own way* **4 get round to** to come to (a task) eventually: *I will get round to paying the bill*

get through *vb* **1** to complete (a task or process) **2** to use up (money or supplies) **3** to succeed in (an examination or test) **4 get through to a** to succeed in making (someone) understand **b** to contact (someone) by telephone

get-together *n* **1** *informal* a small informal social gathering ▷ *vb* **get together 2** to meet socially or in order to have a discussion

Getty *n* **J(ean) Paul** 1892–1976, US oil executive, millionaire, and art collector

get up *vb* **1** to get out of bed **2 get up to** *informal* to be involved in: *I don't know what those guys got up to down there* ▷ *n* **get-up 3** *informal* a costume or outfit

get-up-and-go *n informal* energy or drive

Getz *n* **Stanley,** known as *Stan*. 1927–91, US jazz saxophonist: leader of his own group from 1949

geyser (geez-er) *n* **1** a spring that discharges steam and hot water **2** *Brit & S African* a domestic gas water heater
WORD ORIGIN Icelandic *Geysir*

ghastly ❶ *adj* **-lier, -liest 1** *informal* very unpleasant **2** deathly pale **3** horrible: *a ghastly accident*
WORD ORIGIN Old English *gāstlīc* spiritual

ghat *n* **1** (in India) stairs leading down to a river **2** (in India) a place of cremation **3** (in India) a mountain pass
WORD ORIGIN Hindi

Ghazali *n* **al-** 1058–1111, Muslim theologian, philosopher, and mystic

GHB gamma hydroxybutyrate: a substance with anaesthetic properties, used medically as a sedative and also as a recreational drug

ghee (gee) *n* clarified butter, used in Indian cookery
WORD ORIGIN Hindi *ghī*

Gheorgiu *n* **Angela** born 1965, Romanian soprano: married to Roberto Alagna

gherkin *n* a small pickled cucumber
WORD ORIGIN Dutch *agurkkijn*

ghetto *n, pl* **-tos** *or* **-toes** an area that is inhabited by people of a particular race, religion, nationality, or class
WORD ORIGIN Italian

ghetto blaster *n informal* a large portable CD player or cassette recorder with built-in speakers

ghettoize *or* **-ise** *vb* **-izing, -ized** *or* **-ising, -ised** to confine (someone or something) to a particular area or category: *to ghettoize women as housewives* **ghettoization** *or* **-isation** *n*

Ghiberti *n* **Lorenzo** 1378–1455, Italian sculptor, painter, and goldsmith of the quattrocento: noted esp. for the bronze doors of the baptistry of Florence Cathedral

ghillie *n* ▸ same as **gillie**

Ghirlandaio *or* **Ghirlandajo** *n* **Domenico** original name *Domenico Bigordi*. 1449–94, Italian painter of frescoes

ghost ❶ *n* **1** the disembodied spirit of a dead person, supposed to haunt the living **2** a faint trace: *the ghost of a smile on his face* **3** a faint secondary image in an optical instrument or on a television screen ▷ *vb* **4** ▸ short for **ghostwrite**
WORD ORIGIN Old English *gāst*

ghost gum *n Austral* a eucalyptus with a white trunk and branches

ghostly ❶ *adj* **-lier, -liest** frightening in appearance or effect: *ghostly noises*

ghost town *n* a town that used to be busy but is now deserted

ghostwrite *vb* **-writing, -wrote, -written** to write (an article or book) on behalf of a person who is then credited as author **ghostwriter** *n*

ghoul (gool) *n* **1** a person who is interested in morbid or disgusting things **2** a demon that eats corpses **ghoulish** *adj* **ghoulishly** *adv*
WORD ORIGIN Arabic *ghūl*

GHQ *mil* General Headquarters

GI[1] *n, pl* **GIs** *or* **GI's** *US informal* a soldier in the US Army
WORD ORIGIN abbreviation of *government issue*

GI[2] ▸ see **glycaemic index**

Giacometti *n* **Alberto** 1901–66, Swiss sculptor and painter, noted particularly for his long skeletal statues of isolated figures

Giambologna *n* original name *Giovanni da Bologna* or *Jean de Boulogne*. 1529–1608, Italian mannerist sculptor, born in Flanders: noted for his fountains and such works as *Samson Slaying a Philistine* (1565)

giant ❶ *n* **1** a mythical figure of superhuman size and strength **2** a person or thing of exceptional size, ability, or importance: *industrial giants* ▷ *adj* **3** remarkably large **4** (of an atom or ion or its structure) having large numbers of particles present in a crystal lattice, with each particle exerting a strong force of attraction on those near to it
WORD ORIGIN Greek *gigas*

giant panda *n* ▸ see **panda**

gibber[1] (jib-ber) *vb* to talk in a fast and unintelligible manner
WORD ORIGIN imitative

gibber[2] (gib-ber) *n Austral* **1** a boulder **2** barren land covered with stones
WORD ORIGIN Aboriginal

Gibberd *n* Sir **Frederick** 1908–84, British architect and town planner. His buildings include the Liverpool Roman Catholic cathedral (1960–67) and the Regent's Park Mosque in London (1977). Harlow in the U.K. and Santa Teresa in Venezuela were built to his plans

gibberish *n* rapid incomprehensible talk; nonsense

gibbet (jib-bit) *n* a gallows
WORD ORIGIN Old French *gibet*

gibbon (gib-bon) *n* a small agile ape of the forests of S Asia
WORD ORIGIN French

Gibbon *n* **1 Edward** 1737–94, English historian; author of *The History of the Decline and Fall of the Roman Empire* (1776–88), controversial in its historical criticism of Christianity **2 Lewis Grassic**, real name *James Leslie Mitchell*. 1901–35, Scottish writer: best known for his trilogy of novels *Scots Quair* (1932–34)

Gibbons *n* **1 Grinling** 1648–1721, English sculptor and woodcarver, noted for his delicate carvings of fruit, flowers, birds, etc. **2 Orlando** 1583–1625, English organist and composer, esp. of anthems, motets, and madrigals

gibbous (gib-bus) *adj* (of the moon)

g

THESAURUS

make known, put over, make clear *or* understood

get by *(informal)* **= manage**, survive, cope, fare, get through, exist, make out, get along, make do, subsist, muddle through, keep your head above water, make both ends meet

ghastly *adj* **1** *(informal)* **= horrible**, shocking, terrible, awful, grim, dreadful, horrendous, hideous, from hell *(informal)*, horrid *(informal)*, repulsive, frightful, loathsome, godawful *(slang)* **OPPOSITE:** lovely

ghost *n* **1 = spirit**, soul, phantom, spectre, spook *(informal)*, apparition, wraith, shade *(literary)*, phantasm, atua *(NZ)*, kehua *(NZ)*, wairua *(NZ)* **2 = trace**, shadow, suggestion, hint, suspicion, glimmer, semblance

ghostly *adj* **= unearthly**, weird, phantom, eerie, supernatural, uncanny, spooky *(informal)*, spectral, eldritch *(poetic)*, phantasmal

giant *n* **1 = ogre**, monster, titan, colossus, leviathan, behemoth ▷ *adj* **3 = huge**, great, large, vast, enormous, extensive, tremendous, immense, titanic, jumbo *(informal)*, gigantic, monumental, monstrous, mammoth, colossal, mountainous, stellar *(informal)*, prodigious, stupendous, gargantuan, elephantine, ginormous *(informal)*, Brobdingnagian, humongous *or* humungous *(US slang)*, supersize **OPPOSITE:** tiny

DICTIONARY

more than half but less than fully illuminated
WORD ORIGIN Latin *gibba* hump

Gibbs *n* **1 James** 1682–1754, British architect; his buildings include St Martin's-in-the-Fields, London (1722–26), and the Radcliffe Camera, Oxford (1737–49) **2 Josiah Willard** 1839–1903, US physicist and mathematician: founder of chemical thermodynamics

gibe (jibe) *n, vb* **gibing, gibed** ▸ same as **jibe**[1]
WORD ORIGIN perhaps from Old French *giber* to treat roughly

giblets (jib-lits) *pl n* the gizzard, liver, heart, and neck of a fowl
WORD ORIGIN Old French *gibelet* stew of game birds

g

Gibran *n* **Kahlil** 1883–1931, Syro-Lebanese poet, mystic, and painter, resident in the US after 1910; author of *The Prophet* (1923)

Gibson[1] *n chiefly US* a cocktail consisting of four or more parts dry gin and one part dry vermouth, iced and served with a pickled pearl onion

Gibson[2] *n* **Mel** born 1956, Australian film actor and director: his films include *Mad Max* (1979), *Hamlet* (1990), *Braveheart* (1996; also directed), *What Women Want* (2000), and *The Passion of the Christ* (2004; director only)

gidday, g'day *interj Austral & NZ* an expression of greeting

giddy *adj* **-dier, -diest 1** feeling weak and unsteady on one's feet, as if about to faint **2** happy and excited: *a state of giddy expectation* **giddiness** *n*
WORD ORIGIN Old English *gydig* mad, frenzied, possessed by God

Gide *n* **André** 1869–1951, French novelist, dramatist, critic, diarist, and translator, noted particularly for his exploration of the conflict between self-fulfilment and conventional morality. His novels include *L'Immoraliste* (1902), *La Porte étroite* (1909), and *Les Faux-Monnayeurs* (1926): Nobel prize for literature 1947

Gielgud *n* Sir **John** 1904–2000, English stage, film, and television actor and director

GIF *computers* **a** graphic interchange format: a standard compressed file format used for pictures **b** a picture held in this format

gift ⓣ *n* **1** something given to someone: *a birthday gift* **2** a special ability or power: *a gift for caricature*
WORD ORIGIN Old English: payment for a wife, dowry

gifted ⓣ *adj* having natural talent or aptitude: *that era's most gifted director*

giftwrap *vb* **-wrapping, -wrapped** to wrap (a gift) in decorative wrapping paper

gig[1] *n* **1** a single performance by jazz or pop musicians ▹ *vb* **gigging, gigged 2** to play gigs
WORD ORIGIN origin unknown

gig[2] *n* a light open two-wheeled one-horse carriage
WORD ORIGIN origin unknown

gig[3] *n computers, informal* ▸ short for **gigabyte**

giga- *prefix* **1** denoting 10^9: *gigavolt* **2** *computers* denoting 2^{30}: *gigabyte*
WORD ORIGIN Greek *gigas* giant

gigabyte *n computers* one thousand and twenty-four megabytes

gigantic ⓣ *adj* extremely large: *the most gigantic gold paperweight ever*
WORD ORIGIN Greek *gigantikos*

giggle ⓣ *vb* **-gling, -gled 1** to laugh nervously or foolishly ▹ *n* **2** a nervous or foolish laugh **3** *informal* an amusing person or thing **giggly** *adj*
WORD ORIGIN imitative

Gigli *n* **Beniamino** 1890–1957, Italian operatic tenor

gigolo (jig-a-lo) *n, pl* **-los** a man who is paid by an older woman to be her escort or lover
WORD ORIGIN French

gigot *n chiefly Brit* a leg of lamb or mutton
WORD ORIGIN French

Gilbert and George *n* a team of artists, **Gilbert Proesch,** Italian, born 1942, and **George Passmore,** British, born 1943: noted esp. for their photomontages and performance works

gild *vb* **gilding, gilded** *or* **gilt 1** to cover with a thin layer of gold **2** to make (something) appear golden: *the morning sun gilded the hills* **3 gild the lily a** to adorn unnecessarily something already beautiful **b** to praise someone excessively
WORD ORIGIN Old English *gyldan*

Giles *n* **1 Saint** 7th century AD, Greek hermit in France; patron saint of cripples, beggars, and lepers. Feast day: Sept 1 **2 William Ernest Powell** 1835–97, Australian explorer, born in England. He was noted esp. for his exploration of the western desert (1875–76)

gill (jill) *n* a unit of liquid measure equal to one quarter of a pint (0.14 litres)
WORD ORIGIN Old French *gille* vat, tub

Gill *n* (**Arthur**) **Eric** (**Rowton**) 1882–1940, British sculptor, engraver, and typographer: his sculptures include the *Stations of the Cross* in Westminster Cathedral, London

gillie *or* **ghillie** *n Scot* a sportsman's attendant or guide for hunting or fishing
WORD ORIGIN Scottish Gaelic *gille* boy, servant

Gillray *n* **James** 1757–1815, English caricaturist

gills (gillz) *pl n* the breathing organs of fish and other water creatures
WORD ORIGIN from Old Norse

gilt *vb* **1** ▸ a past of **gild** ▹ *adj* **2** covered with a thin layer of gold ▹ *n* **3** a thin layer of gold, used as decoration

gilt-edged *adj* denoting government securities on which interest payments and final repayments are guaranteed

gilts *pl n* gilt-edged securities

gimcrack (jim-krak) *adj* showy but cheap; shoddy
WORD ORIGIN origin unknown

gimlet (gim-let) *n* **1** a small hand tool with a pointed spiral tip, used for boring holes in wood ▹ *adj* **2** penetrating or piercing: *gimlet eyes*
WORD ORIGIN Old French *guimbelet*

gimmick *n informal* something designed to attract attention or publicity **gimmicky** *adj* **gimmickry** *n*
WORD ORIGIN origin unknown

gin[1] *n* an alcoholic drink distilled from malted grain and flavoured with juniper berries
WORD ORIGIN Dutch *genever* juniper

gin[2] *n* a noose of thin strong wire for catching small mammals
WORD ORIGIN Middle English *gyn*

gin[3] *n Austral offensive* an Aboriginal woman
WORD ORIGIN Aboriginal

ginger *n* **1** the root of a tropical plant, powdered and used as a spice or sugared and eaten as a sweet ▹ *adj* **2** light reddish-brown: *ginger hair* **gingery** *adj*
WORD ORIGIN Old French *gingivre*

ginger ale *n* a nonalcoholic fizzy drink flavoured with ginger extract

THESAURUS

gift *n* **1 = donation**, offering, present, contribution, grant, legacy, hand-out, endowment, boon, bequest, gratuity, prezzie *(informal)*, bonsela *(S African)*, largesse *or* largess, koha *(NZ)* **2 = talent**, ability, capacity, genius, power, bent, faculty, capability, forte, flair, knack, aptitude

gifted *adj* **= talented**, able, skilled, expert, masterly, brilliant, capable, clever, accomplished, proficient, adroit **OPPOSITE:** talentless

gigantic *adj* **= huge**, great, large, giant, massive, vast, enormous, extensive, tremendous, immense, titanic, jumbo *(informal)*, monumental, monstrous, mammoth, colossal, mountainous, stellar *(informal)*, prodigious, stupendous, gargantuan, herculean, elephantine, ginormous *(informal)*, Brobdingnagian, humongous *or* humungous *(US slang)*, supersize **OPPOSITE:** tiny

giggle *vb* **1 = laugh**, chuckle, snigger, chortle, titter, twitter, tee-hee ▹ *n* **2 = laugh**, chuckle, snigger, chortle, titter, twitter

DICTIONARY

ginger beer *n* a drink made by fermenting a mixture of syrup and root ginger
gingerbread *n* a moist brown cake flavoured with ginger
ginger group *n Brit, Austral & NZ* a group within a larger group that agitates for a more active policy
gingerly *adv* carefully or cautiously: *she sat gingerly on the edge of the chair*
WORD ORIGIN perhaps from Old French *gensor* dainty
ginger nut *or* **snap** *n* a hard biscuit flavoured with ginger
gingham *n* a cotton fabric with a checked or striped design
WORD ORIGIN Malay *ginggang* striped cloth
gingivitis (jin-jiv-**vite**-iss) *n* inflammation of the gums
WORD ORIGIN Latin *gingiva* gum
ginormous *adj informal* very large
WORD ORIGIN *gi(gantic)* + *(e)normous*
gin rummy *n* a version of rummy in which a player may finish if the odd cards in his hand total less than ten points
WORD ORIGIN GIN[1] + *rummy*
ginseng (jin-seng) *n* the root of a plant of China and N America, believed to have tonic and energy-giving properties
WORD ORIGIN Mandarin Chinese *jen shen*
Ginzburg *n* **Natalia** 1916–91, Italian writer and dramatist. Her books include *The Road to the City* (1942), *Voices in the Evening* (1961), and *Family Sayings* (1963)
Giorgione *n* **Il** original name *Giorgio Barbarelli*. ?1478–1511, Italian painter of the Venetian school, who introduced a new unity between figures and landscape
gip (jip) *n* ▸ same as **gyp**
Gipsy *n, pl* **-sies** ▸ same as **Gypsy**
giraffe *n* a cud-chewing African mammal with a very long neck and long legs and a spotted yellowy skin
WORD ORIGIN Arabic *zarāfah*
Giraldus Cambrensis *n* literary name of *Gerald de Barri*. ?1146–?1223, Welsh chronicler and churchman, noted for his accounts of his travels in Ireland and Wales
Giraud *n* **Henri Honoré** 1879–1949, French general, who commanded French forces in North Africa (1942–43)
Giraudoux *n* **(Hyppolyte) Jean** 1882–1944, French dramatist. His works include the novel *Suzanne et le Pacifique* (1921) and the plays *Amphitryon 38* (1929) and *La Guerre de Troie n'aura pas lieu* (1935)
gird *vb* **girding, girded** *or* **girt 1** to put a belt or girdle around **2 gird up one's loins** to prepare oneself for action
WORD ORIGIN Old English *gyrdan*
girder *n* a large steel or iron beam used in the construction of bridges and buildings
girdle *n* **1** a woman's elastic corset that covers the stomach and hips **2** anything that surrounds something or someone: *his girdle of supporters* **3** *anat* an encircling arrangement of bones: *the shoulder girdle* ▹ *vb* **-dling, -dled 4** to surround: *a ring of volcanic ash girdling the earth*
WORD ORIGIN Old English *gyrdel*
girl ● *n* **1** a female child **2** a young woman **girlhood** *n* **girlish** *adj*
WORD ORIGIN Middle English *girle*
girlfriend *n* **1** a female friend with whom a person is romantically or sexually involved **2** any female friend
Girl Guide *n* ▸ a former name for **Guide**
girlie *adj informal* **1** featuring naked or scantily dressed women: *girlie magazines* **2** suited to or designed to appeal to young women: *a real girlie night out*
giro (jire-oh) *n, pl* **-ros 1** (in some countries) a system of transferring money within a bank or post office, directly from one account into another **2** *Brit informal* a social-security payment by giro cheque
WORD ORIGIN Greek *guros* circuit
girt *vb* ▸ a past of **gird**
girth *n* **1** the measurement around something **2** a band fastened round a horse's middle to keep the saddle in position
WORD ORIGIN Old Norse *gjörth* belt
Giscard d'Estaing *n* **Valéry** born 1926, French politician; minister of finance and economic affairs (1962–66; 1969–74); president (1974–81)
Gish *n* **1 Dorothy** 1898–1968, US film actress, chiefly in silent films **2** her sister, **Lillian** 1896–1993, US film and stage actress, noted esp. for her roles in such silent films as *The Birth of a Nation* (1915) and *Intolerance* (1916)
Gissing *n* **George (Robert)** 1857–1903, English novelist, noted for his depiction of middle-class poverty. His works include *Demos* (1886) and *New Grub Street* (1891)
gist (jist) *n* the main point or meaning of something: *the gist of the letter*
WORD ORIGIN Anglo-French, as in *cest action gist en* this action consists in
git *n Brit slang* a contemptible person
WORD ORIGIN from *get* (in the sense: to beget, hence a bastard, fool)
Giulini *n* **Carlo Maria** 1914–2005, Italian orchestral conductor, esp. of opera
Giulio Romano *n* ?1499–1546, Italian architect and painter; a founder of mannerism
give ● *vb* **giving, gave, given 1** to present or hand (something) to someone **2** to pay (an amount of money) for a purchase **3** to grant or provide: *to give an answer* **4** to utter (a shout or cry) **5** to perform, make, or do: *the prime minister gave a speech* **6** to host (a party) **7** to sacrifice or devote: *comrades who gave their lives for their country* **8** to concede: *he was very efficient, I have to give him that* **9** to yield or break under pressure: *something has got to give* **10 give or take** plus or minus: *about one hundred metres, give or take five* ▹ *n* **11** a tendency to yield under pressure; elasticity ▸ See also **give away, give in**, etc. **giver** *n*
WORD ORIGIN Old English *giefan*
give-and-take *n* **1** mutual concessions and cooperation **2** a smoothly flowing exchange of ideas and talk: *a relaxed give-and-take about their past involvement*
give away ● *vb* **1** to donate as a gift **2** to reveal (a secret) **3** to present (a bride) formally to her husband in a marriage ceremony **4 give something away** *NZ* to give something up ▹ *n* **giveaway 5** something that reveals hidden feelings or intentions ▹ *adj* **giveaway 6** very cheap or free: *a giveaway rent*
give in ● *vb* to admit defeat
given *vb* **1** ▸ the past participle of **give** ▹ *adj* **2** specific or previously stated: *priorities within the given department* **3** to be assumed: *any given place on the earth* **4 given to** inclined to: *a man not given to undue optimism*
give off ● *vb* to send out (heat, light, or a smell)

g

THESAURUS

girl *n* **1 = female child**, schoolgirl, lass, lassie (*informal*), miss, maiden (*archaic*), maid (*archaic*)
give *vb* **1 = present**, contribute, donate, provide, supply, award, grant, deliver, commit, administer, furnish, confer, bestow, entrust, consign, make over, hand over *or* out **OPPOSITE:** take **4 = communicate**, announce, publish, transmit, pronounce, utter, emit, issue, be a source of, impart **5 = perform**, do, carry out, execute **7 = surrender**, yield, devote, hand over, relinquish, part with, cede **8 = concede**, allow, grant
give away *vb* **2 = reveal**, expose, leak, disclose, betray, uncover, let out, divulge, let slip, let the cat out of the bag (*informal*)
give in *vb* **= admit defeat**, yield, concede, collapse, quit, submit, surrender, comply, succumb, cave in (*informal*), capitulate
give off *vb* **= emit**, produce, release, discharge, send out, throw out, vent, exude, exhale

DICTIONARY

give out *vb* **1** to hand out: *the bloke that was giving out those tickets* **2** to send out (heat, light, or a smell) **3** to make known: *the man who gave out the news* **4** to fail: *the engine gave out*

give over *vb* **1** to set aside for a specific purpose: *the amount of space given over to advertisements* **2** *informal* to stop doing something annoying: *tell him to give over*

give up *vb* **1** to stop (doing something): *I did give up smoking* **2** to resign from (a job or position) **3** to admit defeat or failure **4** to abandon (hope) **5 give oneself up a** to surrender to the police or other authorities **b** to devote oneself completely: *she gave herself up to her work*

g

gizzard *n* the part of a bird's stomach in which hard food is broken up
WORD ORIGIN Old French *guisier* fowl's liver

glacé (glass-say) *adj* preserved in a thick sugary syrup: *glacé cherries*
WORD ORIGIN French: iced

glacial *adj* **1** of glaciers or ice **2** extremely cold **3** cold and unfriendly: *a glacial stare*

glacial period *n* ▸ same as **ice age**

glaciation *n* the process of covering part of the earth's surface with glaciers or masses of ice **glaciated** *adj*

glacier *n* a slowly moving mass of ice formed by an accumulation of snow
WORD ORIGIN Latin *glacies* ice

glad ❶ *adj* **gladder, gladdest 1** happy and pleased **2** very willing: *he was only too glad to help* **3** *archaic* causing happiness: *glad tidings* **gladly** *adv* **gladness** *n* **gladden** *vb*
WORD ORIGIN Old English *glæd*

glade *n* an open space in a forest: *a peaceful and sheltered glade*
WORD ORIGIN origin unknown

gladiator *n* (in ancient Rome) a man trained to fight in arenas to provide entertainment **gladiatorial** *adj*
WORD ORIGIN Latin: swordsman

gladiolus (glad-ee-oh-luss) *n, pl* **-li** (-lie) a garden plant with brightly coloured funnel-shaped flowers
WORD ORIGIN Latin: a small sword

glad rags *pl n informal* one's best clothes

gladsome *adj old-fashioned* joyous or cheerful

gladwrap *Austral, NZ & S African n* **1** *trademark* thin polythene material for wrapping ▹ *vb* **2** to wrap in gladwrap

glamorous ❶ *adj* attractive or fascinating

glamour ❶ *or US* **glamor** *n* exciting or alluring charm or beauty **glamorize** *or* **-ise** *vb*
WORD ORIGIN Scots variant of *grammar* (hence a spell, because occult practices were popularly associated with learning)

glance ❶ *n* **1** a quick look ▹ *vb* **glancing, glanced 2** to look quickly at something **3** to be deflected off an object at an oblique angle: *the ball glanced off a spectator* **glancing** *adj*
WORD ORIGIN Middle English *glacen* to strike obliquely

gland *n* **1** an organ that synthesizes and secretes chemical substances for the body to use or eliminate **2** a similar organ in plants
WORD ORIGIN Latin *glans* acorn

glandular *adj* of or affecting a gland or glands

glandular fever *n* an acute infectious viral disease that causes fever, sore throat, and painful swollen lymph nodes

glare ❶ *vb* **glaring, glared 1** to stare angrily **2** (of light or colour) to be too bright ▹ *n* **3** an angry stare **4** a dazzling light or brilliance **5 in the glare of publicity** receiving a lot of attention from the media or the public
WORD ORIGIN Middle English

glaring ❶ *adj* conspicuous or obvious: *glaring inconsistencies* **glaringly** *adv*

Glaser *n* **Donald Arthur** born 1926, US physicist: invented the bubble chamber; Nobel prize for physics 1960

glasnost *n* a policy of public frankness and accountability, developed in the USSR in the 1980s under Mikhail Gorbachev
WORD ORIGIN Russian: publicity, openness

glass *n* **1** a hard brittle transparent solid, consisting of metal silicates or similar compounds **2** a drinking vessel made of glass **3** the amount contained in a drinking glass: *a glass of wine* **4** objects made of glass, such as drinking glasses and bowls
WORD ORIGIN Old English *glæs*

Glass *n* **Philip** born 1937, US avant-garde composer noted for his minimalist style: his works include *Music in Fifths* (1970), *Akhnaten* (1984), *The Voyage* (1992), and *Monsters of Grace* (1998)

glass-blowing *n* the process of shaping a mass of molten glass by blowing air into it through a tube **glass-blower** *n*

glass ceiling *n* a situation in which progress, esp. promotion, appears to be possible, but restrictions or discrimination create a barrier that prevents it

glasses *pl n* a pair of lenses for correcting faulty vision, in a frame that rests on the nose and hooks behind the ears

glasshouse *n Brit & NZ* ▸ same as **greenhouse**

glassy *adj* **glassier, glassiest 1** smooth, clear, and shiny, like glass: *the glassy sea* **2** expressionless: *that glassy look*

Glaswegian (glaz-weej-an) *adj* **1** of Glasgow, a city in W Scotland ▹ *n* **2** a person from Glasgow **3** the Glasgow dialect

glaucoma *n* an eye disease in which increased pressure in the eyeball causes gradual loss of sight
WORD ORIGIN Greek *glaukos* silvery, bluish-green

glaze ❶ *vb* **glazing, glazed 1** to fit or cover with glass **2** to cover (a piece of pottery) with a protective shiny coating **3** to cover (food) with beaten egg or milk before cooking, in order to produce a shiny coating ▹ *n* **4** a protective shiny coating applied to a piece of pottery **5** a shiny coating of beaten egg or milk applied to food ▸ See also **glaze over** > **glazed** *adj* **glazing** *n*
WORD ORIGIN Middle English *glasen*

THESAURUS

glad *adj* **1 = happy**, pleased, delighted, contented, cheerful, gratified, joyful, overjoyed, chuffed *(slang)*, gleeful **OPPOSITE:** unhappy
3 *(archaic)* **= pleasing**, happy, cheering, pleasant, delightful, cheerful, merry, gratifying, cheery, joyous, felicitous

glamorous *adj* **= attractive**, beautiful, lovely, charming, entrancing, elegant, dazzling, enchanting, captivating, alluring, bewitching **OPPOSITE:** unglamorous

glamour *or US* **glamor** *n* **= charm**, appeal, beauty, attraction, fascination, allure, magnetism, enchantment, bewitchment

glance *n* **1 = peek**, look, glimpse, peep, squint, butcher's *(Brit slang)*, quick look, gander *(informal)*, brief look, dekko *(slang)*, shufti *(Brit slang)*, gink *(NZ slang)* **OPPOSITE:** good look ▹ *vb* **2 = peek**, look, view, check, clock *(Brit informal)*, gaze, glimpse, check out *(informal)*, peep, take a dekko at *(Brit slang)* **OPPOSITE:** scrutinize

glare *vb* **1 = scowl**, frown, glower, look daggers, stare angrily, give a dirty look, lour *or* lower **2 = dazzle**, blaze, flare, flame ▹ *n* **3 = scowl**, frown, glower, dirty look, black look, angry stare, lour *or* lower **4 = dazzle**, glow, blaze, flare, flame, brilliance

glaring *adj* **= obvious**, open, outstanding, patent, visible, gross, outrageous, manifest, blatant, conspicuous, overt, audacious, flagrant, rank, egregious, unconcealed **OPPOSITE:** inconspicuous

glaze *vb* **2 = coat**, polish, gloss, varnish, enamel, lacquer, burnish, furbish ▹ *n* **4 = coat**, finish, polish, shine, gloss, varnish, enamel, lacquer, lustre, patina

DICTIONARY

glaze over *vb* to become dull through boredom or inattention: *the listener's eyes glaze over*

glazier *n* a person who fits windows or doors with glass

Glazunov *n* **Aleksandr Konstantinovich** 1865–1936, Russian composer, in France from 1928. A pupil of Rimsky-Korsakov, he wrote eight symphonies and concertos for piano and for violin among other works

gleam ❶ *n* **1** a small beam or glow of light **2** a brief or dim indication: *a gleam of anticipation in his eye* ▷ *vb* **3** to shine **gleaming** *adj*
WORD ORIGIN Old English *glǣm*

glean *vb* **1** to gather (information) bit by bit **2** to gather the useful remnants of (a crop) after harvesting **gleaner** *n*
WORD ORIGIN Old French *glener*

gleanings *pl n* pieces of information that have been gleaned

glebe *n Austral & Brit* land granted to a member of the clergy as part of his or her benefice
WORD ORIGIN Latin *glaeba*

glee *n* great merriment or joy, esp. caused by the misfortune of another person
WORD ORIGIN Old English *glēo*

gleeful *adj* merry or joyful, esp. over someone else's mistake or misfortune **gleefully** *adv*

glen *n* a deep narrow mountain valley
WORD ORIGIN Scottish Gaelic *gleann*

glengarry *n, pl* **-ries** a brimless Scottish cap with a crease down the crown
WORD ORIGIN after *Glengarry*, Scotland

Glenn *n* **John** born 1921, US astronaut and politician. The first American to orbit the earth (Feb, 1962), he later became a senator (1975–99) and in 1998 returned to space at the age of 77

Glennie *n* Dame **Evelyn** (**Elizabeth Ann**) born 1965, British percussionist

glib *adj* **glibber, glibbest** fluent and easy, often in an insincere or deceptive way: *there were no glib or easy answers* **glibly** *adv* **glibness** *n*
WORD ORIGIN probably from Middle Low German *glibberich* slippery

glide ❶ *vb* **gliding, glided** **1** to move easily and smoothly **2** (of an aircraft) to land without engine power **3** to fly a glider **4** to float on currents of air
WORD ORIGIN Old English *glīdan*

glider *n* **1** an aircraft that does not use an engine, but flies by floating on air currents **2** *Austral* a flying phalanger

glide time *n NZ* ▸ same as **flexitime**

gliding *n* the sport of flying in a glider

glimmer *vb* **1** (of a light) to glow faintly or flickeringly ▷ *n* **2** a faint indication: *a glimmer of hope* **3** a glow or twinkle
WORD ORIGIN Middle English

glimpse ❶ *n* **1** a brief view: *a glimpse of a rare snow leopard* **2** a vague indication: *glimpses of insecurity* ▷ *vb* **glimpsing, glimpsed** **3** to catch sight of momentarily
WORD ORIGIN Germanic

Glinka *n* **Mikhail Ivanovich** 1803–57, Russian composer who pioneered the Russian national school of music. His works include the operas *A Life for the Tsar* (1836) and *Russlan and Ludmilla* (1842)

glint *vb* **1** to gleam brightly ▷ *n* **2** a bright gleam
WORD ORIGIN probably from Old Norse

glissade *n* **1** a gliding step in ballet **2** a controlled slide down a snow slope ▷ *vb* **-sading, -saded** **3** to perform a glissade
WORD ORIGIN French

glissando *n, pl* **-dos** *music* a slide between two notes in which all intermediate notes are played
WORD ORIGIN mock Italian, from French *glisser* to slide

glisten *vb* (of a wet or glossy surface) to gleam by reflecting light: *sweat glistened above his eyes*
WORD ORIGIN Old English *glisnian*

glitch *n* a small problem that stops something from working properly
WORD ORIGIN Yiddish *glitsh* a slip

glitter ❶ *vb* **1** (of a surface) to reflect light in bright flashes **2** (of light) to be reflected in bright flashes **3** to be brilliant in a showy way: *she glitters socially* ▷ *n* **4** a sparkling light **5** superficial glamour: *the trappings and glitter of the European aristocracy* **6** tiny pieces of shiny decorative material **7** *Canad* ice formed from freezing rain **glittering** *adj* **glittery** *adj*
WORD ORIGIN Old Norse *glitra*

glitzy *adj* **glitzier, glitziest** *slang* showily attractive
WORD ORIGIN probably from German *glitzern* to glitter

gloaming *n Scot, poetic* twilight; dusk
WORD ORIGIN Old English *glōmung*

gloat *vb* to regard one's own good fortune or the misfortune of others with smug or malicious pleasure
WORD ORIGIN probably Scandinavian

glob *n informal* a rounded mass of thick fluid
WORD ORIGIN probably from *globe*, influenced by *blob*

global ❶ *adj* **1** of or applying to the whole earth: *global environmental problems* **2** of or applying to the whole of something: *a global total for local-authority revenue* **globally** *adv*

globalize *or* **-lise** *vb* **-izing, -ized** *or* **-ising, -ised** to put (something) into effect worldwide **globalization** *or* **-lisation** *n*

global warming *n* an increase in the overall temperature worldwide believed to be caused by the greenhouse effect

globe ❶ *n* **1** a sphere on which a map of the world is drawn **2 the globe** the earth **3** a spherical object, such as a glass lamp shade or fishbowl **4** *S African* an electric light bulb
WORD ORIGIN Latin *globus*

globetrotter *n* a habitual worldwide traveller **globetrotting** *n, adj*

globular *adj* shaped like a globe or globule

globule *n* a small round drop of liquid
WORD ORIGIN Latin *globulus*

globulin *n* a simple protein found in living tissue

glockenspiel *n* a percussion instrument consisting of tuned metal plates played with a pair of small hammers
WORD ORIGIN German *Glocken* bells + *Spiel* play

gloom ❶ *n* **1** depression or melancholy: *all doom and gloom* **2** partial or total darkness
WORD ORIGIN Middle English *gloumben* to look sullen

THESAURUS

gleam *n* **1 = glimmer**, flash, beam, glow, sparkle **2 = trace**, ray, suggestion, hint, flicker, glimmer, inkling ▷ *vb* **3 = shine**, flash, glow, sparkle, glitter, flare, shimmer, glint, glimmer, glisten, scintillate

glide *vb* **1 = slip**, sail, slide, skim

glimpse *n* **1 = look**, sighting, sight, glance, peep, peek, squint, butcher's *(Brit slang)*, quick look, gander *(informal)*, brief view, shufti *(Brit slang)* ▷ *vb* **3 = catch sight of**, spot, sight, view, clock *(Brit informal)*, spy, espy

glitter *vb* **1, 2 = shine**, flash, sparkle, flare, glare, gleam, shimmer, twinkle, glint, glimmer, glisten, scintillate ▷ *n* **4 = sparkle**, flash, shine, beam, glare, gleam, brilliance, sheen, shimmer, brightness, lustre, radiance, scintillation **5 = glamour**, show, display, gilt, splendour, tinsel, pageantry, gaudiness, showiness

global *adj* **1 = worldwide**, world, international, universal, planetary **2 = comprehensive**, general, total, thorough, unlimited, exhaustive, all-inclusive, all-encompassing, encyclopedic, unbounded
OPPOSITE: limited

globe *n* **1, 2 = planet**, world, earth, sphere, orb

gloom *n* **1 = depression**, despair, misery, sadness, sorrow, blues, woe, melancholy, unhappiness, desolation, despondency, dejection, low spirits, downheartedness

DICTIONARY

gloomy ⓣ *adj* **gloomier, gloomiest** 1 despairing or sad 2 causing depression or gloom: *gloomy economic forecasts* 3 dark or dismal **gloomily** *adv*

gloop *or US* **glop** *n informal* any messy sticky fluid or substance **gloopy** *or US* **gloppy** *adj* **WORD ORIGIN** origin unknown

glorify *vb* **-fies, -fying, -fied** 1 to make (something) seem more important than it really is: *computers are just glorified adding machines* 2 to praise: *few countries have glorified success in business more than the United States* 3 to worship (God) **glorification** *n*

g

glorious ⓣ *adj* 1 brilliantly beautiful: *in glorious colour* 2 delightful or enjoyable: *the glorious summer weather* 3 having or full of glory: *glorious successes* **gloriously** *adv*

glory ⓣ *n, pl* **-ries** 1 fame, praise, or honour: *tales of glory* 2 splendour: *the glory of the tropical day* 3 something worthy of praise: *the Lady Chapel is the great glory of Lichfield* 4 adoration or worship: *the greater glory of God* ▹*vb* **-ries, -rying, -ried** 5 **glory in** to take great pleasure in: *the workers were glorying in their new-found freedom* **WORD ORIGIN** Latin *gloria*

glory box *n Austral & NZ old-fashioned informal* a box in which a young woman stores her trousseau

glory hole *n* an untidy cupboard or storeroom

Glos Gloucestershire

gloss[1] ⓣ *n* 1 a bright shine on a surface 2 a superficially attractive appearance 3 a paint with a shiny finish 4 a cosmetic used to give a shiny appearance: *lip gloss* ▹*vb* 5 to paint with gloss 6 **gloss over** to conceal (an error, failing, or awkward moment) by minimizing it: *don't try to gloss over bad news* **WORD ORIGIN** probably Scandinavian

gloss[2] ⓣ *n* 1 an explanatory comment added to the text of a book ▹*vb* 2 to add a gloss or glosses to **WORD ORIGIN** Latin *glossa* unusual word requiring explanatory note

glossary *n, pl* **-ries** an alphabetical list of technical or specialist words in a book, with explanations **WORD ORIGIN** Late Latin *glossarium;* see GLOSS[2]

glossy ⓣ *adj* **glossier, glossiest** 1 smooth and shiny: *glossy black hair* 2 superficially attractive or sophisticated: *his glossy Manhattan flat* 3 (of a magazine) produced on expensive shiny paper

glottal stop *n phonetics* a speech sound produced by tightly closing and then opening the glottis

glottis *n* the opening at the top of the windpipe, between the vocal cords **WORD ORIGIN** Greek *glōtta* tongue

Gloucester[1] *n* a city in SW England, administrative centre of Gloucestershire, on the River Severn; cathedral (founded 1100). Pop: 123 205 (2001). Latin name: **Glevum**

Gloucester[2] *n* 1 **Humphrey,** Duke of. 1391–1447, English soldier and statesman; son of Henry IV. He acted as protector during Henry VI's minority (1422–29) and was noted for his patronage of humanists 2 ▸ **Duke of** See **Richard III** 3 ▸ **Duke of** See **Thomas of Woodstock**

glove *n* 1 a shaped covering for the hand with individual sheaths for each finger and the thumb 2 a protective hand covering worn in sports such as boxing **WORD ORIGIN** Old English *glōfe*

glove compartment *n* a small storage area in the dashboard of a car

gloved *adj* covered by a glove or gloves: *a gloved hand*

glow ⓣ *n* 1 light produced as a result of great heat 2 a steady light without flames 3 brightness of complexion 4 a feeling of wellbeing or satisfaction ▹*vb* 5 to produce a steady light without flames 6 to shine intensely 7 to experience a feeling of wellbeing or satisfaction: *she glowed with pleasure* 8 (of the complexion) to have a strong bright colour: *his pale face glowing at the recollection* **WORD ORIGIN** Old English *glōwan*

glower (rhymes with **power**) *vb* 1 to stare angrily ▹*n* 2 an angry stare **WORD ORIGIN** origin unknown

glowing ⓣ *adj* full of praise: *a glowing tribute*

glow-worm *n* a European beetle, the females and larvae of which have organs producing a soft greenish light

gloxinia *n* a plant with white, red, or purple bell-shaped flowers **WORD ORIGIN** after Benjamin P. *Gloxin,* botanist

Gluck *n* **Christoph Willibald von** 1714–87, German composer, esp. of operas, including *Orfeo ed Euridice* (1762) and *Alceste* (1767)

glucose *n* a white crystalline sugar found in plant and animal tissues **WORD ORIGIN** Greek *gleukos* sweet wine

glue ⓣ *n* 1 a substance used for sticking things together ▹*vb* **gluing** *or* **glueing, glued** 2 to join or stick together with glue 3 **glued to** paying full attention to: *golf fans will*

THESAURUS

OPPOSITE: happiness
2 = darkness, dark, shadow, cloud, shade, twilight, dusk, obscurity, blackness, dullness, murk, dimness, murkiness, cloudiness, gloominess, duskiness **OPPOSITE:** light

gloomy *adj* **1 = miserable**, down, sad, dismal, low, blue, pessimistic, melancholy, glum, dejected, despondent, dispirited, downcast, joyless, downhearted, down in the dumps *(informal)*, cheerless, down in the mouth, in low spirits **OPPOSITE:** happy
2 = depressing, bad, dismal, dreary, black, saddening, sombre, dispiriting, disheartening, funereal, cheerless, comfortless **3 = dark**, dull, dim, dismal, black, grey, obscure, murky, dreary, sombre, shadowy, overcast, dusky **OPPOSITE:** light

glorious *adj* **1 = splendid**, beautiful, bright, brilliant, shining, superb, divine, gorgeous, dazzling, radiant, resplendent, splendiferous *(facetious)* **OPPOSITE:** dull
2 = delightful, fine, wonderful, excellent, heavenly *(informal)*, marvellous, splendid, gorgeous, pleasurable, splendiferous *(facetious)*
3 = illustrious, famous, celebrated, distinguished, noted, grand, excellent, honoured, magnificent, noble, renowned, elevated, eminent, triumphant, majestic, famed, sublime **OPPOSITE:** ordinary

glory *n* **1 = honour**, praise, fame, celebrity, distinction, acclaim, prestige, immortality, eminence, kudos, renown, exaltation, illustriousness **OPPOSITE:** shame
2 = splendour, majesty, greatness, grandeur, nobility, pomp, magnificence, pageantry, éclat, sublimity ▹*vb* **5 glory in = triumph**, boast, relish, revel, crow, drool, gloat, exult, take delight, pride yourself

gloss[1] *n* **1 = shine**, gleam, sheen, polish, brilliance, varnish, brightness, veneer, lustre, burnish, patina

gloss[2] *n* **1 = interpretation**, comment, note, explanation, commentary, translation, footnote, elucidation ▹*vb* **2 = interpret**, explain, comment, translate, construe, annotate, elucidate

glossy *adj* **1 = shiny**, polished, shining, glazed, bright, brilliant, smooth, sleek, silky, burnished, glassy, silken, lustrous **OPPOSITE:** dull

glow *n* **1, 2 = light**, gleam, splendour, glimmer, brilliance, brightness, radiance, luminosity, vividness, incandescence, phosphorescence **OPPOSITE:** dullness ▹*vb* **5, 6 = shine**, burn, gleam, brighten, glimmer, smoulder

glowing *adj* **= complimentary**, enthusiastic, rave *(informal)*, ecstatic, rhapsodic, laudatory, adulatory **OPPOSITE:** scathing

glue *n* **1 = adhesive**, cement, gum,

DICTIONARY

be glued to their televisions today for the Open Championship **gluey** *adj*
WORD ORIGIN Late Latin *glus*

glue ear *n* an accumulation of fluid in the middle ear of children, caused by infection and causing deafness

glue-sniffing *n* the practice of inhaling glue fumes to produce intoxicating or hallucinatory effects **glue-sniffer** *n*

glum *adj* **glummer, glummest** gloomy and quiet, usually because of a disappointment **glumly** *adv*
WORD ORIGIN variant of *gloom*

glut *n* **1** an excessive supply ▷*vb* **glutting, glutted 2** to supply (a market) with a commodity in excess of the demand for it **3 glut oneself** to eat or drink more than one really needs
WORD ORIGIN probably from Old French *gloutir* to swallow

glute *n* ▸short for **gluteus**

gluten (gloo-ten) *n* a sticky protein found in cereal grains, such as wheat
WORD ORIGIN Latin: glue

gluteus *or* **glutaeus** *n* any of the three muscles of the buttock
WORD ORIGIN Greek *gloutos* rump

glutinous (gloo-tin-uss) *adj* gluelike in texture

glutton *n* **1** someone who eats and drinks too much **2** a person who has a great capacity for something: *a glutton for work* **gluttonous** *adj*
WORD ORIGIN Latin *gluttire* to swallow

gluttony *n* the practice of eating too much

glycaemic index *or US* **glycemic index** *n* an index indicating the effects of various foods on blood sugar. Abbrev: **GI**

glycerine (gliss-ser-reen) *or* **glycerin** *n* ▸a nontechnical name for **glycerol**
WORD ORIGIN Greek *glukeros* sweet

glycerol (gliss-ser-ol) *n* a colourless odourless syrupy liquid obtained from animal and vegetable fats, used as a solvent, antifreeze, and sweetener, and in explosives

glycogen (glike-oh-jen) *n* a starchlike carbohydrate stored in the liver and muscles of humans and animals

glycolysis (glike-**kol**-iss-iss) *n biochem* the breakdown of glucose by enzymes, with the release of energy

gm gram

GM 1 genetically modified **2** *Brit* grant-maintained

G-man *n, pl* **G-men** *US slang* an FBI agent

GMB (in Britain) General, Municipal and Boilermakers (Trade Union)

GMO genetically modified organism

GMT Greenwich Mean Time

gnarled *adj* rough, twisted, and knobbly, usually through age

gnash *vb* to grind (the teeth) together in pain or anger
WORD ORIGIN probably from Old Norse

gnat *n* a small biting two-winged insect
WORD ORIGIN Old English *gnætt*

gnaw *vb* **1** to bite or chew constantly so as to wear away bit by bit **2 gnaw at** to cause constant distress or anxiety to: *uneasiness gnawed at his mind* **gnawing** *adj*
WORD ORIGIN Old English *gnagan*

gneiss *n* a coarse-grained layered metamorphic rock
WORD ORIGIN German *Gneis*

gnome *n* **1** an imaginary creature in fairy tales that looks like a little old man **2** a small statue of a gnome in a garden
WORD ORIGIN French

gnomic (no-mik) *adj literary* of or containing short clever sayings: *gnomic pronouncements*

Gnosticism (noss-tiss-siz-zum) *n* a religious movement involving belief in intuitive spiritual knowledge **Gnostic** *n, adj*

GNP gross national product

gnu (noo) *n, pl* **gnus** *or* **gnu** a sturdy African antelope with an oxlike head
WORD ORIGIN Xhosa *nqu*

go ⓘ *vb* **goes, going, went, gone 1** to move or proceed to or from a place: *go forward* **2** to be in regular attendance at (work, church, or a place of learning) **3** to lead to a particular place: *the path that goes right along the bank* **4** to be kept in a particular place: *where does this go?* **5** to do or become as specified: *he went white; the gun went bang* **6** to be or continue to be in a specified state: *to go to sleep* **7** to operate or function: *the car wouldn't go* **8** to follow a specified course; fare: *I'd hate the meeting to go badly* **9** to be allotted to a particular purpose or recipient: *a third of the total budget goes on the army* **10** to be sold: *the portrait went for a fortune to a telephone bidder* **11** (of words or music) to be expressed or sung: *the song goes like this* **12** to fail or break down: *my eyesight is going; he was on lap 19 when the engine went* **13** to die: *he went quickly at the end* **14** to be spent or finished: *all tension and all hope had gone* **15** to proceed up to or beyond certain limits: *I think this is going too far* **16** to carry authority: *what Daddy says goes* **17** to endure or last out: *they go for eight or ten hours without resting* **18** *not standard* to say: *then she goes, 'shut up'* **19 anything goes** anything is acceptable **20 be going to** to intend or be about to: *she was afraid of what was going to happen next* **21 let go** to relax one's hold on; release **22 let oneself go a** to act in an uninhibited manner **b** to lose interest in one's appearance **23 to go** remaining: *two days to go till the holidays* ▷*n, pl* **goes 24** an attempt: *he had a go at the furniture business* **25** a verbal or physical attack: *he couldn't resist having another go at me* **26** a turn to do something in a game: *'Your go now!' I shouted* **27** *informal* the quality of being active and energetic: *a grand old man, full of go and determination* **28 from the word go** *informal* from the very beginning **29 make a go of** *informal* to be successful in (a business venture or a relationship) **30 on the go** *informal* active and energetic ▸See also **go about, go against**, etc.
WORD ORIGIN Old English *gān*

go about *vb* **1** to tackle (a problem or task): *he went about it in the wrong way* **2** to busy oneself with: *people have been going about their business as usual*

goad *vb* **1** to provoke (someone) to take some kind of action, usually in anger ▷*n* **2** something that provokes someone to take some kind of action **3** a sharp pointed stick for driving cattle
WORD ORIGIN Old English *gād*

go against *vb* **1** to conflict with (someone's wishes or beliefs) **2** to be unfavourable to (a person): *a referendum would almost certainly go against them*

go-ahead *n* **1 give the go-ahead** *informal* to give permission to proceed ▷*adj* **2** enterprising or ambitious: *prosperous and go-ahead republics*

goal ⓘ *n* **1** *sport* the space into which players try to propel the ball or puck to score **2** *sport* **a** a successful attempt at scoring **b** the score so made **3** an aim or purpose: *the goal is to get homeless people on their feet* **goalless** *adj*
WORD ORIGIN origin unknown

g

THESAURUS

paste ▷*vb* **2 = stick**, fix, seal, cement, gum, paste, affix

go *vb* **1 = move**, travel, advance, journey, proceed, pass, fare *(archaic)*, set off **OPPOSITE:** stay **7 = function**, work, run, move, operate, perform **OPPOSITE:** fail **9 = be given**, be spent, be awarded, be allotted ▷*n* **24 = attempt**, try, effort, bid, shot *(informal)*, crack *(informal)*, essay, stab *(informal)*, whirl *(informal)*, whack *(informal)* **26 = turn**, shot *(informal)*, spell, stint **27** *(informal)* **= energy**, life, drive, spirit, pep, vitality, vigour, verve, force, get-up-and-go *(informal)*, oomph *(informal)*, brio, vivacity

goal *n* **3 = aim**, end, target, purpose, object, intention, objective, ambition, destination, Holy Grail *(informal)*

DICTIONARY

goalie *n informal* a goalkeeper
goalkeeper *n sport* a player whose duty is to prevent the ball or puck from entering the goal
goal line *n sport* the line marking each end of the pitch, on which the goals stand
goalpost *n* **1** either of two uprights supporting the crossbar of a goal **2 move the goalposts** to change the aims of an activity to ensure the desired results
goanna *n* a large Australian lizard
WORD ORIGIN from IGUANA
goat *n* **1** an agile cud-chewing mammal with hollow horns **2 act the goat** *informal* to behave in a silly manner **3 get someone's goat** *slang* to annoy someone
WORD ORIGIN Old English *gāt*
goatee *n* a small pointed beard that does not cover the cheeks
goatherd *n* a person who looks after a herd of goats
goatskin *n* leather made from the skin of a goat
goatsucker *n US & Canad* ▸same as **nightjar**
go-away bird *n S African* a grey lourie
WORD ORIGIN imitative
gob[1] *n* a thick mass of a soft substance
WORD ORIGIN Old French *gobe* lump
gob[2] *n Brit, Austral & NZ slang* the mouth
WORD ORIGIN origin unknown
go back on *vb* to fail to fulfil (a promise): *he went back on his promise not to raise taxes*
gobbet *n* a chunk or lump
WORD ORIGIN Old French *gobet*
Gobbi *n* **Tito** 1915–84, Italian operatic baritone
gobble[1] *vb* **-bling, -bled** to eat quickly and greedily
WORD ORIGIN probably from GOB[1]
gobble[2] *n* **1** the loud rapid gurgling sound made by a turkey ▹*vb* **-bling, -bled 2** to make this sound
WORD ORIGIN probably imitative
gobbledegook *or* **gobbledygook** *n* pretentious or unintelligible language
WORD ORIGIN whimsical formation from GOBBLE[2]
gobbler *n informal* a turkey
go-between *n* a person who acts as a messenger between two people or groups
goblet *n* a drinking vessel with a base and stem but without handles
WORD ORIGIN Old French *gobelet* a little cup
goblin *n* a small grotesque creature in fairy tales that causes trouble for people
WORD ORIGIN Old French
gobshite *n Irish taboo slang* a stupid person
WORD ORIGIN GOB[2] + *shite* excrement
gobsmacked *adj Brit, Austral & NZ slang* astonished and astounded
goby *n, pl* **-by** *or* **-bies** a small spiny-finned fish
WORD ORIGIN Latin *gobius* gudgeon
go by *vb* **1** to pass: *as time goes by* **2** to be guided by: *if my experience is anything to go by*
go-cart *n* ▸same as **go-kart**
god ❶ *n* **1** a supernatural being, worshipped as the controller of the universe or some aspect of life or as the personification of some force **2** an image of such a being **3** a person or thing to which excessive attention is given: *the All Blacks are gods in New Zealand* **4 the gods** the top balcony in a theatre **goddess** *fem n*
WORD ORIGIN Old English
God *n* **1** the sole Supreme Being, Creator and ruler of all, in religions such as Christianity, Judaism, and Islam ▹*interj* **2** an oath or exclamation of surprise or annoyance
Godard *n* **Jean-Luc** born 1930, French film director and writer associated with the New Wave of the 1960s. His works include *À bout de souffle* (1960), *Weekend* (1967), *Sauve qui peut* (1980), *Nouvelle Vague* (1990), and *Éloge de l'amour* (2003)
godchild *n, pl* **-children** a person who is sponsored by godparents at baptism
Goddard *n* **Robert Hutchings** 1882–1945, US physicist. He made the first workable liquid-fuelled rocket
goddaughter *n* a female godchild
Godefroy de Bouillon *n* ?1060–1100, French leader of the First Crusade (1096–99), becoming first ruler of the Latin kingdom of Jerusalem
godetia *n* a garden plant with showy flowers
WORD ORIGIN after C. H. *Godet*, botanist
godfather *n* **1** a male godparent **2** the head of a Mafia family or other criminal ring
God-fearing *adj* deeply religious
godforsaken *adj* desolate or dreary: *some godforsaken village in the Himalayas*
Godhead *n* the nature and condition of being God
godless *adj* **1** wicked or unprincipled **2** not religious **godlessness** *n*
godly ❶ *adj* **-lier, -liest** deeply religious **godliness** *n*
godmother *n* a female godparent
Godolphin *n* **Sidney** 1st Earl of Godolphin. 1645–1712, English statesman; as Lord Treasurer, he managed the financing of Marlborough's campaigns in the War of the Spanish Succession
Godoy *n* **Manuel de** 1767–1851, Spanish statesman: Charles IV's unpopular chief minister (1792–97; 1801–08)
godparent *n* a person who promises at a person's baptism to look after his or her religious upbringing
godsend *n* a person or thing that comes unexpectedly but is very welcome
godson *n* a male godchild
Godspeed *interj* an expression of good wishes for a person's safe journey and success
Godunov *n* **Boris Fyodorovich** ?1551–1605, Russian regent (1584–98) and tsar (1598–1605)
Godwin *n* **1** died 1053, Earl of Wessex. He was chief adviser to Canute and Edward the Confessor. His son succeeded Edward to the throne as Harold II **2 Mary** ▸See (Mary) **Wollstonecraft 3 William** 1756–1836, British political philospher and novelist. In *An Enquiry concerning Political Justice* (1793), he rejected government and social institutions, including marriage. His views greatly influenced English romantic writers
goer *n* a person who attends something regularly: *a church goer*
Goes *n* **Hugo van der** ?1440–82, Flemish painter: works include the *Pontinari Altarpiece* and *The Death of a Virgin*
go for *vb* **1** to choose: *any politician will go for the soft option* **2** *informal* to like very much **3** to attack **4** to apply equally to: *the same might go for the other woman*
go-getter *n informal* an ambitious enterprising person **go-getting** *adj*
gogga ❶ (hohh-a) *n S African informal* an insect
WORD ORIGIN Nama (language of southern Africa) *xo xo*
goggle *vb* **-gling, -gled** to stare with wide-open eyes ▸See also **goggles** > **goggle-eyed** *adj*
WORD ORIGIN Middle English *gogelen* to look aside
gogglebox *n Brit slang* a television set
goggles *pl n* close-fitting protective spectacles
go-go *adj* denoting a type of dancing performed to pop music by young women wearing few clothes
Goidelic *n* **1** the group of Celtic languages, consisting of Irish Gaelic, Scottish Gaelic, and Manx ▹*adj* **2** of this group of languages
WORD ORIGIN Old Irish *Goidel* Celt

THESAURUS

god *n* **1 = deity**, immortal, divinity, divine being, supreme being, atua *(NZ)*
godly *adj* **= devout**, religious, holy, righteous, pious, good, saintly, god-fearing
gogga *n (S African informal)* **= insect**, bug, creepy-crawly *(Brit informal)*
golden *adj* **2 = yellow**, bright,

go in for *vb* **1** to enter (a competition) **2** to take up or take part in (an activity)

going *n* **1** the condition of the ground with regard to walking or riding: *the going for the cross-country is perfect* **2** *informal* speed or progress: *not bad going for a lad of 58* ▷ *adj* **3** thriving: *the racecourse was a going concern* **4** current or accepted: *this is the going rate for graduates*

going-over *n, pl* **goings-over** *informal* **1** a thorough examination or investigation **2** a physical beating

goings-on *pl n informal* mysterious or shady activities

go into *vb* to describe or investigate in detail

goitre *or US* **goiter** (goy-ter) *n pathol* a swelling of the thyroid gland in the neck
WORD ORIGIN French

go-kart *n* a small four-wheeled motor vehicle, used for racing

gold *n* **1** a bright yellow precious metal, used as a monetary standard and in jewellery and plating. Symbol: Au **2** jewellery or coins made of this metal **3** ▸ short for **gold medal** ▷ *adj* **4** deep yellow
WORD ORIGIN Old English

Gold *n* **Thomas** 1920–2004, Austrian-born astronomer, working in England and the US: with Bondi and Hoyle he proposed the steady-state theory of the universe

goldcrest *n* a small bird with a bright yellow-and-black crown

gold-digger *n informal* a woman who marries or has a relationship with a man for his money

gold dust *n* **1** gold in the form of small particles or powder **2 like gold dust** in great demand because difficult to obtain: *kidney machines were like gold dust*

golden ❶ *adj* **1** made of gold: *golden bangles* **2** of the colour of gold: *golden corn* **3** *informal* very successful or destined for success: *the golden girl of British athletics* **4** excellent or valuable: *a golden opportunity for peace* **5** (of an anniversary) the fiftieth: *golden wedding; Golden Jubilee*

golden age *n* the most flourishing and outstanding period in the history of an art or nation: *the golden age of Dixieland jazz*

golden eagle *n* a large mountain eagle of the N hemisphere with golden-brown feathers

golden goal *n soccer* (in certain matches) the first goal scored in extra time, which instantly wins the match for the side scoring it

golden handshake *n informal* money given to an employee either on retirement or to compensate for loss of employment

golden hour *n* the first hour after a serious accident, when medical treatment for the victim is crucial

golden mean *n* the middle course between extremes

golden retriever *n* a retriever with silky wavy gold-coloured hair

goldenrod *n* a tall plant with spikes of small yellow flowers

golden rule *n* an important principle: *the golden rule is to start with the least difficult problems*

golden syrup *n* a light golden-coloured treacle used for sweetening food

golden wattle *n* an Australian plant with yellow flowers that yields a useful gum and bark

goldfinch *n* a European finch, the adult of which has yellow-and-black wings

goldfish *n, pl* **-fish** *or* **-fishes** a gold or orange-red freshwater fish, often kept as a pet

gold foil *n* thin gold sheet that is thicker than gold leaf

Golding *n* Sir **William** (**Gerald**) 1911–93, English novelist noted for his allegories of man's proclivity for evil. His novels include *Lord of the Flies* (1954), *Darkness Visible* (1979), *Rites of Passage* (1980), *Close Quarters* (1987), and *Fire Down Below* (1989). Nobel prize for literature 1983

gold leaf *n* very thin gold sheet made by rolling or hammering gold and used for gilding

gold medal *n* a medal made of gold, awarded to the winner of a race or competition

Goldoni *n* **Carlo** 1707–93, Italian dramatist; author of over 250 plays in Italian or French, including *La Locandiera* (1753). His work introduced realistic Italian comedy, superseding the commedia dell'arte

gold-plated *adj* covered with a very thin coating of gold

gold rush *n* a large-scale migration of people to a territory where gold has been found

Goldschmidt *n* **Richard Benedikt** 1878–1958, US geneticist, born in Germany. He advanced the theory that heredity is determined by the chemical configuration of the chromosome molecule rather than by the qualities of the individual genes

goldsmith *n* a person who makes gold jewellery and other articles

Goldsmith *n* **Oliver** ?1730–74, Irish poet, dramatist, and novelist. His works include the novel *The Vicar of Wakefield* (1766), the poem *The Deserted Village* (1770), and the comedy *She Stoops to Conquer* (1773)

gold standard *n* a monetary system in which the basic currency unit equals a specified weight of gold

golf *n* **1** a game in which a ball is struck with clubs into a series of eighteen holes in a grassy course ▷ *vb* **2** to play golf **golfer** *n*
WORD ORIGIN origin unknown

golf club *n* **1** a long-shafted club used to strike a golf ball **2 a** an association of golf players **b** the premises of such an association

golf course *or* **links** *n* an area of ground laid out for golf

golliwog *n* a soft doll with a black face, usually made of cloth
WORD ORIGIN from a doll in a series of American children's books

golly *interj* an exclamation of mild surprise
WORD ORIGIN originally a euphemism for *God*

Gomberg *n* **Moses** 1866–1947, US chemist, born in Russia, noted for his work on free radicals

Gompers *n* **Samuel** 1850–1924, US labour leader, born in England; a founder of the American Federation of Labor and its president (1886–94; 1896–1924)

Gomulka *n* **Władysław** 1905–82, Polish statesman; first secretary of the Polish Communist Party (1956–70)

gonad *n* an organ in which reproductive cells are produced, such as a testis or ovary
WORD ORIGIN Greek *gonos* seed

Goncharov *n* **Ivan Aleksandrovich** 1812–91, Russian novelist: his best-known work is *Oblomov* (1859)

Goncourt *n* **Edmond Louis Antoine Huot de**, 1822–96, and his brother, **Jules Alfred Huot de**, 1830–70, French writers, noted for their collaboration, esp. on their *Journal*, and for the Académie Goncourt founded by Edmond's will

gondola *n* **1** a long narrow flat-bottomed boat with a high ornamented stem, traditionally used on the canals of Venice **2** a moving cabin suspended from a cable, used as a ski lift
WORD ORIGIN Italian

gondolier *n* a person who propels a gondola

gone ❶ *vb* **1** ▸ the past participle of **go** ▷ *adj* **2** no longer present or no longer in existence

THESAURUS

brilliant, blonde *or* blond, flaxen
OPPOSITE: dark
3 *(informal)* = **successful**, glorious, prosperous, best, rich, flourishing, halcyon **OPPOSITE:** worst
4 = **promising**, excellent, valuable, favourable, advantageous, auspicious, opportune, propitious
OPPOSITE: unfavourable

gone *adj* **2a** = **missing**, lost, away, vanished, absent, astray **2b** = **past**, over, ended, finished, elapsed

DICTIONARY

goner *n slang* a person who is about to die or who is beyond help

gong *n* **1** a flat circular metal disc that is hit with a hammer to give out a loud sound **2** *Brit slang* a medal
WORD ORIGIN Malay

gonorrhoea *or esp. US* **gonorrhea** (gon-or-ree-a) *n* a sexually transmitted disease that causes inflammation and a discharge from the genital organs
WORD ORIGIN Greek *gonos* semen + *rhoia* flux

González *n* **Julio** 1876–1942, Spanish sculptor: one of the first to create abstract geometric forms with soldered iron

González Márquez *n* **Felipe** born 1942, Spanish statesman; prime minister of Spain (1982–96)

goo *n informal* a sticky substance
WORD ORIGIN origin unknown

Gooch *n* **Graham** (**Alan**) born 1953, English cricketer; captain of England (1988, 1989–93)

good ❶ *adj* **better, best 1** having admirable, pleasing, or superior qualities: *a good listener* **2** morally excellent; virtuous: *a good person* **3** beneficial: *exercise is good for the heart* **4** kindly or generous: *he is so good to us* **5** competent or talented: *she's good at physics* **6** obedient or well-behaved: *a good boy* **7** reliable or recommended: *a good make* **8** complete or thorough: *she went to have a good look round* **9** appropriate or opportune: *a good time to clear the air* **10** satisfying or enjoyable: *a good holiday* **11** newest or of the best quality: *keep the good dishes for guests* **12** fairly large, extensive, or long: *they contain a good amount of protein* **13 as good as** virtually or practically: *the war was as good as over* ▷ *n* **14** advantage or benefit: *what is the good of it all?* **15** positive moral qualities; virtue **16 for good** for ever; permanently: *his political career was over for good* ▸ See also **goods**
WORD ORIGIN Old English *gōd*

goodbye ❶ *interj* **1** an expression used on parting ▷ *n* **2** the act of saying goodbye: *he said his goodbyes*
WORD ORIGIN from *God be with ye*

good day *interj* an expression of greeting or farewell used during the day

good-for-nothing *n* **1** an irresponsible or worthless person ▷ *adj* **2** irresponsible or worthless

Good Friday *n Christianity* the Friday before Easter, observed as a commemoration of the Crucifixion of Jesus Christ

goodies *pl n* any things considered particularly desirable

goodly *adj* **-lier, -liest** fairly large: *a goodly number of children*

Goodman *n* **Benny,** full name *Benjamin David Goodman*. 1909–86, US jazz clarinetist and bandleader, whose treatment of popular songs created the jazz idiom known as swing

good morning *interj* an expression of greeting or farewell used in the morning

good-natured *adj* tolerant and kindly

goodness ❶ *n* **1** the quality of being good ▷ *interj* **2** an exclamation of surprise

good night *interj* an expression of farewell used in the evening or at night

goods ❶ *pl n* **1** articles produced to be sold: *consumer goods* **2** movable personal property: *houses and goods are insured from fire* **3 deliver the goods** *informal* to do what is expected or required **4 have the goods on someone** *US & Canad slang* to know something incriminating about someone

Good Samaritan *n* a person who helps someone in difficulty or distress
WORD ORIGIN from a parable in Luke 10: 30–37

good-tempered *adj* tolerant and kindly

good turn *n* a helpful and friendly act

goodwill ❶ *n* **1** kindly feelings towards other people **2** the popularity and good reputation of a well-established business, considered as a valuable asset

goody *interj* **1** a child's exclamation of pleasure ▷ *n, pl* **goodies 2** *informal* the hero in a film or book ▸ See **goodies**

Goodyear *n* **Charles** 1800–60, US inventor of vulcanized rubber

goody-goody *informal n, pl* **-goodies 1** a person who behaves well in order to please people in authority ▷ *adj* **2** behaving well in order to please

THESAURUS

good *adj* **1, 10 = excellent**, great, fine, pleasing, capital, choice, crucial *(slang)*, acceptable, pleasant, worthy, first-class, divine, splendid, satisfactory, superb, enjoyable, awesome *(slang)*, dope *(slang)*, world-class, admirable, agreeable, super *(informal)*, pleasurable, wicked *(slang)*, bad *(slang)*, first-rate, tiptop, bitchin' *(US slang)*, booshit *(Austral slang)*, exo *(Austral slang)*, sik *(Austral slang)*, rad *(informal)*, phat *(slang)*, schmick *(Austral informal)*, beaut *(informal)*, barrie *(Scot slang)*, belting *(Brit slang)*, pearler *(Austral slang)* **OPPOSITE:** bad
2 = honourable, moral, worthy, ethical, upright, admirable, honest, righteous, exemplary, right, virtuous, trustworthy, altruistic, praiseworthy, estimable
OPPOSITE: bad
3 = beneficial, useful, healthy, helpful, favourable, wholesome, advantageous, salutary, salubrious
OPPOSITE: harmful
4 = kind, kindly, friendly, obliging, charitable, humane, gracious, benevolent, merciful, beneficent, well-disposed, kind-hearted
OPPOSITE: unkind
5 = proficient, able, skilled, capable, expert, talented, efficient, clever, accomplished, reliable, first-class, satisfactory, competent, thorough, adept, first-rate, adroit, dexterous
OPPOSITE: bad
6 = well-behaved, seemly, mannerly, proper, polite, orderly, obedient, dutiful, decorous, well-mannered
OPPOSITE: naughty
7 = true, real, genuine, proper, reliable, dependable, sound, trustworthy, dinkum *(Austral & NZ informal)* **8 = considerable**, large, substantial, sufficient, adequate, ample **9 = convenient**, timely, fitting, fit, appropriate, suitable, well-timed, opportune
OPPOSITE: inconvenient
12 = full, long, whole, complete, entire, solid, extensive
OPPOSITE: scant
▷ *n* **14 = benefit**, interest, gain, advantage, use, service, profit, welfare, behalf, usefulness, wellbeing **OPPOSITE:** disadvantage
15 = virtue, goodness, righteousness, worth, merit, excellence, morality, probity, rectitude, uprightness
OPPOSITE: evil

goodbye *interj* **1 = farewell**, see you, see you later, ciao *(Italian)*, cheerio, adieu, ta-ta, au revoir *(French)*, auf Wiedersehen *(German)*, adios *(Spanish)*, haere ra *(NZ)* ▷ *n* **2 = farewell**, parting, leave-taking

goodness *n* **1a = virtue**, honour, merit, integrity, morality, honesty, righteousness, probity, rectitude, uprightness **OPPOSITE:** badness **1b = excellence**, value, quality, worth, merit, superiority **1c = nutrition**, benefit, advantage, nourishment, wholesomeness, salubriousness **1d = kindness**, charity, humanity, goodwill, mercy, compassion, generosity, friendliness, benevolence, graciousness, beneficence, kindliness, humaneness, kind-heartedness

goods *pl n* **1 = merchandise**, stock, products, stuff, commodities, wares **2 = property**, things, effects, gear, furniture, movables, possessions, furnishings, belongings, trappings, paraphernalia, chattels, appurtenances

goodwill *n* **1 = friendliness**, favour, friendship, benevolence, amity, kindliness

people in authority

gooey *adj* **gooier, gooiest** *informal* **1** sticky, soft, and often sweet **2** sentimental: *one knows the whole gooey performance is an act*

goof *vb informal* **1** to bungle or botch **2 goof off** *US & Canad* to spend time in a lazy or foolish way: *he's goofing off on the Costa del Sol* WORD ORIGIN probably from dialect *goff* simpleton

go off *vb* **1** to stop functioning: *the heating went off* **2** to make a sudden loud noise: *a bomb went off* **3** to occur as specified: *the actual launch went off perfectly* **4** *informal* (of food) to become stale or rotten **5** *Brit informal* to stop liking

goofy *adj* **goofier, goofiest** *informal* silly or ridiculous

google *vb* **1** to search for (something) on the internet using a search engine **2** to check (someone's credentials) by searching for websites containing his or her name WORD ORIGIN from *Google*, a popular search engine on the internet

googly *n, pl* **-lies** *cricket* a ball bowled like a leg break but spinning from off to leg on pitching WORD ORIGIN Australian English

goon *n* **1** a stupid person **2** *US informal* a hired thug WORD ORIGIN dialect *gooney* fool; influenced by US cartoon character Alice the *goon*

go on *vb* **1** to continue or proceed **2** to take place: *there's a war going on* **3** to talk at length and annoyingly

goosander *n* a duck of Europe and North America with a dark head and white body WORD ORIGIN probably from GOOSE[1] + Old Norse *önd* (genitive *andar*) duck

goose[1] *n, pl* **geese 1** a fairly large web-footed long-necked migratory bird **2** the female of such a bird **3** the flesh of the goose used for food **4** *informal* a silly person WORD ORIGIN Old English *gōs*

goose[2] *vb* **goosing, goosed** *slang* to prod (someone) playfully in the bottom WORD ORIGIN from the jabbing of a goose's bill

gooseberry *n, pl* **-ries 1** a small edible green berry with tiny hairs on the skin **2 play gooseberry** *Brit & NZ informal* to be an unwanted single person accompanying a couple

goose flesh *n* the bumpy condition of the skin due to cold or fear, in which the muscles at the base of the hair follicles contract, making the hair bristle. Also: **goose pimples**

Goosen *n* **Retief** born 1969; South African golfer: won the British Open Championship (2005) and the US Open Championship (2001, 2004)

goose-step *vb* **-stepping, -stepped** to march raising the legs high alternately while keeping the legs straight

Goossens *n* **1** Sir **Eugene** 1893–1962, British composer and conductor, born in Belgium **2** his brother, **Leon** 1896–1988, British oboist

go out *vb* **1** to go to entertainments or social functions **2** to be extinguished or cease to function: *the lights went out* **3** (of information) to be released publicly **4** (of a broadcast) to be transmitted **5 go out with** to have a romantic relationship with

go over *vb* **1** to examine very carefully **2 go over to** to change to: *he went over to the Free Orthodox Church*

gopher (go-fer) *n* an American burrowing rodent with wide cheek pouches WORD ORIGIN origin unknown

Gordian knot *n* **cut the Gordian knot** to solve a complicated problem by bold or forceful action WORD ORIGIN after *Gordius*, in Greek legend, who tied a knot that Alexander the Great cut with a sword

Gordimer *n* **Nadine** born 1923, South African novelist. Her books include *The Lying Days* (1952), *The Conservationist* (1974), which won the Booker prize, *None to Accompany Me* (1994), and *The House Gun* (1998). Her works were banned in South Africa for their condemnation of apartheid. Nobel prize for literature 1991

gore[1] ❶ *n* blood shed from a wound WORD ORIGIN Old English *gor* dirt

gore[2] ❶ *vb* **goring, gored** (of an animal) to pierce or stab (a person or another animal) with a horn or tusk WORD ORIGIN probably from Old English *gār* spear

gore[3] *n* a tapering piece of material in a garment, sail, or umbrella WORD ORIGIN Old English *gāra*

Gore *n* **Al(bert) Jr** born 1948, US Democrat politician; vice president of the US (1993–2001); defeated in the disputed presidential election of 2000; leading environmental campaigner; shared the 2007 Nobel Peace Prize with the Intergovernmental Panel For Climate Change

Górecki *n* **Henryk (Mikołaj)** born 1933, Polish composer, best known for his sombre third symphony (1979)

Gorey *n* **Edward St John** 1925–2000, US illustrator and author, noted for his bizarre humour in such works as *The Unstrung Harp* (1953) and *The Wuggly Ump* (1963)

gorge ❶ *n* **1** a deep narrow steep-sided valley **2 one's gorge rises** one feels disgusted or nauseated ▷ *vb* **gorging, gorged 3** Also: **gorge oneself** to eat greedily WORD ORIGIN Latin *gurges* whirlpool

gorgeous ❶ *adj* **1** strikingly beautiful or attractive **2** *informal* warm, sunny, and very pleasant: *a gorgeous day* **gorgeously** *adv* WORD ORIGIN Old French *gorgias* elegant

Gorgias *n* ?485–?380 BC, Greek sophist and rhetorician, subject of a dialogue by Plato

Gorgon *n* **1** *Greek myth* one of three monstrous sisters who had live snakes for hair, and were so horrifying that anyone who looked at them was turned to stone **2** *informal* a terrifying or repulsive woman WORD ORIGIN Greek *gorgos* terrible

Gorgonzola *n* a sharp-flavoured blue-veined Italian cheese WORD ORIGIN after *Gorgonzola*, Italian town where it originated

gorilla *n* a very large W African ape with coarse black hair WORD ORIGIN Greek *Gorillai*, an African tribe renowned for their hairy appearance

Gorky *n* **Arshile** 1904–48, US abstract expressionist painter, born in Armenia. Influenced by Picasso and Miró, his style is characterized by fluid lines and resonant colours

gormless *adj Brit & NZ informal* stupid or dull-witted WORD ORIGIN obsolete *gaumless*

go round *vb* to be sufficient: *there wasn't enough money to go round*

gorse *n* an evergreen shrub with small yellow flowers and prickles, which grows wild in the countryside WORD ORIGIN Old English *gors*

gory *adj* **gorier, goriest 1** horrific or bloodthirsty: *the gory details* **2** bloody: *gory remains*

gosh *interj* an exclamation of mild surprise or wonder WORD ORIGIN euphemistic for *God*

g

THESAURUS

gore[1] *n* = **blood**, slaughter, bloodshed, carnage, butchery

gore[2] *vb* = **pierce**, wound, stab, spit, transfix, impale

gorge *n* **1** = **ravine**, canyon, pass, clough *(dialect)*, chasm, cleft, fissure, defile, gulch *(US & Canad)* ▷ *vb* **3a** = **overeat**, bolt, devour, gobble, wolf, swallow, gulp, guzzle, pig out *(slang)* **3b** *(usually reflexive)* = **stuff**, fill, feed, cram, glut, surfeit, satiate, sate

gorgeous *adj* **1a** = **magnificent**, grand, beautiful, superb, spectacular, splendid, glittering, dazzling, luxurious, sumptuous, opulent OPPOSITE: shabby **1b** = **beautiful**, attractive, lovely, stunning *(informal)*, elegant, handsome, good-looking, exquisite, drop-dead *(slang)*, ravishing, hot *(informal)*, fit *(Brit informal)*

DICTIONARY

goshawk *n* a large swift short-winged hawk
WORD ORIGIN Old English *gōshafoc*

gosling *n* a young goose
WORD ORIGIN Old Norse *gæslingr*

go-slow *n Brit & NZ* a deliberate slowing of the rate of production by workers as a tactic in industrial conflict

gospel *n* **1 a** the teachings of Jesus Christ **b** the story of Christ's life and teachings **2** a doctrine held to be of great importance: *the gospel of self-help* **3** Also called: **gospel truth** unquestionable truth: *gross inaccuracies which are sometimes taken as gospel* ▹ *adj* **4** denoting a kind of religious music originating in the churches of the Black people in the Southern US
WORD ORIGIN Old English *gōdspell*, from *gōd* good + *spell* message

Gospel *n Christianity* any of the first four books of the New Testament, namely Matthew, Mark, Luke, and John, which tell the story of Jesus Christ

gossamer *n* **1** a very fine fabric **2** a filmy cobweb often seen on foliage or floating in the air
WORD ORIGIN probably Middle English *gos* goose + *somer* summer; referring to *St Martin's summer*, a period in November when goose was eaten and cobwebs abound

Gosse *n* Sir **Edmund William** 1849–1928, English critic and poet, noted particularly for his autobiographical work *Father and Son* (1907)

gossip *n* **1** idle talk, usually about other people's private lives, esp. of a disapproving or malicious nature: *office gossip* **2** an informal conversation, esp. about other people's private lives: *to have a gossip and a giggle* **3** a person who habitually talks about other people, usually maliciously ▹ *vb* **4** to talk idly or maliciously, esp. about other people's private lives **gossipy** *adj*
WORD ORIGIN Old English *godsibb* godparent, applied to a woman's female friends at the birth of a child

got *vb* **1** ▸ the past of **get 2 have got** to possess **3 have got to** must: *you have got to be prepared to work hard*

Gothic *adj* **1** of a style of architecture used in W Europe from the 12th to the 16th centuries, characterized by pointed arches, ribbed vaults, and flying buttresses **2** of a literary style featuring stories of gloom, horror, and the supernatural, popular in the late 18th century **3** of or in a heavy ornate script typeface ▹ *n* **4** Gothic architecture or art
WORD ORIGIN Greek *Gothoi*

go through *vb* **1** to experience (a difficult time or process) **2** to name or describe: *the president went through a list of government ministers* **3** to qualify for the next stage of a competition: *Belgium, Spain and Uruguay all went through from Group E* **4** to be approved: *the bill went through parliament* **5 go through with** to bring to a successful conclusion, often by persistence

gotten *vb chiefly US* ▸ a past participle of **get**

Gottfried von Strassburg *n* early 13th-century German poet; author of the incomplete epic *Tristan and Isolde*, the version of the legend that served as the basis of Wagner's opera

Gottsched *n* **Johann Christoph** 1700–66, German critic, dramatist, and translator

Götz von Berlichingen *n* ▸ See **Berlichingen**

gouache *n* opaque watercolour paint bound with glue
WORD ORIGIN French

Gouda *n* a round mild-flavoured Dutch cheese

gouge (gowj) *vb* **gouging, gouged 1** to scoop or force (something) out of its position **2** to cut (a hole or groove) in something with a pointed object ▹ *n* **3** a mark or groove made by gouging
WORD ORIGIN French

goulash (goo-lash) *n* a rich stew seasoned with paprika, originating in Hungary
WORD ORIGIN Hungarian *gulyás hus* herdsman's meat

Gould *n* **1 Benjamin Apthorp** 1824–96, US astronomer: the first to use the telegraph to determine longitudes; founded the *Astronomical Journal* (1849) **2 Glenn** 1932–82, Canadian pianist

Gounod *n* **Charles François** 1818–93, French composer of the operas *Faust* (1859) and *Romeo and Juliet* (1867)

gourd (goord) *n* **1** a large hard-shelled fruit similar to a cucumber or marrow **2** a container made from a dried gourd shell
WORD ORIGIN Old French *gourde*

gourmand (goor-mand) *n* a person devoted to eating and drinking, usually to excess
WORD ORIGIN Old French *gourmant*

gourmet (goor-may) *n* an expert on good food and drink
WORD ORIGIN French

Gourmont *n* **Remy de** 1858–1915, French symbolist critic and novelist

gout (gowt) *n* a disease that causes painful inflammation of certain joints, for example of the big toe **gouty** *adj*
WORD ORIGIN Latin *gutta* a drop

govern *vb* **1** to direct and control the policy and affairs of (a country or an organization) **2** to control or determine: *the international organizations governing athletics and rugby* **governable** *adj*
WORD ORIGIN Latin *gubernare* to steer

governance *n* government, control, or authority

governess *n* a woman employed in a private household to teach the children

government *n* **1** the executive policy-making body of a country or state **2** the state and its administration: *the assembled heads of state and government* **3** the system by which a country or state is ruled: *the old hard-line government* **governmental** *adj*

governor *n* **1** the chief political administrator of a region, such as a US state or a colony ▸ Related adjective: **gubernatorial 2** *Brit* the senior administrator of a school, prison, or other institution **3** *Brit informal* one's employer or father **governorship** *n*

governor general *n, pl* **governors general** *or* **governor generals** the chief representative of the British government in a Commonwealth country

Gower[1] *n* **the Gower** a peninsula in S Wales, in Swansea county on the

THESAURUS

gospel *n* **1a, 1b, 2 = doctrine**, news, teachings, message, revelation, creed, credo, tidings **3 = truth**, fact, certainty, the last word, verity

gossip *n* **1 = idle talk**, scandal, hearsay, tittle-tattle, buzz, dirt *(US slang)*, goss *(informal)*, jaw *(slang)*, gen *(Brit informal)*, small talk, chitchat, blether, scuttlebutt *(US slang)*, chinwag *(Brit informal)* **3 = busybody**, babbler, prattler, chatterbox *(informal)*, blether, chatterer, scandalmonger, gossipmonger, tattletale *(chiefly US & Canad)* ▹ *vb* **4 = chat**, chatter, blather, schmooze *(slang)*, jaw *(slang)*, dish the dirt *(informal)*, blether, shoot the breeze *(slang, chiefly US)*, chew the fat *or* rag *(slang)*

gourmet *n* **= connoisseur**, foodie *(informal)*, bon vivant *(French)*, epicure, gastronome

govern *vb* **1 = rule**, lead, control, command, manage, direct, guide, handle, conduct, order, reign over, administer, oversee, supervise, be in power over, call the shots, call the tune, hold sway over, superintend

government *n* **1, 2 = administration**, executive, ministry, regime, governing body, powers-that-be **3 = rule**, state, law, authority, administration, sovereignty, governance, dominion, polity, statecraft

governor *n* **1 = leader**, administrator, ruler, head, minister, director, manager, chief, officer, executive, boss *(informal)*, commander,

Bristol Channel: mainly agricultural with several resorts

Gower² *n* **1 David (Ivon)** born 1957, English cricketer **2 John** ?1330–1408, English poet, noted particularly for his tales of love, the *Confessio Amantis*

go with *vb* **1** to blend or harmonize with: *the style goes well with modern art* **2** to be linked with: *respect goes with age*

go without *vb* to be denied or deprived of: *no-one should go without food*

gown ❶ *n* **1** a woman's long formal dress **2** a surgeon's overall **3** a loose wide official robe worn by clergymen, judges, lawyers, and academics
WORD ORIGIN Late Latin *gunna* garment made of fur

goy *n, pl* **goyim** *or* **goys** ▸ a Jewish word for a **Gentile**
WORD ORIGIN Yiddish

Goyen *n* **Jan Josephszoon van** 1596–1656, Dutch landscape painter and etcher

GP general practitioner

GPMU (in Britain) Graphical, Paper and Media Union

GPO (in Britain and Australia) general post office

GPS Global Positioning System: a satellite-based navigation system

Graafian follicle *n anat* a cavity in the ovary that contains a developing egg cell
WORD ORIGIN after R. de *Graaf*, anatomist

grab ❶ *vb* **grabbing, grabbed 1** to seize hold of **2** to take (food, drink, or rest) hurriedly **3** to take (an opportunity) eagerly **4** to seize illegally or unscrupulously: *land grabbing* **5** *informal* to interest or impress ▹*n* **6** the act of grabbing
WORD ORIGIN probably from Middle Dutch *grabben*

grab bag *n* **1** a collection of miscellaneous things **2** *Austral, US & Canad* a bag from which gifts are drawn at random

Gracchus *n* **Tiberius Sempronius** ?163–133 BC, and his younger brother, **Gaius Sempronius**, 153–121 BC, known as *the Gracchi*. Roman tribunes and reformers. Tiberius attempted to redistribute public land among the poor but was murdered in the ensuing riot. Violence again occurred when the reform was revived by Gaius, and he too was killed

grace ❶ *n* **1** elegance and beauty of movement, form, or expression **2** a pleasing or charming quality: *architecture with few redeeming graces* **3** courtesy or decency: *at least she had the grace to laugh* **4** a delay granted for the completion of a task or payment of a debt: *another year's grace* **5** *Christian theol* the free and unmerited favour of God shown towards humankind **6** a short prayer of thanks for a meal **7 airs and graces** an affected manner **8 with bad grace** unwillingly or grudgingly: *independence was granted with bad grace* **9 with good grace** willingly or ungrudgingly: *to accept with good grace* ▹*vb* **gracing, graced 10** to honour or favour: *graced by the presence of Henry Fonda* **11** to decorate or make more attractive: *bedsit walls graced by Che Guevara and James Dean*
WORD ORIGIN Latin *gratia*

Grace *n* **Your** *or* **His** *or* **Her Grace** a title used to address or refer to a duke, duchess, or archbishop

graceful ❶ *adj* having beauty of movement, style, or form **gracefully** *adv* **gracefulness** *n*

graceless *adj* **1** lacking elegance **2** lacking manners

grace note *n music* a note that ornaments a melody

Graces *pl n Greek myth* the three sister goddesses of charm and beauty

gracious ❶ *adj* **1** showing kindness and courtesy **2** characterized by elegance, ease, and indulgence: *gracious living* ▹*interj* **3** an expression of mild surprise or wonder
graciously *adv* **graciousness** *n*

gradation *n* **1** a series of systematic stages; gradual progression **2** a stage in such a series or progression

grade ❶ *n* **1** a place on a scale of quality, rank, or size **2** a mark or rating indicating a student's level of achievement **3** a rank or level of importance in a company or organization **4** *US, Canad, Austral & S African* a class or year in a school **5 make the grade** *informal* to be successful by reaching a required standard ▹*vb* **grading, graded 6** to arrange according to quality or rank: *passes are graded from A down to E* **7** to give a grade to: *senior secretaries will need shorthand and be graded accordingly*
WORD ORIGIN Latin *gradus* step

gradient *n* **1** Also (esp. US): **grade** a sloping part of a railway, road, or path **2** Also (esp. US): **grade** a measure of the steepness of such a slope **3** a measure of the change in something, such as the angle of a curve, over a specified distance
WORD ORIGIN Latin *gradiens* stepping

gradual ❶ *adj* occurring, developing, or moving in small stages: *a gradual handover of power* **gradually** *adv*
WORD ORIGIN Latin *gradus* a step

gradualism *n* the policy of changing something gradually **gradualist** *adj*

graduate ❶ *n* **1** a person who holds a university or college degree **2** *US & Canad* a student who has completed a course of studies at a high school and received a diploma **3** ▸ same as **postgraduate** ▹*vb* **-ating, -ated 4** to receive a degree or diploma **5** to change by degrees: *the winds graduate from tropical storms to cyclones* **6** to mark (a measuring flask or instrument) with units of measurement
WORD ORIGIN Latin *gradus* a step

graduation *n* **1** the act of graduating from university or college **2** *US & Canad* the act of graduating from high school **3** the ceremony at which degrees and diplomas are given to graduating students **4** a

g

THESAURUS

controller, supervisor, superintendent, mandarin, comptroller, functionary, overseer, baas (*S African*)

gown *n* **1, 2 = dress**, costume, garment, robe, frock, garb, habit

grab *vb* **1 = snatch**, catch, seize, capture, bag, grip, grasp, clutch, snap up, pluck, latch on to, catch *or* take hold of

grace *n* **1 = elegance**, finesse, poise, ease, polish, refinement, fluency, suppleness, gracefulness
OPPOSITE: ungainliness
3 = manners, decency, cultivation, etiquette, breeding, consideration, propriety, tact, decorum, mannerliness
OPPOSITE: bad manners
4 = indulgence, mercy, pardon, compassion, quarter, charity, forgiveness, reprieve, clemency, leniency **6 = prayer**, thanks, blessing, thanksgiving, benediction ▹*vb* **10 = honour**, favour, distinguish, elevate, dignify, glorify
OPPOSITE: insult
11 = adorn, enhance, decorate, enrich, set off, garnish, ornament, deck, embellish, bedeck, beautify

graceful *adj* **= elegant**, easy, flowing, smooth, fine, pleasing, beautiful, agile, symmetrical, gracile (*rare*)
OPPOSITE: inelegant

gracious *adj* **1 = courteous**, polite, civil, accommodating, kind, kindly, pleasing, friendly, obliging, amiable, cordial, hospitable, courtly, chivalrous, well-mannered
OPPOSITE: ungracious

grade *n* **1 = class**, condition, quality, brand **2 = mark**, degree, place, order **3 = level**, position, rank, group, order, class, stage, step, station, category, rung, echelon ▹*vb* **6, 7 = classify**, rate, order, class, group, sort, value, range, rank, brand, arrange, evaluate

gradual *adj* **= steady**, even, slow, regular, gentle, moderate, progressive, piecemeal, unhurried
OPPOSITE: sudden

graduate *vb* **6 = mark off**, grade, proportion, regulate, gauge, calibrate, measure out

DICTIONARY

mark indicating measure on an instrument or container

Graeco-Roman *or esp. US* **Greco-Roman** (greek-oh-**rome**-an) *adj* of, or showing the influence of, both Greek and Roman cultures

Graf[1] *n* **Steffi** born 1969, German tennis player: Wimbledon champion 1988, 1989, 1991, 1992, 1993, 1995, and 1996

Graf[2] *German n, pl* ***Grafen*** a German count: often used as a title
WORD ORIGIN German, from Old High German *grāvo*

graffiti (graf-**fee**-tee) *n* drawings or words scribbled or sprayed on walls or posters
WORD ORIGIN Italian: little scratches

graft[1] ⊕ *n* **1** *surgery* a piece of tissue transplanted to an area of the body in need of the tissue **2** a small piece of tissue from one plant that is joined to another plant so that they grow together as one ▹*vb* **3** to transplant (tissue) to an area of the body in need of the tissue **4** to join (part of one plant) onto another plant so that they grow together as one **5** to attach or incorporate: *to graft Japanese production methods onto the American talent for innovation*
WORD ORIGIN Greek *graphein* to write

graft[2] ⊕ *n* **1** *Brit informal* hard work **2** the practice of obtaining money by taking advantage of one's position ▹*vb* **3** *informal* to work hard
WORD ORIGIN origin unknown

Grahame *n* **Kenneth** 1859–1932, Scottish author, noted for the children's classic *The Wind in the Willows* (1908)

Grail *n* ▸see **Holy Grail**

grain ⊕ *n* **1** the small hard seedlike fruit of a cereal plant **2** a mass of such fruits gathered for food **3** cereal plants in general **4** a small hard particle: *a grain of salt* **5** a very small amount: *a grain of compassion* **6 a** the arrangement of the fibres, layers, or particles in wood, leather, or stone **b** the pattern or texture resulting from this **7 go against the grain** to be contrary to one's natural inclinations **grainy** *adj*
WORD ORIGIN Latin *granum*

Grainger *n* **Percy Aldridge** 1882–1961, Australian pianist, composer, and collector of folk music on which many of his works are based

gram *or* **gramme** *n* a metric unit of weight equal to one thousandth of a kilogram
WORD ORIGIN Greek *gramma* small weight

graminivorous *adj* (of an animal) grass-eating
WORD ORIGIN Latin *gramen* grass + *vorare* to swallow

grammar *n* **1** the rules of a language, that show how sentences are formed, or how words are inflected **2** the way in which grammar is used: *the teacher found errors of spelling and grammar* **3** a book on the rules of grammar
WORD ORIGIN Greek *gramma* letter

grammarian *n* a person who studies or writes about grammar for a living

grammar school *n* **1** *Brit* (esp. formerly) a secondary school for children of high academic ability **2** *US* ▸same as **elementary school** **3** *Austral* a private school, usually one controlled by a church

grammatical *adj* **1** of grammar **2** (of a sentence) following the rules of grammar **grammatically** *adv*

gramme *n* ▸same as **gram**

gramophone *n* an old-fashioned type of record player
WORD ORIGIN inversion of *phonogram*

grampus *n, pl* **-puses** a dolphin-like mammal with a blunt snout
WORD ORIGIN Old French *gras* fat + *pois* fish

Gramsci *n* **Antonio** 1891–1937, Italian politician and Marxist theorist: founder (1921) of the Italian Communist party. His important works were written during his imprisonment (1926–37) by the Fascists

gran *n Brit, Austral & NZ informal* a grandmother

Granados *n* **Enrique**, full name *Enrique Granados y Campina*. 1867–1916, Spanish composer, noted for the *Goyescas* (1911) for piano, which formed the basis for an opera of the same name

granary *n, pl* **-ries 1** a building for storing threshed grain **2** a region that produces a large amount of grain
WORD ORIGIN Latin *granarium*

Granary *adj trademark* (of bread or flour) containing malted wheat grain

grand ⊕ *adj* **1** large or impressive in size or appearance; magnificent: *the grand hall* **2** ambitious or important: *grand themes* **3** dignified or haughty **4** *informal* excellent or wonderful **5** comprehensive or complete: *the grand total* ▹*n* **6** *pl* **grand** *slang* a thousand pounds or dollars **7** ▸short for **grand piano** > **grandly** *adv*
WORD ORIGIN Latin *grandis*

grandad, granddad *or US* **granddaddy** *n, pl* **-dads** *or* **-daddies** *informal* a grandfather

grandchild *n, pl* **-children** a son or daughter of one's son or daughter

granddad *or US* **granddaddy** *n informal* ▸see **grandad**

granddaughter *n* a daughter of one's son or daughter

grand duke *n* a prince or nobleman who rules a territory, state, or principality **grand duchess** *fem n* **grand duchy** *n*

grande dame (grond **dam**) *n* a woman regarded as the most prominent or respected member of her profession or group: *the grande dame of international fashion*
WORD ORIGIN French

grandee *n* **1** a high-ranking Spanish nobleman **2** a person who has a high rank or position: *the Party's grandees*
WORD ORIGIN Spanish *grande*

grandeur ⊕ *n* **1** personal greatness, dignity, or nobility: *delusions of grandeur* **2** magnificence or splendour: *cathedral-like grandeur*

grandfather *n* the father of one's father or mother

THESAURUS

graft[1] *n* **2 = shoot**, bud, implant, sprout, splice, scion ▹*vb* **4 = join**, insert, transplant, implant, splice, affix

graft[2] *n* **1** *(Brit informal)* **= labour**, work, industry, effort, struggle, sweat, toil, slog, exertion, blood, sweat, and tears *(informal)* ▹*vb* **3** *(informal)* **= work**, labour, struggle, sweat *(informal)*, grind *(informal)*, slave, strive, toil, drudge

grain *n* **1 = seed**, kernel, grist **2, 3 = cereal**, corn **4, 5 = bit**, piece, trace, spark, scrap, suspicion, molecule, particle, fragment, atom, ounce, crumb, mite, jot, speck, morsel, granule, modicum, mote, whit, iota **6a, 6b = texture**, pattern, surface, fibre, weave, nap

grand *adj* **1 = impressive**, great, large, magnificent, striking, fine, princely, imposing, superb, glorious, noble, splendid, gorgeous, luxurious, eminent, majestic, regal, stately, monumental, sublime, sumptuous, grandiose, opulent, palatial, ostentatious, splendiferous *(facetious)*
OPPOSITE: unimposing
2 = ambitious, great, glorious, lofty, grandiose, exalted, ostentatious **3 = superior**, great, lordly, noble, elevated, eminent, majestic, dignified, stately, lofty, august, illustrious, pompous, pretentious, haughty **4** *(informal)* **= excellent**, great *(informal)*, fine, wonderful, very good, brilliant, outstanding, smashing *(informal)*, superb, first-class, divine, marvellous *(informal)*, terrific *(informal)*, splendid, awesome *(slang)*, world-class, admirable, super *(informal)*, first-rate, splendiferous *(facetious)*
OPPOSITE: bad

grandeur *n* **2 = splendour**, glory, majesty, nobility, pomp, state, magnificence, sumptuousness,

DICTIONARY

grandfather clock *n* an old-fashioned clock in a tall wooden case that stands on the floor
grandiloquent *adj* using pompous or unnecessarily complicated language **grandiloquence** *n*
WORD ORIGIN Latin *grandiloquus*
grandiose *adj* impressive, or meant to impress: *grandiose plans for constructing a new stadium*
WORD ORIGIN French
grand jury *n law, chiefly US* a jury that investigates accusations of crime to decide whether the evidence is adequate to bring a prosecution
grandma *or* **grandmama** *n informal* a grandmother
grand mal *n* a form of epilepsy in which there is loss of consciousness and violent convulsions
WORD ORIGIN French: great illness
grandmaster *n* a person who is exceptionally good at a particular activity or skill, especially chess
grandmother *n* the mother of one's father or mother
Grand National *n* an annual steeplechase for horses, run at Aintree, Liverpool
grandnephew *n* ▸ same as **great-nephew**
grandniece *n* ▸ same as **great-niece**
grand opera *n* an opera that has a serious plot and no spoken dialogue
grandpa *or* **grandpapa** *n informal* a grandfather
grandparent *n* the father or mother of one's father or mother
grand piano *n* a large piano in which the strings are arranged horizontally
Grand Prix (gron **pree**) *n* **1** an international formula motor race **2** a very important international competitive event in other sports, such as athletics
WORD ORIGIN French: great prize
grandsire *n old-fashioned* a grandfather
grand slam *n* **1** the achievement of winning all the games or major tournaments in a sport in one season **2** ▸ see **slam²**
grandson *n* a son of one's son or daughter
grandstand *n* the main block of seats giving the best view at a sports ground
grand tour *n* **1** (formerly) an extended tour of continental Europe **2** *informal* a tour of inspection: *a grand tour of the house*
grange *n Brit* a farmhouse or country house with its farm buildings
WORD ORIGIN Anglo-French *graunge*
granite (**gran**-nit) *n* a very hard rock consisting of quartz and feldspars that is widely used for building
WORD ORIGIN Italian *granito* grained
granivorous *adj* (of an animal) grain-eating
WORD ORIGIN Latin *granum* grain + *vorare* to swallow
granny *or* **grannie** *n, pl* **-nies** *informal* a grandmother
granny flat *n* a flat in or joined on to a house, suitable for an elderly relative to live in
granny knot *n* a reef knot with the ends crossed the wrong way, making it liable to slip or jam
grant ⓣ *vb* **1** to give (a sum of money or a right) formally: *to grant a 38% pay rise; only the President can grant a pardon* **2** to consent to perform or fulfil: *granting the men's request for sanctuary* **3** to admit that (something) is true: *I grant that her claims must be true* **4 take for granted a** to accept that something is true without requiring proof **b** to take advantage of (someone or something) without showing appreciation ▹*n* **5** a sum of money provided by a government or public fund to a person or organization for a specific purpose: *student grants*
WORD ORIGIN Old French *graunter*
Granth (grunt) *n* the sacred scripture of the Sikhs
WORD ORIGIN Hindi
grant-maintained school *n Brit* a school funded directly by central government
granular *adj* of, like, or containing granules: *granular materials such as powders*
granulated *adj* (of sugar) in the form of coarse grains
granule *n* a small grain of something: *gravy granules*
WORD ORIGIN Late Latin *granulum* a small grain
Granville *n* **1 1st Earl,** title of *John Carteret*. 1690–1763, British statesman: secretary of state (1742–44); a leading opponent of Walpole **2 2nd Earl,** title of *Granville George Leveson-Gower*. 1815–91, British Liberal politician: Gladstone's foreign secretary (1870–74; 1880–85) and a supporter of Irish Home Rule
Granville-Barker *n* **Harley** 1877–1946, English dramatist, theatre director, and critic, noted particularly for his *Prefaces to Shakespeare* (1927–47)
grape *n* a small round sweet juicy fruit with a purple or green skin, which can be eaten raw, dried to make raisins, currants, or sultanas, or used to make wine
WORD ORIGIN Old French *grape* bunch of grapes
grapefruit *n, pl* **-fruit** *or* **-fruits** a large round yellow juicy citrus fruit with a slightly bitter taste
grapeshot *n* ammunition for cannons consisting of a cluster of iron balls that scatter after firing
grapevine *n* **1** a vine grown for its grapes **2** *informal* an unofficial means of passing on information from person to person: *he'd doubtless heard rumours on the grapevine*
graph *n* a diagram showing the relation between certain sets of numbers or quantities by means of a series of dots or lines plotted with reference to a set of axes
WORD ORIGIN short for *graphic formula*
-graph *n combining form* **1** an instrument that writes or records: *tachograph* **2** a writing or record: *autograph* **-graphic** *or* **-graphical** *adj combining form* **-graphically** *adv combining form*
WORD ORIGIN Greek *graphein* to write
graphic ⓣ *adj* **1** vividly described: *a graphic account of her three days in captivity* **2** of the graphic arts: *graphic design* **3** Also: **graphical** *maths* of or using a graph: *a graphic presentation* **graphically** *adv*
WORD ORIGIN Greek *graphikos*
graphic arts *pl n* the visual arts based on drawing or the use of line
graphics *n* **1** the art of drawing in accordance with mathematical rules ▹*pl n* **2** the illustrations in a magazine or book, or in a television or film production **3** *computers* information displayed in the form of diagrams or graphs
graphite *n* a soft black form of carbon used in pencils, as a lubricant, and in some nuclear reactors
WORD ORIGIN German *Graphit*
graphology *n* the study of handwriting, usually to analyse the writer's character **graphologist** *n*
graph paper *n* paper printed with a design of small squares for drawing graphs or diagrams on
-graphy *n combining form* **1** indicating a form of writing or representing things: *calligraphy; photography*

g

THESAURUS

sublimity, stateliness
grant *vb* **1 = give,** allow, present, award, accord, permit, assign, allocate, hand out, confer on, bestow on, impart, allot, vouchsafe **3 = accept,** allow, admit, acknowledge, concede, cede, accede ▹*n* **5 = award,** allowance, donation, endowment, gift, concession, subsidy, hand-out, allocation, bounty, allotment, bequest, stipend
graphic *adj* **1 = vivid,** clear, detailed, striking, telling, explicit, picturesque, forceful, expressive, descriptive, illustrative, well-drawn **OPPOSITE:** vague **2, 3 = pictorial,** seen, drawn, visible, visual, representational, illustrative, diagrammatic **OPPOSITE:** impressionistic

DICTIONARY

2 indicating an art or descriptive science: *choreography; topography*
WORD ORIGIN Greek *graphein* to write

grapnel *n* a device with several hooks at one end, which is used to grasp or secure an object, esp. in sailing
WORD ORIGIN Old French *grapin* a little hook

Grappelli *or* **Grappelly** *n* **Stéphane** 1908–97, French jazz violinist: with Django Reinhardt, he led the Quintet of the Hot Club of France between 1934 and 1939

grapple ❶ *vb* **-pling, -pled** ▪ **grapple with a** to try to cope with: *a difficult concept to grapple with* **b** to come to grips with (someone) in hand-to-hand combat
WORD ORIGIN Old French *grappelle* a little hook

g

grappling iron *n* ▸same as **grapnel**

grasp ❶ *vb* **1** to grip firmly **2** to understand: *his failure to grasp the gravity of the crisis* ▹*n* **3** a very firm grip **4** understanding or comprehension: *a good grasp of detail* **5 within someone's grasp** almost certain to be accomplished or won: *he now has that prize within his grasp*
WORD ORIGIN Low German *grapsen*

grasping ❶ *adj* greedy for money

grass *n* **1** a very common green plant with jointed stems and long narrow leaves, eaten by animals such as sheep and cows, and used for lawns and sports fields **2** a particular kind of grass, such as bamboo **3** a lawn **4** *slang* marijuana **5** *Austral & Brit slang* a person who informs, usually on criminals ▹*vb* **6 grass on** *or* **up** *Brit slang* to inform on (someone) to the police or some other authority **7 grass over** to cover with grass **grassy** *adj*
WORD ORIGIN Old English *græs*

grass hockey *n* (in W Canada) field hockey, as contrasted with ice hockey

grasshopper *n* an insect with long hind legs which it uses for leaping

grassland *n* **1** land covered with grass **2** pasture land

grass roots *pl n* **1** ordinary members of a group or organization, as distinct from its leaders ▹*adj* **grassroots 2** of the ordinary members of a group or organization: *the focus of a virulent grassroots campaign*

grass snake *n* a harmless snake with a brownish-green body

grass tree *n* an Australian plant with stiff grass-like leaves and small white flowers

grass widow *n* a woman whose husband is regularly absent for a time
WORD ORIGIN perhaps an allusion to a grass bed as representing an illicit relationship

grate[1] ❶ *vb* **grating, grated 1** to reduce to shreds by rubbing against a rough surface: *grated cheese* **2** to produce a harsh rasping sound by scraping against an object or surface: *the clutch plates grated* **3 grate on** to annoy: *his manner always grated on me*
WORD ORIGIN Old French *grater*

grate[2] *n* **1** a framework of metal bars for holding coal or wood in a fireplace **2** ▸same as **grating**[1]
WORD ORIGIN Latin *cratis* hurdle

grateful ❶ *adj* feeling or showing thanks **gratefully** *adv*
WORD ORIGIN Latin *gratus*

grater *n* a tool with a sharp surface for grating food

Gratian *n* Latin name *Flavius Gratianus.* 359–383 AD, Roman emperor (367–383): ruled with his father Valentinian I (367–375); ruled the Western Roman Empire with his brother Valentinian II (375-83); appointed Theodosius I emperor of the Eastern Roman Empire (379)

gratify *vb* **-fies, -fying, -fied 1** to satisfy or please (someone) **2** to yield to (a desire or whim): *all his wishes were to be gratified* **gratification** *n*
WORD ORIGIN Latin *gratus* grateful + *facere* to make

grating[1] ❶ *n* a framework of metal bars covering an opening in a wall or in the ground

grating[2] ❶ *adj* **1** (of a sound) rough or unpleasant **2** annoying or irritating: *his cringing obsequiousness was grating*

gratis *adv, adj* without payment; free: *the gifts are gratis*
WORD ORIGIN Latin

gratitude ❶ *n* a feeling of being grateful for gifts or favours
WORD ORIGIN Latin *gratus* grateful

Grattan *n* **Henry** 1746–1820, Irish statesman and orator: led the movement that secured legislative independence for Ireland (1782), opposed union with England (1800), and campaigned for Catholic emancipation

gratuitous (grat-tyoo-it-uss) *adj* **1** unjustified or unreasonable: *gratuitous violence* **2** given or received without charge or obligation: *his gratuitous voluntary services* **gratuitously** *adv*
WORD ORIGIN Latin *gratuitus*

gratuity (grat-tyoo-it-ee) *n, pl* **-ties** money given for services rendered; tip

grave[1] ❶ *adj* (rhymes with **save**) **1** serious and worrying: *grave concern* **2** serious and solemn in appearance or behaviour: *the man looked grave and respectful* **3** (rhymes with **halve**) denoting an accent (`) over a vowel in some languages, such as French, which indicates that the vowel is pronounced in a particular way ▹*n* (rhymes with **halve**) **4** a grave accent **gravely** *adv*
WORD ORIGIN Latin *gravis*

grave[2] ❶ (rhymes with **save**) *n* **1** a place where a dead person is buried ▸Related adjective: **sepulchral** **2** death: *people are smoking themselves to an early grave* **3 make someone turn**

THESAURUS

grapple *vb* **a = deal**, tackle, cope, face, fight, battle, struggle, take on, engage, encounter, confront, combat, contend, wrestle, tussle, get to grips, do battle, address yourself to **b = struggle**, fight, combat, wrestle, battle, clash, contend, strive, tussle, scuffle, come to grips

grasp *vb* **1 = grip**, hold, catch, grab, seize, snatch, clutch, clinch, clasp, lay *or* take hold of **2 = understand**, realize, take in, get, see, follow, catch on, comprehend, get the message about, get the picture about, catch *or* get the drift of ▹*n* **3 = grip**, hold, possession, embrace, clutches, clasp **4 = understanding**, knowledge, grip, perception, awareness, realization, mastery, comprehension

grasping *adj* **= greedy**, acquisitive, rapacious, mean, selfish, stingy, penny-pinching *(informal)*, venal, miserly, avaricious, niggardly, covetous, tightfisted, close-fisted, snoep *(S African informal)*
OPPOSITE: generous

grate[1] *vb* **1 = shred**, mince, pulverize **2 = scrape**, grind, rub, scratch, creak, rasp

grateful *adj* **= thankful**, obliged, in (someone's) debt, indebted, appreciative, beholden

grating[1] *n* **= grille**, grid, grate, lattice, trellis, gridiron

grating[2] *adj* **1 = harsh**, grinding, jarring, unpleasant, scraping, raucous, strident, squeaky, rasping, discordant, disagreeable **2 = irritating**, annoying, irksome
OPPOSITE: pleasing

gratitude *n* **= thankfulness**, thanks, recognition, obligation, appreciation, indebtedness, sense of obligation, gratefulness
OPPOSITE: ingratitude

grave[1] *adj* **1 = serious**, important, significant, critical, pressing, threatening, dangerous, vital, crucial, acute, severe, urgent, hazardous, life-and-death, momentous, perilous, weighty, leaden, of great consequence
OPPOSITE: trifling
2 = solemn, sober, gloomy, dull, thoughtful, subdued, sombre, dour, grim-faced, long-faced, unsmiling
OPPOSITE: carefree

grave[2] *n* **1 = tomb**, vault, crypt, mausoleum, sepulchre, pit, last resting place, burying place

DICTIONARY

in his *or* **her grave** to do something that would have shocked a person who is now dead
WORD ORIGIN Old English *græf*
gravel *n* **1** a mixture of rock fragments and pebbles that is coarser than sand **2** *pathol* small rough stones in the kidneys or bladder ▷ *vb* **-elling, -elled** *or US* **-eling, -eled 3** to cover with gravel
WORD ORIGIN Old French *gravele*
gravelly *adj* **1** covered with gravel **2** (of a voice or sound) harsh and grating
graven image *n chiefly bible* a carved image used as an idol
Graves[1] *n* (*sometimes not capital*) a white or red wine from the district around Bordeaux, France
Graves[2] *n* **Robert** (**Ranke**) 1895–1985, English poet, novelist, and critic, whose works include his World War I autobiography, *Goodbye to All That* (1929), and the historical novels I, *Claudius* (1934) and *Claudius the God* (1934)
gravestone *n* a stone marking a grave
graveyard ❶ *n* a place where dead people are buried, esp. one by a church
graveyard slot *n television* the hours from late night until early morning when relatively few people are watching television
gravid (grav-id) *adj med* pregnant
WORD ORIGIN Latin *gravis* heavy
gravimeter (grav-**vim**-it-er) *n* **1** an instrument for measuring the force of gravity **2** an instrument for measuring relative density
WORD ORIGIN French *gravimètre*
gravitas (grav-vit-tass) *n* seriousness or solemnity
WORD ORIGIN Latin: weight
gravitate *vb* **-tating, -tated 1 gravitate towards** to be attracted or influenced by: *the mathematically inclined often gravitate towards computers* **2** *physics* to move under the influence of gravity
gravitation *n physics* **1** the force of attraction that bodies exert on one another as a result of their mass **2** the process or result of this interaction **gravitational** *adj*
gravity ❶ *n, pl* **-ties 1** *physics* **a** the force that attracts bodies towards the centre of the earth, a moon, or any planet **b** ▸ same as **gravitation 2** seriousness or importance: *the gravity of the situation* **3** seriousness or solemnity of appearance or behaviour: *his priestly gravity*
WORD ORIGIN Latin *gravitas* weight
gravy *n, pl* **-vies a** the juices that come from meat during cooking **b** the sauce made by thickening and flavouring these juices
WORD ORIGIN Old French *gravé*
gravy boat *n* a small boat-shaped dish with a spout, used for serving gravy or sauce
gravy train *n slang* a job or scheme that produces a lot of money for little effort
gray *adj, n, vb chiefly US* grey
graze[1] ❶ *vb* **grazing, grazed a** (of an animal) to eat (grass or other growing plants) **b** to feed (animals) on grass or other growing plants
WORD ORIGIN Old English *grasian*
graze[2] ❶ *vb* **grazing, grazed 1** to break the skin of (a part of the body) by scraping **2** to brush against someone gently in passing ▷ *n* **3** an injury on the skin caused by scraping
WORD ORIGIN probably a special use of GRAZE[1]
grazier *n* a rancher or farmer who keeps cattle or sheep on grazing land
grazing *n* land where grass is grown for farm animals to feed upon
grease *n* **1** soft melted animal fat **2** a thick oily substance, such as the kind put on machine parts to make them work smoothly ▷ *vb* **greasing, greased 3** to apply grease to: *lightly grease a baking tin* **4 grease someone's palm** *slang* to bribe someone
WORD ORIGIN Latin *crassus* thick
greasepaint *n* theatrical make-up
greaseproof paper *n* any paper that is resistant to penetration by grease and oil, esp. one used for lining baking dishes or wrapping food
greasy ❶ *adj* **greasier, greasiest 1** covered with or containing grease **2** excessively pleasant or flattering in an insincere manner **greasiness** *n*
great ❶ *adj* **1** large in size **2** large in number or amount: *the great majority* **3** larger than others of its kind: *the great white whale* **4** extreme or more than usual: *great difficulty* **5** of importance or consequence: *a great discovery* **6** of exceptional talents or achievements: *a great artist* **7** skilful: *he's a great storyteller; they are great at problem solving* **8** *informal* excellent ▷ *n* **9 the greats** the most successful people in a particular field: *the all-time greats of golf* ▸ See also **Greats** > **greatly** *adv* **greatness** *n*
WORD ORIGIN Old English *grēat*
great- *prefix* (in expressing relationship) one generation older or younger than: *great-grandmother*
great auk *n* an extinct large auk that could not fly
great-aunt *n* an aunt of one's father or mother
Great Britain *n* the mainland part of the British Isles; England, Scotland, and Wales
great circle *n maths* a circular section of a sphere that has a radius equal to the sphere's radius
greatcoat *n* a heavy overcoat
Great Dane *n* a very large dog with short smooth hair
great-nephew *n* a son of one's nephew or niece
great-niece *n* a daughter of one's nephew or niece
Greats *pl n* **1** the Honours course in classics, ancient history, and philosophy at Oxford University **2** the final examinations at the end of this course
great-uncle *n* an uncle of one's father or mother
Great War *n* ▸ same as **World War I**
greave *n* a piece of armour for the shin
WORD ORIGIN Old French *greve*
Greaves *n* **Jimmy** born 1940, English footballer and television commentator on the sport
grebe *n* a diving water bird
WORD ORIGIN French

g

THESAURUS

graveyard *n* **= cemetery**, churchyard, burial ground, charnel house, necropolis, boneyard (*informal*), God's acre (*literary*)
gravity *n* **2 = seriousness**, importance, consequence, significance, urgency, severity, acuteness, moment, weightiness, momentousness, perilousness, hazardousness OPPOSITE: triviality **3 = solemnity**, gloom, seriousness, gravitas, thoughtfulness, grimness OPPOSITE: frivolity
graze[1] *vb* **a, b = feed**, crop, browse, pasture
graze[2] *vb* **1 = scratch**, skin, bark, scrape, chafe, abrade **2 = touch**, brush, rub, scrape, shave, skim, kiss, glance off ▷ *n* **3 = scratch**, scrape, abrasion
greasy *adj* **1 = fatty**, slick, slippery, oily, slimy, oleaginous
great *adj* **1, 2, 3 = large**, big, huge, vast, enormous, extensive, tremendous, immense, gigantic, mammoth, bulky, colossal, prodigious, stupendous, voluminous, elephantine, ginormous (*informal*), humongous *or* humungous (*US slang*), supersize OPPOSITE: small **8** (*informal*) **= excellent**, good, fine, wonderful, mean (*slang*), topping (*Brit slang*), cracking (*Brit informal*), superb, fantastic (*informal*), tremendous (*informal*), marvellous (*informal*), terrific (*informal*), mega (*slang*), sovereign, awesome (*slang*), dope (*slang*), admirable, first-rate, def (*informal*), brill (*informal*), boffo (*slang*), bitchin', chillin' (*US slang*), booshit (*Austral slang*), exo (*Austral slang*), sik (*Austral slang*), rad (*informal*), phat (*slang*), schmick (*Austral informal*), beaut (*informal*), barrie (*Scot slang*), belting (*Brit slang*), pearler (*Austral slang*) OPPOSITE: poor

DICTIONARY

Grecian (gree-shan) *adj* of ancient Greece

greed ❶ *n* excessive desire for something, such as food or money

greedy ❶ *adj* **greedier, greediest** having an excessive desire for something, such as food or money: *greedy for personal possessions* **greedily** *adv*
WORD ORIGIN Old English *grǣdig*

Greek *adj* **1** of Greece ▷ *n* **2** a person from Greece **3** the language of Greece

Greek cross *n* a cross with each of the four arms of the same length

Greeley *n* **Horace** 1811–72, US journalist and political leader: founder (1841) and editor of the *New York Tribune*, which championed the abolition of slavery

g

green ❶ *adj* **1** of a colour between yellow and blue; of the colour of grass **2** covered with grass, plants, or trees: *green fields* **3** of or concerned with conservation and improvement of the environment: used in a political context: *green issues* **4** (of fruit) fresh, raw, or unripe **5** pale and sick-looking **6** inexperienced or gullible **7** **green with envy** very envious ▷ *n* **8** a colour between yellow and blue **9** anything green, such as green clothing or green ink: *printed in green* **10** a small area of grassy land: *the village green* **11** an area of smooth turf kept for a special purpose: *putting greens* **12** **greens** the leaves and stems of certain plants, eaten as a vegetable: *turnip greens* **13** **Green** a person who supports environmentalist issues **greenish** *or* **greeny** *adj* **greenness** *n*
WORD ORIGIN Old English *grēne*

Green *n* **1** **Henry,** real name *Henry Vincent Yorke*. 1905–73, British novelist: author of *Living* (1929), *Loving* (1945), and *Back* (1946) **2** **John Richard** 1837–83, British historian; author of *A Short History of the English People* (1874) **3** **T(homas) H(ill)** 1836–82, British idealist philosopher. His chief work, *Prolegomena to Ethics*, was unfinished at his death

Greenaway *n* **1** **Kate** 1846–1901, English painter, noted as an illustrator of children's books **2** **Peter** born 1942, British film director; noted for such cerebral films as *The Draughtsman's Contract* (1982), *Prospero's Books* (1990), and *Eight and a Half Women* (1999)

green beans *pl n* long narrow green beans that are cooked and eaten as a vegetable

green belt *n* a protected zone of parkland or open country surrounding a town or city

green card *n* an official permit allowing the holder permanent residence and employment, issued to foreign nationals in the US

Green Cross Code *n Brit* a code for children giving rules on road safety

greenery *n* green leaves or growing plants: *lush greenery*

green-eyed monster *n* jealousy

greenfield *adj* relating to a rural area which has not previously been built on: *greenfield factory sites*

greenfinch *n* a European finch, the male of which has olive-green feathers

green fingers *pl n* skill in growing plants

greenfly *n, pl* **-flies** a green aphid commonly occurring as a pest on plants

greengage *n* a green sweet variety of plum
WORD ORIGIN after Sir W. *Gage*, botanist

Greengrass *n* **Paul** born 1955, English film director and writer; his films include *The Bourne Supremacy* (2004), *United 93* (2006), and *The Bourne Ultimatum* (2007)

greengrocer *n Austral & Brit* a shopkeeper who sells fruit and vegetables

greenhorn *n* an inexperienced person; novice
WORD ORIGIN originally an animal with *green* (that is, young) horns

greenhouse *n* **1** a building with glass walls and roof where plants are grown under controlled conditions ▷ *adj* **2** relating to or contributing to the greenhouse effect: *greenhouse gases such as carbon dioxide*

greenhouse effect *n* the gradual rise in temperature in the earth's atmosphere due to heat being absorbed from the sun and being trapped by gases such as carbon dioxide in the air around the earth

greenkeeper *n* a person responsible for maintaining a golf course or bowling green

green light *n* **1** a signal to go **2** permission to proceed with a project ▷ *vb* **greenlight, -lighting, -lighted** **3** to permit (a project) to proceed

Greenough *n* **George Bellas** 1778–1855, English geologist, founder of the Geological Society of London

green paper *n* a government document containing policy proposals to be discussed

green pepper *n* the green unripe fruit of the sweet pepper, eaten as a vegetable

greenroom *n* (esp. formerly) a backstage room in a theatre where performers rest or receive visitors

greenstick fracture *n* a fracture in which the bone is partly bent and splinters only on the outer side of the bend

greenstone *n NZ* a type of green jade used for Māori carvings and ornaments

greensward *n archaic or literary* an area of fresh green turf

green tea *n* tea made from leaves that have been dried quickly without fermenting

greenway *n US* a corridor of protected open space that is maintained for conservation, recreation, and non-motorized transportation

Greenwich Mean Time (gren-itch) *n* the local time of the 0° meridian passing through Greenwich, England: a basis for calculating times throughout most of the world. Abbrev: **GMT**

greet[1] ❶ *vb* **1** to address or meet with expressions of friendliness or welcome **2** to receive in a specified manner: *a direct request would be greeted coolly* **3** to be immediately noticeable to: *the scene of devastation which greeted him*
WORD ORIGIN Old English *grētan*

greet[2] *vb Scot* to weep
WORD ORIGIN Old English *grǣtan*

greeting ❶ *n* the act or words of welcoming on meeting

greetings *interj* an expression of friendly salutation

gregarious *adj* **1** enjoying the company of others **2** (of animals)

THESAURUS

greed *n* **a** = **gluttony**, voracity, insatiableness, ravenousness **b** = **avarice**, longing, desire, hunger, craving, eagerness, selfishness, acquisitiveness, rapacity, cupidity, covetousness, insatiableness **OPPOSITE:** generosity

greedy *adj* **a** = **gluttonous**, insatiable, voracious, ravenous, piggish, hoggish **b** = **avaricious**, grasping, selfish, insatiable, acquisitive, rapacious, materialistic, desirous, covetous **OPPOSITE:** generous

green *adj* **2** = **verdant**, leafy, grassy **3** = **ecological**, conservationist, environment-friendly, ecologically sound, eco-friendly, ozone-friendly, non-polluting **6** = **inexperienced**, new, innocent, raw, naive, ignorant, immature, gullible, callow, untrained, unsophisticated, credulous, ingenuous, unpolished, wet behind the ears *(informal)* ▷ *n* **10, 11** = **lawn**, common, turf, sward, grassplot

greet[1] *vb* **1a** = **salute**, hail, nod to, say hello to, address, accost, tip your hat to **1b** = **welcome**, meet, receive, karanga *(NZ)*, mihi *(NZ)* **2** = **receive**, take, respond to, react to

greeting *n* = **welcome**, reception, hail, salute, address, salutation, hongi *(NZ)*, kia ora *(NZ)*

DICTIONARY

living together in herds or in flocks
WORD ORIGIN Latin *grex* flock
Gregorian calendar *n* the revision of the calendar introduced in 1582 by Pope Gregory XIII and still widely used
Gregorian chant *n* ▸ same as **plainsong**
Gregory *n* Lady (**Isabella**) **Augusta** (**Persse**) 1852–1932, Irish dramatist; a founder and director of the Abbey Theatre, Dublin
Gregory IX *n* original name *Ugolino of Segni*. ?1148–1241, pope (1227–41). He excommunicated and waged war against Emperor Frederick II
Gregory of Nazianzus *n* **Saint** ?329–89 AD, Cappadocian theologian: bishop of Caesarea (370–79). Feast days: Jan 2, 25, and 30
Gregory of Nyssa *n* **Saint** ?335–394 AD, Cappadocian theologian and brother of St Basil: bishop of Nyssa. Feast day: March 9
Gregory of Tours *n* **Saint** ?538–?594 AD, Frankish bishop and historian. His *Historia Francorum* is the chief source of knowledge of 6th-century Gaul. Feast day: Nov 17
Gregory VII *n* **Saint,** monastic name *Hildebrand*. ?1020–85, pope (1073–85), who did much to reform abuses in the Church. His assertion of papal supremacy and his prohibition (1075) of lay investiture was opposed by the Holy Roman Emperor Henry IV, whom he excommunicated (1076). He was driven into exile when Henry captured Rome (1084). Feast day: May 25
gremlin *n* an imaginary imp jokingly blamed for malfunctions in machinery
WORD ORIGIN origin unknown
grenade *n* a small bomb filled with explosive or gas, thrown by hand or fired from a rifle
WORD ORIGIN Spanish *grenada* pomegranate
grenadier *n mil* **1** (in the British Army) a member of the senior regiment of infantry in the Household Brigade (the **Grenadier Guards**) **2** (formerly) a soldier trained to throw grenades
WORD ORIGIN French
grenadine (gren-a-deen) *n* a syrup made from pomegranate juice, often used as an ingredient in cocktails
Grenfell *n* **Joyce,** real name Joyce Irene Phipps. 1910–79, British comedy actress and writer
Greuze *n* **Jean Baptiste** 1725–1805, French genre and portrait painter
Greville *n* **Fulke,** 1st Baron Brooke. 1554–1628, English poet, writer, politician, and diplomat: Chancellor of the Exchequer (1614–22); author of *The Life of the Renowned Sir Philip Sidney* (1652)
grevillea *n* any of various Australian evergreen trees and shrubs
WORD ORIGIN after C. F. *Greville*, botanist
grew *vb* ▸ the past tense of **grow**
grey ❶ *or US* **gray** *adj* **1** of a colour between black and white; of the colour of ashes **2 a** (of hair) having partly turned white **b** (of a person) having grey hair **3** dismal, dark, or gloomy: *a grey and misty morning* **4** dull or boring: *in 1948 life generally was grey* ▹ *n* **5** a colour between black and white **6** anything grey, such as grey paint or grey clothing: *available in grey or brown* **7** a grey or whitish horse
greyness *n* **greyish** *adj*
WORD ORIGIN Old English *grǣg*
grey area *n* a situation or area that has no clearly defined characteristics or that falls somewhere between two categories
greyed out *adj* (of a navigation button, menu item, etc. on a computer screen) not highlighted, indicating that the function is not available
Grey Friar *n* a Franciscan friar
greyhound *n* a tall slender dog that can run very fast and is used for racing
greying *adj* becoming grey: *greying hair*
greylag *or* **greylag goose** *n* a large grey Eurasian goose
WORD ORIGIN GREY + LAG, because it migrates later than other species
grey matter *n informal* intellect or brains: *those who don't have lots of grey matter*
Grey Owl *n* Grey Owl, original name *Archibald Belaney* (1888–1938). Canadian writer and conservationist, born in England; adopted Native American identity
grey squirrel *n* a grey-furred squirrel, native to E North America but now common in Britain
Grey-Thompson *n* Dame **Tanni** (**Carys Davina**) born 1969, British wheelchair athlete; eleven gold medals in the Paralympics (1988–2004)
grid *n* **1** a network of crossing parallel lines on a map, plan, or graph paper for locating points **2 the grid** the national network of cables or pipes by which electricity, gas, or water is distributed **3** *electronics* an electrode that controls the flow of electrons between the cathode and anode of a valve
WORD ORIGIN from *gridiron*
griddle *n* a thick round iron plate placed on top of a cooker and used to cook food
WORD ORIGIN Old French *gridil*
gridiron *n* **1** a utensil of parallel metal bars, used to grill food **2 a** the field of play in American football **b** *informal* ▸ same as **American football**
WORD ORIGIN Middle English *gredire*
gridlock *n* **1** obstruction of traffic caused by queues of vehicles forming across junctions and so causing queues in intersecting streets **2** a point in a dispute at which no agreement can be reached: *political gridlock* ▹ *vb* **3** (of traffic) to obstruct (an area)
grid reference *n* a series of numbers indicating the location of a point on a map
grief ❶ *n* **1** deep or intense sorrow **2** *informal* trouble or annoyance: *people were giving me grief for leaving ten minutes early* **3 come to grief** to have an unfortunate or unsuccessful end or outcome
grief-stricken *adj* deeply affected by sorrow
Grierson *n* **John** 1898–1972, Scottish film director. He coined the noun *documentary*, of which genre his *Industrial Britain* (1931) and *Song of Ceylon* (1934) are notable examples
grievance ❶ *n* **1** a real or imaginary cause for complaint **2** a feeling of resentment at having been unfairly treated
grieve ❶ *vb* **grieving, grieved** to feel or cause to feel great sorrow or distress **grieved** *adj* **grieving** *adj*
WORD ORIGIN Old French *grever*
grievous *adj* **1** very severe or painful: *grievous injuries* **2** very serious or worrying: *a grievous loss*
grievously *adv*
grievous bodily harm *n criminal law* serious injury caused by one person to another
griffin, griffon *or* **gryphon** *n* a mythical winged monster with an eagle's head and a lion's body
WORD ORIGIN Old French *grifon*
Griffith *n* **1 Arthur** 1872–1922, Irish journalist and nationalist: founder

g

THESAURUS

grey *or US* **gray** *adj* **3 = dull,** dark, dim, gloomy, cloudy, murky, drab, misty, foggy, overcast, sunless **4 = boring,** dull, anonymous, faceless, colourless, nondescript, characterless
grief *n* **1 = sadness,** suffering, pain, regret, distress, misery, agony, mourning, sorrow, woe, anguish, remorse, bereavement, heartache, heartbreak, mournfulness
OPPOSITE: joy
grievance *n* **1 = complaint,** protest, beef *(slang)*, gripe *(informal)*, axe to grind, chip on your shoulder *(informal)*
grieve *vb* **a = mourn,** suffer, weep, ache, lament, sorrow, wail
b = sadden, hurt, injure, distress, wound, crush, pain, afflict, upset, agonize, break the heart of, make your heart bleed **OPPOSITE:** gladden

DICTIONARY

of Sinn Féin (1905); president of the Free State assembly (1922) **2 D**(**avid Lewelyn**) **W**(**ark**) 1875–1948, US film director and producer. He introduced several cinematic techniques, including the flashback and the fade-out, in his masterpiece *The Birth of a Nation* (1915)

Griffith-Joyner *n* **Florence,** known as *Flojo.* 1959–98, US sprinter, winner of two gold medals at the 1988 Olympic Games

griffon *n* **1** a large vulture with pale feathers and black wings **2** a small wire-haired breed of dog
WORD ORIGIN French

g

grill *vb* **1** to cook by direct heat under a grill or over a hot fire **2** *informal* to subject to relentless questioning: *the jury pool was grilled for signs of prejudice* ▷ *n* **3** a device on a cooker that radiates heat downwards for grilling food **4** a gridiron for cooking food **5** a dish of grilled food **6** ▸ see **grillroom**
> **grilled** *adj* **grilling** *n*
WORD ORIGIN Latin *craticula* fine wickerwork

grille *or* **grill** *n* a metal or wooden grating, used as a screen or partition
WORD ORIGIN Latin *craticula* fine hurdlework

Grillparzer *n* **Franz** 1791–1872, Austrian dramatist and poet, noted for his historical and classical tragedies, which include *Sappho* (1818), the trilogy *The Golden Fleece* (1819–22), and *The Jewess of Toledo* (1872)

grillroom *n* a restaurant specializing in grilled foods

grilse (grillss) *n, pl* **grilses** *or* **grilse** a salmon on its first return from the sea to fresh water
WORD ORIGIN origin unknown

grim ⓣ *adj* **grimmer, grimmest 1** unfavourable and worrying: *grim figures on unemployment* **2** harsh and unpleasant: *grim conditions in the detention centres* **3** stern or resolute: *a grim determination to fight on* **4** *informal* unpleasant or disagreeable **grimly** *adv* **grimness** *n*
WORD ORIGIN Old English *grimm*

grimace *n* **1** an ugly or distorted facial expression of disgust, pain, or displeasure ▷ *vb* **-macing, -maced 2** to make a grimace
WORD ORIGIN French

Grimaldi[1] *n* a large crater in the SE quadrant of the moon, about 190 km in diameter, which is conspicuous because of its dark floor
WORD ORIGIN named after Francesco Maria *Grimaldi* (1618–63), Italian physicist

Grimaldi[2] *n* **Joseph** 1779–1837, English actor, noted as a clown in pantomime

grime *n* **1** ingrained dirt ▷ *vb* **griming, grimed 2** to make very dirty: *sweat-grimed faces* **grimy** *adj*
WORD ORIGIN Middle Dutch

grin *vb* **grinning, grinned 1** to smile broadly, showing one's teeth **2 grin and bear it** *informal* to suffer hardship without complaint ▷ *n* **3** a broad smile **grinning** *adj*
WORD ORIGIN Old English *grennian*

grind ⓣ *vb* **grinding, ground 1** to reduce to small particles by pounding or rubbing: *grinding coffee* **2** to smooth, sharpen, or polish by friction **3** (of two objects) to scrape together with a harsh rasping sound **4 an axe to grind** ▸ see **axe** (sense 2) **5 grind one's teeth** to rub one's upper and lower teeth against each other, as if chewing **6 grind to a halt** to come to an end or a standstill: *without enzymes life would grind to a halt* ▷ *n* **7** *informal* hard or tedious work: *the grind of everyday life* ▸ See also **grind down**
WORD ORIGIN Old English *grindan*

grind down *vb* to treat harshly so as to suppress resistance: *to grind down the opposition*

grinder *n* a device for grinding substances: *an electric coffee grinder*

grindstone *n* **1** a revolving stone disc used for sharpening, grinding, or polishing things **2 keep one's nose to the grindstone** to work hard and steadily

grip ⓣ *n* **1** a very tight hold: *he felt a grip at his throat* **2** the style or manner of holding something, such as a golf club or tennis racket **3** power or control over a situation, person, or activity: *rebel forces tighten their grip around the capital* **4** a travelling bag or holdall **5** a small bent clasp used to fasten the hair **6** a handle **7** a person who manoeuvres the cameras in a film or television studio **8 get** *or* **come to grips with** to face up to and deal with (a problem or subject) ▷ *vb* **gripping, gripped 9** to take a tight hold of **10** to affect strongly: *sudden panic gripped her* **11** to hold the interest or attention of: *gripped by the intensity of the film; the story gripped him*
WORD ORIGIN Old English *gripe* grasp

gripe *vb* **griping, griped 1** *informal* to complain persistently **2** to cause sudden intense pain in the bowels ▷ *n* **3** *informal* a complaint **4 the gripes** a sudden intense pain in the bowels
WORD ORIGIN Old English *grīpan*

grippe *n* ▸ a former name for **influenza**
WORD ORIGIN French

gripping ⓣ *adj* very interesting and exciting: *a gripping story*

Gris *n* **Juan** 1887–1927, Spanish cubist painter, resident in France from 1906

Grisham *n* **John** born 1955, US novelist and lawyer; his legal thrillers, many of which have been filmed, include *A Time to Kill* (1989), *The Pelican Brief* (1992), and *The Summons* (2002)

grisly *adj* **-lier, -liest** causing horror or dread: *grisly murders*
WORD ORIGIN Old English *grislic*

grist *n* **1** grain that is to be or that has been ground **2 grist to the mill** anything that can be turned to profit or advantage
WORD ORIGIN Old English *grīst*

gristle *n* tough stringy animal tissue found in meat **gristly** *adj*
WORD ORIGIN Old English

grit ⓣ *n* **1** small hard particles of sand, earth, or stone **2** courage and determination ▷ *vb* **gritting, gritted 3** to cover (an icy road) with grit **4 grit one's teeth a** to rub one's upper and lower teeth against each other, as if chewing **b** to decide to carry on in a difficult situation: *he urged the Cabinet to grit its teeth and continue cutting public spending*
WORD ORIGIN Old English *grēot*

grits *pl n* coarsely ground grain, a popular dish in the Southern US
WORD ORIGIN Old English *grytt*

gritter *n* a vehicle that spreads grit on the roads in icy weather

THESAURUS

grim *adj* **1 = terrible**, shocking, severe, harsh, forbidding, horrible, formidable, sinister, ghastly, hideous, gruesome *(slang)*, grisly, horrid, frightful, godawful

grind *vb* **1 = crush**, mill, powder, grate, pulverize, pound, kibble, abrade, granulate **2 = sharpen**, file, polish, sand, smooth, whet **3 = grate**, scrape, grit, gnash ▷ *n* **7** *(informal)* **= hard work**, labour, effort, task, sweat *(informal)*, chore, toil, drudgery

grip *n* **1 = clasp**, hold, grasp, handclasp *(US)* **3 = control**, rule, influence, command, power, possession, sway, dominance, domination, mastery ▷ *vb* **9 = grasp**, hold, catch, seize, clutch, clasp, latch on to, take hold of **11 = engross**, fascinate, absorb, entrance, hold, catch up, compel, rivet, enthral, mesmerize, spellbind

gripping *adj* **= fascinating**, exciting, thrilling, entrancing, compelling, compulsive, riveting, enthralling, engrossing, spellbinding, unputdownable *(informal)*

grit *n* **1 = gravel**, sand, dust, pebbles **2 = courage**, spirit, resolution, determination, nerve, guts *(informal)*, balls *(taboo slang)*, pluck, backbone, fortitude, toughness, tenacity, perseverance, mettle, doggedness, hardihood

gritty *adj* **1 = courageous**, game, dogged, determined, tough, spirited,

DICTIONARY

gritty ❶ *adj* **-tier, -tiest 1** courageous and tough **2** covered with grit
grizzle *vb* **-zling, -zled** *Brit, Austral & NZ informal* to whine or complain
WORD ORIGIN Germanic
grizzled *adj* **1** (of hair) streaked or mixed with grey **2** (of a person) having grey hair
grizzly *n, pl* **-zlies** a large fierce greyish-brown bear of N America. In full: **grizzly bear**
groan ❶ *n* **1** a long deep cry of pain, grief, or disapproval **2** *informal* a grumble or complaint ▷ *vb* **3** to give a long deep cry of pain, grief, or disapproval **4** *informal* to complain or grumble **5 groan under** to be weighed down by: *chemists' shelves groan under the weight of slimming aids*
groaning *adj, n*
WORD ORIGIN Old English *grānian*
groat *n* a former British coin worth four old pennies
WORD ORIGIN Middle Dutch *groot*
groats *pl n* the crushed grain of various cereals
WORD ORIGIN Old English *grot* particle
grocer *n* a shopkeeper who sells food and other household supplies
WORD ORIGIN Old French *grossier*
groceries *pl n* food and other household supplies
grocery *n, pl* **-ceries** the business or premises of a grocer
Groening *n* **Matt(hew)** born 1954, US cartoonist and writer, creator and producer of *The Simpsons* television series from 1989
grog *n* **1** an alcoholic drink, usually rum, diluted with water **2** *Brit, Austral & NZ informal* any alcoholic drink
WORD ORIGIN after Old *Grog*, nickname of Edward Vernon, British admiral, who in 1740 issued naval rum diluted with water
groggy *adj* **-gier, -giest** *informal* faint, weak, or dizzy
groin *n* **1** the part of the body where the abdomen joins the legs **2** *archit* a curved edge formed where two intersecting vaults meet
WORD ORIGIN origin unknown
grommet *n* **1** a rubber, plastic, or metal ring or eyelet **2** *med* a small tube inserted into the eardrum to drain fluid from the middle ear
WORD ORIGIN obsolete French *gourmer* bridle
Gromyko *n* **Andrei Andreyevich** 1909–89, Soviet statesman and diplomat; foreign minister (1957–85); president (1985–88)
groom ❶ *n* **1** a person employed to clean and look after horses **2** ▸ short for **bridegroom** ▷ *vb* **3** to clean and smarten (a horse or other animal) **4** to keep (oneself or one's appearance) clean and tidy: *carefully groomed hair* **5** to train (someone) for a particular task or occupation: *groomed for future leadership*
grooming *n*
WORD ORIGIN Middle English *grom* manservant
groove ❶ *n* **1** a long narrow furrow cut into a surface **2** the spiral channel in a gramophone record
grooved *adj*
WORD ORIGIN obsolete Dutch *groeve*
groovy *adj* **groovier, grooviest** *slang* attractive, fashionable, or exciting
grope ❶ *vb* **groping, groped 1** to feel about uncertainly for something **2** to find (one's way) by groping **3** to search uncertainly for a solution or expression: *the new democracies are groping for stability* **4** *slang* to fondle (someone) in a rough sexual way ▷ *n* **5** an instance of groping
WORD ORIGIN Old English *grāpian*
Gropius *n* **Walter** 1883–1969, US architect, designer, and teacher, born in Germany. He founded (1919) and directed (1919–28) the Bauhaus in Germany. His influence stemmed from his adaptation of architecture to modern social needs and his pioneering use of industrial materials, such as concrete and steel. His buildings include the Fagus factory at Alfeld (1911) and the Bauhaus at Dessau (1926)
Gros *n* Baron **Antoine Jean** 1771–1835, French painter, noted for his battle scenes
gros point (groh point) *n* **1** a cross-stitch in embroidery **2** work done in this stitch
WORD ORIGIN Old French: large point
gross ❶ *adj* **1** outrageously wrong: *gross violations of human rights* **2** very coarse or vulgar: *gross bad taste* **3** *slang* disgusting or repulsive: *I think beards are gross* **4** repulsively fat **5** with no deductions for tax or the weight of the container; total: *gross income; a gross weight of 20 000 lbs* ▷ *n* **6** *pl* **gross** twelve dozen (144) **7** the entire amount or weight ▷ *vb* **8** to earn as total revenue, before deductions
grossly *adv*
WORD ORIGIN Old French *gros* large
gross domestic product *n* the total value of all goods and services produced domestically by a nation during a year
Grosseteste *n* **Robert** ?1175–1253, English prelate and scholar; bishop of Lincoln (1235–53). He attacked ecclesiastical abuses and wrote commentaries on Aristotle and treatises on theology, philosophy, and science
gross national product *n* the total value of all final goods and services produced annually by a nation: equivalent to gross domestic product plus net investment income from abroad
gross profit *n accounting* the difference between total revenue from sales and the total cost of purchases or materials
Grosz *n* **George** 1893–1959, German painter, in the US from 1932, whose works satirized German militarism and bourgeois society
Grote *n* **George** 1794–1871, English historian, noted particularly for his *History of Greece* (1846–56)

g

THESAURUS

brave, hardy, feisty *(informal, chiefly US & Canad)*, resolute, tenacious, plucky, steadfast, mettlesome, (as) game as Ned Kelly *(Austral slang)* **2 = rough**, sandy, dusty, abrasive, rasping, grainy, gravelly, granular
groan *n* **1 = moan**, cry, sigh, whine **2** *(informal)* **= complaint**, protest, objection, grumble, beef *(slang)*, grouse, gripe *(informal)*, grouch *(informal)* ▷ *vb* **3 = moan**, cry, sigh **4** *(informal)* **= complain**, object, moan, grumble, gripe *(informal)*, beef *(slang)*, carp, bitch *(slang)*, lament, whine, grouse, bemoan, whinge *(informal)*, grouch *(informal)*, bellyache *(slang)*
groom *n* **1 = stableman**, stableboy, hostler *or* ostler *(archaic)* ▷ *vb* **3 = brush**, clean, tend, rub down, curry **4 = smarten up**, dress, clean, turn out, get up *(informal)*, tidy, preen, spruce up, primp, gussy up *(slang, chiefly US)* **5 = train**, prime, prepare, coach, ready, educate, drill, nurture, make ready
groove *n* **1 = indentation**, cut, hollow, score, channel, trench, flute, gutter, trough, furrow, rut
grope *vb* **1 = feel**, search, fumble, flounder, fish, finger, scrabble, cast about, fossick *(Austral & NZ)*
gross *adj* **1 = flagrant**, obvious, glaring, blatant, serious, shocking, rank, plain, sheer, utter, outrageous, manifest, shameful, downright, grievous, unqualified, heinous, egregious, unmitigated, arrant **OPPOSITE:** qualified **2 = vulgar**, offensive, crude, rude, obscene, low, coarse, indecent, improper, unseemly, lewd, X-rated *(informal)*, impure, smutty, ribald, indelicate **OPPOSITE:** decent **4 = fat**, obese, overweight, great, big, large, heavy, massive, dense, bulky, hulking, corpulent, lumpish **OPPOSITE:** slim **5 = total**, whole, entire, aggregate, before tax, before deductions **OPPOSITE:** net ▷ *vb* **8 = earn**, make, take, bring in, rake in *(informal)*

DICTIONARY

grotesque ❶ (groh-tesk) *adj* **1** strangely distorted or bizarre: *a grotesque and pervasive personality cult* **2** ugly or repulsive ▹*n* **3** a grotesque person or thing **4** an artistic style in which parts of human, animal, and plant forms are distorted and mixed, or a work of art in this style
grotesquely *adv*
WORD ORIGIN Old Italian *(pittura) grottesca* cave (painting)

Grotius *n* **Hugo,** original name *Huig de Groot.* 1583–1645, Dutch jurist and statesman, whose *De Jure Belli ac Pacis* (1625) is regarded as the foundation of modern international law
Grotian *adj* **Grotianism** *n*

grotto *n, pl* **-toes** *or* **-tos** a small picturesque cave
WORD ORIGIN Old Italian *grotta*

grotty *adj* **-tier, -tiest** *Brit & NZ slang* **1** nasty or unattractive **2** in bad condition
WORD ORIGIN from *grotesque*

grouch *informal vb* **1** to complain or grumble ▹*n* **2** a person who is always complaining **3** a persistent complaint
WORD ORIGIN Old French *grouchier*

grouchy *adj* **grouchier, grouchiest** bad-tempered

ground[1] ❶ *n* **1** the land surface **2** earth or soil **3** an area used for a particular purpose: *a cricket ground* **4** a matter for consideration or discussion: *there is no need to cover the same ground* **5** an advantage in an argument or competition: *neither side seems willing to give ground in this trial of strength* **6** the background colour of a painting **7** *US & Canad* an electrical earth **8** **grounds** **a** the land around a building **b** reason or justification: *the hostages should be freed on humanitarian grounds* **c** sediment or dregs: *coffee grounds* **9** **break new ground** to do something that has not been done before **10** **common ground** an agreed basis for identifying issues in an argument **11** **get something off the ground** to get something started: *to get the peace conference off the ground* **12** **into the ground** to exhaustion or excess: *he was running himself into the ground* **13** **suit someone down to the ground** *Brit informal* to be totally suitable or appropriate for someone ▹*adj* **14** on the ground: *ground troops* ▹*vb* **15** to confine (an aircraft or pilot) to the ground **16** *naut* to move (a ship) onto the bottom of shallow water, so that it cannot move **17** to instruct in the basics of a subject: *the student who is not grounded in the elements cannot understand the advanced teaching* **18** to provide a basis for; establish: *a scientifically grounded documentation* **19** to forbid (a child) to go out and enjoy himself or herself as a punishment **20** *US & Canad* to connect (a circuit or electrical device) to an earth
WORD ORIGIN Old English *grund*

ground[2] *vb* **1** ▸the past of **grind** ▹*adj* **2** reduced to fine particles by grinding: *ground glass*

ground bass *n music* a short melodic bass line that is repeated over and over again

ground beef *n* finely chopped beef, sometimes used to make hamburgers

ground-breaking *adj* innovative

ground control *n* the people and equipment on the ground that monitor the progress of aircraft or spacecraft

ground cover *n* dense low plants that spread over the surface of the ground

ground floor *n* the floor of a building that is level, or almost level, with the ground

grounding *n* a foundation, esp. the basic general knowledge of a subject

groundless *adj* without reason or justification: *the scare turned out to be groundless*

groundnut *n Brit* a peanut

groundsel (grounce-el) *n* a yellow-flowered weed
WORD ORIGIN Old English *grundeswelge*

groundsheet *n* a waterproof sheet placed on the ground in a tent to keep out damp

groundsman *n, pl* **-men** a person employed to maintain a sports ground or park

groundswell *n* a rapidly developing general feeling or opinion

ground water *n* water that has seeped through from the surface and is held underground

groundwork *n* preliminary work as a foundation or basis

group ❶ *n* **1** a number of people or things considered as a unit **2** a small band of players or singers, esp. of popular music **3** an association of business firms that have the same owner **4** *chem* two or more atoms that are bound together in a molecule and behave as a single unit: *a methyl group* $-CH_3$ **5** *chem* a vertical column of elements in the periodic table that all have similar properties: *the halogen group* ▹*vb* **6** to put into or form into a group
WORD ORIGIN French *groupe*

group captain *n* a middle-ranking officer in some air forces

groupie *n slang* an ardent fan of a celebrity or of a sport or activity: *a polo groupie*

grouping *n* a set of people or organizations who act or work together to achieve a shared aim: *a pro-democracy grouping within China*

group therapy *n psychol* the treatment of people by bringing them together to share their problems in group discussion

grouse[1] *n, pl* **grouse** **1** a game bird with a stocky body and feathered legs and feet **2** the flesh of this bird used for food
WORD ORIGIN origin unknown

grouse[2] *vb* **grousing, groused** **1** to complain or grumble ▹*n* **2** a persistent complaint
WORD ORIGIN origin unknown

grouse[3] *adj Austral & NZ slang* fine or excellent
WORD ORIGIN origin unknown

grout *n* **1** a thin mortar for filling joints between tiles or masonry ▹*vb* **2** to fill with grout
WORD ORIGIN Old English *grūt*

grove ❶ *n* a small wood or group of trees: *orange groves*
WORD ORIGIN Old English *grāf*

grovel (grov-el) *vb* **-elling, -elled** *or US* **-eling, -eled** **1** to behave excessively humbly towards someone, esp. a superior, in an attempt to win his or her favour **2** to crawl on the floor, often in search of something: *grovelling on the floor for missing cards*
grovelling *or US* **groveling** *adj, n*
WORD ORIGIN Middle English *on*

THESAURUS

grotesque *adj* **1a = unnatural,** bizarre, weird, odd, strange, fantastic, distorted, fanciful, deformed, outlandish, whimsical, freakish, misshapen, malformed
OPPOSITE: natural
1b = absurd, ridiculous, ludicrous, preposterous, incongruous
OPPOSITE: natural

ground[1] *n* **1 = earth,** land, dry land, terra firma **3 = arena,** pitch, stadium, park *(informal)*, field, enclosure ▹*pl n* **8a = estate,** holding, land, fields, gardens, property, district, territory, domain **8b = reason,** cause, basis, argument, call, base, occasion, foundation, excuse, premise, motive, justification, rationale, inducement **8c = dregs,** lees, deposit, sediment ▹*vb* **17 = instruct,** train, prepare, coach, teach, inform, initiate, tutor, acquaint with, familiarize with **18 = base,** found, establish, set, settle, fix

group *n* **1 = crowd,** company, party, band, troop, pack, gathering, gang, bunch, congregation, posse *(slang)*, bevy, assemblage ▹*vb* **6 = arrange,** order, sort, class, range, gather, organize, assemble, put together, classify, marshal, bracket, assort

grove *n* **= wood,** woodland, plantation, covert, thicket, copse, brake, coppice, spinney

DICTIONARY

grufe on the face

Groves *n* Sir **Charles** 1915–92, English orchestral conductor

grow ❶ *vb* **growing, grew, grown** **1** (of a person or animal) to increase in size and develop physically **2** (of a plant) to exist and increase in size: *an ancient meadow where wild flowers grow* **3** to produce (a plant) by planting seeds, bulbs, or cuttings, and looking after it: *many farmers have expressed a wish to grow more cotton* **4** to let (one's hair or nails) develop: *to grow a beard* **5** to increase in size or degree: *the gulf between rich and poor is growing* **6** to originate or develop: *Melbourne grew from a sheep-farming outstation and occasional port to a city* **7** to become increasingly as specified: *as the night wore on the audience grew more intolerant* ▸ See also **grow on, grow out of**, etc. **growing** *adj* **grower** *n*
WORD ORIGIN Old English *grōwan*

growing pains *pl n* **1** pains in muscles or joints sometimes experienced by growing children **2** difficulties experienced in the early stages of a new enterprise

growl *vb* **1** (of a dog or other animal) to make a low rumbling sound, usually in anger **2** to say in a gruff or angry manner: *'You're late,' he growled* **3** to make a deep rumbling sound: *his stomach growled* ▹ *n* **4** the act or sound of growling
WORD ORIGIN Old French *grouller* to grumble

grown *adj* developed or advanced: *fully grown; a grown man*

grown-up ❶ *adj* **1** having reached maturity; adult **2** of or suitable for an adult ▹ *n* **3** an adult

grow on *vb* to become progressively more acceptable or pleasant to: *I didn't like that programme at first but it has grown on me*

grow out of *vb* to become too big or mature for: *I used to be into the fifties scene but grew out of it*

growth ❶ *n* **1** the process of growing **2** an increase in size, number, or significance: *the growth of drug trafficking* **3** something grown or growing: *a thick growth of ivy* **4** any abnormal tissue, such as a tumour ▹ *adj* **5** of or relating to growth: *growth hormone*

grow up *vb* to reach maturity; become adult

groyne *n* a wall or breakwater built out from a shore to control erosion
WORD ORIGIN Old French *groign* snout

grub *n* **1** *slang* food **2** the short legless larva of certain insects, such as beetles ▹ *vb* **grubbing, grubbed** **3** to search carefully for something by digging or by moving things about **4** **grub up** to dig (roots or plants) out of the ground
WORD ORIGIN Germanic

grubby *adj* **-bier, -biest** **1** rather dirty **2** unsavoury or morally unacceptable: *grubby activities* **grubbiness** *n*

grudge ❶ *n* **1** a persistent feeling of resentment against a person who has caused harm or upset ▹ *vb* **grudging, grudged** **2** to give unwillingly: *the rich men who grudged pennies for the poor* **3** to resent or envy the success or possessions of: *none of their guests grudged them this celebration* ▹ *adj* **4** planned or carried out in order to settle a grudge: *a grudge match*
WORD ORIGIN Old French *grouchier* to grumble

grudging *adj* felt or done unwillingly: *grudging admiration for his opponent* **grudgingly** *adv*

gruel *n* thin porridge made by boiling oatmeal in water or milk
WORD ORIGIN Old French

gruelling ❶ *or US* **grueling** *adj* extremely severe or tiring: *a gruelling journey*
WORD ORIGIN obsolete *gruel* to punish

gruesome ❶ *adj* inspiring horror and disgust
WORD ORIGIN Scandinavian

gruff *adj* **1** rough or surly in manner or speech **2** (of a voice) low and throaty **gruffly** *adv* **gruffness** *n*
WORD ORIGIN Germanic

grumble ❶ *vb* **-bling, -bled** **1** to complain in a nagging way: *his neighbour grumbled about the long wait* **2** to make low rumbling sounds: *the storm grumbled in the distance* ▹ *n* **3** a complaint **4** a low rumbling sound: *a distant grumble of artillery fire* **grumbling** *adj, n*
WORD ORIGIN Middle Low German *grommelen*

grumpy *adj* **grumpier, grumpiest** sulky and bad-tempered **grumpily** *adv*
WORD ORIGIN imitative

Grünewald *n* **Matthias**, original name *Mathis Gothardt*. ?1470–1528, German painter, the greatest exponent of late Gothic art in Germany. The *Isenheim Altarpiece* is regarded as his masterpiece

grunge *n* **1** a style of rock music with a fuzzy guitar sound **2** a deliberately untidy and uncoordinated fashion style
WORD ORIGIN from US slang: dirt, rubbish

grungy *adj* **grungier, grungiest** **1** *slang, chiefly US & Canad* squalid or seedy **2** *slang* (of pop music) characterized by a loud fuzzy guitar sound

grunt *vb* **1** to make a low short gruff noise, such as the sound made by a pig, or by a person to express annoyance **2** to express (something) gruffly: *he grunted his thanks* ▹ *n* **3** a low short gruff noise, such as the sound made by a pig, or by a person to express annoyance
WORD ORIGIN Old English *grunnettan*

Gruyère (grew-yair) *n* a hard flat pale yellow cheese with holes
WORD ORIGIN after *Gruyère*, Switzerland, where it originated

gryphon *n* ▸ same as **griffin**

g

THESAURUS

grow *vb* **1 = develop**, fill out, get bigger, get taller OPPOSITE: shrink **3 = cultivate**, produce, raise, farm, breed, nurture, propagate **5 = get bigger**, spread, swell, extend, stretch, expand, widen, enlarge, multiply, thicken **6 = originate**, spring, arise, stem, issue **7 = become**, get, turn, come to be

grown-up *adj* **1, 2 = mature**, adult, of age, fully-grown ▹ *n* **3 = adult**, man, woman

growth *n* **1 = increase**, development, expansion, extension, growing, heightening, proliferation, enlargement, multiplication OPPOSITE: decline **2 = progress**, success, improvement, expansion, advance, prosperity, advancement OPPOSITE: failure **4 = tumour**, cancer, swelling, lump, carcinoma *(pathology)*, sarcoma *(medical)*, excrescence

grudge *n* **1 = resentment**, bitterness, grievance, malice, hate, spite, dislike, animosity, aversion, venom, antipathy, enmity, rancour, hard feelings, ill will, animus, malevolence OPPOSITE: goodwill ▹ *vb* **2, 3 = resent**, mind, envy, covet, begrudge OPPOSITE: welcome

gruelling *adj* **= exhausting**, demanding, difficult, tiring, trying, hard, taxing, grinding, severe, crushing, fierce, punishing, harsh, stiff, brutal, fatiguing, strenuous, arduous, laborious, backbreaking OPPOSITE: easy

gruesome *adj* **= horrific**, shocking, terrible, awful, horrible, grim, horrifying, fearful, obscene, horrendous, ghastly, hideous, from hell *(informal)*, grisly, macabre, horrid, repulsive, repugnant, loathsome, abominable, spine-chilling, hellacious *(US slang)* OPPOSITE: pleasant

grumble *vb* **1 = complain**, moan, gripe *(informal)*, whinge *(informal)*, beef *(slang)*, carp, bitch *(slang)*, whine, grouse, bleat, grouch *(informal)*, bellyache *(slang)*, kvetch *(US slang)*, repine **2 = rumble**, growl, gurgle ▹ *n* **3 = complaint**, protest, objection, moan, grievance, grouse, gripe *(informal)*, grouch *(informal)*, beef *(slang)* **4 = rumble**, growl, gurgle

DICTIONARY

GST (in Australia, New Zealand, and Canada) Goods and Services Tax

G-string *n* a strip of cloth worn between the legs and attached to a waistband

G-suit *n* a close-fitting pressurized garment that is worn by the crew of high-speed aircraft
WORD ORIGIN from *g(ravity) suit*

GT gran turismo: a touring car, usually a fast sports car with a hard fixed roof

guano (gwah-no) *n* the dried manure of sea birds, used as a fertilizer
WORD ORIGIN S American Indian *huano* dung

g

guarantee ❶ *n* **1** a formal assurance in writing that a product or service will meet certain standards or specifications **2** something that makes a specified condition or outcome certain: *there was no guarantee that there would not be another military coup* **3** ▸ same as **guaranty** ▹ *vb* **-teeing, -teed 4** to promise or make certain: *to guarantee absolute loyalty* **5** (of a company) to provide a guarantee in writing for (a product or service) **6** to take responsibility for the debts or obligations of (another person)
WORD ORIGIN Germanic

guarantor *n* a person who gives or is bound by a guarantee or guaranty

guaranty *n, pl* **-ties 1** a pledge of responsibility for fulfilling another person's obligations in case of that person's default **2** a thing given or taken as security for a guaranty

guard ❶ *vb* **1** to watch over or shield from danger or harm; protect: *US marines who guard the American embassy* **2** to keep watch over (a prisoner) to prevent escape **3** to protect (a right or privilege) **4** to take precautions: *to guard against a possible coup attempt* ▹ *n* **5** a person or group of people who protect or watch over people or things **6** *Brit, Austral & NZ* the official in charge of a train **7** a device or part of a machine designed to protect the user against injury **8** anything that provides protection: *a guard against future shocks* **9 off guard** having one's defences down; unprepared: *England were caught off guard as the Dutch struck two telling blows* **10 on guard** on duty to protect or watch over people or things **11 on one's guard** prepared to face danger or difficulties: *parents have been warned to be on their guard against kidnappers* **12 stand guard** (of a sentry) to keep watch
WORD ORIGIN Old French *garder* to protect

guarded ❶ *adj* cautious and avoiding any commitment: *a guarded welcome* **guardedly** *adv*

guardhouse *or* **guardroom** *n mil* a military police office in which prisoners can be detained

Guardi *n* **Francesco** 1712–93, Venetian landscape painter

guardian ❶ *n* **1** one who looks after, protects, or defends someone or something: *the nation's moral guardians* **2** someone legally appointed to manage the affairs of another person, such as a child or a person who is mentally ill **guardianship** *n*

guardsman *n, pl* **-men** *mil* a member of a regiment responsible for ceremonial duties

guard's van *n Brit, Austral & NZ* a small railway carriage in which the guard travels

guava (gwah-va) *n* a round tropical fruit with yellow skin and pink pulp
WORD ORIGIN from S American Indian

gubernatorial *adj chiefly US* of or relating to a governor
WORD ORIGIN Latin *gubernator* governor

gudgeon[1] *n* a small slender European freshwater fish, used as bait by anglers
WORD ORIGIN Old French *gougon*

gudgeon[2] *n* the socket of a hinge, which fits round the pin
WORD ORIGIN Old French *goujon*

guelder rose (geld-er) *n* a Eurasian shrub with clusters of white flowers
WORD ORIGIN from *Gelderland*, province of Holland

Guericke *n* **Otto von** 1602–86, German physicist: invented the air pump (1650) and demonstrated the power of a vacuum with the Magdeburg hemispheres

Guernsey (gurn-zee) *n* a breed of dairy cattle that produces rich creamy milk, originating from Guernsey, in the Channel Islands

guerrilla ❶ *or* **guerilla** *n* a member of an irregular, politically motivated, armed force that fights regular forces
WORD ORIGIN Spanish

Guesclin *n* **Bertrand du** ?1320–80, French commander during the Hundred Years' War

guess ❶ *vb* **1** to form an estimate or conclusion about (something), without proper knowledge: *a competition to guess the weight of the cake* **2** to arrive at a correct estimate of (something) by guessing: *I had a notion that he guessed my thoughts* **3** *informal* to think or suppose: *I guess he must have been a great athlete* ▹ *n* **4** an estimate or conclusion arrived at by guessing: *we can hazard a guess at the answer*
WORD ORIGIN probably from Old Norse

guesswork *n* the process of arriving at conclusions or estimates by guessing

guest ❶ *n* **1** a person who receives hospitality at someone else's home **2** a person who is taken out socially by someone else who pays all the expenses **3** a performer or speaker taking part in an event, show, or film by special invitation **4** a person who is staying in a hotel ▹ *vb* **5** to be a guest in an event, show, or film: *he guested in concert with Eric Clapton*
WORD ORIGIN Old English *giest* guest, stranger, enemy

guesthouse *n* a private home or boarding house offering accommodation

guest of honour *n* a famous or important person who is the most important guest at a dinner or other social occasion

guff *n Brit, Austral & NZ slang* ridiculous talk; nonsense
WORD ORIGIN imitative

guffaw *vb* **1** to laugh loudly and raucously ▹ *n* **2** a loud raucous laugh
WORD ORIGIN imitative

GUI (goo-ee) *computers* graphical user interface

guidance ❶ *n* help, advice, or instruction, usually from someone

THESAURUS

guarantee *n* **1 = warranty**, contract, bond, guaranty ▹ *vb* **4a = ensure**, secure, assure, warrant, insure, make certain **4b = promise**, pledge, undertake, swear

guard *vb* **1, 3, 4 = protect**, watch, defend, secure, police, mind, cover, screen, preserve, shelter, shield, patrol, oversee, safeguard, watch over ▹ *n* **8 = shield**, security, defence, screen, protection, pad, safeguard, bumper, buffer, rampart, bulwark

guarded *adj* **= cautious**, reserved, careful, suspicious, restrained, wary, discreet, prudent, reticent, circumspect, cagey *(informal)*, leery *(slang)*, noncommittal

guardian *n* **1, 2 = keeper**, champion, defender, guard, trustee, warden, curator, protector, warder, custodian, preserver

guerrilla *n* **= freedom fighter**, partisan, irregular, underground fighter, member of the underground *or* resistance

guess *vb* **1, 2 = estimate**, predict, work out, speculate, fathom, conjecture, postulate, surmise, hazard a guess, hypothesize **OPPOSITE:** know **3** *(informal)* **= suppose**, think, believe, suspect, judge, imagine, reckon, fancy, conjecture, dare say ▹ *n* **4 = estimate**, reckoning, speculation, judgment, hypothesis, conjecture, surmise, shot in the dark, ballpark figure *(informal)* **OPPOSITE:** certainty

guest *n* **1 = visitor**, company, caller, manu(w)hiri *(NZ)*

guidance *n* **= advice**, direction,

DICTIONARY

more experienced or more qualified: *marriage guidance*

guide ❶ *n* **1** a person who conducts parties of tourists around places of interest, such as museums **2** a person who leads travellers to a place, usually in a dangerous area: *a mountain guide* **3** something that can be used to gauge something or to help in planning one's actions: *starting salary was not an accurate guide to future earnings* **4** ▸same as **guidebook** **5** a book that explains the basics of a subject or skill: *a guide to higher education* ▹*vb* **guiding, guided** **6** to lead the way for (tourists or travellers) **7** to control the movement or course of; steer **8** to direct the affairs of (a person, team, or country): *he will stay with the club he guided to promotion to the First Division* **9** to influence (a person) in his or her actions or opinions: *to be guided by the law* **guiding** *adj*
WORD ORIGIN Germanic

Guide *n* a member of an organization for girls that encourages discipline and practical skills

guidebook *n* a book which gives tourist information on a place

guided missile *n* a missile whose course is controlled electronically

guide dog *n* a dog that has been trained to lead a blind person

guideline *n* a principle put forward to set standards or determine a course of action: *guidelines for arms exporting*

Guido d'Arezzo *n* ?995–?1050 AD, Italian Benedictine monk and musical theorist: reputed inventor of solmization

guild ❶ *n* **1** an organization or club for people with shared interests **2** (in Medieval Europe) an association of men in the same trade or craft
WORD ORIGIN Old Norse *gildi*

guilder *n, pl* **-ders** *or* **-der** a former monetary unit of the Netherlands
WORD ORIGIN Middle Dutch *gulden*

guildhall *n Brit* a hall where members of a guild meet

guile (gile) *n* craftiness or deviousness **guileless** *adj*
WORD ORIGIN Old French

Guillaume de Lorris *n* 13th century, French poet who wrote the first 4058 lines of the allegorical romance, the *Roman de la rose*, continued by Jean de Meung

Guillem *n* **Sylvie** born 1965, French ballet dancer based in Britain; with the Royal Ballet from 1989

guillemot (gil-lee-mot) *n* a northern oceanic black-and-white diving sea bird
WORD ORIGIN French

guillotine *n* **1** a device formerly used, esp. in France, for beheading people, consisting of a weighted blade between two upright posts, which was dropped on the neck **2** a device with a blade for cutting paper ▹*vb* **-tining, -tined** **3** to behead with a guillotine
WORD ORIGIN after J. I. *Guillotin*, who advocated its use

guilt ❶ *n* **1** the fact or state of having done wrong: *the court was unable to establish guilt* **2** remorse or self-reproach caused by feeling that one has done something wrong: *he feels no guilt about the planned cutbacks*
WORD ORIGIN Old English *gylt*

guiltless *adj* free of all responsibility for wrongdoing or crime; innocent

guilty ❶ *adj* **guiltier, guiltiest** **1** *law* judged to have committed a crime: *she has been found guilty of drug trafficking* **2** responsible for doing something wrong: *students who are guilty of cheating* **3** showing, feeling, or indicating guilt: *guilty conscience* **guiltily** *adv*

guinea *n* a former British unit of currency worth £1.05 (21 shillings), sometimes still used in quoting professional fees
WORD ORIGIN the coin was originally made of gold from Guinea

guinea fowl *n* a domestic bird with a heavy rounded body and speckled feathers

guinea pig *n* **1** a tailless S American rodent, commonly kept as a pet or used in scientific experiments **2** a person used in an experiment
WORD ORIGIN origin unknown

Guinness *n* Sir **Alec** 1914–2000, British stage and film actor. His films include *Kind Hearts and Coronets* (1949), *The Bridge on the River Kwai* (1957), for which he won an Oscar, and *Star Wars* (1977); TV roles include Le Carré's George Smiley

guipure (geep-**pure**) *n* heavy lace that has its pattern connected by threads, rather than supported on a net mesh
WORD ORIGIN French

Guiscard *n* **Robert** ?1015–85, Norman conqueror in S Italy

guise ❶ (rhymes with **size**) *n* **1** a false appearance: *in the guise of a wood-cutter* **2** general appearance or form: *haricot beans are best known in Britain in their popular guise of baked beans*
WORD ORIGIN Old French

guitar *n* a stringed instrument with a flat back and a long neck with a fretted fingerboard, which is played by plucking or strumming
guitarist *n*
WORD ORIGIN Spanish *guitarra*

Guitry *n* **Sacha** 1885–1957, French actor, dramatist, and film director, born in Russia: plays include *Nono* (1905)

Guizot *n* **François Pierre Guillaume** 1787–1874, French statesman and historian. As chief minister (1840–48), his reactionary policies contributed to the outbreak of the revolution of 1848

Gulag *n* a system or department that silences dissidents, esp. in the former Soviet Union
WORD ORIGIN Russian *G(lavnoye) U(pravleniye Ispravitelno-Trudovykh) Lag(erei)* Main Administration for Corrective Labour Camps

Gulbenkian *n* **1 Calouste Sarkis** 1869–1955, British industrialist, born in Turkey. He endowed the international Gulbenkian Foundation for the advancement of the arts, science, and education **2** his son, **Nubar Sarkis** 1896–1972, British

THESAURUS

leadership, instruction, government, help, control, management, teaching, counsel, counselling, auspices

guide *n* **1, 2 = escort**, leader, controller, attendant, usher, chaperon, torchbearer, dragoman **3a = pointer**, sign, signal, mark, key, clue, landmark, marker, beacon, signpost, guiding light, lodestar **3b = model**, example, standard, ideal, master, inspiration, criterion, paradigm, exemplar, lodestar **5 = handbook**, manual, guidebook, instructions, catalogue ▹*vb* **6 = lead**, direct, escort, conduct, pilot, accompany, steer, shepherd, convoy, usher, show the way **7 = steer**, control, manage, direct, handle, command, manoeuvre **8, 9 = supervise**, train, rule, teach, influence, advise, counsel, govern, educate, regulate, instruct, oversee, sway, superintend

guild *n* **1 = society**, union, league, association, company, club, order, organization, corporation, lodge, fellowship, fraternity, brotherhood

guilt *n* **1 = culpability**, blame, responsibility, misconduct, delinquency, criminality, wickedness, iniquity, sinfulness, blameworthiness, guiltiness
OPPOSITE: innocence
2 = shame, regret, remorse, contrition, guilty conscience, bad conscience, self-reproach, self-condemnation, guiltiness
OPPOSITE: pride

guilty *adj* **1, 2 = culpable**, responsible, convicted, to blame, offending, erring, at fault, reprehensible, iniquitous, felonious, blameworthy
OPPOSITE: innocent
3 = ashamed, sorry, rueful, sheepish, contrite, remorseful, regretful, shamefaced, hangdog, conscience-stricken OPPOSITE: proud

guise *n* **1 = pretence**, show, mask, disguise, face, front, aspect, façade, semblance **2 = form**, appearance, dress, fashion, shape, aspect, mode, semblance

DICTIONARY

industrialist, diplomat, and philanthropist

gulch ❶ *n US & Canad* a narrow ravine with a stream running through it **WORD ORIGIN** origin unknown

gulf ❶ *n* **1** a large deep bay **2** something that divides or separates people, such as a lack of understanding: *gradually the gulf between father and son has lessened* **WORD ORIGIN** Greek *kolpos*

Gulf War syndrome *n* a group of various debilitating symptoms experienced by many soldiers who served in the Gulf War of 1991, claimed to be associated with damage to the central nervous system

g

gull *n* a large sea bird with white feathers tipped with black or grey **WORD ORIGIN** Celtic

gullet *n* the muscular tube through which food passes from the throat to the stomach **WORD ORIGIN** Latin *gula* throat

gullible *adj* easily tricked; too trusting **gullibility** *n*

gully *or* **gulley** *n, pl* **-lies** *or* **-leys 1** a channel or small valley originally worn away by running water **2** *cricket* a fielding position on the off side, between the slips and point **WORD ORIGIN** French *goulet* neck of a bottle

gulp *vb* **1** to swallow (a drink or food) rapidly in large mouthfuls **2** to gasp or breathe in violently, for example when nervous or when swimming **3 gulp back** to stifle or suppress: *he gulped back the tears as he said his goodbyes* ▹ *n* **4** the act of gulping **5** the quantity taken in a gulp **WORD ORIGIN** imitative

gum[1] ❶ *n* **1** a sticky substance obtained from certain plants, which hardens on exposure to air and dissolves in water **2** a substance used for sticking things together **3** ▸ short for **chewing gum** or **bubble gum 4** *chiefly Brit* a gumdrop ▹ *vb* **gumming, gummed 5** to stick with gum ▸ See also **gum up** **WORD ORIGIN** Old French *gomme*

gum[2] *n* the fleshy tissue that covers the bases of the teeth **WORD ORIGIN** Old English *gōma* jaw

gum arabic *n* a gum obtained from certain acacia trees, used to make ink, food thickeners, and pills

gumboil *n* an abscess on the gum

gumboots *pl n Brit & NZ* long rubber boots, worn in wet or muddy conditions

gumdrop *n* a small hard fruit-flavoured jelly-like sweet

gummy[1] *adj* **-mier, -miest 1** sticky or tacky **2** producing gum

gummy[2] *adj* **-mier, -miest** toothless

gumption *n Brit & NZ informal* common sense or initiative **WORD ORIGIN** origin unknown

gumtree *n* **1** any of various trees that yield gum, such as the eucalyptus **2 up a gumtree** *Brit & NZ informal* in an awkward position; in difficulties

gum up *vb* **gum up the works** *informal* to spoil a plan or hinder progress

gun ❶ *n* **1** a weapon with a metallic tube or barrel from which a missile is fired, usually by force of an explosion **2** a device used to force out (a substance, such as grease or paint) under pressure: *a spray gun* **3 jump the gun** *informal* to act prematurely **4 stick to one's guns** *informal* to stand by one's opinions or intentions in spite of opposition ▹ *vb* **gunning, gunned 5** to press hard on the accelerator of (a vehicle's engine) **6 gun down** to shoot (someone) with a gun ▹ *adj* **7** *NZ slang* expert: *a gun surfer* ▸ See also **gun for** **WORD ORIGIN** Middle English *gonne*

gunboat *n* a small ship carrying mounted guns

gunboat diplomacy *n* diplomacy conducted by threats of military intervention

guncotton *n* a form of cellulose nitrate used as an explosive

gun dog *n* **1** a dog trained to locate or retrieve birds or animals that have been shot in a hunt **2** a dog belonging to any breed traditionally used for these activities

gunfire *n* the repeated firing of guns

gun for *vb informal* to search for (someone) in order to harm him or her in some way

gunge *n informal* a sticky or congealed substance **gungy** *adj* **WORD ORIGIN** imitative

gunk *n informal* a slimy, oily, or dirty substance **WORD ORIGIN** perhaps imitative

gunman ❶ *n, pl* **-men** a man who uses a gun to commit a crime

gunmetal *n* **1** a type of bronze containing copper, tin, and zinc ▹ *adj* **2** dark grey

Gunn *n* **Thom(son William)** 1929–2004, British poet who lived in the USA. His works include *Fighting Terms* (1954), *My Sad Captains* (1961), *Jack Straw's Castle* (1976), *The Man with the Night Sweats* (1992), and *Boss Cupid* (2000)

gunnel (gun-nel) *n* ▸ same as **gunwale**

Gunnell *n* **Sally** born 1966, British athlete: Olympic 400-metre hurdles gold medallist (1992)

gunner *n* a member of the armed forces who works with, uses, or specializes in guns

gunnery *n* the art and science of the efficient design and use of large guns

gunny *n chiefly US* a coarse hard-wearing fabric, made from jute and used for sacks **WORD ORIGIN** Hindi *gōnī*

gunpoint *n* **at gunpoint** being under or using the threat of being shot: *eight tourists have been kidnapped at gunpoint by unidentified men*

gunpowder *n* an explosive mixture of potassium nitrate, charcoal, and sulphur, used to make fireworks

gunrunning *n* the practice of smuggling guns and ammunition into a country **gunrunner** *n*

gunshot *n* **1** bullets fired from a gun **2** the sound of a gun being fired **3** the firing range of a gun: *within gunshot*

gunslinger *n slang* a person who can shoot very accurately and has been involved in many fights using guns, esp. in the frontier days of the American West

gunstock *n* the wooden handle to which the barrel of a rifle is attached

Gunter *n* **Edmund** 1581–1626, English mathematician and astronomer, who invented various measuring instruments, including Gunter's chain

gunwale (gun-nel) *n naut* the top of the side of a ship **WORD ORIGIN** *wale*, ridge of planking originally supporting guns

gunyah *n Austral* a hut or shelter in the bush **WORD ORIGIN** Aboriginal

guppy *n, pl* **-pies** a small brightly coloured tropical fish, often kept in aquariums in people's homes **WORD ORIGIN** after R. J. L. *Guppy*, who gave specimens to the British Museum

Gurdjieff *n* **Georgei Ivanovitch** ?1877–1949, Russian mystic: founded a teaching centre in Paris (1922)

gurdwara (gurd-wah-ra) *n* a Sikh place of worship **WORD ORIGIN** from Sanskrit *guru*

THESAURUS

gulch *n (US & Canad)* = **ravine**, canyon, defile, gorge, gully, pass

gulf *n* **1** = **bay**, bight, sea inlet **2** = **chasm**, opening, split, gap, rent, breach, separation, void, rift, abyss, cleft

gum[1] *n* **1, 2** = **glue**, adhesive, resin, cement, paste ▹ *vb* **5** = **stick**, glue, affix, cement, paste, clog

gun *n* **1** = **firearm**, shooter *(slang)*, piece *(slang)*, rod *(slang)*, heater *(US slang)*, handgun

gunman *n* = **armed man**, hit man *(slang)*, gunslinger *(US slang)*

guru *n* **1** = **teacher**, mentor, sage, master, tutor, mahatma, guiding light, swami, maharishi **2** = **authority**, expert, leader, master, pundit, arbiter, Svengali, torchbearer, fundi *(S African)*

gush *vb* **1** = **flow**, run, rush, flood,

DICTIONARY

teacher + *dvārā* door

gurgle *vb* **-gling, -gled 1** (of water) to make low bubbling noises when flowing **2** to make low throaty bubbling noises: *the baby gurgled in delight* ▹*n* **3** the sound of gurgling
WORD ORIGIN origin unknown

Gurkha *n* **1** a member of a Hindu people living mainly in Nepal **2** a member of a Gurkha regiment in the Indian or British Army
WORD ORIGIN Sanskrit

gurnard *n, pl* **-nard** *or* **-nards** a sea fish with a spiny head and long finger-like pectoral fins
WORD ORIGIN Old French *gornard* grunter

Gurney *n* **Ivor** (**Bertie**) 1890–1937, British poet and composer, noted esp. for his songs and his poems of World War I

guru ❶ *n* **1** a Hindu or Sikh religious teacher or leader **2** a leader or adviser of a person or group of people: *inside a team of advertising gurus are at work*
WORD ORIGIN Hindi

Guru Granth Sahib *n* ▸same as **Granth**

gush ❶ *vb* **1** to pour out suddenly and profusely **2** to speak or behave in an overenthusiastic manner: *I'm not about to start gushing about raspberry coulis* ▹*n* **3** a sudden large flow of liquid **4** a sudden surge of strong feeling: *she felt a gush of pure affection for her mother*
WORD ORIGIN probably imitative

gusher *n* **1** a person who gushes **2** a spurting oil well

gushing *adj* behaving in an overenthusiastic manner: *gushing television commentators*

gusset *n* a piece of material sewn into a garment to strengthen it
WORD ORIGIN Old French *gousset*

gust *n* **1** a sudden blast of wind **2** a sudden surge of strong feeling: *a gust of joviality* ▹*vb* **3** to blow in gusts
gusty *adj*
WORD ORIGIN Old Norse *gustr*

Gustavus Adolphus *or* **Gustavus II** *n* 1594–1632, king of Sweden (1611–32). A brilliant general, he waged successful wars with Denmark, Russia, and Poland and in the Thirty Years' War led a Protestant army against the Catholic League and the Holy Roman Empire (1630–32). He defeated Tilly at Leipzig (1631) and Lech (1632) but was killed at the battle of Lützen

Gustavus I *n* called *Gustavus Vasa.* ?1496–1560, king of Sweden (1523–60). He was elected king after driving the Danes from Sweden (1520–23)

Gustavus II *n* ▸See **Gustavus Adolphus**

Gustavus VI *n* title of *Gustaf Adolf.* 1882–1973, king of Sweden (1950–73)

gusto *n* vigorous enjoyment: *he downed a pint with gusto*
WORD ORIGIN Spanish: taste

gut ❶ *n* **1** ▸same as **intestine 2** *slang* a stomach, esp. a fat one **3** ▸short for **catgut 4** a silky fibrous substance extracted from silkworms and used in the manufacture of fishing tackle ▹*vb* **gutting, gutted 5** to remove the internal organs from (a dead animal or fish) **6** (of a fire) to destroy the inside of (a building): *a local pub was gutted* ▹*adj* **7** *informal* basic, essential, or natural: *I have a gut feeling she's after something* ▸See also **guts**
WORD ORIGIN Old English *gutt*

Guthrie *n* **1 Samuel** 1782–1848, US chemist: invented percussion priming powder and a punch lock for exploding it, and discovered chloroform (1831) **2** Sir (**William**) **Tyrone** 1900–71, English theatrical director **3 Woody,** full name *Woodrow Wilson Guthrie.* 1912–67, US folk singer and songwriter. His songs include "So Long, it's been Good to Know you" (1940) and "This Land is your Land" (1944)

gutless *adj informal* lacking courage or determination

guts *pl n* **1** the internal organs of a person or an animal **2** *informal* courage, willpower, or daring **3** *informal* the inner or essential part: *the new roads have torn apart the guts of the city*

gutsy *adj* **gutsier, gutsiest** *slang* **1** bold or courageous: *the gutsy kid who lost a leg to cancer* **2** robust or vigorous: *a gutsy rendering of 'Bobby Shaftoe'*

gutta-percha *n* a whitish rubber substance, obtained from a tropical Asian tree and used in electrical insulation and dentistry
WORD ORIGIN Malay *getah* gum + *percha* gumtree

gutted *adj Brit, Austral & NZ informal* disappointed and upset: *the supporters will be absolutely gutted if the manager leaves the club*

gutter ❶ *n* **1** a channel on the roof of a building or alongside a kerb, used to collect and carry away rainwater **2** *tenpin bowling* one of the channels on either side of an alley **3 the gutter** a poverty-stricken, degraded, or criminal environment: *he dragged himself up from the gutter* ▹*vb* **4** (of a candle) to flicker and be about to go out **guttering** *n*
WORD ORIGIN Latin *gutta* a drop

gutter press *n informal* the section of the popular press that concentrates on the sensational aspects of the news

guttersnipe *n Brit* a child who spends most of his or her time in the streets, usually in a slum area

guttural (gut-ter-al) *adj* **1** *phonetics* pronounced at the back of the throat **2** harsh-sounding
WORD ORIGIN Latin *guttur* gullet

guy[1] ❶ *n* **1** *informal* a man or boy **2** *informal* a person of either sex: *it's been very nice talking to you guys again* **3** *Brit* a crude model of Guy Fawkes, that is burnt on top of a bonfire on Guy Fawkes Day (November 5)
WORD ORIGIN short for Guy Fawkes, who plotted to blow up the Houses of Parliament

guy[2] *n* a rope or chain for steadying or securing something such as a tent. Also: **guyrope**
WORD ORIGIN probably Low German

Guy *n* **Buddy,** real name *George Guy.* born 1936, US blues singer and guitarist

Guzmán Blanco *n* **Antonio** 1829–99, Venezuelan statesman; president (1873–77; 1879–84; 1886–87). He was virtual dictator of Venezuela from 1870 until his overthrow (1889)

guzzle *vb* **-zling, -zled** to eat or drink quickly or greedily: *the guests guzzled their way through squid with mushrooms*
WORD ORIGIN origin unknown

gybe *or* **jibe** (jibe) *naut vb* **gybing, gybed** *or* **jibing, jibed 1** (of a fore-and-aft sail) to swing suddenly from one side of a ship to the other **2** to change the course of (a ship) by letting the sail gybe ▹*n* **3** an instance of gybing
WORD ORIGIN obsolete Dutch *gijben*

gym *n* ▸short for **gymnasium** or **gymnastics**

gymkhana (jim-**kah**-na) *n Brit, Austral & NZ* an event in which horses and riders take part in various races and contests
WORD ORIGIN Hindi *gend-khānā* ball house

gymnasium *n* a large room containing equipment such as bars, weights, and ropes, for physical exercise
WORD ORIGIN Greek *gumnazein* to exercise naked

g

THESAURUS

pour, jet, burst, stream, cascade, issue, spurt, spout ▹*n* **3 = stream,** flow, rush, flood, jet, burst, issue, outburst, cascade, torrent, spurt, spout, outflow

gut *n* **2** *(slang)* **= paunch** *(informal),* belly, spare tyre *(Brit slang),* potbelly, puku *(NZ)* ▹*vb* **5 = disembowel,** draw, dress, clean, eviscerate **6 = ravage,** strip, empty, sack, rifle, plunder, clean out, ransack, pillage, despoil

gutter *n* **1 = drain,** channel, tube, pipe, ditch, trench, trough, conduit, duct, sluice

guy[1] *n* **1, 2** *(informal)* **= man,** person, fellow, lad, cat *(obsolete slang),* bloke *(Brit informal),* chap

DICTIONARY

gymnast *n* a person who is skilled or trained in gymnastics

gymnastics *n* **1** practice or training in exercises that develop physical strength and agility ▷*pl n* **2** such exercises **gymnastic** *adj*

gym shoes *pl n* ▸same as **plimsolls**

gymslip *n* a tunic formerly worn by schoolgirls as part of school uniform

gynaecology *or US* **gynecology** (guy-nee-kol-la-jee) *n* the branch of medicine concerned with diseases and conditions specific to women **gynaecological** *or US* **gynecological** *adj* **gynaecologist** *or US* **gynecologist** *n*
WORD ORIGIN Greek *gunē* woman + -LOGY

gyp *or* **gip** *n* **give someone gyp** *Brit, Austral & NZ slang* to cause someone severe pain: *her back's still giving her gyp*
WORD ORIGIN probably a contraction of *gee up!*

gypsophila *n* a garden plant with small white flowers

gypsum *n* a mineral used in making plaster of Paris
WORD ORIGIN Greek *gupsos*

Gypsy ❶ *or* **Gipsy** *n, pl* **-sies** a member of a travelling people scattered throughout Europe and North America
WORD ORIGIN from *Egyptian*, since they were thought to have come originally from Egypt

gyrate (jire-rate) *vb* **-rating, -rated** to turn round and round in a circle **gyration** *n*
WORD ORIGIN Greek *guros* circle

gyrfalcon (jur-fawl-kon) *n* a very large rare falcon of northern regions
WORD ORIGIN Old French *gerfaucon*

gyro *n, pl* **-ros** ▸short for **gyroscope**

gyrocompass *n* a nonmagnetic compass that uses a motor-driven gyroscope to indicate true north
WORD ORIGIN Greek *guros* circle + COMPASS

gyroscope (jire-oh-skope) *n* a device containing a disc rotating on an axis that can turn freely in any direction, so that the disc maintains the same position regardless of the movement of the surrounding structure **gyroscopic** *adj*
WORD ORIGIN Greek *guros* circle + *skopein* to watch

g

THESAURUS

Gypsy *or* **Gipsy** *n* = **traveller**, roamer, wanderer, Bohemian, rover, rambler, nomad, vagrant, Romany, vagabond

DICTIONARY

H 1 *chem* hydrogen 2 *physics* henry
h. *or* **H.** 1 height 2 hour
ha[1] *or* **hah** *interj* an exclamation expressing triumph, surprise, or scorn
ha[2] hectare
Ha *chem* hahnium
Haakon IV *n* surnamed *Haakonsson.* 1204–63, king of Norway (1217–63). He strengthened the monarchy and extended Norwegian territory to include Iceland and Greenland
Haakon VII *n* 1872–1957, king of Norway (1905–57). During the Nazi occupation of Norway (1940–45) he led Norwegian resistance from England
Habana[1] *n* ▸the Spanish name for **Havana**
Habana[2] *n* **Bryan** born 1983; South African Rugby Union football player: in national side from 2004
habeas corpus (hay-bee-ass **kor**-puss) *n law* a writ ordering a person to be brought before a judge, so as to decide whether his or her detention is lawful
WORD ORIGIN Latin: you may have the body
haberdasher *n Brit, Austral & NZ* a dealer in small articles used for sewing **haberdashery** *n*
WORD ORIGIN Anglo-French *hapertas* small items of merchandise
Habermas *n* **Jürgen** born 1929, German social theorist: his chief works are *Theory and Practice* (1963) and *Knowledge and Human Interests* (1968)
Haber process (**hah**-ber) *n chem* a method of making ammonia by reacting nitrogen with hydrogen at high pressure in the presence of a catalyst
WORD ORIGIN after Fritz *Haber*, German chemist
habiliments *pl n old-fashioned* clothes
WORD ORIGIN Old French *habillement*
habit ❶ *n* 1 a tendency to act in a particular way 2 established custom or use: *the English habit of taking tea in the afternoon* 3 an addiction to a drug 4 mental disposition or attitude: *deference was a deeply ingrained habit of mind* 5 the costume of a nun or monk 6 a woman's riding costume
WORD ORIGIN Latin *habitus* custom
habitable *adj* fit to be lived in **habitability** *n*
habitant *n* an early French settler in Canada or Louisiana or a descendant of one, esp. a farmer
habitat *n* the natural home of an animal or plant
WORD ORIGIN Latin: it inhabits
habitation *n* 1 occupation of a dwelling place: *unfit for human habitation* 2 *formal* a dwelling place
habit-forming *adj* tending to become a habit or addiction
habitual *adj* 1 done regularly and repeatedly: *habitual behaviour patterns* 2 by habit: *a habitual criminal* **habitually** *adv*
habituate *vb* **-ating, -ated** to accustom; get used to: *habituated to failure* **habituation** *n*
habitué (hab-**it**-yew-ay) *n* a frequent visitor to a place
WORD ORIGIN French
hachure (**hash**-yoor) *n* shading of short lines drawn on a map to indicate the degree of steepness of a hill
WORD ORIGIN French
hacienda (hass-ee-**end**-a) *n* (in Spanish-speaking countries) a ranch or large estate with a house on it
WORD ORIGIN Spanish
hack[1] ❶ *vb* 1 to chop roughly or violently 2 to cut and clear (a way) through undergrowth 3 (in sport) to foul (an opposing player) by kicking his or her shins 4 *Brit & NZ informal* to tolerate 5 to manipulate a computer program skilfully, esp. to gain unauthorized access to another computer system ▹*n* 6 a cut or gash 7 a tool, such as a pick 8 a chopping blow 9 a kick on the shins, such as in rugby
WORD ORIGIN Old English *haccian*
hack[2] ❶ *n* 1 a writer or journalist who produces work fast and on a regular basis 2 a horse kept for riding, often one for hire 3 *Brit* a country ride on horseback ▹*vb* 4 *Brit* to ride (a horse) cross-country for pleasure ▹*adj* 5 unoriginal or of a low standard: *clumsily contrived hack verse*
WORD ORIGIN short for *hackney*
hacker *n slang* a computer enthusiast, esp. one who through a personal computer breaks into the computer system of a company or government **hacking** *or* **hackery** *n*
hacking *adj* (of a cough) dry, painful, and harsh-sounding
hacking jacket *n* a jacket with vents at the side and sloping pockets, originally designed for wearing on horseback
hackles *pl n* 1 the hairs or feathers on the back of the neck of certain animals or birds, which rise when they are angry 2 **raise someone's hackles** make someone feel angry or hostile
WORD ORIGIN Middle English *hakell*
Hackman *n* **Gene** born 1930, US film actor; his films include *The French Connection* (1971), *Mississippi Burning* (1988), *Absolute Power* (1997), and *The Royal Tenenbaums* (2001)
hackney *n* 1 *Brit* a taxi 2 ▸same as **hack**[2] (sense 2)
WORD ORIGIN probably after *Hackney*, London, where horses were formerly raised
hackneyed (**hak**-need) *adj* (of a word or phrase) unoriginal and overused
hacksaw *n* a small saw for cutting metal
had *vb* ▸the past of **have**
haddock *n, pl* **-dock** a North Atlantic food fish
WORD ORIGIN origin unknown
hadedah *or* **hadeda** (**hah**-dee-dah) *n* a large grey-green S African ibis
WORD ORIGIN imitative
Haden *n* **Charles** (**Edward**) born 1937, US jazz bassist
Hades (**hay**-deez) *n Greek myth* 1 the underworld home of the souls of the dead 2 the god of the underworld
Hadith (**had**-dith, hah-**deeth**) *n islam* the body of tradition and legend about Mohammed and his followers, used as a basis of Islamic law
WORD ORIGIN Arabic
hadj *n* ▸same as **hajj**
hadji *n, pl* **hadjis** ▸same as **hajji**
Hadlee *n* Sir **Richard** (**John**) born 1951, New Zealand cricketer
hadn't had not
Haeckel *n* **Ernst Heinrich** 1834–1919, German biologist and philosopher. He formulated the recapitulation theory of evolution and was an exponent of the philosophy of materialistic monism › **Haeckelian** *adj*
haemal *or US* **hemal** (**heem**-al) *adj* of the blood
WORD ORIGIN Greek *haima* blood
haematic *or US* **hematic** (hee-**mat**-ik) *adj* relating to or containing blood
haematite *n* a type of iron ore which is reddish-brown when powdered
haematology *or US* **hematology** *n*

h

THESAURUS

habit *n* 1 = **mannerism**, custom, way, practice, manner, characteristic, tendency, quirk, propensity, foible, proclivity 3 = **addiction**, weakness, obsession, dependence, compulsion, fixation
hack[1] *vb* 1, 2 = **cut**, chop, slash, mutilate, mangle, mangulate *(Austral slang)*, gash, hew, lacerate
hack[2] *n* 1 = **reporter**, writer, correspondent, journalist, scribbler, contributor, literary hack, penny-a-liner, Grub Street writer

DICTIONARY

the branch of medical science concerned with the blood **haematologist** *or US* **hematologist** *n*
WORD ORIGIN Greek *haima* blood + -LOGY

haemoglobin *or US* **hemoglobin** (hee-moh-**globe**-in) *n* a protein in red blood cells that carries oxygen from the lungs to the tissues
WORD ORIGIN Greek *haima* blood + Latin *globus* ball

haemophilia *or US* **hemophilia** (hee-moh-**fill**-lee-a) *n* a hereditary disorder, usually affecting males, in which the blood does not clot properly **haemophiliac** *n*
WORD ORIGIN Greek *haima* blood + *philos* loving

haemorrhage ⊕ *or US* **hemorrhage** (**hem**-or-ij) *n* **1** heavy bleeding from ruptured blood vessels ▷ *vb* **-rhaging, -rhaged 2** to bleed heavily
WORD ORIGIN Greek *haima* blood + *rhēgnunai* to burst

haemorrhoids *or US* **hemorrhoids** (**hem**-or-oydz) *pl n pathol* swollen veins in the wall of the anus
WORD ORIGIN Greek *haimorrhoos* discharging blood

haere mai (hire-a-my) *interj NZ* an expression of greeting or welcome
WORD ORIGIN Māori

Hafiz *n* **Shams al-Din Muhammad** ?1326–90, Persian lyric poet, best known for his many short poems about love and wine, often treated as religious symbols

hafnium *n chem* a metallic element found in zirconium ores. Symbol: Hf
WORD ORIGIN after *Hafnia*, Latin name of Copenhagen

haft *n* the handle of an axe, knife, or dagger
WORD ORIGIN Old English *hæft*

hag *n* **1** an unpleasant or ugly old woman **2** a witch **haggish** *adj*
WORD ORIGIN Old English *hægtesse* witch

Hagen¹ *n* (in the *Nibelungenlied*) Siegfried's killer, who in turn is killed by Siegfried's wife, Kriemhild

Hagen² *n* an industrial city in NW Germany, in North Rhine-Westphalia. Pop: 200 039 (2003 est)

Hagen³ *n* **Walter** 1892–1969, US golfer

haggard *adj* looking tired and ill
WORD ORIGIN Old French *hagard* wild

Haggard *n* Sir (**Henry**) **Rider** 1856–1925, British author of romantic adventure stories, including *King Solomon's Mines* (1885)

haggis *n* a Scottish dish made from sheep's or calf's offal, oatmeal, suet, and seasonings boiled in a skin made from the animal's stomach
WORD ORIGIN origin unknown

haggle *vb* **-gling, -gled** to bargain or wrangle (over a price)
WORD ORIGIN Scandinavian

hagiography *n, pl* **-phies** the writing of lives of the saints **hagiographer** *n*
WORD ORIGIN Greek *hagios* holy + *graphein* to write

hagiology *n, pl* **-gies** literature about the lives and legends of saints
WORD ORIGIN Greek *hagios* holy + -LOGY

hag-ridden *adj* distressed or worried

Hague¹ *n* **The Hague** the seat of government of the Netherlands and capital of South Holland province, situated about 3 km (2 miles) from the North Sea. Pop: 464 000 (2003 est). Dutch names: **'s Gravenhage, Den Haag**

Hague² *n* **William Jefferson** born 1961, British politician; leader of the Conservative party (1997–2001)

hah *interj* ▸ same as **ha¹**

ha-ha¹ *or* **haw-haw** *interj* a written representation of the sound of laughter

ha-ha² *n* a wall set in a ditch so as not to interrupt a view of the landscape
WORD ORIGIN French

Hahnemann *n* (**Christian Friedrich**) **Samuel** 1755–1843, German physician; founder of homeopathy

hahnium *n chem* a transuranic element artificially produced from californium. Symbol: Ha

Haidar Ali *n* ▸ a variant spelling of **Hyder Ali**

haiku (hie-koo) *n, pl* **-ku** a Japanese verse form in 17 syllables
WORD ORIGIN Japanese

hail¹ ⊕ *n* **1** small pellets of ice falling from thunderclouds **2** words, ideas, missiles, etc. directed with force and in great quantity: *a hail of abuse* ▷ *vb* **3** to fall as hail: *it's hailing* **4** to fall like hail: *blows hailed down on him*
WORD ORIGIN Old English *hægl*

hail² ⊕ *vb* **1** to call out to; greet: *a voice from behind hailed him* **2** to praise, acclaim, or acknowledge: *his crew had been hailed as heroes* **3** to stop (a taxi) by shouting or gesturing **4 hail from** to come originally from: *she hails from Nova Scotia* ▷ *n* **5 within hailing distance** within hearing range ▷ *interj* **6** *poetic* an exclamation of greeting
WORD ORIGIN Old Norse *heill* healthy

hail-fellow-well-met *adj* genial and familiar in an offensive way

Hail Mary *n RC church* a prayer to the Virgin Mary

Hailsham of St Marylebone *n* Baron, title of **Quintin** (**McGarel**) **Hogg** 1907–2001, British Conservative politician; Lord Chancellor (1970–74; 1979–87). He renounced his viscountcy in 1963 when he made an unsuccessful bid for the Conservative Party leadership; he became a life peer in 1970

hailstone *n* a pellet of hail

hailstorm *n* a storm during which hail falls

Hailwood *n* **Mike,** full name *Stanley Michael Bailey Hailwood*. 1940–81, English racing motorcyclist: world champion (250 cc.) 1961 and 1966–67; (350 cc.) 1966–67; and (500 cc.) 1962–65

hair ⊕ *n* **1** any of the threadlike outgrowths on the skin of mammals **2** a mass of such outgrowths, such as on a person's head or an animal's body **3** *bot* a threadlike growth from the outer layer of a plant **4** a very small distance or margin: *he missed death by a hair* **5 get in someone's hair** *informal* to annoy someone **6 hair of the dog** an alcoholic drink taken as a cure for a hangover **7 let one's hair down** to enjoy oneself without restraint **8 not turn a hair** to show no reaction **9 split hairs** to make petty and unnecessary distinctions **hairless** *adj*
WORD ORIGIN Old English *hær*

hairclip *n NZ & S African* a small bent metal hairpin

hairdo *n, pl* **-dos** *informal* the style of a person's hair

hairdresser ⊕ *n* **1** a person who cuts and styles hair ▸ Related adjective: **tonsorial 2** a hairdresser's premises **hairdressing** *n*

hairgrip *n chiefly Brit* a small bent clasp used to fasten the hair

hairline *n* **1** the edge of hair at the top of the forehead ▷ *adj* **2** very fine or narrow: *a hairline crack*

hairpiece *n* a section of false hair added to a person's real hair

hairpin *n* a thin U-shaped pin used

THESAURUS

haemorrhage *or US* **hemorrhage** *n* **1 = drain**, outpouring, rapid loss ▷ *vb* **2 = drain**, bleed, flow rapidly

hail¹ *n* **1 = hailstones**, sleet, hailstorm, frozen rain **2 = shower**, rain, storm, battery, volley, barrage, bombardment, pelting, downpour, salvo, broadside ▷ *vb* **3 = rain**, shower, pelt **4 = batter**, rain, barrage, bombard, pelt, rain down on, beat down upon

hail² *vb* **1 = salute**, call, greet, address, welcome, speak to, shout to, say hello to, accost, sing out, halloo
OPPOSITE: snub
2 = acclaim, honour, acknowledge, cheer, applaud, glorify, exalt
OPPOSITE: condemn
3 = flag down, summon, signal to, wave down
4 hail from somewhere = come from, be born in, originate in, be a native of, have your roots in

hair *n* **2 = locks**, mane, tresses, shock, mop, head of hair

hairdresser *n* **1 = stylist**, barber, coiffeur *or* coiffeuse, friseur

DICTIONARY

to fasten the hair

hairpin bend *n* a bend in the road that curves very sharply

hair-raising *adj* very frightening or exciting

hair's-breadth *n* an extremely small margin or distance

hair shirt *n* a shirt made of horsehair cloth worn against the skin as a penance

hair slide *n* a decorative clasp used to fasten the hair

hairsplitting *n* **1** the act of making petty distinctions ▹ *adj* **2** characterized by petty distinctions

hairspring *n* a fine spring in some clocks and watches which regulates the timekeeping

hairstyle *n* the cut and arrangement of a person's hair **hairstylist** *n*

hair trigger *n* a trigger that responds to the slightest pressure

hairy ❶ *adj* **hairier, hairiest 1** covered with hair **2** *slang* dangerous, exciting, and difficult **hairiness** *n*

Haitink *n* **Bernard** born 1929, Dutch orchestral conductor; received an honorary knighthood in 1977

Haji-Ioannou *n* **Stelios** born 1967, British businessman, born in Greece; founder (1995) and chairman (until 2002) of the low-cost airline company Easyjet

hajj *or* **hadj** *n* the pilgrimage a Muslim makes to Mecca
WORD ORIGIN Arabic

hajji *or* **hadji** *n, pl* **hajjis** *or* **hadjis** a Muslim who has made a pilgrimage to Mecca

haka *n NZ* **1** a Māori war chant accompanied by actions **2** a similar chant by a sports team

hake *n, pl* **hake** *or* **hakes 1** an edible fish of the cod family **2** *Austral* ▸ same as **barracuda**
WORD ORIGIN origin unknown

hakea (hah-kee-a) *n* an Australian tree or shrub with hard woody fruit

Hakluyt *n* **Richard** ?1552–1616, English geographer, who compiled *The Principal Navigations, Voyages, and Discoveries of the English Nation* (1589)

hakuna matata *interj African* no problem
WORD ORIGIN from Swahili, there is no problem

halal *or* **hallal** *n* meat from animals that have been slaughtered according to Muslim law
WORD ORIGIN Arabic: lawful

halberd *n history* a tall spear that includes an axe blade and a pick
WORD ORIGIN Middle High German *helm* handle + *barde* axe

halcyon (hal-see-on) *adj* **1** peaceful, gentle, and calm **2 halcyon days** a time, usually in the past, of greatest happiness or success
WORD ORIGIN Greek *alkuōn* kingfisher

Haldane *n* **1 J(ohn) B(urdon) S(anderson)** 1892–1964, Scottish biochemist, geneticist, and writer on science **2** his father, **John Scott** 1860–1936, Scottish physiologist, noted particularly for his research into industrial diseases **3** his brother, **Richard Burdon,** 1st Viscount Haldane of Cloan. 1856–1928, British statesman and jurist. As secretary of state for war (1905–12) he reorganized the army and set up the territorial reserve

hale ❶ *adj* healthy and robust: *hale and hearty*
WORD ORIGIN Old English *hæl* whole

Hale *n* **1 George Ellery** 1868–1938, US astronomer: undertook research into sunspots and invented the spectroheliograph **2** Sir **Matthew** 1609–76, English judge and scholar; Lord Chief Justice (1671–76)

Halévy *n* **1 (Jacques François) Fromental**, original name *Elias Levy*. 1799–1862, French composer, noted for his operas, which include *La Juive* (1835) **2** his nephew, **Ludovic** 1834–1908, French dramatist and novelist, who collaborated with Meilhac on opera libretti

Haley *n* **Bill,** full name *William John Clifton Haley* 1925–81, US rock and roll singer, best known for his recording of "Rock Around the Clock" (1955)

half ❶ *n, pl* **halves 1** either of two equal or corresponding parts that together make up a whole **2** the fraction equal to one divided by two **3** half a pint, esp. of beer **4** *sport* one of two equal periods of play in a game **5** a half-price ticket **6 by half** to an excessive degree: *too clever by half* **7 by halves** without being thorough: *in Italy they rarely do things by halves* **8 go halves** to share expenses ▹ *adj* **9** denoting one of two equal parts: *a half chicken* ▹ *adv* **10** half in degree or quantity: *half as much* **11** partially; to an extent: *half hidden in the trees* **12 not half** *informal* **a** *Brit* very; indeed: *it isn't half hard to look at these charts* **b** yes, indeed
WORD ORIGIN Old English *healf*

half-and-half *adj* half one thing and half another thing

halfback *n rugby* a player positioned immediately behind the forwards

half-baked *adj informal* poorly planned: *half-baked policies*

half board *n Brit* the daily provision by a hotel of bed, breakfast, and evening meal

half-bottle *n* a bottle of spirits or wine that contains half the quantity of a standard bottle

half-breed *n offensive* a person whose parents are of different races

half-brother *n* the son of either one's mother or father by another partner

half-caste *n offensive* a person whose parents are of different races

half-cock *n* **go off at half-cock** *or* **half-cocked** to fail because of lack of preparation

half-crown *or* **half-a-crown** *n* a former British coin worth two shillings and sixpence (12 ½p)

half-cut *adj Brit slang* rather drunk

half-day *n* a day when one works only in the morning or only in the afternoon

half-dozen *n* six

half-hearted *adj* without enthusiasm or determination **half-heartedly** *adv*

half-hitch *n* a knot made by passing the end of a piece of rope around itself and through the loop so made

half-hour *n* **1** a period of 30 minutes **2** the point of time 30 minutes after the beginning of an hour **half-hourly** *adv, adj*

half-life *n* the time taken for radioactive material to lose half its radioactivity

half-light *n* a dim light, such as at dawn or dusk

half-mast *n* the halfway position of a flag on a mast as a sign of mourning

half measures *pl n* inadequate actions or solutions: *the education system cannot be reformed by half measures*

half-moon *n* **1** the moon when half its face is illuminated **2** the time at which a half-moon occurs **3** something shaped like a half-moon

half-nelson *n* a wrestling hold in which a wrestler places an arm under his opponent's arm from behind and exerts pressure with his palm on the back of his opponent's neck

halfpenny *or* **ha'penny** (hayp-nee) *n, pl* **-pennies** a former British coin worth half a penny

half-pie *adj NZ informal* badly planned; not properly thought out: *a half-pie scheme*
WORD ORIGIN Māori *pai* good

h

THESAURUS

hairy *adj* **1 = shaggy**, woolly, furry, stubbly, bushy, bearded, unshaven, hirsute, fleecy, bewhiskered, pileous *(biology)*, pilose *(biology)* **2** *(slang)* **= dangerous**, scary, risky, unpredictable, hazardous, perilous

hale *adj* **= healthy**, well, strong, sound, fit, flourishing, blooming, robust, vigorous, hearty, in the pink, in fine fettle, right as rain *(Brit informal)*, able-bodied

half *n* **1, 2 = fifty per cent**, equal part ▹ *adj* **9 = partial**, limited, fractional, divided, moderate, halved, incomplete ▹ *adv* **11 = partially**, partly, incompletely, slightly, all but, barely, in part, inadequately, after a fashion, pretty nearly

DICTIONARY

half-pipe *n* a structure with a U-shaped cross section, used in skateboarding, snowboarding, Rollerblading, etc.
half-price *adj, adv* for half the normal price: *special half-price tickets; jeans bought half-price in a sale*
half-sister *n* the daughter of either one's mother or father by another partner
half term *n Brit education* a short holiday midway through a term
half-timbered *adj* (of a building) having an exposed timber framework filled with brick or plaster
half-time *n sport* an interval between the two halves of a game
half-title *n* the first right-hand page of a book, with only the title on it
halftone *n* a photographic illustration in which the image is composed of a large number of black and white dots
half-track *n* a vehicle with moving tracks on the rear wheels
half-truth *n* a partially true statement **half-true** *adj*
half volley *n sport* **1** a stroke or shot in which the ball is hit immediately after it bounces ▷ *vb* **half-volley 2** to hit or kick (a ball) immediately after it bounces
halfway ❶ *adv* **1** at or to half the distance **2** at or towards the middle of a period of time or of an event or process **3** rather: *halfway decent* **4 meet someone halfway** to compromise with someone ▷ *adj* **5** at the same distance from two points: *the halfway line*
halfway house *n* **1** a place to rest midway on a journey **2** the halfway stage in any process: *a halfway house between the theatre and cinema is possible*
halfwit *n* a foolish or feeble-minded person **halfwitted** *adj*
halibut *n* a large edible flatfish
WORD ORIGIN Middle English *hali* holy (because it was eaten on holy days) + *butte* flatfish
Halifax[1] *n* **1** a port in SE Canada, capital of Nova Scotia, on the Atlantic: founded in 1749 as a British stronghold. Pop: 276 221 (2001) **2** a town in N England, in Calderdale unitary authority, West Yorkshire: textiles. Pop: 83 570 (2001)
Halifax[2] *n* **1 Charles Montagu,** Earl of Halifax. 1661–1715, British statesman; founder of the National Debt (1692) and the Bank of England (1694) **2 Edward Frederick Lindley Wood,** Earl of Halifax. 1881–1959, British Conservative statesman. He was viceroy of India (1926–31), foreign secretary (1938–40), and ambassador to the US (1941–46) **3 George Savile,** 1st Marquess of Halifax, known as *the Trimmer.* 1633–95, British politician, noted for his wavering opinions. He opposed the exclusion of the Catholic James II from the throne but later supported the Glorious Revolution
halitosis *n* bad-smelling breath
WORD ORIGIN Latin *halitus* breath
hall ❶ *n* **1** an entry area to other rooms in a house **2** a building or room for public meetings, dances, etc. **3** a residential building in a college or university **4** *Brit* a great house of an estate; manor **5** a large dining room in a college or university **6** the large room of a castle or stately home
WORD ORIGIN Old English *heall*
Hall *n* **1 Charles Martin** 1863–1914, US chemist: discovered the electrolytic process for producing aluminium **2** Sir **John** 1824–1907, New Zealand statesman, born in England: prime minister of New Zealand (1879–82) **3** Sir **Peter** born 1930, English stage director: director of the Royal Shakespeare Company (1960–73) and of the National Theatre (1973–88) **4** (**Marguerite**) **Radclyffe** 1883–1943, British novelist and poet. Her frank treatment of a lesbian theme in the novel *The Well of Loneliness* (1928) led to an obscenity trial
Hallé *n* Sir **Charles**, original name *Karl Hallé* 1819–95, German conductor and pianist, in Britain from 1848. In 1857 he founded the Hallé Orchestra in Manchester
hallelujah, halleluiah (hal-ee-**loo**-ya) *or* **alleluia** *interj* an exclamation of praise to God
WORD ORIGIN Hebrew *hellēl* to praise + *yāh* the Lord
Haller *n* **Albrecht von** 1708–77, Swiss biologist: founder of experimental physiology
hallmark ❶ *n* **1** a typical feature: *secrecy became the hallmark of government* **2** *Brit* an official seal stamped on gold, silver, or platinum articles to guarantee purity and date of manufacture **3** a mark of authenticity or excellence ▷ *vb* **4** to stamp with a hallmark
WORD ORIGIN after Goldsmiths' *Hall* in London, where items were stamped
hallo *interj, n* ▸ same as **hello**
halloo *interj chiefly Brit* a shout used to call hounds at a hunt
WORD ORIGIN perhaps variant of *hallow* to encourage hounds by shouting
halloumi *or* **haloumi** *n* a salty white sheep's cheese from Greece or Turkey, usually eaten grilled
WORD ORIGIN from Arabic *haluma* be mild
hallowed *adj* **1** regarded as holy: *hallowed ground* **2** respected and revered because of age, importance, or reputation: *the hallowed pitch at Lord's*
WORD ORIGIN Old English *hālgian* to consecrate
Halloween *or* **Hallowe'en** *n* October 31, celebrated by children by dressing up as ghosts, witches, etc.
WORD ORIGIN *all hallow even* all saints' eve
hallucinate *vb* **-nating, -nated** to seem to see something that is not really there
WORD ORIGIN Latin *alucinari*
hallucination *n* the experience of seeming to see something that is not really there **hallucinatory** *adj*
hallucinogen *n* any drug that causes hallucinations **hallucinogenic** *adj*
hallway *n* an entrance area
halo (**hay**-loh) *n, pl* **-loes** *or* **-los 1** a ring of light around the head of a sacred figure **2** a circle of refracted light around the sun or moon ▷ *vb* **-loes** *or* **-los, -loing, -loed 3** to surround with a halo
WORD ORIGIN Greek *halōs* circular threshing floor
halogen (**hal**-oh-jen) *n chem* any of the nonmetallic chemical elements fluorine, chlorine, bromine, iodine, and astatine, which form salts when combined with metal
WORD ORIGIN Greek *hals* salt + *-genēs* born
Hals *n* **Frans** ?1580–1666, Dutch portrait and genre painter: his works include *The Laughing Cavalier* (1624)
halt ❶ *vb* **1** to come to a stop or bring (someone or something) to a stop ▷ *n* **2** a temporary standstill **3** a military

THESAURUS

halfway *adv* **1, 2 = midway**, to the midpoint, to *or* in the middle ▷ *adj* **5 = midway**, middle, mid, central, intermediate, equidistant
hall *n* **1 = passage**, lobby, corridor, hallway, foyer, entry, passageway, entrance hall, vestibule **2 = meeting place**, chamber, auditorium, concert hall, assembly room
hallmark *n* **1 = trademark**, indication, badge, emblem, sure sign, telltale sign **2, 3 = mark**, sign, device, stamp, seal, symbol, signet, authentication
halt *vb* **1a = stop**, draw up, pull up, break off, stand still, wait, rest, call it a day, belay *(nautical)*
OPPOSITE: continue
1b = come to an end, stop, cease
1c = hold back, end, check, block, arrest, stem, curb, terminate, obstruct, staunch, cut short, impede, bring to an end, stem the flow, nip in the bud **OPPOSITE:** aid
▷ *n* **2 = stop**, end, close, break, stand, arrest, pause, interruption, impasse, standstill, stoppage, termination
OPPOSITE: continuation

DICTIONARY

command to stop **4** *chiefly Brit* a minor railway station without a building: *Deeside Halt* **5 call a halt to** to put an end to
WORD ORIGIN German *halten* to stop

halter *n* **1** a strap around a horse's head with a rope to lead it with ▷*vb* **2** to put a halter on (a horse)
WORD ORIGIN Old English *hælfter*

halterneck *n* a woman's top or dress which fastens behind the neck, leaving the back and arms bare

halting ❶ *adj* hesitant or uncertain: *she spoke halting Italian*

halve ❶ *vb* **halving, halved 1** to divide (something) into two equal parts **2** to reduce (the size or amount of something) by half **3** *golf* to draw with one's opponent on (a hole or round)

halyard *n naut* a line for hoisting or lowering a ship's sail or flag
WORD ORIGIN Middle English *halier*

ham[1] *n* smoked or salted meat from a pig's thigh
WORD ORIGIN Old English *hamm*

ham[2] *n* **1** *informal* an amateur radio operator **2** *theatre informal* an actor who overacts and exaggerates the emotions and gestures of a part ▷*adj* **3** (of actors or their performances) exaggerated and overstated ▷*vb* **hamming, hammed 4 ham it up** *informal* to overact
WORD ORIGIN special use of HAM[1]

hamba *interj S African, usually offensive* go away
WORD ORIGIN Nguni (language group of southern Africa): to go

hamburger *n* a flat round of minced beef, often served in a bread roll
WORD ORIGIN *Hamburger steak*, steak in the fashion of *Hamburg*, Germany

ham-fisted *or* **ham-handed** *adj informal* very clumsy or awkward

Hamilcar Barca *n* died ?228 BC, Carthaginian general; father of Hannibal. He held command (247–41) during the first Punic War and established Carthaginian influence in Spain (237–?228)

hamlet *n* a small village
WORD ORIGIN Old French *hamelet*

Hamlisch *n* **Marvin** born 1944, US composer, best known for the musical *A Chorus Line* (1975)

Hamlyn *n* Baron **Paul** 1926–2001, British businessman and publisher

Hammarskjöld *n* **Dag** (**Hjalmar Agne Carl**) 1905–61, Swedish statesman; secretary-general of the United Nations (1953–61): Nobel peace prize 1961

hammer ❶ *n* **1** a hand tool consisting of a heavy metal head on the end of a handle, used for driving in nails, beating metal, etc. **2** the part of a gun that causes the bullet to shoot when the trigger is pulled **3** *athletics* **a** a heavy metal ball attached to a flexible wire: thrown in competitions **b** the sport of throwing the hammer **4** an auctioneer's mallet **5** the part of a piano that hits a string when a key is pressed **6 come** *or* **go under the hammer** to be on sale at auction **7 hammer and tongs** with great effort or energy ▷*vb* **8** to hit with or as if with a hammer **9** *Brit* to criticize severely **10** *informal* to defeat heavily **11** to feel or sound like hammering: *his heart was hammering* **12 hammer in** to force (facts or ideas) into someone through repetition **13 hammer away at** to work at (something) constantly: *the paper hammered away at the same theme all the way through the campaign* ▸See also **hammer out**
WORD ORIGIN Old English *hamor*

hammer and sickle *n* the emblem on the flag of the former Soviet Union, representing the industrial workers and the peasants

hammerhead *n* a shark with a wide flattened head

hammer out *vb* to produce (an agreement) with great effort

Hammerstein II *n* **Oscar** 1895–1960, US librettist and songwriter: collaborated with the composer Richard Rodgers in musicals such as *South Pacific* (1949) and *The Sound of Music* (1959)

hammertoe *n* a condition in which the toe is permanently bent at the joint

Hammett *n* **Dashiell** 1894–1961, US writer of detective novels. His books include *The Maltese Falcon* (1930) and *The Thin Man* (1932)

hammock *n* a hanging bed made of canvas or net
WORD ORIGIN Spanish *hamaca*

Hammond[1] *n* a city in NW Indiana, adjacent to Chicago. Pop: 80 547 (2003 est)

Hammond[2] *n* **1** Dame **Joan** 1912–96, Australian operatic singer, born in New Zealand **2 Walter Reginald,** known as *Wally*. 1903–65, English cricketer. An all-rounder, he played for England 85 times between 1928 and 1946

Hammurabi *or* **Hammurapi** *n* ?18th century BC, king of Babylonia; promulgator of one of the earliest known codes of law

Hampden *n* **John** 1594–1643, English statesman; one of the leaders of the Parliamentary opposition to Charles I

hamper[1] ❶ *vb* to make it difficult for (someone or something) to move or progress
WORD ORIGIN origin unknown

hamper[2] *n* **1** a large basket with a lid **2** *Brit* a selection of food and drink packed as a gift
WORD ORIGIN Middle English *hanaper* a small basket

Hampshire[1] *n* a county of S England, on the English Channel: crossed by the **Hampshire Downs** and the South Downs, with the New Forest in the southwest and many prehistoric and Roman remains: the geographical and ceremonial county includes Portsmouth and Southampton, which became independent unitary authorities in 1997. Administrative centre: Winchester. Pop (excluding unitary authorities): 1 251 000 (2003 est). Area (excluding unitary authorities): 3679 sq km (1420 sq miles). Abbreviation: **Hants**

Hampshire[2] *n* Sir **Stuart** 1914–2004, British philosopher: his publications include *Thought and Action* (1959), *Two Theories of Morality* (1977), and *Innocence and Experience* (1989)

Hampton[1] *n* **1** a city in SE Virginia, on the harbour of **Hampton Roads** on Chesapeake Bay. Pop: 146 878 (2003 est) **2** a district of the Greater London borough of Richmond-upon-Thames, on the River Thames: famous for **Hampton Court Palace** (built in 1515 by Cardinal Wolsey)

Hampton[2] *n* **1 Christopher James** born 1946, British playwright: his works include *When Did You Last See My Mother?* (1964), the screenplay for the film *Dangerous Liaisons* (1988), and the book for the musical *Sunset Boulevard* (1993) **2 Lionel** 1913–2002, US jazz-band leader and vibraphone player

hamster *n* a small rodent with a stocky body, short tail, and cheek pouches
WORD ORIGIN German

h

THESAURUS

halting *adj* **= faltering**, stumbling, awkward, hesitant, laboured, stammering, imperfect, stuttering

halve *vb* **1 = split in two**, cut in half, bisect, divide in two, share equally, divide equally **2 = cut in half**, reduce by fifty per cent, decrease by fifty per cent, lessen by fifty per cent

hammer *vb* **8 = hit**, drive, knock, beat, strike, tap, bang **10** *(informal)* **= defeat**, beat, thrash, stuff *(slang)*, master, worst, tank *(slang)*, lick *(informal)*, slate *(informal)*, trounce, clobber *(slang)*, run rings around *(informal)*, wipe the floor with *(informal)*, blow out of the water *(slang)*, drub

hamper[1] *vb* **= hinder**, handicap, hold up, prevent, restrict, frustrate, curb, slow down, restrain, hamstring, interfere with, cramp, thwart, obstruct, impede, hobble, fetter, encumber, trammel
OPPOSITE: help

DICTIONARY

hamstring *n* **1** one of the tendons at the back of the knee ▷*vb* **-stringing, -strung 2** to make it difficult for someone to take any action
WORD ORIGIN *ham* (in the sense: leg)

Hamsun *n* **Knut,** pen name of *Knut Pedersen*. 1859–1952, Norwegian novelist, whose works include *The Growth of the Soil* (1917): Nobel prize for literature 1920

hand ❶ *n* **1** the part of the body at the end of the arm, consisting of a thumb, four fingers, and a palm ▸ Related adjective: **manual 2** a person's style of writing: *scrolls written in her own hand* **3** the influence a person or thing has over a particular situation: *the hand of the military in shaping policy was obvious* **4** a part in some activity: *I remember with gratitude Fortune's hand in starting my collection* **5** assistance: *give me a hand with the rice* **6** a round of applause: *give a big hand to the most exciting duo in the game* **7** consent to marry someone: *he asked for her hand in marriage* **8** a manual worker **9** a member of a ship's crew **10** a pointer on a dial or gauge, esp. on a clock **11 a** the cards dealt in one round of a card game **b** one round of a card game **12** a position indicated by its location to the side of an object or the observer: *on the right hand* **13** a contrasting aspect or condition: *on the other hand* **14** source: *I had experienced at first hand many management styles* **15** a person who creates something: *a good hand at baking* **16** a unit of length equalling four inches, used for measuring the height of horses **17 by hand a** by manual rather than mechanical means **b** by messenger: *the letter was delivered by hand* **18 from hand to mouth** with no food or money in reserve: *living from hand to mouth* **19 hand in glove** in close association **20 hand over fist** steadily and quickly: *losing money hand over fist* **21 in hand a** under control **b** receiving attention: *the business in hand* **c** available in reserve: *Pakistan have a game in hand* **22 keep one's hand in** to continue to practise something **23 (near) at hand** very close **24 on hand** close by; available **25 out of hand a** beyond control **b** decisively, without possible reconsideration: *he dismissed the competition out of hand* **26 show one's hand** to reveal one's plans **27 to hand** accessible ▷*vb* **28** to pass or give by the hand or hands **29 hand it to someone** to give credit to someone ▸ See also **hand down, hand on, hands**, etc. **handless** *adj*
WORD ORIGIN Old English

handbag *n* a woman's small bag carried to contain personal articles

handball *n* a game in which two teams of seven players try to throw a ball into their opponent's goal

handbill *n* a small printed notice for distribution by hand

handbook ❶ *n* a reference manual giving practical information on a subject

handbrake *n* a brake in a motor vehicle operated by a hand lever

h & c hot and cold (water)

handcart *n* a simple cart pushed or pulled by hand, used for transporting goods

handcrafted *adj* made by handicraft

handcuff ❶ *n* **1 handcuffs** a linked pair of locking metal rings used for securing prisoners ▷*vb* **2** to put handcuffs on (a person)

hand down *vb* **1** to pass on (knowledge, possessions, or skills) to a younger generation **2** to pass (outgrown clothes) on from one member of a family to a younger one **3** *US & Canad law* to announce (a verdict)

handful ❶ *n, pl* **-fuls 1** the amount that can be held in the hand **2** a small number: *a handful of parents* **3** *informal* a person or animal that is difficult to control: *as a child she was a real handful*

hand-held *adj* **1** held in position by the hand ▷*n* **2** a device, such as a computer, that can be held in the hand

handicap ❶ *n* **1** a physical or mental disability **2** something that makes progress difficult **3 a** a contest in which competitors are given advantages or disadvantages in an attempt to equalize their chances **b** the advantage or disadvantage given **4** *golf* the number of strokes by which a player's averaged score exceeds par for the course ▷*vb* **-capping, -capped 5** to make it difficult for (someone) to do something
WORD ORIGIN probably *hand in cap*, a lottery game in which players drew forfeits from a cap

handicapped *adj* physically or mentally disabled

handicraft *n* **1** a skill performed with the hands, such as weaving **2** the objects produced by people with such skills

handiwork *n* **1** the result of someone's work or activity **2** work produced by hand

handkerchief *n* a small square of fabric used to wipe the nose

handle ❶ *n* **1** the part of an object that is held or operated in order that it may be used **2** a small lever used to open and close a door or window **3** *slang* a person's name **4** a reason for doing something: *trying to get a handle on why companies borrow money* **5 fly off the handle** *informal* to become suddenly extremely angry ▷*vb* **-dling, -dled 6** to hold, move, operate, or touch with the hands **7** to have responsibility for: *she handles all their affairs personally* **8** to manage successfully: *I can handle this challenge* **9** to discuss (a subject) **10** to deal with in a specified way: *the affair was neatly handled* **11** to trade or deal in (specified merchandise): *we handle 1800 properties in Normandy* **12** to react or respond in a specified way to operation or control: *it's light and handles well* **handling** *n*
WORD ORIGIN Old English

handlebars *pl n* a metal tube with handles at each end, used for steering a bicycle or motorcycle

handler *n* **1** a person who trains and controls an animal **2** a person who handles something: *a baggage handler*

Handler *n* **Daniel** born 1970, US

THESAURUS

hand *n* **1 = palm**, fist, paw (*informal*), mitt (*slang*), hook, meathook (*slang*) **2 = writing**, script, handwriting, calligraphy, longhand, penmanship, chirography **6 = round of applause**, clap, ovation, big hand **8 = worker**, employee, labourer, workman, operative, craftsman, artisan, hired man, hireling ▷*vb* **28 = give**, pass, hand over, present to, deliver

handbook *n* **= guidebook**, guide, manual, instruction book, Baedeker, vade mecum

handcuff *pl n* **1 = shackles**, cuffs (*informal*), fetters, manacles, bracelets (*slang*) ▷*vb* **2 = shackle**, secure, restrain, fetter, manacle

handful *n* **2 = few**, sprinkling, small amount, small quantity, smattering, small number **OPPOSITE:** a lot

handicap *n* **1 = disability**, defect, impairment, physical abnormality **2 = disadvantage**, block, barrier, restriction, obstacle, limitation, hazard, drawback, shortcoming, stumbling block, impediment, albatross, hindrance, millstone, encumbrance **OPPOSITE:** advantage **3b = advantage**, penalty, head start ▷*vb* **5 = hinder**, limit, restrict, burden, hamstring, hamper, hold back, retard, impede, hobble, encumber, place at a disadvantage **OPPOSITE:** help

handle *n* **1 = grip**, knob, hilt, haft, stock, handgrip, helve ▷*vb* **6a = control**, manage, direct, operate, guide, use, steer, manipulate, manoeuvre, wield **6b = hold**, feel, touch, pick up, finger, grasp, poke, paw (*informal*), maul, fondle **7 = deal with**, manage, take care of, administer, conduct, supervise **8 = manage**, deal with, tackle, cope with

writer for older children, best known for the macabre humour of his *A Series of Unfortunate Events*, a sequence of books written in the persona of Lemony Snicket

Handley Page *n* **Sir Frederick** ▸See (Sir Frederick Handley) **Page** (sense 2)

handmade *adj* made by hand, not by machine

handmaiden *or* **handmaid** *n* **1** *old-fashioned* a female servant **2** a person or thing that serves a useful but lesser purpose: *these policies resulted in agriculture becoming the poor handmaiden of industry*

hand-me-down *n informal* an item of clothing that someone has finished with and passed on to someone else

hand on *vb* to pass (something) to the next person in a succession

hand-out *n, pl* **hand-outs 1** clothing, food, or money given to a needy person **2** a leaflet, free sample, etc. given out to publicize something **3** a piece of written information given out to the audience at a talk, lecture, etc. ▹*vb* **hand out 4** to distribute

hand over *vb* to give up possession of or transfer (something)

hand-pick *vb* to select (a person) with great care, such as for a special job **hand-picked** *adj*

handrail *n* a rail alongside a stairway, to provide support

hands *pl n* **1 change hands** to pass from the possession of one person to another **2 have one's hands full** to be completely occupied **3 in someone's hands** in someone's control or power: *that's in the hands of the courts* **4 off one's hands** no longer one's responsibility **5 on one's hands** for which one is responsible: *what a problem case I've got on my hands* **6 wash one's hands of** to have nothing more to do with **7 win hands down** to win easily

Hands *n* **Terence David,** known as *Terry.* born 1941, British theatre director: chief executive and artistic director (1986–91) of the Royal Shakespeare Company

handset *n* a telephone mouthpiece and earpiece in a single unit

hands-free *adj, n* (of) a device allowing the user to make and receive phonecalls without holding the handset

handshake *n* the act of grasping and shaking a person's hand, such as in greeting or when agreeing on a deal

handsome ❶ *adj* **1** (esp. of a man) good-looking **2** (of a building, garden, etc.) large, well-made, and with an attractive appearance: *a handsome building* **3** (of an amount of money) generous or large: *a handsome dividend* **handsomely** *adv*

WORD ORIGIN obsolete *handsom* easily handled

hands-on *adj* involving practical experience of equipment: *Navy personnel joined the 1986 expedition for hands-on operating experience*

handspring *n* a gymnastic exercise in which a person leaps forwards or backwards into a handstand and then onto his or her feet

handstand *n* the act of supporting the body on the hands in an upside-down position

hand-to-hand *adj, adv* **1** at close quarters, with fists or knives: *hand-to-hand combat; they fought hand-to-hand*

hand-to-mouth *adj, adv* with barely enough money or food to live on

handwork *n* work done by hand rather than by machine

handwriting *n* **1** writing by hand rather than by typing or printing **2** a person's characteristic writing style **handwritten** *adj*

handy ❶ *adj* **handier, handiest 1** conveniently within reach **2** easy to handle or use **3** good at manual work **handily** *adv*

Handy *n* **W**(illiam) **C**(**hristopher**) 1873–1958, US blues musician and songwriter, esp. noted for the song "St Louis Blues"

handyman *n, pl* **-men** a man skilled at odd jobs

Han Fei Zu *n* died 233 BC, Chinese diplomat and philosopher of law

hang ❶ *vb* **hanging, hung 1** to fasten or be fastened from above **2** to place (something) in position, for instance by a hinge, so as to allow free movement: *to hang a door* **3** to be suspended so as to allow movement from the place where it is attached: *her long hair hung over her face* **4** to decorate with something suspended, such as pictures **5** (of cloth or clothing) to fall or flow in a particular way: *the fine gauge knit hangs loosely with graceful femininity* **6** *pt & pp* **hanged** to suspend or be suspended by the neck until dead **7** to hover: *clouds hung over the mountains* **8** to fasten to a wall: *to hang wallpaper* **9** to exhibit or be exhibited in an art gallery **10** *pt & pp* **hanged** *slang* to damn: used in mild curses or interjections **11 hang fire** to put off doing something **12 hang over** to threaten or overshadow: *the threat of war hung over the Middle East* ▹*n* **13** the way in which something hangs **14 get the hang of something** *informal* to understand the technique of doing something ▸See also **hang about, hang back**, etc.

WORD ORIGIN Old English *hangian*

hang about *or* **around** *vb* **1** to stand about idly somewhere **2** (foll. by *with*) to spend a lot of time in the company (of someone)

hangar *n* a large building for storing aircraft

WORD ORIGIN French: shed

hang back ❶ *vb* to be reluctant to do something

hangdog *adj* dejected, ashamed, or guilty in appearance or manner

hanger *n* ▸same as **coat hanger**

hanger-on *n, pl* **hangers-on** an unwanted follower, esp. of a rich or famous person

hang-glider *n* an unpowered aircraft consisting of a large cloth wing stretched over a light framework from which the pilot hangs in a harness **hang-gliding** *n*

hangi (**hung**-ee) *n NZ* **1** an open-air cooking pit **2** the food cooked in it **3** the social gathering at the resultant meal

WORD ORIGIN Māori

hanging *n* **1** the act or practice of putting a person to death by suspending the body by the neck **2** a large piece of cloth hung on a wall as a decoration

hanging valley *n geog* a tributary valley that enters a main valley high up because the main valley has been deepened through erosion by a glacier

h

THESAURUS

handsome *adj* **1, 2 = good-looking**, attractive, gorgeous, fine, stunning, elegant, personable, nice-looking, dishy *(informal, chiefly Brit)*, comely, fanciable, well-proportioned, hot *(informal)*, fit *(Brit informal)*
OPPOSITE: ugly
3 = generous, large, princely, liberal, considerable, lavish, ample, abundant, plentiful, bountiful, sizable *or* sizeable **OPPOSITE:** mean

handy *adj* **1 = convenient**, close, near, available, nearby, accessible, on hand, at hand, within reach, just round the corner, at your fingertips
OPPOSITE: inconvenient
2 = useful, practical, helpful, neat, convenient, easy to use, manageable, user-friendly, serviceable
OPPOSITE: useless
3 = skilful, skilled, expert, clever, adept, ready, deft, nimble, proficient, adroit, dexterous
OPPOSITE: unskilled

hang *vb* **1 = dangle**, swing, suspend, be pendent **2 = lower**, suspend, dangle, let down, let droop
6 = execute, lynch, string up *(informal)*, gibbet, send to the gallows
14 get the hang of something = grasp, understand, learn, master, comprehend, catch on to, acquire the technique of, get the knack *or* technique

hang back *vb* **= be reluctant**, hesitate, hold back, recoil, demur, be backward

DICTIONARY

hangman *n, pl* **-men** an official who carries out a sentence of hanging

hangnail *n* a piece of skin partly torn away from the base or side of a fingernail

hang on *vb* **1** *informal* to wait: *hang on a minute, will you?* **2** to continue or persist with effort or difficulty **3** to grasp or hold **4** to depend on: *a lot hangs on its success* **5** to listen attentively to: *she hangs on every word our leader says*

hang out *vb* **1** to suspend, be suspended, or lean **2** *informal* to live or spend a lot of time in a place: *fishermen hang out in waterfront bars* **3** **let it all hang out** *informal chiefly US* to relax completely; act or speak freely ▷*n* **hang-out** **4** *informal* a place where someone spends a lot of time

h

hangover ⓘ *n* a feeling of sickness and headache after drinking too much alcohol

hang together *vb* **1** to be united **2** to be consistent: *the story simply did not hang together*

hang up ⓘ *vb* **1** to replace (a telephone receiver) at the end of a conversation **2** to put on a hook or hanger ▷*n* **hang-up** **3** *informal* an emotional or psychological problem

hank ⓘ *n* a loop or coil, esp. of yarn
WORD ORIGIN from Old Norse

hanker *vb* (foll. by *for* or *after*) to have a great desire for **hankering** *n*
WORD ORIGIN probably from Dutch dialect *hankeren*

Hanks *n* **Tom** born 1956, US film actor: his films include *Splash* (1984), *Philadelphia* (1993), *Forrest Gump* (1994), *Saving Private Ryan* (1998), and *The Terminal* (2004)

hanky *or* **hankie** *n, pl* **hankies** *informal* ▸short for **handkerchief**

hanky-panky *n informal* **1** casual sexual relations **2** mischievous behaviour
WORD ORIGIN variant of *hocus-pocus*

Hanna *n* **William** 1910–2001, US animator and film producer who with **Joseph Barbera** (born 1911) created the cartoon characters Tom and Jerry in the 1940s; the Hanna–Barbera company later produced numerous cartoon series for television

Hanoverian (han-no-**veer**-ee-an) *adj* of or relating to the British royal house ruling from 1714 to 1901
WORD ORIGIN after *Hanover*, Germany

Hanratty *n* **James** 1936–62, Englishman executed, despite conflicting evidence, for a murder on the A6 road. Subsequent public concern played a major part in the abolition of capital punishment in Britain. New DNA evidence led to an appeal by Hanratty's supporters being dismissed in 2002

Hansard *n* the official report of the proceedings of the British or Canadian parliament
WORD ORIGIN after L. *Hansard*, its original compiler

Hanseatic League (han-see-**at**-ik) *n history* a commercial organization of towns in N Germany formed in the 14th century to protect and control trade

hansom *n* formerly, a two-wheeled one-horse carriage with a fixed hood. Also called: **hansom cab**
WORD ORIGIN after its designer J. A. *Hansom*

Hants Hampshire

Hanukkah *n* ▸same as **Chanukah**

haphazard *adj* not organized or planned **haphazardly** *adv*
WORD ORIGIN Old Norse *happ* chance, good luck + HAZARD

hapless *adj* unlucky: *the hapless victim of a misplaced murder attempt*
WORD ORIGIN Old Norse *happ* chance, good luck

haploid *adj biol* denoting a cell or organism with unpaired chromosomes
WORD ORIGIN Greek *haplous* single

haplotype *n genetics* a set of alleles inherited by an individual from a single parent

happen ⓘ *vb* **1** to take place; occur **2** to chance (to be or do something): *I happen to know him* **3** to be the case, esp. by chance: *it happens that I know him* **4** **happen to** (of some unforeseen event, such as death) to be the experience or fate of: *if anything happens to me you will know*
WORD ORIGIN obsolete *hap*

happening ⓘ *n* an event that often occurs in a way that is unexpected or hard to explain: *some strange happenings in the village recently*

happy ⓘ *adj* **-pier, -piest** **1** feeling or expressing joy **2** causing joy or gladness: *the happiest day of my life* **3** fortunate or lucky: *it was a happy coincidence* **4** satisfied or content: *he seems happy to let things go on as they are* **5** willing: *I'll be happy to arrange a loan for you* **happily** *adv* **happiness** *n*
WORD ORIGIN Old Norse *happ* chance, good luck

happy-go-lucky *adj* carefree or easy-going

hara-kiri *n* (formerly, in Japan) ritual suicide by disembowelment when disgraced or under sentence of death
WORD ORIGIN Japanese *hara* belly + *kiri* cut

Harald I *n* called *Harald Fairhair* ?850–933, first king of Norway: his rule caused emigration to the British Isles

Harald III *n* surname *Hardraade* 1015–66, king of Norway (1047–66); invaded England (1066) and died at the battle of Stamford Bridge

harangue *vb* **-ranguing, -rangued** **1** to address (a person or group) in an angry or forcefully persuasive way ▷*n* **2** a forceful or angry speech
WORD ORIGIN Old Italian *aringa* public speech

harass ⓘ *vb* to trouble or annoy (someone) by repeated attacks, questions, or problems **harassed** *adj* **harassment** *n*
WORD ORIGIN French *harasser*

harbinger (**har**-binge-er) *n literary* a person or thing that announces or indicates the approach of something: *a harbinger of death*
WORD ORIGIN Old French *herbergere*

harbour ⓘ *or US* **harbor** *n* **1** a sheltered port **2** a place of refuge or safety ▷*vb* **3** to maintain secretly in

THESAURUS

hangover *n* = **aftereffects**, morning after *(informal)*, head *(informal)*, crapulence

hang-up *n* **3** *(informal)* = **preoccupation**, thing *(informal)*, problem, block, difficulty, obsession, mania, inhibition, phobia, fixation

hank *n* = **coil**, roll, length, bunch, piece, loop, clump, skein

happen *vb* **1** = **occur**, take place, come about, follow, result, appear, develop, arise, come off *(informal)*, ensue, crop up *(informal)*, transpire *(informal)*, materialize, present itself, come to pass, see the light of day, eventuate **2** = **chance**, turn out *(informal)*, have the fortune to be

happening *n* = **event**, incident, occasion, case, experience, chance, affair, scene, accident, proceeding, episode, adventure, phenomenon, occurrence, escapade

happy *adj* **1** = **pleased**, delighted, content, contented, thrilled, glad, blessed, blest, sunny, cheerful, jolly, merry, ecstatic, gratified, jubilant, joyous, joyful, elated, over the moon *(informal)*, overjoyed, blissful, rapt, blithe, on cloud nine *(informal)*, cock-a-hoop, walking on air *(informal)*, floating on air, stoked *(Austral & NZ informal)* **2** = **joyful**, blessed, blest, blissful, blithe **OPPOSITE:** sad **3** = **fortunate**, lucky, timely, appropriate, convenient, favourable, auspicious, propitious, apt, befitting, advantageous, well-timed, opportune, felicitous, seasonable **OPPOSITE:** unfortunate

harass *vb* = **annoy**, trouble, bother, worry, harry, disturb, devil *(informal)*, plague, bait, hound, torment, hassle *(informal)*, badger, persecute, exasperate, pester, vex, breathe down someone's neck, chivvy *(Brit)*, give someone grief *(Brit & S African)*, be on your back *(slang)*, beleaguer

harbour *or US* **harbor** *n* **1** = **port**,

the mind: *he might be harbouring a death wish* **4** to give shelter or protection to: *the government accused her of harbouring criminals*
WORD ORIGIN Old English *herebeorg*, from *here* army + *beorg* shelter
harbour master *n* an official in charge of a harbour
hard ❶ *adj* **1** firm, solid, or rigid **2** difficult to do or understand: *a hard sum* **3** showing or requiring a lot of effort or application: *hard work* **4** unkind or unfeeling: *she's very hard, no pity for anyone* **5** causing pain, sorrow, or hardship: *the hard life of a northern settler* **6** tough or violent: *a hard man* **7** forceful: *a hard knock* **8** cool or uncompromising: *we took a long hard look at our profit factor* **9** indisputable and proven to be true: *hard facts* **10** (of water) containing calcium salts which stop soap lathering freely **11** practical, shrewd, or calculating: *he is a hard man in business* **12** harsh: *hard light* **13** (of currency) high and stable in exchange value **14** (of alcoholic drink) being a spirit rather than a wine or beer **15** (of a drug) highly addictive **16** hard-core **17** *phonetics* denoting the consonants *c* and *g* when they are pronounced as in *cat* and *got* **18** politically extreme: *the hard left* **19 hard of hearing** slightly deaf **20 hard up** *informal* in need of money ▷ *adv* **21** with great energy or force: *they fought so hard and well in Spain* **22** with great intensity: *thinking hard about the conversation* **23 hard by** very close to: *Cleveland Place, hard by Bruntsfield Square* **24 hard put (to it)** scarcely having the capacity (to do something) ▷ *n* **25 have a hard on** *taboo slang* to have an erection of the penis **hardness** *n*
WORD ORIGIN Old English *heard*
hard-and-fast *adj* (of rules) fixed and not able to be changed
hardback *n* **1** a book with stiff covers ▷ *adj* **2** of or denoting a hardback
hardball *n US & Canad* **1** baseball as distinct from softball **2 play hardball** *informal* to act in a ruthless or uncompromising way
hard-bitten *adj informal* tough and determined
hardboard *n* stiff board made in thin sheets of compressed sawdust and wood pulp
hard-boiled *adj* **1** (of an egg) boiled until solid **2** *informal* tough, realistic, and unemotional
hard cash *n* money or payment in money, as opposed to payment by cheque, credit, etc.
hard copy *n* computer output printed on paper
hardcore *n* **1** a style of rock music with short fast songs and little melody **2** a type of dance music with a very fast beat
hard core *n* **1** the members of a group who most resist change **2** broken stones used to form a foundation for a road ▷ *adj* **hard-core 3** (of pornography) showing sexual acts in explicit detail **4** extremely committed or fanatical: *a hard-core Communist*
hard disk *n computers* an inflexible disk in a sealed container
hard drive *n computers* the mechanism that handles the reading, writing, and storage of data on the hard disk
Hardecanute *n* ▸ same as **Harthacanute**
harden ❶ *vb* **1** to make or become hard; freeze, stiffen, or set **2** to make or become tough or unfeeling: *life in the camp had hardened her considerably* **3** to make or become stronger or firmer: *they hardened defences* **4** to make or become more determined or resolute: *the government has hardened its attitude to the crisis* **5** *commerce* (of prices or a market) to cease to fluctuate
Hardenberg *n* **Friedrich von** the original name of Novalis ▸ See **Novalis**
Hardenburg *n* **Fürst Karl (August) von** 1750–1822, Prussian statesman: foreign minister (1804–06): prime minister (1807; 1810–22). His reforms enabled Prussia to break away from Napoleonic control in 1813
hardened ❶ *adj* toughened by experience: *a hardened criminal*
hardfill *n NZ & S African* a stone waste material used for landscaping
hard-headed *adj* tough, realistic, or shrewd, esp. in business
hardhearted *adj* unsympathetic and uncaring
hardihood *n* courage or daring
Hardinge *n* **Henry,** 1st Viscount Hardinge of Lahore. 1785–1856, British politician, soldier, and colonial administrator; governor general of India (1844–48)
hard labour *n* difficult and tiring physical work: used as a punishment for a crime in some countries
hard line *n* **1** an uncompromising policy: *a hard line on drugs* ▷ *adj* **hard-line 2** tough and uncompromising: *a hard-line attitude to the refugee problem* **hardliner** *n*
hardly ❶ *adv* **1** scarcely; barely: *he'd hardly sipped his whisky* **2** *ironic* not at all: *it was hardly in the Great Train Robbery league* **3** with difficulty: *their own families would hardly recognize them*
hard pad *n* (in dogs) an abnormal increase in the thickness of the foot pads: a sign of distemper
hard palate *n* the bony front part of the roof of the mouth
hard-pressed *adj* **1** under a great deal of strain and worry: *hard-pressed companies having to cut costs* **2** closely pursued
hard science *n* one of the natural or physical sciences, such as physics, chemistry, or biology
hard sell *n* an aggressive insistent technique of selling

THESAURUS

haven, dock, mooring, marina, pier, wharf, anchorage, jetty, pontoon, slipway ▷ *vb* **3 = hold**, bear, maintain, nurse, retain, foster, entertain, nurture, cling to, cherish, brood over **4 = shelter**, protect, hide, relieve, lodge, shield, conceal, secrete, provide refuge, give asylum to
hard *adj* **1 = tough**, strong, firm, solid, stiff, compact, rigid, resistant, dense, compressed, stony, impenetrable, inflexible, unyielding, rocklike **OPPOSITE:** soft **2 = difficult**, involved, complex, complicated, puzzling, tangled, baffling, intricate, perplexing, impenetrable, thorny, knotty, unfathomable, ticklish **OPPOSITE:** easy **3 = exhausting**, tough, exacting, formidable, fatiguing, wearying, rigorous, uphill, gruelling, strenuous, arduous, laborious, burdensome, Herculean, backbreaking, toilsome **OPPOSITE:** easy **4 = harsh**, severe, strict, cold, exacting, cruel, grim, stern, ruthless, stubborn, unjust, callous, unkind, unrelenting, implacable, unsympathetic, pitiless, unfeeling, obdurate, unsparing, affectless, hardhearted **OPPOSITE:** kind **5 = grim**, dark, painful, distressing, harsh, disastrous, unpleasant, intolerable, grievous, disagreeable, calamitous ▷ *adv* **21 = forcefully**, strongly, heavily, sharply, severely, fiercely, vigorously, intensely, violently, powerfully, forcibly, with all your might, with might and main **OPPOSITE:** softly **22 = intently**, closely, carefully, sharply, keenly
harden *vb* **1 = solidify**, set, freeze, cake, bake, clot, thicken, stiffen, crystallize, congeal, coagulate, anneal **2 = accustom**, season, toughen, train, brutalize, inure, habituate, case-harden
hardened *adj* **= seasoned**, experienced, accustomed, toughened, inured, habituated **OPPOSITE:** naive
hardly *adv* **1 = barely**, only just, scarcely, just, faintly, with difficulty, infrequently, with effort, at a push (*Brit informal*), almost not **OPPOSITE:** completely **3 = only just**, just, only, barely, not quite, scarcely

DICTIONARY

hardship ⊙ *n* **1** conditions of life that are difficult to endure **2** something that causes suffering

hard shoulder *n Brit & NZ* a surfaced verge running along the edge of a motorway and other roads for emergency stops

hardtack *n* a kind of hard saltless biscuit, formerly eaten by sailors

hardware *n* **1** metal tools or implements, esp. cutlery or cooking utensils **2** *computers* the physical equipment used in a computer system **3** heavy military equipment, such as tanks and missiles

hard-wired *adj* (of a circuit or instruction) permanently wired into a computer

hardwood *n* the wood of a deciduous tree such as oak, beech, or ash

hardy ⊙ *adj* **-dier, -diest 1** able to stand difficult conditions **2** (of plants) able to live out of doors throughout the winter **hardiness** *n*
WORD ORIGIN Old French *hardi* emboldened

Hardy *n* **1 Oliver** ▸ See **Laurel and Hardy 2 Thomas** 1840–1928, British novelist and poet. Most of his novels are set in his native Dorset (part of his fictional Wessex) and include *Far from the Madding Crowd* (1874), *The Return of the Native* (1878), *The Mayor of Casterbridge* (1886), *Tess of the d'Urbervilles* (1891), and *Jude the Obscure* (1895), after which his work consisted chiefly of verse **3** Sir **Thomas Masterman** 1769–1839, British naval officer, flag captain under Nelson (1799–1805): 1st Sea Lord (1830)

hare *n, pl* **hares** *or* **hare 1** a mammal like a large rabbit, with longer ears and legs ▹ *vb* **haring, hared 2** (foll. by *off* or *after*) *Austral & Brit informal* to run fast or wildly
WORD ORIGIN Old English *hara*

Hare[1] *n* **1** Sir **David** born 1947, British dramatist and theatre director: his plays include *Plenty* (1978), *Pravda* (with Howard Brenton, 1985), *The Secret Rapture* (1989), *Racing Demon* (1990), and *The Permanent Way* (2003) **2 William** 19th century, Irish murderer and bodysnatcher: associate of William Burke

Hare[2] *n* a member of a Dene Native Canadian people of northern Canada
WORD ORIGIN of Athapascan origin

harebell *n* a blue bell-shaped flower

harebrained *adj* foolish or impractical: *harebrained schemes*

harelip *n* a slight split in the mid line of the upper lip

harem *n* **1** a Muslim man's wives and concubines collectively **2** the part of an Oriental house reserved for wives and concubines
WORD ORIGIN Arabic *harīm* forbidden (place)

Hargreaves *n* **James** died 1778, English inventor of the spinning jenny

haricot bean *or* **haricot** (har-rik-oh) *n* a white edible bean, which can be dried
WORD ORIGIN French *haricot*

Harishchandra *n* also known as *Bharatendu*. 1850–85, Indian poet, dramatist, and essayist, who established Hindi as a literary language

harissa *n* a hot paste or sauce made from chilli peppers, tomatoes, spices, and olive oil, used in North African cuisine

hark *vb old-fashioned* to listen; pay attention: *hark, the cocks are crowing*
WORD ORIGIN Old English *heorcnian*

hark back *vb* to return (to an earlier subject in speech or thought): *he keeps harking back to his music-hall days*

harlequin *n* **1** *theatre* a stock comic character, usually wearing a diamond-patterned multicoloured costume and a black mask ▹ *adj* **2** in varied colours
WORD ORIGIN Old French *Herlequin* leader of a band of demon horsemen

harlequinade *n theatre* a play in which harlequin has a leading role

Harley *n* **Robert,** 1st Earl of Oxford. 1661–1724, British statesman; head of the government (1710–14), negotiated the treaty of Utrecht (1713)

harlot *n literary* a prostitute **harlotry** *n*
WORD ORIGIN Old French *herlot* rascal

Harlow[1] *n* a town in SE England, in W Essex: designated a new town in 1947. Pop: 78 389 (2001 est)

Harlow[2] *n* **Jean,** real name *Harlean Carpentier*. 1911–37, US film actress, whose films include *Hell's Angels* (1930), *Red Dust* (1932), and *Bombshell* (1933)

harm ⊙ *vb* **1** to injure physically, morally, or mentally ▹ *n* **2** physical, moral, or mental injury
WORD ORIGIN Old English *hearm*

harmful ⊙ *adj* causing or tending to cause harm, esp. to a person's health

harmless ⊙ *adj* **1** safe to use, touch, or be near **2** unlikely to annoy or worry people: *a harmless habit*

harmonic *adj* **1** of, producing, or characterized by harmony; harmonious ▹ *n* **2** *music* an overtone of a musical note produced when that note is played, but not usually heard as a separate note ▸ See also **harmonics** > **harmonically** *adv*
WORD ORIGIN Latin *harmonicus* relating to harmony

harmonica *n* a small wind instrument in which reeds enclosed in a narrow oblong box are made to vibrate by blowing and sucking

harmonics *n* the science of musical sounds

harmonious *adj* **1** (esp. of colours or sounds) consisting of parts which blend together well **2** showing agreement, peacefulness, and friendship: *a harmonious relationship* **3** tuneful or melodious

harmonium *n* a musical keyboard instrument in which air from pedal-operated bellows causes the reeds to vibrate

harmonize *or* **-nise** *vb* **-nizing, -nized** *or* **-nising, -nised 1** to sing or play in harmony, such as with another singer or player **2** to make or become harmonious

harmony ⊙ *n, pl* **-nies 1** a state of peaceful agreement and cooperation **2** *music* a pleasant combination of two or more notes sounded at the same time **3** the way parts combine well together or into a whole
WORD ORIGIN Greek *harmonia*

Harnack *n* **Adolf von** 1851–1930, German Protestant theologian,

THESAURUS

hardship *n* **1, 2 = suffering,** want, need, trouble, trial, difficulty, burden, misery, torment, oppression, persecution, grievance, misfortune, austerity, adversity, calamity, affliction, tribulation, privation, destitution **OPPOSITE:** ease

hardy *adj* **1 = strong,** tough, robust, sound, fit, healthy, vigorous, rugged, sturdy, hale, stout, stalwart, hearty, lusty, in fine fettle **OPPOSITE:** frail

harm *vb* **1a = injure,** hurt, wound, abuse, molest, ill-treat, maltreat, lay a finger on, ill-use **OPPOSITE:** heal
1b = damage, hurt, ruin, mar, spoil, impair, blemish ▹ *n* **2 = injury,** suffering, damage, ill, hurt, distress

harmful *adj* **= damaging,** dangerous, negative, evil, destructive, hazardous, unhealthy, detrimental, hurtful, pernicious, noxious, baleful, deleterious, injurious, unwholesome, disadvantageous, baneful, maleficent
OPPOSITE: harmless

harmless *adj* **1 = safe,** benign, wholesome, innocuous, not dangerous, nontoxic, innoxious
OPPOSITE: dangerous
2 = inoffensive, innocent, innocuous, gentle, tame, unobjectionable

harmony *n* **1 = accord,** order, understanding, peace, agreement, friendship, unity, sympathy, consensus, cooperation, goodwill, rapport, conformity, compatibility, assent, unanimity, concord, amity, amicability, like-mindedness
OPPOSITE: conflict
2 *(music)* **= tune,** melody, unison, tunefulness, euphony, melodiousness **OPPOSITE:** discord

DICTIONARY

author of the influential *History of Dogma* (1886–90)

harness ❶ *n* **1** an arrangement of straps for attaching a horse to a cart or plough **2** something resembling this, for attaching something to a person's body: *a parachute harness* **3 in harness** at one's routine work ▷ *vb* **4** to put a harness on (a horse or other animal) **5** to control something in order to make use of it: *learning to harness the power of your own mind*
WORD ORIGIN Old French *harneis* baggage

Harnoncourt *n* **Nikolaus** born 1929, Austrian conductor and cellist, noted for his performances using period instruments

Harold I *n* surname *Harefoot* died 1040, king of England (1037–40); son of Canute

harp *n* **1** a large upright triangular stringed instrument played by plucking the strings with the fingers ▷ *vb* **2 harp on** to speak in a persistent and tedious manner (about a subject) **harpist** *n*
WORD ORIGIN Old English *hearpe*

harpoon *n* **1** a barbed spear attached to a long rope and thrown or fired when hunting whales, etc. ▷ *vb* **2** to spear with a harpoon
WORD ORIGIN probably from Dutch *harpoen*

harpsichord *n* a keyboard instrument, resembling a small piano, with strings that are plucked mechanically **harpsichordist** *n*
WORD ORIGIN Late Latin *harpa* harp + Latin *chorda* string

harpy *n, pl* **-pies** a violent, unpleasant, or greedy woman
WORD ORIGIN from Greek *Harpuiai* the Harpies, literally: snatchers (mythical birdlike female monsters)

harridan *n* a scolding old woman; nag
WORD ORIGIN origin unknown

harrier[1] *n* a cross-country runner
WORD ORIGIN from *hare*

harrier[2] *n* a bird of prey with broad wings and long legs and tail

Harriman *n* **W(illiam) Averell** 1891–1986, US diplomat: negotiated the Nuclear Test Ban Treaty with the Soviet Union (1963); governor of New York (1955–58)

Harrington *n* **James** 1611–77, English republican and writer. He described his ideal form of government in *Oceana* (1656)

Harris[1] *n* the S part of the island of Lewis with Harris, in the Outer Hebrides. Pop: about 3000 (2001). Area: 500 sq km (190 sq miles)

Harris[2] *n* **1** Sir **Arthur Travers,** known as *Bomber Harris.* 1892–1984, British air marshal. He was commander-in-chief of Bomber Command of the RAF (1942–45) **2 Frank** 1856–1931, British writer and journalist; his books include his autobiography *My Life and Loves* (1923–27) and *Contemporary Portraits* (1915–30) **3 Joel Chandler** 1848–1908, US writer; creator of Uncle Remus **4 Roy** 1898–1979, US composer, esp. of orchestral and choral music incorporating American folk tunes

harrow *n* **1** an implement used to break up clods of soil ▷ *vb* **2** to draw a harrow over (land)
WORD ORIGIN from Old Norse

harrowing ❶ *adj* very upsetting or disturbing

harry ❶ *vb* **-ries, -rying, -ried** to keep asking (someone) to do something; pester
WORD ORIGIN Old English *hergian*

harsh ❶ *adj* **1** severe and difficult to cope with: *harsh winters* **2** unkind and showing no understanding: *the judge was very harsh on the demonstrators* **3** excessively hard, bright, or rough: *harsh sunlight* **4** (of sounds) unpleasant and grating **harshly** *adv* **harshness** *n*
WORD ORIGIN probably Scandinavian

hart *n, pl* **harts** *or* **hart** the male of the deer, esp. the red deer
WORD ORIGIN Old English *heorot*

Hart *n* **1 Lorenz** 1895–1943, US lyricist: collaborated with Richard Rodgers in writing musicals **2 Moss** 1904–61, US dramatist: collaborated with George Kaufman on Broadway comedies and wrote libretti for musicals

Harte *n* **(Francis) Bret** 1836–1902, US poet and short-story writer, noted for his sketches of Californian gold miners, such as *The Luck of Roaring Camp* (1870)

hartebeest *n* a large African antelope with curved horns and a fawn-coloured coat
WORD ORIGIN Dutch

Harthacanute, Hardecanute *or* **Hardicanute** *n* ?1019–42, king of Denmark (1035–42) and of England (1040–42); son of Canute

Hartley *n* **1 David** 1705–57, English philosopher and physician. In *Observations of Man* (1749) he introduced the theory of psychological associationism **2 L(eslie) P(oles)** 1895–1972, British novelist. His novels include the trilogy *The Shrimp and the Anemone* (1944), *The Sixth Heaven* (1946), and *Eustace and Hilda* (1947) as well as *The Go-Between* (1953)

Hartnell *n* Sir **Norman** 1901–79, English couturier

harum-scarum *adj* **1** reckless ▷ *adv* **2** recklessly ▷ *n* **3** an impetuous person
WORD ORIGIN origin unknown

Harun al-Rashid *n* ?763–809 AD, Abbasid caliph of Islam (786–809), whose court at Baghdad was idealized in the *Arabian Nights*

harvest ❶ *n* **1** the gathering of a ripened crop **2** the crop itself **3** the season for gathering crops **4** the product of an effort or action ▷ *vb* **5** to gather (a ripened crop) **6** *chiefly US* to remove (an organ) from the body for transplantation
WORD ORIGIN Old English *hærfest*

harvester *n* **1** a harvesting machine, esp. a combine harvester **2** a person who harvests

harvest festival *n* **1** a Christian church service held every year to thank God for the harvest **2** any of various ceremonies celebrating the harvest in other religions

harvest moon *n* the full moon occurring nearest to the autumn equinox

harvest mouse *n* a very small reddish-brown mouse that lives in cornfields or hedgerows

has *vb* ▸ third person singular of the present tense of **have**

h

THESAURUS

harness *n* **1, 2 = equipment**, tackle, gear, tack, trappings ▷ *vb* **5 = exploit**, control, channel, apply, employ, utilize, mobilize, make productive, turn to account, render useful

harrowing *adj* **= distressing**, disturbing, alarming, frightening, painful, terrifying, chilling, traumatic, tormenting, heartbreaking, excruciating, agonizing, nerve-racking, heart-rending, gut-wrenching

harry *vb* **= pester**, trouble, bother, disturb, worry, annoy, plague, tease, torment, harass, hassle *(informal)*, badger, persecute, molest, vex, bedevil, breathe down someone's neck, chivvy, give someone grief *(Brit & S African)*, be on your back *(slang)*, get in your hair *(informal)*

harsh *adj* **1a = severe**, hard, tough, grim, stark, stringent, austere, Spartan, inhospitable, comfortless, bare-bones **1b = bleak**, cold, freezing, severe, bitter, icy **2a = cruel**, savage, brutal, ruthless, relentless, unrelenting, barbarous, pitiless **2b = hard**, sharp, severe, bitter, cruel, stern, unpleasant, abusive, unkind, pitiless, unfeeling **OPPOSITE:** kind **4 = raucous**, rough, jarring, grating, strident, rasping, discordant, croaking, guttural, dissonant, unmelodious **OPPOSITE:** soft

harvest *n* **1 = harvesting**, picking, gathering, collecting, reaping, harvest-time **2 = crop**, yield, year's growth, produce ▷ *vb* **5 = gather**, pick, collect, bring in, pluck, reap

DICTIONARY

Hasan al-Basri *n* died 728 AD, Muslim religious thinker

has-been *n informal* a person who is no longer popular or successful

Hasdrubal *n* died 207 BC, Carthaginian general: commanded the Carthaginian army in Spain (218–211); joined his brother Hannibal in Italy and was killed at the Metaurus

Hašek *n* **Jaroslav** 1883–1923, Czech novelist and short-story writer; author of *The Good Soldier Schweik* (1923)

hash[1] *n* **1** a dish of diced cooked meat, vegetables, etc. reheated: *corned-beef hash* **2** a reworking of old material **3 make a hash of** *informal* to mess up or destroy
WORD ORIGIN Old French *hacher* to chop up

h

hash[2] *n slang* ▸ short for **hashish**

hashish (hash-eesh) *n* a drug made from the hemp plant, smoked for its intoxicating effects
WORD ORIGIN Arabic

hasn't has not

hasp *n* a clasp which fits over a staple and is secured by a pin, bolt, or padlock, used as a fastening
WORD ORIGIN Old English *hæpse*

Hassan II *n* 1929–1999, king of Morocco (1961–99)

hassium *n chem* an element synthetically produced in small quantities by high-energy ion bombardment. Symbol: Hs
WORD ORIGIN Latin, from *Hesse*, the German state where it was discovered

hassle **T** *informal n* **1** a great deal of trouble **2** a prolonged argument ▹ *vb* **-sling, -sled 3** to cause annoyance or trouble to (someone): *stop hassling me!*
WORD ORIGIN origin unknown

hassock *n* a cushion for kneeling on in church
WORD ORIGIN Old English *hassuc* matted grass

haste *n* **1** speed, esp. in an action **2** the act of hurrying in a careless manner **3 make haste** to hurry or rush ▹ *vb* **hasting, hasted 4** *poetic* to hasten
WORD ORIGIN Old French

hasten *vb* **1** to hurry or cause to hurry **2** to be anxious (to say something)

Hastings[1] *n* **1** a port in SE England, in East Sussex on the English Channel: near the site of the **Battle of Hastings** (1066), in which William the Conqueror defeated King Harold; chief of the Cinque Ports. Pop: 85 828 (2001) **2** a town in New Zealand, on E North Island: centre of a rich agricultural and fruit-growing region. Pop: 71 100 (2004 est)

Hastings[2] *n* **1 Gavin** born 1962, Scottish Rugby Union footballer; played for Scotland 1986–95 **2 Warren** 1732–1818, British administrator in India; governor general of Bengal (1773–85). He implemented important reforms but was impeached by parliament (1788) on charges of corruption; acquitted in 1795

hasty *adj* **-tier, -tiest 1** done or happening suddenly or quickly **2** done too quickly and without thought; rash **hastily** *adv*

hat *n* **1** a head covering, often with a brim, usually worn to give protection from the weather **2** *informal* a role or capacity: *I'm wearing my honorary consul's hat* **3 keep something under one's hat** to keep something secret **4 pass the hat round** to collect money for a cause **5 take off one's hat to someone** to admire or congratulate someone
WORD ORIGIN Old English *hætt*

hatband *n* a band or ribbon around the base of the crown of a hat

hatch[1] **T** *vb* **1** to cause (the young of various animals, esp. birds) to emerge from the egg or (of young birds, etc.) to emerge from the egg **2** (of eggs) to break and release the young animal within **3** to devise (a plot or plan)
WORD ORIGIN Germanic

hatch[2] *n* **1** a hinged door covering an opening in a floor or wall **2 a** ▸ short for **hatchway b** a door in an aircraft or spacecraft **3** Also called: **serving hatch** an opening in a wall between a kitchen and a dining area **4** *informal* ▸ short for **hatchback**
WORD ORIGIN Old English *hæcc*

hatch[3] *vb drawing, engraving, etc.* to mark (a figure, etc.) with fine parallel or crossed lines to indicate shading **hatching** *n*
WORD ORIGIN Old French *hacher* to chop

hatchback *n* a car with a single lifting door in the rear

hatchet *n* **1** a short axe used for chopping wood, etc. **2 bury the hatchet** to make peace or resolve a disagreement ▹ *adj* **3** narrow and sharp: *a hatchet face*
WORD ORIGIN Old French *hachette*

hatchet job *n informal* a malicious verbal or written attack

hatchet man *n informal* a person who carries out unpleasant tasks on behalf of an employer

hatchling *n* a young animal that has newly hatched from an egg

hatchway *n* an opening in the deck of a vessel to provide access below

hate **T** *vb* **hating, hated 1** to dislike (someone or something) intensely **2** to be unwilling (to do something): *I hate to trouble you* ▹ *n* **3** intense dislike **4** *informal* a person or thing that is hated: *my own pet hate is restaurants* **hater** *n*
WORD ORIGIN Old English *hatian*

hateful *adj* causing or deserving hate

Hathaway *n* **Anne** ?1557–1623, wife of William Shakespeare

Hathor *n* an Egyptian goddess of creation

hatred **T** *n* intense dislike

Hatshepsut *or* **Hatshepset** *n* queen of Egypt of the 18th dynasty (?1512–1482 BC). She built a great mortuary temple at Deir el Bahri near Thebes

hatter *n* **1** a person who makes and sells hats **2 mad as a hatter** eccentric

Hattersley *n* **Roy** (**Sydney George**), Baron Hattersley of Sparkbrook born 1932, British Labour politician; deputy leader of the Labour Party (1983–92); shadow home secretary (1980–83; 1987–92)

hat trick *n* **1** *cricket* the achievement of a bowler in taking three wickets with three successive balls **2** any achievement of three successive goals, victories, etc.

hauberk *n history* a long sleeveless coat of mail
WORD ORIGIN Old French *hauberc*

THESAURUS

hassle (*informal*) *n* **1 = trouble**, problem, difficulty, upset, bother, grief (*informal*), trial, struggle, uphill (*S African*), inconvenience ▹ *vb* **3 = bother**, bug (*informal*), annoy, harry, hound, harass, badger, pester, get on your nerves (*informal*), be on your back (*slang*), get in your hair (*informal*), breath down someone's neck

hatch[1] (*informal*) *vb* **1 = incubate**, breed, sit on, brood, bring forth **3 = devise**, plan, design, project, scheme, manufacture, plot, invent, put together, conceive, brew, formulate, contrive, dream up (*informal*), concoct, think up, cook up (*informal*), trump up

hate *vb* **1a = detest**, loathe, despise, dislike, be sick of, abhor, be hostile to, recoil from, be repelled by, have an aversion to, abominate, not be able to bear, execrate **OPPOSITE:** love **1b = dislike**, detest, shrink from, recoil from, have no stomach for, not be able to bear **OPPOSITE:** like **2 = be unwilling**, regret, be reluctant, hesitate, be sorry, be loath, feel disinclined ▹ *n* **3 = dislike**, hostility, hatred, loathing, animosity, aversion, antagonism, antipathy, enmity, abomination, animus, abhorrence, odium, detestation, execration **OPPOSITE:** love

hatred *n* **= hate**, dislike, animosity, aversion, revulsion, antagonism, antipathy, enmity, abomination, ill will, animus, repugnance, odium, detestation, execration **OPPOSITE:** love

DICTIONARY

Haughey *n* **Charles James** 1925–2006, Irish politician; leader of the Fianna Fáil party; prime minister of the Republic of Ireland (1979–81; 1982; 1987–92)

haughty *adj* **-tier, -tiest** having or showing excessive pride or arrogance **haughtily** *adv* **haughtiness** *n*
WORD ORIGIN Latin *altus* high

haul ⊙ *vb* **1** to drag or pull (something) with effort **2** to transport, such as in a lorry **3** *naut* to alter the course of (a vessel) ▷*n* **4** the act of dragging with effort **5** a quantity of something obtained: *a good haul of fish; a huge haul of stolen goods* **6 long haul a** a long journey **b** a long difficult process
WORD ORIGIN Old French *haler*

haulage *n* **1** the business of transporting goods **2** a charge for transporting goods

haulier *n Austral & Brit* a person or firm that transports goods by road

haulm (**hawm**) *n* the stalks of beans, peas, or potatoes collectively
WORD ORIGIN Old English *healm*

haunch *n* **1** the human hip or fleshy hindquarter of an animal **2** the leg and loin of an animal, used for food
WORD ORIGIN Old French *hanche*

haunt ⊙ *vb* **1** to visit (a person or place) in the form of a ghost **2** to remain in the memory or thoughts of: *it was a belief which haunted her* **3** to visit (a place) frequently ▷*n* **4** a place visited frequently
WORD ORIGIN Old French *hanter*

haunted ⊙ *adj* **1** (of a place) frequented or visited by ghosts **2** (of a person) obsessed or worried

haunting ⊙ *adj* having a quality of great beauty or sadness so as to be memorable: *a haunting melody*

Hauptmann *n* **Gerhart** 1862–1946, German naturalist, dramatist, novelist, and poet. His works include the historical drama *The Weavers* (1892): Nobel prize for literature 1912

Haussmann *n* **Georges-Eugène,** Baron 1809–91, French town planner, noted for his major rebuilding of Paris in the reign of Napoleon III

hautboy (**oh**-boy) *n old-fashioned* an oboe
WORD ORIGIN French *haut* high + *bois* wood

haute couture (**oat** koo-**ture**) *n* high fashion
WORD ORIGIN French

hauteur (oat-**ur**) *n* haughtiness
WORD ORIGIN French *haut* high

Havana *n* a fine-quality hand-rolled cigar from Cuba

have ⊙ *vb* **has, having, had 1** to possess: *he has a massive collection of old movies; I have an iron constitution* **2** to receive, take, or obtain: *I had a long letter* **3** to hold in the mind: *she always had a yearning to be a schoolteacher* **4** to possess a knowledge of: *I have no German* **5** to experience or be affected by: *a good way to have a change* **6** to suffer from: *to have a blood pressure problem* **7** to gain control of or advantage over: *you have me on that point* **8** *slang* to cheat or outwit: *I've been had* **9** to show: *have mercy on me* **10** to take part in; hold: *I had a telephone conversation* **11** to cause to be done: *have my shoes mended by Friday* **12** to eat or drink **13** *taboo slang* to have sexual intercourse with **14** to tolerate or allow: *I won't have all this noise* **15** to receive as a guest: *we have visitors* **16** to be pregnant with or give birth to (offspring) **17** used to form past tenses: *I have gone; I had gone* **18 have had it** *informal* **a** to be exhausted or killed **b** to have lost one's last chance **19 have it off** *taboo Brit slang* to have sexual intercourse **20 have to** used to express compulsion or necessity: *you'd have to wait six months* ▷*n* **21 haves** *informal* people who have wealth, security, etc.: *the haves and the have-nots* ▸See also **have on, have out**, etc.
WORD ORIGIN Old English *habban*

have-a-go *adj informal* (of people attempting arduous or brave tasks) brave or spirited: *have-a-go pensioner*

Havel[1] *n* a river in E Germany, flowing south to Berlin, then west and north to join the River Elbe. Length: about 362 km (225 miles)

Havel[2] *n* **Václav** born 1936, Czech dramatist and statesman: founder of the Civil Forum movement for political change: president of Czechoslovakia (1989–92) and of the Czech Republic (1993–2003). His plays include *The Garden Party* (1963) and *Redevelopment* (1989)

haven ⊙ *n* **1** a place of safety **2** a harbour for shipping
WORD ORIGIN Old English *hæfen*

haven't have not

have on ⊙ *vb* **1** to wear: *he'd got a long pair of trousers on* **2** to have a commitment: *what do you have on this afternoon?* **3** *informal* to trick or tease: *he's having you on* **4** to have (information, esp. when incriminating) about (a person): *she's got something on him*

have out *vb* to settle (a matter), esp. by fighting or by frank discussion: *I went to Carl's office to have it out with him*

haver *vb* **1** *Scot & N English dialect* to talk nonsense **2** to be unsure and hesitant; dither
WORD ORIGIN origin unknown

haversack *n* a canvas bag carried on the back or shoulder
WORD ORIGIN French *havresac*

have up *vb* to bring to trial: *what, and get me had up for kidnapping?*

havoc ⊙ *n* **1** *informal* chaos, disorder, and confusion **2 play havoc with** to cause a great deal of damage or confusion to
WORD ORIGIN Old French *havot* pillage

haw[1] *n* the fruit of the hawthorn
WORD ORIGIN Old English *haga*

haw[2] *vb* **hum** (*or* **hem**) **and haw** to hesitate in speaking
WORD ORIGIN imitative

Haw-Haw *n* **Lord Haw-Haw** ▸See **Joyce** (sense 2)

hawk[1] *n* **1** a bird of prey with short rounded wings and a long tail **2** a supporter or advocate of warlike policies ▷*vb* **3** to hunt with falcons or hawks **hawkish** *adj* **hawklike** *adj*
WORD ORIGIN Old English *hafoc*

hawk[2] *vb* to offer (goods) for sale in the street or door-to-door
WORD ORIGIN from *hawker* pedlar

hawk[3] *vb* **1** to clear the throat noisily **2** to force (phlegm) up from the throat
WORD ORIGIN imitative

hawker *n* a person who travels from place to place selling goods
WORD ORIGIN probably from Middle Low German *hōken* to peddle

h

THESAURUS

haul *vb* **1 = drag**, draw, pull, hale, heave ▷*n* **5 = yield**, gain, spoils, find, catch, harvest, loot, takings, booty

haunt *vb* **2 = plague**, trouble, obsess, torment, come back to, possess, stay with, recur, beset, prey on, weigh on ▷*n* **4 = meeting place**, resort, hangout *(informal)*, den, rendezvous, stamping ground, gathering place

haunted *adj* **1 = possessed**, ghostly, cursed, eerie, spooky *(informal)*, jinxed **2 = preoccupied**, worried, troubled, plagued, obsessed, tormented

haunting *adj* **= evocative**, poignant, unforgettable, indelible

have *vb* **1 = own**, keep, possess, hold, retain, occupy, boast, be the owner of **2 = get**, obtain, take, receive, accept, gain, secure, acquire, procure, take receipt of **5 = experience**, go through, undergo, meet with, come across, run into, be faced with **6 = suffer**, experience, undergo, sustain, endure, be suffering from **16 = give birth to**, bear, deliver, bring forth, beget, bring into the world

have on *vb (informal)* **3 = tease**, kid *(informal)*, wind up *(Brit slang)*, trick, deceive, take the mickey, pull someone's leg, play a joke on, jerk *or* yank someone's chain *(informal)*

haven *n* **1 = sanctuary**, shelter, retreat, asylum, refuge, oasis, sanctum

havoc *n* **1** *(informal)* **= disorder**, confusion, chaos, disruption, mayhem, shambles

DICTIONARY

hawk-eyed *adj* having extremely keen eyesight

Hawkins *n* **1 Coleman** 1904–69, US pioneer of the tenor saxophone for jazz **2** Sir **John** 1532–95, English naval commander and slave trader, treasurer of the navy (1577–89); commander of a squadron in the fleet that defeated the Spanish Armada (1588)

Hawks *n* **Howard** (**Winchester**) 1896–1977, US film director. His films include *Sergeant York* (1941) and *The Big Sleep* (1946)

Hawksmoor *n* **Nicholas** 1661–1736, English architect. His designs include All Souls', Oxford, and a number of London churches, notably St Anne's, Limehouse

h

Haworth[1] *n* a village in N England, in Bradford unitary authority, West Yorkshire: home of Charlotte, Emily, and Anne Brontë. Pop: 6078 (2001)

Haworth[2] *n* Sir **Walter Norman** 1883–1950, British biochemist, who shared the Nobel prize for chemistry (1937) for being the first to synthesize ascorbic acid (vitamin C)

hawser *n naut* a large heavy rope
WORD ORIGIN Anglo-French *hauceour*

hawthorn *n* a thorny tree or shrub with white or pink flowers and reddish fruits
WORD ORIGIN Old English *haguthorn*

Hawthorne *n* **Nathaniel** 1804–64, US novelist and short-story writer: his works include the novels *The Scarlet Letter* (1850) and *The House of the Seven Gables* (1851) and the children's stories *Tanglewood Tales* (1853)

hay *n* **1** grass cut and dried as fodder **2 hit the hay** *slang* to go to bed **3 make hay while the sun shines** to take full advantage of an opportunity
WORD ORIGIN Old English *hieg*

Hay *n* **Will** 1888–1949, British music-hall comedian, who later starred in films, such as *Oh, Mr Porter!* (1937)

Haydon *n* **Benjamin** (**Robert**) 1786–1846, British historical painter and art critic, best known for his *Autobiography and Journals* (1853)

Hayek *n* **Friedrich August von** 1899–1992, British economist and political philosopher, born in Austria: noted for his advocacy of free-market ideas; shared the Nobel prize for economics 1974

hay fever *n* an allergic reaction to pollen, which causes sneezing, runny nose, and watery eyes

haystack *or* **hayrick** *n* a large pile of hay built in the open and covered with thatch

haywire *adj* **go haywire** *informal* to stop functioning properly

hazard ❶ *n* **1** a thing likely to cause injury, loss, etc. **2** risk or likelihood of injury, loss, etc.: *evaluate the level of hazard in a situation* **3** *golf* an obstacle such as a bunker **4 at hazard** at risk ▷ *vb* **5** to risk: *hazarding the health of his crew* **6 hazard a guess** to make a guess
WORD ORIGIN Arabic *az-zahr* the die

hazard lights *or* **hazard warning lights** *pl n* the indicator lights on a motor vehicle when flashing simultaneously to indicate that the vehicle is stationary

hazardous ❶ *adj* involving great risk

haze ❶ *n* **1** *meteorol* reduced visibility as a result of condensed water vapour, dust, etc. in the air **2** confused or unclear understanding or feeling
WORD ORIGIN from *hazy*

hazel *n* **1** a shrub with edible rounded nuts ▷ *adj* **2** greenish-brown: *hazel eyes*
WORD ORIGIN Old English *hæsel*

hazelnut *n* the nut of a hazel shrub, which has a smooth shiny hard shell

Hazlitt *n* **William** 1778–1830, English critic and essayist: works include *Characters of Shakespeare's Plays* (1817), *Table Talk* (1821), and *The Plain Speaker* (1826)

hazy *adj* **-zier, -ziest 1** (of the sky or a view) unable to be seen clearly because of dust or heat **2** dim or vague: *my memory is a little hazy on this* **hazily** *adv* **haziness** *n*
WORD ORIGIN origin unknown

Hb haemoglobin

HB *Austral & Brit* (of pencil lead) hard-black: denoting a medium-hard lead

H-bomb *n* ▸ short for **hydrogen bomb**

HDD hard disk drive

HD-DVD High Definition DVD: a DVD capable of storing between two and four times as much data as a standard DVD

he *pron* **1** (refers to) a male person or animal **2** (refers to) a person or animal of unknown or unspecified sex: *a member may vote as he sees fit* ▷ *n, adj* **3** (refers to) a male person or animal: *a he-goat*
WORD ORIGIN Old English *hē*

He *chem* helium

HE His *or* Her Excellency

head ❶ *n* **1** the upper or front part of the body that contains the brain, eyes, mouth, nose, and ears **2** a person's mind and mental abilities: *I haven't any head for figures* **3** the most forward part of a thing: *the head of a queue* **4** the highest part of a thing; upper end: *the head of the pass* **5** something resembling a head in form or function, such as the top of a tool **6** the position of leadership or command **7** the person commanding most authority within a group or an organization **8** *bot* the top part of a plant, where the leaves or flowers grow in a cluster **9** a culmination or crisis: *the matter came to a head in December 1928* **10** the froth on the top of a glass of beer **11** the pus-filled tip of a pimple or boil **12** part of a computer or tape recorder that can read, write, or erase information **13** the source of a river or stream **14** the side of a coin that usually bears a portrait of the head of a monarch, etc. **15** a headland or promontory: *Beachy Head* **16** pressure of water or steam in an enclosed space **17** *pl* **head** a person or animal considered as a unit: *the cost per head of Paris's refuse collection; six hundred head of cattle* **18** a headline or heading **19** *informal* ▸ short for **headmaster, headmistress** or **head teacher 20** *informal* ▸ short for **headache 21 give someone his head** to allow someone greater freedom or

THESAURUS

hazard *n* **1, 2 = danger**, risk, threat, problem, menace, peril, jeopardy, pitfall, endangerment, imperilment ▷ *vb* **5 = jeopardize**, risk, endanger, threaten, expose, imperil, put in jeopardy
6 hazard a guess = guess, conjecture, suppose, speculate, presume, take a guess

hazardous *adj* **= dangerous**, risky, difficult, uncertain, unpredictable, insecure, hairy *(slang)*, unsafe, precarious, perilous, parlous *(archaic, humorous)*, dicey *(informal, chiefly Brit)*, fraught with danger, chancy *(informal)* **OPPOSITE:** safe

haze *n (meteorol)* **1 = mist**, film, cloud, steam, fog, obscurity, vapour, smog, dimness, smokiness

head *n* **1 = skull**, crown, pate, bean *(US & Canad slang)*, nut *(slang)*, loaf *(slang)*, cranium, conk *(slang)*, noggin, noddle *(informal, chiefly Brit)* **2 = mind**, reasoning, understanding, thought, sense, brain, brains *(informal)*, intelligence, wisdom, wits, common sense, loaf *(Brit informal)*, intellect, rationality, grey matter, brainpower, mental capacity **4 = top**, crown, summit, height, peak, crest, pinnacle, apex, vertex **7 = leader**, president, director, manager, chief, boss *(informal)*, captain, master, premier, commander, principal, supervisor, superintendent, chieftain, sherang *(Austral & NZ)* **23 head over heels (in love) = completely**, thoroughly, utterly, intensely, wholeheartedly, uncontrollably ▷ *vb* **31a = lead**, precede, be the leader of, be *or* go first, be *or* go at the front of, lead the way **31b = top**, lead, crown, cap **32 = be in charge of**, run, manage, lead, control, rule, direct, guide, command, govern, supervise

DICTIONARY

responsibility **22 go to one's head a** (of an alcoholic drink) to make one slightly drunk **b** to make one conceited: *success has gone to his head* **23 head over heels (in love)** very much (in love) **24 keep one's head** to remain calm **25 not make head nor tail of** not to understand (a problem, etc.) **26 off one's head** *slang* very foolish or insane **27 on one's own head** at one's own risk **28 over someone's head a** to a higher authority: *the taboo of going over the head of their immediate boss* **b** beyond a person's understanding **29 put our** *or* **your** *or* **their heads together** *informal* to consult together **30 turn someone's head** to make someone conceited ▷*vb* **31** to be at the front or top of: *Barnes headed the list* **32** to be in charge of **33** (often foll. by *for*) to go or cause to go (towards): *to head for the Channel ports* **34** *soccer* to propel (the ball) by striking it with the head **35** to provide with a heading ▸See also **head off, heads**
WORD ORIGIN Old English *hēafod*

Head *n* **Edith** 1907–81, US dress designer: won many Oscars for her Hollywood film costume designs

headache ❶ *n* **1** a continuous pain in the head **2** *informal* any cause of worry, difficulty, or annoyance: *financial headaches*

head-banger *n Brit, Austral & NZ slang* **1** a person who shakes his head violently to the beat of heavy-metal music **2** a crazy or stupid person

headboard *n* a vertical board at the head of a bed

headdress *n* any decorative head covering

headed *adj* **1** having a head or heads: *two-headed; bald-headed* **2** having a heading: *headed notepaper*

header *n* **1** *soccer* the action of striking a ball with the head **2** *informal* a headlong fall or dive

headfirst *adv* **1** with the head foremost **2** quickly and without thinking carefully: *she jumped into marriage headfirst*

headgear *n* hats collectively

head-hunting *n* **1** (of companies) the practice of actively searching for new high-level personnel, often from rival companies **2** the practice among certain peoples of removing the heads of enemies they have killed and preserving them as trophies **head-hunter** *n*

heading ❶ *n* **1** a title for a page, chapter, etc. **2** a main division, such as of a speech **3** *mining* a horizontal tunnel

headland *n* a narrow area of land jutting out into a sea

headlight *or* **headlamp** *n* a powerful light on the front of a vehicle

headline *n* **1** a phrase in heavy large type at the top of a newspaper or magazine article indicating the subject **2 headlines** the main points of a television or radio news broadcast

headlong *adv* **1** with the head foremost; headfirst **2** with great haste and without much thought: *they rushed headlong into buying a house* ▷*adj* **3** hasty or reckless

headmaster *or fem* **headmistress** *n* the principal of a school

head off *vb* **1** to intercept and force to change direction: *police head off New Age travellers* **2** to prevent or avert: *trying to head off the prospect of civil war* **3** to depart or set out: *to head off to school*

head-on *adv, adj* **1** front foremost: *a head-on collision* **2** with directness or without compromise: *a head-on confrontation with the unions*

headphones *pl n* two small loudspeakers held against the ears, worn to listen to the radio or recorded music without other people hearing it

headquarters *pl n* any centre from which operations are directed

headroom *or* **headway** *n* the space below a roof or bridge which allows an object to pass or stay underneath it without touching it

heads *adv* with the side of a coin uppermost which has a portrait of a head on it

headship *n* the position or state of being a leader, esp. the head teacher of a school

headshrinker *n slang* a psychiatrist

headstall *n* the part of a bridle that fits round a horse's head

head start *n* an initial advantage in a competitive situation

headstone *n* a memorial stone at the head of a grave

headstrong *adj* determined to do something in one's own way and ignoring the advice of others

head teacher *n* the principal of a school

head-to-head *adv, adj informal* in direct competition

headwaters *pl n* the tributary streams of a river in the area in which it rises

headway *n* **1** progress towards achieving something: *have the police made any headway?* **2** motion forward: *we felt our way out to the open sea, barely making headway* **3** ▸same as **headroom**

headwind *n* a wind blowing directly against the course of an aircraft or ship

heady ❶ *adj* **headier, headiest 1** (of an experience or period of time) extremely exciting **2** (of alcoholic drink, atmosphere, etc.) strongly affecting the physical senses: *a powerful, heady scent of cologne* **3** rash and impetuous

heal ❶ *vb* **1** (of a wound) to repair by natural processes, such as by scar formation **2** to restore (someone) to health **3** to repair (a rift in a personal relationship or an emotional wound) **healer** *n* **healing** *n, adj*
WORD ORIGIN Old English *hǣlan*

Healey *n* **Denis** (**Winston**), Baron Healey born 1917, British Labour politician; Chancellor of the Exchequer (1974–79); deputy leader of the Labour Party (1980–83)

health ❶ *n* **1** the general condition of body and mind: *better health* **2** the state of being bodily and mentally vigorous and free from disease **3** the condition of an organization, society, etc.: *the economic health of the republics*
WORD ORIGIN Old English *hǣlth*

health camp *n NZ* a camp for children with health or behavioural problems

health centre *n Brit* the surgery and offices of the doctors in a district

health farm *n* a residential establishment for people wishing to improve their health by losing weight, exercising, etc.

health food *n* natural food, organically grown and free from additives

healthful *adj* ▸same as **healthy** (senses 1, 2, 3)

health stamp *n NZ* a postage stamp with a small surcharge used to support health camps

health visitor *n* (in Britain) a nurse employed to visit mothers, their preschool children, and the elderly in their homes

h

THESAURUS

headache *n* **1 = migraine**, head (*informal*), neuralgia, cephalalgia (*medical*) **2** (*informal*) **= problem**, worry, trouble, bother, nuisance, inconvenience, bane, vexation

heading *n* **1 = title**, name, caption, headline, rubric

heady *adj* **1 = exciting**, thrilling, stimulating, exhilarating, overwhelming, intoxicating **2 = intoxicating**, strong, potent, inebriating, spirituous

heal *vb* **1 = mend**, get better, get well, cure, regenerate, show improvement **2 = cure**, restore, mend, make better, remedy, make good, make well **OPPOSITE:** injure

health *n* **1 = condition**, state, form, shape, tone, constitution, fettle **2 = wellbeing**, strength, fitness, vigour, good condition, wellness, soundness, robustness, healthiness, salubrity, haleness **OPPOSITE:** illness **3 = state**, condition, shape

DICTIONARY

healthy ❶ *adj* **healthier, healthiest** **1** having or showing good health **2** likely to produce good health: *healthy seaside air* **3** functioning well or being sound: *this is a very healthy business to be in* **4** *informal* considerable: *healthy profits* **5** sensible: *a healthy scepticism about his promises* **healthily** *adv* **healthiness** *n*

Healy *n* **Ian** born 1964, Australian cricketer; holds the record for the highest number of wicketkeeping dismissals in Test matches

heap ❶ *n* **1** a pile of things lying one on top of another **2** (*often pl*) *informal* a large number or quantity ▷ *adv* **3** **heaps** much: *he was heaps better* ▷ *vb* **4** to collect into a pile **5** to give freely (to): *film roles were heaped on her*
WORD ORIGIN Old English *hēap*

h

hear ❶ *vb* **hearing, heard** **1** to perceive (a sound) with the sense of hearing **2** to listen to: *I didn't want to hear what he had to say* **3** to be informed (of something); receive information (about something): *I hear you mean to join the crusade* **4** *law* to give a hearing to (a case) **5** **hear from** to receive a letter or telephone call from **6** **hear! hear!** an exclamation of approval **7** **hear of** to allow: *she wouldn't hear of it* **hearer** *n*
WORD ORIGIN Old English *hieran*

hearing ❶ *n* **1** the sense by which sound is perceived **2** an opportunity for someone to be listened to **3** the range within which sound can be heard; earshot **4** the investigation of a matter by a court of law

hearing aid *n* a small amplifier worn by a partially deaf person in or behind the ear to improve his or her hearing

hearing dog *n* a dog that has been trained to help a deaf person by alerting him or her to various sounds

hearken *vb archaic* to listen
WORD ORIGIN Old English *heorcnian*

hearsay *n* gossip or rumour

hearse *n* a large car used to carry a coffin at a funeral
WORD ORIGIN Latin *hirpex* harrow

heart ❶ *n* **1** a hollow muscular organ whose contractions pump the blood throughout the body **2** this organ considered as the centre of emotions, esp. love **3** tenderness or pity: *my heart went out to her* **4** courage or spirit **5** the most central part or important part: *at the heart of Italian motor racing* **6** (of vegetables such as cabbage) the inner compact part **7** the breast: *she held him to her heart* **8** a shape representing the heart, with two rounded lobes at the top meeting in a point at the bottom **9** **a** a red heart-shaped symbol on a playing card **b** a card with one or more of these symbols or (*when pl*) the suit of cards so marked **10** **break someone's heart** to cause someone to grieve very deeply, esp. by ending a love affair **11** **by heart** by memorizing **12** **have a change of heart** to experience a profound change of outlook or attitude **13** **have one's heart in one's mouth** to be full of apprehension, excitement, or fear **14** **have the heart** to have the necessary will or callousness (to do something): *I didn't have the heart to tell him* **15** **set one's heart on something** to have something as one's ambition **16** **take heart** to become encouraged **17** **take something to heart** to take something seriously or be upset about something **18** **wear one's heart on one's sleeve** to show one's feelings openly **19** **with all one's heart** deeply and sincerely
WORD ORIGIN Old English *heorte*

heartache *n* very great sadness and emotional suffering

heart attack *n* a sudden severe malfunction of the heart

heartbeat *n* one complete pulsation of the heart

heartbreak *n* intense and overwhelming grief, esp. after the end of a love affair **heartbreaking** *adj* **heartbroken** *adj*

heartburn *n* a burning sensation in the chest caused by indigestion

hearten *vb* to encourage or make cheerful **heartening** *adj*

heart failure *n* **1** a condition in which the heart is unable to pump an adequate amount of blood to the tissues **2** sudden stopping of the heartbeat, resulting in death

heartfelt *adj* sincerely and strongly felt: *heartfelt thanks*

hearth *n* **1** the floor of a fireplace **2** this as a symbol of the home
WORD ORIGIN Old English *heorth*

heartland *n* **1** the central region of a country or continent: *we headed west towards the heartland of Tibet* **2** the area where the thing specified is most common or strongest: *Germany's industrial heartland*

heartless *adj* unkind or cruel **heartlessly** *adv*

heart-rending *adj* causing great sadness and pity: *a heart-rending story*

hearts and minds *n* the collective trust or approval of a body of people such as a populace, esp. for a foreign military force: *we must win the hearts and minds of the people*

heart-searching *n* examination of one's feelings or conscience

heartstrings *pl n often facetious* deep emotions: *tugging our heartstrings with pictures of suffering*
WORD ORIGIN originally referring to the tendons supposed to support the heart

heart-throb *n* a man, esp. a film or pop star, who is attractive to a lot of women or girls

heart-to-heart *adj* **1** (of a talk) concerned with personal problems or intimate feelings ▷ *n* **2** an intimate conversation

heart-warming *adj* inspiring feelings of happiness: *the heart-warming spectacle of a family reunion*

THESAURUS

healthy *adj* **1 = well**, sound, fit, strong, active, flourishing, hardy, blooming, robust, vigorous, sturdy, hale, hearty, in good shape (*informal*), in good condition, in the pink, alive and kicking, fighting fit, in fine form, in fine fettle, hale and hearty, fit as a fiddle (*informal*), right as rain (*Brit informal*), physically fit, in fine feather **OPPOSITE:** ill
2a = wholesome, beneficial, nourishing, good for you, nutritious, salutary, hygienic, healthful, salubrious, health-giving **OPPOSITE:** unwholesome
2b = invigorating, bracing, beneficial, good for you, salutary, healthful, salubrious

heap *n* **1 = pile**, lot, collection, store, mountain, mass, stack, rick, mound, accumulation, stockpile, hoard, aggregation **2** (*often pl, informal*) **= a lot**, lots (*informal*), plenty, masses, load(s) (*informal*), ocean(s), great deal, quantities, tons, stack(s), lashings (*Brit informal*), abundance, oodles (*informal*) ▷ *vb* **4 = pile**, store, collect, gather, stack, accumulate, mound, amass, stockpile, hoard, bank

hear *vb* **1 = overhear**, catch, detect **2 = listen to**, heed, attend to, eavesdrop on, listen in to, give attention to, hearken to (*archaic*), hark to, be all ears for (*informal*) **3 = learn**, discover, find out, understand, pick up, gather, be informed, ascertain, be told of, get wind of (*informal*), hear tell (*dialect*) **4** (*law*) **= try**, judge, examine, investigate

hearing *n* **4 = inquiry**, trial, investigation, industrial tribunal

heart *n* **2 = emotions**, feelings, sentiments, love, affection **4 = courage**, will, spirit, mind, purpose, bottle (*Brit informal*), resolution, resolve, nerve, stomach, enthusiasm, determination, guts (*informal*), spine, pluck, bravery, backbone, fortitude, mettle, boldness, spunk (*informal*) **5 = root**, core, essence, centre, nucleus, marrow, hub, kernel, crux, gist, central part, nitty-gritty (*informal*), nub, pith, quintessence **11 by heart = from** *or* **by memory**, verbatim, word for word, pat,

DICTIONARY

heartwood *n* the central core of dark hard wood in tree trunks
hearty *adj* **heartier, heartiest** **1** warm, friendly, and enthusiastic **2** strongly felt: *a hearty dislike* **3** (of a meal) substantial and nourishing **heartily** *adv*
heat ❶ *vb* **1** to make or become hot or warm ▷*n* **2** the state of being hot **3** the energy transferred as a result of a difference in temperature ▸ Related adjectives: **thermal, calorific** **4** hot weather: *he loves the heat of Africa* **5** intensity of feeling: *the heat of their argument* **6** the most intense part: *in the heat of an election campaign* **7** pressure: *political heat on the government* **8** *sport* a preliminary eliminating contest in a competition **9 on** *or* **in heat** (of some female mammals) ready for mating **heating** *n* **WORD ORIGIN** Old English *hǣtu*
heated ❶ *adj* impassioned or highly emotional: *a heated debate* **heatedly** *adv*
heater *n* a device for supplying heat
heath *n* **1** *Brit* a large open area, usually with sandy soil, low shrubs, and heather **2** a low-growing evergreen shrub with small bell-shaped pink or purple flowers **WORD ORIGIN** Old English *hǣth*
heathen *n, pl* **-thens** *or* **-then** *old-fashioned* **1** a person who does not believe in an established religion; pagan ▷*adj* **2** of or relating to heathen peoples **WORD ORIGIN** Old English *hǣthen*
heather *n* a shrub with small bell-shaped flowers growing on heaths and mountains **WORD ORIGIN** origin unknown
Heath Robinson *adj* (of a mechanical device) absurdly complicated in design for a simple function **WORD ORIGIN** after William *Heath Robinson*, cartoonist
heatstroke *n* ▸ same as **sunstroke**
heat wave *n* a spell of unusually hot weather
heave *vb* **heaving, heaved** **1** to lift or move (something) with a great effort **2** to throw (something heavy) with effort **3** to utter (a sigh) noisily or unhappily **4** to rise and fall heavily **5** *pt & pp* **hove** *naut* **a** to move in a specified direction: *heave her bows around and head north* **b** (of a vessel) to pitch or roll **6** to vomit or retch ▷*n* **7** the act of heaving **WORD ORIGIN** Old English *hebban*
heaven ❶ *n* **1** the place where God is believed to live and where those leading good lives are believed to go when they die **2** a place or state of happiness **3 heavens** the sky **4** Also: **heavens** God or the gods, used in exclamatory phrases: *for heaven's sake!* **WORD ORIGIN** Old English *heofon*
heavenly ❶ *adj* **1** *informal* wonderful or very enjoyable: *a heavenly meal* **2** of or occurring in space: *a heavenly body* **3** of or relating to heaven
heave to *vb* to stop (a ship) or (of a ship) to stop
heavy ❶ *adj* **heavier, heaviest** **1** of comparatively great weight **2** with a relatively high density: *lead is a heavy metal* **3** great in degree or amount: *heavy traffic* **4** considerable: *heavy emphasis* **5** hard to fulfil: *an exceptionally heavy demand for this issue* **6** using or consuming a lot of something quickly: *a heavy drinker* **7** deep and loud: *heavy breathing* **8** clumsy and slow: *a heavy lumbering trot* **9** (of a movement or action) with great downward force or pressure: *a heavy blow with a club* **10** solid or fat: *mountain animals acquire a heavy layer of fat* **11** not easily digestible: *a heavy meal* **12** (of cakes or bread) insufficiently raised **13** (of soil) with a high clay content **14** sad or dejected: *you feel heavy or sad afterwards* **15** (of facial features) looking sad and tired **16** (of a situation) serious and causing anxiety or sadness **17** cloudy or overcast: *heavy clouds obscured the sun* **18** (of an industry) engaged in the large-scale manufacture of large objects or extraction of raw materials **19** *mil* (of guns, etc.) large and powerful **20** dull and uninteresting: *Helen finds his friends very heavy going* **21** (of music, literature, etc.) difficult to understand or not immediately appealing **22** *slang* (of rock music) loud and having a powerful beat **23** *slang* using, or prepared to use, violence or brutality ▷*n, pl* **heavies** **24** *slang* a large strong man hired to threaten violence or deter others by his presence **25 a** a villainous role **b** an actor who plays such a part **26 the heavies** *informal* serious newspapers ▷*adv* **27** heavily: *time hung heavy* **heavily** *adv* **heaviness** *n* **WORD ORIGIN** Old English *hefig*
heavy-duty *adj* made to withstand hard wear, bad weather, etc.
heavy-handed *adj* acting forcefully and without care and thought
heavy-hearted *adj* sad and discouraged
heavy hydrogen *n* ▸ same as **deuterium**
heavy metal *n* a type of very loud rock music featuring guitar riffs
heavy water *n* water formed of oxygen and deuterium
heavyweight *n* **1** a professional boxer weighing over 195 pounds (88.5 kg) or an amateur weighing over 91 kg **2** a person who is heavier than average **3** *informal* an important or highly influential person
Heb. *or* **Hebr.** Hebrew (language)
Hebbel *n* **Christian Friedrich** 1813–63, German dramatist and lyric poet, whose historical works were influenced by Hegel; his major plays are *Maria Magdalena* (1844), *Herodes und Marianne* (1850), and the trilogy *Die Nibelungen* (1862)
Hébert *n* **Jacques René** 1755–94, French journalist and revolutionary:

h

THESAURUS

word-perfect, by rote, off by heart, off pat, parrot-fashion *(informal)*
heat *vb* **1 = warm (up)**, cook, boil, roast, reheat, make hot **OPPOSITE:** chill ▷*n* **2 = warmth**, hotness, temperature, swelter, sultriness, fieriness, torridity, warmness, calefaction **OPPOSITE:** cold **4 = hot weather**, warmth, closeness, high temperature, heatwave, warm weather, hot climate, hot spell, mugginess **5 = passion**, excitement, intensity, violence, fever, fury, warmth, zeal, agitation, fervour, ardour, vehemence, earnestness, impetuosity **OPPOSITE:** calmness
heated *adj* **= impassioned**, intense, spirited, excited, angry, violent, bitter, raging, furious, fierce, lively, passionate, animated, frenzied, fiery, stormy, vehement, tempestuous **OPPOSITE:** calm
heaven *n* **1 = paradise**, next world, hereafter, nirvana *(buddhism, hinduism)*, bliss, Zion *(Christianity)*, Valhalla *(Norse myth)*, Happy Valley, happy hunting ground *(native American legend)*, life to come, life everlasting, abode of God, Elysium *or* Elysian fields *(Greek myth)* **2 = happiness**, paradise, ecstasy, bliss, felicity, utopia, contentment, rapture, enchantment, dreamland, seventh heaven, transport, sheer bliss **3 the heavens = sky**, ether, firmament, celestial sphere, welkin *(archaic)*, empyrean *(poetic)*
heavenly *adj* **1** *(informal)* **= wonderful**, lovely, delightful, beautiful, entrancing, divine *(informal)*, glorious, exquisite, sublime, alluring, blissful, ravishing, rapturous **OPPOSITE:** awful **3 = celestial**, holy, divine, blessed, blest, immortal, supernatural, angelic, extraterrestrial, superhuman, godlike, beatific, cherubic, seraphic, supernal *(literary)*, empyrean *(poetic)*, paradisaical **OPPOSITE:** earthly
heavy *adj* **1 = weighty**, large, massive, hefty, bulky, ponderous **OPPOSITE:** light **3 = intensive**, severe, serious, concentrated, fierce, excessive, relentless **4 = considerable**, large,

DICTIONARY

a leader of the sans-culottes during the French Revolution. He was guillotined under Robespierre

Hebraic (hib-**ray**-ik) *adj* of the Hebrews or their language or culture

Hebrew *n* **1** the ancient language of the Hebrews, revived as the official language of Israel **2** a member of an ancient Semitic people; an Israelite ▷*adj* **3** of the Hebrews or their language
WORD ORIGIN Hebrew *'ibhrī* one from beyond (the river)

heck *interj* a mild exclamation of surprise, irritation, etc.
WORD ORIGIN euphemistic for *hell*

heckle *vb* **-ling, -led** to interrupt (a public speaker) with comments, questions, or taunts **heckler** *n*
WORD ORIGIN form of *hackle*

h

hectare *n* a unit of measure equal to one hundred ares (10 000 square metres or 2.471 acres)
WORD ORIGIN French

hectic ❶ *adj* involving a lot of rushed activity
WORD ORIGIN Greek *hektikos* hectic, consumptive

hector *vb* **1** to bully or torment ▷*n* **2** a blustering bully
WORD ORIGIN after *Hector*, legendary Trojan warrior

he'd he had *or* he would

hedge ❶ *n* **1** a row of shrubs or bushes forming a boundary **2** a barrier or protection against something, esp. against the risk of loss on an investment ▷*vb* **hedging, hedged** **3** to avoid making a decision by making noncommittal statements **4 hedge against** to guard against the risk of loss in (a bet or disagreement), by supporting the opposition as well
WORD ORIGIN Old English *hecg*

hedgehog *n* a small mammal with a protective covering of spines

hedgerow *n* a hedge of shrubs or low trees bordering a field

hedge sparrow *n* a small brownish songbird

hedonism *n* the doctrine that the pursuit of pleasure is the most important thing in life **hedonist** *n* **hedonistic** *adj*
WORD ORIGIN Greek *hēdonē* pleasure

heebie-jeebies *pl n* **the heebie-jeebies** *slang* nervous apprehension
WORD ORIGIN coined by W. De Beck, cartoonist

heed ❶ *formal n* **1** careful attention: *he must have taken heed of her warning* ▷*vb* **2** to pay close attention to (a warning or piece of advice)
WORD ORIGIN Old English *hēdan*

heedless *adj* taking no notice; careless or thoughtless **heedlessly** *adv*

heehaw *interj* a representation of the braying sound of a donkey

heel[1] ❶ *n* **1** the back part of the foot **2** the part of a stocking or sock designed to fit the heel **3** the part of a shoe supporting the heel **4** *slang* a contemptible person **5 at one's heels** following closely behind one **6 down at heel** untidy and in poor condition **7 take to one's heels** to run off **8 kick** *or* **cool one's heels** to be kept waiting **9 to heel** under control, such as a dog walking by a person's heel ▷*vb* **10** to repair or replace the heel of (a shoe or boot)
WORD ORIGIN Old English *hēla*

heel[2] *vb* to lean to one side
WORD ORIGIN Old English *hieldan*

heelball *n* **a** a mixture of beeswax and lampblack used by shoemakers **b** a similar substance used to take brass rubbings

heeler *n* *Austral & NZ* a dog that herds cattle by biting at their heels

hefty ❶ *adj* **heftier, heftiest** *informal* **1** large in size, weight, or amount **2** forceful and vigorous: *a hefty slap on the back* **3** involving a large amount of money: *a hefty fine*

hegemony (hig-**em**-on-ee) *n, pl* **-nies** domination of one state, country, or class within a group of others
WORD ORIGIN Greek *hēgemonia*

Hegira *n* the flight of Mohammed from Mecca to Medina in 622 AD, regarded as being the starting point of the Muslim era
WORD ORIGIN Arabic *hijrah* flight

Heidegger *n* **Martin** 1889–1976, German existentialist philosopher: he expounded his ontological system in *Being and Time* (1927)

heifer (**hef**-fer) *n* a young cow
WORD ORIGIN Old English *heahfore*

Heifetz *n* **Jascha** 1901–87, US violinist, born in Russia

height ❶ *n* **1** the vertical distance from the bottom of something to the top **2** the vertical distance of a place above sea level **3** relatively great distance from bottom to top **4** the topmost point; summit **5** the period of greatest intensity: *the height of the shelling* **6** an extreme example: *the height of luxury* **7 heights** extremes: *dizzy heights of success*
WORD ORIGIN Old English *hīehthu*

heighten ❶ *vb* to make or become higher or more intense **heightened** *adj*

height of land *n* *US & Canad* a ridge of high ground dividing two river basins

Heine *n* **Heinrich** 1797–1856, German poet and essayist, whose chief poetic work is *Das Buch der Lieder* (1827). Many of his poems have been set to music, notably by Schubert and Schumann

Heinkel *n* **Ernst Heinrich** 1888–1958, German aircraft designer. His company provided many military aircraft in World Wars I and II, including the first jet-powered plane

heinous *adj* evil and shocking
WORD ORIGIN Old French *haineus*

heir ❶ *n* the person legally succeeding to the property of a deceased person **heiress** *fem n*
WORD ORIGIN Latin *heres*

heir apparent *n, pl* **heirs apparent** **1** *law* a person whose right to succeed to certain property cannot

THESAURUS

huge, substantial, abundant, copious, profuse **OPPOSITE:** slight

hectic *adj* **= frantic**, chaotic, frenzied, heated, wild, excited, furious, fevered, animated, turbulent, flurrying, frenetic, boisterous, feverish, tumultuous, flustering, riotous, rumbustious
OPPOSITE: peaceful

hedge *vb* **3 = prevaricate**, evade, sidestep, duck, dodge, flannel (*Brit informal*), waffle (*informal, chiefly Brit*), quibble, beg the question, pussyfoot (*informal*), equivocate, temporize, be noncommittal
4 hedge against something = protect, insure, guard, safeguard, shield, cover, fortify

heed (*formal*) *n* **1 = thought**, care, mind, note, attention, regard, respect, notice, consideration, watchfulness **OPPOSITE:** disregard ▷*vb* **2 = pay attention to**, listen to, take notice of, follow, mark, mind, consider, note, regard, attend, observe, obey, bear in mind, be guided by, take to heart, give ear to
OPPOSITE: ignore

heel[1] *n* **4** (*slang*) **= swine**, cad (*Brit informal*), scoundrel, scally (*Northwest English dialect*), bounder (*Brit old-fashioned, slang*), rotter (*slang, chiefly Brit*), scumbag (*slang*), blackguard, wrong 'un (*Austral slang*)

hefty *adj* **1 = big**, strong, massive, strapping, robust, muscular, burly, husky (*informal*), hulking, beefy (*informal*), brawny **OPPOSITE:** small

height *n* **1, 2 = altitude**, measurement, highness, elevation, tallness
OPPOSITE: depth
3 = tallness, stature, highness, loftiness **OPPOSITE:** shortness
4 = peak, top, hill, mountain, crown, summit, crest, pinnacle, elevation, apex, apogee, vertex **OPPOSITE:** valley
5 = culmination, climax, zenith, limit, maximum, ultimate, extremity, uttermost, ne plus ultra (*Latin*), utmost degree **OPPOSITE:** low point

heighten *vb* **= intensify**, increase, add to, improve, strengthen, enhance, sharpen, aggravate, magnify, amplify, augment

heir *n* **= successor**, beneficiary, inheritor, heiress (*fem.*), scion, next

DICTIONARY

be defeated **2** a person whose succession to a role or position is extremely likely: *heir apparent to the England captaincy*
heirloom *n* an object that has been in a family for generations
WORD ORIGIN HEIR + *lome* tool
heir presumptive *n property law* a person who expects to succeed to an estate but whose right may be defeated by the birth of an heir nearer in blood to the ancestor
heist *n slang* a robbery
WORD ORIGIN from HOIST
Heitler *n* **Walter** 1904–81, German physicist, noted for his work on chemical bonds
held *vb* ▸ the past of **hold**[1]
Helena[1] *n* a city in W Montana: the state capital. Pop: 26 718 (2003 est)
Helena[2] *n* **Saint** ?248–?328 AD, Roman empress, mother of Constantine I. After converting to Christianity (313) she made a pilgrimage to the Holy Land (?326) where she supposedly discovered the cross on which Christ died. Feast day: May 21
helical *adj* of or like a helix
helicopter *n* an aircraft, powered by rotating overhead blades, that is capable of hovering, vertical flight, and horizontal flight in any direction
WORD ORIGIN Greek *helix* spiral + *pteron* wing
Heliogabalus *or* **Elagabalus** *n* original name *Varius Avitus Bassianus.* ?204–222 AD, Roman emperor (218–222). His reign was notorious for debauchery and extravagance
heliograph *n* an instrument with mirrors and a shutter used for sending messages in Morse code by reflecting the sun's rays
WORD ORIGIN Greek *hēlios* sun + -GRAPHY
heliotrope *n* a plant with small fragrant purple flowers
WORD ORIGIN Greek *hēlios* sun + *trepein* to turn
heliport *n* an airport for helicopters
WORD ORIGIN *heli(copter)* + *port*
helium (heel-ee-um) *n chem* a very light colourless odourless inert gas. Symbol: He
WORD ORIGIN Greek *hēlios* sun, because first detected in the solar spectrum
helix (heel-iks) *n, pl* **helices** (hell-iss-seez) *or* **helixes** a spiral
WORD ORIGIN Greek: spiral
hell ❶ *n* **1** (in Christianity and some other religions) the place or state of eternal punishment of the wicked after death **2** (in various religions and cultures) the abode of the spirits of the dead **3** *informal* a situation that causes suffering or extreme difficulty: *war is hell* **4 come hell or high water** *informal* whatever difficulties may arise **5 for the hell of it** *informal* for the fun of it **6 from hell** *informal* denoting a person or thing that is particularly bad or alarming: *the neighbour from hell* **7 give someone hell** *informal* **a** to give someone a severe reprimand or punishment **b** to be a torment to someone **8 hell for leather** at great speed **9 the hell** *informal* **a** used for emphasis: *what the hell* **b** an expression of strong disagreement: *the hell you do!* ▹ *interj* **10** *informal* an exclamation of anger or surprise
WORD ORIGIN Old English
he'll he will *or* he shall
hellbent *adj informal* rashly intent: *hellbent on revenge*
hellebore *n* a plant with white flowers that bloom in winter
WORD ORIGIN Greek *helleboros*
Hellene *n* a Greek
Hellenic *adj* **1** of the Greeks or their language **2** of or relating to ancient Greece during the classical period (776–323 BC)
Hellenism *n* **1** the principles and ideals of classical Greek civilization **2** the spirit or national character of the Greeks **Hellenist** *n*
Hellenistic *adj* of Greek civilization during the period 323–30 BC
Heller *n* **Joseph** 1923–99, US novelist. His works include *Catch 22* (1961), *God Knows* (1984), *Picture This* (1988), and *Closing Time* (1994)
hellfire *n* the torment of hell, imagined as eternal fire
hellish *adj informal* very unpleasant
Hellman *n* **Lillian** 1905–84, US dramatist. Her works include the plays *The Little Foxes* (1939), *The Searching Wind* (1944), and the autobiographical *Scoundrel Time* (1976)
hello ❶, **hallo** *or* **hullo** *interj* **1** an expression of greeting or surprise **2** a call used to attract attention ▹ *n, pl* **-los 3** the act of saying 'hello'
WORD ORIGIN French *holà*
Hell's Angel *n* a member of a motorcycle gang noted for their lawless behaviour
helm ❶ *n* **1** *naut* the tiller or wheel for steering a ship **2 at the helm** in a position of leadership or control **helmsman** *n*
WORD ORIGIN Old English *helma*
helmet *n* a piece of protective headgear worn by motorcyclists, soldiers, policemen, divers, etc.
WORD ORIGIN Old French
Helmholtz *n* Baron **Hermann Ludwig Ferdinand von** 1821–94, German physiologist, physicist, and mathematician: helped to found the theory of the conservation of energy; invented the ophthalmoscope (1850); and investigated the mechanics of sight and sound
Helmont *n* **Jean Baptiste van** 1577–1644, Flemish chemist and physician. He was the first to distinguish gases and claimed to have coined the word *gas*
Héloïse *n* ?1101–64, pupil, mistress, and wife of Abelard
helot *n* (in ancient Greece) a serf or slave
WORD ORIGIN Greek *Heilōtes* serfs, literally: inhabitants of Helos
help ❶ *vb* **1** to assist (someone to do something) **2** to contribute to: *to help Latin America's economies* **3** to improve a situation: *a felt or rubber underlay will help* **4 a** to refrain from: *I couldn't help feeling foolish* **b** to be responsible for: *you must not blame him, he simply can't help it* **5** to serve (a customer) **6 help oneself** to take something, esp. food or drink, for oneself, without being served ▹ *n* **7** the act of helping **8** a person or thing that helps, esp. a farm worker or domestic servant **9** a remedy: *there's no help for it* ▹ *interj* **10** used to call for assistance ▸ See also **help out** > **helper** *n*
WORD ORIGIN Old English *helpan*

THESAURUS

in line, inheritress *or* inheritrix *(fem.)*
hell *n* **1, 2 = the underworld**, the abyss, Hades *(Greek myth)*, hellfire, the inferno, fire and brimstone, the bottomless pit, Gehenna *(new testament, judaism)*, the nether world, the lower world, Tartarus *(Greek myth)*, the infernal regions, the bad fire *(informal)*, Acheron *(Greek myth)*, Abaddon, the abode of the damned **3** *(informal)* **= torment**, suffering, agony, trial, nightmare, misery, ordeal, anguish, affliction, martyrdom, wretchedness
hello *interj* **1 = hi** *(informal)*, greetings, how do you do?, good morning, good evening, good afternoon, welcome, kia ora *(NZ)*, gidday *or* g'day *(Austral & NZ)*
helm *n* **1** *(nautical)* **= tiller**, wheel, rudder, steering gear
help *vb* **1, 2 = aid**, back, support, second, encourage, promote, assist, relieve, stand by, befriend, cooperate with, abet, lend a hand, succour, lend a helping hand, give someone a leg up *(informal)*
OPPOSITE: hinder
3 = improve, ease, heal, cure, relieve, remedy, facilitate, alleviate, mitigate, ameliorate
OPPOSITE: make worse
4a = resist, refrain from, avoid, control, prevent, withstand, eschew, keep from, abstain from, forbear ▹ *n*
7 = assistance, aid, support, service, advice, promotion, guidance, cooperation, helping hand
OPPOSITE: hindrance

DICTIONARY

helpful ⓘ *adj* giving help **helpfully** *adv* **helpfulness** *n*
helping ⓘ *n* a single portion of food
helpless ⓘ *adj* **1** unable to manage independently **2** made weak: *it reduced her to helpless laughter* **helplessly** *adv* **helplessness** *n*
helpline *n* a telephone line set aside for callers to contact an organization for help with a problem
helpmate *or* **helpmeet** *n* a companion and helper, esp. a husband or wife
help out *vb* to assist (someone) by sharing the burden or cost of something
helter-skelter *adj* **1** hurried or disorganized ▹ *adv* **2** in a hurried or disorganized manner ▹ *n* **3** *Brit* a high spiral slide at a fairground
WORD ORIGIN probably imitative
Helvétius *n* **Claude Adrien** 1715–71, French philosopher. In his chief work *De l'Esprit* (1758), he asserted that the mainspring of human action is self-interest and that differences in human intellects are due only to differences in education
hem[1] ⓘ *n* **1** the bottom edge of a garment, folded under and stitched down ▹ *vb* **hemming, hemmed 2** to provide (a garment) with a hem ▸ See also **hem in**
WORD ORIGIN Old English *hemm*
hem[2] *n* **1** a representation of the sound of clearing the throat, used to gain attention ▹ *vb* **hemming, hemmed 2** to make this sound **3 hem and haw** ▸ see **haw**[2]
he-man *n, pl* **-men** *informal* a strong man, esp. one who shows off his strength
hemi- *prefix* half: *hemisphere*
WORD ORIGIN Greek
hem in *vb* to surround and prevent from moving
hemipterous *or* **hemipteran** *adj* of an order of insects with sucking or piercing mouthparts
WORD ORIGIN Greek *hēmi* half + *pteron* wing
hemisphere *n* one half of a sphere, esp. of the earth (**northern** and **southern hemisphere**) or of the brain **hemispherical** *adj*
hemline *n* the level to which the hem of a skirt or dress hangs: *the hemline debate*
hemlock *n* a poisonous drug derived from a plant with spotted stems and small white flowers
WORD ORIGIN Old English *hymlic*
hemp *n* **1** an Asian plant with tough fibres **2** the fibre of this plant, used to make canvas and rope **3** a narcotic drug obtained from this plant **hempen** *adj*
WORD ORIGIN Old English *hænep*
hen *n* the female of any bird, esp. the domestic fowl
WORD ORIGIN Old English *henn*
henbane *n* a poisonous plant with sticky hairy leaves
hence ⓘ *adv* **1** for this reason; therefore **2** from this time: *two weeks hence* **3** *archaic* from here
WORD ORIGIN Old English *hionane*
henceforth *or* **henceforward** *adv* from now on
henchman *n, pl* **-men** a person employed by someone powerful to carry out orders
WORD ORIGIN Middle English *hengestman*
Henderson *n* **Arthur** 1863–1935, British Labour politician. As foreign secretary (1929–31) he supported the League of Nations and international disarmament; Nobel peace prize 1934
Hendry *n* **Stephen** born 1969, British snooker player: world champion 1990, 1992–96, and 1999
henge *n* a circular monument, often containing a circle of stones, dating from the Neolithic and Bronze Ages
WORD ORIGIN from *Stonehenge*
Hengist *n* died ?488 AD, a leader, with his brother Horsa, of the first Jutish settlers in Britain; he is thought to have conquered Kent (?455)
Henie *n* **Sonja** 1912–69, Norwegian figure-skater
henna *n* **1** a reddish dye, obtained from a shrub or tree of Asia and N Africa which is used to colour hair ▹ *vb* **2** to dye (the hair) with henna
WORD ORIGIN Arabic *hinnā'*
hen night *n* *informal* a party for women only, esp. held for a woman shortly before she is married
hen party *n* *informal* a party at which only women are present
henpecked *adj* (of a man) harassed by the persistent nagging of his wife
Henrietta Maria *n* 1609–69, queen of England (1625–49), the wife of Charles I; daughter of Henry IV of France. Her Roman Catholicism contributed to the unpopularity of the crown in the period leading to the Civil War
henry *n, pl* **-ry, -ries** *or* **-rys** the SI unit of electric inductance
WORD ORIGIN after Joseph *Henry*, physicist
Henry *n* **1 Joseph** 1797–1878, US physicist. He discovered the principle of electromagnetic induction independently of Faraday and constructed the first electromagnetic motor (1829). He also discovered self-induction and the oscillatory nature of electric discharges (1842) **2 Patrick** 1736–99, American statesman and orator, a leading opponent of British rule during the War of American Independence **3 Prince,** known as **Harry** born 1984, second son of Charles, Prince of Wales, and Diana, Princess of Wales
Henryson *n* **Robert** ?1430–?1506, Scottish poet. His works include *Testament of Cresseid* (1593), a sequel to Chaucer's *Troilus and Cressida*, the 13 *Moral Fables of Esope the Phrygian*, and the pastoral dialogue *Robene and Makyne*
Henry the Lion *n* ?1129–95, duke of Saxony (1142–81). His ambitions led to conflict with the Holy Roman Emperors, notably Frederick Barbarossa
Henslowe *n* **Philip** died 1616, English theatre manager, noted also for his diary
Henze *n* **Hans Werner** born 1926, German composer, whose works, in many styles, include the operas *The Stag King* (1956), *The Bassarids* (1965), *The English Cat* (1983), and *Das verratene Meer* (1990) and the oratorio *The Raft of the Medusa* (1968)
hepatic *adj* of the liver
WORD ORIGIN Greek *hēpar* liver
hepatitis *n* inflammation of the liver, causing fever, jaundice, and weakness
Hepburn *n* **1 Audrey** 1929–93, US actress, born in Belgium. Her films include *Roman Holiday* (1955), *Funny Face* (1957), and *My Fair Lady* (1964) **2 Katharine** 1907–2003, US film actress, whose films include *The Philadelphia Story* (1940), *Adam's Rib* (1949), *The African Queen* (1951), *The Lion in Winter* (1968), for which she won an Oscar, and *On Golden Pond* (1981)
Hephaestus *n* *Greek myth* the god of fire
hepta- *combining form* seven: *heptameter*
heptagon *n* *geom* a figure with seven sides **heptagonal** *adj*
WORD ORIGIN Greek *heptagōnos* having seven angles
heptathlon *n* an athletic contest for women in which athletes compete in seven different events
her *pron* **1** (refers to) a female person or animal: *he loves her* **2** (refers to) things personified as feminine, such as ships and nations ▹ *adj* **3** of,

THESAURUS

helpful *adj* **= cooperative**, accommodating, kind, caring, friendly, neighbourly, sympathetic, supportive, benevolent, considerate, beneficent
helping *n* **= portion**, serving, ration, piece, dollop (*informal*), plateful
helpless *adj* **2 = powerless**, weak, disabled, incapable, challenged, paralysed, incompetent, unfit, feeble, debilitated, impotent, infirm
OPPOSITE: powerful
hem[1] *n* **1 = edge**, border, margin, trimming, fringe
hence *adv* **1 = therefore**, thus,

DICTIONARY

belonging to, or associated with her: *her hair*
WORD ORIGIN Old English *hire*
Hera *or* **Here** *n Greek myth* the queen of the gods
Heracleides *or* **Heraclides of Pontus** *n* ?390–?322 BC, Greek astronomer and philosopher: the first to state that the earth rotates on its axis
Heraclitus *n* ?535–?475 BC, Greek philosopher, who held that fire is the primordial substance of the universe and that all things are in perpetual flux
Heraclius *n* ?575–641 AD, Byzantine emperor, who restored the Holy Cross to Jerusalem (629)
herald ⊙ *n* **1** a person who announces important news **2** *often literary* a forerunner ▹*vb* **3** to announce or signal the approach of: *his arrival was heralded by excited barking* **heraldic** *adj*
WORD ORIGIN Germanic
heraldry *n, pl* **-ries** the study of coats of arms and family trees
herb *n* **1** an aromatic plant that is used for flavouring in cookery, and in medicine **2** *bot* a seed-bearing plant whose parts above ground die back at the end of the growing season **herbal** *adj* **herby** *adj*
WORD ORIGIN Latin *herba* grass, green plants
herbaceous *adj* designating plants that are soft-stemmed rather than woody
herbaceous border *n* a flower bed that contains perennials rather than annuals
herbage *n* herbaceous plants collectively, esp. those on which animals graze
herbalist *n* a person who grows or specializes in the use of medicinal herbs
Herbert *n* **1 Edward,** 1st Baron Herbert of Cherbury 1583–1648, English philosopher and poet, noted for his deistic views **2** his brother, **George** 1593–1633, English Metaphysical poet. His chief work is *The Temple: Sacred Poems and Private Ejaculations* (1633) **3 Zbigniew,** 1924–98, Polish poet and dramatist, noted esp. for his dramatic monologues
herbicide *n* a substance used to destroy plants, esp. weeds
WORD ORIGIN Latin *herba* plant + *caedere* to kill
herbivore (her-biv-vore) *n* **1** an animal that feeds only on plants **2** *informal* a liberal or idealistic person **herbivorous** (her-biv-or-uss) *adj*
WORD ORIGIN Latin *herba* plant + *vorare* to swallow
herculean (her-kew-lee-an) *adj* **1** (of a task) requiring tremendous effort or strength **2** resembling Hercules, hero of classical myth, in strength or courage
herd ⊙ *n* **1** a large group of mammals, esp. cattle, living and feeding together **2** *often disparaging* a large group of people ▹*vb* **3** to collect or be collected into or as if into a herd
WORD ORIGIN Old English *heord*
Herder *n* **Johann Gottfried von** 1744–1803, German philosopher, critic, and poet, the leading figure in the *Sturm und Drang* movement in German literature. His chief work is *Outlines of a Philosophy of the History of Man* (1784–91)
herd instinct *n psychol* the inborn tendency to associate with others and follow the group's behaviour
herdsman *n, pl* **-men** *chiefly Brit* a man who looks after a herd of animals
here *adv* **1** in, at, or to this place, point, case, or respect: *I am pleased to be back here* **2 here and there** at several places in or throughout an area **3 here's to** a convention used in proposing a toast **4 neither here nor there** of no relevance ▹*n* **5** this place: *they leave here tonight*
WORD ORIGIN Old English *hēr*
hereabouts *or* **hereabout** *adv* in this region
hereafter *adv* **1** *formal or law* in a subsequent part of this document, matter, or case **2** at some time in the future ▹*n* **3 the hereafter** **a** life after death **b** the future
hereby *adv* (used in official statements and documents) by means of or as a result of this
hereditable *adj* ▸same as **heritable**
hereditary ⊙ *adj* **1** passed on genetically from one generation to another **2** *law* passed on to succeeding generations by inheritance
heredity (hir-red-it-ee) *n, pl* **-ties** the passing on from one generation to another of genetic factors that determine individual characteristics
WORD ORIGIN Latin *hereditas* inheritance
Hereford *n* a hardy breed of beef cattle which has a reddish body with white markings
WORD ORIGIN after *Hereford,* English city
herein *adv formal or law* in this place, matter, or document
hereinafter *adv formal or law* from this point on in this document, matter, or case
hereof *adv formal or law* of or concerning this
heresy (herr-iss-ee) *n, pl* **-sies** **1** an opinion contrary to the principles of a religion **2** any belief thought to be contrary to official or established theory
WORD ORIGIN Greek *hairein* to choose
heretic (herr-it-ik) *n* **1** *now chiefly RC church* a person who maintains beliefs contrary to the established teachings of the Church **2** a person who holds unorthodox opinions in any field **heretical** (hir-ret-ik-kl) *adj*
hereto *adv formal or law* to this place, matter, or document
heretofore *adv formal or law* until now
hereupon *adv* following immediately after this; at this stage
herewith *adv formal* together with this: *a schedule of the event is appended herewith*
Héring *n* **Ewald** 1834–1918, German physiologist and experimental psychologist who studied vision and propounded the doctrine of nativism, the policy of favouring the natives of a country over the immigrants
heritable *adj* capable of being inherited
heritage ⊙ *n* **1** something inherited at birth **2** anything that has been carried over from the past or handed down by tradition **3** the evidence of the past, such as historical sites, considered as the inheritance of present-day society
hermaphrodite (her-maf-roe-dite) *n* an animal, flower, or person that has both male and female reproductive organs **hermaphroditic** *adj*
WORD ORIGIN after *Hermaphroditus,* son of Hermes and Aphrodite, who merged with the nymph Salmacis to form one body
Hermes *n Greek myth* the messenger of the gods
hermetic *adj* sealed so as to be airtight **hermetically** *adv*
WORD ORIGIN after the Greek god *Hermes,* traditionally the inventor of a magic seal

h

THESAURUS

consequently, for this reason, in consequence, ergo, on that account
herald *n* **1 = messenger,** courier, proclaimer, announcer, crier, town crier, bearer of tidings **2** *(often literary)* **= forerunner,** sign, signal, indication, token, omen, precursor, harbinger ▹*vb* **3 = indicate,** promise, precede, pave the way, usher in, harbinger, presage, portend, foretoken
herd *n* **1, 2 = flock,** crowd, collection, mass, drove, crush, mob, swarm, horde, multitude, throng, assemblage, press
hereditary *adj* **1 = genetic,** inborn, inbred, transmissible, inheritable **2** *(law)* **= inherited,** handed down, passed down, willed, family, traditional, transmitted, ancestral, bequeathed, patrimonial
heritage *n* **1 = inheritance,** legacy, birthright, lot, share, estate, tradition, portion, endowment, bequest, patrimony

DICTIONARY

hermit *n* a person living in solitude, esp. for religious reasons **WORD ORIGIN** Greek *erēmos* lonely

hermitage *n* **1** the home of a hermit **2** any retreat

hermit crab *n* a small crab that lives in the empty shells of other shellfish

hernia *n* protrusion of an organ or part through the lining of the body cavity in which it is normally situated **WORD ORIGIN** Latin

hero ❶ *n, pl* **-roes 1** the principal male character in a novel, play, etc. **2** a man of exceptional courage, nobility, etc. **3** a man who is idealized for having superior qualities in any field **WORD ORIGIN** Greek *hērōs*

Hero[1] *n Greek myth* a priestess of Aphrodite, who killed herself when her lover Leander drowned while swimming the Hellespont to visit her

Hero[2] *or* **Heron** *n* 1st century AD, Greek mathematician and inventor

Herod Agrippa I *n* 10 BC–44 AD, king of Judaea (41–44), grandson of Herod (the Great). A friend of Caligula and Claudius, he imprisoned Saint Peter and executed Saint James

Herod Agrippa II *n* died ?93 AD, king of territories in N Palestine (50–?93 AD). He presided (60) at the trial of Saint Paul and sided with the Roman authorities in the Jewish rebellion of 66

Herodias *n* ?14 BC–?40 AD, niece and wife of Herod Antipas and mother of Salome, whom she persuaded to ask for the head of John the Baptist. Her ambition led to the banishment of her husband

heroic ❶ *adj* **1** brave and courageous: *heroic work by the army engineers* **2** of, like, or befitting a hero **heroically** *adv*

heroics *pl n* behaviour or language considered too melodramatic or extravagant for the particular situation in which they are used

heroin *n* a highly addictive drug derived from morphine **WORD ORIGIN** probably from *hero*, referring to its aggrandizing effect on the personality

heroine ❶ *n* **1** the principal female character in a novel, play, etc. **2** a woman of exceptional courage, nobility, etc. **3** a woman who is idealized for having superior qualities in any field

heroism (herr-oh-izz-um) *n* great courage and bravery

heron *n* a wading bird with a long neck, long legs, and grey or white feathers **WORD ORIGIN** Old French *hairon*

Heron *n* **1** ▸ same as **Hero 2 Patrick** 1920–99, British abstract painter and art critic

heronry *n, pl* **-ries** a colony of breeding herons

Herophilus *n* died ?280 BC, Greek anatomist in Alexandria. He was the first to distinguish sensory from motor nerves

hero worship *n* admiration for heroes or idealized people

herpes (her-peez) *n* any of several inflammatory skin diseases, including shingles and cold sores **WORD ORIGIN** Greek *herpein* to creep

herpes simplex *n* an acute viral disease causing clusters of watery blisters **WORD ORIGIN** New Latin: simple herpes

herpes zoster *n* ▸ same as **shingles** **WORD ORIGIN** New Latin: girdle herpes

Herr (hair) *n, pl* **Herren** a German form of address equivalent to *Mr* **WORD ORIGIN** German

Herrick *n* **Robert** 1591–1674, English poet. His chief work is the *Hesperides* (1648), a collection of short, delicate, sacred, and pastoral lyrics

herring *n, pl* **-rings** *or* **-ring** a food fish of northern seas, with a long silver-coloured body **WORD ORIGIN** Old English *hǣring*

herringbone *n* a zigzag pattern consisting of short lines of V shapes, used esp. in fabrics

herring gull *n* a common gull that has white feathers with black-tipped wings

Herriot *n* **1 Édouard** (edwar) 1872–1957, French Radical statesman and writer; premier (1924–25; 1932) **2 James** real name *James Alfred Wight*. 1916–95, British veterinary surgeon and writer. His books based on his experiences in Yorkshire have been adapted for television and films

hers *pron* **1** something belonging to her: *hers is the highest paid part-time job; the money which is rightfully hers* **2 of hers** belonging to her

Herschel *n* **1 Caroline Lucretia** 1750–1848, British astronomer, born in Germany, noted for her catalogue of nebulae and star clusters: sister of Sir William Herschel **2 Sir John Frederick William** 1792–1871, British astronomer. He discovered and catalogued over 525 nebulae and star clusters **3** his father, Sir (**Frederick**) **William,** original name *Friedrich Wilhelm Herschel*. 1738–1822, British astronomer, born in Germany. He constructed a reflecting telescope, which led to his discovery of the planet Uranus (1781), two of its satellites, and two of the satellites of Saturn. He also discovered the motions of binary stars

herself *pron* **1 a** the reflexive form of *she* or *her*: *she busied herself at the stove* **b** used for emphasis: *none other than The Great Mother herself* **2** her normal self: *she hasn't been herself all week*

Herts Hertfordshire

hertz *n, pl* **hertz** the SI unit of frequency, equal to one cycle per second **WORD ORIGIN** after H. R. *Hertz*, physicist

Herzen *n* **Aleksandr** (**Ivanovich**) 1812–70, Russian socialist political philosopher: best known for his autobiography *My Past and Thoughts* (1861–67)

Herzl *n* **Theodor** 1860–1904, Austrian writer, born in Hungary; founder of the Zionist movement. In *The Jewish State* (1896), he advocated resettlement of the Jews in a state of their own

Herzog *n* **1 Roman** born 1934, German politician; president of Germany (1994–99) **2 Werner** born 1942, German film director. His films include *Signs of Life* (1967), *Fata Morgana* (1970), *Fitzcarraldo* (1982), *Little Dieter Needs to Fly* (1997), and *Grizzly Man* (2005)

he's he is *or* he has

hESC human embryonic stem cell

Heseltine *n* **1 Michael** (**Ray Dibden**) Baron born 1933, British Conservative politician; secretary of state for defence (1983–86); secretary of state for the environment (1990–92); secretary of state for trade and industry (1992–95); deputy prime minister (1995–97) **2 Philip Arnold** the real name of composer Peter Warlock ▸ See **Warlock**

Hesiod *n* 8th century BC, Greek poet and the earliest author of didactic verse. His two complete extant works are the *Works and Days*, dealing with the agricultural seasons, and the *Theogony*, concerning the origin of the world and the genealogies of the gods **Hesiodic** *adj*

hesitant *adj* doubtful and unsure in speech or action **hesitancy** *n* **hesitantly** *adv*

THESAURUS

hero *n* **1 = protagonist**, leading man, lead actor, male lead, principal male character **2 = star**, champion, celebrity, victor, superstar, great man, heart-throb *(Brit)*, conqueror, exemplar, celeb *(informal)*, megastar *(informal)*, popular figure, man of the hour **3 = idol**, favourite, pin-up *(slang)*, fave *(informal)*

heroic *adj* **1 = courageous**, brave, daring, bold, fearless, gallant, intrepid, valiant, doughty, undaunted, dauntless, lion-hearted, valorous, stouthearted **OPPOSITE:** cowardly

heroine *n* **1 = protagonist**, leading lady, diva, prima donna, female lead, lead actress, principal female character **3 = idol**, favourite, pin-up

DICTIONARY

hesitate ❶ *vb* **-tating, -tated 1** to be slow and uncertain in acting **2** to be reluctant (to do something): *I hesitate to use the word 'squandered'* **3** to pause during speech because of uncertainty **hesitation** *n*
WORD ORIGIN Latin *haesitare*

Hesse[1] *n* a state of central Germany, formed in 1945 from the former Prussian province of Hesse-Nassau and part of the former state of Hesse; part of West Germany until 1990. Capital: Wiesbaden. Pop: 6 089 000 (2003 est). Area: 21 111 sq km (8151 sq miles). German name: **Hessen**

Hesse[2] *n* **Hermann** 1877–1962, German novelist, short-story writer, and poet. His novels include *Der Steppenwolf* (1927) and *Das Glasperlenspiel* (1943): Nobel prize for literature 1946

hessian *n* a coarse jute fabric similar to sacking
WORD ORIGIN after *Hesse*, Germany

hetero- *combining form* other, another, or different: *heterosexual*
WORD ORIGIN Greek *heteros* other

heterodox *adj* different from established or accepted doctrines or beliefs **heterodoxy** *n*
WORD ORIGIN HETERO- + Greek *doxa* opinion

heterodyne *electronics vb* **-dyning, -dyned 1** to combine (two alternating signals) so as to produce two signals with frequencies corresponding to the sum and the difference of the original frequencies ▷ *adj* **2** produced or operating by heterodyning two signals
WORD ORIGIN HETERO- + Greek *dunamis* power

heterogeneous (het-er-oh-**jean**-ee-uss) *adj* varied in content; composed of different parts: *a heterogeneous collection of art* **heterogeneity** *n*
WORD ORIGIN HETERO- + Greek *genos* sort

heteromorphic *adj biol* **1** differing from the normal form **2** (esp. of insects) having different forms at different stages of the life cycle **heteromorphism** *n*
WORD ORIGIN HETERO- + Greek *morphē* form

heterosexual *n* **1** a person who is sexually attracted to members of the opposite sex ▷ *adj* **2** (of a person) sexually attracted to members of the opposite sex **3** (of a sexual relationship) between a man and a woman **heterosexuality** *n*

heterozygous *adj biol* having two different alleles of the same gene
WORD ORIGIN HETERO- + Greek *zugōtos* yoked

het up *adj informal* agitated or excited: *he was very het up about the traffic*
WORD ORIGIN dialect for *heated*

heuristic (hew-**rist**-ik) *adj* (of a method of teaching) allowing students to learn things for themselves by trial and error
WORD ORIGIN Greek *heuriskein* to discover

Hevelius *n* **Johannes** 1611–87, German astronomer, who published one of the first detailed maps of the lunar surface

Hevesy *n* **Georg von** 1885–1966, Hungarian chemist. He worked on radioactive tracing and, with D. Coster, discovered the element hafnium (1923): Nobel prize for chemistry 1943

hew *vb* **hewing, hewed, hewed** *or* **hewn 1** to chop or cut with an axe **2** to carve (something) from a substance: *a tunnel hewn out of the living rock*
WORD ORIGIN Old English *hēawan*

Hewish *n* **Antony** born 1924, British radio astronomer, noted esp. for his role in the discovery of pulsars (1967): shared the Nobel prize for physics 1974

Hewitt *n* **Lleyton** born 1981, Australian tennis player; US Open champion 2001, Wimbledon singles champion 2002

hex *n* **1** ▸ short for **hexadecimal notation** ▷ *adj* **2** of or relating to hexadecimal notation: *hex code*

hexa- *combining form* six: *hexameter*
WORD ORIGIN Greek *hex* six

hexadecimal notation *n* a number system with a base of 16, the numbers 10–15 being represented by the letters A–F

hexagon *n geom* a figure with six sides **hexagonal** *adj*

hexagram *n geom* a star formed by extending the sides of a regular hexagon to meet at six points

hexameter (hek-**sam**-it-er) *n prosody* a verse line consisting of six metrical feet

hey *interj* **1** an expression of surprise or for catching attention **2 hey presto!** an exclamation used by conjurors at the climax of a trick
WORD ORIGIN imitative

heyday *n* the time of most power, popularity, or success: *the heyday of classical composition*
WORD ORIGIN probably based on *hey*

Heyer *n* **Georgette** 1902–74, British historical novelist and writer of detective stories, noted esp. for her romances of the Regency period

Heywood[1] *n* a town in NW England, in Rochdale unitary authority, Greater Manchester, near Bury. Pop: 28 024 (2001)

Heywood[2] *n* **1 John** ?1497–?1580, English dramatist, noted for his comic interludes **2 Thomas** ?1574–1641, English dramatist, noted esp. for his domestic drama *A Woman Killed with Kindness* (1607)

Hf *chem* hafnium

HFEA *Brit* Human Fertilization and Embryology Authority

Hg *chem* mercury

HGV (in Britain, formerly) heavy goods vehicle

HH 1 His (*or* Her) Highness **2** His Holiness (title of the pope)

hi *interj informal* hello
WORD ORIGIN probably from *how are you?*

HI Hawaii

hiatus (hie-**ay**-tuss) *n, pl* **-tuses** *or* **-tus** a pause or an interruption in continuity: *diplomatic relations restored after a four-year hiatus*
WORD ORIGIN Latin: gap, cleft

hiatus hernia *n* protrusion of the stomach through the diaphragm at the hole for the gullet

Hib *n* Haemophilus influenzae type b: a vaccine against a specific type of bacterial meningitis, administered to children under four years of age

hibernate *vb* **-nating, -nated** (of some animals) to pass the winter in a resting state in which heartbeat, temperature, and breathing rate are very low **hibernation** *n*
WORD ORIGIN Latin *hibernare* to spend the winter

Hibernia *n poetic* Ireland **Hibernian** *adj, n*

hibiscus *n, pl* **-cuses** a tropical plant with large brightly coloured flowers
WORD ORIGIN Greek *hibiskos* marsh mallow

hiccup *n* **1** a spasm of the breathing organs with a sharp coughlike sound **2 hiccups** the state of having such spasms **3** *informal* a minor difficulty ▷ *vb* **-cuping, -cuped** *or* **-cupping, -cupped 4** to make a hiccup or hiccups. Also: **hiccough**
WORD ORIGIN imitative

hick *n US, Austral & NZ informal* an unsophisticated country person
WORD ORIGIN after *Hick*, familiar form of *Richard*

Hickok *n* **James Butler,** known as *Wild Bill Hickok*. 1837–76, US frontiersman and marshal

hickory *n, pl* **-ries 1** a North American tree with edible nuts

h

THESAURUS

(*slang*), fave (*informal*)

hesitate *vb* **1 = waver**, delay, pause, haver (*Brit*), wait, doubt, falter, be uncertain, dither (*chiefly Brit*), vacillate, equivocate, temporize, hum and haw, shillyshally (*informal*), swither (*Scot dialect*) **OPPOSITE:** be decisive **2 = be reluctant**, be unwilling, shrink from, think twice, boggle, scruple, demur, hang back, be disinclined, balk *or* baulk **OPPOSITE:** be determined

DICTIONARY

2 the hard wood of this tree **WORD ORIGIN** Native American *pawcohiccora*

Hickox *n* **Richard** (**Sidney**) born 1948, British conductor; musical director of the City of London Sinfonia and Singers since 1971

hidden ❶ *vb* 1 ▸ a past participle of **hide**[1] ▹ *adj* 2 not easily noticed or obscure: *hidden dangers* 3 difficult to find

hidden agenda *n* a set of motives or intentions concealed from others who might object to them

hide[1] ❶ *vb* **hiding, hid, hidden** *or* **hid** 1 to conceal (oneself or an object) from view or discovery: *in an attempt to hide from his wife* 2 to keep (information or one's feelings) secret 3 to obscure or cover (something) from view: *the collar hid his face* ▹ *n* 4 *Brit* a place of concealment, disguised to appear as part of its surrounding, used by hunters, bird-watchers, etc. **WORD ORIGIN** Old English *hȳdan*

hide[2] ❶ *n* the skin of an animal, either tanned or raw **WORD ORIGIN** Old English *hȳd*

hide-and-seek *n* a game in which one player covers his or her eyes while the others hide, and that player then tries to find them

hideaway *n* a hiding place or secluded spot

hidebound *adj* restricted by petty rules and unwilling to accept new ideas

hideous ❶ (**hid**-ee-uss) *adj* extremely ugly or unpleasant **WORD ORIGIN** Old French *hisdos*

hide-out *n* a hiding place

Hideyoshi Toyotomi *n* 1536–98, Japanese military dictator (1582–98). He unified all Japan (1590)

hiding[1] *n* 1 a state of concealment: *in hiding* 2 **hiding place** a place of concealment

hiding[2] ❶ *n informal* a severe beating

hie *vb* **hieing** *or* **hying, hied** *archaic or poetic* to hurry **WORD ORIGIN** Old English *hīgian* to strive

hierarchy ❶ (**hire**-ark-ee) *n, pl* **-chies** 1 a system of people or things arranged in a graded order 2 **the hierarchy** the people in power in any organization **hierarchical** *adj* **WORD ORIGIN** Late Greek *hierarkhēs* high priest

hieroglyphic (hire-oh-**gliff**-ik) *adj* 1 of or relating to a form of writing using picture symbols, as used in ancient Egypt ▹ *n also* **hieroglyph** 2 a symbol that is difficult to decipher 3 a picture or symbol representing an object, idea, or sound **WORD ORIGIN** Greek *hieros* holy + *gluphein* to carve

hieroglyphics *n* 1 a form of writing, as used in ancient Egypt, in which pictures or symbols are used to represent objects, ideas, or sounds 2 writing that is difficult to decipher

Hieronymus *n* **Eusebius** the Latin name of Saint Jerome ▸ See **Jerome** (sense 1) > **Hieronymic** *or* **Hieronymian** *adj*

hi-fi *n informal* 1 a set of high-quality sound-reproducing equipment 2 ▸ short for **high fidelity** ▹ *adj* 3 producing high-quality sound: *a hi-fi amplifier*

Higgins *n* 1 **Alex,** known as *Hurricane Higgins*. 1949–2010, Northern Irish snooker player 2 **Jack,** real name *Harry Patterson*. born 1929, British novelist; his thrillers include *The Eagle Has Landed* (1975), *Confessional* (1985), and *Midnight Runner* (2002)

higgledy-piggledy *informal adj, adv* 1 in a muddle **WORD ORIGIN** origin unknown

high ❶ *adj* 1 being a relatively great distance from top to bottom: *a high stone wall* 2 being at a relatively great distance above sea level: *a high village* 3 being a specified distance from top to bottom: *three feet high* 4 coming up to a specified level: *waist-high* 5 being at its peak: *high summer* 6 of greater than average height: *a high ceiling* 7 greater than usual in intensity or amount: *high blood pressure; high fees* 8 (of a sound) acute in pitch 9 (of food) slightly decomposed, regarded as enhancing the flavour of game 10 towards the top of a scale of importance or quality: *high fashion* 11 intensely emotional: *high drama* 12 very cheerful: *high spirits* 13 *informal* under the influence of alcohol or drugs 14 luxurious or extravagant: *high life* 15 advanced in complexity: *high finance* 16 formal and elaborate: *High Mass* 17 **high and dry** abandoned in a difficult situation 18 **high and mighty** *informal* too confident and full of self-importance 19 **high opinion** a favourable opinion ▹ *adv* 20 at or to a height: *flying high* ▹ *n* 21 a high level 22 ▸ same as **anticyclone** 23 **on a high** *informal* **a** in a state of intoxication by alcohol or drugs **b** in a state of great excitement and happiness **WORD ORIGIN** Old English *hēah*

High Arctic *n* the regions of Canada, esp. the northern islands, within the Arctic Circle

highball *n chiefly US* a long iced drink consisting of whisky with soda water or ginger ale

highbrow *often disparaging adj* 1 concerned with serious, intellectual subjects ▹ *n* 2 a person with such tastes

highchair *n* a long-legged chair with a table-like tray, used for a child at meal times

High Church *n* 1 the movement within the Church of England stressing the importance of ceremony and ritual ▹ *adj* **High-**

THESAURUS

hidden *adj* 2 = **secret**, veiled, dark, mysterious, obscure, mystical, mystic, shrouded, occult, latent, cryptic, ulterior, abstruse, recondite, hermetic, hermetical 3 = **concealed**, covered, secret, covert, unseen, clandestine, secreted, under wraps, unrevealed

hide[1] *vb* 1a = **conceal**, stash (*informal*), secrete, cache, put out of sight **OPPOSITE:** display
1b = **go into hiding**, take cover, keep out of sight, hole up, lie low, go underground, go to ground, go to earth 2 = **keep secret**, suppress, withhold, keep quiet about, hush up, draw a veil over, keep dark, keep under your hat **OPPOSITE:** disclose
3 = **obscure**, cover, screen, bury, shelter, mask, disguise, conceal, eclipse, veil, cloak, shroud, camouflage, blot out **OPPOSITE:** reveal

hide[2] *n* = **skin**, fell, leather, pelt

hideous *adj* = **ugly**, revolting, ghastly, monstrous, grotesque, gruesome, grisly, unsightly, repulsive **OPPOSITE:** beautiful

hiding[2] *n* (*informal*) = **beating**, whipping, thrashing, tanning (*slang*), caning, licking (*informal*), flogging, spanking, walloping (*informal*), drubbing, lathering (*informal*), whaling, larruping (*Brit dialect*)

hierarchy *n* 1 = **grading**, ranking, social order, pecking order, class system, social stratum

high *adj* 1, 6 = **tall**, towering, soaring, steep, elevated, lofty **OPPOSITE:** short
7 = **extreme**, great, acute, severe, extraordinary, excessive **OPPOSITE:** low
8 = **high-pitched**, piercing, shrill, penetrating, treble, soprano, strident, sharp, acute, piping **OPPOSITE:** deep
10 = **important**, leading, ruling, chief, powerful, significant, distinguished, prominent, superior, influential, notable, big-time (*informal*), eminent, major league (*informal*), exalted, consequential, skookum (*Canad*) **OPPOSITE:** lowly
13 (*informal*) = **intoxicated**, stoned (*slang*), spaced out (*slang*), tripping (*informal*), turned on (*slang*), on a trip (*informal*), delirious, euphoric, freaked out (*informal*), hyped up (*slang*), zonked (*slang*), inebriated ▹ *adv* 20 = **way up**, aloft, far up, to a great height

high-flown *adj* = **extravagant**,

DICTIONARY

Church **2** of or relating to this movement
high commissioner *n* the senior diplomatic representative sent by one Commonwealth country to another
high country *n* **the high country** NZ sheep pastures in the foothills of the Southern Alps
High Court *n* (in England, Wales, Australia, and New Zealand) the supreme court dealing with civil and criminal law cases
high-energy *adj* providing or inspiring a lot of energy: *a high-energy drink; a high-energy workout*
Higher *n* **1** (in Scotland) the advanced level of the Scottish Certificate of Education **2** a pass in a subject at this level: *she has got four Highers*
higher education *n* education and training at colleges, universities, and polytechnics
higher-up *n informal* a person of higher rank
highest common factor *n* the largest number that divides equally into each member of a group of numbers
high explosive *n* an extremely powerful chemical explosive, such as TNT or gelignite
highfalutin (hie-fa-**loot**-in) *adj informal* (of behaviour) excessively grand or pompous
WORD ORIGIN *-falutin* perhaps variant of *fluting*
high fidelity *n* **1** the electronic reproduction of sound with little or no distortion ▷ *adj* **high-fidelity** **2** able to produce sound with little or no distortion: *high-fidelity stereo earphones*
high-five *n slang* a gesture of greeting or congratulation in which two people slap raised palms together
high-flown **T** *adj* extravagant or pretentious: *high-flown language*
high-flyer *or* **high-flier** *n* **1** a person who is extremely ambitious **2** a person of great ability in a career **high-flying** *adj, n*
high frequency *n* a radio frequency between 30 and 3 megahertz
High German *n* the standard German language
high-handed *adj* using authority in an unnecessarily forceful way **high-handedness** *n*
high jump *n* **the high jump** **a** an athletic event in which competitors have to jump over a high bar **b** *Austral & Brit informal* a severe reprimand or punishment: *I was for the high jump again*
Highland *adj* of or denoting the Highlands, a mountainous region of NW Scotland **Highlander** *n*
Highland cattle *n* a breed of cattle with shaggy reddish-brown hair and long horns
Highland fling *n* an energetic Scottish solo dance
highlands *pl n* relatively high ground
high-level language *n* a computer programming language that is close to human language
highlight **T** *n* **1** Also called: **high spot** the most exciting or memorable part of something **2** an area of the lightest tone in a painting or photograph **3** a lightened streak in the hair produced by bleaching ▷ *vb* **4** to give emphasis to: *the prime minister repeatedly highlighted the need for lower pay*
highlighter *n* **1** a cosmetic cream or powder applied to the face to highlight the cheekbones or eyes **2** a fluorescent felt-tip pen used as a marker to emphasize a section of text without obscuring it
highly **T** *adv* **1** extremely: *highly desirable* **2** towards the top of a scale of importance, admiration, or respect: *highly paid doctors*
highly strung *or US & Canad* **high-strung** *adj* tense and easily upset
high-maintenance *adj* **1** (of a piece of equipment, motor vehicle, etc.) requiring regular maintenance to keep it in working order **2** *informal* (of a person) requiring a high level of care and attention; demanding
High Mass *n* a solemn and elaborate Mass
high-minded *adj* having high moral principles
Highness *n* (preceded by *Your, His* or *Her*) a title used to address or refer to a royal person
high-octane *adj* **1** (of petrol) having a high octane number **2** *informal* dynamic or intense: *a high-octane lifestyle*
high-pitched *adj* (of a sound, esp. a voice) pitched high in tone
high-powered *adj* **1** (of machinery or equipment) powerful, advanced, and sophisticated **2** important, successful, or influential: *a high-powered business contact*
high-pressure *adj informal* (of selling) persuasive in an aggressive and persistent manner
high priest *n* the head of a cult or movement **high priestess** *fem n*
high-rise *adj* **1** of or relating to a building that has many storeys: *a high-rise estate* ▷ *n* **2** a building that has many storeys
high-risk *adj* denoting a group or area that is particularly subject to a danger
highroad *n* a main road
high school *n* a secondary school
high seas *pl n* the open seas, which are outside the authority of any one nation
high season *n* the most popular time of year at a holiday resort, etc.
Highsmith *n* **Patricia** 1921–95, US author of crime fiction. Her novels include *Strangers on a Train* (1950) and *Ripley's Game* (1974)
high-spirited *adj* lively and wishing to have fun and excitement
high tea *n Brit* an early evening meal consisting of a cooked dish, bread, cakes, and tea
high-tech *adj* ▸ same as **hi-tech**
high technology *n* any type of sophisticated industrial process, esp. one involving electronics
high-tension *adj* (of electricity cable) carrying a powerful current
high tide *n* the sea at its highest level on the coast
high time *adv informal* the latest possible time: *it was high time she got married*
high treason *n* a serious crime directly affecting a sovereign or state
high-water mark *n* **1** the level reached by sea water at high tide or a river in flood **2** the highest or most successful stage: *the premature high-water mark of his career*
highway *n* **1** a public road that everyone may use **2** *US, Canad, Austral & NZ* a main road, esp. one that connects towns
Highway Code *n* (in Britain) a booklet of regulations and recommendations for all road users
highwayman *n, pl* **-men** (formerly) a robber, usually on horseback, who held up travellers on public roads
hijack **T** *vb* **1** to seize control of or divert (a vehicle or aircraft) while travelling ▷ *n* **2** an instance of hijacking: *Indonesian ferry hijack ends*
hijacker *n*
WORD ORIGIN origin unknown

h

THESAURUS

elaborate, pretentious, exaggerated, inflated, lofty, grandiose, overblown, florid, high-falutin *(informal)*, arty-farty *(informal)*, magniloquent **OPPOSITE:** straightforward
highlight *n* **1 = high point**, peak, climax, feature, focus, best part, focal point, main feature, high spot, memorable part **OPPOSITE:** low point ▷ *vb* **4 = emphasize**, stress, accent, feature, set off, show up, underline, spotlight, play up, accentuate, flag, foreground, focus attention on, call attention to, give prominence to, bring to the fore **OPPOSITE:** play down
highly *adv* **1 = extremely**, very, greatly, seriously *(informal)*, vastly, exceptionally, extraordinarily, immensely, decidedly, tremendously, supremely, eminently
hijack *vb* **1 = seize**, take over, commandeer, expropriate, skyjack

DICTIONARY

hike ⓣ *vb* **hiking, hiked 1** to walk a long way in the country, usually for pleasure **2** to raise (prices) **3** to pull up with a quick movement: *he hiked up his trouser legs* ▷ *n* **4** a long walk **5** a rise in price **hiker** *n*
WORD ORIGIN origin unknown

hilarious ⓣ *adj* very funny **hilariously** *adv* **hilarity** *n*
WORD ORIGIN Greek *hilaros* cheerful

Hilbert *n* **David** 1862–1943, German mathematician, who made outstanding contributions to the theories of number fields and invariants and to geometry

Hildebrand *n* ▸ the monastic name of **Gregory VII** > **Hildebrandian** *adj, n* **Hildebrandine** *adj*

hill ⓣ *n* **1** a natural elevation of the earth's surface, less high than a mountain **2** a heap or mound **3** an incline or slope **hilly** *adj*
WORD ORIGIN Old English *hyll*

Hill *n* **1 Archibald Vivian** 1886–1977, British biochemist, noted for his research into heat loss in muscle contraction: shared the Nobel prize for physiology or medicine (1922) **2 Damon Graham Devereux,** son of Graham Hill. born 1960, British motor-racing driver; Formula One world champion (1996) **3 David Octavius** 1802–70, Scottish painter and portrait photographer, noted esp. for his collaboration with the chemist Robert Adamson (1821–48) **4 Geoffrey** (**William**) born 1932, British poet: his books include *King Log* (1968), *Mercian Hymns* (1971), *The Mystery of the Charity of Charles Péguy* (1983), and *The Orchards of Syon* (2002) **5 Graham** 1929–75, British motor-racing driver: world champion (1962, 1968) **6 Octavia** 1838–1912, British housing reformer; a founder of the National Trust **7** Sir **Rowland** 1795–1879, British originator of the penny postage **8 Susan** (**Elizabeth**) born 1942, British novelist and writer of short stories: her books include *I'm the King of the Castle* (1970) *The Woman in Black* (1983), and *Felix Derby* (2002)

hillbilly *n, pl* **-lies 1** *usually disparaging* an unsophisticated person from the mountainous areas in the southeastern US **2** ▸ same as **country and western**
WORD ORIGIN *hill* + *Billy* (the nickname)

Hillel *n* ?60 BC–?9 AD, rabbi, born in Babylonia; president of the Sanhedrin. He was the first to formulate principles of biblical interpretation

Hiller *n* Dame **Wendy** 1912–2003, British actress. Her many films include *Pygmalion* (1938), *Major Barbara* (1940), and *Separate Tables* (1958)

Hilliard *n* **Nicholas** 1537–1619, English miniaturist, esp. of portraits

hillock *n* a small hill or mound

hilt *n* **1** the handle or shaft of a sword, dagger, or knife **2 to the hilt** to the full: *he plays the role to the hilt*
WORD ORIGIN Old English

Hilton *n* **Walter** died 1396, English mystical writer: author of *The Scale of Perfection*

hilum *n, pl* **-la** *bot* a scar on a seed marking its point of attachment to the seed vessel
WORD ORIGIN Latin: trifle

him *pron* refers to a male person or animal: *I greeted him at the hotel; I must send him a note of congratulation*
WORD ORIGIN Old English

himself *pron* **1 a** the reflexive form of *he* or *him*: *he secretly asked himself* **b** used for emphasis: *approved of by the Creator himself* **2** his normal self: *he was almost himself again*

hind[1] *adj* **hinder, hindmost** situated at the back: *a hind leg*
WORD ORIGIN Old English *hindan* at the back

hind[2] *n, pl* **hinds** *or* **hind** the female of the deer, esp. the red deer
WORD ORIGIN Old English

Hindemith *n* **Paul** (paul) 1895–1963, German composer and musical theorist, who opposed the twelve-tone technique. His works include the song cycle *Das Marienleben* (1923) and the opera *Mathis der Maler* (1938)

hinder[1] ⓣ *vb* to get in the way of (someone or something)
WORD ORIGIN Old English *hindrian*

hinder[2] *adj* situated at the back
WORD ORIGIN Old English

Hindi *n* **1** a language or group of dialects of N central India **2** a formal literary dialect of this language, the official language of India
WORD ORIGIN Old Persian *Hindu* the river Indus

hindmost *adj* furthest back; last

hindquarters *pl n* the rear of a four-legged animal

hindrance *n* **1** an obstruction or snag **2** the act of hindering

hindsight *n* the ability to understand, after something has happened, what should have been done or what caused the event

Hindu *n, pl* **-dus 1** a person who practises Hinduism ▷ *adj* **2** of Hinduism

Hinduism *n* the dominant religion of India, which involves the worship of many gods and belief in reincarnation

Hindustani *n* a group of northern Indian languages that includes Hindi and Urdu

Hines *n* **Earl,** known as *Earl "Fatha" Hines*. 1905–83, US jazz pianist, conductor, and songwriter

hinge *n* **1** a device for holding together two parts, such as a door and its frame, so that one can swing freely ▷ *vb* **hinging, hinged 2** to join or open (something) by means of a hinge **3 hinge on** to depend on: *billions of dollars of western aid hinged on the outcome of the talks* **hinged** *adj*
WORD ORIGIN probably Germanic

Hinglish *n* a variety of English incorporating elements of Hindi
WORD ORIGIN blend of HINDI + ENGLISH

hinny *n, pl* **-nies** the offspring of a male horse and a female donkey
WORD ORIGIN Greek *hinnos*

Hinshelwood *n* Sir **Cyril Norman** 1897–1967, English chemist, who shared the Nobel prize for chemistry (1956) for the study of reaction kinetics

hint ⓣ *n* **1** a suggestion given in an indirect or subtle manner **2** a helpful piece of advice **3** a small amount: *a hint of irony* ▷ *vb* **4** (sometimes foll. by *at*) to suggest indirectly: *a solution has been hinted at by a few politicians*
WORD ORIGIN origin unknown

hinterland *n* **1** land lying behind a coast or the shore of a river **2** an area near and dependent on a large city, esp. a port
WORD ORIGIN German *hinter* behind + LAND

THESAURUS

hike *vb* **1 = walk**, march, trek, ramble, tramp, leg it *(informal)*, back-pack, hoof it *(slang)* ▷ *n* **4 = walk**, march, trek, ramble, tramp, traipse, journey on foot

hilarious *adj* **= funny**, entertaining, amusing, hysterical, humorous, exhilarating, comical, side-splitting

hill *n* **1 = mount**, down *(archaic)*, fell, height, mound, prominence, elevation, eminence, hilltop, tor, knoll, hillock, brae *(Scot)*, kopje *or* koppie *(S African)*

hinder[1] *vb* **= obstruct**, stop, check, block, prevent, arrest, delay, oppose, frustrate, handicap, interrupt, slow down, deter, hamstring, hamper, thwart, retard, impede, hobble, stymie, encumber, throw a spanner in the works, trammel, hold up *or* back **OPPOSITE:** help

hint *n* **1 = clue**, mention, suggestion, implication, indication, reminder, tip-off, pointer, allusion, innuendo, inkling, intimation, insinuation, word to the wise **2 = advice**, help, tip(s), suggestion(s), pointer(s) **3 = trace**, touch, suggestion, taste, breath, dash, whisper, suspicion, tinge, whiff, speck, undertone, soupçon *(French)* ▷ *vb* **4** *(sometimes with* **at***)* **= suggest**, mention, indicate, imply, intimate, tip off, let it be known, insinuate, allude to the fact, tip the wink *(informal)*

hip[1] *n* either side of the body below the waist and above the thigh
WORD ORIGIN Old English *hype*

hip[2] *n* the berry-like brightly coloured fruit of a rose bush. Also called: **rosehip**
WORD ORIGIN Old English *hēope*

hip[3] *interj* an exclamation used to introduce cheers: *hip, hip, hurrah*
WORD ORIGIN origin unknown

hip[4] *adj* **hipper, hippest** *slang* aware of or following the latest trends
WORD ORIGIN variant of earlier *hep*

hip bath *n* a portable bath in which the bather sits

hipbone *n* either of the two bones that form the sides of the pelvis

hip flask *n* a small metal flask for whisky, brandy, etc.

hip-hop *n* a US pop-culture movement originating in the 1980s, comprising rap music, graffiti, and break dancing

Hipparchus[1] *n* **1** 2nd century BC, Greek astronomer. He discovered the precession of the equinoxes, calculated the length of the solar year, and developed trigonometry **2** died 514 BC, tyrant of Athens (527–514)

Hipparchus[2] *n* a large crater in the SW quadrant of the moon, about 130 kilometres in diameter

hippie *n* ▸ same as **hippy**[2]

hippo *n, pl* **-pos** *informal* ▸ short for **hippopotamus**

Hippocratic oath *n* an oath taken by a doctor to observe a code of medical ethics
WORD ORIGIN after *Hippocrates*, Greek physician

hippodrome *n* **1** a music hall, variety theatre, or circus **2** (in ancient Greece or Rome) an open-air course for horse and chariot races
WORD ORIGIN Greek *hippos* horse + *dromos* race

hippopotamus *n, pl* **-muses** *or* **-mi** a very large mammal with thick wrinkled skin and short legs, which lives around the rivers of tropical Africa
WORD ORIGIN Greek *hippopotamos* river horse

hippy[1] *adj* **-pier, -piest** *informal* having large hips

hippy[2] *or* **hippie** *n, pl* **-pies** (esp. during the 1960s) a person whose behaviour and dress imply a rejection of conventional values
WORD ORIGIN from HIP[4]

hipsters *pl n Brit* trousers cut so that the top encircles the hips

Hiram *n* 10th century BC, king of Tyre, who supplied Solomon with materials and craftsmen for the building of the Temple (II Samuel 5:11; I Kings 5:1–18)

hire ⓣ *vb* **hiring, hired 1** to acquire the temporary use of (a thing) or the services of (a person) in exchange for payment **2** to employ (a person) for wages **3** to provide (something) or the services of (oneself or others) for payment **4 hire out** *chiefly Brit* to pay independent contractors for (work to be done) ▷*n* **5** the act of hiring **6 for hire** available to be hired
WORD ORIGIN Old English *hӯrian*

hireling *n disparaging* a person who works only for money

hire-purchase *n* a system in which a buyer takes possession of merchandise on payment of a deposit and completes the purchase by paying a series of instalments while the seller retains ownership until the final instalment is paid

Hiroshige *n* **Ando** 1797–1858, Japanese artist, esp. of colour wood-block prints

hirsute (her-suit) *adj* hairy
WORD ORIGIN Latin *hirsutus* shaggy

his *adj* **1** of, belonging to, or associated with him: *his birthday* ▷*pron* **2** something belonging to him: *his is on the left; that book is his* **3 of his** belonging to him
WORD ORIGIN Old English

Hispanic *adj* **1** of or derived from Spain or the Spanish ▷*n* **2** *US* a US citizen of Spanish or Latin-American descent
WORD ORIGIN Latin *Hispania* Spain

hiss ⓣ *n* **1** a sound like that of a prolonged *s* **2** such a sound as an expression of dislike or disapproval ▷*vb* **3** to utter a hiss **4** to express with a hiss: *she hissed the name* **5** to show dislike or disapproval towards (a speaker or performer) by hissing
WORD ORIGIN imitative

Hiss *n* **Alger** 1904–96, US government official: imprisoned (1950–54) for perjury in connection with alleged espionage activities

hissy fit *n informal* a childish temper tantrum

histamine (hiss-ta-meen) *n* a chemical compound released by the body tissues in allergic reactions
WORD ORIGIN Greek *histos* tissue + *amine*

histogram *n* a statistical graph that represents the frequency of values of a quantity by vertical bars of varying heights and widths
WORD ORIGIN probably *histo(ry)* + Greek *grammē* line

histology *n* the study of the tissues of an animal or plant
WORD ORIGIN Greek *histos* tissue + -LOGY

historian *n* a person who writes or studies history

historic ⓣ *adj* important in history, or likely to be seen as important in the future

historical ⓣ *adj* **1** occurring in the past **2** describing or representing situations or people that existed in the past: *a historical novel* **3** belonging to or typical of the study of history: *historical perspective* **historically** *adv*

historicism *n* **1** the belief that natural laws govern historical events **2** excessive respect for historical institutions, such as traditions or laws

historicity *n* historical authenticity

historiographer *n* a historian employed to write the history of a group or public institution **historiography** *n*

history ⓣ *n, pl* **-ries 1** a record or account of past events and developments **2** all that is preserved of the past, esp. in written form **3** the study of interpreting past events **4** the past events or previous experiences of a place, thing, or person: *he knew the whole history of the place* **5** a play that depicts historical events
WORD ORIGIN Greek *historia* inquiry

histrionic *adj* **1** very dramatic and full of exaggerated emotion: *histrionic bursts of invective* ▷*n* **2 histrionics** behaviour of this kind **histrionically** *adv*
WORD ORIGIN Latin *histrio* actor

hit ⓣ *vb* **hitting, hit 1** to strike or touch (a person or thing) forcefully **2** to come into violent contact with:

h

THESAURUS

hire *vb* **1, 2 = employ**, commission, take on, engage, appoint, sign up, enlist **1, 3 = rent**, charter, lease, let, engage ▷*n* **5 = rental**, hiring, rent, lease

hiss *n* **1 = fizz**, buzz, hissing, fizzing, sibilance, sibilation ▷*vb* **3, 4 = whistle**, wheeze, rasp, whiz, whirr, sibilate **5 = jeer**, mock, ridicule, deride, decry, revile

historic *adj* **= significant**, notable, momentous, famous, celebrated, extraordinary, outstanding, remarkable, ground-breaking, consequential, red-letter, epoch-making **OPPOSITE:** unimportant

historical *adj* **1 = factual**, real, documented, actual, authentic, chronicled, attested, archival, verifiable **OPPOSITE:** contemporary

history *n* **1 = chronicle**, record, story, account, relation, narrative, saga, recital, narration, annals, recapitulation **2 = the past**, the old days, antiquity, yesterday, the good old days, yesteryear, ancient history, olden days, days of old, days of yore, bygone times

hit *vb* **1 = strike**, beat, knock, punch, belt *(informal)*, deck *(slang)*, bang, batter, clip *(informal)*, slap, bash *(informal)*, sock *(slang)*, chin *(slang)*, smack, thump, clout *(informal)*, cuff,

DICTIONARY

a helicopter hit a Volvo **3** to propel (a ball) by striking **4** *cricket* to score (runs) **5** to affect (a person, place, or thing) badly: *the airline says that its revenue will be hit* **6** to reach (a point or place): *the city's crime level hit new heights* **7** **hit the bottle** *slang* to start drinking excessive amounts of alcohol **8** **hit the road** *informal* to set out on a journey ▷*n* **9** an impact or collision **10** a shot or blow that reaches its target **11** *informal* a person or thing that gains wide appeal: *those early collections made her a hit with the club set* **12** *computers, slang* a single visit to a website: *over 500 000 hits a day to its site* ▸See also **hit off, hit on, hit out at**
WORD ORIGIN Old English *hittan*

hit-and-miss *adj informal* happening in an unplanned way: *farming can be very much a hit-and-miss affair*

hit-and-run *adj* denoting a motor-vehicle accident in which the driver does not stop to give assistance or inform the police

hitch ❶ *n* **1** a temporary or minor problem or difficulty **2** a knot that can be undone by pulling against the direction of the strain that holds it ▷*vb* **3** *informal* **a** to obtain (a ride) by hitchhiking **b** to hitchhike **4** to fasten with a knot or tie **5** **get hitched** *slang* to get married **6** **hitch up** to pull up (one's trousers etc.) with a quick jerk
WORD ORIGIN origin unknown

hitchhike *vb* **-hiking, -hiked** to travel by getting free lifts in motor vehicles **hitchhiker** *n*

hi-tech *adj* using sophisticated, esp. electronic, technology

hither *adv old-fashioned* to or towards this place: *come hither*
WORD ORIGIN Old English *hider*

hitherto ❶ *adv formal* until this time: *fundamental questions which have hitherto been ignored*

hit list *n informal* **1** a list of people to be murdered **2** a list of targets to be eliminated: *the Treasury draws up a hit list for spending cuts*

hit man *n* a person hired by terrorists or gangsters to murder someone

hit off ❶ *vb* **hit it off** *informal* to have a good relationship with someone

hit on ❶ *or* **upon** *vb* to think of (an idea or a solution)

hit-or-miss *adj informal* unplanned or unpredictable: *hit-or-miss service*. Also: **hit-and-miss**

hit out at *vb* **1** to direct blows forcefully and vigorously at (someone) **2** to make a verbal attack upon (someone)

hit wicket *n cricket* a batsman breaking the wicket while playing a stroke and so being out

HIV human immunodeficiency virus, the cause of AIDS

hive *n* **1** a structure in which bees live **2** **hive of activity** a busy place with many people working hard
WORD ORIGIN Old English *hȳf*

hive off *vb* **hiving, hived** to transfer (part of a business, esp. the profitable part of a nationalized industry) to new ownership

hives *n pathol* an allergic reaction in which itchy red or whitish raised patches develop on the skin
WORD ORIGIN origin unknown

HM (in Britain) Her (*or* His) Majesty

H.M.A.S. *or* **HMAS** (in Australia) Her (*or* His) Majesty's Australian Ship

HMI (in Britain) Her (*or* His) Majesty's Inspector; a government official who examines and supervises schools

hmm *interj* a sound made when considering or puzzling over something

HMRC (in Britian) Her Majesty's Revenue and Customs: a government department responsible for collecting taxes

H.M.S. *or* **HMS** (in Britain) Her (*or* His) Majesty's Ship

HMSO (in Britain) Her (*or* His) Majesty's Stationery Office

HNC (in Britain) Higher National Certificate; a qualification recognized by many national technical and professional institutions

HND (in Britain) Higher National Diploma; a qualification in a technical subject equivalent to an ordinary degree

ho *n US Black slang* a derogatory term for a woman
WORD ORIGIN from Black or Southern US pronunciation of WHORE

Ho *chem* holmium

hoar *n* ▸short for **hoarfrost**
WORD ORIGIN Old English *hār*

hoard *n* **1** a store of money, food, etc. hidden away for future use ▷*vb* **2** to save or store (money, food, etc.) **hoarder** *n*
WORD ORIGIN Old English *hord*

hoarding *n* a large board at the side of a road, used for displaying advertising posters
WORD ORIGIN Old French *hourd* palisade

hoarfrost *n* a white layer of ice crystals formed on the ground by condensation at temperatures below freezing point

hoarse *adj* **1** (of a voice) rough and unclear through illness or too much shouting **2** having a rough and unclear voice **hoarsely** *adv* **hoarseness** *n*
WORD ORIGIN from Old Norse

hoary *adj* **hoarier, hoariest** **1** having grey or white hair **2** very old: *a hoary old problem*

hoax *n* **1** a deception, esp. a practical joke ▷*vb* **2** to deceive or play a joke on (someone)
WORD ORIGIN probably from *hocus* to trick

hob *n Brit* the flat top part of a cooker, or a separate flat surface, containing hotplates or burners
WORD ORIGIN perhaps from *hub*

Hobbema *n* **Meindert** 1638–1709, Dutch painter of peaceful landscapes, usually including a watermill

hobble *vb* **-bling, -bled** **1** to walk with a lame awkward movement **2** to tie the legs of (a horse) together in order to restrict its movement
WORD ORIGIN probably from Low German

Hobbs *n* Sir **John Berry,** known as *Jack Hobbs.* 1882–1963, English cricketer: scored 197 centuries

hobby ❶ *n, pl* **-bies** an activity pursued in one's spare time for pleasure or relaxation

THESAURUS

flog, whack, clobber (*slang*), smite (*archaic*), wallop (*informal*), swat, lay one on (*slang*), beat *or* knock seven bells out of (*informal*) **2 = collide with**, run into, bump into, clash with, smash into, crash against, bang into, meet head-on **5 = affect**, damage, harm, ruin, devastate, overwhelm, touch, impact on, impinge on, leave a mark on, make an impact *or* impression on **6 = reach**, strike, gain, achieve, secure, arrive at, accomplish, attain ▷*n* **9 = shot**, blow, impact, collision **10 = blow**, knock, stroke, belt (*informal*), rap, slap, bump, smack, clout (*informal*), cuff, swipe (*informal*), wallop (*informal*) **11** (*informal*) **= success**, winner, triumph, smash (*informal*), sensation, sellout, smasheroo (*informal*)

hit off *vb* (*informal*) **= get on (well) with**, take to, click (*slang*), warm to, be on good terms, get on like a house on fire (*informal*)

hit on *or* **upon something** *vb* **= think up**, discover, arrive at, guess, realize, invent, come upon, stumble on, chance upon, light upon, strike upon

hitch *n* **1 = problem**, catch, trouble, check, difficulty, delay, hold-up, obstacle, hazard, drawback, hassle (*informal*), snag, uphill (*S African*), stoppage, mishap, impediment, hindrance ▷*vb* **3b** (*informal*) **= hitchhike**, thumb a lift **4 = fasten**, join, attach, unite, couple, tie, connect, harness, tether, yoke, make fast **6 hitch something up = pull up**, tug, jerk, yank, hoick

hitherto *adv* (*formal*) **= previously**, so far, until now, thus far, up to now, till now, heretofore

hobby *n* **= pastime**, relaxation, leisure pursuit, sideline, diversion,

DICTIONARY

WORD ORIGIN probably variant of the name *Robin*

hobbyhorse *n* **1** a favourite topic about which a person likes to talk at every opportunity: *public transport is his hobbyhorse* **2** a toy consisting of a stick with a figure of a horse's head at one end **3** a figure of a horse attached to a performer's waist in a morris dance

hobgoblin *n* a small, mischievous creature in fairy stories
WORD ORIGIN *hob*, variant of the name *Rob* + GOBLIN

hobnail boots *pl n old-fashioned* heavy boots with short nails in the soles to lessen wear and tear
WORD ORIGIN *hob* (in archaic sense: peg)

hobnob *vb* **-nobbing, -nobbed** to socialize or talk informally: *hobnobbing with the rich*
WORD ORIGIN *hob or nob* to drink to one another in turns

hobo *n, pl* **-bos** *or* **-boes** *US, Canad, Austral & NZ* a tramp or vagrant
WORD ORIGIN origin unknown

Hobson's choice *n* the choice of taking what is offered or nothing at all
WORD ORIGIN after Thomas *Hobson*, liveryman who gave his customers no choice

Hochhuth *n* **Rolf** born 1933, Swiss dramatist. His best-known works are the controversial documentary drama *The Representative* (1963), on the papacy's attitude to the Jews in World War II, *Soldiers* (1967), *German Love Story* (1980), and *Wessis in Weimar* (1992)

hock[1] *n* the joint in the leg of a horse or similar animal that corresponds to the human ankle
WORD ORIGIN Old English *hōhsinu* heel sinew

hock[2] *n* a white wine from the German Rhine
WORD ORIGIN German *Hochheimer*

hock[3] *informal vb* **1** to pawn or pledge ▷*n* **2** **in hock** **a** in debt **b** in pawn
WORD ORIGIN Dutch *hok* prison, debt

hockey *n* **1** a game played on a field by two teams of 11 players who try to hit a ball into their opponents' goal using long sticks curved at the end **2** *US & Canad* ice hockey
WORD ORIGIN origin unknown

Hockney *n* **David** born 1937, English painter, best known for his etchings, such as those to Cavafy's poems (1966), naturalistic portraits such as *Mr and Mrs Clark and Percy* (1971), and for paintings of water, swimmers, and swimming pools

hocus-pocus *n informal* something said or done in order to confuse or trick someone
WORD ORIGIN a dog Latin exclamation used by conjurors

hod *n* an open metal or plastic box attached to a pole, for carrying bricks or mortar
WORD ORIGIN Old French *hotte* pannier

hodgepodge *n chiefly US & Canad* ▸same as **hotchpotch**

Hodgkin's disease *n* a malignant disease that causes enlargement of the lymph nodes, spleen, and liver
WORD ORIGIN after Thomas *Hodgkin*, physician

hoe *n* **1** a long-handled implement used to loosen the soil or to weed ▷*vb* **hoeing, hoed** **2** to scrape or weed with a hoe
WORD ORIGIN Germanic

Hoffman *n* **Dustin** (**Lee**) born 1937, US stage and film actor. His films include *The Graduate* (1967), *Midnight Cowboy* (1969), *All the President's Men* (1976), *Kramer vs Kramer* (1979), *Rain Man* (1989), *Accidental Hero* (1992), and *Moonlight Mile* (2002)

Hofmann *n* **Hans** 1880–1966, US painter, born in Germany: a pioneer of the abstract expressionist style

Hofmannsthal *n* **Hugo von** 1874–1929, Austrian lyric poet and dramatist, noted as the librettist for Richard Strauss' operas, esp. *Der Rosenkavalier* (1911), *Elektra* (1909), and *Ariadne auf Naxos* (1912)

hog *n* **1** a castrated male pig **2** *US & Canad* any mammal of the pig family **3** *informal* a greedy person **4** **go the whole hog** *slang* to do something in the most complete way possible ▷*vb* **hogging, hogged** **5** *slang* to take more than one's share of (something)
WORD ORIGIN Old English *hogg*

Hogan *n* **Ben,** full name *William Benjamin Hogan*. 1912–97, US golfer

Hogg *n* **1** **James,** known as *the Ettrick Shepherd*. 1770–1835, Scottish poet and writer. His works include the volume of poems *The Queen's Wake* (1813) and the novel *The Confessions of a Justified Sinner* (1824) **2** **Quintin** ▸See **Hailsham of St Marylebone**

Hogmanay *n* New Year's Eve in Scotland
WORD ORIGIN probably from Old French *aguillanneuf* a New Year's Eve gift

hogshead *n* a large cask for storing alcoholic drinks
WORD ORIGIN origin unknown

hogwash *n informal* nonsense

Hogwood *n* **Christopher** (**Jarvis Haley**) born 1941, British harpsichordist, conductor, and musicologist; founder and director of the Academy of Ancient Music (1973–2006)

Hohenlohe *n* **Chlodwig,** Prince of Hohenlohe-Schillingsfürst. 1819–1901, Prussian statesman; chancellor of the German empire (1894–1900)

ho-ho *interj* a written representation of the sound of a deep laugh

ho-hum *adj informal* uninteresting or mediocre: *a ho-hum performance*

hoick *vb* **1** to raise abruptly and sharply **2** *NZ* to clear the throat and spit
WORD ORIGIN origin unknown

hoi polloi *pl n* the ordinary people when compared to the rich or well-educated
WORD ORIGIN Greek: the many

hoisin *n* a sweet spicy sauce of soya beans, sugar, garlic, and vinegar, used in Chinese cookery
WORD ORIGIN from Cantonese

hoist ❶ *vb* **1** to raise or lift up, esp. by mechanical means ▷*n* **2** any apparatus or device for lifting things
WORD ORIGIN probably from Low German

hoity-toity *adj informal* arrogant or haughty
WORD ORIGIN obsolete *hoit* to romp

hokey-pokey *n NZ* a brittle toffee sold in lumps

hokum *n slang, chiefly US & Canad* **1** nonsense; bunk **2** obvious sentimental material in a play or film
WORD ORIGIN probably a blend of *hocus-pocus* + *bunkum*

Hokusai *n* **Katsushika** 1760–1849, Japanese artist, noted for the draughtsmanship of his colour wood-block prints, which influenced the impressionists

Holbein *n* **1** **Hans** (hans), known as *Holbein the Elder*. 1465–1524, German painter **2** his son, **Hans,** known as *Holbein the Younger*. 1497–1543, German painter and engraver; court painter to Henry VIII of England (1536–43). He is noted particularly for his portraits, such as those of Erasmus (1524; 1532) and Sir Thomas More (1526)

Holberg *n* **Ludvig,** Baron. 1684–1754, Danish playwright, poet, and historian, born in Norway: considered the founder of modern Danish literature

hold[1] ❶ *vb* **holding, held** **1** to keep (an object or a person) with or within

THESAURUS

avocation, favourite occupation, (leisure) activity

hoist *vb* **1 = raise,** lift, erect, elevate, heave, upraise ▷*n* **2 = lift,** crane, elevator, winch, tackle

hold[1] *vb* **1 = embrace,** grasp, clutch, hug, squeeze, cradle, clasp, enfold **4 = accommodate,** take, contain, seat, comprise, have a capacity for **6 = restrain,** constrain, check, bind, curb, hamper, hinder
OPPOSITE: release

DICTIONARY

the hands or arms **2** to support: *a rope made from 1000 hairs would hold a large adult* **3** to maintain in a specified state or position: *his reputation continued to hold secure* **4** to have the capacity for: *trains designed to hold more than 400* **5** to set aside or reserve: *they will hold our tickets until tomorrow* **6** to restrain or keep back: *designed to hold dangerous criminals* **7** to remain unbroken: *if the elastic holds* **8** (of the weather) to remain dry and bright **9** to keep (the attention of): *a writer holds a reader by his temperament* **10** to arrange and cause to take place: *we must hold an inquiry* **11** to have the ownership or possession of: *she holds a degree in Egyptology* **12** to have responsibility for: *she cannot hold an elective office* **13** to be able to control the outward effects of drinking (alcohol): *he can't hold his liquor* **14** to (cause to) remain committed to (a promise, etc.) **15** to claim or believe: *some Sufis hold that all religious leaders were prophets* **16** to remain valid or true: *the categories are not the same and equivalency does not hold* **17** to consider in a specified manner: *philosophies which we hold so dear* **18** to defend successfully: *the Russians were holding the Volga front* **19** *music* to sustain the sound of (a note) ▹ *n* **20** a way of holding something or the act of holding it **21** something to hold onto for support **22** controlling influence: *drugs will take a hold* **23 with no holds barred** with all limitations removed ▸ See also **hold back, hold down**, etc. **holder** *n*
WORD ORIGIN Old English *healdan*

hold² *n* the space in a ship or aircraft for storing cargo
WORD ORIGIN variant of *hole*

holdall *n Brit* a large strong travelling bag

hold back *vb* **1** to restrain (someone) or refrain from doing something: *managers declined to hold back the crowds; buyers held back in the expectation of further price decreases* **2** to withhold: *holding back the wages*

hold down *vb* **1** to restrain or control someone **2** *informal* to manage to keep (a job) **3** to prevent (wages, prices, etc.) from rising much

Hölderlin *n* **Friedrich** 1770–1843, German lyric poet, whose works include the poems *Menon's Lament for Diotima* and *Bread and Wine* and the novel *Hyperion* (1797–99)

hold forth *vb* to speak for a long time

hold in *vb* to control or conceal (one's feelings)

holding *n* **1** land held under a lease **2** property to which the holder has legal title, such as land, stocks, or shares

holding company *n* a company that holds the controlling shares in one or more other companies

holding paddock *n Austral & NZ* a paddock in which cattle or sheep are kept temporarily, such as when awaiting sale

hold off *vb* **1** to keep (an attacker or attacking force) at a distance **2** to put off (doing something): *he held off distributing weapons*

hold on *vb* **1** to maintain a firm grasp (of something or someone) **2** *informal* to wait, esp. on the telephone **3 hold on to** to keep: *he held on to his world No. 1 ranking*

hold out *vb* **1** to offer (something) **2** to last: *I could hold out until we return home* **3** to continue to stand firm and manage to resist opposition **4 hold out for** to wait patiently for (the fulfilment of one's wishes) **5 hold out on someone** *informal* to keep from telling someone some important information

hold over *vb* to postpone: *several cases had to be held over pending further investigation*

hold-up ❶ *n* **1** an armed robbery **2** a delay: *a traffic hold-up* ▹ *vb* **hold up 3** to delay **4** to support (an object) **5** to stop and rob (someone), using a weapon **6** to exhibit or present (something) as an example: *he was held up as a model professional*

hold with *vb* approve of: *I don't hold with divorce*

hole ❶ *n* **1** an area hollowed out in a solid **2** an opening in or through something **3** an animal's burrow **4** *informal* a fault or error: *this points to a very big hole in parliamentary security* **5** *informal* an unattractive town or other place **6** (on a golf course) any one of the divisions of a course (usually 18) represented by the distance between the tee and the sunken cup on the green into which the ball is to be played **7 in a hole** *slang* in a difficult and embarrassing situation **8 make a hole in** *informal* to use a great amount of (one's money or food supply) **9 pick holes in** to point out faults in ▹ *vb* **holing, holed 10** to make a hole or holes in (something) **11** to hit (a golf ball) into a hole ▸ See **hole up** > **holey** *adj*
WORD ORIGIN Old English *hol*

hole-and-corner *adj informal* furtive or secretive

hole in the heart *n* a congenital defect of the heart, in which there is an abnormal opening in the partition between the left and right halves

hole up *vb informal* to go into hiding

Holi (holl-lee) *n* an annual Hindu spring festival, honouring Krishna

holiday ❶ *n* **1** a period of time spent away from home for enjoyment and relaxation **2** (*often pl*) *chiefly Brit & NZ* a period in which a break is taken from work or studies for rest or recreation **3** a day on which work is suspended by law or custom, such as a bank holiday ▹ *vb* **4** *chiefly Brit* to spend a holiday
WORD ORIGIN Old English *hāligdæg* holy day

Holiday *n* **Billie** real name *Eleanora Fagan*; known as *Lady Day*. 1915–59, US jazz singer

holier-than-thou *adj* offensively self-righteous

Holiness *n* (preceded by *His* or *Your*) a title reserved for the pope

Holinshed or **Holingshed** *n* **Raphael** died ?1580, English chronicler. His *Chronicles of England, Scotland, and Ireland* (1577) provided material for Shakespeare's historical and legendary plays

holism *n* **1** the view that a whole is greater than the sum of its parts **2** (in medicine) consideration of the complete person in the treatment of disease **holistic** *adj*
WORD ORIGIN Greek *holos* whole

hollandaise sauce *n* a rich sauce of egg yolks, butter, vinegar, and lemon juice

THESAURUS

10 = conduct, convene, have, call, run, celebrate, carry on, assemble, preside over, officiate at, solemnize **OPPOSITE:** cancel
12 = occupy, have, fill, maintain, retain, possess, hold down (*informal*)
15 = consider, think, believe, view, judge, regard, maintain, assume, reckon, esteem, deem, presume, entertain the idea **OPPOSITE:** deny
▹ *n* **20 = grip**, grasp, clutch, clasp
22 = control, authority, influence, pull (*informal*), sway, dominance, clout (*informal*), mastery, dominion, ascendancy, mana (*NZ*)

hold-up *n* **1 = robbery**, theft, mugging (*informal*), stick-up (*slang, chiefly US*) **2 = delay**, wait, hitch, trouble, difficulty, setback, snag, traffic jam, obstruction, stoppage, bottleneck

hole *n* **1 = cavity**, depression, pit, hollow, pocket, chamber, cave, shaft, cavern, excavation **2 = opening**, split, crack, break, tear, gap, rent, breach, outlet, vent, puncture, aperture, fissure, orifice, perforation **3 = burrow**, nest, den, earth, shelter, retreat, covert, lair **5** (*informal*) **= hovel**, dump (*informal*), dive (*slang*), slum, joint (*slang*)

holiday *n* **1 = vacation**, leave, break, time off, recess, away day, schoolie (*Austral*), accumulated day off *or* ADO (*Austral*), staycation, stacation (*informal*) **3 = festival**, bank holiday, festivity, public holiday, fête, celebration, anniversary, feast, red-letter day, name day, saint's day, gala

DICTIONARY

WORD ORIGIN French *sauce hollandaise* Dutch sauce

holler *informal vb* **1** to shout or yell ▷ *n* **2** a shout or yell
WORD ORIGIN French *holà* stop!

Holliger *n* **Heinz** (haints) born 1939, Swiss oboist and composer

hollow ⓘ *adj* **1** having a hole or space within; not solid: *a hollow tree* **2** curving inwards: *hollow cheeks* **3** (of sounds) as if echoing in a hollow place **4** without any real value or worth: *a hollow enterprise, lacking purpose, and lacking soul* ▷ *adv* **5 beat someone hollow** *Brit & NZ informal* to defeat someone thoroughly ▷ *n* **6** a cavity or space in something **7** a dip in the land ▷ *vb* **8** (often foll. by *out*) to form a hole or cavity in **hollowly** *adv*
WORD ORIGIN Old English *holh* cave

holly *n* an evergreen tree with prickly leaves and bright red berries, used for Christmas decorations
WORD ORIGIN Old English *holegn*

Holly *n* **Buddy** real name *Charles Harden Holley*. 1936–59, US rock-and-roll singer, guitarist, and songwriter. His hits (all 1956–59) include "That'll be the Day", "Maybe Baby", "Peggy Sue", "Oh, Boy", "Think It Over", and "It Doesn't Matter Anymore"

hollyhock *n* a tall garden plant with spikes of colourful flowers
WORD ORIGIN *holy* + obsolete *hock* mallow

Holmes *n* **1 Oliver Wendell** 1809–94, US author, esp. of humorous essays, such as *The Autocrat of the Breakfast Table* (1858) and its sequels **2** his son, **Oliver Wendell** 1841–1935, US jurist, noted for his liberal judgments **3 Paul** born 1950, New Zealand radio and television broadcaster; presenter of *The Paul Holmes Breakfast*, a popular breakfast radio show, since 1987

holmium *n chem* a silver-white metallic element, the compounds of which are highly magnetic. Symbol: Ho
WORD ORIGIN after *Holmia*, Latin name of Stockholm

holm oak *n* an evergreen oak tree with prickly leaves like holly

holocaust ⓘ *n* **1** destruction or loss of life on a massive scale **2 the Holocaust** mass murder of the Jews in Europe by the Nazis (1940–45)
WORD ORIGIN Greek *holos* whole + *kaiein* to burn

Holocene *adj* of the current geological epoch, which began about 10 000 years ago

hologram *n* a three-dimensional photographic image produced by means of a split laser beam
WORD ORIGIN Greek *holos* whole + *grammē* line

holograph *n* a book or document handwritten by its author
WORD ORIGIN Greek *holos* whole + *graphein* to write

holography *n* the science of using lasers to produce holograms **holographic** *adj* **holographically** *adv*
WORD ORIGIN Greek *holos* whole + -GRAPHY

hols *pl n Brit & S African school slang* holidays

Holst *n* **1 Alison** born 1938, New Zealand chef **2 Gustav** (**Theodore**) 1874–1934, English composer. His works include operas, choral music, and orchestral music such as the suite *The Planets* (1917)

holster *n* a sheathlike leather case for a pistol, worn attached to a belt
WORD ORIGIN Germanic

holt *n* the lair of an otter
WORD ORIGIN from HOLD[2]

holy ⓘ *adj* **-lier, -liest 1** of or associated with God or a deity **2** (of a person) religious and leading a virtuous life **holiness** *n*
WORD ORIGIN Old English *hālig, hǣlig*

Holy Communion *n Christianity* a church service in which people take bread and wine in remembrance of Christ's Last Supper and His atonement for the sins of the world

Holy Ghost *n* **the Holy Ghost** ▸ same as **Holy Spirit**

Holy Grail *n* **1 the Holy Grail** (in medieval legend) the bowl used by Jesus at the Last Supper **2** *informal* any ambition or goal
WORD ORIGIN *grail* from Medieval Latin *gradalis* bowl

Holy Land *n* **the Holy Land** Palestine

holy of holies *n* **1** any sacred place or a place considered as if it were sacred: *the holy of holies they called the Captain's Cabin* **2** the innermost chamber of a Jewish temple

holy orders *pl n* the status of an ordained Christian minister

Holy See *n* **the Holy See** *RC church* the see of the pope as bishop of Rome

Holy Spirit *n* **the Holy Spirit** *Christianity* one of the three aspects of God

Holy Week *n Christianity* the week before Easter Sunday

homage ⓘ *n* a public show of respect or honour towards someone or something: *the master's jazzy-classical homage to Gershwin*
WORD ORIGIN Latin *homo* man

homburg *n* a man's soft felt hat with a dented crown and a stiff upturned brim

home ⓘ *n* **1** the place where one lives **2** the country or area of one's birth **3** a building or organization set up to care for people in a certain category, such as orphans or the aged **4** the place where something is invented or started: *the home of the first aircraft* **5** *sport* a team's own ground: *the match is at home* **6** *baseball, rounders, etc.* the objective towards which a player runs after striking the ball **7 at home a** in one's own home or country **b** at ease: *he felt more at home with the Russians* **c** receiving visitors ▷ *adj* **8** of one's home, birthplace, or native country **9** (of an activity) done in one's house: *home movies* **10** *sport* played on one's own ground: *a home game* **11 home and dry** *Brit slang* definitely safe or successful ▷ *adv* **12** to or at home: *I came home* **13** to or on the point: *the message struck home* **14** to the fullest extent: *they drove their spears home* **15 bring something home to someone** to make something clear to someone ▷ *vb* **homing,**

h

THESAURUS

hollow *adj* **1 = empty**, vacant, void, unfilled, not solid **OPPOSITE:** solid **3 = dull**, low, deep, flat, rumbling, muted, muffled, expressionless, sepulchral, toneless, reverberant **OPPOSITE:** vibrant **4 = worthless**, empty, useless, vain, meaningless, pointless, futile, fruitless, specious, Pyrrhic, unavailing **OPPOSITE:** meaningful ▷ *n* **6 = cavity**, cup, hole, bowl, depression, pit, cave, den, basin, dent, crater, trough, cavern, excavation, indentation, dimple, concavity **OPPOSITE:** mound **7 = valley**, dale, glen, dell, dingle **OPPOSITE:** hill ▷ *vb* **8** *(often foll. by* **out***)* **= scoop out**, dig out, excavate, gouge out, channel, groove, furrow

holocaust *n* **1a = devastation**, destruction, carnage, genocide, inferno, annihilation, conflagration **1b = genocide**, massacre, carnage, mass murder, annihilation, pogrom

holy *adj* **1 = sacred**, blessed, hallowed, dedicated, venerable, consecrated, venerated, sacrosanct, sanctified **OPPOSITE:** unsanctified **2 = devout**, godly, religious, pure, divine, faithful, righteous, pious, virtuous, hallowed, saintly, god-fearing **OPPOSITE:** sinful

homage *n* **= respect**, honour, worship, esteem, admiration, awe, devotion, reverence, duty, deference, adulation, adoration **OPPOSITE:** contempt

home *n* **1 = dwelling**, house, residence, abode, habitation, pad *(slang)*, domicile, dwelling place **2 = birthplace**, household, homeland, home town, homestead, native land, Godzone *(Austral informal)* ▷ *adj* **8 = domestic**, national, local, central, internal, native, inland **15 bring something home to someone = make clear**, emphasize, drive home, press home, impress upon

DICTIONARY

homed 16 (of birds) to return home accurately from a distance **17 home in on** to be directed towards (a goal or target)
WORD ORIGIN Old English *hām*
Home *n* **Baron** ▸ See **Home of the Hirsel**
homeboy *n slang* **1** a close friend **2** a member of a gang
home-brew *n* beer or other alcoholic drink brewed at home
homecoming *n* a return home, esp. after a long absence
Home Counties *pl n* the counties surrounding London
home economics *n* the study of diet, budgeting, child care, and other subjects concerned with running a home
home farm *n Brit* a farm that belonged to and provided food for a large country house
Home Guard *n* a part-time military force of volunteers recruited for the defence of the United Kingdom in the Second World War
home help *n Brit, Austral & NZ* a person employed by a local authority to do housework in an elderly or disabled person's home
homeland ❶ *n* **1** the country from which the ancestors of a person or group came: *defending their homeland* **2** ▸ the official name in S Africa for a **Bantustan**
homeless ❶ *adj* **1** having nowhere to live ▹*pl n* **2 the homeless** people who have nowhere to live: *night shelters for the homeless* **homelessness** *n*
homely ❶ *adj* **-lier, -liest 1** simple, ordinary, and comfortable **2 a** *Brit* (of a person) warm and friendly **b** *chiefly US & Canad* (of a person) plain or unattractive **homeliness** *n*
home-made *adj* (esp. of foods) made at home or on the premises
Home Office *n Brit government* the department responsible for law and order, immigration, and other domestic affairs
homeopathy *or* **homoeopathy** (home-ee-**op**-ath-ee) *n* a method of treating disease by the use of small amounts of a drug that produces symptoms of the disease in healthy people **homeopath** *or* **homoeopath** (home-ee-oh-path) *n* **homeopathic** *or* **homoeopathic** *adj*
WORD ORIGIN Greek *homoios* similar + *patheia* suffering
homeostasis *or* **homoeostasis** (hom-ee-oh-**stass**-iss) *n* the tendency of an organism to achieve a stable metabolic state by compensating automatically for violent changes in the environment and other disruptions
WORD ORIGIN Greek *homoios* similar + *stasis* a standing
homeowner *n* a person who owns the home in which he or she lives
home page *n internet* the introductory information about a website with links to the information or services provided
Homeric (home-**mer**-rik) *adj* of or relating to Homer, Greek epic poet (circa 800 BC)
home rule *n* self-government in domestic affairs
Home Secretary *n Brit government* the head of the Home Office
homesick *adj* depressed by being away from home and family **homesickness** *n*
homespun *adj* (of philosophies or opinions) plain and unsophisticated
homestead *n* **1** a farmhouse and the adjoining land **2** (in the western US & Canada) a house and adjoining tract of land (originally often 160 acres) that was granted by the government for development as a farm
homesteader *n* (in the western US & Canada) a person who lives on and farms a homestead
homestead law *n* (in the western US & Canada) any of various laws granting certain privileges to owners of homesteads
home truths *pl n* unpleasant facts told to a person about himself or herself
home unit *n Austral & NZ* a self-contained residence that is part of a block of such residences
homeward *adj* **1** going home ▹*adv also* **homewards 2** towards home
homework *n* **1** school work done at home **2** research or preparation
homicide ❶ *n* **1** the act of killing someone **2** a person who kills someone **homicidal** *adj*
WORD ORIGIN Latin *homo* man + *caedere* to kill
homie *n slang chiefly US* ▸ short for **homeboy**
homily *n, pl* **-lies** a moralizing talk or piece of writing **homiletic** *adj*
WORD ORIGIN Greek *homilia* discourse
homing *adj* **1** *zool* denoting the ability to return home after travelling great distances **2** (of a missile) capable of guiding itself onto a target
homing pigeon *n* a pigeon developed for its homing instinct, used for racing
hominid *n* **1** any member of the family of primates that includes modern man and the extinct forerunners of man ▹*adj* **2** of or belonging to this family
WORD ORIGIN Latin *homo* man
hominoid *adj* **1** of or like man; manlike ▹*n* **2** a manlike animal
WORD ORIGIN Latin *homo* man
hominy *n chiefly US* coarsely ground maize prepared as a food by boiling in milk or water
WORD ORIGIN probably from a Native American language
homo[1] *n informal, derogatory* ▸ short for **homosexual**
homo[2] *n Canad informal* homogenized milk
homo- *combining form* same or like: *homologous*
WORD ORIGIN Greek *homos* same
homogeneous (home-oh-**jean**-ee-uss) *adj* having parts or members which are all the same or which consist of only one substance: *the Arabs are not a single, homogeneous nation* **homogeneity** *n*
WORD ORIGIN Greek *homos* same + *genos* kind
homogenize *or* **-nise** *vb* **-nizing, -nized** *or* **-nising, -nised 1** to break up the fat globules in (milk or cream) so that they are evenly distributed **2** to make different elements the same or similar: *homogenized products for a mass market*
homogenous (hom-**oj**-in-uss) *adj* having a similar structure because of common ancestry
homograph *n* a word spelt the same as another, but having a different meaning, such as *bear* (to carry) and *bear* (the animal)
WORD ORIGIN Greek *homos* same + *graphein* to write
homologous (hom-**ol**-log-uss) *adj* **1** having a related or similar position or structure **2** *biol* (of organs and parts) having the same origin but different functions: *the wing of a bat and the arm of a monkey are homologous*
WORD ORIGIN Greek *homos* same + *logos* ratio
homology (hom-**ol**-a-jee) *n* the condition of being homologous
homonym *n* a word pronounced and spelt the same as another, but

THESAURUS

homeland *n* **1 = native land,** birthplace, motherland, fatherland, country of origin, mother country, Godzone *(Austral informal)*
homeless *adj* **1 = destitute,** exiled, displaced, dispossessed, unsettled, outcast, abandoned, down-and-out
homely *adj* **1a = comfortable,** welcoming, friendly, domestic, familiar, informal, cosy, comfy *(informal)*, homespun, downhome *(slang, chiefly US)*, homelike, homy **1b = plain,** simple, natural, ordinary, modest, everyday, down-to-earth, unaffected, unassuming, unpretentious, unfussy
OPPOSITE: elaborate
homicide *n* **1 = murder,** killing, manslaughter, slaying, bloodshed
hone *vb* **1 = improve,** better, polish, enhance, upgrade, refine, sharpen,

having a different meaning, such as *novel* (a book) and *novel* (new)

homophobia *n* intense hatred or fear of homosexuals
WORD ORIGIN *homo(sexual)* + *phobia*

homophone *n* a word pronounced the same as another, but having a different meaning or spelling or both, such as *bear* and *bare*
WORD ORIGIN Greek *homos* same + *phōnē* sound

Homo sapiens (home-oh sap-ee-enz) *n* the name for modern man as a species
WORD ORIGIN Latin *homo* man + *sapiens* wise

homosexual *n* **1** a person who is sexually attracted to members of the same sex ▷ *adj* **2** (of a person) sexually attracted to members of the same sex **3** (of a sexual relationship) between members of the same sex
homosexuality *n*
WORD ORIGIN Greek *homos* same

homozygous *adj biol* having two identical alleles of the same gene
WORD ORIGIN Greek *homos* same + *zugōtos* yoked

homy *or esp. US* **homey** *adj* **homier, homiest** like a home; pleasant and cosy

Hon. Honourable (title)

hone ❶ *vb* **honing, honed 1** to develop and improve (a quality or ability): *a workshop to hone interview techniques* **2** to sharpen (a tool) ▷ *n* **3** a fine whetstone used for sharpening edged tools and knives
WORD ORIGIN Old English *hān* stone

Honecker *n* **Erich** 1912–94, German statesman; head of state of East Germany (1976–89)

Honegger *n* **Arthur** 1892–1955, French composer, one of Les Six. His works include the oratorios *King David* (1921) and *Joan of Arc at the Stake* (1935), and *Pacific 231* (1924) for orchestra

honest ❶ *adj* **1** truthful and moral in behaviour; trustworthy **2** open and sincere in relationships and attitudes; without pretensions **3** gained or earned fairly: *an honest income*
WORD ORIGIN Latin *honos* esteem

honestly ❶ *adv* **1** in an honest manner **2** truly: *honestly, that's all I can recall*

honesty ❶ *n, pl* **-ties 1** the quality of being truthful and trustworthy **2** a plant with flattened silvery pods which are used for indoor decoration

honey *n* **1** a sweet edible sticky substance made by bees from nectar **2** *chiefly US & Canad* a term of affection **3** *informal, chiefly US & Canad* something very good of its kind: *a honey of a picture about American family life*
WORD ORIGIN Old English *huneg*

honeybee *n* a bee widely domesticated as a source of honey and beeswax

honeycomb *n* a waxy structure, constructed by bees in a hive, that consists of many six-sided cells in which honey is stored

honeydew *n* a sugary substance excreted by aphids and similar insects

honeydew melon *n* a melon with yellow skin and sweet pale flesh

honeyed *adj poetic* flattering or soothing: *honeyed words*

honeymoon *n* **1** a holiday taken by a newly married couple **2** the early period of an undertaking or activity, such as the start of a new government's term of office, when an attitude of goodwill prevails ▷ *vb* **3** to take a honeymoon
honeymooner *n*
WORD ORIGIN traditionally, referring to the feelings of married couples as changing with the phases of the moon

honeysuckle *n* a climbing shrub with sweet-smelling white, yellow, or pink flowers
WORD ORIGIN Old English *hunigsūce*

honeytrap *n Brit informal* a scheme in which a victim is lured into a compromising sexual situation that provides the opportunity for blackmail

hongi (hong-jee) *n* NZ a Māori greeting in which people touch noses

Hong-wu *or* **Hung-wu** *n* title of *Chu Yuan-Zhang* (or *Chu Yüan-Chang*), 1328–98, first emperor (1368–98) of the Ming dynasty, uniting China under his rule by 1382

Hong Xiu Quan *or* **Hung Hsiu-Ch'uan** *n* 1814–64, Chinese religious leader and revolutionary. Claiming (1851) to be Christ's brother, he led the Taiping rebellion; committed suicide when it was defeated

honk *n* **1** the sound made by a motor horn **2** the sound made by a goose ▷ *vb* **3** to make or cause (something) to make a honking sound

honky-tonk *n* **1** *US & Canad slang* a cheap disreputable nightclub or dance hall **2** a style of ragtime piano-playing, esp. on a tinny-sounding piano
WORD ORIGIN rhyming compound based on HONK

honorarium *n, pl* **-iums** *or* **-ia** a voluntary fee paid for a service which is usually free
WORD ORIGIN Latin *honorarium (donum)* honorary gift

honorary ❶ *adj* **a** held or given as a mark of respect, without the usual qualifications, payment, or work: *an honorary degree* **b** (of a secretary, treasurer, etc.) unpaid

honorific *adj* showing respect: *an honorific title*

honour ❶ *or US* **honor** *n* **1** allegiance to moral principles **2** a person's good reputation and the respect they are given by other people **3 a** fame or glory **b** a person who wins fame or glory for his or her country, school, etc.: *he was an honour to his nation* **4** great respect or esteem, or an outward sign of this **5** a privilege or pleasure: *it was an honour to meet him* **6** *old-fashioned* a woman's virginity **7** *bridge, whist* any of the top four or five cards in a suit **8** *golf* the right to tee off first **9 in honour of** out of respect for **10 on one's honour** under a moral obligation ▷ *vb* **11** to hold someone in respect **12** to give (someone) special praise, attention, or an award **13** to accept and then pay (a cheque or bill) **14** to keep (one's promise); fulfil (a previous agreement)
WORD ORIGIN Latin *honor* esteem

THESAURUS

augment, help **2 = sharpen**, point, grind, edge, file, polish, whet, strop

honest *adj* **1 = trustworthy**, decent, upright, reliable, ethical, honourable, conscientious, reputable, truthful, virtuous, law-abiding, trusty, scrupulous, high-minded, veracious
OPPOSITE: dishonest
2 = open, direct, frank, plain, straightforward, outright, sincere, candid, forthright, upfront *(informal)*, undisguised, round, ingenuous, unfeigned **OPPOSITE:** secretive

honestly *adv* **1 = ethically**, legitimately, legally, in good faith, on the level *(informal)*, lawfully, honourably, by fair means, with clean hands

honesty *n* **1 = integrity**, honour, virtue, morality, fidelity, probity, rectitude, veracity, faithfulness, truthfulness, trustworthiness, straightness, incorruptibility, scrupulousness, uprightness, reputability

honorary *adj* **a = nominal**, unofficial, titular, ex officio, honoris causa *(Latin)*, in name *or* title only

honour *or US* **honor** *n* **1 = integrity**, principles, morality, honesty, goodness, fairness, decency, righteousness, probity, rectitude, trustworthiness, uprightness
OPPOSITE: dishonour
2 = reputation, standing, prestige, image, status, stature, good name, kudos, cachet **3a = prestige**, credit, reputation, glory, fame, distinction, esteem, dignity, elevation, eminence, renown, repute, high standing **OPPOSITE:** disgrace
4 = acclaim, regard, respect, praise, recognition, compliments, homage, accolades, reverence, deference, adoration, commendation, veneration **OPPOSITE:** contempt
5 = privilege, credit, favour, pleasure,

DICTIONARY

Honour *n* (preceded by *Your, His* or *Her*) a title used to address or refer to certain judges

honourable ❶ *or US* **honorable** *adj* **1** principled **2** worthy of respect or esteem **honourably** *adv*

Honourable *adj* **the Honourable** a title of respect placed before a name: used of various officials, of the children of certain peers, and in Parliament by one member speaking of another

honours *or US* **honors** *pl n* **1** (in a university degree course) a rank or mark of the highest academic standard: *an honours degree* **2** observances of respect, esp. at a funeral **3 do the honours** to serve as host or hostess by serving food or pouring drinks

hooch (rhymes with **smooch**) *n informal* alcoholic drink, esp. illegally distilled spirits
WORD ORIGIN from a Native American language

Hooch *or* **Hoogh** *n* **Pieter de** 1629–?1684, Dutch genre painter, noted esp. for his light effects

hood¹ *n* **1** a loose head covering either attached to a coat or made as a separate garment **2** *US, Canad & Austral* the bonnet of a car **3** the folding roof of a convertible car or a pram ▷ *vb* **4** to cover with or as if with a hood **hoodlike** *adj*
WORD ORIGIN Old English *hōd*

hood² *n slang* ▸ short for **hoodlum**

Hood *n* **1 Robin** ▸ See **Robin Hood** **2 Samuel,** 1st Viscount. 1724–1816, British admiral. He fought successfully against the French during the American Revolution and the French Revolutionary Wars **3 Thomas** 1799–1845, British poet and humorist: his work includes protest poetry, such as *The Song of the Shirt* (1843) and *The Bridge of Sighs* (1844)

hooded *adj* **1** (of a garment) having a hood **2** (of eyes) having heavy eyelids that appear to be half-closed

hooded crow *n* a crow that has a grey body and black head, wings, and tail

hoodie *n informal* **1** a hooded sweatshirt **2** a young person who wears a hooded sweatshirt, regarded by some as a potential hooligan

hoodlum *n* a violent criminal, esp. one who is a member of a gang
WORD ORIGIN origin unknown

hoodoo *n, pl* **-doos** **1** *informal* bad luck **2** *informal* a person or thing that brings bad luck **3** *chiefly US* ▸ same as **voodoo**

hoodwink *vb* to trick or deceive
WORD ORIGIN originally, to cover the eyes with a hood

hooey *n slang* nonsense
WORD ORIGIN origin unknown

hoof *n, pl* **hooves** *or* **hoofs** **1** the horny covering of the end of the foot in the horse, deer, and certain other mammals **2 on the hoof a** (of livestock) alive **b** in an impromptu way: *thinking on the hoof* ▷ *vb* **3 hoof it** *slang* to walk **hoofed** *adj*
WORD ORIGIN Old English *hōf*

hoofer *n slang* a professional dancer

Hooft *n* **Pieter Corneliszoon** 1581–1647, Dutch poet, historian, and writer: noted esp. for his love poetry and his 27-volume *History of the Netherlands* (1626–47)

hoo-ha *n* a noisy commotion or fuss
WORD ORIGIN origin unknown

hook ❶ *n* **1** a curved piece of metal or plastic used to hang, hold, or pull something **2** something resembling a hook, such as a sharp bend in a river or a sharply curved strip of land **3** *boxing* a short swinging blow with the elbow bent **4** *cricket, golf* a shot that causes the ball to go to the player's left **5 by hook or by crook** by any means: *get into the charts by hook or by crook* **6 hook, line, and sinker** *informal* completely: *we fell for it hook, line, and sinker* **7 let someone off the hook** *slang* to free someone from an obligation or a difficult situation **8 sling one's hook** *Austral & Brit slang* to leave ▷ *vb* **9** to fasten with or as if with a hook **10** to catch (a fish) on a hook **11** *cricket, golf* to play (a ball) with a hook **12** *rugby* to obtain and pass (the ball) backwards from a scrum, using the feet
WORD ORIGIN Old English *hōc*

hookah *n* an oriental pipe for smoking marijuana or tobacco, with a long flexible stem connected to a container of water through which smoke is drawn and cooled
WORD ORIGIN Arabic *huqqah*

hooked ❶ *adj* **1** bent like a hook **2** (often foll. by *on*) **a** *slang* addicted (to): *hooked on drugs* **b** obsessed with: *hooked on football*

hooker *n* **1** *slang* a prostitute **2** *rugby* a player who uses his feet to get the ball in a scrum

Hooker *n* **1 John Lee** 1917–2001, US blues singer and guitarist **2** Sir **Joseph Dalton** 1817–1911, British botanist; director of Kew Gardens (1865–85) **3 Richard** 1554–1600, British theologian, who influenced Anglican theology with *The Laws of Ecclesiastical Polity* (1593–97) **4** Sir **William Jackson** 1785–1865, British botanist; first director of Kew Gardens: father of Sir Joseph Dalton Hooker

Hooke's law *n physics* the principle that a solid stretches or contracts in proportion to the force placed on it, within the limits of its elasticity
WORD ORIGIN after Robert *Hooke,* physicist

hook-up *n* the linking of broadcasting equipment or stations to transmit a special programme

hookworm *n* a blood-sucking worm with hooked mouthparts

hooligan ❶ *n slang* a young person who behaves in a noisy and violent way in public **hooliganism** *n*
WORD ORIGIN origin unknown

hoon *Austral & NZ slang n* **1** a loutish youth who drives irresponsibly ▷ *vb* **2** to drive irresponsibly

hoop ❶ *n* **1** a rigid circular band of metal, plastic, or wood **2** a child's toy shaped like a hoop and rolled on the ground or whirled around the body **3** *croquet* any of the iron arches through which the ball is driven **4** a large ring through which performers or animals jump **5 go** *or* **be put through the hoops** to go through an ordeal or test ▷ *vb* **6** to surround (something) with a hoop **hooped** *adj*
WORD ORIGIN Old English *hōp*

THESAURUS

compliment, source of pride *or* satisfaction ▷ *vb* **11 = respect**, value, esteem, prize, appreciate, admire, worship, adore, revere, glorify, reverence, exalt, venerate, hallow **OPPOSITE:** scorn **12 = acclaim**, celebrate, praise, decorate, compliment, commemorate, dignify, commend, glorify, exalt, laud, lionize **13 = pay**, take, accept, clear, pass, cash, credit, acknowledge **OPPOSITE:** refuse **14 = fulfil**, keep, carry out, observe, discharge, live up to, be true to, be as good as *(informal)*, be faithful to

honourable *or US* **honorable** *adj* **1 = principled**, moral, ethical, just, true, fair, upright, honest, virtuous, trustworthy, trusty, high-minded, upstanding **2 = proper**, right, respectable, righteous, virtuous, creditable

hook *n* **1 = fastener**, catch, link, lock, holder, peg, clasp, hasp ▷ *vb* **9 = fasten**, fix, secure, catch, clasp, hasp **10 = catch**, land, trap, entrap

hooked *adj* **1 = bent**, curved, beaked, aquiline, beaky, hook-shaped, hamate *(rare)*, hooklike, falcate *(biology)*, unciform *(anat)*, uncinate *(biology)* **2a** *(slang)* **= addicted**, dependent, using *(informal)*, having a habit **2b = obsessed**, addicted, taken, devoted, turned on *(slang)*, enamoured

hooligan *n* **= delinquent**, tough, vandal, casual, ned *(Scot slang)*, rowdy, hoon *(Austral & NZ)*, hoodlum *(chiefly US)*, ruffian, lager lout, yob *or* yobbo *(Brit slang)*, cougan *(Austral slang)*, scozza *(Austral slang)*, bogan *(Austral slang)*, hoodie *(informal)*

hoop *n* **1 = ring**, band, loop, wheel, round, girdle, circlet

DICTIONARY

hoopla *n Austral & Brit* a fairground game in which hoops are thrown over objects in an attempt to win them

hoopoe (hoop-oo) *n* a bird with pinkish-brown plumage with black-and-white wings and a fanlike crest
WORD ORIGIN imitative

hoop pine *n* an Australian tree or shrub with flowers in dense spikes

hooray *interj, n* ▸ same as **hurrah**

Hooray Henry (hoo-ray) *n, pl* **Hooray Henries** *or* **-rys** *Brit informal* a young upper-class man with an affectedly loud and cheerful manner

hoot *n* **1** the sound of a car horn **2** the cry of an owl **3** a high-pitched noise showing disapproval **4** *informal* an amusing person or thing ▹ *vb* **5** *Brit* to blow (a car horn) **6** to make a hoot **7** to jeer or yell contemptuously at someone **8** to drive (speakers or performers on stage) off by hooting
WORD ORIGIN imitative

hooter *n chiefly Brit* **1** a device that hoots, such as a car horn **2** *slang* a nose

Hoover *n* **1** *trademark* a vacuum cleaner ▹ *vb* **hoover 2** to vacuum-clean (a carpet) **3** (often foll. by *up*) to devour (something) quickly and completely

hooves *n* ▸ a plural of **hoof**

hop[1] ● *vb* **hopping, hopped 1** to jump forwards or upwards on one foot **2** (of frogs, birds, etc.) to move forwards in short jumps **3** to jump over something **4** *informal* to move quickly (in, on, out of, etc.): *hop into bed* **5 hop it** *Austral & Brit slang* to go away ▹ *n* **6** an instance of hopping **7** *informal* an informal dance **8** *informal* a short journey, usually in an aircraft **9 on the hop** *informal* **a** active or busy: *he keeps me on the hop* **b** unawares or unprepared: *you caught me on the hop*
WORD ORIGIN Old English *hoppian*

hop[2] *n* a climbing plant with green conelike flowers ▸ See also **hops**
WORD ORIGIN Middle Dutch *hoppe*

hope ● *vb* **hoping, hoped 1** to desire (something), usually with some possibility of fulfilment: *you would hope for their cooperation* **2** to trust or believe: *I hope I've arranged that* ▹ *n* **3** a feeling of desire for something, usually with confidence in the possibility of its fulfilment: *the news was greeted by some as hope for further interest rate cuts* **4** a reasonable ground for this feeling: *there is hope for you yet* **5** the person, thing, situation, or event that gives cause for hope or is desired: *the young are a symbol of hope for the future*
WORD ORIGIN Old English *hopa*

Hope *n* **1 Anthony,** real name *Sir Anthony Hope Hawkins*. 1863–1933, English novelist; author of *The Prisoner of Zenda* (1894) **2 Bob,** real name *Leslie Townes Hope*. 1903–2003, US comedian and comic actor, born in England. His films include *The Cat and the Canary* (1939), *Road to Morocco* (1942), and *The Paleface* (1947). He was awarded an honorary knighthood in 1998 **3 David** (**Michael**) Baron. born 1940, British churchman, Archbishop of York (1995–2005)

hopeful ● *adj* **1** having, inspiring, or expressing hope ▹ *n* **2** a person considered to be on the brink of success: *a young hopeful*

hopefully ● *adv* **1** in a hopeful manner **2** *informal* it is hoped: *hopefully I've got a long career ahead of me*

hopeless ● *adj* **1** having or offering no hope **2** impossible to solve **3** *informal* without skill or ability: *I'm hopeless at maths* **hopelessly** *adv* **hopelessness** *n*

hopper *n* a funnel-shaped device from which solid materials can be discharged into a receptacle below

Hopper *n* **Edward** 1882–1967, US painter, noted for his realistic depiction of everyday scenes

hops *pl n* the dried flowers of the hop plant, used to give a bitter taste to beer

hopscotch *n* a children's game in which a player throws a stone to land in one of a pattern of squares marked on the ground and then hops over to it to pick it up
WORD ORIGIN *hop* + obsolete *scotch* a line, scratch

Horatius Cocles *n* a legendary Roman hero of the 6th century BC, who defended a bridge over the Tiber against Lars Porsena

horde ● *n* a very large crowd, often frightening or unpleasant
WORD ORIGIN Turkish *ordū* camp

Hordern *n* Sir **Michael** (**Murray**) 1911–95, British actor

horehound *n* a plant that produces a bitter juice formerly used as a cough medicine
WORD ORIGIN Old English *hārhūne*

horizon ● *n* **1** the apparent line that divides the earth and the sky **2 horizons** the limits of a person's interests and activities: *seeking to broaden his horizons at college* **3 on the horizon** almost certainly going to happen or be done in the future: *a new type of computer is on the horizon*
WORD ORIGIN Greek *horizein* to limit

horizontal ● *adj* **1** flat and level with the ground or with a line considered as a base **2** affecting or happening at one level in a system or organization: *a horizontal division of labour* ▹ *n* **3** a horizontal plane, position, or line **horizontally** *adv*

Horkheimer *n* **Max** 1895–1973, German social theorist of the Frankfurt school. His books include *Eclipse of Reason* (1947) and *Critical Theory* (1968)

hormone *n* **1** a chemical substance produced in an endocrine gland and transported in the blood to a certain tissue, on which it has a specific effect **2** a similar substance produced by a plant that is essential for growth **3** a synthetic substance having the same effects **hormonal** *adj*
WORD ORIGIN Greek *hormōn*

horn *n* **1** either of a pair of permanent bony outgrowths on the heads of animals such as cattle and antelopes **2** any hornlike projection, such as the eyestalk of a snail **3** the antler of a deer **4** the hard substance of which horns are made **5** a musical wind instrument made from horn **6** any musical instrument consisting of a pipe or tube of brass fitted with a mouthpiece **7** a device, such as on a vehicle, for producing a warning or signalling noise **horned** *adj*
WORD ORIGIN Old English

hornbeam *n* a tree with smooth grey bark

hornbill *n* a tropical bird with a bony

h

THESAURUS

hop[1] *vb* **3 = jump**, spring, bound, leap, skip, vault, caper ▹ *n* **6 = jump**, step, spring, bound, leap, bounce, skip, vault

hope *vb* **2 = believe**, expect, trust, rely, look forward to, anticipate, contemplate, count on, foresee, keep your fingers crossed, cross your fingers ▹ *n* **3 = belief**, confidence, expectation, longing, dream, desire, faith, ambition, assumption, anticipation, expectancy, light at the end of the tunnel
OPPOSITE: despair

hopeful *adj* **1a = optimistic**, confident, assured, looking forward to, anticipating, buoyant, sanguine, expectant **OPPOSITE:** despairing **1b = promising**, encouraging, bright, reassuring, cheerful, rosy, heartening, auspicious, propitious
OPPOSITE: unpromising

hopefully *adv* **1 = optimistically**, confidently, expectantly, with anticipation, sanguinely

hopeless *adj* **1 = impossible**, pointless, futile, useless, vain, forlorn, no-win, unattainable, impracticable, unachievable, not having a prayer

horde *n* **= crowd**, mob, swarm, press, host, band, troop, pack, crew, drove, gang, multitude, throng

horizon *n* **1 = skyline**, view, vista, field *or* range of vision

horizontal *adj* **1 = level**, flat, plane, parallel, supine

DICTIONARY

growth on its large beak

hornblende *n* a green-to-black mineral containing aluminium, calcium, sodium, magnesium, and iron

Hornby *n* **Nick** born 1958, British writer; his books include the memoir *Fever Pitch* (1992; filmed 1997) and the bestselling novels *About a Boy* (1998; filmed 2002) and *How To Be Good* (2001)

hornet *n* **1** a large wasp that can inflict a severe sting **2 hornet's nest** a very unpleasant situation that is difficult to deal with: *you'll stir up a hornet's nest*
WORD ORIGIN Old English *hyrnetu*

horn of plenty *n* ▸ same as **cornucopia**

hornpipe *n* **1** a solo dance, traditionally performed by sailors **2** music for this dance

horny *adj* **hornier, horniest 1** of, like, or hard as horn **2** *slang* **a** sexually aroused **b** provoking sexual arousal **c** sexually eager

horology *n* the art of making clocks and watches or of measuring time **horological** *adj*
WORD ORIGIN Greek *hōra* hour + -LOGY

horoscope *n* **1** the prediction of a person's future based on the positions of the planets, sun, and moon at the time of birth **2** a diagram showing the positions of the planets, sun, and moon at a particular time and place
WORD ORIGIN Greek *hōra* hour + *skopas* observer

Horowitz *n* **Vladimir** 1904–89, Russian virtuoso pianist, in the US from 1928

horrendous *adj* very unpleasant or shocking
WORD ORIGIN Latin *horrendus* fearful

horrible ❶ *adj* **1** disagreeable and unpleasant: *a horrible hotel room* **2** causing fear, shock, or disgust: *he died a horrible death* **horribly** *adv*
WORD ORIGIN Latin *horribilis*

horrid *adj* **1** disagreeable or unpleasant: *it had been a horrid day at school* **2** *informal* (of a person) unkind and nasty: *her horrid parents*
WORD ORIGIN Latin *horridus* prickly

horrific ❶ *adj* provoking horror: *horrific injuries* **horrifically** *adv*

horrify ❶ *vb* **-fies, -fying, -fied** to cause feelings of horror in (someone); shock (someone) greatly

horror ❶ *n* **1** extreme fear or terror **2** intense hatred: *she had a horror of violence* **3** a thing or person causing fear, loathing, or distaste ▹ *adj* **4** having a frightening subject, usually concerned with the supernatural: *a horror film*
WORD ORIGIN Latin: a trembling with fear

horrors *pl n* **the horrors** *slang* a fit of nervousness or anxiety

Horsa *n* died ?455 AD, leader, with his brother Hengist, of the first Jutish settlers in Britain ▸ See also **Hengist**

hors d'oeuvre (or **durv**) *n, pl* **hors d'oeuvre** *or* **hors d'oeuvres** (or **durv**) an appetizer, usually served before the main meal
WORD ORIGIN French

horse ❶ *n* **1** a four-footed mammal with hooves, a mane, and a tail, used for riding and pulling carts, etc. ▸ Related adjectives: **equestrian, equine 2** the adult male of this species; stallion **3** *gymnastics* a padded apparatus on legs, used for vaulting **4 be** *or* **get on one's high horse** *informal* to act in a haughty manner **5 the horses** *informal* horse races on which bets may be placed: *an occasional flutter on the horses* **6 the horse's mouth** the most reliable source: *I'll tell you straight from the horse's mouth.* ▸ See also **horse around**
WORD ORIGIN Old English *hors*

horse around *or* **about** *vb informal* to play roughly or boisterously

horseback *n* a horse's back: *on horseback*

horsebox *n Brit, S African, NZ & Austral* a van or trailer used for transporting horses

horse brass *n* a decorative brass ornament, originally attached to a horse's harness

horse chestnut *n* **1** a tree with broad leaves and brown shiny inedible nuts enclosed in a spiky case **2** the nut of this tree

horseflesh *n* **1** horses collectively: *Ascot's annual parade of fashion and horseflesh* **2** the flesh of a horse as food

horsefly *n, pl* **-flies** a large fly which sucks the blood of horses, cattle, and people

horsehair *n* hair from the tail or mane of a horse, used in upholstery

horse laugh *n* a loud and coarse laugh

horseman *n, pl* **-men 1** a man who is skilled in riding **2** a man riding a horse **horsemanship** *n* **horsewoman** *fem n*

horseplay *n* rough or rowdy play

horsepower *n* a unit of power (equivalent to 745.7 watts), used to measure the power of an engine

horseradish *n* a plant with a white strong-tasting root, which is used to make a sauce

horse sense *n* ▸ same as **common sense**

horseshoe *n* **1** a piece of iron shaped like a U, nailed to the bottom of a horse's hoof to protect the foot **2** an object of similar shape: often regarded as a symbol of good luck

horsetail *n* a plant with small dark toothlike leaves

horsewhip *n* **1** a whip with a long thong, used for managing horses ▹ *vb* **-whipping, -whipped 2** to beat (a person or animal) with such a whip

horsey *or* **horsy** *adj* **horsier, horsiest 1** of or relating to horses: *a horsey smell* **2** devoted to horses: *the horsey set* **3** like a horse: *a horsey face*

Horta[1] *n* a port in the Azores, on the SE coast of Fayal Island

Horta[2] *n* **Victor** 1861–1947, Belgian architect, best known for his early buildings in Art Nouveau style

hortatory *or* **hortative** *adj formal* encouraging
WORD ORIGIN Latin *hortari* to encourage

Horthy *n* **Miklós**, full name *Horthy de Nagybánya*. 1868–1957, Hungarian admiral: suppressed Kun's Communist republic (1919); regent of Hungary (1920–44)

horticulture *n* the art or science of

THESAURUS

horrible *adj* **2a = dreadful**, terrible, awful, nasty, cruel, beastly *(informal)*, mean, unpleasant, ghastly *(informal)*, unkind, horrid, disagreeable
OPPOSITE: wonderful
2b = terrible, awful, appalling, terrifying, shocking, grim, dreadful, revolting, fearful, obscene, ghastly, hideous, shameful, gruesome, from hell *(informal)*, grisly, horrid, repulsive, frightful, heinous, loathsome, abhorrent, abominable, hellacious *(US slang)*

horrific *adj* **= horrifying**, shocking, appalling, frightening, awful, terrifying, grim, dreadful, horrendous, ghastly, from hell *(informal)*, grisly, frightful, hellacious *(US slang)*

horrify *vb* **a = terrify**, alarm, frighten, scare, intimidate, petrify, terrorize, put the wind up *(informal)*, make your hair stand on end, affright
OPPOSITE: comfort
b = shock, appal, disgust, dismay, sicken, outrage, gross out *(US slang)*
OPPOSITE: delight

horror *n* **1 = terror**, fear, alarm, panic, dread, dismay, awe, fright, apprehension, consternation, trepidation **2 = hatred**, disgust, loathing, aversion, revulsion, antipathy, abomination, abhorrence, repugnance, odium, detestation
OPPOSITE: love

horse *n* **1 = nag**, mount, mare, colt, filly, stallion, gelding, jade, pony, yearling, steed *(archaic, literary)*, dobbin, moke *(Austral slang)*, hobby *(archaic, dialect)*, yarraman *or* yarramin *(Austral)*, gee-gee *(slang)*, cuddy *or* cuddie *(dialect, chiefly Scot)*,

cultivating gardens **horticultural** *adj* **horticulturalist** *or* **horticulturist** *n*
WORD ORIGIN Latin *hortus* garden + CULTURE

Horus *n* an Egyptian god with a falcon's head

hosanna *interj* an exclamation of praise to God
WORD ORIGIN Hebrew *hōshi 'āh nnā* save now, we pray

hose¹ *n* **1** a flexible pipe, for conveying a liquid or gas ▹*vb* **hosing, hosed** **2** to wash or water (a person or thing) with a hose
WORD ORIGIN later use of HOSE²

hose² *n* **1** *old-fashioned* stockings, socks, and tights collectively **2** *history* a man's garment covering the legs and reaching up to the waist
WORD ORIGIN Old English *hosa*

hoser *n* **1** *US slang* a person who swindles or deceives others **2** *Canad slang* an unsophisticated, esp. rural, person

hosiery *n* stockings, socks, and knitted underclothing collectively

hospice (hoss-piss) *n* **1** a nursing home that specializes in caring for the terminally ill **2** *archaic* a place of shelter for travellers, esp. one kept by a religious order
WORD ORIGIN Latin *hospes* guest

hospitable *adj* generous, friendly, and welcoming to guests or strangers: *charming and hospitable lodgings* **hospitably** *adv*
WORD ORIGIN Medieval Latin *hospitare* to receive as a guest

hospital *n* an institution for the medical or psychiatric care and treatment of patients
WORD ORIGIN Latin *hospes* guest

hospitality **T** *n, pl* **-ties** kindness in welcoming strangers or guests

hospitalize *or* **-ise** *vb* **-izing, -ized** *or* **-ising, -ised** to admit or send (a person) into a hospital **hospitalization** *or* **-isation** *n*

hospitaller *or US* **hospitaler** *n* a member of a religious order dedicated to hospital work, ambulance services, etc.

host¹ **T** *n* **1** a person who receives or entertains guests, esp. in his own home **2** the organization or country providing the facilities for a function or event: *Barcelona, host of the 1992 Olympic Games* **3** the compere of a radio or television programme **4** *biol* an animal or plant in or on which a parasite lives **5** *computers* a computer connected to a network and providing facilities to other computers and their users **6** *old-fashioned* the owner or manager of an inn ▹*vb* **7** to be the host of (a party, programme, or event): *he's hosting a radio show*
WORD ORIGIN Latin *hospes* guest, host

host² **T** *n* a great number; multitude
WORD ORIGIN Latin *hostis* stranger

Host *n Christianity* the bread used in Holy Communion
WORD ORIGIN Latin *hostia* victim

hostage **T** *n* a person who is illegally held prisoner until certain demands are met by other people
WORD ORIGIN Old French *hoste* guest

hostel *n* **1** a building providing overnight accommodation at a low cost for particular groups of people, such as the homeless **2** ▸same as **youth hostel** **3** *Brit & NZ* a supervised lodging house for nurses, students, etc. **hosteller** *or US* **hosteler** *n*
WORD ORIGIN Medieval Latin *hospitale* hospice

hostelry *n, pl* **-ries** *archaic or facetious* an inn

hostel school *n Canad* ▸same as **residential school**

hostess *n* **1** a woman who receives and entertains guests, esp. in her own house **2** a woman who receives and entertains patrons of a club, restaurant, or dance hall

hostile **T** *adj* **1** unfriendly and aggressive **2** opposed (to): *hostile to the referendum* **3** relating to or involving the enemies of a country
WORD ORIGIN Latin *hostis* enemy

hostility **T** *n, pl* **-ties** **1** unfriendly and aggressive feelings or behaviour **2** **hostilities** acts of warfare

hot **T** *adj* **hotter, hottest** **1** having a relatively high temperature **2** having a temperature higher than desirable **3** spicy or causing a burning sensation on the tongue: *hot chillies* **4** (of a temper) quick to flare up **5** (of a contest or conflict) intense **6** recent or new: *hot from the press* **7** much favoured: *a hot favourite* **8** *informal* having a dangerously high level of radioactivity **9** *slang* stolen or otherwise illegally obtained **10** (of a colour) intense; striking: *hot pink* **11** following closely: *this LP appeared hot on the heels of the debut smash* **12** *informal* dangerous or unpleasant: *they're making it hot for me here* **13** (in various games) very near the answer **14** **hot on** *informal* **a** strict about: *they are extremely hot on sloppy language* **b** particularly knowledgeable about **15** **hot under the collar** *informal* aroused with anger, annoyance, or resentment **16** **in hot water** *informal* in trouble ▸See also **hot up** > **hotly** *adv*
WORD ORIGIN Old English *hāt*

hot air *n informal* empty and usually boastful talk

hotbed *n* a place offering ideal conditions for the growth of an idea or activity: *a hotbed of resistance*

hot-blooded *adj* passionate or excitable

hot-button *adj informal* indicating a controversial subject that is likely to arouse strong emotions: *the hot-button issue of abortion*

hotchpotch *or esp. US & Canad* **hodgepodge** *n* a jumbled mixture
WORD ORIGIN Old French *hochepot* shake pot

hot cross bun *n* a yeast bun marked with a cross and traditionally eaten on Good Friday

hot-desking *n* the practice of not assigning permanent desks in a workplace, so that employees may work at any available desk

hot dog *n* a long roll split lengthways with a hot sausage inside

THESAURUS

studhorse *or* stud

hospitality *n* **= welcome**, warmth, kindness, friendliness, sociability, conviviality, neighbourliness, cordiality, heartiness, hospitableness

host¹ *n* **3 = presenter**, compere *(Brit)*, anchorman *or* anchorwoman **6 = innkeeper**, proprietor, landlord *or* landlady ▹*vb* **7 = present**, introduce, compere *(Brit)*, front *(informal)*

host² *n* **a = multitude**, lot, load *(informal)*, wealth, array, myriad, great quantity, large number **b = crowd**, army, pack, drove, mob, herd, legion, swarm, horde, throng

hostage *n* **= captive**, prisoner, pledge, pawn, security, surety

hostile *adj* **1 = unfriendly**, belligerent, antagonistic, unkind, malevolent, warlike, bellicose, inimical, rancorous, ill-disposed
OPPOSITE: friendly
2 = antagonistic, anti *(informal)*, opposed, opposite, contrary, inimical, ill-disposed

hostility *n* **1 = unfriendliness**, hatred, animosity, spite, bitterness, malice, venom, antagonism, enmity, abhorrence, malevolence, detestation **OPPOSITE:** friendliness ▹*pl n* **2 = warfare**, war, fighting, conflict, combat, armed conflict, state of war **OPPOSITE:** peace

hot *adj* **1 = heated**, burning, boiling, steaming, flaming, roasting, searing, blistering, fiery, scorching, scalding, piping hot **2 = warm**, close, stifling, humid, torrid, sultry, sweltering, balmy, muggy
OPPOSITE: cold
3 = spicy, pungent, peppery, piquant, biting, sharp, acrid **OPPOSITE:** mild
4 = fiery, violent, raging, passionate, stormy, touchy, vehement, impetuous, irascible **OPPOSITE:** calm
5 = fierce, intense, strong, keen, competitive, cut-throat **6 = new**, latest, fresh, recent, up to date, just out, up to the minute, bang up to date *(informal)*, hot off the press
OPPOSITE: old

DICTIONARY

hotel *n* a commercially run establishment providing lodging and meals for guests
WORD ORIGIN French

hotelier *n* an owner or manager of a hotel

Hotere *n* **Ralph** born 1931, New Zealand artist of Māori origin, noted esp. for his minimalist *Black Paintings*

hotfoot *adv* with all possible speed: *hotfoot to the accident*

hot-gospeller *n informal* a revivalist preacher with a highly enthusiastic delivery

hot-headed *adj* impetuous, rash, or hot-tempered **hot-headedness** *n*

hothouse *n* a greenhouse in which the temperature is maintained at a fixed level

hot key *n computers* a single key on a computer keyboard which provides a shortcut to a function in an application

hotline *n* a direct telephone link between heads of government for emergency use

hot money *n* capital that is transferred from one financial centre to another seeking the best opportunity for short-term gain

hotplate *n* **1** a heated metal surface on an electric cooker **2** a portable device on which food can be kept warm

hot pool *n NZ* a geothermally heated pool

hotpot *n* a casserole of meat and vegetables covered with a layer of potatoes

hot rod *n* a car with an engine that has been modified to produce increased power

hot seat *n* **1** *US slang* the electric chair **2** **in the hot seat** *informal* in a difficult and responsible position

hotspot *n* **1** a place where there is a lot of exciting activity or entertainment: *Birmingham's fashionable hot spots* **2** an area where there is fighting or political unrest: *a political hot spot in the Caucasus* **3** a small area of abnormally high temperature or radioactivity **4** *computers* a place (esp. a public building or commercial premises) offering a wireless internet connection

Hotspur *n* **Harry Hotspur** the nickname of Sir Henry Percy ▸ See **Percy** (sense 1)

hot stuff *n informal* **1** a person, object, or activity considered attractive, exciting, or important: *they're still hot stuff* **2** pornographic or erotic books, plays, films, etc.

Hottentot *n* **1** a race of indigenous people of South Africa which is now almost extinct **2** a member of this race **3** Also called: **Khoi Khoi** the language of this race
WORD ORIGIN origin unknown

hotting *n Brit informal* the performing of high-speed stunts in a stolen car **hotter** *n*

hot up *vb* **hotting, hotted** *informal* to make or become more active and exciting

hot-water bottle *n* a rubber container, designed to be filled with hot water and used for warming a bed

Houdon *n* **Jean Antoine** 1741–1828, French neoclassical portrait sculptor

hound ❶ *n* **1** a dog used for hunting: *to ride with the hounds* **2** a despicable person ▹ *vb* **3** to pursue, disturb, or criticize relentlessly: *hounded by the press*
WORD ORIGIN Old English *hund*

Houphouet-Boigny *n* **Félix** 1905–93, Côte d'Ivoire statesman; president of the Côte d'Ivoire (1960–93)

hour *n* **1** a period of time equal to 60 minutes; 1/24 of a day **2** any of the points on the face of a clock or watch that indicate intervals of 60 minutes: *in my hurry I mistook the hour* **3** the time of day **4** the time allowed for or used for something: *a three-and-a-half-hour test* **5** the distance covered in an hour: *an hour from the heart of Tokyo* **6** a special moment: *the decisive hour* ▸ See also **hours**
WORD ORIGIN Latin *hora*

hourglass *n* a device consisting of two transparent sections linked by a narrow channel, containing a quantity of sand that takes an hour to trickle from one section to the other

houri *n, pl* **-ris** (in Muslim belief) any of the nymphs of Paradise
WORD ORIGIN Arabic *haurā'* woman with dark eyes

hourly *adj* **1** of, occurring, or done once every hour **2** measured by the hour: *hourly charges* **3** frequent ▹ *adv* **4** once every hour **5** by the hour: *hourly paid* **6** frequently **7** at any moment: *the arrival of the men was hourly expected*

hours *pl n* **1** an indefinite time: *they play on their bikes for hours* **2** a period regularly appointed for work or business **3** one's times of rising and going to bed: *you keep very late hours* **4** *RC church* prayers recited at seven specified times of the day

Hours *pl n classical myth* the goddesses of the seasons

house ❶ *n* **1** a building used as a home; dwelling **2** the people in a house **3** a building for some specific purpose: *beach house* **4** a family or dynasty: *the House of Windsor* **5** a commercial company: *auction house* **6** a law-making body or the hall where it meets **7** a division of a large school: *he was captain of the house rugby team* **8** the audience in a theatre or cinema **9** *astrol* any of the 12 divisions of the zodiac **10** *informal* a brothel **11** **get on like a house on fire** *informal* (of people) to get on very well together **12** **on the house** (usually of drinks) paid for by the management **13** **put one's house in order** to settle or organize one's affairs ▹ *adj* **14** (of wine) sold unnamed by a restaurant, at a lower price than wines specified on the wine list: *house red* ▹ *vb* **housing, housed** **15** to give accommodation to **16** to contain or cover (something)
WORD ORIGIN Old English *hūs*

house arrest *n* confinement to one's own home rather than in prison

houseboat *n* a stationary boat used as a home

housebound *adj* unable to leave one's house, usually because of illness

housebreaking *n criminal law* the act of entering a building as a trespasser for an unlawful purpose **housebreaker** *n*

housecoat *n* a woman's loose robelike garment for casual wear

housefly *n, pl* **-flies** a common fly often found in houses

household ❶ *n* **1** all the people living together in one house ▹ *adj* **2** relating to the running of a household: *household budget*

householder *n* a person who owns or rents a house

household name *or* **word** *n* a person or thing that is very well known

housekeeper *n* a person employed to run someone else's household

housekeeping *n* **1** the running of a household **2** money allotted for this

house lights *pl n* the lights in the auditorium of a theatre or cinema

THESAURUS

hound *vb* **3 = harass**, harry, bother, provoke, annoy, torment, hassle *(informal)*, prod, badger, persecute, pester, goad, keep after

house *n* **1 = home**, residence, dwelling, building, pad *(slang)*, homestead, edifice, abode, habitation, domicile, whare *(NZ)* **2 = household**, family, ménage **4 = dynasty**, line, race, tribe, clan, ancestry, lineage, family tree, kindred **5 = firm**, company, business, concern, organization, partnership, establishment, outfit *(informal)* **6 = assembly**, parliament, Commons, legislative body **12 on the house = free**, for free *(informal)*, for nothing, free of charge, gratis, without expense ▹ *vb* **15 = accommodate**, board, quarter, take in, put up, lodge, harbour, billet, domicile **16 = contain**, keep, hold, cover, store, protect, shelter

household *n* **1 = family**, home, house, ménage, family circle, ainga *(NZ)*

DICTIONARY

housemaid *n* (esp. formerly) a female servant employed to do housework
housemaid's knee *n* a fluid-filled swelling of the kneecap
houseman *n, pl* **-men** *med* a junior doctor in a hospital
house martin *n* a swallow with a slightly forked tail
House music *or* **House** *n* a type of disco music of the late 1980s, based on funk, with fragments of other recordings edited in electronically
House of Commons *n* (in Britain and Canada) the lower chamber of Parliament
House of Keys *n* the lower chamber of the law-making body of the Isle of Man
House of Lords *n* (in Britain) the upper chamber of Parliament, composed of the peers of the realm
House of Representatives *n* **1** (in the US) the lower chamber of Congress, or of many state legislatures **2** (in Australia) the lower chamber of Parliament **3** the sole chamber of New Zealand's Parliament
house party *n* **1** a party, usually in a country house, at which guests are invited to stay for several days **2** the guests who are invited
house-proud *adj* excessively concerned with the appearance, cleanliness, and tidiness of one's house
houseroom *n* **not give something houseroom** not to want to have something in one's house
house-train *vb* to train (a pet) to urinate and defecate outside
housewares *pl n US & Canad* kitchenware and other utensils for use in the home
house-warming *n* a party given after moving into a new home
housewife *n, pl* **-wives** a woman who runs her own household and does not have a paid job **housewifely** *adj*
housework *n* the work of running a home, such as cleaning, cooking, and shopping
housing ❶ *n* **1** houses collectively **2** the job of providing people with accommodation **3** a part designed to contain and support a component or mechanism: *the inspection panel set within the concrete housing*
Housman *n* **A(lfred) E(dward)** 1859–1936, English poet and classical scholar, author of *A Shropshire Lad* (1896) and *Last Poems* (1922)
hove *vb chiefly naut* ▸ a past of **heave**
hovea *n* an Australian plant with purple flowers
hovel *n* a small house or hut that is dirty or badly in need of repair
WORD ORIGIN origin unknown
hover ❶ *vb* **1** (of a bird, insect, or helicopter) to remain suspended in one place in the air **2** to linger uncertainly in a place **3** to be in an unsettled or uncertain situation or frame of mind: *hovering between two options*
WORD ORIGIN Middle English *hoveren*
hovercraft *n* a vehicle that is able to travel across both land and water on a cushion of air
how *adv* **1** in what way, by what means: *how did you spend the evening?; observing how elderly people coped* **2** to what extent: *they don't know how tough I am* **3** how good, how well, what ... like: *how good are the copies?; so that's how things are* **4 how about?** used to suggest something: *how about some tea?* **5 how are you?** what is your state of health? **6 how's that? a** what is your opinion?: *we'll go out for a late-night supper – how's that?* **b** *cricket* Also written: **howzat** (an appeal to the umpire) is the batsman out?
WORD ORIGIN Old English *hu*
howdah *n* a seat for riding on an elephant's back
WORD ORIGIN Hindi *haudah*
Howe *n* **1 Elias** 1819–67, US inventor of the sewing machine (1846) **2 Gordon**, known as *Gordie*. born 1928, US ice-hockey player, who scored a record 1071 goals in a professional career lasting 32 years **3 Howe of Aberavon**, Baron, title of *(Richard Edward) Geoffrey Howe*. born 1926, British Conservative politician; Chancellor of the Exchequer (1979–83); foreign secretary (1983–89); deputy prime minister (1989–90) **4 Richard,** 4th Viscount Howe. 1726–99, British admiral: served (1776–78) in the War of American Independence and commanded the Channel fleet against France, winning the Battle of the Glorious First of June (1794) **5** his brother, **William,** 5th Viscount Howe. 1729–1814, British general; commander in chief (1776–78) of British forces in the War of American Independence
Howel Dda *n* ▸ See **Hywel Dda**
however ❶ *adv* **1** still; nevertheless: *the book does, however, almost get funny* **2** by whatever means: *get there however you can* **3** (*with an adjective or adverb*) no matter how: *however low we plunge, there is always hope*
howitzer *n* a large gun that fires shells at a steep angle
WORD ORIGIN Czech *houfnice* stone-sling
howl ❶ *n* **1** the long, loud wailing noise made by a wolf or a dog **2** a similar cry of pain or sorrow **3** a loud burst of laughter ▹ *vb* **4** to express (something) in a howl or utter such cries **5** (of the wind, etc.) to make a wailing noise
WORD ORIGIN Middle English *houlen*
howl down *vb* to prevent (a speaker) from being heard by shouting disapprovingly
howler *n informal* a glaring mistake
howling *adj informal* great: *a howling success*
Howlin' Wolf *n* real name *Chester Burnett* 1910–76, US blues singer and songwriter
howzit *sentence substitute S African* an informal word for hello
WORD ORIGIN from the phrase *how is it?*
Hoxha *n* **Enver** 1908–85, Albanian statesman: founded the Albanian Communist Party in 1941 and was its first secretary (1954–85)
hoy *interj* a cry used to attract someone's attention
WORD ORIGIN variant of *hey*
hoyden *n old-fashioned* a wild boisterous girl; tomboy **hoydenish** *adj*
WORD ORIGIN perhaps from Middle Dutch *heidijn* heathen
Hoyle[1] *n* an authoritative book of rules for card games
WORD ORIGIN after Edmond *Hoyle* (1672–1769), English authority on games, its compiler
Hoyle[2] *n* Sir **Fred** 1915–2001, English astronomer and writer: his books include *The Nature of the Universe* (1950) and *Frontiers of Astronomy* (1955), and science-fiction writings
HP *or* **h.p.** **1** *Brit* hire-purchase **2** horsepower
HQ *or* **h.q.** headquarters
hr hour

THESAURUS

housing *n* **1 = accommodation**, homes, houses, dwellings, domiciles **3 = case**, casing, covering, cover, shell, jacket, holder, container, capsule, sheath, encasement
hover *vb* **1 = float**, fly, hang, drift, be suspended, flutter, poise **2 = linger**, loiter, wait nearby, hang about *or* around *(informal)* **3 = waver**, alternate, fluctuate, haver *(Brit)*, falter, dither *(chiefly Brit)*, oscillate, vacillate, seesaw, swither *(Scot dialect)*
however *adv* **1 = but**, nevertheless, still, though, yet, even though, on the other hand, nonetheless, notwithstanding, anyhow, be that as it may
howl *n* **1 = baying**, cry, bay, bark, barking, yelp, yelping, yowl **2 = cry**, scream, roar, bay, wail, outcry, shriek, bellow, clamour, hoot, bawl, yelp, yowl ▹ *vb* **4a = bay**, cry, bark, yelp, quest *(of a hound)* **4b = cry**, shout, scream, roar, weep, yell, cry out, wail, shriek, bellow, bawl, yelp

DICTIONARY

HRH Her (*or* His) Royal Highness
HRT 1 hormone replacement therapy 2 *Austral & NZ* high rising terminal
Hs *chem* hassium
Hsia Kuei *n* ▸ See **Xia Gui**
Hsüan-tsang *n* ▸ a variant transliteration of the Chinese name for **Xuan Zang**
Hsüan-tsung *n* ▸ a variant transliteration of the Chinese name for **Xuan Zong**
Hsün-tzu *n* ▸ a variant transliteration of the Chinese name for **Xun Zi**
HTML *n computers* a text description language that is used on the World Wide Web
WORD ORIGIN *hypertext markup language*
HTTP *n computers* hypertext transfer protocol: a system of rules for transferring files on the internet
Hua Guo Feng *or* **Hua Kuo-feng** *n* born c. 1920, Chinese Communist statesman; prime minister of China 1976–80
Huang Hua *n* born 1913, Chinese Communist statesman; minister for foreign affairs (1976–83)
Huáscar *n* died 1533, Inca ruler (1525–33): murdered by his half brother Atahualpa
hub ⓘ *n* 1 the central portion of a wheel, through which the axle passes 2 the central, most important, or active part of a place or organization
WORD ORIGIN probably variant of *hob*
hubble-bubble *n* 1 ▸ same as **hookah** 2 *archaic* turmoil or confusion
WORD ORIGIN imitative
hubbub *n* 1 a confused noise of many voices 2 great confusion or excitement
WORD ORIGIN probably from Irish *hooboobbes*
hubby *n, pl* **-bies** *informal* a husband
hubcap *n* a metal disc that fits on to and protects the hub of a wheel, esp. on a car
hubris (hew-briss) *n formal* pride or arrogance **hubristic** *adj*
WORD ORIGIN Greek
huckster *n* 1 a person who uses aggressive methods of selling 2 *now rare* a person who sells small articles or fruit in the street
WORD ORIGIN probably from Middle Dutch *hoekster*
huddle ⓘ *n* 1 a small group of people or things standing or lying close together 2 **go into a huddle** *informal* to have a private conference ▹ *vb* **-dling, -dled** 3 (of a group of people) to crowd or nestle closely together 4 to curl up one's arms and legs close to one's body through cold or fear
WORD ORIGIN origin unknown
Huddleston *n* **Trevor** 1913–98, British Anglican prelate; suffragan bishop of Stepney (1968–78) and bishop of Mauritius (1978–83); president of the Anti-Apartheid Movement (1981–94)
Hudson *n* 1 **Henry** died 1611, English navigator: he explored the Hudson River (1609) and Hudson Bay (1610), where his crew mutinied and cast him adrift to die 2 **W**(**illiam**) **H**(**enry**) 1841–1922, British naturalist and novelist, born in Argentina, noted esp. for his romance *Green Mansions* (1904) and the autobiographical *Far Away and Long Ago* (1918)
hue ⓘ *n* 1 the feature of colour that enables an observer to classify it as red, blue, etc. 2 a shade of a colour
WORD ORIGIN Old English *hīw* beauty
hue and cry *n* a loud public outcry
WORD ORIGIN Old French *hue* outcry
huff *n* 1 a passing mood of anger or resentment: *in a huff* ▹ *vb* 2 to blow or puff heavily 3 *draughts* to remove (an opponent's draught) from the board for failure to make a capture 4 **huffing and puffing** empty threats or objections **huffy** *adj* **huffily** *adv*
WORD ORIGIN imitative
hug ⓘ *vb* **hugging, hugged** 1 to clasp (someone or something) tightly, usually with affection 2 to keep close to (a shore or the kerb) ▹ *n* 3 a tight or fond embrace
WORD ORIGIN probably Scandinavian
huge ⓘ *adj* extremely large **hugely** *adv*
WORD ORIGIN Old French *ahuge*
huggermugger *archaic n* 1 confusion or secrecy ▹ *adj, adv* 2 in confusion
WORD ORIGIN origin unknown
Huggins *n* Sir **William** 1824–1910, British astronomer. He pioneered the use of spectroscopy in astronomy and discovered the red shift in the lines of a stellar spectrum
Huguenot (hew-gan-oh) *n* a French Calvinist of the 16th or 17th centuries
WORD ORIGIN French
huh *interj* an exclamation of derision, bewilderment, or inquiry
hui ⓘ (hoo-ee), **huis**, *n NZ* 1 a Māori social gathering 2 a meeting to discuss Māori matters 3 any party
WORD ORIGIN Māori
hula *n* a Hawaiian dance performed by a woman
WORD ORIGIN Hawaiian
Hula Hoop *n trademark* a plastic hoop swung round the body by wiggling the hips
hulk *n* 1 the body of an abandoned ship 2 *disparaging* a large ungainly person or thing
WORD ORIGIN Old English *hulc*
hulking *adj* big and ungainly
hull *n* 1 the main body of a boat 2 the outer covering of a fruit or seed such as a pea or bean 3 the leaves round the stem of a strawberry, raspberry, or similar fruit ▹ *vb* 4 to remove the hulls from (fruit or seeds)
WORD ORIGIN Old English *hulu*
Hull[1] *n* 1 a city and port in NE England, in Kingston upon Hull unitary authority, East Riding of Yorkshire: fishing, food processing; two universities. Pop: 301 416 (2001). Official name: **Kingston upon Hull** 2 a city in SE Canada, in SW Quebec on the River Ottawa: a centre of the timber trade and associated industries. Pop: 66 246 (2001)
Hull[2] *n* **Cordell** 1871–1955, US statesman; secretary of state (1933–44). He helped to found the U.N.: Nobel peace prize 1945
hullabaloo *n, pl* **-loos** a loud confused noise or commotion
WORD ORIGIN *hallo* + Scots *baloo* lullaby
hullo *interj, n* ▸ same as **hello**
Hulme *n* **T**(**homas**) **E**(**rnest**) 1883–1917, English literary critic and poet; a proponent of imagism
hum ⓘ *vb* **humming, hummed** 1 to make a low continuous vibrating sound 2 (of a person) to sing with the lips closed 3 to utter an indistinct sound when hesitating

THESAURUS

hub *n* 2 = **centre**, heart, focus, core, middle, focal point, pivot, nerve centre
huddle *vb* 3 = **crowd**, press, gather, collect, squeeze, cluster, flock, herd, throng 4 = **curl up**, crouch, hunch up, nestle, snuggle, make yourself small
hue *n* 1, 2 = **colour**, tone, shade, dye, tint, tinge, tincture
hug *vb* 1 = **embrace**, hold (onto), cuddle, squeeze, cling, clasp, enfold, hold close, take in your arms ▹ *n* 3 = **embrace**, squeeze, bear hug, clinch *(slang)*, clasp
huge *adj* = **enormous**, great, giant, large, massive, vast, extensive, tremendous, immense, mega *(slang)*, titanic, jumbo *(informal)*, gigantic, monumental, mammoth, bulky, colossal, mountainous, stellar *(informal)*, prodigious, stupendous, gargantuan, elephantine, ginormous *(informal)*, Brobdingnagian, humongous *or* humungous *(US slang)* **OPPOSITE:** tiny
hui *n* 1, 2 *(NZ)* = **meeting**, gathering, assembly, meet, conference, congress, session, rally, convention, get-together *(informal)*, reunion, congregation, conclave, convocation, powwow
hum *vb* 1 = **drone**, buzz, murmur, throb, vibrate, purr, croon, thrum, whir 4 *(informal)* = **be busy**, buzz, bustle, move, stir, pulse, be active,

DICTIONARY

4 *informal* to be in a state of feverish activity: *the town hums with activity and life* 5 *slang* to smell unpleasant 6 **hum and haw** ▸ see **haw²** ▹ *n* 7 a low continuous murmuring sound 8 an unpleasant smell ▹ *interj, n* 9 an indistinct sound of hesitation
WORD ORIGIN imitative

human ❶ *adj* 1 of or relating to people: *human occupants* 2 having the qualities of people as opposed to animals, divine beings, or machines: *human nature* 3 kind or considerate ▹ *n* 4 a human being
WORD ORIGIN Latin *humanus*

human being *n* a man, woman, or child

humane ❶ *adj* 1 showing kindness and sympathy 2 inflicting as little pain as possible: *a humane method of killing minke whales* 3 considered to have a civilizing effect on people: *the humane tradition of a literary education*
WORD ORIGIN variant of *human*

humanism *n* the rejection of religion in favour of a belief in the advancement of humanity by its own efforts **humanist** *n, adj* **humanistic** *adj*

humanitarian ❶ *adj* 1 having the interests of mankind at heart ▹ *n* 2 a person who has the interests of mankind at heart **humanitarianism** *n*

humanity ❶ *n, pl* **-ties** 1 the human race 2 the quality of being human 3 kindness or mercy 4 **humanities** the study of literature, philosophy, and the arts

humanize *or* **-ise** *vb* **-izing, -ized** *or* **-ising, -ised** to make human or humane **humanization** *or* **-isation** *n*

humankind *n* the human race; humanity

humanly *adv* by human powers or means: *as fast as is humanly possible*

humanoid *adj* 1 like a human being in appearance ▹ *n* 2 (in science fiction) a robot or creature resembling a human being

human race *n* all men, women and children collectively

human resources *pl n* 1 the people employed in an organization or for a service 2 (*functioning as sing*) the department in an organization that appoints or keeps records of employees

human rights *pl n* the basic rights of individuals to liberty, justice, etc.

humble ❶ *adj* 1 conscious of one's failings 2 modest and unpretentious: *humble domestic objects* 3 ordinary or not very important: *humble beginnings* ▹ *vb* **-bling, -bled** 4 to cause to become humble; humiliate **humbly** *adv*
WORD ORIGIN Latin *humilis* low

humble pie *n* **eat humble pie** to be forced to behave humbly; be humiliated
WORD ORIGIN earlier *an umble pie*, from *numbles* offal of a deer

Humboldt *n* 1 Baron (**Friedrich Heinrich**) **Alexander von** 1769–1859, German scientist, who made important scientific explorations in Central and South America (1799–1804). In *Kosmos* (1845–62), he provided a comprehensive description of the physical universe 2 his brother, Baron (**Karl**) **Wilhelm von** 1767–1835, German philologist and educational reformer

humbug *n* 1 *Brit* a hard peppermint sweet with a striped pattern 2 a speech or piece of writing that is obviously untrue, dishonest, or nonsense 3 a dishonest person
WORD ORIGIN origin unknown

humdinger *n slang* 1 something unusually large 2 an excellent person or thing
WORD ORIGIN origin unknown

humdrum *adj* ordinary, dull, and uninteresting
WORD ORIGIN probably based on *hum*

humerus (hew-mer-uss) *n, pl* **-meri** (-mer-rye) the bone from the shoulder to the elbow **humeral** *adj*
WORD ORIGIN Latin *umerus*

humid *adj* (of the weather) damp and warm
WORD ORIGIN Latin *umidus*

humidex (hew-mid-ex) *n Canad* a system of measuring discomfort showing the combined effect of humidity and temperature

humidify *vb* **-fies, -fying, -fied** to make the air in (a room) more humid or damp **humidifier** *n*

humidity ❶ *n* 1 dampness 2 a measure of the amount of moisture in the air

humiliate ❶ *vb* **-ating, -ated** to hurt the dignity or pride of: *the English cricket team was humiliated by Australia* **humiliating** *adj* **humiliation** *n*
WORD ORIGIN Latin *humilis* humble

humility *n* the quality of being humble and modest

Hummel *n* **Johann Nepomuk** 1778–1837, German composer and pianist

hummingbird *n* a very small brightly-coloured American bird with a long slender bill, and powerful wings that hum as they vibrate

hummock *n* a very small hill or a mound
WORD ORIGIN origin unknown

hummus *n* a creamy dip originating in the Middle East, made from puréed chickpeas
WORD ORIGIN from Turkish *humus*

humongous ▸ a variant of **humungous**

humorist *n* a person who speaks or writes in a humorous way

humorous ❶ *adj* amusing, esp. in a witty or clever way **humorously** *adv*

THESAURUS

vibrate, pulsate

human *adj* 1 = **mortal**, anthropoid, manlike **OPPOSITE:** nonhuman ▹ *n* 4 = **human being**, person, individual, body, creature, mortal, man *or* woman **OPPOSITE:** nonhuman

humane *adj* 1 = **kind**, compassionate, good, kindly, understanding, gentle, forgiving, tender, mild, sympathetic, charitable, benign, clement, benevolent, lenient, merciful, good-natured, forbearing, kind-hearted **OPPOSITE:** cruel

humanitarian *adj* 1 = **charitable**, philanthropic, public-spirited ▹ *n* 2 = **philanthropist**, benefactor, Good Samaritan, altruist

humanity *n* 1 = **the human race**, man, mankind, people, men, mortals, humankind, Homo sapiens 2 = **human nature**, mortality, humanness 3 = **kindness**, charity, compassion, understanding, sympathy, mercy, tolerance, tenderness, philanthropy, benevolence, fellow feeling, benignity, brotherly love, kind-heartedness

humble *adj* 1, 2 = **modest**, meek, unassuming, unpretentious, submissive, self-effacing, unostentatious **OPPOSITE:** proud 3 = **lowly**, common, poor, mean, low, simple, ordinary, modest, obscure, commonplace, insignificant, unimportant, unpretentious, undistinguished, plebeian, low-born **OPPOSITE:** distinguished ▹ *vb* 4 = **humiliate**, shame, disgrace, break, reduce, lower, sink, crush, put down (*slang*), bring down, subdue, degrade, demean, chagrin, chasten, mortify, debase, put (someone) in their place, abase, take down a peg (*informal*), abash **OPPOSITE:** exalt

humidity *n* 1 = **damp**, moisture, dampness, wetness, moistness, sogginess, dankness, clamminess, mugginess, humidness

humiliate *vb* = **embarrass**, shame, humble, crush, disgrace, put down, subdue, degrade, chagrin, chasten, mortify, debase, discomfit, bring low, put (someone) in their place, take the wind out of someone's sails, abase, take down a peg (*informal*), abash, make (someone) eat humble pie **OPPOSITE:** honour

humorous *adj* = **funny**, comic, amusing, entertaining, witty, merry, hilarious, ludicrous, laughable, farcical, whimsical, comical, droll,

DICTIONARY

humour ❶ *or US* **humor** *n* **1** the quality of being funny **2** the ability to appreciate or express things that are humorous: *a sense of humour* **3** situations, speech, or writings that are humorous **4** a state of mind; mood: *in astoundingly good humour* **5** *archaic* any of various fluids in the body: *aqueous humour* ▷ *vb* **6** to be kind and indulgent to: *he decided the patient needed to be humoured* **humourless** *adj*
WORD ORIGIN Latin *humor* liquid

hump *n* **1** a rounded lump on the ground **2** a rounded deformity of the back **3** a rounded lump on the back of a camel or related animal **4** **the hump** *Brit informal* a fit of sulking: *you've got the hump today* ▷ *vb* **5** *slang* to carry or heave: *who would be responsible if they were injured humping heavy gear around?*
WORD ORIGIN probably from *humpbacked*

humpback *n* **1** ▸ same as **hunchback** **2** Also called: **humpback whale** a large whalebone whale with a hump on its back **3** Also called: **humpback bridge** *Brit* a road bridge with a sharp slope on either side **humpbacked** *adj*

Humperdinck *n* **Engelbert** 1854–1921, German composer, esp. of operas, including *Hansel and Gretel* (1893)

humph *interj* an exclamation of annoyance or scepticism

Humphrey *n* **1** **Duke Humphrey** ▸ See **Gloucester** (sense 1) **2** **Hubert Horatio** 1911–78, US statesman; vice-president of the US under President Johnson (1965–69)

humungous *or esp. US* **humongous** (hew-**mung**-gus) *adj informal* very large; enormous: *it was not a humungous box office hit*
WORD ORIGIN probably from *huge* + *enormous*

humus (hew-muss) *n* a dark brown or black mass of partially decomposed plant and animal matter in the soil
WORD ORIGIN Latin: soil

Humvee *n* a four-wheel drive military vehicle
WORD ORIGIN h(igh-mobility) + m(ulti-purpose) v(ehicle) + -EE

Hun *n, pl* **Huns** *or* **Hun** **1** a member of any of several Asiatic peoples who invaded the Roman Empire in the 4th and 5th centuries AD **2** *offensive informal* (esp. in World War I) a German
WORD ORIGIN Old English *Hūnas*

hunch ❶ *n* **1** a feeling or suspicion not based on facts: *she said that she had had a hunch that the coup would not succeed* **2** ▸ same as **hump** ▷ *vb* **3** to draw (oneself or one's shoulders) up or together
WORD ORIGIN origin unknown

hunchback *n* a person who has an abnormal curvature of the spine **hunchbacked** *adj*

hundred *n, pl* **-dreds** *or* **-dred** **1** the cardinal number that is the product of ten and ten **2** a numeral, 100 or C, representing this number **3** (*often pl*) a large but unspecified number ▷ *adj* **4** amounting to a hundred: *a hundred yards* **hundredth** *adj, n*
WORD ORIGIN Old English

hundreds and thousands *pl n* tiny beads of coloured sugar, used in decorating cakes and sweets

hundredweight *n, pl* **-weights** *or* **-weight** **1** *Brit* a unit of weight equal to 112 pounds or 50.802kg **2** *US & Canad* a unit of weight equal to 100 pounds or 45.359kg **3** a metric unit of weight equal to 50 kilograms

hung *vb* **1** ▸ the past of **hang** ▷ *adj* **2** (of a parliament or jury) with no side having a clear majority **3** **hung over** *informal* suffering the effects of a hangover

Hungarian *adj* **1** of Hungary ▷ *n* **2** a person from Hungary **3** the language of Hungary

hunger ❶ *n* **1** a feeling of emptiness or weakness caused by lack of food **2** a lack of food that causes suffering or death: *refugees dying of hunger and disease* **3** desire or craving: *Europe's hunger for bullion* ▷ *vb* **4** **hunger for** to have a great desire (for)
WORD ORIGIN Old English *hungor*

hunger strike *n* a refusal of all food, usually by a prisoner, as a means of protest

Hung Hsiu-ch'uan *n* ▸ See **Hong Xiu Quan**

hungry ❶ *adj* **-grier, -griest** **1** desiring food **2** (foll. by *for*) having a craving, desire, or need for: *hungry for revenge* **3** expressing greed, craving, or desire: *the media's hungry search for impact* **hungrily** *adv*

Hung-wu *n* ▸ See **Hong-wu**

hunk ❶ *n* **1** a large piece: *a hunk of bread* **2** *slang* a well-built, sexually attractive man
WORD ORIGIN probably related to Flemish *hunke*

hunkers *pl n* haunches
WORD ORIGIN origin unknown

hunt ❶ *vb* **1** to seek out and kill (animals) for food or sport **2** **hunt down** to track in an attempt to capture (someone): *hunting down villains* **3** **hunt for** to search for: *Western companies are hunting for opportunities to invest* ▷ *n* **4** the act or an instance of hunting **5** a party organized for the pursuit of wild animals for sport **6** the members of such a party **hunting** *n*
WORD ORIGIN Old English *huntian*

huntaway *n NZ* a sheepdog trained to drive sheep by barking

hunter *n* **1** a person or animal that seeks out and kills or captures game **2** a person who looks carefully for something: *a house hunter* **3** a horse or dog bred for hunting **4** a watch with a hinged metal lid or case to protect the glass

Hunter *n* **1** **John** 1728–93, British physician, noted for his investigation of venereal and other diseases **2** his brother, **William** 1718–83, British anatomist and obstetrician

hunter-gatherer *n* a member of a society that lives by hunting and gathering naturally occurring resources

Huntingdon[1] *n* a town in E central England, in Cambridgeshire: birthplace of Oliver Cromwell. Pop (with Godmanchester): 20 600 (2001)

Huntingdon[2] *n* **Selina,** Countess of Huntingdon. 1707–91, English religious leader, who founded a

THESAURUS

facetious, jocular, side-splitting, waggish, jocose **OPPOSITE:** serious

humour *or US* **humor** *n* **1 = comedy,** funniness, fun, amusement, funny side, jocularity, facetiousness, ludicrousness, drollery, comical aspect **OPPOSITE:** seriousness **3 = joking,** jokes, comedy, wit, gags (*informal*), farce, jesting, jests, wisecracks (*informal*), witticisms, wittiness **4 = mood,** spirits, temper, disposition, frame of mind ▷ *vb* **6 = indulge,** accommodate, go along with, spoil, flatter, pamper, gratify, pander to, mollify, cosset, fawn on

OPPOSITE: oppose

hunch *n* **1 = feeling,** idea, impression, suspicion, intuition, premonition, inkling, presentiment ▷ *vb* **3 = crouch,** bend, stoop, curve, arch, huddle, draw in, squat, hump

hunger *n* **1 = appetite,** emptiness, voracity, hungriness, ravenousness **2 = starvation,** famine, malnutrition, undernourishment **3 = desire,** appetite, craving, yen (*informal*), ache, lust, yearning, itch, thirst, greediness ▷ *vb* **4** **hunger for something = want,** desire, crave, hope for, long for, wish for, yearn for, pine for, hanker after, ache for, thirst after, itch after

hungry *adj* **1 = starving,** ravenous, famished, starved, empty, hollow, voracious, peckish (*informal, chiefly Brit*), famishing **2, 3 = eager,** keen, craving, yearning, greedy, avid, desirous, covetous, athirst

hunk *n* **1 = lump,** piece, chunk, block, mass, wedge, slab, nugget, wodge (*Brit informal*), gobbet

hunt *vb* **1 = stalk,** track, chase, pursue, trail, hound, gun for ▷ *n* **4 = search,** hunting, investigation, chase, pursuit, quest

DICTIONARY

Calvinistic Methodist sect

huntsman *n, pl* **-men** 1 a person who hunts 2 a person who trains hounds and manages them during a hunt

Hunyadi *n* **János** ?1387–1456, Hungarian general, who led Hungarian resistance to the Turks, defeating them notably at Belgrade (1456)

Hurd *n* **Douglas** (**Richard**), Baron Hurd of Westwell. born 1930, British Conservative politician; home secretary (1985–89); foreign secretary (1989–95)

hurdle ❶ *n* 1 *athletics* one of a number of light barriers over which runners leap in certain events 2 a difficulty or problem: *the main technical hurdle is the environment* 3 **hurdles** a race involving hurdles ▷*vb* **-dling, -dled** 4 to jump over (a hurdle or other obstacle) **hurdler** *n*
WORD ORIGIN Old English *hyrdel*

hurdy-gurdy *n, pl* **hurdy-gurdies** a mechanical musical instrument, such as a barrel organ
WORD ORIGIN probably imitative

hurl ❶ *vb* 1 to throw (something) with great force 2 to utter (something) with force; yell: *onlookers hurled abuse at them*
WORD ORIGIN probably imitative

hurling *or* **hurley** *n* a traditional Irish game resembling hockey

hurly-burly *n* great noise and activity; commotion
WORD ORIGIN obsolete *hurling* uproar

hurrah *or* **hooray** *interj, n* a cheer of joy or victory
WORD ORIGIN probably from German *hurra*

hurricane ❶ *n* a severe, often destructive storm, esp. a tropical cyclone
WORD ORIGIN Spanish *huracán*

hurricane lamp *n* a paraffin lamp with a glass covering

hurried ❶ *adj* done quickly or too quickly **hurriedly** *adv* **hurriedness** *n*

hurry ❶ *vb* **-ries, -rying, -ried** 1 to move or act or cause to move or act in great haste: *the umpires hurried the players off the ground* 2 to speed up the completion or progress of: *eat a small snack rather than hurry a main meal* ▷*n* 3 haste 4 urgency or eagerness 5 **in a hurry** *informal* **a** easily: *a striking old guy, not the sort you'd forget in a hurry* **b** willingly: *he would not ease interest rates again in a hurry*
WORD ORIGIN probably imitative

hurt ❶ *vb* **hurting, hurt** 1 to cause physical or mental injury to: *is she badly hurt?* 2 to cause someone to feel pain: *my head hurt* 3 *informal* to feel pain: *she was hurting* ▷*n* 4 physical or mental pain or suffering ▷*adj* 5 injured or pained: *his hurt head; a hurt expression* **hurtful** *adj*
WORD ORIGIN Old French *hurter* to knock against

hurtle ❶ *vb* **-ling, -led** to move very quickly or violently
WORD ORIGIN Middle English *hurtlen*

Hus *n* **Jan** the Czech name of John Huss ▸ See **Huss**

Husain *n* 1 ?629–680 AD, Islamic caliph, the son of Ali and Fatima and the grandson of Mohammed 2 ▸ same as **Hussein**

husband ❶ *n* 1 a woman's partner in marriage ▷*vb* 2 to use (resources, finances, etc.) economically
WORD ORIGIN Old English *hūsbonda*

husbandry *n* 1 the art or skill of farming 2 management of resources

Husein ibn-Ali *n* 1856–1931, first king of Hejaz (1916–24): initiated the Arab revolt against the Turks (1916–18); forced to abdicate by ibn-Saud

hush ❶ *vb* 1 to make or be silent ▷*n* 2 stillness or silence ▷*interj* 3 a plea or demand for silence ▸ See also **hush up** > **hushed** *adj*
WORD ORIGIN earlier *husht* quiet!

hush-hush *adj informal* (esp. of official work) secret and confidential

hush money *n slang* money given to a person to ensure that something is kept secret

hush up *vb* to suppress information or rumours about (something)

husk *n* 1 the outer covering of certain fruits and seeds ▷*vb* 2 to remove the husk from
WORD ORIGIN probably from Middle Dutch *hūs* house

husky[1] *adj* **huskier, huskiest** 1 (of a voice) slightly hoarse 2 *informal* (of a man) big and strong **huskily** *adv*
WORD ORIGIN probably from *husk*, from the toughness of a corn husk

husky[2] *n, pl* **huskies** an Arctic sledge dog with thick hair and a curled tail
WORD ORIGIN probably based on *eskimo*

Hussain *n* **Nasser** born 1968, British cricketer born in India, captain of England (1999–2003)

hussar (hoo-**zar**) *n history* a member of a light cavalry regiment
WORD ORIGIN Hungarian *huszár*

Husserl *n* **Edmund** 1859–1938, German philosopher; founder of phenomenology

hussy *n, pl* **-sies** *old-fashioned* a woman considered sexually immoral or improper
WORD ORIGIN from *hussif* housewife

hustings *pl n* the campaigns and speeches at a parliamentary election

h

THESAURUS

hurdle *n* 1 = **fence**, wall, hedge, block, barrier, barricade 2 = **obstacle**, block, difficulty, barrier, handicap, hazard, complication, snag, uphill (*S African*), obstruction, stumbling block, impediment, hindrance

hurl *vb* 1 = **throw**, fling, chuck (*informal*), send, fire, project, launch, cast, pitch, shy, toss, propel, sling, heave, let fly (with)

hurricane *n* = **storm**, gale, tornado, cyclone, typhoon, tempest, twister (*US informal*), windstorm, willy-willy (*Austral*)

hurried *adj* **a** = **hasty**, quick, brief, rushed, short, swift, speedy, precipitate, quickie (*informal*), breakneck **b** = **rushed**, perfunctory, hectic, speedy, superficial, hasty, cursory, slapdash

hurry *vb* 1a = **rush**, fly, dash, barrel (along) (*informal, chiefly US & Canad*), scurry, scoot, burn rubber (*informal*)
OPPOSITE: dawdle
1b = **make haste**, rush, lose no time, get a move on (*informal*), step on it (*informal*), get your skates on (*informal*), crack on (*informal*) ▷*n* 3, 4 = **rush**, haste, speed, urgency, bustle, flurry, commotion, precipitation, quickness, celerity, promptitude
OPPOSITE: slowness

hurt *vb* 1a = **injure**, damage, wound, cut, disable, bruise, scrape, impair, gash **OPPOSITE:** heal
1b = **upset**, distress, pain, wound, annoy, sting, grieve, afflict, sadden, cut to the quick, aggrieve 2 = **ache**, be sore, be painful, burn, smart, sting, throb, be tender ▷*n* 4 = **distress**, suffering, pain, grief, misery, agony, sadness, sorrow, woe, anguish, heartache, wretchedness
OPPOSITE: happiness
▷*adj* 5a = **injured**, wounded, damaged, harmed, cut, scratched, bruised, scarred, scraped, grazed
OPPOSITE: healed
5b = **upset**, pained, injured, wounded, sad, crushed, offended, aggrieved, miffed (*informal*), rueful, piqued, tooshie (*Austral slang*)
OPPOSITE: calmed

hurtle *vb* = **rush**, charge, race, shoot, fly, speed, tear, crash, plunge, barrel (along) (*informal, chiefly US & Canad*), scramble, spurt, stampede, scoot, burn rubber (*informal*), rush headlong, go hell for leather (*informal*)

husband *n* 1 = **partner**, man (*informal*), spouse, hubby (*informal*), mate, old man (*informal*), bridegroom, significant other (*US informal*), better half (*humorous*) ▷*vb* 2 = **conserve**, budget, use sparingly, save, store, hoard, economize on, use economically, manage thriftily
OPPOSITE: squander

hush *vb* 1 = **quieten**, still, silence, suppress, mute, muzzle, shush ▷*n* 2 = **quiet**, silence, calm, still (*poetic*), peace, tranquillity, stillness, peacefulness

DICTIONARY

WORD ORIGIN Old Norse *hūsthing*, from *hūs* house + *thing* assembly

hustle *vb* **-tling, -tled 1** to make (someone) move by pushing or jostling them: *he hustled her away* **2** to deal with (something) hurriedly: *they did not heedlessly hustle the tempo* **3** *US & Canad slang* (of a prostitute) to solicit clients ▷*n* **4** lively activity and excitement
WORD ORIGIN Dutch *husselen* to shake

hustler *n US informal* a person who tries to make money or gain an advantage from every situation, often by immoral or dishonest means

Huston *n* **John** 1906–87, US film director. His films include *The Treasure of the Sierra Madre* (1947), for which he won an Oscar, *The African Queen* (1951), *The Man Who Would Be King* (1975), *Prizzi's Honour* (1985), and *The Dead* (1987)

hut Ⓣ *n* a small house or shelter
WORD ORIGIN French *hutte*

hutch *n* a cage for small animals
WORD ORIGIN Old French *huche*

Hutcheson *n* **Francis** 1694–1746, Scottish philosopher: he published books on ethics and aesthetics, including *System of Moral Philosophy* (1755)

Hutton *n* **1 James** 1726–97, Scottish geologist, regarded as the founder of modern geology **2** Sir **Leonard,** known as *Len Hutton*. 1916–90, English cricketer; the first professional captain of England (1953)

Huxley *n* **1 Aldous** (**Leonard**) 1894–1963, British novelist and essayist, noted particularly for his novel *Brave New World* (1932), depicting a scientifically controlled civilization of human robots **2** his half-brother, Sir **Andrew Fielding,** born 1917, English biologist: noted for his research into nerve cells and the mechanism by which nerve impulses are transmitted; Nobel prize for physiology or medicine shared with Alan Hodgkin and John Eccles 1963; president of the Royal Society (1980–85) **3** brother of Aldous, Sir **Julian** (**Sorrel**) 1887–1975, English biologist; first director-general of UNESCO (1946–48). His works include *Essays of a Biologist* (1923) and *Evolution: the Modern Synthesis* (1942) **4** their grandfather, **Thomas Henry** 1825–95, English biologist, the leading British exponent of Darwin's theory of evolution; his works include *Man's Place in Nature* (1863) and *Evolution and Ethics* (1893)

Hu Yaobang *n* 1915–89, Chinese statesman; leader of the Chinese Communist Party (1981–87)

Huygens *n* **Christiaan** 1629–95, Dutch physicist: first formulated the wave theory of light

Huysmans *n* **Joris Karl** 1848–1907, French novelist of the Decadent school, whose works include *À rebours* (1884)

hyacinth *n* a plant with bell-shaped sweet-smelling flowers
WORD ORIGIN Greek *huakinthos*

hyaena *n* ▸same as **hyena**

hybrid Ⓣ *n* **1** an animal or plant resulting from a cross between two different types of animal or plant **2** a vehicle that is powered by an internal-combustion engine and another source of power **3** anything that is a mixture of two different things ▷*adj* **4** of mixed origin **5** (of a vehicle) powered by an internal-combustion engine and another source of power
WORD ORIGIN Latin *hibrida*

hybridize *or* **-ise** *vb* **-izing, -ized** *or* **-ising, -ised** to produce or cause (species) to produce hybrids; crossbreed **hybridization** *or* **-isation** *n*

hydatid disease (**hide**-at-id) *n* a condition caused by the presence of bladder-like cysts (**hydatids**) in the liver, lungs, or brain
WORD ORIGIN Greek *hudatis* watery sac

Hyde[1] *n* a town in NW England, in Tameside unitary authority, Greater Manchester; textiles, footwear, engineering. Pop: 31 253 (2001)

Hyde[2] *n* **1 Douglas** 1860–1949, Irish scholar and author; first president of Eire (1938–45) **2 Edward Hyde** ▸See **Clarendon**

Hyder Ali *or* **Haidar Ali** *n* 1722–82, Indian ruler of Mysore (1766–82), who waged two wars against the British in India (1767–69; 1780–82)

hydra *n* **1** a mythical many-headed serpent **2** a persistent problem: *killing the hydra of drug production is impossible* **3** a microscopic freshwater creature with a slender tubular body and tentacles around the mouth
WORD ORIGIN Greek *hudra* water serpent

hydrangea *n* an ornamental shrub with large clusters of white, pink, or blue flowers
WORD ORIGIN Greek *hudōr* water + *angeion* vessel

hydrant *n* an outlet from a water main, from which water can be tapped for fighting fires

hydrate *chem n* **1** a compound containing water chemically combined with a substance: *chloral hydrate* ▷*vb* **-drating, -drated 2** to treat or impregnate (a substance) with water **hydration** *n*

hydraulic *adj* operated by pressure transmitted through a pipe by a liquid, such as water or oil **hydraulically** *adv*
WORD ORIGIN Greek *hudōr* water + *aulos* pipe

hydraulics *n* the study of the mechanical properties of fluids as they apply to practical engineering

hydride *n chem* a compound of hydrogen with another element

hydro[1] *n, pl* **-dros** *Brit* a hotel offering facilities for hydropathic treatment

hydro[2] *adj* **1** ▸short for **hydroelectric 2** *Canad* electricity as supplied to a residence, business, etc.

hydro- *or before a vowel* **hydr-** *combining form* **1** indicating water or fluid: *hydrodynamics* **2** *chem* indicating hydrogen in a chemical compound: *hydrochloric acid*
WORD ORIGIN Greek *hudōr* water

hydrocarbon *n chem* a compound containing only carbon and hydrogen

hydrocephalus *n* accumulation of fluid in the cavities of the brain, causing enlargement of the head in children **hydrocephalic** *adj*
WORD ORIGIN Greek *hudōr* water + *kephalē* head

hydrochloric acid *n chem* a solution of hydrogen chloride in water: a strong acid used in many industrial and laboratory processes

hydrodynamics *n* the branch of science concerned with the mechanical properties of fluids

hydroelectric *adj* **1** generated by the pressure of falling water: *hydroelectric power* **2** of the generation of electricity by water pressure: *a hydroelectric scheme* **hydroelectricity** *n*

hydrofoil *n* **1** a fast light vessel the hull of which is raised out of the water on one or more pairs of fins **2** any of these fins

hydrogen *n chem* a colourless gas that burns easily and is the lightest element in the universe. It occurs in water and in most organic compounds. Symbol: H **hydrogenous** *adj*
WORD ORIGIN HYDRO- + *-gen* (producing); because its combustion produces water

hydrogenate (**hide**-roj-in-nate) *vb* **-ating, -ated** *chem* to combine (a substance) with hydrogen: *hydrogenated vegetable oil* **hydrogenation** *n*

THESAURUS

hut *n* **a = cabin,** shack, shanty, hovel, whare (NZ) **b = shed,** outhouse, lean-to, lockup

hybrid *n* **1 = crossbreed,** cross, mixture, compound, composite, mule, amalgam, mongrel, half-breed, half-blood **3 = mixture,** compound, composite, amalgam

DICTIONARY

hydrogen bomb *n* an extremely powerful bomb in which energy is released by fusion of hydrogen nuclei to give helium nuclei
hydrogen peroxide *n* a colourless oily unstable liquid chemical used as a hair bleach and as an antiseptic
hydrogen sulphide *n* a colourless poisonous gas with an odour of rotten eggs
hydrography (hide-**rog**-ra-fee) *n* the study of the oceans, seas, and rivers **hydrographer** *n* **hydrographic** *adj*
hydrology *n* the study of the distribution, conservation, and use of the water of the earth and its atmosphere
hydrolysis (hide-**rol**-iss-iss) *n chem* a process of decomposition in which a compound reacts with water to produce other compounds
WORD ORIGIN Greek *hudōr* water + *lusis* a loosening
hydrometer (hide-**rom**-it-er) *n* an instrument for measuring the density of a liquid
hydropathy *n* a method of treating disease by the use of large quantities of water both internally and externally **hydropathic** *adj*
WORD ORIGIN Greek *hudōr* water + *patheia* suffering
hydrophilic *adj chem* tending to dissolve in or mix with water: *a hydrophilic layer*
hydrophobia *n* **1** ▸ same as **rabies** **2** (esp. of a person with rabies) a fear of drinking fluids **hydrophobic** *adj*
hydroplane *n* **1** a motorboat that raises its hull out of the water at high speeds **2** a fin on the hull of a submarine for controlling its vertical motion
hydroponics *n* a method of growing plants in gravel, etc. through which water containing the necessary nutrients is pumped
WORD ORIGIN HYDRO- + *(geo)ponics* science of agriculture
hydrosphere *n* the watery part of the earth's surface
hydrostatics *n* the branch of science concerned with the properties and behaviour of fluids that are not in motion **hydrostatic** *adj*
hydrotherapy *n med* the treatment of certain diseases by exercise in water
hydrous *adj* containing water
hydroxide *n chem* a compound containing a hydroxyl group or ion
hydroxyl *adj chem* of or containing the monovalent group –OH or the ion OH^-: *forming a hydroxyl radical*
hyena *or* **hyaena** *n* a meat-eating doglike mammal of Africa and S Asia
WORD ORIGIN Greek *hus* hog
hygiene ❶ *n* **1** the principles and practices of health and cleanliness: *personal hygiene* **2** Also called: **hygienics** the science concerned with the maintenance of health **hygienic** *adj* **hygienically** *adv* **hygienist** *n*
WORD ORIGIN Greek *hugieinē*
hygrometer (hie-**grom**-it-er) *n* an instrument for measuring humidity
WORD ORIGIN Greek *hugros* wet
hygroscope *n* any device that indicates the humidity of the air without necessarily measuring it, such as an animal or vegetable fibre which contracts with moisture
WORD ORIGIN Greek *hugros* wet + *skopein* to observe
hygroscopic *adj* (of a substance) tending to absorb water from the air
hymen *n anat* a membrane that partly covers the entrance to the vagina and is usually ruptured when sexual intercourse takes place for the first time
WORD ORIGIN Greek: membrane
hymenopterous *adj* of or belonging to an order of insects with two pairs of membranous wings
WORD ORIGIN Greek *humen* membrane + *pteron* wing
hymn ❶ *n* a Christian song of praise sung to God or a saint
WORD ORIGIN Greek *humnos*
hymnal *n* a book of hymns. Also: **hymn book**
hymnody *n* **1** the composition or singing of hymns **2** hymns collectively
hymnology *n* the study of hymn composition **hymnologist** *n*
Hypatia *n* died 415 AD, Neo-Platonist philosopher and politician, who lectured at Alexandria. She was murdered by a Christian mob
hype ❶ *slang n* **1** intensive or exaggerated publicity or sales promotion ▹*vb* **hyping, hyped** **2** to market or promote (a commodity) using intensive or exaggerated publicity
WORD ORIGIN origin unknown
hyped up *adj old-fashioned slang* stimulated or excited by or as if by drugs
hyper *adj informal* overactive or overexcited
hyper- *prefix* above, over, or in excess: *hypercritical*
WORD ORIGIN Greek *huper* over
hyperactive *adj* (of a person) unable to relax and always in a state of restless activity
hyperbola (hie-**per**-bol-a) *n geom* a curve produced when a cone is cut by a plane at a steeper angle to its base than its side
WORD ORIGIN Greek *huperbolē*
hyperbole (hie-**per**-bol-ee) *n* a deliberate exaggeration of speech or writing used for effect, such as *he embraced her a thousand times*
WORD ORIGIN Greek *huper* over + *ballein* to throw
hyperbolic *or* **hyperbolical** *adj* **1** exaggerated **2** of a hyperbola or a hyperbole
hypercritical *adj* excessively critical
hyperglycaemia *or US* **hyperglycemia** (hie-per-glice-**seem**-ee-a) *n pathol* an abnormally large amount of sugar in the blood
WORD ORIGIN Greek *huper* over + *glukus* sweet
hyperlink *computers n* **1** a word, picture, etc. in a computer document on which a user may click to move to another part of the document or to another document ▹*vb* **2** to link (files) in this way
hypermarket *n* a huge self-service store
WORD ORIGIN translation of French *hypermarché*
hypersensitive *adj* **1** unduly emotionally vulnerable **2** abnormally sensitive to an allergen, a drug, or high or low temperatures
hypersexual *adj* **1** excessively interested in sexual activity **2** inappropriately sexualized: *hypersexual and explicit portrayals of women*
hypersonic *adj* having a speed of at least five times the speed of sound
hypertension *n pathol* abnormally high blood pressure
hypertext *n* computer software and hardware that allows users to store and view text and move between related items easily
hypertrophy (hie-**per**-trof-fee) *n, pl* **-phies** enlargement of an organ or part resulting from an increase in the size of the cells
WORD ORIGIN Greek *huper* over + *trophē* nourishment
hyperventilation *n* an increase in the rate of breathing at rest, sometimes resulting in cramp and dizziness **hyperventilate** *vb*
hyphen *n* the punctuation mark (-), used to separate parts of compound words and between syllables of a word split between two consecutive lines
WORD ORIGIN Greek *huphen* together
hyphenate *vb* **-ating, -ated** to

h

THESAURUS

hygiene *n* **1 = cleanliness**, sanitation, disinfection, sterility, sanitary measures, hygienics
hymn *n* **= religious song**, song of praise, carol, chant, anthem, psalm, paean, canticle, doxology
hype *n* **1** *(slang)* **= publicity**, promotion, build-up, plugging *(informal)*, puffing, racket, razzmatazz *(slang)*, brouhaha, ballyhoo *(informal)*

DICTIONARY

separate (words) with a hyphen **hyphenation** *n*

hyphenated *adj* having two words or syllables connected by a hyphen

hypnosis *n* an artificially induced state of relaxation in which the mind is more than usually receptive to suggestion

hypnotherapy *n* the use of hypnosis in the treatment of emotional and mental problems **hypnotherapist** *n*

hypnotic *adj* **1** of or producing hypnosis or sleep **2** having an effect resembling hypnosis: *the film makes for hypnotic viewing* ▹*n* **3** a drug that induces sleep **hypnotically** *adv*
WORD ORIGIN Greek *hupnos* sleep

hypnotism *n* the practice of or process of inducing hypnosis **hypnotist** *n*

h

hypnotize *or* **-tise** *vb* **-tizing, -tized** *or* **-tising, -tised 1** to induce hypnosis in (a person) **2** to hold the attention of (someone) completely; fascinate; mesmerize: *hypnotized by her beauty*

hypo- *or before a vowel* **hyp-** *prefix* beneath; less than: *hypodermic*
WORD ORIGIN Greek *hupo* under

hypoallergenic *adj* not likely to cause an allergic reaction

hypocaust *n* an ancient Roman heating system in which hot air circulated under the floor and between double walls
WORD ORIGIN Latin *hypocaustum*

hypochondria *n* abnormal anxiety concerning one's health
WORD ORIGIN Late Latin: abdomen, supposedly the seat of melancholy

hypochondriac *n* a person abnormally concerned about his or her health

hypocrisy ❶ (hip-ok-rass-ee) *n, pl* **-sies 1** the practice of claiming to have standards or beliefs that are contrary to one's real character or actual behaviour **2** an act or instance of this

hypocrite (**hip**-oh-krit) *n* a person who pretends to be what he or she is not **hypocritical** *adj*
WORD ORIGIN Greek *hupokrinein* to pretend

hypodermic *adj* **1** used for injecting ▹*n* **2** a hypodermic syringe or needle

hypodermic syringe *n med* a syringe consisting of a hollow cylinder, a piston, and a hollow needle, used for withdrawing blood samples or injecting drugs under the skin

hypotension *n pathol* abnormally low blood pressure

hypotenuse (hie-**pot**-a-news) *n* the side in a right-angled triangle that is opposite the right angle
WORD ORIGIN Greek *hupoteinousa grammē* subtending line

hypothalamus *n, pl* **-mi** an area at the base of the brain, which controls hunger, thirst, and other functions

hypothermia *n pathol* an abnormally low body temperature, as a result of exposure to cold weather

hypothesis ❶ (hie-**poth**-iss-iss) *n, pl* **-ses** (-seez) a suggested explanation for a group of facts, accepted either as a basis for further verification or as likely to be true **hypothesize** *or* **-ise** *vb*
WORD ORIGIN Greek *hupotithenai* to propose, literally: put under

hypothetical *adj* based on assumption rather than fact or reality **hypothetically** *adv*

Hypsilantis *or* **Hypsilantes** *n* ▸variants of **Ypsilanti**

hyrax (**hire**-ax) *n, pl* **hyraxes** *or* **hyraces** (**hire**-a-seez) a genus of hoofed rodent-like animals

hyssop *n* **1** an aromatic plant used in herbal medicine **2** a Biblical plant, used for sprinkling in the ritual practices of the Hebrews
WORD ORIGIN Greek *hussōpos*

hysterectomy *n, pl* **-mies** surgical removal of the womb
WORD ORIGIN Greek *hustera* womb + *tomē* a cutting

hysteria ❶ *n* **1** a mental disorder marked by emotional outbursts and, often, symptoms such as paralysis **2** any uncontrolled emotional state, such as of panic, anger, or excitement
WORD ORIGIN Greek *hustera* womb, from the belief that hysteria in women originated in disorders of the womb

hysteric *n* a hysterical person

hysterical ❶ *adj* **1** in a state of uncontrolled panic, anger, or excitement: *a crazy hysterical adolescent* **2** *informal* wildly funny **hysterically** *adv*

hysterics *n* **1** an attack of hysteria **2** *informal* wild uncontrollable bursts of laughter

Hywel Dda *or* **Howel Dda** *n* known as *Hywel the Good*. died 950 AD, Welsh prince. He united S and N Wales and codified Welsh law

Hz hertz

THESAURUS

hypocrisy *n* **1 = insincerity**, pretence, deceit, deception, cant, duplicity, dissembling, falsity, imposture, sanctimoniousness, phoniness (*informal*), deceitfulness, pharisaism, speciousness, two-facedness, phariseeism **OPPOSITE:** sincerity

hypothesis *n* **= theory**, premise, proposition, assumption, thesis, postulate, supposition, premise

hysteria *n* **2 = frenzy**, panic, madness, agitation, delirium, hysterics, unreason

hysterical *adj* **1 = frenzied**, mad, frantic, raving, distracted, distraught, crazed, uncontrollable, berserk, overwrought, convulsive, beside yourself, berko (*Austral slang*) **OPPOSITE:** calm **2** (*informal*) **= hilarious**, uproarious, side-splitting, farcical, comical, wildly funny **OPPOSITE:** serious

Ii

i the imaginary number √−1

I[1] *pron* used by a speaker or writer to refer to himself or herself as the subject of a verb
WORD ORIGIN Old English *ic*

I[2] **1** *chem* iodine **2** the Roman numeral for one

I. **1** Independent **2** Institute **3** International **4** Island; Isle

IA Iowa

iamb (eye-am) *or* **iambus** *n, pl* **iambs** *or* **iambuses** *prosody* a metrical foot of two syllables, a short one followed by a long one
WORD ORIGIN Greek *iambos*

iambic (eye-am-bik) *prosody adj* **1** written in metrical units of one short and one long syllable ▷*n* **2** an iambic foot, line, or stanza

IBA (in Britain) Independent Broadcasting Authority

Ibáñez *n* See **Blasco Ibáñez**

Iberian *adj* **1** of Iberia, the peninsula made up of Spain and Portugal ▷*n* **2** a person from Iberia

Ibert *n* **Jacques (François Antoine)** 1890–1962, French composer; his works include the humorous orchestral *Divertissement* (1930)

Iberville *n* **Pierre le Moyne**, Sieur d' 1661–1706, French-Canadian explorer, who founded (1700) the first French colony in Louisiana

ibex (ibe-eks) *n, pl* **ibexes** *or* **ibex** a wild mountain goat with large backward-curving horns
WORD ORIGIN Latin: chamois

ibid. in the same place: used to refer to a book, page, or passage previously cited
WORD ORIGIN Latin *ibidem*

ibis (ibe-iss) *n, pl* **ibises** *or* **ibis** a large wading bird with a long thin curved bill
WORD ORIGIN Egyptian *hby*

ibn-al-Arabi *n* **Muhyi-l-din** 1165–1240, Muslim mystic and poet, born in Spain, noted for his influence on Sufism

ibn-Batuta *n* 1304–?68, Arab traveller, who wrote the *Rihlah*, an account of his travels (1325–54) in Africa and Asia

ibn-Ezra *n* **Abraham Ben Meir** 1093–1167, Jewish poet, scholar, and traveller, born in Spain

ibn-Gabirol *n* **Solomon** ?1021–?58, Jewish philosopher and poet, born in Spain. His work *The Fountain of Life* influenced Western medieval philosophers

ibn-Khaldun *n* 1332–1406, Arab historian and philosopher. His *Kitab al-'ibar* (*Book of Examples*) is a history of Islam

ibn-Saud *n* **Abdul-Aziz** 1880–1953, first king of Saudi Arabia (1932–53)

Ibo (ee-boh) *n* **1** *pl* **Ibos** *or* **Ibo** a member of an African people of S Nigeria **2** their language

Ibrahim Pasha *n* 1789–1848, Albanian general; son of Mehemet Ali, whom he succeeded as viceroy of Egypt (1848)

ICBM intercontinental ballistic missile

ice *n* **1** water that has frozen and become solid **2** *chiefly Brit* a portion of ice cream **3** **break the ice** to relax the atmosphere, esp. between strangers **4** **on ice** in readiness or reserve **5** **on thin ice** in a dangerous situation: *he knew he was on thin ice* **6** **the Ice** NZ *informal* Antarctica ▷*vb* **icing, iced** **7** (foll. by *up* or *over*) to become covered with ice **8** to cover with icing **9** to cool or chill with ice
WORD ORIGIN Old English *īs*

ice age *n* any period of time during which a large part of the earth's surface was covered with ice, caused by the advance of glaciers

ice beer *n* a beer that is chilled after brewing so that any water is turned to ice and then removed

iceberg *n* **1** a large mass of ice floating in the sea **2** **tip of the iceberg** the small visible part of a problem that is much larger
WORD ORIGIN probably Middle Dutch *ijsberg* ice mountain

iceberg lettuce *n* a type of lettuce with very crisp pale leaves tightly enfolded

iceboat *n* ▸another name for **icebreaker**

icebox *n* **1** *US & Canad* a refrigerator **2** a compartment in a refrigerator for making or storing ice **3** a container packed with ice for keeping food and drink cold

icebreaker *n* a ship designed to break a channel through ice

icecap *n* a thick mass of glacial ice that permanently covers an area

ice cream *n* a sweet frozen food, made from cream, milk, or a custard base, flavoured in various ways

iced *adj* **1** served very cold **2** covered with icing

ice field *n* a large expanse of floating sea ice

ice floe *n* a sheet of ice floating in the sea

ice hockey *n* a game like hockey played on ice by two teams wearing skates

Icelander *n* a person from Iceland

Icelandic *adj* **1** of Iceland ▷*n* **2** the official language of Iceland

ice lolly *n Brit informal* a water ice or an ice cream on a stick

ice pack *n* **1** a bag or folded cloth containing crushed ice, applied to a part of the body to reduce swelling **2** ▸same as **pack ice**

ice skate *n* **1** a boot with a steel blade fitted to the sole which enables the wearer to glide over ice ▷*vb* **ice-skate, -skating, -skated** **2** to glide over ice on ice skates **ice-skater** *n*

icewine *n Canad* a dessert wine made from grapes that have frozen before being harvested

I Ching *n* an ancient Chinese book of divination and a source of Confucian and Taoist philosophy

ichneumon (ik-new-mon) *n* a greyish-brown mongoose

ichthyology (ik-thi-ol-a-jee) *n* the study of fishes **ichthyological** *adj* **ichthyologist** *n*
WORD ORIGIN Greek *ikhthus* fish + -LOGY

icicle *n* a tapering spike of ice hanging where water has dripped
WORD ORIGIN from ICE + Old English *gicel* icicle

icing *n* **1** Also (esp. US and Canad.): **frosting** a mixture of sugar and water or egg whites used to cover and decorate cakes **2** the formation of ice on a ship or aircraft **3** **icing on the cake** any unexpected extra or bonus

icing sugar *n* a very finely ground sugar used for making icing or sweets

icon *or* **ikon** *n* **1** a picture of Christ, the Virgin Mary, or a saint, venerated in the Orthodox Church **2** a picture on a computer screen representing a computer function that can be activated by moving the cursor over it **3** a person or thing regarded as a symbol of a belief or cultural movement: *a feminist icon*
WORD ORIGIN Greek *eikōn* image

iconoclast *n* **1** a person who attacks established or traditional ideas or principles **2** a destroyer of religious images or objects **iconoclastic** *adj* **iconoclasm** *n*

THESAURUS

icy *adj* **1 = cold**, freezing, bitter, biting, raw, chill, chilling, arctic, chilly, frosty, glacial, ice-cold, frozen over, frost-bound
OPPOSITE: hot
2 = slippery, glassy, slippy (*informal, dialect*), like a sheet of glass, rimy
3 = unfriendly, cold, distant, hostile, forbidding, indifferent, aloof, stony, steely, frosty, glacial, frigid, unwelcoming
OPPOSITE: friendly

DICTIONARY

WORD ORIGIN Late Greek *eikōn* icon + *klastēs* breaker

icosahedron (ike-oh-sa-**heed**-ron) *n, pl* **-drons** *or* **-dra** (-dra) a solid figure with 20 faces
WORD ORIGIN Greek *eikosi* twenty + *-edron* -sided

Ictinus *n* 5th century BC, Greek architect, who designed the Parthenon with Callicrates

icy ❶ *adj* **icier, iciest 1** freezing or very cold **2** covered with ice: *an icy runway* **3** cold or reserved in manner **icily** *adv* **iciness** *n*

id *n psychoanal* the primitive instincts and energies in the unconscious mind that underlie all psychological impulses
WORD ORIGIN Latin: it

ID 1 Idaho **2** identification

Id. Idaho

I'd I had *or* I would

i

idea ❶ *n* **1** any product of mental activity; thought **2** a scheme, intention, or plan **3** the thought of something: *the idea excites me* **4** a belief or opinion **5** a vague notion; inkling: *they had no idea of the severity of my injuries* **6** a person's conception of something: *his idea of integrity is not the same as mine* **7** aim or purpose: *the idea is to economize on transport* **8** *philosophy* (in Plato) a universal model of which all things in the same class are only imperfect imitations
WORD ORIGIN Greek: model, outward appearance

ideal ❶ *n* **1** (*often pl*) a principle or model of ethical behaviour **2** a conception of something that is perfect **3** a person or thing considered to represent perfection **4** something existing only as an idea ▷ *adj* **5** most suitable: *they seem to have adopted an ideal man as their candidate* **6** of, involving, or existing only as an idea; imaginary: *an ideal world* **ideally** *adv*

idealism *n* **1** belief in or striving towards ideals **2** the tendency to represent things in their ideal forms, rather than as they are **3** *philosophy* the doctrine that material objects and the external world do not exist in reality, but are creations of the mind **idealist** *n* **idealistic** *adj*

idealize *or* **-ise** *vb* **-izing, -ized** *or* **-ising, -ised** to consider or represent (something) as ideal or more nearly perfect than is true **idealization** *or* **-isation** *n*

idée fixe (ee-day **feeks**) *n, pl* **idées fixes** (ee-day **feeks**) an idea with which a person is obsessed
WORD ORIGIN French

idem *pron, adj* the same: used to refer to an article, chapter, or book already quoted
WORD ORIGIN Latin

identical ❶ *adj* **1** that is the same: *they got the identical motel room as last year* **2** exactly alike or equal **3** (of twins) developed from a single fertilized ovum that has split into two, and thus of the same sex and very much alike **identically** *adv*
WORD ORIGIN Latin *idem* the same

identification parade *n* a group of people, including one suspected of a crime, assembled to discover whether a witness can identify the suspect

identify ❶ *vb* **-fies, -fying, -fied 1** to prove or recognize as being a certain person or thing; determine the identity of **2** (often foll. by *with*) to understand and sympathize with a person or group because one regards oneself as being similar or similarly situated **3** to consider or treat as the same **4** (often foll. by *with*) to connect or associate closely: *he was closely identified with the community charge* **identifiable** *adj* **identification** *n*

Identikit *n* **1** *trademark* a composite picture, assembled from descriptions given, of a person wanted by the police ▷ *adj* **2** artificially created; formulaic: *an identikit pop group* **3** stereotypical: *the identikit Scots midfield mauler*

identity ❶ *n, pl* **-ties 1** the state of being a specified person or thing: *the identity of his murderers was not immediately established* **2** the individual characteristics by which a person or thing is recognized **3** the state of being the same **4** *maths* Also called: **identity element** a member of a set that when combined with any other member of the set, leaves it unchanged: the identity for multiplication of numbers is 1
WORD ORIGIN Latin *idem* the same

identity theft *n* the crime of fraudulently setting up and using bank accounts, credit facilities, etc., in another person's name

ideo- *combining form* of or indicating ideas: *ideology*
WORD ORIGIN from French *idéo-*, from Greek *idea* idea

ideogram *or* **ideograph** *n* a character or symbol that directly represents a concept or thing, rather than the sounds that form its name
WORD ORIGIN Greek *idea* idea + *gramma* a drawing

ideology *n, pl* **-gies** the body of ideas and beliefs of a person, group, or nation **ideological** *adj* **ideologically** *adv* **ideologist** *n*
WORD ORIGIN from IDEO- + -LOGY

ides *n* (in the ancient Roman calendar) the 15th day in March, May, July, and October and the 13th of the other months
WORD ORIGIN Latin *idus*

idiocy *n, pl* **-cies 1** utter stupidity **2** a foolish act or remark

idiom *n* **1** a group of words which, when used together, have a different meaning from the one suggested by the individual words, eg *it was raining cats and dogs* **2** linguistic usage that is grammatical and natural to native speakers **3** the characteristic vocabulary or usage of a person or group **4** the characteristic artistic

THESAURUS

idea *n* **1, 4 = notion**, thought, view, understanding, teaching, opinion, belief, conclusion, hypothesis, impression, conviction, judgment, interpretation, sentiment, doctrine, conception, viewpoint
6 = understanding, thought, view, sense, opinion, concept, impression, judgment, perception, conception, abstraction, estimation
7 = intention, aim, purpose, object, end, plan, reason, goal, design, objective, motive

ideal *n* **2 = model**, example, criterion, prototype, paradigm, archetype, exemplar **3 = epitome**, standard, dream, pattern, perfection, last word, paragon, nonpareil, standard of perfection ▷ *adj* **5 = perfect**, best, model, classic, supreme, ultimate, archetypal, exemplary, consummate, optimal, quintessential
OPPOSITE: imperfect

identical *adj* **1, 2 = alike**, like, the same, matching, equal, twin, equivalent, corresponding, duplicate, synonymous, indistinguishable, analogous, interchangeable, a dead ringer (*slang*), the dead spit (*informal*), like two peas in a pod **OPPOSITE:** different

identify *vb* **1a = recognize**, place, name, remember, spot, label, flag, catalogue, tag, diagnose, classify, make out, pinpoint, recollect, put your finger on (*informal*)
1b = establish, spot, confirm, finger (*informal, chiefly US*), demonstrate, pick out, single out, certify, verify, validate, mark out, substantiate, corroborate, flag up
2 (often foll. by *with*) **= relate to**, understand, respond to, feel for, ally with, empathize with, speak the same language as, put yourself in the place *or* shoes of, see through another's eyes, be on the same wavelength as
4 (often foll. by *with*) **= equate with**, associate with, think of in connection with, put in the same category as

identity *n* **2 = individuality**, self, character, personality, existence, distinction, originality, peculiarity, uniqueness, oneness, singularity, separateness, distinctiveness,

DICTIONARY

style of an individual or school **idiomatic** *adj*
WORD ORIGIN Greek *idios* private, separate

idiosyncrasy *n, pl* **-sies** a personal peculiarity of mind, habit, or behaviour; quirk **idiosyncratic** *adj*
WORD ORIGIN Greek *idios* private, separate + *sunkrasis* mixture

idiot ● *n* **1** a foolish or senseless person **2** *no longer in technical use* a person with severe mental retardation **idiotic** *adj* **idiotically** *adv*
WORD ORIGIN Greek *idiōtēs* private person, ignoramus

idle ● *adj* **1** not doing anything **2** not operating or being used **3** not wanting to work; lazy **4** ineffective or useless: *it would be idle to look for a solution at this stage* **5** frivolous or trivial: *idle pleasures* **6** without basis; unfounded: *idle rumours* ▷ *vb* **idling, idled 7** (often foll. by *away*) to waste or pass (time) in idleness **8** (of an engine) to run at low speed without transmitting any power **idleness** *n* **idler** *n* **idly** *adv*
WORD ORIGIN Old English *īdel*

idol ● (eye-dl) *n* **1** an object of excessive devotion or admiration **2** an image of a god used as an object of worship
WORD ORIGIN Greek *eidōlon* image

idolatry (ide-ol-a-tree) *n* **1** the worship of idols **2** excessive devotion or reverence **idolater** *n* **idolatrous** *adj*

idolize *or* **-ise** *vb* **-izing, -ized** *or* **-ising, -ised 1** to love or admire excessively **2** to worship as an idol **idolization** *or* **-isation** *n*

idyll *or US sometimes* **idyl** (id-ill) *n* **1** a scene or time of peace and happiness **2** a poem or prose work describing a charming rural scene or episode **idyllic** *adj*
WORD ORIGIN Greek *eidullion*

i.e. that is to say
WORD ORIGIN Latin *id est*

IED improvised explosive device

Ieyasu *n* a variant spelling of (Tokugawa) **Iyeyasu**

if ● *conj* **1** in the event that, or on condition that: *if you work hard you'll succeed* **2** used to introduce an indirect question to which the answer is either *yes* or *no*; whether: *it doesn't matter if the play is any good or not* **3** even though: *a splendid if slightly decaying house* **4** used to introduce an unfulfilled wish, with *only*: *if only you had told her* ▷ *n* **5** a condition or stipulation: *there are no hidden ifs or buts*
WORD ORIGIN Old English *gif*

iffy *adj* **iffier, iffiest** *informal* full of uncertainty

igloo *n, pl* **-loos** a dome-shaped Inuit house, built of blocks of solid snow
WORD ORIGIN Inuktitut *igdlu*

Ignatiev *n* Count **Nikolai Pavlovich** 1832–1908, Russian diplomat and politician. As ambassador to Turkey (1864–77), he negotiated the Treaty of San Stefano (1878) ending the Russo-Turkish War

Ignatius *n* **Saint,** surnamed *Theophorus.* died ?110 AD, bishop of Antioch. His seven letters, written on his way to his martyrdom in Rome, give valuable insight into the early Christian Church. Feast day: Oct 17 or Dec 17 or 20

igneous (ig-nee-uss) *adj* **1** (of rocks) formed as molten rock cools and hardens **2** of or like fire
WORD ORIGIN Latin *ignis* fire

ignis fatuus (ig-niss **fat**-yew-uss) *n, pl* **ignes fatui** (ig-neez **fat**-yew-eye) ▸ same as **will-o'-the-wisp**
WORD ORIGIN Medieval Latin, literally: foolish fire

ignite ● *vb* **-niting, -nited 1** to catch fire **2** to set fire to **ignitable** *adj*
WORD ORIGIN Latin *ignis* fire

ignition *n* **1** the system used to ignite the fuel in an internal-combustion engine **2** an igniting or the process of igniting

ignoble *adj* **1** dishonourable **2** of low birth or origins **ignobly** *adv*
WORD ORIGIN Latin *in-* not + *nobilis* noble

ignominy (ig-nom-in-ee) *n, pl* **-minies** disgrace or public shame: *the ignominy of being replaced* **ignominious** *adj*
WORD ORIGIN Latin *ignominia* disgrace

ignoramus *n, pl* **-muses** an ignorant person
WORD ORIGIN Latin, literally: we have no knowledge of

ignorance ● *n* lack of knowledge or education

ignorant ● *adj* **1** lacking in knowledge or education **2** rude through lack of knowledge of good manners: *an ignorant remark* **3** **ignorant of** lacking in awareness or knowledge of: *ignorant of Asian culture*

i

THESAURUS

selfhood, particularity

idiot *n* **1 = fool**, jerk *(slang, chiefly US & Canad)*, ass, plank *(Brit slang)*, charlie *(Brit informal)*, berk *(Brit slang)*, wally *(slang)*, prat *(slang)*, plonker *(slang)*, moron, geek *(slang)*, twit *(informal, chiefly Brit)*, chump, imbecile, cretin, oaf, simpleton, airhead *(slang)*, dimwit *(informal)*, dipstick *(Brit slang)*, gonzo *(slang)*, schmuck *(US slang)*, dork *(slang)*, nitwit *(informal)*, blockhead, divvy *(Brit slang)*, pillock *(Brit slang)*, halfwit, nincompoop, dweeb *(US slang)*, putz *(US slang)*, eejit *(Scot & Irish)*, dumb-ass *(slang)*, dunderhead, numpty *(Scot informal)*, doofus *(slang, chiefly US)*, lamebrain *(informal)*, mooncalf, nerd *or* nurd *(slang)*, numbskull *or* numskull, galah *(Austral & NZ informal)*, dorba *or* dorb *(Austral slang)*, bogan *(Austral slang)*, dill *(Austral & NZ informal)*

idle *adj* **1 = unoccupied**, unemployed, redundant, jobless, out of work, out of action, inactive, at leisure, between jobs, unwaged, at a loose end **OPPOSITE:** occupied
2 = unused, stationary, inactive, out of order, ticking over, gathering dust, mothballed, out of service, out of action *or* operation **3 = lazy**, slow, slack, sluggish, lax, negligent, inactive, inert, lethargic, indolent, lackadaisical, good-for-nothing, remiss, workshy, slothful, shiftless **OPPOSITE:** busy
4 = useless, vain, pointless, hopeless, unsuccessful, ineffective, worthless, futile, fruitless, unproductive, abortive, ineffectual, groundless, of no use, valueless, disadvantageous, unavailing, otiose, of no avail, profitless, bootless **OPPOSITE:** useful ▷ *vb* **7** *(often with* **away***)* **= fritter**, while, waste, fool, lounge, potter, loaf, dally, loiter, dawdle, laze

idol *n* **1 = hero**, superstar, pin-up, favourite, pet, darling, beloved *(slang)*, fave *(informal)* **2 = graven image**, god, image, deity, pagan symbol

if *conj* **1 = provided**, assuming, given that, providing, allowing, admitting, supposing, granting, in case, presuming, on the assumption that, on condition that, as long as

ignite *vb* **1 = catch fire**, burn, burst into flames, fire, inflame, flare up, take fire **2 = set fire to**, light, set alight, torch, kindle, touch off, put a match to *(informal)*

ignorance *n* **a = lack of education**, stupidity, foolishness, blindness, illiteracy, benightedness, unenlightenment, unintelligence, mental darkness **OPPOSITE:** knowledge
b *(with* **of***)* **= unawareness of**, inexperience of, unfamiliarity with, innocence of, unconsciousness of, greenness about, oblivion about, nescience of *(literary)*

ignorant *adj* **1 = uneducated**, unaware, naive, green, illiterate, inexperienced, innocent, untrained, unlearned, unread, untutored, uncultivated, wet behind the ears *(informal)*, unlettered, untaught, unknowledgeable, uncomprehending, unscholarly, as green as grass **OPPOSITE:** educated
2 = insensitive, gross, crude, rude, shallow, superficial, crass **3** *(with* **of***)* **= uninformed of**, unaware of, oblivious to, blind to, innocent of, in the dark about, unconscious of, unschooled in, out of the loop of,

DICTIONARY

ignore ❶ *vb* **-noring, -nored** to refuse to notice; disregard deliberately
WORD ORIGIN Latin *ignorare* not to know

iguana *n* a large tropical tree lizard of the W Indies and S America with a spiny back
WORD ORIGIN S American Indian *iwana*

Ihimaera *n* **Witi**, full name *Witi Tame Ihimaera-Smiler*. born 1944, New Zealand Māori novelist and short-story writer; his novels include *The Whale Rider* (1987) and *The Uncle's Story* (2002)

ikebana (eek-a-**bah**-na) *n* the Japanese art of flower arrangement
WORD ORIGIN Japanese

ikon *n* ▸ same as **icon**

IL Illinois

il- *prefix* ▸ same as **in-**[1] or **in-**[2]

ileum *n* the third and lowest part of the small intestine
WORD ORIGIN Latin: flank, groin

ilex *n* **1** a genus of trees or shrubs that includes holly **2** ▸ same as **holm oak**
WORD ORIGIN Latin

ilium *n, pl* **-ia** the uppermost and widest of the three sections of the hipbone

ilk *n* a type or class: *three or four others of the same ilk*
WORD ORIGIN Old English *ilca* the same family

ill ❶ *adj* **worse, worst 1** not in good health **2** bad, harmful, or hostile: *ill effects* **3** promising an unfavourable outcome: *ill omen* **4 ill at ease** unable to relax ▹ *n* **5** evil or harm ▹ *adv* **6** badly, wrongly: *the title ill befits him* **7** with difficulty; hardly: *we can ill afford another scandal*
WORD ORIGIN Old Norse *illr* bad

ill. **1** illustrated **2** illustration

Ill. Illinois

I'll I will *or* I shall

ill-advised *adj* **1** (of a plan or action) badly thought out **2** (of a person) acting without reasonable care or thought

ill-bred *adj* lacking good manners **ill-breeding** *n*

ill-disposed *adj* unfriendly or unsympathetic

illegal ❶ *adj* against the law **illegally** *adv* **illegality** *n*

illegible *adj* unable to be read or deciphered **illegibility** *n*

illegitimate *adj* **1** born of parents who were not married to each other at the time **2** illegal; unlawful **illegitimacy** *n*

ill-fated *adj* doomed or unlucky

ill-favoured *adj* ugly or unattractive

ill-founded *adj* not based on proper proof or evidence

ill-gotten *adj* obtained dishonestly or illegally: *ill-gotten gains*

ill-health *n* the condition of being unwell

illiberal *adj* **1** narrow-minded or intolerant **2** not generous; mean **3** lacking in culture or refinement **illiberality** *n*

Illich *n* **Ivan** 1926–2002. US teacher and writer, born in Austria. His books include *Deschooling Society* (1971), *Medical Nemesis* (1975), and *In the Mirror of the Past* (1991)

illicit ❶ *adj* **1** ▸ same as **illegal** **2** forbidden or disapproved of by society: *an illicit kiss*

illiterate *adj* **1** unable to read and write **2** uneducated or ignorant: *linguistically illiterate* ▹ *n* **3** an illiterate person **illiteracy** *n*

ill-mannered *adj* having bad manners

illness ❶ *n* **1** a disease or indisposition **2** a state of ill health

illogical *adj* **1** senseless or unreasonable **2** not following logical principles **illogicality** *n* **illogically** *adv*

ill-starred *adj* very unlucky or unfortunate

ill-tempered *adj* having a bad temper

ill-timed *adj* done or happening at an unsuitable time

ill-treat *vb* to treat cruelly or harshly **ill-treatment** *n*

illuminant *n* **1** something that gives off light ▹ *adj* **2** giving off light

illuminate ❶ *vb* **-nating, -nated 1** to light up **2** to make easily understood; explain: *the report obscures rather than illuminates the most relevant facts* **3** to decorate with lights **4** to decorate (an initial letter or manuscript) with designs of gold, silver, or bright colours **illuminating** *adj* **illuminative** *adj*
WORD ORIGIN Latin *illuminare* to light up

illumination *n* **1** an illuminating or being illuminated **2** a source of light **3 illuminations** *chiefly Brit* lights used as decorations in streets or towns **4** the decoration in colours, gold, or silver used on some manuscripts

illumine *vb* **-mining, -mined** *literary* ▸ same as **illuminate**

illusion ❶ *n* **1** a false appearance or deceptive impression of reality: *her upswept hair gave the illusion of above average height* **2** a false or misleading idea or belief: *we may suffer from the illusion that we are special*
WORD ORIGIN Latin *illusio* deceit

THESAURUS

inexperienced in, uninitiated about, unknowing of, unenlightened about **OPPOSITE:** informed

ignore *vb* **a = pay no attention to,** neglect, disregard, slight, overlook, scorn, spurn, rebuff, take no notice of, be oblivious to, dinghy *(Brit slang)* **OPPOSITE:** pay attention to **b = overlook**, discount, disregard, reject, neglect, shrug off, pass over, brush aside, turn a blind eye to, turn a deaf ear to, shut your eyes to

ill *adj* **1 = unwell**, sick, poorly *(informal)*, diseased, funny *(informal)*, weak, crook *(Austral & NZ slang)*, ailing, queer, frail, feeble, unhealthy, seedy *(informal)*, sickly, laid up *(informal)*, queasy, infirm, out of sorts *(informal)*, dicky *(Brit informal)*, nauseous, off-colour, under the weather *(informal)*, at death's door, indisposed, peaky, on the sick list *(informal)*, valetudinarian, green about the gills, not up to snuff *(informal)* **OPPOSITE:** healthy **2 = harmful**, bad, damaging, evil, foul, unfortunate, destructive, unlucky, vile, detrimental, hurtful, pernicious, noxious, ruinous, deleterious, injurious, iniquitous, disadvantageous, maleficent **OPPOSITE:** favourable ▹ *n* **5 = problem**, trouble, suffering, worry, trial, injury, pain, hurt, strain, harm, distress, misery, hardship, woe, misfortune, affliction, tribulation, unpleasantness ▹ *adv* **7 = hardly**, barely, scarcely, just, only just, by no means, at a push **OPPOSITE:** well

illegal *adj* **= unlawful**, banned, forbidden, prohibited, criminal, outlawed, unofficial, illicit, unconstitutional, lawless, wrongful, off limits, unlicensed, under-the-table, unauthorized, proscribed, under-the-counter, actionable *(law)*, felonious **OPPOSITE:** legal

illicit *adj* **1 = illegal**, criminal, prohibited, unlawful, black-market, illegitimate, off limits, unlicensed, unauthorized, bootleg, contraband, felonious **OPPOSITE:** legal **2 = forbidden**, improper, immoral, wrong, guilty, clandestine, furtive

illness *n* **1, 2 = sickness**, ill health, malaise, attack, disease, complaint, infection, disorder, bug *(informal)*, disability, ailment, affliction, poor health, malady, infirmity, indisposition, lurgy *(informal)*

illuminate *vb* **1 = light up**, light, brighten, irradiate, illumine *(literary)* **OPPOSITE:** darken **2 = explain**, interpret, make clear, clarify, clear up, enlighten, shed light on, elucidate, explicate, give insight into **OPPOSITE:** obscure

illusion *n* **1 = false impression**, feeling, appearance, impression, fancy, deception, imitation, sham, pretence, semblance, fallacy **OPPOSITE:** reality **2 = delusion**, misconception, misapprehension, fancy, deception, fallacy, self-deception, false impression, false belief, misbelief

DICTIONARY

illusionist *n* a conjuror
illusory *or* **illusive** *adj* seeming to be true, but actually false: *the economic benefits of such reforms were largely illusory*
illustrate ❶ *vb* **-trating, -trated 1** to clarify or explain by use of examples or comparisons **2** to provide (a book or text) with pictures **3** to be an example of **illustrative** *adj* **illustrator** *n*
WORD ORIGIN Latin *illustrare* to make light, explain
illustration ❶ *n* **1** a picture or diagram used to explain or decorate a text **2** an example: *an illustration of the brutality of the regime* **3** the art of illustrating
illustrious *adj* famous and distinguished
WORD ORIGIN Latin *illustris* bright, famous
ill will *n* unkind feeling; hostility
Ilves *n* **Toomas Hendrik** born 1953, Estonian politician, president of Estonia from 2006
Ilyushin *n* **Sergei Vladimirovich** 1894–1977, Soviet aircraft designer. He designed the dive bomber Il-2 Stormovik and the jet airliner Il-62
IM instant messaging
I'm I am
im- *prefix* ▸ same as **in-**[1] or **in-**[2]
image ❶ *n* **1** a mental picture of someone or something produced by the imagination or memory **2** the appearance or impression given to the public by a person or organization **3** a simile or metaphor **4** a representation of a person or thing in a work of art or literature **5** an optical reproduction of an object, formed by the lens of an eye or camera, or by a mirror **6** a person or thing that resembles another closely **7** a personification of a specified quality; epitome: *the image of good breeding* ▹ *vb* **-aging, -aged 8** to picture in the mind **9** to mirror or reflect an image of **10** to portray or describe
WORD ORIGIN Latin *imago*
imagery *n, pl* **-ries 1** figurative or descriptive language in a literary work **2** mental images **3** images collectively, esp. statues or carvings
imaginary ❶ *adj* **1** existing only in the imagination **2** *maths* relating to the square root of a negative number
imagination ❶ *n* **1** the faculty or action of producing mental images of what is not present or in one's experience **2** creative mental ability
imaginative ❶ *adj* **1** produced by or showing a creative imagination **2** having a vivid imagination
imagine ❶ *vb* **-ining, -ined 1** to form a mental image of **2** to think, believe, or guess: *I would imagine they'll be here soon* **imaginable** *adj*
WORD ORIGIN Latin *imaginari*
imaginings *pl n* speculative thoughts about what might be the case or what might happen; fantasies: *lurid imaginings*
imago (im-**may**-go) *n, pl* **imagoes** *or* **imagines** (im-**maj**-in-eez) a sexually mature adult insect
WORD ORIGIN Latin: likeness
imam *n islam* **1** a leader of congregational prayer in a mosque **2** the title of some Muslim leaders
WORD ORIGIN Arabic
IMAX (**eye**-max) *n* a film projection process that produces an image ten times larger than standard
imbalance *n* a lack of balance, for instance in emphasis or proportion: *a chemical imbalance in the brain*
imbecile (**im**-biss-eel) *n* **1** *informal* an extremely stupid person **2** *old-fashioned* a person of abnormally low intelligence ▹ *adj* **3** stupid or senseless: *imbecile fanaticism* **imbecility** *n*
WORD ORIGIN Latin *imbecillus* feeble
imbed *vb* **-bedding, -bedded** ▸ same as **embed**
imbibe *vb* **-bibing, -bibed** *formal* **1** to drink (alcoholic drinks) **2** to take in or assimilate (ideas): *values she had imbibed as a child*
WORD ORIGIN Latin *imbibere*
imbroglio (imb-**role**-ee-oh) *n, pl* **-glios** a confusing and complicated situation
WORD ORIGIN Italian
imbue *vb* **-buing, -bued** to fill or inspire (with ideals or principles)
WORD ORIGIN Latin *imbuere* to stain
IMF International Monetary Fund
Imhotep *n* c. 2600 BC, Egyptian physician and architect. After his death he was worshipped as a god; the Greeks identified him with Asclepius
imitate ❶ *vb* **-tating, -tated 1** to copy the manner or style of or take as a model: *he remains rock's most imitated guitarist* **2** to mimic or impersonate, esp. for amusement **3** to make a copy or reproduction of; duplicate **imitable** *adj* **imitator** *n*
WORD ORIGIN Latin *imitari*
imitation ❶ *n* **1** a copy of an original or genuine article **2** an instance of imitating someone: *her Coward*

i

THESAURUS

illustrate *vb* **1 = explain**, describe, interpret, sum up, make clear, clarify, summarize, bring home, point up, make plain, elucidate **3 = demonstrate**, show, exhibit, emphasize, exemplify, explicate
illustration *n* **1 = picture**, drawing, painting, image, print, plate, figure, portrait, representation, sketch, decoration, portrayal, likeness, adornment **2 = example**, case, instance, sample, explanation, demonstration, interpretation, specimen, analogy, clarification, case in point, exemplar, elucidation, exemplification
image *n* **1 = thought**, idea, vision, concept, impression, perception, conception, mental picture, conceptualization **3 = figure of speech**, metaphor, simile, conceit, trope **4 = figure**, idol, icon, fetish, talisman **5a = reflection**, appearance, likeness, mirror image **5b = picture**, photo, photograph, representation, reproduction, snapshot **6 = replica**, copy, reproduction, counterpart, spit (*informal, chiefly Brit*), clone, facsimile, spitting image (*informal*), similitude, Doppelgänger, (dead) ringer (*slang*), double
imaginary *adj* **1 = fictional**, made-up, invented, supposed, imagined, assumed, ideal, fancied, legendary, visionary, shadowy, unreal, hypothetical, fanciful, fictitious, mythological, illusory, nonexistent, dreamlike, hallucinatory, illusive, chimerical, unsubstantial, phantasmal, suppositious, imagal (*psychoanalysis*) **OPPOSITE:** real
imagination *n* **1 = mind's eye**, fancy **2 = creativity**, vision, invention, ingenuity, enterprise, insight, inspiration, wit, originality, inventiveness, resourcefulness
imaginative *adj* **1 = creative**, original, inspired, enterprising, fantastic, clever, stimulating, vivid, ingenious, visionary, inventive, fanciful, dreamy, whimsical, poetical **OPPOSITE:** unimaginative
imagine *vb* **1 = envisage**, see, picture, plan, create, project, think of, scheme, frame, invent, devise, conjure up, envision, visualize, dream up (*informal*), think up, conceive of, conceptualize, fantasize about, see in the mind's eye, form a mental picture of, ideate **2 = believe**, think, suppose, assume, suspect, gather, guess (*informal, chiefly US & Canad*), realize, take it, reckon, fancy, deem, speculate, presume, take for granted, infer, deduce, apprehend, conjecture, surmise
imitate *vb* **1 = copy**, follow, repeat, echo, emulate, ape, simulate, mirror, follow suit, duplicate, counterfeit, follow in the footsteps of, take a leaf out of (someone's) book **2 = do an impression of**, take off (*informal*), mimic, do (*informal*), affect, copy, mock, parody, caricature, send up (*Brit informal*), spoof (*informal*), impersonate, burlesque, personate
imitation *n* **1 = replica**, fake, reproduction, sham, forgery, carbon copy (*informal*), counterfeit, counterfeiting, likeness, duplication

DICTIONARY

imitations were not the best thing she did **3** behaviour modelled on the behaviour of someone else: *to learn by imitation* ▷ *adj* **4** made to resemble something which is usually superior or more expensive: *imitation leather*

imitative *adj* **1** imitating or tending to copy **2** copying or reproducing an original, esp. in an inferior manner: *imitative painting* **3** onomatopoeic

immaculate *adj* **1** completely clean or tidy: *an immaculate pinstripe suit* **2** completely flawless: *his equestrian pedigree is immaculate* **immaculately** *adv*
WORD ORIGIN Latin *in-* not + *macula* blemish

immanent *adj* **1** present within and throughout something **2** (of God) present throughout the universe **immanence** *n*
WORD ORIGIN Latin *immanere* to remain in

immaterial *adj* **1** of no real importance or relevance **2** not formed of matter

immature *adj* **1** not fully grown or developed **2** lacking wisdom, insight, or stability because of youth **immaturity** *n*

immeasurable *adj* too great to be measured **immeasurably** *adv*

immediate *adj* **1** taking place without delay: *an immediate cut in interest rates* **2** next or nearest in space, time, or relationship: *our immediate neighbour* **3** present; current: *they had no immediate plans to close it* **immediacy** *n* **immediately** *adv*
WORD ORIGIN Latin *in-* not + *mediare* to be in the middle

immemorial *adj* having existed or happened for longer than anyone can remember: *this has been the custom since time immemorial*

immense *adj* **1** huge or vast **2** *informal* very great **immensely** *adv* **immensity** *n*
WORD ORIGIN Latin *immensus* unmeasured

immerse *vb* **-mersing, -mersed 1** to plunge or dip into liquid **2** to involve deeply: *he immersed himself in the history of Rome* **3** to baptize by dipping the whole body into water **immersion** *n*
WORD ORIGIN Latin *immergere*

immersion heater *n* an electrical device in a domestic hot-water tank for heating water

immigrant *n* a person who comes to a foreign country in order to settle there

immigration *n* the act of coming to a foreign country in order to settle there **immigrate** *vb*
WORD ORIGIN Latin *immigrare* to go into

imminent *adj* likely to happen soon **imminence** *n*
WORD ORIGIN Latin *imminere* to project over

immiscible *adj* (of liquids) incapable of being mixed: *oil and water are immiscible* **immiscibility** *n*

immobile *adj* **1** not moving **2** not able to move or be moved **immobility** *n*

immobilize *or* **-lise** *vb* **-lizing, -lized** *or* **-lising, -lised** to make unable to move or work: *a device for immobilizing steering wheels* **immobilization** *or* **-lisation** *n*

immoderate *adj* excessive or unreasonable: *immoderate consumption of alcohol* **immoderately** *adv*

immodest *adj* **1** behaving in an indecent or improper manner **2** behaving in a boastful or conceited manner **immodesty** *n*

immolate *vb* **-lating, -lated** *literary* to kill or offer as a sacrifice, esp. by fire **immolation** *n*
WORD ORIGIN Latin *immolare*

immoral *adj* **1** morally wrong; corrupt **2** sexually depraved or promiscuous **immorality** *n*

immortal *adj* **1** not subject to death or decay **2** famous for all time **3** everlasting ▷ *n* **4** a person whose fame will last for all time **5** an immortal being **immortality** *n*

immortalize *or* **-ise** *vb* **-izing, -ized** *or* **-ising, -ised 1** to give everlasting fame to: *a name immortalized by countless writers* **2** to give immortality to

immovable *or* **immoveable** *adj* **1** unable to be moved **2** unwilling to change one's opinions or beliefs **3** not affected by feeling; emotionless **4** unchanging **5** *law* (of property) consisting of land or houses **immovability** *or* **immoveability** *n* **immovably** *or* **immoveably** *adv*

immune *adj* **1** protected against a specific disease by inoculation or as the result of natural resistance **2** exempt from obligation or penalty **3 immune to** secure against: *football is not immune to economic recession*
WORD ORIGIN Latin *immunis* exempt from a public service

immune system *n* the mechanism by which a body reacts to foreign materials, involving the production of antibodies

immunity *n, pl* **-ties 1** the ability of

THESAURUS

2 = impression, parody, mockery, takeoff *(informal)*, impersonation **3 = copying**, echoing, resemblance, aping, simulation, mimicry ▷ *adj* **4 = artificial**, mock, reproduction, dummy, synthetic, man-made, simulated, sham, pseudo *(informal)*, ersatz, repro, phoney *or* phony *(informal)* **OPPOSITE:** real

immaculate *adj* **1 = clean**, impeccable, spotless, trim, neat, spruce, squeaky-clean, spick-and-span, neat as a new pin **OPPOSITE:** dirty **2 = perfect**, flawless, impeccable, stainless, faultless, unblemished, unsullied, uncontaminated, unpolluted, untarnished, unexceptionable, undefiled **OPPOSITE:** tainted

immediate *adj* **1 = instant**, prompt, instantaneous, quick, on-the-spot, split-second **OPPOSITE:** later **2 = nearest**, next, direct, close, near, adjacent, contiguous, proximate **OPPOSITE:** far

immense *adj* **1 = huge**, great, massive, vast, large, giant, enormous, extensive, tremendous, mega *(slang)*, titanic, infinite, jumbo *(informal)*, very big, gigantic, monumental, monstrous, mammoth, colossal, mountainous, stellar *(informal)*, prodigious, interminable, stupendous, king-size, king-sized, immeasurable, elephantine, ginormous *(informal)*, Brobdingnagian, illimitable, humongous *or* humungous *(US slang)*, supersize **OPPOSITE:** tiny

immerse *vb* **1 = plunge**, dip, submerge, sink, duck, bathe, douse, dunk, submerse **2 = engross**, involve, absorb, busy, occupy, engage

immigrant *n* **= settler**, incomer, alien, stranger, outsider, newcomer, migrant, emigrant

imminent *adj* **= near**, coming, close, approaching, threatening, gathering, on the way, in the air, forthcoming, looming, menacing, brewing, impending, at hand, upcoming, on the cards, on the horizon, in the pipeline, nigh *(archaic)*, in the offing, fast-approaching, just round the corner, near-at-hand **OPPOSITE:** remote

immoral *adj* **1, 2 = wicked**, bad, wrong, abandoned, evil, corrupt, vicious, obscene, indecent, vile, degenerate, dishonest, pornographic, sinful, unethical, lewd, depraved, impure, debauched, unprincipled, nefarious, dissolute, iniquitous, reprobate, licentious, of easy virtue, unchaste **OPPOSITE:** moral

immortal *adj* **1 = undying**, eternal, perpetual, indestructible, death-defying, imperishable, deathless **OPPOSITE:** mortal **3 = timeless**, eternal, everlasting, lasting, traditional, classic, constant, enduring, persistent, abiding, perennial, ageless, unfading **OPPOSITE:** ephemeral ▷ *n* **4 = hero**, genius, paragon, great **5 = god**, goddess, deity, Olympian, divine being, immortal being, atua *(NZ)*

immunity *n* **1 = resistance**, protection, resilience, inoculation, immunization **OPPOSITE:** susceptibility

DICTIONARY

an organism to resist disease **2** freedom from prosecution, tax, etc.

immunize *or* **-nise** *vb* **-nizing, -nized** *or* **-nising, -nised** to make (someone) immune to a disease, esp. by inoculation **immunization** *or* **-nisation** *n*

immunodeficiency *n* a deficiency in or breakdown of a person's ability to fight diseases

immunology *n* the branch of medicine concerned with the study of immunity **immunological** *adj* **immunologist** *n*

immure *vb* **-muring, -mured 1** *archaic or literary* to imprison **2** to shut (oneself) away from society
WORD ORIGIN Latin *im-* in + *murus* wall

immutable (im-mute-a-bl) *adj* unchangeable or unchanging: *the immutable sequence of night and day* **immutability** *n*

imp *n* **1** a small demon **2** a mischievous child
WORD ORIGIN Old English *impa* bud, hence offspring, child

imp. 1 imperative **2** imperfect

impact ❶ *n* **1** the effect or impression made by something **2** the act of one object striking another; collision **3** the force of a collision ▷*vb* **4** to press firmly against or into **5 impact on** to have an effect on **impaction** *n*
WORD ORIGIN Latin *impactus* pushed against

impacted *adj* (of a tooth) unable to grow out because of being wedged against another tooth below the gum

impair ❶ *vb* to damage or weaken in strength or quality **impairment** *n*
WORD ORIGIN Old French *empeirer* to make worse

impala (imp-ah-la) *n, pl* **-las** *or* **-la** an African antelope with lyre-shaped horns
WORD ORIGIN Zulu

impale *vb* **-paling, -paled** to pierce through or fix with a sharp object: *they impaled his severed head on a spear* **impalement** *n*
WORD ORIGIN Latin *im-* on + *palus* pole

impalpable *adj formal* **1** not able to be felt by touching: *impalpable shadows* **2** difficult to understand **impalpability** *n*

impart *vb* **1** to communicate (information or knowledge) **2** to give (a specified quality): *flavouring to impart a sweet taste*
WORD ORIGIN Latin *im-* in + *partire* to share

impartial *adj* not favouring one side or the other **impartiality** *n* **impartially** *adv*

impassable *adj* (of terrain or roads) not able to be travelled through or over **impassability** *n*

impasse ❶ (am-pass) *n* a situation in which progress or escape is impossible
WORD ORIGIN French

impassible *adj* **1** *rare* not susceptible to pain or injury **2** impassive; unmoved **impassibility** *or* **impassibleness** *n*

impassioned *adj* full of emotion: *an impassioned plea to the United Nations*

impassive *adj* not showing or feeling emotion **impassively** *adv* **impassivity** *n*

impasto *n* the technique of applying paint thickly, so that brush marks are evident
WORD ORIGIN Italian

impatient ❶ *adj* **1** irritable at any delay or difficulty **2** restless to have or do something **impatience** *n* **impatiently** *adv*

impeach *vb* **1** *chiefly US* to charge (a public official) with an offence committed in office **2** *Austral & Brit criminal law* to accuse of treason or serious crime **3** to challenge or question (a person's honesty or honour) **impeachable** *adj* **impeachment** *n*
WORD ORIGIN Late Latin *impedicare* to entangle

impeccable ❶ *adj* without flaw or error: *impeccable manners* **impeccably** *adv*
WORD ORIGIN Latin *in-* not + *peccare* to sin

impecunious *adj formal* without money; penniless
WORD ORIGIN Latin *in-* not + *pecuniosus* wealthy

impedance (imp-eed-anss) *n electronics* the total effective resistance in an electric circuit to the flow of an alternating current

impede *vb* **-peding, -peded** to block or make progress or action difficult
WORD ORIGIN Latin *impedire*

impediment *n* **1** a hindrance or obstruction **2** a physical disability that makes speech or walking difficult

impedimenta *pl n* any objects that impede progress, esp. the baggage and equipment carried by an army

impel *vb* **-pelling, -pelled 1** to urge or force (a person) to do something **2** to push, drive, or force into motion
WORD ORIGIN Latin *impellere* to drive forward

impending ❶ *adj* (esp. of something bad) about to happen
WORD ORIGIN Latin *impendere* to overhang

impenetrable *adj* **1** impossible to get through: *an impenetrable barrier* **2** impossible to understand **3** not receptive to ideas or influence: *impenetrable ignorance* **impenetrability** *n* **impenetrably** *adv*

impenitent *adj* not sorry or penitent **impenitence** *n*

imperative ❶ *adj* **1** extremely urgent; essential **2** commanding or authoritative: *an imperative tone of voice* **3** *grammar* denoting a mood of verbs used in commands ▷*n* **4** *grammar* the imperative mood
WORD ORIGIN Latin *imperare* to command

imperceptible *adj* too slight, subtle, or gradual to be noticed **imperceptibly** *adv*

THESAURUS

2 = exemption, amnesty, indemnity, release, freedom, liberty, privilege, prerogative, invulnerability, exoneration

impact *n* **1 = effect**, influence, consequences, impression, repercussions, ramifications **2 = collision**, force, contact, shock, crash, knock, stroke, smash, bump, thump, jolt ▷*vb* **4 = hit**, strike, crash, clash, crush, ram, smack, collide

impair *vb* **= worsen**, reduce, damage, injure, harm, mar, undermine, weaken, spoil, diminish, decrease, blunt, deteriorate, lessen, hinder, debilitate, vitiate, enfeeble, enervate **OPPOSITE:** improve

impasse *n* **= deadlock**, stalemate, standstill, dead end, standoff, blind alley *(informal)*

impatient *adj* **1 = cross**, tense, annoyed, irritated, prickly, edgy, touchy, bad-tempered, intolerant, petulant, ill-tempered, cantankerous, ratty *(Brit & NZ informal)*, chippy *(informal)*, hot-tempered, quick-tempered, crotchety *(informal)*, ill-humoured, narky *(Brit slang)*, out of humour **2 = eager**, longing, keen, hot, earnest, raring, anxious, hungry, intent, enthusiastic, yearning, greedy, restless, ardent, avid, fervent, zealous, chafing, vehement, fretful, straining at the leash, fervid, keen as mustard, like a cat on hot bricks *(informal)*, athirst **OPPOSITE:** calm

impeccable *adj* **= faultless**, perfect, pure, exact, precise, exquisite, stainless, immaculate, flawless, squeaky-clean, unerring, unblemished, unimpeachable, irreproachable, sinless, incorrupt **OPPOSITE:** flawed

impending *adj* **= looming**, coming, approaching, near, nearing, threatening, forthcoming, brewing, imminent, hovering, upcoming, on the horizon, in the pipeline, in the offing

imperative *adj* **1 = urgent**, essential, pressing, vital, crucial, compulsory, indispensable, obligatory, exigent **OPPOSITE:** unnecessary

DICTIONARY

imperfect *adj* **1** having faults or errors **2** not complete **3** *grammar* denoting a tense of verbs describing continuous, incomplete, or repeated past actions ▷*n* **4** *grammar* the imperfect tense **imperfectly** *adv*

imperfection *n* **1** the state of being imperfect **2** a fault or defect

imperial ⊕ *adj* **1** of an empire, emperor, or empress **2** majestic; commanding **3** exercising supreme authority; imperious **4** (of weights or measures) conforming to the standards of a system formerly official in Great Britain ▷*n* **5** a wine bottle holding the equivalent of eight normal bottles
WORD ORIGIN Latin *imperium* authority

imperialism *n* **1** the policy or practice of extending a country's influence over other territories by conquest, colonization, or economic domination **2** an imperial system, authority, or government **imperialist** *adj, n* **imperialistic** *adj*

imperil *vb* **-illing, -illed** *or US* **-iling, -iled** *formal* to put in danger

imperious *adj* used to being obeyed; domineering **imperiously** *adv*
WORD ORIGIN Latin *imperium* power

imperishable *adj* unable to disappear or be destroyed

impermanent *adj* not permanent; fleeting **impermanence** *n*

impermeable *adj* (of a substance) not allowing fluid to pass through: *an impermeable layer* **impermeability** *n*

impermissible *adj* not allowed

impersonal *adj* **1** without reference to any individual person; objective: *buddhism began as a very impersonal doctrine* **2** without human warmth or sympathy: *an impersonal manner* **3** *grammar* **a** (of a verb) having no subject, as in *it is raining* **b** (of a pronoun) not referring to a person **impersonality** *n* **impersonally** *adv*

impersonate *vb* **-ating, -ated 1** to pretend to be (another person) **2** to imitate the character or mannerisms of (another person) for entertainment **impersonation** *n* **impersonator** *n*

impertinent *adj* disrespectful or rude **impertinence** *n*
WORD ORIGIN Latin *impertinens* not belonging

imperturbable *adj* not easily upset; calm **imperturbability** *n* **imperturbably** *adv*

impervious *adj* **1** not letting water etc. through **2** not influenced by a feeling, argument, etc.

impetigo (imp-it-tie-go) *n* a contagious skin disease causing spots or pimples
WORD ORIGIN Latin: scabby eruption

impetuous *adj* **1** acting without consideration **2** done rashly or hastily **impetuosity** *n*
WORD ORIGIN Late Latin *impetuosus* violent

impetus ⊕ (imp-it-uss) *n, pl* **-tuses 1** an incentive or impulse **2** *physics* the force that starts a body moving or that tends to resist changes in its speed or direction once it is moving
WORD ORIGIN Latin: attack

impi *n, pl* **-pi** *or* **-pies** a group of Zulu warriors
WORD ORIGIN Nguni (language group of southern Africa): regiment, army

impiety *n* lack of respect or religious reverence

impinge *vb* **-pinging, -pinged** (often foll. by *on*) to encroach (on), affect or restrict: *international economic forces impinging on the local economy* **impingement** *n*
WORD ORIGIN Latin *impingere* to dash against

impious (imp-e-uss) *adj* showing a lack of respect or religious reverence

impish *adj* mischievous **impishness** *n*

implacable *adj* **1** incapable of being appeased or pacified **2** unyielding **implacability** *n* **implacably** *adv*

implant ⊕ *vb* **1** to fix firmly in the mind: *to implant sound moral principles* **2** to plant or embed **3** *surgery* to graft or insert (a tissue or hormone) into the body ▷*n* **4** anything implanted in the body, such as a tissue graft **implantation** *n*

implausible *adj* not easy to believe **implausibility** *n*

implement ⊕ *vb* **1** to carry out (instructions etc.): *she refused to implement the agreed plan* ▷*n* **2** a tool or other piece of equipment **implementation** *n*
WORD ORIGIN Late Latin *implementum*, literally: a filling up

implicate ⊕ *vb* **-cating, -cated 1** to show (someone) to be involved, esp. in a crime **2** to imply
WORD ORIGIN Latin *implicare* to involve

implication ⊕ *n* **1** something that is suggested or implied **2** an act or instance of suggesting or implying or being implied **3** a probable consequence (of something)

implicit ⊕ *adj* **1** expressed indirectly: *an implicit agreement* **2** absolute and unquestioning: *implicit trust* **3** contained in, although not stated openly: *this view of the mind was implicit in all his work* **implicitly** *adv*
WORD ORIGIN Latin *implicitus*

implied ⊕ *adj* hinted at or suggested: *an implied criticism*

implode *vb* **-ploding, -ploded** to collapse inwards
WORD ORIGIN *im-* in + *(ex)plode*

implore *vb* **-ploring, -plored** to beg desperately
WORD ORIGIN Latin *implorare*

imply ⊕ *vb* **-plies, -plying, -plied 1** to express or indicate by a hint; suggest **2** to suggest or involve as a necessary consequence: *a spending commitment implies a corresponding tax imposition*
WORD ORIGIN Old French *emplier*

impolite *adj* discourteous; rude **impoliteness** *n*

impolitic *adj* ill-advised; unwise

THESAURUS

imperial *adj* **1 = royal**, regal, kingly, queenly, princely, sovereign, majestic, monarchial, monarchal

impetus *n* **1 = incentive**, push, spur, motivation, impulse, stimulus, catalyst, goad, impulsion **2** *(physics)* **= force**, power, energy, momentum

implant *vb* **1 = instil**, sow, infuse, inculcate, infix **2 = insert**, place, plant, fix, root, sow, graft, embed, ingraft

implement *vb* **1 = carry out**, effect, carry through, complete, apply, perform, realize, fulfil, enforce, execute, discharge, bring about, enact, put into action *or* effect
OPPOSITE: hinder
▷*n* **2 = tool**, machine, device, instrument, appliance, apparatus, gadget, utensil, contraption, contrivance, agent

implicate *vb* **1 = incriminate**, involve, compromise, embroil, entangle, inculpate **OPPOSITE:** dissociate

implication *n* **1, 2 = suggestion**, hint, inference, meaning, conclusion, significance, presumption, overtone, innuendo, intimation, insinuation, signification **3 = consequence**, result, development, ramification, complication, upshot

implicit *adj* **1 = implied**, understood, suggested, hinted at, taken for granted, unspoken, inferred, tacit, undeclared, insinuated, unstated, unsaid, unexpressed
OPPOSITE: explicit
2 = absolute, full, complete, total, firm, fixed, entire, constant, utter, outright, consummate, unqualified, out-and-out, steadfast, wholehearted, unadulterated, unreserved, unshakable, unshaken, unhesitating **3 = inherent**, contained, underlying, intrinsic, latent, ingrained, inbuilt

implied *adj* **= suggested**, inherent, indirect, hinted at, implicit, unspoken, tacit, undeclared, insinuated, unstated, unexpressed

imply *vb* **1 = suggest**, hint, insinuate, indicate, signal, intimate, signify, connote, give (someone) to understand **2 = involve**, mean, entail, include, require, indicate, import, point to, signify, denote, presuppose, betoken

DICTIONARY

imponderable *adj* **1** unable to be weighed or assessed ▹*n* **2** something difficult or impossible to assess

import ❶ *vb* **1** to bring in (goods) from another country **2** *formal* to signify; mean: *to import doom* ▹*n* **3** something imported **4** *formal* importance: *his new work is of great import* **5** meaning **6** *Canad slang* a sportsman who is not native to the area where he plays **importer** *n* **importation** *n*
WORD ORIGIN Latin *importare* to carry in

important ❶ *adj* **1** of great significance, value, or consequence **2** of social significance: *an important man in the company hierarchy* **3** of great concern: *it was important to me to know* **importance** *n* **importantly** *adv*
WORD ORIGIN Medieval Latin *importare* to signify, from Latin: to carry in

importunate *adj formal* persistent or demanding

importune *vb* **-tuning, -tuned** *formal* to harass with persistent requests **importunity** *n*
WORD ORIGIN Latin *importunus* tiresome

impose *vb* **-posing, -posed 1** to establish (a rule, condition, etc.) as something to be obeyed or complied with **2** to force (oneself) on others **3** *printing* to arrange (pages) in the correct order for printing **4** to pass off (something) deceptively on someone **5 impose on** to take advantage of (a person or quality): *she imposed on his kindness*
WORD ORIGIN Latin *imponere* to place upon

imposing ❶ *adj* grand or impressive: *an imposing building*

imposition ❶ *n* **1** the act of imposing **2** something imposed, esp. unfairly on someone **3** the arrangement of pages for printing **4** *old-fashioned* a task set as a school punishment

impossibility *n, pl* **-ties 1** the state or quality of being impossible **2** something that is impossible

impossible ❶ *adj* **1** not able to be done or to happen **2** absurd or unreasonable **3** *informal* intolerable or outrageous: *those children are impossible* **impossibly** *adv*

impostor *or* **imposter** *n* a person who cheats or swindles by pretending to be someone else
WORD ORIGIN Late Latin *impostor* deceiver

imposture *n formal* deception, esp. by pretending to be someone else

impotent (imp-a-tent) *adj* **1** not having the power to influence people or events **2** (of a man) incapable of sexual intercourse **impotence** *n*

impound *vb* **1** to take legal possession of; confiscate **2** to confine (an animal) in a pound

impoverish ❶ *vb* **1** to make (someone) poor **2** weaken the quality of something **impoverished** *adj* **impoverishment** *n*
WORD ORIGIN Old French *empovrir*

impracticable *adj* **1** not able to be put into practice **2** unsuitable for a desired use **impracticability** *n*

impractical *adj* **1** not sensible or workable: *the use of force was viewed as impractical* **2** not having practical skills **impracticality** *n*

imprecation *n formal* a curse **imprecate** *vb*
WORD ORIGIN Latin *imprecari* to invoke

imprecise *adj* inexact or inaccurate **imprecision** *n*

impregnable *adj* **1** unable to be broken into or taken by force: *an impregnable fortress* **2** unable to be affected or overcome: *a confident, impregnable person* **impregnability** *n*
WORD ORIGIN Old French *imprenable*

impregnate *vb* **-nating, -nated 1** to saturate, soak, or fill throughout **2** to make pregnant **3** to imbue or permeate: *the party has been impregnated with an enthusiasm for reform* **impregnation** *n*
WORD ORIGIN Latin *in-* in + *praegnans* pregnant

impresario *n, pl* **-sarios** a person who runs theatre performances, concerts, etc.
WORD ORIGIN Italian

impress ❶ *vb* **1** to make a strong, lasting, or favourable impression on: *he was impressed by the standard of play* **2** to stress or emphasize **3** to imprint or stamp by pressure: *a pattern impressed in paint on the rock* ▹*n* **4** an impressing **5** a mark produced by impressing **impressible** *adj*
WORD ORIGIN Latin *imprimere* to press into

impression ❶ *n* **1** an effect produced in the mind by a person or thing: *she was keen to create a relaxed impression* **2** a vague idea or belief: *he only had a vague impression of how it worked* **3** a strong, favourable, or remarkable effect **4** an impersonation for entertainment **5** an imprint or mark produced by pressing **6** *printing* the number of copies of a publication printed at one time

THESAURUS

import *vb* **1 = bring in**, buy in, ship in, land, introduce ▹*n* **4** *(formal)* **= significance**, concern, value, worth, weight, consequence, substance, moment, magnitude, usefulness, momentousness **5 = meaning**, implication, significance, sense, message, bearing, intention, explanation, substance, drift, interpretation, thrust, purport, upshot, gist, signification

important *adj* **1 = significant**, critical, substantial, grave, urgent, serious, material, signal, primary, meaningful, far-reaching, momentous, seminal, weighty, of substance, salient, noteworthy
OPPOSITE: unimportant
2 = powerful, leading, prominent, commanding, supreme, outstanding, high-level, dominant, influential, notable, big-time *(informal)*, foremost, eminent, high-ranking, authoritative, major league *(informal)*, of note, noteworthy, pre-eminent, skookum *(Canad)*

imposing *adj* **= impressive**, striking, grand, august, powerful, effective, commanding, awesome, majestic, dignified, stately, forcible
OPPOSITE: unimposing

imposition *n* **1 = application**, introduction, levying, decree, laying on **2 = intrusion**, liberty, presumption, cheek *(informal)*, encroachment

impossible *adj* **1a = not possible**, out of the question, impracticable, unfeasible, beyond the bounds of possibility **1b = unachievable**, hopeless, out of the question, vain, unthinkable, inconceivable, far-fetched, unworkable, implausible, unattainable, unobtainable, beyond you, not to be thought of **OPPOSITE:** possible
2 = absurd, crazy *(informal)*, ridiculous, unacceptable, outrageous, ludicrous, unreasonable, unsuitable, intolerable, preposterous, laughable, farcical, illogical, insoluble, unanswerable, inadmissible, ungovernable

impoverish *vb* **1 = bankrupt**, ruin, beggar, break, pauperize **2 = deplete**, drain, exhaust, diminish, use up, sap, wear out, reduce

impress *vb* **1 = excite**, move, strike, touch, affect, influence, inspire, grab *(informal)*, amaze, overcome, stir, overwhelm, astonish, dazzle, sway, awe, overawe, make an impression on *(slang, chiefly US)*

impression *n* **1 = effect**, influence, impact, sway **2 = idea**, feeling, thought, sense, opinion, view, assessment, judgment, reaction, belief, concept, fancy, notion, conviction, suspicion, hunch, apprehension, inkling, funny feeling *(informal)* **4 = imitation**, parody, impersonation, mockery, send-up *(Brit informal)*, takeoff *(informal)* **5 = mark**, imprint, stamp, stamping, depression, outline, hollow, dent, impress, indentation

DICTIONARY

impressionable *adj* easily impressed or influenced: *the promotion of smoking to the impressionable young* **impressionability** *n*

Impressionism *n* a style of painting developed in 19th-century France, with the aim of reproducing the immediate impression or mood of things, especially the effects of light and atmosphere, rather than form or structure

impressionist *n* **1 Impressionist** an artist who painted in the style of Impressionism **2** a person who imitates the character or mannerisms of another person for entertainment

impressionistic *adj* **1 Impressionistic** of or about Impressionism **2** based on subjective observations or impressions rather than systematic study or facts: *Mitchell was making impressionistic documentaries*

impressive ⊕ *adj* capable of impressing, esp. by size, magnificence, or importance **impressively** *adv*

imprimatur (imp-rim-**ah**-ter) *n* official approval for something to be printed, usually given by the Roman Catholic Church

WORD ORIGIN New Latin: let it be printed

imprint ⊕ *n* **1** a mark or impression produced by pressing, printing, or stamping **2** the publisher's name and address, often with the date of publication, printed on the title page of a book ▷ *vb* **3** to produce (a mark) by pressing, printing, or stamping: *T-shirts imprinted with slogans* **4** to establish firmly; impress: *he couldn't dislodge the images imprinted on his brain*

imprison ⊕ *vb* to confine in or as if in prison **imprisonment** *n*

improbable ⊕ *adj* not likely or probable **improbability** *n* **improbably** *adv*

improbity *n, pl* **-ties** *formal* dishonesty or wickedness

impromptu *adj* **1** without planning or preparation; improvised ▷ *adv* **2** in a spontaneous or improvised way: *he spoke impromptu* ▷ *n* **3** a short piece of instrumental music resembling improvisation **4** something that is impromptu

WORD ORIGIN Latin *in promptu* in readiness

improper ⊕ *adj* **1** indecent **2** irregular or incorrect **improperly** *adv*

improper fraction *n* a fraction in which the numerator is greater than the denominator, as $\frac{7}{6}$

impropriety (imp-roe-**pry**-a-tee) *n, pl* **-ties** *formal* unsuitable or slightly improper behaviour

improve ⊕ *vb* **-proving, -proved 1** to make or become better in quality **2 improve on** to achieve a better standard or quality in comparison with: *both had improved on their previous performance* **improvable** *adj*

WORD ORIGIN Anglo-French *emprouer* to turn to profit

improvement ⊕ *n* **1** the act of improving or the state of being improved **2** a change that makes something better or adds to its value: *home improvements* **3** *Austral & NZ* a building on a piece of land, adding to its value

improvident *adj* **1** not providing for the future **2** incautious or rash **improvidence** *n*

improvise ⊕ *vb* **-vising, -vised 1** to do or make quickly from whatever is available, without previous planning **2** to make up (a piece of music, speech, etc.) as one goes along **improvisation** *n*

WORD ORIGIN Latin *improvisus* unforeseen

imprudent *adj* not carefully thought out; rash **imprudence** *n*

impudent *adj* impertinent or insolent **impudence** *n* **impudently** *adv*

WORD ORIGIN Latin *impudens* shameless

impugn (imp-**yoon**) *vb formal* to challenge or attack as false **impugnment** *n*

WORD ORIGIN Latin *impugnare* to fight against

impulse ⊕ *n* **1** a sudden desire or whim **2** an instinctive drive; urge: *the mothering impulse* **3** *physics* **a** the product of a force acting on a body and the time for which it acts **b** the change in the momentum of a body as a result of a force acting upon it **4** *physiol* a stimulus transmitted in a nerve or muscle

WORD ORIGIN Latin *impulsus* incitement

impulsive *adj* **1** tending to act without thinking first: *an impulsive man* **2** done without thinking first **3** forceful or impelling

impunity (imp-**yoon**-it-ee) *n* **with impunity** without punishment or unpleasant consequences

WORD ORIGIN Latin *impunis* unpunished

impure *adj* **1** having unwanted substances mixed in **2** immoral or obscene: *impure thoughts* **3** dirty or unclean

impurity *n, pl* **-ties 1** an impure element or thing: *impurities in the water* **2** the quality of being impure

impute *vb* **-puting, -puted 1** to attribute (blame or a crime) to a person **2** to attribute to a source or cause: *I impute your success to nepotism* **imputation** *n*

WORD ORIGIN Latin *in-* in + *putare* to think

Imran Khan *n* full name *Imran Ahmad Khan Niazi*. born 1952, Pakistani cricketer: played for Worcestershire (1971–76) and Sussex (1977–88); captained Pakistan (1982–84; 1985–87; 1988–92)

in *prep* **1** inside; within: *in the room* **2** at a place where there is: *in the shade* **3** indicating a state, situation, or condition: *in silence* **4** when (a period of time) has elapsed: *come back in one year* **5** using: *written in code*

THESAURUS

impressive *adj* **= grand**, striking, splendid, good, great *(informal)*, fine, affecting, powerful, exciting, wonderful, excellent, dramatic, outstanding, stirring, superb, first-class, marvellous *(informal)*, terrific *(informal)*, awesome, world-class, admirable, first-rate, crash-hot *(Austral)*, forcible **OPPOSITE:** unimpressive

imprint *n* **1 = mark**, print, impression, stamp, indentation ▷ *vb* **3 = engrave**, print, stamp, impress, etch, emboss

imprison *vb* **= jail**, confine, detain, lock up, constrain, put away, intern, incarcerate, send down *(informal)*, send to prison, impound, put under lock and key, immure **OPPOSITE:** free

improbable *adj* **= doubtful**, unlikely, uncertain, unbelievable, dubious, questionable, fanciful, far-fetched, implausible **OPPOSITE:** probable

improper *adj* **1 = indecent**, vulgar, suggestive, unseemly, untoward, risqué, smutty, unbecoming, unfitting, impolite, off-colour, indelicate, indecorous **OPPOSITE:** decent

improve *vb* **1a = enhance**, better, add to, upgrade, amend, mend, augment, embellish, touch up, ameliorate, polish up **1b = get better**, pick up, look up *(informal)*, develop, advance, perk up, take a turn for the better *(informal)* **OPPOSITE:** worsen

improvement *n* **1a = enhancement**, increase, gain, boost, amendment, correction, heightening, advancement, enrichment, face-lift, embellishment, betterment, rectification, augmentation, amelioration **1b = advance**, development, progress, recovery, reformation, upswing, furtherance

improvise *vb* **1 = devise**, contrive, make do, concoct, throw together **2 = ad-lib**, invent, vamp, busk, wing it *(informal)*, play it by ear *(informal)*, extemporize, speak off the cuff *(informal)*

impulse *n* **1, 2 = urge**, longing, desire, drive, wish, fancy, notion, yen *(informal)*, instinct, yearning, inclination, itch, whim, compulsion, caprice

inadequacy *n* **1 = shortage**, poverty, dearth, paucity, insufficiency,

6 wearing: *the man in the blue suit* **7** with regard to (a specified activity or occupation): *in journalism* **8** while performing the action of: *in crossing the street he was run over* **9** having as purpose: *in honour of the president* **10** (of certain animals) pregnant with: *in calf* **11** into: *he fell in the water* **12 have it in one** to have the ability (to do something) **13 in that** *or* **in so far as** because or to the extent that: *it was of great help in that it gave me more confidence* ▷ *adv* **14** in or into a particular place; indoors: *come in* **15** at one's home or place of work: *he's not in at the moment* **16** in office or power: *the Conservatives got in at the last election* **17** so as to enclose: *block in* **18** (in certain games) so as to take one's turn of the play: *you have to get the other side out before you go in* **19** *Brit* (of a fire) alight **20** indicating prolonged activity, esp. by a large number: *teach-in; sit-in* **21 have got it in for** *informal* to wish or intend harm towards **22 in for** about to experience (something, esp. something unpleasant): *they're in for a shock* **23 in on** acquainted with or sharing in: *I was in on all his plans* **24 in with** friendly with ▷ *adj* **25** fashionable; modish: *the in thing to do* ▷ *n* **26 ins and outs** the detailed points or facts (of a situation)
WORD ORIGIN Old English

In *chem* indium

IN Indiana

in. inch(es)

in-[1]**, il-, im-** *or* **ir-** *prefix* **a** not; non: *incredible; illegal; imperfect; irregular* **b** lack of: *inexperience*
WORD ORIGIN Latin

in-[2]**, il-, im-** *or* **ir-** *prefix* in; into; towards; within; on: *infiltrate*
WORD ORIGIN from *in*

inability *n* the fact of not being able to do something

in absentia *adv* in the absence of (someone indicated)
WORD ORIGIN Latin

inaccessible *adj* **1** impossible or very difficult to reach **2** unable to be used or seen: *his works are inaccessible to English-speaking readers* **3** difficult to understand or appreciate: *Webern's music is still considered inaccessible* **inaccessibility** *n*

inaccuracy *n, pl* **-cies 1** lack of accuracy; imprecision **2** an error or mistake **inaccurate** *adj*

inaction *n* lack of action; inertia

inactive *adj* **1** idle; not active **2** *chem* (of a substance) having little or no reactivity **inactivity** *n*

inadequacy ❶ *n, pl* **-cies 1** lack or shortage **2** the state of being or feeling inferior **3** a weakness or failing: *their own failures or inadequacies*

inadequate ❶ *adj* **1** not enough; insufficient **2** not good enough **inadequately** *adv*

inadmissible *adj* not allowable or acceptable

inadvertent *adj* done unintentionally **inadvertence** *n* **inadvertently** *adv*

inadvisable *adj* unwise; not sensible

inalienable *adj* not able to be taken away or transferred to another: *the inalienable rights of the citizen*

inamorata *or masc* **inamorato** *n, pl* **-tas** *or masc* **-tos** *literary* a sweetheart or lover
WORD ORIGIN Italian *innamorata, innamorato*

inane *adj* senseless or silly: *inane remarks* **inanity** *n*
WORD ORIGIN Latin *inanis* empty

inanimate *adj* lacking the qualities of living beings: *inanimate objects*

inanition *n formal* exhaustion or weakness, as from lack of food
WORD ORIGIN Latin *inanis* empty

inapplicable *adj* not suitable or relevant

inapposite *adj* not suitable or appropriate **inappositeness** *n*

inappropriate *adj* not suitable or proper **inappropriately** *adv*

inapt *adj* **1** not apt or fitting **2** lacking skill **inaptitude** *n*

inarticulate *adj* unable to express oneself clearly or well

inasmuch as *conj* **1** since; because **2** in so far as

inattentive *adj* not paying attention **inattention** *n*

inaudible *adj* not loud enough to be heard **inaudibly** *adv*

inaugural ❶ *adj* **1** of or for an inauguration ▷ *n* **2** *US* a speech made at an inauguration

inaugurate *vb* **-rating, -rated 1** to open or celebrate the first public use of ceremonially: *the newest electrified line was inaugurated today* **2** to formally establish (a new leader) in office **3** to begin officially or formally **inauguration** *n* **inaugurator** *n*
WORD ORIGIN Latin *inaugurare* to take omens, hence to install in office after taking auguries

inauspicious *adj* unlucky; suggesting an unfavourable outcome

inboard *adj* **1** (of a boat's motor or engine) situated within the hull **2** situated close to the fuselage of an aircraft ▷ *adv* **3** within the sides of or towards the centre of a vessel or aircraft

inborn *adj* existing from birth: *an inborn sense of optimism*

inbox *n computers* a folder in which incoming messages are stored and displayed

inbred *adj* **1** produced as a result of inbreeding **2** inborn or ingrained: *inbred good manners*

inbreed *vb* **-breeding, -bred** to breed from closely related individuals

inbreeding *n* breeding from closely related individuals

inbuilt *adj* (of a quality or feeling) present from the beginning: *an inbuilt prejudice*

Inc. *US & Austral* (of a company) incorporated

Inca *n* **1** *pl* **Inca** *or* **Incas** a member of a S American indigenous people whose empire, centred on Peru, lasted until the early 1530s **2** the language of this people

incalculable *adj* impossible to estimate or predict **incalculability** *n*

in camera *adv* in private session: *the proceedings were held in camera*
WORD ORIGIN Latin

incandescent *adj* **1** glowing with heat **2** (of artificial light) produced by a glowing filament **incandescence** *n*
WORD ORIGIN Latin *incandescere* to glow

incandescent lamp *n* a lamp that contains a filament which is electrically heated to incandescence

incantation *n* **1** ritual chanting of magic words or sounds **2** a magic spell **incantatory** *adj*
WORD ORIGIN Latin *incantare* to repeat magic formulas

incapable *adj* **1** helpless: *drunk and incapable* **2 incapable of** lacking the ability to

incapacitate *vb* **-tating, -tated** to deprive (a person) of strength, power, or ability; disable

incapacity *n, pl* **-ties 1** lack of power, strength, or ability **2** *law* legal disqualification or ineligibility

incarcerate *vb* **-ating, -ated** *formal* to confine or imprison **incarceration** *n*
WORD ORIGIN Latin *in-* in + *carcer* prison

i

THESAURUS

incompleteness, meagreness, skimpiness, scantiness, inadequateness **2 = incompetence**, inability, deficiency, incapacity, ineffectiveness, incompetency, unfitness, inefficacy, defectiveness, inaptness, faultiness, unsuitableness **3 = shortcoming**, failing, lack, weakness, shortage, defect, imperfection

inadequate *adj* **1 = insufficient**, short, scarce, meagre, poor, lacking, incomplete, scant, sparse, skimpy, sketchy, insubstantial, scanty, niggardly, incommensurate **OPPOSITE:** adequate **2 = incapable**, incompetent, pathetic, faulty, unfitted, defective, unequal, deficient, imperfect, unqualified, not up to scratch (*informal*), inapt **OPPOSITE:** capable

inaugural *adj* **1 = first**, opening, initial, maiden, introductory, dedicatory

DICTIONARY

incarnate *adj* **1** possessing human form: *a devil incarnate* **2** personified or typified: *stupidity incarnate* ▷*vb* **-nating, -nated 3** to give a bodily or concrete form to **4** to be representative or typical of
WORD ORIGIN Late Latin *incarnare* to make flesh

incarnation ❶ *n* **1** the act of embodying or state of being embodied in human form **2** a person or thing that typifies some quality or idea

Incarnation *n Christian theol* God's coming to earth in human form as Jesus Christ

incautious *adj* (of a person or action) careless or rash

incendiary (in-send-ya-ree) *adj* **1** (of bombs etc.) designed to cause fires **2** tending to create strife or violence **3** relating to the illegal burning of property or goods ▷*n, pl* **-aries 4** a bomb that is designed to start fires **5** a person who illegally sets fire to property or goods **incendiarism** *n*
WORD ORIGIN Latin *incendere* to kindle

incense[1] *n* **1** an aromatic substance burnt for its fragrant odour, esp. in religious ceremonies **2** the odour or smoke so produced ▷*vb* **-censing, -censed 3** to burn incense to (a deity) **4** to perfume or fumigate with incense
WORD ORIGIN Church Latin *incensum*

incense[2] ❶ *vb* **-censing, -censed** to make very angry **incensed** *adj*
WORD ORIGIN Latin *incensus* set on fire

incentive ❶ *n* **1** something that encourages effort or action **2** an additional payment made to employees to increase production ▷*adj* **3** encouraging greater effort: *an incentive scheme for workers*
WORD ORIGIN Latin *incentivus* setting the tune

inception *n* the beginning of a project
WORD ORIGIN Latin *incipere* to begin

incessant *adj* never stopping **incessantly** *adv*
WORD ORIGIN Latin *in-* not + *cessare* to cease

incest *n* sexual intercourse between two people who are too closely related to marry **incestuous** *adj*
WORD ORIGIN Latin *in-* not + *castus* chaste

inch *n* **1** a unit of length equal to one twelfth of a foot (2.54cm) **2** *meteorol* the amount of rain or snow that would cover a surface to a depth of one inch **3** a very small distance, degree, or amount: *neither side was prepared to give an inch* **4 every inch** in every way: *she arrived looking every inch a star* **5 inch by inch** gradually **6 within an inch of one's life** almost to death ▷*vb* **7** to move very slowly or gradually: *I inched my way to the bar*
WORD ORIGIN Old English *ynce*

inchoate (in-koe-ate) *adj formal* just begun and not yet properly developed
WORD ORIGIN Latin *incohare* to make a beginning

incidence *n* **1** extent or frequency of occurrence: *the rising incidence of car fires* **2** *physics* the arrival of a beam of light or particles at a surface **3** *geom* the partial overlapping of two figures or a figure and a line

incident ❶ *n* **1** an occurrence or event, esp. a minor one **2** a relatively insignificant event that might have serious consequences **3** a public disturbance ▷*adj* **4** *physics* (of a beam of light or particles) arriving at or striking a surface **5 incident to** *formal* likely to occur in connection with: *the dangers are incident to a policeman's job*
WORD ORIGIN Latin *incidere* to happen

incidental *adj* **1** happening in connection with or resulting from something more important **2** secondary or minor: *incidental expenses* **incidentally** *adv*

incidental music *n* background music for a film or play

incidentals *pl n* minor expenses, events, or action

incinerate *vb* **-ating, -ated** to burn up completely **incineration** *n*
WORD ORIGIN Latin *in-* to + *cinis* ashes

incinerator *n* a furnace for burning rubbish

incipient *adj formal* just starting to be or happen
WORD ORIGIN Latin *incipere* to begin

incise *vb* **-cising, -cised** to cut into with a sharp tool
WORD ORIGIN Latin *incidere* to cut into

incision *n* a cut, esp. one made during a surgical operation

incisive *adj* direct and forceful: *witty and incisive comments*

incisor *n* a sharp cutting tooth at the front of the mouth

incite *vb* **-citing, -cited** to stir up or provoke to action **incitement** *n*
WORD ORIGIN Latin *in-* in, on + *citare* to excite

incivility *n, pl* **-ties 1** rudeness **2** an impolite act or remark

incl. 1 including **2** inclusive

inclement *adj formal* (of weather) stormy or severe **inclemency** *n*

inclination ❶ *n* **1** a liking, tendency, or preference: *he showed no inclination to change his routine* **2** the degree of slope from a horizontal or vertical plane **3** a slope or slant **4** *surveying* the angular distance of the horizon below the plane of observation

incline ❶ *vb* **-clining, -clined 1** to veer from a vertical or horizontal plane; slope or slant **2** to have or cause to have a certain tendency or disposition: *that does not incline me to think that you are right* **3** to bend or lower (part of the body, esp. the head) **4 incline one's ear** to listen favourably ▷*n* **5** an inclined surface or slope **inclined** *adj*
WORD ORIGIN Latin *inclinare* to cause to lean

inclined plane *n* a sloping plane used to enable a load to be raised or lowered by pushing or sliding, which requires less force than lifting

include ❶ *vb* **-cluding, -cluded 1** to have as part of the whole **2** to put in as part of a set, group, or category

THESAURUS

incarnation *n* **2 = embodiment**, manifestation, epitome, type, impersonation, personification, avatar, exemplification, bodily form

incense[2] *vb* **= anger**, infuriate, enrage, excite, provoke, irritate, gall, madden, inflame, exasperate, rile *(informal)*, raise the hackles of, nark *(Brit, Austral & NZ slang)*, make your blood boil *(informal)*, rub you up the wrong way, make your hackles rise, get your hackles up, make you see red *(informal)*

incentive *n* **1 = inducement**, motive, encouragement, urge, come-on *(informal)*, spur, lure, bait, motivation, carrot *(informal)*, impulse, stimulus, impetus, stimulant, goad, incitement, enticement
OPPOSITE: disincentive

incident *n* **1 = happening**, event, affair, business, fact, matter, occasion, circumstance, episode, occurrence, escapade **3 = disturbance**, scene, clash, disorder, confrontation, brawl, uproar, skirmish, mishap, fracas, commotion, contretemps

inclination *n* **1a = desire**, longing, wish, need, aspiration, craving, yearning, hankering **1b = tendency**, liking, taste, turn, fancy, leaning, bent, stomach, prejudice, bias, affection, thirst, disposition, penchant, fondness, propensity, aptitude, predisposition, predilection, proclivity, partiality, turn of mind, proneness **OPPOSITE:** aversion

incline *vb* **2 = predispose**, influence, tend, persuade, prejudice, bias, sway, turn, dispose ▷*n* **5 = slope**, rise, dip, grade, descent, ramp, ascent, gradient, declivity, acclivity

include *vb* **1 = contain**, involve, incorporate, cover, consist of, take in, embrace, comprise, take into account, embody, encompass, comprehend, subsume
OPPOSITE: exclude

DICTIONARY

WORD ORIGIN Latin *in-* in + *claudere* to close
inclusion ❶ *n* **1** an including or being included **2** something included
inclusive ❶ *adj* **1** including everything: *capital inclusive of profit* **2** including the limits specified: *Monday to Friday inclusive* **3** comprehensive
incognito (in-kog-**nee**-toe) *adv, adj* **1** under an assumed name or appearance ▷ *n, pl* **-tos 2** a false identity **3** a person who is incognito
WORD ORIGIN Latin *incognitus* unknown
incognizant *adj* **incognizant of** unaware of **incognizance** *n*
incoherent *adj* **1** unable to express oneself clearly **2** not logically connected or ordered: *an incoherent argument* **incoherence** *n*
income ❶ *n* the total amount of money earned from work or obtained from other sources over a given period of time
income support *n* (in Britain) an allowance paid by the government to people with a very low income
income tax *n* a personal tax levied on annual income
incoming ❶ *adj* **1** about to arrive **2** about to come into office
incommensurable *adj* **1** not able to be judged, measured, or compared **2** *maths* not having a common divisor other than 1, such as 2 and $\sqrt{-5}$ **incommensurability** *n*
incommensurate *adj* **1** inadequate or disproportionate: *gains incommensurate with the risk involved* **2** incommensurable
incommode *vb* **-moding, -moded** *formal* to bother, disturb, or inconvenience
WORD ORIGIN Latin *incommodus* inconvenient
incommodious *adj formal* inconveniently small; cramped
incommunicado *adv, adj* not allowed to communicate with other people, for instance while in solitary confinement
WORD ORIGIN Spanish *incomunicado*
incomparable *adj* so excellent as to be beyond or above comparison **incomparably** *adv*
incompatible ❶ *adj* not able to exist together in harmony; conflicting or inconsistent **incompatibility** *n*
incompetent ❶ *adj* **1** not having the necessary ability or skill to do something **2** *law* not legally qualified: *an incompetent witness* ▷ *n* **3** an incompetent person **incompetence** *n*
incomplete ❶ *adj* not finished or whole
incomprehension *n* inability to understand **incomprehensible** *adj*
inconceivable *adj* so unlikely to be true as to be unthinkable **inconceivability** *n*
inconclusive *adj* not giving a final decision or result
incongruous *adj* out of place; inappropriate: *an incongruous figure among the tourists* **incongruously** *adv* **incongruity** *n*
inconnu (**in**-kon-new) *n Canad* a whitefish of Arctic waters
WORD ORIGIN French, literally: unknown
inconsequential *or* **inconsequent** *adj* **1** unimportant or insignificant **2** not following logically as a consequence **inconsequentially** *adv*
inconsiderable *adj* **1** not worth considering; insignificant **2 not inconsiderable** fairly large: *he gets not inconsiderable royalties from his musicals* **inconsiderably** *adv*
inconsiderate *adj* lacking in care or thought for others; thoughtless **inconsiderateness** *n*
inconsistent ❶ *adj* **1** unstable or changeable in behaviour or mood **2** containing contradictory elements: *an inconsistent argument* **3** not in accordance: *actions inconsistent with high office* **inconsistency** *n*
inconsolable *adj* very distressed **inconsolably** *adv*
inconspicuous *adj* not easily noticed or seen
inconstant *adj* **1** liable to change one's loyalties or opinions **2** variable: *their household income is inconstant* **inconstancy** *n*
incontestable *adj* impossible to deny or argue with
incontinent *adj* **1** unable to control the bladder and bowels **2** lacking self-restraint, esp. sexually **incontinence** *n*
WORD ORIGIN Latin *in-* not + *continere* to restrain
incontrovertible *adj* absolutely certain; undeniable **incontrovertibly** *adv*
inconvenience ❶ *n* **1** a state or instance of trouble or difficulty ▷ *vb* **-iencing, -ienced 2** to cause trouble or difficulty to (someone) **inconvenient** *adj*
incorporate ❶ *vb* **-rating, -rated 1** to include or be included as part of a larger unit **2** to form a united whole or mass **3** to form into a corporation ▷ *adj* **4** incorporated **incorporated** *adj* **incorporation** *n*
WORD ORIGIN Latin *in-* in + *corpus* body

i

THESAURUS

2 = add, enter, put in, insert
inclusion *n* **1 = addition**, incorporation, introduction, insertion **OPPOSITE:** exclusion
inclusive *adj* **1, 3 = comprehensive**, full, overall, general, global, sweeping, all-in, blanket, umbrella, across-the-board, all-together, catch-all *(chiefly US)*, all-embracing, overarching, in toto *(Latin)* **OPPOSITE:** limited
income *n* **= revenue**, gains, earnings, means, pay, interest, returns, profits, wages, rewards, yield, proceeds, salary, receipts, takings
incoming *adj* **1 = arriving**, landing, approaching, entering, returning, homeward **OPPOSITE:** departing **2 = new**, next, succeeding, elected, elect
incompatible *adj* **= inconsistent**, conflicting, contradictory, unsuitable, disparate, incongruous, discordant, antagonistic, irreconcilable, unsuited, mismatched, discrepant, uncongenial, antipathetic, ill-assorted, inconsonant **OPPOSITE:** compatible
incompetent *adj* **1 = inept**, useless, incapable, unable, cowboy *(informal)*, floundering, bungling, unfit, unfitted, ineffectual, incapacitated, inexpert, skill-less, unskilful **OPPOSITE:** competent
incomplete *adj* **= unfinished**, partial, insufficient, wanting, short, lacking, undone, defective, deficient, imperfect, undeveloped, fragmentary, unaccomplished, unexecuted, half-pie *(NZ informal)* **OPPOSITE:** complete
inconsistent *adj* **1 = changeable**, variable, unpredictable, unstable, irregular, erratic, uneven, fickle, capricious, unsteady, inconstant **OPPOSITE:** consistent **3 = incompatible**, conflicting, contrary, at odds, contradictory, in conflict, incongruous, discordant, incoherent, out of step, irreconcilable, at variance, discrepant, inconstant **OPPOSITE:** compatible
inconvenience *n* **1 = trouble**, difficulty, bother, upset, fuss, disadvantage, disturbance, disruption, drawback, hassle *(informal)*, nuisance, downside, annoyance, hindrance, awkwardness, vexation, uphill *(S African)* ▷ *vb* **2 = trouble**, bother, disturb, upset, disrupt, put out, hassle *(informal)*, irk, discommode, give (someone) bother *or* trouble, make (someone) go out of his way, put to trouble
incorporate *vb* **1a = include**, contain, take in, embrace, integrate, embody, encompass, assimilate, comprise of **1b = integrate**, include, absorb, unite, merge, accommodate, knit, fuse, assimilate, amalgamate, subsume, coalesce, harmonize, meld **2 = blend**, mix, combine, compound, consolidate, fuse, mingle, meld

DICTIONARY

incorporeal *adj* without material form, substance, or existence

incorrect ⓣ *adj* **1** wrong: *an incorrect answer* **2** not proper: *incorrect behaviour* **incorrectly** *adv*

incorrigible *adj* (of a person or behaviour) beyond correction or reform; incurably bad **incorrigibility** *n* **incorrigibly** *adv*

incorruptible *adj* **1** too honest to be bribed or corrupted **2** not prone to decay or disintegration **incorruptibility** *n*

increase ⓣ *vb* **-creasing, -creased 1** to make or become greater in size, degree, or frequency ▹ *n* **2** a rise in size, degree, or frequency **3** the amount by which something increases **4 on the increase** becoming more common **increasingly** *adv*
WORD ORIGIN Latin *in-* in + *crescere* to grow

incredible ⓣ *adj* **1** unbelievable **2** *informal* marvellous; amazing **incredibility** *n* **incredibly** *adv*

incredulity *n* unwillingness to believe

incredulous *adj* not prepared or willing to believe something

increment *n* **1** the amount by which something increases **2** a regular salary increase **3** *maths* a small positive or negative change in a variable or function **incremental** *adj*
WORD ORIGIN Latin *incrementum* increase

incriminate *vb* **-nating, -nated 1** to make (someone) seem guilty of a crime **2** to charge (someone) with a crime **incrimination** *n* **incriminatory** *adj*
WORD ORIGIN Late Latin *incriminare* to accuse

incrust *vb* ▸ same as **encrust**

incubate (in-cube-ate) *vb* **-bating, -bated 1** (of birds) to hatch (eggs) by sitting on them **2** to cause (bacteria) to develop, esp. in an incubator or culture medium **3** (of disease germs) to remain inactive in an animal or human before causing disease **4** to develop gradually **incubation** *n*
WORD ORIGIN Latin *incubare*

incubator *n* **1** *med* a heated enclosed apparatus for rearing premature babies **2** an apparatus for hatching birds' eggs or growing bacterial cultures

incubus (in-cube-uss) *n, pl* **-bi** *or* **-buses 1** a demon believed in folklore to have sexual intercourse with sleeping women **2** a nightmarish burden or worry
WORD ORIGIN Latin *incubare* to lie upon

inculcate *vb* **-cating, -cated** to fix in someone's mind by constant repetition **inculcation** *n*
WORD ORIGIN Latin *inculcare* to tread upon

inculpate *vb* **-pating, -pated** *formal* to incriminate
WORD ORIGIN Latin *in-* on + *culpare* to blame

incumbency *n, pl* **-cies** the office, duty, or tenure of an incumbent

incumbent ⓣ *formal n* **1** a person who holds a particular office or position ▹ *adj* **2** morally binding as a duty: *it is incumbent on cricketers to respect the umpire's impartiality*
WORD ORIGIN Latin *incumbere* to lie upon

incur ⓣ *vb* **-curring, -curred** to bring (something undesirable) upon oneself
WORD ORIGIN Latin *incurrere* to run into

incurable *adj* **1** not able to be cured: *an incurable tumour* **2** not able to be changed: *he is an incurable romantic* ▹ *n* **3** a person with an incurable disease **incurability** *n* **incurably** *adv*

incurious *adj* showing no curiosity or interest **incuriously** *adv*

incursion *n* **1** a sudden or brief invasion **2** an inroad or encroachment: *a successful incursion into the American book-shop market* **incursive** *adj*
WORD ORIGIN Latin *incursio* attack

ind. 1 independent **2** index **3** indicative **4** indirect **5** industrial

Ind. 1 Independent **2** India **3** Indian **4** Indiana **5** Indies

indaba (in-dah-ba) *n* **1** (among native peoples of southern Africa) a meeting to discuss a serious topic **2** *S African informal* a matter of concern or for discussion
WORD ORIGIN Zulu

indebted *adj* **1** owing gratitude for help or favours **2** owing money **indebtedness** *n*

indecent ⓣ *adj* **1** morally or sexually offensive **2** unseemly or improper: *indecent haste* **indecency** *n* **indecently** *adv*

indecent assault *n* a sexual attack which does not include rape

indecent exposure *n* the showing of one's genitals in public

indecipherable *adj* impossible to read

indecisive *adj* **1** unable to make decisions **2** not decisive or conclusive: *an indecisive argument* **indecision** *or* **indecisiveness** *n*

indeed ⓣ *adv* **1** certainly; actually: *indeed, the sea featured heavily in his poems* **2** truly, very: *it has become a dangerous place indeed* **3** in fact; what is more:

THESAURUS

incorrect *adj* **1 = false**, wrong, mistaken, flawed, faulty, unfitting, inaccurate, untrue, improper, erroneous, out, wide of the mark (*informal*), specious, inexact, off-base (*US & Canad informal*), off-beam (*informal*), way off-beam (*informal*)
OPPOSITE: correct

increase *vb* **1a = raise**, extend, boost, expand, develop, advance, add to, strengthen, enhance, step up (*informal*), widen, prolong, intensify, heighten, elevate, enlarge, multiply, inflate, magnify, amplify, augment, aggrandize, upscale
OPPOSITE: decrease
1b = grow, develop, spread, mount, expand, build up, swell, wax, enlarge, escalate, multiply, fill out, get bigger, proliferate, snowball, dilate **OPPOSITE:** shrink
▹ *n* **2, 3 = growth**, rise, boost, development, gain, addition, expansion, extension, heightening, proliferation, enlargement, escalation, upsurge, upturn, increment, bounce, intensification, step-up (*informal*), augmentation, aggrandizement

incredible *adj* **1 = unbelievable**, impossible, absurd, unthinkable, questionable, improbable, inconceivable, preposterous, unconvincing, unimaginable, outlandish, far-fetched, implausible, beyond belief, cock-and-bull (*informal*), not able to hold water **2** (*informal*) **= amazing**, great, wonderful, brilliant, stunning, extraordinary, overwhelming, ace (*informal*), astonishing, staggering, marvellous, sensational (*informal*), mega (*slang*), breathtaking, astounding, far-out (*slang*), eye-popping (*informal*), prodigious, awe-inspiring, superhuman, rad (*informal*)

incumbent (*formal*) *n* **1 = holder**, keeper, bearer, custodian ▹ *adj* **2 = obligatory**, required, necessary, essential, binding, compulsory, mandatory, imperative

incur *vb* **= sustain**, experience, suffer, gain, earn, collect, meet with, provoke, run up, induce, arouse, expose yourself to, lay yourself open to, bring upon yourself

indecent *adj* **1 = obscene**, lewd, dirty, blue, offensive, outrageous, inappropriate, rude, gross, foul, crude, coarse, filthy, vile, improper, pornographic, salacious, impure, smutty, immodest, licentious, scatological, indelicate
OPPOSITE: decent
2 = unbecoming, unsuitable, vulgar, improper, tasteless, unseemly, undignified, disreputable, unrefined, discreditable, indelicate, indecorous, unbefitting
OPPOSITE: proper

indeed *adv* **1 = certainly**, yes, definitely, surely, truly, absolutely, undoubtedly, positively, decidedly, without doubt, undeniably, without

it is necessary, indeed indispensable ▹ *interj* **4** an expression of doubt or surprise

indefatigable *adj* never getting tired or giving up: *Mitterrand was an indefatigable organizer* **indefatigably** *adv*
WORD ORIGIN Latin *in-* not + *fatigare* to tire

indefensible *adj* **1** (of behaviour or statements) unable to be justified or supported **2** (of places or buildings) impossible to defend against attack **indefensibility** *n*

indefinable *adj* difficult to describe or explain completely

indefinite *adj* **1** without exact limits: *an indefinite number* **2** vague or unclear **indefinitely** *adv*

indefinite article *n grammar* either of the words 'a' or 'an'

indelible *adj* **1** impossible to erase or remove **2** making indelible marks: *indelible ink* **indelibly** *adv*
WORD ORIGIN Latin *in-* not + *delere* to destroy

indelicate *adj* **1** offensive, embarrassing, or tasteless **2** coarse, crude, or rough **indelicacy** *n*

indemnify *vb* **-fies, -fying, -fied 1** to secure against loss, damage, or liability **2** to compensate for loss or damage **indemnification** *n*

indemnity *n, pl* **-ties 1** insurance against loss or damage **2** compensation for loss or damage **3** legal exemption from penalties incurred
WORD ORIGIN Latin *in-* not + *damnum* damage

indent *vb* **1** to start (a line of writing) further from the margin than the other lines **2** to order (goods) using a special order form **3** to notch (an edge or border) **4** to write out (a document) in duplicate **5** to bind (an apprentice) by indenture ▹ *n* **6** *chiefly Brit* an official order for goods, esp. foreign merchandise
WORD ORIGIN Latin *in-* in + *dens* tooth

indentation *n* **1** a hollow, notch, or cut, as on an edge or on a coastline **2** an indenting or being indented **3** Also: **indention** the leaving of space or the amount of space left between a margin and the start of an indented line

indenture *n* **1** a contract, esp. one binding an apprentice to his or her employer ▹ *vb* **-turing, -tured 2** to bind (an apprentice) by indenture **3** to enter into an agreement by indenture

independent ❶ *adj* **1** free from the influence or control of others **2** not dependent on anything else for function or validity **3** not relying on the support, esp. financial support, of others **4** capable of acting for oneself or on one's own **5** of or having a private income large enough to enable one to live without working: *independent means* **6** *maths* (of a variable) not dependent on another variable ▹ *n* **7** an independent person or thing **8** a politician who does not represent any political party **independence** *n* **independently** *adv*

independent school *n* a school that is neither financed nor controlled by the government or local authorities

in-depth *adj* detailed or thorough: *an in-depth analysis*

indescribable *adj* too intense or extreme for words **indescribably** *adv*

indestructible *adj* not able to be destroyed

indeterminate *adj* **1** uncertain in extent, amount, or nature **2** left doubtful; inconclusive: *an indeterminate reply* **3** *maths* **a** having no numerical meaning, as % **b** (of an equation) having more than one variable and an unlimited number of solutions **indeterminable** *adj* **indeterminacy** *n*

index (in-dex) *n, pl* **-dexes** *or* **-dices 1** an alphabetical list of names or subjects dealt with in a book, indicating where they are referred to **2** a file or catalogue in a library which enables a book or reference to be found **3** a number indicating the level of wages or prices as compared with some standard value **4** an indication or sign: *national birth rate was once an index of military power* **5** *maths* **a** ▸ same as **exponent b** a superscript number placed to the left of a radical sign indicating the root to be extracted: *the index of* $\sqrt[3]{8}$ *is 3* **6** a number or ratio indicating a specific characteristic or property: *refractive index* ▹ *vb* **7** to put an index in (a book) **8** to enter (a word or item) in an index **9** to make index-linked
WORD ORIGIN Latin: pointer

indexation *or* **index-linking** *n* the act of making wages, pensions, or interest rates index-linked

index finger *n* the finger next to the thumb. Also called: **forefinger**

index-linked *adj* (of pensions, wages, or interest rates) rising and falling in line with the cost of living

Indiaman *n, pl* **-men** (formerly) a merchant ship engaged in trade with India

Indian *adj* **1** of India **2** of the original inhabitants of the American continent ▹ *n* **3** a person from India **4** a person descended from the original inhabitants of the American continent

Indian club *n* a heavy bottle-shaped club, usually swung in pairs for exercise

Indian corn *n* ▸ same as **maize**

Indian file *n* ▸ same as **single file**

Indian hemp *n* ▸ same as **hemp**

Indian ink *or esp. US & Canad* **India ink** *n* a black ink made from a fine black soot

Indian summer *n* **1** a period of warm sunny weather in autumn **2** a period of tranquillity or of renewed productivity towards the end of a person's life or career

India paper *n* a thin soft opaque printing paper originally made in the Orient

Indic *adj* **1** of a branch of Indo-European consisting of many of the languages of India, including Sanskrit, Hindi, and Urdu ▹ *n* **2** this group of languages

indicate ❶ *vb* **-cating, -cated 1** to be or give a sign or symptom of: *to concede 18 goals in 7 games indicates a serious malaise* **2** to point out or show **3** to state briefly **4** to switch on the indicators in a motor vehicle to show that one is changing direction **5** (of measuring instruments) to show a reading of **6** (*usually passive*) to recommend or require: *surgery seems to be indicated for this patient* **indication** *n*
WORD ORIGIN Latin *indicare*

indicative (in-dik-a-tiv) *adj* **1** **indicative of** suggesting: *the symptoms aren't indicative of anything serious* **2** *grammar* denoting a mood of

THESAURUS

question, unequivocally, indisputably, assuredly, doubtlessly **3 = really**, actually, in fact, certainly, undoubtedly, genuinely, in reality, to be sure, in truth, categorically, verily (*archaic*), in actuality, in point of fact, veritably

independent *adj* **1 = separate**, unrelated, unconnected, unattached, uncontrolled, unconstrained **OPPOSITE:** controlled **3 = self-sufficient**, free, liberated, unconventional, self-contained, individualistic, unaided, self-reliant, self-supporting **4 = self-governing**, free, autonomous, separated, liberated, sovereign, self-determining, nonaligned, decontrolled, autarchic **OPPOSITE:** subject

indicate *vb* **1a = show**, suggest, reveal, display, signal, demonstrate, point to, imply, disclose, manifest, signify, denote, bespeak, make known, be symptomatic of, evince, betoken, flag up **1b = imply**, suggest, hint, intimate, signify, insinuate, give someone to understand **2 = point to**, point out, specify, gesture towards, designate **5 = register**, show, record, mark, read, express, display, demonstrate

DICTIONARY

verbs used to make a statement ▷ *n* **3** *grammar* the indicative mood

indicator *n* **1** something that acts as a sign or indication: *an indicator of the moral decline of our society* **2** a device for indicating that a motor vehicle is about to turn left or right, esp. two pairs of lights that flash **3** an instrument, such as a gauge, that registers or measures something **4** *chem* a substance used to indicate the completion of a chemical reaction, usually by a change of colour

indices (in-diss-seez) *n* ▶ a plural of **index**

indict (in-**dite**) *vb* to charge (a person) formally with a crime, esp. in writing **indictable** *adj*
WORD ORIGIN Latin *in-* against + *dictare* to declare

indictment *n* **1** *criminal law* a formal charge of crime, esp. in writing: *the indictment contained three similar charges against each of the defendants* **2** a serious criticism: *a scathing indictment of faith healing*

indie *n* *informal* an independent record company

indifference *n* **1** lack of concern or interest: *elite indifference to mass opinion* **2** lack of importance: *a matter of indifference to me*

indifferent *adj* **1** showing no concern or interest: *he was indifferent to politics* **2** of only average standard or quality **3** not at all good: *she had starred in several very indifferent movies* **4** unimportant **5** showing or having no preferences
WORD ORIGIN Latin *indifferens* making no distinction

indigenous (in-dij-in-uss) *adj* originating or occurring naturally in a country or area: *the indigenous population is under threat*
WORD ORIGIN Latin *indigenus*

indigent *adj* *formal* so poor as to lack even necessities: *the indigent widow of a fellow writer* **indigence** *n*
WORD ORIGIN Latin *indigere* to need

indigestible *adj* difficult or impossible to digest **indigestibility** *n*

indigestion *n* difficulty in digesting food, accompanied by stomach pain, heartburn, and belching

indignant *adj* feeling or showing indignation **indignantly** *adv*
WORD ORIGIN Latin *indignari* to be displeased with

indignation *n* anger aroused by something felt to be unfair or wrong

indignity *n, pl* **-ties** embarrassing or humiliating treatment

indigo *adj* **1** deep violet-blue ▷ *n, pl* **-gos** *or* **-goes** **2** a dye of this colour originally obtained from plants
WORD ORIGIN Spanish *indico*, from Greek *Indikos* of India

indirect *adj* **1** done or caused by someone or something else: *indirect benefits* **2** not going in a direct course or line: *he took the indirect route home* **3** not coming straight to the point: *an indirect question* **indirectly** *adv*

indirect object *n* *grammar* the person or thing indirectly affected by the action of a verb and its direct object, as *John* in the sentence *I bought John a newspaper*

indirect speech *n* ▶ same as **reported speech**

indirect tax *n* a tax levied on goods or services which is paid indirectly by being added to the price

indiscernible *adj* not able or scarcely able to be seen

indiscipline *n* lack of discipline

indiscreet *adj* incautious or tactless in revealing secrets

indiscretion *n* **1** the lack of discretion **2** an indiscreet act or remark

indiscriminate *adj* lacking discrimination or careful choice: *an indiscriminate bombing campaign* **indiscriminately** *adv* **indiscrimination** *n*

indispensable *adj* absolutely necessary: *an indispensable guide for any traveller* **indispensability** *n*

indisposed *adj* **1** sick or ill **2** unwilling **indisposition** *n*
WORD ORIGIN Latin *indispositus* disordered

indisputable *adj* beyond doubt

indissoluble *adj* permanent: *joining a political party is not an indissoluble marriage*

indistinct *adj* unable to be seen or heard clearly **indistinctly** *adv*

indistinguishable *adj* so similar as to be difficult to tell apart

indium *n* *chem* a rare soft silvery metallic element. Symbol: In
WORD ORIGIN Latin *indicum* indigo

individual *adj* **1** of, relating to, or meant for a single person or thing: *small sums from individual donors* **2** separate or distinct from others of its kind: *please mark the individual pages* **3** characterized by unusual and striking qualities ▷ *n* **4** a single person, esp. when regarded as distinct from others: *respect for the individual* **5** *informal* a person: *a most annoying individual* **6** *biol* a single animal or plant, esp. as distinct from a species **individually** *adv*
WORD ORIGIN Latin *individuus* indivisible

individualism *n* **1** the principle of leading one's life in one's own way **2** ▶ same as **laissez faire** **3** egotism **individualist** *n* **individualistic** *adj*

individuality *n, pl* **-ties** **1** distinctive or unique character or personality: *a house of great individuality* **2** the qualities that distinguish one person or thing from another **3** a separate existence

individualize *or* **-ise** *vb* **-izing, -ized** *or* **-ising, -ised** to make individual or distinctive in character

indivisible *adj* **1** unable to be divided

THESAURUS

indicator *n* **1 = sign**, mark, measure, guide, display, index, signal, symbol, meter, gauge, marker, benchmark, pointer, signpost, barometer

indict *vb* **= charge**, accuse, prosecute, summon, impeach, arraign, serve with a summons

indictment *n* **1** *(criminal law)* **= charge**, allegation, prosecution, accusation, impeachment, summons, arraignment

indifference *n* **1 = disregard**, apathy, lack of interest, negligence, detachment, coolness, carelessness, coldness, nonchalance, callousness, aloofness, inattention, unconcern, absence of feeling, heedlessness **OPPOSITE:** concern

indifferent *adj* **1 = unconcerned**, distant, detached, cold, cool, regardless, careless, callous, aloof, unimpressed, unmoved, unsympathetic, impervious, uncaring, uninterested, apathetic, unresponsive, heedless, inattentive **OPPOSITE:** concerned **2 = mediocre**, middling, average, fair, ordinary, moderate, insignificant, unimportant, so-so *(informal)*, immaterial, passable, undistinguished, uninspired, of no consequence, no great shakes *(informal)*, half-pie *(NZ informal)* **OPPOSITE:** excellent

indignation *n* **= resentment**, anger, rage, fury, wrath, ire *(literary)*, exasperation, pique, umbrage, righteous anger

indirect *adj* **1 = related**, accompanying, secondary, subsidiary, contingent, collateral, incidental, unintended, ancillary, concomitant **2 = circuitous**, winding, roundabout, curving, wandering, rambling, deviant, meandering, tortuous, zigzag, long-drawn-out, circumlocutory **OPPOSITE:** direct

indispensable *adj* **= essential**, necessary, needed, key, vital, crucial, imperative, requisite, needful, must-have **OPPOSITE:** dispensable

individual *adj* **1 = separate**, single, independent, isolated, lone, solitary, discrete **OPPOSITE:** collective **3 = unique**, special, fresh, novel, exclusive, distinct, singular, idiosyncratic, unorthodox **OPPOSITE:** conventional ▷ *n* **4 = person**, being, human, party, body *(informal)*, type, unit, character, soul, creature, human being, mortal, personage, living soul

DICTIONARY

2 *maths* leaving a remainder when divided by a given number

indoctrinate *vb* **-nating, -nated** to teach (someone) systematically to accept a doctrine or opinion uncritically **indoctrination** *n*

Indo-European *adj* 1 of a family of languages spoken in most of Europe and much of Asia, including English, Russian, and Hindi ▷*n* 2 the Indo-European family of languages

indolent *adj* lazy; idle **indolence** *n*
WORD ORIGIN Latin *indolens* not feeling pain

indomitable *adj* too strong to be defeated or discouraged: *an indomitable work ethic*
WORD ORIGIN Latin *indomitus* untamable

Indonesian *adj* 1 of Indonesia ▷*n* 2 a person from Indonesia

indoor *adj* situated, happening, or used inside a building: *an indoor pool*

indoors *adv, adj* inside or into a building

indrawn *adj* drawn or pulled in: *he heard her indrawn breath*

indubitable (in-dew-bit-a-bl) *adj* beyond doubt; definite **indubitably** *adv*
WORD ORIGIN Latin *in-* not + *dubitare* to doubt

induce ❶ *vb* **-ducing, -duced** 1 to persuade or use influence on 2 to cause or bring about 3 *med* to cause (labour) to begin by the use of drugs or other means 4 *logic obsolete* to draw (a general conclusion) from particular instances 5 to produce (an electromotive force or electrical current) by induction 6 to transmit (magnetism) by induction **inducible** *adj*
WORD ORIGIN Latin *inducere* to lead in

inducement *n* 1 something that encourages someone to do something 2 the act of inducing

induct *vb* 1 to bring in formally or install in a job, rank, or position 2 to initiate in knowledge of (a group or profession): *boys are inducted into the world of men*
WORD ORIGIN Latin *inductus* led in

inductance *n* the property of an electric circuit as a result of which an electromotive force is created by a change of current in the same or in a neighbouring circuit

induction *n* 1 *logic* a process of reasoning by which a general conclusion is drawn from particular instances 2 *med* the process of inducing labour 3 the process by which electrical or magnetic properties are transferred, without physical contact, from one circuit or body to another 4 a formal introduction or entry into an office or position 5 (in an internal-combustion engine) the drawing in of mixed air and fuel from the carburettor to the cylinder **inductional** *adj*

induction coil *n* a transformer for producing a high voltage from a low voltage. It consists of a soft-iron core, a primary coil of few turns, and a concentric secondary coil of many turns

induction course *n* a training course to help familiarize someone with a new job

inductive *adj* 1 *logic* of or using induction: *inductive reasoning* 2 of or operated by electrical or magnetic induction

inductor *n* a device designed to create inductance in an electrical circuit

indulge ❶ *vb* **-dulging, -dulged** 1 (often foll. by *in*) to yield to or gratify (a whim or desire for): *to indulge in new clothes* 2 to allow (someone) to have or do everything he or she wants: *he had given her too much, indulged her in everything* 3 to allow (oneself) the pleasure of something: *he indulged himself* 4 *informal* to take alcoholic drink
WORD ORIGIN Latin *indulgere* to concede

indulgence ❶ *n* 1 something that is allowed because it gives pleasure; extravagance 2 the act of indulging oneself or someone else 3 liberal or tolerant treatment 4 something granted as a favour or privilege 5 *RC church* a remission of the temporal punishment for sin after its guilt has been forgiven

indulgent *adj* kind or lenient, often to excess **indulgently** *adv*

industrial *adj* 1 of, used in, or employed in industry 2 with an economy relying heavily on industry: *northern industrial cities*

industrial action *n* action, such as a strike or work-to-rule, by which workers complain about their conditions

industrial estate *n Brit, Austral, NZ, S African* an area of land set aside for factories and warehouses

industrialism *n* an organization of society characterized by large-scale manufacturing industry rather than trade or farming

industrialist ❶ *n* a person who owns or controls large amounts of money or property in industry

industrialize *or* **-ise** *vb* **-izing, -ized** *or* **-ising, -ised** to develop industry on a large scale in (a country or region) **industrialization** *or* **-isation** *n*

industrial relations *pl n* the relations between management and workers

Industrial Revolution *n* **the Industrial Revolution** the transformation in the 18th and 19th centuries of Britain and other countries into industrial nations

industrious *adj* hard-working

industry ❶ *n, pl* **-tries** 1 the work and process involved in manufacture: *Japanese industry increased output considerably last year* 2 a branch of commercial enterprise concerned with the manufacture of a specified product: *the steel industry* 3 the quality of working hard
WORD ORIGIN Latin *industrius* active

Indy *n* See **d'Indy**

Indy Car racing *n* a form of motor racing around banked oval tracks
WORD ORIGIN after the *Indianapolis 500* motor race

Ine *n* king of Wessex (688–726)

inebriate *n* 1 a person who is habitually drunk ▷*adj* 2 drunk, esp. habitually **inebriation** *n*
WORD ORIGIN Latin *ebrius* drunk

inebriated *adj* drunk

inedible *adj* not fit to be eaten

ineducable (in-ed-yuke-a-bl) *adj* incapable of being educated, esp. on account of mental retardation

ineffable *adj* too great or intense to be expressed in words **ineffably** *adv*
WORD ORIGIN Latin *in-* not + *effabilis* utterable

THESAURUS

induce *vb* 1 = **persuade**, encourage, influence, get, move, press, draw, convince, urge, prompt, sway, entice, coax, incite, impel, talk someone into, prevail upon, actuate
OPPOSITE: dissuade
2 = **cause**, produce, create, begin, effect, lead to, occasion, generate, provoke, motivate, set off, bring about, give rise to, precipitate, incite, instigate, engender, set in motion
OPPOSITE: prevent

indulge *vb* 1 (often foll. by *in*) = **gratify**, satisfy, fulfil, feed, give way to, yield to, cater to, pander to, regale, gladden, satiate 2 = **spoil**, pamper, cosset, baby, favour, humour, give in to, coddle, spoon-feed, mollycoddle, fawn on, overindulge
3 **indulge yourself** = **treat yourself**, splash out, spoil yourself, luxuriate in something, overindulge yourself

indulgence *n* 1, 4 = **luxury**, treat, extravagance, favour, privilege

industrialist *n* = **capitalist**, tycoon, magnate, boss, producer, manufacturer, baron, financier, captain of industry, big businessman

industry *n* 1 = **business**, production, manufacturing, trade, trading, commerce, commercial enterprise 2 = **trade**, world, business, service, line, field, craft, profession, occupation 3 = **diligence**, effort, labour, hard work, trouble, activity, application, striving, endeavour, toil, vigour, zeal, persistence, assiduity, tirelessness

DICTIONARY

ineffective ⓘ *adj* having no effect or an inadequate effect

ineffectual *adj* having no effect or an inadequate effect: *the raids were costly and ineffectual*

inefficient ⓘ *adj* not performing a task or function to the best advantage **inefficiency** *n*

inelegant *adj* lacking elegance or refinement

ineligible *adj* not qualified for or entitled to something

ineluctable *adj formal* impossible to avoid: *the ineluctable collapse of the coalition*
WORD ORIGIN Latin *in-* not + *eluctari* to escape

inept *adj* **1** awkward, clumsy, or incompetent **2** not suitable or fitting; out of place **ineptitude** *n*
WORD ORIGIN Latin *in-* not + *aptus* fitting

inequable *adj* **1** unfair **2** not uniform

inequality ⓘ *n, pl* **-ties 1** the state or quality of being unequal **2** an instance of this **3** lack of smoothness or regularity of a surface **4** *maths* a statement indicating that the value of one quantity or expression is not equal to another

inequitable *adj* unjust or unfair

inequity *n, pl* **-ties 1** injustice or unfairness **2** something which is unjust or unfair

ineradicable *adj* impossible to remove or root out: *an ineradicable distrust of foreigners*

inert *adj* **1** without the power to move or to resist motion **2** inactive or lifeless **3** having only a limited ability to react chemically
WORD ORIGIN Latin *iners* unskilled

inertia *n* **1** a feeling of unwillingness to do anything **2** *physics* the tendency of a body to remain still or continue moving unless a force is applied to it **inertial** *adj*

inertia selling *n Brit* the illegal practice of sending unrequested goods to householders, followed by a bill for the goods if they do not return them

inescapable *adj* not able to be avoided

inessential *adj* **1** not necessary ▷*n* **2** an unnecessary thing

inestimable *adj* too great to be calculated

inevitable ⓘ *adj* **1** unavoidable; sure to happen **2** *informal* so regular as to be predictable: *the inevitable guitar solo* ▷*n* **3** (often preceded by *the*) something that is unavoidable **inevitability** *n* **inevitably** *adv*
WORD ORIGIN Latin *in-* not + *evitare* to avoid

inexact *adj* not exact or accurate

inexcusable *adj* too bad to be justified or tolerated

inexhaustible *adj* incapable of being used up; endless

inexorable *adj* unable to be prevented from continuing or progressing: *an inexorable trend* **inexorably** *adv*
WORD ORIGIN Latin *in-* not + *exorare* to prevail upon

inexpensive ⓘ *adj* not costing a lot of money

inexperienced ⓘ *adj* having no knowledge or experience of a particular situation, activity, etc. **inexperience** *n*

inexpert *adj* lacking skill

inexpiable *adj* (of sin) incapable of being atoned for; unpardonable

inexplicable *adj* impossible to explain

inexpressible *adj* (of a feeling) too strong to be expressed in words

in extremis *adv* **1** in dire straits **2** at the point of death

inextricable *adj* **1** impossible to escape from: *an inextricable dilemma* **2** impossible to disentangle or separate: *an inextricable mass of twisted metal* **inextricably** *adv*

inf. 1 infantry **2** infinitive **3** informal **4** information

infallible *adj* **1** incapable of error **2** always successful: *an infallible cure* **3** (of the Pope) incapable of error in setting forth matters of doctrine on faith and morals **infallibility** *n* **infallibly** *adv*

infamous ⓘ (in-fam-uss) *adj* well-known for something bad

infamy *n, pl* **-mies 1** the state of being infamous **2** an infamous act or event
WORD ORIGIN Latin *infamis* of evil repute

infancy ⓘ *n, pl* **-cies 1** the state or period of being an infant **2** an early stage of growth or development: *virtual reality is in its infancy* **3** *law* the state or period of being a minor

infant ⓘ *n* **1** a very young child; baby **2** *law* ▸ same as **minor** (sense 4) **3** *Brit* a young school child ▷*adj* **4** of, relating to, or designed for young children: *infant school* **5** in an early stage of development: *an infant democracy*
WORD ORIGIN Latin *infans*, literally: speechless

infanta *n* **1** (formerly) a daughter of a king of Spain or Portugal **2** the wife of an infante
WORD ORIGIN Spanish and Portuguese

infante *n* (formerly) any son of a king of Spain or Portugal, except the heir to the throne
WORD ORIGIN Spanish and Portuguese

infanticide *n* **1** the act of killing an infant **2** a person who kills an infant
WORD ORIGIN INFANT + Latin *caedere* to kill

infantile *adj* **1** childishly immature **2** of infants or infancy

infantile paralysis *n* ▸ same as **poliomyelitis**

infantry *n, pl* **-tries** soldiers who fight on foot

THESAURUS

ineffective *adj* **a = unproductive**, useless, futile, vain, unsuccessful, pointless, fruitless, to no avail, ineffectual, unprofitable, to no effect, unavailing, unfruitful, profitless, bootless, inefficacious **OPPOSITE:** effective **b = inefficient**, inadequate, useless, poor, weak, pathetic, powerless, unfit, feeble, worthless, inept, impotent, ineffectual

inefficient *adj* **= wasteful**, uneconomical, profligate, ruinous, improvident, unthrifty, inefficacious

inequality *n* **1, 2 = disparity**, prejudice, difference, bias, diversity, irregularity, unevenness, lack of balance, disproportion, imparity, preferentiality

inevitable *adj* **1 = unavoidable**, inescapable, inexorable, sure, certain, necessary, settled, fixed, assured, fated, decreed, destined, ordained, predetermined, predestined, preordained, ineluctable, unpreventable **OPPOSITE:** avoidable

inexpensive *adj* **= cheap**, reasonable, low-priced, budget, bargain, modest, low-cost, economical **OPPOSITE:** expensive

inexperienced *adj* **= new**, unskilled, untrained, green, fresh, amateur, raw, unfamiliar, unused, callow, immature, unaccustomed, untried, unschooled, wet behind the ears (*informal*), unacquainted, unseasoned, unpractised, unversed, unfledged **OPPOSITE:** experienced

infamous *adj* **= notorious**, base, shocking, outrageous, disgraceful, monstrous, shameful, vile, scandalous, wicked, atrocious, heinous, odious, hateful, loathsome, ignominious, disreputable, egregious, abominable, villainous, dishonourable, nefarious, iniquitous, detestable, opprobrious, ill-famed, flagitious **OPPOSITE:** esteemed

infancy *n* **2 = beginnings**, start, birth, roots, seeds, origins, dawn, early stages, emergence, outset, cradle, inception **OPPOSITE:** end

infant *n* **1 = baby**, child, babe, toddler, tot, wean (*Scot*), little one, bairn (*Scot*), suckling, newborn child, babe in arms, sprog (*slang*), munchkin (*informal, chiefly US*), neonate, rug rat (*slang*), littlie (*Austral informal*), ankle-biter (*Austral slang*), tacker (*Austral slang*)

DICTIONARY

WORD ORIGIN Italian *infanteria*
infant school *n* (in England and Wales) a school for children aged between 5 and 7
infatuate *vb* **-ating, -ated** to inspire or fill with an intense and unreasoning passion **infatuation** *n*
WORD ORIGIN Latin *infatuare*
infatuated *adj* (often foll. by *with*) carried away by an intense and unreasoning passion for someone
infect ● *vb* **1** to contaminate (a person or thing) with a germ or virus or its consequent disease **2** to taint or contaminate **3** to affect with an opinion or feeling as if by contagion: *even she was infected by the excitement*
WORD ORIGIN Latin *inficere* to stain
infection ● *n* **1** an infectious disease **2** contamination of a person or thing by a germ or virus or its consequent disease
infectious ● *adj* **1** (of a disease) capable of being transmitted without actual contact **2** causing or transmitting infection **3** spreading from one person to another: *infectious laughter*
infectious mononucleosis *n* ▸ same as **glandular fever**
infelicity *n, pl* **-ties** *formal* **1** something, esp. a remark or expression, that is inapt **2** the state or quality of being unhappy or unfortunate **infelicitous** *adj*
infer *vb* **-ferring, -ferred 1** to conclude by reasoning from evidence; deduce **2** *not standard* to imply or suggest
WORD ORIGIN Latin *inferre* to bring into
inference *n* **1** the act or process of reaching a conclusion by reasoning from evidence **2** an inferred conclusion or deduction
inferential *adj* of or based on inference
inferior ● *adj* **1** lower in quality, quantity, or usefulness **2** lower in rank, position, or status **3** of poor quality **4** lower in position **5** *printing* (of a character) printed at the foot of an ordinary character ▷ *n* **6** a person inferior to another, esp. in rank
inferiority *n*
WORD ORIGIN Latin: lower
inferiority complex *n psychiatry* a disorder arising from a feeling of inferiority to others, characterized by aggressiveness or extreme shyness
infernal *adj* **1** of or relating to hell **2** *informal* irritating: *stop that infernal noise*
WORD ORIGIN Latin *infernus* lower
inferno *n, pl* **-nos 1** an intense raging fire **2** a place or situation resembling hell, because it is crowded and noisy **3 the inferno** hell
WORD ORIGIN Late Latin *infernus* hell
infertile *adj* **1** not capable of producing offspring **2** (of soil) not productive; barren **infertility** *n*
infest *vb* to inhabit or overrun (a place, plant, etc.) in unpleasantly large numbers: *the area was infested with moles* **infestation** *n*
WORD ORIGIN Latin *infestare* to molest
infidel *n* **1** a person who has no religious belief **2** a person who rejects a specific religion, esp. Christianity or Islam ▷ *adj* **3** of unbelievers or unbelief
WORD ORIGIN Latin *infidelis* unfaithful
infidelity *n, pl* **-ties 1** sexual unfaithfulness to one's husband, wife, or lover **2** an act or instance of unfaithfulness
infield *n* **1** *cricket* the area of the field near the pitch **2** *baseball* the area of the playing field enclosed by the base lines **infielder** *n*
infighting *n* **1** rivalry or quarrelling between members of the same group or organization **2** *boxing* combat at close quarters
infiltrate ● *vb* **-trating, -trated 1** to enter (an organization, area, etc.) gradually and in secret, so as to gain influence or control: *they infiltrated the party structure* **2** to pass (a liquid or gas) through (a substance) by filtering or (of a liquid or gas) to pass through (a substance) by filtering
infiltration *n* **infiltrator** *n*
infinite ● (in-fin-it) *adj* **1** having no limits or boundaries in time, space, extent, or size **2** extremely or immeasurably great or numerous: *infinite wealth* **3** *maths* having an unlimited or uncountable number of digits, factors, or terms **infinitely** *adv*
infinitesimal *adj* **1** extremely small: *an infinitesimal risk* **2** *maths* of or involving a small change in the value of a variable that approaches zero as a limit ▷ *n* **3** *maths* an infinitesimal quantity
infinitive (in-fin-it-iv) *n grammar* a form of the verb which in most languages is not inflected for tense or person and is used without a particular subject: in English, the infinitive usually consists of the word *to* followed by the verb
infinitude *n literary* **1** the state or quality of being infinite **2** an infinite extent or quantity
infinity *n, pl* **-ties 1** an infinitely great number or amount **2** endless time, space, or quantity **3** *maths* the concept of a value greater than any finite numerical value
infirm *adj* physically or mentally weak, esp. from old age
infirmary *n, pl* **-ries** a place for the treatment of the sick or injured; hospital
infirmity *n, pl* **-ties 1** the state of being infirm **2** physical weakness or frailty
infix *vb* **1** to fix firmly in **2** to instil or impress on the mind by repetition **infixation** *or* **infixion** *n*
in flagrante delicto (in flag-**grant**-ee dee-**lick**-toe) *adv chiefly law* while committing the offence
WORD ORIGIN Latin
inflame ● *vb* **-flaming, -flamed 1** to make angry or excited **2** to increase or intensify; aggravate **3** to produce inflammation in or become inflamed **4** to set or be set on fire

i

THESAURUS

infect *vb* **1 = contaminate**, transmit disease to, spread disease to *or* among **2 = pollute**, dirty, poison, foul, corrupt, contaminate, taint, defile, vitiate **3 = affect**, move, touch, influence, upset, overcome, stir, disturb
infection *n* **1 = disease**, condition, complaint, illness, virus, disorder, corruption, poison, pollution, contamination, contagion, defilement, septicity
infectious *adj* **1 = catching**, spreading, contagious, communicable, poisoning, corrupting, contaminating, polluting, virulent, defiling, infective, vitiating, pestilential, transmittable
inferior *adj* **1, 2 = lower**, junior, minor, secondary, subsidiary, lesser, humble, subordinate, lowly, less important, menial **OPPOSITE:** superior ▷ *n* **6 = underling**, junior, subordinate, lesser, menial, minion
infiltrate *vb* **1 = penetrate**, pervade, permeate, creep in, percolate, filter through to, make inroads into, sneak into (*informal*), insinuate yourself, work *or* worm your way into
infinite *adj* **1 = limitless**, endless, unlimited, eternal, perpetual, never-ending, interminable, boundless, everlasting, bottomless, unending, inexhaustible, immeasurable, without end, unbounded, numberless, measureless, illimitable, without number **OPPOSITE:** finite **2 = vast**, enormous, immense, wide, countless, innumerable, untold, stupendous, incalculable, immeasurable, inestimable, numberless, uncounted, measureless, uncalculable
inflame *vb* **1 = enrage**, stimulate, provoke, fire, heat, excite, anger, arouse, rouse, infuriate, ignite, incense, madden, agitate, kindle, rile, foment, intoxicate, make your blood boil, impassion
OPPOSITE: calm

DICTIONARY

inflammable *adj* 1 liable to catch fire 2 easily aroused to anger or passion **inflammability** *n*

inflammation *n* 1 the reaction of living tissue to injury or infection, characterized by heat, redness, swelling, and pain 2 an inflaming or being inflamed

inflammatory *adj* 1 likely to provoke anger 2 characterized by or caused by inflammation

inflatable *adj* 1 capable of being inflated ▷*n* 2 a plastic or rubber object which can be inflated

inflate ❶ *vb* **-flating, -flated** 1 to expand or cause to expand by filling with gas or air 2 to give an impression of greater importance than is justified: *something to inflate their self-esteem* 3 to cause or undergo economic inflation
WORD ORIGIN Latin *inflare* to blow into

i

inflation ❶ *n* 1 an inflating or being inflated 2 *econ* a progressive increase in the general level of prices brought about by an increase in the amount of money in circulation or by increases in costs 3 *informal* the rate of increase of prices **inflationary** *adj*

inflect *vb* 1 to change (the voice) in tone or pitch 2 *grammar* to change (the form of a word) by inflection 3 to bend or curve **inflective** *adj*
WORD ORIGIN Latin *inflectere* to curve, alter

inflection *or* **inflexion** *n* 1 change in the pitch of the voice 2 *grammar* a change in the form of a word, signalling change in such grammatical functions as tense or number 3 an angle or bend 4 an inflecting or being inflected 5 *maths* a change in curvature from concave to convex or vice versa **inflectional** *or* **inflexional** *adj*

inflexible *adj* 1 unwilling to be persuaded; obstinate 2 (of a rule, etc.) firmly fixed: *inflexible schedules* 3 incapable of being bent: *inflexible joints* **inflexibility** *n*

inflict ❶ *vb* 1 to impose (something unpleasant) on 2 to deliver (a blow or wound) **infliction** *n* **inflictor** *n*
WORD ORIGIN Latin *infligere* to strike (something) against

in-flight *adj* happening or provided during flight in an aircraft: *in-flight meals*

inflorescence *n bot* 1 the part of a plant that consists of the flower-bearing stalks 2 the arrangement of the flowers on the stalks 3 the process of flowering; blossoming
WORD ORIGIN Latin *in-* into + *florescere* to bloom

inflow *n* 1 something, such as a liquid or gas, that flows in 2 the act of flowing in; influx

influence ❶ *n* 1 an effect of one person or thing on another 2 the power of a person or thing to have such an effect 3 power resulting from ability, wealth, or position 4 a person or thing with influence 5 **under the influence** *informal* drunk ▷*vb* **-encing, -enced** 6 to have an effect upon (actions or events) 7 to persuade or induce
WORD ORIGIN Latin *influere* to flow into

influential ❶ *adj* having or exerting influence

influenza *n* a highly contagious viral disease characterized by fever, muscular pains, and catarrh
WORD ORIGIN Italian: influence, hence incursion, epidemic

influx ❶ *n* 1 the arrival or entry of many people or things 2 the act of flowing in
WORD ORIGIN Latin *influere* to flow into

info *n informal* ▸ short for **information**

inform ❶ *vb* 1 to give information to; tell: *he informed me that he would be free after lunch* 2 to make knowledgeable (about) or familiar (with): *he'll be informed of his rights* 3 to give incriminating information to the police 4 to impart some essential or formative characteristic to 5 to animate or inspire **informed** *adj*
WORD ORIGIN Latin *informare* to describe

informal ❶ *adj* 1 relaxed and friendly: *an informal interview* 2 appropriate to everyday life or use rather than formal occasions: *informal clothes* 3 (of speech or writing) appropriate to ordinary conversation rather than to formal written language **informality** *n* **informally** *adv*

informant *n* a person who gives information

information ❶ *n* 1 knowledge acquired in any manner; facts 2 *computers* **a** the meaning given to data by the way it is interpreted **b** ▸ same as **data** (sense 2)

information superhighway *n* the concept of a worldwide network of computers transferring information at high speed

information technology *n* the production, storage, and communication of information using computers and electronic technology

THESAURUS

inflate *vb* 1 = **blow up**, pump up, swell, balloon, dilate, distend, aerate, bloat, puff up *or* out **OPPOSITE:** deflate 2a = **increase**, boost, expand, enlarge, escalate, amplify **OPPOSITE:** diminish 2b = **exaggerate**, embroider, embellish, emphasize, enlarge, magnify, overdo, amplify, exalt, overstate, overestimate, overemphasize, blow out of all proportion, aggrandize, hyperbolize

inflation *n* 1 = **increase**, expansion, extension, swelling, escalation, enlargement, intensification

inflict *vb* 1 = **impose**, exact, administer, visit, apply, deliver, levy, wreak, mete *or* deal out

influence *n* 2 = **power**, force, authority, pull *(informal)*, weight, strength, connections, importance, prestige, clout *(informal)*, leverage, good offices 3 = **control**, power, authority, direction, command, domination, supremacy, mastery, ascendancy, mana *(NZ)* ▷*vb* 6 = **affect**, have an effect on, have an impact on, control, concern, direct, guide, impact on, modify, bear upon, impinge upon, act *or* work upon 7 = **persuade**, move, prompt, urge, counsel, induce, incline, dispose, arouse, sway, rouse, entice, coax, incite, instigate, predispose, impel, prevail upon

influential *adj* a = **important**, powerful, moving, telling, leading, strong, guiding, inspiring, prestigious, meaningful, potent, persuasive, authoritative, momentous, weighty **OPPOSITE:** unimportant b = **instrumental**, important, significant, controlling, guiding, effective, crucial, persuasive, forcible, efficacious

influx *n* 1 = **arrival**, flow, rush, invasion, convergence, inflow, incursion, inundation, inrush

inform *vb* 1, 2 = **tell**, advise, let someone know, notify, brief, instruct, enlighten, acquaint, leak to, communicate to, fill someone in, keep someone posted, apprise, clue someone in *(informal)*, put someone in the picture *(informal)*, tip someone off, send word to, give someone to understand, make someone conversant (with)

informal *adj* 1a = **natural**, relaxed, casual, familiar, unofficial, laid-back, easy-going, colloquial, unconstrained, unceremonious 1b = **relaxed**, easy, comfortable, simple, natural, casual, cosy, laid-back *(informal)*, mellow, leisurely, easy-going **OPPOSITE:** formal 2 = **casual**, comfortable, leisure, everyday, simple

information *n* 1 = **facts**, details, material, news, latest *(informal)*, report, word, message, notice, advice, knowledge, data, intelligence, instruction, counsel, the score *(informal)*, gen *(Brit informal)*, dope *(informal)*, info *(informal)*, inside story, blurb, lowdown *(informal)*, tidings, drum *(Austral informal)*, heads up *(US & Canad)*

information theory *n* the study of the processes of communication and the transmission of information

informative ❶ *adj* giving useful information

informer *n* a person who informs to the police

infra dig *adj informal* beneath one's dignity
WORD ORIGIN Latin *infra dignitatem*

infrared *adj* **1** of or using rays with a wavelength just beyond the red end of the visible spectrum ▷*n* **2** the infrared part of the spectrum
WORD ORIGIN Latin *infra* beneath

infrasonic *adj* having a frequency below the range audible to the human ear
WORD ORIGIN Latin *infra* beneath

infrasound *n* infrasonic waves

infrastructure *n* **1** the basic structure of an organization or system **2** the stock of facilities, services, and equipment in a country, including factories, roads, and schools, that are needed for it to function properly
WORD ORIGIN Latin *infra* beneath

infrequent *adj* not happening often **infrequently** *adv*

infringe *vb* **-fringing, -fringed 1** to violate or break (a law or agreement) **2 infringe on** *or* **upon** to encroach or trespass on: *the press infringed on their privacy* **infringement** *n*
WORD ORIGIN Latin *infringere* to break off

infuriate ❶ *vb* **-ating, -ated** to make very angry **infuriating** *adj* **infuriatingly** *adv*
WORD ORIGIN Medieval Latin *infuriare*

infuse *vb* **-fusing, -fused 1** to fill with (an emotion or quality) **2** to soak or be soaked in order to extract flavour
WORD ORIGIN Latin *infundere* to pour into

infusible *adj* unable to be fused or melted **infusibility** *n*

infusion *n* **1** the act of infusing **2** a liquid obtained by infusing

Inge *n* **William Ralph,** known as *the Gloomy Dean*. 1860–1954, English theologian, noted for his pessimism; dean of St Paul's Cathedral (1911–34)

Ingenhousz *n* **Jan** 1730–99, Dutch plant physiologist and physician, who discovered photosynthesis

ingenious ❶ (in-**jean**-ee-uss) *adj* showing cleverness and originality: *a truly ingenious invention*
WORD ORIGIN Latin *ingenium* natural ability

ingenue (**an**-jay-new) *n* an innocent or inexperienced young woman, esp. as a role played by an actress
WORD ORIGIN French

ingenuity (in-jen-**new**-it-ee) *n* cleverness at inventing things
WORD ORIGIN Latin *ingenuitas* a freeborn condition; meaning influenced by INGENIOUS

ingenuous (in-**jen**-new-uss) *adj* **1** unsophisticated and trusting **2** frank and straightforward
WORD ORIGIN Latin *ingenuus* freeborn, virtuous

ingest *vb* to take (food or liquid) into the body **ingestion** *n*
WORD ORIGIN Latin *ingerere* to put into

ingle *n archaic or dialect* a fire in a room or a fireplace
WORD ORIGIN probably Scottish Gaelic *aingeal* fire

inglenook *n Brit* a corner by a fireplace

inglorious *adj* dishonourable or shameful

ingoing *adj* going in; entering

ingot *n* a piece of metal cast in a form suitable for storage, usually a bar
WORD ORIGIN origin unknown

ingrained *or* **engrained** *adj* **1** (of a habit, feeling, or belief) deeply impressed or instilled **2** (of dirt) worked into or through the fibre or pores
WORD ORIGIN *dyed in grain* dyed with kermes through the fibre

ingratiate *vb* **-ating, -ated** to act in order to bring (oneself) into favour (with someone) **ingratiating** *adj*
WORD ORIGIN Latin *in-* in + *gratia* favour

ingratitude *n* lack of gratitude or thanks

ingredient ❶ *n* a component of a mixture or compound, esp. in cooking
WORD ORIGIN Latin *ingrediens* going into

Ingres *n* **Jean Auguste Dominique** 1780–1867, French classical painter, noted for his draughtsmanship

ingress *n formal* **1** the act of going or coming in **2** the right or permission to enter
WORD ORIGIN Latin *ingressus*

ingrowing *adj* (esp. of a toenail) growing abnormally into the flesh **ingrown** *adj*

inhabit ❶ *vb* to live or dwell in **inhabitable** *adj*
WORD ORIGIN Latin *inhabitare*

inhabitant ❶ *n* a person or animal that is a permanent resident of a particular place or region

inhalant (in-**hale**-ant) *n* a medicinal preparation inhaled to help breathing problems

inhale ❶ *vb* **-haling, -haled** to breathe in (air, smoke, or vapour) **inhalation** *n*
WORD ORIGIN Latin *in-* in + *halare* to breathe

inhaler *n* a container used to administer an inhalant

inharmonious *adj* lacking harmony; discordant; disagreeing

inhere *vb* **-hering, -hered** ▪ **inhere in** to be an inseparable part (of)
WORD ORIGIN Latin *inhaerere* to stick in

inherent ❶ *adj* existing as an inseparable part **inherently** *adv*

inherit ❶ *vb* **1** to receive money, property, or a title from someone who has died **2** to receive (a characteristic) from an earlier generation by heredity **3** to receive (a position or situation) from a predecessor: *he inherited a mess* **inheritor** *n*
WORD ORIGIN Old French *enheriter*

inheritable *adj* **1** capable of being transmitted by heredity from one generation to a later one **2** capable of being inherited

inheritance ❶ *n* **1** *law* **a** hereditary succession to an estate or title **b** the right of an heir to succeed on the death of an ancestor **2** something inherited or to be inherited **3** the act of inheriting **4** the fact of receiving

THESAURUS

informative *adj* **= instructive,** revealing, educational, forthcoming, illuminating, enlightening, chatty, communicative, edifying, gossipy, newsy

infuriate *vb* **= enrage,** anger, provoke, irritate, incense, gall, madden, exasperate, rile, nark (*Brit, Austral & NZ slang*), be like a red rag to a bull, make your blood boil, get your goat (*slang*), make your hackles rise, raise your hackles, get your back up, make you see red (*informal*), put your back up **OPPOSITE:** soothe

ingenious *adj* **= creative,** original, brilliant, clever, masterly, bright, subtle, fertile, shrewd, inventive, skilful, crafty, resourceful, adroit, dexterous **OPPOSITE:** unimaginative

ingredient *n* **= component,** part, element, feature, piece, unit, item, aspect, attribute, constituent

inhabit *vb* **= live in,** people, occupy, populate, reside in, tenant, lodge in, dwell in, colonize, take up residence in, abide in, make your home in

inhabitant *n* **= occupant,** resident, citizen, local, native, tenant, inmate, dweller, occupier, denizen, indigene, indweller

inhale *vb* **= breathe in,** gasp, draw in, suck in, respire **OPPOSITE:** exhale

inherent *adj* **= intrinsic,** natural, basic, central, essential, native, fundamental, underlying, hereditary, instinctive, innate, ingrained, elemental, congenital, inborn, inbred, inbuilt, immanent, connate **OPPOSITE:** extraneous

inherit *vb* **1 = be left,** come into, be willed, accede to, succeed to, be bequeathed, fall heir to

inheritance *n* **2 = legacy,** estate, heritage, provision, endowment, bequest, birthright, patrimony

DICTIONARY

characteristics from an earlier generation by heredity

inheritance tax *n* (in Britain) a tax consisting of a percentage levied on the part of an inheritance that exceeds a specified allowance

inhibit ❶ *vb* **1** to restrain or hinder (an impulse or desire) **2** to prohibit or prevent: *an attempt to inhibit nuclear proliferation* **3** *chem* to stop, prevent, or decrease the rate of (a chemical reaction) **inhibited** *adj* **inhibitor** *n*
WORD ORIGIN Latin *inhibere*

inhibition *n* **1** *psychol* a feeling of fear or embarrassment that stops one from behaving naturally **2** an inhibiting or being inhibited **3** the process of stopping or retarding a chemical reaction

inhospitable *adj* **1** not welcoming; unfriendly **2** (of a place or climate) not easy to live in; harsh

inhuman *adj* **1** cruel or brutal **2** not human

inhumane *adj* extremely cruel or brutal

inhumanity *n, pl* **-ties 1** lack of kindness or compassion **2** an inhumane act

inimical *adj* **1** adverse or unfavourable: *inimical to change* **2** unfriendly or hostile
WORD ORIGIN Latin *in-* not + *amicus* friendly

inimitable *adj* impossible to imitate **inimitably** *adv*

iniquity *n, pl* **-ties 1** injustice or wickedness **2** a wicked act **iniquitous** *adj*
WORD ORIGIN Latin *iniquus* unfair

initial ❶ *adj* **1** of or at the beginning ▹*n* **2** the first letter of a word, esp. a person's name **3** *printing* a large letter set at the beginning of a chapter or work ▹*vb* **-tialling, -tialled** *or US* **-tialing, -tialed 4** to sign with one's initials, esp. to indicate approval **initially** *adv*
WORD ORIGIN Latin *initium* beginning

initiate ❶ *vb* **-ating, -ated 1** to begin or set going: *more women initiate divorce today* **2** to accept (new members) into a group, often through secret ceremonies **3** to teach the fundamentals of a skill or knowledge to (someone) ▹*n* **4** a person who has been initiated, esp. recently **5** a beginner **initiation** *n* **initiator** *n*
WORD ORIGIN Latin *initiare*

initiative ❶ *n* **1** a first step; a commencing move: *a peace initiative* **2** the right or power to initiate something: *it forced local people to take the initiative* **3** enterprise: *the drive and initiative to create new products* **4 on one's own initiative** without being prompted

inject ❶ *vb* **1** *med* to put (a fluid) into the body with a syringe **2** to introduce (a new element): *to inject a dose of realism into the assessment* **injection** *n*
WORD ORIGIN Latin *inicere* to throw in

injudicious *adj* showing poor judgment; unwise

injunction ❶ *n* **1** *law* a court order not to do something **2** an authoritative command **injunctive** *adj*
WORD ORIGIN Latin *injungere* to enjoin

injure ❶ *vb* **-juring, -jured 1** to hurt physically or mentally **2** to do wrong to (a person), esp. by an injustice: *the injured party* **3** to damage: *an opportunity to injure your reputation* **injured** *adj*

injurious *adj* **1** causing harm **2** abusive, slanderous, or libellous

injury ❶ *n, pl* **-ries 1** physical hurt **2** a specific instance of this: *a leg injury* **3** harm done to the feelings **4** damage: *inflict no injury on the wealth of the nation*
WORD ORIGIN Latin *injuria* injustice

injury time *n sport* playing time added at the end of a match to compensate for time spent treating injured players. Also called: **stoppage time**

injustice ❶ *n* **1** unfairness **2** an unfair action

ink *n* **1** a black or coloured liquid used for printing, writing, and drawing **2** a dark brown fluid squirted for self-concealment by an octopus or cuttlefish ▹*vb* **3** to mark or cover with ink **4 ink in** to arrange or confirm definitely
WORD ORIGIN Old French *enque*

inkling *n* a vague idea or suspicion
WORD ORIGIN Middle English *inclen* to hint at

inkstand *n* a stand or tray for holding writing tools and containers for ink

inkwell *n* a small container for ink, often fitted into the surface of a desk

inky *adj* **inkier, inkiest 1** dark or black, like ink **2** stained with ink **inkiness** *n*

inlaid *adj* **1** set in another material so that the surface is smooth, such as a

THESAURUS

inhibit *vb* **1 = hinder**, stop, prevent, check, bar, arrest, frustrate, curb, restrain, constrain, obstruct, impede, bridle, stem the flow of, throw a spanner in the works of, hold back *or* in **OPPOSITE:** further **2 = prevent**, stop, bar, frustrate, forbid, prohibit, debar **OPPOSITE:** allow

initial *adj* **1 = opening**, first, early, earliest, beginning, primary, maiden, inaugural, commencing, introductory, embryonic, incipient, inchoate, inceptive **OPPOSITE:** final

initiate *vb* **1 = begin**, start, open, launch, establish, institute, pioneer, kick off *(informal)*, bring about, embark on, originate, set about, get under way, instigate, kick-start, inaugurate, set in motion, trigger off, lay the foundations of, commence on, set going, break the ice on, set the ball rolling on **2 = introduce**, admit, enlist, enrol, launch, establish, invest, recruit, induct, instate ▹*n* **4 = novice**, member, pupil, convert, amateur, newcomer, beginner, trainee, apprentice, entrant, learner, neophyte, tyro, probationer, novitiate, proselyte

initiative *n* **2 = advantage**, start, lead, upper hand **3 = enterprise**, drive, push *(informal)*, energy, spirit, resource, leadership, ambition, daring, enthusiasm, pep, vigour, zeal, originality, eagerness, dynamism, boldness, inventiveness, get-up-and-go *(informal)*, resourcefulness, gumption *(informal)*, adventurousness

inject *vb* **1** *(medical)* **= vaccinate**, shoot *(informal)*, administer, jab *(informal)*, shoot up *(informal)*, mainline *(informal)*, inoculate **2 = introduce**, bring in, insert, instil, infuse, breathe, interject

injunction *n* **2 = order**, ruling, command, instruction, dictate, mandate, precept, exhortation, admonition

injure *vb* **1 = hurt**, wound, harm, break, damage, smash, crush, mar, disable, shatter, bruise, impair, mutilate, maim, mangle, mangulate *(Austral slang)*, incapacitate **2 = undermine**, damage, mar, blight, tarnish, blacken, besmirch, vitiate **3 = damage**, harm, ruin, wreck, weaken, spoil, impair, crool *or* cruel *(Austral slang)*

injury *n* **1 = harm**, suffering, damage, ill, hurt, disability, misfortune, affliction, impairment, disfigurement **2 = wound**, cut, damage, slash, trauma *(pathology)*, sore, gash, lesion, abrasion, laceration **3 = wrong**, abuse, offence, insult, injustice, grievance, affront, detriment, disservice

injustice *n* **1 = unfairness**, discrimination, prejudice, bias, inequality, oppression, intolerance, bigotry, favouritism, inequity, chauvinism, iniquity, partisanship, partiality, narrow-mindedness, one-sidedness, unlawfulness, unjustness **OPPOSITE:** justice **2 = wrong**, injury, crime, abuse, error, offence, sin, grievance, infringement, trespass, misdeed, transgression, infraction, bad *or* evil deed

DICTIONARY

design in wood **2** made in this way: *an inlaid table-top*

inland adj **1** of or in the interior of a country or region, away from a sea or border **2** *chiefly Brit* operating within a country or region; domestic: *inland trade* ▷ *n* **3** the interior of a country or region ▷ *adv* **4** towards or into the interior of a country or region

Inland Revenue *n* (in New Zealand and formerly in Britain) a government department that collects major direct taxes, such as income tax

in-law *n* **1** a relative by marriage ▷ *adj* **2** related by marriage: *his brother-in-law*

inlay *vb* **-laying, -laid 1** to decorate (an article, esp. of furniture) by inserting pieces of wood, ivory, or metal so that the surfaces are smooth and flat ▷ *n* **2** decoration made by inlaying **3** an inlaid article **4** *dentistry* a filling shaped to fit a cavity

inlet *n* **1** a narrow strip of water extending from the sea into the land **2** a passage or valve through which a liquid or gas enters a machine

in-line skate *n* ▸ another name for **Rollerblade**

in loco parentis (par-rent-iss) in place of a parent: said of a person acting for a parent
WORD ORIGIN Latin

inmate *n* a person who is confined to an institution such as a prison or hospital

inmost *adj* ▸ same as **innermost**

inn *n* a pub or small hotel providing food and accommodation
WORD ORIGIN Old English

innards *pl n informal* **1** the internal organs of the body, esp. the entrails **2** the working parts of a machine
WORD ORIGIN variant of *inwards*

innate *adj* existing from birth, rather than acquired; inborn: *his innate decency* **innately** *adv*
WORD ORIGIN Latin *innasci* to be born in

inner *adj* **1** happening or located inside or further inside: *the door to the inner office* **2** of the mind or spirit: *her inner self* **3** exclusive or private: *the inner sanctum of the party secretariat* **4** more profound; less apparent: *the inner meaning* ▷ *n* **5** *archery* **a** the red innermost ring on a target **b** a shot which hits this ring

inner child *n psychol* the part of the psyche that retains the feelings as they were experienced in childhood

inner city *n* the parts of a city in or near its centre, where there are often social and economic problems

inner man *or fem* **inner woman** *n* **1** the mind or soul **2** *jocular* the stomach

innermost *adj* **1** most intimate or private: *innermost secrets* **2** furthest within

inner tube *n* an inflatable rubber tube inside a pneumatic tyre casing

inning *n baseball* a division of the game consisting of a turn at batting and a turn in the field for each side
WORD ORIGIN Old English *innung* a going in

innings *n* **1** *cricket* **a** the batting turn of a player or team **b** the runs scored during such a turn **2** a period of opportunity or action

innkeeper *n* an owner or manager of an inn

innocence *n* the quality or state of being innocent
WORD ORIGIN Latin *innocentia* harmlessness

innocent *adj* **1** not guilty of a particular crime **2** without experience of evil **3** harmless or innocuous **4 innocent of** without or lacking: *innocent of prejudice* ▷ *n* **5** an innocent person, esp. a young child or a naive adult **innocently** *adv*

Innocent II *n* original name *Gregorio Papareschi*. died 1143, pope (1130–43). He condemned Abelard's teachings

Innocent III *n* original name *Giovanni Lotario de' Conti*. ?1161–1216, pope (1198–1216), under whom the temporal power of the papacy reached its height. He instituted the Fourth Crusade (1202) and a crusade against the Albigenses (1208), and called the fourth Lateran Council (1215)

Innocent IV *n* original name *Sinibaldo de' Fieschi*. died 1254, pope (1243–54); an unrelenting enemy of Emperor Frederick II and his heirs

innocuous *adj* having no adverse or harmful effect
WORD ORIGIN Latin *innocuus*

innovate *vb* **-vating, -vated** to introduce new ideas or methods **innovative** *or* **innovatory** *adj* **innovator** *n*
WORD ORIGIN Latin *innovare* to renew

innovation *n* **1** something newly introduced, such as a new method or device **2** the act of innovating

Innu *n* **1** a member of an Algonquian people living in Labrador and northern Quebec **2** the Algonquian language of this people

innuendo *n, pl* **-dos** *or* **-does** an indirect or subtle reference to something rude or unpleasant
WORD ORIGIN Latin: by hinting

Innuit (in-new-it) *n* ▸ same as **Inuit**

innumerable *adj* too many to be counted **innumerably** *adv*

innumerate *adj* having no understanding of mathematics or science **innumeracy** *n*

inoculate *vb* **-lating, -lated 1** to protect against disease by injecting with a vaccine **2** to introduce (microorganisms, esp. bacteria) into (a culture medium) **inoculation** *n*
WORD ORIGIN Latin *inoculare* to implant

inoffensive *adj* causing no harm or annoyance

Inönü *n* **Ismet** 1884–1973, Turkish statesman; president of Turkey (1938–50) and prime minister (1923–37; 1961–65)

inoperable *adj surgery* unable to be safely operated on: *an inoperable tumour*

inoperative *adj* not working or functioning: *continued shelling has rendered the ceasefire inoperative*

inopportune *adj* badly timed or inappropriate

inordinate *adj* **1** excessive: *an inordinate amount of time spent arguing* **2** unrestrained, as in behaviour or emotion: *inordinate anger* **inordinately** *adv*
WORD ORIGIN Latin *inordinatus* disordered

inorganic *adj* **1** not having the structure or characteristics of living organisms **2** *chem* of or denoting chemical compounds that do not contain carbon **3** not resulting from or produced by growth; artificial: *inorganic fertilizers*

inorganic chemistry *n* the branch of chemistry concerned with the elements and compounds which do not contain carbon

i

THESAURUS

inland *adj* **1 = interior**, internal, upcountry

inner *adj* **1 = inside**, internal, interior, inward **OPPOSITE:** outer
4 = hidden, deep, secret, underlying, obscure, repressed, esoteric, unrevealed **OPPOSITE:** obvious

innocence *n* **a = naïveté**, simplicity, inexperience, freshness, credulity, gullibility, ingenuousness, artlessness, unworldliness, guilelessness, credulousness, simpleness, trustfulness, unsophistication, naiveness **OPPOSITE:** worldliness
b = blamelessness, righteousness, clean hands, uprightness, sinlessness, irreproachability, guiltlessness **OPPOSITE:** guilt

innocent *adj* **1 = not guilty**, in the clear, blameless, clear, clean, honest, faultless, squeaky-clean, uninvolved, irreproachable, guiltless, unoffending **OPPOSITE:** guilty
3 = harmless, innocuous, inoffensive, well-meant, unobjectionable, unmalicious, well-intentioned **OPPOSITE:** malicious

innovation *n* **1, 2 = change**, revolution, departure, introduction, variation, transformation, upheaval, alteration

DICTIONARY

inpatient *n* a patient who stays in a hospital for treatment
input *n* **1** resources, such as money, labour, or power, put into a project **2** *computers* the data fed into a computer ▹*vb* **-putting, -put 3** to enter (data) in a computer
inquest ◉ *n* **1** an official inquiry into an unexplained, sudden, or violent death, held by a coroner **2** *informal* an investigation or discussion
WORD ORIGIN Latin *in-* into + *quaesitus* investigation
inquietude *n formal* restlessness or anxiety
inquire ◉ *or* **enquire** *vb* **-quiring, -quired 1** to seek information (about) **2 inquire after** to ask about the health or progress of (a person) **3 inquire into** to make an investigation into **4 inquire of** to ask (a person) for information: *I'll inquire of my aunt when she is coming* **inquirer** *or* **enquirer** *n*
WORD ORIGIN Latin *inquirere*
inquiry ◉ *or* **enquiry** *n, pl* **-ries 1** a question **2** an investigation
inquisition *n* **1** a thorough investigation **2** an official inquiry, esp. one held by a jury before an officer of the Crown **inquisitional** *adj*
Inquisition *n history* an organization within the Catholic Church (1232–1820) for suppressing heresy
inquisitive *adj* **1** excessively curious about other people's business **2** eager to learn **inquisitively** *adv* **inquisitiveness** *n*
inquisitor *n* **1** a person who inquires, esp. deeply or ruthlessly **2 Inquisitor** an officer of the Inquisition
inquisitorial *adj* **1** of or like an inquisition or an inquisitor **2** offensively curious **inquisitorially** *adv*
inquorate *adj* without enough people present to make a quorum
in re (in ray) *prep* in the matter of; concerning
WORD ORIGIN Latin
INRI Jesus of Nazareth, king of the Jews (the inscription placed over Christ's head during the Crucifixion)
WORD ORIGIN Latin *Iesus Nazarenus Rex Iudaeorum*
inroads *pl n* **make inroads into** to start affecting or reducing: *my gambling has made great inroads into my savings*
inrush *n* a sudden and overwhelming inward flow
ins. 1 inches **2** insurance
insane ◉ *adj* **1** mentally ill **2** stupidly irresponsible: *acting on an insane impulse* **insanely** *adv*
insanitary *adj* dirty or unhealthy
insanity *n, pl* **-ties 1** the state of being insane **2** stupidity
insatiable (in-saysh-a-bl) *adj* impossible to satisfy **insatiability** *n* **insatiably** *adv*
inscribe *vb* **-scribing, -scribed 1** to mark or engrave with (words, symbols, or letters) **2** to write one's name, and sometimes a brief dedication, on (a book) before giving to someone **3** to enter (a name) on a list **4** *geom* to draw (a geometric construction) inside another construction so that the two are in contact at as many points as possible but do not intersect
WORD ORIGIN Latin *inscribere*
inscription *n* **1** something inscribed, esp. words carved or engraved on a coin, tomb, or ring **2** a signature or brief dedication in a book or on a work of art
inscrutable *adj* mysterious or enigmatic **inscrutability** *n*
WORD ORIGIN Latin *in-* not + *scrutari* to examine
insect ◉ *n* **1** a small animal that has six legs and usually has wings, such as an ant, fly, or butterfly **2** (loosely) any similar invertebrate, such as a spider, tick, or centipede
WORD ORIGIN Latin *insectum* (animal that has been) cut into
insecticide *n* a substance used to destroy insects
WORD ORIGIN *insect* + Latin *caedere* to kill
insectivore *n* **1** a small mammal, such as a hedgehog or a shrew, that eats invertebrates **2** a plant or animal that eats insects **insectivorous** *adj*
WORD ORIGIN *insect* + Latin *vorare* to swallow
insecure ◉ *adj* **1** anxious or uncertain **2** not adequately protected: *low-paid or insecure employment* **3** unstable or shaky **insecurity** *n*
inseminate *vb* **-nating, -nated** to impregnate (a female) with semen **insemination** *n*
WORD ORIGIN Latin *in-* in + *semen* seed
insensate *adj* **1** lacking sensation or consciousness **2** insensitive or unfeeling **3** foolish
insensible *adj* **1** unconscious **2** without feeling **3** imperceptible **4 insensible of** *or* **to** unaware of or indifferent to: *insensible to suffering* **insensibility** *n*
insensitive *adj* unaware of or ignoring other people's feelings **insensitivity** *n*
inseparable *adj* **1** constantly together because of mutual liking: *they became inseparable companions* **2** too closely connected to be separated **inseparably** *adv*
insert ◉ *vb* **1** to place or fit (something) inside something else **2** to introduce (a clause or comment) into text or a speech ▹*n* **3** something inserted, esp. an advertisement in between the pages of a magazine
WORD ORIGIN Latin *inserere* to plant in
insertion *n* **1** the act of inserting **2** something inserted, such as an advertisement in a newspaper
in-service *adj* denoting training that is given to employees during the course of employment: *an in-service course*

THESAURUS

inquest *n* **1 = inquiry**, investigation, probe, inquisition
inquire *or* **enquire** *vb* **1 = ask**, question, query, quiz, seek information of, request information of **3** (foll. by *into*) **= investigate**, study, examine, consider, research, search, explore, look into, inspect, probe into, scrutinize, make inquiries into
inquiry *or* **enquiry** *n* **1 = question**, query, investigation **2 = investigation**, hearing, study, review, search, survey, analysis, examination, probe, inspection, exploration, scrutiny, inquest
insane *adj* **1 = mad**, crazy, nuts *(slang)*, cracked *(slang)*, mental *(slang)*, barking *(slang)*, crackers *(Brit slang)*, mentally ill, crazed, demented, cuckoo *(informal)*, deranged, loopy *(informal)*, round the bend *(informal)*, barking mad *(slang)*, out of your mind, gaga *(informal)*, screwy *(informal)*, doolally *(slang)*, off your trolley *(slang)*, round the twist *(informal)*, of unsound mind, not right in the head, non compos mentis *(Latin)*, off your rocker *(slang)*, not the full shilling *(informal)*, mentally disordered, buggy *(US slang)*, off the air *(Austral slang)*, porangi *(NZ)* **OPPOSITE:** sane **2 = stupid**, foolish, daft *(informal)*, bizarre, irresponsible, irrational, lunatic, senseless, preposterous, impractical, idiotic, inane, fatuous, dumb-ass *(slang)* **OPPOSITE:** reasonable
insect *n* **2 = bug**, creepy-crawly *(Brit informal)*, gogga *(S African informal)*
insecure *adj* **1 = unconfident**, worried, anxious, afraid, shy, uncertain, unsure, timid, self-conscious, hesitant, meek, self-effacing, diffident, unassertive **OPPOSITE:** confident **2 = unsafe**, dangerous, exposed, vulnerable, hazardous, wide-open, perilous, unprotected, defenceless, unguarded, open to attack, unshielded, ill-protected **OPPOSITE:** safe
insert *vb* **1 = put**, place, set, position, work in, slip, slide, slot, thrust, stick in, wedge, tuck in

DICTIONARY

inset *vb* **-setting, -set 1** to place in or within; insert ▹*n* **2** something inserted **3** *printing* a small map or diagram set within the borders of a larger one ▹*adj* **4** decorated with something inserted

inshore *adj* **1** in or on the water, but close to the shore: *inshore fishermen* ▹*adv, adj* **2** towards the shore from the water: *the boat was forced inshore; a strong wind blowing inshore*

inside ⊕ *prep* **1** in or to the interior of: *a bomb had gone off inside the parliament building* **2** in a period of time less than: *they took the lead inside seven minutes* ▹*adj* **3** on or of the inside: *an article on the paper's inside pages* **4** by or from someone within an organization, esp. illicitly: *inside information* **5** of or being the lane in a road which is nearer the side than other lanes going in the same direction: *all the lorries were in the inside lane* ▹*adv* **6** on, in, or to the inside; indoors: *when the rain started we took our drinks inside* **7** *Brit, Austral & NZ slang* in or into prison ▹*n* **8** the inner side, surface, or part of something **9 inside out** with the inside facing outwards **10 know inside out** to know thoroughly ▸ See also **insides**

inside job *n informal* a crime committed with the assistance of someone employed by or trusted by the victim

insider *n* a member of a group or organization who therefore has exclusive information about it

insider dealing *n* the illegal practice of a person on the stock exchange or in the civil service taking advantage of early confidential information in order to deal in shares for personal profit

insides ⊕ *pl n informal* the stomach and bowels

insidious *adj* working in a subtle or apparently harmless way, but nevertheless dangerous or deadly: *an insidious virus* **insidiously** *adv* **insidiousness** *n*
WORD ORIGIN Latin *insidiae* an ambush

insight ⊕ *n* **1** a penetrating understanding, as of a complex situation or problem **2** the ability to perceive clearly or deeply the inner nature of things

insignia (in-sig-nee-a) *n, pl* **-nias** *or* **-nia** a badge or emblem of membership, office, or honour
WORD ORIGIN Latin: badges

insignificant ⊕ *adj* having little or no importance **insignificance** *n*

insincere *adj* pretending what one does not feel **insincerely** *adv* **insincerity** *n*

insinuate *vb* **-ating, -ated 1** to suggest indirectly by allusion, hints, or innuendo **2** to get (someone, esp. oneself) into a position by gradual manoeuvres: *she insinuated herself into the conversation*
WORD ORIGIN Latin *insinuare* to wind one's way into

insinuation *n* **1** an indirect or devious hint or suggestion **2** an act or the practice of insinuating

insipid *adj* **1** dull and boring **2** lacking flavour **insipidity** *n*
WORD ORIGIN Latin *in-* not + *sapidus* full of flavour

insist ⊕ *vb* (often foll. by *on* or *upon*) **1** to make a determined demand (for): *he insisted on his rights* **2** to express a convinced belief (in) or assertion (of): *she insisted that she had been given permission*
WORD ORIGIN Latin *insistere* to stand upon, urge

insistent *adj* **1** making continual and persistent demands **2** demanding attention: *the chirruping of an insistent bird* **insistence** *n* **insistently** *adv*

in situ *adv, adj* in the original position
WORD ORIGIN Latin

in so far as *or* **insofar as** *prep* to the degree or extent that

insole *n* **1** the inner sole of a shoe or boot **2** a loose inner sole used to give extra warmth or to make a shoe fit

insolent *adj* rude and disrespectful **insolence** *n* **insolently** *adv*
WORD ORIGIN Latin *in-* not + *solere* to be accustomed

insoluble *adj* **1** impossible to solve **2** not able to be dissolved **insolubility** *n*

insolvent *adj* **1** unable to pay one's debts ▹*n* **2** a person who is insolvent **insolvency** *n*

insomnia *n* inability to sleep **insomniac** *n, adj*
WORD ORIGIN Latin *in-* not + *somnus* sleep

insomuch *adv* **1** (foll. by *as* or *that*) to such an extent or degree **2** (foll. by *as*) because of the fact (that)

insouciant *adj* carefree or unconcerned **insouciance** *n*
WORD ORIGIN French

inspan *vb* **-spanning, -spanned** *chiefly S African* **1** to harness (animals) to (a vehicle); yoke **2** to press (people) into service
WORD ORIGIN Middle Dutch *inspannen*

inspect ⊕ *vb* **1** to examine closely, esp. for faults or errors **2** to examine officially **inspection** *n*
WORD ORIGIN Latin *inspicere*

inspector ⊕ *n* **1** an official who checks that things or places meet certain regulations and standards **2** a police officer ranking below a superintendent and above a sergeant

inspectorate *n* **1** a group of inspectors **2** the position or duties of an inspector

inspiration ⊕ *n* **1** stimulation of the mind or feelings to activity or creativity **2** a person or thing that causes this state **3** an inspired idea or action **inspirational** *adj*

i

THESAURUS

inside ▹*adj* **3 = inner**, internal, interior, inward, innermost
OPPOSITE: outside
4 = confidential, private, secret, internal, exclusive, restricted, privileged, classified ▹*n* **8 = interior**, contents, core, nucleus, inner part, inner side ▹*adv* **6 = indoors**, in, within, under cover

insides *pl n* *(informal)* **= stomach**, gut, guts, belly, bowels, internal organs, innards *(informal)*, entrails, viscera, vitals

insight *n* **1 = understanding**, intelligence, perception, sense, knowledge, vision, judgment, awareness, grasp, appreciation, intuition, penetration, comprehension, acumen, discernment, perspicacity

insignificant *adj* **= unimportant**, minor, irrelevant, petty, trivial, meaningless, trifling, meagre, negligible, flimsy, paltry, immaterial, inconsequential, nondescript, measly, scanty, inconsiderable, of no consequence, nonessential, small potatoes, nickel-and-dime *(US slang)*, of no account, nugatory, unsubstantial, not worth mentioning, of no moment **OPPOSITE:** important

insist *vb* (often foll. by *on* or *upon*) **1 = demand**, order, urge, require, command, dictate, entreat
2 = assert, state, maintain, hold, claim, declare, repeat, vow, swear, contend, affirm, reiterate, profess, avow, aver, asseverate

inspect *vb* **1 = examine**, check, look at, view, eye, survey, observe, scan, check out *(informal)*, look over, eyeball *(slang)*, scrutinize, give (something *or* someone) the once-over *(informal)*, take a dekko at *(Brit slang)*, go over *or* through **2 = check**, examine, investigate, study, look at, research, search, survey, assess, probe, audit, vet, oversee, supervise, check out *(informal)*, look over, work over, superintend, give (something *or* someone) the once-over *(informal)*, go over *or* through

inspector *n* **1 = examiner**, investigator, supervisor, monitor, superintendent, auditor, censor, surveyor, scrutinizer, checker, overseer, scrutineer

inspiration *n* **1 = imagination**, creativity, ingenuity, talent, insight, genius, productivity, fertility, stimulation, originality, inventiveness, cleverness, fecundity, imaginativeness **2a = motivation**,

DICTIONARY

inspire ● *vb* **-spiring, -spired 1** to stimulate (a person) to activity or creativity **2** to arouse (an emotion or a reaction): *he inspires confidence*
WORD ORIGIN Latin *in-* into + *spirare* to breathe

inspired ● *adj* **1** brilliantly creative: *his most inspired compositions* **2** very clever and accurate: *an inspired guess*

inst. *old-fashioned* instant (this month)

instability ● *n* lack of steadiness or reliability

install ● *vb* **1** to put in and prepare (equipment) for use **2** to place (a person) formally in a position or rank **3** to settle (a person, esp. oneself) in a position or state: *Tony installed himself in an armchair*
WORD ORIGIN Medieval Latin *installare*

installation ● *n* **1** installing **2** equipment that has been installed **3** a place containing equipment for a particular purpose: *radar installation*

installment plan *n US* Also (*Canad*): **instalment plan**. ▸ Same as **hire-purchase**

instalment ● *or US* **installment** *n* **1** one of the portions into which a debt is divided for payment at regular intervals **2** a portion of something that is issued, broadcast, or published in parts
WORD ORIGIN probably from Old French *estal* something fixed

instance ● *n* **1** a case or particular example **2** urgent request or order: *at the instance of* **3 for instance** as an example **4 in the first instance** in the first place; initially ▹ *vb* **-stancing, -stanced 5** to mention as an example
WORD ORIGIN Latin *instantia* a being close upon

instant ● *n* **1** a very brief time; moment **2** a particular moment: *at the same instant* ▹ *adj* **3** immediate **4** (of foods) able to be prepared very quickly and easily: *instant coffee* **5** urgent or pressing **6** of the present month: *a letter of the 7th instant*
WORD ORIGIN Latin *instans* present, pressing closely

instantaneous *adj* happening at once: *the applause was instantaneous* **instantaneously** *adv*

instantly ● *adv* immediately

instant message *n* **1** an electronic message sent in real time over a computer network ▹ *vb* **instant-message 2** to communicate with (another person) using such messages **instant messaging** *n*

instead ● *adv* **1** as a replacement or substitute for the person or thing mentioned **2 instead of** in place of or as an alternative to
WORD ORIGIN *in stead* in place

instep *n* **1** the middle part of the foot forming the arch between the ankle and toes **2** the part of a shoe or stocking covering this

instigate *vb* **-gating, -gated 1** to cause to happen: *to instigate rebellion* **2** to urge on to some action **instigation** *n* **instigator** *n*
WORD ORIGIN Latin *instigare*

instil *or US* **instill** *vb* **-stilling, -stilled 1** to introduce (an idea or feeling) gradually in someone's mind **2** *rare* to pour in or inject drop by drop **instillation** *n* **instiller** *n*
WORD ORIGIN Latin *instillare* to pour in a drop at a time

instinct ● *n* **1** the inborn tendency to behave in a particular way without the need for thought: *maternal instinct* **2** natural reaction: *my first instinct was to get out of the car* **3** intuition: *Mr Barr's mother said she knew by instinct that her son was safe*
WORD ORIGIN Latin *instinctus* roused

instinctive ● *or* **instinctual** *adj* done or happening without any logical thought: *an instinctive understanding of people* **instinctively** *or* **instinctually** *adv*

institute ● *n* **1** an organization set up for a specific purpose, especially research or teaching **2** the building where such an organization is situated **3** a rule, custom, or precedent ▹ *vb* **-tuting, -tuted 4** to start or establish **5** to install in a position or office

THESAURUS

example, influence, model, boost, spur, incentive, revelation, encouragement, stimulus, catalyst, stimulation, inducement, incitement, instigation, afflatus
OPPOSITE: deterrent
2b = influence, spur, stimulus, muse

inspire *vb* **1 = motivate**, move, cause, stimulate, encourage, influence, persuade, spur, be responsible for, animate, rouse, instil, infuse, hearten, enliven, imbue, spark off, energize, galvanize, gee up, inspirit, fire *or* touch the imagination of
OPPOSITE: discourage

inspired *adj* **1 = brilliant**, wonderful, impressive, exciting, outstanding, thrilling, memorable, dazzling, enthralling, superlative, of genius

instability *n* **= uncertainty**, insecurity, weakness, imbalance, vulnerability, wavering, volatility, unpredictability, restlessness, fluidity, fluctuation, disequilibrium, transience, impermanence, precariousness, mutability, shakiness, unsteadiness, inconstancy **OPPOSITE:** stability

install *vb* **1 = set up**, put in, place, position, station, establish, lay, fix, locate, lodge **2 = institute**, establish, introduce, invest, ordain, inaugurate, induct, instate **3 = settle**, position, plant, establish, lodge, ensconce

installation *n* **1a = setting up**, fitting, instalment, placing, positioning, establishment **1b = appointment**, ordination, inauguration, induction, investiture, instatement

instalment *n* **1 = payment**, repayment, part payment **2 = part**, section, chapter, episode, portion, division

instance *n* **1 = example**, case, occurrence, occasion, sample, illustration, precedent, case in point, exemplification

instant *n* **1 = moment**, second, minute, shake (*informal*), flash, tick (*Brit informal*), no time, twinkling, split second, jiffy (*informal*), trice, twinkling of an eye (*informal*), two shakes (*informal*), two shakes of a lamb's tail (*informal*), bat of an eye (*informal*) **2 = time**, point, hour, moment, stage, occasion, phase, juncture ▹ *adj* **3 = immediate**, prompt, instantaneous, direct, quick, urgent, on-the-spot, split-second **4 = ready-made**, fast, convenience, ready-mixed, ready-cooked, precooked

instantly *adv* **= immediately**, at once, straight away, now, directly, on the spot, right away, there and then, without delay, instantaneously, forthwith, this minute, pronto (*informal*), posthaste, instanter (*law*), tout de suite (*French*)

instead *adv* **1 = rather**, alternatively, preferably, in preference, in lieu, on second thoughts
2 (foll. by *of*) **= in place of**, rather than, in preference to, in lieu of, in contrast with, as an alternative *or* equivalent to

instinct *n* **1 = natural inclination**, feeling, urge, talent, tendency, faculty, inclination, intuition, knack, aptitude, predisposition, sixth sense, proclivity, gut reaction (*informal*), second sight **3 = intuition**, feeling, impulse, gut feeling (*informal*), sixth sense

instinctive *adj* **= natural**, inborn, automatic, unconscious, mechanical, native, inherent, spontaneous, reflex, innate, intuitive, subconscious, involuntary, visceral, unthinking, instinctual, unlearned, unpremeditated, intuitional **OPPOSITE:** acquired

institute *n* **1 = establishment**, body, centre, school, university, society, association, college, institution, organization, foundation, academy, guild, conservatory, fellowship, seminary, seat of learning ▹ *vb* **4 = establish**, start, begin, found, launch, set up, introduce, settle, fix, invest, organize, install, pioneer,

WORD ORIGIN Latin *instituere*, from *statuere* to place

institution ❶ *n* **1** a large important organization such as a university or bank **2** a hospital etc. for people with special needs **3** an established custom, law, or principle: *the institution of marriage* **4** *informal* a well-established person or feature: *the programme has become an institution* **5** an instituting or being instituted

institutional ❶ *adj* **1** of or relating to an institution: *institutional care* **2** dull, routine, and uniform: *institutional meals* **institutionalism** *n*

institutionalize *or* **-ise** *vb* **-izing, -ized** *or* **-ising, -ised 1** (*often passive*) to subject (a person) to institutional life, often causing apathy and dependence on routine **2** to make or become an institution: *institutionalized religion* **3** to place in an institution

instruct ❶ *vb* **1** to order to do something **2** to teach (someone) how to do something **3** to brief (a solicitor or barrister)

WORD ORIGIN Latin *instruere*

instruction ❶ *n* **1** a direction or order **2** the process or act of teaching **instructional** *adj*

instructions ❶ *pl n* information on how to do or use something: *the plane had ignored instructions from air traffic controllers*

instructive *adj* informative or helpful

instructor ❶ *n* **1** a person who teaches something **2** *US & Canad* a college teacher ranking below assistant professor

instrument ❶ *n* **1** a tool or implement, esp. one used for precision work **2** *music* any of various devices that can be played to produce musical sounds **3** a measuring device to show height, speed, etc.: *the pilot's eyes never left his instruments* **4** *informal* a person used by another to gain an end **5** an important factor in something: *her evidence was an instrument in his arrest* **6** a formal legal document

WORD ORIGIN Latin *instrumentum*

instrumental ❶ *adj* **1** helping to cause **2** played by or composed for musical instruments **3** of or done with an instrument: *instrumental error*

instrumentalist *n* a person who plays a musical instrument

instrumentation *n* **1** a set of instruments in a car etc. **2** the arrangement of music for instruments **3** the list of instruments needed for a piece of music

instrument panel *n* a panel holding the instruments in a vehicle or on a machine

insubordinate *adj* not submissive to authority **insubordination** *n*

insubstantial *adj* **1** flimsy, fine, or slight **2** imaginary or unreal

insufferable *adj* unbearable **insufferably** *adv*

insufficient ❶ *adj* not enough for a particular purpose **insufficiency** *n* **insufficiently** *adv*

insular *adj* **1** not open to change or new ideas: *theatre tradition became rather insular* **2** of or like an island **insularity** *n*

WORD ORIGIN Latin *insula* island

insulate ❶ *vb* **-lating, -lated 1** to prevent or reduce the transfer of electricity, heat, or sound by surrounding or lining with a nonconducting material **2** to isolate or set apart **insulator** *n*

WORD ORIGIN Late Latin *insulatus* made into an island

insulation *n* **1** material used to insulate something **2** the act of insulating

insulin (**in**-syoo-lin) *n* a hormone produced in the pancreas which controls the amount of sugar in the blood

WORD ORIGIN Latin *insula* islet (of tissue in the pancreas)

insult ❶ *vb* **1** to treat or speak to rudely: *they insulted us and even threatened to kill us* ▷ *n* **2** an offensive remark or action **3** a person or thing producing the effect of an insult: *their explanation is an insult to our intelligence*

WORD ORIGIN Latin *insultare* to jump upon

insuperable *adj* impossible to overcome; insurmountable **insuperability** *n*

insupportable *adj* **1** impossible to tolerate **2** incapable of being upheld or justified: *an insupportable accusation*

insurance ❶ *n* **1** the agreement by which one makes regular payments to a company who pay an agreed sum if damage, loss, or death occurs **2** the money paid for insurance or by an insurance company **3** a means of protection: *sensible insurance against heart attacks*

insurance policy *n* a contract of insurance

i

constitute, initiate, originate, enact, commence, inaugurate, set in motion, bring into being, put into operation **OPPOSITE:** end

institution *n* **1 = establishment**, body, centre, school, university, society, association, college, institute, organization, foundation, academy, guild, conservatory, fellowship, seminary, seat of learning **3 = custom**, practice, tradition, law, rule, procedure, convention, ritual, fixture, rite

institutional *adj* **1 = conventional**, accepted, established, formal, establishment (*informal*), organized, routine, orthodox, bureaucratic, procedural, societal

instruct *vb* **1 = order**, tell, direct, charge, bid, command, mandate, enjoin **2 = teach**, school, train, direct, coach, guide, discipline, educate, drill, tutor, enlighten, give lessons in

instruction *n* **1 = order**, ruling, command, rule, demand, direction, regulation, dictate, decree, mandate, directive, injunction, behest **2 = teaching**, schooling, training, classes, grounding, education, coaching, lesson(s), discipline, preparation, drilling, guidance, tutoring, tuition, enlightenment, apprenticeship, tutorials, tutelage

instructions *pl n* **= information**, rules, advice, directions, recommendations, guidance, specifications

instructor *n* **1 = teacher**, coach, guide, adviser, trainer, demonstrator, tutor, guru, mentor, educator, pedagogue, preceptor (*rare*), master *or* mistress, schoolmaster *or* schoolmistress

instrument *n* **1 = tool**, device, implement, mechanism, appliance, apparatus, gadget, utensil, contraption (*informal*), contrivance, waldo **5 = agent**, means, force, cause, medium, agency, factor, channel, vehicle, mechanism, organ

instrumental *adj* **1 = active**, involved, influential, useful, helpful, conducive, contributory, of help *or* service

insufficient *adj* **= inadequate**, incomplete, scant, meagre, short, sparse, deficient, lacking, unqualified, insubstantial, incommensurate **OPPOSITE:** ample

insulate *vb* **2 = isolate**, protect, screen, defend, shelter, shield, cut off, cushion, cocoon, close off, sequester, wrap up in cotton wool

insult *vb* **1 = offend**, abuse, injure, wound, slight, outrage, put down, humiliate, libel, snub, slag (off) (*slang*), malign, affront, denigrate, disparage, revile, slander, displease, defame, hurt (someone's) feelings, call names, give offence to **OPPOSITE:** praise ▷ *n* **2 = jibe**, slight, put-down, abuse, snub, barb, affront, indignity, contumely, abusive remark, aspersion **3 = offence**, slight, outrage, snub, slur, affront, rudeness, slap in the face (*informal*), kick in the teeth (*informal*), insolence, aspersion

insurance *n* **1 = assurance**, cover, security, protection, coverage, safeguard, indemnity, indemnification **3 = protection**, security, guarantee, provision, shelter, safeguard, warranty

DICTIONARY

insure ❶ *vb* **-suring, -sured 1** to guarantee or protect (against risk or loss) **2** (often foll. by *against*) to issue (a person) with an insurance policy or take out an insurance policy (on): *the players were insured against accidents* **3** *chiefly US* ▸ same as **ensure** > **insurable** *adj* **insurability** *n*

insured *n* **the insured** the person covered by an insurance policy

insurer *n* a person or company that sells insurance

insurgent *adj* **1** rebellious or in revolt against an established authority ▹ *n* **2** a person who takes part in a rebellion **insurgency** *n*
WORD ORIGIN Latin *insurgens* rising

insurmountable *adj* impossible to overcome: *insurmountable problems*

insurrection *n* the act of rebelling against an established authority **insurrectionist** *n, adj*
WORD ORIGIN Latin *insurgere* to rise up

int. 1 internal **2** Also: **Int** international

intact ❶ *adj* not changed or damaged in any way
WORD ORIGIN Latin *intactus*

intaglio (in-tah-lee-oh) *n, pl* **-lios** *or* **-li 1** a seal or gem decorated with an engraved design **2** an engraved design **intagliated** *adj*
WORD ORIGIN Italian

intake *n* **1** a thing or a quantity taken in: *an intake of students* **2** the act of taking in **3** the opening through which fluid or gas enters a pipe or engine

intangible *adj* **1** difficult for the mind to grasp: *intangible ideas* **2** incapable of being felt by touch **intangibility** *n*

integer *n* any positive or negative whole number or zero, as opposed to a number with fractions or decimals
WORD ORIGIN Latin: untouched

integral ❶ *adj* **1** being an essential part of a whole **2** whole or complete **3** *maths* **a** of or involving an integral **b** involving or being an integer ▹ *n* **4** *maths* the sum of a large number of minute quantities, summed either between stated limits (**definite integral**) or in the absence of limits (**indefinite integral**)

integral calculus *n maths* the branch of calculus concerned with the determination of integrals and their use in solving differential equations

integrand *n maths* a mathematical function to be integrated

integrate ❶ *vb* **-grating, -grated 1** to make or be made into a whole **2** to amalgamate (a racial or religious group) with an existing community **3** to designate (an institution) for use by all races or groups **4** *maths* to determine the integral of a function or variable **integration** *n*
WORD ORIGIN Latin *integrare*

integrated circuit *n* a tiny electronic circuit

integrity ❶ *n* **1** honesty **2** the quality of being whole or united: *respect for a state's territorial integrity* **3** the quality of being unharmed or sound: *the integrity of the cell membrane*
WORD ORIGIN Latin *integritas*

integument *n* any natural protective covering, such as a skin, rind, or shell
WORD ORIGIN Latin *integumentum*

intellect ❶ *n* **1** the ability to understand, think, and reason **2** a particular person's mind or intelligence, esp. a brilliant one: *his intellect is wasted on that job* **3** *informal* a person who has a brilliant mind
WORD ORIGIN Latin *intellectus* comprehension

intellectual ❶ *adj* **1** of, involving, or appealing to the intellect: *intellectual literature* **2** clever or intelligent ▹ *n* **3** a person who has a highly developed intellect **intellectuality** *n* **intellectually** *adv*

intelligence ❶ *n* **1** the ability to understand, learn, and think things out quickly **2** the collection of secret information, esp. for military purposes **3** a group or department collecting military information **4** *old-fashioned* news or information
WORD ORIGIN Latin *intellegere* to understand, literally: to choose between

intelligence quotient *n* a measure of the intelligence of a person calculated by dividing the person's mental age by his or her actual age and multiplying the result by 100

intelligent ❶ *adj* **1** having or showing intelligence: *an intelligent child; an intelligent guess* **2** (of a computerized device) able to initiate or modify action in the light of ongoing events **intelligently** *adv*

intelligent design *n* a theory that rejects the theory of natural selection, arguing for an intelligent cause in the form of a creator

intelligentsia *n* **the intelligentsia** the educated or intellectual people in a society
WORD ORIGIN Russian *intelligentsiya*

intelligible *adj* able to be understood **intelligibility** *n*

intemperate *adj* **1** unrestrained or uncontrolled: *intemperate remarks* **2** drinking alcohol too much or too often **3** extreme or severe: *an intemperate climate* **intemperance** *n*

THESAURUS

insure *vb* **1 = assure**, cover, protect, guarantee, warrant, underwrite, indemnify **2** (often foll. by *against*) **= protect**, cover, safeguard

intact *adj* **= undamaged**, whole, complete, sound, perfect, entire, virgin, untouched, unscathed, unbroken, flawless, unhurt, faultless, unharmed, uninjured, unimpaired, undefiled, all in one piece, together, scatheless, unviolated **OPPOSITE:** damaged

integral *adj* **1 = essential**, basic, fundamental, necessary, component, constituent, indispensable, intrinsic, requisite, elemental **OPPOSITE:** inessential

integrate *vb* **1 = join**, unite, combine, blend, incorporate, merge, accommodate, knit, fuse, mesh, assimilate, amalgamate, coalesce, harmonize, meld, intermix **OPPOSITE:** separate

integrity *n* **1 = honesty**, principle, honour, virtue, goodness, morality, purity, righteousness, probity, rectitude, truthfulness, trustworthiness, incorruptibility, uprightness, scrupulousness, reputability **OPPOSITE:** dishonesty **2 = unity**, unification, cohesion, coherence, wholeness, soundness, completeness **OPPOSITE:** fragility

intellect *n* **1 = intelligence**, mind, reason, understanding, sense, brains *(informal)*, judgment

intellectual *adj* **2 = scholarly**, learned, academic, lettered, intelligent, rational, cerebral, erudite, scholastic, highbrow, well-read, studious, bookish **OPPOSITE:** stupid ▹ *n* **3 = academic**, expert, genius, thinker, master, brain *(informal)*, mastermind, maestro, highbrow, rocket scientist *(informal, chiefly US)*, egghead *(informal)*, brainbox, bluestocking *(usually derogatory)*, pointy-head *(informal, chiefly US)*, master-hand, fundi *(S African)*, acca *(Austral slang)* **OPPOSITE:** idiot

intelligence *n* **1 = intellect**, understanding, brains *(informal)*, mind, reason, sense, knowledge, capacity, smarts *(slang, chiefly US)*, judgment, wit, perception, awareness, insight, penetration, comprehension, brightness, aptitude, acumen, nous *(Brit slang)*, alertness, cleverness, quickness, discernment, grey matter *(informal)*, brain power **OPPOSITE:** stupidity **4** *(old-fashioned)* **= information**, news, facts, report, findings, word, notice, advice, knowledge, data, disclosure, gen *(Brit informal)*, tip-off, low-down *(informal)*, notification, heads up *(US & Canad)* **OPPOSITE:** misinformation

intelligent *adj* **1 = clever**, bright, smart, knowing, quick, sharp, acute, alert, rational, penetrating, enlightened, apt, discerning, knowledgeable, astute, well-informed, brainy *(informal)*, perspicacious, quick-witted, sagacious **OPPOSITE:** stupid

DICTIONARY

intend ⓣ *vb* **1** to propose or plan (something or to do something) **2** to have as one's purpose **3** to mean to express or indicate: *no criticism was intended* **4** (often foll. by *for*) to design or destine (for a certain purpose or person): *the plane was never intended for combat*
WORD ORIGIN Latin *intendere* to stretch forth

intended *adj* **1** planned or future ▷ *n* **2** *informal* a person whom one is to marry

intense ⓣ *adj* **1** of very great force, strength, degree, or amount: *intense heat* **2** characterized by deep or forceful feelings: *an intense person* **intensely** *adv* **intenseness** *n*
WORD ORIGIN Latin *intensus* stretched

intensifier *n* a word, esp. an adjective or adverb, that intensifies the meaning of the word or phrase that it modifies, for example, *very* or *extremely*

intensify ⓣ *vb* **-fies, -fying, -fied** to make or become intense or more intense **intensification** *n*

intensity ⓣ *n, pl* **-ties** **1** the state or quality of being intense **2** extreme force, degree, or amount **3** *physics* the amount or degree of strength of electricity, heat, light, or sound per unit area of volume

intensive ⓣ *adj* **1** of or needing concentrated effort or resources: *intensive training* **2** using one specified factor more than others: *labour-intensive* **3** *agriculture* designed to increase production from a particular area: *intensive farming* **4** *grammar* (of a word) giving emphasis, for example, *very* in *the very same* **intensively** *adv* **intensiveness** *n*

intensive care *n* thorough, continuously supervised treatment of an acutely ill patient in a hospital

intent ⓣ *n* **1** something that is intended **2** *law* the will or purpose to commit a crime: *loitering with intent* **3 to all intents and purposes** in almost every respect; virtually ▷ *adj* **4** having one's attention firmly fixed: *an intent look* **5 intent on** *or* **upon** strongly resolved on: *intent on winning the election* **intently** *adv* **intentness** *n*
WORD ORIGIN Late Latin *intentus* aim

intention ⓣ *n* something intended; a plan, idea, or purpose: *he had no intention of resigning*

intentional *adj* done on purpose **intentionally** *adv*

inter ⓣ (in-**ter**) *vb* **-terring, -terred** to bury (a corpse)
WORD ORIGIN Latin *in-* into + *terra* earth

inter- *prefix* **1** between or among: *international* **2** together, mutually, or reciprocally: *interdependent*
WORD ORIGIN Latin

interact *vb* to act on or in close relation with each other **interaction** *n* **interactive** *adj*

inter alia (in-ter **ale**-ya) *adv* among other things
WORD ORIGIN Latin

interbreed *vb* **-breeding, -bred** **1** to breed within a related group so as to produce particular characteristics in the offspring **2** ▸ same as **crossbreed** (sense 1)

intercede *vb* **-ceding, -ceded** **1** to plead in favour of **2** to act as a mediator in order to end a disagreement: *a policeman was watching the beatings without interceding*
WORD ORIGIN Latin *inter-* between + *cedere* to move

intercept ⓣ *vb* **1** to stop or seize on the way from one place to another **2** *maths* to mark off or include (part of a line, curve, plane, or surface) between two points or lines ▷ *n* **3** *maths* **a** a point at which two figures intersect **b** the distance from the origin to the point at which a line, curve, or surface cuts a coordinate axis **interception** *n* **interceptor** *n*
WORD ORIGIN Latin *intercipere* to seize before arrival

intercession *n* **1** the act of interceding **2** a prayer offered to God on behalf of others **intercessor** *n*

interchange *vb* **-changing, -changed** **1** to change places or cause to change places ▷ *n* **2** the act of interchanging **3** a motorway junction of interconnecting roads and bridges designed to prevent streams of traffic crossing one another **interchangeable** *adj* **interchangeably** *adv*

Intercity *adj trademark* (in Britain) denoting a fast train (service) travelling between cities

intercom *n* an internal communication system with loudspeakers
WORD ORIGIN short for INTERCOMMUNICATION

intercommunicate *vb* **-cating, -cated** **1** to communicate mutually **2** (of two rooms) to interconnect **intercommunication** *n*

intercommunion *n* association between Churches, involving mutual reception of Holy Communion

interconnect *vb* to connect with one another **interconnected** *adj* **interconnection** *n*

intercontinental *adj* travelling between or linking continents

intercourse ⓣ *n* **1** the act of having sex **2** communication or dealings

THESAURUS

intend *vb* **1, 2 = plan**, mean, aim, determine, scheme, propose, purpose, contemplate, envisage, foresee, be resolved *or* determined, have in mind *or* view

intense *adj* **1 = extreme**, great, severe, fierce, serious *(informal)*, deep, powerful, concentrated, supreme, acute, harsh, intensive, excessive, profound, exquisite, drastic, forceful, protracted, unqualified, agonizing, mother of all *(informal)* **OPPOSITE:** mild
2 = passionate, burning, earnest, emotional, keen, flaming, consuming, fierce, eager, enthusiastic, heightened, energetic, animated, ardent, fanatical, fervent, heartfelt, impassioned, vehement, forcible, fervid **OPPOSITE:** indifferent

intensify *vb* **a = increase**, boost, raise, extend, concentrate, add to, strengthen, enhance, compound, reinforce, step up *(informal)*, emphasize, widen, heighten, sharpen, magnify, amplify, augment, redouble **OPPOSITE:** decrease
b = escalate, increase, extend, widen, heighten, deepen, quicken

intensity *n* **1 = passion**, emotion, fervour, force, power, fire, energy, strength, depth, concentration, excess, severity, vigour, potency, extremity, fanaticism, ardour, vehemence, earnestness, keenness, fierceness, fervency, intenseness
2 = force, power, strength, severity, extremity, fierceness

intensive *adj* **1 = concentrated**, thorough, exhaustive, full, demanding, detailed, complete, serious, concerted, intense, comprehensive, vigorous, all-out, in-depth, strenuous, painstaking, all-embracing, assiduous, thoroughgoing

intent *n* **1 = intention**, aim, purpose, meaning, end, plan, goal, design, target, object, resolution, resolve, objective, ambition, aspiration **OPPOSITE:** chance
▷ *adj* **4 = absorbed**, focused, fixed, earnest, committed, concentrated, occupied, intense, fascinated, steady, alert, wrapped up, preoccupied, enthralled, attentive, watchful, engrossed, steadfast, rapt, enrapt **OPPOSITE:** indifferent

intention *n* **= aim**, plan, idea, goal, end, design, target, wish, scheme, purpose, object, objective, determination, intent

inter *vb* **= bury**, lay to rest, entomb, sepulchre, consign to the grave, inhume, inurn

intercept *vb* **1 = catch**, take, stop, check, block, arrest, seize, cut off, interrupt, head off, deflect, obstruct

intercourse *n* **1 = sexual intercourse**, sex *(informal)*, lovemaking, the other *(informal)*, congress, screwing *(taboo,*

DICTIONARY

between individuals or groups **WORD ORIGIN** Latin *intercurrere* to run between

interdenominational *adj* among or involving more than one denomination of the Christian Church

interdepartmental *adj* of or between different departments

interdependent *adj* dependent on one another **interdependence** *n*

interdict *n* **1** *law* an official prohibition or restraint **2** *RC church* the exclusion of a person or place from certain sacraments, although not from communion ▷ *vb* **3** to prohibit or forbid **interdiction** *n* **interdictory** *adj* **WORD ORIGIN** Latin *interdicere* to forbid

interdisciplinary *adj* involving more than one branch of learning

i

interest ⊙ *n* **1** curiosity or concern about something or someone **2** the power of causing this: *to have great interest* **3** (*often pl*) something in which one is interested; a hobby or pursuit **4** (*often pl*) advantage: *in one's own interests* **5** money paid for the use of credit or borrowed money: *she borrowed money at 25 per cent interest* **6** (*often pl*) a right, share, or claim, esp. in a business or property **7** (*often pl*) a group of people with common aims: *foreign interests* ▷ *vb* **8** to arouse the curiosity or concern of **9** to cause to become interested or involved in something **WORD ORIGIN** Latin: it concerns

interested ⊙ *adj* **1** showing or having interest **2** involved in or affected by: *a consultation paper sent to interested parties*

interest group *n* a group of persons who attempt to influence legislators on behalf of a particular interest

interesting ⊙ *adj* causing interest **interestingly** *adv*

interface ⊙ *n* **1** an area where two things interact or link: *the interface between Islamic culture and Western modernity* **2** an electrical circuit linking one device, esp. a computer, with another **3** *physics, chem* a surface that forms the boundary between two liquids or chemical phases that cannot be mixed ▷ *vb* **-facing, -faced 4** to connect or be connected with by interface **interfacial** *adj*

interfacing *n* **1** a piece of fabric sewn beneath the facing of a garment to give shape and firmness **2** ▸ same as **interlining**

interfaith *adj* relating to, between, or involving different religions

interfere ⊙ *vb* **-fering, -fered 1** to try to influence other people's affairs where one is not involved or wanted **2** *physics* to produce or cause to produce interference **3 interfere with a** to clash with or hinder: *child-bearing may interfere with your career* **b** *Brit, Austral & NZ, euphemistic* to abuse sexually **interfering** *adj* **WORD ORIGIN** Old French *s'entreferir* to collide

interference ⊙ *n* **1** the act of interfering **2** any undesired signal that interferes with the reception of radio waves **3** *physics* the meeting of two waves which reinforce or neutralize each other depending on whether they are in or out of phase

interferon *n biochem* a protein made by cells that stops the development of an invading virus

interfuse *vb* **-fusing, -fused 1** to mix or become mixed **2** to blend or fuse together **interfusion** *n*

intergalactic *adj* occurring or located between different galaxies

interim ⊙ *adj* **1** temporary or provisional: *an interim government* ▷ *n* **2 in the interim** during the intervening time **WORD ORIGIN** Latin: meanwhile

interior ⊙ *n* **1** a part or region that is on the inside: *the interior of the earth* **2** the inside of a building or room, with respect to design and decoration **3** the central area of a country or continent, furthest from the sea **4** a picture of the inside of a room or building ▷ *adj* **5** of, situated on, or suitable for the inside **6** mental or spiritual: *interior development* **7** coming or acting from within **8** of a nation's domestic affairs **WORD ORIGIN** Latin

interior angle *n* an angle of a polygon contained between two adjacent sides

interior decoration *n* **1** the decoration and furnishings of the interior of a room or house **2** Also called: **interior design** the art or business of planning this **interior decorator** *n*

interj. interjection

interject *vb* to make (a remark) suddenly or as an interruption **WORD ORIGIN** Latin *interjicere* to place between

interjection *n* a word or phrase which is used on its own and which

THESAURUS

slang), intimacy, shagging (*Brit taboo, slang*), sexual relations, sexual act, nookie (*slang*), copulation, coitus, carnal knowledge, intimate relations, rumpy-pumpy (*slang*), legover (*slang*), coition, rumpo (*slang*) **2 = contact**, relationships, communication, association, relations, trade, traffic, connection, truck, commerce, dealings, correspondence, communion, converse, intercommunication

interest *n* **3** (*often plural*) **= hobby**, activity, pursuit, entertainment, relaxation, recreation, amusement, preoccupation, diversion, pastime, leisure activity **4** (*often plural*) **= advantage**, good, benefit, profit, gain, boot (*dialect*) **6** (*often plural*) **= stake**, investment ▷ *vb* **8, 9 = arouse your curiosity**, engage, appeal to, fascinate, move, involve, touch, affect, attract, grip, entertain, absorb, intrigue, amuse, divert, rivet, captivate, catch your eye, hold the attention of, engross **OPPOSITE:** bore

interested *adj* **1 = curious**, into (*informal*), moved, affected, attracted, excited, drawn, keen, gripped, fascinated, stimulated, intent, responsive, riveted, captivated, attentive **OPPOSITE:** uninterested **2 = involved**, concerned, affected, prejudiced, biased, partial, partisan, implicated, predisposed

interesting *adj* **= intriguing**, fascinating, absorbing, pleasing, appealing, attractive, engaging, unusual, gripping, stirring, entertaining, entrancing, stimulating, curious, compelling, amusing, compulsive, riveting, captivating, enthralling, beguiling, thought-provoking, engrossing, spellbinding **OPPOSITE:** uninteresting

interface *n* **1 = connection**, link, boundary, border, frontier

interfere *vb* **1 = meddle**, intervene, intrude, butt in, get involved, tamper, pry, encroach, intercede, stick your nose in (*informal*), stick your oar in (*informal*), poke your nose in (*informal*), intermeddle, put your two cents in (*US slang*) **3a** (foll. by *with*) **= conflict with**, affect, get in the way of, check, block, clash, frustrate, handicap, hamper, disrupt, cramp, inhibit, thwart, hinder, obstruct, impede, baulk, trammel, be a drag upon (*informal*)

interference *n* **1 = intrusion**, intervention, meddling, opposition, conflict, obstruction, prying, impedance, meddlesomeness, intermeddling

interim *adj* **1 = temporary**, provisional, makeshift, acting, passing, intervening, caretaker, improvised, transient, stopgap, pro tem

interior *n* **1 = inside**, centre, heart, middle, contents, depths, core, belly, nucleus, bowels, bosom, innards (*informal*) ▷ *adj* **5, 7 = inside**, internal, inner **OPPOSITE:** exterior **6 = mental**, emotional, psychological, private, personal, secret, hidden, spiritual, intimate, inner, inward, instinctive, impulsive

intermediary *n* **1 = mediator**, agent,

DICTIONARY

expresses sudden emotion
interlace *vb* **-lacing, -laced** to join by lacing or weaving together: *interlaced fingers*
interlard *vb* to insert in or occur throughout: *to interlard one's writing with foreign phrases*
interlay *vb* **-laying, -laid** to insert (layers) between: *to interlay gold among the silver*
interleaf *n, pl* **-leaves** an extra leaf which is inserted
interleave *vb* **-leaving, -leaved** to insert, as blank leaves in a book, between other leaves
interleukin (in-ter-**loo**-kin) *n biochem* a substance obtained from white blood cells that stimulates their activity against infection and may by used to fight some forms of cancer
interline[1] *vb* **-lining, -lined** to write or print (matter) between the lines of (a text or book)
interline[2] *vb* **-lining, -lined** to provide (a part of a garment) with a second lining
interlining *n* the material used to interline parts of garments
interlink *vb* to connect together
interlock *vb* **1** to join or be joined firmly together ▹*n* **2** a device used to prevent a mechanism from operating independently or unsafely
interlocutor (in-ter-**lock**-yew-ter) *n formal* a person who takes part in a conversation
WORD ORIGIN Latin *inter-* between + *loqui* to talk
interlocutory (in-ter-**lock**-yew-tree) *adj* **1** *law* pronounced during the course of legal proceedings; provisional: *an interlocutory injunction* **2** *formal* of dialogue; conversational
interloper (**in**-ter-lope-er) *n* a person in a place or situation where he or she has no right to be
interlude *n* **1** a period of time or different activity between longer periods or events **2** **a** a pause between the acts of a play **b** a brief piece of music or other entertainment performed during this pause
WORD ORIGIN Latin *inter-* between + *ludus* play
intermarry *vb* **-ries, -rying, -ried** **1** (of different races, religions, or social groups) to become connected by marriage **2** to marry within one's own family or tribe **intermarriage** *n*
intermediary ⓘ *n, pl* **-aries** **1** a person who tries to bring about agreement between others **2** a messenger ▹*adj* **3** acting as an intermediary **4** intermediate
intermediate ⓘ *adj* **1** occurring between two points or extremes **2** (of a class, course, etc.) suitable for learners with some level of skill or competence ▹*n* **3** something intermediate **4** *chem* a substance formed between the first and final stages of a chemical process **intermediation** *n*
WORD ORIGIN Latin *inter-* between + *medius* middle
interment *n* a burial
intermezzo (in-ter-**met**-so) *n, pl* **-zos** *or* **-zi** **1** a short piece of instrumental music performed between the acts of a play or opera **2** **a** a short composition between two longer movements in an extended musical work **b** a similar composition intended for independent performance
WORD ORIGIN Italian
interminable *adj* seemingly endless because boring: *an interminable rambling anecdote* **interminably** *adv*
intermingle *vb* **-gling, -gled** to mix together
intermission *n* an interval between parts of a play, film, etc.
WORD ORIGIN Latin *intermittere* to leave off, cease
intermittent *adj* occurring at intervals **intermittently** *adv*
intern *vb* **1** to imprison, esp. during wartime ▹*n* **2** *chiefly US* a trainee doctor in a hospital **internment** *n*
WORD ORIGIN Latin *internus* internal
internal ⓘ *adj* **1** of, situated on, or suitable for the inside **2** *anat* affecting or relating to the inside of the body: *internal bleeding* **3** of a nation's domestic affairs: *internal politics* **4** coming or acting from within an organization: *an internal reorganization* **5** spiritual or mental: *internal conflict* **internally** *adv*
WORD ORIGIN Latin *internus*
internal-combustion engine *n* an engine in which power is produced by the explosion of a fuel-and-air mixture within the cylinders
international ⓘ *adj* **1** of or involving two or more nations **2** controlling or legislating for several nations: *an international court* **3** available for use by all nations: *international waters* ▹*n* **4** *sport* **a** a game or match between the national teams of different countries **b** a member of a national team **internationally** *adv*
International *n* any of several international socialist organizations
International Date Line *n* the line approximately following the 180° meridian from Greenwich on the east side of which the date is one day earlier than on the west
internationalism *n* the ideal or practice of cooperation and understanding for the good of all nations **internationalist** *n*
International Phonetic Alphabet *n* a series of signs and letters for the representation of human speech sounds
International Style *or* **Modernism** *n* a 20th-century architectural style characterized by undecorated straight forms and the use of glass, steel, and reinforced concrete
internecine *adj formal* destructive to both sides: *internecine war*
WORD ORIGIN Latin *internecare* to destroy
internee *n* a person who is interned
internet ⓘ *n* (*sometimes cap*) a large public access computer network linked to others worldwide
internist *n* a physician who specializes in internal medicine
interpenetrate *vb* **-trating, -trated** **1** to penetrate (something) thoroughly **2** to penetrate each other or one another mutually **interpenetration** *n*
interpersonal *adj* of or relating to relationships between people: *interpersonal conflict at work*
interplanetary *adj* of or linking planets
interplay *n* the action and reaction of things upon each other
Interpol International Criminal Police Organization: an association of over 100 national police forces, devoted chiefly to fighting international crime
interpolate (in-**ter**-pole-ate) *vb* **-lating, -lated** **1** to insert (a comment or passage) into (a conversation or text) **2** *maths* to estimate (a value of a function) between the values already known **interpolation** *n*
WORD ORIGIN Latin *interpolare* to give a new appearance to
interpose *vb* **-posing, -posed** **1** to place (something) between or among other things **2** to interrupt (with comments or questions) **3** to put forward so as to interrupt: *he ended the discussion by interposing a veto* **interposition** *n*
WORD ORIGIN Latin *inter-* between + *ponere* to put

THESAURUS

middleman, broker, entrepreneur, go-between
intermediate *adj* **1 = middle**, mid, halfway, in-between *(informal)*, midway, intervening, transitional, intermediary, median, interposed
internal *adj* **1 = inner**, inside, interior **OPPOSITE:** external
3 = domestic, home, national, local, civic, in-house, intramural
international *adj* **1 = global**, world, worldwide, universal, cosmopolitan, planetary, intercontinental
internet *n* (sometimes cap) **= the information superhighway**, the net *(informal)*, the web *(informal)*, the World Wide Web, cyberspace, blogosphere, the interweb *(facetious)*

DICTIONARY

interpret ❶ *vb* **1** to explain the meaning of **2** to work out the significance of: *his remarks were widely interpreted as a promise not to raise taxes* **3** to convey the meaning of (a poem, song, etc.) in performance **4** to act as an interpreter **interpretive** *adj*
WORD ORIGIN Latin *interpretari*

interpretation ❶ *n* **1** the act or result of interpreting or explaining **2** the particular way in which a performer expresses his or her view of a composition: *an interpretation of Mahler's fourth symphony* **3** explanation, as of a historical site, provided by the use of original objects, visual display material, etc.

interpreter ❶ *n* **1** a person who translates orally from one language into another **2** *computers* a program that translates a statement in a source program to machine language and executes it before translating and executing the next statement

interpretive centre *n* a building situated at a place of interest, such as a country park or historical site, that provides information about the site by showing videos, exhibiting objects, etc.

interracial *adj* between or among people of different races

interregnum *n, pl* **-nums** *or* **-na** a period between the end of one ruler's reign and the beginning of the next **interregnal** *adj*
WORD ORIGIN Latin *inter-* between + *regnum* reign

interrelate *vb* **-lating, -lated** to connect (two or more things) or (of two or more things) to become connected to each other **interrelation** *n* **interrelationship** *n*

interrogate *vb* **-gating, -gated** to question (someone) closely **interrogation** *n* **interrogator** *n*
WORD ORIGIN Latin *interrogare*

interrogative (in-ter-**rog**-a-tiv) *adj* **1** used in asking a question: *an interrogative pronoun* **2** of or like a question: *an interrogative look* ▷ *n* **3** an interrogative word, phrase, sentence, or construction

interrogatory (in-ter-**rog**-a-tree) *adj* **1** expressing or involving a question ▷ *n, pl* **-tories 2** a question or interrogation

interrupt ❶ *vb* **1** to break into (a conversation or discussion) by questions or comment **2** to stop (a process or activity) temporarily **interrupted** *adj* **interruptive** *adj*
WORD ORIGIN Latin *inter-* between + *rumpere* to break

interrupter *or* **interruptor** *n* a device for opening and closing an electric circuit

interruption ❶ *n* **1** something that interrupts, such as a comment or question **2** an interval or intermission **3** the act of interrupting or the state of being interrupted

interscholastic *adj* occurring between two or more schools: *an interscholastic competition*

intersect *vb* **1** (of roads or lines) to cross (each other) **2** to divide or mark off (a place, area, or surface) by passing through or across
WORD ORIGIN Latin *intersecare* to divide

intersection *n* **1** a point at which things intersect, esp. a road junction **2** the act of intersecting or the state of being intersected **3** *maths* **a** a point or set of points common to two or more geometric figures **b** the set of elements that are common to two sets **intersectional** *adj*

intersex *n* **1** the condition of having characteristics in between those of a male and a female **2** an individual exhibiting such characteristics

intersperse *vb* **-spersing, -spersed** **1** to scatter among, between, or on **2** to mix (something) with other things scattered here and there **interspersion** *n*
WORD ORIGIN Latin *inter-* between + *spargere* to sprinkle

interstellar *adj* between or among stars

interstice (in-**ter**-stiss) *n (usually pl)* **1** a small gap or crack between things **2** *physics* the space between adjacent atoms in a crystal lattice
WORD ORIGIN Latin *interstitium* interval

intertwine *vb* **-twining, -twined** to twist together

interval ❶ *n* **1** the period of time between two events **2** *Austral & Brit* a short period between parts of a play, concert, etc. **3** *music* the difference of pitch between two notes **4 at intervals a** now and then: *turn the chicken at intervals* **b** with a certain amount of space between: *the poles were placed at intervals of twenty metres*
WORD ORIGIN Latin *intervallum*, literally: space between two palisades

intervene ❶ *vb* **-vening, -vened** **1** (often foll. by *in*) to involve oneself in a situation, esp. to prevent conflict **2** to interrupt a conversation **3** to happen so as to stop something: *he hoped to play but a serious injury intervened* **4** to come or be among or between: *ten years had intervened since he had seen Joe*
WORD ORIGIN Latin *intervenire* to come between

intervention ❶ *n* the act of intervening, esp. to influence or alter a situation in some way **interventionist** *n, adj*

interview ❶ *n* **1** a formal discussion, esp. one in which an employer assesses a job applicant **2** a conversation in which a well-known person is asked about his or her

THESAURUS

interpret *vb* **1 = explain**, define, clarify, spell out, make sense of, decode, decipher, expound, elucidate, throw light on, explicate **2 = take**, understand, read, explain, regard, construe **3 = portray**, present, perform, render, depict, enact, act out **4 = translate**, convert, paraphrase, adapt, transliterate

interpretation *n* **1a = explanation**, meaning, reading, understanding, sense, analysis, construction, exposition, explication, elucidation, signification **1b = reading**, study, review, version, analysis, explanation, examination, diagnosis, evaluation, exposition, exegesis, explication, elucidation **2 = performance**, portrayal, presentation, rendering, reading, execution, rendition, depiction

interpreter *n* **1 = translator**, linguist, metaphrast, paraphrast

interrupt *vb* **1 = intrude**, disturb, intervene, interfere (with), break in, heckle, butt in, barge in *(informal)*, break (someone's) train of thought **2 = suspend**, break, stop, end, cut, stay, check, delay, cease, cut off, postpone, shelve, put off, defer, break off, adjourn, cut short, discontinue

interruption *n* **2 = disruption**, break, halt, obstacle, disturbance, hitch, intrusion, obstruction, impediment, hindrance **3 = stoppage**, stop, pause, suspension, cessation, severance, hiatus, disconnection, discontinuance

interval *n* **1 = period**, time, spell, term, season, space, stretch, pause, span **2** *(Austral & Brit)* **= break**, interlude, intermission, rest, gap, pause, respite, lull, entr'acte

intervene *vb* **1** (often foll. by *in*) **= step in** *(informal)*, interfere, mediate, intrude, intercede, arbitrate, interpose, take a hand *(informal)* **2 = interrupt**, involve yourself, put your oar in, interpose yourself, put your two cents in *(US slang)* **3 = happen**, occur, take place, follow, succeed, arise, ensue, befall, materialize, come to pass, supervene

intervention *n* **= mediation**, involvement, interference, intrusion, arbitration, conciliation, intercession, interposition, agency

interview *n* **1 = meeting**, examination, evaluation, oral (examination), interrogation **2 = audience**, talk, conference, exchange, dialogue, consultation,

DICTIONARY

views, career, etc. by a reporter ▷ *vb* **3** to question (someone) **interviewee** *n* **interviewer** *n*
WORD ORIGIN Old French *entrevue*

interwar *adj* of or happening in the period between World War I and World War II

interweave *vb* **-weaving, -wove** *or* **-weaved, -woven** *or* **-weaved** to weave together

intestate *adj* **1** (of a person) not having made a will ▷ *n* **2** a person who dies without having made a will **intestacy** *n*
WORD ORIGIN Latin *intestatus*

intestine *n* the part of the alimentary canal between the stomach and the anus ▸ See **large intestine, small intestine** > **intestinal** *adj*
WORD ORIGIN Latin *intestinus* internal

intifada (in-tiff-**ah**-da) *n* the Palestinian uprising against Israel in the West Bank and Gaza Strip
WORD ORIGIN Arabic

intimacy ⊕ *n, pl* **-cies** **1** close or warm friendship **2** (*often pl*) intimate words or acts within a close relationship

intimate[1] ⊕ *adj* **1** characterized by a close or warm personal relationship: *an intimate friend* **2** deeply personal, private, or secret **3** (of knowledge) extensive and detailed **4** *euphemistic* having sexual relations **5** having a friendly quiet atmosphere: *an intimate nightclub* ▷ *n* **6** a close friend **intimately** *adv*
WORD ORIGIN Latin *intimus* innermost

intimate[2] ⊕ *vb* **-mating, -mated** *formal* **1** to make (something) known in an indirect way: *he has intimated his intention to retire* **2** to announce **intimation** *n*
WORD ORIGIN Late Latin *intimare* to proclaim

intimidate ⊕ *vb* **-dating, -dated** to subdue or influence (someone) through fear **intimidating** *adj* **intimidation** *n*
WORD ORIGIN Latin *in-* in + *timidus* fearful

into *prep* **1** to the inner part of: *they went into the house* **2** to the middle of so as to be surrounded by: *into the bushes* **3** against; up against: *he drove into a wall* **4** used to indicate the result of a change: *they turned the theatre into a garage* **5** *maths* used to indicate division: *three into six is two* **6** *informal* interested in: *I'm really into healthy food*

intolerable *adj* more than can be endured **intolerably** *adv*

intolerant *adj* refusing to accept practices and beliefs that differ from one's own **intolerance** *n*

intonation *n* **1** the sound pattern produced by variations in the voice **2** the act of intoning **3** *music* the ability to play or sing in tune **intonational** *adj*

intone *vb* **-toning, -toned** **1** to speak or recite in a monotonous tone **2** to speak with a particular tone
WORD ORIGIN Medieval Latin *intonare*

in toto *adv* totally or entirely
WORD ORIGIN Latin

intoxicant *n* **1** something, such as an alcoholic drink, that causes intoxication ▷ *adj* **2** causing intoxication

intoxicate *vb* **-cating, -cated** **1** (of an alcoholic drink) to make (a person) drunk **2** to stimulate or excite to a point beyond self-control **intoxicated** *adj* **intoxicating** *adj*
WORD ORIGIN Latin *in-* in + *toxicum* poison

intoxication *n* **1** the state of being drunk **2** great excitement and exhilaration

intractable *adj* **1** (of a person) difficult to influence or direct **2** (of a problem or illness) difficult to solve or cure **intractability** *n* **intractably** *adv*

intramural *adj chiefly US & Canad* operating within or involving those within a school or college: *intramural sports*
WORD ORIGIN Latin *intra-* inside + *murus* wall

intranet *n computers* an internal network that makes use of internet technology
WORD ORIGIN *intra-* + INTERNET

intransigent *adj* **1** refusing to change one's attitude ▷ *n* **2** an intransigent person, esp. in politics **intransigence** *n*
WORD ORIGIN Latin *in-* not + *transigere* to settle

intransitive *adj* (of a verb) not taking a direct object: *'to faint' is an intransitive verb* **intransitively** *adv*

intrapreneur *n Brit and US* a person who while remaining within a larger organization uses entrepreneurial skills to develop new services or systems as a subsidiary of the organization
WORD ORIGIN *intra-* inside + *(entre)preneur*

intrauterine *adj* situated within the womb
WORD ORIGIN Latin *intra-* inside + *uterus* womb

intrauterine device *n* a contraceptive device in the shape of a coil, inserted into the womb

intravenous (in-tra-**vee**-nuss) *adj anat* into a vein: *intravenous drug users* **intravenously** *adv*
WORD ORIGIN Latin *intra-* inside + *vena* vein

in-tray *n* a tray used in offices for incoming letters or documents requiring attention

intrepid *adj* fearless or bold **intrepidity** *n* **intrepidly** *adv*
WORD ORIGIN Latin *in-* not + *trepidus* fearful

intricate ⊕ *adj* **1** difficult to sort out: *an intricate problem* **2** full of complicated detail: *intricate Arab*

THESAURUS

press conference ▷ *vb* **3 = question**, interrogate, examine, investigate, ask, pump, grill (*informal*), quiz, cross-examine, cross-question, put the screws on (*informal*), catechize, give (someone) the third degree (*informal*)

intimacy *n* **1 = familiarity**, closeness, understanding, confidence, confidentiality, fraternization
OPPOSITE: aloofness

intimate[1] *adj* **1 = close**, dear, loving, near, warm, friendly, familiar, thick (*informal*), devoted, confidential, cherished, bosom, inseparable, nearest and dearest
OPPOSITE: distant
2 = private, personal, confidential, special, individual, particular, secret, exclusive, privy
OPPOSITE: public
3 = detailed, minute, full, experienced, personal, deep, particular, specific, immediate, comprehensive, exact, elaborate, profound, penetrating, thorough, in-depth, intricate, first-hand, exhaustive **5 = cosy**, relaxed, friendly, informal, harmonious, snug, comfy (*informal*), warm ▷ *n* **6 = friend**, close friend, buddy (*informal*), mate (*informal*), pal, comrade, chum (*informal*), mucker (*Brit slang*), crony, main man (*slang, chiefly US*), china (*Brit slang*), homeboy (*slang, chiefly US*), cobber (*Austral & NZ old-fashioned, informal*), bosom friend, familiar, confidant *or* confidante, (constant) companion, E hoa (*NZ*)
OPPOSITE: stranger

intimate[2] *vb* (*formal*) **1 = suggest**, indicate, hint, imply, warn, allude, let it be known, insinuate, give (someone) to understand, drop a hint, tip (someone) the wink (*Brit informal*) **2 = announce**, state, declare, communicate, impart, make known

intimidate *vb* **= frighten**, pressure, threaten, alarm, scare, terrify, cow, bully, plague, menace, hound, awe, daunt, harass, subdue, oppress, persecute, lean on (*informal*), coerce, overawe, scare off (*informal*), terrorize, pressurize, browbeat, twist someone's arm (*informal*), tyrannize, dishearten, dispirit, affright (*archaic*), domineer

intricate *adj* **1, 2 = complicated**, involved, complex, difficult, fancy, sophisticated, elaborate, obscure,

DICTIONARY

mosaics **intricacy** *n* **intricately** *adv*
WORD ORIGIN Latin *intricare* to entangle

intrigue ❶ *vb* **-triguing, -trigued 1** to make interested or curious: *a question which has intrigued him for years* **2** to plot secretly or dishonestly ▷ *n* **3** secret plotting **4** a secret love affair **intriguing** *adj* **intriguingly** *adv*
WORD ORIGIN French *intriguer*

intrinsic *adj* **1** essential to the real nature of a thing: *hedgerows are an intrinsic part of the countryside* **2** *anat* situated within or peculiar to a part: *intrinsic muscles* **intrinsically** *adv*
WORD ORIGIN Latin *intrinsecus* inwardly

intro *n, pl* **-tros** *informal* ▸ short for **introduction**

introduce ❶ *vb* **-ducing, -duced 1** to present (someone) by name (to another person) **2** to present (a radio or television programme) **3** to present for consideration or approval: *he introduced the bill to Parliament in 1967* **4** to bring into use: *Latvia has introduced its own currency into circulation* **5** to insert **6 introduce to** to cause to experience for the first time: *his father introduced him to golf* **7 introduce with** to start: *he introduced his talk with some music* **introducible** *adj*
WORD ORIGIN Latin *introducere* to bring inside

introduction ❶ *n* **1** the act of introducing something or someone **2** a preliminary part, as of a book or musical composition **3** a book that explains the basic facts about a particular subject to a beginner **4** a presentation of one person to another or others

introductory ❶ *adj* serving as an introduction

introit *n* **1** *RC church* a short prayer said or sung as the celebrant is entering the sanctuary to celebrate Mass **2** *Church of England* a hymn or psalm sung at the beginning of a service
WORD ORIGIN Latin *introitus* entrance

introspection *n* the examining of one's own thoughts, impressions, and feelings **introspective** *adj*
WORD ORIGIN Latin *introspicere* to look within

introversion *n psychol* the directing of interest inwards towards one's own thoughts and feelings rather than towards the external world or making social contacts

introvert *adj* **1** shy and quiet **2** *psychol* concerned more with inner feelings than with external reality ▷ *n* **3** such a person **introverted** *adj*
WORD ORIGIN Latin *intro-* inward + *vertere* to turn

intrude *vb* **-truding, -truded** to come in or join in without being invited
WORD ORIGIN Latin *intrudere* to thrust in

intruder ❶ *n* a person who enters a place without permission

intrusion ❶ *n* **1** the act of intruding; an unwelcome visit, etc.: *an intrusion into her private life* **2** *geol* **a** the forcing of molten rock into spaces in the overlying strata **b** molten rock formed in this way **intrusive** *adj*

intrust *vb* ▸ same as **entrust**

intuition ❶ *n* instinctive knowledge of or belief about something without conscious reasoning: *intuition told her something was wrong* **intuitional** *adj*
WORD ORIGIN Latin *intueri* to gaze upon

intuitive *adj* of, possessing, or resulting from intuition: *an intuitive understanding* **intuitively** *adv*

Inuit *n, pl* **-it** *or* **-its** an indigenous inhabitant of North America or Greenland
WORD ORIGIN Inuktitut, plural of *inuk* person

Inuk *n* a member of the Inuit people

Inuktitut *n* the language of the Inuit

inundate *vb* **-dating, -dated 1** to cover completely with water **2** to overwhelm, as if with a flood: *the police were inundated with calls* **inundation** *n*
WORD ORIGIN Latin *inundare*

inured *adj* able to tolerate something unpleasant because one has become accustomed to it: *he became inured to the casual brutality of his captors* **inurement** *n*
WORD ORIGIN Middle English *enuren* to accustom

invade ❶ *vb* **-vading, -vaded 1** to enter (a country or territory) by military force **2** to enter in large numbers: *the town was invaded by rugby supporters* **3** to disturb (privacy, etc.) **invader** *n*
WORD ORIGIN Latin *invadere*

invalid[1] ❶ *n* **1** a person who is disabled or chronically ill ▷ *adj* **2** sick or disabled ▷ *vb* **3** *chiefly Brit* to dismiss (a soldier, etc.) from active service

THESAURUS

tangled, baroque, perplexing, tortuous, Byzantine, convoluted, rococo, knotty, labyrinthine, daedal (*literary*) **OPPOSITE:** simple

intrigue *vb* **1 = interest**, fascinate, arouse the curiosity of, attract, charm, rivet, titillate, pique, tickle your fancy **2 = plot**, scheme, manoeuvre, conspire, connive, machinate ▷ *n* **3 = plot**, scheme, conspiracy, manoeuvre, manipulation, collusion, ruse, trickery, cabal, stratagem, double-dealing, chicanery, sharp practice, wile, knavery, machination **4 = affair**, romance, intimacy, liaison, amour

introduce *vb* **1 = present**, acquaint, make known, familiarize, do the honours, make the introduction **3 = suggest**, offer, air, table, advance, propose, recommend, float, submit, bring up, put forward, set forth, ventilate, broach, moot **4 = bring in**, establish, set up, start, begin, found, develop, launch, institute, organize, pioneer, initiate, originate, commence, get going, instigate, phase in, usher in, inaugurate, set in motion, bring into being **5 = add**, insert, inject, throw in (*informal*), infuse, interpose, interpolate

introduction *n* **1 = launch**, institution, establishment, start, opening, beginning, pioneering, presentation, initiation, inauguration, induction, commencement, instigation **OPPOSITE:** elimination **2 = opening**, prelude, preface, lead-in, preliminaries, overture, preamble, foreword, prologue, intro (*informal*), commencement, opening remarks, proem, opening passage, prolegomena, prolegomenon, exordium **OPPOSITE:** conclusion

introductory *adj* **a = preliminary**, elementary, first, early, initial, inaugural, preparatory, initiatory, prefatory, precursory **OPPOSITE:** concluding **b = starting**, opening, initial, early

intruder *n* **= trespasser**, burglar, invader, squatter, prowler, interloper, infiltrator, gate-crasher (*informal*)

intrusion *n* **1a = interruption**, interference, infringement, trespass, encroachment **1b = invasion**, breach, infringement, infiltration, encroachment, infraction, usurpation

intuition *n* **a = instinct**, perception, insight, sixth sense, discernment **b = feeling**, idea, impression, suspicion, premonition, inkling, presentiment

invade *vb* **1 = attack**, storm, assault, capture, occupy, seize, raid, overwhelm, violate, conquer, overrun, annex, march into, assail, descend upon, infringe on, burst in on, make inroads on **2 = infest**, swarm, overrun, flood, infect, ravage, beset, pervade, permeate, overspread

invalid[1] *n* **1 = patient**, sufferer, convalescent, valetudinarian ▷ *adj* **2 = disabled**, challenged, ill, sick, poorly (*informal*), weak, ailing, frail, feeble, sickly, infirm, bedridden, valetudinarian

invalid[2] *adj* **1 = null and void**, void, worthless, untrue, null, not binding, inoperative, nugatory **OPPOSITE:** valid **2 = unfounded**, false, untrue,

DICTIONARY

because of illness **invalidism** *n*
WORD ORIGIN Latin *in-* not + *validus* strong
invalid² ❶ *adj* **1** having no legal force: *an invalid cheque* **2** (of an argument, result, etc.) not valid because it has been based on a mistake **invalidity** *n* **invalidly** *adv*
invalidate *vb* **-dating, -dated 1** to make or show (an argument) to be invalid **2** to take away the legal force of (a contract) **invalidation** *n*
invaluable ❶ *adj* having great value that is impossible to calculate
invariable *adj* unchanging **invariably** *adv*
invasion ❶ *n* **1** the act of invading with armed forces **2** any intrusion: *an invasion of privacy* **invasive** *adj*
invective *n* abusive speech or writing
WORD ORIGIN Late Latin *invectivus* scolding
inveigh (in-vay) *vb formal* **inveigh against** to make harsh criticisms against
WORD ORIGIN Latin *invehi*, literally: to be carried in, hence assail
inveigle *vb* **-gling, -gled** to coax or manipulate (someone) into an action or situation **inveiglement** *n*
WORD ORIGIN Old French *avogler* to blind, deceive
invent ❶ *vb* **1** to think up or create (something new) **2** to make up (a story, excuse, etc.) **inventor** *n*
WORD ORIGIN Latin *invenire* to find
invention ❶ *n* **1** something that is invented **2** the act of inventing **3** creative power; inventive skill **4** *euphemistic* a lie: *his story is a malicious invention*
inventive ❶ *adj* creative and resourceful: *her inventive use of colour*
inventory ❶ (in-ven-tree) *n, pl* **-tories 1** a detailed list of the objects in a particular place ▷ *vb* **-tories, -torying, -toried 2** to make a list of
WORD ORIGIN Medieval Latin *inventorium*
inverse *adj* **1** opposite in effect, sequence, direction, etc. **2** *maths* linking two variables in such a way that one increases as the other decreases ▷ *n* **3** the exact opposite: *the inverse of this image* **4** *maths* an inverse element
inversion *n* **1** the act of inverting or state of being inverted **2** something inverted, esp. a reversal of order, functions, etc.: *an inversion of their previous relationship* **inversive** *adj*
invert *vb* **1** to turn upside down or inside out **2** to reverse in effect, sequence, or direction ▷ *n* **3** a homosexual **invertible** *adj*
WORD ORIGIN Latin *in-* in + *vertere* to turn
invertebrate *n* **1** any animal without a backbone, such as an insect, worm, or octopus ▷ *adj* **2** of or designating invertebrates
inverted commas *pl n* ▸ same as **quotation marks**
invest ❶ *vb* **1** (often foll. by *in*) to put (money) into an enterprise with the expectation of profit **2** (often foll. by *in*) to devote (time or effort to a project) **3** to give power or authority to: *invested with the powers of government* **4** (often foll. by *in*) to install someone (in an official position) **5** (foll. by *with* or *in*) to credit or provide (a person with qualities): *he was invested with great common sense* **6** **invest in** to buy: *she invested in some barbecue equipment* **7** **invest with** *usually poetic* to cover, as if with a coat: *when spring invests the trees with leaves* **investor** *n*
WORD ORIGIN Medieval Latin *investire* to clothe
investigate ❶ *vb* **-gating, -gated** to inquire into (a situation or problem) thoroughly in order to discover the truth: *the police are currently investigating the case* **investigative** *adj* **investigator** *n*
WORD ORIGIN Latin *investigare* to search after
investigation ❶ *n* a careful search or examination in order to discover facts
investiture *n* the formal installation of a person in an office or rank
investment ❶ *n* **1** the act of investing **2** money invested **3** something in which money is invested
investment trust *n* a financial enterprise that invests its subscribed capital in a wide range of securities for its investors' benefit
inveterate *adj* **1** deep-rooted or ingrained: *an inveterate enemy of Marxism* **2** confirmed in a habit or practice: *an inveterate gambler* **inveteracy** *n*
WORD ORIGIN Latin *inveteratus* of long standing
invidious *adj* likely to cause

THESAURUS

illogical, irrational, unsound, unscientific, baseless, fallacious, ill-founded **OPPOSITE:** sound
invaluable *adj* = **precious**, valuable, priceless, costly, inestimable, beyond price, worth your *or* its weight in gold **OPPOSITE:** worthless
invasion *n* **1** = **attack**, assault, capture, takeover, raid, offensive, occupation, conquering, seizure, onslaught, foray, appropriation, sortie, annexation, incursion, expropriation, inroad, irruption, arrogation **2** = **intrusion**, breach, violation, disturbance, disruption, infringement, overstepping, infiltration, encroachment, infraction, usurpation
invent *vb* **1** = **create**, make, produce, develop, design, discover, imagine, manufacture, generate, come up with *(informal)*, coin, devise, conceive, originate, formulate, spawn, contrive, improvise, dream up *(informal)*, concoct, think up **2** = **make up**, devise, concoct, forge, fake, fabricate, feign, falsify, cook up *(informal)*, trump up
invention *n* **1** = **creation**, machine, device, design, development, instrument, discovery, innovation, gadget, brainchild *(informal)*, contraption, contrivance **2** = **development**, design, production, setting up, foundation, construction, constitution, creation, discovery, introduction, establishment, pioneering, formation, innovation, conception, masterminding, formulation, inception, contrivance, origination **3** = **creativity**, vision, imagination, initiative, enterprise, inspiration, genius, brilliance, ingenuity, originality, inventiveness, resourcefulness, creativeness, ingeniousness, imaginativeness **4** *(euphemistic)* = **fiction**, story, fantasy, lie, yarn, fabrication, concoction, falsehood, fib *(informal)*, untruth, urban myth, prevarication, tall story *(informal)*, urban legend, figment *or* product of (someone's) imagination
inventive *adj* = **creative**, original, innovative, imaginative, gifted, inspired, fertile, ingenious, groundbreaking, resourceful
OPPOSITE: uninspired
inventory *n* **1** = **list**, record, catalogue, listing, account, roll, file, schedule, register, description, log, directory, tally, roster, stock book
invest *vb* **1, 2** (often foll. by *in*) = **spend**, expend, advance, venture, put in, devote, lay out, sink in, use up, plough in **3** = **empower**, provide, charge, sanction, license, authorize, vest **6** (foll. by *in*) = **buy**, get, purchase, score *(slang)*, pay for, obtain, acquire, procure
investigate *vb* = **examine**, study, research, consider, go into, explore, search for, analyse, look into, inspect, look over, sift, probe into, work over, scrutinize, inquire into, make inquiries about, enquire into
investigation *n* = **examination**, study, inquiry, hearing, research, review, search, survey, analysis, probe, inspection, exploration, scrutiny, inquest, fact finding, recce *(slang)*
investment *n* **1** = **investing**, backing, funding, financing, contribution, speculation, transaction, expenditure, outlay **2** = **stake**, interest, share, concern, portion, ante *(informal)* **3** = **buy**, asset, acquisition, venture, risk, speculation, gamble

DICTIONARY

resentment or unpopularity
WORD ORIGIN Latin *invidia* envy
invigilate (in-vij-il-late) *vb* **-lating, -lated** *Brit* to supervise people who are sitting an examination **invigilation** *n* **invigilator** *n*
WORD ORIGIN Latin *invigilare* to watch over
invigorate *vb* **-ating, -ated** to give energy to or refresh **invigorating** *adj*
WORD ORIGIN Latin *in-* in + *vigor* vigour
invincible *adj* incapable of being defeated: *an army of invincible strength* **invincibility** *n* **invincibly** *adv*
WORD ORIGIN Latin *in-* not + *vincere* to conquer
inviolable *adj* that must not be broken or violated: *an inviolable oath* **inviolability** *n*
inviolate *adj* free from harm or injury **inviolacy** *n*
invisible ❶ *adj* **1** not able to be seen by the eye: *invisible radiation* **2** concealed from sight **3** *econ* relating to services, such as insurance and freight, rather than goods: *invisible earnings* **invisibility** *n* **invisibly** *adv*
invitation ❶ *n* **1** a request to attend a dance, meal, etc. **2** the card or paper on which an invitation is written
invite ❶ *vb* **-viting, -vited 1** to ask (a person) in a friendly or polite way (to do something, attend an event, etc.) **2** to make a request for, esp. publicly or formally: *we invite applications for six scholarships* **3** to bring on or provoke: *his theory invites disaster* **4** to tempt ▷ *n* **5** *informal* an invitation
WORD ORIGIN Latin *invitare*
inviting ❶ *adj* tempting or attractive
in vitro *adv, adj* (of biological processes or reactions) happening outside the body of the organism in an artificial environment
WORD ORIGIN New Latin, literally: in glass
invocation *n* **1** the act of invoking **2** a prayer to God or another deity asking for help, forgiveness, etc. **invocatory** *adj*
invoice *n* **1** a bill for goods and services supplied ▷ *vb* **-voicing, -voiced 2** to present (a customer) with an invoice
WORD ORIGIN Old French *envois*, plural of *envoi* message
invoke ❶ *vb* **-voking, -voked 1** to put (a law or penalty) into use: *chapter 8 of the UN charter was invoked* **2** to bring about: *the hills invoked a feeling of serenity* **3** to call on (God or another deity) for help, inspiration, etc. **4** to summon (a spirit) by uttering magic words
WORD ORIGIN Latin *invocare* to appeal to
involuntary *adj* **1** carried out without one's conscious wishes; unintentional **2** *physiol* (esp. of a movement or muscle) performed or acting without conscious control **involuntarily** *adv*
involute *adj also* **involuted 1** complex, intricate, or involved **2** rolled inwards or curled in a spiral ▷ *n* **3** *geom* the curve described by the free end of a thread as it is wound around another curve on the same plane
WORD ORIGIN Latin *involutus*
involve ❶ *vb* **-volving, -volved 1** to include as a necessary part **2** to have an effect on: *around fifty riders were involved and some were hurt* **3** to implicate: *several people were involved in the crime* **4** to make complicated: *the situation was further involved by her disappearance* **involvement** *n*
WORD ORIGIN Latin *in-* in + *volvere* to roll
involved ❶ *adj* **1** complicated **2 involved in** concerned in
invulnerable *adj* not able to be wounded or damaged **invulnerability** *n*
inward ❶ *adj* **1** directed towards the middle of something **2** situated within **3** of the mind or spirit: *inward meditation* **4** of one's own country or a specific country: *inward investment* ▷ *adv* **5** ▸ same as **inwards**
inwardly *adv* **1** within the private thoughts or feelings: *inwardly troubled, he kept smiling* **2** not aloud: *to laugh inwardly* **3** in or on the inside
inwards *or* **inward** *adv* towards the inside or middle of something
inwrought *adj* worked or woven into material, esp. decoratively
in-your-face *adj slang* aggressive and confrontational: *in-your-face advertising*
Io *chem* ionium
iodide *n chem* a compound containing an iodine atom, such as methyl iodide
iodine *n chem* a bluish-black element found in seaweed and used in medicine, photography, and dyeing. Symbol: I
WORD ORIGIN Greek *iōdēs* rust-coloured, but mistakenly derived from *ion* violet
iodize *or* **-dise** *vb* **-dizing, -dized** *or* **-dising, -dised** to treat with iodine **iodization** *or* **-disation** *n*
IOM Isle of Man
ion *n* an electrically charged atom or group of atoms formed by the loss or gain of one or more electrons
WORD ORIGIN Greek, literally: going
Ionesco *n* **Eugène** 1912–94, French dramatist, born in Romania; a leading exponent of the theatre of the absurd. His plays include *The Bald Prima Donna* (1950) and *Rhinoceros* (1960)
ion exchange *n* the process in which ions are exchanged between a solution and an insoluble solid. It is used to soften water
ionic *adj* of or in the form of ions
Ionic *adj* of a style of classical architecture characterized by fluted columns with scroll-like ornaments on the capital
ionize *or* **-ise** *vb* **-izing, -ized** *or* **-ising, -ised** to change or become changed into ions **ionization** *or* **-isation** *n*
ionosphere *n* a region of ionized layers of air in the earth's upper atmosphere, which reflects radio waves **ionospheric** *adj*
iota (eye-oh-ta) *n* **1** the ninth letter in the Greek alphabet (Ι, ι) **2** a very small amount: *I don't feel one iota of guilt*
IOU *n* a written promise or reminder to pay a debt
WORD ORIGIN representing *I owe you*

THESAURUS

invisible *adj* **1 = unseen**, imperceptible, indiscernible, unseeable, unperceivable
OPPOSITE: visible
invitation *n* **1 = request**, call, invite *(informal)*, bidding, summons
invite *vb* **1 = ask**, bid, summon, request the pleasure of (someone's) company **2 = request**, seek, look for, call for, ask for, bid for, appeal for, petition, solicit **3 = encourage**, attract, cause, draw, lead to, court, ask for *(informal)*, generate, foster, tempt, provoke, induce, bring on, solicit, engender, allure, call forth, leave the door open to
inviting *adj* **= tempting**, appealing, attractive, pleasing, welcoming, warm, engaging, fascinating, intriguing, magnetic, delightful, enticing, seductive, captivating, beguiling, alluring, mouthwatering
OPPOSITE: uninviting
invoke *vb* **1 = apply**, use, implement, call in, initiate, resort to, put into effect **3, 4 = call upon**, appeal to, pray to, petition, conjure, solicit, beseech, entreat, adjure, supplicate
involve *vb* **1 = entail**, mean, demand, require, call for, occasion, result in, imply, give rise to, encompass, necessitate
involved *adj* **1 = complicated**, complex, intricate, hard, difficult, confused, confusing, sophisticated, elaborate, tangled, bewildering, jumbled, entangled, tortuous, Byzantine, convoluted, knotty, unfathomable, labyrinthine
OPPOSITE: straightforward
inward *adj* **1 = incoming**, entering, penetrating, inbound, inflowing, ingoing, inpouring **3 = internal**, inner, private, personal, inside, secret, hidden, interior, confidential, privy, innermost, inmost
OPPOSITE: outward

DICTIONARY

IOW Isle of Wight
IP *computers* internet protocol: a code used to label packets of data sent across the internet, identifying both the sending and the receiving computers
IPA International Phonetic Alphabet
IP address *computers* internet protocol address: a unique code that identifies each computer connected to the internet
Ipatieff *n* **Vladimir Nikolaievich** 1867–1952, US physicist, born in Russia. He discovered the structure of isoprene (1897) and later developed high-octane fuels
ipecacuanha (ip-pee-kak-yew-**ann**-a) *or* **ipecac** (**ip**-pee-kak) *n* a drug made from the dried roots of a S American plant, used to cause vomiting
WORD ORIGIN S American Indian *ipekaaguéne*
iPod *n trademark* a small portable digital audio player capable of storing thousands of tracks in a variety of formats including MP3
ipso facto *adv* by that very fact or act
WORD ORIGIN Latin
IQ intelligence quotient
Iqbal *n* Sir **Muhammad** 1875–1938, Indian Muslim poet, philosopher, and political leader, who advocated the establishment of separate nations for Indian Hindus and Muslims and is generally regarded as the originator of Pakistan
Ir *chem* iridium
IRA Irish Republican Army
Iranian *adj* **1** of Iran ▹*n* **2** a person from Iran **3** a branch of the Indo-European family of languages, including Persian
Iraqi *adj* **1** of Iraq ▹*n* **2** a person from Iraq
irascible *adj* easily angered
irascibility *n* **irascibly** *adv*
WORD ORIGIN Latin *ira* anger
irate *adj* very angry
WORD ORIGIN Latin *iratus* enraged
ire *n literary* anger
WORD ORIGIN Latin *ira*
Ireland[1] *n* **1** an island off NW Europe: part of the British Isles, separated from Britain by the North Channel, the Irish Sea, and St George's Channel; contains large areas of peat bog, with mountains that rise over 900 m (3000 ft) in the southwest and several large lakes. It was conquered by England in the 16th and early 17th centuries and ruled as a dependency until 1801, when it was united with Great Britain until its division in 1921 into the Irish Free State and Northern Ireland. Latin name: **Hibernia** **2 Republic of Ireland, Irish Republic** *or* **Southern Ireland** a republic in NW Europe occupying most of Ireland: established as the Irish Free State (a British dominion) in 1921 and declared a republic in 1949; joined the European Community (now the European Union) in 1973. Official languages: Irish (Gaelic) and English. Currency: euro. Capital: Dublin. Pop: 3 999 000 (2004 est). Area: 70 285 sq km (27 137 sq miles) ▸ Gaelic name: **Eire**. ▸ See also **Northern Ireland**
Ireland[2] *n* **John** (**Nicholson**) 1879–1962, English composer, esp. of songs
Ireton *n* **Henry** 1611–51, English Parliamentarian general in the Civil War; son-in-law of Oliver Cromwell. His plan for a constitutional monarchy was rejected by Charles I (1647), whose death warrant he signed; lord deputy of Ireland (1650–51)
iridaceous (ir-rid-**day**-shuss) *adj* of or belonging to the iris family
iridescent *adj* having shimmering changing colours like a rainbow
iridescence *n*
WORD ORIGIN Latin *irid-* iris
iridium *n chem* a hard yellowish-white chemical element that occurs in platinum ores and is used as an alloy with platinum. Symbol: Ir
WORD ORIGIN Latin *irid-* iris
iris *n* **1** the coloured muscular membrane in the eye that surrounds and controls the size of the pupil **2** a tall plant with long pointed leaves and large flowers
WORD ORIGIN Greek: rainbow
Irish *adj* **1** of Ireland ▹*n* **2** ▸ same as **Irish Gaelic** **3** the dialect of English spoken in Ireland ▹*pl n* **4 the Irish** the people of Ireland
Irish coffee *n* hot coffee mixed with Irish whiskey and topped with double cream
Irish Gaelic *n* the Celtic language of Ireland
Irishman *or fem* **Irishwoman** *n, pl* **-men** *or fem* **-women** a person from Ireland
Irish moss *n* ▸ same as **carrageen**
irk *vb* to irritate or vex
WORD ORIGIN Middle English *irken* to grow weary
irksome *adj* annoying or tiresome
iron ❶ *n* **1** a strong silvery-white metallic element, widely used for structural and engineering purposes. Symbol: Fe **2** a tool made of iron **3** a small electrically heated device with a weighted flat bottom for pressing clothes **4** *golf* a club with an angled metal head **5** a splintlike support for a malformed leg **6** great strength or resolve: *a will of iron* **7 strike while the iron is hot** to act at a suitable moment ▹*adj* **8** made of iron **9** very hard or merciless: *iron determination* **10** very strong: *an iron constitution* ▹*vb* **11** to smooth (clothes or fabric) by removing (creases) with an iron ▸ See also **iron out, irons**
WORD ORIGIN Old English *īren*
Iron Age *n* a phase of human culture that began in the Middle East about 1100 BC, during which iron tools and weapons were used
ironbark *n* an Australian eucalyptus with hard rough bark
ironclad *adj* **1** covered or protected with iron: *an ironclad warship* **2** unable to be contradicted: *ironclad proof* ▹*n* **3** *history* a large wooden 19th-century warship with armoured plating
Iron Curtain *n* (formerly) the guarded border between the countries of the Soviet bloc and the rest of Europe
ironic ❶ *or* **ironical** *adj* of, characterized by, or using irony
ironically *adv*
ironing *n* clothes to be ironed
ironing board *n* a narrow cloth-covered board, usually with folding legs, on which to iron clothes
iron lung *n* an airtight metal cylinder enclosing the entire body up to the neck and providing artificial respiration
iron maiden *n* a medieval instrument of torture, consisting of a hinged case (often shaped in the form of a woman) lined with iron spikes
ironmaster *n Brit history* a manufacturer of iron
ironmonger *n Brit* a shopkeeper or shop dealing in hardware
ironmongery *n*
iron out ❶ *vb* to settle (a problem or difficulty) through negotiation or discussion
iron pyrites *n* ▸ same as **pyrite**
iron rations *pl n* emergency food

THESAURUS

iron *modifier* **8 = ferrous**, ferric, irony ▹*adj* **9, 10 = inflexible**, hard, strong, tough, steel, rigid, adamant, unconditional, steely, implacable, indomitable, unyielding, immovable, unbreakable, unbending, obdurate
OPPOSITE: weak

ironic *or* **ironical** *adj* **a = sarcastic**, dry, sharp, acid, bitter, stinging, mocking, sneering, scoffing, wry, scathing, satirical, tongue-in-cheek, sardonic, caustic, double-edged, acerbic, trenchant, mordant, mordacious **b = paradoxical**, absurd, contradictory, puzzling, baffling, ambiguous, inconsistent, confounding, enigmatic, illogical, incongruous

iron out = settle, resolve, sort out, eliminate, get rid of, reconcile, clear up, simplify, unravel, erase, eradicate, put right, straighten out, harmonize, expedite, smooth over

DICTIONARY

supplies, esp. for military personnel in action

irons *pl n* **1** fetters or chains **2 have several irons in the fire** to have several projects or plans at once

Irons *n* **Jeremy** born 1948, British film and stage actor. His films include *The French Lieutenant's Woman* (1981), *The Mission* (1986), *Reversal of Fortune* (1990), and *Lolita* (1997)

Ironside *n* nickname of Edmund II of England ▸ See **Edmund II**

ironstone *n* **1** any rock consisting mainly of iron ore **2** a tough durable earthenware

ironwood *n* **1** any of various trees, such as hornbeam, with exceptionally hard wood **2** the wood of any of these trees

ironwork *n* work done in iron, esp. decorative work

ironworks *n* a building in which iron is smelted, cast, or wrought

irony ⊙ *n, pl* **-nies 1** the mildly sarcastic use of words to imply the opposite of what they normally mean **2** a situation or result that is the direct opposite of what was expected or intended
WORD ORIGIN Greek *eirōneia*

irradiate *vb* **-ating, -ated 1** *physics* to subject to or treat with light or other electromagnetic radiation **2** to make clear or bright intellectually or spiritually **3** to light up; illuminate **irradiation** *n*

irrational ⊙ *adj* **1** not based on logical reasoning **2** incapable of reasoning **3** *maths* (of an equation or expression) involving radicals or fractional exponents **irrationality** *n* **irrationally** *adv*

irrational number *n maths* any real number that cannot be expressed as the ratio of two integers, such as π

irreconcilable *adj* not able to be resolved or settled: *irreconcilable differences* **irreconcilability** *n*

irrecoverable *adj* not able to be recovered

irredeemable *adj* **1** not able to be reformed, improved, or corrected **2** (of bonds or shares) not able to be bought back directly or paid off **3** (of paper money) not able to be converted into coin **irredeemably** *adv*

irredentist *n* a person in favour of seizing territory that was once part of his or her country **irredentism** *n*
WORD ORIGIN Italian *irredenta* unredeemed

irreducible *adj* impossible to put in a reduced or simpler form **irreducibility** *n*

irrefutable *adj* impossible to deny or disprove

irregular ⊙ *adj* **1** uneven in shape, position, arrangement, etc. **2** not conforming to accepted practice or routine **3** (of a word) not following the usual pattern of formation in a language **4** not occurring at expected or equal intervals: *an irregular pulse* **5** (of troops) not belonging to regular forces ▹ *n* **6** a soldier not in a regular army **irregularity** *n* **irregularly** *adv*

irrelevant ⊙ *adj* not connected with the matter in hand **irrelevance** *or* **irrelevancy** *n*

irreligious *adj* **1** lacking religious faith **2** indifferent or opposed to religion

irremediable *adj* not able to be improved or cured

irremovable *adj* not able to be removed **irremovably** *adv*

irreparable *adj* not able to be repaired or put right: *irreparable damage to his reputation* **irreparably** *adv*

irreplaceable *adj* impossible to replace: *acres of irreplaceable moorland were devastated*

irrepressible *adj* not capable of being repressed, controlled, or restrained **irrepressibility** *n* **irrepressibly** *adv*

irreproachable *adj* blameless or faultless **irreproachability** *n*

irresistible ⊙ *adj* **1** not able to be resisted or refused: *irresistible pressure from the financial markets* **2** extremely attractive: *an irresistible woman* **irresistibility** *n* **irresistibly** *adv*

irresolute *adj* unable to make decisions **irresolution** *n*

irrespective *adj* **irrespective of** without taking account of

irresponsible ⊙ *adj* **1** not showing or done with due care for the consequences of one's actions or attitudes; reckless **2** not capable of accepting responsibility **irresponsibility** *n* **irresponsibly** *adv*

irretrievable *adj* impossible to put right or make good **irretrievability** *n* **irretrievably** *adv*

irreverence *n* **1** lack of due respect **2** a disrespectful remark or act **irreverent** *adj*

irreversible *adj* not able to be reversed or put right again: *irreversible loss of memory* **irreversibly** *adv*

irrevocable *adj* not possible to change or undo **irrevocably** *adv*

irrigate *vb* **-gating, -gated 1** to supply (land) with water through ditches or pipes in order to encourage the growth of crops **2** *med* to bathe (a wound or part of the body) **irrigation** *n* **irrigator** *n*
WORD ORIGIN Latin *irrigare*

irritable *adj* **1** easily annoyed or angered **2** *pathol* abnormally sensitive **3** *biol* (of all living organisms) capable of responding to such stimuli as heat, light, and touch **irritability** *n*

irritant *n* **1** something that annoys or irritates **2** a substance that causes a part of the body to become tender or inflamed ▹ *adj* **3** causing irritation

irritate ⊙ *vb* **-tating, -tated 1** to annoy or anger (someone) **2** *pathol*

THESAURUS

irony *n* **1 = sarcasm**, mockery, ridicule, bitterness, scorn, satire, cynicism, derision, causticity, mordancy **2 = paradox**, ambiguity, absurdity, incongruity, contrariness

irrational *adj* **1 = illogical**, crazy, silly, absurd, foolish, unreasonable, unwise, preposterous, idiotic, nonsensical, unsound, unthinking, injudicious, unreasoning **OPPOSITE:** rational

irregular *adj* **1 = uneven**, broken, rough, twisted, twisting, curving, pitted, ragged, crooked, unequal, jagged, bumpy, lumpy, serpentine, contorted, lopsided, craggy, indented, asymmetrical, serrated, holey, unsymmetrical **OPPOSITE:** even **2 = inappropriate**, unconventional, improper, unethical, odd, unusual, extraordinary, disorderly, exceptional, peculiar, unofficial, abnormal, queer, rum *(Brit slang)*, back-door, unsuitable, unorthodox, out-of-order, unprofessional, anomalous **4 = variable**, inconsistent, erratic, shifting, occasional, random, casual, shaky, wavering, uneven, fluctuating, eccentric, patchy, sporadic, intermittent, haphazard, unsteady, desultory, fitful, spasmodic, unsystematic, inconstant, nonuniform, unmethodical, scattershot **OPPOSITE:** steady **5 = unofficial**, underground, guerrilla, volunteer, resistance, partisan, rogue, paramilitary, mercenary

irrelevant *adj* **= unconnected**, unrelated, unimportant, inappropriate, peripheral, insignificant, negligible, immaterial, extraneous, beside the point, impertinent, neither here nor there, inapplicable, inapt, inapposite, inconsequent **OPPOSITE:** relevant

irresistible *adj* **1 = overwhelming**, compelling, overpowering, urgent, potent, imperative, compulsive, uncontrollable, overmastering

irresponsible *adj* **1 = thoughtless**, reckless, careless, wild, unreliable, giddy, untrustworthy, flighty, ill-considered, good-for-nothing, shiftless, harebrained, undependable, harum-scarum, scatterbrained, featherbrained **OPPOSITE:** responsible

irritate *vb* **1 = annoy**, anger, bother, provoke, offend, needle *(informal)*,

DICTIONARY

to cause (an organ or part of the body) to become inflamed or tender **3** *biol* to stimulate (an organ) to respond in a characteristic manner
irritation *n*
WORD ORIGIN Latin *irritare* to provoke

irrupt *vb* to enter forcibly or suddenly
irruption *n* **irruptive** *adj*
WORD ORIGIN Latin *irrumpere*

Irvine[1] *n* a town on the W coast of Scotland, the administrative centre of North Ayrshire: designated a new town in 1966. Pop: 33 090 (2001)

Irvine[2] *n* **Alexander Andrew Mackay,** Baron, known as *Derry.* born 1940, British lawyer and Labour politician; Lord Chancellor (1997–2003)

Irving *n* **1** Sir **Henry** real name *John Henry Brodribb.* 1838–1905, English actor and manager of the Lyceum Theatre in London (1878–1902) **2 Washington** 1783–1859, US essayist and short-story writer, noted for *The Sketch Book of Geoffrey Crayon* (1820), which contains the stories *Rip Van Winkle* and *The Legend of Sleepy Hollow*

Irwin *n* **Steve,** full name *Stephen Robert Irwin*, known as 'The Crocodile Hunter'. 1962–2006, Australian zoologist, environmentalist and maker of television wildlife documentaries; died following wounding by a stingray

is *vb* ▸ third person singular of the present tense of **be**
WORD ORIGIN Old English

ISA (eye-sa) *n* (in Britain) individual savings account

Isabella[1] *or* **Isabel** *n* **a** a greyish-yellow colour **b** Also: **Isabelline** (*as adjective*): *an Isabella mohair coat*
WORD ORIGIN C17: from the name *Isabella*; original reference uncertain

Isabella[2] *n* original name *Elizabeth Farnese.* 1692–1766, second wife (1714–46) of Philip V of Spain and mother of Charles III of Spain

Isabella II *n* 1830–1904, queen of Spain (1833–68), whose accession precipitated the first Carlist war (1833–39). She was deposed in a revolution

Isabella of France *n* 1292–1358, wife (1308–27) of Edward II of England, whom, aided by her lover, Roger de Mortimer, she deposed; mother of Edward III

isallobar (ice-**sal**-oh-bar) *n* a line on a map connecting places with equal pressure changes
WORD ORIGIN Greek *isos* equal + *allos* other + *baros* weight

ISBN International Standard Book Number

Isherwood *n* **Christopher,** full name *Christopher William Bradshaw-Isherwood.* 1904–86, US novelist and dramatist, born in England. His works include the novel *Goodbye to Berlin* (1939) and three verse plays written in collaboration with W.H. Auden

Ishiguro *n* **Kazuo** born 1954, British novelist, born in Japan. His novels include *An Artist of the Floating World* (1986), the Booker-prizewinning *The Remains of the Day* (1989), and *Never Let Me Go* (2005)

Isidore of Seville *n* **Saint,** Latin name *Isidorus Hispalensis.* ?560–636 AD, Spanish archbishop and scholar, noted for his *Etymologies*, an encyclopedia. Feast day: April 4

isinglass (ize-ing-glass) *n* **1** a gelatine made from the air bladders of freshwater fish **2** ▸ same as **mica**
WORD ORIGIN Middle Dutch *huysenblase* sturgeon bladder

Isis *n* an Egyptian fertility goddess

Iskander Bey *n* the Turkish name for **Scanderbeg**

Isl. **1** Island **2** Isle

Islam *n* **1** the Muslim religion teaching that there is only one God and that Mohammed is his prophet **2** Muslim countries and civilization
Islamic *adj* **Islamist** *adj, n*
WORD ORIGIN Arabic: surrender (to God)

island ❶ *n* **1** a piece of land that is completely surrounded by water **2** something isolated, detached, or surrounded **3** ▸ see **traffic island**
▸ Related adjective: **insular**
WORD ORIGIN Old English *īgland*

islander *n* **1** a person who lives on an island **2** **Islander** NZ a Pacific Islander

isle *n* (except when part of a place name) a poetic name for an island

islet *n* a small island

ism *n informal, often used to show contempt* a doctrine, system, or practice, esp. one whose name ends in *-ism*, such as *communism* or *fascism*

-ism *suffix* **1** indicating a political or religious belief: *socialism; judaism* **2** indicating a characteristic quality: *heroism* **3** indicating an action: *exorcism* **4** indicating prejudice on the basis specified: *sexism*

Ismail Pasha *n* 1830–95, viceroy (1863–66) and khedive (1867–79) of Egypt, who brought his country close to bankruptcy. He was forced to submit to Anglo-French financial control (1876) and to abdicate (1879)

isn't is not

iso- *or before a vowel* **is-** *combining form* equal or identical: *isomagnetic*
WORD ORIGIN Greek *isos* equal

isobar (ice-oh-bar) *n* **1** a line on a map connecting places of equal atmospheric pressure **2** *physics* any of two or more atoms that have the same mass number but different atomic numbers **isobaric** *adj*
isobarism *n*
WORD ORIGIN Greek *isobarēs* of equal weight

isochronal *or* **isochronous** *adj* **1** equal in length of time **2** occurring at equal time intervals **isochronism** *n*
WORD ORIGIN Greek *isos* equal + *khronos* time

Isocrates *n* 436–338 BC, Athenian rhetorician and teacher

isohel *n* a line on a map connecting places with an equal period of sunshine
WORD ORIGIN Greek *isos* equal + *hēlios* sun

isohyet (ice-oh-**hie**-it) *n* a line on a map connecting places having equal rainfall
WORD ORIGIN Greek *isos* equal + *huetos* rain

isolate ❶ *vb* **-lating, -lated** **1** to place apart or alone **2** *chem* to obtain (a substance) in an uncombined form **3** *med* to quarantine (a person or animal) with a contagious disease
isolation *n*
WORD ORIGIN Latin *insulatus*, literally: made into an island

THESAURUS

harass, infuriate, aggravate (*informal*), incense, fret, enrage, gall, ruffle, inflame, exasperate, nettle, pester, vex, irk, pique, rankle with, get under your skin (*informal*), get on your nerves (*informal*), nark (*Brit, Austral & NZ slang*), drive you up the wall (*slang*), rub you up the wrong way (*informal*), get your goat (*slang*), try your patience, get in your hair (*informal*), get on your wick (*informal*), get your dander up (*informal*), raise your hackles, get your back up, get your hackles up, put your back up, hack you off (*informal*)
OPPOSITE: placate
2 (*pathology*) **= inflame**, pain, rub, scratch, scrape, grate, graze, fret, gall, chafe, abrade

island *n* **1 = isle**, inch (*Scot & Irish*), atoll, holm (*dialect*), islet, ait *or* eyot (*dialect*), cay *or* key

isolate *vb* **1 = separate**, break up, cut off, detach, split up, insulate, segregate, disconnect, divorce, sequester, set apart, disunite, estrange **3** (*medical*) **= quarantine**, separate, exclude, cut off, detach, keep in solitude

issue *n* **1 = topic**, point, matter, problem, business, case, question, concern, subject, affair, argument, theme, controversy, can of worms (*informal*) **2 = point**, question, concern, bone of contention, matter of contention, point in question **3 = edition**, printing, copy, impression, publication, number, instalment, imprint, version **5** (*law*) **= children**, young, offspring, babies, kids (*informal*), seed (*chiefly biblical*), successors, heirs,

DICTIONARY

isomer (ice-oh-mer) *n chem* a substance whose molecules contain the same atoms as another but in a different arrangement **isomeric** *adj*

isometric *adj* **1** having equal dimensions or measurements **2** *physiol* relating to muscular contraction that does not produce shortening of the muscle **3** (of a three-dimensional drawing) having the three axes equally inclined and all lines drawn to scale **isometrically** *adv*
WORD ORIGIN Greek *isometria* equal measurement

isometrics *n* a system of isometric exercises

isomorphism *n* **1** *biol* similarity of form, as in different generations of the same life cycle **2** *chem* the existence of two or more substances of different composition in a similar crystalline form **3** *maths* a one-to-one correspondence between the elements of two or more sets **isomorph** *n* **isomorphic** *or* **isomorphous** *adj*

isosceles triangle (ice-soss-ill-eez) *n* a triangle with two sides of equal length
WORD ORIGIN Greek *isos* equal + *skelos* leg

isotherm (ice-oh-therm) *n* a line on a map linking places of equal temperature
WORD ORIGIN Greek *isos* equal + *thermē* heat

isotonic *adj* **1** *physiol* (of two or more muscles) having equal tension **2** (of a drink) designed to replace the fluid and salts lost from the body during exercise

isotope (ice-oh-tope) *n* one of two or more atoms with the same number of protons in the nucleus but a different number of neutrons **isotopic** *adj* **isotopy** *n*
WORD ORIGIN Greek *isos* equal + *topos* place

isotropic *or* **isotropous** *adj* having uniform physical properties, such as elasticity or conduction in all directions **isotropy** *n*

ISP internet service provider: a business providing its customers with connection to the internet

Israeli *adj* **1** of Israel ▹ *n, pl* **-lis** *or* **-li** **2** a person from Israel

Israelite *n bible* a member of the ethnic group claiming descent from Jacob; a Hebrew

Isserlis *n* **Steven** (**John**) born 1958, British cellist

Issigonis *n* Sir **Alec** (**Arnold Constantine**) 1906–88, British car designer born in Smyrna. He is noted for his designs for the Morris Minor (1948) and the Mini (1959)

issue ❶ *n* **1** a topic of interest or discussion **2** an important subject requiring a decision **3** a particular edition of a magazine or newspaper **4** a consequence or result **5** *law* the descendants of a person **6** the act of sending or giving out something **7** the act of emerging; outflow **8** something flowing out, such as a river **9** **at issue** **a** under discussion **b** in disagreement **10** **force the issue** to compel decision on some matter **11** **join issue** to join in controversy **12** **take issue** to disagree ▹ *vb* **-suing, -sued** **13** to make (a statement, etc.) publicly **14** to supply officially (with) **15** to send out or distribute **16** to publish **17** to come forth or emerge **issuable** *adj*
WORD ORIGIN Old French *eissue* way out

isthmus (iss-muss) *n* a narrow strip of land connecting two relatively large land areas
WORD ORIGIN Greek *isthmos*

it *pron* **1** refers to a nonhuman, animal, plant, or inanimate thing, or sometimes to a small baby **2** refers to something unspecified or implied or to a previous or understood clause, phrase, or word: *I knew it* **3** used to represent human life or experience in respect of the present situation: *how's it going?* **4** used as the subject of impersonal verbs: *it is snowing; it's Friday* **5** *informal* the crucial or ultimate point: *the steering failed and I thought that was it* ▹ *n* **6** *informal* **a** sexual intercourse **b** sex appeal **7** a desirable quality or ability
WORD ORIGIN Old English *hit*

IT information technology

ITA initial teaching alphabet: a partly phonetic alphabet used to teach reading

Italian *adj* **1** of Italy ▹ *n* **2** a person from Italy **3** the official language of Italy and one of the official languages of Switzerland

Italianate *adj* Italian in style or character

italic *adj* **1** of a style of printing type in which the characters slant to the right ▹ *pl n* **2** **italics** italic type or print, used for emphasis
WORD ORIGIN Latin *Italicus* of Italy (where it was first used)

italicize *or* **-cise** *vb* **-cizing, -cized** *or* **-cising, -cised** to print (text) in italic type **italicization** *or* **-cisation** *n*

itch ❶ *n* **1** a skin irritation causing a desire to scratch **2** a restless desire **3** any skin disorder, such as scabies, characterized by intense itching ▹ *vb* **4** to feel an irritating or tickling sensation **5** to have a restless desire (to do something): *they were itching to join the fight*
WORD ORIGIN Old English *gīccean* to itch

itchy *adj* **itchier, itchiest** **1** having an itch **2** **have itchy feet** to have a desire to travel **itchiness** *n*

it'd it would *or* it had

item ❶ *n* **1** a single thing in a list or collection **2** a piece of information: *a news item* **3** *book-keeping* an entry in an account **4** *informal* a couple
WORD ORIGIN Latin: in like manner

itemize *or* **-ise** *vb* **-izing, -ized** *or* **-ising, -ised** to put on a list or make a list of **itemization** *or* **-isation** *n*

iterate *vb* **-ating, -ated** to say or do again **iteration** *n* **iterative** *adj*
WORD ORIGIN Latin *iterum* again

itinerant *adj* **1** working for a short time in various places ▹ *n* **2** an itinerant worker or other person
WORD ORIGIN Latin *iter* a journey

itinerary ❶ *n, pl* **-aries** **1** a detailed plan of a journey **2** a record of a journey **3** a guidebook for travellers

-itis *suffix forming nouns* indicating inflammation of a specified part: *tonsillitis*
WORD ORIGIN Greek *-itēs* belonging to

it'll it will *or* it shall

Ito *n* Prince **Hirobumi** 1841–1909, Japanese statesman; premier (1884–88; 1892–96; 1898; 1900–01). He led the movement to modernize Japan and helped to draft the Meiji constitution (1889); assassinated

its *adj* **1** of or belonging to it: *its left rear*

THESAURUS

descendants, progeny, scions
OPPOSITE: parents
12 take issue (foll. by *with*) **= disagree with**, question, challenge, oppose, dispute, object to, argue with, take exception to, raise an objection to ▹ *vb* **13, 15, 16 = give out**, release, publish, announce, deliver, spread, broadcast, distribute, communicate, proclaim, put out, circulate, emit, impart, disseminate, promulgate, put in circulation

itch *n* **1 = irritation**, tingling, prickling, itchiness **2 = desire**, longing, craving, passion, yen (*informal*), hunger, lust, yearning, hankering, restlessness ▹ *vb* **4 = prickle**, tickle, tingle, crawl **5 = long**, ache, crave, burn, pine, pant, hunger, lust, yearn, hanker

item *n* **1a = article**, thing, object, piece, unit, component **1b = matter**, point, issue, case, question, concern, detail, subject, feature, particular, affair, aspect, entry, theme, consideration, topic **2 = report**, story, piece, account, note, feature, notice, article, paragraph, bulletin, dispatch, communiqué, write-up

itinerary *n* **1 = schedule**, line, programme, tour, route, journey, circuit, timetable

wheel; I can see its logical consequence ▷ *pron* **2** something belonging to it: *its is over there*

it's it is *or* it has

itself *pron* **1 a** the reflexive form of *it*: *the cat scratched itself* **b** used for emphasis: *even the money itself won't convince me* **2** its normal or usual self: *my parrot doesn't seem itself these days*

Itúrbide *n* **Agustín de** 1783–1824, Mexican nationalist and emperor (1822–23). He was forced to abdicate and later executed

ITV (in Britain) Independent Television

IUD intrauterine device: a coil-shaped contraceptive fitted into the womb

Ivan III *n* known as *Ivan the Great*. 1440–1505, grand duke of Muscovy (1462–1505). He expanded Muscovy, defeated the Tatars (1480), and assumed the title of Ruler of all Russia (1472)

I've I have

Ives *n* **1 Charles Edward** 1874–1954, US composer, noted for his innovative use of polytonality, polyrhythms, and quarter tones. His works include *Second Piano Sonata: Concord* (1915), five symphonies, chamber music, and songs **2 Frederick Eugene** 1856–1937, US inventor of halftone photography

IVF in vitro fertilization

ivories *pl n slang* **1** the keys of a piano **2** the teeth **3** dice

ivory *n, pl* **-ries 1** a hard smooth creamy white type of bone that makes up a major part of the tusks of elephants ▷ *adj* **2** yellowish-white **ivory-like** *adj*
WORD ORIGIN Latin *ebur*

Ivory *n* **James** born 1928, US film director. With the producer Ismael Merchant, his films include *Shakespeare Wallah* (1964), *Heat and Dust* (1983), *A Room With a View* (1986), and *The Golden Bowl* (2000)

ivory tower *n* remoteness from the realities of everyday life **ivory-towered** *adj*

IVR International Vehicle Registration

ivy *n, pl* **ivies 1** a woody climbing or trailing plant with evergreen leaves and black berry-like fruits **2** any of various other climbing or creeping plants, such as the poison ivy
WORD ORIGIN Old English *īfig*

iwi (ee-wee) *n* NZ a Māori tribe
WORD ORIGIN Māori

ixia *n* a southern African plant of the iris family with showy ornamental funnel-shaped flowers
WORD ORIGIN Greek *ixos* mistletoe

Iyeyasu *or* **Ieyasu** *n* **Tokugawa** 1542–1616, Japanese general and statesman; founder of the Tokugawa shogunate (1603–1867)

Izetbegović *n* **Alija** 1925–2003, Bosnia and Herzegovinian politician: president (1992–2000), he led the country to independence and during the subsequent civil war

J joule(s)

ja *interj S African* yes

jab ❶ *vb* **jabbing, jabbed 1** to poke sharply ▹*n* **2** a quick short punch **3** *informal* an injection: *a flu jab* **4** a sharp poke
WORD ORIGIN variant of *job*

jabber *vb* **1** to speak very quickly and excitedly; chatter ▹*n* **2** quick excited chatter
WORD ORIGIN imitative

Jabir ibn Hayyan *n* ?721–?815. Arab alchemist, whose many works enjoyed enormous esteem among later alchemists, such as Geber

jabiru *n* a large white-and-black Australian stork

jacaranda *n* a tropical American tree with sweet-smelling wood and pale purple flowers
WORD ORIGIN from a Native American langauge

jack *n* **1** a mechanical device used to raise a motor vehicle or other heavy object **2** a playing card with a picture of a pageboy on it **3** *bowls* a small white ball at which the players aim their bowls **4** *electrical engineering* a socket into which a plug can be inserted **5** a flag flown at the bow of a ship, showing nationality **6** one of the pieces used in the game of jacks **7 every man jack** everyone without exception ▸See also **jack in, jacks, jack up**
WORD ORIGIN from short form of *John*

jackal *n* a doglike wild animal of Africa and Asia, which feeds on the decaying flesh of dead animals
WORD ORIGIN Persian *shagāl*

jackanapes *n Brit* a mischievous child
WORD ORIGIN literally: Jack of the ape, nickname of first Duke of Suffolk, whose badge showed an ape's ball and chain

jackaroo, jackeroo *n, pl* **-roos** *Austral* a trainee on a sheep station
WORD ORIGIN from *jack* man + *(kang) aroo*

jackass *n* **1** a fool **2** a male donkey **3 laughing jackass** ▸same as **kookaburra**
WORD ORIGIN *jack* (male) + *ass*

jackboot *n* **1** a leather military boot reaching up to the knee **2** brutal and authoritarian rule

jackdaw *n* a large black-and-grey crowlike bird of Europe and Asia
WORD ORIGIN *jack* + *daw*, obsolete name for jackdaw

jacket *n* **1** a short coat with a front opening and long sleeves **2** the skin of a potato **3** ▸same as **dust jacket**
WORD ORIGIN Old French *jaquet*

jacket potato *n* a potato baked in its skin

Jack Frost *n* frost represented as a person

jack in *vb Brit slang* to abandon (an attempt or enterprise)

jack-in-the-box *n* a toy consisting of a box containing a figure on a compressed spring, which jumps out when the lid is opened

jackknife *vb* **-knifing, -knifed 1** (of an articulated lorry) to go out of control in such a way that the trailer swings round at a sharp angle to the cab ▹*n, pl* **-knives 2** a knife with a blade that can be folded into the handle **3** a dive in which the diver bends at the waist in midair

Jacklin *n* **Tony**, full name *Anthony Jacklin.* born 1944, English golfer: won the British Open Championship (1969) and the US Open Championship (1970)

jack of all trades *n, pl* **jacks of all trades** a person who can do many different kinds of work; handyman

jackpot ❶ *n* **1** the most valuable prize that can be won in a gambling game **2 hit the jackpot** *informal* to be very fortunate or very successful
WORD ORIGIN probably from *jack* (playing card)

jack rabbit *n* a hare of W North America with very long hind legs and large ears
WORD ORIGIN *jackass-rabbit*, referring to its long ears

jacks *n* a game in which metal, bone, or plastic pieces are thrown and then picked up between throws of a small ball
WORD ORIGIN *jackstones*, variant of *checkstones* pebbles

Jack Tar *n chiefly literary* a sailor

jack up *vb* **1** to raise (a motor vehicle) with a jack **2** to increase (prices or salaries) **3** *NZ informal* to organize something through unorthodox channels ▹*n* **jack-up 4** *NZ informal* something achieved dishonestly

Jacobean (jak-a-bee-an) *adj* of or in the reign of James I of England and Ireland (1603–25)
WORD ORIGIN Latin *Jacobus* James

Jacobi *n* **1** Sir **Derek (George)**. born 1938, British actor **2 Karl Gustav Jacob.** 1804–51, German mathematician. Independently of N. H. Abel, he discovered elliptic functions (1829). He also made important contributions to the study of determinants and differential equations

Jacobite *n history* a supporter of James II and his descendants
WORD ORIGIN Latin *Jacobus* James

Jacobsen *n* **Arne** 1902–71, Danish architect and designer. His buildings include the Town Hall at Rodovre (1955)

Jacopo della Quercia *n* ?1374–1438, Italian Renaissance sculptor: best known for his marble reliefs of scenes from Genesis around the portal of S. Petronio, Bologna (1425–35)

Jacquard (jak-ard) *n* a fabric with an intricate design incorporated into the weave
WORD ORIGIN after J. M. *Jacquard*, its inventor

Jacuzzi (jak-oo-zee) *n trademark* a large circular bath with a mechanism that swirls the water

jade *n* **1** an ornamental semiprecious stone, usually green in colour ▹*adj* **2** bluish-green
WORD ORIGIN obsolete Spanish *piedra de ijada* colic stone, because it was believed to cure colic

jaded *adj* tired or bored from overindulgence or overwork

Jaffa *n Brit* a large thick-skinned orange
WORD ORIGIN after *Jaffa*, port in W Israel

jag¹ *n Scot informal* ▸same as **jab** (sense 3)
WORD ORIGIN origin unknown

jag² *n slang* a period of uncontrolled indulgence in an activity: *all-night crying jags*
WORD ORIGIN origin unknown

jagged (jag-gid) *adj* having an uneven edge with sharp points
WORD ORIGIN from *jag* a sharp point

jaguar *n* a large wild cat of south and central America, with a spotted coat
WORD ORIGIN from S American Indian

jail ❶ *or* **gaol** *n* **1** a prison ▹*vb* **2** to confine in prison
WORD ORIGIN Old French *jaiole* cage

jailbird *n informal* a person who is

THESAURUS

jab *vb* **1 = poke**, dig, punch, thrust, tap, stab, nudge, prod, lunge ▹*n* **4 = poke**, dig, punch, thrust, tap, stab, nudge, prod, lunge

jackpot *n* **1 = prize**, winnings, award, pool, reward, pot, kitty, bonanza, pot of gold at the end of the rainbow

jail *n* **1 = prison**, penitentiary *(US)*, jailhouse *(Southern US)*, penal institution, can *(slang)*, inside, cooler *(slang)*, confinement, dungeon, clink *(slang)*, glasshouse *(military informal)*, brig *(chiefly US)*, borstal, calaboose *(US informal)*, choky *(slang)*, pound, nick *(Brit slang)*, stir *(slang)*, jug *(slang)*,

DICTIONARY

or has often been in jail
jailer *or* **gaoler** *n* a person in charge of a jail
jake *adj* **she's jake** *Austral & NZ slang* it is all right
WORD ORIGIN probably from the name *Jake*
Jakobson *n* **Roman** (**Osipovič**) 1896–1982, US linguist, born in Russia. His publications include *Children's Speech* (1941) and *Fundamentals of Language* (1956)
jalopy (jal-lop-ee) *n, pl* **-lopies** *informal* a dilapidated old car
WORD ORIGIN origin unknown
jam[1] ❶ *vb* **jamming, jammed 1** to wedge (an object) into a tight space or against another object: *the table was jammed against the wall* **2** to fill (a place) with people or vehicles: *the surrounding roads were jammed for miles* **3** to make or become stuck or locked: *the window was jammed open* **4** *radio* to prevent the clear reception of (radio communications) by transmitting other signals on the same wavelength **5** *slang* to play in a jam session **6** **jam on the brakes** to apply the brakes of a vehicle very suddenly ▷ *n* **7** a situation where a large number of people or vehicles are crowded into a place: *a traffic jam* **8** *informal* a difficult situation: *you are in a bit of a jam* **9** ▸ same as **jam session**
WORD ORIGIN probably imitative
jam[2] *n* a food made from fruit boiled with sugar until the mixture sets, used for spreading on bread
WORD ORIGIN perhaps from JAM[1] (the act of squeezing)
Jamaican *adj* **1** of Jamaica ▷ *n* **2** a person from Jamaica
jamb *n* a side post of a doorframe or window frame
WORD ORIGIN Old French *jambe* leg, jamb
jamboree *n* a large gathering or celebration
WORD ORIGIN origin unknown
James III *n* 1451–88, king of Scotland (1460–88), son of James II
Jameson *n* Sir **Leander Starr** 1853–1917, British administrator in South Africa, who led an expedition into the Transvaal in 1895 in an unsuccessful attempt to topple its Boer regime (the **Jameson Raid**); prime minister of Cape Colony (1904–08)
James V *n* 1512–42, king of Scotland (1513–42), son of James IV
jammy *adj* **-mier, -miest 1** covered with or tasting like jam **2** *Brit slang* lucky: *jammy so-and-sos!*
jam-packed *adj* filled to capacity
jam session *n slang* an improvised performance by jazz or rock musicians
WORD ORIGIN probably from JAM[1]
Jan. January
Janáček *n* **Leoš** 1854–1928, Czech composer. His music is influenced by Czech folksong and speech rhythms and is remarkable for its integration of melody and language. His works include the operas *Jenufa* (1904) and *The Cunning Little Vixen* (1924), the *Glagolitic Mass* (1927), as well as orchestral and chamber music and songs
jandal *n NZ* a rubber-soled sandal attached to the foot by a thong between the big toe and the next toe
Janet *n* **Pierre Marie Félix** 1859–1947, French psychologist and neurologist, noted particularly for his work on the origins of hysteria
jangle *vb* **-gling, -gled 1** to make a harsh unpleasant ringing noise **2** to produce an irritating or unpleasant effect on: *the caffeine in coffee can jangle the nerves*
WORD ORIGIN Old French *jangler*
janitor *n chiefly Scot, US & Canad* the caretaker of a school or other building
WORD ORIGIN Latin: doorkeeper
janjaweed, janjawid (jan-juh-weed) *n* an armed tribal militia group in the Darfur region of Sudan
WORD ORIGIN Arabic
January *n* the first month of the year
WORD ORIGIN Latin *Januarius*
japan *n* **1** a glossy black lacquer, originally from the Orient, which is used on wood or metal ▷ *vb* **-panning, -panned 2** to varnish with japan
Japanese *adj* **1** of Japan ▷ *n* **2** *pl* **-nese** a person from Japan **3** the language of Japan
jape *n old-fashioned* a joke or prank
WORD ORIGIN origin unknown
japonica *n* **1** a Japanese shrub with red flowers and yellowish fruit **2** ▸ same as **camellia**
WORD ORIGIN New Latin *Japonia* Japan
Jaques-Dalcroze *n* **Émile** 1865–1950, Swiss composer and teacher: invented eurythmics
jar[1] ❶ *n* **1** a wide-mouthed cylindrical glass container, used for storing food **2** *Brit informal* a glass of beer
WORD ORIGIN Arabic *jarrah* large earthen vessel
jar[2] ❶ *vb* **jarring, jarred 1** (usually with *on*) to have an irritating or unpleasant effect: *sometimes a light remark jarred on her father* **2** to be in disagreement or conflict: *their very different temperaments jarred* **3** to jolt or bump ▷ *n* **4** a jolt or shock **jarring** *adj*
WORD ORIGIN probably imitative
jardiniere *n* an ornamental pot or stand for plants
WORD ORIGIN French
jargon ❶ *n* **1** specialized language relating to a particular subject, profession, or group **2** pretentious or unintelligible language
WORD ORIGIN Old French
Jarman *n* **Derek** 1942–94, British film director and writer; his films include *Jubilee* (1977), *Caravaggio* (1986), and *Wittgenstein* (1993)
jarrah *n* an Australian eucalypt yielding valuable timber
Jarrett *n* **Keith** born 1945, US jazz pianist and composer
Jarry *n* **Alfred** 1873–1907, French dramatist and poet, who anticipated the theatre of the absurd with his play *Ubu Roi* (1896)
Jaruzelski *n* **Wojciech** born 1923, Polish statesman and soldier; prime minister (1981–85); head of state 1985–90 (as president from 1989)
jasmine *n* a shrub or climbing plant with sweet-smelling flowers
WORD ORIGIN Persian *yāsmīn*
jasper *n* a kind of quartz, usually red in colour, which is used as a gemstone and for ornamental decoration
WORD ORIGIN Greek *iaspis*
Jaspers *n* **Karl** 1883–1969, German existentialist philosopher
jaundice *n* yellowing of the skin and the whites of the eyes, caused by an

THESAURUS

slammer (*slang*), lockup, reformatory, quod (*slang*), poky *or* pokey (*US & Canad slang*), boob (*Austral slang*) ▷ *vb* **2 = imprison**, confine, detain, lock up, constrain, put away, intern, incarcerate, send down, send to prison, impound, put under lock and key, immure
jam[1] *vb* **1 = pack**, force, press, stuff, squeeze, compact, ram, wedge, cram, compress **2a = crowd**, cram, throng, crush, press, mass, surge, flock, swarm, congregate **2b = congest**, block, clog, stick, halt, stall, obstruct ▷ *n* **8** (*informal*) **= predicament**, tight spot, scrape (*informal*), corner, state, situation, trouble, spot (*informal*), hole (*slang*), fix (*informal*), bind, emergency, mess, dilemma, pinch, plight, strait, hot water, pickle (*informal*), deep water, quandary
jar[1] *n* **1 = pot**, container, flask, receptacle, vessel, drum, vase, jug, pitcher, urn, crock, canister, repository, decanter, carafe, flagon
jar[2] *vb* **1** (*usually with* **on**) **= irritate**, grind, clash, annoy, offend, rattle, gall, nettle, jangle, irk, grate on, get on your nerves (*informal*), nark (*Brit, Austral & NZ slang*), discompose **3 = jolt**, rock, shake, disturb, bump, rattle, grate, agitate, vibrate, rasp, convulse
jargon *n* **1 = parlance**, slang, idiom, patter, tongue, usage, dialect, cant, lingo (*informal*), patois, argot

DICTIONARY

excess of bile pigments in the blood **WORD ORIGIN** French *jaune* yellow
jaundiced *adj* **1** bitter or cynical: *the financial markets are taking a jaundiced view of the Government's motives* **2** having jaundice
jaunt *n* **1** a pleasure trip or outing ▷ *vb* **2** to go on a jaunt **WORD ORIGIN** origin unknown
jaunty *adj* **-tier, -tiest 1** cheerful and energetic: *he was worried beneath the jaunty air* **2** smart and attractive: *a jaunty little hat* **jauntily** *adv* **WORD ORIGIN** French *gentil* noble
Jaurès *n* **Jean Léon** 1859–1914, French politician and writer, who founded the socialist paper *l'Humanité* (1904), and united the French socialist movement into a single party (1905); assassinated
Java *n trademark* a computer programming language that is widely used on the internet **WORD ORIGIN** after *Java* coffee from the Indonesian island, allegedly drunk by its creators
Javanese *adj* **1** of the island of Java, in Indonesia ▷ *n* **2** *pl* **-nese** a person from Java **3** the language of Java
javelin *n* a light spear thrown in a sports competition **WORD ORIGIN** Old French *javeline*
jaw ⓣ *n* **1** either of the bones that hold the teeth and frame the mouth **2** the lower part of the face below the mouth **3** *slang* a long chat ▷ *vb* **4** *slang* to have a long chat **WORD ORIGIN** probably Old French *joue* cheek
Jawara *n* Sir **Dawda** born 1924, Gambian statesman; president of The Gambia (1970–94); overthrown in a military coup
jawbone *n* the bone in the lower jaw of a person or animal
ja well no fine *interj S African* used to indicate reluctant acceptance
jaws ⓣ *pl n* **1** the mouth of a person or animal **2** the parts of a machine or tool that grip an object **3** the narrow opening of a gorge or valley **4** a dangerous or threatening position: *to snatch victory from the jaws of defeat*
jay *n* a bird of Europe and Asia with a pinkish-brown body and blue-and-black wings **WORD ORIGIN** Old French *jai*
Jay *n* **John** 1745–1829, American statesman, jurist, and diplomat; first chief justice of the Supreme Court (1789–95). He negotiated the treaty with Great Britain (**Jay's treaty**, 1794), that settled outstanding disputes
Jayawardene *n* **Junius Richard.** 1906–96, Sri Lankan statesman; prime minister (1977–78) and first president of Sri Lanka (1978–89)
jaywalking *n* crossing the road in a dangerous or careless manner **jaywalker** *n* **WORD ORIGIN** *jay* (in sense: a foolish person)
jazz *n* **1** a kind of popular music of African-American origin that has an exciting rhythm and often involves improvisation **2 and all that jazz** *slang* and other related things **WORD ORIGIN** origin unknown
jazz up *vb informal* **1** to play (a piece of music) in a jazzy style **2** to make (something) appear more interesting or lively: *never seek to jazz up a plain story*
jazzy *adj* **-zier, -ziest 1** colourful and modern: *jazzy shop fronts* **2** of or like jazz
JCB *n trademark, Brit* a large machine used in building, that has a shovel on the front and a digger arm on the back **WORD ORIGIN** initials of Joseph Cyril Bamford, its manufacturer
jealous ⓣ *adj* **1** suspicious or fearful of being displaced by a rival **2** envious: *I was jealous of the girls who had boyfriends* **3** resulting from jealousy: *my jealous tears* **jealously** *adv* **WORD ORIGIN** Late Latin *zelus* emulation
jealousy ⓣ *n, pl* **-ousies** the state of or an instance of feeling jealous
Jean de Meung *n* real name *Jean Clopinel.* ?1250–?1305, French poet, who continued Guillaume de Lorris' *Roman de la Rose.* His portion of the poem consists of some 18 000 lines and contains satirical attacks on women and the Church
Jean Paul *n* real name *Johann Paul Friedrich Richter.* 1763–1825, German novelist
jeans *pl n* casual denim trousers **WORD ORIGIN** from *jean fustian* fabric from Genoa
Jeans *n* Sir **James Hopwood** 1877–1946, English astronomer, physicist, and mathematician, best known for his popular books on astronomy. He made important contributions to the kinetic theory of gases and the theory of stellar evolution
Jeep *n trademark* a small road vehicle with four-wheel drive **WORD ORIGIN** perhaps *general-purpose (vehicle)*, influenced by Eugene the *Jeep*, a creature in a comic strip
Jeeps *n* **Dickie** born 1931, English Rugby Union footballer: halfback for England (1956–62) and the British Lions (1959–62)
jeer ⓣ *vb* **1** to be derisive towards (someone) ▷ *n* **2** a cry of derision **jeering** *adj, n* **WORD ORIGIN** origin unknown
Jefferies *n* **Richard** 1848–87, British writer and naturalist, noted for his observation of English country life: his books include *Bevis* (1882) and collections of essays such as *The Open Air* (1885)
Jeffrey *n* **Francis,** Lord 1773–1850, Scottish judge and literary critic. As editor of the *Edinburgh Review* (1803–29), he was noted for the severity of his criticism of the romantic poets, esp. Wordsworth
Jehovah *n* God **WORD ORIGIN** Hebrew *Yahweh*
Jehovah's Witness *n* a member of a Christian Church whose followers believe that the end of the world is near
jejune *adj* **1** simple and unsophisticated **2** dull and uninteresting **WORD ORIGIN** Latin *jejunus* empty
jejunum (jij-june-um) *n anat* the part of the small intestine between the duodenum and the ileum **jejunal** *adj* **WORD ORIGIN** Latin
Jekyll *n* **Gertrude** 1843–1932, British landscape gardener: noted for her simplicity of design and use of indigenous plants
Jekyll and Hyde *n* a person with two distinct personalities, one good and the other evil **WORD ORIGIN** after the character in a novel by R. L. Stevenson
jell *vb* **1** to take on a definite form: *the changes have had little time to jell* **2** ▸ same as **gel** (sense 2) **WORD ORIGIN** from *jelly*
jellaba *n* a loose robe with a hood, worn by some Arab men **WORD ORIGIN** Arabic *jallabah*
Jellicoe *n* **John Rushworth,** 1st Earl Jellicoe. 1859–1935, British admiral, who commanded the Grand Fleet at the Battle of Jutland (1916), which incapacitated the German fleet for

THESAURUS

jaw *vb* **4** *(slang)* **= talk**, chat, rabbit (on) *(Brit informal)*, gossip, chatter, spout, babble, natter, schmooze *(slang)*, shoot the breeze *(US slang)*, run off at the mouth *(slang)*, chew the fat *or* rag *(slang)*
jaws *pl n* **1, 2, 3 = opening**, gates, entrance, aperture, mouth, abyss, maw, orifice, ingress
jealous *adj* **1 = suspicious**, suspecting, guarded, protective, wary, doubtful, sceptical, attentive, anxious, apprehensive, vigilant, watchful, zealous, possessive, solicitous, distrustful, mistrustful, unbelieving **OPPOSITE:** trusting
2 = envious, grudging, resentful, begrudging, green, intolerant, green-eyed, invidious, green with envy, desirous, covetous, emulous **OPPOSITE:** satisfied
jealousy *n* **= suspicion**, distrust, mistrust, possessiveness, doubt, spite, resentment, wariness,

the rest of World War I

jellied *adj* prepared in a jelly: *jellied eels*

jellies *pl n slang* gelatine capsules of temazepam, dissolved and injected as a recreational drug
WORD ORIGIN from GELATINE

jelly *n, pl* **-lies 1** a fruit-flavoured dessert set with gelatine **2** a food made from fruit juice boiled with sugar until the mixture sets, used for spreading on bread **3** a savoury food preparation set with gelatine ▸ See also **jellies** > **jelly-like** *adj*
WORD ORIGIN Latin *gelare* to freeze

jellyfish *n, pl* **-fish** a small sea creature with a jelly-like umbrella-shaped body and trailing tentacles

jemmy *or US* **jimmy** *n, pl* **-mies** a short steel crowbar, used by burglars to prise open doors and windows
WORD ORIGIN from short form of *James*

Jenkins *n* **Roy** (**Harris**), Baron Jenkins of Hillhead. 1920–2003, British politician and author; Labour home secretary (1965–67, 1974–76) and chancellor of the exchequer (1967–70); president of the European Commission (1977–80); cofounder of the Social Democratic Party (1981); leader of party (1982–83); Chancellor of Oxford University (1987–2003)

jenny *n, pl* **-nies** a female donkey, ass, or wren
WORD ORIGIN from the name *Jenny*

Jensen *n* **Johannes Vilhelm** 1873–1950, Danish novelist, poet, and essayist: best known for his novel sequence about the origins of mankind *The Long Journey* (1908–22). Nobel prize for literature 1944

jeopardize *or* **-ise** *vb* **-izing, -ized** *or* **-ising, -ised** to put (something) at risk: *the escalating violence that is jeopardizing current peace moves*

jeopardy ❶ *n* danger of harm, loss, or death: *the survival of public hospitals is in jeopardy*
WORD ORIGIN Old French *jeu parti*, literally: divided game, hence uncertain issue

jerboa *n* a small rodent of Asia and N Africa with long hind legs used for jumping
WORD ORIGIN Arabic *yarbū'*

jeremiad *n* a long mournful complaint
WORD ORIGIN French *jérémiade*, referring to the Lamentations of Jeremiah in the Bible

jerepigo (jer-ree-pee-go) *n S African* a sweet fortified wine similar to port
WORD ORIGIN Portuguese *jeropiga*

jerk ❶ *vb* **1** to move with an irregular or spasmodic motion **2** to pull or push (something) abruptly or spasmodically ▹ *n* **3** an abrupt or spasmodic movement **4** an irregular jolting motion: *the irritating jerk that heralded a gear change* **5** *slang chiefly US & Canad* a stupid or ignorant person
WORD ORIGIN probably variant of *yerk* to pull stitches tight

jerkin *n* a short jacket
WORD ORIGIN origin unknown

jerky *adj* **jerkier, jerkiest** having an irregular jolting motion: *avoid any sudden or jerky movements* **jerkily** *adv* **jerkiness** *n*

Jerry *n old-fashioned Brit slang* **1** *pl* **-ries** a German, esp. a German soldier **2** Germans collectively

jerry-built *adj* (of houses) built badly with cheap materials

jerry can *n* a flat-sided can used for carrying petrol or water
WORD ORIGIN from *Jerry* German soldier

jersey *n* **1** a knitted garment covering the upper part of the body **2** a soft, slightly stretchy, machine-knitted fabric
WORD ORIGIN after *Jersey*, because of the woollen sweaters worn by the fishermen

Jersey *n* a breed of reddish-brown dairy cattle that produces milk with a high butterfat content
WORD ORIGIN after *Jersey*, island in the English Channel

Jerusalem artichoke *n* a small yellowish-white vegetable that grows underground
WORD ORIGIN altered from Italian *girasole* sunflower

Jespersen *n* (**Jens**) **Otto** (**Harry**) 1860–1943, Danish philologist: author of *Modern English Grammar* (1909–31)

jest *n* **1** something done or said to amuse people **2 in jest** as a joke: *many a true word is spoken in jest* ▹ *vb* **3** to do or say something to amuse people
WORD ORIGIN variant of *gest* exploit

jester *n* a professional clown employed by a king or nobleman during the Middle Ages

Jesuit (jezz-yew-it) *n* a member of the Society of Jesus, a Roman Catholic religious order **Jesuitical** *adj*
WORD ORIGIN New Latin *Jesuita*

Jesus *n* **1** the founder of Christianity, believed by Christians to be the Son of God ▹ *interj* **2** *taboo slang* an oath expressing intense anger or shock

jet[1] ❶ *n* **1** an aircraft driven by jet propulsion **2** a thin stream of liquid or gas forced out of a small hole **3** an outlet or nozzle through which a stream of liquid or gas is forced ▹ *vb* **jetting, jetted 4** to travel by jet aircraft
WORD ORIGIN Old French *jeter* to throw

jet[2] *n* a hard black mineral that is polished and used in jewellery
WORD ORIGIN Old French *jaiet*

jet-black *adj* deep black

jetboat *n* a motorboat propelled by a jet of water

jet engine *n* an aircraft engine that uses jet propulsion for forward motion

jet lag *n* a feeling of fatigue and disorientation often experienced by air passengers who have crossed several time zones in a short space of time

jet-propelled *adj* driven by jet propulsion

jet propulsion *n* a method of propulsion by which an aircraft is moved forward by the force of the exhaust gases ejected from the rear

jetsam *n* **1** goods thrown overboard to lighten a ship during a storm **2 flotsam and jetsam** ▸ see **flotsam** (sense 2)
WORD ORIGIN from *jettison*

jet set *n* rich and fashionable people who travel widely for pleasure **jet-setter** *n* **jet-setting** *adj*

jet ski *n* a small self-propelled vehicle resembling a scooter, which skims across water on a flat keel **jet skiing** *n*

jettison *vb* **1** to abandon or give up: *jettisoning democracy in favour of fascism* **2** to throw overboard
WORD ORIGIN Latin *jactatio* a tossing about

jetty *n, pl* **-ties 1** a landing pier or dock **2** a structure built from a shore out into the water to protect a harbour
WORD ORIGIN Old French *jetee* projecting part

Jevons *n* **William Stanley** 1835–82, English economist and logician: introduced the concept of final or marginal utility in *The Theory of Political Economy* (1871)

Jew *n* **1** a person whose religion is Judaism **2** a descendant of the ancient Hebrews
WORD ORIGIN Hebrew *yehūdāh* Judah

THESAURUS

ill-will, dubiety

jeer *vb* **1 = mock**, hector, deride, heckle, knock *(informal)*, barrack, ridicule, taunt, sneer, scoff, banter, flout, gibe, cock a snook at *(Brit)*, contemn *(formal)* **OPPOSITE:** cheer ▹ *n* **2 = mockery**, abuse, ridicule, taunt, sneer, hiss, boo, scoff, hoot, derision, gibe, catcall, obloquy, aspersion **OPPOSITE:** applause

jeopardy *n* **= danger**, risk, peril, vulnerability, venture, exposure, liability, hazard, insecurity, pitfall, precariousness, endangerment

jerk *vb* **1, 2 = jolt**, bang, bump, lurch, shake ▹ *n* **3, 4 = lurch**, movement, thrust, twitch, jolt, throw

jet[1] *n* **2 = stream**, current, spring, flow, rush, flood, burst, spray, fountain, cascade, gush, spurt, spout, squirt ▹ *vb* **4 = fly**, wing, cruise, soar, zoom

DICTIONARY

jewel ❶ *n* **1** a precious or semiprecious stone **2** a person or thing regarded as precious or special: *a fantastic little car, a real little jewel* **3** a gemstone used as part of the machinery of a watch
WORD ORIGIN Old French *jouel*

jewelled *or US* **jeweled** *adj* decorated with jewels

jeweller *or US* **jeweler** *n* a person who buys, sells, and repairs jewellery

jewellery ❶ *or US* **jewelry** *n* objects such as rings, necklaces, and bracelets, worn for decoration

Jewess *n now often offensive* a woman whose religion is Judaism

jewfish *n Austral* a freshwater catfish

Jewish *adj* of Jews or Judaism

Jewry *n* Jews collectively

jew's-harp *n* a small musical instrument held between the teeth and played by plucking a metal strip with the finger

Jezebel *n* a wicked or shameless woman
WORD ORIGIN after the wife of Ahab, in the Bible

Jhabvala *n* **Ruth Prawer,** original name *Ruth Prawer*. born 1927, British writer living in India and the US, born in Germany to Polish parents: author of the Booker-prizewinning novel *Heat and Dust* (1975) and scripts for films by James Ivory

Jiang Jing Guo *n* See **Chiang Ching-kuo**

Jiang Qing *or* **Chiang Ch'ing** *n* 1913–91, Chinese Communist actress and politician; widow of Mao Tse-tung. She was a leading member of the Gang of Four

Jiang Zemin *n* born 1926, Chinese Communist politician: president (1993–2003)

jib¹ *n* **1** *naut* a triangular sail set in front of the foremast **2 the cut of someone's jib** a person's manner or style
WORD ORIGIN origin unknown

jib² *vb* **jibbing, jibbed** *chiefly Brit* **1** (of an animal) to stop short and refuse to go forwards: *my animal jibbed three times* **2 jib at** to object to: *he jibs at any suggestion that his side are the underdogs*
WORD ORIGIN origin unknown

jib³ *n* the projecting arm of a crane
WORD ORIGIN probably from *gibbet*

jibe¹ *n* **1** an insulting or taunting remark ▷ *vb* **jibing, jibed 2** to make insulting or taunting remarks

jibe² *vb* **jibing, jibed** *informal* to be in accord or be consistent: *their apparent devotion hardly jibed with what he had heard about them*

jibe³ *vb* **jibing, jibed,** *n naut* ▸ same as **gybe**

jiffy *n, pl* **jiffies** *informal* a very short time: *won't be a jiffy!*
WORD ORIGIN origin unknown

Jiffy bag *n trademark* a large padded envelope

jig *n* **1** a lively folk dance **2** music for this dance **3** a mechanical device that holds and locates a part during machining ▷ *vb* **jigging, jigged 4** to dance a jig **5** to move with quick jerky movements
WORD ORIGIN origin unknown

jigger *n* a small whisky glass

jiggered *adj old-fashioned informal* damned or blowed: *well, I'm jiggered, so that's where it went!*
WORD ORIGIN probably euphemism for *buggered*

jiggery-pokery *n informal chiefly Brit* dishonest behaviour; cheating
WORD ORIGIN Scots dialect *joukery-pawkery*

jiggle *vb* **-gling, -gled** to move with quick jerky movements
WORD ORIGIN frequentative of *jig*

jigsaw *n* **1** Also called: **jigsaw puzzle** a puzzle in which the player has to put together a picture that has been cut into irregularly shaped interlocking pieces **2** a mechanical saw with a fine steel blade for cutting along curved or irregular lines in sheets of material
WORD ORIGIN *jig* (to jerk up and down) + SAW¹

jihad *n* Islamic holy war against unbelievers

jilt *vb* to leave or reject (a lover) abruptly or callously
WORD ORIGIN dialect *jillet* flighty girl

Jim Crow *n US* **1** the policy or practice of segregating Black people **2** *offensive* a Black person
WORD ORIGIN from name of song

Jiménez *n* **Juan Ramón** 1881–1958, Spanish lyric poet. His most famous work is *Platero y yo* (1917), a prose poem: Nobel prize for literature 1956

Jiménez de Cisneros *n* **Francisco** 1436–1517, Spanish cardinal and statesman; regent of Castile (1506–07) and Spain (1516–17) and grand inquisitor for Castile and León (1507–17). Also: **Ximenes de Cisneros, Ximenez de Cisneros**

jingle *n* **1** a short catchy song used to advertise a product on radio or television **2** a light ringing sound ▷ *vb* **-gling, -gled 3** to make a light ringing sound
WORD ORIGIN probably imitative

jingoism *n* excessive and aggressive patriotism **jingoistic** *or* **jingoist** *adj*
WORD ORIGIN after the use of *by Jingo!* in a 19th-century song

jink *vb* to move quickly or jerkily in order to dodge someone: *he jinked free and won a race to the line to level the scores*
WORD ORIGIN Scots

jinks *pl n* **high jinks** boisterous or mischievous behaviour
WORD ORIGIN origin unknown

jinni *or* **djinni** *n, pl* **jinn** *or* **djinn** a being or spirit in Muslim belief that could take on human or animal form
WORD ORIGIN Arabic

jinx *n* **1** someone or something believed to bring bad luck ▷ *vb* **2** to bring bad luck to
WORD ORIGIN perhaps from Greek *iunx* wryneck, a bird used in magic

jitterbug *n* **1** a fast jerky American dance that was popular in the 1940s ▷ *vb* **-bugging, -bugged 2** to dance the jitterbug

jitters *pl n* **the jitters** *informal* a feeling of extreme nervousness experienced before an important event: *I had a case of the jitters during my first two speeches*
WORD ORIGIN origin unknown

jittery *adj* nervous

jive *n* **1** a lively jerky dance that was popular in the 1940s and 1950s ▷ *vb* **jiving, jived 2** to dance the jive **jiver** *n*
WORD ORIGIN origin unknown

Jnr Junior

Joachim *n* **1 Joseph** 1831–1907, Hungarian violinist and composer **2 Saint.** 1st century BC, traditionally the father of the Virgin Mary; feast day: July 25 or Sept 9

Joachim of Fiore *n* ?1132–1202 AD, Italian mystic and philosopher, best known for teaching that history can be divided into three ages, those of the Father, Son, and Holy Ghost

Joan *n* **1** known as *the Fair Maid of Kent*. 1328–85, wife of Edward the Black Prince; mother of Richard II **2 Pope** legendary female pope, first mentioned in the 13th century: said to have been elected while disguised as a man and to have died in childbirth

job ❶ *n* **1** a person's occupation or paid employment **2** a piece of work; task **3** the performance of a task: *he made a good job of the repair* **4** *informal* a difficult task: *they are having a job to fill his shoes* **5** *Brit, Austral & NZ informal* a crime, esp. a robbery **6 just the job** *informal* exactly what is required **7 make the best of a bad job** to cope

THESAURUS

jewel *n* **1 = gemstone,** gem, precious stone, brilliant, ornament, trinket, sparkler *(informal)*, rock *(slang)* **2 = treasure,** wonder, prize, darling, pearl, gem, paragon, pride and joy, taonga (NZ)

jewellery *n* **= jewels,** treasure, gems, trinkets, precious stones, ornaments, finery, regalia, bling *(slang)*

job *n* **1 = position,** post, function, capacity, work, posting, calling, place, business, office, trade, field, career, situation, activity, employment, appointment, craft, profession, occupation, placement, vocation, livelihood, métier **2 = task,** concern, duty, charge, work,

as well as possible in unsatisfactory circumstances
WORD ORIGIN origin unknown
jobbing *adj* doing individual jobs for payment: *a jobbing gardener*
Jobcentre *or* **job centre** *n* (in Britain) a government office where advertisements of available jobs are displayed
Jobclub *or* **job club** *n* (in Britain) a group of unemployed people which meets every weekday and is given advice on and help with job seeking
jobless ❶ *adj* **1** unemployed ▷ *pl n* **2** people who are unemployed: *the young jobless*
job lot *n* a miscellaneous collection of articles sold together
Job's comforter *n* a person who adds to someone else's distress while pretending to be sympathetic
WORD ORIGIN after *Job* in the Bible
jobseeker's allowance *n* (in Britain) a social-security payment for unemployed people
job sharing *n* an arrangement by which a job is shared by two part-time workers
Jochum *n* **Eugen** 1902–87, German orchestral conductor
jockey *n* **1** a person who rides horses in races as a profession ▷ *vb* **2 jockey for position** to try to obtain an advantage by skilful manoeuvring
WORD ORIGIN from the name *Jock*
jockstrap *n* an elasticated belt with a pouch to support the genitals, worn by male athletes. Also called: **athletic support**
WORD ORIGIN slang *jock* penis
jocose (joke-**kohss**) *adj old-fashioned* playful or humorous **jocosely** *adv*
WORD ORIGIN Latin *jocus* joke
jocular *adj* **1** (of a person) often joking; good-humoured **2** (of a remark) meant lightly or humorously **jocularity** *n* **jocularly** *adv*
WORD ORIGIN Latin *joculus* little joke
jocund (**jok**-kund) *adj literary* cheerful or merry
WORD ORIGIN Latin *jucundus* pleasant
jodhpurs *pl n* trousers worn for riding, which are loose-fitting around the thighs and tight-fitting below the knees
WORD ORIGIN from *Jodhpur*, town in NW India
Jodl *n* **Alfred** 1890–1946, German general, largely responsible for German strategy during World War II: executed as a war criminal
joey *n Austral* a young kangaroo
Joffre *n* **Joseph Jacques Césaire** 1852–1931, French marshal. He commanded the French army (1914–16) and was largely responsible for the Allies' victory at the Marne (1914), which halted the German advance on Paris
jog ❶ *vb* **jogging, jogged 1** to run at a gentle pace for exercise **2** to nudge slightly **3 jog along** to continue in a plodding way: *many people jog along in second gear for the whole of their lives* **4 jog someone's memory** to remind someone of something ▷ *n* **5** a slow run as a form of exercise **jogger** *n* **jogging** *n*
WORD ORIGIN probably variant of *shog* to shake
joggle *vb* **-gling, -gled** to shake or move with a slightly jolting motion
WORD ORIGIN frequentative of *jog*
jog trot *n* an easy bouncy pace, midway between a walk and a trot
john *n slang chiefly US & Canad* a toilet
WORD ORIGIN special use of the name
John Bull *n* England represented as a man
John Chrysostom *n* **Saint** ?345–407 AD, Greek bishop and theologian; one of the Fathers of the Greek Church, noted for his eloquence. Feast day: Sept 13
John I *n* **1** surnamed *Tzimisces*. 925–976 AD, Byzantine emperor (969–976): extended Byzantine power into Bulgaria and Syria **2** called *the Great*. 1357–1433, king of Portugal (1385–1433). He secured independence for Portugal by his victory over Castile (1385) and initiated Portuguese overseas expansion
John II *n* **1** called *the Good*. 1319–64, king of France (1350–64): captured by the English at Poitiers (1356) and forced to sign treaties (1360) surrendering SW France to England **2** called *the Perfect*. 1455–95, king of Portugal (1481–95): sponsored Portuguese expansion in the New World and reduced the power of the aristocracy **3** surnamed *Casimir Vasa*. 1609–72, king of Poland (1648–68), who lost much territory to neighbouring countries: abdicated
John III *n* **1** 1507–57, king of Portugal (1521–57): his reign saw the expansion of the Portuguese empire overseas but the start of economic decline at home **2** surnamed *Sobieski*. 1624–96, king of Poland (1674–96). He raised the Turkish siege of Vienna (1683)
John IV *n* called *the Fortunate*. 1604–56, king of Portugal (1640–56). As duke of Braganza he led a revolt against Spanish rule and became king: lost most of Portugal's Asian possessions to the Dutch
johnny *n, pl* **-nies** *Brit, old-fashioned informal* a chap: *you legal johnnies*
Johnny Canuck (kan-**nuk**) *n Canad informal* Canada personified as a man
John of Austria *n* called *Don John*. 1547–78, Spanish general: defeated the Turks at Lepanto (1571)
John of Damascus *n* **Saint** ?675–749 AD, Syrian theologian, who defended the veneration of icons and images against the iconoclasts. Feast day: Dec 4
John of Leyden *n* original name *Jan Bockelson*. ?1509–36, Dutch Anabaptist leader. He established a theocracy in Münster (1534) but was tortured to death after the city was recaptured (1535) by its prince bishop
John of Salisbury *n* died 1180, English ecclesiastic and scholar; bishop of Chartres (1176–80). He supported Thomas à Becket against Henry II
John of the Cross *n* **Saint** original name *Juan de Yepis y Alvarez*. 1542–91, Spanish Carmelite monk, poet, and mystic. He founded the Discalced Carmelites with Saint Teresa (1568). Feast day: Dec 14
John Paul I *n* original name *Albino Luciani*. 1912–78, pope (1978) whose brief 33-day reign was characterized by a simpler papal style and anticipated an emphasis on pastoral rather than administrative priorities
Johns *n* **1 Andrew** (**Gary**) born 1974, Australian Rugby League footballer: halfback for Australia (1995–2006) **2 Jasper.** born 1930, US artist, noted for his collages and constructions
John VI *n* ?1769–1826, king of Portugal (1816–26): recognized the independence of Brazil (1825)
John XXII *n* original name *Jacques Duèse*. ?1244–1334, pope (1316–34), residing at Avignon; involved in a long conflict with the Holy Roman Emperor Louis IV and opposed the Franciscan Spirituals
John XXIII *n* original name *Angelo Giuseppe Roncalli*. 1881–1963, pope (1958–63). He promoted ecumenism and world peace and summoned the second Vatican Council (1962–65)
joie de vivre (zhwah de **veev**-ra) *n* enjoyment of life
WORD ORIGIN French, literally: joy of living
join ❶ *vb* **1** to become a member of (a club or organization) **2** to become part of (a queue or list) **3** to meet

j

THESAURUS

business, role, operation, affair, responsibility, function, contribution, venture, enterprise, undertaking, pursuit, assignment, stint, chore, errand
jobless *adj* **1 = unemployed**, redundant, out of work, on the dole (*Brit informal*), inactive, out of a job, unoccupied, idle
jog *vb* **1 = run**, trot, canter, lope, dogtrot **2 = nudge**, push, shake, prod
join *vb* **1 = enrol in**, enter, sign up for, become a member of, enlist in **6 = connect**, unite, couple, link, marry, tie, combine, attach, knit,

DICTIONARY

(someone) as a companion: *join me for a beer* **4** to take part in (an activity): *join the war effort* **5** (of two roads or rivers) to meet and come together **6** to bring into contact: *join hands* **7 join forces** to combine efforts with someone ▹*n* **8** a place where two things are joined together ▸See also **join in, join up**
WORD ORIGIN Latin *jungere* to yoke

joined-up *adj* integrated by an overall strategy: *joined-up government*

joiner *n* a person whose job is making finished woodwork, such as window frames and stairs

joinery *n* the skill or work of a joiner

join in *vb* to take part in (an activity)

joint Ⓣ *adj* **1** shared by or belonging to two or more parties: *the two countries have issued a joint statement* ▹*n* **2** *anat* the junction between two or more bones: *a hip joint* **3** a junction of two or more parts or objects: *a mortar joint* **4** a piece of meat suitable for roasting **5** *slang* a building or place of entertainment: *strip joints* **6** *slang* a cannabis cigarette **7 out of joint a** *informal* out of order or out of keeping: *they find their routine lives out of joint with their training* **b** (of a bone) knocked out of its normal position **8 put someone's nose out of joint** ▸see **nose** (sense 10) ▹*vb* **9** to provide a joint or joints **10** to cut or divide (meat) into joints **jointed** *adj* **jointly** *adv*

joint-stock company *n Brit* a business firm whose capital is owned jointly by shareholders

join up *vb* to become a member of a military organization

Joinville *n* **Jean de** ?1224–1317, French chronicler, noted for his *Histoire de Saint Louis* (1309)

joist *n* a beam made of timber, steel, or concrete, used as a support in the construction of floors and roofs
WORD ORIGIN Old French *giste*

jojoba (hoe-hoe-ba) *n* a shrub whose seeds contain an oil used in cosmetics
WORD ORIGIN Mexican Spanish

joke Ⓣ *n* **1** something that is said or done to amuse people **2** someone or something that is ridiculous: *the country's inexperienced leaders are regarded as something of a joke* **3 no joke** *informal* a serious or difficult matter: *getting over mountain passes at ten thousand feet is no joke* ▹*vb* **joking, joked 4** to say or do something to amuse people **jokey** *adj* **jokingly** *adv*
WORD ORIGIN Latin *jocus*

joker Ⓣ *n* **1** a person who jokes a lot **2** *slang* a person regarded without respect: *waiting for the next jokers to sign up* **3** an extra playing card in a pack, which can replace any other card in some games **4** *Austral & NZ informal* a chap

jol (joll) *S African slang n* **1** a party ▹*vb* **jolling, jolled 2** to have a good time
WORD ORIGIN Dutch

Jolie *n* **Angelina Jolie** (Voight), born 1975, US actor; her films include *Girl Interrupted* (1999), *Lara Croft, Tomb Raider* (2001), and *A Mighty Heart* (2007)

Joliot-Curie *n* **Jean-Frédéric** 1900–58, and his wife, **Irène**, 1897–1956, French physicists: shared the Nobel prize for chemistry in 1935 for discovering artificial radioactivity

Jolliet *n* **Louis** 1645–1700, French-Canadian explorer, with Jaques Marquette, of the Mississippi river

jollification *n* a merry festivity

jollity *n* the condition of being jolly

jolly Ⓣ *adj* **-lier, -liest 1** full of good humour **2** involving a lot of fun: *big jolly birthday parties* ▹*adv* **3** *Brit informal* very: *I'm going to have a jolly good try* ▹*vb* **-lies, -lying, -lied 4 jolly along** *informal* to try to keep (someone) cheerful by flattery or cheerful chat
WORD ORIGIN Old French *jolif*

Jolly Roger *n* the traditional pirate flag, depicting a white skull and crossbones on a black background

Jolson *n* **Al**, real name *Asa Yoelson*. 1886–1950, US singer and film actor, born in Russia; star of the first talking picture *The Jazz Singer* (1927)

jolt Ⓣ *n* **1** a severe shock **2** a sudden violent movement ▹*vb* **3** to surprise or shock: *he was momentarily jolted by the news* **4** to bump against (someone or something) with a sudden violent movement **5** to move in a jerking manner
WORD ORIGIN origin unknown

Jonah *n* a person believed to bring bad luck to those around him or her
WORD ORIGIN after *Jonah* in the Bible

Jongkind *n* **Johann Barthold** 1819–91, Dutch landscape painter and etcher, working in Paris: best known for his atmospheric seascapes

jonquil *n* a narcissus with sweet-smelling yellow or white flowers
WORD ORIGIN French *jonquille*

Jordaens *n* **Jacob** 1593–1678, Flemish painter, noted for his naturalistic depiction of peasant scenes

Jordanian *adj* **1** of Jordan ▹*n* **2** a person from Jordan

Joseph II *n* 1741–90, Holy Roman emperor (1765–90); son of Francis I. He ruled Austria jointly with his mother, Maria Theresa, until her death (1780). He reorganized taxation, abolished serfdom, curtailed the feudal power of the nobles, and asserted his independence from the pope

Josephus *n* **Flavius** real name *Joseph ben Matthias*. ?37–?100 AD, Jewish historian and general; author of *History of the Jewish War* and *Antiquities of the Jews*

josh *vb slang* to joke or tease
WORD ORIGIN origin unknown

Jospin *n* **Lionel** (**Robert**) born 1937, French politician; prime minister (1997–2002)

Josquin des Prés *n* See **des Prés**

joss stick *n* a stick of incense, giving off a sweet smell when burnt
WORD ORIGIN *joss* (a Chinese idol) from Portuguese *deos* god

jostle *vb* **-tling, -tled 1** to bump or push roughly: *television crews filming the scene were jostled by police* **2** to compete with someone: *jostling for power*
WORD ORIGIN Old French *jouster* to joust

THESAURUS

cement, adhere, fasten, annex, add, splice, yoke, append
OPPOSITE: detach

joint *adj* **1 = shared**, mutual, collective, communal, united, joined, allied, combined, corporate, concerted, consolidated, cooperative, reciprocal, collaborative ▹*n* **3 = junction**, union, link, connection, knot, brace, bracket, seam, hinge, weld, linkage, intersection, node, articulation, nexus

joke *n* **1a = jest**, gag (*informal*), wisecrack (*informal*), witticism, crack (*informal*), sally, quip, josh (*slang, chiefly US & Canad*), pun, quirk, one-liner (*informal*), jape **1b = laugh**, jest, fun, josh (*slang, chiefly US & Canad*), lark, sport, frolic, whimsy, jape **2 = laughing stock**, butt, clown, buffoon, simpleton ▹*vb* **4 = jest**, kid (*informal*), fool, mock, wind up (*Brit slang*), tease, ridicule, taunt, quip, josh (*slang, chiefly US & Canad*), banter, deride, frolic, chaff, gambol, play the fool, play a trick

joker *n* **1 = comedian**, comic, wit, clown, wag, kidder (*informal*), jester, prankster, buffoon, trickster, humorist

jolly *adj* **1, 2 = happy**, bright, funny, lively, hopeful, sunny, cheerful, merry, vibrant, hilarious, festive, upbeat (*informal*), bubbly, gay, airy, playful, exuberant, jubilant, cheery, good-humoured, joyous, joyful, carefree, breezy, genial, ebullient, chirpy (*informal*), sprightly, jovial, convivial, effervescent, frolicsome, ludic (*literary*), mirthful, sportive, light-hearted, jocund, gladsome (*archaic*), blithesome
OPPOSITE: miserable

jolt *n* **1 = surprise**, blow, shock, setback, reversal, bombshell, thunderbolt, whammy (*informal, chiefly US*), bolt from the blue **2 = jerk**, start, jump, shake, bump, jar, jog, lurch, quiver ▹*vb* **3 = surprise**, upset, stun, disturb, astonish, stagger, startle, perturb, discompose **4 = jerk**,

DICTIONARY

jot *vb* **jotting, jotted 1 jot down** to write a brief note of: *quickly jot down the answers to these questions* ▹ *n* **2** the least bit: *it makes not one jot of difference*
WORD ORIGIN Greek *iōta* iota, smallest letter
jotter *n* a small notebook
jottings *pl n* notes jotted down
joual (zhwahl) *n* a nonstandard variety of Canadian French
WORD ORIGIN French
joule (jool) *n physics* the SI unit of work or energy
WORD ORIGIN after J. P. *Joule*, physicist
journal ⓣ *n* **1** a newspaper or magazine **2** a daily record of events
WORD ORIGIN Latin *diurnalis* daily
journalese *n* a superficial style of writing regarded as typical of newspapers and magazines
journalism *n* the profession of collecting, writing, and publishing news through newspapers and magazines or by radio and television
journalist ⓣ *n* a person who writes or edits news items for a newspaper or magazine or for radio or television **journalistic** *adj*
journey ⓣ *n* **1** the process of travelling from one place to another **2** the time taken or distance travelled on a journey ▹ *vb* **3** to make a journey
WORD ORIGIN Old French *journee* a day, a day's travelling
journeyman *n, pl* **-men** a qualified craftsman who works for an employer
WORD ORIGIN *journey* (in obsolete sense: a day's work)
joust *history n* **1** a combat with lances between two mounted knights ▹ *vb* **2** to take part in such a tournament
WORD ORIGIN Old French *jouster*
Jove *n* **1** Jupiter (the god) **2 by Jove** *old-fashioned* an exclamation of surprise or for emphasis
jovial *adj* happy and cheerful **joviality** *n* **jovially** *adv*
WORD ORIGIN Latin *jovialis* of (the planet) Jupiter
Jovian[1] *adj* **1** of or relating to the god Jove (Jupiter) **2** of, occurring on, or relating to the planet Jupiter **3** of or relating to the giant planets Jupiter, Saturn, Uranus, and Neptune: *the Jovian planets*
WORD ORIGIN C16: from Old Latin *Jovis* Jupiter
Jovian[2] *n* full name *Flavius Claudius Jovianus*. ?331–364 AD, Roman emperor (363–64): he made peace with Persia, relinquishing Roman provinces beyond the Tigris, and restored privileges to the Christians
Jowett *n* **Benjamin** 1817–93, British classical scholar and educator: translated the works of Plato
jowl[1] *n* **1** the lower jaw **2 cheek by jowl** ▸ see **cheek 3 jowls** cheeks **jowled** *adj*
WORD ORIGIN Old English *ceafl* jaw
jowl[2] *n* fatty flesh hanging from the lower jaw
WORD ORIGIN Old English *ceole* throat
joy ⓣ *n* **1** deep happiness and contentment **2** something that brings deep happiness: *a thing of beauty is a joy for ever* **3** *informal* success or satisfaction: *we checked ports and airports without any joy*
WORD ORIGIN Latin *gaudium*
joyful *adj* feeling or bringing great joy: *joyful crowds; a joyful event* **joyfully** *adv*
joyless *adj* feeling or bringing no joy
joyous *adj* extremely happy and enthusiastic **joyously** *adv*
joyride *n* a drive in a car one has stolen **joyriding** *n* **joyrider** *n*
joystick *n* the control lever of an aircraft or a computer
JP (in Britain) Justice of the Peace
JPEG (jay-peg) *n computers* **a** a standard compressed file format used for pictures **b** a picture held in this file format
Jr Junior
JSA jobseeker's allowance: in Britain, a payment made to unemployed people
Juan Carlos *n* born 1938, king of Spain from 1975: nominated by Franco as the first king of the restored Spanish monarchy that was to follow his death
Juantorena *n* **Alberto** born 1951, Cuban runner: won the 400 metres and the 800 metres in the 1976 Olympic Games
Juárez[1] *n* short for **Ciudad Juárez**
Juárez[2] *n* **Benito Pablo** 1806–72, Mexican statesman. As president (1861–65; 1867–72) he thwarted Napoleon III's attempt to impose an empire under Maximilian and introduced many reforms
jube *n Austral & NZ informal* ▸ same as **jujube**
jubilant *adj* feeling great joy **jubilantly** *adv*
WORD ORIGIN Latin *jubilare* to give a joyful cry
jubilation *n* a feeling of great joy and celebration
jubilee ⓣ *n* a special anniversary, esp. a 25th (**silver jubilee**) or 50th one (**golden jubilee**)
WORD ORIGIN Old French *jubile*, ultimately from Hebrew *yōbhēl* ram's horn, used for proclamation
Judah ha-Levi *n* ?1075–1141, Jewish poet and philosopher, born in Spain; his major works include the collection in *Diwan* and the prose work *Sefer ha-Kuzari*, which presented his philosophy of Judaism in dialogue form
Judah ha-Nasi *n* ?135–?220 AD, rabbi and patriarch of the Sanhedrin, who compiled the Mishnah
Judaic *adj* of Jews or Judaism
Judaism *n* the religion of the Jews, based on the Old Testament and the Talmud
Judas *n* a person who betrays a friend
WORD ORIGIN after *Judas* Iscariot in the Bible
Judas Maccabaeus *n* Jewish leader, whose revolt (166–161 BC) against the Seleucid kingdom of Antiochus IV (Epiphanes) enabled him to recapture Jerusalem and rededicate the Temple
judder *vb informal chiefly Brit* to shake or vibrate violently: *the van juddered before it moved away*
WORD ORIGIN probably blend of *jar* (jolt) + *shudder*
judder bar *n NZ* a raised strip across a road designed to slow down vehicles
judge ⓣ *n* **1** a public official with authority to hear cases and pass sentences in a court of law **2** a

THESAURUS

push, shake, knock, jar, shove, jog, jostle
journal *n* **1a = magazine**, record, review, register, publication, bulletin, chronicle, gazette, periodical, zine *(informal)* **1b = newspaper**, paper, daily, weekly, monthly, tabloid **2 = diary**, record, history, log, notebook, chronicle, annals, yearbook, commonplace book, daybook, blog *(informal)*
journalist *n* **= reporter**, writer, correspondent, newsman *or* newswoman, stringer, commentator, broadcaster, hack *(derogatory)*, columnist, contributor, scribe *(informal)*, pressman, journo *(slang)*, newshound *(informal)*, newspaperman *or* newspaperwoman
journey *n* **1 = trip**, drive, tour, flight, excursion, progress, cruise, passage, trek, outing, expedition, voyage, ramble, jaunt, peregrination, travel ▹ *vb* **3 = travel**, go, move, walk, fly, range, cross, tour, progress, proceed, fare, wander, trek, voyage, roam, ramble, traverse, rove, wend, go walkabout *(Austral)*, peregrinate
joy *n* **1 = delight**, pleasure, triumph, satisfaction, happiness, ecstasy, enjoyment, bliss, transport, euphoria, festivity, felicity, glee, exuberance, rapture, elation, exhilaration, radiance, gaiety, jubilation, hilarity, exaltation, ebullience, exultation, gladness, joyfulness, ravishment
OPPOSITE: sorrow
jubilee *n* **= celebration**, holiday, fête, festival, carnival, festivity, gala
judge *n* **1 = magistrate**, justice, beak *(Brit slang)*, His, Her *or* Your Honour

DICTIONARY

person appointed to determine the result of a competition **3** a person whose opinion on a particular subject is usually reliable: *a fine judge of men* ▷ *vb* **judging, judged 4** to determine the result of (a competition) **5** to appraise critically: *she hopes people judge her on her work rather than her appearance* **6** to decide (something) after inquiry: *we use a means test to judge the most needy cases* **7** to believe or consider: *doctors judged that the benefits of such treatment outweighed the risk*
WORD ORIGIN Latin *judex*

judgment ❶ *or* **judgement** *n* **1** a decision formed after careful consideration: *the editorials reserve their judgment about the new political plan* **2** the verdict pronounced by a court of law **3** the ability to make critical distinctions and achieve a balanced viewpoint: *their judgment was unsound on foreign and defence issues* **4** the formal decision of the judge of a competition **5 against one's better judgment** contrary to what one thinks is sensible: *against my better judgment, I asked for another bourbon* **6 pass judgment** to give one's opinion, usually a critical one, on a matter

judgmental *or* **judgemental** *adj* making judgments, esp. critical ones, about other people's conduct

Judgment Day *n Christianity* the occasion of the Last Judgment by God at the end of the world

judicial ❶ *adj* **1** of judges or the administration of justice **2** showing or using good judgment: *judicial self-restraint* **judicially** *adv*
WORD ORIGIN Latin *judicium* judgment

judiciary *n* the branch of the central authority in a country that administers justice

judicious *adj* having or showing good judgment: *the judicious use of charge cards* **judiciously** *adv*

judo *n* a sport derived from jujitsu, in which the two opponents try to throw or force each other on to the ground
WORD ORIGIN Japanese *jū* gentleness + *dō* way

jug ❶ *n* a container with a handle and a small spout, used for holding and pouring liquids
WORD ORIGIN origin unknown

jugged hare *n* hare stewed in an earthenware pot

juggernaut *n* **1** *Brit* a very large heavy lorry **2** any terrible force that demands complete self-sacrifice
WORD ORIGIN Hindi *Jagannath* lord of the world

juggle ❶ *vb* **-gling, -gled 1** to throw and catch several objects continuously so that most are in the air at the same time **2** to keep (several activities) in progress at the same time: *women who are adept at juggling priorities* **3** to manipulate (facts or figures) to suit one's purpose **juggler** *n*
WORD ORIGIN Old French *jogler* to perform as a jester

jugular *n* a large vein in the neck that carries blood to the heart from the head. Also called: **jugular vein**
WORD ORIGIN Latin *jugulum* throat

juice ❶ *n* **1** a drink made from the liquid part of a fruit or vegetable: *grapefruit juice* **2** *informal* **a** petrol **b** electricity **3 juices a** the fluids in a person's or animal's body: *digestive juices* **b** the liquid that comes out of meat when it is cooked
WORD ORIGIN Old French *jus*

juicy ❶ *adj* **juicier, juiciest 1** full of juice **2** *informal* interesting and exciting: *juicy details*

jujitsu *n* the traditional Japanese system of unarmed self-defence
WORD ORIGIN Japanese *jū* gentleness + *jutsu* art

juju *n* **1** a magic charm or fetish used by some tribes in W Africa **2** the power associated with a juju
WORD ORIGIN probably from W African *djudju* evil spirit, fetish

jujube *n* a chewy sweet made of flavoured gelatine
WORD ORIGIN Medieval Latin *jujuba*

jukebox *n* an automatic coin-operated record player
WORD ORIGIN *juke* (from a Black American language) bawdy

jukskei *n S African* a game in which a peg is thrown over a fixed distance at a stake fixed into the ground
WORD ORIGIN Afrikaans *juk* yoke + *skei* pin

Jul. July

julep *n* a sweet alcoholic drink, usually garnished with sprigs of mint

Juliana *n* full name *Juliana Louise Emma Marie Wilhelmina*. 1909–2004, queen of the Netherlands (1948–80). She abdicated in favour of her eldest daughter Beatrix

Julian calendar *n* the calendar introduced by Julius Caesar, in which leap years occur every fourth year and in every centenary year

Julian of Norwich *n* ?1342–?1413, English mystic and anchoress: best known for the *Revelations of Divine Love* describing her visions

julienne *adj* **1** (of vegetables or meat) cut into thin shreds ▷ *n* **2** a clear soup containing thinly shredded vegetables
WORD ORIGIN French

Julius II *n* original name *Guiliano della Rovere*. 1443–1513, pope (1503–13). He completed the restoration of the Papal States to the Church, began the building of St Peter's, Rome (1506), and patronized Michelangelo, Raphael, and Bramante

July *n, pl* **-lies** the seventh month of the year
WORD ORIGIN after *Julius* Caesar

jumble ❶ *n* **1** a disordered mass or state **2** articles donated for a jumble sale ▷ *vb* **-bling, -bled 3** to mix up
WORD ORIGIN origin unknown

THESAURUS

2 = referee, expert, specialist, umpire, umpie *(Austral slang)*, mediator, examiner, connoisseur, assessor, arbiter, appraiser, arbitrator, moderator, adjudicator, evaluator, authority **3 = critic**, assessor, arbiter, appraiser, evaluator ▷ *vb* **4 = adjudicate**, referee, umpire, mediate, officiate, adjudge, arbitrate **5 = evaluate**, rate, consider, appreciate, view, class, value, review, rank, examine, esteem, criticize, ascertain, surmise **6 = estimate**, guess, assess, calculate, evaluate, gauge, appraise

judgment *n* **1 = opinion**, view, estimate, belief, assessment, conviction, diagnosis, valuation, deduction, appraisal **2 = verdict**, finding, result, ruling, decision, sentence, conclusion, determination, decree, order, arbitration, adjudication, pronouncement **3 = sense**, common sense, good sense, judiciousness, reason, understanding, taste, intelligence, smarts *(slang, chiefly US)*, discrimination, perception, awareness, wisdom, wit, penetration, prudence, sharpness, acumen, shrewdness, discernment, perspicacity, sagacity, astuteness, percipience

judicial *adj* **1 = legal**, official, judiciary, juridical

jug *n* **= container**, pitcher, urn, carafe, creamer *(US & Canad)*, vessel, jar, crock, ewer

juggle *vb* **3 = manipulate**, change, doctor *(informal)*, fix *(informal)*, alter, modify, disguise, manoeuvre, tamper with, misrepresent, falsify

juice *n* **1 = liquid**, extract, fluid, liquor, sap, nectar **3a = secretion**, serum

juicy *adj* **1 = moist**, lush, watery, succulent, sappy **2 = interesting**, colourful, sensational, vivid, provocative, spicy *(informal)*, suggestive, racy, risqué

jumble *n* **2 = muddle**, mixture, mess, disorder, confusion, chaos, litter, clutter, disarray, medley, mélange *(French)*, miscellany, mishmash, farrago, hotchpotch *(US)*, hodgepodge, gallimaufry, pig's breakfast *(informal)*, disarrangement ▷ *vb* **3 = mix**, mistake, confuse,

DICTIONARY

jumble sale *n* a sale, usually of second-hand articles, often in aid of charity

jumbo ❶ *adj* **1** *Brit, Austral & NZ informal* very large: *jumbo prawns* ▷ *n, pl* **-bos** **2** ▸ short for **jumbo jet**
WORD ORIGIN after a famous elephant exhibited by P. T. Barnum

jumbo jet *n informal* a very large jet-propelled airliner

jumbuck *n Austral old-fashioned slang* sheep
WORD ORIGIN from a native Australian language

jump ❶ *vb* **1** to move suddenly up into the air by using the muscles in the legs and feet **2** to move quickly: *he jumps on a No. 6 bus* **3** to jerk with astonishment or shock: *he jumped when he heard a loud noise* **4** (of prices) to rise suddenly or abruptly **5** to change quickly from one subject to another: *any other comments before I jump on to the next section?* **6** *informal* to attack without warning: *the officer was jumped by three prisoners who broke his jaw* **7** **jump down someone's throat** *informal* to speak sharply to someone **8** **jump the gun** ▸ see **gun** (sense 3) **9** **jump the queue** **a** to take a place in a queue ahead of people who are already queuing **b** to have an unfair advantage over other people: *squatters should not be able to jump the queue for housing* **10** **jump to it** *informal* to begin doing something immediately ▷ *n* **11** the act or an instance of jumping **12** *sport* any of several contests that involve jumping: *the long jump* **13** a sudden rise: *a 78% jump in taxable profits* **14** a sudden change from one subject to another: *stunning jumps from thought to thought* **15** a step or degree: *one jump ahead of the competition* **16** **take a running jump** *informal* a contemptuous expression of dismissal ▸ See also **jump at, jump on**
WORD ORIGIN probably imitative

jump at *vb* to accept eagerly: *I jumped at the chance to return to English county cricket*

jumped-up ❶ *adj informal* having suddenly risen in significance and appearing arrogant: *a jumped-up bunch of ex-student-leaders*

jumper[1] ❶ *n* **1** *Austral & Brit* a knitted garment covering the upper part of the body **2** *US & Canad* a pinafore dress
WORD ORIGIN obsolete *jump* man's loose jacket

jumper[2] *n* a person or animal that jumps

jump jet *n informal* a fixed-wing jet aircraft that can land and take off vertically

jump leads *pl n* two heavy cables used to start a motor vehicle with a flat battery by connecting the flat battery to the battery of another vehicle

jump on *vb informal* to make a sudden physical or verbal attack on: *the press really jumped on him*

jump-start *vb* **1** to start the engine of (a motor vehicle) by pushing or rolling it and then engaging the gears ▷ *n* **2** the act of starting a motor vehicle in this way

jump suit *n* a one-piece garment combining trousers and top

jumpy *adj* **jumpier, jumpiest** nervous or apprehensive

Jun. **1** June **2** Junior

junction *n* a place where roads or railway lines meet, link, or cross each other
WORD ORIGIN Latin *junctio* a joining

juncture *n* a point in time, esp. a critical one: *trade has been halted at a crucial juncture*

June *n* the sixth month of the year
WORD ORIGIN probably from Latin *Junius* of the goddess Juno

jungle *n* **1** a forest area in a hot country with luxuriant vegetation **2** a confused or confusing situation: *the administrative jungle* **3** a situation where there is an intense struggle for survival: *the economic jungle* **4** a type of fast electronic dance music
WORD ORIGIN Hindi *jangal*

junior ❶ *adj* **1** lower in rank or position: *junior officers* **2** younger: *world junior champion* **3** (in England and Wales) of school children between the ages of 7 and 11 approximately **4** *US* of the third year of a four-year course at college or high school ▷ *n* **5** a person holding a low rank or position **6** a person who is younger than another person: *the man she is to marry is 20 years her junior* **7** (in England and Wales) a junior school child **8** *US* a junior student
WORD ORIGIN Latin: younger

Junior *adj* the younger of two: usually used after a name to distinguish between two people of the same name: *Harry Connick Junior*

junior lightweight *n* a professional boxer weighing up to 130 pounds (59 kg)

juniper *n* an evergreen shrub with purple berries which are used to make gin
WORD ORIGIN Latin *juniperus*

Junius *n* pen name of the anonymous author of a series of letters (1769–72) attacking the ministries of George III of England: now generally believed to have been written by Sir Philip Francis

junk[1] ❶ *n* **1** old or unwanted objects **2** *informal* rubbish: *the sheer junk written about astrology* **3** *slang* narcotic drugs, esp. heroin
WORD ORIGIN Middle English *jonke* old useless rope

junk[2] *n* a Chinese sailing boat with a flat bottom and square sails
WORD ORIGIN Portuguese *junco*, from Javanese *jon*

junk bond *n finance* a security that offers a high yield but often involves a high risk of default

Junkers *n* **Hugo** 1859–1935, German aircraft designer. His military aircraft were used in both World Wars

junket *n* **1** an excursion made by a public official and paid for out of public funds **2** a sweet dessert made of flavoured milk set with rennet **3** a feast **junketing** *n*
WORD ORIGIN Middle English: rush basket, hence custard served on rushes

junk food *n* food with a low nutritional value

junkie *n informal* a drug addict

junk mail *n* unsolicited mail advertising goods or services

Juno *n* the queen of the Roman gods

junta *n* a group of military officers holding the power in a country after a revolution
WORD ORIGIN Spanish: council

Jupiter *n* **1** the king of the Roman

j

THESAURUS

disorder, shuffle, tangle, muddle, confound, entangle, ravel, disorganize, disarrange, dishevel

jumbo *adj* **1** *(Brit, Austral & NZ informal)* = **giant**, large, huge, immense, mega *(informal)*, gigantic, oversized, elephantine, ginormous *(informal)*, humongous *or* humungous *(US slang)*, supersize **OPPOSITE:** tiny

jump *vb* **1** = **leap**, dance, spring, bound, bounce, hop, skip, caper, prance, gambol **3** = **recoil**, start, jolt, flinch, shake, jerk, quake, shudder, twitch, wince **4** = **increase**, rise, climb, escalate, gain, advance, boost, mount, soar, surge, spiral, hike, ascend ▷ *n* **11** = **leap**, spring, skip, bound, buck, hop, vault, caper **13** = **rise**, increase, escalation, upswing, advance, boost, elevation, upsurge, upturn, increment, augmentation

jumped-up *adj (informal)* = **conceited**, arrogant, pompous, stuck-up, cocky, overbearing, puffed up, presumptuous, insolent, immodest, toffee-nosed, self-opinionated, too big for your boots *or* breeches

jumper[1] *n* **1** *(Austral & Brit)* = **sweater**, top, jersey, cardigan, woolly, pullover

junior *adj* **1** = **minor**, lower, secondary, lesser, subordinate, inferior **2** = **younger** **OPPOSITE:** senior

junk[1] *n* **1, 2** = **rubbish**, refuse, waste, scrap, litter, debris, crap *(slang)*, garbage *(chiefly US)*, trash, clutter,

DICTIONARY

gods **2** the largest planet
Jurassic *adj geol* of the geological period about 180 million years ago, during which dinosaurs flourished **WORD ORIGIN** after the *Jura* (Mountains) in W central Europe
juridical *adj* of law or the administration of justice **WORD ORIGIN** Latin *jus* law + *dicere* to say
jurisdiction ❶ *n* **1** the right or power to administer justice and to apply laws **2** the exercise or extent of such right or power **3** authority in general: *under the jurisdiction of the referee* **WORD ORIGIN** Latin *jurisdictio*
jurisprudence *n* the science or philosophy of law **WORD ORIGIN** Latin *juris prudentia*
jurist *n* a person who is an expert on law **WORD ORIGIN** French *juriste*
juror *n* a member of a jury **WORD ORIGIN** Old French *jurer* to take an oath

j

jury *n, pl* **-ries** **1** a group of, usually, twelve people, sworn to deliver a true verdict according to the evidence upon a case presented in a court of law **2** a group of people appointed to judge a competition **WORD ORIGIN** Old French *jurer* to swear
jury box *n* an enclosure where the jury sits in a court of law
jury-rigged *adj chiefly naut* set up in a makeshift manner **WORD ORIGIN** origin unknown
just ❶ *adv* **1** very recently: *the results have just been published* **2** at this very instant or in the very near future: *news is just coming in of a nuclear explosion* **3** no more than; only: *nothing fancy, just solid German fare* **4** exactly: *just the opposite* **5** barely: *the swimmers arrived just in time for the opening ceremony* **6 just about** practically or virtually: *just about everyone* **7 just about to** very soon going to: *it was just about to explode* **8 just a moment** *or* **second** *or* **minute** an expression requesting someone to wait for a short time **9 just now** **a** a short time ago: *as you said just now* **b** at the present time: *he needs all the support he can get just now* **c** *S African informal* in a little while **10 just so** arranged with precision: *a cottage with the gardens and rooms all just so* ▷ *adj* **11** fair and right: *a just war* **justly** *adv* **justness** *n* **WORD ORIGIN** Latin *jus* justice
justice ❶ *n* **1** the quality of being just **2** the administration of law according to prescribed and accepted principles **3** a judge **4 bring to justice** to capture, try, and punish (a criminal) **5 do justice to** to show to full advantage: *she wore white slacks and a sleeveless blouse that did full justice to her trim figure* **WORD ORIGIN** Latin *justitia*
justice of the peace *n* **1** (in Britain) a magistrate who is authorized to act as a judge in a local court of law **2** (in New Zealand) a person authorized to act in a limited judicial capacity
justifiable *adj* having a good cause or reason: *I reacted with justifiable indignation* **justifiably** *adv*
justify ❶ *vb* **-fies, -fying, -fied** **1** to prove (something) to be just or valid: *the idea of the end justifying the means* **2** to defend (an action) as being warranted: *an essay justifying his conversion to Catholicism* **3** to arrange (text) when typing or printing so that both margins are straight **justification** *n* **WORD ORIGIN** Latin *justificare*
Justinian II *n* 669–711 AD, Byzantine emperor (685–95, 705–11). Banished (695) after a revolt against his oppressive rule, he regained the throne with the help of the Bulgars. He was killed in a second revolt
Justin Martyr *n* **Saint** ?100–?165 AD, Christian apologist and philosopher. Feast day: June 1
jute *n* a fibre that comes from the bark of an East Indian plant, used in making rope, sacks, and mats **WORD ORIGIN** Bengali *jhuto*
jut out *vb* **jutting, jutted** to stick out **WORD ORIGIN** variant of JET[1]
Juvenal *n* Latin name *Decimus Junius Juvenalis*. ?60–?140 AD, Roman satirist. In his 16 verse satires, he denounced the vices of imperial Rome
juvenile ❶ *adj* **1** young; not fully adult: *juvenile offenders* **2** of or for young people: *juvenile court* **3** immature in behaviour ▷ *n* **4** a young person **WORD ORIGIN** Latin *juvenilis*
juvenile delinquent *n* a young person who is guilty of a crime **juvenile delinquency** *n*
juvenilia *pl n* works produced in an artist's youth
juxtapose *vb* **-posing, -posed** to place (two objects or ideas) close together or side by side **juxtaposition** *n* **WORD ORIGIN** Latin *juxta* next to + POSITION

THESAURUS

rummage, dross, odds and ends, space junk, oddments, flotsam and jetsam, leavings, dreck *(slang, chiefly US)*
jurisdiction *n* **1, 2, 3 = authority**, say, power, control, rule, influence, command, sway, dominion, prerogative, mana *(NZ)*
just *adv* **1, 2 = recently**, lately, only now **3 = merely**, but, only, simply, solely, no more than, nothing but **4 = exactly**, really, quite, completely, totally, perfectly, entirely, truly, absolutely, precisely, altogether, positively **5 = barely**, hardly, only just, scarcely, at most, by a whisker, at a push, by the skin of your teeth ▷ *adj* **11 = fair**, good, legitimate, honourable, right, square, pure, decent, upright, honest, equitable, righteous, conscientious, impartial, virtuous, lawful, blameless, unbiased, fair-minded, unprejudiced **OPPOSITE:** unfair
justice *n* **1a = fairness**, equity, integrity, honesty, decency, impartiality, rectitude, reasonableness, uprightness, justness, rightfulness, right **OPPOSITE:** injustice **1b = justness**, fairness, legitimacy, reasonableness, right, integrity, honesty, legality, rectitude, rightfulness **3 = judge**, magistrate, beak *(Brit slang)*, His, Her *or* Your Honour
justify *vb* **1, 2 = explain**, support, warrant, bear out, legitimize, establish, maintain, confirm, defend, approve, excuse, sustain, uphold, acquit, vindicate, validate, substantiate, exonerate, legalize, absolve, exculpate
juvenile *adj* **1 = young**, junior, adolescent, youthful, immature **OPPOSITE:** adult **3 = immature**, childish, infantile, puerile, young, youthful, inexperienced, boyish, callow, undeveloped, unsophisticated, girlish, babyish, jejune ▷ *n* **4 = child**, youth, minor, girl, boy, teenager, infant, adolescent **OPPOSITE:** adult

K 1 kelvin(s) 2 *chess* king 3 *chem* potassium
WORD ORIGIN New Latin *kalium*
4 one thousand
WORD ORIGIN from KILO- 5 *computers* a unit of 1024 words, bits, or bytes

kabaddi *n* a game in which players try to touch opposing players but avoid being captured by them

Kabila *n* **Laurent** (*French* lorã) 1940–2001, Congolese politician and guerrilla leader: he overthrew the Mobutu regime in Zaïre, becoming president of the renamed Democratic Republic of Congo (1997–2001): assassinated

Kabir *n* 1440–1518, Indian religious leader who pioneered a religious movement that combined elements of Islam and Hinduism and is considered the precursor of Sikhism

kabloona *n* a person who is not of Inuit ancestry, esp. a white person

Kaczynski *n* **Lech** 1949–2010, Polish politician, president of Poland from 2005

Kádár *n* **János** 1912–89, Hungarian statesman; Communist prime minister of Hungary (1956–58; 1961–65) and first secretary of the Communist Party (1956–88)

Kaddish *n, pl* **Kaddishim** *Judaism* an ancient Jewish liturgical prayer, recited esp. by mourners
WORD ORIGIN Aramaic *qaddīsh* holy

Kaffir (kaf-fer) *n S African, offensive obsolete* a Black African
WORD ORIGIN Arabic *kāfir* infidel

kaftan *or* **caftan** *n* 1 a long loose garment worn by men in eastern countries 2 a woman's dress resembling this
WORD ORIGIN Turkish *qaftān*

kahawai *n* a food and game fish of New Zealand
WORD ORIGIN Māori

Kahn *n* 1 **Herman** 1922–83, US mathematician and futurologist; director of the Hudson Institute (1961–83) 2 **Louis I(sadore)**. 1901–74, US architect, noted for his art museums at Yale (1951–53), Fort Worth (1966–72), and New Haven (1969–74)

kai ❶ *n NZ informal* food
WORD ORIGIN Māori

kail *n* ▸ same as **kale**

kaiser (kize-er) *n history* a German or Austro-Hungarian emperor
WORD ORIGIN German, from Latin *Caesar* emperor

Kaiser[1] *n* (*sometimes not capital*) *history* 1 any German emperor, esp. Wilhelm II (ruled 1888–1918) 2 *obsolete* any Austro-Hungarian emperor
WORD ORIGIN C16: from German, ultimately from Latin *Caesar* emperor, from the cognomen of Gaius Julius CAESAR

Kaiser[2] *n* **Georg** 1878–1945, German expressionist dramatist

kak ❶ (kuck) *n S African, taboo* 1 faeces 2 rubbish
WORD ORIGIN Afrikaans

kaka *n* a parrot of New Zealand
WORD ORIGIN Māori

kakapo *n, pl* **-pos** a ground-living nocturnal New Zealand parrot that resembles an owl
WORD ORIGIN Māori

Kalashnikov *n* a Russian-made automatic rifle
WORD ORIGIN after M *Kalashnikov*, its designer

kale *n* a type of cabbage with crinkled leaves
WORD ORIGIN Old English *cāl*

kaleidoscope *n* 1 a tube-shaped toy lined with angled mirrors and containing loose pieces of coloured paper that form intricate patterns when viewed through a hole in the end 2 any complicated or rapidly changing set of colours, circumstances, etc.: *a kaleidoscope of shifting political groups and alliances*
kaleidoscopic *adj*
WORD ORIGIN Greek *kalos* beautiful + *eidos* form + *skopein* to look at

kalends *pl n* ▸ same as **calends**

kaleyard *n Scot* a vegetable garden
WORD ORIGIN literally: cabbage garden

Kalidasa *n* ?5th century AD, Indian dramatist and poet, noted for his romantic verse drama *Sakuntala*

Kalinin[1] *n* the former name (until 1991) of **Tver**

Kalinin[2] *n* **Mikhail Ivanovich** 1875–1946, Soviet statesman: titular head of state (1919–46); a founder of *Pravda* (1912)

Kamasutra (kah-ma-soo-tra) *n* **the Kamasutra** an ancient Hindu text on sex
WORD ORIGIN Sanskrit *kāma* love + *sūtra* thread, rule

Kamerlingh-Onnes *n* **Heike** 1853–1926, Dutch physicist: a pioneer of the physics of low-temperature materials and discoverer (1911) of superconductivity. Nobel prize for physics 1913

kamik *n* a traditional Inuit boot made of caribou hide or sealskin

kamikaze (kam-mee-kah-zee) *n* 1 (in World War II) a Japanese pilot who performed a suicidal mission ▹ *adj* 2 (of an action) undertaken in the knowledge that it will result in the death or injury of the person performing it: *a kamikaze attack*
WORD ORIGIN Japanese *kami* divine + *kaze* wind

Kamloops trout *n* a bright silvery rainbow trout common in British Columbia, Canada

Kammerer *n* **Paul** 1880–1926, Austrian zoologist: noted for his controversial experiments, esp. with the midwife toad, apparently demonstrating the inheritance of acquired characteristics. Accused of fraud, he committed suicide

Kandinsky *n* **Vasili** 1866–1944, Russian expressionist painter and theorist, regarded as the first to develop an entirely abstract style: a founder of *der Blaue Reiter*

kangaroo *n, pl* **-roos** a large Australian marsupial with powerful hind legs used for leaping
WORD ORIGIN probably Aboriginal

kangaroo court *n* an unofficial court set up by a group to discipline its members

kangaroo paw *n* an Australian plant with green-and-red flowers

Kang-de *or* **Kang-te** *n* title as emperor of Manchukuo of (Henry) **Pu-yi**

kaolin *n* a fine white clay used in making porcelain and in some medicines
WORD ORIGIN *Kaoling*, Chinese mountain where supplies for Europe were first obtained

kapa haka *n NZ* the traditional Māori performing arts, often performed competitively
WORD ORIGIN Māori

ka pai *interj NZ* good! well done!
WORD ORIGIN Māori

Kapil Dev *n* **(Ramlal) Nikhanj** born 1959, Indian cricketer: captain

THESAURUS

kai *n* (*NZ informal*) **= food**, grub (*slang*), provisions, fare, board, commons, eats (*slang*), feed, diet, meat, bread, tuck (*informal*), tucker (*Austral & NZ informal*), rations, nutrition, tack (*informal*), refreshment, scoff (*slang*), nibbles, foodstuffs, nourishment, chow (*informal*), sustenance, nosh (*slang*), daily bread, victuals, edibles, comestibles, provender, nosebag (*slang*), pabulum (*rare*), nutriment, vittles (*obsolete, dialect*), viands, aliment, eatables (*slang*)

kak *n* 1 **= faeces**, excrement, stool, muck, manure, dung, droppings, waste matter 2 **= rubbish**, nonsense, malarkey, garbage (*informal*), rot, crap (*taboo, slang*), drivel, tripe (*informal*), claptrap (*informal*), poppycock (*informal*), pants, bizzo (*Austral slang*), bull's wool (*Austral & NZ slang*)

DICTIONARY

of India (1983–84)

Kapitza *n* **Piotr Leonidovich** 1894–1984, Russian physicist. He worked in England and the USSR, doing research in several areas, particularly cryogenics; Nobel prize for physics in 1978

kapok *n* a fluffy fibre from a tropical tree, used for stuffing pillows and padding sleeping bags
WORD ORIGIN Malay

kaput (kap-**poot**) *adj informal* ruined or broken: *the chronometer, incidentally, is kaput*
WORD ORIGIN German *kaputt*

Karadžić *n* **Radovan** born 1945, Bosnian Serb political leader and psychiatrist; charged with genocide by the International War Crimes Tribunal for his role in the Bosnian civil war of 1992–95; in hiding

Karajan *n* **Herbert von** 1908–89, Austrian conductor

karakul *n* **1** a sheep of central Asia, the lambs of which have soft curled dark hair **2** the fur prepared from these lambs
WORD ORIGIN Russian

Karamanlis *n* **Konstantinos** 1907–98, Greek statesman; prime minister of Greece (1955–58; 1958–61; 1961–63; 1974–80): president of Greece (1980–85; 1990–95)

Karan *n* **Donna** born 1948, US fashion designer

karaoke *n* a form of entertainment in which members of the public sing well-known songs over a prerecorded backing tape
WORD ORIGIN Japanese *kara* empty + *ōkesutora* orchestra

karate *n* a Japanese system of unarmed combat, in which punches, chops, and kicks are made with the hands, feet, elbows, and legs
WORD ORIGIN Japanese: empty hand

Karloff *n* **Boris**, real name *William Pratt* 1887–1969, English film actor, famous for his roles in horror films, esp. *Frankenstein* (1931)

karma *n Hinduism, Buddhism* a person's actions affecting his or her fate in the next reincarnation
WORD ORIGIN Sanskrit: action, effect

karoo *or* **karroo** *n, pl* **-roos** *S African* an arid semidesert plateau of Southern Africa
WORD ORIGIN Khoi (language of southern Africa) *karo* dry

kaross (ka-**ross**) *n S African* a blanket made of animal skins sewn together
WORD ORIGIN Khoi (language of southern Africa) *karos* animal-skin blanket

Karpov *n* **Anatoly** born 1951, Russian chess player: world champion (1975–85); FIDE world champion (1993–99)

karri *n, pl* **-ris** **1** an Australian eucalypt **2** its wood, used for building

Karsh *n* **Yousuf** 1908–2002, Canadian photographer noted for portraits, especially of famous subjects

kart *n* ▸ same as **go-kart**

Karzai *n* **Hamid** born 1957, Afghan military and political leader: president from 2002

kasbah *n* ▸ same as **casbah**

katipo *n, pl* **-pos** a small venomous New Zealand spider, commonly black with a red or orange stripe on the abdomen
WORD ORIGIN Māori

katydid *n* a large green grasshopper of North America
WORD ORIGIN imitative

Katz *n* Sir **Bernard** 1911–2003, British neurophysiologist, born in Germany. Shared the Nobel prize for physiology or medicine (1970) with Julius Axelrod and Ulf von Euler

Kauffmann *n* **Angelica** 1741–1807, Swiss painter, who worked chiefly in England

Kaufman *n* **George S(imon)** 1889–1961, US dramatist who, with Moss Hart, collaborated on many Broadway comedy hits

kauri *n* a large New Zealand conifer grown for its valuable wood and resin
WORD ORIGIN Māori

Kawabata *n* **Yasunari** 1899–1972, Japanese novelist, author of *Yukiguni* (*Snow Country*, 1948) and *Yama no oto* (*The Sound of the Mountain*, 1954): Nobel prize for literature 1968

kayak *n* **1** an Inuit canoe-like boat consisting of a frame covered with animal skins **2** a fibreglass or canvas-covered canoe of similar design
WORD ORIGIN Inuktitut

Kazan[1] *n* a city in W Russia, capital of the Tatar Autonomous Republic on the River Volga: capital of an independent khanate in the 15th century; university (1804); a major industrial centre. Pop: 1 108 000 (2005 est)

Kazan[2] *n* **Elia**, real name *Elia Kazanjoglous* 1909–2003, US stage and film director and writer, born in Turkey. His films include *Gentleman's Agreement* (1947) and *On the Waterfront* (1954) for both of which he won Oscars, and *East of Eden* (1955)

Kazantzakis *n* **Nikos** 1885–1957, Greek novelist, poet, and dramatist, noted esp. for his novels *Zorba the Greek* (1946) and *Christ Recrucified* (1954) and his epic poem *The Odyssey* (1938)

kazoo *n, pl* **-zoos** a cigar-shaped metal musical instrument that produces a buzzing sound when the player hums into it
WORD ORIGIN probably imitative

KBE (in Britain) Knight (Commander of the Order) of the British Empire

kbps *computers* kilobits per second

kbyte *computers* kilobyte

kcal kilocalorie

KCB (in Britain) Knight Commander of the Bath

kea *n* a large brown-green parrot of New Zealand
WORD ORIGIN Māori

kebab *n* a dish consisting of small pieces of meat and vegetables, usually threaded onto skewers and grilled
WORD ORIGIN Arabic *kabāb* roast meat

Keble *n* **John** 1792–1866, English clergyman. His sermon on national apostasy (1833) is considered to have inspired the Oxford Movement

kecks *or* **keks** *pl n N English dialect* trousers
WORD ORIGIN from dialect *kicks* breeches

kedge *naut vb* **kedging, kedged** **1** to move (a ship) along by hauling in on the cable of a light anchor ▹*n* **2** a light anchor used for kedging
WORD ORIGIN Middle English *caggen* to fasten

kedgeree *n chiefly Brit* a dish consisting of rice, fish, and eggs
WORD ORIGIN Hindi *khicarī*

Keegan *n* **Kevin** born 1951, English footballer; manager of Newcastle United (1992–97; 2008); England coach (1999–2000)

keek *vb, n Scot* ▸ same as **peep**[1]
WORD ORIGIN probably from Middle Dutch *kīken* to look

keel *n* **1** one of the main lengthways steel or timber pieces along the base of a ship, to which the frames are fastened **2** **on an even keel** working or progressing smoothly without any sudden changes
WORD ORIGIN Old Norse *kjölr*

keelhaul *vb* **1** to reprimand (someone) harshly **2** *history* to drag (someone) under the keel of a ship as a punishment

keel over *vb* **1** (of an object) to turn upside down **2** *informal* (of a person) to collapse suddenly

keelson *or* **kelson** *n* a lengthways beam fastened to the keel of a ship for strength
WORD ORIGIN probably from Low German *kielswin* keel swine

keen[1] ❶ *adj* **1** eager or enthusiastic: *a keen gardener* **2** intense or strong:

THESAURUS

keen[1] *adj* **1, 8 = eager**, earnest, spirited, devoted, intense, fierce, enthusiastic, passionate, ardent, avid, fervent, impassioned, zealous, ebullient, wholehearted, fervid, bright-eyed and bushy-tailed (*informal*) **OPPOSITE:** unenthusiastic **2 = earnest**, fierce, intense, vehement, burning, flaming,

DICTIONARY

a keen interest in environmental issues **3** intelligent, quick, and perceptive: *a keen sense of humour* **4** (of sight, smell, or hearing) capable of recognizing fine distinctions **5** (of a knife or blade) having a sharp cutting edge **6** very strong and cold: *a keen wind* **7** very competitive: *keen prices* **8** **keen on** fond of; devoted to: *he is very keen on sport* **keenly** *adv* **keenness** *n*

WORD ORIGIN Old English *cēne*

keen² *vb* **1** to lament the dead ▷*n* **2** a lament for the dead

WORD ORIGIN Irish Gaelic *caoine*

keep ● *vb* **keeping, kept 1** to have or retain possession of (something) **2** to have temporary charge of: *he'd kept my broken beads in his pocket for me all evening* **3** to store in a customary place: *I keep it at the back of the drawer with my journal* **4** to remain or cause (someone or something) to remain in a specified state or condition: *keep still* **5** to continue or cause (someone) to continue: *keep going straight on* **6** to stay (in, on, or at a place or position): *keep to the paths* **7** to have as part of normal stock: *they keep a small stock of first-class German wines* **8** to support (someone) financially **9** to detain (someone) **10** to be faithful to (something): *to keep a promise* **11** (of food) to stay in good condition for a certain time: *fish doesn't keep very well* **12** to observe (a religious festival) with rites or ceremonies **13** to maintain by writing regular records in: *he keeps a nature diary in his spare time* **14** to look after or maintain for use, pleasure, or profit: *an old man who kept goats and cows* **15** to associate with: *she has started keeping bad company* **16** **how are you keeping?** are you well? **17** **keep in with** to stay friendly with someone as they may be useful to you ▷*n* **18** the cost of food and other everyday expense: *I have to earn my keep* **19** the main tower within the walls of a medieval castle or fortress **20** **for keeps** *informal* permanently ▸See also **keep at, keep away**, etc.

WORD ORIGIN Old English *cēpan* to observe

keep at *vb* **1** to persist in (an activity) **2** to compel (a person) to continue doing (a task)

keep away *vb* (often foll. by *from*) to prevent (someone) from going (somewhere)

keep back *vb* to refuse to reveal (something)

keep down *vb* **1** to hold (a group of people) under control **2** to cause (numbers or costs) not to increase **3** to lie low **4** to cause (food) to stay in the stomach; not vomit

keeper ● *n* **1** a person in charge of animals in a zoo **2** a person in charge of a museum, collection, or section of a museum **3** a person who supervises a person or thing: *the self-appointed keeper of the village conscience* **4** ▸short for **gamekeeper, goalkeeper** or **wicketkeeper**

keep fit *n* exercises designed to promote physical fitness if performed regularly

keep from *vb* **1** to restrain (oneself or someone else) from (doing something) **2** to preserve or protect (someone) from (something): *this will keep you from falling asleep*

keeping *n* **1** **in keeping with** suitable or appropriate to or for **2** **out of keeping with** unsuitable or inappropriate to or for

keep off *vb* **1** to stay or cause (someone) to stay at a distance (from) **2** to avoid or cause to avoid (something): *to keep off alcohol; to keep babies off sugar* **3** to avoid or cause (someone) to avoid (a topic)

keep on *vb* **1** to persist in (doing something): *petrol consumption keeps on rising* **2** to continue to employ: *a skeleton staff of 20 is being kept on* **3** **keep on about** to persist in talking about **4** **keep on at** to nag (a person)

keep out *vb* **1** to remain or cause (someone) to remain outside **2** **keep out of a** to cause (someone) to remain unexposed to (an unpleasant situation) **b** to avoid: *to keep out of trouble*

keepsake *n* a gift kept in memory of the giver

keep to *vb* **1** to do exactly what was expected of one: *he kept to his normal schedule* **2** to be confined to: *she kept to her bed until her flu had cleared up* **3** **keep oneself to oneself** to avoid the company of others **4** **keep to oneself a** to avoid the company of others **b** to avoid giving away (information)

keep up *vb* **1** to maintain at the present level **2** to maintain in good condition **3** **keep up with a** to maintain a pace set by (someone) **b** to remain informed about: *he liked to think he kept up with current musical trends* **c** to remain in contact with (someone) **4** **keep up with the Joneses** *informal* to compete with one's friends or neighbours in material possessions

keg *n* a small barrel in which beer is transported and stored

WORD ORIGIN Scandinavian

Keitel *n* **Wilhelm** 1882–1946, German field marshal; chief of the supreme command of the armed forces (1938–45). He was convicted at the Nuremberg trials and executed

Kekkonen *n* **Urho** (1900–86), Finnish statesman; president (1956–81)

Kekulé von Stradonitz *n* **(Friedrich) August** 1829–96, German chemist. His elucidation of the concepts of valence and single, double, and triple bonds enabled him to suggest the structure of many molecules, notably benzene (**Kekulé structure**)

kelp *n* a large brown seaweed rich in iodine and potash

WORD ORIGIN origin unknown

kelpie *n* **1** (in Scottish folklore) a

THESAURUS

consuming, eager, passionate, heightened, energetic, ardent, fanatical, fervent, impassioned, fervid **3 = perceptive**, quick, sharp, brilliant, acute, smart, wise, clever, subtle, piercing, penetrating, discriminating, shrewd, discerning, ingenious, astute, intuitive, canny, incisive, insightful, observant, perspicacious, sapient **OPPOSITE:** obtuse

5 = sharp, satirical, incisive, trenchant, pointed, cutting, biting, edged, acute, acid, stinging, piercing, penetrating, searing, tart, withering, scathing, pungent, sarcastic, sardonic, caustic, astringent, vitriolic, acerbic, mordant, razor-like, finely honed **OPPOSITE:** dull

7 = intense, strong, fierce, relentless, cut-throat

keep *vb* **1a** *(usually with* **from***)* **= prevent**, hold back, deter, inhibit, block, stall, restrain, hamstring, hamper, withhold, hinder, retard, impede, shackle, keep back **1b = hold on to**, maintain, retain, keep possession of, save, preserve, nurture, cherish, conserve **OPPOSITE:** lose

2, 3 = store, put, place, house, hold, deposit, pile, stack, heap, amass, stow **7 = carry**, stock, have, hold, sell, supply, handle, trade in, deal in

8 = support, maintain, sustain, provide for, mind, fund, board, finance, feed, look after, foster, shelter, care for, take care of, nurture, safeguard, cherish, nourish, subsidize **9 = delay**, detain, hinder, impede, stop, limit, check, arrest, curb, constrain, obstruct, retard, set back **OPPOSITE:** release

14a = raise, own, maintain, tend, farm, breed, look after, rear, care for, bring up, nurture, nourish

14b = manage, run, administer, be in charge (of), rule, direct, handle, govern, oversee, supervise, preside over, superintend ▷*n* **18 = board**, food, maintenance, upkeep, means, living, support, nurture, livelihood, subsistence, kai (*NZ informal*), nourishment, sustenance

19 = tower, castle, stronghold, dungeon, citadel, fastness, donjon

keeper *n* **2 = curator**, guardian, steward, superintendent, attendant, caretaker, overseer, preserver

DICTIONARY

water spirit in the form of a horse **2** an Australian sheepdog with a smooth coat and upright ears
WORD ORIGIN origin unknown

kelson *n* ▸ same as **keelson**

kelt *n* a salmon that has recently spawned
WORD ORIGIN origin unknown

Kelt *n* ▸ same as **Celt**

kelvin *n physics* the basic SI unit of thermodynamic temperature
WORD ORIGIN after W. T. *Kelvin*, physicist

Kelvin scale *n physics* a thermodynamic temperature scale starting at absolute zero

Kemble *n* **1 Frances Anne,** known as *Fanny.* 1809–93, English actress, in the US from 1832 **2** her uncle, **John Philip**. 1757–1823, English actor and theatrical manager

Kempe *n* **1 Margery** ?1373–?1440, English mystic. Her autobiography, *The Book of Margery Kempe*, describes her mystical experiences and pilgrimages in Europe and Palestine **2 Rudolf** 1910–76, German orchestral conductor, noted esp. for his interpretations of Wagner

ken *n* **1 beyond one's ken** beyond one's range of knowledge ▹ *vb* **kenning, kenned** *or* **kent 2** *Scot & N English dialect* to know
WORD ORIGIN Old English *cennan*

Kendall *n* **Edward Calvin** 1886–1972, US biochemist, who isolated the hormone thyroxine (1916). He shared the Nobel prize for physiology or medicine (1950) with Phillip Hench and Tadeus Reichstein for their work on hormones

kendo *n* the Japanese sport of fencing using wooden staves
WORD ORIGIN Japanese

Kendrew *n* Sir **John Cowdery** 1917–97, British biochemist. Using X-ray diffraction he discovered the structure of myoglobin, for which he shared a Nobel Prize (1962) with Max Perutz

Keneally *n* **Thomas** (**Michael**) born 1935, Australian writer. His novels include the Booker prizewinner *Schindler's Ark* (1982); other works are *The Playmaker* (1987), *The Great Shame* (1998), and *The Woman and Her Hero* (2007)

kennel *n* **1** a hutlike shelter for a dog **2 kennels** a place where dogs are bred, trained, or boarded ▹ *vb* **-nelling, -nelled** *or US* **-neling, -neled** to keep (a dog) in a kennel
WORD ORIGIN Latin *canis* dog

Kennelly *n* **Arthur Edwin** 1861–1939, US electrical engineer: independently of Heaviside, he predicted the existence of an ionized layer in the upper atmosphere, known as the Kennelly-Heaviside layer or E region

Kenny *n* **1 Brett** born 1961, Australian rugby league player **2 Yvonne,** born 1950, Australian opera singer

Kent[1] *n* a county of SE England, on the English Channel: the first part of Great Britain to be colonized by the Romans; one of the seven kingdoms of Anglo-Saxon England until absorbed by Wessex in the 9th century AD. Apart from the Downs it is mostly low-lying and agricultural, specializing in fruit and hops. The Medway towns of Rochester and Gillingham became an independent unitary authority in 1998. Administrative centre: Maidstone. Pop (excluding Medway): 1 348 800 (2003 est). Area (excluding Medway): 3526 sq km (1361 sq miles)

Kent[2] *n* **William** ?1685–1748, English architect, landscape gardener, and interior designer

Kenyan *adj* **1** from Kenya ▹ *n* **2** a person from Kenya

kepi *n* a French military cap with a flat top and a horizontal peak
WORD ORIGIN French

kept *vb* **1** ▸ the past of **keep 2 kept woman** *or* **man** a person financially supported by someone in return for sexual favours

keratin *n* a fibrous protein found in the hair and nails

kerb *or US & Canad* **curb** *n* a line of stone or concrete forming an edge between a pavement and a roadway
WORD ORIGIN Old French *courbe* bent

kerb crawling *n Brit* the act of driving slowly beside a kerb to pick up a prostitute **kerb crawler** *n*

kerbstone *or US & Canad* **curbstone** *n* one of a series of stones that form a kerb

kerchief *n* a piece of cloth worn over the head or round the neck
WORD ORIGIN Old French *cuevrechef*

Kerenski *or* **Kerensky** *n* **Aleksandr Fyodorovich** 1881–1970, Russian liberal revolutionary leader; prime minister (July–October 1917): overthrown by the Bolsheviks

kerfuffle *n informal* a noisy and disorderly incident
WORD ORIGIN Scots *curfuffle, carfuffle*

kermes (**kur**-meez) *n* the dried bodies of female scale insects, used as a red dyestuff
WORD ORIGIN Arabic *qirmiz*

Kern *n* **Jerome** (**David**) 1885–1945, US composer of musical comedies, esp. *Show Boat* (1927)

kernel *n* **1** the edible seed of a nut or fruit within the shell or stone **2** the grain of a cereal, such as wheat, consisting of the seed in a hard husk **3** the central or essential part of something: *there is a kernel of truth in these remarks*
WORD ORIGIN Old English *cyrnel* a little seed

kerosene *n US, Canad, Austral & NZ* ▸ same as **paraffin** (sense 1)
WORD ORIGIN Greek *kēros* wax

Kerr *n* Sir **John Robert** 1914–91, Australian public servant. As governor general of Australia (1974–77), he dismissed the Labor prime minister Gough Whitlam (1975) amid great controversy

Kerry *n, pl* **-ries** a small black breed of dairy cattle, originally from Ireland
WORD ORIGIN after *Kerry*, county in SW Ireland

Kerry[1] *n* **John Forbes** born 1943, US politician; Democratic Party candidate in the presidential election of 2004

Kerry[2] *n* **1** a county of SW Republic of Ireland, in W Munster province: mostly mountainous (including the highest peaks in Ireland), with a deeply indented coast and many offshore islands. County town: Tralee. Pop: 132 527 (2002). Area: 4701 sq km (1815 sq miles) **2** a small black breed of dairy cattle, originally from Kerry

Kesey *n* **Ken** 1935–2001, US novelist, best-known for *One Flew Over the Cuckoo's Nest* (1962)

Kesselring *n* **Albert** 1885–1960, German field marshal. He commanded the Luftwaffe attacks on Poland, France, and Britain (1939–40), and was supreme commander in Italy (1943–45) and on the western front (1945)

kestrel *n* a small falcon that feeds on small animals such as mice
WORD ORIGIN Old French *cresserele*

ketch *n* a two-masted sailing ship
WORD ORIGIN Middle English *cache*

ketchup *n* a thick cold sauce, usually made of tomatoes
WORD ORIGIN Chinese *kōetsiap* brine of pickled fish

ketone (**kee**-tone) *n chem* any of a class of compounds with the general formula R´COR, where R and R´ are alkyl or aryl groups
WORD ORIGIN German *Keton*, from *Aketon* acetone

kettle *n* **1** a metal container with a handle and spout, for boiling water **2** any of various metal containers for heating liquid, cooking, etc. **3 a different kettle of fish** a different matter entirely **4 a fine kettle of fish**

THESAURUS

key[1] *n* **1 = opener**, door key, latchkey **6 = answer**, means, secret, solution, path, formula, passage, clue, cue, pointer, sign ▹ *adj* **9 = essential**, leading, major, main, important, chief, necessary, basic, vital, crucial, principal, fundamental, decisive, indispensable, pivotal, must-have **OPPOSITE:** minor

a difficult or awkward situation **WORD ORIGIN** Old Norse *ketill*

kettledrum *n* a large bowl-shaped metal drum that can be tuned to play specific notes

key[1] ❶ *n* **1** a specially shaped metal instrument for moving the bolt of a lock so as to lock or unlock a door, suitcase, etc. **2** an instrument that is turned to operate a valve, clock winding mechanism, etc. **3** any of a set of levers pressed to operate a typewriter, computer, or musical keyboard instrument **4** a scale of musical notes that starts at one specific note **5** something that is crucial in providing an explanation or interpretation **6** a means of achieving a desired end: *education is the key to success in most walks of life today* **7** a list of explanations of symbols, codes, or abbreviations **8** pitch: *he spoke in a low key* ▹ *adj* **9** of great importance: *key prosecution witnesses have been giving evidence* ▹ *vb* **10** to harmonize with: *training and educational programmes uniquely keyed for local needs* **11** to adjust or fasten (something) with a key or some similar device **12** ▸ same as **keyboard** ▸ See also **key in** **WORD ORIGIN** Old English *cǣg*

key[2] *n* ▸ same as **cay**

keyboard *n* **1** a set of keys on a typewriter, computer, or piano **2** a musical instrument played using a keyboard ▹ *vb* **3** to enter (text) in type using a keyboard **keyboarder** *n*

keyed up *adj* very excited or nervous

key grip *n* the person in charge of moving and setting up camera tracks and scenery in a film or television studio

keyhole *n* an opening for inserting a key into a lock

keyhole surgery *n* surgery carried out using very small instruments, performed through a narrow hole cut in the body rather than through a major incision

key in *vb* to enter (information or instructions) into a computer by means of a keyboard

key money *n Brit* a sum of money required from a new tenant of a house or flat before he or she moves in

Keynesian (cane-zee-an) *adj* of the economic theories of J M Keynes, who argued that governments should fund public works to maintain full employment, accepting if necessary the consequence of inflation

keynote *n* **1** a central or dominant idea in a speech or literary work **2** the note on which a scale or key is based ▹ *adj* **3** central or dominating: *his keynote speech to the party conference*

keypad *n* a small panel with a set of buttons for operating a Teletext system, electronic calculator, etc.

keyring *n* a metal ring, often decorative, for keeping keys on

key signature *n music* a group of sharps or flats at the beginning of each stave line to indicate the key

keystone *n* **1** the most important part of a process, organization, etc.: *the keystone of the government's economic policy* **2** the central stone at the top of an arch

keyword *n computers* a word or phrase that a computer will search for in order to locate the information or file that the computer user has requested

key worker *n chiefly Brit* **1** a social worker, mental health worker, or nursery nurse assigned to an individual case, patient or child **2** (in Britain) a worker in a public sector profession considered by the government to be essential to society

kg kilogram

KG (in Britain) Knight of the Order of the Garter

KGB (formerly) the Soviet secret police **WORD ORIGIN** Russian *Komitet Gosudarstvennoi Bezopasnosti* State Security Committee

Khachaturian *n* **Aram Ilich** 1903–78, Russian composer. His works, which often incorporate Armenian folk tunes, include a piano concerto and the ballets *Gayaneh* (1942) and *Spartacus* (1954)

Khadijah *n* 554–619 AD, the first wife of the Prophet Mohammed, regarded as the first convert to Islam

Khafre *n* Greek name *Chephren.* king of Egypt (*c.* 2550 BC) of the 4th dynasty. He built the second pyramid and is thought to have built the Sphinx at Giza

khaki *adj* **1** dull yellowish-brown ▹ *n* **2** a hard-wearing fabric of this colour, used for military uniforms **WORD ORIGIN** Urdu, from Persian: dusty

Khalid ibn Abdul Aziz *n* 1913–82, king and President of the Council of Ministers of Saudi Arabia (1975–82)

Khamenei *n* Ayatollah **Seyed Ali** born 1940, Iranian political and religious leader: president of Iran (1981–89); leader of the Islamic Republic from 1989

khan *n* a title of respect in Afghanistan and central Asia **WORD ORIGIN** Turkish

Khan *n* See **Imran Khan**

Khatami *n* **Seyed Mohammad** born 1943, Iranian politician: president of Iran (1997–2005)

Khayyám *n* See **Omar Khayyám**

kHz kilohertz

kia ora ❶ *interj* NZ a Māori greeting **WORD ORIGIN** Māori

kibbutz *n, pl* **kibbutzim** a farm, factory, or other workplace in Israel, owned and run communally by its members **WORD ORIGIN** Modern Hebrew *qibbūs* gathering

kibosh *n* **put the kibosh on** *slang* to put a stop to **WORD ORIGIN** origin unknown

kick ❶ *vb* **1** to drive, push, or hit with the foot or feet **2** to strike out with the feet, as in swimming **3** to raise a leg high, as in dancing **4** *rugby* to score (a conversion, drop kick, or penalty) with a kick: *he kicked his third penalty* **5** (of a firearm) to recoil when fired **6** *informal* to object or resist: *school uniforms give children something to kick against* **7** *informal* to free oneself of (an addiction): *smokers who want to kick the habit* **8** **alive and kicking** *informal* active and in good health **9** **kick someone upstairs** to promote someone to a higher but effectively powerless position ▹ *n* **10** a thrust or blow with the foot **11** any of certain rhythmic leg movements used in swimming **12** the recoil of a firearm **13** *informal* an exciting effect: *we get a kick out of attacking opposing fans and overturning their buses; a few small bets just for kicks* **14** *informal* the intoxicating effect of an alcoholic drink: *a cocktail with a kick in it* **15** **kick in the teeth** *slang* a humiliating rebuff ▸ See also **kick about, kick off**, etc. **WORD ORIGIN** Middle English *kiken*

kick about *or* **around** *vb informal* **1** to treat (someone) harshly **2** to discuss (ideas) informally **3** to lie neglected or forgotten: *there's a copy of that book kicking about somewhere*

kickback *n* **1** part of an income paid to a person in return for an opportunity to make a profit, often by some illegal arrangement **2** a strong reaction

kick in *vb* to start or become activated

kick off ❶ *vb* **1** to start play in a game of football by kicking the ball from the centre of the field **2** *informal* to commence (a discussion, event, etc.) ▹ *n* **kick-off 3 a** the kick that

THESAURUS

kia ora *interj (NZ)* = **hello**, hi *(informal)*, greetings, gidday *or* g'day *(Austral & NZ)*, how do you do?, good morning, good evening, good afternoon, welcome

kick *vb* **1** = **boot**, strike, knock, punt, put the boot in(to) *(slang)* **7** *(informal)* = **give up**, break, stop, abandon, quit, cease, eschew, leave off, desist from, end ▹ *n* **13** *(informal)* = **thrill**, glow, buzz *(slang)*, tingle, high *(slang)*, sensation

kick off *(informal)* = **begin**, start, open, commence, launch, initiate, get under way, kick-start, get on the road

DICTIONARY

officially starts a game of football **b** the time when the first kick is due to take place **4** *informal* the time when an event is due to begin

kick out ⓣ *vb informal* to dismiss (someone) or throw (someone) out forcefully

kickstand *n* a short metal bar on a motorcycle, which when kicked into a vertical position holds the cycle upright when stationary

kick-start *n* **1** Also: **kick-starter** a pedal on a motorcycle that is kicked downwards to start the engine **2** an action or event that reactivates something ▹*vb* **3** to start (a motorcycle) with a kick-start **4** to do something bold or drastic in order to begin or improve the performance of something: *to kick-start the economy*

kick up *vb informal* to cause (trouble)

kid[1] ⓣ *n* **1** *informal* a young person; child **2** a young goat **3** soft smooth leather made from the hide of a kid ▹*adj* **4** younger: *my kid sister* ▹*vb* **kidding, kidded 5** (of a goat) to give birth to (young)

WORD ORIGIN from Old Norse

kid[2] ⓣ *vb* **kidding, kidded** *informal* **1** to tease or deceive (someone) for fun **2** to fool (oneself) into believing something: *don't kid yourself that no-one else knows* **kidder** *n*

WORD ORIGIN probably from KID[1]

Kid *n* a variant spelling of (Thomas) **Kyd**

Kidd *n* **William,** known as *Captain Kidd.* 1645–1701, Scottish privateer, pirate, and murderer; hanged

kiddie *n informal* a child

kid gloves *pl n* **handle someone with kid gloves** to treat someone with great tact in order not to upset them

Kidman *n* **Nicole** born 1967, Australian film actress, born in Hawaii. Her films include *To Die For* (1995), *Eyes Wide Shut* (1999), *The Hours* (2002), and *The Golden Compass* (2007): formerly married to Tom Cruise

kidnap ⓣ *vb* **-napping, -napped** *or US* **-naping, -naped** to capture and hold (a person), usually for ransom **kidnapper** *or US* **-naper** *n* **kidnapping** *or US* **-naping** *n*

WORD ORIGIN KID[1] + obsolete *nap* to steal

kidney *n* **1** either of two bean-shaped organs at the back of the abdominal cavity. They filter waste products from the blood, which are excreted as urine **2** the kidneys of certain animals used as food

WORD ORIGIN origin unknown

kidney bean *n* a reddish-brown kidney-shaped bean, edible when cooked

kidney machine *n* a machine carrying out the functions of damaged human kidneys

kidology *n informal* the practice of bluffing or deception in order to gain a psychological advantage over someone

Kieślowski *n* **Krzysztof** 1941–96, Polish film director, whose later films were made in France; his work includes the television series *Decalogue* (1988–89) and the film trilogy *Three Colours* (1993–94)

kill ⓣ *vb* **1** to cause the death of (a person or animal) **2** *informal* to cause (someone) pain or discomfort: *my feet are killing me* **3** to put an end to: *his infidelity had killed his marriage* **4** *informal* to quash or veto: *the main opposition party tried to kill the bill* **5** *informal* to overwhelm (someone) completely with laughter, attraction, or surprise: *her jokes really kill me* **6 kill oneself** *informal* to overexert oneself **7 kill time** to spend time on something unimportant or trivial while waiting for something: *I'm just killing time until I can talk to the other witnesses* **8 kill two birds with one stone** to achieve two results with one action ▹*n* **9** the act of causing death at the end of a hunt or bullfight **10** the animal or animals killed during a hunt **11 in at the kill** present when something comes to a dramatic end with unpleasant results for someone else **killer** *n*

WORD ORIGIN Middle English *cullen*

killer whale *n* a black-and-white toothed whale, most common in cold seas

killing ⓣ *adj* **1** *informal* very tiring: *a killing pace* **2** *informal* extremely funny **3** causing death; fatal ▹*n* **4** the act of causing death; slaying **5 make a killing** *informal* to have a sudden financial success

killjoy *n* a person who spoils other people's pleasure

kiln *n* a large oven for burning, drying, or processing pottery, bricks, etc.

WORD ORIGIN Latin *culina* kitchen

kilo *n, pl* **kilos** ▸short for **kilogram** or **kilometre**

kilo- *combining form* **1** denoting one thousand (10^3): *kilometre* **2** (in computers) denoting 2^{10} (1024): *kilobyte*. In computer usage, *kilo-* is restricted to sizes of storage (e.g. *kilobit*) when it means 1024: in other computer contexts it retains its usual meaning of 1000

WORD ORIGIN Greek *khilioi* thousand

kilobit *n computers* 1024 bits

kilobyte *n computers* 1024 bytes

kilocalorie *n* one thousand calories

kilocycle *n* ▸an old word for **kilohertz**

kilogram *or* **kilogramme** *n* **1** one thousand grams **2** the basic SI unit of mass

kilohertz *n, pl* **kilohertz** one thousand hertz; one thousand cycles per second

kilojoule *n* one thousand joules

THESAURUS

kick out *(informal)* **= dismiss**, remove, reject, get rid of, discharge, expel, oust, eject, evict, toss out, give the boot *(slang)*, sack *(informal)*, kiss off *(slang, chiefly US & Canad)*, give (someone) their marching orders, give the push, give the bum's rush *(slang)*, show someone the door, throw someone out on their ear *(informal)*, kennet *(Austral slang)*, jeff *(Austral slang)*

kid[1] *n* **1** *(informal)* **= child**, girl, boy, baby, lad, teenager, youngster, infant, adolescent, juvenile, toddler, tot, lass, wean, little one, bairn, stripling, sprog *(slang)*, munchkin *(informal, chiefly US)*, rug rat *(US & Canad informal)*, littlie *(Austral informal)*, ankle-biter *(Austral slang)*, tacker *(Austral slang)*

kid[2] *(informal) vb* **1 = tease**, joke, trick, fool, pretend, mock, rag *(Brit)*, wind up *(Brit slang)*, ridicule, hoax, beguile, gull *(archaic)*, delude, jest, bamboozle, hoodwink, cozen, jerk *or* yank someone's chain *(informal)*

kidnap *vb* **= abduct**, remove, steal, capture, seize, snatch *(slang)*, hijack, run off with, run away with, make off with, hold to ransom

kill *vb* **1 = slay**, murder, execute, slaughter, destroy, waste *(informal)*, do in *(slang)*, take out *(slang)*, massacre, butcher, wipe out *(informal)*, dispatch, cut down, erase, assassinate, eradicate, whack *(informal)*, do away with, blow away *(slang, chiefly US)*, obliterate, knock off *(slang)*, liquidate, decimate, annihilate, neutralize, exterminate, terminate *(slang)*, croak, mow down, take (someone's) life, bump off *(slang)*, extirpate, wipe from the face of the earth *(informal)* **3, 4** *(informal)* **= destroy**, defeat, crush, scotch, still, stop, total *(slang)*, ruin, halt, cancel, wreck, shatter, veto, suppress, dismantle, stifle, trash *(slang)*, ravage, eradicate, smother, quash, quell, extinguish, annihilate, put paid to

killing *adj* **1** *(informal)* **= tiring**, hard, testing, taxing, difficult, draining, exhausting, punishing, crippling, fatiguing, gruelling, sapping, debilitating, strenuous, arduous, laborious, enervating, backbreaking ▹*n* **4 = murder**, massacre, slaughter, execution, dispatch, manslaughter, elimination, slaying, homicide, bloodshed, carnage, fatality, liquidation, extermination, annihilation, eradication, butchery **5 make a killing** *(informal)* **= profit**, gain, clean up *(informal)*, be lucky, be successful, make a fortune, strike it

DICTIONARY

kilolitre *or US* **kiloliter** *n* a measure of volume equivalent to one thousand litres

kilometre *or US* **kilometer** *n* a unit of length equal to one thousand metres

kiloton *n* **1** one thousand tons **2** an explosive power, esp. of a nuclear weapon, equal to the power of 1000 tons of TNT

kilovolt *n* one thousand volts

kilowatt *n* one thousand watts

kilowatt-hour *n* a unit of energy equal to the work done by a power of 1000 watts in one hour

kilt *n* **1** a knee-length pleated tartan skirt-like garment, worn by men in Highland dress and by women and girls ▹*vb* **2** to put pleats in (cloth) **kilted** *adj*
WORD ORIGIN Scandinavian

Kilvert *n* **Francis** 1840–79, British clergyman and diarist. His diary (published 1938–40) gives a vivid account of life in the Welsh Marches in the 1870s

kimono (kim-**moan**-no) *n, pl* **-nos** **1** a loose wide-sleeved Japanese robe, fastened with a sash **2** a European dressing gown resembling this
WORD ORIGIN Japanese: clothing

kin *n* **1** a person's relatives collectively **2** ▸ see **next of kin**
WORD ORIGIN Old English *cyn*

kind¹ ❶ *adj* **1** considerate, friendly, and helpful: *a good, kind man; a few kind words* **2** cordial; courteous: *reprinted by kind permission*
WORD ORIGIN Old English *gecynde* natural, native

kind² ❶ *n* **1** a class or group having characteristics in common: *what kind of music do you like?* **2** essential nature or character: *differences of degree rather than of kind* **3** **in kind** **a** (of payment) in goods or services rather than in money **b** with something of the same sort: *the government threatened to retaliate in kind to any use of nuclear weapons* **4** **kind of** to a certain extent; loosely: *kind of hard; a kind of socialist* **5** **of a kind** of a poorer quality or standard than is wanted or expected: *a few farmers wrest subsistence of a kind from the thin topsoil*
WORD ORIGIN Old English *gecynd* nature

kindergarten *n* a class or school for children under six years old
WORD ORIGIN from German, literally: children's garden

kind-hearted *adj* considerate and sympathetic

kindle *vb* **-dling, -dled** **1** to set (a fire) alight or (of a fire) to start to burn **2** to arouse or be aroused: *his passions were kindled as quickly as her own*
WORD ORIGIN Old Norse *kynda*

kindling *n* material for starting a fire, such as dry wood or straw

kindly ❶ *adj* **-lier, -liest** **1** having a warm-hearted and caring nature **2** pleasant or agreeable: *a kindly climate* ▹*adv* **3** in a considerate or humane way **4** please: *will you kindly stop prattling on about it!* **5** **not take kindly to** to react unfavourably towards **kindliness** *n*

kindness ❶ *n* **1** the quality of being kind **2** a kind or helpful act

kindred *adj* **1** having similar qualities: *cholera, and other kindred diseases* **2** related by blood or marriage **3** **kindred spirit** a person with whom one has something in common ▹*n* **4** relationship by blood or marriage **5** similarity in character **6** a person's relatives collectively
WORD ORIGIN Middle English *kinred*

kindy, kindie *n, pl* **-dies** *Austral & NZ informal* a kindergarten

kine *pl n archaic* cows or cattle
WORD ORIGIN Old English *cȳna* of cows

kinematics (kin-nim-**mat**-iks) *n physics* the study of the motion of bodies without reference to mass or force **kinematic** *adj*
WORD ORIGIN Greek *kinēma* movement

kinetic (kin-**net**-ik) *adj* relating to or caused by motion **kinetically** *adv*
WORD ORIGIN Greek *kinein* to move

kinetic art *n* art, such as sculpture, that moves or has moving parts

kinetic energy *n physics* the energy of motion of a body equal to the work it would do if it were brought to rest

kinetics *n physics* the branch of mechanics concerned with the study of bodies in motion

king ❶ *n* **1** a male ruler of a country who has inherited the throne from his parents **2** a ruler or chief: *the king of the fairies* **3** a person, animal, or thing considered as the best or most important of its kind: *the king of rock and roll* **4** a playing card with a picture of a king on it **5** a chessman, able to move one square in any direction: the object of the game is to checkmate one's opponent's king **6** *draughts* a piece which has moved entirely across the board and been crowned and which may therefore move backwards as well as forwards **kingship** *n*
WORD ORIGIN Old English *cyning*

kingcup *n Brit* a yellow-flowered plant; marsh marigold

kingdom ❶ *n* **1** a territory or state ruled by a king or queen **2** any of the three groups into which natural objects may be divided: the animal, plant, and mineral kingdoms **3** a place or area considered to be under the total power and control of a person, organization, or thing: *the kingdom of God*

kingfisher *n* a fish-eating bird with a greenish-blue and orange plumage
WORD ORIGIN originally *king's fisher*

kingklip *n* an edible eel-like marine fish of S Africa
WORD ORIGIN Afrikaans

king-of-arms *n, pl* **kings-of-arms** a person holding the highest rank of heraldic office

kingpin *n* **1** the most important person in an organization: *a Mexican narcotics kingpin* **2** a pivot pin that

THESAURUS

rich *(informal)*, make a bomb *(slang)*, rake it in *(informal)*, have a windfall

kind¹ *adj* **1 = considerate**, good, loving, kindly, understanding, concerned, friendly, neighbourly, gentle, generous, mild, obliging, sympathetic, charitable, thoughtful, benign, humane, affectionate, compassionate, clement, gracious, indulgent, benevolent, attentive, amiable, courteous, amicable, lenient, cordial, congenial, philanthropic, unselfish, propitious, beneficent, kind-hearted, bounteous, tender-hearted
OPPOSITE: unkind

kind² *n* **1a = class**, sort, type, variety, brand, grade, category, genre, classification, league **1b = sort**, set, type, ilk, family, race, species, breed, genus

kindly *adj* **1 = benevolent**, kind, caring, nice, warm, gentle, helpful, pleasant, mild, sympathetic, beneficial, polite, favourable, benign, humane, compassionate, hearty, cordial, considerate, genial, affable, good-natured, beneficent, well-disposed, kind-hearted, warm-hearted **OPPOSITE:** cruel ▹*adv* **3 = benevolently**, politely, generously, thoughtfully, tenderly, lovingly, cordially, affectionately, helpfully, graciously, obligingly, agreeably, indulgently, selflessly, unselfishly, compassionately, considerately **OPPOSITE:** unkindly

kindness *n* **1 = goodwill**, understanding, charity, grace, humanity, affection, patience, tolerance, goodness, compassion, hospitality, generosity, indulgence, decency, tenderness, clemency, gentleness, philanthropy, benevolence, magnanimity, fellow-feeling, amiability, beneficence, kindliness
OPPOSITE: malice

king *n* **1, 2 = ruler**, monarch, sovereign, crowned head, leader, lord, prince, Crown, emperor, majesty, head of state, consort, His Majesty, overlord

kingdom *n* **1 = country**, state, nation, land, division, territory, province, empire, commonwealth, realm, domain, tract, dominion, sovereign state

DICTIONARY

provides a steering joint in a motor vehicle

king post *n building* a vertical post connecting the apex of a triangular roof truss to the tie beam

king prawn *n* a large prawn, fished commercially in Australian waters

king-size *or* **king-sized** *adj* larger than a standard size

Kingsley *n* **1** Sir **Ben** born 1943, British actor. He won an Oscar for his performance in the title role of the film *Gandhi* (1982) **2 Charles** 1819–75, British clergyman and author. His works include the historical romances *Westward Ho!* (1855) and *Hereward the Wake* (1866) and the children's story *The Water Babies* (1863) **3** his brother, **Henry** 1830–76, British novelist, editor, and journalist, who spent some time in Australia. His works include *Ravenshoe* (1861) and the Anglo-Australian novels *The Recollections of Geoffrey Hamlyn* (1859) and *The Hillyars and the Burtons* (1865)

King-Smith *n* **Ronald Gordon**, known as *Dick*. born 1922, British writer for children; his numerous books include *The Sheep Pig* (1984) and the *Sophie* series

kink *n* **1** a twist or bend in something such as a rope or hair **2** *informal* a flaw or quirk in someone's personality ▹*vb* **3** to form or cause to form a kink

WORD ORIGIN Dutch

kinky *adj* **kinkier, kinkiest 1** *slang* given to unusual sexual practices **2** tightly looped or curled

Kinnock *n* **Neil** (**Gordon**) Baron. born 1942, British Labour politician, born in Wales; leader of the Labour Party (1983–92); a European commissioner from 1994 and vice-president of the European Commission (1999–2004)

Kinsey *n* **Alfred Charles** 1894–1956, US zoologist, who directed a survey of human sexual behaviour

kinsfolk *pl n* one's family or relatives

kinship *n* **1** blood relationship **2** the state of having common characteristics

kinsman *n, pl* **-men** a relation by blood or marriage **kinswoman** *fem n*

kiosk *n* **1** a small booth from which cigarettes, newspapers, and sweets are sold **2** *chiefly Brit* a public telephone box

WORD ORIGIN French *kiosque* bandstand, from Persian *kūshk* pavilion

kip *Brit slang n* **1** sleep: *a couple of hours' kip* **2** a bed ▹*vb* **kipping, kipped 3** to sleep or take a nap **4 kip down** to sleep in a makeshift bed

WORD ORIGIN origin unknown

kipper *n* **1** a herring that has been cleaned, salted, and smoked ▹*vb* **2** to cure (a herring) by salting and smoking it

WORD ORIGIN Old English *cypera*

Kirchhoff *n* **Gustav Robert** 1824–87, German physicist. With Bunsen he developed the method of spectrum analysis that led to their discovery of caesium (1860) and rubidium (1861): also worked on electrical networks

Kirchner *n* **Ernst Ludwig** 1880–1938, German expressionist painter and printmaker; a founder of the group *die Brücke* (1905)

kirk *n Scot* a church

WORD ORIGIN Old Norse *kirkja*

Kirk[1] *n* **the Kirk** *informal* the Presbyterian Church of Scotland

Kirk[2] *n* **Norman** 1923–74, prime minister of New Zealand (1972–74)

Kirkby[1] *n* a town in NW England, in Knowsley unitary authority, Merseyside. Pop: 40 006 (2001)

Kirkby[2] *n* Dame **Emma** born 1949, British soprano, specializing in performances of early music with period instruments

Kirov[1] *n* a city in NW Russia, on the Vyatka River: an early trading centre; engineering industries. Pop: 454 000 (2005 est). Former name (1780–1934): **Vyatka**

Kirov[2] *n* **Sergei Mironovich** 1888–1934, Soviet politician; one of Stalin's chief aides. His assassination was the starting point for Stalin's purge of the Communist Party (1934–38)

Kirsch *or* **Kirschwasser** *n* a brandy distilled from black cherries

WORD ORIGIN German *Kirschwasser* cherry water

kismet *n* fate or destiny

WORD ORIGIN Persian *qismat*

kiss ❶ *vb* **1** to touch with the lips as an expression of love, greeting, or respect **2** to join lips with another person as an act of love or desire **3** *literary* to touch lightly: *a long high free kick that kissed the top of the crossbar* ▹*n* **4** a caress with the lips **5** a light touch **kissable** *adj*

WORD ORIGIN Old English *cyssan*

kissagram *n Brit, Austral & NZ* a greetings service in which a person is employed to present greetings by kissing the person celebrating

kiss curl *n* a circular curl of hair pressed flat against the cheek or forehead

kisser *n slang* the mouth or face

kissing crust *n NZ* the soft end of a loaf of bread where two loaves have been separated

kiss of life *n* **the kiss of life** mouth-to-mouth resuscitation in which a person blows gently into the mouth of an unconscious person

kist *n Scot & S African* a large wooden chest

kit[1] ❶ *n* **1** a set of tools or supplies for use together or for a purpose: *a first-aid kit* **2** the container for such a set **3** a set of parts sold ready to be assembled: *a model aircraft kit* **4** *NZ* a flax basket **5** clothing and other personal effects, such as those of a soldier: *a complete set of school team kit* ▸ See also **kit out**

WORD ORIGIN Middle Dutch *kitte* tankard

kit[2] *n NZ* a shopping bag made of string

WORD ORIGIN Māori *kete*

Kitagawa Utamaro *n* See **Utamaro**

Kitaj *n* **R. B.** 1932–2007, US painter working in Britain, noted for such large figurative works as *If Not, Not* (1976)

kitbag *n* a canvas or other bag for a serviceman's kit

kitchen *n* a room equipped for preparing and cooking food

WORD ORIGIN Late Latin *coquina*

kitchenette *n* a small kitchen or part of a room equipped for use as a kitchen

kitchen garden *n* a garden for growing vegetables, herbs, etc.

kitchen tea *n Austral & NZ* a party held before a wedding to which guests bring kitchen equipment as presents

kite *n* **1** a light frame covered with a thin material flown in the wind at the end of a length of string **2** a bird of prey with a long forked tail and large wings **3** a four-sided geometrical shape in which each side is equal in length to one of the sides joining it

WORD ORIGIN Old English *cȳta*

Kite mark *n Brit* the official mark in the form of a kite on articles approved by the British Standards Institution

kith *n* **kith and kin** *old-fashioned* one's friends and relations

WORD ORIGIN Old English *cȳthth*

kit out ❶ *or* **up** *vb* **kitting, kitted** *chiefly Brit* to provide with clothes or

THESAURUS

kiss *vb* **1, 2 = peck** (*informal*), osculate, snog (*Brit slang*), neck (*informal*), smooch (*informal*), canoodle (*slang*) **3 = brush**, touch, shave, scrape, graze, caress, glance off, stroke ▹*n* **4 = peck** (*informal*), snog (*Brit slang*), smacker (*slang*), smooch (*informal*), French kiss, osculation

kit[1] *n* **1 = equipment**, supplies, materials, tackle, tools, instruments, provisions, implements, rig, apparatus, trappings, utensils, paraphernalia, accoutrements, appurtenances **5 = gear**, things, effects, dress, clothes, clothing, stuff, equipment, uniform, outfit, rig, costume, garments, baggage, equipage

kit out *or* **up** (*chiefly Brit*), **= equip**, fit, supply, provide with, arm, stock, outfit, costume, furnish, fix up, fit

DICTIONARY

equipment needed for a particular activity

kitsch *n* tawdry or sentimental art or literature **kitschy** *adj*
WORD ORIGIN from German

kitten *n* **1** a young cat **2** **have kittens** *informal* to react with disapproval or anxiety: *she had kittens when she discovered the price*
WORD ORIGIN Old French *caton*

kittenish *adj* lively and flirtatious

kittiwake *n* a type of seagull with pale grey black-tipped wings and a square-cut tail
WORD ORIGIN imitative

kitty[1] *n, pl* **-ties** ▸ a diminutive or affectionate name for a **kitten** or **cat**

kitty[2] *n, pl* **-ties** **1** any shared fund of money **2** the pool in certain gambling games
WORD ORIGIN probably from KIT[1]

kiwi *n, pl* **kiwis** **1** a flightless bird of New Zealand with a long beak, stout legs, and no tail **2** a New Zealander
WORD ORIGIN Māori

kiwi fruit *n* an edible fruit with a fuzzy brown skin and green flesh

kJ kilojoule(s)

kl kilolitre(s)

Klaus *n* **Vaclav** born 1941, Czech politician, president of Czech Republic from 2003

klaxon *n* a type of loud horn used on fire engines and ambulances as a warning signal
WORD ORIGIN former trademark

Kléber *n* **Jean Baptiste** 1753–1800, French general, who succeeded Napoleon as commander in Egypt (1799); assassinated

Klee *n* **Paul** 1879–1940, Swiss painter and etcher. A founder member of *der Blaue Reiter*, he subsequently evolved an intensely personal style of unusual fantasy and wit

Klein *n* **1** **Calvin** (**Richard**) born 1942, US fashion designer **2** **Melanie** 1882–1960, Austrian psychoanalyst resident in England (from 1926), noted for her work on child behaviour

kleinhuisie (klayn-hay-see) *n S African* an outside toilet
WORD ORIGIN Afrikaans, literally: little house

Kleist *n* (**Bernd**) **Heinrich** (**Wilhelm**) **von** 1777–1811, German dramatist, poet, and short-story writer. His plays include *The Broken Pitcher* (1808), *Penthesilea* (1808), and *The Prince of Homburg* (published 1821)

Klemperer *n* **Otto** 1885–1973, orchestral conductor, born in Germany. He was best known for his interpretations of Beethoven

kleptomania *n psychol* a strong impulse to steal **kleptomaniac** *n*
WORD ORIGIN Greek *kleptein* to steal + *mania* madness

Klimt *n* **Gustav** 1862–1918, Austrian painter. He founded the Vienna Sezession (1897), a group of painters influenced by Art Nouveau

Kline *n* **Franz** 1910–62, US abstract expressionist painter. His works are characterized by heavy black strokes on a white or grey background

Klint *n* **Kaara** 1888–1954, Danish furniture designer; founder of the contemporary Scandinavian style

klipspringer *n* a small agile antelope of rocky regions of Africa south of the Sahara
WORD ORIGIN Afrikaans: rock jumper

kloof *n S African* a mountain pass or gorge
WORD ORIGIN Afrikaans

Klopstock *n* **Friedrich Gottlieb** 1724–1803, German poet, noted for his religious epic *Der Messias* (1748–73) and for his odes

km kilometre(s)

km/h kilometres per hour

knack ⊙ *n* **1** a skilful way of doing something **2** an ability to do something difficult with apparent ease
WORD ORIGIN probably from Middle English *knak* sharp knock

knacker *n Brit* a person who buys up old horses for slaughter
WORD ORIGIN origin unknown

knackered *adj slang* **1** extremely tired: *they'd been marching for three hours and were absolutely knackered* **2** broken or no longer functioning: *a knackered TV set*

knapsack *n* a canvas or leather bag carried strapped on the back or shoulder
WORD ORIGIN Low German *knappen* to eat + *sack* bag

knapweed *n* a plant with purplish thistle-like flowers
WORD ORIGIN Middle English *knopwed*

knave *n* **1** *cards* the jack **2** *archaic* a dishonest man **knavish** *adj*
WORD ORIGIN Old English *cnafa*

knavery *n, pl* **-eries** *old-fashioned* dishonest behaviour

knead *vb* **1** to work and press (a soft substance, such as dough) into a smooth mixture with the hands **2** to squeeze or press with the hands **kneader** *n*
WORD ORIGIN Old English *cnedan*

knee *n* **1** the joint of the leg between the thigh and the lower leg **2** the area around this joint **3** the upper surface of a sitting person's thigh: *a little girl being cuddled on her father's knee* **4** the part of a garment that covers the knee **5** **bring someone to his knees** to force someone into submission ▹ *vb* **kneeing, kneed** **6** to strike, nudge, or push with the knee
WORD ORIGIN Old English *cnēow*

kneecap *n* **1** *anat* a small flat triangular bone in front of and protecting the knee ▹ *vb* **-capping, -capped** **2** (of terrorists) to shoot (a person) in the kneecap

knee-deep *adj* **1** so deep as to reach or cover the knees **2** **a** sunk to the knees: *knee-deep in mud* **b** deeply involved: *knee-deep in work*

knee-high *adj* as high as the knee

knee-jerk *n* **1** *physiol* a sudden involuntary kick of the lower leg caused by a sharp tap on the tendon just below the kneecap ▹ *adj* **kneejerk** **2** made or occurring as a predictable and automatic response: *a kneejerk reaction*

kneel ⊙ *vb* **kneeling, knelt** *or* **kneeled** **1** to rest, fall, or support oneself on one's knees ▹ *n* **2** the act or position of kneeling
WORD ORIGIN Old English *cnēowlian*

knees-up *n Brit informal* a party

knell *n* **1** the sound of a bell rung to announce a death or a funeral **2** something that indicates death or destruction ▹ *vb* **3** to ring a knell **4** to proclaim by a tolling bell
WORD ORIGIN Old English *cnyll*

Kneller *n* Sir **Godfrey** ?1646–1723, portrait painter at the English court, born in Germany

knelt *vb* ▸ the past tense of **kneel**

knew *vb* ▸ the past tense of **know**

knickerbockers *pl n* loose-fitting short trousers gathered in at the knee or calf
WORD ORIGIN after Diedrich *Knickerbocker*, fictitious author of Washington Irving's *History of New York*

knickers ⊙ *pl n* a woman's or girl's undergarment covering the lower trunk and having separate legs or leg-holes
WORD ORIGIN contraction of *knickerbockers*

knick-knack *n* a small ornament or trinket
WORD ORIGIN reduplication of obsolete *knack* a toy

THESAURUS

out, deck out, accoutre

knack *n* **1, 2 = skill**, art, ability, facility, talent, gift, capacity, trick, bent, craft, genius, expertise, forte, flair, competence, ingenuity, propensity, aptitude, dexterity, cleverness, quickness, adroitness, expertness, handiness, skilfulness
OPPOSITE: ineptitude

kneel *vb* **1 = genuflect**, bow, stoop, curtsy *or* curtsey, bow down, kowtow, get down on your knees, make obeisance

knickers *pl n* **= underwear**, smalls, briefs, drawers, panties, bloomers

DICTIONARY

knife ⓣ *n, pl* **knives** **1** a cutting instrument or weapon consisting of a sharp-edged blade of metal fitted into a handle ▹ *vb* **knifing, knifed** **2** to stab or kill with a knife **knifelike** *adj*
WORD ORIGIN Old English *cnīf*

knife edge *n* **1** the sharp cutting edge of a knife **2** a critical point in the development of a situation: *and at this point the election result is still poised on a knife edge*

knight *n* **1** a man who has been given a knighthood in recognition of his achievements **2 a** (in medieval Europe) a person who served his lord as a mounted and heavily armed soldier **b** (in medieval Europe) a devoted male admirer of a noblewoman, esp. her champion in a jousting tournament **3** a chessman shaped like a horse's head, able to move either two squares horizontally and one square vertically or two squares vertically and one square horizontally ▹ *vb* **4** to make (a man) a knight
WORD ORIGIN Old English *cniht* servant

Knight *n* Dame **Laura** 1887–1970, British painter, noted for her paintings of Gypsies, the ballet, and the circus

knight errant *n, pl* **knights errant** (esp. in medieval romance) a knight who wanders in search of deeds of courage, chivalry, etc. **knight errantry** *n*

knighthood *n* an honorary title given to a man by the British sovereign in recognition of his achievements

knightly *adj* of, resembling, or appropriate for a knight **knightliness** *n*

knit ⓣ *vb* **knitting, knitted** *or* **knit** **1** to make (a garment) by looping (wool) using long eyeless needles or a knitting machine **2** to join together closely **3** to draw (one's eyebrows) together ▹ *n* **4** a fabric made by knitting **knitter** *n*
WORD ORIGIN Old English *cnyttan* to tie in

knitting *n* knitted work or the process of producing it

knitwear *n* knitted clothes, such as sweaters

knives *n* ▸ the plural of **knife**

knob ⓣ *n* **1** a rounded projection from a surface, such as a rotating switch on a radio **2** a rounded handle of a door or drawer **3** a small amount of butter or margarine **knoblike** *adj*
WORD ORIGIN Middle Low German *knobbe* knot in wood

knobbly *adj* having or covered with small bumps: *a curious knobbly root vegetable*

knobkerrie *n S African* a club or a stick with a rounded end
WORD ORIGIN Khoi (language of southern Africa) *kirri* stick

knock ⓣ *vb* **1** to give a blow or push to **2** to rap sharply with the knuckles: *he knocked on the door of the guest room* **3** to make by striking: *he knocked a hole in the wall* **4** to collide (with) **5** to bring into a certain condition by hitting: *he was knocked unconscious in a collision* **6** *informal* to criticize adversely **7** to emit a regular banging sound as a result of a fault: *the engine was knocking badly* **8 knock on the head** to prevent the further development of (a plan) ▹ *n* **9 a** a blow, push, or rap: *he gave the table a knock* **b** the sound so caused **10** the sound of knocking in an engine or bearing **11** *informal* a misfortune, rejection, or setback **12** *informal* criticism ▸ See also **knock about, knock back,** etc.
WORD ORIGIN Old English *cnocian*

knock about ⓣ *or* **around** *vb* **1** to wander or travel about: *I have knocked about the world through three continents* **2** (foll. by *with*) to associate **3** to treat brutally: *she looked knocked about, with bruises and cuts to her head* **4** to consider or discuss informally ▹ *adj* **knockabout** **5** (of comedy) lively, boisterous, and physical

knock back *vb informal* **1** to drink quickly: *he fell over after knocking back eight pints of lager* **2** to cost: *lunch for two here will knock you back £50* **3** to reject or refuse: *I don't know any man who'd knock back an offer like that* ▹ *n* **knockback** **4** *slang* a refusal or rejection

knock down *vb* **1** to strike to the ground with a blow, such as in boxing **2** (in auctions) to declare an article sold **3** to demolish **4** *informal* to reduce (a price) ▹ *adj* **knockdown** **5** powerful: *a knockdown argument* **6** *chiefly Brit* (of a price) very cheap **7** easily dismantled: *knockdown furniture*

knocker *n* **1** a metal object attached to a door by a hinge and used for knocking **2 knockers** *slang* a woman's breasts

knock-knees *pl n* legs that are bent inwards at the knees **knock-kneed** *adj*

knock off ⓣ *vb* **1** *informal* to finish work: *around ten, the day shift knocked off* **2** *informal* to make or do hastily or easily: *she knocked off 600 books in all during her long life* **3** *informal* to take (an amount) off the price of (an article): *I'll knock off 10% if you pay cash* **4** *Brit, Austral & NZ informal* to steal **5** *slang* to kill **6** *slang* to stop doing something; used as a command: *knock it off!*

knock-on *rugby n* **1** the foul of playing the ball forward with the hand or arm ▹ *vb* **knock on** **2** to play (the ball)

K

THESAURUS

knife *n* **1 = blade,** carver, cutter, cutting tool ▹ *vb* **2 = cut,** wound, stab, slash, thrust, gore, pierce, spear, jab, bayonet, impale, lacerate

knit *vb* **2a = join,** unite, link, tie, bond, ally, combine, secure, bind, connect, merge, weave, fasten, meld **2b = heal,** unite, join, link, bind, connect, loop, mend, fasten, intertwine, interlace **3 = furrow,** tighten, knot, wrinkle, crease, screw up, pucker, scrunch up

knob *n* **1 = ball,** stud, nub, protuberance, boss, bunch, swell, knot, bulk, lump, bump, projection, snag, hump, protrusion, knurl

knock *vb* **1 = hit,** strike, punch, belt *(informal)*, slap, chin *(slang)*, smack, thump, clap, cuff, smite *(archaic)*, thwack, lay one on *(slang)*, beat *or* knock seven bells out of *(informal)* **2 = bang,** beat, strike, tap, rap, bash *(informal)*, thump, buffet, pummel **6** *(informal)* **= criticize,** condemn, put down, run down, abuse, blast, pan *(informal)*, slam *(slang)*, slate *(informal)*, have a go (at) *(informal)*, censure, slag (off) *(slang)*, denigrate, belittle, disparage, deprecate, diss *(slang, chiefly US)*, find fault with, carp at, lambast(e), pick holes in, cast aspersions on, cavil at, pick to pieces, give (someone *or* something) a bad press, nit-pick *(informal)* **9a = bang,** blow, impact, jar, collision, jolt, smash **9b = knocking,** pounding, beating, tap, hammering, bang, banging, rap, thump, thud **11** *(informal)* **= setback,** check, defeat, blow, upset, reverse, disappointment, hold-up, hitch, reversal, misfortune, rebuff, whammy *(informal, chiefly US)*, bummer *(slang)*

knock about *or* **around** (foll. by *with*) *vb* **1 = wander,** travel, roam, rove, range, drift, stray, ramble, straggle, traipse, go walkabout *(Austral)*, stravaig *(Scot & Northern English dialect)* **2 = mix with,** associate with, mingle with, hang out with *(informal)*, hang with *(informal, chiefly US)*, be friends with, consort with, run around with *(informal)*, hobnob with, socialize with, accompany, hang about with, fraternize with **3 knock someone about** *or* **around = hit,** attack, beat, strike, damage, abuse, hurt, injure, wound, assault, harm, batter, slap, bruise, thrash, beat up *(informal)*, buffet, maul, work over *(slang)*, clobber *(slang)*, mistreat, manhandle, maltreat, lambast(e), slap around *(informal)*, beat *or* knock seven bells out of *(informal)*

knock off *vb (informal)* **1 = stop work,** get out, conclude, shut down, terminate, call it a day *(informal)*, finish work, clock off, clock out

DICTIONARY

forward with the hand or arm

knock-on effect *n* the indirect result of an action or decision

knockout ❶ *n* **1** the act of rendering someone unconscious **2** *boxing* a blow that renders an opponent unable to continue after the referee has counted to ten **3** a competition in which competitors are eliminated progressively **4** *informal* a person or thing that is very impressive or attractive: *at my youngest sister's wedding she was a knockout in navy and scarlet* ▷ *vb* **knock out 5** to render (someone) unconscious **6** *boxing* to defeat (an opponent) by a knockout **7** to destroy: *communications in many areas were knocked out by the earthquake* **8** to eliminate from a knockout competition **9** *informal* to amaze: *the fantastic audience reaction knocked me out*

knock up *vb* **1** Also: **knock together** *informal* to make or assemble quickly: *my boyfriend can knock up a wonderful lasagne* **2** *Brit informal* to waken: *to knock someone up early* **3** *slang* to make pregnant **4** to practise before a game of tennis, squash, or badminton ▷ *n* **knock-up 5** a practice session at tennis, squash, or badminton

knoll *n* a small rounded hill
WORD ORIGIN Old English *cnoll*

knot ❶ *n* **1** a fastening formed by looping and tying pieces of rope, cord, or string **2** a tangle, such as in hair **3** a decorative bow, such as of ribbon **4** a small cluster or huddled group: *a knot of passengers gathered on the platform* **5** a bond: *to tie the knot of friendship* **6 a** a hard mass of wood where a branch joins the trunk of a tree **b** a cross section of this visible in timber **7** a feeling of tightness, caused by tension or nervousness: *a dull knot of anxiety that sat in the pit of her stomach* **8** a unit of speed used by ships and aircraft, equal to one nautical mile per hour **9 at a rate of knots** very fast **10 tie someone in knots** to confuse someone completely ▷ *vb* **knotting, knotted 11** to tie or fasten in a knot **12** to form into a knot **13** to entangle or become entangled **knotted** *adj* **knotless** *adj*
WORD ORIGIN Old English *cnotta*

knothole *n* a hole in a piece of wood where a knot has been

knotty *adj* **-tier, -tiest 1** full of knots **2** extremely difficult or puzzling: *a knotty problem*

know ❶ *vb* **knowing, knew, known 1** to be or feel certain of the truth or accuracy of (a fact, answer, or piece of information) **2** to be acquainted with: *I'd known him for many years, since I was seventeen* **3** to have a grasp of or understand (a skill or language) **4** to understand or be aware of (something, or how to do or be something): *she knew how to get on with people* **5** to experience: *you had to have known poverty before you could give money its true value, he claimed* **6** to be intelligent, informed, or sensible enough (to do something): *how did he know to send the letter in the first place?* **7** to be able to distinguish: *I don't know one flower from another* **8 know what's what** to know how one thing or things in general work **9 you never know** things are uncertain ▷ *n* **10 in the know** *informal* aware or informed **knowable** *adj*
WORD ORIGIN Old English *gecnāwan*

know-all *n informal, disparaging* a person who pretends or appears to know a lot more than other people

know-how ❶ *n informal* the ability to do something that is difficult or technical

knowing ❶ *adj* **1** suggesting secret knowledge: *Paul saw the knowing look that passed between them* **2** cunning or shrewd **3** deliberate **knowingly** *adv* **knowingness** *n*

knowledge ❶ *n* **1** the facts or experiences known by a person or group of people **2** the state of knowing **3** specific information about a subject **4 to my knowledge** as I understand it

knowledgeable ❶ *or* **knowledgable** *adj* intelligent or well-informed **knowledgeably** *or* **knowledgably** *adv*

Knowles *n* **Beyoncé** born 1981, US singer, songwriter, and actress. A member of the hugely successful Destiny's Child, she later found solo success with *Dangerously in Love* (2003) and the single "Crazy in Love" (2003)

known ❶ *vb* **1** ▸ the past participle of **know** ▷ *adj* **2** identified: *consorting with known criminals*

Knox-Johnston *n* Sir **Robin** (**William Robert Patrick**) born 1939, British yachtsman. He was the first to sail round the world alone nonstop (1968–69)

knuckle *n* **1** a joint of a finger **2** the knee joint of a calf or pig **3 near the knuckle** *informal* likely to offend people because of frankness or rudeness ▸ See also **knuckle down, knuckle under**
WORD ORIGIN Middle English

knuckle down *vb* **-ling, -led** *informal* to apply oneself conscientiously: *he's never been able to knuckle down and study anything for long*

knuckle-duster *n* a metal appliance worn over the knuckles to add force to a blow

knuckle under *vb* **-ling, -led** to give way under pressure or authority

knurl *n* a small ridge, often one of a series
WORD ORIGIN probably from *knur* a knot in wood

THESAURUS

knockout *n* **1, 2, 3 = killer blow**, coup de grâce *(French)*, kayo *(slang)*, KO *or* K.O. *(slang)* **4** *(informal)* **= success**, hit, winner, triumph, smash, sensation, smash hit, stunner *(informal)*, smasheroo *(informal)*
OPPOSITE: failure

knot *n* **1, 3 = connection**, tie, bond, joint, bow, loop, braid, splice, rosette, ligature ▷ *vb* **11 = tie**, secure, bind, complicate, weave, loop, knit, tether, entangle

know *vb* **1 = have knowledge of**, see, understand, recognize, perceive, be aware of, be conscious of **2 = be acquainted with**, recognize, associate with, be familiar with, be friends with, be friendly with, have knowledge of, have dealings with, socialize with, fraternize with, be pals with **OPPOSITE:** be unfamiliar with
3, 4, 5 *(sometimes with* **about** *or* **of***)* **= be familiar with**, experience, understand, ken *(Scot)*, comprehend, fathom, apprehend, have knowledge of, be acquainted with, feel certain of, have dealings in, be versed in
OPPOSITE: be ignorant of

know-how *n (informal)* **= expertise**, experience, ability, skill, knowledge, facility, talent, command, craft, grasp, faculty, capability, flair, knack, ingenuity, aptitude, proficiency, dexterity, cleverness, deftness, savoir-faire, adroitness, ableness

knowing *adj* **1 = meaningful**, significant, expressive, eloquent, enigmatic, suggestive

knowledge *n* **1 = learning**, schooling, education, science, intelligence, instruction, wisdom, scholarship, tuition, enlightenment, erudition
OPPOSITE: ignorance
2a = understanding, sense, intelligence, judgment, perception, awareness, insight, grasp, appreciation, penetration, comprehension, discernment
2b = acquaintance, information, notice, intimacy, familiarity, cognizance **OPPOSITE:** unfamiliarity

knowledgeable *adj* **a = well-informed**, acquainted, conversant, au fait *(French)*, experienced, understanding, aware, familiar, conscious, in the know *(informal)*, cognizant, in the loop, au courant *(French)*, clued-up *(informal)*, across, down with **b = intelligent**, lettered, learned, educated, scholarly, erudite

known *adj* **2 = famous**, well-known, celebrated, popular, common, admitted, noted, published, obvious, familiar, acknowledged, recognized, plain, confessed, patent, manifest, avowed **OPPOSITE:** unknown

k

DICTIONARY

Knussen *n* **(Stuart) Oliver** born 1952, British composer and conductor. His works include the opera *Where the Wild Things Are* (1981) and three symphonies

KO *or* **k.o.** *vb* **KO'ing, KO'd** *or* **k.o.'ing, k.o.'d 1** to knock out ▷ *n, pl* **KO's** *or* **k.o.'s 2** a knockout

koala *or* **koala bear** *n* a tree-dwelling Australian marsupial with dense grey fur
WORD ORIGIN Aboriginal

Kobe beef (koh-bi) *n* a grade of beef from cattle raised in Kobe, Japan, which is extremely tender and full-flavoured

Koch *n* **Robert** 1843–1910, German bacteriologist, who isolated the anthrax bacillus (1876), the tubercle bacillus (1882), and the cholera bacillus (1883): Nobel prize for physiology or medicine 1905

Kodály *n* **Zoltán** 1882–1967, Hungarian composer. His works were often inspired by native folk songs and include the comic opera *Háry János* (1926) and *Psalmus Hungaricus* (1923) for chorus and orchestra

koeksister (kook-sist-er) *n S African* a plaited doughnut deep-fried and soaked in syrup
WORD ORIGIN Afrikaans

Koestler *n* **Arthur** 1905–83, British writer, born in Hungary. Of his early antitotalitarian novels *Darkness at Noon* (1940) is outstanding. His later works, *The Sleepwalkers* (1959), *The Act of Creation* (1964), and *The Ghost in the Machine* (1967) reflect his interest in science, philosophy, and psychology. He committed suicide

kohanga reo, kohanga *n NZ* an infant class where children are taught in Māori
WORD ORIGIN Māori: language nest

kohl *n* a cosmetic powder used to darken the area around the eyes
WORD ORIGIN Arabic

Köhler *n* **Wolfgang** 1887–1967, German psychologist, a leading exponent of Gestalt psychology

kohlrabi (kole-rah-bee) *n, pl* **-bies** a type of cabbage with an edible stem
WORD ORIGIN Italian *cavolo* cabbage + *rapa* turnip

Koizumi *n* **Junichiro** born 1941, Japanese politician; prime minister (2001–06)

kokanee (coke-can-ee) *n* a freshwater salmon of lakes and rivers in W North America
WORD ORIGIN after *Kokanee* Creek, in British Columbia

Kokoschka *n* **Oskar** 1886–1980, Austrian expressionist painter and dramatist, noted for his landscapes and portraits

kola *n* ▸ same as **cola**

kolkhoz (kol-hawz) *n* (formerly) a collective farm in the Soviet Union
WORD ORIGIN Russian

Kollwitz *n* **Käthe** 1867–1945, German lithographer and sculptress

Kolmogorov *n* **Andrei Nikolaevich** (1903–87), Soviet mathematician, who made important contributions to the theoretical foundations of probability

komatik (koh-ma-tik) *n Canad* a sledge with wooden runners and crossbars bound with animal hides
WORD ORIGIN Inuktitut

kook *n US & Canad informal* an eccentric or foolish person **kooky** *or* **kookie** *adj*
WORD ORIGIN probably from *cuckoo*

kookaburra *n* a large Australian kingfisher with a cackling cry
WORD ORIGIN Aboriginal

Koolhaas *n* **Rem** Dutch architect and theorist, co-founder of the Office for Metropolitan Architecture (1975); buildings include the Grand Palais and associated developments in Lille, France (1989–96); books include *S, M, L, XL* (1996)

Kooning *n* See **de Kooning**

koori *n, pl* **-ris** an Australian Aborigine

kopeck *n* a former Russian monetary unit worth one hundredth of a rouble
WORD ORIGIN Russian *kopeika*

kopje ⓣ, **koppie** (kop-ee) *n S African* a small isolated hill
WORD ORIGIN Afrikaans

Koran *n* the sacred book of Islam, believed by Muslims to be the infallible word of God dictated to Mohammed **Koranic** *adj*
WORD ORIGIN Arabic *qur'ān* reading, book

Korchnoi *n* **Victor** born 1931, Soviet-born chess player: Soviet champion 1960, 1962, and 1964: defected to the West in 1976

Korda *n* Sir **Alexander**, real name *Sandor Kellner*. 1893–1956, British film producer and director, born in Hungary: his films include *The Scarlet Pimpernel* (1934), *Anna Karenina* (1948), and *The Third Man* (1949)

Korean *adj* **1** of Korea ▷ *n* **2** a person from Korea **3** the official language of North and South Korea

korma *n* a type of mild Indian dish consisting of meat or vegetables cooked in water, yoghurt, or cream
WORD ORIGIN from Urdu

Korzybski *n* **Alfred (Habdank Skarbek)** 1879–1950, US originator of the theory and study of general semantics, born in Poland

Kosciusko *n* **Thaddeus,** Polish name *Tadeusz Kociusko*. 1746–1817, Polish general: fought for the colonists in the American War of Independence and led an unsuccessful revolt against the partitioning of Poland (1794)

kosher (koh-sher) *adj* **1** *Judaism* **a** conforming to religious law **b** (of food) prepared in accordance with the dietary laws **2** *informal* legitimate, genuine, or proper ▷ *n* **3** kosher food
WORD ORIGIN Yiddish

Kossoff *n* **Leon** born 1926, British painter, esp. of London scenes

Kossuth *n* **Lajos** 1802–94, Hungarian statesman. He led the revolution against Austria (1848) and was provisional governor (1849), but he fled when the revolt was suppressed (1849)

Kostunica *n* **Vojislav** born 1944, Serbian politician; president of the Federal Republic of Yugoslavia (2000–03); prime minister of Serbia and Montenegro (2004–06); prime minister of Serbia from 2006

Kosygin *n* **Aleksei Nikolayevich** 1904–80, Soviet statesman; premier of the Soviet Union (1964–80)

kowhai (koh-wye, koh-fye) *n* a small tree of New Zealand and Chile with clusters of yellow flowers
WORD ORIGIN Māori

kowtow *vb* **1** to be humble and very respectful (towards): *the senior editors accused each other of kowtowing to his demands* **2** to touch the forehead to the ground in deference ▷ *n* **3** the act of kowtowing
WORD ORIGIN Chinese *k'o* to strike, knock + *t'ou* head

kph kilometres per hour

Kr *chem* krypton

kraal *n* **1** a Southern African hut village surrounded by a strong fence **2** *S African* an enclosure for livestock
WORD ORIGIN Afrikaans, from Portuguese *curral* enclosure

Krafft-Ebing *n* **Richard**, Baron von Krafft-Ebing. 1840–1902, German neurologist and psychiatrist who pioneered the systematic study of sexual behaviour in *Psychopathia Sexualis* (1886)

kraken *n* a legendary sea monster
WORD ORIGIN Norwegian

krans (krahnss) *n S African* a sheer rock face
WORD ORIGIN Afrikaans

Krebs *n* Sir **Hans Adolf** 1900–81, British biochemist, born in Germany, who shared a Nobel prize for physiology or medicine (1953) for the discovery of the **Krebs cycle**

Kreisler *n* **Fritz** 1875–1962, US violinist, born in Austria

Kremer *n* **Gidon** born 1947, Latvian

THESAURUS

kopje *or* **koppie** *n* (*S African*) **= hill**, down (*archaic*), fell, mount, height, mound, prominence, elevation, eminence, hilltop, tor, knoll, hillock, brae (*Scot*)

violinist, now based in the US

kremlin *n* the citadel of any Russian city
WORD ORIGIN Russian *kreml*

Kremlin *n* the central government of Russia and, formerly, the Soviet Union

krill *n, pl* **krill** a small shrimplike crustacean
WORD ORIGIN Norwegian *kril* young fish

Krishna *n* a Hindu god, the incarnation of Vishnu

Krishna Menon *n* See **Menon**

Kristeva *n* **Julia** born 1941, French semiotician, born in Bulgaria. Her works include *La Révolution du langage poétique* (1974), *Histoires d'amour* (1983), and the autobiographical novel *Les Samourais* (1990)

Kristiansen *n* **Ingrid** born 1956, Norwegian long-distance runner: former London marathon winner: world 10 000 metres record holder (1986–93)

krona *n, pl* **-nor** the standard monetary unit of Sweden
WORD ORIGIN Swedish, from Latin *corona* crown

krone (kroh-na) *n, pl* **-ner** (-ner) the standard monetary unit of Norway and Denmark
WORD ORIGIN Danish or Norwegian, from Latin *corona* crown

Kropotkin *n* Prince **Peter,** Russian name *Pyotr Alexeyevich.* 1842–1921, Russian anarchist: his books include *Mutual Aid* (1902) and *Modern Science and Anarchism* (1903)

krugerrand *n* a one-ounce gold coin minted in South Africa
WORD ORIGIN Paul *Kruger,* Boer statesman + *rand*

Krupp *n* a German family of steel and armaments manufacturers, including **Alfred,** 1812–87, his son **Friedrich Alfred,** 1854–1902, and the latter's son-in-law, **Gustav Krupp von Bohlen und Halbach,** 1870–1950

krypton *n chem* an inert gaseous element occurring in trace amounts in air and used in fluorescent lights and lasers. Symbol: Kr
WORD ORIGIN Greek *kruptos* hidden

KS Kansas

Kt Knight

KT (in Britain) Knight of the Order of the Thistle

kt. kiloton

Kubelik *n* **Raphael** 1914–96, Czech conductor and composer

Kubrick *n* **Stanley** 1928–99, US film writer, director, and producer. He directed *Lolita* (1962), *Dr Strangelove* (1963), *2001: A Space Odyssey* (1968), *A Clockwork Orange* (1971), *The Shining* (1980), *Full Metal Jacket* (1987), and *Eyes Wide Shut* (1999)

kudos (kew-doss) *n* personal fame or glory
WORD ORIGIN Greek

kudu *or* **koodoo** *n* a spiral-horned African antelope
WORD ORIGIN Afrikaans, from Khoi (language of southern Africa)

kugel (koog-el) *n S African* a rich, fashion-conscious, materialistic young Jewish woman
WORD ORIGIN from Yiddish *kugel,* a type of savoury pudding popular in Jewish cookery

Ku Klux Klan *n* a secret organization of White Protestant Americans who use violence against black and Jewish people **Ku Klux Klanner** *n*
WORD ORIGIN probably based on Greek *kuklos* circle + CLAN

kukri *n* a heavy, curved knife used by Gurkhas
WORD ORIGIN Hindi

kulak *n* (formerly) a property-owning Russian peasant
WORD ORIGIN Russian

Kumaratunge *n* **Chandrika Bandaranaike** born 1945, Sri Lankan politician: prime minister (1994); president (1994–2005)

kumera *or* **kumara** *n NZ* a tropical root vegetable with yellow flesh
WORD ORIGIN Māori

kümmel *n* a German liqueur flavoured with aniseed and cumin
WORD ORIGIN from German

kumquat (kumm-kwott) *n* a citrus fruit resembling a tiny orange
WORD ORIGIN Cantonese Chinese *kam kwat* golden orange

Kun *n* **Béla** 1886–?1937, Hungarian Communist leader, president of the short-lived Communist republic in Hungary (1919). He was forced into exile and died in a Stalinist purge

Kundera *n* **Milan** born 1929, Czech novelist living in France. His novels include *The Book of Laughter and Forgetting* (1979), *The Unbearable Lightness of Being* (1984), and *Ignorance* (2002)

Küng *n* **Hans** born 1928, Swiss Roman Catholic theologian, who questioned the doctrine of infallibility: his licence to teach was withdrawn in 1979. His books include *Global Responsibility* (1991)

kung fu *n* any of various Chinese systems of martial art, esp. unarmed combat in which punches, chops, and kicks are made with the hands and feet; certain styles involve the use of weapons
WORD ORIGIN Chinese: skill; accomplishment

kura kaupapa Māori *n NZ* a primary school where the teaching is done in Māori

kurrajong *n* an Australian tree or shrub with tough fibrous bark
WORD ORIGIN from a native Australian language

Kutuzov *n* Prince **Mikhail Ilarionovich** 1745–1813, Russian field marshal, who harried the French army under Napoleon throughout their retreat from Moscow (1812–13)

Kuznets *n* **Simon** 1901–85, US economist born in Russia. His books include *National Income and its Composition (1919–1938)* (1941) and *Economic Growth of Nations* (1971). He was awarded the Nobel Prize for economics in 1971

kV kilovolt

kvetch *vb slang chiefly US* to complain or grumble
WORD ORIGIN Yiddish

kW kilowatt

Kwanzaa *n* an African-American festival held from December 26 through January 1
WORD ORIGIN from Swahili *(matunda ya) kwanza* first (fruits)

kwashiorkor *n* severe malnutrition of young children, caused by not eating enough protein
WORD ORIGIN native word in Ghana

kWh kilowatt-hour

KWIC *computers* keyword in context

KWOC *computers* keyword out of context

Ky *n* **Nguyen Kao** born 1930, Vietnamese military and political leader; premier of South Vietnam (1965–67); vice president (1967–71)

KY Kentucky

Kyd *or* **Kid** *n* **Thomas** 1558–94, English dramatist, noted for his revenge play *The Spanish Tragedy* (1586)

kyle *n Scot* a narrow strait or channel: *Kyle of Lochalsh*
WORD ORIGIN Gaelic *caol* narrow

Kynewulf *n* a variant spelling of **Cynewulf**

Ll

DICTIONARY

l litre(s)
L **1** large **2** Latin **3** learner driver **4** Usually written: **£** pound **WORD ORIGIN** Latin *libra* **5** the Roman numeral for 50
L. *or* **l.** **1** lake **2** left **3** length **4** *pl* **LL** *or* **ll** lines
la *n music* ▸ same as **lah**
La *chem* lanthanum
LA **1** Los Angeles **2** Louisiana
laager *n* (in Africa) a camp defended by a circular formation of wagons **WORD ORIGIN** Afrikaans *lager*
lab *n informal* ▸ short for **laboratory**
Lab *politics* Labour
label ⊕ *n* **1** a piece of card or other material attached to an object to show its contents, ownership, use, or destination **2** a brief descriptive term given to a person, group, or school of thought: *we would need a handy label to explain the new company* ▹ *vb* **-belling, -belled** *or US* **-beling, -beled** **3** to attach a label to **4** to describe or classify in a word or phrase **WORD ORIGIN** Old French: ribbon
labial (lay-bee-al) *adj* **1** of or near the lips **2** *phonetics* relating to a speech sound made using the lips ▹ *n* **3** *phonetics* a speech sound such as English *p* or *m*, that involves the lips **WORD ORIGIN** Latin *labium* lip
labiate (lay-bee-ate) *n* **1** any of a family of plants with square stems, aromatic leaves, and a two-lipped flower, such as mint or thyme ▹ *adj* **2** of this family **WORD ORIGIN** Latin *labium* lip
Labiche *n* **Eugène Marin** 1815–88, French dramatist, noted for his farces of middle-class life, which include *Le Chapeau de paille d'Italie* (1851) and *Le Voyage de Monsieur Perrichon* (1860)
labium (lay-bee-um) *n, pl* **-bia** (-bee-a) **1** a lip or liplike structure **2** any one of the four lip-shaped folds of the vulva **WORD ORIGIN** Latin: lip
labor *n US, Austral & sometimes Canad* ▸ same as **labour**
laboratory *n, pl* **-ries** a building or room equipped for conducting scientific research or for teaching practical science **WORD ORIGIN** Latin *laborare* to work
Labor Day *n* **1** (in the US and Canada) public holiday in honour of labour, held on the first Monday in September **2** (in Australia) public holiday observed on different days in different states
laborious *adj* involving great exertion or prolonged effort **laboriously** *adv*
Labor Party *n* the main left-wing political party in Australia
labour ⊕ *or US, Austral & sometimes Canad* **labor** *n* **1** productive work, esp. physical work done for wages **2** the people involved in this, as opposed to management **3** the final stage of pregnancy, leading to childbirth **4** difficult work or a difficult job ▹ *vb* **5** to do physical work: *the girls were labouring madly on it* **6** to work hard (for something) **7** to make one's way with difficulty: *she was now labouring down the return length* **8** to emphasize too persistently: *I have laboured the point* **9** (usually foll. by *under*) to be at a disadvantage because of a mistake or false belief: *she laboured under the illusion that I understood her* **WORD ORIGIN** Latin *labor*
Labour Day *n* **1** a public holiday in honour of work, held in Britain on May 1 **2** (in New Zealand) a public holiday commemorating the introduction of the eight-hour day, held on the 4th Monday in October
laboured ⊕ *or US, Austral & sometimes Canad* **labored** *adj* undertaken with difficulty: *laboured breathing*
labourer ⊕ *or US, Austral & sometimes Canad* **laborer** *n* a person engaged in physical work
labour exchange *n Brit* the former name for a Jobcentre
Labour Party *n* **1** the main left-wing political party in a number of countries including Britain and New Zealand **2** any similar party in various other countries
labour-saving *adj* (of a method or piece of equipment) reducing the amount of work or effort needed to carry out a task
Labrador *or* **Labrador retriever** *n* a powerfully built dog with short dense usually black or golden hair
La Bruyère *n* **Jean de** 1645–96, French moralist, noted for his *Caractères* (1688), satirical character studies, including portraits of contemporary public figures
laburnum *n* a small ornamental tree that has clusters of yellow drooping flowers. It is highly poisonous **WORD ORIGIN** Latin
labyrinth (lab-er-inth) *n* **1** a mazelike network of tunnels or paths, either natural or man-made **2** any complex or confusing system **3** the interconnecting cavities of the internal ear **labyrinthine** *adj* **WORD ORIGIN** Greek *laburinthos*
lac *n* a resinous substance secreted by certain insects (**lac insects**), used in the manufacture of shellac **WORD ORIGIN** Hindi *lākh* resin
lace ⊕ *n* **1** a delicate decorative fabric made from threads woven in an open web of patterns **2** a cord or string drawn through eyelets to fasten a shoe or garment ▹ *vb* **lacing, laced** **3** to fasten (shoes) with a lace **4** to draw (a cord or thread) through holes as when tying shoes **5** to add a small amount of alcohol, a drug, or poison to (food or drink) **6** to intertwine; interlace **WORD ORIGIN** Latin *laqueus* noose
lacerate (lass-er-rate) *vb* **-ating, -ated** **1** to tear (the flesh) jaggedly **2** to hurt (the feelings): *it would only lacerate an overburdened conscience* **laceration** *n*

l

THESAURUS

label *n* **1 = tag**, ticket, tab, marker, flag, tally, sticker, docket *(chiefly Brit)* ▹ *vb* **3 = tag**, mark, stamp, ticket, flag, tab, tally, sticker, docket *(chiefly Brit)*
labour *n* **1 = work**, effort, employment, toil, industry **2 = workers**, employees, workforce, labourers, hands, workmen **3 = childbirth**, birth, delivery, contractions, pains, throes, travail, labour pains, parturition ▹ *vb* **5 = work**, toil, strive, work hard, grind *(informal)*, sweat *(informal)*, slave, endeavour, plod away, drudge, travail, slog away *(informal)*, exert yourself, peg along *or* away *(chiefly Brit)*, plug along *or* away *(informal)* **OPPOSITE:** rest **6 = struggle**, work, strain, work hard, strive, go for it *(informal)*, grapple, toil, make an effort, make every effort, do your best, exert yourself, work like a Trojan **8 = overemphasize**, stress, elaborate, exaggerate, strain, dwell on, overdo, go on about, make a production (out) of *(informal)*, make a federal case of *(US informal)* **9** *(usually with* **under***)* **= be disadvantaged by**, suffer from, be a victim of, be burdened by
laboured *adj* **= difficult**, forced, strained, heavy, awkward
labourer *n* **= worker**, workman, working man, manual worker, hand, blue-collar worker, drudge, unskilled worker, navvy *(Brit informal)*, labouring man
lace *n* **1 = netting**, net, filigree, tatting, meshwork, openwork **2 = cord**, tie, string, lacing, thong, shoelace, bootlace ▹ *vb* **3 = fasten**, tie, tie up, do up, secure, bind, close, attach, thread **5 = mix**, drug, doctor, add to, spike, contaminate, fortify, adulterate **6 = intertwine**, interweave, entwine, twine, interlink

DICTIONARY

WORD ORIGIN Latin *lacerare* to tear

lace up *vb* **1** to fasten (clothes or footwear) with laces ▷ *adj* **lace-up** **2** (of footwear) to be fastened with laces ▷ *n* **lace-up** **3** a shoe or boot which fastens with a lace

lachrymal *adj* ▸ same as **lacrimal**

lachrymose *adj* **1** given to weeping; tearful **2** mournful; sad
WORD ORIGIN Latin *lacrima* a tear

lacing *n chiefly Brit informal* a severe beating

lack ❶ *n* **1** shortage or absence of something required or desired: *a lack of confidence* ▷ *vb* **2** (often foll. by *in*) to be short (of) or have need (of): *lacking in sparkle*
WORD ORIGIN related to Middle Dutch *laken* to be wanting

lackadaisical *adj* **1** lacking vitality and purpose **2** lazy and careless in a dreamy way
WORD ORIGIN earlier *lackadaisy*

lackey *n* **1** a servile follower; hanger-on **2** a liveried male servant or valet
WORD ORIGIN Catalan *lacayo, alacayo*

lacklustre *or US* **lackluster** *adj* lacking brilliance, force, or vitality

Laclos *n* **Pierre Choderlos de** 1741–1803, French soldier and writer, noted for his novel in epistolary form *Les Liaisons dangereuses* (1782)

laconic *adj* (of a person's speech) using few words **laconically** *adv*
WORD ORIGIN Greek *Lakōnikos* Spartan; referring to the Spartans' terseness of speech

lacquer *n* **1** a hard glossy coating made by dissolving natural or synthetic resins in a solvent that evaporates quickly **2** a black resin, obtained from certain trees, used to give a hard glossy finish to wooden furniture **3** a clear sticky substance for spraying onto the hair to hold a style in place
WORD ORIGIN Portuguese *laca* lac

lacquered *adj* coated with lacquer

lacrimal *or* **lachrymal** (lack-rim-al) *adj* of tears or the glands that secrete tears
WORD ORIGIN Latin *lacrima* a tear

lacrosse *n* a sport in which two teams try to propel a ball into each other's goal using long-handled sticks with a pouched net at the end
WORD ORIGIN Canadian French: the hooked stick

lactate[1] *vb* **-tating, -tated** (of mammals) to secrete milk

lactate[2] *n* an ester or salt of lactic acid

lactation *n* **1** the secretion of milk from the mammary glands **2** the period during which milk is secreted

lacteal *adj* **1** of or like milk **2** (of lymphatic vessels) conveying or containing chyle ▷ *n* **3** any of the lymphatic vessels that convey chyle from the small intestine to the blood
WORD ORIGIN Latin *lacteus* of milk

lactic *adj* relating to or derived from milk
WORD ORIGIN Latin *lac* milk

lactic acid *n* a colourless syrupy acid found in sour milk and used as a preservative (**E270**) for foodstuffs

lactose *n* a white crystalline sugar occurring in milk

lacuna (lak-kew-na) *n, pl* **-nae** (-nee) a gap or space in a book or manuscript
WORD ORIGIN Latin: pool, cavity

lacy *adj* **lacier, laciest** of or like lace

lad ❶ *n* **1** a boy or young man **2** *informal* any male **3** **the lads** *informal* a group of males
WORD ORIGIN perhaps from Old Norse

ladder *n* **1** a portable frame consisting of two long parallel supports connected by steps, for climbing up or down **2** any system thought of as having a series of ascending stages: *the career ladder* **3** *chiefly Brit* a line of connected stitches that have come undone in tights or stockings ▷ *vb* **4** *chiefly Brit* to have or cause to have a line of undone stitches
WORD ORIGIN Old English *hlǣdder*

ladder back *n* a chair in which the back is made of horizontal slats between two uprights

laddish *adj Brit, Austral & NZ informal, often derogatory* characteristic of young men, esp. by being rowdy or immature

lade *vb* **lading, laded, laden** *or* **laded** **1** to put cargo on board (a ship) or (of a ship) to take on cargo **2** (foll. by *with*) to burden or load
WORD ORIGIN Old English *hladen* to load

laden ❶ *adj* **1** loaded **2** burdened

la-di-da *or* **lah-di-dah** *adj informal* affected or pretentious in speech or manners
WORD ORIGIN mockingly imitative of affected speech

ladies *or* **ladies' room** *n informal* a women's public toilet

lading *n* a load; cargo; freight

Ladislaus I *or* **Ladislas I** *n* **Saint** 1040–95, king of Hungary (1077–95) He extended his country's boundaries and suppressed paganism. Feast day: June 27

ladle *n* **1** a long-handled spoon with a deep bowl for serving soup, stew, etc. ▷ *vb* **-dling, -dled** **2** to serve out as with a ladle
WORD ORIGIN Old English *hlædel*

ladle out *vb informal* to distribute (money, gifts, etc.) generously

lad mag *n* a magazine aimed at or appealing to men, focusing on fashion, gadgets, and often featuring scantily dressed women

lady ❶ *n, pl* **-dies** **1** a woman regarded as having the characteristics of a good family, such as dignified manners **2** a polite name for a woman ▷ *adj* **3** female: *a lady chef*
WORD ORIGIN Old English *hlǣfdīge*

Lady *n, pl* **-dies** **1** (in Britain) a title borne by various classes of women of the peerage **2** **Our Lady** a title of the Virgin Mary

ladybird *n* a small red beetle with black spots
WORD ORIGIN after Our *Lady*, the Virgin Mary

ladyboy *n informal* a transvestite or transsexual, esp. one from the Far East

Lady Day *n* March 25, the feast of the Annunciation of the Virgin Mary: a quarter day in England, Wales, and Ireland

lady-in-waiting *n, pl* **ladies-in-waiting** a lady who attends a queen or princess

lady-killer *n informal* a man who is or believes he is irresistible to women

ladylike *adj* refined and fastidious

Ladyship *n* (preceded by *Your* or *Her*) a title used to address or refer to any peeress except a duchess

lady's-slipper *n* an orchid with reddish or purple flowers

Laënnec *n* **René Théophile Hyacinthe** 1781–1826, French physician, who invented the stethoscope

Lafayette *or* **La Fayette** *n* **1** **Marie Joseph Paul Yves Roch Gilbert du Motier**, Marquis de Lafayette. 1757–1834, French general and statesman. He fought on the side of the colonists in the War of American Independence and, as commander of the National Guard (1789–91; 1830),

THESAURUS

lack *n* **1 = shortage**, want, absence, deficiency, need, shortcoming, deprivation, inadequacy, scarcity, dearth, privation, shortness, destitution, insufficiency, scantiness, debt
OPPOSITE: abundance
▷ *vb* **2** (often foll. by *in*) **= miss**, want, need, require, not have, be without, be short of, be in need of, be deficient in **OPPOSITE:** have

lad *n* **1 = boy**, kid *(informal)*, guy *(informal)*, youth, fellow, youngster, chap *(informal)*, juvenile, shaver *(informal)*, nipper *(informal)*, laddie *(Scot)*, stripling

laden *adj* **1, 2 = loaded**, burdened, hampered, weighted, full, charged, taxed, oppressed, fraught, weighed down, encumbered

lady *n* **1 = gentlewoman**, duchess, noble, dame, baroness, countess, aristocrat, viscountess, noblewoman, peeress **2 = woman**, female, girl, miss, maiden *(archaic)*, maid *(archaic)*, lass, damsel, lassie *(informal)*, charlie *(Austral slang)*, chook *(Austral slang)*, wahine *(NZ)*

l

DICTIONARY

he played a leading part in the French Revolution and the revolution of 1830 **2 Marie-Madeleine**, Comtesse de Lafayette. 1634–93, French novelist, noted for her historical romance *La Princesse de Clèves* (1678)

La Fontaine *n* **Jean de** 1621–95, French poet, famous for his *Fables* (1668–94)

Laforgue *n* **Jules** 1860–87, French symbolist poet. An originator of free verse, he had a considerable influence on modern poetry

lag[1] ❶ *vb* **lagging, lagged 1** (often foll. by *behind*) to hang (back) or fall (behind) in movement, progress, or development **2** to fall away in strength or intensity ▹*n* **3** a slowing down or falling behind **4** the interval of time between two events, esp. between an action and its effect: *the time lag between mobilization and combat*
WORD ORIGIN origin unknown

lag[2] *vb* **lagging, lagged 1** to wrap (a pipe, cylinder, or boiler) with insulating material to prevent heat loss ▹*n* **2** the insulating casing of a steam cylinder or boiler
WORD ORIGIN Scandinavian

lag[3] *n* **old lag** *Brit, Austral & NZ slang* a convict or ex-convict
WORD ORIGIN origin unknown

lager *n* a light-bodied effervescent beer, fermented in a closed vessel using yeasts that sink to the bottom of the brew
WORD ORIGIN German *Lagerbier* beer for storing

Lagerfeld *n* **Karl (Otto)** born 1938, German fashion designer working mainly in Paris

Lagerkvist *n* **Pär (Fabian)** 1891–1974, Swedish novelist and dramatist. His works include the novels *The Dwarf* (1944) and *Barabbas* (1950): Nobel prize for literature 1951

Lagerlöf *n* **Selma** 1858–1940, Swedish novelist, noted esp. for her children's classic *The Wonderful Adventures of Nils* (1906–07): Nobel prize for literature 1909

laggard *n* a person who lags behind

lagging *n* insulating material wrapped around pipes, boilers, or tanks to prevent loss of heat

lagoon *n* a body of water cut off from the open sea by coral reefs or sand bars
WORD ORIGIN Latin *lacuna* pool

Lagrange *n* Comte **Joseph Louis** 1736–1813, French mathematician and astronomer, noted particularly for his work on harmonics, mechanics, and the calculus of variations ▹ **Lagrangian** *adj*

La Guardia *n* **Fiorello H(enry)** 1882–1947, US politician. As mayor of New York (1933–45), he organized slum-clearance and labour safeguard schemes and suppressed racketeering

lah *n music* (in tonic sol-fa) the sixth note of any ascending major scale

laid *vb* ▸ the past of **lay**[1]

laid-back ❶ *adj* relaxed in style or character

laid paper *n* paper with a regular pattern of lines impressed upon it

lain *vb* ▸ the past participle of **lie**[2]

Laine *n* **Cleo**, full name *Clementina Dinah Laine*. born 1927, British jazz singer, noted esp. for her recordings with her husband John Dankworth

lair *n* **1** the resting place of a wild animal **2** *informal* a place of seclusion or hiding
WORD ORIGIN Old English *leger*

laird *n Scot* a landowner, esp. of a large estate
WORD ORIGIN Scots variant of *lord*

laissez faire *or* **laisser faire** (less-ay fair) *n* the policy of nonintervention, esp. by a government in commerce
WORD ORIGIN French, literally: let (them) act

laity (lay-it-ee) *n* **1** people who are not members of the clergy **2** all the people who do not belong to a specific profession
WORD ORIGIN from LAY[3]

lake[1] ❶ *n* an expanse of water entirely surrounded by land
WORD ORIGIN Latin *lacus*

lake[2] *n* **1** a bright pigment produced by combining organic colouring matter with an inorganic compound **2** a red dye obtained by combining a metallic compound with cochineal
WORD ORIGIN variant of *lac*

Lake District *n* a region of lakes and mountains in NW England. Also called: **Lakeland, the Lakes**

lake trout *n* a yellow-spotted trout of the Great Lakes region of Canada

lakh (lahk) *n* (in India) 100 000, esp. referring to this sum of rupees
WORD ORIGIN Hindi *lākh*

Lalique *n* **René (Jules)** 1860–1945, French Art- Nouveau jeweller, glass-maker, and designer: noted esp. for his frosted glassware

Lalo *n* **(Victor-Antoine-)Édouard** 1823–92, French composer of Spanish descent. His works include the *Symphonie espagnole* (1873) and the ballet *Namouna* (1882)

lam[1] *vb* **lamming, lammed** *slang* to attack vigorously
WORD ORIGIN Scandinavian

lam[2] *n* **on the lam** *US & Canad slang* **a** making an escape **b** in hiding
WORD ORIGIN origin unknown

lama *n* a Buddhist priest or monk in Mongolia or Tibet
WORD ORIGIN Tibetan *blama*

Lamartine *n* **Alphonse Marie Louis de Prat de** 1790–1869, French romantic poet, historian, and statesman: his works include *Méditations poétiques* (1820) and *Histoire des Girondins* (1847)

lamb *n* **1** the young of a sheep **2** the meat of a young sheep eaten as food **3** someone who is innocent, gentle, and good ▹*vb* **4** (of a ewe) to give birth
WORD ORIGIN Old English

Lamb[1] *n* **the Lamb** a title given to Christ in the New Testament

Lamb[2] *n* **1 Charles**, pen name *Elia*. 1775–1834, English essayist and critic. He collaborated with his sister Mary on *Tales from Shakespeare* (1807). His other works include *Specimens of English Dramatic Poets* (1808) and the largely autobiographical essays collected in *Essays of Elia* (1823; 1833) **2** ▸ **William** See (2nd Viscount) **Melbourne 3 Willis Eugene** 1913–2008, US physicist. He detected the small difference in energy between two states of the hydrogen atom (**Lamb shift**). Nobel prize for physics 1955

lambast *or* **lambaste** *vb* **1** to beat severely **2** to reprimand severely
WORD ORIGIN LAM[1] + BASTE[3]

lambent *adj* **1** (of a flame or light) flickering softly over a surface **2** (of wit or humour) light or brilliant
lambency *n*
WORD ORIGIN Latin *lambere* to lick

Lambert *n* **Constant** 1905–51, English composer and conductor. His works include much ballet music and *The Rio Grande* (1929), a work for chorus, orchestra, and piano, using jazz idioms

lambing *n* **1** the birth of lambs at the end of winter **2** the shepherd's work of tending the ewes and newborn lambs at this time

lamb's fry *n Austral & NZ* lamb's liver for cooking

lambskin *n* the skin of a lamb, usually with the wool still on, used to make coats, slippers, etc.

THESAURUS

lag[1] *vb* **1** (often foll. by *behind*) **= hang back**, delay, drag (behind), trail, linger, be behind, idle, saunter, loiter, straggle, dawdle, tarry, drag your feet *(informal)*

laid-back *adj* **= relaxed**, calm, casual, together *(slang)*, at ease, easy-going, unflappable *(informal)*, unhurried, free and easy, easy-peasy *(slang)*, chilled *(informal)* **OPPOSITE:** tense

lake[1] *n* **= pond**, pool, reservoir, loch *(Scot)*, lagoon, mere, lough *(Irish)*, tarn

lame *adj* **1 = disabled**, handicapped, crippled, limping, defective, hobbling, game, halt *(archaic)* **2 = unconvincing**, poor, pathetic, inadequate, thin, weak, insufficient, feeble, unsatisfactory, flimsy

DICTIONARY

lame ❶ *adj* **1** disabled or crippled in the legs or feet **2** weak; unconvincing: *lame arguments* ▷ *vb* **laming, lamed 3** to make lame **lamely** *adv* **lameness** *n*
WORD ORIGIN Old English *lama*

lamé (lah-may) *n* a fabric interwoven with gold or silver threads
WORD ORIGIN Old French *lame* gold or silver thread

lame duck *n* a person who is unable to cope without the help of other people

lament ❶ *vb* **1** to feel or express sorrow or regret (for or over) ▷ *n* **2** an expression of sorrow **3** a poem or song in which a death is lamented **lamentation** *n*
WORD ORIGIN Latin *lamentum*

lamentable *adj* very unfortunate or disappointing **lamentably** *adv*

lamented *adj* grieved for: usually said of someone dead

Lamerie *n* **Paul de** 1688–1751, English silversmith of French Huguenot descent, noted for his lavish rococo designs

lamina *n, pl* **-nae** a thin plate, esp. of bone or mineral **laminar** *adj*
WORD ORIGIN Latin: thin plate

laminate *vb* **-nating, -nated 1** to make (material in sheet form) by sticking together thin sheets **2** to cover with a thin sheet of material **3** to split or be split into thin sheets ▷ *n* **4** a material made by sticking sheets together ▷ *adj* **5** composed of lamina; laminated **lamination** *n*

laminated *adj* **1** composed of many layers stuck together **2** covered with a thin protective layer of plastic

lamington *n Austral & NZ* a sponge cake covered with a sweet coating

Lammas *n* August 1, formerly observed in England as a harvest festival: a quarter day in Scotland
WORD ORIGIN Old English *hlāfmæsse* loaf mass

lamp *n* **1** a device that produces light: *an electric lamp; a gas lamp; an oil lamp* **2** a device that produces radiation, esp. for therapeutic purposes: *an ultraviolet lamp*
WORD ORIGIN Greek *lampein* to shine

lampblack *n* a fine black soot used as a pigment in paint and ink

Lampedusa[1] *n* an island in the Mediterranean, between Malta and Tunisia. Area: about 21 sq km (8 sq miles)

Lampedusa[2] *n* **Giuseppe Tomasi di** 1896–1957, Italian novelist: author of the historical novel *The Leopard* (1958)

lampoon *n* **1** a piece of writing ridiculing a person ▷ *vb* **2** to ridicule and criticize (someone) in a lampoon **lampooner** *or* **lampoonist** *n*
WORD ORIGIN French *lampon*

lamppost *n* a metal or concrete pole supporting a lamp in a street

lamprey *n* an eel-like fish with a round sucking mouth
WORD ORIGIN Late Latin *lampreda*

LAN *computers* local area network

Lancastrian *n* **1** a person from Lancashire or Lancaster **2** a supporter of the house of Lancaster in the Wars of the Roses (1455–85) ▷ *adj* **3** of Lancashire or Lancaster **4** of the house of Lancaster

lance *n* **1** a long weapon with a pointed head used by horsemen ▷ *vb* **lancing, lanced 2** to pierce (an abscess or boil) with a lancet **3** to pierce with or as with a lance
WORD ORIGIN Latin *lancea*

lance corporal *n* a noncommissioned officer of the lowest rank

lanceolate *adj* narrow and tapering to a point at each end, like some leaves
WORD ORIGIN Latin *lanceola* small lance

lancer *n* (formerly) a cavalryman armed with a lance

lancet *n* **1** a pointed surgical knife with two sharp edges **2** ▸ short for **lancet arch** or **lancet window**
WORD ORIGIN Old French *lancette* small lance

lancet arch *n* a narrow acutely pointed arch

lancet window *n* a narrow window with a lancet arch

lancewood *n* a New Zealand tree with slender leaves

Lancs Lancashire

land ❶ *n* **1** the solid part of the surface of the earth as distinct from seas and lakes ▸ Related adjective: **terrestrial 2** ground, esp. with reference to its use or quality: *agricultural land* **3** rural or agricultural areas: *he couldn't leave the land* **4** *law* ground owned as property **5** a country, region, or area: *to bring peace and riches to your land* ▷ *vb* **6** to come down or bring (something) down to earth after a flight or jump **7** to transfer (something) or go from a ship to the shore: *sacks of malt were landed from barges* **8** to come to or touch shore **9** *informal* to obtain: *he landed a handsomely paid job at Lloyd's* **10** *angling* to retrieve (a hooked fish) from the water **11** *informal* to deliver (a blow or punch) ▸ See also **land up** > **landless** *adj*
WORD ORIGIN Old English

Land[1] *n* **Edwin Herbert** 1909–91, US inventor of the Polaroid Land camera

Land[2] *German n, pl* **Länder a** any of the federal states of Germany **b** any of the provinces of Austria

land agent *n* a person in charge of a landed estate

landau (lan-daw) *n* a four-wheeled horse-drawn carriage with two folding hoods
WORD ORIGIN after *Landau*, a town in Germany, where first made

Landau *n* **Lev Davidovich** 1908–68, Soviet physicist, noted for his researches on quantum theory and his work on the theories of solids and liquids: Nobel prize for physics 1962

landed *adj* **1** owning land: *landed gentry* **2** consisting of land: *landed property*

landfall *n* the act of sighting or nearing land, esp. from the sea

landfill *n* disposing of rubbish by covering it with earth

land girl *n* a girl or woman who does farm work, esp. in wartime

land-holder *n* a person who owns or occupies land **land-holding** *adj, n*

landing *n* **1** the floor area at the top of a flight of stairs **2** the act of coming to land, esp. after a flight or sea voyage **3** a place of disembarkation

landing field *n* an area of land on which aircraft land and from which they take off

landing gear *n* the undercarriage of an aircraft

landlady *n, pl* **-dies 1** a woman who owns and leases property **2** a woman who owns or runs a lodging house or pub

land line *n* a telecommunications wire or cable laid over land

landlocked *adj* (of a country) completely surrounded by land

landlord ❶ *n* **1** a man who owns and leases property **2** a man who owns or runs a lodging house or pub

landlubber *n naut* any person without experience at sea

l

THESAURUS

lament *vb* **1 = bemoan**, grieve, mourn, weep over, complain about, regret, wail about, deplore, bewail ▷ *n* **2 = complaint**, moaning, moan, keening, wail, wailing, lamentation, plaint, ululation **3 = dirge**, requiem, elegy, threnody, monody, coronach (*Scot & Irish*)

land *n* **1 = ground**, earth, dry land, terra firma **2 = soil**, ground, earth, clay, dirt, sod, loam **3 = countryside**, farming, farmland, rural districts **4** (*law*) **= property**, grounds, estate, acres, real estate, realty, acreage, real property, homestead (*US & Canad*) **5 = country**, nation, region, state, district, territory, province, kingdom, realm, tract, motherland, fatherland ▷ *vb* **8 = arrive**, dock, put down, moor, berth, alight, touch down, disembark, come to rest, debark **9** (*informal*) **= gain**, get, win, score (*slang*), secure, obtain, acquire

landlord *n* **1 = owner**, landowner, proprietor, freeholder, lessor, landholder **2 = innkeeper**, host, hotelier, hotel-keeper

DICTIONARY

landmark ❶ *n* **1** a prominent object in or feature of a particular landscape **2** an important or unique event or development: *a landmark in scientific progress*

landmass *n* a large continuous area of land

land mine *n mil* an explosive device placed in the ground, usually detonated when someone steps on it or drives over it

Landor *n* **Walter Savage** 1775–1864, English poet, noted also for his prose works, including *Imaginary Conversations* (1824–29)

landowner *n* a person who owns land **landowning** *n, adj*

Landowska *n* **Wanda** 1877–1959, US harpsichordist, born in Poland

landscape ❶ *n* **1** an extensive area of land regarded as being visually distinct **2** a painting, drawing, or photograph depicting natural scenery ▷ *vb* **-scaping, -scaped 3** to improve the natural features of (an area of land)
WORD ORIGIN Middle Dutch *lantscap* region

landscape gardening *n* the art of laying out grounds in imitation of natural scenery **landscape gardener** *n*

Landseer *n* Sir **Edwin Henry** 1802–73, English painter, noted for his studies of animals

landside *n* the part of an airport farthest from the aircraft

landslide ❶ *n* **1** Also called: **landslip a** the sliding of a large mass of rocks and soil down the side of a mountain or cliff **b** the material dislodged in this way **2** an overwhelming electoral victory

Landsteiner *n* **Karl** 1868–1943, Austrian immunologist, who discovered (1900) human blood groups and introduced the ABO classification system. He also discovered (1940) the Rhesus (Rh) factor in blood and researched into poliomyelitis. Nobel prize for physiology or medicine (1930)

land up ❶ *vb* to arrive at a final point or condition

landward *adj* **1** lying, facing, or moving towards land **2** in the direction of the land ▷ *adv also* **landwards 3** towards land

lane ❶ *n* **1** a narrow road, esp. in the country **2** one of the parallel strips into which the carriageway of a major road or motorway is divided **3** any well-defined route or course, such as for ships or aircraft **4** one of the parallel strips into which a running track or swimming bath is divided for races
WORD ORIGIN Old English *lane, lanu*

Lanfranc *n* ?1005–89, Italian ecclesiastic and scholar; archbishop of Canterbury (1070–89) and adviser to William the Conqueror. He instituted many reforms in the English Church

lang. language

Lang *n* **1 Cosmo Gordon,** 1st Baron Lang of Lambeth. 1864–1945, British churchman; archbishop of Canterbury (1928–42) **2 Fritz** 1890–1976, Austrian film director, later in the US, most notable for his silent films, such as *Metropolis* (1926), *M* (1931), and *The Testament of Dr. Mabuse* (1932) **3 Jack (John Thomas)** 1876–1975, controversial Labor premier of New South Wales from 1925–27 and from 1930–32, who introduced much social welfare legislation and was dismissed by the governor, Sir Philip Game, in 1932 for acting unconstitutionally

Langer *n* **Bernhard** born 1957, German professional golfer: won the US Masters Championship (1985, 1993)

Langland *n* **William** ?1332–?1400, English poet. The allegorical religious poem in alliterative verse, *The Vision of William concerning Piers the Plowman,* is attributed to him

Langley *n* **Samuel Pierpont** 1834–1906, US astronomer and physicist: invented the bolometer (1878) and pioneered the construction of heavier-than-air flying machines

Langmuir *n* **Irving** 1881–1957, US chemist. He developed the gas-filled tungsten lamp and the atomic hydrogen welding process: Nobel prize for chemistry 1932

Langton *n* **Stephen** ?1150–1228, English cardinal; archbishop of Canterbury (1213–28). He was consecrated archbishop by Pope Innocent III in 1207 but was kept out of his see by King John until 1213. He was partly responsible for the Magna Carta (1215)

Langtry *n* **Lillie,** known as *the Jersey Lily,* real name *Émilie Charlotte le Breton*. 1852–1929, English actress, noted for her beauty and for her friendship with Edward VII

language ❶ *n* **1** a system of spoken sounds or conventional symbols for communicating thought **2** the language of a particular nation or people **3** the ability to use words to communicate **4** any other means of communicating: *body language* **5** the specialized vocabulary used by a particular group: *legal language* **6** a particular style of verbal expression: *rough language* **7** *computers* ▸ see **programming language**
WORD ORIGIN Latin *lingua* tongue

language laboratory *n* a room in a school or college equipped with tape recorders etc. for learning foreign languages

languid *adj* lacking energy; dreamy and inactive **languidly** *adv*
WORD ORIGIN Latin *languere* to languish

languish ❶ *vb literary* **1** to suffer deprivation, hardship, or neglect: *she won't languish in jail for it* **2** to lose or diminish in strength or energy: *the design languished into oblivion* **3** (often foll. by *for*) to be listless with desire; pine **languishing** *adj*
WORD ORIGIN Latin *languere*

languor (lang-ger) *n literary* a pleasant state of dreamy relaxation **languorous** *adj*
WORD ORIGIN Latin *languere* to languish

lank *adj* **1** (of hair) straight and limp **2** thin or gaunt: *a lank bespectacled boy*
WORD ORIGIN Old English *hlanc* loose

Lankester *n* Sir **Edwin Ray** 1847–1929, English zoologist, noted particularly for his work in embryology and study of protozoans

lanky *adj* **lankier, lankiest** ungracefully tall and thin **lankiness** *n*

lanolin *n* a yellowish sticky substance extracted from wool: used in some ointments
WORD ORIGIN Latin *lana* wool + *oleum* oil

Lansbury *n* **George** 1859–1940, British Labour politician, who led

THESAURUS

landmark *n* **1 = feature**, spectacle, monument **2 = milestone**, turning point, watershed, critical point, tipping point

landscape *n* **1 = scenery**, country, view, land, scene, prospect, countryside, outlook, terrain, panorama, vista

landslide *n* **1a, 1b = landslip**, avalanche, mudslide, rockfall

land up = end up, arrive, turn up, wind up, finish up, fetch up *(informal)*

lane *n* **1 = road**, street, track, path, strip, way, passage, trail, pathway, footpath, passageway, thoroughfare

language *n* **1, 2 = tongue**, speech, vocabulary, dialect, idiom, vernacular, patter, lingo *(informal)*, patois, lingua franca **3 = speech**, communication, expression, speaking, talk, talking, conversation, discourse, interchange, utterance, parlance, vocalization, verbalization

languish *vb (literary)* **1 = decline**, waste away, fade away, wither away, flag, weaken, wilt, sicken **OPPOSITE:** flourish **2 = waste away**, suffer, rot, be abandoned, be neglected, be disregarded **OPPOSITE:** thrive **3** *(often with* **for***)* **= pine**, want, long, desire, sigh, hunger, yearn, hanker, eat your heart out over, suspire

DICTIONARY

the Labour Party in opposition (1931–35). A committed pacifist, he resigned over the party's reaction to Mussolini's seizure of Ethiopia

lantana (lan-**tay**-na) *n* a shrub with orange or yellow flowers, considered a weed in Australia

lantern *n* **1** a light with a transparent protective case **2** a raised part on top of a dome or roof which lets in light or air **3** the upper part of a lighthouse that houses the light **WORD ORIGIN** Greek *lampein* to shine

lantern jaw *n* a long hollow jaw that gives the face a drawn appearance **lantern-jawed** *adj*

lanthanide series *n chem* a class of 15 chemically related elements (**lanthanides**) with atomic numbers from 57 (lanthanum) to 71 (lutetium)

lanthanum *n chem* a silvery-white metallic element of the lanthanide series: used in electronic devices and glass manufacture. Symbol: La **WORD ORIGIN** Greek *lanthanein* to lie unseen

lanyard *n* **1** a cord worn round the neck to hold a whistle or knife **2** *naut* a line for extending or tightening rigging **WORD ORIGIN** Old French *lasne* strap

laodicean (lay-oh-**diss**-see-an) *adj* indifferent, esp. in religious matters **WORD ORIGIN** referring to the early Christians of Laodicea (Revelation 3:14–16)

lap[1] *n* **1** the area formed by the upper surface of the thighs of a seated person **2** a protected place or environment: *in the lap of luxury* **3** the part of a person's clothing that covers the lap **4 drop in someone's lap** to give someone the responsibility of **WORD ORIGIN** Old English *læppa* flap

lap[2] ❶ *n* **1** one circuit of a racecourse or track **2** a stage or part of a journey **3 a** an overlapping part **b** the extent of overlap ▹*vb* **lapping, lapped 4** to overtake (an opponent) in a race so as to be one or more circuits ahead **5** to enfold or wrap around **6** to place or lie partly or completely over or project beyond: *deep-pile carpet that lapped against his ankles* **7** to envelop or surround with comfort, love, or peace: *she was lapped by the luxury of Seymour House* **WORD ORIGIN** probably same as LAP[1]

lap[3] ❶ *vb* **lapping, lapped 1** (of small waves) to wash against (the shore or a boat) with light splashing sounds **2** (often foll. by *up*) (esp. of animals) to scoop (a liquid) into the mouth with the tongue ▹*n* **3** the act or sound of lapping ▸See also **lap up** **WORD ORIGIN** Old English *lapian*

laparoscopy *n* an investigative surgical procedure in which an optical instrument is inserted through a small incision in the abdomen **laparoscopic** *adj* **WORD ORIGIN** Greek *lapara* flank + *skopos* target

lap dancing *n* a form of entertainment in which scantily dressed women dance erotically for individual members of the audience

lapdog *n* a small pet dog

lapel (lap-**pel**) *n* the part on the front of a jacket or coat that folds back towards the shoulders **WORD ORIGIN** from LAP[1]

lapidary *n, pl* **-daries 1** a person who cuts, polishes, sets, or deals in gemstones ▹*adj* **2** of or relating to gemstones or the work of a lapidary **WORD ORIGIN** Latin *lapidarius*, from *lapis* stone

lapis lazuli (**lap**-iss **lazz**-yew-lie) *n* a brilliant blue mineral used as a gemstone **WORD ORIGIN** Latin *lapis* stone + Medieval Latin *lazulum* azure

lap joint *n* a joint made by fastening together overlapping parts

lap of honour *n* a ceremonial circuit of a racing track by the winner of a race

Lapp *n* **1** Also: **Laplander** a member of a nomadic people living chiefly in N Scandinavia **2** the language of this people ▹*adj* **3** of this people or their language

lappet *n* **1** a small hanging flap or piece of lace **2** *zool* a flap of flesh or membrane, such as the ear lobe or a bird's wattle **WORD ORIGIN** LAP[1] + *-et* (diminutive suffix)

lapse ❶ *n* **1** a temporary drop in standard as a result of forgetfulness or lack of concentration **2** a moment or instance of bad behaviour, esp. by someone who is usually well-behaved **3** a period of time sufficient for a change to take place: *the lapse between phone call and now* **4** a gradual decline to a lower degree, condition, or state: *its lapse from the tradition of Disraeli* **5** *law* the loss of some right by neglecting to exercise or renew it ▹*vb* **lapsing, lapsed 6** to drop in standard or fail to maintain a standard **7** to decline gradually in status, condition, or degree **8** to allow to end or become no longer valid, esp. through negligence: *a bid that lapsed last July* **9** (usually foll. by *into*) to drift (into a condition): *she appeared to lapse into a brief reverie* **10** (often foll. by *from*) to turn away (from beliefs or standards) **11** (of time) to slip away **lapsed** *adj* **WORD ORIGIN** Latin *lapsus* error

laptop *adj* (of a computer) small and light enough to be held on the user's lap

lap up ❶ *vb* **1** to eat or drink **2** to accept (information or attention) eagerly: *the public are lapping up the scandal*

lapwing *n* a bird of the plover family with a crested head. Also called: **peewit** **WORD ORIGIN** Old English *hlēapewince* plover

Lara *n* **Brian Charles** born 1970, Trinidadian cricketer: holder of records for highest individual score in first-class cricket and for highest Test innings score

larboard *n naut* ▸an old word for **port**[2] (sense 1) **WORD ORIGIN** Middle English *laddeborde*

larceny *n, pl* **-nies** *law* theft **larcenist** *n* **WORD ORIGIN** Old French *larcin*

larch *n* **1** a coniferous tree with deciduous needle-like leaves and egg-shaped cones **2** the wood of this tree **WORD ORIGIN** Latin *larix*

lard *n* **1** the soft white fat obtained from pigs and prepared for use in cooking ▹*vb* **2** to prepare (lean meat or poultry) by inserting small strips of bacon or fat before cooking **3** to add unnecessary material to (speech or writing) **WORD ORIGIN** Latin *laridum* bacon fat

larder *n* a room or cupboard used for storing food **WORD ORIGIN** Old French *lardier*

Lardner *n* **Ring**(**old Wilmer**) 1885–1933, US short-story writer and journalist, whose best-known works are collected in *How to Write Short Stories* (1924) and *The Love Nest* (1926)

lardy cake *n Brit* a sweet cake made of bread dough, lard, sugar, and dried fruit

large ❶ *adj* **1** having a relatively great size, quantity, or extent; big **2** of

l

THESAURUS

lap[2] *n* **1 = circuit**, course, round, tour, leg, distance, stretch, circle, orbit, loop

lap[3] *vb* **1 = ripple**, wash, splash, slap, swish, gurgle, slosh, purl, plash

lapse *n* **1 = mistake**, failing, fault, failure, error, slip, negligence, omission, oversight, indiscretion **2, 4 = decline**, fall, drop, descent, deterioration, relapse, backsliding **3 = interval**, break, gap, passage, pause, interruption, lull, breathing space, intermission ▹*vb* **6, 7 = slip**, fall, decline, sink, drop, slide, deteriorate, degenerate **8 = end**, stop, run out, expire, terminate, become obsolete, become void

lap up *vb* **2 = relish**, like, enjoy, appreciate, delight in, savour, revel in, wallow in, accept eagerly **2b = drink**, sip, lick, swallow, gulp, sup

large *adj* **1a = big**, great, huge, heavy, giant, massive, vast, enormous, tall,

DICTIONARY

wide or broad scope, capacity, or range; comprehensive: *a large effect* ▹*n* **3 at large a** as a whole; in general: *both the Navy and the country at large* **b** (of a dangerous criminal or wild animal) out of captivity; free **c** in full detail ▹*vb* **larging, larged 4 large it** *Brit slang* to enjoy oneself or celebrate in an extravagant way **largeness** *n*
WORD ORIGIN Latin *largus* ample

large intestine *n* the part of the alimentary canal consisting of the caecum, colon, and rectum

largely *adv* principally; to a great extent

large-scale *adj* **1** wide-ranging or extensive **2** (of maps and models) constructed or drawn to a big scale

largesse *or* **largess** (lar-**jess**) *n* the generous giving of gifts, favours, or money
WORD ORIGIN Old French

largish *adj* fairly large

largo *music adv* **1** in a slow and stately manner ▹*n, pl* **-gos 2** a piece or passage to be performed in a slow and stately manner
WORD ORIGIN Italian

lariat *n US & Canad* **1** a lasso **2** a rope for tethering animals
WORD ORIGIN Spanish *la reata* the lasso

lark[1] *n* a small brown songbird, esp. the skylark
WORD ORIGIN Old English *lāwerce, lǣwerce*

lark[2] *informal n* **1** a carefree adventure or frolic **2** a harmless piece of mischief **3** an activity or job viewed with disrespect ▹*vb* **4 lark about** to have a good time frolicking or playing pranks **larky** *adj*
WORD ORIGIN origin unknown

larkspur *n* a plant with blue, pink, or white flowers with slender spikes at the base
WORD ORIGIN LARK[1] + SPUR

La Rochefoucauld *n* **François** Duc de La Rochefoucauld. 1613–80, French writer. His best-known work is *Réflexions ou sentences et maximes morales* (1665), a collection of epigrammatic and cynical observations on human nature

Larousse *n* **Pierre Athanase** 1817–75, French grammarian, lexicographer, and encyclopedist. He edited and helped to compile the *Grand Dictionnaire universel du XIX siècle* (1866–76)

larrikin *n Austral & NZ old-fashioned slang* a mischievous or unruly person

larva *n, pl* **-vae** the immature form of many insects before it develops into its adult form **larval** *adj*
WORD ORIGIN New Latin

Larwood *n* **Harold** 1904–95, English cricketer. An outstanding fast bowler, he played 21 times for England between 1926 and 1932

laryngeal *adj* of or relating to the larynx

laryngitis *n* inflammation of the larynx, causing huskiness or loss of voice

larynx (**lar**-rinks) *n, pl* **larynges** (lar-**rin**-jeez) *or* **larynxes** a hollow organ forming part of the air passage to the lungs: it contains the vocal cords
WORD ORIGIN Greek *larunx*

lasagne *or* **lasagna** (laz-**zan**-ya) *n* **1** a form of pasta in wide flat sheets **2** a dish made from layers of lasagne, meat, and cheese
WORD ORIGIN Italian, from Latin *lasanum* cooking pot

La Salle[1] *n* a city in SE Canada, in Quebec: a S suburb of Montreal. Pop (with Émard): 100 327 (2006)

La Salle[2] *n* Sieur **Robert Cavelier de** 1643–87, French explorer and fur trader in North America; founder of Louisiana (1682)

lascar *n* an East Indian seaman

lascivious (lass-**iv**-ee-uss) *adj* showing or producing sexual desire; lustful **lasciviously** *adv*
WORD ORIGIN Latin *lascivia* wantonness

Lasdun *n* Sir **Denys** 1914–2001, British architect. He is best known for the University of East Anglia (1968) and the National Theatre in London (1976)

laser (**lay**-zer) *n* **1** a device that produces a very narrow intense beam of light, which is used for cutting very hard materials and in surgery etc. ▹*vb* **2** to use a laser on (something), esp. as part of medical treatment **3** Also: **laser off** to remove (a tattoo, fat, etc.) with laser treatment
WORD ORIGIN from *l*ight *a*mplification by *s*timulated *e*mission of *r*adiation

laser printer *n* a computer printer that uses a laser beam to produce characters which are then transferred to paper

lash[1] *n* **1** an eyelash **2** a sharp cutting blow from a whip **3** the flexible end of a whip ▹*vb* **4** to hit (a person or thing) sharply with a whip, esp. formerly as punishment **5** (of rain or waves) to beat forcefully against **6** to attack (someone) with words of ridicule or scolding **7** to flick or wave sharply to and fro: *his tail lashing in irritation* **8** to urge as with a whip: *to lash the audience into a violent mood* ▸See also **lash out**
WORD ORIGIN perhaps imitative

lash[2] *vb* to bind or secure with rope, string, or cord
WORD ORIGIN Latin *laqueus* noose

lashing[1] *n* **1** a flogging **2** a scolding

lashing[2] *n* rope, string, or cord used for binding or securing

lashings *pl n old-fashioned, informal* large amounts; lots: *lashings of cream*

lash out *vb* **1** to make a sudden verbal or physical attack **2** *informal* to spend extravagantly

Lasker *n* **Emanuel** 1868–1941, German chess player: world champion (1894–1921)

Laski *n* **Harold (Joseph)** 1893–1950, English political scientist and socialist leader

lass *n* a girl or young woman
WORD ORIGIN origin unknown

Lassa fever *n* a serious viral disease of Central West Africa, characterized by high fever and muscular pains
WORD ORIGIN after *Lassa*, the Nigerian village where it was first identified

Lassalle *n* **Ferdinand** 1825–64, German socialist and writer: a founder of the first German workers' political party (1863), which later

THESAURUS

considerable, substantial, strapping, immense (*informal*), hefty, gigantic, monumental, bulky, chunky, burly, colossal, hulking, goodly, man-size, brawny, elephantine, thickset, ginormous (*informal*), humongous *or* humungous (*US slang*), sizable *or* sizeable, supersize **OPPOSITE:** small **1b = massive**, great, big, huge, giant, vast, enormous, considerable, substantial, immense, tidy (*informal*), jumbo (*informal*), gigantic, monumental, mammoth, colossal, gargantuan, stellar (*informal*), king-size, ginormous (*informal*), humongous *or* humungous (*US slang*), sizable *or* sizeable, supersize
OPPOSITE: small

largely *adv* **= mainly**, generally, chiefly, widely, mostly, principally, primarily, considerably, predominantly, extensively, by and large, as a rule, to a large extent, to a great extent

large-scale *adj* **1 = wide-ranging**, global, sweeping, broad, wide, vast, extensive, wholesale, far-reaching

lash[1] *n* **2 = blow**, hit, strike, stroke, stripe, swipe (*informal*) ▹*vb* **4 = whip**, beat, thrash, birch, flog, lam (*slang*), scourge, chastise, lambast(e), flagellate, horsewhip **5 = pound**, beat, strike, hammer, drum, smack (*dialect*) **6 = censure**, attack, blast, put down, criticize, slate (*informal, chiefly Brit*), ridicule, scold, berate, castigate, lampoon, tear into (*informal*), flay, upbraid, satirize, lambast(e), belabour

lash[2] *vb* **= fasten**, join, tie, secure, bind, rope, strap, make fast

last[1] *adj* **1 = hindmost**, furthest, final,

DICTIONARY

became the Social Democratic Party

lassie *n Scot & N English informal* a little lass; girl

lassitude *n* physical or mental weariness
WORD ORIGIN Latin *lassus* tired

lasso (lass-oo) *n, pl* **-sos** *or* **-soes** **1** a long rope with a noose at one end used for catching horses and cattle ▷ *vb* **-soing, -soed** **2** to catch as with a lasso **lassoer** *n*
WORD ORIGIN Spanish, from Latin *laqueus* noose

Lassus *n* **Roland de** Italian name *Orlando di Lasso.* ?1532–94, Flemish composer, noted for his mastery in both sacred and secular music

last[1] ❶ *adj* **1** being, happening, or coming at the end or after all others **2** most recent: *last April* **3** only remaining: *that's the last one* **4** most extreme; utmost **5** least suitable or likely: *China was the last place on earth he intended to go* ▷ *adv* **6** after all others **7** most recently: *we last saw him on Thursday night* **8** as the last or latest item ▷ *n* **9** **the last** **a** a person or thing that is last **b** the final moment; end **10** the final appearance, mention, or occurrence: *the last of this season's visitors* **11** **at last** in the end; finally **12** **at long last** finally, after difficulty or delay
WORD ORIGIN variant of Old English *latest, lætest*

last[2] ❶ *vb* **1** to continue to exist for a length of time: *the soccer war lasted 100 hours* **2** to be sufficient for the needs of (a person) for a length of time: *I shall make a couple of bottles to last me until next summer* **3** to remain fresh, uninjured, or unaltered for a certain time: *the flowers haven't lasted well* ▸ See also **last out**
WORD ORIGIN Old English *lǣstan*

last[3] *n* the wooden or metal form on which a shoe or boot is made or repaired
WORD ORIGIN Old English *lāst* footprint

last-ditch *adj* done as a final resort: *a last-ditch attempt*

lasting ❶ *adj* existing or remaining effective for a long time

Last Judgment *n* **the Last Judgment** *theol* God's verdict on the destinies of all human beings at the end of the world

lastly *adv* **1** at the end or at the last point **2** finally

last-minute *adj* given or done at the latest possible time: *last-minute changes*

last name *n* ▸ same as **surname**

last out *vb* **1** to be sufficient for one's needs: *if the energy supply lasts out* **2** to endure or survive: *I might not last out my hours of duty*

last post *n mil* **1** a bugle call used to signal the time to retire at night **2** a similar call sounded at military funerals

last rites *pl n Christianity* religious rites for those close to death

last straw *n* a small incident, irritation, or setback that coming after others is too much to cope with

Last Supper *n* **the Last Supper** the meal eaten by Christ with his disciples on the night before his Crucifixion

lat. latitude

Lat. Latin

latch ❶ *n* **1** a fastening for a gate or door that consists of a bar that may be slid or lowered into a groove, hole, or notch **2** a spring-loaded door lock that can only be opened by a key from outside ▷ *vb* **3** to fasten, fit, or be fitted with a latch
WORD ORIGIN Old English *læccan* to seize

latchkey child *n Brit, Austral & NZ* a child who has to let himself or herself in at home after school, as both parents are out at work

latch on *vb informal* **1** (often foll. by *to*) to attach oneself (to): *he should latch on to a man with a deal to do* **2** to understand: *it took a while to latch on to what he was trying to say*

late ❶ *adj* **1** occurring or arriving after the correct or expected time: *the plane will be late* **2** towards or near the end: *the late afternoon* **3** occurring or being at a relatively advanced time: *a late starter, his first novel was effectively his last* **4** at an advanced time in the evening or at night: *it's late, I have to get back* **5** having died recently: *her late father* **6** recent: *recollect the late defeats which your enemies have experienced* **7** former: *the late manager of the team* **8** **of late** recently ▷ *adv* **9** after the correct or expected time: *Mark Wright arrived late* **10** at a relatively advanced age: *coming late to motherhood* **11** recently: *as late as in 1983, only 9 per cent of that labour force was unionized* **12** **late in the day** **a** at a late or advanced stage **b** too late **lateness** *n*
WORD ORIGIN Old English *læt*

lateen *adj naut* denoting a rig with a triangular sail bent to a yard hoisted to the head of a low mast
WORD ORIGIN French *voile latine* Latin sail

Late Greek *n* the Greek language from about the 3rd to the 8th centuries AD

Late Latin *n* the form of written Latin used from the 3rd to the 7th centuries AD

lately ❶ *adv* in recent times; of late

latent *adj* lying hidden and not yet developed within a person or thing **latency** *n*
WORD ORIGIN Latin *latere* to lie hidden

later ❶ *adj, adv* **1** ▸ the comparative of **late** ▷ *adv* **2** afterwards

lateral (lat-ter-al) *adj* of or relating to the side or sides **laterally** *adv*
WORD ORIGIN Latin *latus* side

lateral thinking *n* a way of solving problems by apparently illogical methods

latest ❶ *adj, adv* **1** ▸ the superlative of **late** ▷ *adj* **2** most recent, modern, or new: *the latest fashions* ▷ *n* **3** **at the latest** no later than the time specified

latex *n* a milky fluid produced by many plants: latex from the rubber plant is used in the manufacture of rubber
WORD ORIGIN Latin: liquid

lath *n, pl* **laths** one of several thin narrow strips of wood used as a

THESAURUS

at the end, remotest, furthest behind, most distant, rearmost, aftermost **OPPOSITE:** foremost **2 = most recent**, latest, previous **3, 4 = final**, closing, concluding, ultimate, utmost **OPPOSITE:** first ▷ *adv* **6, 8 = in** *or* **at the end**, after, behind, in the rear, bringing up the rear

last[2] *vb* **1, 3 = continue**, keep, remain, survive, wear, carry on, endure, hold on, persist, keep on, hold out, abide **OPPOSITE:** end

lasting *adj* **= continuing**, long-term, permanent, enduring, remaining, eternal, abiding, long-standing, perennial, lifelong, durable, perpetual, long-lasting, deep-rooted, indelible, unending, undying, unceasing **OPPOSITE:** passing

latch *n* **1 = fastening**, catch, bar, lock, hook, bolt, clamp, hasp, sneck *(dialect)* ▷ *vb* **3 = fasten**, bar, secure, lock, bolt, make fast, sneck *(dialect)*

late *adj* **1 = overdue**, delayed, last-minute, belated, tardy, behind time, unpunctual, behindhand **OPPOSITE:** early **5 = dead**, deceased, departed, passed on, old, former, previous, preceding, defunct **OPPOSITE:** alive **6 = recent**, new, advanced, fresh **OPPOSITE:** old ▷ *adv* **9 = behind time**, belatedly, tardily, behindhand, dilatorily, unpunctually **OPPOSITE:** early

lately *adv* **= recently**, of late, just now, in recent times, not long ago, latterly

later *adv* **2 = afterwards**, after, next, eventually, in time, subsequently, later on, thereafter, in a while, in due course, at a later date, by and by, at a later time

latest *adj* **2 = up-to-date**, current, fresh, newest, happening *(informal)*, modern, most recent, up-to-the-minute

DICTIONARY

supporting framework for plaster or tiles
WORD ORIGIN Old English *lætt*
lathe *n* a machine for shaping metal or wood by turning it against a fixed tool
WORD ORIGIN perhaps from Old Norse
lather *n* **1** foam formed by soap or detergent in water **2** foamy sweat, as produced by a horse **3** *informal* a state of agitation ▹*vb* **4** to coat or become coated with lather **5** to form a lather **6** *informal* to beat; flog
lathery *adj*
WORD ORIGIN Old English *lēathor* soap
Latin *n* **1** the language of ancient Rome and the Roman Empire **2** a member of any of those peoples whose languages are derived from Latin ▹*adj* **3** of the Latin language **4** of those peoples whose languages are derived from Latin **5** of the Roman Catholic Church
WORD ORIGIN Latin *Latinus* of Latium
Latin America *n* those areas of South and Central America whose official languages are Spanish and Portuguese **Latin American** *adj, n*
latish *adj, adv* rather late
latitude ❶ *n* **1 a** an angular distance measured in degrees north or south of the equator **b** (*often pl*) a region considered with regard to its distance from the equator **2** scope for freedom of action and thought
latitudinal *adj*
WORD ORIGIN Latin *latus* broad
latitudinarian *adj* **1** liberal, esp. in religious matters ▹*n* **2** a person with latitudinarian views
Latour *n* **Maurice Quentin de** 1704–88, French pastelist noted for the vivacity of his portraits
La Tour *n* **Georges de** ?1593–1652, French painter, esp. of candlelit religious scenes
latrine *n* a toilet in a barracks or camp
WORD ORIGIN Latin *lavatrina* bath
latter ❶ *n* **1 the latter** the second or second mentioned of two ▹*adj* **2** near or nearer the end: *the latter half of the season* **3** more advanced in time or sequence; later
WORD ORIGIN Old English *lætra*
latter-day *adj* present-day; modern
latterly *adv* recently; lately
lattice (lat-iss) *n* **1** Also called: **latticework** a framework of strips of wood or metal interlaced in a diagonal pattern **2** a gate, screen, or fence formed of such a framework **3** an array of atoms, ions, or molecules in a crystal or an array of points indicating their positions in space ▹*vb* **-ticing, -ticed 4** to make, adorn, or supply with a lattice
latticed *adj*
WORD ORIGIN Old French *latte* lath
Latvian *adj* **1** from Latvia ▹*n* **2** a person from Latvia **3** the language of Latvia
laud *literary vb* **1** to praise or glorify ▹*n* **2** praise or glorification
WORD ORIGIN Latin *laudare* to praise
Lauda *n* **Niki** born 1949, Austrian motor-racing driver: world champion 1975, 1977, 1984
laudable *adj* deserving praise; commendable **laudability** *n* **laudably** *adv*
laudanum (lawd-a-num) *n* a sedative extracted from opium
WORD ORIGIN New Latin
laudatory *adj* (of speech or writing) expressing praise
Lauder *n* Sir **Harry** real name *Hugh MacLennan*. 1870–1950, Scottish ballad singer and music-hall comedian
Laue *n* **Max Theodor Felix von** 1879–1960, German physicist. He pioneered the technique of measuring the wavelengths of X-rays by their diffraction by crystals and contributed to the theory of relativity: Nobel prize for physics 1914
laugh ❶ *vb* **1** to express amusement or happiness by producing a series of inarticulate sounds **2** to utter or express with laughter: *he laughed his derision at the play* **3** to bring or force (oneself) into a certain condition by laughter: *laughing herself silly* **4 laugh at** to make fun of; jeer at **5 laugh up one's sleeve** to laugh secretly ▹*n* **6** the act or an instance of laughing **7** *informal* a person or thing that causes laughter: *he's a laugh, that one* **8 the last laugh** final success after previous defeat ▸See also **laugh off** > **laughingly** *adv*
WORD ORIGIN Old English *læhan, hliehhen*
laughable *adj* ridiculous because so obviously inadequate or unsuccessful
laughing gas *n* nitrous oxide used as an anaesthetic: it may cause laughter and exhilaration when inhaled
laughing stock *n* a person or thing that is treated with ridicule
laugh off ❶ *vb* to treat (something serious or difficult) lightly
laughter ❶ *n* the action or noise of laughing
WORD ORIGIN Old English *hleahtor*
Laughton *n* **Charles** 1899–1962, US actor, born in England: noted esp. for his films of the 1930s, such as *The Private Life of Henry VIII* (1933), for which he won an Oscar, and *Mutiny on the Bounty* (1935)
launch[1] ❶ *vb* **1** to move (a vessel) into the water, esp. for the first time **2 a** to start off or set in motion: *to launch an appeal* **b** to put (a new product) on the market **3** to set (a rocket, missile, or spacecraft) into motion **4** to involve (oneself) totally and enthusiastically: *Francis launched himself into the transfer market with gusto* **5 launch into** to start talking or writing (about) **6** (usually foll. by *out*) to start (out) on a new enterprise ▹*n* **7** an act or instance of launching
launcher *n*
WORD ORIGIN Late Latin *lanceare* to use a lance, hence to set in motion
launch[2] *n* an open motorboat
WORD ORIGIN Malay *lancharan* boat, from *lanchar* speed
launch pad *or* **launching pad** *n* a platform from which a spacecraft, rocket, or missile is launched
launder *vb* **1** to wash and iron (clothes and linen) **2** to make (money illegally obtained) appear to be legally gained by passing it through foreign banks or legitimate enterprises
WORD ORIGIN Latin *lavare* to wash

THESAURUS

latitude *n* **2 = scope**, liberty, indulgence, freedom, play, room, space, licence, leeway, laxity, elbowroom, unrestrictedness
latter *n* **1 = second**, last, last-mentioned, second-mentioned ▹*adj* **2, 3 = last**, later, latest, ending, closing, final, concluding
OPPOSITE: earlier
laugh *vb* **1 = chuckle**, giggle, snigger, crack up (*informal*), cackle, chortle, guffaw, titter, roar, bust a gut (*informal*), be convulsed (*informal*), be in stitches, crease up (*informal*), split your sides, be rolling in the aisles (*informal*) ▹*n* **6 = chortle**, giggle, chuckle, snigger, guffaw, titter, belly laugh, roar, shriek **7a** (*informal*) **= joke**, scream (*informal*), hoot (*informal*), lark, prank **7b** (*informal*) **= clown**, character (*informal*), scream (*informal*), comic, caution (*informal*), wit, comedian, entertainer, card (*informal*), wag, joker, hoot (*informal*), humorist
laugh off = disregard, ignore, dismiss, overlook, shrug off, minimize, brush aside, make light of, pooh-pooh
laughter *n* **= amusement**, entertainment, humour, glee, fun, mirth, hilarity, merriment
launch[1] *vb* **2a = begin**, start, open, initiate, introduce, found, set up, originate, commence, get under way, instigate, inaugurate, embark upon **3 = propel**, fire, dispatch, discharge, project, send off, set in motion, send into orbit **5** (foll. by *into*) **= start enthusiastically**, begin, initiate, embark on, instigate, inaugurate, embark upon

l

DICTIONARY

Launderette *n Brit, Austral & NZ trademark* an establishment where clothes can be washed and dried, using coin-operated machines. Also called (US, Canad, Austral, NZ): **Laundromat**

laundry *n, pl* **-dries** **1** the clothes or linen to be laundered or that have been laundered **2** a place where clothes and linen are washed and ironed

laundry list *n US & Canad* a list of items perceived as being long

laureate (lor-ee-at) *adj* **1** *literary* crowned with laurel leaves as a sign of honour ▷ *n* **2** ▸ short for **poet laureate** > **laureateship** *n*
WORD ORIGIN Latin *laurea* laurel

laurel ❶ *n* **1** a small Mediterranean evergreen tree with glossy leaves **2** **laurels** a wreath of laurel, worn on the head as an emblem of victory or honour in classical times **3** **laurels** honour, distinction, or fame **4** **look to one's laurels** to be on guard against one's rivals **5** **rest on one's laurels** to be satisfied with what one has already achieved and stop striving for further success
WORD ORIGIN Latin *laurus*

Lauren *n* **Ralph** born 1939, US fashion designer

Laurence *n* Margaret, full name *Jean Margaret Laurence*, 1926–87, Canadian novelist and short story writer; her novels include *The Stone Angel* (1964)

lav *n Brit informal* ▸ short for **lavatory**

lava *n* **1** molten rock discharged by volcanoes **2** any rock formed by the solidification of lava
WORD ORIGIN Latin *lavare* to wash

Laval[1] *n* a city in SE Canada, in Quebec: a NW suburb of Montreal. Pop: 343 005 (2001)

Laval[2] *n* **Pierre** 1883–1945, French statesman. He was premier of France (1931–32; 1935–36) and premier of the Vichy government (1942–44). He was executed for collaboration with Germany

lavatorial *adj* characterized by frequent reference to excretion: *lavatorial humour*

lavatory *n, pl* **-ries** ▸ same as **toilet**
WORD ORIGIN Latin *lavare* to wash

lavender *n* **1** a plant grown for its bluish-purple flowers and as the source of a sweet-smelling oil **2** its dried flowers, used to perfume clothes ▷ *adj* **3** pale bluish-purple
WORD ORIGIN Medieval Latin *lavendula*

lavender water *n* a light perfume made from lavender

Laver *n* **Rod(ney)** (**George**) born 1938, Australian tennis player: Wimbledon champion 1961, 1962, 1968, 1969; US champion 1962, 1969

Lavigne *n* **Avril** born 1984, Canadian rock singer and songwriter; her recordings include *Let Go* (2002), *Under My Skin* (2004) and *The Best Damn Thing* (2007)

lavish ❶ *adj* **1** great in quantity or richness: *lavish banquets* **2** very generous in giving **3** extravagant; wasteful: *lavish spending habits* ▷ *vb* **4** to give or to spend very generously or in great quantities **lavishly** *adv*
WORD ORIGIN Old French *lavasse* torrent

law ❶ *n* **1** a rule or set of rules regulating what may or may not be done by members of a society or community **2** a rule or body of rules made by the legislature or other authority ▸ Related adjectives: **legal, judicial, juridical** **3** the control enforced by such rules: *scant respect for the rule of law* **4** **the law** **a** the legal or judicial system **b** the profession or practice of law **c** *informal* the police or a policeman **5** **law and order** the policy of strict enforcement of the law, esp. against crime and violence **6** a rule of behaviour: *an unwritten law that Nanny knows best* **7** Also called: **law of nature** a generalization based on a recurring fact or event **8** the science or knowledge of law; jurisprudence **9** a general principle, formula, or rule in mathematics, science, or philosophy: *the law of gravity* **10** **the Law** the laws contained in the first five books of the Old Testament **11** **go to law** to resort to legal proceedings on some matter **12** **lay down the law** to speak in an authoritative manner
WORD ORIGIN Old English *lagu*

law-abiding *adj* obeying the laws: *a law-abiding citizen*

lawbreaker *n* a person who breaks the law **lawbreaking** *n, adj*

Lawes *n* **1** **Henry** 1596–1662, English composer, noted for his music for Milton's masque *Comus* (1634) and for his settings of some of Robert Herrick's poems **2** his brother, **William** 1602–45, English composer, noted for his harmonically experimental instrumental music

lawful *adj* allowed, recognized, or sanctioned by law; legal **lawfully** *adv*

lawgiver *n* **1** the giver of a code of laws **2** Also called: **lawmaker** a maker of laws **lawgiving** *n, adj*

lawless *adj* **1** breaking the law, esp. in a wild or violent way: *lawless butchery* **2** not having laws **lawlessness** *n*

Law Lords *pl n* (in Britain) members of the House of Lords who sit as the highest court of appeal

lawn[1] *n* an area of cultivated and mown grass
WORD ORIGIN Old French *lande*

lawn[2] *n* a fine linen or cotton fabric
WORD ORIGIN probably from *Laon*, town in France where made

lawn mower *n* a hand-operated or power-operated machine for cutting grass

lawn tennis *n* **1** tennis played on a grass court **2** ▸ same as **tennis**

lawrencium *n chem* an element artificially produced from californium. Symbol: Lr
WORD ORIGIN after E. O. *Lawrence*, physicist

Lawson *n* **1** **Henry Archibald** 1867–1922, Australian poet and short-story writer, whose work is taken as being most representative of the Australian outback, esp. in *While the Billy Boils* (1896) and *Joe Wilson and his Mates* (1901) **2** **Nigel**, Baron. born 1932, British Conservative politician; Chancellor of the Exchquer (1983–89). **3** his daughter, **Nigella** born 1959, British journalist, broadcaster, and cookery writer

lawsuit ❶ *n* a case in a court of law brought by one person or group against another

lawyer ❶ *n* a member of the legal profession who can advise clients about the law and represent them in court

THESAURUS

laurel *n* **5** **rest on your laurels** = **sit back**, relax, take it easy, relax your efforts

lavish *adj* **1** = **grand**, magnificent, splendid, lush, abundant, sumptuous, exuberant, opulent, copious, luxuriant, profuse **OPPOSITE:** stingy
2 = **generous**, free, liberal, bountiful, effusive, open-handed, unstinting, munificent **OPPOSITE:** stingy
3 = **extravagant**, wild, excessive, exaggerated, unreasonable, wasteful, prodigal, unrestrained, intemperate, immoderate, improvident, thriftless **OPPOSITE:** thrifty
▷ *vb* **4** = **shower**, pour, heap, deluge, dissipate **OPPOSITE:** stint

law *n* **1** = **statute**, act, bill, rule, demand, order, command, code, regulation, resolution, decree, canon, covenant, ordinance, commandment, enactment, edict **2, 8** = **constitution**, code, legislation, charter, jurisprudence **4b** = **the legal profession**, the bar, barristers **6, 9** = **principle**, standard, code, formula, criterion, canon, precept, axiom, kaupapa *(NZ)*

lawsuit *n* = **case**, cause, action, trial, suit, argument, proceedings, dispute, contest, prosecution, legal action, indictment, litigation, industrial tribunal, legal proceedings

lawyer *n* = **legal adviser**, attorney, solicitor, counsel, advocate, barrister, counsellor, legal representative

l

DICTIONARY

lax *adj* lacking firmness; not strict **laxity** *n*
WORD ORIGIN Latin *laxus* loose

laxative *n* **1** a medicine that induces the emptying of the bowels ▷ *adj* **2** easing the emptying of the bowels
WORD ORIGIN Latin *laxare* to loosen

Laxness *n* **Halldór (Kiljan)** 1902–98, Icelandic novelist, noted for his treatment of rural working life in Iceland. His works include *Salka Valka* (1932) and *Independent People* (1935). Nobel prize for literature 1955

lay[1] ❶ *vb* **lays, laying, laid 1** to put in a low or horizontal position; cause to lie: *Mary laid a clean square of white towelling carefully on the grass* **2** to establish as a basis: *ready to lay your new fashion foundations?* **3** to place or be in a particular state or position: *underneath lay a key* **4** to regard as the responsibility of: *ridiculous attempts to lay the loss at the door of the Admiralty* **5** to put forward: *ruses by which we lay claim on one another* **6** to arrange or prepare: *she would lay her plans* **7** to place in position: *he laid a wreath* **8** (of birds, esp. the domestic hen) to produce (eggs) **9** to make (a bet) with (someone): *I'll lay money he's already gone home* **10** to arrange (a table) for a meal **11** to prepare (a fire) by arranging fuel in the grate **12** *taboo slang* to have sexual intercourse with **13 lay bare** to reveal or explain: *a century of neurophysiology has now laid bare the structures of the brain* **14 lay hold of** to seize or grasp **15 lay oneself open** to make oneself vulnerable (to criticism or attack) **16 lay open** to reveal or disclose **17 lay waste** to destroy completely ▷ *n* **18** the manner or position in which something lies or is placed **19** *taboo, slang* **a** an act of sexual intercourse **b** a sexual partner ▶ See also **lay aside, lay down**, etc.
WORD ORIGIN Old English *lecgan*

lay[2] *vb* ▶ the past tense of **lie**[2]

lay[3] ❶ *adj* **1** of or involving people who are not members of the clergy **2** nonprofessional or nonspecialist
WORD ORIGIN Greek *laos* people

lay[4] *n* a short narrative poem intended to be sung
WORD ORIGIN Old French *lai*

layabout *n* a lazy person

Layamon *or* **Lawman** *n* 12th-century English poet and priest; author of the *Brut*, a chronicle providing the earliest version of the Arthurian story in English

Layard *n* Sir **Austen Henry** 1817–94, English archaeologist, noted for his excavations at Nimrud and Nineveh

lay aside *vb* **1** to abandon or reject **2** to put aside (one thing) in order to take up another **3** to store or reserve for future use

lay-by *n* **1** *Brit* a place where drivers can stop by the side of a main road **2** *Austral & NZ* a system of payment whereby a buyer pays a deposit on an article, which is reserved for him or her until he or she has paid the full price

lay down *vb* **1** to place on the ground or a surface **2** to sacrifice: *willing to lay down their lives for the truth* **3** to formulate (a rule or principle) **4** to record (plans) on paper **5** to store or stock: *the speed with which we lay down extra, unwanted fat*

layer *n* **1** a single thickness of something, such as a cover or a coating on a surface **2** a laying hen **3** *horticulture* a shoot that forms its own root while still attached to the parent plant ▷ *vb* **4** to form or make a layer or layers
WORD ORIGIN from LAY[1]

layette *n* a complete set of clothing, bedclothes, and other accessories for a newborn baby
WORD ORIGIN Middle Dutch *laege* box

lay figure *n* **1** an artist's jointed dummy, used esp. for studying effects of drapery **2** a person considered to be subservient or unimportant
WORD ORIGIN Dutch *leeman*, literally: joint-man

lay in *vb* to accumulate and store: *they've already laid in five hundred bottles of great vintages*

lay into *vb informal* to attack or scold severely

layman *or fem* **laywoman** *n, pl* **-men** *or* **-women 1** a person who is not a member of the clergy **2** a person who does not have specialized knowledge of a subject: *the layman's guide to nuclear power*

lay off ❶ *vb* **1** to suspend (staff) during a slack period at work **2** *informal* to leave (a person, thing, or activity) alone: *'Lay off the defence counsel bit!' he snapped* ▷ *n* **lay-off 3** a period of imposed unemployment

lay on *vb* **1** to provide or supply: *they laid on a treat for the entourage* **2 lay it on thick** *slang* to exaggerate, esp. when flattering

lay out ❶ *vb* **1** to arrange or spread out **2** to plan or design: *the main streets were laid out on a grid system* **3** to prepare (a corpse) for burial or cremation **4** *informal* to spend (money), esp. lavishly **5** *informal* to knock (someone) unconscious ▷ *n* **layout 6** the arrangement or plan of something, such as a building **7** the arrangement of printed material

lay reader *n* **1** *Church of England* a person licensed to conduct religious services other than the Eucharist **2** *RC church* a layman chosen to read the epistle at Mass

lay up *vb* **1** *informal* to confine through illness: *laid up with a bad cold* **2** to store for future use

laze *vb* **lazing, lazed 1** to be idle or lazy **2** (often foll. by *away*) to spend (time) in idleness ▷ *n* **3** time spent lazing
WORD ORIGIN from *lazy*

lazy ❶ *adj* **lazier, laziest 1** not inclined to work or exert oneself **2** done in a relaxed manner with little effort **3** moving in a sluggish manner: *the lazy drift of the bubbles* **lazily** *adv* **laziness** *n*
WORD ORIGIN origin unknown

lazybones *n informal* a lazy person

lb 1 pound (weight)
WORD ORIGIN Latin *libra* **2** *cricket* leg bye

lbw *cricket* leg before wicket

lc 1 in the place cited
WORD ORIGIN Latin *loco citato* **2** *printing* lower case

LCD 1 liquid crystal display **2** Also: **lcd** lowest common denominator

lcm *or* **LCM** lowest common multiple

THESAURUS

lay[1] *vb* **1, 3, 7 = place**, put, set, spread, plant, establish, settle, leave, deposit, put down, set down, posit **4 = attribute**, charge, assign, allocate, allot, ascribe, impute **5 = put forward**, offer, present, advance, lodge, submit, bring forward **6a = devise**, plan, design, prepare, work out, plot, hatch, contrive, concoct **6b = arrange**, prepare, make, organize, position, locate, set out, devise, put together, dispose, draw up **8 = produce**, bear, deposit **9 = bet**, stake, venture, gamble, chance, risk, hazard, wager, give odds

lay[3] *adj* **1 = nonclerical**, secular, non-ordained, laic, laical **2 = nonspecialist**, amateur, unqualified, untrained, inexpert, nonprofessional

lay off 1 = dismiss, fire *(informal)*, release, drop, sack *(informal)*, pay off, discharge, oust, let go, make redundant, give notice to, give the boot to *(slang)*, give the sack to *(informal)*, give someone their cards, kennet *(Austral slang)*, jeff *(Austral slang)*

lay out *(informal) vb* **5 = knock out**, fell, floor, knock unconscious, knock for six, kayo *(slang)* ▷ *n* **6 = arrangement**, design, draft, outline, format, plan, formation, geography

lazy *adj* **1 = idle**, inactive, indolent, slack, negligent, inert, remiss, workshy, slothful, shiftless
OPPOSITE: industrious
2, 3 = lethargic, languorous, slow-moving, languid, sleepy, sluggish, drowsy, somnolent, torpid
OPPOSITE: quick

DICTIONARY

lea *n* **1** *poetic* a meadow or field **2** grassland
WORD ORIGIN Old English *lēah*

LEA (in Britain) Local Education Authority

leach ❶ *vb* **1** to remove or be removed from a substance by a liquid passing through it **2** to lose soluble substances by the action of a liquid passing through
WORD ORIGIN perhaps Old English *leccan* to water

Leach *n* **Bernard** (**Howell**) 1887–1979, British potter, born in Hong Kong

Leacock *n* **Stephen Butler** 1869–1944, Canadian humorist and economist: his comic works include *Literary Lapses* (1910) and *Frenzied Fiction* (1917)

lead[1] ❶ *vb* **leading, led 1** to show the way to (an individual or a group) by going with or ahead: *he led her into the house* **2** to guide, control, or direct: *he dismounted and led his horse back* **3** to influence someone to act, think, or behave in a certain way: *researching our family history has led her to correspond with relatives abroad* **4** to have the principal part in (something): *planners led the development of policy* **5** to go at the head of or have the top position in (something): *the pair led the field by almost two minutes* **6** (of a road or way) to be the means of reaching a place: *the footbridge leads on to a fine promenade* **7** to pass or spend: *I've led a happy life* **8** to guide or be guided by physical means: *he took her firmly by the arm and led her home* **9** to direct the course of (water, a rope, or wire) along or as if along a channel **10** (foll. by *with*) to have as the most important item: *the Review leads with a critique of A Place of Greater Safety* **11** *Brit music* to play first violin in (an orchestra) **12** to begin a round of cards by putting down the first card ▹*n* **13** the first or most prominent place **14** example or leadership: *some of his children followed his lead* **15** an advantage over others: *Essex have a lead of 24 points* **16** an indication; clue: *we've got a lead on how the body got into the water* **17** a length of leather, nylon, or chain used to walk or control a dog **18** the principal role in a play, film, or other production, or the person playing such a role **19** the most important news story in a newspaper: *the shooting makes the lead in the Times* **20** the act of playing the first card in a round of cards or the card so played **21** a wire, cable, or other conductor for making an electrical connection ▹*adj* **22** acting as a leader or lead: *lead singer* ▸See also **lead off, lead on**, etc.
WORD ORIGIN Old English *lǣdan*

lead[2] *n* **1** a heavy toxic bluish-white metallic element: used in alloys, cable sheaths, paints, and as a radiation shield. Symbol: Pb **2 a** graphite used for drawing **b** a thin stick of this as the core of a pencil **3** a lead weight suspended on a line, used to take soundings of the depth of water **4** lead weights or shot, as used in cartridges or fishing lines **5** a thin strip of lead for holding small panes of glass or pieces of stained glass **6 leads a** thin sheets or strips of lead used as a roof covering **b** a roof covered with such sheets **7** Also called: **leading** *printing* a thin strip of metal, formerly used for spacing between lines of type ▹*adj* **8** of, relating to, or containing lead ▹*vb* **9** to surround, cover, or secure with lead or leads
WORD ORIGIN Old English *lēad*

Leadbelly *n* real name *Huddie Ledbetter.* 1888–1949, US blues singer and guitarist

leaded *adj* (of windows) made from many small panes of glass held together by lead strips

leaden *adj* **1** heavy or sluggish: *my limbs felt leaden* **2** of a dull greyish colour: *leaden November sky* **3** made of lead **4** gloomy, spiritless, or lifeless: *hollow characters and leaden dialogue*

leader ❶ *n* **1** a person who rules, guides, or inspires others; head **2** *Austral & Brit* the leading editorial in a newspaper. Also: **leading article 3** *music* the principal first violinist of an orchestra who acts as the conductor's deputy **4** the person or animal who is leading in a race **5** the best or the most successful of its kind: *the company is a world leader in its field* **6** the leading horse or dog in a team **7** a strip of blank film or tape at the beginning of a reel **8** *bot* any of the long slender shoots that grow from the stem or branch of a tree
leadership *n*

leaderboard *n* a board displaying the current scores of the leading competitors, esp. in a golf tournament

lead-in *n* an introduction to a subject

leading ❶ *adj* **1** principal or primary: *the leading designers* **2** in the first position: *the leading driver*

leading aircraftman *n* the rank above aircraftman in the British air force **leading aircraftwoman** *fem n*

leading light *n* an important and influential person in an organization or campaign

leading question *n* a question worded to suggest the desired answer, such as *What do you think of the horrible effects of pollution?*

leading rating *n* a rank in the Royal Navy comparable to a corporal in the army

lead off *vb* to begin

lead on ❶ *vb* to trick (someone) into believing or doing something wrong

lead pencil *n* a pencil containing a

THESAURUS

leach *vb* **1 = extract**, strain, drain, filter, seep, percolate, filtrate, lixiviate *(chemistry)*

lead[1] *vb* **1 = go in front (of)**, head, be in front, be at the head (of), walk in front (of) **2, 8 = guide**, conduct, steer, escort, precede, usher, pilot, show the way **3 = cause**, prompt, persuade, move, draw, influence, motivate, prevail, induce, incline, dispose **4 = command**, rule, govern, preside over, head, control, manage, direct, supervise, be in charge of, head up **5 = be ahead (of)**, be first, exceed, be winning, excel, surpass, come first, transcend, outstrip, outdo, blaze a trail **6 = connect to**, link, open onto **7 = live**, have, spend, experience, pass, undergo ▹*n* **13 = first place**, winning position, primary position, vanguard, van **14 = example**, direction, leadership, guidance, model, pattern **15 = advantage**, start, advance, edge, margin, winning margin **16 = clue**, tip, suggestion, trace, hint, guide, indication, pointer, tip-off **17 = leash**, line, cord, rein, tether **18 = leading role**, principal, protagonist, title role, star part, principal part ▹*adj* **22 = main**, prime, top, leading, first, head, chief, premier, primary, most important, principal, foremost

leader *n* **1 = principal**, president, head, chief, boss *(informal)*, director, manager, chairman, captain, chair, premier, governor, commander, superior, ruler, conductor, controller, counsellor, supervisor, superintendent, big name, big gun *(informal)*, chairwoman, chieftain, bigwig *(informal)*, ringleader, chairperson, big shot *(informal)*, overseer, big cheese *(slang, old-fashioned)*, big noise *(informal)*, big hitter *(informal)*, baas *(S African)*, torchbearer, number one, sherang *(Austral & NZ)*
OPPOSITE: follower

leading *adj* **1 = principal**, top, major, main, first, highest, greatest, ruling, chief, prime, key, primary, supreme, most important, outstanding, governing, superior, dominant, foremost, pre-eminent, unsurpassed, number one
OPPOSITE: minor

lead on = entice, tempt, lure, mislead, draw on, seduce, deceive, beguile, delude, hoodwink, inveigle, string along *(informal)*

lead up to = introduce, approach, prepare for, intimate, pave the way for, prepare the way, make advances, make overtures, work round to

DICTIONARY

thin stick of a graphite compound
lead poisoning *n* acute or chronic poisoning by lead
lead time *n manufacturing* the time between the design of a product and its production
lead up to ❶ *vb* **1** to act as a preliminary or introduction to **2** to approach (a topic) gradually or cautiously
leaf ❶ *n, pl* **leaves 1** one of the flat usually green blades attached to the stem of a plant **2** the foliage of a tree or plant: *shrubs have been planted for their leaf interest* **3 in leaf** (of shrubs or trees) with all its leaves fully opened **4** a very thin sheet of metal **5** one of the sheets of paper in a book **6** a hinged, sliding, or detachable part, such as an extension to a table **7 take a leaf out of someone's book** to imitate someone in a particular course of action **8 turn over a new leaf** to begin a new and improved course of behaviour ▷ *vb* **9** (usually foll. by *through*) to turn pages casually or hurriedly without reading them **10** (of plants) to produce leaves **leafless** *adj*
WORD ORIGIN Old English *lēaf*
leafage *n* the leaves of plants
leaflet ❶ *n* **1** a sheet of printed matter distributed, usually free, for advertising or information **2** any small leaf **3** one of the divisions of a compound leaf ▷ *vb* **-leting, -leted 4** to distribute leaflets (to)
leaf mould *n* a rich soil consisting of decayed leaves
leafy ❶ *adj* **leafier, leafiest 1** covered with leaves **2** having many trees or shrubs: *a leafy suburb*
league[1] ❶ *n* **1** an association of people or nations formed to promote the interests of its members **2** an association of sporting clubs that organizes matches between member teams **3** *informal* a class or level: *the guy is not even in the same league* **4 in league (with)** working or planning together with ▷ *vb* **leaguing, leagued 5** to form or be formed into a league
WORD ORIGIN Latin *ligare* to bind
league[2] *n* an obsolete unit of distance of varying length: commonly equal to 3 miles (4.8 km)
WORD ORIGIN Late Latin *leuga, leuca*
leak ❶ *n* **1 a** a crack or hole that allows the accidental escape or entrance of liquid, gas, radiation, etc. **b** such escaping or entering liquid, etc. **2** a disclosure of secret information **3** the loss of current from an electrical conductor because of faulty insulation **4** the act or an instance of leaking **5** *slang* urination ▷ *vb* **6** to enter or escape or allow to enter or escape through a crack or hole **7** to make (secret information) public, esp. deliberately **leaky** *adj*
WORD ORIGIN from Old Norse
leakage *n* the act or an instance or the result of leaking: *the leakage of 60 tonnes of oil*
Leakey *n* **1 Louis Seymour Bazett** 1903–72, British anthropologist and archaeologist, settled in Kenya. He discovered fossil remains of manlike apes in E Africa **2** his son **Richard** born 1944, Kenyan anthropologist, who discovered the remains of primitive man over 2 million years old in E Africa
lean[1] ❶ *vb* **leaning, leaned** *or* **leant 1** (foll. by *against, on* or *upon*) to rest or put (something) so that it rests against a support **2** to bend or make (something) bend from an upright position **3** (foll. by *to* or *towards*) to have or express a tendency or preference ▷ *n* **4** the condition of bending from an upright position ▸ See also **lean on**
WORD ORIGIN Old English *hleonian, hlinian*
lean[2] ❶ *adj* **1** (esp. of a person) having a trim body with no surplus flesh **2** (of meat) having little or no fat **3** (of a period) sparse, difficult, or causing hardship: *these are lean days in Baghdad* ▷ *n* **4** the part of meat that contains little or no fat **leanness** *n*
WORD ORIGIN Old English *hlǣne*
leaning ❶ *n* a tendency or inclination
lean on *vb* **1** *informal* to try to influence (someone) by using threats **2** to depend on (someone) for help and advice
leant *vb* ▸ a past of **lean**[1]
lean-to *n, pl* **-tos** a building with a sloping roof attached to another building or a wall
leap ❶ *vb* **leaping, leapt** *or* **leaped 1** to jump suddenly from one place to another **2** (often foll. by *at*) to move or react quickly **3** to jump over ▷ *n* **4** the act of jumping **5** an abrupt or important change or increase: *a leap to full European union* **6 a leap in the dark** an action performed without knowledge of the consequences **7 by leaps and bounds** with unexpectedly rapid progress
WORD ORIGIN Old English *hlēapan*
leapfrog *n* **1** a children's game in which each player in turn leaps over the others' bent backs ▷ *vb* **-frogging, -frogged 2 a** to play leapfrog **b** to leap over (something) **3** to advance by jumps or stages
leap year *n* a calendar year of 366 days, February 29 (**leap day**) being the additional day, that occurs every four years
learn ❶ *vb* **learning; learned** *or* **learnt 1** to gain knowledge (of something) or acquire skill in (some art or practice) **2** to memorize (something) **3** to gain by experience, example, or practice: *I learned everything the hard way*

THESAURUS

leaf *n* **1 = frond**, flag, needle, pad, blade, bract, cotyledon, foliole **5 = page**, sheet, folio **9** (usually foll. by *through*) **= skim**, glance, scan, browse, look through, dip into, flick through, flip through, thumb through, riffle
leaflet *n* **1 = booklet**, notice, advert (*Brit informal*), brochure, bill, circular, flyer, tract, pamphlet, handout, mailshot, handbill
leafy *adj* **1, 2 = green**, leaved, leafed, shaded, shady, summery, verdant, bosky (*literary*), springlike, in foliage
league[1] *n* **1 = association**, union, alliance, coalition, group, order, band, corporation, combination, partnership, federation, compact, consortium, guild, confederation, fellowship, fraternity, confederacy **3** (*informal*) **= class**, group, level, category, ability group
leak *n* **1a = hole**, opening, crack, puncture, aperture, chink, crevice, fissure, perforation **1b, 4 = leakage**, leaking, discharge, drip, oozing, seepage, percolation **2 = disclosure**, exposé, exposure, admission, revelation, uncovering, betrayal, unearthing, divulgence ▷ *vb* **6 = escape**, pass, spill, release, discharge, drip, trickle, ooze, seep, exude, percolate **7 = disclose**, tell, reveal, pass on, give away, make public, divulge, let slip, make known, spill the beans (*informal*), blab (*informal*), let the cat out of the bag, blow wide open (*slang*)
lean[1] *vb* **1** (foll. by *against, on,* or *upon*) **= rest**, prop, be supported, recline, repose **2 = bend**, tip, slope, incline, tilt, heel, slant **3** (foll. by *to* or *towards*) **= tend**, prefer, favour, incline, be prone to, gravitate, be disposed to, have a propensity to
lean[2] *adj* **1 = thin**, slim, slender, skinny, angular, trim, spare, gaunt, bony, lanky, wiry, emaciated, scrawny, svelte, lank, rangy, scraggy, macilent (*rare*) **OPPOSITE:** fat
leaning *n* **= tendency**, liking for, bias, inclination, taste, bent, disposition, penchant, propensity, aptitude, predilection, proclivity, partiality, proneness
leap *vb* **1 = jump**, spring, bound, bounce, hop, skip, caper, cavort, frisk, gambol ▷ *n* **4 = jump**, spring, bound, hop, skip, vault, caper, frisk **5 = rise**, change, increase, soaring, surge, escalation, upsurge, upswing
learn *vb* **1, 3 = master**, grasp, acquire, pick up, take in, attain, become able, familiarize yourself with **2 = memorize**, commit to memory, learn by heart, learn by rote, get

4 (often foll. by *of* or *about*) to become informed; find out: *Captain Nelson learned of the disaster from his wireless* **learnable** *adj* **learner** *n*
WORD ORIGIN Old English *leornian*

learned ❶ (lurn-id) *adj* **1** having great knowledge **2** involving or characterized by scholarship: *your learned paper on the subject*

learning ❶ *n* knowledge gained by studying

lease ❶ *n* **1** a contract by which an owner rents buildings or land to another person for a specified period **2 a new lease of life** a prospect of renewed energy, health, or happiness ▹ *vb* **leasing, leased 3** to let or rent (land or buildings) by lease
WORD ORIGIN Old French *laissier* to let go

leasehold *n* **1** land or property held under a lease **2** the holding of such property under lease **leaseholder** *n*

leash *n* **1** a dog's lead **2 straining at the leash** eagerly impatient to begin something ▹ *vb* **3** to put a leash on
WORD ORIGIN Old French *laissier* to loose (hence to let a dog run on a leash)

least ❶ *adj, adv* **1 the least** ▸ the superlative of **little**: *without encountering the least sign of civilization; he is the least well-educated prime minister* ▹ *adj* **2** of very little importance **3** smallest ▹ *adv* **4 at least** if nothing else: *at least I wrote* **5 at the least** at the minimum: *at the very least you should have some self respect* **6 not in the least** not at all: *you're not detaining me, not in the least*
WORD ORIGIN Old English *lǣst*, superlative of *lǣssa* less

leastways *or US & Canad* **leastwise** *adv informal* at least; anyway

leather *n* **1** the skin of an animal made smooth and flexible by tanning and removing the hair **2 leathers** leather clothes, esp. as worn by motorcyclists ▹ *adj* **3** made of leather ▹ *vb* **4** to whip as if with a leather strap **5** to dress in leather
WORD ORIGIN Old English *lether-* (in compound words)

leatherjacket *n* **1** any of various tropical fishes having a leathery skin **2** the tough-skinned larva of certain crane flies, which destroy the roots of grasses

leathery *adj* looking or feeling like leather, esp. in toughness

leave[1] ❶ *vb* **leaving, left 1** to go away (from a person or place) **2** to cause to remain behind, often by mistake, in a place: *I left the paper under the table* **3** to cause to be or remain in a specified state: *the poll leaves the parties neck-and-neck* **4** to stop attending or belonging to a particular organization or institution: *at seventeen she left the convent* **5** to not eat something or not deal with something: *he left a half-eaten lunch* **6** to result in; cause: *I have been terribly hurt by women, it leaves indelible marks* **7** to allow (someone) to do something without interfering: *the governor left them to it for a further few hours* **8** to be survived by (members of one's family): *he leaves a widow and one daughter* **9** to bequeath: *her adored son left his millions to an unknown half-sister* **10** to have as a remainder: *37 – 14 leaves 23* **11 leave (someone) alone a** to stop annoying (someone) **b** to permit to stay or be alone ▸ See also **leave off, leave out**
WORD ORIGIN Old English *lǣfan*

leave[2] ❶ *n* **1** permission to be absent, for instance from work: *so I asked for leave* **2** the length of such absence: *weekend leave* **3** permission to do something: *they were refused leave to appeal* **4 on leave** officially excused from work or duty **5 take (one's) leave of** to say farewell to
WORD ORIGIN Old English *lēaf*

leaven (lev-ven) *n also* **leavening 1** any substance, such as yeast, that produces fermentation in dough and makes it rise **2** an influence that produces a gradual change ▹ *vb* **3** to cause fermentation in (dough) **4** to spread through, causing a gradual change
WORD ORIGIN Latin *levare* to raise

leave off *vb* **1** to stop; cease **2** to stop wearing or using

leave out ❶ *vb* to omit or exclude: *leave out everything not necessary to living*

leaves *n* ▸ the plural of **leaf**

leave-taking *n* a departing; a farewell

leavings *pl n* things left behind unwanted, such as food on a plate

Lebanese *adj* **1** from the Lebanon ▹ *n, pl* **-nese 2** a person from the Lebanon

Lebensraum (lay-benz-rowm) *n* territory claimed by a nation or state because it is necessary for survival or growth
WORD ORIGIN German: living space

Leblanc *n* **Nicolas** ?1742–1806, French chemist, who invented a process for the manufacture of soda from common salt

Lebrun *n* **1 Albert** 1871–1950, French statesman; president (1932–40) **2** Also: **Le Brun Charles** 1619–90, French historical painter. He was court painter to Louis XIV and executed much of the decoration of the palace of Versailles

Le Carré *n* **John,** real name *David John Cornwell*. born 1931, English novelist, esp. of spy thrillers such as *The Spy who came in from the Cold* (1963), *Tinker, Tailor, Soldier, Spy* (1974), *Smiley's People* (1980), *The Tailor of Panama* (1996), and *The Mission Song* (2006)

lecherous (letch-er-uss) *adj* (of a man) having or showing strong and uncontrolled sexual desire **lecher** *n* **lechery** *n*
WORD ORIGIN Old French *lechier* to lick

lecithin (less-sith-in) *n biochem* a yellow-brown compound found in

THESAURUS

(something) word-perfect, learn parrot-fashion, get off pat, con *(archaic)* **4 = discover**, hear, understand, gain knowledge, find out about, become aware, discern, ascertain, come to know, suss (out) *(slang)*

learned *adj* **1, 2 = scholarly**, experienced, lettered, cultured, skilled, expert, academic, intellectual, versed, literate, well-informed, erudite, highbrow, well-read **OPPOSITE:** uneducated

learning *n* **= knowledge**, study, education, schooling, research, scholarship, tuition, enlightenment

lease *vb* **3 = hire**, rent, let, loan, charter, rent out, hire out

least *adj* **3 = smallest**, meanest, fewest, minutest, lowest, tiniest, minimum, slightest, minimal

leave[1] *vb* **1a = depart from**, withdraw from, go from, escape from, desert, quit, flee, exit, pull out of, retire from, move out of, disappear from, run away from, forsake, flit *(informal)*, set out from, go away from, hook it *(slang)*, pack your bags *(informal)*, make tracks, abscond from, decamp from, sling your hook *(Brit slang)*, slope off from, take your leave of, do a bunk from *(Brit slang)*, take yourself off from *(informal)* **OPPOSITE:** arrive **1b = give up**, abandon, desert, dump *(informal)*, drop, surrender, ditch *(informal)*, chuck *(informal)*, discard, relinquish, renounce, jilt *(informal)*, cast aside, forbear, leave in the lurch **OPPOSITE:** stay with **1, 4 = quit**, give up, get out of, resign from, drop out of **2 = forget**, lay down, leave behind, mislay **6 = cause**, produce, result in, generate, deposit **7 = entrust**, commit, delegate, refer, hand over, assign, consign, allot, cede, give over **9 = bequeath**, will, transfer, endow, transmit, confer, hand down, devise *(law)*, demise

leave[2] *n* **1, 2 = holiday**, break, vacation, time off, sabbatical, leave of absence, furlough, schoolie *(Austral)*, accumulated day off *or* ADO *(Austral)* **3 = permission**, freedom, sanction, liberty, concession, consent, allowance, warrant, authorization, dispensation **OPPOSITE:** refusal

leave out = omit, exclude, miss out, forget, except, reject, ignore, overlook, neglect, skip, disregard, bar, cast aside, count out

DICTIONARY

plant and animal tissues, esp. egg yolk: used in making cosmetics and inks, and as an emulsifier and stabilizer (**E322**) in foods
WORD ORIGIN Greek *lekithos* egg yolk

Lecky *n* **William Edward Hartpole** 1838–1903, Irish historian; author of *The History of England in the 18th Century* (1878–90)

Leconte de Lisle *n* **Charles Marie René** 1818–94, French Parnassian poet

lectern *n* a sloping reading desk, esp. in a church
WORD ORIGIN Latin *legere* to read

lecture *n* **1** a talk on a particular subject delivered to an audience **2** a lengthy scolding ⊳ *vb* **-turing, -tured** **3** to deliver a lecture (to an audience or class) **4** to scold (someone) at length **lecturer** *n* **lectureship** *n*
WORD ORIGIN Latin *legere* to read

led *vb* ▸ the past of **lead**[1]

LED *electronics* light-emitting diode: a semiconductor that gives out light when an electric current is applied to it

Lederberg *n* **Joshua** 1925–2008, US geneticist, who discovered the phenomenon of transduction in bacteria. Nobel prize for physiology or medicine 1958 with George Beadle and Edward Tatum

ledge *n* **1** a narrow horizontal surface that projects from a wall or window **2** a narrow shelflike projection on a cliff or mountain
WORD ORIGIN perhaps Middle English *leggen* to lay

ledger *n* *book-keeping* the principal book in which the commercial transactions of a company are recorded
WORD ORIGIN perhaps Middle English *leggen* to lay (because kept in a specific place)

Ledger *n* **Heath(cliffe) Andrew** 1979–2008, Australian film actor. His films include *The Patriot* (2000), *A Knight's Tale* (2001) and *Brokeback Mountain* (2005)

ledger line *n* *music* a short line above or below the staff used to indicate the pitch of notes higher or lower than the range of the staff

Led Zeppelin *n* British rock group (1968–80); comprised Jimmy Page (born 1944), Robert Plant (born 1948), John Paul Jones (born 1946), and John Bonham (1948–80): recordings include *Led Zeppelin I* (1969), *Led Zeppelin IV* (1971), and *Physical Graffiti* (1975)

lee *n* **1** a sheltered part or side; the side away from the direction from which the wind is blowing ⊳ *adj* **2** *naut* on, at, or towards the side away from the wind: *her lee rail was awash*
WORD ORIGIN Old English *hlēow* shelter

leech *n* **1** a worm which has a sucker at each end of the body and feeds on the blood or tissues of other animals **2** a person who lives off another person; parasite
WORD ORIGIN Old English *lǣce*

leek *n* a vegetable of the onion family with a slender white bulb and broad flat green overlapping leaves: the national emblem of Wales
WORD ORIGIN Old English *lēac*

leer *vb* **1** to give a sneering or suggestive look or grin ⊳ *n* **2** such a look
WORD ORIGIN Old English *hlēor* cheek

leery *adj* **leerier, leeriest** **1** *slang* (foll. by *of*) suspicious or wary **2** *now chiefly dialect* knowing or sly
WORD ORIGIN perhaps obsolete sense (to look askance) of *leer*

lees *pl n* the sediment from an alcoholic drink
WORD ORIGIN plural of obsolete *lee*, from Old French

leet *n* *Scot* a list of candidates for an office
WORD ORIGIN perhaps Anglo-French *litte*, variant of LIST[1]

leeward *chiefly naut adj* **1** of, in, or moving in the direction towards which the wind blows ⊳ *n* **2** the side towards the lee ⊳ *adv* **3** towards the lee

leeway *n* **1** flexibility of action or expenditure: *he gave me a lot of leeway in the work I did* **2** sideways drift of a boat or aircraft

Le Fanu *n* (**Joseph**) **Sheridan** 1814–73, Irish writer, best known for his stories of mystery and the supernatural, esp. *Uncle Silas* (1864) and the collection *In a Glass Darkly* (1872)

left[1] *adj* **1** denoting the side of something or someone that faces west when the front is turned towards the north **2** on the left side of the body: *I grabbed it with my left hand* **3** liberal, radical, or socialist ⊳ *adv* **4** on or in the direction of the left ⊳ *n* **5** a left side, direction, position, area, or part **6** **the left** the people in a political party or society who have more socialist or liberal views: *the biggest party of the French Left* **7** *boxing* **a** a blow with the left hand **b** the left hand
WORD ORIGIN Old English: idle, weak

left[2] *vb* ▸ the past of **leave**[1]

left field *n* **1** *baseball* **a** the area of the outfield to the batter's left **b** the fielder who covers this area **2** **out of left field** unexpected or surprising: *Their proposal came out of left field* ⊳ *adj* **3** *US & Canad informal* unconventional or outside the mainstream

left-hand *adj* **1** of, on, or towards the left **2** for the left hand

left-handed *adj* **1** better at using the left hand than the right **2** done with the left hand **3** designed for use by the left hand **4** awkward or clumsy **5** ambiguous or insincere: *a left-handed compliment* **6** turning from right to left; anticlockwise ⊳ *adv* **7** with the left hand: *I write left-handed* **left-hander** *n*

leftist *adj* **1** of or relating to the political left or its principles ⊳ *n* **2** a person who supports the political left **leftism** *n*

left-luggage office *n* *Brit* a place at a railway station or airport where luggage may be left for a small charge

leftover *n* **1** (*often pl*) an unused portion, esp. of cooked food ⊳ *adj* **2** left as an unused portion

leftward *adj, adv also* **leftwards** on or towards the left

left-wing *adj* **1** socialist or radical: *the party ditched many of its more left-wing policies* **2** belonging to the more radical part of a political party: *a group of left-wing Conservatives* ⊳ *n* **left wing** **3** (*often cap*) the more radical or progressive section, esp. of a political party: *the Left Wing of the Labour Party* **4** *sport* **a** the left-hand side of the field of play **b** a player positioned in this area in certain games **left-winger** *n*

lefty *n, pl* **lefties** *informal* **1** *Brit, Austral & NZ* a left-winger **2** *chiefly US & Canad*

THESAURUS

lecture *n* **1 = talk**, address, speech, lesson, instruction, presentation, discourse, sermon, exposition, harangue, oration, disquisition **2 = telling-off** (*informal*), rebuke, reprimand, talking-to (*informal*), heat (*slang, chiefly US & Canad*), going-over (*informal*), wigging (*Brit slang*), censure, scolding, chiding, dressing-down (*informal*), reproof, castigation ⊳ *vb* **3 = talk**, speak, teach, address, discourse, spout, expound, harangue, give a talk, hold forth, expatiate **4 = tell off** (*informal*), berate, scold, reprimand, carpet (*informal*), censure, castigate, chide, admonish, tear into (*informal*), read the riot act, reprove, bawl out (*informal*), chew out (*US & Canad informal*), tear (someone) off a strip (*Brit informal*), give a rocket (*Brit & NZ informal*), give someone a talking-to (*informal*), give someone a dressing-down (*informal*), give someone a telling-off (*informal*)

lees *pl n* **= sediment**, grounds, refuse, deposit, precipitate, dregs, settlings

left[1] *adj* **1, 2 = left-hand**, port, larboard (*nautical*) **3** (*of politics*) **= socialist**, liberal, radical, progressive, left-wing, leftist

left-wing *adj* **1 = socialist**, communist, red (*informal*), radical, leftist, liberal, revolutionary, militant, Marxist, Bolshevik, Leninist, collectivist, Trotskyite

leg *n* **1 = limb**, member, shank, lower

a left-handed person

leg ⓣ *n* **1** either of the two lower limbs in humans, or any similar structure in animals that is used for movement or support **2** the part of a garment that covers the leg **3** a lower limb of an animal, esp. the thigh, used for food: *leg of lamb* **4** something similar to a leg in appearance or function, such as one of the supports of a chair **5** a section of a journey **6** a single stage, lap, or length in a relay race **7** one of a series of games, matches, or parts of games **8** *cricket* the side of the field to the left of a right-handed batsman as he faces the bowler **9 not have a leg to stand on** *informal* to have no reasonable basis for an opinion or argument **10 on one's last legs** worn out or exhausted **11 to pull someone's leg** *informal* to tease or make fun of someone **12 shake a leg** *informal* to hurry up **13 stretch one's legs** to stand up or walk around, esp. after sitting for some time ▷*vb* **legging, legged 14 leg it** *informal* to walk, run, or hurry
WORD ORIGIN Old Norse *leggr*

legacy ⓣ *n, pl* **-cies 1** money or personal property left to someone by a will **2** something handed down to a successor
WORD ORIGIN Medieval Latin *legatia* commission

legal ⓣ *adj* **1** established by or permitted by law; lawful **2** of or relating to law **3** relating to or characteristic of lawyers **legally** *adv*
WORD ORIGIN Latin *legalis*

legal aid *n* financial assistance available to people who are unable to meet the full cost of legal proceedings

legalese *n* the conventional language in which legal documents are written

legalism *n* strict adherence to the letter of the law **legalist** *n, adj* **legalistic** *adj*

legality *n, pl* **-ties** the state or quality of being legal or lawful

legalize *or* **-ise** *vb* **-izing, -ized** *or* **-ising, -ised** to make lawful or legal **legalization** *or* **-isation** *n*

legal tender *n* currency that a creditor must by law accept to pay a debt

legate *n* a messenger, esp. one representing the Pope
WORD ORIGIN Latin *legare* to delegate

legatee *n* the recipient of a legacy

legation *n* **1** a diplomatic mission headed by a minister **2** the official residence and office of a diplomatic minister

legato (leg-ah-toe) *music adv* **1** smoothly and evenly ▷*n, pl* **-tos 2** a style of playing with no gaps between notes
WORD ORIGIN Italian

leg before wicket *n cricket* a dismissal on the grounds that a batsman has been struck on the leg by a bowled ball that otherwise would have hit the wicket. Abbrev: **lbw**

leg break *n cricket* a bowled ball that spins from leg to off on pitching

leg bye *n cricket* a run scored after the ball has hit the batsman's leg or some other part of his body, except his hand, without touching the bat. Abbrev: **lb**

legend ⓣ *n* **1** a popular story handed down from earlier times which may or may not be true **2** such stories collectively **3** a person whose fame makes him or her seem exceptional: *he is a living legend* **4** modern stories about a famous person which may or may not be true: *no Garland fan could complain about sordid revelations tarnishing the legend* **5** words written on something to explain it: *a pub mirror spelling out the legend 'Saloon Bar'* **6** an explanation on a table, map, or chart, of the symbols used
WORD ORIGIN Medieval Latin *legenda* passages to be read

legendary ⓣ *adj* **1** very famous: *the legendary beauty of the Alps* **2** of or relating to legend **3** described in legend: *the legendary birthplace of Aphrodite*

Legendre *n* **Adrien Marie** 1752–1833, French mathematician, noted for his work on the theory of numbers, the theory of elliptical functions, and the method of least squares

Léger *n* **Fernand** 1881–1955, French cubist painter, influenced by industrial technology

legerdemain (lej-er-de-**main**) *n* **1** ▸same as **sleight of hand** **2** cunning deception
WORD ORIGIN Old French: light of hand

leger line *n* ▸same as **ledger line**

leggings *pl n* **1** an extra outer covering for the lower legs **2** close-fitting trousers for women or children

leggy *adj* **1** having unusually long legs **2** (of a plant) having a long weak stem

leghorn *n* **1** a type of Italian wheat straw that is woven into hats **2** any hat made from this straw
WORD ORIGIN English name for *Livorno*, in Italy

Leghorn (leg-**gorn**) *n* a breed of domestic fowl

legible *adj* (of handwriting) able to be read **legibility** *n* **legibly** *adv*
WORD ORIGIN Latin *legere* to read

legion ⓣ *n* **1** any large military force: *the French Foreign Legion* **2** (*often pl*) any very large number **3** an infantry unit in the ancient Roman army of three to six thousand men **4** an association of veterans **legionary** *adj, n*
WORD ORIGIN Latin *legio*

legionnaire *n* (*often cap*) a member of a legion

Legionnaire's disease *n* a serious bacterial infection, with symptoms similar to pneumonia
WORD ORIGIN after the outbreak at a meeting of the American Legion in Philadelphia in 1976

legislate *vb* **-lating, -lated 1** to make or pass laws **2** to bring into effect by legislation **legislator** *n*
WORD ORIGIN Latin *lex, legis* law + *latus*, past participle of *ferre* to bring

legislation ⓣ *n* **1** the act or process of making laws **2** the laws so made

legislative ⓣ *adj* **1** of or relating to the process of making laws **2** having the power or function of making laws:

I

THESAURUS

limb, pin (*informal*), stump (*informal*)
4 = support, prop, brace, upright
5, 6 = stage, part, section, stretch, lap, segment, portion
11 pull someone's leg (*informal*) **= tease**, joke, trick, fool, kid (*informal*), have (someone) on, rag, rib (*informal*), wind up (*Brit slang*), deceive, hoax, make fun of, poke fun at, twit, chaff, lead up the garden path, jerk *or* yank someone's chain (*informal*)

legacy *n* **1 = bequest**, inheritance, endowment, gift, estate, devise (*law*), heirloom

legal *adj* **1 = lawful**, allowed, sanctioned, constitutional, proper, valid, legitimate, authorized, rightful, permissible, legalized, allowable, within the law, licit
2, 3 = judicial, judiciary, forensic, juridical, jurisdictive

legend *n* **1 = myth**, story, tale, fiction, narrative, saga, fable, folk tale, urban myth, urban legend, folk story
3 = celebrity, star, phenomenon, genius, spectacle, wonder, big name, marvel, prodigy, luminary, celeb (*informal*), megastar (*informal*)
5 = inscription, title, caption, device, motto, rubric

legendary *adj* **1 = famous**, celebrated, well-known, acclaimed, renowned, famed, immortal, illustrious
OPPOSITE: unknown
2, 3 = mythical, fabled, traditional, romantic, fabulous, fanciful, fictitious, storybook, apocryphal
OPPOSITE: factual

legion *n* **1 = army**, company, force, division, troop, brigade
2 = multitude, host, mass, drove, number, horde, myriad, throng

legislation *n* **1 = lawmaking**, regulation, prescription, enactment, codification **2 = law**, act, ruling, rule, bill, measure, regulation, charter, statute

legislative *adj* **2 = law-making**,

DICTIONARY

the election to Singapore's new legislative assembly

legislature ⓣ *n* a body of people authorized to make, amend, and repeal laws

legitimate ⓣ *adj* **1** authorized by or in accordance with law: *legitimate accounting practices* **2** based on correct or acceptable principles of reasoning: *a legitimate argument* **3** (of a child) born of parents legally married to each other **4** of, relating to, or ruling by hereditary right: *under their legitimate ruling house* **5** of or relating to serious drama as distinct from films, television, or vaudeville ▷ *vb* **-mating, -mated 6** to make, pronounce, or show to be legitimate **legitimacy** *n* **legitimately** *adv*
WORD ORIGIN Medieval Latin *legitimatus* made legal

legitimize *or* **-mise** *vb* **-mizing, -mized** *or* **-mising, -mised** to make legitimate; legalize **legitimization** *or* **-misation** *n*

legless *adj* **1** without legs **2** *slang* very drunk

Lego *n trademark* a construction toy consisting of plastic bricks and other components that fit together
WORD ORIGIN Danish *leg godt* play well

leg-pull *n Brit informal* a practical joke

legroom *n* space to move one's legs comfortably, as in a car

leguaan *n* a large amphibious S African lizard
WORD ORIGIN Dutch, from French *l'iguane* the iguana

legume *n* **1** the pod of a plant of the pea or bean family **2** the seed from such pods, esp. beans or peas
WORD ORIGIN Latin *legere* to pick (a crop)

leguminous *adj* of or relating to any family of flowering plants having pods (or legumes) as fruits

Lehár *n* **Franz** 1870–1948, Hungarian composer of operettas, esp. *The Merry Widow* (1905)

Lehmann *n* **1 Lilli** 1848–1929, German soprano **2 Lotte** 1888–1976, US soprano, born in Germany **3 Rosamond** (**Nina**) 1903–90, British novelist. Her books include *Dusty Answer* (1927), *Invitation to the Waltz* (1932), and *The Echoing Grove* (1953)

Lehmbruck *n* **Wilhelm** 1881–1919, German sculptor and graphic artist

lei *n* (in Hawaii) a garland of flowers, worn around the neck
WORD ORIGIN Hawaiian

Leibovitz *n* **Annie** born 1949, US photographer, known for her portraits of celebrities

Leicester[1] *n* **1** a city in central England, in Leicester unitary authority, on the River Soar: administrative centre of Leicestershire: Roman remains and a ruined Norman castle; two universities (1957, 1992); light engineering, hosiery, and footwear industries. Pop: 283 900 (2003 est) **2** a unitary authority in central England, in Leicestershire. Pop: 330 574 (2001). Area: 73 sq km (28 sq miles) **3** ▸ short for **Leicestershire** **4** a breed of sheep with long wool, originally from Leicestershire **5** a fairly mild dark orange whole-milk cheese, similar to Cheddar

Leicester[2] *n* **Earl of** title of *Robert Dudley*. ?1532–88, English courtier; favourite of Elizabeth I. He led an unsuccessful expedition to the Netherlands (1585–87)

Leichhardt *n* **Friedrich Wilhelm Ludwig** 1813–48, Australian explorer, born in Prussia. He disappeared during an attempt to cross Australia from East to West

Leics Leicestershire

Leigh[1] *n* a town in NW England, in Wigan unitary authority, Greater Manchester: engineering industries. Pop: 43 006 (2001)

Leigh[2] *n* **1 Mike** born 1943, British dramatist and theatre, film, and television director, noted for his use of improvisation. His plays include *Abigail's Party* (1977), and his films include *High Hopes* (1988), *Secrets and Lies* (1996), and *Vera Drake* (2004) **2 Vivien,** real name *Vivian Hartley*. 1913–67, English stage and film actress. Her films include *Gone with the Wind* (1939) and *A Streetcar Named Desire* (1951), for both of which she won Oscars

Leigh Fermor *n* See **Fermor**

Leighton *n* **Frederic,** 1st Baron Leighton of Stretton. 1830–96, British painter and sculptor of classical subjects: president of the Royal Academy (1878)

leisure ⓣ *n* **1** time or opportunity for relaxation or hobbies **2 at leisure a** having free time **b** not occupied **3 at one's leisure** when one has free time **leisured** *adj*
WORD ORIGIN Old French *leisir*

leisure centre *n* a building providing facilities, such as a swimming pool, gym, and café, for a range of leisure pursuits

leisurely *adj* **1** unhurried; relaxed ▷ *adv* **2** in a relaxed way **leisureliness** *n*

leitmotif *or* **leitmotiv** (lite-mote-eef) *n* **1** *music* a recurring melodic phrase used to suggest a character, thing, or idea **2** an often repeated image in a literary work
WORD ORIGIN German: leading motif

lekgotla (leh-hot-luh), **kgotla** (hot-luh) *n S African* **1** a meeting place for village assemblies, court cases, and meetings of village leaders **2** a conference or business meeting
WORD ORIGIN Sotho, Tswana

lekker ⓣ *adj S African slang* pleasing, enjoyable, or tasty
WORD ORIGIN Afrikaans, from Dutch

Lely *n* Sir **Peter** Dutch name *Pieter van der Faes*. 1618–80, Dutch portrait painter in England

Lemaître *n* Abbé **Georges** (**Édouard**) 1894–1966, Belgian astronomer and priest, who first proposed the big-bang theory of the universe (1927)

Lemalu *n* **Jonathan** (**Fa'afetai**) born 1976, New Zealand singer of Samoan descent; a bass-baritone noted esp. for his lieder recitals

lemming *n* **1** a small rodent of northern and arctic regions, reputed to rush into the sea in large groups and drown **2** a member of any group following an unthinking course towards destruction
WORD ORIGIN Norwegian

lemon *n* **1** a yellow oval edible fruit with juicy acidic flesh that grows on an evergreen tree in warm and tropical regions **2** *slang* a person or thing considered to be useless or defective ▷ *adj* **3** light yellow **lemony** *adj*
WORD ORIGIN Arabic *laymūn*

THESAURUS

parliamentary, congressional, judicial, ordaining, law-giving, juridical, jurisdictive

legislature *n* **= parliament**, house, congress, diet, senate, assembly, chamber, law-making body

legitimate *adj* **1 = lawful**, real, true, legal, acknowledged, sanctioned, genuine, proper, authentic, statutory, authorized, rightful, kosher *(informal)*, dinkum *(Austral & NZ informal)*, legit *(slang)*, licit
OPPOSITE: unlawful
2 = reasonable, just, correct, sensible, valid, warranted, logical, justifiable, well-founded, admissible
OPPOSITE: unreasonable
▷ *vb* **6 = legitimize**, allow, permit, sanction, authorize, legalize, give the green light to, legitimatize, pronounce lawful

leisure *n* **1 = spare time**, free time, rest, holiday, quiet, ease, retirement, relaxation, vacation, recreation, time off, breathing space, spare moments **OPPOSITE:** work

lekker *adj (S African slang)* **= delicious**, tasty, luscious, choice, savoury, palatable, dainty, delectable, mouthwatering, yummy *(slang)*, scrumptious *(informal)*, appetizing, toothsome, ambrosial, yummo *(Austral slang)*

DICTIONARY

lemonade *n* a drink made from lemon juice, sugar, and water or from carbonated water, citric acid, and sweetener

lemon sole *n* an edible European flatfish

Lemper *n* **Ute** born 1963, German singer and actress, noted esp. for her performances of songs by Kurt Weill

lemur *n* a nocturnal animal, related to the monkey, with a foxy face and long tail, found on Madagascar
WORD ORIGIN Latin *lemures* ghosts

lend ⓣ *vb* **lending, lent 1** to permit the temporary use of **2** to provide (money) temporarily, often at interest **3** to contribute (some abstract quality): *a painted trellis lends a classical air to any garden* **4 lend an ear** to listen **5 lend oneself** *or* **itself** to be appropriate for: *the building lends itself to loft conversion* **lender** *n*
WORD ORIGIN Old English *lǣnan*

Lendl *n* **Ivan** born 1960, Czech tennis player; US Open champion (1985–87)

Lenglen *n* **Suzanne** 1899–1938, French tennis player: Wimbledon champion (1919–25)

length ⓣ *n* **1** the extent or measurement of something from end to end **2** a specified distance, esp. between two positions: *the length of a cricket-pitch* **3** a period of time, as between specified limits or moments **4** the quality, state, or fact of being long rather than short **5** a piece of something, usually longer than it is wide: *a length of twine* **6** (*usually pl*) the amount of trouble taken in doing something: *to go to great lengths* **7** *prosody, phonetics* the duration of a vowel or syllable **8 at length a** after a long interval or period of time **b** in great detail
WORD ORIGIN Old English *lengthu*

lengthen ⓣ *vb* to make or become longer

lengthways *or* **lengthwise** *adv, adj* in, according to, or along the direction of length

lengthy ⓣ *adj* **lengthier, lengthiest** very long or tiresome **lengthily** *adv* **lengthiness** *n*

lenient (lee-nee-ent) *adj* tolerant, not strict or severe **leniency** *n* **leniently** *adv*
WORD ORIGIN Latin *lenis* soft

lenity *n, pl* **-ties** mercy or clemency

Leno *n* **Dan,** original name *George Galvin.* 1860–1904, British music-hall entertainer, noted esp. for his pantomime performances: he died insane

Le Nôtre *n* **André** 1613–1700, French landscape gardener, who created the gardens at Versailles for Louis XIV

lens *n* **1** a piece of glass or other transparent material with a curved surface or surfaces, used to bring together or spread rays of light passing through it: used in cameras, telescopes, and spectacles **2** *anat* a transparent structure in the eye, behind the iris, that focuses images on the retina
WORD ORIGIN Latin: lentil

lent *vb* ▸ the past of **lend**

Lent *n Christianity* the period from Ash Wednesday to Easter Saturday, during which some Christians give up doing something they enjoy **Lenten** *adj*
WORD ORIGIN Old English *lencten, lengten* spring, literally: lengthening (of hours of daylight)

lentil *n* any of the small edible seeds of a leguminous Asian plant
WORD ORIGIN Latin *lens*

lento *music adv* **1** slowly ▹ *n, pl* **-tos 2** a movement or passage performed slowly
WORD ORIGIN Italian

Lenya *n* **Lotte,** original name *Caroline Blamauer.* 1900–81, Austrian singer and actress, associated esp. with the songs of her husband Kurt Weill

Leo *n astrol* the fifth sign of the zodiac; the Lion
WORD ORIGIN Latin

Leo III *n* **1** called *the Isaurian.* ?675–741 AD, Byzantine emperor (717–41): he checked Arab expansionism and began the policy of iconoclasm, which divided the empire for the next century **2 Saint** ?750–816 AD, pope (795–816). He crowned Charlemagne emperor of the Romans (800). Feast day: June 12

Leonard *n* **Sugar Ray,** real name *Ray Charles Leonard.* born 1956, US boxer: the first man to have won world titles at five officially recognized weights

Leoncavallo *n* **Ruggiero** 1858–1919, Italian composer of operas, notably *I Pagliacci* (1892)

leonine *adj* of or like a lion
WORD ORIGIN Latin *leo* lion

Leonov *n* **Aleksei Arkhipovich** born 1934, Soviet cosmonaut; the first man to walk in space (1965)

leopard *or fem* **leopardess** *n* a large African and Asian mammal of the cat family, which has a tawny yellow coat with black spots. Also called: **panther**
WORD ORIGIN Greek *leōn* lion + *pardos* panther

Leopardi *n* Count **Giacomo** 1798–1837, Italian poet and philosopher, noted esp. for his lyrics, collected in *I Canti* (1831)

Leopold I *n* **1** 1640–1705, Holy Roman Emperor (1658–1705). His reign was marked by wars with Louis XIV of France and with the Turks **2** 1790–1865, first king of the Belgians (1831–65)

Leopold II *n* **1** 1747–92, Holy Roman Emperor (1790–92). He formed an alliance with Prussia against France (1792) after the downfall of his brother-in-law Louis XVI **2** 1835–1909, king of the Belgians (1865–1909); son of Leopold I. He financed Stanley's explorations in Africa, becoming first sovereign of the Congo Free State (1885)

Leopold III *n* 1901–83, king of the Belgians (1934–51); son of Albert I. His surrender to the Nazis (1940) forced his eventual abdication in favour of his son, Baudouin

leotard *n* a tight-fitting garment covering the body from the shoulders to the thighs and worn by acrobats, ballet dancers, and people doing exercises
WORD ORIGIN after Jules *Léotard,* acrobat

Leo X *n* original name *Giovanni de' Medici.* 1475–1521, pope (1513–21): noted for his patronage of Renaissance art and learning; excommunicated Luther (1521)

Le Pen *n* **Jean-Marie** born 1928, French politician; leader of the extreme right-wing Front National from 1972; runner-up in the presidential election of 2002

leper *n* **1** a person who has leprosy **2** a person who is avoided
WORD ORIGIN Greek *lepros* scaly

lepidopteran *n, pl* **-terans** *or* **-tera 1** an insect that has two pairs of fragile wings and develops from a caterpillar; a butterfly or moth ▹ *adj*

L

THESAURUS

lend *vb* **1, 2 = loan,** advance, sub (*Brit informal*), accommodate one with **3 = give,** provide, add, present, supply, grant, afford, contribute, hand out, furnish, confer, bestow, impart **5 lend oneself or itself = be appropriate for,** suit, be suitable for, fit, be appropriate to, be adaptable to, present opportunities of, be serviceable for

length *n* **1 = distance,** reach, measure, extent, span, longitude **3 = duration,** term, period, space, stretch, span, expanse **5 = piece,** measure, section, segment, portion

lengthen *vb* **a = extend,** continue, increase, stretch, expand, elongate, make longer **OPPOSITE:** shorten **b = protract,** extend, prolong, draw out, spin out, make longer **OPPOSITE:** cut down

lengthy *adj* **a = protracted,** long, prolonged, very long, tedious, lengthened, diffuse, drawn-out, interminable, long-winded, long-drawn-out, overlong, verbose, prolix **b = very long,** rambling, interminable, long-winded, wordy, discursive, extended, overlong, verbose, prolix **OPPOSITE:** brief

DICTIONARY

also **lepidopterous** **2** denoting such an insect
WORD ORIGIN Greek *lepis* scale + *pteron* wing

lepidopterist *n* a person who studies or collects moths and butterflies

Lepidus *n* **Marcus Aemilius** died ?13 BC, Roman statesman: formed the Second Triumvirate with Octavian (later Augustus) and Mark Antony

Leppard *n* **Raymond** born 1927, British conductor and musicologist, in the US from 1977: noted esp. for his revivals of early opera

leprechaun *n* (in Irish folklore) a mischievous elf
WORD ORIGIN Irish Gaelic *leipreachān*

leprosy *n pathol* a chronic infectious disease, characterized by painful inflamed lumps beneath the skin and disfigurement and wasting away of affected parts **leprous** *adj*

lepton *n physics* any of a group of elementary particles with weak interactions
WORD ORIGIN Greek *leptos* thin

Lermontov *n* **Mikhail Yurievich** 1814–41, Russian novelist and poet: noted esp. for the novel *A Hero of Our Time* (1840)

Lerner *n* **Alan Jay** 1914–86, US songwriter and librettist. With Frederick Loewe he wrote *My Fair Lady* (1956) and *Camelot* (1960) as well as a number of film scripts, including *Gigi* (1958)

Le Sage *or* **Lesage** *n* **Alain-René** 1668–1747, French novelist and dramatist, author of the picaresque novel *Gil Blas* (1715–35)

lesbian ❶ *n* **1** a female homosexual ▹*adj* **2** of or characteristic of lesbians **lesbianism** *n*
WORD ORIGIN *Lesbos*, Greek Aegean island

lese-majesty (lezz-maj-ist-ee) *n* **1** an offence against the sovereign power in a state; treason **2** an act of disrespect towards authority
WORD ORIGIN from Latin *laesa majestas* wounded majesty

lesion *n* **1** any structural change in an organ or tissue resulting from injury or disease **2** an injury or wound
WORD ORIGIN Late Latin *laesio* injury

less ❶ *adj* **1** ▸the comparative of **little**: *less fibre* **2** *not standard* fewer ▹*adv* **3** ▸the comparative of **little**: *eat less* **4** **less of** to a smaller extent or degree: *it would become less of a problem* **5** **no less** *sometimes ironic* used to indicate admiration or surprise: *sculpted by a famous Frenchman, Rodin no less* ▹*prep* **6** minus: *a two pounds-a-week rise (less tax)*
WORD ORIGIN Old English *lǣssa, lǣs*

lessee *n* a person to whom a lease is granted
WORD ORIGIN Old French *lesser* to lease

lessen ❶ *vb* to make or become less

Lesseps *n* See **de Lesseps**

lesser ❶ *adj* not as great in quantity, size, or worth

Lessing *n* **1 Doris** (**May**) born 1919, English novelist and short-story writer, brought up in Rhodesia: her novels include the five-novel sequence *Children of Violence* (1952–69), *The Golden Notebook* (1962), a series of science-fiction works (1979–83), *The Good Terrorist* (1985), and *The Sweetest Dream* (2001). Nobel prize for literature 2007 **2 Gotthold Ephraim** 1729–81, German dramatist and critic. His plays include *Miss Sara Sampson* (1755), the first German domestic tragedy, and *Nathan der Weise* (1779). He is noted for his criticism of French classical dramatists, and for his treatise on aesthetics *Laokoon* (1766)

lesson ❶ *n* **1 a** a single period of instruction in a subject **b** the content of such a period **2** material assigned for individual study **3** something from which useful knowledge or principles can be learned: *one could still learn an important lesson from these masters* **4** an experience that serves as a warning or example: *the experience will prove a sobering lesson for the military* **5** a passage of Scripture read during a church service
WORD ORIGIN Old French *leçon*

lessor *n* a person who grants a lease of property

lest *conj* **1** so as to prevent any possibility that: *one grabbed it lest a neighbour got there first* **2** for fear that: *his anxiety lest anything mar the family event*
WORD ORIGIN Old English *thȳ lǣs the*, literally: whereby less that

let[1] ❶ *vb* **letting, let 1** to allow: *a child lets a friend play with his favourite toy* **2 a** an auxiliary expressing a request, proposal, or command, or conveying a warning or threat: *well, let's try it; just let me catch you here again!* **b** an auxiliary expressing an assumption or hypothesis: *let 'a' equal 'b'* **c** an auxiliary used to convey resigned acceptance of the inevitable: *let the worst happen* **3** to allow someone to rent (property or accommodation) **4** to cause the movement of (something) in a specified direction: *this lets aluminium creep into the brain* **5** **let alone** not to mention: *I could hardly think, let alone find words to say* **6** **let alone** *or* **be** stop annoying or interfering with: *let the poor cat alone* **7** **let go** to relax one's hold (on) **8** **let loose a** to allow (a person or animal) to leave or escape **b** *informal* to make (a sound) suddenly: *he let loose a laugh* **c** *informal* to fire (ammunition) from a gun ▹*n* **9** *Austral & Brit* the act of letting property or accommodation ▸See also **let down, let off**, etc.
WORD ORIGIN Old English *lǣtan* to permit

let[2] *n* **1** *tennis, squash* a minor infringement or obstruction of the ball, requiring a point to be replayed **2** **without let or hindrance** without obstruction
WORD ORIGIN Old English *lettan* to hinder

let down ❶ *vb* **1** to fail to satisfy the expectations of (someone); disappoint **2** to lower **3** to lengthen a garment by decreasing the hem **4** to deflate: *to let down a tyre* ▹*n* **letdown 5** a disappointment

lethal ❶ *adj* capable of causing death **lethally** *adv*
WORD ORIGIN Latin *letum* death

lethargy *n, pl* **-gies 1** sluggishness or dullness **2** an abnormal lack of energy **lethargic** *adj* **lethargically** *adv*

THESAURUS

lesbian *adj* **2 = homosexual**, gay, les *(slang)*, butch *(slang)*, sapphic, lesbo *(slang)*, tribadic

less *adj* **1 = smaller**, shorter, slighter, not so much

lessen *vb* **a = reduce**, lower, diminish, decrease, relax, ease, narrow, moderate, dial down, weaken, erode, impair, degrade, minimize, curtail, lighten, wind down, abridge, de-escalate **OPPOSITE:** increase **b = grow less**, diminish, decrease, contract, ease, weaken, shrink, slow down, dwindle, lighten, wind down, die down, abate, slacken

lesser *adj* **= lower**, slighter, secondary, subsidiary, subordinate, inferior, less important **OPPOSITE:** greater

lesson *n* **1a, 1b = class**, schooling, period, teaching, coaching, session, instruction, lecture, seminar, tutoring, tutorial **3, 4 = example**, warning, model, message, moral, deterrent, precept, exemplar **5 = Bible reading**, reading, text, Bible passage, Scripture passage

let[1] *vb* **1a = allow**, grant, permit, warrant, authorize, give the go-ahead, give permission, suffer *(archaic)*, give the green light, give leave, give the O.K. *or* okay *(informal)* **3 = lease**, hire, rent, rent out, hire out, sublease **let down 4 = deflate**, empty, exhaust, flatten, puncture

let down *vb* **1 = disappoint**, fail, abandon, desert, disillusion, fall short, leave stranded, leave in the lurch, disenchant, dissatisfy

lethal *adj* **= deadly**, terminal, fatal, deathly, dangerous, devastating, destructive, mortal, murderous, poisonous, virulent, pernicious, noxious, baneful **OPPOSITE:** harmless

DICTIONARY

WORD ORIGIN Greek *lēthargos* drowsy

let off ❶ *vb* **1** to excuse from (work or duties): *I'll let you off homework for a week* **2** *informal* to spare (someone) the expected punishment: *lots were let off because they couldn't be bothered to prosecute anybody* **3** to explode or fire (a bomb, gun, or firework) **4** to release (liquid, air, or steam)

let on *vb informal* **1** to reveal (a secret) **2** to pretend: *he let on that he was a pilgrim*

let out *vb* **1** to emit: *he let out a scream* **2** to allow to leave; release **3** to make (property) available for people to rent **4** to make (a garment) wider by reducing the seams **5** to reveal (a secret) ▹*n* **let-out 6** a chance to escape

letter ❶ *n* **1** a written or printed message, usually enclosed in an envelope and sent by post **2** any of a set of conventional symbols used in writing or printing a language: character of the alphabet **3** the strict meaning of an agreement or document; exact wording: *the letter of the law* **4 to the letter** precisely: *you have to follow treatment to the letter for it to be effective* ▹*vb* **5** to write or mark letters on (a sign) **lettering** *n*

WORD ORIGIN Latin *littera* letter of the alphabet

letter bomb *n* an explosive device in an envelope or parcel that explodes when the envelope or parcel is opened

letter box *n chiefly Brit* **1** a slot in a door through which letters are delivered **2** Also called: **pillar box, postbox** a public box into which letters and postcards are put for collection

lettered *adj* **1** well educated **2** printed or marked with letters

letterhead *n* a printed heading on stationery giving the name and address of the sender

letter of credit *n* a letter issued by a bank entitling the bearer to draw money from other banks

letterpress *n* a method of printing in which ink is transferred from raised surfaces to paper by pressure

letters *pl n* **1** literary knowledge or ability: *a man of letters* **2** literary culture in general

letters patent *pl n* ▸see **patent** (senses 1, 3)

lettuce *n* a plant cultivated for its large edible leaves, which are used in salads

WORD ORIGIN Latin *lactuca*, from *lac* milk, because of its milky juice

let up ❶ *vb* **1** to diminish or stop **2** (foll. by *on*) *informal* to be less harsh (towards someone) ▹*n* **let-up 3** *informal* a lessening: *there has been no let-up in the war*

Leucippus *n* 5th century BC Greek philosopher, who originated the atomist theory of matter, developed by his disciple, Democritus

leucocyte (loo-koh-site) *n* any of the various large white cells in the blood of vertebrates

WORD ORIGIN Greek *leukos* white + *kutos* vessel

leukaemia *or esp. US* **leukemia** (loo-kee-mee-a) *n* an acute or chronic disease characterized by extreme overproduction of white blood cells

WORD ORIGIN Greek *leukos* white + *haima* blood

levee[1] *n US* **1** a natural or artificial river embankment **2** a quay

WORD ORIGIN French, from Latin *levare* to raise

levee[2] *n* a formal reception held by a sovereign just after rising from bed

WORD ORIGIN French, from Latin *levare* to raise

level ❶ *adj* **1** on a horizontal plane **2** having an even surface **3** being of the same height as something else: *the floor of the lean-to was level with the patio* **4** equal to or even with (something or someone else): *Johnson was level with the overnight leader* **5** not exceeding the upper edge of (a spoon etc.) **6** consistent or regular: *a level pulse* **7 one's level best** the best one can do ▹*vb* **-elling, -elled** *or US* **-eling, -eled 8** (sometimes foll. by *off*) to make horizontal or even **9** to make equal in position or status **10** to direct (an accusation or criticism) emphatically at someone **11** to focus (a look) directly at someone **12** to aim (a weapon) horizontally **13** to demolish completely ▹*n* **14** a horizontal line or plane **15** a device, such as a spirit level, for determining whether a surface is horizontal **16** position or status in a scale of values: *a high-level delegation* **17** stage or degree of progress: *primary school level* **18** a specified vertical position: *floor level* **19** the topmost horizontal line or plane from which the height of something is calculated: *sea level* **20** a flat even surface or area of land **21** a degree or intensity reached on a measurable or notional scale: *noise level* **22 on the level** *informal* sincere or genuine

WORD ORIGIN Latin *libella*, diminutive of *libra* scales

level crossing *n Brit, Austral, & NZ* a point at which a railway line and a road cross

level-headed *adj* calm and sensible

lever ❶ *n* **1** a handle used to operate machinery **2** a bar used to move a heavy object or to prise something open **3** a rigid bar that turns on a fixed support (fulcrum) to transfer effort and motion, for instance to move a load **4** a means of exerting pressure in order to achieve an aim: *using the hostages as a lever to gain concessions from the west* ▹*vb* **5** to open or move with a lever

WORD ORIGIN Latin *levare* to raise

leverage ❶ *n* **1** the mechanical advantage gained by using a lever **2** the ability to influence people or events: *information gives leverage*

leveraged buyout *n* a takeover bid in which a small company uses its assets, and those of the target company, to raise the loans required to finance the takeover

leveret (lev-ver-it) *n* a young hare

WORD ORIGIN Latin *lepus* hare

Leverhulme *n* **William Hesketh,** 1st Viscount. 1851–1925, English soap manufacturer and philanthropist, who founded (1881) the model industrial town Port Sunlight

l

THESAURUS

let off *(informal)* **1,2 = excuse**, release, discharge, pardon, spare, forgive, exempt, dispense, exonerate, absolve, grant an amnesty to

letter *n* **1 = message**, line, answer, note, reply, communication, dispatch, acknowledgment, billet *(archaic)*, missive, epistle, e-mail **2 = character**, mark, sign, symbol

let up 1 = stop, diminish, decrease, subside, relax, ease (up), moderate, lessen, abate, slacken

level *adj* **1, 2 = horizontal**, even, flat, plane, smooth, uniform, as flat as a pancake **OPPOSITE:** slanted **3 = equal**, in line, aligned, balanced, on a line, at the same height **4 = even**, tied, equal, drawn, neck and neck, all square, level pegging ▹*vb* **8** (sometimes foll. by *off*) **= flatten**, plane, smooth, make flat, even off *or* out **9 = equalize**, balance, even up **10, 11, 12 = direct**, point, turn, train, aim, focus, beam **13 = destroy**, devastate, wreck, demolish, flatten, knock down, pull down, tear down, bulldoze, raze, lay waste to, kennet *(Austral slang)*, jeff *(Austral slang)* **OPPOSITE:** build ▹*n* **16, 17 = position**, standard, degree, grade, standing, stage, rank, status **22 on the level** *(informal)* **= honest**, genuine, sincere, open, straight, fair, square, straightforward, up front *(slang)*, dinkum *(Austral & NZ informal)*, above board

lever *n* **1, 2, 3 = handle**, bar, crowbar, jemmy, handspike ▹*vb* **5 = prise**, move, force, raise, pry (US), jemmy

leverage *n* **1 = force**, hold, pull, strength, grip, grasp **2 = influence**, authority, pull *(informal)*, weight, rank, clout *(informal)*, purchasing power, ascendancy

DICTIONARY

Leverrier *n* **Urbain Jean Joseph** 1811–77, French astronomer: calculated the existence and position of the planet Neptune

Levi[1] *n* **1** *Old Testament* **a** the third son of Jacob and Leah and the ancestor of the tribe of Levi (Genesis 29:34) **b** the priestly tribe descended from this patriarch (Numbers 18:21–24) **2** *new testament* another name for Matthew the apostle

Levi[2] *n* **1 Carlo** 1902–75, Italian physician, painter, and writer. Best known for his novel *Christ Stopped at Eboli* (1947), his other works include *The Watch* (1952) and *Words are Stones* (1958) **2 Primo** 1919–87, Italian novelist. His book *If This is a Man* (1947) relates his experiences in Auschwitz. Other books include *The Periodic Table* (1956) and *The Drowned and the Saved* (1988), published after his suicide

Levi[3] *or* **Levite** *n judaism* a descendant of the tribe of Levi who has certain privileges in the synagogue service

leviathan (lev-vie-ath-an) *n* any huge or powerful thing
WORD ORIGIN Hebrew *liwyāthān*, a Biblical sea monster

Levis *pl n trademark* denim jeans

Lévi-Strauss *n* **Claude** (klod) (1908–2009) French anthropologist, leading exponent of structuralism. His books include *The Elementary Structures of Kinship* (1969), *Totemism* (1962), *The Savage Mind* (1966), *Mythologies* (1964–71), and *Saudades do Brazil* (Memories of Brazil; 1994)

levitate *vb* **-tating, -tated** to rise or cause to rise, suspended, in the air **levitation** *n*
WORD ORIGIN Latin *levis* light

levity *n, pl* **-ties** a frivolous or too light-hearted attitude to serious matters
WORD ORIGIN Latin *levis* light

levy ⊕ (lev-vee) *vb* **levies, levying, levied 1** to impose and collect (a tax, tariff, or fine) **2** to conscript troops for service ▷ *n, pl* **levies 3 a** the imposition and collection of taxes, tariffs, or fines **b** the money so raised **4** troops conscripted for service
WORD ORIGIN Latin *levare* to raise

Lévy-Bruhl *n* **Lucien** 1857–1939, French anthropologist and philosopher, noted for his study of the psychology of primitive peoples

lewd *adj* indecently vulgar; obscene **lewdly** *adv* **lewdness** *n*
WORD ORIGIN Old English *lǣwde* lay, ignorant

lexical *adj* **1** relating to the vocabulary of a language **2** relating to a lexicon **lexically** *adv*

lexicography *n* the process or profession of compiling dictionaries **lexicographer** *n*

lexicon *n* **1** a dictionary, esp. one of an ancient language such as Greek **2** the vocabulary of a language or of an individual
WORD ORIGIN Greek *lexis* word

ley *n* land temporarily under grass
WORD ORIGIN variant of *lea*

Leyden[1] *n* a variant spelling of **Leiden**

Leyden[2] *n* See **Lucas van Leyden**

Leyden jar (lide-en) *n physics* an early type of capacitor consisting of a glass jar with the lower part of the inside and outside coated with tinfoil
WORD ORIGIN from *Leiden*, city in the Netherlands

LGBT lesbian, gay, bisexual, and transgender

LGV (in Britain) large goods vehicle

Li *chem* lithium

liability ⊕ *n, pl* **-ties 1** someone or something that is a problem or embarrassment **2** the state of being legally responsible **3** (*often pl*) sums of money owed by an organization

liable ⊕ *adj* **1** probable or likely: *weak and liable to give way* **2** commonly suffering a condition: *he's liable to get colds in his chest* **3** legally obliged or responsible; answerable
WORD ORIGIN Old French *lier* to bind

liaise *vb* **-aising, -aised** (usually foll. by *with*) to communicate and maintain contact with

liaison ⊕ *n* **1** communication and cooperative contact between groups **2** a secretive or adulterous sexual relationship
WORD ORIGIN Old French *lier* to bind

liana *n* a woody climbing and twining plant of tropical forests
WORD ORIGIN French

liar ⊕ *n* a person who tells lies

lib *n informal* liberation: used in the name of certain movements: *women's lib; gay lib*

Lib *Brit, Austral & S African politics* Liberal

libation (lie-bay-shun) *n* **a** the pouring out of wine in honour of a deity **b** the wine so poured out
WORD ORIGIN Latin *libare* to pour an offering of drink

Libby *n* **Willard Frank** 1908–80, US chemist, who devised the technique of radiocarbon dating: Nobel prize for chemistry 1960

libel ⊕ *n* **1** *law* the publication of something false which damages a person's reputation **2** any damaging or unflattering representation or statement ▷ *vb* **-belling, -belled** *or US* **-beling, -beled 3** *law* to make or publish a false damaging statement or representation about (a person) **libellous** *or* **libelous** *adj*
WORD ORIGIN Latin *libellus* a little book

liberal ⊕ *adj* **1** having social and political views that favour progress and reform **2** generous in temperament or behaviour **3** tolerant of other people **4** using or existing in large quantities; lavish: *the world's finest gadgetry, in liberal quantities* **5** not rigid; free: *a more liberal interpretation* **6** (of an education) designed to develop general cultural interests and intellectual ability **7 Liberal** of or relating to a Liberal Party ▷ *n* **8** a person who has liberal ideas or opinions **liberalism** *n* **liberally** *adv*
WORD ORIGIN Latin *liber* free

THESAURUS

levy *vb* **1 = impose**, charge, tax, collect, gather, demand, exact ▷ *n* **3a, 3b = tax**, fee, toll, tariff, duty, assessment, excise, imposition, impost, exaction

liability *n* **1 = disadvantage**, burden, drawback, inconvenience, drag, handicap, minus *(informal)*, nuisance, impediment, albatross, hindrance, millstone, encumbrance
2 = responsibility, accountability, culpability, obligation, onus, answerability

liable *adj* **1 = likely**, tending, inclined, disposed, prone, apt **2 = vulnerable**, subject, exposed, prone, susceptible, open, at risk of **3 = responsible**, accountable, amenable, answerable, bound, obligated, chargeable

liaison *n* **1 = contact**, communication, connection, interchange **2 = affair**, romance, intrigue, fling, love affair, amour, entanglement, illicit romance

liar *n* **= falsifier**, storyteller *(informal)*, perjurer, fibber, fabricator, prevaricator

libel *n* **1, 2 = defamation**, slander, misrepresentation, denigration, smear, calumny, vituperation, obloquy, aspersion ▷ *vb* **3 = defame**, smear, slur, blacken, malign, denigrate, revile, vilify, slander, traduce, derogate, calumniate, drag (someone's) name through the mud

liberal *adj* **1a = tolerant**, enlightened, open-minded, permissive, advanced, catholic, humanitarian, right-on *(informal)*, indulgent, easy-going, unbiased, high-minded, broad-minded, unprejudiced, unbigoted, politically correct *or* PC
OPPOSITE: intolerant
1b = progressive, radical, reformist, libertarian, advanced, right-on *(informal)*, forward-looking, humanistic, free-thinking, latitudinarian, politically correct *or* PC **OPPOSITE:** conservative
2 = generous, kind, charitable, extravagant, free-handed, prodigal, altruistic, open-hearted, bountiful, magnanimous, open-handed, unstinting, beneficent, bounteous
OPPOSITE: stingy
4 = abundant, generous, handsome, lavish, ample, rich, plentiful,

DICTIONARY

Liberal Democrat *n* a member or supporter of the Liberal Democrats, a British centrist political party that advocates proportional representation

liberality *n, pl* **-ties** **1** generosity **2** the quality of being broad-minded

liberalize *or* **-ise** *vb* **-izing, -ized** *or* **-ising, -ised** to make (a law) less strict **liberalization** *or* **-isation** *n*

Liberal Party *n* **1** *history* a British non-Socialist political party which advocated progress and reform **2** any similar party in various other countries **3** the main right-wing political party in Australia

liberate ⊙ *vb* **-ating, -ated** **1** to free (someone) from social prejudices or injustices **2** to give liberty to; make free **3** to release (a country) from enemy occupation **liberation** *n* **liberator** *n*

liberated *adj* **1** not bound by traditional sexual and social roles: *a liberated woman* **2** given liberty **3** released from enemy occupation

libertarian *n* **1** a person who believes in freedom of thought and action ▹ *adj* **2** believing in freedom of thought and action

libertine (lib-er-teen) *n* **1** a person who is promiscuous and unscrupulous ▹ *adj* **2** promiscuous and unscrupulous
WORD ORIGIN Latin *libertus* freed

liberty ⊙ *n, pl* **-ties** **1** the freedom to choose, think, and act for oneself **2** the right of unrestricted movement and access; freedom **3** (*often pl*) a social action regarded as being forward or improper **4 at liberty** free or unconfined **5 at liberty to** unrestricted or authorized: *I am not at liberty to divulge his name* **6 take liberties (with)** to be overfamiliar (towards someone)
WORD ORIGIN Latin *libertas*

Libeskind *n* **Daniel** born 1946, US architect, born in Poland. Based in Berlin, he designed the Jewish Museum there (1999), the Imperial War Museum in Manchester (2000), the proposed spiral extension to London's Victoria and Albert Museum, and the "Freedom Tower" that will replace the World Trade Center in New York

libidinous *adj* characterized by excessive sexual desire **libidinously** *adv*

libido (lib-ee-doe) *n, pl* **-dos** **1** *psychoanal* psychic energy from the id **2** sexual urge or desire **libidinal** *adj*
WORD ORIGIN Latin: desire

Libra *n astrol* the seventh sign of the zodiac; the Scales
WORD ORIGIN Latin

librarian *n* a person in charge of or assisting in a library **librarianship** *n*

library *n, pl* **-braries** **1** a room or building where books and other literary materials are kept **2** a collection of literary materials, films, tapes, or records, kept for borrowing or reference **3** the building or institution that houses such a collection **4** a set of books published as a series, often in a similar format **5** *computers* a collection of standard programs, usually stored on disk
WORD ORIGIN Latin *liber* book

libretto *n, pl* **-tos** *or* **-ti** a text written for an opera **librettist** *n*
WORD ORIGIN Italian: little book

Libyan *adj* **1** from Libya ▹ *n* **2** a person from Libya

lice *n* ▸ the plural of **louse**

licence ⊙ *or US* **license** *n* **1** a document giving official permission to do, use, or own something **2** formal permission or exemption **3** intentional disregard of conventional rules to achieve a certain effect: *poetic licence* **4** excessive freedom
WORD ORIGIN Latin *licet* it is allowed

license ⊙ *vb* **-censing, -censed** **1** to grant a licence to or for **2** to give permission to or for **licensable** *adj*

licensee *n* a person who holds a licence, esp. one to sell alcoholic drink

license plate *n* ▸ the US and Canadian term for **numberplate**

licentiate *n* a person who holds a certificate of competence to practise a certain profession

licentious *adj* sexually unrestrained or promiscuous **licentiousness** *n*
WORD ORIGIN Latin *licentia* licence

lichee *n* ▸ same as **lychee**

lichen *n* any of various small mossy plants that grow in patches on tree trunks, bare ground, rocks, and stone walls
WORD ORIGIN Greek *leikhein* to lick

lich gate *n* ▸ same as **lych gate**

Lichtenstein *n* **Roy** 1923–97, US pop artist

licit *adj formal* lawful; permitted
WORD ORIGIN Latin *licere* to be permitted

lick ⊙ *vb* **1** to pass the tongue over in order to taste, wet, or clean **2** to flicker over or round (something): *flames licked the gutters* **3** *informal* **a** to defeat **b** to thrash **4 lick into shape** to put into a satisfactory condition **5 lick one's wounds** to retire after a defeat ▹ *n* **6** an instance of passing the tongue over something **7** a small amount: *a lick of paint* **8** *informal* a blow **9** *informal* a fast pace: *a pulsating rhythm taken at a lick* **10 a lick and a promise** something hastily done, esp. a hurried wash
WORD ORIGIN Old English *liccian*

licorice *n US & Canad* ▸ same as **liquorice**

lid *n* **1** a removable or hinged cover: *a saucepan lid* **2** ▸ short for **eyelid** **3 put the (tin) lid on** *informal* to put an end to **lidded** *adj*
WORD ORIGIN Old English *hlid*

Liddell Hart *n* Sir **Basil Henry** 1895–1970, British military strategist and historian: he advocated the development of mechanized warfare before World War II

lido (lee-doe) *n, pl* **-dos** *Brit* an open-air swimming pool or a part of a beach used by the public for swimming and sunbathing

L

THESAURUS

copious, bountiful, profuse, munificent **OPPOSITE:** limited

liberate *vb* **2, 3 = free**, release, rescue, save, deliver, discharge, redeem, let out, set free, let loose, untie, emancipate, unchain, unbind, manumit **OPPOSITE:** imprison

liberty *n* **1 = independence**, sovereignty, liberation, autonomy, immunity, self-determination, emancipation, self-government, self-rule
6 take liberties (*with*) **= not show enough respect**, show disrespect, act presumptuously, behave too familiarly, behave impertinently

licence *n* **1 = certificate**, document, permit, charter, warrant
2 = permission, the right, authority, leave, sanction, liberty, privilege, immunity, entitlement, exemption, prerogative, authorization, dispensation, a free hand, carte blanche, blank cheque
OPPOSITE: denial
3 = freedom, creativity, latitude, independence, liberty, deviation, leeway, free rein, looseness
OPPOSITE: restraint
4 = laxity, abandon, disorder, excess, indulgence, anarchy, lawlessness, impropriety, irresponsibility, profligacy, licentiousness, unruliness, immoderation
OPPOSITE: moderation

license *vb* **1, 2 = permit**, commission, enable, sanction, allow, entitle, warrant, authorize, empower, certify, accredit, give a blank cheque to **OPPOSITE:** forbid

lick *vb* **1 = taste**, lap, tongue, touch, wash, brush **2 = flicker**, touch, flick, dart, ripple, ignite, play over, kindle
3a (*informal*) **= beat**, defeat, overcome, best, top, stuff (*slang*), tank (*slang*), undo, rout, excel, surpass, outstrip, outdo, trounce, clobber (*slang*), vanquish, run rings around (*informal*), wipe the floor with (*informal*), blow out of the water (*slang*) ▹ *n* **7 = dab**, little (bit), touch, taste, sample, stroke, brush, speck **9** (*informal*) **= pace**, rate, speed, clip

DICTIONARY

WORD ORIGIN *Lido*, island bathing beach near Venice

lie[1] ❶ *vb* **lying, lied 1** to speak untruthfully with the intention of deceiving **2** to convey a false impression: *the camera cannot lie* ▷ *n* **3** an untrue statement deliberately used to mislead **4** something that is deliberately intended to deceive **5 give the lie to a** to disprove **b** to accuse of lying

WORD ORIGIN Old English *lyge*, *lēogan*

lie[2] ❶ *vb* **lying, lay, lain 1** (often foll. by *down*) to place oneself or be in a horizontal position **2** to be situated: *I left the money lying on the table; Nepal became the only country lying between China and India* **3** to be and remain (in a particular state or condition): *others of their species lie asleep* **4** to stretch or extend: *an enormous task lies ahead* **5** (usually foll. by *in*) to exist or comprise: *her charm lies in her inner beauty* **6** (foll. by *with*) to rest (with): *the fault lies with them* ▷ *n* **7** the manner, place, or style in which something is situated **8** an animal's lair **9 lie of the land** the way in which a situation is developing ▸ See also **lie down, lie in**

WORD ORIGIN Old English *licgan*

Lie *n* **Trygve Halvdan** 1896–1968, Norwegian statesman; first secretary-general of the United Nations (1946–52)

Liebfraumilch (leeb-frow-milk) *n* a sweet white wine from the German Rhine

WORD ORIGIN German: from *Liebfrau* the Virgin Mary + *Milch* milk

lied (leed) *n, pl* **lieder** *music* a musical setting for solo voice and piano of a romantic or lyrical poem

WORD ORIGIN German: song

lie detector *n informal* a device used to measure any increase in blood pressure, pulse rate, etc. of someone being questioned, which is thought to indicate that the person is lying

lie down *vb* **1** to place oneself or be in a horizontal position in order to rest **2** to yield to: *never take any attack on your candidate lying down* ▷ *n* **lie-down 3** a rest

liege (leej) *adj* **1** (of a lord) owed feudal allegiance: *their liege lord* **2** (of a vassal or subject) owing feudal allegiance: *a liege subject* **3** faithful; loyal ▷ *n* **4** a liege lord **5** a subject

WORD ORIGIN Old French *lige*

lie in *vb* **1** to remain in bed late into the morning ▷ *n* **lie-in 2** a long stay in bed in the morning

lien *n law* a right to retain possession of someone else's property until a debt is paid

WORD ORIGIN Latin *ligamen* bond

lieu (lyew) *n* **in lieu of** instead of

WORD ORIGIN Old French

Lieut. lieutenant

lieutenant (lef-ten-ant, loo-ten-ant) *n* **1** a junior officer in the army, navy, or the US police force **2** a person who acts as principal assistant

lieutenancy *n*

WORD ORIGIN Old French, literally: place-holding

lieutenant colonel *n* an officer in an army, air force, or marine corps immediately junior to a colonel

lieutenant commander *n* an officer in a navy immediately junior to a commander

lieutenant general *n* a senior officer in an army, air force, or marine corps

lieutenant governor *n* **1** a deputy governor **2** (in Canada) the representative of the Crown in a province

Lifar *n* **Serge** 1905–86, Russian ballet dancer and choreographer: ballet master at the Paris Opera Ballet (1932–58). His ballets include *Prométhée* (1929), *Icare* (1935), and *Phèdre* (1950)

life ❶ *n, pl* **lives 1** the state or quality that identifies living beings, characterized chiefly by growth, reproduction, and response to stimuli **2** the period between birth and death or between birth and the present time **3** a living person or being: *riots which claimed 22 lives* **4** the remainder or extent of one's life: *with that lady for the rest of her life* **5** the process of living: *rituals gave his life stability* **6** *informal* a sentence of life imprisonment, usually approximating to fifteen years **7** a characteristic state or mode of existence: *country life is best* **8** the length of time that something is active or functioning: *the life of a battery* **9** a present condition or mode of existence: *they are leading a joyous life* **10** a biography **11** the sum or course of human events and activities **12** liveliness or high spirits: *full of life* **13** a source of strength, animation, or vitality: *he was the life of the show* **14** all living things collectively: *there is no life on Mars; marine life* **15 a matter of life and death** a matter of extreme urgency **16 as large as life** *informal* real and living **17 not on your life** *informal* certainly not **18 to the life** (of a copy of a painting or drawing) resembling the original exactly **19 true to life** faithful to reality

WORD ORIGIN Old English *līf*

life assurance *n* insurance that provides for a sum of money to be paid to the insured person at a certain age or to the spouse or children on the death of the insured. Also called: **life insurance**

life belt *n* an inflatable ring used to keep a person afloat when in danger of drowning

lifeblood *n* **1** the blood vital to life **2** something that is essential for existence, development, or success

lifeboat *n* a boat used for rescuing people at sea

life buoy *n* a buoyant device to keep people afloat in an emergency

life coach *n* a person whose job it is to improve the quality of his or her client's life, by offering advice on professional and personal matters, such as careers, health, personal relationships, etc.

life cycle *n* the series of changes occurring in each generation of an animal or plant

lifeguard *n* a person at a beach or pool whose job is to rescue people in danger of drowning

life jacket *n* an inflatable sleeveless jacket worn to keep a person afloat when in danger of drowning

lifeless *adj* **1** inanimate; dead **2** lacking liveliness or animation **3** unconscious

lifelike *adj* closely resembling or representing life

lifeline *n* **1** a single means of contact or support on which a person or an area relies **2** a rope used for life-saving

THESAURUS

lie[1] *vb* **1, 2 = fib**, fabricate, invent, misrepresent, falsify, tell a lie, prevaricate, perjure, not tell the truth, equivocate, dissimulate, tell untruths, not speak the truth, say something untrue, forswear yourself ▷ *n* **3, 4 = falsehood**, deceit, fabrication, fib, fiction, invention, deception, untruth, porky *(Brit slang)*, pork pie *(Brit slang)*, white lie, falsification, prevarication, falsity, mendacity **5a give the lie to = disprove**, expose, discredit, contradict, refute, negate, invalidate, rebut, make a nonsense of, prove false, controvert, confute

lie[2] *vb* **1** (often foll. by *down*) **= recline**, rest, lounge, couch, sprawl, stretch out, be prone, loll, repose, be prostrate, be supine, be recumbent **2a = be placed**, be, rest, exist, extend, be situated **2b = be situated**, sit, be located, be positioned

life *n* **1 = being**, existence, breath, entity, vitality, animation, viability, sentience **2, 4 = existence**, being, lifetime, time, days, course, span, duration, continuance **5, 7, 9 = way of life**, situation, conduct, behaviour, life style **10 = biography**, story, history, career, profile, confessions, autobiography, memoirs, life story **12 = liveliness**, activity, energy, spirit, go *(informal)*, pep, sparkle, vitality, animation, vigour, verve, zest, high spirits, get-up-and-go *(informal)*, oomph *(informal)*, brio, vivacity

DICTIONARY

lifelong ❶ *adj* lasting for a lifetime
life peer *n Brit* a peer whose title ceases at his or her death
life preserver *n* **1** *Brit* a bludgeon kept for self-defence **2** *US & Canad* a life belt or life jacket
lifer *n informal* a prisoner sentenced to life imprisonment
life raft *n* a raft for emergency use at sea
life-saver *n* **1** ▸same as **lifeguard** **2** *informal* a person or thing that gives help in time of need **life-saving** *adj, n*
life science *n* any of the sciences concerned with the structure and behaviour of living organisms, such as biology, botany, or zoology
life-size *or* **life-sized** *adj* representing actual size
lifestyle *n* a set of attitudes, habits, and possessions regarded as typical of a particular group or an individual
life-support *adj* (of equipment or treatment) necessary to sustain life
lifetime ❶ *n* **1** the length of time a person is alive **2** **of a lifetime** (of an opportunity or experience) the most important or memorable
lift ❶ *vb* **1** to rise or raise upwards to a higher place: *the breakdown truck was lifting the lorry* **2** to move upwards: *he slowly lifted his hand* **3** to raise in status or estimation: *lifted from poverty* **4** to revoke or cancel: *the government lifted its restrictions on imported beef* **5** to remove (plants or underground crops) from the ground for harvesting **6** to disappear or disperse: *the tension lifted* **7** *informal* to plagiarize (music or writing) ▹*n* **8 a** a compartment raised or lowered in a vertical shaft to transport people or goods to another floor in a building **b** ▸see **chairlift, ski lift** **9** a ride in a car or other vehicle as a passenger **10** a rise in morale or feeling of cheerfulness **11** the act of lifting **12** the force that lifts airborne objects **WORD ORIGIN** from Old Norse
liftoff *n* the initial movement of a rocket as it leaves its launch pad
lig *Brit slang n* **1** (esp. in the media) a function with free entertainment and refreshments ▹*vb* **ligging, ligged** **2** to attend such a function **ligger** *n* **ligging** *n*
ligament *n anat* a band of tough tissue that connects various bones or cartilage
WORD ORIGIN Latin *ligare* to bind
ligature *n* **1** a link, bond, or tie **2** *printing* a character of two or more joined letters, such as ff **3** *music* a slur or the group of notes connected by it ▹*vb* **-turing, -tured** **4** to bind with a ligature
WORD ORIGIN Latin *ligare* to bind
Ligeti *n* **György** 1923–2006, Hungarian composer, resident in Vienna. His works, noted for their experimentalism, include *Atmospheres* (1961) for orchestra, *Volumina* (1962) for organ, and a requiem mass (1965)
light[1] ❶ *n* **1** the natural medium, electromagnetic radiation, that makes sight possible **2** anything that illuminates, such as a lamp or candle **3** ▸see **traffic light** **4** a particular type of light: *dim yellow light* **5 a** daylight **b** daybreak; dawn **6** anything that lets in light, such as a window **7** an aspect or view: *we have seen the world in a new light* **8** mental understanding or spiritual insight: *suddenly he saw the light* **9** an outstanding person: *a leading light of the movement* **10** brightness of countenance, esp. a sparkle in the eyes **11 a** something that ignites, such as a spark or flame **b** something used for igniting, such as a match **12** ▸see **lighthouse** **13** **come to light** to become known or visible **14** **in (the) light of** taking into account **15** **see the light** to understand **16** **see the light (of day)** **a** to come into being **b** to come to public notice ▹*adj* **17** full of light **18** (of a colour) pale: *light blue* ▹*vb* **lighting, lighted** *or* **lit** **19** to ignite **20** (often foll. by *up*) to illuminate or cause to illuminate **21** to guide by light ▸See also **light up** > **lightish** *adj*
WORD ORIGIN Old English *lēoht*
light[2] ❶ *adj* **1** not heavy; weighing relatively little **2** relatively low in density, strength, amount, degree, etc.: *light oil; light alloy* **3** lacking sufficient weight **4** not bulky or clumsy: *light bedclothes* **5** not serious or difficult to understand; entertaining: *light music* **6** graceful or agile: *light movements* **7** without strong emphasis or serious meaning: *he gazed about with a light inattentive smile* **8** easily digested: *a light lunch* **9** relatively low in alcohol: *a light wine* **10** without burdens, difficulties, or problems: *a light heart lives longest* **11** dizzy or unclear: *a light head* **12** (of bread or cake) spongy or well risen **13 a** (of transport) designed to carry light loads **b** (of a vessel, aircraft, or other transport) not loaded **14** carrying light arms or equipment: *light infantry* **15** (of an industry) producing small consumer goods using light machinery **16** **make light of** to treat as insignificant or unimportant ▹*adv* **17** with little equipment or luggage: *travelling light* ▹*vb* **lighting, lighted** *or* **lit** **18** (esp. of birds) to settle or land after flight **19** (foll. by *on* or *upon*) to discover by chance ▸See also **lights** > **lightish** *adj* **lightly** *adv* **lightness** *n*
WORD ORIGIN Old English *lēoht*
light bulb *n* a hollow rounded glass fitting containing a gas and a thin

l

THESAURUS

lifelong *adj* **= long-lasting**, enduring, lasting, permanent, constant, lifetime, for life, persistent, long-standing, perennial, deep-rooted, for all your life
lifetime *n* **1 = existence**, time, day(s), course, period, span, life span, your natural life, all your born days
lift *vb* **1, 2 = raise**, pick up, hoist, draw up, elevate, uplift, heave up, buoy up, raise high, bear aloft, upheave, upraise **OPPOSITE:** lower **4 = revoke**, end, remove, withdraw, stop, relax, cancel, terminate, rescind, annul, countermand **OPPOSITE:** impose **6 = disappear**, clear, vanish, disperse, dissipate, rise, be dispelled ▹*n* **8a = elevator** *(chiefly US)*, hoist, paternoster **9 = ride**, run, drive, transport, hitch *(informal)*, car ride **10 = boost**, encouragement, stimulus, reassurance, uplift, pick-me-up, fillip, shot in the arm *(informal)*, gee-up **OPPOSITE:** blow
light[1] *n* **1 = brightness**, illumination, luminosity, luminescence, ray of light, flash of light, shining, glow, blaze, sparkle, glare, gleam, brilliance, glint, lustre, radiance, incandescence, phosphorescence, scintillation, effulgence, lambency, refulgence **OPPOSITE:** dark **2 = lamp**, bulb, torch, candle, flare, beacon, lighthouse, lantern, taper **7 = aspect**, approach, attitude, context, angle, point of view, interpretation, viewpoint, slant, standpoint, vantage point **11a, 11b = match**, spark, flame, lighter ▹*adj* **17 = bright**, brilliant, shining, glowing, sunny, illuminated, luminous, well-lighted, well-lit, lustrous, aglow, well-illuminated **OPPOSITE:** dark **18 = pale**, fair, faded, blonde, blond, bleached, pastel, light-coloured, whitish, light-toned, light-hued **OPPOSITE:** dark ▹*vb* **19 = ignite**, inflame, fire, torch, kindle, touch off, set alight, set a match to **OPPOSITE:** put out **20** (often foll. by *up*) **= illuminate**, light up, brighten, lighten, put on, turn on, clarify, switch on, floodlight, irradiate, illumine, flood with light **OPPOSITE:** darken
light[2] *adj* **1, 4 = insubstantial**, thin, delicate, lightweight, easy, slight, portable, buoyant, airy, flimsy, underweight, not heavy, transportable, lightsome, imponderous **OPPOSITE:** heavy **2a = weak**, soft, gentle, moderate, slight, mild, faint, indistinct **OPPOSITE:** strong

DICTIONARY

metal filament that gives out light when an electric current is passed through it

lighten[1] ❶ *vb* **1** to make less dark **2** to shine; glow **3** (of lightning) to flash

lighten[2] ❶ *vb* **1** to make or become less heavy **2** to make or become less burdensome **3** to make or become more cheerful or lively

lighter[1] *n* a small portable device for lighting cigarettes, etc.

lighter[2] *n* a flat-bottomed barge used in loading or unloading a ship
WORD ORIGIN probably from Middle Dutch

light-fingered *adj* skilful at thieving, esp. by picking pockets

light flyweight *n* a professional boxer weighing up to 108 pounds (49 kg) or an amateur boxer weighing up to 48 kg

Lightfoot *n* **Gordon** born 1938, Canadian singer and short songwriter; his recordings include 'If You Could Read My Mind' (1970), *Dream Street Rose* (1980) and *Harmony* (2004)

light-footed *adj* having a light tread

light-headed *adj* giddy; feeling faint

light-hearted *adj* cheerful or carefree in mood or disposition **light-heartedly** *adv*

light heavyweight *n* a professional boxer weighing up to 175 pounds (79.5 kg) or an amateur weighing up to 81 kg

lighthouse *n* a tower with a light to guide ships and warn of obstructions

lighting *n* **1** the apparatus for and design of artificial light effects to a stage, film, or television set **2** the act or quality of illumination

lighting-up time *n* the time when vehicles are required by law to have their lights on

light middleweight *n* a professional boxer weighing up to 154 pounds (70 kg) or an amateur boxer weighing up to 71 kg

lightning *n* **1** a flash of light in the sky caused by a discharge of electricity ▷*adj* **2** fast and sudden: *a lightning attack*
WORD ORIGIN variant of *lightening*

lightning conductor *or* **rod** *n* a metal rod attached to the highest part of a building to divert lightning safely to earth

light pen *n* a penlike photoelectric device that in conjunction with a computer can be used to draw lines or identify symbols on a VDU screen

light pollution *n* the glow from the lighting in streets and buildings that obscures the night sky

light rail *n* a transport system using small trains or trams

lights *pl n* the lungs of sheep, bullocks, and pigs, used for feeding pets
WORD ORIGIN because of the light weight of the lungs

lightship *n* a moored ship equipped as a lighthouse

lights out *n* the time when residents of an institution are expected to retire to bed

light up *vb* **1** to illuminate **2** to make or become cheerful or animated: *their faces lit up and one dug the other in the ribs* **3** to light a cigarette or pipe

lightweight ❶ *adj* **1** not serious **2** of relatively light weight ▷*n* **3** *informal* a person of little importance or influence. **4** a person or animal of relatively light weight **5** a professional boxer weighing up to 135 pounds (61 kg) or an amateur weighing up to 60 kg

light welterweight *n* a professional or an amateur boxer weighing up to 140 pounds (63.5 kg)

light year *n astron* the distance travelled by light in one mean solar year, i.e. 9.4607×10^{15} metres

ligneous *adj* of or like wood
WORD ORIGIN Latin *lignum* wood

lignite (lig-nite) *n* a brown sedimentary rock with a woody texture: used as a fuel

lignum vitae (lig-num vite-ee) *n* a tropical American tree with heavy resinous wood
WORD ORIGIN Late Latin, literally: wood of life

like[1] ❶ *adj* **1** resembling ▷*prep* **2** in the manner of; similar to: *she was like a child; it looks like a traffic cone* **3** such as: *a modern material, like carbon fibre* **4** characteristic of ▷*adv* **5** in the manner of: *cheering like mad* **6** *dialect* likely ▷*conj* **7** *not standard* as though; as if: *I don't want to make it seem like I had this bad childhood* **8** in the same way that: *she doesn't dance like you do* ▷*n* **9** the equal or counterpart of a person or thing **10 the like** similar things: *magic, supernormal powers and the like* **11 the likes** *or* **like of** people or things similar to (someone or something specified): *the theatre was not meant for the likes of him*
WORD ORIGIN Old English *gelīc*

like[2] ❶ *vb* **liking, liked 1** to find enjoyable **2** to be fond of **3** to prefer or choose: *I'd like to go home* **4** to feel disposed or inclined; choose; wish: *do as you like* ▷*n* **5** (*usually pl*) a favourable feeling, desire, or preference: *tell me your likes and dislikes* **likeable** *or* **likable** *adj*
WORD ORIGIN Old English *līcian*

likelihood ❶ *n* chance; probability

likely ❶ *adj* **1** tending or inclined: *likely to win* **2** probable: *the likely effects of the tunnel* **3** appropriate for a purpose or activity: *a likely candidate* ▷*adv* **4** probably or presumably **5 not likely** *informal* definitely not
WORD ORIGIN Old Norse *līkligr*

like-minded *adj* sharing similar opinions

liken ❶ *vb* to compare

likeness *n* **1** resemblance **2** portrait **3** an imitative appearance;

THESAURUS

2b = insignificant, small, minute, tiny, slight, petty, trivial, trifling, inconsequential, inconsiderable, unsubstantial **OPPOSITE:** serious
5 = light-hearted, pleasing, funny, entertaining, amusing, diverting, witty, trivial, superficial, humorous, gay, trifling, frivolous, unserious **OPPOSITE:** serious
6 = nimble, graceful, airy, deft, agile, sprightly, lithe, limber, lissom, light-footed, sylphlike **OPPOSITE:** clumsy
8 = digestible, small, restricted, modest, frugal, not rich, not heavy **OPPOSITE:** substantial

lighten[1] *vb* **1, 2 = brighten**, flash, shine, illuminate, gleam, light up, irradiate, become light, make bright

lighten[2] *vb* **3a = ease**, relieve, alleviate, allay, reduce, facilitate, lessen, mitigate, assuage **OPPOSITE:** intensify
3b = cheer, lift, revive, brighten, hearten, perk up, buoy up, gladden, elate **OPPOSITE:** depress

lightweight *adj* **1 = unimportant**, shallow, trivial, insignificant, slight, petty, worthless, trifling, flimsy, paltry, inconsequential, undemanding, insubstantial, nickel-and-dime (*US slang*), of no account **OPPOSITE:** significant
2 = thin, fine, delicate, sheer, flimsy, gossamer, diaphanous, filmy, unsubstantial

like[1] *adj* **1 = similar to**, same as, allied to, equivalent to, parallel to, resembling, identical to, alike, corresponding to, comparable to, akin to, approximating, analogous to, cognate to **OPPOSITE:** different

like[2] *vb* **1, 2 = enjoy**, love, adore (*informal*), delight in, go for, dig (*slang*), relish, savour, revel in, be fond of, be keen on, be partial to, have a preference for, have a weakness for **OPPOSITE:** dislike
3, 4 = wish, want, choose, prefer, desire, select, fancy, care, feel inclined

likelihood *n* **= probability**, chance, possibility, prospect, liability, good chance, strong possibility, reasonableness, likeliness

likely *adj* **1 = inclined**, disposed, prone, liable, tending, apt **2 = probable**, expected, anticipated, odds-on, on the cards, to be expected

liken *vb* **= compare**, match, relate, parallel, equate, juxtapose, mention

semblance: *in the likeness of a dragon*
likewise ❶ *adv* **1** in addition; also **2** similarly
liking ❶ *n* **1** fondness **2** what one likes or prefers: *if it's not to your liking, do let me know*
lilac *n* **1** a small tree with large sprays of purple or white sweet-smelling flowers ▷*adj* **2** pale purple
WORD ORIGIN Persian *nīlak* bluish
Lilburn *n* **Douglas** (**Gordon**) 1915–2001, New Zealand composer; noted esp. for his pioneering use of electronic music in combination with more traditional orchestration
Lilburne *n* **John** ?1614–57, English Puritan pamphleteer and leader of the Levellers, a radical group prominent during the Civil War
Lilienthal *n* **Otto** 1848–96, German aeronautical engineer, a pioneer of glider design
Liliuokalani *n* **Lydia Kamekeha** 1838–1917, queen and last sovereign of the Hawaiian Islands (1891–95)
Lillee *n* **Dennis** (**Keith**) born 1949, Australian cricketer who, by the end of the 1982–83 season, had taken what was then the world record total of 355 wickets in 65 tests
Lilliputian (lil-lip-pew-shun) *n* **1** a tiny person or being ▷*adj* **2** tiny; very small
WORD ORIGIN from *Lilliput*, an imaginary country of tiny people in Swift's *Gulliver's Travels*
Lilo *n, pl* **-los** *trademark* a type of inflatable plastic mattress
lilt *n* **1** a pleasing musical quality in a speaking voice **2** (in music) a jaunty rhythm **3** a graceful rhythmic motion ▷*vb* **4** (of a voice, tune, or song) to rise and fall in a pleasant way **5** to move gracefully and rhythmically **lilting** *adj*
WORD ORIGIN origin unknown
lily *n, pl* **lilies 1** a perennial plant, such as the tiger lily, with scaly bulbs and showy white or coloured flowers **2** a water lily
WORD ORIGIN Latin *lilium*
lily-livered *adj old-fashioned* cowardly
lily of the valley *n, pl* **lilies of the valley** a small plant with spikes of sweet-smelling white bell-shaped flowers
limb[1] ❶ *n* **1** an arm, leg, or wing **2** any of the main branches of a tree **3 out on a limb a** in a precarious or questionable position **b** *Brit & NZ* isolated, esp. because of unpopular opinions **limbless** *adj*
WORD ORIGIN Old English *lim*
limb[2] *n* the apparent outer edge of the sun, a moon, or a planet
WORD ORIGIN Latin *limbus* edge
limber[1] *adj* **1** pliant; supple **2** able to move or bend the body freely; agile
WORD ORIGIN origin unknown
limber[2] *n* **1** part of a gun carriage, consisting of an axle, pole, and two wheels ▷*vb* **2** to attach the limber (to a gun)
WORD ORIGIN Middle English *lymour* shaft of a gun carriage
limber up *vb* to loosen stiff muscles by exercise
limbo[1] *n, pl* **-bos 1** (*often cap*) *RC church* (formerly) the supposed region intermediate between heaven and hell for the unbaptized **2 in limbo** not knowing the result or next stage of something and powerless to influence it
WORD ORIGIN Medieval Latin *in limbo* on the border (of hell)
limbo[2] *n, pl* **-bos** a West Indian dance in which dancers lean backwards and pass under a horizontal bar which is gradually lowered
WORD ORIGIN origin unknown
Limburg[1] *n* **1** a medieval duchy of W Europe: divided between the Netherlands and Belgium in 1839 **2** a province of the SE Netherlands: contains a coalfield and industrial centres. Capital: Maastricht. Pop: 1 142 000 (2003 est). Area: 2253 sq km (809 sq miles) **3** a province of NE Belgium: contains the industrial regions of the Kempen coalfield. Capital: Hasselt. Pop: 805 786 (2004 est). Area: 2422 sq km (935 sq miles). French name: **Limbourg**
Limburg[2] *or* **Limbourg** *n* **de** active ?1400–?1416, a Dutch family of manuscript illuminators. The three brothers Pol, Herman, and Jehanequin are best known for illustrating the *Très Riches Heures du Duc de Berry*, one of the finest examples of the International Gothic style
lime[1] *n* **1** *agriculture* calcium hydroxide spread as a dressing on acidic land ▷*vb* **liming, limed 2** to spread a calcium compound upon (land)
WORD ORIGIN Old English *līm*
lime[2] *n* the green oval fruit of a small Asian citrus tree with acid fleshy pulp rich in vitamin C
WORD ORIGIN Arabic *līmah*
lime[3] *n* a European linden tree planted for ornament
WORD ORIGIN Old English *lind* linden
lime-green *adj* light yellowish-green
limekiln *n* a kiln in which calcium carbonate is burned to produce quicklime
limelight ❶ *n* **1 the limelight** glare of publicity: *this issue will remain in the limelight* **2 a** a type of lamp, formerly used in stage lighting, in which lime is heated to white heat **b** brilliant white light produced in this way
limerick (lim-mer-ik) *n* a form of comic verse consisting of five lines
WORD ORIGIN allegedly from *will you come up to Limerick?* a refrain sung between nonsense verses at a party
limestone *n* rock consisting mainly of calcium carbonate: used as a building stone and in making cement
limey *n US, Canad & Austral slang* **1** a British person **2** a British sailor or ship
WORD ORIGIN from *lime-juicer*, because British sailors drank lime juice as a protection against scurvy
limit ❶ *n* **1** (*sometimes pl*) the ultimate extent or amount of something: *each soloist was stretched to his or her limit by the demands of the vocal writing* **2** (*often pl*) the boundary of a specific area: *beyond the city limits* **3** the largest quantity or amount allowed **4 the limit** *informal* a person or thing that is intolerably exasperating ▷*vb* **-iting, -ited 5** to restrict **limitable** *adj*
WORD ORIGIN Latin *limes* boundary
limitation ❶ *n* **1** a restriction or controlling of quantity, quality, or achievement **2 limitations** the limit or extent of an ability to achieve something: *learn your own limitations*

THESAURUS

in the same breath, set beside
likewise *adv* **2 = similarly**, the same, in the same way, in similar fashion, in like manner
liking *n* **1, 2 = fondness**, love, taste, desire, bent, stomach, attraction, weakness, tendency, preference, bias, affection, appreciation, inclination, thirst, affinity, penchant, propensity, soft spot, predilection, partiality, proneness
OPPOSITE: dislike
limb[1] *n* **1 = part**, member, arm, leg, wing, extension, extremity, appendage **2 = branch**, spur, projection, offshoot, bough
limelight *n* **1 = publicity**, recognition, fame, the spotlight, attention, prominence, stardom, public eye, public notice, glare of publicity
limit *n* **1** (sometimes *pl*) **= end**, bound, ultimate, deadline, utmost, breaking point, termination, extremity, greatest extent, the bitter end, end point, cutoff point, furthest bound **2** (often *pl*) **= boundary**, end, edge, border, extent, pale, confines, frontier, precinct, perimeter, periphery ▷*vb* **5 = restrict**, control, check, fix, bound, confine, specify, curb, restrain, ration, hinder, circumscribe, hem in, demarcate, delimit, put a brake on, keep within limits, straiten
limitation *n* **1 = restriction**, control, check, block, curb, restraint, constraint, obstruction, impediment
limited *adj* **1, 3 = restricted**, controlled, fixed, defined, checked, bounded, confined, curbed, hampered, constrained, finite, circumscribed
OPPOSITE: unlimited

DICTIONARY

limited ● *adj* **1** having a limit; restricted **2** without fullness or scope; narrow **3** (of governing powers or sovereignty) restricted by a constitution, laws, or an assembly: *limited government* **4** *Brit & NZ* (of a business enterprise) owned by shareholders whose liability for the enterprise's debts is restricted

limited edition *n* an edition of something, such as a book, which has been restricted to a particular number of copies

limn *vb old-fashioned* to represent in drawing or painting
WORD ORIGIN Latin *inluminare* to brighten

limousine *n* any large luxurious car
WORD ORIGIN French, literally: cloak

limp[1] ● *vb* **1** to walk with an uneven step, esp. with a weak or injured leg **2** to advance in a labouring or faltering manner ▷ *n* **3** an uneven walk or progress **limping** *adj, n*
WORD ORIGIN Old English *lempheallt* lame

limp[2] ● *adj* **1** lacking firmness or stiffness **2** not energetic or vital **3** (of the binding of a book) paperback **limply** *adv*
WORD ORIGIN probably Scandinavian

l

limpet *n* **1** a conical shellfish that clings tightly to rocks with its muscular foot ▷ *adj* **2** denoting certain weapons that are magnetically attached to their targets and resist removal: *limpet mines*
WORD ORIGIN Old English *lempedu*

limpid *adj* **1** clear or transparent **2** (of speech or writing) clear and easy to understand **limpidity** *n*
WORD ORIGIN Latin *limpidus* clear

limy[1] *adj* **limier, limiest** of, like, or smeared with birdlime

limy[2] *adj* **limier, limiest** of or tasting of lime (the fruit)

Linacre *n* **Thomas** ?1460–1524, English humanist and physician: founded the Royal College of Physicians (1518)

linage *n* **1** the number of lines in written or printed matter **2** payment according to the number of lines

Lin Biao *n* See **Lin Piao**

linchpin *or* **lynchpin** *n* **1** a pin inserted through an axle to keep a wheel in position **2** an essential person or thing: *she was the linchpin of the experiment*
WORD ORIGIN Old English *lynis*

Lincs Lincolnshire

linctus *n, pl* **-tuses** a soothing syrupy cough mixture
WORD ORIGIN Latin *lingere* to lick

Lind *n* **1 James** 1716–94, British physician. He demonstrated (1754) that citrus fruits can cure and prevent scurvy, a remedy adopted by the British navy in 1796 **2 Jenny,** original name *Johanna Maria Lind Goldschmidt*. 1820–87, Swedish coloratura soprano

Lindemann *n* **Frederick Alexander,** 1st Viscount Cherwell. 1886–1957, British physicist, born in Germany; Churchill's scientific adviser during World War II

linden *n* a large tree with heart-shaped leaves and fragrant yellowish flowers ▸ See also **lime**[3]
WORD ORIGIN Old English *linde* lime tree

Lindsay *n* **1** ▸ See (Sir David) **Lyndsay** **2** (**Nicholas**) **Vachel** 1879–1931, US poet; best known for *General William Booth* (1913) and *The Congo* (1914) **3 Norman Alfred William** 1879–1969, Australian artist and writer

Lindwall *n* **Ray**(**mond Russell**) 1921–96, Australian cricketer. A fast bowler, he played for Australia 61 times between 1946 and 1958

line[1] ● *n* **1** a narrow continuous mark, such as one made by a pencil or brush **2** a thin indented mark or wrinkle on skin **3** a continuous length without breadth **4** a boundary: *the United Nations established a provisional demarcation line* **5** *sport* **a** a white band indicating a division on a field or track **b** a mark or imaginary mark at which a race begins or ends **6** a boundary or limit: *the invidious dividing line between universities and polytechnics* **7** the edge or contour of a shape: *the shoulder line* **8** a wire or string with a particular function: *a long washing line* **9** a telephone connection: *it was a very bad line* **10** a conducting wire, cable, or circuit for electric-power transmission or telecommunications **11** a system of travel or transportation: *a shipping line* **12** a route between two points on a railway **13** a railway track **14** a course or direction of movement: *the birds' line of flight* **15** a course of action or behaviour: *to adopt a more aggressive line* **16** a policy or prescribed way of thinking: *city commentators supported the CBI line* **17** a field of interest or activity: *heroin – that was their line* **18** straight or orderly alignment: *stand in line* **19** one kind of product or article: *a line of smart suits* **20** a row of people or things **21** a row of printed or written words **22** a unit of verse consisting of words in a single row **23** one of a number of narrow horizontal bands forming a television picture **24** *music* any of the five horizontal marks that make up the stave **25** the most forward defensive position: *the front line* **26** a formation of ships or soldiers abreast of each other **27** the combatant forces of certain armies and navies **28** *US & Canad* a queue **29 all along the line** at every stage in a series **30 draw the line (at)** to object (to) or set a limit (on): *I'm not a killer, I draw the line at that* **31 drop someone a line** to send someone a short note **32 get a line on** *informal* to obtain information about **33 in line for** likely to receive: *high achievers are in line for cash bonuses* **34 in line with** conforming to **35 lay** *or* **put on the line a** to speak frankly and directly **b** to risk (one's career or reputation) on something ▷ *vb* **lining, lined 36** to mark with a line or lines **37** to be or form a border: *the square was lined with stalls selling snacks* **38** to place in or form a row, series, or alignment ▸ See also **lines, line-up** > **lined** *adj*
WORD ORIGIN Old French *ligne* + Old English *līn*

line[2] *vb* **lining, lined 1** to attach an inside layer to **2** to cover the inside of: *the works of Shakespeare lined his walls* **3 line one's pockets** to make a lot of money, esp. dishonestly
WORD ORIGIN Latin *linum* flax

lineage (lin-ee-ij) *n* direct descent from an ancestor

lineal *adj* **1** being in a direct line of

THESAURUS

limp[1] *vb* **1 = hobble**, stagger, stumble, shuffle, halt *(archaic)*, hop, falter, shamble, totter, dodder, hirple *(Scot)* ▷ *n* **3 = lameness**, hobble, hirple *(Scot)*

limp[2] *adj* **1 = floppy**, soft, relaxed, loose, flexible, slack, lax, drooping, flabby, limber, pliable, flaccid
OPPOSITE: stiff

line[1] *n* **1, 3 = stroke**, mark, rule, score, bar, band, channel, dash, scratch, slash, underline, streak, stripe, groove **2 = wrinkle**, mark, crease, furrow, crow's foot **4, 6 = boundary**, mark, limit, edge, border, frontier, partition, borderline, demarcation **8 = string**, cable, wire, strand, rope, thread, cord, filament, wisp **14 = trajectory**, way, course, track, channel, direction, route, path, axis **17 = occupation**, work, calling, interest, business, job, area, trade, department, field, career, activity, bag *(slang)*, employment, province, profession, pursuit, forte, vocation, specialization **20 = row**, queue, rank, file, series, column, sequence, convoy, procession, crocodile *(Brit)* ▷ *vb* **33 in line for = due for**, being considered for, a candidate for, shortlisted for, in the running for, on the short list for, next in succession to **36 = mark**, draw, crease, furrow, cut, rule, score, trace, underline, inscribe **37 = border**, edge, bound, fringe, rank, skirt, verge, rim

DICTIONARY

descent from an ancestor **2** of or derived from direct descent **3** linear
WORD ORIGIN Latin *linea* line
lineament *n (often pl)* a facial outline or feature
WORD ORIGIN Latin *lineare* to draw a line
linear (lin-ee-er) *adj* **1** of or in lines **2** of or relating to length **3** represented by a line or lines **linearity** *n*
linear measure *n* a unit or system of units for the measurement of length
lineation (lin-ee-ay-shun) *n* **1** the act of marking with lines **2** an arrangement of lines
line dancing *n* a form of dancing performed by rows of people to country and western music
line drawing *n* a drawing formed with lines only
Lineker *n* **Gary Winston** born 1960, English footballer: played for England (1986–92; captain 1991–92); his clubs included Barcelona (1986–89) and Tottenham Hotspur (1989–92)
linen *n* **1** a hard-wearing fabric woven from the spun fibres of flax **2** articles, such as sheets or tablecloths, made from linen cloth or from cotton
WORD ORIGIN Latin *linum* flax
line of fire *n* the flight path of a bullet discharged from a firearm
line printer *n* an electromechanical device that prints a line of characters at a time: used in printing and in computer systems
liner[1] *n* **1** a passenger ship or aircraft, esp. one that is part of a commercial fleet **2** Also called: **eyeliner** a cosmetic used to outline the eyes
liner[2] *n* something used as a lining: *a plastic bin liner*
lines *pl n* **1** the words of a theatrical role: *shaky sets, fluffed lines, and wooden plots* **2** *informal chiefly Brit* a marriage certificate: *marriage lines* **3** a school punishment of writing out the same sentence or phrase a specified number of times **4** **read between the lines** to find an implicit meaning in addition to the obvious one
linesman *n, pl* **-men** **1** an official who helps the referee or umpire in various sports, by indicating when the ball has gone out of play **2** a person who maintains railway, electricity, or telephone lines
line-up ❶ *n* **1** people or things assembled for a particular purpose: *Christmas TV line-up* **2** the members of such an assembly ▷ *vb* **line up** **3** to form or organize a line-up
ling[1] *n, pl* **ling** *or* **lings** a fish with a long slender body
WORD ORIGIN probably Low German
ling[2] *n* heather
WORD ORIGIN Old Norse *lyng*
linger ❶ *vb* **1** to delay or prolong departure **2** to survive in a weakened condition for some time before death **3** to spend a long time doing or considering something **lingering** *adj*
WORD ORIGIN Old English *lengan* prolong
lingerie (lan-zher-ee) *n* women's underwear and nightwear
WORD ORIGIN French, from Latin *lineus* linen
lingo *n, pl* **-goes** *informal* any foreign or unfamiliar language or jargon
WORD ORIGIN perhaps from LINGUA FRANCA
lingua franca *n, pl* **lingua francas** *or* **linguae francae** **1** a language used for communication among people of different mother tongues **2** any system of communication providing mutual understanding
WORD ORIGIN Italian: Frankish tongue
lingual *adj* **1** *anat* of the tongue **2** articulated with the tongue **3** *rare* of language or languages **lingually** *adv*
linguist *n* **1** a person who is skilled in foreign languages **2** a person who studies linguistics
WORD ORIGIN Latin *lingua* tongue
linguistic *adj* **1** of language **2** of linguistics **linguistically** *adv*
linguistics *n* the scientific study of language
liniment *n* a medicated oily liquid applied to the skin to relieve pain or stiffness
WORD ORIGIN Latin *linere* to smear
lining *n* **1** material used to line a garment or curtain **2** any interior covering: *the lining of the womb*
link ❶ *n* **1** any of the separate rings that form a chain **2** an emotional or logical relationship between people or things; association **3** a connecting part or episode **4** a type of communications connection: *a rail link; radio link* ▷ *vb* **5** (often foll. by *up*) to connect with or as if with links **6** to connect by association
WORD ORIGIN from Old Norse
linkage *n* **1** the act of linking or the state of being linked **2** a system of links
linkman *n, pl* **-men** a presenter of a television or radio programme consisting of a number of items broadcast from different locations
links *pl n* a golf course
WORD ORIGIN Old English *hlincas*, plural of *hlinc* ridge
link-up *n* a joining together of two systems or groups
linnet *n* a brownish finch: the male has a red breast and forehead
WORD ORIGIN Old French *linotte*, from Latin *līnum* flax (because the bird feeds on flaxseeds)
lino *n* ▸ short for **linoleum**
linocut *n* **1** a design cut in relief in linoleum mounted on a block of wood **2** a print made from such a block
linoleum *n* a floor covering made of hessian or jute with a smooth decorative coating of powdered cork
WORD ORIGIN Latin *linum* flax + *oleum* oil
Linotype *n trademark* a typesetting machine that casts an entire line of text on one piece of metal
Lin Piao *or* **Lin Biao** *n* 1908–71, Chinese Communist general and statesman. He became minister of defence (1959) and second in rank to Mao Tse-tung (1966). He fell from grace and is reported to have died in an air crash while attempting to flee to the Soviet Union
linseed *n* the seed of the flax plant
WORD ORIGIN Old English *līn* flax + *sǣd* seed
linseed oil *n* a yellow oil extracted from flax seeds and used in making paints, inks, linoleum, and varnish
lint *n* **1** an absorbent material with raised fibres on one side, used to dress wounds **2** tiny shreds of yarn or cloth; fluff
WORD ORIGIN probably Latin *linteus* made of linen, from *linum* flax
lintel *n* a horizontal beam over a door or window
WORD ORIGIN probably ultimately from Latin *limes* boundary
lion *n* **1** a large animal of the cat family found in Africa and India, with a tawny yellow coat and, in the male, a shaggy mane **2** a courageous and strong person **3** **the lion's share** the largest portion **lioness** *fem n*
WORD ORIGIN Latin *leo*
lion-hearted *adj* very brave; courageous

THESAURUS

line-up *n* **1, 2 = arrangement**, team, row, selection, array
linger *vb* **1 = stay**, remain, stop, wait, delay, lag, hang around, idle, dally, loiter, take your time, wait around, dawdle, hang in the air, procrastinate, tarry, drag your feet or heels
link *n* **2a = connection**, relationship, association, tie-up, affinity, affiliation, vinculum
2b = relationship, association, tie, bond, connection, attachment, liaison, affinity, affiliation
3 = component, part, piece, division, element, constituent ▷ *vb* **5** (often foll. by *up*) **= connect**, join, unite, couple, tie, bind, attach, fasten, yoke
OPPOSITE: separate
6 = associate, relate, identify, connect, bracket

DICTIONARY

lionize *or* **-ise** *vb* **-izing, -ized** *or* **-ising, -ised** to treat as a celebrity

lip ❶ *n* **1** *anat* either of the two fleshy folds surrounding the mouth **2** any structure resembling a lip, such as the rim of a jug **3** *slang* impudent talk or backchat **4 bite one's lip** to avoid showing feelings of anger or distress **5 keep a stiff upper lip** to maintain one's composure during a time of trouble **6 lick** *or* **smack one's lips** to anticipate or recall something with glee or relish
WORD ORIGIN Old English *lippa*

lipase *n biochem* any of a group of enzymes that digest fat and are produced in the stomach and pancreas and occur in seeds

Lipchitz *n* **Jacques** 1891–1973, US sculptor, born in Lithuania: he pioneered cubist sculpture

Li Peng *n* born 1928, Chinese Communist politician: premier (1988–98)

lipid *n biochem* any of a group of organic compounds including fats, oils, waxes, and sterols
WORD ORIGIN Greek *lipos* fat

lipo *n informal* ▸ short for **liposuction**

Li Po *or* **Li T'ai-po** *n* ?700–762 AD, Chinese poet. His lyrics deal mostly with wine, nature, and women and are remarkable for their imagery

lipogram *n* a piece of writing in which all words containing a particular letter have been deliberately omitted

liposuction *n* a cosmetic surgical operation in which fat is removed from the body by suction

Lippershey *or* **Lippersheim** *n* **Hans** died ?1619, Dutch lens grinder, who built the first telescope

Lippi *n* **1 Filippino** ?1457–1504, Italian painter of the Florentine school **2** his father, **Fra Filippo** ?1406–69, Italian painter of the Florentine school, noted particularly for his frescoes at Prato Cathedral (1452–64)

Lippmann *n* **Gabriel** 1845–1921, French physicist. He devised the earliest process of colour photography: Nobel prize for physics 1908

lip-read *vb* **-reading, -read** to interpret speech by lip-reading

lip-reading *n* a method used by deaf people to understand spoken words by interpreting movements of the speaker's lips **lip-reader** *n*

lip service *n* **pay lip service to** to appear to support or obey something publicly while actually disregarding it

lipstick *n* a cosmetic in the form of a stick, for colouring the lips

liquefy *vb* **-fies, -fying, -fied** (esp. of a gas) to make or become liquid **liquefaction** *n*
WORD ORIGIN Latin *liquefacere* to make liquid

liqueur (lik-**cure**) *n* a highly flavoured sweetened alcoholic spirit, intended to be drunk after a meal
WORD ORIGIN French

liquid ❶ *n* **1** a substance in a physical state which can change shape but not size ▹ *adj* **2** of or being a liquid: *liquid medicines* **3** shining and clear: *liquid sunlight days* **4** flowing, fluent, or smooth **5** (of assets) in the form of money or easily convertible into money
WORD ORIGIN Latin *liquere* to be fluid

liquidate *vb* **-dating, -dated 1** to settle or pay off (a debt or claim) **2** to dissolve a company and divide its assets among creditors **3** to convert (assets) into cash **4** to eliminate or kill

liquidation *n* **1 a** the dissolving of a company by selling its assets to pay off its debts **b go into liquidation** (of a business firm) to have its affairs so terminated **2** destruction; elimination

liquidator *n* an official appointed to liquidate a business

liquid-crystal display *n* a display of numbers, characters, or images, esp. on a calculator, using cells containing a liquid with crystalline properties, that change their reflectivity when an electric field is applied to them

liquidity *n* the state of being able to meet financial obligations

liquidize *or* **-dise** *vb* **-izing, -ized** *or* **-ising, -ised 1** to make or become liquid; liquefy **2** to process (food) in a liquidizer to make it liquid

liquidizer *or* **-diser** *n* a kitchen appliance with blades for liquidizing food

liquid measure *n* a unit or system of units for measuring volumes of liquids or their containers

liquid oxygen *n* oxygen liquefied by cooling: used in rocket fuels

liquid paraffin *n* an oily liquid obtained by petroleum distillation and used as a laxative

liquor ❶ *n* **1** spirits or other alcoholic drinks **2** any liquid in which food has been cooked
WORD ORIGIN Latin *liquere* to be liquid

liquorice *or US & Canad* **licorice** (**lik**-ker-iss) *n* **1** a chewy black sweet with a strong flavour **2** the dried black root of a Mediterranean plant, used as a laxative and in confectionery
WORD ORIGIN Greek *glukus* sweet + *rhiza* root

lira *n, pl* **lire** *or* **liras 1** a former monetary unit of Italy **2** the standard monetary unit of Turkey
WORD ORIGIN Italian, from Latin *libra* pound

lisle (rhymes with **mile**) *n* a strong fine cotton thread or fabric, formerly used to make stockings
WORD ORIGIN after *Lisle* (now Lille), in France

lisp *n* **1** a speech defect in which *s* and *z* are pronounced like the *th* sounds in English *thin* and *then* respectively ▹ *vb* **2** to speak with a lisp
WORD ORIGIN Old English *wlisp* lisping (imitative)

LISP *n* a high-level computer programming language suitable for work in artificial intelligence
WORD ORIGIN *lis(t) p(rocessing)*

lissom *or* **lissome** *adj* slim and graceful and agile in movement
WORD ORIGIN variant of *lithesome*, from *lithe* + *-some* of a specific nature

list[1] ❶ *n* **1** an item-by-item record of names or things, usually written one below the other ▹ *vb* **2** to make a list of **3** to include in a list
WORD ORIGIN Old English *līste*

list[2] ❶ *vb* **1** (esp. of ships) to lean to one side ▹ *n* **2** a leaning to one side: *developed a list to starboard*
WORD ORIGIN origin unknown

listed building *n* (in Britain, Australia, and New Zealand) a building protected from demolition or alteration because of its special historical or architectural interest

listen ❶ *vb* **1** to concentrate on hearing something **2** to take heed or

THESAURUS

lip *n* **2 = edge**, rim, brim, margin, brink, flange **3** *(slang)* **= impudence**, rudeness, insolence, impertinence, sauce *(informal)*, cheek *(informal)*, effrontery, backchat *(informal)*, brass neck *(informal)*

liquid *n* **1 = fluid**, solution, juice, liquor, sap ▹ *adj* **2 = fluid**, running, flowing, wet, melted, thawed, watery, molten, runny, liquefied, aqueous **5 = convertible**, disposable, negotiable, realizable

liquor *n* **1 = alcohol**, drink, spirits, booze *(informal)*, grog, hard stuff *(informal)*, strong drink, Dutch courage *(informal)*, intoxicant, juice *(informal)*, hooch *or* hootch *(informal, chiefly US & Canad)* **2 = juice**, stock, liquid, extract, gravy, infusion, broth

list[1] *n* **1 = inventory**, record, listing, series, roll, file, schedule, index, register, catalogue, directory, tally, invoice, syllabus, tabulation, leet *(Scot)* ▹ *vb* **2, 3 = itemize**, record, note, enter, file, schedule, index, register, catalogue, write down, enrol, set down, enumerate, note down, tabulate

list[2] *vb* **1 = lean**, tip, heel, incline, tilt, cant, heel over, careen ▹ *n* **2 = tilt**, leaning, slant, cant

listen *vb* **1 = hear**, attend, pay attention, hark, be attentive, be all

DICTIONARY

pay attention: *listen, let me explain* **listener** *n*
WORD ORIGIN Old English *hlysnan*
listen in *vb* (often foll. by *on* or *to*) to listen secretly to; eavesdrop
listeriosis *n* a serious form of food poisoning, caused by bacteria of the genus *Listeria*
WORD ORIGIN after Joseph *Lister*, surgeon
listing *n* **1** a list or an entry in a list **2 listings** lists of films, concerts, etc. printed in newspapers and magazines, and showing details such as times and venues
listless *adj* lacking interest or energy **listlessly** *adv*
WORD ORIGIN obsolete *list* desire
Liston *n* **Sonny,** real name *Charles*. 1922–70, US boxer: former world heavyweight champion
list price *n* the selling price of merchandise as quoted in a catalogue or advertisement
lists *pl n* **1** *history* the enclosed field of combat at a tournament **2 enter the lists** to engage in a conflict or controversy
WORD ORIGIN plural of Old English *līste* border
lit *vb* ▸ a past of **light**[1] or **light**[2]
lit. **1** literal(ly) **2** literary **3** literature
Li T'ai-po *n* See **Li Po**
litany *n, pl* **-nies** **1** *Christianity* a prayer consisting of a series of invocations, each followed by the same response **2** any tedious recital: *a litany of complaints*
WORD ORIGIN Late Greek *litaneia* prayer
litchi *n* ▸ same as **lychee**
lite *adj* **1** (of food or drink) containing few calories or little alcohol or fat **2** denoting a less extreme version of a person or thing: *reggae lite*
WORD ORIGIN variant spelling of LIGHT[2]
liter *n* US ▸ same as **litre**
literacy ❶ *n* **1** the ability to read and write **2** the ability to use language effectively
literal ❶ *adj* **1** in exact accordance with the explicit meaning of a word or text **2** word for word: *a literal translation* **3** dull or unimaginative: *she's very, very literal and flat in how she interprets what she sees* **4** true; actual ▹ *n* **5** a misprint or misspelling in a text **literally** *adv*
WORD ORIGIN Latin *littera* letter
literalism *n* the tendency to take words and statements in their literal sense **literalist** *n*
literary ❶ *adj* **1** of or characteristic of literature: *literary criticism* **2** knowledgeable about literature **3** (of a word) used chiefly in written work; not colloquial **literariness** *n*
WORD ORIGIN Latin *litterarius* concerning reading and writing
literate ❶ *adj* **1** able to read and write **2** educated ▹ *n* **3** a literate person
WORD ORIGIN Latin *litteratus* learned
literati *pl n* literary or scholarly people
WORD ORIGIN Latin
literature ❶ *n* **1** written material such as poetry, novels, or essays **2** the body of written work of a particular culture, people, or era: *Elizabethan literature* **3** written or printed matter of a particular type or genre: *medical literature* **4** the art or profession of a writer **5** *informal* printed matter on any subject
WORD ORIGIN Latin *litteratura* writing
lithe *adj* attractively graceful and supple in movement
WORD ORIGIN Old English *līthe* (in the sense: gentle; later: supple)
lithium *n chem* a soft silvery element of the alkali metal series: the lightest known metal. Symbol: Li
WORD ORIGIN Greek *lithos* stone
litho *n, pl* **-thos**, *adj, adv* ▸ short for **lithography, lithograph, lithographic** or **lithographically**
lithograph *n* **1** a print made by lithography ▹ *vb* **2** to reproduce (pictures or text) by lithography **lithographic** *adj* **lithographically** *adv*
lithography (lith-og-ra-fee) *n* a method of printing from a metal or stone surface on which the printing areas are made ink-receptive **lithographer** *n*
WORD ORIGIN Greek *lithos* stone + *graphein* to write
Lithuanian *adj* **1** from Lithuania ▹ *n* **2** a person from Lithuania **3** the language of Lithuania
litigant *n* a person involved in a lawsuit
litigate *vb* **-gating, -gated** **1** to bring or contest a lawsuit **2** to engage in legal proceedings **litigator** *n*
WORD ORIGIN Latin *lis, lit-* lawsuit + *agere* to carry on
litigation ❶ *n* the process of bringing or contesting a lawsuit
litigious (lit-ij-uss) *adj* frequently going to law
litmus *n* a soluble powder obtained from lichens, which is turned red by acids and blue by alkalis. Paper treated with it (**litmus paper**) is used as an indicator in chemistry
WORD ORIGIN perhaps Scandinavian
litmus test *n* something which is regarded as a simple and accurate test of a particular thing, such as a person's attitude to an issue
litotes *n, pl* **-tes** understatement used for effect, for example 'She was not a little upset' meaning 'She was extremely upset'
WORD ORIGIN Greek *litos* small
litre *or US* **liter** *n* a measure of volume equivalent to 1 cubic decimetre
WORD ORIGIN Greek *litra* a unit of weight
litter ❶ *n* **1** small items of rubbish carelessly dropped in public places **2** a disordered or untidy collection of objects **3** a group of animals produced at one birth **4** straw or hay used as bedding for animals **5** dry material used to line a receptacle in which a domestic cat can urinate and defecate **6** (esp. formerly) a bed or seat held between parallel poles and used for carrying people ▹ *vb* **7** to strew with litter **8** to scatter or be scattered in an untidy fashion **9** (of animals) to give birth to offspring **10** to provide (an animal) with straw or hay for bedding
WORD ORIGIN Latin *lectus* bed
litter lout *Brit or US, Canad, Austral & NZ* **litterbug** *n slang* a person who drops refuse in public places
little ❶ *adj* **1** of small or less than average size **2** young: *a little boy* **3** endearingly familiar: *he was a sweet*

THESAURUS

ears, lend an ear, hearken *(archaic)*, prick up your ears, give ear, keep your ears open, pin back your ears *(informal)* **2 = pay attention**, observe, obey, mind, concentrate, heed, take notice, take note of, take heed of, do as you are told, give heed to
literacy *n* **1, 2 = education**, learning, knowledge, scholarship, cultivation, proficiency, articulacy, ability to read and write, articulateness
literal *adj* **1, 2 = exact**, close, strict, accurate, faithful, verbatim, word for word **4 = actual**, real, true, simple, plain, genuine, gospel, bona fide, unvarnished, unexaggerated
literary *adj* **1, 2 = well-read**, lettered, learned, formal, intellectual, scholarly, literate, erudite, bookish
literate *adj* **1, 2 = educated**, lettered, learned, cultured, informed, scholarly, cultivated, knowledgeable, well-informed, erudite, well-read
literature *n* **1, 2 = writings**, letters, compositions, lore, creative writing, written works, belles-lettres
litigation *n* **= lawsuit**, case, action, process, disputing, prosecution, contending
litter *n* **1 = rubbish**, refuse, waste, fragments, junk, debris, shreds, garbage *(chiefly US)*, trash, muck, detritus, grot *(slang)* **3 = brood**, family, young, offspring, progeny ▹ *vb* **7 = clutter**, mess up, clutter up, be scattered about, disorder, disarrange, derange, muss *(US & Canad)* **8 = scatter**, spread, shower, strew
little *adj* **1 = small**, minute, short, tiny, mini, wee, compact, miniature, dwarf, slender, diminutive, petite,

DICTIONARY

little man **4** contemptible, mean, or disagreeable: *some of my best friends were little squirts* **5** of small quantity, extent, or duration: *there was little money circulating; I could see little evidence of it* ▹ *adv* **6** (usually preceded by *a*) to a small extent or degree; not a lot: *to sleep a little* **7** not at all, or hardly: *army life varied little as the years passed* **8** not much or often: *we go there very little now* **9 little by little** by small degrees ▹ *n* **10 make little of** to treat as insignificant: *one episode in their history is made little of in the guide books* **11 think little of** to have a low opinion of ▸ See also **less, lesser, least**
WORD ORIGIN Old English *lȳtel*

little people *pl n folklore* small supernatural beings, such as elves

Littlewood *n* **(Maud) Joan** 1914–2002, British theatre director, who founded the Theatre Workshop Company (1945) with the aim of bringing theatre to the working classes: noted esp. for her production of *Oh, What a Lovely War!* (1963)

littoral *adj* **1** of or by the shore ▹ *n* **2** a coastal region
WORD ORIGIN Latin *litus* shore

liturgy *n, pl* **-gies** the forms of public services officially prescribed by a Church **liturgical** *adj*
WORD ORIGIN Greek *leitourgia*

l

Liu Shao Qi *or* **Liu Shao-ch'i** *n* 1898–1974, Chinese Communist statesman; chairman of the People's Republic of China (1959–68); deposed during the Cultural Revolution

livable *or* **liveable** *adj* (foll. by *with*) tolerable or pleasant to live (with)

live¹ ❶ *vb* **living, lived 1** to show the characteristics of life; be alive **2** to remain alive or in existence **3** to exist in a specified way: *to live at ease* **4** to have one's home: *he went to live in Switzerland* **5** to continue or last: *his childhood had always lived inside him* **6** (foll. by *on, upon* or *by*) to support one's style of life: *forest dwellers who live by extracting rubber* **7** (foll. by *with*) to endure the effects (of a crime or mistake); tolerate **8** to pass or spend (one's life) **9** to enjoy life to the full: *he likes to live every day to the full* **10** to put into practice in one's daily life: *the freedom to live his own life as he chooses* **11 live and let live** to be tolerant ▸ See also **live down, live in**, etc.
WORD ORIGIN Old English *libban, lifian*

live² ❶ *adj* **1** alive; living **2** *radio, television* transmitted at the time of performance, rather than being prerecorded: *a live broadcast* **3** actual: *I was able to speak to a real live Hurricane pilot* **4** (of a record) recorded during a performance **5** connected to a source of electric power: *a live cable* **6** of current interest; controversial: *the document has become a live political issue* **7** loaded or capable of exploding: *a live firing exercise with a 4.5in gun* **8** (of a coal or ember) glowing or burning ▹ *adv* **9** during, at, or in the form of a live performance
WORD ORIGIN shortened from *on live* alive

live down *vb* to withstand people's reactions to a crime or mistake until they forget it

live in *vb* **1** to have one's home at the place where one works ▹ *adj* **live-in 2** resident: *a live-in nanny is a must; her live-in girlfriend*

livelihood ❶ *n* one's job or other source of income

livelong (liv-long) *adj chiefly poetic* long or seemingly long: *all the livelong day*

lively ❶ *adj* **-lier, -liest 1** full of life or vigour **2** vivacious or animated **3** vivid **liveliness** *n*

liven *vb* (usually foll. by *up*) to make or become lively; enliven

liver¹ *n* **1** a large glandular organ which secretes bile, balances nutrients, and removes certain poisons from the body **2** the liver of certain animals used as food
WORD ORIGIN Old English *lifer*

liver² *n* a person who lives in a specified way: *a fast liver*

liveried *adj* wearing livery

liverish *adj* **1** *informal* having a disorder of the liver **2** feeling disagreeable and slightly irritable

Liverpudlian *adj* **1** of Liverpool, a city in NW England ▹ *n* **2** a person from Liverpool

liver sausage *n* a sausage containing liver

liverwort *n* a plant growing in wet places and resembling green seaweeds or leafy mosses
WORD ORIGIN late Old English *liferwyrt*

livery *n, pl* **-eries 1** the identifying uniform of a servant **2** distinctive dress or outward appearance **3** the stabling, keeping, or hiring out of horses for money
WORD ORIGIN Old French *livrée* allocation

lives *n* ▸ the plural of **life**

livestock *n* animals kept on a farm

live together *vb* (of an unmarried couple) to live in the same house; cohabit

live up to *vb* to fulfil (an expectation, obligation, or principle)

live wire *n* **1** *informal* an energetic person **2** a wire carrying an electric current

Livia Drusilla *n* 58 BC–29 AD, Roman noblewoman: wife (from 39 BC) of Emperor Augustus and mother of Emperor Tiberius

livid *adj* **1** *informal* extremely angry **2** of a dark grey or purple colour: *livid bruises*
WORD ORIGIN Latin *livere* to be black and blue

living ❶ *adj* **1** possessing life; not dead or inanimate **2** currently in use or valid: *a living alliance* **3** seeming to be

THESAURUS

dainty, elfin, bijou, infinitesimal, teeny-weeny, Lilliputian, munchkin *(informal, chiefly US)*, teensy-weensy, pygmy *or* pigmy **OPPOSITE:** big
2 = young, small, junior, infant, immature, undeveloped, babyish
▹ *n* **6** (usually preceded by *a*) **= to a small extent**, slightly, to some extent, to a certain extent, to a small degree ▹ *adv* **7 = hardly**, barely, not quite, not much, only just, scarcely **OPPOSITE:** much
8 = rarely, seldom, scarcely, not often, infrequently, hardly ever **OPPOSITE:** always

live¹ *vb* **1, 2 = exist**, last, prevail, be, have being, breathe, persist, be alive, have life, draw breath, remain alive
4 = dwell, board, settle, lodge, occupy, abide, inhabit, hang out *(informal)*, stay *(chiefly Scot)*, reside, have as your home, have your home in
6 = survive, remain alive, feed yourself, get along, make a living, earn a living, make ends meet, subsist, eke out a living, support yourself, maintain yourself
9 = thrive, be happy, flourish, prosper, have fun, enjoy life, enjoy yourself, luxuriate, live life to the full, make the most of life

live² *adj* **1 = living**, alive, breathing, animate, existent, vital, quick *(archaic)* **5, 7 = active**, connected, switched on, unexploded **6 = topical**, important, pressing, current, hot, burning, active, vital, controversial, unsettled, prevalent, pertinent

livelihood *n* **= occupation**, work, employment, means, living, job, maintenance, subsistence, bread and butter *(informal)*, sustenance, (means of) support, (source of) income

lively *adj* **1, 2 = animated**, spirited, quick, keen, active, alert, dynamic, sparkling, vigorous, cheerful, energetic, outgoing, merry, upbeat *(informal)*, brisk, bubbly, nimble, agile, perky, chirpy *(informal)*, sparky, sprightly, vivacious, frisky, gay, alive and kicking, spry, chipper *(informal)*, blithe, full of beans *(informal)*, frolicsome, full of pep *(informal)*, blithesome, bright-eyed and bushy-tailed **OPPOSITE:** dull
3 = vivid, strong, striking, bright, exciting, stimulating, bold, colourful, refreshing, forceful, racy, invigorating **OPPOSITE:** dull

living *adj* **1, 4, 7 = alive**, existing, moving, active, vital, breathing, lively, vigorous, animated, animate,

DICTIONARY

real: *a living doll* **4** (of people or animals) existing in the present age **5** very: *the living image* **6** of or like everyday life: *living costs* **7** of or involving those now alive: *one of our greatest living actors* ▷ *n* **8** the condition of being alive **9** the manner of one's life: *high living* **10** one's financial means **11** *Church of England* a benefice

living room *n* a room in a private house or flat used for relaxation and entertainment

living wage *n* a wage adequate for a worker to live on and support a family in reasonable comfort

living will *n* a document that states that a person who becomes terminally ill does not want their life to be prolonged by artificial means

Livy *n* Latin name *Titus Livius*. 59 BC–17 AD, Roman historian; of his history of Rome in 142 books, only 35 survive

lizard *n* a reptile with an elongated body, four limbs, and a long tail
WORD ORIGIN Latin *lacerta*

ll. lines (of written matter)

llama *n* a South American mammal of the camel family, that is used as a beast of burden and is valued for its woolly fleece
WORD ORIGIN from a Native American language

LLB Bachelor of Laws
WORD ORIGIN Latin *Legum Baccalaureus*

LLD Doctor of Laws
WORD ORIGIN Latin *Legum Doctor*

Llewellyn *n* Colonel **Harry** 1911–99, Welsh show-jumping rider: on Foxhunter, he was a member of the British team that won the gold medal at the 1952 Olympic Games

Llewelyn I *n* See **Llywelyn ap Iorwerth**

Llewelyn II *n* See **Llywelyn ap Gruffudd**

LLM Master of Laws
WORD ORIGIN Latin *Legum Magister*

Lloyd *n* **1 Clive** (**Hubert**) born 1944, West Indian (Guyanese) cricketer; captained the West Indies (1974–88) **2 Harold** (**Clayton**) 1893–1971, US comic film actor **3 Marie,** real name *Matilda Alice Victoria Wood*. 1870–1922, English music-hall entertainer

Llywelyn ap Iorwerth *n* called *Llywelyn the Great*. died 1240, prince of Gwynedd, N Wales (1194–1238), who extended his rule over most of Wales

lo *interj old-fashioned* look! see!: *lo and behold*
WORD ORIGIN Old English *lā*

loach *n* a freshwater fish with a long narrow body and barbels around the mouth
WORD ORIGIN Old French *loche*

Loach *n* **Ken**(**neth**) born 1936, British television and film director; his works for television include *Cathy Come Home* (1966) and his films include *Kes* (1970), *Riff-Raff* (1991), *Bread and Roses* (2000), and *The Wind that Shakes the Barley* (2006)

load ⓣ *n* **1** something to be borne or conveyed; weight **2** the amount borne or conveyed **3** something that weighs down or burdens: *I have enough of a load to carry right now* **4** *electronics* the power delivered by a machine, generator, or circuit **5** an external force applied to a component or mechanism **6 a load of** *informal* a quantity of: *a load of half-truths* **7 get a load of** *informal* to pay attention to ▷ *vb* **8** to place cargo or goods upon (a ship or vehicle) **9** to burden or oppress **10** to supply in abundance: *other treats are loaded with fat* **11** to cause to be biased: *the dice are loaded* **12** to put ammunition into (a firearm) **13** *photog* to insert film in (a camera) **14** to weight or bias (a roulette wheel or dice) **15** *computers* to transfer (a program) to a memory ▸ See also **loads** > **loader** *n*
WORD ORIGIN Old English *lād* course; in meaning, influenced by LADE

loaded ⓣ *adj* **1** carrying a load **2** charged with ammunition **3** (of a question or statement) containing a hidden trap or implication **4** (of dice or a roulette wheel) weighted or otherwise biased **5** *slang* wealthy **6** *slang chiefly US & Canad* drunk

loads *pl n informal* (often foll. by *of*) a lot

loadstar *n* ▸ same as **lodestar**

loadstone *n* ▸ same as **lodestone**

loaf[1] ⓣ *n, pl* **loaves 1** a shaped mass of baked bread **2** any shaped or moulded mass of food, such as cooked meat **3** *slang* the head; common sense: *use your loaf!*
WORD ORIGIN Old English *hlāf*

loaf[2] ⓣ *vb* to loiter or lounge around in an idle way
WORD ORIGIN perhaps from *loafer*

loafer *n* **1** a person who avoids work; idler **2** a moccasin-like shoe
WORD ORIGIN perhaps German *Landläufer* vagabond

loam *n* fertile soil consisting of sand, clay, and decaying organic material **loamy** *adj*
WORD ORIGIN Old English *lām*

loan ⓣ *n* **1** money lent at interest for a fixed period of time **2** the act of lending: *I am grateful to her for the loan of her book* **3** property lent **4 on loan** lent out; borrowed ▷ *vb* **5** to lend (something, esp. money)
WORD ORIGIN Old Norse *lān*

loan shark *n* a person who lends money at an extremely high interest rate, esp. illegally

loath *or* **loth** (rhymes with **both**) *adj* (usually foll. by *to*) reluctant or unwilling
WORD ORIGIN Old English *lāth* (in the sense: hostile)

loathe ⓣ *vb* **loathing, loathed** to feel strong disgust for
WORD ORIGIN Old English *lāthiān*

loathing ⓣ *n* strong disgust

loathsome *adj* causing loathing

loaves *n* ▸ the plural of **loaf**[1]

lob *sport n* **1** a ball struck or bowled in a high arc ▷ *vb* **lobbing, lobbed 2** to hit or kick (a ball) in a high arc **3** *informal* to throw
WORD ORIGIN probably Low German

Lobachevsky *n* **Nikolai Ivanovich** 1793–1856, Russian mathematician; a founder of non-Euclidean geometry

lobar (loh-ber) *adj* of or affecting a lobe

THESAURUS

alive and kicking, in the land of the living *(informal)*, quick *(archaic)* **OPPOSITE:** dead
2 = current, continuing, present, developing, active, contemporary, persisting, ongoing, operative, in use, extant **OPPOSITE:** obsolete
▷ *n* **9 = lifestyle**, ways, situation, conduct, behaviour, customs, way of life, mode of living

load *n* **1, 2 = cargo**, lading, delivery, haul, shipment, batch, freight, bale, consignment **3 = oppression**, charge, pressure, worry, trouble, weight, responsibility, burden, affliction, onus, albatross, millstone, encumbrance, incubus ▷ *vb* **8 = fill**, stuff, pack, pile, stack, heap, cram, freight, lade **12 = make ready**, charge, prime, prepare to fire

loaded *adj* **3 = tricky**, charged, sensitive, delicate, manipulative, emotive, insidious, artful, prejudicial, tendentious **5** *(slang)* **= rich**, wealthy, affluent, well off, rolling *(slang)*, flush *(informal)*, well-heeled *(informal)*, well-to-do, moneyed, minted *(Brit slang)*

loaf[1] *n* **1, 2 = lump**, block, cake, cube, slab **3** *(slang)* **= head**, mind, sense, common sense, block *(informal)*, nous *(Brit slang)*, chump *(Brit slang)*, gumption *(Brit informal)*, noddle *(informal, chiefly Brit)*

loaf[2] *vb* **= idle**, hang around, take it easy, lie around, loiter, loll, laze, lounge around, veg out *(slang, chiefly US)*, be indolent

loan *n* **1 = advance**, credit, mortgage, accommodation, allowance, touch *(slang)*, overdraft ▷ *vb* **5 = lend**, allow, credit, advance, accommodate, let out

loathe *vb* **= hate**, dislike, despise, detest, abhor, abominate, have a strong aversion to, find disgusting, execrate, feel repugnance towards, not be able to bear *or* abide

loathing *n* **= hatred**, hate, horror, disgust, aversion, revulsion, antipathy, abomination, repulsion, abhorrence, repugnance, odium, detestation, execration

L

DICTIONARY

lobate *adj* with or like lobes
lobby ⓘ *n, pl* **-bies** **1** a room or corridor used as an entrance hall or vestibule **2** a group which attempts to influence legislators on behalf of a particular interest **3** *chiefly Brit* a hall in a legislative building used for meetings between legislators and members of the public **4** *chiefly Brit* one of two corridors in a legislative building in which members vote ▷ *vb* **-bies, -bying, -bied** **5** to attempt to influence (legislators) in the formulation of policy
WORD ORIGIN Old High German *lauba* arbor
lobbyist *n* a person who lobbies on behalf of a particular interest
lobe *n* **1** any rounded projection **2** the fleshy lower part of the external ear **3** any subdivision of a bodily organ
WORD ORIGIN Greek *lobos* lobe of the ear or of the liver
lobelia *n* a plant with blue, red, white, or yellow five-lobed flowers
WORD ORIGIN Matthias de *Lobel*, botanist
Lobengula *n* ?1836–94, last Matabele king (1870–93); his kingdom was destroyed by the British
lobola ⓘ *n S African* (in southern Africa) an African custom by which a bridegroom's family makes a payment in cattle or cash to the bride's family shortly before the marriage
WORD ORIGIN Nguni (language group of southern Africa) *ukulobola* to give bride price
lobotomy *n, pl* **-mies** the surgical cutting of nerves in the frontal lobe of the brain to treat severe mental disorders
WORD ORIGIN Greek *lobos* lobe + *tomē* a cutting
lobscouse *n* a sailor's stew of meat, vegetables, and hardtack
WORD ORIGIN perhaps dialect *lob* to boil + *scouse* broth
lobster *n, pl* **-sters** *or* **-ster** **1** a large edible crustacean with large pincers and a long tail, which turns red when boiled **2** its edible flesh **3** *Austral informal* a $20 note
WORD ORIGIN Old English *loppestre*, from *loppe* spider
lobster pot *n* a round basket made of open slats, used to catch lobsters
local ⓘ *adj* **1** of or concerning a particular area **2** restricted to a particular place **3** *med* of, affecting, or confined to a limited area or part: *a local anaesthetic* **4** (of a train or bus) stopping at all stations or stops ▷ *n* **5** an inhabitant of a specified locality: *we swim, sunbathe, meet the locals, unwind* **6** *Brit informal* a pub close to one's home **locally** *adv*
WORD ORIGIN Latin *locus* place
local anaesthetic *n med* ▸ see **anaesthesia**
local authority *n* the governing body of a county, district, or region
locale (loh-**kahl**) *n* the place where something happens or has happened
WORD ORIGIN French, from Latin *locus* place
local government *n* the government of the affairs of counties, towns, and districts by locally elected political bodies
locality *n, pl* **-ties** **1** a neighbourhood or area **2** the site or scene of an event
localize *or* **-ise** *vb* **-izing, -ized** *or* **-ising, -ised** to restrict (something) to a particular place
locate ⓘ *vb* **-cating, -cated** **1** to discover the whereabouts of; find **2** to situate or build: *located around the corner from the church* **3** to become established or settled
location ⓘ *n* **1** a site or position; situation **2** the act of locating or the state of being located: *make their location and rescue a top priority* **3** a place outside a studio where filming is done: *shot on location* **4** (in South Africa) a Black African or Coloured township
WORD ORIGIN Latin *locare* to place
loc. cit. (in textual annotation) in the place cited
WORD ORIGIN Latin *loco citato*
loch *n Scot* **1** a lake **2** a long narrow arm of the sea
WORD ORIGIN Gaelic
loci (**loh**-sigh) *n* ▸ the plural of **locus**
lock[1] ⓘ *n* **1** a device for fastening a door, drawer, lid, etc. and preventing unauthorized access **2** a section of a canal or river closed off by gates between which the water level can be altered to aid boats moving from one level to the next **3** *Brit & NZ* the extent to which a vehicle's front wheels will turn: *they adopted more steering lock* **4** the interlocking of parts **5** a mechanism that fires a gun **6** **lock, stock, and barrel** completely; entirely **7** a wrestling hold **8** Also called: **lock forward** *rugby* a player in the second row of the scrum ▷ *vb* **9** to fasten or become fastened to prevent entry or exit **10** to secure (a building) by locking all doors and windows **11** to fix or become fixed together securely **12** to become or cause to become immovable: *just before your knees lock* **13** to clasp or entangle in a struggle or embrace ▸ See also **lock out, lock up**
WORD ORIGIN Old English *loc*
lock[2] ⓘ *n* **1** a strand or curl of hair **2** **locks** *chiefly literary* hair
WORD ORIGIN Old English *loc*
locker *n* a small compartment with a lock, used for temporarily storing clothes, valuables, or luggage
locket *n* a small hinged ornamental pendant that holds a picture or keepsake
WORD ORIGIN French *loquet* latch
lockjaw *n pathol* ▸ a nontechnical name for **trismus** or **tetanus**
lock out *vb* **1** to prevent from entering by locking a door **2** to prevent (employees) from working during an industrial dispute, by shutting them out of the premises ▷ *n* **lockout** **3** the closing of a place of employment by an employer, in order to force employees to accept terms
locksmith *n* a person who makes or repairs locks
lock up ⓘ *vb* **1** to imprison **2** to secure a building by locking all the doors and windows ▷ *n* **lockup** **3** a jail **4** *Brit* a garage or store separate from the main premises **5** *Brit* a small shop with no attached quarters for the owner ▷ *adj* **lock-up** **6** *Brit & NZ* (of premises) without living

THESAURUS

lobby *n* **1 = corridor**, hall, passage, entrance, porch, hallway, foyer, passageway, entrance hall, vestibule **2 = pressure group**, group, camp, faction, lobbyists, interest group, special-interest group, ginger group, public-interest group *(US & Canad)* ▷ *vb* **5 = campaign**, press, pressure, push, influence, promote, urge, persuade, appeal, petition, pull strings *(Brit informal)*, exert influence, bring pressure to bear, solicit votes
lobola *n (S African)* **= dowry**, portion, marriage settlement, dot *(archaic)*
local *adj* **1 = community**, district, regional, provincial, parish, neighbourhood, small-town *(chiefly US)*, parochial, parish pump **2, 3 = confined**, limited, narrow, restricted ▷ *n* **5 = resident**, native, inhabitant, character *(informal)*, local yokel *(derogatory)*
locate *vb* **1 = find**, discover, detect, come across, track down, pinpoint, unearth, pin down, lay your hands on, run to earth *or* ground **2 = place**, put, set, position, seat, site, establish, settle, fix, situate
location *n* **1 = place**, point, setting, position, situation, spot, venue, whereabouts, locus, locale
lock[1] *n* **1 = fastening**, catch, bolt, clasp, padlock ▷ *vb* **9, 10 = fasten**, close, secure, shut, bar, seal, bolt, latch, sneck *(dialect)* **11 = unite**, join, link, engage, mesh, clench, entangle, interlock, entwine **13 = embrace**, press, grasp, clutch, hug, enclose, grapple, clasp, encircle
lock[2] *n* **1 = strand**, curl, tuft, tress, ringlet
lock up = imprison, jail, confine, cage, detain, shut up, incarcerate, send down *(informal)*, send to prison, put behind bars

DICTIONARY

quarters: *a lock-up garage*

Lockyer *n* Sir **Joseph Norman** 1836–1920, English astronomer: a pioneer in solar spectroscopy, he was the first to observe helium in the sun's atmosphere (1868)

loco[1] *n informal* a locomotive

loco[2] *adj slang chiefly US* insane
WORD ORIGIN Spanish: crazy

locomotion *n* the act or power of moving
WORD ORIGIN Latin *loco* from a place + MOTION

locomotive *n* **1** a self-propelled engine for pulling trains ▹*adj* **2** of locomotion

locum *n* a person who stands in temporarily for a doctor or clergyman
WORD ORIGIN Medieval Latin *locum tenens* (someone) holding the place (of another)

locus (loh-kuss) *n, pl* **loci 1** an area or place where something happens **2** *maths* a set of points or lines whose location satisfies or is determined by one or more specified conditions: *the locus of points equidistant from a given point is a circle*
WORD ORIGIN Latin

locust *n* **1** an African insect, related to the grasshopper, which travels in vast swarms, stripping large areas of vegetation **2** a North American leguminous tree with prickly branches; the carob tree
WORD ORIGIN Latin *locusta*

locution *n* **1** manner or style of speech **2** a word, phrase, or expression
WORD ORIGIN Latin *locutio* an utterance

lode *n* a vein of metallic ore
WORD ORIGIN Old English *lād* course

lodestar *n* **1** a star, esp. the North Star, used in navigation or astronomy as a point of reference **2** something that serves as a guide

lodestone *n* **1 a** magnetic iron ore **b** a piece of this, used as a magnet **2** a person or thing regarded as a focus of attraction

lodge ❶ *n* **1** *chiefly Brit* the gatekeeper's house at the entrance to the grounds of a country mansion **2** a house or cabin used occasionally by hunters, skiers, etc.: *a hunting lodge* **3** *chiefly Brit* a room used by porters in a university or college **4** a local branch of certain societies **5** a beaver's home ▹*vb* **lodging, lodged 6** to provide or be provided with rented accommodation **7** to live temporarily in rented accommodation **8** to embed or be embedded: *the bullet lodged in his brain* **9** to leave for safety or storage: *he lodged his wages in the bank* **10** to bring (a charge or accusation) against someone: *the Brazilians lodged a complaint* **11** (often foll. by *in* or *with*) to place (authority or power) in the control (of someone)
WORD ORIGIN Old French *loge*

Lodge[1] *n* **1 David** (**John**) born 1935, British novelist and critic. His books include *Changing Places* (1975), *Small World* (1984), *Nice Work* (1988), *Therapy* (1995), and *Thinks...* (2001) **2** Sir **Oliver** (**Joseph**) 1851–1940, British physicist, who made important contributions to electromagnetism, radio reception, and attempted to detect the ether. He also studied allegedly psychic phenomena **3 Thomas** ?1558–1625, English writer. His romance *Rosalynde* (1590) supplied the plot for Shakespeare's *As You Like It*

Lodge[2] *n* **the Lodge** the official Canberra residence of the Australian Prime Minister

lodger *n* a person who pays rent in return for accommodation in someone else's home

lodging ❶ *n* **1** a temporary residence: *where might I find a night's lodging?* **2 lodgings** a rented room or rooms in another person's home

Loeb *n* **Jacques** 1859–1924, US physiologist, born in Germany, noted esp. for his pioneering work on artificial parthenogenesis

loess (loh-iss) *n* a fine-grained soil, found mainly in river valleys, originally deposited by the wind
WORD ORIGIN Swiss German *lösch* loose

Loewe[1] *n* **Frederick** 1904–88, US composer of such musical comedies as *Brigadoon* (1947), *My Fair Lady* (1956), and *Camelot* (1960), all with librettos by Alan Jay Lerner

Loewe[2] *or* **Löwe** *n* (**Johann**) **Karl** (**Gottfried**) 1796–1869, German composer, esp. of songs, such as *Der Erlkönig* (1818)

Loewi *n* **Otto** 1873–1961, US pharmacologist, born in Germany. He shared a Nobel prize for physiology or medicine (1936) with Dale for their work on the chemical transmission of nerve impulses

loft *n* **1** the space inside a roof **2** a gallery in a church **3** a room over a stable used to store hay **4** a raised house or coop in which pigeons are kept **5** *golf* **a** the angle of the face of the club used to elevate a ball **b** the height reached by a struck ball ▹*vb* **6** *sport* to strike or kick (a ball) high in the air
WORD ORIGIN Old Norse *lopt* air, ceiling

lofty ❶ *adj* **loftier, loftiest 1** of majestic or imposing height **2** morally admirable: *lofty ideals* **3** unpleasantly superior: *a lofty contempt* **loftily** *adv* **loftiness** *n*

log[1] ❶ *n* **1** a section of a felled tree stripped of branches **2 a** a detailed record of a voyage of a ship or aircraft **b** a record of the hours flown by pilots and aircrews **c** a book in which these records are made; logbook **3** a device consisting of a float with an attached line, formerly used to measure the speed of a ship **4 sleep like a log** to sleep without stirring ▹*vb* **logging, logged 5** to saw logs from (trees) **6** to enter (a distance or event) in a logbook or log ▸See also **log in, log out**
WORD ORIGIN origin unknown

log[2] *n* ▸short for **logarithm**

loganberry *n, pl* **-ries** a purplish-red fruit, similar to a raspberry, that grows on a trailing prickly plant
WORD ORIGIN after J. H. *Logan*, who first grew it

logarithm *n* the exponent indicating the power to which a fixed number, the base, must be raised to obtain a given number or variable **logarithmic** *adj*
WORD ORIGIN Greek *logos* ratio + *arithmos* number

logbook *n* **1** a book containing the official record of trips made by a ship

THESAURUS

lodge *n* **2 = cabin**, house, shelter, cottage, hut, chalet, gatehouse, hunting lodge **4 = society**, group, club, association, section, wing, chapter, branch, assemblage ▹*vb* **6, 7 = stay**, room, stop (*Brit informal*), board, reside, sojourn **8 = stick**, remain, catch, implant, come to rest, become fixed, imbed **10 = register**, put, place, set, lay, enter, file, deposit, submit, put on record

lodging *n* **1, 2** (*often plural*) **= accommodation**, rooms, boarding, apartments, quarters, digs (*Brit informal*), shelter, residence, dwelling, abode, habitation, bachelor apartment (*Canad*)

lofty *adj* **1 = high**, raised, towering, tall, soaring, elevated, sky-high
OPPOSITE: low
2 = noble, grand, distinguished, superior, imposing, renowned, elevated, majestic, dignified, stately, sublime, illustrious, exalted
OPPOSITE: humble
3 = haughty, lordly, proud, arrogant, patronizing, condescending, snooty (*informal*), disdainful, supercilious, high and mighty (*informal*), toffee-nosed (*slang, chiefly Brit*)
OPPOSITE: modest

log[1] *n* **1 = stump**, block, branch, chunk, trunk, bole, piece of timber **2a, 2b, 2c = record**, listing, account, register, journal, chart, diary, tally, logbook, daybook, blog (*informal*) ▹*vb* **6 = record**, report, enter, book, note, register, chart, put down, tally, set down, make a note of

DICTIONARY

or aircraft **2** *Brit informal* the registration document of a car

loggerhead *n* **1** a large-headed turtle occurring in most seas **2 at loggerheads** engaged in dispute or confrontation
WORD ORIGIN probably dialect *logger* wooden block + HEAD

loggia (loj-ya) *n* a covered gallery on the side of a building
WORD ORIGIN Italian

logging *n* the work of felling, trimming, and transporting timber **logger** *n*

logic ❶ *n* **1** the branch of philosophy that analyses the patterns of reasoning **2** a particular system of reasoning **3** reasoned thought or argument, as distinguished from irrationality **4** the interdependence of a series of events or facts **5** *electronics, computers* the principles underlying the units in a computer system that produce results from data
WORD ORIGIN Greek *logikos* concerning speech or reasoning

logical ❶ *adj* **1** relating to or characteristic of logic **2** using or deduced from the principles of logic: *a logical conclusion* **3** capable of or using clear and valid reasoning **4** reasonable because of facts or events: *the logical choice* **logically** *adv*

logic gate *n electronics* ▸same as **gate** (sense 4)

logician *n* a person who specializes in or is skilled at logic

log in *or* **on** *vb* to gain entrance to a computer system by keying in a special command

logistics *n* the detailed planning and organization of a large complex operation, such as a military campaign **logistical** *or* **logistic** *adj* **logistically** *adv*
WORD ORIGIN French *loger* to lodge

logjam *n chiefly US & Canad* **1** a blockage caused by the crowding together of logs floating in a river **2** a deadlock

logo (loh-go) *n, pl* **-os** a special design that identifies a company or an organization and appears on all its products, printed material, etc.
WORD ORIGIN shortened from *logotype* badge, symbol

log out *vb* to exit from a computer system by keying in a special command

-logy *n combining form* **1** indicating the science or study of: *musicology* **2** indicating writing or discourse: *trilogy; phraseology* **-logical** *or* **-logic** *adj combining form* **-logist** *n combining form*
WORD ORIGIN Greek *logos* word

loin *n* **1** the part of the body between the pelvis and the ribs **2** a cut of meat from this part of an animal ▸See also **loins**
WORD ORIGIN Old French *loigne*

loincloth *n* a piece of cloth covering only the loins

loins *pl n* **1** the hips and the inner surface of the legs where they join the body **2** *euphemistic* the genitals

loiter *vb* to stand or wait aimlessly or idly
WORD ORIGIN perhaps Middle Dutch *löteren* to wobble

Lolita (low-lee-ta) *n* a sexually precocious young girl
WORD ORIGIN after the character in Nabokov's novel *Lolita*

loll *vb* **1** to lounge in a lazy manner **2** to hang loosely: *a wet lolling tongue; his head lolled back and forth*
WORD ORIGIN perhaps imitative

lollipop *n* **1** a boiled sweet stuck on a small wooden stick **2** *Brit* an ice lolly
WORD ORIGIN perhaps dialect *lolly* the tongue + POP²

lollipop man *or* **lady** *n Brit informal* a person holding a circular sign on a pole who stops traffic to enable children to cross the road safely

lollop *vb chiefly Brit* to walk or run with a clumsy or relaxed bouncing movement
WORD ORIGIN probably LOLL + *-op*, as in *gallop*

lolly *n, pl* **-lies 1** *informal* a lollipop **2** *Brit* ▸short for **ice lolly 3** *Brit, Austral, & NZ slang* money **4** *Austral & NZ informal* a sweet
WORD ORIGIN shortened from *lollipop*

Lomax *n* **Alan** born 1915, and his father **John Avery** (1867–1948), US folklorists

Lombard¹ *n* **1** a native or inhabitant of Lombardy **2** Also called: **Langobard** a member of an ancient Germanic people who settled in N Italy after 568 AD ▷ *adj* Also **Lombardic 3** of or relating to Lombardy or the Lombards

Lombard² *n* **Peter** ?1100–?60, Italian theologian, noted for his *Sententiarum libri quatuor*

Lombardi *n* **Vincent Thomas** 1913–70, American football coach, whose team won the first two Superbowls, and after whom the Superbowl trophy is named

Lombroso *n* **Cesare** 1836–1909, Italian criminologist: he postulated the existence of a criminal type

Lomu *n* **Jonah** born 1975, New Zealand Rugby Union football player

London¹ *n* **1** the capital of the United Kingdom, a port in S England on the River Thames near its estuary on the North Sea: consists of the **City** (the financial quarter), the **West End** (the entertainment and major shopping centre), the **East End** (the industrial and former dock area), and extensive suburbs. Latin name: **Londinium.** ▸See also **City 2 Greater London** the administrative area of London, consisting of the City of London and 32 boroughs (13 Inner London boroughs and 19 Outer London boroughs): formed in 1965 from the City, parts of Surrey, Kent, Essex, and Hertfordshire, and almost all of Middlesex, and abolished for administrative purposes in 1996: a Mayor of London and a new London Assembly took office in 2000. Pop: 7 387 900 (2003 est). Area: 1579 sq km (610 sq miles) **3** a city in SE Canada, in SE Ontario on the Thames River: University of Western Ontario (1878). Pop: 337 318 (2001) **4 it's London to a brick** *Austral & NZ slang* it is certain

London² *n* **Jack,** full name *John Griffith London.* 1876–1916, US novelist, short-story writer, and adventurer. His works include *Call of the Wild* (1903), *The Sea Wolf* (1904), *The Iron Heel* (1907), and the semiautobiographical *John Barleycorn* (1913)

Londoner *n* a person from London

London pride *n* a rock plant with a rosette of leaves and pink flowers

lone ❶ *adj* **1** solitary: *a lone figure* **2** isolated: *a lone isle guarded by the great Atlantic swell* **3** *Brit* unmarried or widowed: *a lone parent*
WORD ORIGIN from the mistaken division of *alone* into *a lone*

lonely ❶ *adj* **-lier, -liest 1** unhappy as a result of solitude **2** resulting from the state of being alone: *command can be a lonely business* **3** isolated and not much visited by people: *a lonely beach* **loneliness** *n*

THESAURUS

logic *n* **3 = reason**, reasoning, sense, good reason, good sense, sound judgment

logical *adj* **1, 2, 3 = rational**, clear, reasoned, reasonable, sound, relevant, consistent, valid, coherent, pertinent, well-organized, cogent, well-reasoned, deducible
OPPOSITE: illogical
4 = reasonable, obvious, sensible, most likely, natural, necessary, wise, plausible, judicious
OPPOSITE: unlikely

lone *adj* **1 = solitary**, single, separate, one, only, sole, by yourself, unaccompanied

lonely *adj* **1 = solitary**, alone, isolated, abandoned, lone, withdrawn, single, estranged, outcast, forsaken, forlorn, destitute, by yourself, lonesome (*chiefly US & Canad*), friendless, companionless
OPPOSITE: accompanied
3 = desolate, deserted, remote, isolated, solitary, out-of-the-way, secluded, uninhabited, sequestered, off the beaten track (*informal*), godforsaken, unfrequented
OPPOSITE: crowded

DICTIONARY

lonely hearts *adj* of or for people seeking a congenial companion or marriage partner: *lonely hearts ads*

loner *n informal* a person who prefers to be alone

lonesome ⓣ *adj* **1** *chiefly US & Canad* lonely **2** causing feelings of loneliness: *it was lonesome up here on the mountain*

long[1] ⓣ *adj* **1** having relatively great length in space or time **2** having greater than the average or expected range, extent, or duration: *a long session of talks* **3** seeming to occupy a greater time than is really so: *she was quiet a long moment* **4** of a specified extent or duration: *trimmed to about two cms long* **5** consisting of a large number of parts: *a long list* **6** *phonetics, prosody* (of a vowel) of relatively considerable duration **7** from end to end; lengthwise **8** *finance* having large holdings of securities or commodities in anticipation of rising prices **9 in the long run** ultimately; after or over a period of time **10 long on** *informal* plentifully supplied or endowed with: *long on show-biz gossip* ▷ *adv* **11** for a certain time or period: *how long have we got?* **12** for or during an extensive period of time: *to talk long into the night* **13** a considerable amount of time: *long after I met you; long ago* **14 as** *or* **so long as a** for or during the same length of time that **b** provided that; if ▷ *n* **15** anything that is long **16 before long** soon **17 for long** for a long time **18 the long and the short of it** the essential points or facts **longish** *adj*
WORD ORIGIN Old English *lang*

long[2] ⓣ *vb* to have a strong desire for something or to do something: *I longed for a baby; the more I think of him the more I long to see him*
WORD ORIGIN Old English *langian*

long. longitude

long- *adv (in combination)* for or lasting a long time: *long-established; long-lasting*

Long *n* **Crawford Williamson** 1815–78, US surgeon. He was the first to use ether as an anaesthetic

longboat *n* **1** the largest boat carried aboard a commercial ship **2** ▸ same as **longship**

longbow *n* a large powerful hand-drawn bow

long-distance *adj* **1** covering relatively long distances: *a long-distance race* **2** (of a telephone call) connecting points relatively far apart

longevity (lon-jev-it-ee) *n* long life
WORD ORIGIN Latin *longus* long + *aevum* age

long face *n* a glum expression

Longfellow *n* **Henry Wadsworth** 1807–82, US poet, noted particularly for his long narrative poems *Evangeline* (1847) and *The Song of Hiawatha* (1855)

longhand *n* ordinary handwriting, as opposed to typing or shorthand

longhorn *n* a British breed of beef cattle with long curved horns

longing ⓣ *n* **1** a strong feeling of wanting something one is unlikely ever to have ▷ *adj* **2** having or showing desire: *longing glances*
longingly *adv*

Longinus *n* **Dionysius** ?2nd century AD, supposed author of the famous Greek treatise on literary criticism, *On the Sublime* > **Longinean** *adj*

longitude *n* distance in degrees east or west of the prime meridian at 0°
WORD ORIGIN Latin *longitudo* length

longitudinal *adj* **1** of longitude or length **2** placed or extended lengthways

long johns *pl n informal* long underpants

long jump *n* an athletic contest of jumping the greatest length from a fixed mark

long-life *adj* (of milk, batteries, etc.) lasting longer than the regular kind

long-lived *adj* living or lasting for a long time

long-playing *adj old-fashioned* of or relating to an LP

long-range *adj* **1** of or extending into the future: *a long-range economic forecast* **2** (of vehicles, aircraft, or weapons) capable of covering great distances

longship *n* a narrow open boat with oars and a square sail, used by the Vikings

longshore drift *n* the movement of material along a beach, due to waves approaching the shore at an oblique angle

longshoreman *n, pl* **-men** *US & Canad* a docker

long shot *n* **1** an undertaking, guess, or possibility with little chance of success **2** a bet against heavy odds **3 not by a long shot** not by any means: *she wasn't beaten, not by a long shot*

long-sighted *adj* **1** able to see only distant objects in focus **2** far-sighted

long-standing ⓣ *adj* existing for a long time

long-suffering *adj* enduring trouble or unhappiness without complaint

long-term *adj* **1** lasting or extending over a long time: *a long-term commitment* ▷ *n* **long term 2 in the long term** over a long period of time: *in the long term the cost of energy will have to go up*

longtime *adj* of long standing: *his longtime colleague; his longtime relationship with Sue*

Longus *n* ?3rd century AD, Greek author of the prose romance *Daphnis and Chloe*

long wave *n* a radio wave with a wavelength greater than 1000 metres

longways *or US & Canad* **longwise** *adv* lengthways

long-winded *adj* tiresomely long
long-windedness *n*

loo *n, pl* **loos** *Brit & NZ informal* a toilet
WORD ORIGIN perhaps from French *lieux d'aisance* water closet

loofah *n* a long rough-textured bath sponge made from the dried pod of a gourd
WORD ORIGIN Arabic *lūf*

look ⓣ *vb* **1** (often foll. by *at*) to direct the eyes (towards): *he turned to look at her* **2** (often foll. by *at*) to consider: *let's look at the issues involved* **3** to give the impression of being; seem: *Luxembourg's timetable looks a winner* **4** to face in a particular direction: *Morgan's Rock looks south* **5** (foll. by *for*) to search or seek: *the department looks for reputable firms* **6** (foll. by *into*) to carry out an investigation **7** to direct a look at (someone) in a specified way: *she looks at Teresina suspiciously* **8** to match in appearance with

l

THESAURUS

lonesome *adj* **1, 2** *(chiefly US & Canad)* = **lonely**, deserted, isolated, lone, gloomy, dreary, desolate, forlorn, friendless, cheerless, companionless

long[1] *adj* **1** = **elongated**, extended, stretched, expanded, extensive, lengthy, far-reaching, spread out
OPPOSITE: short
2, 3 = **prolonged**, slow, dragging, sustained, lengthy, lingering, protracted, interminable, spun out, long-drawn-out **OPPOSITE:** brief

long[2] *vb* = **desire**, want, wish, burn, dream of, pine, hunger, ache, lust, crave, yearn, covet, itch, hanker, set your heart on, eat your heart out over

longing *n* **1** = **desire**, hope, wish, burning, urge, ambition, hunger, yen *(informal)*, hungering, aspiration, ache, craving, yearning, coveting, itch, thirst, hankering
OPPOSITE: indifference

long-standing *adj* = **established**, fixed, enduring, abiding, long-lasting, long-lived, long-established, time-honoured

look *vb* **1, 7** (often foll. by *at*) = **see**, view, consider, watch, eye, study, check, regard, survey, clock *(Brit slang)*, examine, observe, stare, glance, gaze, scan, check out *(informal)*, inspect, gape, peep, behold *(archaic)*, goggle, eyeball *(slang)*, scrutinize, ogle, gawp *(Brit slang)*, gawk, recce *(slang)*, get a load of *(informal)*, take a gander at *(informal)*, rubberneck *(slang)*, take a dekko at *(Brit slang)*, feast your eyes upon
2 (often foll. by *at*) **consider**,

DICTIONARY

(something): *looking your best* **9** to expect or hope (to do something): *we would look to derive a procedure that would account for most cases* **10** **look alive** *or* **lively** *or* **sharp** *or* **smart** to hurry up; get busy **11** **look here** an expression used to attract someone's attention or add emphasis to a statement ▷ *n* **12** an instance of looking: *a look of icy contempt* **13** a view or sight (of something): *take a look at my view* **14** (*often pl*) appearance to the eye or mind; aspect: *I'm not happy with the look of things here; better than you by the looks of it* **15** style or fashion: *the look made famous by the great Russian* ▷ *conj* **16** an expression demanding attention or showing annoyance: *look, I won't be coming back* ▶ See also **look after, look back**, etc. **looker** *n*
WORD ORIGIN Old English *lōcian*

look after ⊕ *vb* to take care of

lookalike *n* a person or thing that is the double of another, often well-known, person or thing

look back *vb* **1** to think about the past **2** **never looked back** was extremely successful: *he became the station's first major signing and never looked back*

look down ⊕ *vb* (foll. by *on* or *upon*) to treat as inferior or unimportant

look forward to ⊕ *vb* to anticipate with pleasure

look-in *informal n* **1** a chance to be chosen or participate: *before anyone else gets a look-in* ▷ *vb* **look in** **2** to pay a short visit

looking glass *n* a mirror

look on *vb* **1** to be a spectator **2** to consider or regard: *I just looked on her as a friend* **looker-on** *n*

lookout ⊕ *n* **1** the act of watching for danger or for an opportunity: *on the lookout for attack* **2** a person or people keeping such a watch **3** a viewpoint from which a watch is kept **4** *informal* worry or concern: *that is my lookout rather than theirs* **5** *chiefly Brit* chances or prospect: *it's a bad lookout for Europe* ▷ *vb* **look out** **6** to be careful **7** to watch out for: *look out particularly for oils that have been flavoured* **8** to find and take out: *little time to look out clothes that she might need* **9** (foll. by *on* or *over*) to face in a particular direction: *looking out over the courtyard*

look over *vb* **1** to inspect or examine ▷ *n* **look-over** **2** an inspection

look-see *n slang* a brief inspection

look up ⊕ *vb* **1** to discover or confirm by checking in a reference book **2** to improve: *things were looking up* **3** **look up to** to have respect for: *she looked up to him as a kind of father* **4** to visit (a person): *I'll look you up when I'm in town*

loom[1] *n* a machine for weaving yarn into cloth
WORD ORIGIN variant of Old English *gelōma* tool

loom[2] ⊕ *vb* **1** to appear indistinctly, esp. as a tall and threatening shape **2** (of an event) to seem ominously close
WORD ORIGIN perhaps East Frisian *lomen* to move slowly

loon[1] *n US & Canad* ▶ same as **diver** (sense 3)
WORD ORIGIN Scandinavian

loon[2] *n informal* a simple-minded or stupid person

loonie *n Canad slang* **1** a Canadian dollar coin with a loon bird on one of its faces **2** the Canadian currency

loony *slang adj* **loonier, looniest** **1** insane **2** foolish or ridiculous ▷ *n, pl* **loonies** **3** a foolish or insane person
WORD ORIGIN shortened from *lunatic*

loop ⊕ *n* **1** the rounded shape formed by a curved line that crosses itself: *a loop of the highway* **2** any round or oval-shaped thing that is closed or nearly closed **3** *electronics* a closed circuit through which a signal can circulate **4** a flight manoeuvre in which an aircraft flies vertically in a complete circle **5** a continuous strip of film or tape **6** *computers* a series of instructions in a program, performed repeatedly until some specified condition is satisfied ▷ *vb* **7** to make into a loop **8** to fasten or encircle with a loop **9** Also: **loop the loop** to fly or be flown vertically in a complete circle
WORD ORIGIN origin unknown

loophole ⊕ *n* an ambiguity or omission in the law, which enables one to evade it

loopy *adj* **loopier, loopiest** *informal* slightly mad or crazy

Loos *n* **Adolf** 1870–1933, Austrian architect: a pioneer of modern architecture, noted for his plain austere style in such buildings as Steiner House, Vienna (1910)

loose ⊕ *adj* **1** (of clothing) not close-fitting: *the jacket loose and unbuttoned* **2** free or released from confinement or restraint **3** not tight, fastened, fixed, or tense **4** not bundled, fastened, or put in a container: *loose tobacco* **5** inexact or imprecise: *a loose translation* **6** (of cash) accessible: *a lot of the loose money is floating around the city* **7** *old-fashioned*

THESAURUS

contemplate **3 = seem**, appear, display, seem to be, look like, exhibit, manifest, strike you as **4 = face**, overlook, front on, give onto **5** (foll. by *for*) **= search**, seek, hunt, forage, fossick (*Austral & NZ*) **9 = hope**, expect, await, anticipate, reckon on ▷ *n* **12, 13 = glimpse**, view, glance, observation, review, survey, sight, examination, gaze, inspection, peek, squint (*informal*), butcher's (*Brit slang*), gander (*informal*), once-over (*informal*), recce (*slang*), eyeful (*informal*), look-see (*slang*), shufti (*Brit slang*) **14, 15** (often *pl*) **appearance**, effect, bearing, face, air, style, fashion, cast, aspect, manner, expression, impression, complexion, guise, countenance, semblance, demeanour, mien (*literary*)

look after = take care of, mind, watch, protect, tend, guard, nurse, care for, supervise, sit with, attend to, keep an eye on, take charge of

look down (foll. by *on* or *upon*) **disdain**, despise, scorn, sneer at, spurn, hold in contempt, treat with contempt, turn your nose up (at) (*informal*), contemn (*formal*), look down your nose at (*informal*), misprize

look forward to = anticipate, expect, look for, wait for, await, hope for, long for, count on, count the days until, set your heart on

lookout *n* **1 = watch**, guard, vigil, qui vive **2 = watchman**, guard, sentry, sentinel, vedette (*military*) **3 = watchtower**, post, tower, beacon, observatory, citadel, observation post **4** (*informal*) **= concern**, business, worry, funeral (*informal*), pigeon (*Brit informal*) **7 = be careful of**, beware, watch out for, pay attention to, be wary of, be alert to, be vigilant about, keep an eye out for, be on guard for, keep your eyes open for, keep your eyes peeled for, keep your eyes skinned for, be on the qui vive for

look up = research, find, search for, hunt for, track down, seek out **2 = improve**, develop, advance, pick up, progress, come along, get better, shape up (*informal*), perk up, ameliorate, show improvement **3 look up to = respect**, honour, admire, esteem, revere, defer to, have a high opinion of, regard highly, think highly of **4 = visit**, call on, go to see, pay a visit to, drop in on (*informal*), look in on

loom[2] *vb* **1 = appear**, emerge, hover, take shape, threaten, bulk, menace, come into view, become visible

loop *n* **1, 2 = curve**, ring, circle, bend, twist, curl, spiral, hoop, coil, loophole, twirl, kink, noose, whorl, eyelet, convolution ▷ *vb* **7 = twist**, turn, join, roll, circle, connect, bend, fold, knot, curl, spiral, coil, braid, encircle, wind round, curve round

loophole *n* **= let-out**, escape, excuse, plea, avoidance, evasion, pretence, pretext, subterfuge, means of escape

loose *adj* **1 = slack**, easy, hanging, relaxed, loosened, not fitting, sloppy, baggy, slackened, loose-fitting, not tight **OPPOSITE:** tight **3 = free**, detached, insecure, unfettered, released, floating, wobbly, unsecured, unrestricted, untied, unattached, movable,

DICTIONARY

sexually promiscuous **8** lacking a sense of propriety: *loose talk* **9** **at a loose end** bored because one has nothing to do ▹*n* **10** **on the loose** free from confinement or restraint **11** **the loose** *rugby* the part of play when the forwards close round the ball in a ruck or loose scrum ▹*adv* **12** in a loose manner; loosely ▹*vb* **loosing, loosed** **13** to free or release from restraint or obligation: *he loosed the dogs* **14** to unfasten or untie: *the guards loosed his arms* **15** to make or become less strict, tight, firmly attached, or compact **16** to let fly (a bullet, arrow, or other missile) **loosely** *adv* **looseness** *n*
WORD ORIGIN Old Norse *lauss* free

loosebox *n* an enclosed stall with a door in which an animal can be kept

loose cannon *n* a person or thing, with the potential to cause considerable damage, that appears to be out of control

loose-jointed *adj* supple and lithe

loose-leaf *adj* (of a binder) allowing the removal and addition of pages

loosen ⊙ *vb* **1** to make or become less tight: *loosen and relax the ankle* **2** (often foll. by *up*) to make or become less firm, compact, or rigid: *massage is used first to loosen up the muscles* **3** to untie **4** (often foll. by *up*) to make or become less strict: *the churches loosen up on sexual teachings*

loot ⊙ *n* **1** goods stolen in wartime or during riots; plunder **2** *informal* money ▹*vb* **3** to plunder (a city) during war or riots **4** to steal (money or goods) during war or riots **looter** *n*
WORD ORIGIN Hindi *lūt*

lop *vb* **lopping, lopped** (usually foll. by *off*) **1** to cut (parts) off a tree or body **2** to cut out or eliminate any unnecessary parts: *some parts of the legislature were lopped off*
WORD ORIGIN Middle English *loppe* branches cut off

lope *vb* **loping, loped** **1** to move or run with a long easy stride ▹*n* **2** a long steady gait or stride
WORD ORIGIN Old Norse *hlaupa* to leap

lop-eared *adj* (of animals) having ears that droop

Lopez *n* **Jennifer** born 1970, Puerto Rican singer and film actress, known as *J-Lo*; her films include *Out of Sight* (1997) and *The Wedding Planner* (2001) and her records include *On the 6* (1999) and *This is Me…Then* (2002)

lopsided *adj* greater in weight, height, or size on one side

loquacious *adj* talkative **loquacity** *n*
WORD ORIGIN Latin *loqui* to speak

lord ⊙ *n* **1** a person with power or authority over others, such as a monarch or master **2** a male member of the nobility **3** (in medieval Europe) a feudal superior **4** **my lord** a respectful form of address used to a judge, bishop, or nobleman ▹*vb* **5** **lord it over someone** to act in a superior manner towards someone
WORD ORIGIN Old English *hlāford* bread keeper

Lord ⊙ *n* **1** *Christianity* a title given to God or Jesus Christ **2** *Brit* a title given to certain male peers **3** *Brit* a title given to certain high officials and judges ▹*interj* **4** an exclamation of dismay or surprise: *Good Lord!*

Lord Chancellor *n* *Brit government* the cabinet minster who is head of the judiciary and Speaker of the House of Lords

Lord Chief Justice *n* (in England and Wales) the judge who is second only to the Lord Chancellor and president of one division of the High Court of Justice

Lord Lieutenant *n* **1** (in Britain) the representative of the Crown in a county **2** (formerly) the British viceroy in Ireland

lordly *adj* **-lier, -liest** **1** haughty or arrogant **2** of or suitable to a lord **lordliness** *n*

Lord Mayor *n* the mayor in the City of London, in certain other English boroughs, and in some Australian cities

Lord Privy Seal *n* (in Britain) the senior cabinet minister without official duties

Lords *n* **the Lords** ▸short for **House of Lords**

lordship *n* the position or authority of a lord

Lordship *n* (preceded by *Your* or *His*) *Brit* a title used to address or refer to a bishop, a judge of the high court, or any peer except a duke

Lord's Prayer *n* **the Lord's Prayer** the prayer taught by Jesus Christ to his disciples

Lords Spiritual *pl n* (in Britain) the Anglican archbishops and senior bishops who are members of the House of Lords

Lord's Supper *n* **the Lord's Supper** ▸same as **Holy Communion**

Lords Temporal *pl n* (in Britain) the peers other than bishops in their capacity as members of the House of Lords

lore *n* collective knowledge or wisdom on a particular subject
WORD ORIGIN Old English *lār*

Lorenz *n* **Konrad Zacharias** 1903–89, Austrian zoologist, who founded ethology. His works include *On Aggression* (1966): shared the Nobel prize for physiology or medicine 1973

lorgnette (lor-**nyet**) *n* a pair of spectacles or opera glasses mounted on a long handle
WORD ORIGIN French, from *lorgner* to squint

lorikeet *n* a small brightly coloured Australian parrot

Lorrain *n* See **Claude Lorrain**

Lorris *n* See **Guillaume de Lorris**

lorry *n, pl* **-ries** *Brit & S African* a large motor vehicle for transporting heavy loads
WORD ORIGIN perhaps dialect *lurry* to pull

los Angeles *n* See **de los Angeles**

lose ⊙ *vb* **losing, lost** **1** to come to be without, through carelessness or by accident or theft **2** to fail to keep or

THESAURUS

unfastened, unbound, unconfined **5 = vague**, random, inaccurate, disordered, rambling, diffuse, indefinite, disconnected, imprecise, ill-defined, indistinct, inexact
OPPOSITE: precise
7 *(old-fashioned)* **= promiscuous**, fast, abandoned, immoral, dissipated, lewd, wanton, profligate, disreputable, debauched, dissolute, libertine, licentious, unchaste
OPPOSITE: chaste
▹*vb* **13, 14 = free**, release, ease, liberate, detach, unleash, let go, undo, loosen, disconnect, set free, slacken, untie, disengage, unfasten, unbind, unloose, unbridle
OPPOSITE: fasten

loosen *vb* **3 = untie**, undo, release, separate, detach, let out, unstick, slacken, unbind, work free, work loose, unloose
4 (often foll. by *up*) **= relax**, chill *(slang)*, soften, unwind, go easy *(informal)*, lighten up *(slang)*, hang loose, outspan *(S African)*, ease up *or* off

loot *n* **1 = plunder**, goods, prize, haul, spoils, booty, swag *(slang)* ▹*vb* **3, 4 = plunder**, rob, raid, sack, rifle, ravage, ransack, pillage, despoil

lord *n* **1a = ruler**, leader, chief, king, prince, master, governor, commander, superior, monarch, sovereign, liege, overlord, potentate, seigneur ▹*vb* **5 lord it over someone = boss around** *or* **about** *(informal)*, order around, threaten, bully, menace, intimidate, hector, bluster, browbeat, ride roughshod over, pull rank on, tyrannize, put on airs, be overbearing, act big *(slang)*, overbear, play the lord, domineer

Lord *n* **1b the Lord** *or* **Our Lord = Jesus Christ**, God, Christ, Messiah, Jehovah, the Almighty, the Galilean, the Good Shepherd, the Nazarene **2 = peer**, nobleman, count, duke, gentleman, earl, noble, baron, aristocrat, viscount, childe *(archaic)*

lose *vb* **1, 10 = mislay**, miss, drop, forget, displace, be deprived of, fail to keep, lose track of, suffer loss,

DICTIONARY

maintain: *to lose control* **3** to suffer the loss of: *he will lose his redundancy money* **4** to get rid of: *I've lost a stone this summer* **5** to fail to get or make use of: *Lysenko never lost a chance to show his erudition* **6** to be defeated in a fight or competition **7** to fail to see, hear, or understand: *she lost sight of him* **8** to waste: *so I'd lost a fortune* **9** to go astray from: *psychologists lose the trail* **10** to allow to go astray or out of sight: *he lost, at the Gare de Lyon, a case with most of his early manuscripts* **11** to cause the loss of: *I came in to have the gear attended to, which lost me a lap* **12** to absorb or engross: *lost in thought* **13** to die or cause the death of: *two lost as yacht sinks in storm* **14** to outdistance or escape from: *there's some satisfaction in knowing that they've lost us* **15** (of a timepiece) to run slow (by a specified amount)
WORD ORIGIN Old English *losian* to perish

lose out *vb informal* **1** to be defeated or unsuccessful **2** **lose out on** to fail to secure or make use of: *the yard has already lost out on a number of valuable orders this year*

loser ❶ *n* **1** a person or thing that loses **2** *informal* a person or thing that seems destined to fail: *he's a bit of a loser*

Losey *n* **Joseph** 1909–84, US film director, in Britain from 1952. His films include *The Servant* (1963), *The Go-Between* (1971), and *Don Giovanni* (1979)

losing *adj* unprofitable or failing: *a losing streak that cost him millions*

loss ❶ *n* **1** the act or an instance of losing **2** (sometimes *pl*) the person, thing, or amount lost: *the only loss was a sleeping-bag* **3** the disadvantage or deprivation resulting from losing: *a loss of sovereignty* **4** **at a loss** **a** uncertain what to do; bewildered **b** with income less than outlay: *they cannot afford to run branches at a loss*
WORD ORIGIN Old English *lōsian* to be destroyed

loss leader *n* an article offered at a low price to attract customers

lost ❶ *vb* **1** ▸ the past of **lose** ▹ *adj* **2** unable to find one's way **3** unable to be found or recovered **4** confused or bewildered: *she seemed a bit lost* **5** (sometimes foll. by *on*) not used, noticed, or understood by: *not that the propaganda value of the game was lost on the authorities* **6** no longer possessed or existing: *lost credit* **7** (foll. by *in*) engrossed (in): *he remained lost in his own thoughts* **8** morally fallen: *a lost woman* **9** damned: *a lost soul*

lost cause *n* something with no chance of success

lot ❶ *pron* **1** **a lot** a great number or quantity: *not that there was a lot to tell; a lot of people* ▹ *n* **2** a collection of things or people: *your lot have wasted enough time* **3** destiny or fortune: *the refugees did not choose their lot* **4** any object, such as a straw or slip of paper, drawn from others at random to make a selection or choice: *they could only be split by the drawing of lots; the casting by lots* **5** the use of lots in making a choice: *chosen by lot* **6** an item or set of items for sale in an auction **7** *US, Canad, Austral & NZ* an area of land: *to the parking lot* **8** **a bad lot** an unpleasant or disreputable person **9** **cast** *or* **throw in one's lot with someone** to join with voluntarily and share the fortunes of someone **10** **the lot** the entire amount or number ▹ *adv* **11** (preceded by *a*) *informal* to a considerable extent, degree, or amount: *steroids are used a lot in weightlifting* ▸ See also **lots**
WORD ORIGIN Old English *hlot*

loth (rhymes with **both**) *adj* ▸ same as **loath**

Lothair I *n* ?795–855 AD, Frankish ruler and Holy Roman Emperor (823–30, 833–34, 840–55); son of Louis I, whom he twice deposed from the throne

Lothair II *n* called *the Saxon*. ?1070–1137, German king (1125–37) and Holy Roman Emperor (1133–37). He was elected German king over the hereditary Hohenstaufen claimant

Lothario (loh-**thah**-ree-oh) *n, pl* **-os** a seducer
WORD ORIGIN after a character in a play

lotion ❶ *n* a liquid preparation having a soothing, cleansing, or antiseptic action, applied to the skin
WORD ORIGIN Latin *lotio* a washing

lots *informal pl n* **1** (often foll. by *of*) great numbers or quantities: *lots of friends; you can read lots into Nostradamus* ▹ *adv* **2** a great deal

lottery ❶ *n, pl* **-teries** **1** a method of raising money by selling tickets by which a winner is selected at random **2** a venture whose outcome is a matter of luck: *hospital treatment is a lottery*
WORD ORIGIN Middle Dutch *loterije*

lotto *n* **1** a game of chance similar to bingo **2** **Lotto** (in certain countries) the national lottery
WORD ORIGIN Italian

lotus *n* **1** (in Greek mythology) a fruit that induces dreamy forgetfulness in those who eat it **2** any of several water lilies of tropical Africa and Asia, regarded as sacred **3** a symbolic representation of such a plant
WORD ORIGIN Greek *lōtos*

lotus-eater *n* a person who lives in lazy forgetfulness

lotus position *n* a seated cross-legged position with each foot on top of the opposite thigh, used in yoga and meditation

loud ❶ *adj* **1** (of sound) relatively great in volume: *loud applause* **2** making or able to make sounds of relatively great volume: *a loud voice* **3** insistent and emphatic: *loud appeals* **4** (of colours or patterns) harsh to look at **5** noisy, vulgar, and offensive ▹ *adv* **6** in a loud manner **7** **out loud**

THESAURUS

misplace **3 = forfeit**, miss, fail, yield, default, be deprived of, pass up (*informal*), lose out on (*informal*) **6 = be defeated**, be beaten, lose out, be worsted, come to grief, come a cropper (*informal*), be the loser, suffer defeat, get the worst of, take a licking (*informal*), crash out

loser *n* **1, 2 = failure**, flop (*informal*), underdog, also-ran, no-hoper (*Austral slang*), dud (*informal*), lemon (*slang*), clinker (*slang, chiefly US*), washout (*informal*), non-achiever

loss *n* **1 = losing**, waste, disappearance, deprivation, squandering, drain, forfeiture **OPPOSITE:** gain
2 (*sometimes plural*) **= deficit**, debt, deficiency, debit, depletion, shrinkage, losings **OPPOSITE:** gain
3 = damage, cost, injury, hurt, harm, disadvantage, detriment, impairment **OPPOSITE:** advantage
4a at a loss = confused, puzzled, baffled, bewildered, stuck (*informal*), helpless, stumped, perplexed, mystified, nonplussed, at your wits' end

lost *adj* **3 = missing**, missed, disappeared, vanished, strayed, wayward, forfeited, misplaced, mislaid

lot *n* **2 = bunch** (*informal*), group, crowd, crew, set, band, quantity, assortment, consignment
3 = destiny, situation, circumstances, fortune, chance, accident, fate, portion, doom, hazard, plight

lotion *n* **= cream**, solution, balm, salve, liniment, embrocation

lottery *n* **1 = raffle**, draw, lotto (*Brit, NZ & S African*), sweepstake **2 = gamble**, chance, risk, venture, hazard, toss-up (*informal*)

loud *adj* **1, 2, 3 = noisy**, strong, booming, roaring, piercing, thundering, forte (*music*), turbulent, resounding, deafening, thunderous, rowdy, blaring, strident, boisterous, tumultuous, vociferous, vehement, sonorous, ear-splitting, obstreperous, stentorian, clamorous, ear-piercing, high-sounding
OPPOSITE: quiet
4 = garish, bold, glaring, flamboyant, vulgar, brash, tacky (*informal*), flashy, lurid, tasteless, naff (*Brit slang*), gaudy, tawdry, showy, ostentatious, brassy **OPPOSITE:** sombre

DICTIONARY

audibly **loudly** *adv* **loudness** *n*
WORD ORIGIN Old English *hlud*

loud-hailer *n* a portable loudspeaker with a built-in amplifier and microphone

loudmouth *n* a person who talks too much, esp. in a boastful or indiscreet way **loudmouthed** *adj*

loudspeaker *n* a device for converting electrical signals into sounds

lough *n Irish* **1** a lake **2** a long narrow arm of the sea
WORD ORIGIN Irish *loch* lake

Louis I *n* known as *Louis the Pious* or *Louis the Debonair.* 778–840 AD, king of France and Holy Roman Emperor (814–23, 830–33, 834–40): he was twice deposed by his sons

Louis II *n* **1** known as *Louis the German.* ?804–876 AD, king of Germany (843–76); son of Louis I **2** 1845–86, king of Bavaria (1864–86): noted for his extravagant castles and his patronage of Wagner. Declared insane (1886), he drowned himself **3** ▸ **de Bourbon** See (Prince de) **Condé**

Louis IV *n* known as *Louis the Bavarian.* ?1287–1347, king of Germany (1314–47) and Holy Roman Emperor (1328–47)

Louis IX *n* known as *Saint Louis.* 1214–70, king of France (1226–70): led the Sixth Crusade (1248–54) and was held to ransom (1250); died at Tunis while on another crusade

Louis Napoleon *n* the original name of **Napoleon III**

Louis of Nassau *n* 1538–74, a leader (1568–74) of the revolt of the Netherlands against Spain: died in battle

Louis Philippe *n* known as the *Citizen King.* 1773–1850, king of the French (1830–48). His régime became excessively identified with the bourgeoisie and he was forced to abdicate by the revolution of 1848

Louis V *n* known as *Louis le Fainéant.* ?967–987 AD, last Carolingian king of France (986–87)

Louis VII *n* known as *Louis le Jeune.* *c.* 1120–80, king of France (1137–80). He engaged in frequent hostilities (1152–74) with Henry II of England

Louis VIII *n* known as *Coeur-de-Lion.* 1187–1226, king of France (1223–26). He was offered the English throne by opponents of King John but his invasion failed (1216)

Louis XI *n* 1423–83, king of France (1461–83); involved in a struggle with his vassals, esp. the duke of Burgundy, in his attempt to unite France under an absolute monarchy

Louis XII *n* 1462–1515, king of France (1498–1515), who fought a series of unsuccessful wars in Italy

Louis XVII *n* 1785–95, titular king of France (1793–95) during the Revolution, after the execution of his father Louis XVI; he died in prison

Louis XVIII *n* 1755–1824, king of France (1814–24); younger brother of Louis XVI. He became titular king after the death of Louis XVII (1795) and ascended the throne at the Bourbon restoration in 1814. He was forced to flee during the Hundred Days

lounge ❶ *n* **1** a living room in a private house **2** ▸ same as **lounge bar** **3** a communal room in a hotel, ship, or airport, used for waiting or relaxing in **4** the act of lounging ▹ *vb* **lounging, lounged 5** (often foll. by *about* or *around*) to sit or lie in a relaxed manner **6** to pass time lazily or idly
WORD ORIGIN origin unknown

lounge bar *n* a more expensive and comfortable bar in a pub or hotel

lounge suit *n* a man's suit for daytime wear

lour *vb* ▸ same as **lower**[2]

lourie (rhymes with **dowry**) *or* **loerie** *n* a type of African bird with either crimson or grey plumage
WORD ORIGIN Afrikaans, from Malay

louse *n* **1** *pl* **lice** a wingless blood-sucking insect which feeds off man and some animals **2** *pl* **louses** *slang* an unpleasant or dishonourable person
WORD ORIGIN Old English *lūs*

louse up *vb* **lousing, loused** *slang* to ruin or spoil

lousy *adj* **lousier, lousiest 1** *slang* very mean or unpleasant **2** *slang* inferior or bad **3** *slang* ill or unwell **4** infested with lice

lout *n* a crude or oafish person; boor **loutish** *adj*
WORD ORIGIN perhaps Old English *lūtan* to stoop

louvre *or US* **louver** (loo-ver) *n* **a** any of a set of horizontal slats in a door or window, slanted to admit air but not rain **b** the slats and frame supporting them **louvred** *or US* **louvered** *adj*
WORD ORIGIN Old French *lovier*

lovage *n* a European herb with greenish-white flowers
WORD ORIGIN Old French *luvesche,* from Latin *ligusticum,* literally: Ligurian (plant)

love ❶ *vb* **loving, loved 1** to have a great affection for a person or thing **2** to have passionate desire for someone **3** to like (to do something) very much ▹ *n* **4** an intense emotion of affection towards a person or thing **5** a deep feeling of sexual attraction **6** wholehearted liking for or pleasure in something **7** a beloved person: often used as an endearment **8** *Brit informal* a commonplace term of address, not necessarily restricted to people one knows or has regard for **9** (in tennis, squash, etc.) a score of zero **10 fall in love** to become in love **11 for love or money** in any circumstances **12 in love** feeling a strong emotional and sexual attraction **13 make love to a** to have sexual intercourse with **b** *now archaic* to court **lovable** *or* **loveable** *adj*
WORD ORIGIN Old English *lufu*

love affair ❶ *n* a romantic or sexual relationship between two people who are not married to each other

lovebird *n* any of several small African parrots often kept as cage birds

lovebite *n* a temporary red mark left on a person's skin by a partner biting or sucking it during lovemaking

love child *n euphemistic* a child whose parents have not been married to each other

THESAURUS

lounge *n* **1 = sitting room,** living room, parlour, drawing room, front room, reception room, television room ▹ *vb* **5, 6** (often foll. by *about* or *around*) **= relax,** pass time, hang out *(informal),* idle, loaf, potter, sprawl, lie about, waste time, recline, take it easy, saunter, loiter, loll, dawdle, laze, kill time, make yourself at home, veg out *(slang, chiefly US),* outspan *(S African),* fritter time away

love *vb* **1, 2 = adore,** care for, treasure, cherish, prize, worship, be devoted to, be attached to, be in love with, dote on, hold dear, think the world of, idolize, feel affection for, have affection for, adulate **OPPOSITE:** hate **3 = enjoy,** like, desire, fancy, appreciate, relish, delight in, savour, take pleasure in, have a soft spot for, be partial to, have a weakness for **OPPOSITE:** dislike ▹ *n* **4, 5 = passion,** liking, regard, friendship, affection, warmth, attachment, intimacy, devotion, tenderness, fondness, rapture, adulation, adoration, infatuation, ardour, endearment, aroha *(NZ),* amity **OPPOSITE:** hatred **6 = liking,** taste, delight in, bent for, weakness for, relish for, enjoyment, devotion to, penchant for, inclination for, zest for, fondness for, soft spot for, partiality to **7 = beloved,** dear, dearest, sweet, lover, angel, darling, honey, loved one, sweetheart, truelove, dear one, leman *(archaic),* inamorata *or* inamorato **OPPOSITE:** enemy **13a make love** (foll. by *to*) **= have sexual intercourse,** have sex, go to bed, sleep together, do it *(informal),* mate, have sexual relations, have it off *(slang),* have it away *(slang)*

love affair *n* **= romance,** relationship, affair, intrigue, liaison, amour, affaire de coeur *(French)*

DICTIONARY

Lovelace *n* **1 Countess of,** title of *Ada Augusta King.* 1815–52, English mathematician and personal assistant to Charles Babbage: daughter of Lord Byron. She wrote the first computer program **2 Richard** 1618–58, English Cavalier poet, noted for *To Althea from Prison* (1642) and *Lucasta* (1649)

loveless *adj* without love: *a loveless marriage*

love-lies-bleeding *n* a plant with drooping spikes of small red flowers

love life *n* a person's romantic or sexual relationships

Lovell *n* Sir **Bernard** born 1913, English radio astronomer; founder (1951) and director of Jodrell Bank

lovelorn *adj* miserable because of unreturned love or unhappiness in love

lovely ⓣ *adj* **-lier, -liest 1** very attractive or beautiful **2** highly pleasing or enjoyable: *thanks for a lovely evening* ▷ *n, pl* **-lies 3** *slang* an attractive woman: *curvaceous lovelies* **loveliness** *n*

lovemaking *n* **1** sexual play and activity between lovers, including sexual intercourse **2** *archaic* courtship

lover ⓣ *n* **1** a person having a sexual relationship with another person outside marriage **2** *(often pl)* either of the people involved in a love affair **3** someone who loves a specified person or thing: *an animal-lover*

lovesick *adj* pining or languishing because of love **lovesickness** *n*

lovey-dovey *adj* making a sentimental or showy display of affection

loving ⓣ *adj* feeling or showing love and affection **lovingly** *adv*

loving cup *n* a large two-handled cup out of which people drink in turn

low[1] ⓣ *adj* **1** having a relatively small distance from base to top: *a low wall* **2** of less than usual amount, degree, quality, or cost: *low score; low inflation* **3** situated at a relatively short distance above the ground, sea level, or the horizon: *heavy weather with low driving cloud* **4** (of numbers) small **5** involving or containing a relatively small amount of something: *low-alcohol summer drinks* **6** having little value or quality: *it sounds as if your self-confidence is low* **7** coarse or vulgar: *low comedy* **8** unworthy or contemptible: *Oh, that's low, Justin* **9** inferior in culture or status **10** in a weakened physical or mental state **11** with a hushed tone: *in a low, scared voice* **12** low-necked: *a low evening gown* **13** *music* of or having a relatively low pitch **14** (of latitudes) situated not far north or south of the equator **15** having little or no money **16** unfavourable: *he has a low opinion of Ford* **17** deep: *a low bow* **18** (of a gear) providing a relatively low speed ▷ *adv* **19** in a low position, level, or degree: *the pilot flew low over the area* **20** at a low pitch; deeply: *he's singing very low* **21** cheaply: *the bank is having to buy high and sell low* **22 lay low a** to make (someone) fall by a blow **b** to overcome or destroy **23 lie low** to keep or be concealed or quiet ▷ *n* **24** a low position, level, or degree: *shares hit new low* **25** an area of low atmospheric pressure; depression **lowness** *n*
WORD ORIGIN Old Norse *lāgr*

low[2] *n* **1** Also: **lowing** the sound uttered by cattle; moo ▷ *vb* **2** to make a mooing sound
WORD ORIGIN Old English *hlōwan*

Low *n* Sir **David** 1891–1963, British political cartoonist, born in New Zealand: created Colonel Blimp ▸ See **blimp**

low-alcohol *adj* (of beer or wine) containing only a small amount of alcohol

lowborn *adj now rare* of ignoble or common parentage

lowbrow *disparaging n* **1** a person with uncultivated or nonintellectual tastes ▷ *adj* **2** of or for such a person

Low Church *n* a section of the Church of England which stresses evangelical beliefs and practices **Low-Church** *adj*

low comedy *n* comedy characterized by slapstick and physical action

Low Countries *pl n* Belgium, Luxembourg, and the Netherlands

low-down *informal adj* **1** mean, underhand, and dishonest ▷ *n* **lowdown 2 the lowdown** information

Lowell *n* **1 Amy** (**Lawrence**) 1874–1925, US imagist poet and critic **2 James Russell** 1819–91, US poet, essayist, and diplomat, noted for his series of poems in Yankee dialect, *Biglow Papers* (1848; 1867) **3 Robert** (**Traill Spence**) 1917–77, US poet. His volumes of verse include *Lord Weary's Castle* (1946), *Life Studies* (1959), *For the Union Dead* (1964), and a book of free translations of European poems, *Imitations* (1961)

lower[1] ⓣ *adj* **1** being below one or more other things: *the lower branches* **2** reduced in amount or value: *lower rates* **3 Lower** *geol* denoting the early part of a period or formation ▷ *vb* **4** to cause or allow to move down: *she lowered her head* **5** to behave in a way that damages one's respect: *she'd never lowered herself enough to make a call* **6** to lessen or become less: *the cholesterol was lowered by medication* **7** to make quieter or reduce the pitch of

lower[2] *or* **lour** *vb* (of the sky or weather) to be overcast and menacing **lowering** *or* **louring** *adj*
WORD ORIGIN Middle English *louren* to scowl

THESAURUS

lovely *adj* **1 = beautiful**, appealing, attractive, charming, winning, pretty, sweet, handsome, good-looking, exquisite, admirable, enchanting, graceful, captivating, amiable, adorable, comely, fit *(Brit informal)* **OPPOSITE:** ugly
2 = wonderful, pleasing, nice, pleasant, engaging, marvellous, delightful, enjoyable, gratifying, agreeable **OPPOSITE:** horrible

lover *n* **1, 2** (often *pl*) **= sweetheart**, beloved, loved one, beau, flame *(informal)*, mistress, admirer, suitor, swain *(archaic)*, woman friend, lady friend, man friend, toy boy, paramour, leman *(archaic)*, fancy bit *(slang)*, boyfriend *or* girlfriend, fancy man *or* fancy woman *(slang)*, fiancé *or* fiancée, inamorata *or* inamorato, Wag *(Brit informal)*

loving *adj* **a = affectionate**, kind, warm, dear, friendly, devoted, tender, fond, ardent, cordial, doting, amorous, solicitous, demonstrative, warm-hearted **OPPOSITE:** cruel
b = tender, kind, caring, warm, gentle, sympathetic, considerate

low[1] *adj* **1 = small**, little, short, stunted, squat, fubsy *(archaic, dialect)* **OPPOSITE:** tall
7 = coarse, common, rough, gross, crude, rude, obscene, disgraceful, vulgar, undignified, disreputable, unbecoming, unrefined, dishonourable, ill-bred
10a = dejected, down, blue, sad, depressed, unhappy, miserable, fed up, moody, gloomy, dismal, forlorn, glum, despondent, downcast, morose, disheartened, downhearted, down in the dumps *(informal)*, sick as a parrot *(informal)*, cheesed off *(informal)*, brassed off *(Brit slang)* **OPPOSITE:** happy
10b = ill, weak, exhausted, frail, dying, reduced, sinking, stricken, feeble, debilitated, prostrate **OPPOSITE:** strong
11 = quiet, soft, gentle, whispered, muted, subdued, hushed, muffled **OPPOSITE:** loud

lower[1] *adj* **1 = subordinate**, under, smaller, junior, minor, secondary, lesser, low-level, inferior, second-class **2 = reduced**, cut, diminished, decreased, lessened, curtailed, pared down **OPPOSITE:** increased
▷ *vb* **4 = drop**, sink, depress, let down, submerge, take down, let fall, make lower **OPPOSITE:** raise
6 = lessen, cut, reduce, moderate, diminish, slash, decrease, prune, minimize, curtail, abate **OPPOSITE:** increase

DICTIONARY

lower case *n* (in printing) small letters, as opposed to capital letters **lower-case** *adj*
lower class *n* the class with the lowest position in society **lower-class** *adj*
lower house *n* one of the houses of a parliament that has two chambers: usually the larger and more representative
lowest common denominator *n maths* the smallest integer or polynomial that is exactly divisible by each denominator of a set of fractions
lowest common multiple *n maths* the smallest number or quantity that is exactly divisible by each member of a set of numbers or quantities
low frequency *n* any radio frequency lying between 300 and 30 kilohertz
Low German *n* a language of N Germany, spoken in rural areas
low-key ❶ *or* **low-keyed** *adj* **1** restrained or subdued **2** having a low intensity or tone
lowland *n* **1** relatively low ground **2** (*often pl*) a low generally flat region ▹ *adj* **3** of a lowland or lowlands **lowlander** *n*
Lowland *adj* of the Lowlands or the dialects of English spoken there **Lowlander** *n*
Lowlands *pl n* a low generally flat region of S Central Scotland
lowlight *n* **1** an unenjoyable or unpleasant part of an event **2** (*usually pl*) a streak of darker colour artificially applied to the hair
lowly *adj* **-lier, -liest 1** humble in position or status **2** simple and unpretentious **lowliness** *n*
Low Mass *n* a simplified form of Mass that is spoken rather than sung
low-minded *adj* having a vulgar or crude mind **low-mindedness** *n*
low-pitched *adj* **1** pitched low in tone **2** (of a roof) with a shallow slope
low profile *n* a deliberate shunning of publicity: *he kept a low profile* **low-profile** *adj*
low-spirited *adj* depressed or dejected
low-tech *adj* **1** of or using low technology **2** in the style of interior design that uses items associated with low technology
low technology *n* unsophisticated technology that is limited to the production of basic necessities
low tide *n* the tide at its lowest level or the time at which it reaches this
low water *n* **1** low tide **2** the lowest level which a stretch of water reaches
loyal ❶ *adj* **1** faithful to one's friends, country, or government **2** of or expressing loyalty: *the loyal toast* **loyally** *adv*
WORD ORIGIN Latin *legalis* legal
loyalist *n* a patriotic supporter of the sovereign or government **loyalism** *n*
Loyalist *n* (in Northern Ireland) any of the Protestants wishing to retain Ulster's link with Britain
loyalty ❶ *n, pl* **-ties 1** the quality of being loyal **2** a feeling of friendship or duty towards someone or something
loyalty card *n* a swipe card issued by a supermarket or chain store to a customer, used to record credit points awarded for money spent in the store
lozenge *n* **1** *med* a medicated tablet held in the mouth until it has dissolved **2** *geom* a rhombus
WORD ORIGIN Old French *losange*
LP *n* a gramophone record of 12 inches in diameter, which holds about 20 or 25 minutes of sound on each side
WORD ORIGIN shortened from *long player*
L-plate *n Austral & Brit* a red 'L' on a white square attached to a motor vehicle to indicate that the driver is a learner
Lr *chem* lawrencium
LSD *n* lysergic acid diethylamide; an illegal hallucinogenic drug
L.S.D., £.s.d. *or* **l.s.d.** pounds, shillings, pence
WORD ORIGIN Latin *librae, solidi, denarii*
Lt Lieutenant
Ltd *Brit* Limited (Liability)
Lu *chem* lutetium
lubber *n* **1** a big, awkward, or stupid person **2** ▸ short for **landlubber** > **lubberly** *adj, adv* **lubberliness** *n*
WORD ORIGIN probably from Old Norse
Lubitsch *n* **Ernst** 1890–1947, US film director, born in Germany; best known for such sophisticated comedies as *Forbidden Paradise* (1924) and *Ninotchka* (1939)
lubricant *n* a lubricating substance, such as oil
lubricate (loo-brik-ate) *vb* **-cating, -cated 1** to cover with an oily substance to lessen friction **2** to make greasy, slippery, or smooth **lubrication** *n*
WORD ORIGIN Latin *lubricare* to make slippery
lubricious (loo-**brish**-uss) *adj formal or literary* lewd
WORD ORIGIN Latin *lubricus* slippery
Lucan[1] *n* Latin name *Marcus Annaeus Lucanus*. 39–65 AD, Roman poet. His epic poem *Pharsalia* describes the civil war between Caesar and Pompey
Lucan[2] *adj* of or relating to St Luke or St Luke's gospel
Lucas van Leyden *n* ?1494–1533, Dutch painter and engraver
lucerne *n Austral & Brit* ▸ same as **alfalfa**
Lucian *n* 2nd century AD, Greek writer, noted esp. for his satirical *Dialogues of the Gods* and *Dialogues of the Dead*
lucid *adj* **1** clear and easily understood **2** capable of clear thought, particularly between periods of insanity or delirium **3** shining or glowing **lucidity** *n* **lucidly** *adv*
WORD ORIGIN Latin *lucidus* full of light
Lucifer *n* Satan
WORD ORIGIN Latin: light-bearer, from *lux* light + *ferre* to bear
Lucilius *n* **Gaius** ?180–102 BC, Roman satirist, regarded as the originator of poetical satire
luck ❶ *n* **1** events that are subject to chance; fortune, good or bad **2** success or good fortune **3 down on one's luck** lacking good fortune to the extent of suffering hardship **4 no such luck** *informal* unfortunately not **5 try one's luck** to attempt something that is uncertain
WORD ORIGIN Middle Dutch *luc*
luckless *adj* unfortunate or unlucky
lucky ❶ *adj* **luckier, luckiest 1** having or bringing good fortune **2** happening by chance, esp. as desired **luckily** *adv*
lucky dip *n Brit, Austral, & NZ* a box filled with sawdust containing small prizes for which children search
lucrative ❶ *adj* profitable
lucre (loo-ker) *n usually facetious*

THESAURUS

low-key *adj* **1, 2 = subdued**, quiet, restrained, muted, played down, understated, muffled, toned down, low-pitched
loyal *adj* **1 = faithful**, true, devoted, dependable, constant, attached, patriotic, staunch, trustworthy, trusty, steadfast, dutiful, unwavering, true-blue, immovable, unswerving, tried and true, true-hearted **OPPOSITE:** disloyal
loyalty *n* **1, 2 = faithfulness**, commitment, devotion, allegiance, reliability, fidelity, homage, patriotism, obedience, constancy, dependability, trustworthiness, steadfastness, troth (*archaic*), fealty, staunchness, trueness, trustiness, true-heartedness
luck *n* **1 = fortune**, lot, stars, chance, accident, fate, hazard, destiny, hap (*archaic*), twist of fate, fortuity **2 = good fortune**, success, advantage, prosperity, break (*informal*), stroke of luck, blessing, windfall, good luck, fluke, godsend, serendipity
lucky *adj* **1 = fortunate**, successful, favoured, charmed, blessed, prosperous, jammy (*Brit slang*), serendipitous **OPPOSITE:** unlucky
lucrative *adj* **= profitable**, rewarding, productive, fruitful, paying,

l

DICTIONARY

money or wealth: *filthy lucre*
WORD ORIGIN Latin *lucrum* gain

Lucy *n* **Saint** died ?303 AD, a virgin martyred by Diocletian in Syracuse. Feast day: Dec 13

Luddite *n Brit history* **1** any of the textile workers opposed to mechanization, who organized machine-breaking between 1811 and 1816 **2** any opponent of industrial change or innovation ▷ *adj* **3** of the Luddites
WORD ORIGIN after Ned *Ludd*, who destroyed machinery

Ludendorff *n* **Erich Friedrich Wilhelm von** 1865–1937, German general, Hindenburg's aide in World War I

luderick *n* an Australian fish, usually black or dark brown in colour

ludicrous ❶ *adj* absurd or ridiculous **ludicrously** *adv*
WORD ORIGIN Latin *ludus* game

ludo *n Austral & Brit* a simple board game in which players move counters forward by throwing dice
WORD ORIGIN Latin: I play

luff *vb* **1** *naut* to sail (a ship) into the wind **2** to move the jib of a crane in order to shift a load
WORD ORIGIN Old French *lof*

lug[1] *vb* **lugging, lugged** to carry or drag with great effort
WORD ORIGIN probably from Old Norse

lug[2] *n* **1** a projecting piece by which something is connected, supported, or lifted **2** *informal & Scot* an ear
WORD ORIGIN Scots: ear

luggage ❶ *n* suitcases, trunks, and bags
WORD ORIGIN perhaps LUG[1] + *-age*, as in *baggage*

lugger *n naut* a small working boat with an oblong sail
WORD ORIGIN origin unknown

lugubrious (loo-goo-bree-uss) *adj* mournful or gloomy
WORD ORIGIN Latin *lugere* to grieve

lugworm *n* a large worm which lives in burrows on sandy shores and is often used as bait by fishermen
WORD ORIGIN origin unknown

Luhrmann *n* **Baz (Mark Anthony)** born 1962, Australian film director and screenwriter; his films include *Strictly Ballroom* (1992), *Romeo and Juliet* (1996), and *Moulin Rouge* (2001)

Lukács *n* **Georg**, original name *György*. 1885–1971, Hungarian Marxist philosopher and literary critic, whose works include *History and Class Consciousness* (1923), *Studies in European Realism* (1946), and *The Historical Novel* (1955)

lukewarm *adj* **1** (of a liquid) moderately warm; tepid **2** lacking enthusiasm or conviction
WORD ORIGIN probably from Old English *hlēow* warm

lull ❶ *vb* **1** to soothe (a person or animal) by soft sounds or motions **2** to calm (fears or suspicions) by deception ▷ *n* **3** a short period of calm
WORD ORIGIN perhaps imitative of crooning sounds

lullaby *n, pl* **-bies** a quiet song to lull a child to sleep
WORD ORIGIN perhaps a blend of *lull* + *goodbye*

Lully *n* **1 Jean Baptiste**, Italian name *Giovanni Battista Lulli*. 1632–87, French composer, born in Italy; founder of French opera. With Philippe Quinault as librettist, he wrote operas such as *Alceste* (1674) and *Armide* (1686); as superintendent of music at the court of Louis XIV, he wrote incidental music to comedies by Molière **2** Also: **Lull Raymond** *or* **Ramón** ?1235–1315, Spanish philosopher, mystic, and missionary. His chief works are *Ars generalis sive magna* and the Utopian novel *Blaquerna*

lumbago (lum-bay-go) *n* pain in the lower back; low backache
WORD ORIGIN Latin *lumbus* loin

lumbar *adj* relating to the lower back
WORD ORIGIN Latin *lumbus* loin

lumbar puncture *n med* insertion of a hollow needle into the lower spinal cord to withdraw fluid for diagnosis

lumber[1] ❶ *n* **1** *Brit* unwanted disused household articles **2** *chiefly US & Canad* logs; sawn timber ▷ *vb* **3** *Brit informal* to burden with something unpleasant: *somebody gets lumbered with the extra costs* **4** to fill up with useless household articles **5** *chiefly US & Canad* to convert trees into marketable timber
WORD ORIGIN perhaps from LUMBER[2]

lumber[2] ❶ *vb* to move awkwardly and heavily **lumbering** *adj*
WORD ORIGIN Middle English *lomeren*

lumberjack *n* (esp. in North America) a person who fells trees and prepares the timber for transport

luminary *n, pl* **-naries 1 a** a famous person **b** an expert in a particular subject **2** *literary* something, such as the sun or moon, that gives off light

luminescence *n physics* the emission of light at low temperatures by any process other than burning **luminescent** *adj*

luminous *adj* **1** reflecting or giving off light: *luminous colours* **2** *not in technical use* luminescent: *luminous sparklers* **3** enlightening or wise **luminosity** *n*
WORD ORIGIN Latin *lumen* light

lump[1] ❶ *n* **1** a small solid mass without definite shape **2** *pathol* any small swelling or tumour **3** *informal* an awkward, heavy, or stupid person **4 a lump in one's throat** a tight dry feeling in one's throat, usually caused by great emotion **5 the lump** *Brit* self-employed workers in the building trade considered collectively ▷ *adj* **6** in the form of a lump or lumps: *lump sugar* ▷ *vb* **7** (often foll. by *together*) to consider as a single group, often without justification **8** to grow into lumps or become lumpy
WORD ORIGIN probably related to Scandinavian dialect: block

lump[2] *vb* **lump it** *informal* to accept something irrespective of personal preference: *if you don't like it, you can lump it*
WORD ORIGIN origin unknown

lumpectomy *n, pl* **-mies** surgical removal of a tumour in a breast
WORD ORIGIN *lump* + Greek *tomē* a cutting

lumpish *adj* stupid, clumsy, or heavy **lumpishness** *n*

lump sum *n* a relatively large sum of money, paid at one time

lumpy *adj* **lumpier, lumpiest** full of or having lumps **lumpiness** *n*

lunacy *n, pl* **-cies 1** foolishness **2** (formerly) any severe mental illness

lunar *adj* relating to the moon: *lunar eclipse*

THESAURUS

high-income, well-paid, money-making, advantageous, gainful, remunerative

ludicrous *adj* **= ridiculous**, crazy, absurd, preposterous, odd, funny, comic, silly, laughable, farcical, outlandish, incongruous, comical, zany, nonsensical, droll, burlesque, cockamamie *(slang, chiefly US)*
OPPOSITE: sensible

luggage *n* **= baggage**, things, cases, bags, gear, trunks, suitcases, paraphernalia, impedimenta

lull *vb* **1, 2 = calm**, soothe, subdue, still, quiet, compose, hush, quell, allay, pacify, lullaby, tranquillize, rock to sleep ▷ *n* **3 = respite**, pause, quiet, silence, calm, hush, tranquillity, stillness, let-up *(informal)*, calmness

lumber[1] *n* **1** *(Brit)* **= junk**, refuse, rubbish, discards, trash, clutter, jumble, white elephants, castoffs, trumpery ▷ *vb* **3** *(Brit informal)* **= burden**, land, load, saddle, impose upon, encumber

lumber[2] *vb* **= plod**, shuffle, shamble, trudge, stump, clump, waddle, trundle, lump along

lump[1] *n* **1 = piece**, group, ball, spot, block, mass, cake, bunch, cluster, chunk, wedge, dab, hunk, nugget, gob, clod, gobbet **2** *(pathology)* **= swelling**, growth, bump, tumour, bulge, hump, protuberance, protrusion, tumescence ▷ *vb* **7** (often foll. by *together*) **= group**, throw, mass, combine, collect, unite, pool, bunch, consolidate, aggregate, batch, conglomerate, coalesce, agglutinate

DICTIONARY

WORD ORIGIN Latin *luna* the moon

lunatic ❶ *adj* **1** foolish; eccentric **2** *archaic* insane ▷*n* **3** a foolish or annoying person **4** *archaic* a person who is insane
WORD ORIGIN Latin *luna* moon

lunatic asylum *n offensive* a home or hospital for the mentally ill

lunatic fringe *n* the members of a group who adopt views regarded as extreme

lunch *n* **1** a meal eaten during the middle of the day ▷*vb* **2** to eat lunch
WORD ORIGIN shortened from *luncheon*

luncheon *n* a lunch, often a formal one
WORD ORIGIN probably variant of *nuncheon*, from Middle English *none* noon + *schench* drink

luncheon meat *n* a ground mixture of meat (often pork) and cereal, usually tinned

luncheon voucher *n Brit* a voucher for a specified amount issued to employees and accepted by some restaurants as payment for food

lunchroom *n US & Canad* a room where lunch is served or where students or employees may eat lunches they bring

lung *n* the part of the body that allows an animal or bird to breathe air. Humans have two lungs, contained within the chest cavity
WORD ORIGIN Old English *lungen*

lunge ❶ *n* **1** a sudden forward motion **2** *fencing* a thrust made by advancing the front foot and straightening the back leg ▷*vb* **lunging, lunged 3** to move with a lunge **4** *fencing* to make a lunge
WORD ORIGIN French *allonger* to stretch out (one's arm)

lungfish *n, pl* **-fish** *or* **-fishes** a freshwater fish with an air-breathing lung

lupin *n* a garden plant with large spikes of brightly coloured flowers and flattened pods
WORD ORIGIN Latin *lupinus* wolfish; from the belief that it ravenously exhausted the soil

lupine *adj* of or like a wolf
WORD ORIGIN Latin *lupus* wolf

lupus *n* an ulcerous skin disease
WORD ORIGIN Latin: wolf; so called because it rapidly eats away the affected part

lurch[1] ❶ *vb* **1** to lean or tilt suddenly to one side **2** to stagger ▷*n* **3** a lurching movement
WORD ORIGIN origin unknown

lurch[2] *n* **leave someone in the lurch** to abandon someone in trouble
WORD ORIGIN French *lourche*, a game similar to backgammon

lure ❶ *vb* **luring, lured 1** (sometimes foll. by *away* or *into*) to tempt or attract by the promise of reward ▷*n* **2** a person or thing that lures **3** *angling* a brightly coloured artificial spinning bait **4** *falconry* a feathered decoy to which small pieces of meat can be attached
WORD ORIGIN Old French *loirre* falconer's lure

Luria *n* **1 Alexander Romanovich** 1902–77, Russian psychologist, a pioneer of modern neuropsychology. His most important work concerns the psychological effects of brain tumours **2 Isaac** (**ben Solomon**) 1534–72, Jewish mystic living in Egypt and Palestine: noted for his interpretation of the Cabbala

lurid *adj* **1** vivid in shocking detail; sensational: *magazines whose lurid covers sickened him* **2** glaring in colour: *a lurid red tartan* **3** horrible in savagery or violence: *reporting lurid crimes* **luridly** *adv*
WORD ORIGIN Latin *luridus* pale yellow

Lurie *n* **Alison** born 1926, US novelist. Her novels include *Imaginary Friends* (1967), *The War Between the Tates* (1974), *Foreign Affairs* (1985), and *The Last Resort* (1998)

lurk ❶ *vb* **1** to move stealthily or be concealed, esp. for evil purposes **2** to be present in an unobtrusive way; be latent
WORD ORIGIN probably frequentative of *lour*

lurking *adj* lingering but almost unacknowledged: *it confirms a lurking suspicion*

luscious (**lush**-uss) *adj* **1** extremely pleasurable to taste or smell **2** very attractive
WORD ORIGIN perhaps short for *delicious*

lush[1] ❶ *adj* **1** (of vegetation) growing thickly and healthily **2** luxurious, elaborate, or opulent
WORD ORIGIN Latin *laxus* loose

lush[2] *n slang* an alcoholic
WORD ORIGIN origin unknown

lust ❶ *n* **1** a strong sexual desire **2** a strong desire or drive: *a lust for power* ▷*vb* **3** (often foll. by *after* or *for*) to have a passionate desire (for) **lustful** *adj* **lustfully** *adv*
WORD ORIGIN Old English

lustre *or US* **luster** *n* **1** soft shining light reflected from a surface; sheen **2** great splendour or glory **3** a shiny metallic surface on some pottery and porcelain **lustrous** *adj*
WORD ORIGIN Latin *lustrare* to make bright

lusty *adj* **lustier, lustiest 1** healthy and full of strength and energy **2** strong or invigorating **lustily** *adv* **lustiness** *n*

lute *n* an ancient plucked stringed instrument with a long fingerboard and a body shaped like a half pear
WORD ORIGIN Arabic *al 'ūd*, literally: the wood

lutetium (loo-tee-shee-um) *n chem* a silvery-white metallic element of the lanthanide series. Symbol: Lu
WORD ORIGIN *Lutetia*, ancient name of Paris

Lutheran *n* **1** a follower of Martin Luther (1483–1546), German leader of the Reformation, or a member of a Lutheran Church ▷*adj* **2** of or

THESAURUS

lunatic *adj* **1, 2 = mad**, crazy, insane, irrational, nuts *(slang)*, barking *(slang)*, daft, demented, barmy *(slang)*, deranged, bonkers *(slang, chiefly Brit)*, unhinged, loopy *(informal)*, crackpot *(informal)*, out to lunch *(informal)*, barking mad *(slang)*, maniacal, gonzo *(slang)*, up the pole *(informal)*, crackbrained, wacko *or* whacko *(informal)*, off the air *(Austral slang)* ▷*n* **3, 4 = madman**, maniac, psychopath, nut *(slang)*, loony *(slang)*, nutter *(Brit slang)*, nutcase *(slang)*, headcase *(informal)*, headbanger *(informal)*, crazy *(informal)*

lunge *n* **1 = thrust**, charge, pounce, pass, spring, swing, jab, swipe *(informal)* ▷*vb* **3 = pounce**, charge, bound, dive, leap, plunge, dash, thrust, poke, jab

lurch[1] *vb* **1 = tilt**, roll, pitch, list, rock, lean, heel **2 = stagger**, reel, stumble, weave, sway, totter

lure *vb* **1** (sometimes foll. by *away* or *into*) **= tempt**, draw, attract, invite, trick, seduce, entice, beckon, lead on, allure, decoy, ensnare, inveigle ▷*n* **2 = temptation**, attraction, incentive, bait, carrot *(informal)*, magnet, inducement, decoy, enticement, siren song, allurement

lurk *vb* **1, 2 = hide**, sneak, crouch, prowl, snoop, lie in wait, slink, skulk, conceal yourself, move with stealth, go furtively

lush[1] *adj* **1 = abundant**, green, flourishing, lavish, dense, prolific, rank, teeming, overgrown, verdant **2 = luxurious**, grand, elaborate, lavish, extravagant, sumptuous, plush *(informal)*, ornate, opulent, palatial, ritzy *(slang)*

lust *n* **1 = lechery**, sensuality, licentiousness, carnality, the hots *(slang)*, libido, lewdness, wantonness, salaciousness, lasciviousness, concupiscence, randiness *(informal, chiefly Brit)*, pruriency **2 = desire**, longing, passion, appetite, craving, greed, thirst, cupidity, covetousness, avidity, appetence **3** (often foll. by *after* or *for*) **= desire**, want, crave, need, yearn for, covet, slaver over, lech after *(informal)*, be consumed with desire for, hunger for *or* after

DICTIONARY

relating to Luther, his doctrines, or any of the Churches that follow these doctrines **Lutheranism** *n*

Lutosławski *n* **Witold** 1913–94, Polish composer, whose works frequently juxtapose aleatoric and notated writing

Lutyens *n* **1** Sir **Edwin** 1869–1944, British architect, noted for his neoclassical country houses and his planning of New Delhi, India **2** his daughter, **Elisabeth** 1906–83, British composer

luvvie *or* **luvvy** *n, pl* **-vies** *facetious* a person who is involved in acting or the theatre

lux *n, pl* **lux** the SI unit of illumination
WORD ORIGIN Latin: light

luxe *n* ▸ see **de luxe**

Luxembourger *n* a person from Luxembourg

Luxemburg *n* **Rosa** 1871–1919, German socialist leader, led an unsuccessful Communist revolt (1919) with Karl Liebknecht and was assassinated

luxuriant *adj* **1** rich and abundant; lush: *luxuriant foliage* **2** very elaborate or ornate **luxuriance** *n* **luxuriantly** *adv*
WORD ORIGIN Latin *luxuriare* to abound to excess

luxuriate *vb* **-ating, -ated 1 luxuriate in** to take self-indulgent pleasure in; revel in **2** to flourish profusely

luxurious ⊕ *adj* **1** characterized by luxury **2** enjoying or devoted to luxury **luxuriously** *adv*

luxury ⊕ *n, pl* **-ries 1** indulgence in rich and sumptuous living **2** something considered an indulgence rather than a necessity ▹ *adj* **3** relating to, indicating, or supplying luxury: *a luxury hotel*
WORD ORIGIN Latin *luxuria* excess

LV (in Britain) luncheon voucher

lx lux

Lyautey *n* **Louis Hubert Gonzalve** 1854–1934, French marshal and colonial administrator; resident general in Morocco (1912–25)

lyceum *n* (now chiefly in the names of buildings) a public building for events such as concerts and lectures
WORD ORIGIN Latin: a school in ancient Athens

lychee (lie-chee) *n* a Chinese fruit with a whitish juicy pulp
WORD ORIGIN Cantonese *lai chi*

lych gate *or* **lich gate** *n* a roofed gate to a churchyard, formerly used as a temporary shelter for a coffin
WORD ORIGIN Old English *līc* corpse

Lycra *n trademark* a synthetic elastic fabric used for tight-fitting garments, such as swimsuits

Lycurgus *n* 9th century BC, Spartan lawgiver. He is traditionally regarded as the founder of the Spartan constitution, military institutions, and educational system

Lydgate *n* **John** ?1370–?1450, English poet and monk. His vast output includes devotional works and translations, such as that of a French version of Boccaccio's *The Fall of Princes* (1430–38)

lye *n* **1** a caustic solution obtained from wood ash **2** a concentrated solution of sodium hydroxide or potassium hydroxide
WORD ORIGIN Old English *lēag*

Lyell *n* Sir **Charles** 1797–1875, Scottish geologist. In *Principles of Geology* (1830–33) he advanced the theory of uniformitarianism, refuting the doctrine of catastrophism

lying *vb* ▸ the present participle of **lie**[1] or **lie**[2]

lying-in *n, pl* **lyings-in** *old-fashioned* confinement in childbirth

Lyle *n* **Sandy,** full name *Alexander Walter Barr Lyle.* born 1958, Scottish professional golfer: won the British Open Championship (1985) and the US Masters (1988)

Lyly *n* **John** ?1554–1606, English dramatist and novelist, noted for his two romances, *Euphues, or the Anatomy of Wit* (1578) and *Euphues and his England* (1580), written in an elaborate style ▸ See also **euphuism**

lymph *n* the almost colourless body fluid containing chiefly white blood cells **lymphatic** *adj*
WORD ORIGIN Latin *lympha* water

lymphatic system *n* a network of fine vessels by which lymph circulates throughout the body

lymph node *n* any of many bean-shaped masses of tissue in the lymphatic system that help to protect against infection

lymphocyte *n* a type of white blood cell
WORD ORIGIN *lymph* + Greek *kutos* vessel

Lynagh *n* **Michael** born 1963, Australian Rugby Union football player; captain of Australia 1987, 1992–95

lynch *vb* (of a mob) to kill (a person) for some supposed offence without a trial **lynching** *n*
WORD ORIGIN after Captain William *Lynch* of Virginia, US

Lynch *n* **1 David** born 1946, US film director; his work includes the films *Eraserhead* (1977), *Blue Velvet* (1986), *Wild at Heart* (1990), and *Mulholland Drive* (2001) and the television series *Twin Peaks* (1990) **2 John,** known as *Jack Lynch.* 1917–99, Irish statesman; prime minister of the Republic of Ireland (1966–73; 1977–79)

lynchpin *n* ▸ same as **linchpin**

Lyndsay *or* **Lindsay** *n* Sir **David** 1486–1554, Scottish poet and courtier, author of *Ane Pleasant Satyre of the Three Estates* (1552)

lynx *n, pl* **lynxes** *or* **lynx** a mammal of the cat family, with grey-brown mottled fur, tufted ears, and a short tail
WORD ORIGIN Greek *lunx*

lynx-eyed *adj* having keen sight

lyre *n* an ancient Greek U-shaped stringed instrument, similar to a harp but plucked with a plectrum
WORD ORIGIN Greek *lura*

lyrebird *n* an Australian bird, the male of which spreads its tail into the shape of a lyre during courtship

lyric *adj* **1 a** (of poetry) expressing the writer's personal feelings **b** (of poetry) having the form and manner of a song **2** of or relating to such poetry **3** (of a singing voice) light and melodic ▹ *n* **4** a short poem of songlike quality **5 lyrics** the words of a popular song: *Cole invests all her lyrics with a touch of drama* **lyrically** *adv*
WORD ORIGIN Greek *lura* lyre

lyrical ⊕ *adj* **1** ▸ same as **lyric** (senses 1, 2) **2** enthusiastic or effusive

lyricism *n* **1** the quality or style of lyric poetry **2** emotional outpouring

lyricist *n* a person who writes the words for a song, opera, or musical

Lysander *n* died 395 BC, Spartan naval commander of the Peloponnesian War

Lysias *n* ?450–?380 BC, Athenian orator

Lysimachus *n* ?360–281 BC, Macedonian general under Alexander the Great; king of Thrace (323–281); killed in battle by Seleucus I

Lysippus *n* 4th century BC, Greek sculptor. He introduced a new naturalism into Greek sculpture

Lyttelton *n* **Humphrey** 1921–2008, British jazz trumpeter and band leader who influenced the British revival of New Orleans jazz

Lytton *n* **1st Baron,** title of *Edward George Earle Lytton Bulwer-Lytton.* 1803–73, British novelist, dramatist, and statesman, noted particularly for his historical romances

THESAURUS

luxurious *adj* **1 = sumptuous,** expensive, comfortable, magnificent, costly, splendid, lavish, plush *(informal)*, opulent, ritzy *(slang)*, de luxe, well-appointed

luxury *n* **1 = opulence,** splendour, richness, extravagance, affluence, hedonism, a bed of roses, voluptuousness, the life of Riley, sumptuousness **OPPOSITE:** poverty **2 = extravagance,** treat, extra, indulgence, frill, nonessential **OPPOSITE:** necessity

lyrical *adj* **2 = enthusiastic,** emotional, inspired, poetic, carried away, ecstatic, expressive, impassioned, rapturous, effusive, rhapsodic

Mm

m 1 metre(s) **2** mile(s) **3** milli- **4** million **5** minute(s)

M 1 mach **2** *currency* mark(s) **3** medium **4** mega- **5** (in Britain) motorway **6** the Roman numeral for 1000

m. 1 male **2** married **3** masculine **4** meridian **5** month

M. 1 Majesty **2** Master **3** (in titles) Member **4** *pl* **MM.** *or* **MM** Monsieur

ma *n* an informal word for mother

Ma *n* **Yo-Yo** born 1955, US cellist, born in France to Chinese parents

MA 1 Massachusetts **2** Master of Arts

ma'am *n* ▸ short for **madam** (sense 1)

maas (**mahs**) *n S African* thick soured milk
WORD ORIGIN Nguni (language group of southern Africa) *amasi* milk

Mabuse *n* **Jan** original name *Jan Gossaert*. ?1478–?1533, Flemish painter

mac *or* **mack** *n Brit informal* a mackintosh

Mac *n chiefly US & Canad* an informal term of address to a man
WORD ORIGIN Gaelic *mac* son of

macabre (mak-**kahb**-ra) *adj* strange and horrible; gruesome
WORD ORIGIN French

macadam *n* a road surface made of compressed layers of small broken stones, esp. one bound together with tar or asphalt
WORD ORIGIN after John *McAdam*, engineer

macadamia (mak-a-**day**-mee-a) *n* an Australian tree with edible nuts
WORD ORIGIN after John *Macadam*, Australian chemist

macadamize *or* **-ise** *vb* **-izing, -ized** *or* **-ising, -ised** to pave a road with macadam

Macapagal Arroyo *n* **Gloria** ▸ See **Arroyo**

macaque (mak-**kahk**) *n* any of various Asian and African monkeys with cheek pouches and either a short tail or no tail
WORD ORIGIN W African *makaku*

macaroni *n, pl* **-nis** *or* **-nies 1** pasta tubes made from wheat flour **2** (in 18th-century Britain) a man who was excessively concerned with his clothes and appearance
WORD ORIGIN Italian (dialect) *maccarone*

macaroon *n* a sweet biscuit made of ground almonds
WORD ORIGIN French *macaron*

Macaulay *n* **1** Dame **Rose** 1881–1958, British novelist. Her books include *Dangerous Ages* (1921) and *The Towers of Trebizond* (1956) **2 Thomas Babington,** 1st Baron. 1800–59, English historian, essayist, and statesman. His *History of England from the Accession of James the Second* (1848–61) is regarded as a classic of the Whig interpretation of history

macaw *n* a large tropical American parrot with a long tail and brightly coloured feathers
WORD ORIGIN Portuguese *macau*

MacBride *n* **Sean** 1904–88, Irish statesman; minister for external affairs (1948–51); chairman of Amnesty International (1961–75); Nobel Peace Prize 1974; UN commissioner for Namibia (1974–76)

MacDiarmid *n* **Hugh,** pen name of *Christopher Murray Grieve*. 1892–1978, Scottish poet; a founder of the Scottish National Party. His poems include *A Drunk Man Looks at the Thistle* (1926)

mace[1] *n* **1** a ceremonial staff carried by certain officials **2** a club with a spiked metal head used in the Middle Ages
WORD ORIGIN probably Vulgar Latin *mattea*

mace[2] *n* a spice made from the dried outer casing of the nutmeg
WORD ORIGIN Latin *macir*

macebearer *n* a person who carries a mace in processions or ceremonies

macerate (**mass**-er-ate) *vb* **-ating, -ated** to soften or be softened by soaking **macerated** *adj* **maceration** *n*
WORD ORIGIN Latin *macerare* to soften

MacGregor *n* **Joanna** (**Clare**) born 1959, British concert pianist and broadcaster; recordings include the "crossover" album *Play* (2001)

Mach (**mak**) *n* a unit for expressing the speed of an aircraft as a multiple of the speed of sound: *an airliner capable of cruising at Mach 2*. ▸ See also **Mach number**

Machado *n* **Joaquim Maria** 1839–1908, Brazilian author of novels and short stories, whose novels include *Epitaph of a Small Winner* (1881) and *Dom Casmurro* (1899)

Machaut *n* **Guillaume de** *c.* 1300–77, French composer and poet; a leading exponent of ars nova

Machel *n* **Samora** (**Moises**) 1933–86, Mozambique statesman; president of Mozambique from 1975–86

machete (mash-**ett**-ee) *n* a broad heavy knife used for cutting or as a weapon
WORD ORIGIN Spanish

Machiavellian (mak-ee-a-**vel**-yan) *adj* cleverly deceitful and unscrupulous **Machiavellianism** *n*
WORD ORIGIN after *Machiavelli*, political philosopher

machinations (mak-in-**nay**-shuns) *pl n* cunning schemes or plots to gain power or harm an opponent: *the machinations of a power-hungry institution*
WORD ORIGIN Latin *machinari* to plan

machine ❶ *n* **1** an assembly of components arranged so as to perform a particular task and usually powered by electricity **2** a vehicle, such as a car or aircraft **3** a system within an organization that controls activities and policies: *the party machine* ▹ *vb* **-chining, -chined 4** to shape, cut, or make something using a machine **machinable** *adj*
WORD ORIGIN Latin *machina*

machine code *or* **language** *n* instructions for a computer in binary or hexadecimal code that require no conversion or translation by the computer

machine gun *n* **1** a rapid-firing automatic gun, using small-arms ammunition ▹ *vb* **machine-gun, -gunning, -gunned 2** to shoot or fire at with a machine gun

machine-readable *adj* in a form suitable for processing by a computer

machinery ❶ *n, pl* **-eries 1** machines, machine parts, or machine systems collectively **2** the mechanism of a machine **3** the organization and procedures by which a system functions: *the machinery of international politics*

machine shop *n* a workshop in which machine tools are operated

machine tool *n* a power-driven machine, such as a lathe, for cutting and shaping metal, wood, or plastic

machinist *n* **1** a person who operates machines to cut or process materials **2** a maker or repairer of machines

machismo (mak-**izz**-moh) *n* strong or exaggerated masculinity
WORD ORIGIN Spanish *macho* male

Mach number (**mak**) *n* the ratio of the speed of a body in a particular medium to the speed of sound in that medium
WORD ORIGIN after Ernst *Mach*, physicist

macho ❶ (**match**-oh) *adj* **1** strongly or

m

machine *n* **1 = appliance**, device, apparatus, engine, tool, instrument, mechanism, gadget, contraption, gizmo (*informal*), contrivance **3 = system**, agency, structure, organization, machinery, setup (*informal*)

machinery *n* **1, 2 = equipment**, gear, instruments, apparatus, works, technology, tackle, tools, mechanism(s), gadgetry

macho *adj* **1 = manly**, masculine,

DICTIONARY

exaggeratedly masculine ▷ *n* **2** strong or exaggerated masculinity
WORD ORIGIN from *machismo*

mack *n Brit informal* ▸ same as **mac**

mackerel *n, pl* **-rel** *or* **-rels** an edible sea fish
WORD ORIGIN Old French *maquerel*

Mackerras *n* **Charles** born 1925, Australian conductor, esp. of opera; resident in England

mackinaw *n chiefly US & Canad* a thick short double-breasted plaid coat
WORD ORIGIN from a variant of *Mackinac*, an island in N Michigan

Mackinder *n* Sir **Halford John** 1861–1947, British geographer noted esp. for his work in political geography. His writings include *Democratic Ideas and Reality* (1919)

mackintosh *or* **macintosh** *n Brit* **1** a raincoat made of rubberized cloth **2** any raincoat
WORD ORIGIN after Charles *Macintosh*, who invented it

Maclean *n* **1 Donald** 1913–83, British civil servant, who spied for the Russians: fled to the former Soviet Union (with Guy Burgess) in 1951 **2 Sorley** 1911–96, Scottish Gaelic poet. His works include *Dàin do Eimhir agus Dàin Eile* (1943) and *Spring Tide and Neap Tide* (1977)

Macleish *n* **Archibald** 1892–1982, US poet and public official; his works include *Collected Poems* (1952) and *J.B.* (1958)

Macleod *n* **John James Rickard** 1876–1935, Scottish physiologist: shared the Nobel prize for physiology or medicine (1923) with Banting for their part in discovering insulin

Macmahon *n* **Marie Edme Patrice Maurice**, Comte de Macmahon. 1808–93, French military commander. He commanded the troops that suppressed the Paris Commune (1871) and was elected president of the Third Republic (1873–79)

MacNeice *n* **Louis** 1907–63, British poet, born in Northern Ireland. His works include *Autumn Journal* (1939) and *Solstices* (1961) and a translation of *Agamemnon* (1936)

Maconchy *n* Dame **Elizabeth**, married name *Elizabeth LeFanu*. 1907–94, British composer of Irish parentage; noted esp. for her chamber music, which includes 13 string quartets and *Romanza* (1980) for viola and ensemble

Macpherson *n* **James** 1736–96, Scottish poet and translator. He published supposed translations of the legendary Gaelic poet Ossian, in reality largely his own work

macramé (mak-**rah**-mee) *n* **1** the art of knotting and weaving coarse thread into patterns **2** ornaments made in this way
WORD ORIGIN Turkish *makrama* towel

Macready *n* **William Charles** 1793–1873, English actor and theatre manager

macro- *or before a vowel* **macr-** *combining form* large, long, or great: *macroscopic*
WORD ORIGIN Greek *makros*

macrobiotics *n* a dietary system which advocates whole grains and vegetables grown without chemical additives **macrobiotic** *adj*
WORD ORIGIN Greek *makros* long + *biotos* life

macrocarpa *n* a large Californian coniferous tree, used in New Zealand and elsewhere as a windbreak on farms and for rough timber
WORD ORIGIN Greek *makros* large + *karpos* fruit

macrocosm *n* a complex structure, such as the universe or society, regarded as a whole
WORD ORIGIN Greek *makros kosmos* great world

macroeconomics *n* the branch of economics concerned with the relationships between aggregates, such as consumption and investment, in a large economic system **macroeconomic** *adj*

macromolecule *n* any very large molecule, such as a protein or synthetic polymer

macron *n* a mark (¯) placed over a letter to represent a long vowel
WORD ORIGIN Greek *makros* long

macroscopic *adj* **1** large enough to be visible to the naked eye **2** concerned with large units
WORD ORIGIN Greek *makros* large + *skopein* to look at

macula (**mak**-kew-la) *n, pl* **-ulae** (-yew-lee) *anat* a small spot or area of distinct colour, such as a freckle
WORD ORIGIN Latin

mad ❶ *adj* **madder, maddest** **1** mentally deranged; insane **2** extremely foolish; senseless: *that was a mad thing to do!* **3** *informal* angry or annoyed: *he's mad at her for the unjust accusation* **4** extremely excited or confused: *a mad rush* **5 a** (of animals) unusually ferocious: *a mad bear* **b** (of animals) afflicted with rabies **6 like mad** *informal* with great energy, enthusiasm, or haste **7 mad about** *or* **on** *or* **over** wildly enthusiastic about or fond of **madness** *n*
WORD ORIGIN Old English *gemǣded* made insane

madam *n, pl* **madams 1** *pl* **mesdames** a polite term of address for a woman **2** a woman who runs a brothel **3** *Austral & Brit informal* a spoilt or pert girl: *she is a thoroughly precocious little madam if ever there was one*
WORD ORIGIN Old French *ma dame* my lady

madame (**mad**-dam) *n, pl* **mesdames** (may-**dam**) a French form of address equivalent to *Mrs*

madcap *adj* **1** impulsive, reckless, or unlikely to succeed: *a madcap expansion of council bureaucracy* ▷ *n* **2** an impulsive or reckless person

mad cow disease *n informal* ▸ same as **BSE**

THESAURUS

butch *(slang)*, two-fisted, tough, chauvinist, virile, he-man

mad *adj* **1 = insane**, mental *(slang)*, crazy *(informal)*, nuts *(slang)*, bananas *(slang)*, barking *(slang)*, raving, distracted, frantic, frenzied, unstable, crackers *(Brit slang)*, batty *(slang)*, crazed, lunatic, loony *(slang)*, psychotic, demented, cuckoo *(informal)*, unbalanced, barmy *(slang)*, nutty *(slang)*, deranged, delirious, rabid, bonkers *(slang, chiefly Brit)*, flaky *(US slang)*, unhinged, loopy *(informal)*, crackpot *(informal)*, out to lunch *(informal)*, round the bend *(Brit slang)*, aberrant, barking mad *(slang)*, out of your mind, gonzo *(slang)*, screwy *(informal)*, doolally *(slang)*, off your head *(slang)*, off your trolley *(slang)*, round the twist *(Brit slang)*, up the pole *(informal)*, of unsound mind, as daft as a brush *(informal, chiefly Brit)*, lost your marbles *(informal)*, not right in the head, non compos mentis *(Latin)*, off your rocker *(slang)*, not the full shilling *(informal)*, off your nut *(slang)*, off your chump *(slang)*, wacko *or* whacko *(informal)*, off the air *(Austral slang)* **OPPOSITE:** sane
2 = foolish, absurd, wild, stupid, daft *(informal)*, ludicrous, unreasonable, irrational, unsafe, senseless, preposterous, foolhardy, nonsensical, unsound, inane, imprudent, asinine
OPPOSITE: sensible
3 *(informal)* **= angry**, cross, furious, irritated, fuming, choked, infuriated, raging, ape *(slang)*, incensed, enraged, exasperated, irate, livid *(informal)*, berserk, seeing red *(informal)*, incandescent, wrathful, fit to be tied *(slang)*, in a wax *(informal, chiefly Brit)*, berko *(Austral slang)*, tooshie *(Austral slang)*, off the air *(Austral slang)*
OPPOSITE: calm
4 = frenzied, wild, excited, energetic, abandoned, agitated, frenetic, uncontrolled, boisterous, full-on *(informal)*, ebullient, gay, riotous, unrestrained
7 *(usually with* **about***)* **= enthusiastic**, wild, crazy *(informal)*, nuts *(slang)*, keen, hooked, devoted, in love with, fond, daft *(informal)*, ardent, fanatical, avid, impassioned, zealous, infatuated, dotty *(slang, chiefly Brit)*, enamoured
OPPOSITE: nonchalant

DICTIONARY

madden ❶ *vb* to make or become mad or angry **maddening** *adj*

madder *n* **1** a plant with small yellow flowers and a red fleshy root **2** a dark reddish-purple dye formerly obtained from its root **3** an artificial pigment of this colour
WORD ORIGIN Old English *mædere*

made *vb* **1** ▸ the past of **make** ▹ *adj* **2** produced or shaped as specified: *handmade* **3 get** *or* **have it made** *informal* to be assured of success

Madeira (mad-**deer**-a) *n* a fortified white wine from Madeira, an island in the N Atlantic

Madeira cake *n* a type of rich sponge cake

mademoiselle (mad-mwah-**zel**) *n, pl* **mesdemoiselles** (maid-mwah-**zel**) **1** a French form of address equivalent to *Miss* **2** a French teacher or governess

made-to-measure *adj* (of a piece of clothing) made specifically to fit the person who has ordered it

made-up *adj* **1** invented or fictitious **2** wearing make-up **3** put together: *some made-up carpet shampoo* **4** (of a road) surfaced with tarmac or concrete

madhouse *n informal* **1** a state of uproar or confusion **2** *old-fashioned* a mental hospital

madly ❶ *adv* **1** in an insane or foolish manner **2** with great speed and energy **3** *informal* extremely or excessively: *she was madly in love with him*

madman *or fem* **madwoman** *n, pl* **-men** *or* **-women** a person who is insane

Madonna *n* **1** *chiefly RC church* the Virgin Mary **2** a picture or statue of the Virgin Mary
WORD ORIGIN Italian: my lady

madras *n* a medium-hot curry: *chicken madras*
WORD ORIGIN after the *Madras* area of India

madrigal *n* a type of 16th- or 17th-century part song for unaccompanied voices **madrigalist** *n*
WORD ORIGIN Medieval Latin *matricale* primitive

maelstrom (**male**-strom) *n* **1** a large powerful whirlpool **2** any confused, violent, and destructive turmoil: *a maelstrom of adulterous passion*
WORD ORIGIN Old Dutch *malen* to whirl round + *stroom* stream

maenad (**mean**-ad) *n* **1** *classical history* a female disciple of Dionysus, the Greek god of wine **2** a frenzied woman
WORD ORIGIN Greek *mainas* madwoman

maestro (**my**-stroh) *n, pl* **-tri** *or* **-tros** **1** a distinguished musician or conductor **2** any master of an art: *Milan's maestro of minimalism*
WORD ORIGIN Italian: master

Maeterlinck *n* Comte **Maurice** 1862–1949, Belgian poet and dramatist, noted particularly for his symbolist plays, such as *Pelléas et Mélisande* (1892), which served as the basis for an opera by Debussy, and *L'Oiseau bleu* (1909). Nobel prize for literature 1911

mae west *n slang* an inflatable life jacket
WORD ORIGIN after *Mae West*, actress renowned for her large bust

Mafia *n* **the Mafia** a secret criminal organization founded in Sicily, and carried to the US by Italian immigrants
WORD ORIGIN Sicilian dialect, literally: hostility to the law

mafioso (maf-fee-**oh**-so) *n, pl* **-sos** *or* **-si** (-see) a member of the Mafia

mag *n* ▸ short for **magazine** (sense 1)

magazine ❶ *n* **1** a periodic paperback publication containing written pieces and illustrations **2** a television or radio programme made up of short nonfictional items **3** a metal case holding several cartridges used in some firearms **4** a rack for automatically feeding slides through a projector **5** a place for storing weapons, explosives, or military equipment
WORD ORIGIN Arabic *makhāzin* storehouses

magenta (maj-**jen**-ta) *adj* deep purplish-red
WORD ORIGIN after *Magenta*, Italy

maggot *n* the limbless larva of various insects, esp. the housefly and blowfly **maggoty** *adj*
WORD ORIGIN earlier *mathek*

magi (**maje**-eye) *pl n, sing* **magus** (**may**-guss) **1** ▸ see **magus 2 the three Magi** *Christianity* the wise men from the East who came to worship the infant Jesus (Matthew 2:1–12)
WORD ORIGIN see MAGUS

magic ❶ *n* **1** the supposed power to make things happen by using supernatural means **2** tricks done to entertain; conjuring **3** any mysterious or extraordinary quality or power: *the magic of Placido Domingo* **4 like magic** very quickly ▹ *adj also* **magical 5** of magic **6** possessing or considered to possess mysterious powers **7** unaccountably enchanting **8** *informal* wonderful or marvellous ▹ *vb* **-icking, -icked 9** to transform or produce as if by magic: *he had magicked up a gourmet meal at a moment's notice* **magically** *adv*
WORD ORIGIN Greek *magikē* witchcraft

magic away *vb* to cause to disappear as if by magic: *to magic away pollution*

magic carpet *n* (in fairy stories) a carpet which can carry people through the air

magician ❶ *n* **1** a conjuror **2** a person with magic powers

magic lantern *n* an early type of slide projector

magisterial *adj* **1** commanding and authoritative **2** of a magistrate **magisterially** *adv*
WORD ORIGIN Latin *magister* master

m

THESAURUS

madden *vb* **= infuriate**, irritate, incense, enrage, upset, provoke, annoy, aggravate *(informal)*, gall, craze, inflame, exasperate, vex, unhinge, drive you crazy, nark *(Brit, Austral & NZ slang)*, drive you round the bend *(Brit slang)*, make your blood boil, drive you to distraction *(informal)*, get your goat *(slang)*, drive you round the twist *(Brit slang)*, get your dander up *(informal)*, make your hackles rise, raise your hackles, drive you off your head *(slang)*, drive you out of your mind, get your back up, get your hackles up, make you see red *(informal)*, put your back up, hack you off *(informal)* **OPPOSITE:** calm

madly *adv* **1a = foolishly**, wildly, absurdly, ludicrously, unreasonably, irrationally, senselessly, nonsensically **1b = insanely**, frantically, hysterically, crazily, deliriously, distractedly, rabidly, frenziedly, dementedly **2 = energetically**, quickly, wildly, rapidly, hastily, furiously, excitedly, hurriedly, recklessly, speedily, like mad *(informal)*, hell for leather, like lightning, hotfoot, like the clappers *(Brit informal)*, like nobody's business *(informal)*, like greased lightning *(informal)* **3** *(informal)* **= passionately**, wildly, desperately, intensely, exceedingly, extremely, excessively, to distraction, devotedly

magazine *n* **1 = journal**, paper, publication, supplement, rag *(informal)*, issue, glossy *(informal)*, pamphlet, periodical, fanzine *(informal)*

magic *n* **1 = sorcery**, wizardry, witchcraft, enchantment, occultism, black art, spells, necromancy, sortilege, theurgy **2 = conjuring**, illusion, trickery, sleight of hand, hocus-pocus, jiggery-pokery *(informal, chiefly Brit)*, legerdemain, prestidigitation, jugglery **3 = charm**, power, glamour, fascination, magnetism, enchantment, allurement, mojo *(US slang)* ▹ *adj* **7 = miraculous**, entrancing, charming, fascinating, marvellous, magical, magnetic, enchanting, bewitching, spellbinding, sorcerous

magician *n* **1 = conjuror**, illusionist, prestidigitator **2 = sorcerer**, witch, wizard, illusionist, warlock, necromancer, thaumaturge *(rare)*, theurgist, archimage *(rare)*, enchanter *or* enchantress

DICTIONARY

magistracy *n, pl* **-cies** 1 the office or function of a magistrate 2 magistrates collectively

magistrate ❶ *n* 1 a public officer concerned with the administration of law 2 ▸ same as **justice of the peace** 3 *Austral & NZ* ▸ a former name for **district court judge**
WORD ORIGIN Latin *magister* master

magistrates' court *n* (in England) a court that deals with minor crimes, certain civil actions, and preliminary hearings

magma *n, pl* **-mas** *or* **-mata** hot molten rock within the earth's crust which sometimes finds its way to the surface where it solidifies to form igneous rock
WORD ORIGIN Greek: salve made by kneading

Magna Carta *n English history* the charter granted by King John at Runnymede in 1215, recognizing the rights and privileges of the barons, church, and freemen
WORD ORIGIN Medieval Latin: great charter

magnanimous *adj* generous and forgiving, esp. towards a defeated enemy **magnanimity** *n* **magnanimously** *adv*
WORD ORIGIN Latin *magnanimus* great-souled

m

magnate *n* an influential or wealthy person, esp. in industry
WORD ORIGIN Late Latin *magnates* great men

magnesia *n* a white tasteless substance used as an antacid and laxative; magnesium oxide
WORD ORIGIN Greek *Magnēsia* of *Magnēs*, ancient mineral-rich region

magnesium *n chem* a light silvery-white metallic element that burns with a very bright white flame. Symbol: Mg
WORD ORIGIN from *magnesia*

magnet *n* 1 a piece of iron, steel, or lodestone that has the property of attracting iron to it 2 a person or thing that exerts a great attraction: *these woods are a magnet for bird watchers*
WORD ORIGIN Greek *magnēs*

magnetic ❶ *adj* 1 of, producing, or operated by means of magnetism 2 of or like a magnet 3 capable of being made into a magnet 4 exerting a powerful attraction: *political leaders of magnetic appeal* **magnetically** *adv*

magnetic disk *n* a computer storage disk

magnetic field *n* an area around a magnet in which its power of attraction is felt

magnetic mine *n* a mine which detonates when a magnetic field such as that generated by the metal of a ship's hull is detected

magnetic needle *n* a slender magnetized rod used in certain instruments, such as the magnetic compass, for indicating the direction of a magnetic field

magnetic north *n* the direction in which a compass needle points, at an angle from the direction of true (geographic) north

magnetic pole *n* either of two variable points on the earth's surface towards which a magnetic needle points

magnetic storm *n* a sudden severe disturbance of the earth's magnetic field, caused by emission of charged particles from the sun

magnetic tape *n* a long plastic strip coated with a magnetic substance, used to record sound or video signals or to store information in computers

magnetism *n* 1 the property of attraction displayed by magnets 2 powerful personal charm 3 the branch of physics concerned with magnetic phenomena

magnetite *n* a black magnetizable mineral that is an important source of iron

magnetize *or* **-ise** *vb* **-izing, -ized** *or* **-ising, -ised** 1 to make a substance or object magnetic 2 to attract strongly: *he was magnetized by her smile* **magnetizable** *or* **-isable** *adj* **magnetization** *or* **-isation** *n*

magneto (mag-nee-toe) *n, pl* **-tos** a small electric generator in which the magnetic field is produced by a permanent magnet, esp. one used to provide the spark in an internal-combustion engine
WORD ORIGIN short for *magnetoelectric generator*

magnetron *n* an electronic valve used with a magnetic field to generate microwave oscillations, used. esp. in radar
WORD ORIGIN *magnet + electron*

Magnificat *n Christianity* the hymn of the Virgin Mary (Luke 1:46–55), used as a canticle
WORD ORIGIN from its opening word

magnification *n* 1 the act of magnifying or the state of being magnified 2 the degree to which something is magnified 3 a magnified copy of something

magnificent ❶ *adj* 1 splendid or impressive in appearance 2 superb or very fine: *a magnificent performance* **magnificence** *n* **magnificently** *adv*
WORD ORIGIN Latin *magnificus* great in deeds

magnify ❶ *vb* **-fies, -fying, -fied** 1 to make something look bigger than it really is, for instance by using a lens or microscope 2 to make something seem more important than it really is; exaggerate: *you are magnifying the problem out of all proportion* 3 to make something sound louder than it really is: *the stethoscope magnifies internal body sounds* 4 *archaic* to glorify or praise **magnified** *adj*
WORD ORIGIN Latin *magnificare* to praise

magnifying glass *or* **magnifier** *n* a convex lens used to produce an enlarged image of an object

magniloquent *adj* (of speech) excessively grand, literary, and pompous **magniloquence** *n*
WORD ORIGIN Latin *magnus* great + *loqui* to speak

magnitude ❶ *n* 1 relative importance: *an evil of the first magnitude* 2 relative size or extent 3 *astron* the apparent brightness of a celestial body expressed on a numerical scale on which bright stars have a low value
WORD ORIGIN Latin *magnitudo* size

magnolia *n* an Asian and North American tree or shrub with white,

THESAURUS

magistrate *n* 1 = **judge**, justice, provost *(Scot)*, bailie *(Scot)*, justice of the peace, J.P.

magnetic *adj* 4 = **attractive**, irresistible, seductive, captivating, charming, fascinating, entrancing, charismatic, enchanting, hypnotic, alluring, mesmerizing
OPPOSITE: repulsive

magnificent *adj* 1 = **splendid**, striking, grand, impressive, august, rich, princely, imposing, elegant, divine *(informal)*, glorious, noble, gorgeous, lavish, elevated, luxurious, majestic, regal, stately, sublime, sumptuous, grandiose, exalted, opulent, transcendent, resplendent, splendiferous *(facetious)*
OPPOSITE: ordinary
2 = **brilliant**, fine, excellent, outstanding, superb, superior, splendid

magnify *vb* 1 = **enlarge**, increase, boost, expand, intensify, blow up *(informal)*, heighten, amplify, augment, dilate **OPPOSITE:** reduce
2a = **make worse**, exaggerate, intensify, worsen, heighten, deepen, exacerbate, aggravate, increase, inflame, fan the flames of
2b = **exaggerate**, overdo, overstate, build up, enhance, blow up, inflate, overestimate, dramatize, overrate, overplay, overemphasize, blow up out of all proportion, aggrandize, make a production (out) of *(informal)*, make a federal case of *(US informal)*
OPPOSITE: understate

magnitude *n* 1 = **importance**, consequence, significance, mark, moment, note, weight, proportion, dimension, greatness, grandeur, eminence **OPPOSITE:** unimportance
2 = **immensity**, size, extent, enormity, strength, volume,

DICTIONARY

pink, purple, or yellow showy flowers
WORD ORIGIN after Pierre *Magnol*, botanist
magnox *n* an alloy composed mainly of magnesium, used in fuel elements of some nuclear reactors (**magnox reactors**)
WORD ORIGIN from *mag(nesium) n(o) ox(idation)*
magnum *n, pl* **-nums** a wine bottle of twice the normal size, holding 1.5 litres
WORD ORIGIN Latin: a big thing
magnum opus *n* a great work of art or literature, esp. the greatest single work of an artist
WORD ORIGIN Latin
magpie *n* **1** a bird of the crow family with black-and-white plumage, a long tail, and a chattering call **2** any of various similar Australian birds, eg the butcherbird **3** *Brit* a person who hoards small objects
WORD ORIGIN from *Mag*, diminutive of *Margaret* + *pie*, obsolete name for the magpie
magus (may-guss) *n, pl* **magi** (**maje**-eye) **1** a Zoroastrian priest **2** an astrologer or magician of ancient times
WORD ORIGIN Old Persian: magician
Magyar *n* **1** a member of the main ethnic group of Hungary **2** the Hungarian language ▷ *adj* **3** of the Magyars
maharaja *or* **maharajah** *n* the head of one of the royal families which formerly ruled parts of India
WORD ORIGIN Hindi: great raja
maharani *or* **maharanee** *n* the wife of a maharaja
WORD ORIGIN Hindi: great rani
maharishi *n hinduism* a teacher of religious and mystical knowledge
WORD ORIGIN Hindi: great sage
mahatma *n* a person revered for his holiness or wisdom: often used as a title or form of address: *Mahatma Gandhi*
WORD ORIGIN Sanskrit *mahā* great + *ātman* soul
Mahavira *n* the title of **Vardhamana** 599–527 BC, Indian ascetic and religious teacher, regarded as the founder of Jainism
Mahfouz *or* **Mahfuz** *n* **Naguib** 1911–2006, Egyptian novelist and writer, author of the trilogy of novels *Bain al-Kasrain* (1945–57). His novel *Children of Gebelawi* (1959) was banned by the Muslim authorities in Egypt Nobel prize for literature 1988
mah jong *or* **mah-jongg** *n* a game of Chinese origin, played using tiles bearing various designs, in which the players try to obtain a winning combination of tiles
WORD ORIGIN Chinese, literally: sparrows
mahogany *n, pl* **-nies 1** the hard reddish-brown wood of any of several tropical trees ▷ *adj* **2** reddish-brown: *wonderful mahogany tones*
WORD ORIGIN origin unknown
mahout (ma-**howt**) *n* (in India and the East Indies) an elephant driver or keeper
WORD ORIGIN Hindi *mahāut*
Mahy *n* **Margaret** born 1936, New Zealand writer for children. Her books include *A Lion in the Meadow* (1969), *The Changeover* (1984), and *Alchemy* (2002)
maid ❶ *n* **1** a female servant **2** *archaic or literary* a young unmarried girl; maiden
WORD ORIGIN form of *maiden*
maiden ❶ *n* **1** *archaic or literary* a young unmarried girl, esp. a virgin **2** *horse racing* a horse that has never won a race ▷ *adj* **3** unmarried: *a maiden aunt* **4** first or earliest: *maiden voyage* **maidenhood** *n* **maidenly** *adj*
WORD ORIGIN Old English *mægden*
maidenhair fern *n* a fern with delicate hairlike fronds of small pale green leaflets
maidenhead *n* **1** the hymen **2** virginity or maidenhood
maiden name *n* a woman's surname before marriage
maiden over *n cricket* an over in which no runs are scored
maid of honour *n* **1** an unmarried lady attending a queen or princess **2** *US & Canad* the principal unmarried attendant of a bride
maidservant *n* a female servant
mail[1] ❶ *n* **1** letters and packages transported and delivered by the post office **2** the postal system **3** a single collection or delivery of mail **4** a train, ship, or aircraft that carries mail **5** ▸ short for **e-mail** ▷ *vb* **6** *chiefly US & Canad* to send by mail **7** to contact or send by e-mail
WORD ORIGIN Old French *male* bag
mail[2] *n* flexible armour made of riveted metal rings or links **mailed** *adj*
WORD ORIGIN Old French *maille* mesh
mailbag *n* a large bag for transporting or delivering mail
mailbox *n* **1** *US, Canad & Austral* a box outside a house into which the postman puts letters for the occupiers of the house **2** (on a computer) the directory in which e-mail messages are stored
mail coach *n history* a fast stagecoach designed primarily for carrying mail
mailing list *n* a register of names and addresses to which information or advertising matter is sent by post or e-mail
Maillol *n* **Aristide** 1861–1944, French sculptor, esp. of monumental female nudes
mailman *n, pl* **-men** *US & Canad* a postman
mail merge *n computers* a word-processing facility that can produce personalized letters by combining data from two different files
mail order *n* a system of buying and selling goods by post
mailshot *n* a posting of circulars, leaflets, or other advertising to a selected large number of people at once
maim *vb* to injure badly or cruelly, with some permanent damage resulting
WORD ORIGIN Old French *mahaignier* to wound
Maimonides *n* also called Rabbi *Moses ben Maimon*. 1135–1204, Jewish philosopher, physician, and jurist, born in Spain. He codified Jewish law in *Mishneh Torah* (1180) › **Maimonidean** *adj, n*
main ❶ *adj* **1** chief or principal ▷ *n* **2** a principal pipe or line in a system used to distribute water, electricity, or gas **3** **mains** the main distribution network for water, gas, or electricity **4** great strength or force: *with might and main* **5** *literary* the open ocean **6** **in the main** on the whole

m

THESAURUS

vastness, bigness, largeness, hugeness **OPPOSITE:** smallness
maid *n* **1** = **servant**, chambermaid, housemaid, menial, handmaiden (*archaic*), maidservant, female servant, domestic (*archaic*), parlourmaid, serving-maid **2** (*archaic, literary*) = **girl**, maiden, lass, miss, nymph (*poetic*), damsel, lassie (*informal*), wench
maiden *n* **1** (*archaic, literary*) = **girl**, maid, lass, damsel, miss, virgin, nymph (*poetic*), lassie (*informal*), wench ▷ *adjective* **3** = **unmarried**, pure, virgin, intact, chaste, virginal, unwed, undefiled **4** = **first**, initial, inaugural, introductory, initiatory
mail[1] *n* **1** = **letters**, post, packages, parcels, correspondence ▷ *vb* **6** = **post**, send, forward, dispatch, send by mail *or* post **7** = **e-mail**, send, forward
main *adj* **1** = **chief**, leading, major, prime, head, special, central, particular, necessary, essential, premier, primary, vital, critical, crucial, supreme, outstanding, principal, cardinal, paramount, foremost, predominant, pre-eminent, must-have **OPPOSITE:** minor ▷ *pl n* **2** = **pipeline**, channel, pipe, conduit, duct **3** = **cable**, line, electricity supply, mains supply **6** **in the main** = **on the whole**, generally, mainly, mostly, in general, for the most part

DICTIONARY

WORD ORIGIN Old English *mægen* strength

mainbrace *n naut* **1** the rope that controls the movement of the spar of a ship's mainsail **2 splice the mainbrace** ▸ see **splice**

main clause *n grammar* a clause that can stand alone as a sentence

mainframe *n computers* a high-speed general-purpose computer, with a large store capacity

mainland *n* the main part of a land mass as opposed to an island

main line *n* **1** *railways* the chief route between two points, usually fed by branch lines ▹ *vb* **mainline 2** *slang* to inject a drug into a vein

mainly ⓣ *adv* for the most part; principally

mainmast *n naut* the chief mast of a sailing vessel with two or more masts

mainsail *n naut* the largest and lowermost sail on the mainmast

mainspring *n* **1** the chief cause or motive of something: *the mainspring of a dynamic economy* **2** the chief spring of a watch or clock

mainstay *n* **1** a chief support **2** *naut* a rope securing a mainmast

mainstream ⓣ *n* **1** the people or things representing the most common or generally accepted ideas and styles in a society, art form, etc.: *the mainstream of academic life* **2** the main current of a river ▹ *adj* **3** belonging to the social or cultural mainstream: *mainstream American movies*

mainstreeting *n Canad* the practice of a politician walking about a town or city to try to gain votes

maintain ⓣ *vb* **1** to continue or keep in existence: *we must maintain good relations with them* **2** to keep in proper or good condition: *an expensive car to maintain* **3** to sustain or keep up a particular level or speed: *he set off at a high speed, but couldn't maintain it all the way* **4** to enable a person to have the money, food and other things he or she needs to live: *the money maintained us for a month* **5** to assert: *he had always maintained that he never wanted children* **6** to defend against contradiction: *he maintained his innocence*

WORD ORIGIN from Latin *manu tenere* to hold in the hand

maintenance ⓣ *n* **1** the act of maintaining or the state of being maintained **2** the process of keeping a car, building, etc. in good condition **3** *law* financial provision ordered to be made by way of periodical payments or a lump sum, usually for a separated or divorced spouse

Maintenon *n* **Marquise de,** title of *Françoise d'Aubigné*. 1635–1719, the mistress and, from about 1685, second wife of Louis XIV

maisonette *n Brit & S African* a flat with more than one floor

WORD ORIGIN French, diminutive of *maison* house

Maistre *n* **Josephe de** 1753–1821, French writer and diplomat, noted for his extreme reactionary views, expounded in such works as *Les Soirées de St Petersbourg* (1821)

Maitland[1] *n* a town in SE Australia, in E New South Wales: industrial centre of an agricultural region. Pop: 53 470 (2001)

Maitland[2] *n* **Frederic William** 1850–1906, English legal historian

maitre d'hotel (met-ra dote-tell) *n, pl* **maitres d'hotel** a head waiter

WORD ORIGIN French

maize *n* a type of corn grown for its large yellow edible grains, which are used for food and as a source of oil ▸ See also **sweet corn**

WORD ORIGIN Spanish *maiz*

Maj. Major

majestic ⓣ *adj* beautiful, dignified, and impressive **majestically** *adv*

majesty ⓣ *n* **1** great dignity and grandeur **2** supreme power or authority

WORD ORIGIN Latin *majestas*

Majesty *n, pl* **-ties** (preceded by *Your, His, Her* or *Their*) a title used to address or refer to a sovereign or the wife or widow of a sovereign

Maj. Gen. Major General

majolica *or* **maiolica** *n* a type of porous pottery glazed with bright metallic oxides. It was extensively made in Renaissance Italy

WORD ORIGIN Italian, from Late Latin *Majorica* Majorca

major ⓣ *adj* **1** greater in size, frequency, or importance than others of the same kind: *the major political parties* **2** very serious or significant: *a major investigation* **3** main or principal: *a major road* **4** *music* **a** (of a scale) having notes separated by a whole tone, except for the third and fourth notes, and seventh and eighth notes, which are separated by a semitone **b** of or based on the major scale: *the key of D major* ▹ *n* **5** a middle-ranking military officer **6** *music* a major key, chord, mode, or scale **7** a person who has reached the age of legal majority **8** *US, Canad, S African, Austral & NZ* the principal field of study of a student ▹ *vb* **9** *US, Canad, S African, Austral & NZ* to study as one's principal subject: *he majored in economics*

WORD ORIGIN Latin: greater

major-domo *n, pl* **-mos** the chief steward or butler of a great household

WORD ORIGIN Medieval Latin *major domus* head of the household

majorette *n* one of a group of girls who practise formation marching and baton twirling

major general *n* a senior military officer

majority ⓣ *n, pl* **-ties 1** the greater number or part of something **2** (in an election) the number of votes or seats by which the strongest party or candidate beats the combined

m

THESAURUS

mainly *adv* = **chiefly**, mostly, largely, generally, usually, principally, in general, primarily, above all, substantially, on the whole, predominantly, in the main, for the most part, most of all, first and foremost, to the greatest extent

mainstream *adj* **3** = **conventional**, general, established, received, accepted, central, current, core, prevailing, orthodox, lamestream *(informal)* **OPPOSITE:** unconventional

maintain *vb* **1, 3** = **continue**, retain, preserve, sustain, carry on, keep, keep up, prolong, uphold, nurture, conserve, perpetuate **OPPOSITE:** end **2** = **look after**, care for, take care of, finance, conserve, keep in good condition **5** = **assert**, state, hold, claim, insist, declare, allege, contend, affirm, profess, avow, aver, asseverate **OPPOSITE:** disavow

maintenance *n* **1** = **continuation**, carrying-on, continuance, support, perpetuation, prolongation, sustainment, retainment **2** = **upkeep**, keeping, care, supply, repairs, provision, conservation, nurture, preservation **3** = **allowance**, living, support, keep, food, livelihood, subsistence, upkeep, sustenance, alimony, aliment

majestic *adj* = **grand**, magnificent, impressive, superb, kingly, royal, august, princely, imposing, imperial, noble, splendid, elevated, awesome, dignified, regal, stately, monumental, sublime, lofty, pompous, grandiose, exalted, splendiferous *(facetious)* **OPPOSITE:** modest

majesty *n* **1** = **grandeur**, glory, splendour, magnificence, dignity, nobility, sublimity, loftiness, impressiveness, awesomeness, exaltedness **OPPOSITE:** triviality

major *adj* **1, 3** = **main**, higher, greater, bigger, lead, leading, head, larger, better, chief, senior, supreme, superior, elder, uppermost **OPPOSITE:** minor **2** = **important**, vital, critical, significant, great, serious, radical, crucial, outstanding, grave, extensive, notable, weighty, pre-eminent

majority *n* **1** = **most**, more, mass, bulk, best part, better part, lion's share, preponderance, plurality, greater number **4** = **adulthood**,

opposition or the runner-up **3** the largest party or group that votes together in a meeting, council or parliament **4** the age at which a person legally becomes an adult **5 in the majority** forming or part of the group of people or things made up of more than half of a larger group
WORD ORIGIN Medieval Latin *majoritas*

make ⓘ *vb* **making, made 1** to create, construct, establish, or draw up; bring into being: *houses made of stone; he will have to make a will* **2** to cause to do or be; compel or induce: *please make her go away* **3** to bring about or produce: *don't make a noise* **4** to carry out or perform: *he made his first trip to China in 1987; she made an obscene gesture* **5** to appoint: *they made him caretaker manager* **6** to come into a specified state or condition: *to make merry* **7** to become: *she will make a good diplomat* **8** to cause or ensure the success of: *that news has made my day* **9** to amount to: *5 and 5 make 10* **10** to earn or be paid: *they must be making a fortune* **11** to have the qualities of or be suitable for: *what makes this book such a good read?* **12** to prepare for use: *she forgot to make her bed* **13** to be the essential element in: *confidence makes a good salesman* **14** to use for a specified purpose: *they will make this town their base* **15** to deliver: *he made a very good speech* **16** to consider to be: *what time do you make it?* **17** to cause to seem or represent as being: *her girlish pigtails made her look younger than she was; she made the experience sound most unpleasant* **18** to acquire: *she doesn't make friends easily* **19** to engage in: *they made war on the Turks* **20** to travel a certain distance or to a certain place: *we can make at least three miles before it gets dark* **21** to arrive in time for: *he didn't make the first act of the play* **22** to win or score: *he made a break of 125* **23** *informal* to gain a place or position on or in: *to make the headlines* **24 make a day** *or* **night of it** to cause an activity to last a day or night **25 make eyes at** *old-fashioned* to flirt with or ogle **26 make it** *informal* **a** to be able to attend: *I'm afraid I can't make it to your party* **b** to be successful **27 make like** *slang chiefly US & Canad* **a** to imitate **b** to pretend **28 make to** *or* **as if to** *or* **as though to** to act with the intention or with a show of doing something: *she made as if to hit him* ▷ *n* **29** manufacturer; brand: *what make of car is that?* **30** the way in which something is made **31 on the make** *slang* out for profit or conquest ▸ See also **make away, make for**, etc. **maker** *n*
WORD ORIGIN Old English *macian*

make away *vb* **1** to depart in haste **2 make away with a** to steal **b** to kill or get rid of

Makeba *n* **Miriam** 1932–2008, South African singer and political activist; banned from South Africa from 1960 to 1990

make believe *vb* **1** to pretend ▷ *n* **make-believe 2** a fantasy or pretence

make do *vb* to manage with an inferior alternative

make for *vb* **1** to head towards **2** to prepare to attack **3** to help bring about: *this will make for a spectacular race*

make of *vb* to interpret as the meaning of: *what did she make of it all?*

make off ⓘ *vb* **1** to go or run away in haste **2 make off with** to steal or abduct

make out *vb* **1** to manage to see or hear **2** to understand **3** to write out: *how shall I make out the cheque?* **4** to attempt to establish or prove: *she made me out to be a crook* **5** to pretend: *he made out that he could play the piano* **6** to manage or get on: *how did you make out in the exam?*

make over *vb* **1** to renovate or remodel: *she made over the dress to fit her sister* ▷ *n* **makeover 2** a complete remodelling **3** a series of alterations, including beauty treatments and new clothes, intended to make an improvement to someone's appearance

Maker *n* a title given to God

makeshift ⓘ *adj* serving as a temporary substitute

make-up ⓘ *n* **1** cosmetics, such as powder or lipstick **2** the cosmetics used by an actor to adapt his or her appearance **3** the arrangement of the parts of something **4** mental or physical constitution ▷ *vb* **make up 5** to form or constitute: *these arguments make up the case for the defence* **6** to devise or compose, sometimes with the intent to deceive: *she was well known for making up stories about herself* **7** to supply what is lacking in; complete: *I'll make up the difference* **8** Also: **make it up** to settle differences amicably **9 make up for** to compensate for: *one good year can make up for several bad ones* **10** to apply cosmetics to the face **11 make up to** *informal* **a** to make friendly overtures to **b** to flirt with

makeweight *n* an unimportant person or thing added to make up a lack

making ⓘ *n* **1** the act or process of producing something **2 be the making of** to cause the success of **3 in the making** in the process of becoming or being made

makings *pl n* **have the makings of** to have the potentials, qualities, or materials necessary to make or become something: *it had the makings of a classic showdown*

mako *n, pl* **makos** a powerful shark of the Atlantic and Pacific Oceans
WORD ORIGIN Māori

mal- *combining form* bad or badly; wrong or wrongly: *maladjusted; malfunction*

maturity, age of consent, seniority, manhood *or* womanhood

make *vb* **1 = create**, build, produce, manufacture, form, model, fashion, shape, frame, construct, assemble, compose, forge, mould, put together, originate, fabricate **1, 3 = produce**, cause, create, effect, lead to, occasion, generate, bring about, give rise to, engender, beget **2 = force**, cause, press, compel, drive, require, oblige, induce, railroad *(informal)*, constrain, coerce, impel, dragoon, pressurize, prevail upon **4 = perform**, do, act out, effect, carry out, engage in, execute, prosecute **9 = amount to**, total, constitute, add up to, count as, tot up to *(informal)* **10 = earn**, get, gain, net, win, clear, secure, realize, obtain, acquire, bring in, take in, fetch **29 = brand**, sort, style, model, build, form, mark, kind, type, variety, construction, marque

make off *n* **1 = flee**, clear out *(informal)*, abscond, fly, bolt, decamp, hook it *(slang)*, do a runner *(slang)*, run for it *(informal)*, slope off, cut and run *(informal)*, beat a hasty retreat, fly the coop *(US & Canad informal)*, make away, skedaddle *(informal)*, take a powder *(US & Canad slang)*, take to your heels, run away *or* off

makeshift *adj* **= temporary**, provisional, make-do, substitute, jury *(chiefly nautical)*, expedient, rough and ready, stopgap

make-up *n* **1, 2 = cosmetics**, paint *(informal)*, powder, face *(informal)*, greasepaint *(theatre)*, war paint *(informal)*, maquillage *(French)* **3 = structure**, organization, arrangement, form, construction, assembly, constitution, format, formation, composition, configuration **4 = nature**, character, constitution, temperament, make, build, figure, stamp, temper, disposition, frame of mind, cast of mind ▷ *vb* **make up 6 = invent**, create, construct, compose, write, frame, manufacture, coin, devise, hatch, originate, formulate, dream up, fabricate, concoct, cook up *(informal)*, trump up **8 = settle your differences**, shake hands, make peace, bury the hatchet, call it quits, forgive and forget, mend fences, become reconciled, declare a truce, be friends again

making *n* **1 = creation**, production, manufacture, construction, assembly, forging, composition, fabrication

DICTIONARY

WORD ORIGIN Latin *malus* bad, *male* badly

malachite (mal-a-kite) *n* a green mineral used as a source of copper, and for making ornaments
WORD ORIGIN Greek *molokhitis*

Malachy *n* **Saint** 1094–1148, Irish prelate; he became Archbishop of Armagh (1132) and founded (1142) the first Cistercian abbey in Ireland. Feast day: Nov 3

maladjustment *n psychol* a failure to meet the demands of society, such as coping with problems and social relationships **maladjusted** *adj*

maladminister *vb* to administer badly, inefficiently, or dishonestly **maladministration** *n*

maladroit (mal-a-**droyt**) *adj* clumsy, awkward, or tactless **maladroitly** *adv* **maladroitness** *n*
WORD ORIGIN French *mal* badly + ADROIT

malady (mal-a-dee) *n, pl* **-dies** *old-fashioned* any disease or illness
WORD ORIGIN Vulgar Latin *male habitus* in poor condition

malaise (mal-**laze**) *n* **1** a vague feeling of unease, illness, or depression **2** a complex of problems affecting a country, economy, etc.: *Belgium's political malaise*
WORD ORIGIN Old French *mal* bad + *aise* ease

m

Malamud *n* **Bernard** 1914–86, US novelist and short-story writer. His works include *The Fixer* (1966) and *Dubin's Lives* (1979)

malapropism *n* the comic misuse of a word by confusion with one which sounds similar, for example *under the affluence of alcohol*
WORD ORIGIN after Mrs *Malaprop* in Sheridan's play *The Rivals*

malaria *n* a disease with recurring attacks of fever, caused by the bite of some types of mosquito **malarial** *adj*
WORD ORIGIN Italian *mala aria* bad air

malarkey *n slang* nonsense or rubbish
WORD ORIGIN origin unknown

Malay *n* **1** a member of a people living chiefly in Malaysia and Indonesia **2** the language of this people ▷ *adj* **3** of the Malays or their language

Malayan *adj* **1** of Malaya ▷ *n* **2** a person from Malaya

Malaysian *adj* **1** of Malaysia ▷ *n* **2** a person from Malaysia

Malcolm *n* **George** 1917–97, British harpsichordist

malcontent *n* a person who is discontented with the existing situation
WORD ORIGIN Old French

male ❶ *adj* **1** of the sex that can fertilize female reproductive cells **2** of or characteristic of a man **3** for or composed of men or boys: *a male choir* **4** (of flowers) bearing stamens but lacking a pistil **5** *electronics, engineering* having a projecting part or parts that fit into a hollow counterpart: *a male plug* ▷ *n* **6** a male person, animal, or plant **maleness** *n*
WORD ORIGIN Latin *masculus* masculine

Malebranche *n* **Nicolas** 1638–1715, French philosopher. Originally a follower of Descartes, he developed the philosophy of occasionalism, esp. in *De la recherche de la vérité* (1674)

male chauvinism *n* the belief, held by some men, that men are better and more important than women **male chauvinist** *n, adj*

malediction (mal-lid-**dik**-shun) *n* the utterance of a curse against someone or something **maledictory** *adj*
WORD ORIGIN Latin *maledictio* a reviling

malefactor (mal-if-act-or) *n* a criminal or wrongdoer **malefaction** *n*
WORD ORIGIN Latin *malefacere* to do evil

Malenkov *n* **Georgi Maksimilianovich** 1902–88, Soviet politician; prime minister (1953–55). He was removed from the party presidium (1957) for plotting against Khrushchev; expelled from the Communist Party (1961)

Malevich *n* **Kasimir** 1878–1935, Russian painter. He founded the abstract art movement known as Suprematism

malevolent (mal-**lev**-a-lent) *adj* wishing evil to others; malicious **malevolence** *n* **malevolently** *adv*
WORD ORIGIN Latin *malevolens*

malfeasance (mal-**fee**-zanss) *n law* wrongful or illegal behaviour, esp. by a public official
WORD ORIGIN Old French *mal faisant* evil-doing

malformation *n* **1** the condition of being faulty or abnormal in form or shape **2** *pathol* a deformity, esp. when congenital **malformed** *adj*

malfunction *vb* **1** to fail to function properly or fail to function at all ▷ *n* **2** failure to function properly or failure to function at all

Malherbe *n* **François de** 1555–1628, French poet and critic. He advocated the classical ideals of clarity and concision of meaning

malice (**mal**-iss) *n* the desire to do harm or cause mischief to others **malicious** *adj* **maliciously** *adv*
WORD ORIGIN Latin *malus* evil

malice aforethought *n law* a deliberate intention to do something unlawful

malign (mal-**line**) *vb* **1** to say unpleasant and untrue things about someone; slander ▷ *adj* **2** evil in influence or effect
WORD ORIGIN Latin *malignus* spiteful

malignant (mal-**lig**-nant) *adj* **1** seeking to harm others **2** tending to cause great harm; injurious **3** *pathol* (of a tumour) uncontrollable or resistant to therapy **malignancy** *n*
WORD ORIGIN Late Latin *malignare* to behave spitefully

malignity (mal-**lig**-nit-ee) *n* the condition of being malign or deadly

malinger (mal-**ling**-ger) *vb* to pretend to be ill, or exaggerate how ill one is, to avoid work **malingerer** *n*
WORD ORIGIN French *malingre* sickly

Malinowski *n* **Bronislaw Kasper** 1884–1942, Polish anthropologist in England and the US, who researched into the sexual behaviour of primitive people in New Guinea and Melanesia

mall (mawl) *n* **1** *US, Canad, Austral, & NZ* ▸ short for **shopping mall** **2** a shaded avenue, esp. one open to the public
WORD ORIGIN after *the Mall*, an avenue in St James's Park, London

mallard *n, pl* **-lard** *or* **-lards** a common N hemisphere duck, the male of which has a dark green head
WORD ORIGIN Old French *mallart*

Mallarmé *n* **Stéphane** (stefan) 1842–98, French symbolist poet, noted for his free verse, in which he chooses words for their evocative qualities; his works include *L'Après-midi d'un Faune* (1876), *Vers et Prose* (1893), and *Divagations* (1897)

Malle *n* **Louis** 1932–95, French film director: his films include *Le Feu follet* (1963), *Au revoir les enfants* (1987), and *Vanya on 42nd Street* (1994)

malleable (**mal**-lee-a-bl) *adj* **1** (esp. of metal) capable of being hammered or pressed into shape without breaking **2** able to be influenced **malleability** *n* **malleably** *adv*
WORD ORIGIN Medieval Latin *malleabilis*

mallee *n* a low-growing eucalypt found in dry regions of Australia

mallet *n* **1** a hammer with a large wooden head **2** a long stick with a head like a hammer used to strike the ball in croquet or polo
WORD ORIGIN Old French *maillet* wooden hammer

mallow *n* any of a group of plants, with purple, pink, or white flowers
WORD ORIGIN Latin *malva*

THESAURUS

male *adj* **2 = masculine**, manly, macho, virile, manlike, manful
OPPOSITE: female

mammoth *adj* **2 = colossal**, huge, giant, massive, vast, enormous, mighty, immense, titanic, jumbo (*informal*), gigantic, monumental, mountainous, stellar (*informal*), prodigious, stupendous,

DICTIONARY

malnourished *adj* physically weak due to lack of healthy food
malnutrition *n* physical weakness resulting from insufficient food or an unbalanced diet
malodorous (mal-**lode**-or-uss) *adj* having an unpleasant smell: *the malodorous sludge of Boston harbour*
Malouf *n* **David** born 1934, Australian novelist, short-story writer, and poet. His novels include *An Imaginary Life* (1978), *Remembering Babylon* (1993), and *The Conversations at Curlow Creek* (1996)
malpractice *n* illegal, unethical, or negligent professional conduct
Malraux *n* **André** 1901–76, French writer and statesman. His novels include *La Condition humaine* (1933) on the Kuomintang revolution (1927–28) and *L'Espoir* (1937) on the Spanish Civil War, in both of which events he took part. He also wrote on art, notably in *Les Voix du silence* (1951)
malt *n* **1** grain, such as barley, that is kiln-dried after it has been germinated by soaking in water **2** ▸see **malt whisky** ▹*vb* **3** to make into or become malt **4** to make from malt or to add malt to **malted** *adj* **malty** *adj*
WORD ORIGIN Old English *mealt*
Maltese *adj* **1** of Malta ▹*n* **2** *pl* **-tese** a person from Malta **3** the language of Malta
Maltese cross *n* a cross with triangular arms that taper towards the centre, sometimes with the outer sides curving in
Malthusian (malth-**yew**-zee-an) *adj* of the theory stating that increases in population tend to exceed increases in the food supply and that therefore sexual restraint should be exercised
WORD ORIGIN after T. R. *Malthus*, economist
maltose *n* a sugar formed by the action of enzymes on starch
WORD ORIGIN *malt* + *-ose* indicating a sugar
maltreat *vb* to treat badly, cruelly, or violently **maltreatment** *n*
WORD ORIGIN French *maltraiter*
malt whisky *n* whisky made from malted barley
malversation *n rare* professional or public misconduct
WORD ORIGIN French *malverser* to behave badly
malware *n* a computer program designed specifically to damage or disrupt a system, such as a virus
mam *n informal or dialect* ▸same as **mother**
mama *or esp. US* **mamma** (mam-**mah**) *n old-fashioned, informal* ▸same as **mother**
WORD ORIGIN reduplication of childish syllable *ma*
mamba *n* a very poisonous tree snake found in tropical and Southern Africa
WORD ORIGIN Zulu *im-amba*
mambo *n, pl* **-bos** a Latin American dance resembling the rumba
WORD ORIGIN American Spanish
Mamet *n* **David** born 1947, US dramatist and film director. His plays include *Sexual Perversity in Chicago* (1974), *American Buffalo* (1976), *Glengarry Glen Ross* (1983), and *Oleanna* (1992); films include *House of Games* (1987) and *Spartan* (2004)
mammal *n* a warm-blooded animal, such as a human being, dog or whale, the female of which produces milk to feed her babies **mammalian** *adj, n*
WORD ORIGIN Latin *mamma* breast
mammary *adj* of the breasts or milk-producing glands
WORD ORIGIN Latin *mamma* breast
mammary gland *n* any of the milk-producing glands in mammals, such as a woman's breast or a cow's udder
mammon *n* wealth regarded as a source of evil and corruption, personified in the New Testament as a false god (**Mammon**)
WORD ORIGIN New Testament Greek *mammōnas* wealth
mammoth ❶ *n* **1** a large extinct elephant with a hairy coat and long curved tusks ▹*adj* **2** gigantic
WORD ORIGIN Russian *mamot*
mammy *n, pl* **-mies** *informal or dialect* ▸same as **mother**
man ❶ *n, pl* **men 1** an adult male human being, as distinguished from a woman **2** a human being of either sex; person: *all men are born equal* **3** human beings collectively; mankind ▸Related adjective: **anthropoid 4** a human being regarded as representative of a particular period or category: *Neanderthal man* **5** an adult male human being with qualities associated with the male, such as courage or virility: *take it like a man* **6** an employee, servant, or representative **7** a member of the armed forces who is not an officer **8** a member of a group or team **9** a husband, boyfriend, or male lover **10** a movable piece in various games, such as draughts **11** *S African slang* any person: used as a term of address **12 as one man** with unanimous action or response **13 he's your man** he's the person needed **14 man and boy** from childhood **15 sort out the men from the boys** to discover who can cope with difficult or dangerous situations and who cannot **16 to a man** without exception ▹*vb* **manning, manned 17** to provide with sufficient people for operation or defence **18** to take one's place at or near in readiness for action **manhood** *n*
WORD ORIGIN Old English *mann*
Man. Manitoba
mana ❶ *n* NZ authority, influence and prestige
manacle (**man**-a-kl) *n* **1** a metal ring or chain put round the wrists or ankles, used to restrict the movements of a prisoner or convict ▹*vb* **-cling, -cled 2** to put manacles on
WORD ORIGIN Latin *manus* hand
manage ❶ *vb* **-aging, -aged 1** to succeed in doing something: *we finally managed to sell our old house* **2** to be in charge of; administer: *the company is badly managed* **3** to have room or time for: *can you manage lunch tomorrow?* **4** to keep under control: *she disapproved of taking drugs to manage stress* **5** to struggle on despite difficulties, esp. financial ones: *most people cannot manage on a cleaner's salary* **manageable** *adj*
WORD ORIGIN Italian *maneggiare* to train (esp. horses)
management ❶ *n* **1** the people responsible for running an

m

THESAURUS

gargantuan, elephantine, ginormous *(informal)*, Brobdingnagian, humongous *or* humungous *(US slang)*, supersize
OPPOSITE: tiny
man *n* **1 = male**, guy *(informal)*, fellow *(informal)*, gentleman, bloke *(Brit informal)*, chap *(Brit informal)*, dude *(US informal)*, geezer *(informal)*, adult male **2 = human**, human being, body, person, individual, adult, being, somebody, soul, personage **3 = mankind**, humanity, people, mortals, human race, humankind, Homo sapiens ▹*vb* **17 = staff**, people, fill, crew, occupy, garrison, furnish with men
mana *n* (NZ) **= authority**, influence, power, might, force, weight, strength, domination, sway, standing, status, importance, esteem, stature, eminence
manage *vb* **2a = be in charge of**, run, handle, rule, direct, conduct, command, govern, administer, oversee, supervise, preside over, be head of, call the shots in, superintend, call the tune in **2b = organize**, use, handle, govern, regulate **4 = control**, influence, guide, handle, master, dominate, manipulate **5 = cope**, survive, shift, succeed, get on, carry on, fare, get through, make out, cut it *(informal)*, get along, make do, get by *(informal)*, crack it *(informal)*, muddle through
management *n* **1, 2 = directors**, board, executive(s), bosses *(informal)*, administration, employers,

DICTIONARY

organization or business **2** managers or employers collectively **3** the technique or practice of managing or controlling

manager ⓘ *n* **1** a person who manages an organization or business **2** a person in charge of a sports team **3** a person who controls the business affairs of an actor or entertainer **manageress** *fem n*

managerial *adj* of a manager or management

managing director *n* the senior director of a company, who has overall responsibility for the way it is run

mañana (man-yah-na) *n, adv* **a** tomorrow **b** some other and later time
WORD ORIGIN Spanish

man-at-arms *n, pl* **men-at-arms** a soldier, esp. a medieval soldier

manatee *n* a large plant-eating mammal occurring in tropical coastal waters of the Atlantic
WORD ORIGIN Carib *Manattouï*

Manchu *n, pl* **-chus** *or* **-chu** a member of a Mongoloid people of Manchuria, a region of NE China, who conquered China in the 17th century, ruling until 1912

Mancunian (man-kew-nee-an) *adj* **1** of Manchester, a city in NW England ▷*n* **2** a person from Manchester
WORD ORIGIN Medieval Latin *Mancunium* Manchester

mandala *n Hindu and Buddhist art* a circular design symbolizing the universe
WORD ORIGIN Sanskrit: circle

mandarin *n* **1** (in the Chinese Empire) a member of a senior grade of the bureaucracy **2** a high-ranking official with extensive powers **3** a person of standing and influence, esp. in literary or intellectual circles **4** a small citrus fruit resembling the tangerine
WORD ORIGIN Sanskrit *mantrin* counsellor

Mandarin Chinese *or* **Mandarin** *n* the official language of China since 1917

mandate ⓘ *n* **1** an official or authoritative command to carry out a particular task: *the UN force's mandate does not allow it to intervene* **2** *politics* the political authority given to a government or an elected representative through an electoral victory **3** Also: **mandated territory** (formerly) a territory administered by one country on behalf of an international body ▷*vb* **-dating, -dated 4** to delegate authority to **5** to assign territory to a nation under a mandate
WORD ORIGIN Latin *mandare* to command

mandatory ⓘ *adj* **1** obligatory; compulsory **2** having the nature or powers of a mandate **mandatorily** *adv*

Mandelstam *or* **Mandelshtam** *n* **1 Nadezhda** (**Yakovlevna**), born *Nadezhda Khazina*. 1899–1980, Soviet writer, wife of Osip Mandelstam: noted for her memoirs *Hope against Hope* (1971) and *Hope Abandoned* (1973) describing life in Stalin's Russia **2 Osip** (**Emilyevich**) 1891–?1938, Soviet poet and writer, born in Warsaw; he was persecuted by Stalin and died in a labour camp. His works include *Tristia* (1922), *Poems* (1928), and the autobiographical *Journey to Armenia* (1933)

Mandeville *n* **1 Bernard de** ?1670–1733, English author, born in Holland, noted for his satire *The Fable of the Bees* (1723) **2** Sir **John** 14th century, English author of *The Travels of Sir John Mandeville*. The book claims to be an account of the author's journeys in the East but is largely a compilation from other works

mandible *n* **1** the lower jawbone of a vertebrate **2** either of the jawlike mouthparts of an insect **3** either part of the bill of a bird, esp. the lower part
WORD ORIGIN Late Latin *mandibula* jaw

mandolin *n* a musical instrument with four pairs of strings stretched over a small light body, usually played with a plectrum
WORD ORIGIN Italian *mandolino* small lute

mandrake *n* a plant with a forked root. It was formerly thought to have magic powers and a narcotic was prepared from its root
WORD ORIGIN Latin *mandragoras*

mandrel *or* **mandril** *n* **1** a spindle on which the object being worked on is supported in a lathe **2** a shaft on which a machining tool is mounted
WORD ORIGIN perhaps from French *mandrin* lathe

mandrill *n* a monkey of W Africa. The male has red and blue markings on its face and buttocks
WORD ORIGIN *man* + *drill* an Old-World monkey

mane *n* **1** the long hair that grows from the neck in such mammals as the lion and horse **2** long thick human hair **maned** *adj*
WORD ORIGIN Old English *manu*

manège (man-nayzh) *n* **1** the art of training horses and riders **2** a riding school
WORD ORIGIN Italian *maneggiare* to manage

maneuver *n, vb US* ▸same as **manoeuvre**

man Friday *n* **1** a loyal male servant or assistant **2** Also: **girl Friday, person Friday** any person who does all the odd jobs that arise, esp. in an office
WORD ORIGIN after the native in *Robinson Crusoe*

manful *adj* determined and brave **manfully** *adv*

manganese *n chem* a brittle greyish-white metallic element used in making steel. Symbol: Mn
WORD ORIGIN probably altered form of Medieval Latin *magnesia*

mange *n* a skin disease of domestic animals, characterized by itching and loss of hair
WORD ORIGIN Old French *mangeue* itch

mangelwurzel *n* a variety of beet with a large yellowish root
WORD ORIGIN German *Mangold* beet + *Wurzel* root

manger *n* a trough in a stable or barn from which horses or cattle feed
WORD ORIGIN Old French *maingeure*

mangetout (mawnzh-too) *n* a variety of garden pea with an edible pod
WORD ORIGIN French: eat all

mangle[1] *vb* **-gling, -gled 1** to destroy or damage by crushing and twisting **2** to spoil **mangled** *adj*
WORD ORIGIN Norman French *mangler*

mangle[2] *n* **1** a machine for pressing or squeezing water out of washed clothes, consisting of two heavy rollers between which the clothes are passed ▷*vb* **-gling, -gled 2** to put through a mangle
WORD ORIGIN Dutch *mangel*

mango *n, pl* **-goes** *or* **-gos** the egg-shaped edible fruit of a tropical Asian tree, with a smooth rind and sweet juicy flesh

THESAURUS

directorate **3 = administration**, control, rule, government, running, charge, care, operation, handling, direction, conduct, command, guidance, supervision, manipulation, governance, superintendence

manager *n* **1 = supervisor**, head, director, executive, boss *(informal)*, governor, administrator, conductor, controller, superintendent, gaffer *(informal, chiefly Brit)*, proprietor, organizer, comptroller, overseer, baas *(S African)*, sherang *(Austral & NZ)*

mandate *n* **1 = command**, order, charge, authority, commission, sanction, instruction, warrant, decree, bidding, canon, directive, injunction, fiat, edict, authorization, precept

mandatory *adj* **1 = compulsory**, required, binding, obligatory, requisite **OPPOSITE:** optional

DICTIONARY

WORD ORIGIN Malay *mangā*

mangrove *n* a tropical evergreen tree or shrub with intertwining aerial roots that forms dense thickets along coasts
WORD ORIGIN older *mangrow* (changed through influence of *grove*), from Portuguese *mangue*

mangy *adj* **-gier, -giest 1** having mange **2** scruffy or shabby **mangily** *adv* **manginess** *n*

manhandle *vb* **-handling, -handled 1** to handle or push someone about roughly **2** to move something by manpower rather than by machinery

Manhire *n* **Bill** born 1946, New Zealand poet and writer. His poetry collections include *How to Take Off Your Clothes at the Picnic* (1977), *Zoetropes* (1984), and *Sunshine* (1996)

manhole *n* a hole with a detachable cover, through which a person can enter a sewer or pipe to inspect or repair it

man-hour *n* a unit of work in industry, equal to the work done by one person in one hour

manhunt *n* an organized search, usually by police, for a wanted man or fugitive

mania *n* **1** an obsessional enthusiasm or liking **2** a mental disorder characterized by great or violent excitement
WORD ORIGIN Greek: madness

-mania *n combining form* indicating extreme or abnormal excitement aroused by something: *kleptomania*

maniac *n* **1** a wild disorderly person **2** a person who has a great craving or enthusiasm for something **maniacal** (man-eye-ak-kl) *adj*
WORD ORIGIN Late Latin *maniacus* belonging to madness

manic *adj* **1** extremely excited or energetic; frenzied: *manic, cavorting dancers* **2** of, involving, or affected by mania: *deep depression broken by periods of manic excitement*

manic-depressive *psychiatry adj* **1** denoting a mental disorder characterized by an alternation between extreme euphoria and deep depression ▷*n* **2** a person afflicted with this disorder

manicure *n* **1** cosmetic care of the hands and fingernails ▷*vb* **-curing, -cured 2** to care for the fingernails and hands **manicurist** *n*
WORD ORIGIN Latin *manus* hand + *cura* care

manifest ⊙ *adj* **1** easily noticed, obvious ▷*vb* **2** to reveal or display: *an additional symptom now manifested itself* **3** to show by the way one behaves: *he manifested great personal bravery* **4** (of a disembodied spirit) to appear in visible form ▷*n* **5** a customs document containing particulars of a ship and its cargo **6** a list of the cargo and passengers on an aeroplane **manifestation** *n*
WORD ORIGIN Latin *manifestus* plain

manifesto *n, pl* **-tos** *or* **-toes** a public declaration of intent or policy issued by a group of people, for instance by a political party
WORD ORIGIN Italian

manifold *adj formal* **1** numerous and varied: *her talents are manifold* ▷*n* **2** a pipe with a number of inlets or outlets, esp. one in a car engine
WORD ORIGIN Old English *manigfeald*

manikin *n* **1** a little man; dwarf or child **2** a model of the human body
WORD ORIGIN Dutch *manneken*

manila *or* **manilla** *n* a strong usually brown paper used to make envelopes
WORD ORIGIN after *Manila*, in the Philippines

man in the street *n* the average person

manioc *n* ▸ same as **cassava**
WORD ORIGIN S American Indian *mandioca*

manipulate ⊙ *vb* **-lating, -lated 1** to handle or use skilfully **2** to control something or someone cleverly or deviously **manipulation** *n* **manipulator** *n* **manipulative** *adj*
WORD ORIGIN Latin *manipulus* handful

mankind ⊙ *n* **1** human beings collectively **2** men collectively

manly ⊙ *adj* **-lier, -liest 1** possessing qualities, such as vigour or courage, traditionally regarded as appropriate to a man; masculine **2** characteristic of a man **manliness** *n*

man-made ⊙ *adj* made by humans; artificial

manna *n* **1** *bible* the miraculous food which sustained the Israelites in the wilderness (Exodus 16:14–36) **2** a windfall: *manna from heaven*
WORD ORIGIN Hebrew *mān*

manned *adj* having a human staff or crew: *thirty years of manned space flight*

mannequin *n* **1** a woman who wears the clothes displayed at a fashion show; model **2** a life-size dummy of the human body used to fit or display clothes
WORD ORIGIN French

manner ⊙ *n* **1** the way a thing happens or is done **2** a person's bearing and behaviour **3** the style or customary way of doing something: *sculpture in the Greek manner* **4** type or kind **5 in a manner of speaking** in a way; so to speak **6 to the manner born** naturally fitted to a specified role or activity
WORD ORIGIN Old French *maniere*

mannered ⊙ *adj* **1** (of speech or behaviour) unnaturally formal and put on to impress others **2** having manners as specified: *ill-mannered*

Mannerheim *n* Baron **Carl Gustaf Emil** 1867–1951, Finnish soldier and statesman; president of Finland (1944–46)

mannerism *n* **1** a distinctive and individual gesture way or way of speaking **2** excessive use of a distinctive or affected manner, esp. in art or literature

mannerly *adj* well-mannered and polite **mannerliness** *n*

m

THESAURUS

manifest *adj* **1 = obvious**, apparent, patent, evident, open, clear, plain, visible, bold, distinct, glaring, noticeable, blatant, conspicuous, unmistakable, palpable, salient
OPPOSITE: concealed
▷*vb* **2, 3 = display**, show, reveal, establish, express, prove, declare, demonstrate, expose, exhibit, set forth, make plain, evince
OPPOSITE: conceal

manipulate *vb* **1 = work**, use, operate, handle, employ, wield **2 = influence**, control, direct, guide, conduct, negotiate, exploit, steer, manoeuvre, do a number on (*chiefly US*), twist around your little finger

mankind *n* **1 = people**, man, humanity, human race, humankind, Homo sapiens

manly *adj* **1 = virile**, male, masculine, macho, strong, powerful, brave, daring, bold, strapping, hardy, heroic, robust, vigorous, muscular, courageous, fearless, butch (*slang*), resolute, gallant, valiant, well-built, red-blooded (*informal*), dauntless, stout-hearted, valorous, manful
OPPOSITE: effeminate

man-made *adj* **= artificial**, manufactured, plastic (*slang*), mock, synthetic, ersatz

manner *n* **1, 3 = style**, way, fashion, method, means, form, process, approach, practice, procedure, habit, custom, routine, mode, genre, tack, tenor, usage, wont **2 = behaviour**, look, air, bearing, conduct, appearance, aspect, presence, tone, demeanour, deportment, mien (*literary*), comportment **4 = type**, form, sort, kind, nature, variety, brand, breed, category ▷*pl n* **1 = conduct**, bearing, behaviour, breeding, carriage, demeanour, deportment, comportment **2a = politeness**, courtesy, etiquette, refinement, polish, decorum, p's and q's **2b = protocol**, ceremony, customs, formalities, good form, proprieties, the done thing, social graces, politesse

mannered *adj* **1 = affected**, put-on, posed, artificial, pseudo (*informal*), pretentious, stilted, arty-farty (*informal*) **OPPOSITE:** natural

DICTIONARY

manners *pl n* **1** a person's social conduct viewed in the light of whether it is regarded as polite or acceptable or not: *his manners leave something to be desired; shockingly bad manners* **2** a socially acceptable way of behaving: *it's not manners to point*

Mannheim[1] *n* a city in SW Germany, in Baden-Württemberg at the confluence of the Rhine and Neckar: one of Europe's largest inland harbours; a cultural and musical centre. Pop: 308 353 (2003 est)

Mannheim[2] *n* **Karl** (karl) 1893–1947, Hungarian sociologist, living in Britain from 1933: author of *Ideology and Utopia* (1929) and *Man and Society in an Age of Reconstruction* (1941)

Manning *n* **1 Henry Edward** 1808–92, British churchman. Originally an Anglican, he was converted to Roman Catholicism (1851) and made archbishop of Westminster (1865) and cardinal (1875) **2 Olivia** 1908–80, British novelist and short-story writer, best known for her novel sequence *Fortunes of War*, comprising the *Balkan Trilogy* (1960–65) and the *Levant Trilogy* (1977–80)

mannish *adj* (of a woman) displaying qualities regarded as typical of a man

manoeuvre ❶ *or US* **maneuver** (man-noo-ver) *vb* **-vring, -vred** *or* **-vering, -vered 1** to move or do something with dexterity and skill: *she manoeuvred the car easily into the parking space* **2** to manipulate a situation in order to gain some advantage **3** to perform a manoeuvre or manoeuvres ▷ *n* **4** a movement or action requiring dexterity and skill **5** a contrived, complicated, and possibly deceptive plan or action **6 manoeuvres** military or naval exercises, usually on a large scale **7** a change in course of a ship or aircraft, esp. a complicated one **8 room for manoeuvre** the possibility of changing one's plans or behaviour if it becomes necessary or desirable **manoeuvrable** *or US* **maneuverable** *adj* **manoeuvrability** *or US* **maneuverability** *n*
WORD ORIGIN French, from Medieval Latin *manuopera* manual work

manoeuvring *or US* **maneuvering** *n* the skilful manipulation of a situation to gain some advantage

man-of-war *n, pl* **men-of-war 1** a warship **2** ▸ short for **Portuguese man-of-war**

Manolete *n* original name *Manuel Rodriguez y Sánchez.* 1917–47, Spanish bullfighter

manor *n* **1** (in medieval Europe) the lands and property controlled by a lord **2** *Brit* a large country house and its lands **3** *Brit slang* an area of operation, esp. of a local police force **manorial** *adj*
WORD ORIGIN Old French *manoir* dwelling

manor house *n chiefly Brit* a large country house, esp. one that was originally part of a medieval manor

manpower *n* the number of people needed or available for a job

manqué (mong-kay) *adj* unfulfilled; would-be: *an actor manqué*
WORD ORIGIN French, literally: having missed

mansard *n* a roof with two slopes on both sides and both ends, the lower slopes being steeper than the upper
WORD ORIGIN after François *Mansart*, architect

manse *n* the house provided for a minister of some Christian denominations
WORD ORIGIN Medieval Latin *mansus* dwelling

Mansell *n* **Nigel** born 1953, English motor-racing driver: world champion in 1992

manservant *n, pl* **menservants** a male servant, esp. a valet

Mansholt *n* **Sicco Leendert** 1908–95, Dutch economist and politician; vice president (1958–72) and president (1972–73) of the European Economic Community Commission. He was the author of the Mansholt Plan for the agricultural organization of the European Economic Community

mansion ❶ *n* **1** a large and imposing house **2 Mansions** *Brit* a name given to some blocks of flats as part of their address: *18 Wilton Mansions*
WORD ORIGIN Latin *mansio* a remaining

manslaughter *n law* the unlawful but not deliberately planned killing of one human being by another

Manson *n* Sir **Patrick** 1844–1922, British physician, who established that mosquitoes transmit certain parasites responsible for human diseases

Mansur *n* **Abu Ja'far al-** 712–75 AD, 2nd caliph of the Abbasid dynasty (754–75). He founded Baghdad (762) and made it the Islamic capital

Mantegna *n* **Andrea** 1431–1506, Italian painter and engraver, noted esp. for his frescoes, such as those in the Ducal Palace, Mantua

mantel *n* a wooden, stone, or iron frame around a fireplace
WORD ORIGIN variant of *mantle*

mantelpiece *n* a shelf above a fireplace often forming part of the mantel. Also: **mantel shelf, chimneypiece**

manticore *n* a mythical beast with a lion's body, a scorpion's tail, and a man's head with three rows of teeth
WORD ORIGIN Persian *mardkhora* man-eater

mantilla *n* a woman's lace or silk scarf covering the shoulders and head, worn esp. in Spain
WORD ORIGIN Spanish *manta* cloak

mantis *n, pl* **-tises** *or* **-tes** a carnivorous insect resembling a grasshopper, that rests with the first pair of legs raised as if in prayer. Also: **praying mantis**
WORD ORIGIN Greek: prophet

mantissa *n* the part of a common logarithm consisting of the decimal point and the figures following it: *the mantissa of 2.4771 is .4771*
WORD ORIGIN Latin: something added

mantle ❶ *n* **1** *old-fashioned* a loose wrap or cloak **2** anything that covers completely or envelops: *a mantle of snow covered the ground* **3** the responsibilities and duties which go with a particular job or position: *he refuses to accept the mantle of leader* **4** a small mesh dome used to increase illumination in a gas or oil lamp by becoming incandescent **5** *geol* the part of the earth between the crust and the core ▷ *vb* **-tling, -tled 6** to spread over or become spread over: *mountains mantled in lush vegetation*
WORD ORIGIN Latin *mantellum* little cloak

man-to-man *adj* characterized by frankness and sincerity: *a man-to-man discussion*

mantra *n* **1** *hinduism, buddhism* any sacred word or syllable used as an object of concentration **2** *hinduism* a Vedic psalm of praise
WORD ORIGIN Sanskrit: speech, instrument of thought

manual ❶ *adj* **1** of a hand or hands: *manual dexterity* **2** physical as opposed

THESAURUS

manoeuvre *vb* **2a = scheme**, plot, plan, intrigue, wangle *(informal)*, machinate **2b = manipulate**, arrange, organize, devise, manage, set up, engineer, fix, orchestrate, contrive, stage-manage ▷ *n* **5 = stratagem**, move, plan, action, movement, scheme, trick, plot, tactic, intrigue, dodge, ploy, ruse, artifice, subterfuge, machination **6** *(often plural)* **= movement**, operation, exercise, deployment, war game

mansion *n* **1 = residence**, manor, hall, villa, dwelling, abode, habitation, seat

mantle *n* **1** *(archaic)* **= cloak**, wrap, cape, hood, shawl **2 = covering**, cover, screen, cloud, curtain, envelope, blanket, veil, shroud, canopy, pall

manual *adj* **2 = physical**, human, done by hand **3 = hand-operated**, hand, non-automatic ▷ *n* **4 = handbook**,

to mental: *manual labour* **3** operated or done by human labour rather than automatic or computer-aided means: *a manual gearbox* ▷ *n* **4** a book of instructions or information **5** *music* one of the keyboards on an organ **manually** *adv*
WORD ORIGIN Latin *manus* hand

Manuel I *n* called *the Fortunate* 1469–1521, king of Portugal (1495–1521); his reign saw the discovery of Brazil and the beginning of Portuguese trade with India and the East

manufacture ❶ *vb* **-turing, -tured** **1** to process or make goods on a large scale, esp. using machinery **2** to invent or concoct evidence, an excuse, etc. ▷ *n* **3** the production of goods, esp. by industrial processes **manufacturer** *n* **manufacturing** *n, adj*
WORD ORIGIN Latin *manus* hand + *facere* to make

manuka (mah-nook-a) *n* a New Zealand tree with strong elastic wood and aromatic leaves
WORD ORIGIN Māori

manuka honey *n* honey from the nectar of the manuka tree; its antibacterial agent is used for medicinal purposes ▸ See also **UMF**

manumit (man-new-mit) *vb* **-mitting, -mitted** to free from slavery **manumission** *n*
WORD ORIGIN Latin *manumittere* to release

manure *n* **1** animal excrement used as a fertilizer ▷ *vb* **-nuring, -nured** **2** to spread manure upon fields or soil
WORD ORIGIN Anglo-French *mainoverer*

manuscript *n* **1** a book or other document written by hand **2** the original handwritten or typed version of a book or article submitted by an author for publication
WORD ORIGIN Medieval Latin *manuscriptus* handwritten

Manutius *n* See **Aldus Manutius**

Manx *adj* **1** of the Isle of Man ▷ *n* **2** an almost extinct Celtic language of the Isle of Man ▷ *pl n* **3** **the Manx** the people of the Isle of Man **Manxman** *n* **Manxwoman** *n*
WORD ORIGIN Scandinavian

Manx cat *n* a short-haired breed of cat without a tail

many ❶ *adj* **1** a large number of; numerous: *many times; many people think the government is incompetent* ▷ *pron* **2** a number of people or things, esp. a large one: *his many supporters; have as many as you want* **3** **many a** each of a considerable number of: *many a man* ▷ *n* **4** **the many** the majority of mankind, esp. the common people
WORD ORIGIN Old English *manig*

Manzoni *n* **Alessandro** 1785–1873, Italian romantic novelist and poet, famous for his historical novel *I Promessi sposi* (1825–27)

Maoism *n* Communism as interpreted in the theories and policies of Mao Tse-tung (1893–1976), Chinese statesman **Maoist** *n, adj*

Māori *n* **1** *pl* **-ri** *or* **-ris** a member of the Polynesian people living in New Zealand since before the arrival of European settlers **2** the language of this people ▷ *adj* **3** of this people or their language

map *n* **1** a diagrammatic representation of the earth's surface or part of it, showing the geographical distributions or positions of features such as roads, towns, relief, and rainfall **2** a diagrammatic representation of the stars or of the surface of a celestial body **3** *maths* ▸ same as **function** **4** **put on the map** to make (a town or company) well-known: *William Morris put Kelmscott on the map* ▷ *vb* **mapping, mapped** **5** to make a map of **6** *maths* to represent or transform (a function, figure, or set) ▸ See also **map out**
WORD ORIGIN Latin *mappa* cloth

Map *or* **Mapes** *n* **Walter** ?1140–?1209, Welsh ecclesiastic and satirical writer. His chief work is the miscellany *De Nugis curialium*

maple *n* **1** any of various trees or shrubs with five-pointed leaves and winged seeds borne in pairs **2** the hard wood of any of these trees ▸ See also **sugar maple**
WORD ORIGIN Old English *mapeltrēow* maple tree

maple leaf *n* the leaf of the maple tree, the national emblem of Canada

maple syrup *n* a very sweet syrup made from the sap of the sugar maple

map out *vb* to plan or design

mapping *n maths* ▸ same as **function**

maquis (mah-kee) *n, pl* **-quis** (-kee) **1** the French underground movement that fought against the German occupying forces in World War II **2** a type of shrubby, mostly evergreen, vegetation found in coastal regions of the Mediterranean area
WORD ORIGIN French

mar ❶ *vb* **marring, marred** to spoil or be the one bad feature of: *Sicily's coastline is marred by high-rise hotels*
WORD ORIGIN Old English *merran*

Mar. March

marabou *n* **1** a large black-and-white African stork **2** the soft white down of this bird, used to trim hats etc.
WORD ORIGIN Arabic *murābit* holy man

maraca (mar-rak-a) *n* a shaken percussion instrument, usually one of a pair, consisting of a gourd or plastic shell filled with dried seeds or pebbles
WORD ORIGIN Brazilian Portuguese

marae (mar-rye) *n NZ* **1** an enclosed space in front of a Māori meeting house **2** a Māori meeting house and its buildings
WORD ORIGIN Māori

maraschino (mar-rass-kee-no) *n* a liqueur made from a type of sour cherry having a taste like bitter almonds
WORD ORIGIN Italian

maraschino cherry *n* a cherry preserved in maraschino

Marat *n* **Jean Paul** 1743–93, French revolutionary leader and journalist. He founded the radical newspaper *L'Ami du peuple* and was elected to the National Convention (1792). He was instrumental in overthrowing the Girondists (1793); he was stabbed to death in his bath by Charlotte Corday

marathon *n* **1** a race on foot of 26 miles 385 yards (42.195 kilometres) **2** any long or arduous task or event ▷ *adj* **3** of or relating to a race on foot of 26 miles 385 yards (42.195 kilometres): *marathon runners* **4** long and arduous: *a marathon nine hour meeting*
WORD ORIGIN referring to the feat of the messenger said to have run 26

THESAURUS

guide, instructions, bible, guidebook, workbook

manufacture *vb* **1 = make**, build, produce, construct, form, create, process, shape, turn out, assemble, compose, forge, mould, put together, fabricate, mass-produce **2 = concoct**, make up, invent, devise, hatch, fabricate, think up, cook up *(informal)*, trump up ▷ *n* **3 = making**, production, construction, assembly, creation, produce, fabrication, mass-production

many *adj* **1 = numerous**, various, varied, countless, abundant, myriad, innumerable, sundry, copious, manifold, umpteen *(informal)*, profuse, multifarious, multitudinous, multifold, divers *(archaic)* ▷ *pron* **2 = a lot**, lots *(informal)*, plenty, a mass, scores, piles *(informal)*, tons *(informal)*, heaps *(informal)*, large numbers, a multitude, umpteen *(informal)*, a horde, a thousand and one, a gazillion *(informal)*

mar *vb* **a = harm**, damage, hurt, spoil, stain, blight, taint, tarnish, blot, sully, vitiate, put a damper on **b = ruin**, injure, spoil, scar, flaw, impair, mutilate, detract from, maim, deform, blemish, mangle, disfigure, deface **OPPOSITE:** improve

DICTIONARY

miles from Marathon to Athens to bring the news of victory in 490 BC

maraud *vb* to wander or raid in search of plunder **marauder** *n* **marauding** *adj*
WORD ORIGIN French *marauder* to prowl

marble *n* **1** a hard limestone rock, which usually has a mottled appearance and can be given a high polish **2** a block of marble or work of art made of marble **3** a small round glass ball used in playing marbles ▷*vb* **-bling, -bled 4** to mottle with variegated streaks in imitation of marble **marbled** *adj*
WORD ORIGIN Greek *marmaros*

marbles *n* a game in which marbles are rolled at one another

marbling *n* **1** a mottled effect or pattern resembling marble **2** the streaks of fat in lean meat

marc *n* **1** the remains of grapes or other fruit that have been pressed for wine-making **2** a brandy distilled from these
WORD ORIGIN French

Marc *n* **Franz** 1880–1916, German expressionist painter; cofounder with Kandinsky of the *Blaue Reiter* group (1911). He is noted for his symbolic compositions of animals

marcasite *n* **1** a pale yellow form of iron pyrites used in jewellery **2** a cut and polished form of steel used for making jewellery
WORD ORIGIN Arabic *marqashītā*

Marcel *n* **Gabriel (Honoré)** 1889–1973, French Christian existentialist philosopher and dramatist, whose philosophical works include *Being and Having* (1949) and *The Mystery of Being* (1951)

Marcellus *n* **Marcus Claudius** ?268–208 BC, Roman general and consul, who captured Syracuse (212) in the Second Punic War

march¹ ⊙ *vb* **1** to walk with very regular steps, like a soldier **2** to walk in a quick and determined manner, esp. when angry: *he marched into the kitchen without knocking* **3** to make a person or group proceed: *he was marched back to his cell* **4** (of an army, procession, etc.) to walk as an organized group: *the demonstrators marched down the main street* **5** to advance or progress steadily: *time marches on* ▷*n* **6** a regular stride **7** a long or exhausting walk **8** the steady development or progress of something: *the continuous march of industrial development* **9** a distance covered by marching **10** an organized protest in which a large group of people walk somewhere together: *a march against racial violence* **11** a piece of music suitable for marching to **12 steal a march on** to gain an advantage over, esp. by a trick **marcher** *n* **marching** *adj*
WORD ORIGIN Old French *marchier* to tread

march² *n* **1** a border or boundary **2** the land lying along a border or boundary, often of disputed ownership
WORD ORIGIN Old French *marche*

March *n* the third month of the year
WORD ORIGIN Latin *Martius* (month) of Mars

March hare *n* a hare during its breeding season in March, noted for its wild and excitable behaviour

marching girl *n NZ* a girl who does team formation marching as a sport

marching orders *pl n* **1** *informal* dismissal, esp. from employment **2** military orders, giving instructions about a march

marchioness (marsh-on-**ness**) *n* **1** a woman who holds the rank of marquis or marquess **2** the wife or widow of a marquis or marquess
WORD ORIGIN Medieval Latin *marchionissa*

marchpane *n archaic* marzipan
WORD ORIGIN French

Marcuse *n* **Herbert** 1898–1979, US philosopher, born in Germany. In his later works he analysed the situation of man under monopoly capitalism and the dehumanizing effects of modern technology. His works include *Eros and Civilization* (1958) and *One Dimensional Man* (1964)

Mardi Gras (**mar-dee grah**) *n* the festival of Shrove Tuesday, celebrated in some cities with great revelry
WORD ORIGIN French: fat Tuesday

mare¹ *n* the adult female of a horse or zebra
WORD ORIGIN Old English *mere*

mare² (**mar**-ray) *n, pl* **maria** one of many huge dry plains on the surface of the moon or Mars, visible as dark markings
WORD ORIGIN Latin: sea

Marenzio *n* **Luca** 1553–99, Italian composer of madrigals

mare's-nest *n* a discovery imagined to be important but proving to be worthless

Margaret *n* **1** called the *Maid of Norway.* ?1282–90, queen of Scotland (1286–90); daughter of Eric II of Norway. Her death while sailing to England to marry the future Edward II led Edward I to declare dominion over Scotland **2** 1353–1412, queen of Sweden (1388–1412) and regent of Norway and Denmark (1380–1412), who united the three countries under her rule **3 Princess** 1930–2002, younger sister of Queen Elizabeth II of Great Britain and Northern Ireland

Margaret of Anjou *n* 1430–82, queen of England. She married the mentally unstable Henry VI of England in 1445 to confirm the truce with France during the Hundred Years' War. She became a leader of the Lancastrians in the Wars of the Roses and was defeated at Tewkesbury (1471) by Edward IV

Margaret of Navarre *n* Also: **Margaret of Angoulême** 1492–1549, queen of Navarre (1544–49) by marriage to Henry II of Navarre; sister of Francis I of France. She was a poet, a patron of humanism, and author of the *Heptaméron* (1558)

Margaret of Scotland *n* **Saint** 1045–93, queen consort of Malcolm III of Scotland. Her piety and benefactions to the church led to her canonization (1250). Feast days: June 10, Nov 16

Margaret of Valois *n* 1553–1615, daughter of Henry II of France and Catherine de' Medici; queen of Navarre (1572) by marriage to Henry of Navarre. The marriage was dissolved (1599) after his accession as Henry IV of France: noted for her *Mémoires*

margarine *n* a butter substitute made from vegetable and animal fats
WORD ORIGIN Greek *margaron* pearl

marge *n Austral & Brit informal* margarine

margin ⊙ *n* **1** an edge, rim, or border: *we came to the margin of the wood; people on the margin of society* **2** the blank space surrounding the text on a page **3** an additional amount or one beyond the minimum necessary: *the margin of victory was seven lengths; a small margin of error* **4** *chiefly Austral* a payment made in addition to a basic wage, esp. for special skill or responsibility **5** a limit beyond which something can no longer exist or function: *the margin of physical survival* **6** *econ* the minimum return below which an enterprise becomes unprofitable
WORD ORIGIN Latin *margo* border

marginal ⊙ *adj* **1** of, in, on, or forming a margin **2** not important;

m

THESAURUS

march¹ *vb* **1, 4 = parade**, walk, file, pace, stride, tread, tramp, swagger, footslog **2 = walk**, strut, storm, sweep, stride, stalk, flounce ▷*n* **7 = walk**, trek, hike, tramp, slog, yomp (*Brit informal*), routemarch **8 = progress**, development, advance, evolution, progression

margin *n* **1 = edge**, side, limit, border, bound, boundary, confine, verge, brink, rim, brim, perimeter, periphery

marginal *adj* **2 = insignificant**, small, low, minor, slight, minimal, negligible **3 = borderline**, bordering,

DICTIONARY

insignificant: *he remained a rather marginal political figure* **3** close to a limit, esp. a lower limit: *marginal legal ability* **4** *econ* relating to goods or services produced and sold at the margin of profitability: *marginal cost* **5** *politics* of or designating a constituency in which elections tend to be won by small margins: *a marginal seat* **6** designating agricultural land on the edge of fertile areas ▷ *n* **7** *politics chiefly Brit & NZ* a marginal constituency
marginally *adv*

marginalia *pl n* notes in the margin of a book, manuscript, or letter

Margolis *n* **Donald** born 1955, US playwright; plays include *The Loman Family Picnic* (1989) and the Pulitzer Prize-winning *Dinner with Friends* (1999)

margrave *n* (formerly) a German nobleman ranking above a count
WORD ORIGIN Middle Dutch *markgrave* count of the frontier

Margrethe II *n* born 1940, queen of Denmark from 1972

marguerite *n* a garden plant with flowers resembling large daisies
WORD ORIGIN French: daisy

Marie *n* 1875–1938, queen consort of Ferdinand I of Romania. A granddaughter of Queen Victoria, she secured Romania's support for the Allies in World War I

Marie de France *n* 12th century AD, French poet, who probably lived in England; noted for her *lais* (verse narratives) based on Celtic tales

Marie Louise *n* 1791–1847, empress of France (1811–15) as the second wife of Napoleon I; daughter of Francis I of Austria. On Napoleon's abdication (1815) she became Duchess of Parma

marigold *n* any of various plants cultivated for their yellow or orange flowers
WORD ORIGIN from *Mary* (the Virgin) + *gold*

marijuana ❶ *or* **marihuana** (mar-ree-**wah**-na) *n* the dried leaves and flowers of the hemp plant, used as a drug, esp. in cigarettes
WORD ORIGIN Mexican Spanish

marimba *n* a percussion instrument consisting of a set of hardwood plates placed over tuned metal resonators, played with soft-headed sticks
WORD ORIGIN West African

Marin *n* **John** 1870–1953, US painter, noted esp. for his watercolour landscapes and seascapes

marina *n* a harbour for yachts and other pleasure boats
WORD ORIGIN Latin: marine

marinade *n* **1** a mixture of oil, wine, vinegar, etc. in which meat or fish is soaked before cooking ▷ *vb* **-nading, -naded 2** ▸ same as **marinate**
WORD ORIGIN French

marinate *vb* **-nating, -nated** to soak in marinade **marinated** *adj*
WORD ORIGIN Italian *marinare* to pickle

marine ❶ *adj* **1** of, found in, or relating to the sea **2** of shipping or navigation **3** used or adapted for use at sea ▷ *n* **4** (esp. in Britain and the US) a soldier trained for land and sea combat **5** a country's shipping or navy collectively: *the merchant marine*
WORD ORIGIN Latin *marinus* of the sea

mariner ❶ (**mar**-in-er) *n* a sailor

Marinetti *n* **Filippo Tommaso** 1876–1944, Italian poet; founder of futurism (1909)

marionette *n* a puppet whose limbs are moved by strings
WORD ORIGIN French, from the name *Marion*

Maritain *n* **Jacques** 1882–1973, French neo-Thomist Roman Catholic philosopher

marital ❶ *adj* of or relating to marriage **maritally** *adv*
WORD ORIGIN Latin *maritus* married

maritime ❶ *adj* **1** of or relating to shipping **2** of, near, or living near the sea
WORD ORIGIN Latin *maritimus* of the sea

Marius *n* **Gaius** ?155–86 BC, Roman general and consul. He defeated Jugurtha, the Cimbri, and the Teutons (107–101), but his rivalry with Sulla caused civil war (88). He was exiled but returned (87) and took Rome

Marivaux *n* **Pierre Carlet de Chamblain de** 1688–1763, French dramatist and novelist, noted particularly for his comedies, such as *Le jeu de l'amour et du hasard* (1730) and *La Vie de Marianne* (1731–41)

marjoram *n* a plant with sweet-scented leaves, used for seasoning food and in salads
WORD ORIGIN Medieval Latin *marjorana*

mark[1] ❶ *n* **1** a visible impression on a surface, such as a spot or scratch **2** a sign, symbol, or other indication that distinguishes something **3** a written or printed symbol, as used for punctuation **4** a letter, number, or percentage used to grade academic work **5** a thing that indicates position; marker **6** an indication of some quality: *a mark of respect* **7** a target or goal **8** impression or influence: *this book displays the mark of its author's admiration of Kafka* **9** (in trade names) a particular model or type of a vehicle, machine, etc.: *the Ford Escort Mark Two* **10** one of the temperature settings at which a gas oven can work: *bake at gas mark 5 for thirty minutes* **11 make one's mark** to achieve recognition **12 on your mark** *or* **marks** a command given to runners in a race to prepare themselves at the starting line **13 up to the mark** meeting the desired standard ▷ *vb* **14** to make a visible impression, trace, or stain on **15** to have a tendency to become dirty, scratched, or damaged: *this material marks easily* **16** to characterize or distinguish: *the gritty determination that has marked his career* **17** to designate someone as a particular type of person: *she would now be marked*

m

THESAURUS

on the edge, peripheral

marijuana *n* **= cannabis**, pot *(slang)*, weed *(slang)*, dope *(slang)*, blow *(slang)*, smoke *(informal)*, stuff *(slang)*, leaf *(slang)*, tea *(US slang)*, grass *(slang)*, chronic *(US slang)*, hemp, hash *(slang)*, gage *(US obsolete, slang)*, hashish, mary jane *(US slang)*, ganja, bhang, kif, wacky baccy *(slang)*, sinsemilla, dagga *(S African)*, charas

marine *adj* **1, 2 = nautical**, sea, maritime, oceanic, naval, saltwater, seafaring, ocean-going, seagoing, pelagic, thalassic

mariner *n* **= sailor**, seaman, sea dog, seafarer, hand, salt, tar, navigator, gob *(US slang)*, matelot *(slang, chiefly Brit)*, Jack Tar, seafaring man, bluejacket

marital *adj* **= matrimonial**, married, wedded, nuptial, conjugal, spousal, connubial

maritime *adj* **1 = nautical**, marine, naval, sea, oceanic, seafaring **2 = coastal**, seaside, littoral

mark[1] *n* **1 = spot**, stain, streak, smudge, line, nick, impression, scratch, bruise, scar, dent, blot, blemish, blotch, pock, splotch, smirch **2a = characteristic**, feature, symptom, standard, quality, measure, stamp, par, attribute, criterion, norm, trait, badge, hallmark, yardstick, peculiarity **2b = brand**, impression, label, stamp, print, device, flag, seal, symbol, token, earmark, emblem, insignia, signet, handprint **6 = indication**, sign, note, evidence, symbol, proof, token **7 = target**, goal, aim, purpose, end, object, objective ▷ *vb* **14 = scar**, scratch, dent, imprint, nick, brand, impress, stain, bruise, streak, blot, smudge, blemish, blotch, splotch, smirch **16 = distinguish**, show, illustrate, exemplify, denote, evince, betoken **17 = label**, identify, brand, flag, stamp, characterize **20, 21 = observe**, mind, note, regard, notice, attend to, pay attention to, pay heed to, hearken to *(archaic)* **22 = grade**, correct, assess, evaluate, appraise

DICTIONARY

as a troublemaker **18** to label, esp. to indicate price **19** to celebrate or commemorate an occasion or its anniversary: *a series of concerts to mark the 200th anniversary of Mozart's death* **20** to pay attention to: *mark my words* **21** to observe or notice **22** to grade or evaluate academic work **23** *sport* to stay close to an opponent to hamper his or her play **24 mark off** *or* **out** to set boundaries or limits on **25 mark time a** to move the feet alternately as in marching but without advancing **b** to wait for something more interesting to happen ▸See also **markdown, mark-up**
WORD ORIGIN Old English *mearc*

mark² *n* ▸see **Deutschmark**
WORD ORIGIN Old English *marc* unit of weight of precious metal

markdown *n* **1** a price reduction ▹*vb* **mark down 2** to reduce in price **3** to make a written note of: *she marked down the number of the getaway car*

marked ❶ *adj* **1** obvious or noticeable: *a marked improvement* **2** singled out, esp. as the target of attack: *a marked man* **markedly** (mark-id-lee) *adv*

marker *n* **1** an object used to show the position of something **2** Also called: **marker pen** a thick felt-tipped pen used for drawing and colouring

m

market ❶ *n* **1** an occasion at which people meet to buy and sell merchandise **2** a place at which a market is held **3** the buying and selling of goods and services, esp. when unrestrained by political or social considerations: *the market has been brought into health care* **4** the trading opportunities provided by a particular group of people: *the youth market* **5** demand for a particular product **6** ▸short for **stock market** **7 be in the market for** to wish to buy **8 on the market** available for purchase **9 seller's** *or* **buyer's market** a market characterized by excess demand (or supply) and thus favourable to sellers (or buyers) ▹*adj* **10** of, relating to, or controlled by the buying and selling of goods and services, esp. when unrestrained by political or social considerations: *a market economy* ▹*vb* **-keting, -keted 11** to offer or produce for sale **marketable** *adj*
WORD ORIGIN Latin *mercari* to trade

market forces *pl n* the effect of supply and demand on trading within a free market

market garden *n chiefly Brit & NZ* a place where fruit and vegetables are grown for sale **market gardener** *n*

marketing *n* the part of a business which controls the way that goods or services are sold

market maker *n stock Exchange* a dealer in securities on the London Stock Exchange who can also deal with the public as a broker

marketplace *n* **1** a place where a public market is held **2** the commercial world of buying and selling

market price *n* the prevailing price at which goods may be bought or sold

market research *n* the study of customers' wants and purchases, and of the forces influencing them

market-test *vb* to put (a section of a public-sector service) out to tender, often before full privatization

market town *n chiefly Brit* the main town in an agricultural area, usually one where a market is regularly held

Markiewicz *n* **Constance,** Countess, original name *Constance Gore-Booth.* 1868–1927, Irish nationalist, married to a Polish count. She fought in the Easter Rising (1916) and was sentenced to death but reprieved. The first woman elected to the British parliament (1918), she refused to take her seat

marking *n* **1** the arrangement of colours on an animal or plant **2** the assessment and correction of pupils' or students' written work by teachers

Markova *n* Dame **Alicia** real name *Lilian Alicia Marks.* (1910–2004), English ballerina

marksman *n, pl* **-men** a person skilled in shooting **marksmanship** *n*

mark-up *n* **1** an amount added to the cost of something to provide the seller with a profit ▹*vb* **mark up 2** to increase the cost of something by an amount or percentage in order to make a profit

marl *n* a fine-grained rock consisting of clay, limestone, and silt used as a fertilizer **marly** *adj*
WORD ORIGIN Late Latin *margila*

marlin *n, pl* **-lin** *or* **-lins** a large fish with a long spear-like upper jaw, found in warm and tropical seas
WORD ORIGIN after *marlinspike* (because of its long jaw)

marlinspike *or* **marlinespike** (mar-lin-spike) *n naut* a pointed metal tool used in separating strands of rope
WORD ORIGIN Dutch *marlijn* light rope + SPIKE

marmalade *n* a jam made from citrus fruits, esp. oranges
WORD ORIGIN Portuguese *marmelo* quince

marmoreal (mar-more-ee-al) *adj* of or like marble
WORD ORIGIN Latin *marmoreus*

marmoset *n* a small South American monkey with a long bushy tail
WORD ORIGIN Old French *marmouset* grotesque figure

marmot *n* any of various burrowing rodents of Europe, Asia, and North America. They are heavily built and have coarse fur
WORD ORIGIN French *marmotte*

maroon¹ ❶ *vb* **1** to abandon someone in a deserted area, esp. on an island **2** to isolate in a helpless situation: *we're marooned here until the snow stops* **marooned** *adj*
WORD ORIGIN American Spanish *cimarrón* wild

maroon² *adj* **1** dark purplish-red ▹*n* **2** an exploding firework or flare used as a warning signal
WORD ORIGIN French: chestnut

Marprelate *n* **Martin,** the pen name of the anonymous author or authors of a series of satirical Puritan tracts (1588–89), attacking the bishops of the Church of England

Marquand *n* **J(ohn) P(hillips)** 1893–1960, US novelist, noted for his stories featuring the Japanese detective Mr Moto and for his satirical comedies of New England life, such as *The Late George Apley* (1937)

marque (mark) *n* a brand of product, esp. of a car
WORD ORIGIN French

marquee *n* a large tent used for a party, exhibition, etc.
WORD ORIGIN invented singular form of MARQUISE

marquess (mar-kwiss) *n* **1** (in the British Isles) a nobleman ranking between a duke and an earl **2** ▸see **marquis**

marquetry *n, pl* **-quetries** a pattern of inlaid veneers of wood or metal used chiefly as ornamentation in furniture
WORD ORIGIN Old French *marqueter* to inlay

Marquette *n* **Jacques**, known as *Père Marquette.* 1637–75, French Jesuit missionary and explorer, with Louis Jolliet, of the Mississippi river

marquis *n, pl* **-quises** *or* **-quis** (in various countries) a nobleman ranking above a count, corresponding to a British marquess
WORD ORIGIN Old French *marchis* count of the frontier

Marquis *n* **Don(ald Robert Perry)**

THESAURUS

marked *adj* **1 = noticeable**, clear, decided, striking, noted, obvious, signal, dramatic, considerable, outstanding, remarkable, apparent, prominent, patent, evident, distinct, pronounced, notable, manifest, blatant, conspicuous, salient
OPPOSITE: imperceptible

market *n* **1, 2 = fair**, mart, bazaar, souk (*Arabic*) ▹*vb* **11 = sell**, promote, retail, peddle, vend, offer for sale

maroon¹ *vb* **1, 2 = abandon**, leave, desert, strand, leave high and dry (*informal*), cast away, cast ashore

1878–1937, US humorist; author of *archy* and *mehitabel* (1927)
marquise (mar-**keez**) *n* **1** (in various countries) a marchioness **2** a gemstone cut in a pointed oval shape
WORD ORIGIN French
marram grass *n* a grass that grows on sandy shores: often planted to stabilize sand dunes
WORD ORIGIN Old Norse *marálmr*
marriage ❶ *n* **1** the state or relationship of being husband and wife: *the institution of marriage* **2** the contract made by a man and woman to live as husband and wife ▸ Related adjectives: **connubial, nuptial 3** the ceremony formalizing this union; wedding **4** a close union or relationship: *the marriage of scientific knowledge and industry*
marriageable *adj* suitable for marriage, usually with reference to age
marriage guidance *n* advice given by trained counsellors to couples who have problems in their married life
married *adj* **1** having a husband or wife **2** of marriage or married people: *married life* ▹*n* **3 marrieds** married people: *young marrieds*
Marriner *n* Sir **Neville** born 1924, British conductor and violinist; founder (1956) and director of the Academy of St Martin in the Fields, which specializes in baroque music
marrow *n* **1** the fatty tissue that fills the cavities of bones **2** ▸ short for **vegetable marrow**
WORD ORIGIN Old English *mærg*
marrowfat *or* **marrow pea** *n* a variety of large pea
marry[1] ❶ *vb* **-ries, -rying, -ried 1** to take (someone) as one's husband or wife **2** to join or give in marriage **3** Also: **marry up** to fit together or unite; join: *their playing marries Irish traditional music and rock*
WORD ORIGIN Latin *maritare*
marry[2] *interj archaic* an exclamation of surprise or anger
WORD ORIGIN euphemistic for the Virgin *Mary*
Marryat *n* **Frederick,** known as *Captain Marryat*. 1792–1848, English novelist and naval officer; author of novels of sea life, such as *Mr Midshipman Easy* (1836), and children's stories, such as *The Children of the New Forest* (1847)
Mars *n* **1** the Roman god of war **2** the fourth planet from the sun
Marsalis *n* **Wynton** born 1962, US jazz and classical trumpeter
Marseillaise (mar-say-**yaze**) *n* **the Marseillaise** the French national anthem
WORD ORIGIN French *(chanson) marseillaise* (song) of Marseilles (first sung in Paris by the battalion of Marseilles)
marsh ❶ *n* low poorly drained land that is wet, muddy, and sometimes flooded **marshy** *adj*
WORD ORIGIN Old English *merisc*
Marsh *n* **1** Dame (**Edith**) **Ngaio** 1899–1981, New Zealand crime writer, living in Britain (from 1928). Her many detective novels include *Final Curtain* (1947) and *Last Ditch* (1977) **2 Rodney** (**William**) born 1947, Australian cricketer. He finished his career with a world record of 355 Test match dismissals
marshal ❶ *n* **1** (in some armies and air forces) an officer of the highest rank: *Field Marshall* **2** an officer who organizes or controls ceremonies or public events **3** *US* the chief police or fire officer in some states **4** (formerly in England) an officer of the royal family or court ▹*vb* **-shalling, -shalled** *or US* **-shaling, -shaled 5** to arrange in order: *she marshalled her facts and came to a conclusion* **6** to assemble and organize people or vehicles in readiness for onward movement **7** to guide or lead, esp. in a ceremonious way: *she marshalled them towards the lecture theatre* **marshalcy** *n*
WORD ORIGIN Old French *mareschal*
marshalling yard *n railways* a place where railway wagons are shunted and made up into trains
Marshal of the Royal Air Force *n* the highest rank in the Royal Air Force
marsh gas *n* a gas largely composed of methane formed when plants decay in the absence of air
marshland *n* land consisting of marshes
marshmallow *n* a spongy pink or white sweet
marsh mallow *n* a plant that grows in salt marshes and has pale pink flowers. It was formerly used to make marshmallows
Marsilius of Padua *n* Italian name *Marsiglio dei Mainardini*. ?1290–?1343, Italian political philosopher, best known as the author of the *Defensor pacis* (1324), which upheld the power of the temporal ruler over that of the church
Marston *n* **John** ?1576–1634, English dramatist and satirist. His works include the revenge tragedies *Antonio and Mellida* (1602) and *Antonio's Revenge* (1602) and the satirical comedy *The Malcontent* (1604)
marsupial (mar-**soop**-ee-al) *n* **1** a mammal, such as a kangaroo or an opossum, the female of which carries her babies in a pouch at the front of her body until they reach a mature state ▹*adj* **2** of or like a marsupial
WORD ORIGIN Latin *marsupium* purse
mart *n* a market or trading centre
WORD ORIGIN Middle Dutch: market
Martello tower *n* a round tower used for coastal defence, formerly much used in Europe
WORD ORIGIN after Cape *Mortella* in Corsica
marten *n, pl* **-tens** *or* **-ten 1** any of several agile weasel-like mammals with bushy tails and golden-brown to blackish fur **2** the fur of these animals
WORD ORIGIN Middle Dutch *martren*
Martha *n* **Saint Martha** *new testament* a sister of Mary and Lazarus, who lived at Bethany and ministered to Jesus (Luke 10:38–42). Feast day: July 29 or June 4
martial ❶ *adj* of or characteristic of war, soldiers, or the military life: *martial music*
WORD ORIGIN Latin *martialis* of Mars, god of war
Martial[1] *adj* of or relating to Mars
Martial[2] *n* full name *Marcus Valerius Martialis*. ?40–?104 AD, Latin epigrammatist and poet, born in Spain
martial art *n* any of various philosophies and techniques of self-defence originating in the Far East, such as judo or karate
martial law *n* rule of law maintained by military forces in the absence of civil law
Martian (**marsh**-an) *adj* **1** of the planet Mars ▹*n* **2** an inhabitant of Mars, in science fiction
martin *n* a bird of the swallow family with a square or slightly forked tail
WORD ORIGIN probably after St *Martin*, because the birds were believed to migrate at Martinmas
Martin du Gard *n* **Roger** 1881–1958,

m

THESAURUS

marriage *n* **1, 3 = wedding**, match, nuptials, wedlock, wedding ceremony, matrimony, espousal, nuptial rites
marry[1] *vb* **2 = tie the knot** *(informal)*, wed, take the plunge *(informal)*, walk down the aisle *(informal)*, get hitched *(slang)*, get spliced *(informal)*, become man and wife, plight your troth *(old-fashioned)* **3 = unite**, match, join, link, tie, bond, ally, merge, knit, unify, splice, yoke
marsh *n* **= swamp**, moss *(Scot & Northern English dialect)*, bog, slough, fen, quagmire, morass, muskeg *(Canad)*
marshal *vb* **5, 6 = arrange**, group, order, collect, gather, line up, organize, assemble, deploy, array, dispose, draw up, muster, align **7 = conduct**, take, lead, guide, steer, escort, shepherd, usher
martial *adj* **= military**, soldierly, brave, heroic, belligerent, warlike, bellicose

DICTIONARY

French novelist, noted for his series of novels, *Les Thibault* (1922–40): Nobel prize for literature 1937

Martineau *n* **1 Harriet** 1802–76, English author of books on political economy and of novels and children's stories **2** her brother, **James** 1805–1900, English Unitarian theologian and minister

martinet *n* a person who maintains strict discipline
WORD ORIGIN after General *Martinet*, drillmaster under Louis XIV

martingale *n* a strap from the reins to the girth of a horse, preventing it from carrying its head too high
WORD ORIGIN French

martini *n* **1** *(often cap) trademark* an Italian vermouth **2** a cocktail of gin and vermouth

Martini[1] *n, pl* **-nis 1** *trademark* an Italian vermouth **2** a cocktail of gin and vermouth
WORD ORIGIN C19 (sense 2): perhaps from the name of the inventor

Martini[2] *n* **Simone** ?1284–1344, Sienese painter

Martinmas *n* the feast of St Martin on November 11: a quarter day in Scotland

Martinů *n* **Bohuslav** 1890–1959, Czech composer

Martin V *n* original name *Oddone Colonna*. 1368–1431, pope (1417–31). His election at the Council of Constance brought to an end the Great Schism

martyr *n* **1** a person who chooses to die rather than renounce his or her religious beliefs **2** a person who suffers greatly or dies for a cause or belief **3 a martyr to** suffering constantly from: *a martyr to arthritis* ▷ *vb* **4** to make a martyr of **martyrdom** *n*
WORD ORIGIN Late Greek *martur-* witness

marvel ⊕ *vb* **-velling, -velled** *or US* **-veling, -veled 1** to be filled with surprise or wonder ▷ *n* **2** something that causes wonder
WORD ORIGIN Old French *merveille*

Marvell *n* **Andrew** 1621–78, English poet and satirist. He is noted for his lyrical poems and verse and prose satires attacking the government after the Restoration

marvellous ⊕ *or US* **marvelous** *adj* **1** excellent or splendid: *a marvellous idea* **2** causing great wonder or surprise; extraordinary: *electricity is a marvellous thing* **marvellously** *or US* **marvelously** *adv*

Marxism *n* the economic and political theories of Karl Marx (1818–83), German political philosopher, which argue that class struggle is the basic agency of historical change, and that capitalism will be superseded by communism **Marxist** *n, adj*

marzipan *n* a mixture made from ground almonds, sugar, and egg whites that is put on top of cakes or used to make sweets
WORD ORIGIN Italian *marzapane*

Masaccio *n* original name *Tommaso Guidi*. 1401–28, Florentine painter. He was the first to apply to painting the laws of perspective discovered by Brunelleschi. His chief work is the frescoes in the Brancacci chapel in the church of Sta. Maria del Carmine, Florence

masala *n Indian cookery* a mixture of spices ground into a paste

Masaryk *n* **1 Jan** (jan) 1886–1948, Czech statesman; foreign minister (1941–48). He died in mysterious circumstances after the Communists took control of the government **2** his father, **Tomáš Garrigue** 1850–1937, Czech philosopher and statesman; a founder of Czechoslovakia (1918) and its first president (1918–35)

masc. masculine

Mascagni *n* **Pietro** 1863–1945, Italian composer of operas, including *Cavalleria rusticana* (1890)

mascara *n* a cosmetic for darkening the eyelashes
WORD ORIGIN Spanish: mask

mascarpone (mass-car-po-nee) *n* a soft Italian cream cheese
WORD ORIGIN from Italian dialect *mascherpa* ricotta

mascot *n* a person, animal, or thing considered to bring good luck
WORD ORIGIN French *mascotte*

masculine ⊕ *adj* **1** possessing qualities or characteristics considered typical of or appropriate to a man; manly **2** unwomanly; not feminine **3** *grammar* denoting a gender of nouns that includes some male animate things **4** *prosody* denoting a rhyme between pairs of single final stressed syllables **masculinity** *n*
WORD ORIGIN Latin *masculinus*

Masefield *n* **John** 1878–1967, English poet, novelist, and critic; poet laureate (1930–67)

maser *n* a device for amplifying microwaves, working on the same principle as a laser
WORD ORIGIN *m(icrowave) a(mplification by) s(timulated) e(mission of) r(adiation)*

mash *n* **1** a soft pulpy mass **2** *agriculture* bran, meal, or malt mixed with warm water and used as food for horses, cattle, or poultry **3** *Brit informal* mashed potatoes ▷ *vb* **4** to beat or crush into a mash **mashed** *adj*
WORD ORIGIN Old English *mǣsc-*

Masinissa *or* **Massinissa** *n* ?238–?149 BC, king of Numidia (?210–149), who fought as an ally of Rome against Carthage in the Second Punic War

mask ⊕ *n* **1** any covering for the whole or a part of the face worn for amusement, protection, or disguise **2** behaviour that hides one's true feelings: *his mask of detachment* **3** *surgery* a sterile gauze covering for the nose and mouth worn to minimize the spread of germs **4** a device placed over the nose and mouth to facilitate or prevent inhalation of a gas **5** a moulded likeness of a face or head, such as a death mask **6** the face or head of an animal such as a fox ▷ *vb* **7** to cover with or put on a mask **8** to hide or disguise: *a high brick wall that masked the front of the building* **9** to cover so as to protect **masked** *adj*
WORD ORIGIN Arabic *maskharah* clown

masking tape *n* an adhesive tape used to protect surfaces surrounding an area to be painted

masochism (mass-oh-kiz-zum) *n* **1** *psychiatry* a condition in which pleasure, esp. sexual pleasure, is obtained from feeling pain or from

THESAURUS

marvel *vb* **1 = be amazed**, wonder, gaze, gape, goggle, be awed, be filled with surprise ▷ *n* **2 = wonder**, phenomenon, miracle, portent

marvellous *adj* **1 = excellent**, great *(informal)*, mean *(slang)*, topping *(Brit slang)*, wonderful, brilliant, bad *(slang)*, cracking *(Brit informal)*, amazing, crucial *(slang)*, extraordinary, remarkable, smashing *(informal)*, superb, spectacular, fantastic *(informal)*, magnificent, astonishing, fabulous *(informal)*, divine *(informal)*, glorious, terrific *(informal)*, splendid, sensational *(informal)*, mega *(slang)*, sovereign, awesome *(slang)*, breathtaking, phenomenal, astounding, singular, miraculous, colossal, super *(informal)*, wicked *(informal)*, def *(slang)*, prodigious, wondrous *(archaic, literary)*, brill *(informal)*, stupendous, jaw-dropping, eye-popping, bodacious *(slang, chiefly US)*, boffo *(slang)*, jim-dandy *(slang)*, chillin' *(US slang)*, booshit *(Austral slang)*, exo *(Austral slang)*, sik *(Austral slang)*, rad *(informal)*, phat *(slang)*, schmick *(Austral informal)* OPPOSITE: terrible

masculine *adj* **1, 2 = male**, manly, mannish, manlike, virile, manful

mask *n* **2 = façade**, disguise, show, front, cover, screen, blind, cover-up, veil, cloak, guise, camouflage, veneer, semblance, concealment ▷ *vb* **8 = disguise**, hide, conceal, obscure, cover (up), screen, blanket, veil, cloak, mantle, camouflage, enshroud

being humiliated **2** a tendency to take pleasure from one's own suffering **masochist** *n, adj* **masochistic** *adj*
WORD ORIGIN after Leopold von Sacher *Masoch*, novelist

mason *n* a person skilled in building with stone
WORD ORIGIN Old French *masson*

Mason *n* a Freemason

Masonic *adj* of Freemasons or Freemasonry

masonry *n* **1** stonework or brickwork **2** the craft of a mason

Masonry *n* Freemasonry

masque (mask) *n* a dramatic entertainment of the 16th to 17th centuries, consisting of dancing, dialogue, and song **masquer** *n*
WORD ORIGIN variant of *mask*

masquerade (mask-er-aid) *vb* **-ading, -aded 1** to pretend to be someone or something else ▹*n* **2** an attempt to keep secret the real identity or nature of something: *he was unable to keep up his masquerade as the war's victor* **3** a party at which the guests wear masks and costumes
WORD ORIGIN Spanish *mascara* mask

mass ❶ *n* **1** a large body of something without a definite shape **2** a collection of the component parts of something: *a mass of fibres* **3** a large amount or number, as of people **4** the main part or majority **5** the size of a body; bulk **6** *physics* a physical quantity expressing the amount of matter in a body **7** (in painting or drawing) an area of unified colour, shade, or intensity ▹*adj* **8** done or occurring on a large scale: *mass hysteria* **9** consisting of a mass or large number, esp. of people: *a mass meeting* ▹*vb* **10** to join together into a mass ▸See also **masses** > **massed** *adj*
WORD ORIGIN Latin *massa*

Mass *n* **1** (in the Roman Catholic Church and certain other Christian churches) a service in which bread and wine are consecrated to represent the body and blood of Christ **2** a musical setting of parts of this service
WORD ORIGIN Church Latin *missa*

massacre ❶ (mass-a-ker) *n* the wanton or savage killing of large numbers of people **2** *informal* an overwhelming defeat ▹*vb* **-cring, -cred 3** to kill people indiscriminately in large numbers **4** *informal* to defeat overwhelmingly
WORD ORIGIN Old French

massage ❶ (mass-ahzh) *n* **1** the kneading or rubbing of parts of the body to reduce pain or stiffness or help relaxation ▹*vb* **-saging, -saged 2** to give a massage to **3** to manipulate statistics or evidence to produce a desired result
WORD ORIGIN French *masser* to rub

massage parlour *n* **1** a commercial establishment providing massages **2** *euphemistic* a place where men pay to have sex with prostitutes

massasauga (mass-a-saw-ga) *n* a North American venomous snake with a horny rattle at the end of the tail
WORD ORIGIN after the *Missisauga* River, Ontario, Canada

Massasoit *n* died 1661, Wampanoag Indian chief, who negotiated peace with the Pilgrim Fathers (1621)

Masséna *n* **André**, Prince d'Essling. 1758–1817, French marshal under Napoleon I: victories at Saorgio (1794), Loano (1795), Rivoli (1797), Zürich (1799), and Caldiero (1805): defeated by Wellington in the Peninsular War (1810–11)

Massenet *n* **Jules Émile Frédéric** 1842–1912, French composer of operas, including *Manon* (1884), *Werther* (1892), and *Thais* (1894)

masses *pl n* **1 the masses** ordinary people as a group **2 masses of** *informal chiefly Brit* a great number or quantity of: *masses of food*

masseur (mass-ur) *or fem* **masseuse** (mass-**uhz**) *n* a person who gives massages

massif (mass-seef) *n* a series of connected masses of rock forming a mountain range
WORD ORIGIN French

Massine *n* **Léonide** 1896–1979, US ballet dancer and choreographer, born in Russia

Massinger *n* **Philip** 1583–?1640, English dramatist, noted esp. for his comedy *A New Way to pay Old Debts* (1633)

Massinissa *n* a variant spelling of **Masinissa**

massive ❶ *adj* **1** (of objects) large, bulky, heavy, and usually solid **2** impressive or imposing **3** intensive or considerable: *a massive overdose* **massively** *adv*
WORD ORIGIN French *massif*

mass-market *adj* of, for, or appealing to a large number of people; popular: *mass-market newspapers*

mass media *pl n* the means of communication that reach large numbers of people, such as television, newspapers, and radio

mass noun *n* a noun that refers to an extended substance rather than to each of a set of objects, eg, *water* as opposed to *lake*

mass number *n* the total number of protons and neutrons in the nucleus of an atom

mass-produce *vb* **-producing, -produced** to manufacture standardized goods on a large scale by extensive use of machinery **mass-produced** *adj* **mass-production** *n*

mass spectrometer *n* an instrument for analysing the composition of a sample of material, in which ions, produced from the sample, are separated by electric or magnetic fields according to their ratios of charge to mass

Massys, Matsys, *or* **Metsys** *n* **Quentin** 1466–1530, Flemish painter, based in Antwerp; noted for his portraits and scenes of everyday life

mast[1] *n* **1** *naut* a vertical pole for supporting sails, radar equipment, etc. above the deck of a ship **2** a tall upright pole used as an aerial for radio or television broadcasting: *a television mast* **3 before the mast** *naut* as an apprentice seaman
WORD ORIGIN Old English *mæst*

mass *n* **1 = piece**, block, lump, chunk, hunk, concretion **2 = lot**, collection, load, combination, pile, quantity, bunch, stack, heap, rick, batch, accumulation, stockpile, assemblage, aggregation, conglomeration **5 = size**, matter, weight, extent, dimensions, bulk, magnitude, greatness ▹*adj* **8 = large-scale**, general, popular, widespread, extensive, universal, wholesale, indiscriminate, pandemic ▹*vb* **10 = gather**, assemble, accumulate, collect, rally, mob, muster, swarm, amass, throng, congregate, foregather

massacre *n* **1 = slaughter**, killing, murder, holocaust, carnage, extermination, annihilation, butchery, mass slaughter, blood bath ▹*vb* **3 = slaughter**, kill, murder, butcher, take out *(slang)*, wipe out, slay, blow away *(slang, chiefly US)*, annihilate, exterminate, mow down, cut to pieces

massage *n* **1 = rub-down**, rubbing, manipulation, kneading, reflexology, shiatsu, acupressure, chiropractic treatment, palpation ▹*vb* **2 = rub down**, rub, manipulate, knead, pummel, palpate **3 = manipulate**, alter, distort, doctor, cook *(informal)*, fix *(informal)*, rig, fiddle *(informal)*, tamper with, tinker with, misrepresent, fiddle with, falsify

massive *adj* **1 = huge**, great, big, heavy, imposing, vast, enormous, solid, impressive, substantial, extensive, monster, immense, hefty, titanic, gigantic, monumental, whacking *(informal)*, mammoth, bulky, colossal, whopping *(informal)*, weighty, stellar *(informal)*, hulking, ponderous, gargantuan, elephantine, ginormous *(informal)*, humongous *or* humungous *(US slang)*, supersize **OPPOSITE:** tiny

DICTIONARY

mast² *n* the fruit of forest trees, such as beech or oak, used as food for pigs **WORD ORIGIN** Old English *mæst*
mastaba *n* a mud-brick superstructure above tombs in ancient Egypt **WORD ORIGIN** Arabic: bench
mastectomy (mass-tek-tom-ee) *n, pl* **-mies** surgical removal of a breast **WORD ORIGIN** Greek *mastos* breast + *tomē* a cutting
master ❶ *n* **1** the man who has authority over others, such as the head of a household, the employer of servants, or the owner of slaves or animals **2** a person with exceptional skill at a certain thing: *B.B. King is a master of the blues* **3** a person who has complete control of a situation: *the master of his portfolio* **4** an original copy or tape from which duplicates are made **5** a craftsman fully qualified to practise his trade and to train others **6** a player of a game, esp. chess or bridge, who has won a specified number of tournament games **7** a highly regarded teacher or leader **8** a graduate holding a master's degree **9** the chief officer aboard a merchant ship **10** *chiefly Brit* a male teacher **11** the superior person or side in a contest **12** the heir apparent of a Scottish viscount or baron: *the Master of Ballantrae* ▷ *adj* **13** (of a craftsman) fully qualified to practise and to train others **14** overall or controlling: *master plan* **15** designating a mechanism that controls others: *master switch* **16** main or principal: *master bedroom* ▷ *vb* **17** to become thoroughly proficient in **18** to overcome or defeat **WORD ORIGIN** Latin *magister* teacher
Master *n* a title of address for a boy who is not old enough to be called *Mr*
master aircrew *n* a rank in the Royal Air Force, equal to warrant officer
masterful *adj* **1** showing great skill **2** domineering or authoritarian **masterfully** *adv*
master key *n* a key that opens all the locks of a set; passkey
masterly ❶ *adj* showing great skill; expert
mastermind ❶ *vb* **1** to plan and direct a complex task or project ▷ *n* **2** a person who plans and directs a complex task or project
Master of Arts *n* a degree, usually postgraduate in a nonscientific subject, or a person holding this degree
master of ceremonies *n* a person who presides over a public ceremony, formal dinner, or entertainment, introducing the events and performers
Master of Science *n* a degree, usually postgraduate in a scientific subject, or a person holding this degree
Master of the Rolls *n* (in England) the senior civil judge in the country and the head of the Public Record Office
masterpiece ❶ *or* **masterwork** *n* **1** an outstanding work or performance **2** the most outstanding piece of work of an artist or craftsman
Masters *n* **Edgar Lee** 1868–1950, US poet; best known for *Spoon River Anthology* (1915)
masterstroke *n* an outstanding piece of strategy, skill, or talent
mastery ❶ *n, pl* **-teries 1** outstanding skill or expertise **2** complete power or control: *he had complete mastery over the country*
masthead *n* **1** *naut* the highest part of a mast **2** the name of a newspaper or periodical printed at the top of the front page
mastic *n* **1** an aromatic resin obtained from a Mediterranean tree and used to make varnishes and lacquers **2** any of several putty-like substances used as a filler, adhesive, or seal **WORD ORIGIN** Greek *mastikhē*
masticate *vb* **-cating, -cated** to chew food **mastication** *n* **WORD ORIGIN** Greek *mastikhan* to grind the teeth
mastiff *n* a large powerful short-haired dog, usually fawn or brown with dark streaks **WORD ORIGIN** Latin *mansuetus* tame
mastitis *n* inflammation of the breast
mastodon *n* an extinct elephant-like mammal **WORD ORIGIN** New Latin, literally: breast-tooth, referring to the nipple-shaped projections on the teeth
mastoid *adj* **1** shaped like a nipple or breast ▷ *n* **2** a nipple-like projection of bone behind the ear **3** *informal* mastoiditis **WORD ORIGIN** Greek *mastos* breast
mastoiditis *n* inflammation of the mastoid
Mastroianni *n* **Marcello** 1924–96, Italian film actor; his films include *Le notti bianche* (1957), *La dolce vita* (1960), *Ginger and Fred* (1985), and *Prêt à Porter* (1995)
masturbate *vb* **-bating, -bated** to fondle one's own genitals, or those of someone else, to cause sexual pleasure **masturbation** *n* **WORD ORIGIN** Latin *masturbari*
mat¹ *n* **1** a thick flat piece of fabric used as a floor covering, a place to wipe one's shoes, etc. **2** a small pad of material used to protect a surface from heat or scratches from an object placed upon it **3** a large piece of thick padded material put on the floor as a surface for wrestling, gymnastics, etc. ▷ *vb* **matting, matted 4** to tangle or become tangled into a dense mass **WORD ORIGIN** Old English *matte*
mat² *adj* ▸ same as **matt** **WORD ORIGIN** French, literally: dead
matador *n* the bullfighter armed

THESAURUS

master *n* **1 = lord**, ruler, commander, chief, director, manager, boss *(informal)*, head, owner, captain, governor, employer, principal, skipper *(informal)*, controller, superintendent, overlord, overseer, baas *(S African)* **OPPOSITE:** servant **2 = expert**, maestro, pro *(informal)*, ace *(informal)*, genius, wizard, adept, virtuoso, grandmaster, doyen, past master, dab hand *(Brit informal)*, wonk *(informal)*, maven *(US)*, fundi *(S African)* **OPPOSITE:** amateur **10 = teacher**, tutor, instructor, schoolmaster, pedagogue, preceptor **OPPOSITE:** student ▷ *adj* **16 = main**, principal, chief, prime, grand, great, foremost, predominant **OPPOSITE:** lesser ▷ *vb* **17 = learn**, understand, pick up, acquire, grasp, get the hang of *(informal)*, become proficient in, know inside out, know backwards **18 = overcome**, defeat, suppress, conquer, check, curb, tame, lick *(informal)*, subdue, overpower, quash, quell, triumph over, bridle, vanquish, subjugate **OPPOSITE:** give in to
masterly *adj* **= skilful**, skilled, expert, finished, fine, excellent, crack *(informal)*, supreme, clever, superior, world-class, exquisite, adept, consummate, first-rate, superlative, masterful, adroit, dexterous
mastermind *vb* **1 = plan**, manage, direct, organize, devise, conceive, be the brains behind *(informal)* ▷ *n* **2 = organizer**, director, manager, authority, engineer, brain(s) *(informal)*, architect, genius, planner, intellect, virtuoso, rocket scientist *(informal, chiefly US)*, brainbox
masterpiece *n* **1, 2 = classic**, tour de force *(French)*, pièce de résistance *(French)*, magnum opus, master work, jewel, chef-d'oeuvre *(French)*
mastery *n* **1 = understanding**, knowledge, comprehension, ability, skill, know-how, command, grip, grasp, expertise, prowess, familiarity, attainment, finesse, proficiency, virtuosity, dexterity, cleverness, deftness, acquirement **2 = control**, authority, command, rule, victory, triumph, sway, domination, superiority, conquest, supremacy, dominion, upper hand, ascendancy, pre-eminence, mana

DICTIONARY

with a sword, who attempts to kill the bull
WORD ORIGIN Spanish, from *matar* to kill

matai *n* a New Zealand tree, the wood of which is used for timber for building
WORD ORIGIN Māori

match¹ ❶ *n* **1** a formal game or sports event in which people or teams compete **2** a person or thing able to provide competition for another: *he has met his match* **3** a person or thing that resembles, harmonizes with, or is equivalent to another: *the colours aren't a perfect match, but they're close enough; white wine is not a good match for steak* **4** a person or thing that is an exact copy or equal of another **5** a partnership between a man and a woman, as in marriage **6** a person regarded as a possible partner in marriage: *for any number of men she would have been a good match* ▹ *vb* **7** to fit parts together **8** to resemble, harmonize with, or equal one another or something else: *our bedroom curtains match the bedspread; she walked at a speed that he could barely match* **9** to find a match for **10 match with** *or* **against a** to compare in order to determine which is the superior **b** to arrange a competition between **matching** *adj*
WORD ORIGIN Old English *gemæcca* spouse

match² *n* **1** a thin strip of wood or cardboard tipped with a chemical that ignites when scraped against a rough or specially treated surface **2** a fuse used to fire cannons' explosives
WORD ORIGIN Old French *meiche*

matchbox *n* a small box for holding matches

match-fit *adj sport* in good physical condition for competing in a match

matchless *adj* unequalled

matchmaker *n* a person who introduces people in the hope that they will form a couple
matchmaking *n, adj*

match play *n golf* scoring according to the number of holes won and lost

match point *n sport* the final point needed to win a match

matchstick *n* **1** the wooden part of a match ▹ *adj* **2** (esp. of drawn figures) thin and straight: *little matchstick men*

matchwood *n* **1** wood suitable for making matches **2** splinters

mate¹ ❶ *n* **1 a** *informal chiefly Brit, Austral, & NZ* a friend: often used as a term of address between males: *I spotted my mate Jimmy McCrae at the other end of the bar; that's all right, mate* **b** an associate or colleague: *a classmate; the governor's running mate* **2** the sexual partner of an animal **3** a marriage partner **4** *naut* any officer below the master on a commercial ship **5** (in some trades) an assistant: *a plumber's mate* **6** one of a pair of matching items ▹ *vb* **mating, mated 7** to pair (a male and female animal) or (of animals) to pair for breeding **8** to marry **9** to join as a pair
WORD ORIGIN Low German

mate² *n, vb* **mating, mated** *chess* ▸ same as **checkmate**

mater *n Brit, humorous* mother: often used facetiously
WORD ORIGIN Latin

material ❶ *n* **1** the substance of which a thing is made **2** cloth **3** ideas or notes that a finished work may be based on: *the material of the story resembles an incident in his own life* ▹ *adj* **4** concerned with or composed of physical matter or substance; not relating to spiritual or abstract things: *the material universe* **5** of or affecting economic or physical wellbeing: *material prosperity* **6** relevant or pertinent: *material evidence* ▸ See also **materials**
WORD ORIGIN Latin *materia* matter

materialism *n* **1** excessive interest in and desire for money or possessions **2** the belief that only the material world exists **materialist** *n, adj* **materialistic** *adj*

materialize *or* **-ise** *vb* **-izing, -ized** *or* **-ising, -ised 1** *not standard* to become fact; actually happen: *the promised pay rise never materialized* **2** to appear after being invisible: *trees materialized out of the gloom* **3** to take shape: *after hours of talks, a plan began to materialize*
materialization *or* **-isation** *n*

materially ❶ *adv* to a significant extent: *we were not materially affected*

materials *pl n* the equipment necessary for a particular activity: *building materials*

materiel (mat-ear-ee-ell) *n* the materials and equipment of an organization, esp. of a military force
WORD ORIGIN French

maternal ❶ *adj* **1** of or characteristic of a mother **2** related through the mother's side of the family: *his maternal uncle* **maternally** *adv*
WORD ORIGIN Latin *mater* mother

maternity ❶ *n* **1** motherhood **2** motherliness ▹ *adj* **3** relating to women during pregnancy or childbirth: *maternity leave*

mate's rates *pl n NZ informal* reduced charges offered to a friend or colleague

matey *adj Brit informal* friendly or intimate

math *n US & Canad informal* ▸ short for **mathematics**

mathematical *adj* **1** using, used in, or relating to mathematics **2** having the precision of mathematics
mathematically *adv*

mathematician *n* an expert or specialist in mathematics

mathematics *n* **1** a group of related sciences, including algebra, geometry, and calculus, which use a

m

THESAURUS

(NZ), whip hand

match¹ *n* **1 = game**, test, competition, trial, tie, contest, fixture, bout, head-to-head **2 = equal**, rival, equivalent, peer, competitor, counterpart **5 = marriage**, union, couple, pair, pairing, item *(informal)*, alliance, combination, partnership, duet, affiliation ▹ *vb* **8a = correspond with**, suit, go with, complement, fit with, accompany, team with, blend with, tone with, harmonize with, coordinate with **8b = correspond**, agree, accord, square, coincide, tally, conform, match up, be compatible, harmonize, be consonant **8c = rival**, equal, compete with, compare with, emulate, contend with, measure up to

mate¹ *n* **1a** *(informal)* **= friend**, pal *(informal)*, companion, buddy *(informal)*, china *(Brit slang)*, cock *(Brit informal)*, comrade, chum *(informal)*, mucker *(Brit informal)*, crony, main man *(slang, chiefly US)*, homeboy *(slang, chiefly US)*, cobber *(Austral & NZ old-fashioned, informal)*, E hoa *(NZ)* **1b = colleague**, associate, companion, co-worker, fellow-worker, compeer **3 = partner**, lover, companion, spouse, consort, significant other *(US informal)*, better half *(humorous)*, helpmeet, husband *or* wife **5 = assistant**, subordinate, apprentice, helper, accomplice, sidekick *(informal)* ▹ *vb* **7 = pair**, couple, breed, copulate

material *n* **1 = substance**, body, matter, stuff, elements, constituents **2 = cloth**, stuff, fabric, textile **3 = information**, work, details, facts, notes, evidence, particulars, data, info *(informal)*, subject matter, documentation ▹ *adj* **4 = physical**, worldly, solid, substantial, concrete, fleshly, bodily, tangible, palpable, corporeal, nonspiritual **6 = relevant**, important, significant, essential, vital, key, serious, grave, meaningful, applicable, indispensable, momentous, weighty, pertinent, consequential, apposite, apropos, germane

materially *adv* **= significantly**, much, greatly, considerably, essentially, seriously, gravely, substantially
OPPOSITE: insignificantly

maternal *adj* **1 = motherly**, protective, nurturing, maternalistic

maternity *n* **1, 2 = motherhood**, parenthood, motherliness

matted *adj* **= tangled**, knotted,

DICTIONARY

specialized notation to study number, quantity, shape, and space **2** numerical calculations involved in the solution of a problem
WORD ORIGIN Greek *mathēma* a science

maths *n Austral & Brit informal* ▸ short for **mathematics**

matinee (mat-in-nay) *n* an afternoon performance of a play or film
WORD ORIGIN French

matins *n* an early morning service in various Christian Churches
WORD ORIGIN Latin *matutinus* of the morning

matriarch (mate-ree-ark) *n* the female head of a tribe or family **matriarchal** *adj*
WORD ORIGIN Latin *mater* mother + Greek *arkhein* to rule

matriarchy *n, pl* **-chies** a form of social organization in which a female is head of the family or society, and descent and kinship are traced through the female line

matrices (may-triss-seez) *n* ▸ a plural of **matrix**

matricide *n* **1** the act of killing one's mother **2** a person who kills his or her mother **matricidal** *adj*
WORD ORIGIN Latin *mater* mother + *caedere* to kill

matriculate *vb* **-lating, -lated** to enrol or be enrolled in a college or university **matriculation** *n*
WORD ORIGIN Medieval Latin *matriculare* to register

matrilineal (mat-rill-in-ee-al) *adj* relating to descent through the female line

matrimony *n* the state of being married **matrimonial** *adj*
WORD ORIGIN Latin *matrimonium* wedlock

matrix (may-trix) *n, pl* **-trices** *or* **matrixes 1** the context or framework in which something is formed or develops: *a highly complex matrix of overlapping interests* **2** the rock in which fossils or pebbles are embedded **3** a mould, esp. one used in printing **4** *maths* a rectangular array of elements set out in rows and columns
WORD ORIGIN Latin: womb

matron *n* **1** a staid or dignified married woman **2** a woman in charge of the domestic or medical arrangements in an institution **3** *Brit* (formerly) the administrative head of the nursing staff in a hospital **matronly** *adj*
WORD ORIGIN Latin *matrona*

matron of honour *n, pl* **matrons of honour** a married woman attending a bride

Matsuo Basho *n* See **Basho**

Matsys *n* a variant spelling of (Quentin) **Massys**

matt *or* **matte** *adj* having a dull surface rather than a shiny one

matted ❶ *adj* tangled into a thick mass

matter ❶ *n* **1** the substance of which something, esp. a physical object, is made; material **2** substance that occupies space and has mass, as distinguished from substance that is mental or spiritual **3** substance of a specified type: *vegetable matter* **4** an event, situation, or subject: *a matter of taste; the break-in is a matter for the police* **5** a quantity or amount: *a matter of a few pounds* **6** the content of written or verbal material as distinct from its style or form **7** written material in general: *advertising matter* **8** a secretion or discharge, such as pus **9 for that matter** as regards that **10 no matter** regardless of; irrespective of: *you have to leave, no matter what she thinks* **11 the matter** wrong; the trouble: *there's nothing the matter* ▹ *vb* **12** to be of importance ▹ *interj* **no matter 13** it is unimportant
WORD ORIGIN Latin *materia* cause, substance

matter of fact ❶ *n* **1 as a matter of fact** actually; in fact ▹ *adj* **matter-of-fact 2** unimaginative or emotionless: *he conducted the executions in a completely matter-of-fact manner*

Matthew Paris *n* See **Paris** (sense 2)

Matthias *n* **1** 1557–1619, Holy Roman Emperor (1612–19); king of Hungary (1608–18) and Bohemia (1611–17) **2 Saint Matthias** *new testament* the disciple chosen by lot to replace Judas as one of the 12 apostles (Acts 1:15–26). Feast day: May 14 or Aug 9

Matthias I Corvinus *n* ?1440–90, king of Hungary (1458–90): built up the most powerful kingdom in Central Europe. A patron of Renaissance art, he founded the Corvina library, one of the finest in Europe. Hungarian name: **Mátyás Hollós**

matting *n* a coarsely woven fabric used as a floor covering

mattock *n* a type of large pick that has one flat, horizontal end to its blade, used for loosening soil
WORD ORIGIN Old English *mattuc*

mattress *n* a large flat cushion with a strong cover, filled with cotton, foam rubber, etc. and often including coiled springs, used as a bed
WORD ORIGIN Arabic *almatrah* place where something is thrown

maturation *n* the process of becoming mature

mature ❶ *adj* **1** fully developed physically or mentally; grown-up **2** (of plans or theories) fully considered and thought-out **3** sensible and balanced in personality and emotional behaviour **4** due or payable: *a mature insurance policy* **5** (of fruit, wine, or cheese) ripe or fully aged ▹ *vb* **-turing, -tured 6** to make or become mature **7** (of bills or bonds) to become due for payment or repayment **maturity** *n*
WORD ORIGIN Latin *maturus* early, developed

matzo *n, pl* **matzos** a large very thin biscuit of unleavened bread, traditionally eaten by Jews during Passover
WORD ORIGIN Hebrew *matsāh*

maudlin *adj* foolishly or tearfully sentimental, esp. as a result of drinking
WORD ORIGIN Middle English *Maudelen* Mary Magdalene, often shown weeping

maul ❶ *vb* **1** to tear with the claws: *she was badly mauled by a lion* **2** to criticize a play, performance, etc. severely: *the film was mauled by the critics* **3** to handle roughly or clumsily ▹ *n* **4** *rugby* a loose scrum
WORD ORIGIN Latin *malleus* hammer

maunder *vb* to move, talk, or act aimlessly or idly
WORD ORIGIN origin unknown

Maundy Thursday *n Christianity* the Thursday before Easter observed as a commemoration of the Last Supper

THESAURUS

unkempt, knotty, tousled, ratty, uncombed

matter *n* **1 = substance**, material, body, stuff **4 = situation**, thing, issue, concern, business, question, event, subject, affair, incident, proceeding, episode, topic, transaction, occurrence ▹ *vb* **12 = be important**, make a difference, count, be relevant, make any difference, mean anything, have influence, carry weight, cut any ice *(informal)*, be of consequence, be of account

matter-of-fact *adj* **2 = unsentimental**, flat, dry, plain, dull, sober, down-to-earth, mundane, lifeless, prosaic, deadpan, unimaginative, unvarnished, emotionless, unembellished

mature *adj* **1 = grown-up**, adult, grown, of age, full-blown, fully fledged, fully-developed, full-grown **OPPOSITE:** immature **5 = matured**, seasoned, ripe, mellow, ripened ▹ *vb* **6 = develop**, grow up, bloom, blossom, come of age, become adult, age, reach adulthood, maturate

maul *vb* **1 = mangle**, claw, lacerate, tear, mangulate *(Austral slang)* **3 = ill-treat**, beat, abuse, batter, thrash, beat up *(informal)*, molest, work over *(slang)*, pummel, manhandle, rough up, handle roughly, knock about *or* around, beat *or* knock seven bells out of *(informal)*

DICTIONARY

WORD ORIGIN Latin *mandatum* commandment

Maupertuis *n* **Pierre Louis Moreau de** 1698–1759, French mathematician, who originated the principle of least action (or Maupertuis principle)

Mauriac *n* **François** 1885–1970, French novelist, noted esp. for his psychological studies of the conflict between religious belief and human desire. His works include *Le désert de l'amour* (1925), *Thérèse Desqueyroux* (1927), and *Le nœud de vipères* (1932): Nobel prize for literature 1952

Maurice *n* **1** 1521–53, duke of Saxony (1541–53) and elector of Saxony (1547–53). He was instrumental in gaining recognition of Protestantism in Germany **2** known as *Maurice of Nassau*. 1567–1625, prince of Orange and count of Nassau; the son of William the Silent, after whose death he led the United Provinces of the Netherlands in their struggle for independence from Spain (achieved by 1609) **3 Frederick Denison** 1805–72, English Anglican theologian and pioneer of Christian socialism

Maurois *n* **André**, pen name of *Émile Herzog*. 1885–1967, French writer, best known for his biographies, such as those of Shelley, Byron, and Proust

Maurras *n* **Charles** 1868–1952, French writer and political theorist, who founded (1899) the extreme right-wing group L'Action Français: sentenced (1945) to life imprisonment for supporting Pétain during World War II

Maury *n* **Matthew Fontaine** 1806–73, US pioneer hydrographer and oceanographer

mausoleum (maw-so-lee-um) *n* a large stately tomb
WORD ORIGIN Greek *mausōleion* the tomb of king *Mausolus*

mauve *adj* light purple
WORD ORIGIN Latin *malva* mallow

maverick ❶ *n* **1** a person of independent or unorthodox views **2** (in the US and Canada) an unbranded stray calf ▷ *adj* **3** (of a person or his or her views) independent and unorthodox
WORD ORIGIN after Samuel A. *Maverick*, Texas rancher

maw *n* the mouth, throat, or stomach of an animal
WORD ORIGIN Old English *maga*

mawkish *adj* foolishly or embarrassingly sentimental **mawkishness** *n*
WORD ORIGIN obsolete *mawk* maggot

Mawson *n* Sir **Douglas** 1882–1958, Australian Antarctic explorer, born in England

max *n informal* **1** the most significant or greatest thing **2 to the max** to the ultimate extent

max. maximum

maxi *adj* **1** (of a garment) very long **2** large or considerable
WORD ORIGIN from *maximum*

maxilla *n, pl* **-lae 1** the upper jawbone of a vertebrate **2** any part of the mouth in insects and other arthropods **maxillary** *adj*
WORD ORIGIN Latin: jaw

maxim *n* a brief expression of a general truth, principle, or rule of conduct
WORD ORIGIN Latin *maxima*, in the phrase *maxima propositio* basic axiom

Maxim *n* Sir **Hiram Stevens** 1840–1916, British inventor of the first automatic machine gun (1884), born in the US

maximal *adj* of or being a maximum; the greatest possible

Maximilian I *n* 1459–1519, king of Germany (1486–1519) and Holy Roman Emperor (1493–1519)

maximize *or* **-ise** *vb* **-izing, -ized** *or* **-ising, -ised** to make as high or great as possible; increase to a maximum **maximization** *or* **-isation** *n*

maximum ❶ *n, pl* **-mums** *or* **-ma 1** the greatest possible amount or degree: *he gave the police the maximum of cooperation* **2** the greatest amount recorded, allowed, or reached: *keep to a maximum of two drinks a day* ▷ *adj* **3** of, being, or showing a maximum or maximums: *maximum speed*
WORD ORIGIN Latin: greatest

maxwell *n* the cgs unit of magnetic flux
WORD ORIGIN after J. C. *Maxwell*, physicist

may[1] *vb, past* **might 1** used as an auxiliary to indicate that permission is requested by or granted to someone: *she may leave* **2** used as an auxiliary to indicate the possibility that something could happen: *problems which may well have tragic consequences* **3** used as an auxiliary to indicate ability or capacity, esp. in questions: *may I help you?* **4** used as an auxiliary to indicate a strong wish: *long may she reign*
WORD ORIGIN Old English *mæg*, from *magan* to be able

may[2] *or* **may tree** *n Brit* ▸ same as **hawthorn**
WORD ORIGIN from *May*

May *n* the fifth month of the year
WORD ORIGIN probably from *Maia*, Roman goddess

May[1] *n* the fifth month of the year, consisting of 31 days
WORD ORIGIN from Old French, from Latin *Maius*, probably from *Maia*, Roman goddess, identified with the Greek goddess MAIA

May[2] *n* **Robert McCredie Baron** born 1936, Australian biologist and ecologist

Maya *n* **1** *pl* **-ya** *or* **-yas** a member of an indigenous people of Central America, who once had an advanced civilization **2** the language of this people **Mayan** *n, adj*

Mayakovski *or* **Mayakovsky** *n* **Vladimir Vladimirovich** 1893–1930, Russian Futurist poet and dramatist. His poems include *150 000 000* (1921) and *At the Top of my Voice* (1930); his plays include *Vladimir Mayakovsky—a Tragedy* (1913) and *The Bedbug* (1929)

maybe ❶ *adv* perhaps

Mayday *n* the international radio distress signal
WORD ORIGIN phonetic spelling of French *m'aidez* help me

May Day *n* the first day of May, traditionally a celebration of the coming of spring: in some countries now a holiday in honour of workers

Mayer *n* **1 Julius Robert von** 1814–78, German physicist whose research in thermodynamics (1842) contributed to the discovery of the law of conservation of energy **2 Louis B(urt)** 1885–1957, US film producer, born in Russia; founder and first head (1924–48) of the Metro-Goldwyn-Mayer (MGM) film company

mayfly *n, pl* **-flies** a short-lived insect with large transparent wings

mayhem ❶ *n* **1** any violent destruction or confusion: *a driver caused motorway mayhem* **2** *law* the maiming of a person
WORD ORIGIN Anglo-French *mahem* injury

Mayhew *n* **Henry** 1812–87, British social commentator, journalist, and writer; a founder of *Punch* (1841): best known for *London Labour and the London Poor* (1851–62)

mayn't may not

Mayo[1] *n* a county of NW Republic of Ireland, in NW Connacht province, on the Atlantic: has many offshore islands and several large lakes. County town: Castlebar. Pop: 117 446

m

THESAURUS

maverick *n* **1 = rebel,** radical, dissenter, individualist, protester, eccentric, heretic, nonconformist, iconoclast, dissentient **OPPOSITE:** traditionalist ▷ *adj* **3 = rebel,** radical, dissenting, individualistic, eccentric, heretical, iconoclastic, nonconformist

maximum *n* **2 = top,** most, peak, ceiling, crest, utmost, upper limit, uttermost **OPPOSITE:** minimum ▷ *adj* **3 = greatest,** highest, supreme, paramount, utmost, most, maximal, topmost **OPPOSITE:** minimal

maybe *adv* **= perhaps,** possibly, it could be, conceivably, perchance (*archaic*), mayhap (*archaic*), peradventure (*archaic*)

mayhem *n* **1 = chaos,** trouble, violence, disorder, destruction, confusion, havoc, fracas, commotion

DICTIONARY

(2002). Area: 5397 sq km (2084 sq miles)

Mayo² *n* a family of US medical practitioners. They pioneered group practice and established (1903) the **Mayo Clinic** in Rochester, Minnesota. Foremost among them were **William Worrall Mayo** (1819–1911), his sons **William James Mayo** (1861–1939) and **Charles Horace Mayo** (1865–1939), and Charles's son, **Charles William Mayo** (1898–1968)

mayonnaise *n* a thick creamy sauce made from egg yolks, oil, and vinegar
WORD ORIGIN French

mayor *n* the civic head of a municipal council in many countries **mayoral** *adj*
WORD ORIGIN Latin *maior* greater

mayoralty *n, pl* **-ties** the office or term of office of a mayor

mayoress *n* **1** *chiefly Brit* the wife of a mayor **2** a female mayor

maypole *n* a tall pole around which people dance during May-Day celebrations

May queen *n* a girl chosen to preside over May-Day celebrations

maze ⊙ *n* **1** a complex network of paths or passages designed to puzzle people who try and find their way through or out of it **2** a puzzle in which the player must trace a path through a complex network of lines without touching or crossing any of them **3** any confusing network or system: *a maze of regulations*
WORD ORIGIN from *amaze*

mazurka *n* **1** a lively Polish dance in triple time **2** music for this dance
WORD ORIGIN Polish

Mazzini *n* **Giuseppe** 1805–72, Italian nationalist. In 1831, in exile, he established the Young Italy association in Marseille, which sought to unite Italy as a republic. In 1849 he was one of the triumvirate that ruled the short-lived Roman republic

mb millibar

Mb *computers* megabyte

MB **1** Bachelor of Medicine **2** Manitoba

MBE (in Britain) Member of the Order of the British Empire

MC **1** Master of Ceremonies **2** (in the US) Member of Congress **3** (in Britain) Military Cross

McBride *n* **Willie John** born 1940, Irish Rugby Union footballer. A forward, he played for Ireland (1962–75) and the British Lions (1962–74)

MCC (in Britain) Marylebone Cricket Club

McCahon *n* **Colin** 1919–87, influential New Zealand painter; noted esp. for landscapes and bold abstract paintings, many featuring lettering and Christian imagery

McCall *n* **Davina (Lucy Pascale)**, born 1967, English television presenter, especially of *Big Brother* (from 2000)

McConnell *n* **Jack** born 1960, Scottish Labour politician; first minister of the Scottish Parliament (2001–07)

McCormack *n* **John** 1884–1945, Irish tenor: became US citizen 1919

McCormick *n* **Cyrus Hall** 1809–84, US inventor of the reaping machine (1831)

McCoy¹ *n slang* the genuine person or thing (esp in the phrase **the real McCoy**)
WORD ORIGIN c20: perhaps after Kid *McCoy*, professional name of Norman Selby (1873–1940), American boxer, who was called "the real McCoy" to distinguish him from another boxer of that name

McCoy² *n* **Tony,** full name *Anthony Peter McCoy*. born 1974, Northern Irish jockey; winner of seven consecutive riders' titles in 2001–02

McCullers *n* **Carson** 1917–67, US writer, whose novels include *The Heart is a Lonely Hunter* (1940)

McDonald *n* Sir **Trevor** born 1939, British television journalist, born in Trinidad; presenter of ITV's *News at Ten* (1990–99)

McEwan *n* **Ian** (**Russell**) born 1948, British novelist and short-story writer. His books include *First Love, Last Rites* (1975), *The Child in Time* (1987), *The Innocent* (1990), *Amsterdam* (1998), *Atonement* (2001), and *Saturday* (2005)

McGonagall *n* **William** 1830–?1902, Scottish writer of doggerel, noted for its bathos, repetitive rhymes, poor scansion, and ludicrous effect

McGrath *n* **Glenn** (**Donald**) born 1970, Australian cricketer; played for Australia from 1993

McGregor *n* **Ewan** born 1971, Scottish actor; his films include *Shallow Grave* (1994), *Trainspotting* (1996), *The Phantom Menace* (1999), *Moulin Rouge* (2001), *Big Fish* (2004), and *Revenge of the Sith* (2005)

McGwire *n* **Mark** (**David**) born 1963, US baseball player

MCh Master of Surgery
WORD ORIGIN Latin *Magister Chirurgiae*

McIndoe *n* Sir **Archibald Hector** 1900–60, New Zealand plastic surgeon; noted for his pioneering work with wounded World War II airmen

McKean *n* **Tom** born 1963, Scottish athlete: European 800 metres gold medallist (1990)

McKellen *n* Sir **Ian** (**Murray**) born 1939, British actor, noted esp. for his Shakespearean roles; films include *The Lord of the Rings* trilogy (2001–03)

McKenna *n* **Siobhán** 1923–86, Irish actress, whose notable roles included Pegeen Mike in Synge's *The Playboy of the Western World* and Shaw's Saint Joan

McKinnon *n* **Don**(**ald**) (**Charles**) born 1939, New Zealand politician; secretary-general of the Commonwealth (2000–08); deputy prime minister of New Zealand (1990–96)

McMillan *n* **Edwin M**(**attison**) 1907–91, US physicist; Nobel prize for chemistry 1951 (with Glenn Seaborg) for the discovery of transuranic elements

McPartlin *n* **Antony** born 1975, British television presenter, who appears with Declan Donnelly as Ant and Dec

McPherson *n* **Conor** born 1972, Irish playwright and theatre director; his plays include *The Weir* (1997) and *Port Authority* (2001)

Md *chem* mendelevium

MD **1** Doctor of Medicine
WORD ORIGIN Latin *Medicinae Doctor*
2 Managing Director **3** Maryland

MDF medium density fibreboard: a wood-substitute material used in interior decoration

MDMA methylenedioxy-methamphetamine: the chemical name for the drug ecstasy

MDT (in the US and Canada) Mountain Daylight Time

me¹ *pron (objective)* **1** refers to the speaker or writer: *that hurts me* ▸ *n* **2** *informal* the personality of the speaker or writer or something that expresses it: *the real me*
WORD ORIGIN Old English *mē*

me² *or* **mi** *n music* (in tonic sol-fa) the third note of any ascending major scale

ME **1** Maine **2** Middle English **3** ▸ myalgic encephalomyelitis: see **chronic fatigue syndrome**

mea culpa (may-ah cool-pah) an acknowledgment of guilt
WORD ORIGIN Latin, literally: my fault

mead¹ *n* a wine-like alcoholic drink made from honey, often with spices added
WORD ORIGIN Old English *meodu*

mead² *n archaic or poetic* a meadow
WORD ORIGIN Old English *mǣd*

Mead¹ *n* **Lake Mead** a reservoir in NW Arizona and SE Nevada, formed by

THESAURUS

maze *n* **3 = web**, puzzle, confusion, tangle, snarl, mesh, labyrinth, imbroglio, convolutions, complex network

meadow *n* **1, 2 = field**, pasture, grassland, ley, lea *(poetic)*

mean¹ *vb* **1 = imply**, suggest, intend, indicate, refer to, intimate, get at *(informal)*, hint at, have in mind, drive

DICTIONARY

the Hoover Dam across the Colorado River: one of the largest man-made lakes in the world. Area: 588 sq km (227 sq miles)

Mead[2] *n* **Margaret** 1901–78, US anthropologist. Her works include *Coming of Age in Samoa* (1928) and *Male and Female* (1949)

Meade *n* **George Gordon** 1815–72, Union general in the American Civil War. He commanded the Army of the Potomac, defeating the Confederates at Gettysburg (1863)

meadow *n* **1** a grassy field used for hay or for grazing animals **2** a low-lying piece of grassland, often near a river
WORD ORIGIN Old English *mædwe*

meadowsweet *n* a plant with dense heads of small fragrant cream-coloured flowers

Meads *n* **Colin** born 1935, New Zealand Rugby Union footballer. A forward, he played for the All Blacks (1957–71)

meagre *or US* **meager** *adj* **1** not enough in amount or extent: *meagre wages* **2** thin or emaciated
WORD ORIGIN Old French *maigre*

meal[1] *n* **1** any of the regular occasions, such as breakfast or dinner, when food is served and eaten **2** the food served and eaten **3 make a meal of** *informal* to perform a task with unnecessarily great effort
WORD ORIGIN Old English *mǣl* measure, set time, meal

meal[2] *n* **1** the edible part of a grain or bean pulse (excluding wheat) ground to a coarse powder **2** *Scot* oatmeal **3** *chiefly US* maize flour **mealy** *adj*
WORD ORIGIN Old English *melu*

mealie *or* **mielie** *n (often pl) S African* ▸ same as **maize**
WORD ORIGIN Afrikaans, from Latin *milium* millet

meals-on-wheels *n* a service taking hot meals to the elderly or infirm in their own homes

meal ticket *n slang* a person or situation providing a source of livelihood or income
WORD ORIGIN from original US sense of ticket entitling holder to a meal

mealy-mouthed *adj* unwilling or afraid to speak plainly

mean[1] *vb* **meaning, meant 1** to intend to convey or express: *what do you mean by that?* **2** to denote, represent, or signify: *a red light means 'stop!'; 'gravid' is a technical term meaning 'pregnant'* **3** to intend: *I meant to phone you earlier, but didn't have time* **4** to say or do in all seriousness: *the boss means what she says* **5** to have the importance specified: *music means everything to him* **6** to destine or design for a certain person or purpose: *those sweets weren't meant for you* **7** to produce, cause, or result in: *major road works will mean long traffic delays* **8** to foretell: *those black clouds mean rain* **9 mean well** to have good intentions
WORD ORIGIN Old English *mǣnan*

mean[2] *adj* **1** not willing to give or use much of something, esp. money: *she was noticeably mean; don't be mean with the butter* **2** unkind or spiteful: *a mean trick* **3** *informal* ashamed: *she felt mean about not letting the children stay out late* **4** *informal chiefly US, Canad & Austral* bad-tempered or vicious **5** shabby and poor: *a mean little room* **6** *slang* excellent or skilful: *he plays a mean trumpet* **7 no mean a** of high quality: *no mean player* **b** difficult: *no mean feat* **meanly** *adv* **meanness** *n*
WORD ORIGIN Old English *gemǣne* common

mean[3] *n* **1** the middle point, state, or course between limits or extremes **2** *maths* **a** the mid-point between the highest and lowest number in a set **b** the average ▹ *adj* **3** intermediate in size or quantity **4** occurring halfway between extremes or limits; average
WORD ORIGIN Late Latin *medianus* median

meander (mee-and-er) *vb* **1** (of a river, road, etc.) to follow a winding course **2** to wander without definite aim or direction ▹ *n* **3** a curve or bend, as in a river **4** a winding course or movement
WORD ORIGIN Greek *Maiandros* the River Maeander

mean deviation *n statistics* the difference between an observed value of a variable and its mean

meanie *or* **meany** *n informal* **1** *chiefly Brit* a miserly person **2** *chiefly US* a nasty ill-tempered person

meaning *n* **1** the sense or significance of a word, sentence, or symbol **2** the inner, symbolic, or true interpretation or message: *the meaning of the New Testament*

meaningful *adj* **1** serious and important: *a meaningful relationship* **2** intended to express a feeling or opinion: *a meaningful pause*

meaningless *adj* having no meaning or purpose; futile

means *n* **1** the medium, method, or instrument used to obtain a result or achieve an end: *a means of transport* ▹ *pl n* **2** income: *a man of means* **3 by all means** without hesitation or doubt; certainly **4 by means of** with the use or help of **5 by no** *or* **not by any means** on no account; in no way

means test *n* the checking of a person's income to determine whether he or she qualifies for financial aid **means-tested** *adj*

meant *vb* ▸ the past of **mean**[1]

meantime *n* **1** the intervening period: *in the meantime* ▹ *adv* **2** ▸ same as **meanwhile**

mean time *or* **mean solar time** *n* the times, at a particular place, measured so as to give 24-hour days (mean solar days) throughout a year

m

THESAURUS

at *(informal)*, allude to, insinuate **2 = signify**, say, suggest, indicate, represent, express, stand for, convey, spell out, purport, symbolize, denote, connote, betoken **3 = intend**, want, plan, expect, design, aim, wish, think, propose, purpose, desire, set out, contemplate, aspire, have plans, have in mind

mean[2] *adj* **1 = miserly**, stingy, parsimonious, niggardly, close *(informal)*, near *(informal)*, tight, selfish, beggarly, mercenary, skimpy, penny-pinching, ungenerous, penurious, tight-fisted, mingy *(Brit informal)*, snoep *(S African informal)* **OPPOSITE:** generous
3 = dishonourable, base, petty, degraded, disgraceful, shameful, shabby, vile, degenerate, callous, sordid, abject, despicable, narrow-minded, contemptible, wretched, scurvy, ignoble, hard-hearted, scungy *(Austral & NZ)*, low-minded **OPPOSITE:** honourable

mean[3] *n* **1, 2a, 2b = average**, middle, balance, norm, median, midpoint ▹ *adj* **3, 4 = average**, middle, middling, standard, medium, normal, intermediate, median, medial

meaning *n* **1a = significance**, message, explanation, substance, value, import, implication, drift, interpretation, essence, purport, connotation, upshot, gist, signification **1b = definition**, sense, interpretation, explication, elucidation, denotation

meaningful *adj* **1 = significant**, important, serious, material, useful, relevant, valid, worthwhile, purposeful **OPPOSITE:** trivial

meaningless *adj* **= nonsensical**, senseless, inconsequential, inane, insubstantial **OPPOSITE:** worthwhile

means *pl n* **1 = method**, way, course, process, medium, measure, agency, channel, instrument, avenue, mode, expedient **2 = money**, funds, capital, property, riches, income, resources, estate, fortune, wealth, substance, affluence, wherewithal
3 by all means = certainly, surely, of course, definitely, absolutely, positively, doubtlessly
5 by no means = in no way, no way, not at all, definitely not, not in the least, on no account, not in the slightest, not the least bit, absolutely not

meantime *or* **meanwhile** *adv* **2 = at the same time**, in the meantime,

DICTIONARY

meanwhile ⓣ *adv* **1** during the intervening period **2** at the same time, esp. in another place

meany *n, pl* **meanies** ▸same as **meanie**

measles *n* a highly contagious viral disease common in children, characterized by fever and a rash of small red spots ▸See also **German measles**
WORD ORIGIN Low German *masele* spot on the skin

measly *adj* **-slier, -sliest** **1** *informal* too small in quantity or value **2** having or relating to measles

measure ⓣ *n* **1** the size, quantity, or degree of something, as discovered by measurement or calculation **2** a device for measuring distance, volume, etc. such as a graduated scale or container **3** a system or unit of measurement: *the joule is a measure of energy* **4** an amount of alcoholic drink, esp. that served as standard in a bar **5** degree or extent: *a measure of success* **6** a particular action intended to achieve an effect: *radical measures are needed to cut unemployment* **7** a legislative bill, act, or resolution **8** *music* ▸same as **bar**[1] (sense 9) **9** *prosody* poetic rhythm or metre **10** *prosody* a metrical foot **11** *old-fashioned* a dance **12** **for good measure** as an extra precaution or beyond requirements ▹*vb* **-uring, -ured** **13** to determine the size, amount, etc. of by measurement: *he measured the room for a new carpet* **14** to indicate or record the size, speed, force, etc. of: *this dial measures the pressure in the pipe* **15** to have the size, quantity, etc. specified: *the room measures six feet* **16** to estimate or assess: *you cannot measure intelligence purely by exam results* **17** to function as a measurement of: *the ohm measures electrical resistance* **18** to bring into competition or conflict with: *he measured his strength against that of his opponent* ▸See also **measure out, measures, measure up** >**measurable** *adj*
WORD ORIGIN Latin *mensura*

measured ⓣ *adj* **1** slow or stately **2** carefully considered; deliberate

measurement ⓣ *n* **1** the act or process of measuring **2** an amount, extent, or size determined by measuring **3** a system or unit used for measuring: *the kilometre is the standard measurement of distance in most countries* **4** **measurements** the size of a person's waist, chest, hips, etc. used when buying clothes

measure out *vb* to carefully pour or put the required amount of (something) into a container: *she measured out a large whisky*

measures *pl n* rock strata that contain a particular type of deposit: *coal measures*

measure up *vb* **1** to take the measurement of (an area): *we went round and measured up for curtains* **2** **measure up to** to fulfil (expectations or standards)

measuring *adj* used to measure quantities, esp. in cooking: *a measuring jug*

meat *n* **1** the flesh of animals used as food **2** the essence or gist: *get to the meat of your lecture as quickly as possible* **meatless** *adj*
WORD ORIGIN Old English *mete*

meatball *n* minced beef, shaped into a ball before cooking

meaty *adj* **meatier, meatiest** **1** of, like, or full of meat **2** heavily built; fleshy or brawny **3** full of import or interest: *a meaty historical drama*

Mecca *n* **1** the holy city of Islam **2** a place that attracts many visitors

mech. **1** mechanical **2** mechanics

mechanic *n* a person skilled in maintaining or operating machinery or motors
WORD ORIGIN Greek *mēkhanē* machine

mechanical ⓣ *adj* **1** made, performed, or operated by machinery **2** able to understand how machines work and how to repair or maintain them **3 a** (of an action) done without thought or feeling **b** (of a task) not requiring any thought; routine or repetitive **4** of or involving the science of mechanics **mechanically** *adv*

mechanical drawing *n* a drawing to scale of a machine or architectural plan from which dimensions can be taken

mechanical engineering *n* the branch of engineering concerned with the design, construction, and operation of machines

mechanics *n* **1** the scientific study of motion and force **2** the science of designing, constructing, and operating machines ▹*pl n* **3** the technical aspects of something

mechanism ⓣ *n* **1** a system of moving parts that performs some function, esp. in a machine **2** any mechanical device or part of such a device **3** a process or technique: *the body's defence mechanisms* **mechanistic** *adj*

mechanize *or* **-nise** *vb* **-nizing, -nized** *or* **-nising, -nised** **1** to equip a factory or industry with machinery **2** to make mechanical or automatic **3** *mil* to equip an army with armoured vehicles **mechanization** *or* **-nisation** *n*

MEd Master of Education

med. **1** medical **2** medicine **3** medieval **4** medium

medal *n* a small flat piece of metal bearing an inscription or image, given as an award or in commemoration of some outstanding event
WORD ORIGIN French *médaille*

medallion *n* **1** a disc-shaped ornament worn on a chain round the neck **2** a large medal **3** a circular decorative device used in architecture
WORD ORIGIN Italian *medaglia* medal

medallist *or US* **medalist** *n chiefly sport* a winner of a medal or medals

Medawar *n* Sir **Peter Brian** 1915–87, English zoologist, who shared the Nobel prize for physiology or medicine (1960) with Sir Macfarlane

m

THESAURUS

simultaneously, for the present, concurrently, in the meanwhile

meanwhile *or* **meantime** *adv* **1 = for now**, in the meantime, for the moment, in the interim, for then, in the interval, in the meanwhile, in the intervening time

measure *n* **1 = quantity**, share, amount, degree, reach, range, size, capacity, extent, proportion, allowance, portion, scope, quota, ration, magnitude, allotment, amplitude **2 = gauge**, rule, scale, metre, ruler, yardstick **6 = action**, act, step, procedure, means, course, control, proceeding, initiative, manoeuvre, legal action, deed, expedient **7 = law**, act, bill, legislation, resolution, statute, enactment ▹*vb* **13, 14, 16 = quantify**, rate, judge, determine, value, size, estimate, survey, assess, weigh, calculate, evaluate, compute, gauge, mark out, appraise, calibrate

measured *adj* **1 = steady**, even, slow, regular, dignified, stately, solemn, leisurely, sedate, unhurried **2 = considered**, planned, reasoned, studied, calculated, deliberate, sober, premeditated, well-thought-out

measurement *n* **1 = calculation**, assessment, evaluation, estimation, survey, judgment, valuation, appraisal, computation, calibration, mensuration, metage

mechanical *adj* **1 = automatic**, automated, mechanized, power-driven, motor-driven, machine-driven **OPPOSITE:** manual **3a, 3b = unthinking**, routine, automatic, matter-of-fact, cold, unconscious, instinctive, lacklustre, involuntary, impersonal, habitual, cursory, perfunctory, unfeeling, machine-like, emotionless, spiritless **OPPOSITE:** conscious

mechanism *n* **1 = machine**, system, structure, device, tool, instrument, appliance, apparatus, contrivance **3 = process**, workings, way, means, system, performance, operation, medium, agency, method, functioning, technique, procedure, execution, methodology

Burnet for work on immunology

meddle *vb* **-dling, -dled** to interfere annoyingly **meddler** *n* **meddlesome** *adj*
WORD ORIGIN Old French *medler*

media *n* **1** ▸ a plural of **medium** **2** **the media** the mass media collectively ▹ *adj* **3** of or relating to the mass media: *media hype*

mediaeval (med-ee-eve-al) *adj* ▸ same as **medieval**

media event *n* an event that is staged for or exploited by the mass media

medial (mee-dee-al) *adj* of or situated in the middle **medially** *adv*
WORD ORIGIN Latin *medius* middle

median *n* **1** a middle point, plane, or part **2** *geom* a straight line joining one corner of a triangle to the midpoint of the opposite side **3** *statistics* the middle value in a frequency distribution, below and above which lie values with equal total frequencies
WORD ORIGIN Latin *medius* middle

median strip *n US, Canad & NZ* the strip that separates the two sides of a motorway or dual carriageway

mediate ➊ (mee-dee-ate) *vb* **-ating, -ated** **1** to intervene between people or in a dispute in order to bring about agreement **2** to resolve differences by mediation **3** to be changed slightly by (an experience or event): *clients' attitudes to social workers have often been mediated by their past experiences* **mediation** *n* **mediator** *n*
WORD ORIGIN Late Latin *mediare* to be in the middle

medic *n informal* a doctor, medical orderly, or medical student
WORD ORIGIN from MEDICAL

medical *adj* **1** of or relating to the science of medicine or to the treatment of patients without surgery ▹ *n* **2** *informal* a medical examination **medically** *adv*
WORD ORIGIN Latin *medicus* physician

medical certificate *n* **1** a doctor's certificate giving evidence of a person's unfitness for work **2** a document stating the result of a satisfactory medical examination

medicament (mid-dik-a-ment) *n* a medicine

medicate *vb* **-cating, -cated** **1** to treat a patient with a medicine **2** to add a medication to a bandage, shampoo, etc. **medicative** *adj*
WORD ORIGIN Latin *medicare* to heal

medication *n* **1** treatment with drugs or remedies **2** a drug or remedy

medicinal (mid-diss-in-al) *adj* relating to or having therapeutic properties **medicinally** *adv*

medicine ➊ *n* **1** any substance used in treating or alleviating the symptoms of disease **2** the science of preventing, diagnosing, or curing disease **3** any nonsurgical branch of medical science **4** **take one's medicine** to accept a deserved punishment
WORD ORIGIN Latin *medicina (ars)* (art) of healing

medicine man *n* (among certain peoples) a person believed to have supernatural powers of healing

medico *n, pl* **-cos** *informal* a doctor or medical student

medieval *or* **mediaeval** (med-ee-eve-al) *adj* **1** of, relating to, or in the style of the Middle Ages **2** *informal* old-fashioned or primitive **medievalist** *or* **mediaevalist** *n*
WORD ORIGIN New Latin *medium aevum* the middle age

Medieval Greek *n* the Greek language from the 7th to 13th century AD

Medieval Latin *n* the Latin language as used throughout Europe in the Middle Ages

mediocre ➊ (mee-dee-oak-er) *adj* not very high quality; average or second rate **mediocrity** (mee-dee-ok-rit-ee) *n*
WORD ORIGIN Latin *mediocris* moderate

meditate *vb* **-tating, -tated** **1** to think about something deeply: *he meditated on the problem* **2** to reflect deeply on spiritual matters **3** to plan, consider, or think of doing something **meditative** *adj* **meditator** *n*
WORD ORIGIN Latin *meditari* to reflect upon

meditation ➊ *n* **1** the act of meditating; reflection **2** contemplation of spiritual matters, esp. as a religious practice

Mediterranean *adj* of the Mediterranean Sea, lying between S Europe, N Africa, and SW Asia, or the surrounding region
WORD ORIGIN Latin *medius* middle + *terra* land

medium ➊ *adj* **1** midway between extremes of size, amount, or degree: *fry over a medium heat; a man of medium height* ▹ *n, pl* **-dia** *or* **-diums** **2** a middle state, degree, or condition: *the happy medium* **3** a substance which has a particular effect or can be used for a particular purpose: *linseed oil is used as a thinning medium for oil paint* **4** a means for communicating information or news to the public **5** a person who can supposedly communicate with the dead **6** the substance or surroundings in which an organism naturally lives or grows **7** *art* the category of a work of art, as determined by its materials: *his works in the photographic medium*
WORD ORIGIN Latin *medius* middle

medium wave *n* a radio wave with a wavelength between 100 and 1000 metres

medlar *n* the apple-like fruit of a small Eurasian tree, which is not edible until it has begun to decay
WORD ORIGIN Old French *medlier*

medley *n* **1** a mixture of various elements **2** a musical composition consisting of various tunes arranged as a continuous whole **3** *swimming* a race in which a different stroke is used for each length
WORD ORIGIN Old French, from *medler* to mix, quarrel

medulla (mid-dull-la) *n, pl* **-las** *or* **-lae** (-lee) **1** *anat* the innermost part of an organ or structure **2** *anat* the lower stalklike section of the brain **3** *bot* the central pith of a plant stem **medullary** *adj*
WORD ORIGIN Latin: marrow

medusa (mid-dew-za) *n, pl* **-sas** *or* **-sae** (-zee) jellyfish
WORD ORIGIN *Medusa*, in Greek mythology, who had snakes for hair

meek *adj* quiet, and ready to do what other people say **meekly** *adv*
WORD ORIGIN related to Old Norse *mjūkr* amenable

meerkat *n* a South African mongoose
WORD ORIGIN Dutch: sea-cat

meerschaum (meer-shum) *n* **1** a

THESAURUS

mediate *vb* **1 = intervene**, moderate, step in *(informal)*, intercede, settle, referee, resolve, umpire, reconcile, arbitrate, interpose, conciliate, make peace, restore harmony, act as middleman, bring to terms, bring to an agreement

medicine *n* **1 = remedy**, drug, cure, prescription, medication, nostrum, physic, medicament

mediocre *adj* **= second-rate**, average, ordinary, indifferent, middling, pedestrian, inferior, commonplace, vanilla *(slang)*, insignificant, so-so *(informal)*, banal, tolerable, run-of-the-mill, passable, undistinguished, uninspired, bog-standard *(Brit & Irish slang)*, no great shakes *(informal)*, half-pie *(NZ informal)*, fair to middling *(informal)*, meh *(slang)*
OPPOSITE: excellent

meditation *n* **1 = reflection**, thought, concentration, study, musing, pondering, contemplation, reverie, ruminating, rumination, cogitation, cerebration, a brown study

medium *adj* **1 = average**, mean, middle, middling, fair, intermediate, midway, mediocre, median, medial
OPPOSITE: extraordinary
▹ *n* **2 = middle**, mean, centre, average, compromise, middle ground, middle way, midpoint, middle course, middle path
5 = spiritualist, seer, clairvoyant, fortune teller, spiritist, channeller

DICTIONARY

white, heat-resistant, claylike mineral **2** a tobacco pipe with a bowl made of this mineral
WORD ORIGIN German *Meerschaum*, literally: sea foam

meet[1] ❶ *vb* **meeting, met 1** to be in or come to the same place at the same time as, either by arrangement or by accident: *I met him in town* **2** to come into contact with something or each other: *his head met the ground with a crack; the town where the Rhine and the Moselle meet* **3** to come to or be at the place of arrival of: *he met his train at noon* **4** to make the acquaintance of or be introduced to someone or each other **5** (of people) to gather together for a purpose: *the board meets once a week* **6** to compete, play, or fight against **7** to cope with effectively; satisfy: *they were unable to meet his demands* **8** to pay for (something): *it is difficult to meet the cost of medical insurance* **9** Also: **meet with** to experience or suffer: *he met his death at the Somme* **10 there is more to this than meets the eye** there is more involved in this than appears ▹*n* **11** a sports meeting **12** *chiefly Brit* the assembly of hounds and huntsmen prior to a hunt
WORD ORIGIN Old English *mētan*

meet[2] *adj archaic* proper, fitting, or correct: *meet and proper*
WORD ORIGIN Old English *gemǣte*

m

meeting ❶ *n* **1** an act of coming together: *a meeting was fixed for the following day* **2** an assembly or gathering of people: *the meeting voted in favour* **3** a sporting competition, as of athletes, or of horse racing

meg *n computers informal* ▸short for **megabyte**

mega *adj slang* extremely good, great, or successful

mega- *combining form* **1** denoting 10^6: *megawatt* **2** (in computer technology) denoting 2^{20} (1 048 576): *megabyte* **3** large or great: *megalith* **4** *informal* very great: *megastar*
WORD ORIGIN Greek *megas* huge, powerful

megabyte *n computers* 2^{20} or 1 048 576 bytes

megadeath *n* the death of a million people, esp. in a nuclear war or attack

megahertz *n, pl* **megahertz** one million hertz; one million cycles per second

megajoule *n* one million joules

megalith *n* a very large stone, esp. one forming part of a prehistoric monument **megalithic** *adj*

megalomania *n* **1** a mental illness characterized by delusions of power **2** *informal* a craving for power **megalomaniac** *adj, n*
WORD ORIGIN Greek *megas* great + *mania* madness

megaphone *n* a funnel-shaped instrument used to make someone's voice sound louder, esp. out of doors

megapixel *n* one million pixels: used to describe the resolution of digital images

megapode *n* any of various ground-living birds of Australia, New Guinea, and adjacent islands. Their eggs incubate in mounds of sand or rotting vegetation
WORD ORIGIN Greek *megas* great + *-podos* -footed

megaton *n* **1** one million tons **2** an explosive power, esp. of a nuclear weapon, equal to the power of one million tons of TNT

megavolt *n* one million volts

megawatt *n* one million watts

Mehemet Ali *or* **Mohammed Ali** *n* 1769–1849, Albanian commander in the service of Turkey. He was made viceroy of Egypt (1805) and its hereditary ruler (1841), founding a dynasty that ruled until 1952

Mehta *n* **Zubin** born 1936, Indian conductor; musical director of the Israel Philharmonic orchestra from 1969

Meilhac *n* **Henri** 1831–97, French dramatist, who collaborated with Halévy on opera libretti, esp. Offenbach's *La Belle Hélène* (1865) and *La Vie parisienne* (1867)

meiosis (my-oh-siss) *n, pl* **-ses** (-seez) a type of cell division in which reproductive cells are produced, each containing half the chromosome number of the parent nucleus
WORD ORIGIN Greek *meiōn* less

meitnerium *n chem* an element artificially produced in small quantities by high-energy ion bombardment. Symbol: Mt
WORD ORIGIN after Lise *Meitner*, physicist

melaleuca (mel-a-loo-ka) *n* an Australian shrub or tree with a white trunk and black branches
WORD ORIGIN Greek *melas* black + *leukos* white

melamine *n* a colourless crystalline compound used in making synthetic resins
WORD ORIGIN German *Melamin*

melancholia (mel-an-kole-lee-a) *n* ▸an old name for **depression** (sense 1)

melancholy ❶ (mel-an-kol-lee) *n, pl* **-cholies 1** a tendency to gloominess or depression **2** a sad thoughtful state of mind ▹*adj* **3** characterized by, causing, or expressing sadness **melancholic** *adj, n*
WORD ORIGIN Greek *melas* black + *kholē* bile

Melanchthon *n* **Philipp** original surname *Schwarzerd*. 1497–1560, German Protestant reformer. His *Loci Communes* (1521) was the first systematic presentation of Protestant theology and in the Augsburg Confession (1530) he stated the faith of the Lutheran churches. He also reformed the German educational system

melange (may-**lahnzh**) *n* a mixture or assortment: *a melange of historical facts and legends*
WORD ORIGIN French *mêler* to mix

melanin *n* a black pigment present in the hair, skin, and eyes of humans and animals
WORD ORIGIN Greek *melas* black

melanoma *n, pl* **-mas** *or* **-mata** *pathol* a tumour composed of dark-coloured cells, occurring in some skin cancers
WORD ORIGIN Greek *melas* black + *-oma*, modelled on *carcinoma*

Melba toast *n* very thin crisp toast

THESAURUS

meet[1] *vb* **1 = encounter**, come across, run into, happen on, find, contact, confront, bump into *(informal)*, run across, chance on, come face to face with **OPPOSITE:** avoid
2 = converge, unite, join, cross, touch, connect, come together, link up, adjoin, intersect, abut
OPPOSITE: diverge
5 = gather, collect, assemble, get together, rally, come together, muster, convene, congregate, foregather **OPPOSITE:** disperse
7 = fulfil, match (up to), answer, perform, handle, carry out, equal, satisfy, cope with, discharge, comply with, come up to, conform to, gratify, measure up to **OPPOSITE:** fall short of
9 = experience, face, suffer, bear, go through, encounter, endure, undergo

meeting *n* **1 = encounter**, introduction, confrontation, engagement, rendezvous, tryst, assignation **2 = conference**, gathering, assembly, meet, congress, session, rally, convention, get-together *(informal)*, reunion, congregation, hui *(NZ)*, conclave, convocation, powwow

melancholy *n* **1, 2 = sadness**, depression, misery, gloom, sorrow, woe, blues, unhappiness, despondency, the hump *(Brit informal)*, dejection, low spirits, gloominess, pensiveness
OPPOSITE: happiness
▹*adj* **3 = sad**, down, depressed, unhappy, low, blue, miserable, moody, gloomy, dismal, sombre, woeful, glum, mournful, dejected, despondent, dispirited, melancholic, downcast, lugubrious, pensive, sorrowful, disconsolate, joyless, doleful, downhearted, heavy-hearted, down in the dumps *(informal)*, woebegone, down in the mouth, low-spirited
OPPOSITE: happy

DICTIONARY

WORD ORIGIN after Dame Nellie *Melba*, singer

Melchior[1] *n* **1** (in Christian tradition) one of the Magi, the others being Balthazar and Caspar **2 Lauritz** 1890–1973, US operatic tenor, born in Denmark

Melchior[2] *n* (in Christian tradition) one of the Magi, the others being Balthazar and Caspar

meld *vb* to merge or blend
WORD ORIGIN blend of *melt* + *weld*

melee (mel-lay) *n* a noisy riotous fight or crowd
WORD ORIGIN French, from *mêler* to mix

Méliès *n* **Georges** 1861–1938, French pioneer film director

mellifluous (mel-**lif**-flew-uss) *adj* (of sound) smooth and sweet
WORD ORIGIN Latin *mel* honey + *fluere* to flow

mellow ❶ *adj* **1** (esp. of colours, light, or sounds) soft or rich: *the mellow stillness of a sunny Sunday morning* **2** kind-hearted, esp. through maturity or old age **3** genial and relaxed, for instance through the effects of alcohol or good food **4** (esp. of fruits) sweet, ripe and full-flavoured **5** (esp. of wine or cheese) having developed a full, smooth flavour as a result of maturing **6** (of soil) soft and loamy ▷ *vb* **7** to make or become mellow **8** (foll. by *out*) to make or become calm and relaxed
WORD ORIGIN origin unknown

melodeon *n* **1** a small accordion **2** a keyboard instrument like a harmonium
WORD ORIGIN German *Melodie* melody

melodic (mel-**lod**-ik) *adj* **1** of or relating to melody **2** tuneful and pleasant to the ear; melodious **melodically** *adv*

melodious (mel-**lode**-ee-uss) *adj* **1** pleasant to the ear: *he gave a melodious chuckle* **2** tuneful and melodic **melodiousness** *n*

melodrama *n* **1** a play or film full of extravagant action and emotion **2** overdramatic emotion or behaviour **melodramatic** *adj* **melodramatics** *pl n*
WORD ORIGIN Greek *melos* song + *drama* drama

melody ❶ *n, pl* **-dies 1** *music* a succession of notes forming a distinctive sequence; tune **2** sounds that are pleasant because of their tone or arrangement, esp. words of poetry
WORD ORIGIN Greek *melōidia*

melon *n* any of various large edible fruits which have a hard rind and juicy flesh
WORD ORIGIN Greek *mēlon* apple

Melpomene (mel-**pom**-in-nee) *n* *Greek myth* the Muse of tragedy

melt ❶ *vb* **1** to change from a solid into a liquid as a result of the action of heat **2** to dissolve: *these sweets melt in the mouth* **3** Also: **melt away** to diminish and finally disappear; fade away: *he felt his inner doubts melt away* **4** to blend so that it is impossible to tell where one thing ends and another begins: *they melted into the trees until the gamekeeper had passed* **5** to make or become emotional or sentimental; soften: *she melted into tears* **meltingly** *adv*
WORD ORIGIN Old English *meltan* to digest

meltdown *n* **1** (in a nuclear reactor) the melting of the fuel rods, with the possible escape of radioactivity **2** *informal* a sudden disastrous failure **3** *informal* a process of irreversible decline

melting point *n* the temperature at which a solid turns into a liquid

melting pot *n* a place or situation in which many races, ideas, etc. are mixed

meltwater *n* melted snow or ice

member ❶ *n* **1** a person who belongs to a group or organization such as a club or political party **2** any part of a plant or animal, such as a limb or petal **3** a Member of Parliament: *the member for Glasgow Central* ▷ *adj* **4** (of a country or group) belonging to an organization or alliance: *a summit of the member countries' heads of state is due*
WORD ORIGIN Latin *membrum* limb, part

Member of Parliament *n* a person who has been elected to the House of Commons or the equivalent assembly in another country

membership ❶ *n* **1** the members of an organization collectively **2** the number of members **3** the state of being a member

membrane *n* a thin flexible tissue that covers, lines, or connects plant and animal organs or cells **membranous** *adj*
WORD ORIGIN Latin *membrana* skin covering a part of the body

memento *n, pl* **-tos** *or* **-toes** something that reminds one of past events; a souvenir
WORD ORIGIN Latin, imperative of *meminisse* to remember

memento mori *n, pl* **memento mori** an object intended to remind people of death
WORD ORIGIN Latin: remember you must die

Memling *or* **Memlinc** *n* **Hans** ?1430–94, Flemish painter of religious works and portraits

memo *n, pl* **memos** ▸ short for **memorandum**

memoir ❶ (**mem**-wahr) *n* a biography or historical account based on personal knowledge
WORD ORIGIN Latin *memoria* memory

memoirs ❶ *pl n* **1** a collection of reminiscences about a period or series of events, written from personal experience **2** an autobiography

memorabilia *pl n, sing* **-rabile** objects connected with famous people or events

memorable ❶ *adj* worth remembering or easily remembered because it is very special or important **memorably** *adv*
WORD ORIGIN Latin *memorare* to remember

memorandum ❶ *n, pl* **-dums** *or* **-da** **1** a note sent by one person or department to another within a business organization **2** a note of things to be remembered **3** *law* a short written summary of the terms of a transaction
WORD ORIGIN Latin: (something) to be remembered

m

THESAURUS

mellow *adj* **4, 5a = full-flavoured**, rounded, rich, sweet, smooth, delicate, juicy **4, 5b = ripe**, perfect, mature, ripened, well-matured
OPPOSITE: unripe
▷ *vb* **7 = season**, develop, improve, perfect, ripen **8 = relax**, improve, settle, calm, mature, soften, sweeten

melody *n* **1 = tune**, song, theme, refrain, air, music, strain, descant **2 = tunefulness**, music, harmony, musicality, euphony, melodiousness

melt *vb* **1, 2 = dissolve**, run, soften, fuse, thaw, diffuse, flux, defrost, liquefy, unfreeze, deliquesce **5 = soften**, touch, relax, disarm, mollify

member *n* **1 = representative**, associate, supporter, fellow, subscriber, comrade, disciple

membership *n* **1 = members**, body, associates, fellows **3 = participation**, belonging, fellowship, enrolment

memoir *n* **= account**, life, record, register, journal, essay, biography, narrative, monograph

memoirs *pl n* **1, 2 = autobiography**, diary, life story, life, experiences, memories, journals, recollections, reminiscences

memorable *adj* **= noteworthy**, celebrated, impressive, historic, important, special, striking, famous, significant, signal, extraordinary, remarkable, distinguished, haunting, notable, timeless, unforgettable, momentous, illustrious, catchy, indelible, unfading **OPPOSITE:** forgettable

memorandum *n* **1, 2 = note**, minute, message, communication, reminder, memo, jotting, e-mail

DICTIONARY

memorial ❶ *n* **1** something, such as a statue, built or displayed to preserve the memory of someone or something: *a war memorial* ▷ *adj* **2** in memory of someone or something: *a memorial service*
WORD ORIGIN Late Latin *memoriale* a reminder

memorize *or* **-rise** *vb* **-rizing, -rized** *or* **-rising, -rised** to commit to memory; learn by heart

memory ❶ *n, pl* **-ries 1** the ability of the mind to store and recall past sensations, thoughts, and knowledge: *she can do it from memory* **2** the sum of everything retained by the mind **3** a particular recollection of an event or person: *he started awake with a sudden memory* **4** the length of time one can remember: *my memory doesn't go that far back* **5** commemoration: *in memory of our leader* **6** a person's reputation after death: *a conductor of fond memory* **7** a part of a computer in which information is stored
WORD ORIGIN Latin *memoria*

memory card *n* a small removable data storage device, used in mobile phones, digital cameras, etc.

Memory Stick *n computers* **1** *trademark* a standard format for memory cards **2 memory stick** also: **USB memory stick.** ▶ Same as **USB drive**

memsahib *n* (formerly, in India) a term of respect used for a European married woman
WORD ORIGIN *ma'am* + *sahib*

men *n* ▶ the plural of **man**

menace ❶ *vb* **-acing, -aced 1** to threaten with violence or danger ▷ *n* **2** a threat; a source of danger **3** *informal* an annoying person or thing; nuisance **menacing** *adj*
WORD ORIGIN Latin *minax* threatening

ménage (may-nahzh) *n* a household
WORD ORIGIN French

ménage à trois (ah trwah) *n, pl* **ménages à trois** a sexual arrangement involving a married couple and the lover of one of them
WORD ORIGIN French, literally: household of three

menagerie (min-naj-er-ee) *n* a collection of wild animals kept for exhibition
WORD ORIGIN French

Menander *n* **1** ?160 BC–?120 BC, Greek king of the Punjab. A Buddhist convert, he reigned over much of NW India **2** ?342–?292 BC, Greek comic dramatist. The *Dyskolos* is his only complete extant comedy but others survive in adaptations by Terence and Plautus

Mencius *n* Chinese name *Mengzi* or *Meng-tze.* ?372–?289 BC, Chinese philosopher, who propounded the ethical system of Confucius

Mencken *n* **H**(**enry**) **L**(**ouis**) 1880–1956, US journalist and literary critic, noted for *The American Language* (1919): editor of the *Smart Set* and the *American Mercury*, which he founded (1924)

mend ❶ *vb* **1** to repair something broken or not working **2** to heal or recover: *a wound like that will take a while to mend* **3** (esp. of behaviour) to improve; make or become better: *if you don't mend your ways you'll be in serious trouble* ▷ *n* **4** a mended area, esp. on a garment **5 on the mend** regaining one's health
WORD ORIGIN from *amend*

mendacity *n* the tendency to be untruthful **mendacious** *adj*
WORD ORIGIN Latin *mendax* untruthful

mendelevium *n chem* an artificially produced radioactive element. Symbol: Md
WORD ORIGIN after D. I. *Mendeleyev*, chemist

Mendel's laws *pl n* the principles of heredity proposed by Gregor Mendel (1822–84), Austrian monk and botanist **Mendelism** *n*

Mendes *n* **Sam**(**uel**) (**Alexander**) born 1965, British theatre and film director, who made his name as artistic director of the Donmar Warehouse, London (1992–2002) before directing the films *American Beauty* (1999) and *The Road to Perdition* (2002). He is married to the actress Kate Winslet

Mendès-France *n* **Pierre** 1907–82, French statesman; prime minister (1954–55). He concluded the war in Indochina and granted independence to Tunisia

mendicant *adj* **1** begging **2** (of a monk, nun, etc.) dependent on charity for food ▷ *n* **3** a mendicant friar **4** a beggar
WORD ORIGIN Latin *mendicus* beggar

Mendoza[1] *n* a city in W central Argentina, in the foothills of the Sierra de los Paramillos: largely destroyed by an earthquake in 1861; commercial centre of an intensively cultivated irrigated region; University of Cuyo (1939). Pop: 1 072 000 (2005 est)

Mendoza[2] *n* **Pedro de** died 1537, Spanish soldier and explorer; founder of Buenos Aires (1536)

Menelik II *n* 1844–1913, emperor of Abyssinia (1889–1910). He defeated the Italians at Aduwa (1896), maintaining the independence of Abyssinia in an era of European expansion in Africa

Menes *n* the first king of the first dynasty of Egypt (?3100 BC). He is said to have united Upper and Lower Egypt and founded Memphis

menfolk *pl n* men collectively, esp. the men of a particular family

Mengelberg *n* (**Josef**) **Willem** 1871–1951, Dutch orchestral conductor, noted for his performances of the music of Mahler

Mengistu Haile Mariam *n* born 1937, Ethiopian soldier and statesman; head of state from 1977 until 1991 when rebels seized power and he fled into exile

Mengzi *or* **Meng-tze** *n* the Chinese name for **Mencius**

menhir (men-hear) *n* a single standing stone, dating from prehistoric times
WORD ORIGIN Breton *men* stone + *hir* long

menial (mean-nee-al) *adj* **1** involving or doing boring work of low status ▷ *n* **2** a domestic servant
WORD ORIGIN Old French *meinie* household

Meninga *n* **Mal** born 1960, Australian rugby league player

meninges (min-in-jeez) *pl n, sing* **meninx** (**mean-inks**) the three membranes that surround the brain and spinal cord
WORD ORIGIN Greek, plural of *meninx* membrane

meningitis (men-in-jite-iss) *n* inflammation of the meninges, caused by infection and causing severe headache, fever, and rigidity of the neck muscles

THESAURUS

memorial *n* **1 = monument**, cairn, shrine, plaque, cenotaph ▷ *adj* **2 = commemorative**, remembrance, monumental

memory *n* **1 = recall**, mind, retention, ability to remember, powers of recall, powers of retention **3 = recollection**, reminder, reminiscence, impression, echo, remembrance **5 = commemoration**, respect, honour, recognition, tribute, remembrance, observance

menace *vb* **1 = bully**, threaten, intimidate, terrorize, alarm, frighten, scare, browbeat, utter threats to ▷ *n* **2 = threat**, warning, intimidation, ill-omen, ominousness, commination **3** (*informal*) **= nuisance**, plague, pest, annoyance, troublemaker, mischief-maker

mend *vb* **1a = repair**, fix, restore, renew, patch up, renovate, refit, retouch **1b = darn**, repair, patch, stitch, sew **2 = heal**, improve, recover, cure, remedy, get better, be all right, be cured, recuperate, pull through, convalesce **3 = improve**, better, reform, correct, revise, amend, rectify, ameliorate, emend **5 on the mend = convalescent**, improving, recovering, getting better, recuperating, convalescing

DICTIONARY

meniscus *n, pl* **-nisci** *or* **-niscuses 1** the curved upper surface of a liquid standing in a tube, produced by the surface tension **2** a crescent-shaped lens
WORD ORIGIN Greek *mēniskos* crescent

Menon *n* **Vengalil Krishnan Krishna** 1897–1974, Indian diplomat and politician, who was a close associate of Nehru and played a key role in the Indian nationalist movement

menopause *n* the period during which a woman's menstrual cycle ceases, normally at an age of 45 to 50 **menopausal** *adj*
WORD ORIGIN Greek *mēn* month + *pausis* halt

menorah (min-or-a) *n judaism* a seven-branched candelabrum used as an emblem of Judaism
WORD ORIGIN Hebrew: candlestick

Menotti *n* **Gian Carlo** 1911–2007, Italian composer, in the US from 1928. His works include the operas *The Medium* (1946), *The Consul* (1950), *Amahl and the Night Visitors* (1951), and *Giorno di Nozze* (1988)

menses (men-seez) *n* ▸ same as **menstruation**
WORD ORIGIN Latin, plural of *mensis* month

menstrual *adj* of or relating to menstruation: *the menstrual cycle*

menstruate *vb* **-ating, -ated** to undergo menstruation
WORD ORIGIN Latin *menstruare*, from *mensis* month

menstruation *n* the approximately monthly discharge of blood from the womb in women of childbearing age who are not pregnant

mensuration *n* **1** the study of the measurement of geometric magnitudes such as length **2** the act or process of measuring
WORD ORIGIN Latin *mensura* measure

menswear *n* clothing for men

mental ❶ *adj* **1** of, done by, or involving the mind: *mental alertness* **2** done in the mind without using speech or writing: *mental arithmetic* **3** affected by mental illness: *a mental patient* **4** concerned with mental illness: *a mental hospital* **5** *slang* extremely foolish or eccentric **mentally** *adv*
WORD ORIGIN Latin *mens* mind

mental age *n* the age which a person is considered to have reached in thinking ability, judged by comparing his or her ability with the average for people of various ages: *a twenty-one-year-old woman with a mental age of only ten*

mental handicap *n* any intellectual disability resulting from injury to or abnormal development of the brain **mentally handicapped** *adj*

mental illness *n* any of various disorders in which a person's thoughts, emotions, or behaviour are so abnormal as to cause suffering to himself, herself, or other people

mentality ❶ *n, pl* **-ties** a particular attitude or way of thinking: *the traditional civil service mentality*

menthol *n* an organic compound found in peppermint oil and used as an antiseptic, decongestant, and painkiller **mentholated** *adj*
WORD ORIGIN Latin *mentha* mint

mention ❶ *vb* **1** to refer to or speak about briefly or incidentally **2** to include in a report, list etc. because of high standards or an outstanding achievement: *the hotel is mentioned in all the guidebooks; he was twice mentioned in dispatches during the war* **3 not to mention (something)** to say nothing of (something too obvious to mention) ▹*n* **4** a slight reference or allusion **5** a recognition or acknowledgment of high quality or an outstanding achievement
WORD ORIGIN Latin *mentio* a calling to mind

mentor ❶ *n* an adviser or guide
WORD ORIGIN *Mentor*, adviser of Telemachus in Homer's *Odyssey*

menu ❶ *n* **1** a list of dishes served at a meal or that can be ordered in a restaurant **2** a list of options displayed on a visual display unit from which the operator can choose
WORD ORIGIN French: small, detailed (list)

meow *or* **miaow** (mee-ow) *n* **1** the characteristic high-pitched cry of a cat; mew ▹*vb* **2** to make such a sound

MEP (in Britain) Member of the European Parliament

Mephistopheles (mef-iss-**stoff**-ill-eez) *n* a devil in medieval mythology to whom Faust sold his soul **Mephistophelean** *adj*

mercantile *adj* of trade or traders; commercial
WORD ORIGIN Italian *mercante* merchant

Mercator projection (mer-**kate**-er) *n* a way of drawing maps in which latitude and longitude form a rectangular grid, scale being exaggerated with increasing distance from the equator
WORD ORIGIN after G. *Mercator*, cartographer

mercenary *n, pl* **-naries 1** a soldier who fights for a foreign army for money ▹*adj* **2** motivated by greed or the desire for gain: *calculating and mercenary businessmen* **3** of or relating to a mercenary or mercenaries
WORD ORIGIN Latin *merces* wages

Mercer *n* **Johnny**, full name *John Herndon Mercer*. 1909–76, US popular songwriter and singer. His most popular songs include "Blues in the Night" (1941) and "Moon River" (1961)

mercerized *or* **-ised** *adj* (of cotton) treated with an alkali to make it strong and shiny
WORD ORIGIN after John *Mercer*, maker of textiles

merchandise ❶ *n* **1** goods for buying, selling, or trading with; commodities ▹*vb* **-dising, -dised 2** to engage in the commercial purchase and sale of goods or services; trade

merchandising *n* **1** the selection and display of goods in a retail outlet **2** commercial goods, esp. ones issued to exploit the popularity of a pop group, sporting event, etc.

merchant ❶ *n* **1** a person who buys and sells goods in large quantities and usually of one type: *a wine merchant* **2** *chiefly Scot, US, & Canad* a person engaged in retail trade; shopkeeper **3** *slang* a person dealing in something undesirable: *a gossip merchant* ▹*adj* **4** of ships involved in

m

THESAURUS

mental *adj* **1 = intellectual**, rational, theoretical, cognitive, brain, conceptual, cerebral **3** *(slang)* **= insane**, mad, disturbed, unstable, mentally ill, lunatic, psychotic, unbalanced, deranged, round the bend *(Brit slang)*, as daft as a brush *(informal, chiefly Brit)*, not right in the head

mentality *n* **= attitude**, character, personality, psychology, make-up, outlook, disposition, way of thinking, frame of mind, turn of mind, cast of mind

mention *vb* **1 = refer to**, point out, acknowledge, bring up, state, report, reveal, declare, cite, communicate, disclose, intimate, tell of, recount, hint at, impart, allude to, divulge, broach, call attention to, make known, touch upon, adduce, speak about *or* of ▹*n* **4** *(often with* **of***)* **= reference**, announcement, observation, indication, remark, notification, allusion **5 = acknowledgment**, recognition, tribute, citation, honourable mention

mentor *n* **= guide**, teacher, coach, adviser, tutor, instructor, counsellor, guru

menu *n* **1 = bill of fare**, tariff *(chiefly Brit)*, set menu, table d'hôte, carte du jour *(French)*

merchandise *n* **1 = goods**, produce, stock, products, truck, commodities, staples, wares, stock in trade, vendibles

merchant *n* **1, 2 = tradesman**, dealer, trader, broker, retailer, supplier, seller, salesman, vendor, shopkeeper, trafficker, wholesaler, purveyor

DICTIONARY

commercial trade or their crews: *a merchant sailor; the British merchant fleet*
WORD ORIGIN Latin *mercari* to trade

Merchant *n* **Ismail** 1936–2005, Indian film producer, noted for his collaboration with James Ivory on such films as *Shakespeare Wallah* (1965), *The Europeans* (1979), *A Room with a View* (1986), *The Remains of the Day* (1993), and *The Golden Bowl* (2000)

merchant bank *n* a financial institution that deals primarily with foreign trade and business finance **merchant banker** *n*

merchantman *n, pl* **-men** a merchant ship

merchant navy *n* the ships or crew engaged in a nation's commercial shipping

merciful *adj* **1** (of an act or event) giving relief from pain or suffering: *after months of illness, death came as a merciful release* **2** showing or giving mercy; compassionate **mercifully** *adv*

merciless *adj* without mercy; pitiless, cruel, or heartless **mercilessly** *adv*

Merckx *n* **Eddy** born 1945, Belgian professional cyclist: five times winner of the Tour de France, including four consecutive victories (1969–72)

m

Mercouri *n* **Melina** 1925–94, Greek actress and politician: her films include *Never on Sunday* (1960); minister of culture (1981–85 and 1993–94)

mercurial (mer-cure-ee-al) *adj* **1** lively and unpredictable: *a mercurial and temperamental chess player* **2** of or containing mercury
WORD ORIGIN Latin *mercurialis*

mercuric *adj* of or containing mercury in the divalent state

mercurous *adj* of or containing mercury in the monovalent state

mercury *n, pl* **-ries** *chem* a silvery toxic metal, the only element liquid at normal temperatures, used in thermometers, barometers, lamps, and dental amalgams. Symbol: Hg
WORD ORIGIN Latin *Mercurius*, messenger of Jupiter

Mercury *n* **1** *Roman myth* the messenger of the gods **2** the second smallest planet and the one nearest the sun

mercy ❶ *n, pl* **-cies** **1** compassionate treatment of or attitude towards an offender or enemy who is in one's power **2** the power to show mercy: *they threw themselves on the King's mercy* **3** a relieving or welcome occurrence or act: *it was a mercy you turned up when you did* **4** **at the mercy of** in the power of ▹ *adj* **5** done or undertaken in an attempt to relieve suffering or bring help: *a mercy mission*
WORD ORIGIN Latin *merces* recompense

mercy killing *n* ▸ same as **euthanasia**

mere[1] ❶ *adj* nothing more than: *the election in Slovenia seems a mere formality* **merely** *adv*
WORD ORIGIN Latin *merus* pure

mere[2] *n Brit dialect or archaic* a lake
WORD ORIGIN Old English: sea, lake

Meredith *n* **George** 1828–1909, English novelist and poet. His works, notable for their social satire and analysis of character, include the novels *Beauchamp's Career* (1876) and *The Egoist* (1879) and the long tragic poem *Modern Love* (1862)

meretricious *adj* superficially or garishly attractive but of no real value
WORD ORIGIN Latin *meretrix* prostitute

merganser (mer-gan-ser) *n, pl* **-sers** *or* **-ser** a large crested marine diving duck
WORD ORIGIN Latin *mergere* to plunge + *anser* goose

merge ❶ *vb* **merging, merged** **1** to combine, esp. so as to become part of a larger whole: *the two airlines merged in 1983* **2** to blend gradually, without any sudden change being apparent: *late afternoon merged imperceptibly into early evening*
WORD ORIGIN Latin *mergere* to plunge

merger ❶ *n* the act of merging, esp. the combination of two or more companies

meridian *n* **1** one of the imaginary lines joining the north and south poles at right angles to the equator, designated by degrees of longitude from 0° at Greenwich to 180° **2** (in acupuncture etc.) any of various channels through which vital energy is believed to circulate round the body

WORD ORIGIN Latin *meridies* midday

meridional *adj* **1** of or along a meridian **2** of or in the south, esp. the south of Europe

Mérimée *n* **Prosper** 1803–70, French novelist, dramatist, and short-story writer, noted particularly for his short novels *Colomba* (1840) and *Carmen* (1845), on which Bizet's opera was based

meringue (mer-rang) *n* **1** stiffly beaten egg whites mixed with sugar and baked **2** a small cake made from this mixture
WORD ORIGIN French

merino *n, pl* **-nos** **1** a sheep with long fine wool, originally reared in Spain **2** the yarn made from this wool
WORD ORIGIN Spanish

merit ❶ *n* **1** worth or superior quality; excellence: *the film had two sequels, neither of much merit* **2** an admirable or advantageous quality: *the relative merits of film and video as a medium of communication* **3** **have the merit of** to have a positive feature or advantage that the alternatives do not have: *the first version has the merit of being short* **4** **on its merits** on its intrinsic qualities or virtues ▹ *vb* **-iting, -ited** **5** to be worthy of; deserve: *the issue merits much fuller discussion*
WORD ORIGIN Latin *meritum* reward

meritocracy (mer-it-tok-rass-ee) *n, pl* **-cies** a social system in which power is held by the most talented or intelligent people **meritocrat** *n* **meritocratic** *adj*

meritorious *adj* deserving praise for being good or worthwhile
WORD ORIGIN Latin *meritorius* earning money

Merleau-Ponty *n* **Maurice** 1908–61, French phenomenological philosopher

merlin *n* a small falcon with dark plumage
WORD ORIGIN Old French *esmerillon*

mermaid *n* an imaginary sea creature with a woman's head and upper body and a fish's tail **merman** *masc n*
WORD ORIGIN *mere* sea + *maid*

merry ❶ *adj* **-rier, -riest** **1** cheerful and jolly **2** *Austral & Brit informal* slightly drunk **3** **make merry** to take part in noisy, cheerful celebrations or fun **merrily** *adv* **merriment** *n*

THESAURUS

mercy *n* **1,2 = compassion**, charity, pity, forgiveness, quarter, favour, grace, kindness, clemency, leniency, benevolence, forbearance
OPPOSITE: cruelty
3 = blessing, relief, boon, godsend, piece of luck, benison *(archaic)*

mere[1] *adj* **= simple**, merely, no more than, nothing more than, just, common, plain, pure, pure and simple, unadulterated, unmitigated, unmixed

merge *vb* **1a = combine**, blend, fuse, amalgamate, unite, join, mix, consolidate, mingle, converge, coalesce, melt into, meld, intermix
OPPOSITE: separate
1b = join, unite, combine, consolidate, fuse **OPPOSITE:** separate
2 = melt, blend, incorporate, mingle, tone with, be swallowed up by, become lost in

merger *n* **= union**, fusion, consolidation, amalgamation, combination, coalition, incorporation

merit *n* **2 = advantage**, value, quality, worth, strength, asset, virtue, good point, strong point, worthiness ▹ *vb* **5 = deserve**, warrant, be entitled to, earn, incur, have a right to, be worthy of, have a claim to

merry *adj* **1 = cheerful**, happy, upbeat *(informal)*, carefree, glad, jolly, festive, joyous, joyful, genial, fun-loving, chirpy *(informal)*, vivacious,

WORD ORIGIN Old English *merige* agreeable

merry-go-round *n* **1** a fairground roundabout **2** a whirl of activity

merrymaking *n* noisy, cheerful celebrations or fun **merrymaker** *n*

Merton[1] *n* a borough in SW Greater London. Pop: 191 400 (2003 est). Area: 38 sq km (15 sq miles)

Merton[2] *n* **Thomas** (**Feverel**) 1915–68, US writer, monk, and mystic; noted esp. for his autobiography *The Seven Storey Mountain* (1948)

mesa *n* a flat-topped hill found in arid regions
WORD ORIGIN Spanish: table

mésalliance (mez-**zal**-ee-anss) *n* a marriage with a person of lower social status
WORD ORIGIN French

mescal (mess-**kal**) *n* **1** a globe-shaped cactus without spines found in Mexico and the southwestern US **2** a Mexican alcoholic spirit similar to tequila
WORD ORIGIN Mexican Indian *mexcalli*

mescaline *n* a hallucinogenic drug derived from the button-like top of the mescal cactus

mesdames (may-**dam**) *n* ▸ the plural of **madame** or **madam** (sense 1)

mesdemoiselles (maid-mwah-**zel**) *n* ▸ the plural of **mademoiselle**

mesembryanthemum *n* a low-growing plant with fleshy leaves and bright daisy-like flowers
WORD ORIGIN Greek *mesēmbria* noon + *anthemon* flower

mesh ❶ *n* **1** a material resembling a net made from intersecting strands with a space between each strand **2** an open space between the strands of a net or network: *the minimum permitted size of fishing net mesh* **3** (*often pl*) the strands surrounding these spaces **4** anything that ensnares or holds like a net ▹ *adj* **5** made from mesh: *a wire mesh fence* ▹ *vb* **6** to entangle or become entangled **7** (of gear teeth) to engage or interlock **8** to fit together closely or work in harmony: *she schedules her holidays to mesh with theirs*
WORD ORIGIN probably Dutch *maesche*

mesmerize *or* **-ise** *vb* **-izing, -ized** *or* **-ising, -ised** **1** to fascinate and hold spellbound: *his voice had the entire audience mesmerized* **2** *archaic* to hypnotize **mesmerism** *n* **mesmerizing** *adj*

Mesolithic (mess-oh-**lith**-ik) *adj* of the middle period of the Stone Age, in Europe from about 12 000 to 3000 BC
WORD ORIGIN Greek *misos* middle + *lithos* stone

mesomorph *n physiol* a person with a muscular body build ▸ See also **ectomorph, endomorph** > **mesomorphic** *adj*
WORD ORIGIN Greek *misos* middle + *morphē* shape

meson (**mee**-zon) *n physics* any of a group of elementary particles that has a mass between those of an electron and a proton
WORD ORIGIN Greek *misos* middle + *-on*, indicating an elementary particle

mesosphere (**mess**-oh-sfeer) *n* the atmospheric layer above the stratosphere

Mesozoic (mess-oh-**zoh**-ik) *adj geol* of the geological era that began 225 million years ago and lasted about 155 million years, during which the dinosaurs emerged, flourished, then became extinct
WORD ORIGIN Greek *misos* middle + *zōion* animal

mess ❶ *n* **1** a state of untidiness or confusion, esp. a dirty or unpleasant one: *the house was in a mess* **2** a confused and difficult situation; muddle: *the firm is in a terrible financial mess* **3** *informal* a dirty or untidy person or thing: *there was a nasty burnt mess in the saucepan* **4** a building providing catering, and sometimes recreation, facilities for service personnel **5** a group of service personnel who regularly eat together **6** *old-fashioned* a portion of soft or runny food: *a mess of pottage* ▹ *vb* **7** (of service personnel) to eat in a group ▸ See also **mess about, mess up, mess with**
WORD ORIGIN Old French *mes* dish of food

mess about *or* **around** *vb* **1** to pass the time doing trivial or silly things without any particular purpose or plan: *messing about in boats* **2** to interfere or meddle: *you have no business messing around here* **3** *chiefly US* to engage in adultery

message ❶ *n* **1** a communication from one person or group to another **2** an implicit meaning or moral, as in a work of art **3** a religious or political belief that someone attempts to communicate to others: *paintings with a fierce feminist message* **4** **get the message** *informal* to understand
WORD ORIGIN Old French, from Latin *mittere* to send

message board *n* an internet discussion forum

Messager *n* **André** (**Charles Prosper**) 1853–1929, French composer and conductor

messages *pl n Scot & NE English dialect* household shopping

messaging *n* the sending of a message by any form of electronic communication: *text messaging*

Messalina *n* **Valeria** died 48 AD, wife of the Roman emperor Claudius, notorious for her debauchery and cruelty

messenger ❶ *n* a person who takes messages from one person or group to another
WORD ORIGIN Old French *messagier*

Messerschmitt *n* **Willy** 1898–1978, German aeronautical engineer. His military planes figured prominently in World War II, including the Me-262, the first jet fighter

Messiaen *n* **Olivier** 1908–92, French composer and organist. His music is distinguished by its rhythmic intricacy; he was influenced by Hindu and Greek rhythms and bird song

Messiah *n* **1** *judaism* the awaited king of the Jews, who will be sent by God to free them **2** *Christianity* Jesus Christ, when regarded in this role **3** a liberator of a country or people
WORD ORIGIN Hebrew *māshīach* anointed

Messianic *adj* **1** of or relating to a Messiah, or the arrival on Earth of a Messiah **2** **messianic** of or relating

THESAURUS

rollicking, convivial, gleeful, blithe, frolicsome, mirthful, sportive, light-hearted, jocund, gay, blithesome **OPPOSITE:** gloomy **2** (*Brit informal*) = **tipsy**, happy, elevated (*informal*), mellow, tiddly (*slang, chiefly Brit*), squiffy (*Brit informal*)

mesh *n* **1** = **net**, netting, network, web, tracery ▹ *vb* **8** = **engage**, combine, connect, knit, come together, coordinate, interlock, dovetail, fit together, harmonize

mess *n* **1** = **untidiness**, disorder, confusion, chaos, turmoil, litter, clutter, disarray, jumble, disorganization, grot (*slang*), dirtiness **2a** = **shambles**, botch, hash, cock-up (*Brit slang*), state, bodge (*informal*), pig's breakfast (*informal*) **2b** = **difficulty**, dilemma, plight, spot (*informal*), hole (*informal*), fix (*informal*), jam (*informal*), hot water (*informal*), stew (*informal*), mix-up, muddle, pickle (*informal*), uphill (*S African*), predicament, deep water, perplexity, tight spot, imbroglio, fine kettle of fish (*informal*)

message *n* **1** = **communication**, note, bulletin, word, letter, notice, memo, dispatch, memorandum, communiqué, missive, intimation, tidings, e-mail, text **2** = **point**, meaning, idea, moral, theme, import, purport

messenger *n* = **courier**, agent, runner, carrier, herald, envoy, bearer, go-between, emissary, harbinger, delivery boy, errand boy

DICTIONARY

to the belief that someone or something will bring about a complete transformation of the existing social order: *a messianic zeal for the free market*

messieurs (may-syuh) *n* ▸ the plural of **monsieur**

mess jacket *n* a waist-length jacket, worn by officers in the mess for formal dinners

mess kit *n* a soldier's eating utensils for use in the field

Messrs (mess-erz) *n* ▸ the plural of **Mr**

mess up *vb informal* **1** to make untidy or dirty **2** to spoil something, or do something badly: *he messed up his driving test*

mess with ⓣ *vb informal chiefly US* to interfere in, or become involved with, a dangerous person, thing, or situation: *he had started messing with drugs*

messy ⓣ *adj* **messier, messiest** **1** untidy **2** dirty **3** unpleasantly confused or complicated: *the messy, uncontrollable world of real life* **messily** *adv* **messiness** *n*

Meštrović *n* **Ivan** 1883–1962, US sculptor, born in Austria: his works include portraits of Sir Thomas Beecham and Pope Pius XI

met *vb* ▸ the past of **meet**[1]

Met *adj* **1** Meteorological: *the Met Office* ▹ *n* **2 the Met** the Metropolitan Police, who operate in London

metabolic syndrome *n* a condition associated with obesity, which increases the risk of cardiovascular disease and diabetes

metabolism (met-**tab**-ol-liz-zum) *n* the chemical processes that occur in living organisms, resulting in growth, production of energy, and elimination of waste **metabolic** *adj*
WORD ORIGIN Greek *metaballein* to change

metabolize *or* **-lise** *vb* **-lizing, -lized** *or* **-lising, -lised** to produce or be produced by metabolism

metacarpus *n, pl* **-pi** the set of five long bones in the hand between the wrist and the fingers **metacarpal** *adj, n*
WORD ORIGIN Greek *meta* after + *karpos* wrist

metal *n* **1 a** *chem* a chemical element, such as iron or copper, that reflects light and can be shaped, forms positive ions, and is a good conductor of heat and electricity **b** an alloy, such as brass or steel, containing one or more of these elements **2** ▸ short for **road metal** **3** *informal* ▸ short for **heavy metal** **4 metals** the rails of a railway ▹ *adj* **5** made of metal
WORD ORIGIN Greek *metallon* mine

metalanguage *n* the language or system of symbols used to discuss another language or system

metalled *or US* **metaled** *adj* (of a road) surfaced with crushed rock or small stones: *a metalled driveway*

metallic *adj* **1** of or consisting of metal **2** sounding like two pieces of metal hitting each other: *a metallic click* **3** (of a voice) harsh, unpleasant, and unemotional **4** shining like metal: *metallic paint* **5** (of a taste) unpleasantly harsh and bitter

metalliferous *adj* containing a metallic element
WORD ORIGIN Latin *metallum* metal + *ferre* to bear

metallography *n* the study of the composition and structure of metals

metalloid *n chem* a nonmetallic element, such as arsenic or silicon, that has some of the properties of a metal

metallurgy *n* the scientific study of the structure, properties, extraction, and refining of metals **metallurgical** *adj* **metallurgist** *n*
WORD ORIGIN *metal* + Greek *-urgia*, from *ergon* work

metal road *n NZ* an unsealed road covered in gravel

metalwork *n* **1** the craft of making articles from metal **2** articles made from metal **3** the metal part of something **metalworker** *n*

metamorphic *adj* **1** (of rocks) altered considerably from the original structure and composition by pressure and heat **2** of metamorphosis or metamorphism

metamorphism *n* the process by which metamorphic rocks are formed

metamorphose *vb* **-phosing, -phosed** to change from one state or thing into something different: *the media personality metamorphosed into society hostess*

metamorphosis (met-a-**more**-foss-is) *n, pl* **-ses** (-seez) **1** a complete change of physical form or substance **2** a complete change of character or appearance **3** *zool* the change of form that accompanies transformation into an adult in certain animals, for example the butterfly or frog
WORD ORIGIN Greek: transformation, from *meta* after + *morphē* form

metaphor ⓣ *n* a figure of speech in which a word or phrase is applied to an object or action that it does not literally apply to in order to imply a resemblance, for example *he is a lion in battle* **metaphorical** *adj* **metaphorically** *adv*
WORD ORIGIN Greek *metapherein* to transfer

metaphysical *adj* **1** of metaphysics **2** abstract, abstruse, or unduly theoretical

Metaphysical *adj* denoting certain 17th-century poets who combined intense feeling with elaborate imagery

metaphysics *n* **1** the philosophical study of the nature of reality **2** abstract or subtle discussion or reasoning
WORD ORIGIN Greek *ta meta ta phusika* the things after the physics, from the arrangement of subjects treated in the works of Aristotle

Metastasio *n* **Pietro**, original name *Pietro Antonio Domenico Trapassi*. 1698–1782, Italian poet and librettist; Viennese court poet (from 1730). His works include *La clemenza di Tito* (1732)

metastasis (mit-**tass**-tiss-iss) *n, pl* **-ses** (-seez) **1** *pathol* the spreading of a disease, esp. cancer, from one part of the body to another **2** the spreading of a problem into new areas **metastasize** *or* **-sise** *vb*
WORD ORIGIN Greek: transition

metatarsus *n, pl* **-si** the set of five long bones in the foot between the toes and the ankle **metatarsal** *adj, n*
WORD ORIGIN Greek *meta* after + *tarsos* instep

metathesis (mit-**tath**-iss-iss) *n, pl* **-ses** (-seez) the transposition of two sounds or letters in a word
WORD ORIGIN Greek *metatithenai* to transpose

metazoan (met-a-**zoh**-an) *n* **1** any animal having a body composed of many cells: includes all animals except sponges and protozoans ▹ *adj* **2** of the metazoans
WORD ORIGIN New Latin *Metazoa*

Metchnikoff *n* **Élie** 1845–1916, Russian bacteriologist in France. He formulated the theory of phagocytosis and shared the Nobel prize for physiology or medicine 1908

meteor *n* **1** a small piece of rock or metal that has entered the earth's atmosphere from space **2** Also:

m

THESAURUS

mess with something *or* **someone** ▹ *vb* **= interfere with**, play with, fiddle with *(informal)*, tamper with, tinker with, meddle with

messy *adj* **1a = disorganized**, sloppy *(informal)*, untidy, slovenly **1b = untidy**, disordered, littered, chaotic, muddled, cluttered, shambolic, disorganized, daggy *(Austral & NZ informal)* **OPPOSITE:** tidy **2a = dirty**, grubby, grimy, scuzzy *(slang, chiefly US)* **2b = dishevelled**, ruffled, untidy, rumpled, bedraggled, unkempt, tousled, uncombed, daggy *(Austral & NZ informal)* **3 = confusing**, difficult, complex, confused, tangled, chaotic,

DICTIONARY

shooting star the bright streak of light appearing in the sky due to a piece of rock or metal burning up because of friction as it falls through the atmosphere
WORD ORIGIN Greek *meteōros* lofty
meteoric (meet-ee-or-rik) *adj* **1** of or relating to meteors **2** brilliant and very rapid: *his meteoric rise to power* **meteorically** *adv*
meteorite *n* the rocklike remains of a meteoroid that has collided with the earth
meteoroid *n* any of the small celestial bodies that are thought to orbit the sun. When they enter the earth's atmosphere, they become visible as meteors
meteorol. *or* **meteor.** **1** meteorological **2** meteorology
meteorology *n* the study of the earth's atmosphere and weather-forming processes, esp. for weather forecasting **meteorological** *adj* **meteorologist** *n*
mete out *vb* **meting, meted** to impose or deal out something, usually something unpleasant: *the sentence meted out to him has proved controversial*
WORD ORIGIN Old English *metan* to measure
meter¹ *n* **1** any device that measures and records the quantity or number of units of something that was used during a specified period or is being used at that moment: *a gas meter* **2** ▸ short for **parking meter** **3** ▸ short for **taximeter** ▹ *vb* **4** to measure the amount of something used or a rate of flow with a meter
WORD ORIGIN Old English *metan* to measure
meter² *n US* ▸ same as **metre¹** or **metre²**
-meter *n combining form* **1** indicating an instrument for measuring: *barometer* **2** *prosody* indicating a verse having a specified number of feet: *pentameter*
WORD ORIGIN Greek *metron* measure
methadone *n* a drug similar to morphine, sometimes prescribed as a heroin substitute
WORD ORIGIN *(di)meth(yl)* + *a(mino)* + *d(iphenyl)* + *-one*, indicating a ketone
methamphetamine *n* a variety of amphetamine used for its stimulant action
methanal *n* ▸ same as **formaldehyde**
methane *n* a colourless odourless flammable gas, the main constituent of natural gas
WORD ORIGIN *meth(yl)* + *-ane*, indicating an alkane
methane series *n* a series of saturated hydrocarbons with the general formula C_nH_{2n+2}
methanol *n* a colourless poisonous liquid used as a solvent and fuel. Also: **methyl alcohol**
WORD ORIGIN *methane* + *-ol*, indicating alcohol
methicillin *n* a semisynthetic penicillin used to treat various infections
methinks *vb, past* **methought** *archaic* it seems to me that
method ⓘ *n* **1** a way of doing something, esp. a systematic or regular one **2** orderliness of thought or action **3** the techniques of a particular field or subject
WORD ORIGIN Greek *methodos*, literally: a going after
Method *n* an acting technique in which the actor bases his or her role on the inner motivation of the character played
methodical *adj* careful, well-organized, and systematic **methodically** *adv*
Methodist *n* **1** a member of any of the Christian Nonconformist denominations that derive from the beliefs and practices of John Wesley and his followers ▹ *adj* **2** of or relating to Methodists or their Church **Methodism** *n*
Methodius *n* **Saint,** with his younger brother Saint Cyril called *the Apostles of the Slavs*. 815–885 AD, Greek Christian theologian sent as a missionary to the Moravians. Feast day: Feb 14 or May 11
methodology *n, pl* **-gies** **1** the system of methods and principles used in a particular discipline **2** the philosophical study of method **methodological** *adj*
methought *vb archaic* ▸ the past tense of **methinks**
meths *n Brit, Austral & NZ informal* methylated spirits
methyl *adj* of or containing the monovalent saturated hydrocarbon group of atoms CH_3–: *methyl mercury*
WORD ORIGIN from *methylene*
methyl alcohol *n* ▸ same as **methanol**
methylate *vb* **-ating, -ated** to mix with methanol
methylated spirits *n* alcohol that has been rendered undrinkable by the addition of methanol and a violet dye, used as a solvent or as a fuel for small lamps or heaters. Also: **methylated spirit**
methylene *adj* of, consisting of, or containing the divalent group of atoms $-CH_2-$: *a methylene group or radical*
WORD ORIGIN Greek *methu* wine + *hulē* wood + *-ene*, indicating a double bond
meticulous *adj* very precise about details; careful and thorough **meticulously** *adv* **meticulousness** *n*
WORD ORIGIN Latin *meticulosus* fearful
métier (met-ee-ay) *n* **1** a profession or trade **2** a person's strong point or speciality
WORD ORIGIN French
Métis (met-teess) *n, pl* **-tis** (-teess, -teez) a person of mixed parentage, esp. the offspring of a Native American and a French Canadian **Métisse** *fem n*
WORD ORIGIN French
metonymy (mit-on-im-ee) *n, pl* **-mies** a figure of speech in which one thing is replaced by another associated with it, for instance the use of *Downing Street* to mean *the British government*
WORD ORIGIN Greek *meta-*, indicating change + *onoma* name
metre¹ *or US* **meter** *n* the basic SI unit of length, equal to 100 centimetres (39.37 inches): *the majority of people are between one and a half and two metres tall*
WORD ORIGIN same as METRE²
metre² *or US* **meter** *n* **1** *prosody* the rhythmic arrangement of syllables in verse, usually according to the number and kind of feet in a line **2** *music chiefly US* the rhythmic arrangement of the beat in a piece of music
WORD ORIGIN Greek *metron* measure
metre-kilogram-second *n* ▸ see **mks units**
metric *adj* of or relating to the metre or metric system: *use either all metric or all imperial measurements*
metrical *or* **metric** *adj* **1** of or relating to measurement **2** of or in poetic metre **metrically** *adv*
metricate *vb* **-cating, -cated** to convert a measuring system or instrument to metric units **metrication** *n*
metric system *n* any decimal system of units based on the metre. For scientific purposes SI units are used
metric ton *n* (not in technical use) a tonne
metro *n, pl* **-ros** an urban, usually underground, railway system in certain cities, such as Paris
WORD ORIGIN French, from *chemin de fer métropolitain* metropolitan railway
metronome *n* a device which indicates the speed music should be

m

THESAURUS

tortuous
metaphor *n* = **figure of speech,** image, symbol, analogy, emblem, conceit *(literary)*, allegory, trope, figurative expression
method *n* **1** = **manner,** process, approach, technique, way, plan, course, system, form, rule, programme, style, practice, fashion, scheme, arrangement, procedure, routine, mode, modus operandi **2** = **orderliness,** planning, order, system, form, design, structure, purpose, pattern, organization, regularity

played at by producing a clicking sound from a pendulum with an adjustable period of swing
WORD ORIGIN Greek *metron* measure + *nomos* law

metropolis (mit-trop-oh-liss) *n* the main city of a country or region
WORD ORIGIN Greek *mētēr* mother + *polis* city

metropolitan *adj* **1** of or characteristic of a metropolis **2** of or consisting of a city and its suburbs: *the Tokyo metropolitan region* **3** of or belonging to the home territories of a country, as opposed to overseas territories: *metropolitan France* ▹*n* **4** *Christianity* the senior clergyman, esp. an archbishop, in charge of an ecclesiastical province **5** an inhabitant of a large city

-metry *n combining form* indicating the process or science of measuring: *geometry* **-metric** *adj combining form*
WORD ORIGIN Greek *metron* measure

Metsys *n* a variant spelling of (Quentin) **Massys**

mettle *n* **1** courage or spirit: *the lack of mettle evident among British politicians* **2** character or abilities: *the mettle saints are made of* **3 on one's mettle** roused to making one's best efforts
WORD ORIGIN variant of *metal*

Meung *n* See **Jean de Meung**

MeV million electronvolts (10^6 electronvolts)

mew[1] *n* **1** the characteristic high-pitched cry of a cat; meow ▹*vb* **2** to make such a sound
WORD ORIGIN imitative

mew[2] *n* a seagull
WORD ORIGIN Old English *mǣw*

mewl *vb* **1** (esp. of a baby) to cry weakly; whimper ▹*n* **2** a weak or whimpering cry
WORD ORIGIN imitative

mews *n chiefly Brit* **1** a yard or street lined by buildings originally used as stables but now often converted into dwellings ▹*adj* **2** (of a flat or house) located in a mews: *a mews cottage*
WORD ORIGIN plural of *mew*, originally referring to royal stables built on the site of hawks' mews (cages)

Mex. 1 Mexican **2** Mexico

Mexican *adj* **1** of Mexico ▹*n* **2** a person from Mexico

Mexican wave *n* the rippling effect produced when the spectators in successive sections of a sports stadium stand up while raising their arms and then sit down
WORD ORIGIN first seen at the World Cup finals in *Mexico* in 1986

Meyerbeer *n* **Giacomo**, real name *Jakob Liebmann Beer*. 1791–1864, German composer, esp. of operas, such as *Robert le diable* (1831) and *Les Huguenots* (1836)

Meyerhof *n* **Otto (Fritz)** 1884–1951, German physiologist, noted for his work on the metabolism of muscles. He shared the Nobel prize for physiology or medicine 1922

Meyerhold *n* **Vsevolod Emilievich**, original name *Karl Theodor Kasimir*. 1874–*c*. 1940, Russian theatre director, noted for his experimental nonrealistic productions. He was arrested in 1939 and died in custody

mezzanine (mez-zan-een) *n* an intermediate storey, esp. one between the ground and first floor
WORD ORIGIN Italian *mezzano* middle

mezzo (met-so) *adv* **1** *music* moderately; quite: *mezzo-forte* ▹*n, pl* **-zos 2** ▸short for **mezzo-soprano**
WORD ORIGIN Italian: half

mezzo-soprano *n, pl* **-nos 1** a female voice lower than soprano but higher than contralto **2** a singer with such a voice

mezzotint (met-so-tint) *n* **1** a method of engraving done by scraping and burnishing the roughened surface of a copper plate **2** a print made from a plate so treated
WORD ORIGIN Italian *mezzotinto* half tint

mg milligram

Mg *chem* magnesium

M. Glam Mid Glamorgan

Mgr 1 manager **2** monseigneur **3** monsignor

MHz megahertz

mi *n music* ▸same as **me**[2]

MI Michigan

MI5 Military Intelligence, section five; the part of the British security services which combats spying and subversion in Britain

MI6 Military Intelligence, section six; the part of the British security services which spies on other countries. Also called: **SIS**

Miandad *n* **Javed** born 1957, Pakistani cricketer, a famous batsman; played for Pakistan 1976–94; national team coach 1999–2001

miasma (mee-azz-ma) *n, pl* **-mata** *or* **-mas** an unwholesome or foreboding atmosphere
WORD ORIGIN Greek: defilement

mica (my-ka) *n* any of a group of minerals consisting of flakelike crystals of aluminium or potassium silicates. They have a high resistance to electricity and heat
WORD ORIGIN Latin: crumb

mice *n* ▸the plural of **mouse**

Michael *n* **1** 1596–1645, tsar of Russia (1613–45); founder of the Romanov dynasty **2** born 1921, king of Romania (1927–30, as part of a three-part regency; 1940–47), who relinquished the throne (1930–40) in favour of his father, Carol II. He led the coup d'état that overthrew (1944) Antonescu but was forced to abdicate (1947) by the Communists **3 Saint Michael** *bible* one of the archangels. Feast day: Sept 29 or Nov 8

Michaelmas (mik-kl-mass) *n* Sept 29, the feast of St Michael the archangel: one of the four quarter days in England, Ireland, and Wales

Michaelmas daisy *n Brit* a garden plant with small daisy-shaped purple, pink, or white flowers in autumn

Michael VIII *n* surnamed *Palaeologus*. 1224–82, Byzantine emperor (1259–82); founder of the Palaeologan dynasty. His reign saw the recovery of Constantinople from the Latins (1261) and the reunion (1274) of the Greek and Roman churches

Michelet *n* **Jules** 1798–1874, French historian, noted esp. for his *Histoire de France* (17 vols, 1833–67)

Michelin *n* **André** 1853–1931, French industrialist; founder, with his brother **Édouard Michelin** (1859–1940), of the Michelin Tyre Company (1888): the first to use demountable pneumatic tyres on motor vehicles

Michelozzo *n* full name *Michelozzo di Bartolommeo*. 1396–1472, Italian architect and sculptor. His most important design was the Palazzo Riccardo for the Medici family in Florence (1444–59)

Michelson *n* **Albert Abraham** 1852–1931, US physicist, born in Germany: noted for his part in the Michelson-Morley experiment: Nobel prize for physics 1907

Mick *n offensive slang* an Irishman
WORD ORIGIN nickname for *Michael*

mickey *n* **take the mickey (out of)** *informal* to tease (someone)
WORD ORIGIN origin unknown

Mickey Finn *n slang* a drink containing a drug to make the drinker unconscious
WORD ORIGIN origin unknown

Mickey Mouse *adj slang* trivial, insignificant, or amateurish: *a Mickey Mouse survey*
WORD ORIGIN after the cartoon character created by Walt Disney

Mickiewicz *n* **Adam** 1798–1855, Polish poet, whose epic *Thaddeus* (1834) is regarded as a masterpiece of Polish literature

mickle *or* **muckle** *Archaic or Scot & N English dialect adj* **1** large or abundant ▹*adv* **2** much; greatly ▹*n* **3** a great amount
WORD ORIGIN Old Norse *mikell*

micro *n, pl* **micros** ▸short for **microcomputer** or **microprocessor**

micro- *or* **micr-** *combining form* **1** small or minute: *microdot* **2** involving the use of a microscope: *microscopy* **3** denoting 10^{-6}: *microsecond*
WORD ORIGIN Greek *mikros* small

microbe *n* any microscopic organism, esp. a disease-causing bacterium **microbial** *or* **microbic** *adj*
WORD ORIGIN MICRO- + Greek *bios* life

microbiology *n* the branch of biology involving the study of microorganisms

DICTIONARY

microblog *n* a blog in which there is a limitation on the length of individual postings **microblogger** *n* **microblogging** *n*
microchemistry *n* chemical experimentation with minute quantities of material
microchip *n* a tiny wafer of semiconductor material, such as silicon, containing an integrated circuit. Often shortened to: **chip**
microcircuit *n* a miniature electronic circuit in which a number of permanently connected components are contained in one small chip of semiconducting material
microcomputer *n* a compact computer in which the central processing unit is contained in one or more silicon chips
microcosm *n* **1** a miniature representation of something: *this area is a microcosm of France as a whole* **2** man regarded as epitomizing the universe **3 in microcosm** on a small scale **microcosmic** *adj*
WORD ORIGIN Greek *mikros kosmos* little world
microdot *n* a greatly reduced photographic copy (about the size of a pinhead) of a document
microeconomics *n* the branch of economics concerned with particular commodities, firms, or individuals and the relationships between them
microelectronics *n* the branch of electronics concerned with microcircuits
microfiche (my-kroh-feesh) *n* ▸ same as **fiche**
WORD ORIGIN French, from MICRO- + *fiche* small card
microfilm *n* **1** a strip of film on which books or documents can be recorded in miniaturized form ▹ *vb* **2** to photograph a page or document on microfilm
microlight *or* **microlite** *n* a very small private aircraft with large wings
micrometer (my-krom-it-er) *n* an instrument for the accurate measurement of small distances or angles
microminiaturization *or* **-isation** *n* the production and use of very small electronic components
micron (my-kron) *n* a unit of length equal to one millionth of a metre
WORD ORIGIN Greek *mikros* small
microorganism *n* any organism of microscopic size, such as a virus or bacterium
microphone *n* a device for converting sound into electrical energy
microprocessor *n computers* a single integrated circuit which acts as the central processing unit in a small computer
microscope *n* **1** an optical instrument that uses a lens or combination of lenses to produce a greatly magnified image of a small, close object **2** any instrument, such as the electron microscope, for producing a greatly magnified visual image of a small object
microscopic *adj* **1** too small to be seen except with a microscope **2** very small; minute **3** of or using a microscope **microscopically** *adv*
microscopy *n* the use of microscopes
microsecond *n* one millionth of a second
microstructure *n* a structure on a microscopic scale, such as that of a metal or a cell
microsurgery *n* intricate surgery performed using a special microscope and miniature precision instruments
microwave *n* **1** an electromagnetic wave with a wavelength of between 0.3 and 0.001 metres: used in radar and cooking **2** ▸ short for **microwave oven** ▹ *vb* **-waving, -waved 3** to cook in a microwave oven
microwave detector *n* a device used by police for recording the speed of a motorist
microwave oven *n* a type of cooker which uses microwaves to cook food quickly
micturate *vb* **-rating, -rated** to urinate **micturition** *n*
WORD ORIGIN Latin *micturire* to desire to urinate
mid[1] *n archaic* the middle
WORD ORIGIN Old English
mid[2] *or* **'mid** *prep poetic* amid
mid- *combining form* indicating a middle part, point, time, or position: *midday; mid-June; mid-Victorian*
midair *n* some point above ground level, in the air
midday ❶ *n* **1** twelve o'clock in the day; noon **2** the middle part of the day, from late morning to early afternoon: *the midday sun*
midden *n Austral & Brit* a dunghill or pile of refuse
WORD ORIGIN from Old Norse
middle ❶ *n* **1** an area or point equal in distance from the ends or edges of a place: *a hotel in the middle of town* **2** the time between the first part and last part of an event or period of time: *the middle of June; the film got a bit boring in the middle* **3** the part of the body around the stomach; waist **4 in the middle of** busy doing something: *I'm in the middle of washing the dishes* ▹ *adj* **5** equally distant from the ends or outer edges of something; central: *the middle finger* **6** having an equal number of elder and younger brothers and sisters: *he was the middle child of three* **7** intermediate in status or situation: *middle management* **8** avoiding extremes; moderate: *we must find a middle course between authoritarianism and anarchy*
WORD ORIGIN Old English *middel*
middle age *n* the period of life between youth and old age, usually considered to occur between the ages of 40 and 60 **middle-aged** *adj*
Middle Ages *n European history* **1** (broadly) the period from the fall of the W Roman Empire in 476 AD to the Italian Renaissance **2** (narrowly) the period from about 1000 AD to the 15th century
middle-age spread *or* **middle-aged spread** *n* the fat that appears round many people's waists when they become middle-aged
Middle America *n* the US middle class, esp. those groups that are politically conservative
middlebrow *disparaging n* **1** a person with conventional tastes and limited cultural appreciation ▹ *adj* **2** of or appealing to middlebrows
middle C *n music* the note written on the first ledger line below the treble staff or the first ledger line above the bass staff. On a piano it is near the middle of the keyboard
middle class ❶ *n* **1** the social class between the working and upper classes. It consists of business and professional people ▹ *adj* **middle-class 2** of or characteristic of the middle class
middle-distance *adj* **1** *athletics* of or being a race of a length between the sprints and the distance events, esp. the 800 or 1500 metres: *a middle-distance runner* ▹ *n* **middle distance 2** the part of a painting between the foreground and the far distance
middle ear *n* the sound-conducting part of the ear immediately inside the eardrum
Middle East *n* the area around the E Mediterranean, esp. Israel and the Arab countries from Turkey to North Africa and eastwards to Iran **Middle Eastern** *adj*
Middle England *n* a characterization of a predominantly middle-class,

m

THESAURUS

midday *n* **1 = noon**, twelve o'clock, noonday, noontime, twelve noon, noontide
middle *n* **1 = centre**, heart, inside, thick, core, midst, nucleus, hub, halfway point, midpoint, midsection ▹ *adj* **5 = central**, medium, inside, mid, intervening, inner, halfway, intermediate, median, medial **7 = intermediate**, inside, intervening, inner
middle-class *adj* **2 = bourgeois**, traditional, conventional, suburban, petit-bourgeois

DICTIONARY

middle-income section of British society, living mainly in suburban and rural England

Middle English *n* the English language from about 1100 to about 1450

Middle High German *n* High German from about 1200 to about 1500

Middle Low German *n* Low German from about 1200 to about 1500

middleman *n, pl* **-men 1** a trader who buys from the producer and sells to the consumer **2** an intermediary or go-between

middle name *n* **1** a name between a person's first name and surname **2** a characteristic quality for which a person is known: *danger is my middle name*

middle-of-the-road *adj* **1** not extreme, esp. in political views; moderate **2** of or denoting popular music of wide general appeal

middle school *n* (in England and Wales) a school for children aged between 8 or 9 and 12 or 13

Middleton[1] *n* a town in NW England, in Rochdale Unitary Authority, Greater Manchester. Pop: 45 314 (2001)

Middleton[2] *n* **1 Kate**, real name *Catherine Elizabeth*. born 1985, English fiancée of Prince William, to marry him in 2011 **2 Thomas** ?1570–1627, English dramatist. His plays include the tragedies *Women beware Women* (1621) and, in collaboration with William Rowley (?1585–?1642), *The Changeling* (1622) and the political satire *A Game at Chess* (1624)

middleweight *n* a professional boxer weighing up to 160 pounds (72.5 kg) or an amateur weighing up to 75 kg

middling ❶ *adj* **1** neither very good nor very bad **2** moderate in size **3 fair to middling** neither good nor bad, esp. in health ▹*adv* **4** *informal* moderately: *middling well*

Middx Middlesex

midfield *n soccer* the area between the two opposing defences

midge *n* a small mosquito-like biting insect occurring in dancing swarms, esp. near water
WORD ORIGIN Old English *mycge*

midget *n* **1** a dwarf whose skeleton and features are of normal proportions ▹*adj* **2** much smaller than normal: *a midget submarine*
WORD ORIGIN *midge* + *-et* small

MIDI *n* a system for transmitting information to electronic musical instruments
WORD ORIGIN *m(usical) i(nstrument) d(igital) i(nterface)*

midi- *combining form* of medium or middle size or length: *a midi-skirt*

midi system *n* a complete set of compact hi-fi sound equipment designed as a single unit

midland *n* the central or inland part of a country

Midlands *n* **1 the Midlands** the central counties of England ▹*adj* **2** of, in, or from the central counties of England: *a Midlands engineering firm*

midmost *adj, adv* in the middle or midst

midnight ❶ *n* **1** the middle of the night; 12 o'clock at night ▹*adj* **2** happening or apparent at midnight or in the middle of the night: *midnight Mass* **3 burn the midnight oil** to work or study late into the night

midnight sun *n* the sun visible at midnight during the summer inside the Arctic and Antarctic circles

mid-off *n cricket* the fielding position on the off side closest to the bowler

mid-on *n cricket* the fielding position on the on side closest to the bowler

midpoint *n* **1** the point on a line equally distant from either end **2** a point in time halfway between the beginning and end of an event

midriff *n* **1** the middle part of the human body between waist and chest **2** *anat* ▸same as **diaphragm** (sense 1)
WORD ORIGIN Old English *midhrif* mid belly

midshipman *n, pl* **-men** a naval officer of the lowest commissioned rank

midships *adv, adj naut* ▸see **amidships**

midst *n* **1 in our midst** among us **2 in the midst of a** surrounded by **b** at a point during

midsummer *n* **1** the middle or height of summer **2** ▸same as **summer solstice**

Midsummer's Day *or* **Midsummer Day** *n* June 24, the feast of St John the Baptist: one of the four quarter days in England, Ireland, and Wales

midtown *n US & Canad* the centre of a town

midway ❶ *adj* **1** in or at the middle of the distance; halfway: *the midway point* ▹*adv* **2** to the middle of the distance

midweek *n* the middle of the week

Midwest *n* the N central part of the US **Midwestern** *adj*

mid-wicket *n cricket* the fielding position on the on side, roughly the same distance from both wickets, and halfway towards the boundary

midwife *n, pl* **-wives** a person qualified to deliver babies and to care for women before, during, and after childbirth **midwifery** (mid-wiff-fer-ree) *n*
WORD ORIGIN Old English *mid* with + *wīf* woman

midwinter *n* **1** the middle or depth of winter **2** ▸same as **winter solstice**

mien (mean) *n literary* a person's manner, bearing, or appearance
WORD ORIGIN probably from obsolete *demean* appearance

Mies van der Rohe *n* **Ludwig** 1886–1969, US architect, born in Germany. He directed the Bauhaus (1929–33) and developed a functional style, characterized by geometrical design. His works include the Seagram building, New York (1958)

mifepristone (mi-fep-riss-tone) *n* ▸a technical name for **abortion pill**

miffed *adj informal* offended or upset
WORD ORIGIN perhaps imitative of bad temper

might[1] *vb* **1** ▸the past tense or subjunctive mood of **may**[1]: *he might have come* **2** (used as an auxiliary) expressing possibility: *he might well have gone already*. ▸See **may**[1] (sense 2)
WORD ORIGIN Old English *mihte*

might[2] ❶ *n* **1** great power, strength, or vigour **2 with all one's might** using all one's strength and energy **3 (with) might and main** ▸see **main**
WORD ORIGIN Old English *miht*

mighty ❶ *adj* **mightier, mightiest 1** powerful or strong **2** very great in extent or importance ▹*adv* **3** *informal chiefly US, Canad & Austral* very: *mighty hungry* **mightily** *adv* **mightiness** *n*

mignonette (min-yon-net) *n* a plant with spikes of small fragrant greenish-white flowers
WORD ORIGIN French, diminutive of *mignon* dainty

migraine (mee-grain) *n* a throbbing headache usually affecting only one side of the head and commonly accompanied by nausea and visual disturbances
WORD ORIGIN French, from Greek *hemi* half + *kranion* skull

migrant ❶ *n* **1** a person or animal that

THESAURUS

middling *adj* **1 = mediocre**, all right, indifferent, so-so *(informal)*, unremarkable, tolerable, run-of-the-mill, passable, serviceable, unexceptional, half-pie *(NZ informal)*, O.K. *or* okay *(informal)* **2 = moderate**, medium, average, fair, ordinary, modest, adequate, bog-standard *(Brit & Irish slang)*

midnight *n* **1 = twelve o'clock**, middle of the night, dead of night, twelve o'clock at night, the witching hour

midway *adv* **2 = halfway**, in the middle of, part-way, equidistant, at the midpoint, betwixt and between

might[2] *n* **1, 2 = power**, force, energy, ability, strength, capacity, efficiency, capability, sway, clout *(informal)*, vigour, prowess, potency, efficacy, valour, puissance, hard power

mighty *adj* **1 = powerful**, strong, strapping, robust, hardy, vigorous, potent, sturdy, stout, forceful, stalwart, doughty, lusty, indomitable, manful, puissant
OPPOSITE: weak

migrant *n* **1 = wanderer**, immigrant,

DICTIONARY

moves from one place to another ▹ *adj* **2** moving from one place to another: *migrant farm labourers*

migrate ❶ *vb* **-grating, -grated 1** to go from one place to settle in another, esp. in a foreign country **2** (of living creatures, esp. birds) to journey between different habitats at specific times of the year **migration** *n* **migratory** *adj*
WORD ORIGIN Latin *migrare* to change one's abode

mikado *n, pl* **-dos** *archaic* the Japanese emperor
WORD ORIGIN Japanese

mike *n informal* a microphone

mil *n photog* ▸ short for **millimetre**: *35-mil film*
WORD ORIGIN Latin *millesimus* thousandth

milady *n, pl* **-dies** (formerly) a continental title for an English gentlewoman

milch (miltch) *adj chiefly Brit* (esp. of cattle) kept for milk
WORD ORIGIN Old English *-milce* (in compounds)

mild ❶ *adj* **1** (of a taste or sensation) not strong; bland **2** gentle or temperate in character, climate, or behaviour **3** not extreme; moderate: *mild criticism of senior officers* **4** feeble; unassertive: *a mild protest* ▹ *n* **5** *Brit* a dark beer flavoured with fewer hops than bitter
WORD ORIGIN Old English *milde*

mildew *n* **1** a disease of plants caused by a parasitic fungus **2** ▸ same as **mould²** ▹ *vb* **3** to affect or become affected with mildew **mildewy** *adj*
WORD ORIGIN Old English *mildēaw* honey dew

mild steel *n* strong tough steel containing a small quantity of carbon

mile *n* **1** Also: **statute mile** a unit of length used in the UK, the US and certain other countries, equal to 1760 yards. 1 mile is equivalent to 1.60934 kilometres **2** ▸ see **nautical mile 3** Also: **miles** *informal* a great distance; great deal: *he missed by miles* **4** a race extending over a mile ▹ *adv* **5 miles** very much: *it's miles better than their first album*
WORD ORIGIN Latin *milia (passuum)* a thousand (paces)

mileage *n* **1** a distance expressed in miles **2** the total number of miles that a motor vehicle has travelled **3** the number of miles a motor vehicle will travel on one gallon of fuel **4** *informal* the usefulness or benefit of something: *the opposition is trying to make political mileage out of the issue*

mileometer *or* **milometer** (mile-om-it-er) *n Brit* a device that records the number of miles that a vehicle has travelled

milepost *n chiefly US & Canad* a signpost that shows the distance in miles to or from a place

miler *n* an athlete, horse, etc. that specializes in races of one mile

Miles *n* **Bernard,** Baron Miles of Blackfriars. 1907–91, British actor and theatre manager. He founded the Mermaid Theatre in London, and was known as a character actor

milestone *n* **1** a stone pillar that shows the distance in miles to or from a place **2** a significant event in a life or history: *a milestone in Turkish-Bulgarian relations*

milfoil *n* ▸ same as **yarrow**
WORD ORIGIN Latin *mille* thousand + *folium* leaf

Milhaud *n* **Darius** (darjys) 1892–1974, French composer; member of Les Six. A notable exponent of polytonality, his large output includes operas, symphonies, ballets, string quartets, and songs

milieu (meal-yuh) *n, pl* **milieux** *or* **milieus** (meal-yuhz) the social and cultural environment in which a person or thing exists: *the film takes for its milieu an apparently wholesome small town*
WORD ORIGIN French

militant ❶ *adj* **1** very active or aggressive in the support of a cause **2** *formal* warring; engaged in warfare ▹ *n* **3** a militant person **militancy** *n* **militantly** *adv*
WORD ORIGIN Latin *militare* to be a soldier

militarism *n* the pursuit of policies intended to create and maintain aggressive and influential armed forces **militarist** *n, adj* **militaristic** *adj*

militarized *or* **-ised** *adj* occupied by armed forces: *one of the most heavily militarized borders in the world* **militarization** *or* **-isation** *n*

military ❶ *adj* **1** of or relating to the armed forces or war **2** of or characteristic of soldiers ▹ *n* **3 the military** the armed services, esp. the army **militarily** *adv*
WORD ORIGIN Latin *miles* soldier

military police *n* a corps within an army that performs police duties

militate *vb* **-tating, -tated** (of facts or events) to have a strong influence or effect: *our position militated against counter-attacks*

militia (mill-ish-a) *n* a military force of trained civilians enlisted for use in emergency only **militiaman** *n*
WORD ORIGIN Latin: soldiery

milk ❶ *n* **1 a** a whitish fluid secreted by the mammary glands of mature female mammals and used for feeding their young **b** the milk of cows, goats, etc. used by humans as a food and to make cheese, butter, and yogurt **2** any similar fluid, such as the juice of a coconut ▹ *vb* **3** to draw milk from the udder of a cow or other animal **4** to extract as much money, help, or value as possible from: *he was accused of milking the situation for his own ends* **milker** *n* **milkiness** *n* **milky** *adj*
WORD ORIGIN Old English *milc*

milk-and-water *adj* weak, feeble, or insipid

milk bar *n* (formerly) a snack bar at which milk drinks and light refreshments are served

milk chocolate *n* chocolate that has been made with milk, having a creamy taste

milk float *n Brit* a small electrically powered vehicle used to deliver milk to houses

milkmaid *n* a girl or woman who milks cows

milkman *n, pl* **-men** *Brit, Austral & NZ* a man who delivers milk to people's houses

milk of magnesia *n* a suspension of magnesium hydroxide in water, used as an antacid and laxative

milk pudding *n* a pudding made by cooking milk with a grain, esp. rice

milk round *n* **1** *Brit & NZ* a route along which a milkman regularly delivers milk **2** *Brit* a regular series of visits

THESAURUS

traveller, gypsy, tinker, rover, transient, nomad, emigrant, itinerant, drifter, vagrant ▹ *adj* **2 = itinerant**, wandering, drifting, roving, travelling, shifting, immigrant, gypsy, transient, nomadic, migratory, vagrant

migrate *vb* **1 = move**, travel, journey, wander, shift, drift, trek, voyage, roam, emigrate, rove

mild *adj* **1 = bland**, thin, smooth, tasteless, insipid, flavourless **2a = gentle**, kind, easy, soft, pacific, calm, moderate, forgiving, tender, pleasant, mellow, compassionate, indulgent, serene, easy-going, amiable, meek, placid, docile, merciful, peaceable, forbearing, equable, easy-oasy *(slang)*, chilled *(informal)* **OPPOSITE:** harsh **2b = temperate**, warm, calm, moderate, clement, tranquil, balmy **OPPOSITE:** cold

militant *adj* **1, 2 = aggressive**, warring, fighting, active, combating, contending, vigorous, two-fisted, assertive, in arms, embattled, belligerent, combative **OPPOSITE:** peaceful

military *adj* **1, 2 = warlike**, armed, soldierly, martial, soldierlike **3 the military = the armed forces**, the forces, the services, the army

milk *vb* **4 = exploit**, use, pump, squeeze, drain, take advantage of, bleed, impose on, wring, fleece, suck dry

DICTIONARY

made by recruitment officers from industry to colleges

milk shake *n* a cold frothy drink made of milk, flavouring, and sometimes ice cream, whisked or beaten together

milksop *n* a feeble or ineffectual man or youth

milk tooth *n* any of the first set of teeth in young children

Milky Way *n* **1** the diffuse band of light stretching across the night sky that consists of millions of distant stars in our galaxy **2** the galaxy in which the Earth is situated
WORD ORIGIN translation of Latin *via lactea*

mill ❶ *n* **1** a building where grain is crushed and ground to make flour **2** a factory, esp. one which processes raw materials: *a steel mill* **3** any of various processing or manufacturing machines, esp. one that grinds, presses, or rolls **4** a small device for grinding solids: *a pepper mill* **5 go** *or* **be put through the mill** to have an unpleasant experience or ordeal ▹ *vb* **6** to grind, press, or process in or as if in a mill **7** to groove or flute the edge of a coin **8** to move about in a confused manner: *the corridor was full of people milling about*
WORD ORIGIN Latin *molere* to grind

Millay *n* **Edna St Vincent** 1892–1950, US poet, noted esp. for her sonnets; her collections include *The Buck in the Snow* (1928) and *Fatal Interview* (1931)

milled *adj* **1** crushed or ground in a mill: *freshly milled black pepper* **2** (of a coin) having a grooved and often raised edge

millennium (mill-en-nee-um) *n, pl* **-nia** (-nee-a) *or* **-niums 1** a period of one thousand years **2 the Millennium** *Christianity* the period of a thousand years of Christ's awaited reign upon earth **3** a future period of peace and happiness **millennial** *adj*
WORD ORIGIN Latin *mille* thousand + *annus* year

millennium bug *n computers* any software problem arising from the change in date at the start of the 21st century

millepede *n* ▸ same as **millipede**

miller *n history* a person who owns or operates a mill, esp. a corn mill

miller's thumb *n* a small freshwater European fish with a flattened body
WORD ORIGIN from the alleged likeness of the fish's head to a thumb

millesimal (mill-less-im-al) *adj* **1** denoting or consisting of a thousandth ▹ *n* **2** a thousandth part of something
WORD ORIGIN Latin *millesimus*

millet *n* a cereal grass cultivated for its edible grain and as animal fodder
WORD ORIGIN Latin *milium*

Millet *n* **Jean François** 1814–75, French painter of the Barbizon school, noted for his studies of peasants at work

Millett *n* **Kate** full name *Katherine Murray Millett.* born 1934, US feminist writer and artist; books include *Sexual Politics* (1969) and *The Politics of Cruelty* (1994)

milli- *combining form* denoting 10^{-3}: *millimetre*
WORD ORIGIN Latin *mille* thousand

milliard *n Brit* (no longer in technical use) a thousand million
WORD ORIGIN French

millibar *n* a unit of atmospheric pressure equal to 100 newtons per square metre

milligram *or* **milligramme** *n* one thousandth of a gram
WORD ORIGIN French

Millikan *n* **Robert Andrews** 1868–1953, US physicist. He measured the charge of an electron (1910), verified Einstein's equation for the photoelectric effect (1916), and studied cosmic rays; Nobel prize for physics 1923

millilitre *or US* **milliliter** *n* a measure of volume equivalent to one thousandth of a litre

millimetre *or US* **millimeter** *n* a unit of length equal to one thousandth of a metre

milliner *n* a person who makes or sells women's hats **millinery** *n*
WORD ORIGIN originally *Milaner* a native of *Milan,* once famous for its fancy goods

million *n, pl* **-lions** *or* **-lion 1** the number equal to one thousand thousands: 1 000 000 or 10^6 **2** (*often pl*) *informal* an extremely large but unspecified number: *I've got a million things to do today* **millionth** *n, adj*
WORD ORIGIN early Italian *millione*

millionaire *n* a person who has money or property worth at least a million pounds, dollars, etc. **millionairess** *fem n*

millipede *or* **millepede** *n* a small crawling animal with a cylindrical many-segmented body, each segment of which bears two pairs of legs
WORD ORIGIN Latin *mille* thousand + *pes* foot

millisecond *n* one thousandth of a second

millpond *n* a pool which provides water to turn a millwheel

millrace *n* the current of water that turns a millwheel

Mills *n* **1 Hayley** born 1946, British actress. Her films include *Pollyanna* (1960) and *The Parent Trap* (1961) **2** her father, Sir **John** 1908–2005, British actor. His films include *This Happy Breed* (1944), *Great Expectations* (1946), and *Ryan's Daughter* (1971)

millstone *n* **1** one of a pair of heavy flat stones that are rotated one against the other to grind grain **2** a heavy burden of responsibility or obligation: *the debt had become a millstone round his neck*

millstream *n* a stream of water used to turn a millwheel

millwheel *n* a water wheel that drives a mill

milometer (mile-om-it-er) *n* ▸ same as **mileometer**

milord *n* (formerly) a continental title used for an English gentleman
WORD ORIGIN from *my lord*

Miłosz *n* **Czeslaw** 1911–2004, US poet and writer, born in Lithuania, writing in Polish; author of *The Captive Mind* (1953). Nobel prize for literature 1980

Milstein *n* **Nathan** 1904–92, US violinist, born in Ukraine

milt *n* the male reproductive gland, sperm, or semen of a fish
WORD ORIGIN Old English *milte* spleen

Miltiades *n* ?540–?489 BC, Athenian general, who defeated the Persians at Marathon (490)

mime *n* **1** a style of acting using only gesture and bodily movement and not words **2** a performer specializing in this **3** a performance in this style ▹ *vb* **miming, mimed 4** to express or describe something in actions or gestures without using speech **5** (of musicians) to pretend to be singing or playing music that is actually prerecorded **mimer** *n*
WORD ORIGIN Greek *mimos* imitator

Mimeograph (mim-ee-oh-grahf) *n* **1** *trademark* an office machine for printing multiple copies from a stencil ▹ *vb* **2** to print copies using this machine

mimetic (mim-met-ik) *adj* **1** imitating or representing something: *most photographs are mimetic representations of the real world* **2** *biol* of or showing mimicry
WORD ORIGIN Greek *mimeisthai* to imitate

mimic ❶ *vb* **-icking, -icked 1** to imitate a person or a way of acting or speaking, esp. to entertain or make

m

THESAURUS

mill *n* **2 = factory**, works, shop, plant, workshop, foundry **4 = grinder**, crusher, quern ▹ *vb* **6 = grind**, pound, press, crush, powder, grate, pulverize, granulate, comminute **8 mill about** *or* **around = swarm**, crowd, stream, surge, seethe, throng

mimic *vb* **1 = imitate**, do (*informal*), take off (*informal*), ape, parody, caricature, impersonate ▹ *n* **4 = imitator**, impressionist, copycat (*informal*), impersonator, caricaturist,

DICTIONARY

fun of **2** to take on the appearance of: *certain flies mimic wasps* **3** to copy closely or in a servile manner: *social climbers in the colonies began to mimic their conquerors* ▹ *n* **4** a person or an animal, such as a parrot, that is clever at mimicking
WORD ORIGIN Greek *mimikos*

mimicry *n, pl* **-ries 1** the act or art of copying or imitating closely **2** *biol* the resemblance shown by one animal species to another dangerous or inedible one, which protects it from predators

mimosa *n* a tropical shrub with ball-like clusters of yellow flowers and leaves sensitive to touch and light
WORD ORIGIN Latin *mimus* mime, because the plant's sensitivity to touch imitates the similar reaction of animals

min. 1 minimum **2** minute *or* minutes

Min. 1 Minister **2** Ministry

Minamoto Yoritomo *n* 1147–99, Japanese nobleman; the first shogun (1192–99) of the feudal era

minaret *n* a slender tower of a mosque with one or more balconies
WORD ORIGIN Arabic *manārat* lamp

minatory *adj* threatening or menacing
WORD ORIGIN Latin *minari* to threaten

mince ❶ *vb* **mincing, minced 1** to chop, grind, or cut into very small pieces **2** to walk or speak in an affected dainty manner **3 not mince one's words** be direct and to the point rather than making an effort to avoid upsetting people ▹ *n* **4** *chiefly Brit & NZ* minced meat **minced** *adj* **mincer** *n*
WORD ORIGIN Old French *mincier*, from Late Latin *minutia* smallness

mincemeat *n* **1** a mixture of dried fruit and spices used for filling pies **2 make mincemeat of** *informal* to defeat completely

mince pie *n* a small round pastry tart filled with mincemeat

mincing ❶ *adj* (of a person or their style of walking or speaking) affectedly elegant

mind ❶ *n* **1** the part of a person responsible for thought, feelings, and intention ▸ Related adjective: **mental 2** intelligence as opposed to feelings or wishes **3** memory or recollection: *his name didn't spring to mind immediately* **4** a person considered as an intellectual being: *one of Europe's greatest minds* **5** the condition or state of a person's feelings or thoughts: *a confused state of mind* **6** an intention or desire: *I have a mind to go* **7** attention or thoughts: *keep your mind on the job* **8** a sound mental state; sanity: *he's out of his mind* **9 change one's mind** to alter one's decision or opinion **10 give someone a piece of one's mind** to scold someone severely **11 in two minds** undecided or wavering **12 make up one's mind** to reach a decision **13 on one's mind** in one's thoughts **14 to my mind** in my opinion ▹ *vb* **15** to take offence at: *do you mind if I open a window?* **16** to pay attention to: *to mind one's own business* **17** to make certain; ensure: *mind you tell him* **18** to take care of: *mind the shop* **19** to be cautious or careful about: *mind how you go* **20** *dialect* to remember ▸ See also **mind out**
WORD ORIGIN Old English *gemynd*

mind-boggling *adj* so large, complicated, or surprising that it causes surprise and shock: *mind-boggling wealth*

minded *adj* having a mind or inclination as specified: *commercially minded*

minder *n* **1** *slang* an aide or assistant, esp. one employed as a bodyguard or public relations officer for someone **2** ▸ short for **child minder**

mindful *adj* **mindful of** being aware of and taking into account: *the company is ever mindful of the need to find new markets*

mindless *adj* **1** stupid or careless **2** requiring little or no intellectual effort **3** heedless: *mindless of the risks involved* **mindlessly** *adv* **mindlessness** *n*

Mind Map *n trademark* a method of representing ideas in a diagram, with related concepts arranged around a core concept

mind out *vb* to be careful or pay attention

mind-reader *n* a person seemingly able to make out the thoughts of another

mind's eye *n* **in one's mind's eye** in one's imagination

Mindszenty *n* **Joseph** 1892–1975, Hungarian cardinal. He was sentenced to life imprisonment on a charge of treason (1949) but released during the 1956 Revolution

mine[1] *pron* **1** something or someone belonging to or associated with me: *it's a great favourite of mine* **2 of mine** belonging to or associated with me ▹ *adj* **3** *archaic* ▸ same as **my**: *mine eyes; mine host*
WORD ORIGIN Old English *mīn*

mine[2] ❶ *n* **1** a place where minerals, esp. coal, ores, or precious stones, are dug from the ground **2** a type of bomb placed in water or under the ground, and designed to destroy ships, vehicles, or people passing over or near it **3** a profitable source or abundant supply: *a mine of information* ▹ *vb* **mining, mined 4** to dig minerals from the ground: *lead has been mined here for over three centuries* **5** to dig a hole or tunnel, esp. in order to obtain minerals **6** to place explosive mines in or on: *the retreating troops had mined the bridge*
WORD ORIGIN Old French

mine dump *n S African* a large mound of waste material from gold-mining operations

minefield *n* **1** an area of ground or water containing explosive mines **2** a subject or situation full of hidden problems

minelayer *n* a warship or aircraft for carrying and laying mines

miner ❶ *n* a person who works in a mine, esp. a coal mine

mineral *n* **1** a naturally occurring solid inorganic substance with a characteristic chemical composition and structure **2** any inorganic matter **3** any substance obtained by mining, esp. a metal ore **4** *Brit* a soft

m

THESAURUS

parodist, parrot

mince *vb* **1 = cut**, grind, crumble, dice, hash, chop up

mincing *adj* **= affected**, nice, camp *(informal)*, precious, pretentious, dainty, sissy, effeminate, foppish, poncy *(slang)*, arty-farty *(informal)*, lah-di-dah *(informal)*, niminy-piminy

mind *n* **2 = intelligence**, reason, reasoning, understanding, sense, spirit, brain(s) *(informal)*, wits, mentality, intellect, grey matter *(informal)*, ratiocination **3 = memory**, recollection, remembrance, powers of recollection **6 = intention**, will, wish, desire, urge, fancy, purpose, leaning, bent, notion, tendency, inclination, disposition **8 = sanity**, reason, senses, judgment, wits, marbles *(informal)*, rationality, mental balance ▹ *vb* **15 = take offence at**, dislike, care about, object to, resent, disapprove of, be bothered by, look askance at, be affronted by **16 = pay attention to**, follow, mark, watch, note, regard, respect, notice, attend to, listen to, observe, comply with, obey, heed, adhere to, take heed of, pay heed to ▸ *related adjectives:* mental **18 = look after**, watch, protect, tend, guard, take care of, attend to, keep an eye on, have *or* take charge of **19 = be careful**, watch, take care, be wary, be cautious, be on your guard

mine[2] *n* **1 = pit**, deposit, shaft, vein, colliery, excavation, coalfield, lode **3 = source**, store, fund, stock, supply, reserve, treasury, wealth, abundance, hoard ▹ *vb* **4 = dig up**, extract, quarry, unearth, delve, excavate, hew, dig for

miner *n* **= coalminer**, pitman *(Brit)*, collier *(Brit)*

DICTIONARY

drink containing carbonated water and flavourings ▷ *adj* **5** of, containing, or resembling minerals **WORD ORIGIN** Medieval Latin *minera* mine, ore

mineralogy (min-er-al-a-jee) *n* the scientific study of minerals **mineralogical** *adj* **mineralogist** *n*

mineral water *n* water containing dissolved mineral salts or gases

Minerva *n* the Roman goddess of wisdom

minestrone (min-ness-strone-ee) *n* a soup made from a variety of vegetables and pasta **WORD ORIGIN** Italian, from *minestrare* to serve

minesweeper *n* a naval vessel equipped to clear mines

Ming *adj* of or relating to Chinese porcelain from the time of the Ming dynasty, which ruled China from 1368 to 1644

minger *n Brit informal* unattractive person

minging *n Brit informal* unattractive or unpleasant

mingle ❶ *vb* **-gling, -gled 1** to mix or blend **2** to associate or mix with a group of people: *the performers mingled with the audience after the show* **WORD ORIGIN** Old English *mengan* to mix

Mingus *n* **Charles,** known as *Charlie Mingus*. 1922–79, US jazz double bassist, composer, and band leader

mingy *adj* **-gier, -giest** *Brit & NZ informal* mean or miserly **WORD ORIGIN** probably a blend of *mean* + *stingy*

mini *adj* **1** small; miniature **2** (of a skirt or dress) very short ▷ *n, pl* **minis 3** something very small of its kind, esp. a miniskirt

mini- *combining form* smaller or shorter than the standard size: *minibus; miniseries* **WORD ORIGIN** from *miniature* + *minimum*

miniature ❶ *n* **1** a model or representation on a very small scale **2** a very small painting, esp. a portrait **3** a very small bottle of whisky or other spirits, which can hold 50 millilitres **4 in miniature** on a small scale ▷ *adj* **5** much smaller than usual; small-scale **miniaturist** *n* **WORD ORIGIN** Medieval Latin *miniare* to paint red (in illuminating manuscripts), from *minium* red lead

miniaturize *or* **-ise** *vb* **-izing, -ized** *or* **-ising, -ised** to make a very small version of something, esp. electronic components **miniaturization** *or* **-isation** *n*

minibus *n* a small bus

minicab *n Brit* an ordinary car used as a taxi

minicomputer *n* a small digital computer which is more powerful than a microcomputer

minidisc *n* a small recordable compact disc

minim *n* **1** a unit of fluid measure equal to one sixtieth of a drachm **2** *music* a note with the time value of half a semibreve **WORD ORIGIN** Latin *minimus* smallest

minimal ❶ *adj* of the least possible quantity or degree

minimalism *n* **1** a type of music based on the repetition of simple elements **2** a design or style using the simplest and fewest elements to create the maximum effect **minimalist** *adj, n*

minimize ❶ *or* **-mise** *vb* **-mizing, -mized** *or* **-mising, -mised 1** to reduce to the lowest possible degree or amount: *these measures should help minimize our costs* **2** to regard or treat as less important than it really is; belittle: *I don't want to minimize the importance of her contribution*

minimum ❶ *n, pl* **-mums** *or* **-ma 1** the least possible amount, degree, or quantity: *fry the burgers in the minimum of oil* **2** the least amount recorded, allowed, or reached: *soak the beans for a minimum of eight hours* ▷ *adj* **3** of, being, or showing a minimum or minimums: *the minimum age* **WORD ORIGIN** Latin *minimus* least

minimum lending rate *n* (formerly) the minimum rate at which the Bank of England would lend money: replaced in 1981 by the base rate

minimum wage *n* the lowest wage that an employer is permitted to pay by law or union contract

mining *n* **1** the act, process, or industry of extracting coal or ores from the earth **2** *mil* the process of laying mines

minion *n* a servile assistant **WORD ORIGIN** French *mignon* darling

miniseries *n, pl* **-series** a television programme in several parts that is shown on consecutive days over a short period

miniskirt *n* a very short skirt

minister ❶ *n* **1** (esp. in Presbyterian and some Nonconformist Churches) a member of the clergy **2** a head of a government department **3** a diplomat with a lower rank than an ambassador ▷ *vb* **4 minister to** to attend to the needs of **ministerial** *adj* **WORD ORIGIN** Latin: servant

minister of state *n* (in the British Parliament) a minister, usually below cabinet rank, appointed to assist a senior minister

Minister of the Crown *n Brit* any Government minister of cabinet rank

ministrations *pl n* the giving of help or service: *the ministrations of the chaplain* **WORD ORIGIN** Latin *ministrare* to wait upon

ministry ❶ *n, pl* **-tries 1** the profession or duties of a minister of religion **2** ministers considered as a group **3 a** a government department headed by a minister **b** the buildings of such a department

mink *n, pl* **mink** *or* **minks 1** a mammal of Europe, Asia, and North America, resembling a large stoat **2** its highly valued fur **3** a garment made of this, esp. a woman's coat or stole **WORD ORIGIN** Scandinavian

Minkowski *n* **Hermann** 1864–1909, German mathematician, born in Russia. His concept of a four-dimensional space-time continuum (1907) proved crucial for the general theory of relativity developed by Einstein

m

THESAURUS

mingle *vb* **1 = mix**, combine, blend, merge, unite, join, marry, compound, alloy, interweave, coalesce, intermingle, meld, commingle, intermix, admix **OPPOSITE:** separate **2 = associate**, circulate, hang out *(informal)*, consort, socialize, rub shoulders *(informal)*, hobnob, fraternize, hang about *or* around **OPPOSITE:** dissociate

miniature *adj* **5 = small**, little, minute, baby, reduced, tiny, pocket, toy, mini, wee, dwarf, scaled-down, diminutive, minuscule, midget, teeny-weeny, Lilliputian, teensy-weensy, pygmy *or* pigmy **OPPOSITE:** giant

minimal *adj* **= minimum**, smallest, least, slightest, token, nominal, negligible, least possible, littlest

minimize *vb* **1 = reduce**, decrease, shrink, diminish, prune, curtail, attenuate, downsize, miniaturize **OPPOSITE:** increase **2 = play down**, discount, underestimate, belittle, disparage, decry, underrate, deprecate, depreciate, make light *or* little of **OPPOSITE:** praise

minimum *n* **1 = lowest**, least, depth, slightest, lowest level, nadir, bottom level ▷ *adj* **3 = lowest**, smallest, least, slightest, minimal, least possible, littlest **OPPOSITE:** maximum

minister *n* **1 = clergyman**, priest, divine, vicar, parson, preacher, pastor, chaplain, cleric, rector, curate, churchman, padre *(informal)*, ecclesiastic **4 minister to = attend to**, serve, tend to, answer to, accommodate, take care of, cater to, pander to, administer to, be solicitous of

ministry *n* **1 = the priesthood**, the church, the cloth, the pulpit, holy orders **2 = administration**, government, council, cabinet

DICTIONARY

minneola *n* a juicy citrus fruit that is a cross between a tangerine and a grapefruit

minnow *n, pl* **-nows** *or* **-now** a small slender European freshwater fish
WORD ORIGIN Old English *myne*

Minoan (min-**no**-an) *adj* of or denoting the Bronze Age culture of Crete from about 3000 BC to about 1100 BC
WORD ORIGIN *Minos*, in Greek mythology, king of Crete

Minogue *n* **Kylie** born 1968, Australian singer and actress: appeared in the television series *Neighbours* from 1986; records include "I Should Be So Lucky" (1988), *Kylie Minogue* (1994), *Fever* (2001), and *X* (2007)

minor ❶ *adj* **1** lesser or secondary in size, frequency, or importance than others of the same kind: *a minor poet* **2** not very serious or significant: *minor injuries* **3** *music* **a** (of a scale) having a semitone between the second and third and fifth and sixth notes (**natural minor**) **b** of or based on the minor scale: *his quintet in C minor; a minor third* ▷ *n* **4** a person below the age of legal majority **5** *US, Canad & Austral education* a subsidiary subject **6** *music* a minor key, chord, mode, or scale ▷ *vb* **7 minor in** *US education* to study as a subsidiary subject: *to minor in politics*
WORD ORIGIN Latin: less, smaller

minority *n, pl* **-ties 1** the smaller of two parts, factions, or groups **2** a group that is different, esp. racially or politically, from a larger group of which it is a part **3 in the minority** forming or part of the group of people or things made up of less than half of a larger group ▷ *adj* **4** relating to or being a minority: *a minority sport*

Minotaur *n Greek myth* a monster with the head of a bull and the body of a man
WORD ORIGIN Greek *Minōtauros*

minster *n Brit* any of certain cathedrals and large churches, usually originally connected to a monastery
WORD ORIGIN Church Latin *monasterium* monastery

minstrel *n* **1** a medieval singer and musician **2** a performer in a minstrel show
WORD ORIGIN Old French *menestral*

minstrel show *n* a theatrical entertainment consisting of songs and dances performed by actors wearing black face make-up

mint[1] *n* **1** any of various plants with aromatic leaves used for seasoning and flavouring **2** a sweet flavoured with mint **minty** *adj*
WORD ORIGIN Greek *minthē*

mint[2] ❶ *n* **1** a factory where the official coins of a country are made **2** a very large amount of money ▷ *adj* **3 in mint condition** in perfect condition; as if new ▷ *vb* **4** to make coins by stamping metal **5** to invent or create: *no-one knows who first minted the term 'yuppie'*
WORD ORIGIN Latin *moneta* money, mint

minuet (min-new-**wet**) *n* **1** a stately court dance of the 17th and 18th centuries in triple time **2** music for this dance
WORD ORIGIN French *menuet* dainty

minus *prep* **1** reduced by the subtraction of: *six minus two equals four* **2** *informal* without or lacking: *he returned minus his jacket* ▷ *adj* **3** indicating or involving subtraction: *a minus sign* **4** Also: **negative** less than zero: *it's minus eight degrees in Montreal today* **5** *education* slightly below the standard of a particular grade: *a C minus for maths* ▷ *n* **6** ▸ short for **minus sign 7** a negative quantity **8** *informal* something detrimental or negative
WORD ORIGIN Latin, neuter of *minor* less

minuscule (min-niss-skyool) *adj* very small
WORD ORIGIN Latin *(littera) minuscula* very small (letter)

minus sign *n* the symbol –, indicating subtraction, a negative quantity, or a negative electrical charge

minute[1] ❶ *n* **1** 60 seconds; one sixtieth of an hour **2** any very short period of time; moment: *I'll be with you in a minute* **3** the distance that can be travelled in a minute: *it's about ten minutes away* **4** a measure of angle equal to one sixtieth of a degree **5 up to the minute** the very latest or newest ▷ *vb* **-uting, -uted 6** to record in minutes: *the decision was minuted in 1990* ▸ See also **minutes**
WORD ORIGIN Medieval Latin *minuta*, noun use of Latin *minutus* minute (small)

minute[2] ❶ *adj* **1** very small; tiny **2** precise or detailed: *a minute examination* **minutely** *adv*
WORD ORIGIN Latin *minutus*, past participle of *minuere* to diminish

minutes ❶ *pl n* an official record of the proceedings of a meeting or conference

minute steak *n* a small piece of steak that can be cooked quickly

minutiae (my-**new**-shee-eye) *pl n, sing* **-tia** trifling or precise details
WORD ORIGIN Late Latin, plural of *minutia* smallness

minx *n* a bold or flirtatious girl
WORD ORIGIN origin unknown

Miocene (**my**-oh-seen) *adj geol* of the epoch of geological time about 25 million years ago
WORD ORIGIN Greek *meiōn* less + *kainos* new

Mirabeau *n* **Comte de,** title of *Honoré-Gabriel Riqueti*. 1749–91, French Revolutionary politician

miracle ❶ *n* **1** an event contrary to the laws of nature and attributed to a supernatural cause **2** any amazing and fortunate event: *it's a miracle that no-one was killed in the accident* **3** a marvellous example of something: *a miracle of organization*
WORD ORIGIN Latin *mirari* to wonder at

miracle play *n* a medieval play based on a biblical story or the life of a saint

miraculous ❶ *adj* **1** like a miracle **2** surprising or remarkable

mirage (mir-**rahzh**) *n* **1** an image of a distant object or sheet of water, often inverted or distorted, caused by atmospheric refraction by hot air **2** something illusory: *the mirage of economic recovery*
WORD ORIGIN French, from *(se) mirer* to be reflected

Miranda[1] *n* one of the larger satellites of the planet Uranus

m

THESAURUS

3a = department, office, bureau, government department

minor *adj* **2 = small**, lesser, subordinate, smaller, light, slight, secondary, petty, inferior, trivial, trifling, insignificant, negligible, unimportant, paltry, inconsequential, inconsiderable, nickel-and-dime *(US slang)* **OPPOSITE:** major

mint[2] *vb* **4 = make**, produce, strike, cast, stamp, punch, coin

minute[1] *n* **2 = moment**, second, bit, shake *(informal)*, flash, instant, tick *(Brit informal)*, sec *(informal)*, short time, little while, jiffy *(informal)*, trice

minute[2] *adj* **1 = small**, little, tiny, miniature, slender, fine, microscopic, diminutive, minuscule, infinitesimal, teeny-weeny, Lilliputian, teensy-weensy **OPPOSITE:** huge
2 = precise, close, detailed, critical, exact, meticulous, exhaustive, painstaking, punctilious **OPPOSITE:** imprecise

minutes *pl n* **= record**, notes, proceedings, transactions, transcript, memorandum

miracle *n* **3 = wonder**, phenomenon, sensation, marvel, amazing achievement, astonishing feat

miraculous *adj* **2 = wonderful**, amazing, extraordinary, incredible, astonishing, marvellous, magical, unbelievable, phenomenal, astounding, eye-popping *(informal)*, inexplicable, wondrous *(archaic, literary)*, unaccountable, superhuman **OPPOSITE:** ordinary

DICTIONARY

Miranda² *n* **Francisco de** 1750–1816, Venezuelan revolutionary, who planned to liberate South and Central America from Spain. A leader (1811–12) of the Venezuelan uprising, he surrendered to Spain and died in prison

mire *n* **1** a boggy or marshy area **2** mud, muck, or dirt **3** an unpleasant or difficult situation that is difficult to get out of: *the country sank deeper into the economic mire* ▹*vb* **miring, mired 4** to sink or be stuck in a mire: *the company has been mired in financial scandal*
WORD ORIGIN Old Norse *mýrr*

Miró *n* **Joan** (xwan) 1893–1983, Spanish surrealist painter

Mirren *n* Dame **Helen**, original name *Ilyena Vasilievna Mironov*, born 1945, English actor; her films include *Savage Messiah* (1972), *The Long Good Friday* (1980), *The Cook, The Thief, His Wife and Her Lover* (1989) and *The Queen* (2006), for which she won an Academy Award for Best Actress

mirror ❶ *n* **1** a sheet of glass with a metal coating on its back, that reflects an image of an object placed in front of it **2** a thing that reflects or depicts something else ▹*vb* **3** to reflect or represent faithfully: *the book inevitably mirrors my own interests*
WORD ORIGIN Latin *mirari* to wonder at

mirror ball *n* a large revolving ball covered with small pieces of mirror glass so that it reflects light in changing patterns: used in discos and ballrooms

mirror image *n* an image or object that has left and right reversed as if seen in a mirror

mirth *n* laughter, gaiety, or merriment **mirthful** *adj* **mirthless** *adj*
WORD ORIGIN Old English *myrgth*

MIRV multiple independently targeted re-entry vehicle: a missile that has several warheads, each one being aimed at a different target

mis- *prefix* **1** wrong or bad; wrongly or badly: *misunderstanding; mislead* **2** lack of; not: *mistrust*
WORD ORIGIN Old English *mis(se)-*

misadventure *n* **1** an unlucky event; misfortune **2** *law* accidental death not due to crime or negligence

misaligned *adj* not properly aligned; out of true **misalignment** *n*

misalliance *n* an unsuitable alliance or marriage

misanthrope (miz-zan-thrope) *or* **misanthropist** (miz-zan-throp-ist) *n* a person who dislikes or distrusts people in general **misanthropic** (miz-zan-throp-ik) *adj* **misanthropy** (miz-zan-throp-ee) *n*
WORD ORIGIN Greek *misos* hatred + *anthrōpos* man

misapply *vb* **-plies, -plying, -plied** to use something for a purpose for which it is not intended or is not suited **misapplication** *n*

misapprehend *vb* to misunderstand **misapprehension** *n*

misappropriate *vb* **-ating, -ated** to take and use money dishonestly **misappropriation** *n*

misbegotten *adj* **1** planned or designed badly or with dishonourable motives or aims **2** *literary or dialect* illegitimate; bastard

misbehave *vb* **-having, -haved** to behave badly **misbehaviour** *or US* **misbehavior** *n*

miscalculate *vb* **-lating, -lated** to calculate or judge wrongly: *we miscalculated the strength of the opposition* **miscalculation** *n*

miscall *vb* to call by the wrong name

miscarriage ❶ *n* **1** spontaneous premature expulsion of a fetus from the womb, esp. before the 20th week of pregnancy **2** an act of mismanagement or failure: *a miscarriage of justice*

miscarry *vb* **-ries, -rying, -ried 1** to expel a fetus prematurely from the womb **2** to fail

miscast *vb* **-casting, -cast** to cast a role or an actor in a play or film inappropriately: *the role of the avaricious boss was miscast; she was miscast as Cassandra*

miscegenation (miss-ij-in-nay-shun) *n* interbreeding of races, esp. where differences of colour are involved
WORD ORIGIN Latin *miscere* to mingle + *genus* race

miscellaneous (miss-sel-lane-ee-uss) *adj* composed of or containing a variety of things; mixed or assorted
WORD ORIGIN Latin *miscere* to mix

miscellany (miss-sell-a-nee) *n, pl* **-nies** a mixed assortment of items

mischance *n* **1** bad luck **2** an unlucky event or accident

mischief *n* **1** annoying but not malicious behaviour that causes trouble or irritation **2** an inclination to tease **3** injury or harm caused by a person or thing
WORD ORIGIN Old French *meschief*, from *mes-* mis- + *chef* end

mischief-maker *n* someone who deliberately causes trouble **mischief-making** *n*

mischievous (miss-chiv-uss) *adj* **1** full of mischief **2** teasing; slightly malicious **3** intended to cause harm: *a purveyor of mischievous disinformation* **mischievously** *adv*

miscible (miss-sib-bl) *adj* able to be mixed: *miscible with water* **miscibility** *n*
WORD ORIGIN Latin *miscere* to mix

misconceived *adj* false, mistaken, or badly thought-out: *a misconceived conception of loyalty*

misconception *n* a false or mistaken view, idea, or belief

misconduct ❶ *n* behaviour, such as adultery or professional negligence, that is regarded as immoral or unethical

misconstrue *vb* **-struing, -strued** to interpret mistakenly **misconstruction** *n*

miscreant (miss-kree-ant) *n* a wrongdoer or villain
WORD ORIGIN Old French *mescreant* unbelieving

misdeal *vb* **-dealing, -dealt 1** to deal out cards incorrectly ▹*n* **2** a faulty deal

misdeed *n* an evil or illegal action

misdemeanour *or US* **misdemeanor** *n* **1** a minor wrongdoing **2** *criminal law* (formerly) an offence less serious than a felony

misdirect *vb* to give someone wrong directions or instructions **misdirection** *n*

mise en scène (meez on sane) *n* **1** the stage setting and scenery in a play **2** the environment of an event
WORD ORIGIN French

miser *n* a person who hoards money and hates spending it: *I'm married to a miser* **miserly** *adj*
WORD ORIGIN Latin: wretched

miserable ❶ *adj* **1** unhappy or depressed; wretched **2** causing misery or discomfort: *a miserable existence* **3** sordid or squalid: *miserable living conditions* **4** mean or

THESAURUS

mirror *n* **1 = looking-glass**, glass *(Brit)*, reflector, speculum ▹*vb* **3 = reflect**, show, follow, match, represent, copy, repeat, echo, parallel, depict, reproduce, emulate

miscarriage *n* **2 = failure**, error, breakdown, mismanagement, undoing, thwarting, mishap, botch *(informal)*, perversion, misfire, mischance, nonsuccess

misconduct *n* **= immorality**, wrongdoing, mismanagement, malpractice, misdemeanour, delinquency, impropriety, transgression, misbehaviour, dereliction, naughtiness, malfeasance *(Law)*, unethical behaviour, malversation *(rare)*

miserable *adj* **1 = sad**, down, low, depressed, distressed, gloomy, dismal, afflicted, melancholy, heartbroken, desolate, forlorn, mournful, dejected, broken-hearted, despondent, downcast, sorrowful, wretched, disconsolate, crestfallen, doleful, down in the dumps *(informal)*, woebegone, down in the mouth *(informal)* **OPPOSITE:** happy **4 = pathetic**, low, sorry, disgraceful, mean, shameful, shabby, abject,

DICTIONARY

ungenerous: *a miserable pension*
miserableness *n* **miserably** *adv*
WORD ORIGIN Latin *miserabilis*
misericord *n* a ledge projecting from the underside of the hinged seat of a choir stall in a church, which the occupant can rest against while standing
WORD ORIGIN Latin *miserere* to pity + *cor* heart
misery ❶ *n, pl* **-eries 1** intense unhappiness or suffering **2** something which causes such unhappiness **3** squalid or poverty-stricken conditions **4** *Brit informal* a person who is habitually depressed: *he is such a misery*
WORD ORIGIN Latin *miser* wretched
misfire *vb* **-firing, -fired 1** (of a firearm) to fail to fire as expected **2** (of a motor engine or vehicle) to fail to fire at the appropriate time **3** to fail to have the intended result; go wrong: *he was injured when a practical joke misfired* ▷ *n* **4** the act or an instance of misfiring
misfit *n* a person who is not suited to the role, social group, etc. he or she finds himself or herself in
misfortune ❶ *n* **1** bad luck **2** an unfortunate event
misgivings *pl n* feelings of uncertainty, fear, or doubt
misgovern *vb* to govern badly
misgovernment *n*
misguided ❶ *adj* mistaken or unwise
mishandle *vb* **-dling, -dled** to handle or treat badly or inefficiently
mishap *n* a minor accident
mishear *vb* **-hearing, -heard** to fail to hear what someone says correctly
Mishima *n* **Yukio** 1925–70, Japanese novelist and short-story writer, whose works reflect a preoccupation with homosexuality and death. He committed harakiri in protest at the decline of traditional Japanese values
mishit *sport n* **1** a faulty shot, kick, or stroke ▷ *vb* **-hitting, -hit 2** to hit or kick a ball with a faulty stroke
mishmash *n* a confused collection or mixture
WORD ORIGIN reduplication of *mash*
misinform *vb* to give incorrect information to **misinformation** *n*
misinterpret *vb* to understand or represent something wrongly: *the press misinterpreted the President's remarks*
misinterpretation *n*
misjudge *vb* **-judging, -judged** to judge wrongly or unfairly
misjudgment *or* **misjudgement** *n*
mislay *vb* **-lays, -laying, -laid** to lose something temporarily, esp. by forgetting where it is
mislead ❶ *vb* **-leading, -led** to give false or confusing information to
misleading ❶ *adj* giving a false or confusing impression: *misleading use of statistical data*
mismanage *vb* **-aging, -aged** to organize or run something badly
mismanagement *n*
mismatch *vb* **1** to form an unsuitable partner, opponent, or set ▷ *n* **2** an unsuitable match **mismatched** *adj*
misnamed *adj* having an inappropriate or misleading name: *the grotesquely misnamed Freedom Party*
misnomer (miss-no-mer) *n* **1** an incorrect or unsuitable name for a person or thing **2** the use of the wrong name
WORD ORIGIN Old French *mesnommer* to misname
misogyny (miss-oj-in-ee) *n* hatred of women **misogynist** *n*
misogynous *adj*
WORD ORIGIN Greek *misos* hatred + *gunē* woman
misplace *vb* **-placing, -placed 1** to lose something temporarily by forgetting where it was placed **2** to put something in the wrong place
misplaced *adj* **1** (of an emotion or action) directed towards a person or thing that does not deserve it: *misplaced optimism* **2** put in the wrong place: *a scrappy game dominated by misplaced kicking*
misprint *n* **1** an error in printing ▷ *vb* **2** to print a letter incorrectly
misprision *n law* the concealment of the commission of a felony or an act of treason
WORD ORIGIN Old French *mesprision* error
mispronounce *vb* **-nouncing, -nounced** to pronounce a word or name wrongly **mispronunciation** *n*
misquote *vb* **-quoting, -quoted** to quote inaccurately **misquotation** *n*
misread *vb* **-reading, -read 1** to misinterpret or misunderstand: *he misread her politeness as approval* **2** to read incorrectly
misrepresent *vb* to represent wrongly or inaccurately
misrepresentation *n*
misrule *vb* **-ruling, -ruled 1** to govern inefficiently or without justice ▷ *n* **2** inefficient or unjust government **3** disorder or lawlessness
miss[1] ❶ *vb* **1** to fail to notice, see, or hear: *it's right at the top of the hill, so you can't miss it; I missed what he said because I was talking at the time* **2** to fail to hit something aimed at: *he threw a stone at the dog but missed* **3** to fail to achieve or reach: *they narrowly missed promotion last season* **4** to fail to take advantage of: *he never missed a chance to make money* **5** to fail or be unable to be present: *he had missed the last three meetings* **6** to be too late for: *we missed the bus and had to walk* **7** to discover or regret the loss or absence of: *the boys miss their father when he's away on business* **8** to escape or avoid narrowly: *it missed the helicopter's rotors by inches* ▷ *n* **9** a failure to hit, reach, etc.: *an easy miss in the second frame gave his opponent the advantage* **10 give something a miss**

m

THESAURUS

despicable, deplorable, lamentable, contemptible, scurvy, pitiable, detestable, piteous
OPPOSITE: respectable
misery *n* **1 = unhappiness**, distress, despair, grief, suffering, depression, torture, agony, gloom, sadness, discomfort, torment, hardship, sorrow, woe, anguish, melancholy, desolation, wretchedness
OPPOSITE: happiness
4 (*Brit informal*) **= moaner**, pessimist, killjoy, spoilsport, grouch (*informal*), prophet of doom, wet blanket (*informal*), sourpuss (*informal*), wowser (*Austral & NZ slang*)
misfortune *n* **1** (*often plural*) **= bad luck**, adversity, hard luck, ill luck, infelicity, evil fortune, bad trot (*Austral slang*)
2 = mishap, loss, trouble, trial, blow, failure, accident, disaster, reverse, tragedy, harm, misery, setback, hardship, calamity, affliction, tribulation, whammy (*informal, chiefly US*), misadventure, bummer (*slang*), mischance, stroke of bad luck, evil chance **OPPOSITE:** good luck
misguided *adj* **= unwise**, mistaken, foolish, misled, misplaced, deluded, ill-advised, imprudent, injudicious, labouring under a delusion *or* misapprehension
mislead *vb* **= deceive**, fool, delude, take someone in (*informal*), bluff, beguile, misdirect, misinform, hoodwink, lead astray, pull the wool over someone's eyes (*informal*), take someone for a ride (*informal*), misguide, give someone a bum steer (*informal, chiefly US*)
misleading *adj* **= confusing**, false, ambiguous, deceptive, spurious, evasive, disingenuous, tricky (*informal*), deceitful, specious, delusive, delusory, sophistical, casuistical, unstraightforward
OPPOSITE: straightforward
miss[1] *vb* **1 = fail to notice**, mistake, overlook, pass over **5 = not go to**, skip, cut, omit, be absent from, fail to attend, skive off (*informal*), play truant from, bludge (*Austral & NZ informal*), absent yourself from
7 = long for, wish for, yearn for, want, need, hunger for, pine for, long to see, ache for, feel the loss of, regret the absence of **8 = avoid**, beat, escape, skirt, duck, cheat, bypass, dodge, evade, get round, elude, steer clear of, sidestep, circumvent, find a way round, give a wide berth to ▷ *n*
9 = mistake, failure, fault, error, blunder, omission, oversight

DICTIONARY

to decide not to do, go to, or take part in something: *I'll give the pub a miss and have a quiet night in* ▸ See also **miss out**
WORD ORIGIN Old English *missan*

miss² *n informal* an unmarried woman or girl
WORD ORIGIN from *mistress*

Miss *n* a title of a girl or unmarried woman, usually used before the surname: *Miss Brown to you*

missal *n RC church* a book containing the prayers and rites of the Masses for a complete year
WORD ORIGIN Church Latin *missale*, from *missa* Mass

misshapen *adj* badly shaped; deformed

missile ❶ *n* **1** a rocket with an exploding warhead, used as a weapon **2** an object or weapon that is thrown, launched, or fired at a target
WORD ORIGIN Latin *mittere* to send

missing ❶ *adj* **1** not in its proper or usual place and unable to be found **2** not able to be traced and not known to be dead: *seven men were reported missing after the raid* **3** not included in something although it perhaps should have been: *two things are missing from the report*

missing link *n* **1** any missing section or part in a series **2 the missing link** a hypothetical extinct animal, formerly thought to be intermediate between the apes and man

mission ❶ *n* **1** a specific task or duty assigned to a person or group of people **2** a task or duty that a person believes he or she must achieve; vocation: *he felt it was his mission to pass on his knowledge to other people* **3** a group of people representing or working for a particular country or organization in a foreign country: *the UN peacekeeping mission* **4** a group of people sent by a church to a foreign country to do religious and social work **5** the place in which a church or government mission is based **6** the dispatch of aircraft or spacecraft to achieve a particular task **7** a charitable centre that offers shelter or aid to the poor or needy **8** *S African* a long and difficult process
WORD ORIGIN Latin *mittere* to send

missionary ❶ *n, pl* **-aries 1** a person sent abroad by a church to do religious and social work ▹ *adj* **2** of or relating to missionaries: *missionary work* **3** resulting from a desire to convert people to one's own beliefs: *missionary zeal*

mission statement *n* an official statement of the aims and objectives of a business or other organization

missive *n* a formal or official letter
WORD ORIGIN Latin *mittere* to send

miss out *vb* **1** to leave out or overlook **2 miss out on** to fail to take part in (something enjoyable or beneficial): *she'd missed out on going to university*

misspell *vb* **-spelling, -spelt** *or* **-spelled** to spell a word wrongly
misspelling *n*

misspend *vb* **-spending, -spent** to waste or spend unwisely
misspent *adj*

missus *or* **missis** *n* **1** *Brit, Austral & NZ informal* one's wife or the wife of the person addressed or referred to: *the missus is a fabulous cook* **2** an informal term of address for a woman
WORD ORIGIN spoken version of *mistress*

missy *n, pl* **missies** *informal* an affectionate or disparaging form of address to a girl

mist ❶ *n* **1** a thin fog **2** a fine spray of liquid, such as that produced by an aerosol container **3** condensed water vapour on a surface **4** something that causes haziness or lack of clarity, such as a film of tears ▹ *vb* **5** to cover or be covered with mist: *the windscreen has misted up again; his eyes misted over and he shook with rage* **misty** *adj* **mistiness** *n*
WORD ORIGIN Old English

mistake ❶ *n* **1** an error or blunder **2** a misconception or misunderstanding ▹ *vb* **-taking, -took, -taken 3** to misunderstand or misinterpret: *the chaplain quite mistook her meaning* **4** to confuse a person or thing with another: *they saw the HMS Sheffield and mistook her for the Bismarck* **5** to choose badly or incorrectly: *he mistook his path*
WORD ORIGIN Old Norse *mistaka* to take erroneously

mistaken ❶ *adj* **1** wrong in opinion or judgment **2** arising from error in opinion or judgment: *a mistaken viewpoint*

mister *n* an informal form of address for a man
WORD ORIGIN variant of *master*

Mister *n* ▸ the full form of **Mr**

mistime *vb* **-timing, -timed** to do or say at the wrong time

Mistinguett *n* original name *Jeanne-Marie Bourgeois*. 1875–1956, French dancer, chanteuse, and entertainer

mistle thrush *or* **missel thrush** *n* a large European thrush with a brown back and spotted breast
WORD ORIGIN Old English *mistel* mistletoe

mistletoe *n* a Eurasian evergreen shrub with waxy white berries, which grows as a parasite on various trees
WORD ORIGIN Old English *misteltān*, from *mistel* mistletoe + *tān* twig

mistook *vb* ▸ the past tense of **mistake**

mistral *n* a strong cold dry northerly wind of S France
WORD ORIGIN Provençal, from Latin *magistralis* masterful

Mistral *n* **1 Frédéric** 1830–1914, French Provençal poet, who led a movement to revive Provençal language and literature: shared the Nobel prize for literature 1904 **2 Gabriela**, pen name of *Lucila Godoy de Alcayaga*. 1889–1957, Chilean poet, educationalist, and diplomatist. Her poetry includes the collection *Desolación* (1922): Nobel prize for literature 1945

mistreat *vb* to treat badly
mistreatment *n*

THESAURUS

missile *n* **1, 2 = projectile**, weapon, shell, rocket

missing *adj* **1 = lost**, misplaced, not present, gone, left behind, astray, unaccounted for, mislaid, nowhere to be found

mission *n* **2 = task**, work, calling, business, job, office, charge, goal, operation, commission, trust, aim, purpose, duty, undertaking, pursuit, quest, assignment, vocation, errand

missionary *n* **1 = evangelist**, preacher, apostle, converter, propagandist, proselytizer

mist *n* **1, 2 = fog**, cloud, steam, spray, film, haze, vapour, drizzle, smog, dew, condensation, haar *(Eastern Brit)*, smur *or* smir *(Scot)*

mistake *n* **1 = error**, blunder, oversight, slip, misunderstanding, boob *(Brit slang)*, misconception, gaffe *(informal)*, slip-up *(informal)*, bloomer *(Brit informal)*, clanger *(informal)*, miscalculation, error of judgment, faux pas, false move, boo-boo *(informal)*, barry *or* Barry Crocker *(Austral slang)* **2 = oversight**, error, slip, inaccuracy, fault, slip-up *(informal)*, howler *(informal)*, goof, solecism, erratum, barry *or* Barry Crocker *(Austral slang)* ▹ *vb* **3 = misunderstand**, misinterpret, misjudge, misread, misconstrue, get wrong, misapprehend, misconceive **4 mistake something** *or* **someone for something** *or* **someone = confuse with**, accept as, take for, mix up with, misinterpret as, confound with

mistaken *adj* **1 = wrong**, incorrect, misled, in the wrong, misguided, off the mark, off target, wide of the mark, misinformed, off base *(US & Canad informal)*, barking up the wrong tree *(informal)*, off beam *(informal)*, getting the wrong end of the stick *(informal)*, way off beam *(informal)*, labouring under a misapprehension
OPPOSITE: correct
2 = inaccurate, false, inappropriate, faulty, unfounded, erroneous, unsound, fallacious
OPPOSITE: accurate

mistress *n* **1 = lover**, girlfriend,

DICTIONARY

mistress ❶ *n* **1** a woman who has a continuing sexual relationship with a man who is usually married to somebody else **2** a woman in a position of authority, ownership, or control **3** a woman having control over something specified: *she is a mistress of disguise* **4** *chiefly Brit* a female teacher
WORD ORIGIN Old French *maistresse*

mistrial *n law* a trial which is invalid because of some error

mistrust *vb* **1** to have doubts or suspicions about ▷ *n* **2** lack of trust **mistrustful** *adj* **mistrustfully** *adv*

misunderstand ❶ *vb* **-standing, -stood** to fail to understand properly

misunderstanding ❶ *n* **1** a failure to understand properly **2** a disagreement

misunderstood *adj* not properly or sympathetically understood: *a misunderstood adolescent*

misuse ❶ *n* **1** incorrect, improper, or careless use: *misuse of drugs* **2** cruel or inhumane treatment ▷ *vb* **-using, -used 3** to use wrongly **4** to treat badly or harshly

Mitchell *n* **1 Joni,** original name *Roberta Joan Anderson.* born 1943, Canadian folk-rock singer and songwriter. Her albums include *Blue* (1971), *Court and Spark* (1974), *Mingus* (1979), *Turbulent Indigo* (1994), and *Shine* (2007) **2 Margaret** 1900–49, US novelist; author of *Gone with the Wind* (1936) **3 Reginald Joseph** 1895–1937, British aeronautical engineer; designer of the Spitfire fighter **4 Sir Thomas Livingstone**, known as *Major Mitchell.* 1792–1855, Australian explorer born in Scotland

Mitchum *n* **Robert** 1917–97, US film actor. His many films include *Night of the Hunter* (1955) and *Farewell my Lovely* (1975)

mite[1] *n* any of numerous very small creatures of the spider family, some of which live as parasites
WORD ORIGIN Old English *mīte*

mite[2] *n* **1** a very small creature or thing **2** a very small sum of money **3 a mite** *informal* somewhat: *the main course was a mite bland*
WORD ORIGIN Middle Dutch *mīte*

mitigate *vb* **-gating, -gated** to make less severe or harsh **mitigating** *adj* **mitigation** *n*
WORD ORIGIN Latin *mitis* mild + *agere* to make

mitochondrion *n, pl* **-dria** *biol* a small spherical or rodlike body found in the cytoplasm of most cells
WORD ORIGIN Greek *mitos* thread + *khondrion* grain

mitosis *n* a type of cell division in which the nucleus divides into two nuclei each containing the same number of chromosomes as the parent nucleus
WORD ORIGIN Greek *mitos* thread

mitre *or US* **miter** (my-ter) *n* **1** *Christianity* the headdress of a bishop or abbot, consisting of a tall pointed cleft cap **2** Also: **mitre joint** a corner joint formed by cutting bevels of equal angles at the ends of each piece of material ▷ *vb* **-tring, -tred** *or* **-tering, -tered 3** to join with a mitre joint
WORD ORIGIN Greek *mitra* turban

mitt *n* **1** a glovelike hand covering that does not cover the fingers **2** ▸ short for **mitten 3** *slang* a hand **4** a baseball glove
WORD ORIGIN from *mitten*

mitten *n* a glove with one section for the thumb and a single section for the fingers
WORD ORIGIN Old French *mitaine*

mix ❶ *vb* **1** to combine or blend into one mass or substance: *mix the water, yeast, and flour into a smooth dough* **2** to be able to combine into one substance: *oil and water do not mix* **3** to form by combining different substances: *to mix cement* **4** to do at the same time: *to mix business and pleasure* **5** to be outgoing in social situations: *he mixed well* **6** *music* to balance and adjust individual performers' parts to make an overall sound by electronic means ▷ *n* **7** something produced by mixing; mixture **8** a mixture of ingredients, esp. one commercially prepared for making a cake **9** *music* the sound produced by mixing ▸ See also **mix-up** > **mixed** *adj*
WORD ORIGIN Latin *miscere*

mixed bag *n informal* something made up of different elements, characteristics, or people

mixed blessing *n* an event or situation with both advantages and disadvantages

mixed doubles *pl n tennis, badminton* a doubles game with a man and a woman as partners on each side

mixed economy *n* an economy in which some companies are privately owned and others are owned by the government

mixed farming *n* farming involving both the growing of crops and the keeping of livestock **mixed farm** *n*

mixed grill *n* a dish of several kinds of grilled meat, tomatoes, and mushrooms

mixed marriage *n* a marriage between people of different races or religions

mixed metaphor *n* a combination of incongruous metaphors, such as *when the Nazi jackboots sing their swan song*

mixed-up ❶ *adj* in a state of mental confusion

mixer *n* **1** a kitchen appliance, usually electrical, used for mixing foods **2** any of various other devices or machines used for mixing things: *a cement mixer* **3** a nonalcoholic drink such as tonic water or ginger ale that is mixed with an alcoholic drink **4** *informal* a person considered in relation to his or her ability to mix socially: *he's not a good mixer*

mixture ❶ *n* **1** something produced by blending or combining other things: *top with the cheese and breadcrumb mixture* **2** a combination of different things, such as feelings: *he*

THESAURUS

concubine, kept woman, paramour, floozy *(slang)*, fancy woman *(slang)*, inamorata, doxy *(archaic)*, fancy bit *(slang)*, ladylove *(rare)*

misunderstand *vb* **a = misinterpret**, misread, get the wrong idea (about), mistake, misjudge, misconstrue, mishear, misapprehend, be at cross-purposes with, misconceive **b = miss the point**, get the wrong end of the stick, get your wires crossed, get your lines crossed

misunderstanding *n* **1 = mistake**, error, mix-up, misconception, misreading, misapprehension, false impression, misinterpretation, misjudgment, wrong idea, misconstruction

misuse *n* **1a = waste**, embezzlement, squandering, dissipation, fraudulent use, misemployment, misusage **1b = abuse**, corruption, exploitation **1c = misapplication**, abuse, illegal use, wrong use **1d = perversion**, distortion, desecration, profanation **1e = misapplication**, solecism, malapropism, catachresis ▷ *vb* **3 = abuse**, misapply, misemploy, prostitute

mix *vb* **1 = combine**, blend, merge, unite, join, cross, compound, incorporate, put together, fuse, mingle, jumble, alloy, amalgamate, interweave, coalesce, intermingle, meld, commingle, commix **4** *(often with* **up**) **= combine**, marry, blend, integrate, amalgamate, coalesce, meld, commix **5 = socialize**, associate, hang out *(informal)*, mingle, circulate, come together, consort, hobnob, fraternize, rub elbows *(informal)* ▷ *n* **7 = mixture**, combination, blend, fusion, compound, jumble, assortment, alloy, medley, concoction, amalgam, mixed bag *(informal)*, meld, melange, miscellany

mixed-up *adj* **= confused**, disturbed, puzzled, bewildered, at sea, upset, distraught, muddled, perplexed, maladjusted

mixture *n* **1a = composite**, union, compound, alloy **1b = concoction**, union, compound, blend, brew,

m

DICTIONARY

speaks of her with a mixture of loyalty and regret **3** *chem* a substance consisting of two or more substances mixed together without any chemical bonding between them

mix-up ❶ *n* **1** a confused condition or situation ▷ *vb* **mix up 2** to make into a mixture **3** to confuse: *he mixes Ryan up with Lee* **4** **mixed up in** involved in (an activity or group, esp. one that is illegal): *she's mixed up in a drugs racket*

Mizoguchi *n* **Kenji** 1898–1956, Japanese film director. His films include *A Paper Doll's Whisper of Spring* (1925), *Woman of Osaka* (1940), and *Ugetsu Monogatari* (1952)

mizzenmast *n naut* (on a vessel with three or more masts) the third mast from the bow
WORD ORIGIN Italian *mezzano* middle + MAST

MJ megajoule

Mk (in trade names) mark

mks units *pl n* a metric system of units based on the metre, kilogram, and second: it forms the basis of the SI units

ml **1** millilitre(s) **2** mile(s)

ML Medieval Latin

Mladic *n* **Ratko** born 1943, Bosnian military figure, commander of the Bosnian Serb forces during the civil war of 1992–95; indicted by the U.N. for war crimes, including the massacre of 6000 Bosnian Muslims at Srebrenica (1995)

MLitt Master of Letters
WORD ORIGIN Latin *Magister Litterarum*

Mlle *or* **Mlle.** *pl* **Mlles** *or* **Mlles.** the French equivalent of *Miss*
WORD ORIGIN from *Mademoiselle*

MLR minimum lending rate

mm millimetre(s)

Mme *pl* **Mmes** the French equivalent of *Mrs*
WORD ORIGIN from *Madame, Mesdames*

MMORPG (more-peg) massive(ly) multi-player online role-playing game: an internet-based computer game set in a virtual world, where many people can play at the same time and interact with each other

MMR a combined vaccine against measles, mumps, and rubella, given to very young children

MMus Master of Music

Mn *chem* manganese

MN Minnesota

mnemonic (nim-on-ik) *n* **1** something, for instance a verse, intended to help the memory ▷ *adj* **2** aiding or meant to aid one's memory **mnemonically** *adv*
WORD ORIGIN Greek *mnēmōn* mindful

mo *n informal chiefly Brit* ▸ short for **moment** (sense 1)

Mo *chem* molybdenum

MO **1** Medical Officer **2** Missouri

m.o. *or* **MO** **1** mail order **2** money order

moa *n* a recently extinct large flightless bird of New Zealand that resembled the ostrich
WORD ORIGIN Māori

moan ❶ *n* **1** a low prolonged cry of pain or suffering **2** any similar sound, esp. that made by the wind **3** *informal* a grumble or complaint ▷ *vb* **4** to make a low cry of, or talk in a way suggesting, pain or suffering: *he moaned in pain* **5** to make a sound like a moan: *the wind moaned through the trees* **6** *informal* to grumble or complain **moaner** *n*
WORD ORIGIN Old English *mǣnan* to grieve over

moat *n* a wide ditch, originally filled with water, surrounding a fortified place such as a castle
WORD ORIGIN Old French *motte* mound

mob ❶ *n* **1** a riotous or disorderly crowd of people **2** *informal* any group of people **3** the masses **4** *slang* a gang of criminals ▷ *vb* **-bing, -bed** **5** to attack in a group resembling a mob **6** to surround in a crowd to acclaim or attack: *she was mobbed by her fans when she left the theatre*
WORD ORIGIN shortened from Latin *mobile vulgus* the fickle populace

mobcap *n* a woman's 18th-century cotton cap with a pouched crown
WORD ORIGIN obsolete *mob* woman, esp. loose-living + CAP

mobile ❶ *adj* **1** able to move or be moved: *mobile toilets* **2** changing quickly in expression: *a mobile face* **3** *sociol* (of individuals or social groups) moving within and between classes, occupations, and localities ▷ *n* **4** a light structure suspended in midair with delicately balanced parts that are set in motion by air currents **5** ▸ short for **mobile phone** > **mobility** *n*
WORD ORIGIN Latin *mobilis*

mobile home *n* a large caravan, usually staying in one place, which people live in permanently

mobile phone *n* a portable telephone powered by batteries

mobilize ❶ *or* **-lise** *vb* **-lizing, -lized** *or* **-lising, -lised** **1** to prepare for war or another emergency by organizing resources and the armed services **2** to organize for a purpose: *we must mobilize local residents behind our campaign* **mobilization** *or* **-lisation** *n*

mobster *n US* a member of a criminal organization; gangster

Mobutu[1] *n* the former name (until 1997) of **Lake Albert.** ▸ See **Albert**

Mobutu[2] *n* **Sese Seko**, original name *Joseph.* 1930–97, Zaïrese statesman; president of Zaïre (now the Democratic Republic of Congo) (1970–97); accused of corruption and overthrown by rebels in 1997; died in exile

moccasin *n* **1** a type of soft leather shoe traditionally worn by some Native American peoples **2** a soft leather shoe with a raised seam at the front above the toe
WORD ORIGIN American Indian

mocha (mock-a) *n* **1** a dark brown coffee originally imported from the port of Mocha in Arabia **2** a flavouring made from coffee and chocolate

mock ❶ *vb* **1** to behave with scorn or contempt towards a person or thing:

m

THESAURUS

composite, amalgam, conglomeration **2a = blend**, mix, variety, fusion, assortment, combine, brew, jumble, medley, concoction, amalgam, amalgamation, mixed bag *(informal)*, meld, potpourri, mélange *(French)*, miscellany, conglomeration, hotchpotch, admixture, salmagundi **2b = cross**, combination, blend, association

mix-up *n* **1 = confusion**, mistake, misunderstanding, mess, tangle, muddle, jumble, fankle *(Scot)*

moan *n* **1 = groan**, sigh, sob, lament, wail, grunt, whine, lamentation **3** *(informal)* **= complaint**, protest, grumble, beef *(slang)*, bitch *(slang)*, whine, grouse, gripe *(informal)*, grouch *(informal)*, kvetch *(US slang)* ▷ *vb* **4 = groan**, sigh, sob, whine, keen, lament, deplore, bemoan, bewail **6** *(informal)* **= grumble**, complain, groan, whine, beef *(slang)*, carp, bitch *(slang)*, grouse, gripe *(informal)*, whinge *(informal)*, bleat, moan and groan, grouch *(informal)*

mob *n* **1 = crowd**, pack, collection, mass, body, press, host, gathering, drove, gang, flock, herd, swarm, horde, multitude, throng, assemblage **2 = gang**, company, group, set, lot, troop, crew *(informal)* ▷ *vb* **6 = surround**, besiege, overrun, jostle, fall on, set upon, crowd around, swarm around

mobile *adj* **1 = movable**, moving, travelling, wandering, portable, locomotive, itinerant, peripatetic, ambulatory, motile

mobilize *vb* **1 = deploy**, prepare, ready, rally, assemble, call up, marshal, muster, call to arms, get *or* make ready **2 = rally**, organize, stimulate, excite, prompt, marshal, activate, awaken, animate, muster, foment, put in motion

mock *vb* **1 = laugh at**, insult, tease, ridicule, taunt, scorn, sneer, scoff, deride, flout, make fun of, wind someone up *(Brit slang)*, poke fun at,

her husband mocked her attempts to educate herself **2** to imitate or mimic, esp. in fun **3** to defy or frustrate: *the team mocked the visitors' attempts to score* ▹ *n* **4 mocks** *informal* (in England and Wales) school examinations taken as practice before public exams ▹ *adj* **5** sham or imitation: *mock Georgian windows* **6** serving as an imitation or substitute, esp. for practice purposes: *a mock battle* ▸ See also **mock-up** > **mocking** *n, adj*
WORD ORIGIN Old French *mocquer*

mockers *pl n* **put the mockers on** *Brit, Austral & NZ informal* to ruin the chances of success of
WORD ORIGIN perhaps from *mock*

mockery *n, pl* **-eries 1** ridicule, contempt, or derision **2** a person, thing, or action that is so worthless that it seems like a parody: *the interview was a mockery from start to finish* **3 make a mockery of something** to make something appear worthless or foolish: *the judge's decision makes a mockery of the law*

mock-heroic *adj* (of a literary work, esp. a poem) imitating the style of heroic poetry in order to satirize an unheroic subject

mockingbird *n* an American songbird which can mimic the song of other birds

mock orange *n* a shrub with white fragrant flowers like those of the orange

mock turtle soup *n* an imitation turtle soup made from a calf's head

mock-up *n* a working full-scale model of a machine or apparatus for test or research purposes

mod[1] *n Brit* a member of a group of teenagers, originally in the mid-1960s, who were very clothes-conscious and rode motor scooters
WORD ORIGIN from *modernist*

mod[2] *n* an annual Highland Gaelic meeting with musical and literary competitions
WORD ORIGIN Gaelic *mōd* assembly

MOD (in Britain) Ministry of Defence

mod. 1 moderate **2** modern

modal (**mode**-al) *adj* **1** of or relating to mode or manner **2** *grammar* (of a verb form or auxiliary verb) expressing possibility, intention, or necessity rather than actuality: 'can', 'might', and 'will' are examples of modal verbs in English **3** *music* of or relating to a mode **modality** *n*

mod cons *pl n informal* modern conveniences, such as hot water and heating

mode ❶ *n* **1** a manner or way of doing, acting, or existing **2** a particular fashion or style **3** *music* any of the various scales of notes within one octave **4** *maths* the most frequently occurring of a range of values
WORD ORIGIN Latin *modus* manner

model ❶ *n* **1** a three-dimensional representation, usually on a smaller scale, of a device or structure: *an architect's model of the proposed new housing estate* **2** an example or pattern that people might want to follow: *her success makes her an excellent role model for other young Black women* **3** an outstanding example of its kind: *the report is a model of clarity* **4** a person who poses for a sculptor, painter, or photographer **5** a person who wears clothes to display them to prospective buyers; mannequin **6** a design or style of a particular product: *the cheapest model of this car has a 1300cc engine* **7** a theoretical description of the way a system or process works: *a working model of the human immune system* ▹ *adj* **8** excellent or perfect: *a model husband* **9** being a small-scale representation of: *a model aeroplane* ▹ *vb* **-elling, -elled** *or US* **-eling, -eled 10** to make a model of: *he modelled a plane out of balsa wood* **11** to plan or create according to a model or models: *it had a constitution modelled on that of the United States* **12** to display (clothing and accessories) as a mannequin **13** to pose for a sculptor, painter, or photographer
WORD ORIGIN Latin *modulus*, diminutive of *modus* mode

modem (**mode**-em) *n computers* a device for transmitting information between two computers by a telephone line, consisting of a modulator that converts computer signals into audio signals and a corresponding demodulator
WORD ORIGIN from *mo(dulator) dem(odulator)*

moderate ❶ *adj* **1** not extreme or excessive: *a man of moderate views; moderate consumption of alcohol* **2** (of a size, rate, intensity, etc.) towards the middle of the range of possible values: *a moderate-sized garden; a moderate breeze* **3** of average quality or extent: *moderate success* ▹ *n* **4** a person who holds moderate views, esp. in politics ▹ *vb* **-ating, -ated 5** to make or become less extreme or violent: *he has moderated his opinions since then* **6** to preside over a meeting, discussion, etc. **moderately** *adv*
WORD ORIGIN Latin *moderari* to restrain

moderation *n* **1** the quality of being moderate **2** the act of moderating **3 in moderation** within moderate or reasonable limits

moderato (mod-er-**ah**-toe) *adv music* **1** at a moderate speed **2** with restraint: *allegro moderato*
WORD ORIGIN Italian

moderator *n* **1** *Presbyterian Church* a minister appointed to preside over a Church court, synod, or general assembly **2** a person who presides over a public or legislative assembly **3** a material, such as heavy water, used for slowing down neutrons in nuclear reactors

modern ❶ *adj* **1** of the present or a recent time; contemporary: *there have been very few outbreaks of the disease in modern times* **2** using the latest techniques, equipment, etc.; up-to-date: *modern and efficient railways*

m

THESAURUS

chaff, take the mickey out of *(informal)*, jeer at, show contempt for, make a monkey out of, laugh to scorn **OPPOSITE:** respect
▹ *adj* **5, 6 = imitation**, pretended, artificial, forged, fake, false, faked, dummy, bogus, sham, fraudulent, pseudo *(informal)*, counterfeit, feigned, spurious, ersatz, phoney or phony *(informal)* **OPPOSITE:** genuine

mode *n* **1 = method**, way, plan, course, system, form, state, process, condition, style, approach, quality, practice, fashion, technique, manner, procedure, custom, vein **2 = fashion**, style, trend, rage, vogue, look, craze

model *n* **1 = representation**, image, copy, miniature, dummy, replica, imitation, duplicate, lookalike, facsimile, mock-up **2 = pattern**, example, design, standard, type, original, ideal, mould, norm, gauge, prototype, paradigm, archetype, exemplar, lodestar **4 = sitter**, subject, poser ▹ *vb* **10 = shape**, form, design, fashion, cast, stamp, carve, mould, sculpt **12 = show off** *(informal)*, wear, display, sport

moderate *adj* **1 = mild**, reasonable, controlled, limited, cool, calm, steady, modest, restrained, deliberate, sober, middle-of-the-road, temperate, judicious, peaceable, equable **OPPOSITE:** extreme
2, 3 = average, middling, medium, fair, ordinary, indifferent, mediocre, so-so *(informal)*, passable, unexceptional, fairish, half-pie (NZ *informal*), fair to middling *(informal)*
▹ *vb* **5a = soften**, control, calm, temper, regulate, quiet, diminish, decrease, curb, restrain, tame, subdue, play down, lessen, repress, mitigate, tone down, pacify, modulate, soft-pedal *(informal)*
5b = lessen, relax, ease, wane, abate **OPPOSITE:** intensify

modern *adj* **1 = current**, present, contemporary, recent, late, present-day, latter-day **2 = up-to-date**, latest, fresh, new, novel, with it *(informal)*, up-to-the-minute, newfangled, neoteric *(rare)* **OPPOSITE:** old-fashioned

DICTIONARY

3 of contemporary styles or schools of art, literature, and music, esp. those of an experimental kind ▹ *n* 4 a contemporary person **modernity** *n*
WORD ORIGIN Late Latin *modernus*, from *modus* mode

Modern English *n* the English language since about 1450

modernism *n* a early- and mid-twentieth century movement in art, literature, and music that rejected traditional styles and techniques **modernist** *n, adj*

modernize *or* **-ise** *vb* **-izing, -ized** *or* **-ising, -ised** 1 to make modern in style, methods, or equipment: *a commitment to modernizing industry* 2 to adopt modern ways or ideas **modernization** *or* **-isation** *n*

modern languages *n* the languages spoken in present-day Europe, with the exception of English

modern pentathlon *n* an athletic contest consisting of five different events: horse riding with jumps, fencing with electric épée, freestyle swimming, pistol shooting, and cross-country running

modest ⊕ *adj* 1 having a humble opinion of oneself or one's accomplishments 2 not extreme or excessive: *a modest increase in inflation* 3 not ostentatious or pretentious: *a modest flat in the suburbs* 4 shy or easily embarrassed 5 *old-fashioned* (esp. of clothes) not revealing much of the body: *a modest dress* **modestly** *adv* **modesty** *n*
WORD ORIGIN Latin *modestus* moderate

modicum *n* a small amount
WORD ORIGIN Latin: a little way

modifier *n grammar* a word or phrase that makes the sense of another word more specific: for example, the noun *garage* is a modifier of *door* in *garage door*

modify ⊕ *vb* **-fies, -fying, -fied** 1 to change or alter slightly 2 to make less extreme or uncompromising 3 *grammar* (of a word or phrase) to act as a modifier to another word or phrase **modification** *n*
WORD ORIGIN Latin *modus* measure + *facere* to make

Modigliani *n* **Amedeo** 1884–1920, Italian painter and sculptor, noted esp. for the elongated forms of his portraits

modish (mode-ish) *adj* in the current fashion or style **modishly** *adv*

modiste (mode-east) *n* a fashionable dressmaker or milliner
WORD ORIGIN French

modulate *vb* **-lating, -lated** 1 to change the tone, pitch, or volume of (one's voice) 2 to adjust or regulate the degree of: *the hormone which modulates the development of the sexual organs* 3 *music* to change from one key to another 4 *physics, electronics* to superimpose the amplitude, frequency, or phase of a wave or signal onto another wave or signal **modulation** *n* **modulator** *n*
WORD ORIGIN Latin *modulari* to modulate

module *n* 1 a standard self-contained unit, such as an assembly of electronic components or a standardized piece of furniture, that can be used in combination with other units 2 *astronautics* a self-contained separable unit making up a spacecraft 3 *education* a short course of study that together with other such courses counts towards a qualification **modular** *adj*
WORD ORIGIN Latin *modulus*, diminutive of *modus* mode

modulus *n, pl* **-li** *physics* a coefficient expressing a specified property, for instance elasticity, of a specified substance
WORD ORIGIN Latin

modus operandi (mode-uss op-er-an-die) *n, pl* **modi operandi** (mode-eye) method of operating
WORD ORIGIN Latin

modus vivendi (mode-uss viv-venn-die) *n, pl* **modi vivendi** (mode-eye) a working arrangement between conflicting interests
WORD ORIGIN Latin: way of living

moggy *or* **mog** *n, pl* **moggies** *or* **mogs** *Brit, Austral & NZ slang* a cat
WORD ORIGIN dialect *mog*, originally a pet name for a cow

mogul ⊕ (moh-gl) *n* an important or powerful person

Mogul *adj* of or relating to a Muslim dynasty of Indian emperors established in 1526
WORD ORIGIN Persian *mughul* Mongolian

MOH (in Britain) Medical Officer of Health

mohair *n* 1 the long soft silky hair of the Angora goat 2 a fabric made from yarn of this hair and cotton or wool
WORD ORIGIN Arabic *mukhayyar*, literally: choice

Mohammed *or* **Muhammad** *n* the prophet who founded Islam

Mohammed Ali *n* ▸ See **Muhammad Ali**

Mohammed II *n* ?1430–81, Ottoman sultan of Turkey (1451–81). He captured Constantinople (1453) and conquered large areas of the Balkans

Mohawk *n* 1 a member of a N American Indian people formerly living along the Mohawk river 2 the language of this people

mohican *n* a punk hairstyle in which the head is shaved at the sides and the remaining strip of hair is worn stiffly erect and often brightly coloured
WORD ORIGIN after the *Mohicans*, a Native American people

Mohican *n* 1 *pl* **-cans** *or* **-can** a member of a N American Indian people formerly living along the Hudson river 2 the language of this people

Moholy-Nagy *n* **Laszlo** *or* **Ladislaus** 1895–1946, US painter and teacher, born in Hungary. He worked at the Bauhaus (1923–29)

moiety (moy-it-ee) *n, pl* **-ties** *archaic* 1 a half 2 one of two parts or divisions of something
WORD ORIGIN Old French *moitié*

moire (mwahr) *n* a fabric, usually silk, with a watered effect
WORD ORIGIN French

moiré (mwahr-ray) *adj* 1 having a watered or wavelike pattern ▹ *n* 2 such a pattern, impressed on fabrics 3 a fabric, usually silk, with such a pattern 4 Also: **moiré pattern** a pattern seen when two geometrical patterns, such as grids, are visually superimposed
WORD ORIGIN French

moist ⊕ *adj* slightly damp or wet
WORD ORIGIN Old French

moisten *vb* to make or become moist

moisture ⊕ *n* water diffused as vapour or condensed on or in objects

moisturize *or* **-ise** *vb* **-izing, -ized** *or* **-ising, -ised** to add moisture to the air or the skin **moisturizer** *or* **-iser** *n*

THESAURUS

modest *adj* 2 = **moderate**, small, limited, fair, ordinary, middling, meagre, frugal, scanty, unexceptional 3, 4 = **unpretentious**, simple, reserved, retiring, quiet, shy, humble, discreet, blushing, self-conscious, coy, meek, reticent, unassuming, self-effacing, demure, diffident, bashful, aw-shucks

modify *vb* 1 = **change**, reform, vary, convert, transform, alter, adjust, adapt, revise, remodel, rework, tweak (*informal*), reorganize, recast, reshape, redo, refashion 2 = **tone down**, limit, reduce, lower, qualify, relax, ease, restrict, moderate, temper, soften, restrain, lessen, abate

mogul *n* = **tycoon**, lord, baron, notable, magnate, big gun (*informal*), big shot (*informal*), personage, nob (*slang, chiefly Brit*), potentate, big wheel (*slang*), big cheese (*slang, old-fashioned*), big noise (*informal*), big hitter (*informal*), heavy hitter (*informal*), nabob (*informal*), bashaw, V.I.P.

moist *adj* = **damp**, wet, dripping, rainy, soggy, humid, dank, clammy, dewy, not dry, drizzly, dampish, wettish

moisture *n* = **damp**, water, liquid, sweat, humidity, dew, perspiration,

DICTIONARY

mojo *n, pl* **mojos** *or* **mojoes** *US slang* **1** a charm or magic spell **2** the art of casting magic spells **3** uncanny personal power or influence, esp. the power to attract sexually
WORD ORIGIN from West African
moke *n* **1** *Brit slang* a donkey **2** *Austral & NZ* a horse of inferior quality
WORD ORIGIN origin unknown
mol *chem* mole
mol. **1** molecular **2** molecule
molar *n* **1** a large back tooth specialized for crushing and chewing food ▷ *adj* **2** of any of these teeth
WORD ORIGIN Latin *mola* millstone
molasses *n* **1** the thick brown bitter syrup obtained from sugar during refining **2** *US & Canad* ▸ same as **treacle**
WORD ORIGIN Portuguese *melaço*
mold *n, vb US* ▸ same as **mould**
mole[1] *n* a small dark raised spot on the skin
mole[2] *n* **1** a small burrowing mammal with velvety dark fur and forelimbs specialized for digging **2** *informal* a spy who has infiltrated an organization and become a trusted member of it
WORD ORIGIN Middle Dutch *mol*
mole[3] *n chem* the basic SI unit of amount of substance: the amount that contains as many elementary entities as there are atoms in 0.012 kilogram of carbon-12
WORD ORIGIN German *Mol*, short for *Molekül* molecule
mole[4] *n* **1** a breakwater **2** a harbour protected by a breakwater
WORD ORIGIN Latin *moles* mass
molecular (mol-**lek**-yew-lar) *adj* of or relating to molecules
molecular formula *n chem* a chemical formula indicating the number and type of atoms in a molecule, but not its structure: NH_3 *is the molecular formula of ammonia*
molecular weight *n chem* the sum of all the atomic weights of the atoms in a molecule
molecule ❶ (**mol**-lik-kyool) *n* **1** the simplest unit of a chemical compound that can exist, consisting of two or more atoms held together by chemical bonds **2** a very small particle
WORD ORIGIN New Latin *molecula*, diminutive of Latin *moles* mass
molehill *n* **1** the small mound of earth thrown up by a burrowing mole **2** **make a mountain out of a molehill** to exaggerate an unimportant matter out of all proportion
molest *vb* **1** to accost or attack someone, esp. a woman or child with the intention of assaulting her or him sexually **2** to disturb or injure, esp. by using or threatening violence: *killing, capturing, or molesting the local wildlife was strictly forbidden*
molestation *n* **molester** *n*
WORD ORIGIN Latin *molestare* to annoy
Molina *n* See **de Molina**
moll *n slang* a gangster's female accomplice or girlfriend
WORD ORIGIN from *Moll*, familiar form of *Mary*
mollify *vb* **-fies, -fying, -fied** to make someone less angry or upset; soothe: *he sought to mollify his critics*
mollification *n*
WORD ORIGIN Latin *mollis* soft + *facere* to make
mollusc *or US* **mollusk** *n* an invertebrate with a soft unsegmented body and often a shell, such as a snail, mussel, or octopus
WORD ORIGIN Latin *molluscus*
mollycoddle *vb* **-coddling, -coddled** to give an excessive amount of care and protection to
WORD ORIGIN from *Molly*, girl's name + *coddle*
Molnár *n* **Ferenc.** 1878–1952, Hungarian dramatist and novelist. His plays include *Liliom* (1909)
Molotov cocktail *n* a simple bomb made from a bottle filled with petrol and a cloth wick; petrol bomb
WORD ORIGIN after V. M. *Molotov*, Soviet statesman
molt *vb, n US* ▸ same as **moult**
molten *adj* so hot that it has melted and formed a liquid: *molten metal*
Moltke *n* **1** Count **Helmuth Johannes Ludwig von** 1848–1916, German general; chief of the German general staff (1906–14) **2** his uncle Count **Helmuth Karl Bernhard von** 1800–91, German field marshal; chief of the Prussian general staff (1858–88)
molto *adv music* very: *allegro molto; molto adagio*
WORD ORIGIN Italian
molybdenum (mol-**lib**-din-um) *n chem* a very hard silvery-white metallic element used in alloys, esp. to harden and strengthen steels. Symbol: Mo
WORD ORIGIN Greek *molubdos* lead
mom ❶ *n informal chiefly US, Canad & S African* ▸ same as **mother**
moment ❶ *n* **1** a short period of time **2** a specific instant or point in time: *at that moment the phone rang* **3** **the moment** the present point of time: *for the moment he is out of prison* **4** importance, significance, or value: *a matter of greatest moment* **5** *physics* **a** a tendency to produce motion, esp. rotation about a point or axis **b** the product of a physical quantity, such as force or mass, and its distance from a fixed reference point
WORD ORIGIN Latin *momentum* movement
momentary *adj* lasting for only a moment; temporary
momentarily *adv*
moment of truth *n* a moment when a person or thing is put to the test
momentous ❶ (moh-**men**-tuss) *adj* of great significance
momentousness *n*
momentum ❶ (moh-**men**-tum) *n* **1** the impetus to go forward, develop, or get stronger: *the campaign steadily gathered support and momentum* **2** the impetus of a moving body: *the sledge gathered momentum as it slid ever faster down the slope* **3** *physics* the product of a body's mass and its velocity
WORD ORIGIN Latin: movement
momma *n chiefly US* ▸ an informal or childish word for **mother**
Mommsen *n* **Theodor** 1817–1903, German historian, noted esp. for *The History of Rome* (1854–56): Nobel prize for literature 1902
Mon. Monday
mon- *combining form* ▸ see **mono-**
monad *n* **1** *philosophy* any fundamental singular metaphysical entity **2** a single-celled organism **3** an atom, ion, or radical with a valency of one
WORD ORIGIN Greek *monas* unit
monandrous *adj* **1** *biol* having only one stamen in each flower **2** having only one male sexual partner over a period of time
WORD ORIGIN Greek *monos* sole + *anēr* man
monarch ❶ *n* a sovereign head of state, esp. a king, queen, or emperor,

m

THESAURUS

dampness, wetness, dankness, wateriness
molecule *n* **2 = particle**, atom, mite, jot, speck, mote, iota
mom *n* (*US & Canad*) **= mum**, mother, ma
moment *n* **1 = instant**, second, minute, flash, shake (*informal*), tick (*Brit informal*), no time, twinkling, split second, jiffy (*informal*), trice, two shakes (*informal*), two shakes of a lamb's tail (*informal*), bat of an eye (*informal*) **2 = time**, point, stage, instant, point in time, hour, juncture
momentous *adj* **= significant**, important, serious, vital, critical, crucial, grave, historic, decisive, pivotal, fateful, weighty, consequential, of moment, earth-shaking (*informal*)
OPPOSITE: unimportant
momentum *n* **1 = impetus**, force, power, drive, push, energy, strength, thrust, propulsion, go-forward
monarch *n* **= ruler**, king *or* queen, sovereign, tsar, potentate, crowned head, emperor *or* empress, prince *or* princess

DICTIONARY

who rules by hereditary right **monarchical** *or* **monarchic** *adj* **WORD ORIGIN** Greek *monos* sole + *arkhos* ruler

monarchism *n* the belief that a country should have a hereditary ruler, such as a king, rather than an elected one **monarchist** *n, adj*

monarchy ❶ *n, pl* **-chies** 1 a form of government in which supreme authority is held by a single hereditary ruler, such as a king 2 a country reigned over by a monarch

monastery ❶ *n, pl* **-teries** the building or group of buildings where a community of monks lives **WORD ORIGIN** Greek *monazein* to live alone

monastic *adj* 1 of or relating to monasteries, monks, or nuns 2 (of a way of life) simple and austere; ascetic **monasticism** *n*

monatomic *adj chem* 1 (of an element) consisting of single atoms 2 (of a compound or molecule) having only one atom or group that can be replaced in a reaction

Monck *n* **George** 1st Duke of Albemarle. 1608–70, English general. In the Civil War he was a Royalist until captured (1644) and persuaded to support the Commonwealth. After Cromwell's death he was instrumental in the restoration of Charles II (1660)

Mondale *n* **Walter** (**Frederick**) born 1928, US Democratic politician; vice president of the US (1977–81)

Monday *n* the second day of the week, and the first day of the working week **WORD ORIGIN** Old English *mōnandæg* moon's day

monetarism *n* 1 the theory that inflation is caused by an excess quantity of money in an economy 2 an economic policy based on this theory and a belief in the efficiency of free market forces **monetarist** *n, adj*

monetary ❶ *adj* of money or currency **WORD ORIGIN** Latin *moneta* money

money ❶ *n* 1 a means of payment and measure of value: *some cultures used to use shells as money* 2 the official currency, in the form of banknotes or coins, issued by a government 3 **moneys** *or* **monies** *law old-fashioned* a financial sum or income 4 an unspecified amount of wealth: *money to lend* 5 *informal* a rich person or rich people: *he married money* 6 **for my money** in my opinion 7 **one's money's worth** full value for the money one has paid for something 8 **put money on** to place a bet on ▸ Related adjective: **pecuniary** **WORD ORIGIN** Latin *moneta*

moneybags *n informal* a very rich person

moneychanger *n* a person engaged in the business of exchanging currencies or money

moneyed *or* **monied** *adj* having a great deal of money; rich

money-grubbing *adj informal* seeking greedily to obtain money **money-grubber** *n*

moneylender *n* a person who lends money at interest as a living

moneymaker *n* 1 a person whose chief concern is to make money 2 a person or thing that is or might be profitable **moneymaking** *adj, n*

money-spinner *n informal* an enterprise, idea, or thing that is a source of wealth

-monger *n combining form* 1 indicating a trader or dealer: *an ironmonger* 2 indicating a promoter of something: *a warmonger* **WORD ORIGIN** Old English *mangere*

mongol *n offensive* (not in technical use) a person affected by Down's syndrome **mongoloid** *n, adj*

Mongolian *adj* 1 of Mongolia ▹*n* 2 a person from Mongolia 3 the language of Mongolia

mongolism *n offensive* ▸ a former name (not in technical use) for **Down's syndrome** **WORD ORIGIN** the condition produces facial features similar to those of the Mongoloid peoples

Mongoloid *adj* of a major racial group of mankind, characterized by yellowish skin, straight black hair, and slanting eyes: includes most of the people of SE Asia, E Asia, and the Arctic area of N America

mongoose *n, pl* **-gooses** a small long-tailed predatory mammal of Asia and Africa that kills snakes **WORD ORIGIN** from Marathi (a language of India) *mangūs*

mongrel *n* 1 a dog of mixed breeding 2 something made up of things from a variety of sources: *despite using components from three other cars, this new model is no mongrel* ▹*adj* 3 of mixed breeding or origin: *a mongrel race* **WORD ORIGIN** from obsolete *mong* mixture

monied *adj* ▸ same as **moneyed**

monies *n law old-fashioned* ▸ a plural of **money**

moniker *or* **monicker** *n slang* a person's name or nickname **WORD ORIGIN** Shelta *munnik*, altered from Irish Gaelic *ainm* name

monism *n philosophy* the doctrine that reality consists of only one basic substance or element, such as mind or matter **monist** *n, adj* **WORD ORIGIN** Greek *monos* sole

monition *n* a warning or caution **WORD ORIGIN** Latin *monere* to warn

monitor ❶ *n* 1 a person or device that warns, checks, controls, or keeps a continuous record of something 2 *Brit, Austral & NZ* a pupil assisting a teacher with various duties 3 a screen used to display certain kinds of information, for example in airports or television studios 4 a large predatory lizard inhabiting warm regions of Africa, Asia, and Australia ▹*vb* 5 to act as a monitor of 6 to observe or record the condition or performance of a person or thing 7 to check a broadcast for acceptable quality or content **monitorial** *adj* **WORD ORIGIN** Latin *monere* to advise

monitory *adj* acting as or giving a warning

monk ❶ *n* a male member of a religious community bound by vows of poverty, chastity, and obedience ▸ Related adjective: **monastic** **monkish** *adj* **WORD ORIGIN** Greek *monos* alone

Monk *n* 1 **Thelonious** (**Sphere**) 1920–82, US jazz pianist and composer 2 ▸ a variant spelling of (George) **Monck**

monkey ❶ *n* 1 any long-tailed primate that is not a lemur or tarsier

THESAURUS

monarchy *n* 1 **= sovereignty**, despotism, autocracy, kingship, absolutism, royalism, monocracy 2 **= kingdom**, empire, realm, principality

monastery *n* **= abbey**, house, convent, priory, cloister, religious community, nunnery, friary

monetary *adj* **= financial**, money, economic, capital, cash, fiscal, budgetary, pecuniary

money *n* 1, 2 **= cash**, funds, capital, currency, hard cash, green (*slang*), readies (*informal*), riches, necessary (*informal*), silver, bread (*slang*), coin, tin (*slang*), brass (*Northern English dialect*), loot (*informal*), dough (*slang*), the ready (*informal*), banknotes, dosh (*Brit & Austral slang*), lolly (*Brit slang*), the wherewithal, legal tender, megabucks (*US & Canad slang*), needful (*informal*), specie, shekels (*informal*), dibs (*slang*), filthy lucre (*facetious*), moolah (*slang*), ackers (*slang*), gelt (*slang, chiefly US*), spondulicks (*slang*), pelf (*derogatory*), mazuma (*slang, chiefly US*), kembla (*Austral slang*)see:

monitor *n* 1 **= guide**, observer, supervisor, overseer, invigilator 2 **= prefect** (*Brit*), head girl, head boy, senior boy, senior girl ▹*vb* 5, 6 **= check**, follow, record, watch, survey, observe, scan, oversee, supervise, keep an eye on, keep track of, keep tabs on

monk *n* **= friar**, brother, religious, novice, monastic, oblate ▸ *related adjective:* monastic

DICTIONARY

2 (loosely) any primate that is not a human **3** a naughty or mischievous child **4** *slang* £500 or $500 **5 give a monkey's** *Brit slang* to care about or regard as important: *who gives a monkey's what he thinks?* ▹ *vb* **6 monkey around** *or* **about with** to meddle or tinker with
WORD ORIGIN origin unknown
monkey business *n informal* mischievous or dishonest behaviour or acts
monkey nut *n Brit* a peanut
monkey puzzle *n* a South American coniferous tree with branches shaped like a candelabrum and stiff sharp leaves
monkey tricks *or US* **monkey shines** *pl n informal* mischievous behaviour or acts
monkey wrench *n chiefly Brit* a wrench with adjustable jaws
monkshood *n* a poisonous plant with hooded blue-purple flowers
Monmouth[1] *n* a market town in E Wales, in Monmouthshire: Norman castle, where Henry V was born in 1387. Pop: 8547 (2001)
Monmouth[2] *n* **James Scott,** Duke of Monmouth. 1649–85, the illegitimate son of Charles II of England, he led a rebellion against James II in support of his own claim to the Crown; captured and beheaded
Monnet *n* **Jean** 1888–1979, French economist and public servant, regarded as founding father of the European Economic Community. He was first president (1952–55) of the European Coal and Steel Community
mono *adj* **1** ▸ short for **monophonic** ▹ *n* **2** monophonic sound
mono- *or before a vowel* **mon-** *combining form* **1** one; single: *monorail; monolingual* **2** *chem* indicating that a chemical compound contains a single specified atom or group: *monoxide*
WORD ORIGIN Greek *monos* alone
monobasic *adj chem* (of an acid, such as hydrogen chloride) having only one replaceable hydrogen atom per molecule
monochromatic *adj* (of light or other electromagnetic radiation) having only one wavelength
monochrome *adj* **1** *photog, television* black-and-white ▹ *n* **2** a painting or drawing done in a range of tones of a single colour
WORD ORIGIN Greek *monokhrōmos* of one colour
monocle (mon-a-kl) *n* (formerly) a lens worn for correcting defective sight in one eye only, held in position by the facial muscles **monocled** *adj*
WORD ORIGIN MONO- + Latin *oculus* eye
monocline *n* a fold in stratified rocks in which the strata are inclined in the same direction from the horizontal **monoclinal** *adj, n*
WORD ORIGIN MONO- + Greek *klinein* to lean
monoclinic *adj crystallog* of the crystal system characterized by three unequal axes, one pair of which are not at right angles to each other
monoclonal antibody *n* an antibody produced from a single clone of cells grown in a culture
monocoque (mon-a-cock) *n* a vehicle body moulded from a single piece of material with no separate load-bearing parts
WORD ORIGIN French
monocotyledon (mon-no-kot-ill-leed-on) *n* any flowering plant with a single embryonic seed leaf, such as the grasses, lilies, palms, and orchids
monocular *adj* having or intended for the use of only one eye
WORD ORIGIN Late Latin *monoculus* one-eyed
monoculture *n* the continuous growing of one type of crop
monody *n, pl* **-dies 1** (in Greek tragedy) an ode sung by a single actor **2** *music* a style of composition consisting of a single vocal part, usually with accompaniment **monodist** *n*
WORD ORIGIN MONO- + Greek *aeidein* to sing
monoecious (mon-ee-shuss) *adj* **1** (of some flowering plants) having the male and female reproductive organs in separate flowers on the same plant **2** (of some animals and lower plants) hermaphrodite
WORD ORIGIN MONO- + Greek *oikos* house
monogamy *n* the state or practice of having only one husband or wife at a time **monogamous** *adj*
WORD ORIGIN MONO- + Greek *gamos* marriage
monogram *n* a design of one or more letters, esp. initials, on clothing, stationery, etc.
WORD ORIGIN Greek *monogrammatos* consisting of one letter
monograph *n* a paper, book, or other work concerned with a single subject or aspect of a subject
monolingual *adj* knowing or expressed in only one language
monolith *n* **1** a large block of stone **2** a statue, obelisk, or column cut from one block of stone **3** something which can be regarded as forming one large, single, whole: *the Christian religion should not be thought of as a monolith* **monolithic** *adj*
WORD ORIGIN Greek *monolithos* made from a single stone
monologue *n* **1** a long speech made by one actor in a play or film; soliloquy **2** a dramatic piece for a single performer **3** any long speech by one person, esp. one which prevents other people talking or expressing their views
WORD ORIGIN Greek *monologos* speaking alone
monomania *n* an obsession with one thing or idea **monomaniac** *n, adj*
monomer *n chem* a compound whose molecules can join together to form a polymer
monomial *n maths* an expression consisting of a single term, such as 5*ax*
WORD ORIGIN MONO- + (BIN)OMIAL
mononucleosis (mon-oh-new-klee-oh-siss) *n* **infectious mononucleosis** ▸ same as **glandular fever**
monophonic *adj* (of a system of broadcasting, recording, or reproducing sound) using only one channel between source and loudspeaker. Short form: **mono**
monoplane *n* an aeroplane with only one pair of wings
monopolize *or* **-lise** *vb* **-lizing, -lized** *or* **-lising, -lised 1** to have full control or use of, to the exclusion of others **2** to hold exclusive control of a market or supply
monopoly *n, pl* **-lies 1** exclusive control of the market supply of a product or service **2 a** an enterprise exercising this control **b** the product or service so controlled **3** *law* the exclusive right granted to a person or company by the state to trade in a specified commodity or area **4** exclusive control, possession, or use of something **monopolist** *n* **monopolistic** *adj*
WORD ORIGIN MONO- + Greek *pōlein* to sell
Monopoly *n trademark* a board game for two to six players who deal in 'property' as they move tokens around the board
monorail *n* a single-rail railway
monosaccharide *n* a simple sugar, such as glucose, that cannot be broken down into other sugars
monosodium glutamate *n* a substance which enhances protein flavours: used as a food additive
monosyllable *n* a word of one syllable **monosyllabic** *adj*
monotheism *n* the belief or doctrine that there is only one God **monotheist** *n, adj* **monotheistic** *adj*
monotone *n* **1** a single unvaried pitch

THESAURUS

monkey *n* **1, 2 = simian**, ape, primate, jackanapes *(archaic)* **3 = rascal**, horror, devil, rogue, imp, tyke, scallywag, mischief maker, scamp, nointer *(Austral slang)* ▸ *related adjective:* simian

DICTIONARY

level in speech or sound **2** a way of speaking which lacks variety of pitch or expression: *he rambled on in a dull monotone* **3** lack of variety in style or expression ▹*adj* **4** unvarying

monotonous *adj* tedious because of lack of variety **monotonously** *adv*

monotony *n, pl* **-nies 1** wearisome routine; dullness **2** lack of variety in pitch or tone

monounsaturated *adj* of a group of vegetable oils, such as olive oil, that have a neutral effect on cholesterol in the body

monovalent *adj chem* **1** having a valency of one **2** having only one valency **monovalence** *or* **monovalency** *n*

monoxide *n* an oxide that contains one oxygen atom per molecule

Monseigneur (mon-sen-**nyur**) *n, pl* **Messeigneurs** (may-sen-**nyur**) a title given to French prelates and princes
WORD ORIGIN French, literally: my lord

monsieur (muss-**syuh**) *n, pl* **messieurs** (may-**syuh**) a French form of address equivalent to *sir* or *Mr*
WORD ORIGIN French, literally: my lord

Monsignor *n, pl* **Monsignors** *or* **Monsignori** *RC church* a title given to certain senior clergymen
WORD ORIGIN Italian

monsoon *n* **1** a seasonal wind of S Asia which blows from the southwest in summer and from the northeast in winter **2** the rainy season when the SW monsoon blows, from about April to October
WORD ORIGIN Arabic *mawsim* season

monsoon bucket *n NZ* a large container for water carried by helicopter and used to extinguish bush and scrub fires

mons pubis (monz **pew**-biss) *n, pl* **montes pubis** (**mon**-teez) the fatty flesh in human males over the junction of the pubic bones
WORD ORIGIN New Latin: hill of the pubes

monster ❶ *n* **1** an imaginary beast, usually frightening in appearance **2** a very large person, animal, or thing **3** an exceptionally cruel or wicked person **4** a person, animal, or plant with a marked deformity
WORD ORIGIN Latin *monstrum* portent

monstrance *n RC church* a vessel in which the consecrated Host is exposed for adoration
WORD ORIGIN Latin *monstrare* to show

monstrosity *n, pl* **-ties 1** an outrageous or ugly person or thing **2** the state or quality of being monstrous

monstrous ❶ *adj* **1** hideous or unnatural in size or character **2** atrocious, unjust, or shocking: *the President described the invasion as monstrous* **3** huge **4** of or like a monster **5** (of plants and animals) abnormal in structure **monstrously** *adv*

mons veneris (monz **ven**-er-iss) *n, pl* **montes veneris** (**mon**-teez) the fatty flesh in human females over the junction of the pubic bones
WORD ORIGIN New Latin: hill of Venus

montage (mon-**tahzh**) *n* **1** a picture made by combining material from various sources, such as other pictures or photographs **2** the technique of producing pictures in this way **3** a method of film editing by juxtaposition or partial superimposition of several shots to form a single image **4** a film sequence of this kind
WORD ORIGIN French

Montagu *n* **1 Charles** See (Earl of) **Halifax** (sense 2) (sense 2) **2 Lady Mary Wortley** 1689–1762, English writer, noted for her *Letters from the East* (1763)

Montaigne *n* **Michel Eyquem de** 1533–92, French writer. His life's work, the *Essays* (begun in 1571), established the essay as a literary genre and record the evolution of his moral ideas

Montale *n* **Eugenio** 1896–1981, Italian poet: Nobel prize for literature 1975

Montana[1] *n* a state of the western US: consists of the Great Plains in the east and the Rocky Mountains in the west. Capital: Helena. Pop: 917 621 (2003 est). Area: 377 070 sq km (145 587 sq miles). Abbreviation: **Mont,** (with zip code) **MT**

Montana[2] *n* **Joe** born 1958, American football quarterback

Montcalm *n* **Louis Joseph**, Marquis de Montcalm de Saint-Véran. 1712–59, French general in Canada (1756); killed in Quebec by British forces under General Wolfe

Montefeltro *n* an Italian noble family who ruled Urbino from the 13th to the 16th century. **Federigo Montefeltro**, duke of Urbino (1422–82), was a noted patron of the arts and military leader

Montespan *n* **Marquise de,** title of *Françoise Athénaïs de Rochechouart*. 1641–1707, French noblewoman; mistress of Louis XIV of France

Montesquieu *n* **Baron de la Brède et de**, title of *Charles Louis de Secondat*. 1689–1755, French political philosopher. His chief works are the satirical *Lettres persanes* (1721) and *L'Esprit des lois* (1748), a comparative analysis of various forms of government, which had a profound influence on political thought in Europe and the US

Monteux *n* **Pierre** 1875–1964, US conductor, born in France

Monteverdi *n* **Claudio** ?1567–1643, Italian composer, noted esp. for his innovations in opera and for his expressive use of dissonance. His operas include *Orfeo* (1607) and *L'Incoronazione di Poppea* (1642) and he also wrote many motets and madrigals

Montez *n* **Lola**, original name *Marie Gilbert*. 1818–61, Irish dancer; mistress of Louis I of Bavaria (1786–1868; reigned 1825–48)

month *n* **1** one of the twelve divisions (**calendar months**) of the calendar year **2** a period of time extending from one date to a corresponding date in the next calendar month **3** a period of four weeks or of 30 days
WORD ORIGIN Old English *mōnath*

Montherlant *n* **Henri** (**Millon**) **de** 1896–1972, French novelist and dramatist: his novels include *Les Jeunes Filles* (1935–39) and *Le Chaos et la nuit* (1963)

monthly *adj* **1** happening or payable once every month: *a monthly magazine* **2** lasting or valid for a month: *a monthly travel pass* ▹*adv* **3** once a month ▹*n, pl* **-lies 4** a magazine published once a month

Montrose *n* **James Graham,** 1st Marquess and 5th Earl of Montrose. 1612–50, Scottish general, noted for his victories in Scotland for Charles I in the Civil War. He was later

THESAURUS

monster *n* **2 = giant**, mammoth, titan, colossus, monstrosity, leviathan, behemoth **3 = brute**, devil, savage, beast, demon, villain, barbarian, fiend, ogre, ghoul, bogeyman

monstrous *adj* **1 = unnatural**, terrible, horrible, dreadful, abnormal, obscene, horrendous, hideous, grotesque, gruesome, frightful, hellish, freakish, fiendish, miscreated **OPPOSITE:** normal **2 = outrageous**, shocking, evil, horrifying, vicious, foul, cruel, infamous, intolerable, disgraceful, scandalous, atrocious, inhuman, diabolical, heinous, odious, loathsome, devilish, egregious, fiendish, villainous **OPPOSITE:** decent **3 = huge**, giant, massive, great, towering, vast, enormous, tremendous, immense, titanic, gigantic, mammoth, colossal, stellar *(informal)*, prodigious, stupendous, gargantuan, elephantine, ginormous *(informal)*, humongous *or* humungous *(US slang)* **OPPOSITE:** tiny

captured and hanged

monument *n* **1** something, such as a statue or building, erected in commemoration of a person or event **2** an ancient building which is regarded as an important part of a country's history **3** an exceptional example of the results of something: *the whole town is a monument to bad sixties' architecture*
WORD ORIGIN Latin *monumentum*

monumental *adj* **1** large, impressive, or likely to last or be remembered for a long time: *a monumental three-volume biography* **2** of or being a monument **3** *informal* extreme: *a monumental gamble*

moo *n* **1** the characteristic deep long sound made by a cow ▹ *vb* **2** to make this sound; low

mooch *vb slang* **1** to loiter or walk aimlessly **2** to cadge or scrounge
WORD ORIGIN perhaps Old French *muchier* to skulk

mood[1] *n* **1** a temporary state of mind or temper: *a happy mood* **2** a sullen or gloomy state of mind, esp. when temporary: *she's in a mood* **3** a prevailing atmosphere or feeling: *the current mood of disenchantment with politics* **4 in the mood** inclined to do or have (something)
WORD ORIGIN Old English *mōd* mind, feeling

mood[2] *n grammar* a form of a verb indicating whether the verb expresses a fact (indicative mood), a wish or supposition (subjunctive mood), or a command (imperative mood)
WORD ORIGIN same as MOOD[1]

moody *adj* **moodier, moodiest** **1** sullen, sulky, or gloomy **2** temperamental or changeable **moodily** *adv* **moodiness** *n*

Moody *n* **Dwight Lyman** 1837–99, US evangelist and hymnodist, noted for his revivalist campaigns in Britain and the US with I. D. Sankey

Moog *n music trademark* a type of synthesizer
WORD ORIGIN after Robert *Moog*, engineer

mooi *adj S African slang* pleasing or nice
WORD ORIGIN Afrikaans

mooli *n* a type of large white radish
WORD ORIGIN E African native name

moon *n* **1** the natural satellite of the earth ▸ Related adjective: **lunar** **2** this satellite as it is seen during its revolution around the earth, esp. at one of its phases: *new moon; full moon* **3** any natural satellite of a planet **4** a month **5 over the moon** *informal* extremely happy; ecstatic ▹ *vb* **6 moon about** *or* **around** to be idle in a listless or dreamy way **moonless** *adj*
WORD ORIGIN Old English *mōna*

Moon[1] *n* a system of embossed alphabetical signs for blind readers, the fourteen basic characters of which can, by rotation, mimic most of the letters of the Roman alphabet, thereby making learning easier for those who learned to read before going blind ▸ Compare **Braille**

Moon[2] *n* **William** 1818–94, British inventor of the Moon writing system in 1847, who, himself blind, taught blind children in Brighton and printed mainly religious works from stereotyped plates of his own designing

moonbeam *n* a ray of moonlight

moon-faced *adj* having a round face

moonlight *n* **1** light from the sun received on earth after reflection by the moon ▹ *adj* **2** illuminated by the moon: *a moonlight walk* ▹ *vb* **-lighting, -lighted 3** *informal* to work at a secondary job, esp. illegally **moonlighter** *n*

moonlight flit *n Austral & Brit informal* a hurried departure at night to avoid paying rent

moonlit *adj* illuminated by the moon

moonscape *n* the surface of the moon or a picture or model of it

moonshine *n* **1** *US & Canad* illegally distilled or smuggled whisky **2** foolish or nonsensical talk or thought

moonshot *n* the launching of a spacecraft to the moon

moonstone *n* a white translucent form of feldspar, used as a gem

moonstruck *adj* slightly mad or odd, as if affected by the moon

moony *adj* **moonier, mooniest** *Brit, Austral & NZ informal* dreamy or listless

moor[1] *n Brit* an expanse of open uncultivated ground covered with heather, coarse grass, and bracken
WORD ORIGIN Old English *mōr*

moor[2] *vb* to secure a ship or boat with cables, ropes, or anchors so that it remains in one place **moorage** *n*
WORD ORIGIN Germanic

Moor *n* a member of a Muslim people of North Africa who ruled Spain between the 8th and 15th centuries
WORD ORIGIN Greek *Mauros*

moorhen *n* a waterfowl with black plumage and a red bill

mooring *n* a place where a ship or boat can be tied up or anchored

moorings *pl n naut* the ropes and anchors used in mooring a vessel

Moorish *adj* **1** of or relating to the Moors **2** of a style of architecture used in Spain from the 13th to the 16th century, characterized by the horseshoe arch

moorland *n Brit* an area of moor

moose *n, pl* **moose** a large North American deer with large flattened antlers; the American elk
WORD ORIGIN from a Native American language

moot *adj* **1** subject or open to debate: *a moot point* ▹ *vb* **2** to suggest or bring up for debate: *a compromise proposal, involving building fewer flats, was mooted* ▹ *n* **3** (in Anglo-Saxon England) a

THESAURUS

monument *n* **1 = memorial**, cairn, statue, pillar, marker, shrine, tombstone, mausoleum, commemoration, headstone, gravestone, obelisk, cenotaph

monumental *adj* **1 = important**, classic, significant, outstanding, lasting, enormous, historic, enduring, memorable, awesome, majestic, immortal, unforgettable, prodigious, stupendous, awe-inspiring, epoch-making **OPPOSITE:** unimportant ▹ *adj* **3** *(informal)* **= immense**, great, massive, terrible, tremendous, horrible, staggering, catastrophic, gigantic, colossal, whopping *(informal)*, indefensible, unforgivable, egregious **OPPOSITE:** tiny

mood[1] *n* **1 = state of mind**, spirit, humour, temper, vein, tenor, disposition, frame of mind

moody *adj* **1a = sulky**, cross, wounded, angry, offended, irritable, crabbed, crusty, temperamental, touchy, curt, petulant, ill-tempered, irascible, cantankerous, tetchy, testy, chippy *(informal)*, in a huff, short-tempered, waspish, piqued, crabby, huffy, splenetic, crotchety *(informal)*, ill-humoured, huffish, tooshie *(Austral slang)* **OPPOSITE:** cheerful **1b = gloomy**, sad, miserable, melancholy, frowning, dismal, dour, sullen, glum, introspective, in the doldrums, out of sorts *(informal)*, downcast, morose, lugubrious, pensive, broody, crestfallen, doleful, down in the dumps *(informal)*, saturnine, down in the mouth *(informal)*, mopish, mopy **OPPOSITE:** cheerful **2 = changeable**, volatile, unpredictable, unstable, erratic, fickle, temperamental, impulsive, mercurial, capricious, unsteady, fitful, flighty, faddish, inconstant **OPPOSITE:** stable

moon *n* **3 = satellite** ▹ *vb* **6 = idle**, drift, loaf, languish, waste time, daydream, mope, mooch *(Brit slang)* ▸ *related adjective:* lunar

moor[1] *n* **= moorland**, fell *(Brit)*, heath, muir *(Scot)*

moor[2] *vb* **= tie up**, fix, secure, anchor, dock, lash, berth, fasten, make fast

mop *n* **1, 2 = squeegee**, sponge, swab **3 = mane**, shock, mass, tangle, mat, thatch ▹ *vb* **4 = clean**, wash, wipe, sponge, swab, squeegee

DICTIONARY

local administrative assembly
WORD ORIGIN Old English *gemōt*
mop ➊ *n* **1** a tool with a head made of twists of cotton or sponge and a long handle used for washing or polishing floors **2** a similar tool, except smaller and without a long handle, used to wash dishes **3** a thick untidy mass of hair ▹ *vb* **mopping, mopped 4** to clean or soak up with or as if with a mop: *she mopped her brow with a handkerchief* ▸ See also **mop up**
WORD ORIGIN Latin *mappa* napkin
mope *vb* **moping, moped 1** to be gloomy or apathetic **2** to walk around in a gloomy and aimless manner
WORD ORIGIN perhaps from obsolete *mope* fool
moped *n* a light motorcycle not over 50cc
WORD ORIGIN *motor* + *pedal*
mopes *pl n* **the mopes** low spirits
mopoke *n* **1** a small spotted owl of Australia and New Zealand **2** *Austral slang* a slow or lugubrious person
WORD ORIGIN imitative of the bird's cry
moppet *n* ▸ same as **poppet**
WORD ORIGIN obsolete *mop* rag doll
mop up *vb* **1** to clean with a mop **2** *informal* to complete the last remaining stages of a job **3** *mil* to clear remaining enemy forces after a battle, by killing them or taking them prisoner
moquette *n* a thick velvety fabric used for carpets and upholstery
WORD ORIGIN French
moraine *n* a ridge or mound formed from debris deposited by a glacier
WORD ORIGIN French
moral ➊ *adj* **1** concerned with or relating to the distinction between good and bad or right and wrong behaviour: *moral sense* **2** based on a sense of right and wrong according to conscience: *moral duty* **3** displaying a sense of right and wrong; (of support or a victory) psychological rather than practical ▹ *n* **4** a lesson about right or wrong behaviour that is shown in a fable or event **5 morals** principles of behaviour in accordance with standards of right and wrong **morally** *adv*
WORD ORIGIN Latin *moralis* relating to morals or customs
morale ➊ (mor-**rahl**) *n* the degree of confidence or optimism of a person or group
WORD ORIGIN French
moralist *n* **1** a person who has a strong sense of right and wrong **2** someone who criticizes other people for not doing what he or she thinks is morally correct **moralistic** *adj*
morality ➊ *n, pl* **-ties 1** good moral conduct **2** the degree to which something is morally acceptable: *we discussed the morality of fox-hunting* **3** a system of moral principles
morality play *n* a medieval type of drama concerned with the conflict between personified virtues and vices
moralize *or* **-ise** *vb* **-izing, -ized** *or* **-ising, -ised 1** to discuss or consider something in the light of one's own moral beliefs, esp. with disapproval **2** to interpret or explain in a moral sense **3** to improve the morals of
moral philosophy *n* the branch of philosophy dealing with ethics
morass *n* **1** a tract of swampy low-lying land **2** a disordered, confusing, or muddled state of affairs
WORD ORIGIN Old French *marais* marsh
moratorium ➊ *n, pl* **-ria** *or* **-riums 1** a legally authorized postponement of the payment of a debt **2** an agreed suspension of activity
WORD ORIGIN Latin *mora* delay
Moravia[1] *n* a region of the Czech Republic around the Morava River, bounded by the Bohemian-Moravian Highlands, the Sudeten Mountains, and the W Carpathians: became a separate Austrian crownland in 1848; part of Czechoslovakia 1918–92; valuable mineral resources. Czech name: **Morava**. German name: **Mähren**
Moravia[2] *n* **Alberto**, pen name of *Alberto Pincherle*. 1907–90, Italian novelist and short-story writer: his works include *The Time of Indifference* (1929), *The Woman of Rome* (1949), *The Lie* (1966), and *Erotic Tales* (1985)
moray *n* a large marine eel marked with brilliant colours
WORD ORIGIN Greek *muraina*
Moray[1] *n* a council area and historical county of NE Scotland: part of Grampian region from 1975 to 1996: mainly hilly, with the Cairngorm mountains in the S. Administrative centre: Elgin. Pop: 87 460 (2003 est). Area: 2238 sq km (874 sq miles). Former name: **Elgin**
Moray[2] *or* **Murray** *n* **1st Earl of,** title of *James Stuart*. ?1531–70, regent of Scotland (1567–70) following the abdication of Mary, Queen of Scots, his half-sister. He defeated Mary and Bothwell at Langside (1568); assassinated by a follower of Mary
morbid *adj* **1** having an unusual interest in death or unpleasant events **2** *med* relating to or characterized by disease **morbidity** *n* **morbidly** *adv*
WORD ORIGIN Latin *morbus* illness
mordant *adj* **1** sarcastic or caustic: *mordant wit* ▹ *n* **2** a substance used in dyeing to fix colours **3** an acid or other corrosive fluid used to etch lines on a printing plate
WORD ORIGIN Latin *mordere* to bite
Mordecai[1] *n Old Testament* the cousin of Esther who averted a massacre of the Jews (Esther 2–9)
Mordecai[2] *n Old Testament* the cousin of Esther who averted a massacre of the Jews (Esther 2–9)
more ➊ *adj* **1** ▸ the comparative of **much** or **many**: *more joy than you know; even more are leaving the country* **2** additional or further: *no more apples* **3 more of** to a greater extent or degree: *more of a nuisance* ▹ *adv* **4** used to form the comparative of some adjectives and adverbs: *more quickly* **5** ▸ the comparative of **much**: *people listen to the radio more now* **6 more or less a** as an estimate; approximately **b** to an unspecified extent or degree: *the film was a disaster, more or less*
WORD ORIGIN Old English *māra*
Moreau *n* **1 Gustave** 1826–98, French symbolist painter **2 Jean Victor** 1763–1813, French general in the Revolutionary and Napoleonic Wars **3 Jeanne** born 1928, French stage and film actress. Her films include *Jules et Jim* (1961), *Diary of a Chambermaid* (1964), and *The Proprietor* (1996)
moreish *or* **morish** *adj informal* (of food) causing a desire for more
morel *n* an edible mushroom with a pitted cap

THESAURUS

moral *adj* **3 = good**, just, right, principled, pure, decent, innocent, proper, noble, ethical, upright, honourable, honest, righteous, virtuous, blameless, high-minded, chaste, upstanding, meritorious, incorruptible **OPPOSITE:** immoral ▹ *n* **4 = lesson**, meaning, point, message, teaching, import, significance, precept ▹ *pl n* **5 = morality**, standards, conduct, principles, behaviour, manners, habits, ethics, integrity, mores, scruples
morale *n* **= confidence**, heart, spirit, temper, self-esteem, team spirit, mettle, esprit de corps
morality *n* **1 = virtue**, justice, principles, morals, honour, integrity, goodness, honesty, decency, fair play, righteousness, good behaviour, propriety, chastity, probity, rectitude, rightness, uprightness **2 = rights and wrongs**, ethics, ethicality **3 = ethics**, conduct, principles, ideals, morals, manners, habits, philosophy, mores, moral code
moratorium *n* **1, 2 = postponement**, stay, freeze, halt, suspension, respite, standstill
more *det* **2 = extra**, additional, spare, new, other, added, further, fresh, new-found, supplementary

DICTIONARY

WORD ORIGIN French *morille*
morello *n, pl* **-los** a variety of small very dark sour cherry
WORD ORIGIN Italian: blackish
moreover ❶ *adv* in addition to what has already been said
morepork *n chiefly NZ* ▸ same as **mopoke**
mores (more-rayz) *pl n* the customs and conventions embodying the fundamental values of a community
WORD ORIGIN Latin: customs
Moreton Bay bug *n* an Australian flattish edible shellfish
Morgan[1] *n* an American breed of small compact saddle horse
WORD ORIGIN C19: named after Justin *Morgan* (1747–98), American owner of the original sire
Morgan[2] *n* **1 Edwin (George)** (1920–2010), Scottish poet, noted esp. for his collection *The Second Life* (1968) and his many concrete and visual poems; appointed Scottish national poet 2004 **2** Sir **Henry** 1635–88, Welsh buccaneer, who raided Spanish colonies in the West Indies for the English **3 John Pierpont** 1837–1913, US financier, philanthropist, and art collector **4 (Hywel) Rhodri** born 1939, Welsh Labour politician; first minister of Wales from 2000 **5 Thomas Hunt** 1866–1945, US biologist. He formulated the chromosome theory of heredity. Nobel prize for physiology or medicine 1933
morganatic *adj* of or designating a marriage between a person of high rank and a person of low rank, by which the latter is not elevated to the higher rank and any children have no rights to inherit the higher party's titles or property
WORD ORIGIN Medieval Latin *morganaticum* morning-gift after consummation representing the husband's only liability
morgue *n* **1** a mortuary **2** *informal* a store of clippings and back numbers used for reference in a newspaper
WORD ORIGIN French
moribund *adj* **1** near death **2** no longer performing effectively or usefully: *Romania's moribund economy*
WORD ORIGIN Latin *mori* to die
Mörike *n* **Eduard** 1804–75, German poet, noted for his lyrics, such as *On a Winter's Morning before Sunrise* and *At Midnight*
morish *adj* ▸ same as **moreish**
Morisot *n* **Berthe** 1841–95, French impressionist painter; noted for her studies of women and children
Morley[1] *n* an industrial town in N England, in Leeds unitary authority, West Yorkshire. Pop: 54 051 (2001)
Morley[2] *n* **1 Edward Williams** 1838–1923, US chemist who collaborated with A. A. Michelson in the Michelson-Morley experiment **2 John,** Viscount Morley of Blackburn. 1838–1923, British Liberal statesman and writer; secretary of state for India (1905–10) **3 Robert** 1908–92, British actor. His many films include *Major Barbara* (1940), *Oscar Wilde* (1960), and *The Blue Bird* (1976) **4 Thomas** ?1557–?1603, English composer and organist, noted for his madrigals and his textbook on music, *A Plaine and Easie Introduction to Practicall Musicke* (1597)
Mormon *n* **1** a member of the Church of Jesus Christ of Latter-day Saints, founded in 1830 in New York by Joseph Smith ▹ *adj* **2** of the Mormons, their Church, or their beliefs **Mormonism** *n*
morn *n poetic* morning
WORD ORIGIN Old English *morgen*
mornay *adj* served with a cheese sauce: *haddock mornay*
WORD ORIGIN after Philippe de *Mornay*, Huguenot leader
Mornay *n* **Philippe de,** Seigneur du Plessis-Marly. 1549–1623, French Huguenot leader. Also: **Duplessis-Mornay**
morning ❶ *n* **1** the first part of the day, ending at noon **2** daybreak; dawn **3 the morning after** *informal* the aftereffects of excess, esp. a hangover ▹ *adj* **4** of or in the morning: *morning coffee*
WORD ORIGIN from *morn*, on the model of *evening*
morning dress *n* formal daytime dress for men, consisting of a frock coat with the front cut away (**morning coat**), usually with grey trousers and top hat
morning-glory *n, pl* **-ries** a tropical climbing plant with trumpet-shaped blue, pink, or white flowers, which close in late afternoon
mornings *adv informal* in the morning, esp. regularly, or during every morning
morning sickness *n* nausea occurring shortly after rising in early pregnancy
morning star *n* a planet, usually Venus, seen just before sunrise
Moro[1] *n* **1** (*pl* **-ros** *or* **-ro**) a member of a group of predominantly Muslim peoples of the S Philippines: noted for their manufacture of weapons **2** the language of these peoples, belonging to the Malayo-Polynesian family
WORD ORIGIN C19: via Spanish from Latin *Maurus* MOOR
Moro[2] *n* **Aldo** 1916–78, Italian Christian Democrat statesman; prime minister of Italy (1963–68; 1974–76) and minister of foreign affairs (1965–66; 1969–72; 1973–74). He negotiated the entry of the Italian Communist Party into coalition government before being kidnapped by the Red Brigades in 1978 and murdered
Moroccan *adj* **1** of Morocco ▹ *n* **2** a person from Morocco
morocco *n* a fine soft leather made from goatskins
WORD ORIGIN after *Morocco*, where it was originally made
moron *n* **1** *informal, derogatory* a foolish or stupid person **2** (formerly) a person having an intelligence quotient of between 50 and 70 **moronic** *adj*
WORD ORIGIN Greek *mōros* foolish
morose (mor-**rohss**) *adj* ill-tempered, sullen, and unwilling to talk very much **morosely** *adv*
WORD ORIGIN Latin *morosus* peevish
morpheme *n linguistics* a speech element having a meaning or grammatical function that cannot be subdivided into further such elements
morphine *or* **morphia** *n* a drug extracted from opium: used in medicine as an anaesthetic and sedative
WORD ORIGIN *Morpheus*, in Greek mythology, the god of sleep and dreams
morphing *n* a computer technique used for graphics and in films, in which one image is gradually transformed into another image without individual changes being noticeable in the process
WORD ORIGIN from METAMORPHOSIS
morphology *n* the science of forms and structures of organisms or words **morphological** *adj*
Morphy *n* **Paul** 1837–84, US chess player, widely considered to have been the world's greatest player
morris dance *n* an old English folk dance performed by men (**morris men**) who wear a traditional costume decorated with bells
WORD ORIGIN Middle English *moreys daunce* Moorish dance
morrow *n* **the morrow** *old-fashioned or poetic* **1** the next day **2** the morning
WORD ORIGIN Old English *morgen* morning
Morse code *n* a code formerly used internationally for transmitting messages, in which letters and numbers are represented by groups

THESAURUS

moreover *adv* **= furthermore**, also, further, in addition, too, as well, besides, likewise, what is more, to boot, additionally, into the bargain, withal (*literary*)
morning *n* **1 = before noon**, forenoon, morn (*poetic*), a.m. **2 = dawn**, sunrise, morrow (*archaic*), first light, daybreak, break of day

DICTIONARY

of dots and dashes, or by shorter and longer sounds
WORD ORIGIN after Samuel *Morse*, inventor

morsel *n* a small piece of something, esp. of food
WORD ORIGIN Old French *mors* a bite

mortal ❶ *adj* **1** (of living beings, esp. humans) destined to die sometime rather than living forever **2** causing death; fatal: *a mortal wound* **3** deadly or unrelenting: *he is my mortal enemy* **4** of or resulting from the fear of death: *mortal terror* **5** of or involving life or the world: *the hangman's noose ended his mortal existence* **6** great or very intense: *mortal pain* **7** *informal* conceivable or possible: *there was no mortal reason to leave* **8** *slang* long and tedious: *for three mortal hours* ▹*n* **9** a human being **mortally** *adv*
WORD ORIGIN Latin *mors* death

mortality ❶ *n, pl* **-ties 1** the condition of being mortal **2** great loss of life, as in war or disaster **3** the number of deaths in a given period

mortal sin *n Christianity* a sin that will lead to damnation unless repented of

mortar *n* **1** a small cannon that fires shells in high arcs **2** a mixture of cement or lime or both with sand and water, used to hold bricks or stones together **3** a vessel, usually bowl-shaped, in which substances are crushed with a pestle ▹*vb* **4** to fire on with mortars **5** to join bricks or stones with mortar
WORD ORIGIN Latin *mortarium* basin in which mortar is mixed

mortarboard *n* **1** a black tasselled academic cap with a flat square top **2** a small square board with a handle on the underside for carrying mortar

mortgage *n* **1** an agreement under which a person borrows money to buy property, esp. a house, and the lender can take possession of the property if the borrower fails to repay the money **2** a loan obtained under such an agreement: *a mortgage of three times one's income* **3** a regular repayment of money borrowed under such an agreement: *the monthly mortgage on the building* ▹*vb* **-gaging, -gaged 4** to pledge a house or other property as security for the repayment of a loan ▹*adj* **5** of or relating to a mortgage: *a mortgage payment*
WORD ORIGIN Old French, literally: dead pledge

mortgagee *n* the person or organization who lends money in a mortgage agreement

mortgagor *or* **-ger** *n* the person who borrows money in a mortgage agreement

mortice *or* **mortise** (more-tiss) *n* **1** a slot or recess cut into a piece of wood or stone to receive a matching projection (tenon) on another piece, or a mortice lock ▹*vb* **-ticing, -ticed** *or* **-tising, -tised 2** to cut a slot or recess in a piece of wood or stone **3** to join two pieces of wood or stone by means of a mortice and tenon
WORD ORIGIN Old French *mortoise*

mortice lock *n* a lock set into the edge of a door so that the mechanism of the lock is enclosed by the door

mortician *n chiefly US* ▸ same as **undertaker**

mortify *vb* **-fies, -fying, -fied 1** to make someone feel ashamed or embarrassed **2** *Christianity* to subdue one's emotions, the body, etc. by self-denial **3** (of flesh) to become gangrenous **mortification** *n* **mortifying** *adj*
WORD ORIGIN Latin *mors* death + *facere* to do

Mortimer *n* **1** Sir **John** (**Clifford**) born 1923, British barrister, playwright, and novelist, best known for the television series featuring the barrister Horace Rumpole. His novels include *Paradise Postponed* (1985) and *The Sound of Trumpets* (1998) **2 Roger de,** 8th Baron of Wigmore and 1st Earl of March. 1287–1330, lover of Isabella, the wife of Edward II of England: they invaded England in 1326 and compelled the king to abdicate in favour of his son, Edward III; executed

Morton *n* **1 4th Earl of,** title of *James Douglas*. 1516–81, regent of Scotland (1572–78) for the young James VI. He was implicated in the murders of Rizzio (1566) and Darnley (1567) and played a leading role in ousting Mary, Queen of Scots; executed **2 Jelly Roll,** real name *Ferdinand Joseph La Menthe Morton*. 1885–1941, US jazz pianist, singer, and songwriter; one of the creators of New Orleans jazz

mortuary *n, pl* **-aries** a building or room where dead bodies are kept before cremation or burial
WORD ORIGIN Latin *mortuarius* of the dead

mosaic (moh-zay-ik) *n* a design or decoration made up of small pieces of coloured glass or stone
WORD ORIGIN Greek *mouseios* of the Muses

Mosaic *adj* of or relating to Moses or the laws and traditions ascribed to him

Moseley *n* **Henry Gwyn-Jeffreys** 1887–1915, English physicist. He showed that the wavelengths of X-rays emitted from the elements are related to their atomic numbers

moselle *n* a German white wine from the valley of the river Moselle

mosey *vb* **mosey along** *or* **on** *informal* to walk slowly and casually; amble
WORD ORIGIN origin unknown

Moshesh *or* **Moshoeshoe** *n* died 1870, African chief, who founded the Basotho nation, now Lesotho

Moslem *n, pl* **-lems** *or* **-lem** *adj* ▸ same as **Muslim**

Mosley *n* Sir **Oswald Ernald** 1896–1980, British politician; founder of the British Union of Fascists (1932)

mosque *n* a Muslim place of worship
WORD ORIGIN Arabic *masjid* temple

mosquito *n, pl* **-toes** *or* **-tos** a two-winged insect, the females of which pierce the skin of humans and animals to suck their blood
WORD ORIGIN Spanish, diminutive of *mosca* fly

mosquito net *n* a fine curtain or net to keep mosquitoes away, esp. hung over a bed

moss *n* **1** a very small flowerless plant typically growing in dense mats on trees, rocks, or moist ground **2** *Scot & N English* a peat bog or marsh **mossy** *adj*
WORD ORIGIN Old English *mos* swamp

Moss *n* **1 Kate** born 1974, British supermodel. **2** Sir **Stirling** born 1929, English racing driver

mossie *n S African* the common sparrow
WORD ORIGIN Afrikaans

moss rose *n* a variety of rose that has a mossy stem and fragrant pink flowers

most *n* **1** the greatest number or degree: *the most I can ever remember being paid* **2** the majority: *most of his records are dreadful* **3 at (the) most** at the maximum: *she is fifteen at the most* **4 make the most of** to use to the best advantage: *they made the most of their chances* ▹*adj* **5** of or being the majority of a group of things or people or the largest part of something: *most people don't share your views* **6 the most** ▸ the superlative of **many** or **much**: *he has the most talent* ▹*adv* **7 the most** used to form the superlative of some adjectives and adverbs: *the most beautiful women in the*

THESAURUS

mortal *adj* **1, 5 = human**, worldly, passing, earthly, fleshly, temporal, transient, ephemeral, perishable, corporeal, impermanent, sublunary **2 = fatal**, killing, terminal, deadly, destructive, lethal, murderous, death-dealing ▹*n* **9 = human being**, being, man, woman, body, person, human, individual, earthling

mortality *n* **1 = humanity**, transience, impermanence, ephemerality, temporality, corporeality, impermanency **2, 3 = death**, dying, fatality, loss of life

m

DICTIONARY

world **8** ▸ the superlative of **much**: *what do you like most about your job?* **9** very; exceedingly: *a most unfortunate accident*
WORD ORIGIN Old English *māst* or *mǣst*

mostly ❶ *adv* **1** almost entirely; generally: *the men at the party were mostly young* **2** on many or most occasions; usually: *rattlesnakes mostly hunt at night*

Most Reverend *n* (in Britain) a courtesy title applied to archbishops

mot (moh) *n* ▸ short for **bon mot**
WORD ORIGIN French: word

MOT **1** *Brit* ▸ short for **MOT test** **2** *Brit* the certificate showing that a vehicle has passed its MOT test **3** *NZ* Ministry of Transport

mote *n* a tiny speck
WORD ORIGIN Old English *mot*

motel *n* a roadside hotel for motorists
WORD ORIGIN *mo(tor)* + *(ho)tel*

motet (moh-tet) *n* a religious song for a choir in which several voices, usually unaccompanied, sing contrasting parts simultaneously
WORD ORIGIN Old French, diminutive of *mot* word

moth *n* any of numerous chiefly nocturnal insects resembling butterflies, that typically have stout bodies and do not have club-shaped antennae
WORD ORIGIN Old English *moththe*

mothball *n* **1** a small ball of camphor or naphthalene placed in stored clothing to repel clothes moths **2 put in mothballs** to postpone work on ▹ *vb* **3** to take something out of operation but maintain it for future use **4** to postpone work on

moth-eaten *adj* **1** decayed or scruffy **2** eaten away by or as if by moths: *a moth-eaten suit*

mother ❶ *n* **1** a female who has given birth to offspring **2** a person's own mother **3** a title given to certain members of female religious orders **4** motherly qualities, such as maternal affection: *it appealed to the mother in her* **5 the mother of** a female or thing that creates, founds, or protects something: *the mother of modern feminism; necessity is the mother of invention* **6 the mother of all** *informal* the greatest example of its kind: *the mother of all parties* ▹ *adj* **7** of or relating to a female or thing that creates, founds, or protects something: *our mother company is in New York* **8** native or innate: *mother wit* ▹ *vb* **9** to give birth to or produce **10** to nurture or protect **motherless** *adj* **motherly** *adj*
WORD ORIGIN Old English *mōdor*

Mother Carey's chicken *n* ▸ same as **stormy petrel**
WORD ORIGIN origin unknown

mother country *n* **1** the original country of colonists or settlers **2** a person's native country

motherhood *n* the state of being a mother

Mothering Sunday *n* **1** (in Britain and S Africa) the fourth Sunday in Lent, when mothers traditionally receive presents from their children **2** (in Australia) the second Sunday in May, when mothers traditionally receive presents from their children. Also called: **Mother's Day**

mother-in-law *n, pl* **mothers-in-law** the mother of one's wife or husband

motherland *n* a person's native country

mother-of-pearl *n* a hard iridescent substance that forms the inner layer of the shells of certain molluscs, such as the oyster

Mother's Day *n* **1** ▸ see **Mothering Sunday** **2** *US & Canad* the second Sunday in May, observed as a day in honour of mothers

mother superior *n, pl* **mother superiors** *or* **mothers superior** the head of a community of nuns

mother tongue *n* the language first learned by a child

mothproof *adj* **1** (esp. of clothes) chemically treated so as to repel clothes moths ▹ *vb* **2** to make mothproof

motif ❶ (moh-teef) *n* **1** a distinctive idea, esp. a theme elaborated on in a piece of music or literature **2** a recurring shape in a design **3** a single decoration, such as a symbol or name on a piece of clothing
WORD ORIGIN French

motile *adj* capable of independent movement **motility** *n*
WORD ORIGIN Latin *movere* to move

motion ❶ *n* **1** the process of continual change in the position of an object; movement: *the motion of the earth round the sun* ▸ Related adjective: **kinetic** **2** a movement or gesture: *he made stabbing motions with the spear* **3** a way or style of moving: *massage the back with steady circular motions* **4** a formal proposal to be discussed and voted on in a debate or meeting **5** *Brit* **a** the evacuation of the bowels **b** excrement **6 go through the motions** to do something mechanically or without sincerity **7 set in motion** to make operational or start functioning ▹ *vb* **8** to signal or direct a person by a movement or gesture: *she motioned to me to sit down* **motionless** *adj*
WORD ORIGIN Latin *movere* to move

Motion *n* **Andrew** born 1952, British poet and biographer; his collections include *Pleasure Steamers* (1978) and *Public Property* (2002): poet laureate from 1999

motion picture *n US & Canad* a film; movie

motivate ❶ *vb* **-vating, -vated** **1** to give a reason or inspiration for a course of action to someone: *he was motivated purely by greed* **2** to inspire and encourage someone to do something: *a good teacher must motivate her pupils* **motivation** *n*

motive ❶ *n* **1** the reason, whether conscious or unconscious, for a certain course of action **2** ▸ same as **motif** (sense 2) ▹ *adj* **3** of or causing motion: *a motive force*
WORD ORIGIN Late Latin *motivus* moving

motive power *n* **1** any source of energy used to produce motion **2** the means of supplying power to an engine or vehicle

mot juste (moh **zhoost**) *n, pl* **mots justes** the appropriate word or expression
WORD ORIGIN French

motley *adj* **1** made up of people or things of different types: *a motley assortment of mules, donkeys, and camels*

m

THESAURUS

mostly *adv* **1 = mainly**, largely, chiefly, principally, primarily, above all, on the whole, predominantly, for the most part, almost entirely **2 = generally**, usually, on the whole, most often, as a rule, customarily

mother *n* **1, 2 = female parent**, mum *(Brit informal)*, ma *(informal)*, mater, dam, old woman *(informal)*, mom *(US & Canad)*, mummy *(Brit informal)*, old lady *(informal)*, foster mother, birth mother, biological mother ▹ *modifier* **8 = native**, natural, innate, inborn, connate ▸ *related adjective:* maternal ▹ *vb* **10 = nurture**, raise, protect, tend, nurse, rear, care for, cherish

motif *n* **1 = theme**, idea, subject, concept, leitmotif **2, 3 = design**, form, shape, decoration, ornament

motion *n* **1 = movement**, action, mobility, passing, travel, progress, flow, passage, locomotion, motility, kinesics **4 = proposal**, suggestion, recommendation, proposition, submission ▹ *vb* **8 = gesture**, direct, wave, signal, nod, beckon, gesticulate

motivate *vb* **1 = inspire**, drive, stimulate, provoke, lead, move, cause, prompt, stir, trigger, set off, induce, arouse, prod, get going, instigate, impel, actuate, give incentive to, inspirit **2 = stimulate**, drive, inspire, stir, arouse, get going, galvanize, incentivize

motive *n* **1 = reason**, motivation, cause, ground(s), design, influence, purpose, object, intention, spur, incentive, inspiration, stimulus, rationale, inducement, incitement, mainspring, the why and wherefore

DICTIONARY

2 multicoloured ▷*n* **3** *history* the costume of a jester
WORD ORIGIN perhaps Old English *mot* speck

motocross *n* the sport of motorcycle racing across rough ground
WORD ORIGIN *moto(r) + cross(-country)*

motor *n* **1** the engine, esp. an internal-combustion engine, of a vehicle **2** a machine that converts energy, esp. electrical energy, into mechanical energy **3** *chiefly Brit informal* a car ▷*adj* **4** *chiefly Brit* of or relating to cars and other vehicles powered by petrol or diesel engines: *the motor industry* **5** powered by or relating to a motor: *a new synthetic motor oil* **6** *physiol* producing or causing motion ▷*vb* **7** to travel by car **8** *informal* to move fast
motorized or **-ised** *adj*
WORD ORIGIN Latin *movere* to move

motorbicycle *n* **1** a motorcycle **2** a moped

motorbike *n informal* a motorcycle

motorboat *n* any boat powered by a motor

motorcade *n* a procession of cars carrying an important person or people
WORD ORIGIN *motor + (caval)cade*

motorcar *n* ▸a more formal word for **car**

motorcycle *n* a two-wheeled vehicle driven by an engine **motorcyclist** *n*

motorist *n* a driver of a car

motorman *n, pl* **-men** *Brit, Austral & NZ* the driver of an electric train

motor scooter *n* a light motorcycle with small wheels and an enclosed engine

motor vehicle *n* a road vehicle driven by an engine

motorway *n Brit, Austral, & NZ* a dual carriageway for fast-moving traffic, with no stopping permitted and no crossroads

Motown *n trademark* music combining rhythm and blues and pop
WORD ORIGIN *Mo(tor) Town,* nickname for Detroit

motte *n history* a mound on which a castle was built
WORD ORIGIN Old French

MOT test *n* (in Britain) a compulsory annual test of the roadworthiness of motor vehicles over 3 years old

mottled *adj* coloured with streaks or blotches of different shades
mottling *n*
WORD ORIGIN from *motley*

motto ❶ *n, pl* **-toes** or **-tos** **1** a short saying expressing the guiding maxim or ideal of a family or organization, esp. when part of a coat of arms **2** a verse or maxim contained in a paper cracker **3** a quotation prefacing a book or chapter of a book
WORD ORIGIN Italian

mould[1] ❶ *or US* **mold** *n* **1** a shaped hollow container into which a liquid material is poured so that it can set in a particular shape: *pour the mixture into a buttered mould, cover, and steam for two hours* **2** a shape, nature, or type: *an orthodox Communist in the Stalinist mould* **3** a framework around which something is constructed or shaped: *the heated glass is shaped round a mould inside a kiln* **4** something, esp. a food, made in or on a mould: *salmon mould* ▷*vb* **5** to make in a mould **6** to shape or form: *a figure moulded out of clay* **7** to influence or direct: *cultural factors moulding our everyday life*
WORD ORIGIN Latin *modulus* a small measure

mould[2] ❶ *or US* **mold** *n* a coating or discoloration caused by various fungi that develop in a damp atmosphere on food, fabrics, and walls
WORD ORIGIN Northern English dialect *mowlde* mouldy

mould[3] *or US* **mold** *n* loose soil, esp. when rich in organic matter: *leaf mould*
WORD ORIGIN Old English *molde*

mouldboard *or US* **moldboard** *n* the curved blade of a plough, which turns over the furrow

moulder *or US* **molder** *vb* to crumble or cause to crumble, as through decay: *John Brown's body lies mouldering in the grave*
WORD ORIGIN from MOULD[3]

moulding *or US* **molding** *n* a shaped ornamental edging

mouldy *or US* **moldy** *adj* **-dier, -diest** **1** covered with mould **2** stale or musty, esp. from age or lack of use **3** *slang* dull or boring

Moulin *n* **Jean** 1899–1943, French lawyer and Resistance hero; Chairman of the National Council of the Resistance (1943): tortured to death by the Nazis

moult *or US* **molt** *vb* **1** (of birds and animals) to shed feathers, hair, or skin so that they can be replaced by a new growth ▷*n* **2** the periodic process of moulting
WORD ORIGIN Latin *mutare* to change

mound ❶ *n* **1** a heap of earth, debris, etc. **2** any heap or pile **3** a small natural hill
WORD ORIGIN origin unknown

mount[1] ❶ *vb* **1** to climb or ascend: *he mounted the stairs to his flat* **2** to get up on a horse, a platform, etc. **3** Also: **mount up** to increase or accumulate: *costs do mount up; the tension mounted* **4** to fix onto a backing, setting, or support: *sensors mounted on motorway bridges* **5** to organize and stage a campaign, a play, etc.: *the Allies mounted a counter attack on the eastern front* ▷*n* **6** a backing, setting, or support onto which something is fixed: *a diamond set in a gold mount* **7** a horse for riding: *none of his mounts at yesterday's race meeting finished better than third*
WORD ORIGIN same as MOUNT[2]

mount[2] *n* a mountain or hill: used in literature and (when cap.) in proper names: *Mount Etna*
WORD ORIGIN Latin *mons* mountain

mountain ❶ *n* **1** a very large, high, and steep hill: *the highest mountain in the Alps* **2** a huge heap or mass: *a mountain of papers* **3** a surplus of a commodity, esp. in the European Union: *a butter mountain* ▷*adj* **4** of, found on, or for use on a mountain or mountains: *a mountain village*
WORD ORIGIN Latin *mons*

mountain ash *n* a tree with clusters of small white flowers and bright red berries; rowan

mountain bike *n* a type of bicycle

THESAURUS

motto *n* **1 = saying**, slogan, maxim, rule, cry, formula, gnome, adage, proverb, dictum, precept, byword, watchword, tag-line

mould[1] *n* **1 = cast**, form, die, shape, pattern, stamp, matrix **2 = nature**, character, sort, kind, quality, type, stamp, kidney, calibre, ilk ▷*vb* **6 = shape**, make, work, form, create, model, fashion, cast, stamp, construct, carve, forge, sculpt **7 = influence**, make, form, control, direct, affect, shape

mould[2] *n* **= fungus**, blight, mildew, mustiness, mouldiness

mound *n* **1, 2 = heap**, bing *(Scot)*, pile, drift, stack, rick **3 = hill**, bank, rise, dune, embankment, knoll, hillock, kopje *or* koppie *(S African)*

mount[1] *vb* **1 = ascend**, scale, climb (up), go up, clamber up, make your way up **OPPOSITE:** descend **2 = get (up) on**, jump on, straddle, climb onto, climb up on, hop on to, bestride, get on the back of, get astride **OPPOSITE:** get off **3a = increase**, build, grow, swell, intensify, escalate, multiply **OPPOSITE:** decrease **3b = accumulate**, increase, collect, gather, build up, pile up, amass, cumulate **5 = display**, present, stage, prepare, put on, organize, get up *(informal)*, exhibit, put on display ▷*n* **6 = backing**, setting, support, stand, base, mounting, frame, fixture, foil **7 = horse**, steed *(literary)*

mountain *n* **1 = peak**, mount, height, ben *(Scot)*, horn, ridge, fell *(Brit)*, berg *(S African)*, alp, pinnacle, elevation, Munro, eminence **2 = heap**, mass, masses, pile, a great deal, ton, stack, abundance, mound, profusion, shedload *(Brit informal)*

mourn *vb* **a** *(often with* **for***)* **= grieve for,**

with straight handlebars and heavy-duty tyres, originally designed for use over rough hilly ground

mountain cat *n* any of various wild animals of the cat family, such as the bobcat, lynx, or puma

mountaineer *n* **1** a person who climbs mountains ▹*vb* **2** to climb mountains **mountaineering** *n*

mountain goat *n* a wild goat inhabiting mountainous regions

mountain lion *n* a puma

mountainous *adj* **1** having many mountains: *a mountainous region* **2** like a mountain or mountains, esp. in size: *mountainous waves*

mountain oyster *n NZ informal* a sheep's testicle eaten as food

mountain sickness *n* nausea, headache, and shortness of breath caused by climbing to high altitudes

Mountbatten *n* **Louis** (**Francis Albert Victor Nicholas**), 1st Earl Mountbatten of Burma 1900–79, British naval commander; great-grandson of Queen Victoria. During World War II he was supreme allied commander in SE Asia (1943–46). He was the last viceroy of India (1947) and governor general (1947–48); killed by an IRA bomb

mountebank *n* **1** (formerly) a person who sold quack medicines in public places **2** a charlatan or fake
WORD ORIGIN Italian *montambanco* a climber on a bench

mounted *adj* riding horses: *mounted police*

Mountie *or* **Mounty** *n, pl* **Mounties** *informal* a member of the Royal Canadian Mounted Police
WORD ORIGIN from *mounted*

mounting *n* ▸same as **mount**[1] (sense 6)

mourn ❶ *vb* to feel or express sadness for the death or loss of someone or something **mourner** *n*
WORD ORIGIN Old English *murnan*

mournful *adj* **1** feeling or expressing grief and sadness: *he stood by, a mournful expression on his face* **2** (of a sound) suggestive or reminiscent of grief or sadness: *the locomotive gave a mournful bellow* **mournfully** *adv*

mourning ❶ *n* **1** sorrow or grief, esp. over a death **2** the conventional symbols of grief for a death, such as the wearing of black **3** the period of time during which a death is officially mourned ▹*adj* **4** of or relating to mourning

mouse *n, pl* **mice 1** a small long-tailed rodent similar to but smaller than a rat **2** a quiet, timid, or cowardly person **3** *computers* a hand-held device used to control cursor movements and computing functions without keying ▹*vb* **mousing, moused 4** *rare* to stalk and catch mice
WORD ORIGIN Old English *mūs*

mouser *n* a cat or other animal that is used to catch mice

mousetrap *n* **1** a spring-loaded trap for killing mice **2** *Brit informal* cheese of mediocre quality

moussaka *n* a dish originating in the Balkan States, consisting of meat, aubergines, and tomatoes, topped with cheese sauce
WORD ORIGIN Modern Greek

mousse *n* **1** a light creamy dessert made with eggs, cream, and fruit set with gelatine **2** a similar dish made from fish or meat **3** ▸short for **styling mousse**
WORD ORIGIN French: froth

moustache *or US* **mustache** *n* unshaved hair growing on the upper lip
WORD ORIGIN French, from Italian *mostaccio*

mousy *or* **mousey** *adj* **mousier, mousiest 1** (of hair) dull light brown in colour **2** shy or ineffectual **mousiness** *n*

mouth ❶ *n, pl* **mouths 1** the opening through which many animals take in food and issue sounds **2** the visible part of the mouth; lips **3** a person regarded as a consumer of food: *three mouths to feed* **4** a particular manner of speaking: *a foul mouth* **5** *informal* boastful, rude, or excessive talk: *she is all mouth* **6** the point where a river issues into a sea or lake **7** an opening, such as that of a bottle, tunnel, or gun **8 down in the mouth** in low spirits ▹*vb* **9** to form words with movements of the lips but without speaking **10** to speak or say something insincerely, esp. in public: *ministers mouthing platitudes*
WORD ORIGIN Old English *mūth*

mouthful *n, pl* **-fuls 1** the amount of food or drink put into the mouth at any one time when eating or drinking **2** a long word, phrase, or name that is difficult to say **3** *Brit informal* an abusive response: *I asked him to move and he just gave me a mouthful*

mouth organ *n* ▸same as **harmonica**

mouthpiece *n* **1** the part of a wind instrument into which the player blows **2** the part of a telephone receiver into which a person speaks **3** a person or publication expressing the views of an organization

mouthwash *n* a medicated solution for gargling and cleansing the mouth

mouthwatering *adj* (of food) making one want to eat it, because it looks or smells delicious

movable *or* **moveable** *adj* **1** able to be moved; not fixed **2** (of a festival, esp. Easter) varying in date from year to year ▹*n* **3 movables** movable articles, esp. furniture

move ❶ *vb* **moving, moved 1** to go or take from one place to another; change in position: *I moved your books off the table* **2** to start to live or work in a different place: *I moved to Brighton from Bristol last year* **3** to be or cause to be in motion: *the trees were moving in the wind; the car moved slowly down the road* **4** to act or begin to act: *the government plans to move to reduce crime* **5** to cause or prompt to do something: *public opinion moved the President to act* **6** to change the time when something is scheduled to happen: *can I move the appointment to Friday afternoon, please?* **7** to arouse affection, pity, or

m

miss, lament, keen for, weep for, sorrow for, wail for, wear black for **b = bemoan**, rue, deplore, bewail

mourning *n* **1 = grieving**, grief, bereavement, weeping, woe, lamentation, keening **2 = black**, weeds, sackcloth and ashes, widow's weeds

mouth *n* **1, 2 = lips**, trap (*slang*), chops (*slang*), jaws, gob (*slang, esp. Brit*), maw, yap (*slang*), cakehole (*Brit slang*) **6 = inlet**, outlet, estuary, firth, outfall, debouchment **7a = entrance**, opening, gateway, cavity, door, aperture, crevice, orifice **7b = opening**, lip, rim

move *vb* **1 = go**, walk, march, advance, progress, shift, proceed, stir, budge, make a move, change position **1, 6 = transfer**, change, carry, transport, switch, shift, transpose **2 = relocate**, leave, remove, quit, go away, migrate, emigrate, move house, flit (*Scot & Northern English dialect*), decamp, up sticks (*Brit informal*), pack your bags (*informal*), change residence **5 = drive**, lead, cause, influence, persuade, push, shift, inspire, prompt, stimulate, motivate, induce, shove, activate, propel, rouse, prod, incite, impel, set going **OPPOSITE:** discourage **7 = touch**, affect, excite, impress, stir, agitate, disquiet, make an impression on, tug at your heartstrings (*often facetious*) **9 = propose**, suggest, urge, recommend, request, advocate, submit, put forward ▹*n* **17 = action**, act, step, movement, shift, motion, manoeuvre, deed **18 = ploy**, action, measure, step, initiative, stroke, tactic, manoeuvre, deed, tack, ruse, gambit, stratagem **19 = transfer**, posting, shift, removal, migration, relocation, flit (*Scot & Northern English dialect*), flitting (*Scot & Northern English dialect*), change of address **20a, 20b = turn**, go, play, chance, shot (*informal*), opportunity

DICTIONARY

compassion in; touch: *her story moved me to tears* **8** to change, progress, or develop in a specified way: *the conversation moved to more personal matters* **9** to suggest a proposal formally, as in a debate: *to move a motion* **10** to spend most of one's time with a specified social group: *they both move in theatrical, arty circles* **11** (in board games) to change the position of a piece **12** (of machines) to work or operate **13** **a** (of the bowels) to excrete waste **b** to cause the bowels to excrete waste **14** (of merchandise) to be disposed of by being bought **15** to travel quickly: *this car can really move* **16** **move heaven and earth** do everything possible to achieve a result ▸ *n* **17** the act of moving; movement **18** one of a sequence of actions, usually part of a plan: *the first real move towards disarmament* **19** the act of moving one's home or place of business **20** **a** (in a boardgame) a player's turn to move his piece **b** (in a boardgame) a manoeuvre of a piece **21** **get a move on** *informal* to hurry up **22** **make a move** *informal* **a** to prepare or begin to leave a place to go somewhere else: *we'd better make a move if we want to be home before dark* **b** to do something which will produce a response: *neither of us wanted to make the first move* **23** **on the move** travelling from place to place
WORD ORIGIN Latin *movere*

move in *vb* **1** Also: **move into** to start to live in a different house or flat **2** to start to live in the same house or flat as: *he moved in with his girlfriend* **3** to attack a person or place, or try to gain influence or control over a person or activity: *the police moved in to break up the demonstration*

movement ⓣ *n* **1** the act, process, or an instance of moving **2** the manner of moving: *their movement is jerky* **3** **a** a group of people with a common ideology **b** the organized action and campaigning of such a group: *a successful movement to abolish child labour* **4** a trend or tendency: *a movement towards shorter working hours* **5** *finance* a change in the price or value of shares, a currency, etc.: *adverse currency movements* **6** *music* a principal self-contained section of a large-scale work, such as a symphony **7** **movements** a person's location and activities during a specific time: *police were trying to piece together the recent movements of the two men* **8** **a** the evacuation of the bowels **b** the matter evacuated **9** the mechanism which drives and regulates a watch or clock

move on *vb* **1** to leave one place in order to go elsewhere: *we spent three days in Perth before moving on towards Inverness* **2** to order (someone) to leave and go elsewhere: *we were moved on by the police* **3** to finish one thing and turn one's attention to something else: *can we move on to the next question?*

move over *vb* **1** to change one's position in order to make room for someone else: *if you moved over there'd be room for us both on the couch* **2** to leave one's job so that someone else can have it: *she decided to move over to let someone younger onto the board*

mover *n* **1** a person or animal that moves in a particular way: *a slow mover* **2** the person who first puts forward a proposal **3** *US & Canad* a removal firm or a person who works for one

movie ⓣ *n* **1** *informal* a cinema film **2** **the movies** the cinema: *I want to go to the movies tonight*

moving ⓣ *adj* **1** arousing or touching the emotions: *a moving account of her son's death* **2** changing or capable of changing position: *a moving target* **movingly** *adv*

moving staircase *or* **stairway** *n* an escalator

mow ⓣ *vb* **mowing, mowed, mowed** *or* **mown** **1** to cut down grass or crops: *a tractor chugged along, mowing hay* **2** to cut the growing vegetation of a field or lawn: *to mow a meadow* **mower** *n*
WORD ORIGIN Old English *māwan*

mow down ⓣ *vb* to kill in large numbers, esp. by gunfire

Mowlam *n* **Mo,** full name *Marjorie Mowlam.* 1949–2005, British Labour politician; secretary of state for Northern Ireland (1997–99) and minister for the cabinet office (1999–2001)

mown *vb* ▸ the past participle of **mow**

Moya *n* **(John) Hidalgo** 1920–94, British architect: in partnership with Philip Powell, his designs include Skylon, Festival of Britain (1950), Wolfson College, Oxford (1974), and the Queen Elizabeth Conference Centre, Westminster (1986)

mozzarella (mot-sa-**rel**-la) *n* a moist white curd cheese originally made in Italy from buffalo milk
WORD ORIGIN Italian

MP **1** Member of Parliament **2** Military Police **3** Mounted Police

MP3 *n computers* an audio or video file created using MPEG-1 Audio Layer-3, trade name of a file compression system

MPEG (**em**-peg) *n computers* **a** a standard compressed file format used for audio and video files **b** a file in this format
WORD ORIGIN from *Motion Picture Experts Group*

mpg miles per gallon

mph miles per hour

MPhil Master of Philosophy

MPV multipurpose vehicle

Mr *n, pl* **Messrs** a title used before a man's name or before some office that he holds: *Mr Pickwick; Mr President*
WORD ORIGIN from *mister*

MRI *med* magnetic resonance imaging: a diagnostic scanning technique which gives detailed images of internal tissue by analysing its response to being bombarded with high-frequency radio waves within a strong magnetic field

Mrs *n, pl* **Mrs** *or* **Mesdames** a title used before the name of a married woman
WORD ORIGIN from *mistress*

ms millisecond(s)

Ms (**mizz**) *n* a title used before the name of a woman to avoid indicating whether she is married or not

MS **1** Mississippi **2** multiple sclerosis

MS. *or* **ms.** *pl* **MSS** *or* **mss** manuscript

MSc Master of Science

MSF Manufacturing, Science, and Finance (Union)

MSG monosodium glutamate

MSM mainstream media

MSP (in Britain) Member of the Scottish Parliament

MST Mountain Standard Time

mt megaton

Mt[1] Mount: *Mt Everest*

Mt[2] *chem* meitnerium

MT Montana

mt. megaton

MTech (in the US) Master of Technology

THESAURUS

movement *n* **1 = activity**, moving, stirring, bustle, agitation **1, 2 = move**, act, action, operation, motion, gesture, manoeuvre
3a = group, party, organization, grouping, front, camp, faction
3b = campaign, drive, push, crusade
5 = development, change, shift, variation, fluctuation **6** *(music)* **= section**, part, division, passage

movie *n* **1 = film**, picture, feature, flick *(slang)*, motion picture, moving picture *(US)*

moving *adj* **1 = emotional**, touching, affecting, exciting, inspiring, stirring, arousing, poignant, emotive, impelling
OPPOSITE: unemotional
2 = mobile, running, active, going, operational, in motion, driving, kinetic, movable, motile, unfixed
OPPOSITE: stationary

mow *vb* **1, 2 = cut**, crop, trim, shear, scythe

mow something *or* **someone down** *vb* **= massacre**, butcher, slaughter, cut down, shoot down, blow away

DICTIONARY

Mu'awiyah I *n* ?602–680 AD, first caliph (661–80) of the Omayyad dynasty of Damascus; regarded as having secularized the caliphate
Mubarak *n* **(Muhammad) Hosni** born 1928, Egyptian statesman; president of Egypt from 1981
much ❶ *adj* **more, most 1** a large amount or degree of: *there isn't much wine left* ▹ *n* **2** a large amount or degree **3 a bit much** *informal* rather excessive **4 make much of a** to make sense of: *he couldn't make much of her letter* **b** to give importance to: *the press made much of the story* **5 not much of** not to any appreciable degree or extent: *he's not much of a cook* **6 not up to much** *informal* of a low standard: *this beer is not up to much* ▹ *adv* **7** considerably: *I'm much better now* **8** practically or nearly: *it's much the same* **9** often or a great deal: *that doesn't happen much these days* **10 (as) much as** even though; although: *much as I'd like to, I can't come* ▸ See also **more, most**
WORD ORIGIN Old English *mycel*
muchness *n* **much of a muchness** *Brit & NZ* very similar
mucilage (mew-sill-ij) *n* **1** a sticky substance used as an adhesive, such as gum or glue **2** a glutinous substance secreted by certain plants **mucilaginous** *adj*
WORD ORIGIN Late Latin *mucilago* mouldy juice
muck ❶ *n* **1** dirt or filth **2** farmyard dung or decaying vegetable matter **3** *slang chiefly Brit & NZ* something of poor quality; rubbish: *I don't want to eat this muck* **4 make a muck of** *slang chiefly Brit & NZ* to ruin or spoil ▹ *vb* **5** to spread manure upon ▸ See also **muck about, muck in,** etc.
WORD ORIGIN probably Old Norse
muck about *or* **around** *vb slang* **1** to waste time by misbehaving or being silly **2 muck about with** to interfere with, annoy, or waste the time of
muck in *vb Brit & NZ slang* to share duties or work with other people
muck out *vb* to clean (a barn, stable, etc.)
muckraking *n* seeking out and exposing scandal relating to well-known people **muckraker** *n*
mucksweat *n Brit informal* profuse sweat
muck up *vb informal* to ruin, spoil, or do very badly: *I mucked up my driving test*
mucky *adj* **1** dirty or muddy: *don't come in here with your mucky boots on!* **2** sexually explicit; obscene: *a mucky book*
mucosa *n* ▸ same as **mucous membrane** > **mucosal** *adj*
WORD ORIGIN Latin *mucosus* slimy
mucous membrane *n* a mucus-secreting tissue that lines body cavities or passages
mucus (mew-kuss) *n* the slimy protective secretion of the mucous membranes **mucosity** *n* **mucous** *adj*
WORD ORIGIN Latin: nasal secretions
mud ❶ *n* **1** soft wet earth, as found on the ground after rain or at the bottom of ponds **2 (someone's) name is mud** *informal* (someone) is disgraced **3 throw mud at** *informal* to slander or vilify ▹ *adj* **4** made from mud or dried mud: *a mud hut*
WORD ORIGIN probably Low German *mudde*
mud bath *n* **1** a medicinal bath in heated mud **2** a dirty or muddy place, occasion, or state: *heavy rain turned the pitch into a mud bath*
muddle ❶ *n* **1** a state of untidiness or confusion: *the files are in a terrible muddle* **2** a state of mental confusion or uncertainty: *the government are in a muddle over the economy* ▹ *vb* **-dling, -dled 3** Also: **muddle up** to mix up or confuse (objects or items): *you've got your books all muddled up with mine* **4** to make (someone) confused: *don't muddle her with too many suggestions* **muddled** *adj*
WORD ORIGIN perhaps Middle Dutch *moddelen* to make muddy
muddleheaded *adj* mentally confused or vague
muddle through *vb* to succeed in spite of lack of organization
muddy ❶ *adj* **-dier, -diest 1** covered or filled with mud **2** not clear or bright: *muddy colours* **3** cloudy: *a muddy liquid* **4** (esp. of thoughts) confused or vague ▹ *vb* **-dies, -dying, -died 5** to make muddy **6** to make a situation or issue less clear: *the allegations of sexual misconduct only serve to muddy the issue* **muddily** *adv*
mud flat *n* an area of low muddy land that is covered at high tide but not at low tide
mud flow *n* the rapid downhill movement of a mass of mud, typically in the shape of a tongue
mudguard *n* a curved part of a bicycle or other vehicle attached above the wheels to reduce the amount of water or mud thrown up by them
mudpack *n* a cosmetic paste applied to the face to improve the complexion
mudpie *n* a mass of mud moulded into a pielike shape by a child
mudslinging *n* the making of malicious personal attacks on an opponent, esp. in politics **mudslinger** *n*
muesli (mewz-lee) *n* a mixture of rolled oats, nuts, and dried fruit, usually eaten with milk
WORD ORIGIN Swiss German
muezzin (moo-ezz-in) *n islam* the official of a mosque who calls the faithful to prayer from the minaret
WORD ORIGIN Arabic *mu'adhdhin*
muff[1] *n* a tube of fur or cloth into which the hands are placed for warmth
WORD ORIGIN probably Dutch *mof*
muff[2] *vb* **1** to do (something) badly: *I muffed my chance to make a good impression* **2** to bungle (a shot or catch)
WORD ORIGIN origin unknown
muffin *n* **1** a small cup-shaped sweet bread roll, usually eaten hot with butter **2** a thick round baked yeast roll, usually toasted and served with butter
WORD ORIGIN origin unknown
muffle *vb* **-fling, -fled 1** to deaden (a sound or noise), esp. by wrapping the source of it in something: *the sound was muffled by the double glazing* **2** to wrap up in a scarf or coat for warmth **3** to censor or restrict: *an*

m

THESAURUS

(slang, chiefly US), cut to pieces
much *adj* **1 = great**, a lot of, plenty of, considerable, substantial, piles of *(informal)*, ample, abundant, copious, oodles of *(informal)*, plenteous, sizable or sizeable amount, shedful *(slang)*
OPPOSITE: little
▹ *adv* **7 = greatly**, a lot, considerably, decidedly, exceedingly, appreciably
OPPOSITE: hardly
9 = often, a lot, regularly, routinely, a great deal, frequently, many times, habitually, on many occasions, customarily ▹ *noun* **2 = a lot**, plenty, a great deal, lots *(informal)*, masses *(informal)*, loads *(informal)*, tons *(informal)*, heaps *(informal)*, a good deal, an appreciable amount
OPPOSITE: little
muck *n* **1 = dirt**, mud, filth, crap *(taboo, slang)*, sewage, ooze, scum, sludge, mire, slime, slob *(Irish)*, gunk *(informal)*, gunge *(informal)*, crud *(slang)*, kak *(S African informal)*, grot *(slang)* **2 = manure**, crap *(taboo, slang)*, dung, ordure
mud *n* **1 = dirt**, clay, ooze, silt, sludge, mire, slime, slob *(Irish)*, gloop *(informal)*
muddle *n* **1, 2 = confusion**, mess, disorder, chaos, plight, tangle, mix-up, clutter, disarray, daze, predicament, jumble, ravel, perplexity, disorganization, hotchpotch, hodgepodge *(US)*, pig's breakfast *(informal)*, fankle *(Scot)* ▹ *vb* **3 = jumble**, confuse, disorder, scramble, tangle, mix up, make a mess of **4 = confuse**, bewilder, daze, confound, perplex, disorient, stupefy, befuddle
muddy *adj* **1a = boggy**, swampy, marshy, miry, quaggy **1b = dirty**, soiled, grimy, mucky, mud-caked, bespattered, clarty *(Scot & Northern English dialect)*

DICTIONARY

attempt to muffle criticism **muffled** *adj*
WORD ORIGIN probably Old French *moufle* mitten

muffler *n* **1** *Brit* a thick scarf worn for warmth **2** a device to deaden sound, esp. one on a car exhaust; silencer

mufti *n* civilian clothes worn by a person who normally wears a military uniform
WORD ORIGIN from *Mufti*, Muslim religious leader

mug¹ ❶ *n* **1** a large drinking cup with a handle **2** the quantity held by a mug or its contents: *a mug of coffee*
WORD ORIGIN probably Scandinavian

mug² ❶ *n* **1** *slang* a person's face or mouth: *keep your ugly mug out of this* **2** *slang* a gullible person, esp. one who is swindled easily **3 a mug's game** a worthless activity
WORD ORIGIN perhaps same as MUG¹

mug³ ❶ *vb* **mugging, mugged** to attack someone in order to rob them **mugger** *n* **mugging** *n*

muggins *n slang* **a** a stupid or gullible person **b** a title used humorously to refer to oneself
WORD ORIGIN probably from surname *Muggins*

muggy *adj* **-gier, -giest** (of weather or air) unpleasantly warm and humid **mugginess** *n*
WORD ORIGIN dialect *mug* drizzle

mug shot *n informal* a photograph of a person's face, esp. one resembling a police-file picture

mug up ❶ *vb Brit slang* to study a subject hard, esp. for an exam
WORD ORIGIN origin unknown

Muhammad *n* ▸ same as **Mohammed**

Muir *n* **Edwin** 1887–1959, Scottish poet, novelist, and critic

mujaheddin *or* **mujahedeen** (moo-ja-hed-**deen**) *pl n* fundamentalist Muslim guerrillas
WORD ORIGIN Arabic *mujāhidīn* fighters

mukluk *n* a soft boot, usually of sealskin, worn in the American Arctic
WORD ORIGIN Yupik (native language of Siberia and Alaska) *muklok* large seal

mulatto (mew-**lat**-toe) *n, pl* **-tos** *or* **-toes** a person with one Black and one White parent
WORD ORIGIN Spanish *mulato* young mule

mulberry *n, pl* **-ries 1** a tree with edible blackberry-like fruit, the leaves of which are used to feed silkworms **2** the fruit of any of these trees ▹*adj* **3** dark purple
WORD ORIGIN Latin *morum*

mulch *n* **1** a mixture of half-rotten vegetable matter and peat used to protect the roots of plants or enrich the soil ▹*vb* **2** to cover soil with mulch
WORD ORIGIN obsolete *mulch* soft

mule¹ *n* **1** the sterile offspring of a male donkey and a female horse **2** a machine that spins cotton into yarn
WORD ORIGIN Latin *mulus*

mule² *n* a backless shoe or slipper
WORD ORIGIN Latin *mulleus* a magistrate's shoe

muleteer *n* a person who drives mules

mulga *n* **1** an Australian acacia shrub growing in desert regions **2** *Austral* the outback
WORD ORIGIN Aboriginal

mulish *adj* stubborn; obstinate

mull *n Scot* a promontory or headland: *the Mull of Galloway*
WORD ORIGIN probably Gaelic *maol*

mullah *n* (formerly) a Muslim scholar, teacher, or religious leader
WORD ORIGIN Arabic *mawlā* master

mulled *adj* (of wine or ale) flavoured with sugar and spices and served hot
WORD ORIGIN origin unknown

Muller *n* **Hermann Joseph** 1890–1967, US geneticist, noted for his work on the transmutation of genes by X-rays: Nobel prize for physiology or medicine 1946

Müller *n* **1 Friedrich Max** 1823–1900, British Sanskrit scholar born in Germany **2 Johann** ▸ See **Regiomontanus 3 Johannes Peter** 1801–58, German physiologist, anatomist, and experimental psychologist **4 Paul Hermann** 1899–1965, Swiss chemist. He synthesized DDT (1939) and discovered its use as an insecticide: Nobel prize for physiology or medicine 1948

mullet *n, pl* **mullets** *or* **mullet** any of various marine food fishes
WORD ORIGIN Greek *mullos*

Mulligan *n* **Gerry**, full name *Gerald Joseph Mulligan*. 1927–96, US jazz saxophonist, who pioneered the cool jazz style of the 1950s

mulligatawny *n* a curry-flavoured soup of Anglo-Indian origin
WORD ORIGIN Tamil *milakutanni* pepper water

Mulliken *n* **Robert Sanderson** 1896–1986, US physicist and chemist, who won the Nobel prize for chemistry (1966) for his work on bonding and the electronic structure of molecules

mullion *n* a slender vertical bar between the casements or panes of a window **mullioned** *adj*
WORD ORIGIN Old French *moinel*

mull over *vb* to study or ponder: *he mulled over the arrangements*
WORD ORIGIN probably from *muddle*

mulloway *n* a large Australian sea fish, valued for sport and food

multi- *combining form* **1** many or much: *multimillion* **2** more than one: *multistorey*
WORD ORIGIN Latin *multus* much, many

multicoloured *adj* having many colours: *multicoloured balls of wool*

multicultural *adj* of or for the cultures of several different races

multifarious (mull-tee-**fare**-ee-uss) *adj* many and varied: *multifarious religious movements and political divisions sprang up around this time*
WORD ORIGIN Late Latin *multifarius* manifold

multiflora rose *n* a climbing rose with clusters of small fragrant flowers

multiform *adj* having many shapes or forms

multilateral *adj* of or involving more than two nations or parties: *multilateral trade negotiations*

multilingual *adj* **1** able to speak more than two languages **2** written or expressed in more than two languages: *a multilingual leaflet*

multimedia *pl n* **1** the combined use of media such as television and slides **2** *computers* of or relating to systems that can manipulate data in a variety of forms, such as sound, graphics, or text

multimillionaire *n* a person who has money or property worth several million pounds, dollars, etc.

multinational *adj* **1** (of a large business company) operating in several countries **2** involving people from several countries: *a multinational peacekeeping force* ▹*n* **3** a large company operating in several countries

multiparous (mull-**tip**-a-russ) *adj* producing many offspring at one birth
WORD ORIGIN New Latin *multiparus*

THESAURUS

mug¹ *n* **1, 2 = cup**, pot, jug, beaker, tankard, stein, flagon, toby jug

mug² *n* **1** *(slang)* **= face**, features, countenance, visage, clock *(Brit slang)*, kisser *(slang)*, dial *(slang)*, mush *(Brit slang)*, puss *(slang)*, phiz *or* phizog *(Brit slang)* **2** *(Brit slang)* **= fool**, innocent, sucker *(slang)*, charlie *(Brit informal)*, gull *(archaic)*, chump *(informal)*, simpleton, putz *(US slang)*, weenie *(US informal)*, muggins *(Brit slang)*, easy *or* soft touch *(slang)*, dorba *or* dorb *(Austral slang)*, bogan *(Austral slang)*

mug³ *vb (informal)* **= attack**, assault, beat up, rob, steam *(informal)*, hold up, do over *(Brit, Austral & NZ slang)*, work over *(slang)*, assail, lay into *(informal)*, put the boot in *(slang)*, duff up *(Brit slang)*, set about *or* upon, beat *or* knock seven bells out of *(informal)*

mug up (on) something *vb* **= study**, cram *(informal)*, bone up on *(informal)*, swot up on *(Brit informal)*, get up *(informal)*

DICTIONARY

multiple ⓘ *adj* **1** having or involving more than one part, individual, or element ▷ *n* **2** a number or polynomial which can be divided by another specified one an exact number of times: *6 is a multiple of 2* **multiply** *adv*
WORD ORIGIN Latin *multiplus*

multiple-choice *adj* (of a test or question) giving a number of possible answers out of which the correct one must be chosen

multiple sclerosis *n* a chronic progressive disease of the central nervous system, resulting in speech and visual disorders, tremor, muscular incoordination, and partial paralysis

multiplex *n, pl* **-plexes 1** a purpose-built complex containing several cinemas and usually restaurants and bars ▷ *adj* **2** having many elements; complex
WORD ORIGIN Latin: having many folds

multiplicand *n* a number to be multiplied by another number (the **multiplier**)

multiplication *n* **1** a mathematical operation, equivalent to adding a number to itself a specified number of times. For instance, 4 multiplied by 3 equals 12 (i.e. 4+4+4) **2** the act of multiplying or state of being multiplied

multiplication sign *n* the symbol ×, placed between numbers to be multiplied

multiplication table *n* a table giving the results of multiplying two numbers together

multiplicity *n, pl* **-ties 1** a large number or great variety **2** the state of being multiple

multiplier *n* a number by which another number (the **multiplicand**) is multiplied

multiply ⓘ *vb* **-plies, -plying, -plied 1** to increase or cause to increase in number, quantity, or degree **2** to combine numbers or quantities by multiplication **3** to increase in number by reproduction
WORD ORIGIN Latin *multiplicare*

multipurpose *adj* having many uses: *a giant multipurpose enterprise*

multipurpose vehicle *n* a large car, similar to a van, designed to carry up to eight passengers

multiracial *adj* consisting of or involving people of many races: *a multiracial society* **multiracialism** *n*

multistage *adj* (of a rocket or missile) having several stages, each of which can be jettisoned after it has burnt out

multistorey *adj* (of a building) having many storeys

multitrack *adj* (in sound recording) using tape containing two or more tracks

multitude ⓘ *n* **1** a large number of people or things: *a multitude of different pressure groups* **2 the multitude** the common people **multitudinous** *adj*
WORD ORIGIN Latin *multitudo*

multi-user *adj* (of a computer) capable of being used by several people at once

mum[1] *n chiefly Brit informal* ▸ same as **mother**
WORD ORIGIN a child's word

mum[2] *adj* **1 keep mum** remain silent **2 mum's the word** keep quiet (about something)
WORD ORIGIN suggestive of closed lips

mumble *vb* **-bling, -bled 1** to speak or say something indistinctly, with the mouth partly closed: *I could hear him mumbling under his breath* ▷ *n* **2** an indistinct or low utterance or sound
WORD ORIGIN Middle English *momelen*, from MUM[2]

mumbo jumbo *n* **1** meaningless language; nonsense or gibberish **2** foolish religious ritual or incantation
WORD ORIGIN probably from West African *mama dyumbo*, name of a tribal god

Mumford *n* **Lewis** 1895–1990, US sociologist, whose works are chiefly concerned with the relationship between man and his environment. They include *The City in History* (1962) and *Roots of Contemporary Architecture* (1972)

mummer *n* one of a group of masked performers in a folk play or mime
WORD ORIGIN Old French *momer* to mime

mummery *n, pl* **-meries 1** a performance by mummers **2** hypocritical or ostentatious ceremony

mummified *adj* (of a body) preserved as a mummy **mummification** *n*

mummy[1] *n, pl* **-mies** *chiefly Brit* an embalmed body as prepared for burial in ancient Egypt
WORD ORIGIN Persian *mūm* wax

mummy[2] *n, pl* **-mies** ▸ a child's word for **mother**
WORD ORIGIN variant of MUM[1]

mumps *n* an infectious viral disease in which the glands below the ear become swollen and painful
WORD ORIGIN obsolete *mump* to grimace

munch *vb* to chew noisily and steadily
WORD ORIGIN imitative

mundane ⓘ *adj* **1** everyday, ordinary, and therefore not very interesting **2** relating to the world or worldly matters
WORD ORIGIN Latin *mundus* world

mung bean *n* an E Asian bean plant grown for its edible seeds which are used as a source of bean sprouts
WORD ORIGIN Tamil *mūngu*

municipal ⓘ *adj* of or relating to a town or city or its local government
WORD ORIGIN Latin *municipium* a free town

municipality *n, pl* **-ties 1** a city, town, or district enjoying local self-government **2** the governing body of such a unit

munificent (mew-**niff**-fiss-sent) *adj* very generous **munificence** *n*
WORD ORIGIN Latin *munus* gift + *facere* to make

muniments (**mew**-nim-ments) *pl n law* the title deeds and other documentary evidence relating to the title to land
WORD ORIGIN Latin *munire* to defend

munitions (mew-**nish**-unz) *pl n* military equipment and stores, esp. ammunition

Munnings *n* Sir **Alfred** 1878–1959, British painter, best known for his horse paintings

Munro[1] *n, pl* **Munros** *mountaineering* any separate mountain peak over 3000 feet high: originally used of Scotland only but now sometimes extended to other parts of the British Isles
WORD ORIGIN C20: named after Hugh Thomas *Munro* (1856–1919), who published a list of these in 1891

Munro[2] *n* **1 Alice,** original name *Alice Laidlaw.* born 1931, Canadian short-story writer; her books include

THESAURUS

multiple *adj* **1 = many**, several, various, numerous, collective, sundry, manifold, multitudinous

multiply *vb* **1 = increase**, extend, expand, spread, build up, accumulate, augment, proliferate **OPPOSITE:** decrease **3 = reproduce**, breed, propagate

multitude *n* **1a = great number**, lot, host, collection, army, sea, mass, assembly, legion, horde, myriad, concourse, assemblage **1b = crowd**, host, mass, mob, congregation, swarm, sea, horde, throng, great number

mundane *adj* **1 = ordinary**, routine, commonplace, banal, everyday, day-to-day, vanilla *(slang)*, prosaic, humdrum, workaday **OPPOSITE:** extraordinary **2 = earthly**, worldly, human, material, fleshly, secular, mortal, terrestrial, temporal, sublunary **OPPOSITE:** spiritual

municipal *adj* **= civic**, city, public, local, community, council, town, district, urban, metropolitan, borough

m

DICTIONARY

Lives of Girls and Women (1971), *The Moons of Jupiter* (1982), and *The Love of a Good Woman* (1999) **2 H**(**ector**) **H**(**ugh**), pen name Saki. 1870–1916, Scottish author, born in Burma (now Myanmar), noted for his collections of satirical short stories, such as *Reginald* (1904) and *Beasts and Superbeasts* (1914)

Münsterberg *n* **Hugo** 1863–1916, German psychologist, in the US from 1897, noted for his pioneering work in applied psychology

munted *adj NZ slang* **1** destroyed or ruined **2** abnormal or peculiar

Müntzer *n* **Thomas** c. 1490–1525, German radical religious and political reformer; executed for organizing the Peasants' War (1524–25)

muon (mew-on) *n* a positive or negative elementary particle with a mass 207 times that of an electron
WORD ORIGIN short for *mu meson*

mural (myoor-al) *n* **1** a large painting on a wall ▹*adj* **2** of or relating to a wall **muralist** *n*
WORD ORIGIN Latin *murus* wall

Muralitharan *n* **Muttiah** born 1972, Sri Lankan cricketer, a famous spin bowler; has played for Sri Lanka since 1992

Murasaki Shikibu *n* 11th-century Japanese court lady, author of *The Tale of Genji*, perhaps the world's first novel

Murat *n* **Joachim** 1767–1815, French marshal, during the Napoleonic Wars; king of Naples (1808–15)

Murchison *n* Sir **Roderick Impey** 1792–1871, Scottish geologist: played a major role in establishing parts of the geological time scale, esp. the Silurian, Permian, and Devonian periods

murder ❶ *n* **1** the unlawful intentional killing of one human being by another **2** *informal* something dangerous, difficult, or unpleasant: *shopping on Christmas Eve is murder* **3 cry blue murder** *informal* to make an outcry **4 get away with murder** *informal* to do as one pleases without ever being punished ▹*vb* **5** to kill someone intentionally and unlawfully **6** *informal* to ruin a piece of music or drama by performing it very badly: *he absolutely murdered that song* **7** *informal* to beat decisively **murderer** *n* **murderess** *fem n* **murderous** *adj*
WORD ORIGIN Old English *morthor*

Murillo *n* **Bartolomé Esteban** 1618–82, Spanish painter, esp. of religious subjects and beggar children

murk *n* thick gloomy darkness
WORD ORIGIN Old Norse *myrkr* darkness

murky ❶ *adj* **murkier, murkiest** **1** gloomy or dark **2** cloudy or hard to see through: *a murky stagnant pond* **3** obscure and suspicious; shady: *murky goings-on; his murky past* **murkily** *adv* **murkiness** *n*

murmur ❶ *vb* **1** to speak or say in a quiet indistinct way **2** to complain ▹*n* **3** a continuous low indistinct sound, such as that of a distant conversation **4** an indistinct utterance: *a murmur of protest* **5** a complaint or grumble: *he left without a murmur* **6** *med* any abnormal soft blowing sound heard usually over the chest: *a heart murmur* **murmuring** *n, adj* **murmurous** *adj*
WORD ORIGIN Latin *murmurare* to rumble

Murphy *n* **1 Alex** born 1939, British rugby league player and coach **2 Eddie,** full name *Edward Regan Murphy.* born 1951, US film actor and comedian. His films include *48 Hours* (1982), *Beverly Hills Cop* (1984), *Coming to America* (1988), and *Dr Dolittle* (1998) **3 William Parry** 1892–1987, US physician: with G. R. Minot, he discovered the liver treatment for anaemia and they shared, with G. H. Whipple, the Nobel prize for physiology or medicine in 1934

Murphy-O'Connor *n* **Cormac** born 1932, British cardinal, Archbishop of Westminster from 2000

Murphy's Law *n* ▸same as **Sod's Law**

murrain (murr-rin) *n* any plaguelike disease in cattle
WORD ORIGIN Old French *morir* to die

Murray[1] *n* a river in SE Australia, rising in New South Wales and flowing northwest into SE South Australia, then south into the sea at Encounter Bay: the main river of Australia, important for irrigation and power. Length: 2590 km (1609 miles)

Murray[2] *n* **1 1st Earl of** See (1st Earl of) **Moray** **2** Sir (**George**) **Gilbert** (**Aimé**) 1866–1957, British classical scholar, born in Australia: noted for his verse translations of Greek dramatists, esp. Euripides **3** Sir **James Augustus Henry** 1837–1915, Scottish lexicographer; one of the original editors (1879–1915) of what became the *Oxford English Dictionary* **4 Les,** full name *Leslie Allan Murray.* born 1938, Australian poet; his collections include *The Weatherboard Cathedral* (1969), *The Daylight Moon* (1987), *Subhuman Redneck Poems* (1996), and *The Biplane Houses* (2007) **5 Murray of Epping Forest,** Baron, title of *Lionel Murray,* known as *Len.* 1922–2004, British trades union leader; general secretary of the Trades Union Congress (1973–84)

mus. **1** museum **2** music **3** musical

MusB *or* **MusBac** Bachelor of Music

muscle ❶ *n* **1** a tissue in the body composed of bundles of elongated cells which produce movement in an organ or part by contracting or relaxing **2** an organ composed of muscle tissue: *the heart is essentially just another muscle* **3** strength or force: *we do not have the political muscle to force through these reforms* ▹*vb* **-cling, -cled** **4 muscle in** to force one's way into a situation; intrude: *I don't like the way he's trying to muscle in here*
WORD ORIGIN Medical Latin *musculus* little mouse

muscle-bound *adj* having overdeveloped and inelastic muscles

muscleman *n, pl* **-men** **1** a man with highly developed muscles **2** a henchman employed to intimidate or use violence upon victims

Muscovite *adj* **1** of Moscow, a city in Russia ▹*n* **2** a person from Moscow

muscular ❶ *adj* **1** having well-developed muscles; brawny **2** of or consisting of muscle: *great muscular effort is needed* **3** forceful or powerful: *a muscular account of Schumann's Fourth Symphony* **muscularity** *n*

muscular dystrophy *n* a hereditary disease in which the muscles gradually weaken and waste away

musculature *n* the arrangement of

THESAURUS

murder *n* **1 = killing,** homicide, massacre, assassination, slaying, bloodshed, carnage, butchery ▹*vb* **5 = kill,** massacre, slaughter, assassinate, hit *(slang)*, destroy, waste *(informal)*, do in *(informal)*, eliminate *(slang)*, take out *(slang)*, terminate *(slang)*, butcher, dispatch, slay, blow away *(slang, chiefly US)*, bump off *(slang)*, rub out *(US slang)*, take the life of, do to death, murk *(slang)*

murky *adj* **1 = dark,** gloomy, dismal, grey, dull, obscure, dim, dreary, cloudy, misty, impenetrable, foggy, overcast, dusky, nebulous, cheerless
OPPOSITE: bright
2 = dark, obscure, cloudy, impenetrable

murmur *vb* **1 = mumble,** whisper, mutter, drone, purr, babble, speak in an undertone ▹*n* **4 = whisper,** whispering, mutter, mumble, drone, purr, babble, undertone

muscle *n* **1 = tendon,** sinew, muscle tissue, thew **3 = strength,** might, force, power, weight, stamina, potency, brawn, sturdiness
4 muscle in *(informal)* **= impose yourself,** encroach, butt in, force your way in, elbow your way in

muscular *adj* **1, 3 = strong,** powerful, athletic, strapping, robust, vigorous, sturdy, stalwart, husky *(informal)*, beefy *(informal)*, lusty, sinewy, muscle-bound, brawny, powerfully built, thickset, well-knit

DICTIONARY

muscles in an organ, part, or organism

musculoskeletal *adj* of or relating to the skeleton and musculature taken together

MusD *or* **MusDoc** Doctor of Music

muse[1] ❶ *vb* **musing, mused** to think deeply and at length about: *she mused unhappily on how right her sister had been*
WORD ORIGIN Old French *muser*

muse[2] *n* **the muse** a force or person, esp. a woman, that inspires a creative artist
WORD ORIGIN Greek *Mousa* a Muse

Muses *pl n Greek myth* the nine sister goddesses, each of whom was the protector of a different art or science

museum *n* a building where objects of historical, artistic, or scientific interest are exhibited and preserved
WORD ORIGIN Greek *Mouseion* home of the Muses

museum piece *n informal* a very old or old-fashioned object or building

Museveni *n* **Yoweri** born 1944, Ugandan politician; president of Uganda from 1986

Musgrave *n* **Thea** born 1928, Scottish composer, noted esp. for her operas

mush[1] *n* **1** a soft pulpy mass **2** *informal* cloying sentimentality
WORD ORIGIN obsolete *moose* porridge

mush[2] *Canad interj* **1** an order to dogs in a sled team to start up or go faster ▹*vb* **2** to travel by or drive a dogsled
WORD ORIGIN perhaps from imperative of French *marcher* to advance

Musharraf *n* **Pervez** born 1943, Pakistani general and politician; became military leader of Pakistan following a coup in 2001; president from 2002

mushroom *n* **1** an edible fungus consisting of a cap at the end of a stem **2** something resembling a mushroom in shape or rapid growth ▹*vb* **3** to grow rapidly: *consumer debt mushroomed rapidly in 1989*
WORD ORIGIN Late Latin *mussirio*

mushroom cloud *n* the large mushroom-shaped cloud produced by a nuclear explosion

mushy *adj* **mushier, mushiest 1** soft and pulpy **2** *informal* excessively sentimental

music *n* **1** an art form consisting of sequences of sounds organized melodically, harmonically, and rhythmically **2** such sounds, esp. when produced by singing or musical instruments **3** any written or printed representation of musical sounds: *I can't read music* **4** any sequence of sounds perceived as pleasing or harmonious **5 face the music** *informal* to confront the consequences of one's actions **6 music to one's ears** something, such as a piece of news, that one is pleased to hear
WORD ORIGIN Greek *mousikē (tekhnē)* (art) in the protection of the Muses

musical ❶ *adj* **1** of or used in music **2** talented in or fond of music **3** pleasant-sounding; harmonious: *musical laughter* **4** involving or set to music: *a musical biography of Judy Garland* ▹*n* **5** a play or film that has dialogue interspersed with songs and dances **musicality** *n* **musically** *adv*

musical box *n* a box containing a mechanical instrument that plays tunes when the box is opened

musical chairs *n* **1** a game in which the players run round a row of chairs while music plays. There is one more player than there are chairs, and when the music stops the player who cannot find a chair to sit on is out **2** any situation involving a number of people in a series of interrelated changes: *the dismissal of the Chancellor started a game of musical chairs in the Cabinet*

music centre *n Brit* a single hi-fi unit containing a turntable, radio, compact disc player, and cassette player

music hall *n chiefly Brit* **1** (formerly) a variety entertainment consisting of songs and comic turns **2** a theatre at which such entertainments were staged

musician *n* a person who plays or composes music, esp. as a profession

musicianship *n* the technical and interpretive skills involved in singing or playing music: *the piano part is simple but performed with great musicianship*

musicology *n* the scholarly study of music **musicologist** *n*

Musil *n* **Robert** 1880–1942, Austrian novelist, whose novel *The Man Without Qualities* (1930–42) is an ironic examination of contemporary ills

musk *n* **1** a strong-smelling glandular secretion of the male musk deer, used in perfumery **2** any similar substance produced by animals or plants, or manufactured synthetically
WORD ORIGIN Persian *mushk*

musk deer *n* a small central Asian mountain deer

muskeg ❶ *n chiefly Canad* an area of undrained boggy land
WORD ORIGIN Native American: grassy swamp

musket *n* a long-barrelled muzzle-loading gun fired from the shoulder, a forerunner of the rifle **musketeer** *n*
WORD ORIGIN Italian *moschetto* arrow, earlier: sparrow hawk

Muskie *n* **Edmund (Sixtus)** 1914–96, US Democratic politician: Governor of Maine (1955–59): senator for Maine (1959–80): Secretary of State (1980–81)

muskmelon *n* any of several varieties of melon, such as the cantaloupe and honeydew

musk ox *n* a large ox, which has a dark shaggy coat, downward-curving horns, and emits a musky smell

muskrat *n, pl* **-rats** *or* **-rat 1** a North American beaver-like amphibious rodent **2** the brown fur of this animal

musk rose *n* a Mediterranean rose, cultivated for its white musk-scented flowers

musky *adj* **muskier, muskiest** having a heady sweet smell **muskiness** *n*

Muslim *or* **Moslem** *n, pl* **-lims** *or* **-lim 1** a follower of the religion of Islam ▹*adj* **2** of or relating to Islam
WORD ORIGIN Arabic, literally: one who surrenders

muslin *n* a very fine plain-weave cotton fabric
WORD ORIGIN French *mousseline*

musquash *n* muskrat fur
WORD ORIGIN from a Native American language

muss ❶ *vb US & Canad informal* to make untidy; rumple: *watch you don't muss up my hair!*
WORD ORIGIN probably a blend of *mess* + *fuss*

mussel *n* an edible shellfish, with a dark slightly elongated hinged shell, which lives attached to rocks
WORD ORIGIN Latin *musculus*, diminutive of *mus* mouse

Musset *n* **Alfred de** 1810–57, French romantic poet and dramatist: his works include the play *Lorenzaccio* (1834) and the lyrics *Les Nuits* (1835–37), tracing his love affair with George Sand

must[1] ❶ *vb* **1** used as an auxiliary to express or indicate the need or

THESAURUS

muse[1] *vb* = **ponder**, consider, reflect, contemplate, think, weigh up, deliberate, speculate, brood, meditate, mull over, think over, ruminate, cogitate, be lost in thought, be in a brown study

musical *adj* **3** = **melodious**, lyrical, harmonious, melodic, lilting, tuneful, dulcet, sweet-sounding, euphonious, euphonic
OPPOSITE: discordant

muskeg *n (Canad)* = **swamp**, bog, marsh, quagmire, moss *(Scot & Northern English dialect)*, slough, fen, mire, morass, everglade(s) *(US)*, pakihi *(NZ)*

muss *vb* = **mess (up)**, disarrange, dishevel, ruffle, rumple, make untidy, tumble

must[1] *n* **7** = **necessity**, essential, requirement, duty, fundamental,

m

DICTIONARY

necessity to do something: *I must go to the shops* **2** used as an auxiliary to express or indicate obligation or requirement: *you must not smoke in here* **3** used as an auxiliary to express or indicate the probable correctness of a statement: *he must be finished by now* **4** used as an auxiliary to express or indicate inevitability: *all good things must come to an end* **5** used as an auxiliary to express or indicate determination: *I must try and finish this* **6** used as an auxiliary to express or indicate conviction or certainty on the part of the speaker: *you must be kidding!* ▷*n* **7** an essential or necessary thing: *strong boots are a must for hill walking*
WORD ORIGIN Old English *mōste*, past tense of *mōtan* to be allowed or obliged

must[2] *n* the pressed juice of grapes or other fruit ready for fermentation
WORD ORIGIN Latin *mustum* new wine

mustache *n US* ▸same as **moustache**

mustachio *n, pl* **-chios** *often humorous* a moustache, esp. a bushy or elaborate one **mustachioed** *adj*
WORD ORIGIN Italian *mostaccio*

mustang *n* a small breed of horse, often wild or half wild, found in the southwestern US
WORD ORIGIN Mexican Spanish *mestengo*

mustard *n* **1** a hot, spicy paste made from the powdered seeds of any of a family of plants **2** any of these plants, which have yellow flowers and slender pods ▷*adj* **3** brownish-yellow
WORD ORIGIN Old French *moustarde*

mustard and cress *n* seedlings of white mustard and garden cress, used in salads and as a garnish

mustard gas *n* an oily liquid with poisonous vapour used in chemical warfare, esp. in World War I, which can cause blindness, burns, and sometimes death

mustard plaster *n med* a mixture of powdered black mustard seeds applied to the skin

muster ❶ *vb* **1** to summon or gather: *I put as much disbelief in my expression as I could muster* **2** to call or be called together for duty or inspection: *the battalion mustered on the bank of the river* ▷*n* **3** an assembly of military personnel for duty or inspection **4** a collection, assembly, or gathering **5 pass muster** to be acceptable
WORD ORIGIN Latin *monstrare* to show

musty *adj* **-tier, -tiest** **1** smelling or tasting old, stale, or mouldy **2** old-fashioned, dull, or hackneyed: *musty ideas* **mustily** *adv* **mustiness** *n*
WORD ORIGIN perhaps variant of obsolete *moisty*

mutable (mew-tab-bl) *adj* able to or tending to change **mutability** *n*
WORD ORIGIN Latin *mutare* to change

mutagen (mew-ta-jen) *n* any substance that can induce genetic mutation **mutagenic** *adj*
WORD ORIGIN MUTATION + *-gen* (suffix) producing

mutagenesis (mew-ta-jen-iss-iss) *n* the origin and development of a genetic mutation
WORD ORIGIN MUTATION + GENESIS

mutant (mew-tant) *n* **1** an animal, organism, or gene that has undergone mutation ▷*adj* **2** of or resulting from mutation

mutate (mew-tate) *vb* **-tating, -tated** to undergo or cause to undergo mutation
WORD ORIGIN Latin *mutare* to change

mutation ❶ (mew-tay-shun) *n* **1** a change or alteration **2** a change in the chromosomes or genes of a cell which may affect the structure and development of the resultant offspring **3** a physical characteristic in an organism resulting from this type of chromosomal change

mute ❶ *adj* **1** not giving out sound or speech; silent **2** unable to speak; dumb **3** unspoken or unexpressed: *she shot him a look of mute entreaty* **4** (of a letter in a word) silent: *the 'k' in 'know' is mute* ▷*n* **5** a person who is unable to speak **6** any of various devices used to soften the tone of stringed or brass instruments ▷*vb* **muting, muted** **7** to reduce the volume or soften the tone of a musical instrument by means of a mute or soft pedal **8** to reduce the volume of a sound: *the double glazing muted the noise* **mutely** *adv* **muteness** *n*
WORD ORIGIN Latin *mutus* silent

muted *adj* **1** (of a sound or colour) softened: *a muted pink shirt* **2** (of an emotion or action) subdued or restrained: *his response was muted* **3** (of a musical instrument) being played while fitted with a mute: *muted trumpet*

mute swan *n* the swan most commonly seen in Britain, which has a pure white plumage and an orange-red bill

muti (moo-tee) *n S African* medicine, esp. herbal
WORD ORIGIN Zulu

Muti *n* **Riccardo** born 1941, Italian conductor: musical director of Philharmonia Orchestra, London (1979–82), Philadelphia Orchestra (1980–92), and La Scala, Milan (1986–2005)

mutilate (mew-till-ate) *vb* **-lating, -lated** **1** to injure by tearing or cutting off a limb or essential part; maim **2** to damage a book or text so as to render it unintelligible **3** to spoil or damage severely: *why did he mutilate his favourite tapes and leave ours alone?* **mutilated** *adj* **mutilation** *n* **mutilator** *n*
WORD ORIGIN Latin *mutilare* to cut off

mutineer *n* a person who mutinies

mutinous *adj* **1** openly rebellious **2** characteristic or indicative of mutiny

mutiny (mew-tin-ee) *n, pl* **-nies** **1** open rebellion against authority, esp. by sailors or soldiers against their officers ▷*vb* **-nies, -nying, -nied** **2** to engage in mutiny: *soldiers who had mutinied and taken control*
WORD ORIGIN Old French *mutin* rebellious

mutt *n slang* **1** a foolish or stupid person **2** a mongrel dog
WORD ORIGIN from *muttonhead*

mutter ❶ *vb* **1** to say something or speak in a low and indistinct tone: *he muttered an excuse* **2** to grumble ▷*n* **3** a muttered sound or complaint **muttering** *n, adj*
WORD ORIGIN Middle English *moteren*

Mutter *n* **Anne-Sophie** born 1963, German violinist

mutton *n* **1** the flesh of mature sheep, used as food **2 mutton dressed as lamb** an older woman dressed up to look young
WORD ORIGIN Medieval Latin *multo* sheep

mutton bird *n* **1** *Austral* a migratory sea bird with dark plumage **2** *NZ*

m

THESAURUS

obligation, imperative, requisite, prerequisite, sine qua non *(Latin)*, necessary thing, must-have

muster *vb* **1 = summon up**, collect, call up, marshal **2a = rally**, group, gather, assemble, round up, marshal, mobilize, call together **2b = assemble**, meet, come together, convene, congregate, convoke ▷*n* **4 = assembly**, meeting, collection, gathering, rally, convention, congregation, roundup, mobilization, hui (NZ), concourse, assemblage, convocation, runanga (NZ)

mutation *n* **1, 2 = change**, variation, evolution, transformation, modification, alteration, deviation, metamorphosis, transfiguration **3 = anomaly**, variation, deviant, freak of nature

mute *adj* **1 = close-mouthed**, silent, taciturn, tongue-tied, tight-lipped, unspeaking **2 = dumb**, speechless, voiceless, unspeaking, aphasic, aphonic **3 = silent**, dumb, unspoken, tacit, wordless, voiceless, unvoiced

mutter *vb* **1, 2 = grumble**, complain, murmur, rumble, whine, mumble, grouse, bleat, grouch *(informal)*, talk

DICTIONARY

any of a number of migratory sea birds, the young of which are a Māori delicacy
muttonchops *pl n* side whiskers trimmed in the shape of chops
mutual ❶ (mew-chew-al) *adj* **1** experienced or expressed by each of two or more people about the other; reciprocal: *mutual respect* **2** common to or shared by two or more people: *a mutual friend* **3** denoting an organization, such as an insurance company, in which the policyholders or investors share the profits and expenses and there are no shareholders **mutuality** *n* **mutually** *adv*
WORD ORIGIN Latin *mutuus* reciprocal
mutual fund *n US & Canad* an investment trust that issues units for public sale and invests the money in many different businesses
Muybridge *n* **Eadweard**, original name *Edward James Muggeridge*. 1830–1904, US photographer, born in England; noted for his high-speed photographic studies of animals and people in motion
Muzak *n trademark* recorded light music played in places such as restaurants and shops
Muzorewa *n* **Abel** (**Tendekayi**) born 1925, Zimbabwean Methodist bishop and politician; president of the African National Council (1971–85). He was one of the negotiators of an internal settlement (1978–79); prime minister of Rhodesia (1979)
muzzle *n* **1** the projecting part of an animal's face, usually the jaws and nose **2** a guard, made of plastic or strap of strong material, fitted over an animal's nose and jaws to prevent it biting or eating **3** the front end of a gun barrel ▷ *vb* **-zling, -zled 4** to prevent from being heard or noticed: *an attempt to muzzle the press* **5** to put a muzzle on an animal
WORD ORIGIN Old French *muse* snout
muzzy *adj* **-zier, -ziest 1** confused and groggy: *he felt muzzy and hung over* **2** blurred or hazy: *the picture was muzzy and out of focus* **muzzily** *adv* **muzziness** *n*
WORD ORIGIN origin unknown
MV megavolt
MW 1 megawatt **2** *radio* medium wave
mwah *interj* a representation of the sound of a kiss
Mx *physics* maxwell
my *adj* **1** of, belonging to, or associated with the speaker or writer (me): *my own way of doing things* **2** used in various forms of address: *my lord* ▷ *interj* **3** an exclamation of surprise or awe: *my, how you've grown!*
WORD ORIGIN variant of Old English *mīn*
myall *n* an Australian acacia with hard scented wood
WORD ORIGIN Aboriginal
mycelium (mice-eel-lee-um) *n, pl* **-lia** (-lee-a) the mass forming the body of a fungus
WORD ORIGIN Greek *mukēs* mushroom + *hēlos* nail
Mycenaean (mice-in-ee-an) *adj* of or relating to the Aegean civilization of Mycenae, a city in S Greece (1400–1100 BC)
mycology *n* the study of fungi
WORD ORIGIN Greek *mukēs* mushroom + -LOGY
myelin (my-ill-in) *n* a white tissue forming an insulating sheath around certain nerve fibres
WORD ORIGIN Greek *muelos* marrow
myeloma (my-ill-oh-ma) *n, pl* **-mas** *or* **-mata** (-ma-ta) a tumour of the bone marrow
WORD ORIGIN Greek *muelos* marrow + *-oma*, modelled on *carcinoma*
Myers *n* **L**(**eopold**) **H**(**amilton**) 1881–1944, British novelist, best known for his novel sequence *The Near and the Far* (1929–40)
mynah *or* **myna** *n* a tropical Asian starling which can mimic human speech
WORD ORIGIN Hindi *mainā*
Mynheer (min-near) *n* a Dutch title of address equivalent to *Sir* or *Mr*
WORD ORIGIN Dutch *mijnheer* my lord
myocardium *n, pl* **-dia** the muscular tissue of the heart **myocardial** *adj*
WORD ORIGIN Greek *mus* muscle + *kardia* heart
myopia (my-oh-pee-a) *n* inability to see distant objects clearly because the images are focused in front of the retina; short-sightedness **myopic** (my-op-ik) *adj*
WORD ORIGIN Greek *muōps* short-sighted
myriad ❶ (mir-ree-ad) *adj* **1** innumerable: *the myriad demands of the modern world* ▷ *n* **2** a large indefinite number: *myriads of tiny yellow flowers*
WORD ORIGIN Greek *murias* ten thousand
myriapod *n* an invertebrate with a long segmented body and many legs, such as a centipede
WORD ORIGIN Greek *murias* ten thousand + *pous* foot
myrmidon *n* a follower or henchman
WORD ORIGIN after the followers of Achilles in Greek myth
Myron *n* 5th century BC, Greek sculptor. He worked mainly in bronze and introduced a greater variety of pose into Greek sculpture, as in his *Discobolus*
myrrh (mur) *n* the aromatic resin of an African or Asian shrub or tree, used in perfume, incense, and medicine
WORD ORIGIN Greek *murrha*
myrtle (mur-tl) *n* an evergreen shrub with pink or white flowers and aromatic blue-black berries
WORD ORIGIN Greek *murtos*
myself *pron* **1** the reflexive form of I or *me*: *I really enjoyed myself at the party* **2** I or me in person, as distinct from anyone else: *I myself know of no answer* **3** my usual self: *I'm not myself today*
mysterious ❶ *adj* **1** of unknown cause or nature: *a mysterious illness* **2** creating a feeling of strangeness, curiosity, or wonder: *a fascinating and mysterious old woman* **mysteriously** *adv*
mystery ❶ *n, pl* **-teries 1** an unexplained or inexplicable event or phenomenon **2** a person or thing that arouses curiosity or suspense because of an unknown, obscure, or enigmatic quality **3** a story or film which arouses suspense and curiosity because of facts concealed **4** a religious rite, such as the Eucharist in Christianity
WORD ORIGIN Greek *mustērion* secret rites
mystery play *n* (in the Middle Ages) a type of drama based on the life of Christ
mystery tour *n* an excursion to an unspecified destination
mystic *n* **1** a person who achieves mystical experience ▷ *adj* **2** ▸ same as **mystical**
WORD ORIGIN Greek *mustēs* one who has been initiated

m

THESAURUS

under your breath
mutual *adj* **1, 2 = shared**, common, joint, interactive, returned, communal, reciprocal, interchangeable, reciprocated, correlative, requited
myriad *adj* **1 = innumerable**, countless, untold, incalculable, immeasurable, a thousand and one, multitudinous ▷ *n* **2 = multitude**, millions, scores, host, thousands, army, sea, mountain, flood, a million, a thousand, swarm, horde
mysterious *adj* **1 = strange**, unknown, puzzling, curious, secret, hidden, weird, concealed, obscure, baffling, veiled, mystical, perplexing, uncanny, incomprehensible, mystifying, impenetrable, arcane, inexplicable, cryptic, insoluble, unfathomable, abstruse, recondite **OPPOSITE:** clear **2 = secretive**, enigmatic, evasive, discreet, covert, reticent, furtive, inscrutable, non-committal, surreptitious, cloak-and-dagger, sphinx-like
mystery *n* **1, 2 = puzzle**, problem, question, secret, riddle, enigma, conundrum, teaser, poser (*informal*), closed book

DICTIONARY

mystical ❶ *adj* **1** relating to or characteristic of mysticism **2** *Christianity* having a sacred significance that is beyond human understanding **3** having occult or metaphysical significance **mystically** *adv*

mysticism *n* **1** belief in or experience of a reality beyond normal human understanding or experience **2** the use of prayer and meditation in an attempt to achieve direct intuitive experience of the divine

mystify *vb* **-fies, -fying, -fied 1** to confuse, bewilder, or puzzle: *his success mystifies many in the fashion industry* **2** to make obscure: *it is important for us not to mystify the function of the scientist* **mystification** *n* **mystifying** *adj*

mystique (miss-**steek**) *n* an aura of mystery, power, and awe that surrounds a person or thing

myth ❶ *n* **1 a** a story about superhuman beings of an earlier age, usually of how natural phenomena or social customs came into existence **b** ▸ same as **mythology** (senses 1, 2) **2 a** an idea or explanation which is widely held but untrue or unproven: *the myth that the USA is a classless society* **b** a person or thing whose existence is fictional or unproven: *the Loch Ness Monster is a myth*

WORD ORIGIN Greek *muthos* fable

myth. 1 mythological **2** mythology

mythical *or* **mythic** *adj* **1** of or relating to myth **2** imaginary or fictitious **mythically** *adv*

mythology ❶ *n, pl* **-gies 1** myths collectively, esp. those associated with a particular culture or person **2** a body of stories about a person, institution, etc. **3** the study of myths **mythological** *adj*

myxoedema *or US* **myxedema** (mix-id-**deem**-a) *n* a disease caused by an underactive thyroid gland, characterized by puffy eyes, face, and hands, and mental sluggishness

WORD ORIGIN Greek *muxa* mucus + *oidēma* swelling

myxomatosis (mix-a-mat-**oh**-siss) *n* an infectious and usually fatal viral disease of rabbits causing swellings and tumours

WORD ORIGIN Greek *muxa* mucus + *-ōma* denoting tumour + *-osis* denoting disease

THESAURUS

mystical *or* **mystic** *adj* **1, 3 = supernatural**, mysterious, transcendental, esoteric, occult, arcane, metaphysical, paranormal, inscrutable, otherworldly, abstruse, cabalistic, preternatural, nonrational

myth *n* **1a = legend**, story, tradition, fiction, saga, fable, parable, allegory, fairy story, folk tale, urban myth, urban legend **2a, 2b = illusion**, story, fancy, fantasy, imagination, invention, delusion, superstition, fabrication, falsehood, figment, tall story, cock and bull story *(informal)*

mythology *n* **1, 2 = legend**, myths, folklore, stories, tradition, lore, folk tales, mythos

m

Nn

DICTIONARY

n¹ 1 nano- 2 neutron
n² *n* 1 *maths* a number whose value is not stated: *two to the power n* ▷ *adj* 2 an indefinite number of: *there are n objects in the box* **nth** *adj*
N 1 *chess* knight 2 *chem* nitrogen 3 *physics* newton(s) 4 North(ern) 5 nuclear: *N plant*
n. 1 neuter 2 noun 3 number
N. 1 National(ist) 2 Navy 3 New 4 Norse
Na *chem* sodium
WORD ORIGIN Latin *natrium*
NA North America
n/a not applicable: used to indicate that a question on a form is not relevant to the person filling it in
Naafi *n* 1 *Brit* Navy, Army, and Air Force Institutes 2 a canteen or shop run by this organization, esp. for military personnel
naan *n* ▸ same as **nan bread**
naartjie (nahr-chee) *n S African* a tangerine
WORD ORIGIN Afrikaans
nab ❶ *vb* **nabbing, nabbed** *informal* 1 to arrest (someone) 2 to catch (someone) doing something wrong
WORD ORIGIN perhaps Scandinavian
nabob (nay-bob) *n informal* a rich or important person
WORD ORIGIN Hindi *nawwāb*; see NAWAB
nacelle (nah-sell) *n* a streamlined enclosure on an aircraft, esp. one housing an engine
WORD ORIGIN French: small boat
nacho *n, pl* **nachos** *Mexican cookery* a snack of a piece of tortilla topped with cheese, peppers, etc.
nacre (nay-ker) *n* mother-of-pearl **nacreous** *adj*
WORD ORIGIN Arabic *naqqārah* shell, drum
Nadar *n* real name *Gaspard Félix Tournachon*. 1820–1910, French photographer, writer, and caricaturist: noted for his portrait photographs of artists and writers and for taking the first aerial photographs (1858)
Nader *n* **Ralph** born 1934, US lawyer and campaigner for consumer rights and the environment: a candidate for president in 1996, 2000, and 2004
nadir *n* 1 the point in the sky directly below an observer and opposite the zenith 2 the lowest or worst point of anything: *I had touched the very nadir of despair*
WORD ORIGIN Arabic *nazīr as-samt*, literally: opposite the zenith
naevus *or US* **nevus** (nee-vuss) *n, pl* **-vi** a birthmark or mole
WORD ORIGIN Latin
naff *adj Brit slang* in poor taste: *naff frocks and trouser suits* **naffness** *n*
WORD ORIGIN perhaps back slang from *fan*, short for FANNY
nag¹ ❶ *vb* **nagging, nagged** 1 to scold or find fault constantly 2 **nag at** to be a constant source of discomfort or worry to ▷ *n* 3 a person who nags **nagging** *adj, n*
WORD ORIGIN Scandinavian
nag² ❶ *n* 1 *often disparaging* an old horse 2 a small riding horse
WORD ORIGIN Germanic
Nagarjuna *n* c. 150–c. 250 AD, Indian Buddhist monk, founder of the Madhyamika (Middle Path) school of Mahayana Buddhism: noted for his philosophical writings
Nagy *n* **Imre** 1896–1958, Hungarian statesman; prime minister (1953–55; 1956). He was removed from office and later executed when Soviet forces suppressed the revolution of 1956; reburied with honours in 1989
naiad (nye-ad) *n, pl* **naiads** *or* **naiades** (nye-ad-deez) *Greek myth* a water nymph
WORD ORIGIN Greek *nāias*
nail ❶ *n* 1 a piece of metal with a point at one end and a head at the other, hit with a hammer to join two objects together 2 the hard covering of the upper tips of the fingers and toes 3 **hit the nail on the head** to say something exactly correct or accurate 4 **on the nail** at once: *he paid always in cash, always on the nail* ▷ *vb* 5 to attach (something) with nails 6 *informal* to arrest or catch (someone)
WORD ORIGIN Old English *nægl*
nail down *vb* 1 to secure or fasten down with nails or as if with nails 2 to force an agreement from 3 to settle in a definite way: *a compromise was agreed in principle but has not yet been nailed down*
nailfile *n* a small metal file used to shape and smooth the nails
nail varnish *or* **polish** *n* a thick liquid applied to the nails as a cosmetic
Naipaul *n* Sir **V(idiadhar) S(urajprasad)** born 1932, Trinidadian novelist of Indian descent, living in Britain. His works include *A House for Mr Biswas* (1961), *In a Free State* (1971), which won the Booker Prize, *A Bend in the River* (1979), *The Enigma of Arrival* (1987), and *Beyond Belief* (1998): Nobel prize for literature 2001
Naismith *n* **James** 1861–1939, Canadian sportsman and coach; inventor of basketball
naive ❶ *or* **naïve** *or* **naïf** (nye-eev) *adj* 1 innocent and gullible 2 simple and lacking sophistication: *naive art* **naively** *adv*
WORD ORIGIN French, from Latin *nativus* native
naivety (nye-eev-tee) *or* **naïveté** *n* the state or quality of being naive
naked ❶ *adj* 1 without clothes 2 not concealed: *naked aggression* 3 without any covering: *it was dimly lit by naked bulbs* 4 **the naked eye** the eye unassisted by any optical instrument: *difficult to spot with the naked eye* **nakedly** *adv* **nakedness** *n*
WORD ORIGIN Old English *nacod*
namby-pamby *adj Brit, Austral & NZ* excessively sentimental or prim
WORD ORIGIN nickname of Ambrose Phillips, 18th-century pastoral poet
name ❶ *n* 1 a word or term by which a person or thing is known ▸ Related

n

THESAURUS

nab *vb* **1 = catch**, arrest, apprehend, seize, lift *(slang)*, nick *(slang, chiefly Brit)*, grab, capture, nail *(informal)*, collar *(informal)*, snatch, catch in the act, feel your collar *(slang)*
nag¹ *vb* **1 = scold**, harass, badger, pester, worry, harry, plague, hassle *(informal)*, vex, berate, breathe down someone's neck, upbraid, chivvy, bend someone's ear *(informal)*, be on your back *(slang)*, henpeck ▷ *n* **3 = scold**, complainer, grumbler, virago, shrew, tartar, moaner, harpy, harridan, termagant, fault-finder
nag² *n* **1, 2** *(often derog.)* **= horse** (US), hack, jade, plug
nail *n* **1 = tack**, spike, rivet, hobnail, brad *(Technical)* **2 = fingernail**, toenail, talon, thumbnail, claw ▷ *vb* **5 = fasten**, fix, secure, attach, pin, hammer, tack **6** *(informal)* **= catch**, arrest, capture, apprehend, lift *(slang)*, trap, nab *(informal)*, snare, ensnare, entrap, feel your collar *(slang)*
naive *or* **naïve** *or* **naïf** *adj* **1 = gullible**, trusting, credulous, unsuspicious, green, simple, innocent, childlike, callow, unsophisticated, unworldly, artless, ingenuous, guileless, wet behind the ears *(informal)*, jejune, as green as grass **OPPOSITE:** worldly
naked *adj* **1 = nude**, stripped, exposed, bare, uncovered, undressed, in the raw *(informal)*, starkers *(informal)*, stark-naked, unclothed, in the buff *(informal)*, in the altogether *(informal)*, buck naked *(slang)*, undraped, in your birthday suit *(informal)*, scuddy *(slang)*, without a stitch on *(informal)*, in the bare scud *(slang)*, naked as the day you were born *(informal)* **OPPOSITE:** dressed
name *n* **1 = title**, nickname, designation, appellation, term, handle *(slang)*, denomination,

DICTIONARY

adjective: **nominal** **2** reputation, esp. a good one: *he was making a name for himself* **3** a famous person: *she's a big name now* **4** **call someone names** *or* **a name** to insult someone by using rude words to describe him or her **5** **in name only** not possessing the powers or status implied by one's title: *a leadership in name only* **6** **in the name of** **a** for the sake of: *in the name of decency* **b** by the authority of: *in the name of the law* **7** **name of the game** the most significant or important aspect of something: *survival is the name of the game in wartime* **8** **to one's name** in one's possession: *she hasn't a penny to her name* ▷ *vb* **naming, named** **9** to give a name to **10** to refer to by name: *he refused to name his source* **11** to fix or specify: *he named a time for the meeting* **12** to appoint: *she was named Journalist of the Year* **13** to ban (an MP) from the House of Commons by mentioning him or her formally by name as being guilty of disorderly conduct **14** **name names** to cite people in order to blame or accuse them
WORD ORIGIN Old English *nama*

namecheck *vb* **1** to mention (someone) by name ▷ *n* **2** a mention of someone's name, for example on a radio programme

name day *n* *RC church* the feast day of a saint whose name one bears

name-dropping *n* *informal* the practice of referring to famous people as though they were friends, in order to impress others

nameless *adj* **1** without a name **2** unspecified: *the individual concerned had better remain nameless* **3** too horrible to speak about: *the nameless dread*

namely ● *adv* that is to say

nameplate *n* a small sign on or next to a door giving the occupant's name and, sometimes, profession

namesake *n* a person or thing with the same name as another
WORD ORIGIN probably originally *for the name's sake*

Namier *n* Sir **Lewis Bernstein,** original name *Ludwik Bernsztajn vel Niemirowski*. 1888–1960, British historian, born in Poland: noted esp. for his studies of 18th-century British politics

Nana Sahib *n* real name *Dandhu Panth*. ?1825–?1860, Indian nationalist, who led the uprising at Cawnpore during the Indian Mutiny

nan bread *or* **naan** *n* a slightly leavened Indian bread in a large flat leaf shape
WORD ORIGIN Hindi

nancy *n, pl* **-cies** *Brit, Austral & NZ offensive slang* an effeminate or homosexual boy or man. Also called: **nancy boy**
WORD ORIGIN from the girl's name

nanny *n, pl* **-nies** **1** a woman whose job is looking after young children ▷ *vb* **nannies, nannying, nannied** **2** to nurse or look after someone else's children **3** to be too protective towards (someone)
WORD ORIGIN child's name for a nurse

nanny goat *n* a female goat

nano- *combining form* denoting one thousand millionth (10^{-9}): *nanosecond*
WORD ORIGIN Latin *nanus* dwarf

nanometre *n* one thousand-millionth of a metre. Symbol: **nm**

nanotechnology *n* a branch of technology dealing with the manufacture of objects with dimensions of less than 100 nanometres and the manipulation of individual molecules and atoms

nap[1] ● *n* **1** a short sleep ▷ *vb* **napping, napped** **2** to have a short sleep **3** **catch someone napping** to catch someone unprepared: *they don't want to be caught napping when the army moves again*
WORD ORIGIN Old English *hnappian*

nap[2] ● *n* the raised fibres of velvet or similar cloth
WORD ORIGIN probably Middle Dutch *noppe*

nap[3] *n* **1** a card game similar to whist **2** *horse racing* a tipster's choice for a certain winner ▷ *vb* **napping, napped** **3** *horse racing* to name (a horse) as a likely winner
WORD ORIGIN shortened from *Napoleon*

napalm *n* **1** a highly inflammable jellied petrol, used in firebombs and flame-throwers ▷ *vb* **2** to attack (people or places) with napalm
WORD ORIGIN *na(phthene)* + *palm(itate)* salt of palmitic acid

nape *n* the back of the neck
WORD ORIGIN origin unknown

naphtha *n* *chem* a liquid mixture distilled from coal tar or petroleum: used as a solvent and in petrol
WORD ORIGIN Greek

naphthalene *n* *chem* a white crystalline substance distilled from coal tar or petroleum, used in mothballs, dyes, and explosives
WORD ORIGIN *naphtha* + *alcohol* + *-ene*

napkin ● *n* **1** a piece of cloth or paper for wiping the mouth or protecting the clothes while eating **2** ▸ same as **sanitary towel**
WORD ORIGIN Latin *mappa* cloth

nappy *n, pl* **-pies** *Brit & NZ* a piece of soft absorbent material, usually disposable, wrapped around the waist and between the legs of a baby to absorb its urine and excrement
WORD ORIGIN from *napkin*

Narayan *n* **R(asipuram) K(rishnaswamy)** 1906–2001, Indian novelist writing in English. His books include *Swami and Friends* (1938), *The Man-Eater of Malgudi* (1961), *Under the Banyan Tree* (1985), and *Grandmother's Tale* (1993)

narcissism *n* an exceptional interest in or admiration for oneself **narcissistic** *adj*
WORD ORIGIN after *Narcissus*, a youth in Greek mythology, who fell in love with his reflection

narcissus (nahr-**siss**-uss) *n, pl* **-cissi** (-**siss**-eye) a yellow, orange, or white flower related to the daffodil
WORD ORIGIN Greek *narkissos*, perhaps from *narkē* numbness, because of narcotic properties attributed to the plant

narcosis *n* unconsciousness caused by a narcotic or general anaesthetic
WORD ORIGIN Greek *narkē* numbness

narcotic ● *n* **1** a drug, such as opium or morphine, that produces numbness and drowsiness, used

THESAURUS

epithet, sobriquet, cognomen, moniker *or* monicker *(slang)* ▷ *vb* **9 = call**, christen, baptize, dub, term, style, label, entitle, denominate **11, 12 = nominate**, choose, commission, mention, identify, select, appoint, specify, designate

namely *adv* **= specifically**, that is to say, to wit, i.e., viz.

nap[1] *n* **1 = sleep**, rest, kip *(Brit slang)*, siesta, catnap, forty winks *(informal)*, shuteye *(slang)*, zizz *(Brit informal)*, nana nap *(informal)* ▷ *vb* **2 = sleep**, rest, nod, drop off *(informal)*, doze, kip *(Brit slang)*, snooze *(informal)*, nod off *(informal)*, catnap, drowse, zizz *(Brit informal)*

nap[2] *n* **= pile**, down, fibre, weave, shag, grain

napkin *n* **1 = serviette**, cloth

narcotic *n* **1 = drug**, anaesthetic, painkiller, sedative, opiate, tranquillizer, anodyne, analgesic ▷ *adj* **2 = sedative**, calming, dulling, numbing, hypnotic, analgesic, stupefying, soporific, painkilling

narrative *n* **1 = story**, report, history, detail, account, statement, tale, chronicle

narrow *adj* **1 = thin**, fine, slim, pinched, slender, tapering, attenuated **OPPOSITE:** broad **2a = limited**, restricted, confined, tight, close, near, cramped, meagre, constricted, circumscribed, scanty, straitened, incapacious **OPPOSITE:** wide **2b = insular**, prejudiced, biased, partial, reactionary, puritan, bigoted, dogmatic, intolerant, narrow-minded, small-minded, illiberal **OPPOSITE:** broad-minded ▷ *vb* **4 = get narrower**, taper, shrink, tighten, constrict **5** *(often with* **down***)* **= restrict**, limit, reduce, diminish,

n

medicinally but addictive ▷*adj* **2** of narcotics or narcosis
WORD ORIGIN Greek *narkē* numbness
nark *slang vb* **1** to annoy ▷*n* **2** an informer or spy: *copper's nark* **3** *Brit* someone who complains in an irritating or whining manner
WORD ORIGIN probably from Romany *nāk* nose
narky *adj* **narkier, narkiest** *slang* irritable, complaining, or sarcastic
narrate *vb* **-rating, -rated 1** to tell (a story); relate **2** to speak the words accompanying and telling what is happening in a film or TV programme **narrator** *n*
WORD ORIGIN Latin *narrare* to recount
narration *n* **1** a narrating **2** a narrated account or story
narrative *n* **1** an account of events **2** the part of a literary work that relates events ▷*adj* **3** telling a story: *a narrative account of the main events* **4** of narration: *narrative clarity*
narrow *adj* **1** small in breadth in comparison to length **2** limited in range, extent, or outlook: *a narrow circle of academics* **3** with little margin: *a narrow advantage* ▷*vb* **4** to make or become narrow **5 narrow down** to restrict or limit: *the search can be narrowed down to a single room* ▸ See also **narrows** > **narrowly** *adv* **narrowness** *n*
WORD ORIGIN Old English *nearu*
narrow boat *n Brit* a long bargelike canal boat
narrow gauge *n* **1** a railway track with less than 56<fract>(1/2) inches (1.435 metres) between the lines ▷*adj* **narrow-gauge 2** denoting a railway with a narrow gauge
narrow-minded *adj* bigoted, intolerant, or prejudiced **narrow-mindedness** *n*
narrows *pl n* a narrow part of a strait, river, or current
narwhal *n* an arctic whale with a long spiral tusk
WORD ORIGIN Old Norse *nāhvalr*, from *nār* corpse + *hvalr* whale
NASA (in the US) National Aeronautics and Space Administration
nasal *adj* **1** of the nose **2** (of a sound) pronounced with air passing through the nose **3** (of a voice) characterized by nasal sounds **nasally** *adv*
WORD ORIGIN Latin *nasus* nose
nascent *adj formal* starting to grow or develop
WORD ORIGIN Latin *nasci* to be born
NASDAQ US National Association of Securities Dealers Automated Quotations (System)
Nash *n* **1 John** 1752–1835, English town planner and architect. He designed Regent's Park, Regent Street, and the Marble Arch in London **2 Ogden** 1902–71, US humorous poet **3 Paul** 1889–1946, English painter, noted esp. as a war artist in both World Wars and for his landscapes **4 Richard,** known as *Beau Nash.* 1674–1762, English dandy **5** ▸ See (Thomas) **Nashe 6** Sir **Walter** 1882–1968, New Zealand Labour statesman, born in England: prime minister of New Zealand (1957–60)
Nashe *or* **Nash** *n* **Thomas** 1567–1601, English pamphleteer, satirist, and novelist, author of the first picaresque novel in English, *The Unfortunate Traveller, or the Life of Jack Wilton* (1594)
Nasmyth *n* **James** 1808–90, British engineer; inventor of the steam hammer (1839)
Nastase *n* **Ilie** born 1946, Romanian tennis player
nasturtium *n* a plant with yellow, red, or orange trumpet-shaped flowers
WORD ORIGIN Latin: kind of cress
nasty *adj* **-tier, -tiest 1** unpleasant: *a nasty odour* **2** dangerous or painful: *a nasty burn* **3** (of a person) spiteful or ill-natured ▷*n, pl* **-ties 4** something unpleasant: *video nasties* **nastily** *adv* **nastiness** *n*
WORD ORIGIN probably related to Dutch *nestig* dirty
nat. 1 national **2** nationalist
natal (nay-tl) *adj* of or relating to birth
WORD ORIGIN Latin *natalis* of one's birth
nation *n* a large body of people of one or more cultures or races, organized into a single state: *a major industrialized nation*
WORD ORIGIN Latin *natio* birth, tribe
national *adj* **1** of or serving a nation as a whole **2** characteristic of a particular nation: *the national character* ▷*n* **3** a citizen of a particular country: *Belgian nationals* **4** a national newspaper **nationally** *adv*
national anthem *n* a patriotic song adopted by a nation for use on public occasions
National Curriculum *n* (in England and Wales) the curriculum of subjects taught in state schools since 1989
national debt *n* the total outstanding borrowings of a nation's central government
national grid *n Brit & NZ* **1** a network of high-voltage power lines linking major electric power stations **2** the arrangement of vertical and horizontal lines on an ordnance survey map
National Health Service *n* (in Britain) the system of national medical services financed mainly by taxation
national hunt *n Brit (often cap)* horse racing over courses with fences
national insurance *n* (in Britain) state insurance based on contributions from employees and employers, providing payments to the unemployed, the sick, and the retired
nationalism *n* **1** a policy of national independence **2** patriotism, sometimes to an excessive degree **nationalist** *n, adj* **nationalistic** *adj*
nationality *n, pl* **-ties 1** the fact of being a citizen of a particular nation **2** a group of people of the same race: *young men of all nationalities*
nationalize *or* **-ise** *vb* **-izing, -ized** *or* **-ising, -ised** to put (an industry or a company) under state control **nationalization** *or* **-isation** *n*
national park *n* an area of countryside protected by a national government for its scenic or environmental importance and visited by the public
national service *n chiefly Brit* compulsory military service
National Socialism *n German history* the doctrines and practices of the Nazis, involving the supremacy of Hitler, anti-Semitism, state control of the economy, and national expansion **National Socialist** *n, adj*
national superannuation *n NZ* a

n

THESAURUS

constrict, circumscribe, straiten
nasty *adj* **1a = unpleasant**, ugly, disagreeable **OPPOSITE:** pleasant **1b = disgusting**, unpleasant, dirty, offensive, foul, horrible, polluted, filthy, sickening, vile, distasteful, repellent, obnoxious, objectionable, disagreeable, nauseating, odious, repugnant, loathsome, grotty *(slang)*, malodorous, noisome, unappetizing, yucky *or* yukky *(slang)*, festy *(Austral slang)*, yucko *(Austral slang)* **2 = serious**, bad, dangerous, critical, severe, painful **3 = spiteful**, mean, offensive, annoying, vicious, unpleasant, abusive, vile, malicious, bad-tempered, despicable, disagreeable **OPPOSITE:** pleasant
nation *n* **a = country**, state, commonwealth, realm, micronation **b = public**, people, community, society, population
national *adj* **1 = nationwide**, state, public, civil, widespread, governmental, countrywide ▷*n* **3 = citizen**, subject, resident, native, inhabitant
nationalism *n* **2 = patriotism**, loyalty to your country, chauvinism, jingoism, nationality, allegiance, fealty
nationality *n* **1 = citizenship**, birth **2 = race**, nation, ethnic group

DICTIONARY

government pension paid to people of 65 years and over; retirement pension

National Trust *n* (in Britain) an organization concerned with the preservation of historic buildings and areas of natural beauty

nationwide ❶ *adj* covering or available to the whole of a nation

native ❶ *adj* **1** relating to a place where a person was born: *native land* **2** born in a specified place: *a native New Yorker* **3** **native to** originating in: *a plant native to alpine regions* **4** natural or inborn: *native genius* **5** relating to the original inhabitants of a country: *archaeology may uncover magnificent native artefacts* **6** **go native** (of a settler) to adopt the lifestyle of the local population ▹*n* **7** a person born in a specified place: *a native of Palermo* **8** an indigenous animal or plant: *the saffron crocus is a native of Asia Minor* **9** a member of the original race of a country, as opposed to colonial immigrants
WORD ORIGIN Latin *nativus* innate, natural, from *nasci* to be born

Native American *n* ▸same as **American Indian**

native bear *n Austral* ▸same as **koala**

native companion *n Austral* ▸same as **brolga**

native dog *n Austral* ▸same as **dingo**

nativity *n, pl* **-ties** birth or origin
WORD ORIGIN Late Latin *nativitas* birth

Nativity *n Christianity* **1** the birth of Jesus Christ **2** the feast of Christmas celebrating this

NATO *or* **Nato** North Atlantic Treaty Organization: an international organization established for purposes of collective security

natter *Brit & NZ informal vb* **1** to talk idly and at length ▹*n* **2** a long idle chat
WORD ORIGIN dialect *gnatter* to grumble, imitative

natterjack *n* a greyish-brown toad with reddish warty lumps
WORD ORIGIN origin unknown

natty *adj* **-tier, -tiest** *informal* smart and spruce **nattily** *adv*
WORD ORIGIN dialect *net* neat

natural ❶ *adj* **1** as is normal or to be expected: *the natural consequence* **2** genuine or spontaneous: *talking in a relaxed, natural manner* **3** of, according to, existing in, or produced by nature: *natural disasters* **4** not acquired; inborn: *their natural enthusiasm* **5** not created by human beings **6** not synthetic: *natural fibres such as wool* **7** (of a parent) not adoptive **8** (of a child) illegitimate **9** *music* not sharp or flat: *F natural* ▹*n* **10** *informal* a person with an inborn talent or skill: *she's a natural at bridge* **11** *music* a note that is neither sharp nor flat **naturalness** *n*

natural gas *n* a gaseous mixture, consisting mainly of methane, found below ground; used widely as a fuel

natural history *n* the study of animals and plants in the wild

naturalism *n* a movement in art and literature advocating detailed realism **naturalistic** *adj*

naturalist *n* **1** a student of natural history **2** a person who advocates or practises naturalism

naturalize *or* **-ise** *vb* **-izing, -ized** *or* **-ising, -ised** **1** to give citizenship to (a person born in another country) **2** to introduce (a plant or animal) into another region **3** to cause (a foreign word or custom) to be adopted **naturalization** *or* **-isation** *n*

natural logarithm *n* a logarithm which has the irrational number *e* as a base

naturally ❶ *adv* **1** of course; surely **2** in a natural or normal way **3** instinctively

natural number *n* a positive integer, such as 1, 2, 3, 4 etc.

natural philosophy *n old-fashioned* physics

natural resources *pl n* naturally occurring materials such as coal, oil, and minerals

natural science *n* any of the sciences dealing with the study of the physical world, such as biology, physics, chemistry, and geology

natural selection *n* a process by which only those creatures and plants well adapted to their environment survive

natural wastage *n chiefly Brit* a reduction in the number of employees through not replacing those who leave, rather than by dismissing employees or making them redundant

nature ❶ *n* **1** the whole system of the existence, forces, and events of the physical world that are not controlled by human beings **2** fundamental or essential qualities: *the theory and nature of science* **3** kind or sort: *problems of a financial nature* **4** temperament or personality: *an amiable and pleasant nature* **5** **by nature** essentially: *he was by nature a cautious man* **6** **in the nature of** essentially; by way of: *it was in the nature of a debate rather than an argument*
WORD ORIGIN Latin *natura*, from *nasci* to be born

nature reserve *n* an area of land that is preserved and managed in order to protect its animal and plant life

nature study *n* the study of animals and plants by direct observation

nature trail *n* a path through countryside, signposted to draw attention to natural features of interest

naturism *n* ▸same as **nudism** > **naturist** *n, adj*

naught *n* **1** *archaic or literary* nothing **2** *chiefly US* the figure 0 ▹*adv* **3** *archaic or literary* not at all: *I care naught*
WORD ORIGIN Old English *nāwiht*

naughty ❶ *adj* **-tier, -tiest** **1** (of children) mischievous or disobedient **2** mildly indecent: *naughty lingerie* **naughtily** *adv* **naughtiness** *n*
WORD ORIGIN (originally: needy, poor) from *naught*

nausea ❶ (naw-zee-a) *n* **1** the feeling of being about to vomit **2** disgust

THESAURUS

nationwide *adj* **= national**, general, widespread, countrywide, overall

native *n* **7, 9** *(usually with* **of***)* **= inhabitant**, national, resident, citizen, countryman, aborigine *(often offensive)*, dweller

natural *adj* **1a = logical**, reasonable, valid, legitimate **1b = normal**, common, regular, usual, ordinary, typical, everyday
OPPOSITE: abnormal
2 = unaffected, open, frank, genuine, spontaneous, candid, unpretentious, unsophisticated, dinkum *(Austral & NZ informal)*, artless, ingenuous, real, simple, unstudied
OPPOSITE: affected
4 = innate, native, characteristic, indigenous, inherent, instinctive, intuitive, congenital, inborn, immanent, in your blood, essential
6 = pure, plain, organic, whole, unrefined, unbleached, unpolished, unmixed **OPPOSITE:** processed

naturally *adv* **1 = of course**, certainly, as a matter of course, as anticipated **2 = typically**, simply, normally, spontaneously, customarily

nature *n* **1 = creation**, world, earth, environment, universe, cosmos, natural world **2 = quality**, character, make-up, constitution, attributes, essence, traits, complexion, features **3 = kind**, sort, style, type, variety, species, category, description **4 = temperament**, character, personality, disposition, outlook, mood, humour, temper

naughty *adj* **1 = disobedient**, bad, mischievous, badly behaved, wayward, playful, wicked, sinful, fractious, impish, roguish, refractory **OPPOSITE:** good **2 = obscene**, blue, vulgar, improper, lewd, risqué, X-rated *(informal)*, bawdy, smutty, off-colour, ribald **OPPOSITE:** clean

nausea *n* **1 = sickness**, vomiting, retching, squeamishness, queasiness, biliousness

naval *adj* **= nautical**, marine, maritime

DICTIONARY

WORD ORIGIN Greek: seasickness, from *naus* ship

nauseate *vb* **-ating, -ated 1** to cause (someone) to feel sick **2** to arouse feelings of disgust in (someone) **nauseating** *adj*

nauseous *adj* **1** as if about to be sick: *he felt nauseous* **2** sickening

nautical *adj* of the sea, ships, or navigation
WORD ORIGIN Greek *nautikos*, from *naus* ship

nautical mile *n* a unit of length, used in navigation, standardized as 6080 feet

nautilus *n, pl* **-luses** *or* **-li** a sea creature with a shell and tentacles
WORD ORIGIN Greek *nautilos* sailor

naval ❶ *adj* of or relating to a navy or ships
WORD ORIGIN Latin *navis* ship

nave[1] *n* the long central part of a church
WORD ORIGIN Latin *navis* ship, from the similarity in shape

nave[2] *n* the hub of a wheel
WORD ORIGIN Old English *nafu, nafa*

navel *n* the slight hollow in the centre of the abdomen, where the umbilical cord was attached
WORD ORIGIN Old English *nafela*

navel orange *n* a sweet orange that has a navel-like hollow at the top

navigable *adj* **1** wide, deep, or safe enough to be sailed through: *the navigable portion of the Nile* **2** able to be steered: *the boat has to be watertight and navigable*

navigate *vb* **-gating, -gated 1** to direct or plot the course or position of a ship or aircraft **2** to travel over or through safely: *your cousin, who's just navigated the Amazon* **3** *informal* to direct (oneself) carefully or safely: *he navigated his unsteady way to the bar* **4** (of a passenger in a vehicle) to read the map and give directions to the driver **navigation** *n* **navigational** *adj* **navigator** *n*
WORD ORIGIN Latin *navis* ship + *agere* to drive

Navratilova *n* **Martina** born 1956, Czech-born US tennis player: Wimbledon champion 1978, 1979, 1982–87, 1990; world champion 1980 and 1984

navvy *n, pl* **-vies** *Austral & Brit informal* a labourer on a building site or road
WORD ORIGIN from *navigator* builder of a *navigation* (in the sense: canal)

navy ❶ *n, pl* **-vies 1** the branch of a country's armed services comprising warships with their crews, and all their supporting services **2** the warships of a nation ▷ *adj* **3** ▸ short for **navy-blue**
WORD ORIGIN Latin *navis* ship

navy-blue *adj* very dark blue
WORD ORIGIN from the colour of the British naval uniform

nawab (na-**wahb**) *n* (formerly) a Muslim ruler or powerful landowner in India
WORD ORIGIN Hindi *nawwāb*, from Arabic *nuwwāb*, plural of *na'ib* viceroy

nay *interj* **1** *old-fashioned* no ▷ *n* **2** a person who votes against a motion ▷ *adv* **3** used for emphasis: *I want, nay, need to know*
WORD ORIGIN Old Norse *nei*

Nazarene *n* **1 the Nazarene** Jesus Christ **2** *old-fashioned* a Christian **3** a person from Nazareth, a town in N Israel ▷ *adj* **4** of Nazareth

Nazi *n, pl* **-zis 1** a member of the fascist National Socialist German Workers' Party, which came to power in Germany in 1933 under Adolf Hitler ▷ *adj* **2** of or relating to the Nazis **Nazism** *n*
WORD ORIGIN German, phonetic spelling of the first two syllables of *Nationalsozialist* National Socialist

nb *cricket* no-ball

Nb *chem* niobium

NB 1 New Brunswick **2** note well
WORD ORIGIN Latin *nota bene*

NC 1 North Carolina **2** *Brit education* National Curriculum

NCO noncommissioned officer

Nd *chem* neodymium

ND North Dakota

N'Dour *n* **Youssou** born 1959, Senegalese singer and musician, whose work has popularized African music in the West; recordings include *Nelson Mandela* (1986), *Eyes Open* (1992), and *Nothing's in Vain* (2002)

NDT Newfoundland Daylight Time

Ne *chem* neon

NE 1 Nebraska **2** northeast(ern)

ne- *combining form*: *Nearctic*. ▸ Same as **neo-**

Neanderthal (nee-**ann**-der-tahl) *adj* **1** of a type of primitive man that lived in Europe before 12 000 BC **2** *informal* with excessively conservative views: *his notoriously Neanderthal attitude to women*
WORD ORIGIN after *Neandertal*, a valley in Germany

neap *n* ▸ short for **neap tide**
WORD ORIGIN Old English, as in *nēpflōd* neap tide

Neapolitan *adj* **1** of Naples, a city in SW Italy ▷ *n* **2** a person from Naples
WORD ORIGIN Greek *Neapolis* new town

neap tide *n* a tide that occurs at the first and last quarter of the moon when there is the smallest rise and fall in tidal level

near ❶ *prep* **1** at or to a place or time not far away from ▷ *adv* **2** at or to a place or time not far away **3** ▸ short for **nearly**: *the pain damn near crippled him* ▷ *adj* **4** at or in a place or time not far away: *in the near future* **5** closely connected or intimate: *a near relation* **6** almost being the thing specified: *a mood of near rebellion* ▷ *vb* **7** to draw close (to): *the participants are nearing agreement* ▷ *n* **8** the left side of a horse or vehicle **nearness** *n*
WORD ORIGIN Old English *nēar*, comparative of *nēah* close

nearby ❶ *adj* **1** not far away: *a nearby village* ▷ *adv* **2** close at hand: *I live nearby*

Near East *n* ▸ same as **Middle East**

nearly ❶ *adv* **1** almost **2 not nearly** nowhere near: *it's not nearly as easy as it looks*

near miss *n* **1** any attempt that just fails to succeed **2** an incident in which two aircraft or vehicles narrowly avoid collision **3** a bomb or shot that does not quite hit the target

nearside *n* **1** *chiefly Brit* the side of a vehicle that is nearer the kerb **2** the left side of an animal

near-sighted *adj* ▸ same as **short-sighted**

near thing *n* *informal* an event whose outcome is nearly a failure or a disaster, or only just a success

neat ❶ *adj* **1** clean and tidy **2** smoothly or competently done: *a neat answer* **3** (of alcoholic drinks) undiluted **4** *slang chiefly US & Canad*

n

THESAURUS

navy *n* **2 = fleet**, warships, flotilla, armada

near *adj* **4a = close**, bordering, neighbouring, nearby, beside, adjacent, adjoining, close by, at close quarters, just round the corner, contiguous, proximate, within sniffing distance *(informal)*, a hop, skip and a jump away *(informal)* **OPPOSITE:** far
4b = imminent, forthcoming, approaching, looming, impending, upcoming, on the cards *(informal)*, nigh, in the offing, near-at-hand, next **OPPOSITE:** far-off

nearby *adj* **1 = neighbouring**, adjacent, adjoining

nearly *adv* **1a = practically**, about, almost, virtually, all but, just about, not quite, as good as, well-nigh **1b = almost**, about, approaching, roughly, just about, approximately

neat *adj* **1a = tidy**, nice, straight, trim, orderly, spruce, uncluttered, shipshape, spick-and-span **OPPOSITE:** untidy
1b = methodical, tidy, systematic, fastidious **OPPOSITE:** disorganized
1c = smart, trim, tidy, spruce, dapper, natty *(informal)*, well-groomed, well-turned out **2a = graceful**, elegant, adept, nimble, agile, adroit, efficient **OPPOSITE:** clumsy
2b = clever, efficient, handy, apt, well-judged **OPPOSITE:** inefficient

DICTIONARY

admirable; excellent **neatly** *adv* **neatness** *n*
WORD ORIGIN Latin *nitidus* clean

neaten *vb* to make neat

neath *prep archaic* ▸short for **beneath**

neb *n archaic or dialect* the beak of a bird or the nose of an animal
WORD ORIGIN Old English *nebb*

nebula (neb-yew-la) *n, pl* **-lae** (-lee) *astron* a hazy cloud of particles and gases **nebular** *adj*
WORD ORIGIN Latin: mist, cloud

nebulize *or* **-ise** *vb* **-izing, -ized** *or* **-ising, -ised** to turn (a liquid) into a fine spray

nebulizer *or* **-iser** *n* a device which turns a drug from a liquid into a fine spray which can be inhaled

nebulous *adj* vague and unclear: *a nebulous concept*

NEC (in Britain) National Executive Committee

necessaries *pl n* essential items: *the necessaries and comforts of life*

necessarily ❶ *adv* **1** as a certainty: *the factors were not necessarily connected with one another* **2** inevitably: *tourism is an industry that has a necessarily close connection with governments*

necessary ❶ *adj* **1** needed in order to obtain the desired result: *the necessary skills* **2** certain or unavoidable: *the necessary consequences* ▹*n* **3 do the necessary** *informal* to do something that is necessary in a particular situation **4 the necessary** *informal* the money required for a particular purpose ▸See also **necessaries**
WORD ORIGIN Latin *necessarius* indispensable

necessitate *vb* **-tating, -tated** to compel or require

necessitous *adj literary* very needy

necessity *n, pl* **-ties 1** a set of circumstances that inevitably requires a certain result: *the necessity to maintain safety standards* **2** something needed: *the daily necessities* **3** great poverty **4 of necessity** inevitably

neck *n* **1** the part of the body connecting the head with the rest of the body **2** the part of a garment around the neck **3** the long narrow part of a bottle or violin **4** the length of a horse's head and neck taken as the distance by which one horse beats another in a race: *to win by a neck* **5** *informal* impudence **6 by a neck** by a very small margin: *she held on to win by a neck* **7 get it in the neck** *informal* to be reprimanded or punished severely **8 neck and neck** absolutely level in a race or competition **9 neck of the woods** *informal* a particular area: *how did they get to this neck of the woods?* **10 stick one's neck out** *informal* to risk criticism or ridicule by speaking one's mind **11 up to one's neck in** *informal* to be deeply involved in: *he was up to his neck in the scandal* ▹*vb* **12** *informal* (of two people) to kiss each other passionately
WORD ORIGIN Old English *hnecca*

neckband *n* a band around the neck of a garment

Necker *n* **Jacques** 1732–1804, French financier and statesman, born in Switzerland; finance minister of France (1777–81; 1788–90). He attempted to reform the fiscal system and in 1789 he recommended summoning the States General. His subsequent dismissal was one of the causes of the storming of the Bastille (1789)

neckerchief *n* a piece of cloth worn tied round the neck
WORD ORIGIN *neck + kerchief*

necklace *n* **1** a decorative piece of jewellery worn round the neck **2** (in South Africa) a tyre soaked in petrol, placed round a person's neck, and set on fire in order to burn the person to death

neckline *n* the shape or position of the upper edge of a dress or top

necktie *n US* ▸same as **tie** (sense 5)

necromancy (neck-rome-man-see) *n* **1** communication with the dead **2** sorcery **necromancer** *n*
WORD ORIGIN Greek *nekros* corpse + *mantis* prophet

necrophilia *n* sexual attraction for or sexual intercourse with dead bodies
WORD ORIGIN Greek *nekros* corpse + *philos* loving

necropolis (neck-rop-pol-liss) *n* a cemetery
WORD ORIGIN Greek *nekros* dead + *polis* city

necrosis *n* **1** *biol, med* the death of cells in the body, as from an interruption of the blood supply **2** *bot* death of plant tissue due to disease or frost **necrotic** *adj*
WORD ORIGIN Greek *nekros* corpse

nectar *n* **1** a sugary fluid produced by flowers and collected by bees **2** *classical myth* the drink of the gods **3** any delicious drink
WORD ORIGIN Greek *nektar*

nectarine *n* a smooth-skinned variety of peach
WORD ORIGIN apparently from *nectar*

ned *n Scot slang* a hooligan
WORD ORIGIN origin unknown

NEDC (formerly) National Economic Development Council. Also (informal): **Neddy**

née *prep* indicating the maiden name of a married woman: *Jane Gray (née Blandish)*
WORD ORIGIN French, past participle (feminine) of *naître* to be born

need ❶ *vb* **1** to require or be in want of: *they desperately need success* **2** to be obliged: *the government may need to impose a statutory levy* **3** used to express necessity or obligation and does not add -s when used with singular nouns or pronouns: *need he go?* ▹*n* **4** the condition of lacking something: *he has need of a new coat* **5** a requirement: *the need for closer economic co-operation* **6** necessity: *there was no need for an explanation* **7** poverty or destitution: *the money will go to those areas where need is greatest* **8** distress: *help has been given to those in need* ▸See also **needs**
WORD ORIGIN Old English *nēad, nied*

needful *adj* **1** necessary or required ▹*n* **2 the needful** *informal* what is necessary, usually money

THESAURUS

3 *(of an alcoholic drink)* = **undiluted**, straight, pure, unmixed **4** *(chiefly US & Canad slang)* = **cool**, great *(informal)*, excellent, brilliant, cracking *(Brit informal)*, smashing *(informal)*, superb, fantastic *(informal)*, tremendous, ace *(informal)*, fabulous *(informal)*, marvellous, terrific, awesome *(slang)*, mean *(slang)*, super *(informal)*, brill *(informal)*, bodacious *(slang, chiefly US)*, boffo *(slang)*, chillin' *(US slang)*, booshit *(Austral slang)*, exo *(Austral slang)*, sik *(Austral slang)*, rad *(informal)*, phat *(slang)*, schmick *(Austral informal)*, beaut *(informal)*, barrie *(Scot slang)*, belting *(Brit slang)*, pearler *(Austral slang)* **OPPOSITE:** terrible

necessarily *adv* **1** = **automatically**, naturally, definitely, undoubtedly, accordingly, by definition, of course, certainly **2** = **inevitably**, of necessity, unavoidably, perforce, incontrovertibly, nolens volens *(Latin)*

necessary *adj* **1** = **needed**, required, essential, vital, compulsory, mandatory, imperative, indispensable, obligatory, requisite, de rigueur *(French)*, needful, must-have **OPPOSITE:** unnecessary **2** = **inevitable**, certain, unavoidable, inescapable **OPPOSITE:** avoidable

necessity *n* **2** = **essential**, need, necessary, requirement, fundamental, requisite, prerequisite, sine qua non *(Latin)*, desideratum, want, must-have

need *vb* **1a** = **want**, miss, require, lack, have to have, demand **1b** = **require**, want, demand, call for, entail, necessitate, have occasion to *or* for **2** = **have to**, be obliged to ▹*n* **5** = **requirement**, demand, essential, necessity, requisite, desideratum, must-have **6** = **necessity**, call, demand, requirement, obligation **7** = **poverty**, deprivation, destitution, neediness, distress, extremity, privation, penury, indigence, impecuniousness **8** = **emergency**, want, necessity, urgency, exigency

needle *n* **1** a pointed slender piece of metal with a hole in it through which thread is passed for sewing **2** a long pointed rod used in knitting **3** ▸ same as **stylus** **4** *med* the long hollow pointed part of a hypodermic syringe, which is inserted into the body **5** a pointer on the scale of a measuring instrument **6** a long narrow stiff leaf: *pine needles* **7** *Brit informal* intense rivalry or ill-feeling in a sports match **8** ▸ short for **magnetic needle** **9** **have** *or* **get the needle** *Brit informal* to be annoyed ▷ *vb* **-dling, -dled** **10** *informal* to goad or provoke
WORD ORIGIN Old English *nǣdl*

needlecord *n* a fine-ribbed corduroy fabric

needlepoint *n* **1** embroidery done on canvas **2** lace made by needles on a paper pattern

needless *adj* not required; unnecessary **needlessly** *adv*

needlewoman *n, pl* **-women** a woman who does needlework

needlework *n* sewing and embroidery

needs *adv* **1** necessarily: *they must needs be admired* ▷ *pl n* **2** what is required: *he provides them with their needs*

needy *adj* **needier, neediest** in need of financial support

Néel *n* **Louis** (lwi) 1904–2000, French physicist, noted for his research on magnetism; shared the Nobel prize for physics in 1970

ne'er *adv poetic* never

ne'er-do-well *n* **1** an irresponsible or lazy person ▷ *adj* **2** useless; worthless: *his ne'er-do-well brother*

nefarious (nif-fair-ee-uss) *adj literary* evil; wicked
WORD ORIGIN Latin *ne* not + *fas* divine law

neg. negative

negate *vb* **-gating, -gated** **1** to cause to have no value or effect: *his prejudices largely negate his accomplishments* **2** to deny the existence of
WORD ORIGIN Latin *negare*

negation *n* **1** the opposite or absence of something **2** a negative thing or condition **3** a negating

negative *adj* **1** expressing a refusal or denial: *a negative response* **2** lacking positive qualities, such as enthusiasm or optimism **3** *med* indicating absence of the condition for which a test was made **4** *physics* **a** (of an electric charge) having the same electrical charge as an electron **b** (of a body or system) having a negative electric charge; having an excess of electrons **5** ▸ same as **minus** (sense 4) **6** measured in a direction opposite to that regarded as positive **7** ▸ short for **electronegative** **8** of a photographic negative ▷ *n* **9** a statement or act of denial or refusal **10** *photog* a piece of photographic film, exposed and developed, bearing an image with a reversal of tones or colours, from which positive prints are made **11** a word or expression with a negative meaning, such as *not* **12** a quantity less than zero **13** **in the negative** indicating denial or refusal
negatively *adv*

negative equity *n* the holding of a property of fallen value which is worth less than the amount of mortgage still unpaid

negativism *n* a tendency to be unconstructively critical
negativist *n, adj*

neglect *vb* **1** to fail to give due care or attention to: *she had neglected her child* **2** to fail (to do something) through carelessness: *he neglected to greet his guests* **3** to disregard: *he neglected his duty* ▷ *n* **4** lack of due care or attention: *the city had a look of shabbiness and neglect* **5** the state of being neglected
WORD ORIGIN Latin *neglegere*

neglectful *adj* not paying enough care or attention: *abusive and neglectful parents*

negligee (neg-lee-zhay) *n* a woman's light, usually lace-trimmed dressing gown
WORD ORIGIN French

negligence *n* neglect or carelessness **negligent** *adj* **negligently** *adv*

negligible *adj* so small or unimportant as to be not worth considering

negotiable *adj* **1** able to be changed or agreed by discussion: *the prices were negotiable* **2** (of a bill of exchange or promissory note) legally transferable

negotiate *vb* **-ating, -ated** **1** to talk with others in order to reach (an agreement) **2** to succeed in passing round or over (a place or a problem)
negotiation *n* **negotiator** *n*
WORD ORIGIN Latin *negotium* business, from *nec* not + *otium* leisure

Negro *old-fashioned* *n, pl* **-groes** **1** a member of any of the Black peoples originating in Africa ▷ *adj* **2** of Negroes
WORD ORIGIN Latin *niger* black

Negroid *adj* of or relating to the Negro race

neigh *n* **1** the high-pitched sound made by a horse ▷ *vb* **2** to make this sound
WORD ORIGIN Old English *hnǣgan*

neighbour *or US* **neighbor** *n* **1** a person who lives near or next to another **2** a person, thing, or country near or next to another
WORD ORIGIN Old English *nēah* near + *būr, gebūr* dweller

neighbourhood *or US* **neighborhood** *n* **1** a district where people live **2** the immediate

THESAURUS

needle *vb* **10 = irritate**, provoke, annoy, sting, bait, harass, taunt, nag, hassle *(informal)*, aggravate *(informal)*, prod, gall, ruffle, spur, prick, nettle, goad, irk, rile, get under your skin *(informal)*, get on your nerves *(informal)*, nark *(Brit, Austral & NZ slang)*, hack you off *(informal)*, get in your hair *(informal)*

needless *adj* **= unnecessary**, excessive, pointless, gratuitous, useless, unwanted, redundant, superfluous, groundless, expendable, uncalled-for, dispensable, nonessential, undesired **OPPOSITE:** essential

needy *adj* **= poor**, deprived, disadvantaged, impoverished, penniless, destitute, poverty-stricken, underprivileged, indigent, down at heel *(informal)*, impecunious, dirt-poor, on the breadline *(informal)* **OPPOSITE:** wealthy

negative *adj* **1 = dissenting**, contradictory, refusing, denying, rejecting, opposing, resisting, contrary **OPPOSITE:** assenting **2 = pessimistic**, cynical, unwilling, gloomy, antagonistic, jaundiced, uncooperative, contrary **OPPOSITE:** optimistic ▷ *n* **9 = denial**, no, refusal, rejection, contradiction

neglect *vb* **1 = disregard**, ignore, leave alone, turn your back on, fail to look after **OPPOSITE:** look after **2a = shirk**, forget, overlook, omit, evade, pass over, skimp, procrastinate over, let slide, be remiss in *or* about **2b = fail**, forget, omit ▷ *n* **4a = negligence**, inattention, unconcern **OPPOSITE:** care **4b = shirking**, failure, oversight, carelessness, dereliction, forgetfulness, slackness, laxity, laxness, slovenliness, remissness

negligence *n* **= carelessness**, failure, neglect, disregard, shortcoming, omission, oversight, dereliction, forgetfulness, slackness, inattention, laxity, thoughtlessness, laxness, inadvertence, inattentiveness, heedlessness, remissness

negotiate *vb* **1 = bargain**, deal, contract, discuss, debate, consult, confer, mediate, hold talks, arbitrate, cut a deal, conciliate, parley, discuss terms **2a = arrange**, manage, settle, work out, bring about, transact **2b = get round**, clear, pass, cross, pass through, get over, get past, surmount

neighbourhood *or (US)* **neighborhood** *n* **1 = district**, community, quarter, region,

DICTIONARY

environment; surroundings **3** the people in a district **4 in the neighbourhood of** approximately ▹ *adj* **5** in and for a district: *our neighbourhood cinema*

neighbouring ⓣ *or US* **neighboring** *adj* situated nearby: *the neighbouring island*

neighbourly ⓣ *or US* **neighborly** *adj* kind, friendly, and helpful

Neill *n* **1 A**(**lexander**) **S**(**utherland**) 1883–1973, Scottish educationalist and writer, who put his progressive educational theories into practice at Summerhill school (founded 1921) **2 Sam** born 1947, New Zealand film and television actor; his work includes the television series *Reilly, Ace of Spies*, and the films *My Brilliant Career* (1979), *Dead Calm* (1989), and *Jurassic Park* (1993)

neither *adj* **1** not one nor the other (of two): *neither enterprise went well* ▹ *pron* **2** not one nor the other (of two): *neither completed the full term* ▹ *conj* **3 a** used preceding alternatives joined by *nor*; not: *sparing neither strength nor courage* **b** ▸ same as **nor** (sense 2) ▹ *adv* **4** *not standard* ▸ same as **either** (sense 4)
WORD ORIGIN Old English *nāwther*

Nekrasov *n* **Nikolai Alekseyevich** 1821–77, Russian poet, who wrote chiefly about the sufferings of the peasantry

nelson *n* a wrestling hold in which a wrestler places his arm or arms under his opponent's arm or arms from behind and exerts pressure with his palms on the back of his opponent's neck
WORD ORIGIN from a proper name

nematode *n* a slender unsegmented cylindrical worm
WORD ORIGIN Greek *nēma* thread + *eidos* shape

nemesis (nem-miss-iss) *n, pl* **-ses** (-seez) a means of retribution or vengeance
WORD ORIGIN Greek *nemein* to distribute what is due

neo- *combining form* new, recent, or a modern form of: *neoclassicism; neo-Nazi*
WORD ORIGIN Greek *neos* new

neoclassicism *n* a late 18th- and early 19th-century style of art and architecture, based on ancient Roman and Greek models **neoclassical** *adj*

neocolonialism *n* political control wielded by one country over another through control of its economy **neocolonial** *adj*

neocon *n, adj chiefly US* ▸ short for **neoconservative**

neoconservative *adj* **1** favouring a return to a set of established (esp. political) conservative values which have been updated to suit current conditions ▹ *n* **2** a person subscribing to neoconservative philosophy

neodymium *n chem* a toxic silvery-white metallic element of the lanthanide series. Symbol: Nd
WORD ORIGIN NEO- + *didymium*, a compound originally thought to be an element

Neolithic *adj* of the period that lasted in Europe from about 4000 to 2400 BC, characterized by primitive farming and the use of polished stone and flint tools and weapons
WORD ORIGIN NEO- + Greek *lithos* stone

neologism (nee-ol-a-jiz-zum) *n* a newly coined word, or an established word used in a new sense
WORD ORIGIN NEO- + Greek *logos* word

neon *n* **1** *chem* a colourless odourless rare gas, used in illuminated signs and lights. Symbol: Ne ▹ *adj* **2** of or illuminated by neon: *a flashing neon sign*
WORD ORIGIN Greek: new

neonatal *adj* relating to the first few weeks of a baby's life **neonate** *n*

neon light *n* a glass tube containing neon, which gives a pink or red glow when a voltage is applied

neophyte *n formal* **1** a beginner **2** a person newly converted to a religious faith **3** a novice in a religious order
WORD ORIGIN Greek *neos* new + *phuton* a plant

Nepali (nip-paw-lee) *or* **Nepalese** (nep-pal-leez) *adj* **1** of Nepal ▹ *n* **2** *pl* **-pali, -palis** *or* **-palese** a person from Nepal **3** the language of Nepal

nephew *n* a son of one's sister or brother
WORD ORIGIN Latin *nepos*

nephritis (nif-frite-tiss) *n* inflammation of the kidney
WORD ORIGIN Greek *nephros* kidney

Nepos *n* **Cornelius** ?100–?25 BC, Roman historian and biographer; author of *De Viris illustribus*

nepotism (nep-a-tiz-zum) *n* favouritism shown to relatives and friends by those with power
WORD ORIGIN Italian *nepote* nephew

Neptune *n* **1** the Roman god of the sea **2** the eighth planet from the sun

neptunium *n chem* a silvery metallic element synthesized in the production of plutonium. Symbol: Np
WORD ORIGIN after *Neptune*, the planet

nerd *or* **nurd** *n slang* **1** a boring or unpopular person, esp. one who is obsessed with a particular subject: *a computer nerd* **2** a stupid and feeble person **nerdish** *or* **nurdish** *adj*
WORD ORIGIN origin unknown

Neri *n* **Saint Philip** Italian name *Filippo de' Neri*. 1515–95, Italian priest; founder of the Congregation of the Oratory (1564). Feast day: May 26

Nernst *n* **Walther Hermann** 1864–1941, German physical chemist who formulated the third law of thermodynamics: Nobel prize for chemistry 1920

Neruda *n* **Pablo**, real name *Neftali Ricardo Reyes*. 1904–73, Chilean poet. His works include *Veinte poemas de amor y una canción desesperada* (1924) and *Canto general* (1950), an epic history of the Americas: Nobel prize for literature 1971

Nerva *n* full name *Marcus Cocceius Nerva*. ?30–98 AD, Roman emperor (96–98), who introduced some degree of freedom after the repressive reign of Domitian. He adopted Trajan as his son and successor

Nerval *n* **Gérard de**, real name *Gérard Labrunie*. 1808–55, French poet, noted esp. for the sonnets of mysticism, myth, and private passion in *Les Chimères* (1854)

nervate *adj* (of leaves) with veins

nerve ⓣ *n* **1** a cordlike bundle of fibres that conducts impulses between the brain and other parts of the body **2** bravery and determination **3** *informal* impudence: *you've got a nerve!* **4 lose one's nerve** to lose self-confidence and become afraid about what one is doing **5 strain every nerve** to make every effort (to do something) ▹ *vb* **nerving, nerved**

THESAURUS

surroundings, locality, locale **2 = vicinity**, confines, proximity, precincts, environs, purlieus

neighbouring *or (US)* **neighboring** *adj* **= nearby**, next, near, bordering, surrounding, connecting, adjacent, adjoining, abutting, contiguous, nearest **OPPOSITE:** remote

neighbourly *or (US)* **neighborly** *adj* **= helpful**, kind, social, civil, friendly, obliging, harmonious, amiable, considerate, sociable, genial, hospitable, companionable, well-disposed

nerve *n* **2 = bravery**, courage, spirit, bottle *(Brit slang)*, resolution, daring, determination, guts *(informal)*, pluck, grit, fortitude, vigour, coolness, balls *(taboo, slang)*, mettle, firmness, spunk *(informal)*, fearlessness, steadfastness, intrepidity, hardihood, gameness **3** *(informal)* **= impudence**, face *(informal)*, front, neck *(informal)*, sauce *(informal)*, cheek *(informal)*, brass *(informal)*, gall, audacity, boldness, temerity, chutzpah *(US & Canad informal)*, insolence, impertinence, effrontery, brass neck *(Brit informal)*, brazenness, sassiness *(US slang)* **6 nerve yourself = brace yourself**, pr epare yourself, steel yourself, fortify yourself, gear yourself up, gee yourself up

DICTIONARY

6 nerve oneself to prepare oneself (to do something difficult or unpleasant) ▸ See also **nerves**
WORD ORIGIN Latin *nervus*
nerve cell *n* ▸ same as **neuron**
nerve centre *n* **1** a place from which a system or organization is controlled: *an underground nerve centre of intelligence* **2** a group of nerve cells associated with a specific function
nerve gas *n* a poisonous gas which affects the nervous system
nerveless *adj* **1** (of fingers or hands) without feeling; numb **2** (of a person) fearless
nerve-racking *or* **nerve-wracking** *adj* very distressing or harrowing
nerves ⓘ *pl n informal* **1** anxiety or tension: *nerves can often be the cause of wedding-day hitches* **2** the ability or inability to remain calm in a difficult situation: *his nerves are in a shocking state* **3 get on someone's nerves** to irritate someone
Nervi *n* **Pier Luigi** 1891–1979, Italian engineer and architect; noted for his pioneering use of reinforced concrete as a decorative material. He codesigned the UNESCO building in Paris (1953)
nervous ⓘ *adj* **1** apprehensive or worried **2** excitable; highly strung **3** of or relating to the nerves: *the nervous system* **nervously** *adv* **nervousness** *n*
nervous breakdown *n* a mental illness in which the sufferer ceases to function properly, and experiences symptoms including tiredness, anxiety, and deep depression
nervous system *n* the brain, spinal column, and nerves, which together control thought, feeling, and movement ▸ See **neuron**
nervy *adj* **nervier, nerviest** *Austral & Brit informal* excitable or nervous
Nesbit *n* **E(dith)** 1858–1924, British writer of children's books, including *The Phoenix and the Carpet* (1904) and *The Railway Children* (1906)
ness *n Brit* a headland or cape
WORD ORIGIN Old English *næs*
-ness *suffix* indicating state, condition, or quality: *greatness; selfishness*
WORD ORIGIN Old English *-nes*
Nesselrode *n* Count **Karl Robert** 1780–1862, Russian diplomat: as foreign minister (1822–56), he negotiated the Treaty of Paris after the Crimean War (1856)
nest ⓘ *n* **1** a place or structure in which birds or other animals lay eggs or give birth to young **2** a cosy or secluded place **3** a set of things of graduated sizes designed to fit together: *a nest of tables* ▹ *vb* **4** to make or inhabit a nest **5** (of a set of objects) to fit one inside another **6** *computers* to position (data) within other data at different ranks or levels
WORD ORIGIN Old English
nest egg *n* a fund of money kept in reserve
nestle ⓘ *vb* **-tling, -tled 1** to snuggle or cuddle closely **2** to be in a sheltered position: *honey-coloured stone villages nestling in wooded valleys*
WORD ORIGIN Old English *nestlian*
nestling ⓘ *n* a young bird not yet able to fly
net¹ ⓘ *n* **1** a very fine fabric made from intersecting strands of material with a space between each strand **2** a piece of net, used to protect or hold things or to trap animals **3** (in certain sports) a strip of net over which the ball or shuttlecock must be hit **4** the goal in soccer or hockey **5** a strategy intended to trap people: *innocent fans were caught in the police net* **6** *informal* ▸ short for **internet** ▹ *vb* **netting, netted 7** to catch (a fish or other animal) in a net
WORD ORIGIN Old English *net(t)*
net² ⓘ *or* **nett** *adj* **1** remaining after all deductions, as for taxes and expenses: *net income* **2** (of weight) excluding the weight of wrapping or container **3** final or conclusive: *the net effect* ▹ *vb* **netting, netted 4** to yield or earn as a clear profit
WORD ORIGIN French: neat
Netanyahu *n* **Benjamin** born 1949, Israeli politician: leader of the Likud party (1993–99); prime minister (1996–99)
netball *n* a team game, usually played by women, in which a ball has to be thrown through a net hanging from a ring at the top of a pole
nether *adj old-fashioned* lower or under: *nether regions*
WORD ORIGIN Old English *nithera*, literally: further down
nethermost *adj* lowest
nether world *n* **1** the underworld **2** hell. Also called: **nether regions**
net profit *n* gross profit minus all operating expenses such as wages and overheads
Netrebko *n* **Anna** born 1971, Russian operatic soprano
nett *adj, vb* ▸ same as **net²**
netting *n* a fabric or structure made of net
nettle *n* **1** a plant with stinging hairs on the leaves **2 grasp the nettle** to attempt something unpleasant with boldness and courage
WORD ORIGIN Old English *netele*
nettled *adj* irritated or annoyed
nettle rash *n* a skin condition, usually caused by an allergy, in which itchy red or white raised patches appear
network ⓘ *n* **1** a system of intersecting lines, roads, veins, etc. **2** an interconnecting group or system: *a network of sympathizers and safe-houses* **3** *radio, television* a group of broadcasting stations that all transmit the same programme at the same time **4** *electronics, computers* a system of interconnected components or circuits ▹ *vb* **5** *radio, television* to broadcast (a programme) over a network
Neumann *n* **1 Johann Balthasar** 1687–1753, German rococo architect. His masterpiece is the church of Vierzehnheiligen in Bavaria **2** ▸ See (John) **von Neumann**
neural *adj* of a nerve or the nervous system
neuralgia *n* severe pain along a nerve **neuralgic** *adj*
neuritis (nyoor-**rite**-tiss) *n* inflammation of a nerve or nerves, often causing pain and loss of function in the affected part
neurology *n med* the scientific study of the nervous system **neurological** *adj* **neurologist** *n*
neuron *or* **neurone** *n* a cell specialized to conduct nerve impulses
WORD ORIGIN Greek
neurosis (nyoor-**oh**-siss) *n, pl* **-ses** (-seez) a mental disorder producing

n

THESAURUS

nerves *pl n* **1** *(informal)* **= tension**, stress, strain, anxiety, butterflies (in your stomach) *(informal)*, nervousness, cold feet *(informal)*, heebie-jeebies *(slang)*, worry
nervous *adj* **1** *(often with* **of***)* **= apprehensive**, anxious, uneasy, edgy, worried, wired *(slang)*, tense, fearful, shaky, hysterical, neurotic, agitated, ruffled, timid, hyper *(informal)*, jittery *(informal)*, uptight *(informal)*, flustered, on edge, excitable, nervy *(Brit informal)*, jumpy, twitchy *(informal)*, fidgety, timorous, highly strung, antsy *(informal)*, toey *(Austral slang)*, adrenalized
OPPOSITE: calm
nest *n* **2 = refuge**, resort, retreat, haunt, den, hideaway
nestle *vb* **1** *(often with* **up** *or* **down***)* **= snuggle**, cuddle, huddle, curl up, nuzzle
nestling *n* **= chick**, fledgling, baby bird
net¹ *n* **1, 2 = mesh**, netting, network, web, lattice, lacework, openwork ▹ *vb* **7 = catch**, bag, capture, trap, nab *(informal)*, entangle, ensnare, enmesh
net² *or* **nett** *adj* **1 = after taxes**, final, clear, take-home ▹ *vb* **4 = earn**, make, clear, gain, realize, bring in, accumulate, reap
network *n* **1a = web**, system, arrangement, grid, mesh, lattice, circuitry, nexus, plexus, interconnection, net **1b = maze**, warren, labyrinth

DICTIONARY

hysteria, anxiety, depression, or obsessive behaviour

neurosurgery *n med* the branch of surgery concerned with the nervous system **neurosurgeon** *n* **neurosurgical** *adj*

neurotic ⊕ *adj* **1** tending to be emotionally unstable **2** afflicted by neurosis ▷*n* **3** a person afflicted with a neurosis or tending to be emotionally unstable

neurotransmitter *n biochem* a chemical by which a nerve cell communicates with another nerve cell or with a muscle

neuter *adj* **1** *grammar* denoting a gender of nouns which are neither male nor female **2** (of animals and plants) sexually underdeveloped ▷*n* **3** *grammar* **a** the neuter gender **b** a neuter noun **4** a sexually underdeveloped female insect, such as a worker bee **5** a castrated animal ▷*vb* **6** to castrate (an animal)
WORD ORIGIN Latin *ne* not + *uter* either (of two)

neutral ⊕ *adj* **1** not taking any side in a war or dispute **2** of or belonging to a neutral party or country **3** not displaying any emotions or opinions **4** (of a colour) not definite or striking **5** *chem* neither acidic nor alkaline **6** *physics* having zero charge or potential ▷*n* **7** a neutral person or nation **8** the position of the controls of a gearbox that leaves the gears unconnected to the engine **neutrality** *n*
WORD ORIGIN Latin *neutralis* of neuter gender

neutralize *or* **-ise** *vb* **-izing, -ized** *or* **-ising, -ised 1** to make electrically or chemically neutral **2** to make ineffective by counteracting **3** to make (a country) neutral by international agreement: *the great powers neutralized Belgium in the 19th century* **neutralization** *or* **-isation** *n*

neutrino (new-tree-no) *n, pl* **-nos** *physics* an elementary particle with no mass or electrical charge
WORD ORIGIN Italian diminutive of *neutrone* neutron

neutron *n physics* a neutral elementary particle of about the same mass as a proton
WORD ORIGIN from *neutral*, on the model of *electron*

neutron bomb *n* a nuclear weapon designed to kill people and animals while leaving buildings virtually undamaged

never ⊕ *adv* **1** at no time; not ever **2** certainly not; not at all **3** Also: **well I never!** surely not!
WORD ORIGIN Old English *nǣfre*

never-ending *adj* long and boring

nevermore *adv literary* never again

never-never *n* **the never-never** *informal* hire-purchase: *they are buying it on the never-never*

never-never land *n* an imaginary idyllic place

nevertheless ⊕ *adv* in spite of that

new ⊕ *adj* **1** recently made, brought into being, or acquired: *a new car* **2** of a kind never before existing; novel: *a new approach to monetary policy* **3** recently discovered: *testing new drugs* **4** recently introduced to or inexperienced in a place or situation: *new to this game* **5** fresh; additional: *you can acquire new skills* **6** unknown: *this is new to me* **7** (of a cycle) beginning again: *a new era* **8** (of crops) harvested early: *new potatoes* **9** changed for the better: *she returned a new woman* ▷*adv* **10** recently, newly: *new-laid eggs* ▸ See also **news** ▸ **newish** *adj* **newness** *n*
WORD ORIGIN Old English *nīowe*

New Age *n* **1** a philosophy, originating in the late 1980s, characterized by a belief in alternative medicine, astrology, and spiritualism ▷*adj* **2** of the New Age: *New Age therapies* **New Ager** *n*

New Age Music *n* a type of gentle melodic largely instrumental popular music originating in the USA in the late 1980s

New Australian *n Austral* an Australian name for a recent immigrant, esp. one from Europe

newbie *n informal* a person new to a job, club, etc.

newborn *adj* recently or just born

New Canadian *n Canad* a recent immigrant to Canada

new chum *n Austral & NZ, archaic informal* a recent British immigrant

Newcomb *n* **Simon** 1835–1909, US astronomer, noted for his tables of celestial bodies and astronomical constants

Newcombe *n* **John** (**David**) born 1944, Australian tennis player; winner of seven Grand Slam singles titles (1967–74)

newcomer ⊕ *n* a recent arrival or participant

newel *n* **1** Also called: **newel post** the post at the top or bottom of a flight of stairs that supports the handrail **2** the central pillar of a winding staircase
WORD ORIGIN Old French *nouel* knob

newfangled *adj* objectionably or unnecessarily modern
WORD ORIGIN Middle English *newefangel* liking new things

new-found *adj* newly or recently discovered: *new-found confidence*

Ne Win *n* **U** 1911–2002, Burmese statesman and general; prime minister (1958–60), head of the military government (1962–74), and president (1974–81)

New Jerusalem *n Christianity* heaven

Newlands *n* **John Alexander** 1838–98, British chemist: classified the elements in order of their atomic weight, noticing similarities in every eighth and thus discovering his law of octaves

New Latin *n* the form of Latin used since the Renaissance, mainly for scientific names

newly *adv* **1** recently **2** again; anew: *newly interpreted*

newlyweds *pl n* a recently married couple

New Man *n* **the New Man** *chiefly Brit* a type of modern man who allows the caring side of his nature to show by being supportive and by sharing

THESAURUS

neurotic *adj* **1, 2 = unstable**, nervous, disturbed, anxious, abnormal, obsessive, compulsive, manic, unhealthy, hyper *(informal)*, twitchy *(informal)*, overwrought, maladjusted **OPPOSITE:** rational

neutral *adj* **1, 2 = unbiased**, impartial, disinterested, even-handed, dispassionate, sitting on the fence, uninvolved, noncommittal, nonpartisan, unprejudiced, nonaligned, unaligned, noncombatant, nonbelligerent **OPPOSITE:** biased **3a = expressionless**, dull, blank, deadpan, toneless **3b = uncontroversial** *or* noncontroversial, safe, inoffensive **4 = colourless**, achromatic

never *adv* **1 = at no time**, not once, not ever **OPPOSITE:** always **2 = under no circumstances**, no way, not at all, on no account, not on your life *(informal)*, not on your nelly *(Brit slang)*, not for love nor money *(informal)*, not ever

nevertheless *adv* **= even so**, still, however, yet, regardless, nonetheless, notwithstanding, in spite of that, (even) though, but

new *adj* **1 = brand new**, unused **3 = modern**, recent, contemporary, up-to-date, latest, happening *(informal)*, different, current, advanced, original, fresh, novel, topical, state-of-the-art, ground-breaking, modish, newfangled, modernistic, ultramodern, all-singing, all-dancing **OPPOSITE:** old-fashioned **4, 6 = unfamiliar**, unaccustomed, strange, unknown **5 = extra**, more, added, new-found, supplementary **9 = renewed**, changed, improved, restored, altered, rejuvenated, revitalized

newcomer *n* **a = new arrival**, incomer, immigrant, stranger, foreigner, alien, settler **b = beginner**, stranger, outsider, novice, new arrival, parvenu, Johnny-come-lately

DICTIONARY

child care and housework
new maths *n Brit* an approach to mathematics in which basic set theory is introduced at an elementary level
new moon *n* the moon when it appears as a narrow crescent at the beginning of its cycle
news ❶ *n* **1** important or interesting new happenings **2** information about such events, reported in the mass media **3 the news** a television or radio programme presenting such information **4** interesting or important new information: *it's news to me* **5** a person or thing widely reported in the mass media: *reggae is suddenly big news again*
news agency *n* an organization that collects news reports and sells them to newspapers, magazines, and TV and radio stations
newsagent *n Brit* a shopkeeper who sells newspapers and magazines
newscast *n* a radio or television broadcast of the news **newscaster** *n*
WORD ORIGIN *news* + *(broad)cast*
news conference *n* ▸same as **press conference**
newsflash *n* a brief item of important news, which interrupts a radio or television programme
newsgroup *n computers* a forum where subscribers exchange information about a specific subject by e-mail
newsletter *n* a periodical bulletin issued to members of a group
newspaper *n* a weekly or daily publication consisting of folded sheets and containing news, features, and advertisements
newspeak *n* the language of politicians and officials regarded as deliberately ambiguous and misleading
WORD ORIGIN from the novel *1984* by George Orwell
newsprint *n* an inexpensive wood-pulp paper used for newspapers
newsreader *n* a news announcer on radio or television
newsreel *n* a short film with a commentary which presents current events
newsroom *n* a room in a newspaper office or radio or television station where news is received and prepared for publication or broadcasting: *a journalist who was in the newsroom at the time*
newsstand *n* a portable stand from which newspapers are sold
New Style *n* the present method of reckoning dates using the Gregorian calendar
newsworthy *adj* sufficiently interesting to be reported as news
newsy *adj* **newsier, newsiest** (of a letter) full of news
newt *n* a small amphibious creature with a long slender body and tail and short legs
WORD ORIGIN mistaken division of *an ewt*; *ewt* from Old English *efeta*
New Testament *n* the second part of the Christian Bible, dealing with the life and teachings of Christ and his followers
newton *n* the SI unit of force that gives an acceleration of 1 metre per second per second to a mass of 1 kilogram
WORD ORIGIN after Sir Isaac *Newton*, scientist
new town *n* (in Britain) a town planned as a complete unit and built with government sponsorship
new wave *n* a movement in politics, the arts, or music that consciously breaks with traditional values
New World *n* **the New World** the western hemisphere of the world, esp. the Americas
New Year *n* the first day or days of the year in various calendars, usually a holiday
New Year's Day *n* January 1, celebrated as a holiday in many countries
New Year's Eve *n* December 31
New Zealander *n* a person from New Zealand
Nexø *n* **Martin Andersen** 1869–1954, Danish novelist. His chief works are the novels *Pelle the Conqueror* (1906–10), which deals with the labour movement, and *Ditte, Daughter of Man* (1917–21)
next ❶ *adj* **1** immediately following: *the next generation* **2** immediately adjoining: *in the next room* **3** closest to in degree: *the next-best thing* ▹*adv* **4** at a time immediately to follow: *the patient to be examined next* **5 next to a** adjacent to: *the house next to ours* **b** following in degree: *next to my wife, I love you most* **c** almost: *the evidence is next to totally useless*
WORD ORIGIN Old English *nēhst*, superlative of *nēah* near
next door *adj, adv* in, at, or to the adjacent house or flat: *the Cabinet retired next door; the people next door*
next of kin *n* a person's closest relative
nexus *n, pl* **nexus 1** a connection or link **2** a connected group or series
WORD ORIGIN Latin, from *nectere* to bind
Ney *n* **Michel**, Duc d'Elchingen 1769–1815, French marshal, who earned the epithet *Bravest of the Brave* at the battle of Borodino (1812) in the Napoleonic Wars. He rallied to Napoleon on his return from Elba and was executed for treason (1815)
NF Newfoundland
Nfld. Newfoundland
ngati (nah-tee) *n, pl* **ngati** *NZ* (occurring as part of the tribe name) a tribe or clan
WORD ORIGIN Māori
NH New Hampshire
NHS (in Britain) National Health Service
Ni *chem* nickel
NI 1 (in Britain) National Insurance **2** Northern Ireland
niacin *n* a vitamin of the B complex that occurs in milk, liver, and yeast. Also called: **nicotinic acid**
WORD ORIGIN from *ni(cotinic) ac(id)* + *-in* denoting a chemical substance
Niarchos *n* **Stavros Spyro** 1909–96, Greek shipowner. He pioneered the use of supertankers in the 1950s
nib *n* the writing point of a pen
WORD ORIGIN origin unknown
nibble *vb* **-bling, -bled 1** to take little bites (of) **2** to bite gently: *she nibbled at her lower lip* ▹*n* **3** a little bite **4** a light hurried meal
WORD ORIGIN related to Low German *nibbelen*
nibs *n* **his** *or* **her nibs** *slang* a mock title used of an important or self-important person
WORD ORIGIN origin unknown
NICAM near-instantaneous companding system: a technique for coding audio signals into digital form
nice ❶ *adj* **1** pleasant **2** kind: *it's really nice of you to worry about me* **3** good or satisfactory: *a nice clean operation* **4** subtle: *a nice distinction* **nicely** *adv* **niceness** *n*
WORD ORIGIN Old French: simple, silly

THESAURUS

(informal), noob *(derogatory, slang)*
news *n* **1, 2 = information**, latest *(informal)*, report, word, story, release, account, statement, advice, exposé, intelligence, scandal, rumour, leak, revelation, buzz, gossip, dirt *(US slang)*, goss *(informal)*, disclosure, bulletin, dispatch, gen *(Brit informal)*, communiqué, hearsay, tidings, news flash, scuttlebutt *(US slang)*
next *adj* **1 = following**, later, succeeding, subsequent
2 = adjacent, closest, nearest, neighbouring, adjoining ▹*adv*
4 = afterwards, then, later, following, subsequently, thereafter
nice *adj* **1a = pleasant**, delightful, agreeable, good, attractive, charming, pleasurable, enjoyable
OPPOSITE: unpleasant
1b = likable *or* **likeable**, friendly, engaging, charming, pleasant, agreeable, amiable, prepossessing
2 = kind, helpful, obliging, considerate **OPPOSITE:** unkind
4 = precise, fine, careful, strict, accurate, exact, exacting, subtle,

DICTIONARY

nicety *n, pl* **-ties 1** a subtle point: *the niceties of our arguments* **2** a refinement or delicacy: *social niceties* **3 to a nicety** precisely

niche (neesh) *n* **1** a recess in a wall for a statue or ornament **2** a position exactly suitable for the person occupying it: *perhaps I will find my niche in a desk job* ▷ *adj* **3** of or aimed at a specialist group or market: *niche retailing ventures*
WORD ORIGIN Old French *nichier* to nest

Nicholas I *n* **1 Saint,** called *the Great.* died 867 AD, Italian ecclesiastic; pope (858–867). He championed papal supremacy. Feast day: Nov 13 **2** 1796–1855, tsar of Russia (1825–55). He gained notoriety for his autocracy and his emphasis on military discipline and bureaucracy

Nicholas of Cusa *n* 1401–64, German cardinal, philosopher, and mathematician: anticipated Copernicus in asserting that the earth revolves around the sun

Nicholas V *n* original name *Tommaso Parentucelli.* 1397–1455, Italian ecclesiastic; pope (1447–55). He helped to found the Vatican Library

Nichols *n* **Peter** (**Richard**) born 1927, British dramatist, whose works include *A Day in the Death of Joe Egg* (1967), the musical *Privates on Parade* (1977), and *Blue Murder* (1995)

Nicias *n* died 414 BC, Athenian statesman and general. He ended the first part of the Peloponnesian War by making peace with Sparta (421)

nick *vb* **1** to make a small cut in **2** *chiefly Brit slang* to steal **3** *chiefly Brit slang* to arrest ▷ *n* **4** a small notch or cut **5** *slang* a prison or police station **6** *informal* condition: *in good nick* **7 in the nick of time** just in time
WORD ORIGIN perhaps Middle English *nocke* nock

nickel *n* **1** *chem* a silvery-white metallic element that is often used in alloys. Symbol: Ni **2** a US or Canadian coin worth five cents
WORD ORIGIN German *Kupfernickel* nickel ore, literally: copper demon; it was mistakenly thought to contain copper

nickelodeon *n US* an early type of jukebox
WORD ORIGIN *nickel* + *(mel)odeon*

nickel silver *n* an alloy containing copper, zinc, and nickel

nicker *n, pl* **nicker** *Brit slang* a pound sterling
WORD ORIGIN origin unknown

nick-nack *n* ▸ same as **knick-knack**

nickname *n* **1** a familiar, pet, or derisory name given to a person or place ▷ *vb* **-naming, -named 2** to call (a person or place) by a nickname: *Gaius Caesar Augustus Germanicus, nicknamed Caligula*
WORD ORIGIN mistaken division of *an ekename* an additional name

Nicolai *n* **Carl Otto Ehrenfried** 1810–49, German composer: noted for his opera *The Merry Wives of Windsor* (1849)

Nicolson *n* Sir **Harold** (**George**) 1886–1968, British diplomat, politician, and author: married to Vita Sackville-West

nicotine *n* a poisonous alkaloid found in tobacco **nicotinic** *adj*
WORD ORIGIN after J. *Nicot,* who introduced tobacco into France

nictitating membrane *n* (in reptiles, birds, and some mammals) a thin fold of skin under the eyelid that can be drawn across the eye

Niebuhr *n* **1 Barthold Georg** 1776–1831, German historian, noted for his critical approach to sources, esp. in *History of Rome* (1811–32) **2 Reinhold** 1892–1971, US Protestant theologian. His works include *Moral Man and Immoral Society* (1932) and *The Nature and Destiny of Man* (1941–43)

niece *n* a daughter of one's sister or brother
WORD ORIGIN Latin *neptis* granddaughter

Nielsen *n* **Carl** (**August**) (karl) 1865–1931, Danish composer. His works include six symphonies and the opera *Masquerade* (1906)

Niemeyer *n* **Oscar.** born 1907, Brazilian architect. His work includes many buildings in Brasília, esp. the president's palace (1959) and the cathedral (1964)

Niemöller *n* **Martin** 1892–1984, German Protestant theologian, who was imprisoned (1938–45) for his opposition to Hitler

niff *Brit slang n* **1** a stink ▷ *vb* **2** to stink **niffy** *adj*
WORD ORIGIN perhaps from *sniff*

nifty *adj* **-tier, -tiest** *informal* neat or smart
WORD ORIGIN origin unknown

Nigerian *adj* **1** of Nigeria ▷ *n* **2** a person from Nigeria

niggard *n* a stingy person
WORD ORIGIN perhaps from Old Norse

niggardly *adj* not generous: *it pays its staff on a niggardly scale* **niggardliness** *n*

nigger *n offensive* a Black person
WORD ORIGIN Spanish *negro*

niggle *vb* **-gling, -gled 1** to worry slightly **2** to find fault continually ▷ *n* **3** a small worry or doubt **4** a trivial objection or complaint **niggling** *adj*
WORD ORIGIN Scandinavian

nigh *archaic, poetic adv* **1** nearly ▷ *adj* **2** near ▷ *prep* **3** close to
WORD ORIGIN Old English *nēah, nēh*

night *n* **1** the period of darkness that occurs each 24 hours, between sunset and sunrise **2** the period between sunset and bedtime; evening **3** the time between bedtime and morning **4** nightfall or dusk **5** an evening designated for a specific activity: *opening night* **6 make a night of it** to celebrate the whole evening ▸ Related adjective: **nocturnal** *adj* **7** of, occurring, or working at night: *the night sky* ▸ See also **nights**
WORD ORIGIN Old English *niht*

nightcap *n* **1** a drink taken just before bedtime **2** a soft cap formerly worn in bed

nightclub *n* a place of entertainment open until late at night, usually offering drink, a floor show, and dancing

nightdress *n* a loose dress worn in bed by women or girls

nightfall *n* the approach of darkness; dusk

nightgown *n* ▸ same as **nightdress**

nightie *n informal* ▸ short for **nightdress**

nightingale *n* a small bird with a musical song, usually heard at night
WORD ORIGIN Old English *nihtegale,* literally: night singer

nightjar *n* a nocturnal bird with a harsh cry
WORD ORIGIN *night* + JAR[2] (so called from its discordant cry)

nightlife *n* the entertainment and social activities available at night in a town or city: *New York nightlife*

night-light *n* a dim light left on overnight

nightlong *adj, adv* throughout the night

nightly *adj* **1** happening each night ▷ *adv* **2** each night

THESAURUS

delicate, discriminating, rigorous, meticulous, scrupulous, fastidious
OPPOSITE: vague

niche *n* **1 = recess**, opening, corner, hollow, nook, alcove **2 = position**, calling, place, slot *(informal)*, vocation, pigeonhole *(informal)*

nick *vb* **1 = cut**, mark, score, damage, chip, scratch, scar, notch, dent, snick **2** *(slang, chiefly Brit)* **= steal**, pinch *(informal)*, swipe *(slang)*, pilfer, snitch *(slang)* ▷ *n* **4 = cut**, mark, scratch, score, chip, scar, notch, dent, snick

nickname *n* **1 = pet name**, label, diminutive, epithet, sobriquet, familiar name, moniker *or* monicker *(slang)*, handle *(slang)*

night *n* **1 = darkness**, dark, night-time, dead of night, night watches, hours of darkness ▸ *related adjective:* nocturnal

nightly *adj* **1 = nocturnal**, night-time ▷ *adv* **2 = every night**, nights *(informal)*, each night, night after night

DICTIONARY

nightmare ❶ *n* **1** a terrifying or deeply distressing dream **2** a terrifying or unpleasant experience **3** a thing that is feared: *wheels and loose straps are a baggage handler's nightmare* **nightmarish** *adj*
WORD ORIGIN *night* + Old English *mare, mære* evil spirit

nights *adv informal* at night or on most nights: *he works nights*

night safe *n* a safe built into the outside wall of a bank, in which customers can deposit money when the bank is closed

night school *n* an educational institution that holds classes in the evening

nightshade *n* a plant which produces poisonous berries with bell-shaped flowers
WORD ORIGIN Old English *nihtscada*

nightshirt *n* a long loose shirtlike garment worn in bed

night soil *n archaic* human excrement collected at night from cesspools or privies

nightspot *n informal* a nightclub

night-time *n* the time from sunset to sunrise

night watch *n* **1** a watch or guard kept at night for security **2** the period of time this watch is kept

night watchman *n* a person who keeps guard at night on a factory or other building

nihilism (nye-ill-liz-zum) *n* a total rejection of all established authority and institutions **nihilist** *n, adj* **nihilistic** *adj*
WORD ORIGIN Latin *nihil* nothing

-nik *suffix forming nouns* indicating a person associated with a particular state or quality: *refusenik*
WORD ORIGIN Russian

nil ❶ *n* nothing: esp. as a score in games
WORD ORIGIN Latin

Nilsson *n* **Birgit** 1918–2006, Swedish operatic soprano

nimble *adj* **1** agile and quick in movement **2** mentally alert or acute **nimbly** *adv*
WORD ORIGIN Old English *nǣmel* quick to grasp + *numol* quick at seizing

nimbus *n, pl* **-bi** *or* **-buses** **1** a dark grey rain cloud **2** a halo
WORD ORIGIN Latin: cloud

NIMBY not in my back yard: used of people who are opposed to any building or changes that will affect them directly

Nimitz *n* **Chester William** 1885–1966, US admiral; commander in chief of the US Pacific fleet in World War II (1941–45)

Nimzowitsch *n* **Aaron Isayevich** 1886–1935, Latvian chess player and theorist; influential in enunciating the principles of the hypermodern school, of which he was the main instigator

nincompoop *n informal* a stupid person
WORD ORIGIN origin unknown

nine *n* **1** the cardinal number that is the sum of one and eight **2** a numeral, 9 or IX, representing this number **3** something representing or consisting of nine units **4** **dressed up to the nines** *informal* elaborately dressed **5** **999** (in Britain) the telephone number of the emergency services ▹ *adj* **6** amounting to nine: *nine men* **ninth** *adj, n*
WORD ORIGIN Old English *nigon*

nine-days wonder *n* something that arouses great interest, but only for a short period

nine-eleven, 9-11, *or* **9/11** *n* the 11th of September 2001, the day on which the twin towers of the World Trade Center in New York were flown into and destroyed by aeroplanes hijacked by Islamic fundamentalists. Also called: **September eleven**
WORD ORIGIN from the US custom of expressing dates in figures, the day of the month following the number of the month

ninefold *adj* **1** having nine times as many or as much **2** having nine parts ▹ *adv* **3** by nine times as much or as many

ninepins *n* the game of skittles

nineteen *n* **1** the cardinal number that is the sum of ten and nine **2** a numeral, 19 or XIX, representing this number **3** something representing or consisting of nineteen units **4** **talk nineteen to the dozen** to talk very fast ▹ *adj* **5** amounting to nineteen: *nineteen years* **nineteenth** *adj, n*

nineteenth hole *n golf slang* the bar in a golf clubhouse
WORD ORIGIN from its being the next objective after a standard 18-hole round

ninety *n, pl* **-ties** **1** the cardinal number that is the product of ten and nine **2** a numeral, 90 or XC, representing this number **3** something representing or consisting of ninety units **4** **nineties** the numbers 90 to 99, esp. when used to refer to a year of someone's life or of a century ▹ *adj* **5** amounting to ninety: *ninety degrees* **ninetieth** *adj, n*

Ninian *n* **Saint** ?360–?432 AD, the first known apostle of Scotland; built a stone church (*candida casa*) at Whithorn on his native Solway; preached to the Picts. Feast day: Sept 16

ninja *n, pl* **-ja** *or* **-jas** a person skilled in ninjutsu, a Japanese martial art characterized by stealthy movement and camouflage
WORD ORIGIN Japanese

ninny *n, pl* **-nies** a stupid person
WORD ORIGIN perhaps from *an innocent*

Ninus *n* a king of Assyria and the legendary founder of Nineveh, husband of Semiramis

niobium *n chem* a white superconductive metallic element. Symbol: Nb
WORD ORIGIN Latin after *Niobe* (daughter of Tantalus); because it occurred in tantalite

nip[1] ❶ *vb* **nipping, nipped** **1** *informal* to hurry **2** to pinch or squeeze **3** to bite lightly **4** (of the cold) to affect (someone) with a stinging sensation **5** to check the growth of (something): *a trite script nips all hope in the bud* ▹ *n* **6** a pinch or light bite **7** sharp coldness: *a nip in the air*
WORD ORIGIN perhaps from Old Norse

nip[2] ❶ *n* a small drink of spirits
WORD ORIGIN from *nipperkin* a vessel holding a half-pint or less

nipper *n Brit, Austral & NZ informal* a small child

nipple *n* **1** the small projection in the centre of each breast, which in females contains the outlet of the milk ducts **2** a small projection through which oil or grease can be put into a machine or component
WORD ORIGIN perhaps from *neb* peak, tip

nippy *adj* **-pier, -piest** **1** (of weather) frosty or chilly **2** *informal* quick or nimble **3** (of a motor vehicle) small and relatively powerful

Nirenberg *n* **Marshall Warren** born 1927, US biochemist; shared the Nobel prize for physiology or medicine (1968) for his role in deciphering the genetic code

nirvana ❶ (near-vah-na) *n buddhism, hinduism* the ultimate state of

THESAURUS

nightmare *n* **1 = bad dream,** hallucination, night terror **2 = ordeal,** trial, hell, horror, torture, torment, tribulation, purgatory, hell on earth

nil *n* **a = nothing,** love, zero, zip (*US slang*) **b = zero,** nothing, none, naught, zilch (*slang*), zip (*US slang*)

nip[1] *vb* **1** (*with* **along, up, out**) (*Brit informal*)**= pop,** go, run, rush, dash **2, 6 = pinch,** catch, grip, squeeze, clip, compress, tweak **3 = bite,** snap, nibble

nip[2] *n* **= dram,** shot (*informal*), drop, taste, finger, swallow, portion, peg (*Brit*), sip, draught, sup, mouthful, snifter (*informal*), soupçon (*French*)

nirvana *n* **= paradise,** peace, joy, bliss, serenity, tranquillity

DICTIONARY

spiritual enlightenment and bliss attained by extinction of all desires and individual existence
WORD ORIGIN Sanskrit: extinction

nisi (nye-sigh) *adj* ▸ see **decree nisi**

Nissen hut *n chiefly Brit* a tunnel-shaped military shelter made of corrugated steel
WORD ORIGIN after Lt Col. Peter *Nissen,* mining engineer

nit[1] *n* the egg or larva of a louse
WORD ORIGIN Old English *hnitu*

nit[2] *n informal* ▸ short for **nitwit**

nit-picking *informal n* **1** a concern with insignificant details, usually with the intention of finding fault ▹ *adj* **2** showing such concern

nitrate *chem n* **1** a salt or ester of nitric acid **2** a fertilizer containing nitrate salts ▹ *vb* **-trating, -trated 3** to treat with nitric acid or a nitrate **4** to convert or be converted into a nitrate **nitration** *n*

nitre *or US* **niter** *n chem* ▸ same as **potassium nitrate**
WORD ORIGIN Latin *nitrum*

nitric *adj chem* of or containing nitrogen

nitric acid *n chem* a colourless corrosive liquid widely used in industry

nitride *n chem* a compound of nitrogen with a more electropositive element

nitrify *vb* **-fies, -fying, -fied** *chem* **1** to treat (a substance) or cause (a substance) to react with nitrogen **2** to treat (soil) with nitrates **3** to convert (ammonium compounds) into nitrates by oxidation **nitrification** *n*

nitrite *n chem* a salt or ester of nitrous acid

nitro- *or before a vowel* **nitr-** *combining form* **1** indicating that a chemical compound contains the univalent group, $-NO_2$: *nitrobenzene* **2** indicating that a chemical compound is a nitrate ester: *nitrocellulose*
WORD ORIGIN Greek *nitron* nitre

nitrogen (nite-roj-jen) *n chem* a colourless odourless gas that forms four-fifths of the air and is an essential part of all animal and plant life. Symbol: N **nitrogenous** *adj*

nitrogen cycle *n* the natural cycle by which nitrates in the soil, derived from dead organic matter, are absorbed by plants and reduced to nitrates again when the plants and the animals feeding on them die and decay

nitrogen fixation *n* the conversion of atmospheric nitrogen into nitrogen compounds by soil bacteria

nitroglycerine *or* **nitroglycerin** *n chem* a thick pale yellow explosive liquid made from glycerol and nitric and sulphuric acids

nitrous *adj chem* derived from or containing nitrogen in a low valency state

nitrous acid *n chem* a weak acid known only in solution and in the form of nitrite salts

nitrous oxide *n chem* a colourless gas used as an anaesthetic

nitty-gritty *n* **the nitty-gritty** *informal* the basic facts of a matter or situation
WORD ORIGIN perhaps rhyming compound from *grit*

nitwit *n informal* a stupid person
WORD ORIGIN perhaps NIT[1] + WIT[1]

Niven *n* **David** 1909–83, British film actor and author. His films include *The Prisoner of Zenda* (1937), *Around the World in 80 Days* (1956), *Casino Royale* (1967), and *Paper Tiger* (1975). He wrote the autobiographical *The Moon's a Balloon* (1972) and *Bring on the Empty Horses* (1975)

Nizam al-Mulk *n* title of *Abu Ali Hasan Ibn Ali*. ?1018–92, Persian statesman; vizier of Persia (1063–92) for the Seljuk sultans: assassinated

NJ New Jersey

Nkomo *n* **Joshua** 1917–99, Zimbabwean politician; coleader, with Robert Mugabe, of the Patriotic Front (1976–80) against the government of Ian Smith in Rhodesia; minister (1980–82; 1988–99) and vice-president (1990–96)

nkosi (ing-koss-ee) *n S African* a term of address to a superior; master; chief
WORD ORIGIN Nguni (language group of southern Africa) *inkosi* chief, lord

nm nanometre

NM New Mexico

no[1] ❶ *interj* **1** used to express denial, disagreement, or refusal ▹ *n, pl* **noes** *or* **nos 2** an answer or vote of *no* **3** a person who answers or votes *no*
WORD ORIGIN Old English *nā*

no[2] *adj* **1** not any, not a, or not one: *I have no money; no comment* **2** not at all: *he's no exception* **3** not: *no taller than a child* **4 no way!** an expression of emphatic refusal or denial
WORD ORIGIN Old English *nān* none

No[1] *or* **Noh** *n, pl* **No** *or* **Noh** the stylized classical drama of Japan, using music and dancing
WORD ORIGIN Japanese *nō* talent

No[2] *chem* nobelium

No. *or* **no.** *pl* **Nos.** *or* **nos.** number
WORD ORIGIN French *numéro*

n.o. *cricket* not out

nob *n chiefly Brit slang* a person of wealth or social distinction
WORD ORIGIN origin unknown

no-ball *n cricket* an improperly bowled ball, for which the batting side scores a run. Abbrev: **nb**

nobble *vb* **-bling, -bled** *chiefly Brit, Austral, & NZ slang* **1** to bribe or threaten **2** to disable (a racehorse) to stop it from winning **3** to steal
WORD ORIGIN *a nobbler,* a false division of *an hobbler* one who hobbles horses

nobelium *n chem* a radioactive element produced artificially from curium. Symbol: No
WORD ORIGIN after *Nobel* Institute, Stockholm, where it was discovered

Nobel prize (no-bell) *n* a prize for outstanding contributions to chemistry, physics, physiology and medicine, literature, economics, and peace that may be awarded annually
WORD ORIGIN after Alfred *Nobel,* chemist & philanthropist

Nobile *n* **Umberto** 1885–1978, Italian aeronautical engineer and aviator. He flew his *Norge* airship over the North Pole (1926) with Amundsen and his *Italia* airship over the Pole in 1928, crashing on the return

nobility *n* **1** the quality of being noble; dignity **2** the class of people who hold titles and high social rank

noble ❶ *adj* **1** having or showing high moral qualities: *a noble cause* **2** belonging to a class of people who hold titles and high social rank **3** impressive and magnificent: *a noble beast* **4** *chem* (of certain metals) resisting oxidation ▹ *n* **5** a person who holds a title and high social rank **nobly** *adv*
WORD ORIGIN Latin *nobilis,* originally capable of being known, hence well-known

noble gas *n* any of the unreactive gases helium, neon, argon, krypton, xenon, and radon

nobleman *or fem* **noblewoman** *n, pl* **-men** *or* **-women** a person of noble rank

THESAURUS

no[1] *sentence substitute* **1 = not at all,** certainly not, of course not, absolutely not, never, no way, nay **OPPOSITE:** yes ▹ *n* **2 = refusal,** rejection, denial, negation, veto **OPPOSITE:** consent

noble *adj* **1 = worthy,** generous, upright, honourable, virtuous, magnanimous **OPPOSITE:** despicable **2 = aristocratic,** lordly, titled, gentle *(archaic)*, patrician, blue-blooded, highborn **OPPOSITE:** humble **3 = dignified,** great, august, imposing, impressive, distinguished, magnificent, splendid, stately **OPPOSITE:** lowly ▹ *n* **5 = lord,** peer, aristocrat, nobleman, aristo *(informal)* **OPPOSITE:** commoner

nobody *pron* **1 = no-one** ▹ *n* **2 = nonentity,** nothing *(informal)*, lightweight *(informal)*, zero, no-mark *(Brit slang)*, cipher **OPPOSITE:** celebrity

nod *vb* **2 = signal,** indicate, motion, gesture **3 = incline,** bob, bow, duck,

noblesse oblige (no-bless oh-bleezh) *n often ironic* the supposed obligation of the nobility to be honourable and generous
WORD ORIGIN French, lit: nobility obliges

nobody ❶ *pron* **1** no person; no-one ▷ *n, pl* **-bodies 2** a person of no importance

no-brainer *n slang* something that requires little or no mental effort

Nobunaga *n* See **Oda Nobunaga**

nock *n* **1** a notch on an arrow that fits on the bowstring **2** a groove at either end of a bow that holds the bowstring
WORD ORIGIN related to Swedish *nock* tip

no-claims bonus *or* **no-claim bonus** *n* a reduction in the cost of an insurance policy made if no claims have been made in a specified period

nocturnal *adj* **1** of the night **2** (of animals) active at night
WORD ORIGIN Latin *nox* night

nocturne *n* a short dreamy piece of music

nod ❶ *vb* **nodding, nodded 1** to lower and raise (one's head) briefly, to express agreement or greeting **2** to express by nodding: *he nodded his approval* **3** to sway or bend forwards and back **4** to let one's head fall forward with sleep **5 nodding acquaintance** a slight knowledge (of a subject or person) ▷ *n* **6** a quick down-and-up movement of the head, in agreement **7 land of Nod** an imaginary land of sleep
WORD ORIGIN origin unknown

noddle *n chiefly Brit informal* the head or brains
WORD ORIGIN origin unknown

noddy *n, pl* **-dies 1** a tropical tern with a dark plumage **2** a fool
WORD ORIGIN perhaps from obsolete *noddy* foolish, drowsy

node *n* **1** *bot* the point on a plant stem from which the leaves grow **2** *maths* a point at which a curve crosses itself **3** a knot or knob **4** *physics* a point in a vibrating body at which there is practically no vibration **5** *anat* any natural bulge or swelling: *lymph node* **6** *astron* either of the two points at which the orbit of a body intersects the path of the sun or the orbit of another body **nodal** *adj*
WORD ORIGIN Latin *nodus* knot

nod off *vb informal* to fall asleep

nodule *n* **1** a small rounded lump, knot, or node **2** a rounded mineral growth on the root of a plant such as clover **nodular** *adj*
WORD ORIGIN Latin *nodulus*

Noel *or* **Noël** *n* ▸ same as **Christmas**
WORD ORIGIN French, from Latin *natalis* a birthday

nog *n* an alcoholic drink containing beaten egg
WORD ORIGIN origin unknown

noggin *n* **1** *informal* the head **2** a small quantity of spirits
WORD ORIGIN origin unknown

no-go area *n* a district that is barricaded off so that the police or army can enter only by force

Noguchi *n* **Hideyo** 1876–1928, Japanese bacteriologist, active in the US. He made important discoveries in the treatment of syphilis

noise ❶ *n* **1** a sound, usually a loud or disturbing one **2** loud shouting; din **3** an undesired electrical disturbance in a signal **4** unwanted or irrelevant elements in a visual image: *removing noise from pictures* **5 noises** conventional utterances conveying a reaction: *he made the appropriate noises* ▷ *vb* **noising, noised 6 be noised abroad** (of news or gossip) to be spread
WORD ORIGIN Latin *nausea* seasickness

noiseless *adj* making little or no sound **noiselessly** *adv*

noise pollution *n* annoying or harmful noise in an environment

noisette (nwah-zett) *n* a hazelnut chocolate
WORD ORIGIN French

noisome *adj formal* **1** (of smells) offensive **2** extremely unpleasant
WORD ORIGIN obsolete *noy*, variant of *annoy*

noisy ❶ *adj* **noisier, noisiest 1** making a lot of noise **2** (of a place) full of noise **noisily** *adv*

Nolde *n* **Emil** 1867–1956, German painter and engraver, noted particularly for his violent use of colour and the primitive masklike quality of his figures

Nollekens *n* **Joseph** 1737–1823, British neoclassical sculptor of portrait busts, tombs, and mythological subjects

nomad *n* **1** a member of a tribe who move from place to place to find pasture and food **2** a wanderer **nomadic** *adj*
WORD ORIGIN Greek *nomas* wandering for pasture

no-man's-land *n* land between boundaries, esp. an unoccupied zone between opposing forces

nom de plume *n, pl* **noms de plume** ▸ same as **pen name**
WORD ORIGIN French

nomenclature (no-men-klatch-er) *n formal* the system of names used in a particular subject
WORD ORIGIN Latin *nomenclatura* list of names

nominal ❶ *adj* **1** in name only: *nominal independence* **2** very small in comparison with real worth: *a nominal amount of aid* **nominally** *adv*
WORD ORIGIN Latin *nomen* name

nominalism *n* the philosophical theory that a general word, such as *dog*, is merely a name and does not denote a real object **nominalist** *n*

nominal value *n* ▸ same as **par value**

nominate ❶ *vb* **-nating, -nated 1** to propose (someone) as a candidate **2** to appoint (someone) to an office or position **nomination** *n*
WORD ORIGIN Latin *nomen* name

nominative *n grammar* a grammatical case in some languages that identifies the subject of a verb
WORD ORIGIN Latin *nominativus* belonging to naming

nominee ❶ *n* a person who is nominated to an office or as a candidate

non- *prefix* **1** indicating negation: *nonexistent* **2** indicating refusal or failure: *noncooperation* **3** indicating exclusion from a specified class: *nonfiction* **4** indicating lack or absence: *nonevent*
WORD ORIGIN Latin *non* not

nonaddictive *adj* not causing addiction

nonage *n* **1** *law* the state of being under full legal age for various actions **2** a period of immaturity

nonagenarian *n* a person who is from 90 to 99 years old
WORD ORIGIN Latin *nonaginta* ninety

nonaggression *n* the policy of not attacking other countries

nonagon *n geom* a figure with nine sides **nonagonal** *adj*

nonalcoholic *adj* containing no alcohol

n

THESAURUS

dip ▷ *n* **6 = signal**, sign, motion, gesture, indication

noise *n* **1, 2 = sound**, talk, row, racket, outcry, clamour, din, clatter, uproar, babble, blare, fracas, commotion, pandemonium, rumpus, cry, tumult, hubbub **OPPOSITE:** silence

noisy *adj* **1a = rowdy**, chattering, strident, boisterous, vociferous, riotous, uproarious, obstreperous, clamorous **OPPOSITE:** quiet **1b = loud**, piercing, deafening, tumultuous, ear-splitting, cacophonous, clamorous **OPPOSITE:** quiet

nominal *adj* **1 = titular**, formal, purported, in name only, supposed, so-called, pretended, theoretical, professed, ostensible **2 = token**, small, symbolic, minimal, trivial, trifling, insignificant, inconsiderable

nominate *vb* **1 = propose**, suggest, recommend, submit, put forward **2 = appoint**, name, choose, commission, select, elect, assign, designate, empower

nominee *n* **= candidate**, applicant, entrant, contestant, aspirant, runner

DICTIONARY

nonaligned *adj* (of a country) not part of a major alliance or power bloc **nonalignment** *n*

nonbeliever *n* a person who does not follow a particular religious movement

nonbelligerent *adj* (of a country) not taking part in a war

nonce *n* **for the nonce** for the present
WORD ORIGIN a mistaken division of *for then anes*, for the once

nonce word *n* a word coined for a single occasion

nonchalant (non-shall-ant) *adj* casually unconcerned or indifferent **nonchalance** *n* **nonchalantly** *adv*
WORD ORIGIN French, from *nonchaloir* to lack warmth

non-com *n* ▸short for **noncommissioned officer**

noncombatant *n* a member of the armed forces whose duties do not include fighting, such as a chaplain or surgeon

noncombustible *adj* not capable of igniting and burning

noncommissioned officer *n* (in the armed forces) a person who is appointed as a subordinate officer, from the lower ranks, rather than by a commission

noncommittal *adj* not committing oneself to any particular opinion

noncompliance *n* failure or refusal to do as requested

non compos mentis *adj* of unsound mind
WORD ORIGIN Latin: not in control of one's mind

nonconductor *n* a substance that is a poor conductor of heat, electricity, or sound

nonconformist *n* **1** a person who does not conform to generally accepted patterns of behaviour or thought ▹*adj* **2** (of behaviour or ideas) not conforming to accepted patterns: *men who pride themselves on their nonconformist past* **nonconformity** *n*

Nonconformist *n* **1** a member of a Protestant group separated from the Church of England ▹*adj* **2** of or relating to Nonconformists

noncontributory *adj Brit* denoting a pension scheme for employees, the premiums of which are paid entirely by the employer

non-cooperation *n* the refusal to do more than is legally or contractually required of one

noncustodial *adj* not involving imprisonment: *a noncustodial sentence*

nondescript *adj* lacking outstanding features
WORD ORIGIN NON- + Latin *descriptus*, past participle of *describere* to copy

non-domicile *n Brit* a UK resident who claims another country as his or her permanent home, esp. to escape certain taxes. Also shortened to: **non-dom**

non-domiciled *adj Brit* of or denoting a person who is resident in the UK but who claims domicile in another country

nondrinker *n* a person who does not drink alcohol

none ❶ *pron* **1** not any: *none of the men was represented by a lawyer; none of it meant anything to him* **2** no-one; nobody: *none could deny it* **3 none the** in no degree: *her parents were none the wiser*
WORD ORIGIN Old English *nān*, literally: not one

nonentity (non-enn-tit-tee) *n, pl* **-ties** an insignificant person or thing

non-essential *adj* not absolutely necessary

nonetheless ❶ *adv* despite that; however

nonevent *n* a disappointing or insignificant occurrence which was expected to be important

nonexistent ❶ *adj* not existing in a particular place **nonexistence** *n*

nonferrous *adj* **1** denoting a metal other than iron **2** not containing iron

nonfiction *n* writing that deals with facts or real events

nonflammable *adj* not easily set on fire

nonfunctional *adj* having no practical function

nonintervention *n* refusal to intervene in the affairs of others

noniron *adj* not requiring ironing

nonmember *n* a person who is not a member of a particular club or organization

nonmetal *n chem* a chemical element that forms acidic oxides and is a poor conductor of heat and electricity **nonmetallic** *adj*

nonmoral *adj* not involving morality; neither moral nor immoral

non-native *adj* not originating in a particular place

non-nuclear *adj* not involving or using nuclear power or weapons

Nono *n* **Luigi** 1924–90, Italian composer of 12-tone music

no-nonsense *adj* sensible, practical, and straightforward: *a no-nonsense approach to crime*

nonpareil (non-par-rail) *n* a person or thing that is unsurpassed
WORD ORIGIN French, from NON- + *pareil* similar

non-partisan *adj* not supporting any single political party

non-payment *n* failure to pay money owed

nonplussed *or US* **nonplused** *adj* perplexed
WORD ORIGIN Latin *non plus* no further

nonprofessional *adj* not earning a living at a specified occupation: *nonprofessional investors*

non-profit-making *adj* not intended to make a profit

nonproliferation *n* limitation of the production or spread of something such as nuclear or chemical weapons

nonrepresentational *adj art* ▸same as **abstract**

nonresident *n* a person who does not live in a particular country or place

nonsectarian *adj* not confined to any specific subdivision of a religious group

nonsense ❶ *n* **1** something that has or makes no sense **2** unintelligible language **3** foolish behaviour: *she'll stand no nonsense* **nonsensical** *adj*

non sequitur (sek-wit-tur) *n* a statement having little or no relation to what preceded it
WORD ORIGIN Latin: it does not follow

nonslip *adj* designed to prevent slipping: *a nonslip mat*

nonsmoker *n* **1** a person who does not smoke **2** a train carriage or compartment in which smoking is forbidden

nonsmoking *or* **no-smoking** *adj* denoting an area in which smoking is forbidden

nonstandard *adj* denoting words, expressions, or pronunciations that

THESAURUS

none *pron* **1 = not any**, nothing, zero, not one, nil, no part, not a bit, zilch *(slang, chiefly US & Canad)*, diddly *(US slang)* **2 = no-one**, nobody, not one

nonetheless *adv* **= nevertheless**, however, yet, even so, despite that, in spite of that

nonexistent *adj* **= imaginary**, imagined, fancied, fictional, mythical, unreal, hypothetical, illusory, insubstantial, hallucinatory
OPPOSITE: real

nonsense *n* **1 = rubbish**, hot air *(informal)*, waffle *(informal, chiefly Brit)*, twaddle, pants *(slang)*, rot, crap *(slang)*, garbage *(informal)*, trash, bunk *(informal)*, tosh *(slang, chiefly Brit)*, rhubarb, pap, foolishness, bilge *(informal)*, drivel, tripe *(informal)*, gibberish, guff *(slang)*, bombast, moonshine, claptrap *(informal)*, hogwash, hokum *(slang, chiefly US & Canad)*, blather, double Dutch *(Brit informal)*, piffle *(informal)*, poppycock *(informal)*, balderdash, bosh *(informal)*, eyewash *(informal)*, stuff and nonsense, tommyrot, horsefeathers *(US slang)*, bunkum *or* buncombe *(chiefly US)*, bizzo *(Austral slang)*, bull's wool *(Austral & NZ slang)*
OPPOSITE: sense
3 = idiocy, folly, stupidity, absurdity, silliness, inanity, senselessness,

DICTIONARY

are not regarded as correct by educated native speakers of a language
nonstarter *n* a person or an idea that has little chance of success
nonstick *adj* (of cooking utensils) coated with a substance that food will not stick to when cooked
nonstop ❶ *adj* **1** without a stop: *two weeks of nonstop rain* ▹ *adv* **2** without a stop: *most days his phone rings nonstop*
nontoxic *adj* not poisonous
non-U *adj Brit informal* (of language or behaviour) not characteristic of the upper classes
nonunion *adj* **1** (of a company) not employing trade union members: *a nonunion shop* **2** (of a person) not belonging to a trade union
nonverbal *adj* not involving the use of language
non-violent *adj* using peaceful methods to bring about change **nonviolence** *n*
nonvoting *adj finance* (of shares in a company) not entitling the holder to vote at company meetings
non-White *adj* **1** belonging to a race of people not European in origin ▹ *n* **2** a member of one of these races
noodle *n* a simpleton
WORD ORIGIN a blend of *noddle* + *noodles*
noodles *pl n* ribbon-like strips of pasta
WORD ORIGIN German *Nudeln*
nook *n* **1** a corner or recess **2** a secluded or sheltered place
WORD ORIGIN origin unknown
noon ❶ *n* the middle of the day; 12 o'clock
WORD ORIGIN Latin *nona (hora)* ninth hour (originally 3 pm, the ninth hour from sunrise)
noonday *adj* happening or appearing at noon
no-one *or* **no one** *pron* no person; nobody
noose *n* a loop in the end of a rope, tied with a slipknot, such as one used to hang people
WORD ORIGIN Latin *nodus* knot
nope *interj informal* no
nor *conj* **1** used to join alternatives, the first of which is preceded by *neither*; and not: *neither willing nor able* **2** and not ... either: *he had not arrived yet, nor had any of the models*
WORD ORIGIN contraction of Old English *nōther*
Nordau *n* **Max Simon**, original name *Max Simon Südfeld*. 1849–1923, German author, born in Hungary; a leader of the Zionist movement
Nordenskjöld *n* Baron **Nils Adolf Erik** 1832–1901, Swedish Arctic explorer and geologist, born in Finland. He was the first to navigate the Northeast Passage (1878–79)
nordic *adj skiing* of competitions in cross-country racing and ski-jumping
Nordic *adj* of Scandinavia or its typically tall, blond, and blue-eyed people
WORD ORIGIN French *nordique* of the north
norm ❶ *n* a standard that is required or regarded as normal
WORD ORIGIN Latin *norma* carpenter's square
normal ❶ *adj* **1** usual, regular, or typical: *the study of normal behaviour* **2** free from mental or physical disorder **3** *geom* ▸ same as **perpendicular** (sense 1) ▹ *n* **4** the usual, regular, or typical state, degree, or form **5** *geom* a perpendicular line or plane **normality** *or esp. US* **normalcy** *n*
WORD ORIGIN Latin *normalis* conforming to the carpenter's square
normalize *or* **-ise** *vb* **-izing, -ized** *or* **-ising, -ised 1** to make or become normal **2** to bring into conformity with a standard **normalization** *or* **-isation** *n*
normally ❶ *adv* **1** as a rule; usually **2** in a normal manner
Norman *n* **1** a person from Normandy in N France, esp. one of the people who conquered England in 1066 **2** ▸ same as **Norman French** ▹ *adj* **3** of the Normans or their dialect of French **4** of Normandy **5** of a style of architecture used in Britain from the Norman Conquest until the 12th century, with rounded arches and massive masonry walls
Norman[1] *n* **1** (in the Middle Ages) a member of the people of Normandy descended from the 10th-century Scandinavian conquerors of the country and the native French **2** a native or inhabitant of Normandy **3** ▸ another name for **Norman French** ▹ *adj* **4** of, relating to, or characteristic of the Normans, esp. the Norman kings of England, the Norman people living in England, or their dialect of French **5** of, relating to, or characteristic of Normandy or its inhabitants **6** denoting, relating to, or having the style of Romanesque architecture used in Britain from the Norman Conquest until the 12th century. It is characterized by the rounded arch, the groin vault, massive masonry walls, etc.
Norman[2] *n* **1 Greg.** born 1955, Australian golfer **2 Jessye** born 1945, US Black soprano
Norman French *n* the medieval Norman and English dialect of Old French
normative *adj* of or establishing a norm or standard: *a normative model*
Norn *n Norse myth* any of the three virgin goddesses of fate
WORD ORIGIN Old Norse
Norrington *n* Sir **Roger** (**Arthur Carver**) born 1934, British conductor; noted for period performances of early music
Norse *adj* **1** of ancient and medieval Scandinavia **2** of Norway ▹ *n* **3 a** the N group of Germanic languages spoken in Scandinavia **b** any one of these languages, esp. in their ancient or medieval forms
Norseman *n, pl* **-men** ▸ same as **Viking**
north ❶ *n* **1** one of the four cardinal points of the compass, at 0° or 360° **2** the direction along a meridian towards the North Pole **3** the direction in which a compass needle points; magnetic north **4 the north** any area lying in or towards the north ▹ *adj* **5** in or towards the north **6** (esp. of the wind) from the north ▹ *adv* **7** in, to, or towards the north
WORD ORIGIN Old English

n

THESAURUS

ridiculousness, ludicrousness, fatuity
nonstop *adj* **1 = continuous**, constant, relentless, uninterrupted, steady, endless, unbroken, interminable, incessant, unending, ceaseless, unremitting, unfaltering
OPPOSITE: occasional
▹ *adv* **2 = continuously**, constantly, steadily, endlessly, relentlessly, perpetually, incessantly, without stopping, ceaselessly, interminably, unremittingly, uninterruptedly, unendingly, unfalteringly, unbrokenly
noon *n* **= midday**, high noon, noonday, noontime, twelve noon, noontide
norm *n* **= standard**, rule, model, pattern, mean, type, measure, average, par, criterion, benchmark, yardstick
normal *adj* **1 = usual**, common, standard, average, natural, regular, ordinary, acknowledged, typical, conventional, routine, accustomed, habitual, run-of-the-mill
OPPOSITE: unusual
2 = sane, reasonable, rational, lucid, well-adjusted, compos mentis (*Latin*), in your right mind, mentally sound, in possession of all your faculties
normally *adv* **1 = usually**, generally, commonly, regularly, typically, ordinarily, as a rule, habitually **2 = as usual**, naturally, properly, conventionally, in the usual way
north *adj* **5, 6 = northern**, polar, arctic, boreal, northerly ▹ *adv* **7 = northward(s)**, in a northerly direction

DICTIONARY

North *n* **1 the North a** the northern part of England, generally regarded as reaching the southern boundaries of Yorkshire, Derbyshire, and Cheshire **b** (in the US) the states north of the Mason-Dixon Line that were known as the Free States during the Civil War **c** the economically and technically advanced countries of the world ▹ *adj* **2** of or denoting the northern part of a country or area

Northants Northamptonshire

northbound *adj* going towards the north

Northcliffe *n* **Viscount** title of *Alfred Charles William Harmsworth.* 1865–1922, British newspaper proprietor. With his brother, 1st Viscount Rothermere, he built up a vast chain of newspapers. He founded the *Daily Mail* (1896), the *Daily Mirror* (1903), and acquired *The Times* (1908)

North Country *n* **the North Country** ▸ same as **North** (sense 1a)

northeast *n* **1** the direction midway between north and east **2 the northeast** any area lying in or towards the northeast ▹ *adj also* **northeastern 3** (*sometimes cap*) of or denoting that part of a country or area which lies in the northeast **4** situated in, moving towards, or facing the northeast **5** (esp. of the wind) from the northeast ▹ *adv* **6** in, to, or towards the northeast **northeasterly** *adj, adv, n*

Northeast *n* **the Northeast** the northeastern part of England, esp. Northumberland and Durham

northeaster *n* a strong wind or storm from the northeast

northerly *adj* **1** of or in the north ▹ *adv, adj* **2** towards the north **3** from the north: *a cold northerly wind*

northern *adj* **1** situated in or towards the north **2** facing or moving towards the north **3** (*sometimes cap*) of or characteristic of the north or North **northernmost** *adj*

Northerner *n* a person from the north of a country or area, esp. England

northern hemisphere *n* that half of the globe lying north of the equator

northern lights *pl n* ▸ same as **aurora borealis**

northings *pl n* a series of numbers in a grid reference indicating the distance northwards from a given latitude

Northman *n, pl* **-men** ▸ same as **Viking**

North Pole *n* the northernmost point on the earth's axis, at a latitude of 90°N, which has very low temperatures

North Star *n* **the North Star** ▸ same as **Pole Star**

Northumb. Northumberland

Northumberland[1] *n* the northernmost county of England, on the North Sea; became a unitary authority in 2009: hilly in the north (the Cheviots) and west (the Pennines), with many Roman remains, notably Hadrian's Wall; shipbuilding, coal mining. Administrative centre: Morpeth. Pop: 310 600 (2007 est). Area: 5032 sq km (1943 sq miles). Abbreviation: **Northd**

Northumberland[2] *n* **1st Duke of,** title of *John Dudley.* 1502–53, English statesman and soldier, who governed England (1549–53) during the minority of Edward VI. His attempt (1553) to gain the throne for his daughter-in-law, Lady Jane Grey, led to his execution

northward *adj, adv also* **northwards 1** towards the north ▹ *n* **2** the northward part or direction

northwest *n* **1** the direction midway between north and west **2 the northwest** any area lying in or towards the northwest ▹ *adj also* **northwestern 3** (*sometimes cap*) of or denoting that part of a country or area which lies in the northwest **4** situated in, moving towards, or facing the northwest **5** (esp. of the wind) from the northwest ▹ *adv* **6** in, to, or towards the northwest **northwesterly** *adj, adv, n*

Northwest *n* **the Northwest** the northwestern part of England, esp. Lancashire and the Lake District

northwester *n* a strong wind or storm from the northwest

Norton *n* **Graham,** real name *Graham Walker.* born 1963, Irish comedian noted for his camp humour

Norwegian *adj* **1** of Norway ▹ *n* **2** a person from Norway **3** the language of Norway

nor'wester *n NZ* a hot dry wind

Nos. *or* **nos.** numbers

nose ❶ *n* **1** the organ situated above the mouth, used for smelling and breathing **2** the sense of smell **3** the front part of a vehicle **4** the distinctive smell of a wine or perfume **5** instinctive skill in finding something: *he had a nose for media events* **6 get up someone's nose** *informal* to annoy someone **7 keep one's nose clean** to stay out of trouble **8 look down one's nose at** *informal* to be haughty towards **9 pay through the nose** *informal* to pay a high price **10 put someone's nose out of joint** *informal* to make someone envious by doing what he would have liked to do or had expected to do **11 rub someone's nose in it** *informal* to remind someone unkindly of a failing or error **12 turn up one's nose at** *informal* to show contempt for **13 win by a nose** to win by a narrow margin ▹ *vb* **nosing, nosed 14** to move forward slowly and carefully: *a motorboat nosed out of the mist* **15** to pry or snoop **16 nose out** to discover by searching or prying

WORD ORIGIN Old English *nosu*

nosebag *n* a bag containing feed, fastened around the head of a horse

noseband *n* the part of a horse's bridle that goes around the nose

nosebleed *n* bleeding from the nose

nose cone *n* the cone-shaped front section of a missile or spacecraft

nose dive *n* **1** (of an aircraft) a sudden plunge with the nose pointing downwards **2** *informal* a sudden drop: *when we fail our self-confidence takes a nose dive* ▹ *vb* **nose-dive, -diving, -dived 3** to take a nose dive

nosegay *n* a small bunch of flowers

WORD ORIGIN *nose + gay* (archaic) toy

nosey *or* **nosy** *adj* **nosier, nosiest** *informal* prying or inquisitive **nosiness** *n*

nosey parker *n Brit & S African informal* a prying person

WORD ORIGIN arbitrary use of surname *Parker*

nosh *Brit, Austral & NZ slang n* **1** food ▹ *vb* **2** to eat

WORD ORIGIN Yiddish

nosh-up *n Brit slang* a large meal

nostalgia ❶ *n* **1** a sentimental yearning for the past **2** homesickness **nostalgic** *adj* **nostalgically** *adv*

WORD ORIGIN Greek *nostos* a return home + *algios* pain

nostril *n* either of the two openings at the end of the nose

WORD ORIGIN Old English *nosu* nose + *thyrel* hole

nostrum *n* **1** a quack medicine **2** a favourite remedy

WORD ORIGIN Latin: our own (make)

nosy *adj* **nosier, nosiest** ▸ same as **nosey**

not *adv* **1** used to negate the sentence, phrase, or word that it modifies: *I will*

THESAURUS

nose *n* **1 = snout,** bill, beak, hooter *(slang)*, snitch *(slang)*, conk *(slang)*, neb *(archaic, dialect)*, proboscis, schnozzle *(slang, chiefly US)* ▹ *vb* **14 = ease forward,** push, edge, shove, nudge

nostalgia *n* **1 = reminiscence,** longing, regret, pining, yearning, remembrance, homesickness, wistfulness

notable *adj* **1 = remarkable,** marked, striking, unusual, extraordinary, outstanding, evident, pronounced, memorable, noticeable, uncommon, conspicuous, salient, noteworthy **OPPOSITE:** imperceptible ▹ *n* **2 = celebrity,** worthy, big name, dignitary, luminary, celeb *(informal)*, personage, megastar *(informal)*,

DICTIONARY

not stand for it **2 not that** which is not to say that: *not that I've ever heard him complain*
WORD ORIGIN Old English *nāwiht*, from *nā* no + *wiht* creature, thing

nota bene (note-a ben-nay) note well; take note
WORD ORIGIN Latin

notable (note-a-bl) *adj* **1** worthy of being noted; remarkable ▷*n* **2** a person of distinction **notability** *n* **notably** *adv*
WORD ORIGIN Latin *notare* to note

notary *or* **notary public** (note-a-ree) *n, pl* **notaries** *or* **notaries public** a public official, usually a solicitor, who is legally authorized to attest and certify documents
WORD ORIGIN Latin *notarius* one who makes notes, a clerk

notation (no-tay-shun) *n* **1** representation of numbers or quantities in a system by a series of symbols **2** a set of such symbols
WORD ORIGIN Latin *notare* to note

notch *n* **1** a V-shaped cut **2** *informal* a step or level: *the economy moved up another notch* ▷*vb* **3** to cut a notch in **4 notch up** *informal* to score or achieve: *he notched up a hat trick of wins*
WORD ORIGIN mistaken division of *an otch*, from Old French *oche* notch

note *n* **1** a brief informal letter **2** a brief record in writing for future reference **3** a critical comment or explanation in a book **4** an official written communication, as from a government or from a doctor **5** ▸short for **banknote 6** *Brit & NZ* a musical sound of a particular pitch **7** a written symbol representing the pitch and duration of a musical sound **8** *chiefly Brit* a key on a piano, organ, or other keyboard instrument **9** a particular feeling or atmosphere: *an optimistic note* **10** a distinctive vocal sound, as of a type of animal **11** a sound used as a signal or warning: *the note to retreat was sounded* **12** ▸short for **promissory note 13 of note a** distinguished or famous **b** important: *nothing of note* **14 strike the right note** to behave appropriately **15 take note of** to pay attention to ▷*vb* **noting, noted 16** to notice; pay attention to: *such criticism should be noted* **17** to make a written note of: *he noted it in his diary* **18** to remark upon: *I note that you do not wear shoes*
WORD ORIGIN Latin *nota* sign

notebook *n* a book for writing in

notebook computer *n* a portable computer approximately the size of a sheet of A4 paper

notecase *n* ▸same as **wallet**

noted *adj* well-known: *a noted scholar*

notelet *n* a folded card with a printed design on the front, for writing informal letters

notepad *n* a number of sheets of paper fastened together along one edge, used for writing notes or letters on

notepaper *n* paper used for writing letters

noteworthy *adj* worth noting; remarkable

nothing *pron* **1** not anything: *I felt nothing* **2** a matter of no importance: *don't worry, it's nothing* **3** absence of meaning, value, or worth: *the industry shrank to almost nothing* **4** the figure 0 **5 have** *or* **be nothing to do with** to have no connection with **6 nothing but** not something other than; only **7 nothing doing** *informal* an expression of dismissal or refusal **8 nothing less than** downright: *nothing less than complete withdrawal* **9 think nothing of something** to regard something as easy or natural ▷*adv* **10** not at all: *he looked nothing like his brother* ▷*n* **11** *informal* a person or thing of no importance or significance
WORD ORIGIN Old English *nāthing, nān thing*

nothingness *n* **1** nonexistence **2** total insignificance

notice *n* **1** observation or attention: *to attract notice* **2** a displayed placard or announcement giving information **3** advance notification of something such as intention to end a contract of employment: *she handed in her notice* **4** a theatrical or literary review: *the film reaped ecstatic notices* **5 at short notice** with very little notification **6 take no notice of** to ignore or disregard **7 take notice** to pay attention ▷*vb* **-ticing, -ticed 8** to become aware (of) **9** to point out or remark upon
WORD ORIGIN Latin *notus* known

noticeable *adj* easily seen or detected **noticeably** *adv*

notice board *n* a board on which notices are displayed

notifiable *adj* having to be reported to the authorities: *a notifiable disease*

notification *n* **1** the act of notifying someone of something **2** a formal announcement

notify *vb* **-fies, -fying, -fied** to inform: *notify gas and electricity companies of your moving date*
WORD ORIGIN Latin *notus* known + *facere* to make

notion *n* **1** an idea or opinion **2** a whim
WORD ORIGIN Latin *notio* a becoming acquainted (with)

notional *adj* hypothetical, imaginary, or unreal: *a notional dividend payment*

notorious *adj* well known for some bad reason **notoriety** *n* **notoriously** *adv*

n

THESAURUS

notability, V.I.P.

notch *n* **1 = cut**, nick, incision, indentation, mark, score, cleft **2** *(informal)* **= level**, step, degree, grade, cut *(informal)* ▷*vb* **3 = cut**, mark, score, nick, scratch, indent

note *n* **1 = message**, letter, communication, memo, memorandum, epistle, e-mail, text **2 = record**, reminder, memo, memorandum, jotting, minute **3 = annotation**, comment, remark, gloss **4 = document**, form, record, certificate **7 = symbol**, mark, sign, indication, token **9 = tone**, touch, trace, hint, sound ▷*vb* **16 = notice**, see, observe, perceive **17 = write down**, record, scribble, take down, set down, jot down, put in writing, put down in black and white **18 = mention**, record, mark, indicate, register, remark

notebook *n* **= notepad**, record book, exercise book, jotter, journal, diary, Filofax®, memorandum book

noted *adj* **= famous**, celebrated, recognized, distinguished, well-known, prominent, notorious, acclaimed, notable, renowned, eminent, conspicuous, illustrious
OPPOSITE: unknown

nothing *pron* **1, 4 = nought**, zero, nil, naught, not a thing, zilch *(slang)*, sod all *(slang)*, damn all *(slang)*, zip *(US slang)* **2 = a trifle**, no big deal, a mere bagatelle **3 = void**, emptiness, nothingness, nullity, nonexistence ▷*n* **11** *(informal)* **= nobody**, cipher, nonentity

notice *n* **1 = attention**, interest, note, regard, consideration, observation, scrutiny, heed, cognizance
OPPOSITE: oversight
3 = notification, warning, advice, intimation, news, communication, intelligence, announcement, instruction, advance warning, wake-up call, heads up *(US & Canad)* ▷*vb* **8, 9 = observe**, see, mind, note, spot, remark, distinguish, perceive, detect, heed, discern, behold *(archaic, literary)*, mark, eyeball *(slang)*
OPPOSITE: overlook

noticeable *adj* **= obvious**, clear, striking, plain, bold, evident, distinct, manifest, conspicuous, unmistakable, salient, observable, perceptible, appreciable

notify *vb* **= inform**, tell, advise, alert to, announce, warn, acquaint with, make known to, apprise of

notion *n* **1 = idea**, view, opinion, belief, concept, impression, judgment, sentiment, conception, apprehension, inkling, mental image *or* picture, picture **2 = whim**, wish, desire, fancy, impulse, inclination, caprice

notorious *adj* **= infamous**, disreputable, opprobrious

DICTIONARY

WORD ORIGIN Medieval Latin *notorius* well-known
not proven *adj* a verdict in Scottish courts, given when there is insufficient evidence to convict the accused
no-trump *cards n* **1** a bid or hand without trumps ▷*adj* **2** (of a hand) suitable for playing without trumps
Notts Nottinghamshire
notwithstanding ⊙ *prep* **1** in spite of ▷*adv* **2** nevertheless
nougat *n* a hard chewy pink or white sweet containing chopped nuts
WORD ORIGIN French, from Latin *nux* nut
nought ⊙ *n* **1** the figure 0 ▷*n, adv* **2** ▸same as **naught**
WORD ORIGIN Old English *nōwiht*, from *ne* not, no + *ōwiht* something
noughties *pl n informal* the decade from 2000 to 2009
noughts and crosses *n Brit* a game in which two players, one using a nought, the other a cross, alternately mark squares formed by two pairs of crossed lines, the winner being the first to get three of his or her symbols in a row
noun *n* a word that refers to a person, place, or thing
WORD ORIGIN Latin *nomen* name
nourish ⊙ *vb* **1** to provide with the food necessary for life and growth **2** to encourage or foster (an idea or feeling) **nourishing** *adj*
WORD ORIGIN Latin *nutrire* to feed
nourishment *n* the food needed to nourish the body
nous *n old-fashioned, slang* common sense
WORD ORIGIN Greek: mind
nouveau riche (noo-voh **reesh**) *n, pl* **nouveaux riches** (noo-voh **reesh**) a person who has become wealthy recently and is regarded as vulgar
WORD ORIGIN French: new rich
nouvelle cuisine (noo-vell kwee-**zeen**) *n* a style of preparing and presenting food with light sauces and unusual combinations of flavours
WORD ORIGIN French: new cooking
Nov. November
nova *n, pl* **-vae** *or* **-vas** a star that undergoes an explosion and fast increase of brightness, then gradually decreases to its original brightness
WORD ORIGIN New Latin *nova (stella)* new (star)
Novalis *n* real name *Friedrich von Hardenberg*. 1772–1801, German romantic poet. His works include the mystical *Hymnen an die Nacht* (1797; published 1800) and *Geistliche Lieder* (1799)
novel[1] ⊙ *n* a long fictional story in book form
WORD ORIGIN Latin *novella (narratio)* new (story)
novel[2] ⊙ *adj* fresh, new, or original: *a novel approach*
WORD ORIGIN Latin *novus* new
novelette *n* a short novel, usually one regarded as trivial or sentimental
novelist ⊙ *n* a writer of novels
novella *n, pl* **-las** a short narrative tale or short novel
WORD ORIGIN Italian
Novello *n* **Ivor,** real name *Ivor Novello Davies*. 1893–1951, Welsh actor, composer, songwriter, and dramatist
novelty ⊙ *n, pl* **-ties** **1** the quality of being new and interesting **2** a new or unusual experience or thing **3** a small cheap toy or trinket
November *n* the eleventh month of the year
WORD ORIGIN Latin: ninth month
novena (no-**vee**-na) *n, pl* **-nas** *or* **-nae** (-nee) *RC church* a set of prayers or services on nine consecutive days
WORD ORIGIN Latin *novem* nine
novice ⊙ (**nov**-viss) *n* **1** a beginner **2** a person who has entered a religious order but has not yet taken vows
WORD ORIGIN Latin *novus* new
novitiate *or* **noviciate** *n* **1** the period of being a novice **2** the part of a monastery or convent where the novices live
now ⊙ *adv* **1** at or for the present time **2** immediately: *bring it now* **3** in these times; nowadays **4** given the present circumstances: *now do you understand why?* **5 a** used as a hesitation word: *now, I can't really say* **b** used for emphasis: *now listen to this* **c** used at the end of a command: *run along now* **6 just now a** very recently: *he left just now* **b** very soon: *I'm going just now* **7 now and again** *or* **then** occasionally **8 now now!** an exclamation used to tell someone off or to calm someone ▷*conj* **9** Also: **now that** seeing that: *now you're here, you can help me* ▷*n* **10** the present time: *now is the time to go*
WORD ORIGIN Old English *nū*
nowadays ⊙ *adv* in these times: *nowadays his work is regarded as out-of-date*
Nowell *n* ▸same as **Noel**
nowhere *adv* **1** in, at, or to no place **2 getting nowhere** *informal* making no progress **3 nowhere near** far from: *the stadium is nowhere near completion* ▷*n* **4 in the middle of nowhere** (of a place) completely isolated
no-win *adj* with no possibility of a favourable outcome: *a no-win situation*
nowt *n N English dialect* nothing
WORD ORIGIN from *naught*
noxious *adj* **1** poisonous or harmful **2** extremely unpleasant
WORD ORIGIN Latin *noxius* harmful
nozzle *n* a projecting spout from which fluid is discharged
WORD ORIGIN diminutive of *nose*
Np *chem* neptunium
nr near
NS **1** New Style (method of reckoning dates) **2** Nova Scotia
NSPCC (in Britain) National Society for the Prevention of Cruelty to Children
NST Newfoundland Standard Time
NSW New South Wales
NT **1** (in Britain) National Trust **2** New Testament **3** Northern Territory **4** Nunavut
-n't not: added to *be* or *have*, or auxiliary verbs: *can't; don't; isn't*
nth *adj* ▸see **n**[2]
Nu *n* **U,** original name *Thakin Nu*. 1907–95, Burmese statesman and writer; prime minister (1948–56, 1957–58, 1960–62). He attempted to establish parliamentary democracy, but was ousted (1962) by Ne Win
nuance (**new**-ahnss) *n* a subtle difference, as in colour, meaning, or tone

n

THESAURUS

notwithstanding *prep* **1 = despite**, in spite of, regardless of
nought *or* **naught** *or* **ought** *or* **aught** *n* **1 = zero**, nothing, nil
nourish *vb* **1 = feed**, supply, sustain, nurture **2 = encourage**, support, maintain, promote, sustain, foster, cultivate
novel[1] *n* **= story**, tale, fiction, romance, narrative
novel[2] *adj* **= new**, different, original, fresh, unusual, innovative, uncommon, singular, ground-breaking, left-field (*informal*)
OPPOSITE: ordinary
novelist *n* **= author**, writer
novelty *n* **1 = newness**, originality, freshness, innovation, surprise, uniqueness, strangeness, unfamiliarity **2 = curiosity**, marvel, rarity, oddity, wonder **3 = trinket**, souvenir, memento, bauble, bagatelle, gimcrack, trifle, gewgaw, knick-knack
novice *n* **1 = beginner**, pupil, amateur, newcomer, trainee, apprentice, learner, neophyte, tyro, probationer, proselyte **OPPOSITE:** expert
now *adv* **2 = immediately**, presently (*Scot & US*), promptly, instantly, at once, straightaway **3 = nowadays**, at the moment, these days
7 now and then *or* **again** **= occasionally**, sometimes, at times, from time to time, on and off, on occasion, once in a while, intermittently, infrequently, sporadically
nowadays *adv* **= now**, today, at the moment, these days, in this day and age
nucleus *n* **2, 3 = centre**, heart, focus,

DICTIONARY

WORD ORIGIN French

nub *n* the point or gist: *this is the nub of his theory*
WORD ORIGIN Middle Low German *knubbe* knob

nubble *n* a small lump **nubbly** *adj*
WORD ORIGIN from *nub*

nubile (new-bile) *adj* **1** (of a young woman) sexually attractive **2** (of a young woman) old enough or mature enough for marriage
WORD ORIGIN Latin *nubere* to marry

nubuck (new-buk) *n* (*sometimes cap*) leather that has been rubbed on the flesh side of the skin to give it a fine velvet-like finish

nuclear *adj* **1** of nuclear weapons or energy **2** of an atomic nucleus: *nuclear fission*

nuclear bomb *n* a bomb whose force is due to uncontrolled nuclear fusion or fission

nuclear energy *n* energy released during a nuclear reaction as a result of fission or fusion

nuclear family *n sociol, anthropol* a family consisting only of parents and their offspring

nuclear fission *n nuclear physics* the splitting of an atomic nucleus, either spontaneously or by bombardment by a neutron: used in atomic bombs and nuclear power plants

nuclear-free *adj* (of an area) barred, esp. by local authorities, from being supplied with nuclear-generated electricity and from storing nuclear waste or weapons

nuclear fusion *n nuclear physics* the combination of two nuclei to form a heavier nucleus with the release of energy: used in hydrogen bombs

nuclear physics *n* the branch of physics concerned with the structure of the nucleus and the behaviour of its particles

nuclear power *n* power produced by a nuclear reactor

nuclear reaction *n physics* a process in which the structure and energy content of an atomic nucleus is changed by interaction with another nucleus or particle

nuclear reactor *n nuclear physics* a device in which a nuclear reaction is maintained and controlled to produce nuclear energy

nuclear winter *n* a theoretical period of low temperatures and little light that has been suggested would occur after a nuclear war

nucleate *adj* **1** having a nucleus ▷ *vb* **-ating, -ated 2** to form a nucleus

nuclei (new-klee-eye) *n* ▸ the plural of **nucleus**

nucleic acid *n biochem* a complex compound, such as DNA or RNA, found in all living cells

nucleon *n physics* a proton or neutron

nucleonics *n* the branch of physics concerned with the applications of nuclear energy **nucleonic** *adj*

nucleus ❶ *n, pl* **-clei 1** *physics* the positively charged centre of an atom, made of protons and neutrons, about which electrons orbit **2** a central thing around which others are grouped **3** a centre of growth or development: *the nucleus of a new relationship* **4** *biol* the part of a cell that contains the chromosomes and associated molecules that control the characteristics and growth of the cell **5** *chem* a fundamental group of atoms in a molecule serving as the base structure for related compounds
WORD ORIGIN Latin: kernel

nude ❶ *adj* **1** completely undressed ▷ *n* **2** a naked figure in painting, sculpture, or photography **3 in the nude** naked **nudity** *n*
WORD ORIGIN Latin *nudus*

nudge ❶ *vb* **nudging, nudged 1** to push (someone) gently with the elbow to get attention **2** to push (something or someone) lightly: *the dog nudged the stick with its nose* **3** to persuade (someone) gently ▷ *n* **4** a gentle poke or push
WORD ORIGIN origin unknown

nudism *n* the practice of not wearing clothes, for reasons of health **nudist** *n, adj*

nugatory (new-gat-tree) *adj formal* **1** of little value **2** not valid: *their rejection rendered the treaty nugatory*
WORD ORIGIN Latin *nugae* trifling things

nugget *n* **1** a small lump of gold in its natural state **2** something small but valuable: *a nugget of useful knowledge* ▷ *vb* **3** *NZ & S African* to polish footwear
WORD ORIGIN origin unknown

nuisance ❶ *n* **1** a person or thing that causes annoyance or bother ▷ *adj* **2** causing annoyance or bother: *nuisance calls*
WORD ORIGIN Old French *nuire* to injure

NUJ (in Britain) National Union of Journalists

nuke *slang vb* **nuking, nuked 1** to attack with nuclear weapons ▷ *n* **2** a nuclear bomb

null *adj* **1 null and void** not legally valid **2 null set** *maths* a set with no members **nullity** *n*
WORD ORIGIN Latin *nullus* none

nulla-nulla *n* a wooden club used by Australian Aborigines

nullify *vb* **-fies, -fying, -fied 1** to make (something) ineffective **2** to make (something) legally void **nullification** *n*
WORD ORIGIN Latin *nullus* of no account + *facere* to make

NUM (in Britain & S Africa) National Union of Mineworkers

Numa Pompilius *n* the legendary second king of Rome (?715–?673 BC), said to have instituted religious rites

numb ❶ *adj* **1** deprived of feeling through cold, shock, or fear **2** unable to move; paralysed ▷ *vb* **3** to make numb **numbly** *adv* **numbness** *n*
WORD ORIGIN Middle English *nomen*, literally: taken (with paralysis)

numbat *n* a small Australian marsupial with a long snout and tongue

number ❶ *n* **1** a concept of quantity that is or can be derived from a single unit, a sum of units, or zero **2** the word or symbol used to represent a number **3** a numeral or

n

THESAURUS

basis, core, pivot, kernel, nub

nude *adj* **1 = naked**, stripped, exposed, bare, uncovered, undressed, stark-naked, in the raw (*informal*), disrobed, starkers (*informal*), unclothed, in the buff (*informal*), au naturel (*French*), in the altogether (*informal*), buck naked (*slang*), unclad, undraped, in your birthday suit (*informal*), scuddy (*slang*), without a stitch on (*informal*), in the bare scud (*slang*), naked as the day you were born (*informal*) **OPPOSITE:** dressed

nudge *vb* **1, 2 = push**, touch, dig, jog, prod, elbow, shove, poke **3 = prompt**, influence, urge, persuade, spur, prod, coax, prevail upon ▷ *n* **4 = push**, touch, dig, elbow, bump, shove, poke, jog, prod

nuisance *n* **1 = trouble**, problem, trial, bore, drag (*informal*), bother, plague, pest, irritation, hassle (*informal*), inconvenience, annoyance, pain (*informal*), pain in the neck (*informal*), pain in the backside (*informal*), pain in the butt (*informal*) **OPPOSITE:** benefit

numb *adj* **1a = unfeeling**, dead, frozen, paralysed, insensitive, deadened, immobilized, torpid, insensible **OPPOSITE:** sensitive **1b = stupefied**, deadened, unfeeling, insensible ▷ *vb* **3a = stun**, knock out, paralyse, daze, stupefy **3b = deaden**, freeze, dull, paralyse, immobilize, benumb

number *n* **2 = numeral**, figure, character, digit, integer **5 = amount**, quantity, collection, total, count, sum, aggregate **OPPOSITE:** shortage **6 = issue**, copy, edition, imprint, printing **8 = group**, company, set, band, crowd, gang, coterie ▷ *vb* **15 = calculate**, account, reckon, compute, enumerate **OPPOSITE:** guess **17 = amount to**, come to, total, add up to **18 = include**, count

DICTIONARY

string of numerals used to identify a person or thing: *an account number* **4** the person or thing so identified: *he was seeded number two* **5** sum or quantity: *a very large number of people have telephoned* **6** one of a series, as of a magazine **7** a self-contained piece of pop or jazz music **8** a group of people: *one of their number might be willing* **9** *informal* an admired article: *that little number is by Dior* **10** *grammar* classification of words depending on how many people or things are referred to **11 any number of** many **12 beyond** *or* **without number** innumerable **13 have someone's number** *informal* to have discovered someone's true character or intentions **14 one's number is up** *Austral & Brit informal* one is about to die ▹*vb* **15** to count **16** to assign a number to: *numbered seats* **17** to add up to: *the illustrations numbered well over fifty* **18** to include in a group: *he numbered several Americans among his friends* **19 one's days are numbered** something unpleasant, such as death, is likely to happen to one soon
WORD ORIGIN Latin *numerus*

number crunching *n computers* the large-scale processing of numerical data

numberless *adj* too many to be counted

number one *n* **1** *informal* oneself: *he looks after number one* **2** *informal* the bestselling pop record in any one week ▹*adj* **3** first in importance, urgency, or quality: *he's their number one suspect*

numberplate *n* a plate on a motor vehicle showing the registration number

Number Ten *n* 10 Downing Street, the British prime minister's official London residence

numbskull *or* **numskull** *n* a stupid person

numeral *n* a word or symbol used to express a sum or quantity
WORD ORIGIN Latin *numerus* number

numerate *adj* able to do basic arithmetic **numeracy** *n*

numeration *n* **1** the act or process of numbering or counting **2** a system of numbering

numerator *n maths* the number above the line in a fraction

numerical *or* **numeric** *adj* measured or expressed in numbers: *record the severity of your symptoms in numerical form*
numerically *adv*

numerology *n* the study of numbers and of their supposed influence on human affairs

numerous ❶ *adj* **1** many: *they carried out numerous bombings* **2** consisting of a large number of people or things: *the cast is not as numerous as one might suppose*

numinous *adj formal* **1** arousing spiritual or religious emotions **2** mysterious or awe-inspiring
WORD ORIGIN Latin *numen* divine will

numismatics *n* the study or collection of coins or medals
numismatist *n*
WORD ORIGIN Greek *nomisma* piece of currency

numskull *n* ▸same as **numbskull**

nun *n* a female member of a religious order
WORD ORIGIN Late Latin *nonna*

nuncio *n, pl* **-cios** *RC church* a papal ambassador
WORD ORIGIN Latin *nuntius* messenger

Nunn *n* Sir **Trevor** (**Robert**) born 1940, British theatre director; artistic director (1968–86) and chief executive (1968–86) of the Royal Shakespeare Company; artistic director of the Royal National Theatre (1997–2003). His productions include *Nicholas Nickleby* (1980), *Cats* (1981), and *Les Misérables* (1985)

nunnery *n, pl* **-neries** a convent

nunny bag *n Canad* (in Newfoundland) a small sealskin knapsack
WORD ORIGIN probably from Scots dialect *noony* lunch

nuptial *adj* relating to marriage: *a nuptial blessing*
WORD ORIGIN Latin *nuptiae* marriage

nuptials *pl n* a wedding

nurd *n slang* ▸same as **nerd**

Nurhachi *n* 1559–1626, Manchurian leader, who unified the Manchurian state and began (1618) the Manchurian conquest of China

Nuri as-Said *n* 1888–1958, Iraqi soldier and statesman: prime minister of Iraq 14 times between 1930 and 1958: he died during a military coup

Nurmi *n* **Paavo**, known as *The Flying Finn*. 1897–1973, Finnish runner, winner of the 1500, 5000, and 10 000 metres' races at the 1924 Olympic Games in Paris

nurse ❶ *n* **1** a person trained to look after sick people, usually in a hospital **2** ▸short for **nursemaid** ▹*vb* **nursing, nursed 3** to look after (a sick person) **4** to breast-feed (a baby) **5** (of a baby) to feed at its mother's breast **6** to try to cure (an ailment) **7** to harbour or foster (a feeling) **8** to clasp fondly: *she nursed her drink*
nursing *n, adj*
WORD ORIGIN Latin *nutrire* to nourish

nursemaid *or* **nurserymaid** *n* a woman employed to look after children

nursery ❶ *n, pl* **-ries 1** a room in a house where children sleep or play **2** a place where children are taken care of when their parents are at work **3** a place where plants and young trees are grown for sale

nurseryman *n, pl* **-men** a person who raises plants and trees for sale

nursery nurse *n* a person trained to look after children of pre-school age

nursery rhyme *n* a short traditional verse or song for children

nursery school *n* a school for young children from three to five years old

nursery slopes *pl n* gentle slopes used by beginners in skiing

nursery stakes *pl n* a race for two-year-old horses

nursing home *n* a private hospital or home for people who are old or ill

nursing officer *n* (in Britain) the administrative head of the nursing staff of a hospital

nurture ❶ *n* **1** the act or process of promoting the development of a child or young plant ▹*vb* **-turing, -tured 2** to promote or encourage the development of
WORD ORIGIN Latin *nutrire* to nourish

nut ❶ *n* **1** a dry one-seeded fruit that grows inside a hard shell **2** the edible inner part of such a fruit **3** a small piece of metal with a hole in it, that screws on to a bolt **4** *slang* an eccentric or insane person **5** *slang* the head **6** *slang* an enthusiast: *a health nut* **7** *Brit* a small piece of coal **8 a hard** *or* **tough nut to crack** a person or thing that presents difficulties **9 do one's nut** *Austral & Brit slang* to be very angry ▸See also **nuts**
WORD ORIGIN Old English *hnutu*

NUT (in Britain & S Africa) National Union of Teachers

nutcase *n slang* an insane person

nutcracker *n* a device for cracking the shells of nuts. Also: **nutcrackers**

n

THESAURUS

numerous *adj* **1, 2 = many**, several, countless, lots, abundant, plentiful, innumerable, copious, manifold, umpteen *(informal)*, profuse, thick on the ground **OPPOSITE:** few

nurse *vb* **3 = look after**, treat, tend, care for, take care of, minister to **4 = breast-feed**, feed, nurture, nourish, suckle, wet-nurse **7 = harbour**, have, maintain, preserve, entertain, cherish, keep alive

nursery *n* **2 = crèche**, kindergarten, playgroup, play-centre *(NZ)*

nurture *n* **1 = upbringing**, training, education, instruction, rearing, development ▹*vb* **2 = bring up**, raise, look after, rear, care for, develop **OPPOSITE:** neglect

nut *n* **4** *(slang)* **= madman**, eccentric, flake *(slang, chiefly US)*, psycho *(slang)*,

DICTIONARY

nuthatch *n* a songbird that feeds on insects, seeds, and nuts
WORD ORIGIN Middle English *notehache* nut hatchet, from its habit of splitting nuts

nutmeg *n* a spice made from the seed of a tropical tree
WORD ORIGIN Old French *nois muguede* musk-scented nut

nutraceutical *n* ▸ see **functional food**

nutria (new-tree-a) *n* the fur of the coypu
WORD ORIGIN Latin *lutra* otter

nutrient (new-tree-ent) *n* **1** a substance that provides nourishment: *their only source of nutrient* ▹ *adj* **2** providing nourishment
WORD ORIGIN Latin *nutrire* to nourish

nutriment (new-tree-ment) *n* the food or nourishment required by all living things to grow and stay healthy
WORD ORIGIN Latin *nutrimentum*

nutrition ❶ (new-**trish**-un) *n* **1** the process of taking in and absorbing nutrients **2** the process of being nourished **3** the study of nutrition **nutritional** *adj* **nutritionist** *n*
WORD ORIGIN Latin *nutrire* to nourish

nutritious *adj* providing nourishment
WORD ORIGIN Latin *nutrix* nurse

nutritive *adj* of nutrition; nutritious

nuts *adj slang* **1** insane **2 nuts about** very fond of or enthusiastic about

nuts and bolts *pl n informal* the essential or practical details: *the nuts and bolts of photography*

nutshell *n* **in a nutshell** in essence; briefly

nutter *n Brit & NZ slang* an insane person

nutty *adj* **-tier, -tiest 1** containing or resembling nuts **2** *slang* insane or eccentric **nuttiness** *n*

nux vomica *n* the seed of a tree, containing strychnine
WORD ORIGIN Medieval Latin: vomiting nut

nuzzle *vb* **-zling, -zled** to push or rub gently with the nose or snout
WORD ORIGIN from *nose*

NV Nevada

nvCJD new-variant Creutzfeldt-Jakob disease

NW northwest(ern)

NWT Northwest Territories (of Canada)

NY *or* **N.Y.** New York

NYC New York City

nylon *n* a synthetic material used for clothing and many other products
WORD ORIGIN originally a trademark

nylons *pl n* stockings made of nylon

Nyman *n* **Michael** born 1944, British composer; works include the opera *The Man Who Mistook His Wife For a Hat* (1986) and scores for films, including *The Piano* (1992) and several films by Peter Greenaway

nymph *n* **1** *myth* a spirit of nature, represented as a beautiful young woman **2** the larva of certain insects, resembling the adult form **3** *chiefly poetic* a beautiful young woman
WORD ORIGIN Greek *numphē*

nymphet *n* a girl who is sexually precocious and desirable

nympho *n, pl* **-phos** *informal* ▸ short for **nymphomaniac**

nymphomaniac *n* a woman with an abnormally intense sexual desire **nymphomania** *n*
WORD ORIGIN Greek *numphē* nymph + *mania* madness

NZ, N.Z. New Zealand

NZE New Zealand English

NZRFU New Zealand Rugby Football Union

NZSE40 Index New Zealand Stock Exchange 40 Index

THESAURUS

crank *(informal)*, lunatic, maniac, loony *(slang)*, nutter *(Brit slang)*, oddball *(informal)*, crackpot *(informal)*, wacko *(slang)*, nutcase *(slang)*, headcase *(informal)*, crazy *(informal)*
5 *(slang)* = **head**, skull, noggin

nutrition *n* **1** = **food**, nourishment, sustenance, nutriment

n

Oo

DICTIONARY

O[1] **1** *chem* oxygen **2** Old **3** ▸same as **nought**
O[2] *interj* ▸same as **oh**
o. *or* **O.** old
o' *prep informal or old-fashioned* of: *a cup o' tea*
OA Order of Australia
oaf *n* a stupid or clumsy person
oafish *adj*
WORD ORIGIN variant of Old English *ælf* elf
oak *n* **1** a large forest tree with hard wood, acorns as fruits, and leaves with rounded projections **2** the wood of this tree, used as building timber and for making furniture
oaken *adj*
WORD ORIGIN Old English *āc*
oak apple *or* **gall** *n* a brownish round lump or ball produced on oak trees by certain wasps
Oakley *n* **Annie,** real name *Phoebe Anne Oakley Mozee.* 1860–1926, US markswoman
Oaks *n* **the Oaks** an annual horse race for three-year-old fillies, run at Epsom
WORD ORIGIN named after an estate near Epsom
oakum *n* loose fibre obtained by unravelling old rope, used for filling cracks in wooden ships
WORD ORIGIN Old English *ācumba*, literally: off-combings
OAM Medal of the Order of Australia
OAP (in Britain) old age pensioner
oar *n* **1** a long pole with a broad blade, used for rowing a boat **2** **put** *or* **stick one's oar in** to interfere or interrupt
WORD ORIGIN Old English *ār*
oarsman *or fem* **oarswoman** *n, pl* **-men** *or* **-women** a person who rows
oarsmanship *n*
oasis *n, pl* **-ses** **1** a fertile patch in a desert **2** a place or situation offering relief in the midst of difficulty
WORD ORIGIN Greek
oast *n chiefly Brit* an oven for drying hops
WORD ORIGIN Old English *āst*
oast house *n chiefly Brit* a building containing ovens for drying hops
Oastler *n* **Richard** 1789–1861, British social reformer; he campaigned against child labour and helped achieve the ten-hour day (1847)
oat *n* **1** a hard cereal grown as food **2** **oats** the edible grain of this cereal **3** **sow one's wild oats** to have casual sexual relationships while young
oaten *adj*
WORD ORIGIN Old English *āte*
oatcake *n* a thin unsweetened biscuit made of oatmeal
oath ❶ *n, pl* **oaths** **1** a solemn promise, esp. to tell the truth in a court of law **2** an offensive or blasphemous expression; a swearword **3** **on** *or* **under oath** having made a solemn promise to tell the truth, esp. in a court of law
WORD ORIGIN Old English *āth*
oatmeal *n* **1** a coarse flour made by grinding oats ▹*adj* **2** greyish-yellow
ob. (on tombstones) he *or* she died
WORD ORIGIN Latin *obiit*
Obasanjo *n* **Olusegun** born 1937, Nigerian politician and general; head of the military government (1976–79); president (1999–2007)
obbligato (ob-lig-**gah**-toe) *music adj* **1** not to be omitted in performance ▹*n, pl* **-tos** **2** an essential part or accompaniment: *an aria with bassoon obbligato*
WORD ORIGIN Italian
obdurate *adj* not to be persuaded; hardhearted or obstinate
obduracy *n*
WORD ORIGIN Latin *obdurare* to make hard
OBE (in Britain) Officer of the Order of the British Empire
obedient *adj* obeying or willing to obey **obedience** *n* **obediently** *adv*
WORD ORIGIN Latin *oboediens*
obeisance (oh-**bay**-sanss) *n formal* **1** an attitude of respect or humble obedience **2** a bow or curtsy showing this attitude **obeisant** *adj*
WORD ORIGIN Old French *obéissant* obeying
obelisk (**ob**-bill-isk) *n* **1** a four-sided stone pillar that tapers to a pyramid at the top **2** *printing* ▸same as **dagger** (sense 2)
WORD ORIGIN Greek *obeliskos* a little spit
obese (oh-**beess**) *adj* very fat
obesity *n*
WORD ORIGIN Latin *obesus*
obey ❶ *vb* **1** to carry out instructions or orders; be obedient **2** to act in accordance with one's feelings, an impulse, etc.: *I had obeyed the impulse to open the gate and had walked up the drive*
WORD ORIGIN Latin *oboedire*
obfuscate *vb* **-cating, -cated** *formal* to make something unnecessarily difficult to understand **obfuscation** *n* **obfuscatory** *adj*
WORD ORIGIN Latin *ob-* (intensive) + *fuscare* to blacken
obituary *n, pl* **-aries** a published announcement of a death, usually with a short biography of the dead person **obituarist** *n*
WORD ORIGIN Latin *obitus* death
obj. **1** objection **2** *grammar* object(ive)
object[1] ❶ *n* **1** a thing that can be touched or seen **2** a person or thing seen as a focus for feelings, actions, or thought: *she had become for him an object of compassion* **3** an aim or purpose: *the main object of the exercise* **4** *philosophy* that which can be perceived by the mind, as contrasted with the thinking subject **5** *grammar* a noun, pronoun, or noun phrase that receives the action of a verb or is governed by a preposition, such as *the bottle* in *she threw the bottle* **6** **no object** not a hindrance or obstacle: *money's no object*
WORD ORIGIN Late Latin *objectus* something thrown before (the mind)
object[2] ❶ *vb* **1** to express disapproval or opposition: *my colleagues objected strongly to further delays* **2** to state as one's reason for opposing: *he objected that his small staff would be unable to handle the added work* **objector** *n*
WORD ORIGIN Latin *ob-* against + *jacere* to throw
objection ❶ *n* **1** an expression or feeling of opposition or disapproval

THESAURUS

oath *n* **1 = promise**, bond, pledge, vow, word, compact, covenant, affirmation, sworn statement, avowal, word of honour **2 = swear word**, curse, obscenity, blasphemy, expletive, four-letter word, cuss *(informal)*, profanity, strong language, imprecation, malediction
obey *vb* **1 = carry out**, follow, perform, respond to, implement, fulfil, execute, discharge, act upon, carry through **OPPOSITE:** disregard **2 = abide by**, keep, follow, comply with, observe, mind, embrace, hold to, heed, conform to, keep to, adhere to, be ruled by
object[1] *n* **1 = thing**, article, device, body, item, implement, entity, gadget, contrivance **2 = target**, victim, focus, butt, recipient **3 = purpose**, aim, end, point, plan, idea, reason, goal, design, target, principle, function, intention, objective, intent, motive, end in view, end purpose, the why and wherefore
object[2] *vb* **1a** *(often with* **to**) **= protest against**, oppose, say no to, kick against *(informal)*, argue against, draw the line at, take exception to, raise objections to, cry out against, complain against, take up the cudgels against, expostulate against **OPPOSITE:** accept **1b = disagree**, demur, remonstrate, expostulate, express disapproval **OPPOSITE:** agree
objection *n* **1, 2 = protest**, opposition, complaint, doubt, exception,

2 a reason for opposing something: *the planning officer had raised no objection to the proposals*

objectionable *adj* offensive or unacceptable

objective ❶ *n* **1** an aim or purpose: *the objective is to highlight the environmental threat to the planet* **2** *grammar* a grammatical case in some languages that identifies the direct object of a verb or preposition **3** *optics* the lens nearest to the object observed in an optical instrument ▷ *adj* **4** not distorted by personal feelings or bias: *I have tried to be as objective as possible in my presentation* **5** of or relating to actual facts as opposed to thoughts or feelings: *stand back and try to take a more objective view of your life as a whole* **6** existing independently of the mind; real **objectival** *adj* **objectively** *adv* **objectivity** *n*

object lesson *n* a practical demonstration of some principle or ideal

objet d'art (ob-zhay **dahr**) *n, pl* **objets d'art** (ob-zhay **dahr**) a small object considered to be of artistic worth
WORD ORIGIN French: object of art

oblate *adj geom* (of a sphere) flattened at the poles: *the oblate spheroid of the earth*
WORD ORIGIN New Latin *oblatus* lengthened

oblation *n* **1** *Christianity* the offering of bread and wine to God at Communion **2** any offering made for religious purposes **oblational** *adj*
WORD ORIGIN Medieval Latin *oblatus* offered

obligated *adj* being morally or legally bound to do something: *they are obligated to provide temporary accommodation* **obligative** *adj*

obligation ❶ *n* **1** a moral or legal duty **2** the binding power of such a duty: *I feel under some obligation to help you with your education* **3** a sense of being in debt because of a service or favour: *I don't want him marrying me out of obligation*

obligatory *adj* required or compulsory because of custom or law

oblige ❶ *vb* **obliging, obliged** **1** to compel someone by legal, moral, or physical means to do something **2** to make (someone) indebted or grateful for a favour: *I am obliged to you for your help* **3** to do a favour to someone: *she obliged the guests with a song*
WORD ORIGIN Latin *ob-* towards + *ligare* to bind

obliging ❶ *adj* willing to be helpful **obligingly** *adv*

oblique (oh-**bleak**) *adj* **1** at an angle; slanting **2** *geom* (of lines or planes) neither perpendicular nor parallel to one another **3** indirect or evasive: *only oblique references have been made to the anti-government unrest* ▷ *n* **4** ▸ same as **solidus** > **obliquely** *adv* **obliqueness** *n*
WORD ORIGIN Latin *obliquus*

oblique angle *n* an angle that is not a right angle or any multiple of a right angle

obliterate *vb* **-rating, -rated** to destroy every trace of; wipe out completely **obliteration** *n*
WORD ORIGIN Latin *oblitterare* to erase

oblivion *n* **1** the condition of being forgotten or disregarded: *the Marxist-Leninist wing of the party looks set to sink into oblivion* **2** the state of being unaware or unconscious: *guests seemed to feel a social obligation to drink themselves into oblivion*
WORD ORIGIN Latin *oblivio* forgetfulness

oblivious *adj* unaware or unconscious: *oblivious of her soaking clothes; I was oblivious to the beauty* **obliviousness** *n*

oblong *adj* **1** having an elongated, rectangular shape ▷ *n* **2** a figure or object having this shape
WORD ORIGIN Latin *oblongus*

obloquy (ob-lock-wee) *n, pl* **-quies** *formal* **1** abusive statements or blame: *the British press was held up to moral obloquy* **2** disgrace brought about by this: *the punishment of lifelong public obloquy and private embarrassment*
WORD ORIGIN Latin *obloquium* contradiction

obnoxious *adj* extremely unpleasant **obnoxiousness** *n*
WORD ORIGIN Latin *obnoxius*

oboe *n* a double-reeded woodwind instrument with a penetrating nasal tone **oboist** *n*
WORD ORIGIN French *haut bois*, literally: high wood (referring to its pitch)

Obote *n* (**Apollo**) **Milton** 1924–2005, Ugandan politician; prime minister of Uganda (1962–66) and president (1966–71; 1980–85). He was deposed by Amin in 1971 and remained in exile until 1980; deposed again in 1985 by the Acholi army

O'Brien *n* **1 Conor Cruise** 1917–2008, Irish diplomat and writer. As an Irish Labour MP he served in the coalition government of 1973–77, becoming a senator (1977–79). He edited the *Observer* (1978–81) **2 Edna** born 1936, Irish novelist. Her books include *The Country Girls* (1960), *Johnny I Hardly Knew You* (1977), and *In the Forest* (2002) **3 Flann,** real name *Brian O'Nolan*. 1911–66, Irish novelist and journalist. His novels include *At Swim-Two-Birds* (1939) and the posthumously published *The Third Policeman* (1967). As Myles na Gopaleen he wrote a satirical column for the *Irish Times* **4 Kerry** born 1945. Australian journalist and broadcaster

obs. obsolete

obscene ❶ *adj* **1** offensive to accepted standards of decency or modesty **2** *law* tending to deprave or corrupt: *an obscene publication* **3** disgusting: *a great dark obscene pool of blood* **obscenity** *n*
WORD ORIGIN Latin *obscenus* inauspicious

O

THESAURUS

dissent, outcry, censure, disapproval, niggle *(informal)*, protestation, scruple, demur, formal complaint, counter-argument, cavil, remonstrance, demurral
OPPOSITE: agreement

objective *n* **1 = purpose**, aim, goal, end, plan, hope, idea, design, target, wish, scheme, desire, object, intention, ambition, aspiration, Holy Grail *(informal)*, end in view, why and wherefore ▷ *adj* **4, 5 = unbiased**, detached, just, fair, judicial, open-minded, equitable, impartial, impersonal, disinterested, even-handed, dispassionate, unemotional, uninvolved, unprejudiced, uncoloured
OPPOSITE: subjective
6 = factual, real, circumstantial

obligation *n* **1a = duty**, compulsion **1b = task**, job, duty, work, calling, business, charge, role, function, mission, province, assignment, pigeon *(informal)*, chore
2 = responsibility, duty, liability, accountability, culpability, answerability, accountableness

oblige *vb* **1 = compel**, make, force, require, bind, railroad *(informal)*, constrain, necessitate, coerce, impel, dragoon, obligate **3 = help**, assist, serve, benefit, please, favour, humour, accommodate, indulge, gratify, do someone a service, put yourself out for, do (someone) a favour *or* a kindness, meet the wants *or* needs of **OPPOSITE:** bother

obliging *adj* **= accommodating**, kind, helpful, willing, civil, friendly, polite, cooperative, agreeable, amiable, courteous, considerate, hospitable, unselfish, good-natured, eager to please, complaisant
OPPOSITE: unhelpful

obscene *adj* **1 = indecent**, dirty, offensive, gross, foul, coarse, filthy, vile, improper, immoral, pornographic, suggestive, blue, loose, shameless, lewd, depraved, X-rated *(informal)*, bawdy, salacious, prurient, impure, lascivious, smutty, ribald, unwholesome, scabrous, immodest, licentious, indelicate,

DICTIONARY

obscure ⓣ *adj* **1** not well-known: *the concerts feature several obscure artists* **2** not easily understood: *the contracts are written in obscure language* **3** unclear or indistinct ▷ *vb* **-scuring, -scured** **4** to make unclear or vague; hide: *no amount of bluster could obscure the fact that the prime minister had run out of excuses* **5** to cover or cloud over **obscuration** *n* **obscurity** *n*
WORD ORIGIN Latin *obscurus* dark

obsequies (ob-sick-weez) *pl n, sing* **-quy** *formal* funeral rites
WORD ORIGIN Medieval Latin *obsequiae*

obsequious (ob-seek-wee-uss) *adj* being overattentive in order to gain favour **obsequiousness** *n*
WORD ORIGIN Latin *obsequiosus* compliant

observance *n* **1** the observing of a law or custom **2** a ritual, ceremony, or practice, esp. of a religion

observant *adj* quick to notice details around one; sharp-eyed

observation ⓣ *n* **1** the act of watching or the state of being watched **2** a comment or remark **3** detailed examination of something before analysis, diagnosis, or interpretation: *you may be admitted to hospital for observation and rest* **4** the facts learned from observing **5** the ability to notice things: *she has good powers of observation* **observational** *adj*

observatory *n, pl* **-ries** a building specially designed and equipped for studying the weather and the stars

observe ⓣ *vb* **-serving, -served** **1** to see or notice: *after some hours I observed a change in the animal's behaviour* **2** to watch (something) carefully **3** to make scientific examinations of **4** to remark: *the speaker observed that times had changed* **5** to keep (a law or custom) **observable** *adj* **observer** *n*
WORD ORIGIN Latin *observare*

obsessed ⓣ *adj* thinking about someone or something all the time: *he had become obsessed with her* **obsessive** *adj, n*
WORD ORIGIN Latin *obsessus* besieged

obsession ⓣ *n* **1** something that preoccupies a person to the exclusion of other things: *his principal obsession was with trying to economize* **2** *psychiatry* a persistent idea or impulse, often associated with anxiety and mental illness **obsessional** *adj*

obsidian *n* a dark glassy volcanic rock
WORD ORIGIN after *Obsius*, the discoverer of a stone resembling obsidian

obsolescent *adj* becoming obsolete or out of date **obsolescence** *n*

obsolete ⓣ *adj* no longer used; out of date
WORD ORIGIN Latin *obsoletus* worn out

obstacle ⓣ *n* **1** a situation or event that prevents something being done: *there are obstacles which could slow the development of a vaccine* **2** a person or thing that hinders movement
WORD ORIGIN Latin *obstaculum*, from *ob-* against + *stare* to stand

obstetrician *n* a doctor who specializes in obstetrics

obstetrics *n* the branch of medicine concerned with pregnancy and childbirth **obstetric** *adj*
WORD ORIGIN Latin *obstetrix* a midwife

obstinate *adj* **1** keeping stubbornly to a particular opinion or course of action **2** difficult to treat or deal with: *obstinate weeds* **obstinacy** *n* **obstinately** *adv*
WORD ORIGIN Latin *obstinatus*

obstreperous *adj* noisy and difficult to control: *her obstreperous teenage son*

THESAURUS

unchaste **OPPOSITE:** decent
3 = offensive, shocking, evil, disgusting, outrageous, revolting, sickening, vile, wicked, repellent, atrocious, obnoxious, heinous, nauseating, odious, loathsome, abominable, detestable

O

obscure *adj* **1 = unknown**, minor, little-known, humble, unfamiliar, out-of-the-way, unseen, lowly, unimportant, unheard-of, unsung, nameless, undistinguished, inconspicuous, unnoted, unhonoured, unrenowned
OPPOSITE: famous
2 = abstruse, involved, complex, confusing, puzzling, subtle, mysterious, deep, vague, unclear, doubtful, mystical, intricate, ambiguous, enigmatic, esoteric, perplexing, occult, opaque, incomprehensible, arcane, cryptic, unfathomable, recondite, clear as mud *(informal)*
OPPOSITE: straightforward
3a = unclear, hidden, uncertain, confused, mysterious, concealed, doubtful, indefinite, indeterminate
OPPOSITE: well-known
3b = indistinct, vague, blurred, dark, clouded, faint, dim, gloomy, veiled, murky, fuzzy, shadowy, cloudy, misty, hazy, indistinguishable, indeterminate, dusky, undefined, out of focus, ill-defined, obfuscated, indiscernible, tenebrous
OPPOSITE: clear
▷ *vb* **4 = hide**, cover (up), screen, mask, disguise, conceal, veil, cloak, shroud, camouflage, envelop, encase, enshroud **OPPOSITE:** expose
5 = obstruct, hinder, block out

observation *n* **1, 3 = watching**, study, survey, review, notice, investigation, monitoring, attention, consideration, examination, inspection, scrutiny, surveillance, contemplation, cognition, perusal
2a = comment, finding, thought, note, statement, opinion, remark, explanation, reflection, exposition, utterance, pronouncement, annotation, elucidation, obiter dictum *(Latin)* **2b = remark**, thought, comment, statement, opinion, reflection, assertion, utterance, animadversion

observe *vb* **1 = notice**, see, note, mark, discover, spot, regard, witness, clock *(Brit slang)*, distinguish, perceive, detect, discern, behold *(archaic, literary)*, eye, eyeball *(slang)*, peer at, espy, get a load of *(informal)*
2 = watch, study, view, look at, note, check, regard, survey, monitor, contemplate, check out *(informal)*, look on, keep an eye on *(informal)*, gaze at, pay attention to, keep track of, scrutinize, keep tabs on *(informal)*, recce *(slang)*, keep under observation, watch like a hawk, take a dekko at *(Brit slang)* **4 = remark**, say, comment, state, note, reflect, mention, declare, opine, pass comment, animadvert
5 = comply with, keep, follow, mind, respect, perform, carry out, honour, fulfil, discharge, obey, heed, conform to, adhere to, abide by
OPPOSITE: disregard

obsessed *adj* **= absorbed**, dominated, gripped, caught up, haunted, distracted, hung up *(slang)*, preoccupied, immersed, beset, in the grip, infatuated, fixated, having a one-track mind
OPPOSITE: indifferent

obsession *n* **1, 2 = preoccupation**, thing *(informal)*, complex, enthusiasm, addiction, hang-up *(informal)*, mania, phobia, fetish, fixation, infatuation, ruling passion, pet subject, hobbyhorse, idée fixe *(French)*, bee in your bonnet *(informal)*

obsolete *adj* **= outdated**, old, passé, ancient, antique, old-fashioned, dated, discarded, extinct, past it, out of date, archaic, disused, out of fashion, out, antiquated, anachronistic, outmoded, musty, old hat, behind the times, superannuated, antediluvian, outworn, démodé *(French)*, out of the ark *(informal)*, vieux jeu *(French)*
OPPOSITE: up-to-date

obstacle *n* **1 = hindrance**, check, bar, block, difficulty, barrier, handicap, hurdle, hitch, drawback, snag, deterrent, uphill *(S African)*, obstruction, stumbling block, impediment **OPPOSITE:** help
2 = obstruction, block, barrier, hurdle, hazard, snag, impediment, blockage, hindrance

DICTIONARY

WORD ORIGIN Latin *ob-* against + *strepere* to roar

obstruct ❶ *vb* **1** to block a way with an obstacle **2** to make progress or activity difficult: *this government will never obstruct the course of justice* **3** to block a clear view of

WORD ORIGIN Latin *obstructus* built against

obstruction *n* **1** a person or thing that obstructs **2** the act of obstructing or being obstructed **3** *sport* the act of unfairly impeding an opposing player

obstructionist *n* a person who deliberately obstructs legal or parliamentary business **obstructionism** *n*

obstructive *adj* deliberately causing difficulties or delays **obstructively** *adv* **obstructiveness** *n*

obtain ❶ *vb* **1** to gain possession of; get **2** *formal* to be customary or accepted: *silence obtains from eight in the evening* **obtainable** *adj*

WORD ORIGIN Latin *obtinere* to take hold of

obtrude *vb* **-truding, -truded 1** to push oneself or one's opinions on others in an unwelcome way **2** to be or make unpleasantly noticeable **obtrusion** *n*

WORD ORIGIN Latin *obtrudere*

obtrusive *adj* unpleasantly noticeable: *the music should fit your mood, it shouldn't be too obtrusive* **obtrusiveness** *n*

obtuse *adj* **1** mentally slow or emotionally insensitive **2** *maths* (of an angle) between 90° and 180° **3** not sharp or pointed; blunt **obtuseness** *n*

WORD ORIGIN Latin *obtusus* dulled

obverse *n* **1** a counterpart or opposite: *his true personality being the obverse of his outer image* **2** the side of a coin that bears the main design **3** the front, top, or main surface of anything

WORD ORIGIN Latin *obversus* turned towards

obviate *vb* **-ating, -ated** *formal* to avoid or prevent (a need or difficulty): *a mediator will obviate the need for independent legal advice*

WORD ORIGIN Latin *obviare*

obvious ❶ *adj* **1** easy to see or understand ▷ *n* **2 state the obvious** to say something that is unnecessary or already known: *he is prone to stating the obvious* **obviously** *adv* **obviousness** *n*

WORD ORIGIN Latin *obvius*

ocarina *n* a small egg-shaped wind instrument with a mouthpiece and finger holes

WORD ORIGIN Italian: little goose

O'Casey *n* **Sean** 1880–1964, Irish dramatist. His plays include *Juno and the Paycock* (1924) and *The Plough and the Stars* (1926), which are realistic pictures of Dublin slum life

occasion ❶ *n* **1** a particular event or the time at which it happens **2** a need or reason to do or be something: *we barely knew him and never had occasion to speak of him* **3** a suitable time or opportunity to do something **4** a special event, time, or celebration: *a wedding day is a truly special occasion* **5 on occasion** every so often **6 rise to the occasion** to meet the special demands of a situation ▷ *vb* **7** *formal* to cause, esp. incidentally

WORD ORIGIN Latin *occasio* a falling down

occasional ❶ *adj* happening from time to time; not frequent or regular **occasionally** *adv*

occasional table *n* a small table with no regular use

Occident *n* the western hemisphere, esp. Europe and America **Occidental** *adj*

WORD ORIGIN Latin *occidere* to fall (with reference to the setting sun)

occiput (ox-sip-putt) *n anat* the back of the head or skull **occipital** *adj*

WORD ORIGIN Latin *ob-* at the back of + *caput* head

occlude *vb* **-cluding, -cluded** *formal* **1** to block or stop up a passage or opening: *the arteries are occluded by deposits of plaque* **2** to shut in or out: *slowly occluding him from Nash's vision* **3** *chem* (of a solid) to absorb and retain a gas or other substance **occlusion** *n*

WORD ORIGIN Latin *occludere*

occluded front *n meteorol* the front formed when the cold front of a depression overtakes a warm front, raising the warm air from ground level

occult ❶ *adj* **1** involving mystical or supernatural phenomena or powers **2** beyond ordinary human understanding **3** secret or mysterious ▷ *n* **4 the occult** the knowledge and study of occult phenomena and powers

WORD ORIGIN Latin *occultus* hidden, secret

occupancy *n, pl* **-cies 1** the act of occupying a property **2** the period of time during which one is an occupant of a property

occupant ❶ *n* a person occupying a property, position, or place

O

THESAURUS

obstruct *vb* **1 = block**, close, bar, cut off, plug, choke, clog, barricade, shut off, stop up, bung up *(informal)* **2a = hold up**, stop, check, bar, block, prevent, arrest, restrict, interrupt, slow down, hamstring, interfere with, hamper, inhibit, clog, hinder, retard, impede, get in the way of, bring to a standstill, cumber **2b = impede**, prevent, frustrate, hold up, slow down, hamstring, interfere with, hamper, hold back, thwart, hinder, retard, get in the way of, trammel, cumber **OPPOSITE:** help **3 = obscure**, screen, cut off, cover, hide, mask, shield

obtain *vb* **1a = get**, gain, acquire, land, net, pick up, bag, secure, get hold of, come by, procure, get your hands on, score *(slang)*, come into possession of **OPPOSITE:** lose **1b = achieve**, get, gain, realize, accomplish, attain **2** *(formal)* **= prevail**, hold, stand, exist, be the case, abound, predominate, be in force, be current, be prevalent

obvious *adj* **1 = clear**, open, plain, apparent, visible, bold, patent, evident, distinct, pronounced, straightforward, explicit, manifest, transparent, noticeable, blatant, conspicuous, overt, unmistakable, palpable, unequivocal, undeniable, salient, recognizable, unambiguous, self-evident, indisputable, perceptible, much in evidence, unquestionable, open-and-shut, cut-and-dried *(informal)*, undisguised, incontrovertible, self-explanatory, unsubtle, unconcealed, clear as a bell, staring you in the face *(informal)*, right under your nose *(informal)*, sticking out a mile *(informal)*, plain as the nose on your face *(informal)* **OPPOSITE:** unclear

occasion *n* **1 = time**, moment, point, stage, incident, instance, occurrence, juncture **2 = reason**, cause, call, ground(s), basis, excuse, incentive, motive, warrant, justification, provocation, inducement **3 = opportunity**, chance, time, opening, window **4 = function**, event, affair, do *(informal)*, happening, experience, gathering, celebration, occurrence, social occasion ▷ *vb* **7** *(formal)* **= cause**, begin, produce, create, effect, lead to, inspire, result in, generate, prompt, provoke, induce, bring about, originate, evoke, give rise to, precipitate, elicit, incite, engender

occasional *adj* **= infrequent**, odd, rare, casual, irregular, sporadic, intermittent, few and far between, desultory, periodic **OPPOSITE:** constant

occult *adj* **1 = supernatural**, dark, magical, mysterious, psychic, mystical, mystic, unearthly, unnatural, esoteric, uncanny, arcane, paranormal, abstruse, recondite, preternatural, cabbalistic, supranatural ▷ *n* **4 the occult = magic**, witchcraft, sorcery, wizardry, enchantment, occultism, black art, necromancy, theurgy

occupant *n* **= occupier**, resident, tenant, user, holder, inmate, inhabitant, incumbent, dweller, denizen, addressee, lessee, indweller

DICTIONARY

occupation ⓣ *n* **1** a person's job or profession **2** any activity on which someone's time is spent: *a pleasant and rewarding occupation* **3** the control of a country by a foreign military power **4** the act of occupying or the state of being occupied: *the occupation of Kuwait* **occupational** *adj*

occupational hazard *n* something unpleasant that occurs due to your job: *frequent colds are an occupational hazard in teaching*

occupational therapy *n* treatment of people with physical, emotional, or social problems using purposeful activity to help them overcome or learn to accept their problems

occupier *n Brit* the person who lives in a particular house, whether as owner or tenant

occupy ⓣ *vb* **-pies, -pying, -pied 1** to live, stay, or work in (a house, flat, or office) **2** to keep (someone or someone's mind) busy **3** to take up (time or space) **4** to move in and take control of (a country or other place): *soldiers have occupied the country's television station* **5** to fill or hold (a position or office)
WORD ORIGIN Latin *occupare* to seize hold of

occur ⓣ *vb* **-curring, -curred 1** to happen **2** to be found or be present; exist **3 occur to** to come into the mind of
WORD ORIGIN Latin *occurrere* to run up to

occurrence ⓣ *n* **1** something that happens **2** the fact of occurring: *the likelihood of its occurrence increases with age*

ocean *n* **1** the vast area of salt water covering about 70 per cent of the earth's surface **2** one of the five principal divisions of this, the Atlantic, Pacific, Indian, Arctic, and Antarctic **3** *informal* a huge quantity or expanse: *oceans of replies* **4** *literary* the sea **oceanic** *adj*
WORD ORIGIN from *Oceanus*, Greek god of the stream believed to flow round the earth

ocean-going *adj* (of a ship or boat) suited for travel on the open ocean

oceanography *n* the study of oceans and their environment **oceanographer** *n* **oceanographic** *adj*

ocelot (oss-ill-lot) *n* a large cat of Central and South America with a dark-spotted yellow-grey coat
WORD ORIGIN Mexican Indian *ocelotl* jaguar

och *interj Scot & Irish* an expression of surprise, annoyance, or disagreement

oche (ok-kee) *n darts* a mark on the floor behind which a player must stand when throwing a dart
WORD ORIGIN origin unknown

ochre *or US* **ocher** (oak-er) *n* **1** a yellow or reddish-brown earth used in paints or dyes ▷ *adj* **2** moderate yellow-orange to orange
WORD ORIGIN Greek *ōkhros* pale yellow

Ockeghem *or* **Okeghem** *n* **Johannes, Jean d'** or **Jan van** Flemish composer. Also: **Ockenheim**

o'clock *adv* used after a number between one and twelve to specify an hour: *five o'clock in the morning*

O'Connell *n* **Daniel** 1775–1847, Irish nationalist leader and orator, whose election to the British House of Commons (1828) forced the acceptance of Catholic emancipation (1829)

O'Connor *n* **1 Feargus** 1794–1855, Irish politician and journalist, a leader of the Chartist movement **2 (Mary) Flannery** 1925–64, US novelist and short-story writer, author of *Wise Blood* (1952) and *The Violent Bear it Away* (1960) **3 Frank,** real name *Michael O'Donovan*. 1903–66, Irish short-story writer and critic **4 Thomas Power,** known as *Tay Pay*. 1848–1929, Irish journalist and nationalist leader

OCR optical character recognition: the ability (through a computer device) for letters and numbers to be optically scanned and input to a storage device

Oct. October

octagon *n* a geometric figure with eight sides **octagonal** *adj*
WORD ORIGIN Greek *oktagōnos* having eight angles

octahedron (ok-ta-**heed**-ron) *n, pl* **-drons** *or* **-dra** a solid figure with eight plane faces

octane *n* a liquid hydrocarbon found in petroleum

octane number *or* **rating** *n* a number indicating the quality of a petrol

octave *n* **1 a** the musical interval between the first note and the eighth note of a major or minor scale **b** the higher of these two notes **c** the series of notes filling this interval **2** *prosody* a rhythmic group of eight lines of verse
WORD ORIGIN Latin *octo* eight

Octavia *n* died 11 BC, wife of Mark Antony; sister of Augustus

octavo *n, pl* **-vos 1** a book size resulting from folding a sheet of paper of a standard size to form eight leaves **2** a book or sheet of this size
WORD ORIGIN New Latin *in octavo* in an eighth (of a sheet)

octet *n* **1** a group of eight instrumentalists or singers **2** a piece of music for eight performers
WORD ORIGIN Latin *octo* eight

October *n* the tenth month of the year
WORD ORIGIN Latin *octo* eight, since it was originally the eighth month in Roman reckoning

octogenarian *n* **1** a person between 80 and 89 years old ▷ *adj* **2** between 80 and 89 years old
WORD ORIGIN Latin *octogenarius* containing eighty

octopus *n, pl* **-puses** a sea creature with a soft oval body and eight long tentacles with suckers
WORD ORIGIN Greek *oktōpous* having eight feet

ocular *adj* of or relating to the eyes or sight
WORD ORIGIN Latin *oculus* eye

THESAURUS

occupation *n* **1 = job**, work, calling, business, line (of work), office, trade, position, post, career, situation, activity, employment, craft, profession, pursuit, vocation, livelihood, walk of life **2 = hobby**, pastime, diversion, relaxation, sideline, leisure pursuit, (leisure) activity **3, 4 = invasion**, seizure, conquest, incursion, subjugation, foreign rule

occupy *vb* **1 = inhabit**, own, live in, stay in *(Scot)*, be established in, dwell in, be in residence in, establish yourself in, ensconce yourself in, tenant, reside in, lodge in, take up residence in, make your home, abide in **OPPOSITE:** vacate **2** *(often passive)* **= engage**, interest, involve, employ, busy, entertain, absorb, amuse, divert, preoccupy, immerse, hold the attention of, engross, keep busy *or* occupied **3 = take up**, consume, tie up, use up, monopolize, keep busy *or* occupied **4 = invade**, take over, capture, seize, conquer, keep, hold, garrison, overrun, annex, take possession of, colonize **OPPOSITE:** withdraw **5 = hold**, control, dominate, possess

occur *vb* **1 = happen**, take place, come about, follow, result, chance, arise, turn up *(informal)*, come off *(informal)*, ensue, crop up *(informal)*, transpire *(informal)*, befall, materialize, come to pass *(archaic)*, betide, eventuate **2 = exist**, appear, be found, develop, obtain, turn up, be present, be met with, manifest itself, present itself, show itself **3 occur to someone = come to mind**, strike someone, dawn on someone, come to someone, spring to mind, cross someone's mind, present itself to someone, enter someone's head, offer itself to someone, suggest itself to someone

occurrence *n* **1 = incident**, happening, event, fact, matter, affair, proceeding, circumstance, episode, adventure, phenomenon, transaction **2 = existence**, instance, appearance, manifestation, materialization

DICTIONARY

oculist *n old-fashioned* an ophthalmologist
OD *informal n* **1** an overdose of a drug ▷*vb* **OD'ing, OD'd 2** to take an overdose of a drug
odalisque (ode-a-lisk) *n* a female slave in a harem
WORD ORIGIN Turkish *ōdalik*
Oda Nobunaga *n* 1534–82, Japanese general and feudal leader, who unified much of Japan under his control: assassinated
odd ❶ *adj* **1** unusual or peculiar: *his increasingly odd behaviour* **2** occasional or incidental: *the odd letter from a friend abroad, the occasional postcard from a chum* **3** leftover or additional: *we use up odd pieces of fabric to make up jerseys in wild designs* **4** (of a number) not divisible by two **5** being part of a pair or set when the other or others are missing: *the drawer was full of odd socks* **6** somewhat more than the round numbers specified: *I had known him for the past twenty-odd years* **7 odd man** *or* **one out** a person or thing excluded from others forming a group or unit ▸See also **odds** > **oddly** *adv* **oddness** *n*
WORD ORIGIN Old Norse *oddi* angle, point, third or odd number
oddball *n informal* a strange or eccentric person
oddity *n, pl* **-ties 1** an odd person or thing **2** a peculiar characteristic **3** the quality of being or appearing unusual or strange
odd-man rush *n ice hockey* an attacking move when the defence is outnumbered by the opposing team
oddments *pl n* odd pieces or things; leftovers: *oddments of wool*
odds ❶ *pl n* **1** the probability, expressed as a ratio, that something will or will not happen: *the odds against an acquittal had stabilized at six to four* **2** the difference, expressed as a ratio, between the money placed on a bet and the amount that would be received as winning payment: *the current odds are ten to one* **3** the likelihood that a certain state of affairs will be so: *the odds are that you are going to fail* **4** the advantage that one contender is judged to have over another: *the odds are in his favour* **5 it makes no odds** *Austral & Brit* it does not matter **6 at odds** on bad terms **7** at variance **8 over the odds** more than is expected or necessary
odds and ends ❶ *pl n* small, usually unimportant, objects, jobs to be done, etc.: *I have brought a few odds and ends with me*
odds-on *adj* having a better than even chance of winning
ode *n* a lyric poem, usually addressed to a particular subject, with lines of varying lengths and metres
WORD ORIGIN Greek *ōidē* song
Odets *n* **Clifford** 1906–63, US dramatist; founder member of the Group Theatre. His plays include *Waiting for Lefty* (1935) and *Golden Boy* (1937)
Odin *n* the chief god in Norse mythology
odious *adj* offensive or hateful: *I steeled myself for the odious task*
odiousness *n*
WORD ORIGIN see ODIUM
odium (oh-dee-um) *n formal* widespread dislike or disapproval of a person or action
WORD ORIGIN Latin
Odoacer *or* **Odovacar** *n* ?434–493 AD, barbarian ruler of Italy (476–493); assassinated by Theodoric
odometer (odd-om-it-er) *n US & Canad* ▸same as **mileometer**
WORD ORIGIN Greek *hodos* way + -METER
odoriferous *adj formal* having or giving off a pleasant smell
odour ❶ *or US* **odor** *n* a particular and distinctive scent or smell **odorous** *adj* **odourless** *adj*
WORD ORIGIN Latin *odor*
Odovacar *n* same as **Odoacer**
odyssey ❶ (odd-iss-ee) *n* a long eventful journey
OE *NZ informal* overseas experience: *he's away on his OE*
Oë *n* **Kenzaburo** born 1932, Japanese novelist and writer; his books include *The Catch* (1958), *A Personal Matter* (1964), and *Silent Cry* (1989): Nobel prize for literature 1994
OECD Organization for Economic Cooperation and Development
oedema *or* **edema** (id-deem-a) *n, pl* **-mata** *pathol* an abnormal accumulation of fluid in the tissues of the body, causing swelling
WORD ORIGIN Greek *oidēma* swelling
Oedipus complex (ee-dip-puss) *n psychoanal* the usually unconscious sexual desire of a child, esp. a male child, for the parent of the opposite sex **oedipal** *adj*
Oehlenschläger *or* **Öhlenschläger** *n* **Adam Gottlob** 1779–1850, Danish romantic poet and dramatist
o'er *prep, adv poetic* over
oesophagus (ee-soff-a-guss) *n, pl* **-gi** (-guy) the tube through which food travels from the throat to the stomach; gullet **oesophageal** *adj*
WORD ORIGIN Greek *oisophagos*
oestrogen (ee-stra-jen) *n* a female sex hormone that controls the reproductive cycle, and prepares the body for pregnancy
WORD ORIGIN from *oestrus* + *-gen* (suffix) producing
oestrus (ee-struss) *n* a regularly occurring period of fertility and sexual receptivity in the reproductive cycle of most female mammals, except humans; heat
WORD ORIGIN Greek *oistros* gadfly, hence frenzy
of *prep* **1** belonging to; situated in or coming from; because of: *the inhabitants of former East Germany; I saw five people die of chronic hepatitis* **2** used after words or phrases expressing quantities: *a pint of milk* **3** specifying an amount or value: *we had to release the bombs at a height of 400 metres* **4** made up of, containing, or characterized by: *a length of rope; she is a woman of enviable beauty* **5** used to link a verbal noun with a following noun or noun phrase that is either the subject or the object of the verb: *the sudden slipping of the plates of the Earth's crust; the bombing of civilian targets* **6** at a given distance or space of time

O

THESAURUS

odd *adj* **1a = peculiar**, strange, unusual, different, funny, extraordinary, bizarre, weird, exceptional, eccentric, abnormal, queer, rum *(Brit slang)*, deviant, unconventional, far-out *(slang)*, quaint, kinky *(informal)*, off-the-wall *(slang)*, outlandish, whimsical, oddball *(informal)*, out of the ordinary, offbeat, left-field *(informal)*, freakish, freaky *(slang)*, wacko *(slang)*, outré, daggy *(Austral & NZ informal)*
1b = unusual, different, strange, rare, funny *(slang)*, extraordinary, remarkable, bizarre, fantastic, curious, weird, exceptional, peculiar, abnormal, queer, irregular, uncommon, singular, uncanny, outlandish, out of the ordinary, freakish, atypical, freaky
OPPOSITE: normal
2 = occasional, various, varied, random, casual, seasonal, irregular, periodic, miscellaneous, sundry, incidental, intermittent, infrequent
OPPOSITE: regular
3 = spare, remaining, extra, surplus, single, lone, solitary, uneven, leftover, unmatched, unpaired
OPPOSITE: matched
odds *pl n* **3 = probability**, chances, likelihood
odds and ends *pl n* **= scraps**, bits, pieces, remains, rubbish, fragments, litter, debris, shreds, remnants, bits and pieces, bric-a-brac, bits and bobs, oddments, odds and sods, leavings, miscellanea, sundry *or* miscellaneous items
odour *or (US)* **odor** *n* **= smell**, scent, perfume, fragrance, stink, bouquet, aroma, whiff, stench, pong *(Brit informal)*, niff *(Brit slang)*, redolence, malodour, fetor
odyssey *n (often cap.)* **= journey**, tour, trip, passage, quest, trek, expedition, voyage, crusade, excursion, pilgrimage, jaunt, peregrination

DICTIONARY

from: *you can still find wood within a mile of the village; he had been within hours of leaving for Romania* **7** used to specify or give more information about: *the city of Glasgow; a meeting on the subject of regional security* **8** about or concerning: *speaking of boycotts* **9** *US* before the hour of: *about quarter of eight in the evening*
WORD ORIGIN Old English

Ofcom *n* (in Britain) Office of Communications: a government body regulating the telecommunications industries

off ⓣ *prep* **1** so as to be no longer in contact with: *take the wok off the heat* **2** so as to be no longer attached to or associated with: *making use of benefit disqualification to terrorize the unemployed off the register* **3** away from: *he was driven off the road* **4** situated near to or leading away from: *they were laying out a bombing range off the coast* **5** no longer having a liking for: *she's gone off you lately* **6** no longer using: *he was off heroin for a year* ▷ *adv* **7** so as to deactivate or disengage: *turn off the gas supply* **8 a** so as to get rid of: *he was flying at midnight so he had to sleep off his hangover* **b** as a reduction in price: *she took twenty per cent off* **9** spent away from work or other duties: *it was the assistant manager's day off* **10** away; at a distance: *the men dashed back to their car and sped off* **11** away in the future: *the date was six weeks off* **12** so as to be no longer taking place: *the investigation was hastily called off* **13** removed from contact with something: *he took the jacket off* **14 off and on** occasionally; not regularly or continuously: *we lived together off and on* ▷ *adj* **15** not on; no longer operating: *her bedroom light was off* **16** cancelled or postponed: *the deal is off and your deposit will be returned in full* **17** in a specified condition, esp. regarding money or provisions: *a married man with four children is better off on the dole; how are you off for money?* **18** not up to the usual standard: *an off year for good wine* **19** no longer on the menu: *haddock is off* **20** (of food or drink) having gone bad or sour: *this milk is off* ▷ *n* **21** *cricket* the side of the field to the right of a right-handed batsman when he is facing the bowler
WORD ORIGIN variant of *of*

offal *n* the edible internal parts of an animal, such as the heart or liver
WORD ORIGIN *off* + *fall*, referring to parts cut off

offal pit *or* **hole** *n NZ* a place on a farm for the disposal of animal offal

offbeat *adj* unusual, unconventional, or eccentric

off-break *n cricket* a bowled ball that spins from off to leg on pitching

off colour *adj* **1** slightly ill; unwell **2** slightly indecent: *an off colour joke*

offcut *n* a piece of paper, wood, or fabric remaining after the main pieces have been cut; remnant

Offenbach[1] *n* a city in central Germany, on the River Main in Hesse opposite Frankfurt am Main: leather-goods industry. Pop: 119 208 (2003 est)

Offenbach[2] *n* **Jacques** 1819–80, German-born French composer of many operettas, including *Orpheus in the Underworld* (1858), and of the opera *The Tales of Hoffmann* (1881)

offence ⓣ *or US* **offense** *n* **1** a breaking of a law or rule; crime **2** annoyance or anger **3** a cause of annoyance or anger **4 give offence** to cause to feel upset or angry **5 take offence** to feel hurt or offended

offend ⓣ *vb* **1** to hurt the feelings of (a person); insult **2** to be disagreeable to; disgust: *the lady was offended by what she saw* **3** to commit a crime **offender** *n* **offending** *adj*
WORD ORIGIN Latin *offendere*

offensive ⓣ *adj* **1** unpleasant or disgusting to the senses: *there was an offensive smell of beer* **2** causing annoyance or anger; insulting **3** for the purpose of attack rather than defence ▷ *n* **4** an attitude or position of aggression: *to go on the offensive* **5** an attack or hostile action: *troops had launched a major offensive against the rebel forces* **offensively** *adv*

offer ⓣ *vb* **1** to present for acceptance or rejection: *I offered her a lift* **2** to provide: *this department offers a wide range of courses* **3** to present itself: *if an opportunity should offer* **4** to be willing (to do something): *his father offered to pay his tuition* **5** to put forward (a proposal, information, or opinion) for consideration: *may I offer a different view?* **6** to present for sale **7** to propose as payment; bid **8** to present (a prayer or sacrifice) as an act of worship **9** to show readiness for: *to offer resistance* ▷ *n* **10** something that is offered **11** the act of offering
WORD ORIGIN Latin *offerre* to present

O

THESAURUS

off *adv* **9 = absent**, gone, unavailable, not present, inoperative, nonattendant **10 = away**, out, apart, elsewhere, aside, hence, from here ▷ *adj* **16 = cancelled**, abandoned, postponed, shelved **20 = bad**, rotten, rancid, mouldy, high, turned, spoiled, sour, decayed, decomposed, putrid

offence *or (US)* **offense** *n* **1 = crime**, wrong, sin, lapse, fault, violation, wrongdoing, trespass, felony, misdemeanour, delinquency, misdeed, transgression, peccadillo, unlawful act, breach of conduct **2 = outrage**, shock, anger, trouble, bother, grief *(informal)*, resentment, irritation, hassle *(informal)*, wrath, indignation, annoyance, ire *(literary)*, displeasure, pique, aggravation, hard feelings, umbrage, vexation, wounded feelings **3 = insult**, injury, slight, hurt, harm, outrage, put-down *(slang)*, injustice, snub, affront, indignity, displeasure, rudeness, slap in the face *(informal)*, insolence

offend *vb* **1 = distress**, upset, outrage, pain, wound, slight, provoke, insult, annoy, irritate, put down, dismay, snub, aggravate *(informal)*, gall, agitate, ruffle, disconcert, vex, affront, displease, rile, pique, give offence, hurt (someone's) feelings, nark *(Brit, Austral & NZ slang)*, cut to the quick, miff *(informal)*, tread on (someone's) toes *(informal)*, put (someone's) nose out of joint, put (someone's) back up, disgruntle, get (someone's) goat *(slang)*, hack someone off *(informal)*
OPPOSITE: please
3 = break the law, sin, err, do wrong, fall, fall from grace, go astray

offensive *adj* **1 = disgusting**, gross, nasty, foul, unpleasant, revolting, stinking, sickening, vile, repellent, unsavoury, obnoxious, unpalatable, objectionable, disagreeable, nauseating, odious, repugnant, loathsome, abominable, grotty *(slang)*, detestable, noisome, yucky *or* yukky *(slang)*, festy *(Austral slang)*, yucko *(Austral slang)*
OPPOSITE: pleasant
2 = insulting, rude, abusive, embarrassing, slighting, annoying, irritating, degrading, affronting, contemptuous, disparaging, displeasing, objectionable, disrespectful, scurrilous, detestable, discourteous, uncivil, unmannerly
OPPOSITE: respectful
3 = attacking, threatening, aggressive, striking, hostile, invading, combative
OPPOSITE: defensive
▷ *n* **5 = attack**, charge, campaign, strike, push *(informal)*, rush, assault, raid, drive, invasion, onslaught, foray, incursion

offer *vb* **2 = provide**, present, furnish, make available, afford, place at (someone's) disposal
OPPOSITE: withhold
4 = volunteer, come forward, offer your services, be at (someone's) service **5 = propose**, suggest, advance, extend, submit, put forward, put forth **6 = put up for sale**, sell, put on the market, put under the hammer **7 = bid**, submit, propose, extend, tender, proffer **9 = give**, show, bring, provide, render, impart ▷ *n* **10a = proposal**, suggestion, proposition, submission, attempt, endeavour, overture **10b = bid**, tender, bidding price

DICTIONARY

offering ❶ *n* **1** something that is offered **2** a contribution to the funds of a religious organization **3** a sacrifice to a god
offertory *n, pl* **-tories** *Christianity* **1** the part of a church service when the bread and wine for communion are offered for consecration **2** the collection of money at this service **3** the prayers said or sung while the worshippers' offerings are being brought to the altar
off-grid *adj* not involving or requiring the use of mainstream sources of energy
offhand *adj also* **offhanded** **1** curt or casual in manner: *I felt calm enough to adopt a casual offhand manner* ▷ *adv* **2** without preparation: *I don't know offhand why that should be so* **offhandedly** *adv* **offhandedness** *n*
Offiah *n* **Martin** born 1965, English Rugby League football player
office ❶ *n* **1** a room, set of rooms, or building in which business, professional duties, or clerical work are carried out **2** a department of an organization dealing with particular business: *cheque books were sent from the printer to the bank's sorting office* **3** the group of people working in an office: *she assured him that the office was running smoothly* **4** a government department or agency: *Office of Fair Trading* **5** a position of trust or authority, as in a government: *he would not seek a second term of office* **6** a place where tickets, information, or some service can be obtained: *why don't you give the ticket office a ring?* **7** *Christianity* a religious ceremony or service **8** **good offices** the help given by someone to someone else: *Syria's good offices finally led to the release of two western hostages* **9** **in** *or* **out of office** (of a government) in *or* out of power
WORD ORIGIN Latin *officium* service, duty
officer ❶ *n* **1** a person in the armed services, or on a non-naval ship, who holds a position of authority **2** a policeman or policewoman **3** a person holding a position of authority in a government or organization
official ❶ *adj* **1** of an office or position of authority: *I'm not here in any official capacity* **2** approved by or derived from authority: *there has been no official announcement* **3** formal or ceremonial: *he was speaking at an official dinner in Warsaw* ▷ *n* **4** a person holding a position of authority **officially** *adv*
officialdom *n* officials or bureaucrats collectively
officialese *n* language typical of official documents, esp. when wordy or pompous
Official Receiver *n Brit* an officer appointed by the government to deal with the affairs of a bankrupt person or company
officiate *vb* **-ating, -ated** **1** to perform the duties of an office; act in an official capacity: *the referee will officiate at the match* **2** to conduct a religious or other ceremony: *the priest officiated at the wedding* **officiation** *n* **officiator** *n*
officious *adj* offering unwanted advice or services; interfering **officiousness** *n*
WORD ORIGIN Latin *officiosus* kindly
offing *n* **1** the part of the sea that can be seen from the shore **2** **in the offing** *Brit, Austral & NZ* not far off; likely to occur soon
off key *adj music* **1** out of tune: *an off-key rendition* ▷ *adv* **2** out of tune: *he sings off key*
off-licence *n Brit* a shop or a counter in a shop where alcoholic drink is sold for drinking elsewhere
off-line *adj* (of computer equipment) not directly connected to or controlled by the central processing unit of a computer
off-load *vb* to get rid of (something unpleasant), usually by giving it to someone else: *you take all the credit and off-load all the blame*
off-peak *adj* (of services) used at times other than those of greatest demand
off-putting *adj informal* rather unpleasant or disturbing: *it can be very off-putting when you first visit a social security office*
off-road *adj* (of a motor vehicle) designed for use away from public roads
off-roader *n* a motor vehicle designed for use away from public roads
offset ❶ *vb* **-setting, -set** **1** to cancel out or compensate for **2** to print (something) using the offset process ▷ *n* **3** a printing method in which the impression is made onto a surface, such as a rubber roller, which transfers it to the paper **4** *bot* a short runner in certain plants that produces roots and shoots at the tip
offshoot *n* **1** a shoot growing from the main stem of a plant **2** something that has developed from something else
offshore *adj, adv* **1** away from or at some distance from the shore ▷ *adj* **2** sited or conducted at sea: *he reversed his position on offshore drilling*
offside *adj, adv* **1** *sport* (of a player) in a position illegally ahead of the ball when it is played ▷ *n* **2** *chiefly Brit* the side of a vehicle nearest the centre of the road
off spin *n cricket* a method of spin bowling delivery in which the ball spins from off to leg after bouncing **off-spinner** *n*
offspring ❶ *n* **1** the immediate descendant or descendants of a person or animal **2** a product, outcome, or result: *the women's liberation movement was the offspring of the 1960s*
off-the-peg *adj* (of clothing) ready to wear; not produced especially for the person buying

O

THESAURUS

offering *n* **2 = contribution**, gift, donation, present, subscription, hand-out, stipend, widow's mite **3 = sacrifice**, tribute, libation, burnt offering, oblation *(in religious contexts)*
office *n* **1 = place of work**, workplace, base, workroom, place of business **2 = branch**, department, division, section, wing, subdivision, subsection **5 = post**, place, role, work, business, service, charge, situation, commission, station, responsibility, duty, function, employment, capacity, appointment, occupation
officer *n* **2 = police officer**, detective, PC, police constable, police man, police woman **3 = official**, executive, agent, representative, bureaucrat, public servant, appointee, dignitary, functionary, office-holder, office bearer
official *adj* **1, 2 = authorized**, approved, formal, sanctioned, licensed, proper, endorsed, warranted, legitimate, authentic, ratified, certified, authoritative, accredited, bona fide, signed and sealed, ex officio, ex cathedra, straight from the horse's mouth *(informal)* **OPPOSITE:** unofficial **3 = formal**, prescribed, bureaucratic, ceremonial, solemn, ritualistic ▷ *n* **4 = officer**, executive, agent, representative, bureaucrat, public servant, appointee, dignitary, functionary, office-holder, office bearer
offset *vb* **1 = cancel out**, balance, set off, make up for, compensate for, redeem, counteract, neutralize, counterbalance, nullify, obviate, balance out, counterpoise, countervail
offspring *n* **1a = child**, baby, kid *(informal)*, youngster, infant, successor, babe, toddler, heir, issue, tot, descendant, wean *(Scot)*, little one, brat, bairn *(Scot)*, nipper *(informal)*, chit, scion, babe in arms *(informal)*, sprog *(slang)*, munchkin *(informal, chiefly US)*, rug rat *(slang)*, littlie *(Austral informal)*, ankle-biter *(Austral slang)*, tacker *(Austral slang)* **OPPOSITE:** parent **1b = children**, kids *(informal)*, young, family, issue, stock, seed *(chiefly biblical)*, fry, successors, heirs, spawn, descendants, brood, posterity, lineage, progeny, scions

DICTIONARY

Ofgem *n* (in Britain) Office of Gas and Electricity Markets: the body which regulates the power supply industries

Ofili *n* **Chris(topher)** born 1968, British painter, noted esp. for his brightly coloured collages using elephant dung: Turner Prize 1998

O'Flaherty *n* **Liam** 1897–1984, Irish novelist and short-story writer. His novels include *The Informer* (1925) and *Famine* (1937)

Oflot *n* (in Britain) Office of the National Lottery: the body which oversees the running of the National Lottery

Ofsted *n* (in Britain) Office for Standards in Education: the body which assesses the educational standards of schools in England and Wales

oft *adv old-fashioned or poetic* ▸ short for **often**
WORD ORIGIN Old English

often ❶ *adv* **1** frequently; much of the time **2 as often as not** quite frequently **3 every so often** occasionally **4 more often than not** in more than half the instances
WORD ORIGIN Middle English variant of *oft*

Ofwat *n* (in Britain) Office of Water Services: the body which regulates the activities of the water companies in England and Wales

Ogden *n* **C(harles) K(ay)** 1889–1957, English linguist, who, with I. A. Richards, devised Basic English

Ogdon *n* **John (Andrew Howard)** 1937–89, British pianist and composer

ogee arch (oh-jee) *n* a pointed arch made with an S-shaped curve on each side
WORD ORIGIN probably from Old French

ogle *vb* **ogling, ogled** to stare at (someone) lustfully
WORD ORIGIN probably from Low German *oegeln*

Oglethorpe *n* **James Edward** 1696–1785, English general and colonial administrator; founder of the colony of Georgia (1733)

O grade *n* **1** (formerly) the basic level of the Scottish Certificate of Education **2** a pass in a particular subject at O grade: *she has eight O grades*

ogre *n* **1** (in folklore) a man-eating giant **2** any monstrous or cruel person **ogreish** *adj* **ogress** *fem n*
WORD ORIGIN French

oh *interj* an exclamation of surprise, pain, pleasure, fear, or annoyance

OH Ohio

O. Henry *n* pen name of *William Sidney Porter*. 1862–1910, US short-story writer. His collections of stories, characterized by his use of caricature and surprising endings, include *Cabbages and Kings* (1904) and *The Four Million* (1906)

O'Higgins *n* **1 Ambrosio** ?1720–1801, Irish soldier, who became viceroy of Chile (1789–96) and of Peru (1796–1801) **2** his son, **Bernardo** 1778–1842, Chilean revolutionary. He was one of the leaders in the struggle for independence from Spain and was Chile's first president (1817–23)

Öhlenschläger *n* a variant spelling of **Oehlenschläger**

ohm *n* the SI unit of electrical resistance
WORD ORIGIN after Georg Simon *Ohm*, physicist

OHMS (in Britain and the Commonwealth) On Her (*or* His) Majesty's Service

oil ❶ *n* **1** any of a number of viscous liquids with a smooth sticky feel, which are usually flammable, insoluble in water, and are obtained from plants, animals, or mineral deposits by synthesis **2** ▸ same as **petroleum 3** a substance derived from petroleum and used for lubrication **4** *Brit* paraffin as a domestic fuel **5** oil colour or paint **6** an oil painting ▹ *vb* **7** to lubricate with oil or apply oil to **8 oil the wheels** to make things run smoothly
WORD ORIGIN Latin *oleum* (olive) oil

oilcloth *n* a cotton fabric treated with oil or a synthetic resin to make it waterproof, formerly used esp. for tablecloths

oilfield *n* an area containing reserves of oil

oilfired *adj* using oil as fuel

oil paint *n* a thick paint made of pigment ground in linseed oil

oil painting *n* **1** a picture painted with oil paints **2** the art of painting with oil paints

oil rig *n* a structure used as a base when drilling an oil well

oil-seed rape *n* ▸ same as **rape²**

oilskin *n* **1** a thick cotton fabric treated with oil to make it waterproof **2** a protective outer garment made of this fabric

oil slick *n* a mass of floating oil covering an area of water

oil well *n* a well bored into the earth or sea bed to a supply of oil

oily ❶ *adj* **oilier, oiliest 1** soaked or covered with oil **2** of, containing, or like oil **3** attempting to gain favour by insincere behaviour and flattery **oiliness** *n*

oink *n* the grunt of a pig or an imitation of this

ointment *n* a smooth greasy substance applied to the skin to heal or protect, or as a cosmetic: *home-made creams and ointments*
WORD ORIGIN Latin *unguentum* unguent

Oistrakh *n* **1 David** 1908–74, Russian violinist **2** his son, **Igor** born 1931, Russian violinist

OK Oklahoma

O.K. *or* **okay** ❶ *informal interj* **1** an expression of approval or agreement ▹ *adj* **2** in good or satisfactory condition ▹ *adv* **3** reasonably well or in a satisfactory manner ▹ *vb* **O.K.ing, O.K.ed 4** to approve or endorse ▹ *n, pl* **O.K.s 5** approval or agreement
WORD ORIGIN perhaps from *o(ll) k(orrect)*, jocular alteration of *all correct*

okapi (oh-kah-pee) *n, pl* **-pis** *or* **-pi** an African mammal related to the giraffe, but with a shorter neck, a reddish coat, and white stripes on the legs
WORD ORIGIN from a Central African word

okay *interj, adj, adv, vb, n* ▸ same as **O.K.**

O'Keeffe *n* **Georgia** 1887–1986, US painter, best known for her semiabstract still lifes, esp. of flowers: married the photographer Alfred Stieglitz

Okeghem *n* a variant spelling of **Ockeghem**

THESAURUS

often *adv* **1 = frequently**, much, generally, commonly, repeatedly, again and again, very often, oft (*archaic, poetic*), over and over again, time and again, habitually, time after time, customarily, oftentimes (*archaic*), not infrequently, many a time, ofttimes (*archaic*)
OPPOSITE: never

oil *n* **3 = lubricant**, grease, lubrication, fuel oil ▹ *vb* **7 = lubricate**, grease, make slippery

oily *adj* **1, 2 = greasy**, slick, slimy, fatty, slippery, oleaginous, smeary

O.K. *or* **okay** *sentence substitute* **1 = all right**, right, yes, agreed, very good, roger, very well, ya (*S African*), righto (*Brit informal*), okey-dokey (*informal*), chur (*NZ informal*), yebo (*S African informal*) ▹ *adj* **2a** (*informal*) **= all right**, fine, fitting, fair, in order, correct, approved, permitted, suitable, acceptable, convenient, allowable
OPPOSITE: unacceptable
2b = well, all right, safe, sound, healthy, hale, unharmed, uninjured, unimpaired ▹ *vb* **4 = approve**, allow, pass, agree to, permit, sanction, second, endorse, authorize, ratify, go along with, consent to, validate, countenance, give the go-ahead, rubber-stamp (*informal*), say yes to, give the green light, assent to, give the thumbs up (*informal*), concur in, give your consent to, give your blessing to ▹ *n* **5 = authorization**, agreement, sanction, licence, approval, go-ahead (*informal*), blessing, permission, consent, say-so

DICTIONARY

okra *n* a tall plant with long green pods that are used as food
WORD ORIGIN West African

Okri *n* **Ben** born 1959, Nigerian writer; his books include the Booker-prizewinning *The Famished Road* (1991), *Dangerous Love* (1996), and *In Arcadia* (2002)

Olaf I *or* **Olav I** *n* known as *Olaf Tryggvesson.* ?965–?1000 AD, king of Norway (995–?1000). He began the conversion of Norway to Christianity

Olaf II *or* **Olav II** *n* **Saint** 995–1030 AD, king of Norway (1015–28), who worked to complete the conversion of Norway to Christianity; deposed by Canute; patron saint of Norway. Feast day: July 29

Olaf V *or* **Olav V** *n* 1903–91, king of Norway 1957–91; son of Haakon VII

old ❶ *adj* **1** having lived or existed for a long time: *the old woman; burning witches is one old custom I've no desire to see revived* **2** of or relating to advanced years or a long life: *I twisted my knee as I tried to squat and cursed old age* **3** worn with age or use: *the old bathroom fittings* **4** having lived or existed for a specified period: *he is 60 years old* **5** the earlier or earliest of two or more things with the same name: *the old edition; the Old Testament* **6** designating the form of a language in which the earliest known records are written: *Old English* **7** familiar through long acquaintance or repetition: *an old acquaintance; the legalization argument is an old and familiar one* **8** dear: used as a term of affection or familiarity: *always rely on old Tom to turn out* **9** out of date; unfashionable **10** former or previous: *my old housekeeper lent me some money* **11** of long standing: *he's an old and respected member of staff* **12** **good old days** an earlier period of time regarded as better than the present ▷*n* **13** an earlier or past time: *in days of old* **oldish** *adj*
WORD ORIGIN Old English *eald*

old age pension *n* ▸a former name for **retirement pension** > **old age pensioner** *n*

Old Bailey *n* the Central Criminal Court of England

old boy *n* **1** a male ex-pupil of a school **2** *informal chiefly Brit* **a** a familiar form of address used to refer to a man **b** an old man

Oldcastle *n* Sir **John,** Baron Cobham. ?1378–1417, Lollard leader. In 1411 he led an English army in France but in 1413 he was condemned as a heretic and later hanged and burnt. He is thought to have been a model for Shakespeare's character Falstaff in *Henry IV*

old country *n* the country of origin of an immigrant or an immigrant's ancestors

olde *adj facetious* quaint
WORD ORIGIN from the former spelling of old

olden *adj archaic or poetic* old: *in the olden days the girls were married young*

Oldenbarneveldt *n* **Johan van.** 1547–1619, Dutch statesman, regarded as a founder of Dutch independence; the leading figure (from 1586) in the United Provinces of the Netherlands: executed by Maurice of Nassau

Oldenburg[1] *n* **1** a city in NW Germany, in Lower Saxony: former capital of Oldenburg state. Pop: 158 340 (2003 est) **2** a former state of NW Germany: became part of Lower Saxony in 1946

Oldenburg[2] *n* **Claes** born 1929, US pop sculptor and artist, born in Sweden

Old English *n* the English language of the Anglo-Saxons, spoken from the fifth century AD to about 1100. Also called: **Anglo-Saxon**

Old English sheepdog *n* a large sheepdog with thick shaggy hair

old-fashioned ❶ *adj* **1** in the style of a previous period; outdated: *she wore her hair in a strangely old-fashioned tight hairdo* **2** favouring or denoting the styles or ideas of a former time: *old-fashioned values*

Oldfield *n* **Bruce** born 1950, British fashion designer

old flame *n informal, old-fashioned* a person with whom one once had a romantic relationship

Old French *n* the French language in its earliest forms, from about the 9th century up to about 1400

old girl *n* **1** a female ex-pupil of a school **2** *informal chiefly Brit* **a** a familiar form of address used to refer to a woman **b** an old woman

old guard *n* a group of people in an organization who have traditional values: *the company's old guard is making way for a new, more youthful team*
WORD ORIGIN after Napoleon's imperial guard

old hand *n* a skilled or experienced person

old hat *adj* old-fashioned or dull

Old High German *n* a group of West Germanic dialects that developed into modern German; High German up to about 1200

old identity *n* NZ a well-known local person who has lived in an area for a long time

oldie *n informal* an old song, film, or person

old lady *n informal* one's mother or wife

old maid *n* **1** a woman regarded as unlikely ever to marry; spinster **2** *informal* a prim, fussy, or excessively cautious person

old man *n* **1** *informal* one's father **2** one's husband **3** an affectionate form of address used to a man

old master *n* **1** one of the great European painters of the period 1500 to 1800 **2** a painting by one of these

old moon *n* a phase of the moon between last quarter and new moon, when it appears as a waning crescent

Old Nick *n informal* Satan

old school *n* a group of people favouring traditional or conservative ideas or practices

old school tie *n* the system of mutual help supposed to operate among the former pupils of independent schools

Old Style *n* the former method of reckoning dates using the Julian calendar

Old Testament *n* the first part of the Christian Bible, containing the sacred Scriptures of the Hebrews

old-time *adj* of or relating to a former time; old-fashioned: *an old-time waltz*

old wives' tale *n* a belief, usually superstitious or foolish, passed on by word of mouth as a piece of traditional wisdom

old woman *n* **1** *informal* one's mother or wife **2** a timid, fussy, or cautious person **old-womanish** *adj*

Old World *n* that part of the world that was known to Europeans before the discovery of the Americas; the eastern hemisphere

old-world *adj* of or characteristic of former times; quaint or traditional

O

THESAURUS

(informal), confirmation, mandate, endorsement, green light, ratification, assent, seal of approval, approbation

old *adj* **1a = aged,** elderly, ancient, getting on, grey, mature, past it *(informal)*, venerable, patriarchal, grey-haired, antiquated, over the hill *(informal)*, senile, grizzled, decrepit, hoary, senescent, advanced in years, full of years, past your prime
OPPOSITE: young
1b = long-standing, established, fixed, enduring, abiding, long-lasting, long-established, time-honoured **5, 10 = former,** earlier, past, previous, prior, one-time, erstwhile, late, quondam, whilom *(archaic)*, ex-

old-fashioned *adj* **1 = out of date,** ancient, dated, outdated, unfashionable, antiquated, outmoded, passé, old hat, behind the times, fusty, out of style, démodé *(French)*, out of the ark *(informal)*, not with it *(informal)*, (old-)fogeyish
OPPOSITE: up-to-date
2 = oldfangled, square *(informal)*, outdated, old, past, dead, past it *(informal)*, obsolete, old-time, archaic, unfashionable, superannuated, obsolescent, out of the ark *(informal)*

DICTIONARY

oleaginous (oh-lee-**aj**-in-uss) *adj* like or producing oil; oily
WORD ORIGIN Latin *oleaginus*

oleander (oh-lee-**ann**-der) *n* an evergreen Mediterranean shrub with fragrant white, pink, or purple flowers
WORD ORIGIN Medieval Latin

O level *n* **1** (formerly, in Britain) the basic level of the General Certificate of Education **2** a pass in a particular subject at O level: *a very intelligent young woman with ten O levels*

olfactory *adj* of the sense of smell
WORD ORIGIN Latin *olere* to smell + *facere* to make

oligarchy (**ol**-lee-gark-ee) *n, pl* **-chies** **1** government by a small group of people **2** a state governed this way **3** a small group of people governing such a state **oligarchic** *or* **oligarchical** *adj*
WORD ORIGIN Greek *oligos* few + *arkhein* to rule

Oligocene (**ol**-lig-go-seen) *adj geol* of the epoch of geological time about 35 million years ago
WORD ORIGIN Greek *oligos* little + *kainos* new

oligopoly *n, pl* **-lies** *econ* a market situation in which control over the supply of a commodity is held by a small number of producers
WORD ORIGIN Greek *oligos* few + *pōlein* to sell

Oliphant *n* Sir **Mark Laurence Elwin** 1901–2000, British nuclear physicist, born in Australia

Olivares *n* **Conde-Duque de,** title of *Gaspar de Guzmán y Pimental*. 1587–1645, Spanish statesman: court favourite and prime minister (1621–43) of Philip IV. His attempts to establish Hapsburg domination of Europe ended in failure

olive *n* **1** an evergreen Mediterranean tree **2** the small green or black bitter-tasting fruit of this tree ▷ *adj* **3** ▸ short for **olive-green**
WORD ORIGIN Latin *oliva*

olive branch *n* a peace offering: *I should offer some kind of olive branch and get in touch with them*

olive-green *adj* deep yellowish-green

olive oil *n* a yellowish-green oil pressed from ripe olives and used in cooking and medicines

Oliver *n* **1** one of Charlemagne's 12 paladins ▸ See also **Roland** **2** **Isaac** ?1556–1617, English portrait miniaturist, born in France: he studied under Hilliard and worked at James I's court **3** **Jamie** (**Trevor**) born 1975, British chef and presenter of television cookery programmes **4** **Joseph,** known as *King Oliver.* 1885–1938, US pioneer jazz cornetist

oloroso (ol-ler-**roh**-so) *n* a golden-coloured sweet sherry
WORD ORIGIN Spanish: fragrant

Olsen *n* **Mary-Kate** and **Ashley** born 1986, US twin juvenile act who became famous sharing a role in the sitcom *Full House* (1987–95); now known for their videos, CDs, and numerous branded products

Olympiad *n* **1** a staging of the modern Olympic Games **2** an international contest in chess or other games

Olympian *adj* **1** of Mount Olympus or the classical Greek gods **2** majestic or godlike ▷ *n* **3** a competitor in the Olympic Games **4** a god of Mount Olympus

Olympic *adj* of the Olympic Games

Olympic Games *n* **1** an ancient Greek festival, held every fourth year in honour of Zeus, consisting of games and festivities **2** Also called: **the Olympics** the modern revival of these games, consisting of international athletic and sporting contests held every four years in a selected country

OM Order of Merit (a Brit. title)

Omar *or* **Umar** *n* died 644 AD, the second caliph of Islam (634–44). During his reign Islamic armies conquered Syria and Mesopotamia: murdered

ombudsman *n, pl* **-men** an official who investigates citizens' complaints against the government or its servants
WORD ORIGIN Swedish: commissioner

omega *n* **1** the 24th and last letter of the Greek alphabet (Ω, ω) **2** the ending or last of a series

omega-3 *n* an unsaturated fatty acid that occurs naturally in fish oil, valuable in reducing blood cholesterol

omelette *or esp. US* **omelet** *n* a dish of beaten eggs cooked in a flat pan and often folded round a savoury filling
WORD ORIGIN French

omen *n* **1** a thing or occurrence regarded as a sign of future happiness or disaster **2** prophetic significance: *birds of ill omen*
WORD ORIGIN Latin

OMG Oh my God!: used esp. in emails, text messages, etc.

ominous **T** *adj* warning of evil **ominously** *adv*
WORD ORIGIN Latin *ominosus*

omission **T** *n* **1** something that has been left out or passed over **2** an act of missing out or failing to do something: *we regret the omission of these and the names of the other fine artists*

omit **T** *vb* **omitting, omitted** **1** to fail to include; leave out **2** to fail (to do something)
WORD ORIGIN Latin *omittere*

omnibus *n, pl* **-buses** **1** a collection of works by one author or several works on a similar topic, reprinted in one volume **2** Also called: **omnibus edition** a television or radio programme consisting of two or more episodes of a serial broadcast earlier in the week **3** *old-fashioned* a bus ▷ *adj* **4** consisting of or dealing with several different things at once: *this year's version of an omnibus crime bill*
WORD ORIGIN Latin, literally: for all

omnipotent (om-**nip**-a-tent) *adj* having very great or unlimited power **omnipotence** *n*
WORD ORIGIN Latin *omnipotens* all-powerful

omnipresent *adj* (esp. of a god) present in all places at the same time **omnipresence** *n*
WORD ORIGIN Latin *omnis* all + *praesens* present

omniscient (om-**niss**-ee-ent) *adj formal* knowing or seeming to know everything **omniscience** *n*
WORD ORIGIN Latin *omnis* all + *scire* to know

omnivore (**om**-niv-vore) *n* an animal that eats any type of food

omnivorous (om-**niv**-or-uss) *adj* **1** eating any type of food **2** taking in everything indiscriminately: *his omnivorous sociability has meant constant hard work for his wife*
WORD ORIGIN Latin *omnivorus* all-devouring

on *prep* **1** in contact with or at the surface of: *let the cakes stand in the tins on a wire rack; she had dirt on her dress* **2** attached to: *a piece of paper on a clipboard* **3** carried with: *the message found on her* **4** near to or along the side of: *the hotel is on the coast* **5** within the time limits of (a day or date): *they returned to Moscow on 22nd September* **6** being performed upon or relayed through the medium of: *a construction of refined sounds played on special musical instruments; what's on television?* **7** at the

THESAURUS

ominous *adj* **= threatening,** menacing, sinister, dark, forbidding, grim, fateful, foreboding, unpromising, portentous, baleful, inauspicious, premonitory, unpropitious, minatory, bodeful
OPPOSITE: promising

omission *n* **1 = gap,** space, blank, exclusion, lacuna **2 = exclusion,** removal, leaving out, elimination, deletion, excision, noninclusion
OPPOSITE: inclusion

omit *vb* **1 = leave out,** miss (out), drop, exclude, eliminate, skip, give (something) a miss (*informal*)
OPPOSITE: include
2 = forget, fail, overlook, neglect, pass over, lose sight of, leave (something) undone, let (something) slide

once *adv* **1 = on one occasion,** one

DICTIONARY

occasion of: *she had received numerous letters congratulating her on her election* **8** immediately after or at the same time as: *check with the tourist office on arrival* **9** through the use of: *an extraordinarily vigorous man who thrives on physical activity; the program runs on the Unix operating system* **10** regularly taking (a drug): *she's on the pill* **11** by means of (a mode of transport): *his only way up the hill had to be on foot; they get around on bicycles* **12** in the process or course of: *he is away on a climbing expedition; coal miners have been on strike for six weeks* **13** concerned with or relating to: *ten million viewers watched the recent series on homelessness* **14** (of a statement or action) having as basis or grounds: *I have it on good authority* **15** charged to: *all drinks are on the house for the rest of the evening* **16** staked as a bet: *I'll have a bet on the favourite* ▷ *adv* **17** in operation; functioning: *the lights had been left on all night* **18** attached to, surrounding, or placed in contact with something: *they escaped with nothing on except sleeveless shirts and shorts* **19** taking place: *what do you have on tonight?* **20** continuously or persistently: *the crisis must not be allowed to drag on indefinitely* **21** forwards or further: *they trudged on* **22 on and off** occasionally; not regularly or continuously **23 on and on** without ceasing; continually ▷ *adj* **24** *informal* performing: *who's on next?* **25** *informal* definitely taking place: *is the party still on?* **26** *informal* tolerable, practicable, or acceptable: *I'm not going, that's just not on* **27 on at** *informal* nagging: *he was always on at her to stop smoking* ▷ *n* **28** *cricket* the side of the field to the left of a right-handed batsman when he is facing the bowler
WORD ORIGIN Old English *an, on*

ON Ontario

onager *n, pl* **-gri** *or* **-gers** a wild ass of Persia
WORD ORIGIN Greek *onagros*

onanism *n* **1** withdrawal in sexual intercourse before ejaculation **2** masturbation
WORD ORIGIN after *Onan*: see Genesis 38:9

ONC (in Britain) Ordinary National Certificate

once ❶ *adv* **1** one time; on one occasion only **2** at some past time, but no longer: *I was in love once* **3** by one degree (of relationship): *he was Deirdre's cousin once removed* **4 once and for all** conclusively; for the last time **5 once in a while** occasionally; now and then **6 once or twice** a few times **7 once upon a time** used to begin fairy tales and children's stories ▷ *conj* **8** as soon as: *once you have learned good grammar you can leave it to nature and forget it* ▷ *n* **9** one occasion or case: *once is enough* **10 all at once a** suddenly **b** simultaneously **11 at once a** immediately **b** simultaneously **12 for once** this time, even if at no other time
WORD ORIGIN Middle English *ones, anes*

once-over *n informal* a quick examination or appraisal

oncogene (ong-koh-jean) *n* a gene present in all cells, that when abnormally activated can cause cancer
WORD ORIGIN Greek *onkos* tumour + *-gen* (suffix) producing

oncoming *adj* coming nearer in space or time; approaching: *oncoming traffic*

OND (in Britain) Ordinary National Diploma

Ondaatje *n* **Michael** born 1943, Sri Lankan-born Canadian writer: his works include the poetry collection *There's a Trick with a Knife I'm Learning to Do* (1979), the Booker-prizewinning novel *The English Patient* (1992, filmed 1997), *Anil's Ghost* (2000), and *Divisadero* (2007)

one *adj, n* **1** single or lone (person or thing); not two or more: *one civilian has died and thirty-three have been injured* **2** only or unique (person or thing): *he is the one to make correct judgments and influence the public; she was unique, inimitable, one of a kind* **3** a specified (person or thing) as distinct from another or others of its kind: *place one hand under the knee and the other under the ankle; which one is correct?* **4 one or two** a few ▷ *adj* **5** a certain, indefinite, or unspecified (time): *one day he would learn the truth about her* **6** *informal, emphatic* a: *we're on to one hell of a story* ▷ *pron* **7** an indefinite person regarded as typical of every person: *one can always hope that there won't be an accident* **8** any indefinite person: *one can catch fine trout in this stream* **9** I or me: *one only wonders what he has against the dogs* ▷ *n* **10** the smallest natural number and first cardinal number **11** a numeral, 1 or I, representing this number **12** something representing or consisting of one unit **13** *informal* a joke or story: *have you heard the one about the actress and the bishop?* **14 (all) in one** combined or united **15 all one** of no consequence: *leave if you want to, it's all one to me* **16 at one with** in agreement or harmony with **17 one and all** everyone, without exception **18 one by one** one at a time; individually
WORD ORIGIN Old English *ān*

one another *pron* each other: *they seem to genuinely care for one another*

one-armed bandit *n informal* a fruit machine operated by pulling down a lever at one side

one-dimensional *adj* **1** having one dimension **2** completely lacking in depth or complexity: *the production staging is one-dimensional and the direction rigid*

one-horse *adj informal* small or insignificant: *a dusty one-horse town in the foothills of the Karakoram mountain range*

one-liner *n informal* a short joke or witty remark

oneness *n* **1** agreement **2** uniqueness **3** sameness

one-night stand *n* **1** *informal* a sexual encounter lasting only one evening or night **2** a performance given only once at any one place

one-off *n* something that happens or is made only once

onerous (own-er-uss) *adj* (of a task) difficult to carry out **onerousness** *n*
WORD ORIGIN Latin *onus* load

oneself *pron* **1** the reflexive form of *one* **2** one's normal or usual self: *one doesn't feel oneself after such an experience*

one-sided ❶ *adj* **1** considering or favouring only one side of a matter: *a one-sided version of events* **2** having all the advantage on one side: *it was a one-sided match with Brazil missing a succession of chances*

one-stop *adj* having or providing a range of services or goods in one place: *one-stop shopping*

One Thousand Guineas *n* **the One Thousand Guineas** an annual horse race for three-year-old fillies, run at Newmarket

one-time *adj* at some time in the past; former

one-to-one *adj* **1** (of two or more things) corresponding exactly **2** denoting a relationship or encounter in which someone is involved with only one other person: *one-to-one meetings* **3** *maths* involving the pairing of each member of one set with only one member of another set, without remainder

one-track *adj informal* obsessed with one idea or subject: *she's got a one-track mind*

one-up *adj informal* having an advantage or lead over someone else **one-upmanship** *n*

O

THESAURUS

time, one single time **2 = at one time**, in the past, previously, formerly, long ago, in the old days, once upon a time, in times past, in times gone by ▷ *conj* **8 = as soon as**, when, after, the moment, immediately, the instant

one-sided *adj* **1 = biased**, prejudiced, weighted, twisted, coloured, unfair, partial, distorted, partisan, warped, slanted, unjust, discriminatory, lopsided **OPPOSITE:** unbiased **2 = unequal**, unfair, uneven, unjust, unbalanced, lopsided, inequitable, ill-matched **OPPOSITE:** equal

DICTIONARY

one-way *adj* **1** moving or allowing travel in one direction only: *the town centre has a baffling one-way system* **2** involving no reciprocal obligation or action: *he does not get anything back out of the one-way relationship*

ongoing ⊕ *adj* in progress; continuing: *there are still ongoing discussions about the future role of NATO*

onion *n* **1** a vegetable with an edible bulb with a strong smell and taste **2 know one's onions** *Brit & NZ slang* to be fully acquainted with a subject **oniony** *adj*
WORD ORIGIN Latin *unio*

Onions *n* **Charles Talbut** 1873–1965, English lexicographer; an editor of the *Oxford English Dictionary*

on-line *or* **online** *adj* **1** (of computer equipment) directly connected to and controlled by the central processing unit of a computer **2** of or relating to the internet: *online shopping*

onlooker ⊕ *n* a person who observes without taking part **onlooking** *adj*

only ⊕ *adj* **1** alone of its or their kind: *I will be talking to the only journalist to have been inside the prison* **2** (of a child) having no brothers or sisters **3** unique by virtue of superiority; best: *first class is the only way to travel* **4 one and only** incomparable: *the one and only Diana Ross* ▷ *adv* **5** without anyone or anything else being included; alone: *only you can decide if you can abide by this compromise* **6** merely or just: *it's only Henry* **7** no more or no greater than: *I was talking to a priest only a minute ago* **8** merely: *they had only to turn up to win the competition* **9** not earlier than; not until: *I've only found out today why you wouldn't come* **10 if only** *or* **if ... only** used to introduce a wish or hope **11 only too** extremely: *they were only too willing to do anything to help* ▷ *conj* **12** but or however: *those countries are going through the same cycle, only a little later than us*
WORD ORIGIN Old English *ānlīc*

o.n.o. or near(est) offer

onomatopoeia (on-a-mat-a-pee-a) *n* use of a word which imitates the sound it represents, such as *hiss* **onomatopoeic** *or* **onomatopoetic** *adj*
WORD ORIGIN Greek *onoma* name + *poiein* to make

onrush *n* a forceful forward rush or flow; surge

onset ⊕ *n* a start; beginning

onshore *adj, adv* **1** towards the land: *a stiff onshore wind* **2** on land; not at sea

onside *adj, adv sport* (of a player) in a legal position, for example, behind the ball or with a required number of opponents between oneself and the opposing team's goal line

onslaught ⊕ *n* a violent attack
WORD ORIGIN Middle Dutch *aenslag*

Ont. Ontario

onto *or* **on to** *prep* **1** to a position that is on: *step onto the train* **2** having discovered or become aware of: *the police are onto us* **3** into contact with: *get onto the factory*

ontology *n philosophy* the study of the nature of being **ontological** *adj*
WORD ORIGIN Greek *ōn* being + -LOGY

onus (own-uss) *n, pl* **onuses** a responsibility, task, or burden: *the courts put the onus on parents*
WORD ORIGIN Latin: burden

onward ⊕ *adj* **1** directed or moving forward ▷ *adv also* **onwards** **2** continuing; progressing

onyx *n* a kind of quartz with alternating coloured layers, used as a gemstone
WORD ORIGIN Greek: fingernail (so called from its veined appearance)

oodles *pl n informal* great quantities: *he has shown he can raise oodles of cash*
WORD ORIGIN origin unknown

oolite (oh-a-lite) *n* a limestone made up of tiny grains of calcium carbonate **oolitic** *adj*
WORD ORIGIN New Latin *oolites*, literally: egg stone

oom *n S African* a title of respect used to refer to an elderly man
WORD ORIGIN Afrikaans, literally: uncle

oomiak *or* **oomiac** *n* ▸ same as **umiak**

oompah *n* a representation of the sound made by a deep brass instrument, esp. in brass band music

oomph *n informal* enthusiasm, vigour, or energy
WORD ORIGIN origin unknown

oops *interj* an exclamation of surprise or of apology when someone has a slight accident or makes a mistake

OOS occupational overuse syndrome: pain caused by repeated awkward movements while at work

ooze[1] ⊕ *vb* **oozing, oozed** **1** to flow or leak out slowly; seep **2** (of a substance) to discharge moisture **3** to overflow with (a feeling or quality): *he oozes confidence* ▷ *n* **4** a slow flowing or leaking **oozy** *adj*
WORD ORIGIN Old English *wōs* juice

ooze[2] ⊕ *n* a soft thin mud, such as that found at the bottom of a lake, river, or sea
WORD ORIGIN Old English *wāse* mud

op. opus

opacity (ohp-ass-it-tee) *n, pl* **-ties** **1** the state or quality of being opaque **2** the quality of being difficult to understand; unintelligibility

opal *n* a precious stone, usually milky or bluish in colour, with shimmering changing reflections
WORD ORIGIN Greek *opallios*

opalescent *adj* having shimmering changing reflections, like opal **opalescence** *n*

opaque *adj* **1** not able to be seen through; not transparent or translucent **2** hard to understand; unintelligible
WORD ORIGIN Latin *opacus* shady

op. cit. (op sit) (in textual annotations) in the work cited
WORD ORIGIN Latin *opere citato*

OPEC Organization of Petroleum-Exporting Countries

open ⊕ *adj* **1** not closed, fastened, or blocked up: *the doctor's office was open* **2** not enclosed, covered, or wrapped: *the parcel was open* **3** extended, expanded, or unfolded: *an open flower* **4** ready for business: *some of the crafts rooms and photography shops are open all night* **5** (of a job) available: *all the positions on the council should be open to*

O

THESAURUS

ongoing *adj* **= in progress**, current, growing, developing, advancing, progressing, evolving, unfolding, unfinished, extant

onlooker *n* **= spectator**, witness, observer, viewer, looker-on, watcher, eyewitness, bystander

only *adj* **1 = sole**, one, single, individual, exclusive, unique, lone, solitary, one and only ▷ *adv* **6, 8 = just**, simply, purely, merely, no more than, nothing but, but, at most, at a push **7 = hardly**, just, barely, only just, scarcely, at most, at a push

onset *n* **= beginning**, start, rise, birth, kick-off (*informal*), outbreak, starting point, inception, commencement
OPPOSITE: end

onslaught *n* **= attack**, charge, campaign, strike, rush, assault, raid, invasion, offensive, blitz, onset, foray, incursion, onrush, inroad
OPPOSITE: retreat

onward *or* **onwards** *adv* **2 = forward**, on, forwards, ahead, beyond, in front, forth

ooze[1] *vb* **1 = seep**, well, drop, escape, strain, leak, drain, sweat, filter, bleed, weep, drip, trickle, leach, dribble, percolate **2 = emit**, release, leak, sweat, bleed, discharge, drip, leach, give out, dribble, exude, give off, excrete, overflow with, pour forth **3 = exude**, emit, radiate, display, exhibit, manifest, emanate, overflow with

ooze[2] *n* **= mud**, clay, dirt, muck, silt, sludge, mire, slime, slob (*Irish*), gloop (*informal*), alluvium

open *adj* **1 = unclosed**, unlocked, ajar, unfastened, yawning, gaping, unlatched, unbolted, partly open, unbarred, off the latch
OPPOSITE: closed
2 = unsealed, unstoppered
OPPOSITE: unopened
3 = extended, expanded, unfolded,

females **6** unobstructed by buildings or trees: *we lived in a small market town surrounded by open countryside* **7** free to all to join in, enter, or use: *there was an open competition and I was appointed* **8** (of a season or period) not restricted for purposes of hunting game of various kinds **9** not decided or finalized: *the legality of these sales is still an open question* **10** ready to consider new ideas: *I was able to approach their problem with an open mind* **11** honest and frank **12** generous: *she has given me love and the open hand* **13** exposed to view; blatant: *there has never been such sustained and open criticism of the President* **14** unprotected; susceptible: *a change of policy which would leave vulnerable youths open to exploitation* **15** having spaces or gaps: *open ranks; an open texture* **16** *computers* designed to an internationally agreed standard to allow communication between computers irrespective of size or manufacturer **17** *music* **a** (of a string) not stopped with the finger **b** (of a note) played on such a string **18** *sport* (of a goal or court) unguarded or relatively unprotected **19** (of a wound) exposed to the air ▷ *vb* **20** to make or become open: *it was easy to open the back door and to slip noiselessly outside; she knelt and tried to open the drawer* **21** to set or be set in action; start: *the US will have to open talks on Palestinian rights; I want to open a dress shop* **22** to arrange for (a bank account), usually by making an initial deposit **23** to declare open ceremonially or officially ▷ *n* **24** *sport* a competition which anyone may enter **25 the open** any wide or unobstructed area **opener** *n* **openly** *adv* **openness** *n*

WORD ORIGIN Old English

open air *n* the place or space where the air is unenclosed; outdoors

open-and-shut *adj* easily decided or solved; obvious: *an open-and-shut case*

opencast mining *n* mining by excavating from the surface

WORD ORIGIN *open* + archaic *cast* ditch, cutting

open day *n* a special occasion on which a school, university, or other institution is open for the public to visit

open-ended *adj* **1** without definite limits; unrestricted: *the schedule is open-ended* **2** (of an activity) done without the aim of attaining a particular result or decision: *the dangers of open-ended military involvement*

open-eyed *adj* **1** with the eyes wide open, as in amazement **2** watchful; alert

open-handed *adj* generous

open-hearted *adj* **1** kind or generous **2** willing to speak one's mind; candid

open-heart surgery *n* surgical repair of the heart during which the heart is exposed and the blood circulation is maintained mechanically

open house *n* a situation in which people allow friends or visitors to come to their house whenever they want to

opening ● *n* **1** the beginning or first part of something **2** the first performance of a theatrical production **3** a chance or opportunity: *an opening into show business* **4** a hole or gap

opening time *n Austral & Brit* the time at which public houses can legally open for business

open letter *n* a letter, esp. one of protest, addressed to an individual but published in a newspaper or magazine for all to read

open market *n* a process by which prices are decided by supply and demand and goods are sold anywhere

open-minded ● *adj* willing to consider new ideas; unprejudiced

open-mouthed *adj* gaping in surprise

open-plan *adj* having no or few dividing walls between areas: *the house includes an open-plan living room and dining area*

open prison *n* a prison in which the prisoners are not locked up, thus extending the range of work they can do

open secret *n* something that is supposed to be secret but is widely known

open source *n* **1** intellectual property, esp. computer source code, made freely available to the public by its creators ▷ *adj* **2** relating to this code: *open-source software*

open-standard *adj* (of computer programs, codes, etc.) freely available to all users

Open University *n* (in Britain) a university teaching by means of television and radio lectures, correspondence courses, and summer schools

open up *vb* **1** to make or become accessible: *the Berlin Wall came down and opened up new territory for dramatists* **2** to speak freely or without self-restraint **3** to start firing a gun or guns **4** *informal* to increase the speed of (a vehicle)

open verdict *n* a finding by a coroner's jury of death without stating the cause

O

stretched out, spread out, unfurled, straightened out, unrolled
OPPOSITE: shut
5 = vacant, free, available, empty, up for grabs *(informal)*, unoccupied, unfilled, unengaged **6 = clear**, free, passable, uncluttered, unhindered, unimpeded, navigable, unobstructed, unhampered
OPPOSITE: obstructed
7 = general, public, free, catholic, broad, universal, blanket, unconditional, across-the-board, unqualified, all-inclusive, unrestricted, overarching, free to all, nondiscriminatory, one-size-fits-all
OPPOSITE: restricted
9 = unresolved, unsettled, undecided, debatable, up in the air, moot, arguable, yet to be decided
10 = receptive, welcoming, sympathetic, responsive, amenable
11 = frank, direct, natural, plain, innocent, straightforward, sincere, transparent, honest, candid, truthful, upfront *(informal)*, plain-spoken, above board, unreserved, artless, ingenuous, guileless, straight from the shoulder *(informal)*
OPPOSITE: sly
▷ *vb* **20a = unfasten**, unlock, unclasp, throw wide, unbar, unclose
OPPOSITE: close
20b = unwrap, uncover, undo, unravel, untie, unstrap, unseal, unlace **OPPOSITE:** wrap
20c = uncork, crack (open)
20d = unfold, spread (out), expand, stretch out, unfurl, unroll
OPPOSITE: fold
20e = clear, unblock **OPPOSITE:** block
20f = undo, loosen, unbutton, unfasten **OPPOSITE:** fasten
21a = start, begin, launch, trigger, kick off *(informal)*, initiate, commence, get going, instigate, kick-start, inaugurate, set in motion, get (something) off the ground *(informal)*, enter upon **OPPOSITE:** end
21b = begin, start, commence
OPPOSITE: end

opening *n* **1 = beginning**, start, launch, launching, birth, dawn, outset, starting point, onset, overture, initiation, inauguration, inception, commencement, kickoff *(informal)*, opening move
OPPOSITE: ending
3 = opportunity, chance, break *(informal)*, time, place, moment, window, occasion, look-in *(informal)*
4 = hole, break, space, tear, split, crack, gap, rent, breach, slot, outlet, vent, puncture, rupture, aperture, cleft, chink, fissure, orifice, perforation, interstice
OPPOSITE: blockage

open-minded *adj* **= unprejudiced**, liberal, free, balanced, catholic, broad, objective, reasonable, enlightened, tolerant, impartial, receptive, unbiased, even-handed, dispassionate, fair-minded, broad-minded, undogmatic
OPPOSITE: narrow-minded

DICTIONARY

opera[1] *n* **1** a dramatic work in which most or all of the text is sung to orchestral accompaniment **2** the branch of music or drama relating to operas **3** a group that produces or performs operas **4** a theatre where opera is performed
WORD ORIGIN Latin: work

opera[2] *n* ▸ a plural of **opus**

operable *adj* **1** capable of being treated by a surgical operation **2** capable of being operated or put into practice **operability** *n*

opera glasses *pl n* small low-powered binoculars used by audiences in theatres

opera house *n* a theatre specially designed for the performance of operas

operand *n maths* a quantity, variable, or function upon which an operation is performed

operate T *vb* **-ating, -ated 1** to work **2** to control the working of (a machine) **3** to manage, direct, or run (a business or system) **4** to perform a surgical operation (upon a person or animal) **5** to conduct military or naval operations
WORD ORIGIN Latin *operari* to work

operatic *adj* **1** of or relating to opera **2** overdramatic or exaggerated: *he was about to go out with his operatic strut*

operating system *n* the software controlling a computer

operating theatre *or US* **room** *n* a room in which surgical operations are performed

operation T *n* **1** the act or method of operating **2** the condition of being in action: *there are twenty teleworking centres in operation around the country* **3** an action or series of actions done to produce a particular result: *a large-scale police operation has been in place to manage the heavy traffic* **4** *surgery* a surgical procedure carried out to remove, replace, or repair a diseased or damaged part of the body **5** a military or naval manoeuvre **6** *maths* any procedure, such as addition, in which a number is derived from another number or numbers by applying specific rules

operational T *adj* **1** in working order and ready for use **2** of or relating to an action done to produce a particular result

operations research *n* the analysis of problems in business and industry. Also called: **operational research**

operative T (op-rat-tiv) *adj* **1** in force, effect, or operation: *these pension provisions became operative from 1978* **2** (of a word) particularly relevant or significant: *'if' is the operative word* **3** of or relating to a surgical operation ▷ *n* **4** a worker with a special skill

operator T *n* **1** a person who operates a machine or instrument, esp. a telephone switchboard **2** a person who runs a business: *your tour operator will arrange a visa for you* **3** *informal* a person who manipulates affairs and other people: *she considered him a shrewd operator who only liked to appear to be simple* **4** *maths* any symbol, term, or letter used to indicate or express a specific operation or process

operculum (oh-perk-yew-lum) *n, pl* **-la** (-la) *or* **-lums** a covering flap or lidlike structure in animals or plants
WORD ORIGIN Latin: lid

operetta *n* a type of comic or light-hearted opera

ophthalmia *n* inflammation of the eyeball or conjunctiva
WORD ORIGIN Greek *ophthalmos* eye

ophthalmic *adj* of or relating to the eye

ophthalmic optician *n* ▸ see **optician** (sense 1)

ophthalmology *n* the branch of medicine concerned with the eye and its diseases **ophthalmologist** *n*

ophthalmoscope *n* an instrument for examining the interior of the eye

Ophüls *n* **Max** (maks) 1902–57, German film director, whose films include *Liebelei* (1932), *La Signora di tutti* (1934), *La Ronde* (1950), *Le Plaisir* (1952), and *Lola Montes* (1955)

opiate (oh-pee-ate) *n* **1** a narcotic or sedative drug containing opium **2** something that causes mental dullness or inactivity

opine *vb* **opining, opined** *formal* to hold or express an opinion: *he opined that the navy would have to start again from the beginning*
WORD ORIGIN Latin *opinari*

opinion T *n* **1** belief not founded on certainty or proof but on what seems probable **2** evaluation or estimation of a person or thing: *they seemed to share my high opinion of her* **3** a judgment given by an expert: *medical opinion* **4 a matter of opinion** a point open to question
WORD ORIGIN Latin *opinio* belief

opinionated *adj* holding very strong opinions which one is convinced are right

opinion poll *n* ▸ same as **poll** (sense 1)

opium (oh-pee-um) *n* an addictive narcotic drug made from the seed capsules of the opium poppy and used in medicine as a painkiller and sedative
WORD ORIGIN Latin: poppy juice

opossum *n, pl* **-sums** *or* **-sum 1** a thick-furred American marsupial, with a long snout and a hairless prehensile tail **2** *Austral & NZ* a similar Australian animal, such as a phalanger
WORD ORIGIN Native American *aposoum*

opponent T *n* a person who opposes another in a contest, battle, or argument
WORD ORIGIN Latin *opponere* to oppose

opportune *adj formal* **1** happening at a time that is suitable or advantageous: *there was an opportune knock at the door* **2** (of time) suitable for a particular purpose: *I have arrived at a very opportune moment*
WORD ORIGIN Latin *opportunus*, from *ob-* to + *portus* harbour (originally: coming to the harbour, obtaining timely protection)

opportunist *n* **1** a person who adapts his or her actions to take advantage of opportunities and circumstances without regard for principles ▷ *adj* **2** taking advantage of opportunities and circumstances in this way **opportunism** *n* **opportunistic** *adj*

O

THESAURUS

operate *vb* **1a = function**, work, act, be in business, be in action **1b = work**, go, run, perform, function **OPPOSITE:** break down **2 = run**, work, use, control, drive, manoeuvre **3 = manage**, run, direct, handle, govern, oversee, supervise, preside over, be in charge of, call the shots in, superintend, call the tune in

operation *n* **1 = performance**, working, running, action, movement, functioning, motion, manipulation

operational *adj* **1 = working**, going, running, ready, functioning, operative, viable, functional, up and running, workable, usable, in working order **OPPOSITE:** inoperative

operative *adj* **1 = in force**, current, effective, standing, functioning, active, efficient, in effect, in business, operational, functional, in operation, workable, serviceable **OPPOSITE:** inoperative ▷ *n* **4 = worker**, hand, employee, mechanic, labourer, workman, artisan, machinist, working man *or* working woman

operator *n* **1 = worker**, hand, driver, mechanic, operative, conductor, technician, handler, skilled employee

opinion *n* **1 = belief**, feeling, view, idea, theory, notion, conviction, point of view, sentiment, viewpoint, persuasion, conjecture **2, 3 = estimation**, view, impression, assessment, judgment, evaluation, conception, appraisal, considered opinion

opponent *n* **a = adversary**, rival, enemy, the opposition, competitor, challenger, foe, contestant, antagonist **OPPOSITE:** ally **b = opposer**, dissident, objector, dissentient, disputant **OPPOSITE:** supporter

DICTIONARY

opportunity ❶ *n, pl* **-ties 1** a favourable combination of circumstances **2** a good chance or prospect
opportunity shop *n Austral & NZ* a shop selling second-hand clothes, sometimes for charity. Sometimes shortened to: **op-shop**
opposable *adj zool* (of the thumb) capable of touching the tip of all the other fingers
oppose ❶ *vb* **-posing, -posed 1** Also: **be opposed to** to be against (something or someone) in speech or action **2 as opposed to** in strong contrast with: *I'm a realist as opposed to a theorist* **opposing** *adj*
WORD ORIGIN Latin *opponere*
opposite ❶ *adj* **1** situated on the other or further side **2** facing or going in contrary directions: *he saw another small craft heading the opposite way* **3** completely different: *I have a different, in fact, opposite view on this subject* **4** *maths* (of a side in a triangle) facing a specified angle ▷*n* **5** a person or thing that is opposite; antithesis ▷*prep* **6** facing; across from ▷*adv* **7** in an opposite position: *fragments smashed through the windows of the house opposite*
opposite number *n* a person holding an equivalent position in another group or organization: *a ritual exchange of insults with an opposite number*
opposition ❶ *n* **1** the act of opposing or being opposed **2** hostility, resistance, or disagreement **3** a person or group antagonistic or opposed to another **4** a political party or group opposed to the ruling party or government **5** *astrol* a diametrically opposite position of two heavenly bodies
oppress ❶ *vb* **1** to put down or control by cruelty or force **2** to make anxious or uncomfortable
oppression *n* **oppressor** *n*
WORD ORIGIN Latin *ob-* against + *premere* to press
oppressive ❶ *adj* **1** cruel, harsh, or tyrannical **2** uncomfortable or depressing: *a small flat can become rather oppressive* **3** (of weather) hot and humid **oppressiveness** *n*
opprobrium (op-probe-ree-um) *n formal* **1** the state of being abused or scornfully criticized **2** a cause of disgrace or shame **opprobrious** *adj*
WORD ORIGIN Latin *ob-* against + *probrum* a shameful act
oppugn (op-pewn) *vb formal* to call into question; dispute
WORD ORIGIN Latin *ob-* against + *pugnare* to fight
op-shop *n Austral & NZ* ▸ short for **opportunity shop**
opt ❶ *vb* to show preference (for) or choose (to do something)
WORD ORIGIN Latin *optare* to choose
optic *adj* of the eye or vision
WORD ORIGIN Greek *optos* visible
optical *adj* **1** of or involving light or optics **2** of the eye or the sense of sight; optic **3** (of a lens) helping vision
optical fibre *n* a thin flexible glass fibre used in fibre optics to transmit information
optician *n* **1** Also called: **ophthalmic optician** a person who is qualified to examine the eyes and prescribe and supply spectacles and contact lenses **2** Also called: **dispensing optician** a person who supplies and fits spectacle frames and lenses, but is not qualified to prescribe lenses
optic nerve *n* a cranial nerve of vertebrates that conducts nerve impulses from the retina of the eye to the brain
optics *n* the science dealing with light and vision
optimal *adj* best or most favourable
optimism *n* **1** the tendency to take the most hopeful view in all matters **2** *philosophy* the doctrine of the ultimate triumph of good over evil
optimist *n* **optimistic** *adj* **optimistically** *adv*
WORD ORIGIN Latin *optimus* best
optimize *or* **-mise** *vb* **-mizing, -mized** *or* **-mising, -mised** to make the most of
optimum ❶ *n, pl* **-ma** *or* **-mums 1** the most favourable conditions or best compromise possible ▷*adj* **2** most favourable or advantageous; best: *balance is a critical part of an optimum diet*
WORD ORIGIN Latin: the best (thing)
option ❶ *n* **1** the power or liberty to choose: *we have no option other than to fully comply* **2** something that is or may be chosen: *the menu includes a vegetarian option* **3** an exclusive right, usually for a limited period, to buy or sell something at a future date: *a producer could extend his option on the material for another six months* **4 keep** *or* **leave one's options open** not to

THESAURUS

opportunity *n* **2 = chance**, opening, time, turn, hour, break *(informal)*, moment, window, possibility, occasion, slot, scope, look-in *(informal)*
oppose *vb* **1 = be against**, fight (against), check, bar, block, prevent, take on, counter, contest, resist, confront, face, combat, defy, thwart, contradict, withstand, stand up to, hinder, struggle against, obstruct, fly in the face of, take issue with, be hostile to, counterattack, speak (out) against, be in opposition to, be in defiance of, strive against, set your face against, take *or* make a stand against **OPPOSITE:** support
opposite *adj* **1, 2 = facing**, other, opposing **3 = different**, conflicting, opposed, contrasted, contrasting, unlike, differing, contrary, diverse, adverse, at odds, contradictory, inconsistent, dissimilar, divergent, irreconcilable, at variance, poles apart, diametrically opposed, antithetical, streets apart **OPPOSITE:** alike
▷*n* **5 = reverse**, contrary, converse, antithesis, the other extreme, contradiction, inverse, the other side of the coin *(informal)*, obverse
▷*prep* **6** *(often with* **to***)* **= facing**, face to face with, across from, eyeball to eyeball with *(informal)*
opposition *n* **2 = hostility**, resistance, resentment, disapproval, obstruction, animosity, aversion, antagonism, antipathy, obstructiveness, counteraction, contrariety **OPPOSITE:** support
3 = opponent(s), competition, rival(s), enemy, competitor(s), other side, challenger(s), foe, contestant(s), antagonist(s)
oppress *vb* **1 = subjugate**, abuse, suppress, wrong, master, overcome, crush, overwhelm, put down, subdue, overpower, persecute, rule over, enslave, maltreat, hold sway over, trample underfoot, bring someone to heel, tyrannize over, rule with an iron hand, bring someone under the yoke **OPPOSITE:** liberate
2 = depress, burden, discourage, torment, daunt, harass, afflict, sadden, vex, weigh down, dishearten, cast someone down, dispirit, take the heart out of, deject, lie *or* weigh heavy upon, make someone despondent
oppressive *adj* **1 = tyrannical**, severe, harsh, heavy, overwhelming, cruel, brutal, authoritarian, unjust, repressive, Draconian, autocratic, inhuman, dictatorial, coercive, imperious, domineering, overbearing, burdensome, despotic, high-handed, peremptory, overweening, tyrannous **OPPOSITE:** merciful
3 = stifling, close, heavy, sticky, overpowering, suffocating, stuffy, humid, torrid, sultry, airless, muggy
opt *vb* **= choose**, decide, prefer, select, elect, see fit, make a selection **OPPOSITE:** reject
optimum *adj* **2 = ideal**, best, highest, finest, choicest, perfect, supreme, peak, outstanding, first-class, foremost, first-rate, flawless, superlative, pre-eminent, most excellent, A1 *or* A-one *(informal)*, most favourable *or* advantageous **OPPOSITE:** worst
option *n* **1 = choice**, alternative, selection, preference, freedom of choice, power to choose, election

DICTIONARY

commit oneself **5** **soft option** an easy alternative ▷ *vb* **6** to obtain or grant an option on: *the film rights are optioned by an international film director*
WORD ORIGIN Latin *optare* to choose

optional ⓣ *adj* possible but not compulsory; open to choice

optometrist (op-**tom**-met-trist) *n* a person qualified to examine the eyes and prescribe and supply spectacles and contact lenses **optometry** *n*

opt out *vb* **1** (often foll. by *of*) to choose not to be involved (in) or part (of), used esp. of schools and hospitals that leave the public sector ▷ *n* **opt-out** **2** the act of opting out, esp. of a local authority administration

opulent (**op**-pew-lent) *adj* **1** having or indicating wealth **2** abundant or plentiful **opulence** *n*
WORD ORIGIN Latin *opulens*

opus ⓣ (**oh**-puss) *n, pl* **opuses** *or* **opera** an artistic creation, esp. a musical work by a particular composer, numbered in order of publication: *Beethoven's opus 61*
WORD ORIGIN Latin: a work

or *conj* **1** used to join alternatives: *do you want to go out or stay at home?* **2** used to join rephrasings of the same thing: *twelve, or a dozen*
WORD ORIGIN Middle English contraction of *other*

OR Oregon

oracle *n* **1** a shrine in ancient Greece or Rome at which gods were consulted through the medium of a priest or priestess for advice or prophecy **2** a prophecy or statement made by an oracle **3** any person believed to indicate future action with infallible authority
WORD ORIGIN Latin *oraculum*

oracular *adj* **1** of or like an oracle **2** wise and prophetic **3** mysterious or ambiguous

oral ⓣ *adj* **1** spoken or verbal; using spoken words **2** of or for use in the mouth: *an oral thermometer* **3** (of a drug) to be taken by mouth: *an oral contraceptive* ▷ *n* **4** an examination in which the questions and answers are spoken rather than written **orally** *adv*
WORD ORIGIN Latin *os, oris* mouth

orange *n* **1** a round reddish-yellow juicy citrus fruit **2** the evergreen tree on which it grows **3** a colour between red and yellow; the colour of an orange ▷ *adj* **4** of a colour between red and yellow
WORD ORIGIN Arabic *nāranj*

orangeade *n Brit* a usually fizzy orange-flavoured drink

orange blossom *n* the flowers of the orange tree, traditionally worn by brides

Orangeman *n, pl* **-men** a member of a political society founded in Ireland in 1795 to uphold Protestantism
WORD ORIGIN after William, prince of *Orange*, later William III

orangery *n, pl* **-eries** a conservatory or greenhouse in which orange trees are grown in cooler climates

orangey *adj* slightly orange

orang-utan *or* **orang-utang** *n* a large ape of the forests of Sumatra and Borneo, with shaggy reddish-brown hair and long arms
WORD ORIGIN Malay *ōrang* man + *hūtan* forest

oration *n* a formal or ceremonial public speech
WORD ORIGIN Latin *oratio*

orator (**or**-rat-tor) *n* a person who gives an oration, esp. one skilled in persuasive public speaking

oratorio (or-rat-**tor**-ee-oh) *n, pl* **-rios** a musical composition for soloists, chorus, and orchestra, based on a religious theme
WORD ORIGIN Italian

oratory[1] (**or**-rat-tree) *n* the art or skill of public speaking
WORD ORIGIN Latin *(ars) oratoria* (the art of) public speaking

oratory[2] *n, pl* **-ries** a small room or building set apart for private prayer
WORD ORIGIN Latin *orare* to pray

orb *n* **1** an ornamental sphere with a cross on top, carried by a king or queen in important ceremonies **2** a sphere; globe **3** *poetic* the eye **4** *obsolete or poetic* a heavenly body, such as the sun
WORD ORIGIN Latin *orbis* circle, disc

Orbison *n* **Roy** (**Kelton**) 1936–89, US pop singer and songwriter. His records include the singles "Only the Lonely" (1960) and "Oh Pretty Woman" (1964) and the album *Mystery Girl* (1989)

orbit ⓣ *n* **1** the curved path followed by something, such as a heavenly body or spacecraft, in its motion around another body **2** a range or sphere of action or influence **3** *anat* the eye socket ▷ *vb* **-biting, -bited** **4** to move around (a heavenly body) in an orbit **5** to send (a satellite or spacecraft) into orbit **orbital** *adj*
WORD ORIGIN Latin *orbis* circle

Orcadian *n* **1** a person from Orkney ▷ *adj* **2** of Orkney
WORD ORIGIN Latin *Orcades* the Orkney Islands

Orcagna *n* **Andrea**, original name *Andrea di Cione*. ?1308–68, Florentine painter, sculptor, and architect

orchard *n* an area of land on which fruit trees are grown
WORD ORIGIN Old English *orceard*

orchestra *n* **1** a large group of musicians whose members play a variety of different instruments **2** Also called: **orchestra pit** the space, in front of or under the stage, reserved for musicians in a theatre **orchestral** *adj*
WORD ORIGIN Greek: the space in the theatre for the chorus

orchestrate ⓣ *vb* **-trating, -trated** **1** to score or arrange (a piece of music) for orchestra **2** to arrange (something) in order to produce a particular result: *he had orchestrated today's meeting* **orchestration** *n*

orchid *n* a plant having flowers of unusual shapes and beautiful colours, usually with one lip-shaped petal which is larger than the other two
WORD ORIGIN Greek *orkhis* testicle, because of the shape of its roots

Orczy *n* Baroness **Emmuska** 1865–1947, British novelist, born in Hungary; author of *The Scarlet Pimpernel* (1905)

ordain ⓣ *vb* **1** to make (someone) a member of the clergy **2** *formal* to decree or order with authority **ordainment** *n*
WORD ORIGIN Late Latin *ordinare*

ordeal ⓣ *n* **1** a severe or trying experience **2** *history* a method of trial in which the accused person was subjected to physical danger
WORD ORIGIN Old English *ordāl, ordēl* verdict

O

THESAURUS

optional *adj* **= voluntary**, open, discretionary, possible, extra, elective, up to the individual, noncompulsory
OPPOSITE: compulsory

opus *n* **= work**, piece, production, creation, composition, work of art, brainchild, oeuvre *(French)*

oral *adj* **1 = spoken**, vocal, verbal, unwritten, viva voce

orbit *n* **1 = path**, course, track, cycle, circle, revolution, passage, rotation, trajectory, sweep, ellipse, circumgyration **2 = sphere of influence**, reach, range, influence, province, scope, sphere, domain, compass, ambit ▷ *vb* **4 = circle**, ring, go round, compass, revolve around, encircle, circumscribe, gird, circumnavigate

orchestrate *vb* **1 = score**, set, arrange, adapt **2 = organize**, plan, run, set up, arrange, be responsible for, put together, see to *(informal)*, marshal, coordinate, concert, stage-manage

ordain *vb* **1 = appoint**, call, name, commission, select, elect, invest, install, nominate, anoint, consecrate, frock **2** *(formal)* **= order**, will, rule, demand, require, direct, establish, command, dictate, prescribe, pronounce, lay down, decree, instruct, enact, legislate, enjoin

ordeal *n* **1 = hardship**, trial, difficulty, test, labour, suffering, trouble(s), nightmare, burden, torture, misery,

DICTIONARY

order ❶ *n* 1 an instruction that must be obeyed; command 2 a state in which everything is arranged logically, comprehensibly, or naturally: *she strove to keep more order in the house* 3 an arrangement of things in succession; sequence: *group them by letter and then put them in numerical order* 4 an established or customary system of society: *there is an opportunity here for a new world order* 5 a peaceful or harmonious condition of society: *riot police were called in to restore order* 6 **a** an instruction to supply something in return for payment: *the waitress came to take their order* **b** the thing or things supplied 7 a written instruction to pay money: *post the coupon below with a cheque or postal order* 8 a social class: *the result will be harmful to society as a whole and to the lower orders in particular* 9 *biol* one of the groups into which a class is divided, containing one or more families 10 kind or sort: *the orchestra played superbly and the singing was of the highest order* 11 Also called: **religious order** a religious community of monks or nuns 12 a group of people who have been awarded a particular honour: *the Order of the Garter* 13 the office or rank of a Christian minister: *he studied for the priesthood as a young man, but never took Holy Orders* 14 the procedure and rules followed by an assembly or meeting: *a point of order* 15 one of the five major classical styles of architecture, classified by the type of columns used 16 **a tall order** something difficult or demanding 17 **in order a** in sequence **b** properly arranged: *everything is in order for your trip* **c** appropriate or fitting 18 **in order that** so that 19 **in order to** so that it is possible to: *a healthy diet is necessary in order to keep fit* 20 **in** *or* **of the order of** amounting approximately to: *summer temperatures are usually in the order of thirty-five degrees* 21 **keep order** to ensure that people obey the law or behave in an acceptable manner 22 **on order** having been ordered but not yet delivered 23 **out of order a** not in sequence **b** not working: *the lift was out of order, so we had to use the stairs* **c** not following the rules or customary procedure: *the chairperson ruled the motion out of order* 24 **to order** according to a buyer's specifications ▷ *vb* 25 to command or instruct (to do something): *she ordered her son to wash the dishes; the police ordered her into the house* 26 to request (something) to be supplied in return for payment: *I ordered a new car three weeks ago, but it hasn't been delivered yet* 27 to arrange (things) methodically or in their proper places ▷ *interj* 28 an exclamation demanding that orderly behaviour be restored
WORD ORIGIN Latin *ordo*

order around *or* **about** *vb* to repeatedly tell (someone) what to do in a bossy or unsympathetic way: *it was intolerable that those two fat slobs could order her around*

orderly ❶ *adj* 1 tidy or well-organized: *they evacuated the building in an orderly manner* 2 well-behaved; law-abiding ▷ *n, pl* **-lies** 3 *med* a male hospital attendant 4 *mil* a soldier whose duty is to carry orders or perform minor tasks for a more senior officer
orderliness *n*

Order of Merit *n Brit* an order awarded for outstanding achievement in any field

order paper *n* a list indicating the order of business, esp. in Parliament

ordinal number *n* a number indicating position in a sequence, such as *first, second, third*

ordinance *n* an official rule or order
WORD ORIGIN Latin *ordinare* to set in order

ordinarily *adv* in ordinary or usual practice; usually; normally

ordinary ❶ *adj* 1 usual or normal: *it was an ordinary working day for them* 2 not special or different in any way: *what do ordinary Germans feel about reunification?* 3 dull or unexciting: *the restaurant charged very high prices for very ordinary cooking* ▷ *n, pl* **-naries** 4 *RC church* the parts of the Mass that do not vary from day to day 5 **out of the ordinary** unusual
WORD ORIGIN Latin *ordinarius* orderly

Ordinary level *n* ▸ (in Britain) the formal name for **O level**

ordinary rating *n* a rank in the Royal Navy equivalent to that of a private in the army

ordinary seaman *n Brit, Austral & NZ* a seaman of the lowest rank

ordinary shares *pl n Austral & Brit* shares issued by a company entitling their holders to a dividend according to the profits of the company and to a claim on net assets

ordinate *n maths* the vertical coordinate of a point in a two-dimensional system of coordinates
WORD ORIGIN Latin *ordinare* to arrange in order

ordination *n* the act or ceremony of making someone a member of the clergy

ordnance *n* 1 weapons and other military supplies 2 **the ordnance** a government department dealing with military supplies
WORD ORIGIN variant of *ordinance*

Ordnance Survey *n* the British government organization that produces detailed maps of Britain and Ireland

THESAURUS

agony, torment, anguish, toil, affliction, tribulation(s), baptism of fire **OPPOSITE:** pleasure

order *n* 1 **= instruction**, ruling, demand, direction, command, say-so *(informal)*, dictate, decree, mandate, directive, injunction, behest, stipulation 2 **= organization**, system, method, plan, pattern, arrangement, harmony, symmetry, regularity, propriety, neatness, tidiness, orderliness **OPPOSITE:** chaos 3 **= sequence**, grouping, ordering, line, series, structure, chain, arrangement, line-up, succession, disposal, array, placement, classification, layout, progression, disposition, setup *(informal)*, categorization, codification 5 **= peace**, control, law, quiet, calm, discipline, law and order, tranquillity, peacefulness, lawfulness 6a **= request**, booking, demand, commission, application, reservation, requisition 8 **= class**, set, rank, degree, grade, sphere, caste 9 *(biology)* **= kind**, group, class, family, form, sort, type, variety, cast, species, breed, strain, category, tribe, genre, classification, genus, ilk, subdivision, subclass, taxonomic group 12 **= society**, company, group, club, union, community, league, association, institute, organization, circle, corporation, lodge, guild, sect, fellowship, fraternity, brotherhood, sisterhood, sodality ▷ *vb* 25 **= command**, instruct, direct, charge, demand, require, bid, compel, enjoin, adjure **OPPOSITE:** forbid 26 **= request**, ask (for), book, demand, seek, call for, reserve, engage, apply for, contract for, solicit, requisition, put in for, send away for 27 **= arrange**, group, sort, class, position, range, file, rank, line up, organize, set out, sequence, catalogue, sort out, classify, array, dispose, tidy, marshal, lay out, tabulate, systematize, neaten, put in order, set in order, put to rights **OPPOSITE:** disarrange

orderly *adj* 1 **= well-organized**, ordered, regular, in order, organized, trim, precise, neat, tidy, systematic, businesslike, methodical, well-kept, shipshape, systematized, well-regulated, in apple-pie order *(informal)* **OPPOSITE:** disorganized 2 **= well-behaved**, controlled, disciplined, quiet, restrained, law-abiding, nonviolent, peaceable, decorous **OPPOSITE:** disorderly

ordinary *adj* 1 **= usual**, standard, normal, common, established, settled, regular, familiar, household, typical, conventional, routine, stock, everyday, prevailing, accustomed, customary, habitual, quotidian,

DICTIONARY

Ordovician (or-doe-**vish**-ee-an) *adj geol* of the period of geological time about 500 million years ago
WORD ORIGIN Latin *Ordovices*, ancient Celtic tribe in N Wales
ordure *n* excrement; dung
WORD ORIGIN Old French *ord* dirty
ore *n* rock or mineral from which valuable substances such as metals can be extracted
WORD ORIGIN Old English *ār, ōra*
oregano (or-rig-**gah**-no) *n* a sweet-smelling herb used as seasoning
WORD ORIGIN Greek *origanon* an aromatic herb
Oresme *n* **Nicole d'** ?1320–82, French economist, mathematician, and cleric: bishop of Lisieux (1378–82)
Orff *n* **Carl** (karl) 1895–1982, German composer. His works include the secular oratorio *Carmina Burana* (1937) and the opera *Antigone* (1949)
organ *n* **1** a part in animals and plants that is adapted to perform a particular function, for example the heart or lungs **2 a** a musical keyboard instrument which produces sound by forcing air through pipes of a variety of lengths **b** Also called: **electric organ** a keyboard instrument which produces similar sounds electronically **3** a means of communication, such as a newspaper issued by a specialist group or party **4** *euphemistic* a penis
WORD ORIGIN Greek *organon* tool
organdie *n* a fine, slightly stiff cotton fabric
WORD ORIGIN French *organdi*
organ-grinder *n* (formerly) an entertainer who played a barrel organ in the streets
organic *adj* **1** of, produced by, or found in plants or animals: *the rocks were carefully searched for organic remains* **2** not using, or grown without, artificial fertilizers or pesticides: *organic vegetables; an organic farm* **3** *chem* of or belonging to the class of chemical compounds that are formed from carbon **4** (of change or development) gradual and natural rather than sudden or forced **5** made up of many different parts which contribute to the way in which the whole society or structure works: *an organic whole* **organically** *adv*
organic chemistry *n chem* the branch of chemistry dealing with carbon compounds
organism *n* **1** an animal or plant **2** anything resembling a living creature in structure, behaviour, or complexity: *cities are more complicated organisms than farming villages*
organist *n* a person who plays the organ
organization *or* **-isation** *n* **1** an organized group of people, such as a club, society, union, or business **2** the act of organizing: *setting up the European tour took a lot of organization* **3** the structure and arrangement of the different parts of something: *the report recommended radical changes in the organization of the social services department* **4** the state of being organized: *the material in this essay lacks any sort of organization* **organizational** *or* **-isational** *adj*
organize *or* **-ise** *vb* **-izing, -ized** *or* **-ising, -ised 1** to plan and arrange (something): *we organized a protest meeting in the village hall* **2** to arrange systematically: *the files are organized in alphabetical order and by date* **3** to form, join, or recruit (people) into a trade union: *the seasonal nature of tourism makes it difficult for hotel workers to organize* **organizer** *or* **-iser** *n*
WORD ORIGIN Medieval Latin *organizare*
organized *or* **-ised** *adj* **1** planned and controlled on a large scale and involving many people: *organized crime* **2** orderly and efficient: *a highly organized campaign* **3** (of the workers in a factory or office) belonging to a trade union: *socialism is especially popular among organized labour*
organza *n* a thin stiff fabric of silk, cotton, or synthetic fibre
WORD ORIGIN origin unknown
orgasm *n* the most intense point of pleasure and excitement during sexual activity **orgasmic** *adj*
WORD ORIGIN Greek *orgasmos*
orgy *n, pl* **-gies 1** a wild party involving promiscuous sexual activity and excessive drinking **2** an act of immoderate or frenzied indulgence: *the rioters were engaged in an orgy of destruction* **orgiastic** *adj*
WORD ORIGIN Greek *orgia* secret rites
oriel window *or* **oriel** *n* a window built out from the wall of a house at an upper level
WORD ORIGIN Old French *oriol* gallery
orient *vb* **1 2** to position or set (for example a map or chart) with relation to the points of the compass or other specific directions **3 orient oneself** to adjust or align oneself or one's ideas according to new surroundings or circumstances: *new employees can take some time to orient themselves to the company's procedures* **4 be oriented to** *or* **towards** to work or act with a particular aim, idea, or person in mind: *many people feel that Britain is too much oriented to the Americans* ▷ *n* **5** *poetic* the east
WORD ORIGIN Latin *oriens* rising (sun)

O

THESAURUS

wonted **2 = commonplace**, plain, modest, humble, stereotyped, pedestrian, mundane, vanilla *(slang)*, stale, banal, unremarkable, prosaic, run-of-the-mill, humdrum, homespun, uninteresting, workaday, common or garden *(informal)*, unmemorable
organ *n* **1 = body part**, part of the body, member, element, biological structure **3 = newspaper**, paper, medium, voice, agency, channel, vehicle, journal, publication, rag *(informal)*, gazette, periodical, mouthpiece
organic *adj* **1 = natural**, biological, living, live, vital, animate, biotic **5 = systematic**, ordered, structured, organized, integrated, orderly, standardized, methodical, well-ordered, systematized
organism *n* **1 = creature**, being, thing, body, animal, structure, beast, entity, living thing, critter *(US dialect)*
organization *or* **organisation** *n* **1 = group**, company, party, body, concern, league, association, band, institution, gathering, circle, corporation, federation, outfit *(informal)*, faction, consortium, syndicate, combine, congregation, confederation **2 = management**, running, planning, making, control, operation, handling, structuring, administration, direction, regulation, construction, organizing, supervision, governance, formulation, coordination, methodology, superintendence **3, 4 = structure**, grouping, plan, system, form, design, method, pattern, make-up, arrangement, construction, constitution, format, formation, framework, composition, chemistry, configuration, conformation, interrelation of parts
organize *or* **organise** *vb* **1 = arrange**, run, plan, form, prepare, establish, set up, shape, schedule, frame, look after, be responsible for, construct, constitute, devise, put together, take care of, see to *(informal)*, get together, marshal, contrive, get going, coordinate, fix up, straighten out, lay the foundations of, lick into shape, jack up *(NZ informal)*
OPPOSITE: disrupt
2 = put in order, arrange, group, list, file, index, catalogue, classify, codify, pigeonhole, tabulate, inventory, systematize, dispose
OPPOSITE: muddle
orient *or* **orientate** *vb* **1 = adjust**, settle, adapt, tune, convert, alter, compose, accommodate, accustom, reconcile, align, harmonize, familiarize, acclimatize, find your feet *(informal)*
3 orient yourself = get your bearings, get the lie of the land, establish your location

DICTIONARY

Orient *n* **the Orient** East Asia
oriental *adj* eastern
Oriental *adj* **1** of the Orient ▷*n* **2** a person from the Orient
orientate *vb* **-tating, -tated** ▸ same as **orient**
-orientated or **-oriented** *adj combining form* interested in or directed towards the thing specified: *career-orientated women*
orientation ❶ *n* **1** the activities and aims that a person or organization is interested in: *the course has a practical rather than theoretical orientation* **2** the position of an object with relation to the points of the compass or other specific directions: *the room's southerly orientation means that it receives a lot of light* ▷*adj* **3** of or providing information or training needed to understand a new situation or environment: *nearly every college has an orientation programme*
orienteering *n* a sport in which contestants race on foot over a cross-country course consisting of checkpoints found with the aid of a map and compass
WORD ORIGIN Swedish *orientering*
orifice (or-rif-fiss) *n* an opening or hole through which something can pass, esp. one in the body such as the mouth or anus
WORD ORIGIN Latin *os* mouth + *facere* to make
orig. 1 origin **2** original(ly)
origami (or-rig-**gah**-mee) *n* the art, originally Japanese, of folding paper intricately into decorative shapes
WORD ORIGIN Japanese *ori* a fold + *kami* paper
Origen *n* ?185–?254 AD, Christian theologian, born in Alexandria. His writings include *Hexapla*, a synopsis of the Old Testament, *Contra Celsum*, a defence of Christianity, and *De principiis*, a statement of Christian theology
origin ❶ *n* **1** the point, source, or event from which something develops: *the origin of the term 'jazz' is obscure; the war had its origin in the clash between rival nationalists* **2** the country, race, or social class of a person's parents or ancestors: *an Australian of Greek origin; he was proud of his working-class origins* **3** *maths* the point at which the horizontal and vertical axes intersect
WORD ORIGIN Latin *origo* beginning
original ❶ *adj* **1** first or earliest: *the dining room also has attractive original beams* **2** fresh and unusual; not copied from or based on something else: *the composer's work has created some original and attractive choreography* **3** able to think of or carry out new ideas or concepts: *he is an excitingly original writer* **4** being the first and genuine form of something, from which a copy or translation is made: *all French recipes were translated from the original abridged versions* ▷*n* **5** the first and genuine form of something, from which others are copied or translated: *the original is in the British Museum* **6** a person or thing used as a model in art or literature: *she claimed to be the original on whom Lawrence based Lady Chatterley* **originality** *n* **originally** *adv*
original sin *n* a state of sin believed by some Christians to be inborn in all human beings as a result of Adam's disobedience
originate ❶ *vb* **-nating, -nated** to come or bring (something) into existence: *humans probably originated in East Africa* **origination** *n* **originator** *n*
oriole *n* a songbird with a long pointed bill and a mostly yellow-and-black plumage
WORD ORIGIN Latin *aureolus* golden
Orléans[1] *n* a city in N central France, on the River Loire: famous for its deliverance by Joan of Arc from the long English siege in 1429; university (1305); an important rail and road junction. Pop: 113 126 (1999)
Orléans[2] *n* **1 Charles,** Duc d'Orléans 1394–1465, French poet; noted for the poems written during his imprisonment in England; father of Louis XII **2 Louis Philippe Joseph,** Duc d'Orléans, known as *Philippe Égalité* (after 1792). 1747–93, French nobleman, who supported the French Revolution and voted for the death of his cousin, Louis XVI, but was executed after his son, the future king Louis-Philippe, defected to the Austrians
Orlov *n* Count **Grigori Grigorievich** 1734–83, Russian soldier and a lover of Catherine II. He led (with his brother, Count **Aleksey Grigorievich Orlov,** 1737–1808) the coup that brought Catherine to power
Ormandy *n* **Eugene** 1899–1985, US conductor, born in Hungary
ormolu *n* a gold-coloured alloy of copper, tin, or zinc, used to decorate furniture and other articles
WORD ORIGIN French *or moulu* ground gold
Ormonde *n* **1st Duke of,** title of *James Butler.* 1610–88, Anglo-Irish general; commander (1641–50) of the royalist forces in Ireland; Lord Lieutenant of Ireland (1661–69; 1677–84)
ornament ❶ *n* **1** anything that adorns someone or something; decoration: *the room's only ornament was a dim, oily picture of the Holy Family* **2** decorations collectively: *he had no watch, nor ornament of any kind* **3** a small decorative object: *I hit a garden ornament while parking* **4** a person whose character or talent makes

O

THESAURUS

orientation *n* **1 = inclination,** tendency, bias, leaning, bent, disposition, predisposition, predilection, proclivity, partiality, turn of mind **2 = position,** situation, location, site, bearings, direction, arrangement, whereabouts, disposition, coordination
origin *n* **1a = beginning,** start, birth, source, launch, foundation, creation, dawning, early stages, emergence, outset, starting point, onset, genesis, initiation, inauguration, inception, font *(poetic)*, commencement, fountain, fount, origination, fountainhead, mainspring **OPPOSITE:** end
1b = root, source, basis, beginnings, base, cause, spring, roots, seed, foundation, nucleus, germ, provenance, derivation, wellspring, fons et origo *(Latin)*
original *adj* **1a = first,** earliest, early, initial, aboriginal, primitive, pristine, primordial, primeval, autochthonous **1b = initial,** first, starting, opening, primary, inaugural, commencing, introductory **OPPOSITE:** final
2 = new, fresh, novel, different, unusual, unknown, unprecedented, innovative, unfamiliar, unconventional, seminal, ground-breaking, untried, innovatory, newfangled **OPPOSITE:** unoriginal
3 = creative, inspired, imaginative, artistic, fertile, ingenious, visionary, inventive, resourceful ▷*n*
5 = prototype, master, pattern **OPPOSITE:** copy
originate *vb* **a = begin,** start, emerge, come, issue, happen, rise, appear, spring, flow, be born, proceed, arise, dawn, stem, derive, commence, emanate, crop up *(informal)*, come into being, come into existence **OPPOSITE:** end
b = invent, produce, create, form, develop, design, launch, set up, introduce, imagine, institute, generate, come up with *(informal)*, pioneer, evolve, devise, initiate, conceive, bring about, formulate, give birth to, contrive, improvise, dream up *(informal)*, inaugurate, think up, set in motion
ornament *n* **1 = decoration,** trimming, accessory, garnish, frill, festoon, trinket, bauble, flounce, gewgaw, knick-knack, furbelow, falderal **2 = embellishment,** trimming, decoration, embroidery, elaboration, adornment, ornamentation ▷*vb* **6 = decorate,** trim, adorn, enhance, deck, array, dress up, enrich, brighten, garnish, gild, do up *(informal)*, embellish, emblazon, festoon, bedeck, beautify, prettify, bedizen *(archaic)*, engarland

DICTIONARY

them an asset to society or the group to which they belong: *an ornament of the firm* **5** *music* a note or group of notes which embellishes the melody but is not an integral part of it, for instance a trill ▷*vb* **6** to decorate or adorn: *the hall had a high ceiling, ornamented with plaster fruits and flowers* **ornamental** *adj* **ornamentation** *n* **ornamented** *adj*
WORD ORIGIN Latin *ornamentum*

ornate *adj* **1** heavily or elaborately decorated: *an ornate ceiling painted with allegorical figures* **2** (of style in writing) overelaborate; using many literary expressions **ornately** *adv*
WORD ORIGIN Latin *ornare* to decorate

ornithology *n* the study of birds **ornithological** *adj* **ornithologist** *n*
WORD ORIGIN Greek *ornis* bird

orotund *adj* **1** (of the voice) resonant and booming **2** (of speech or writing) pompous; containing many long or formal words
WORD ORIGIN Latin *ore rotundo* with rounded mouth

Orozco *n* **José Clemente** 1883–1949, Mexican painter, noted for his monumental humanistic murals

orphan *n* **1** a child whose parents are dead ▷*vb* **2** to cause (someone) to become an orphan: *she was orphaned at 16 when her parents died in a car crash*
WORD ORIGIN Greek *orphanos*

orphanage *n* a children's home for orphans and abandoned children

orphaned *adj* having no living parents

Orr *n* **Robert Gordon**, known as *Bobby.* born 1948, Canadian ice-hockey player

orrery *n, pl* **-ries** a mechanical model of the solar system in which the planets can be moved around the sun
WORD ORIGIN originally made for Earl of *Orrery*

orris *n* **1** a kind of iris that has fragrant roots **2** Also: **orrisroot** the root of this plant prepared and used as perfume
WORD ORIGIN variant of *iris*

Ortega *n* **Daniel,** full surname *Ortega Saavedra.* born 1945, Nicaraguan politician and former resistance leader; president of Nicaragua (1985–90) and from 2007

Ortega y Gasset *n* **José** 1883–1955, Spanish essayist and philosopher. His best-known work is *The Revolt of the Masses* (1930)

orthodontics *n* the branch of dentistry concerned with correcting irregularities of the teeth

orthodontic *adj* **orthodontist** *n*
WORD ORIGIN Greek *orthos* straight + *odōn* tooth

orthodox ❶ *adj* conforming to traditional or established standards in religion, behaviour, or attitudes: *orthodox medicine; the concerto has a more orthodox structure than is usual for this composer* **orthodoxy** *n*
WORD ORIGIN Greek *orthos* correct + *doxa* belief

Orthodox *adj* **1** of the Orthodox Church of Eastern Europe **2** of or being the form of Judaism characterized by traditional interpretation of and strict adherence to Mosaic Law: *an Orthodox Jew*

Orthodox Church *n* the Christian Church dominant in Eastern Europe, which has the Greek Patriarch of Constantinople as its head

orthography *n* **1** spelling considered to be correct: *British and American orthography is different in many cases* **2** the study of spelling **orthographic** *adj*
WORD ORIGIN Greek *orthos* correct + *graphein* to write

orthopaedics *or US* **orthopedics** *n* the branch of surgery concerned with disorders of the bones and joints **orthopaedic** *or US* **orthopedic** *adj* **orthopaedist** *or US* **orthopedist** *n*
WORD ORIGIN Greek *orthos* straight + *pais* child

ortolan *n* a small European songbird eaten as a delicacy
WORD ORIGIN Latin *hortulus* a little garden

Orton *n* **Joe (Kingsley)** 1933–67, British dramatist, noted for his black comedies: these include *Entertaining Mr Sloane* (1964), *Loot* (1966), and *What the Butler Saw* (1969)

oryx *n* any of various large straight-horned African antelopes

Os *chem* osmium

OS **1** (in Britain) Ordnance Survey **2** outsize(d)

Osborne *n* **John (James)** 1929–94, British dramatist. His plays include *Look Back in Anger* (1956), containing the prototype of the angry young man, Jimmy Porter, *The Entertainer* (1957), and *Inadmissible Evidence* (1964)

Oscar *n* an award in the form of a small gold statuette awarded annually in the US for outstanding achievements in various aspects of the film industry: *he won an Oscar for Best Supporting Actor in 1974*
WORD ORIGIN said to have been named after a remark made by an official that it reminded her of her uncle Oscar

Oscar II *n* 1829–1907, king of Sweden (1872–1907) and of Norway (1872–1905)

oscillate (oss-ill-late) *vb* **-lating, -lated** **1** to swing repeatedly back and forth: *its wings oscillate up and down many times a second* **2** to waver between two extremes of opinion, attitude, or behaviour: *the government oscillates between a desire for reform and a desire to keep its powers intact* **3** *physics* (of an electric current) to vary between minimum and maximum values **oscillation** *n* **oscillator** *n*
WORD ORIGIN Latin *oscillare* to swing

oscilloscope (oss-**sill**-oh-scope) *n* an instrument that produces a visual representation of an oscillating electric current on the screen of a cathode-ray tube

osier (oh-zee-er) *n* **1** a willow tree whose flexible branches or twigs are used for making baskets and furniture **2** a twig or branch from this tree
WORD ORIGIN Old French

Osiris *n* an Egyptian god of the underworld

Osler *n* **Sir William** 1849–1919, Canadian physician, pioneer of residency in medical training

osmium *n chem* a very hard brittle bluish-white metal, the heaviest known element. Symbol: Os
WORD ORIGIN Greek *osmē* smell, from its penetrating odour

osmoregulation *n zool* the adjustment of the osmotic pressure of a cell or organism in relation to the surrounding fluid

osmosis *n* **1** the diffusion of liquids through a membrane until they are mixed **2** the process by which people or ideas influence each other gradually and subtly **osmotic** *adj*
WORD ORIGIN Greek *ōsmos* push

osprey *n* a large fish-eating bird of prey, with a dark back and whitish head and underparts
WORD ORIGIN Old French *ospres*, apparently from Latin *ossifraga*, literally: bone-breaker

osseous *adj* consisting of or like bone
WORD ORIGIN Latin *os* bone

Ossian *n* a legendary Irish hero and bard of the 3rd century AD ▸ See also **Macpherson** > **Ossi'anic** *adj*

Ossietzky *n* **Carl von** 1889–1938, German pacifist leader. He was imprisoned for revealing Germany's secret rearmament (1931–32) and again under Hitler (1933–36): Nobel peace prize 1935

ossify *vb* **-fies, -fying, -fied** **1** to change into bone; harden **2** to become rigid, inflexible, or

THESAURUS

orthodox *adj* **a = established,** official, accepted, received, common, popular, traditional, normal, regular, usual, ordinary, approved, familiar, acknowledged, conventional, routine, customary, well-established, kosher *(informal)*
OPPOSITE: unorthodox
b = conformist, conservative, traditional, strict, devout, observant, doctrinal
OPPOSITE: nonconformist

O

DICTIONARY

unprogressive: *ossified traditions* **ossification** *n*
WORD ORIGIN Latin *os* bone + *facere* to make

ostensible *adj* apparent or seeming; alleged: *our ostensible common interest is boats* **ostensibly** *adv*
WORD ORIGIN Latin *ostendere* to show

ostensive *adj* directly showing or pointing out: *he gave ostensive definitions to things*
WORD ORIGIN Latin *ostendere* to show

ostentation *n* pretentious, showy, or vulgar display: *she felt the gold taps in the bathroom were tasteless ostentation* **ostentatious** *adj* **ostentatiously** *adv*

osteoarthritis (ost-ee-oh-arth-**rite**-iss) *n* chronic inflammation of the joints, causing pain and stiffness **osteoarthritic** *adj*
WORD ORIGIN Greek *osteon* bone + ARTHRITIS

osteopathy *n* a system of healing based on the manipulation of bones or muscle **osteopath** *n*
WORD ORIGIN Greek *osteon* bone + *patheia* suffering

osteoporosis (ost-ee-oh-pore-**oh**-siss) *n* brittleness of the bones, caused by lack of calcium
WORD ORIGIN Greek *osteon* bone + *poros* passage

ostinato *n, pl* **-tos** *music* a persistently repeated phrase or rhythm
WORD ORIGIN Italian, from Latin *obstinatus* obstinate

ostler *n* (formerly) a stableman at an inn
WORD ORIGIN variant of *hostler*, from *hostel*

ostracize *or* **-cise** *vb* **-cizing, -cized** *or* **-cising, -cised** to exclude or banish (a person) from a particular group or from society: *he was ostracized from his family when his affair became known* **ostracism** *n*
WORD ORIGIN Greek *ostrakizein* to select someone for banishment by voting on potsherds

ostrich *n* **1** a large African bird which runs fast but cannot fly, and has a long neck, long legs, and soft dark feathers **2** a person who refuses to recognize an unpleasant truth: *he accused the Minister of being 'an ostrich with its head stuck in the sand, while all around him unemployment soars'*
WORD ORIGIN Greek *strouthion*

Ostrovsky *n* **Aleksandr Nikolayevich** 1823–86, Russian dramatist, noted for his satirical comedies about the bourgeoisie. His plays include *The Bankrupt* (1849) and *The Storm* (1859), a tragedy

Ostwald *n* **Wilhelm** 1853–1932, German chemist, noted for his pioneering work in catalysis. He also invented a process for making nitric acid from ammonia and developed a new theory of colour: Nobel prize for chemistry 1909

Oswald *n* **1 Lee Harvey** 1939–63, presumed assassin (1963) of US president John F. Kennedy; murdered by Jack Ruby two days later **2 Saint** ?605–41 AD, king of Northumbria (634–41); with St Aidan he restored Christianity to the region. He was killed in battle by Penda of Mercia. Feast day: Aug 5

OT Old Testament

OTC (in Britain) Officers' Training Corps

OTE *chiefly Brit* (esp. in job adverts) on target earnings: the minimum amount of money a salesman is expected to make

other ● *adj* **1** remaining (one or ones) in a group of which one or some have been specified: *she wasn't getting on with the other children* **2** being a different one or ones from the one or ones already specified or understood: *other people might not be so tolerant of your behaviour; are you sure it's not in your other pocket?* **3** refers to a place or time which is not the one the speaker or writer is in: *results in other countries have been most encouraging* **4** additional; further: *there is one other thing for the government to do* **5 every other** every alternate: *the doctor sees me every other week* **6 other than a** apart from: *he knew little of the country other than it was Muslim* **b** different from: *treatment other than a hearing aid will be possible for those with inner ear deafness* **7 or other** used to add vagueness to the preceding word or phrase: *he could take some evening course or other which could lead to an extra qualification; he was called away from the house on some pretext or other* **8 the other day** a few days ago ▷ *n* **9** an additional person or thing: *show me one other* **10 others** people apart from the person who is being spoken or written about: *she devoted her entire life to helping others* **11 the others** the people or things remaining in a group of which one or some have been specified: *I can't speak for the others* ▷ *adv* **12** otherwise; differently: *they couldn't behave other than they do* **otherness** *n*
WORD ORIGIN Old English *ōther*

other ranks *pl n Austral & Brit* (in the armed forces) all those who do not hold a commissioned rank

otherwise ● *conj* **1** or else; if not, then: *I was fifty but said I was forty, otherwise I'd never have got a job* ▷ *adv* **2** differently: *it was fruitless to pretend or to hope otherwise* **3** in other respects: *shrewd psychological twists perk up an otherwise predictable story line* ▷ *adj* **4** different: *circumstances beyond our control dictated that it should be otherwise* ▷ *pron* **5 or otherwise** or not; or the opposite: *he didn't want company, talkative or otherwise*

otherworldly *adj* **1** concerned with spiritual rather than practical matters: *his otherworldly manner concealed a ruthless business mind* **2** mystical or supernatural: *this part of Italy has an otherworldly beauty*

Otho I *n* same as **Otto I**

otiose (oh-tee-oze) *adj* serving no useful purpose: *such a strike is almost otiose*
WORD ORIGIN Latin *otiosus* leisured

O'Toole *n* **Peter** born 1932, British actor, born in Ireland. His films include *Lawrence of Arabia* (1962), *The Lion in Winter* (1968), *High Spirits* (1988), and *Fairytale* (1998); stage appearances include *Jeffrey Bernard is Unwell* (1989)

OTT *slang* over the top

otter *n* a small freshwater fish-eating animal with smooth brown fur, a streamlined body, and webbed feet
WORD ORIGIN Old English *otor*

Otto *n* **Rudolf** 1869–1937, German theologian: his best-known work is *The Idea of the Holy* (1923)

Otto I *or* **Otho I** *n* called *the Great*. 912–73 AD, king of Germany (936–73); Holy Roman Emperor (962–73)

Otto IV *n* ?1175–1218 German king and Holy Roman Emperor (1198–1215): invaded S Italy (1210) but was later (1214) defeated by France and deposed

ottoman *n, pl* **-mans** a storage chest with a padded lid for use as a seat
WORD ORIGIN French *ottomane*, feminine of *Ottoman*

Ottoman *adj* **1** *history* of the Ottomans or the Ottoman Empire, the Turkish empire which lasted from the late 13th century until the end of World War I, and at its height included the Balkans and much of N Africa ▷ *n, pl* **-mans 2** a member of a Turkish people who formed the basis of this empire
WORD ORIGIN Arabic *Othmānī*

Otway *n* **Thomas** 1652–85, English dramatist, noted for *The Orphan* (1680) and *Venice Preserv'd* (1682)

ou (oh) *n S African slang* a man, bloke, or chap
WORD ORIGIN Afrikaans

THESAURUS

other *det* **2, 3 = different**, alternative, contrasting, distinct, diverse, dissimilar, separate, alternative, substitute, alternate, unrelated, variant **4 = additional**, more, further, new, added, extra, fresh, spare, supplementary, auxiliary

otherwise *sentence connector* **1 = or else**, or, if not, or then ▷ *adv* **2 = differently**, any other way, in another way, contrarily, contrastingly, in contrary fashion **3 = apart from that**, in other ways, in (all) other respects

O

DICTIONARY

OU **1** the Open University **2** Oxford University

oubaas (oh-bahss) *n S African* a man in authority
WORD ORIGIN Afrikaans *ou* man + *baas* boss

oubliette (oo-blee-ett) *n history* a dungeon, the only entrance to which is a trap door in the ceiling
WORD ORIGIN French *oublier* to forget

ouch *interj* an exclamation of sharp sudden pain

Oudry *n* **Jean-Baptiste** 1686–1755, French rococo painter and tapestry designer, noted esp. for animal and hunting scenes

ought *vb* **1** used to express duty or obligation: *she ought to tell this to the police* **2** used to express advisability: *we ought to get the roof repaired before the attics get any damper* **3** used to express probability or expectation: *a good lawyer ought to be able to fix it for you* **4** used to express a desire on the part of the speaker: *you ought to have a good breakfast before you hit the road*
WORD ORIGIN Old English *āhte*, past tense of *āgan* to owe

oughtn't ought not

Ouida *n* real name *Marie Louise de la Ramée* 1839–1908, British popular novelist, best known for *Under Two Flags* (1867)

Ouija board *or* **Ouija** (weej-a) *n trademark* a board on which are marked the letters of the alphabet. Answers to questions are spelt out by a pointer, which is supposedly guided by spirits
WORD ORIGIN French *oui* yes + German *ja* yes

O

ouma (oh-mah) *n S African* **1** grandmother, often as a title with a surname **2** *slang* any elderly woman
WORD ORIGIN Afrikaans

ounce ❶ *n* **1** a unit of weight equal to one sixteenth of a pound or 28.4 grams **2** ▸short for **fluid ounce** **3** a small amount: *you haven't got one ounce of control over her*
WORD ORIGIN Latin *uncia* a twelfth

OUP (in Northern Ireland) Official Unionist Party

oupa (oh-pah) *n S African* **1** grandfather, often as a title with a surname **2** *slang* any elderly man
WORD ORIGIN Afrikaans

our *adj* **1** of, belonging to, or associated with us: *our daughter* **2** a formal word for *my* used by monarchs
WORD ORIGIN Old English *ūre*

Our Father *n* ▸same as the **Lord's Prayer**

ours *pron* **1** something belonging to us: *ours are smaller guns than those; the money is ours* **2** **of ours** belonging to or associated with us: *my wife and a friend of ours had both deserted me*

ourself *pron archaic* a formal word for *myself* used by monarchs

ourselves *pron* **1** **a** the reflexive form of *we* or *us*: *we humiliated ourselves* **b** used for emphasis: *we ourselves will finish it* **2** our usual selves: *we've not been feeling quite ourselves since the accident* **3** *not standard* used instead of *we* or *us* in compound noun phrases: *other people and ourselves*

ousel *n* ▸same as **ouzel**

oust ❶ *vb* to force (someone) out of a position; expel: *the coup which ousted the President*
WORD ORIGIN Anglo-Norman *ouster*

ouster *n US* an act or instance of forcing someone out of a position: *the demonstrators called for the ouster of the police chief*

out ❶ *adv, adj* **1** away from the inside of a place: *she took her purse out; inspection of the eggs should be done when the hen is out of the nest* **2** away from one's home or place of work for a short time: *I called earlier but you were out; a search party is out looking for survivors* **3** no longer burning, shining, or functioning: *he switched the light out; the living-room fire went out while we were next door eating* **4** used up; not having any more of: *their supplies ran out after two weeks; we're out of milk* **5** public; revealed: *our dirty little secret is out* **6** available to the public: *her biography will be out in December* **7** (of the sun, stars, or moon) visible **8** in bloom: *the roses are out early this year* **9** not in fashion or current usage: *trying to be trendy is out* **10** excluded from consideration: *cost cutting is out of the question* **11** not allowed: *smoking on duty is out* **12** **out for** *or* **to** wanting or intent on (something or doing something): *the young soldiers were out for revenge; they're out to get me* **13** *sport* (of a player in a sport like cricket or baseball) no longer batting because he or she has been dismissed by being caught, bowled, etc. **14** on strike **15** in or into a state of unconsciousness: *he went outside and passed out in an alley* **16** used to indicate a burst of activity as indicated by a verb: *war broke out in the Gulf* **17** out of existence: *the mistakes were scored out* **18** to the fullest extent: *spread out* **19** loudly; clearly: *he cried out in shock and pain* **20** to a conclusion; completely: *she'd worked it out for herself* **21** existing: *the friendliest dog out* **22** inaccurate or incorrect: *the estimate was out by sixty pounds* **23** not in office or authority: *she was finally voted out as party leader* **24** (of a period of time) completed: *before the year is out* **25** openly homosexual: *I came out as a lesbian when I was still in my teens* **26** *old-fashioned* (of a young woman) in or into upper-class society life: *Lucinda had a large party when she came out* **27** **out of** **a** at or to a point outside: *the train pulled out of the station* **b** away from; not in: *they're out of touch with reality; out of focus* **c** because of; motivated by: *out of jealousy* **d** from (a material or source): *made out of plastic* **e** no longer in a specified state or condition: *out of work; out of practice* ▹*adj* **28** *informal* not concealing one's homosexuality ▹*prep* **29** *US or not standard* out of; out through: *he ran out the door* ▹*interj* **30** **a** an exclamation of dismissal **b** (in signalling and radio) an expression used to signal that the speaker is signing off: *over and out!* ▹*vb* **31** *informal* (of homosexuals) to expose (a public figure) as being a fellow homosexual **32** *informal* to reveal something embarrassing or unknown about (a person): *he was outed as a talented goal scorer*
WORD ORIGIN Old English *ūt*

out- *prefix* **1** excelling or surpassing in a particular action: *outlast; outlive* **2** at or from a point away, outside: *outpost; outpatient* **3** going away, outward: *outcrop; outgrowth*

outage *n* a period of power failure

out and about *adj* regularly going out of the house to work, take part in social activity, etc. esp. after an illness

out-and-out *adj* absolute; thorough: *it's an out-and-out lie*

outback *n* the remote bush country of Australia

outbid *vb* **-bidding, -bidded** *or* **-bid** to offer a higher price than (another person)

outboard motor *n* a portable petrol

THESAURUS

ounce *n* **3 = shred**, bit, drop, trace, scrap, grain, particle, fragment, atom, crumb, snippet, speck, whit, iota

oust *vb* **= expel**, turn out, dismiss, exclude, exile, discharge, throw out, relegate, displace, topple, banish, eject, depose, evict, dislodge, unseat, dispossess, send packing, turf out *(informal)*, disinherit, drum out, show someone the door, give the bum's rush *(slang)*, throw out on your ear *(informal)*

out *adj* **2 = not in**, away, elsewhere, outside, gone, abroad, from home, absent, not here, not there, not at home **3 = extinguished**, ended, finished, dead, cold, exhausted, expired, used up, doused, at an end **OPPOSITE:** alight **5 = revealed**, exposed, common knowledge, public knowledge, (out) in the open **OPPOSITE:** kept secret **6 = available**, on sale, in the shops, at hand, to be had, purchasable, procurable **8 = in bloom**, opening, open, flowering, blooming, in flower, in full bloom ▹*vb* **31 = expose**, uncover, unmask

DICTIONARY

engine that can be attached externally to the stern of a boat to propel it

outbox *n computers* a folder in which outgoing messages are stored

outbreak ❶ *n* a sudden occurrence of disease or war

outbuilding *n* ▸ same as **outhouse**

outburst ❶ *n* **1** a sudden strong expression of emotion, esp. of anger: *such emotional outbursts do nothing to help calm discussion of the matter* **2** a sudden period of violent activity: *this sudden outburst of violence has come as a shock*

outcast *n* a person who is rejected or excluded from a particular group or from society

outclass *vb* to surpass (someone) in performance or quality

outcome ❶ *n* the result or consequence of something

outcrop *n* part of a rock formation that sticks out of the earth

outcry ❶ *n, pl* **-cries** a widespread or vehement protest: *there was great popular outcry against the plan for a dual carriageway*

outdated ❶ *adj* old-fashioned or obsolete

outdistance *vb* **-tancing, -tanced** **1** to surpass (someone) in a particular activity **2** to leave (other competitors) behind in a race

outdo *vb* **-does, -doing, -did, -done** to be more successful or better than (someone or something) in performance: *this car easily outdoes its rivals when it comes to comfort*

outdoor ❶ *adj* **1** taking place, existing, or intended for use in the open air: *have a swim at the beach or outdoor pool; she was just taking off her outdoor clothing* **2** fond of the outdoors: *Paul was a butch outdoor type*

outdoors *adv* **1** in the open air; outside: *he hardly ever went outdoors* ▹ *n* **2** the world outside or far away from buildings; the open air: *he'd forgotten his fear of the outdoors*

outer ❶ *adj* **1** on the outside; external: *the building's outer walls were painted pale pink* **2** further from the middle: *the outer suburbs* ▹ *n* **3** *archery* **a** the white outermost ring on a target **b** a shot that hits this ring

outermost *adj* furthest from the centre or middle

outer space *n* space beyond the atmosphere of the earth

outface *vb* **-facing, -faced** to subdue or disconcert (someone) by staring

outfall *n Brit, Austral & NZ* the mouth of a river, drain, or pipe: *the survey measured pollution levels near sewer outfalls*

outfield *n* **1** *cricket* the area of the field far from the pitch **2** *baseball* the area of the playing field beyond the lines connecting first, second, and third bases **outfielder** *n*

outfit ❶ *n* **1** a set of clothes worn together **2** *informal* a group of people working together as a unit **3** a set of equipment for a particular task; kit: *a complete anti-snakebite outfit*

outfitter *n old-fashioned* a shop or person that sells men's clothes

outflank *vb* **1** to go around and beyond the side of (an enemy army) **2** to get the better of (someone)

outflow *n* **1** anything that flows out, such as liquid or money **2** the amount that flows out

outfox *vb* to defeat or foil (someone) by being more cunning; outsmart

outgoing ❶ *adj* **1** leaving: *some members of the outgoing government continued to attend the peace talks* **2** friendly and sociable

outgoings ❶ *pl n* expenses

outgrow *vb* **-growing, -grew, -grown** **1** to grow too large for (clothes or shoes): *it's amazing how quickly children outgrow their clothes* **2** to lose (a way of behaving or thinking) in the course of becoming more mature: *most teenagers outgrow their moodiness as they near adulthood* **3** to grow larger or faster than (someone or something): *the weeds threatened to outgrow and choke the rice plants*

outgrowth *n* **1** a natural development or consequence: *he argued that religion was an outgrowth of magic* **2** a thing growing out of a main body; offshoot

outhouse *n* a building near to, but separate from, a main building

outing ❶ *n* **1** a trip or excursion **2** *informal* the naming by homosexuals of other prominent homosexuals, often against their will

outlandish *adj* extremely unconventional; bizarre

outlast *vb* to last longer than

outlaw ❶ *n* **1** *history* a criminal who has been deprived of legal protection and rights ▹ *vb* **2** to make (something) illegal: *racial discrimination was formally outlawed* **3** *history* to make (someone) an outlaw **outlawed** *adj*

outlay *n* the money, effort, or time spent on something

outlet ❶ *n* **1** a means of expressing one's feelings: *the shock would give her an outlet for her own grief* **2** **a** a market for a product: *there is a huge sales outlet for personal computers* **b** a shop or

THESAURUS

outbreak *n* = **eruption**, burst, explosion, epidemic, rash, outburst, flare-up, flash, spasm, upsurge

outburst *n* **1** = **explosion**, surge, outbreak, eruption, flare-up **2** = **fit**, storm, attack, gush, flare-up, eruption, spasm, outpouring, paroxysm

outcome *n* = **result**, end, consequence, conclusion, end result, payoff *(informal)*, upshot

outcry *n* = **protest**, complaint, objection, cry, dissent, outburst, disapproval, clamour, uproar, commotion, protestation, exclamation, formal complaint, hue and cry, hullaballoo, demurral

outdated *adj* = **old-fashioned**, dated, obsolete, out of date, passé, antique, archaic, unfashionable, antiquated, outmoded, behind the times, out of style, obsolescent, démodé *(French)*, out of the ark *(informal)*, oldfangled **OPPOSITE:** modern

outdoor *adj* **1** = **open-air**, outside, out-of-door(s), alfresco **OPPOSITE:** indoor

outer *adj* **1** = **external**, outside, outward, exterior, exposed, outermost **OPPOSITE:** inner **2** = **outlying**, remote, distant, provincial, out-of-the-way, peripheral, far-flung **OPPOSITE:** central

outfit *n* **1** = **costume**, dress, clothes, clothing, suit, gear *(informal)*, get-up *(informal)*, kit, ensemble, apparel, attire, garb, togs *(informal)*, threads *(slang)*, schmutter *(slang)*, rigout *(informal)* **2** *(informal)* = **group**, company, team, set, party, firm, association, unit, crowd, squad, organization, crew, gang, corps, setup *(informal)*, galère *(French)*

outgoing *adj* **1** = **leaving**, last, former, past, previous, retiring, withdrawing, prior, departing, erstwhile, late, ex- **OPPOSITE:** incoming **2** = **sociable**, open, social, warm, friendly, accessible, expansive, cordial, genial, affable, extrovert, approachable, gregarious, communicative, convivial, demonstrative, unreserved, companionable **OPPOSITE:** reserved

outgoings *pl n* = **expenses**, costs, payments, expenditure, overheads, outlay

outing *n* **1** = **journey**, run, trip, tour, expedition, excursion, spin *(informal)*, ramble, jaunt, pleasure trip

outlaw *n* **1** = **bandit**, criminal, thief, crook, robber, fugitive, outcast, delinquent, felon, highwayman, desperado, marauder, brigand, lawbreaker, footpad *(archaic)* ▹ *vb* **2** = **ban**, bar, veto, forbid, condemn, exclude, embargo, suppress, prohibit, banish, disallow, proscribe, make illegal, interdict **OPPOSITE:** legalise **3** = **banish**, excommunicate, ostracize, put a price on (someone's) head

outlet *n* **1** = **channel**, release, medium, avenue, vent, conduit, safety valve, means of expression **2b** = **shop**,

DICTIONARY

organization selling the goods of a particular producer or wholesaler or manufacturer: *her own brand is now sold to outlets throughout the world* **3** an opening permitting escape or release: *make sure the exhaust outlet is not blocked*

outline ⓣ *n* **1** a general explanation or description of something, which does not give all the details: *the course gave a brief outline of twentieth-century music* **2 outlines** the important features of something: *the outlines of his theory are correct, we just need to fill in the details* **3** the general shape of something, esp. when only the profile and not the details are visible: *it was still light enough to see the outline of the distant mountains* **4** a drawing showing only the external lines of an object ▷ *vb* **-lining, -lined** **5** to give the main features or general idea of (something): *I outlined what we had done and what we had still to do* **6** to show the general shape of an object but not its details, as light does coming from behind an object: *we could see the towers of the city outlined against the night sky*

outlive *vb* **-living, -lived** **1** to live longer than (someone): *she only outlived her husband by a few months* **2** to live beyond (a date or period): *the sparrow outlived the winter* **3 outlive its usefulness** to be no longer useful or necessary: *some argued that the organization had outlived its usefulness*

outlook ⓣ *n* **1** a general attitude to life: *my whole outlook on life had changed* **2** the probable condition or outcome of something: *the economic outlook is not good* **3** the weather forecast for the next few days: *the outlook for the weekend* **4** the view from a place: *a dreary outlook of chimneys and smoke*

outlying *adj* far away from the main area

outmanoeuvre *or US* **outmaneuver** *vb* **-vring, -vred** *or* **-vering, -vered** to gain an advantage over (someone) by skilful dealing: *the management outmanoeuvred us into accepting redundancies*

outmatch *vb* to surpass or outdo (someone)

outmoded *adj* no longer fashionable or accepted

outnumber *vb* to exceed in number: *they were outnumbered by fifty to one*

out of bounds *adj, adv* **1** (often foll. by *to*) not to be entered (by): *the area has been out of bounds to foreign journalists and closed to tourists* **2** (in a sport such as golf) outside the boundaries of the course or playing area

out-of-date ⓣ *adj* **1** old-fashioned; outmoded ▷ *adv* **2** old-fashioned; outmoded

out of doors *adv* in the open air; outside

out of pocket *adj* having lost or spent money: *I was ten pounds out of pocket after paying for their drinks*

out-of-the-way *adj* remote and isolated: *an out-of-the-way village in the Bavarian Forest*

out-of-work *adj* unemployed: *an out-of-work engineer*

outpace *vb* **-pacing, -paced** **1** to go faster than (someone) **2** to surpass or outdo (someone or something) in growth, development, etc.: *the increase in the number of households is outpacing the number of houses being built*

outpatient *n* a patient who visits a hospital for treatment but does not stay there overnight

outport *n Canad* an isolated fishing village, esp. in Newfoundland

outpost *n* a small settlement in a distant part of the country or in a foreign country, which is used for military or trading purposes

outpouring *n* **1** a great amount of something that is produced very rapidly: *a prolific outpouring of ideas and energy* **2** a passionate outburst: *the hysterical outpourings of fanatics*

output ⓣ *n* **1** the amount of something that is made or produced: *our weekly output has increased by 240 tonnes* **2** *electronics* the power, voltage, or current delivered by a circuit or component **3** *computers* the information produced by a computer ▷ *vb* **-putting, -putted** *or* **-put** **4** *computers* to produce (data) at the end of a process

outrage ⓣ *n* **1** deep indignation, anger, or resentment: *she felt a sense of outrage that he should abandon her like that* **2** an extremely vicious or cruel act; gross violation of decency, morality, or honour: *there have been reports of another bombing outrage in the capital* ▷ *vb* **-raging, -raged** **3** to cause deep indignation, anger, or resentment in (someone): *they were outraged by the news of the assassination*
WORD ORIGIN French *outré* beyond

outrageous ⓣ *adj* **1** unusual and shocking: *his sense of humour made him say and do the most outrageous things* **2** shocking and socially or morally unacceptable: *I will fight these outrageous accusations of corruption in the courts if necessary* **outrageously** *adv*

Outram *n* Sir **James** 1803–63, British soldier and administrator in India; he participated in the relief of Lucknow (1857) during the Indian Mutiny

outrank *vb* to be of higher rank than (someone)

outré (oo-tray) *adj* eccentric and rather shocking

THESAURUS

store, supermarket, market, mart, boutique, emporium, hypermarket **3 = pipe**, opening, channel, passage, tube, exit, canal, way out, funnel, conduit, duct, orifice, egress

outline *n* **1 = summary**, review, résumé, abstract, summing-up, digest, rundown, compendium, main features, synopsis, rough idea, précis, bare facts, thumbnail sketch, recapitulation, abridgment **3 = shape**, lines, form, figure, profile, silhouette, configuration, contour(s), delineation, lineament(s) ▷ *vb* **5 = summarize**, review, draft, plan, trace, sketch (in), sum up, encapsulate, delineate, rough out, adumbrate **6 = silhouette**, etch, delineate

outlook *n* **1 = attitude**, views, opinion, position, approach, mood, perspective, point of view, stance, viewpoint, disposition, standpoint, frame of mind **2 = prospect(s)**, future, expectations, forecast, prediction, projection, probability, prognosis

out-of-date *adj* **2 = old-fashioned**, ancient, dated, discarded, extinct, outdated, stale, obsolete, démodé *(French)*, archaic, unfashionable, superseded, antiquated, outmoded, passé, old hat, behind the times, superannuated, out of style, outworn, obsolescent, out of the ark *(informal)*, oldfangled **OPPOSITE:** modern

output *n* **1 = production**, manufacture, manufacturing, yield, productivity, outturn *(rare)*

outrage *n* **1 = indignation**, shock, anger, rage, fury, hurt, resentment, scorn, wrath, ire *(literary)*, exasperation, umbrage, righteous anger ▷ *vb* **3 = offend**, shock, upset, pain, wound, provoke, insult, infuriate, incense, gall, madden, vex, affront, displease, rile, scandalize, give offence, nark *(Brit, Austral & NZ slang)*, cut to the quick, make your blood boil, put (someone's) nose out of joint, put (someone's) back up, disgruntle

outrageous *adj* **1 = atrocious**, shocking, terrible, violent, offensive, appalling, cruel, savage, horrible, beastly, horrifying, vicious, ruthless, infamous, disgraceful, scandalous, wicked, barbaric, unspeakable, inhuman, diabolical, heinous, flagrant, egregious, abominable, infernal, fiendish, villainous, nefarious, iniquitous, execrable, godawful *(slang)*, hellacious *(US slang)* **OPPOSITE:** mild **2 = unreasonable**, unfair, excessive, steep *(informal)*, shocking, over the top *(slang)*, extravagant, too great, scandalous, preposterous, unwarranted, exorbitant, extortionate, immoderate, O.T.T. *(slang)* **OPPOSITE:** reasonable

DICTIONARY

WORD ORIGIN French: having gone beyond
outrider *n* a person who rides a motorcycle or horse in front of or beside an official vehicle as an attendant or guard
outrigger *n* **1** a stabilizing framework projecting from the side of a boat or canoe **2** a boat or canoe equipped with such a framework
outright ⓣ *adj* **1** complete; total: *he is close to an outright victory* **2** straightforward and direct: *outright hostility* ▷ *adv* **3** completely: *the film was banned outright* **4** instantly: *my driver was killed outright* **5** openly: *ask her outright why she treated you as she did*
outrun *vb* **-running, -ran, -run 1** to run faster or further than (someone) **2** to develop faster than (something): *the population of the city is in danger of outrunning the supply of houses*
outsell *vb* **-selling, -sold** to be sold in greater quantities than: *CDs are now outselling cassettes*
outset ⓣ *n* a start; beginning: *we never really hit it off from the outset*
outshine *vb* **-shining, -shone** to be better than (someone) at something: *by university she had begun to outshine me in sports*
outside ⓣ *prep* **1** on or to the exterior of: *a crowd gathered outside the court* **2** beyond the limits of: *it was outside my experience and beyond my ability* **3** apart from; other than: *no-one knows outside us* ▷ *adj* **4** on or of the outside: *an outside light is also a good idea* **5** remote; unlikely: *I still had an outside chance of the title* **6** coming from outside a particular group or organization: *the patient had been subjected to outside influences* **7** of or being the lane in a road which is further from the side than other lanes going in the same direction: *he was doing 120 in the outside lane* ▷ *adv* **8** outside a specified thing or place; out of doors: *we went outside to get some fresh air* **9** *slang* not in prison ▷ *n* **10** the external side or surface of something **11 at the outside** *informal* at the very most: *I'll be away four days at the outside*
outside broadcast *n radio, television* a broadcast not made from a studio
outsider ⓣ *n* **1** a person excluded from a group **2** a contestant thought unlikely to win
outsize *adj* **1** Also: **outsized** very large or larger than normal ▷ *n* **2** an outsize garment
outskirts ⓣ *pl n* the parts of a town or city that are furthest from the centre: *an office in the northernmost outskirts of Glasgow*
outsmart *vb informal* ▸ same as **outwit**
outsource *vb* **1** to subcontract (work) to another company **2** to buy (components for a product) rather than manufacture them
outspan ⓣ *S African n* **1** an area on a farm kept available for travellers to rest and refresh their animals ▷ *vb* **-spanning, -spanned 2** to unharness or unyoke (animals) **3** to relax
WORD ORIGIN Afrikaans *uit* out + *spannen* to stretch
outspoken ⓣ *adj* **1** saying exactly what one thinks: *an outspoken critic of human rights abuses* **2** spoken candidly: *she is known for her outspoken views*
outspokenness *n*
outspread *adj* spread or stretched out as far as possible: *a gull glided by with outspread wings*
outstanding ⓣ *adj* **1** very good; excellent: *an outstanding performance* **2** still to be dealt with or paid: *outstanding bills; a few outstanding problems have to be put right* **3** very obvious or important: *there are significant exceptions, of which oil is the outstanding example* **outstandingly** *adv*
outstation *n* a station or post in a remote region
outstay *vb* ▸ same as **overstay**
outstretched *adj* extended or stretched out as far as possible: *he pushed a wad of drachma notes into the young man's outstretched hand*
outstrip *vb* **-stripping, -stripped 1** to surpass (someone) in a particular activity: *his newspapers outstrip all others in vulgarity* **2** to go faster than (someone)
outtake *n* an unreleased take from a recording session, film, or television programme
out there *adj slang* unconventional or eccentric

THESAURUS

outright *adj* **1 = absolute**, complete, total, direct, perfect, pure, sheer, utter, thorough, wholesale, unconditional, downright, consummate, unqualified, undeniable, out-and-out, unadulterated, unmitigated, thoroughgoing, unalloyed, arrant, deep-dyed *(usually derogatory)* **2 = definite**, clear, certain, straight, flat, absolute, black-and-white, decisive, straightforward, clear-cut, unmistakable, unequivocal, unqualified, unambiguous, cut-and-dried *(informal)*, incontrovertible, uncontestable ▷ *adv* **3 = absolutely**, completely, totally, fully, entirely, thoroughly, wholly, utterly, to the full, without hesitation, to the hilt, one hundred per cent, straightforwardly, without restraint, unmitigatedly, lock, stock and barrel **5 = openly**, frankly, plainly, face to face, explicitly, overtly, candidly, unreservedly, unhesitatingly, forthrightly, straight from the shoulder *(informal)*
outset *n* **= beginning**, start, opening, early days, starting point, onset, inauguration, inception, commencement, kickoff *(informal)*
OPPOSITE: finish
outside *adj* **4 = external**, outer, exterior, surface, extreme, outdoor, outward, superficial, extraneous, outermost, extramural
OPPOSITE: inner
5 = remote, small, unlikely, slight, slim, poor, distant, faint, marginal, doubtful, dubious, slender, meagre, negligible, inconsiderable ▷ *adv* **8 = outdoors**, out, out of the house, out-of-doors ▷ *n* **10 = exterior**, face, front, covering, skin, surface, shell, coating, finish, façade, topside
outsider *n* **1 = stranger**, incomer, visitor, foreigner, alien, newcomer, intruder, new arrival, unknown, interloper, odd one out, nonmember, outlander
outskirts *pl n* **= edge**, borders, boundary, suburbs, fringe, perimeter, vicinity, periphery, suburbia, environs, purlieus, faubourgs
outspan *vb* **3** *(S African)* **= relax**, chill out *(slang, chiefly US)*, take it easy, loosen up, laze, lighten up *(slang)*, put your feet up, hang loose *(slang)*, let yourself go *(informal)*, let your hair down *(informal)*, mellow out *(informal)*, make yourself at home
outspoken *adj* **1, 2 = forthright**, open, free, direct, frank, straightforward, blunt, explicit, downright, candid, upfront *(informal)*, unequivocal, undisguised, plain-spoken, unreserved, unconcealed, unceremonious, free-spoken, straight from the shoulder *(informal)*, undissembling **OPPOSITE:** reserved
outstanding *adj* **1 = excellent**, good, great, important, special, fine, noted, champion, celebrated, brilliant, impressive, superb, distinguished, well-known, prominent, superior, first-class, exceptional, notable, world-class, exquisite, admirable, eminent, exemplary, first-rate, stellar *(informal)*, superlative, top-notch *(informal)*, mean *(slang)*, pre-eminent, meritorious, estimable, tiptop, A1 *or* A-one *(informal)*, booshit *(Austral slang)*, exo *(Austral slang)*, sik *(Austral slang)*, rad *(informal)*, phat *(slang)*, schmick *(Austral informal)*, beaut *(informal)*, barrie *(Scot slang)*, belting *(Brit slang)*, pearler *(Austral slang)*
OPPOSITE: mediocre
2a = unpaid, remaining, due, owing, ongoing, pending, payable, unsettled, unresolved, uncollected
2b = undone, left, not done, omitted, unfinished, incomplete, passed over, unfulfilled, not completed, unperformed, unattended to

DICTIONARY

out-tray *n* a shallow basket in an office for collecting letters and documents that are to be sent out

outvote *vb* **-voting, -voted** to defeat (someone) by getting more votes than him or her

outward ❶ *adj* **1** apparent or superficial: *to outward appearances the house is largely unchanged today* **2** of or relating to the outside: *outward shape* **3** (of a journey) away from a place to which one intends to return ▹ *adv also* **outwards 4** in an outward direction; towards the outside
outwardly *adv*

outweigh ❶ *vb* **1** to be more important, significant, or influential than: *these niggles are outweighed by the excellent cooking and service* **2** to be heavier than

outwit *vb* **-witting, -witted** to gain an advantage over (someone) by cunning or ingenuity

outworks *pl n mil* defences which lie outside the main fortifications of a fort etc.

outworn *adj* (of a belief or custom) old-fashioned and no longer of any use or relevance: *there is no point in pandering to outworn superstition*

ouzel *or* **ousel** (ooze-el) *n* ▸ same as **dipper** (sense 2)
WORD ORIGIN Old English *ōsle*

ouzo (ooze-oh) *n, pl* **ouzos** a strong aniseed-flavoured alcoholic drink from Greece
WORD ORIGIN Modern Greek *ouzon*

ova *n* ▸ the plural of **ovum**

oval ❶ *adj* **1** egg-shaped ▹ *n* **2** anything that is oval in shape, such as a sports ground
WORD ORIGIN Latin *ovum* egg

ovary *n, pl* **-ries 1** a reproductive organ in women and female animals in which eggs are produced **2** *bot* the lower part of a pistil, containing the ovules **ovarian** *adj*
WORD ORIGIN Latin *ovum* egg

ovate *adj* shaped like an egg: *the tree has bluish-green, ovate leaves*
WORD ORIGIN Latin *ovatus* egg-shaped

ovation ❶ *n* an enthusiastic round of applause
WORD ORIGIN Latin *ovatio* rejoicing

oven *n* **1** an enclosed heated compartment or container for baking or roasting food, or for drying or firing ceramics ▹ *vb* **2** to cook in an oven
WORD ORIGIN Old English *ofen*

over ❶ *prep* **1** directly above; across the top or upper surface of: *set the frying pan over a low heat* **2** on or to the other side of: *the pilot flew over the blue waters* **3** during or throughout (a period of time): *over the next few months it became clear what was happening* **4** throughout the whole extent of: *the effects are being felt all over the country now* **5** by means of (an instrument of telecommunication): *there was an announcement over the Tannoy system* **6** more than: *she had met him over a year ago* **7** concerning; about: *there has been much argument over these figures* **8** while occupied in: *I'll tell you over dinner tonight* **9** having recovered from the effects of: *he appeared to be over his niggling injury problems* **10 all over someone** *informal* extremely affectionate or attentive towards someone **11 over and above** added to; in addition to ▹ *adv* **12** in a state, condition, or position over something: *to climb over* **13** onto its side: *the jug toppled over* **14** at or to a point across an intervening space: *she carried him over to the other side of the river* **15** covering the whole area: *there's poverty the world over* **16** from beginning to end: *to read a document over* **17 all over a** finished **b** over one's entire body **c** typically: *that's him all over* **18 over again** once more **19 over and over (again)** repeatedly ▹ *interj* **20** (in signalling and radio) it is now your turn to speak ▹ *adj* **21** finished; no longer in progress: *the second round of voting is over* ▹ *adv* **22** remaining: *there wasn't any money left over* ▹ *adj* **23** surplus ▹ *n* **24** *cricket* **a** a series of six balls bowled by a bowler from the same end of the pitch **b** the play during this
WORD ORIGIN Old English *ofer*

over- *prefix* **1** excessive or excessively: *overcharge; overdue* **2** superior in rank: *overlord* **3** indicating location or movement above: *overhang* **4** downwards from above: *overthrow*

overabundance *n* more than is really needed; excess

overact *vb* to act in an exaggerated way

overactive *adj* more active than is normal or desirable: *an overactive thyroid gland*

overall ❶ *adj* **1** from one end to the other: *the overall length* **2** including everything; total: *the overall cost* ▹ *adv* **3** in general; on the whole: *overall, I think this is the better car* ▹ *n* **4** *Brit & NZ* a coat-shaped work garment worn over ordinary clothes as a protection against dirt **5 overalls** work trousers with a bib and braces or jacket attached, worn over ordinary clothes as a protection against dirt and wear

overambitious *adj* attempting more than one has the ability to do well: *good plain cookery marred by overambitious sauces*

overarching *adj* overall or all-encompassing: *an overarching concept*

overarm *sport adj* **1** bowled, thrown, or performed with the arm raised above the shoulder ▹ *adv* **2** with the arm raised above the shoulder

overawe *vb* **-awing, -awed** to affect (someone) with an overpowering sense of awe: *he was overawed by the prospect of meeting the Prime Minister*

overbalance *vb* **-ancing, -anced** to lose one's balance

overbearing *adj* **1** imposing one's views in an unpleasant or forceful manner **2** of particular or overriding importance: *an overbearing need*

overblown *adj* inflated or excessive: *humiliation comes from having overblown expectations for yourself*

overboard *adv* **1** from a boat or ship into the water: *many passengers drowned when they jumped overboard to escape the flames* **2 go overboard** *informal* **a** to be extremely enthusiastic **b** to go to extremes **3 throw overboard** to reject or abandon (an idea or a plan)

overburden *vb* to have more of

THESAURUS

outward *adj* **1 = apparent**, seeming, outside, surface, external, outer, superficial, ostensible
OPPOSITE: inward

outweigh *vb* **1 = override**, cancel (out), eclipse, offset, make up for, compensate for, redeem, supersede, neutralize, counterbalance, nullify, take precedence over, prevail over, obviate, balance out, preponderate, outbalance

oval *adj* **1 = elliptical**, egg-shaped, ovoid, ovate, ellipsoidal, oviform

ovation *n* **= applause**, hand, cheering, cheers, praise, tribute, acclaim, clapping, accolade, plaudits, big hand, commendation, hand-clapping, acclamation, laudation **OPPOSITE:** derision

over *prep* **1a = above**, on top of, atop **1b = on top of**, on, across, upon **2 = across**, past, (looking) onto **6 = more than**, above, exceeding, in excess of, upwards of **7 = about**, regarding, relating to, with respect to, re, concerning, apropos of, anent (*Scot*) ▹ *adj* **21 = finished**, by, done (with), through, ended, closed, past, completed, complete, gone, in the past, settled, concluded, accomplished, wrapped up (*informal*), bygone, at an end, ancient history (*informal*), over and done with ▹ *adv* **22 = extra**, more, other, further, beyond, additional, in addition, surplus, in excess, left over, unused, supplementary, auxiliary

overall *adj* **2 = total**, full, whole, general, complete, long-term, entire, global, comprehensive, gross, blanket, umbrella, long-range, inclusive, all-embracing, overarching ▹ *adv* **3 = in general**, generally, mostly, all things considered, on average, in (the) large, on the whole, predominantly, in the main, in the long term, by and large, all in all, on balance, generally

something than it is possible to cope with: *the city's streets are already overburdened by rush-hour motorists*

overcast *adj* (of the sky or weather) cloudy

overcharge *vb* **-charging, -charged** to charge too high a price

overcoat *n* a warm heavy coat worn in cold weather

overcome ⊙ *vb* **-coming, -came, -come 1** to deal successfully with or control (a problem or feeling): *once I'd overcome my initial nerves I discovered hang-gliding was great fun* **2** (of an emotion or a feeling) to affect (someone) strongly or make (someone) powerless: *he was overcome by a sudden surge of jealousy* **3** to defeat (someone) in a conflict

overcompensate *vb* **-sating, -sated** to attempt to make up for or cancel out (something) to an unnecessary degree: *when bookings dropped slightly, the company overcompensated by slashing the price of its holidays by 50%*

overconfident *adj* having more belief in one's abilities than is justified

overcook *vb* to spoil food by cooking it for too long

overcrowded *adj* containing more people or things than is desirable: *overcrowded commuter trains*

overcrowding *n* the cramming of too many people into too small a space: *prison overcrowding and poor conditions*

overdo *vb* **-does, -doing, -did, -done 1** to do (something) to excess **2** to exaggerate (something) **3** to cook (something) too long **4 overdo it** *or* **things** to something to a greater degree than is advisable or healthy

overdose *n* **1** a larger dose of a drug than is safe: *she tried to kill herself with an overdose of alcohol and drugs* ▷ *vb* **-dosing, -dosed 2** to take more of a drug than is safe, either accidentally or deliberately: *this drug is rarely prescribed because it is easy to overdose fatally on it*

overdraft *n* **1** the withdrawal of more money from a bank account than there is in it **2** the amount of money withdrawn thus

overdraw *vb* **-drawing, -drew, -drawn** to withdraw more money from a bank account than is in it

overdrawn *adj* **1** having overdrawn one's bank account **2** (of an account) in debit

overdressed *adj* wearing clothes which are too elaborate or formal for the occasion

overdrive *n* **1** a very high gear in a motor vehicle, used at high speeds to reduce wear **2** a state of great activity or excitement: *the government propaganda machine went into overdrive to try to play down the Minister's comments*

overdub *vb* **-dubbing, -dubbed 1** to add (new sounds) to a tape in such a way that the old and the new sounds can be heard ▷ *n* **2** a sound or series of sounds added by this method

overdue ⊙ *adj* **1** not having arrived or happened by the time expected or desired: *a reassessment of policy on this issue is long overdue* **2** (of money) not having been paid by the required date: *by this time his rent was three weeks overdue* **3** (of a library book) not having been returned to the library by the required date

overeat *vb* **-eating, -ate, -eaten** to eat more than is necessary or healthy

overemphasize *or* **-sise** *vb* **-sizing, -sized** *or* **-sising, -sised** to give (something) more importance than is necessary or appropriate

overestimate *vb* **-mating, -mated** to believe something or someone to be bigger, more important, or better than is the case **overestimation** *n*

overexcited *adj* excessively enthusiastic or agitated

overexert *vb* to exhaust or injure oneself by doing too much **overexertion** *n*

overexposed *adj* (of a photograph) too light in colour because the film has been exposed to light for too long

overfeed *vb* **-feeding, -fed** to give (a person, plant, or animal) more food than is necessary or healthy

overfill *vb* to put more into (something) than there is room for

overflow ⊙ *vb* **-flowing, -flowed** *or formerly* **-flown 1** to flow over (a brim) **2** to be filled beyond capacity so as to spill over **3 overflow with** to be filled with (an emotion): *a letter overflowing with passion and ardour* ▷ *n* **4** something that overflows, usually a liquid **5** an outlet that enables surplus liquid to be drained off **6** the amount by which a limit or capacity is exceeded ▷ *adj* **7** of or being a subsidiary thing for use when there is no room left in the main one: *an overflow car park*

overgraze *vb* **-grazing, -grazed** to graze (land) too intensively so that it is damaged and no longer provides nourishment

overgrown *adj* covered over with plants or weeds: *they headed up the overgrown and winding trail*

overhang *vb* **-hanging, -hung 1** to project or hang over beyond (something) ▷ *n* **2** an overhanging part or object

overhaul ⊙ *vb* **1** to examine (a system or an idea) carefully for faults **2** to make repairs or adjustments to (a vehicle or machine) **3** to overtake (a vehicle or person) ▷ *n* **4** a thorough examination and repair

overhead ⊙ *adj* **1** situated or operating above head height: *overhead compartments* ▷ *adv* **2** over or above head height: *the missile streaked overhead*

overhead projector *n* a projector that throws an enlarged image of a transparency onto a surface above and behind the person using it

overheads ⊙ *pl n* the general costs of running a business, such as rent, electricity, and stationery

overhear *vb* **-hearing, -heard** to hear (a speaker or remark) unintentionally or without the knowledge of the speaker

O

THESAURUS

speaking, taking everything into consideration

overcome *vb* **1 = conquer**, beat, master, survive, weather, curb, suppress, subdue, rise above, quell, triumph over, get the better of, vanquish **3 = defeat**, beat, conquer, master, tank *(slang)*, crush, overwhelm, overthrow, lick *(informal)*, undo, subdue, rout, overpower, quell, triumph over, best, get the better of, trounce, worst, clobber *(slang)*, stuff *(slang)*, vanquish, surmount, subjugate, prevail over, wipe the floor with *(informal)*, make mincemeat of *(informal)*, blow (someone) out of the water *(slang)*, come out on top of *(informal)*, bring (someone) to their knees *(informal)*, render incapable, render powerless, be victorious over, render helpless

overdue *adj* **1 = delayed**, belated, late, late in the day, long delayed, behind schedule, tardy, not before time *(informal)*, behind time, unpunctual, behindhand **OPPOSITE:** early **2 = unpaid**, owing

overflow *vb* **2 = spill over**, discharge, well over, run over, pour over, pour out, bubble over, brim over, surge over, slop over, teem over ▷ *n* **4 = flood**, flooding, spill, discharge, spilling over, inundation **6 = surplus**, extra, excess, overspill, inundation, overabundance, additional people *or* things

overhaul *vb* **1, 2 = check**, service, maintain, examine, restore, tune (up), repair, go over, inspect, fine tune, do up *(informal)*, re-examine, recondition **3 = overtake**, pass, leave behind, catch up with, get past, outstrip, get ahead of, draw level with, outdistance ▷ *n* **4 = check**, service, examination, going-over *(informal)*, inspection, once-over *(informal)*, checkup, reconditioning

overhead *adj* **1 = raised**, suspended, elevated, aerial, overhanging ▷ *adv* **2 = above**, in the sky, on high, aloft, up above **OPPOSITE:** underneath

overheads *pl n* **= running costs**, expenses, outgoings, operating costs, oncosts

DICTIONARY

overheat *vb* **1** to make or become too hot **2** to cause (an economy) to tend towards inflation **3 become overheated** (of a person, discussion, etc.) to become angry or agitated: *the Colonel becomes overheated if he sees the term 'Ms' in the newspaper*

overindulge *vb* **-dulging, -dulged** to do too much of something pleasant, such as eating or drinking: *nobody ever wants a hangover, but we all overindulge occasionally* **overindulgence** *n*

overjoyed *adj* extremely pleased

overkill *n* any treatment that is greater than that required: *the overkill in negative propaganda resulted in this upsurge*

overlap *vb* **-lapping, -lapped 1** (of two things) to share part of the same space as or lie partly over (each other): *slice the meat and lay it in overlapping slices in a serving dish* **2** to coincide partly in time or subject: *their careers have overlapped for the last ten years* ▷ *n* **3** a part that overlaps **4** the amount or length of something overlapping

overlay *vb* **-laying, -laid 1** to cover (a surface) with an applied decoration: *a woollen cloth overlaid with gold and silver embroidery* ▷ *n* **2** something that is laid over something else; a covering **3** an applied decoration or layer, for example of gold leaf

overleaf *adv* on the other side of the page

overlie *vb* **-lying, -lay, -lain** to lie on or cover (something or someone): *a thin layer of black dust overlay everything*

overload *vb* **1** to put too large a load on or in (something): *the aircraft was dangerously overloaded* **2** to cause (a transport system) to be unable to function properly because too many people or vehicles are using it: *Heathrow Airport was already overloaded by 1972* **3** to try to put more electricity through a system than the system can cope with ▷ *n* **4** an excessive load

overlook ❶ *vb* **1** to fail to notice (something) **2** to disregard or ignore (misbehaviour or a fault): *I'm prepared to overlook your failure, but don't do it again* **3** to give a view of (something) from above: *a cliff overlooking the Atlantic*

overlord *n* a supreme lord or master

overly *adv* too; excessively

overman *vb* **-manning, -manned** to provide with too many staff: *the company is not overmanned overall, but it has too many managers and not enough productive workers* **overmanned** *adj* **overmanning** *n*

overmuch *adv, adj* too much; very much

overnight *adv* **1** during the night **2** in or as if in the course of one night; suddenly: *we are not saying that a change like this would happen overnight* ▷ *adj* **3** done in, occurring in, or lasting the night: *the army has ordered an overnight curfew* **4** staying for one night: *overnight guests* **5** for use during a single night: *should I pack an overnight case?* **6** happening very quickly; sudden: *he doesn't expect the programme to be an overnight success*

overpaid *adj* earning more money than one deserves

overpass *n* ▸ same as **flyover**

overplay *vb* **1** to overemphasize (something) **2 overplay one's hand** to overestimate the worth or strength of one's position

overpopulated *adj* (of a town or country) having more people living in it than it can support

overpopulation *n* the state of being overpopulated

overpower ❶ *vb* **1** to conquer or subdue (someone) by superior force **2** to have such a strong effect on (someone) as to make him or her helpless or ineffective: *I was so appalled, so overpowered by my guilt and my shame that I was unable to speak* **overpowering** *adj*

overpriced *adj* costing more than it is thought to be worth

overprint *vb* **1** to print (additional matter or another colour) onto (something already printed) ▷ *n* **2** additional matter or another colour printed onto something already printed

overqualified *adj* having more professional or academic qualifications than are required for a job

overrate *vb* to have too high an opinion of: *the director's role was seriously overrated*

overreach *vb* **overreach oneself** to fail by trying to be too clever or achieve too much: *he built up a successful media empire before he overreached himself and lost much of his fortune*

overreact *vb* to react more strongly or forcefully than is necessary: *allergies happen when the body overreacts to a harmless substance* **overreaction** *n*

override ❶ *vb* **-riding, -rode, -ridden 1** to set aside or disregard (a person or a person's decisions) by having superior authority or power: *the managing director can override any decision he doesn't like* **2** to be more important than or replace (something): *unsurprisingly the day-to-day struggle for survival overrode all moral considerations* **overriding** *adj*

overripe *adj* (of a fruit or vegetable) so ripe that it has started to decay or go soft

overrule *vb* **-ruling, -ruled 1** to reverse the decision of (a person or organization with less power): *the President overruled the hardliners in the party who wanted to use force* **2** to rule or decide against (an argument or decision): *the initial judgment was overruled by the Supreme Court*

overrun ❶ *vb* **-running, -ran, -run 1** to conquer (territory) rapidly by force of number **2** to spread over (a place) rapidly: *dirty tenements, overrun by lice, rats, and roaches* **3** to extend or run beyond a set limit: *Tuesday's lunch overran by three-quarters of an hour*

overseas *adv* **1** across the sea; abroad ▷ *adj* **2** of, to, from, or in a distant country or countries ▷ *n* **3** *informal* a foreign country or foreign countries collectively

oversee *vb* **-seeing, -saw, -seen** to watch over and direct (someone or something); supervise **overseer** *n*

O

THESAURUS

overlook *vb* **1 = miss**, forget, neglect, omit, disregard, pass over, fail to notice, leave undone, slip up on, leave out of consideration
OPPOSITE: notice
2 = ignore, excuse, forgive, pardon, disregard, condone, turn a blind eye to, wink at, blink at, make allowances for, let someone off with, let pass, let ride, discount, pass over, take no notice of, be oblivious to, pay no attention to, turn a deaf ear to, shut your eyes to **3 = look over** *or* **out on**, have a view of, command a view of, front on to, give upon, afford a view of

overpower *vb* **1 = overcome**, master, overwhelm, overthrow, subdue, quell, get the better of, subjugate, prevail over, immobilize, bring (someone) to their knees *(informal)*, render incapable, render powerless, render helpless, get the upper hand over **2 = overwhelm**, overcome, bowl over *(informal)*, stagger

override *vb* **1a = overrule**, reverse, cancel, overturn, set aside, repeal, quash, revoke, disallow, rescind, upset, rule against, invalidate, annul, nullify, ride roughshod over, outvote, countermand, trample underfoot, make null and void
1b = ignore, reject, discount, overlook, set aside, disregard, pass over, take no notice of, take no account of, pay no attention to, turn a deaf ear to **2 = outweigh**, overcome, eclipse, supersede, take precedence over, prevail over, outbalance

overrun *vb* **1 = overwhelm**, attack, assault, occupy, raid, invade, penetrate, swamp, rout, assail, descend upon, run riot over
2 = spread over, overwhelm, choke, swamp, overflow, infest, inundate, permeate, spread like wildfire, swarm over, surge over, overgrow

DICTIONARY

oversell *vb* **-selling, -sold** to exaggerate the merits or abilities of

oversew *vb* **-sewing, -sewed, -sewn** *or* **-sewed** to sew (two edges) with stitches that pass over them both

oversexed *adj* more interested in sex than is thought decent

overshadow ❶ *vb* **1** to make (someone or something) seem insignificant or less important by comparison **2** to sadden the atmosphere of: *news of their team-mate's injury overshadowed the victory celebrations*

overshoe *n* a protective shoe worn over an ordinary shoe

overshoot *vb* **-shooting, -shot** to go beyond (a mark or target): *the plane overshot the main runway*

overshot *adj* (of a water wheel) driven by a flow of water that passes over the wheel

oversight *n* a mistake caused by not noticing something

oversimplify *vb* **-fies, -fying, -fied** to make something seem simpler than it really is: *the Nationalists' analysis oversimplifies the problems facing the country today*

oversized *adj* much larger than the usual size

oversleep *vb* **-sleeping, -slept** to sleep beyond the intended time for getting up

overspend *vb* **-spending, -spent** to spend more than one can afford

overspill *n Brit* the rehousing of people from crowded cities in smaller towns

overstate *vb* **-stating, -stated** to state (something) too strongly; overemphasize **overstatement** *n*

overstay *vb* **overstay one's welcome** to stay as a guest longer than one's host or hostess would like

overstayer *n NZ* a person who remains in New Zealand after their permit has expired

overstep *vb* **-stepping, -stepped 1** to go beyond the limits of what is thought acceptable: *he had overstepped his authority by acting without consulting his superiors* **2 overstep the mark** to go too far and behave in an unacceptable way

overstretch *vb* **1** to attempt to do more than there is time or capability for: *for the first time in her career she may have overstretched her talents* **2** to damage (something) by stretching it further than it can safely go: *he overstretched his Achilles tendon* **overstretched** *adj*

overstrung *adj* too highly strung; tense

overt ❶ *adj* done or shown in an open and obvious way: *jurors were now looking at the defendant with overt hostility* **overtly** *adv*
WORD ORIGIN Old French

overtake ❶ *vb* **-taking, -took, -taken 1** *chiefly Brit* to move past (another vehicle or person) travelling in the same direction **2** to do better than (someone) after catching up with him or her **3** to come upon (someone) suddenly or unexpectedly: *a mortal tiredness overtook him*

overtax *vb* **1** to impose too great a strain on: *a singer who had overtaxed her voice* **2** to tax (people) too heavily

over-the-top *adj slang* excessive; beyond the usual or acceptable bounds of behaviour

overthrow ❶ *vb* **-throwing, -threw, -thrown 1** to defeat and replace (a ruler or government) by force **2** to replace (standards or values) ▷ *n* **3** downfall or destruction: *the overthrow of the US-backed dictatorship*

overtime *n* **1** work at a regular job done in addition to regular working hours **2** pay for such work ▷ *adv* **3** in addition to one's regular working hours: *she had been working overtime and she fell asleep at the wheel*

overtone *n* **1** an additional meaning or hint: *I don't want to deny that from time to time there are political overtones* **2** *music, acoustics* any of the tones, with the exception of the principal or lowest one, that make up a musical sound

overture *n* **1** *music* **a** a piece of orchestral music played at the beginning of an opera, oratorio, ballet, musical comedy, or film, often containing the main musical themes of the work **b** a one-movement orchestral piece, usually having a descriptive or evocative title: *the 1812 Overture* **2 overtures** opening moves towards a new relationship or agreement: *the German government made a variety of friendly overtures towards the French*
WORD ORIGIN Late Latin *apertura* opening

overturn ❶ *vb* **1** to turn over or upside down **2** to overrule or reverse (a legal decision) **3** to overthrow or destroy (a government)

overuse *vb* **1** to use excessively ▷ *n* **2** excessive use

overvalue *vb* **-valuing, -valued** to regard (someone or something) as much more important or valuable than is the case: *his approach overvalues hard work and undervalues true skill* **overvalued** *adj*

overview *n* a general survey

overweening *adj* (of opinions or qualities) excessive or immoderate: *your modesty is a cover for your overweening conceit*
WORD ORIGIN obsolete *ween* to think

overweight ❶ *adj* **1** (of a person) weighing more than is healthy **2** weighing more than is usual or permitted

THESAURUS

3 = exceed, go beyond, surpass, overshoot, outrun, run over *or* on

overshadow *vb* **1 = outshine**, eclipse, surpass, dwarf, rise above, take precedence over, tower above, steal the limelight from, leave *or* put in the shade, render insignificant by comparison, throw into the shade **2 = spoil**, ruin, mar, wreck, scar, blight, crool *or* cruel *(Austral slang)*, mess up, take the edge off, put a damper on, cast a gloom upon, take the pleasure *or* enjoyment out of

overt *adj* **= open**, obvious, plain, public, clear, apparent, visible, patent, evident, manifest, noticeable, blatant, downright, avowed, flagrant, observable, undisguised, barefaced, unconcealed
OPPOSITE: hidden

overtake *vb* **1 = pass**, leave behind, overhaul, catch up with, get past, draw level with, outdistance, go by *or* past **2 = outdo**, top, exceed, eclipse, surpass, outstrip, get the better of, outclass, outshine, best, go one better than *(informal)*, outdistance, be one up on **3 = befall**, hit, happen to, come upon, take by surprise, catch off guard, catch unawares, catch unprepared

overthrow *vb* **1 = defeat**, beat, master, overcome, crush, overwhelm, conquer, bring down, oust, lick *(informal)*, topple, subdue, rout, overpower, do away with, depose, trounce, unseat, vanquish, subjugate, dethrone
OPPOSITE: uphold
▷ *n* **3 = downfall**, end, fall, defeat, collapse, ruin, destruction, breakdown, ousting, undoing, rout, suppression, displacement, subversion, deposition, unseating, subjugation, dispossession, disestablishment, dethronement
OPPOSITE: preservation

overturn *vb* **1a = tip over**, spill, topple, upturn, capsize, upend, keel over, overbalance **1b = knock over** *or* **down**, upset, upturn, tip over, upend **2 = reverse**, change, alter, cancel, abolish, overthrow, set aside, repeal, quash, revoke, overrule, override, negate, rescind, invalidate, annul, nullify, obviate, countermand, declare null and void, overset **3 = overthrow**, defeat, destroy, overcome, crush, bring down, oust, topple, do away with, depose, unseat, dethrone

overweight *adj* **1 = fat**, heavy, stout, huge, massive, solid, gross, hefty, ample, plump, bulky, chunky, chubby, obese, fleshy, beefy *(informal)*, tubby *(informal)*, portly, outsize,

DICTIONARY

overwhelm ❶ *vb* **1** to overpower the thoughts, emotions, or senses of (someone): *we were overwhelmed with grief* **2** to overcome (people) with irresistible force: *gang violence has overwhelmed an ailing police force* **overwhelming** *adj* **overwhelmingly** *adv*

overwork *vb* **1** to work too hard or too long **2** to use (something) too much: *anti-communism was already being overworked by others* ▷ *n* **3** excessive work

overwrite *vb* **-writing, -wrote, -written 1** to record on a storage medium, such as a magnetic disk, thus destroying what was originally recorded there **2** to write (something) in an excessively ornate style

overwrought *adj* tense, nervous, and agitated

Ovett *n* **Steve** born 1955, British middle-distance runner: winner of the 800 metres in the 1980 Olympic Games

oviduct *n anat* the tube through which eggs are conveyed from an ovary
WORD ORIGIN Latin *ovum* egg + *ducere* to lead

oviform *adj biol* shaped like an egg
WORD ORIGIN Latin *ovum* egg + *forma* shape

ovine *adj* of or like a sheep
WORD ORIGIN Latin *ovis* sheep

oviparous (oh-vip-par-uss) *adj zool* producing eggs that hatch outside the body of the mother
WORD ORIGIN Latin *ovum* egg + *-parus* bearing

ovoid (oh-void) *adj* egg-shaped

ovulate (ov-yew-late) *vb* **-lating, -lated** *biol* to produce or release eggs from an ovary **ovulation** *n*

ovule *n* **1** *bot* the part of a plant that contains the egg cell and develops into the seed after fertilization **2** *zool* an immature ovum
WORD ORIGIN Latin *ovum* egg

ovum (oh-vum) *n, pl* **ova** an unfertilized female egg cell
WORD ORIGIN Latin: egg

owe ❶ *vb* **owing, owed 1** to be under an obligation to pay an amount of money to (someone): *he owes me a lot of money* **2** to feel an obligation to do or give: *I think I owe you an apology* **3 owe something to** to have something as a result of: *many serving officers owe their present position to the former president*
WORD ORIGIN Old English *āgan* to have

owing ❶ *adj* **1** not yet paid; due: *the bailiffs seized goods worth far more than the amount owing* **2 owing to** because of; as a result of: *the flight was delayed owing to fog*

owl *n* a bird of prey which has a flat face, large eyes, and a small hooked beak, and which is active at night **owlish** *adj*
WORD ORIGIN Old English *ūle*

own ❶ *adj* (*preceded by a possessive*) **1** used to emphasize that something belongs to a particular person: *rely on your own instincts* ▷ *pron* (*preceded by a possessive*) **2** the one or ones belonging to a particular person: *I had one of my own* **3** the people that someone feels loyalty to, esp. relations: *we all look after our own around here* **4 come into one's own** to fulfil one's potential **5 hold one's own** to have the necessary ability to deal successfully with a situation: *he chose a partner who could hold her own with the best* **6 on one's own a** without help: *you'll never manage to lift that on your own* **b** by oneself; alone: *he lives on his own in a flat in town* ▷ *vb* **7** to have (something) as one's possession: *he owns homes in four countries* **8** Also: **own up to** to confess or admit: *I own I could not bear to think of it; I though she was going to own up to an affair* **owner** *n* **ownership** *n*
WORD ORIGIN Old English *āgen*

owner-occupier *n* someone who owns the house in which he or she lives

ownership flat *n NZ* a flat owned by the occupier

own goal *n* **1** *soccer* a goal scored by a player accidentally playing the ball into his or her own team's net **2** *informal* any action that results in disadvantage to the person who took it or to his or her associates: *the minister's admission was the latest in a series of own goals by the government*

ox *n, pl* **oxen** a castrated bull used for pulling heavy loads and for meat
WORD ORIGIN Old English *oxa*

oxalic acid *n* a colourless poisonous acid found in many plants
WORD ORIGIN Latin *oxalis* garden sorrel

oxbow lake *n* a crescent-shaped lake on the flood plain of a river and constituting remnant of a former meander

Oxbridge *n Brit* the British universities of Oxford and Cambridge considered together

oxen *n* ▸ the plural of **ox**

Oxenstierna *or* **Oxenstjerna** *n* **Count Axel** 1583–1654, Swedish statesman. He was chancellor (1612–54) and successfully directed Swedish foreign policy for most of the Thirty Years' War

Oxfam Oxford Committee for Famine Relief

oxidation *n* the act or process of oxidizing

oxide *n chem* a compound of oxygen with another element
WORD ORIGIN French

oxidize *or* **-dise** *vb* **-dizing, -dized** *or* **-dising, -dised** to react chemically with oxygen, as in burning or rusting **oxidization** *or* **-disation** *n*

Oxon Oxfordshire

Oxon. (in degree titles) of Oxford University
WORD ORIGIN Latin *Oxoniensis*

oxtail *n* the tail of an ox, used in soups and stews

oxyacetylene *n* a mixture of oxygen and acetylene, used in blowlamps for cutting or welding metals at high temperatures

oxygen *n chem* a colourless odourless gaseous element essential to life processes and to combustion. Symbol: O
WORD ORIGIN Greek *oxus* sharp + *-genēs* producing: from former belief that all acids contained oxygen

oxygenate *vb* **-ating, -ated** to add oxygen to: *to oxygenate blood*

oxygen mask *n* a small bowl-shaped object which is connected via a pipe to an cylinder of oxygen and can be placed over a person's nose and mouth to help him or her breathe

oxygen tent *n med* a transparent enclosure covering a bedridden patient, into which oxygen is released to aid breathing

O

THESAURUS

buxom, roly-poly, rotund, podgy, corpulent, elephantine, well-padded (*informal*), well-upholstered (*informal*), broad in the beam (*informal*), on the plump side **OPPOSITE:** underweight

overwhelm *vb* **1 = overcome**, overpower, devastate, stagger, get the better of, bowl over (*informal*), prostrate, knock (someone) for six (*informal*), render speechless, render incapable, render powerless, render helpless, sweep (someone) off his *or* her feet, take (someone's) breath away **2 = destroy**, beat, defeat, overcome, smash, crush, massacre, conquer, wipe out, overthrow, knock out, lick (*informal*), subdue, rout, eradicate, overpower, quell, annihilate, put paid to, vanquish, subjugate, immobilize, make mincemeat of (*informal*), cut to pieces

owe *vb* **1 = be in debt (to)**, be in arrears (to), be overdrawn (by), be beholden to, be under an obligation to, be obligated *or* indebted (to)

owing *adj* **1 = unpaid**, due, outstanding, owed, payable, unsettled, overdue
2 owing to = because of, thanks to, as a result of, on account of, by reason of

own *adj* **1 = personal**, special, private, individual, particular, exclusive ▷ *vb* **7 = possess**, have, keep, hold, enjoy, retain, be responsible for, be in possession of, have to your name

oxymoron (ox-see-**more**-on) *n* a figure of speech that combines two apparently contradictory terms, for example *cruel kindness*
WORD ORIGIN Greek *oxus* sharp + *mōros* stupid

oyez *or* **oyes** *interj* a cry usually uttered three times by a public crier or court official calling for silence and attention
WORD ORIGIN Old French *oiez!* hear!

oyster *n* **1** an edible shellfish, some types of which produce pearls **2 the world is your oyster** you are in a position where there is every possible chance of personal advancement and satisfaction ▷*adj* **3** greyish-white
WORD ORIGIN Greek *ostreon*

oystercatcher *n* a wading bird with black-and-white plumage and a long stout red bill

oz *or* **oz.** ounce
WORD ORIGIN Italian *onza*

Oz *n slang* Australia

Özal *n* **Turgut** 1927–93, Turkish statesman: prime minister of Turkey (1983–89); president (1989–93)

ozone *n* **1** a form of oxygen with a strong odour, formed by an electric discharge in the atmosphere **2** *informal* clean bracing air, as found at the seaside
WORD ORIGIN Greek *ozein* to smell

ozone layer *n* a layer of ozone in the upper atmosphere that absorbs harmful ultraviolet rays from the sun

O

Pp

DICTIONARY

p *or* **P** *n, pl* **p's, P's** *or* **Ps 1** the 16th letter of the English alphabet **2 mind one's p's and q's** to be careful to behave correctly and use polite language

p 1 *Brit, Austral & NZ* penny **2** *Brit* pence

P 1 *chem* phosphorus **2** (on road signs) parking **3** *chess* pawn

p. 1 *pl* **pp.** page **2** per

pa[1] *n informal* father

pa[2] *n* NZ (formerly) a fortified Māori settlement

Pa 1 *chem* protactinium **2** *physics* pascal

PA 1 Pennsylvania **2** personal assistant **3** public-address system

p.a. yearly
WORD ORIGIN Latin *per annum*

Pabst *n* **G**(**eorge**) **W**(**ilhelm**) 1885–1967, German film director, whose films include *Joyless Street* (1925), *Pandora's Box* (1929), and *The Last Act* (1954)

pace[1] *n* **1 a** a single step in walking **b** the length of a step **2** speed of walking or running **3** speed of doing some other activity: *efforts to accelerate the pace of change are unlikely to succeed* **4** manner of walking **5 keep pace with** to advance at the same speed as **6 put someone through his** *or* **her paces** to test someone's ability **7 set the pace** to determine the speed at which a group advances ▹ *vb* **pacing, paced 8** to walk with regular steps, often in anxiety or impatience: *he paced up and down the foyer impatiently* **9** to set the speed for (the competitors) in a race **10 pace out** to measure by paces
WORD ORIGIN Latin *passus* step

pace[2] *prep* with due respect to: used to express polite disagreement
WORD ORIGIN Latin, from *pax* peace

pacemaker *n* **1** an electronic device positioned in the body, next to the heart, to regulate the heartbeat **2** a competitor who, by leading a race, causes it to be run at a particular speed

Pachelbel *n* **Johann** 1653–1706, German organist and composer, noted esp. for his popular *Canon in D Major*

Pachomius *n* **Saint** ?290–346 AD, Egyptian hermit; founder of the first Christian monastery (318). Feast day: May 14 or 15

pachyderm (**pak**-ee-durm) *n* a large thick-skinned mammal, such as an elephant or rhinoceros
WORD ORIGIN Greek *pakhus* thick + *derma* skin

pacific *adj formal* tending to bring peace; non-aggressive; peaceful
WORD ORIGIN Latin *pax* peace + *facere* to make

Pacific *adj* of the Pacific Ocean, the world's largest and deepest ocean, lying between Asia and Australia and America, or its islands

pacifier *n US & Canad* a baby's dummy

pacifist *n* a person who is totally opposed to violence and refuses to take part in war **pacifism** *n*

pacify *vb* **-fies, -fying, -fied** to soothe or calm **pacification** *n*
WORD ORIGIN Old French *pacifier;* see PACIFIC

Pacino *n* **Al,** full name *Alfredo James Pacino.* born 1940, US film actor; his films include *The Godfather* (1972), *Dog Day Afternoon* (1975), *Scent of a Woman* (1992), for which he won an Oscar, and *Insomnia* (2002)

pack[1] *n* **1** a bundle or load carried on the back **2** *Brit & NZ* a complete set of playing cards **3** a group of animals that hunt together: *a pack of hounds* **4** *rugby* the forwards of a team **5** any collection of people or things: *a pack of lies* **6** *chiefly US & Canad* ▸ same as **packet** (sense 1) **7** an organized group of Cub Scouts or Brownie Guides **8** ▸ same as **rucksack** or **backpack 9** Also called: **face pack** a cream treatment that cleanses and tones the skin ▹ *vb* **10** to put (articles) in a case or container for moving **11** to roll (articles) up into a bundle **12** to press tightly together; cram: *thousands of people packed into the city's main square* **13** (foll. by *off*) to send away hastily: *their young son came in to say good night and was packed off to bed* **14** *slang* to be able to deliver a specified amount of unexpected or violent force or power: *the film's unexpected ending packs quite a punch* **15** *US informal* to carry (a gun) habitually **16 send someone packing** *informal* to dismiss someone abruptly ▸ See also **pack in, pack up**
WORD ORIGIN origin unknown

pack[2] *vb* to fill (a committee, jury, or audience) with one's own supporters
WORD ORIGIN perhaps from *pact*

package *n* **1** a small parcel **2** Also: **package deal** a deal in which separate items are presented together as a unit **3** *US & Canad* ▸ same as **packet** (sense 1) ▹ *vb* **-aging, -aged 4** to put (something) into a package **packaging** *n*

package holiday *n* a holiday in which everything is arranged by one company for a fixed price

packet *n* **1** a container, together with its contents: *a packet of crisps* **2** a small parcel **3** Also: **packet boat** a boat that transports mail, passengers, or goods on a fixed short route **4** *slang* a large sum of money: *she was paid a packet* **5** *computers* a unit into which a larger piece of data is broken down for more efficient transmission
WORD ORIGIN Old French *pacquet*

packhorse *n* a horse used to carry goods

pack ice *n* a large area of floating ice, consisting of pieces that have become massed together

pack in *vb informal* to stop doing (something): *I'm going to pack it in and resign*

packing *n* material, such as paper or plastic, used to protect packed goods

packsack *n* ▸ the US and Canadian word for **haversack**

THESAURUS

pace[1] *n* **1a = footstep**, step, stride **3 = speed**, rate, momentum, tempo, progress, motion, clip *(informal)*, lick *(informal)*, velocity **4 = step**, walk, stride, tread, gait ▹ *vb* **8 = stride**, walk, pound, patrol, walk up and down, march up and down, walk back and forth

pack[1] *n* **1 = bundle**, kit, parcel, load, burden, bale, rucksack, truss, knapsack, back pack, kitbag, fardel *(archaic)* **5 = group**, crowd, collection, company, set, lot, band, troop, crew, drove, gang, deck, bunch, mob, flock, herd, assemblage **6** *(chiefly US & Canad)* **= packet**, box, package, carton ▹ *vb* **10 = package**, load, store, bundle, batch, stow **12 = cram**, charge, crowd, press, fill, stuff, jam, compact, mob, ram, wedge, compress, throng, tamp **13** (*with* **off**) **= send away**, dismiss, send packing *(informal)*, bundle out, hustle out

package *n* **1 = parcel**, box, container, packet, carton **2 = collection**, lot, unit, combination, compilation ▹ *vb* **4 = pack**, box, wrap up, parcel (up), batch

packet *n* **1 = container**, box, package, wrapping, poke *(dialect)*, carton, wrapper **2 = package**, parcel **4** *(slang)* **= a fortune**, lot(s), pot(s) *(informal)*, a bomb *(Brit slang)*, a pile *(informal)*, big money, a bundle *(slang)*, big bucks *(informal, chiefly US)*, a small fortune, a mint, a wad *(US & Canad slang)*, megabucks *(US & Canad slang)*, an arm and a leg *(informal)*, a bob or two *(Brit informal)*, a tidy sum *(informal)*, a king's ransom *(informal)*, a pretty penny *(informal)*, top whack *(informal)*

pact *n* **= agreement**, contract, alliance, treaty, deal, understanding, league, bond, arrangement, bargain, convention, compact, protocol,

DICTIONARY

packthread *n* a strong thread for sewing or tying up packages

pack up *vb* **1** to put (articles) in a bag or case before leaving **2** *informal* to stop doing (something) **3** (of a machine) to break down

pact ❶ *n* a formal agreement between two or more parties
WORD ORIGIN Latin *pactum*

pad[1] ❶ *n* **1** a thick piece of soft material used for comfort, shape, protection, or absorption **2** a number of sheets of paper fastened together along one edge **3** the fleshy cushioned underpart of an animal's paw **4** a level area or flat-topped structure, from which rockets are launched or helicopters take off **5** the floating leaf of the water lily **6** *slang* a person's residence ▷*vb* **padding, padded 7** to fill (something) out with soft material for comfort, shape, or protection **8 pad out** to lengthen (a speech or piece of writing) with unnecessary words or pieces of information
WORD ORIGIN origin unknown

pad[2] ❶ *vb* **padding, padded 1** to walk with a soft or muffled step **2** to travel (a route) on foot: *men padding the streets in cheap sneakers*
WORD ORIGIN Middle Dutch *pad* path

padded cell *n* a room with padded walls in a psychiatric hospital, in which patients who are likely to injure themselves are placed

padding ❶ *n* **1** any soft material used to pad something **2** unnecessary information put into a speech or written work to make it longer

paddle[1] ❶ *n* **1** a short light oar with a flat blade at one or both ends **2** a paddle wheel used to move a boat **3** a blade of a water wheel or paddle wheel ▷*vb* **-dling, -dled 4** to move (a boat) with a paddle **5** to swim with short rapid strokes, like a dog **6** *US & Canad informal* to spank
WORD ORIGIN origin unknown

paddle[2] ❶ *vb* **-dling, -dled 1** to walk barefoot in shallow water **2** to dabble (one's fingers, hands, or feet) in water ▷*n* **3** the act of paddling in water
WORD ORIGIN origin unknown

paddle steamer *n* a ship propelled by paddle wheels turned by a steam engine

paddle wheel *n* a large wheel fitted with paddles, turned by an engine to propel a ship

paddock *n* **1** a small enclosed field for horses **2** (in horse racing) the enclosure in which horses are paraded and mounted before a race **3** *Austral & NZ* any area of fenced land
WORD ORIGIN Old English *pearruc* enclosure

paddy[1] *n, pl* **-dies 1** Also: **paddy field** a field planted with rice **2** rice as a growing crop or when harvested but not yet milled
WORD ORIGIN Malay *pādī*

paddy[2] *n, pl* **-dies** *Brit & NZ informal* a fit of temper
WORD ORIGIN from *Paddy*, informal name for an Irishman

pademelon, paddymelon (pad-ee-mel-an) *n* a small Australian wallaby

Paderewski *n* **Ignace Jan** 1860–1941, Polish pianist, composer, and statesman; prime minister (1919)

padkos (pudd-koss) *n S African* snacks and provisions for a journey
WORD ORIGIN Afrikaans, literally: road food

padlock *n* **1** a detachable lock with a hinged hoop fastened through a ring on the object to be secured ▷*vb* **2** to fasten (something) with a padlock
WORD ORIGIN origin unknown

padre (pah-dray) *n informal* a chaplain to the armed forces
WORD ORIGIN via Spanish or Italian from Latin *pater* father

paean (pee-an) *n literary* an expression of praise or joy
WORD ORIGIN Greek *paian* hymn to Apollo

paediatrician *or US* **pediatrician** *n* a doctor who specializes in children's diseases

paediatrics *or US* **pediatrics** *n* the branch of medicine concerned with children and their diseases **paediatric** *or US* **pediatric** *adj*
WORD ORIGIN Greek *pais, paid-* child + *iatros* physician

paedophile *or US* **pedophile** *n* a person who is sexually attracted to children

paedophilia *or US* **pedophilia** *n* the condition of being sexually attracted to children
WORD ORIGIN Greek *pais, paid-* child + *philos* loving

paella (pie-ell-a) *n* a Spanish dish made from rice, shellfish, chicken, and vegetables
WORD ORIGIN Catalan

Páez *n* **José Antonio** 1790–1873, Venezuelan revolutionary leader; first president (1831–46) of independent Venezuela

pagan ❶ *adj* **1** having, being, or relating to religious beliefs, esp. ancient ones, which are not part of any of the world's major religions: *this was the site of a pagan temple to the sun* **2** irreligious ▷*n* **3** a person who does not belong to any of the world's major religions **4** a person without any religion **paganism** *n*
WORD ORIGIN Church Latin *paganus* civilian (hence not a soldier of Christ)

page[1] ❶ *n* **1** one side of one of the leaves of a book, newspaper, or magazine **2** one of the leaves of a book, newspaper, or magazine **3** *literary* a period or event: *a new page in the country's political history* **4** a screenful of information from a website or teletext service
WORD ORIGIN Latin *pagina*

page[2] ❶ *n* **1** a small boy who attends a bride at her wedding **2** a youth employed to run errands for the guests in a hotel or club **3** *medieval history* a boy in training for knighthood ▷*vb* **paging, paged 4** to summon (a person), by bleeper or loudspeaker, in order to pass on a message
WORD ORIGIN Greek *pais* child

pageant *n* **1** an outdoor show portraying scenes from history **2** any magnificent display or procession
WORD ORIGIN perhaps from Latin *pagina* scene of a play

pageantry *n* spectacular display or ceremony

pageboy *n* **1** a hairstyle in which the hair is smooth and the same medium length with the ends curled under **2** ▸ same as **page**[2] (senses 1, 2)

pagination *n* the numbering in sequence of the pages of a book or manuscript **paginate** *vb*

Paglia *n* **Camille** born 1947, US writer and academic, noted for provocative cultural studies such as *Sexual Personae* (1990) and *Vamps and Tramps* (1995)

P

THESAURUS

covenant, concord, concordat

pad[1] *n* **1a = wad**, dressing, pack, padding, compress, wadding **1b = cushion**, filling, stuffing, pillow, bolster, upholstery **2 = notepad**, block, tablet, notebook, jotter, writing pad **3 = paw**, foot, sole **6** (*slang*) **= home**, flat, apartment, place, room, quarters, hang-out (*informal*), bachelor apartment (*Canad*) ▷*vb* **7 = pack**, line, fill, protect, shape, stuff, cushion

pad[2] *vb* **1 = sneak**, creep, steal, pussyfoot (*informal*), go barefoot

padding *n* **1 = filling**, stuffing, packing, wadding **2 = waffle** (*informal, chiefly Brit*), hot air (*informal*), verbiage, wordiness, verbosity, prolixity

paddle[1] *n* **1 = oar**, sweep, scull ▷*vb* **4 = row**, pull, scull

paddle[2] *vb* **1 = wade**, splash (about), slop, plash

pagan *adj* **1, 2 = heathen**, infidel, irreligious, polytheistic, idolatrous, heathenish ▷*n* **3, 4 = heathen**, infidel, unbeliever, polytheist, idolater

page[1] *n* **1, 2 = folio**, side, leaf, sheet

page[2] *n* **1 = servant**, attendant, squire, pageboy, footboy **2 = attendant**, bellboy (*US*), pageboy, footboy ▷*vb* **4 = call**, seek, summon, call out for, send for

DICTIONARY

Pagnol *n* **Marcel** (**Paul**) 1895–1974, French dramatist, film director, and novelist, noted for his depiction of Provençal life in such films as *Manon des Sources* (1952; remade 1986)

pagoda *n* a pyramid-shaped Asian temple or tower
WORD ORIGIN Portuguese *pagode*

paid *vb* **1** ▸ past of **pay** **2** **put paid to** to end or destroy: *a knee injury put paid to his promising sporting career*

pail *n* **1** a bucket **2** Also called: **pailful** the amount contained in a pail: *a pail of water*
WORD ORIGIN Old English *pægel*

pain ❶ *n* **1** physical hurt or discomfort caused by injury or illness **2** emotional suffering **3** Also called: **pain in the neck** *informal* a person or thing that is annoying or irritating **4** **on pain of** subject to the penalty of: *orders which their soldiers were bound to follow on pain of death* ▹ *vb* **5** to cause (a person) physical or mental suffering **6** *informal* to annoy; irritate ▸ See also **pains** > **painless** *adj*
WORD ORIGIN Latin *poena* punishment

pained *adj* having or suggesting pain or distress: *a pained look*

painful ❶ *adj* **1** causing pain or distress: *painful inflammation of the joints; he began the painful task of making funeral arrangements* **2** affected with pain: *the symptoms include fever and painful joints* **3** tedious or difficult: *the hours passed with painful slowness* **4** *informal* extremely bad: *a painful so-called comedy* **painfully** *adv*

painkiller *n* a drug that relieves pain

pains ❶ *pl n* care or trouble: *they are at great pains to appear realistic and responsible*

painstaking *adj* extremely careful and thorough **painstakingly** *adv*

paint ❶ *n* **1** a coloured substance, spread on a surface with a brush or a roller, that forms a hard coating **2** a dry film of paint on a surface **3** *informal* face make-up ▹ *vb* **4** to apply paint to paper or canvas to make (a picture) of **5** to coat (a surface) with paint **6** to describe vividly in words: *the survey paints a dismal picture of growing hunger and disease* **7** to apply make-up to (the face) **8** to apply (liquid) to (a surface): *paint the varnish on and leave it to dry for at least four hours* **9** **paint the town red** *informal* to celebrate in a lively way
WORD ORIGIN Latin *pingere* to paint

paintbrush *n* a brush used to apply paint

painted lady *n* a butterfly with pale brownish-red mottled wings

painter[1] *n* **1** an artist who paints pictures **2** a person who paints surfaces of buildings as a trade

painter[2] *n* a rope attached to the bow of a boat for tying it up
WORD ORIGIN probably from Old French *penteur* strong rope

painting *n* **1** a picture produced by using paint **2** the art of producing pictures by applying paints to paper or canvas **3** the act of applying paint to a surface

paintwork *n* the covering of paint on parts of a vehicle, building, etc.: *someone had damaged the Porsche by scraping a key along its paintwork*

pair ❶ *n* **1** two identical or similar things matched for use together: *a pair of shoes* **2** two people, animals, or things used or grouped together: *a pair of tickets* **3** an object consisting of two identical or similar parts joined together: *a pair of jeans* **4** a male and a female animal of the same species kept for breeding purposes **5** *parliament* two opposed members who both agree not to vote on a specified motion **6** two playing cards of the same denomination **7** one member of a matching pair: *I can't find the pair to this glove* ▹ *vb* **8** to group (people or things) in twos **9** **pair off** to separate into groups of two
WORD ORIGIN Latin *par* equal

paisley pattern *or* **paisley** *n* a detailed pattern of small curving shapes, used in fabric
WORD ORIGIN after *Paisley*, town in Scotland

pajamas *pl n US* pyjamas

pakeha (pah-kee-hah) *n*, *pl* **pakeha** *or* **pakehas** *NZ* a person of European descent, as distinct from a Māori
WORD ORIGIN Māori

Paki *Brit slang, offensive* *n* **1** a Pakistani or person of Pakistani descent ▹ *adj* **2** Pakistani or of Pakistani descent

Pakistani *adj* **1** of Pakistan ▹ *n* **2** a person from Pakistan

pal ❶ *informal* *n* **1** a close friend ▹ *vb* **palling, palled** **2** **pal up with** to become friends with
WORD ORIGIN Romany: brother

palace *n* **1** the official residence of a king, queen, president, or archbishop **2** a large and richly furnished building
WORD ORIGIN Latin *Palatium* Palatine, the site of the palace of the emperors in Rome

Palacio Valdés *n* **Armando** 1853–1938, Spanish novelist and critic

paladin *n* **1** one of the legendary twelve peers of Charlemagne's court **2** (formerly) a knight who did battle for a king or queen
WORD ORIGIN Italian *paladino*

palaeo- *or US* **paleo-** *combining form* old, ancient, or prehistoric: *palaeobotany*

Palaeocene *or US* **Paleocene** (pal-ee-oh-seen) *adj geol* of the epoch of geological time about 65 million years ago
WORD ORIGIN Greek *palaeo-* ancient + *kainos* new

palaeography *or US* **paleography** (pal-ee-og-ra-fee) *n* the study of ancient handwriting
WORD ORIGIN Greek *palaeo-* ancient + -GRAPHY

Palaeolithic *or US* **Paleolithic** (pal-ee-oh-lith-ik) *adj* of the period from about 2.5 to 3 million years ago until about 12 000 BC, during which primitive man emerged and unpolished chipped stone tools were made
WORD ORIGIN Greek *palaeo-* ancient + *lithos* stone

palaeontology *or US* **paleontology**

THESAURUS

pain *n* **1a = suffering**, discomfort, trouble, hurt, irritation, tenderness, soreness **1b = ache**, smarting, stinging, aching, cramp, throb, throbbing, spasm, pang, twinge, shooting pain **2 = sorrow**, suffering, torture, distress, despair, grief, misery, agony, sadness, torment, hardship, bitterness, woe, anguish, heartache, affliction, tribulation, desolation, wretchedness ▹ *vb* **5a = distress**, worry, hurt, wound, torture, grieve, torment, afflict, sadden, disquiet, vex, agonize, cut to the quick, aggrieve **5b = hurt**, chafe, cause pain to, cause discomfort to

painful *adj* **1 = distressing**, unpleasant, harrowing, saddening, grievous, distasteful, agonizing, disagreeable, afflictive **OPPOSITE:** pleasant **2 = sore**, hurting, smarting, aching, raw, tender, throbbing, inflamed, excruciating **OPPOSITE:** painless **3 = difficult**, arduous, trying, hard, severe, troublesome, laborious, vexatious **OPPOSITE:** easy

pains *pl n* **= trouble**, labour, effort, industry, care, bother, diligence, special attention, assiduousness

paint *n* **1 = colouring**, colour, stain, dye, tint, pigment, emulsion ▹ *vb* **4 = depict**, draw, portray, figure, picture, represent, sketch, delineate, catch a likeness **5 = colour**, cover, coat, decorate, stain, whitewash, daub, distemper, apply paint to

pair *n* **1 = set**, match, combination, doublet, matched set, two of a kind **2 = couple**, brace, duo, twosome ▹ *vb* **8 = team**, match (up), join, couple, marry, wed, twin, put together, bracket, yoke, pair off

pal *n* **1** (*informal*) **= friend**, companion, mate (*informal*), buddy (*informal*), comrade, chum (*informal*), crony, cock (*Brit informal*), main man (*slang, chiefly US*), homeboy (*slang, chiefly US*), cobber (*Austral & NZ old-fashioned, informal*), boon companion, E hoa (*NZ*)

DICTIONARY

(pal-ee-on-**tol**-a-jee) *n* the study of past geological periods and fossils **palaeontologist** *or US* **paleontologist** *n*
WORD ORIGIN Greek *palaeo-* ancient + *ōn, ont-* being + -LOGY

Palaeozoic *or US* **Paleozoic** (pal-ee-oh-**zoh**-ik) *adj geol* of the geological era that lasted from about 600 million years ago to 230 million years ago
WORD ORIGIN Greek *palaeo-* ancient + *zōion* animal

Palagi (pa-**lang**-gee) *n, pl* **-gis** *NZ* the Samoan name for a Pakeha

palanquin (pal-an-**keen**) *n* (formerly, in the Orient) a covered bed in which someone could be carried on the shoulders of four men
WORD ORIGIN Portuguese *palanquim*

palatable *adj* **1** (of food or drink) pleasant to taste **2** (of an experience or idea) acceptable or satisfactory

palate *n* **1** the roof of the mouth **2** the sense of taste: *a range of dishes to tempt every palate*
WORD ORIGIN Latin *palatum*

palatial *adj* like a palace; magnificent: *his palatial home*

palatinate *n* a territory ruled by a palatine prince or noble or a count palatine

palatine *adj* possessing royal prerogatives: *a count palatine*
WORD ORIGIN Latin *palatium* palace

palaver (pal-**lah**-ver) *n* time-consuming fuss: *all the palaver involved in obtaining a visa*
WORD ORIGIN Portuguese *palavra* talk

palazzo pants *pl n* women's trousers with very wide legs
WORD ORIGIN Italian *palazzo* palace

pale[1] ❶ *adj* **1** (of a colour) whitish and not very strong: *pale yellow* **2** (of a complexion) having a whitish appearance, usually because of illness, shock, or fear **3** lacking brightness or colour: *the pale, chill light of an October afternoon* ▹*vb* **paling, paled 4** to become pale or paler: *the girl paled at the news* **paleness** *n*
WORD ORIGIN Latin *pallidus*

pale[2] *n* **1** a wooden post used in fences **2 a** a fence made of pales **b** a boundary **3 beyond the pale** outside the limits of social convention: *the destruction of forests is beyond the pale*
WORD ORIGIN Latin *palus* stake

paleface *n* an offensive term for a White person, said to have been used by Native Americans of N America

Palestinian *adj* **1** of Palestine, an area in the Middle East between the Jordan River and the Mediterranean ▹*n* **2** an Arab from this area, esp. one living in Israel or Israeli-occupied territory or as a refugee

Palestrina *n* **Giovanni Pierluigi da** ?1525–94, Italian composer and master of counterpoint. His works, nearly all for unaccompanied choir and religious in nature, include the *Missa Papae Marcelli* (1555)

palette *n* **1** a flat board used by artists to mix paints **2** the range of colours characteristic of a particular artist or school of painting: *he uses a cool palette with no strong red* **3** the range of colours or patterns that can be displayed on the visual display unit of a computer
WORD ORIGIN French

palette knife *n* a spatula with a thin flexible blade used in painting or cookery

Paley *n* **William** 1743–1805, English theologian and utilitarian philosopher. His chief works are *The Principles of Moral and Political Philosophy* (1785), *Horae Paulinae* (1790), *A View of the Evidences of Christianity* (1794), and *Natural Theology* (1802)

Palgrave *n* **Francis Turner** 1824–97, British critic and poet, editor of the poetry anthology *The Golden Treasury* (1861)

palindrome *n* a word or phrase that reads the same backwards or forwards, such as *able was I ere I saw Elba*
WORD ORIGIN Greek *palindromos* running back again

paling *n* **1** a fence made of pales **2** pales collectively **3** a single pale

palisade *n* **1** a fence made of stakes driven into the ground **2** one of the stakes used in such a fence
WORD ORIGIN Latin *palus* stake

Palissy *n* **Bernard** 1510–89, French Huguenot potter and writer on natural history, noted for his rustic glazed earthenware: died in the Bastille

pall[1] *n* **1** a cloth spread over a coffin **2** a coffin at a funeral ceremony **3** a dark heavy covering: *a pall of smoke and dust hung in the air* **4** a depressing atmosphere: *a pall hung on them all after his death*
WORD ORIGIN Latin *pallium* cloak

pall[2] *vb* to become boring or uninteresting, esp. by continuing for too long: *any pleasure had palled long before the two-hour programme was over*
WORD ORIGIN variant of *appal*

Palladian *adj* of a style of architecture characterized by symmetry and the revival and development of ancient Roman styles
WORD ORIGIN after Andrea *Palladio*, Italian architect

palladium *n chem* a rare silvery-white element of the platinum metal group, used in jewellery. Symbol: Pd
WORD ORIGIN after the asteroid *Pallas*

pallbearer *n* a person who helps to carry or who escorts the coffin at a funeral

pallet[1] *n* a straw-filled mattress or bed
WORD ORIGIN Latin *palea* straw

pallet[2] *n* **1** a tool with a flat, sometimes flexible, blade used for shaping pottery **2** a portable platform for storing and moving goods
WORD ORIGIN Latin *pala* spade

palliasse *n* a straw-filled mattress; pallet
WORD ORIGIN French *paillasse*

palliate *vb* **-ating, -ated 1** to lessen the severity of (pain or disease) without curing it **2** to cause (an offence) to seem less serious
WORD ORIGIN Latin *pallium* a cloak

palliative *adj* **1** relieving without curing ▹*n* **2** something that palliates, such as a sedative drug **3** something that alleviates or lessens a problem: *equal pay was a palliative for the growing unrest among women*

pallid *adj* **1** lacking colour, brightness, or vigour: *a pallid autumn sun* **2** lacking energy or vitality; insipid: *many militants find the party's socialism too pallid*
WORD ORIGIN Latin *pallidus*

pallor *n* paleness of complexion, usually because of illness, shock, or fear
WORD ORIGIN Latin: whiteness

pally *adj* **-lier, -liest** *informal* on friendly terms

palm[1] *n* **1** the inner surface of the hand from the wrist to the base of the fingers **2** the part of a glove that covers the palm **3 in the palm of one's hand** at one's mercy or command: *he had the jury in the palm of his hand* ▹*vb* **4** to hide (something) in the hand: *he palmed the key* ▸ See also **palm off**
WORD ORIGIN Latin *palma*

palm[2] *or* **palm tree** *n* a tropical or subtropical tree with a straight unbranched trunk crowned with long pointed leaves
WORD ORIGIN Latin *palma*, from the likeness of its spreading fronds to a hand

Palma[1] *n* the capital of the Balearic Islands, on the SW coast of Majorca: a tourist centre. Pop: 367 277 (2003 est). Official name: **Palma de Mallorca**

P

THESAURUS

pale[1] *adj* **1 = light**, soft, faded, subtle, muted, bleached, pastel, light-coloured **2 = white**, pasty, bleached, washed-out, wan, bloodless, colourless, pallid, anaemic, ashen, sallow, whitish, ashy, like death warmed up (*informal*) **OPPOSITE:** rosy-cheeked **3 = dim**, weak, faint, feeble, thin, wan, watery ▹*vb* **4 = become pale**, blanch, whiten, go white, lose colour

DICTIONARY

Palma[2] *n* **Jacopo**, known as *Palma Vecchio*, original name *Jacopo Negretti*. ?1480–1528, Venetian painter, noted esp. for his portraits of women

palmate *adj* shaped like an open hand: *palmate leaves*

Palme *n* (**Sven**) **Olof** (**Joachim**) 1927–86, Swedish Social Democratic statesman; prime minister (1969–76, 1982–86); assassinated

Palmer *n* **1 Arnold** born 1929, US professional golfer: won the US Open Championship (1960) and the British Open Championship (1961; 1962) **2 Samuel** 1805–81, English painter of visionary landscapes, influenced by William Blake

Palmer-Tomkinson *n* **Tara** born 1971, British socialite, television personality, and journalist

palmetto *n, pl* **-tos** a small palm tree with fan-shaped leaves
WORD ORIGIN Spanish *palmito* a little palm

palmistry *n* fortune-telling by examining the lines and bumps of the hand **palmist** *n*

palm off *vb* **1** to get rid of (someone or something) by passing it on to another: *the risk has to be shared with subcontractors, not simply palmed off on them* **2** to divert (someone) by a lie or excuse: *Mark was palmed off with a series of excuses*

palm oil *n* an oil obtained from the fruit of certain palm trees, used as an edible fat and in soap

Palm Sunday *n* the Sunday before Easter

palmtop *adj* (of a computer) small enough to be held in the hand

palmy *adj* **palmier, palmiest** **1** successful, prosperous and happy: *the palmy days of youth* **2** covered with palm trees: *palmy beaches*

palomino *n, pl* **-nos** a golden or cream horse with a white mane and tail
WORD ORIGIN Spanish: dovelike

palpable *adj* **1** obvious: *palpable nonsense* **2** (of a feeling or an atmosphere) so intense that it seems capable of being touched: *an air of palpable gloom hung over him* **palpably** *adv*
WORD ORIGIN Latin *palpare* to touch

palpate *vb* **-pating, -pated** *med* to examine (an area of the body) by touching **palpation** *n*
WORD ORIGIN Latin *palpare* to stroke

palpitate *vb* **-tating, -tated** **1** (of the heart) to beat rapidly **2** to flutter or tremble **palpitation** *n*
WORD ORIGIN Latin *palpitare*

palsy (pawl-zee) *n pathol* paralysis of a specified type: *cerebral palsy* **palsied** *adj*
WORD ORIGIN Old French *paralisie*

Paltrow *n* **Gwyneth** (**Kate**) born 1973, US film actress; her films include *Emma* (1996), *Sliding Doors* (1998), *Shakespeare in Love* (1998), and *Sylvia* (2003)

paltry *adj* **-trier, -triest** insignificant
WORD ORIGIN Low Germanic *palter*, *paltrig* ragged

pampas *n* the extensive grassy plains of South America
WORD ORIGIN Native American *bamba* plain

pampas grass *n* a South American grass with large feathery silver-coloured flower branches

pamper ❶ *vb* to treat (someone) with excessive indulgence or care; spoil
WORD ORIGIN Germanic

pamphlet ❶ *n* a thin paper-covered booklet, often on a subject of current interest
WORD ORIGIN Medieval Latin *Pamphilus*, title of a poem

pamphleteer *n* a person who writes or issues pamphlets

Pamuk *n* **Orhan** born 1952, Turkish novelist and writer; author of *The Black Book* (1990), *My Name is Red* (1998), *Snow* (2002) and *Istanbul: Memories of a City* (2003). Nobel prize for literature 2006

pan[1] ❶ *n* **1** a wide long-handled metal container used in cooking **2** any of various similar containers used in industry, etc. **3** either of the two dishes on a set of scales **4** *Brit* the bowl of a lavatory **5** a natural or artificial hollow in the ground: *a saltpan* ▷ *vb* **panning, panned** **6** to sift gold from (a river) in a shallow pan **7** *informal* to criticize harshly: *his first film was panned by the critics* ▸ See also **pan out**
WORD ORIGIN Old English *panne*

pan[2] ❶ *vb* **panning, panned** **1** to move (a film camera) or (of a film camera) to be moved to follow a moving object or to take in a whole scene ▷ *n* **2** the act of panning
WORD ORIGIN from *panoramic*

pan- *combining form* including or relating to all parts or members: *Pan-American*
WORD ORIGIN Greek

panacea (pan-a-see-a) *n* a remedy for all diseases or problems
WORD ORIGIN Greek *pan-* all + *akēs* remedy

panache (pan-ash) *n* a confident and stylish manner: *the orchestra played with great panache*
WORD ORIGIN Old Italian *pennacchio* feather

panama hat *or* **panama** *n* a straw hat with a rounded crown and a wide brim

Pan-American *adj* of North, South, and Central America collectively

panatella *n* a long slender cigar
WORD ORIGIN American Spanish *panetela* long thin biscuit

pancake *n* **1** a thin flat circle of fried batter **2** Also called: **pancake landing** an aircraft landing made by levelling out a few feet from the ground and then dropping onto it

Pancake Day *n* Shrove Tuesday, when people traditionally eat pancakes

panchromatic *adj photog* (of an emulsion or film) sensitive to light of all colours

pancreas (pang-kree-ass) *n* a large gland behind the stomach, that produces insulin and aids digestion **pancreatic** *adj*
WORD ORIGIN Greek *pan-* all + *kreas* flesh

panda *n* **1** Also called: **giant panda** a large black-and-white bearlike animal from the high mountain bamboo forests of China **2** Also called: **lesser panda, red panda** a raccoon-like animal of the mountain forests of S Asia, with a reddish-brown coat and ringed tail
WORD ORIGIN Nepalese

panda car *n Brit* a police patrol car

pandemic *adj* (of a disease) occurring over a wide geographical area
WORD ORIGIN Greek *pandēmos* general

pandemonium *n* wild confusion; uproar
WORD ORIGIN Greek *pan-* all + *daimōn* demon

pander *vb* **1** (foll. by *to*) to indulge (a person or his or her desires): *he pandered to popular fears* ▷ *n* **2** *chiefly archaic* a person who procures a sexual partner for someone
WORD ORIGIN after *Pandarus*, in legend, the procurer of Cressida for Troilus

pandit *n hinduism* ▸ same as **pundit** (sense 2)

Pandit *n* **Vijaya Lakshmi** 1900–90, Indian politician and diplomat; sister of Jawaharlal Nehru

Pandora's box *n* a source of many unforeseen difficulties

THESAURUS

pamper *vb* = **spoil**, indulge, gratify, baby, pet, humour, pander to, fondle, cosset, coddle, mollycoddle, wait on (someone) hand and foot, cater to your every whim

pamphlet *n* = **booklet**, leaflet, brochure, circular, tract, folder

pan[1] *n* **1** = **pot**, vessel, container, saucepan ▷ *vb* **6** = **sift out**, look for, wash, search for **7** *(informal)* = **criticize**, knock, blast, hammer *(Brit informal)*, slam *(slang)*, rubbish *(informal)*, roast *(informal)*, put down, slate *(informal)*, censure, slag (off) *(slang)*, tear into *(informal)*, flay, lambast(e), throw brickbats at *(informal)*

pan[2] *vb* **1** = **move along** *or* **across**, follow, track, sweep, scan, traverse, swing across

panic *n* **1** = **fear**, alarm, horror, terror,

DICTIONARY

WORD ORIGIN a box, in Greek myth, from which all human problems were released
p & p *Brit* postage and packing
pane *n* a sheet of glass in a window or door
WORD ORIGIN Latin *pannus* rag
panegyric (pan-ee-**jirr**-rik) *n* a formal speech or piece of writing that praises a person or event
WORD ORIGIN Greek *panēguris* public gathering
panel *n* **1** a distinct section of a larger surface area, such as that in a door **2** any distinct section of something formed from a sheet of material, such as part of a car body **3** a piece of material inserted in a garment **4** a group of people acting as a team, such as in a quiz or a discussion before an audience **5** *law* **a** a list of jurors **b** the people on a jury **6** ▸ short for **instrument panel** ▹ *adj* **7** of a group acting as a panel: *a panel game* ▹ *vb* **-elling, -elled** *or US* **-eling, -eled 8** to cover or decorate with panels
WORD ORIGIN Old French: portion
panel beater *n* a person who repairs damage to car bodies
panelling *or US* **paneling** *n* panels collectively, such as on a wall or ceiling
panellist *or US* **panelist** *n* a member of a panel, usually on radio or television
panel van *n* *Austral & NZ* a small van
pang *n* a sudden sharp feeling of pain or sadness
WORD ORIGIN Germanic
pangolin *n* an animal of tropical countries with a scaly body and a long snout for feeding on ants and termites. Also called: **scaly anteater**
WORD ORIGIN Malay *peng-gōling*
Pan Gu *or* **P'an Ku** *n* 32–92 AD, Chinese historian and court official, noted for his history of the Han dynasty: died in prison
panic ❶ *n* **1** a sudden overwhelming feeling of terror or anxiety, sometimes affecting a whole group of people ▹ *adj* **2** of or resulting from such terror: *panic measures* ▹ *vb* **-icking, -icked 3** to feel or cause to feel panic **panicky** *adj*
WORD ORIGIN Greek *panikos* emanating from *Pan*, god of the fields
panicle *n* *bot* a loose, irregularly branched cluster of flowers, such as in the oat
WORD ORIGIN Latin *panicula* tuft
panic-stricken *adj* affected by panic
panini *n, pl* **-ni** *or* **-nis** a type of Italian bread usually served grilled with a variety of fillings
panjandrum *n* a pompous self-important official
WORD ORIGIN after a character in a nonsense work
pannier *n* **1** one of a pair of bags fixed on either side of the back wheel of a bicycle or motorcycle **2** one of a pair of large baskets slung over a beast of burden
WORD ORIGIN Old French *panier*
panoply (**pan**-a-plee) *n* a magnificent array: *ambassadors equipped with the full panoply of diplomatic bags, codes and cyphers*
WORD ORIGIN Greek *pan-* all + *hopla* armour
panorama ❶ *n* **1** a wide unbroken view in all directions: *the beautiful panorama of the Cornish coast* **2** a wide or comprehensive survey of a subject: *the panorama of American life* **3** a picture of a scene unrolled before spectators a part at a time so as to appear continuous **panoramic** *adj*
WORD ORIGIN Greek *pan-* all + *horama* view
pan out *vb* **1** *informal* to work out; result: *Parker's research did not pan out too well* **2** (of gravel) to yield gold by panning
panpipes *pl n* a musical wind instrument made of tubes of decreasing lengths joined together
pansy *n, pl* **-sies 1** a garden plant whose flowers have rounded white, yellow, or purple velvety petals **2** *offensive slang* an effeminate or homosexual man or boy
WORD ORIGIN Old French *pensée* thought
pant ❶ *vb* **1** to breathe with noisy gasps after exertion **2** to say (something) while breathing in this way **3** (foll. by *for*) to have a frantic desire for ▹ *n* **4** the act of panting
WORD ORIGIN Greek *phantasioun* to have visions
pantaloons *pl n* baggy trousers gathered at the ankles
WORD ORIGIN French *pantalon* trousers
pantechnicon *n* *Brit* a large van used for furniture removals
WORD ORIGIN Greek *pan-* all + *tekhnē* art; originally a London bazaar later used as a furniture warehouse
pantheism *n* **1** the belief that God is present in everything **2** readiness to worship all gods **pantheist** *n* **pantheistic** *adj*
pantheon *n* **1** (in ancient Greece or Rome) a temple built to honour all the gods **2** all the gods of a particular creed: *the Celtic pantheon of horse gods* **3** a group of very important people: *he deserves a place in the pantheon of social reformers*
WORD ORIGIN Greek *pan-* all + *theos* god
panther *n* a leopard, usually a black one
WORD ORIGIN Greek
panties *pl n* women's or children's underpants
pantihose *pl n* *US & Austral* women's tights
pantile *n* a roofing tile, with an S-shaped cross section
WORD ORIGIN PAN[1] + *tile*
panto *n, pl* **-tos** *Brit informal* ▸ short for **pantomime** (sense 1)
pantograph *n* **1** an instrument for copying drawings or maps to any scale **2** a device on the roof of an electric train to carry the current from an overhead wire
WORD ORIGIN Greek *pant-* all + *graphein* to write
pantomime *n* **1** (in Britain) a play based on a fairy tale and performed at Christmas time **2** a theatrical entertainment in which words are replaced by gestures and bodily actions **3** *informal chiefly Brit* a confused or farcical situation
WORD ORIGIN Greek *pantomimos*
pantry *n, pl* **-tries** a small room or large cupboard in which food is kept
WORD ORIGIN Latin *panis* bread
pants ❶ *pl n* **1** *Brit* an undergarment with two leg holes, covering the body from the waist or hips to the thighs **2** *US, Canad, Austral & NZ* trousers or shorts **3 bore** *or* **scare the pants off someone** *informal* to bore or scare someone very much
WORD ORIGIN shortened from *pantaloons*
pantyhose *pl n* *Austral & NZ* women's tights
Panufnik *n* Sir **Andrzej** 1914–91, British composer and conductor, born in Poland. His works include nine symphonies, the cantata *Winter Solstice* (1972), Polish folk-song settings, and ballet music
Paolozzi *n* Sir **Eduardo** (**Luigi**) born 1924, British sculptor and designer, noted esp. for his semiabstract metal figures

THESAURUS

anxiety, dismay, hysteria, fright, agitation, consternation, trepidation, a flap *(informal)* ▹ *vb* **3a = go to pieces**, overreact, become hysterical, have kittens *(informal)*, lose your nerve, be terror-stricken, lose your bottle *(Brit slang)* **3b = alarm**, scare, terrify, startle, unnerve
panorama *n* **1 = view**, prospect, scenery, vista, bird's-eye view, scenic view **2 = survey**, perspective, overview, overall picture
pant *vb* **1 = puff**, blow, breathe, gasp, throb, wheeze, huff, heave, palpitate
pants *pl n* **1** *(Brit)* **= underpants**, briefs, drawers, knickers, panties, boxer shorts, Y-fronts®, broekies *(S African)*, underdaks *(Austral slang)* **2** *(US, Canad, Austral & NZ)* **= trousers**, slacks

DICTIONARY

pap[1] *n* **1** a soft food for babies or invalids **2** worthless or oversimplified entertainment or information **3** *S African* maize porridge
WORD ORIGIN Latin *pappare* to eat

pap[2] *n old-fashioned Scot & N English dialect* a nipple or teat
WORD ORIGIN from Old Norse

papa (pap-**pah**) *n old-fashioned, informal* father
WORD ORIGIN French

papacy (pay-pa-see) *n, pl* **-cies** **1** the office or term of office of a pope **2** the system of government in the Roman Catholic Church that has the pope as its head
WORD ORIGIN Medieval Latin *papa* pope

Papadopoulos *n* **1 Georgios** 1919–99, Greek army officer and statesman; prime minister (1967–73) and president (1973) in Greece's military government **2 Tassos Nikolaou.** born 1934, Cypriot politician: president of Cyprus from 2003

papal *adj* of the pope or the papacy

Papandreou *n* **Andreas** (**George**) 1919–96, Greek economist and socialist politician; prime minister (1981–89; 1993–96)

paparazzo (pap-a-**rat**-so) *n, pl* **-razzi** (**-rat**-see) a freelance photographer who specializes in taking shots of famous people without their knowledge or consent
WORD ORIGIN Italian

papaya (pap-**pie**-a) *n* a large green fruit with a sweet yellow flesh, that grows in the West Indies
WORD ORIGIN Spanish

Papen *n* **Franz von** 1879–1969, German statesman; chancellor (1932) and vice chancellor (1933–34) under Hitler, whom he was instrumental in bringing to power

paper ⊕ *n* **1** a flexible material made in sheets from wood pulp or other fibres and used for writing on, decorating walls, or wrapping parcels **2** ▸short for **newspaper** or **wallpaper** **3 papers** documents, such as a passport, which can identify the bearer **4** a set of examination questions **5 papers** the collected diaries or letters of someone's private or public life **6** a lecture or an essay on a specific subject **7 on paper** in theory, as opposed to fact: *countless ideas which look good on paper just don't work in practice* ▹*adj* **8** made of paper: *paper towels; a paper bag* **9** recorded on paper but not yet existing in practice: *a paper profit of more than $50 million* ▹*vb* **10** to cover (walls) with wallpaper ▸See also **paper over** > **papery** *adj*
WORD ORIGIN Latin *papyrus*

paperback *n* **1** a book with covers made of flexible card ▹*adj* **2** of a paperback or publication of paperbacks: *a paperback novel*

paperboy *or* **papergirl** *n* a boy or girl employed to deliver newspapers to people's homes

paper chase *n* a former type of cross-country run in which a runner lays a trail of paper for others to follow

paperclip *n* a bent wire clip for holding sheets of paper together

paperhanger *n* a person who hangs wallpaper as an occupation

paperknife *n, pl* **-knives** a knife-shaped object with a blunt blade for opening sealed envelopes

paper money *n* banknotes, rather than coins

paper over *vb* to conceal (something unpleasant or difficult)

paperweight *n* a small heavy object placed on top of loose papers to prevent them from scattering

paperwork *n* clerical work, such as the writing of reports or letters

papier-mâché (pap-yay **mash**-ay) *n* **1** a hard substance made of layers of paper mixed with paste and moulded when moist ▹*adj* **2** made of papier-mâché
WORD ORIGIN French, literally: chewed paper

papilla (pap-**pill**-a) *n, pl* **-lae** (-lee) *biol* a small projection of tissue at the base of a hair, tooth, or feather **papillary** *adj*
WORD ORIGIN Latin: nipple

papist *n, adj usually offensive* ▸same as **Roman Catholic**
WORD ORIGIN Church Latin *papa* pope

papoose *n* a Native American baby
WORD ORIGIN Native American *papoos*

Pappus of Alexandria *n* 3rd century BC, Greek mathematician, whose eight-volume *Synagoge* is a valuable source of information about Greek mathematics

paprika *n* a mild powdered seasoning made from red peppers
WORD ORIGIN Hungarian

Pap test *or* **smear** *n med* ▸same as **cervical smear**
WORD ORIGIN after George *Papanicolaou*, anatomist

papyrus (pap-**ire**-uss) *n, pl* **-ri** (-rye) *or* **-ruses** **1** a tall water plant of Africa **2** a kind of paper made from the stem of this plant, used by the ancient Egyptians, Greeks, and Romans **3** an ancient document written on this paper
WORD ORIGIN Greek *papuros* reed

par *n* **1** the usual or average condition: *I feel slightly below par most of the time* **2** *golf* a standard score for a hole or course that a good player should make: *four under par with two holes to play* **3** *finance* the established value of the unit of one national currency in terms of the unit of another **4** *commerce* ▸short for **par value** **5 on a par with** equal or equivalent to: *an environmental disaster on a par with Chernobyl* **6 par for the course** to be expected: *random acts of violence were par for the course in the capital*
WORD ORIGIN Latin: equal

par. **1** paragraph **2** parenthesis

para *n informal* **1** a paratrooper **2** a paragraph

para- *or before a vowel* **par-** *prefix* **1** beside or near: *parameter* **2** beyond: *parapsychology* **3** resembling: *paratyphoid fever*
WORD ORIGIN Greek

parable *n* a short story that uses familiar situations to illustrate a religious or moral point
WORD ORIGIN Greek *parabolē* analogy

parabola (par-**ab**-bol-a) *n geom* an open plane curve formed by the intersection of a cone by a plane parallel to its side **parabolic** *adj*
WORD ORIGIN Greek *parabolē* a setting alongside

paracetamol *n* a mild pain-relieving drug
WORD ORIGIN from *para-acetamidophenol*

parachute *n* **1** a large fabric canopy connected by a harness, that slows the descent of a person or package from an aircraft ▹*vb* **-chuting, -chuted** **2** to land or to drop (supplies or troops) by parachute from an aircraft **parachutist** *n*
WORD ORIGIN French

parade ⊕ *n* **1** an ordered march or procession **2** a public promenade or street of shops **3** a blatant but sometimes insincere display: *a man who made a parade of liking his own company best* ▹*vb* **-rading, -raded** **4** to exhibit or flaunt: *he neither paraded nor*

THESAURUS

paper *n* **2 = newspaper**, news, daily, journal, organ, rag (*informal*), tabloid, gazette, broadsheet **3 = documents**, records, certificates, identification, deeds, identity papers, I.D. (*informal*) **4 = examination**, test, exam **5 = letters**, records, documents, file, diaries, archive, paperwork, dossier **6 = essay**, study, article, analysis, script, composition, assignment, thesis, critique, treatise, dissertation, monograph ▹*vb* **10 = wallpaper**, line, hang, paste up, cover with paper

parade *n* **1 = procession**, march, ceremony, pageant, train, review, column, spectacle, tattoo, motorcade, cavalcade, cortège ▹*vb* **4 = flaunt**, show, display, exhibit, show off (*informal*), air, draw attention to, brandish, vaunt, make

DICTIONARY

disguised his devout faith **5** to walk or march, esp. in a procession
WORD ORIGIN French: a making ready

parade ground *n* a place where soldiers assemble regularly for inspection or display

paradigm ❶ (par-a-dime) *n* a model or example: *his experience is a paradigm for the young artist*
WORD ORIGIN Greek *paradeigma* pattern

paradise ❶ *n* **1** heaven; where the good go after death **2** the Garden of Eden **3** any place or condition that fulfils a person's desires
WORD ORIGIN Greek *paradeisos* garden

paradise duck *n* a New Zealand duck with bright feathers

paradox ❶ *n* **1** a statement that seems self-contradictory but may be true: *it's a strange paradox that a musician must practise improvising to become a good improviser* **2** a self-contradictory proposition, such as *I always tell lies* **3** a person or thing that is made up of contradictory elements
paradoxical *adj* **paradoxically** *adv*
WORD ORIGIN Greek *paradoxos* opposed to existing notions

paraffin *n* **1** *Brit* a liquid mixture distilled from petroleum or shale and used as a fuel or solvent **2** *chem* ▸ the former name for **alkane**
WORD ORIGIN Latin *parum* too little + *affinis* adjacent; so called from its chemical inertia

paraffin wax *n* a white waxlike substance distilled from petroleum and used to make candles and as a sealing agent

paragon *n* a model of perfection: *a paragon of female integrity and determination*
WORD ORIGIN Old Italian *paragone* comparison

paragraph ❶ *n* **1** a section of a piece of writing, usually devoted to one idea, which begins on a new line and is often indented **2** *printing* the character ¶, used to indicate the beginning of a new paragraph ▹*vb* **3** to put (a piece of writing) into paragraphs
WORD ORIGIN Greek *paragraphos* line drawing attention to part of a text

parakeet *n* a small colourful parrot with a long tail
WORD ORIGIN Spanish *periquito* parrot

paralegal *n* a person trained to assist lawyers but not qualified to practise law

parallax *n* an apparent change in an object's position due to a change in the observer's position
WORD ORIGIN Greek *parallaxis* change

parallel ❶ *adj* **1** separated by an equal distance at every point: *parallel lines; a path parallel to the main road* **2** precisely corresponding: *we decide our salaries by comparison with parallel jobs in other charities* **3** *computers* operating on several items of information or instructions at the same time ▹*n* **4** *maths* one of a set of parallel lines or planes **5** something with similar features to another **6** a comparison; similarity between two things: *she attempted to excuse herself by drawing a parallel between her behaviour and ours* **7** Also called: **parallel of latitude** any of the imaginary lines around the earth parallel to the equator, marking degrees of latitude **8** *printing* the character ||, used as a reference mark ▹*vb* **9** to correspond to: *the increase in smoking is paralleled by an increase in lung cancer*
WORD ORIGIN Greek *parallēlos* alongside one another

parallel bars *pl n gymnastics* a pair of wooden bars on upright posts used for various exercises

parallelepiped (par-a-lel-ee-**pipe**-ed) *n geom* a solid shape whose six faces are parallelograms
WORD ORIGIN Greek *parallēlos* parallel + *epipedon* plane surface

parallelism *n* **1** the state of being parallel **2** a close likeness

parallelogram *n geom* a plane figure whose opposite sides are parallel and equal in length
WORD ORIGIN Greek *parallēlos* parallel + *grammē* line

paralyse ❶ *or US* **-lyze** *vb* **-lysing, -lysed** *or* **-lyzing, -lyzed** **1** *pathol* to affect with paralysis **2** to make immobile: *he was paralysed by fear*
WORD ORIGIN French *paralyser*

paralysis ❶ *n* **1** *pathol* inability to move all or part of the body due to damage to the nervous system **2** a state of inactivity: *the economic chaos and political paralysis into which the country has sunk*
WORD ORIGIN Greek *paralusis*, from *para-* beyond + *lusis* a loosening

paralytic *adj* **1** of or relating to paralysis **2** *Brit informal* very drunk ▹*n* **3** a person who is paralysed

paramecium (par-a-**mee**-see-um) *n, pl* **-cia** (-see-a) a single-celled animal which lives in ponds, puddles, and sewage filters and swims by means of cilia

paramedic *n* a person, such as a member of an ambulance crew, whose work supplements that of the medical profession **paramedical** *adj*

parameter ❶ (par-**am**-it-er) *n* **1** *maths* an arbitrary constant that determines the specific form of a mathematical expression, such as *a* and *b* in $y = ax^2 + b$ **2** *informal* any limiting factor: *exchange rates are allowed to fluctuate only within designated parameters*
WORD ORIGIN Greek *para* beside + *metron* measure

paramilitary *adj* denoting a group of people organized on military lines

paramount ❶ *adj* of the greatest importance
WORD ORIGIN Old French *par* by + *-amont* above

paramour *n old-fashioned* an adulterous lover

P

THESAURUS

a show of **5 = march**, process, file, promenade

paradigm *n* **= model**, example, original, pattern, ideal, norm, prototype, archetype, exemplar

paradise *n* **1 = heaven**, Promised Land, Zion (*Christianity*), Happy Valley (*Islam*), City of God, Elysian fields, garden of delights, divine abode, heavenly kingdom **3 = bliss**, delight, heaven, felicity, utopia, seventh heaven

paradox *n* **1, 2, 3 = contradiction**, mystery, puzzle, ambiguity, anomaly, inconsistency, enigma, oddity, absurdity

paragraph *n* **1 = section**, part, notice, item, passage, clause, portion, subdivision

parallel *adj* **1 = equidistant**, alongside, aligned, side by side, coextensive
OPPOSITE: divergent
2 = matching, correspondent, corresponding, like, similar, uniform, resembling, complementary, akin, analogous
OPPOSITE: different
▹*n* **5 = equivalent**, counterpart, match, equal, twin, complement, duplicate, analogue, likeness, corollary **OPPOSITE:** opposite
6 = similarity, correspondence, correlation, comparison, analogy, resemblance, likeness, parallelism
OPPOSITE: difference

paralyse *vb* **1 = disable**, cripple, lame, debilitate, incapacitate **2a = freeze**, stun, numb, petrify, transfix, stupefy, halt, stop dead, immobilize, anaesthetize, benumb
2b = immobilize, freeze, halt, disable, cripple, arrest, incapacitate, bring to a standstill

paralysis *n* **1 = immobility**, palsy, paresis (*pathology*) **2 = standstill**, breakdown, stoppage, shutdown, halt, stagnation, inactivity

parameter *n* **2** (*informal*) **= limit**, constant, restriction, guideline, criterion, framework, limitation, specification

paramount *adj* **= principal**, prime, first, chief, main, capital, primary, supreme, outstanding, superior, dominant, cardinal, foremost, eminent, predominant, pre-eminent
OPPOSITE: secondary

DICTIONARY

WORD ORIGIN Old French, literally: through love

paranoia *n* **1** a mental disorder which causes delusions of grandeur or of persecution **2** *informal* intense fear or suspicion, usually unfounded **paranoid** *or* **paranoiac** *adj, n*
WORD ORIGIN Greek *para-* beyond + *noos* mind

paranormal *adj* **1** beyond normal scientific explanation ▷*n* **2 the paranormal** paranormal happenings or matters generally

parapet *n* **1** a low wall or railing along the edge of a balcony or roof **2** *mil* a mound of sandbags in front of a trench to conceal and protect troops from fire
WORD ORIGIN Italian *parapetto*

paraphernalia *n* various articles or bits of equipment
WORD ORIGIN Greek *para-* beyond + *phernē* dowry

paraphrase *n* **1** an expression of a statement or text in other words ▷*vb* **-phrasing, -phrased 2** to put (a statement or text) into other words
WORD ORIGIN Greek *paraphrazein* to recount

paraplegia (par-a-**pleej**-ya) *n pathol* paralysis of the lower half of the body **paraplegic** *adj, n*
WORD ORIGIN Greek: a blow on one side

parapsychology *n* the study of mental phenomena such as telepathy

Paraquat *n trademark* an extremely poisonous weedkiller

parasite ❶ *n* **1** an animal or plant that lives in or on another from which it obtains nourishment **2** a person who habitually lives at the expense of others; sponger **parasitic** *adj*
WORD ORIGIN Greek *para-* beside + *sitos* grain

parasol *n* an umbrella-like sunshade
WORD ORIGIN French

paratrooper *n* a member of the paratroops

paratroops *pl n* troops trained to be dropped by parachute into a battle area

paratyphoid fever *n* a disease resembling but less severe than typhoid fever

parboil *vb* to boil (food) until partially cooked
WORD ORIGIN Late Latin *perbullire* to boil thoroughly; modern meaning due to confusion of *par-* with *part*

parcel ❶ *n* **1** something wrapped up; a package **2** a group of people or things sharing something in common: *a parcel of fools* **3** a distinct portion of land: *he was the recipient of a substantial parcel of land* ▷*vb* **-celling, -celled** *or US* **-celing, -celed 4** (often foll. by *up*) to wrap (something) up into a parcel **5** (foll. by *out*) to divide (something) into portions: *the children were parcelled out to relatives*
WORD ORIGIN Old French *parcelle*

parch *vb* **1** to deprive (something) of water; dry up: *the summer sun parched the hills* **2** to make (someone) very thirsty: *I'm parched. Have we got any lemonade?*
WORD ORIGIN origin unknown

parchment *n* **1** a thick smooth material made from animal skin and used for writing on **2** a manuscript made of this material **3** a stiff yellowish paper resembling parchment
WORD ORIGIN Greek *pergamēnē*, from *Pergamēnos* of Pergamum (where parchment was made)

pardon ❶ *vb* **1** to forgive or excuse (a person) for (an offence, mistake etc.): *I hope you'll pardon the wait; to pardon someone* ▷*n* **2** forgiveness **3** official release from punishment for a crime ▷*interj* **4** Also: **pardon me, I beg your pardon a** sorry; excuse me **b** what did you say? **pardonable** *adj*
WORD ORIGIN Medieval Latin *perdonare* to forgive freely

pare *vb* **paring, pared 1** to peel (the outer layer) from (something): *thinly pare the rind from the grapefruit* **2** to trim or cut the edge of **3** to decrease bit by bit: *the government is prepared to pare down the armed forces*
WORD ORIGIN Latin *parare* to make ready

Paré *n* **Ambroise** 1510–90, French surgeon. He reintroduced ligature of arteries following amputation instead of cauterization

parent ❶ *n* **1** a father or mother **2** a person acting as a father or mother; guardian **3** a plant or animal that has produced one or more plants or animals **parental** *adj* **parenthood** *n*
WORD ORIGIN Latin *parens*, from *parere* to bring forth

parentage *n* ancestry or family

parent company *n* a company that owns a number of smaller companies

parenthesis (par-**en**-thiss-iss) *n, pl* **-ses** (-seez) **1** a word or phrase inserted into a passage, and marked off by brackets or dashes **2** Also called: **bracket** either of a pair of characters ( ), used to enclose such a phrase **parenthetical** *adj* **parenthetically** *adv*
WORD ORIGIN Greek: something placed in besides

parenting *n* the activity of bringing up children

parent-teacher association *n* an organization consisting of the parents and teachers of school pupils formed to organize activities on behalf of the school

par excellence *adv* beyond comparison: *this book justifies its claim to be a reference work par excellence*
WORD ORIGIN French

parfait (par-**fay**) *n* a dessert consisting of layers of ice cream, fruit, and sauce, topped with whipped cream, and served in a tall glass: *a blackberry and apricot parfait*
WORD ORIGIN French: perfect

pariah (par-**rye**-a) *n* a social outcast: *the man they regard as a pariah*
WORD ORIGIN Tamil *paraiyan* drummer

parietal (par-**rye**-it-al) *adj anat, biol* of or forming the walls of a body cavity: *the parietal bones of the skull*
WORD ORIGIN Latin *paries* wall

paring *n* something that has been cut off something

parish ❶ *n* **1** an area that has its own church and a priest or pastor ▸Related adjective: **parochial 2** the people who live in a parish **3** (in England and, formerly, Wales) the smallest unit of local government
WORD ORIGIN Greek *paroikos* neighbour

parish clerk *n* an official who performs various (esp. administrative) duties for a church or civil parish

parish council *n* (in England and, formerly, Wales) the administrative body of a parish ▸See **parish** (sense 3)

parishioner *n* a person who lives in a particular parish

THESAURUS

parasite *n* **2 = sponger** *(informal)*, sponge *(informal)*, drone *(Brit)*, leech, hanger-on, scrounger *(informal)*, bloodsucker *(informal)*, cadger, quandong *(Austral slang)*

parcel *n* **1 = package**, case, box, pack, packet, bundle, carton ▷*vb* **4** *(often with* **up***)* **= wrap**, pack, package, tie up, do up, gift-wrap, box up, fasten together
5 parcel something out = distribute, divide, portion, allocate, split up, dispense, allot, carve up, mete out, dole out, share out, apportion, deal out

pardon *vb* **1 = acquit**, free, release, liberate, reprieve, remit, amnesty, let off *(informal)*, exonerate, absolve, exculpate **OPPOSITE:** punish ▷*n* **2 = forgiveness**, mercy, indulgence, absolution, grace **OPPOSITE:** condemnation **3 = acquittal**, release, discharge, amnesty, reprieve, remission, exoneration **OPPOSITE:** punishment ▷*interj* **4a = pardon me**, forgive me, excuse me

parent *n* **1 = father** *or* **mother**, sire, progenitor, begetter, procreator, old *(Austral & NZ informal)*, oldie *(Austral informal)*, patriarch

parish *n* **2 = community**, fold, flock, church, congregation, parishioners, churchgoers **3 = district**, community

DICTIONARY

parish register *n* a book in which the births, baptisms, marriages, and deaths in a parish are recorded

parity *n* **1** equality, for example of rank or pay **2** close or exact equivalence: *the company maintained parity with the competition* **3** *finance* equivalence between the units of currency of two countries
WORD ORIGIN Latin *par* equal

park ❶ *n* **1** a large area of open land for recreational use by the public **2** a piece of open land for public recreation in a town **3** *Brit* a large area of private land surrounding a country house **4** an area designed to accommodate a number of related enterprises: *a science park* **5** *US & Canad* a playing field or sports stadium **6 the park** *Brit informal* the pitch in soccer ▷ *vb* **7** to stop and leave (a vehicle) temporarily: *I parked between the two cars already outside; police vans were parked on every street corner* **8** *informal* to leave or put (someone or something) somewhere: *she parked herself on the sofa and stayed there all evening* **parking** *n*
WORD ORIGIN Germanic

parka *n* a long jacket with a quilted lining and a fur-trimmed hood
WORD ORIGIN from Aleutian (language of Aleutian Islands, off Alaska): skin

parkade *n Canad* a building used as a car park

park and ride *n* a transportation scheme in which drivers park some distance away from a city centre, tourist attraction, etc. and complete their journey by public transport

Parker Bowles *n* **Camilla** (née *Shand*). born 1947, became the second wife of Prince Charles in 2005; created Duchess of Cornwall

parkette *n Canad* a small public car park

parkin *n Brit* a moist spicy ginger cake usually containing oatmeal
WORD ORIGIN origin unknown

parking lot *n US & Canad* area or building where vehicles may be left for a time

parking meter *n* a coin-operated device beside a parking space that indicates how long a vehicle may be left parked

parking ticket *n* the notice of a fine served on a motorist for a parking offence

Parkinson's disease *or* **Parkinsonism** *n* a progressive disorder of the central nervous system which causes tremor, rigidity, and impaired muscular coordination
WORD ORIGIN after J. *Parkinson*, surgeon

Parkinson's law *n* the notion that work expands to fill the time available for its completion
WORD ORIGIN after C. N. *Parkinson*, historian and writer

parkland *n* grassland with scattered trees

parky *adj* **parkier, parkiest** *Brit informal* (of the weather) chilly
WORD ORIGIN origin unknown

parlance *n* the manner of speaking associated with a particular group or subject: *he had, in Marxist parlance, a 'petit bourgeois' mentality*
WORD ORIGIN French *parler* to talk

parley *old-fashioned n* **1** a discussion between members of opposing sides to decide terms of agreement ▷ *vb* **2** to have a parley
WORD ORIGIN French *parler* to talk

parliament ❶ *n* a law-making assembly of a country
WORD ORIGIN Old French *parlement*, from *parler* to speak

Parliament *n* **1** the highest law-making authority in Britain, consisting of the House of Commons, the House of Lords, and the sovereign **2** the equivalent law-making authority in another country

parliamentarian *n* an expert in parliamentary procedures

parliamentary ❶ *adj* **1** of or from a parliament: *parliamentary elections* **2** conforming to the procedures of a parliament: *parliamentary language*

parlour ❶ *or US* **parlor** *n* **1** *old-fashioned* a living room for receiving visitors **2** a room or shop equipped as a place of business: *an ice-cream parlour*
WORD ORIGIN Old French *parler* to speak

parlous *adj archaic or humorous* dangerously bad; dire: *the parlous state of the economy*
WORD ORIGIN variant of *perilous*

Parmenides *n* 5th century BC, Greek Eleatic philosopher, born in Italy. He held that the universe is single and unchanging and denied the existence of change and motion. His doctrines are expounded in his poem *On Nature*, of which only fragments are extant

Parmesan (par-miz-zan) *n* a hard strong-flavoured cheese used grated on pasta dishes and soups
WORD ORIGIN Italian *parmegiano* of Parma, Italy

Parmigianino *n* real name *Girolamo Francesco Maria Mazzola* 1503–40, Italian painter, one of the originators of mannerism. Also: **Parmigiano**

parochial *adj* **1** narrow in outlook; provincial **2** of or relating to a parish **parochialism** *n*
WORD ORIGIN see PARISH

parody ❶ *n, pl* **-dies 1** a piece of music or literature that mimics the style of another composer or author in a humorous way **2** something done so badly that it seems like an intentional mockery ▷ *vb* **-dies, -dying, -died 3** to make a parody of **parodist** *n*
WORD ORIGIN Greek *paroidia* satirical poem

parole *n* **1** the freeing of a prisoner before his or her sentence has run out, on condition that he or she behaves well **2** a promise given by a prisoner to behave well if granted liberty or partial liberty **3 on parole** conditionally released from prison ▷ *vb* **-roling, -roled 4** to place (a person) on parole
WORD ORIGIN Old French *parole d'honneur* word of honour

parotid gland *n anat* either of a pair of salivary glands in front of and below the ears
WORD ORIGIN Greek *para-* near + *ous* ear

paroxysm *n* **1** an uncontrollable outburst of emotion: *a paroxysm of grief* **2** *pathol* **a** a sudden attack or recurrence of a disease **b** a fit or convulsion **paroxysmal** *adj*
WORD ORIGIN Greek *paroxunein* to goad

parquet (par-kay) *n* **1** a floor covering made of blocks of wood ▷ *vb* **2** to cover (a floor) with parquetry
WORD ORIGIN Old French: small enclosure

parquetry (par-kit-tree) *n* pieces of wood arranged in a geometric pattern, used to cover floors

parr *n* a salmon up to two years of age
WORD ORIGIN origin unknown

Parr *n* **Catherine** 1512–48, sixth wife of Henry VIII of England

P

THESAURUS

park *n* **1 = recreation ground**, garden, playground, pleasure garden, playpark, domain (NZ), forest park (NZ) **2, 3 = parkland**, grounds, estate, lawns, woodland, grassland **5** (*US & Canad*) **= field**, pitch, playing field

parliament *n* **= assembly**, council, congress, senate, convention, legislature, talking shop (*informal*), convocation

parliamentary *adj* **1 = governmental**, congressional, legislative, law-making, law-giving, deliberative

parlour *or (US)* **parlor** *n* **1** (*old-fashioned*) **= sitting room**, lounge, living room, drawing room, front room, reception room, best room **2 = establishment**, shop, store, salon

parody *n* **1 = takeoff** (*informal*), imitation, satire, caricature, send-up (*Brit informal*), spoof (*informal*), lampoon, skit, burlesque ▷ *vb* **3 = take off** (*informal*), mimic, caricature, send up (*Brit informal*), spoof (*informal*), travesty, lampoon, poke fun at, burlesque, satirize, do a takeoff of (*informal*)

DICTIONARY

parricide *n* **1** a person who kills one of his or her parents **2** the act of killing either of one's parents **parricidal** *adj*
WORD ORIGIN Latin *parricidium* murder of a parent or relative

parrot ❶ *n* **1** a tropical bird with a short hooked beak, bright plumage, and an ability to mimic human speech **2** a person who repeats or imitates someone else's words **3 sick as a parrot** *usually facetious* extremely disappointed ▹ *vb* **-roting, -roted 4** to repeat or imitate (someone else's words) without understanding them
WORD ORIGIN probably from French *paroquet*

parrot fever *n* ▸ same as **psittacosis**

parrotfish *n* a brightly coloured sea fish

parry ❶ *vb* **-ries, -rying, -ried 1** to ward off (an attack) **2** to avoid answering (questions) in a clever way ▹ *n, pl* **-ries 3** an instance of parrying **4** a skilful evasion of a question
WORD ORIGIN French *parer* to ward off

Parry *n* **1** Sir (**Charles**) **Hubert** (**Hastings**) 1848–1918, English composer, noted esp. for his choral works **2** Sir **William Edward** 1790–1855, English arctic explorer, who searched for the Northwest Passage (1819–25) and attempted to reach the North Pole (1827)

parse (parz) *vb* **parsing, parsed** to analyse (a sentence or the words in a sentence) grammatically
WORD ORIGIN Latin *pars (orationis)* part (of speech)

parsec *n* a unit of astronomical distance equivalent to 3.0857 × 10^{16} metres or 3.262 light years
WORD ORIGIN *parallax* + *second* (of time)

parsimony *n formal* extreme caution in spending **parsimonious** *adj*
WORD ORIGIN Latin *parcimonia*

parsley *n* a herb with curled pleasant-smelling leaves, used for seasoning and decorating food
WORD ORIGIN Middle English *persely*

parsnip *n* a long tapering cream-coloured root vegetable
WORD ORIGIN Latin *pastinaca*

parson ❶ *n* **1** a parish priest in the Church of England **2** any clergyman **3** NZ a nonconformist minister
WORD ORIGIN Latin *persona* personage

parsonage *n* the residence of a parson, provided by the parish

Parsons *n* **1** Sir **Charles Algernon** 1854–1931, English engineer, who developed the steam turbine **2 Gram,** real name *Cecil Connor.* 1946–73 US country-rock singer and songwriter; founder of the Flying Burrito Brothers (1968–70), he later released the solo albums *G.P.* (1973) and *Grievous Angel* (1974) **3 Talcott** 1902–79, US sociologist, author of *The Structure of Social Action* (1937) and *The Social System* (1951)

parson's nose *n* the rump of a fowl when cooked

part ❶ *n* **1** a piece or portion **2** one of several equal divisions: *a salad dressing made with two parts oil to one part vinegar* **3** *(theatre)* an actor's role in a play **4** a person's duty: *his ancestors had done their part nobly and well at Bannockburn* **5** an involvement in or contribution to something: *he was jailed for his part in the fraud* **6** a region or area: *he's well known in these parts; the weather in this part of the country is extreme* **7** *anat* an area of the body **8** a component that can be replaced in a vehicle or machine **9** *US, Canad & Austral* ▸ same as **parting** (sense 2) **10** *music* a melodic line assigned to one or more instrumentalists or singers **11 for my part** as far as I am concerned **12 for the most part** generally **13 in part** to some degree; partly **14 on the part of** on behalf of **15 part and parcel of** an essential ingredient of **16 play a part a** to pretend to be what one is not **b** (foll. by *in*) to have something to do with: *examinations play a large part in education and in schools* **17 take part in** to participate in **18 take someone's part** to support someone, for example in an argument **19 take something in good part** to respond to (teasing or criticism) with good humour ▹ *vb* **20** to divide or separate from one another: *her lips parted in laughter; the cord parted with a pop* **21** to go away from one another: *we parted with handshakes all round* **22** to split: *the path parts here* **23** to arrange (the hair) in such a way that a line of scalp is left showing ▹ *adv* **24** to some extent; partly: *this book is part history, part travelogue* **25 part from** to cause (someone) to give up: *I was astonished at the way Henry parted his audience from their money* **26 part with** to give up: *check carefully before you part with your cash* ▸ See also **parts**
WORD ORIGIN Latin *pars* a part

partake ❶ *vb* **-taking, -took, -taken 1 partake in** to take part in **2 partake of** to take (food or drink)
WORD ORIGIN from earlier *part taker*

parterre *n* **1** a formally patterned flower garden **2** the pit of a theatre
WORD ORIGIN French

Parthian shot *n* a hostile remark or gesture delivered while departing
WORD ORIGIN from the custom of archers from Parthia, an ancient Asian empire, who shot their arrows backwards while retreating

partial ❶ *adj* **1** relating to only a part; not complete: *partial deafness* **2** biased: *religious programmes can be as partial as they like* **3 be partial to** to have a particular liking for **partiality** *n* **partially** *adv*
WORD ORIGIN Latin *pars* part

participate *vb* **-pating, -pated** ▪ **participate in** to become actively involved in **participant** *n* **participation** *n* **participatory** *adj*
WORD ORIGIN Latin *pars* part + *capere* to take

participle *n grammar* a form of a verb that is used in compound tenses or as an adjective ▸ See also **present participle, past participle** > **participial** *adj*
WORD ORIGIN Latin *pars* part + *capere* to take

particle ❶ *n* **1** an extremely small piece or amount: *clean thoroughly to remove all particles of dirt* **2** *grammar* an

P

THESAURUS

parrot *vb* **4 = repeat**, echo, imitate, copy, reiterate, mimic

parry *vb* **1 = ward off**, block, deflect, repel, rebuff, fend off, stave off, repulse, hold at bay **2 = evade**, avoid, fence off, dodge, duck *(informal)*, shun, sidestep, circumvent, fight shy of

parson *n* **2 = clergyman**, minister, priest, vicar, divine, incumbent, reverend *(informal)*, preacher, pastor, cleric, rector, curate, churchman, man of God, man of the cloth, ecclesiastic

part *n* **1 = piece**, share, proportion, percentage, lot, bit, section, sector, slice, scrap, particle, segment, portion, fragment, lump, fraction, chunk, wedge **OPPOSITE:** entirety **2, 8 = component**, bit, piece, unit, element, ingredient, constituent, module **3a** *(theatre)* **= role**, representation, persona, portrayal, depiction, character part **3b** *(theatre)* **= lines**, words, script, dialogue **6 = region**, area, district, territory, neighbourhood, quarter, vicinity, neck of the woods *(informal)*, airt *(Scot)* **7** *(anat)* **= organ**, member, limb ▹ *vb* **20 = divide**, separate, break, tear, split, rend, detach, sever, disconnect, cleave, come apart, disunite, disjoin **OPPOSITE:** join **21 = part company**, separate, break up, split up, say goodbye, go (their) separate ways **OPPOSITE:** meet

partial *adj* **1 = incomplete**, limited, unfinished, imperfect, fragmentary, uncompleted **OPPOSITE:** complete **2 = biased**, prejudiced, discriminatory, partisan, influenced, unfair, one-sided, unjust, predisposed, tendentious **OPPOSITE:** unbiased

particle *n* **1 = bit**, piece, scrap, grain, molecule, atom, shred, crumb, mite, jot, speck, mote, whit, tittle, iota

DICTIONARY

uninflected part of speech, such as an interjection or preposition **3** *physics* a minute piece of matter, such as an electron or proton
WORD ORIGIN Latin *pars* part

parti-coloured *or US* **particolored** *adj* having different colours in different parts
WORD ORIGIN from obsolete *party* of more than one colour

particular ❶ *adj* **1** of, belonging to, or being one person or thing; specific: *the particular type of tuition on offer* **2** exceptional or special: *the report voices particular concern over the state of the country's manufacturing industry* **3** providing specific details or circumstances: *a particular account* **4** difficult to please; fussy ▷ *n* **5** a separate distinct item as opposed to a generalization: *moving from the general to the particular* **6** an item of information; detail: *she refused to go into particulars* **7 in particular** especially or exactly: *three painters in particular were responsible for these developments* **particularly** *adv*
WORD ORIGIN Latin *particula* a small part

particularity *n, pl* **-ties 1** great attentiveness to detail **2** the state of being particular as opposed to general; individuality

particularize *or* **-ise** *vb* **-izing, -ized** *or* **-ising, -ised** to give details about (something) **particularization** *or* **-isation** *n*

parting ❶ *n* **1** a departure or leave-taking **2** *Brit & NZ* the line of scalp showing when sections of hair are combed in opposite directions **3** the act of dividing (something): *the parting of the Red Sea*

parting shot *n* a hostile remark or gesture delivered while departing

partisan ❶ *n* **1** a person who supports a particular cause or party **2** a member of an armed resistance group within occupied territory ▷ *adj* **3** prejudiced or one-sided **partisanship** *n*
WORD ORIGIN Old Italian *partigiano*

partition ❶ *n* **1** a large screen or thin wall that divides a room **2** the division of a country into two or more independent countries ▷ *vb* **3** to separate (a room) into sections: *the shower is partitioned off from the rest of the bathroom* **4** to divide (a country) into separate self-governing parts: *the subcontinent was partitioned into India and Pakistan*
WORD ORIGIN Latin *partire* to divide

partitive *grammar adj* **1** (of a noun) referring to part of something. The phrase *some of the butter* is a partitive construction ▷ *n* **2** a partitive word, such as *some* or *any*
WORD ORIGIN Latin *partire* to divide

partly ❶ *adv* not completely

partner ❶ *n* **1** either member of a couple in a relationship **2** a member of a business partnership **3** one of a pair of dancers or of players on the same side in a game: *her bridge partner* **4** an ally or companion: *the country's main European trading partner* ▷ *vb* **5** to be the partner of (someone)
WORD ORIGIN Middle English *parcener* joint inheritor

partnership ❶ *n* **1** a relationship in which two or more people or organizations work together in a business venture **2** the condition of being a partner

part of speech *n grammar* a class of words, such as a noun, verb, or adjective, sharing important syntactic or semantic features

Parton *n* **Dolly** born 1946, US country and pop singer and songwriter

partook *vb* ▸ the past tense of **partake**

partridge *n, pl* **-tridges** *or* **-tridge** a game bird with an orange-brown head, greyish neck, and a short rust-coloured tail
WORD ORIGIN Latin *perdix*

Partridge *n* **Eric (Honeywood)** 1894–1979, British lexicographer, born in New Zealand; author of works on English usage, idiom, slang, and etymology

parts *pl n literary* abilities or talents: *a man of many parts*

part song *n* a song composed in harmonized parts

part-time *adj* **1** for less than the normal full working time: *a part-time job* ▷ *adv* **part time 2** on a part-time basis: *he works part time* **part-timer** *n*

parturient *adj formal* giving birth
WORD ORIGIN Latin *parturire* to be in labour

parturition *n* the process of giving birth
WORD ORIGIN Latin *parturire* to be in labour

party ❶ *n, pl* **-ties 1** a social gathering for pleasure **2** a group of people involved in the same activity: *a search party* **3** a group of people sharing a common political aim **4** the person or people who take part in or are involved in something, esp. a legal action or dispute: *a judge in a wig and gown who will decide who the guilty party is* **5** *informal, humorous* a person: *he's an odd old party* ▷ *vb* **-ties, -tying, -tied 6** *informal* to celebrate; have a good time
WORD ORIGIN Old French *partie* part

party line *n* **1** the policies of a political party **2** a telephone line shared by two or more subscribers

party wall *n property law* a common

P

THESAURUS

particular *adj* **1 = specific**, special, express, exact, precise, distinct, peculiar **OPPOSITE:** general **2 = special**, exceptional, notable, uncommon, marked, unusual, remarkable, singular, noteworthy, especial **4 = fussy**, demanding, critical, exacting, discriminating, meticulous, fastidious, dainty, choosy *(informal)*, picky *(informal)*, finicky, pernickety *(informal)*, overnice, nit-picky *(informal)* **OPPOSITE:** indiscriminate ▷ *n* **6 = detail**, fact, feature, item, circumstance, specification

parting *n* **1 = farewell**, departure, goodbye, leave-taking, adieu, valediction **3 = division**, breaking, split, separation, rift, partition, detachment, rupture, divergence

partisan *n* **1 = supporter**, champion, follower, backer, disciple, stalwart, devotee, adherent, upholder, votary **OPPOSITE:** opponent **2 = underground fighter**, guerrilla, irregular, freedom fighter, resistance fighter ▷ *adj* **3 = prejudiced**, one-sided, biased, partial, sectarian, factional, tendentious **OPPOSITE:** unbiased

partition *n* **1 = screen**, wall, barrier, divider, room divider **2 = division**, splitting, dividing, separation, segregation, severance ▷ *vb* **3 = separate**, screen, divide, fence off, wall off

partly *adv* **= partially**, relatively, somewhat, slightly, in part, halfway, not fully, in some measure, incompletely, up to a certain point, to a certain degree *or* extent **OPPOSITE:** completely

partner *n* **1 = spouse**, consort, bedfellow, significant other *(US informal)*, mate, better half *(Brit informal)*, helpmate, husband *or* wife **2 = associate**, colleague, collaborator, copartner **4 = companion**, collaborator, accomplice, ally, colleague, associate, mate, team-mate, participant, comrade, confederate, bedfellow, copartner

partnership *n* **1 = cooperation**, association, alliance, sharing, union, connection, participation, copartnership

party *n* **1 = get-together** *(informal)*, celebration, do *(informal)*, social, at-home, gathering, function, reception, bash *(informal)*, rave *(Brit slang)*, festivity, knees-up *(Brit informal)*, beano *(Brit slang)*, social gathering, shindig *(informal)*, soirée, rave-up *(Brit slang)*, hooley *or* hoolie *(chiefly Irish & NZ)* **2 = group**, team, band, company, body, unit, squad, gathering, crew, gang, bunch *(informal)*, detachment *(military)* **3 = faction**, association, alliance, grouping, set, side, league, camp, combination, coalition, clique, coterie, schism, confederacy, cabal

DICTIONARY

wall separating two properties

Parumov *n* **Georgi** born 1957, Bulgarian politician, president of Bulgaria from 2002

par value *n* the value printed on a share certificate or bond at the time of its issue

parvenu *or fem* **parvenue** (par-ven-new) *n* a person newly risen to a position of power or wealth who is considered to lack culture or education
WORD ORIGIN French

pascal *n* the SI unit of pressure; the pressure exerted on an area of 1 square metre by a force of 1 newton
WORD ORIGIN after B. *Pascal*, mathematician & scientist

Pascal *n* a high-level computer programming language developed as a teaching language
WORD ORIGIN after B. *Pascal*, mathematician & scientist

paschal (**pask**-l) *adj* **1** of or relating to the Passover **2** of or relating to Easter
WORD ORIGIN Hebrew *pesah* Passover

pas de deux (pah de **duh**) *n, pl* **pas de deux** *ballet* a dance for two people
WORD ORIGIN French: step for two

pasha *n* (formerly) a high official of the Ottoman Empire: placed after a name when used as a title
WORD ORIGIN Turkish *paşa*

pashmina (pash-**mee**-na) *n* a type of cashmere scarf or shawl made from the underfur of Tibetan goats
WORD ORIGIN Persian *pashm* wool

Pašić *n* **Nicola** 1845–1926, Serbian statesman; prime minister of Serbia (1891–92; 1904–05; 1906–08; 1909–11; 1912–18) and of the Kingdom of Serbs, Croats, and Slovenes (1921–24; 1924–26)

Pasionaria *n* **La** (la), real name *Dolores Ibarruri* 1895–1989, Spanish Communist leader, who lived in exile in the Soviet Union (1939–75)

Pasmore *n* **Victor** 1908–98, British artist. Originally a figurative painter, he devoted himself to abstract paintings and reliefs after 1947

paso doble (**pass**-so **dobe**-lay) *n* **1** a modern ballroom dance in fast duple time **2** music for this dance
WORD ORIGIN Spanish: double step

Pasolini *n* **Pier Paolo** 1922–75, Italian film director His films include *The Gospel according to St Matthew* (1964), *Oedipus Rex* (1967), *Theorem* (1968), *Pigsty* (1969), and *Decameron* (1970)

pas op (pass op) *interj S African* beware
WORD ORIGIN Afrikaans

paspalum (pass-**pale**-um) *n Austral & NZ* a type of grass with wide leaves

pasqueflower *n* a small purple-flowered plant of Europe and Asia
WORD ORIGIN French *passefleur*, changed to *pasqueflower* Easter flower, because it blooms at Easter

pass *vb* **1** to go by or past (a person or thing) **2** to continue or extend in a particular direction: *the road to Camerino passes through some fine scenery* **3** to go through or cause (something) to go through (an obstacle or barrier): *the bullet passed through his head* **4** to be successful in (a test or examination) **5** to spend (time) or (of time) go by: *the time passed surprisingly quickly* **6** to hand over or be handed over: *she passed me her glass* **7** to be inherited by: *his mother's small estate had passed to him after her death* **8** *sport* to hit, kick, or throw (the ball) to another player **9** (of a law-making body) to agree to (a law or proposal): *the bill was passed by parliament last week* **10** to pronounce (judgment): *the court is expected to pass sentence later today* **11** to move onwards or over: *a flicker of amusement passed over his face* **12** to exceed: *Australia's population has just passed the seventeen million mark* **13** to go without comment: *the insult passed unnoticed* **14** to choose not to answer a question or not to make a bid or a play in card games **15** to discharge (urine etc.) from the body **16** to come to an end or disappear: *the madness will soon pass* **17** (foll. by *for* or *as*) to be likely to be mistaken for (someone or something else): *the few sunny days that pass for summer in this country* **18** *old-fashioned* to take place: *what passed at the meeting?* **19 pass away** *or* **on** *euphemistic* to die ▷ *n* **20** a successful result in an examination or test **21** *sport* the transfer of a ball from one player to another **22** a route through a range of mountains where there is a gap between peaks **23** a permit or licence **24** *mil* a document authorizing leave of absence **25** *bridge, etc.* an instance of choosing not to answer a question or not to make a bid or a play in card games **26 a pretty pass** a bad state of affairs **27 make a pass at** *informal* to try to persuade (someone) to have sex: *he made a pass at his secretary* ▸ See also **pass off, pass out**, etc.
WORD ORIGIN Latin *passus* step

pass. passive

passable *adj* **1** adequate or acceptable: *passable if hardly faultless German* **2** (of a road, path, etc.) capable of being travelled along: *most main roads are passable with care despite the snow*
passably *adv*

passage ❶ *n* **1** a channel or opening providing a way through **2** a hall or corridor **3** a section of a written work, speech, or piece of music **4** a journey by ship **5** the act of passing from one place or condition to another: *Ireland faced a tough passage to qualify for the World Cup finals* **6** the right or freedom to pass: *the aid convoys were guaranteed safe passage through rebel-held areas* **7** the establishing of a law by a law-making body
WORD ORIGIN Old French *passer* to pass

passageway *n* corridor or passage

passbook *n* **1** a book issued by a bank or building society for recording deposits and withdrawals **2** *S African* formerly, an official identity document

passé (**pas**-say) *adj* out-of-date: *smoking is a bit passé these days*
WORD ORIGIN French

passenger ❶ *n* **1** a person travelling in a vehicle driven by someone else **2** *Brit & NZ* a member of a team who does not take an equal share of the work: *you'll have to pull your weight – we can't afford passengers*
WORD ORIGIN Old French *passager* passing

passer-by ❶ *n, pl* **passers-by** a person who is walking past someone or something

passerine *adj* **1** belonging to an order of perching birds that includes the larks, finches, and starlings ▷ *n* **2** any bird of this order
WORD ORIGIN Latin *passer* sparrow

passim *adv* throughout: used to indicate that what is referred to occurs frequently in a particular piece of writing
WORD ORIGIN Latin

passing ❶ *adj* **1** momentary or short-lived: *a passing fad* **2** casual or superficial: *a passing resemblance* ▷ *n* **3** *euphemistic* death **4** the ending of something: *the passing of the old order in Eastern Europe* **5 in passing** briefly and without going into detail; incidentally: *this fact is only noted in passing*

P

THESAURUS

passage *n* **1 = alley**, way, opening, close (*Brit*), course, road, channel, route, path, lane, avenue, thoroughfare **2 = corridor**, hallway, passageway, hall, lobby, entrance, exit, doorway, aisle, entrance hall, vestibule **3 = extract**, reading, piece, section, sentence, text, clause, excerpt, paragraph, verse, quotation **4 = journey**, crossing, tour, trip, trek, voyage **6 = safe-conduct**, right to travel, freedom to travel, permission to travel, authorization to travel

passenger *n* **1 = traveller**, rider, fare, commuter, hitchhiker, pillion rider, fare payer

passer-by *n* **= bystander**, witness, observer, viewer, spectator, looker-on, watcher, onlooker, eyewitness

passing *adj* **1 = momentary**, fleeting, short-lived, transient, ephemeral, short, brief, temporary, transitory, evanescent, fugacious (*rare*) **2 = superficial**, short, quick, slight,

DICTIONARY

passion ❶ *n* **1** intense sexual love **2** any strongly felt emotion **3** a strong enthusiasm for something: *a passion for football* **4** the object of an intense desire or enthusiasm: *flying is his abiding passion* **passionless** *adj*
WORD ORIGIN Latin *pati* to suffer
Passion *n* the sufferings of Christ from the Last Supper to his death on the cross
passionate ❶ *adj* **1** showing intense sexual desire **2** capable of or revealing intense emotion: *a passionate speech* **passionately** *adv*
passionflower *n* a tropical plant with brightly coloured showy flowers
WORD ORIGIN parts of the flowers are said to resemble the instruments of the Crucifixion
passion fruit *n* the edible egg-shaped fruit of the passionflower
Passion play *n* a play about the Passion of Christ
passive ❶ *adj* **1** not taking an active part **2** submissive and receptive to outside forces **3** *grammar* denoting a form of verbs used to indicate that the subject is the recipient of the action, as *was broken* in *The glass was broken by that boy over there* **4** *chem* (of a substance) chemically unreactive ▷ *n* **5** *grammar* the passive form of a verb **passively** *adv* **passivity** *n*
WORD ORIGIN Latin *passivus* capable of suffering
passive resistance *n* resistance to a government or the law by nonviolent acts such as fasting, peaceful demonstrations, or refusing to cooperate
passive smoking *n* the unwilling inhalation of smoke from other people's cigarettes by a nonsmoker
passkey *n* **1** a private key **2** ▶ same as **master key** or **skeleton key**
pass law *n* (formerly in South Africa) a law restricting the movement of Black Africans
pass off *vb* **1** to present (something or oneself) under false pretences: *women who passed themselves off effectively as men* **2** to come to a gradual end: *the effects of the gas passed off relatively peacefully* **3** to take place: *the main demonstration passed off peacefully*
pass out *vb* **1** *informal* to become unconscious; faint **2** *Brit* (of an officer cadet) to qualify for a military commission
pass over *vb* **1** to take no notice of; disregard: *she claims she had been passed over for promotion because she is a woman* **2** to ignore or not discuss: *this disaster can not be passed over lightly*
Passover *n* an eight-day Jewish festival commemorating the sparing of the Israelites in Egypt
WORD ORIGIN *pass over*, translation of Hebrew *pesah*
passport *n* **1** an official document issued by a government, which identifies the holder and grants him or her permission to travel abroad **2** an asset that gains a person admission or acceptance: *good qualifications are no automatic passport to a job*
WORD ORIGIN French *passer* to pass + *port* port
pass up *vb informal* to let (something) go by; disregard: *am I passing up my one chance to be really happy?*
password *n* a secret word or phrase that ensures admission by proving identity or membership
Passy *n* **Frédéric** (frederik) 1822–1912, French politician and economist, who campaigned for international arbitration to prevent war: shared the first Nobel peace prize 1901
past ❶ *adj* **1** of the time before the present: *the past history of the world* **2** no longer in existence: *past happiness* **3** immediately previous: *the past year* **4** former: *a past president* **5** *grammar* indicating a tense of verbs used to describe actions that have been begun or completed at the time of speaking ▷ *n* **6 the past** the period of time before the present: *a familiar face from the past* **7** the history of a person or nation **8** an earlier disreputable period of someone's life: *a woman with a bit of a past* **9** *grammar* **a** the past tense **b** a verb in the past tense ▷ *adv* **10** on or onwards: *I called but he just walked past* **11** at a time before the present; ago: *three years past* ▷ *prep* **12** beyond in time: *it's past midnight* **13** beyond in place: *a procession of mourners filed past the coffin* **14** beyond the limit of: *riches past his wildest dreams* **15 not put it past someone** to consider someone capable of (a particular action): *I wouldn't put it past him to double-cross us* **16 past it** *informal* unable to do the things one could do when younger
WORD ORIGIN from *pass*
pasta *n* a type of food, such as spaghetti, that is made from a dough of flour and water and formed into different shapes
WORD ORIGIN Italian
paste ❶ *n* **1** a soft moist mixture, such as toothpaste **2** an adhesive made from water and flour or starch, for use with paper **3** a smooth creamy preparation of fish, meat, or vegetables for spreading on bread: *sausage paste* **4** *Brit & NZ* dough for making pastry **5** a hard shiny glass used to make imitation gems ▷ *vb* **pasting, pasted 6** to attach by paste: *she bought a scrapbook and carefully pasted in it all her clippings* **7** *slang* to beat or defeat (someone)
WORD ORIGIN Greek *pastē* barley porridge
pasteboard *n* a stiff board made by pasting layers of paper together
pastel ❶ *n* **1 a** a crayon made of ground pigment bound with gum **b** a picture drawn with such crayons

P

THESAURUS

glancing, casual, summary, shallow, hasty, cursory, perfunctory, desultory
passion *n* **1 = love**, desire, affection, lust, the hots *(slang)*, attachment, itch, fondness, adoration, infatuation, ardour, keenness, concupiscence **2 = emotion**, feeling, fire, heat, spirit, transport, joy, excitement, intensity, warmth, animation, zeal, zest, fervour, eagerness, rapture, ardour **OPPOSITE:** indifference **3, 4 = mania**, fancy, enthusiasm, obsession, bug *(informal)*, craving, fascination, craze, infatuation
passionate *adj* **1 = loving**, erotic, hot, sexy *(informal)*, aroused, sensual, ardent, steamy *(informal)*, wanton, amorous, lustful, desirous **OPPOSITE:** cold **2 = emotional**, excited, eager, enthusiastic, animated, strong, warm, wild, intense, flaming, fierce, frenzied, ardent, fervent, heartfelt, impassioned, zealous, impulsive, vehement, impetuous, fervid **OPPOSITE:** unemotional
passive *adj* **1 = inactive**, inert, uninvolved, non-participating **OPPOSITE:** active **2 = submissive**, resigned, compliant, receptive, lifeless, docile, nonviolent, quiescent, acquiescent, unassertive, unresisting **OPPOSITE:** spirited
past *adj* **1 = former**, late, early, recent, previous, ancient, prior, long-ago, preceding, foregoing, erstwhile, bygone, olden **OPPOSITE:** future **2 = over**, done, ended, spent, finished, completed, gone, forgotten, accomplished, extinct, elapsed, over and done with **3 = last**, recent, previous, preceding **4 = previous**, former, one-time, sometime, erstwhile, quondam, ex- ▷ *n* **6 = former times**, history, long ago, antiquity, the good old days, yesteryear *(literary)*, times past, the old times, days gone by, the olden days, days of yore **OPPOSITE:** future **7 = background**, life, experience, history, past life, life story, career to date ▷ *adv* **10 = on**, by, along ▷ *prep* **12 = after**, beyond, later than, over, outside, farther than, in excess of, subsequent to **13 = by**, across, in front of
paste *n* **2 = adhesive**, glue, cement, gum, mucilage **3 = purée**, pâté, spread ▷ *vb* **6 = stick**, fix, glue, cement, gum, fasten
pastel *adj* **3 = pale**, light, soft, delicate, muted, soft-hued **OPPOSITE:** bright

DICTIONARY

2 a pale delicate colour ▹*adj* 3 (of a colour) pale and delicate: *pastel pink*
WORD ORIGIN Latin *pasta* paste

pastern *n* the part of a horse's foot between the fetlock and the hoof
WORD ORIGIN Old French *pasture* a tether

paste-up *n printing* a sheet of paper or board with artwork and proofs pasted on it, which is photographed prior to making a plate

pasteurize *or* **-ise** *vb* **-izing, -ized** *or* **-ising, -ised** to destroy bacteria (in beverages or solid foods) by a special heating process **pasteurization** *or* **-isation** *n*
WORD ORIGIN after Louis *Pasteur*, chemist

pastiche (past-**eesh**) *n* a work of art that mixes styles or copies the style of another artist
WORD ORIGIN French

pastille *n* a small fruit-flavoured and sometimes medicated sweet
WORD ORIGIN Latin *pastillus* small loaf

pastime ❶ *n* an activity which makes time pass pleasantly

pasting *n* 1 *slang* a thrashing or heavy defeat 2 *informal* strong criticism

past master *n* a person with a talent for or experience in a particular activity: *a past master at manipulating the media*

pastor ❶ *n* a member of the clergy in charge of a congregation
WORD ORIGIN Latin: shepherd

pastoral ❶ *adj* 1 of or depicting country life or scenery 2 (of land) used for pasture 3 of or relating to a member of the clergy or his or her duties 4 of or relating to shepherds or their work ▹*n* 5 a literary work, picture, or piece of music portraying country life 6 a letter from a bishop to the clergy or people of his diocese
WORD ORIGIN Latin *pastor* shepherd

pastorale (past-or-**ahl**) *n, pl* **-rales** a musical composition that suggests country life
WORD ORIGIN Italian

pastoralism *n* a system of agriculture in dry grassland regions based on raising stock such as cattle, sheep, or goats **pastoralist** *n*

past participle *n grammar* a form of verb used to form compound past tenses and passive forms of the verb and to modify nouns: *spoken is the past participle of speak*

pastrami *n* highly seasoned smoked beef
WORD ORIGIN Yiddish

pastry *n* 1 a dough of flour, water, and fat 2 *pl* **-tries** an individual cake or pie 3 baked foods, such as tarts, made with this dough
WORD ORIGIN from *paste*

pasturage *n* 1 the business of grazing cattle 2 ▸same as **pasture**

pasture ❶ *n* 1 land covered with grass, suitable for grazing by farm animals 2 the grass growing on this land
WORD ORIGIN Latin *pascere* to feed

pasty[1] (**pay**-stee) *adj* **pastier, pastiest** (of the complexion) pale and unhealthy-looking

pasty[2] (**past**-ee) *n, pl* **pasties** a round of pastry folded over a filling of meat and vegetables
WORD ORIGIN Old French *pastée*

pat[1] ❶ *vb* **patting, patted** 1 to tap (someone or something) lightly with the hand 2 to shape (something) with a flat instrument or the palm of the hand 3 **pat someone on the back** *informal* to congratulate someone ▹*n* 4 a gentle tap or stroke 5 a small shaped lump of something soft, such as butter 6 **pat on the back** *informal* an indication of approval
WORD ORIGIN probably imitative

pat[2] *adv* 1 Also: **off pat** thoroughly learned: *he had all his answers off pat* 2 **stand pat** *chiefly US & Canad* to stick firmly to a belief or decision ▹*adj* 3 quick, ready, or glib: *a pat generalization*
WORD ORIGIN perhaps adverbial use ('with a light stroke') of PAT[1]

patch ❶ *n* 1 a piece of material used to cover a hole in a garment 2 a small contrasting section: *there was a bald patch on the top of his head* 3 a small plot of land 4 *med* a protective covering for an injured eye 5 a scrap or remnant 6 the area under someone's supervision, such as a policeman or social worker 7 **a bad patch** a difficult time 8 **not a patch on** not nearly as good as ▹*vb* 9 to mend (a garment) with a patch 10 **patch together** to produce (something) by piecing parts together hurriedly or carelessly 11 **patch up** a to mend (something) hurriedly or carelessly b to make up (a quarrel)
WORD ORIGIN perhaps from French *pieche* piece

patchwork *n* 1 needlework done by sewing together pieces of different materials 2 something made up of various parts

patchy *adj* **patchier, patchiest** 1 of uneven quality or intensity: *since then her career has been patchy* 2 having or forming patches

pate *n old-fashioned or humorous* the head or the crown of the head
WORD ORIGIN origin unknown

pâté (**pat**-ay) *n* a spread of finely minced meat, fish, or vegetables often served as a starter
WORD ORIGIN French

pâté de foie gras (de fwah **grah**) *n* a smooth rich paste made from the liver of specially fattened geese
WORD ORIGIN French: pâté of fat liver

patella (pat-**tell**-a) *n, pl* **-lae** (-lee) *anat* kneecap **patellar** *adj*
WORD ORIGIN Latin

paten (**pat**-in) *n* a plate, usually made of silver or gold, used for the bread at Communion
WORD ORIGIN Latin *patina* pan

patent ❶ *n* 1 a an official document granting the exclusive right to make, use, and sell an invention for a limited period b the right granted by such a document 2 an invention protected by a patent ▹*adj* 3 open or available for inspection: *letters patent* 4 obvious: *their scorn was patent to everyone* 5 concerning protection of or appointment by a patent 6 (of food, drugs, etc.) made or held under a patent ▹*vb* 7 to obtain a patent for (an invention)
WORD ORIGIN Latin *patere* to lie open

patent leather *n* leather processed with lacquer to give a hard glossy surface

patently *adv* clearly and obviously: *an outdated and patently absurd promise*

patent medicine *n* a medicine with a patent, available without a prescription

Patent Office *n* a government department that issues patents

pater *n Brit, humorous* father
WORD ORIGIN Latin

THESAURUS

pastime *n* = **activity**, game, sport, entertainment, leisure, hobby, relaxation, recreation, distraction, amusement, diversion

pastor *n* = **clergyman**, minister, priest, vicar, divine, parson, rector, curate, churchman, ecclesiastic

pastoral *adj* 1 = **rustic**, country, simple, rural, idyllic, bucolic, Arcadian, georgic *(literary)*, agrestic 3 = **ecclesiastical**, priestly, ministerial, clerical

pasture *n* 1 = **grassland**, grass, meadow, grazing, lea *(poetic)*, grazing land, pasturage, shieling *(Scot)*

pat[1] *vb* 1 = **stroke**, touch, tap, pet, slap, dab, caress, fondle ▹*n* 4 = **tap**, stroke, slap, clap, dab, light blow

patch *n* 1 = **reinforcement**, piece of fabric, piece of cloth, piece of material, piece sewn on 2, 5 = **spot**, bit, stretch, scrap, shred, small piece 3 = **plot**, area, ground, land, tract ▹*vb* 9 = **sew (up)**, mend, repair, reinforce, stitch (up) 11a *(with up)* = **mend**, cover, fix, reinforce

patent *n* 1a, 1b = **copyright**, licence, franchise, registered trademark ▹*adj* 4 = **obvious**, apparent, evident, blatant, open, clear, glaring, manifest, transparent, conspicuous, downright, unmistakable, palpable, unequivocal, flagrant, indisputable, unconcealed

DICTIONARY

Pater *n* **Walter** (**Horatio**) 1839–94, English essayist and critic, noted for his prose style and his advocation of the "love of art for its own sake". His works include the philosophical romance *Marius the Epicurean* (1885), *Studies in the History of the Renaissance* (1873), and *Imaginary Portraits* (1887)

paternal *adj* **1** fatherly: *paternal authority* **2** related through one's father: *his paternal grandmother* **paternally** *adv*
WORD ORIGIN Latin *pater* father

paternalism *n* authority exercised in a way that limits individual responsibility **paternalistic** *adj*
WORD ORIGIN Latin *pater* father

paternity *n* **1** the fact or state of being a father **2** descent or derivation from a father

paternity suit *n* legal proceedings, usually brought by an unmarried mother, in order to gain legal recognition that a particular man is the father of her child

Paternoster *n RC church* the Lord's Prayer
WORD ORIGIN Latin *pater noster* our father

path ❶ *n, pl* **paths 1** a road or way, often a narrow trodden track **2** a surfaced walk, such as through a garden **3** the course or direction in which something moves: *his car skidded into the path of an oncoming lorry* **4** a course of conduct: *the path of reconciliation and forgiveness*
WORD ORIGIN Old English *pæth*

pathetic ❶ *adj* **1** arousing pity or sympathy **2** distressingly inadequate: *his pathetic attempt to maintain a stiff upper lip failed* **pathetically** *adv*
WORD ORIGIN Greek *pathos* suffering

pathetic fallacy *n* (in literature) the presentation of inanimate objects in nature as possessing human feelings

pathname *n computers* the name of a file or directory together with its position in relation to other directories

pathogen *n* any agent, such as a bacterium, that can cause disease **pathogenic** *adj*
WORD ORIGIN Greek *pathos* suffering + *-gen* (suffix) producing

pathological *adj* **1** of or relating to pathology **2** *informal* compulsively motivated: *pathological jealousy*

pathology *n* the branch of medicine that studies diseases **pathologist** *n*
WORD ORIGIN Greek *pathos* suffering + -LOGY

pathos *n* the power, for example in literature, of arousing feelings of pity or sorrow
WORD ORIGIN Greek: suffering

pathway *n* a path

patience ❶ *n* **1** the capacity for calmly enduring difficult situations: *the endless patience of the nurses* **2** the ability to wait calmly for something to happen without complaining or giving up: *he urged the international community to have patience to allow sanctions to work* **3** *Brit & NZ* a card game for one player only
WORD ORIGIN Latin *pati* to suffer

patient ❶ *adj* **1** enduring difficult situations with an even temper **2** persevering or diligent: *his years of patient work may finally pay off* ▷ *n* **3** a person who is receiving medical care **patiently** *adv*

patina *n* **1** a film formed on the surface of a metal **2** the sheen on the surface of an old object, caused by age and much handling
WORD ORIGIN Italian: coating

Patinir *or* **Patenier** *n* **Joachim** ?1485–1524, Flemish painter, noted esp. for the landscapes in his paintings on religious themes

patio *n, pl* **-tios 1** a paved area adjoining a house: *a barbecue on the patio* **2** an open inner courtyard in a Spanish or Spanish-American house
WORD ORIGIN Spanish: courtyard

patisserie (pat-**eess**-er-ee) *n* **1** a shop where fancy pastries are sold **2** such pastries
WORD ORIGIN French

Patmore *n* **Coventry** (**Kersey Dighton**) 1823–96, English poet. His works, celebrating both conjugal and divine love, include *The Angel in the House* (1854–62) and *The Unknown Eros* (1877)

patois (**pat**-wah) *n, pl* **patois** (**pat**-wahz) **1** a regional dialect of a language **2** the jargon of a particular group
WORD ORIGIN Old French: rustic speech

Paton *n* **Alan** (**Stewart**) 1903–88, South African writer, noted esp. for his novel dealing with racism and apartheid in South Africa, *Cry, the Beloved Country* (1965)

patrial *n* (in Britain, formerly) a person with a right by statute to live in the United Kingdom, and so not subject to immigration control
WORD ORIGIN Latin *patria* native land

patriarch *n* **1** the male head of a tribe or family **2** *bible* any of the men regarded as the fathers of the human race or of the Hebrew people **3 a** *RC church* the pope **b** *Eastern Orthodox Church* a highest-ranking bishop **4** an old man who is respected **patriarchal** *adj*
WORD ORIGIN Church Latin *patriarcha*

patriarchate *n* the office, jurisdiction, or residence of a patriarch

patriarchy *n* **1** a form of social organization in which males hold most of the power **2** *pl* **-chies** a society governed by such a system

patrician *n* **1** a member of the nobility of ancient Rome **2** an aristocrat **3** a person of refined conduct and tastes ▷ *adj* **4** (in ancient Rome) of or relating to patricians **5** aristocratic
WORD ORIGIN Latin *patricius* noble

patricide *n* **1** the act of killing one's father **2** a person who kills his or her father **patricidal** *adj*
WORD ORIGIN Latin *pater* father + *caedere* to kill

patrimony *n, pl* **-nies** an inheritance from one's father or other ancestor
WORD ORIGIN Latin *patrimonium* paternal inheritance

patriot ❶ *n* a person who loves his or her country and passionately supports its interests **patriotic** *adj* **patriotically** *adv* **patriotism** *n*
WORD ORIGIN Greek *patris* native land

patrol ❶ *n* **1** the action of going round an area or building at regular intervals for purposes of security or observation **2** a person or group that

THESAURUS

path *n* **1, 2 = way**, road, walk, track, trail, avenue, pathway, footpath, walkway (*chiefly US*), towpath, footway, berm (*NZ*) **3 = route**, way, course, direction, passage **4 = course**, way, road, track, route, procedure

pathetic *adj* **1 = sad**, moving, touching, affecting, distressing, tender, melting, poignant, harrowing, heartbreaking, plaintive, heart-rending, gut-wrenching, pitiable OPPOSITE: funny

patience *n* **1 = forbearance**, tolerance, composure, serenity, cool (*slang*), restraint, calmness, equanimity, toleration, sufferance, even temper, imperturbability
OPPOSITE: impatience
2 = endurance, resignation, submission, fortitude, persistence, long-suffering, perseverance, stoicism, constancy

patient *adj* **1 = forbearing**, understanding, forgiving, mild, accommodating, tolerant, indulgent, lenient, even-tempered
OPPOSITE: impatient
2 = long-suffering, resigned, calm, enduring, quiet, composed, persistent, philosophical, serene, persevering, stoical, submissive, self-possessed, uncomplaining, untiring ▷ *n* **3 = sick person**, case, sufferer, invalid

patriot *n* **= nationalist**, loyalist, chauvinist, flag-waver (*informal*), lover of your country

patrol *n* **2 = guard**, watch, garrison, watchman, sentinel, patrolman ▷ *vb* **5 = police**, guard, keep watch (on), pound, range (over), cruise, inspect,

DICTIONARY

carries out such an action **3** a group of soldiers or ships involved in patrolling a particular area **4** a division of a troop of Scouts or Guides ▷ *vb* **-trolling, -trolled 5** to engage in a patrol of (a place): *peacekeepers patrolled several areas of the city*
WORD ORIGIN French *patrouiller*

patrol car *n* a police car used for patrolling streets

patron ❶ *n* **1** a person who financially supports artists, writers, musicians, or charities **2** a regular customer of a shop, hotel, etc.
WORD ORIGIN Latin *patronus* protector

patronage ❶ *n* **1** the support or custom given by a patron **2** (in politics) the ability or power to appoint people to jobs **3** a condescending manner

patronize *or* **-ise** *vb* **-izing, -ized** *or* **-ising, -ised 1** to treat (someone) in a condescending way **2** to be a patron of **patronizing** *or* **-ising** *adj* **patronizingly** *or* **-isingly** *adv*

patron saint *n* a saint regarded as the particular guardian of a country or a group of people

patronymic *n* a name derived from one's father's or a male ancestor
WORD ORIGIN Greek *patēr* father + *onoma* name

patter[1] *vb* **1** to make repeated light tapping sound **2** to walk with quick soft steps ▷ *n* **3** a quick succession of light tapping sounds, such as by feet: *the steady patter of rain against the window*
WORD ORIGIN from PAT[1]

patter[2] *n* **1** the glib rapid speech of comedians or salesmen **2** chatter **3** the jargon of a particular group ▷ *vb* **4** to speak glibly and rapidly
WORD ORIGIN Latin *pater* in *Pater Noster* Our Father

pattern ❶ *n* **1** an arrangement of repeated parts or decorative designs **2** a regular recognizable way that something is done: *I followed a normal eating pattern* **3** a plan or diagram used as a guide to making something: *a knitting pattern* **4** a model worthy of imitation: *a pattern of kindness* **5** a representative sample ▷ *vb* **6** (foll. by *after* or *on*) to model: *an orchestra patterned after Count Basie's*
WORD ORIGIN Medieval Latin *patronus* example

patterned *n* having a decorative pattern on it: *a selection of plain and patterned fabrics*

Patti *n* **Adelina** 1843–1919, Italian operatic coloratura soprano, born in Spain

patty *n, pl* **-ties** a small round pie filled with meat or vegetables
WORD ORIGIN French *pâté*

paua (pah-ooh-uh) *n* an edible shellfish of New Zealand, which has a pearly shell used for jewellery
WORD ORIGIN Māori

paucity *n formal* **1** scarcity **2** smallness of amount or number
WORD ORIGIN Latin *paucus* few

Paul *n* **1 Saint** Also called: **Paul the Apostle, Saul of Tarsus** original name *Saul*. died ?67 AD, one of the first Christian missionaries to the Gentiles, who died a martyr in Rome. Until his revelatory conversion he had assisted in persecuting the Christians. He wrote many of the Epistles in the New Testament. Feast day: June 29. Related adjective: **Pauline 2** ▸ **Jean** See **Jean Paul 3 Les,** real name *Lester Polfuss*. 1915–2009, US guitarist: creator of the solid-body electric guitar and pioneer in multitrack recording

Paul I *n* **1** 1754–1801, tsar of Russia (1796–1801); son of Catherine II; assassinated **2** 1901–64, king of the Hellenes (1947–64); son of Constantine I

Paul III *n* original name *Alessandro Farnese* 1468–1549, Italian ecclesiastic; pope (1534–49). He excommunicated Henry VIII of England (1538) and inaugurated the Counter-Reformation by approving the establishment of the Jesuits (1540), instituting the Inquisition in Italy, and convening the Council of Trent (1545)

Paulinus *n* **Saint** died 644 AD, Roman missionary to England; first bishop of York and archbishop of Rochester. Feast day: Oct 10

Paulinus of Nola *n* **Saint** ?353–431 AD, Roman consul and Christian poet; bishop of Nola (409–431). Feast day: June 22

Paul VI *n* original name *Giovanni Battista Montini*. 1897–1978, Italian ecclesiastic; pope (1963–1978)

paunch *n* a protruding belly or abdomen **paunchy** *adj*
WORD ORIGIN Latin *pantices* bowels

pauper *n old-fashioned* **1** a person who is extremely poor **2** (formerly) a person supported by public charity
WORD ORIGIN Latin: poor

Pausanias *n* 2nd century AD, Greek geographer and historian. His *Description of Greece* gives a valuable account of the topography of ancient Greece

pause ❶ *vb* **pausing, paused 1** to stop doing (something) for a short time **2** to hesitate: *she answered him without pausing* ▷ *n* **3** a temporary stop or rest in speech or action **4** *music* a continuation of a note or rest beyond its normal length **5 give someone pause** to cause someone to hesitate: *it gave him pause for reflection*
WORD ORIGIN Greek *pausis*

pavane (pav-van) *n* **1** a slow and stately dance of the 16th and 17th centuries **2** music for this dance
WORD ORIGIN Spanish *pavana*

pave ❶ *vb* **paving, paved 1** to cover (a road or area of ground) with a firm surface to make it suitable for walking or travelling on **2 pave the way for** to prepare or make easier: *the arrests paved the way for the biggest-ever Mafia trial*
WORD ORIGIN Old French *paver*

pavement *n* **1** a hard-surfaced path for pedestrians, alongside and a little higher than a road **2** the material used in paving **3** *US* the surface of a road
WORD ORIGIN Latin *pavimentum* hard floor

Pavese *n* **Cesare** 1908–50, Italian writer and translator. His works include collections of poems, such as *Verrà la morte e avra i tuoi occhi* (1953), short stories, such as the collection *Notte di festa* (1953), and the novel *La Luna e i falò* (1950)

pavilion *n* **1** a building at a sports ground, esp. a cricket pitch, in which players can wash and change **2** an

THESAURUS

safeguard, make the rounds (of), keep guard (on), walk *or* pound the beat (of)

patron *n* **1 = supporter**, friend, champion, defender, sponsor, guardian, angel *(informal)*, advocate, backer, helper, protagonist, protector, benefactor, philanthropist **2 = customer**, client, buyer, frequenter, shopper, habitué

patronage *n* **1 = support**, promotion, sponsorship, backing, help, aid, championship, assistance, encouragement, espousal, benefaction

pattern *n* **1 = design**, arrangement, motif, figure, device, decoration, ornament, decorative design **2 = order**, plan, system, method, arrangement, sequence, orderliness **3 = plan**, design, original, guide, instructions, diagram, stencil, template

pause *vb* **1, 2 = stop briefly**, delay, hesitate, break, wait, rest, halt, cease, interrupt, deliberate, waver, take a break, discontinue, desist, have a breather *(informal)*
OPPOSITE: continue
▷ *n* **3 = stop**, break, delay, interval, hesitation, stay, wait, rest, gap, halt, interruption, respite, lull, stoppage, interlude, cessation, let-up *(informal)*, breathing space, breather *(informal)*, intermission, discontinuance, entr'acte, caesura
OPPOSITE: continuance

pave *vb* **1 = cover**, floor, surface, flag, concrete, tile, tar, asphalt, macadamize

DICTIONARY

open building or temporary structure used for exhibitions **3** a summerhouse or other decorative shelter **4** a large ornate tent
WORD ORIGIN Latin *papilio* butterfly, tent

paving *n* **1** a paved surface **2** material used for a pavement

pavlova *n* a meringue cake topped with whipped cream and fruit
WORD ORIGIN after Anna *Pavlova*, ballerina

paw ❶ *n* **1** a four-legged mammal's foot with claws and pads **2** *informal* a hand ▷*vb* **3** to scrape or hit with the paws **4** *informal* to touch or caress (someone) in a rough or overfamiliar manner
WORD ORIGIN Germanic

pawl *n* a pivoted lever shaped to engage with a ratchet to prevent motion in a particular direction
WORD ORIGIN Dutch *pal*

pawn[1] *vb* **1** to deposit (an article) as security for money borrowed **2** to stake or risk: *I will pawn my honour on this matter* ▷*n* **3** an article deposited as security **4** the condition of being so deposited: *in pawn*
WORD ORIGIN Old French *pan* security

pawn[2] *n* **1** a chessman of the lowest value, usually able to move only one square forward at a time **2** a person or thing manipulated by someone else: *our city is just a pawn in their power games*
WORD ORIGIN Anglo-Norman *poun*, from Medieval Latin *pedo* infantryman

pawnbroker *n* a person licensed to lend money on goods deposited
pawnbroking *n*

Pawnee *n, pl* **Pawnees** *or* **Pawnee 1** a member of a group of Native American peoples, formerly living in Nebraska and Kansas, now chiefly in Oklahoma **2** the language of these peoples

pawnshop *n* the premises of a pawnbroker

pawpaw (paw-paw) *n* ▸same as **papaya**

pax *n* **1** *chiefly RC church* the kiss of peace ▷*interj* **2** *Brit school slang* a call signalling a desire to end hostilities
WORD ORIGIN Latin: peace

Paxman *n* **Jeremy** (**Dickson**) born 1950, British journalist, broadcaster, and author, noted esp. for his political interviews

Paxton *n* Sir **Joseph** 1801–65, English architect, who designed Crystal Palace (1851), the first large structure of prefabricated glass and iron parts

pay ❶ *vb* **pays, paying, paid 1** to give (money) in return for goods or services: *Willie paid for the drinks; nurses are not very well paid* **2** to settle (a debt or obligation) by giving or doing something: *he has paid his debt to society* **3** to suffer: *she paid dearly for her mistake* **4** to give (a compliment, regards, attention, etc.) **5** to profit or benefit (someone): *it doesn't always pay to be honest* **6** to make (a visit or call) **7** to yield a return of: *the account pays 5% interest* **8 pay one's way a** to contribute one's share of expenses **b** to remain solvent without outside help ▷*n* **9** money given in return for work or services; a salary or wage **10 in the pay of** employed by ▸See also **pay back, pay for**, etc.
WORD ORIGIN Latin *pacare* to appease

payable ❶ *adj* **1** (often foll. by *on*) due to be paid: *the instalments are payable on the third of each month* **2** that is capable of being paid: *pensions are payable to those disabled during the wars*

pay back *vb* **1** to repay (a loan) **2** to make (someone) suffer for a wrong he or she has done you: *I want to pay him back for all the suffering he's caused me*

PAYE (in Britain, Australia and New Zealand) pay as you earn; a system by which income tax is deducted by employers and paid directly to the government

payee *n* the person to whom a cheque or money order is made out

pay for *vb* **1** to make payment for **2** to suffer or be punished for (a mistake)

paying guest *n euphemistic* a lodger

payload *n* **1** the amount of passengers, cargo, or bombs which an aircraft can carry **2** the part of a cargo which earns revenue **3** the explosive power of a warhead or bomb carried by a missile or aircraft

paymaster *n* an official responsible for the payment of wages and salaries

payment ❶ *n* **1** the act of paying **2** a sum of money paid **3** something given in return; punishment or reward

pay off *vb* **1** to pay the complete amount of (a debt) **2** to pay (someone) all that is due in wages and dismiss him or her from employment **3** to turn out successfully: *her persistence finally paid off* **4** *informal* to give a bribe to ▷*n* **payoff 5** *informal* the climax or outcome of events **6** *informal* a bribe **7** the final payment of a debt **8** the final settlement, esp. in retribution: *the payoff came when the gang besieged the squealer's house*

payola *n informal* a bribe to secure special treatment, esp. to promote a commercial product

pay out *vb* **1** to spend (money) on a particular thing **2** to release (a rope) gradually, bit by bit ▷*n* **payout 3** a sum of money paid out

pay-per-view *n* a television broadcasting system where a charge is made for receiving a specific programme

payphone *n* a coin-operated telephone

payroll *n* a list of employees, giving the salary or wage of each

payslip *n* a note given to an employee stating his or her salary or wage and detailing the deductions

Payton *n* **Walter** 1954–99, American footballer and sports administrator

pay up *vb* to pay (money) promptly or in full

Paz *n* **Octavio** 1914–98, Mexican poet and essayist. His poems include the cycle *Piedra de Sol* (1957) and *Blanco* (1967). Nobel prize for literature 1990

Pb *chem* lead
WORD ORIGIN New Latin *plumbum*

pc 1 per cent **2** postcard

PC 1 personal computer **2** (in Britain) Police Constable **3** *informal* ▸short for **politically correct 4** (in Britain) Privy Council *or* Counsellor **5** (in Canada) Progressive Conservative

PCOS polycystic ovary syndrome

PCV (in Britain) passenger carrying vehicle

pd paid

Pd *chem* palladium

PDA personal digital assistant

PDF portable document format: a format in which documents may be viewed

PDSA (in Britain) People's Dispensary for Sick Animals

P

THESAURUS

paw *vb* **4** *(informal)* **= manhandle**, grab, maul, molest, handle roughly

pay *vb* **1a = reward**, compensate, reimburse, recompense, requite, remunerate, front up **1b = spend**, offer, give, fork out *(informal)*, remit, cough up *(informal)*, shell out *(informal)* **2 = settle**, meet, clear, foot, honour, discharge, liquidate, square up **4 = give**, extend, present with, grant, render, hand out, bestow, proffer **5a = be profitable**, make money, make a return, provide a living, be remunerative **5b = benefit**, serve, repay, be worthwhile, be advantageous **7 = bring in**, earn, return, net, yield ▷*n* **9 = wages**, income, payment, earnings, fee, reward, hire, salary, compensation, allowance, remuneration, takings, reimbursement, hand-outs, recompense, stipend, emolument, vacation pay *(Canad)*, meed *(archaic)*

payable *adj* **1 = due**, outstanding, owed, owing, mature, to be paid, obligatory, receivable

payment *n* **1 = settlement**, paying, discharge, outlay, remittance, defrayal **2 = remittance**, advance, deposit, premium, portion, instalment **3 = wages**, fee, reward, hire, remuneration

DICTIONARY

PDT Pacific Daylight Time
PE 1 physical education **2** Prince Edward Island
pea *n* **1** an annual climbing plant with green pods containing green seeds **2** the seed of this plant, eaten as a vegetable
WORD ORIGIN from *pease* (incorrectly assumed to be a plural)
Peabody *n* **George** 1795–1869, US merchant, banker, and philanthropist in the US and England
peace *n* **1** stillness or silence **2** absence of mental anxiety: *peace of mind* **3** absence of war **4** harmony between people or groups **5** a treaty marking the end of a war **6** law and order within a state: *a breach of the peace* **7 at peace a** dead: *the old lady is at peace now* **b** in a state of harmony or serenity **8 hold** *or* **keep one's peace** to keep silent **9 keep the peace** to maintain law and order
WORD ORIGIN Latin *pax*
peaceable *adj* **1** inclined towards peace **2** tranquil or calm
peace dividend *n* additional money available to a government from cuts in defence expenditure because of the end of a period of hostilities
peaceful *adj* **1** not in a state of war or disagreement **2** calm or tranquil
peacefully *adv*
peacemaker *n* a person who brings about peace, esp. between others
peace offering *n* something given or said in order to restore peace: *I bought Mum some flowers as a peace offering*
peace pipe *n* a long decorated pipe smoked by Native Americans, esp. as a token of peace
peacetime *n* a period without war
peach *n* **1** a soft juicy fruit with a downy skin, yellowish-orange sweet flesh, and a single stone **2** *informal* a person or thing that is especially pleasing: *a peach of a goal* ▷ *adj* **3** pale pinkish-orange
WORD ORIGIN Latin *Persicum malum* Persian apple
peach melba *n* a dessert made of halved peaches, vanilla ice cream, and raspberries
WORD ORIGIN after Dame Nellie *Melba*, singer
peachy *adj* **peachier, peachiest** of or like a peach, esp. in colour or texture
peacock *n, pl* **-cocks** *or* **-cock 1** a large male bird of the pheasant family with a crested head and a very large fanlike tail with blue and green eyelike spots **2** a vain strutting person **peahen** *fem n*
WORD ORIGIN Latin *pavo* peacock + COCK
Peacock *n* **Thomas Love** 1785–1866, English novelist and poet, noted for his satirical romances, including *Headlong Hall* (1816) and *Nightmare Abbey* (1818)
peafowl *n* a peacock or peahen
peak *n* **1** a pointed tip or projection: *the peak of the roof* **2 a** the pointed summit of a mountain **b** a mountain with a pointed summit **3** the point of greatest success or achievement: *the peak of his career* **4** a projecting piece on the front of some caps ▷ *vb* **5** to form or reach a peak ▷ *adj* **6** of or relating to a period of greatest demand: *hotels are generally dearer in peak season*
WORD ORIGIN perhaps from *pike* (the weapon)
Peake *n* **Mervyn** 1911–68, English novelist, poet, and illustrator. In his trilogy *Gormenghast* (1946–59), he creates, with vivid imagination, a grotesque Gothic world
peaked *adj* having a peak
peak load *n* the maximum load on an electrical power-supply system
peaky *adj* **peakier, peakiest** pale and sickly
WORD ORIGIN origin unknown
peal *n* **1** a long loud echoing sound, such as of bells or thunder ▷ *vb* **2** to sound with a peal or peals
WORD ORIGIN Middle English *pele*
peanut *n* a plant with edible nutlike seeds which ripen underground ▸ See also **peanuts**
peanut butter *n* a brownish oily paste made from peanuts
peanuts *n slang* a trifling amount of money
pear *n* **1** a sweet juicy fruit with a narrow top and a rounded base **2 go pear-shaped** *informal* to go wrong: *the plan started to go pear-shaped*
WORD ORIGIN Latin *pirum*
pearl *n* **1** a hard smooth greyish-white rounded object found inside the shell of a clam or oyster and much valued as a gem **2** ▸ see **mother-of-pearl 3** a person or thing that is like a pearl in beauty or value ▷ *adj* **4** of, made of, or set with pearl or mother-of-pearl ▷ *vb* **5** to set with or as if with pearls **6** to shape into or assume a pearl-like form or colour **7** to dive for pearls
WORD ORIGIN Latin *perna* sea mussel
pearl barley *n* barley ground into small round grains, used in soups and stews
pearly *adj* **pearlier, pearliest 1** resembling a pearl, esp. in lustre **2** decorated with pearls or mother-of-pearl
Pearly Gates *pl n informal* the entrance to heaven
pearly king *or fem* **pearly queen** *n* the London barrow vendor whose ceremonial clothes display the most lavish collection of pearl buttons
Pears *n* Sir **Peter** 1910–86, British tenor, associated esp. with the works of Benjamin Britten
Pearse *n* **Patrick (Henry)**, Irish name *Pádraic*. 1879–1916, Irish nationalist, who planned and led the Easter Rising (1916): executed by the British
Peary *n* **Robert Edwin** 1856–1920, US arctic explorer, generally regarded as the first man to reach the North Pole (1909)
peasant *n* **1** a member of a low social class employed in agricultural labour **2** *informal* an uncouth or uncultured person
WORD ORIGIN Old French *païsant*
peasantry *n* peasants as a class
pease *n, pl* **pease** *archaic or dialect* ▸ same as **pea**
WORD ORIGIN Old English *pise, peose*
pease pudding *n* (esp. in Britain) a dish of split peas that have been soaked and boiled
peasouper *n informal chiefly Brit* thick dirty yellowish fog
peat *n* decaying vegetable matter found in uplands and bogs and used as a fuel (when dried) and as a fertilizer
WORD ORIGIN perhaps Celtic
pebble *n* **1** a small smooth rounded stone, esp. one worn by the action of water ▷ *vb* **-bling, -bled 2** to cover with pebbles **pebbly** *adj*

P

THESAURUS

peace *n* **1 = stillness**, rest, quiet, silence, calm, hush, tranquillity, seclusion, repose, calmness, peacefulness, quietude, restfulness **2 = serenity**, calm, relaxation, composure, contentment, repose, equanimity, peacefulness, placidity, harmoniousness **4 = harmony**, accord, agreement, concord, amity **5 = truce**, ceasefire, treaty, armistice, pacification, conciliation, cessation of hostilities
OPPOSITE: war
peaceful *adj* **1 = at peace**, friendly, harmonious, amicable, cordial, nonviolent, without hostility, free from strife, on friendly *or* good terms
OPPOSITE: hostile
2a = calm, still, quiet, gentle, pleasant, soothing, tranquil, placid, restful, chilled *(informal)*
OPPOSITE: agitated
2b = serene, placid, undisturbed, untroubled, unruffled
peak *n* **1, 2a = point**, top, tip, summit, brow, crest, pinnacle, apex, aiguille **3 = high point**, crown, climax, culmination, zenith, maximum point, apogee, acme, ne plus ultra *(Latin)* ▷ *vb* **5 = culminate**, climax, come to a head, be at its height, reach its highest point, reach the zenith
peasant *n* **1 = rustic**, countryman, hind *(obsolete)*, swain *(archaic)*, son of the soil, churl *(archaic)*

DICTIONARY

WORD ORIGIN Old English *papolstān* pebble stone

pebble dash *n Austral & Brit* a finish for external walls consisting of small stones set in plaster

pec *n informal* a pectoral muscle: *a gigolo with flowing blond locks and rippling pecs*

pecan (pee-kan) *n* a smooth oval nut with a sweet oily kernel that grows on hickory trees in the Southern US
WORD ORIGIN Native American *paccan*

peccadillo *n, pl* **-loes** *or* **-los** a trivial misdeed
WORD ORIGIN Spanish *pecadillo*, from Latin *peccare* to sin

peccary *n, pl* **-ries** *or* **-ry** a piglike animal of American forests
WORD ORIGIN Carib

peck[1] ❶ *vb* **1** to strike or pick up with the beak **2** *informal* to kiss (a person) quickly and lightly **3** **peck at** to eat slowly and reluctantly: *pecking away at your lunch* ▷ *n* **4** a quick light blow from a bird's beak **5** a mark made by such a blow **6** *informal* a quick light kiss
WORD ORIGIN origin unknown

peck[2] *n* an obsolete unit of liquid measure equal to one quarter of a bushel or 2 gallons (9.1 litres)
WORD ORIGIN Anglo-Norman

Peck *n* **Gregory** 1916–2003, US film actor; his films include *Keys of the Kingdom* (1944), *The Gunfighter* (1950), *The Big Country* (1958), *To Kill a Mockingbird* (1963), *The Omen* (1976), and *Other People's Money* (1991)

pecker *n* **keep one's pecker up** *Brit & NZ slang* to remain cheerful

pecking order *n* the order of seniority or power in a group: *she came from a family low in the social pecking order*

Peckinpah *n* **Sam(uel David)** 1926–84, US film director, esp. of Westerns, such as *The Wild Bunch* (1969). Among his other films are *Straw Dogs* (1971), *Bring me the Head of Alfredo Garcia* (1974), and *Cross of Iron* (1977)

peckish *adj informal* feeling slightly hungry

pectin *n biochem* a water-soluble carbohydrate that occurs in ripe fruit: used in the manufacture of jams because of its ability to gel
WORD ORIGIN Greek *pēktos* congealed

pectoral *adj* **1** of or relating to the chest, breast, or thorax: *pectoral fins* **2** worn on the breast or chest: *a pectoral cross* ▷ *n* **3** a pectoral organ or part, esp. a muscle or fin
WORD ORIGIN Latin *pectus* breast

pectoral fin *n* a fin, just behind the head in fishes, that helps to control the direction of movement

peculate *vb* **-lating, -lated** *literary* to embezzle (public money)
peculation *n*
WORD ORIGIN Latin *peculari*

peculiar ❶ *adj* **1** strange or odd: *a peculiar idea* **2** distinct or special **3** (foll. by *to*) belonging exclusively (to): *a fish peculiar to these waters*
WORD ORIGIN Latin *peculiaris* concerning private property

peculiarity *n, pl* **-ties** **1** a strange or unusual habit; eccentricity **2** a distinguishing trait **3** the state or quality of being peculiar

pecuniary *adj* **1** of or relating to money **2** *law* (of an offence) involving a monetary penalty
WORD ORIGIN Latin *pecunia* money

pedagogue *or US sometimes* **pedagog** *n* a teacher, esp. a pedantic one
pedagogic *adj*
WORD ORIGIN Greek *pais* boy + *agōgos* leader

pedagogy (**ped**-a-goj-ee) *n* the principles, practice, or profession of teaching

pedal[1] *n* **1** a foot-operated lever used to control a vehicle or machine, or to modify the tone of a musical instrument ▷ *vb* **-alling, -alled** *or US* **-aling, -aled** **2** to propel (a bicycle) by operating the pedals **3** to operate the pedals of an organ or piano
WORD ORIGIN Latin *pedalis*, from *pes* foot

pedal[2] *adj* of or relating to the foot or the feet
WORD ORIGIN Latin *pedalis*, from *pes* foot

pedant *n* a person who is concerned chiefly with insignificant detail or who relies too much on academic learning **pedantic** *adj* **pedantically** *adv*
WORD ORIGIN Italian *pedante* teacher

pedantry *n, pl* **-ries** the practice of being a pedant, esp. in the minute observance of petty rules or details

peddle ❶ *vb* **-dling, -dled** **1** to sell (goods) from place to place **2** to sell illegal drugs **3** to advocate (an idea or information) persistently: *the version of events being peddled by his opponents*
WORD ORIGIN from *pedlar*

pederast *or* **paederast** *n* a man who has homosexual relations with boys
pederasty *or* **paederasty** *n*
WORD ORIGIN Greek *pais* boy + *erastēs* lover

pedestal *n* **1** a base that supports something, such as a statue **2** **put someone on a pedestal** to admire someone very much
WORD ORIGIN Old Italian *piedestallo*

pedestrian ❶ *n* **1** a person who travels on foot ▷ *adj* **2** dull or commonplace: *a pedestrian performance*
WORD ORIGIN Latin *pes* foot

pedestrian crossing *n Austral & Brit* a path across a road marked as a crossing for pedestrians

pedestrianize *or* **-ise** *vb* **-izing, -ized** *or* **-ising, -ised** to convert (a street or shopping area) into an area for pedestrians only

pedestrian precinct *n Brit* an area of a town for pedestrians only, esp. an area of shops

pedicure *n* medical or cosmetic treatment of the feet
WORD ORIGIN Latin *pes* foot + *curare* to care for

pedigree ❶ *n* **1** the line of descent of a purebred animal **2** a document recording this **3** a genealogical table, esp. one indicating pure ancestry
WORD ORIGIN Old French *pie de grue* crane's foot, alluding to the spreading lines used in a genealogical chart

pediment *n* a triangular part over a door, as used in classical architecture
WORD ORIGIN obsolete *periment*, perhaps workman's corruption of *pyramid*

pedlar *or esp. US* **peddler** *n* a person who peddles
WORD ORIGIN Middle English *ped* basket

pedometer (pid-**dom**-it-er) *n* a device that measures the distance

THESAURUS

peck[1] *vb* **1 = pick**, bite, hit, strike, tap, poke, jab, prick, nibble **2** *(informal)* **= kiss**, plant a kiss, give someone a smacker, give someone a peck *or* kiss ▷ *n* **6** *(informal)* **= kiss**, smacker, osculation *(rare)*

peculiar *adj* **1 = odd**, strange, unusual, bizarre, funny, extraordinary, curious, weird, exceptional, eccentric, abnormal, out-of-the-way, queer, uncommon, singular, unconventional, far-out *(slang)*, quaint, off-the-wall *(slang)*, outlandish, offbeat, freakish, wacko *(slang)*, outré, daggy *(Austral & NZ informal)* **OPPOSITE:** ordinary **2 = special**, private, individual, personal, particular, unique, characteristic, distinguishing, distinct, idiosyncratic **OPPOSITE:** common

peddle *vb* **1 = sell**, trade, push *(informal)*, market, hawk, flog *(slang)*, vend, huckster, sell door to door

pedestrian *n* **1 = walker**, foot-traveller, footslogger **OPPOSITE:** driver ▷ *adj* **2 = dull**, flat, ordinary, boring, commonplace, mundane, mediocre, plodding, banal, prosaic, run-of-the-mill, humdrum, unimaginative, uninteresting, uninspired, ho-hum *(informal)*, no great shakes *(informal)*, half-pie *(NZ informal)* **OPPOSITE:** exciting

pedigree *n* **1 = lineage**, family, line, race, stock, blood, breed, heritage, descent, extraction, ancestry, family tree, genealogy, derivation

P

DICTIONARY

walked by recording the number of steps taken
WORD ORIGIN Latin *pes* foot + METER
Pedro I *n* 1798–1834, first emperor of Brazil (1822–31); son of John VI of Portugal: declared Brazilian independence (1822)
Pedro II *n* 1825–91, last emperor of Brazil (1831–89); son of Pedro I. He was deposed when Brazil became a republic (1889)
peduncle *n* **1** *bot* a plant stalk bearing a flower cluster or solitary flower **2** *anat, pathol* any stalklike structure **peduncular** *adj*
WORD ORIGIN Latin *pediculus* little foot
pee *informal vb* **peeing, peed 1** to urinate ▷*n* **2** urine **3** the act of urinating
WORD ORIGIN euphemistic for *piss*
peek *vb* **1** to glance quickly or secretly ▷*n* **2** such a glance
WORD ORIGIN Middle English *pike*
peel ❶ *vb* **1** to remove the skin or rind of (a fruit or vegetable) **2** to come off in flakes **3** (of a person or part of the body) to shed skin in flakes as a result of sunburn ▷*n* **4** the skin or rind of a fruit, etc. ▸See also **peel off**
WORD ORIGIN Latin *pilare* to make bald
Peele *n* **George** ?1556–?96, English dramatist and poet. His works include the pastoral drama *The Arraignment of Paris* (1584) and the comedy *The Old Wives' Tale* (1595)
peelings *pl n* strips of skin or rind that have been peeled off: *potato peelings*
peel off *vb* **1** to remove or be removed by peeling: *this softens the paint, which can then be peeled off* **2** *slang* to take off one's clothes or a piece of clothing **3** to leave a group of moving people, vehicles, etc. by taking a course that curves away to one side: *two aircraft peeled off to attack the enemy bombers*
peen *n* the end of a hammer head opposite the striking face, often rounded or wedge-shaped
WORD ORIGIN origin unknown
peep[1] ❶ *vb* **1** to look slyly or quickly, such as through a small opening or from a hidden place **2** to appear partially or briefly: *the sun peeped through the clouds* ▷*n* **3** a quick or sly look **4** the first appearance: *the peep of dawn*
WORD ORIGIN variant of *peek*
peep[2] *vb* **1** (esp. of young birds) to make small shrill noises ▷*n* **2** a peeping sound
WORD ORIGIN imitative
Peeping Tom *n* a man who furtively observes women undressing
WORD ORIGIN after the tailor who, according to legend, peeped at Lady Godiva when she rode naked through Coventry
peepshow *n* a box containing a series of pictures that can be seen through a small hole
peer[1] ❶ *n* **1** a member of a nobility **2** a person who holds any of the five grades of the British nobility: duke, marquess, earl, viscount, and baron **3** a person of equal social standing, rank, age, etc.: *he is greatly respected by his peers in the arts world*
WORD ORIGIN Latin *par* equal
peer[2] ❶ *vb* **1** to look intently or as if with difficulty: *Walter peered anxiously at his father's face* **2** to appear dimly: *the sun peered through the fog*
WORD ORIGIN Flemish *pieren* to look with narrowed eyes
peerage *Brit n* **1** the whole body of peers; aristocracy **2** the position, rank, or title of a peer
peeress *n* **1** (in Britain) a woman holding the rank of a peer **2** the wife or widow of a peer
peer group *n* a social group composed of people of similar age and status
peerless *adj* having no equals; unsurpassed
peer pressure *n* influence from one's peer group
peeve *informal vb* **peeving, peeved 1** to irritate or annoy: *the way he looked at her peeved her* ▷*n* **2** something that irritates: *my pet peeve* **peeved** *adj*
WORD ORIGIN from *peevish*
peevish *adj* fretful or irritable **peevishly** *adv*
WORD ORIGIN origin unknown
peewee *n* a black-and-white Australian bird
peewit *or* **pewit** *n* ▸same as **lapwing**
WORD ORIGIN imitative of its call
peg ❶ *n* **1** a small pin or bolt used to join two parts together, to fasten, or to mark **2** a hook or knob for hanging things on **3** *music* a pin on a stringed instrument which can be turned to tune the string wound around it **4** Also called: **clothes peg** a split or hinged pin for fastening wet clothes to a line to dry **5** *Brit* a small drink of spirits **6** an opportunity or pretext for doing something: *the play's subject matter provides a perfect peg for a discussion of issues like morality and faith* **7 bring** *or* **take (someone) down a peg** to lower the pride of (someone) **8 off the peg** *Brit & NZ* (of clothes) ready-to-wear, as opposed to tailor-made ▷*vb* **pegging, pegged 9** to insert a peg into **10** to secure with pegs: *the balloon was pegged down to stop it drifting away* **11** to mark (a score) with pegs, as in some card games **12** *chiefly Brit* to work steadily: *he pegged away at his job for years* **13** to fix or maintain something, such as prices, at a particular level or value: *a fixed rate mortgage, pegged at 9.6 per cent.* ▸See also **peg out**
WORD ORIGIN Low Germanic *pegge*
pegboard *n* **1** a board with a pattern of holes into which small pegs can be fitted, used for playing certain games or keeping a score **2** hardboard with rows of holes from which articles may be hung for display
peggy square *n NZ* a small hand-knitted square
peg leg *n informal* **1** an artificial leg **2** a person with an artificial leg
peg out *vb* **1** *informal* to collapse or die **2** to mark or secure with pegs: *the scientists pegged out a hectare of land in order to study every plant in it*
Péguy *n* **Charles** 1873–1914, French poet and essayist, whose works include *Le Mystère de la charité de Jeanne d'Arc* (1910); founder of the journal *Cahiers de la quinzaine* (1900–14): killed in World War I
Pei *n* **I(eoh) M(ing)** born 1917, US architect, born in China. His buildings include the E wing of the National Museum of Art, Washington DC (1978), a glass and steel pyramid at the Louvre, Paris (1989), and the Rock and Roll Hall of Fame, Cleveland, USA (1995)
PEI Prince Edward Island
peignoir (pay-nwahr) *n* a woman's light dressing gown
WORD ORIGIN French
Peirce *n* **Charles Sanders** 1839–1914, US logician, philosopher, and mathematician; pioneer of pragmatism
pejorative (pij-jor-a-tiv) *adj* **1** (of a word or expression) having an insulting or critical sense ▷*n* **2** a pejorative word or expression
WORD ORIGIN Late Latin *pejorare* to make worse

THESAURUS

peel *vb* **1 = skin**, scale, strip, pare, shuck, flake off, decorticate *(rare)*, take the skin *or* rind off ▷*n* **4 = rind**, skin, peeling, epicarp, exocarp
peep[1] *vb* **1 = peek**, look, peer, spy, eyeball *(slang)*, sneak a look, steal a look, keek *(Scot)*, look surreptitiously, look from hiding ▷*n* **3 = look**, glimpse, peek, butcher's *(Brit slang)*, gander *(informal)*, look-see *(slang)*, shufti *(Brit slang)*, keek *(Scot)*
peer[1] *n* **1, 2 = noble**, lord, count, duke, earl, baron, aristocrat, viscount, marquess, marquis, nobleman, aristo *(informal)* **3 = equal**, like, match, fellow, contemporary, coequal, compeer
peer[2] *vb* **1 = squint**, look, spy, gaze, scan, inspect, peep, peek, snoop, scrutinize, look closely
peg *n* **1 = pin**, spike, rivet, skewer, dowel, spigot ▷*vb* **10 = fasten**, join, fix, secure, attach, make fast
pen[1] *vb* **3 = write (down)**, draft,

DICTIONARY

peke *n informal* a Pekingese dog
Pekingese *or* **Pekinese** *n* **1** *pl* **-ese** a small dog with a long straight coat, curled plumed tail, and short wrinkled muzzle **2** the dialect of Mandarin Chinese spoken in Beijing
pelargonium *n* a plant with circular leaves and red, pink, or white flowers: includes many cultivated geraniums
WORD ORIGIN Greek *pelargos* stork
pelf *n contemptuous* money or wealth
WORD ORIGIN Old French *pelfre* booty
pelican *n* a large water bird with a pouch beneath its long bill for holding fish
WORD ORIGIN Greek *pelekan*
pelican crossing *n* (in Britain) a type of road crossing with a pedestrian-operated traffic-light system
WORD ORIGIN from *pe(destrian) li(ght) con(trolled) crossing*, with *-con* adapted to *-can* of *pelican*
pelisse (pel-leess) *n* a cloak or loose coat which is usually fur-trimmed
WORD ORIGIN Old French, from Latin *pellis* skin
pellagra *n pathol* a disease caused by a diet lacking in vitamin B, which results in scaling of the skin, diarrhoea and mental disorder
WORD ORIGIN Italian, from *pelle* skin + Greek *agra* paroxysm
pellet *n* **1** a small round ball, esp. of compressed matter **2 a** an imitation bullet used in toy guns **b** a piece of small shot **3** a small pill
WORD ORIGIN Latin *pila* ball
Pelletier *n* **Pierre Joseph** 1788–1842, French chemist, who isolated quinine, chlorophyll, and other chemical substances
pell-mell *adv* **1** in a confused headlong rush: *the hounds ran pell-mell into the yard* **2** in a disorderly manner: *the things were piled pell-mell in the room*
WORD ORIGIN Old French *pesle-mesle*
pellucid *adj literary* **1** transparent or translucent **2** extremely clear in style and meaning
WORD ORIGIN Latin *pellucidus*
pelmet *n* a board or piece of fabric used to conceal the curtain rail
WORD ORIGIN probably from French *palmette* palm-leaf decoration on cornice moulding
pelota *n* a game played by two players who use a basket strapped to their wrists or a wooden racket to propel a ball against a specially marked wall
WORD ORIGIN Spanish: ball
pelt[1] *vb* **1** to throw (missiles) at **2** (foll. by *along* etc.) to hurry **3** to rain heavily ▷ *n* **4** a blow **5 at full pelt** very quickly: *she ran down the street at full pelt*
WORD ORIGIN origin unknown
pelt[2] *n* the skin or fur of an animal, esp. as material for clothing or rugs: *the lucrative international trade in beaver pelts*
WORD ORIGIN probably from Latin *pellis* skin
pelvis *n, pl* **-vises** *or* **-ves** **1** the framework of bones at the base of the spine, to which the hips are attached **2** the bones that form this structure **pelvic** *adj*
WORD ORIGIN Latin: basin
pen[1] **T** *n* **1** an instrument for writing or drawing using ink ▸ See also **ballpoint, fountain pen** **2 the pen** writing as an occupation ▷ *vb* **penning, penned** **3** to write or compose
WORD ORIGIN Latin *penna* feather
pen[2] **T** *n* **1** an enclosure in which domestic animals are kept **2** any place of confinement ▷ *vb* **penning, penned** *or* **pent** **3** to enclose (animals) in a pen **4 penned in** being or feeling trapped or confined: *she stood penned in by bodies at the front of the crowd*
WORD ORIGIN Old English *penn*
pen[3] *n US & Canad informal* ▸ short for **penitentiary** (sense 1)
pen[4] *n* a female swan
WORD ORIGIN origin unknown
Pen. Peninsula
penal (pee-nal) *adj* **1** of or relating to punishment **2** used as a place of punishment: *a penal colony* **penally** *adv*
WORD ORIGIN Latin *poena* penalty
penal code *n* the body of laws relating to crime and punishment
penalize *or* **-ise** *vb* **-izing, -ized** *or* **-ising, -ised** **1** to impose a penalty on (someone) for breaking a law or rule **2** to inflict a disadvantage on: *why should I be penalized just because I'm a woman?* **penalization** *or* **-isation** *n*
penalty **T** *n, pl* **-ties** **1** a legal punishment for a crime or offence **2** loss or suffering as a result of one's own action: *we are now paying the penalty for neglecting to keep our equipment up to date* **3** *sport, games, etc.* a handicap awarded against a player or team for illegal play, such as a free shot at goal by the opposing team
WORD ORIGIN Latin *poena*
penalty box *n* **1** Also called: **penalty area** *soccer* a rectangular area in front of the goal, within which a penalty is awarded for a serious foul by the defending team **2** *ice hockey* a bench for players serving time penalties
penalty corner *n hockey* a free hit from the goal line taken by the attacking side
penalty shoot-out *n sport* a method of deciding the winner of a drawn match, in which players from each team attempt to score with a penalty shot
penance *n* **1** voluntary self-punishment to make amends for a sin **2** *RC church* a sacrament in which repentant sinners are forgiven provided they confess their sins to a priest and perform a penance
WORD ORIGIN Latin *paenitentia* repentance
pence *n* ▸ a plural of **penny**
penchant (pon-shon) *n* strong inclination or liking: *a stylish woman with a penchant for dark glasses*
WORD ORIGIN French
pencil *n* **1** a rod of graphite encased in wood which is used for writing or drawing ▷ *vb* **-cilling, -cilled** *or US* **-ciling, -ciled** **2** to draw, colour, write, or mark with a pencil **3 pencil in** to note, arrange, or include provisionally or tentatively
WORD ORIGIN Latin *penicillus* painter's brush
Penda *n* died 655 AD, king of Mercia (?634–55)
pendant *n* **a** an ornament worn on a chain round the neck: *a beautiful pearl pendant* **b** an ornament that hangs from a piece of jewellery
WORD ORIGIN Latin *pendere* to hang down
pendent *adj literary* **1** dangling **2** jutting
WORD ORIGIN see PENDANT
Penderecki *n* **Krzystof** born 1933, Polish composer, noted for his highly individual orchestration. His works include *Threnody for the Victims of Hiroshima* for strings (1960), *Stabat Mater* (1962), *Polish Requiem* (1983–84), and the opera *Ubu Rex* (1991)
pending **T** *prep* **1** while waiting for ▷ *adj* **2** not yet decided or settled **3** imminent: *these developments have been pending for some time*
pendulous *adj literary* hanging downwards and swinging freely
WORD ORIGIN Latin *pendere* to hang down
pendulum *n* **1** a weight suspended so it swings freely under the influence of gravity **2** such a device used to

THESAURUS

compose, pencil, draw up, scribble, take down, inscribe, scrawl, jot down, dash off, commit to paper
pen[2] *n* **1 = enclosure**, pound, fold, cage, coop, hutch, corral *(chiefly US & Canad)*, sty ▷ *vb* **3 = enclose**, confine, cage, pound, mew (up), fence in, impound, hem in, coop up, hedge in, shut up *or* in
penalty *n* **1 = punishment**, price, fine, handicap, forfeit, retribution, forfeiture
pending *prep* **1 = awaiting**, until, waiting for, till ▷ *adj* **2 = undecided**, unsettled, in the balance, up in the air, undetermined **3 = forthcoming**, imminent, prospective, impending, in the wind, in the offing

P

DICTIONARY

regulate a clock mechanism **3** a movement from one attitude or belief towards its opposite: *the pendulum has swung back to more punitive measures*

penetrate ❶ *vb* **-trating, -trated 1** to find or force a way into or through **2** to diffuse through; permeate: *the smell of cooking penetrated through to the sitting room* **3** to see through: *the sunlight did not penetrate the thick canopy of leaves* **4** (of a man) to insert the penis into the vagina of (a woman) **5** to grasp the meaning of (a principle, etc.) **penetrable** *adj* **penetrative** *adj*
WORD ORIGIN Latin *penetrare*

penetrating ❶ *adj* tending to or able to penetrate: *a penetrating mind; a penetrating voice*

penetration ❶ *n* **1** the act or an instance of penetrating **2** the ability or power to penetrate **3** keen insight or perception

pen friend *n* a person with whom one exchanges letters, often a person in another country whom one has not met

penguin *n* a flightless black-and-white sea bird with webbed feet and wings modified as flippers for swimming
WORD ORIGIN origin unknown

penicillin *n* an antibiotic used to treat diseases caused by bacteria
WORD ORIGIN Latin *pencillus* tuft of hairs

peninsula *n* a narrow strip of land projecting from the mainland into a sea or lake **peninsular** *adj*
WORD ORIGIN Latin, literally: almost an island

P

penis *n, pl* **-nises** *or* **-nes** the organ of copulation in higher vertebrates, also used for urinating in many mammals **penile** *adj*
WORD ORIGIN Latin

penitent *adj* **1** feeling regret for one's sins; repentant ▹*n* **2** a person who is penitent **penitence** *n*
WORD ORIGIN Church Latin *paenitens* regretting

penitential *adj* of, showing, or as a penance

penitentiary *n, pl* **-ries 1** (in the US and Canada) a state or federal prison ▹*adj* **2** of or for penance **3** used for punishment and reformation: *the penitentiary system*
WORD ORIGIN Latin *paenitens* penitent

penknife *n, pl* **-knives** a small knife with one or more blades that fold into the handle

penmanship *n formal* style or technique of writing by hand

pen name *n* a name used by a writer instead of his or her real name; nom de plume

pennant *n* **1** a long narrow flag, esp. one used by ships as identification or for signalling **2** *chiefly US, Canad, & Austral* a flag indicating the winning of a championship in certain sports
WORD ORIGIN probably a blend of *pendant* + *pennon*

Penney *n* **William George,** Baron Penney of East Hendred. 1909–91, British mathematician. He worked on the first atomic bomb and became chairman of the UK Atomic Energy Authority (1964–67)

penniless *adj* very poor

pennon *n* **1** a long flag, often tapering and divided at the end, originally a knight's personal flag **2** a small tapering or triangular flag flown by a ship or boat
WORD ORIGIN Latin *penna* feather

penny *n, pl* **pennies** *or* **pence 1** a British bronze coin worth one hundredth of a pound **2** a former British and Australian coin worth one twelfth of a shilling **3** *pl* **pennies** *US & Canad* a cent **4** *informal chiefly Brit* the least amount of money: *I don't have a penny* **5 a pretty penny** *informal* a considerable sum of money **6 spend a penny** *Brit & NZ informal* to urinate **7 the penny dropped** *informal* the explanation of something was finally understood
WORD ORIGIN Old English *penig, pening*

Penny Black *n* the first adhesive postage stamp, issued in Britain in 1840

penny-dreadful *n, pl* **-fuls** *Brit informal* a cheap, often lurid book or magazine

penny-farthing *n Brit* an early type of bicycle with a large front wheel and a small rear wheel

penny-pinching *adj* **1** excessively careful with money; miserly ▹*n* **2** miserliness **penny-pincher** *n*

pennyroyal *n* a Eurasian plant with hairy leaves and small mauve flowers, which provides an aromatic oil used in medicine
WORD ORIGIN Old French *pouliol* pennyroyal + *real* royal

penny-wise *adj* **penny-wise and pound-foolish** careful or thrifty in small matters but wasteful in large ventures

pennywort *n* a Eurasian rock plant with whitish-green tubular flowers and rounded leaves

pennyworth *n* **1** the amount that can be bought for a penny **2** a small or insignificant amount of something: *they'd thrown in their pennyworth of opinion*

penology (pee-nol-a-jee) *n* the study of the punishment of criminals and of prison management
WORD ORIGIN Greek *poinē* punishment

pen pal *n informal* ▸same as **pen friend**

penpusher *n* a person whose work involves a lot of boring paperwork **penpushing** *adj, n*

Penrose *n* Sir **Roger** born 1931, British mathematician and theoretical physicist, noted for his investigation of black holes

pension[1] ❶ *n* **1** a regular payment made by the state or a former employer to a person who has retired or to a widowed or disabled person ▹*vb* **2** to grant a pension to ▸See also **pension off** > **pensionable** *adj* **pensioner** *n*
WORD ORIGIN Latin *pensio* a payment

pension[2] (pon-syon) *n* (in France and some other countries) a relatively cheap boarding house
WORD ORIGIN French: extended meaning of *pension* grant

pension off *vb* to cause (someone) to retire from a job and pay him or her a pension

pensive *adj* deeply thoughtful, often with a tinge of sadness **pensively** *adv*
WORD ORIGIN Latin *pensare* to consider

pent *vb* ▸a past of **pen**[2]

penta- *combining form* five: *pentagon; pentameter*
WORD ORIGIN Greek *pente*

pentacle *n* ▸same as **pentagram**
WORD ORIGIN Italian *pentacolo* something having five corners

pentagon *n geom* a figure with five

THESAURUS

penetrate *vb* **1 = pierce**, enter, go through, bore, probe, stab, prick, perforate, impale **5 = grasp**, understand, work out, figure out *(informal)*, unravel, discern, comprehend, fathom, decipher, suss (out) *(slang)*, get to the bottom of

penetrating *adj* **a = sharp**, harsh, piercing, carrying, piping, loud, intrusive, strident, shrill, high-pitched, ear-splitting
OPPOSITE: sweet
b = pungent, biting, strong, powerful, sharp, heady, pervasive, aromatic **c = piercing**, cutting, biting, sharp, freezing, fierce, stinging, frosty, bitterly cold, arctic **d = intelligent**, quick, sharp, keen, critical, acute, profound, discriminating, shrewd, discerning, astute, perceptive, incisive, sharp-witted, perspicacious, sagacious
OPPOSITE: dull
e = perceptive, searching, sharp, keen, alert, probing, discerning
OPPOSITE: unperceptive

penetration *n* **1a = piercing**, entry, entrance, invasion, puncturing, incision, perforation **1b = entry**, entrance, inroad

pension[1] *n* **1 = allowance**, benefit, welfare, annuity, superannuation

DICTIONARY

sides **pentagonal** *adj*

Pentagon *n* a five-sided building that houses the headquarters of the US Department of Defense

pentagram *n* a star-shaped figure with five points

pentameter (pen-**tam**-it-er) *n* a line of poetry consisting of five metrical feet

Pentateuch (**pent**-a-tyuke) *n* the first five books of the Old Testament **Pentateuchal** *adj*
WORD ORIGIN Greek *pente* five + *teukhos* scroll case

pentathlon *n* an athletic contest consisting of five different events ▸ See also **modern pentathlon**
WORD ORIGIN Greek *pente* five + *athlon* contest

pentatonic scale *n music* a scale consisting of five notes

pentavalent *adj chem* having a valency of five

Pentecost *n* a Christian festival occurring on Whit Sunday celebrating the descent of the Holy Ghost to the apostles
WORD ORIGIN Greek *pentēkostē* fiftieth (day after the Resurrection)

Pentecostal *adj* relating to any of the Christian groups that have a charismatic and fundamentalist approach to Christianity

penthouse *n* a luxurious flat built on the top floor or roof of a building
WORD ORIGIN Middle English *pentis*, later *penthouse*, from Latin *appendere* to hang from

pent-up *adj* not released; repressed: *full of pent-up emotional violence*

penultimate *adj* second last

penumbra *n, pl* **-brae** *or* **-bras 1** the partially shadowed region which surrounds the full shadow in an eclipse **2** *literary* a partial shadow **penumbral** *adj*
WORD ORIGIN Latin *paene* almost + *umbra* shadow

penurious *adj formal* **1** niggardly with money **2** lacking money or means

penury *n formal* **1** extreme poverty **2** extreme scarcity
WORD ORIGIN Latin *penuria*

Penzias *n* **Arno Allan** born 1933, US astrophysicist, who shared the Nobel prize for physics (1978) with Robert W. Wilson for their discovery of cosmic microwave background radiation

peon *n* a Spanish-American farm labourer or unskilled worker
WORD ORIGIN Spanish

peony *n, pl* **-nies** a garden plant with showy pink, red, white, or yellow flowers
WORD ORIGIN Greek *paiōnia*

people ❶ *pl n* **1** persons collectively or in general **2** a group of persons considered together: *old people suffer from anaemia more often than younger people do* **3** *pl* **-ples** the persons living in a particular country: *the American people* **4** one's family or ancestors: *her people originally came from Skye* **5 the people a** the mass of ordinary persons without rank or privileges **b** the body of persons in a country who are entitled to vote ▹ *vb* **-pling, -pled 6** to provide with inhabitants: *the centre of the continent is sparsely peopled*
WORD ORIGIN Latin *populus*

people carrier *n* ▸ same as **multipurpose vehicle**

people mover *n Brit, Austral & NZ* ▸ same as **multipurpose vehicle**

pep *n* **1** high spirits, energy, or vitality ▹ *vb* **pepping, pepped 2 pep up** to make more lively or interesting: *the company has spent thousands trying to pep up its image*
WORD ORIGIN short for *pepper*

peplum *n, pl* **-lums** *or* **-la** a flared ruffle attached to the waist of a garment
WORD ORIGIN Greek *peplos* shawl

pepper ❶ *n* **1** a sharp hot condiment obtained from the fruit of an East Indian climbing plant **2** Also called: **capsicum** a colourful tropical fruit used as a vegetable and a condiment ▹ *vb* **3** to season with pepper **4** to sprinkle liberally: *his speech is heavily peppered with Americanisms* **5** to pelt with small missiles
WORD ORIGIN Greek *peperi*

pepper-and-salt *adj* **1** (of a fabric) marked with a fine mixture of black and white **2** (of hair) streaked with grey

peppercorn *n* the small dried berry of the pepper plant

peppercorn rent *n Brit* a rent that is very low or nominal

pepper mill *n* a small hand mill used to grind peppercorns

peppermint *n* **1** a mint plant which produces a pungent oil, used as a flavouring **2** a sweet flavoured with peppermint

pepperoni *n* a dry sausage of pork and beef spiced with pepper
WORD ORIGIN Italian *peperoni* peppers

pepper spray *n* a defence spray agent derived from hot cayenne peppers, which causes temporary blindness and breathing difficulty

peppery *adj* **1** tasting of pepper **2** irritable

pep pill *n informal* a tablet containing a stimulant drug

pepsin *n* an enzyme produced in the stomach, which, when activated by acid, breaks down proteins
WORD ORIGIN Greek *peptein* to digest

pep talk *n informal* a talk designed to increase confidence and enthusiasm

peptic *adj* **1** of or relating to digestion **2** of or caused by pepsin or the action of the digestive juices: *a peptic ulcer*
WORD ORIGIN Greek *peptein* to digest

peptic ulcer *n* an ulcer in the stomach or duodenum

peptide *n chem* a compound consisting of two or more amino acids linked by chemical bonding between the amino group of one and the carboxyl group of another

per *prep* **1** for every: *three pence per pound; 30 pounds per week* **2** by; through **3 as per** according to: *proceed as per the instructions* **4 as per usual** *or* **as per normal** *informal* as usual
WORD ORIGIN Latin: by, for each

peradventure *archaic adv* **1** by chance; perhaps ▹ *n* **2** chance or doubt
WORD ORIGIN Old French *par aventure* by chance

perambulate *vb* **-lating, -lated** *formal* to walk about (a place) **perambulation** *n*
WORD ORIGIN Latin *per-* through + *ambulare* to walk

perambulator *n formal* ▸ same as **pram**

per annum *adv* in each year
WORD ORIGIN Latin

per capita *adj, adv* of or for each person: *the average per capita wage has increased*
WORD ORIGIN Latin, literally: according to heads

perceive ❶ *vb* **-ceiving, -ceived 1** to become aware of (something) through the senses **2** to understand or grasp **perceivable** *adj*
WORD ORIGIN Latin *percipere* to seize entirely

P

THESAURUS

people *pl n* **1 = persons**, humans, individuals, folk *(informal)*, men and women, human beings, humanity, mankind, mortals, the human race, Homo sapiens **3 = nation**, public, community, subjects, population, residents, citizens, folk, inhabitants, electors, populace, tax payers, citizenry, (general) public **4a = race**, tribe, ethnic group **4b = family**, parents, relations, relatives, folk, folks *(informal)*, clan, kin, next of kin, kinsmen, nearest and dearest, kith and kin, your own flesh and blood, rellies *(Austral slang)* ▹ *vb* **6 = inhabit**, occupy, settle, populate, colonize

pepper *n* **1 = seasoning**, flavour, spice ▹ *vb* **4 = sprinkle**, spot, scatter, dot, stud, fleck, intersperse, speck, spatter, freckle, stipple, bespatter **5 = pelt**, hit, shower, scatter, blitz, riddle, rake, bombard, assail, strafe, rain down on

perceive *vb* **1 = see**, notice, note, identify, discover, spot, observe, remark, recognize, distinguish, glimpse, make out, pick out, discern, behold, catch sight of, espy, descry **2 = understand**, sense, gather, get *(informal)*, know, see, feel, learn,

DICTIONARY

per cent *adv* **1** in each hundred. Symbol: % ▷ *n also* **percent 2** a percentage or proportion
WORD ORIGIN Medieval Latin *per centum* out of every hundred

percentage *n* **1** proportion or rate per hundred parts **2** any proportion in relation to the whole: *a small percentage of the population* **3** *informal* profit or advantage

percentile *n* one of 99 actual or notional values of a variable dividing its distribution into 100 groups with equal frequencies

perceptible *adj* able to be perceived; recognizable **perceptibly** *adv*

perception ⊤ *n* **1** the act of perceiving **2** insight or intuition: *his acute perception of other people's emotions* **3** the ability to perceive **4** way of viewing: *advertising affects the customer's perception of a product* **perceptual** *adj*
WORD ORIGIN Latin *perceptio* comprehension

perceptive *adj* **1** observant **2** able to perceive **perceptively** *adv* **perceptiveness** *n*

perch[1] ⊤ *n* **1** a branch or other resting place above ground for a bird **2** any raised resting place: *from his perch on the bar stool* ▷ *vb* **3** (of birds) to alight or rest on a perch: *it fluttered to the branch and perched there for a moment* **4** to place or position precariously: *he was perched uneasily on the edge of his chair*
WORD ORIGIN Latin *pertica* long staff

perch[2] *n, pl* **perch** *or* **perches 1** a spiny-finned edible freshwater fish of Europe and North America **2** any of various similar or related fishes
WORD ORIGIN Greek *perkē*

P

perchance *adv archaic or poetic* **1** perhaps **2** by chance
WORD ORIGIN Anglo-French *par chance*

percipient *adj formal* quick at perceiving; observant **percipience** *n*
WORD ORIGIN Latin *percipiens* observing

percolate *vb* **-lating, -lated 1** to pass or filter through very small holes: *the light percolating through the stained-glass windows cast coloured patterns on the floor* **2** to spread gradually: *his theories percolated through the academic community* **3** to make (coffee) or (of coffee) to be made in a percolator **percolation** *n*
WORD ORIGIN Latin *per-* through + *colare* to strain

percolator *n* a coffeepot in which boiling water is forced up through a tube and filters down through the coffee grounds into a container

percussion *n* **1** the striking of one thing against another **2** *music* percussion instruments collectively **percussive** *adj*
WORD ORIGIN Latin *percutere* to hit

percussion cap *n* a detonator which contains material that explodes when struck

percussion instrument *n* a musical instrument, such as the drums, that produces a sound when struck directly

percussionist *n music* a person who plays percussion instruments

perdition *n* **1** *Christianity* final and unalterable spiritual ruin; damnation **2** ▸ same as **hell**
WORD ORIGIN Late Latin *perditio* ruin

peregrinate *vb* **-nating, -nated** *formal* to travel or wander about from place to place **peregrination** *n*
WORD ORIGIN Latin *peregrinari* to travel

peregrine falcon *n* a European falcon with dark plumage on the back and wings and lighter underparts
WORD ORIGIN Latin *peregrinus* foreign

Perelman *n* **S**(**idney**) **J**(**oseph**) 1904–79, US humorous writer. After scriptwriting for the Marx Brothers, he published many collections of articles, including *Crazy Like a Fox* (1944) and *Eastward, Hi!* (1977)

peremptory *adj* **1** urgent or commanding: *a peremptory knock on the door* **2** expecting immediate obedience without any discussion: *he gave peremptory instructions to his son* **3** dogmatic **peremptorily** *adv*
WORD ORIGIN Latin *peremptorius* decisive

perennial ⊤ *adj* **1** lasting throughout the year or through many years ▷ *n* **2** a plant that continues its growth for at least three years
WORD ORIGIN Latin *per-* through + *annus* year

Peres *n* **Shimon** born 1923, Israeli statesman, born in Poland: prime minister (1984–86; 1995–96); president from 2007; Nobel peace prize 1994 jointly with Yasser Arafat and Yitzhak Rabin

perestroika *n* (in the late 1980s) the policy of restructuring the Soviet economy and political system
WORD ORIGIN Russian: reconstruction

Pérez de Cuéllar *n* **Javier** born 1920, Peruvian diplomat and UN secretary-general (1982–91)

Pérez Galdós *n* **Benito** 1843–1920, Spanish novelist. His works include the *Episodios nacionales* (1873–1912), a series of historical novels, and *Fortunata y Jacinta* (1886–87)

Perez-Reverte *n* **Arturo** born 1952, Spanish novelist and writer; his books include *The Fencing Master* (1988), *The Dumas Club* (1993), *The Queen of the South* (2002) and the historical 'Captain Alatriste' series, beginning with *Captain Alatriste* (1996)

perfect ⊤ *adj* **1** having all essential elements **2** faultless: *a perfect circle* **3** correct or precise: *perfect timing* **4** utter or absolute: *a perfect stranger* **5** excellent in all respects: *a perfect day* **6** *maths* exactly divisible into equal integral or polynomial roots: *36 is a perfect square* **7** *grammar* denoting a tense of verbs used to describe a completed action ▷ *n* **8** *grammar* the perfect tense ▷ *vb* **9** to improve to one's satisfaction: *he is in Paris to perfect his French* **10** to make fully accomplished: *he perfected the system* **perfectly** *adv*
WORD ORIGIN Latin *perficere* to complete

perfectible *adj* capable of becoming or being made perfect **perfectibility** *n*

perfection ⊤ *n* the state or quality of being perfect
WORD ORIGIN Latin *perfectio* a completing

THESAURUS

realize, conclude, appreciate, grasp, comprehend, get the message about, deduce, apprehend, suss (out) *(slang)*, get the picture about

perception *n* **2 = understanding**, intelligence, observation, discrimination, insight, sharpness, cleverness, keenness, shrewdness, acuity, discernment, perspicacity, astuteness, incisiveness, perceptiveness, quick-wittedness, perspicuity **4 = awareness**, understanding, sense, impression, feeling, idea, taste, notion, recognition, observation, consciousness, grasp, sensation, conception, apprehension

perch[1] *n* **1 = resting place**, post, branch, pole, roost ▷ *vb* **3a = sit**, rest, balance, settle **3b = land**, alight, roost **4 = place**, put, rest, balance

perennial *adj* **1 = continual**, lasting, continuing, permanent, constant, enduring, chronic, persistent, abiding, lifelong, perpetual, recurrent, never-ending, incessant, unchanging, inveterate

perfect *adj* **1, 2 = faultless**, correct, pure, accurate, faithful, impeccable, exemplary, flawless, foolproof, blameless **OPPOSITE:** deficient **3 = exact**, true, accurate, precise, right, close, correct, strict, faithful, spot-on *(Brit informal)*, on the money *(US)*, unerring **4 = complete**, absolute, sheer, utter, consummate, out-and-out, unadulterated, unmitigated, unalloyed **OPPOSITE:** partial **5 = excellent**, ideal, supreme, superb, splendid, sublime, superlative ▷ *vb* **9 = improve**, develop, polish, elaborate, refine, cultivate, hone **OPPOSITE:** mar

perfection *n* **= excellence**, integrity, superiority, purity, wholeness, sublimity, exquisiteness, faultlessness, flawlessness,

DICTIONARY

perfectionism *n* the demand for the highest standard of excellence **perfectionist** *n, adj*
perfect pitch *n* ▸ same as **absolute pitch**
perfidious *adj literary* treacherous or deceitful **perfidy** *n*
WORD ORIGIN Latin *perfidus*
perforate *vb* **-rating, -rated 1** to make a hole or holes in **2** to punch rows of holes between (stamps) for ease of separation **perforable** *adj* **perforator** *n*
WORD ORIGIN Latin *per-* through + *forare* to pierce
perforation *n* **1** a hole or holes made in something **2** a series of punched holes, such as that between individual stamps
perforce *adv formal* of necessity
WORD ORIGIN Old French *par force*
perform ❶ *vb* **1** to carry out (an action): *the hospital performs more than a hundred such operations each year* **2** to present (a play or concert): *he performed a couple of songs from his new album* **3** to fulfil: *you have performed the first of two conditions* **performable** *adj* **performer** *n*
WORD ORIGIN Old French *parfournir*
performance ❶ *n* **1** the act or process of performing **2** an artistic or dramatic production: *the concert includes the first performance of a new trumpet concerto* **3** manner or quality of functioning: *the car's overall performance is excellent* **4** *informal* conduct or behaviour, esp. when distasteful: *what did you mean by that performance at the restaurant?*
perfume ❶ *n* **1** a liquid cosmetic worn for its pleasant smell **2** a fragrant smell ▹ *vb* **-fuming, -fumed 3** to impart a perfume to **perfumed** *adj*
WORD ORIGIN French *parfum*, from Latin *per* through + *fumare* to smoke
perfumer *n* a person who makes or sells perfume **perfumery** *n*
perfunctory *adj formal* done only as a matter of routine: *he gave his wife a perfunctory kiss* **perfunctorily** *adv* **perfunctoriness** *n*
WORD ORIGIN Late Latin *perfunctorius* negligent
perfuse *vb* **-fusing, -fused 1** to permeate (a liquid, colour, etc.) through or over (something) **2** *surgery* to pass (a fluid) through tissue
pergola *n* an arched trellis or framework that supports climbing plants
WORD ORIGIN Italian
Pergolesi *n* **Giovanni Battista** 1710–36, Italian composer: his works include the operetta *La Serva padrona* (1733) and the *Stabat Mater* (1736) for women's voices
perhaps ❶ *adv* **1** possibly; maybe **2** approximately; roughly: *it would have taken perhaps three or four minutes*
WORD ORIGIN earlier *perhappes*, from *per* by + *happes* chance
perianth *n bot* the outer part of a flower
WORD ORIGIN Greek *peri-* around + *anthos* flower
pericardium *n, pl* **-dia** the membranous sac enclosing the heart **pericardial** *adj*
WORD ORIGIN Greek *peri-* around + *kardia* heart
pericarp *n bot* the part of a fruit enclosing the seed that develops from the wall of the ovary
WORD ORIGIN Greek *peri-* around + *karpos* fruit
perigee *n astron* the point in its orbit around the earth when the moon or a satellite is nearest the earth
WORD ORIGIN Greek *peri-* near + *gea* earth
perihelion *n, pl* **-lia** *astron* the point in its orbit around the sun when a planet or comet is nearest the sun
WORD ORIGIN Greek *peri-* near + *hēlios* sun
peril ❶ *n* great danger or jeopardy **perilous** *adj*
WORD ORIGIN Latin *periculum*
perimeter ❶ (per-rim-it-er) *n* **1** *maths* **a** the curve or line enclosing a plane area **b** the length of this curve or line **2** any boundary around something
WORD ORIGIN Latin *perimetros*
perinatal *adj* of or occurring in the period from about three months before to one month after birth
WORD ORIGIN Greek *peri-* around + Latin *natus* born
perineum (per-rin-nee-um) *n, pl* **-nea** (-nee-a) *anat* the region of the body between the anus and the genitals **perineal** *adj*
WORD ORIGIN Greek *perinaion*
period ❶ *n* **1** a portion of time: *six inches of rain fell in a 24-hour period* **2** a portion of time specified in some way: *the President's first period of office* **3** an occurrence of menstruation **4** *geol* a unit of geological time during which a system of rocks is formed: *the Jurassic period* **5** a division of time at school, college, or university when a particular subject is taught **6** *physics, math* the time taken to complete one cycle of a regularly recurring phenomenon **7** *chem* one of the horizontal rows of elements in the periodic table **8** *chiefly US & Canad* ▸ same as **full stop** ▹ *adj* **9** dating from or in the style of an earlier time: *a performance on period instruments*
WORD ORIGIN Greek *periodos* circuit
periodic ❶ *adj* recurring at intervals **periodically** *adv* **periodicity** *n*
periodical *n* **1** a publication issued at regular intervals, usually monthly or weekly ▹ *adj* **2** of or relating to such publications **3** periodic or occasional
periodic law *n chem* the principle that the chemical properties of the elements are periodic functions of their atomic numbers
periodic table *n chem* a table of the elements, arranged in order of increasing atomic number, based on the periodic law
peripatetic (per-rip-a-tet-ik) *adj* **1** travelling from place to place **2** *Brit* employed in two or more educational establishments and travelling from one to another: *a peripatetic violin teacher* ▹ *n* **3** a peripatetic person
WORD ORIGIN Greek *peripatein* to pace to and fro

P

THESAURUS

perfectness, immaculateness
perform *vb* **1 = do**, achieve, carry out, effect, complete, satisfy, observe, fulfil, accomplish, execute, bring about, pull off, act out, transact **2 = present**, act (out), stage, play, produce, represent, put on, render, depict, enact, appear as **3 = fulfil**, carry out, execute, discharge
performance *n* **1a = presentation**, playing, acting (out), staging, production, exhibition, interpretation, representation, rendering, portrayal, rendition **1b = carrying out**, practice, achievement, discharge, execution, completion, accomplishment, fulfilment, consummation **2 = show**, appearance, concert, gig *(informal)*, recital
perfume *n* **1 = fragrance**, scent, essence, incense, cologne, eau de toilette, eau de cologne, attar **2 = scent**, smell, fragrance, bouquet, aroma, odour, sweetness, niff *(Brit slang)*, redolence, balminess
perhaps *adv* **1 = maybe**, possibly, it may be, it is possible (that), conceivably, as the case may be, perchance *(archaic)*, feasibly, for all you know, happen *(Northern English dialect)*
peril *n* **= danger**, risk, threat, hazard, menace, jeopardy, perilousness
perimeter *n* **2 = boundary**, edge, border, bounds, limit, margin, confines, periphery, borderline, circumference, ambit
OPPOSITE: centre
period *n* **1 = time**, term, season, space, run, stretch, spell, phase, patch *(Brit informal)*, interval, span
periodic *adj* **= recurrent**, regular, repeated, occasional, periodical, seasonal, cyclical, sporadic, intermittent, every so often, infrequent, cyclic, every once in a while, spasmodic, at fixed intervals

DICTIONARY

peripheral ❶ (per-**if**-er-al) *adj* **1** not relating to the most important part of something; incidental **2** of or relating to a periphery ▷ *n* **3** *computers* any device, such as a disk or modem, concerned with input/output or storage

periphery (per-**if**-er-ee) *n, pl* **-eries** **1** the boundary or edge of an area or group: *slums sprouted up on the periphery of the city* **2** fringes of a field of activity: *less developed countries on the periphery of the capitalist system*
WORD ORIGIN Greek *peri-* around + *pherein* to bear

periphrasis (per-**if**-ra-siss) *n, pl* **-rases** (-ra-seez) a roundabout way of expressing something; circumlocution
WORD ORIGIN Greek *peri-* around + *phrazein* to declare

periscope *n* an optical instrument used, esp. in submarines, to give a view of objects on a different level
WORD ORIGIN Greek *periskopein* to look around

perish ❶ *vb* **1** to be destroyed or die **2** to cause to suffer: *we were perished with cold* **3** to rot or cause to rot: *to prevent your swimsuit from perishing, rinse it in clean water before it dries*
WORD ORIGIN Latin *perire* to pass away entirely

perishable *adj* **1** liable to rot ▷ *n* **2** (*often pl*) a perishable article, esp. food

perishing *adj* **1** *informal* (of weather) extremely cold **2** *slang* confounded or blasted: *get rid of the perishing lot!*

peristalsis (per-riss-**tal**-siss) *n, pl* **-ses** (-seez) *physiol* the wavelike involuntary muscular contractions of the walls of the digestive tract **peristaltic** *adj*
WORD ORIGIN Greek *peri-* around + *stalsis* compression

peritoneum (per-rit-toe-**nee**-um) *n, pl* **-nea** (-**nee**-a) *or* **-neums** a serous sac that lines the walls of the abdominal cavity and covers the abdominal organs **peritoneal** *adj*
WORD ORIGIN Greek *peritonos* stretched around

peritonitis (per-rit-tone-**ite**-iss) *n* inflammation of the peritoneum, causing severe abdominal pain

periwig *n historical* a wig formerly worn by men
WORD ORIGIN French *perruque*

periwinkle[1] *n* ▸ same as **winkle** (sense 1)
WORD ORIGIN origin unknown

periwinkle[2] *n* a Eurasian evergreen plant with trailing stems and blue flowers
WORD ORIGIN Old English *perwince*

perjure *vb* **-juring, -jured** ▪ **perjure oneself** *criminal law* to deliberately give false evidence while under oath **perjurer** *n*
WORD ORIGIN Latin *perjurare*

perjury (**per**-jer-ee) *n, pl* **-juries** *criminal law* the act of deliberately giving false evidence while under oath
WORD ORIGIN Latin *perjurium* a false oath

perk[1] ❶ *n informal* an incidental benefit gained from a job, such as a company car
WORD ORIGIN short for *perquisite*

perk[2] *vb informal* ▸ short for **percolate** (sense 3)

perk up *vb* **1** to make or become more cheerful **2** to rise or cause to rise briskly: *the dog's ears perked up suddenly*
WORD ORIGIN origin unknown

perky *adj* **perkier, perkiest** **1** jaunty or lively **2** confident or spirited

Perl *n* a computer programming language that is used for text manipulation, esp. on the World Wide Web
WORD ORIGIN practical extraction and report language

perlemoen (**per**-la-moon) *n S African* ▸ same as **abalone**
WORD ORIGIN Afrikaans, from Dutch

Perlman *n* **Itzhak** born 1945, Israeli violinist; polio victim

perm[1] *n* **1** a hairstyle with long-lasting waves or curls produced by treating the hair with chemicals ▷ *vb* **2** to give a perm to (hair)

perm[2] *n informal* ▸ short for **permutation** (sense 4)

permafrost *n* ground that is permanently frozen
WORD ORIGIN *perma(nent)* + *frost*

permanent ❶ *adj* **1** existing or intended to exist forever: *a permanent solution* **2** not expected to change: *a permanent condition* **permanence** *n* **permanently** *adv*
WORD ORIGIN Latin *permanens* continuing

permanent wave *n* ▸ same as **perm**[1] (sense 1)

permanent way *n chiefly Brit* the track of a railway, including the sleepers and rails

permanganate *n* a salt of an acid containing manganese, used as a disinfectant

permeable *adj* capable of being permeated, esp. by liquids **permeability** *n*

permeate *vb* **-ating, -ated** **1** to penetrate or spread throughout (something): *his mystical philosophy permeates everything he creates* **2** to pass through or cause to pass through by osmosis or diffusion: *the rain permeated her anorak* **permeation** *n*
WORD ORIGIN Latin *permeare*

Permian *adj geol* of the period of geological time about 280 million years ago
WORD ORIGIN after *Perm*, Russian port

permissible *adj* permitted or allowable **permissibility** *n*

permission ❶ *n* authorization to do something

permissive *adj* tolerant or lenient, esp. in sexual matters: *the so-called permissive society* **permissiveness** *n*

permit ❶ *vb* **-mitting, -mitted** **1** to allow (something) to be done or to happen: *smoking is not permitted in the office* **2** to allow (someone) to do something: *her father does not permit her to eat sweets* **3** to allow the possibility (of): *they saw each other as often as time and circumstances permitted* ▷ *n* **4** an official document granting permission to do something
WORD ORIGIN Latin *permittere*

THESAURUS

peripheral *adj* **1 = secondary**, beside the point, minor, marginal, irrelevant, superficial, unimportant, incidental, tangential, inessential **2 = outermost**, outside, external, outer, exterior, borderline, perimetric

perish *vb* **1a = die**, be killed, be lost, expire, pass away, lose your life, decease, cark it (*Austral & NZ slang*) **1b = be destroyed**, fall, decline, collapse, disappear, vanish, go under **3 = rot**, waste away, break down, decay, wither, disintegrate, decompose, moulder

perk[1] *n* (*Brit informal*) **= bonus**, benefit, extra, plus, dividend, icing on the cake, fringe benefit, perquisite

permanent *adj* **1 = lasting**, fixed, constant, enduring, persistent, eternal, abiding, perennial, durable, perpetual, everlasting, unchanging, immutable, indestructible, immovable, invariable, imperishable, unfading **OPPOSITE:** temporary **2 = long-term**, established, secure, stable, steady, long-lasting **OPPOSITE:** temporary

permission *n* **= authorization**, sanction, licence, approval, leave, freedom, permit, go-ahead (*informal*), liberty, consent, allowance, tolerance, green light, assent, dispensation, carte blanche, blank cheque, sufferance **OPPOSITE:** prohibition

permit *vb* **1, 2 = allow**, admit, grant, sanction, let, suffer, agree to, entitle, endure, license, endorse, warrant, tolerate, authorize, empower, consent to, give the green light to, give leave *or* permission **OPPOSITE:** forbid **3 = enable**, let, allow, cause ▷ *n* **4 = licence**, pass, document, certificate, passport, visa, warrant, authorization **OPPOSITE:** prohibition

DICTIONARY

permutate *vb* **-tating, -tated** to alter the sequence or arrangement (of): *endlessly permutating three basic designs*
permutation *n* **1** *maths* an ordered arrangement of the numbers or terms of a set into specified groups: *the permutations of a, b, and c, taken two at a time, are ab, ba, ac, ca, bc, cb* **2** a combination of items made by reordering **3** a transformation **4** a fixed combination for selections of results on football pools
WORD ORIGIN Latin *permutare* to change thoroughly
pernicious *adj formal* **1** wicked or malicious: *pernicious lies* **2** causing grave harm; deadly
WORD ORIGIN Latin *pernicies* ruin
pernicious anaemia *n* a severe form of anaemia resulting in a reduction of the red blood cells, weakness, and a sore tongue
pernickety *adj informal* **1** excessively fussy about details **2** (of a task) requiring close attention
WORD ORIGIN origin unknown
peroration *n formal* the concluding part of a speech which sums up the points made previously
WORD ORIGIN Latin *peroratio*
peroxide *n* **1** hydrogen peroxide used as a hair bleach **2** any of a class of metallic oxides, such as sodium peroxide, Na_2O_2 ▷ *adj* **3** bleached with or resembling peroxide: *a peroxide blonde* ▷ *vb* **-iding, -ided 4** to bleach (the hair) with peroxide
perp *n US & Canad informal* a person who has committed a crime
WORD ORIGIN short for *perpetrator*
perpendicular *adj* **1** at right angles to a given line or surface **2** upright; vertical **3** denoting a style of English Gothic architecture characterized by vertical lines ▷ *n* **4** *geom* a line or plane perpendicular to another
perpendicularity *n*
WORD ORIGIN Latin *perpendiculum* a plumb line
perpetrate *vb* **-trating, -trated** to perform or be responsible for (a deception or crime) **perpetration** *n* **perpetrator** *n*
WORD ORIGIN Latin *perpetrare*
perpetual ❶ *adj* **1** never ending or never changing: *Mexico's colourful scenery and nearly perpetual sunshine* **2** continually repeated: *his mother's perpetual worries about his health*
perpetually *adv*
WORD ORIGIN Latin *perpetualis*
perpetual motion *n* motion of a hypothetical mechanism that continues indefinitely without any external source of energy
perpetuate ❶ *vb* **-ating, -ated** to cause to continue: *images that perpetuate stereotypes of Black people as illiterate, happy-go-lucky entertainers*
perpetuation *n*
WORD ORIGIN Latin *perpetuare* to continue without interruption
perpetuity *n, pl* **-ties 1** eternity **2** the state of being perpetual **3** something perpetual, such as a pension that is payable indefinitely **4 in perpetuity** forever
WORD ORIGIN Latin *perpetuitas* continuity
perplex *vb* **1** to puzzle or bewilder **2** to complicate: *this merely perplexes the issue* **perplexing** *adj*
WORD ORIGIN Latin *perplexus* entangled
perplexity *n, pl* **-ties 1** the state of being perplexed **2** something that perplexes
perquisite *n formal* ▸ same as **perk**[1]
WORD ORIGIN Latin *perquirere* to seek earnestly for something
Perrault *n* **Charles** 1628–1703, French author, noted for his *Contes de ma mère l'oye* (1697), which contains the fairy tales *Little Red Riding Hood*, *Cinderella*, and *The Sleeping Beauty*
Perrin *n* **Jean Baptiste** 1870–1942, French physicist. His researches on the distribution and diffusion of particles in colloids (1911) gave evidence for the physical reality of molecules, confirmed the explanation of Brownian movement in terms of kinetic theory, and determined the magnitude of the Avogadro constant. He also studied cathode rays: Nobel prize for physics 1926
perry *n, pl* **-ries** an alcoholic drink made from fermented pear juice
WORD ORIGIN Old French *peré*
Perry *n* **1 Fred(erick John)** 1909–95, English tennis and table-tennis player; world singles table-tennis champion (1929); Wimbledon singles champion (1934–36) **2 Grayson** born 1960, British potter. A transvestite, he won the Turner Prize (2003). **3 Matthew Calbraith** 1794–1858, US naval officer, who led a naval expedition to Japan that obtained a treaty (1854) opening up Japan to western trade **4** his brother, **Oliver Hazard** 1785–1819, US naval officer. His defeat of a British squadron on Lake Erie (1813) was the turning point in the War of 1812, leading to the recapture of Detroit
per se (per **say**) *adv* in itself
WORD ORIGIN Latin
Perse *n* **Saint-John**, real name *Alexis Saint-Léger*. 1887–1975, French poet, born in Guadeloupe. His works include *Anabase* (1922) and *Chronique* (1960). Nobel prize for literature 1960
persecute ❶ *vb* **-cuting, -cuted 1** to oppress or maltreat (someone), because of race or religion **2** to harass (someone) persistently
persecution *n* **persecutor** *n*
WORD ORIGIN Latin *persequi* to take vengeance upon
perseverance *n* continued steady belief or efforts; persistence
persevere *vb* **-severing, -severed** (often foll. by *with* or *in*) to continue to make an effort despite difficulties
WORD ORIGIN Latin *perseverus* very strict
Persian *adj* **1** of ancient Persia or modern Iran ▷ *n* **2** a person from Persia (now Iran) **3** the language of Iran or of Persia
Persian carpet *n* a hand-made carpet or rug with flowing or geometric designs in rich colours
Persian cat *n* a long-haired variety of domestic cat
Persian lamb *n* **1** a black loosely curled fur from the karakul lamb **2** a karakul lamb
persiflage (per-sif-flahzh) *n literary* light frivolous conversation or writing
WORD ORIGIN French
persimmon *n* a sweet red tropical fruit
WORD ORIGIN from a Native American language
persist ❶ *vb* **1** to continue without interruption: *if the symptoms persist, see your doctor* **2** (often foll. by *in* or *with*) to continue obstinately despite opposition: *she persisted in using these controversial methods*
WORD ORIGIN Latin *persistere*

THESAURUS

perpetual *adj* **1 = everlasting**, permanent, endless, eternal, lasting, enduring, abiding, perennial, infinite, immortal, never-ending, unending, unchanging, undying, sempiternal *(literary)*
OPPOSITE: temporary
2 = continual, repeated, constant, endless, continuous, persistent, perennial, recurrent, never-ending, uninterrupted, interminable, incessant, ceaseless, unremitting, unfailing, unceasing **OPPOSITE:** brief
perpetuate *vb* **= maintain**, preserve, sustain, keep up, keep going, continue, keep alive, immortalize, eternalize **OPPOSITE:** end
persecute *vb* **1 = victimize**, hunt, injure, pursue, torture, hound, torment, martyr, oppress, pick on, molest, ill-treat, maltreat
OPPOSITE: mollycoddle
2 = harass, bother, annoy, bait, tease, worry, hassle *(informal)*, badger, pester, vex, be on your back *(slang)*
OPPOSITE: leave alone
persist *vb* **1 = continue**, last, remain, carry on, endure, keep up, linger, abide **2** *(often foll. by* **in** *or* **with)** with) **= persevere**, continue, go on, carry on, hold on *(informal)*, keep on, keep going, press on, not give up, stand firm, soldier on *(informal)*, stay

DICTIONARY

persistent ❶ *adj* **1** unrelenting: *persistent rain* **2** showing persistence: *she was a persistent woman* **persistence** *n* **persistently** *adv*

persistent vegetative state *n med* an irreversible condition, resulting from brain damage, characterized by lack of consciousness, thought, and feeling, although reflex activities continue

person ❶ *n, pl* **people** *or* **persons** **1** an individual human being **2** the body of a human being: *he was found to have a knife concealed about his person* **3** *grammar* a category into which pronouns and forms of verbs are subdivided to show whether they refer to the speaker, the person addressed, or some other individual or thing **4 in person** actually doing something or being somewhere oneself: *I had the chance to hear her speak in person*
WORD ORIGIN Latin *persona* mask

-person *n combining form* sometimes used instead of *man* and *woman* or *lady*: *chairperson*

persona (per-soh-na) *n, pl* **-nae** (-nee) the personality that a person adopts and presents to other people
WORD ORIGIN Latin: mask

personable *adj* pleasant in appearance and personality

personage *n* **1** an important or distinguished person **2** any person

personal ❶ *adj* **1** of the private aspects of a person's life: *redundancy can put an enormous strain on personal relationships* **2** of a person's body: *personal hygiene* **3** belonging to, or for the sole use of, a particular individual: *he disappeared, leaving his passport, diary and other personal belongings in his flat* **4** undertaken by an individual: *the sponsorship deal requires him to make a number of personal appearances for publicity purposes* **5** offensive in respect of an individual's personality or intimate affairs: *he has suffered a lifetime of personal remarks about his weight* **6** having the attributes of an individual conscious being: *a personal God* **7** *grammar* of person **8** *law* of movable property, such as money

personal assistant *n* a person who is employed to help someone with his or her work, esp. the secretarial and administrative aspects of it

personal column *n* a newspaper column containing personal messages and advertisements

personal computer *n* a small computer used for word processing or computer games

personality ❶ *n, pl* **-ties** **1** *psychol* the distinctive characteristics which make an individual unique **2** the distinctive character of a person which makes him or her socially attractive: *some people find him lacking in personality and a bit colourless* **3** a well-known person in a certain field; celebrity **4** a remarkable person: *she is a personality to be reckoned with* **5** *(often pl)* an offensive personal remark: *the argument never degenerated into personalities*

personalize *or* **-ise** *vb* **-izing, -ized** *or* **-ising, -ised** **1** to base (an argument or discussion) around people's characters rather than on abstract arguments **2** to mark (stationery or clothing) with a person's initials or name **3** ▸ same as **personify**

personally ❶ *adv* **1** without the help of others: *she had seen to it personally that permission was granted* **2** in one's own opinion: *personally, I think it's overrated* **3** as if referring to oneself: *yes, he was rather rude but it's not worth taking it personally* **4** as a person: *I don't like him personally, but he's fine to work with*

personal organizer *n* **1** a diary for storing personal records, appointments, etc. **2** a pocket-sized electronic device that performs the same functions

personal pronoun *n* a pronoun such as *I, you, he, she, it, we,* and *they* that represents a definite person or thing

personal stereo *n chiefly Brit* a small portable audio cassette player used with lightweight headphones

persona non grata (non grah-ta) *n, pl* **personae non gratae** (grah-tee) an unacceptable person
WORD ORIGIN Latin

personate *vb* **-ating, -ated** *criminal law* to assume the identity of (another person) with intent to deceive **personation** *n*

personify *vb* **-fies, -fying, -fied** **1** to give human characteristics to (a thing or abstraction) **2** to represent (an abstract quality) in human or animal form **3** (of a person or thing) to represent (an abstract quality), as in art **4** to be the embodiment of: *she can be charm personified* **personification** *n*

personnel ❶ *n* **1** the people employed in an organization or for a service **2** the department in an organization that appoints or keeps records of employees **3** (in the armed forces) people, as opposed to machinery or equipment
WORD ORIGIN French

perspective ❶ *n* **1** a way of regarding situations or facts and judging their relative importance: *the female perspective on sex and love* **2** objectivity: *Kay's problems helped me put my minor worries into perspective* **3** a method of drawing that gives the effect of solidity and relative distances and sizes **4** the appearance of objects or buildings relative to each other, determined by their distance from the viewer
WORD ORIGIN Latin *perspicere* to inspect carefully

Perspex *n trademark* a clear acrylic resin used as a substitute for glass

perspicacious *adj formal* acutely perceptive or discerning **perspicacity** *n*
WORD ORIGIN Latin *perspicax*

perspicuous *adj literary* (of speech or

p

THESAURUS

the course, plough on, be resolute, stick to your guns *(informal)*, show determination, crack on *(informal)*

persistent *adj* **1 = continuous**, constant, relentless, lasting, repeated, endless, perpetual, continual, never-ending, interminable, unrelenting, incessant, unremitting
OPPOSITE: occasional
2 = determined, dogged, fixed, steady, enduring, stubborn, persevering, resolute, tireless, tenacious, steadfast, obstinate, indefatigable, immovable, assiduous, obdurate, stiff-necked, unflagging, pertinacious
OPPOSITE: irresolute

person *n* **1 = individual**, being, body, human, soul, creature, human being, mortal, living soul, man *or* woman

personal *adj* **1 = private**, intimate, confidential **3a = own**, special, private, individual, particular, peculiar, privy **3b = individual**, special, particular, exclusive **5 = offensive**, critical, slighting, nasty, insulting, rude, belittling, disparaging, derogatory, disrespectful, pejorative

personality *n* **1 = nature**, character, make-up, identity, temper, traits, temperament, psyche, disposition, individuality **2 = character**, charm, attraction, charisma, attractiveness, dynamism, magnetism, pleasantness, likableness *or* likeableness **3 = celebrity**, star, big name, notable, household name, famous name, celeb *(informal)*, personage, megastar *(informal)*, well-known face, well-known person

personally *adv* **1 = by yourself**, alone, independently, solely, on your own, in person, in the flesh **2 = in your opinion**, for yourself, in your book, for your part, from your own viewpoint, in your own view

personnel *n* **1 = employees**, people, members, staff, workers, men and women, workforce, human resources, helpers, liveware

perspective *n* **1 = outlook**, attitude, context, angle, overview, way of looking, frame of reference, broad view **2 = objectivity**, proportion, relation, relativity, relative importance

DICTIONARY

writing) easily understood; lucid **perspicuity** *n*
WORD ORIGIN Latin *perspicuus* transparent

perspiration *n* **1** the salty fluid secreted by the sweat glands of the skin; sweat **2** the act of sweating

perspire *vb* **-spiring, -spired** to sweat
WORD ORIGIN Latin *per-* through + *spirare* to breathe

persuade ⊕ *vb* **-suading, -suaded 1** to make (someone) do something by reason or charm: *we tried to persuade him not to come up the mountain with us* **2** to cause to believe; convince: *persuading people of the need for enforced environmental protection may be difficult* **persuadable** *adj*
WORD ORIGIN Latin *persuadere*

persuasion ⊕ *n* **1** the act of persuading **2** the power to persuade **3** a set of beliefs; creed: *the Roman Catholic persuasion; literary intellectuals of the modernist persuasion*

persuasive ⊕ *adj* able to persuade: *a persuasive argument* **persuasively** *adv*

pert *adj* **1** saucy or impudent **2** attractive in a neat way: *pert buttocks*
WORD ORIGIN Latin *apertus* open

pertain *vb* (often foll. by *to*) **1** to have reference or relevance: *the notes pertaining to the case* **2** to be appropriate: *the product pertains to real user needs* **3** to belong (to) or be a part (of)
WORD ORIGIN Latin *pertinere*

pertinacious *adj* **1** doggedly resolute in purpose or belief **2** stubbornly persistent **pertinacity** *n*
WORD ORIGIN Latin *per-* (intensive) + *tenax* clinging

pertinent *adj* relating to the matter at hand; relevant **pertinence** *n*
WORD ORIGIN Latin *pertinens*

perturb *vb* **1** to disturb the composure of **2** to throw into disorder
WORD ORIGIN Latin *perturbare* to confuse

perturbation *n literary* anxiety or worry

Perugino *n* **II**, real name *Pietro Vannucci*. 1446–1523, Italian painter; master of Raphael. His works include the fresco *Christ giving the Keys to Peter* in the Sistine Chapel, Rome

peruke *n historical* a wig for men worn in the 17th and 18th centuries
WORD ORIGIN French *perruque*

peruse *vb* **-rusing, -rused 1** to read or examine with care **2** to browse or read in a leisurely way **perusal** *n*
WORD ORIGIN *per-* (intensive) + *use*

Perutz *n* **Max Ferdinand** 1914–2002, British biochemist, born in Austria. With J. C. Kendrew, he worked on the structure of haemoglobin and shared the Nobel prize for chemistry 1962

Peruzzi *n* **Baldassare Tommaso** 1481–1536, Italian architect and painter of the High Renaissance. The design of the Palazzo Massimo, Rome, is attributed to him

pervade *vb* **-vading, -vaded** to spread through or throughout (something) **pervasion** *n* **pervasive** *adj*
WORD ORIGIN Latin *per-* through + *vadere* to go

perverse ⊕ *adj* **1** deliberately acting in a way different from what is regarded as normal or proper **2** wayward or contrary; obstinate **perversely** *adv* **perversity** *n*
WORD ORIGIN Latin *perversus* turned the wrong way

perversion *n* **1** any abnormal means of obtaining sexual satisfaction **2** the act of perverting

pervert ⊕ *vb* **1** to use wrongly or badly **2** to interpret wrongly or badly; distort **3** to lead (someone) into abnormal behaviour, esp. sexually; corrupt **4** to debase ▷ *n* **5** a person who practises sexual perversion **perverted** *adj*
WORD ORIGIN Latin *pervertere* to turn the wrong way

pervious *adj* **1** able to be penetrated; permeable: *the thin walls were pervious to the slightest sound* **2** receptive to new ideas; open-minded
WORD ORIGIN Latin *per-* through + *via* a way

Pesach *or* **Pesah** (pay-sahk) *n* ▸ same as **Passover**

peseta (pess-say-ta) *n* a former monetary unit of Spain
WORD ORIGIN Spanish

pesky *adj* **peskier, peskiest** *informal chiefly US & Canad* troublesome
WORD ORIGIN probably changed from *pesty*

peso (pay-so) *n, pl* **-sos** the standard monetary unit of Chile, Colombia, Cuba, the Dominican Republic, Mexico, the Philippines, and Uruguay
WORD ORIGIN Spanish: weight

pessary *n, pl* **-ries** *med* **1** a device worn in the vagina, either as a support for the uterus or as a contraceptive **2** a vaginal suppository
WORD ORIGIN Greek *pessos* plug

pessimism *n* **1** the tendency to expect the worst in all things **2** the doctrine of the ultimate triumph of evil over good **pessimist** *n* **pessimistic** *adj* **pessimistically** *adv*
WORD ORIGIN Latin *pessimus* worst

Pessoa *n* **Fernando** 1888–1935, Portuguese poet, who ascribed much of his work to three imaginary poets, Alvaro de Campos, Alberto Caeiro, and Ricardo Reis

pest ⊕ *n* **1** an annoying person or thing; nuisance **2** any organism that damages crops, or injures or irritates livestock or man
WORD ORIGIN Latin *pestis* plague

Pestalozzi *n* **Johann Heinrich** 1746–1827, Swiss educational reformer. His emphasis on learning by observation exerted a wide influence on elementary education

pester *vb* to annoy or nag continually
WORD ORIGIN Old French *empestrer* to hobble (a horse)

pesticide *n* a chemical used to

THESAURUS

persuade *vb* **1a = talk (someone) into**, urge, advise, prompt, influence, counsel, win (someone) over, induce, sway, entice, coax, incite, prevail upon, inveigle, bring (someone) round *(informal)*, twist (someone's) arm, argue (someone) into **OPPOSITE:** dissuade **1b = cause**, prompt, lead, move, influence, motivate, induce, incline, dispose, impel, actuate **2 = convince**, satisfy, assure, prove to, convert to, cause to believe

persuasion *n* **1 = urging**, influencing, conversion, inducement, exhortation, wheedling, enticement, cajolery, blandishment, inveiglement **3 = belief**, views, opinion, party, school, side, camp, faith, conviction, faction, cult, sect, creed, denomination, tenet, school of thought, credo, firm belief, certitude, fixed opinion

persuasive *adj* **= convincing**, telling, effective, winning, moving, sound, touching, impressive, compelling, influential, valid, inducing, logical, credible, plausible, forceful, eloquent, weighty, impelling, cogent **OPPOSITE:** unconvincing

perverse *adj* **1 = abnormal**, incorrect, unhealthy, improper, deviant, depraved **2 = stubborn**, contrary, unreasonable, dogged, contradictory, troublesome, rebellious, wayward, delinquent, intractable, wilful, unyielding, obstinate, intransigent, headstrong, unmanageable, cussed *(informal)*, obdurate, stiff-necked, disobedient, wrong-headed, refractory, pig-headed, miscreant, mulish, cross-grained, contumacious **OPPOSITE:** cooperative

pervert *vb* **1, 2 = distort**, abuse, twist, misuse, warp, misinterpret, misrepresent, falsify, misconstrue **3, 4 = corrupt**, degrade, subvert, deprave, debase, desecrate, debauch, lead astray ▷ *n* **5 = deviant**, degenerate, sicko *(informal)*, sleazeball *(slang)*, debauchee, weirdo *or* weirdie *(informal)*

pest *n* **1 = nuisance**, bore, trial, pain *(informal)*, drag *(informal)*, bother, irritation, gall, annoyance, bane, pain in the neck *(informal)*, vexation, thorn in your flesh **2 = infection**, bug, insect, plague, epidemic, blight, scourge, bane, pestilence, gogga *(S African informal)*

DICTIONARY

destroy pests, esp. insects
WORD ORIGIN *pest* + Latin *caedere* to kill

pestilence *n literary* any deadly epidemic disease, such as the plague

pestilent *adj* **1** annoying or irritating **2** highly destructive morally or physically **3** likely to cause infectious disease **pestilential** *adj*
WORD ORIGIN Latin *pestis* plague

pestle *n* a club-shaped instrument for grinding or pounding substances in a mortar
WORD ORIGIN Old French *pestel*

pet[1] ❶ *n* **1** a tame animal kept for companionship or pleasure **2** a person who is favoured or indulged: *teacher's pet* ▷ *adj* **3** kept as a pet: *a pet hamster* **4** of or for pet animals: *pet food* **5** strongly felt or particularly cherished: *a pet hatred; he would not stand by and let his pet project be abandoned* ▷ *vb* **petting, petted 6** to treat as a pet; pamper **7** to pat or stroke affectionately **8** *informal* (of two people) to caress each other in an erotic manner
WORD ORIGIN origin unknown

pet[2] *n* a fit of sulkiness
WORD ORIGIN origin unknown

Pétain *n* **Henri Philippe Omer** 1856–1951, French marshal, noted for his victory at Verdun (1916) in World War I and his leadership of the pro-Nazi government of unoccupied France at Vichy (1940–44); imprisoned for treason (1945)

petal *n* any of the brightly coloured leaflike parts which form the head of a flower **petalled** *adj*
WORD ORIGIN Greek *petalon* leaf

P

petard *n* **1** (formerly) a device containing explosives used to break through a wall or door **2 hoist with one's own petard** being the victim of one's own schemes
WORD ORIGIN French: firework

Peter III *n* 1728–62, grandson of Peter I and tsar of Russia (1762): deposed in a coup d'état led by his wife (later Catherine II); assassinated

peter out *vb* to come gradually to an end: *the road petered out into a rutted track*
WORD ORIGIN origin unknown

Peter Pan *n* a youthful or immature man
WORD ORIGIN after the main character in *Peter Pan*, a play

Peterson *n* **Oscar** (**Emmanuel**) 1925–2007, Canadian jazz pianist and singer, who led his own trio from the early 1950s

Peter the Hermit *n* ?1050–1115, French monk and preacher of the First Crusade

pethidine (**peth**-id-een) *n* a white crystalline water-soluble drug used to relieve pain
WORD ORIGIN perhaps a blend of *piperidine* + *ethyl*

petiole *n bot* the stalk which attaches a leaf to a plant
WORD ORIGIN Latin *petiolus* little foot

Petipa *n* **Marius** 1819–1910, French ballet dancer and choreographer of the Russian imperial ballet: collaborated with Tchaikovsky on *The Sleeping Beauty* (1890)

Petit *n* **Roland** born 1924, French ballet dancer and choreographer. His innovative ballets include *Carmen* (1949), *Kraanerg* (1969), and *The Blue Angel* (1985); he also choreographed films, such as *Anything Goes* (1956) and *Black Tights* (1960)

petit bourgeois (pet-ee **boor**-zhwah) *n, pl* **petits bourgeois** (pet-ee **boor**-zhwahz) the lower middle class
WORD ORIGIN French

petite (pit-**eat**) *adj* (of a woman) small and dainty
WORD ORIGIN French

petit four (pet-ee **four**) *n, pl* **petits fours** (pet-ee **fours**) a very small fancy cake or biscuit
WORD ORIGIN French, literally: little oven

petition ❶ *n* **1** a written document signed by a large number of people demanding some form of action from a government or other authority **2** any formal request to a higher authority **3** *law* a formal application in writing made to a court asking for some specific judicial action: *she filed a petition for divorce* ▷ *vb* **4** to address or present a petition to (a government or to someone in authority): *he petitioned the Crown for mercy* **5** (foll. by *for*) to seek by petition: *the firm's creditors petitioned for liquidation* **petitioner** *n*
WORD ORIGIN Latin *petere* to seek

petit mal (pet-ee **mal**) *n* a mild form of epilepsy in which there are periods of loss of consciousness for up to 30 seconds
WORD ORIGIN French: little illness

petit point (pet-ee **point**) *n* **1** a small diagonal needlepoint stitch used for fine detail **2** work done with such stitches
WORD ORIGIN French: small point

pet name *n* an affectionate nickname for a close friend or family member

Petöfi *n* **Sándor** 1823–49, Hungarian lyric poet and patriot

petrel *n* a sea bird with a hooked bill and tubular nostrils, such as the albatross, storm petrel, or shearwater
WORD ORIGIN variant of earlier *pitteral*

Petri dish (**pet**-ree) *n* a shallow dish used in laboratories, esp. for producing cultures of bacteria
WORD ORIGIN after J. R. *Petri*, bacteriologist

Petrie *n* Sir (**William Matthew**) **Flinders** 1853–1942, British Egyptologist and archaeologist

petrify *vb* **-fies, -fying, -fied 1** to stun or daze with fear: *he was petrified of going to jail* **2** (of organic material) to turn to stone **3** to make or become unable to change or develop: *a society petrified by outmoded conventions* **petrification** *n*
WORD ORIGIN Greek *petra* stone

petrochemical *n* a substance, such as acetone, obtained from petroleum **petrochemistry** *n*

petrodollar *n* money earned by a country by exporting petroleum

petrol *n* a volatile flammable liquid obtained from petroleum and used as a fuel for internal-combustion engines
WORD ORIGIN see PETROLEUM

petrolatum (pet-rol-**late**-um) *n* a translucent jelly-like substance obtained from petroleum: used as a lubricant and in medicine as an ointment base

petrol bomb *n* a simple grenade consisting of a bottle filled with petrol. A piece of cloth is put in the neck of the bottle and set alight just before the bomb is thrown

petroleum *n* a dark-coloured thick flammable crude oil occurring in sedimentary rocks, consisting mainly of hydrocarbons: the source of petrol and paraffin
WORD ORIGIN Latin *petra* stone + *oleum* oil

petroleum jelly *n* ▸ same as **petrolatum**

petrol station *n Brit* ▸ same as **filling station**

Petronius *n* **Gaius**, known as *Petronius Arbiter*. died 66 AD, Roman satirist, supposed author of the *Satyricon*, a picaresque account of the licentiousness of contemporary society

THESAURUS

pet[1] *n* **2 = favourite**, treasure, darling, jewel, idol, fave (*informal*), apple of your eye, blue-eyed boy or girl (*Brit informal*) ▷ *adj* **5 = favourite**, chosen, special, personal, particular, prized, preferred, favoured, dearest, cherished, fave (*informal*), dear to your heart ▷ *vb* **6 = pamper**, spoil, indulge, cosset, baby, dote on, coddle, mollycoddle, wrap in cotton wool **7 = fondle**, pat, stroke, caress **8** (*informal*) **= cuddle**, kiss, snog (*Brit slang*), smooch (*informal*), neck (*informal*), canoodle (*slang*)

petition *n* **1 = appeal**, round robin, list of signatures **2, 3 = entreaty**, appeal, address, suit, application, request, prayer, plea, invocation, solicitation, supplication ▷ *vb* **4 = appeal**, press, plead, call (upon), ask, urge, sue, pray, beg, crave, solicit, beseech,

DICTIONARY

Petrosian *n* **Tigran** 1929–84, Soviet chess player; world champion (1963–69)

petticoat *n* a woman's underskirt
WORD ORIGIN from *petty* + *coat*

pettifogging *adj* excessively concerned with unimportant detail **pettifogger** *n*
WORD ORIGIN origin unknown

pettish *adj* peevish or fretful **pettishness** *n*
WORD ORIGIN from PET[2]

petty ❶ *adj* **-tier, -tiest 1** trivial or unimportant: *petty details* **2** small-minded: *petty spite* **3** low in importance: *petty criminals* **pettily** *adv* **pettiness** *n*
WORD ORIGIN French *petit* little

petty cash *n* a small cash fund for minor incidental expenses

petty officer *n* a noncommissioned officer in the navy

petulant *adj* unreasonably irritable or peevish **petulance** *n* **petulantly** *adv*
WORD ORIGIN Latin *petulans* bold

petunia *n* a tropical American plant with pink, white, or purple funnel-shaped flowers
WORD ORIGIN obsolete French *petun* variety of tobacco

Pevsner *n* **1 Antoine** 1886–1962, French constructivist sculptor and painter, born in Russia; brother of Naum Gabo **2** Sir **Nikolaus** 1902–83, British architectural historian, born in Germany: his series *Buildings of England* (1951–74) describes every structure of account in the country

pew *n* **1 a** (in a church) a long benchlike seat with a back, used by the congregation **b** (in a church) an enclosed compartment reserved for the use of a family or group **2 take a pew** take a seat
WORD ORIGIN Greek *pous* foot

pewter *n* **1** an alloy containing tin, lead, and sometimes copper and antimony **2** dishes or kitchen utensils made from pewter
WORD ORIGIN Old French *peaultre*

pfennig (fen-ig) *n* a former German monetary unit worth one hundredth of a mark
WORD ORIGIN German: penny

PG indicating a film certified for viewing by anyone, but which contains scenes that may be unsuitable for children, for whom parental guidance is necessary

pH *n* potential of hydrogen; a measure of the acidity or alkalinity of a solution

Phaedrus *n* ?15 BC–?50 AD, Roman author of five books of Latin verse fables, based chiefly on Aesop

phaeton (fate-on) *n* a light four-wheeled horse-drawn carriage with or without a top
WORD ORIGIN from French, after *Phaëthon*, character in Greek myth

phagocyte (fag-go-site) *n* a cell or protozoan that engulfs particles, such as microorganisms
WORD ORIGIN Greek *phagein* to eat + *kutos* vessel

phalanger *n* an Australian marsupial with dense fur and a long tail
WORD ORIGIN Greek *phalaggion* spider's web, referring to its webbed hind toes

phalanx (fal-lanks) *n, pl* **phalanxes** *or* **phalanges** (fal-lan-jeez) **1** any closely grouped mass of people: *a solid phalanx of reporters and photographers* **2** a number of people united for a common purpose **3** an ancient Greek battle formation of infantry in close ranks
WORD ORIGIN Greek

phallic *adj* of or resembling a phallus: *a phallic symbol*

phallus (fal-luss) *n, pl* **-luses** *or* **-li** (-lie) **1** ▸ same as **penis 2** an image of the penis as a symbol of reproductive power
WORD ORIGIN Greek *phallos*

phantasm *n* **1** a phantom **2** an unreal vision; illusion **phantasmal** *adj*
WORD ORIGIN Greek *phantasma*

phantasmagoria *n* a shifting medley of dreamlike figures **phantasmagoric** *adj*
WORD ORIGIN probably from French *fantasmagorie* production of phantoms

phantasy *n, pl* **-sies** *archaic* ▸ same as **fantasy**

phantom ❶ *n* **1** an apparition or spectre **2** the visible representation of something abstract, such as in a dream or hallucination: *the phantom of liberty* ▹ *adj* **3** deceptive or unreal: *she regularly took days off for what her bosses considered phantom illnesses*
WORD ORIGIN Latin *phantasma*

Pharaoh (fare-oh) *n* the title of the ancient Egyptian kings
WORD ORIGIN Egyptian *pr-'o* great house

Pharisee *n* **1** a member of an ancient Jewish sect teaching strict observance of Jewish traditions **2** (*often not cap*) a self-righteous or hypocritical person **Pharisaic** *adj*
WORD ORIGIN Hebrew *pārūsh* separated

pharmaceutical *adj* of or relating to drugs or pharmacy

pharmaceutics *n* ▸ same as **pharmacy** (sense 1)

pharmacist *n* a person qualified to prepare and dispense drugs

pharmacology *n* the science or study of drugs **pharmacological** *adj* **pharmacologist** *n*

pharmacopoeia (far-ma-koh-pee-a) *n* an authoritative book containing a list of medicinal drugs along with their uses, preparation and dosages
WORD ORIGIN Greek *pharmakopoiia* art of preparing drugs

pharmacy *n* **1** the preparation and dispensing of drugs **2** *pl* **-cies** a dispensary
WORD ORIGIN Greek *pharmakon* drug

pharyngitis (far-rin-jite-iss) *n* inflammation of the pharynx, causing a sore throat

pharynx (far-rinks) *n, pl* **pharynges** (far-rin-jeez) *or* **pharynxes** the part of the alimentary canal between the mouth and the oesophagus **pharyngeal** *adj*
WORD ORIGIN Greek *pharunx* throat

phase ❶ *n* **1** any distinct or characteristic stage in a sequence of events: *these two CDs sum up two distinct phases in the singer's career* **2** *astron* one of the recurring shapes of the portion of the moon, Mercury, or Venus illuminated by the sun **3** *physics* a particular stage in a periodic process or phenomenon **4** *physics* **in** *or* **out of phase** (of two waves or signals) reaching or not reaching corresponding phases at the same time ▹ *vb* **phasing, phased 5** to do or introduce gradually: *the redundancies will be phased over two years.* ▸ See also **phase in, phase out**
WORD ORIGIN Greek *phasis* aspect

phase in *vb* to introduce in a gradual or cautious manner: *the scheme was phased in over seven years*

phase out *vb* to discontinue gradually: *rent subsidies are being phased out*

PhD Doctor of Philosophy

pheasant *n* a long-tailed bird with a brightly coloured plumage in the male: native to Asia but introduced elsewhere
WORD ORIGIN Latin *phasianus*

Phelps *n* **Michael** (**Fred**) born 1985, US swimmer, who won six gold medals at the 2004 Olympic Games and

THESAURUS

entreat, adjure, supplicate

petty *adj* **1 = trivial**, inferior, insignificant, little, small, slight, trifling, negligible, unimportant, paltry, measly (*informal*), contemptible, piddling (*informal*), inconsiderable, inessential, nickel-and-dime (*US slang*)
OPPOSITE: important
2 = small-minded, mean, cheap, grudging, shabby, spiteful, stingy, ungenerous, mean-minded
OPPOSITE: broad-minded

phantom *n* **1 = spectre**, ghost, spirit, shade (*literary*), spook (*informal*), apparition, wraith, revenant, phantasm

phase *n* **1 = stage**, time, state, point, position, step, development, condition, period, chapter, aspect, juncture

DICTIONARY

eight gold medals at the 2008 Olympic Games

phenobarbitone *or* **phenobarbital** *n* a sedative used to treat insomnia and epilepsy

phenol *n* a white crystalline derivative of benzene, used as an antiseptic and disinfectant and in the manufacture of resins, explosives, and pharmaceutical substances
WORD ORIGIN Greek *phaino-* shining; because originally prepared from illuminating gas

phenomena *n* ▸a plural of **phenomenon**

phenomenal ⊕ *adj* **1** extraordinary or outstanding: *a phenomenal success* **2** of or relating to a phenomenon **phenomenally** *adv*

phenomenalism *n philosophy* the doctrine that all knowledge comes from sense perception **phenomenalist** *n, adj*

phenomenon ⊕ *n, pl* **-ena** *or* **-enons** **1** anything that can be perceived as an occurrence or fact **2** any remarkable occurrence or person
WORD ORIGIN Greek *phainomenon*, from *phainesthai* to appear

phenotype *n* the physical form of an organism as determined by the interaction of its genetic make-up and its environment

phenyl (fee-nile) *adj* of, containing, or consisting of the monovalent group C_6H_5, derived from benzene: *a phenyl group*

phew *interj* an exclamation of relief, surprise, disbelief, or weariness

phial *n* a small bottle for liquid medicine
WORD ORIGIN Greek *phialē* wide shallow vessel

phil. **1** philharmonic **2** philosophy

philadelphus *n* a shrub grown for its strongly scented showy flowers
WORD ORIGIN Greek *philadelphon*, literally: loving one's brother

philander *vb* (of a man) to flirt or have many casual love affairs with women **philanderer** *n* **philandering** *adj, n*
WORD ORIGIN Greek *philandros* fond of men, used as a name for a lover in literary works

philanthropy *n, pl* **-pies** **1** the practice of helping people less well-off than oneself **2** love of mankind in general **philanthropic** *adj* **philanthropist** *n*
WORD ORIGIN Greek *philanthrōpia* love of mankind

philately (fill-lat-a-lee) *n* the collection and study of postage stamps **philatelist** *n*
WORD ORIGIN Greek *philos* loving + *ateleia* exemption from tax

Philby *n* **1 Harold Adrian Russell,** known as *Kim*. 1912–88, English double agent; defected to the Soviet Union (1963) **2** his father, **H(arry) Saint John** (**Bridger**) 1885–1960, British explorer, civil servant, and Arabist

philharmonic *adj* **1** fond of music ▹*n* **2** a specific choir, orchestra, or musical society: *the Vienna Philharmonic*
WORD ORIGIN French *philharmonique*

Philip I *n* **1** known as *Philip the Handsome* 1478–1506, king of Castile (1506); father of Emperor Charles V and founder of the Hapsburg dynasty in Spain **2** title of Philip II of Spain as king of Portugal

Philip IV *n* known as *Philip the Fair* 1268–1314, king of France (1285–1314): he challenged the power of the papacy, obtaining the elevation of Clement V as pope residing at Avignon (the beginning of the Babylonian captivity of the papacy)

philippic *n* a bitter verbal attack
WORD ORIGIN after the orations of Demosthenes against Philip of Macedon

Philippine *adj, n* ▸same as **Filipino**

Philip the Bold *n* 1342–1404, duke of Burgundy (1363–1404), noted for his courage at Poitiers (1356) in the Hundred Years' War: regent of France for his nephew Charles VI (1368–88, 1392–1404)

Philip the Good *n* 1396–1467, duke of Burgundy (1419–67), under whose rule Burgundy was one of the most powerful states in Europe

Philip the Magnanimous *n* 1504–67, German prince; landgrave of Hesse (1509–67). He helped to crush (1525) the Peasants' Revolt and formed (1531) the League of Schmalkaden, an alliance of German Protestant rulers

Philip V *n* 1683–1746, king of Spain (1700–46) and founder of the Bourbon dynasty in Spain. His accession began the War of Spanish Succession (1701–13)

Philip VI *n* 1293–1350, first Valois king of France (1328–50). Edward III of England claimed his throne, which with other disputes led to the beginning of the Hundred Years' War (1337)

philistine *n* **1** a person who is hostile towards culture and the arts ▹*adj* **2** boorishly uncultured **philistinism** *n*

Philistine *n* a member of the non-Semitic people who inhabited ancient Palestine

Phillip *n* **Arthur** 1738–1814, English naval commander; captain general of the First Fleet, which carried convicts from Portsmouth to Sydney Cove, Australia, where he founded New South Wales

Phillips *n* Captain **Mark** born 1948, English three-day-event horseman; married to Anne, the Princess Royal, divorced 1992

Philo Judaeus *n* ?20 BC–?50 AD, Jewish philosopher, born in Alexandria. He sought to reconcile Judaism with Greek philosophy

philology *n* the science of the structure and development of languages **philological** *adj* **philologist** *n*
WORD ORIGIN Greek *philologia* love of language

philosopher ⊕ *n* **1** a person who studies philosophy **2** a person who remains calm and stoical in the face of difficulties or disappointments

philosopher's stone *n* a substance thought by alchemists to be capable of changing base metals into gold

philosophical ⊕ *or* **philosophic** *adj* **1** of or relating to philosophy or philosophers **2** calm and stoical in the face of difficulties or disappointments **philosophically** *adv*

philosophize *or* **-phise** *vb* **-phizing, -phized** *or* **-phising, -phised** to discuss in a philosophical manner **philosophizer** *or* **-phiser** *n*

philosophy ⊕ *n, pl* **-phies** **1** the academic study of knowledge, thought, and the meaning of life

P

THESAURUS

phenomenal *adj* **1 = extraordinary**, outstanding, remarkable, fantastic, unique, unusual, marvellous, exceptional, notable, sensational, uncommon, singular, miraculous, stellar *(informal)*, prodigious, unparalleled, wondrous *(archaic, literary)* **OPPOSITE:** unremarkable

phenomenon *n* **1 = occurrence**, happening, fact, event, incident, circumstance, episode **2 = wonder**, sensation, spectacle, sight, exception, miracle, marvel, prodigy, rarity, nonpareil

philosopher *n* **1 = thinker**, theorist, sage, wise man, logician, metaphysician, dialectician, seeker after truth

philosophical *or* **philosophic** *adj* **1 = theoretical**, abstract, learned, wise, rational, logical, thoughtful, erudite, sagacious **OPPOSITE:** practical **2 = stoical**, calm, composed, patient, cool, collected, resigned, serene, tranquil, sedate, impassive, unruffled, imperturbable **OPPOSITE:** emotional

philosophy *n* **1, 2 = thought**, reason, knowledge, thinking, reasoning, wisdom, logic, metaphysics **3, 4 = outlook**, values, principles, convictions, thinking, beliefs, doctrine, ideology, viewpoint, tenets, world view, basic idea, attitude to life, Weltanschauung *(German)*

2 the particular doctrines of a specific individual or school relating to these issues: *the philosophy of John Locke* 3 any system of beliefs or values 4 a personal outlook or viewpoint
WORD ORIGIN Greek *philosophia* love of wisdom

philtre *or US* **philter** *n* a drink supposed to arouse desire
WORD ORIGIN Greek *philtron* love potion

phishing *n* the practice of using fraudulent e-mails and copies of legitimate websites to extract financial data from computer users for criminal purposes

Phiz *n* real name *Hablot Knight Browne* 1815–82, English painter, noted for his illustrations for Dickens' novels

phlebitis (fleb-bite-iss) *n* inflammation of a vein, usually in the legs **phlebitic** *adj*
WORD ORIGIN Greek *phleps* vein

phlegm ⓣ (flem) *n* 1 the thick yellowish substance secreted by the walls of the respiratory tract 2 apathy or stolidity 3 calmness **phlegmy** *adj*
WORD ORIGIN Greek *phlegma*

phlegmatic (fleg-mat-ik) *adj* having an unemotional disposition

phloem (flow-em) *n bot* the plant tissue that acts as a path for the distribution of food substances to all parts of the plant
WORD ORIGIN Greek *phloos* bark

phlox *n, pl* **phlox** *or* **phloxes** a plant with clusters of white, red, or purple flowers
WORD ORIGIN Greek, literally: flame

phobia *n psychiatry* an intense and irrational fear of a given situation or thing **phobic** *adj, n*
WORD ORIGIN Greek *phobos* fear

Phoenician (fon-nee-shun) *adj* 1 of Phoenicia, an ancient E Mediterranean country ▷*n* 2 a person from Phoenicia

phoenix *n* a legendary Arabian bird said to set fire to itself and rise anew from the ashes every 500 years
WORD ORIGIN Greek *phoinix*

Phomvihane *n* **Kaysone** 1920–92, Laotian Communist statesman; prime minister of Laos (1975–91); president (1991–92)

phone *n, vb* **phoning, phoned** ▸short for **telephone**

phonecard *n* a card used instead of coins to operate certain public telephones

phone-in *n* a radio or television programme in which telephone questions or comments from the public are broadcast live as part of a discussion

phoneme *n linguistics* one of the set of speech sounds in any given language that serve to distinguish one word from another **phonemic** *adj*
WORD ORIGIN Greek *phōnēma* sound, speech

phonemics *n* the classification and analysis of the phonemes of a language

phonetic *adj* 1 of phonetics 2 denoting any perceptible distinction between one speech sound and another 3 conforming to pronunciation: *phonetic spelling* **phonetically** *adv*
WORD ORIGIN Greek *phōnein* to make sounds, speak

phonetics *n* the study of speech processes, including the production, perception, and analysis of speech sounds

phoney *or esp. US* **phony** *informal adj* **-nier, -niest** 1 not genuine: *a phoney Belgian 50-franc coin* 2 (of a person) insincere or pretentious ▷*n, pl* **-neys** *or esp. US* **-nies** 3 an insincere or pretentious person 4 something that is not genuine
WORD ORIGIN origin unknown

phonograph *n* 1 an early form of record player capable of recording and reproducing sound on wax cylinders 2 *US & Canad* a record player
WORD ORIGIN Greek *phonē* sound + *graphein* to write

phonology *n, pl* **-gies** 1 the study of the sound system in a language 2 such a sound system **phonological** *adj*
WORD ORIGIN Greek *phonē* sound, voice + -LOGY

phooey *interj informal* an exclamation of scorn or contempt
WORD ORIGIN probably variant of *phew*

phosgene (foz-jean) *n* a poisonous gas used in warfare
WORD ORIGIN Greek *phōs* light + *-genēs* born

phosphate *n* 1 any salt or ester of any phosphoric acid 2 (*often pl*) chemical fertilizer containing phosphorous compounds **phosphatic** *adj*

phosphor *n* a substance capable of emitting light when irradiated with particles of electromagnetic radiation
WORD ORIGIN Greek *phōsphoros* phosphorus

phosphoresce *vb* **-rescing, -resced** to exhibit phosphorescence

phosphorescence *n* 1 *physics* a fluorescence that persists after the bombarding radiation producing it has stopped 2 the light emitted in phosphorescence **phosphorescent** *adj*

phosphoric *adj* of or containing phosphorus in the pentavalent state

phosphorous *adj* of or containing phosphorus in the trivalent state

phosphorus *n chem* a toxic flammable nonmetallic element which appears luminous in the dark. It exists in two forms, white and red. Symbol: P
WORD ORIGIN Greek *phōsphoros* light-bringing

photo *n, pl* **-tos** ▸short for **photograph**

photo- *combining form* 1 of or produced by light: *photosynthesis* 2 indicating a photographic process: *photolithography*
WORD ORIGIN Greek *phōs, phōt-* light

photocell *n* a cell which produces a current or voltage when exposed to light or other electromagnetic radiation

photocopier *n* a machine using light-sensitive photographic materials to reproduce written, printed, or graphic work

photocopy *n, pl* **-copies** 1 a photographic reproduction of written, printed, or graphic work ▷*vb* **-copies, -copying, -copied** 2 to reproduce on photographic material

photoelectric *adj* of or concerned with electric or electronic effects caused by light or other electromagnetic radiation **photoelectricity** *n*

P

THESAURUS

phlegm *n* **1 = mucus**, catarrh, sputum, mucous secretion

photograph *n* **1 = picture**, photo (*informal*), shot, image, print, slide, snap (*informal*), snapshot, transparency, likeness ▷ *vb* **2 = take a picture of**, record, film, shoot, snap (*informal*), take (someone's) picture, capture on film, get a shot of

photographic *adj* **1 = pictorial**, visual, graphic, cinematic, filmic **2 = accurate**, minute, detailed, exact, precise, faithful, retentive

phrase *n* **1, 2 = expression**, saying, remark, motto, construction, tag, quotation, maxim, idiom, utterance, adage, dictum, way of speaking, group of words, locution ▷ *vb* **4 = express**, say, word, put, term, present, voice, frame, communicate, convey, utter, couch, formulate, put into words

physical *adj* **1 = corporal**, fleshly, bodily, carnal, somatic, corporeal **2 = earthly**, fleshly, mortal, incarnate, unspiritual **2, 3 = material**, real, substantial, natural, solid, visible, sensible, tangible, palpable

physician *n* **1 = doctor**, specialist, doc (*informal*), healer, medic (*informal*), general practitioner, medical practitioner, medico (*informal*), doctor of medicine, sawbones (*slang*), G.P., M.D.

photoengraving *n* **1** a photomechanical process for producing letterpress printing plates **2** a print made from such a plate **photoengrave** *vb*

photo finish *n* a finish of a race in which contestants are so close that a photograph is needed to decide the result

Photofit *n trademark* a picture of someone wanted by the police which has been made by combining photographs of different facial features resembling those of the wanted person

photoflash *n* ▸ same as **flashbulb**

photoflood *n* a highly incandescent electric lamp used for indoor photography and television

photogenic *adj* **1** (esp. of a person) always looking attractive in photographs **2** *biol* producing or emitting light

photograph ❶ *n* **1** a picture made by the chemical action of light on sensitive film ▹ *vb* **2** to take a photograph of

photographic ❶ *adj* **1** of or like photography or a photograph **2** (of a person's memory) able to retain facts or appearances in precise detail **photographically** *adv*

photography *n* **1** the process of recording images on sensitized material by the action of light **2** the practice of taking photographs **photographer** *n*

photogravure *n* a process in which an etched metal plate for printing is produced by photography
WORD ORIGIN PHOTO- + French *gravure* engraving

photolithography *n* a lithographic printing process using photographically made plates **photolithographer** *n*

photometer (foe-**tom**-it-er) *n* an instrument used to measure the intensity of light

photometry (foe-**tom**-it-tree) *n* the branch of physics concerned with the measurement of the intensity of light **photometrist** *n*

photomontage (foe-toe-mon-**tahzh**) *n* **1** the combination of several photographs to produce one picture **2** a picture produced in this way

photon *n physics* a quantum of electromagnetic radiation energy, such as light, having both particle and wave behaviour

photosensitive *adj* sensitive to electromagnetic radiation, esp. light

Photoshop *n* **1** *trademark* a software application for managing and editing digital images ▹ *vb* **2** *informal* to alter (a digital image) using Photoshop or a similar application

photostat *n* **1** a type of photocopying machine or process **2** any copy made by such a machine ▹ *vb* **-statting, -statted** *or* **-stating, -stated 3** to make a photostat copy (of)

photosynthesis *n* (in plants) the process by which a green plant uses sunlight to build up carbohydrate reserves **photosynthesize** *or* **-sise** *vb* **photosynthetic** *adj*

phototropism (foe-toe-**trope**-iz-zum) *n* the growth of plants towards a source of light **phototropic** *adj*
WORD ORIGIN PHOTO- + Greek *tropos* turn

phrasal verb *n* a phrase that consists of a verb plus an adverb or preposition, esp. one whose meaning cannot be deduced from its parts, such as *take in* meaning *deceive*

phrase ❶ *n* **1** a group of words forming a unit of meaning in a sentence **2** an idiomatic or original expression **3** *music* a small group of notes forming a coherent unit of melody ▹ *vb* **phrasing, phrased 4** to express orally or in a phrase: *I could have phrased that better* **5** *music* to divide (a melodic line or part) into musical phrases, esp. in performance **phrasal** *adj*
WORD ORIGIN Greek *phrasis* speech

phrase book *n* a book containing frequently used expressions and their equivalent in a foreign language

phraseology *n, pl* **-gies** the manner in which words or phrases are used

phrasing *n* **1** the exact words used to say or write something **2** the way in which someone who is performing a piece of music or reading aloud divides up the work being performed by pausing slightly in appropriate places

phrenology *n* (formerly) the study of the shape and size of the skull as a means of finding out a person's character and mental ability **phrenological** *adj* **phrenologist** *n*
WORD ORIGIN Greek *phrēn* mind + -LOGY

Phryne *n* real name *Muesarete* 4th century BC, Greek courtesan; lover of Praxiteles and model for Apelles' painting *Aphrodite Rising from the Waves*

phut *informal n* **1** a representation of a muffled explosive sound ▹ *adv* **2 go phut** to break down or collapse
WORD ORIGIN imitative

phylactery *n, pl* **-teries** *judaism* either of the pair of square cases containing biblical passages, worn by Jewish men on the left arm and head during weekday morning prayers
WORD ORIGIN Greek *phulaktērion* safeguard

phylum *n, pl* **-la** *biol* one of the major groups into which the animal and plant kingdoms are divided, containing one or more classes
WORD ORIGIN Greek *phulon* race

physical ❶ *adj* **1** of the body, as distinguished from the mind or spirit **2** of material things or nature: *the physical world* **3** of or concerned with matter and energy **4** of or relating to physics **physically** *adv*

physical education *n* training and practice in sports and gymnastics

physical geography *n* the branch of geography that deals with the natural features of the earth's surface

physical jerks *pl n Austral & Brit informal* repetitive keep-fit exercises

physical science *n* any of the sciences concerned with nonliving matter, such as physics, chemistry, astronomy, and geology

physician ❶ *n* **1** a medical doctor **2** *archaic* a healer
WORD ORIGIN Greek *phusis* nature

physicist *n* a person versed in or studying physics

physics *n* **1** the branch of science concerned with the properties of matter and energy and the relationships between them **2** physical properties of behaviour: *the physics of the electron*
WORD ORIGIN translation of Greek *ta phusika* natural things

physio *n* **1** ▸ short for **physiotherapy** **2** *pl* **physios** ▸ short for **physiotherapist**

physiognomy (fiz-ee-**on**-om-ee) *n* **1** a person's face considered as an indication of personality **2** the outward appearance of something: *the changed physiognomy of the forests*
WORD ORIGIN Greek *phusis* nature + *gnōmōn* judge

physiography *n* ▸ same as **physical geography**
WORD ORIGIN Greek *phusis* nature + -GRAPHY

physiology *n* **1** the branch of science concerned with the functioning of organisms **2** the processes and functions of all or part of an organism **physiologist** *n* **physiological** *adj*
WORD ORIGIN Greek *phusis* nature + -LOGY

physiotherapy *n* the treatment of disease or injury by physical means, such as massage or exercises, rather than by drugs **physiotherapist** *n*
WORD ORIGIN *physio-* (prefix) physical + *therapy*

physique *n* person's bodily build and muscular development
WORD ORIGIN French

pi *n, pl* **pis 1** the 16th letter in the Greek alphabet (Π, π) **2** *maths* a number that is the ratio of the circumference of a circle to its diameter; approximate value: 3.141 592.... Symbol: π

Piaget *n* **Jean** 1896–1980, Swiss psychologist, noted for his work on the development of the cognitive functions in children

pianissimo *adj, adv music* to be performed very quietly
WORD ORIGIN Italian

P

DICTIONARY

pianist *n* a person who plays the piano

piano[1] *n, pl* **-anos** a musical instrument played by depressing keys that cause hammers to strike strings and produce audible vibrations
WORD ORIGIN short for *pianoforte*

piano[2] *adj, adv music* to be performed softly
WORD ORIGIN Italian

Piano *n* **Renzo** born 1937, Italian architect; buildings include the Pompidou Centre, Paris (1977; with Richard Rogers) and the Potsdamer Platz redevelopment, Berlin (1998)

piano accordion *n* an accordion in which the right hand plays a piano-like keyboard **piano accordionist** *n*

pianoforte (pee-ann-oh-for-tee) *n* ▸ the full name for **piano**[1]
WORD ORIGIN Italian *piano e forte* soft and loud

Pianola (pee-an-**oh**-la) *n trademark* a type of mechanical piano, the music for which is encoded in perforations in a paper roll

piazza *n* **1** a large open square in an Italian town **2** *chiefly Brit* a covered passageway or gallery
WORD ORIGIN Italian: marketplace

pibroch (**pee**-brok) *n* a form of music for Scottish bagpipes, consisting of a theme and variations
WORD ORIGIN Gaelic *piobaireachd*

pic *n, pl* **pics** *or* **pix** *informal* a photograph or illustration

pica (**pie**-ka) *n* **1** a size of printer's type giving 6 lines to the inch **2** a size of typewriter type that has 10 characters to the inch
WORD ORIGIN Latin *pica* magpie; sense connection obscure

Picabia *n* **Francis** 1879–1953, French painter, designer, and writer, associated with the cubist, Dadaist, and surrealist movements

picador *n bullfighting* a horseman who wounds the bull with a lance to weaken it
WORD ORIGIN Spanish

Picard *n* **Jean** 1620–82, French astronomer. He was the first to make a precise measurement of a longitude line, enabling him to estimate the earth's radius

picaresque *adj* of or relating to a type of fiction in which the hero, a rogue, goes through a series of episodic adventures
WORD ORIGIN Spanish *pícaro* a rogue

picayune (pick-a-**yoon**) *US & Canad informal adj* **1** of small value or importance **2** mean or petty ▹ *n* **3** any coin of little value, such as a five-cent piece **4** an unimportant person or thing
WORD ORIGIN French *picaillon* coin from Piedmont

piccalilli *n* a pickle of mixed vegetables in a mustard sauce
WORD ORIGIN origin unknown

piccanin *n S African, offensive* a Black African child
WORD ORIGIN variant of *piccaninny*

piccaninny *or esp. US* **pickaninny** *n, pl* **-nies** *offensive* a small Black or Aboriginal child
WORD ORIGIN perhaps from Portuguese *pequenino* tiny one

Piccard *n* **1 Auguste** 1884–1962, Swiss physicist, whose study of cosmic rays led to his pioneer balloon ascents in the stratosphere (1931–32) **2** his twin brother, **Jean Félix** 1884–1963, US chemist and aeronautical engineer, born in Switzerland, noted for his balloon ascent into the stratosphere (1934)

piccolo *n, pl* **-los** a woodwind instrument an octave higher than the flute
WORD ORIGIN Italian: small

pick[1] ❶ *vb* **1** to choose or select **2** to gather (fruit, berries, or crops) from (a tree, bush, or field) **3** to remove loose particles from: *she picked some bits of fluff off her sleeve* **4** (foll. by *at*) to nibble (at) without appetite **5** to provoke (an argument or fight) deliberately **6** to separate (strands or fibres), as in weaving **7** to steal from (someone's pocket) **8** to open (a lock) with an instrument other than a key **9** to make (one's way) carefully on foot: *they picked their way through the rubble* **10 pick and choose** to select fastidiously or fussily ▹ *n* **11** choice: *take your pick* **12** the best: *the pick of the country's young cricketers* ▸ See also **pick off, pick on**, etc.
WORD ORIGIN Middle English *piken*

pick[2] *n* **1** a tool with a handle and a long curved steel head, used for loosening soil or breaking rocks **2** any tool used for picking, such as an ice pick or toothpick **3** a plectrum ▹ *vb* **4** to pierce or break up (a hard surface) with a pick
WORD ORIGIN perhaps a variant of PIKE[2]

pickaback *n, adv* ▸ same as **piggyback**

pickaxe *or US* **pickax** *n* a large pick

Pickering *n* **1 Edward Charles** 1846–1919, US astronomer, who invented the meridian photometer **2** his brother, **William Henry** 1858–1938, US astronomer, who discovered Phoebe, the ninth satellite of Saturn, and predicted (1919) the existence and position of Pluto

picket ❶ *n* **1** a person or group standing outside a workplace to dissuade strikebreakers from entering **2** a small unit of troops posted to give early warning of attack **3** a pointed stake that is driven into the ground to support a fence ▹ *vb* **-eting, -eted 4** to act as pickets outside (a workplace)
WORD ORIGIN Old French *piquer* to prick

picket fence *n* a fence consisting of pickets driven into the ground

picket line *n* a line of people acting as pickets

Pickford *n* **Mary,** real name *Gladys Mary Smith.* 1893–1979, US actress in silent films, born in Canada

pickings *pl n* money or profits acquired easily

pickle ❶ *n* **1** (*often pl*) food, esp. vegetables preserved in vinegar or brine **2** a liquid or marinade, such as spiced vinegar, for preserving vegetables, meat, or fish **3** *informal* an awkward or difficult situation: *to be in a pickle; they are in a pickle over what to do with toxic waste* ▹ *vb* **-ling, -led 4** to preserve or treat in a pickling liquid
WORD ORIGIN probably Middle Dutch *pekel*

pickled *adj* **1** (of food) preserved in a pickling liquid **2** *informal* drunk

pick-me-up *n informal* a tonic, esp. a special drink taken as a stimulant

pick off *vb* to aim at and shoot (people or things) one by one

THESAURUS

pick[1] *vb* **1 = select**, choose, identify, elect, nominate, sort out, specify, opt for, single out, mark out, plump for, hand-pick, decide upon, cherry-pick, fix upon, settle on *or* upon, sift out, flag up OPPOSITE: reject **2 = gather**, cut, pull, collect, take in, harvest, pluck, garner, cull **5 = provoke**, start, cause, stir up, incite, instigate, foment **8 = open**, force, crack (*informal*), break into, break open, prise open, jemmy (*informal*) ▹ *n* **11 = choice**, decision, choosing, option, selection, preference **12 = best**, prime, finest, tops (*slang*), choicest, flower, prize, elect, pride, elite, cream, jewel in the crown, crème de la crème (*French*)

picket *n* **1 = protester**, demonstrator, picketer, flying picket **2 = lookout**, watch, guard, patrol, scout, spotter, sentry, sentinel, vedette (*military*) **3 = stake**, post, pale, paling, peg, upright, palisade, stanchion ▹ *vb* **4 = blockade**, boycott, demonstrate outside

pickle *n* **1 = chutney**, relish, piccalilli **3** (*informal*) **= predicament**, spot (*informal*), fix (*informal*), difficulty, bind (*informal*), jam (*informal*), dilemma, scrape (*informal*), hot water (*informal*), uphill (*S African*), quandary, tight spot ▹ *vb* **4 = preserve**, marinade, keep, cure, steep

P

DICTIONARY

pick on *vb* to continually treat someone unfairly

pick out *vb* **1** to select for use or special consideration: *she picked out a wide gold wedding ring* **2** to distinguish (an object from its surroundings), such as in painting: *the wall panels are light brown, with their edges picked out in gold* **3** to recognize (a person or thing): *the culprit was picked out at a police identification parade* **4** to play (a tune) tentatively, as by ear

pickpocket *n* a person who steals from the pockets of others in public places

pick up *vb* **1** to lift or raise: *he picked up his glass* **2** to obtain or purchase: *a couple of pictures she had picked up in a flea market in Paris* **3** to improve in health or condition: *the tourist trade has picked up after the slump caused by the Gulf War* **4** to learn as one goes along: *she had a good ear and picked up languages quickly* **5** to raise (oneself) after a fall or setback: *she picked herself up and got on with her life* **6** to resume; return to **7** to accept the responsibility for paying (a bill) **8** to collect or give a lift to (passengers or goods) **9** *informal* to become acquainted with for a sexual purpose **10** *informal* to arrest **11** to receive (sounds or signals)

pick-up *n* **1** a small truck with an open body used for light deliveries **2** *informal* a casual acquaintance made for a sexual purpose **3** *informal* **a** a stop to collect passengers or goods **b** the people or things collected **4** a device which converts vibrations into electrical signals, such as that to which a record player stylus is attached

picky *adj* **pickier, pickiest** *Brit, Austral & NZ informal* fussy; finicky

picnic ❶ *n* **1** an excursion on which people bring food to be eaten in the open air **2** an informal meal eaten out-of-doors **3 no picnic** *informal* a hard or disagreeable task ▷ *vb* **-nicking, -nicked 4** to eat or take part in a picnic **picnicker** *n*

WORD ORIGIN French *piquenique*

pico- *combining form* denoting 10^{-12}: *picofarad*

WORD ORIGIN Spanish *pico* small quantity

Pico della Mirandola *n* Count **Giovanni** 1463–94, Italian Platonist philosopher. His attempt to reconcile the ideas of classical, Christian, and Arabic writers in a collection of 900 theses, prefaced by his *Oration on the Dignity of Man* (1486), was condemned by the pope

picot (peek-oh) *n* any of a pattern of small loops, for example on lace

Pict *n* a member of any of the peoples who lived in N Britain in the first to the fourth centuries AD **Pictish** *adj*

WORD ORIGIN Late Latin *Picti* painted men

pictograph *n* **1** a picture or symbol standing for a word or group of words, as in written Chinese **2** Also called: **pictogram** a chart on which symbols are used to represent values **pictographic** *adj*

WORD ORIGIN Latin *pingere* to paint

pictorial *adj* **1** relating to or expressed by pictures ▷ *n* **2** a periodical containing many pictures

WORD ORIGIN Latin *pingere* to paint

picture ❶ *n* **1** a visual representation produced on a surface, such as in a photograph or painting **2** a mental image: *neither had any clear picture of whom they were looking for* **3** a description or account of a situation considered as an observable scene: *the reports do not provide an accurate picture of the spread of AIDS* **4** a person or thing resembling another: *he is the picture of a perfect host* **5** a person or scene typifying a particular state: *his face was a picture of dejection* **6** the image on a television screen **7** a cinema film **8 in the picture** informed about a situation **9 the pictures** a cinema or film show ▷ *vb* **-turing, -tured 10** to visualize or imagine **11** to describe or depict vividly: *a documentary that had pictured the police as good-natured dolts* **12** to put in a picture or make a picture of: *the women pictured above are all the same age*

WORD ORIGIN Latin *pingere* to paint

picture rail *n* the rail near the top of a wall from which pictures are hung

picturesque ❶ *adj* **1** visually pleasing, as in being striking or quaint: *a small picturesque harbour* **2** (of language) graphic or vivid

WORD ORIGIN French *pittoresque*

picture window *n* a large window with a single pane of glass, usually facing a view

piddle *vb* **-dling, -dled 1** *informal* to urinate **2 piddle about** *or* **around** *or* **away** to spend (one's time) aimlessly: *we have been piddling around for seven months*

WORD ORIGIN origin unknown

piddling *adj informal* petty or trivial: *piddling amounts of money*

pidgin *n* a language made up of elements of two or more languages and used between the speakers of the languages involved

WORD ORIGIN supposed Chinese pronunciation of *business*

pidgin English *n* a pidgin in which one of the languages involved is English

pie *n* **1** a sweet or savoury filling baked in pastry **2 pie in the sky** illusory hope or promise of some future good

WORD ORIGIN origin unknown

piebald *adj* **1** marked in two colours, esp. black and white ▷ *n* **2** a black-and-white horse

WORD ORIGIN dialect *pie* magpie + BALD

piece ❶ *n* **1** a separate bit or part **2** an instance or occurrence: *a piece of luck* **3** an example or specimen of a style or type: *each piece of furniture is crafted from native red pine by traditional methods* **4** a literary, musical, or artistic composition **5** a coin: *a fifty-pence piece* **6** a firearm or cannon **7** a small object used in playing various games: *a chess piece* **8 go to pieces** (of a person) to lose control of oneself; have a breakdown ▷ *vb* **piecing,**

P

THESAURUS

picnic *n* **1, 2 = excursion**, fête champêtre *(French)*, barbecue, barbie *(informal)*, cookout *(US & Canad)*, alfresco meal, déjeuner sur l'herbe *(French)*, clambake *(US & Canad)*, outdoor meal, outing

picture *n* **1a = representation**, drawing, painting, portrait, image, print, illustration, sketch, portrayal, engraving, likeness, effigy, delineation, similitude **1b = photograph**, photo, still, shot, image, print, frame, slide, snap, exposure, portrait, snapshot, transparency, enlargement **2 = idea**, vision, concept, impression, notion, visualization, mental picture, mental image **3 = description**, impression, explanation, report, account, image, sketch, depiction, re-creation **5 = personification**, model, embodiment, soul, essence, archetype, epitome, perfect example, exemplar, quintessence, living example **7 = film**, movie *(US informal)*, flick *(slang)*, feature film, motion picture ▷ *vb* **10 = imagine**, see, envision, visualize, conceive of, fantasize about, conjure up an image of, see in the mind's eye **11 = represent**, show, describe, draw, paint, illustrate, portray, sketch, render, depict, delineate **12 = show**, photograph, capture on film

picturesque *adj* **1 = interesting**, pretty, beautiful, attractive, charming, scenic, quaint
OPPOSITE: unattractive
2 = vivid, striking, graphic, colourful, memorable **OPPOSITE:** dull

piece *n* **1a = bit**, section, slice, part, share, division, block, length, quantity, scrap, segment, portion, fragment, fraction, chunk, wedge, shred, slab, mouthful, morsel, wodge *(Brit informal)* **1b = component**, part, section, bit, unit, segment, constituent, module **4a = composition**, work, production, opus **4b = work of art**, work, creation

pier *n* **1 = jetty**, wharf, quay,

DICTIONARY

pieced **9** (often foll. by *together*) to fit or assemble bit by bit **10** (often foll. by *up*) to patch or make up (a garment) by adding pieces
WORD ORIGIN Middle English *pece*
pièce de résistance (pyess de ray-zeest-onss) *n* the most outstanding item in a series
WORD ORIGIN French
piece goods *pl n* goods, esp. fabrics, made in standard widths and lengths
piecemeal *adv* **1** bit by bit; gradually ▹*adj* **2** fragmentary or unsystematic: *a piecemeal approach*
WORD ORIGIN Middle English *pece* piece + *-mele* a measure
piece of eight *n, pl* **pieces of eight** a former Spanish coin worth eight reals
piecework *n* work paid for according to the quantity produced
pie chart *n* a circular graph divided into sectors proportional to the sizes of the quantities represented
pied *adj* having markings of two or more colours
WORD ORIGIN dialect *pie* magpie
pied-à-terre (pyay-da-tair) *n, pl* **pieds-à-terre** (pyay-da-tair) a flat or other lodging for occasional use
WORD ORIGIN French, literally: foot on (the) ground
pie-eyed *adj slang* drunk
Pienaar *n* **(Jacobus) Francois** born 1967, South African Rugby Union footballer; captain of the South African team that won the Rugby World Cup in 1995
pier ❶ *n* **1** a structure with a deck that is built out over water and used as a landing place or promenade **2** a pillar or support that bears heavy loads **3** the part of a wall between two adjacent openings
WORD ORIGIN Middle English *per*
pierce ❶ *vb* **piercing, pierced** **1** to make a hole in (something) with a sharp point **2** to force (a way) through (something) **3** (of light) to shine through (darkness) **4** (of sounds or cries) to sound sharply through (the silence) **5** to penetrate: *the cold pierced the air* **piercing** *adj*
WORD ORIGIN Old French *percer*
pier glass *n* a tall narrow mirror, designed to hang on the wall between windows
Piero della Francesca *n* ?1420–92, Italian painter, noted particularly for his frescoes of the *Legend of the True Cross* in San Francesco, Arezzo
Piero di Cosimo *n* 1462–1521, Italian painter, noted for his mythological works
Pierrot (pier-roe) *n* a male character from French pantomime with a whitened face, white costume, and pointed hat
pietism *n* exaggerated piety
Pietro da Cortona *n* real name *Pietro Berrettini* 1596–1669, Italian baroque painter and architect
piety *n, pl* **-ties** **1** dutiful devotion to God and observance of religious principles **2** the quality of being pious **3** a pious action or saying
WORD ORIGIN Latin *pietas*
piezoelectric effect (pie-eez-oh-ill-ek-trik) *or* **piezoelectricity** *n physics* **a** the production of electricity by applying a mechanical stress to certain crystals **b** the converse effect in which stress is produced in a crystal as a result of an applied voltage
WORD ORIGIN Greek *piezein* to press
piffle *n informal* nonsense
WORD ORIGIN origin unknown
piffling *adj informal* worthless; trivial
pig ❶ *n* **1** a mammal with a long head, a snout, and bristle-covered skin, which is kept and killed for pork, ham, and bacon ▸ Related adjective: **porcine** **2** *informal* a dirty, greedy, or bad-mannered person **3** *offensive slang* a policeman **4** a mass of metal cast into a simple shape **5** *Brit informal* something that is difficult or unpleasant: *the coast is a pig for little boats* **6** **a pig in a poke** something bought or received without previous sight or knowledge **7** **make a pig of oneself** *informal* to overeat ▹*vb* **pigging, pigged** **8** (of a sow) to give birth **9** (often foll. by *out*) *slang* to eat greedily or to excess: *she had pigged out on pizza before the show*
WORD ORIGIN Middle English *pigge*
pigeon¹ *n* **1** a bird which has a heavy body, small head, and short legs, and is usually grey in colour **2** *slang* a victim or dupe
WORD ORIGIN Old French *pijon* young dove
pigeon² *n informal* concern or responsibility: *this is our pigeon – there's nothing to keep you*
WORD ORIGIN from *pidgin*
pigeonhole *n* **1** a small compartment, such as in a bureau, for filing papers ▹*vb* **-holing, -holed** **2** to classify or categorize **3** to put aside
pigeon-toed *adj* with the toes or feet turned inwards
piggery *n, pl* **-geries** a place where pigs are kept
piggish *adj* **1** like a pig in appetite or manners **2** stubborn **piggishness** *n*
Piggott *n* **Lester (Keith)** born 1935, English flat-racing jockey: he won the Derby nine times
piggy *n, pl* **-gies** **1** ▸ a child's word for a **pig** ▹*adj* **-gier, -giest** **2** ▸ same as **piggish**
piggyback *or* **pickaback** *n* **1** a ride on the back and shoulders of another person ▹*adv, adj* **2** on the back and shoulders of another person
piggy bank *n* a child's bank shaped like a pig with a slot for coins
pig-headed *adj* stupidly stubborn
pig iron *n* crude iron produced in a blast furnace and poured into moulds
piglet *n* a young pig
pigment ❶ *n* **1** any substance which gives colour to paint or dye **2** a substance which occurs in plant or animal tissue and produces a characteristic colour **pigmentary** *adj*
WORD ORIGIN Latin *pigmentum*
pigmentation *n* colouring in plants, animals, or humans, caused by the presence of pigments
Pigmy *n, pl* **-mies** ▸ same as **Pygmy**
pigskin *n* **1** the skin of the domestic pig **2** leather made of this skin **3** *US & Canad informal* a football
pigsty *or US & Canad* **pigpen** *n, pl* **-sties** **1** a pen for pigs **2** an untidy place
pigswill *n* waste food or other edible matter fed to pigs
pigtail *n* a plait of hair or one of two plaits on either side of the face
pike¹ *n, pl* **pike** *or* **pikes** a large predatory freshwater fish with a broad flat snout, strong teeth, and a long body covered with small scales
WORD ORIGIN Old English *pīc* point, from the shape of its jaw
pike² *n* a medieval weapon consisting of a metal spearhead on a long pole **pikeman** *n*
WORD ORIGIN Old English *pīc* point
pikelet *n Austral & NZ* a small thick pancake
piker *n Austral & NZ slang* shirker
pikestaff *n* **1** the wooden handle of a pike **2** **plain as a pikestaff** very obvious or noticeable
pikey *n Brit slang, derogatory* **1** a gypsy or vagrant **2** a member of the underclass
pilaster *n* a shallow rectangular column attached to the face of a wall **pilastered** *adj*
WORD ORIGIN Latin *pila* pillar
pilau *or* **pilaf** *n* a Middle Eastern dish, consisting of rice flavoured with

P

THESAURUS

promenade, landing place **2 = pillar**, support, post, column, pile, piling, upright, buttress
pierce *vb* **1 = penetrate**, stab, spike, enter, bore, probe, drill, run through, lance, puncture, prick, transfix, stick into, perforate, impale
pig *n* **1 = hog**, sow, boar, piggy, swine, grunter, piglet, porker, shoat
2a *(informal)* **= slob**, hog *(informal)*, guzzler *(slang)*, glutton, gannet *(informal)*, sloven, greedy guts *(slang)*
2b *(informal)* **= brute**, monster, scoundrel, animal, beast, rogue, swine, rotter, boor
pigment *n* **1 = colour**, colouring, paint, stain, dye, tint, tincture, colouring matter, colorant, dyestuff

DICTIONARY

spices and cooked in stock, to which meat, poultry, or fish may be added
WORD ORIGIN Turkish *pilāw*

pilchard *n* a small edible sea fish of the herring family, with a rounded body covered with large scales
WORD ORIGIN origin unknown

pile[1] ⓣ *n* **1** a collection of objects laid on top of one another **2** *informal* a large amount: *boxing has made him a pile of money; I've got piles of work to do* **3** ▸ same as **pyre** **4** a large building or group of buildings **5** *physics* a nuclear reactor ▹ *vb* **piling, piled** **6** (often foll. by *up*) to collect or be collected into a pile: *snow piled up in the drive* **7** (foll. by *in, into, off* or *out* etc.) to move in a group, often in a hurried manner: *the crew piled into the van* **8** **pile it on** *informal* to exaggerate ▸ See also **pile up**
WORD ORIGIN Latin *pila* stone pier

pile[2] ⓣ *n* a long heavy beam driven into the ground as a foundation for a structure
WORD ORIGIN Latin *pilum*

pile[3] ⓣ *n* the fibres in a fabric that stand up or out from the weave, such as in carpeting or velvet
WORD ORIGIN Latin *pilus* hair

pile-driver *n* a machine that drives piles into the ground

piles *pl n* swollen veins in the rectum; haemorrhoids
WORD ORIGIN Latin *pilae* balls

pile up *vb* **1** to gather or be gathered in a pile ▹ *n* **pile-up** **2** *informal* a traffic accident involving several vehicles

pilfer *vb* to steal (minor items) in small quantities
WORD ORIGIN Old French *pelfre* booty

pilgrim ⓣ *n* **1** a person who journeys to a holy place **2** any wayfarer
WORD ORIGIN Latin *peregrinus* foreign

pilgrimage ⓣ *n* **1** a journey to a shrine or other holy place **2** a journey or long search made for sentimental reasons: *a sentimental pilgrimage to the poet's birthplace*

Pilgrim Fathers *pl n* the English Puritans who founded Plymouth Colony in SE Massachusetts (1620)

pill ⓣ *n* **1** a small mass of medicine intended to be swallowed whole **2** **the pill** *informal* an oral contraceptive taken by a woman **3** something unpleasant that must be endured: *her reinstatement was a bitter pill to swallow; the pill was sweetened by a reduction in interest*
WORD ORIGIN Latin *pilula* a little ball

pillage *vb* **-laging, -laged** **1** to steal property violently, often in war ▹ *n* **2** the act of pillaging **3** something obtained by pillaging; booty
WORD ORIGIN Old French *piller* to despoil

pillar ⓣ *n* **1** an upright support of stone, brick, or metal; column **2** something resembling this: *a pillar of smoke* **3** a prominent supporter or member: *a pillar of society* **4** **from pillar to post** from one place to another
WORD ORIGIN Latin *pila*

pillar box *n* (in Britain) a red pillar-shaped public letter box situated in the street

pillbox *n* **1** a box for pills **2** a small enclosed fort of reinforced concrete **3** a small round hat

pillion *n* **1** a seat for a passenger behind the rider of a motorcycle or horse ▹ *adv* **2** on a pillion: *the motorbike on which he was riding pillion*
WORD ORIGIN from Gaelic

pillock *n slang* a stupid or annoying person
WORD ORIGIN Scandinavian dialect *pillicock* penis

pillory *n, pl* **-ries** **1** *historical* a wooden frame in which offenders were locked by the neck and wrists and exposed to public abuse and ridicule ▹ *vb* **-ries, -rying, -ried** **2** to expose to public ridicule **3** to punish by putting in a pillory
WORD ORIGIN Old French *pilori*

pillow *n* **1** a cloth bag stuffed with feathers, polyester fibre, or pieces of foam rubber used to support the head in bed ▹ *vb* **2** to rest (one's head) on or as if on a pillow: *he pillowed his head in her lap*
WORD ORIGIN Old English *pylwe*

pillowcase *or* **pillowslip** *n* a removable washable cover for a pillow

pilot ⓣ *n* **1** a person who is qualified to fly an aircraft or spacecraft **2** a person employed to steer a ship into or out of a port **3** a person who acts as a guide ▹ *adj* **4** serving as a test or trial: *a pilot scheme* **5** serving as a guide: *a pilot beacon* ▹ *vb* **-loting, -loted** **6** to act as pilot of **7** to guide or lead (a project or people): *the legislation was piloted through its committee stage*
WORD ORIGIN French *pilote*

pilot light *n* a small flame that lights the main burner of a gas appliance

pilot officer *n* the most junior commissioned rank in certain air forces

Piłsudski *n* **Józef** 1867–1935, Polish nationalist leader and statesman; president (1918–21) and premier (1926–28; 1930)

pimento *n, pl* **-tos** ▸ same as **allspice** or **pimiento**
WORD ORIGIN Spanish *pimiento* pepper plant

pimiento (pim-yen-toe) *n, pl* **-tos** a Spanish pepper with a red fruit used as a vegetable
WORD ORIGIN variant of PIMENTO

pimp *n* **1** a man who obtains customers for a prostitute, in return for a share of his or her earnings ▹ *vb* **2** to act as a pimp
WORD ORIGIN origin unknown

pimpernel *n* a plant, such as the scarlet pimpernel, typically having small star-shaped flowers
WORD ORIGIN Old French *pimpernelle*

pimple *n* a small swollen infected spot on the skin **pimpled** *adj* **pimply** *adj*
WORD ORIGIN Middle English

pimp up, pimp out *vb* to make (someone or something, esp. a car) more extravagantly decorated, as with flashy accessories, etc. **pimped-up** *or* **pimped-out** *adj*

pin ⓣ *n* **1** a short stiff straight piece of wire with a pointed end and a

THESAURUS

pile[1] *n* **1 = heap**, collection, mountain, mass, stack, rick, mound, accumulation, stockpile, hoard, assortment, assemblage **2** *(informal)* **= lot(s)**, mountain(s), load(s) *(informal)*, oceans, wealth, great deal, stack(s), abundance, large quantity, oodles *(informal)*, shedload *(Brit informal)* **4 = mansion**, building, residence, manor, country house, seat, big house, stately home, manor house **6 = load**, stuff, pack, stack, charge, heap, cram, lade **7 = crowd**, pack, charge, rush, climb, flood, stream, crush, squeeze, jam, flock, shove

pile[2] *n* **= foundation**, support, post, column, piling, beam, upright, pier, pillar

pile[3] *n* **= nap**, fibre, down, hair, surface, fur, plush, shag, filament

pilgrim *n* **1, 2 = traveller**, crusader, wanderer, devotee, palmer, haji *(islam)*, wayfarer

pilgrimage *n* **2 = journey**, tour, trip, mission, expedition, crusade, excursion, hajj *(islam)*

pill *n* **1 = tablet**, capsule, pellet, bolus, pilule

pillar *n* **1 = support**, post, column, piling, prop, shaft, upright, pier, obelisk, stanchion, pilaster **3 = supporter**, leader, rock, worthy, mainstay, leading light *(informal)*, tower of strength, upholder, torchbearer

pilot *n* **1 = airman**, captain, flyer, aviator, aeronaut **2, 3 = helmsman**, guide, navigator, leader, director, conductor, coxswain, steersman ▹ *adj* **4 = trial**, test, model, sample, experimental ▹ *vb* **6a = fly**, control, operate, be at the controls of **6b = navigate**, drive, manage, direct, guide, handle, conduct, steer **7 = direct**, lead, manage, conduct, steer

pin *n* **1 = tack**, nail, needle, safety pin **3 = peg**, rod, brace, bolt ▹ *vb* **9 = fasten**, stick, attach, join, fix, secure, nail, clip, staple, tack, affix **10 = hold fast**, hold down, press,

DICTIONARY

rounded head: used mainly for fastening **2** ▸ short for **cotter pin, hairpin, rolling pin** or **safety pin** **3** a wooden or metal peg **4** a pin-shaped brooch **5** (in various bowling games) a club-shaped wooden object set up in groups as a target **6** a clip that prevents a hand grenade from exploding until it is removed or released **7** *golf* the flagpole marking the hole on a green **8** *informal* a leg ▹ *vb* **pinning, pinned** **9** to fasten with a pin or pins **10** to seize and hold fast: *they pinned his arms behind his back* **11** **pin something on someone** *informal* to place the blame for something on someone: *corruption charges are the easiest to pin on former dictators* ▸ See also **pin down**
WORD ORIGIN Old English *pinn*

PIN Personal Identity Number: a code number used in conjunction with a bank card to enable an account holder to use certain computerized systems, such as cash dispensers

pinafore *n* **1** *chiefly Brit* an apron with a bib **2** a dress with a sleeveless bodice or bib top, worn over a jumper or blouse
WORD ORIGIN *pin* + *afore* in front

pinball *n* an electrically operated table game in which the player shoots a small ball through several hazards

pince-nez (panss-nay) *n, pl* **pince-nez** glasses that are held in place only by means of a clip over the bridge of the nose
WORD ORIGIN French, literally: pinch-nose

pincers *pl n* **1** a gripping tool consisting of two hinged arms and curved jaws **2** the jointed grasping arms of crabs and lobsters
WORD ORIGIN Old French *pincier* to pinch

pinch ❶ *vb* **1** to squeeze (something, esp. flesh) between a finger and thumb **2** to squeeze by being too tight: *shoes that pinch* **3** to cause stinging pain to: *the cold pinched his face* **4** to make thin or drawn-looking, such as from grief or cold **5** *informal* to steal **6** *informal* to arrest **7** (usually foll. by *out* or *back*) to remove the tips of (a plant shoot) to correct or encourage growth ▹ *n* **8** a squeeze or sustained nip **9** the quantity that can be taken up between a thumb and finger: *a pinch of ground ginger* **10** extreme stress or need: *most companies are feeling the pinch of recession* **11** **at a pinch** if absolutely necessary **12** **feel the pinch** to be forced to economize
WORD ORIGIN probably from Old French

pinchbeck *n* **1** an alloy of copper and zinc, used as imitation gold ▹ *adj* **2** sham or cheap
WORD ORIGIN after C. *Pinchbeck*, watchmaker who invented the alloy

Pinckney *n* **1** **Charles** 1757–1824, US statesman, who was a leading member of the convention that framed the US Constitution (1787) **2** his cousin, **Charles Cotesworth** 1746–1825, US soldier, statesman, and diplomat, who also served at the Constitutional Convention **3** his brother, **Thomas** 1750–1828, US soldier and politician. He was US minister to Britain (1792–96) and special envoy to Spain (1795–96)

Pincus *n* **Gregory Goodwin** 1903–67, US physiologist, whose work on steroid hormones led to the development of the first contraceptive pill

pincushion *n* a small cushion in which pins are stuck ready for use

pin down *vb* **1** to force (someone) to make a decision or carry out a promise **2** to define clearly: *the courts have found it difficult to pin down what exactly obscenity is*

pine[1] *n* **1** an evergreen tree with long needle-shaped leaves and brown cones **2** the light-coloured wood of this tree
WORD ORIGIN Latin *pinus*

pine[2] ❶ *vb* **pining, pined** **1** (often foll. by *for*) to feel great longing (for) **2** (often foll. by *away*) to become ill or thin through grief or longing
WORD ORIGIN Old English *pīnian* to torture

Pine *n* **Courtney** born 1964, British jazz saxophonist

pineal gland *or* **body** (pin-ee-al) *n* a small cone-shaped gland at the base of the brain
WORD ORIGIN Latin *pinea* pine cone

pineapple *n* a large tropical fruit with juicy flesh and a thick hard skin
WORD ORIGIN Middle English *pinappel* pine cone

pine cone *n* the woody seed case of a pine tree

pine marten *n* a mammal of N European and Asian coniferous woods, with dark brown fur and a creamy-yellow patch on the throat

Pinero *n* Sir **Arthur Wing** 1855–1934, English dramatist. His works include the farce *Dandy Dick* (1887) and the problem play *The Second Mrs Tanqueray* (1893)

ping *n* **1** a short high-pitched sound, such as of a bullet striking metal ▹ *vb* **2** to make such a noise
WORD ORIGIN imitative

pinger *n* a device that makes a pinging sound, esp. a timer

Ping-Pong *n trademark* ▸ same as **table tennis**

pinhead *n* **1** the head of a pin **2** *informal* a stupid person **pinheaded** *adj*

pinhole *n* a small hole made with or as if with a pin

pinion[1] *n* **1** *chiefly poetic* a bird's wing **2** the outer part of a bird's wing including the flight feathers ▹ *vb* **3** to immobilize (someone) by holding or tying his or her arms **4** to confine
WORD ORIGIN Latin *pinna* wing

pinion[2] *n* a cogwheel that engages with a larger wheel or rack
WORD ORIGIN French *pignon*

pink[1] ❶ *n* **1** a colour between red and white **2** anything pink, such as pink paint or pink clothing: *packaged in pink* **3** a garden plant with pink, red, or white fragrant flowers **4** **in the pink** in good health ▹ *adj* **5** of a colour between red and white **6** *informal* having mild left-wing sympathies **7** *informal* relating to homosexuals or homosexuality: *the pink vote* ▹ *vb* **8** ▸ same as **knock** (sense 7) > **pinkish** *or* **pinky** *adj*
WORD ORIGIN origin unknown

pink[2] *vb* to cut with pinking shears
WORD ORIGIN perhaps from Low German

Pinkerton *n* **Allan** 1819–84, US private detective, born in Scotland. He founded the first detective agency in the US (1850) and organized an intelligence system for the Federal States of America (1861)

Pink Floyd *n* British rock group, formed in 1966: originally comprised Syd Barrett (1946–2006), Roger Waters (born 1944), Rick Wright (1945–2008), and Nick Mason (born 1945); Barrett was replaced by Dave Gilmour (born 1944) in 1968 and Waters left in 1986. Recordings include *The Piper at the Gates of Dawn*

P

THESAURUS

restrain, constrain, immobilize, pinion

pinch *vb* **1 = nip**, press, squeeze, grasp, compress, tweak **2 = hurt**, crush, squeeze, pain, confine, cramp, chafe **5** *(informal)* **= steal**, rob, snatch, lift *(informal)*, nick *(slang, chiefly Brit)*, swipe *(slang)*, knock off *(slang)*, blag *(slang)*, pilfer, snitch *(slang)*, purloin, filch, snaffle *(Brit informal)* ▹ *n* **8 = nip**, squeeze, tweak **9 = dash**, bit, taste, mite, jot, speck, small quantity, smidgen *(informal)*, soupçon *(French)* **10 = emergency**, crisis, difficulty, plight, scrape *(informal)*, strait, uphill *(S African)*, predicament, extremity, hardship

pine[2] *vb* **2** *(often with* **away***)* **= waste**, decline, weaken, sicken, sink, flag, fade, decay, dwindle, wither, wilt, languish, droop

pink[1] *adj* **5 = rosy**, rose, salmon, flushed, reddish, flesh coloured, roseate

DICTIONARY

(1967), *Dark Side of the Moon* (1973), *Wish You Were Here* (1975), and *The Wall* (1979)

pinkie *or* **pinky** *n, pl* **-ies** *Scot, US, Canad & NZ* the little finger
WORD ORIGIN Dutch *pinkje*

pinking shears *pl n* scissors with a serrated edge that give a wavy edge to material cut and so prevent fraying

pin money *n* a small amount of extra money earned to buy small luxuries

pinna *n anat* the external part of the ear

pinnace *n* a ship's boat
WORD ORIGIN French *pinace*

pinnacle ❶ *n* **1** the highest point of fame or success **2** a towering peak of a mountain **3** a slender spire
WORD ORIGIN Latin *pinna* wing

pinnate *adj bot* (of compound leaves) having leaflets growing opposite each other in pairs
WORD ORIGIN Latin *pinna* feather

pinny *n, pl* **-nies** ▸ an informal or child's name for **pinafore** (sense 1)

pinotage (pin-oh-tazh) *n* a red wine blended from the Pinot Noir and Hermitage grapes that is unique to South Africa

pinpoint ❶ *vb* **1** to locate or identify exactly: *we've pinpointed the fault* ▹ *adj* **2** exact: *pinpoint accuracy*

pinprick *n* a small irritation or annoyance

pins and needles *n informal* a tingling sensation in a part of the body

Pinsent *n* **Matthew** (**Clive**) born 1970, British oarsman; won four gold medals in rowing events at consecutive Olympic Games (1992, 1996, 2000, 2004)

pinstripe *n* (in textiles) a very narrow stripe in fabric or the fabric itself

pint *n* **1** *Brit* a unit of liquid measure equal to one eighth of an Imperial gallon (0.568 litre) **2** *US* a unit of liquid measure equal to one eighth of a US gallon (0.473 litre) **3** *Brit informal* a pint of beer
WORD ORIGIN Old French *pinte*

pinta *n Brit informal* a pint of milk
WORD ORIGIN phonetic rendering of *pint of*

pintail *n, pl* **-tails** *or* **-tail** a greyish-brown duck with a pointed tail

pintle *n* a pin or bolt forming the pivot of a hinge
WORD ORIGIN Old English *pintel* penis

pinto *US & Canad adj* **1** marked with patches of white; piebald ▹ *n, pl* **-tos** **2** a pinto horse
WORD ORIGIN American Spanish

pint-size *or* **pint-sized** *adj informal* very small

pin tuck *n* a narrow, ornamental fold used on shirt fronts and dress bodices

Pinturicchio *or Italian* **Pintoricchio** *n* real name *Bernardino di Betto* ?1454–1513, Italian painter of the Umbrian school

pin-up *n* **1** *informal* a picture of a sexually attractive person, often partially or totally undressed **2** *slang* a person who has appeared in such a picture: *your favourite pin-up* **3** a photograph of a famous personality

pinwheel *n* ▸ same as **Catherine wheel**

Pinyin *n* a system of spelling used to represent Chinese in Roman letters

Pinzón *n* **1** **Martín Alonzo** ?1440–93, Spanish navigator, who commanded the *Pinta* on Columbus' first expedition (1492–93), which he abandoned in a vain attempt to be the first to arrive back in Spain **2** his brother, **Vicente Yáñez** ?1460–?1524, Spanish navigator, who commanded the *Niña* on Columbus' first expedition (1492–93)

pion *or* **pi meson** *n physics* any of three subatomic particles which are classified as mesons

pioneer ❶ *n* **1** an explorer or settler of a new land or region **2** an originator or developer of something new ▹ *vb* **3** to be a pioneer (in or of) **4** to initiate or develop: *the new technique was pioneered in France*
WORD ORIGIN Old French *paonier* infantryman

pious *adj* **1** religious or devout **2** insincerely reverent; sanctimonious **piousness** *n*
WORD ORIGIN Latin *pius*

pip[1] *n* the seed of a fleshy fruit, such as an apple or pear
WORD ORIGIN short for *pippin*

pip[2] *n* **1** a short high-pitched sound used as a time signal on radio **2** any of the spots on a playing card, dice, or domino **3** *informal* the emblem worn on the shoulder by junior officers in the British Army, indicating their rank
WORD ORIGIN imitative

pip[3] *n* **1** a contagious disease of poultry **2** *facetious slang* a minor human ailment **3** **get** *or* **have the pip** *NZ slang* to sulk **4** **give someone the pip** *Brit, NZ & S African slang* to annoy someone: *it really gives me the pip*
WORD ORIGIN Middle Dutch *pippe*

pip[4] *vb* **pipping, pipped** ■ **pip someone at the post** *Brit & NZ slang* to defeat someone whose success seems certain
WORD ORIGIN probably from PIP[2]

pipe ❶ *n* **1** a long tube for conveying water, oil, or gas **2** **a** a tube with a small bowl at the end for smoking tobacco **b** the amount of tobacco that fills the bowl of a pipe **3** *zool, bot* any of various hollow organs, such as the respiratory passage of certain animals **4** **a** a tubular instrument in which air vibrates and produces a musical sound **b** any of the tubular devices on an organ **5** a boatswain's whistle **6** **put that in your pipe and smoke it** *informal* accept that fact if you can **7** **the pipes** ▸ see **bagpipes** ▹ *vb* **piping, piped** **8** to play (music) on a pipe **9** to summon or lead by a pipe: *to pipe in the haggis* **10** **a** to signal orders to (the crew) by a boatswain's pipe **b** to signal the arrival or departure of: *he piped his entire ship's company on deck* **11** to utter in a shrill tone **12** to convey (water, oil, or gas) by pipe **13** to force cream or icing through a shaped nozzle to decorate food ▸ See also **pipe down, pipe up**
WORD ORIGIN Old English *pīpe*

pipeclay *n* a fine white pure clay, used in tobacco pipes and pottery and to whiten leather and similar materials

pipe cleaner *n* a short length of wire covered with tiny tufts of yarn: used to clean the stem of a tobacco pipe

piped music *n* light music played as background music in public places

pipe down ❶ *vb informal* to stop talking or making noise

pipe dream *n* a fanciful or impossible plan or hope
WORD ORIGIN alluding to dreams produced by smoking an opium pipe

pipeline ❶ *n* **1** a long pipe for transporting oil, water, or gas **2** a

THESAURUS

pinnacle *n* **1 = height**, top, crown, crest, meridian, zenith, apex, apogee, acme, vertex **2 = summit**, top, height, peak, eminence

pinpoint *vb* **1a = identify**, discover, spot, define, distinguish, put your finger on **1b = locate**, find, spot, identify, home in on, zero in on, get a fix on

pioneer *n* **1 = settler**, explorer, colonist, colonizer, frontiersman **2 = founder**, leader, developer, innovator, founding father, trailblazer ▹ *vb* **4 = develop**, create, launch, establish, start, prepare, discover, institute, invent, open up, initiate, originate, take the lead on, instigate, map out, show the way on, lay the groundwork on

pipe *n* **1 = tube**, drain, canal, pipeline, line, main, passage, cylinder, hose, conduit, duct, conveyor ▹ *vb* **12 = convey**, channel, supply, conduct, bring in, transmit, siphon

pipe down *vb (informal)* **= be quiet**, shut up *(informal)*, hush, stop talking, quieten down, shush, button it *(slang)*, belt up *(slang)*, shut your mouth, hold your tongue, put a sock in it *(Brit slang)*, button your lip *(slang)*

pipeline *n* **1 = tube**, passage, pipe, line, conduit, duct, conveyor

DICTIONARY

means of communication **3 in the pipeline** in preparation

pipe organ *n* ▸ same as **organ** (sense 2a)

piper *n* a person who plays a pipe or bagpipes

Piper *n* **John** 1903–92, British artist. An official war artist in World War II, he is known esp. for his watercolours of bombed churches and his stained glass in Coventry Cathedral

pipette *n* a slender glass tube for transferring or measuring out liquids
WORD ORIGIN French: little pipe

pipe up *vb* to speak up unexpectedly

pipi *n, pl* **pipi** *or* **pipis** *Austral & NZ* an edible mollusc of Australia and New Zealand
WORD ORIGIN Māori

piping *n* **1** a system of pipes **2** a string of icing or cream used to decorate cakes and desserts **3** a thin strip of covered cord or material, used to edge hems or cushions **4** the sound of a pipe or bagpipes **5** a shrill voice or whistling sound: *a dove's cool piping* ▹ *adj* **6** making a shrill sound ▹ *adv* **7 piping hot** extremely hot

pipistrelle *n* a type of small brownish bat found throughout the world
WORD ORIGIN Italian *pipistrello*

pipit *n* a small songbird with a brownish speckled plumage and a long tail
WORD ORIGIN probably imitative

pippin *n* a type of eating apple
WORD ORIGIN Old French *pepin*

pipsqueak *n informal* an insignificant or contemptible person

piquant (**pee**-kant) *adj* **1** having a spicy taste **2** stimulating to the mind: *love was a forbidden piquant secret*
piquancy *n*
WORD ORIGIN French, literally: prickling

pique (**peek**) *n* **1** a feeling of resentment or irritation, such as from hurt pride ▹ *vb* **piquing, piqued 2** to hurt (someone's) pride **3** to excite (curiosity or interest)
WORD ORIGIN French *piquer* to prick

piqué (**pee**-kay) *n* a stiff ribbed fabric of cotton, silk, or spun rayon
WORD ORIGIN French: pricked

piquet (pik-**ket**) *n* a card game for two people played with a reduced pack
WORD ORIGIN French

piracy *n, pl* **-cies 1** *Brit & NZ* robbery on the seas **2** a crime, such as hijacking, committed aboard a ship or aircraft **3** the unauthorized use of patented or copyrighted material

Piranesi *n* **Giambattista** 1720–78, Italian etcher and architect: etchings include *Imaginary Prisons* and *Views of Rome*

piranha *n* a small fierce freshwater fish of tropical America, with strong jaws and sharp teeth
WORD ORIGIN S American Indian: fish with teeth

pirate ⊕ *n* **1** a person who commits piracy **2** a vessel used by pirates **3** a person who illegally sells or publishes someone else's literary or artistic work **4** a person or group of people who broadcast illegally ▹ *vb* **-rating, -rated 5** to sell or reproduce (artistic work, ideas, etc.) illegally
piratical *adj*
WORD ORIGIN Greek *peira* an attack

piri-piri *n* a hot sauce, of Portuguese colonial origin, made from red chilli peppers
WORD ORIGIN from a Bantu language: pepper

pirouette *n* **1** a body spin performed on the toes or the ball of the foot ▹ *vb* **-etting, -etted 2** to perform a pirouette
WORD ORIGIN French

Pisanello *n* **Antonio** ?1395–?1455, Italian painter and medallist; a major exponent of the International Gothic style. He is best known for his portrait medals and drawings of animals

Pisano *n* **1 Andrea**, real name *Andrea de Pontedera*. ?1290–1348, Italian sculptor and architect, noted for his bronze reliefs on the door of the baptistry in Florence **2 Giovanni** ?1250–?1320, Italian sculptor, who successfully integrated classical and Gothic elements in his sculptures, esp. in his pulpit in St Andrea, Pistoia **3** his father, **Nicola** ?1220–?84, Italian sculptor, who pioneered the classical style and is often regarded as a precursor of the Italian Renaissance: noted esp. for his pulpit in the baptistry of Pisa Cathedral

piscatorial *adj formal* of or relating to fish, fishing, or fishermen
WORD ORIGIN Latin *piscatorius*

Pisces *n astrol* the twelfth sign of the zodiac; the Fishes
WORD ORIGIN Latin

pisciculture (**piss**-ee-cult-cher) *n formal* the rearing and breeding of fish under controlled conditions
WORD ORIGIN Latin *piscis* fish

piscine (**piss**-sign) *adj* of or resembling a fish
WORD ORIGIN Latin *piscis* fish

Pisistratus *n* ?600–527 BC, tyrant of Athens: he established himself in firm control of the city following his defeat of his aristocratic rivals at Pallene (546)

piss *taboo vb* **1** to urinate **2** to discharge as or in one's urine: *to piss blood* ▹ *n* **3** an act of urinating **4** urine **5 take the piss** to make fun of or mock someone ▸ See also **piss down, piss off**
WORD ORIGIN probably imitative

pissant *US, derogatory slang n* **1** an insignificant or contemptible person ▹ *adj* **2** insignificant or contemptible
WORD ORIGIN from PISS + ANT

Pissarro *n* **Camille** 1830–1903, French impressionist painter, esp. of landscapes

piss down *vb taboo slang* to rain heavily

pissed *adj slang* **1** *Brit, Austral, S Africa & NZ* drunk **2** *US & Canad* angry

piss off *vb taboo slang* **1** to annoy or disappoint **2** to go away: often used to dismiss a person

pistachio *n, pl* **-chios** a Mediterranean nut with a hard shell and an edible green kernel
WORD ORIGIN Persian *pistah*

piste (**peest**) *n* a slope or course for skiing
WORD ORIGIN French

pistil *n* the seed-bearing part of a flower
WORD ORIGIN Latin *pistillum* pestle

pistillate *adj bot* (of plants) having pistils

pistol *n* a short-barrelled handgun
WORD ORIGIN Czech *pišťala*

pistol-whip *vb* **-whipping, -whipped** *US* to beat or strike with a pistol barrel

piston *n* a cylindrical part that slides to and fro in a hollow cylinder: in an engine it is attached by a rod to other parts, thus its movement causes the other parts to move
WORD ORIGIN Old Italian *pistone*

pit[1] ⊕ *n* **1** a large deep opening in the ground **2** a coal mine **3** *anat* **a** a small natural depression on the surface of a body or organ **b** the floor of any natural bodily cavity: *the pit of the stomach* **4** *pathol* a pockmark **5** a concealed danger or difficulty **6** an area at the side of a motor-racing track for servicing or refuelling vehicles **7** the area occupied by the orchestra in a theatre **8** an enclosure for fighting animals or birds **9** the back of the ground floor of a theatre **10** ▸ same as **pitfall** (sense 2) **11 the pit** hell ▹ *vb* **pitting, pitted 12** (often

THESAURUS

pirate *n* **1 = buccaneer**, raider, rover, filibuster, marauder, corsair, sea wolf, freebooter, sea robber, sea rover ▹ *vb* **5 = copy**, steal, reproduce, bootleg, lift *(informal)*, appropriate, borrow, poach, crib *(informal)*, plagiarize

pit[1] *n* **1 = hole**, gulf, depression, hollow, trench, crater, trough, cavity, abyss, chasm, excavation, pothole **2 = coal mine**, mine, shaft, colliery, mine shaft ▹ *vb* **13 = scar**, mark, hole, nick, notch, dent, gouge, indent, dint, pockmark

P

DICTIONARY

foll. by *against*) to match in opposition, esp. as antagonists: *sister pitted against sister* **13** to mark with small dents or scars **14** to place or bury in a pit **15** **pit one's wits against** to compete against in a test or contest ▸ See also **pits**
WORD ORIGIN Old English *pytt*

pit² *chiefly US & Canad* *n* **1** the stone of various fruits ▹ *vb* **pitting, pitted** **2** to remove the stone from (a fruit)
WORD ORIGIN Dutch: kernel

pitapat *adv* **1** with quick light taps ▹ *n* **2** such taps
WORD ORIGIN imitative

pit bull terrier *n* a strong muscular terrier with a short coat

pitch¹ ❶ *vb* **1** to hurl or throw **2** to set up (a tent or camp) **3** to slope or fall forwards or downwards: *she pitched forwards like a diver* **4** (of a ship or plane) to dip and raise its back and front alternately **5** to set the level or tone of: *his ambitions were pitched too high* **6** to aim to sell (a product) to a specified market or on a specified basis **7** *music* to sing or play (a note or interval) accurately ▹ *n* **8** *chiefly Brit* (in many sports) the field of play **9** a level of emotion: *children can wind their parents up to a pitch of anger and guilt* **10** the degree or angle of slope **11** the distance between corresponding points or adjacent threads on a screw thread **12** the pitching motion of a ship or plane **13** *music* the highness or lowness of a note in relation to other notes: *low pitch* **14** the act or manner of pitching a ball **15** *chiefly Brit* the place where a street or market trader regularly sells **16** *slang* a persuasive sales talk, esp. one routinely repeated ▸ See also **pitch in, pitch into**
WORD ORIGIN Middle English *picchen*

pitch² *n* **1** a thick sticky substance formed from coal tar and used for paving or waterproofing **2** any similar substance, such as asphalt, occurring as a natural deposit ▹ *vb* **3** to apply pitch to
WORD ORIGIN Old English *pic*

pitch-black *adj* extremely dark; unlit: *it was a wild night, pitch-black, with howling gales*

pitchblende *n* a blackish mineral which is the principal source of uranium and radium
WORD ORIGIN German *Pechblende*

pitch-dark *adj* extremely or completely dark

pitched battle *n* a fierce fight

pitcher¹ *n* a large jug, usually rounded with a narrow neck
WORD ORIGIN Old French *pichier*

pitcher² *n baseball* the player on the fielding team who throws the ball to the batter

pitcher plant *n* a plant with pitcher-like leaves that attract and trap insects, which are then digested

pitchfork *n* **1** a long-handled fork with two or three long curved prongs for tossing hay ▹ *vb* **2** to use a pitchfork on (something)

pitch in *vb* to cooperate or contribute

pitch into *vb informal* to attack (someone) physically or verbally

pitch pine *n* a pine tree of North America: a source of turpentine and pitch

pitch pipe *n* a small pipe that sounds a note to establish the correct starting note for unaccompanied singing

piteous *adj* arousing or deserving pity: *the piteous mewing of an injured kitten* **piteousness** *n*

pitfall ❶ *n* **1** an unsuspected difficulty or danger **2** a trap in the form of a concealed pit, designed to catch men or wild animals
WORD ORIGIN Old English *pytt* pit + *fealle* trap

pith *n* **1** the soft white lining inside the rind of fruits such as the orange **2** the essential part: *policy, though, isn't the pith of what happened yesterday* **3** the soft spongy tissue in the centre of the stem of certain plants
WORD ORIGIN Old English *pitha*

pithead *n* the top of a mine shaft and the buildings and hoisting gear around it

pith helmet *n* a lightweight hat made of the pith of the sola, an E Indian swamp plant, that is worn for protection from the sun

pithy *adj* **pithier, pithiest** **1** terse and full of meaning **2** of, resembling, or full of pith **pithiness** *n*

pitiable *adj* arousing or deserving pity or contempt **pitiableness** *n*

pitiful *adj* arousing or deserving great pity or contempt **pitifully** *adv* **pitifulness** *n*

pitiless *adj* feeling no pity or mercy **pitilessly** *adv*

Pitman *n* Sir **Isaac** 1813–97, English inventor of a system of phonetic shorthand (1837)

piton (peet-on) *n mountaineering* a metal spike that may be driven into a crack and used to secure a rope
WORD ORIGIN French

pits *pl n* **the pits** *slang* the worst possible person, place, or thing
WORD ORIGIN perhaps from *armpits*

pitta bread *or* **pitta** *n* a flat rounded slightly leavened bread, originally from the Middle East
WORD ORIGIN Modern Greek *pitta* a cake

pittance *n* a very small amount of money
WORD ORIGIN Old French *pietance* ration

pitter-patter *n* **1** the sound of light rapid taps or pats, such as of rain drops ▹ *vb* **2** to make such a sound

Pitt-Rivers *n* **Augustus Henry Lane Fox** 1827–1900, British archaeologist; first inspector of ancient monuments (1882): assembled a major anthropological collection of tools and weapons (now in the **Pitt-Rivers Museum,** Oxford)

pituitary *or* **pituitary gland** *n* the gland at the base of the brain which secretes hormones that affect skeletal growth, development of the sex glands, and other functions of the body
WORD ORIGIN Late Latin *pituitarius* slimy

pity ❶ *n, pl* **pities** **1** sorrow felt for the sufferings of others **2** a cause of regret: *it's a great pity he did not live longer* **3** **have** *or* **take pity on** to have sympathy or show mercy for ▹ *vb* **pities, pitying, pitied** **4** to feel pity for **pitying** *adj*
WORD ORIGIN Latin *pietas* duty

Pius II *n* pen name *Aeneas Silvius*, original name *Enea Silvio de' Piccolomini*. 1405–64, Italian ecclesiastic, humanist, poet, and historian; pope (1458–64)

Pius IV *n* original name *Giovanni Angelo de' Medici*. 1499–1565, pope (1559–65). He reconvened the Council of Trent

THESAURUS

pitch¹ *vb* **1 = throw**, launch, cast, toss, hurl, fling, chuck *(informal)*, sling, lob *(informal)*, bung *(Brit slang)*, heave **2 = set up**, place, station, locate, raise, plant, settle, fix, put up, erect **3 = fall**, drop, plunge, dive, stagger, tumble, topple, plummet, fall headlong, (take a) nosedive **4 = toss (about)**, roll, plunge, flounder, lurch, wallow, welter, make heavy weather ▹ *n* **8** *(chiefly Brit)* **= sports field**, ground, stadium, arena, park, field of play **9 = level**, point, degree, summit, extent, height, intensity, high point **13** *(music)* **= tone**, sound, key, frequency, timbre, modulation **16** *(slang)* **= talk**, line, patter, spiel *(informal)*

pitfall *n* **1 = danger**, difficulty, peril, catch, trap, hazard, drawback, snag, uphill *(S African)*, banana skin *(informal)*

pity *n* **1 = compassion**, understanding, charity, sympathy, distress, sadness, sorrow, kindness, tenderness, condolence, commiseration, fellow feeling **OPPOSITE:** mercilessness **2 = shame**, crime *(informal)*, sin *(informal)*, misfortune, bad luck, sad thing, bummer *(slang)*, crying shame, source of regret ▹ *vb* **4 = feel sorry for**, feel for, sympathize with, grieve for, weep for, take pity on, empathize with, bleed for, commiserate with, have compassion for, condole with

(1562), confirming its final decrees
Pius V *n* **Saint** original name *Michele Ghislieri*. 1504–72, Italian ecclesiastic; pope (1566–72). He attempted to enforce the reforms decreed by the Council of Trent, excommunicated Elizabeth I of England (1570), and organized the alliance that defeated the Turks at Lepanto (1571). Feast day: 30 April
Pius VI *n* original name *Giovanni Angelico Braschi* 1717–99, Italian ecclesiastic; pope (1775–99). He opposed French attempts to limit papal authority and denounced (1791) the French Revolution: he died a prisoner of the French in the Revolutionary Wars
Pius VII *n* original name *Luigi Barnaba Chiaramonti* 1740–1823, Italian ecclesiastic; pope (1800–23). He concluded a concordat with Napoleon (1801) and consecrated him as emperor of France (1804), but resisted his annexation of the Papal States (1809)
Pius X *n* **Saint** original name *Giuseppe Sarto* 1835–1914, Italian ecclesiastic; pope (1903–14). He condemned Modernism (1907) and initiated a new codification of canon law. Feast day: Aug 21
Pius XI *n* original name *Achille Ratti* 1857–1939, Italian ecclesiastic; pope (1922–39). He signed the Lateran Treaty (1929), by which the Vatican City was recognized as an independent state. His encyclicals condemned Nazism and Communism
Pius XII *n* original name *Eugenio Pacelli* 1876–1958, Italian ecclesiastic; pope (1939–58): his attitude towards Nazi German anti-Semitism has been a matter of controversy
pivot *n* **1** a central shaft around which something turns **2** the central person or thing necessary for progress or success ▹ *vb* **-oting, -oted 3** to turn on or provide with a pivot
WORD ORIGIN Old French
pivotal ❶ *adj* **1** of crucial importance **2** of or acting as a pivot
pix *n* *informal* ▸ a plural of **pic**
pixel *n* the smallest constituent unit of an image, as on a visual display unit
WORD ORIGIN from *pix* pictures + *el(ement)*
pixie *or* **pixy** *n, pl* **pixies** (in folklore) a fairy or elf
pizza *n* a dish of Italian origin consisting of a baked disc of dough covered with a wide variety of savoury toppings
WORD ORIGIN Italian
pizzazz *or* **pizazz** *n* *informal* an attractive combination of energy and style
WORD ORIGIN origin obscure
pizzicato (pit-see-**kah**-toe) *adj, adv* *music* (in music for the violin family) to be plucked with the finger
WORD ORIGIN Italian: pinched
Pl. (in street names) Place
plaas *n* *S African* a farm
WORD ORIGIN Afrikaans
placard *n* **1** a notice that is paraded in public ▹ *vb* **2** to attach placards to
WORD ORIGIN Old French *plaquart*
placate *vb* **-cating, -cated** to calm (someone) to stop him or her feeling angry or upset **placatory** *adj*
WORD ORIGIN Latin *placare*
place ❶ *n* **1** a particular part of a space or of a surface **2** a geographical point, such as a town or city **3** a position or rank in a sequence or order **4** an open square lined with houses in a city or town **5** space or room **6** a house or living quarters: *he's buying his own place* **7** any building or area set aside for a specific purpose **8** the point reached in reading or speaking: *her finger was pressed to the page as if marking her place* **9** right or duty: *it's not my place to do their job for them* **10** appointment, position, or job: *she won a place at university* **11** position, condition, or state: *you know what your place in the world is* **12** a space or seat, as at a dining table **13** *maths* the relative position of a digit in a number **14 all over the place** in disorder or disarray **15 go places** *informal* to become successful **16 in** *or* **out of place** in or out of the proper or customary position **17 in place of a** instead of: *leeks can be used in place of the broccoli* **b** in exchange for: *he gave her it in place of her ring* **18 know one's place** to be aware of one's inferior position **19 put someone in his** *or* **her place** to humble someone who is arrogant, conceited, etc. **20 take place** to happen or occur **21 take the place of** to be a substitute for ▹ *vb* **placing, placed 22** to put in a particular or appropriate place **23** to find or indicate the place of: *I bet you the media couldn't have placed Neath on the map before the by-election* **24** to identify or classify by linking with an appropriate context: *I felt I should know him, but could not quite place him* **25** to make (an order or bet) **26** to find a home or job for (someone) **27** (often foll. by *with*) to put under the care (of) **28** (of a racehorse, greyhound, athlete, etc.) to arrive in first, second, third, or sometimes fourth place
WORD ORIGIN Latin *platea* courtyard
Place *n* **Francis** 1771–1854, British radical, who campaigned for the repeal (1824) of the Combination Acts, which forbade the forming of trade unions, and for parliamentary reform
placebo (plas-**see**-bo) *n, pl* **-bos** *or* **-boes** *med* an inactive substance given to a patient usually to compare its effects with those of a real drug but sometimes for the psychological benefit gained by the patient through believing that he or she is receiving treatment
WORD ORIGIN Latin: I shall please
place kick *n* *rugby, American football, etc.* a kick in which the ball is placed in position before it is kicked
placement *n* **1** arrangement or position **2** a temporary job which someone is given as part of a training course: *many pupils have been on work placements with local businesses* **3** the act or an instance of finding someone a job or a home: *the main task of the adoption agency is to find the best family placement for each child*
placenta (plass-**ent**-a) *n, pl* **-tas** *or* **-tae** the organ formed in the womb of most mammals during pregnancy, providing oxygen and nutrients for the fetus **placental** *adj*
WORD ORIGIN Latin, from Greek *plakoeis* flat cake
place setting *n* the cutlery, crockery, and glassware laid for one person at a dining table
placid *adj* having a calm appearance or nature: *placid waters; a placid temperament* **placidity** *or* **placidness** *n* **placidly** *adv*
WORD ORIGIN Latin *placidus* peaceful
placket *n* *dressmaking* an opening at

THESAURUS

pivotal *adj* **1 = crucial**, central, determining, vital, critical, decisive, focal, climactic
place *n* **1, 7 = spot**, point, position, site, area, situation, station, location, venue, whereabouts, locus **2 = region**, city, town, quarter, village, district, neighbourhood, hamlet, vicinity, locality, locale, dorp *(S African)* **3 = position**, point, spot, location **12 = space**, position, seat, chair ▹ *vb* **20 take place = happen**, occur, go on, go down *(US & Canad)*, arise, come about, crop up, transpire *(informal)*, befall, materialize, come to pass *(archaic)*, betide **22 = lay (down)**, leave, put (down), set (down), stand, sit, position, rest, plant, station, establish, stick *(informal)*, settle, fix, arrange, lean, deposit, locate, set out, install, prop, dispose, situate, stow, bung *(Brit slang)*, plonk *(informal)*, array **24a = classify**, class, group, put, order, sort, rank, arrange, grade, assign, categorize **24b = identify**, remember, recognize, pin someone down, put your finger on, put a name to, set someone in context **26, 27 = entrust to**, give to, assign to, appoint to, allocate to, find a home for

DICTIONARY

the waist of a dress or skirt for buttons or zips or for access to a pocket
WORD ORIGIN perhaps from Medieval Dutch *plackaet* breastplate

plagiarize *or* **-rise** (play-jer-ize) *vb* **-rizing, -rized** *or* **-rising, -rised** to steal ideas or passages from (another's work) and present them as one's own **plagiarism** *n* **plagiarizer** *or* **-riser** *n*
WORD ORIGIN Latin *plagium* kidnapping

plague ❶ *n* **1** any widespread and usually highly contagious disease with a high fatality rate **2** an infectious disease of rodents transmitted to man by the bite of the rat flea; bubonic plague **3** something that afflicts or harasses: *a plague of locusts* **4** *informal* a nuisance ▷ *vb* **plaguing, plagued 5** to afflict or harass: *a playing career plagued by injury* **6** *informal* to annoy or pester
WORD ORIGIN Latin *plaga* a blow

plaice *n, pl* **plaice** *or* **plaices** an edible European flatfish with a brown body marked with red or orange spots
WORD ORIGIN Greek *platus* flat

plaid *n* **1** a long piece of tartan cloth worn over the shoulder as part of Highland costume **2** a crisscross weave or cloth
WORD ORIGIN Scottish Gaelic *plaide*

Plaid Cymru (plide **kumm**-ree) *n* the Welsh nationalist party
WORD ORIGIN Welsh

plain ❶ *adj* **1** flat or smooth **2** easily understood: *he made it plain what he wanted from me* **3** honest or blunt: *the plain fact is that my mother has no time for me* **4** without adornment: *a plain brown envelope* **5** not good-looking **6** (of fabric) without pattern or of simple weave **7** lowly, esp. in social rank or education: *the plain people of Ireland* **8** *knitting* of or done in plain stitch ▷ *n* **9** a level stretch of country **10** a simple stitch in knitting made by passing the wool round the front of the needle ▷ *adv* **11** clearly or simply: *that's just plain stupid!* **plainly** *adv* **plainness** *n*
WORD ORIGIN Latin *planus* level, clear

plainchant *n* ▸ same as **plainsong**

plain chocolate *n Brit* chocolate with a slightly bitter flavour and dark colour

plain clothes *pl n* ordinary clothes, as opposed to uniform, worn by a detective on duty

plain flour *n* flour to which no raising agent has been added

plain sailing *n* **1** *informal* smooth or easy progress **2** *naut* sailing in a body of water that is unobstructed; clear sailing

plainsong *n* the style of unaccompanied choral music used in the medieval Church, esp. in Gregorian chant
WORD ORIGIN translation of Medieval Latin *cantus planus*

plain speaking *n* saying exactly what one thinks **plain-spoken** *adj*

plaint *n* **1** *archaic* a complaint or lamentation **2** *law* a statement in writing of grounds of complaint made to a court of law
WORD ORIGIN Old French *plainte*

plaintiff *n* a person who sues in a court of law
WORD ORIGIN Old French *plaintif* complaining

plaintive *adj* sad and mournful **plaintively** *adv*
WORD ORIGIN Old French *plaintif* grieving

plait (platt) *n* **1** a length of hair that has been plaited ▷ *vb* **2** to intertwine (strands or strips) in a pattern
WORD ORIGIN Latin *plicare* to fold

plan ❶ *n* **1** a method thought out for doing or achieving something **2** a detailed drawing to scale of a horizontal section through a building **3** an outline or sketch ▷ *vb* **planning, planned 4** to form a plan (for) **5** to make a plan of (a building) **6** to intend
WORD ORIGIN Latin *planus* flat

planchette *n* a device on which messages are written under supposed spirit guidance
WORD ORIGIN French: little board

plane[1] ❶ *n* **1** an aeroplane **2** *maths* a flat surface in which a straight line joining any two of its points lies entirely on that surface **3** a level surface: *an inclined plane* **4** a level of existence or attainment: *her ambition was set on a higher plane than pulling pints in a pub* ▷ *adj* **5** level or flat **6** *maths* lying entirely in one plane ▷ *vb* **planing, planed 7** to glide or skim: *they planed over the ice*
WORD ORIGIN Latin *planum* level surface

plane[2] *n* **1** a tool with a steel blade for smoothing timber ▷ *vb* **planing, planed 2** to smooth (timber) using a plane **3** (often foll. by *away* or *off*) to remove using a plane
WORD ORIGIN Latin *planare* to level

planet *n* any of the nine celestial bodies, Mercury, Venus, Earth, Mars, Jupiter, Saturn, Uranus, Neptune, or Pluto, that revolve around the sun in oval-shaped orbits **planetary** *adj*
WORD ORIGIN Greek *planaein* to wander

P

THESAURUS

plague *n* **1 = disease**, infection, epidemic, contagion, pandemic, pestilence, lurgy *(informal)* **3 = infestation**, invasion, epidemic, influx, host, swarm, multitude ▷ *vb* **5 = torment**, trouble, pain, torture, haunt, afflict **6** *(informal)* **= pester**, trouble, bother, disturb, annoy, tease, harry, harass, hassle, fret, badger, persecute, molest, vex, bedevil, get on your nerves *(informal)*, give someone grief *(Brit & S African)*, be on your back *(slang)*, get in your hair *(informal)*

plain *adj* **2 = clear**, obvious, patent, evident, apparent, visible, distinct, understandable, manifest, transparent, overt, unmistakable, lucid, unambiguous, comprehensible, legible
OPPOSITE: hidden
3 = straightforward, open, direct, frank, bold, blunt, sincere, outspoken, honest, downright, candid, forthright, upfront *(informal)*, artless, ingenuous, guileless
OPPOSITE: roundabout
4 = unadorned, simple, basic, severe, pure, bare, modest, stark, restrained, muted, discreet, austere, spartan, unfussy, unvarnished, unembellished, unornamented, unpatterned, bare-bones
OPPOSITE: ornate
5 = ugly, ordinary, unattractive, homely *(US & Canad)*, not striking, unlovely, unprepossessing, not beautiful, no oil painting *(informal)*, ill-favoured, unalluring
OPPOSITE: attractive
7 = ordinary, homely, common, simple, modest, everyday, commonplace, lowly, unaffected, unpretentious, frugal, workaday
OPPOSITE: sophisticated
▷ *n* **9 = flatland**, plateau, prairie, grassland, mesa, lowland, steppe, open country, pampas, tableland, veld, llano

plan *n* **1 = scheme**, system, design, idea, programme, project, proposal, strategy, method, suggestion, procedure, plot, device, scenario, proposition, contrivance **2, 3 = diagram**, map, drawing, chart, illustration, representation, sketch, blueprint, layout, delineation, scale drawing ▷ *vb* **4 = devise**, arrange, prepare, scheme, frame, plot, draft, organize, outline, invent, formulate, contrive, think out, concoct **5 = design**, outline, draw up a plan of **6 = intend**, aim, mean, propose, purpose, contemplate, envisage, foresee

plane[1] *n* **1 = aeroplane**, aircraft, jet, airliner, jumbo jet **3 = flat surface**, the flat, horizontal, level surface **4 = level**, position, stage, footing, condition, standard, degree, rung, stratum, echelon ▷ *adj* **5 = level**, even, flat, regular, plain, smooth, uniform, flush, horizontal ▷ *vb* **7 = skim**, sail, skate, glide

planetarium *n, pl* **-iums** *or* **-ia 1** an instrument for projecting images of the sun, moon, stars, and planets onto a domed ceiling **2** a building in which such an instrument is housed

planetoid (plan-it-oid) *n* ▸ see **asteroid**

plane tree *or* **plane** *n* a tree with rounded heads of fruit and leaves with pointed lobes
WORD ORIGIN Greek *platos* wide (because of its broad leaves)

plangent (plan-jent) *adj* (of sounds) mournful and resounding

plank *n* **1** a long flat piece of sawn timber **2** one of the policies in a political party's programme **3 walk the plank** to be forced by sailors to walk to one's death off the end of a plank jutting out from the side of a ship
WORD ORIGIN Late Latin *planca* board

planking *n* a number of planks

plankton *n* the small drifting plants and animals on the surface layer of a sea or lake
WORD ORIGIN Greek *planktos* wandering

planner *n* **1** a person who makes plans, esp. for the development of a town, building, etc. **2** a chart for recording future appointments, etc.

planning permission *n* formal permission granted by a local authority for the construction, alteration, or change of use of a building

plant ❶ *n* **1** a living organism that grows in the ground and lacks the power of movement **2** the land, building, and equipment used in an industry or business **3** a factory or workshop **4** mobile mechanical equipment for construction or road-making **5** *informal* a thing positioned secretly for discovery by someone else, often in order to incriminate an innocent person ▹ *vb* **6** to set (seeds or crops) into the ground to grow: *it's the wrong time of year for planting roses* **7** to place firmly in position: *I planted my chair beside hers* **8** to introduce into someone's mind: *once Wendy had planted the idea in the minds of the owners, they quite fancied selling* **9** *slang* to deliver (a blow or kiss) **10** *informal* to position or hide (someone) in order to deceive or observe **11** *informal* to hide or secrete (something), usually for some illegal purpose or in order to incriminate someone
WORD ORIGIN Old English

plantain[1] *n* a plant with a rosette of broad leaves and a slender spike of small greenish flowers
WORD ORIGIN Latin *planta* sole of the foot

plantain[2] *n* **1** a large tropical fruit like a green-skinned banana **2** the tree on which this fruit grows
WORD ORIGIN Spanish *platano*

plantation *n* **1** an estate, esp. in tropical countries, where cash crops such as rubber or coffee are grown on a large scale **2** a group of cultivated trees or plants **3** (formerly) a colony of settlers

planter *n* **1** the owner or manager of a plantation **2** a decorative pot for house plants

plantigrade *adj* walking on the entire sole of the foot, as humans and bears do
WORD ORIGIN Latin *planta* sole of the foot + *gradus* a step

plaque *n* **1** a commemorative inscribed stone or metal plate **2** Also called: **dental plaque** a filmy deposit on teeth consisting of mucus, bacteria, and food, that causes decay
WORD ORIGIN French

plasma *n* **1** the clear yellowish fluid portion of blood which contains the corpuscles and cells **2** a sterilized preparation of such fluid, taken from the blood, for use in transfusions **3** ▸ a former name for **protoplasm 4** *physics* a hot ionized gas containing positive ions and free electrons
WORD ORIGIN Greek: something moulded

plasma screen *n* a type of flat screen on a television or a visual display unit in which the image is created by electric current passing through many gas-filled cells

plaster ❶ *n* **1** a mixture of lime, sand, and water that is applied to a wall or ceiling as a soft paste and dries as a hard coating **2** *Brit, Austral, & NZ* an adhesive strip of material for dressing a cut or wound **3** ▸ short for **mustard plaster** or **plaster of Paris** ▹ *vb* **4** to coat (a wall or ceiling) with plaster **5** to apply like plaster: *he plastered his face with shaving cream* **6** to cause to lie flat or to adhere: *his hair was plastered to his forehead* **plasterer** *n*
WORD ORIGIN Greek *emplastron* healing dressing

plasterboard *n* a thin rigid board, made of plaster compressed between two layers of fibreboard, used to form or cover interior walls

plastered *adj slang* drunk

plaster of Paris *n* a white powder that sets to a hard solid when mixed with water, used for making sculptures and casts for setting broken limbs

plastic ❶ *n* **1** any of a large number of synthetic materials that can be moulded when soft and then set **2** *informal* Also called: **plastic money** credit cards etc. as opposed to cash ▹ *adj* **3** made of plastic **4** easily influenced **5** capable of being moulded or formed **6** of moulding or modelling: *the plastic arts* **7** *slang* superficially attractive yet artificial or false: *glamorous models with plastic smiles* **plasticity** *n*
WORD ORIGIN Greek *plastikos* mouldable

plastic bullet *n* a solid PVC cylinder fired by the police in riot control

plastic explosive *n* an adhesive jelly-like explosive substance

Plasticine *n trademark* a soft coloured material used, esp. by children, for modelling

plasticize *or* **-cise** *vb* **-cizing, -cized** *or* **-cising, -cised** to make or become plastic

plasticizer *or* **-ciser** *n* a substance added to a plastic material to soften it and improve flexibility

plastic surgery *n* the branch of surgery concerned with the repair or reconstruction of missing, injured, or malformed tissues or parts **plastic surgeon** *n*

plate ❶ *n* **1** a shallow dish made of porcelain, earthenware, glass, etc. on which food is served **2** Also called: **plateful** the contents of a plate **3** a shallow dish for receiving a collection in church **4** flat metal of even thickness obtained by rolling **5** a thin coating of metal usually on another metal **6** dishes or cutlery made of gold or silver **7** a sheet of metal, plastic, or rubber having a printing surface produced by a

P

THESAURUS

plant *n* **1 = flower**, bush, vegetable, herb, weed, shrub **3 = factory**, works, shop, yard, mill, foundry **4 = machinery**, equipment, gear, apparatus **6 = sow**, scatter, set out, transplant, implant, put in the ground **7 = place**, put, set, settle, fix **8 = place**, put, establish, found, fix, institute, root, lodge, insert, sow the seeds of, imbed **10, 11 = hide**, put, place, conceal

plaster *n* **1 = mortar**, stucco, gypsum, plaster of Paris, gesso **2 = bandage**, dressing, sticking plaster, Elastoplast®, adhesive plaster ▹ *vb* **5 = cover**, spread, coat, smear, overlay, daub, besmear, bedaub

plastic *adj* **5 = pliant**, soft, flexible, supple, pliable, tensile, ductile, mouldable, fictile **OPPOSITE:** rigid

plate *n* **1 = platter**, dish, dinner plate, salver, trencher *(archaic)* **2 = helping**, course, serving, dish, portion, platter, plateful **5 = layer**, panel, sheet, slab **8 = illustration**, picture, photograph, print, engraving, lithograph ▹ *vb* **18 = coat**, gild, laminate, face, cover, silver, nickel, overlay, electroplate, anodize, platinize

DICTIONARY

process such as stereotyping **8** a print taken from such a sheet or from a woodcut **9** a thin flat sheet of a substance, such as glass **10** a small piece of metal or plastic with an inscription, fixed to another surface: *a brass name plate* **11** *photog* a sheet of glass coated with photographic emulsion on which an image can be formed by exposure to light **12** *informal* ▸ same as **denture** **13** *anat* any flat platelike structure **14** a cup awarded to the winner of a sporting contest, esp. a horse race **15** any of the rigid layers of the earth's crust **16** **have a lot on one's plate** to have many pressing things to deal with **17** **on a plate** acquired without trouble: *he got the job handed to him on a plate* ▹ *vb* **plating, plated** **18** to coat (a metal surface) with a thin layer of another metal **19** to cover with metal plates, usually for protection **20** to form (metal) into plate, usually by rolling
WORD ORIGIN Old French: something flat

plateau ❶ (plat-oh) *n, pl* **-eaus** *or* **-eaux** (-ohs) **1** a wide level area of high land **2** a relatively long period of stability: *the body temperature rises to a plateau that it keeps until shortly before bedtime* ▹ *vb* **3** to remain stable for a long period
WORD ORIGIN French

plated *adj* coated with a layer of metal

plate glass *n* glass produced in thin sheets, used for windows and mirrors

platelayer *n Brit* a workman who lays and maintains railway track

platelet *n* a minute particle occurring in the blood of vertebrates and involved in the clotting of the blood

platen *n* **1** the roller on a typewriter, against which the keys strike **2** a flat plate in a printing press that presses the paper against the type
WORD ORIGIN Old French *platine*

platform ❶ *n* **1** a raised floor **2** a raised area at a railway station where passengers get on or off the trains **3** ▸ see **drilling platform** **4** the declared aims of a political party **5** the thick raised sole of some shoes **6** a type of computer hardware or operating system
WORD ORIGIN French *plat* flat + *forme* layout

platform game *n* a type of computer game that is played by moving a figure on the screen through a series of obstacles

platform ticket *n* a ticket for admission to railway platforms but not for travel

plating *n* **1** a coating of metal **2** a layer or covering of metal plates

Platini *n* **Michel** born 1955, French football player and sports administrator

platinum *n* a silvery-white metallic element, very resistant to heat and chemicals: used in jewellery, laboratory apparatus, electrical contacts, dentistry, electroplating, and as a catalyst. Symbol: Pt
WORD ORIGIN Spanish *platina* silvery element

platinum blonde *n* a girl or woman with silvery-blonde hair

platitude *n* a trite or unoriginal remark: *it's a platitude, but people need people* **platitudinous** *adj*
WORD ORIGIN French: flatness

platonic *adj* friendly or affectionate but without physical desire: *platonic love*

Platonic *adj* of the philosopher Plato or his teachings

Platonism (plate-on-iz-zum) *n* the teachings of Plato (?427–?347 BC), Greek philosopher, and his followers **Platonist** *n*

platoon *n mil* a subunit of a company, usually comprising three sections of ten to twelve men
WORD ORIGIN French *peloton* little ball, group of men

platteland *n* **the platteland** (in South Africa) the country districts or rural areas
WORD ORIGIN Afrikaans

platter *n* a large shallow, usually oval, dish
WORD ORIGIN Anglo-Norman *plater*

platypus *or* **duck-billed platypus** *n, pl* **-puses** an Australian egg-laying amphibious mammal, with dense fur, webbed feet, and a ducklike bill
WORD ORIGIN Greek *platus* flat + *pous* foot

plaudit *n* (*usually pl*) an expression of enthusiastic approval
WORD ORIGIN Latin *plaudite* applaud!

plausible ❶ *adj* **1** apparently reasonable or true: *a plausible excuse* **2** apparently trustworthy or believable: *he is an extraordinarily plausible liar* **plausibility** *n* **plausibly** *adv*
WORD ORIGIN Latin *plausibilis* worthy of applause

Plautus *n* **Titus Maccius** ?254–?184 BC, Roman comic dramatist. His 21 extant works, adapted from Greek plays, esp. those by Menander, include *Menaechmi* (the basis of Shakespeare's *The Comedy of Errors*), *Miles Gloriosus*, *Rudens*, and *Captivi*

play ❶ *vb* **1** to occupy oneself in (a sport or recreation) **2** to compete against (someone) in a sport or game: *I saw Brazil play Argentina recently* **3** to fulfil (a particular role) in a team game: *he usually plays in midfield* **4** (often foll. by *about* or *around*) to behave carelessly: *he's only playing with your affections, you know* **5** to act the part (of) in a dramatic piece: *he has played Hamlet to packed Broadway houses* **6** to perform (a dramatic piece) **7** **a** to perform (music) on an instrument **b** to be able to perform on (a musical instrument): *she plays the bassoon* **8** to send out (water) or cause to send out water: *they played a hose across the wrecked building* **9** to cause (a radio etc.) to emit sound **10** to move freely or quickly: *the light played across the water* **11** *stock Exchange* to speculate for gain in (a market) **12** *angling* to tire (a hooked fish) by alternately letting out and reeling in the line **13** to put (a card) into play **14** to gamble **15** **play fair** *or* **false with** to act fairly *or* unfairly with **16** **play for time** to gain time to one's advantage by the use of delaying tactics **17** **play into the hands of** to act unwittingly to the advantage of (an opponent) **18** **play politics** **a** to negotiate politically **b** to exploit an important issue merely for political gain **c** to make something into a political issue ▹ *n* **19** **a** a dramatic piece

THESAURUS

plateau *n* **1 = upland**, table, highland, mesa, tableland **2 = levelling off**, level, stage, stability

platform *n* **1 = stage**, stand, podium, rostrum, dais, soapbox **4 = policy**, programme, principle, objective(s), manifesto, tenet(s), party line

plausible *adj* **1 = believable**, possible, likely, reasonable, credible, probable, persuasive, conceivable, tenable, colourable, verisimilar
OPPOSITE: unbelievable
2 = glib, smooth, specious, smooth-talking, smooth-tongued, fair-spoken

play *vb* **1a = amuse yourself**, have fun, frolic, sport, fool, romp, revel, trifle, caper, frisk, gambol, entertain yourself, engage in games **1b = take part in**, be involved in, engage in, participate in, compete in, be in a team for **2 = compete against**, challenge, take on, rival, oppose, vie with, contend against **5 = act**, portray, represent, perform, impersonate, act the part of, take the part of, personate **7a = perform on**, strum, make music on ▹ *n* **19a, 19b = drama**, show, performance, piece, comedy, entertainment, tragedy, farce, soap opera, soapie *or* soapy *(Austral slang)*, pantomime, stage show, television drama, radio play, masque, dramatic piece **20 = amusement**, pleasure, leisure, games, sport, fun, entertainment, relaxation, a good time, recreation, enjoyment, romping, larks, capering, frolicking, junketing, fun and games, revelry, skylarking, living it up *(informal)*, gambolling, horseplay, merrymaking, me-time

p

DICTIONARY

written for performance by actors **b** the performance of such a piece **20** games or other activity undertaken for pleasure **21** the playing of a game or the time during which a game is in progress: *rain stopped play* **22** conduct: *fair play* **23** gambling **24** activity or operation: *radio allows full play to your imagination* **25** scope for freedom of movement: *there was a lot of play in the rope* **26** free or rapidly shifting motion: *the play of light on the water* **27** fun or jest: *I used to throw cushions at her in play* **28 in** *or* **out of play** (of a ball in a game) in *or* not in a position for continuing play according to the rules **29 make a play for** *informal* to make an obvious attempt to gain (something) ▸ See also **play along, playback**, etc. **playable** *adj*
WORD ORIGIN Old English *plega, plegan*

play along *vb* to cooperate (with) temporarily: *I'll play along with them for the moment*

playback *n* **1** the playing of a recording on magnetic tape ▹ *vb* **play back 2** to listen to or watch (something recorded)

playbill *n* a poster or bill advertising a play

playboy ⊙ *n* a rich man who devotes himself to such pleasures as nightclubs and female company

playcentre *n NZ* a centre for preschool children run by parents

play down *vb* to minimize the importance of: *she played down the problems of the company*

player ⊙ *n* **1** a person who takes part in a game or sport **2** a person who plays a musical instrument **3** *informal* a leading participant in a particular field or activity: *one of the key players in Chinese politics* **4** an actor

Player *n* **Gary** born 1935, South African professional golfer: won the British Open Championship (1959; 1968; 1974) and the US Open Championship (1965)

player piano *n* a mechanical piano; Pianola

playful *adj* **1** good-natured and humorous: *a playful remark* **2** full of high spirits and fun: *a playful child* **playfully** *adv*

playgoer *n* a person who goes often to the theatre

playground *n* **1** an outdoor area for children's play, either with swings and slides, or adjoining a school **2** a place or activity enjoyed by a specified person or group: *they oppose turning the island into a tourist playground*

playgroup *n* a regular meeting of infants for supervised creative play

playhouse *n* a theatre

playing field *n* (*sometimes pl*) *Brit & NZ* a field or open space used for sport

playlist *n* a list of records chosen for playing, such as on a radio station

play-lunch *n Austral & NZ* a child's mid-morning snack at school

playmaker *n sport* a player who creates scoring opportunities for his or her team-mates

playmate *n* a companion in play

play off *vb* **1** to set (two people) against each other for one's own ends: *she delighted in playing one parent off against the other* **2** to take part in a play-off ▹ *n* **play-off 3** *sport* an extra contest to decide the winner when there is a tie **4** *chiefly US & Canad* a contest or series of games to determine a championship

play on *vb* to exploit (the feelings or weakness of another): *he played on my sympathy*

play on words *n* ▸ same as **pun**

playpen *n* a small portable enclosure in which a young child can safely be left to play

playschool *n* a nursery group for preschool children

PlayStation *n trademark* a video games console

plaything *n* **1** a toy **2** a person regarded or treated as a toy

playtime *n* a time for play or recreation, such as a school break

play up *vb* **1** to highlight: *the temptation is to play up the sensational aspects of the story* **2** *Austral & Brit informal* to behave in an unruly way **3** to give (one) trouble or not be working properly: *my back's playing me up again; the photocopier's started to play up* **4 play up to** to try to please by flattery

playwright *n* a person who writes plays

plaza *n* **1** an open public square, usually in Spain **2** *chiefly US & Canad* a modern shopping complex
WORD ORIGIN Spanish

PLC *or* **plc** (in Britain) Public Limited Company

plea ⊙ *n* **1** an emotional appeal **2** *law* a statement by or on behalf of a defendant **3** an excuse: *his plea of poverty rings a little hollow*
WORD ORIGIN Anglo-Norman *plai*

plead ⊙ *vb* **pleading, pleaded, plead** *or esp. Scot & US* **pled 1** (sometimes foll. by *with*) to ask with deep feeling **2** to give as an excuse: *whenever she invites him to dinner, he pleads a prior engagement* **3** *law* to declare oneself to be (guilty or not guilty) of the charge made against one **4** *law* to present (a case) in a court of law
WORD ORIGIN Latin *placere* to please

pleadings *pl n law* the formal written statements presented by the plaintiff and defendant in a lawsuit

pleasant ⊙ *adj* **1** pleasing or enjoyable: *what a pleasant surprise* **2** having pleasing manners or appearance: *he was a pleasant boy* **pleasantly** *adv*
WORD ORIGIN Old French *plaisant*

pleasantry *n, pl* **-ries 1** (*often pl*) a polite or jocular remark: *we exchanged pleasantries about the weather* **2** agreeable jocularity
WORD ORIGIN French *plaisantérie*

please ⊙ *vb* **pleasing, pleased 1** to give pleasure or satisfaction to (a person) **2** to regard as suitable or satisfying: *he can get almost anyone he pleases to work with him* **3 if you please** if you wish, sometimes used in ironic exclamation **4 pleased with** happy because of **5 please oneself** to do as one likes ▹ *adv* **6** used in making polite requests or pleading: *please sit down* **7 yes please** a polite phrase used to accept an offer or invitation **pleased** *adj*
WORD ORIGIN Latin *placere*

Pleasence *n* **Donald** 1919–95, British actor. His films include *Dr Crippen* (1962) and *Cul de Sac* (1966)

pleasing ⊙ *adj* giving pleasure

P

THESAURUS

playboy *n* **= womanizer**, philanderer, rake, socialite, man about town, pleasure seeker, lady-killer (*informal*), roué, lover boy (*slang*), ladies' man

player *n* **1 = sportsman** *or* **sportswoman**, competitor, participant, contestant, team member **2 = musician**, artist, performer, virtuoso, instrumentalist, music maker **4 = performer**, entertainer, Thespian, trouper, actor *or* actress

plea *n* **1 = appeal**, request, suit, prayer, begging, petition, overture, entreaty, intercession, supplication **3 = excuse**, claim, defence, explanation, justification, pretext, vindication, extenuation

plead *vb* **1 = appeal**, ask, request, beg, petition, crave, solicit, implore, beseech, entreat, importune, supplicate

pleasant *adj* **1 = pleasing**, nice, welcome, satisfying, fine, lovely, acceptable, amusing, refreshing, delightful, enjoyable, gratifying, agreeable, pleasurable, delectable, lekker (*S African slang*)
OPPOSITE: horrible
2 = friendly, nice, agreeable, likable *or* likeable, engaging, charming, cheerful, cheery, good-humoured, amiable, genial, affable, congenial
OPPOSITE: disagreeable

please *vb* **1 = delight**, entertain, humour, amuse, suit, content, satisfy, charm, cheer, indulge, tickle, gratify, gladden, give pleasure to, tickle someone pink (*informal*)
OPPOSITE: annoy

pleasing *adj* **= enjoyable**, satisfying, attractive, charming, entertaining,

DICTIONARY

pleasurable *adj* enjoyable or agreeable **pleasurably** *adv*

pleasure ❶ *n* **1** a feeling of happiness and contentment: *the pleasure of hearing good music* **2** something that gives enjoyment: *his garden was his only pleasure* **3** the activity of enjoying oneself: *business before pleasure* **4** *euphemistic* sexual gratification: *he took his pleasure of her* **5** a person's preference
WORD ORIGIN Old French *plaisir*

pleat *n* **1** a fold formed by doubling back fabric and pressing or stitching into place ▹ *vb* **2** to arrange (material) in pleats
WORD ORIGIN variant of *plait*

pleb *n Brit informal, often offensive* a common vulgar person

plebeian (pleb-**ee**-an) *adj* **1** of the lower social classes **2** unrefined: *plebeian tastes* ▹ *n* **3** one of the common people, usually of ancient Rome **4** a coarse or unrefined person
WORD ORIGIN Latin *plebs* the common people of ancient Rome

plebiscite (**pleb**-iss-ite) *n* a direct vote by all the electorate on an issue of national importance
WORD ORIGIN Latin *plebiscitum* decree of the people

plectrum *n, pl* **-trums** *or* **-tra** an implement for plucking the strings of a guitar or similar instrument
WORD ORIGIN Greek *plektron*

pled *vb US & Scot* ▸ a past (esp. in legal usage) of **plead**

pledge ❶ *n* **1** a solemn promise **2 a** something valuable given as a guarantee that a promise will be kept or a debt paid **b** the condition of being used as security: *in pledge* **3** a token: *a pledge of good faith* **4** an assurance of support or goodwill, given by drinking a toast: *we drank a pledge to their success* **5 take** *or* **sign the pledge** to vow not to drink alcohol ▹ *vb* **pledging, pledged 6** to promise solemnly **7** to promise to give (money to charity, etc.) **8** to bind by or as if by a pledge: *I was pledged to secrecy* **9** to give (one's word or property) as a guarantee **10** to drink a toast to (a person or cause)
WORD ORIGIN Old French *plege*

Pleiocene *adj, n* ▸ same as **Pliocene**

Pleistocene (**ply**-stow-seen) *adj geol* of the epoch of geological time from about 1.6 million to 10 000 years ago
WORD ORIGIN Greek *pleistos* most + *kainos* recent

Plekhanov *n* **Georgi Valentinovich** 1857–1918, Russian revolutionary; founder of Russian Marxism and leader of the Russian Social Democratic Workers' Party

plenary *adj* **1** (of an assembly) attended by all the members **2** full or complete: *plenary powers*
WORD ORIGIN Latin *plenus* full

plenipotentiary *adj* **1** (usually of a diplomat) invested with full authority ▹ *n, pl* **-aries 2** a diplomat or representative who has full authority to transact business
WORD ORIGIN Latin *plenus* full + *potentia* power

plenitude *n literary* **1** abundance **2** fullness or completeness
WORD ORIGIN Latin *plenus* full

plenteous *adj literary* **1** abundant: *a plenteous supply* **2** producing abundantly: *a plenteous harvest*

plentiful ❶ *adj* existing in large amounts or numbers **plentifully** *adv*

plenty ❶ *n, pl* **-ties 1** (often foll. by *of*) a great number or amount: *plenty of time* **2** abundance: *an age of plenty* ▹ *adj* **3** very many: *there's plenty more fish in the sea* ▹ *adv* **4** *informal* more than adequately: *that's plenty fast enough for me*
WORD ORIGIN Latin *plenus* full

pleonasm *n rhetoric* **1** the use of more words than necessary, such as *a tiny little child* **2** an unnecessary word or phrase **pleonastic** *adj*
WORD ORIGIN Greek *pleonasmos* excess

plethora *n* an excess
WORD ORIGIN Greek *plēthōrē* fullness

pleura (**ploor**-a) *n, pl* **pleurae** (**ploor**-ee) *anat* the thin transparent membrane enveloping the lungs **pleural** *adj*
WORD ORIGIN Greek: side, rib

pleurisy *n* inflammation of the pleura, making breathing painful **pleuritic** *adj, n*

plexus *n, pl* **-uses** *or* **-us** a complex network of nerves or blood vessels
WORD ORIGIN Latin *plectere* to braid

pliable *adj* **1** easily bent: *pliable branches* **2** easily influenced: *his easy and pliable nature* **pliability** *n*

pliant *adj* **1** easily bent; supple: *pliant young willow and hazel twigs* **2** easily influenced: *he was a far more pliant subordinate than his predecessor* **pliancy** *n*
WORD ORIGIN Old French *plier* to fold

pliers *pl n* a gripping tool consisting of two hinged arms usually with serrated jaws
WORD ORIGIN from PLY[1]

plight[1] ❶ *n* a dangerous or difficult situation: *the plight of the British hostages*
WORD ORIGIN Old French *pleit* fold, and probably influenced by Old English *pliht* peril

plight[2] *vb* **plight one's troth** *old-fashioned* to make a promise to marry
WORD ORIGIN Old English *pliht* peril

Plimsoll line *n* a line on the hull of a ship showing the level that the water should reach if the ship is properly loaded
WORD ORIGIN after Samuel *Plimsoll*, who advocated its adoption

plimsolls *pl n Brit* light rubber-soled canvas sports shoes
WORD ORIGIN from the resemblance of the sole to a Plimsoll line

plinth *n* **1** a base on which a statue stands **2** the slab that forms the base of a column or pedestal
WORD ORIGIN Greek *plinthos* brick

Pliocene *or* **Pleiocene** (**ply**-oh-seen) *adj geol* of the epoch of geological time about 10 million years ago
WORD ORIGIN Greek *pleiōn* more + *kainos* recent

PLO Palestine Liberation Organization

plod *vb* **plodding, plodded 1** to walk with heavy slow steps **2** to work slowly and steadily ▹ *n* **3** the act of plodding **4** *Brit slang* a policeman **plodder** *n*
WORD ORIGIN imitative

Plomer *n* **William** (**Charles Franklyn**) 1903–73, British poet, novelist, and short-story writer, born in South Africa. His novels include *Turbott Wolfe* (1926) and *The Case is Altered* (1932)

THESAURUS

delightful, gratifying, agreeable, pleasurable **OPPOSITE:** unpleasant

pleasure *n* **1 = happiness**, delight, satisfaction, enjoyment, bliss, gratification, contentment, gladness, delectation **OPPOSITE:** displeasure **2 = amusement**, joy, recreation, diversion, solace, jollies *(slang)*, beer and skittles *(informal)* **OPPOSITE:** duty

pledge *n* **1 = promise**, vow, assurance, word, undertaking, warrant, oath, covenant, word of honour **2a, 2b = guarantee**, security, deposit, bail, bond, collateral, earnest, pawn, gage, surety ▹ *vb* **6 = promise**, vow, vouch, swear, contract, engage, undertake, give your word, give your word of honour, give your oath

plentiful *adj* **= abundant**, liberal, generous, lavish, complete, ample, infinite, overflowing, copious, inexhaustible, bountiful, profuse, thick on the ground, bounteous *(literary)*, plenteous **OPPOSITE:** scarce

plenty *n* **1** *(often with* **of***)* **= lots of** *(informal)*, enough, a great deal of, masses of, quantities of, piles of *(informal)*, mountains of, a good deal of, stacks of, heaps of *(informal)*, a mass of, a volume of, an abundance of, a plethora of, a quantity of, a fund of, oodles of *(informal)*, a store of, a mine of, a sufficiency of **2 = abundance**, wealth, luxury, prosperity, fertility, profusion, affluence, opulence, plenitude, fruitfulness, copiousness, plenteousness, plentifulness

plight[1] *n* **= difficulty**, condition, state, situation, trouble, circumstances, dilemma, straits, predicament,

DICTIONARY

plonk[1] *vb* **1** to put down heavily and carelessly: *he plonked himself down on the sofa* ▹*n* **2** the act or sound of plonking
WORD ORIGIN variant of *plunk*

plonk[2] *n informal* cheap inferior wine
WORD ORIGIN origin unknown

plonker *n Brit slang* a stupid person
WORD ORIGIN origin unknown

plop *n* **1** the sound made by an object dropping into water without a splash ▹*vb* **plopping, plopped 2** to drop with such a sound: *a tear rolled down his cheek and plopped into his soup* **3** to fall or be placed heavily or carelessly: *we plopped down on the bed and went straight to sleep*
WORD ORIGIN imitative

plosive *phonetics adj* **1** pronounced with a sudden release of breath ▹*n* **2** a plosive consonant
WORD ORIGIN French *explosif* explosive

plot[1] **T** *n* **1** a secret plan for an illegal purpose **2** the story of a play, novel, or film ▹*vb* **plotting, plotted 3** to plan secretly; conspire **4** to mark (a course) on a map **5** to make a plan or map of **6 a** to locate (points) on a graph by means of coordinates **b** to draw (a curve) through these points **7** to construct the plot of (a play, novel, or film) **plotter** *n*
WORD ORIGIN from PLOT[2], influenced by obsolete *complot* conspiracy

plot[2] **T** *n* a small piece of land: *there was a small vegetable plot in the garden*
WORD ORIGIN Old English

Plotinus *n* ?205–?270 AD, Roman Neo-Platonist philosopher, born in Egypt

plough T *or esp. US* **plow** *n* **1** an agricultural tool for cutting or turning over the earth **2** a similar tool used for clearing snow ▹*vb* **3** to turn over (the soil) with a plough **4** to make (furrows or grooves) in (something) with or as if with a plough **5** (sometimes foll. by *through*) to move (through something) in the manner of a plough: *the ship ploughed through the water* **6** (foll. by *through*) to work at slowly or perseveringly **7** to invest (money): *he ploughed the profits back into the business* **8 plough into** (of a vehicle, plane, etc.) to run uncontrollably into (something): *the aircraft ploughed into a motorway embankment*
WORD ORIGIN Old English *plōg* plough land

Plough *n* **the Plough** the group of the seven brightest stars in the constellation Ursa Major

ploughman *or esp. US* **plowman** *n, pl* **-men** a man who ploughs

ploughman's lunch *n* a snack lunch consisting of bread and cheese with pickle

ploughshare *or esp. US* **plowshare** *n* the cutting blade of a plough

plover *n* a shore bird with a round head, straight bill, and long pointed wings
WORD ORIGIN Old French *plovier* rainbird

plow *n, vb US* ▸same as **plough**

Plowright *n* Dame **Joan** born 1929, British actress, married to Laurence Olivier (1961–89)

ploy T *n* a manoeuvre designed to gain an advantage in a situation: *a cheap political ploy*
WORD ORIGIN from obsolete noun sense of *employ*, meaning an occupation

pluck T *vb* **1** to pull or pick off **2** to pull out the feathers of (a bird for cooking) **3** (foll. by *off* or *away* etc.) *archaic* to pull (something) forcibly or violently (from something or someone) **4** to sound the strings of (a musical instrument) with the fingers or a plectrum **5** *slang* to swindle ▹*n* **6** courage **7** a pull or tug **8** the heart, liver, and lungs of an animal used for food ▸See also **pluck up**
WORD ORIGIN Old English *pluccian*

pluck up *vb* to summon up (courage)

plucky *adj* **pluckier, pluckiest** courageous **pluckily** *adv* **pluckiness** *n*

plug T *n* **1** an object used to block up holes or waste pipes **2** a device with one or more pins which connects an appliance to an electricity supply **3** *informal* a favourable mention of a product etc. for example on television, to encourage people to buy it **4** ▸see **spark plug 5** a piece of tobacco for chewing ▹*vb* **plugging, plugged 6** to block or seal (a hole or gap) with a plug **7** *informal* to make frequent favourable mentions of (a product etc.), for example on television **8** *slang* to shoot: *he lifted the rifle and plugged the deer* **9** *slang* to punch **10** (foll. by *along* or *away* etc.) *informal* to work steadily ▸See also **plug in**
WORD ORIGIN Middle Dutch *plugge*

plug in *vb* to connect (an electrical appliance) to a power source by pushing a plug into a socket

plum T *n* **1** an oval dark red or yellow fruit with a stone in the middle, that grows on a small tree **2** a raisin, as used in a cake or pudding **3** *informal* something of a superior or desirable kind ▹*adj* **4** made from plums: *plum cake* **5** dark reddish-purple **6** very desirable: *plum targets for attack*
WORD ORIGIN Old English *plūme*

plumage *n* the feathers of a bird
WORD ORIGIN Old French *plume* feather

plumb T *vb* **1** to understand (something obscure): *to plumb a mystery* **2** to test the alignment of or make vertical with a plumb line **3** (foll. by *in* or *into*) to connect (an appliance or fixture) to a water pipe or drainage system: *the shower should be plumbed in professionally* **4 plumb the depths** (usually foll. by *of*) to experience the worst extremes (of something): *to plumb the depths of despair* ▹*n* **5** a lead weight hanging at the end of a string and used to test the depth of water or to test whether something is vertical **6 out of plumb** not vertical ▹*adv* **7** vertical or

P

THESAURUS

extremity, perplexity

plot[1] *n* **1 = plan**, scheme, intrigue, conspiracy, cabal, stratagem, machination, covin *(law)* **2 = story**, action, subject, theme, outline, scenario, narrative, thread, story line ▹*vb* **3 = plan**, scheme, conspire, intrigue, manoeuvre, contrive, collude, cabal, hatch a plot, machinate **4 = chart**, mark, draw, map, draft, locate, calculate, outline, compute **7 = devise**, design, project, lay, imagine, frame, conceive, brew, hatch, contrive, concoct, cook up *(informal)*

plot[2] *n* **= patch**, lot, area, ground, parcel, tract, allotment

plough *or* **plow** *(US) vb* **3, 4 = turn over**, dig, till, ridge, cultivate, furrow, break ground **5** *(sometimes with* **through***)* **= forge**, cut, drive, press, push, plunge, surge, stagger, wade, flounder, trudge, plod

ploy *n* **= tactic**, move, trick, device, game, scheme, manoeuvre, dodge, ruse, gambit, subterfuge, stratagem, contrivance, wile

pluck *vb* **1, 4 = tug**, catch, snatch, clutch, jerk, yank, tweak, pull at **2 = pull out** *or* **off**, pick, draw, collect, gather, harvest ▹*n* **6 = courage**, nerve, heart, spirit, bottle *(Brit slang)*, resolution, determination, guts *(informal)*, grit, bravery, backbone, mettle, boldness, spunk *(informal)*, intrepidity, hardihood

plug *n* **1 = stopper**, cork, bung, spigot, stopple **3** *(informal)* **= mention**, advertisement, advert *(Brit informal)*, push, promotion, publicity, puff, hype, good word ▹*vb* **6 = seal**, close, stop, fill, cover, block, stuff, pack, cork, choke, stopper, bung, stop up, stopple **7** *(informal)* **= mention**, push, promote, publicize, advertise, build up, puff, hype, write up **10** *(with* **along** *or* **away** *etc.) (informal)* **= slog away**, labour, toil away, grind away *(informal)*, peg away, plod away, drudge away

plum *adj* **6 = choice**, prize, first-class

plumb *adv (informal)* **= exactly**, precisely, bang, slap, spot-on *(Brit informal)*

DICTIONARY

perpendicular **8** *informal chiefly US* utterly: *plumb stupid* **9** *informal* exactly: *plumb in the centre*
WORD ORIGIN Latin *plumbum* lead

plumber *n* a person who fits and repairs pipes and fixtures for water, drainage, or gas systems
WORD ORIGIN Old French *plommier* worker in lead

plumbing *n* **1** the pipes and fixtures used in a water, drainage, or gas system **2** the trade or work of a plumber

plumb line *n* a string with a metal weight at one end, used to test the depth of water or to test whether something is vertical

plume *n* **1** a large ornamental feather **2** a group of feathers worn as a badge or ornament on a hat **3** something like a plume: *a plume of smoke* ▷ *vb* **pluming, plumed 4** to adorn with plumes **5** (of a bird) to preen (its feathers) **6 plume oneself** (foll. by *on* or *upon*) to be proud of oneself or one's achievements, esp. unjustifiably: *she was pluming herself on her figure*
WORD ORIGIN Old French

plummet ❶ *vb* **-meting, -meted 1** to drop down; plunge ▷ *n* **2** the weight on a plumb line or fishing line
WORD ORIGIN Old French *plommet* ball of lead

plummy *adj* **-mier, -miest 1** of, full of, or like plums: *a red wine full of ripe plummy fruit* **2** *Brit informal* (of a voice) deep, rich, and usually upper-class in manner: *his plummy condescending voice* **3** *Brit informal* desirable: *they lived plummy lives in the hills of Tuscany*

plump¹ ❶ *adj* **1** full or rounded: *until puberty I was really quite plump* ▷ *vb* **2** (often foll. by *up* or *out*) to make (something) fuller or rounded: *she plumped up the cushions on the couch*
plumpness *n*
WORD ORIGIN Middle Dutch *plomp* blunt

plump² *vb* **1** (often foll. by *down* or *into* etc.) to drop or sit suddenly and heavily: *he plumped down on the seat* **2 plump for** to choose one from a selection ▷ *n* **3** a heavy abrupt fall or the sound of this ▷ *adv* **4** suddenly or heavily **5** directly: *the plane landed plump in the middle of the field* **6** in a blunt, direct, or decisive manner
WORD ORIGIN probably imitative

plum pudding *n* a boiled or steamed pudding made with flour, suet, and dried fruit

plumy *adj* **plumier, plumiest 1** like a feather **2** covered or adorned with feathers

plunder ❶ *vb* **1** to seize (valuables or goods) from (a place) by force, usually in wartime; loot ▷ *n* **2** anything plundered; booty **3** the act of plundering; pillage
WORD ORIGIN probably from Dutch *plunderen*

plunge ❶ *vb* **plunging, plunged 1** (usually foll. by *into*) to thrust or throw (something or oneself) forcibly or suddenly: *they plunged into the sea; he plunged the knife in to the hilt* **2** to throw or be thrown into a certain condition: *the room was plunged into darkness* **3** (usually foll. by *into*) to involve or become involved deeply (in) **4** to move swiftly or impetuously **5** to descend very suddenly or steeply: *temperatures were plunging* **6** *informal* to gamble recklessly ▷ *n* **7** a leap or dive **8** *informal* a swim **9** a pitching motion **10 take the plunge** *informal* to make a risky decision which cannot be reversed later
WORD ORIGIN Old French *plongier*

plunger *n* **1** a rubber suction cup used to clear blocked drains **2** a device with a plunging motion; piston

plunk *vb* **1** to pluck the strings of (an instrument) to produce a twanging sound **2** (often foll. by *down*) to drop or be dropped heavily ▷ *n* **3** the act or sound of plunking
WORD ORIGIN imitative

Plunket *or* **Plunkett** *n* **Saint Oliver** 1629–81, Irish Roman Catholic churchman and martyr; wrongly executed as a supposed conspirator in the Popish Plot (1678). Feast day: July 11

Plunket baby *n* NZ a baby brought up according to the principles of the Plunket Society

Plunket nurse *n* NZ a nurse working for the Plunket Society

Plunket Society *n* NZ an organization for the care of mothers and babies

pluperfect *grammar adj* **1** denoting a tense of verbs used to describe an action completed before a past time. In English this is a compound tense formed with *had* plus the past participle ▷ *n* **2** the pluperfect tense
WORD ORIGIN Latin *plus quam perfectum* more than perfect

plural *adj* **1** of or consisting of more than one **2** *grammar* denoting a word indicating more than one ▷ *n* **3** *grammar* **a** the plural number **b** a plural form
WORD ORIGIN Latin *plus* more

pluralism *n* **1** the existence and toleration in a society of a variety of groups of different ethnic origins, cultures, or religions **2** the holding of more than one office by a person
pluralist *n, adj* **pluralistic** *adj*

plurality *n, pl* **-ties 1** the state of being plural **2** *maths* a number greater than one **3** a large number **4** a majority

pluralize *or* **-ise** *vb* **-izing, -ized** *or* **-ising, -ised** to make or become plural

plus ❶ *prep* **1** increased by the addition of: *four plus two* **2** with the addition of: *a good salary, plus a company car* ▷ *adj* **3** indicating addition: *a plus sign* **4** *maths* ▸ same as **positive** (sense 7) **5** on the positive part of a scale **6** indicating the positive side of an electrical circuit **7** involving advantage: *a plus factor* **8** *informal* having a value above the value stated: *it must be worth a thousand pounds plus* **9** slightly above a specified standard: *he received a B plus for his essay* ▷ *n* **10** a plus sign (+), indicating addition **11** a positive quantity **12** *informal* something positive or an advantage **13** a gain, surplus, or advantage
WORD ORIGIN Latin: more

plus fours *pl n* men's baggy knickerbockers gathered in at the knee, now only worn for hunting or golf
WORD ORIGIN because made with four inches of material to hang over at the knee

p

THESAURUS

plummet *vb* **1 = plunge**, fall, drop, crash, tumble, swoop, stoop, nosedive, descend rapidly

plump¹ *adj* **1 = chubby**, fat, stout, full, round, burly, obese, fleshy, beefy *(informal)*, tubby, portly, buxom, dumpy, roly-poly, well-covered, rotund, podgy, corpulent, well-upholstered *(informal)*
OPPOSITE: scrawny

plunder *vb* **1a = loot**, strip, sack, rob, raid, devastate, spoil, rifle, ravage, ransack, pillage, despoil **1b = steal**, rob, take, nick *(informal)*, pinch *(informal)*, embezzle, pilfer, thieve ▷ *n* **2 = loot**, spoils, prey, booty, swag *(slang)*, ill-gotten gains **3 = pillage**, sacking, robbery, marauding, rapine, spoliation

plunge *vb* **1a = submerge**, sink, duck, dip, immerse, douse, dunk **1b = throw**, cast, pitch, propel **4 = hurtle**, charge, career, jump, tear, rush, dive, dash, swoop, lurch **5a = descend**, fall, drop, crash, pitch, sink, go down, dive, tumble, plummet, nosedive **5b = fall steeply**, drop, crash *(informal)*, go down, slump, plummet, take a nosedive *(informal)* ▷ *n* **7 = dive**, jump, duck, swoop, descent, immersion, submersion **9 = fall**, crash *(informal)*, slump, drop, tumble

plus *prep* **2 = and**, with, added to, coupled with, with the addition of ▷ *n* **12, 13** *(informal)* **= advantage**, benefit, asset, gain, extra, bonus, perk *(Brit informal)*, good point, icing on the cake ▷ *adj* **7 = additional**,

DICTIONARY

plush ⊕ *n* **1** a velvety fabric with a long soft pile, used for furniture coverings ▹ *adj* **2** Also: **plushy** *informal* luxurious
WORD ORIGIN French *pluche*

plus-one *n informal* someone who accompanies an invited person to a social function

Pluto *n* **1** *classical myth* the god of the underworld **2** the smallest planet and the one farthest from the sun

plutocracy *n, pl* **-cies** **1** government by the wealthy **2** a state ruled by the wealthy **3** a group that exercises power on account of its wealth **plutocratic** *adj*
WORD ORIGIN Greek *ploutos* wealth + *-kratia* rule

plutocrat *n* a person who is powerful because of being very rich

plutonic *adj* (of igneous rocks) formed from molten rock that has cooled and solidified below the earth's surface
WORD ORIGIN after the Greek god *Pluto*

plutonium *n chem* a toxic radioactive metallic element, used in nuclear reactors and weapons. Symbol: Pu
WORD ORIGIN after *Pluto*, because Pluto lies beyond Neptune and plutonium was discovered soon after neptunium

pluvial *adj geog, geol* of or due to the action of rain
WORD ORIGIN Latin *pluvia* rain

ply[1] ⊕ *vb* **plies, plying, plied** **1** to work at (a job or trade) **2** to use (a tool) **3** (usually foll. by *with*) to provide (with) or subject (to) persistently: *he plied us with drink; he plied me with questions* **4** to work steadily **5** (of a ship) to travel regularly along (a route): *to ply the trade routes*
WORD ORIGIN Middle English *plye*, short for *aplye* to apply

ply[2] *n, pl* **plies** **1** a layer or thickness, such as of fabric or wood **2** one of the strands twisted together to make rope or yarn
WORD ORIGIN Old French *pli* fold

Plymouth Brethren *pl n* a Puritanical religious sect with no organized ministry

plywood *n* a board made of thin layers of wood glued together under pressure, with the grain of one layer at right angles to the grain of the next

Pm *chem* promethium

PM **1** Prime Minister **2** Postmaster **3** Paymaster

p.m. **1** after noon
WORD ORIGIN Latin *post meridiem*
2 postmortem (examination)

PMG **1** Postmaster General **2** Paymaster General

PMS premenstrual syndrome

PMT premenstrual tension

pneumatic *adj* **1** operated by compressed air: *pneumatic drill* **2** containing compressed air: *a pneumatic tyre* **3** of or concerned with air, gases, or wind
WORD ORIGIN Greek *pneuma* breath, wind

pneumatics *n* the branch of physics concerned with the mechanical properties of air and other gases

pneumonia *n* inflammation of one or both lungs
WORD ORIGIN Greek *pneumōn* lung

po *n, pl* **pos** *Brit, old-fashioned informal* a chamber pot
WORD ORIGIN from POT[1]

Po *chem* polonium

PO **1** Also: **p.o.** *Brit* postal order **2** Post Office **3** petty officer **4** Pilot Officer

poach[1] *vb* **1** to catch (game or fish) illegally on someone else's land **2** **a** to encroach on (someone's rights or duties) **b** to steal (an idea, employee, or player) **poacher** *n*
WORD ORIGIN Old French *pocher*

poach[2] *vb* to simmer (food) very gently in liquid
WORD ORIGIN Old French *pochier* to enclose in a bag

pock *n* **1** a pus-filled blister resulting from smallpox **2** a pockmark
WORD ORIGIN Old English *pocc*

pocket ⊕ *n* **1** a small pouch sewn into clothing for carrying small articles **2** any pouchlike container, esp. for catching balls at the edge of a snooker table **3** a small isolated area or group: *a pocket of resistance* **4** a cavity in the earth, such as one containing ore **5** **in one's pocket** under one's control **6** **out of pocket** having made a loss ▹ *vb* **-eting, -eted** **7** to put into one's pocket **8** to take secretly or dishonestly **9** *billiards, etc.* to drive (a ball) into a pocket **10** to conceal or suppress: *he pocketed his pride and asked for help* ▹ *adj* **11** small: *a pocket edition*
WORD ORIGIN Anglo-Norman *poket* a little bag

pocketbook *n chiefly US* a small case for money and papers

pocket borough *n* (before the Reform Act of 1832) an English borough constituency controlled by one person or family

pocketful *n, pl* **-fuls** as much as a pocket will hold

pocketknife *n, pl* **-knives** a small knife with one or more blades that fold into the handle; penknife

pocket money *n* **1** a small weekly sum of money given to children by parents **2** money for small personal expenses

pockmarked *adj* **1** (of the skin) marked with pitted scars after the healing of smallpox **2** (of a surface) covered in many small hollows: *the building is pockmarked with bullet holes* **pockmark** *n*

pod ⊕ *n* **1** **a** a long narrow seedcase containing peas, beans, etc. **b** the seedcase as distinct from the seeds ▹ *vb* **podding, podded** **2** to remove the pod from
WORD ORIGIN origin unknown

podcast *n* **1** an audio file similar to a radio broadcast, which can be downloaded and listened to on a computer, iPod™, etc. ▹ *vb* **-casts, -casting, -cast** *or* **-casted** **2** to create such files and make them available for downloading **3** to make (music, interviews, etc.) available using this format **podcaster** *n* **podcasting** *n*

podgy *adj* **podgier, podgiest** short and fat **podginess** *n*
WORD ORIGIN from *podge* a short plump person

podiatry (pod-eye-a-tree) *n* ▸ another word for **chiropody** > **podiatrist** *n*

podium ⊕ *n, pl* **-diums** *or* **-dia** **1** a small raised platform used by conductors or speakers **2** a plinth that supports a colonnade or wall
WORD ORIGIN Latin: platform

poem ⊕ *n* **1** a literary work, often in verse, usually dealing with emotional or descriptive themes in a rhythmic form **2** a literary work that is not in verse but deals with emotional or descriptive themes in a rhythmic form: *a prose poem* **3** anything like a poem in beauty or effect: *his painting is a poem on creation*
WORD ORIGIN Greek *poiēma* something created

poep (poop) *n S African, taboo* **1** an emission of intestinal gas from the anus **2** a mean or despicable person
WORD ORIGIN Afrikaans

poesy *n archaic* poetry

poet ⊕ *n* **1** a writer of poetry **2** a person with great imagination and creativity

P

THESAURUS

added, extra, positive, supplementary, add-on

plush *adj* **2** *(informal)* **= luxurious**, luxury, costly, lavish, rich, sumptuous, opulent, palatial, ritzy *(slang)*, de luxe **OPPOSITE:** cheap

ply[1] *vb* **1 = work at**, follow, exercise, pursue, carry on, practise

pocket *n* **2 = pouch**, bag, sack, hollow, compartment, receptacle ▹ *vb* **8 = steal**, take, lift *(informal)*, appropriate, pilfer, purloin, filch, help yourself to, snaffle *(Brit informal)* ▹ *adj* **11 = small**, compact, miniature, portable, little, potted *(informal)*, concise, pint-size(d) *(informal)*, abridged

pod *n* **1b = shell**, case, hull, husk, shuck

podium *n* **1 = platform**, stand, stage, rostrum, dais

poem *n* **1 = verse**, song, lyric, rhyme, sonnet, ode, verse composition

poet *n* **1 = bard**, rhymer, lyricist, lyric poet, versifier, maker *(archaic)*, elegist

DICTIONARY

WORD ORIGIN Greek *poiētēs* maker, poet

poetaster *n* a writer of inferior verse

poetic ❶ *or* **poetical** *adj* **1** like poetry, by being expressive or imaginative **2** of poetry or poets **3** recounted in verse

poetic justice *n* an appropriate punishment or reward for previous actions

poetic licence *n* freedom from the normal rules of language or truth, as in poetry

poet laureate *n, pl* **poets laureate** *Brit* the poet selected by the British sovereign to write poems on important occasions

poetry ❶ *n* **1** poems in general **2** the art or craft of writing poems **3** a poetic quality that prompts an emotional response: *her acting was full of poetry*
WORD ORIGIN Latin *poeta* poet

po-faced *adj* wearing a disapproving stern expression
WORD ORIGIN perhaps from PO + POKER-FACED

pogey ❶ *or* **pogy** (**pohg**-ee) *n, pl* **pogeys** *or* **pogies** *Canad slang* **1** financial or other relief given to the unemployed by the government; dole **2** unemployment insurance
WORD ORIGIN from earlier *pogie* workhouse

pogo stick *n* a pole with steps for the feet and a spring at the bottom, so that the user can bounce up, down, and along on it
WORD ORIGIN origin unknown

pogrom *n* an organized persecution and massacre
WORD ORIGIN Russian: destruction

poi *n NZ* a ball of woven flax swung rhythmically by Māori women during poi dances
WORD ORIGIN Māori

poi dance *n NZ* a women's formation dance that involves singing and twirling a poi

poignant ❶ *adj* **1** sharply painful to the feelings: *a poignant reminder* **2** cutting: *poignant wit* **3** pertinent in mental appeal: *a poignant subject*
poignancy *n*
WORD ORIGIN Latin *pungens* pricking

Poincaré *n* **1 Jules Henri** 1854–1912, French mathematician, physicist, and philosopher. He made important contributions to the theory of functions and to astronomy and electromagnetic theory **2** his cousin, **Raymond** 1860–1934, French statesman; premier of France (1912–13; 1922–24; 1926–29); president (1913–20)

poinsettia *n* a shrub of Mexico and Central America, widely grown for its showy scarlet bracts, which resemble petals
WORD ORIGIN after J. P. *Poinsett*, US Minister to Mexico

point ❶ *n* **1** the essential idea in an argument or discussion: *I agreed with the point he made* **2** a reason or aim: *what is the point of this exercise?* **3** a detail or item **4** a characteristic: *he has his good points* **5** a location or position **6** a dot or tiny mark **7** a dot used as a decimal point or a full stop **8** the sharp tip of anything: *the point of the spear* **9** a headland: *the soaring cliffs at Dwerja Point in the southwest of the island* **10** *maths* a geometric element having a position located by coordinates, but no magnitude **11** a specific condition or degree: *freezing point* **12** a moment: *at that point he left* **13** (*often pl*) any of the extremities, such as the tail, ears, or feet, of a domestic animal **14** (*often pl*) *ballet* the tip of the toes **15** a single unit for measuring something such as value, or of scoring in a game **16** *printing* a unit of measurement equal to one twelfth of a pica **17** *navigation* one of the 32 direction marks on the compass **18** *cricket* a fielding position at right angles to the batsman on the off side **19** either of the two electrical contacts that make or break the circuit in the distributor of a motor vehicle **20** *Brit, Austral, & NZ* (*often pl*) a movable section of railway track used to direct a train from one line to another **21** *Brit* ▸ short for **power point** **22** *boxing* a mark awarded for a scoring blow or knockdown **23 beside the point** irrelevant **24 make a point of a** to make a habit of (something) **b** to do (something) because one thinks it important **25 on** *or* **at the point of** about to; on the verge of: *on the point of leaving* **26 to the point** relevant **27 up to a point** not completely ▹ *vb* **28** (usually foll. by *at* or *to*) to show the position or direction of something by extending a finger or other pointed object towards it **29** (usually foll. by *at* or *to*) to single out one person or thing from among several: *all the symptoms pointed to epilepsy* **30** to direct or face in a specific direction: *point me in the right direction* **31** to finish or repair the joints in brickwork with mortar or cement **32** (of gun dogs) to show where game is lying by standing rigidly with the muzzle turned towards it ▸ See also **point out**
WORD ORIGIN Latin *pungere* to pierce

point-blank *adj* **1** fired at a very close target **2** plain or blunt: *a point-blank refusal to discuss the matter* ▹ *adv* **3** directly or bluntly: *the Minister was asked point-blank if he intended to resign*
WORD ORIGIN *point* + *blank* (centre spot of an archery target)

point duty *n* the control of traffic by a policeman at a road junction

pointed ❶ *adj* **1** having a sharp tip **2** cutting or incisive: *pointed wit* **3** obviously directed at a particular person: *a pointed remark* **4** emphasized or obvious: *pointed ignorance*
pointedly *adv*

pointer ❶ *n* **1** something that is a helpful indicator of how a situation has arisen or may turn out: *a significant pointer to the likely resumption of talks* **2** an indicator on a measuring instrument **3** a long stick used by teachers, to point out particular

THESAURUS

poetic *adj* **1 = figurative**, creative, lyric, symbolic, lyrical, rhythmic, rhythmical, songlike **2 = lyrical**, lyric, rhythmic, elegiac, rhythmical, metrical

poetry *n* **1, 2 = verse**, poems, rhyme, rhyming, poesy (*archaic*), verse composition, metrical composition

pogey *n* **1** (*Canad slang*) **= benefits**, the dole (*Brit & Austral*), welfare, social security, unemployment benefit, state benefit, allowance

poignant *adj* **1 = moving**, touching, affecting, upsetting, sad, bitter, intense, painful, distressing, pathetic, harrowing, heartbreaking, agonizing, heart-rending, gut-wrenching

point *n* **1 = essence**, meaning, subject, question, matter, heart, theme, import, text, core, burden, drift, thrust, proposition, marrow, crux, gist, main idea, nub, pith **2 = purpose**, aim, object, use, end, reason, goal, design, intention, objective, utility, intent, motive, usefulness **3, 4 = aspect**, detail, feature, side, quality, property, particular, respect, item, instance, characteristic, topic, attribute, trait, facet, peculiarity, nicety **5 = place**, area, position, station, site, spot, location, locality, locale **6 = pinpoint**, mark, spot, dot, fleck, speck **8 = end**, tip, sharp end, top, spur, spike, apex, nib, tine, prong **11 = stage**, level, position, condition, degree, pitch, circumstance, extent **12 = moment**, time, stage, period, phase, instant, juncture, moment in time, very minute **15 = score**, tally, mark ▹ *vb* **30a = aim**, level, train, direct **30b = face**, look, direct

pointed *adj* **1 = sharp**, edged, acute, barbed **2 = cutting**, telling, biting, sharp, keen, acute, accurate, penetrating, pertinent, incisive, trenchant

pointer *n* **1 = hint**, tip, suggestion, warning, recommendation, caution, piece of information, piece of advice **2 = indicator**, hand, guide, needle, arrow

features on a map, chart, etc. **4** a large smooth-coated gun dog

pointillism (pwan-till-iz-zum) *n* a technique used by some impressionist painters, in which dots of colour are placed side by side so that they merge when seen from a distance **pointillist** *n, adj*
WORD ORIGIN French

pointing *n* the insertion of mortar between the joints in brickwork

pointless ❶ *adj* without meaning or purpose

point of no return *n* a point at which one is committed to continuing with an action

point of order *n, pl* **points of order** an objection in a meeting to the departure from the proper procedure

point of view *n, pl* **points of view** **1** a mental viewpoint or attitude: *she refuses to see the other person's point of view* **2** a way of considering something: *a scientific point of view*

point out *vb* to draw someone's attention to

point-to-point *n Brit* a steeplechase organized by a hunt

poise *n* **1** dignified manner **2** physical balance: *the poise of a natural model* **3** mental balance: *he recovered his poise* ▹*vb* **poising, poised** **4** to be balanced or suspended **5** to be held in readiness: *the cats were poised to spring on her*
WORD ORIGIN Old French *pois* weight

poised ❶ *adj* **1** absolutely ready **2** behaving with or showing poise

poison ❶ *n* **1** a substance that causes death or injury when swallowed or absorbed **2** something that destroys or corrupts: *the poison of Nazism* ▹*vb* **3** to give poison to someone **4** to add poison to something **5** to have a harmful or evil effect on **6** (foll. by *against*) to turn (a person's mind) against: *he poisoned her mind against me* **poisoner** *n*
WORD ORIGIN Latin *potio* a drink, esp. a poisonous one

poison ivy *n* a North American climbing plant that causes an itching rash if it touches the skin

poisonous ❶ *adj* **1** of or like a poison **2** malicious

poison-pen letter *n* a malicious anonymous letter

poke[1] ❶ *vb* **poking, poked** **1** to jab or prod with an elbow, finger, etc. **2** to make a hole by poking **3** (sometimes foll. by *at*) to thrust (at): *she poked at the food with her fork* **4** (usually foll. by *in* or *through* etc.) to thrust forward or out: *yellow hair poked from beneath his cap* **5** to stir (a fire) by poking **6** (often foll. by *about* or *around*) to search or pry **7** **poke one's nose into** to meddle in ▹*n* **8** a jab or prod
WORD ORIGIN Low German & Middle Dutch *poken*

poke[2] *n* **1** *dialect* a pocket or bag **2** **a pig in a poke** ▸see **pig**
WORD ORIGIN Old French *poque*

poker[1] *n* a metal rod with a handle for stirring a fire

poker[2] *n* a card game of bluff and skill in which players bet on the hands dealt
WORD ORIGIN origin unknown

poker face *n informal* an expressionless face, such as that of a poker player trying to hide the value of his or her cards **poker-faced** *adj*

pokerwork *n* the art of producing pictures or designs on wood by burning it with a heated metal point

poky *adj* **pokier, pokiest** (of a room) small and cramped **pokiness** *n*
WORD ORIGIN from POKE[1] (in slang sense: to confine)

pol. **1** political **2** politics

Polanski *n* **Roman** born 1933, Polish film director with a taste for the macabre, as in *Repulsion* (1965) and *Rosemary's Baby* (1968): later films include *Tess* (1980), *Death and the Maiden* (1995), and *The Pianist* (2002)

polar *adj* **1** of or near either of the earth's poles or the area inside the Arctic or Antarctic Circles **2** of or having a pole or polarity **3** directly opposite in tendency or nature: *polar opposites*

polar bear *n* a white bear of coastal regions of the North Pole

polar circle *n* the Arctic or Antarctic Circle

polarity *n, pl* **-ties** **1** the state of having two directly opposite tendencies or opinions **2** the condition of a body which has opposing physical properties, usually magnetic poles or electric charge **3** the particular state of a part with polarity: *an electrode with positive polarity*

polarization *or* **-isation** *n* **1** the condition of having or giving polarity **2** *physics* the condition in which waves of light or other radiation are restricted to certain directions of vibration

polarize *or* **-ise** *vb* **-izing, -ized** *or* **-ising, -ised** **1** to cause people to adopt directly opposite opinions: *political opinion had polarized since the restoration of democracy* **2** to have or give polarity or polarization

Polaroid *n trademark* **1** a type of plastic that polarizes light: used in sunglasses to eliminate glare **2** **Polaroid camera** a camera that produces a finished print by developing and processing it inside the camera within a few seconds **3** **Polaroids** sunglasses with Polaroid plastic lenses

polder *n* a stretch of land reclaimed from the sea
WORD ORIGIN Middle Dutch *polre*

pole[1] ❶ *n* **1** a long slender rounded piece of wood, metal, or other material **2** **up the pole** *Brit, Austral & NZ informal* **a** slightly mad **b** in a predicament
WORD ORIGIN Latin *palus* a stake

pole[2] *n* **1** either end of the earth's axis of rotation ▸See also **North Pole, South Pole** **2** *physics* **a** either of the opposite forces of a magnet **b** either of two points at which there are opposite electric charges **3** either of two directly opposite tendencies or opinions **4** **poles apart** having widely divergent opinions or tastes
WORD ORIGIN Greek *polos* pivot

Pole *n* a person from Poland

Pole[1] *n* a native, inhabitant, or citizen of Poland or a speaker of Polish

Pole[2] *n* **Reginald** 1500–58, English cardinal; last Roman Catholic archbishop of Canterbury (1556–58)

poleaxe *or US* **poleax** *vb* **-axing, -axed** **1** to hit or stun with a heavy blow ▹*n* **2** an axe formerly used in

P

pointless *adj* **= senseless,** meaningless, futile, fruitless, unproductive, stupid, silly, useless, absurd, irrelevant, in vain, worthless, ineffectual, unprofitable, nonsensical, aimless, inane, unavailing, without rhyme or reason OPPOSITE: worthwhile

poised *adj* **1 = ready,** waiting, prepared, standing by, on the brink, in the wings, all set **2 = composed,** calm, together *(informal)*, collected, dignified, graceful, serene, suave, urbane, self-confident, unfazed *(informal)*, debonair, unruffled, nonchalant, self-possessed OPPOSITE: agitated

poison *n* **1 = toxin,** venom, bane *(archaic)* ▹*vb* **3 = murder,** kill, give someone poison, administer poison to **5 = contaminate,** foul, infect, spoil, pollute, blight, taint, adulterate, envenom, befoul **6** *(with* **against)** **= corrupt,** colour, undermine, bias, sour, pervert, warp, taint, subvert, embitter, deprave, defile, jaundice, vitiate, envenom

poisonous *adj* **1 = toxic,** fatal, deadly, lethal, mortal, virulent, noxious, venomous, baneful *(archaic)*, mephitic **2 = evil,** vicious, malicious, corrupting, pernicious, baleful, baneful *(archaic)*, pestiferous

poke[1] *vb* **1 = jab,** hit, push, stick, dig, punch, stab, thrust, butt, elbow, shove, nudge, prod **4** *(usually with* **in** *or* **through** *etc.)* **= protrude,** stick, thrust, jut ▹*n* **8 = jab,** hit, dig, punch, thrust, butt, nudge, prod

pole[1] *n* **1 = rod,** post, support, staff, standard, bar, stick, stake, paling, shaft, upright, pillar, mast, picket, spar, stave

DICTIONARY

battle or used by a butcher
WORD ORIGIN Middle English *pollax* battle-axe

polecat *n, pl* **-cats** *or* **-cat 1** a dark brown mammal like a weasel that gives off a foul smell **2** *US* a skunk
WORD ORIGIN origin unknown

pole dancing *n* a form of entertainment in which a scantily dressed woman dances erotically, turning on and posing against a vertically fixed pole on stage **pole dancer** *n*

polemic (pol-**em**-ik) *n* **1** a fierce attack on or defence of a particular opinion, belief, etc.: *anti-capitalist polemic* ▹ *adj also* **polemical 2** of or involving dispute or controversy **polemicist** *n*
WORD ORIGIN Greek *polemos* war

polemics *n* the art of dispute

pole position *n* **1** (in motor racing) the starting position on the inside of the front row, generally considered the best one **2** an advantageous starting position

pole star *n* a guiding principle or rule

Pole Star *n* **the Pole Star** the star closest to the N celestial pole

pole vault *n* **1 the pole vault** a field event in which competitors try to clear a high bar with the aid of a very flexible long pole ▹ *vb* **pole-vault 2** to perform or compete in the pole vault **pole-vaulter** *n*

Poliakoff *n* **Stephen** born 1952, British playwright and film director; work includes the stage plays *Breaking the Silence* (1984) and *Blinded by the Sun* (1996) and the television serials *The Lost Prince* (2003) and *Friends and Crocodiles* (2005)

P

police ⓣ *n* **1** (often preceded by *the*) the organized civil force in a state which keeps law and order **2** the men and women who are members of such a force **3** an organized body with a similar function: *security police* ▹ *vb* **-licing, -liced 4** to maintain order or control by means of a police force or similar body
WORD ORIGIN French, from Latin *politia* administration

police dog *n* a dog trained to help the police

policeman *or fem* **policewoman** *n, pl* **-men** *or fem* **-women** a member of a police force

police procedural *n* a novel, film, or television drama that deals with police work

police state *n* a state in which a government controls people's freedom through the police

police station *n* the office of the police force of a district

policy¹ ⓣ *n, pl* **-cies 1** a plan of action adopted by a person, group, or government **2** *archaic* wisdom or prudence
WORD ORIGIN Old French *policie*, from Latin *politia* administration

policy² *n, pl* **-cies** a document containing an insurance contract **policyholder** *n*
WORD ORIGIN Old French *police* certificate

Polignac *n* **Prince de,** title of *Auguste Jules Armand Marie de Polignac*. 1780–1847, French statesman; prime minister (1829–30) to Charles X: his extreme royalist and ultramontane policies provoked the 1830 revolution and cost Charles X the throne

polio *n* ▸ short for **poliomyelitis**

poliomyelitis (pole-ee-oh-my-el-**lite**-iss) *n* a viral disease which affects the brain and spinal cord, often causing paralysis
WORD ORIGIN Greek *polios* grey + *muelos* marrow

polish ⓣ *vb* **1** to make smooth and shiny by rubbing **2** to perfect or complete: *media experts he had hired to polish his image* **3** to make or become elegant or refined: *not having polished his south London accent didn't help his career* ▹ *n* **4** a substance used for polishing **5** a shine or gloss **6** elegance or refinement ▸ See also **polish off, polish up**
WORD ORIGIN Latin *polire* to polish

Polish *adj* **1** of Poland ▹ *n* **2** the language of Poland

polished ⓣ *adj* **1** accomplished: *a polished actor* **2** done or performed well or professionally: *a polished performance*

polish off *vb informal* **1** to finish completely **2** to dispose of or kill

polish up *vb* **1** to make smooth and shiny by polishing **2** to improve (a skill or ability) by working at it: *I'm going to evening classes to polish up my German*

Politburo *n* formerly, the chief decision-making committee of a Communist country
WORD ORIGIN Russian

polite ⓣ *adj* **1** having good manners; courteous **2** cultivated or refined: *polite society* **3** socially correct but insincere: *he smiled a polite response and stifled an urge to scream* **politely** *adv* **politeness** *n*
WORD ORIGIN Latin *politus* polished

Politian *n* Italian name *Angelo Polliziano;* original name *Angelo Ambrogini*. 1454–94, Florentine humanist and poet

politic ⓣ *adj* **1** wise or possibly advantageous: *I didn't feel it was politic to mention it* **2** artful or shrewd: *a politic manager* **3** crafty; cunning: *a politic old scoundrel* **4** *archaic* political ▸ See also **body politic**
WORD ORIGIN Old French *politique*, from Greek *polis* city

political ⓣ *adj* **1** of the state, government, or public administration **2** relating to or interested in politics: *she was always a very political person* **3** of the parties and the partisan aspects of politics: *the government blames political opponents for fanning the unrest* **politically** *adv*

politically correct *adj* displaying progressive attitudes, esp. in using vocabulary which is intended to avoid any implied prejudice

political prisoner *n* a person imprisoned for holding particular political beliefs

THESAURUS

police *n* **1, 2 = the law** *(informal)*, police force, constabulary, fuzz *(slang)*, law enforcement agency, boys in blue *(informal)*, the Old Bill *(slang)*, rozzers *(slang)* ▹ *vb* **4 = control**, patrol, guard, watch, protect, regulate, keep the peace, keep in order

policy¹ *n* **1 = procedure**, plan, action, programme, practice, scheme, theory, code, custom, stratagem

polish *vb* **1 = shine**, wax, clean, smooth, rub, buff, brighten, burnish, furbish **2, 3 = perfect**, improve, enhance, refine, finish, correct, cultivate, brush up, touch up, emend ▹ *n* **4 = varnish**, wax, glaze, lacquer, japan **5 = sheen**, finish, sparkle, glaze, gloss, brilliance, brightness, veneer, lustre, smoothness **6 = style**, class *(informal)*, finish, breeding, grace, elegance, refinement, finesse, urbanity, suavity, politesse

polished *adj* **1, 2 = accomplished**, professional, masterly, fine, expert, outstanding, skilful, adept, impeccable, flawless, superlative, faultless **OPPOSITE:** amateurish

polite *adj* **1 = mannerly**, civil, courteous, affable, obliging, gracious, respectful, well-behaved, deferential, complaisant, well-mannered **OPPOSITE:** rude **2 = refined**, cultured, civilized, polished, sophisticated, elegant, genteel, urbane, courtly, well-bred **OPPOSITE:** uncultured

politic *adj* **1 = wise**, diplomatic, sensible, discreet, prudent, advisable, expedient, judicious, tactful, sagacious, in your best interests

political *adj* **1 = governmental**, government, state, parliamentary, constitutional, administrative, legislative, civic, ministerial, policy-making, party political

politician *n* **= statesman** *or* **stateswoman**, representative, senator *(US)*, congressman *(US)*, Member of Parliament, legislator, public servant, congresswoman *(US)*, politico *(informal, chiefly US)*, lawmaker, office bearer, M.P., elected offical

DICTIONARY

political science *n* the study of the state, government, and politics **political scientist** *n*

politician ❶ *n* a person actively engaged in politics, esp. a member of parliament

politicize *or* **-cise** *vb* **-cizing, -cized** *or* **-cising, -cised** 1 to make political or politically aware 2 to take part in political discussion or activity **politicization** *or* **-cisation** *n*

politics ❶ *n* 1 (*functioning as sing*) the art and science of government 2 (*functioning as pl*) political opinions or sympathies: *his conservative politics* 3 (*functioning as pl*) political activities or affairs: *party politics* 4 (*functioning as sing*) the business or profession of politics 5 (*functioning as sing or pl*) any activity concerned with the acquisition of power: *company politics are often vicious*

polity *n, pl* **-ties** *formal* 1 a politically organized state, church, or society 2 a form of government of a state, church, or society
WORD ORIGIN Greek *politeia* citizenship, from *polis* city

polka *n* 1 a lively 19th-century dance 2 music for this dance ▷ *vb* **-kaing, -kaed** 3 to dance a polka
WORD ORIGIN Czech *pulka* half-step

polka dots *pl n* a regular pattern of small bold spots on a fabric

poll ❶ *n* 1 Also called: **opinion poll** the questioning of a random sample of people to find out the general opinion 2 the casting, recording, or counting of votes in an election 3 the result of such a voting: *a marginal poll* 4 the head ▷ *vb* 5 to receive (a certain number of votes) 6 to record the votes of: *he polled the whole town* 7 to question (a person, etc.) as part of an opinion poll 8 to vote in an election 9 to clip or shear 10 to remove or cut short the horns of (cattle)
WORD ORIGIN Middle Low German *polle* hair, head, top of a tree

pollack *or* **pollock** *n, pl* **-lacks, -lack, -locks** *or* **-lock** a food fish related to the cod, found in northern seas
WORD ORIGIN origin unknown

Pollack *n* **Sydney** born 1934, US film director. His films include *Tootsie* (1982), *Out of Africa* (1986), and *The Firm* (1993)

Pollaiuolo *n* 1 **Antonio** ?1432–98, Florentine painter, sculptor, goldsmith, and engraver: his paintings include the *Martyrdom of St Sebastian* 2 his brother **Piero** ?1443–96, Florentine painter and sculptor

pollard *n* 1 an animal that has shed its horns or has had them removed 2 a tree with its top cut off to encourage a more bushy growth ▷ *vb* 3 to cut off the top of (a tree) to make it grow **pollarded** *adj*
WORD ORIGIN see POLL

pollen *n* a fine powder produced by flowers to fertilize other flowers of the same species
WORD ORIGIN Latin: powder

Pollen *n* **Daniel** 1813–96, New Zealand statesman, born in Ireland: prime minister of New Zealand (1876)

pollen count *n* a measure of the amount of pollen in the air over a 24-hour period, often published as a warning to hay fever sufferers

pollinate *vb* **-nating, -nated** to fertilize by the transfer of pollen **pollination** *n*

polling booth *n* a compartment in which a voter can mark his or her ballot paper in private during an election

polling station *n* a building where voters go during an election to cast their votes

pollock *n* ▸ same as **pollack**

pollster *n* a person who conducts opinion polls

poll tax *n* any tax levied per head of adult population, esp. the tax which replaced domestic rates (in Scotland from 1989 and England and Wales from 1990, until 1993)

pollutant *n* a substance that pollutes, usually the chemical waste of an industrial process

pollute ❶ *vb* **-luting, -luted** 1 to contaminate with poisonous or harmful substances 2 to corrupt morally **pollution** *n*
WORD ORIGIN Latin *polluere* to defile

polo *n* 1 a game like hockey played on horseback with long-handled mallets and a wooden ball 2 ▸ short for **water polo**
WORD ORIGIN Tibetan *pulu* ball

polonaise *n* 1 a stately Polish dance 2 music for this dance
WORD ORIGIN French *danse polonaise* Polish dance

polo neck *n* a sweater with a high tight turned-over collar

polonium *n chem* a rare radioactive element found in trace amounts in uranium ores. Symbol: Po
WORD ORIGIN Medieval Latin *Polonia* Poland; in honour of the nationality of its discoverer, Marie Curie

polo shirt *n* a cotton short-sleeved shirt with a collar and three-button opening at the neck

poltergeist *n* a spirit believed to be responsible for noises and acts of mischief, such as throwing objects about
WORD ORIGIN German *poltern* to be noisy + *Geist* ghost

poltroon *n obsolete* a complete coward
WORD ORIGIN Old Italian *poltrone* lazy good-for-nothing

poly *n, pl* **polys** *informal* ▸ short for **polytechnic**

poly- *combining form* many or much: *polyhedron; polysyllabic*
WORD ORIGIN Greek *polus*

polyandry *n* the practice of having more than one husband at the same time **polyandrous** *adj*
WORD ORIGIN Greek *polus* many + *anēr* man

polyanthus *n, pl* **-thuses** a hybrid garden primrose with brightly coloured flowers
WORD ORIGIN Greek: having many flowers

Polybius *n* ?205–?123 BC, Greek historian. Under the patronage of Scipio the Younger, he wrote in 40 books a history of Rome from 264 BC to 146 BC

Polycarp *n* **Saint** ?69–?155 AD, Christian martyr and bishop of Smyrna, noted for his letter to the church at Philippi. Feast day: Feb 23

polychromatic *adj* 1 having many colours 2 (of radiation) containing more than one wavelength

Polyclitus, Polycleitus, *or* **Polycletus** *n* 5th-century BC Greek sculptor, noted particularly for his idealized bronze sculptures of the male nude, such as the *Doryphoros*

Polycrates *n* died ?522 BC, Greek tyrant of Samos, who was crucified by a Persian satrap

polycystic ovary syndrome *n* a hormonal disorder preventing ovulation, leading to reduced fertility, hirsutism, and weight gain. abbreviation: **PCOS**

polyester *n* a synthetic material used to make plastics and textile fibres

polyethylene *n* ▸ same as **polythene**

polygamy (pol-ig-a-mee) *n* the practice of having more than one wife or husband at the same time

P

THESAURUS

politics *n* **1a = affairs of state**, government, government policy, public affairs, civics **1b = political science**, polity, statesmanship, civics, statecraft **2 = political beliefs**, party politics, political allegiances, political leanings, political sympathies

poll *n* **1 = survey**, figures, count, sampling, returns, ballot, tally, census, canvass, Gallup Poll, (public) opinion poll **2 = election**, vote, voting, referendum, ballot, plebiscite ▷ *vb* **5 = gain**, return, record, register, tally **7 = question**, interview, survey, sample, ballot, canvass

pollute *vb* **1 = contaminate**, dirty, mar, poison, soil, foul, infect, spoil, stain, taint, adulterate, make filthy, smirch, befoul
OPPOSITE: decontaminate
2 = defile, violate, corrupt, sully, deprave, debase, profane, desecrate, dishonour, debauch, besmirch
OPPOSITE: honour

DICTIONARY

polygamist *n* **polygamous** *adj*
WORD ORIGIN Greek *polus* many + *gamos* marriage

polyglot *adj* **1** able to speak many languages **2** written in or using many languages ▷ *n* **3** a person who can speak many languages
WORD ORIGIN Greek *poluglōttos* many-tongued

Polygnotus *n* 5th century BC, Greek painter: associated with Cimon in rebuilding Athens

polygon *n* a geometrical figure with three or more sides and angles **polygonal** *adj*
WORD ORIGIN Greek *polugōnon* figure with many angles

polygraph *n* an instrument for recording pulse rate and perspiration, often used as a lie detector
WORD ORIGIN Greek *polugraphos* writing copiously

polygyny *n* the practice of having more than one wife at the same time **polygynous** *adj*
WORD ORIGIN Greek *polus* many + *gunē* woman

polyhedron *n, pl* **-drons** *or* **-dra** a solid figure with four or more sides **polyhedral** *adj*
WORD ORIGIN Greek *polus* many + *hedron* side

Polyhymnia *n Greek myth* the Muse of singing, mime, and sacred dance

polymath *n* a person of great and varied learning
WORD ORIGIN Greek *polumathēs* having much knowledge

polymer *n* a natural or synthetic compound with large molecules made up of simple molecules of the same kind

polymeric *adj* of or being a polymer: *polymeric materials such as PVC*
WORD ORIGIN Greek *polumerēs* having many parts

polymerization *or* **-isation** *n* the process of forming a polymer **polymerize** *or* **-ise** *vb*

polymorphous *or* **polymorphic** *adj* having, or passing through many different forms or stages
WORD ORIGIN Greek *polus* many + *morphē* form

Polynesian *adj* **1** of Polynesia ▷ *n* **2** a person from Polynesia **3** any of the languages of Polynesia

polynomial *maths adj* **1** consisting of two or more terms ▷ *n* **2** an algebraic expression consisting of the sum of a number of terms

polyp *n* **1** *zool* a small sea creature that has a hollow cylindrical body with a ring of tentacles around the mouth **2** *pathol* a small growth on the surface of a mucous membrane
WORD ORIGIN Greek *polupous* having many feet

polyphonic *adj music* consisting of several melodies played together

polyphony (pol-if-on-ee) *n, pl* **-nies** polyphonic style of composition or a piece of music using it
WORD ORIGIN Greek *poluphōnia* diversity of tones

polysaccharide *n* a carbohydrate which consists of a number of linked sugar molecules, such as starch or cellulose

polystyrene *n* a synthetic material used esp. as white rigid foam for insulating and packing

polysyllable *n* a word having more than two syllables **polysyllabic** *adj*

polytechnic *n* **1** *Brit* (in New Zealand and formerly in Britain) college offering courses in many subjects at and below degree level ▷ *adj* **2** of or relating to technical instruction
WORD ORIGIN Greek *polutekhnos* skilled in many arts

polytheism *n* belief in more than one god **polytheistic** *adj* **polytheist** *n*

polythene *n* a light plastic material made from ethylene, usually made into thin sheets or bags

polyunsaturated *adj* of a group of fats that are less likely to contribute to the build-up of cholesterol in the body

polyurethane *n* a synthetic material used esp. in paints

polyvinyl chloride *n* ▸ see **PVC**

pom *n Austral & NZ slang* person from England **pommy**

pomace (pumm-iss) *n* apple pulp left after pressing for juice
WORD ORIGIN Latin *pomum* apple

pomade *n* a perfumed oil put on the hair to make it smooth and shiny, esp. formerly
WORD ORIGIN French *pommade*

pomander *n* **1** a mixture of sweet-smelling substances in a container, used to perfume drawers or cupboards **2** a container for such a mixture
WORD ORIGIN Medieval Latin *pomum ambrae* apple of amber

Pombal *n* **Marquês de** title of *Sebastião José de Carvalho e Mello.* 1699–1782, Portuguese statesman, who dominated Portuguese government from 1750 to 1777 and instituted many administrative and economic reforms

pomegranate *n* a round tropical fruit with a tough reddish rind containing many seeds in a juicy red pulp
WORD ORIGIN Latin *pomum* apple + *granatus* full of seeds

pomelo (pom-ill-oh) *n, pl* **-los** the edible yellow fruit, like a grapefruit, of a tropical tree
WORD ORIGIN Dutch *pompelmoes*

Pomeranian *n* a toy dog with a long straight silky coat
WORD ORIGIN after *Pomerania*, region of N central Europe

pomfret (pum-frit) *or* **pomfret-cake** *n* a small black rounded liquorice sweet
WORD ORIGIN from *Pomfret*, earlier form of *Pontefract*, Yorks., where originally made

pommel *n* **1** the raised part on the front of a saddle **2** a knob at the top of a sword handle ▷ *vb* **-melling, -melled** *or US* **-meling, -meled** **3** ▸ same as **pummel**
WORD ORIGIN Old French *pomel* knob

pommy *n, pl* **-mies** (*sometimes cap*) *slang* a word used by Australians and New Zealanders for a British person. Sometimes shortened to: **pom**
WORD ORIGIN origin unknown

pomp *n* **1** stately display or ceremony **2** ostentatious display
WORD ORIGIN Greek *pompē* procession

Pompidou *n* **Georges** 1911–74, French statesman; president of France (1969–74)

pompom *n* **1** a decorative ball of tufted silk or wool **2** the small round flower head of some dahlias and chrysanthemums
WORD ORIGIN French

pom-pom *n* an automatic rapid-firing gun
WORD ORIGIN imitative

pompous *adj* **1** foolishly dignified or self-important **2** foolishly grand in style: *a pompous speech* **pomposity** *n* **pompously** *adv*

ponce *offensive slang chiefly Brit n* **1** an effeminate man **2** ▸ same as **pimp** ▷ *vb* **poncing, ponced** **3** (often foll. by *around* or *about*) *Austral & Brit* to act stupidly or waste time
WORD ORIGIN from Polari, an English slang derived from the Mediterranean ports

Ponce de León *n* **Juan** ?1460–1521, Spanish explorer. He settled (1509) and governed (1510–12) Puerto Rico and discovered (1513) Florida

poncho *n, pl* **-chos** a type of cloak made of a piece of cloth with a hole in the middle for the head
WORD ORIGIN American Spanish

pond ❶ *n* a pool of still water
WORD ORIGIN Middle English *ponde* enclosure

ponder ❶ *vb* (sometimes foll. by *on* or *over*) to consider thoroughly or deeply **ponderable** *adj*

THESAURUS

pond *n* = **pool**, tarn, small lake, fish pond, duck pond, millpond, lochan (*Scot*), dew pond

ponder *vb* = **think about**, consider, study, reflect on, examine, weigh up, contemplate, deliberate about, muse on, brood on, meditate on, mull over, puzzle over, ruminate on, give thought to, cogitate on, rack your

WORD ORIGIN Latin *ponderare* to weigh, consider
ponderous *adj* **1** serious and dull: *much of the film is ponderous and pretentious* **2** heavy or huge **3** (of movement) slow and clumsy
WORD ORIGIN Latin *ponderosus* of great weight
pondok *or* **pondokkie** *n* (in southern Africa) a crudely made house or shack
WORD ORIGIN Malay *pondók* leaf house
pondweed *n* a plant which grows in ponds and slow streams
pong *Austral & Brit informal* *n* **1** a strong unpleasant smell ▹*vb* **2** to give off a strong unpleasant smell **pongy** *adj*
WORD ORIGIN origin unknown
ponga (pong-a) *n* a tall New Zealand tree fern with large leathery leaves
WORD ORIGIN Māori
poniard (pon-yerd) *n* a small slender dagger
WORD ORIGIN Old French *poignard*
Pontiac *n* died 1769, chief of the Ottawa Indians, who led a rebellion against the British (1763–66)
pontiff *n* the Pope
WORD ORIGIN Latin *pontifex* high priest
pontifical *adj* **1** of a pontiff **2** pompous or dogmatic in manner
pontificate *vb* **-cating, -cated 1** to speak in a dogmatic manner **2** to officiate as a pontiff ▹*n* **3** the term of office of a Pope
Ponting *n* **Ricky (Thomas)** born 1974, Australian cricketer; a batsman, he played for Australia (from 1995), captaining the side from 2004
pontoon¹ *n* a floating platform used to support a bridge
WORD ORIGIN Latin *ponto* punt
pontoon² *n* a card game in which players try to obtain sets of cards worth 21 points
WORD ORIGIN probably an alteration of French *vingt-et-un* twenty-one
Pontoppidan *n* **Henrik** 1857–1943, Danish novelist and short-story writer, author of the novel sequences *The Promised Land* (1891–95), *Lykke-Per* (1898–1904), and *The Empire of Death* (1912–16). Nobel prize for literature 1917
Pontormo *n* **Jacopo da** original name *Jacopo Carrucci*. 1494–1556, Italian mannerist painter
pony *n, pl* **-nies** a breed of small horse
WORD ORIGIN Scots *powney*, perhaps from Latin *pullus* young animal, foal
ponytail *n* a hairstyle in which the hair is tied in a bunch at the back of the head and hangs down like a tail
pony trekking *n* the pastime of riding ponies cross-country
poodle *n* a dog with curly hair, which is sometimes clipped
WORD ORIGIN German *Pudel*
poof *n Brit, Austral & NZ offensive slang* a male homosexual **poofy** *adj*
WORD ORIGIN French *pouffe* puff
pooh *interj* an exclamation of disdain, scorn, or disgust
pooh-pooh *vb* to express disdain or scorn for
pool¹ ❶ *n* **1** a small body of still water **2** a small body of spilt liquid: *a pool of blood* **3** ▸see **swimming pool 4** a deep part of a stream or river
WORD ORIGIN Old English *pōl*
pool² ❶ *n* **1** a shared fund of resources or workers: *a typing pool* **2** a billiard game in which all the balls are potted with the cue ball **3** the combined stakes of those betting in many gambling games **4** *commerce* a group of producers who agree to maintain output levels and high prices ▹*vb* **5** to put into a common fund
WORD ORIGIN French *poule*, literally: hen used to signify stakes in a card game
pools *pl n* **the pools** *chiefly Brit* a nationwide mainly postal form of gambling which bets on the results of football matches
poop *n naut* a raised part at the back of a sailing ship
WORD ORIGIN Latin *puppis*
pooped *adj US, Canad, Austral & NZ slang* exhausted or tired: *if I wasn't so pooped I'd run and have a look at it*
WORD ORIGIN Middle English *poupen* to blow
poor ❶ *adj* **1** having little money and few possessions **2** less than is necessary or expected: *it was a poor reward for all his effort* **3** (sometimes foll. by *in*) lacking in (something): *a food which is rich in energy but poor in vitamins* **4** inferior: *poor quality* **5** disappointing or disagreeable: *a poor play* **6** pitiable; unlucky: *poor John is ill* **7 poor man's (something)** a cheaper substitute for (something): *pewter, sometimes known as poor man's silver*
WORD ORIGIN Latin *pauper*
poorhouse *n* ▸same as **workhouse**
poor law *n English history* a law providing for support of the poor from parish funds
poorly ❶ *adv* **1** badly ▹*adj* **2** *informal* rather ill
poor White *n often offensive* a poverty-stricken White person, usually in the southern US or South Africa
pop¹ ❶ *vb* **popping, popped 1** to make or cause to make a small explosive sound **2** (often foll. by *in* or *out* etc.) *informal* to enter or leave briefly or suddenly: *his mother popped out to buy him an ice cream* **3** to place suddenly or unexpectedly: *Benny popped a sweet into his mouth* **4** to burst with a small explosive sound **5** (of the eyes) to protrude **6** *informal* to pawn **7 pop the question** *informal* to propose marriage ▹*n* **8** a light sharp explosive sound **9** *Brit informal* a nonalcoholic fizzy drink ▹*adv* **10** with a pop ▸See also **pop off**
WORD ORIGIN imitative
pop² *n* **1** music of general appeal, esp. to young people, that usually has a

P

brains about, excogitate
pool¹ *n* **1 = pond**, lake, mere, tarn **2 = puddle**, drop, patch, splash
pool² *n* **1 = supply**, reserve, fall-back **3 = kitty**, bank, fund, stock, store, pot, jackpot, stockpile, hoard, cache ▹*vb* **5 = combine**, share, merge, put together, amalgamate, lump together, join forces on
poor *adj* **1 = impoverished**, broke (*informal*), badly off, hard up (*informal*), short, in need, needy, on the rocks, penniless, destitute, poverty-stricken, down and out, skint (*Brit slang*), in want, indigent, down at heel, impecunious, dirt-poor (*informal*), on the breadline, flat broke (*informal*), penurious, on your uppers, stony-broke (*Brit slang*), necessitous, in queer street, without two pennies to rub together (*informal*), on your beam-ends **OPPOSITE:** rich
2, 3 = meagre, inadequate, insufficient, reduced, lacking, slight, miserable, pathetic, incomplete, scant, sparse, deficient, skimpy, measly, scanty, pitiable, niggardly, straitened, exiguous **OPPOSITE:** ample
4, 5 = inferior, unsatisfactory, mediocre, second-rate, sorry, weak, pants (*informal*), rotten (*informal*), faulty, feeble, worthless, shabby, shoddy, low-grade, below par, substandard, low-rent (*informal*), crappy (*slang*), valueless, no great shakes (*informal*), rubbishy, poxy (*slang*), not much cop (*Brit slang*), half-pie (*NZ informal*), bodger or bodgie (*Austral slang*)
OPPOSITE: excellent
6 = unfortunate, pathetic, miserable, unlucky, hapless, pitiful, luckless, wretched, ill-starred, pitiable, ill-fated **OPPOSITE:** fortunate
poorly *adv* **1 = badly**, incompetently, inadequately, crudely, inferiorly, unsuccessfully, insufficiently, shabbily, unsatisfactorily, inexpertly **OPPOSITE:** well
▹*adj* **2** (*informal*) **= ill**, sick, ailing, unwell, crook (*Austral & NZ informal*), seedy (*informal*), below par, out of sorts, off colour, under the weather (*informal*), indisposed, feeling rotten (*informal*) **OPPOSITE:** healthy
pop¹ *n* **8 = bang**, report, crack, noise, burst, explosion ▹*vb* **1, 4 = burst**, crack, snap, bang, explode, report, go off (with a bang) **3 = put**, insert,

DICTIONARY

strong rhythm and uses electrical amplification ▷ *adj* **2** relating to pop music: *a pop concert* **3** *informal* ▶ short for **popular**

pop[3] *n informal* **1** father **2** an old man

POP 1 point of presence: a device that enables access to the internet **2** post office protocol: a protocol which brings e-mail to and from a mail server

pop. 1 population **2** popular(ly)

pop art *n* a movement in modern art that uses the methods, styles, and themes of popular culture and mass media

popcorn *n* grains of maize heated until they puff up and burst

Pope ⓣ *n* the bishop of Rome as head of the Roman Catholic Church
WORD ORIGIN Greek *pappas* father

popery (pope-er-ee) *n offensive* Roman Catholicism

popeyed *adj* **1** staring in astonishment **2** having bulging eyes

popgun *n* a toy gun that fires a pellet or cork by means of compressed air

popinjay *n* a conceited, foppish, or overly talkative person
WORD ORIGIN Arabic *babaghā* parrot

popish (pope-ish) *adj offensive* relating to Roman Catholicism

poplar *n* a tall slender tree with light soft wood, triangular leaves, and catkins
WORD ORIGIN Latin *populus*

poplin *n* a strong plain-woven fabric, usually of cotton, with fine ribbing
WORD ORIGIN French *papeline*

pop off *vb informal* **1** to depart suddenly **2** to die suddenly

Popov *n* **1 Alexander Stepanovich** 1859–1906, Russian physicist, the first to use an aerial in experiments with radio waves **2 Oleg (Konstantinovich)** born 1930, Russian clown, a member of the Moscow Circus

poppadom *or* **poppadum** *n* a thin round crisp fried Indian bread
WORD ORIGIN Hindi

popper *n Brit informal* a press stud

poppet *n* a term of affection for a small child or sweetheart
WORD ORIGIN variant of *puppet*

popping crease *n cricket* a line in front of and parallel with the wicket where the batsman stands
WORD ORIGIN from obsolete *pop* to hit

poppy *n, pl* **-pies 1** a plant with showy red, orange, or white flowers **2** a drug, such as opium, obtained from these plants **3** an artificial red poppy worn to mark Remembrance Sunday and in New Zealand to mark Anzac Day ▷ *adj* **4** reddish-orange
WORD ORIGIN Old English *popæg*

poppycock *n informal* nonsense
WORD ORIGIN Dutch dialect *pappekak*, literally: soft excrement

Poppy Day *n informal* Remembrance Sunday

Popsicle *n trademark* ▶ the US and Canadian term for **ice lolly**

populace *n* the common people; masses
WORD ORIGIN Latin *populus*

popular ⓣ *adj* **1** widely liked or admired **2** (often foll. by *with*) liked by a particular person or group: *the bay is popular with windsurfers and water-skiers* **3** common among the general public: *the groundswell of popular feeling* **4** designed to appeal to a mass audience: *an attack on him in the popular press* **popularity** *n* **popularly** *adv*
WORD ORIGIN Latin *popularis* of the people

popular front *n* a left-wing group or party opposed to fascism

popularize *or* **-ise** *vb* **-izing, -ized** *or* **-ising, -ised 1** to make popular **2** to make easily understandable **popularization** *or* **-isation** *n*

populate ⓣ *vb* **-lating, -lated 1** (*often passive*) to live in: *a mountainous region populated mainly by Armenians* **2** to provide with inhabitants **populated** *adj*
WORD ORIGIN Latin *populus* people

population ⓣ *n* **1** all the inhabitants of a place **2** the number of such inhabitants **3** all the people of a particular class in a place: *the bulk of the rural population lives in poverty* **4** *ecology* a group of individuals of the same species inhabiting a given area: *a population of grey seals*

populism *n* a political strategy based on a calculated appeal to the interests or prejudices of ordinary people: *the Islamic radicals preach a heady message of populism and religion* **populist** *adj, n*

populous *adj* containing many inhabitants

pop-up *adj* **1** (of an appliance) characterized by or having a mechanism that pops up **2** (of a book) having pages that rise when opened to simulate a three-dimensional form **3** *computers* (of a menu on a computer screen, etc.) suddenly appearing when an option is selected ▷ *n computers* **4** something that appears over or above the open window on a computer screen

porangi (pore-ang-ee) *adj NZ informal* crazy; mad
WORD ORIGIN Māori

porbeagle *n* a kind of shark

porcelain *n* **1** a delicate type of china **2** an object or objects made of this
WORD ORIGIN French *porcelaine*, from Italian *porcellana* cowrie shell

porch *n* a covered approach to the entrance of a building
WORD ORIGIN French *porche*

porcine *adj* of or like a pig
WORD ORIGIN Latin *porcus* a pig

porcupine *n* a large rodent covered with long pointed quills
WORD ORIGIN Middle English *porc despyne* pig with spines

pore[1] *vb* **poring, pored ▪ pore over** to examine or study intently: *a wife who pored over account books and ledgers all day*
WORD ORIGIN Middle English *pouren*

pore[2] ⓣ *n* **1** a small opening in the skin or surface of an animal or plant **2** any small hole, such as a tiny gap in a rock
WORD ORIGIN Greek *poros* passage, pore

poriferan (por-riff-er-an) *n biol* a sponge
WORD ORIGIN from New Latin *porifer* bearing pores

pork *n* the flesh of pigs used as food
WORD ORIGIN Latin *porcus* pig

porker *n* a pig fattened for food

pork pie *n* a pie with a minced pork filling

porky *adj* **porkier, porkiest 1** of or like pork **2** *informal* fat or obese

porn *or* **porno** *n, adj informal* ▶ short for **pornography** or **pornographic**

pornography ⓣ *n* writings, pictures, or films designed to be sexually exciting **pornographer** *n* **pornographic** *adj*
WORD ORIGIN Greek *pornographos* writing of prostitutes

porous *adj* **1** allowing air and liquids to be absorbed **2** *biol, geol* having pores **porosity** *n*
WORD ORIGIN Late Latin *porus* passage, pore

porphyry (por-fir-ee) *n, pl* **-ries** a reddish-purple rock with large

THESAURUS

push, stick, slip, thrust, tuck, shove

Pope *n* **= Holy Father**, pontiff, His Holiness, Bishop of Rome, Vicar of Christ

popular *adj* **1, 2 = well-liked**, liked, favoured, celebrated, in, accepted, favourite, famous, approved, in favour, fashionable, in demand, sought-after, fave (*informal*)
OPPOSITE: unpopular
3 = common, general, standard, widespread, prevailing, stock, current, public, conventional, universal, prevalent, ubiquitous
OPPOSITE: rare

populate *vb* **1** (*often passive*) **= inhabit**, people, live in, occupy, reside in, dwell in (*formal*) **2 = settle**, people, occupy, pioneer, colonize

population *n* **1 = inhabitants**, people, community, society, residents, natives, folk, occupants, populace, denizens, citizenry

pore[2] *n* **1, 2 = opening**, hole, outlet, orifice, stoma

pornography *n* **= obscenity**, porn (*informal*), erotica, dirt, filth,

DICTIONARY

crystals of feldspar in it
porphyritic *adj*
WORD ORIGIN Greek *porphuros* purple

Porphyry *n* original name *Malchus* 232–305 AD, Greek Neo-Platonist philosopher, born in Syria; disciple and biographer of Plotinus

porpoise *n, pl* **-poises** *or* **-poise** a small mammal of the whale family with a blunt snout
WORD ORIGIN Latin *porcus* pig + *piscis* fish

porridge *n* **1** a dish made of oatmeal or other cereal, cooked in water or milk **2** *chiefly Brit slang* a term of imprisonment
WORD ORIGIN variant of *pottage*

porringer *n* a small dish, often with a handle, used esp. formerly for soup or porridge
WORD ORIGIN Middle English *potinger*

Porson *n* **Richard** 1759–1808, English classical scholar, noted for his editions of Aeschylus and Euripides

port[1] ❶ *n* a town with a harbour where ships can load and unload
WORD ORIGIN Latin *portus*

port[2] *n* **1** the left side of an aircraft or ship when facing the front of it ▷*vb* **2** to turn or be turned towards the port
WORD ORIGIN origin unknown

port[3] *n* a strong sweet fortified wine, usually dark red
WORD ORIGIN after *Oporto*, Portugal, from where it came originally

port[4] *n* **1** *naut* **a** an opening with a watertight door in the side of a ship, used for loading, etc. **b** ▸see **porthole 2** *electronics* a logical circuit for the input and output of data
WORD ORIGIN Latin *porta* gate

port[5] *vb computers* to change (programs) from one system to another
WORD ORIGIN probably from PORT[4]

portable ❶ *adj* **1** easily carried ▷*n* **2** an article designed to be easily carried, such as a television or typewriter **portability** *n*
WORD ORIGIN Latin *portare* to carry

portage *n* **1** the transporting of boats and supplies overland between navigable waterways **2** the route used for such transport ▷*vb* **-taging, -taged 3** to transport (boats and supplies) in this way
WORD ORIGIN French

portal *n* **1** *literary* a large and impressive gateway or doorway **2** *computers* an internet site providing links to other sites
WORD ORIGIN Latin *porta* gate

portcullis *n* an iron grating suspended in a castle gateway, that can be lowered to bar the entrance
WORD ORIGIN Old French *porte coleïce* sliding gate

portend *vb* to be an omen of: *the 0.5 percent increase certainly portends higher inflation ahead*
WORD ORIGIN Latin *portendere* to indicate

portent *n* **1** a sign of a future event **2** great or ominous significance: *matters of great portent* **3** a marvel
WORD ORIGIN Latin *portentum* sign

portentous *adj* **1** of great or ominous significance **2** self-important or pompous: *there was nothing portentous or solemn about him*

porter[1] ❶ *n* **1** a man employed to carry luggage at a railway station or hotel **2** a hospital worker who transfers patients between rooms **porterage** *n*
WORD ORIGIN Latin *portare* to carry

porter[2] ❶ *n chiefly Brit* a doorman or gatekeeper of a building
WORD ORIGIN Latin *porta* door

porter[3] *n Brit* a dark sweet ale brewed from black malt
WORD ORIGIN short for *porter's ale*

porterhouse *n* a thick choice beef steak. Also called: **porterhouse steak**
WORD ORIGIN formerly, a place that served porter, beer, and sometimes meals

portfolio *n, pl* **-os 1** a flat case for carrying maps, drawings, or papers **2** selected examples, such as drawings or photographs, that show an artist's recent work **3** the area of responsibility of the head of a government department: *the defence portfolio* **4** a list of investments held by an investor **5 Minister without portfolio** a cabinet minister without responsibility for a government department
WORD ORIGIN Italian *portafoglio*

porthole *n* a small round window in a ship or aircraft

portico *n, pl* **-coes** *or* **-cos** a porch or covered walkway with columns supporting the roof
WORD ORIGIN Italian, from Latin *porticus*

portion ❶ *n* **1** a part of a whole **2** a part belonging to a person or group **3** a helping of food served to one person **4** *law* a dowry **5** *literary* someone's fate or destiny: *utter disaster was my portion* ▷*vb* **6** to divide (something) into shares **portion out**
WORD ORIGIN Latin *portio*

portion out *vb* to distribute or share (something) among a group of people: *the British portioned out the oil-rich lands to various sheikhs*

portly *adj* **-lier, -liest** stout or rather fat
WORD ORIGIN from *port* (in the sense: deportment)

portmanteau *n, pl* **-teaus** *or* **-teaux** *old-fashioned* a large suitcase made of stiff leather that opens out into two compartments
WORD ORIGIN French: cloak carrier

portmanteau word *n* a word made by joining together the beginning and end of two other words, such as *brunch*. Also called: **blend**

portrait ❶ *n* **1** a painting, drawing, or photograph of a person, often only of the face **2** a description **portraitist** *n*
WORD ORIGIN French

portraiture *n* **1** the art of making portraits **2** a description **3 a** a portrait **b** portraits collectively

portray ❶ *vb* to describe or represent (someone) by artistic means, such as in writing or on film **portrayal** *n*
WORD ORIGIN Old French *portraire* to depict

Portuguese *adj* **1** of Portugal ▷*n* **2** *pl* **-guese** a person from Portugal **3** the language of Portugal and Brazil

Portuguese man-of-war *n* a large sea creature like a jellyfish, with long stinging tentacles

pose ❶ *vb* **posing, posed 1** to take up a particular position to be photographed or drawn **2** to behave in an affected way in order to impress others **3** (often foll. by *as*) to pretend to be (someone one is not) **4** to create or be (a problem, threat,

P

THESAURUS

indecency, porno *(informal)*, smut

port[1] *n* **= harbour**, haven, anchorage, seaport, roadstead

portable *adj* **1 = light**, compact, convenient, handy, lightweight, manageable, movable, easily carried, portative

porter[1] *n* **1 = baggage attendant**, carrier, bearer, baggage-carrier

porter[2] *n (chiefly Brit)* **= doorman**, caretaker, janitor, concierge, gatekeeper

portion *n* **1 = part**, bit, piece, section, scrap, segment, fragment, fraction, chunk, wedge, hunk, morsel **2 = share**, division, allowance, lot, measure, quantity, quota, ration, allocation, allotment **3 = helping**, serving, piece, plateful

portrait *n* **1 = picture**, painting, image, photograph, representation, sketch, likeness, portraiture **2 = description**, account, profile, biography, portrayal, depiction, vignette, characterization, thumbnail sketch

portray *vb* **a = play**, take the role of, act the part of, represent, personate *(rare)* **b = describe**, present, depict, evoke, delineate, put in words **c = represent**, draw, paint, illustrate, sketch, figure, picture, render, depict, delineate **d = characterize**, describe, represent, depict, paint a mental picture of

pose *vb* **1 = position yourself**, sit, model, strike a pose, arrange yourself **2 = put on airs**, affect, posture, show off *(informal)*, strike an

DICTIONARY

etc.): *dressing complicated wounds has always posed a problem for doctors* **5** to put forward or ask: *the question you posed earlier* ▹*n* **6** a position taken up for an artist or photographer **7** behaviour adopted for effect **WORD ORIGIN** Old French *poser* to set in place

Poseidon *n Greek myth* the god of the sea

poser[1] *n* **1** *Brit, Austral & NZ informal* a person who likes to be seen in trendy clothes in fashionable places **2** a person who poses

poser[2] *n* a baffling question

poseur *n* a person who behaves in an affected way in order to impress others
WORD ORIGIN French

posh ❶ *adj informal chiefly Brit* **1** smart or elegant **2** upper-class
WORD ORIGIN probably from obsolete slang *posh* a dandy

posit (pozz-it) *vb* **-iting, -ited** to lay down as a basis for argument: *the archetypes posited by modern psychology*
WORD ORIGIN Latin *ponere* to place

position ❶ *n* **1** place or location: *the hotel is in an elevated position above the River Wye* **2** the proper or usual place **3** the way in which a person or thing is placed or arranged: *an upright position* **4** point of view; attitude: *the Catholic Church's position on contraception* **5** social status, esp. high social standing **6** a job; appointment **7** *sport* a player's allotted role or place in the playing area **8** *mil* a place occupied for tactical reasons **9 in a position to** able to: *you were not in a position to repay the money* ▹*vb* **10** to put in the proper or usual place; locate **positional** *adj*
WORD ORIGIN Latin *ponere* to place

positive ❶ *adj* **1** expressing certainty: *a positive answer* **2** definite or certain: *are you absolutely positive about the date?* **3** tending to emphasize what is good; constructive: *positive thinking* **4** tending towards progress or improvement: *investment that could have a positive impact on the company's fortunes* **5** *philosophy* constructive rather than sceptical **6** *informal* complete; downright: *a positive delight* **7** *maths* having a value greater than zero: *a positive number* **8** *grammar* denoting the unmodified form of an adjective as opposed to its comparative or superlative form **9** *physics* (of an electric charge) having an opposite charge to that of an electron **10** *physics* ▸short for **electropositive 11** *med* (of the result of an examination or test) indicating the presence of a suspected condition or organism ▹*n* **12** something positive **13** *maths* a quantity greater than zero **14** *photog* a print showing an image whose colours and tones correspond to those of the original subject **15** *grammar* the positive degree of an adjective or adverb **16** a positive object, such as a terminal in a cell **positively** *adv* **positiveness** *or* **positivity** *n*
WORD ORIGIN Late Latin *positivus*

positive discrimination *n* the provision of special opportunities for a disadvantaged group

positive vetting *n Brit* the thorough checking of all aspects of a person's life to ensure his or her suitability for a position that may involve national security

positivism *n* a system of philosophy that accepts only things that can be seen or proved **positivist** *n, adj*

positron *n physics* the antiparticle of the electron, having the same mass but an equal and opposite charge
WORD ORIGIN *posi(tive)* + *(elec)tron*

poss. 1 possible **2** possession **3** possessive **4** possibly

posse (poss-ee) *n* **1** *US* a selected group of men on whom the sheriff may call for assistance **2** *informal* a group of friends or associates: *a posse of reporters* **3** (in W Canada) a troop of horses and riders who perform at rodeos
WORD ORIGIN Latin: to be able

possess ❶ *vb* **1** to have as one's property; own **2** to have as a quality or attribute: *he possessed an innate elegance, authority, and wit on screen* **3** to gain control over or dominate: *absolute terror possessed her* **possessor** *n*
WORD ORIGIN Latin *possidere*

possessed *adj* **1** (foll. by *of*) owning or having: *he is possessed of a calm maturity far beyond his years* **2** under the influence of a powerful force, such as a spirit or strong emotion: *possessed by the devil; she was possessed by a frenzied urge to get out of Moscow*

possession ❶ *n* **1** the state of possessing; ownership: *how had this compromising picture come into the possession of the press?* **2** anything that is possessed **3 possessions** wealth or property **4** the state of being controlled by or as if by evil spirits **5** the occupancy of land or property: *troops had taken possession of the airport*

P

THESAURUS

attitude, attitudinize ▹*n* **3** (*often with* **as**) **= impersonate**, pretend to be, sham, feign, profess to be, masquerade as, pass yourself off as **6 = posture**, position, bearing, attitude, stance, mien (*literary*) **7 = act**, role, façade, air, front, posturing, pretence, masquerade, mannerism, affectation, attitudinizing

posh *adj* **1 = smart**, grand, exclusive, luxury, elegant, fashionable, stylish, luxurious, classy (*slang*), swish (*informal, chiefly Brit*), up-market, swanky (*informal*), ritzy (*slang*), schmick (*Austral informal*) **2 = upper-class**, high-class, top-drawer, plummy, high-toned, la-di-da (*informal*)

position *n* **1 = location**, place, point, area, post, situation, station, site, spot, bearings, reference, orientation, whereabouts, locality, locale **3 = posture**, attitude, arrangement, pose, stance, disposition **4 = attitude**, view, perspective, point of view, standing, opinion, belief, angle, stance, outlook, posture, viewpoint, slant, way of thinking, standpoint **5 = status**, place, standing, class, footing, station, rank, reputation, importance, consequence, prestige, caste, stature, eminence, repute **6 = job**, place, post, opening, office, role, situation, duty, function, employment, capacity, occupation, berth (*informal*), billet (*informal*) ▹*vb* **10 = place**, put, set, stand, stick (*informal*), settle, fix, arrange, locate, sequence, array, dispose, lay out

positive *adj* **1 = definite**, real, clear, firm, certain, direct, express, actual, absolute, concrete, decisive, explicit, affirmative, clear-cut, unmistakable, conclusive, unequivocal, indisputable, categorical, incontrovertible, nailed-on (*slang*) **OPPOSITE:** inconclusive **2 = certain**, sure, convinced, confident, satisfied, assured, free from doubt **OPPOSITE:** uncertain **4 = beneficial**, effective, useful, practical, helpful, progressive, productive, worthwhile, constructive, pragmatic, efficacious **OPPOSITE:** harmful **6** (*informal*) **= absolute**, complete, perfect, right (*Brit informal*), real, total, rank, sheer, utter, thorough, downright, consummate, veritable, unqualified, out-and-out, unmitigated, thoroughgoing, unalloyed

possess *vb* **1 = own**, have, hold, be in possession of, be the owner of, have in your possession, have to your name **2 = be endowed with**, have, enjoy, benefit from, be born with, be blessed with, be possessed of, be gifted with **3 = seize**, hold, control, dominate, occupy, haunt, take someone over, bewitch, take possession of, have power over, have mastery over

possession *n* **1 = ownership**, control, custody, hold, hands, tenure, occupancy, proprietorship ▹*pl n* **3 = property**, things, effects, estate, assets, wealth, belongings, chattels, goods and chattels

DICTIONARY

6 a territory subject to a foreign state 7 the criminal offence of having something illegal on one's person: *arrested for drug dealing and possession* 8 *sport* control of the ball by a team or player: *City had most of the possession, but couldn't score*

possessive *adj* 1 of possession 2 desiring excessively to possess or dominate: *a possessive husband* 3 *grammar* denoting a form of a noun or pronoun used to convey possession, as *my* or *Harry's*: *a possessive pronoun* ▹*n* 4 *grammar* a the possessive case b a word in the possessive case **possessiveness** *n*

possibility ❶ *n, pl* **-ties** 1 the state of being possible 2 anything that is possible 3 a competitor or candidate with a chance of success 4 a future prospect or potential: *all sorts of possibilities began to open up*

possible ❶ *adj* 1 capable of existing, happening, or proving true: *the earliest possible moment* 2 capable of being done: *I am grateful to the library staff for making this work possible* 3 having potential: *a possible buyer* 4 feasible but less than probable: *it's possible that's what he meant, but I doubt it* ▹*n* 5 ▸same as **possibility** (sense 3)
WORD ORIGIN Latin *possibilis*

possibly ❶ *adv* 1 perhaps or maybe 2 by any means; at all: *he can't possibly come*

possum *n* 1 *informal* an opossum 2 *Austral & NZ* a phalanger 3 **play possum** to pretend to be dead, ignorant, or asleep in order to deceive an opponent

post¹ ❶ *n* 1 an official system of mail delivery 2 letters or packages that are transported and delivered by the Post Office; mail 3 a single collection or delivery of mail 4 a postbox or post office: *take this to the post* 5 *computers* an item of e-mail made publicly available ▹*vb* 6 to send by post 7 *computers* to make (e-mail) publicly available 8 *book-keeping* a to enter (an item) in a ledger b (often foll. by *up*) to enter all paper items in (a ledger) 9 **keep someone posted** to inform someone regularly of the latest news
WORD ORIGIN Latin *posita* something placed

post² ❶ *n* 1 a length of wood, metal, or concrete fixed upright to support or mark something 2 *horse racing* a either of two upright poles marking the beginning and end of a racecourse b the finish of a horse race ▹*vb* 3 (sometimes foll. by *up*) to put up (a notice) in a public place 4 to publish (a name) on a list
WORD ORIGIN Latin *postis*

post³ ❶ *n* 1 a position to which a person is appointed; job 2 a position to which a soldier or guard is assigned for duty 3 a permanent military establishment 4 *Brit* either of two military bugle calls (**first post** and **last post**) giving notice of the time to retire for the night ▹*vb* 5 *Austral & Brit* to send (someone) to a new place to work 6 to assign to or station at a particular place or position: *guards were posted at the doors*
WORD ORIGIN French *poste*, from Latin *ponere* to place

post- *prefix* 1 after in time: *postgraduate* 2 behind: *postdated*
WORD ORIGIN Latin

postage *n* the charge for sending a piece of mail by post

postage stamp *n* ▸same as **stamp** (sense 1)

postal *adj* of a Post Office or the mail-delivery service

postal order *n* a written money order sent by post and cashed at a post office by the person who receives it

postbag *n* 1 *chiefly Brit* a mailbag 2 the mail received by a magazine, radio programme, or public figure

postbox *n* ▸same as **letter box** (sense 2)

postcard *n* a card, often with a picture on one side, for sending a message by post without an envelope

post chaise (shaze) *n old-fashioned* a four-wheeled horse-drawn coach formerly used as a rapid means of carrying mail and passengers

postcode *n* a system of letters and numbers used to aid the sorting of mail

post-consumer *adj* (of a consumer item) discarded for disposal or recovery having been recycled: *made from 75% post-consumer waste*

postdate *vb* **-dating, -dated** 1 to write a future date on (a cheque or document) 2 to occur at a later date than 3 to assign a date to (an event or period) that is later than its previously assigned date

poster ❶ *n* 1 a large notice displayed in a public place as an advertisement 2 a large printed picture

poste restante *n* a post-office department where mail is kept until it is called for
WORD ORIGIN French, literally: mail remaining

posterior *n* 1 *formal or humorous* the buttocks ▹*adj* 2 at the back of or behind something: *posterior leg muscles* 3 coming after in a series or time
WORD ORIGIN Latin: latter

posterity *n* 1 future generations 2 all of one's descendants
WORD ORIGIN Latin *posterus* coming after

postern *n* a small back door or gate
WORD ORIGIN Old French *posterne*

post-free *adv, adj* 1 *Austral & Brit* with the postage prepaid 2 free of postal charge

postgraduate *n* 1 a person who is studying for a more advanced qualification after obtaining a degree ▹*adj* 2 of or for postgraduates

posthaste *adv* with great speed

posthumous (poss-tume-uss) *adj* 1 happening after one's death 2 born after the death of one's father 3 (of a book) published after the

P

THESAURUS

possibility *n* 1a = **feasibility**, likelihood, plausibility, potentiality, practicability, workableness 1b = **likelihood**, chance, risk, odds, prospect, liability, hazard, probability 4 = **potential**, promise, prospects, talent, capabilities, potentiality

possible *adj* 1 = **likely**, potential, anticipated, probable, odds-on, on the cards OPPOSITE: improbable 1, 2 = **feasible**, viable, workable, achievable, within reach, on (*informal*), practicable, attainable, doable, realizable OPPOSITE: unfeasible 3 = **aspiring**, would-be, promising, hopeful, prospective, wannabe (*informal*) 4 = **conceivable**, likely, credible, plausible, hypothetical, imaginable, believable, thinkable OPPOSITE: inconceivable

possibly *adv* 1 = **perhaps**, maybe, God willing, perchance (*archaic*), mayhap (*archaic*), peradventure (*archaic*), haply (*archaic*)

post¹ *n* 1 = **mail**, collection, delivery, postal service, snail mail (*informal*) 2 = **correspondence**, letters, cards, mail ▹*vb* 6 = **send (off)**, forward, mail, get off, transmit, dispatch, consign 9 **keep someone posted** = **notify**, brief, advise, inform, report to, keep someone informed, keep someone up to date, apprise, fill someone in on (*informal*)

post² *n* 1 = **support**, stake, pole, stock, standard, column, pale, shaft, upright, pillar, picket, palisade, newel ▹*vb* 3 = **put up**, announce, publish, display, advertise, proclaim, publicize, promulgate, affix, stick something up, make something known, pin something up

post³ *n* 1 = **job**, place, office, position, situation, employment, appointment, assignment, berth (*informal*), billet (*informal*) 2 = **position**, place, base, beat, station ▹*vb* 5, 6 = **station**, assign, put, place, position, establish, locate, situate, put on duty

poster *n* 1 = **notice**, bill, announcement, advertisement, sticker, placard, public notice, affiche (*French*)

DICTIONARY

author's death **posthumously** *adv*
WORD ORIGIN Latin *postumus* the last

postie *n Scot, Austral & NZ informal* a postman

postilion *or* **postillion** *n* (esp. formerly) a person who rides one of a pair of horses drawing a coach
WORD ORIGIN French *postillon*

postimpressionism *n* a movement in painting in France at the end of the 19th century which rejected Impressionism but adapted its use of pure colour to paint with greater subjective emotion
postimpressionist *n, adj*

posting *n* **1** a job to which someone is assigned by his or her employer, which involves moving to a particular town or country: *Bonn was his third posting overseas* **2** *computers* an e-mail message that is publicly available

postman *or fem* **postwoman** *n, pl* **-men** *or fem* **-women** a person who collects and delivers mail as a profession

postmark *n* **1** an official mark stamped on mail, showing the place and date of posting ▹*vb* **2** to put such a mark on (mail)

postmaster *n* **1** Also (fem): **postmistress** an official in charge of a post office **2** the person who manages the e-mail at a site

postmaster general *n, pl* **postmasters general** the executive head of the postal service

postmeridian *adj* occurring after noon
WORD ORIGIN Latin *postmeridianus*

postmortem *n* **1** In full: **postmortem examination** medical examination of a dead body to discover the cause of death **2** analysis of a recent event: *a postmortem on the party's recent appalling by-election results* ▹*adj* **3** occurring after death
WORD ORIGIN Latin, literally: after death

postnatal *adj* occurring after childbirth: *postnatal depression*

post office *n* a building where stamps are sold and postal business is conducted

Post Office *n* a government department responsible for postal services

postoperative *adj* of or occurring in the period after a surgical operation

postpaid *adv, adj* with the postage prepaid

postpone ❶ *vb* **-poning, -poned** to put off until a future time
postponement *n*
WORD ORIGIN Latin *postponere* to put after

postpositive *adj grammar* (of an adjective) placed after the word it modifies

postprandial *adj formal* after dinner
WORD ORIGIN Latin *post-* after + *prandium* midday meal

postscript *n* a message added at the end of a letter, after the signature
WORD ORIGIN Late Latin *postscribere* to write after

post-traumatic stress disorder *n* a psychological condition, characterized by anxiety, withdrawal, and a proneness to physical illness, that may follow a traumatic experience

postulant *n* an applicant for admission to a religious order
WORD ORIGIN Latin *postulare* to ask

postulate *formal vb* **-lating, -lated** **1** to assume to be true as the basis of an argument or theory **2** to ask, demand, or claim ▹*n* **3** something postulated **postulation** *n*
WORD ORIGIN Latin *postulare* to ask for

posture ❶ *n* **1** a position or way in which a person stands, walks, etc.: *good posture* **2** a mental attitude: *a cooperative posture* **3** an affected attitude: *an intellectual posture* ▹*vb* **-turing, -tured** **4** to behave in an exaggerated way to attract attention **5** to assume an affected attitude
postural *adj*
WORD ORIGIN Latin *positura*

postviral fatigue syndrome *or* **postviral syndrome** *n* ▸same as **chronic fatigue syndrome**

postwar *adj* occurring or existing after a war

posy *n, pl* **-sies** a small bunch of flowers
WORD ORIGIN variant of *poesy*

pot[1] ❶ *n* **1** a round deep container, often with a handle and lid, used for cooking **2** the amount that a pot will hold **3** ▸short for **flowerpot** or **teapot** **4** a handmade piece of pottery **5** *billiards, etc.* a shot by which a ball is pocketed **6** a chamber pot **7** the money in the pool in gambling games **8** *(often pl) informal* a large sum of money **9** *informal* a cup or other trophy **10** ▸see **potbelly** **11** **go to pot** to go to ruin ▹*vb* **potting, potted** **12** to put (a plant) in soil in a flowerpot **13** *billiards, etc.* to pocket (a ball) **14** to preserve (food) in a pot **15** to shoot (game) for food rather than for sport **16** to shoot casually or without careful aim **17** *informal* to capture or win
WORD ORIGIN Old English *pott*

pot[2] *n slang* cannabis
WORD ORIGIN perhaps from Mexican Indian *potiguaya*

potable (pote-a-bl) *adj formal* drinkable
WORD ORIGIN Latin *potare* to drink

potage (po-tahzh) *n* thick soup
WORD ORIGIN French

potash *n* **1** potassium carbonate, used as fertilizer **2** a compound containing potassium: *permanganate of potash*
WORD ORIGIN from *pot ashes,* because originally obtained by evaporating the lye of wood ashes in pots

potassium *n chem* a light silvery element of the alkali metal group. Symbol: K
WORD ORIGIN New Latin *potassa* potash

potassium nitrate *n* a crystalline compound used in gunpowders, fertilizers, and as a preservative for foods (E252)

potation *n formal* **1** the act of drinking **2** a drink, usually alcoholic
WORD ORIGIN Latin *potare* to drink

potato *n, pl* **-toes** **1** a starchy vegetable that grows underground **2** the plant from which this vegetable is obtained
WORD ORIGIN Spanish *patata,* from a Native American language

potato beetle *n* ▸same as **Colorado beetle**

potato chip *n* ▸the US and Canadian term for **crisp** (sense 7)

potato crisp *n* ▸same as **crisp** (sense 7)

potbelly *n, pl* **-lies** **1** a bulging belly **2** a person with such a belly

potboiler *n informal* an inferior work of art produced quickly to make money

pot-bound *adj* (of a pot plant) having roots too big for its pot, so that it is unable to grow further

poteen *or* **poitín** *n* (in Ireland) illegally made alcoholic drink
WORD ORIGIN Irish *poitín* little pot

potent ❶ *adj* **1** having great power or influence **2** (of arguments) persuasive or forceful **3** highly effective: *a potent poison* **4** (of a male) capable of having sexual intercourse
potency *n*

THESAURUS

postpone *vb* **= put off**, delay, suspend, adjourn, table, shelve, defer, put back, hold over, put on ice *(informal)*, put on the back burner *(informal)*, take a rain check on *(US & Canad informal)* **OPPOSITE:** go ahead with

posture *n* **1 = bearing**, set, position, attitude, pose, stance, carriage, disposition, mien *(literary)* ▹*vb* **4 = show off** *(informal)*, pose, affect, hot-dog *(chiefly US)*, make a show, put on airs, try to attract attention, attitudinize, do something for effect

pot[1] *n* **1, 4 = container**, bowl, pan, vessel, basin, vase, jug, cauldron, urn, utensil, crock, skillet

potent *adj* **1 = powerful**, commanding, dynamic, dominant, influential, authoritative **3 = strong**, powerful, mighty, vigorous, forceful, efficacious, puissant **OPPOSITE:** weak

DICTIONARY

WORD ORIGIN Latin *potens* able
potentate *n* a ruler or monarch
WORD ORIGIN Latin *potens* powerful
potential ❶ *adj* **1 a** possible but not yet actual: *potential buyers* **b** capable of being or becoming; latent: *potential danger* ▷*n* **2** ability or talent not yet in full use: *she has great potential as a painter* **3** In full: **electric potential** the work required to transfer a unit positive electric charge from an infinite distance to a given point **potentially** *adv*
WORD ORIGIN Latin *potentia* power
potential difference *n* the difference in electric potential between two points in an electric field, measured in volts
potential energy *n* the energy which an object has stored up because of its position
potentiality *n, pl* **-ties** latent capacity for becoming or developing
pother (rhymes with **bother**) *n literary* a fuss or commotion
WORD ORIGIN origin unknown
potherb *n* a plant whose leaves, flowers, or stems are used in cooking
pothole *n* **1** a hole in the surface of a road **2** a deep hole in a limestone area
potholing *n* the sport of exploring underground caves **potholer** *n*
pothook *n* **1** an S-shaped hook for suspending a pot over a fire **2** an S-shaped mark in handwriting
potion *n* a drink of medicine, poison, or some supposedly magic liquid
WORD ORIGIN Latin *potio* a drink, esp. a poisonous one
pot luck *n* **take pot luck** *informal* to accept whatever happens to be available: *we'll take pot luck at whatever restaurant might still be open*
potoroo *n, pl* **-roos** an Australian leaping rodent
potpourri (po-poor-ee) *n, pl* **-ris 1** a fragrant mixture of dried flower petals **2** an assortment or medley
WORD ORIGIN French, literally: rotten pot
pot roast *n* meat cooked slowly in a covered pot with very little liquid
potsherd *n* a broken piece of pottery
WORD ORIGIN *pot* + *schoord* piece of broken crockery
pot shot *n* **1** a shot taken without careful aim **2** a shot fired at an animal within easy range
pottage *n* a thick soup or stew
WORD ORIGIN Old French *potage* contents of a pot
potted *adj* **1** grown in a pot: *potted plant* **2** cooked or preserved in a pot: *potted shrimps* **3** *informal* shortened or abridged: *a potted history*
potter[1] *n* a person who makes pottery
potter[2] ❶ *or esp. US & Canad* **putter** *vb* **1** to move with little energy or direction: *I saw him pottering off to see to his canaries* **2 potter about** *or* **around** *or* **away** to be busy in a pleasant but aimless way: *he potters away doing God knows what all day*
WORD ORIGIN Old English *potian* to thrust
Potteries *n* **the Potteries** a region of W central England, in Staffordshire, where many china industries are situated
potter's wheel *n* a flat spinning disc on which clay is shaped by hand
pottery ❶ *n, pl* **-teries 1** articles made from baked clay **2** a place where such articles are made **3** the craft of making such articles
potting shed *n* a garden hut in which plants are put in flowerpots and potting materials are stored
potty[1] *adj* **-tier, -tiest** *informal* **1** slightly crazy **2** trivial or insignificant **3** (foll. by *about*) very keen (on) **pottiness** *n*
WORD ORIGIN origin unknown
potty[2] *n, pl* **-ties** a bowl used as a toilet by a small child
pouch *n* **1** a small bag **2** a baglike pocket in various animals, such as the cheek fold in hamsters ▷*vb* **3** to place in or as if in a pouch **4** to make or be made into a pouch
WORD ORIGIN Old French *poche* bag
pouf *or* **pouffe** (poof) *n* a large solid cushion used as a seat
WORD ORIGIN French
Poulenc *n* **Francis** 1899–1963, French composer; a member of Les Six. His works include the operas *Les Mamelles de Tirésias* (1947) and *Dialogues des Carmélites* (1957), and the ballet *Les Biches* (1924)
poulterer *n Brit* a person who sells poultry
poultice (pole-tiss) *n med* a moist dressing, often heated, applied to painful and swollen parts of the body
WORD ORIGIN Latin *puls* a thick porridge
poultry *n* domestic fowls
WORD ORIGIN Old French *pouletrie*
pounce ❶ *vb* **pouncing, pounced 1** (often foll. by *on* or *upon*) to spring upon suddenly to attack or capture ▷*n* **2** the act of pouncing; a spring or swoop
WORD ORIGIN origin unknown
pound[1] *n* **1** the standard monetary unit of the United Kingdom and some other countries, made up of 100 pence. Official name: **pound sterling 2** the standard monetary unit of various other countries, such as Cyprus and Malta **3** a unit of weight made up of 16 ounces and equal to 0.454 kilograms
WORD ORIGIN Old English *pund*
pound[2] ❶ *vb* **1** (sometimes foll. by *on* or *at*) to hit heavily and repeatedly **2** to crush to pieces or to powder **3** (foll. by *out*) to produce, by typing heavily **4** (of the heart) to throb heavily **5** to run with heavy steps
WORD ORIGIN Old English *pūnian*
pound[3] ❶ *n* an enclosure for stray dogs or officially removed vehicles
WORD ORIGIN Old English *pund-*
poundage *n* **1** a charge of so much per pound of weight **2** a charge of so much per pound sterling
-pounder *n combining form* **1** something weighing a specified number of pounds: *a 200-pounder* **2** something worth a specified number of pounds: *a ten-pounder* **3** a gun that discharges a shell weighing a specified number of pounds: *a two-pounder*
pour ❶ *vb* **1** to flow or cause to flow out in a stream **2** to rain heavily **3** to be given or obtained in large amounts: *foreign aid is pouring into Iran* **4** to move together in large numbers: *the fans poured onto the pitch*
WORD ORIGIN origin unknown
pourboire (poor-bwahr) *n* a tip or gratuity

P

THESAURUS

potential *adj* **1a, 1b = possible**, future, likely, promising, budding, embryonic, undeveloped, unrealized, probable **1b = hidden**, possible, inherent, dormant, latent ▷*n* **2 = ability**, possibilities, capacity, capability, the makings, what it takes *(informal)*, aptitude, wherewithal, potentiality
potter[2] *vb* **2** *(usually with* **about** *or* **around** *or* **away***)* **= mess about**, fiddle *(informal)*, tinker, dabble, fritter, footle *(informal)*, poke along, fribble
pottery *n* **1 = ceramics**, terracotta, crockery, earthenware, stoneware
pounce *vb* **1** *(often followed by* **on** *or* **upon***)* **= attack**, strike, jump, leap, swoop
pound[2] *vb* **1** *(sometimes with* **on** *or* **at***)* **= beat**, strike, hammer, batter, thrash, thump, pelt, clobber *(slang)*, pummel, belabour, beat *or* knock seven bells out of *(informal)*, beat the living daylights out of **2 = crush**, powder, bruise, bray *(dialect)*, pulverize **4 = pulsate**, beat, pulse, throb, palpitate, pitapat **5 = stomp**, tramp, march, thunder *(informal)*, clomp
pound[3] *n* **= enclosure**, yard, pen, compound, kennels, corral *(chiefly US & Canad)*
pour *vb* **1a = let flow**, spill, splash, dribble, drizzle, slop *(informal)*, slosh *(informal)*, decant **1b = flow**, stream, run, course, rush, emit, cascade, gush, spout, spew **2 = rain**, sheet, pelt (down), teem, bucket down *(informal)*, rain cats and dogs *(informal)*, come down in torrents, rain hard *or* heavily **4 = stream**, crowd, flood, swarm, gush, throng, teem

DICTIONARY

WORD ORIGIN French, literally: for drinking

pout ⊙ *vb* **1** to thrust out (the lips) sullenly or provocatively **2** to swell out; protrude ▷ *n* **3** a pouting
WORD ORIGIN origin unknown

pouter *n* a breed of domestic pigeon that can puff out its crop

poutine (poo-**teen**) *n Canad* a dish of chipped potatoes topped with curd cheese and a tomato-based sauce

poverty ⊙ *n* **1** the state of lacking adequate food or money **2** lack or scarcity: *a poverty of information* **3** inferior quality or inadequacy: *the poverty of political debate in this country*
WORD ORIGIN Old French *poverté*

poverty-stricken *adj* extremely poor

poverty trap *n* the situation of being unable to raise one's living standard because any extra income would result in state benefits being reduced or withdrawn

pow *interj* an exclamation to indicate that a collision or explosion has taken place

POW prisoner of war

powder ⊙ *n* **1** a substance in the form of tiny loose particles **2** a medicine or cosmetic in this form ▷ *vb* **3** to cover or sprinkle with powder
powdery *adj*
WORD ORIGIN Old French *poldre*, from Latin *pulvis* dust

powdered *adj* **1** sold in the form of a powder, esp. one which has been formed by grinding or drying the original material: *powdered milk* **2** covered or made up with a cosmetic in the form of a powder: *liveried footmen in powdered wigs*

powder keg *n* **1** a potential source of violence or disaster: *a political powder keg* **2** a small barrel for holding gunpowder

powder puff *n* a soft pad used to apply cosmetic powder to the skin

powder room *n* a ladies' cloakroom or toilet

power ⊙ *n* **1** ability to do something **2** (*often pl*) a specific ability or faculty **3** political, financial, or social force or authority: *men's use of power over women in a subordinate position in the workforce; economic power is the bedrock of political power* **4** a position of control, esp. over the running of a country: *he seized power in a coup in 1966* **5** a state with political, industrial, or military strength **6** a person or group having authority **7** a prerogative or privilege: *the power of veto* **8** official or legal authority **9** *maths* the value of a number or quantity raised to some exponent **10** *physics, engineering* a measure of the rate of doing work expressed as the work done per unit time **11** the rate at which electrical energy is fed into or taken from a device or system, measured in watts **12** mechanical energy as opposed to manual labour **13** a particular form of energy: *nuclear power* **14** the magnifying capacity of a lens or optical system **15** *informal* a great deal: *a power of good* **16 the powers that be** established authority ▷ *vb* **17** to supply with power ▷ *adj* **18** producing or using electrical energy: *a large selection of power tools*
WORD ORIGIN Anglo-Norman *poer*

powerboat *n* a fast powerful motorboat

power cut *n* a temporary interruption in the supply of electricity

powerful ⊙ *adj* **1** having great power or influence **2** having great physical strength **3** extremely effective: *a powerful drug* **powerfully** *adv* **powerfulness** *n*

powerhouse *n* **1** *informal* a forceful person or thing **2** an electrical generating station

powerless ⊙ *adj* without power or authority; unable to act **powerlessly** *adv* **powerlessness** *n*

power of attorney *n* **1** legal authority to act for another person **2** the document conferring such authority

power play *n* **1** behaviour or tactics intended to magnify a person's influence or power **2** the use of brute strength or force of numbers in order to achieve an objective

power point *n* an electrical socket fitted into a wall for plugging in electrical appliances

power pole *n Austral & NZ* a pole carrying an overhead power line

power-sharing *n* a political arrangement in which opposing groups in a society participate in government

power station *n* an installation for generating and distributing electricity

power steering *n* a type of steering in vehicles in which the turning of the steering wheel is assisted by power from the engine

Powhatan *n* American Indian name *Wahunsonacock*. died 1618, American Indian chief of a confederacy of tribes; father of Pocahontas

powwow *n* **1** a talk or meeting **2** a meeting of Native Americans of N America ▷ *vb* **3** to hold a powwow
WORD ORIGIN from a Native American language

Powys[1] *n* a county in E Wales, formed in 1974 from most of Breconshire, Montgomeryshire, and Radnorshire. Administrative centre: Llandrindod Wells. Pop: 129 300 (2003 est). Area: 5077 sq km (1960 sq miles)

Powys[2] *n* **1 John Cowper** 1872–1963, British novelist, essayist, and poet, who spent much of his life in the US His novels include *Wolf Solent* (1929), *A Glastonbury Romance* (1932), and *Owen Glendower* (1940) **2** his brother, **Llewelyn** 1884–1939, British essayist and journalist **3** his brother, **T(heodore) F(rancis)** 1875–1953, British novelist and short-story writer, noted for such religious fables as *Mr Weston's Good Wine* (1927) and *Unclay* (1931)

pox *n* **1** a disease in which pus-filled blisters or pimples form on the skin **2 the pox** *informal* syphilis

THESAURUS

pout *vb* **1 = sulk**, glower, mope, look sullen, purse your lips, look petulant, pull a long face, lour *or* lower, make a moue, turn down the corners of your mouth ▷ *n* **3 = sullen look**, glower, long face, moue (*French*)

poverty *n* **1 = pennilessness**, want, need, distress, necessity, hardship, insolvency, privation, penury, destitution, hand-to-mouth existence, beggary, indigence, pauperism, necessitousness
OPPOSITE: wealth
2 = scarcity, lack, absence, want, deficit, shortage, deficiency, inadequacy, dearth, paucity, insufficiency, sparsity
OPPOSITE: abundance

powder *n* **1 = dust**, pounce (*rare*), talc, fine grains, loose particles ▷ *vb* **3 = dust**, cover, scatter, sprinkle, strew, dredge

power *n* **1 = ability**, capacity, faculty, property, potential, capability, competence, competency
OPPOSITE: inability
3a = strength, might, energy, weight, muscle, vigour, potency, brawn **OPPOSITE:** weakness
3b = forcefulness, force, strength, punch (*informal*), intensity, potency, eloquence, persuasiveness, cogency, powerfulness **4 = control**, authority, influence, command, sovereignty, sway, dominance, domination, supremacy, mastery, dominion, ascendancy, mana (*NZ*)
7 = authority, right, licence, privilege, warrant, prerogative, authorization

powerful *adj* **1 = influential**, dominant, controlling, commanding, supreme, prevailing, sovereign, authoritative, puissant, skookum (*Canad*)
OPPOSITE: powerless
2 = strong, strapping, mighty, robust, vigorous, potent, energetic, sturdy, stalwart **OPPOSITE:** weak

powerless *adj* **= defenceless**, vulnerable, dependent, subject, tied, ineffective, unarmed, disenfranchised, over a barrel (*informal*), disfranchised

DICTIONARY

WORD ORIGIN changed from *pocks*, plural of *pock*

pp 1 past participle 2 (in signing documents on behalf of someone else) by delegation to
WORD ORIGIN Latin *per procurationem*

pp. pages

PPS 1 parliamentary private secretary 2 additional postscript
WORD ORIGIN Latin *post postscriptum*

PPTA (in New Zealand) Post Primary Teachers Association

PQ 1 Province of Quebec 2 (in Canada) Parti Québecois

PQE, Pqe post-qualification experience

pr *pl* **prs** pair

Pr *chem* praseodymium

PR 1 proportional representation 2 public relations

pr. 1 price 2 pronoun

practicable *adj* 1 capable of being done 2 usable **practicability** *n*
WORD ORIGIN French *praticable*

practical ❶ *adj* 1 involving experience or actual use rather than theory 2 concerned with everyday matters: *the kind of practical and emotional upheaval that divorce can bring* 3 sensible, useful, and effective rather than fashionable or attractive: *it's a marvellous design, because it's comfortable, it's practical, and it actually looks good* 4 involving the simple basics: *practical skills* 5 being very close to (a state); virtual: *it's a practical certainty* ▷*n* 6 an examination or lesson in which something has to be made or done **practicality** *n* **practically** *adv*
WORD ORIGIN Greek *praktikos*, from *prassein* to experience

practical joke *n* a trick intended to make someone look foolish **practical joker** *n*

practice ❶ *n* 1 something done regularly or repeatedly 2 repetition of an activity in order to gain skill: *regular practice is essential if you want to play an instrument well* 3 the business or surgery of a doctor or lawyer 4 the act of doing something: *I'm not sure how effective these methods will be when put into practice* 5 **in practice** a what actually happens as distinct from what is supposed to happen: *many ideas which look good on paper just don't work in practice* b skilled in something through having had a lot of regular recent experience at it: *I still go shooting, just to keep in practice* 6 **out of practice** not having had much regular recent experience at an activity: *although out of practice, I still love playing my violin*
WORD ORIGIN Greek *praktikē* practical work

practise ❶ *or US* **practice** *vb* **-tising, -tised** *or* **-ticing, -ticed** 1 to do repeatedly in order to gain skill 2 to take part in or follow (a religion etc.): *none of them practise Islam* 3 to work at (a profession): *he originally intended to practise medicine* 4 to do regularly: *they practise meditation*
WORD ORIGIN Greek *prattein* to do

practised ❶ *adj* expert or skilled because of long experience in a skill or field: *the doctor answered with a practised smoothness*

practising *adj* taking part in an activity or career on a regular basis: *a practising barrister*

practitioner *n* a person who practises a profession

praetor (pree-tor) *n* (in ancient Rome) a senior magistrate ranking just below the consuls **praetorian** *adj, n*
WORD ORIGIN Latin

Praetorius *n* **Michael** 1571–1621, German composer and musicologist, noted esp. for his description of contemporary musical practices and instruments, *Syntagma musicum* (1615–19)

pragmatic ❶ *adj* 1 concerned with practical consequences rather than theory 2 *philosophy* of pragmatism **pragmatically** *adv*
WORD ORIGIN Greek *pragmatikos*

pragmatism *n* 1 policy dictated by practical consequences rather than by theory 2 *philosophy* the doctrine that the content of a concept consists only in its practical applicability **pragmatist** *n, adj*

prairie *n* (*often pl*) a large treeless area of grassland of North America
WORD ORIGIN French, from Latin *pratum* meadow

prairie dog *n* a rodent that lives in burrows in the N American prairies

praise ❶ *vb* **praising, praised** 1 to express admiration or approval for 2 to express thanks and worship to (one's God) ▷*n* 3 the expression of admiration or approval 4 **sing someone's praises** to praise someone highly
WORD ORIGIN Latin *pretium* prize

praiseworthy *adj* deserving praise; commendable

praline (prah-leen) *n* a sweet made of nuts with caramelized sugar
WORD ORIGIN French

pram *n* a four-wheeled carriage for a baby, pushed by a person on foot
WORD ORIGIN altered from *perambulator*

prance *vb* **prancing, pranced** 1 to walk with exaggerated movements 2 (of an animal) to move with high springing steps ▷*n* 3 the act of prancing
WORD ORIGIN origin unknown

Prandtl *n* **Ludwig** 1875–1953, German physicist, who made important contributions to aerodynamics and aeronautics

prang *old-fashioned slang n* 1 a crash in an aircraft or car ▷*vb* 2 to crash or

THESAURUS

practical *adj* **1 = empirical**, real, applied, actual, hands-on, in the field, experimental, factual **OPPOSITE:** theoretical **2 = sensible**, ordinary, realistic, down-to-earth, mundane, matter-of-fact, no-nonsense, businesslike, hard-headed, workaday, grounded **OPPOSITE:** impractical **3 = functional**, efficient, realistic, pragmatic **OPPOSITE:** impractical **4 = useful**, ordinary, appropriate, sensible, everyday, functional, utilitarian, serviceable

practice *n* **1 = custom**, use, way, system, rule, method, tradition, habit, routine, mode, usage, wont, praxis, usual procedure, tikanga (*NZ*) **2 = training**, study, exercise, work-out, discipline, preparation, drill, rehearsal, repetition **3a = profession**, work, business, career, occupation, pursuit, vocation **3b = business**, company, office, firm, enterprise, partnership, outfit (*informal*) **4 = use**, experience, action, effect, operation, application, enactment

practise *vb* **1 = rehearse**, study, prepare, perfect, repeat, go through, polish, go over, refine, run through **2 = carry out**, follow, apply, perform, observe, engage in, live up to, put into practice **3 = work at**, pursue, carry on, undertake, specialize in, ply your trade **4 = do**, train, exercise, work out, drill, warm up, keep your hand in

practised *adj* **= skilled**, trained, experienced, seasoned, able, expert, qualified, accomplished, versed, proficient **OPPOSITE:** inexperienced

pragmatic *adj* **1 = practical**, efficient, sensible, realistic, down-to-earth, matter-of-fact, utilitarian, businesslike, hard-headed **OPPOSITE:** idealistic

praise *vb* **1 = acclaim**, approve of, honour, cheer, admire, applaud, compliment, congratulate, pay tribute to, laud, extol, sing the praises of, pat someone on the back, cry someone up, big up (*slang, chiefly Caribbean*), eulogize, take your hat off to, crack someone up (*informal*) **OPPOSITE:** criticize **2 = give thanks to**, bless, worship, adore, magnify (*archaic*), glorify, exalt, pay homage to ▷*n* **3 = approval**, acclaim, applause, cheering, tribute, compliment, congratulations, ovation, accolade, good word, kudos, eulogy, commendation, approbation, acclamation, panegyric, encomium, plaudit, laudation **OPPOSITE:** criticism

DICTIONARY

damage (an aircraft or car)
WORD ORIGIN perhaps imitative

prank *n* a mischievous trick
prankster *n*
WORD ORIGIN origin unknown

Prasad *n* **Rajendra** 1884–1963, Indian statesman and journalist; first president of India (1950–62)

praseodymium (pray-zee-oh-**dim**-ee-um) *n chem* a silvery-white element of the lanthanide series of metals. Symbol: Pr
WORD ORIGIN New Latin

prat *n Brit, Austral & NZ slang* an incompetent or ineffectual person
WORD ORIGIN probably special use of earlier *prat* buttocks, origin unknown

Pratchett *n* **Terence (David John)**, known as *Terry*. born 1948, British writer, noted for his comic fantasy novels in the *Discworld* series

prate *vb* **prating, prated 1** to talk idly and at length ▷*n* **2** chatter
WORD ORIGIN Germanic

prattle *vb* **-tling, -tled 1** to chatter in a foolish or childish way ▷*n* **2** foolish or childish talk
WORD ORIGIN Middle Low German *pratelen* to chatter

prawn *n* a small edible shellfish
WORD ORIGIN origin unknown

praxis *n* **1** practice as opposed to the theory **2** accepted practice or custom
WORD ORIGIN Greek: deed, action

pray ❶ *vb* **1** to say prayers (to one's God) **2** to ask earnestly; beg ▷*adv* **3** *archaic* I beg you; please: *pray, leave us alone*
WORD ORIGIN Latin *precari* to implore

prayer[1] ❶ *n* **1** a thanksgiving or an appeal spoken to one's God **2** a set form of words used in praying: *the Lord's Prayer* **3** an earnest request **4** the practice of praying: *call the faithful to prayer* **5** *(often pl)* a form of devotion spent mainly praying: *morning prayers* **6** something prayed for

prayer[2] *n* a person who prays

prayer book *n* a book of prayers used in church or at home

prayer mat *or* **prayer rug** *n* the small carpet on which a Muslim performs his or her daily prayers

prayer wheel *n buddhism* (in Tibet) a cylinder inscribed with prayers, each turning of which is counted as an uttered prayer

praying mantis *n* ▸same as **mantis**

pre- *prefix* before in time or position: *predate; pre-eminent*
WORD ORIGIN Latin *prae*

preach ❶ *vb* **1** to talk on a religious theme as part of a church service **2** to speak in support of (something) in a moralizing way
WORD ORIGIN Latin *praedicare* to proclaim

preacher ❶ *n* a person who preaches

preamble *n* an introduction that comes before something spoken or written
WORD ORIGIN Latin *prae* before + *ambulare* to walk

prearranged *adj* arranged beforehand **prearrangement** *n*

prebend *n* **1** the allowance paid by a cathedral or collegiate church to a canon or member of the chapter **2** the land or tithe from which this is paid **prebendal** *adj*
WORD ORIGIN Old French *prébende*

prebendary *n, pl* **-daries** a clergyman who is a member of the chapter of a cathedral

Precambrian *or* **Pre-Cambrian** *adj geol* of the earliest geological era, lasting from about 4500 million years ago to 600 million years ago

precancerous *adj* relating to cells that show signs that they may develop cancer

precarious ❶ *adj* (of a position or situation) dangerous or insecure **precariously** *adv*
WORD ORIGIN Latin *precarius* obtained by begging

precaution ❶ *n* an action taken in advance to prevent an undesirable event **precautionary** *adj*
WORD ORIGIN Latin *prae* before + *cavere* to beware

precede ❶ *vb* **-ceding, -ceded** to go or be before (someone or something) in time, place, or rank
WORD ORIGIN Latin *praecedere*

precedence (**press**-ee-denss) *n* formal order of rank or position

precedent ❶ *n* **1** a previous occurrence used to justify taking the same action in later similar situations **2** *law* a judicial decision that serves as an authority for deciding a later case ▷*adj* **3** preceding

precentor *n* a person who leads the singing in church services
WORD ORIGIN Latin *prae* before + *canere* to sing

precept *n* **1** a rule of conduct **2** a rule for morals **3** *law* a writ or warrant **preceptive** *adj*
WORD ORIGIN Latin *praeceptum*

preceptor *n rare* an instructor **preceptorial** *adj*

precession *n* **1** the act of preceding **2** the motion of a spinning body, in which the axis of rotation sweeps out a cone **3** **precession of the equinoxes** the slightly earlier occurrence of the equinoxes each year
WORD ORIGIN Latin *praecedere* to precede

precinct ❶ *n* **1** *Brit, Austral & S African* an area in a town closed to traffic: *a shopping precinct* **2** *Brit, Austral & S African* an enclosed area around a building **3** *US* an administrative area of a city
WORD ORIGIN Latin *praecingere* to surround

precincts *pl n* the surrounding region

preciosity (presh-ee-**oss**-it-ee) *n, pl* **-ties** affectation

precious ❶ *adj* **1** very costly or valuable: *precious jewellery* **2** loved and treasured **3** very affected in speech, manners, or behaviour **4** *informal* worthless: *nothing is too good for his precious dog* ▷*adv* **5** *informal* very:

P

THESAURUS

pray *vb* **1 = say your prayers**, offer a prayer, recite the rosary **2 = beg**, ask, plead, petition, urge, request, sue, crave, invoke, call upon, cry, solicit, implore, beseech, entreat, importune, adjure, supplicate

prayer[1] *n* **1 = orison**, litany, invocation, intercession **3 = plea**, appeal, suit, request, petition, entreaty, supplication **5 = supplication**, devotion, communion

preach *vb* **1 = deliver a sermon**, address, exhort, evangelize, preach a sermon, orate **2 = urge**, teach, champion, recommend, advise, counsel, advocate, exhort

preacher *n* **= clergyman**, minister, parson, missionary, evangelist, revivalist

precarious *adj* **a = insecure**, dangerous, uncertain, tricky, risky, doubtful, dubious, unsettled, dodgy *(Brit, Austral & NZ informal)*, unstable, unsure, hazardous, shaky, hairy *(slang)*, perilous, touch and go, dicey *(informal, chiefly Brit)*, chancy *(informal)*, built on sand, shonky *(Austral & NZ informal)* **OPPOSITE:** secure **b = dangerous**, unstable, shaky, slippery, insecure, unsafe, unreliable, unsteady **OPPOSITE:** stable

precaution *n* **= safeguard**, insurance, protection, provision, safety measure, preventative measure, belt and braces *(informal)*

precede *vb* **a = go before**, introduce, herald, pave the way for, usher in, antedate, antecede, forerun **b = go ahead of**, lead, head, go before, take precedence

precedent *n* **1 = instance**, example, authority, standard, model, pattern, criterion, prototype, paradigm, antecedent, exemplar, previous example

precinct *n* **3** *(US)* **= area**, quarter, section, sector, district, zone

precious *adj* **1 = valuable**, expensive, rare, fine, choice, prized, dear, costly, high-priced, exquisite, invaluable, priceless, recherché, inestimable **OPPOSITE:** worthless **2 = loved**, valued, favourite, prized,

DICTIONARY

there's precious little to do in this town
WORD ORIGIN Latin *pretiosus* valuable

precious metal *n* gold, silver, or platinum

precious stone *n* a rare mineral, such as diamond, ruby, or opal, that is highly valued as a gem

precipice *n* the very steep face of a cliff
WORD ORIGIN Latin *praecipitium* steep place

precipitant *adj* **1** hasty or rash **2** rushing or falling rapidly ▷*n* **3** something which helps bring about an event or condition: *stressful events are often the precipitant for a manic attack*

precipitate ❶ *vb* **-tating, -tated 1** to cause to happen earlier than expected: *the scandal could bring the government down, precipitating a general election* **2** to condense or cause to condense and fall as snow or rain **3** *chem* to cause to be deposited in solid form from a solution **4** to throw from a height: *the encircled soldiers chose to precipitate themselves into the ocean* ▷*adj* **5** done rashly or hastily **6** rushing ahead ▷*n* **7** *chem* a precipitated solid
WORD ORIGIN Latin *praecipitare* to throw down headlong

precipitation *n* **1** the formation of a chemical precipitate **2** *meteorol* **a** rain, hail, snow, or sleet formed by condensation of water vapour in the atmosphere **b** the falling of these **3** rash haste: *they decamped with the utmost precipitation*

precipitous *adj* **1** very steep: *precipitous cliffs* **2** very quick and severe: *a precipitous decline* **3** rapid and unplanned; hasty: *European governments urged the Americans not to make a precipitous decision*

précis (**pray**-see) *n, pl* **précis 1** a short summary of a longer text ▷*vb* **2** to make a précis of
WORD ORIGIN French

precise ❶ *adj* **1** particular or exact: *this precise moment* **2** strictly correct in amount or value: *precise measurements* **3** working with total accuracy: *precise instruments* **4** strict in observing rules or standards **precisely** *adv*
WORD ORIGIN Latin *prae* before + *caedere* to cut

precision ❶ *n* **1** the quality of being precise ▷*adj* **2** accurate: *precision engineering*

preclude *vb* **-cluding, -cluded** *formal* to make impossible to happen
WORD ORIGIN Latin *prae* before + *claudere* to close

precocious *adj* having developed or matured early or too soon
precocity *n*
WORD ORIGIN Latin *prae* early + *coquere* to ripen

precognition *n psychol* the alleged ability to foresee future events
WORD ORIGIN Latin *praecognoscere* to foresee

preconceived *adj* (of ideas etc.) formed without real experience or reliable information
preconception *n*

precondition *n* something that is necessary before something else can come about

precursor *n* **1** something that comes before and signals something to follow; a forerunner **2** a predecessor
WORD ORIGIN Latin *praecursor* one who runs in front

pred. predicate

predacious *adj* (of animals) habitually hunting and killing other animals for food
WORD ORIGIN Latin *praeda* plunder

predate *vb* **-dating, -dated 1** to occur at an earlier date than **2** to write a date on (a document) that is earlier than the actual date

predator *n* an animal that kills and eats other animals

predatory (**pred**-a-tree) *adj* **1** (of animals) habitually hunting and killing other animals for food **2** eager to gain at the expense of others
WORD ORIGIN Latin *praedari* to pillage

predecease *vb* **-ceasing, -ceased** to die before (someone else)

predecessor ❶ *n* **1** a person who precedes another in an office or position **2** an ancestor **3** something that precedes something else: *the library will be more extravagant than its predecessors*
WORD ORIGIN Latin *prae* before + *decedere* to go away

predestination *n Christian theol* the belief that future events have already been decided by God

predestined *adj Christian theol* determined in advance by God
WORD ORIGIN Latin *praedestinare* to resolve beforehand

predetermine *vb* **-mining, -mined 1** to determine beforehand **2** to influence or bias **predetermined** *adj*

predicable *adj* capable of being predicated

predicament ❶ *n* an embarrassing or difficult situation
WORD ORIGIN see PREDICATE

predicant (**pred**-ik-ant) *adj* **1** of preaching ▷*n* **2** a member of a religious order founded for preaching, usually a Dominican
WORD ORIGIN Latin *praedicans* preaching

predicate *n* **1** *grammar* the part of a sentence in which something is said about the subject **2** *logic* something that is asserted about the subject of a proposition ▷*vb* **-cating, -cated 3** to base or found: *political aims which are predicated upon a feminist view of women's oppression* **4** to declare or assert: *it has been predicated that if we continue with our current sexual behaviour every family will have an AIDS victim* **5** *logic* to assert (something) about the subject of a proposition **predication** *n*
predicative *adj*
WORD ORIGIN Latin *praedicare* to assert publicly

predict ❶ *vb* to tell about in advance; prophesy **predictable** *adj*
predictably *adv* **predictor** *n*
WORD ORIGIN Latin *praedicere*

P

THESAURUS

dear, dearest, treasured, darling, beloved, adored, cherished, fave *(informal)*, idolized, worth your *or* its weight in gold **3 = affected**, artificial, fastidious, twee *(Brit informal)*, chichi, overrefined, overnice

precipitate *vb* **1 = quicken**, trigger, accelerate, further, press, advance, hurry, dispatch, speed up, bring on, hasten, push forward, expedite **4 = throw**, launch, cast, discharge, hurl, fling, let fly, send forth ▷*adj* **5 = hasty**, hurried, frantic, rash, reckless, impulsive, madcap, ill-advised, precipitous, impetuous, indiscreet, heedless, harum-scarum **6 = sudden**, quick, brief, rushing, violent, plunging, rapid, unexpected, swift, abrupt, without warning, headlong, breakneck

precise *adj* **1 = exact**, specific, actual, particular, express, fixed, correct, absolute, accurate, explicit, definite, clear-cut, literal, unequivocal
OPPOSITE: vague
4 = strict, particular, exact, nice, formal, careful, stiff, rigid, meticulous, inflexible, scrupulous, fastidious, prim, puritanical, finicky, punctilious, ceremonious
OPPOSITE: inexact

precision *n* **1 = exactness**, care, accuracy, fidelity, correctness, rigour, nicety, particularity, exactitude, meticulousness, definiteness, dotting the i's and crossing the t's, preciseness

predecessor *n* **1 = previous job holder**, precursor, forerunner, antecedent, former job holder, prior job holder **2 = ancestor**, forebear, antecedent, forefather, tupuna *or* tipuna *(NZ)*

predicament *n* **= fix** *(informal)*, state, situation, spot *(informal)*, corner, hole *(slang)*, emergency, mess, jam *(informal)*, dilemma, pinch, plight, scrape *(informal)*, hot water *(informal)*, pickle *(informal)*, how-do-you-do *(informal)*, quandary, tight spot

predict *vb* **= foretell**, forecast, divine, foresee, prophesy, call, augur, presage, portend, prognosticate, forebode, soothsay, vaticinate *(rare)*

DICTIONARY

prediction ❶ *n* **1** the act of forecasting in advance **2** something that is forecast in advance

predictive *adj* **1** relating to or able to make predictions **2** (of a word processor) able to complete words after only part of a word has been keyed

predikant (pred-ik-**ant**) *n* a minister in the Dutch Reformed Church in South Africa
WORD ORIGIN Dutch

predilection *n formal* a preference or liking
WORD ORIGIN French *prédilection*

predispose *vb* **-posing, -posed** (often foll. by *to*) **1** to influence (someone) in favour of something: *some scientists' social class background predisposes them to view the natural world in a certain way* **2** to make (someone) susceptible to something: *a high-fat diet appears to predispose men towards heart disease* **predisposition** *n*

predominant *adj* being more important or noticeable than others: *improved living conditions probably played the predominant role in reducing disease in the nineteenth century* **predominance** *n* **predominantly** *adv*

predominate *vb* **-nating, -nated 1** to be the most important or controlling aspect or part: *the image of brutal repression that has tended to predominate since the protests were crushed* **2** to form the greatest part or be most common: *women predominate in this gathering*
WORD ORIGIN Latin *prae* before + *dominari* to rule

pre-eminent *adj* outstanding **pre-eminence** *n*

pre-empt *vb* to prevent an action by doing something which makes it pointless or impossible: *he pre-empted his expulsion from the party by resigning*

pre-emption *n law* the purchase of or right to buy property in advance of others
WORD ORIGIN Medieval Latin *praeemere* to buy beforehand

pre-emptive *adj mil* designed to damage or destroy an enemy's attacking strength before it can be used: *a pre-emptive strike*

preen *vb* **1** (of birds) to clean or trim (feathers) with the beak **2** to smarten (oneself) carefully **3 preen oneself** (often foll. by *on*) to be self-satisfied
WORD ORIGIN Middle English *preinen*

pref. 1 preface **2** prefatory **3** preference **4** preferred **5** prefix

prefab *n* a prefabricated house

prefabricated *adj* (of a building) made in shaped sections for quick assembly

preface (**pref**-iss) *n* **1** an introduction to a book, usually explaining its intention or content **2** anything introductory ▷*vb* **-acing, -aced 3** to say or do something before proceeding to the main part **4** to act as a preface to
WORD ORIGIN Latin *praefari* to say in advance

prefatory *adj* concerning a preface
WORD ORIGIN Latin *praefari* to say in advance

prefect *n* **1** *Brit, Austral, & NZ* a senior pupil in a school with limited power over the behaviour of other pupils **2** (in some countries) the chief administrative officer in a department
WORD ORIGIN Latin *praefectus* one put in charge

prefecture *n* the office or area of authority of a prefect

prefer ❶ *vb* **-ferring, -ferred 1** to like better: *most people prefer television to reading books* **2** *law* to put (charges) before a court for judgment **3** (*often passive*) to promote over another or others
WORD ORIGIN Latin *praeferre* to carry in front, prefer

preferable ❶ *adj* more desirable or suitable **preferably** *adv*

preference ❶ *n* **1** a liking for one thing above the rest **2** a person or thing preferred

preference shares *pl n* shares issued by a company which give their holders a priority over ordinary shareholders to payment of dividend

preferential *adj* **1** showing preference: *preferential treatment* **2** indicating a special favourable status in business affairs: *the President is to renew China's preferential trading status* **3** indicating a voting system which allows voters to rank candidates in order of preference: *a multi-option referendum with preferential voting*

preferment *n* promotion to a higher position

prefigure *vb* **-uring, -ured 1** to represent or suggest in advance **2** to imagine beforehand

prefix *n* **1** *grammar* a letter or group of letters put at the beginning of a word to make a new word, such as *un-* in *unhappy* **2** a title put before a name, such as *Mr* ▷*vb* **3** *grammar* to add (a letter or group of letters) as a prefix to the beginning of a word **4** to put before

pregnant ❶ *adj* **1** carrying a fetus or fetuses within the womb **2** full of meaning or significance: *a pregnant pause* **pregnancy** *n*
WORD ORIGIN Latin *praegnans*

prehensile *adj* capable of curling round objects and grasping them: *a prehensile tail*
WORD ORIGIN Latin *prehendere* to grasp

prehistoric *adj* of man's development before the appearance of the written word **prehistory** *n*

preindustrial *adj* of a time before the mechanization of industry

prejudge *vb* **-judging, -judged** to judge before knowing all the facts

prejudice ❶ *n* **1** an unreasonable or unfair dislike or preference **2** intolerance of or dislike for people because they belong to a specific race, religion, or group: *class prejudice* **3** the act or condition of holding such opinions **4** harm or detriment: *conduct to the prejudice of good order and military discipline* **5 without prejudice** *law* without harm to an existing right or claim ▷*vb* **-dicing, -diced 6** to cause (someone) to have a prejudice **7** to harm: *the incident prejudiced his campaign*
WORD ORIGIN Latin *prae* before + *judicium* sentence

prejudicial *adj* harmful; damaging

prelacy *n, pl* **-cies 1 a** the office or status of a prelate **b** prelates

p

THESAURUS

prediction *n* **1, 2 = prophecy**, forecast, prognosis, divination, prognostication, augury, soothsaying, sortilege

prefer *vb* **1 = like better**, favour, go for, pick, select, adopt, fancy, opt for, single out, plump for, incline towards, be partial to

preferable *adj* **= better**, best, chosen, choice, preferred, recommended, favoured, superior, worthier, more suitable, more desirable, more eligible **OPPOSITE:** undesirable

preference *n* **1 = liking**, wish, taste, desire, bag (*slang*), leaning, bent, bias, cup of tea (*informal*), inclination, penchant, fondness, predisposition, predilection, proclivity, partiality **2 = first choice**, choice, favourite, election, pick, option, selection, top of the list, fave (*informal*)

pregnant *adj* **1 = expectant**, expecting (*informal*), with child, in the club (*Brit slang*), in the family way (*informal*), gravid, preggers (*Brit informal*), enceinte, in the pudding club (*slang*), big *or* heavy with child **2 = meaningful**, pointed, charged, significant, telling, loaded, expressive, eloquent, weighty, suggestive

prejudice *n* **1 = bias**, preconception, partiality, preconceived notion, warp, jaundiced eye, prejudgment **2, 3 = discrimination**, racism, injustice, sexism, intolerance, bigotry, unfairness, chauvinism, narrow-mindedness ▷*vb* **6 = bias**, influence, colour, poison, distort, sway, warp, slant, predispose, jaundice, prepossess **7 = harm**, damage, hurt, injure, mar, undermine, spoil, impair, hinder,

DICTIONARY

collectively **2** *often offensive* government of the Church by prelates

prelate (prel-it) *n* a clergyman of high rank, such as a bishop
WORD ORIGIN Church Latin *praelatus*, from Latin *praeferre* to hold in special esteem

preliminaries *pl n* ▸ same as **prelims**

preliminary ⊙ *adj* **1** occurring before or in preparation; introductory ▹ *n, pl* **-naries 2** an action or event occurring before or in preparation for an activity: *the discussions are a preliminary to the main negotiations* **3** a qualifying contest held before a main competition
WORD ORIGIN Latin *prae* before + *limen* threshold

prelims *pl n* **1** the pages of a book, such as the title page and contents, which come before the main text **2** the first public examinations in some universities
WORD ORIGIN a contraction of *preliminaries*

prelude ⊙ (prel-yewd) *n* **1 a** an introductory movement in music **b** a short piece of music for piano or organ **2** an event introducing or preceding the main event ▹ *vb* **-uding, -uded 3** to act as a prelude to (something) **4** to introduce by a prelude
WORD ORIGIN Latin *prae* before + *ludere* to play

premarital *adj* occurring before marriage: *premarital sex*

premature ⊙ *adj* **1** happening or done before the normal or expected time: *premature ageing* **2** impulsive or hasty: *a premature judgment* **3** (of a baby) born weeks before the date when it was due to be born **prematurely** *adv*
WORD ORIGIN Latin *prae* in advance + *maturus* ripe

premedication *n surgery* any drugs given to prepare a patient for a general anaesthetic

premeditated *adj* planned in advance **premeditation** *n*

premenstrual *adj* occurring or experienced before a menstrual period

premenstrual syndrome *or* **tension** *n* symptoms, such as nervous tension, that may be experienced because of hormonal changes in the days before a menstrual period starts

premier ⊙ *n* **1** a prime minister **2** a head of government of a Canadian province or Australian state ▹ *adj* **3** first in importance or rank: *Torbay, Devon's premier resort* **4** first in occurrence **premiership** *n*
WORD ORIGIN Latin *primus* first

premiere ⊙ *n* **1** the first public performance of a film, play, or opera ▹ *vb* **-ering, -ered 2** to give, or (of a film, play, or opera) be, a premiere: *the play was premiered last year in Johannesburg; the movie premieres tomorrow*
WORD ORIGIN French, feminine of *premier* first

Preminger *n* **Otto** (**Ludwig**) 1906–86, US film director, born in Austria. His films include *Carmen Jones* (1954) and *Anatomy of a Murder* (1959)

premise ⊙ *or* **premiss** *n logic* a statement that is assumed to be true and is used as a basis for an argument
WORD ORIGIN Medieval Latin *praemissa* sent on before

premises ⊙ *pl n* **1** a piece of land together with its buildings **2** *law* (in a deed) the matters referred to previously

premium ⊙ *n* **1** an extra sum of money added to a standard rate, price, or wage: *the superior taste persuades me to pay the premium for bottled water* **2** the (regular) amount paid for an insurance policy **3** the amount above the usual value at which something sells: *some even pay a premium of up to 15 per cent for the privilege* **4** great value or regard: *we do put a very high premium on common sense* **5 at a premium a** in great demand, usually because of scarcity **b** at a higher price than usual
WORD ORIGIN Latin *praemium* prize

Premium Savings Bonds *pl n* (in Britain) savings certificates issued by the government, on which no interest is paid, but there is a monthly draw for cash prizes. Also called: **premium bonds**

premolar *n* a tooth between the canine and first molar in adult humans

premonition *n* a feeling that something unpleasant is going to happen; foreboding **premonitory** *adj*
WORD ORIGIN Latin *prae* before + *monere* to warn

prenatal *adj* before birth; during pregnancy

preoccupy *vb* **-pies, -pying, -pied** to fill the thoughts or mind of (someone) to the exclusion of other things **preoccupation** *n*
WORD ORIGIN Latin *praeoccupare* to capture in advance

preordained *adj* decreed or determined in advance

preowned *adj euphemistic* already used; second-hand

prep *n Brit informal* ▸ short for **preparation** (sense 4)

prep. 1 preparation **2** preparatory **3** preposition

prepacked *adj* (of goods) sold already wrapped

prepaid *adj* paid for in advance

preparation ⊙ *n* **1** the act of preparing or being prepared **2** (*often pl*) something done in order to prepare for something else: *to make preparations for a wedding* **3** something that is prepared, such as a medicine **4** *Brit, old-fashioned* **a** homework **b** the period reserved for this

preparatory (prip-par-a-tree) *adj* **1** preparing for: *a preparatory meeting to*

P

THESAURUS

crool or cruel *(Austral slang)*

preliminary *adj* **1 = first**, opening, trial, initial, test, pilot, prior, introductory, preparatory, exploratory, initiatory, prefatory, precursory ▹ *n* **2 = introduction**, opening, beginning, foundation, start, preparation, first round, prelude, preface, overture, initiation, preamble, groundwork, prelims

prelude *n* **1a = overture**, opening, introduction, introductory movement **2 = introduction**, beginning, preparation, preliminary, start, commencement, curtain-raiser

premature *adj* **1 = early**, untimely, before time, unseasonable **2 = hasty**, rash, too soon, precipitate, impulsive, untimely, ill-considered, jumping the gun, ill-timed, inopportune, overhasty

premier *n* **1 = head of government**, prime minister, chancellor, chief minister, P.M. ▹ *adj* **3 = chief**, leading, top, first, highest, head, main, prime, primary, principal, arch, foremost

premiere *n* **1 = first night**, opening, debut, first showing, first performance

premise *n* **= assumption**, proposition, thesis, ground, argument, hypothesis, assertion, postulate, supposition, presupposition, postulation

premises *pl n* **1 = building(s)**, place, office, property, site, establishment

premium *n* **1 = surcharge**, extra charge, additional fee *or* charge **2 = fee**, charge, payment, instalment **3 = bonus**, reward, prize, percentage *(informal)*, perk *(Brit informal)*, boon, bounty, remuneration, recompense, perquisite
5a, 5b at a premium = in great demand, valuable, expensive, rare, costly, scarce, in short supply, hard to come by, like gold dust, beyond your means, not to be had for love or money

preparation *n* **1 = groundwork**, development, preparing, arranging, devising, getting ready, thinking-up, putting in order **2** *(often pl)* **= arrangement**, plan, measure, provision **3 = mixture**, cream, medicine, compound, composition, lotion, concoction, amalgam, ointment, tincture

DICTIONARY

organize the negotiations **2** introductory **3 preparatory to** before: *Jack cleared his throat preparatory to speaking*

preparatory school *n* **1** *Brit & S African* a private school for children between the ages of 6 and 13, generally preparing pupils for public school **2** (in the US) a private secondary school preparing pupils for college

prepare ❶ *vb* **-paring, -pared 1** to make or get ready: *the army prepared for battle* **2** to put together using parts or ingredients: *he had spent most of the afternoon preparing the meal* **3** to equip or outfit, as for an expedition **4 be prepared to** to be willing and able to: *I'm not prepared to say*
WORD ORIGIN Latin *prae* before + *parare* to make ready

prepay *vb* **-paying, -paid** to pay for in advance **prepayment** *n*

preponderant *adj* greater in amount, force, or influence **preponderance** *n*

preponderate *vb* **-ating, -ated** to be more powerful, important, or numerous (than): *the good preponderate over the bad*
WORD ORIGIN Late Latin *praeponderare* to be of greater weight

preposition *n* a word used before a noun or pronoun to relate it to the other words, for example *in* in *he is in the car* **prepositional** *adj*
WORD ORIGIN Latin *praepositio* a putting before

prepossess *vb* **1** to make a favourable impression in advance **2** to preoccupy or engross mentally **prepossession** *n*

prepossessing *adj* making a favourable impression; attractive

P

preposterous *adj* utterly absurd
WORD ORIGIN Latin *praeposterus* reversed

prep school *n informal* ▸ see **preparatory school**

prepuce (pree-pyewss) *n* **1** the retractable fold of skin covering the tip of the penis; foreskin **2** the retractable fold of skin covering the tip of the clitoris
WORD ORIGIN Latin *praeputium*

Pre-Raphaelite (pree-raff-a-lite) *n* **1** a member of a group of painters in the nineteenth century who revived the style considered typical of Italian painting before Raphael ▹ *adj* **2** of or in the manner of Pre-Raphaelite painting and painters

prerecord *vb* to record (music or a programme) in advance so that it can be played or broadcast later **prerecorded** *adj*

prerequisite *n* **1** something that is required before something else is possible ▹ *adj* **2** required before something else is possible

prerogative *n* a special privilege or right
WORD ORIGIN Latin *praerogativa* privilege

pres. 1 present (time) **2** presidential

Pres. President

presage (press-ij) *vb* **-aging, -aged 1** to be a warning or sign of something about to happen: *the windless air presaged disaster* ▹ *n* **2** an omen **3** a misgiving
WORD ORIGIN Latin *praesagire* to perceive beforehand

presbyopia *n med* a gradual inability of the eye to focus on nearby objects
WORD ORIGIN Greek *presbus* old man + *ōps* eye

presbyter *n* **1** (in some episcopal Churches) an official with administrative and priestly duties **2** (in the Presbyterian Church) an elder **presbyterial** *adj*
WORD ORIGIN Greek *presbuteros* an older man

presbyterian *adj* **1** of or designating Church government by lay elders ▹ *n* **2** someone who supports this type of Church government **presbyterianism** *n*

Presbyterian *adj* **1** of any of the Protestant Churches governed by lay elders ▹ *n* **2** a member of a Presbyterian Church **Presbyterianism** *n*

presbytery *n, pl* **-teries 1** *Presbyterian Church* a local Church court **2** *RC church* the residence of a parish priest **3** elders collectively **4** the part of a church east of the choir; a sanctuary
WORD ORIGIN see PRESBYTER

preschool *adj* of or for children below the age of five: *a preschool playgroup*

prescience (press-ee-enss) *n formal* knowledge of events before they happen **prescient** *adj*
WORD ORIGIN Latin *praescire* to know beforehand

Prescott *n* **1 John Leslie** born 1938, British politician: deputy leader of the Labour Party from 1994; deputy prime minister (1997–2007); secretary of state for the environment, transport, and the regions (1997–2001); minister for local government and the regions (2002–07) **2 William Hickling** 1796–1859, US historian, noted for his work on the history of Spain and her colonies

prescribe ❶ *vb* **-scribing, -scribed 1** *med* to recommend the use of (a medicine or other remedy) **2** to lay down as a rule
WORD ORIGIN Latin *praescribere* to write previously

prescript *n* something laid down or prescribed

prescription ❶ *n* **1 a** written instructions from a doctor for the preparation and use of a medicine **b** the medicine prescribed **2** written instructions from an optician specifying the lenses needed to correct bad eyesight **3** a prescribing
WORD ORIGIN Legal Latin *praescriptio* an order

prescriptive *adj* **1** laying down rules **2** based on tradition

presence ❶ *n* **1** the fact of being in a specified place: *the test detects the presence of sugar in the urine* **2** impressive personal appearance or bearing: *a person of dignified and commanding presence* **3** the company or nearness of a person: *she seemed completely unaware of my presence* **4** *mil* a force stationed in another country: *the American-led military presence in the Gulf* **5** an invisible spirit felt to be nearby: *I felt a presence in the room*
WORD ORIGIN Latin *praesentia* a being before

presence of mind ❶ *n* the ability to stay calm and act sensibly in a crisis

present[1] ❶ *adj* **1** being in a specified place: *he had been present at the birth of his*

THESAURUS

prepare *vb* **1a = make** *or* **get ready**, arrange, draw up, form, fashion, get up *(informal)*, construct, assemble, contrive, put together, make provision, put in order, jack up *(NZ informal)* **1b = get ready**, plan, anticipate, make provision, lay the groundwork, make preparations, arrange things, get everything set **2 = make**, cook, put together, get, produce, assemble, muster, concoct, fix up, dish up, rustle up *(informal)*

prescribe *vb* **1** *(medical)* **= specify**, order, direct, stipulate, write a prescription for **2 = ordain**, set, order, establish, rule, require, fix, recommend, impose, appoint, command, define, dictate, assign, lay down, decree, stipulate, enjoin

prescription *n* **1a = instruction**, direction, formula, script *(informal)*, recipe **1b = medicine**, drug, treatment, preparation, cure, mixture, dose, remedy

presence *n* **1 = being**, existence, company, residence, attendance, showing up, companionship, occupancy, habitation, inhabitance **2 = personality**, bearing, appearance, aspect, air, ease, carriage, aura, poise, demeanour, self-assurance, mien *(literary)*, comportment

presence of mind *n* **= level-headedness**, assurance, composure, poise, cool *(slang)*, wits, countenance, coolness, aplomb, alertness, calmness, equanimity, self-assurance, phlegm, quickness, sang-froid, self-possession, unflappability *(informal)*, imperturbability, quick-wittedness, self-command, collectedness

present[1] *adj* **1 = here**, there, near, available, ready, nearby, accounted for, to hand, at hand, in attendance

DICTIONARY

son **2** existing or happening now **3** current: *the present exchange rate* **4** *grammar* of a verb tense used when the action described is happening now ▷*n* **5** *grammar* the present tense **6 at present** now **7 for the present** for now; temporarily **8 the present** the time being; now ▸See also **presents**
WORD ORIGIN Latin *praesens*

present² ❶ *n* (prez-int) **1** a gift ▷*vb* (pri-zent) **2** to introduce (a person) formally to another **3** to introduce to the public: *the Museum of Modern Art is presenting a retrospective of his work* **4** to introduce and compere (a radio or television show) **5** to show or exhibit: *they took advantage of every tax dodge that presented itself* **6** to bring about: *the case presented a large number of legal difficulties* **7** to put forward or submit: *they presented a petition to the Prime Minister* **8** to give or offer formally: *he was presented with a watch to celebrate his twenty-five years with the company* **9** to hand over for action or payment: *to present a bill* **10** to portray in a particular way: *her lawyer presented her as a naive woman who had got into bad company* **11** to aim (a weapon) **12 present arms** to salute with one's weapon
WORD ORIGIN Latin *praesentare* to exhibit

presentable *adj* **1** fit to be seen by or introduced to other people **2** acceptable: *the team reached a presentable total* **presentability** *n*

presentation ❶ *n* **1** the act of presenting or being presented **2** the manner of presenting **3** a talk or lecture; the manner of presenting **4** a formal ceremony in which an award is made **5** a public performance, such as a play or a ballet

present-day *adj* of the modern day; current: *even by present-day standards these were large aircraft*

presenter *n* a person who introduces a radio or television show and links the items in it

presentiment (priz-zen-tim-ent) *n* a sense that something unpleasant is about to happen; premonition
WORD ORIGIN obsolete French *pressentir* to sense beforehand

presently ❶ *adv* **1** soon: *you will understand presently* **2** *chiefly Scot, US, & Canad* at the moment: *these methods are presently being developed*

present participle *n grammar* a form of verb, ending in *-ing*, which is used to describe action that is happening at the same time as that of the main verb

present perfect *adj, n grammar* ▸same as **perfect** (senses 7, 8)

presents *pl n law* used in a deed or document to refer to itself: *know all men by these presents*

preservative *n* **1** a chemical added to foods to prevent decay ▷*adj* **2** preventing decay

preserve ❶ *vb* **-serving, -served 1** to keep safe from change or extinction; protect: *we are interested in preserving world peace* **2** to protect from decay or damage: *the carefully preserved village of Cregneish* **3** to treat (food) in order to prevent it from decaying **4** to maintain; keep up: *the 1.2% increase in earnings needed to preserve living standards* ▷*n* **5** an area of interest restricted to a particular person or group: *working-class preserves such as pigeon racing* **6** (*usually pl*) fruit preserved by cooking in sugar **7** an area where game is kept for private hunting or fishing **preservation** *n*
WORD ORIGIN Latin *prae* before + *servare* to keep safe

preset *vb* **-setting, -set 1** to set the timer on a piece of equipment so that it starts to work at a specific time ▷*adj* **2** (of equipment) with the controls set in advance

preshrunk *adj* (of fabric or a garment) having been shrunk during manufacture so that further shrinkage will not occur when washed

preside ❶ *vb* **-siding, -sided 1** to chair a meeting **2** to exercise authority: *he presided over the burning of the books*
WORD ORIGIN Latin *praesidere* to superintend

presidency *n, pl* **-cies** the office or term of a president

president *n* **1** the head of state of a republic, esp. of the US **2** the head of a company, society, or institution **3** a person who presides over a meeting **4** the head of certain establishments of higher education **presidential** *adj*
WORD ORIGIN Late Latin *praesidens* ruler

presidium *n* (in Communist countries) a permanent administrative committee
WORD ORIGIN Russian *prezidium*

press¹ ❶ *vb* **1** to apply weight or force to: *he pressed the button on the camera* **2** to squeeze: *she pressed his hand* **3** to compress to alter in shape **4** to smooth out creases by applying pressure or heat **5** to make (objects) from soft material by pressing with a mould **6** to crush to force out (juice) **7** to urge (someone) insistently: *they pressed for an answer* **8** to force or compel: *I was pressed into playing rugby at school* **9** to plead or put forward strongly: *they intend to press their claim for damages in the courts* **10** to be urgent: *time presses* **11** (sometimes foll. by *on* or *forward*) to continue in a determined way: *they pressed on with their journey* **12** to crowd; push: *shoppers press along the pavements* **13 pressed for** short of: *pressed for time* ▷*n* **14** any machine that exerts pressure to form or cut materials or to extract

P

THESAURUS

OPPOSITE: absent
2, 3 = current, existing, immediate, contemporary, instant, present-day, existent, extant
8 the present = now, today, the time being, here and now, this day and age, the present moment

present² *n* **1 = gift**, offering, grant, favour, donation, hand-out, endowment, boon, bounty, gratuity, prezzie (*informal*), benefaction, bonsela (*S African*), koha (*NZ*), largesse or largess ▷*vb* **2 = introduce**, make known, acquaint someone with **3a = put on**, stage, perform, give, show, mount, render, put before the public **3b = launch**, display, demonstrate, parade, exhibit, unveil **8 = give**, award, hand over, offer, grant, donate, hand out, furnish, confer, bestow, entrust, proffer, put at someone's disposal

presentation *n* **1 = giving**, award, offering, donation, investiture, bestowal, conferral **3 = appearance**, look, display, packaging, arrangement, layout **5 = performance**, staging, production, show, arrangement, representation, portrayal, rendition

presently *adv* **1 = soon**, shortly, directly, before long, momentarily (*US & Canad*), in a moment, in a minute, pretty soon (*informal*), anon (*archaic*), by and by, in a short while, in a jiffy (*informal*), erelong (*archaic, poetic*) **2** (*chiefly Scot, US & Canad*) **= at present**, currently, now, today, these days, nowadays, at the present time, in this day and age, at the minute (*Brit informal*)

preserve *vb* **1 = protect**, keep, save, maintain, guard, defend, secure, shelter, shield, care for, safeguard, conserve **OPPOSITE:** attack
4 = maintain, keep, continue, retain, sustain, keep up, prolong, uphold, conserve, perpetuate, keep alive **OPPOSITE:** end
▷*n* **5 = area**, department, field, territory, province, arena, orbit, sphere, realm, domain, specialism

preside *vb* **1 = officiate**, chair, moderate, be chairperson

press¹ *vb* **1 = push (down)**, depress, lean on, bear down, press down, force down **2 = hug**, squeeze, embrace, clasp, crush, encircle, enfold, hold close, fold in your arms **3 = compress**, grind, reduce, mill, crush, pound, squeeze, tread, pulp, mash, trample, condense, pulverize, tamp, macerate **4 = steam**, finish,

DICTIONARY

liquids or compress solids **15** ▸see **printing press 16** the art or process of printing **17** the opinions and reviews in the newspapers: *the government is not receiving a good press at the moment* **18** the act of pressing or state of being pressed: *at the press of a button* **19** a crowd: *a press of people at the exit* **20** a cupboard for storing clothes or linen **21 go to press** to go to be printed: *when is this book going to press?* **22 the press a** news media collectively, esp. newspapers **b** journalists collectively
WORD ORIGIN Old French *presser*

press² *vb* **1** to recruit (men) forcibly for military service **2** to use for a purpose other than intended: *press into service*
WORD ORIGIN from *prest* to recruit soldiers

press agent *n* a person employed to obtain favourable publicity for an individual or organization

press box *n* a room at a sports ground reserved for reporters

Pressburger *n* **Emeric** 1902–88, Hungarian film writer and producer, living in Britain: best known for his collaboration (1942–57) with Michael Powell. Films include *The Life and Death of Colonel Blimp* (1943), *I Know Where I'm Going* (1945), and *A Matter of Life and Death* (1946)

press conference *n* an interview for reporters given by a famous person

press gallery *n* an area for newspaper reporters, esp. in a parliament

press gang *n* **1** (formerly) a group of men used to capture men and boys and force them to join the navy ▹*vb* **press-gang 2** to force (a person) to join the navy by a press gang **3** to persuade (someone) to do something that he or she does not want to do: *he was press-ganged into joining the family business*

pressing ⓘ *adj* **1** demanding immediate attention ▹*n* **2** a large number of gramophone records produced at one time

press stud *n Brit* a fastener in which one part with a projecting knob snaps into a hole on another part

press-up *n* an exercise in which the body is raised from and lowered to the floor by straightening and bending the arms

pressure ⓘ *n* **1** the state of pressing or being pressed **2** the application of force by one body on the surface of another **3** urgent claims or demands: *to work under pressure* **4** a condition that is hard to bear: *the pressure of grief* **5** *physics* the force applied to a unit area of a surface **6 bring pressure to bear on** to use influence or authority to persuade ▹*vb* **-suring, -sured 7** to persuade forcefully: *he was pressured into resignation*
WORD ORIGIN Late Latin *pressura* a pressing, from Latin *premere* to press

pressure cooker *n* an airtight pot which cooks food quickly by steam under pressure **pressure-cook** *vb*

pressure group *n* a group that tries to influence policies or public opinion

pressurize *or* **-ise** *vb* **-izing, -ized** *or* **-ising, -ised 1** to increase the pressure in (an aircraft cabin, etc.) in order to maintain approximately atmospheric pressure when the external pressure is low **2** to make insistent demands of (someone): *do not be pressurized into making a decision* **pressurization** *or* **-isation** *n*

prestidigitation *n formal* ▸same as **sleight of hand** > **prestidigitator** *n*
WORD ORIGIN French

prestige ⓘ *n* **1** high status or respect resulting from success or achievements: *a symbol of French power and prestige* **2** the power to impress: *a humdrum family car with no prestige* **prestigious** *adj*
WORD ORIGIN Latin *praestigiae* tricks

presto *music adv* **1** very fast ▹*n, pl* **-tos 2** a passage to be played very quickly
WORD ORIGIN Italian

presumably ⓘ *adv* one supposes or guesses; probably: *he emerged from what was presumably the kitchen carrying a tray*

presume ⓘ *vb* **-suming, -sumed 1** to take (something) for granted: *I presume he's dead* **2** to dare (to): *I would not presume to lecture you on medical matters, Dr Jacobs* **3** (foll. by *on* or *upon*) to rely or depend: *don't presume on his agreement* **4** (foll. by *on* or *upon*) to take advantage (of): *I'm afraid I presumed on Aunt Ginny's generosity* **presumedly** *adv* **presuming** *adj*
WORD ORIGIN Latin *praesumere* to take in advance

presumption *n* **1** the act of presuming **2** a basis on which an assumption is made **3** bold insolent behaviour **4** a belief or assumption based on reasonable evidence **presumptive** *adj*

presumptuous *adj* bold and insolent

presuppose *vb* **-posing, -posed 1** to require as a previous condition in order to be true: *the idea of integration presupposes a disintegrated state* **2** to take for granted **presupposition** *n*

preteen *n* a boy or girl approaching his or her teens

pretence *or US* **pretense** *n* **1** an action or claim that could mislead people into believing something which is not true: *Daniel made a pretence of carefully reading it; the pretence that many of the unemployed are on 'training schemes'* **2** a false display; affectation: *she abandoned all pretence of work and watched me* **3** a claim, esp. a false one, to a right, title, or distinction **4** make-believe **5** a pretext: *they were placed in a ghetto on the pretence that they would be safe there*

pretend ⓘ *vb* **1** to claim or give the appearance of (something untrue): *he pretended to be asleep* **2** to make believe: *one of the actresses pretended to urinate into a bucket* **3** (foll. by *to*) to present a claim, esp. a doubtful one: *to pretend to the throne*
WORD ORIGIN Latin *praetendere* to stretch forth, feign

pretender *n* a person who makes a false or disputed claim to a throne or title

THESAURUS

iron, smooth, flatten, put the creases in **8 = urge**, force, beg, petition, sue, enforce, insist on, compel, constrain, exhort, implore, enjoin, pressurize, entreat, importune, supplicate **9 = plead**, present, lodge, submit, tender, advance insistently **12a = push**, squeeze, jam, thrust, ram, wedge, shove **12b = crowd**, push, gather, rush, surge, mill, hurry, cluster, flock, herd, swarm, hasten, seethe, throng

pressing *adj* **1 = urgent**, serious, burning, vital, crucial, imperative, important, constraining, high-priority, now or never, importunate, exigent **OPPOSITE:** unimportant

pressure *n* **1, 2 = force**, crushing, squeezing, compressing, weight, compression, heaviness **3 = stress**, demands, difficulty, strain, press, heat, load, burden, distress, hurry, urgency, hassle (*informal*), uphill (*S African*), adversity, affliction, exigency **4 = power**, influence, force, obligation, constraint, sway, compulsion, coercion

prestige *n* **1 = status**, standing, authority, influence, credit, regard, weight, reputation, honour, importance, fame, celebrity, distinction, esteem, stature, eminence, kudos, cachet, renown, Brownie points, mana (*NZ*)

presumably *adv* **= it would seem**, probably, likely, apparently, most likely, seemingly, doubtless, on the face of it, in all probability, in all likelihood, doubtlessly

presume *vb* **1 = believe**, think, suppose, assume, guess (*informal, chiefly US & Canad*), take it, take for granted, infer, conjecture, postulate, surmise, posit, presuppose **2 = dare**, venture, undertake, go so far as, have the audacity, take the liberty, make bold, make so bold as

pretend *vb* **1 = feign**, affect, assume, allege, put on, fake, make out, simulate, profess, sham, counterfeit, falsify, impersonate, dissemble, dissimulate, pass yourself off as **2 = make believe**, suppose, imagine, play, act, make up, play the part of

DICTIONARY

pretension *n* **1** *(often pl)* a false claim to merit or importance **2** the quality of being pretentious

pretentious *adj* **1** making (unjustified) claims to special merit or importance: *many critics thought her work and ideas pretentious and empty* **2** vulgarly showy; ostentatious: *a family restaurant with no pretentious furnishing*

preterite *or esp. US* **preterit** (pret-er-it) *grammar n* **1** a past tense of verbs, such as *jumped, swam* **2** a verb in this tense ▷ *adj* **3** expressing such a past tense
WORD ORIGIN Late Latin *praeteritum (tempus)* past (time)

preternatural *adj* beyond what is natural; supernatural
WORD ORIGIN Latin *praeter naturam* beyond the scope of nature

pretext *n* a false reason given to hide the real one: *delivering the book had been a good pretext for seeing her again*
WORD ORIGIN Latin *praetextum* disguise, from *praetexere* to weave in front

prettify *vb* **-fies, -fying, -fied** to make pretty

pretty ⊙ *adj* **-tier, -tiest 1** attractive in a delicate or graceful way **2** pleasant to look at **3** *informal, often ironic* excellent or fine: *well, this is a pretty state of affairs to have got into* ▷ *adv* **4** *informal* fairly: *I think he and Nicholas got on pretty well* **5 sitting pretty** *informal* in a favourable state **prettily** *adv* **prettiness** *n*
WORD ORIGIN Old English *prættig* clever

pretty-pretty *adj informal* excessively pretty

pretzel *n* a brittle salted biscuit in the shape of a knot
WORD ORIGIN from German

prevail ⊙ *vb* **1** (often foll. by *over* or *against*) to prove superior; gain mastery: *moderate nationalists have until now prevailed over the radicals* **2** to be the most important feature: *a casual good-natured mood prevailed* **3** to be generally established: *this attitude has prevailed for many years* **4 prevail on** *or* **upon** to succeed in persuading: *he had easily been prevailed upon to accept a lift*
WORD ORIGIN Latin *praevalere* to be superior in strength

prevailing ⊙ *adj* **1** widespread: *the prevailing mood* **2** most usual: *the prevailing wind is from the west*

prevalent ⊙ *adj* widespread or common **prevalence** *n*

prevaricate *vb* **-cating, -cated** to avoid giving a direct or truthful answer **prevarication** *n* **prevaricator** *n*
WORD ORIGIN Latin *praevaricari* to walk crookedly

prevent ⊙ *vb* **1** to keep from happening: *vitamin C prevented scurvy* **2** (often foll. by *from*) to keep (someone from doing something): *circumstances prevented her from coming* **preventable** *adj* **prevention** *n*
WORD ORIGIN Latin *praevenire*

preventive *adj* **1** intended to prevent or hinder **2** *med* tending to prevent disease ▷ *n* **3** something that serves to prevent **4** *med* any drug or agent that tends to prevent disease. Also: **preventative**

Prévert *n* **Jacques** 1900–77, Parisian poet, satirist, and writer of film scripts, noted esp. for his song poems. He was a member of the surrealist group from 1925 to 1929

preview ⊙ *n* **1** an opportunity to see a film, exhibition, or play before it is shown to the public ▷ *vb* **2** to view in advance

Previn *n* **André** born 1929, US orchestral conductor, born in Germany; living in Britain

previous ⊙ *adj* **1** coming or happening before **2** *informal* happening too soon; premature: *such criticism is a bit previous because no definite decision has yet been taken* **3 previous to** before **previously** *adv*
WORD ORIGIN Latin *praevius* leading the way

Prévost d'Exiles *n* **Antoine François** known as *Abbé Prévost*. 1697–1763, French novelist, noted for his romance *Manon Lescaut* (1731), which served as the basis for operas by Puccini and Massenet

prewar *adj* relating to the period before a war, esp. before World War I or II

prey ⊙ *n* **1** an animal hunted and killed for food by another animal **2** the victim of a hostile person, influence, emotion, or illness: *children are falling prey to the disease* **3 bird** *or* **beast of prey** a bird *or* animal that kills and eats other birds or animals ▷ *vb* (often foll. by *on* or *upon*) **4** to hunt and kill for food **5** to worry or obsess: *it preyed on his conscience* **6** to make a victim (of others), by profiting at their expense
WORD ORIGIN Old French *preie*

price ⊙ *n* **1** the amount of money for which a thing is bought or sold **2** the cost at which something is obtained: *the price of making the wrong decision* **3 at any price** whatever the price or cost **4 at a price** at a high price **5** *gambling* odds **6 what price (something)?** what are the chances of (something) happening now? ▷ *vb* **pricing, priced 7** to fix the price of **8** to discover the price of
WORD ORIGIN Latin *pretium*

price-fixing *n* the setting of prices by agreement among producers and distributors

priceless ⊙ *adj* **1** extremely valuable **2** *informal* extremely amusing

P

THESAURUS

pretty *adj* **1 = attractive**, appealing, beautiful, sweet, lovely, charming, fair, fetching, good-looking, cute, graceful, bonny, personable, comely, prepossessing, fit *(Brit informal)* **OPPOSITE:** plain ▷ *adv* **4** *(informal)* **= fairly**, rather, quite, kind of *(informal)*, somewhat, moderately, reasonably

prevail *vb* **1** *(often with* **over** *or* **against***)* **= win**, succeed, triumph, overcome, overrule, be victorious, carry the day, prove superior, gain mastery **3 = be widespread**, abound, predominate, be current, be prevalent, preponderate, exist generally

prevailing *adj* **1 = widespread**, general, established, popular, common, set, current, usual, ordinary, fashionable, in style, customary, prevalent, in vogue **2 = predominating**, ruling, main, existing, principal

prevalent *adj* **= common**, accepted, established, popular, general, current, usual, widespread, extensive, universal, frequent, everyday, rampant, customary, commonplace, ubiquitous, rife, habitual **OPPOSITE:** rare

prevent *vb* **1, 2 = stop**, avoid, frustrate, restrain, check, bar, block, anticipate, hamper, foil, inhibit, head off, avert, thwart, intercept, hinder, obstruct, preclude, impede, counteract, ward off, balk, stave off, forestall, defend against, obviate, nip in the bud **OPPOSITE:** help

preview *n* **1 = sample**, sneak preview, trailer, sampler, taster, foretaste, advance showing

previous *adj* **1a = earlier**, former, past, prior, one-time, preceding, sometime, erstwhile, antecedent, anterior, quondam, ex- **OPPOSITE:** later **1b = preceding**, past, prior, foregoing

prey *n* **1 = quarry**, game, kill **2 = victim**, target, mark, mug *(Brit slang)*, dupe, fall guy *(informal)*

price *n* **1 = cost**, value, rate, charge, bill, figure, worth, damage *(informal)*, amount, estimate, fee, payment, expense, assessment, expenditure, valuation, face value, outlay, asking price **2 = consequences**, penalty, cost, result, sacrifice, toll, forfeit ▷ *vb* **7 = evaluate**, value, estimate, rate, cost, assess, put a price on

priceless *adj* **1 = valuable**, expensive, precious, invaluable, rich, prized, dear, rare, treasured, costly, cherished, incomparable, irreplaceable, incalculable, inestimable, beyond price, worth a

DICTIONARY

pricey *adj* **pricier, priciest** *informal* expensive

prick ❶ *vb* **1** to pierce lightly with a sharp point **2** to cause a piercing sensation (in): *a needle pricked her finger* **3** to cause a sharp emotional pain (in): *the film pricked our consciences about the plight of the Afghan refugees* **4 prick up one's ears a** (of a dog) to make the ears stand erect **b** (of a person) to listen attentively ▷ *n* **5** a sudden sharp pain caused by pricking **6** a mark made by a sharp point **7** a sharp emotional pain: *a prick of conscience* **8** *slang taboo* a penis **9** *slang offensive* a man who provokes contempt
WORD ORIGIN Old English *prica* point, puncture

prickle *n* **1** *bot* a thorn or spike on a plant **2** a pricking or stinging sensation ▷ *vb* **-ling, -led 3** to feel a stinging sensation
WORD ORIGIN Old English *pricel*

prickly ❶ *adj* **-lier, -liest 1** having prickles **2** tingling or stinging: *he had a prickly feeling down his back* **3** touchy or irritable: *Canadians are notoriously prickly about being taken for Americans*

prickly heat *n* an itchy rash that occurs in very hot moist weather

prickly pear *n* **1** a tropical cactus with edible oval fruit **2** the fruit of this plant

pride ❶ *n* **1** satisfaction in one's own or another's success or achievements: *his obvious pride in his son's achievements* **2** an excessively high opinion of oneself **3** a sense of dignity and self-respect: *he must swallow his pride and ally himself with his political enemies* **4** one of the better or most admirable parts of something: *the pride of the main courses is the Japanese fish and vegetable tempura* **5** a group of lions **6 pride and joy** the main source of pride: *the car was his pride and joy* **7 pride of place** the most important position ▷ *vb* **priding, prided 8** (foll. by *on* or *upon*) to take pride in (oneself) for
WORD ORIGIN Old English *prȳde*

prie-dieu (pree-**dyuh**) *n* an upright frame with a ledge for kneeling upon, for use when praying
WORD ORIGIN French *prier* to pray + *Dieu* God

priest ❶ *n* **1** (in the Christian Church) a person ordained to administer the sacraments and preach **2** a minister of any religion **3** an official who performs religious ceremonies **priestess** *fem n* **priesthood** *n* **priestly** *adj*
WORD ORIGIN Old English *prēost*, apparently from *presbyter*

prig *n* a person who is smugly self-righteous and narrow-minded **priggish** *adj* **priggishness** *n*
WORD ORIGIN origin unknown

Prigogine *n* Viscount **Ilya** 1917–2003, Belgian chemist, born in Russia: Nobel prize for chemistry 1977 for his work on nonequilibrium thermodynamics

prim *adj* **primmer, primmest** affectedly proper, or formal, and rather prudish **primly** *adv*
WORD ORIGIN origin unknown

prima ballerina *n* a leading female ballet dancer
WORD ORIGIN Italian: first ballerina

primacy *n, pl* **-cies 1** the state of being first in rank, grade, or order **2** *Christianity* the office of an archbishop

prima donna *n, pl* **prima donnas 1** a leading female opera singer **2** *informal* a temperamental person
WORD ORIGIN Italian: first lady

primaeval *adj* ▸ same as **primeval**

prima facie (**prime**-a **fay**-shee) *adv* as it seems at first
WORD ORIGIN Latin

primal *adj* **1** of basic causes or origins **2** chief or most important
WORD ORIGIN Latin *primus* first

primarily ❶ *adv* **1** chiefly or mainly **2** originally

primary ❶ *adj* **1** first in importance **2** first in position or time, as in a series: *he argued that the country was only in the primary stage of socialism* **3** fundamental or basic: *the new policy will put the emphasis on primary health care rather than hospital care* **4** being the first stage; elementary: *all new recruits participated in the same primary training courses* **5** relating to the education of children up to the age of 11 or 12 **6** (of an industry) involving the obtaining of raw materials **7** (of the flight feathers of a bird's wing) outer and longest **8** being the part of an electric circuit in which a changing current causes a current in a neighbouring circuit: *a primary coil* ▷ *n, pl* **-ries 9** a person or thing that is first in position, time, or importance **10** (in the US) an election in which the voters of a state choose a candidate for office. Full name: **primary election 11** a primary school **12** a primary colour **13** any of the outer and longest flight feathers of a bird's wing **14** a primary part of an electric circuit
WORD ORIGIN Latin *primarius* principal

primary accent *or* **stress** *n linguistics* the strongest accent in a word

primary colours *pl n* **1** *physics* the colours red, green, and blue from which all other colours can be obtained by mixing **2** *art* the colours red, yellow, and blue from which all other colours can be obtained by mixing

primary school *n* **1** (in England and Wales) a school for children between the ages of 5 and 11 **2** (in Scotland, Australia and New Zealand) a school for children between the ages of 5 and 12 **3** (in the US and Canada) a school equivalent to the first three or four grades of elementary school

primate[1] *n* a mammal with flexible hands and feet and a highly developed brain, such as a monkey, an ape, or a human being

primate[2] *n* an archbishop
WORD ORIGIN Latin *primas* principal

prime ❶ *adj* **1** first in importance: *the prime aim* **2** of the highest quality: *prime beef* **3** typical: *a prime example* ▷ *n* **4** the time when a thing is at its best **5** a period of power, vigour, and activity: *he was in the prime of life*

THESAURUS

king's ransom, worth your *or* its weight in gold **OPPOSITE:** worthless

prick *vb* **1 = pierce**, stab, puncture, bore, pink, punch, lance, jab, perforate, impale ▷ *n* **6 = puncture**, cut, hole, wound, gash, perforation, pinhole

prickly *adj* **1 = spiny**, barbed, thorny, bristly, brambly, briery **2 = itchy**, sharp, smarting, stinging, crawling, pricking, tingling, scratchy, prickling

pride *n* **1 = satisfaction**, achievement, fulfilment, delight, content, pleasure, joy, gratification **2 = conceit**, vanity, arrogance, pretension, presumption, snobbery, morgue *(French)*, hubris, smugness, self-importance, egotism, self-love, hauteur, pretentiousness, haughtiness, loftiness, vainglory, superciliousness, bigheadedness *(informal)* **OPPOSITE:** humility **3 = self-respect**, honour, ego, dignity, self-esteem, self-image, self-worth, amour-propre *(French)*

priest *n* **1, 2 = clergyman**, minister, father, divine, vicar, pastor, cleric, curate, churchman, padre *(informal)*, holy man, man of God, man of the cloth, ecclesiastic, father confessor

primarily *adv* **1 = chiefly**, largely, generally, mainly, especially, essentially, mostly, basically, principally, fundamentally, above all, on the whole, for the most part **2 = at first**, originally, initially, in the first place, in the beginning, first and foremost, at *or* from the start

primary *adj* **1 = chief**, leading, main, best, first, highest, greatest, top, prime, capital, principal, dominant, cardinal, paramount
OPPOSITE: subordinate

prime *adj* **1 = main**, leading, chief, central, major, ruling, key, senior, primary, supreme, principal, ultimate, cardinal, paramount,

DICTIONARY

6 *maths* ▸ short for **prime number** ▹ *vb* **priming, primed 7** to give (someone) information in advance to prepare him or her **8** to prepare (a surface) for painting **9** to prepare (a gun or mine) before detonating or firing **10** to fill (a pump) with its working fluid, to expel air from it before starting **11** to prepare (something)
WORD ORIGIN Latin *primus* first

prime meridian *n* the 0° meridian from which the other meridians are worked out, usually taken to pass through Greenwich

Prime Minister *n* the leader of a government

prime mover *n* a person or thing which was important in helping create an idea, situation, etc.: *he was the prime mover behind the coup*

prime number *n* an integer that cannot be divided into other integers but is only divisible by itself or 1, such as 2, 3, 5, 7, and 11

primer[1] *n* **1** a substance applied to a surface as a base coat or sealer **2** a device for detonating the main charge in a gun or mine
WORD ORIGIN see PRIME (verb)

primer[2] *n* an introductory text, such as a school textbook
WORD ORIGIN Medieval Latin *primarius (liber)* a first (book)

prime stock *n NZ* livestock in peak condition and ready for killing

primeval (prime-ee-val) *adj* of the earliest age of the world
WORD ORIGIN Latin *primus* first + *aevum* age

primitive ● *adj* **1** of or belonging to the beginning **2** *biol* of an early stage in development: *primitive amphibians* **3** characteristic of an early simple state, esp. in being crude or basic: *a primitive dwelling* ▹ *n* **4** a primitive person or thing **5** a painter of any era whose work appears childlike or untrained **6** a work by such an artist
WORD ORIGIN Latin *primitivus* earliest of its kind

Primo de Rivera *n* **1 José Antonio** 1903–36, Spanish politician; founded Falangism **2** his father, **Miguel**. 1870–1930, Spanish general; dictator of Spain (1923–30)

primogeniture *n* **1** *formal* the state of being the first-born child **2** *law* the right of an eldest son to inherit all the property of his parents
WORD ORIGIN Medieval Latin *primogenitura* birth of a first child

primordial *adj formal* existing at or from the beginning
WORD ORIGIN Late Latin *primordialis* original

primp *vb* to tidy (one's hair or clothes) fussily
WORD ORIGIN probably from *prim*

primrose *n* **1** a wild plant which has pale yellow flowers in spring ▹ *adj* **2** Also: **primrose yellow** pale yellow **3** of primroses
WORD ORIGIN Medieval Latin *prima rosa* first rose

primrose path *n* (often preceded by *the*) a pleasurable way of life

primula *n* a type of primrose with brightly coloured funnel-shaped flowers
WORD ORIGIN Medieval Latin *primula (veris)* little first one (of the spring)

Primus *n trademark* a portable paraffin cooking stove, used esp. by campers

prince ● *n* **1** a male member of a royal family, esp. the son of the king or queen **2** the male ruler of a small country **3** an outstanding member of a specified group: *Dryden, that prince of poets*
WORD ORIGIN Latin *princeps* first man, ruler

Prince *n* full name *Prince Rogers Nelson* born 1958, US rock singer, songwriter, record producer, and multi-instrumentalist. His albums include *Dirty Mind* (1981), *Purple Rain* (1984), *Parade* (1986), and *Emancipation* (1996); in 2007 he released his latest album *Planet Earth* as a free gift with a British newspaper

prince consort *n* the husband of a queen, who is himself a prince

princely ● *adj* **-lier, -liest 1** of or characteristic of a prince **2** generous or lavish

Prince of Wales *n* the eldest son of the British sovereign

princess ● *n* **1** a female member of a royal family, esp. the daughter of the king or queen **2** the wife of a prince

Princess Royal *n* a title sometimes given to the eldest daughter of the British sovereign

principal ● *adj* **1** first in importance, rank, or value: *salt is the principal source of sodium in our diets; the Republic's two principal parties* ▹ *n* **2** the head of a school or other educational institution **3** a person who holds one of the most important positions in an organization: *she became a principal in the home finance department* **4** the leading actor in a play **5** *law* **a** a person who engages another to act as his or her agent **b** a person who takes an active part in a crime **c** the person held responsible for fulfilling an obligation **6** *finance* **a** capital or property, as contrasted with income **b** the original amount of a debt on which interest is calculated **principally** *adv*
WORD ORIGIN Latin *principalis* chief

principal boy *n Brit* the leading male role in a pantomime, traditionally played by a woman

principality *n, pl* **-ties** a territory ruled by a prince

principal parts *pl n grammar* the main verb forms, from which all other verb forms may be deduced

principle ● *n* **1** a moral rule guiding personal conduct: *he'd stoop to anything – he has no principles* **2** a set of such moral rules: *a man of principle* **3** a basic

P

THESAURUS

overriding, foremost, predominant, pre-eminent, number-one *(informal)* **2 = best**, top, select, highest, capital, quality, choice, selected, excellent, superior, first-class, first-rate, grade-A ▹ *n* **4, 5 = peak**, flower, bloom, maturity, height, perfection, best days, heyday, zenith, full flowering ▹ *vb* **7 = inform**, tell, train, coach, brief, fill in *(informal)*, groom *(informal)*, notify, clue in *(informal)*, gen up *(Brit informal)*, give someone the lowdown, clue up *(informal)* **9, 11 = prepare**, set up, load, equip, get ready, make ready

primitive *adj* **1 = early**, first, earliest, original, primary, elementary, pristine, primordial, primeval
OPPOSITE: modern
3 = crude, simple, rough, rude, rudimentary, unrefined
OPPOSITE: elaborate

prince *n* **2 = ruler**, lord, monarch, sovereign, crown prince, liege, potentate, prince regent, crowned head, dynast

princely *adj* **1 = regal**, royal, imposing, magnificent, august, grand, imperial, noble, sovereign, majestic, dignified, stately, lofty, high-born **2 = substantial**, considerable, goodly, large, huge, massive, enormous, tidy *(informal)*, whopping (great) *(informal)*, sizable *or* sizeable

princess *n* **2 = ruler**, lady, monarch, sovereign, liege, crowned head, crowned princess, dynast, princess regent

principal *adj* **1 = main**, leading, chief, prime, first, highest, controlling, strongest, capital, key, essential, primary, most important, dominant, arch, cardinal, paramount, foremost, pre-eminent
OPPOSITE: minor
▹ *n* **2 = headmaster** *or* **headmistress**, head *(informal)*, director, dean, head teacher, rector, master *or* mistress **4 = star**, lead, leader, prima ballerina, first violin, leading man *or* lady, coryphée **6a = capital**, money, assets, working capital, capital funds

principle *n* **2 = morals**, standards, ideals, honour, virtue, ethics, integrity, conscience, morality, decency, scruples, probity, rectitude, moral standards, sense of duty, moral law, sense of honour, uprightness, kaupapa *(NZ)* **3, 4,**

DICTIONARY

or general truth: *the principle of freedom of expression* **4** a basic law or rule underlying a particular theory or philosophy: *the government has been deceitful and has violated basic principles of democracy* **5** a general law in science: *the principle of the conservation of mass* **6** *chem* a constituent of a substance that determines its characteristics **7 in principle** in theory though not always in practice **8 on principle** because of one's beliefs
WORD ORIGIN Latin *principium* beginning, basic tenet

principled *adj* (of a person or action) guided by moral rules: *principled opposition to the war*

prink *vb* **1** to dress (oneself) finely **2** to preen oneself
WORD ORIGIN probably changed from *prank* to adorn

print ❶ *vb* **1** to reproduce (a newspaper, book, etc.) in large quantities by mechanical or electronic means **2** to reproduce (text or pictures) by applying ink to paper **3** to write in letters that are not joined up **4** to stamp (fabric) with a design **5** to produce (a photograph) from a negative **6** to fix in the mind or memory ▷*n* **7** printed content, such as newsprint **8** a printed publication, such as a book **9** a picture printed from an engraved plate or wood block **10** printed text, with regard to the typeface: *italic print* **11** a photograph produced from a negative **12** a fabric with a printed design **13** a mark made by pressing something onto a surface **14** ▸see **fingerprint 15 in print a** in printed or published form **b** (of a book) available from a publisher **16 out of print** no longer available from a publisher ▸See also **print out**
WORD ORIGIN Old French *preindre* to make an impression

printed circuit *n* an electronic circuit in which the wiring is a metallic coating printed on a thin insulating board

printer *n* **1** a person or business engaged in printing **2** a machine that prints **3** *computers* a machine that prints out results on paper

printing *n* **1** the process of producing printed matter **2** printed text **3** all the copies of a book printed at one time **4** a form of writing in which the letters are not joined together

printing press *n* a machine used for printing

print out *vb* **1** *computers* to produce (printed information) ▷*n* **print-out, printout 2** printed information from a computer

prior[1] ❶ *adj* **1** previous: *prior knowledge* **2 prior to** before
WORD ORIGIN Latin: previous

prior[2] *n* **1** the head monk in a priory **2** the abbot's deputy in a monastery **prioress** *fem n*
WORD ORIGIN Late Latin: head

Prior *n* **Matthew** 1664–1721, English poet and diplomat, noted for his epigrammatic occasional verse

priority ❶ *n, pl* **-ties 1** the most important thing that must be dealt with first **2** the right to be or go before others

priory *n, pl* **-ories** a religious house where certain orders of monks or nuns live

Priscian *n* Latin name *Priscianus Caesariensis*. 6th century AD, Latin grammarian

prise ❶ *or* **prize** *vb* **prising, prised** *or* **prizing, prized** to force open or out by levering
WORD ORIGIN Old French *prise* a taking

prism *n* **1** a transparent block, often with triangular ends and rectangular sides, used to disperse light into a spectrum or refract it in optical instruments **2** *maths* a polyhedron with parallel bases and sides that are parallelograms
WORD ORIGIN Greek *prisma* something shaped by sawing

prismatic *adj* **1** of or shaped like a prism **2** exhibiting bright spectral colours; rainbow-like: *prismatic light*

prison ❶ *n* **1** a public building used to hold convicted criminals and accused people awaiting trial **2** any place of confinement
WORD ORIGIN Old French *prisun*, from Latin *prensio* a capturing

prisoner ❶ *n* **1** a person kept in prison as a punishment for a crime, or while awaiting trial **2** a person confined by any restraints: *he's a prisoner of his own past* **3 take (someone) prisoner** to capture and hold (someone) as a prisoner

prisoner of war *n* a serviceman captured by an enemy in wartime

prissy *adj* **-sier, -siest** prim and prudish **prissily** *adv*
WORD ORIGIN probably from *prim* + *sissy*

pristine *adj* **1** completely new, clean, and pure: *pristine white plates* **2** of or involving the original, unchanged, and unspoilt period or state: *the viewing of wild game in its pristine natural state*
WORD ORIGIN Latin *pristinus* primitive

Pritchett *n* Sir **V(ictor) S(awdon)** 1900–97, British short-story writer, novelist, essayist, and autobiographer; his works include *Mr Beluncle* (1951) and *A Careless Widow* (1989)

privacy ❶ *n* **1** the condition of being private **2** secrecy

private ❶ *adj* **1** not for general or public use: *a private bathroom* **2** confidential or secret: *a private conversation* **3** involving someone's domestic and personal life rather than his or her work or business: *what I do in my private life is none of your business* **4** owned or paid for by individuals rather than by the government: *private enterprise* **5** not publicly known: *they had private reasons for the decision* **6** having no public office, rank, or position: *the Red Cross received donations from private citizens* **7** (of a place) quiet and secluded: *the*

THESAURUS

5 = rule, idea, law, theory, basis, truth, concept, formula, fundamental, assumption, essence, proposition, verity, golden rule, precept

print *vb* **1 = publish**, release, circulate, issue, disseminate **2 = run off**, publish, copy, reproduce, issue, engrave, go to press, put to bed *(informal)* **4 = mark**, impress, stamp, imprint ▷*n* **9a = picture**, plate, etching, engraving, lithograph, woodcut, linocut **9b = copy**, picture, reproduction, replica **11 = photograph**, photo, snap

prior[1] *adj* **1 = earlier**, previous, former, preceding, foregoing, antecedent, aforementioned, pre-existing, anterior, pre-existent **2 prior to = before**, preceding, earlier than, in advance of, previous to

priority *n* **1 = prime concern**, first concern, primary issue, most pressing matter **2 = precedence**, preference, greater importance, primacy, predominance

prise *or* **prize** *vb* **= force**, pull, lever

prison *n* **1 = jail**, confinement, can *(slang)*, pound, nick *(Brit slang)*, stir *(slang)*, cooler *(slang)*, jug *(slang)*, dungeon, clink *(slang)*, glasshouse *(military) (informal)*, gaol, penitentiary *(US)*, slammer *(slang)*, lockup, quod *(slang)*, penal institution, calaboose *(US informal)*, choky *(slang)*, poky *or* pokey *(US & Canad slang)*, boob *(Austral slang)*

prisoner *n* **1 = convict**, con *(slang)*, lag *(slang)*, jailbird

privacy *n* **1 = seclusion**, isolation, solitude, retirement, retreat, separateness, sequestration, privateness

private *adj* **1 = exclusive**, individual, privately owned, own, special, particular, reserved **OPPOSITE:** public **2 = secret**, confidential, covert, inside, closet, unofficial, privy *(archaic)*, clandestine, off the record, hush-hush *(informal)*, in camera **OPPOSITE:** public **5 = personal**, individual, secret, intimate, undisclosed, unspoken, innermost, unvoiced **7 = secluded**,

DICTIONARY

garden is completely private **8** (of a person) quiet and retiring: *she was private – her life was her own* ▹ *n* **9** a soldier of the lowest rank in the army **10 in private** in secret **privately** *adv*
WORD ORIGIN Latin *privatus* belonging to one individual, withdrawn from public life

private bill *n* a bill presented to Parliament on behalf of a private individual or corporation

private company *n* a limited company that does not issue shares for public subscription

private detective *n* a person hired by a client to do detective work

privateer *n* **1** a privately owned armed vessel authorized by the government to take part in a war **2** a captain of such a ship

private eye *n informal* a private detective

private income *n* income from sources other than employment, such as investment

private member *n* a Member of Parliament who is not a government minister

private member's bill *n* a law proposed by a Member of Parliament who is not a government minister

private parts *or* **privates** *pl n euphemistic* the genitals

private school *n* a school controlled by a private body, accepting mostly fee-paying pupils

private sector *n* the part of a country's economy that consists of privately owned enterprises

privation *n formal* loss or lack of the necessities of life
WORD ORIGIN Latin *privatio* deprivation

privative (priv-a-tiv) *adj* **1** causing privation **2** *grammar* expressing lack or absence, for example *-less* and *un-*

privatize *or* **-ise** *vb* **-izing, -ized** *or* **-ising, -ised** to sell (a state-owned company) to individuals or a private company **privatization** *or* **-isation** *n*

privet *n* a bushy evergreen shrub used for hedges
WORD ORIGIN origin unknown

privilege ❶ *n* **1** a benefit or advantage granted only to certain people: *a privilege of rank* **2** the opportunity to do something which gives you great satisfaction and which most people never have the chance to do: *I had the privilege of meeting the Queen when she visited our school* **3** the power and advantages that come with great wealth or high social class: *the use of violence to protect class privilege and thwart popular democracy*
WORD ORIGIN Latin *privilegium* law relevant to rights of an individual

privileged ❶ *adj* enjoying a special right or immunity

privy *adj* **privier, priviest 1** *archaic* secret **2 privy to** sharing in the knowledge of something secret ▹ *n, pl* **privies 3** *obsolete* a toilet, esp. an outside one
WORD ORIGIN Old French *privé* something private

Privy Council *n* **1** the private council of the British king or queen **2** (in Canada) a formal body of advisers of the governor general **Privy Counsellor** *n*

privy purse *n* an allowance voted by Parliament for the private expenses of the king or queen

privy seal *n* (in Britain) a seal affixed to certain documents of state

prize[1] ❶ *n* **1** something of value, such as a trophy, given to the winner of a contest or game **2** something given to the winner of any game of chance, lottery, etc. **3** something striven for ▹ *adj* **4** winning or likely to win a prize: *a prize bull*
WORD ORIGIN Old French *prise* a capture

prize[2] ❶ *vb* **prizing, prized** to value highly
WORD ORIGIN Old French *preisier* to praise

prizefight *n* a boxing match for a prize or purse **prizefighter** *n*

pro[1] *adv* **1** in favour of a motion etc. ▹ *prep* **2** in favour of ▹ *n, pl* **pros 3** (*usually pl*) an argument or vote in favour of a proposal or motion ▸ See also **pros and cons**
WORD ORIGIN Latin: in favour of

pro[2] *n, pl* **pros**, *adj informal* **1** ▸ short for **professional 2** a prostitute

PRO public relations officer

pro-[1] *prefix* **1** in favour of; supporting: *pro-Chinese* **2** acting as a substitute for: *pronoun*
WORD ORIGIN Latin

pro-[2] *prefix* before in time or position: *proboscis*
WORD ORIGIN Greek

proactive *adj* tending to initiate change rather than reacting to events

probability ❶ *n, pl* **-ties 1** the condition of being probable **2** an event or other thing that is likely to happen or be true **3** *statistics* a measure of the likelihood of an event happening

probable ❶ *adj* **1** likely to happen or be true **2** most likely: *the probable cause of the accident* ▹ *n* **3** a person who is likely to be chosen for a team, event, etc.
WORD ORIGIN Latin *probabilis* that may be proved

probably ❶ *adv* in all likelihood or probability: *the wedding's probably going to be in late August*

probate *n* **1** the process of officially proving the validity of a will **2** the official certificate stating that a will is genuine
WORD ORIGIN Latin *probare* to inspect

probation *n* **1** a system of dealing with offenders, esp. juvenile ones, by placing them under supervision **2 on probation a** under the supervision of a probation officer **b** undergoing a test or trial period, such as at the start of a new job **probationary** *adj*
WORD ORIGIN Latin *probare* to test

probationer *n* **1** a person on a trial period in a job **2** a person under the supervision of a probation officer

probation officer *n* an officer of a court who supervises offenders placed on probation

probe ❶ *vb* **probing, probed 1** to investigate, or look into, closely **2** to poke or examine (something) with or as if with a probe: *he probed carefully*

THESAURUS

secret, separate, isolated, concealed, retired, sequestered, not overlooked **OPPOSITE:** busy
8 = solitary, reserved, retiring, withdrawn, discreet, secretive, self-contained, reclusive, reticent, insular, introvert, uncommunicative **OPPOSITE:** sociable

privilege *n* **1 = right**, benefit, due, advantage, claim, freedom, sanction, liberty, concession, franchise, entitlement, prerogative, birthright

privileged *adj* **= special**, powerful, advantaged, favoured, ruling, honoured, entitled, elite, indulged

prize[1] *n* **1 = reward**, cup, award, honour, premium, medal, trophy, accolade **2 = winnings**, haul, jackpot, stakes, purse, windfall ▹ *adj* **4 = champion**, best, winning, top, outstanding, award-winning, first-rate, top-notch (*informal*)

prize[2] *vb* **= value**, appreciate, treasure, esteem, cherish, hold dear, regard highly, set store by

probability *n* **1 = likelihood**, prospect, chance, odds, expectation, liability, presumption, likeliness **3** (*statistics*) **= chance**, odds, possibility, likelihood

probable *adj* **1, 2 = likely**, possible, apparent, reasonable to think, most likely, presumed, credible, plausible, feasible, odds-on, on the cards, presumable **OPPOSITE:** unlikely

probably *adv* **= likely**, perhaps, maybe, possibly, presumably, most likely, doubtless, in all probability, in all likelihood, perchance (*archaic*), as likely as not

probe *vb* **1 = examine**, research, go into, investigate, explore, test, sound, search, look into, query, verify, sift, analyze, dissect, delve into, work over, scrutinize

DICTIONARY

with his fingertips ▷*n* **3** *surgery* a slender instrument for exploring a wound etc. **4** a thorough inquiry, such as one into corrupt practices **5** ▸see **space probe**
WORD ORIGIN Latin *probare* to test

probiotic *n* **1** a bacterium that protects the body from harmful bacteria ▷*adj* **2** of or relating to probiotics: *probiotic yogurts*

probity *n* *formal* honesty; integrity
WORD ORIGIN Latin *probitas* honesty

problem ⊙ *n* **1** something or someone that is difficult to deal with **2** a puzzle or question set for solving **3** *maths* a statement requiring a solution usually by means of several operations ▷*adj* **4** of a literary work that deals with difficult moral questions: *a problem play* **5** difficult to deal with or creating difficulties for others: *a problem child*
WORD ORIGIN Greek *problēma* something put forward

problematic ⊙ *or* **problematical** *adj* difficult to solve or deal with

proboscis (pro-**boss**-iss) *n* **1** a long flexible trunk or snout, such as an elephant's **2** the elongated mouth part of certain insects
WORD ORIGIN Greek *proboskis* trunk of an elephant

procedure ⊙ *n* **1** a way of doing something, esp. an established method **2** the established form of conducting the business of a legislature **procedural** *adj*

proceed ⊙ *vb* **1** to advance or carry on, esp. after stopping **2** (often foll. by *with*) to start or continue doing: *he proceeded to pour himself a large whisky* **3** *formal* to walk or go **4** (often foll. by *against*) to start a legal action **5** *formal* to arise (from): *their mutual dislike proceeded from differences of political opinion*
WORD ORIGIN Latin *procedere* to advance

proceeding ⊙ *n* **1** an act or course of action **2** **proceedings** the events of an occasion: *millions watched the proceedings on television* **3** **proceedings** the minutes of the meetings of a society **4** **proceedings** legal action

proceeds ⊙ *pl n* the amount of money obtained from an event or activity

process[1] ⊙ *n* **1** a series of actions or changes: *a process of genuine national reconciliation* **2** a series of natural developments which result in an overall change: *the ageing process* **3** a method of doing or producing something: *the various production processes use up huge amounts of water* **4** **a** a summons to appear in court **b** an action at law **5** a natural outgrowth or projection of a part or organism **6** **in the process of** during or in the course of ▷*vb* **7** to handle or prepare by a special method of manufacture **8** *computers* to perform operations on (data) in order to obtain the required information
WORD ORIGIN Latin *processus* an advancing

process[2] *vb* to move in an orderly or ceremonial group: *the cult members processed through the streets to the music of tambourines*

processed *adj* (of food) treated by adding colouring, preservatives, etc. to improve its appearance or the period it will stay edible: *processed cheese*

procession ⊙ *n* **1** a line of people or vehicles moving forwards in an orderly or ceremonial manner **2** the act of proceeding in a regular formation
WORD ORIGIN Latin *processio* a marching forwards

processional *adj* **1** of or suitable for a procession: *the processional route* ▷*n* **2** *Christianity* a hymn sung as the clergy enter church

processor *n* **1** *computers* ▸same as **central processing unit** **2** a person or thing that carries out a process

proclaim ⊙ *vb* **1** to announce publicly; declare: *Greece was proclaimed an independent kingdom in 1832* **2** to indicate plainly: *the sharp hard glint in the eye proclaimed her determination*
proclamation *n*
WORD ORIGIN Latin *proclamare* to shout aloud

proclivity *n, pl* **-ties** *formal* a tendency or inclination
WORD ORIGIN Latin *proclivitas*

Proclus *n* ?410–485 AD, Greek Neo-Platonist philosopher

Procopius *n* ?490–?562 AD, Byzantine historian, noted for his account of the wars of Justinian I against the Persians, Vandals, and Ostrogoths

procrastinate *vb* **-nating, -nated** to put off (an action) until later; delay
procrastination *n* **procrastinator** *n*
WORD ORIGIN Latin *procrastinare* to postpone until tomorrow

procreate *vb* **-ating, -ated** *formal* to produce (offspring) **procreative** *adj*
procreation *n*
WORD ORIGIN Latin *procreare*

Procrustean *adj* ruthlessly enforcing uniformity
WORD ORIGIN after *Procrustes*, robber in Greek myth who fitted travellers into his bed by stretching or lopping off their limbs

proctor *n* a member of the staff of certain universities having duties including the enforcement of discipline **proctorial** *adj*
WORD ORIGIN syncopated variant of *procurator*

procurator fiscal *n* (in Scotland) a legal officer who acts as public

P

THESAURUS

2 = explore, examine, poke, prod, feel around ▷*n* **4 = investigation**, study, research, inquiry, analysis, examination, exploration, scrutiny, inquest, scrutinization

problem *n* **1 = difficulty**, trouble, dispute, plight, obstacle, dilemma, headache (*informal*), disagreement, complication, predicament, quandary **2 = puzzle**, question, riddle, enigma, conundrum, teaser, poser, brain-teaser (*informal*)

problematic *adj* **= tricky**, puzzling, uncertain, doubtful, dubious, unsettled, questionable, enigmatic, debatable, moot, problematical, chancy (*informal*), open to doubt
OPPOSITE: clear

procedure *n* **1 = method**, policy, process, course, system, form, action, step, performance, operation, practice, scheme, strategy, conduct, formula, custom, routine, transaction, plan of action, modus operandi (*Latin*)

proceed *vb* **1 = continue**, go on, progress, carry on, go ahead, get on, press on, crack on (*informal*)
OPPOSITE: discontinue
2 (*often with* **with**) **= begin**, go ahead, get going, make a start, get under way, set something in motion **3** (*formal*) **= go on**, continue, advance, progress, carry on, go ahead, move on, move forward, press on, push on, make your way, crack on (*informal*)
OPPOSITE: stop
5 (*formal*) **= arise**, come, follow, issue, result, spring, flow, stem, derive, originate, ensue, emanate

proceeding *n* **1 = action**, process, procedure, move, act, step, measure, venture, undertaking, deed, occurrence, course of action

proceeds *pl n* **= income**, profit, revenue, returns, produce, products, gain, earnings, yield, receipts, takings

process[1] *n* **1 = procedure**, means, course, system, action, performance, operation, measure, proceeding, manner, transaction, mode, course of action **2 = development**, growth, progress, course, stage, step, movement, advance, formation, evolution, unfolding, progression **3 = method**, system, practice, technique, procedure

procession *n* **1 = parade**, train, march, file, column, motorcade, cavalcade, cortege

proclaim *vb* **1 = pronounce**, announce, declare **2 = announce**, declare, advertise, show, publish, indicate, blaze (abroad), herald, circulate, trumpet, affirm, give out, profess, promulgate, make known, enunciate, blazon (abroad), shout from the housetops (*informal*)
OPPOSITE: keep secret

DICTIONARY

prosecutor and coroner

procure *vb* **-curing, -cured 1** to get or provide: *it remained very difficult to procure food and fuel* **2** to obtain (people) to act as prostitutes **procurement** *n*
WORD ORIGIN Latin *procurare* to look after

procurer *n* a person who obtains people to act as prostitutes

prod ❶ *vb* **prodding, prodded 1** to poke with a pointed object **2** to rouse (someone) to action ▷ *n* **3** the act of prodding **4** a reminder
WORD ORIGIN origin unknown

Prodi *n* **Romano** born 1939, Italian politician; prime minister (1996–98) and from 2006; president of the European Commission (1999–2004)

prodigal *adj* **1** recklessly wasteful or extravagant **2 prodigal of** lavish with: *you are prodigal of both your toil and your talent* ▷ *n* **3** a person who squanders money **prodigality** *n*
WORD ORIGIN Latin *prodigere* to squander

prodigious *adj* **1** very large or immense **2** wonderful or amazing
WORD ORIGIN Latin *prodigiosus* marvellous

prodigy ❶ *n, pl* **-gies 1** a person, esp. a child, with marvellous talent **2** anything that is a cause of wonder
WORD ORIGIN Latin *prodigium* an unnatural happening

produce ❶ *vb* **-ducing, -duced 1** to bring (something) into existence **2** to present to view: *he produced his passport* **3** to make: *this area produces much of Spain's best wine* **4** to give birth to **5** to present on stage, film, or television: *the girls and boys write and produce their own plays* **6** to act as producer of ▷ *n* **7** food grown for sale: *farm produce* **8** something produced **producible** *adj*
WORD ORIGIN Latin *producere* to bring forward

producer ❶ *n* **1** a person with the financial and administrative responsibility for a film or television programme **2** a person responsible for the artistic direction of a play **3** a person who supervises the arrangement, performance, and mixing of a recording **4** a person or thing that produces

product ❶ *n* **1** something produced **2** a consequence: *their skill was the product of hours of training* **3** *maths* the result achieved by multiplication

production ❶ *n* **1** the act of producing **2** anything that is produced **3** the amount produced or the rate at which it is produced **4** *econ* the creation or manufacture of goods and services **5** any work created as a result of literary or artistic effort **6** the presentation of a play, opera, etc. **7** the artistic direction of a play **8** the overall sound of a recording

production line *n* a system in a factory in which an item being manufactured is moved from machine to machine by conveyor belt, and each machine carries out one step in the manufacture of the item

productive ❶ *adj* **1** producing or having the power to produce **2** yielding favourable results **3** *econ* producing goods and services that have exchange value: *the country's productive capacity* **4** (foll. by *of*) resulting in: *a period highly productive of books and ideas* **productivity** *n*

product placement *n* the practice of a company of paying for its product to appear prominently in a film or television programme

proem (pro-em) *n formal* an introduction or preface
WORD ORIGIN Greek *pro-* before + *hoimē* song

Prof. Professor

profane *adj* **1** showing disrespect for religion or something sacred **2** secular **3** coarse or blasphemous: *profane language* ▷ *vb* **-faning, -faned 4** to treat (something sacred) with irreverence **5** to put to an unworthy use **profanation** *n*
WORD ORIGIN Latin *profanus* outside the temple

profanity *n, pl* **-ties 1** the quality of being profane **2** coarse or blasphemous action or speech

profess ❶ *vb* **1** to claim (something as true), often falsely: *he professes not to want the job of prime minister* **2** to acknowledge openly: *he professed great relief at getting some rest* **3** to have as one's belief or religion: *most Indonesians profess the Islamic faith* **professed** *adj*
WORD ORIGIN Latin *profiteri* to confess openly

profession ❶ *n* **1** a type of work that requires special training, such as in law or medicine **2** the people employed in such an occupation **3** a declaration of a belief or feeling: *a profession of faith*
WORD ORIGIN Latin *professio* public acknowledgment

professional ❶ *adj* **1** of a profession **2** taking part in an activity, such as sport or music, as a means of livelihood **3** displaying a high level

P

THESAURUS

prod *vb* **1 = poke**, push, dig, shove, propel, nudge, jab, prick **2 = prompt**, move, urge, motivate, spur, stimulate, rouse, stir up, incite, egg on, goad, impel, put a bomb under (*informal*) ▷ *n* **3 = poke**, push, boost, dig, elbow, shove, nudge, jab **4 = prompt**, boost, signal, cue, reminder, stimulus

prodigy *n* **1 = genius**, talent, wizard, mastermind, whizz (*informal*), whizz kid (*informal*), wunderkind, brainbox, child genius, wonder child, up-and-comer (*informal*)

produce *vb* **1 = cause**, lead to, result in, effect, occasion, generate, trigger, make for, provoke, set off, induce, bring about, give rise to, engender **2 = display**, show, present, proffer **3 = make**, build, create, develop, turn out, manufacture, construct, invent, assemble, put together, originate, fabricate, mass-produce **4 = bring forth**, bear, deliver, breed, give birth to, beget, bring into the world **5 = present**, stage, direct, put on, do, show, mount, exhibit, put before the public ▷ *n* **7, 8 = fruit and vegetables**, goods, food, products, crops, yield, harvest, greengrocery (*Brit*)

producer *n* **1, 2 = director**, promoter, impresario, régisseur (*French*) **4 = maker**, manufacturer, builder, creator, fabricator

product *n* **1 = goods**, produce, production, creation, commodity, invention, merchandise, artefact, concoction **2 = result**, fruit, consequence, yield, returns, issue, effect, outcome, legacy, spin-off, end result, offshoot, upshot

production *n* **1 = producing**, making, manufacture, manufacturing, construction, assembly, preparation, formation, fabrication, origination **6 = presentation**, staging, mounting **7 = management**, administration, direction

productive *adj* **1 = creative**, dynamic, vigorous, energetic, inventive **2 = useful**, rewarding, valuable, profitable, effective, worthwhile, beneficial, constructive, gratifying, fruitful, advantageous, gainful **OPPOSITE:** useless **4 = fertile**, rich, producing, prolific, plentiful, fruitful, teeming, generative, fecund **OPPOSITE:** barren

profess *vb* **1 = claim**, allege, pretend, fake, make out, sham, purport, feign, act as if, let on, dissemble **2 = state**, admit, announce, maintain, own, confirm, declare, acknowledge, confess, assert, proclaim, affirm, certify, avow, vouch, aver, asseverate

profession *n* **1 = occupation**, calling, business, career, employment, line, office, position, sphere, vocation, walk of life, line of work, métier

professional *adj* **1 = qualified**, trained, skilled, white-collar **3 = expert**, experienced, finished, skilled, masterly, efficient, crack (*slang*), polished, practised, ace (*informal*), accomplished, slick, competent, adept, proficient **OPPOSITE:** amateurish

DICTIONARY

of competence or skill: *a professional and polished performance* **4** undertaken or performed by people who are paid: *professional golf* ▷*n* **5** a professional person **professionalism** *n* **professionally** *adv*

professor ⓘ *n* **1** the highest rank of teacher in a university **2** *chiefly US & Canad* any teacher in a university or college **3** *rare* a person who professes his or her opinions or beliefs **professorial** *adj* **professorship** *n*
WORD ORIGIN Latin: a public teacher

proffer *vb formal* to offer for acceptance
WORD ORIGIN Old French *proffrir*

proficient *adj* skilled; expert **proficiency** *n*
WORD ORIGIN Latin *proficere* to make progress

profile ⓘ *n* **1** an outline, esp. of the human face, as seen from the side **2** a short biographical sketch
WORD ORIGIN Italian *profilo*

profiling *n* the practice of categorizing people and predicting their behaviour according to particular characteristics such as race or age

profit ⓘ *n* **1** (*often pl*) money gained in business or trade **2** a benefit or advantage ▷*vb* **-iting, -ited 3** to gain a profit or advantage: *we do not want to profit from someone else's problems*
WORD ORIGIN Latin *proficere* to make progress

profitable ⓘ *adj* making money or gaining an advantage or benefit **profitability** *n* **profitably** *adv*

profit and loss *n book-keeping* an account showing the year's income and expense items and indicating gross and net profit or loss

profiteer *n* **1** a person who makes excessive profits at the expense of the public ▷*vb* **2** to make excessive profits **profiteering** *n*

profit-sharing *n* a system in which a portion of the net profit of a business is shared among its employees

profligate *adj* **1** recklessly extravagant **2** shamelessly immoral ▷*n* **3** a profligate person **profligacy** *n*
WORD ORIGIN Latin *profligatus* corrupt

pro forma *adj* **1** laying down a set form ▷*adv* **2** performed in a set manner
WORD ORIGIN Latin: for form's sake

profound ⓘ *adj* **1** showing or needing great knowledge: *a profound knowledge of Greek literature* **2** strongly felt; intense: *profound relief* **3** extensive: *profound changes* **4** situated at or having a great depth **profoundly** *adv* **profundity** *n*
WORD ORIGIN Latin *profundus* deep

profuse *adj* **1** plentiful or abundant: *he broke out in a profuse sweat* **2** (often foll. by *in*) generous in the giving (of): *he was profuse in his apologies* **profusely** *adv* **profusion** *n*
WORD ORIGIN Latin *profundere* to pour lavishly

progenitor (pro-**jen**-it-er) *n* **1** a direct ancestor **2** an originator or founder
WORD ORIGIN Latin: ancestor

progeny (**proj**-in-ee) *n, pl* **-nies 1** offspring; descendants **2** an outcome
WORD ORIGIN Latin *progenies* lineage

progesterone *n* a hormone, produced in the ovary, that prepares the womb for pregnancy and prevents further ovulation
WORD ORIGIN PRO-[1] + *ge(station)* + *ster(ol)* + *-one*

prognathous *adj* having a projecting lower jaw

prognosis *n, pl* **-noses 1** *med* a forecast about the course or outcome of an illness **2** any forecast
WORD ORIGIN Greek: knowledge beforehand

prognosticate *vb* **-cating, -cated 1** to foretell (future events) **2** to indicate or suggest beforehand **prognostication** *n* **prognosticator** *n*
WORD ORIGIN Medieval Latin *prognosticare* to predict

program *n* **1** a sequence of coded instructions which enables a computer to perform various tasks ▷*vb* **-gramming, -grammed 2** to arrange (data) so that it can be processed by a computer **3** to feed a program into (a computer) **programmer** *n*

programmable *or* **programable** *adj* capable of being programmed for computer processing

programme ⓘ *or US* **program** *n* **1** a planned series of events **2** a broadcast on radio or television **3** a printed list of items or performers in an entertainment ▷*vb* **-gramming, -grammed** *or US* **-graming, -gramed 4** to schedule (something) as a programme **programmatic** *adj*
WORD ORIGIN Greek *programma* written public notice

programming language *n* a language system by which instructions to a computer are coded, that is understood by both user and computer

progress ⓘ *n* **1** improvement or development **2** movement forward or advance **3 in progress** taking place ▷*vb* **4** to become more advanced or skilful **5** to move forward
WORD ORIGIN Latin *progressus* a going forwards

progression ⓘ *n* **1** the act of

THESAURUS

▷*n* **5 = expert**, authority, master, pro (*informal*), specialist, guru, buff (*informal*), wizard, adept, whizz (*informal*), maestro, virtuoso, hotshot (*informal*), past master, dab hand (*Brit informal*), wonk (*informal*), maven (*US*), fundi (*S African*)

professor *n* **1 = don** (*Brit*), fellow (*Brit*), prof (*informal*), head of faculty

profile *n* **1 = outline**, lines, form, figure, shape, silhouette, contour, side view **2 = biography**, sketch, vignette, characterization, thumbnail sketch, character sketch

profit *n* **1** (*often pl*) **= earnings**, winnings, return, revenue, gain, boot (*dialect*), yield, proceeds, percentage (*informal*), surplus, receipts, bottom line, takings, emoluments **OPPOSITE:** loss **2 = benefit**, good, use, interest, value, gain, advantage, advancement, mileage (*informal*), avail **OPPOSITE:** disadvantage ▷*vb* **3 = benefit**, help, serve, aid, gain, promote, contribute to, avail, be of advantage to

profitable *adj* **a = money-making**, lucrative, paying, commercial, rewarding, worthwhile, cost-effective, fruitful, gainful, remunerative **b = beneficial**, useful, rewarding, valuable, productive, worthwhile, fruitful, advantageous, expedient, serviceable **OPPOSITE:** useless

profound *adj* **1 = wise**, learned, serious, deep, skilled, subtle, penetrating, philosophical, thoughtful, sage, discerning, weighty, insightful, erudite, abstruse, recondite, sagacious **OPPOSITE:** uninformed **2 = sincere**, acute, intense, great, keen, extreme, hearty, heartfelt, abject, deeply felt, heartrending **OPPOSITE:** insincere

programme *n* **1 = schedule**, plan, agenda, timetable, listing, list, line-up, calendar, order **2 = show**, performance, production, broadcast, episode, presentation, transmission, telecast, podcast

progress *n* **1 = development**, increase, growth, advance, gain, improvement, promotion, breakthrough, step forward, advancement, progression, headway, betterment, amelioration **OPPOSITE:** regression **2 = movement forward**, passage, advancement, progression, course, advance, headway, onward movement **OPPOSITE:** movement backward **3 in progress = going on**, happening, continuing, being done, occurring, taking place, proceeding, under way, ongoing, being performed, in operation ▷*vb* **4 = develop**, improve, advance, better, increase, grow, gain, get on, come on, mature, blossom,

DICTIONARY

progressing; advancement **2** the act or an instance of moving from one thing in a sequence to the next **3** *maths* a sequence of numbers in which each term differs from the succeeding term by a fixed ratio

progressive ❶ *adj* **1** favouring political or social reform **2** happening gradually: *a progressive illness* **3** (of a dance, card game, etc.) involving a regular change of partners ▷*n* **4** a person who favours political or social reform **progressively** *adv*

prohibit ❶ *vb* **-iting, -ited 1** to forbid by law or other authority **2** to hinder or prevent: *the paucity of information prohibits us from drawing reliable conclusions* **prohibitor** *n*
WORD ORIGIN Latin *prohibere* to prevent

prohibition ❶ *n* **1** the act of forbidding **2** a legal ban on the sale or drinking of alcohol **3** an order or decree that forbids **prohibitionist** *n*

Prohibition *n* the period (1920–33) when making, selling, and transporting alcohol was banned in the US **Prohibitionist** *n*

prohibitive *adj* **1** (esp. of prices) too high to be affordable **2** prohibiting or tending to prohibit: *a prohibitive distance*

project ❶ *n* **1** a proposal or plan **2** a detailed study of a particular subject ▷*vb* **3** to make a prediction based on known data and observations **4** to cause (an image) to appear on a surface **5** to communicate (an impression): *he wants to project an image of a deep-thinking articulate gentleman* **6** to jut out **7** to cause (one's voice) to be heard clearly at a distance **8** to transport in the imagination: *it's hard to project oneself into his situation*
WORD ORIGIN Latin *proicere* to throw down

projectile *n* **1** an object thrown as a weapon or fired from a gun ▷*adj* **2** designed to be thrown forwards **3** projecting forwards
WORD ORIGIN New Latin *projectilis* jutting forwards

projection ❶ *n* **1** a part that juts out **2** a forecast based on known data **3** the process of showing film on a screen **4** the representation on a flat surface of a three-dimensional figure or curved line

projectionist *n* a person who operates a film projector

projector *n* an apparatus for projecting photographic images, film, or slides onto a screen

prolapse *pathol n* **1** Also: **prolapsus** the slipping down of an internal organ of the body from its normal position ▷*vb* **-lapsing, -lapsed 2** (of an internal organ) to slip from its normal position
WORD ORIGIN Latin *prolabi* to slide along

prolapsed *adj pathol* (of an internal organ) having slipped from its normal position

prolate *adj geom* having a polar diameter which is longer than the equatorial diameter
WORD ORIGIN Latin *prolatus* enlarged

prole *n chiefly Brit offensive slang* a proletarian

proletarian (pro-lit-air-ee-an) *adj* **1** of the proletariat ▷*n* **2** a member of the proletariat

proletariat (pro-lit-air-ee-at) *n* the working class
WORD ORIGIN Latin *proletarius* one whose only contribution to the state was his offspring

proliferate *vb* **-ating, -ated 1** to increase rapidly in numbers **2** to grow or reproduce (new parts, such as cells) rapidly **proliferation** *n*
WORD ORIGIN Latin *proles* offspring + *ferre* to bear

prolific ❶ *adj* **1** producing a constant creative output: *a prolific author* **2** producing fruit or offspring in abundance **3** (often foll. by *in* or *of*) rich or fruitful **prolifically** *adv*
WORD ORIGIN Latin *proles* offspring

prolix *adj* (of a speech or piece of writing) overlong and boring **prolixity** *n*
WORD ORIGIN Latin *prolixus* stretched out widely

prologue *or US often* **prolog** *n* **1** an introduction to a play or book **2** an event that comes before another: *this success was a happy prologue to their transatlantic tour*
WORD ORIGIN Greek *pro-* before + *logos* discourse

prolong ❶ *vb* to make (something) last longer **prolongation** *n*
WORD ORIGIN Late Latin *prolongare*

prom *n* **1** *Brit* ▸short for **promenade** (sense 1) or **promenade concert 2** *US & Canad informal* a formal dance held at a high school or college

PROM *n computers* Programmable Read Only Memory

promenade *n* **1** *chiefly Brit* a paved walkway along the seafront at a holiday resort **2** *old-fashioned* a leisurely walk for pleasure or display ▷*vb* **-nading, -naded 3** *old-fashioned* to take a leisurely walk
WORD ORIGIN French

promenade concert *n* a concert at which some of the audience stand rather than sit

promethium (pro-meeth-ee-um) *n chem* an artificial radioactive element of the lanthanide series. Symbol: Pm
WORD ORIGIN from *Prometheus*, in Greek mythology, the Titan who gave fire to mankind

prominent ❶ *adj* **1** standing out from the surroundings; noticeable

P

THESAURUS

ameliorate **OPPOSITE:** get behind **5 = move on**, continue, travel, advance, proceed, go forward, gain ground, forge ahead, make inroads (into), make headway, make your way, cover ground, make strides, gather way, crack on *(informal)* **OPPOSITE:** move back

progression *n* **1 = progress**, advance, advancement, gain, headway, furtherance, movement forward **3 = sequence**, course, order, series, chain, cycle, string, succession

progressive *adj* **1 = enlightened**, liberal, modern, advanced, radical, enterprising, go-ahead, revolutionary, dynamic, avant-garde, reformist, up-and-coming, forward-looking **2 = growing**, continuing, increasing, developing, advancing, accelerating, ongoing, continuous, intensifying, escalating

prohibit *vb* **1 = forbid**, ban, rule out, veto, outlaw, disallow, proscribe, debar, interdict **OPPOSITE:** permit **2 = prevent**, restrict, rule out, stop, hamper, hinder, constrain, obstruct, preclude, impede, make impossible **OPPOSITE:** allow

prohibition *n* **3 = ban**, boycott, embargo, bar, veto, prevention, exclusion, injunction, disqualification, interdiction, interdict, proscription, disallowance, forbiddance, restraining order *(US) (law)*

project *n* **1 = scheme**, plan, job, idea, design, programme, campaign, operation, activity, proposal, venture, enterprise, undertaking, occupation, proposition, plan of action **2 = assignment**, task, homework, piece of research ▷*vb* **3 = forecast**, expect, estimate, predict, reckon, calculate, gauge, extrapolate, predetermine **6 = stick out**, extend, stand out, bulge, beetle, protrude, overhang, jut

projection *n* **2 = forecast**, estimate, reckoning, prediction, calculation, estimation, computation, extrapolation

prolific *adj* **1 = productive**, creative, fertile, inventive, copious **3** *(often with* **in** *or* **of***)* **= fruitful**, fertile, abundant, rich, rank, teeming, bountiful, luxuriant, generative, profuse, fecund **OPPOSITE:** unproductive

prolong *vb* **= lengthen**, continue, perpetuate, draw out, extend, delay, stretch out, carry on, spin out, drag out, make longer, protract **OPPOSITE:** shorten

prominent *adj* **1 = noticeable**, striking, obvious, outstanding,

DICTIONARY

2 widely known; famous **3** jutting or projecting outwards: *prominent eyes* **prominence** *n* **prominently** *adv*
WORD ORIGIN Latin *prominere* to jut out

promiscuous *adj* **1** taking part in many casual sexual relationships **2** *formal* consisting of different elements mingled indiscriminately **promiscuity** *n*
WORD ORIGIN Latin *promiscuus* indiscriminate

promise ❶ *vb* **-ising, -ised 1** to say that one will definitely do or not do something: *I promise I'll have it finished by the end of the week* **2** to undertake to give (something to someone): *he promised me a car for my birthday* **3** to show signs of; seem likely: *she promises to be a fine singer* **4** to assure (someone) of the certainty of something: *everything's fine, I promise you* ▷ *n* **5** an undertaking to do or not do something **6** indication of future success: *a young player who shows great promise*
WORD ORIGIN Latin *promissum* a promise

Promised Land *n* **1** *bible* the land of Canaan **2** any longed-for place where one expects to find greater happiness

promising ❶ *adj* likely to succeed or turn out well

promissory note *n commerce chiefly US* a written promise to pay a stated sum of money to a particular person on a certain date or on demand

promo *n, pl* **-mos** *informal* an item produced to promote a product, esp. a video used to promote a pop record

promontory *n, pl* **-ries** a point of high land that juts out into the sea
WORD ORIGIN Latin *promunturium* headland

promote ❶ *vb* **-moting, -moted 1** to encourage the progress or success of: *all attempts to promote a lasting ceasefire have failed* **2** to raise to a higher rank or position **3** to encourage the sale of (a product) by advertising **4** to work for: *he actively promoted reform* **promotion** *n* **promotional** *adj*
WORD ORIGIN Latin *promovere* to push onwards

promoter *n* **1** a person who helps to organize and finance an event, esp. a sports one **2** a person or thing that encourages the progress or success of: *a promoter of terrorism*

prompt ❶ *vb* **1** to cause (an action); bring about: *the killings prompted an anti-Mafia crackdown* **2** to motivate or cause someone to do something: I *still don't know what prompted me to go* **3** to remind (an actor) of lines forgotten during a performance **4** to refresh the memory of ▷ *adj* **5** done without delay **6** quick to act ▷ *adv* **7** *informal* punctually: *at 8 o'clock prompt* ▷ *n* **8** anything that serves to remind **promptly** *adv* **promptness** *n*
WORD ORIGIN Latin *promptus* evident

prompter *n* **a** a person offstage who reminds the actors of forgotten lines **b** a device which performs a similar function for public speakers, TV presenters, etc.

promulgate *vb* **-gating, -gated 1** to put (a law or decree) into effect by announcing it officially **2** to make widely known **promulgation** *n* **promulgator** *n*
WORD ORIGIN Latin *promulgare*

pron. 1 pronoun **2** pronunciation

prone ❶ *adj* **1** having a tendency to be affected by or do something: *I am prone to indigestion* **2** lying face downwards; prostrate
WORD ORIGIN Latin *pronus* bent forward

prong *n* a long pointed projection from an instrument or tool such as a fork
WORD ORIGIN Middle English

pronominal *adj grammar* relating to or playing the part of a pronoun

pronoun *n* a word, such as *she* or *it*, that replaces a noun or noun phrase that has already been or is about to be mentioned
WORD ORIGIN Latin *pronomen*

pronounce ❶ *vb* **-nouncing, -nounced 1** to speak (a sound or sounds), esp. clearly or in a certain way **2** to announce or declare officially: *I now pronounce you man and wife* **3** to declare as one's judgment: *he pronounced the wine drinkable* **pronounceable** *adj*
WORD ORIGIN Latin *pronuntiare* to announce

pronounced ❶ *adj* very noticeable: *he speaks with a pronounced lisp*

pronouncement *n* a formal announcement

pronto *adv informal* at once
WORD ORIGIN Spanish: quick

pronunciation *n* **1** the recognized way to pronounce sounds in a given language **2** the way in which

P

THESAURUS

remarkable, pronounced, blatant, conspicuous, to the fore, unmistakable, eye-catching, salient, in the foreground, easily seen, obtrusive **OPPOSITE:** inconspicuous
2 = famous, leading, top, chief, important, main, noted, popular, respected, celebrated, outstanding, distinguished, well-known, notable, renowned, big-time *(informal)*, foremost, eminent, major league *(informal)*, pre-eminent, well-thought-of **OPPOSITE:** unknown

promise *vb* **1, 2 = guarantee**, pledge, vow, swear, contract, assure, undertake, warrant, plight, stipulate, vouch, take an oath, give an undertaking to, cross your heart, give your word **3 = seem likely**, look like, hint at, show signs of, bespeak, augur, betoken, lead you to expect, hold out hopes of, give hope of, bid fair, hold a probability of ▷ *n* **5 = guarantee**, word, bond, vow, commitment, pledge, undertaking, assurance, engagement, compact, oath, covenant, word of honour **6 = potential**, ability, talent, capacity, capability, flair, aptitude

promising *adj* **a = encouraging**, likely, bright, reassuring, hopeful, favourable, rosy, auspicious, propitious, full of promise **OPPOSITE:** unpromising **b = talented**, able, gifted, rising, likely, up-and-coming

promote *vb* **1, 4 = help**, back, support, further, develop, aid, forward, champion, encourage, advance, work for, urge, boost, recommend, sponsor, foster, contribute to, assist, advocate, stimulate, endorse, prescribe, speak for, nurture, push for, espouse, popularize, gee up **OPPOSITE:** impede **2 = raise**, upgrade, elevate, honour, dignify, exalt, kick upstairs *(informal)*, aggrandize **OPPOSITE:** demote **3 = advertise**, sell, hype, publicize, push, plug *(informal)*, puff, call attention to, beat the drum for *(informal)*

prompt *vb* **1, 2 = cause**, move, inspire, stimulate, occasion, urge, spur, provoke, motivate, induce, evoke, give rise to, elicit, incite, instigate, impel, call forth **OPPOSITE:** discourage **3, 4 = remind**, assist, cue, help out, prod, jog the memory, refresh the memory ▷ *adj* **5 = immediate**, quick, rapid, instant, timely, early, swift, on time, speedy, instantaneous, punctual, pdq *(slang)*, unhesitating **OPPOSITE:** slow ▷ *adv* **7** *(informal)* **= exactly**, sharp, promptly, on the dot, punctually

prone *adj* **1 = liable**, given, subject, inclined, tending, bent, disposed, susceptible, apt, predisposed **OPPOSITE:** disinclined **2 = face down**, flat, lying down, horizontal, prostrate, recumbent, procumbent **OPPOSITE:** face up

pronounce *vb* **1 = say**, speak, voice, stress, sound, utter, articulate, enunciate, vocalize **2, 3 = declare**, announce, judge, deliver, assert, proclaim, decree, affirm

pronounced *adj* **= noticeable**, clear, decided, strong, marked, striking, obvious, broad, evident, distinct, definite, conspicuous, unmistakable, salient **OPPOSITE:** imperceptible

proof *n* **1 = evidence**, demonstration, testimony, confirmation,

DICTIONARY

someone pronounces words
proof ◐ *n* **1** any evidence that confirms that something is true or exists **2** *law* the total evidence upon which a court bases its verdict **3** *maths, logic* a sequence of steps or statements that establishes the truth of a proposition **4** the act of testing the truth of something **5** an early copy of printed matter for checking before final production **6** *photog* a trial print from a negative **7** (esp. formerly) a defined level of alcoholic content used as a standard measure for comparing the alcoholic strength of other liquids: *Moldavian ruby port, seventeen degrees proof* ▹ *adj* **8** (foll. by *against*) able to withstand: *proof against tears* **9** (esp. formerly) having a level of alcoholic content used as a standard measure for comparing the alcoholic strength of other liquids ▹ *vb* **10** to take a proof from (type matter) **11** to render (something) proof, esp. to waterproof
WORD ORIGIN Old French *preuve* a test
proofread *vb* **-reading, -read** to read and correct (printer's proofs) **proofreader** *n*
proof spirit *n* (in Britain) an alcoholic beverage that contains a standard percentage of alcohol
prop[1] ◐ *vb* **propping, propped** (often foll. by *up*) **1** to support (something or someone) in an upright position: *she was propped up by pillows* **2** to sustain or support: *the type of measures necessary to prop up the sagging US economy* **3** (often foll. by *against*) to place or lean ▹ *n* **4** something that gives rigid support, such as a pole **5** a person or thing giving moral support
WORD ORIGIN perhaps from Middle Dutch *proppe*
prop[2] *n* a movable object used on the set of a film or play
prop[3] *n informal* a propeller
prop. **1** proper(ly) **2** property **3** proposition **4** proprietor
propaganda ◐ *n* **1** the organized promotion of information to assist or damage the cause of a government or movement **2** such information **propagandist** *n, adj*
WORD ORIGIN Italian
propagate *vb* **-gating, -gated** **1** to spread (information or ideas) **2** *biol* to reproduce or breed **3** *horticulture* to produce (plants) **4** *physics* to transmit, esp. in the form of a wave: *the electrical signal is propagated through a specialized group of conducting fibres* **propagation** *n* **propagator** *n*
WORD ORIGIN Latin *propagare* to increase (plants) by cuttings
propane *n* a flammable gas found in petroleum and used as a fuel
WORD ORIGIN from *propionic (acid)*
propel ◐ *vb* **-pelling, -pelled** to cause to move forwards **propellant** *n, adj*
WORD ORIGIN Latin *propellere*
propeller *n* a revolving shaft with blades to drive a ship or aircraft
propene *n* ▸ same as **propylene**
propensity *n, pl* **-ties** *formal* a natural tendency: *his problem had always been a propensity to live beyond his means*
WORD ORIGIN Latin *propensus* inclined to
proper ◐ *adj* **1** real or genuine: *a proper home* **2** appropriate or usual: *good wine must have the proper balance of sugar and acid* **3** suited to a particular purpose: *they set out without any proper climbing gear* **4** correct in behaviour: *in many societies it is not considered proper for a woman to show her legs* **5** excessively moral: *she was very strait-laced and proper* **6** being or forming the main or central part of something: *a suburb some miles west of the city proper* **7** *Brit, Austral & NZ informal* complete: *you made him look a proper fool* **properly** *adv*
WORD ORIGIN Latin *proprius* special
proper fraction *n* a fraction in which the numerator has a lower absolute value than the denominator, for example ½
proper noun *or* **name** *n* the name of a person or place, for example *Iceland* or *Patrick*
Propertius *n* **Sextus** ?50–?15 BC, Roman elegiac poet
property ◐ *n, pl* **-ties** **1** something owned **2** *law* the right to possess, use, and dispose of anything **3** possessions collectively **4** land or buildings owned by someone **5** a quality or attribute: *the oils have healing properties* **6** ▸ same as **prop**[2]
WORD ORIGIN Latin *proprius* one's own
prophecy ◐ *n, pl* **-cies** **1** a prediction **2** **a** a message revealing God's will **b** the act of uttering such a message **3** the function or activity of a prophet
prophesy *vb* **-sies, -sying, -sied** to foretell
prophet ◐ *n* **1** a person supposedly chosen by God to pass on His message **2** a person who predicts the future: *a prophet of doom* **3** a spokesman for, or advocate of, some cause: *a prophet of revolution* **prophetess** *fem n*
WORD ORIGIN Greek *prophētēs* one who declares the divine will
Prophet *n* **the** the main name used of Mohammed, the founder of Islam
prophetic *adj* **1** foretelling what will happen **2** of the nature of a prophecy **prophetically** *adv*
prophylactic *adj* **1** preventing disease ▹ *n* **2** a drug or device that prevents disease **3** *chiefly US* a condom
WORD ORIGIN Greek *prophulassein* to guard by taking advance measures
propinquity *n formal* nearness in time, place, or relationship
WORD ORIGIN Latin *propinquus* near
propitiate *vb* **-ating, -ated** to appease (someone, esp. a god or spirit); make well disposed **propitiable** *adj* **propitiation** *n* **propitiator** *n* **propitiatory** *adj*
WORD ORIGIN Latin *propitiare*

P

THESAURUS

verification, certification, corroboration, authentication, substantiation, attestation ▹ *adj* **8** (*with* **against**) **= impervious**, strong, tight, resistant, impenetrable, repellent
prop[1] *vb* **1, 2** (*often with* **up**) **= support**, maintain, sustain, shore, hold up, brace, uphold, bolster, truss, buttress **3** (*often with* **against**) **= lean**, place, set, stand, position, rest, lay, balance, steady ▹ *n* **4 = support**, stay, brace, mainstay, truss, buttress, stanchion **5 = mainstay**, support, sustainer, anchor, backbone, cornerstone, upholder
propaganda *n* **1, 2 = information**, advertising, promotion, publicity, hype, brainwashing, disinformation, ballyhoo (*informal*), agitprop, newspeak, boosterism
propel *vb* **= drive**, launch, start, force, send, shoot, push, thrust, shove, set in motion **OPPOSITE:** stop
proper *adj* **1 = real**, actual, genuine, true, bona fide, kosher (*informal*), dinkum (*Austral & NZ informal*) **2, 3 = correct**, accepted, established, appropriate, right, formal, conventional, accurate, exact, precise, legitimate, orthodox, apt **OPPOSITE:** improper **4 = polite**, right, becoming, seemly, fitting, fit, mannerly, suitable, decent, gentlemanly, refined, respectable, befitting, genteel, de rigueur (*French*), ladylike, meet (*archaic*), decorous, punctilious, comme il faut (*French*) **OPPOSITE:** unseemly
property *n* **3 = possessions**, goods, means, effects, holdings, capital, riches, resources, estate, assets, wealth, belongings, chattels **4 = land**, holding, title, estate, acres, real estate, freehold, realty, real property **5 = quality**, feature, characteristic, mark, ability, attribute, virtue, trait, hallmark, peculiarity, idiosyncrasy
prophecy *n* **1 = prediction**, forecast, revelation, prognosis, foretelling, prognostication, augury, sortilege, vaticination (*rare*) **3 = second sight**, divination, augury, telling the future, soothsaying
prophet *n* **2 = soothsayer**, forecaster, diviner, oracle, seer, clairvoyant, augur, sibyl, prognosticator, prophesier

DICTIONARY

propitious *adj* **1** favourable or auspicious: *a propitious moment* **2** likely to prove favourable; advantageous: *his origins were not propitious for a literary career*
WORD ORIGIN Latin *propitius* well disposed

proponent *n* a person who argues in favour of something
WORD ORIGIN Latin *proponere* to propose

proportion ⓣ *n* **1** relative size or extent: *a large proportion of our revenue comes from advertisements* **2** correct relationship between parts **3** a part considered with respect to the whole: *the proportion of women in the total workforce* **4 proportions** dimensions or size: *a building of vast proportions* **5** *maths* a relationship between four numbers in which the ratio of the first pair equals the ratio of the second pair **6 in proportion a** comparable in size, rate of increase, etc. **b** without exaggerating ▹*vb* **7** to adjust in relative amount or size: *the size of the crops are very rarely proportioned to the wants of the inhabitants* **8** to cause to be harmonious in relationship of parts
WORD ORIGIN Latin *pro portione*, literally: for (its, one's) portion

proportional ⓣ *adj* **1** being in proportion ▹*n* **2** *maths* an unknown term in a proportion, for example in *a/b = c/x, x* is the fourth proportional **proportionally** *adv*

proportional representation *n* the representation of political parties in parliament in proportion to the votes they win

proportionate *adj* being in proper proportion **proportionately** *adv*

proposal ⓣ *n* **1** the act of proposing **2** a suggestion put forward for consideration **3** an offer of marriage

propose ⓣ *vb* **-posing, -posed 1** to put forward (a plan) for consideration **2** to nominate (someone) for a position **3** to intend (to do something): *I don't propose to waste any more time discussing it* **4** to ask people to drink a toast **5** (often foll. by *to*) to make an offer of marriage
WORD ORIGIN Old French *proposer*, from Latin *proponere* to display

proposition ⓣ *n* **1** a proposal or offer **2** *logic* a statement that affirms or denies something and is capable of being true or false **3** *maths* a statement or theorem, usually containing its proof **4** *informal* a person or matter to be dealt with: *even among experienced climbers the mountain is considered a tough proposition* **5** *informal* an invitation to engage in sexual intercourse ▹*vb* **6** to invite (someone) to engage in sexual intercourse
WORD ORIGIN Latin *propositio* a setting forth

propound *vb* to put forward for consideration
WORD ORIGIN Latin *proponere* to set forth

proprietary *adj* **1** denoting a product manufactured and distributed under a trade name **2** possessive: *she watched them with a proprietary eye* **3** privately owned and controlled
WORD ORIGIN Late Latin *proprietarius* an owner

proprietor ⓣ *n* an owner of a business establishment **proprietress** *fem n* **proprietorial** *adj*

propriety *n, pl* **-ties 1** the quality or state of being appropriate or fitting **2** correct conduct **3 the proprieties** the standards of behaviour considered correct by polite society
WORD ORIGIN Old French *propriété*, from Latin *proprius* one's own

propulsion *n* **1** a force that moves (something) forward **2** the act of propelling or the state of being propelled **propulsive** *adj*
WORD ORIGIN Latin *propellere* to propel

propylene *or* **propene** *n* a gas found in petroleum and used to produce many organic compounds
WORD ORIGIN from *propionic (acid)*

pro rata *adv, adj* in proportion
WORD ORIGIN Medieval Latin

prorogue *vb* **-roguing, -rogued** to suspend (parliament) without dissolving it **prorogation** *n*
WORD ORIGIN Latin *prorogare*, literally: to ask publicly

prosaic (pro-**zay**-ik) *adj* **1** lacking imagination; dull **2** having the characteristics of prose **prosaically** *adv*

pros and cons *pl n* the advantages and disadvantages of a situation
WORD ORIGIN Latin *pro* for + *con(tra)* against

proscenium *n, pl* **-nia** *or* **-niums** the arch in a theatre separating the stage from the auditorium
WORD ORIGIN Greek *pro* before + *skēnē* scene

proscribe *vb* **-scribing, -scribed 1** to prohibit (something) **2** to condemn (something); to outlaw or banish **proscription** *n* **proscriptive** *adj*
WORD ORIGIN Latin *proscribere* to put up a public notice

prose *n* **1** ordinary spoken or written language in contrast to poetry **2** a passage set for translation into a foreign language **3** commonplace or dull talk ▹*vb* **prosing, prosed 4** to speak or write in a tedious style
WORD ORIGIN Latin *prosa oratio* straightforward speech

prosecute ⓣ *vb* **-cuting, -cuted 1** to bring a criminal charge against (someone) **2** to continue to do (something): *the business of prosecuting a cold war through propaganda* **3 a** to seek redress by legal proceedings **b** to institute or conduct a prosecution **prosecutor** *n*
WORD ORIGIN Latin *prosequi* to follow

prosecution *n* **1** the act of bringing criminal charges against someone

THESAURUS

proportion *n* **1 = part**, share, cut (*informal*), amount, measure, division, percentage, segment, quota, fraction **2 = balance**, agreement, harmony, correspondence, symmetry, concord, congruity **3 = relative amount**, relationship, distribution, ratio **4 = dimensions**, size, volume, capacity, extent, range, bulk, scope, measurements, magnitude, breadth, expanse, amplitude

proportional *or* **proportionate** *adj* **1 = correspondent**, equivalent, corresponding, even, balanced, consistent, comparable, compatible, equitable, in proportion, analogous, commensurate
OPPOSITE: disproportionate

proposal *n* **2 = suggestion**, plan, programme, scheme, offer, terms, design, project, bid, motion, recommendation, tender, presentation, proposition, overture

propose *vb* **1 = put forward**, present, suggest, advance, come up with, submit, tender, proffer, propound **2 = nominate**, name, present, introduce, invite, recommend, put up **3 = intend**, mean, plan, aim, design, scheme, purpose, have in mind, have every intention **5** (*often with* **to**) **= offer marriage**, pop the question (*informal*), ask for someone's hand (in marriage), pay suit

proposition *n* **1 = proposal**, plan, suggestion, scheme, bid, motion, recommendation **2 = theory**, idea, argument, concept, thesis, hypothesis, theorem, premise, postulation **4 = task**, problem, activity, job, affair, venture, undertaking **5 = advance**, pass (*informal*), proposal, overture, improper suggestion, come-on (*informal*) ▹*vb* **6 = make a pass at**, solicit, accost, make an indecent proposal to, make an improper suggestion to

proprietor *or* **proprietress** *n* **= owner**, landowner, freeholder, possessor, titleholder, deed holder, landlord *or* landlady

prosecute *vb* **1 = take someone to court**, try, sue, summon, indict, do (*slang*), arraign, seek redress, put someone on trial, litigate, bring suit against, bring someone to trial, put someone in the dock, bring action against, prefer charges against

DICTIONARY

2 the institution and conduct of legal proceedings against a person 3 the lawyers acting for the Crown to put the case against a person 4 the carrying out of something begun

proselyte (pross-ill-ite) *n* a recent convert **proselytism** *n*
WORD ORIGIN Greek *prosēlutos* recent arrival, convert

proselytize *or* **-ise** (pross-ill-it-ize) *vb* **-izing, -ized** *or* **-ising, -ised** to attempt to convert (someone)

prosody (pross-a-dee) *n* 1 the study of poetic metre and techniques 2 the vocal patterns in a language **prosodic** *adj* **prosodist** *n*
WORD ORIGIN Greek *prosōidia* song set to music

prospect ❶ *n* 1 (*pl*) chances or opportunities for future success: *a job with impossible workloads and poor career prospects* 2 expectation, or something anticipated: *she was terrified at the prospect of bringing up two babies on her own* 3 *old-fashioned* a view or scene: *a prospect of spires, domes, and towers* ▷ *vb* 4 (sometimes foll. by *for*) to search for gold or other valuable minerals
WORD ORIGIN Latin *prospectus* distant view

prospective ❶ *adj* 1 future: *prospective customers* 2 expected or likely: *the prospective loss* **prospectively** *adv*

prospector *n* a person who searches for gold or other valuable minerals

prospectus ❶ *n, pl* **-tuses** a booklet produced by a university, company, etc. giving details about it and its activities

prosper ❶ *vb* to be successful
WORD ORIGIN Latin *prosperare* to succeed

prosperity ❶ *n* success and wealth

prosperous ❶ *adj* wealthy and successful

Prost *n* **Alain** born 1955, French motor-racing driver: world champion 1985, 1986, 1989, and 1993

prostate *n* a gland in male mammals that surrounds the neck of the bladder. Also called: **prostate gland**
WORD ORIGIN Greek *prostatēs* something standing in front (of the bladder)

prosthesis (pross-theess-iss) *n, pl* **-ses** (-seez) *surgery* **a** the replacement of a missing body part with an artificial substitute **b** an artificial body part such as a limb, eye, or tooth **prosthetic** *adj*
WORD ORIGIN Greek: an addition

prostitute ❶ *n* 1 a person who offers sexual intercourse in return for payment ▷ *vb* **-tuting, -tuted** 2 to offer (oneself or another) in sexual intercourse for money 3 to offer (oneself or one's talent) for unworthy purposes **prostitution** *n*
WORD ORIGIN Latin *pro-* in public + *statuere* to cause to stand

prostrate *adj* 1 lying face downwards 2 physically or emotionally exhausted ▷ *vb* **-trating, -trated** 3 **prostrate oneself** to cast (oneself) face downwards, as in submission 4 to exhaust physically or emotionally **prostration** *n*
WORD ORIGIN Latin *prosternere* to throw to the ground

prosy *adj* **prosier, prosiest** dull and long-winded **prosily** *adv*

Prot. 1 Protectorate 2 Protestant

protactinium *n chem* a toxic radioactive metallic element. Symbol: Pa

protagonist ❶ *n* 1 a supporter of a cause: *a great protagonist of the ideas and principles of mutuality* 2 the leading character in a play or story
WORD ORIGIN Greek *prōtos* first + *agōnistēs* actor

Protagoras *n* ?485–?411 BC, Greek philosopher and sophist, famous for his dictum "Man is the measure of all things."

protea (pro-tee-a) *n* an African shrub with showy heads of flowers
WORD ORIGIN after *Proteus*, a sea god who could take many shapes

protean (pro-tee-an) *adj* capable of constantly changing shape or form: *he is a protean stylist who can move from blues to ballads with consummate ease*
WORD ORIGIN after *Proteus*; see PROTEA

protect ❶ *vb* 1 to defend from trouble, harm, or loss 2 *econ* to assist (domestic industries) by taxing imports
WORD ORIGIN Latin *protegere* to cover before

protection ❶ *n* 1 the act of protecting or the condition of being protected 2 something that keeps (one) safe 3 **a** the charging of taxes on imports, to protect domestic industries **b** Also called: **protectionism** the policy of such taxation 4 *informal* Also called: **protection money** money paid to gangsters to avoid attack or damage **protectionism** *n* **protectionist** *n, adj*

protective ❶ *adj* 1 giving protection: *protective clothing* 2 tending or wishing to protect someone **protectively** *adv* **protectiveness** *n*

P

THESAURUS

prospect *n* 1 (*pl*) **= possibilities**, openings, chances, future, potential, expectations, outlook, scope 2 **= idea**, thought, outlook, contemplation 3 (*old-fashioned*) **= view**, perspective, landscape, scene, sight, vision, outlook, spectacle, panorama, vista ▷ *vb* 4 **= look**, search, seek, survey, explore, drill, go after, dowse

prospective *adj* 1 **= potential**, possible, to come, about to be, upcoming, soon-to-be 2 **= expected**, coming, future, approaching, likely, looked-for, intended, awaited, hoped-for, anticipated, forthcoming, imminent, destined, eventual, on the cards

prospectus *n* **= catalogue**, plan, list, programme, announcement, outline, brochure, handbook, syllabus, synopsis, conspectus

prosper *vb* **= succeed**, advance, progress, thrive, make it (*informal*), flower, get on, do well, flourish, bloom, make good, be fortunate, grow rich, fare well

prosperity *n* **= success**, riches, plenty, ease, fortune, wealth, boom, luxury, well-being, good times, good fortune, the good life, affluence, life of luxury, life of Riley (*informal*), prosperousness OPPOSITE: poverty

prosperous *adj* **a = wealthy**, rich, affluent, well-off, in the money (*informal*), blooming, opulent, well-heeled (*informal*), well-to-do, moneyed, in clover (*informal*), minted (*Brit slang*) OPPOSITE: poor **b = successful**, booming, thriving, flourishing, doing well, prospering, on a roll, on the up and up (*Brit*), palmy OPPOSITE: unsuccessful

prostitute *n* 1 **= whore**, hooker (*US slang*), pro (*slang*), brass (*slang*), tart (*informal*), hustler (*US & Canad slang*), moll (*slang*), call girl, courtesan, working girl (*facetious, slang*), harlot, streetwalker, camp follower, loose woman, fallen woman, scrubber (*Brit & Austral slang*), strumpet, trollop, white slave, bawd (*archaic*), cocotte, fille de joie (*French*) ▷ *vb* 3 **= cheapen**, sell out, pervert, degrade, devalue, squander, demean, debase, profane, misapply

protagonist *n* 1 **= supporter**, leader, champion, advocate, exponent, mainstay, prime mover, standard-bearer, moving spirit, torchbearer 2 **= leading character**, lead, principal, central character, hero *or* heroine

protect *vb* 1 **= keep someone safe**, defend, keep, support, save, guard, secure, preserve, look after, foster, shelter, shield, care for, harbour, safeguard, watch over, stick up for (*informal*), cover up for, chaperon, give someone sanctuary, take someone under your wing, mount *or* stand guard over OPPOSITE: endanger

protection *n* 1 **= safety**, charge, care, defence, protecting, security, guarding, custody, safeguard, preservation, aegis, guardianship, safekeeping 2a **= safeguard**, cover, guard, shelter, screen, barrier, shield, refuge, buffer, bulwark 2b **= armour**, cover, screen, barrier, shelter, shield, bulwark

protective *adj* 1 **= protecting**, covering, sheltering, shielding,

DICTIONARY

protector ❶ *n* **1** a person or thing that protects **2** *history* a person who acts for the king or queen during his or her childhood, absence, or incapacity **protectress** *fem n*

protectorate *n* **1** a territory largely controlled by a stronger state **2** the office or term of office of a protector

protégé *or fem* **protégée** (pro-tizh-ay) *n* a person who is protected and helped by another
WORD ORIGIN French *protéger* to protect

protein *n* any of a large group of nitrogenous compounds that are essential for life
WORD ORIGIN Greek *prōteios* primary

pro tempore *adv, adj* for the time being. Often shortened to: **pro tem**

protest ❶ *n* **1** public, often organized, demonstration of objection **2** a strong objection **3** a formal statement declaring that a debtor has dishonoured a bill **4** the act of protesting ▷ *vb* **5** to take part in a public demonstration to express one's support for or disapproval of an action, proposal, etc.: *the workers marched through the city to protest against the closure of their factory* **6** to disagree or object: *'I'm OK,' she protested* **7** to assert in a formal or solemn manner: *all three repeatedly protested their innocence* **8** *US & NZ* to object forcefully to: *students and teachers have protested the budget reductions* **protestant** *adj, n* **protester** *n*
WORD ORIGIN Latin *protestari* to make a formal declaration

Protestant *n* **1** a follower of any of the Christian Churches that separated from the Roman Catholic Church in the sixteenth century ▷ *adj* **2** of or relating to any of these Churches or their followers **Protestantism** *n*

protestation *n formal* a strong declaration

protium *n* the most common isotope of hydrogen, with a mass number of 1
WORD ORIGIN from Greek *prōtos* first

proto- *or sometimes before a vowel* **prot-** *combining form* **1** first: *protomartyr* **2** original: *prototype*
WORD ORIGIN Greek *prōtos* first

protocol ❶ *n* **1** the rules of behaviour for formal occasions **2** a record of an agreement in international negotiations **3** *computers* a standardized format for exchanging data, esp. between different computer systems
WORD ORIGIN Late Greek *prōtokollon* sheet glued to the front of a manuscript

proton (pro-ton) *n* a positively charged elementary particle, found in the nucleus of an atom
WORD ORIGIN Greek *prōtos* first

protoplasm *n biol* a complex colourless substance forming the living contents of a cell **protoplasmic** *adj*
WORD ORIGIN Greek *prōtos* first + *plasma* form

prototype ❶ *n* **1** an early model of a product, which is tested so that the design can be changed if necessary **2** a person or thing that serves as an example of a type

protozoan (pro-toe-zoe-an) *n, pl* **-zoa** a very tiny single-celled invertebrate, such as an amoeba. Also: **protozoon**
WORD ORIGIN Greek *prōtos* first + *zoion* animal

protract *vb* to lengthen or extend (a situation etc.) **protracted** *adj* **protraction** *n*
WORD ORIGIN Latin *protrahere* to prolong

protractor *n* an instrument for measuring angles, usually a flat semicircular piece of plastic

protrude *vb* **-truding, -truded** to stick out or project **protrusion** *n* **protrusive** *adj*
WORD ORIGIN PRO-[2] + Latin *trudere* to thrust

protuberant *adj* swelling out; bulging **protuberance** *n*
WORD ORIGIN Late Latin *protuberare* to swell

proud ❶ *adj* **1** feeling pleasure or satisfaction: *she was proud of her daughter's success* **2** feeling honoured **3** haughty or arrogant **4** causing pride: *the city's proud history* **5** dignified: *too proud to accept charity* **6** (of a surface or edge) projecting or protruding ▷ *adv* **7** **do someone proud** to entertain someone on a grand scale: *Mum did us all proud last Christmas* **proudly** *adv*
WORD ORIGIN Old French *prud, prod* brave

proud flesh *n* a mass of tissue formed around a healing wound

Proudhon *n* **Pierre Joseph** 1809–65, French socialist, whose pamphlet *What is Property?* (1840) declared that property is theft

Prout *n* **1 Ebenezer** 1835–1909, English musicologist and composer, noted for his editions of works by Handel and J. S. Bach **2 William** 1785–1850, English chemist, noted for his modification of the atomic theory

prove ❶ *vb* **proving, proved; proved** *or* **proven** **1** to establish the truth or validity of: *such a claim is difficult to prove scientifically* **2** *law* to establish the genuineness of (a will) **3** to show (oneself) to be: *he proved equal to the task* **4** to be found to be: *it proved to be a trap* **5** (of dough) to rise in a warm place before baking **provable** *adj*
WORD ORIGIN Latin *probare* to test

proven ❶ *vb* **1** ▸ a past participle of **prove** **2** ▸ see **not proven** ▷ *adj* **3** known from experience to work: *a proven ability to make money*

provenance (prov-in-anss) *n* a place of origin
WORD ORIGIN French

Provençal (prov-on-sahl) *adj* **1** of Provence, in SE France ▷ *n* **2** a language of Provence **3** a person from Provence

THESAURUS

safeguarding, insulating **2 = caring**, defensive, motherly, fatherly, warm, careful, maternal, vigilant, watchful, paternal, possessive

protector *n* **1a = defender**, champion, guard, guardian, counsel, advocate, patron, safeguard, bodyguard, benefactor, guardian angel, tower of strength, knight in shining armour **1b = guard**, screen, protection, shield, pad, cushion, buffer

protest *n* **1 = demonstration**, march, rally, sit-in, demo *(informal)*, hikoi *(NZ)* **2 = objection**, complaint, declaration, dissent, outcry, disapproval, protestation, demur, formal complaint, remonstrance, demurral ▷ *vb* **7 = assert**, argue, insist, maintain, declare, vow, testify, contend, affirm, profess, attest, avow, asseverate

protocol *n* **1 = code of behaviour**, manners, courtesies, conventions, customs, formalities, good form, etiquette, propriety, decorum, rules of conduct, politesse, p's and q's

prototype *n* **1, 2 = original**, model, precedent, first, example, standard, paradigm, archetype, mock-up

proud *adj* **1 = satisfied**, pleased, content, contented, honoured, thrilled, glad, gratified, joyful, appreciative, well-pleased **OPPOSITE:** dissatisfied **3 = conceited**, vain, arrogant, stuck-up *(informal)*, lordly, imperious, narcissistic, overbearing, snooty *(informal)*, haughty, snobbish, egotistical, self-satisfied, disdainful, self-important, presumptuous, boastful, supercilious, high and mighty *(informal)*, toffee-nosed *(slang, chiefly Brit)*, too big for your boots *or* breeches **OPPOSITE:** humble

prove *vb* **1 = verify**, establish, determine, show, evidence, confirm, demonstrate, justify, ascertain, bear out, attest, substantiate, corroborate, authenticate, evince, show clearly **OPPOSITE:** disprove **4 = turn out**, come out, end up, be found to be

proven *adj* **3 = established**, accepted, proved, confirmed, tried, tested, checked, reliable, valid, definite, authentic, certified, verified, attested, undoubted,

DICTIONARY

provender *n old-fashioned* fodder for livestock
WORD ORIGIN Old French *provendre*
proverb *n* a short memorable saying that expresses a truth or gives a warning, for example *is half a loaf is better than no bread*
WORD ORIGIN Latin *proverbium*
proverbial *adj* **1** well-known because commonly or traditionally referred to **2** of a proverb **proverbially** *adv*
provide ⊕ *vb* **-viding, -vided 1** to make available **2** to afford; yield: *social activities providing the opportunity to meet new people* **3** (often foll. by *for* or *against*) to take careful precautions: *we provide for the possibility of illness in the examination regulations* **4** (foll. by *for*) to support financially: *both parents should be expected to provide for their children* **5** *formal* **provide for** (of a law, treaty, etc.) to make possible: *a bill providing for stiffer penalties for racial discrimination* **provider** *n*
WORD ORIGIN Latin *providere* to provide for
providence *n* **1** God or nature seen as a protective force that oversees people's lives **2** the foresight shown by a person in the management of his or her affairs
Providence *n Christianity* God, esp. as showing foreseeing care of his creatures
provident *adj* **1** thrifty **2** showing foresight
WORD ORIGIN Latin *providens* foreseeing
providential *adj* fortunate, as if through divine involvement
provident society *n* ▸ same as **friendly society**
providing ⊕ *or* **provided** *conj* on condition (that): *the deal is on, providing he passes his medical*
province ⊕ *n* **1** a territory governed as a unit of a country or empire **2** an area of learning, activity, etc. **3 the provinces** those parts of a country lying outside the capital
WORD ORIGIN Latin *provincia* conquered territory
provincewide *Canad adj* **1** relating to the whole of a province: *a provincewide referendum* ▹ *adv* **2** throughout a province: *an advertising campaign to go provincewide*
provincial ⊕ *adj* **1** of a province **2** unsophisticated or narrow-minded **3** *NZ* denoting a football team representing a province ▹ *n* **4** an unsophisticated person **5** a person from a province or the provinces **provincialism** *n*
provision ⊕ *n* **1** the act of supplying something **2** something supplied **3 provisions** food and other necessities **4** a condition incorporated in a document **5 make provision for** to make arrangements for beforehand: *many restaurants still make no provision for non-smokers* ▹ *vb* **6** to supply with provisions
WORD ORIGIN Latin *provisio* a providing
provisional ⊕ *adj* temporary or conditional: *a provisional diagnosis* **provisionally** *adv*
Provisional *n* a member of the Provisional IRA or Sinn Féin
proviso (pro-**vize**-oh) *n, pl* **-sos** *or* **-soes** a condition or stipulation **provisory** *adj*
WORD ORIGIN Medieval Latin *proviso quod* it being provided that
provocation ⊕ *n* **1** the act of provoking or inciting **2** something that causes indignation or anger
provocative ⊕ *adj* provoking or inciting, esp. to anger or sexual desire: *a provocative remark* **provocatively** *adv*
provoke ⊕ *vb* **-voking, -voked 1** to deliberately act in a way intended to anger someone: *waving a red cape, Delgado provoked the animal into charging* **2** to incite or stimulate: *the army seems to have provoked this latest confrontation* **3** (often foll. by *into*) to cause a person to react in a particular, often angry, way: *keeping your true motives hidden may provoke others into being just as two-faced with you* **4** to bring about: *the case has provoked furious public debate* **provoking** *adj*
WORD ORIGIN Latin *provocare* to call forth
provost *n* **1** the head of certain university colleges or schools **2** the chief councillor of a Scottish town
WORD ORIGIN Old English *profost*
provost marshal *n* the officer in charge of military police in a camp or city
prow *n* the bow of a vessel
WORD ORIGIN Greek *prōra*

THESAURUS

dependable, trustworthy
provide *vb* **1 = supply**, give, contribute, provision, distribute, outfit, equip, accommodate, donate, furnish, dispense, part with, fork out *(informal)*, stock up, cater to, purvey **OPPOSITE:** withhold
2 = give, bring, add, produce, present, serve, afford, yield, lend, render, impart
4 (*with* **for**) **= support**, look after, care for, keep, maintain, sustain, take care of, fend for
providing *or* **provided** *conj* **= on condition that**, if, subject to, given that, on the assumption that, in the event that, with the proviso that, contingent upon, with the understanding that, as long as, if and only if, upon these terms
province *n* **1 = region**, section, county, district, territory, zone, patch, colony, domain, dependency, tract
provincial *adj* **1 = regional**, state, local, county, district, territorial, parochial
2 = parochial, insular, narrow-minded, unsophisticated, limited, narrow, small-town *(chiefly US)*, uninformed, inward-looking, small-minded, parish-pump, upcountry **OPPOSITE:** cosmopolitan
provision *n* **1 = supplying**, giving, providing, supply, delivery, distribution, catering, presentation, equipping, furnishing, allocation, fitting out, purveying, accoutrement
4 = condition, term, agreement, requirement, demand, rider, restriction, qualification, clause, reservation, specification, caveat, proviso, stipulation **3 = food**, supplies, stores, feed, fare, rations, eats *(slang)*, groceries, tack *(informal)*, grub *(slang)*, foodstuff, kai *(NZ informal)*, sustenance, victuals, edibles, comestibles, provender, nosebag *(slang)*, vittles *(obsolete, dialect)*, viands, eatables
provisional *adj* **a = temporary**, interim, transitional, stopgap, pro tem **OPPOSITE:** permanent
b = conditional, limited, qualified, contingent, tentative, provisory
OPPOSITE: definite
provocation *n* **1 = cause**, reason, grounds, motivation, justification, stimulus, inducement, incitement, instigation, casus belli *(Latin)*
2 = offence, challenge, insult, taunt, injury, dare, grievance, annoyance, affront, indignity, red rag, vexation
provocative *adj* **= offensive**, provoking, insulting, challenging, disturbing, stimulating, annoying, outrageous, aggravating *(informal)*, incensing, galling, goading
provoke *vb* **1 = anger**, insult, annoy, offend, irritate, infuriate, hassle *(informal)*, aggravate *(informal)*, incense, enrage, gall, put someone out, madden, exasperate, vex, affront, chafe, irk, rile, pique, get on someone's nerves *(informal)*, get someone's back up, put someone's back up, try someone's patience, nark *(Brit, Austral & NZ slang)*, make someone's blood boil, get in someone's hair *(informal)*, rub someone up the wrong way, hack someone off *(informal)*
OPPOSITE: pacify
4 = rouse, cause, produce, lead to, move, fire, promote, occasion, excite, inspire, generate, prompt, stir, stimulate, motivate, induce, bring about, evoke, give rise to, precipitate, elicit, inflame, incite, instigate, kindle, foment, call forth, draw forth, bring on *or* down
OPPOSITE: curb

DICTIONARY

prowess ❶ *n* **1** superior skill or ability **2** bravery or fearlessness
WORD ORIGIN Old French *proesce*

prowl *vb* **1** (sometimes foll. by *around* or *about*) to move stealthily around (a place) as if in search of prey or plunder ▷*n* **2** the act of prowling **3 on the prowl** moving around stealthily **prowler** *n*
WORD ORIGIN origin unknown

prox. proximo (next month)

proximate *adj* **1** next or nearest in space or time **2** very near **3** immediately coming before or following in a series **4** approximate
WORD ORIGIN Latin *proximus* next

proximity ❶ *n* **1** nearness in space or time **2** nearness or closeness in a series
WORD ORIGIN Latin *proximitas* closeness

proxy ❶ *n, pl* **proxies 1** a person authorized to act on behalf of someone else: *the firm's creditors can vote either in person or by proxy* **2** the authority to act on behalf of someone else
WORD ORIGIN Latin *procuratio* procuration

proxy server *n computers* a computer that acts as an intermediary between a client machine and a server, caching information to save access time

Prozac *n trademark* an antidepressant drug

prude *n* a person who is excessively modest or prim, esp. regarding sex **prudery** *n* **prudish** *adj*
WORD ORIGIN Old French *prode femme* respectable woman

prudent ❶ *adj* **1** sensible and careful **2** discreet or cautious **3** exercising good judgment **prudence** *n* **prudently** *adv*
WORD ORIGIN Latin *prudens* far-sighted

prudential *adj old-fashioned* showing prudence: *prudential reasons* **prudentially** *adv*

Prudentius *n* **Aurelius Clemens** 348–410 AD, Latin Christian poet, born in Spain. His works include the allegory *Psychomachia*

Prud'hon *n* **Pierre Paul** 1758–1823, French painter, noted for the romantic and mysterious aura of his portraits

prune[1] *n* a purplish-black partially dried plum
WORD ORIGIN Latin *prunum* plum

prune[2] ❶ *vb* **pruning, pruned 1** to cut off dead or surplus branches of (a tree or shrub) **2** to shorten or reduce
WORD ORIGIN Old French *proignier* to clip

prurient *adj* **1** excessively interested in sexual matters **2** exciting lustfulness **prurience** *n*
WORD ORIGIN Latin *prurire* to lust after, itch

Prussian *adj* **1** of Prussia, a former German state ▷*n* **2** a person from Prussia

prussic acid *n* the extremely poisonous solution of hydrogen cyanide
WORD ORIGIN French *acide prussique* Prussian acid

pry *vb* **pries, prying, pried** (often foll by *into*) to make an impertinent or uninvited inquiry (about a private matter)
WORD ORIGIN origin unknown

Prynne *n* **William** 1600–69, English Puritan leader and pamphleteer, whose ears were cut off in punishment for his attacks on Laud

PS 1 Also: **ps** postscript **2** private secretary

PSA (in New Zealand) Public Service Association

psalm *n* (*often cap*) any of the sacred songs that make up a book (Psalms) of the Old Testament
WORD ORIGIN Greek *psalmos* song accompanied on the harp

psalmist *n* a writer of psalms

psalmody *n, pl* **-dies** the singing of sacred music

Psalter *n* **1** the Book of Psalms **2** a book containing a version of Psalms
WORD ORIGIN Greek *psaltērion* stringed instrument

psaltery *n, pl* **-teries** an ancient musical instrument played by plucking strings

PSBR (in Britain) public sector borrowing requirement: the money needed by the public sector of the economy for items not paid for by income

psephology (sef-fol-a-jee) *n* the statistical and sociological study of elections **psephologist** *n*
WORD ORIGIN Greek *psephos* pebble, vote + -LOGY

pseud *n informal* a pretentious person

pseudo *adj informal* not genuine

pseudo- *or sometimes before a vowel* **pseud-** *combining form* false, pretending, or unauthentic: *pseudo-intellectual*
WORD ORIGIN Greek *pseudēs* false

pseudonym *n* a fictitious name adopted, esp. by an author **pseudonymity** *n* **pseudonymous** *adj*
WORD ORIGIN Greek *pseudēs* false + *onoma* name

psittacosis *n* a viral disease of parrots that can be passed on to humans
WORD ORIGIN Greek *psittakos* a parrot

psoriasis (so-rye-a-siss) *n* a skin disease with reddish spots and patches covered with silvery scales
WORD ORIGIN Greek: itching disease

psst *interj* a sound made to attract someone's attention, esp. without others noticing

PST Pacific Standard Time

PSV (in Britain, formerly) public service vehicle

psyche ❶ *n* the human mind or soul
WORD ORIGIN Greek *psukhē* breath, soul

psychedelic *adj* **1** denoting a drug that causes hallucinations **2** *informal* having vivid colours and complex patterns similar to those experienced during hallucinations
WORD ORIGIN Greek *psukhē* mind + *delos* visible

psychiatry *n* the branch of medicine concerned with the study and treatment of mental disorders **psychiatric** *adj* **psychiatrist** *n*

psychic ❶ *adj* **1** relating to or having powers (especially mental powers) which cannot be explained by natural laws **2** relating to the mind ▷*n* **3** a person who has psychic powers **psychical** *adj*

THESAURUS

prowess *n* **1 = skill**, ability, talent, expertise, facility, command, genius, excellence, accomplishment, mastery, attainment, aptitude, dexterity, adroitness, adeptness, expertness **OPPOSITE:** inability **2 = bravery**, daring, courage, heroism, mettle, boldness, gallantry, valour, fearlessness, intrepidity, hardihood, valiance, dauntlessness, doughtiness **OPPOSITE:** cowardice

proximity *n* **1, 2 = nearness**, closeness, vicinity, neighbourhood, juxtaposition, contiguity, propinquity, adjacency

proxy *n* **1 = representative**, agent, deputy, substitute, factor, attorney, delegate, surrogate

prudent *adj* **1, 2 = cautious**, careful, wary, discreet, canny, vigilant, circumspect **OPPOSITE:** careless **3 = wise**, politic, sensible, sage, shrewd, discerning, judicious, sagacious **OPPOSITE:** unwise

prune[2] *vb* **1 = cut**, trim, clip, dock, shape, cut back, shorten, snip, lop, pare down **2 = reduce**, cut, cut back, trim, cut down, pare down, make reductions in

psyche *n* **= soul**, mind, self, spirit, personality, individuality, subconscious, true being, anima, essential nature, pneuma (*philosophy*), innermost self, inner man, wairua (*NZ*)

psychic *adj* **1a = supernatural**, mystic, occult, clairvoyant, telepathic, extrasensory, preternatural, telekinetic **1b = mystical**, spiritual, magical, other-worldly, paranormal, preternatural **2 = psychological**, emotional, mental, spiritual, inner, psychiatric, cognitive, psychogenic ▷*n* **3 = clairvoyant**, fortune teller

DICTIONARY

psycho *informal* *n, pl* **-chos** **1** ▸ same as **psychopath** ▹ *adj* **2** ▸ same as **psychopathic**

psycho- *or sometimes before a vowel* **psych-** *combining form* indicating the mind or mental processes: *psychology; psychosomatic*
WORD ORIGIN Greek *psukhē* spirit, breath

psychoactive *adj* capable of affecting mental activity: *a psychoactive drug*

psychoanalyse *or esp. US* **-lyze** *vb* **-lysing, -lysed** *or* **-lyzing, -lyzed** to examine or treat (a person) by psychoanalysis

psychoanalysis *n* a method of treating mental and emotional disorders by discussion and analysis of the patient's thoughts and feelings **psychoanalyst** *n* **psychoanalytical** *or* **psychoanalytic** *adj*

psychogenic *adj psychol* (esp. of disorders or symptoms) of mental, rather than organic, origin

psychological ❶ *adj* **1** relating to the mind or mental activity **2** relating to psychology **3** having its origin in the mind: *his backaches are purely psychological* **psychologically** *adv*

psychological moment *n* the best time for achieving the desired response or effect

psychological warfare *n* the military application of psychology, esp. to influence morale in time of war

psychology ❶ *n, pl* **-gies** **1** the scientific study of all forms of human and animal behaviour **2** *informal* the mental make-up of a person **psychologist** *n*

psychopath *n* a person afflicted with a personality disorder which causes him or her to commit antisocial and sometimes violent acts **psychopathic** *adj*

psychopathology *n* the scientific study of mental disorders

psychopathy (sike-**op**-ath-ee) *n* any mental disorder or disease

psychosis (sike-**oh**-siss) *n, pl* **-ses** (-seez) a severe mental disorder in which the sufferer's contact with reality becomes highly distorted: *a classic case of psychosis* **psychotic** *adj*

psychosomatic *adj* (of a physical disorder) thought to have psychological causes, such as stress

psychotherapy *n* the treatment of nervous disorders by psychological methods **psychotherapeutic** *adj* **psychotherapist** *n*

psych up *vb* to prepare (oneself or another) mentally for a contest or task

pt **1** part **2** past tense **3** point **4** port **5** pro tempore

Pt *chem* platinum

PT *old-fashioned* physical training

pt. pint

PTA Parent-Teacher Association

ptarmigan (**tar**-mig-an) *n* a bird of the grouse family that turns white in winter

Pte. *mil* private

pterodactyl (terr-roe-**dak**-til) *n* an extinct flying reptile with batlike wings
WORD ORIGIN Greek *pteron* wing + *daktulos* finger

PTO *or* **pto** please turn over

Ptolemaic (tol-lim-**may**-ik) *adj* relating to Ptolemy, the 2nd-century AD Greek astronomer, or to his belief that the earth was in the centre of the universe

ptomaine *or* **ptomain** (**toe**-main) *n* any of a group of poisonous alkaloids found in decaying matter
WORD ORIGIN Greek *ptoma* corpse

PTSD post-traumatic stress disorder

Pty *Austral & S African* Proprietary

Pu *chem* plutonium

pub ❶ *n* **1** *chiefly Brit* a building with a licensed bar where alcoholic drinks may be bought and drunk **2** *Austral & NZ* a hotel

pub. **1** public **2** publication **3** published **4** publisher **5** publishing

pub-crawl *n informal* a drinking tour of a number of pubs

puberty (**pew**-ber-tee) *n* the beginning of sexual maturity **pubertal** *adj*
WORD ORIGIN Latin *pubertas* maturity

pubes (**pew**-beez) *n, pl* **pubes** **1** the region above the genitals **2** pubic hair **3** ▸ the plural of **pubis**
WORD ORIGIN Latin

pubescent *adj* **1** arriving or arrived at puberty **2** covered with down, as some plants and animals **pubescence** *n*
WORD ORIGIN Latin *pubescere* to reach manhood

pubic (**pew**-bik) *adj* of or relating to the pubes or pubis: *pubic hair*

pubis *n, pl* **-bes** one of the three sections of the hipbone that forms part of the pelvis
WORD ORIGIN New Latin *os pubis* bone of the pubes

public ❶ *adj* **1** relating to the people as a whole **2** provided by the government: *public service* **3** open to all: *public gardens* **4** well-known: *a public figure* **5** performed or made openly: *public proclamation* **6** maintained by and for the community: *a public library* **7** open, acknowledged, or notorious: *a public scandal* **8** **go public** **a** (of a private company) to offer shares for sale to the public: *few German firms have gone public in recent years* **b** to make information, plans, etc. known: *the group would not have gone public with its suspicions unless it was fully convinced of them* ▹ *n* **9** the community or people in general **10** a particular section of the community: *the racing public* **publicly** *adv*
WORD ORIGIN Latin *publicus*

public-address system *n* a system of microphones, amplifiers, and loudspeakers for increasing the sound level of speech or music at public gatherings

publican *n Brit, Austral & NZ* a person who owns or runs a public house

publication ❶ *n* **1** the publishing of a printed work **2** any printed work offered for sale **3** the act of making information known to the public

P

THESAURUS

psychological *adj* **1 = mental**, emotional, intellectual, inner, cognitive, cerebral **3 = imaginary**, psychosomatic, unconscious, subconscious, subjective, irrational, unreal, all in the mind

psychology *n* **1 = behaviourism**, study of personality, science of mind **2** *(informal)* **= way of thinking**, attitude, behaviour, temperament, mentality, thought processes, mental processes, what makes you tick, mental make-up

pub *or* **public house** *n* **1** *(chiefly Brit)* **= tavern**, bar, inn, local *(Brit informal)*, saloon, watering hole *(facetious, slang)*, boozer *(Brit, Austral & NZ informal)*, beer parlour *(Canad)*, beverage room *(Canad)*, roadhouse, hostelry *(archaic, facetious)*, alehouse *(archaic)*, taproom

public *adj* **1 = general**, popular, national, shared, common, widespread, universal, collective **2 = civic**, government, state, national, local, official, community, social, federal, civil, constitutional, municipal **3 = open**, community, accessible, communal, open to the public, unrestricted, free to all, not private **OPPOSITE:** private **4 = well-known**, leading, important, respected, famous, celebrated, recognized, distinguished, prominent, influential, notable, renowned, eminent, famed, noteworthy, in the public eye **7 = known**, published, exposed, open, obvious, acknowledged, recognized, plain, patent, notorious, overt, in circulation **OPPOSITE:** secret ▹ *n* **9 = people**, society, country, population, masses, community, nation, everyone, citizens, voters, electorate, multitude, populace, hoi polloi, Joe Public *(slang)*, Joe Six-Pack *(US slang)*, commonalty

publication *n* **2 = pamphlet**, book, newspaper, magazine, issue, title, leaflet, brochure, booklet, paperback, hardback, periodical, zine *(informal)*,

DICTIONARY

public bar *n* a bar in a hotel or pub which is cheaper and more basically furnished than the lounge or saloon bar

public company *or* **public limited company** *n* a limited company whose shares may be purchased by the public

public convenience *n* a public toilet

public enemy *n* a notorious person who is considered a danger to the public

public house *n* **1** *Brit* a pub **2** *US & Canad* an inn or small hotel

publicist *n* a person, such as a press agent or journalist, who publicizes something

publicity ❶ *n* **1** the process or information used to arouse public attention **2** the public interest so aroused

publicize *or* **-cise** *vb* **-cizing, -cized** *or* **-cising, -cised** to bring to public attention

public lending right *n* the right of authors to receive payment when their books are borrowed from public libraries

public prosecutor *n law* an official in charge of prosecuting important cases

public relations *n* the practice of gaining the public's goodwill and approval for an organization

public school *n* **1** (in England and Wales) a private independent fee-paying secondary school **2** (in certain Canadian provinces) a public elementary school as distinguished from a separate school **3** (in the US) any school that is part of a free local educational system

public sector *n* the part of a country's economy that consists of state-owned industries and services

public servant *n* **1** an elected or appointed holder of a public office **2** *Austral & NZ* a civil servant

public service *n Austral & NZ* the civil service

public-spirited *adj* having or showing an active interest in the good of the community

public utility *n* an organization that supplies water, gas, or electricity to the public

publish ❶ *vb* **1** to produce and issue (printed matter) for sale **2** to have one's written work issued for publication **3** to announce formally or in public **publishing** *n*
WORD ORIGIN Latin *publicare* to make public

publisher *n* **1** a company or person that publishes books, periodicals, music, etc. **2** *US & Canad* the proprietor of a newspaper

puce *adj* dark brownish-purple: *his face suddenly turned puce with futile rage*
WORD ORIGIN French *couleur puce* flea colour

puck[1] *n* a small disc of hard rubber used in ice hockey
WORD ORIGIN origin unknown

puck[2] *n* a mischievous or evil spirit **puckish** *adj*
WORD ORIGIN Old English *pūca*

pucker *vb* **1** to gather into wrinkles ▷ *n* **2** a wrinkle or crease
WORD ORIGIN origin unknown

pudding ❶ *n* **1** a dessert, esp. a cooked one served hot **2** a savoury dish with pastry or batter: *steak-and-kidney pudding* **3** a sausage-like mass of meat: *black pudding*
WORD ORIGIN Middle English *poding*

puddle *n* **1** a small pool of water, esp. of rain **2** a worked mixture of wet clay and sand that is impervious to water ▷ *vb* **-dling, -dled 3** to make (clay etc.) into puddle **4** to subject (iron) to puddling **puddly** *adj*
WORD ORIGIN Middle English *podel*

pudenda *pl n* the human genitals, esp. of a female
WORD ORIGIN Latin: the shameful (parts)

pudgy *adj* **pudgier, pudgiest** *chiefly US* podgy **pudginess** *n*
WORD ORIGIN origin unknown

Pudovkin *n* **Vsevolod.** 1893–1953, Russian film director; noted for his silent films, such as *Mother* (1926) and *Storm over Asia* (1928)

puerile *adj* silly and childish **puerility** *n*
WORD ORIGIN Latin *puer* a boy

puerperal (pew-er-per-al) *adj* concerning the period following childbirth
WORD ORIGIN Latin *puerperium* childbirth

puerperal fever *n* a serious, formerly widespread, form of blood poisoning caused by infection during childbirth

puerperium (pure-peer-ee-um) *n* the period after childbirth

Pufendorf *n* **Samuel von** 1632–94, German jurist and philosopher, who lived in Sweden and Denmark. His *De Jure naturae et gentium* (1672) was an important contribution to the philosophy of natural and international law

puff ❶ *n* **1** a short quick blast of breath, wind, or smoke **2** the amount of wind or smoke released in a puff **3** the sound made by a puff **4** an act of inhaling and expelling cigarette smoke **5** a light pastry usually filled with cream and jam **6 out of puff** out of breath: *by the third flight of stairs she was out of puff* ▷ *vb* **7** to blow or breathe in short quick blasts **8** (often foll. by *out*) to cause to be out of breath **9** to take draws at (a cigarette) **10** to move with or by the emission of puffs: *the steam train puffed up the incline* **11** (often foll. by *up* or *out*) to swell **puffy** *adj*
WORD ORIGIN Old English *pyffan*

puff adder *n* a large venomous African viper whose body swells when alarmed

puffball *n* a ball-shaped fungus that sends out a cloud of brown spores when mature

puffin *n* a black-and-white sea bird with a brightly coloured beak
WORD ORIGIN origin unknown

puff pastry *or US* **puff paste** *n* a light flaky pastry

pug *n* a small dog with a smooth coat, lightly curled tail, and a short wrinkled nose
WORD ORIGIN origin unknown

Pugachov *n* **Yemelyan Ivanovich** 1726–75, Russian Cossack rebel, leader of a major revolt against the government of Catherine II: executed

Puget *n* **Pierre** 1620–94, French Baroque sculptor, best known for his *Milo of Crotona* (c. 1680)

pugilist (pew-jil-ist) *n* a boxer **pugilism** *n* **pugilistic** *adj*
WORD ORIGIN Latin *pugil* a boxer

Pugin *n* **Augustus** (**Welby Northmore**) 1812–52, British architect; a leader of the Gothic Revival. He collaborated with Sir Charles Barry on the Palace of Westminster (begun 1836)

THESAURUS

handbill, blog *(informal)* **3 = announcement**, publishing, broadcasting, reporting, airing, appearance, declaration, advertisement, disclosure, proclamation, notification, dissemination, promulgation

publicity *n* **1 = advertising**, press, promotion, hype, boost, build-up, plug *(informal)*, puff, ballyhoo *(informal)*, puffery *(informal)*, boosterism **2 = attention**, exposure, fame, celebrity, fuss, public interest, limelight, notoriety, media attention, renown, public notice

publish *vb* **1 = put out**, issue, produce, print, bring out **3 = announce**, reveal, declare, spread, advertise, broadcast, leak, distribute, communicate, disclose, proclaim, circulate, impart, publicize, divulge, promulgate, shout from the rooftops *(informal)*, blow wide open *(slang)*

pudding *n* **1 = dessert**, afters *(Brit informal)*, sweet, pud *(informal)*, second course, last course

puff *n* **1, 2 = blast**, breath, flurry, whiff, draught, gust, emanation **4 = drag**, pull *(slang)*, smoke ▷ *vb* **7 = breathe heavily**, pant, exhale, blow, gasp, gulp, wheeze, fight for breath, puff and pant **9 = smoke**, draw, drag *(slang)*, suck, inhale, pull at *or* on

DICTIONARY

pugnacious *adj* ready and eager to fight **pugnacity** *n*
WORD ORIGIN Latin *pugnax*

pug nose *n* a short stubby upturned nose **pug-nosed** *adj*
WORD ORIGIN from *pug* (the dog)

puissance *n* a showjumping competition that tests a horse's ability to jump large obstacles
WORD ORIGIN see PUISSANT

puissant (pew-iss-sant) *adj archaic or poetic* powerful
WORD ORIGIN Old French, from Latin *potens* mighty

puke *slang vb* **puking, puked 1** to vomit ▷*n* **2** the act of vomiting **3** the matter vomited
WORD ORIGIN probably imitative

pukeko (poo-kek-oh) *n, pl* **-kos** a brightly coloured New Zealand wading bird
WORD ORIGIN Māori

pukka *adj* **1** properly done, constructed, etc. **2** genuine or real
WORD ORIGIN Hindi *pakkā* firm

pulchritude *n formal or literary* physical beauty **pulchritudinous** *adj*
WORD ORIGIN Latin *pulchritudo*

Pulci *n* **Luigi** 1432–84, Italian poet. His masterpiece is the comic epic poem *Morgante* (1483)

pule *vb* **puling, puled** *literary* to whine or whimper
WORD ORIGIN imitative

pull ❶ *vb* **1** to exert force on (an object) to draw it towards the source of the force **2** to strain or stretch **3** to remove or extract: *he pulled a crumpled tenner from his pocket* **4** *informal* to draw out (a weapon) for use: *he pulled a knife on his attacker* **5** *informal* to attract: *the game is expected to pull a large crowd* **6** *slang* to attract a sexual partner **7** (usually foll. by *on* or *at*) to drink or inhale deeply: *he pulled on his pipe* **8** to possess or exercise the power to move: *this car doesn't pull well on hills* **9** to withdraw or remove: *the board pulled their support* **10** *printing* to take (a proof) from type **11** *golf, baseball, etc.* to hit (a ball) away from the direction in which the player intended to hit it **12** *cricket* to hit (a ball) to the leg side **13** to row (a boat) or take a stroke of (an oar) in rowing **14 pull a face** to make a grimace **15 pull a fast one** *slang* (often foll. by *on*) to play a sly trick **16 pull apart** *or* **to pieces** to criticize harshly **17 pull (one's) punches** to limit the force of one's criticisms or blows ▷*n* **18** the act of pulling **19** the force used in pulling: *the pull of the moon affects the tides* **20** the act of taking in drink or smoke **21** *printing* a proof taken from type **22** something used for pulling, such as a handle **23** *informal* power or influence: *his uncle is chairman of the company, so he has quite a lot of pull* **24** *informal* the power to attract attention or support **25** a single stroke of an oar in rowing **26** the act of pulling the ball in golf, cricket, etc. ▸See also **pull down, pull in**, etc.
WORD ORIGIN Old English *pullian*

pull down *vb* to destroy or demolish: *the old houses were pulled down*

pullet *n* a hen less than one year old
WORD ORIGIN Old French *poulet* chicken

pulley *n* a wheel with a grooved rim in which a belt, chain, or piece of rope runs in order to lift weights by a downward pull
WORD ORIGIN Old French *polie*

pull in *vb* **1** Also: **pull over** (of a motor vehicle) to draw in to the side of the road **2** (often foll. by *to*) to reach a destination: *the train pulled in to the station* **3** to attract: *his appearance will pull in the crowds* **4** *Brit, Austral & NZ slang* to arrest **5** to earn (money): *he pulls in at least thirty thousand a year*

Pullman[1] *n, pl* **-mans** a luxurious railway coach, esp. a sleeping car. Also called: **Pullman car**
WORD ORIGIN C19: named after George M. Pullman (1831–97), the US inventor who first manufactured such coaches

Pullman[2] *n* **Philip** born 1946, British author. Writing primarily for older children, he is best known for the fantasy trilogy *His Dark Materials* (1997–2000)

pull off *vb informal* to succeed in accomplishing (something difficult): *super-heroes who pull off the impossible*

pull out *vb* **1 a** (of a motor vehicle) to draw away from the side of the road **b** (of a motor vehicle) to move out from behind another vehicle to overtake **2** to depart: *the train pulled out of the station* **3** to withdraw: *several companies have pulled out of the student market* **4** to remove by pulling **5** to abandon a situation

pullover *n* a sweater that is pulled on over the head

pull through *vb* to survive or recover, esp. after a serious illness

pull together *vb* **1** to cooperate or work in harmony **2 pull oneself together** *informal* to regain one's self-control

pull up *vb* **1** (of a motor vehicle) to stop **2** to remove by the roots **3** to rebuke

pulmonary *adj* **1** of or affecting the lungs **2** having lungs or lunglike organs
WORD ORIGIN Latin *pulmo* a lung

pulp ❶ *n* **1** a soft wet substance made from matter which has been crushed or beaten: *mash the strawberries to a pulp* **2** the soft fleshy part of a fruit or vegetable: *halve the tomatoes then scoop the seeds and pulp into a bowl* **3** printed or recorded material with little depth or designed to shock: *pulp fiction; a tape player churned out disco pulp* ▷*vb* **4** to reduce a material to pulp: *he began to pulp the orange in his fingers* **pulpy** *adj*
WORD ORIGIN Latin *pulpa*

pulpit *n* **1** a raised platform in churches used for preaching **2** (usually preceded by *the*) preaching or the clergy
WORD ORIGIN Latin *pulpitum* a platform

pulpwood *n* pine, spruce, or any other soft wood used to make paper

pulsar *n* a very small star which emits regular pulses of radio waves
WORD ORIGIN from *puls(ating st)ar*

pulsate *vb* **-sating, -sated 1** to expand and contract rhythmically, like a heartbeat **2** to quiver or vibrate: *the images pulsate with energy and light* **3** *physics* to vary in intensity or magnitude **pulsation** *n*
WORD ORIGIN Latin *pulsare* to push

pulse[1] ❶ *n* **1** *physiol* **a** the regular beating of blood through the arteries at each heartbeat **b** a single such beat **2** *physics, electronics* a sudden change in a quantity, such as a voltage, that is normally constant in a system **3** a regular beat or vibration **4** bustle or excitement: *the lively pulse of a city* **5** the feelings or thoughts of a group as they can be measured: *the political pulse of the capital* ▷*vb* **pulsing, pulsed 6** to beat, throb, or vibrate
WORD ORIGIN Latin *pulsus* a beating

pulse[2] *n* the edible seeds of pod-bearing plants, such as peas, beans, and lentils

P

THESAURUS

pull *vb* **1 = draw**, haul, drag, trail, tow, tug, jerk, yank, prise, wrench, lug, wrest **OPPOSITE:** push **2 = strain**, tear, stretch, rend, rip, wrench, dislocate, sprain **3 = extract**, pick, remove, gather, take out, weed, pluck, cull, uproot, draw out **OPPOSITE:** insert **5, 6** *(informal)* **= attract**, draw, bring in, tempt, lure, interest, entice, pull in, magnetize **OPPOSITE:** repel ▷*n* **18 = tug**, jerk, yank, twitch, heave **OPPOSITE:** shove **20 = puff**, drag *(slang)*, inhalation **23** *(informal)* **= influence**, power, authority, say, standing, weight, advantage, muscle, sway, prestige, clout *(informal)*, leverage, kai *(NZ informal)*

pulp *n* **1 = paste**, mash, pap, mush, semisolid, pomace, semiliquid **2 = flesh**, meat, marrow, soft part ▷*vb* **4 = crush**, squash, mash, pulverize

pulse[1] *n* **3 = beat**, rhythm, vibration, beating, stroke, throb, throbbing, oscillation, pulsation ▷*vb* **6 = beat**, tick, throb, vibrate, pulsate

DICTIONARY

WORD ORIGIN Latin *puls* pottage of pulse

pulverize *or* **-ise** *vb* **-izing, -ized** *or* **-ising, -ised** **1** to reduce to fine particles by crushing or grinding **2** to destroy completely **pulverization** *or* **-isation** *n*
WORD ORIGIN Latin *pulvis* dust

puma *n* a large American wild cat with a plain greyish-brown coat and a long tail
WORD ORIGIN S American Indian

pumice (pumm-iss) *n* a light porous stone used for scouring and for removing hard skin. Also called: **pumice stone**
WORD ORIGIN Old French *pomis*

pummel *vb* **-melling, -melled** *or US* **-meling, -meled** to strike repeatedly with the fists
WORD ORIGIN see POMMEL

pump¹ ❶ *n* **1** a device to force a gas or liquid to move in a particular direction ▷ *vb* **2** (sometimes foll. by *from* or *out* etc.) to raise or drive (air, liquid, etc.) with a pump, esp. into or from something **3** (usually foll. by *in* or *into*) to supply in large amounts: *pumping money into the economy* **4** to operate (a handle etc.) in the manner of a pump: *he was warmly applauded, and his hand was pumped by well-wishers* **5** to obtain information from (someone) by persistent questioning **6 pump iron** *slang* to exercise with weights; do body-building exercises
WORD ORIGIN Middle Dutch *pumpe* pipe

pump² *n* **1** *chiefly Brit* a shoe with a rubber sole, used in games such as tennis; plimsoll **2** *chiefly Brit* a low-cut low-heeled shoe, worn for dancing
WORD ORIGIN origin unknown

pumpernickel *n* a slightly sour black bread made of coarse rye flour
WORD ORIGIN from German

pumpkin *n* **1** a large round fruit with a thick orange rind, pulpy flesh, and many seeds **2** the creeping plant that bears this fruit
WORD ORIGIN Greek *pepōn* ripe

pun *n* **1** the use of words to exploit double meanings for humorous effect, for example *my dog's a champion boxer* ▷ *vb* **punning, punned** **2** to make puns
WORD ORIGIN origin unknown

punch¹ ❶ *vb* **1** to strike at with a clenched fist ▷ *n* **2** a blow with the fist **3** *informal* point or vigour: *the jokes are mildly amusing but lack any real punch*
WORD ORIGIN probably variant of *pounce* to stamp

punch² ❶ *n* **1** a tool or machine for shaping, piercing, or engraving **2** *computers* a device for making holes in a card or paper tape ▷ *vb* **3** to pierce, cut, stamp, shape, or drive with a punch
WORD ORIGIN Latin *pungere* to prick

punch³ *n* a mixed drink containing fruit juice and, usually, alcoholic liquor, generally hot and spiced
WORD ORIGIN origin unknown

Punch *n* the main character in the children's puppet show, Punch and Judy

punchbag *n* a stuffed or inflated bag suspended by a flexible rod, that is punched for exercise, esp. boxing training

punchball *n* a stuffed or inflated ball supported by a flexible rod, that is punched for exercise, esp. boxing training

punchbowl *n* a large bowl for serving punch

punch-drunk *adj* dazed and confused through suffering repeated blows to the head

punched card *or esp. US* **punch card** *n* *computers* a card on which data can be coded in the form of punched holes

Punchinello *n, pl* **-los** *or* **-loes** a clown from Italian puppet shows, the origin of Punch
WORD ORIGIN Italian *Polecenella*

punch line *n* the last line of a joke or funny story that gives it its point

punch-up *n* *informal* a fight or brawl

punchy *adj* **punchier, punchiest** *informal* effective or forceful: *learn to compose short concise punchy letters*

punctilious *adj formal* **1** paying careful attention to correct social behaviour **2** attentive to detail **punctiliously** *adv*
WORD ORIGIN Latin *punctum* a point

punctual *adj* **1** arriving or taking place at an arranged time **2** (of a person) always keeping exactly to arranged times **punctuality** *n* **punctually** *adv*
WORD ORIGIN Medieval Latin *punctualis* concerning detail

punctuate ❶ *vb* **-ating, -ated** **1** to insert punctuation marks into (a written text) **2** to interrupt at frequent intervals: *the meeting was punctuated by heckling* **3** to emphasize: *he punctuated the question by pressing the muzzle into the pilot's neck*
WORD ORIGIN Latin *pungere* to puncture

punctuation *n* **1** the use of symbols, such as commas, to indicate speech patterns and meaning not otherwise shown by the written language **2** the symbols used for this purpose

punctuation mark *n* any of the signs used in punctuation, such as a comma

puncture ❶ *n* **1** a small hole made by a sharp object **2** a tear and loss of pressure in a tyre **3** the act of puncturing or perforating ▷ *vb* **-turing, -tured** **4** to pierce a hole in (something) with a sharp object **5** to cause (a tyre etc.) to lose pressure by piercing
WORD ORIGIN Latin *pungere* to prick

pundit *n* **1** an expert on a subject who often speaks or writes about it for a non-specialist audience: *Spain's leading sports pundit, who hosts two TV programmes* **2** a Hindu scholar learned in Sanskrit, religion, philosophy, or law
WORD ORIGIN Hindi *pandit*

pungent *adj* **1** having a strong sharp bitter smell or taste **2** (of speech or writing) biting; critical **pungency** *n*
WORD ORIGIN Latin *pungens* piercing

punish ❶ *vb* **1** to force (someone) to undergo a penalty for some crime or misbehaviour **2** to inflict punishment for (some crime or misbehaviour) **3** to treat harshly, esp. by overexertion: *he continued to punish himself in the gym* **punishable** *adj* **punishing** *adj*
WORD ORIGIN Latin *punire*

punishment ❶ *n* **1** a penalty for a crime or offence **2** the act of punishing or state of being punished **3** *informal* rough physical treatment:

THESAURUS

pump¹ *vb* **3 = supply**, send, pour, inject **5 = interrogate**, probe, quiz, cross-examine, grill *(informal)*, worm out of, give someone the third degree, question closely

punch¹ *vb* **1 = hit**, strike, box, smash, belt *(informal)*, slam, plug *(slang)*, bash *(informal)*, sock *(slang)*, clout *(informal)*, slug, swipe *(informal)*, biff *(slang)*, bop *(informal)*, wallop *(informal)*, pummel ▷ *n* **2 = blow**, hit, knock, bash *(informal)*, plug *(slang)*, sock *(slang)*, thump, clout *(informal)*, jab, swipe *(informal)*, biff *(slang)*, bop *(informal)*, wallop *(informal)* **3** *(informal)* **= effectiveness**, force, bite, impact, point, drive, vigour, verve, forcefulness

punch² *vb* **3 = pierce**, cut, bore, drill, pink, stamp, puncture, prick, perforate

punctuate *vb* **2 = interrupt**, break, pepper, sprinkle, intersperse, interject

puncture *n* **1 = hole**, opening, break, cut, nick, leak, slit, rupture, perforation **2 = flat tyre**, flat, flattie *(NZ)* ▷ *vb* **4 = pierce**, cut, nick, penetrate, prick, rupture, perforate, impale, bore a hole (in)

punish *vb* **1 = discipline**, correct, castigate, chastise, beat, sentence, whip, lash, cane, flog, scourge, chasten, penalize, bring to book, slap someone's wrist, throw the book at, rap someone's knuckles, give someone the works *(slang)*, give a lesson to

punishment *n* **1 = penalty**, reward, sanction, penance, comeuppance

DICTIONARY

the boxer's face could not withstand further punishment

punitive ❶ (pew-nit-tiv) *adj* relating to punishment: *punitive measures*

punk *n* **1** a worthless person **2** a youth movement of the late 1970s, characterized by anti-Establishment slogans, short spiky hair, and the wearing of worthless articles such as safety pins for decoration **3** ▸ short for **punk rock 4** a follower of the punk movement or of punk rock ▹ *adj* **5** relating to the punk youth movement of the late 1970s: *a punk band* **6** worthless or insignificant
WORD ORIGIN origin unknown

punkah *or* **punka** *n* (in India) a ceiling fan made of a cloth stretched over a rectangular frame
WORD ORIGIN Hindi *pankhā*

punk rock *n* rock music of the punk youth movement of the late 1970s, characterized by energy and aggressive lyrics and performance **punk rocker** *n*

punnet *n* a small basket for fruit
WORD ORIGIN origin unknown

punster *n* a person who is fond of making puns

punt[1] *n* **1** an open flat-bottomed boat, propelled by a pole ▹ *vb* **2** to propel (a punt) by pushing with a pole on the bottom of a river
WORD ORIGIN Latin *ponto*

punt[2] *n* **1** a kick in certain sports, such as rugby, in which the ball is dropped and kicked before it hits the ground ▹ *vb* **2** to kick (a ball) using a punt
WORD ORIGIN origin unknown

punt[3] ❶ *chiefly Brit vb* **1** to gamble or bet ▹ *n* **2** a gamble or bet, esp. against the bank, such as in roulette **3 take a punt at** *Austral & NZ* to make an attempt at
WORD ORIGIN French *ponter*

punt[4] *n* a former monetary unit of the Republic of Ireland

punter ❶ *n* **1** a person who places a bet **2** *Brit, Austral & NZ informal* any member of the public, esp. when a customer: *the punters are flocking into the sales*

puny *adj* **-nier, -niest** small and weakly
WORD ORIGIN Old French *puisné* born later

pup *n* **1 a** a young dog; puppy **b** the young of various other animals, such as the seal ▹ *vb* **pupping, pupped 2** (of dogs, seals, etc.) to give birth to pups

pupa (pew-pa) *n, pl* **-pae** (-pee) *or* **-pas** an insect at the stage of development between larva and adult **pupal** *adj*
WORD ORIGIN Latin: a doll

pupil[1] ❶ *n* a student who is taught by a teacher
WORD ORIGIN Latin *pupus* a child

pupil[2] *n* the dark circular opening at the centre of the iris of the eye
WORD ORIGIN Latin *pupilla*, diminutive of *pupa* doll; from the tiny reflections in the eye

puppet ❶ *n* **1** a small doll or figure moved by strings attached to its limbs or by the hand inserted in its cloth body **2** a person or state that appears independent but is controlled by another: *the former cabinet ministers have denied that they are puppets of a foreign government*
WORD ORIGIN Latin *pupa* doll

puppeteer *n* a person who operates puppets

puppy *n, pl* **-pies 1** a young dog **2** *informal, contemptuous* a brash or conceited young man **puppyish** *adj*
WORD ORIGIN Old French *popée* doll

puppy fat *n* fatty tissue that develops in childhood or adolescence and usually disappears with maturity

purblind *adj* **1** partly or nearly blind **2** lacking in understanding
WORD ORIGIN *pure* (that is, utterly) *blind*

purchase ❶ *vb* **-chasing, -chased 1** to obtain (goods) by payment **2** to obtain by effort or sacrifice: *he had purchased his freedom at the expense of his principles* ▹ *n* **3** something that is bought **4** the act of buying **5** the mechanical advantage achieved by a lever **6** a firm leverage or grip **purchaser** *n*
WORD ORIGIN Old French *porchacier* to strive to obtain

purdah *n* the custom in some Muslim and Hindu communities of keeping women in seclusion, with clothing that conceals them completely when they go out
WORD ORIGIN Hindi *parda* veil

pure ❶ *adj* **1** not mixed with any other materials or elements: *pure wool* **2** free from tainting or polluting matter: *pure water* **3** innocent: *pure love* **4** complete: *Pamela's presence on that particular flight was pure chance* **5** (of a subject) studied in its theoretical aspects rather than for its practical applications: *pure mathematics* **6** of unmixed descent **purely** *adv* **pureness** *n*
WORD ORIGIN Latin *purus* unstained

purebred *adj* denoting a pure strain obtained through many generations of controlled breeding

puree (pure-ray) *n* **1** a smooth thick pulp of sieved fruit, vegetables, meat, or fish ▹ *vb* **-reeing, -reed 2** to make (foods) into a puree
WORD ORIGIN French

purgative *med n* **1** a medicine for emptying the bowels ▹ *adj* **2** causing emptying of the bowels

purgatory *n* **1** *chiefly RC church* a place in which the souls of those who have died undergo limited suffering for their sins on earth before they go to heaven **2** a situation of temporary suffering or torment: *it was purgatory living in the same house as him* **purgatorial** *adj*
WORD ORIGIN Latin *purgare* to purify

purge ❶ *vb* **purging, purged 1** to rid (something) of undesirable qualities **2** to rid (an organization etc.) of undesirable people: *the party was*

P

THESAURUS

(slang) **2 = penalizing**, discipline, correction, retribution, what for *(informal)*, chastening, just deserts, chastisement, punitive measures

punitive *adj* **= retaliatory**, in retaliation, vindictive, in reprisal, revengeful, retaliative, punitory

punt[3] *vb* **1 = bet**, back, stake, gamble, lay, wager ▹ *n* **2 = bet**, stake, gamble, wager

punter *n* **1 = gambler**, better, backer, punt *(chiefly Brit)*

pupil[1] *n* **= student**, scholar, schoolboy *or* schoolgirl, schoolchild
OPPOSITE: teacher

puppet *n* **1 = marionette**, doll, glove puppet, finger puppet **2 = pawn**, tool, instrument, creature, dupe, gull *(archaic)*, figurehead, mouthpiece, stooge, cat's-paw

purchase *vb* **1 = buy**, pay for, obtain, get, score *(slang)*, gain, pick up, secure, acquire, invest in, shop for, get hold of, come by, procure, make a purchase **OPPOSITE:** sell
▹ *n* **3 = acquisition**, buy, investment, property, gain, asset, possession
6 = grip, hold, support, footing, influence, edge, advantage, grasp, lever, leverage, foothold, toehold

pure *adj* **1 = unmixed**, real, clear, true, simple, natural, straight, perfect, genuine, neat, authentic, flawless, unalloyed **OPPOSITE:** adulterated
2 = clean, immaculate, sterile, wholesome, sanitary, spotless, sterilized, squeaky-clean, unblemished, unadulterated, untainted, disinfected, uncontaminated, unpolluted, pasteurized, germ-free
OPPOSITE: contaminated
3 = innocent, virgin, modest, good, true, moral, maidenly, upright, honest, immaculate, impeccable, righteous, virtuous, squeaky-clean, blameless, chaste, virginal, unsullied, guileless, uncorrupted, unstained, undefiled, unspotted
OPPOSITE: corrupt
4 = complete, total, perfect, absolute, mere, sheer, patent, utter, outright, thorough, downright, palpable, unqualified, out-and-out, unmitigated **OPPOSITE:** qualified

purge *vb* **1 = rid**, clear, cleanse, strip, empty, void ▹ *n* **7 = removal**,

DICTIONARY

purged **3 a** to empty (the bowels) **b** to cause (a person) to empty his or her bowels **4 a** *law* to clear (a person) of a charge **b** to free (oneself) of guilt by showing repentance **5** to be purified ▹ *n* **6** the act or process of purging **7** the removal of undesirables from a state, organization, or political party **8** a medicine that empties the bowels
WORD ORIGIN Latin *purgare* to purify

purify *vb* **-fies, -fying, -fied 1** to free (something) of harmful or inferior matter **2** to free (a person) from sin or guilt **3** to make clean, for example in a religious ceremony
purification *n*
WORD ORIGIN Latin *purus* pure + *facere* to make

purism *n* strict insistence on the correct usage or style, such as in grammar or art **purist** *adj, n*
puristic *adj*

puritan *n* **1** a person who follows strict moral or religious principles ▹ *adj* **2** of or like a puritan: *he maintained a streak of puritan self-denial*
puritanism *n*
WORD ORIGIN Late Latin *puritas* purity

Puritan *history n* **1** a member of the extreme English Protestants who wished to strip the Church of England of most of its rituals ▹ *adj* **2** of or relating to the Puritans
Puritanism *n*

puritanical *adj* **1** *usually disparaging* strict in moral or religious outlook **2** (*sometimes cap*) of or relating to a puritan or the Puritans
puritanically *adv*

purity ❶ *n* the state or quality of being pure

purl[1] *n* **1** a knitting stitch made by doing a plain stitch backwards **2** a decorative border, such as of lace ▹ *vb* **3** to knit in purl stitch
WORD ORIGIN dialect *pirl* to twist into a cord

purl[2] *vb literary* (of a stream) to flow with a gentle movement and a murmuring sound
WORD ORIGIN probably imitative

purlieu (**per**-lyoo) *n* **1** *English history* land on the edge of a royal forest **2** (*usually pl*) *literary* a neighbouring area; outskirts **3** (*often pl*) *literary* a place one frequents: *the committee was the purlieu of civil servants*
WORD ORIGIN Anglo-French *puralé* a going through

purlin *or* **purline** *n* a horizontal beam that supports the rafters of a roof
WORD ORIGIN origin unknown

purloin *vb formal* to steal
WORD ORIGIN Old French *porloigner* to put at a distance

purple *n* **1** a colour between red and blue **2** cloth of this colour, often used to symbolize royalty or nobility **3** the official robe of a cardinal **4** anything purple, such as purple paint or purple clothing: *a large lady, unwisely dressed in purple* ▹ *adj* **5** of a colour between red and blue **6** (of writing) excessively elaborate: *purple prose* **purplish** *adj*
WORD ORIGIN Greek *porphura* the purple fish (murex)

purple heart *n informal chiefly Brit* a heart-shaped purple tablet consisting mainly of amphetamine

Purple Heart *n* a decoration awarded to members of the US Armed Forces wounded in action

purport ❶ *vb* **1** to claim to be or do something, esp. falsely: *painkillers may actually cause the headaches they purport to cure* **2** (of speech or writing) to signify or imply ▹ *n* **3** meaning or significance
WORD ORIGIN Old French *porporter* to convey

purpose ❶ *n* **1** the reason for which anything is done, created, or exists **2** a fixed design or idea that is the object of an action **3** determination: *his easy manner only lightly conceals a clear sense of purpose* **4** practical advantage or use: *we debated senseless points of dogma for hours to no fruitful purpose* **5 on purpose** intentionally ▹ *vb* **-posing, -posed 6** to intend or determine to do (something)
WORD ORIGIN Old French *porposer* to plan

purpose-built *adj* made to serve a specific purpose

purposeful *adj* with a fixed and definite purpose; determined
purposefully *adv*

purposely ❶ *adv* on purpose

purposive *adj formal* **1** having or showing a definite intention: *the establishment of the camps lacks a purposive trend towards a solution* **2** useful

purr *vb* **1** (esp. of cats) to make a low vibrant sound, usually considered as expressing pleasure **2** to express (pleasure) by this sound or by a sound suggestive of purring ▹ *n* **3** a purring sound
WORD ORIGIN imitative

purse ❶ *n* **1** a small pouch for carrying money **2** *US, Canad, Austral & NZ* a woman's handbag **3** wealth or resources: *the public purse appeared bottomless* **4** a sum of money that is offered as a prize ▹ *vb* **pursing, pursed 5** to pull (the lips) into a small rounded shape
WORD ORIGIN Old English *purs*

purser *n* an officer aboard a ship who keeps the accounts

purse strings *pl n* **hold the purse strings** to control the spending of a particular family, group, etc.

pursuance *n formal* the carrying out of an action or plan: *the pursuance of duty had taken him abroad*

pursue ❶ *vb* **-suing, -sued 1** to follow (a person, vehicle, or animal) in order to capture or overtake **2** to try hard to achieve (some desire or aim) **3** to follow the guidelines of (a plan or policy) **4** to apply oneself to (studies or interests) **5** to follow persistently or seek to become acquainted with: *was his desire to pursue and marry Carol based purely on her looks?*

THESAURUS

elimination, crushing, expulsion, suppression, liquidation, cleanup, witch hunt, eradication, ejection

purity *n* = **cleanness**, clarity, cleanliness, brilliance, genuineness, wholesomeness, fineness, clearness, pureness, faultlessness, immaculateness, untaintedness **OPPOSITE:** impurity

purport *vb* **1** = **claim**, allege, proclaim, maintain, declare, pretend, assert, pose as, profess

purpose *n* **1** = **reason**, point, idea, goal, grounds, design, aim, basis, principle, function, object, intention, objective, motive, motivation, justification, impetus, the why and wherefore **2** = **aim**, end, plan, hope, view, goal, design, project, target, wish, scheme, desire, object, intention, objective, ambition, aspiration, Holy Grail (*informal*) **3** = **determination**, commitment, resolve, will, resolution, initiative, enterprise, ambition, conviction, motivation, persistence, tenacity, firmness, constancy, single-mindedness, steadfastness
5 on purpose = **deliberately**, purposely, consciously, intentionally, knowingly, wilfully, by design, wittingly, calculatedly, designedly

purposely *adv* = **deliberately**, expressly, consciously, intentionally, knowingly, with intent, on purpose, wilfully, by design, calculatedly, designedly **OPPOSITE:** accidentally

purse *n* **1** = **pouch**, wallet, money-bag **2** (*US, Canad, Austral & NZ*) = **handbag**, bag, shoulder bag, pocket book, clutch bag **3** = **funds**, means, money, resources, treasury, wealth, exchequer, coffers, wherewithal ▹ *vb* **5** = **pucker**, close, contract, tighten, knit, wrinkle, pout, press together

pursue *vb* **1** = **follow**, track, hunt, chase, dog, attend, shadow, accompany, harry, tail (*informal*), haunt, plague, hound, stalk, harass, go after, run after, hunt down, give chase to **OPPOSITE:** flee **2** = **try for**, seek, desire, search for, aim for, aspire to, work towards, strive for, have as a goal **3** = **engage in**, follow, perform, conduct, wage, tackle, take up, work at, carry on,

DICTIONARY

6 to continue to discuss or argue (a point or subject) **pursuer** *n*
WORD ORIGIN Old French *poursivre*

pursuit ❶ *n* **1** the act of pursuing **2** an occupation or pastime

pursuivant (purse-iv-ant) *n* the lowest rank of heraldic officer
WORD ORIGIN Old French

purulent (pure-yew-lent) *adj* of, relating to, or containing pus **purulence** *n*
WORD ORIGIN Latin *purulentus*

purvey *vb* **1** to sell or provide (foodstuffs) **2** to provide or make available: *the foreign ministry used him to purvey sensitive items of diplomatic news* **purveyor** *n*
WORD ORIGIN Old French *porveeir* to provide

purview *n* **1** scope of operation: *each designation falls under the purview of a different ministry* **2** breadth or range of outlook: *he hopes that the purview of science will be widened*
WORD ORIGIN Anglo-Norman *purveu*

pus *n* the yellowish fluid that comes from inflamed or infected tissue
WORD ORIGIN Latin

push ❶ *vb* **1** (sometimes foll. by *off* or *away* etc.) to apply steady force to in order to move **2** to thrust (one's way) through something, such as a crowd **3** (sometimes foll. by *for*) to be an advocate or promoter (of): *there are many groups you can join to push for change* **4** to spur or drive (oneself or another person) in order to achieve more effort or better results: *you must be careful not to push your children too hard* **5** *informal* to sell (narcotic drugs) illegally ▷ *n* **6** the act of pushing; thrust **7** *informal* drive or determination: *everything depends on him having the push to obtain the money* **8** *informal* a special effort to achieve something: *when this push spent itself it was obvious the bid had failed* **9 the push** *Brit & NZ informal* dismissal from employment ▸ See also **push about, push off**, etc.
WORD ORIGIN Latin *pulsare*

push about *or* **around** *vb informal* to bully: *don't let them push you around*

push-bike *n Brit, Austral & NZ informal* a bicycle

push button *n* **1** an electrical switch operated by pressing a button ▷ *adj* **push-button 2** operated by a push button: *a push-button radio*

pushchair *n Brit* a small folding chair on wheels in which a small child can be wheeled around: *escalators are difficult with pushchairs*

pushed *adj* (often foll. by *for*) *informal* short of: *pushed for time*

pusher *n informal* a person who sells illegal drugs

pushing *prep* **1** almost or nearly (a certain age, speed, etc.): *pushing fifty* ▷ *adj* **2** aggressively ambitious

push off *vb informal* to go away; leave

pushover *n informal* **1** something that is easily achieved **2** a person, team, etc. that is easily taken advantage of or defeated

push-start *vb* **1** to start (a motor vehicle) by pushing it, thus turning the engine ▷ *n* **2** this process

push through *vb* to force to accept: *the President wants to push through his economic package*

pushy *adj* **pushier, pushiest** *informal* offensively assertive or ambitious

pusillanimous *adj formal* timid and cowardly: *pusillanimous behaviour* **pusillanimity** *n*
WORD ORIGIN Latin *pusillus* weak + *animus* courage

Puskas *n* **Ferenc** 1927–2006, Hungarian footballer; played for Hungary (1945–56) and Real Madrid (1958–66)

puss *n* **1** *informal* a cat **2** *slang* a girl or woman
WORD ORIGIN probably Low German

pussy[1] *n, pl* **pussies 1** Also called: **pussycat** *informal* a cat **2** *taboo slang* the female genitals
WORD ORIGIN from *puss*

pussy[2] *adj* **-sier, -siest** containing or full of pus

pussyfoot *vb informal* **1** to move about stealthily **2** to avoid committing oneself: *don't let's pussyfoot about naming the hit man*

pussy willow *n* a willow tree with silvery silky catkins

pustulate *vb* **-lating, -lated** to form into pustules

pustule *n* a small inflamed raised area of skin containing pus **pustular** *adj*
WORD ORIGIN Latin *pustula* a blister

put ❶ *vb* **putting, put 1** to cause to be (in a position or place): *he put the book on the table* **2** to cause to be (in a state or condition): *what can be done to put things right?* **3** to lay (blame, emphasis, etc.) on a person or thing: *don't try to put the blame on someone else!* **4** to set or commit (to an action, task, or duty), esp. by force: *she put him to work weeding the garden* **5** to estimate or judge: *I wouldn't put him in the same class as Verdi as a composer* **6** (foll. by *to*) to utilize: *he put his culinary skills to good use when he opened a restaurant* **7** to express: *he didn't put it quite as crudely as that* **8** to make (an end or limit): *opponents claim the scheme will put an end to much of the sailing and boating in the area* **9** to present for consideration; propose: *he put the question to the committee* **10** to invest (money) in or expend (time or energy) on: *they put a lot of money into the sport* **11** to throw or cast: *put the shot* ▷ *n* **12** a throw, esp. in putting the shot ▸ See also **put about, put across**, etc.
WORD ORIGIN Middle English *puten* to push

put about *vb* **1** to make widely known: *a rumour was put about that he had been drunk* **2** *naut* to change course

put across *vb* to communicate successfully: *he's not very good at putting his ideas across*

put aside *vb* **1** to save: *try to put some money aside in case of emergencies* **2** to disregard: *put aside adolescent fantasies of romance*

putative (pew-tat-iv) *adj formal* **1** commonly regarded as being: *the desire of the putative father to establish his possible paternity* **2** considered to exist or have existed; inferred:

P

THESAURUS

practise, participate in, prosecute, ply, go in for, apply yourself to **6 = continue**, maintain, carry on, keep on, hold to, see through, adhere to, persist in, proceed in, persevere in

pursuit *n* **1a = quest**, seeking, search, aim, aspiration, striving towards **1b = pursuing**, seeking, tracking, search, hunt, hunting, chase, trail, trailing **2 = occupation**, activity, interest, line, pleasure, hobby, pastime, vocation

push *vb* **1** (*sometimes with* **off** *or* **away** *etc.*) **= shove**, force, press, thrust, drive, knock, sweep, plunge, elbow, bump, ram, poke, propel, nudge, prod, jostle, hustle, bulldoze, impel, manhandle **OPPOSITE:** pull **2 = make** or **force your way**, move, shoulder, inch, squeeze, thrust, elbow, shove, jostle, work your way, thread your way **4 = urge**, encourage, persuade, spur, drive, press, influence, prod, constrain, incite, coerce, egg on, impel, browbeat, exert influence on **OPPOSITE:** discourage ▷ *n* **6 = shove**, thrust, butt, elbow, poke, nudge, prod, jolt **OPPOSITE:** pull **7** (*informal*) **= drive**, go (*informal*), energy, initiative, enterprise, ambition, determination, pep, vitality, vigour, dynamism, get-up-and-go (*informal*), gumption (*informal*) **9 the push** (*Brit & NZ informal*) **= dismissal**, the sack (*informal*), discharge, the boot (*slang*), your cards (*informal*), your books (*informal*), marching orders (*informal*), the kiss-off (*slang, chiefly US & Canad*), the (old) heave-ho (*informal*), the order of the boot (*slang*)

put *vb* **1 = place**, leave, set, position, rest, park (*informal*), plant, establish, lay, stick (*informal*), settle, fix, lean, deposit, dump (*informal*), prop, lay down, put down, situate, set down, stow, bung (*informal*), plonk (*informal*) **7 = express**, state, word, phrase, set, pose, utter

DICTIONARY

a putative earlier form
WORD ORIGIN Latin *putare* to consider

put away *vb* **1** to save: *it takes a lot of discipline to put away something for your old age* **2** *informal* to lock up in a prison, mental institution, etc.: *we have enough evidence to put him away for life* **3** *informal* to eat or drink in large amounts: *he put away three beers and three huge shots of brandy*

put back *vb* **1** to return to its former place **2** to move to a later time: *the finals could be put back until Monday*

put down *vb* **1** to make a written record of **2** to repress: *the rising was put down with revolting cruelty* **3** to consider: *I'd put him down as a complete fool* **4** to attribute: *the government's defeat in the election can be put down to a general desire for change* **5** to put (an animal) to death **6** *slang* to belittle or humiliate ▹*n* **put-down 7** *informal* a cruelly crushing remark

put forward *vb* **1** to propose or suggest **2** to offer the name of; nominate

put in *vb* **1** to devote (time or effort): *the competitors who did best were the ones who had put in some practice* **2** (often foll. by *for*) to apply (for a job) **3** to submit: *they have put in an official complaint* **4** *naut* to bring a vessel into port

Putnam *n* **1 Israel** 1718–90, American general in the War of Independence **2** his cousin **Rufus** 1738–1824, American soldier in the War of Independence; surveyor general of the US (1796–1803)

put off *vb* **1** to postpone: *ministers have put off making a decision until next month* **2** to evade (a person) by delay: *they tried to put him off, but he came anyway* **3** to cause dislike in: *he was put off by her appearance* **4** to cause to lose interest in: *the accident put him off sailing* **5** to distract: *a swerving cycle may have put off the driver*

put on *vb* **1** to dress oneself in **2** to adopt (an attitude or feeling) insincerely: *I don't see why you have to put on that fake American accent* **3** to present (a play or show) **4** to add: *I've put on nearly a stone since September* **5** to cause (an electrical device) to function: *she put on the light* **6** to bet (money) on a horse race or game **7** to impose: *the government has put a tax on gas*

put out *vb* **1 a** to annoy or anger **b** to disturb or confuse **2** to extinguish (a fire, light, etc.) **3** to inconvenience (someone): *I hope I'm not putting you out* **4** to select or lay out for use: *she put out two clean cloths in the kitchen* **5** to publish or broadcast: *she put out a statement denying the rumours* **6** to dislocate: *he put his back out digging the garden*

put over *vb informal* to communicate (facts or information)

putrefy *vb* **-fies, -fying, -fied** *formal* (of organic matter) to rot and produce an offensive smell
putrefaction *n*
WORD ORIGIN Latin *putrefacere*

putrescent *adj formal* becoming putrid; rotting: *putrescent toadstools*
putrescence *n*
WORD ORIGIN Latin *putrescere* to become rotten

putrid *adj* **1** (of organic matter) rotting: *putrid meat* **2** sickening or foul: *a putrid stench* **3** *informal* deficient in quality or value: *a penchant for putrid puns* **4** morally corrupt **putridity** *n*
WORD ORIGIN Latin *putrere* to be rotten

putsch *n* a violent and sudden political revolt: *an attempted putsch against the general*
WORD ORIGIN from German

putt *golf n* **1** a stroke on the green with a putter to roll the ball into or near the hole ▹*vb* **2** to strike (the ball) in this way
WORD ORIGIN Scot

puttee *n* (*usually pl*) (esp. as part of a military uniform) a strip of cloth worn wound around the leg from the ankle to the knee
WORD ORIGIN Hindi *paṭṭī*

putter *n golf* a club, usually with a short shaft, for putting

put through *vb* **1** to connect by telephone: *I'm sorry, you've been put through to the wrong extension* **2** to carry out to a conclusion

putting green *n* (on a golf course) the area of closely mown grass around the hole

Puttnam *n* **David,** Baron born 1941, British film producer. Films include *Chariots of Fire* (1981), *The Killing Fields* (1984), *Memphis Belle* (1990), and *My Life So Far* (1999)

putty *n, pl* **-ties 1** a stiff paste used to fix glass into frames and fill cracks in woodwork ▹*vb* **-ties, -tying, -tied 2** to fix or fill with putty
WORD ORIGIN French *potée* a potful

put up *vb* **1** to build or erect: *I want to put up a fence round the garden* **2** to display (a poster, sign, etc.) **3** to accommodate or be accommodated at: *can you put me up for tonight?* **4** to increase (prices) **5** to submit (a plan, case, etc.) **6** to offer: *the factory is being put up for sale* **7** to give: *they put up a good fight* **8** to provide (money) for: *they put up 35 per cent of the film's budget* **9** to nominate or be nominated as a candidate: *the party have yet to decide whether to put up a candidate* **10 put up to** to incite to: *I wonder who put them up to it?* **11 put up with** *informal* to endure or tolerate ▹*adj* **put-up 12** *informal* dishonestly or craftily prearranged: *a put-up job*

put upon *vb* to take advantage of (someone): *he's always being put upon*

putz *n US slang* a despicable or stupid person
WORD ORIGIN Yiddish *puts* ornament

Puvis de Chavannes *n* **Pierre Cécile** 1824–98, French mural painter

Pu-yi *n* **Henry** 1906–67, last emperor of China as Xuan-Tong (1908–12); emperor of the Japanese puppet state of Manchukuo as Kang-de (1934–45)

puzzle ⓣ *vb* **-zling, -zled 1** to baffle or bewilder **2 puzzle out** to solve (a problem) by mental effort **3 puzzle over** to think deeply about in an attempt to understand: *he puzzled over the squiggles and curves on the paper* ▹*n* **4** a problem that cannot be easily solved **5** a toy, game, or question presenting a problem that requires skill or ingenuity for its solution
puzzlement *n* **puzzled** *adj* **puzzler** *n* **puzzling** *adj*
WORD ORIGIN origin unknown

PVC polyvinyl chloride

PVS persistent vegetative state

PW policewoman

PWR pressurized-water reactor

pyaemia *or* **pyemia** *n med* blood poisoning with pus-forming microorganisms in the blood
WORD ORIGIN Greek *puon* pus + *haima* blood

pye-dog *or* **pi-dog** *n* a half-wild Asian dog with no owner
WORD ORIGIN Hindi *pāhī* outsider

pygmy *n, pl* **-mies 1** something that is a very small example of its type **2** an abnormally undersized person **3** a person of little importance or significance ▹*adj* **4** very small: *the pygmy anteater*
WORD ORIGIN Greek *pugmaios* undersized

Pygmy *n, pl* **-mies** a member of one of the very short peoples of Equatorial Africa

pyjamas *or US* **pajamas** *pl n* a loose-fitting jacket or top and trousers worn to sleep in
WORD ORIGIN Persian *pai* leg + *jāma* garment

pylon *n* **1** *chiefly Brit* a large vertical steel tower-like structure supporting high-tension electrical cables **2** *US & Canad* a plastic cone used to

P

THESAURUS

puzzle *vb* **1 = perplex,** beat *(slang)*, confuse, baffle, stump, bewilder, confound, mystify, faze, flummox, bemuse, nonplus ▹*n* **4 = mystery,** problem, paradox, enigma, conundrum **5 = problem,** riddle, maze, labyrinth, question, conundrum, teaser, poser, brain-teaser *(informal)*

demarcate areas, esp. on public roads
WORD ORIGIN Greek *pulōn* a gateway

Pym *n* **1 Barbara** (**Mary Crampton**) 1913–80, British novelist, noted for such comedies of middle-class English life as *Excellent Women* (1952), *A Glass of Blessings* (1958), and *The Sweet Dove Died* (1978) **2 John** ?1584–1643, leading English parliamentarian during the events leading to the Civil War. He took a prominent part in the impeachment of Buckingham (1626) and of Strafford and Laud (1640)

Pynchon *n* **Thomas** born 1937, US novelist, author of V (1963), *The Crying of Lot 49* (1967), *Gravity's Rainbow* (1973), *Mason and Dixon* (1997), and *Against the Day* (2006)

pyorrhoea *or esp. US* **pyorrhea** (pire-**ree**-a) *n med* a discharge of pus, esp. in diseases of the gums or tooth sockets
WORD ORIGIN Greek *puon* pus + *rhein* to flow

pyramid *n* **1** a huge stone building with a square base and four sloping triangular sides meeting in a point, such as the royal tombs built by the ancient Egyptians **2** *maths* a solid figure with a polygonal base and triangular sides that meet in a common vertex **pyramidal** *adj*
WORD ORIGIN Greek *puramis*

pyramid selling *n* the practice of selling distributors batches of goods which they then subdivide and sell to other distributors, this process continuing until the final distributors are left with a stock that is unsaleable except at a loss

pyre *n* a pile of wood for cremating a corpse
WORD ORIGIN Greek *pur* fire

pyrethrum (pie-**reeth**-rum) *n* **1** a Eurasian chrysanthemum with white, pink, red, or purple flowers **2** an insecticide prepared from dried pyrethrum flowers
WORD ORIGIN Greek *purethron*

pyretic (pie-**ret**-ik) *adj pathol* of, relating to, or characterized by fever
WORD ORIGIN Greek *puretos* fever

Pyrex *n trademark* a variety of heat-resistant glassware used in cookery and chemical apparatus

pyrite (**pie**-rite) *n* a yellow mineral consisting of iron sulphide in cubic crystalline form. Formula: FeS_2
WORD ORIGIN Latin *pyrites* flint

pyrites (pie-**rite**-eez) *n, pl* **-tes** **1** ▸ same as **pyrite** **2** a disulphide of a metal, esp. of copper and tin

pyromania *n psychiatry* the uncontrollable impulse and practice of setting things on fire **pyromaniac** *n, adj*
WORD ORIGIN Greek *pur* fire + *mania* madness

pyrotechnics *n* **1** the art of making fireworks **2** a firework display **3** a brilliant display of skill: *all those courtroom pyrotechnics* **pyrotechnic** *adj*
WORD ORIGIN Greek *pur* fire + *tekhnē* art

Pyrrhic victory (**pir**-ik) *n* a victory in which the victor's losses are as great as those of the defeated
WORD ORIGIN after *Pyrrhus,* who defeated the Romans in 279 BC but suffered heavy losses

Pythagoras' theorem (pie-**thag**-or-ass) *n* the theorem that in a right-angled triangle the square of the length of the hypotenuse equals the sum of the squares of the other two sides
WORD ORIGIN after *Pythagoras,* Greek philosopher and mathematician

Pytheas *n* 4th century BC, Greek navigator. He was the first Greek to visit and describe the coasts of Spain, France, and the British Isles and may have reached Iceland

python *n* a large nonpoisonous snake of Australia, Africa, and S Asia which kills its prey by crushing it with its body
WORD ORIGIN after *Python,* a dragon killed by Apollo

pyx *n Christianity* any receptacle in which the bread used in Holy Communion is kept
WORD ORIGIN Latin *pyxis* small box

Qq

DICTIONARY

Q 1 *chess* queen 2 question
q. 1 quart 2 quarter 3 question 4 quire
Q. 1 Queen 2 question
Qaboos bin Said *n* born 1940, Sultan of Oman from 1970
QC 1 Queen's Counsel 2 Quebec
QED which was to be shown or proved
WORD ORIGIN Latin *quod erat demonstrandum*
Qian Long *or* **Ch'ien-lung** *n* original name *Hong-li*. 1711–99, Chinese emperor of the Qing dynasty. He expanded the Chinese empire and was a patron of the arts
QLD *or* **Qld** Queensland
QM Quartermaster
qr. *pl* **qrs** 1 quarter 2 quire
qt *pl* **qt** *or* **qts** quart
q.t. *n* **on the q.t.** *informal* secretly
qua (kwah) *prep* in the capacity of; by virtue of being
WORD ORIGIN Latin
quack[1] *vb* 1 (of a duck) to utter a harsh guttural sound 2 to make a noise like a duck ▷*n* 3 the sound made by a duck
WORD ORIGIN imitative
quack[2] *n* 1 an unqualified person who claims medical knowledge 2 *Brit, Austral & NZ informal* a doctor **quackery** *n*
WORD ORIGIN short for *quacksalver*, from Dutch
quad[1] *n* ▸short for **quadrangle** (sense 1)
quad[2] *n informal* a quadruplet
quad[3] *n* 1 quadraphonics ▷*adj* 2 quadraphonic
quad bike *or* **quad** *n* a vehicle like a small motorcycle, with four large wheels, designed for agricultural and sporting uses
quadrangle *n* 1 a rectangular courtyard with buildings on all four sides 2 *geom* a figure consisting of four points connected by four lines **quadrangular** *adj*
WORD ORIGIN Late Latin *quadrangulum*
quadrant *n* 1 *geom* **a** a quarter of the circumference of a circle **b** the area enclosed by two perpendicular radii of a circle 2 a piece of a mechanism in the form of a quarter circle 3 an instrument formerly used in astronomy and navigation for measuring the altitudes of stars
WORD ORIGIN Latin *quadrans* a quarter
quadraphonic *adj* using four independent channels to reproduce or record sound **quadraphonics** *n*
quadrate *n* 1 a cube or square, or a square or cubelike object ▷*vb* **-rating, -rated** 2 to make square or rectangular
WORD ORIGIN Latin *quadrare* to make square
quadratic *maths n* 1 Also called: **quadratic equation** an equation in which the variable is raised to the power of two, but nowhere raised to a higher power: *solve the quadratic equation* $2x^2-3x-6=3$ ▷*adj* 2 of or relating to the second power
quadrennial *adj* 1 occurring every four years 2 lasting four years
quadri- *or before a vowel* **quadr-** *combining form* four: *quadrilateral*
WORD ORIGIN Latin
quadriceps *n anat* a muscle at the front of the thigh
WORD ORIGIN New Latin
quadrilateral *adj* 1 having four sides ▷*n* 2 a polygon with four sides
quadrille *n* 1 a square dance for four couples 2 music for this dance
WORD ORIGIN Spanish *cuadrilla*
quadrillion *n, pl* **-lions** *or* **-lion** 1 (in Britain, France, and Germany) the number represented as one followed by 24 zeros (10^{24}) 2 (in the US and Canada) the number represented as one followed by 15 zeros (10^{15})
WORD ORIGIN French *quadrillon*
quadriplegia *n* paralysis of all four limbs **quadriplegic** *adj, n*
WORD ORIGIN QUADRI- + Greek *plēssein* to strike
quadruped (kwod-roo-ped) *n* an animal, esp. a mammal, that has four legs
WORD ORIGIN Latin *quadru-* four + *pes* foot
quadruple *vb* **-pling, -pled** 1 to multiply by four ▷*adj* 2 four times as much or as many 3 consisting of four parts 4 *music* having four beats in each bar ▷*n* 5 a quantity or number four times as great as another
WORD ORIGIN Latin *quadru-* four + *-plus* -fold
quadruplet *n* one of four children born at one birth
quadruplicate *adj* 1 fourfold or quadruple ▷*vb* **-cating, -cated** 2 to multiply or be multiplied by four
WORD ORIGIN Latin *quadruplicare* to increase fourfold
quaff (kwoff) *vb old-fashioned* to drink heartily or in one draught
WORD ORIGIN perhaps imitative
quagga *n, pl* **-gas** *or* **-ga** a recently extinct zebra, striped only on the head and shoulders
WORD ORIGIN Hottentot *qüagga*
quagmire (kwog-mire) *n* a soft wet area of land that gives way under the feet; bog
WORD ORIGIN from *quag* bog + *mire*
quail[1] *n, pl* **quails** *or* **quail** a small game bird of the partridge family
WORD ORIGIN Old French *quaille*
quail[2] *vb* to shrink back with fear; cower
WORD ORIGIN origin unknown
quaint *adj* attractively unusual, esp. in an old-fashioned style
WORD ORIGIN Old French *cointe*, from Latin *cognitus* known
quake ❶ *vb* **quaking, quaked** 1 to shake or tremble with or as if with fear 2 to shudder because of instability ▷*n* 3 *informal* an earthquake
WORD ORIGIN Old English *cwacian*
Quaker *n* a member of a Christian sect, the Religious Society of Friends **Quakerism** *n*
WORD ORIGIN originally an offensive nickname
qualification ❶ *n* 1 an official record of achievement awarded on the successful completion of a course of training or passing of an examination 2 an ability, quality, or attribute, esp. one that fits a person to perform a particular job or task 3 a condition that modifies or limits; restriction 4 the act of qualifying or being qualified
qualified ❶ *adj* 1 having successfully completed a training course or passed the exams necessary in order to be entitled to work in a particular profession: *a qualified lawyer* 2 having

q

THESAURUS

quake *vb* **1, 2 = shake**, tremble, quiver, move, rock, shiver, throb, shudder, wobble, waver, vibrate, pulsate, quail, totter, convulse
qualification *n* **2 = eligibility**, quality, ability, skill, capacity, fitness, attribute, capability, endowment(s), accomplishment, achievement, aptitude, suitability, suitableness
3 = condition, restriction, proviso, requirement, rider, exception, criterion, reservation, allowance, objection, limitation, modification, exemption, prerequisite, caveat, stipulation
qualified *adj* **1, 2, 3 = capable**, trained, experienced, seasoned, able, fit, expert, talented, chartered, efficient, practised, licensed, certificated, equipped, accomplished, eligible, competent, skilful, adept, knowledgeable, proficient
OPPOSITE: untrained
4 = restricted, limited, provisional, conditional, reserved, guarded, bounded, adjusted, moderated, adapted, confined, modified,

the abilities, qualities, or attributes necessary to perform a particular job or task **3** having completed a training or degree course and gained the relevant certificates **4** limited or restricted; not wholehearted: *the mission was only a qualified success*

qualify ❶ *vb* **-fies, -fying, -fied 1** to have the abilities or attributes required in order to do or have something, such as a job: *he qualified as a teacher; she did not qualify for a State pension at that time* **2** to moderate or restrict (a statement one has made) **3** to describe or be described as having a particular quality: *it was neither witty nor subtle enough to qualify as a spoof* **4** to be successful in one stage of a competition and as a result progress to the next stage: *Lewis failed to qualify for the 100 metres* **5** *grammar* to modify the sense of (a word)
qualifier *n*
WORD ORIGIN Latin *qualis* of what kind + *facere* to make

qualitative *adj* involving or relating to distinctions based on quality

qualitative analysis *n chem* analysis of a substance to determine its constituents

quality ❶ *n, pl* **-ties 1** degree or standard of excellence **2** a distinguishing characteristic or attribute **3** the basic character or nature of something **4** a feature of personality **5** (formerly) high social status ▷*adj* **6** excellent or superior: *a quality product*
WORD ORIGIN Latin *qualis* of what sort

quality assurance *n commerce* the process of verifying that a product conforms to required standards, often performed by an independent assessor

quality control *n* checking of the relative quality of a manufactured product, usually by testing samples

qualm (kwahm) *n* **1** a pang of conscience; scruple **2** a sudden sensation of misgiving **3** a sudden feeling of sickness or nausea
WORD ORIGIN Old English *cwealm* death or plague

quandary *n, pl* **-ries** a situation in which it is difficult to decide what to do; predicament; dilemma
WORD ORIGIN origin unknown

quandong (kwon-dong) *n* **1** a small Australian tree with edible fruit and nuts used in preserves **2** an Australian tree with pale timber

quango *n, pl* **-gos** a semipublic government-financed administrative body whose members are appointed by the government
WORD ORIGIN *qu(asi-)a(utonomous) n(on)g(overnmental) o(rganization)*

Quant *n* **Mary.** born 1934, British fashion designer, whose Chelsea Look of miniskirts and geometrically patterned fabrics dominated London fashion in the 1960s

quantify *vb* **-fies, -fying, -fied** to discover or express the quantity of
quantifiable *adj* **quantification** *n*
WORD ORIGIN Latin *quantus* how much + *facere* to make

quantitative *adj* **1** involving considerations of amount or size **2** capable of being measured

quantitative analysis *n chem* analysis of a substance to determine the proportions of its constituents

quantitative easing *or* **quantitive easing** *n* the practice of increasing the supply of money in order to stimulate economic activity

quantity ❶ *n, pl* **-ties 1** a specified or definite amount or number **2** the aspect of anything that can be measured, weighed, or counted **3** a large amount **4** *maths* an entity having a magnitude that may be denoted by a numerical expression
WORD ORIGIN Latin *quantus* how much

quantity surveyor *n* a person who estimates the cost of the materials and labour necessary for a construction job

quantum *n, pl* **-ta 1** an amount or quantity, esp. a specific amount **2** *physics* the smallest quantity of some physical property that a system can possess ▷*adj* **3** of or designating a major breakthrough or sudden advance: *a quantum leap in business computing*
WORD ORIGIN Latin *quantus* how much

quantum theory *n* a theory concerning the behaviour of physical systems based on the idea that they can only possess certain properties, such as energy and angular momentum, in discrete amounts (quanta)

quarantine *n* **1** a period of isolation, esp. of people or animals arriving from abroad, to prevent the spread of disease ▷*vb* **-tining, -tined 2** to isolate in or as if in quarantine
WORD ORIGIN Italian *quarantina* period of forty days

quark *n physics* the hypothetical elementary particle supposed to be a fundamental unit of all baryons and mesons
WORD ORIGIN special use of a word coined by James Joyce in the novel *Finnegans Wake*

Quarles *n* **Francis.** 1592–1644, English poet

quarrel ❶ *n* **1** an angry disagreement; argument **2** a cause of dispute; grievance ▷*vb* **-relling, -relled** *or US* **-reling, -reled** (often foll. by *with*) **3** to engage in a disagreement or dispute; argue **4** to find fault; complain
WORD ORIGIN Latin *querella* complaint

quarrelsome *adj* inclined to quarrel or disagree

quarry[1] *n, pl* **-ries 1** a place where stone is dug from the surface of the earth ▷*vb* **-ries, -rying, -ried 2** to extract (stone) from a quarry
WORD ORIGIN Old French *quarriere*

quarry[2] ❶ *n, pl* **-ries 1** an animal that is being hunted; prey **2** anything pursued

THESAURUS

tempered, cautious, refined, amended, contingent, tentative, hesitant, circumscribed, equivocal **OPPOSITE:** unconditional

qualify *vb* **2 = restrict**, limit, reduce, vary, ease, moderate, adapt, modify, regulate, diminish, temper, soften, restrain, lessen, mitigate, abate, tone down, assuage, modulate, circumscribe

quality *n* **1a = standard**, standing, class, condition, value, rank, grade, merit, classification, calibre **1b = excellence**, status, merit, position, value, worth, distinction, virtue, superiority, calibre, eminence, pre-eminence **2, 4 = characteristic**, feature, attribute, point, side, mark, property, aspect, streak, trait, facet, quirk, peculiarity, idiosyncrasy **3 = nature**, character, constitution, make, sort, kind, worth, description, essence

quantity *n* **1 = amount**, lot, total, sum, part, portion, quota, aggregate, number, allotment **2 = size**, measure, mass, volume, length, capacity, extent, bulk, magnitude, greatness, expanse

quarrel *n* **1 = disagreement**, fight, row, difference (of opinion), argument, dispute, controversy, breach, scrap *(informal)*, disturbance, misunderstanding, contention, feud, fray, brawl, spat, squabble, strife, wrangle, skirmish, vendetta, discord, fracas, commotion, tiff, altercation, broil, tumult, dissension, affray, shindig *(informal)*, disputation, dissidence, shindy *(informal)*, bagarre *(French)*, biffo *(Austral slang)* **OPPOSITE:** accord
▷*vb* **3 = disagree**, fight, argue, row, clash, dispute, scrap *(informal)*, differ, fall out *(informal)*, brawl, squabble, spar, wrangle, bicker, be at odds, lock horns, cross swords, fight like cat and dog, go at it hammer and tongs, altercate **OPPOSITE:** get on *or* along (with)

quarry[2] *n* **1, 2 = prey**, victim, game, goal, aim, prize, objective

DICTIONARY

WORD ORIGIN Middle English *quirre* entrails offered to the hounds
quarry tile *n* an unglazed floor tile
quart *n* a unit of liquid measure equal to one quarter of a gallon or two pints (1.136 litres)
WORD ORIGIN Latin *quartus* fourth
quarter ● *n* **1** one of four equal parts of something such as an object or quantity **2** the fraction equal to one divided by four (¼) **3** a fourth part of a year; three months **4** *Brit informal* a unit of weight equal to four ounces (113.4 grams) **5** a region or district of a town or city: *the French quarter of New Orleans* **6** a region, direction, or point of the compass **7** *US & Canad* a coin worth 25 cents **8** ▸short for **quarter-hour** **9** *astron* **a** one fourth of the moon's period of revolution around the earth **b** either of two phases of the moon when half of the lighted surface is visible **10** (*sometimes pl*) an unspecified person or group of people: *it met stiff opposition in some quarters* **11** mercy or pity shown to a defeated opponent: *no quarter was asked or given* **12** any of the four limbs of a quadruped ▹*vb* **13** to divide into four equal parts **14** (formerly) to dismember (a human body) **15** to billet or be billeted in lodgings **16** *heraldry* to divide (a shield) into four separate bearings ▹*adj* **17** being or consisting of one of four equal parts ▸See also **quarters**
WORD ORIGIN Latin *quartus* fourth
quarterback *n* a player in American football who directs attacking play
quarter day *n* *Brit* any of four days in the year when certain payments become due
quarterdeck *n* *naut* the rear part of the upper deck of a ship, traditionally for official or ceremonial use
quarterfinal *n* the round before the semifinal in a competition
quarter-hour *n* **1** a period of 15 minutes **2** either of the points of time 15 minutes before or after the hour
quarterlight *n* *Brit* a small pivoted window in the door of a car for ventilation
quarterly *adj* **1** occurring, done, due, or issued at intervals of three months ▹*n, pl* **-lies** **2** a periodical issued every three months ▹*adv* **3** once every three months
quartermaster *n* **1** a military officer responsible for accommodation, food, and equipment **2** a naval officer responsible for navigation
quarters ● *pl n* accommodation, esp. as provided for military personnel
quarter sessions *n* (formerly) a court with limited jurisdiction, held four times a year
quarterstaff *n, pl* **-staves** a stout iron-tipped wooden staff about 6ft long, formerly used as a weapon
WORD ORIGIN origin unknown
quartet *n* **1** a group of four singers or instrumentalists **2** a piece of music for four performers **3** any group of four
WORD ORIGIN Italian *quarto* fourth
quartile *n* **1** one of three values of a variable dividing its distribution into four groups with equal frequencies ▹*adj* **2** of a quartile
quarto *n, pl* **-tos** a book size resulting from folding a sheet of paper into four leaves or eight pages
WORD ORIGIN New Latin *in quarto* in quarter
quartz *n* a hard glossy mineral consisting of crystalline silicon dioxide
WORD ORIGIN German *Quarz*
quartz clock *or* **watch** *n* a very accurate clock or watch that is operated by a vibrating quartz crystal
quartz crystal *n* a thin plate or rod cut from a piece of quartz and ground so that it vibrates at a particular frequency
quasar (**kway**-zar) *n* any of a class of extremely distant starlike objects that are powerful sources of radio waves and other forms of energy
WORD ORIGIN *quas(i-stell)ar (radio source)*
quash ● *vb* **1** to officially reject (something, such as a judgment or decision) as invalid **2** to defeat or suppress forcefully and completely
WORD ORIGIN Latin *quassare* to shake
quasi- (**kway**-zie) *combining form* **1** almost but not really; seemingly: *a quasi-religious cult* **2** resembling but not actually being; so-called: *a quasi-scholar*
WORD ORIGIN Latin: as if
quassia (**kwosh**-a) *n* **1** a tropical American tree with bitter bark and wood **2** the wood of this tree or a bitter compound extracted from it, used in insecticides
WORD ORIGIN after Graman *Quassi*, who discovered its medicinal value
quaternary *adj* consisting of four parts
WORD ORIGIN Latin *quaterni* by fours
Quaternary *adj* *geol* of the most recent period of geological time, which started about one million years ago
quatrain *n* a stanza or poem of four lines
WORD ORIGIN French, from Latin *quattuor* four
quatrefoil *n* **1** a leaf composed of four leaflets **2** *archit* a carved ornament of four arcs about a common centre
WORD ORIGIN Old French *quatre* four + *-foil* leaflet
quattrocento (kwat-roe-**chen**-toe) *n* the 15th century, esp. in reference to Renaissance Italian art
WORD ORIGIN Italian: four hundred (short for fourteen hundred)
quaver *vb* **1** (esp. of the voice) to quiver or tremble **2** to say or sing (something) with a trembling voice ▹*n* **3** *music* a note having the time value of an eighth of a semibreve **4** a tremulous sound or note **quavering** *adj*
WORD ORIGIN Germanic
quay (**kee**) *n* a wharf built parallel to the shoreline
WORD ORIGIN Old French *kai*
Quayle *n* Sir (**John**) **Anthony**. 1913–89, British actor and theatrical producer: director (1948–56) of the Shakespeare Memorial Theatre
Que. Quebec
queasy *adj* **-sier, -siest** **1** having the feeling that one is about to vomit; nauseous **2** feeling or causing uneasiness **queasily** *adv* **queasiness** *n*
WORD ORIGIN origin unknown
queen ● *n* **1** a female sovereign who is the official ruler or head of state **2** the wife of a king **3** a woman, thing, or place considered the best or most important of her or its kind: *the rose is considered the queen of garden flowers* **4** *slang* an effeminate male homosexual **5** the only fertile

q

THESAURUS

quarter *n* **5 = district**, region, neighbourhood, place, point, part, side, area, position, station, spot, territory, zone, location, province, colony, locality **11 = mercy**, pity, compassion, favour, charity, sympathy, tolerance, kindness, forgiveness, indulgence, clemency, leniency, forbearance, lenity ▹*vb* **15 = accommodate**, house, lodge, place, board, post, station, install, put up, billet, give accommodation, provide with accommodation
quarters *pl n* **= lodgings**, rooms, accommodation, post, station, chambers, digs (*Brit informal*), shelter, lodging, residence, dwelling, barracks, abode, habitation, billet, domicile, cantonment (*military*)
quash *vb* **1 = annul**, overturn, reverse, cancel, overthrow, set aside, void, revoke, overrule, rescind, invalidate, nullify, declare null and void **2 = suppress**, crush, put down, beat, destroy, overthrow, squash, subdue, repress, quell, extinguish, quench, extirpate
queen *n* **1, 2 = sovereign**, ruler, monarch, leader, Crown, princess, majesty, head of state, Her Majesty, empress, crowned head **3 = leading light**, star, favourite, celebrity, darling, mistress, idol,

DICTIONARY

female in a colony of bees, wasps, or ants **6** a playing card with a picture of a queen on it **7** a chessman, able to move in a straight line in any direction ▷*vb* **8** *chess* to promote (a pawn) to a queen when it reaches the eighth rank **9 queen it** *informal* to behave in an overbearing manner: *she is more beautiful than ever and still queening it over everybody* **queenly** *adj*
WORD ORIGIN Old English *cwēn*
Queen *n* **Ellery**. pseudonym of *Frederic Dannay* (1905–82) and *Manfred B. Lee* (1905–71), US co-authors of detective novels featuring a sleuth also called Ellery Queen
Queen Anne *adj* **1** of or in an 18th-century style of furniture characterized by the use of curves **2** of or in an early 18th-century English architectural style characterized by the use of red bricks and classical ornamentation
queen consort *n* the wife of a reigning king
queen mother *n* the widow of a former king who is also the mother of the reigning sovereign
queen post *n building* one of a pair of vertical posts that connect the tie beam of a truss to the principal rafters of a roof
Queen's Bench *n* (in Britain) one of the divisions of the High Court of Justice
Queensberry rules *pl n* **1** the code of rules followed in modern boxing **2** *informal* gentlemanly conduct, esp. in a dispute
WORD ORIGIN after the ninth Marquess of *Queensberry*, who originated the rules
Queen's Counsel *n* **1** (in Britain, Australia and New Zealand) a barrister or advocate appointed Counsel to the Crown **2** (in Canada and New Zealand) an honorary title bestowed on lawyers with long experience
Queen's English *n* correctly spoken and written British English
queen's evidence *n English law* evidence given for the Crown against former associates in crime by an accomplice
Queen's Guide *or* **Scout** *n* a Guide or Scout who has passed the highest tests of proficiency
queen's highway *n* **1** (in Britain) any public road or right of way **2** (in Canada) a main road maintained by the provincial government
queer ❶ *adj* **1** not normal or usual; odd or strange **2** dubious; shady **3** *Brit* faint, giddy, or queasy **4** *informal, usually offensive* homosexual **5** *informal* eccentric or slightly mad ▷*n* **6** *informal, usually offensive* a homosexual ▷*vb* **7 queer someone's pitch** *informal* to spoil or thwart someone's chances of something
WORD ORIGIN origin unknown
queer street *n* **in queer street** *informal* in a difficult financial situation, esp. debt or bankruptcy
quell *vb* **1** to suppress (rebellion or unrest); subdue **2** to overcome or allay
WORD ORIGIN Old English *cwellan* to kill
quench *vb* **1** to satisfy (one's thirst) **2** to put out; extinguish **3** to suppress or subdue **4** *metallurgy* to cool (hot metal) by plunging it into cold water
WORD ORIGIN Old English *ācwencan* to extinguish
Queneau *n* **Raymond**. 1903–76. French writer, influenced in the 1920s by surrealism. His novels include *Zazie dans le métro* (1959)
quern *n* a stone hand mill for grinding corn
WORD ORIGIN Old English *cweorn*
querulous (kwer-yew-luss) *adj* complaining; whining or peevish **querulously** *adv*
WORD ORIGIN Latin *queri* to complain
query ❶ *n, pl* **-ries 1** a question, esp. one expressing doubt **2** a question mark ▷*vb* **-ries, -rying, -ried 3** to express uncertainty, doubt, or an objection concerning (something) **4** to express as a query; ask
WORD ORIGIN Latin *quaere* ask!
quesadilla *n Mexican cookery* a toasted tortilla filled with cheese and sometimes other ingredients
WORD ORIGIN Spanish, diminutive of *queso* cheese
Quesnay *n* **François** 1694–1774, French political economist, encyclopedist, and physician. He propounded the theory championed by the physiocrats in his *Tableau économique* (1758)
quest ❶ *n* **1** a looking for or seeking; search **2** the object of a search; a goal or target ▷*vb* **3 quest for** to go in search of **4** (of dogs) to search for game
WORD ORIGIN Old French *queste*
question ❶ *n* **1** a form of words addressed to a person in order to obtain an answer; interrogative sentence **2** a point at issue: *they were silent on the question of social justice* **3** a difficulty or uncertainty **4 a** an act of asking **b** an investigation into some problem **5** a motion presented for debate **6 beyond (all) question** beyond (any) doubt **7 call something into question a** to make something the subject of disagreement **b** to cast doubt upon the validity or truth of something **8 in question** under discussion: *the area in question was not contaminated* **9 out of the question** beyond consideration; impossible ▷*vb* **10** to put a question or questions to (a person); interrogate **11** to make (something) the subject of dispute **12** to express uncertainty; doubt
WORD ORIGIN Latin *quaestio*
questionable ❶ *adj* **1** (esp. of a person's morality or honesty) doubtful **2** of disputable value or

q

THESAURUS

big name, doyenne
queer *adj* **1, 2 = strange**, odd, funny, unusual, extraordinary, remarkable, curious, weird, peculiar, abnormal, rum *(Brit slang)*, uncommon, erratic, singular, eerie, unnatural, unconventional, uncanny, disquieting, unorthodox, outlandish, left-field *(informal)*, anomalous, droll, atypical, outré
OPPOSITE: normal
3 = faint, dizzy, giddy, queasy, light-headed, reeling
query *n* **1a = question**, inquiry, enquiry, problem, demand
1b = doubt, suspicion, reservation, objection, hesitation, scepticism ▷*vb*
3 = question, challenge, doubt, suspect, dispute, object to, distrust, mistrust, call into question, disbelieve, feel uneasy about, throw doubt on, harbour reservations about **4 = ask**, inquire *or* enquire, question
quest *n* **1 = search**, hunt, mission, enterprise, undertaking, exploration, crusade
question *n* **1 = inquiry**, enquiry, query, investigation, examination, interrogation **OPPOSITE:** answer
2 = issue, point, matter, subject, problem, debate, proposal, theme, motion, topic, proposition, bone of contention, point at issue
3 = difficulty, problem, doubt, debate, argument, dispute, controversy, confusion, uncertainty, query, contention, misgiving, can of worms *(informal)*, dubiety ▷*vb* **9 out of the question = impossible**, unthinkable, inconceivable, not on *(informal)*, hopeless, unimaginable, unworkable, unattainable, unobtainable, not feasible, impracticable, unachievable, unrealizable, not worth considering, not to be thought of
10 = interrogate, cross-examine, interview, examine, investigate, pump *(informal)*, probe, grill *(informal)*, quiz, ask questions, sound out, catechize **11, 12 = dispute**, challenge, doubt, suspect, oppose, query, distrust, mistrust, call into question, disbelieve, impugn, cast aspersions on, cast doubt upon, controvert
OPPOSITE: accept
questionable *adj* **1, 2 = dubious**, suspect, doubtful, controversial, uncertain, suspicious, dodgy *(Brit,*

DICTIONARY

authority **questionably** *adv*
questioner *n* a person who asks a question
questioning *adj* **1** proceeding from or characterized by doubt or uncertainty **2** intellectually inquisitive: *a questioning mind* ▷ *n* **3** interrogation
question mark *n* **1** the punctuation mark (?), used at the end of questions **2** a doubt or uncertainty: *a question mark still hangs over their success*
question master *n Brit* the person chairing a radio or television quiz or panel game
questionnaire ❶ *n* a set of questions on a form, used to collect statistical information or opinions from people
question time *n* (in parliamentary bodies of the British type) the time set aside each day for questions to government ministers
queue ❶ *n* **1** a line of people or vehicles waiting for something ▷ *vb* **queuing** *or* **queueing, queued 2** (often foll. by *up*) to form or remain in a line while waiting
WORD ORIGIN Latin *cauda* tail
Quevedo y Villegas *n* **Francisco Gómez de.** 1580–1645, Spanish poet and writer, noted for his satires and the picaresque novel *La historia de la vida del Buscón* (1626)
Quezon y Molina *n* **Manuel Luis.** 1878–1944, Philippine statesman: first president of the Philippines (from 1935) and head of the government in exile after the Japanese conquest of the islands in World War II
quibble *vb* **-bling, -bled 1** to make trivial objections ▷ *n* **2** a trivial objection or equivocation, esp. one used to avoid an issue **3** *archaic* a pun
WORD ORIGIN origin unknown
quiche (keesh) *n* a savoury flan with an egg custard filling to which cheese, bacon, or vegetables are added
WORD ORIGIN French
quick ❶ *adj* **1** characterized by rapidity of movement or action; fast **2** lasting or taking a short time **3** immediate or prompt: *her quick action minimized the damage* **4** eager or ready to perform (an action): *quick to condemn* **5** responsive to stimulation; alert; lively: *they were impressed by his quick mind* **6** easily excited or aroused: *he is impulsive and has a quick temper* **7** nimble in one's movements or actions; deft: *she has quick hands* ▷ *n* **8** any area of sensitive flesh, esp. that under a nail **9 cut someone to the quick** to hurt someone's feelings deeply **10 the quick** *archaic* living people ▷ *adv* **11** in a rapid manner; swiftly **quickly** *adv* **quickness** *n*
WORD ORIGIN Old English *cwicu* living
quick-change artist *n* an actor or entertainer who undertakes several rapid changes of costume during a performance
quicken ❶ *vb* **1** to make or become faster; accelerate **2** to impart to or receive vigour or enthusiasm: *science quickens the imagination* **3 a** (of a fetus) to begin to show signs of life **b** (of a pregnant woman) to reach the stage of pregnancy at which movements of the fetus can be felt
quick-freeze *vb* **-freezing, -froze, -frozen** to preserve (food) by subjecting it to rapid refrigeration
quickie *informal n* **1** anything made or done rapidly ▷ *adj* **2** made or done rapidly: *a quickie divorce*
quicklime *n* a white caustic solid, mainly composed of calcium oxide, used in the manufacture of glass and steel
quicksand *n* a deep mass of loose wet sand that submerges anything on top of it
quickset *chiefly Brit adj* **1** (of plants or cuttings) planted so as to form a hedge ▷ *n* **2** a hedge composed of such plants
quicksilver *n* the metal mercury
quickstep *n* **1** a modern ballroom dance in rapid quadruple time **2** music for this dance
quick-tempered *adj* easy to anger
quick-witted *adj* having a keenly alert mind **quick-wittedness** *n*
quid[1] *n, pl* **quid** *Brit slang* **1** a pound (sterling) **2 be quids in** to be in a very favourable or advantageous position
WORD ORIGIN origin unknown
quid[2] *n* a piece of tobacco for chewing
WORD ORIGIN Old English *cwidu* chewing resin
quiddity *n, pl* **-ties 1** the essential nature of something **2** a petty or trifling distinction
WORD ORIGIN Latin *quid* what
quid pro quo *n, pl* **quid pro quos** one thing, esp. an advantage or object, given in exchange for another
WORD ORIGIN Latin: something for something
quiescent (kwee-ess-ent) *adj formal* quiet, inactive, or dormant **quiescence** *n*
WORD ORIGIN Latin *quiescere* to rest
quiet ❶ *adj* **1** characterized by an absence of noise **2** calm or tranquil: *the sea is quiet today* **3** untroubled: *a quiet life* **4** not busy: *business is quiet this morning* **5** private or secret: *I had a quiet word with her* **6** free from anger, impatience, or other extreme emotion **7** not showy: *quiet colours; a quiet wedding* **8** modest or reserved: *quiet humour* ▷ *n* **9** the state of being silent, peaceful, or untroubled **10 on**

q

THESAURUS

Austral & NZ informal), unreliable, shady (*informal*), debatable, unproven, fishy (*informal*), moot, arguable, iffy (*informal*), equivocal, problematical, disputable, controvertible, dubitable, shonky (*Austral & NZ informal*)
OPPOSITE: indisputable
questionnaire *n* **= set of questions**, form, survey form, question sheet
queue *n* **1 = line**, row, file, train, series, chain, string, column, sequence, succession, procession, crocodile (*Brit informal*), progression, cavalcade, concatenation
quick *adj* **1 = fast**, swift, speedy, express, active, cracking (*Brit informal*), smart, rapid, fleet, brisk, hasty, headlong, nippy (*informal*), pdq (*slang*) **OPPOSITE:** slow
2 = brief, passing, hurried, flying, fleeting, summary, lightning, short-lived, hasty, cursory, perfunctory **OPPOSITE:** long
3 = immediate, instant, prompt, sudden, abrupt, instantaneous, expeditious **4, 6 = excitable**, passionate, impatient, abrupt, hasty, irritable, touchy, curt, petulant, irascible, testy **OPPOSITE:** calm
5 = intelligent, bright (*informal*), alert, sharp, acute, smart, clever, all there (*informal*), shrewd, discerning, astute, receptive, perceptive, quick-witted, quick on the uptake (*informal*), nimble-witted **OPPOSITE:** stupid
quicken *vb* **1 = speed up**, hurry, accelerate, hasten, gee up (*informal*)
2 = stimulate, inspire, arouse, excite, strengthen, revive, refresh, activate, animate, rouse, incite, resuscitate, energize, revitalize, kindle, galvanize, invigorate, reinvigorate, vitalize, vivify
quiet *adj* **1a = soft**, low, muted, lowered, whispered, faint, suppressed, stifled, hushed, muffled, inaudible, indistinct, low-pitched **OPPOSITE:** loud
1b = peaceful, silent, hushed, soundless, noiseless **OPPOSITE:** noisy
1c = silent, dumb **2, 6 = calm**, peaceful, tranquil, contented, gentle, mild, serene, pacific, placid, restful, untroubled, chilled (*informal*)
OPPOSITE: exciting
3 = still, motionless, calm, peaceful, tranquil, untroubled
OPPOSITE: troubled
8 = reserved, retiring, shy, collected, gentle, mild, composed, serene, sedate, meek, placid, docile, unflappable (*informal*), phlegmatic, peaceable, imperturbable, equable, even-tempered, unexcitable
OPPOSITE: excitable
▷ *n* **9 = peace**, rest, tranquillity, ease, silence, solitude, serenity, stillness, repose, calmness, quietness,

DICTIONARY

the quiet without other people knowing ▷*vb* **11** to make or become calm or silent **quietly** *adv* **quietness** *n*
WORD ORIGIN Latin *quies* repose
quieten *vb Brit & NZ* **1** (often foll. by *down*) to make or become calm or silent **2** to allay (fear or doubts)
quietism *n formal* passivity and calmness of mind towards external events **quietist** *n, adj*
quietude *n formal* quietness, peace, or tranquillity
quietus *n, pl* **-tuses 1** *literary* a release from life; death **2** the discharge or settlement of debts or duties
WORD ORIGIN Latin *quietus est*, literally: he is at rest
quiff *n Brit* a tuft of hair brushed up above the forehead
WORD ORIGIN origin unknown
quill *n* **1** Also called: **quill pen** a feather made into a pen **2 a** any of the large stiff feathers of the wing or tail of a bird **b** the hollow stem of a feather **3** any of the stiff hollow spines of a porcupine or hedgehog
WORD ORIGIN origin unknown
Quiller-Couch *n* Sir **Arthur** (**Thomas**), known as Q. 1863–1944, British critic and novelist, who edited the *Oxford Book of English Verse* (1900)
quilling *n* a decorative craftwork in which material such as glass, fabric or paper is formed into small bands or rolls that form the basis of a design
quilt ❶ *n* **1** a cover for a bed, consisting of a soft filling sewn between two layers of material, usually with crisscross seams **2** a continental quilt; duvet ▷*vb* **3** to stitch together two layers of (fabric) with padding between them **quilted** *adj*
WORD ORIGIN Old French *coilte* mattress
quin *n* a quintuplet
quince *n* the acid-tasting pear-shaped fruit of an Asian tree, used in preserves
WORD ORIGIN Greek *kudōnion*
quincunx *n* a group of five objects arranged in the shape of a rectangle with one at each corner and the fifth in the centre
WORD ORIGIN Latin: five twelfths; in ancient Rome, this was a coin marked with five spots
Quine *n* **Willard van Orman.** 1908–2000, US philosopher. His works include *Word and Object* (1960), *Philosophy of Logic* (1970), *The Roots of Reference* (1973), and *The Logic of Sequences* (1990)
quinine *n* a bitter drug extracted from cinchona bark, used as a tonic and formerly in malaria therapy
WORD ORIGIN Spanish *quina* cinchona bark
Quinn *n* **Anthony.** 1915–2001, US film actor, born in Mexico: noted esp. for his performances in *La Strada* (1954) and *Zorba the Greek* (1964)
quinquennial *adj* occurring once every five years or over a period of five years
quinquereme *n* an ancient Roman galley with five banks of oars
WORD ORIGIN Latin *quinque* five + *remus* oar
quinsy *n* inflammation of the tonsils and throat, with abscesses
WORD ORIGIN Greek *kuōn* dog + *ankhein* to strangle
quint *n US & Canad* a quintuplet
quintal *n* **1** a unit of weight equal to (esp. in Britain) 112 pounds (50.85 kg) or (esp. in US) 100 pounds (45.36 kg) **2** a unit of weight equal to 100 kilograms
WORD ORIGIN Arabic *qintār*
quintessence *n* **1** the perfect representation of a quality or state **2** an extract of a substance containing its central nature in its most concentrated form **quintessential** *adj*
WORD ORIGIN Medieval Latin *quinta essentia* the fifth essence
quintet *n* **1** a group of five singers or instrumentalists **2** a piece of music for five performers **3** any group of five
WORD ORIGIN Italian *quintetto*
Quintilian *n* Latin name *Marcus Fabius Quintilianus*. ?35–?96 AD, Roman rhetorician and teacher
quintillion *n, pl* **-lions** *or* **-lion 1** (in Britain, France, and Germany) the number represented as one followed by 30 zeros (10^{30}) **2** (in the US and Canada) the number represented as one followed by 18 zeros (10^{18})
WORD ORIGIN Latin *quintus* fifth
quintuple *vb* **-pling, -pled 1** to multiply by five ▷*adj* **2** five times as much or as many **3** consisting of five parts ▷*n* **4** a quantity or number five times as great as another
WORD ORIGIN Latin *quintus* fifth + *-plus* -fold
quintuplet *n* one of five children born at one birth
quip ❶ *n* **1** a witty saying ▷*vb* **quipping, quipped 2** to make a quip
WORD ORIGIN probably from Latin *quippe* indeed, to be sure
quire *n* a set of 24 or 25 sheets of paper
WORD ORIGIN Old French *quaier*
quirk *n* **1** a peculiarity of character; mannerism or foible **2** an unexpected twist or turn: *a strange quirk of fate* **quirky** *adj*
WORD ORIGIN origin unknown
quisling *n* a traitor who aids an occupying enemy force; collaborator
WORD ORIGIN after Vidkun *Quisling*, Norwegian collaborator with the Nazis
quit ❶ *vb* **quitting, quit 1** to stop (doing something) **2** to resign (from): *the Prime Minister's decision to quit; he quit his job as a salesman* **3** to leave (a place) **quitter** *n*
WORD ORIGIN Old French *quitter*
quitch *or* **quitch grass** *n* ▸ same as **couch grass**
quite ❶ *adv* **1** (*not used with a negative*) to a greater than average extent; somewhat: *he found her quite attractive* **2** absolutely: *you're quite right* **3** in actuality; truly **4 quite a** *or* **an** of an exceptional kind: *she is quite a girl* **5 quite something** a remarkable thing or person ▷*interj* **6** an expression used to indicate agreement
WORD ORIGIN adverbial use of *quite* (adjective) quit, free of
quits *adj informal* **1** on an equal footing **2 call it quits** to end a dispute or contest, agreeing that honours are even
quittance *n* **1** release from debt or other obligation **2** a document certifying this
WORD ORIGIN Old French *quitter* to release from obligation
quiver[1] *vb* **1** to shake with a tremulous movement; tremble ▷*n* **2** a shaking or trembling **quivering** *adj*
WORD ORIGIN obsolete *cwiver* quick, nimble

q

THESAURUS

peacefulness, restfulness
OPPOSITE: noise
quilt *n* **1, 2 = bedspread**, duvet, comforter (*US*), downie (*informal*), coverlet, eiderdown, counterpane, doona (*Austral*), continental quilt
quip *n* **1 = joke**, sally, jest, riposte, wisecrack (*informal*), retort, counterattack, pleasantry, repartee, gibe, witticism, bon mot, badinage
quit *vb* **1 = stop**, give up, cease, end, drop, abandon, suspend, halt, discontinue, belay (*nautical*)
OPPOSITE: continue
2 = resign (from), leave, retire (from), pull out (of), surrender, chuck (*informal*), step down (from) (*informal*), relinquish, renounce, pack in (*informal*), abdicate **3 = leave**, depart from, go out of, abandon, desert, exit, withdraw from, forsake, go away from, pull out from, decamp from
quite *adv* **1 = somewhat**, rather, fairly, reasonably, kind of (*informal*), pretty (*informal*), relatively, moderately, to some extent, comparatively, to some degree, to a certain extent **2 = absolutely**, perfectly, completely, totally, fully, entirely, precisely, considerably, wholly, in all respects, without reservation

DICTIONARY

quiver² *n* a case for holding or carrying arrows
WORD ORIGIN Old French *cuivre*

quixotic (kwik-**sot**-ik) *adj* unrealistically optimistic or chivalrous **quixotically** *adv*
WORD ORIGIN after Don *Quixote* in Cervantes' romance

quiz ⓣ *n, pl* **quizzes** **1** an entertainment in which the knowledge of the players is tested by a series of questions **2** any set of quick questions designed to test knowledge **3** an investigation by close questioning ▷ *vb* **quizzing, quizzed** **4** to investigate by close questioning; interrogate
WORD ORIGIN origin unknown

quizzical *adj* questioning and mocking or supercilious: *the question elicits a quizzical expression* **quizzically** *adv*

quod *n Brit slang* a jail
WORD ORIGIN origin unknown

quoin *n* **1** an external corner of a wall **2** the stone forming the outer corner of a wall; a cornerstone **3** a wedge
WORD ORIGIN variant of *coin* (in former sense of corner)

quoit *n* a large ring used in the game of quoits
WORD ORIGIN origin unknown

quoits *n* a game in which quoits are tossed at a stake in the ground in attempts to encircle it

quokka *n* a small Australian wallaby

quondam *adj formal* of an earlier time; former: *her quondam employers*
WORD ORIGIN Latin

quorate *adj* having or being a quorum: *the meeting is now quorate*

Quorn *n trademark* a vegetable protein used as a meat substitute

quorum *n* the minimum number of members required to be present in a meeting or assembly before any business can be transacted
WORD ORIGIN Latin, literally: of whom

quota ⓣ *n* **1** the share that is due from, due to, or allocated to a person or group **2** the prescribed number or quantity allowed, required, or admitted
WORD ORIGIN Latin *quotus* of what number

quotation ⓣ *n* **1** a written or spoken passage repeated exactly in a later work, speech, or conversation, usually with an acknowledgment of its source **2** the act of quoting **3** an estimate of costs submitted by a contractor to a prospective client

quotation marks *pl n* the punctuation marks used to begin and end a quotation, either "and" or 'and'

quote ⓣ *vb* **quoting, quoted** **1** to repeat (words) exactly from (an earlier work, speech, or conversation), usually with an acknowledgment of their source **2** to state a price for goods or a job of work **3** to put quotation marks round (words) ▷ *n* **4** *informal* a quotation **5** **quotes** *informal* quotation marks ▷ *interj* **6** an expression used to indicate that the words that follow are a quotation **quotable** *adj*
WORD ORIGIN Medieval Latin *quotare* to assign reference numbers to passages

quoth *vb archaic* (foll. by *I, he or she*) said
WORD ORIGIN Old English *cwæth*

quotidian *adj* **1** daily **2** *literary* commonplace **3** (esp. of fever) recurring daily
WORD ORIGIN Latin *quotidianus*

quotient *n* the result of the division of one number or quantity by another
WORD ORIGIN Latin *quotiens* how often

Qu Qiu Bai *or* **Ch'ü Ch'iu-pai** *n* 1889–1935, Chinese communist leader who was also an important literary figure: executed by the Nationalist forces in Shanghai

Quran (koo-**rahn**) *n* ▸ same as **Koran**

q.v. (denoting a cross-reference) which (word, item, etc.) see
WORD ORIGIN New Latin *quod vide*

qwerty *or* **QWERTY keyboard** *n* the standard English language typewriter or computer keyboard with the characters q, w, e, r, t, and y at the top left of the keyboard

THESAURUS

quiz *n* **3 = examination**, questioning, interrogation, interview, investigation, grilling *(informal)*, cross-examination, cross-questioning, the third degree *(informal)* ▷ *vb* **4 = question**, ask, interrogate, examine, investigate, pump *(informal)*, grill *(informal)*, catechize

quota *n* **1, 2 = share**, allowance, ration, allocation, part, cut *(informal)*, limit, proportion, slice, quantity, portion, assignment, whack *(informal)*, dispensation

quotation *n* **1, 2 = passage**, quote *(informal)*, excerpt, cutting, selection, reference, extract, citation **3 = estimate**, price, tender, rate, cost, charge, figure, quote *(informal)*, bid price

quote *vb* **1a = repeat**, recite, reproduce, recall, echo, extract, excerpt, proclaim, parrot, paraphrase, retell **1b = refer to**, cite, give, name, detail, relate, mention, instance, specify, spell out, recount, recollect, make reference to, adduce

q

Rr

DICTIONARY

r **1** radius **2** ratio **3** right **4** *cricket* run(s)

R **1** *chem* radical **2** Regina **3** Registered Trademark **4** *physics, electronics* resistance **5** Rex **6** River **7** *chess* rook

Ra *chem* radium

RA **1** rear admiral **2** (in Britain) Royal Academy **3** (in Britain) Royal Artillery

RAAF Royal Australian Air Force

rabbi (rab-bye) *n, pl* **-bis** **1** the spiritual leader of a Jewish congregation **2** an expert in or teacher of Jewish Law **rabbinical** *adj*
WORD ORIGIN Hebrew: my master

rabbit *n, pl* **-bits** *or* **-bit** **1** a common burrowing mammal with long ears and a short fluffy tail ▷ *vb* **-biting, -bited** **2** *informal* to talk too much: *he keeps rabbiting on about interrogation*
WORD ORIGIN origin unknown

rabbit ears *pl n Austral & NZ* an indoor television aerial

rabbit fence *n* a fence to prevent the spread of rabbits

rabbiting *n* **go rabbiting** to hunt rabbits

rabbit punch *n* a short sharp blow to the back of the neck

rabble *n* **1** a disorderly crowd of noisy people **2** **the rabble** *contemptuous* the common people
WORD ORIGIN origin unknown

rabble-rouser *n* a person who stirs up the feelings of the mob **rabble-rousing** *adj, n*

Rabelaisian *adj* characterized by broad, often bawdy humour and sharp satire
WORD ORIGIN after the work of the French writer, François *Rabelais*

Rabi *n* **Isidor Isaac** 1898–1988, US physicist, born in Austria, who devised the atomic and molecular beam resonance method of observing atomic spectra. Nobel prize for physics 1944

Rabia[1] *n* either the third or the fourth month of the Muslim year, known as **Rabia I** and **Rabia II** respectively; the Muslim spring

Rabia[2] *or* **Rabiah** *n* full name *Rabia al-Adawiyyah* c. 713–801 AD, Islamic saint, mystic, and religious leader; her teachings inspired the Sufi movement

rabid *adj* **1** fanatical: *a rabid separatist* **2** having rabies **rabidity** *n*
WORD ORIGIN Latin *rabidus* frenzied

rabies (ray-beez) *n pathol* a fatal infectious viral disease of the nervous system transmitted by dogs and certain other animals
WORD ORIGIN Latin: madness

RAC (in Britain) Royal Automobile Club

raccoon *or* **racoon** *n, pl* **-coons** *or* **-coon** a small American mammal with a long striped tail
WORD ORIGIN from a Native American language

race[1] *n* **1** a contest of speed **2** any competition or rivalry: *the arms race* **3** a rapid current of water **4** a channel of a stream: *a mill race* **5** *Austral & NZ* a narrow passage through which sheep pass individually, as to a sheep dip ▷ *vb* **racing, raced** **6** to take part in a contest of speed with (someone) **7** to enter (an animal or vehicle) in a race: *to race greyhounds* **8** to travel as fast as possible **9** (of an engine) to run faster than normal **10** (of the heart) to beat faster than normal ▸ See also **races** > **racer** *n* **racing** *adj, n*
WORD ORIGIN Old Norse *rās* running

race[2] *n* **1** a group of people of common ancestry with distinguishing physical features, such as skin colour or build **2** **the human race** human beings collectively **3** a group of animals or plants having common characteristics that distinguish them from other members of the same species
WORD ORIGIN Italian *razza*

race caller *n* a professional horse-racing commentator

racecourse *n* a long broad track on which horses are raced

racehorse *n* a horse specially bred for racing

raceme (rass-eem) *n bot* a cluster of flowers along a central stem, as in the foxglove
WORD ORIGIN Latin *racemus* bunch of grapes

race meeting *n* a series of horse or greyhound races held at the same place

race relations *pl n* the relations between members of two or more races within a single community

race riot *n* a riot involving violence between people of different races

races *pl n* **the races** a series of contests of speed between horses or greyhounds over a fixed course

racetrack *n* **1** a circuit used for races between cars, bicycles, or runners **2** *US & Canad* a racecourse

racial *adj* **1** relating to the division of the human species into races **2** typically associated with any such group **racially** *adv*

racism *or* **racialism** *n* **1** hostile or oppressive behaviour towards people because they belong to a different race **2** the belief that some races are innately superior to others because of hereditary characteristics **racist** *or* **racialist** *n, adj*

rack[1] *n* **1** a framework for holding particular articles, such as coats or luggage **2** a straight bar with teeth on its edge, to work with a cogwheel **3** **the rack** *history* an instrument of torture that stretched the body of the victim ▷ *vb* **4** to cause great suffering to: *Germany was racked by food riots* **5** **rack one's brains** to try very hard to think of something
WORD ORIGIN probably from Middle Dutch *rec* framework

rack[2] *n* **go to rack and ruin** to be destroyed through neglect
WORD ORIGIN variant of WRACK[1]

rack[3] *vb* to clear (wine or beer) by siphoning it off from the dregs

rack[4] *n* the neck or rib part of a joint of meat

rack-and-pinion *n* a device for converting rotary into linear motion and vice versa, in which a gearwheel (the pinion) engages with a flat toothed bar (the rack)

racket[1] *n* **1** a noisy disturbance **2** an illegal activity done to make money **3** *slang* a business or

r

THESAURUS

race[1] *n* **1 = competition**, contest, chase, dash, pursuit, contention **2 = contest**, competition, rivalry, contention ▷ *vb* **6a = compete against**, run against **6b = compete**, run, contend, take part in a race **8 = run**, fly, career, speed, tear, dash, hurry, barrel (along) *(informal, chiefly US & Canad)*, dart, gallop, zoom, hare *(Brit informal)*, hasten, burn rubber *(informal)*, go like a bomb *(Brit & NZ informal)*, run like mad *(informal)*

race[2] *n* **1 = people**, ethnic group, nation, blood, house, family, line, issue, stock, type, seed *(chiefly biblical)*, breed, folk, tribe, offspring, clan, kin, lineage, progeny, kindred

racial *adj* **1 = ethnic**, ethnological, national, folk, genetic, tribal, genealogical

rack[1] *n* **1 = frame**, stand, structure, framework ▷ *vb* **4 = torture**, distress, torment, harass, afflict, oppress, harrow, crucify, agonize, pain, excruciate

racket[1] *n* **1 = noise**, row, shouting, fuss, disturbance, outcry, clamour, din, uproar, commotion, pandemonium, rumpus, babel, tumult, hubbub, hullabaloo, ballyhoo *(informal)* **2 = fraud**, scheme, criminal activity, illegal enterprise

DICTIONARY

occupation: *I've been in the racket since I was sixteen* ▷ *vb* **-eting, -eted 4** to make a commotion **rackety** *adj*
WORD ORIGIN probably imitative

racket[2] *or* **racquet** *n* a bat consisting of an oval frame surrounding a mesh of strings, with a handle, used in tennis, badminton, and squash ▸ See also **rackets**
WORD ORIGIN French *raquette*

racketeer *n* a person who makes money from illegal activities **racketeering** *n*

rackets *n* a game similar to squash, played by two or four people

Rackham *n* **Arthur** 1867–1939, English artist, noted for his book illustrations, esp. of fairy tales

rack-rent *n* an extortionate rent

raclette *n* a Swiss dish of melted cheese, usually served on boiled potatoes
WORD ORIGIN French

raconteur (rak-on-tur) *n* a person skilled in telling stories
WORD ORIGIN French

racoon *n, pl* **-coons** *or* **-coon** ▸ same as **raccoon**

racquet *n* ▸ same as **racket**[2]

racy *adj* **racier, raciest 1** slightly shocking **2** spirited or lively **racily** *adv* **raciness** *n*

rad radian

RADA (in Britain) Royal Academy of Dramatic Art

radar *n* **1** a method of detecting the position and velocity of a distant object by bouncing a narrow beam of extremely high-frequency radio pulses off it **2** the equipment used in this
WORD ORIGIN *ra(dio) d(etecting) a(nd) r(anging)*

radar trap *n* a device which uses radar to detect motorists who break the speed limit

Radcliffe *n* **1 Ann** 1764–1823, British novelist, noted for her Gothic romances *The Mysteries of Udolpho* (1794) and *The Italian* (1797) **2 Paula (Jane)** born 1973, British athlete, winner of the London Marathon (2002, 2003, 2005), gold medalist in the marathon at the World Championships (2005), and European Record holder for the 10000m

raddle *vb Austral & NZ* to mark sheep for identification

raddled *adj* (of a person) untidy or rundown in appearance
WORD ORIGIN from *rud* red ochre

Radek *n* **Karl (Bernhardovich)**, original name *Karl Sobelsohn*. 1885–?1939, Soviet politician and journalist who was secretary of Comintern (1920–24). He was accused of treason (1937) and probably died in a labour camp

Radetzky *n* Count **Joseph** 1766–1858, Austrian field marshal: served in the war against Sardinia (1848–9), winning brilliant victories at Custozza (1848) and Novara (1849): governor of Lombardy-Venetia in N Italy (1849-57)

radial *adj* **1** spreading out from a common central point **2** of a radius or ray **3** ▸ short for **radial-ply** ▷ *n* **4** a radial-ply tyre **radially** *adv*

radial-ply *adj* (of a tyre) having the fabric cords in the outer casing running radially to enable the sidewalls to be flexible

radian *n* an SI unit of plane angle; the angle between two radii of a circle that cut off on the circumference an arc equal in length to the radius

radiant *adj* **1** characterized by health and happiness: *radiant good looks* **2** shining **3** emitted as radiation: *radiant heat* **4** sending out heat by radiation: *radiant heaters* **radiance** *n* **radiantly** *adv*
WORD ORIGIN Latin *radiare* to shine

radiant energy *n* energy that is emitted or propagated in the form of particles or electromagnetic radiation

radiate ❶ *vb* **-ating, -ated 1** to spread out from a central point **2** to show (an emotion or quality) to a great degree: *she radiated competence and composure* **3** to emit or be emitted as radiation ▷ *adj* **4** having rays or a radial structure
WORD ORIGIN Latin *radiare* to emit rays

radiation *n* **1** *physics* **a** the emission of energy as particles, electromagnetic waves or sound **b** the particles or waves emitted **2** the process of radiating

radiation sickness *n* illness caused by overexposure to radioactive material or X-rays

radiator *n* **1** *Brit* a device for heating a room or building, consisting of a series of pipes containing hot water **2** a device for cooling an internal-combustion engine, consisting of thin-walled tubes containing water **3** *Austral & NZ* an electric fire

radical ❶ *adj* **1** favouring fundamental change in political or social conditions: *a radical student movement* **2** of the essential nature of a person or thing; fundamental: *a radical fault* **3** searching or thorough: *a radical interpretation* **4** *maths* of or containing roots of numbers or quantities ▷ *n* **5** a person who favours fundamental change in existing institutions or in political, social, or economic conditions **6** *maths* a root of a number or quantity, such as $\sqrt[3]{5}$, $\sqrt{x}$ **7** *chem* an atom or group of atoms that acts as a unit during chemical reactions **radicalism** *n* **radically** *adv*
WORD ORIGIN Latin *radix* a root

radicalize *or* **-ise** *vb* **-izing, -ized** *or* **-ising, -ised** to make (a person, group, or situation) radical or more radical: *the feelings of its own radicalized population*

radical sign *n* the symbol √ placed before a number or quantity to indicate the extraction of a root, esp. a square root. The value of a higher root is indicated by a raised digit in front of the symbol, as in $\sqrt[3]{}$

radicchio (rad-**deek**-ee-oh) *n, pl* **-chios** an Italian variety of chicory, with purple leaves streaked with white that are eaten raw in salads

radicle *n bot* **a** the part of the embryo of seed-bearing plants that develops into the main root **b** a very small root or rootlike part
WORD ORIGIN Latin *radix* root

Radiguet *n* **Raymond** 1903–23, French novelist; the author of *The Devil in the Flesh* (1923) and *Count d'Orgel* (1924)

radii *n* ▸ a plural of **radius**

radio *n, pl* **-dios 1** the use of electromagnetic waves for broadcasting or two-way communication without the use of linking wires **2** an electronic device for converting radio signals into sounds **3** a communications device for sending and receiving messages using radio waves **4** sound broadcasting ▷ *vb* **5** to transmit (a message) by radio ▷ *adj* **6** of, relating to, or using radio broadcasting or radio signals: *a radio interview* **7** using or producing electromagnetic waves in the range used for radio signals: *radio astronomy*
WORD ORIGIN Latin *radius* ray

radio- *combining form* **1** (denoting) radio **2** (denoting) radioactivity or radiation: *radiocarbon*

radioactive *adj* showing or using radioactivity

radioactivity *n* the spontaneous emission of radiation from atomic

r

THESAURUS

radiate *vb* **1a = emit**, spread, send out, disseminate, pour, shed, scatter, glitter, gleam **1b = spread out**, diverge, branch out **2 = show**, display, demonstrate, exhibit, emanate, give off *or* out **3 = shine**, emanate, be diffused

radical *adj* **1 = revolutionary**, extremist, fanatical **2, 3 = fundamental**, natural, basic, essential, native, constitutional, organic, profound, innate, deep-seated, thoroughgoing
OPPOSITE: superficial
▷ *n* **5 = extremist**, revolutionary, militant, fanatic
OPPOSITE: conservative

rage *n* **1a = fury**, temper, frenzy,

DICTIONARY

nuclei. The radiation can consist of alpha or beta particles, or gamma rays
radio astronomy *n* astronomy using a radio telescope to analyse signals received from radio sources in space
radiocarbon *n* a radioactive isotope of carbon, esp. carbon-14
radiocarbon dating *n* ▸ same as **carbon dating**
radiochemistry *n* the chemistry of radioactive substances
radio-controlled *adj* controlled by signals sent by radio
radio frequency *n* any electromagnetic frequency that lies in the range 10 kilohertz to 300 000 megahertz and can be used for broadcasting
radiogram *n Brit* an old-fashioned combined radio and record player
radiograph *n* an image produced on a special photographic film or plate by radiation, usually by X-rays
radiography (ray-dee-og-ra-fee) *n* the production of radiographs for use in medicine or industry **radiographer** *n*
radioisotope *n* a radioactive isotope
radiology (ray-dee-ol-a-jee) *n* the use of X-rays and radioactive substances in the diagnosis and treatment of disease **radiologist** *n*
radioscopy (ray-dee-oss-kop-ee) *n* examination of a person or object by means of a fluorescent screen and an X-ray source
radiosonde *n* an airborne instrument to send meteorological information back to earth by radio
WORD ORIGIN RADIO- + French *sonde* sounding line
radiotelegraphy *n* telegraphy in which messages are transmitted by radio waves
radiotelephone *n* a telephone which sends and receives messages using radio waves rather than wires **radiotelephony** *n*
radio telescope *n* an instrument used in radio astronomy to pick up and analyse radio waves from space
radiotherapy *n* the treatment of disease, esp. cancer, by radiation
radio wave *n* an electromagnetic wave of radio frequency
radish *n* a small hot-flavoured red root vegetable eaten raw in salads
WORD ORIGIN Latin *radix* root
radium *n chem* a highly radioactive luminescent metallic element, found in pitchblende. Symbol: Ra
WORD ORIGIN Latin *radius* ray
radius (ray-dee-uss) *n, pl* **-dii** (-dee-eye) *or* **-diuses** **1** a straight line joining the centre of a circle to any point on the circumference **2** the length of this line **3** *anat* the outer, slightly shorter of the two bones of the forearm **4** a circular area of a specified size round a central point: *within a seven-mile radius of the club*
WORD ORIGIN Latin: ray, spoke
radon (ray-don) *n chem* a colourless radioactive element of the noble gas group. Symbol: Rn
WORD ORIGIN from *radium*
Raeburn *n* Sir **Henry** 1756–1823, Scottish portrait painter
RAF (in Britain) Royal Air Force
Rafferty *or* **Rafferty's rules** *pl n Austral & NZ slang* no rules at all
WORD ORIGIN origin unknown
raffia *n* a fibre obtained from the leaves of a palm tree, used for weaving
WORD ORIGIN Malagasy
raffish *adj* unconventional or slightly disreputable
WORD ORIGIN obsolete *raff* rubbish
raffle *n* **1** a lottery, often to raise money for charity, in which the prizes are goods rather than money ▹ *vb* **-fling, -fled** **2** to offer as a prize in a raffle
WORD ORIGIN Old French
Rafsanjani *n* **Hojatoleslam Hashemi Ali Akbar** born 1934, Iranian politician: president of Iran (1989–97)
raft *n* a floating platform of logs or planks tied together
WORD ORIGIN Old Norse *raptr* rafter
rafter *n* any of the parallel sloping beams that form the framework of a roof
WORD ORIGIN Old English
rag[1] *n* **1** a small piece of cloth **2** *Brit, Austral & NZ informal* a newspaper **3 rags** old tattered clothing **4 from rags to riches** from being extremely poor to being extremely wealthy
WORD ORIGIN probably formed from *ragged*, from Old English *raggig*
rag[2] *Brit vb* **ragging, ragged** **1** to tease **2** to play rough practical jokes on ▹ *n* **3** a boisterous practical joke ▹ *adj* **4** (in British universities and colleges) of various events organized to raise money for charity: *a rag week*
WORD ORIGIN origin unknown
rag[3] *n* a piece of ragtime music
ragamuffin *n* **1** a ragged dirty child **2** ▸ same as **ragga**
WORD ORIGIN probably from RAG[1]
rag-and-bone man *n Brit* a man who goes from street to street buying old clothes and furniture
ragbag *n* a confused mixture: *the traditional ragbag of art traders*
rage **T** *n* **1** intense anger or passion **2** a fashion or craze: *the dance was the rage of Europe* **3** aggressive behaviour associated with a specified activity or environment: *road rage; school rage* **4 all the rage** *informal* very popular **5** *Austral & NZ informal* a dance or party ▹ *vb* **raging, raged** **6** to feel or show intense anger **7** to proceed violently and without restraint: *the argument was still raging*
WORD ORIGIN Latin *rabies* madness
ragga *n* a dance-oriented style of reggae
WORD ORIGIN from RAGAMUFFIN
ragged **T** (rag-gid) *adj* **1** dressed in shabby or torn clothes **2** (of clothes) tattered and torn **3** having a rough or uneven surface or edge **4** neglected or untidy: *the ragged stone-built village*
ragged robin *n* a plant that has pink or white flowers with ragged petals
raglan *adj* **1** (of a sleeve) joined to the garment by diagonal seams from the collar to the underarm **2** (of a garment) with this style of sleeve
WORD ORIGIN after Lord *Raglan*
ragout (rag-goo) *n* a richly seasoned stew of meat and vegetables
WORD ORIGIN French
ragtag *n* **ragtag and bobtail** the common people
ragtime *n* a style of jazz piano music with a syncopated melody
WORD ORIGIN probably *ragged time*
rag trade *n informal* the clothing business
ragwort *n* a plant with ragged leaves and yellow flowers
raid **T** *n* **1** a sudden surprise attack: *a bombing raid* **2** a surprise visit by police searching for people or goods:

r

THESAURUS

rampage, tantrum, foulie (*Austral slang*), hissy fit (*informal*), strop (*Brit informal*) OPPOSITE: calmness
1b = anger, violence, passion, obsession, madness, raving, wrath, mania, agitation, ire, vehemence, high dudgeon **2 = craze**, fashion, enthusiasm, vogue, fad (*informal*), latest thing ▹ *vb* **6 = be furious**, rave, blow up (*informal*), fume, lose it (*informal*), fret, seethe, crack up (*informal*), see red (*informal*), chafe, lose the plot (*informal*), go ballistic (*slang, chiefly US*), rant and rave, foam at the mouth, lose your temper, blow a fuse (*slang, chiefly US*), fly off the handle (*informal*), be incandescent, go off the deep end (*informal*), throw a fit (*informal*), wig out (*slang*), go up the wall (*slang*), blow your top, lose your rag (*slang*), be beside yourself, flip your lid (*slang*) OPPOSITE: stay calm
ragged *adj* **1, 2 = tatty**, worn, poor, torn, rent, faded, neglected, rundown, frayed, shabby, worn-out, seedy, scruffy, in tatters, dilapidated, tattered, threadbare, unkempt, in rags, down at heel, the worse for wear, in holes, having seen better days, scraggy OPPOSITE: smart
3 = rough, fragmented, crude, rugged, notched, irregular, unfinished, uneven, jagged, serrated
raid *n* **1 = attack**, invasion, seizure, onset, foray, sortie, incursion, surprise attack, hit-and-run attack,

DICTIONARY

a drugs raid ▹ *vb* **3** to make a raid on **4** to sneak into (a place) in order to steal **raider** *n*
WORD ORIGIN Old English *rād* military expedition

rail¹ *n* **1** a horizontal bar supported by vertical posts, used as a fence or barrier **2** a horizontal bar on which to hang things: *a curtain rail* **3** one of a pair of parallel bars that serve as a running surface for the wheels of a train **4** railway: *by car or by rail* **5 go off the rails** to start behaving improperly or eccentrically ▹ *vb* **6** to fence (an area) with rails
WORD ORIGIN Old French *raille* rod

rail² *vb* **rail against** *or* **at** to complain bitterly or loudly about
WORD ORIGIN Old French *railler* to mock

rail³ *n* a small wading marsh bird
WORD ORIGIN Old French *raale*

railcard *n Brit* an identity card, which pensioners or young people can buy, entitling them to cheaper rail travel

railhead *n* **1** a terminal of a railway **2** the farthest point reached by completed track on an unfinished railway

railing ⊙ *n* a fence made of rails supported by posts

raillery *n, pl* **-leries** good-natured teasing
WORD ORIGIN French *railler* to tease

railroad *n* **1** *US* a railway ▹ *vb* **2** *informal* to force (a person) into an action with haste or by unfair means

railway *n* **1** a track composed of a line of parallel metal rails fixed to sleepers, on which trains run **2** any track on which the wheels of a vehicle may run: *a cable railway* **3** the rolling stock, buildings, and tracks used in such a transport system **4** the organization responsible for operating a railway network

raiment *n archaic or poetic* clothing
WORD ORIGIN from *arrayment*

rain ⊙ *n* **1 a** water falling from the sky in drops formed by the condensation of water vapour in the atmosphere **b** a fall of rain ▸ Related adjective: **pluvial** **2** a large quantity of anything falling rapidly: *a rain of stones descended on the police* **3 (come) rain or shine** regardless of circumstances **4 right as rain** *informal* perfectly all right ▹ *vb* **5** to fall as rain: *it's raining back home* **6** to fall rapidly and in large quantities: *steel rungs and sawdust raining down* **7 rained off** cancelled or postponed because of rain. US and Canad term: **rained out** ▸ See also **rains** > **rainy** *adj*
WORD ORIGIN Old English *regn*

rainbird *n S African* a common name for **Burchell's coucal**, a bird whose call is believed to be a sign of impending rain

rainbow *n* an arched display in the sky of the colours of the spectrum, caused by the refraction and reflection of the sun's rays through rain

rainbow nation *n* the South African nation

rainbow trout *n* a freshwater trout with black spots and two red stripes

rain check *n* **take a rain check** *informal* to request or accept the postponement of an offer

raincoat *n* a coat made of a waterproof material

rainfall *n* the amount of rain, hail, or snow in a specified place and time

rainforest *n* dense forest found in tropical areas of heavy rainfall

Rainier III *n* full name *Rainier Louis Henri Maxence Bertrand de Grimaldi*. 1923–2005, ruling prince of Monaco from 1949. He married (1956) the US actress Grace Kelly (1929–82)

rains *pl n* **the rains** the season in the tropics when there is a lot of rain

rainstorm *n* a storm with heavy rain

rainwater *n* water from rain

rainy day *n* a future time of need, esp. financial need

Rais *or* **Retz** *n* **Gilles de** 1404–40, French nobleman who fought with Joan of Arc: marshal of France (1429–40). He was executed for the torture and murder of more than 140 children

raise ⊙ *vb* **raising, raised** **1** to lift to a higher position or level **2** to place in an upright position **3** to increase in amount, quality, or intensity: *to raise interest rates* **4** to collect or gather together: *to raise additional capital; to raise an army* **5** to cause to be expressed: *to raise a smile* **6** to stir up **7** to bring up: *to raise a family* **8** to grow: *to raise a crop* **9** to put forward for consideration: *they raised controversial issues* **10** to arouse from sleep or death **11** to build: *to raise a barn* **12** to bring to an end: *to raise a siege* **13** to establish radio communications with: *we raised Moscow last night* **14** to advance in rank; promote **15** *maths* to multiply (a number) by itself a specified number of times: *8 is 2 raised to the power 3* **16** to cause (dough) to rise, as by the addition of yeast **17** *cards* to bet more than the previous player **18 raise Cain a** to create a disturbance **b** to protest vehemently ▹ *n* **19** *US, Canad & NZ* an increase in pay
WORD ORIGIN Old Norse *reisa*

raised *adj* higher than the surrounding area: *a small raised platform*

raisin *n* a dried grape
WORD ORIGIN Old French: grape

raison d'être (ray-zon det-ra) *n, pl* **raisons d'être** (ray-zon det-ra) reason or justification for existence
WORD ORIGIN French

raita (rye-ta) *n* an Indian dish of chopped cucumber, mint, etc. in yogurt, served with curry
WORD ORIGIN Hindi

Raj *n* **the Raj** the British government in India before 1947
WORD ORIGIN Hindi

raja *or* **rajah** *n history* an Indian prince or ruler
WORD ORIGIN Hindi

rake¹ ⊙ *n* **1** a farm or garden tool consisting of a row of teeth set in a headpiece attached to a long shaft and used for gathering leaves or straw, or for smoothing loose earth **2** any of various implements similar

r

THESAURUS

sally, inroad, irruption **2 = bust** *(informal)*, swoop, descent, surprise search ▹ *vb* **3a = attack**, invade, assault, rifle, forage *(military)*, fall upon, swoop down upon, reive *(dialect)* **3b = make a search of**, search, bust *(informal)*, descend on, make a raid on, make a swoop on **3, 4 = steal from**, break into, plunder, pillage, sack

railing *n* **= fence**, rails, barrier, paling, balustrade

rain *n* **1a, 1b = rainfall**, fall, showers, deluge, drizzle, downpour, precipitation, raindrops, cloudburst ▹ *vb* **5 = pour**, pelt (down), teem, bucket down *(informal)*, fall, shower, drizzle, rain cats and dogs *(informal)*, come down in buckets *(informal)* **6 = fall**, shower, be dropped, sprinkle, be deposited

raise *vb* **1 = lift**, move up, elevate, uplift, heave **2 = set upright**, lift, elevate **3a = increase**, reinforce, intensify, heighten, advance, boost, strengthen, enhance, put up, exaggerate, hike (up) *(informal)*, enlarge, escalate, inflate, aggravate, magnify, amplify, augment, jack up **OPPOSITE:** reduce **3b = make louder**, heighten, amplify, louden **4 = collect**, get, gather, obtain **5 = cause**, start, produce, create, occasion, provoke, bring about, originate, give rise to, engender **7 = bring up**, develop, rear, nurture **9 = put forward**, suggest, introduce, advance, bring up, broach, moot **11 = build**, construct, put up, erect **OPPOSITE:** demolish

rake¹ *vb* **3 = gather**, collect, scrape together, scrape up, remove **7 = search**, hunt, examine, scan, comb, scour, ransack, forage, scrutinize, fossick *(Austral & NZ)*

rake² *n* **= libertine**, playboy, swinger *(slang)*, profligate, lecher, roué, sensualist, voluptuary, debauchee, rakehell *(archaic)*, dissolute man, lech *or* letch *(informal)* **OPPOSITE:** puritan

rally¹ *n* **1 = gathering**, mass meeting,

DICTIONARY

in shape or function ▹*vb* **raking, raked 3** to scrape or gather with a rake **4** to smooth (a surface) with a rake **5** Also: **rake out** to clear (ashes) from (a fire) **6 rake together** *or* **up** to gather (items or people) with difficulty, as from a limited supply **7** to search or examine carefully: *raking over the past is not always popular* **8** to direct (gunfire) along the length of (a target): *the machine guns raked up and down their line* **9** to scrape or graze: *he raked the tip of his shoe across the pavement* ▸See also **rake in, rake-off,** etc.
WORD ORIGIN Old English *raca*

rake² ⓣ *n* an immoral man
WORD ORIGIN short for *rakehell*

rake³ *n* **1** the degree to which an object slopes ▹*vb* **raking, raked 2** to slope from the vertical, esp. (of a ship's mast) towards the stern **3** to construct with a backward slope
WORD ORIGIN origin unknown

raked *adj* (of a surface) sloping so that it is higher at the back than at the front

rake in *vb informal* to acquire (money) in large amounts

rake-off *n slang* a share of profits, esp. an illegal one

rake up *vb* to bring back memories of (a forgotten unpleasant event): *she doesn't want to rake up the past*

rakish¹ (ray-kish) *adj* dashing or jaunty: *a hat which he wore at a rakish angle*
WORD ORIGIN probably from RAKE³

rakish² *adj* immoral: *a rakish life of drinking and womanizing* **rakishly** *adv*
WORD ORIGIN from RAKE²

rallentando *music adj, adv* **1** becoming slower ▹*n* **2** a passage in which the music becomes slower
WORD ORIGIN Italian

rally¹ ⓣ *n, pl* **-lies 1** a large gathering of people for a meeting **2** a marked recovery of strength, as during illness **3** *stock Exchange* a sharp increase in price or trading activity after a decline **4** *tennis, squash, etc.* an exchange of several shots before one player wins the point **5** a car-driving competition on public roads ▹*vb* **-lies, -lying, -lied 6** to bring or come together after being dispersed **7** to bring or come together for a common cause **8** to summon up (one's strength or spirits) **9** to recover (sometimes only temporarily) from an illness **10** *stock Exchange* to increase sharply after a decline
WORD ORIGIN Old French *rallier*

rally² *vb* **-lies, -lying, -lied** to mock or tease (someone) in a good-natured way
WORD ORIGIN Old French *railler* to tease

rally round *vb* to group together to help someone

ram ⓣ *n* **1** an uncastrated adult male sheep **2** a hydraulically or pneumatically driven piston **3** the falling weight of a pile driver **4** ▸short for **battering ram** ▹*vb* **ramming, rammed 5** to strike against with force **6** to force or drive: *he rammed his sword into the man's belly* **7** to stuff or cram **8 ram something home** to make something clear or obvious: *to ram home the message* **9 ram something down someone's throat** to put forward or emphasize an argument or idea with excessive force
WORD ORIGIN Old English *ramm*

RAM *computers* random access memory: a temporary storage space which loses its contents when the computer is switched off

Rama *n* a Hindu god, the incarnation of Vishnu

Ramadan *n* **1** the ninth month of the Muslim year, 30 days long, during which strict fasting is observed from sunrise to sunset **2** the fast itself

Ramakrishna *n* **Sri** 1834–86, Hindu yogi and religious reformer. He preached the equal value of all religions as different paths to God

Ramanuja *n* 11th century AD, Indian Hindu philosopher and theologian

Ramaphosa *n* **(Matamela) Cyril** born 1952, Black South African statesman and trade unionist

ramble ⓣ *vb* **-bling, -bled 1** to walk for relaxation, sometimes with no particular direction **2** to speak or write in a confused style **3** to grow or develop in a random fashion ▹*n* **4** a walk, esp. in the countryside
WORD ORIGIN Middle English *romblen*

rambler *n* **1** a person who takes country walks **2** a climbing rose

rambling *adj* **1** long and irregularly shaped: *a rambling fourteenth-century church* **2** (of speech or writing) confused and long-winded ▹*n* **3** the activity of going for long walks in the country

RAMC Royal Army Medical Corps

Rameau *n* **Jean Philippe** 1683–1764, French composer. His works include the opera *Castor et Pollux* (1737), chamber music, harpsichord pieces, church music, and cantatas. His *Traité de l'harmonie* (1722) was of fundamental importance in the development of modern harmony

ramekin (ram-ik-in) *n* a small container for baking and serving one portion of food
WORD ORIGIN French *ramequin*

ramification *n* **1 ramifications** the consequences or complications resulting from an action **2** a structure of branching parts

ramify *vb* **-fies, -fying, -fied 1** to become complex **2** to spread in branches; subdivide
WORD ORIGIN French *ramifier*

ramjet *n* **a** a type of jet engine in which fuel is burned in a duct using air compressed by the forward speed of the aircraft **b** an aircraft powered by such an engine

ramp ⓣ *n* **1** a slope that joins two surfaces at different levels **2** a place where the level of a road surface changes because of roadworks **3** a movable stairway by which passengers enter and leave an aircraft **4** *Brit* a small hump on a road to make traffic slow down
WORD ORIGIN Old French *ramper* to crawl, rear

rampage ⓣ *vb* **-paging, -paged 1** to rush about violently ▹*n* **2 on the rampage** behaving violently or destructively
WORD ORIGIN Scots

r

THESAURUS

convention, convocation, meeting, conference, congress, assembly, congregation, muster, hui (NZ) **2 = recovery**, improvement, comeback (*informal*), revival, renewal, resurgence, recuperation, turn for the better **OPPOSITE:** relapse ▹*vb* **6, 7 = gather together**, unite, bring together, regroup, reorganize, reassemble, re-form **9 = recover**, improve, pick up, revive, get better, come round, perk up, recuperate, turn the corner, pull through, take a turn for the better, regain your strength, get your second wind
OPPOSITE: get worse

ram *vb* **5 = hit**, force, drive into, strike, crash, impact, smash, slam, dash, run into, butt, collide with **6, 7 = cram**, pound, force, stuff, pack, hammer, jam, thrust, tamp

ramble *vb* **1 = walk**, range, drift, wander, stroll, stray, roam, rove, amble, saunter, straggle, traipse (*informal*), go walkabout (*Austral*), perambulate, stravaig (*Scot & Northern English dialect*), peregrinate **2 = babble**, wander, rabbit (on) (*Brit informal*), chatter, waffle (*informal, chiefly Brit*), digress, rattle on, maunder, witter on (*informal*), expatiate, run off at the mouth (*slang*) ▹*n* **4 = walk**, tour, trip, stroll, hike, roaming, excursion, roving, saunter, traipse (*informal*), peregrination, perambulation

ramp *n* **1 = slope**, grade, incline, gradient, inclined plane, rise

rampage *vb* **1 = go berserk**, tear, storm, rage, run riot, run amok, run wild, go ballistic (*slang*), go ape (*slang*) **2 on the rampage = berserk**, wild, violent, raging, destructive, out of control, rampant, amok, riotous, berko (*Austral slang*)

DICTIONARY

rampant ❶ *adj* **1** growing or spreading uncontrollably **2** *heraldry* (of a beast) standing on the hind legs, the right foreleg raised above the left: *a lion rampant*
WORD ORIGIN Old French *ramper* to crawl, rear

rampart *n* a mound of earth or a wall built to protect a fort or city
WORD ORIGIN Old French

Ramphal *n* Sir **Shridath Surendranath**, known as *Sunni* born 1928, Guyanese diplomat and Commonwealth Secretary-General (1975–90)

Ramphele *n* **Mamphela** born 1947, Black South African political activist: partner of Steve Biko; a director of the World Bank from 2000

rampike *n Canad* a tall tree that has been burned bare of branches

ramp up *vb* **1** to increase or cause to increase **2** to increase the effort involved in a process

ram raid *n informal* a raid on a shop in which a stolen car is driven into the window **ram raider** *n*

ramrod *n* **1** a long thin rod for cleaning the barrel of a gun or forcing gunpowder into an old-fashioned gun ▹ *adj* **2** (of someone's posture) very straight and upright

Ramsay *n* **1 Allan** ?1686–1758, Scottish poet, editor, and bookseller, noted particularly for his pastoral comedy *The Gentle Shepherd* (1725): first person to introduce the circulating library in Scotland **2** his son, **Allan** 1713–84, Scottish portrait painter **3 James Andrew Broun Ramsay** ▸ See **Dalhousie** (sense 2) **4 Gordon** born 1963, British chef and restaurateur; achieved a third Michelin star (2001) **5** Sir **William** 1852–1916, Scottish chemist. He discovered argon (1894) with Rayleigh, isolated helium (1895), and identified neon, krypton, and xenon: Nobel prize for chemistry 1904

Ramses III *or* **Rameses III** *n* died ?1167 BC, king of ancient Egypt (?1198–?67). His reign was marked by wars in Libya and Syria

Ramsey *n* Sir **Alf(red)** (**Ernest**) 1922–99, English footballer and football manager, who played for England 32 times and managed England when they won the World Cup (1966)

ramshackle *adj* badly made or cared for: *a curious ramshackle building*
WORD ORIGIN obsolete *ransackle* to ransack

Ram Singh *n* 1816–85, Indian leader of a puritanical Sikh sect, the Kukas, who tried to remove the British from India through a policy of noncooperation

ran *vb* ▸ the past tense of **run**

RAN Royal Australian Navy

ranch *n* **1** a large cattle farm in the American West **2** *chiefly US & Canad* a large farm for the rearing of a particular kind of livestock or crop: *he owned a yak ranch in Tibet* ▹ *vb* **3** to run a ranch **rancher** *n*
WORD ORIGIN Mexican Spanish *rancho* small farm

ranchslider *n NZ* a glazed sliding door usually opening onto an outside terrace

rancid *adj* (of fatty foods) stale and having an offensive smell **rancidity** *n*
WORD ORIGIN Latin *rancidus*

rancour *or US* **rancor** *n* deep bitter hate **rancorous** *adj*
WORD ORIGIN Old French

rand *n* the standard monetary unit of the Republic of South Africa
WORD ORIGIN from *Witwatersrand*, S Transvaal, referring to the gold-mining there

R & B rhythm and blues

R & D research and development

Randolph *n* **1 Edmund Jennings**, 1753–1813, US politician. He was a member of the convention that framed the US constitution (1787), attorney general (1789–94), and secretary of state (1794–95) **2 John**, called *Randolph of Roanoke*. 1773–1833, US politician, noted for his eloquence: in 1820 he opposed the Missouri Compromise that outlawed slavery **3** Sir **Thomas**; 1st Earl of Moray. Died 1332, Scottish soldier: regent after the death of Robert the Bruce (1329)

random ❶ *adj* **1** lacking any definite plan or prearranged order: *a random sample* ▹ *n* **2 at random** not following any prearranged order **randomly** *adv* **randomness** *n*
WORD ORIGIN Old French *randir* to gallop

random access *n* a method of reading data from a computer file without having to read through the file from the beginning

randy ❶ *adj* **randier, randiest** *informal* sexually aroused **randily** *adv* **randiness** *n*
WORD ORIGIN probably from obsolete *rand* to rant

ranee *n* ▸ same as **rani**

rang *vb* ▸ the past tense of **ring¹**

rangatira (rung-a-teer-a) *n NZ* a Māori chief of either sex
WORD ORIGIN Māori

range ❶ *n* **1** the limits within which a person or thing can function effectively: *academic ability range* **2 a** the maximum effective distance of a projectile fired from a weapon **b** the distance between a target and a weapon **3** the total distance which a ship, aircraft, or vehicle can travel without taking on fresh fuel **4** the difference in pitch between the highest and lowest note of a voice or musical instrument **5** a whole set of related things: *a range of treatments was available* **6** the total products of a manufacturer, designer, or stockist: *the latest skin-care range* **7** the limits within which something can lie: *a range of prices* **8** *US & Canad* an extensive tract of open land on which livestock can graze **9** a chain of mountains **10** an area set aside for shooting practice or rocket testing **11** a large cooking stove with one or more ovens **12** *maths* the set of values that a function or variable can take ▹ *vb* **ranging, ranged 13** to vary between one point and another **14** to cover a specified period or specified things: *attitudes ranged from sympathy to indifference* **15** to roam (over) **16** to establish or be situated in a line or series **17** to put into a specific category: *they ranged themselves with the opposition*
WORD ORIGIN Old French: row

rangefinder *n* an instrument for finding how far away an object is

THESAURUS

rampant *adj* **1 = widespread**, rank, epidemic, prevalent, rife, exuberant, uncontrolled, unchecked, unrestrained, luxuriant, profuse, spreading like wildfire **2** *(heraldry)* **= upright**, standing, rearing, erect

random *adj* **1a = chance**, spot, casual, stray, accidental, arbitrary, incidental, indiscriminate, haphazard, unplanned, fortuitous, aimless, desultory, hit or miss, purposeless, unpremeditated, adventitious **OPPOSITE:** planned **1b = casual**, arbitrary, indiscriminate, unplanned, aimless, purposeless, unpremeditated
2 at random = haphazardly, randomly, arbitrarily, casually, accidentally, irregularly, by chance, indiscriminately, aimlessly, willy-nilly, unsystematically, purposelessly, adventitiously

randy *adj (informal)* **= lustful**, hot, sexy *(informal)*, turned-on *(slang)*, aroused, raunchy *(slang)*, horny *(slang)*, amorous, lascivious, lecherous, sexually excited, concupiscent, satyric

range *n* **1, 7 = limits**, reach, distance, sweep, extent, pale, confines, parameters *(informal)*, ambit
5 = series, variety, selection, assortment, lot, collection, gamut
▹ *vb* **13 = vary**, run, reach, extend, go, stretch, fluctuate **15 = roam**, explore, wander, rove, sweep, cruise, stroll, ramble, traverse

rank¹ *n* **1 = status**, level, position, grade, order, standing, sort, quality,

r

DICTIONARY

ranger *n* **1** an official in charge of a park or nature reserve **2** *US* an armed trooper employed to police a State or district: *a Texas ranger*
Ranger *or* **Ranger Guide** *n Austral & Brit* a member of the senior branch of the Guides
rangy (**rain**-jee) *adj* **rangier, rangiest** having long slender limbs
rani *or* **ranee** *n* the wife or widow of a raja
WORD ORIGIN Hindi
Ranjit Singh *n* called *the Lion of the Punjab*. 1780–1839; founder of the Sikh kingdom in the Punjab
rank[1] ❶ *n* **1** a position within a social organization: *the rank of superintendent* **2** high social or other standing: *accusations were made against people of high rank* **3** a person's social class: *it was too grand for someone of his lowly rank* **4** the position of an item in any ordering or sequence **5** a line or row of people or things **6** a place where taxis wait to be hired **7** a line of people, esp. soldiers, positioned one beside the other **8** any of the eight horizontal rows of squares on a chessboard **9 close ranks** to maintain solidarity **10 pull rank** to get one's own way by virtue of one's superior position **11 rank and file** the ordinary people or members of a group **12 the ranks** the common soldiers ▷ *vb* **13** to give or hold a specific position in an organization or group **14** to arrange in rows or lines **15** to arrange in sequence: *to rank students according to their grades* **16** to be important: *the legendary coronation stone ranks high in the hearts of patriots*
WORD ORIGIN Old French *ranc*
rank[2] ❶ *adj* **1** complete or absolute: *rank incompetence* **2** smelling offensively strong **3** growing too quickly: *rank weeds*
WORD ORIGIN Old English *ranc* straight, proud
Rank *n* **1 J(oseph) Arthur**, 1st Baron. 1888–1972, British industrialist and film executive, whose companies dominated the British film industry in the 1940s and 1950s **2 Otto** 1884–1939, Austrian psychoanalyst, noted for his theory that the trauma of birth may be reflected in certain forms of mental illness
Rankin *n* **Ian** born 1960, Scottish novelist; best known for his series of novels featuring Edinburgh detective Inspector Rebus, beginning with *Knots and Crosses* (1987)
rankle *vb* **-kling, -kled** to continue to cause resentment or bitterness
WORD ORIGIN Old French *draoncle* ulcer
ransack *vb* **1** to search through every part of (a place or thing) **2** to plunder or pillage
WORD ORIGIN Old Norse *rann* house + *saka* to search
ransom ❶ *n* **1** the money demanded in return for the release of someone who has been kidnapped **2 hold to ransom a** to keep (a prisoner) in confinement until payment is received **b** to attempt to force (a person) to do something ▷ *vb* **3** to pay money to obtain the release of (a prisoner) **4** to set free (a prisoner) in return for money **ransomer** *n*
WORD ORIGIN Old French *ransoun*
Ransom *n* **John Crowe** 1888–1974, US poet and critic
Ransome *n* **Arthur** 1884–1967, English writer, best known for his books for children, including *Swallows and Amazons* (1930) and *Great Northern?* (1947)
rant ❶ *vb* **1** to talk in a loud and excited way ▷ *n* **2** loud excited speech **ranting** *adj, n*
WORD ORIGIN Dutch *ranten* to rave
ranunculus *n, pl* **-luses** *or* **-li** a genus of plants including the buttercup
WORD ORIGIN Latin *rana* frog
RAOC Royal Army Ordnance Corps
rap[1] ❶ *vb* **rapping, rapped 1** to hit with a sharp quick blow **2** to knock loudly and sharply **3 rap out** to utter in sharp rapid speech: *he rapped out his address* **4** to perform a rhythmic monologue with musical backing **5** *slang* to talk in a relaxed and friendly way **6** to rebuke or criticize sharply **7 rap over the knuckles** to reprimand ▷ *n* **8** a sharp quick blow or the sound produced by it **9** a fast rhythmic monologue over a musical backing **10** a sharp rebuke or criticism **11** *slang* a legal charge: *a murder rap* **12 take the rap** *slang* to suffer the punishment for a crime, whether guilty or not **rapper** *n*
WORD ORIGIN probably from Old Norse
rap[2] *n* **not care a rap** to not care in the least: *she didn't care a rap for us*
WORD ORIGIN probably from *ropaire*, counterfeit coin formerly current in Ireland
rapacious *adj* **1** greedy or grasping **2** (of animals or birds) living by catching prey **rapacity** *n*
WORD ORIGIN Latin *rapax*
Rapacki *n* **Adam** 1909–70, Polish politician: foreign minister (1956–68): proposed (1957) the denuclearization of Poland, Czechoslovakia, East Germany, and West Germany (the **Rapacki Plan**): rejected by the West because of Soviet predominance in conventional weapons
rape[1] ❶ *vb* **raping, raped 1** to force (someone) to submit to sexual intercourse ▷ *n* **2** the act of raping **3** any violation or abuse: *the rape of the country's natural resources* **rapist** *n*
WORD ORIGIN Latin *rapere* to seize
rape[2] *n* a yellow-flowered plant cultivated for its seeds, **rapeseed**, which yield a useful oil, **rape oil**, and as a fodder plant
WORD ORIGIN Latin *rapum* turnip
rapid ❶ *adj* **1** (of an action) taking or lasting a short time **2** acting or moving quickly: *a rapid advance* **rapidly** *adv* **rapidity** *n*
WORD ORIGIN Latin *rapidus*
rapid eye movement *n* the movement of the eyeballs while a person is dreaming
rapids *pl n* part of a river where the water is very fast and turbulent
rapier (**ray**-pyer) *n* a long narrow two-edged sword
WORD ORIGIN Old French *espee rapiere* rasping sword
rapine (**rap**-pine) *n* pillage or plundering
WORD ORIGIN Latin *rapina*
rapport (rap-**pore**) *n* a sympathetic relationship or understanding
WORD ORIGIN French

r

THESAURUS

type, station, division, degree, classification, echelon **3 = class**, dignity, caste, nobility, stratum **5, 7 = row**, line, file, column, group, range, series, formation, tier ▷ *vb* **13 = order**, class, grade, classify, dispose **14, 15 = arrange**, sort, position, range, line up, locate, sequence, array, marshal, align
rank[2] *adj* **2 = foul**, off, bad, offensive, disgusting, revolting, stinking, stale, pungent, noxious, disagreeable, musty, rancid, fetid, putrid, fusty, strong-smelling, gamey, noisome, mephitic, olid, yucky *or* yukky *(slang)*, festy *(Austral slang)* **3 = abundant**, flourishing, lush, luxuriant, productive, vigorous, dense, exuberant, profuse, strong-growing
ransom *n* **1 = payment**, money, price, payoff
rant *vb* **1 = shout**, roar, yell, rave, bellow, cry, spout *(informal)*, bluster, declaim, vociferate
rap[1] *vb* **1, 2 = hit**, strike, knock, crack, tap ▷ *n* **8 = blow**, knock, crack, tap, clout *(informal)* **10 = rebuke**, sentence, blame, responsibility, punishment, censure, chiding
rape[1] *vb* **1 = sexually assault**, violate, abuse, ravish, force, outrage ▷ *n* **2 = sexual assault**, violation, ravishment, outrage
rapid *adj* **1 = sudden**, prompt, speedy, precipitate, express, fleet, swift, quickie *(informal)*, expeditious
OPPOSITE: gradual
2 = quick, fast, hurried, swift, brisk, hasty, flying, pdq *(slang)*
OPPOSITE: slow

DICTIONARY

rapprochement (rap-**prosh**-mong) *n* a re-establishment of friendly relations: *the policy of rapprochement with Eastern Europe*
WORD ORIGIN French

rapscallion *n old-fashioned* a rascal or rogue
WORD ORIGIN earlier *rascallion*

rap sheet *n chiefly US & Canad informal* a police record of an individual's criminal history

rapt *adj* **1** totally engrossed: *rapt attention* **2** arising from or showing rapture: *with a rapt look on his face*
WORD ORIGIN Latin *raptus* carried away

raptor *n* any bird of prey **raptorial** *adj*
WORD ORIGIN Latin: robber

rapture *n* **1** extreme happiness or delight **2** **raptures** ecstatic joy: *they will be in raptures over the rugged scenery* **rapturous** *adj*
WORD ORIGIN Latin *raptus* carried away

rare[1] ❶ *adj* **1** uncommon or unusual: *a rare plant* **2** not happening or done very often: *a rare appearance in London* **3** of uncommonly high quality: *a rare beauty* **4** (of air at high altitudes) having low density; thin
WORD ORIGIN Latin *rarus* sparse

rare[2] *adj* (of meat) very lightly cooked
WORD ORIGIN Old English *hrēr*

rarebit *n* ▸ short for **Welsh rarebit**

rare earth *n chem* **1** any oxide of a lanthanide **2** Also called: **rare-earth element** any element of the lanthanide series

rarefied (**rare**-if-ide) *adj* **1** highly specialized: *the rarefied world of classical ballet* **2** (of air) thin **3** exalted in character: *the rarefied heights of academic excellence*

rarely ❶ *adv* **1** hardly ever **2** to an unusual degree; exceptionally

raring ❶ *adj* **raring to do something** keen and willing to do something
WORD ORIGIN *rare*, variant of REAR[2]

rarity ❶ *n, pl* **-ties** **1** something that is valuable because it is unusual **2** the state of being rare

rascal *n* **1** a scoundrel or rogue **2** a mischievous child **rascally** *adj*
WORD ORIGIN Old French *rascaille* rabble

rase *vb* **rasing, rased** ▸ same as **raze**

rash[1] ❶ *adj* acting or done without proper thought or consideration; hasty: *rash actions* **rashly** *adv* **rashness** *n*
WORD ORIGIN Old High German *rasc* hurried, clever

rash[2] ❶ *n* **1** an outbreak of spots or patches on the skin, caused by illness or allergy **2** an outbreak of occurrences: *a rash of censorship trials*
WORD ORIGIN Old French *rasche*

rasher *n* a thin slice of bacon
WORD ORIGIN origin unknown

Rask *n* **Rasmus Christian** 1787–1832, Danish philologist. He pioneered comparative philology with his work on Old Norse (1818)

Rasmussen *n* **Knud Johan Victor** 1879–1933, Danish arctic explorer and ethnologist. He led several expeditions through the Arctic in support of his theory that the North American Indians were originally migrants from Asia

rasp *n* **1** a harsh grating noise **2** a coarse file with rows of raised teeth ▹ *vb* **3** to say or speak in a grating voice **4** to make a harsh grating noise **5** to scrape or rub (something) roughly **6** to irritate (one's nerves)
WORD ORIGIN Old French *raspe*

raspberry *n, pl* **-ries** **1** the red fruit of a prickly shrub of Europe and North America **2** *informal* a spluttering noise made with the tongue and lips to express contempt: *she blew a loud raspberry*
WORD ORIGIN origin unknown

Rastafarian *or* **Rasta** *n* **1** a believer in a religion of Jamaican origin that regards Ras Tafari, the former emperor of Ethiopia, Haile Selassie, as God ▹ *adj* **2** of Rastafarians

raster *n* **1** an image consisting of rows of pixel information, such as a JPEG, GIF etc. **2** a pattern of horizontal scanning lines traced by an electron beam, esp. on a television screen
WORD ORIGIN from German *Raster* screen

rasterize *vb* to convert (a digitized image) into a form that can be printed or represented on a VDU

rat *n* **1** a long-tailed rodent, similar to but larger than a mouse **2** *informal* someone who is disloyal or treacherous **3** **smell a rat** to detect something suspicious ▹ *vb* **ratting, ratted** **4** **rat on** **a** to betray (someone): *good friends don't rat on each other* **b** to go back on (an agreement): *his ex-wife claims he ratted on their divorce settlement* **5** to hunt and kill rats
WORD ORIGIN Old English *ræt*

ratafia (rat-a-**fee**-a) *n* **1** a liqueur made from fruit **2** an almond-flavoured biscuit
WORD ORIGIN West Indian Creole French

rat-arsed *adj Austral & Brit slang* drunk

rat-a-tat *or* **rat-a-tat-tat** *n* a repeated knocking or tapping sound

ratatouille (rat-a-**twee**) *n* a vegetable casserole made of stewed tomatoes, aubergines, etc.
WORD ORIGIN French

ratbag *n slang* an eccentric, stupid, or unreliable person

ratchet *n* **1** a device in which a toothed rack or wheel is engaged by a pivoted lever which permits motion in one direction only **2** the toothed rack or wheel in such a device **3** to operate using a ratchet **4** (usually foll. by *up* or *down*) to increase or decrease, esp. irreversibly: *Hitchcock ratchets up the tension once again*
WORD ORIGIN French *rochet*

rate[1] ❶ *n* **1** a quantity or amount considered in relation to or measured against another quantity or amount: *he was publishing at the rate of about 10 books a year* **2** a price or charge with reference to a standard or scale: *an exchange rate* **3** the speed of progress or change: *crime is increasing at an alarming rate* **4** a charge made per unit for a commodity or

THESAURUS

rare[1] *adj* **2 = uncommon**, unusual, exceptional, out of the ordinary, few, strange, scarce, singular, sporadic, sparse, infrequent, thin on the ground, recherché
OPPOSITE: common
3 = superb, great, fine, excellent, extreme, exquisite, admirable, superlative, choice, incomparable, peerless

rarely *adv* **1 = seldom**, hardly, almost never, hardly ever, little, once in a while, infrequently, on rare occasions, once in a blue moon *(informal)*, only now and then, scarcely ever **OPPOSITE:** often

raring *adj* **raring to = eager to**, impatient to, longing to, yearning to, willing to, ready to, keen to, desperate to, enthusiastic to, avid to, champing at the bit to *(informal)*, keen as mustard to, athirst to

rarity *n* **1 = curio**, find, treasure, pearl, one-off, curiosity, gem, collector's item **2 = uncommonness**, scarcity, infrequency, unusualness, shortage, strangeness, singularity, sparseness

rash[1] *adj* **= reckless**, hasty, impulsive, imprudent, premature, adventurous, careless, precipitate, brash, audacious, headlong, madcap, ill-advised, foolhardy, unwary, thoughtless, unguarded, headstrong, impetuous, indiscreet, unthinking, helter-skelter, ill-considered, hot-headed, heedless, injudicious, incautious, venturesome, harebrained, harum-scarum **OPPOSITE:** cautious

rash[2] *n* **1 = outbreak of spots**, (skin) eruption **2 = spate**, series, wave, flood, succession, plague, outbreak, epidemic

rate[1] *n* **1 = degree**, standard, scale, proportion, percentage, ratio **2, 4 = charge**, price, cost, fee, tax, figure, dues, duty, hire, toll, tariff **3 = speed**, pace, tempo, velocity, time, measure, gait, frequency **7 at any rate = in any case**, anyway, nevertheless, anyhow, at all events

DICTIONARY

service **5** ▸ see **rates** **6** relative quality: *a third-rate power* **7** **at any rate** in any case ▹ *vb* **rating, rated** **8** to assign a position on a scale of relative values: *he is rated as one of the top caterers in the country* **9** to estimate the value of: *we rate your services highly* **10** to consider or regard: *it could hardly be rated a success* **11** to be worthy of: *it barely rates a mention* **12** *informal* to have a high opinion of: *the cognoscenti have always rated his political skills*
WORD ORIGIN Medieval Latin *rata*

rate[2] *vb* **rating, rated** to scold or criticize severely
WORD ORIGIN origin unknown

rateable *adj* **1** able to be rated or evaluated **2** liable to payment of rates

rateable value *n* (in Britain) a fixed value assigned to a property, used to assess the rates due on it

rate-cap *vb* **-capping, -capped** (formerly in Britain) to put an upper limit on the rates charged by a local council **rate-capping** *n*

ratepayer *n* a person who pays local rates on a building

rates *pl n* (in some countries) a tax on property levied by a local authority

Rathenau *n* **Walther** 1867–1922, German industrialist and statesman: he organized the German war industries during World War I, became minister of reconstruction (1921) and of foreign affairs (1922), and was largely responsible for the treaty of Rapallo with Russia. His assassination by right-wing extremists caused a furore

rather ❶ *adv* **1** fairly: *that was a rather narrow escape* **2** to a limited extent: *I rather thought that was the case* **3** more truly or appropriately: *they tend to be cat rather than dog people* **4** more willingly: *I would rather go straight home* ▹ *interj* **5** an expression of strong affirmation: *Is it worth seeing?* — *Rather!*
WORD ORIGIN Old English *hrathor*, comparative of *hrathe* ready, quick

ratify ❶ *vb* **-fies, -fying, -fied** to give formal approval to **ratification** *n*
WORD ORIGIN Latin *ratus* fixed + *facere* to make

rating ❶ *n* **1** a valuation or assessment **2** a classification according to order or grade **3** a noncommissioned sailor **4** **ratings** the size of the audience for a TV or radio programme

ratio ❶ *n, pl* **-tios** **1** the relationship between two numbers or amounts expressed as a proportion: *a ratio of one instructor to every five pupils* **2** *maths* a quotient of two numbers or quantities
WORD ORIGIN Latin: a reckoning

ration ❶ *n* **1** a fixed allowance of something that is scarce, such as food or petrol in wartime **2** **rations** a fixed daily allowance of food, such as that given to a soldier ▹ *vb* **3** to restrict the distribution of (something): *the government has rationed petrol* **4** to distribute a fixed amount of something to each person in a group **rationing** *n*
WORD ORIGIN Latin *ratio* reckoning

rational ❶ *adj* **1** reasonable or sensible **2** using reason or logic in thinking out a problem **3** capable of reasoning: *man is a rational being* **4** sane: *rational behaviour* **5** *maths* able to be expressed as a ratio of two integers: *a rational number* **rationality** *n* **rationally** *adv*
WORD ORIGIN Latin *rationalis*

rationale ❶ (rash-a-**nahl**) *n* the reason for an action or belief

rationalism *n* the philosophy that regards reason as the only basis for beliefs or actions **rationalist** *n* **rationalistic** *adj*

rationalize *or* **-ise** *vb* **-izing, -ized** *or* **-ising, -ised** **1** to find reasons to justify or explain (one's actions) **2** to apply logic or reason to (something) **3** to get rid of unnecessary equipment or staff to make (a business) more efficient **rationalization** *or* **-isation** *n*

rational number *n* any real number that can be expressed in the form *a*/*b*, where *a* and *b* are integers and *b* is not zero, as ⅔

ratpack *n slang* the members of the press who pursue celebrities and give wide coverage of their private lives: *the royal ratpack*

rat race *n* a continual routine of hectic competitive activity: *get out of the rat race for a while*

rattan *n* a climbing palm with tough stems used for wickerwork and canes
WORD ORIGIN Malay *rōtan*

ratter *n* a dog or cat that catches and kills rats

Rattigan *n* Sir **Terence Mervyn** 1911–77, English playwright. His plays include *The Winslow Boy* (1946), *Separate Tables* (1954), and *Ross* (1960)

rattle ❶ *vb* **-tling, -tled** **1** to make a rapid succession of short sharp sounds, such as when loose pellets are shaken in a container **2** to send, move, or drive with such a sound: *rain rattled against the window* **3** to shake briskly causing sharp sounds **4** *informal* to frighten or confuse **5** **rattle off** *or* **out** to recite perfunctorily or rapidly **6** **rattle on** *or* **away** to talk quickly and at length about something unimportant **7** **rattle through** to do (something) very quickly: *she rattled through a translation* ▹ *n* **8** a rapid succession of short sharp sounds **9** a baby's toy filled with small pellets that rattle when shaken **rattly** *adj*
WORD ORIGIN Middle Dutch *ratelen*

Rattle *n* Sir **Simon** born 1955, British conductor. Principal conductor (1980–91) and music director (1991–98) of the City of Birmingham Symphony Orchestra; chief conductor of the Berlin Philharmonic Orchestra from 2002

rattlesnake *n* a poisonous snake with loose horny segments on the tail that make a rattling sound

rattletrap *n informal* a broken-down old vehicle

rattling *adv informal, old-fashioned* very: *a rattling good yarn*

ratty *adj* **-tier, -tiest** *informal* **1** cross and irritable **2** (of the hair) straggly and greasy **rattily** *adv* **rattiness** *n*

THESAURUS

▹ *vb* **8, 9, 10 = evaluate**, consider, rank, reckon, class, value, measure, regard, estimate, count, grade, assess, weigh, esteem, classify, appraise, adjudge **11 = deserve**, merit, be entitled to, be worthy of

rather *adv* **1, 2 = to some extent**, quite, sort of *(informal)*, kind of *(informal)*, a little, a bit, pretty *(informal)*, fairly, relatively, somewhat, slightly, moderately, to some degree **4 = preferably**, sooner, instead, more readily, more willingly

ratify *vb* **= approve**, sign, establish, confirm, bind, sanction, endorse, uphold, authorize, affirm, certify, consent to, validate, bear out, corroborate, authenticate
OPPOSITE: annul

rating *n* **2 = position**, evaluation, classification, placing, rate, order, standing, class, degree, estimate, rank, status, grade, designation

ratio *n* **1 = proportion**, rate, relationship, relation, arrangement, percentage, equation, fraction, correspondence, correlation

ration *n* **1 = allowance**, quota, allotment, provision, helping, part, share, measure, dole, portion ▹ *vb* **3 = limit**, control, restrict, save, budget, conserve

rational *adj* **1 = sensible**, sound, wise, reasonable, intelligent, realistic, logical, enlightened, sane, lucid, judicious, sagacious, grounded

rationale *n* **= reason**, grounds, theory, principle, philosophy, logic, motivation, exposition, raison d'être *(French)*

rattle *vb* **1, 2 = clatter**, bang, jangle **3 = shake**, jiggle, jolt, vibrate, bounce, jar, jounce **4** *(informal)* **= fluster**, shake, upset, frighten, scare, disturb, disconcert, perturb, faze, discomfit, discountenance, put (someone) off his stride, discompose, put (someone) out of countenance

DICTIONARY

Ratushinskaya *n* **Irina** born 1954, Russian poet and writer: imprisoned (1983–86) in a Soviet labour camp on charges of subversion. Her publications include *Poems* (1984), *Grey is the Colour of Hope* (1988), and *The Odessans* (1992)

raucous *adj* loud and harsh
WORD ORIGIN Latin *raucus*

raunchy *adj* **-chier, -chiest** *slang* sexy or earthy
WORD ORIGIN origin unknown

Rauschenberg *n* **Robert** born 1925, US artist; one of the foremost exponents of pop art

ravage ❶ *vb* **-aging, -aged** 1 to cause extensive damage to ▷ *n* 2 **ravages** the damaging effects: *the ravages of weather and pollution*
WORD ORIGIN Old French *ravir* to snatch away

rave ❶ *vb* **raving, raved** 1 to talk in a wild or incoherent manner 2 *informal* to write or speak (about) with great enthusiasm ▷ *n* 3 *informal* an enthusiastically favourable review 4 *slang* a professionally organized large-scale party with electronic dance music 5 a name given to various types of dance music, such as techno, that feature a fast electronic rhythm
WORD ORIGIN probably from Old French *resver* to wander

ravel *vb* **-elling, -elled** *or US* **-eling, -eled** 1 to tangle or become entangled 2 (of a fabric) to fray out in loose ends; unravel
WORD ORIGIN Middle Dutch *ravelen*

raven *n* 1 a large bird of the crow family with shiny black feathers ▷ *adj* 2 (of hair) shiny black
WORD ORIGIN Old English *hrǣfn*

ravening *adj* (of animals) hungrily searching for prey

ravenous *adj* 1 very hungry 2 ravening **ravenously** *adv*
WORD ORIGIN Old French *ravineux*

raver *n slang* 1 *Brit, Austral & S African* a person who leads a wild or uninhibited social life 2 a person who enjoys rave music and goes to raves

ravine (rav-**veen**) *n* a deep narrow steep-sided valley worn by a stream
WORD ORIGIN Old French: torrent

raving ❶ *adj* 1 delirious 2 *informal* great or exceptional: *a raving beauty* ▷ *adv* 3 to an excessive degree: *raving mad* ▷ *n* 4 **ravings** frenzied or wildly extravagant talk

ravioli *pl n* small squares of pasta with a savoury filling, such as meat or cheese
WORD ORIGIN Italian

ravish *vb* 1 to enrapture or delight: *tourists ravished by our brilliant costumes* 2 *literary* to rape **ravishment** *n*
WORD ORIGIN Latin *rapere* to seize

ravishing *adj* lovely or delightful **ravishingly** *adv*

raw ❶ *adj* 1 (of food) not cooked 2 in an unfinished or unrefined state: *raw sewage* 3 not selected or modified: *raw data* 4 (of the skin or a wound) painful, with the surface scraped away 5 untrained or inexperienced: *a raw recruit* 6 (of the weather) harshly cold and damp 7 frank or realistic: *a raw reality* 8 **raw deal** *informal* unfair or dishonest treatment ▷ *n* 9 **in the raw a** *informal* naked **b** in a natural and uncivilized state: *to see life in the raw* 10 **on the raw** *Brit informal* sensitive to upset: *my nerves are on the raw today*
WORD ORIGIN Old English *hrēaw*

rawboned *adj* having a lean bony physique

rawhide *n* 1 untanned hide 2 a whip or rope made of strips of this

Rawlplug *n trademark* a short fibre or plastic tube used to provide a fixing in a wall for a screw

Rawsthorne *n* **Alan** 1905–71, English composer, whose works include three symphonies, several concertos, and a set of *Symphonic Studies* (1939)

ray[1] ❶ *n* 1 a narrow beam of light 2 any of a set of lines spreading from a central point 3 a slight indication: *a ray of hope* 4 *maths* a straight line extending from a point 5 a thin beam of electromagnetic radiation or particles 6 any of the spines that support the fin of a fish
WORD ORIGIN Old French *rai*

ray[2] *n* a sea fish related to the sharks, with a flattened body and a long whiplike tail
WORD ORIGIN Old French *raie*

ray[3] *n music* (in tonic sol-fa) the second note of any ascending major scale

Ray[1] *n* **Cape Ray** a promontory in SW Newfoundland, Canada

Ray[2] *n* 1 **John** 1627–1705, English naturalist. He originated natural botanical classification and the division of flowering plants into monocotyledons and dicotyledons 2 **Man**, real name *Emmanuel Rudnitsky*. 1890–1976, US surrealist photographer 3 **Satyajit** 1921–92, Indian film director, noted for his *Apu* trilogy (1955–59)

rayon *n* a textile fibre or fabric made from cellulose
WORD ORIGIN French

raze *or* **rase** *vb* **razing, razed** *or* **rasing, rased** to destroy (buildings or a town) completely
WORD ORIGIN Old French *raser*

razoo *n, pl* **-zoos** *Austral & NZ informal* an imaginary coin: *we haven't got a brass razoo*
WORD ORIGIN origin unknown

razor *n* an implement with a sharp blade, used for shaving
WORD ORIGIN Old French *raseor*

razorbill *n* a black-and-white sea bird with a stout sideways flattened bill

razor shell *n* 1 a burrowing shellfish with a long narrow shell 2 this shell

razor wire *n* strong wire with pieces of sharp metal set across it at intervals

razzle-dazzle *or* **razzmatazz** *n slang* 1 noisy or showy fuss or activity 2 a spree or frolic
WORD ORIGIN rhyming compound from *dazzle*

Rb *chem* rubidium

RC 1 Red Cross 2 Roman Catholic

Rd road

re[1] ❶ *prep* with reference to
WORD ORIGIN Latin *res* thing

re[2] *n music* ▸ same as **ray**[3]

Re *chem* rhenium

THESAURUS

ravage *vb* 1 = **destroy**, ruin, devastate, wreck, shatter, gut, spoil, loot, demolish, plunder, desolate, sack, ransack, pillage, raze, lay waste, wreak havoc on, despoil, leave in ruins ▷ *n* 2 *(pl)* = **damage**, destruction, devastation, desolation, waste, ruin, havoc, demolition, plunder, pillage, depredation, ruination, rapine, spoliation

rave *vb* 1 = **rant**, rage, roar, thunder, fume, go mad *(informal)*, babble, splutter, storm, be delirious, talk wildly 2 *(informal)* = **enthuse**, praise, gush, be delighted by, be mad about *(informal)*, big up *(slang, chiefly Caribbean)*, rhapsodize, be wild about *(informal)*, cry up

raving *adj* 1 = **mad**, wild, raging, crazy, furious, frantic, frenzied, hysterical, insane, irrational, crazed, berserk, delirious, rabid, out of your mind, gonzo *(slang)*, berko *(Austral slang)*, off the air *(Austral slang)*

raw *adj* 1 = **uncooked**, natural, fresh, bloody *(of meat)*, undressed, unprepared **OPPOSITE:** cooked 2 = **unrefined**, natural, crude, unprocessed, basic, rough, organic, coarse, unfinished, untreated, unripe **OPPOSITE:** refined 5 = **inexperienced**, new, green, ignorant, immature, unskilled, callow, untrained, untried, undisciplined, unseasoned, unpractised **OPPOSITE:** experienced 6 = **chilly**, biting, cold, freezing, bitter, wet, chill, harsh, piercing, damp, unpleasant, bleak, parky *(Brit informal)*

ray *n* 1 = **beam**, bar, flash, shaft, gleam

re[1] *prep* = **concerning**, about, regarding, respecting, with regard to, on the subject of, in respect of, with reference to, apropos, anent *(Scot)*

DICTIONARY

RE 1 (in Britain) Religious Education 2 Royal Engineers

re- *prefix* 1 (used with many main words to mean) repetition of an action: *remarry* 2 (used with many main words to mean) return to a previous condition: *renew*
WORD ORIGIN Latin

reach ❶ *vb* 1 to arrive at or get to (a place) 2 to make a movement (towards), as if to grasp or touch: *she reached for her bag* 3 to succeed in touching: *I can't reach that shelf unless I stand on a chair* 4 to make contact or communication with: *to reach a wider audience* 5 to extend as far as (a point or place): *to reach the ceiling* 6 to come to (a certain condition or situation): *to reach a compromise* 7 to arrive at or amount to (an amount or value): *temperatures in Greece reached 35° yesterday* 8 *informal* to give (something to a person) with the outstretched hand ▹*n* 9 the extent or distance of reaching: *within easy reach* 10 the range of influence or power: *it symbolized America's global reach* 11 **reaches** a section of river, land, or sky: *the quieter reaches of the upper Thames* **reachable** *adj*
WORD ORIGIN Old English *rǣcan*

reach-me-down *adj Brit informal* cheap and ready-made or second-hand: *a reach-me-down suit*

reacquaint *vb* **reacquaint oneself with** *or* **become reacquainted with** to get to know (someone) again

react ❶ *vb* 1 (of a person or thing) to act in response to another person, a stimulus, or a situation 2 **react against** to act in an opposing or contrary manner 3 *chem* to undergo a chemical reaction 4 *physics* to exert an equal force in the opposite direction to an acting force
WORD ORIGIN Late Latin *reagere*

reactance *n electronics* the resistance to the flow of an alternating current caused by the inductance or capacitance of the circuit

reactant *n* a substance that participates in a chemical reaction

reaction ❶ *n* 1 a physical or emotional response to a stimulus 2 any action resisting another 3 opposition to change 4 *med* any effect produced by a drug or by a substance (allergen) to which a person is allergic 5 *chem* a process that involves changes in the structure and energy content of atoms, molecules, or ions 6 the equal and opposite force that acts on a body whenever it exerts a force on another body 7 **reactions** someone's ability to act in response to something that happens

reactionary ❶ *adj* 1 opposed to political or social change ▹*n, pl* **-aries** 2 a person opposed to radical change

reactivate *vb* **-vating, -vated** to make (something) active again **reactivation** *n*

reactive *adj* 1 readily taking part in chemical reactions: *ozone is a highly reactive form of oxygen gas* 2 of or having a reactance 3 responsive to stimulus **reactively** *adv* **reactivity** *n*

reactor *n* ▸short for **nuclear reactor**

read ❶ *vb* **reading, read** 1 to look at and understand or take in (written or printed matter) 2 to look at and say aloud 3 to have a certain wording: *the memorandum read as follows* 4 to interpret in a specified way: *it can be read as satire* 5 to interpret the significance or meaning of: *an astrologer who reads Tarot* 6 to register or show: *the meter reads 100* 7 to make out the true nature or mood of: *she had read his thoughts* 8 to interpret (signs, characters, etc.) other than by visual means: *to read Braille* 9 to have sufficient knowledge of (a language) to understand the written word 10 to undertake a course of study in (a subject): *to read economics* 11 to gain knowledge by reading: *he read about the war* 12 to hear and understand, esp. when using a two-way radio: *we are reading you loud and clear* 13 *computers* to obtain (data) from a storage device, such as magnetic tape ▹*n* 14 matter suitable for reading: *this book is a very good read* 15 a spell of reading ▸See also **read into, read out**, etc.
WORD ORIGIN Old English *rǣdan* to advise, explain

readable *adj* 1 enjoyable to read 2 (of handwriting or print) legible

Reade *n* **Charles** 1814–84, English novelist: author of *The Cloister and the Hearth* (1861), a historical romance

reader *n* 1 a person who reads 2 a person who reads aloud in public 3 a person who reads and judges manuscripts sent to a publisher 4 a book of texts for those learning a foreign language 5 *Brit* a member of staff below a professor but above a senior lecturer at a university 6 a proofreader 7 ▸short for **lay reader**

readership *n* all the readers collectively of a publication or author: *a new format would alienate its readership*

reading ❶ *n* 1 the act of reading 2 ability to read: *disputes over methods of teaching reading* 3 material for reading 4 a public recital of a literary work 5 a measurement indicated by a gauge or dial 6 *parliamentary procedure* one of the three stages in the passage of a bill through a legislative assembly 7 the form of a particular word or passage in a given text 8 an interpretation of a situation or something said ▹*adj* 9 of or for reading: *reading glasses*

read into *vb* to discover in a statement (meanings not intended by the speaker or writer): *one of the implications we must read into the work*

readjust *vb* to adapt to a new situation **readjustment** *n*

readmit *vb* **-mitting, -mitted** to let (a person or country) back into a place or organization **readmission** *n*

read out *vb* 1 to read (something) aloud 2 to retrieve information from a computer memory ▹*n* **read-out** 3 the information retrieved from a computer memory

read up *vb* to read intensively about (a subject) in order to get information: *he had read up on the cases*

read-write head *n computers* an electromagnet that can both read and write information on a magnetic tape or disk

r

THESAURUS

reach *vb* 1 = **arrive at**, get to, get as far as, make, attain, land at 2, 3 = **touch**, grasp, extend to, get (a) hold of, stretch to, go as far as, contact 4 = **contact**, get in touch with, get through to, make contact with, get, find, communicate with, get hold of, establish contact with 7 = **attain**, get to, amount to ▹*n* 9 = **grasp**, range, distance, stretch, sweep, capacity, extent, extension, scope 10 = **jurisdiction**, power, influence, command, compass, mastery, ambit

react *vb* 1 = **respond**, act, proceed, behave, conduct yourself

reaction *n* 1 = **response**, acknowledgment, feedback, answer, reply 2 = **counteraction**, compensation, backlash, recoil, counterbalance, counterpoise 3 = **conservatism**, the right, counter-revolution, obscurantism

reactionary *adj* 1 = **conservative**, right-wing, counter-revolutionary, obscurantist, blimpish
OPPOSITE: radical
▹*n* 2 = **conservative**, die-hard, right-winger, rightist, counter-revolutionary, obscurantist, Colonel Blimp OPPOSITE: radical

read *vb* 1 = **scan**, study, look at, refer to, glance at, pore over, peruse, run your eye over 1, 9 = **understand**, interpret, comprehend, construe, decipher, perceive the meaning of, see, discover 6 = **register**, show, record, display, indicate

reading *n* 1 = **perusal**, study, review, examination, inspection, scrutiny 4 = **recital**, performance, rendering, rendition, lesson, lecture, sermon, homily 8 = **interpretation**, take (*informal, chiefly US*), understanding, treatment, version, construction, impression, grasp, conception

DICTIONARY

ready ❶ *adj* **readier, readiest** **1** prepared for use or action **2** prompt or eager: *the ready use of corporal punishment* **3** quick or intelligent: *a ready wit* **4 ready to** on the point of or liable to: *ready to pounce* **5** easily available: *his ready tears* ▷ *n* **6** *informal* ▶ same as **ready money** **7 at the ready** poised for use: *with pen at the ready* ▷ *vb* **readies, readying, readied** **8** to make ready; prepare **readily** *adv* **readiness** *n*
WORD ORIGIN Old English *(ge)rǣde*

ready-made *adj* **1** for immediate use by any customer **2** extremely convenient or ideally suited: *a ready-made audience*

ready money *n* cash for immediate use. Also: **the ready, the readies**

reaffirm *vb* to state again **reaffirmation** *n*

reafforest *vb* to plant new trees in (an area that was formerly forested) **reafforestation** *n*

reagent (ree-age-ent) *n* a chemical substance that reacts with another, used to detect the presence of the other

real[1] ❶ *adj* **1** existing or occurring in the physical world **2** actual: *the real agenda* **3** important or serious: *the real challenge* **4** rightly so called: *a real friend* **5** genuine: *the council has no real authority* **6** (of food or drink) made in a traditional way to ensure the best flavour **7** *maths* involving or containing real numbers alone **8** relating to immovable property such as land or buildings: *real estate* **9** *econ* (of prices or incomes) considered in terms of purchasing power rather than nominal currency value **10 the real thing** the genuine article, not a substitute or imitation
WORD ORIGIN Latin *res* thing

real[2] *n* a former small Spanish or Spanish-American silver coin
WORD ORIGIN Spanish, literally: royal

real ale *n chiefly Brit* beer that has fermented in the barrel

real estate *n* immovable property, esp. land and houses

realignment (ree-a-line-ment) *n* a new arrangement or organization: *there will be a realignment of party allegiances*

realism *n* **1** awareness or acceptance of things as they are, as opposed to the abstract or ideal **2** a style in art or literature that attempts to show the world as it really is **3** *philosophy* the theory that physical objects continue to exist whether they are perceived or not **realist** *n* **realistic** *adj* **realistically** *adv*

reality ❶ *n, pl* **-ties** **1** the state of things as they are or appear to be, rather than as one might wish them to be **2** something that is real **3** the state of being real **4 in reality** in fact

reality TV *n* television programmes focusing on members of the public living in conditions created especially by the programme makers

realize ❶ *or* **-ise** *vb* **-izing, -ized** *or* **-ising, -ised** **1** to be aware of or grasp the significance of **2** to achieve (a plan or ambition) **3** to convert (property or goods) into cash **4** (of goods or property) to sell for (a certain sum): *this table realized a large sum at auction* **5** to produce a complete work of art from an idea or draft **realizable** *or* **-isable** *adj* **realization** *or* **-isation** *n*

really ❶ *adv* **1** truly: *really boring* **2** in reality: *it's really quite harmless* ▷ *interj* **3** an exclamation of dismay, doubt, or surprise

realm ❶ *n* **1** a kingdom **2** a field of interest or study: *the realm of science*
WORD ORIGIN Old French *reialme*

real number *n* any rational or irrational number

real tennis *n* an ancient form of tennis played in a four-walled indoor court

real-time *adj* (of a computer system) processing data as it is received

realtor *n US & Canad* an estate agent
WORD ORIGIN from a trademark

realty *n* ▶ same as **real estate**

ream *n* **1** a number of sheets of paper, now equal to 500 or 516 sheets (20 quires) **2 reams** *informal* a large quantity (of written material): *reams of verse*
WORD ORIGIN Arabic *rizmah* bale

reap ❶ *vb* **1** to cut and gather (a harvest) **2** to receive as the result of a previous activity: *reap the benefits of our efforts*
WORD ORIGIN Old English *riopan*

reaper *n* **1** a person who reaps or a machine for reaping **2 the grim reaper** death

reappear *vb* to come back into view **reappearance** *n*

reappraise *vb* **-praising, -praised** to consider or review (something) to see if changes are needed **reappraisal** *n*

rear[1] ❶ *n* **1** the back part **2** the area or position that lies at the back **3** *informal* the buttocks **4 bring up the rear** to come last ▷ *adj* **5** of or in the rear: *the rear carriage*
WORD ORIGIN Old French *rer*

rear[2] ❶ *vb* **1** to care for and educate (children) until maturity **2** to breed (animals) or grow (plants) **3** (of a horse) to lift the front legs in the air and stand nearly upright **4** to place or lift (something) upright
WORD ORIGIN Old English *rǣran*

rear admiral *n* a high-ranking naval officer

THESAURUS

ready *adj* **1a = prepared**, set, primed, organized, all set, in readiness **OPPOSITE:** unprepared **1b = completed**, arranged **2 = willing**, happy, glad, disposed, game *(informal)*, minded, keen, eager, inclined, prone, have-a-go *(informal)*, apt, agreeable, predisposed **OPPOSITE:** reluctant **3 = prompt**, smart, quick, bright, sharp, keen, acute, rapid, alert, clever, intelligent, handy, apt, skilful, astute, perceptive, expert, deft, resourceful, adroit, quick-witted, dexterous **OPPOSITE:** slow **5 = available**, handy, at the ready, at your fingertips, present, near, accessible, convenient, on call, on tap *(informal)*, close to hand, at *or* on hand **OPPOSITE:** unavailable

real[1] *adj* **1, 2 = true**, genuine, sincere, honest, factual, existent, dinkum *(Austral & NZ informal)*, unfeigned **2, 5 = true**, actual **4 = proper**, true, valid, legitimate **5a = genuine**, authentic, bona fide, dinkum *(Austral & NZ informal)* **OPPOSITE:** fake **5b = typical**, true, genuine, sincere, unaffected, dinkum *(Austral & NZ informal)*, unfeigned

reality *n* **1, 3 = fact**, truth, certainty, realism, validity, authenticity, verity, actuality, materiality, genuineness, verisimilitude, corporeality **2 = truth**, fact, actuality

realize *vb* **1 = become aware of**, understand, recognize, appreciate, take in, grasp, conceive, catch on *(informal)*, comprehend, twig *(Brit informal)*, get the message, apprehend, become conscious of, be cognizant of **2 = fulfil**, achieve, accomplish, make real **5 = achieve**, do, effect, complete, perform, fulfil, accomplish, bring about, consummate, incarnate, bring off, make concrete, bring to fruition, actualize, make happen, effectuate, reify, carry out *or* through

really *adv* **2 = truly**, actually, in fact, indeed, in reality, in actuality

realm *n* **1 = kingdom**, state, country, empire, monarchy, land, province, domain, dominion, principality **2 = field**, world, area, province, sphere, department, region, branch, territory, zone, patch, orbit, turf *(US slang)*

reap *vb* **1 = collect**, gather, bring in, harvest, garner, cut **2 = get**, win, gain, obtain, acquire, derive

rear[1] *n* **1 = back part**, back **OPPOSITE:** front **2 = back**, end, tail, rearguard, tail end, back end ▷ *adj* **5 = back**, aft, hind, hindmost, after *(naut)*, last, following, trailing **OPPOSITE:** front

rear[2] *vb* **1 = bring up**, raise, educate, care for, train, nurse, foster, nurture **2 = breed**, keep

Reardon *n* **Ray** born 1932, Welsh snooker player: world champion 1970, 1973–76, 1978
rearguard *n* **1** the troops who protect the rear of a military formation ▷ *adj* **2 rearguard action** an effort to prevent or postpone something that is unavoidable
rear light *or* **rear lamp** *n* a red light, usually one of a pair, attached to the rear of a vehicle. Also called: **tail-light, tail lamp**
rearm *vb* **1** to arm again **2** to equip with better weapons **rearmament** *n*
rearmost *adj* nearest the back
rearrange *vb* **-ranging, -ranged** to organize differently **rearrangement** *n*
rear-view mirror *n* a mirror on a motor vehicle enabling the driver to see the traffic behind
rearward *adj* **1** in the rear ▷ *adv also* **rearwards 2** towards the rear
reason ❶ *n* **1** a cause or motive for a belief or action: *he had two reasons for his dark mood* **2** the ability to think or argue rationally **3** an argument in favour of or a justification for something: *there is every reason to encourage people to keep fit* **4** sanity **5 by reason of** because of **6 within reason** within moderate or justifiable bounds **7 it stands to reason** it is logical or obvious ▷ *vb* **8** to think logically in forming conclusions **9 reason with** to persuade by logical arguments into doing something **10 reason out** to work out (a problem) by reasoning **WORD ORIGIN** Latin *reri* to think
reasonable ❶ *adj* **1** sensible **2** not making unfair demands **3** logical: *a reasonable explanation* **4** moderate in price **5** average: *a reasonable amount of luck* **reasonably** *adv* **reasonableness** *n*
reasoned *adj* well thought out or well presented: *a reasoned explanation*
reasoning *n* **1** the process of drawing conclusions from facts or evidence **2** the conclusions reached in this way
reassemble *vb* **-bling, -bled** to put back together again
reassert *vb* **1** to state or declare again **2 reassert oneself** to become significant or noticeable again: *reality had reasserted itself*
reassess *vb* to reconsider the value or importance of **reassessment** *n*
reassure ❶ *vb* **-assuring, -assured** to relieve (someone) of anxieties **reassurance** *n* **reassuring** *adj*
rebate[1] ❶ *n* a refund or discount **WORD ORIGIN** Old French *rabattre* to beat down
rebate[2] *or* **rabbet** *n* **1** a groove cut into a piece of timber into which another piece fits ▷ *vb* **-bating, -bated** *or* **-beting, -beted 2** to cut a rebate in **3** to join (pieces of timber) with a rebate **WORD ORIGIN** Old French *rabattre* to beat down
rebel ❶ *vb* **-belling, -belled 1** to fight against the ruling power **2** to reject accepted conventions of behaviour ▷ *n* **3** a person who rebels **4** a person who rejects accepted conventions of behaviour ▷ *adj* **5** rebelling: *rebel councillors* **WORD ORIGIN** Latin *re-* again + *bellum* war
rebellion ❶ *n* **1** organized opposition to a government or other authority involving the use of violence **2** nonviolent opposition to a government or other authority: *a Tory backbenchers' rebellion* **3** rejection of accepted conventions of behaviour **WORD ORIGIN** Latin *rebellio*
rebellious ❶ *adj* rebelling or showing a tendency towards rebellion **rebelliously** *adv*
rebirth *n* a revival or renaissance: *the rebirth of their nation*
reboot *vb* to shut down and then restart (a computer system)
rebore *or* **reboring** *n* the boring of a cylinder to restore its true shape
reborn *adj* active again after a period of inactivity
rebound ❶ *vb* **1** to spring back from a sudden impact **2** (of a plan or action) to misfire so as to hurt the person responsible ▷ *n* **3** the act of rebounding **4 on the rebound** *informal* while recovering from rejection: *she married him on the rebound*
rebrand *vb* to change or update the image of (an organization or product)
rebuff ❶ *vb* **1** to snub and reject an offer or suggestion ▷ *n* **2** a blunt refusal; snub **WORD ORIGIN** Old French *rebuffer*
rebuild *vb* **-building, -built 1** to build (a building or town) again, after severe damage **2** to develop (something such as a business or

THESAURUS

reason *n* **1 = cause**, grounds, purpose, motive, end, goal, design, target, aim, basis, occasion, object, intention, incentive, warrant, impetus, inducement, why and wherefore *(informal)* **2, 4 = sense**, mind, reasoning, understanding, brains, judgment, logic, mentality, intellect, comprehension, apprehension, sanity, rationality, soundness, sound mind, ratiocination **OPPOSITE:** emotion ▷ *vb* **8 = deduce**, conclude, work out, solve, resolve, make out, infer, draw conclusions, think, ratiocinate, syllogize
9 reason with = persuade, debate with, remonstrate with, bring round, urge, win over, argue with, dispute with, dissuade, prevail upon *(informal)*, expostulate with, show (someone) the error of his ways, talk into *or* out of
reasonable *adj* **1 = within reason**, fit, proper **OPPOSITE:** impossible **1, 3 = sensible**, reasoned, sound, practical, wise, intelligent, rational, logical, sober, credible, plausible, sane, judicious, grounded **OPPOSITE:** irrational **2 = fair**, just, right, acceptable, moderate, equitable, justifiable, well-advised, well-thought-out, tenable **OPPOSITE:** unfair **4 = low**, cheap, competitive, moderate, modest, inexpensive, tolerable **5 = average**, fair, moderate, modest, tolerable, O.K. *or* okay *(informal)*
reassure *vb* **= encourage**, comfort, bolster, hearten, cheer up, buoy up, gee up, restore confidence to, inspirit, relieve (someone) of anxiety, put *or* set your mind at rest
rebate[1] *n* **= refund**, discount, reduction, bonus, allowance, deduction
rebel *vb* **1 = revolt**, resist, rise up, mutiny, take to the streets, take up arms, man the barricades **2 = defy**, dissent, disobey, come out against, refuse to obey, dig your heels in *(informal)* ▷ *n* **3 = revolutionary**, resistance fighter, insurgent, secessionist, mutineer, insurrectionary, revolutionist **4 = nonconformist**, dissenter, heretic, apostate, schismatic ▷ *adj* **5 = rebellious**, revolutionary, insurgent, mutinous, insubordinate, insurrectionary
rebellion *n* **1 = resistance**, rising, revolution, revolt, uprising, mutiny, insurrection, insurgency, insurgence **2, 3 = nonconformity**, dissent, defiance, heresy, disobedience, schism, insubordination, apostasy
rebellious *adj* **a = defiant**, difficult, resistant, intractable, recalcitrant, obstinate, unmanageable, incorrigible, refractory, contumacious **OPPOSITE:** obedient **b = revolutionary**, rebel, disorderly, unruly, turbulent, disaffected, insurgent, recalcitrant, disloyal, seditious, mutinous, disobedient, ungovernable, insubordinate, insurrectionary **OPPOSITE:** obedient
rebound *vb* **1 = bounce**, ricochet, spring back, return, resound, recoil **2 = misfire**, backfire, recoil, boomerang
rebuff *vb* **1 = reject**, decline, refuse, turn down, cut, check, deny, resist, slight, discourage, put off, snub, spurn, knock back *(slang)*, brush off *(slang)*, repulse, cold-shoulder

DICTIONARY

relationship) again after destruction or damage

rebuke ❶ *vb* **-buking, -buked** 1 to scold sternly ▷*n* 2 a stern scolding
WORD ORIGIN Old French *rebuker*

rebus (ree-buss) *n, pl* **-buses** a puzzle consisting of pictures and symbols representing syllables and words
WORD ORIGIN Latin: by things

rebut *vb* **-butting, -butted** to prove that (a claim) is untrue **rebuttal** *n*
WORD ORIGIN Old French *reboter*

rec *n* ▸short for **recreation**

recalcitrant *adj* wilfully disobedient **recalcitrance** *n*
WORD ORIGIN Latin *re-* again + *calcitrare* to kick

recall ❶ *vb* 1 to bring back to mind 2 to order to return 3 to annul or cancel ▷*n* 4 the ability to remember things 5 an order to return

recant *vb* to take back (a former belief or statement) publicly **recantation** *n*
WORD ORIGIN Latin *re-* again + *cantare* to sing

recap *informal vb* **-capping, -capped** 1 to recapitulate ▷*n* 2 a recapitulation

recapitulate *vb* **-lating, -lated** to restate the main points of (an argument or speech)
WORD ORIGIN Late Latin *recapitulare*, literally: to put back under headings

recapitulation *n* 1 the act of recapitulating 2 *music* the repeating of earlier themes, esp. in the final section of a movement

recapture *vb* **-turing, -tured** 1 to relive vividly (a former experience or sensation): *recaptured some of those first feelings* 2 to capture again ▷*n* 3 the act of recapturing

recast *vb* **-casting, -cast** 1 to give a new form or shape to: *he found the organization wholly recast* 2 to change the actors or singers in (a play, musical, or opera) 3 to rework (a piece of writing or music): *she has recast most of my book*

recce *chiefly Brit slang vb* **-ceing, -ced** *or* **-ceed** 1 to reconnoitre ▷*n* 2 reconnaissance

recede ❶ *vb* **-ceding, -ceded** 1 to withdraw from a point or limit: *the tide had receded* 2 to become more distant: *the threat of intervention had receded* 3 (of a man's hair) to stop growing at the temples and above the forehead 4 to slope backwards: *a receding chin*
WORD ORIGIN Latin *recedere* to go back

receipt ❶ *n* 1 a written acknowledgment that money or goods have been received 2 the act of receiving 3 **receipts** money taken in over a particular period by a shop or business
WORD ORIGIN Old French *receite*

receive ❶ *vb* **-ceiving, -ceived** 1 to get (something offered or sent to one) 2 to experience: *he received a knife wound* 3 to greet (guests) 4 to have (an honour) bestowed: *he received the Order of the Garter* 5 to admit (a person) to a society or condition: *he was received into the Church* 6 to convert (incoming radio or television signals) into sounds or pictures 7 to be informed of (news) 8 to react to: *the article was well received* 9 to support or sustain (the weight of something) 10 *tennis, etc.* to play at the other end from the server 11 *Brit & NZ* to buy and sell stolen goods
WORD ORIGIN Latin *recipere*

received *adj* generally accepted or believed: *contrary to received wisdom*

Received Pronunciation *n* the accent of standard Southern British English

receiver *n* 1 the detachable part of a telephone that is held to the ear 2 the equipment in a telephone, radio, or television that converts the incoming signals into sound or pictures 3 a person appointed by a court to manage property of a bankrupt 4 a person who receives stolen goods knowing they have been stolen

receivership *n law* the state of being administered by a receiver: *the company went into receivership*

recent ❶ *adj* 1 having happened lately 2 new **recently** *adv*
WORD ORIGIN Latin *recens* fresh

Recent *adj* ▸same as **Holocene**

receptacle *n* 1 an object used to contain something 2 *bot* the enlarged or modified tip of the flower stalk that bears the flower
WORD ORIGIN Latin *receptaculum* store-place

reception ❶ *n* 1 an area in an office, hotel, etc. where visitors are received or reservations dealt with 2 a formal party for guests, esp. after a wedding 3 the manner in which something is received: *an enthusiastic reception* 4 the act of formally welcoming 5 *radio, television* the quality of a received broadcast: *the reception was poor*

receptionist *n* a person employed to receive guests or clients and deal with reservations and appointments

reception room *n* a room in a private house suitable for entertaining guests

receptive *adj* willing to consider and accept new ideas or suggestions **receptivity** *or* **receptiveness** *n*

receptor *n physiol* a sensory nerve ending that changes specific stimuli into nerve impulses

recess ❶ *n* 1 a space, such as an

THESAURUS

OPPOSITE: encourage
▷*n* **2 = rejection**, defeat, snub, knock-back, check, opposition, slight, refusal, denial, brush-off *(slang)*, repulse, thumbs down, cold shoulder, slap in the face *(informal)*, kick in the teeth *(slang)*, discouragement
OPPOSITE: encouragement

rebuke *vb* **1 = scold**, censure, reprimand, reproach, blame, lecture, carpet *(informal)*, berate, tick off *(informal)*, castigate, chide, dress down *(informal)*, admonish, tear into *(informal)*, tell off *(informal)*, take to task, read the riot act, reprove, upbraid, bawl out *(informal)*, haul (someone) over the coals *(informal)*, chew out *(US & Canad informal)*, tear (someone) off a strip *(informal)*, give a rocket *(Brit & NZ informal)*, reprehend
OPPOSITE: praise
▷*n* **2 = scolding**, censure, reprimand, reproach, blame, row, lecture, wigging *(Brit slang)*, ticking-off *(informal)*, dressing-down *(informal)*, telling-off *(informal)*, admonition, tongue-lashing, reproof, castigation, reproval **OPPOSITE:** praise

recall *vb* **1 = recollect**, remember, call up, evoke, reminisce about, call to mind, look *or* think back to, mind *(dialect)* **2 = call back 3 = annul**, withdraw, call in, take back, cancel, repeal, call back, revoke, retract, rescind, nullify, countermand, abjure ▷*n* **4 = recollection**, memory, remembrance

recede *vb* **1 = fall back**, withdraw, retreat, draw back, return, go back, retire, back off, regress, retrogress, retrocede

receipt *n* **1 = sales slip**, proof of purchase, voucher, stub, acknowledgment, counterfoil **2 = receiving**, delivery, reception, acceptance, recipience

receive *vb* **1, 4 = get**, accept, be given, pick up, collect, obtain, acquire, take, derive, be in receipt of, accept delivery of **2 = experience**, suffer, bear, go through, encounter, meet with, sustain, undergo, be subjected to **3 = greet**, meet, admit, welcome, entertain, take in, accommodate, be at home to

recent *adj* **2 = new**, modern, contemporary, up-to-date, late, young, happening *(informal)*, current, fresh, novel, latter, present-day, latter-day **OPPOSITE:** old

reception *n* **2 = party**, gathering, get-together, social gathering, do *(informal)*, social, function, entertainment, celebration, bash *(informal)*, festivity, knees-up *(Brit informal)*, shindig *(informal)*, soirée, levee, rave-up *(Brit slang)* **3 = response**, reaction, acknowledgment, recognition, treatment, welcome, greeting

recess *n* **1 = alcove**, corner, bay,

DICTIONARY

alcove, set back in a wall **2** a holiday between sessions of work **3 recesses** secret hidden places: *the recesses of her brain* **4** *US & Canad* a break between classes at a school
WORD ORIGIN Latin *recessus* a retreat
recessed *adj* hidden or placed in a recess
recession ❶ *n* **1** a period of economic difficulty when little is being bought or sold **2** the act of receding
recessional *n* a hymn sung as the clergy and choir withdraw after a church service
recessive *adj* **1** tending to recede **2** *genetics* (in a pair of genes) designating a gene that has a characteristic which will only be passed on if the other gene has the same characteristic
recharge *vb* **-charging, -charged** to cause (a battery) to take in and store electricity again **rechargeable** *adj*
recherché (rish-air-shay) *adj* **1** studiedly refined or elegant **2** known only to connoisseurs
WORD ORIGIN French: thoroughly sought after
recidivism *n* habitual relapse into crime **recidivist** *n, adj*
WORD ORIGIN Latin *recidivus* falling back
recipe ❶ *n* **1** a list of ingredients and directions for making a particular dish **2** a method for achieving something: *a recipe for industrial chaos*
WORD ORIGIN Latin, literally: take (it)!
recipient *n* a person who receives something
reciprocal (ris-sip-pro-kl) *adj* **1** done or felt by each of two people or groups to or about the other: *a reciprocal agreement* **2** given or done in return: *a reciprocal invitation* **3** *grammar* (of a pronoun) indicating that action is given and received by each subject, for example, *each other* in *they started to shout at each other* ▷ *n* **4** Also called: **inverse** *maths* a number or quantity that when multiplied by a given number or quantity gives a product of one: *the reciprocal of 2 is 0.5* **reciprocally** *adv*
WORD ORIGIN Latin *reciprocus* alternating
reciprocate *vb* **-cating, -cated** **1** to give or feel in return: *not everyone reciprocated his enthusiasm* **2** (of a machine part) to move backwards and forwards **reciprocation** *n*
reciprocity *n* **1** reciprocal action or relation **2** a mutual exchange of commercial or other privileges
recital ❶ (ris-site-al) *n* **1** a musical performance by a soloist or soloists **2** the act of reciting something learned or prepared **3** a narration or description: *she plagued her with the recital of constant ailments and illnesses*
recitation *n* **1** the act of reciting poetry or prose from memory **2** something recited
recitative (ress-it-a-teev) *n* a narrative passage in an opera or oratorio, reflecting the natural rhythms of speech
WORD ORIGIN Italian *recitativo*
recite ❶ *vb* **-citing, -cited** **1** to repeat (a poem or passage) aloud from memory before an audience **2** to give a detailed account of
WORD ORIGIN Latin *recitare*
reckless ❶ *adj* having no regard for danger or consequences: *reckless driving*
WORD ORIGIN Old English *recceleās*
reckon ❶ *vb* **1** *informal* to be of the opinion: *she reckoned she could find them* **2** to consider: *he reckoned himself a failure* **3** to calculate or compute **4** to expect **5 reckon with** to take into account: *there is this ancestral hatred to reckon with* **6 reckon without** to fail to take into account **7 reckon on** *or* **upon** to rely on or expect: *they can't reckon on your automatic support*
WORD ORIGIN Old English *(ge) recenian* recount
reckoning ❶ *n* **1** counting or calculating: *by his reckoning, he owed him money* **2** retribution for one's actions: *the moment of reckoning came* **3** settlement of an account or bill
reclaim ❶ *vb* **1** to get back possession of: *the club is now trying to reclaim the money from the blockaders* **2** to convert (unusable or submerged land) into land suitable for farming or building on **3** to recover (useful substances) from waste products **reclamation** *n*
WORD ORIGIN Latin *reclamare* to cry out
recline *vb* **-clining, -clined** to rest in a leaning position
WORD ORIGIN Latin *reclinare*
reclining *adj* (of a seat) with a back that can be adjusted to slope at various angles
recluse *n* a person who lives alone and avoids people **reclusive** *adj*
WORD ORIGIN Late Latin *recludere* to shut away
recognition ❶ *n* **1** the act of recognizing **2** acceptance or acknowledgment **3** formal acknowledgment of a government or of the independence of a country **4 in recognition of** as a token of thanks for
recognizance *or* **recognisance** (rik-og-nizz-anss) *n law* **a** an undertaking made before a court or magistrate to do something specified, such as to appear in court on a stated day **b** a sum of money promised as a guarantee of this undertaking
WORD ORIGIN Old French *reconoissance*
recognize ❶ *or* **-nise** *vb* **-nizing, -nized** *or* **-nising, -nised** **1** to identify (a person or thing) as someone or something already known **2** to

r

THESAURUS

depression, hollow, niche, cavity, nook, oriel, indentation **2 = break**, rest, holiday, closure, interval, vacation, respite, intermission, cessation of business, schoolie *(Austral)*
recession *n* **1 = depression**, drop, decline, slump, downturn
OPPOSITE: boom
recipe *n* **1 = directions**, instructions, ingredients, receipt *(obsolete)*
recital *n* **1 = performance**, rendering, rehearsal, reading **2 = recitation**, repetition **3 = account**, telling, story, detailing, statement, relation, tale, description, narrative, narration, enumeration, recapitulation
recite *vb* **1 = perform**, relate, deliver, repeat, rehearse, declaim, recapitulate, do your party piece *(informal)*
reckless *adj* **= careless**, wild, rash, irresponsible, precipitate, hasty, mindless, negligent, headlong, madcap, ill-advised, regardless, foolhardy, daredevil, thoughtless, indiscreet, imprudent, heedless, devil-may-care, inattentive, incautious, harebrained, harum-scarum, overventuresome
OPPOSITE: cautious
reckon *vb* **1** *(informal)* **= think**, believe, suppose, imagine, assume, guess *(informal, chiefly US & Canad)*, fancy, conjecture, surmise, be of the opinion **2 = consider**, hold, rate, account, judge, think of, regard, estimate, count, evaluate, esteem, deem, gauge, look upon, appraise **3 = count**, figure, total, calculate, compute, add up, tally, number, enumerate*(used in negative constructions)*
reckoning *n* **1 = count**, working, estimate, calculation, adding, counting, addition, computation, summation
reclaim *vb* **1 = retrieve**, get *or* take back, rescue, regain, reinstate **2 = regain**, restore, salvage, recapture, regenerate
recognition *n* **1 = identification**, recall, recollection, discovery, detection, remembrance **2 = acceptance**, acknowledgment, understanding, admission, perception, awareness, concession, allowance, confession, realization, avowal
recognize *vb* **1 = identify**, know, place, remember, spot, notice, recall, make out, recollect, know again, put your finger on **2 = acknowledge**, see,

DICTIONARY

accept or be aware of (a fact or problem): *to recognize change* **3** to acknowledge formally the status or legality of (something or someone): *an organization recognized by the UN* **4** to show approval or appreciation of (something) **5** to make formal acknowledgment of (a claim or duty): *I must ask for her to be recognized as a hostile witness* **recognizable** *or* **-isable** *adj*
WORD ORIGIN Latin *re-* again + *cognoscere* to know

recoil *vb* **1** to jerk or spring back **2** to draw back in fear or horror **3** (of an action) to go wrong so as to hurt the person responsible ▷ *n* **4** the backward movement of a gun when fired **5** the act of recoiling
WORD ORIGIN Old French *reculer*

recollect *vb* to remember
recollection *n*
WORD ORIGIN Latin *recolligere* to gather again

recombinant (ree-**kom**-bin-ant) *adj genetics* produced by the combining of genetic material from more than one origin

recommend ❶ *vb* **1** to advise as the best course or choice **2** to praise or commend: *I would wholeheartedly recommend his books* **3** to make attractive or advisable: *she has everything to recommend her*
recommendation *n*
WORD ORIGIN Latin *re-* again + *commendare* to commend

recompense *vb* **-pensing, -pensed** **1** to pay or reward for work or help **2** to compensate or make up for loss or injury ▷ *n* **3** compensation for loss or injury **4** reward or repayment
WORD ORIGIN Latin *re-* again + *compensare* to balance

reconcile ❶ *vb* **-ciling, -ciled** **1** to make (two apparently conflicting things) compatible or consistent with each other: *in many cases science and religion are reconciled* **2** to re-establish friendly relations with (a person or people) or between (people) **3** to accept or cause to accept (an unpleasant situation): *we reconciled ourselves to a change*
WORD ORIGIN Latin *reconciliare*

reconciliation ❶ *n* **1** the state of being reconciled **2** the act of reconciling people or groups **3** *S African* a political term emphasizing the need to acknowledge the wrongs of the past

recondite *adj formal* **1** requiring special knowledge **2** dealing with abstruse or profound subjects
WORD ORIGIN Latin *reconditus* hidden away

recondition *vb* to restore to good condition or working order: *a reconditioned engine* **reconditioned** *adj*

reconnaissance (rik-**kon**-iss-anss) *n* **1** the process of obtaining information about the position and movements of an enemy **2** a preliminary inspection
WORD ORIGIN French

reconnoitre *or US* **reconnoiter** (rek-a-**noy**-ter) *vb* to make a reconnaissance of
WORD ORIGIN obsolete French *reconnoître*

reconsider ❶ *vb* to think about again, with a view to changing one's policy or course of action **reconsideration** *n*

reconstitute *vb* **-tuting, -tuted** **1** to reorganize in a slightly different form **2** to restore (dried food) to its former state by adding water
reconstitution *n*

reconstruct ❶ *vb* **1** to build again **2** to reorganize: *three works proved useful in reconstructing the training routine* **3** to form a picture of (a past event, esp. a crime) by piecing together evidence
reconstruction *n*

reconvene *vb* to gather together again after an interval: *we reconvene tomorrow*

record ❶ *n* (**rek**-ord) **1** a document or other thing that preserves information **2** **records** information or data on a subject collected over a long period: *dental records* **3** a thin disc of a plastic material upon which sound has been recorded in a continuous spiral groove on each side **4** the best recorded achievement in some field: *her score set a Games record* **5** the known facts about a person's achievements **6** a list of crimes of which an accused person has previously been convicted **7** anything serving as evidence or as a memorial: *the First World War is a record of human folly* **8** *computers* a group of data or piece of information preserved as a unit in machine-readable form **9** **for the record** for the sake of strict factual accuracy **10** **go on record** to state one's views publicly **11** **have a record** to have previous criminal convictions **12** **off the record** not for publication **13** **on record** **a** stated in a public document **b** publicly known ▷ *adj* **14** being the highest or lowest, or best or worst ever achieved: *record losses* ▷ *vb* (rik-**kord**) **15** to put in writing to preserve the true facts: *to record the minutes of a meeting* **16** to preserve (sound, TV programmes, etc.) on plastic disc, magnetic tape, etc. for reproduction on a playback device **17** to show or register
WORD ORIGIN Latin *recordari* to remember

recorded delivery *n* a postal service by which an official receipt is obtained for the posting and delivery of a letter or parcel

r

THESAURUS

allow, understand, accept, admit, grant, realize, concede, perceive, confess, be aware of, take on board, avow **OPPOSITE:** ignore
4 = appreciate, respect, notice, salute

recommend *vb* **1a = advocate**, suggest, propose, approve, endorse, commend **OPPOSITE:** disapprove of
1b = put forward, approve, endorse, commend, vouch for, praise, big up *(slang)*, speak well of, put in a good word for **1c = advise**, suggest, advance, propose, urge, counsel, advocate, prescribe, put forward, exhort, enjoin

reconcile *vb* **1 = resolve**, settle, square, adjust, compose, rectify, patch up, harmonize, put to rights
2a = reunite, bring back together, make peace between, pacify, conciliate **2b = make peace between**, reunite, propitiate, bring to terms, restore harmony between, re-establish friendly relations between

reconciliation *n* **1 = reunion**, conciliation, rapprochement *(French)*, appeasement, détente, pacification, propitiation, understanding, reconcilement **OPPOSITE:** separation

reconsider *vb* **= rethink**, review, revise, think again, think twice, reassess, re-examine, have second thoughts, change your mind, re-evaluate, think over, think better of, take another look at

reconstruct *vb* **1 = rebuild**, reform, restore, recreate, remake, renovate, remodel, re-establish, regenerate, reorganize, reassemble **3 = build up a picture of**, build up, piece together, deduce

record *n* **1, 2 = document**, file, register, log, report, minute, account, entry, journal, diary, memorial, archives, memoir, chronicle, memorandum, annals, blog *(informal)* **3 = disc**, recording, single, release, album, waxing *(informal)*, LP, vinyl, EP, forty-five, platter *(US slang)*, seventy-eight, gramophone record, black disc **5, 6 = background**, history, performance, career, track record *(informal)*, curriculum vitae
7 = evidence, trace, documentation, testimony, witness, memorial, remembrance ▷ *vb* **15 = set down**, report, minute, note, enter, document, register, preserve, log, put down, chronicle, write down, enrol, take down, inscribe, transcribe, chalk up *(informal)*, put on record, put on file **16 = make a recording of**, cut, video, tape, lay down *(slang)*, wax *(informal)*, video-tape, tape-record, put on wax *(informal)* **17 = register**, show, read, contain, indicate, give evidence of

recorder *n* **1 = chronicler**, archivist,

DICTIONARY

recorder ❶ *n* **1** a person or machine that records, esp. a video, cassette, or tape recorder **2** *music* a wind instrument, blown through the end, with finger-holes and a reedlike tone **3** (in England and Wales) a barrister or solicitor appointed to sit as a part-time judge in the crown court

recording ❶ *n* **1** something that has been recorded **2** the process of storing sounds or visual signals for later use

record player *n* a device for reproducing the sounds stored on a record

recount ❶ *vb* to tell the story or details of
WORD ORIGIN Old French *reconter*

re-count *vb* **1** to count again ▷*n* **2** a second or further count, esp. of votes in an election

recoup (rik-**koop**) *vb* **1** to regain or make good (a loss) **2** to reimburse or compensate (someone) for a loss **recoupment** *n*
WORD ORIGIN Old French *recouper* to cut back

recourse *n* **1** **have recourse to** to turn to a source of help or course of action **2** a source of help or course of action that is turned to when in difficulty
WORD ORIGIN Latin *re-* back + *currere* to run

recover ❶ *vb* **1** (of a person) to regain health, spirits, or composure **2** to regain a former and better condition: *real wages have recovered from the recession* **3** to find again or obtain the return of (something lost) **4** to get back or make good (expense or loss) **5** to obtain (useful substances) from waste **6** *law* to gain (something) by the judgment of a court: *it should be possible to recover damages* **recoverable** *adj*
WORD ORIGIN Latin *recuperare*

recovery ❶ *n, pl* **-eries** **1** the act of recovering from sickness, a shock, or a setback **2** restoration to a former and better condition **3** the regaining of something lost **4** the extraction of useful substances from waste

recreant *n archaic* a disloyal or cowardly person
WORD ORIGIN Old French *recroire* to surrender

re-create *vb* **-creating, -created** to make happen or exist again **re-creation** *n*

recreation ❶ *n* an activity done for pleasure or relaxation **recreational** *adj*
WORD ORIGIN Latin *recreare* to refresh

recreation ground *n* an area of publicly owned land where sports and games may be played

recrimination *n* accusations made by two people or groups about each other: *bitter recrimination* **recriminatory** *adj*
WORD ORIGIN Latin *re-* back + *criminari* to accuse

recrudescence *n literary* an outbreak of trouble or a disease after a period of quiet
WORD ORIGIN Latin *re-* again + *crudus* bloody, raw

recruit ❶ *vb* **1** to enlist (people) for military service **2** to enrol or obtain (members or support) ▷*n* **3** a newly joined member of a military service **4** a new member or supporter **recruitment** *n*
WORD ORIGIN French *recrute* new growth

rectal *adj* of the rectum

rectangle *n* an oblong shape with four straight sides and four right angles **rectangular** *adj*
WORD ORIGIN Latin *rectus* straight + *angulus* angle

rectify *vb* **-fies, -fying, -fied** **1** to put right; correct **2** *chem* to separate (a substance) from a mixture by distillation **3** *electronics* to convert (alternating current) into direct current **rectification** *n* **rectifier** *n*
WORD ORIGIN Latin *rectus* straight + *facere* to make

rectilinear (rek-tee-**lin**-ee-er) *adj formal* **1** in a straight line **2** bounded by or formed of straight lines

rectitude *n* moral or religious correctness: *a model of rectitude*
WORD ORIGIN Latin *rectus* right

recto *n, pl* **-tos** **1** the right-hand page of a book **2** the front of a sheet of printed paper
WORD ORIGIN Latin: on the right

rector *n* **1** *Church of England* a clergyman in charge of a parish **2** *RC church* a cleric in charge of a college or congregation **3** *chiefly Brit* the head of certain academic institutions **4** (in Scotland) a high-ranking official in a university, elected by the students **rectorship** *n*
WORD ORIGIN Latin: director

rectory *n, pl* **-ries** the house of a rector

rectum *n, pl* **-tums** *or* **-ta** the lower part of the alimentary canal, ending in the anus
WORD ORIGIN Latin: straight

recumbent *adj* lying down
WORD ORIGIN Latin *recumbere* to lie back

recuperate *vb* **-ating, -ated** to recover from illness or exhaustion **recuperation** *n* **recuperative** *adj*
WORD ORIGIN Latin *recuperare*

recur ❶ *vb* **-curring, -curred** **1** to happen or occur again **2** (of a thought or feeling) to come back to the mind **recurrence** *n* **recurrent** *adj* **recurring** *adj*
WORD ORIGIN Latin *re-* again + *currere* to run

recurring decimal *n* a rational number that contains a pattern of digits repeated indefinitely after the decimal point: *1 divided by 11 gives the recurring decimal 0.09090909...*

recusant (**rek**-yew-zant) *n* **1** *history* a Roman Catholic who did not attend the services of the Church of England **2** a person who refuses to obey authority **recusancy** *n*
WORD ORIGIN Latin *recusans* refusing

recycle ❶ *vb* **-cling, -cled** **1** to reprocess (something already used) for further use: *public demand for*

THESAURUS

historian, scorer, clerk, registrar, scribe, diarist, scorekeeper, annalist

recording *n* **1 = record**, video, tape, disc, gramophone record, cut *(informal)*

recount *vb* **= tell**, report, detail, describe, relate, repeat, portray, depict, rehearse, recite, tell the story of, narrate, delineate, enumerate, give an account of

recover *vb* **1 = get better**, improve, get well, recuperate, pick up, heal, revive, come round, bounce back, mend, turn the corner, pull through, convalesce, be on the mend, take a turn for the better, get back on your feet, feel yourself again, regain your health *or* strength **OPPOSITE:** relapse **2 = rally 3, 6 = recoup**, restore, repair, get back, regain, make good, retrieve, reclaim, redeem, recapture, win back, take back, repossess, retake, find again **OPPOSITE:** lose **4 = save**, rescue, retrieve, salvage, reclaim **OPPOSITE:** abandon

recovery *n* **1 = improvement**, return to health, rally, healing, revival, mending, recuperation, convalescence, turn for the better **3 = retrieval**, repossession, reclamation, restoration, repair, redemption, recapture

recreation *n* **= leisure**, play, sport, exercise, fun, relief, pleasure, entertainment, relaxation, enjoyment, distraction, amusement, diversion, refreshment, beer and skittles *(informal)*, me-time

recruit *vb* **1 = enlist**, draft, impress, enrol **OPPOSITE:** dismiss **2a = gather**, take on, obtain, engage, round up, enrol, procure, proselytize **2b = assemble**, raise, levy, muster, mobilize ▷*n* **4 = beginner**, trainee, apprentice, novice, convert, initiate, rookie *(informal)*, helper, learner, neophyte, tyro, greenhorn *(informal)*, proselyte

recur *vb* **1 = happen again**, return, come back, repeat, persist, revert, reappear, come and go, come again

recycle *vb* **1 = reprocess**, reuse, salvage, reclaim, save

r

DICTIONARY

recycled paper **2** to pass (a substance) through a system again for further use **recyclable** *adj*

red ❶ *adj* **redder, reddest 1** of a colour varying from crimson to orange; of the colour of blood **2** reddish in colour or having parts or marks that are reddish: *red deer* **3** flushed in the face from anger or shame **4** (of the eyes) bloodshot **5** (of wine) made from black grapes and coloured by their skins ▷*n* **6** the colour red; the colour of blood **7** anything red, such as red clothing or red paint: *she had dressed in red* **8 in the red** *informal* in debt **9 see red** *informal* to become very angry **redness** *n* **reddish** *adj* **WORD ORIGIN** Old English *rēad*

Red *informal n* **1** a Communist or socialist ▷*adj* **2** Communist or socialist

red admiral *n* a butterfly with black wings with red and white markings

redback spider *n* a small venomous Australian spider with a red stripe on the back of the abdomen

red blood cell *n* ▸same as **erythrocyte**

red-blooded *adj informal* vigorous or virile

redbreast *n* a robin

redbrick *adj* (of a British university) founded in the late 19th or early 20th century

red card *soccer n* **1** a piece of red pasteboard raised by a referee to indicate that a player has been sent off ▷*vb* **red-card 2** to send off (a player)

red carpet *n* very special treatment given to an important guest

redcoat *n* **1** *history* a British soldier **2** *Canad informal* a Mountie

Red Crescent *n* the name and symbol used by the Red Cross in Muslim countries

Red Cross *n* an international organization (**Red Cross Society**) which helps victims of war or natural disaster

redcurrant *n* a very small red edible fruit that grows in bunches on a bush

red deer *n* a large deer of Europe and Asia, which has a reddish-brown coat and a short tail

redden *vb* **1** to make or become red or redder **2** to blush

Redding *n* **Otis** 1941–67, US soul singer and songwriter. His recordings include "Respect" (1965), *Dictionary of Soul* (1966), and "(Sittin' on) The Dock of the Bay" (1968)

redecorate *vb* to paint or wallpaper (a room) again **redecoration** *n*

redeem ❶ *vb* **1** to make up for **2** to reinstate (oneself) in someone's good opinion: *he missed a penalty but redeemed himself by setting up the winning goal* **3** *Christianity* (of Christ as Saviour) to free (humanity) from sin by death on the Cross **4** to buy back: *she didn't have the money to redeem it* **5** to pay off (a loan or debt) **6** to convert (bonds or shares) into cash **7** to exchange (coupons) for goods **8** to fulfil (a promise): *I vowed to abide by the bill and have redeemed my pledge* **redeemable** *adj* **redeemer** *n* **WORD ORIGIN** Latin *re-* back + *emere* to buy

Redeemer *n* **the Redeemer** *Christianity* Jesus Christ

redeeming *adj* making up for faults or deficiencies: *the soundtrack is the film's only redeeming feature*

redemption ❶ *n* **1** the act of redeeming **2** the state of being redeemed **3** *Christianity* deliverance from sin through the incarnation and death of Christ **redemptive** *adj*

redeploy *vb* to assign (people) to new positions or tasks **redeployment** *n*

redevelop *vb* to rebuild or renovate (an area or building) **redeveloper** *n* **redevelopment** *n*

redfish *n, pl* **-fish** *or* **-fishes** *Canad* ▸same as **kokanee**

red flag *n* **1** a symbol of revolution **2** a warning of danger

Redford *n* **Robert** born 1937, US film actor and director. His films include (as actor) *Barefoot in the Park* (1966), *Butch Cassidy and the Sundance Kid* (1969), *The Sting* (1973), *All the President's Men* (1976), *Up Close and Personal* (1996) and (as director) *Ordinary People* (1980), *A River Runs Through It* (1992), and *The Horse Whisperer* (1998)

red-handed *adj* **catch someone red-handed** to catch someone in the act of doing something wrong or illegal

red hat *n* the broad-brimmed crimson hat given to cardinals as the symbol of their rank

redhead *n* a person with reddish hair **redheaded** *adj*

red herring *n* something which diverts attention from the main issue

red-hot *adj* **1** (of metal) glowing hot **2** extremely hot **3** very keen or excited **4** furious: *one of those red-hot blazes of temper* **5** very recent or topical: *red-hot information*

red-hot poker *n* a garden plant with spikes of red or yellow flowers

Red Indian *n, adj offensive* Native American

redirect *vb* **1** to send in a new direction or course **2** to send (mail) to a different address

redistribute *vb* **-uting, -uted** to share out in a different way: *to redistribute the world's wealth*

redistribution *n* **1** the act of redistributing **2** a revision of the number of seats that each province has in the Canadian House of Commons, made every ten years

red lead *n* a bright-red poisonous insoluble oxide of lead

red-letter day *n* a memorably important or happy occasion **WORD ORIGIN** from the red letters in ecclesiastical calendars to indicate saints' days

red light *n* **1** a traffic signal to stop **2** a danger signal

red-light district *n* an area where many prostitutes work

red meat *n* meat, such as beef or lamb, that is dark brown when cooked

Redmond *n* **John Edward** 1856–1918, Irish politician. He led the Parnellites from 1891 and helped to procure the Home Rule bill of 1912, but was considered too moderate by extreme nationalists

redo *vb* **-doing, -did, -done 1** to do over again in order to improve **2** *informal* to redecorate: *we should consider redoing some of the rooms*

THESAURUS

red *adj* **1 = crimson**, scarlet, ruby, vermilion, rose, wine, pink, cherry, cardinal, coral, maroon, claret, carmine **2 = chestnut**, flaming, reddish, flame-coloured, bay, sandy, foxy, Titian, carroty, ginger **3 = flushed**, embarrassed, blushing, suffused, florid, shamefaced, rubicund ▷*n* **6 = crimson**, scarlet, ruby, vermilion, rose, wine, pink, cherry, cardinal, coral, maroon, claret, carmine **8 in the red** *(informal)* **= in debt**, bankrupt, on the rocks, insolvent, in arrears, overdrawn, owing money, in deficit, showing a loss, in debit **9 see red** *(informal)* **= lose your temper**, boil, lose it *(informal)*, seethe, go mad *(informal)*, crack up *(informal)*, lose the plot *(informal)*, go ballistic *(slang, chiefly US)*, blow a fuse *(slang, chiefly US)*, fly off the handle *(informal)*, become enraged, go off the deep end *(informal)*, wig out *(slang)*, go up the wall *(slang)*, blow your top, lose your rag *(slang)*, be beside yourself with rage *(informal)*, be *or* get very angry, go off your head *(slang)*

redeem *vb* **1 = make up for**, offset, make good, compensate for, outweigh, redress, atone for, make amends for, defray **2 = reinstate**, absolve, restore to favour, rehabilitate **4 = buy back**, recover, regain, retrieve, reclaim, win back, repossess, repurchase, recover possession of

redemption *n* **1 = compensation**, amends, reparation, atonement, expiation **3** *(Christianity)* **= salvation**, release, rescue, liberation, ransom,

DICTIONARY

redolent *adj* **redolent of** *or* **with** **1** reminiscent or suggestive of: *a castle redolent of historical novels* **2** smelling of: *the warm heavy air was redolent of sea and flowers* **redolence** *n*
WORD ORIGIN Latin *redolens*

Redon *n* **Odilon** 1840–1916, French symbolist painter and etcher. He foreshadowed the surrealists in his paintings of fantastic dream images

redouble *vb* **-bling, -bled** **1** to make or become much greater: *the party will have to redouble its efforts* **2** *bridge* to double (an opponent's double)

redoubt *n* **1** a small fort defending a hill top or pass **2** a stronghold
WORD ORIGIN French *redoute*

redoubtable *adj* to be feared and respected: *the redoubtable Mr Brooks* **redoubtably** *adv*
WORD ORIGIN Old French *redouter* to dread

redound *vb* **1** **redound to** to have an advantageous or disadvantageous effect on: *individual rights redound to the common good* **2** **redound on** *or* **upon** to recoil or rebound on
WORD ORIGIN Latin *redundare* to stream over

redox *n* a chemical reaction between two substances, in which one is oxidized and the other reduced

red pepper *n* **1** the red ripe fruit of the sweet pepper, eaten as a vegetable **2** ▸ same as **cayenne pepper**

redraft *vb* to write a second copy of (a letter, proposal, essay, etc.)

red rag *n* something that infuriates or provokes: *a red rag to businessmen*
WORD ORIGIN so called because red objects supposedly infuriate bulls

redress ● *vb* **1** to make amends for **2** to adjust in order to make fair or equal: *to redress the balance* ▹ *n* **3** compensation or reparation **4** the setting right of a wrong
WORD ORIGIN Old French *redrecier* to set up again

red salmon *n* a salmon with reddish flesh

redshank *n* a large common European sandpiper with red legs

red shift *n* the appearance of lines in the spectrum of distant stars nearer the red end of the spectrum than on earth: used to calculate the velocity of objects in relation to the earth

redskin *n informal, offensive* a Native American
WORD ORIGIN so called because one now extinct tribe painted themselves with red ochre

red squirrel *n* a reddish-brown squirrel of Europe and Asia

redstart *n* **1** a European songbird of the thrush family, the male of which has an orange-brown tail and breast **2** a North American warbler
WORD ORIGIN Old English *rēad* red + *steort* tail

red tape *n* time-consuming official rules or procedure
WORD ORIGIN from the red tape used to bind official government documents

reduce ● *vb* **-ducing, -duced** **1** to bring down or lower: *monitoring could reduce the number of perinatal deaths* **2** to weaken or lessen: *vegetarian diets reduce cancer risk* **3** to bring by force or necessity to some state or action: *it reduced her to helpless laughter* **4** to slim **5** to set out systematically as an aid to understanding: *reducing the problem to three main issues* **6** *cookery* to thicken (a sauce) by boiling away some of its liquid **7** to impoverish: *to be in reduced circumstances* **8** *chem* **a** to undergo a chemical reaction with hydrogen **b** to lose oxygen atoms **c** to increase the number of electrons **9** *maths* to simplify the form of (an expression or equation), esp. by substitution of one term by another **reducible** *adj*
WORD ORIGIN Latin *reducere* to bring back

reduction *n* **1** the act of reducing **2** the amount by which something is reduced **3** a reduced form of an original, such as a copy of a document on a smaller scale **reductive** *adj*

redundant ● *adj* **1** deprived of one's job because it is no longer necessary or sufficiently profitable **2** surplus to requirements **redundancy** *n*
WORD ORIGIN Latin *redundans* overflowing

reduplicate *vb* **-cating, -cated** to make double; repeat

redwood *n* a giant Californian conifer with reddish bark

re-echo *vb* **-oing, -oed** to echo over and over again

reed *n* **1** a tall grass that grows in swamps and shallow water **2** a straight hollow stem of this plant **3** *music* **a** a thin piece of cane or metal in certain wind instruments, which vibrates producing a musical note when the instrument is blown **b** a wind instrument or organ pipe that sounds by means of a reed
WORD ORIGIN Old English *hrēod*

Reed *n* **1** Sir **Carol** 1906–76, English film director. His films include *The Third Man* (1949), *An Outcast of the Islands* (1951), and *Oliver!* (1968), for which he won an Oscar **2** **Lou** born 1942, US rock singer, songwriter, and guitarist: member of the Velvet Underground (1965–70). His albums include *Transformer* (1972), *Berlin* (1973), *Street Hassle* (1978), *New York* (1989), *Set the Twilight Reeling* (1996), and *The Raven* (2003) **3** **Walter** 1851–1902, US physician, who proved that yellow fever is transmitted by mosquitoes (1900)

reedy *adj* **reedier, reediest** **1** harsh or thin in tone: *his reedy, hesitant voice* **2** (of a place) full of reeds **reedily** *adv* **reediness** *n*

reef[1] *n* **1** a ridge of rock, sand, or coral, lying just beneath the surface of the sea: *a coral reef* **2** a vein of ore
WORD ORIGIN Middle Dutch *ref*

reef[2] *naut n* **1** the part of a sail which can be rolled up to reduce its area ▹ *vb* **2** to reduce the area of (sail) by taking in a reef
WORD ORIGIN Middle Dutch *rif*

reefer *n* **1** Also called: **reefer jacket** a man's short heavy double-breasted woollen jacket **2** *old-fashioned, slang* a hand-rolled cigarette containing cannabis
WORD ORIGIN from the cigarette's resemblance to the rolled reef of a sail

reef knot *n* a knot consisting of two overhand knots turned opposite ways

reek *vb* **1** to give off a strong unpleasant smell **2** **reek of** to give a strong suggestion of: *the scene had reeked of insincerity* **3** *dialect* to give off smoke or fumes ▹ *n* **4** a strong unpleasant smell **5** *dialect* smoke or steam
WORD ORIGIN Old English *rēocan*

reel[1] *n* **1** a cylindrical object or frame that turns on an axis and onto

r

THESAURUS

emancipation, deliverance

redress *vb* **1 = make amends for**, pay for, make up for, compensate for, put right, recompense for, make reparation for, make restitution for **2 = put right**, reform, balance, square, correct, ease, repair, relieve, adjust, regulate, remedy, amend, mend, rectify, even up, restore the balance ▹ *n* **3 = amends**, payment, compensation, reparation, restitution, atonement, recompense, requital, quittance

reduce *vb* **1, 2 = lessen**, cut, contract, lower, depress, moderate, weaken, diminish, turn down, decrease, slow down, cut down, shorten, dilute, impair, curtail, wind down, abate, tone down, debase, truncate, abridge, downsize, kennet *(Austral slang)*, jeff *(Austral slang)*
OPPOSITE: increase

redundant *adj* **2 = superfluous**, extra, surplus, excessive, unnecessary, unwanted, inordinate, inessential, supernumerary, de trop *(French)*, supererogatory
OPPOSITE: essential

reel[2] *vb* **1a = stagger**, rock, roll, pitch, stumble, sway, falter, lurch, wobble, waver, totter **1b = whirl**, swim, spin, revolve, swirl, twirl, go round and round

DICTIONARY

which film, tape, wire, or thread is wound **2** a winding device attached to a fishing rod, used for casting and winding in the line **3** a roll of film for projection ▹ *vb* **4 reel in** to wind or draw in on a reel
WORD ORIGIN Old English *hrēol*

reel[2] ● *vb* **1** to move unsteadily or spin round, as if about to fall **2** to be in a state of confusion or stress: *my mind was still reeling*
WORD ORIGIN probably from REEL[1]

reel[3] *n* **1** a lively Scottish dance **2** music for this dance
WORD ORIGIN from REEL[2]

re-elect *vb* to vote for (someone) to retain his or her position, for example as a Member of Parliament **re-election** *n*

reel off *vb* to recite or write fluently or quickly

re-enact *vb* to act out (a previous event) again **re-enactment** *n*

re-enter *vb* **1** to come back into (a place, esp. a country) **2** (of a spacecraft) to return into (the earth's atmosphere) **re-entry** *n*

re-equip *vb* **-equipping, -equipped** to provide with fresh supplies, components, etc.

re-establish *vb* to create or set up (an organization, link, etc.) again **re-establishment** *n*

reeve *n* **1** *English history* the local representative of the king in a shire until the early 11th century **2** (in medieval England) a steward who supervised the daily affairs of a manor **3** *Canad government* (in some provinces) a president of a local council
WORD ORIGIN Old English *gerēfa*

re-examine *vb* **-examining, -examined** to inspect or investigate again **re-examination** *n*

ref *n informal* the referee in a sport

refectory *n, pl* **-ries** a dining hall in a religious or academic institution
WORD ORIGIN Latin *refectus* refreshed

refectory table *n* a long narrow dining table supported by two trestles

refer ● *vb* **-ferring, -ferred** ■ **refer to** **1** to mention or allude to **2** to be relevant or relate (to): *the word cancer refers to many quite specific different diseases* **3** to seek information (from): *he referred to his notes* **4** to direct the attention of (someone) for information: *the reader is referred to the introduction* **5** to direct (a patient or client) to another doctor or agency: *her GP referred her to a specialist* **6** to hand over for consideration or decision: *to refer a complaint to another department* **referable** *or* **referrable** *adj* **referral** *n*
WORD ORIGIN Latin *re-* back + *ferre* to carry

referee ● *n* **1** the umpire in various sports, such as football and boxing **2** a person who is willing to provide a reference for someone for a job **3** a person referred to for a decision or opinion in a dispute ▹ *vb* **-eeing, -eed 4** to act as a referee

reference ● *n* **1** the act of referring **2** a mention: *this book contains several references to the Civil War* **3** direction to a passage elsewhere in a book or to another book **4** a book or passage referred to **5** a written testimonial regarding one's character or capabilities **6** a person referred to for such a testimonial **7** relation or restriction, esp. to or by membership of a specific group: *without reference to sex or age* **8 with reference to** concerning ▹ *adj* **9** containing information or facts: *reference books* **referential** *adj*

referendum ● *n, pl* **-dums** *or* **-da** a direct vote of the electorate on a question of importance
WORD ORIGIN Latin: something to be carried back

refill *vb* **1** to fill (something) again ▹ *n* **2** a second or subsequent filling: I *held out my glass for a refill* **3** a replacement supply of something in a permanent container **refillable** *adj*

refine ● *vb* **-fining, -fined 1** to make free from impurities; purify **2** to improve: *surgical techniques are constantly being refined* **3** to separate (a mixture) into pure constituents: *molasses is a residual syrup obtained during sugar refining*

refined ● *adj* **1** cultured or polite **2** freed from impurities **3** highly developed and effective: *refined intelligence tests*

refinement *n* **1** an improvement to something, such as a piece of equipment **2** fineness of taste or manners **3** a subtle point or distinction **4** the act of refining

refinery *n, pl* **-eries** a factory for purifying a raw material, such as sugar or oil

refit *vb* **-fitting, -fitted 1** to make (a ship) ready for use again by repairing or re-equipping ▹ *n* **2** a repair or re-equipping for further use

reflation *n* an increase in the supply of money and credit designed to encourage economic activity **reflate** *vb* **reflationary** *adj*
WORD ORIGIN RE- + *-flation*, as in *inflation*

reflect ● *vb* **1** (of a surface or object) to throw back (light, heat, or sound) **2** (of a mirror) to form an image of (something) by reflection **3** to show: *many of her books reflect her obsession with fine art* **4** to consider carefully **5 reflect on** *or* **upon** to cause to be regarded in a specified way: *the incident reflects very badly on me* **6** to bring as a consequence: *the programme reflected great credit on the technicians*
WORD ORIGIN Latin *re-* back + *flectere* to bend

reflecting telescope *n* a telescope in which the initial image is formed by a concave mirror

reflection ● *n* **1** the act of reflecting **2** the return of rays of light, heat, or sound **3** an image of an object given back in a mirror **4** careful or long consideration **5 on reflection** after careful consideration or reconsideration **6** discredit or blame: *it's a sad reflection on modern morality* **7** *maths* a transformation of

THESAURUS

refer *vb* **4 = direct**, point, send, guide, recommend

referee *n* **1 = umpire**, umpie (*Austral slang*), judge, ref (*informal*), arbiter, arbitrator, adjudicator ▹ *vb* **4 = umpire**, judge, mediate, adjudicate, arbitrate

reference *n* **2 = allusion**, note, mention, remark, quotation **4 = citation 5 = testimonial**, recommendation, credentials, endorsement, certification, good word, character reference

referendum *n* **= public vote**, popular vote, plebiscite

refine *vb* **1 = purify**, process, filter, cleanse, clarify, distil, rarefy **2 = improve**, perfect, polish, temper, elevate, hone

refined *adj* **1 = cultured**, civil, polished, sophisticated, gentlemanly, elegant, polite, cultivated, gracious, civilized, genteel, urbane, courtly, well-bred, ladylike, well-mannered
OPPOSITE: coarse
2 = purified, processed, pure, filtered, clean, clarified, distilled
OPPOSITE: unrefined
3 = discerning, fine, nice, sensitive, exact, subtle, delicate, precise, discriminating, sublime, fastidious, punctilious

reflect *vb* **1, 2 = throw back**, return, mirror, echo, reproduce, imitate, give back **3 = show**, reveal, express, display, indicate, demonstrate, exhibit, communicate, manifest, bear out, bespeak, evince **4** (*with/or upon*) **= consider**, think, contemplate, deliberate, muse, ponder, meditate, mull over, ruminate, cogitate, wonder

reflection *n* **3 = image**, echo, counterpart, mirror image **4 = consideration**, thinking, pondering, deliberation, thought, idea, view, study, opinion, impression, observation, musing, meditation, contemplation, rumination, perusal,

DICTIONARY

a shape in which right and left, or top and bottom, are reversed
reflective ❶ *adj* **1** characterized by quiet thought or contemplation **2** capable of reflecting: *a reflective coating*
reflector *n* **1** a polished surface for reflecting light **2** a reflecting telescope
reflex *n* **1** an immediate involuntary response to a given stimulus **2** a mechanical response to a particular situation, involving no conscious decision **3** an image produced by reflection ▷ *adj* **4** of or caused by a reflex: *a reflex action* **5** reflected **6** *maths* (of an angle) between 180° and 360°
WORD ORIGIN Latin *reflexus* bent back
reflex camera *n* a camera which uses a mirror to channel light from a lens to the viewfinder, so that the image seen is the same as the image photographed
reflexive *adj* **1** *grammar* denoting a pronoun that refers back to the subject of a sentence or clause. Thus, in *that man thinks a great deal of himself*, the pronoun *himself* is reflexive **2** *grammar* denoting a verb used with a reflexive pronoun as its direct object, as in *to dress oneself* **3** *physiol* of or relating to a reflex ▷ *n* **4** a reflexive pronoun or verb
reflexology *n* foot massage as a therapy in alternative medicine **reflexologist** *n*
reform ❶ *n* **1** correction of abuses or malpractices: *a programme of economic reforms* **2** improvement of morals or behaviour ▷ *vb* **3** to improve (a law or institution) by correcting abuses **4** to give up or cause to give up a bad habit or way of life **reformative** *adj* **reformer** *n*
WORD ORIGIN Latin *reformare* to form again
reformation (ref-fer-**may**-shun) *n* **1** a reforming **2 the Reformation** a religious movement in 16th-century Europe that began as an attempt to reform the Roman Catholic Church and resulted in the establishment of the Protestant Churches
reformatory *n, pl* **-ries** (formerly) a place where young offenders were sent to be reformed
Reformed *adj* of a Protestant Church, esp. a Calvinist one
reformist *adj* **1** advocating reform rather than abolition, esp. of a religion or a political movement ▷ *n* **2** a person advocating reform
refract *vb* to cause light, heat, or sound to undergo refraction **refractive** *adj* **refractor** *n*
WORD ORIGIN Latin *re-* back + *frangere* to break
refracting telescope *n* a type of telescope in which the image is formed by a set of lenses. Also called: **refractor**
refraction *n* *physics* **1** the change in direction of a wave, such as light or sound, in passing from one medium to another in which it has a different velocity **2** the amount by which a wave is refracted
refractory *adj* **1** *formal* stubborn or rebellious **2** *med* not responding to treatment **3** (of a material) able to withstand high temperatures without fusion or decomposition
refrain[1] ❶ *vb* **refrain from** to keep oneself from doing
WORD ORIGIN Latin *refrenare* to check with a bridle
refrain[2] ❶ *n* **1** a frequently repeated part of a song **2** a much repeated saying or idea
WORD ORIGIN Latin *refringere* to break into pieces
refrangible *adj* capable of being refracted
refresh ❶ *vb* **1** to revive or reinvigorate, for example through rest, drink, or food **2** to stimulate (the memory) **refresher** *n*
WORD ORIGIN Old French *refreschir*
refresher course *n* a course designed to improve or update a person's knowledge of a subject
refreshing ❶ *adj* **1** having a reviving effect **2** pleasantly different or new: *refreshing candour*
refreshment ❶ *n* **1** the act of refreshing **2 refreshments** snacks and drinks served as a light meal
refrigerant *n* **1** a fluid capable of vaporizing at low temperatures, used in refrigerators ▷ *adj* **2** causing cooling or freezing
refrigerate *vb* **-ating, -ated** to chill or freeze in order to preserve **refrigeration** *n*
WORD ORIGIN Latin *refrigerare* to make cold
refrigerator *n* ▸ the full name for **fridge**
refuel *vb* **-elling, -elled** *or US* **-eling, -eled** to supply or be supplied with fresh fuel
refuge ❶ *n* **1** shelter or protection from danger or hardship **2** a place, person, or thing that offers protection or help
WORD ORIGIN Latin *re-* back + *fugere* to escape
refugee ❶ *n* a person who has fled from some danger, such as war or political persecution
refulgent *adj* *literary* shining brightly **refulgence** *n*
WORD ORIGIN Latin *refulgere* to reflect
refund ❶ *vb* **1** to give back (money) **2** to pay back (a person) ▷ *n* **3** return of money to a purchaser or the amount returned **refundable** *adj*
WORD ORIGIN Latin *re-* back + *fundere* to pour
refurbish ❶ *vb* to renovate and brighten up **refurbishment** *n*
refusal ❶ *n* **1** the act of refusing **2** the opportunity to reject or accept: *he was*

r

THESAURUS

cogitation, cerebration
reflective *adj* **1 = thoughtful**, contemplative, meditative, pensive, reasoning, pondering, deliberative, ruminative, cogitating
reform *n* **1 = improvement**, amendment, correction, rehabilitation, renovation, betterment, rectification, amelioration ▷ *vb* **3 = improve**, better, correct, restore, repair, rebuild, amend, reclaim, mend, renovate, reconstruct, remodel, rectify, rehabilitate, regenerate, reorganize, reconstitute, revolutionize, ameliorate, emend **4 = mend your ways**, go straight *(informal)*, shape up *(informal)*, get it together *(informal)*, turn over a new leaf, get your act together *(informal)*, clean up your act *(informal)*, pull your socks up *(Brit informal)*, get back on the straight and narrow *(informal)*
refrain[1] *vb* *(with* **from***)* **= stop**, avoid, give up, cease, do without, renounce, abstain, eschew, leave off, desist, forbear, kick *(informal)*
refrain[2] *n* **1 = chorus**, song, tune, melody
refresh *vb* **1 = revive**, cool, freshen, revitalize, cheer, stimulate, brace, rejuvenate, kick-start *(informal)*, enliven, breathe new life into, invigorate, revivify, reanimate, inspirit **2 = stimulate**, prompt, renew, jog, prod, brush up *(informal)*
refreshing *adj* **1 = stimulating**, fresh, cooling, bracing, invigorating, revivifying, thirst-quenching, inspiriting **OPPOSITE:** tiring **2 = new**, different, original, novel
refreshment *n* **2** *(pl)* **= food and drink**, drinks, snacks, titbits, kai *(NZ informal)*
refuge *n* **1 = protection**, security, shelter, harbour, asylum **2 = haven**, resort, retreat, sanctuary, hide-out, bolt hole
refugee *n* **= exile**, émigré, displaced person, runaway, fugitive, escapee
refund *vb* **1 = repay**, return, restore, make good, pay back, reimburse, give back ▷ *n* **3 = repayment**, reimbursement, return
refurbish *vb* **= renovate**, restore, repair, clean up, overhaul, revamp, mend, remodel, do up *(informal)*, refit, fix up *(informal, chiefly US & Canad)*, spruce up, pimp up, pimp out, re-equip, set to rights
refusal *n* **1 = rejection**, denial, defiance, rebuff, knock-back *(slang)*, thumbs down, repudiation, kick in

DICTIONARY

given first refusal on all three scripts

refuse¹ ❶ *vb* **-fusing, -fused 1** to be determined not (to do something): *he refuses to consider it* **2** to decline to give or allow (something) to (someone): *if the judge refuses bail, he'll appeal* **3** to decline to accept (something offered): *he refused the captaincy* **4** (of a horse) to be unwilling to jump a fence
WORD ORIGIN Latin *refundere* to pour back

refuse² ❶ *n* anything thrown away; rubbish
WORD ORIGIN Old French *refuser* to refuse

refusenik *n* **1** (formerly) a Jew in the USSR who was refused permission to emigrate **2** a person who refuses to obey a law or cooperate with the government because of strong beliefs

refute *vb* **-futing, -futed** to prove (a statement or theory) to be false or incorrect **refutation** *n*
WORD ORIGIN Latin *refutare*

regain ❶ *vb* **1** to get back or recover **2** to reach again: *to regain the shore*

regal ❶ *adj* **1** of or fit for a king or queen **2** splendid and dignified; magnificent: *a luxury cruise liner on her serene and regal way around the better ports* **regality** *n* **regally** *adv*
WORD ORIGIN Latin *regalis*

regale *vb* **-galing, -galed 1** to give delight or amusement to: *she would regale her friends with stories* **2** to provide with abundant food or drink
WORD ORIGIN French *régaler*

regalia *n* the ceremonial emblems or robes of royalty or high office
WORD ORIGIN Medieval Latin: royal privileges

regard ❶ *vb* **1** to look upon or think of in a specified way: *angina can therefore be regarded as heart cramp* **2** to look closely or attentively at (something or someone) **3** to take notice of: *he has never regarded the conventions* **4 as regards** on the subject of ▷ *n* **5** respect or affection: *you haven't a high regard for her opinion* **6** attention: *he eats what he wants with no regard to health* **7** a gaze or look **8** reference or connection: *with regard to my complaint* **9 regards** an expression of goodwill: *give her my regards*
WORD ORIGIN Old French *regarder* to look at, care about

regardful *adj* **regardful of** paying attention to

regarding ❶ *prep* on the subject of; relating to

regardless ❶ *adj* **1 regardless of** taking no notice of: *the illness can affect anyone regardless of their social class* ▷ *adv* **2** in spite of everything: *I carried on regardless*

regatta *n* a series of races of boats or yachts
WORD ORIGIN obsolete Italian *rigatta* contest

regency *n, pl* **-cies 1** government by a regent **2** the status of a regent **3** a period when a regent is in power
WORD ORIGIN Latin *regere* to rule

Regency *adj* of the regency (1811–20) of the Prince of Wales (later George IV) or the styles of architecture or furniture produced during it

regenerate *vb* (ri-jen-er-ate), **-ating, -ated 1** to undergo or cause to undergo physical, economic, or spiritual renewal **2** to come or bring into existence once again **3** to replace (lost or damaged tissues or organs) by new growth ▷ *adj* (ri-jen-er-it) **4** physically, economically, or spiritually renewed **regeneration** *n* **regenerative** *adj*

regent *n* **1** the ruler of a country during the childhood, absence, or illness of its monarch **2** *US & Canad* a member of the governing board of certain schools and colleges ▷ *adj* **3** acting as a regent: *the Prince Regent*
WORD ORIGIN Latin *regere* to rule

Reger *n* **Max** 1873–1916, German composer, noted esp. for his organ works

reggae *n* a type of popular music of Jamaican origin with a strong beat
WORD ORIGIN West Indian

regicide *n* **1** the killing of a king **2** a person who kills a king
WORD ORIGIN Latin *rex* king + *caedere* to kill

regifting *n* the practice of giving an unwanted gift to another person

regime ❶ (ray-**zheem**) *n* **1** a system of government **2** a particular administration: *the corrupt regime* **3** *med* a regimen
WORD ORIGIN French

regimen *n* a prescribed system of diet and exercise
WORD ORIGIN Latin: guidance

regiment *n* **1** an organized body of troops as a unit in the army **2** a large number or group **regimental** *adj*
WORD ORIGIN Late Latin *regimentum* government

regimentals *pl n* **1** the uniform and insignia of a regiment **2** military uniform

regimental sergeant major *n mil* the senior warrant officer in a regiment or battalion

regimented *adj* very strictly controlled: *the regimented confines of the school* **regimentation** *n*

Regina *n* queen: now used chiefly in documents and inscriptions
WORD ORIGIN Latin

Regiomontanus *n* original name *Johann Müller*. 1436–76, German mathematician and astronomer, who furthered the development of trigonometry

region ❶ *n* **1** an administrative division of a country **2** an area considered as a unit for geographical or social reasons **3** a sphere of activity or interest **4** a part of the

r

THESAURUS

the teeth *(slang)*, negation, no

refuse¹ *vb* **1, 3 = decline**, reject, turn down, say no to, repudiate **2 = deny**, decline, withhold **OPPOSITE:** allow

refuse² *n* **= rubbish**, waste, sweepings, junk *(informal)*, litter, garbage *(chiefly US)*, trash, sediment, scum, dross, dregs, leavings, dreck *(slang, chiefly US)*, offscourings, lees

regain *vb* **1 = recover**, get back, retrieve, redeem, recapture, win back, take back, recoup, repossess, retake **2 = get back to**, return to, reach again, reattain

regal *adj* **1, 2 = royal**, majestic, kingly *or* queenly, noble, princely, proud, magnificent, sovereign, fit for a king *or* queen

regard *vb* **1 = consider**, see, hold, rate, view, value, account, judge, treat, think of, esteem, deem, look upon, adjudge **2 = look at**, view, eye, watch, observe, check, notice, clock *(Brit slang)*, remark, check out *(informal)*, gaze at, behold, eyeball *(US slang)*, scrutinize, get a load of *(informal)*, take a dekko at *(Brit slang)* **4 as regards = concerning**, regarding, relating to, pertaining to ▷ *n* **5 = respect**, esteem, deference, store, thought, love, concern, care, account, note, reputation, honour, consideration, sympathy, affection, attachment, repute **7 = look**, gaze, scrutiny, stare, glance **9** *(pl)* **= good wishes**, respects, greetings, compliments, best wishes, salutations, devoirs

regarding *prep* **= concerning**, about, as to, on the subject of, re, respecting, in respect of, as regards, with reference to, in re, in the matter of, apropos, in *or* with regard to

regardless *adj* **1** *(with* **of***)* **= irrespective of**, disregarding, unconcerned about, heedless of, unmindful of ▷ *adv* **2 = in spite of everything**, anyway, nevertheless, nonetheless, in any case, no matter what, for all that, rain or shine, despite everything, come what may

regime *n* **1, 2 = government**, rule, management, administration, leadership, establishment, reign **3 = plan**, course, system, policy, programme, scheme, regimen

region *n* **1, 2 = area**, country, place, part, land, quarter, division, section, sector, district, territory, zone, province, patch, turf *(US slang)*, tract, expanse, locality

DICTIONARY

body: *the lumbar region* **5** **in the region of** approximately: *in the region of 100 000 troops* **6** **the regions** the parts of a country away from the capital: *discord between Moscow and the regions*
regional *adj*
WORD ORIGIN Latin *regio*

regionalism *n* **1** the division of a country or organization into geographical regions each having some autonomy **2** loyalty to one's home region

register ❶ *n* **1** an official list recording names, events, or transactions **2** the book in which such a list is written **3** a device that records data, totals sums of money, etc.: *a cash register* **4** a style of speaking or writing, such as slang, used in particular circumstances or social situations **5** *music* **a** the timbre characteristic of a certain manner of voice production **b** any of the stops on an organ in respect of its tonal quality: *the flute register* ▹*vb* **6** to enter (an event, person's name, ownership, etc.) in a register **7** to show on a scale or other measuring instrument **8** to show in a person's face or bearing: *his face registered surprise* **9** *informal* to have an effect or make an impression: *the news did not register at first* **10** to have a letter or parcel insured against loss by the Post Office: *registered mail*
registration *n*
WORD ORIGIN Medieval Latin *registrum*

register office *n Brit* a government office where civil marriages are performed and births, marriages, and deaths are recorded

registrar *n* **1** a person who keeps official records **2** an official responsible for student records and enrolment in a college **3** a hospital doctor senior to a houseman but junior to a consultant

registration document *n Austral & Brit* a document giving identification details of a vehicle, including its owner's name

registration number *n* a sequence of letters and numbers given to a motor vehicle when it is registered, displayed on numberplates at the front and rear

registry *n, pl* **-tries** **1** a place where official records are kept **2** the registration of a ship's country of origin: *a ship of Liberian registry*

registry office *n Brit & NZ* ▸same as **register office**

Regius professor (reej-yuss) *n Brit* a person appointed by the Crown to a university chair founded by a royal patron
WORD ORIGIN Latin *regius* royal

regress *vb* **1** to return to a former and worse condition ▹*n* **2** return to a former and worse condition
regressive *adj*
WORD ORIGIN Latin *regredi* to go back

regression *n* **1** the act of regressing **2** *psychol* the use by an adult of behaviour more appropriate to a child

regret ❶ *vb* **-gretting, -gretted** **1** to feel sorry or upset about **2** to express apology or distress: *we regret any misunderstanding caused* ▹*n* **3** a feeling of repentance, guilt, or sorrow **4** **regrets** a polite expression of refusal: *she had sent her regrets*
regretful *adj* **regretfully** *adv*
regrettable *adj* **regrettably** *adv*
WORD ORIGIN Old French *regreter*

regroup *vb* **1** to reorganize (military forces) after an attack or a defeat **2** to rearrange into a new grouping

regular ❶ *adj* **1** normal, customary, or usual **2** symmetrical or even: *regular features* **3** according to a uniform principle, arrangement, or order **4** occurring at fixed or prearranged intervals: *we run regular advertisements in the press* **5** following a set rule or normal practice **6** *grammar* following the usual pattern of formation in a language: *regular verbs* **7** of or serving in the permanent military services: *the regular armed forces* **8** *maths* (of a polygon) having all its sides and angles the same **9** officially qualified or recognized: *he's not a regular doctor* **10** *informal* not constipated: *eating fresh vegetables helps keep you regular* **11** *US & Canad informal* likeable: *a regular guy* **12** complete or utter: *a regular fool* **13** subject to the rule of an established religious community: *canons regular* ▹*n* **14** a professional long-term serviceman in a military unit **15** *informal* a frequent customer or visitor
regularity *n* **regularize** *or* **-ise** *vb*
regularly *adv*
WORD ORIGIN Latin *regula* ruler, model

regulate ❶ *vb* **-lating, -lated** **1** to control by means of rules: *a code of practice to regulate advertising by schools* **2** to adjust slightly: *he had to take drugs to regulate his heartbeat* **regulatory** *adj*
WORD ORIGIN Late Latin *regulare* to control

regulation ❶ *n* **1** a rule that governs procedure or behaviour **2** the act of regulating ▹*adj* **3** in accordance with rules or conventions: *dressed in the orchestra's regulation black tie*

regulator *n* **1** a mechanism that automatically controls pressure, temperature, etc. **2** the mechanism by which the speed of a clock is regulated

Regulus[1] *n* **Marcus Atilius** died ?250 BC, Roman general; consul (267; 256). Captured by the Carthaginians in the First Punic War, he was sent to Rome on parole to deliver the enemy's peace terms, advised the Senate to refuse them, and was tortured to death on his return to Carthage

Regulus[2] *n* the brightest star in the constellation Leo. Visual magnitude: 1.3; spectral type: B8; distance: 69 light years

regurgitate *vb* **-tating, -tated** **1** to vomit **2** (of some birds and animals) to bring back (partly digested food) to the mouth to feed the young **3** to reproduce (ideas or facts) without understanding them
regurgitation *n*
WORD ORIGIN Medieval Latin *re-* back + *gurgitare* to flood

rehabilitate *vb* **-tating, -tated** **1** to

r

THESAURUS

register *n* **1, 2 = list**, record, roll, file, schedule, diary, catalogue, log, archives, chronicle, memorandum, roster, ledger, annals ▹*vb* **6a = enrol**, sign on *or* up, enlist, list, note, enter, check in, inscribe, set down **6b = record**, catalogue, chronicle, take down **7 = indicate**, show, record, read **8 = show**, mark, record, reflect, indicate, betray, manifest, bespeak

regret *vb* **1a = be** *or* **feel sorry about**, feel remorse about, be upset about, rue, deplore, bemoan, repent (of), weep over, bewail, cry over spilt milk **OPPOSITE:** be satisfied with **1b = mourn**, miss, grieve for *or* over ▹*n* **3a = remorse**, compunction, self-reproach, pang of conscience, bitterness, repentance, contrition, penitence, ruefulness **3b = sorrow**, disappointment, grief, lamentation **OPPOSITE:** satisfaction

regular *adj* **1, 5 = normal**, common, established, usual, ordinary, typical, routine, everyday, customary, commonplace, habitual, unvarying **OPPOSITE:** infrequent **2 = even**, level, balanced, straight, flat, fixed, smooth, uniform, symmetrical **OPPOSITE:** uneven **4a = frequent**, daily **4b = steady**, consistent

regulate *vb* **1 = control**, run, order, rule, manage, direct, guide, handle, conduct, arrange, monitor, organize, govern, administer, oversee, supervise, systematize, superintend **2 = moderate**, control, modulate, settle, fit, balance, tune, adjust

regulation *n* **1 = rule**, order, law, direction, procedure, requirement, dictate, decree, canon, statute, ordinance, commandment, edict, precept, standing order **2 = control**, government, management, administration, direction, arrangement, supervision, governance, rule

DICTIONARY

help (a person) to readapt to society after illness or imprisonment **2** to restore to a former position or rank **3** to restore the good reputation of **rehabilitation** *n*
WORD ORIGIN Medieval Latin *rehabilitare* to restore

rehash *vb* **1** to use (old or already used ideas) in a slightly different form without real improvement ▷ *n* **2** old ideas presented in a new form
WORD ORIGIN *re-* again + *hash* to chop into pieces

rehearse ⊕ *vb* **-hearsing, -hearsed** **1** to practise (a play, concert, etc.) for public performance **2** to repeat aloud: *he rehearsed his familiar views on the press* **3** to train (a person) for public performance **rehearsal** *n* **rehearser** *n*
WORD ORIGIN Old French *rehercier* to harrow a second time

rehouse *vb* **-housing, -housed** to provide with a new and better home

Reich (rike) *n* the former German state, esp. the Nazi dictatorship in Germany from 1933–45 (**Third Reich**)
WORD ORIGIN German: kingdom

reign ⊕ *n* **1** the period during which a monarch is the official ruler of a country **2** a period during which a person or thing is dominant: *a reign of terror* ▷ *vb* **3** to rule (a country) **4** to be supreme: *a sense of confusion reigns in the capital*
WORD ORIGIN Old French *reigne*

reigning *adj* currently holding a title or championship: *the reigning world champion*

reimburse *vb* **-bursing, -bursed** to repay (someone) for (expenses or losses) **reimbursement** *n*
WORD ORIGIN Medieval Latin *imbursare* to put in a moneybag

rein ⊕ *n* **1 reins a** a long narrow straps attached to a bit to control a horse **b** narrow straps attached to a harness to control a young child **c** means of control: *to take up the reins of government* **2 give (a) free rein** to allow a considerable amount of freedom **3 keep a tight rein on** to control carefully: *we have to keep a tight rein on expenditure* ▷ *vb* **4** to restrain or halt with reins **5** to control or limit: *public spending was reined in* ▶ See also **rein in**
WORD ORIGIN Old French *resne*

reincarnate *vb* **-nating, -nated** to be born again in a different body: *souls may be reincarnated in human forms*

reincarnation ⊕ *n* **1** the belief that after death the soul is reborn in another body **2** an instance of rebirth in another body **3** reappearance in a new form of a principle or idea: *he was the reincarnation of the old Republican Party isolationist*

reindeer *n, pl* **-deer** *or* **-deers** a deer with large branched antlers that lives in the arctic regions
WORD ORIGIN Old Norse *hreindýri*

reinforce ⊕ *vb* **-inforcing, -inforced** **1** to give added emphasis to (an idea or feeling): *his tired face reinforced his own weariness* **2** to make physically stronger or harder: *the plastic panels were reinforced with carbon fibre* **3** to give added support to (a military force) by providing more men or equipment: *the army garrison had been reinforced with helicopters* **reinforcement** *n*
WORD ORIGIN French *renforcer*

reinforced concrete *n* concrete with steel bars or mesh embedded in it to strengthen it

rein in *vb* **1** to stop (a horse) by pulling on the reins **2** to restrict or stop: *either prices or wage packets had to be reined in*

reinstate ⊕ *vb* **-stating, -stated** **1** to restore to a former rank or status **2** to cause to exist or be important again: *reinstate some semblance of order* **reinstatement** *n*

reinvigorate *vb* to give renewed energy to; refresh

reissue *n* **1** a book, CD, etc. that is published or released again after being unavailable for a time ▷ *vb* **2** to publish or release (a book, CD, etc.) again after a period of unavailability

reiterate ⊕ *vb* **-ating, -ated** *formal* to repeat again and again **reiteration** *n*
WORD ORIGIN Latin *reiterare*

reject ⊕ *vb* **1** to refuse to accept, use, or believe **2** to deny to (a person) the feelings hoped for: *the boy had been rejected by his mother* **3** to pass over or throw out as useless **4** (of an organism) to fail to accept (a tissue graft or organ transplant) ▷ *n* **5** a person or thing rejected as not up to standard **rejection** *n*
WORD ORIGIN Latin *reicere* to throw back

rejig *vb* **-jigging, -jigged** **1** to re-equip (a factory or plant) **2** *informal* to rearrange or manipulate, sometimes in an unscrupulous way: *the promoter hastily rejigged the running order*

rejoice ⊕ *vb* **-joicing, -joiced** to feel or express great happiness **rejoicing** *n*
WORD ORIGIN Old French *resjoir*

rejoin[1] *vb* to come together with (someone or something) again

rejoin[2] ⊕ *vb* to reply in a sharp or witty way
WORD ORIGIN Old French *rejoindre*

rejoinder *n* a sharp or witty reply

rejuvenate *vb* **-nating, -nated** to give back youth or vitality to **rejuvenation** *n*
WORD ORIGIN Latin *re-* again + *juvenis* young

rekindle *vb* **-dling, -dled** to arouse (former emotions or interests)

relapse *vb* **-lapsing, -lapsed** **1** to fall back into bad habits or illness ▷ *n* **2** the act of relapsing **3** the return of ill health after an apparent or partial recovery
WORD ORIGIN Latin *re-* back + *labi* to slip

relate ⊕ *vb* **-lating, -lated** **1** to establish a relation between **2** to have reference or relation to **3** to have an understanding (of people or

r

THESAURUS

rehearse *vb* **1 = practise**, prepare, run through, go over, train, act, study, ready, repeat, drill, try out, recite

reign *n* **1 = rule**, sovereignty, supremacy, power, control, influence, command, empire, monarchy, sway, dominion, hegemony, ascendancy ▷ *vb* **3 = rule**, govern, be in power, occupy *or* sit on the throne, influence, command, administer, hold sway, wear the crown, wield the sceptre **4 = be supreme**, prevail, predominate, hold sway, be rife, be rampant

rein *n* **1a, 1b** *(pl)* **= control**, harness, bridle, hold, check, restriction, brake, curb, restraint

reincarnation *n* **1 = rebirth**, metempsychosis, transmigration of souls

reinforce *vb* **2 = support**, strengthen, fortify, toughen, stress, prop, supplement, emphasize, underline, harden, bolster, stiffen, shore up, buttress **3 = increase**, extend, add to, strengthen, supplement, augment

reinstate *vb* **1 = restore**, recall, bring back, re-establish, return, rehabilitate

reiterate *vb (formal)* **= repeat**, restate, say again, retell, do again, recapitulate, iterate

reject *vb* **1 = deny**, decline, abandon, exclude, veto, discard, relinquish, renounce, spurn, eschew, leave off, throw off, disallow, forsake, retract, repudiate, cast off, disown, forgo, disclaim, forswear, swear off, wash your hands of **OPPOSITE:** approve **2 = rebuff**, drop, jilt, desert, turn down, ditch *(slang)*, break with, spurn, refuse, say no to, repulse, throw over **OPPOSITE:** accept **3 = discard**, decline, eliminate, scrap, bin, jettison, cast aside, throw away *or* out **OPPOSITE:** accept ▷ *n* **5a = castoff**, second, discard, flotsam, clunker *(informal)* **OPPOSITE:** treasure **5b = failure**, loser, flop

rejoice *vb* **= be glad**, celebrate, delight, be happy, joy, triumph, glory, revel, be overjoyed, exult, jump for joy, make merry **OPPOSITE:** lament

rejoin *vb* **= reply**, answer, respond, retort, come back with, riposte, return

relate *vb* **4 = tell**, recount, report, present, detail, describe, chronicle,

DICTIONARY

ideas): *the inability to relate to others* **4** to tell (a story) or describe (an event) **WORD ORIGIN** Latin *relatus* brought back
related ❶ *adj* **1** linked by kinship or marriage **2** connected or associated: *salts and related compounds*
relation ❶ *n* **1** the connection between things or people **2** a person who is connected by blood or marriage **3** connection by blood or marriage **4** an account or narrative **5 in** *or* **with relation to** with reference to: *an inquiry into export controls in relation to Iraq*
relations ❶ *pl n* **1** social or political dealings between individuals or groups **2** family or relatives **3** *euphemistic* sexual intercourse
relationship ❶ *n* **1** the dealings and feelings that exist between people or groups **2** an emotional or sexual affair **3** the connection between two things: *the relationship between exercise and mental health* **4** association by blood or marriage
relative ❶ *adj* **1** true to a certain degree or extent: *a zone of relative affluence* **2** having significance only in relation to something else: *time is relative* **3 relative to** in proportion to: *it will benefit from high growth in earnings relative to prices* **4** respective: *the relative qualities of speed and accuracy* **5** relevant: *the facts relative to the enquiry* **6** *grammar* of a clause (**relative clause**) that modifies a noun or pronoun occurring earlier in the sentence **7** *grammar* of or belonging to a class of words, such as *who, which,* or *that,* which function as conjunctions introducing relative clauses ▷*n* **8** a person who is related by blood or marriage **relatively** *adv*
relative atomic mass *n* ▸same as **atomic weight**
relativity *n* **1** either of two theories developed by Albert Einstein, the **special theory of relativity**, which requires that the laws of physics shall be the same as seen by any two different observers in uniform relative motion, and the **general theory of relativity**, which considers observers with relative acceleration and leads to a theory of gravitation **2** the state of being relative
relax ❶ *vb* **1** to make or become less tense, looser, or less rigid **2** to ease up from effort or attention **3** to make (rules or discipline) less strict **4** to become more friendly **5** to lessen the intensity of: *he relaxed his vigilance in the lulls between attacks* **relaxed** *adj*
WORD ORIGIN Latin *relaxare* to loosen
relaxation ❶ *n* **1** rest after work or effort **2** a form of recreation: *his favoured form of relaxation was walking on the local moors* **3** the act of relaxing
relay ❶ *n* **1** a fresh set of people or animals relieving others **2** ▸short for **relay race** **3** an automatic device that controls a valve or switch, esp. one in which a small change in current or voltage controls the switching on or off of circuits **4** *radio* a combination of a receiver and transmitter designed to receive radio signals and retransmit them ▷*vb* **5** to pass on (a message) **6** to retransmit (a signal) by means of a relay **7** *Brit* to broadcast (a performance or event) as it happens **WORD ORIGIN** Old French *relaier* to leave behind
relay race *n* a race between teams in which each contestant covers a specified portion of the distance
release ❶ *vb* **-leasing, -leased** **1** to free (a person or animal) from captivity or imprisonment **2** to free (someone) from obligation or duty **3** to free (something) from (one's grip) **4** to allow news or information to be made public or available **5** to allow (something) to move freely: *she released the handbrake* **6** to issue (a CD, film, or book) for sale or public showing: *the CD was originally released six years ago* **7** to give out heat, energy, radiation, etc.: *the explosion released a cloud of toxic gas* ▷*n* **8** the act of freeing or state of being freed **9** a statement to the press **10** the act of issuing for sale or publication **11** something issued for sale or public showing
WORD ORIGIN Old French *relesser*
relegate ❶ *vb* **-gating, -gated** **1** to put in a less important position **2** to demote (a sports team) to a lower division: *four clubs were relegated from the first division* **relegation** *n*
WORD ORIGIN Latin *re-* back + *legare* to send
relent *vb* **1** to change one's mind about some decision **2** to become milder or less severe: *the weather relented*
WORD ORIGIN Latin *re-* back + *lentare* to bend
relentless ❶ *adj* **1** never stopping or

THESAURUS

rehearse, recite, impart, narrate, set forth, give an account of
related *adj* **1 = akin**, kin, kindred, cognate, consanguineous, agnate **OPPOSITE:** unrelated
2 = associated, linked, allied, joint, accompanying, connected, affiliated, akin, correlated, interconnected, concomitant, cognate, agnate
OPPOSITE: unconnected
relation *n* **1 = similarity**, link, bearing, bond, application, comparison, tie-in, correlation, interdependence, pertinence, connection **2 = relative**, kin, kinsman *or* kinswoman, rellie *(Austral slang)*
relations *pl n* **2 = family**, relatives, tribe, clan, kin, kindred, kinsmen, kinsfolk, ainga *(NZ)*, rellies *(Austral slang)*
relationship *n* **1 = association**, bond, communications, connection, conjunction, affinity, rapport, kinship **2 = affair**, romance, liaison, amour, intrigue **3 = connection**, link, proportion, parallel, ratio, similarity, tie-up, correlation
relative *adj* **1 = comparative** **3** *(with* **to***)* **= in proportion to**, corresponding to, proportionate to, proportional to **4 = corresponding**, respective, reciprocal ▷*n* **8 = relation**, connection, kinsman *or* kinswoman, member of your *or* the family, rellie *(Austral slang)*
relax *vb* **1 = make less tense**, soften, loosen up, unbend, rest **1, 4 = be** *or* **feel at ease**, chill out *(slang, chiefly US)*, take it easy, loosen up, laze, lighten up *(slang)*, put your feet up, hang loose *(slang)*, let yourself go *(informal)*, let your hair down *(informal)*, mellow out *(informal)*, make yourself at home, outspan *(S African)*, take your ease **OPPOSITE:** be alarmed
2 = calm down, calm, unwind, loosen up, tranquillize **3 = moderate**, ease, relieve, weaken, diminish, mitigate, slacken **OPPOSITE:** tighten up
5 = lessen, reduce, ease, relieve, weaken, loosen, let up, slacken
OPPOSITE: tighten
relaxation *n* **1, 2 = leisure**, rest, fun, pleasure, entertainment, recreation, enjoyment, amusement, refreshment, beer and skittles *(informal)*, me-time
relay *vb* **6, 7 = broadcast**, carry, spread, communicate, transmit, send out
release *vb* **1 = set free**, free, discharge, liberate, drop, deliver, loose, let go, undo, let out, extricate, untie, disengage, emancipate, unchain, unfasten, turn loose, unshackle, unloose, unfetter, unbridle, manumit **OPPOSITE:** imprison
2 = acquit, excuse, exempt, let go, dispense, let off, exonerate, absolve
4 = issue, publish, make public, make known, break, present, launch, distribute, unveil, put out, circulate, disseminate
OPPOSITE: withhold
▷*n* **8 = liberation**, freedom, delivery, liberty, discharge, emancipation, deliverance, manumission, relief
OPPOSITE: imprisonment
9 = issue, announcement, publication, proclamation, offering
relegate *vb* **1, 2 = demote**, degrade, downgrade, declass
relentless *adj* **1 = unremitting**, sustained, punishing, persistent,

DICTIONARY

reducing in severity: *relentless deterioration in standards* **2** (of a person) determined and pitiless

relevant *adj* to do with the matter in hand **relevance** *n*
WORD ORIGIN Medieval Latin *relevans*

reliable *adj* able to be trusted **reliability** *n* **reliably** *adv*

reliance *n* the state of relying on or trusting (a person or thing) **reliant** *adj*

relic *n* **1** an object or custom that has survived from the past **2** something valued for its past associations **3 relics** remaining parts or traces **4** *RC church, eastern church* a body part or possession of a saint, venerated as holy
WORD ORIGIN Latin *reliquiae* remains

relict *n archaic* **1** a relic **2** a widow
WORD ORIGIN Latin *relictus* left behind

relief *n* **1** a feeling of cheerfulness that follows the removal of anxiety, pain, or distress **2** a temporary pause in anxiety, pain, or distress **3** money, food, or clothing given to people in special need: *disaster relief* **4** the act of freeing a besieged town or fortress: *the relief of Mafeking* **5** a person who replaces another at some task or duty **6** a bus, plane, etc. that carries additional passengers when a scheduled service is full **7** Also called: **relievo** *sculpture, archit* the projection of a carved design from the surface **8** any vivid effect resulting from contrast: *a welcome relief* **9** the difference between the highest and lowest level: *study the map of relief and the rainfall map* **10 on relief** *US & Canad* (of people) in receipt of government aid because of personal need
WORD ORIGIN Old French *relever* to relieve

relief map *n* a map showing the shape and height of the land surface by contours and shading

relieve *vb* **-lieving, -lieved 1** to lessen (pain, distress, boredom, etc.) **2** to bring assistance to (someone in need): *a plan to relieve those facing hunger* **3** to free (someone) from an obligation: *a further attempt to relieve the taxpayers of their burdens* **4** to take over the duties of (someone): *the night nurse came in to relieve her* **5** to free (a besieged town or fort) **6 relieve oneself** to urinate or defecate **7** to set off by contrast: *painted walls are marginally relieved by some abstract prints* **8** *informal* to take from: *the prince had relieved him of his duties* **relieved** *adj*
WORD ORIGIN Latin *re-* again + *levare* to lighten

religion *n* **1** belief in or worship of a supernatural power or powers considered to be divine or to have control of human destiny **2** any formal expression of such belief: *the Christian religion* **3** *chiefly RC church* the way of life entered upon by monks and nuns: *to enter religion*
WORD ORIGIN Latin *religio*

religious *adj* **1** of religion **2** pious or devout **3** scrupulous or conscientious: *religious attention to detail* **4** *Christianity* relating to the way of life of monks and nuns ▷ *n* **5** *Christianity* a monk or nun **religiously** *adv*

relinquish *vb formal* **1** to give up: *that hope has to be relinquished* **2** to renounce (a claim or right) **3** to release one's hold on **relinquishment** *n*
WORD ORIGIN Latin *relinquere*

reliquary (rel-lik-wer-ee) *n, pl* **-quaries** a container for relics of saints

relish *vb* **1** to savour or enjoy (an experience) to the full **2** to anticipate eagerly ▷ *n* **3** liking or enjoyment: *he has an enormous relish for life* **4** pleasurable anticipation: *his early relish for a new challenge* **5** an appetizing or spicy food, such as a pickle, added to a main dish to improve its flavour **6** a zestful quality: *he tells stories with great relish*
WORD ORIGIN earlier *reles* aftertaste

relive *vb* **-living, -lived** to experience (a sensation or event) again, esp. in the imagination

reload *vb* to put fresh ammunition into (a firearm)

relocate *vb* **-cating, -cated** to move or be moved to a new place of work **relocation** *n*

reluctance *n* **1** unwillingness to do something **2** *physics* a measure of the resistance of a closed magnetic circuit to a magnetic flux
WORD ORIGIN Latin *reluctari* to resist

reluctant *adj* unwilling or disinclined **reluctantly** *adv*

THESAURUS

unstoppable, unbroken, unrelenting, incessant, unabated, nonstop, unrelieved, unflagging, unfaltering **2 = merciless**, hard, fierce, harsh, cruel, grim, ruthless, uncompromising, unstoppable, inflexible, unrelenting, unforgiving, inexorable, implacable, unyielding, remorseless, pitiless, undeviating
OPPOSITE: merciful

relevant *adj* **= significant**, appropriate, proper, related, fitting, material, suited, relative, to the point, apt, applicable, pertinent, apposite, admissible, germane, to the purpose, appurtenant, ad rem *(Latin)* OPPOSITE: irrelevant

reliable *adj* **a = dependable**, trustworthy, honest, responsible, sure, sound, true, certain, regular, stable, faithful, predictable, upright, staunch, reputable, trusty, unfailing, tried and true
OPPOSITE: unreliable
b = definitive, sound, dependable, trustworthy

reliance *n* **a = dependency**, dependence **b = trust**, confidence, belief, faith, assurance, credence, credit

relic *n* **1, 2 = remnant**, vestige, memento, trace, survival, scrap, token, fragment, souvenir, remembrance, keepsake

relief *n* **1 = ease**, release, comfort, cure, remedy, solace, balm, deliverance, mitigation, abatement, alleviation, easement, palliation, assuagement **2 = rest**, respite, let-up, relaxation, break, diversion, refreshment *(informal)*, remission, breather *(informal)* **3 = aid**, help, support, assistance, sustenance, succour

relieve *vb* **1 = ease**, soothe, alleviate, allay, relax, comfort, calm, cure, dull, diminish, soften, console, appease, solace, mitigate, abate, assuage, mollify, salve, palliate
OPPOSITE: intensify
2 = help, support, aid, sustain, assist, succour, bring aid to

religion *n* **1, 2 = belief**, faith, theology, creed

religious *adj* **1 = spiritual**, holy, sacred, divine, theological, righteous, sectarian, doctrinal, devotional, scriptural **3 = conscientious**, exact, faithful, rigid, rigorous, meticulous, scrupulous, fastidious, unerring, unswerving, punctilious

relinquish *vb* **1, 2** *(formal)* **= give up**, leave, release, drop, abandon, resign, desert, quit, yield, hand over, surrender, withdraw from, let go, retire from, renounce, waive, vacate, say goodbye to, forsake, cede, repudiate, cast off, forgo, abdicate, kiss (something) goodbye, lay aside

relish *vb* **1 = enjoy**, like, prefer, taste, appreciate, savour, revel in, luxuriate in OPPOSITE: dislike
2 = look forward to, fancy, delight in, lick your lips over ▷ *n* **3 = enjoyment**, liking, love, taste, fancy, stomach, appetite, appreciation, penchant, zest, fondness, gusto, predilection, zing *(informal)*, partiality
OPPOSITE: distaste
5 = condiment, seasoning, sauce, appetizer

reluctance *n* **1 = unwillingness**, dislike, loathing, distaste, aversion, backwardness, hesitancy, disinclination, repugnance, indisposition, disrelish

reluctant *adj* **= unwilling**, slow, backward, grudging, hesitant, averse, recalcitrant, loath, disinclined, unenthusiastic,

DICTIONARY

rely ❶ *vb* **-lies, -lying, -lied** ▪ **rely on** *or* **upon a** to be dependent on: *the organization relies on voluntary contributions* **b** to have trust or confidence in: *you can rely on his judgment*
WORD ORIGIN Old French *relier* to fasten together

REM rapid eye movement

remain ❶ *vb* **1** to continue to be: *the situation remains alarming* **2** to stay behind or in the same place: *to remain at home* **3** to be left after use or the passage of time **4** to be left to be done, said, etc.: *whether this will be a long-term trend remains to be seen*
WORD ORIGIN Latin *remanere*

remainder ❶ *n* **1** a part or portion that is left after use or the passage of time: *we ate some biscuits and the remainder of the jam* **2** *maths* **a** the amount left over when one quantity cannot be exactly divided by another: *for 10 ÷ 3, the remainder is 1* **b** the amount left over when one quantity is subtracted from another **3** a number of copies of a book sold cheaply because it has been impossible to sell them at full price ▷ *vb* **4** to sell (copies of a book) as a remainder

remains ❶ *pl n* **1** parts left over from something after use or the passage of time: *the remains of the old Roman fortress* **2** a corpse

remake *vb* **-making, -made 1** to make again in a different way ▷ *n* **2** a new version of an old film

remand *vb* **1** *law* to send (a prisoner or accused person) back into custody or put on bail before trial ▷ *n* **2** the sending of a person back into custody or putting on bail before trial **3 on remand** in custody or on bail awaiting trial
WORD ORIGIN Latin *re-* back + *mandare* to command

remand centre *n* a place where accused people are detained while awaiting trial

remark ❶ *vb* **1** to pass a casual comment (about) **2** to say **3** to observe or notice ▷ *n* **4** a brief casually expressed thought or opinion
WORD ORIGIN Old French *remarquer* to observe

remarkable ❶ *adj* **1** worthy of note or attention: *a remarkable career* **2** striking or extraordinary: *a thing of remarkable beauty* **remarkably** *adv*

Remarque *n* **Erich Maria** 1898–1970, US novelist, born in Germany, noted for his novel of World War I, *All Quiet on the Western Front* (1929)

remarry *vb* **-ries, -rying, -ried** to marry again following a divorce or the death of one's previous spouse **remarriage** *n*

REME Royal Electrical and Mechanical Engineers

remedial *adj* **1** providing or intended as a remedy **2** of special teaching for slow learners: *remedial classes* **remedially** *adv*

remedy ❶ *n, pl* **-edies 1** a drug or treatment for curing pain or disease **2** a way of solving a problem: *every statesman promised a remedy for unemployment* ▷ *vb* **-edies, -edying, -edied 3** to put right or improve **remediable** *adj*
WORD ORIGIN Latin *remedium* a cure

remember ❶ *vb* **1** to become aware of (something forgotten) again **2** to keep (an idea, intention, etc.) in one's mind: *remember to write* **3** to give money to (someone), as in a will or in tipping **4 remember to** to mention (a person's name) to another person, by way of greeting: *remember me to her* **5** to commemorate: *we are here to remember the dead*
WORD ORIGIN Latin *re-* again + *memor* mindful

remembrance ❶ *n* **1** a memory **2** a memento or keepsake **3** the act of honouring some past event or person

Remembrance Day *n* **1** (in Britain) Remembrance Sunday **2** (in Canada and Australia) a statutory holiday observed on November 11 in memory of the dead of both World Wars

Remembrance Sunday *n* (in Britain) the Sunday closest to November 11, on which the dead of both World Wars are commemorated

remind ❶ *vb* **1** to cause to remember: *remind her that she was on duty* **2** to put in mind (of someone or something): *you remind me of Alice in Wonderland*

reminder *n* **1** something that recalls the past **2** a note to remind a person of something not done

reminisce *vb* **-niscing, -nisced** to talk or write about old times or past experiences

reminiscence *n* **1** the act of recalling or narrating past experiences **2** something remembered from the past **3 reminiscences** stories about a person's life, often presented in a book

reminiscent ❶ *adj* **1 reminiscent of** reminding or suggestive of **2** characterized by reminiscence
WORD ORIGIN Latin *reminisci* to call to mind

remiss *adj formal* careless in attention to duty or responsibility
WORD ORIGIN Latin *remissus*

remission *n* **1** a reduction in the length of a prison term **2** forgiveness for sin **3** easing of

THESAURUS

indisposed **OPPOSITE:** willing

rely *vb* (*with* **on** *or* **upon**) **a = depend on**, lean on **b = be confident of**, bank on, trust, count on, bet on, reckon on, lean on, be sure of, have confidence in, swear by, repose trust in

remain *vb* **1a = stay**, continue, go on, stand, dwell, bide **1b = continue**, be left, endure, persist, linger, hang in the air, stay **2 = stay behind**, wait, delay, stay put, tarry **OPPOSITE:** go

remainder *n* **1 = rest**, remains, balance, trace, excess, surplus, butt, remnant, relic, residue, stub, vestige(s), tail end, dregs, oddment, leavings, residuum

remains *pl n* **1a = remnants**, leftovers, remainder, scraps, rest, pieces, balance, traces, fragments, debris, residue, crumbs, vestiges, detritus, dregs, odds and ends, oddments, leavings **1b = relics 2 = corpse**, body, carcass, cadaver

remark *vb* **1, 2 = comment**, say, state, reflect, mention, declare, observe, pass comment, animadvert **3 = notice**, note, observe, perceive, see, mark, regard, make out, heed, espy, take note *or* notice of ▷ *n* **4 = comment**, observation, reflection, statement, thought, word, opinion, declaration, assertion, utterance

remarkable *adj* **1, 2 = extraordinary**, striking, outstanding, famous, odd, strange, wonderful, signal, rare, unusual, impressive, surprising, distinguished, prominent, notable, phenomenal, uncommon, conspicuous, singular, miraculous, noteworthy, pre-eminent **OPPOSITE:** ordinary

remedy *n* **1 = cure**, treatment, specific, medicine, therapy, antidote, panacea, restorative, relief, nostrum, physic (*rare*), medicament, counteractive ▷ *vb* **3 = put right**, redress, rectify, reform, fix, correct, solve, repair, relieve, ameliorate, set to rights

remember *vb* **1 = recall**, think back to, recollect, reminisce about, retain, recognize, call up, summon up, call to mind **OPPOSITE:** forget **2 = bear in mind**, keep in mind **5 = look back (on)**, commemorate

remembrance *n* **1 = memory**, recollection, thought, recall, recognition, retrospect, reminiscence, anamnesis **2 = souvenir**, token, reminder, monument, relic, remembrancer (*archaic*), memento, keepsake **3 = commemoration**, memorial, testimonial

remind *vb* **1 = jog your memory**, prompt, refresh your memory, make you remember

reminiscent *adj* **1** (*with* **of**) **= suggestive**, evocative, redolent, remindful, similar

DICTIONARY

intensity of the symptoms of a disease **4** a release from an obligation

remit (rim-mitt) *vb* **-mitting, -mitted** **1** to send (money) for goods or services **2** to cancel (a punishment or debt) **3** *law* to send back (a case) to a lower court for further consideration **4** to slacken or ease off **5** *archaic* to forgive (crime or sins) ▷*n* (ree-mitt) **6** area of authority: *within the review body's remit*
WORD ORIGIN Latin *re-* back + *mittere* to send

remittance *n* money sent as payment

remittent *adj* (of a disease) periodically less severe

remix *vb* **1** to change the relative prominence of each performer's part of (a recording) ▷*n* **2** a remixed version of a recording

remnant ❶ *n* **1** a part left over **2** a piece of material from the end of a roll **3** a surviving trace or vestige: *the authorities drafted in the military to crush any remnant of protest*
WORD ORIGIN Old French *remenant* remaining

remodel *vb* **-elling, -elled** to give a different shape or form to: *a renaissance of boutiques and remodelled apartments; the country is planning to remodel its armed forces*

remonstrance *n formal* a strong protest about something

remonstrate *vb* **-strating, -strated** *formal* to argue in protest or objection: *the player remonstrated loudly with the official* **remonstration** *n*
WORD ORIGIN Latin *re-* again + *monstrare* to show

remorse ❶ *n* a sense of deep regret and guilt for something one did

remorseful *adj*
WORD ORIGIN Medieval Latin *remorsus* a gnawing

remorseless *adj* **1** constantly unkind and lacking pity: *remorseless fate* **2** continually intense: *the superintendent's remorseless gaze*

remote ❶ *adj* **1** far away **2** far from civilization **3** distant in time **4** not relevant: *the issues seem remote from the general population* **5** (of a person's manner) aloof or abstracted **6** slight or faint: *a remote possibility* **7** operated from a distance; remote-controlled: *a remote manipulator arm* **remotely** *adv*
WORD ORIGIN Latin *remotus* far removed

remote control *n* control of an apparatus from a distance by radio or electrical signals **remote-controlled** *adj*

remould *vb* **1** to change completely: *to remould the country* **2** *Brit* to bond a new tread onto the casing of (a worn pneumatic tyre) ▷*n* **3** *Brit* a tyre made by this process

removable *adj* capable of being removed from a place or released from another object: *a farmer's truck with removable wooden sides*

removal ❶ *n* **1** the act of removing or state of being removed **2** the process of moving one's possessions from a previous address to a new one

remove ❶ *vb* **-moving, -moved** **1** to take away and place elsewhere **2** to take (clothing) off **3** to get rid of **4** to dismiss (someone) from office **5** *formal* to change the location of one's home or place of business ▷*n* **6** the degree of difference: *one remove away from complete rebuttal* **7** *Brit* (in certain schools) a class or form designed to prepare pupils for senior classes
WORD ORIGIN Old French *removoir*

removed *adj* **1** very different or distant: *madness seemed far removed from the sunny order of things* **2** separated by a degree of descent: *the child of a person's first cousin is their first cousin once removed*

remunerate *vb* **-ating, -ated** *formal* to reward or pay for work or service **remuneration** *n* **remunerative** *adj*
WORD ORIGIN Latin *remunerari*

renaissance ❶ *n* a renewal of interest or creativity in an area: *a complete renaissance in maze building*
WORD ORIGIN French

Renaissance *n* **1** **the Renaissance** the great revival of art, literature, and learning in Europe in the 14th, 15th, and 16th centuries ▷*adj* **2** of or from the Renaissance

renal (ree-nal) *adj* of the kidneys
WORD ORIGIN Latin *renes* kidneys

Renan *n* **(Joseph) Ernest** (ernest) 1823–92, French philosopher, theologian, and historian; best known for his *Life of Jesus* (1863), which discounted the supernatural aspects of the Gospels

renascent *adj literary* becoming active or vigorous again: *renascent nationalism* **renascence** *n*
WORD ORIGIN Latin *renasci* to be born again

rend ❶ *vb* **rending, rent** *literary* **1** to tear violently **2** (of a sound) to break (the silence) with a shrill or piercing tone
WORD ORIGIN Old English *rendan*

Rendell *n* **Ruth (Barbara)**, Baroness born 1930, British crime writer: author of detective novels, such as

THESAURUS

r

remnant *n* **1, 3 = remainder**, remains, trace, fragment, end, bit, rest, piece, balance, survival, scrap, butt, shred, hangover, residue, rump, leftovers, stub, vestige, tail end, oddment, residuum

remorse *n* **= regret**, shame, guilt, pity, grief, compassion, sorrow, anguish, repentance, contrition, compunction, penitence, self-reproach, pangs of conscience, ruefulness, bad *or* guilty conscience

remote *adj* **1, 2 = distant**, far, isolated, lonely, out-of-the-way, far-off, secluded, inaccessible, faraway, outlying, in the middle of nowhere, off the beaten track, backwoods, godforsaken **OPPOSITE:** nearby
3 = far, distant, obscure, far-off
5 = aloof, cold, removed, reserved, withdrawn, distant, abstracted, detached, indifferent, faraway, introspective, uninterested, introverted, uninvolved, unapproachable, uncommunicative, standoffish **OPPOSITE:** outgoing
6 = slight, small, outside, poor, unlikely, slim, faint, doubtful, dubious, slender, meagre, negligible, implausible, inconsiderable **OPPOSITE:** strong

removal *n* **1a = extraction**, stripping, withdrawal, purging, abstraction, uprooting, displacement, eradication, erasure, subtraction, dislodgment, expunction, taking away *or* off *or* out **1b = dismissal**, expulsion, elimination, ejection, dispossession **2 = move**, transfer, departure, relocation, flitting *(Scot & Northern English dialect)*

remove *vb* **1a = take out**, withdraw, extract, abstract **OPPOSITE:** insert
1b = take away, move, pull, transfer, detach, displace, do away with, dislodge, cart off *(slang)*, carry off *or* away **OPPOSITE:** put back
2 = take off, doff **OPPOSITE:** put on
3a = erase, eliminate, take out
3b = get rid of, wipe out, erase, eradicate, blow away *(slang, chiefly US)*, blot out, expunge **3c = delete**, shed, get rid of, erase, excise, strike out, efface, expunge **4 = dismiss**, eliminate, get rid of, discharge, abolish, expel, throw out, oust, relegate, purge, eject, do away with, depose, unseat, see the back of, dethrone, show someone the door, give the bum's rush *(slang)*, throw out on your ear *(informal)* **OPPOSITE:** appoint
5 *(formal)* **= move**, transfer, transport, shift, quit, depart, move away, relocate, vacate, flit *(Scot & Northern English dialect)*

renaissance *n* **= rebirth**, revival, restoration, renewal, awakening, resurrection, regeneration, resurgence, reappearance, new dawn, re-emergence, reawakening, new birth

rend *vb* **1, 2** *(literary)* **= tear**, break, split, rip, pull, separate, divide, crack, burst, smash, disturb, shatter, pierce, fracture, sever, wrench, splinter, rupture, cleave, lacerate, rive, tear to pieces, sunder *(literary)*, dissever

DICTIONARY

Wolf to the Slaughter (1967), and psychological thrillers, such as *The Lake of Darkness* (1980) and (under the name **Barbara Vine**) *A Fatal Inversion* (1987) and *The Chimney Sweeper's Boy* (1998)

render ❶ *vb* **1** to cause to become: *he was rendered unconscious by his wound* **2** to give or provide (aid, a service, etc.) **3** *formal* to present or submit (a bill) **4** to translate **5** to represent in painting, music, or acting **6** to yield or give: *he rendered up his soul to God* **7** to cover with plaster **8** to melt down (fat) **rendering** *n*
WORD ORIGIN Old French *rendre*

rendezvous (ron-day-voo) *n, pl* **-vous** (-vooz) **1** an appointment to meet at a specified time and place **2** a place where people meet ▷ *vb* **3** to meet at a specified time or place
WORD ORIGIN French

rendition *n formal* **1** a performance of a piece of music or a dramatic role **2** a translation

renegade *n* a person who deserts a cause for another
WORD ORIGIN Spanish *renegado*

renege (rin-nayg) *vb* **-neging, -neged** to go back (on an agreement or promise): *the politicians reneged on every promise*
WORD ORIGIN Medieval Latin *renegare* to renounce

renew ❶ *vb* **1** to begin again **2** to take up again after a break: *they wanted to renew diplomatic ties* **3** to make valid again: *we didn't renew the lease* **4** to grow again **5** to restore to a new or fresh condition **6** to replace (an old or worn-out part or piece) **7** to restate or reaffirm (a promise) **renewal** *n*

renewable *adj* **1** able to be renewed **2** (of energy or an energy source) inexhaustible or capable of being perpetually replenished ▷ *pl n* **renewables 3** renewable energy sources, such as wind and wave power

Reni *n* **Guido** 1575–1642, Italian baroque painter and engraver

rennet *n* a substance prepared from the stomachs of calves and used for curdling milk to make cheese
WORD ORIGIN Old English *gerinnan* to curdle

Rennie *n* **John** 1761–1821, British civil engineer who designed bridges, canals, docks, and harbours, including three London bridges and the London and East India docks

renounce ❶ *vb* **-nouncing, -nounced 1** to give up (a belief or habit) voluntarily **2** to give up formally (a claim or right): *he would renounce his rights to the throne*
WORD ORIGIN Latin *renuntiare*

renovate ❶ *vb* **-vating, -vated** to restore to good condition **renovation** *n* **renovator** *n*
WORD ORIGIN Latin *re-* again + *novare* to make new

renown *n* widespread good reputation
WORD ORIGIN Old French *renom*

renowned ❶ *adj* famous

rent[1] ❶ *vb* **1** to give or have use of (land, a building, a machine, etc.) in return for periodic payments ▷ *n* **2** a payment made periodically for the use of land, a building, a machine, etc.
WORD ORIGIN Old French *rente* revenue

rent[2] ❶ *n* **1** a slit made by tearing ▷ *vb* **2** ▸ the past of **rend**

rental *n* **1** the amount paid or received as rent ▷ *adj* **2** of or relating to rent

rent boy *n* a young male prostitute

rentier (ron-tee-ay) *n* a person who lives off unearned income such as rents or interest

renunciation *n* **1** the act or an instance of renouncing **2** a formal declaration renouncing something

reo *n* NZ a language
WORD ORIGIN Māori

reopen *vb* to open again after a period of being closed or suspended: *the Supreme Court has agreed to reopen the case*

reorder *vb* to change the order of; organize differently

reorganize *or* **-ise** *vb* **-izing, -ized** *or* **-ising, -ised** to organize in a new and more efficient way **reorganization** *or* **-isation** *n*

rep[1] *n theatre* ▸ short for **repertory company**

rep[2] *n* **1** a sales representative **2** someone elected to represent a group of people: *the union rep* **3** NZ *informal* a rugby player selected to represent his district

repair[1] ❶ *vb* **1** to restore (something damaged or broken) to good condition or working order **2** to make up for (a mistake or injury) **3** to heal (a breach or division) in (something): *he is attempting to repair his country's relations with America* ▷ *n* **4** the act, task, or process of repairing **5** a part that has been repaired **6** state or condition: *many museums may have to close because they are in such bad repair* **repairable** *adj*
WORD ORIGIN Latin *re-* again + *parare* to make ready

repair[2] *vb* **repair to** to go to (a place)
WORD ORIGIN Latin *re-* back + *patria* fatherland

reparable (rep-rab-bl) *adj* able to be repaired or remedied

reparation *n* **1** the act of making up for loss or injury **2 reparations** compensation paid by a defeated nation after a war for the damage and injuries it caused
WORD ORIGIN Latin *reparare* to repair

repartee *n* **1** conversation consisting of witty remarks **2** a sharp witty remark made as a reply
WORD ORIGIN French *repartie*

repast *n literary* a meal
WORD ORIGIN Old French *repaistre* to feed

repatriate *vb* **-ating, -ated 1** to send back (a person) to the country of his or her birth or citizenship ▷ *n* **2** a

r

THESAURUS

render *vb* **1 = make**, cause to become, leave **2 = provide**, give, show, pay, present, supply, deliver, contribute, yield, submit, tender, hand out, furnish, turn over, make available **5 = represent**, interpret, portray, depict, do, give, play, act, present, perform

renew *vb* **1, 2 = recommence**, continue, extend, repeat, resume, prolong, reopen, recreate, reaffirm, re-establish, rejuvenate, regenerate, restate, begin again, revitalize, bring up to date **2 = reaffirm**, resume, breathe new life into, recommence **5 = restore**, repair, transform, overhaul, mend, refurbish, renovate, refit, fix up *(informal, chiefly US & Canad)*, modernize **6 = replace**, refresh, replenish, restock

renounce *vb* **1 = disown**, reject, abandon, quit, discard, spurn, eschew, leave off, throw off, forsake, retract, repudiate, cast off, abstain from, recant, forswear, abjure, swear off, wash your hands of **2 = disclaim**, deny, decline, give up, resign, relinquish, waive, renege, forgo, abdicate, abjure, abnegate
OPPOSITE: assert

renovate *vb* **= restore**, repair, refurbish, do up *(informal)*, reform, renew, overhaul, revamp, recreate, remodel, rehabilitate, refit, fix up *(informal, chiefly US & Canad)*, modernize, reconstitute, recondition

renowned *adj* **= famous**, noted, celebrated, well-known, distinguished, esteemed, acclaimed, notable, eminent, famed, illustrious
OPPOSITE: unknown

rent[1] *vb* **1a = hire**, lease **1b = let**, lease ▷ *n* **2 = hire**, rental, lease, tariff, fee, payment

rent[2] *n* **1 = tear**, split, rip, slash, slit, gash, perforation, hole

repair[1] *vb* **1 = mend**, fix, recover, restore, heal, renew, patch, make good, renovate, patch up, put back together, restore to working order
OPPOSITE: damage
2 = put right, make up for, compensate for, rectify, square, retrieve, redress ▷ *n* **4 = mend**, restoration, overhaul, adjustment **5 = darn**, mend, patch **6 = condition**,

DICTIONARY

person who has been repatriated: *Algerian repatriates* **repatriation** *n*
WORD ORIGIN Latin *re-* back + *patria* fatherland

repay ❶ *vb* **-paying, -paid 1** to refund or reimburse **2** to make a return for (something): *to repay hospitality*
repayable *adj* **repayment** *n*

repeal ❶ *vb* **1** to cancel (a law) officially ▷ *n* **2** the act of repealing: *the repeal of repressive legislation*
repealable *adj*
WORD ORIGIN Old French *repeler*

repeat ❶ *vb* **1** to say, write, or do again **2** to tell to another person (the secrets told to one by someone else) **3** to recite (a poem, etc.) from memory **4** to occur more than once: *this pattern repeats itself many times* **5** (of food) to be tasted again after eating as the result of belching **6** to say (the words or sounds) uttered by someone else; echo ▷ *n* **7** the act or an instance of repeating **8** a word, action, pattern, etc. that is repeated **9** *radio, television* a broadcast of a programme which has been broadcast before **10** *music* a passage that is an exact restatement of the passage preceding it **repeated** *adj* **repeatedly** *adv* **repeatable** *adj*
WORD ORIGIN Latin *repetere* to seek again

repeater *n* **1** a gun capable of firing several shots without reloading **2** a clock or watch which strikes the hour or quarter-hour just past, when a spring is pressed

repel ❶ *vb* **-pelling, -pelled 1** to cause (someone) to feel disgusted **2** to force or drive back (someone or something) **3** to be effective in keeping away or controlling: *these buzzers are claimed to repel female mosquitoes* **4** to fail to mix with or absorb: *water and oil repel each other* **5** to reject or spurn: *she repelled his advances*
WORD ORIGIN Latin *re-* back + *pellere* to push

repellent *adj* **1** disgusting or distasteful **2** resisting water etc. ▷ *n* **3** a chemical used to keep insects or other creatures away

repent *vb* to feel regret for (something bad one has done)
repentance *n* **repentant** *adj*
WORD ORIGIN Old French *repentir*

repercussion *n* **1 repercussions** results or consequences of an action or event **2** an echo or reverberation
WORD ORIGIN Latin *repercutere* to strike back

repertoire ❶ *n* **1** all the works that a company or performer can perform **2** the entire stock of skills or techniques that someone or something, such as a computer, is capable of: *a superb repertoire of shots*
WORD ORIGIN French

repertory *n, pl* **-ries 1** ▸ same as **repertoire** (sense 2) **2** ▸ short for **repertory company**
WORD ORIGIN Late Latin *repertorium* storehouse

repertory company *n* a permanent theatre company producing a succession of plays

repetition ❶ *n* **1** the act of repeating **2** a thing that is repeated **3** a replica or copy **repetitious** *adj* **repetitive** *adj*

rephrase *vb* **-phrasing, -phrased** to express in different words
rephrasing *n*

repine *vb* **-pining, -pined** *literary* to be worried or discontented
WORD ORIGIN RE- + PINE[2]

replace ❶ *vb* **-placing, -placed 1** to take the place of **2** to substitute a person or thing for (another): *we need to replace that chair* **3** to put (something) back in its rightful place

replacement ❶ *n* **1** the act or process of replacing **2** a person or thing that replaces another

replay *n* **1** a showing again of a sequence of action immediately after it happens **2** a second sports match played because an earlier game was drawn ▷ *vb* **3** to play (a recording, match, etc.) again

replenish *vb* to make full or complete again by supplying what has been used up **replenishment** *n*
WORD ORIGIN Old French *replenir*

replete *adj* **1** pleasantly full of food and drink **2** well supplied: *a world replete with true horror* **repletion** *n*
WORD ORIGIN Latin *repletus*

replica ❶ *n* an exact copy
WORD ORIGIN Italian, literally: a reply

replicate ❶ *vb* **-cating, -cated** to make or be an exact copy of; reproduce
replication *n*
WORD ORIGIN Latin *replicatus* bent back

reply ❶ *vb* **-plies, -plying, -plied 1** to make answer (to) in words or writing or by an action **2** to say (something) in answer: *she replied that she did not believe him* ▷ *n, pl* **-plies 3** an answer or response
WORD ORIGIN Old French *replier* to fold again

report ❶ *vb* **1** to give an account (of)

THESAURUS

state, form, shape (*informal*), nick (*informal*), fettle

repay *vb* **1 = pay back**, refund, settle up, return, square, restore, compensate, reimburse, recompense, requite, remunerate

repeal *vb* **1 = abolish**, reverse, revoke, annul, recall, withdraw, cancel, set aside, rescind, invalidate, nullify, obviate, abrogate, countermand, declare null and void **OPPOSITE:** pass ▷ *n* **2 = abolition**, withdrawal, cancellation, rescinding, annulment, revocation, nullification, abrogation, rescission, invalidation, rescindment **OPPOSITE:** passing

repeat *vb* **1 = reiterate**, restate, recapitulate, iterate **2 = retell**, relate, quote, renew, echo, replay, reproduce, rehearse, recite, duplicate, redo, rerun, reshow ▷ *n* **7 = repetition**, echo, duplicate, reiteration, recapitulation **9** (*radio, television*) **= rerun**, replay, reproduction, reshowing

repel *vb* **1 = disgust**, offend, revolt, sicken, nauseate, put you off, make you sick, gross out (*US slang*), turn you off (*informal*), make you shudder, turn your stomach, give you the creeps (*informal*) **OPPOSITE:** delight **2, 3 = drive off**, fight, refuse, check, decline, reject, oppose, resist, confront, parry, hold off, rebuff, ward off, beat off, repulse, keep at arm's length, put to flight **OPPOSITE:** submit to

repertoire *n* **2 = range**, list, stock, supply, store, collection, repertory, repository

repetition *n* **1 = recurrence**, repeating, reappearance, duplication, echo **2 = repeating**, redundancy, replication, duplication, restatement, iteration, reiteration, tautology, recapitulation, repetitiousness

replace *vb* **1 = take the place of**, follow, succeed, oust, take over from, supersede, supplant, stand in lieu of, fill (someone's) shoes *or* boots, step into (someone's) shoes *or* boots **2 = substitute**, change, exchange, switch, swap, commute **3 = put back**, restore

replacement *n* **1 = replacing** **2 = successor**, double, substitute, stand-in, fill-in, proxy, surrogate, understudy

replica *n* **a = reproduction**, model, copy, imitation, facsimile, carbon copy **OPPOSITE:** original **b = duplicate**, copy, carbon copy

replicate *vb* **= copy**, follow, repeat, reproduce, recreate, ape, mimic, duplicate, reduplicate

reply *vb* **1, 2 = answer**, respond, retort, return, come back, counter, acknowledge, react, echo, rejoin, retaliate, write back, reciprocate, riposte, make answer ▷ *n* **3 = answer**, response, reaction, counter, echo, comeback (*informal*), retort, retaliation, acknowledgment, riposte, counterattack, return, rejoinder, reciprocation

report *vb* **1 = inform of**, communicate, announce, mention, declare, recount, give an account of, bring word on **2, 3 = communicate**,

DICTIONARY

2 to give an account of the results of an investigation (into): *the commission is to report on global warming* **3** to make a formal report on (a subject) **4** to make a formal complaint about **5** to present (oneself) at an appointed place or for a specific purpose: *report to the manager's office* **6** **report to** to be responsible to and under the authority of **7** to act as a reporter ▷*n* **8** an account prepared after investigation and published or broadcast **9** an account of the discussions of a committee or other group of people: *I have the report of the mining union* **10** a story for which there is no absolute proof: *according to report, he is not dead* **11** *Brit & NZ* a statement on the progress of a school child **12** a loud bang made by a gun or explosion **13** comment on a person's character or actions: *he is of good report here* **reportedly** *adv*
WORD ORIGIN Latin *re-* back + *portare* to carry

reported speech *n* a report of what someone said that gives the content of the speech without repeating the exact words

reporter ⊕ *n* a person who gathers news for a newspaper or broadcasting organization

repose¹ *n* **1** a state of quiet restfulness **2** calmness or composure **3** sleep ▷*vb* **-posing, -posed** **4** to lie or lay down at rest **5** to lie when dead
WORD ORIGIN Old French *reposer*

repose² *vb* **-posing, -posed** to put (trust) in a person or thing
WORD ORIGIN Latin *reponere* to store up

reposition *vb* to place in a different position

repository *n, pl* **-ries** **1** a place or container in which things can be stored for safety: *a repository for national treasures* **2** a person to whom a secret is entrusted
WORD ORIGIN Latin *repositorium*

repossess *vb* (of a lender) to take back (property) from a customer who is behind with payments, for example mortgage repayments **repossession** *n*

reprehend *vb* to find fault with
WORD ORIGIN Latin *reprehendere*

reprehensible *adj* deserving criticism: *Willie's reprehensible behaviour*

represent ⊕ *vb* **1** to act as the authorized delegate for (a person, country, etc.): *she represented her country at the Olympic Games* **2** to act as a substitute (for) **3** to stand as an equivalent of **4** to be a means of expressing: *the lights are relit to represent resurrection* **5** to display the characteristics of: *romanticism in music is represented by Liszt* **6** to describe as having a specified character or quality: *the magical bird was often represented as having two heads* **7** to state or explain **8** to present an image of through a picture or sculpture **9** to bring clearly before the mind
WORD ORIGIN Latin *repraesentare* to exhibit

representation ⊕ *n* **1** the state of being represented **2** anything that represents, such as a pictorial portrait **3** **representations** formal statements made to an official body by a person making a complaint **representational** *adj*

representative ⊕ *n* **1** a person chosen to act for or represent a group **2** a person who tries to sell the products or services of a firm **3** a typical example ▷*adj* **4** typical of a class or kind **5** representing **6** including examples of all the interests or types in a group **7** acting as deputy for another **8** of a political system in which people choose a person to make decisions on their behalf

repress ⊕ *vb* **1** to keep (feelings) under control **2** to restrict the freedom of: *he continued to repress his people* **3** *psychol* to banish (unpleasant thoughts) from one's conscious mind **repression** *n* **repressive** *adj*
WORD ORIGIN Latin *reprimere* to press back

reprieve ⊕ *vb* **-prieving, -prieved** **1** to postpone the execution of (a condemned person) **2** to give temporary relief to ▷*n* **3** a postponement or cancellation of a punishment **4** a warrant granting a postponement or cancellation **5** a temporary relief from pain or harm
WORD ORIGIN Old French *repris* (something) taken back

reprimand *vb* **1** to blame (someone) officially for a fault ▷*n* **2** an instance of blaming someone officially
WORD ORIGIN French *réprimande*

reprint *vb* **1** to print further copies of (a book) ▷*n* **2** a reprinted copy

reprisal *n* an act of taking revenge: *many residents say they are living in fear of reprisals by the army*
WORD ORIGIN Old French *reprisaille*

reprise (rip-**preez**) *music n* **1** the repeating of an earlier theme ▷*vb* **-prising, -prised** **2** to repeat an earlier theme

reproach *n* **1** blame or rebuke **2** a scolding **3** **beyond reproach** beyond criticism ▷*vb* **4** to express disapproval (of someone's actions) **reproachful** *adj*
WORD ORIGIN Old French *reprochier*

reprobate (**rep**-roh-bate) *n* **1** an unprincipled bad person ▷*adj* **2** morally unprincipled

THESAURUS

publish, record, announce, tell, state, air, detail, describe, note, cover, document, give an account of, relate, broadcast, pass on, proclaim, circulate, relay, recite, narrate, write up **5 = present yourself**, come, appear, arrive, turn up, be present, show up *(informal)*, clock in *or* on ▷*n* **8a = article**, story, dispatch, piece, message, communiqué, write-up **8b = news**, word, information, announcement, tidings **9 = account**, record, detail, note, statement, relation, version, communication, tale, description, declaration, narrative, summary, recital **10 = rumour**, talk, buzz, gossip, goss *(informal)*, hearsay, scuttlebutt *(US slang)* **12 = bang**, sound, crash, crack, noise, blast, boom, explosion, discharge, detonation, reverberation

reporter *n* **= journalist**, writer, correspondent, newscaster, hack *(derogatory)*, announcer, pressman, journo *(slang)*, newshound *(informal)*, newspaperman *or* newspaperwoman

represent *vb* **1 = act for**, speak for **2 = stand for**, substitute for, play the part of, assume the role of, serve as **3 = express**, equal, correspond to, symbolize, equate with, mean, betoken **4, 8 = depict**, show, describe, picture, express, illustrate, outline, portray, sketch, render, designate, reproduce, evoke, denote, delineate **5 = exemplify**, embody, symbolize, typify, personify, epitomize

representation *n* **2a = picture**, model, image, portrait, illustration, sketch, resemblance, likeness **2b = portrayal**, depiction, account, relation, description, narrative, narration, delineation

representative *n* **1 = delegate**, member, agent, deputy, commissioner, councillor, proxy, depute *(Scot)*, spokesman *or* spokeswoman **2 = agent**, salesman, rep, traveller, commercial traveller ▷*adj* **4, 6 = typical**, characteristic, archetypal, exemplary, illustrative **OPPOSITE:** uncharacteristic **5 = symbolic**, evocative, emblematic, typical

repress *vb* **1 = control**, suppress, hold back, bottle up, check, master, hold in, overcome, curb, restrain, inhibit, overpower, keep in check **OPPOSITE:** release **2 = subdue**, abuse, crush, quash, wrong, persecute, quell, subjugate, maltreat, trample underfoot, tyrannize over, rule with an iron hand **OPPOSITE:** liberate

reprieve *vb* **1 = grant a stay of execution to**, pardon, let off the hook *(slang)*, postpone *or* remit the punishment of ▷*n* **3 = stay of execution**, suspension, amnesty, pardon, remission, abeyance, deferment, postponement of punishment

DICTIONARY

WORD ORIGIN Late Latin *reprobatus* held in disfavour

reprobation *n literary* disapproval or blame

reproduce ❶ *vb* **-ducing, -duced 1** to make a copy or representation of **2** *biol* to produce offspring **3** to re-create **reproducible** *adj*

reproduction ❶ *n* **1** *biol* a process by which an animal or plant produces one or more individuals similar to itself **2** a copy of a work of art **3** the quality of sound from an audio system **4** the act or process of reproducing ▷*adj* **5** made in imitation of an earlier style: *reproduction furniture* **reproductive** *adj*

reproof *n* a severe blaming of someone for a fault

reprove *vb* **-proving, -proved** to speak severely to (someone) about a fault **reprovingly** *adv*

WORD ORIGIN Old French *reprover*

reptile *n* **1** a cold-blooded animal, such as a tortoise, snake, or crocodile, that has an outer covering of horny scales or plates and lays eggs **2** a contemptible grovelling person **reptilian** *adj*

WORD ORIGIN Late Latin *reptilis* creeping

Repton *n* **Humphry** 1752–1818, English landscape gardener

republic *n* **1** a form of government in which the people or their elected representatives possess the supreme power **2** a country in which the head of state is an elected or nominated president

WORD ORIGIN Latin *respublica*, literally: the public thing

republican *adj* **1** of or supporting a republic ▷*n* **2** a person who supports or advocates a republic **republicanism** *n*

Republican ❶ *adj* **1** belonging to the Republican Party, the more conservative of the two main political parties in the US **2** belonging to the Irish Republican Army ▷*n* **3** a member or supporter of the Republican Party in the US **4** a member or supporter of the Irish Republican Army **Republicanism** *n*

repudiate (rip-pew-dee-ate) *vb* **-ating, -ated 1** to reject the authority or validity of **2** to disown (a person) **3** to refuse to acknowledge or pay (a debt) **repudiation** *n*

WORD ORIGIN Latin *repudium* divorce

repugnant *adj* offensive or disgusting **repugnance** *n*

WORD ORIGIN Latin *repugnans* resisting

repulse *vb* **-pulsing, -pulsed 1** to be disgusting to: *this act of feminist rage repulsed as many as it delighted* **2** to drive (an army) back **3** to reject with coldness or discourtesy: *she repulsed his advances* ▷*n* **4** a driving back **5** a cold discourteous rejection or refusal

WORD ORIGIN Latin *repellere*

repulsion *n* **1** a feeling of disgust or aversion **2** *physics* a force separating two objects, such as the force between two like electric charges

repulsive *adj* **1** disgusting or distasteful **2** *physics* of repulsion **repulsively** *adv*

reputable (rep-pew-tab-bl) *adj* trustworthy or respectable **reputably** *adv*

reputation ❶ *n* **1** the opinion generally held of a person or thing **2** a high opinion generally held about a person or thing **3** notoriety or fame, esp. for some specified characteristic

WORD ORIGIN Latin *reputatio*

repute *n* good reputation: *a sculptor of international repute*

WORD ORIGIN Latin *reputare* to think over

reputed *adj* supposed or rumoured: *the island was reputed to have held a Roman temple; the reputed murderess* **reputedly** *adv*

request ❶ *vb* **1** to ask for or politely demand: *we requested a formal meeting with the committee* ▷*n* **2** the act or an instance of asking for something: *a polite request* **3** something asked for **4 on request** if asked for: *most companies will send samples on request*

WORD ORIGIN Old French *requeste*

Requiem (rek-wee-em) *n* **1** *RC church* a Mass celebrated for the dead **2** a musical setting of this Mass

WORD ORIGIN Latin *requies* rest

require ❶ *vb* **-quiring, -quired 1** to need **2** to be a necessary condition: *the decision requires a logical common-sense approach* **3** to insist upon **4** to order or command: *family doctors are required to produce annual reports*

WORD ORIGIN Latin *requirere* to seek to know

requirement ❶ *n* **1** something demanded or imposed as an obligation **2** a specific need or want

requisite (rek-wizz-it) *adj* **1** absolutely essential ▷*n* **2** something essential

WORD ORIGIN Latin *requisitus* sought after

requisition *vb* **1** to demand and take for use, esp. for military or public use ▷*n* **2** a formal request or demand for the use of something **3** the act of taking something over, esp. for military or public use **4** a formal written demand

requite *vb* **-quiting, -quited** to return to someone (the same treatment or feeling as received): *an Australian who requites her love* **requital** *n*

WORD ORIGIN *re-* back + obsolete *quite* to repay

reredos (rear-doss) *n* a screen or wall decoration at the back of an altar

WORD ORIGIN Old French *arere* behind + *dos* back

reroute *vb* **-routing, -routed** to send or direct by a different route

rerun *n* **1** a film or programme that is broadcast again **2** a race that is run again ▷*vb* **-running, -ran, -run 3** to put on (a film or programme) again **4** to run (a race) again

resale *n* the selling again of something purchased

reschedule *vb* **-uling, -uled 1** to change the time, date, or schedule of: *the show has been rescheduled for August* **2** to arrange a revised schedule for repayment of (a debt)

rescind *vb* to annul or repeal **rescission** *n*

WORD ORIGIN Latin *rescindere* to cut off

rescue ❶ *vb* **-cuing, -cued 1** to bring

THESAURUS

reproduce *vb* **1a = copy**, recreate, replicate, duplicate, match, represent, mirror, echo, parallel, imitate, emulate **1b = print**, copy, transcribe **2** *(biology)* **= breed**, produce young, procreate, generate, multiply, spawn, propagate, proliferate

reproduction *n* **1** *(biology)* **= breeding**, procreation, propagation, increase, generation, proliferation, multiplication **2 = copy**, picture, print, replica, imitation, duplicate, facsimile **OPPOSITE:** original

Republican *adj* **1 = right-wing**, Conservative

reputation *n* **1 = name**, standing, credit, character, honour, fame, distinction, esteem, stature, eminence, renown, repute

request *vb* **1a = ask for**, apply for, appeal for, put in for, demand, desire, pray for, beg for, requisition, beseech **1b = invite**, call for, beg, petition, beseech, entreat, supplicate **1c = seek**, ask (for), sue for, solicit ▷*n* **2a = appeal**, call, demand, plea, desire, application, prayer, petition, requisition, solicitation, entreaty, supplication, suit **2b = asking**, plea, begging

require *vb* **1 = need**, crave, depend upon, have need of, want, miss, lack, wish, desire, stand in need of **3 = order**, demand, direct, command, compel, exact, oblige, instruct, call upon, constrain, insist upon **4 = ask**, enjoin

requirement *n* **1, 2 = necessity**, demand, specification, stipulation, want, need, must, essential, qualification, precondition, requisite, prerequisite, sine qua non *(Latin)*, desideratum, must-have

rescue *vb* **1a = save**, get out, save the life of, extricate, free, release, deliver,

DICTIONARY

(someone or something) out of danger or trouble ▷ *n* **2** the act or an instance of rescuing **rescuer** *n*
WORD ORIGIN Old French *rescourre*

reseal *vb* to close or secure tightly again

research ❶ *n* **1** systematic investigation to establish facts or collect information on a subject ▷ *vb* **2** to carry out investigations into (a subject) **researcher** *n*
WORD ORIGIN Old French *recercher* to search again

resemble ❶ *vb* **-bling, -bled** to be or look like **resemblance** *n*
WORD ORIGIN Old French *resembler*

resent ❶ *vb* to feel bitter or indignant about **resentful** *adj* **resentment** *n*
WORD ORIGIN French *ressentir*

reservation ❶ *n* **1** a doubt: *his only reservation was, did he have the stamina?* **2** an exception or limitation that prevents one's wholehearted acceptance: *work I admire without reservation* **3** a seat, room, etc. that has been reserved **4** (esp. in the US) an area of land set aside for American Indian peoples: *the Cherokee reservation* **5** *Brit* ▸ short for **central reservation**

reserve ❶ *vb* **-serving, -served** **1** to keep back or set aside for future use **2** to obtain by arranging beforehand: *I phoned to reserve two tickets* **3** to keep for oneself: *the association reserves the right to charge a fee* **4** to delay announcing (a legal judgment) ▷ *n* **5** something kept back or set aside for future use **6** the state or condition of being reserved: *we're keeping these two in reserve* **7** *sport* a substitute **8** an area of publicly owned land used for sport, etc.: *a wildlife reserve* **9** the hiding of one's feelings and personality **10** the part of a nation's armed services not in active service **11** **reserves** *finance* money or assets held by a bank or business to meet future expenses **12** *Canad* an Indian reservation
WORD ORIGIN Latin *reservare* to keep

reserved ❶ *adj* **1** not showing one's feelings **2** set aside for use by a particular person

reserve price *n* the minimum price acceptable to the owner of property being auctioned or sold

reservist *n* a member of a nation's military reserve

reservoir ❶ *n* **1** a natural or artificial lake for storing water for community use **2** a large supply of something: *a vast reservoir of youthful enthusiasm*
WORD ORIGIN French *réservoir*

resettle *vb* **-tling, -tled** to settle to live in a different place **resettlement** *n*

reshuffle *n* **1** a reorganization of jobs in a government or company ▷ *vb* **-fling, -fled** **2** to reorganize jobs or duties in a government or company

reside ❶ *vb* **-siding, -sided** *formal* **1** to live permanently (in a place): *my daughter resides in Europe* **2** to be present (in): *desire resides in the unconscious*
WORD ORIGIN Latin *residere* to sit back

residence ❶ *n* **1** a person's home or house **2** a large imposing house **3** the fact of residing in a place **4** a period of residing in a place **5** **in residence** **a** living in a particular place: *the Monarch was not in residence* **b** (of an artist) working for a set period at a college, gallery, etc.: *composer in residence*

resident ❶ *n* **1** a person who lives in a place **2** a bird or animal that does not migrate ▷ *adj* **3** living in a place **4** living at a place in order to carry out a job: *a resident custodian* **5** employed for one's specialized abilities: *the Museum's resident expert on seventeenth-century Dutch art* **6** (of birds and animals) not in the habit of migrating

residential *adj* **1** (of a part of a town) consisting mainly of houses **2** providing living accommodation: *residential clubs for homeless boys*

residential school *n* a government boarding school in N Canada for Indian and Inuit students

residual *adj* **1** of or being a remainder ▷ *n* **2** something left over as a residue

residue ❶ *n* **1** what is left over after something has been removed **2** *law* what is left of an estate after the discharge of debts and distribution of specific gifts
WORD ORIGIN Latin *residuus* remaining over

residuum *n, pl* **-ua** ▸ same as **residue**

resign ❶ *vb* **1** to give up office or a job **2** to accept (an unpleasant fact): *he resigned himself to the inevitable* **3** to give

THESAURUS

recover, liberate, set free, save (someone's) bacon (*Brit informal*)
OPPOSITE: desert
1b = salvage, deliver, redeem, come to the rescue of ▷ *n* **2 = saving**, salvage, deliverance, extrication, release, relief, recovery, liberation, salvation, redemption

research *n* **1 = investigation**, study, inquiry, analysis, examination, probe, exploration, scrutiny, experimentation, delving, groundwork, fact-finding ▷ *vb* **2 = investigate**, study, examine, experiment, explore, probe, analyse, look into, work over, scrutinize, make inquiries, do tests, consult the archives

resemble *vb* **= be like**, look like, favour (*informal*), mirror, echo, parallel, be similar to, duplicate, take after, remind you of, bear a resemblance to, put you in mind of

resent *vb* **= be bitter about**, dislike, object to, grudge, begrudge, take exception to, be offended by, be angry about, take offence at, take umbrage at, harbour a grudge against, take as an insult, bear a grudge about, be in a huff about, take amiss to, have hard feelings about **OPPOSITE:** be content with

reservation *n* **1 = doubt**, scepticism, scruples, demur, hesitancy **4 = reserve**, territory, preserve, homeland, sanctuary, tract, enclave

reserve *vb* **1, 3 = keep**, hold, save, husband, store, retain, preserve, set aside, withhold, hang on to, conserve, stockpile, hoard, lay up, put by, keep back **2 = book**, prearrange, pre-engage, engage, bespeak ▷ *n* **5 = store**, fund, savings, stock, capital, supply, reservoir, fall-back, stockpile, hoard, backlog, cache **7** (*sport*) **= substitute**, extra, spare, alternative, fall-back, auxiliary **8 = park**, reservation, preserve, sanctuary, tract, forest park (*NZ*) **9 = shyness**, silence, restraint, constraint, reluctance, formality, modesty, reticence, coolness, aloofness, secretiveness, taciturnity

reserved *adj* **1 = uncommunicative**, cold, cool, retiring, formal, silent, modest, shy, cautious, restrained, secretive, aloof, reticent, prim, demure, taciturn, unresponsive, unapproachable, unsociable, undemonstrative, standoffish, close-mouthed, unforthcoming
OPPOSITE: uninhibited
2 = set aside, taken, kept, held, booked, retained, engaged, restricted, spoken for

reservoir *n* **1 = lake**, pond, basin **2 = store**, stock, source, supply, reserves, fund, pool, accumulation, stockpile

reside *vb* **1** (*formal*) **= live**, lodge, dwell, have your home, remain, stay, settle, abide, hang out (*informal*), sojourn
OPPOSITE: visit

residence *n* **1 = home**, house, household, dwelling, place, quarters, flat, lodging, pad (*slang*), abode, habitation, domicile

resident *n* **1a = inhabitant**, citizen, denizen, indweller, local
OPPOSITE: nonresident
1b = tenant, occupant, lodger

residue *n* **1 = remainder**, remains, remnant, leftovers, rest, extra, balance, excess, surplus, dregs, residuum

resign *vb* **1 = quit**, leave, step down (*informal*), vacate, abdicate, call it a day *or* night, give *or* hand in your notice **2 = accept**, reconcile yourself to, succumb to, submit to, bow to,

DICTIONARY

up (a right or claim)
WORD ORIGIN Latin *resignare* to unseal, destroy

resignation ⓣ *n* **1** the act of resigning **2** a formal document stating one's intention to resign **3** passive endurance of difficulties: *full of quiet resignation*

resigned ⓣ *adj* content to endure something unpleasant **resignedly** *adv*

resilient *adj* **1** (of a person) recovering easily and quickly from misfortune or illness **2** (of an object) capable of regaining its original shape or position after bending or stretching **resilience** *n*
WORD ORIGIN Latin *resilire* to jump back

resin (rezz-in) *n* **1** a solid or semisolid substance obtained from certain plants: *cannabis resin* **2** a similar substance produced synthetically **resinous** *adj*
WORD ORIGIN Latin *resina*

resist ⓣ *vb* **1** to stand firm against or oppose: *the party's old guard continue to resist economic reform* **2** to refrain from in spite of temptation: *I couldn't resist a huge portion of almond cake* **3** to refuse to comply with: *to resist arrest* **4** to be proof against: *airport design should be strengthened to help resist explosion* **resistible** *adj*
WORD ORIGIN Latin *resistere*

resistance ⓣ *n* **1** the act of resisting **2** the capacity to withstand something, esp. the body's natural capacity to withstand disease **3** *electronics* the opposition to a flow of electric current through a circuit, component, or substance **4** any force that slows or hampers movement: *wind resistance* **5 line of least resistance** the easiest, but not necessarily the best, course of action **resistant** *adj, n*

Resistance *n* **the Resistance** an illegal organization fighting for national liberty in a country under enemy occupation

resistor *n* an electrical component designed to introduce a known value of resistance into a circuit

resit *vb* **-sitting, -sat 1** to sit (an examination) again ▷*n* **2** an examination which one must sit again

reskill *vb* to train (workers) to acquire new skills **reskilling** *n*

Resnais *n* **Alain** born 1922, French film director, whose films include *Hiroshima mon amour* (1959), *L'Année dernière à Marienbad* (1961), *La Vie est un roman* (1983), and *On Connaît la Chanson* (1998)

resolute *adj* firm in purpose or belief **resolutely** *adv*
WORD ORIGIN Latin *resolutus*

resolution ⓣ *n* **1** firmness or determination **2** a decision to do something **3** a formal expression of opinion by a meeting **4** the act of resolving **5** *music* the process in harmony whereby a dissonant note or chord is followed by a consonant one **6** the ability of a television to reproduce fine detail **7** *physics* Also called: **resolving power** the ability of a telescope or microscope to produce separate images of closely placed objects

resolvable *or* **resoluble** *adj* able to be resolved or analysed

resolve ⓣ *vb* **-solving, -solved 1** to decide or determine firmly **2** to express (an opinion) formally by a vote **3** to separate or cause to separate into (constituent parts) **4** to find the answer or solution to **5** to explain away or dispel: *to resolve the controversy* **6** *music* to follow (a dissonant note or chord) by one producing a consonance **7** *physics* to distinguish between (separate parts) of (an image) as in a microscope, telescope, or other optical instrument ▷*n* **8** absolute determination: *he spoke of his resolve to deal with the problem of terrorism*
WORD ORIGIN Latin *resolvere* to unfasten, reveal

resolved *adj* determined

resonance *n* **1** the condition or quality of being resonant **2** sound produced by a body vibrating in sympathy with a neighbouring source of sound
WORD ORIGIN Latin *resonare* to resound

resonant *adj* **1** resounding or re-echoing **2** producing resonance: *the resonant cavities of the mouth* **3** full of resonance: *his voice is a resonant baritone*

resonate *vb* **-nating, -nated** to resound or cause to resound **resonator** *n*

resort ⓣ *vb* **1 resort to** to have recourse (to) for help, use, etc.: *some people have resorted to begging for food* **2** to go, esp. often or habitually: *to resort to the beach* ▷*n* **3** a place to which many people go for holidays **4** the use of something as a means or aid **5 last resort** the last possible course of action open to a person
WORD ORIGIN Old French *resortir* to come out again

resound ⓣ (riz-**zownd**) *vb* **1** to ring or echo with sound **2** (of sounds) to echo or ring **3** to be widely known: *his fame resounded throughout India*
WORD ORIGIN Latin *resonare* to sound again

resounding ⓣ *adj* **1** echoing **2** clear

THESAURUS

give in to, yield to, acquiesce to **3 = give up**, abandon, yield, hand over, surrender, turn over, relinquish, renounce, forsake, cede, forgo

resignation *n* **1 = leaving**, notice, retirement, departure, surrender, abandonment, abdication, renunciation, relinquishment **3 = acceptance**, patience, submission, compliance, endurance, fortitude, passivity, acquiescence, forbearing, sufferance, nonresistance **OPPOSITE:** resistance

resigned *adj* **= stoical**, patient, subdued, long-suffering, compliant, submissive, acquiescent, unresisting, unprotesting

resist *vb* **1 = oppose**, fight, battle against, refuse, check, weather, dispute, confront, combat, defy, curb, thwart, stand up to, hinder, contend with, counteract, hold out against, put up a fight (against), countervail **OPPOSITE:** accept **2 = refrain from**, refuse, avoid, turn down, leave alone, keep from, forgo, abstain from, forbear, prevent yourself from **OPPOSITE:** indulge in **4 = withstand**, repel, be proof against

resistance *n* **1a = opposition**, hostility, aversion **1b = fighting**, fight, battle, struggle, combat, contention, defiance, obstruction, impediment, intransigence, hindrance, counteraction

resolution *n* **1 = determination**, energy, purpose, resolve, courage, dedication, fortitude, sincerity, tenacity, perseverance, willpower, boldness, firmness, staying power, stubbornness, constancy, earnestness, obstinacy, steadfastness, doggedness, relentlessness, resoluteness, staunchness **2 = decision**, resolve, intention, aim, purpose, determination, intent **3 = declaration**, motion, verdict, judgment

resolve *vb* **1 = decide**, determine, undertake, make up your mind, agree, design, settle, purpose, intend, fix, conclude **4 = work out**, answer, solve, find the solution to, clear up, crack, fathom, suss (out) *(slang)*, elucidate ▷*n* **8 = determination**, resolution, courage, willpower, boldness, firmness, earnestness, steadfastness, resoluteness **OPPOSITE:** indecision

resort *n* **3 = holiday centre**, spot, retreat, haunt, refuge, tourist centre, watering place *(Brit)*

resound *vb* **1, 2 = echo**, resonate, reverberate, fill the air, re-echo, **ring**

resounding *adj* **1 = echoing**, full, sounding, rich, ringing, powerful, booming, vibrant, reverberating, resonant, sonorous

resource *n* **1** *(pl)* **= reserves**, supplies,

DICTIONARY

and emphatic: *he won a resounding victory* **resoundingly** *adv*

resource ❶ *n* **1 resources** sources of economic wealth, esp. of a country or business enterprise: *mineral resources* **2 resources** money available for use **3** something resorted to for aid or support: *he saw the university as a resource for the community* **4** the ability to deal with problems: *a man of resource* **5** a means of doing something: *resistance was their only resource*
WORD ORIGIN Old French *resourdre* to spring up again

resourceful *adj* capable and full of initiative **resourcefulness** *n*

respect ❶ *n* **1** consideration: *respect for my feelings* **2** an attitude of deference or esteem **3** the state of being honoured or esteemed **4** a detail or characteristic: *in virtually all respects boys develop more slowly than girls* **5 in respect of** *or* **with respect to** in reference or relation to **6 respects** polite greetings: *he paid his respects to her and left* ▷ *vb* **7** to have an attitude of esteem towards: *she is the person I most respect and wish to emulate* **8** to pay proper attention or consideration to: *he called on rebel groups to respect a cease-fire* **respecter** *n*
WORD ORIGIN Latin *respicere* to pay attention to

respectable ❶ *adj* **1** worthy of respect **2** having good social standing or reputation **3** relatively or fairly good: *they obtained respectable results* **4** fit to be seen by other people **respectability** *n* **respectably** *adv*

respectful *adj* full of or showing respect **respectfully** *adv*

respecting *prep* on the subject of

respective ❶ *adj* relating separately to each of several people or things: *the culprits will be repatriated to their respective countries*

respectively *adv* (in listing things that refer to another list) separately in the order given: *Diotema and Mantinea were tutors to Pythagoras and Socrates respectively*

Respighi *n* **Ottorino** 1879–1936, Italian composer, noted esp. for his suites *The Fountains of Rome* (1917) and *The Pines of Rome* (1924)

respiration (ress-per-ray-shun) *n* **1** breathing **2** the process in living organisms of taking in oxygen and giving out carbon dioxide **3** the breakdown of complex organic substances that takes place in the cells of animals and plants, producing energy and carbon dioxide **respiratory** *adj*

respirator *n* **1** a device worn over the mouth and nose to prevent the breathing in of poisonous fumes **2** an apparatus for providing artificial respiration

respire *vb* **-spiring, -spired 1** to breathe **2** to undergo respiration
WORD ORIGIN Latin *respirare* to exhale

respite ❶ *n* **1** an interval of rest: *I allowed myself a six month respite to enjoy my family* **2** a temporary delay
WORD ORIGIN Old French *respit*

resplendent *adj* **1** brilliant or splendid in appearance **2** shining **resplendence** *n*
WORD ORIGIN Latin *re-* again + *splendere* to shine

respond ❶ *vb* **1** to state or utter (something) in reply **2** to act in reply: *the government must respond accordingly to our recommendations* **3** to react favourably: *most headaches will respond to the use of relaxants*
WORD ORIGIN Old French *respondre*

respondent *n law* a person against whom a petition is brought

response ❶ *n* **1** the act of responding **2** a reply or reaction **3** a reaction to stimulation of the nervous system **4 responses** *Christianity* the words recited or sung in reply to the priest at a church service

responsibility ❶ *n, pl* **-ties 1** the state of being responsible **2** a person or thing for which one is responsible

responsible ❶ *adj* **1 responsible for** having control or authority over **2** being the agent or cause (of some action): *only a small number of students were responsible for the disturbances* **3 responsible to** being accountable for one's actions and decisions to: *management should be made more responsible to shareholders* **4** rational and accountable for one's own actions **5** (of a position or duty) involving decision and accountability **responsibly** *adv*
WORD ORIGIN Latin *respondere* to respond

responsive ❶ *adj* reacting quickly or favourably to something **responsiveness** *n*

respray *n* a new coat of paint applied to a vehicle

THESAURUS

stocks **2** (*pl*) **= funds**, means, holdings, money, capital, wherewithal, riches, materials, assets, wealth, property *n* **3 = facility 5 = means**, course, resort, device, expedient

respect *n* **1 = consideration**, kindness, deference, friendliness, tact, thoughtfulness, solicitude, kindliness, considerateness **2 = regard**, honour, recognition, esteem, appreciation, admiration, reverence, estimation, veneration, approbation **OPPOSITE:** contempt **4 = particular**, way, point, matter, sense, detail, feature, aspect, characteristic, facet ▷ *vb* **7 = think highly of**, value, regard, honour, recognize, appreciate, admire, esteem, adore, revere, reverence, look up to, defer to, venerate, set store by, have a good *or* high opinion of **8a = show consideration for**, regard, notice, honour, observe, heed, attend to, pay attention to **8b = abide by**, follow, observe, comply with, obey, heed, keep to, adhere to **OPPOSITE:** disregard

respectable *adj* **1, 2 = honourable**, good, respected, decent, proper, worthy, upright, admirable, honest, dignified, venerable, reputable, decorous, estimable **OPPOSITE:** disreputable **3 = reasonable**, considerable, substantial, fair, tidy (*informal*), ample, tolerable, presentable, appreciable, fairly good, sizable *or* sizeable, goodly **OPPOSITE:** small **4 = decent**, neat, tidy (*informal*), spruce

respective *adj* **= specific**, own, several, individual, personal, particular, various, separate, relevant, corresponding

respite *n* **1 = pause**, break, rest, relief, halt, interval, relaxation, recess, interruption, lull, cessation, let-up (*informal*), breathing space, breather (*informal*), hiatus, intermission

respond *vb* **1 = answer**, return, reply, come back, counter, acknowledge, retort, rejoin **OPPOSITE:** remain silent **2 = react**, retaliate, reciprocate, take the bait, rise to the bait, act in response

response *n* **1, 2 = answer**, return, reply, reaction, comeback (*informal*), feedback, retort, acknowledgment, riposte, counterattack, rejoinder, counterblast

responsibility *n* **1 = fault**, blame, liability, guilt, culpability, burden **2a = duty**, business, job, role, task, accountability, answerability **2b = job**, task, function, role, pigeon (*informal*)

responsible *adj* **1** (*with* **for**) **= in charge**, in control, at the helm, in authority, carrying the can (*informal*) **2 = to blame**, guilty, at fault, culpable **3 = accountable**, subject, bound, liable, amenable, answerable, duty-bound, chargeable, under obligation **OPPOSITE:** unaccountable **4 = sensible**, sound, adult, stable, mature, reliable, rational, sober, conscientious, dependable, trustworthy, level-headed **OPPOSITE:** unreliable

responsive *adj* **= sensitive**, open, aware, sharp, alive, forthcoming, sympathetic, awake, susceptible, receptive, reactive, perceptive, impressionable, quick to react **OPPOSITE:** unresponsive

r

DICTIONARY

rest¹ ❶ *n* **1** relaxation from exertion or labour **2** a period of inactivity **3** relief or refreshment **4** calm **5** death regarded as repose: *now he has gone to his eternal rest* **6 at rest a** not moving **b** calm **c** dead **d** asleep **7** a pause or interval **8** a mark in a musical score indicating a pause lasting a specific time **9** a thing or place on which to put something for support or to steady it **10 lay to rest** to bury (a dead person) ▷ *vb* **11** to become or make refreshed **12** to position (oneself, etc.) for rest or relaxation **13** to place for support or steadying: *he slumped forward to rest his head on his forearms* **14** to depend or rely: *his presidency rested on the outcome of the crisis* **15** to direct (one's eyes) or (of one's eyes) to be directed: *she rested her gaze on the face of the statue* **16** to be at ease **17** to cease or cause to cease from motion or exertion **18** to remain without further attention or action: *she refused to let the matter rest* **19** *law* to finish the introduction of evidence in (a case) **20** to put (pastry) in a cool place to allow the gluten to contract
WORD ORIGIN Old English *ræst, reste*

rest² ❶ *n* **1 the rest a** something left; remainder **b** the others: *the rest of the world* ▷ *vb* **2** to continue to be (as specified): *your conscience can rest easy*
WORD ORIGIN Old French *rester* to remain

rest area *n Austral & NZ* a motorist's stopping place off a highway, equipped with tables and seats

restart *vb* to commence (something) or set (something) in motion again

restate *vb* to state or affirm (something) again or in a different way **restatement** *n*

restaurant ❶ *n* a place where meals are prepared and served to customers
WORD ORIGIN French

restaurant car *n* a railway coach in which meals are served

restaurateur (rest-er-a-**tur**) *n* a person who owns or runs a restaurant

rest-cure *n* a rest taken as part of a course of medical treatment

restful *adj* relaxing or soothing

restitution *n* **1** the act of giving back something that has been lost or stolen **2** *law* compensation for loss or injury
WORD ORIGIN Latin *restituere* to rebuild

restive *adj* **1** restless or uneasy **2** impatient of control or authority
WORD ORIGIN Old French *restif* balky

restless ❶ *adj* **1** bored or dissatisfied **2** unable to stay still or quiet **3** not restful: *a restless sleep* **restlessly** *adv* **restlessness** *n*

restoration ❶ *n* **1** the act of restoring to a former or original condition, place, etc. **2** the giving back of something lost or stolen **3** something restored, replaced, or reconstructed **4** a model or representation of a ruin or extinct animal **5 the Restoration** *Brit* the re-establishment of the monarchy in 1660 or the reign of Charles II (1660–85)

restorative (rist-**or**-a-tiv) *adj* **1** giving back health or good spirits ▷ *n* **2** a food or medicine that gives back health or good spirits

restore ❶ *vb* **-storing, -stored 1** to return (something) to its original or former condition **2** to bring back to health or good spirits **3** to return (something lost or stolen) to its owner **4** to re-enforce or re-establish: *he must restore confidence in himself and his government; they worked to restore the monarchy* **5** to reconstruct (a ruin, extinct animal, etc.) **restorer** *n*
WORD ORIGIN Latin *restaurare* to rebuild

restrain ❶ *vb* **1** to hold (someone) back from some action **2** to limit or restrict: *restrain any tendency to impulse-buy* **3** to deprive (someone) of liberty
WORD ORIGIN Latin *re-* back + *stringere* to draw

restrained ❶ *adj* not displaying emotion

restraint ❶ *n* **1** something that restrains **2** the ability to control one's impulses or passions **3** a restraining or being restrained

THESAURUS

rest¹ *n* **1 = relaxation**, repose, leisure, idleness, me-time **OPPOSITE:** work **3 = refreshment**, release, relief, ease, comfort, cure, remedy, solace, balm, deliverance, mitigation, abatement, alleviation, easement, palliation, assuagement **4 = calm**, tranquillity, stillness, somnolence **7 = pause**, break, breather, time off, stop, holiday, halt, interval, vacation, respite, lull, interlude, cessation, breathing space *(informal)*, intermission ▷ *vb* **11, 16 = relax**, sleep, take it easy, lie down, idle, nap, be calm, doze, sit down, slumber, kip *(Brit slang)*, snooze *(informal)*, laze, lie still, be at ease, put your feet up, take a nap, drowse, mellow out *(informal)*, have a snooze *(informal)*, refresh yourself, outspan *(S African)*, zizz *(Brit informal)*, have forty winks *(informal)*, take your ease **OPPOSITE:** work **13 = place**, lay, repose, stretch out, stand, sit, lean, prop **17 = stop**, have a break, break off, take a breather *(informal)*, stay, halt, cease, discontinue, knock off *(informal)*, desist, come to a standstill **OPPOSITE:** keep going

rest² *n* **1a = remainder**, remains, excess, remnants, others, balance, surplus, residue, rump, leftovers, residuum

restaurant *n* **= café**, diner *(chiefly US & Canad)*, bistro, cafeteria, trattoria, tearoom, eatery *or* eaterie

restless *adj* **2 = unsettled**, worried, troubled, nervous, disturbed, anxious, uneasy, agitated, unruly, edgy, fidgeting, on edge, ill at ease, restive, jumpy, fitful, fretful, fidgety, unquiet, antsy *(informal)* **OPPOSITE:** relaxed

restoration *n* **1a = reinstatement**, return, revival, restitution, re-establishment, reinstallation, replacement **OPPOSITE:** abolition **1b = repair**, recovery, reconstruction, renewal, rehabilitation, refurbishing, refreshment, renovation, rejuvenation, revitalization **OPPOSITE:** demolition

restore *vb* **1, 5 = repair**, refurbish, renovate, reconstruct, fix (up), recover, renew, rebuild, mend, rehabilitate, touch up, recondition, retouch, set to rights **OPPOSITE:** demolish **2 = revive**, build up, strengthen, bring back, refresh, rejuvenate, revitalize, revivify, reanimate **OPPOSITE:** make worse **3 = return**, replace, recover, bring back, send back, hand back **4 = reinstate**, re-establish, reintroduce, reimpose, re-enforce, reconstitute **OPPOSITE:** abolish

restrain *vb* **1 = hold back**, hold, control, check, contain, prevent, restrict, handicap, confine, curb, hamper, rein, harness, subdue, hinder, constrain, curtail, bridle, debar, keep under control, have on a tight leash, straiten **OPPOSITE:** encourage **2 = control**, keep in, limit, govern, suppress, inhibit, repress, muzzle, keep under control

restrained *adj* **= controlled**, reasonable, moderate, self-controlled, soft, calm, steady, mild, muted, reticent, temperate, undemonstrative **OPPOSITE:** hot-headed

restraint *n* **1 = limitation**, limit, check, ban, boycott, embargo, curb, rein, taboo, bridle, disqualification, interdict, restraining order *(US) (law)* **OPPOSITE:** freedom **2 = self-control**, self-discipline, self-restraint, self-possession, pulling your punches **OPPOSITE:** self-indulgence **3 = constraint**, limitation, inhibition, moderation, hold, control, restriction, prevention, suppression, hindrance, curtailment

restrict *vb* **= limit**, fix, regulate, specify, curb, ration, keep within

DICTIONARY

restrict ❶ *vb* to confine or keep within certain limits **restrictive** *adj*
WORD ORIGIN Latin *restrictus* bound up
restriction ❶ *n* a rule or situation that limits or controls something or someone: *operating under severe financial restrictions*
restrictive practice *n* **1** a trading agreement against the public interest **2** a practice of a union or other group tending to limit the freedom of other workers or employers
rest room *n US, Canad & Austral* a toilet in a public building
restructure *vb* **-turing, -tured** to organize in a different way: *to restructure the world economy*
result ❶ *n* **1** the outcome or consequence of an action, policy, etc. **2** the final score of a sporting contest **3** a number or value obtained by solving a mathematical problem **4** a favourable result, esp. a victory or success: *the best chance of a result is at Cheltenham* **5 results** the marks or grades obtained in an examination ▷ *vb* **6 result from** to be the outcome or consequence of: *poverty resulting from high unemployment* **7 result in** to end in (a specified way): *negotiations which resulted in the Treaty of Paris*
WORD ORIGIN Latin *resultare* to spring from
resultant *adj* **1** arising as a result: *the resultant publicity* ▷ *n* **2** *maths, physics* a single vector that is the vector sum of two or more other vectors, such as a force which results from two other forces acting on a single point
resume ❶ *vb* **-suming, -sumed 1** to begin again or go on with (something interrupted) **2** to occupy again or recover: *he will resume his party posts today*
WORD ORIGIN Latin *resumere*
résumé ❶ (rezz-yew-may) *n* **1** a short descriptive summary **2** *US, Canad & Austral* a curriculum vitae
WORD ORIGIN French
resumption ❶ *n* the act of resuming or beginning again
resurgence ❶ *n* a rising again to vigour: *worldwide religious resurgence* **resurgent** *adj*
WORD ORIGIN Latin *resurgere* to rise again
resurrect ❶ *vb* **1** to bring or be brought back to life from death **2** to bring back into use or activity
resurrection ❶ *n* **1** a return to life by a dead person **2** revival or renewal **3 the Resurrection a** *Christian theol* the rising again of Christ from the tomb three days after his death **b** the rising again from the dead of all people at the Last Judgment
WORD ORIGIN Latin *resurgere* to rise again
resuscitate (ris-suss-it-tate) *vb* **-tating, -tated** to restore to consciousness **resuscitation** *n*
WORD ORIGIN Latin *re-* again + *suscitare* to raise
retail *n* **1** the sale of goods individually or in small quantities to the public ▷ *adj* **2** of or engaged in such selling: *auctioneers have been successful in cornering the retail market* ▷ *adv* **3** in small amounts or at a retail price ▷ *vb* **4** to sell or be sold in small quantities to the public **5** to relate (gossip or scandal) in detail: *he gleefully retailed the story* **retailer** *n*
WORD ORIGIN Old French *re-* again + *taillier* to cut
retail therapy *n* the action of shopping for clothes, etc. esp. to cheer oneself up
retain ❶ *vb* **1** to keep in one's possession **2** to be able to hold or contain: *with this method the salmon retains its flavour and texture* **3** *law* to engage the services of (a barrister) by payment of a preliminary fee **4** (of a person) to be able to remember (something) without difficulty **5** to hold in position
WORD ORIGIN Latin *retinere* to hold back
retainer *n* **1** a fee paid in advance to engage someone's services **2** *Brit, Austral & NZ* a reduced rent paid for a room or flat to reserve it for future use **3** a servant who has been with a family for a long time
retaining wall *n* a wall constructed to hold back earth, loose rock, etc.
retake *vb* **-taking, -took, -taken 1** to recapture: *to retake Jerusalem* **2** to take something, such as an examination or vote, again ▷ *n* **3** *films* a rephotographed scene
retaliate ❶ *vb* **-ating, -ated 1** to repay some injury or wrong in kind **2** to cast (accusations) back upon a person **retaliation** *n* **retaliatory** *adj*
WORD ORIGIN Latin *re-* back + *talis* of such kind
retard ❶ *vb* to delay or slow down (the progress or development) **retardant** *n, adj* **retardation** *n*
WORD ORIGIN Latin *retardare*
retarded *adj* underdeveloped mentally
retch *vb* **1** to undergo spasms of the stomach as if one is vomiting ▷ *n* **2** an involuntary spasm of the stomach
WORD ORIGIN Old English *hrǣcan*
retention *n* **1** the act of retaining or state of being retained **2** the capacity to remember **3** *pathol* the abnormal holding of something within the body, esp. fluid
retentive *adj*
rethink *vb* **-thinking, -thought 1** to think about (something) again with a view to changing one's tactics ▷ *n* **2** the act or an instance of thinking again

r

THESAURUS

bounds *or* limits **OPPOSITE:** widen
restriction *n* = **control**, rule, condition, check, regulation, curb, restraint, constraint, confinement, containment, demarcation, stipulation
result *n* **1a** = **consequence**, effect, outcome, end result, issue, event, development, product, reaction, fruit, sequel, upshot **OPPOSITE:** cause **1b** = **outcome**, conclusion, end, decision, termination ▷ *vb* **6** *(with* **from)** = **arise**, follow, issue, happen, appear, develop, spring, flow, turn out, stem, derive, ensue, emanate, eventuate
resume *vb* **1** = **begin again**, continue, go on with, proceed with, carry on, reopen, restart, recommence, reinstitute, take up *or* pick up where you left off **OPPOSITE:** discontinue
résumé *n* **1** = **summary**, synopsis, abstract, précis, review, digest, epitome, rundown, recapitulation
resumption *n* = **continuation**, carrying on, reopening, renewal, restart, resurgence, new beginning, re-establishment, fresh outbreak
resurgence *n* = **revival**, return, renaissance, resurrection, resumption, rebirth, re-emergence, recrudescence, renascence
resurrect *vb* **1** = **restore to life**, raise from the dead **2** = **revive**, renew, bring back, kick-start *(informal)*, reintroduce, breathe new life into
resurrection *n* **1, 3a, 3b** = **raising** *or* **rising from the dead**, return from the dead **OPPOSITE:** demise **2** = **revival**, restoration, renewal, resurgence, return, comeback *(informal)*, renaissance, rebirth, reappearance, resuscitation, renascence **OPPOSITE:** killing off
retain *vb* **1a** = **maintain**, keep, reserve, preserve, keep up, uphold, nurture, continue to have, hang *or* hold onto **1b** = **keep**, keep possession of, hang *or* hold onto, save **OPPOSITE:** let go
retaliate *vb* **1** = **pay someone back**, hit back, strike back, reciprocate, take revenge, get back at someone, get even with *(informal)*, even the score, get your own back *(informal)*, wreak vengeance, exact retribution, give as good as you get *(informal)*, take an eye for an eye, make reprisal, give (someone) a taste of his *or* her own medicine, give tit for tat, return like for like **OPPOSITE:** turn the other cheek
retard *vb* = **slow down**, check, arrest, delay, handicap, stall, brake, detain, defer, clog, hinder, obstruct, impede, set back, encumber, decelerate, hold back *or* up **OPPOSITE:** speed up

DICTIONARY

Réti *n* **Richard** 1889–1929, Hungarian chess player and theorist; influential in enunciating the theories of the hypermodern school

reticent *adj* not willing to say or tell much **reticence** *n*
WORD ORIGIN Latin *reticere* to keep silent

reticulate *adj* in the form of a network or having a network of parts: *a reticulate leaf* **reticulation** *n*
WORD ORIGIN Late Latin *reticulatus* like a net

retina *n, pl* **-nas** *or* **-nae** the light-sensitive inner lining of the back of the eyeball **retinal** *adj*
WORD ORIGIN Medieval Latin

retinopathy *n* any of various noninflammatory diseases of the retina, which may have serious effects on vision

retinue *n* a band of attendants accompanying an important person
WORD ORIGIN Old French *retenue*

retire ❶ *vb* **-tiring, -tired 1** to give up or to cause (a person) to give up work, esp. on reaching pensionable age **2** to go away into seclusion **3** to go to bed **4** to withdraw from a sporting contest, esp. because of injury **5** to pull back (troops) from battle or (of troops) to fall back **retired** *adj* **retirement** *n*
WORD ORIGIN French *retirer*

retirement pension *n Brit* a regular payment made by the state or a former employee to a retired person over a specified age

retiring ❶ *adj* very shy

retort[1] ❶ *vb* **1** to reply quickly, wittily, or angrily **2** to use (an argument) against its originator ▹*n* **3** a sharp, angry, or witty reply **4** an argument used against its originator
WORD ORIGIN Latin *re-* back + *torquere* to twist, wrench

retort[2] *n* **1** a glass vessel with a long tapering neck that is bent down, used for distillation **2** a vessel used for heating ores in the production of metals or heating coal to produce gas
WORD ORIGIN see RETORT[1]

retouch *vb* to restore or improve (a painting or photograph) with new touches

retrace *vb* **-tracing, -traced 1** to go back over (one's steps or a route) **2** to go over (a story) from the beginning

retract *vb* **1** to withdraw (a statement, charge, etc.) as invalid or unjustified **2** to go back on (a promise or agreement) **3** to draw in (a part or appendage): *the rear wheels are retracted for tight spaces* **retraction** *n*
WORD ORIGIN Latin *retractare* to withdraw

retractile *adj* capable of being drawn in: *the retractile claws of a cat*

retrain *vb* to train to do a new or different job **retraining** *n*

retread *vb* **-treading, -treaded 1** to bond a new tread onto (a worn tyre) ▹*n* **2** a remoulded tyre

retreat ❶ *vb* **1** *mil* to withdraw or retire in the face of or from action with an enemy **2** to retire or withdraw to seclusion or shelter **3** to alter one's opinion about something ▹*n* **4** the act of retreating or withdrawing **5** *mil* **a** a withdrawal or retirement in the face of the enemy **b** a bugle call signifying withdrawal or retirement **6** a place to which one may retire, esp. for religious contemplation **7** a period of seclusion, esp. for religious contemplation **8** the act of altering one's opinion about something
WORD ORIGIN Old French *retret*

retrench *vb* to reduce expenditure **retrenchment** *n*
WORD ORIGIN Old French *re-* off + *trenchier* to cut

retrial *n* a second trial of a defendant in a court of law

retribution *n* punishment or vengeance for evil deeds **retributive** *adj*
WORD ORIGIN Latin *re-* back + *tribuere* to pay

retrieve ❶ *vb* **-trieving, -trieved 1** to get or fetch back again **2** to bring back to a more satisfactory state: *his attempt to retrieve the situation* **3** to rescue or save **4** to recover (stored information) from a computer system **5** (of dogs) to find and fetch (shot birds and animals) **6** to remember ▹*n* **7** the chance of being retrieved: *beyond retrieve* **retrievable** *adj* **retrieval** *n*
WORD ORIGIN Old French *retrover*

retriever *n* a dog trained to retrieve shot birds and animals

retro *adj* associated with or revived from the past: *swap sandals for heeled mules to complete the retro look*

retro- *prefix* **1** back or backwards: *retroactive* **2** located behind: *retrochoir*
WORD ORIGIN Latin

retroactive *adj* effective from a date in the past: *justice through retroactive legislation is never justice*

retrograde *adj* **1** tending towards an earlier worse condition **2** moving or bending backwards **3** (esp. of order) reverse or inverse ▹*vb* **-grading, -graded 4** to go backwards or deteriorate
WORD ORIGIN Latin *retro-* backwards + *gradi* to walk

retrogress *vb* to go back to an earlier worse condition **retrogression** *n* **retrogressive** *adj*
WORD ORIGIN Latin *retrogressus* having moved backwards

retrorocket *n* a small rocket on a larger rocket or a spacecraft, that produces thrust in the opposite direction to the direction of flight in order to slow down

retrospect ❶ *n* **in retrospect** when looking back on the past
WORD ORIGIN Latin *retrospicere* to look back

retrospective *adj* **1** looking back in time **2** applying from a date in the past: *retrospective legislation* ▹*n* **3** an exhibition of an artist's life's work

retroussé (rit-**troo**-say) *adj* (of a nose) turned upwards
WORD ORIGIN French

retsina *n* a Greek wine flavoured with resin
WORD ORIGIN Modern Greek

return ❶ *vb* **1** to come back to a former place or state **2** to give, put, or send back **3** to repay with something of equivalent value: *she returned the*

THESAURUS

retire *vb* **1 = stop working**, give up work, be pensioned off, (be) put out to grass *(informal)* **2 = withdraw**, leave, remove, exit, go away, depart, absent yourself, betake yourself
3 = go to bed, turn in *(informal)*, go to sleep, hit the sack *(slang)*, go to your room, kip down *(Brit slang)*, hit the hay *(slang)*

retiring *adj* **= shy**, reserved, quiet, modest, shrinking, humble, timid, coy, meek, reclusive, reticent, unassuming, self-effacing, demure, diffident, bashful, aw-shucks, timorous, unassertive
OPPOSITE: outgoing

retort[1] *vb* **1, 2 = reply**, return, answer, respond, counter, rejoin, retaliate, come back with, riposte, answer back ▹*n* **3 = reply**, answer, response, comeback, riposte, rejoinder

retreat *vb* **1** *(mil)* **= withdraw**, retire, back off, draw back, leave, go back, shrink, depart, fall back, recede, pull back, back away, recoil, give ground, turn tail **OPPOSITE:** advance
▹*n* **4, 5a = flight**, retirement, departure, withdrawal, evacuation
OPPOSITE: advance
6 = refuge, haven, resort, retirement, shelter, haunt, asylum, privacy, den, sanctuary, hideaway, seclusion

retrieve *vb* **1 = get back**, regain, repossess, fetch back, recall, recover, restore, recapture **2, 3 = redeem**, save, rescue, repair, salvage, win back, recoup

retrospect *n* **= hindsight**, review, afterthought, re-examination, survey, recollection, remembrance, reminiscence **OPPOSITE:** foresight

return *vb* **1, 6 = come back**, go back, repair, retreat, turn back, revert, reappear **OPPOSITE:** depart
2 = put back, replace, restore, render, transmit, convey, send back, reinstate, take back, give back, carry back, retrocede **OPPOSITE:** keep

DICTIONARY

compliment **4** to hit, throw, or play (a ball) back **5** to recur or reappear: *as he relaxed his appetite returned* **6** to come back or revert in thought or speech: *let's return to what he said* **7** to earn or yield (profit or interest) **8** to answer or reply **9** to vote into office **10** *law* (of a jury) to deliver (a verdict) ▷ *n* **11** the act or an instance of coming back **12** the act of being returned **13** replacement or restoration: *the return of law and order* **14** something that is given or sent back **15** *sport* the act of playing or throwing a ball back **16** a recurrence or reappearance: *the return of tuberculosis* **17** the yield or profit from an investment or venture **18** a statement of one's taxable income (a **tax return**) **19** an answer or reply **20** *Brit, Austral, & NZ* ▸ short for **return ticket 21 in return** in exchange **22 returns** statement of the votes counted at an election **23 by return (of post)** *Brit* by the next post back to the sender **24 many happy returns (of the day)** a conventional birthday greeting ▷ *adj* **25** of or being a return: *the team is keen on a return match* **returnable** *adj*
WORD ORIGIN Old French *retorner*

returning officer *n* an official in charge of conducting an election in a constituency

return ticket *n* a ticket allowing a passenger to travel to a place and back

Retz *n* **Gilles de Retz** ▸ See **Rais**

Reuchlin *n* **Johann** 1455–1522, German humanist, who promoted the study of Greek and Hebrew

reunify *vb* **-fies, -fying, -fied** to bring together again something previously divided **reunification** *n*

reunion *n* **1** a gathering of people who have been apart **2** the act of coming together again

reunite *vb* **-niting, -nited** to bring or come together again after a separation

reuse *n* **1** the act of using something again ▷ *vb* **-using, -used 2** to use again **reusable** *adj*

Reuter *n* Baron **Paul Julius von** original name *Israel Beer Josaphat.* 1816–99, German telegrapher, who founded a news agency in London (1851)

rev *informal n* **1** revolution per minute (of an engine) ▷ *vb* **revving, revved 2** to increase the speed of revolution of (an engine)

rev. 1 revise(d) **2** revision

Rev. Reverend

revalue *vb* **-valuing, -valued** to adjust the exchange value of (a currency) upwards **revaluation** *n*

revamp ❶ *vb* to patch up or renovate

Revd. Reverend

reveal ❶ *vb* **1** to disclose or divulge (a secret) **2** to expose to view or show (something concealed) **3** (of God) to disclose (divine truths)
WORD ORIGIN Latin *revelare* to unveil

revealing *adj* **1** disclosing information that one did not know: *she made several revealing remarks during the interview* **2** (of clothes) showing more of the body than is usual

reveille (riv-val-ee) *n* a signal given by a bugle or drum to awaken soldiers or sailors in the morning
WORD ORIGIN French *réveillez!* awake!

revel ❶ *vb* **-elling, -elled** *or US* **-eling, -eled 1 revel in** to take pleasure or wallow in: *he would revel in his victory* **2** to take part in noisy festivities ▷ *n* **3 revels** noisy merrymaking **reveller** *n*
WORD ORIGIN Old French *reveler*

revelation ❶ *n* **1** the act of making known a truth which was previously secret **2** a fact newly made known **3** a person or experience that proves to be different from expectations: *New York State could prove a revelation to first-time visitors* **4** *Christianity* God's disclosure of his own nature and his purpose for mankind

Revelation *or* **Revelations** *n informal* the last book of the New Testament, containing visionary descriptions of heaven, and of the end of the world

revelry *n, pl* **-ries** noisy or unrestrained merrymaking

revenge ❶ *n* **1** vengeance for wrongs or injury received **2** something done as a means of vengeance ▷ *vb* **-venging, -venged 3** to inflict equivalent injury or damage for (injury received) **4** to take vengeance for (oneself or another) **revengeful** *adj*
WORD ORIGIN Old French *revenger*

revenue ❶ *n* **1** income, esp. that obtained by a government from taxation **2** a government department responsible for collecting taxes
WORD ORIGIN Old French *revenir* to return

reverberate *vb* **-ating, -ated 1** to resound or re-echo **2** to reflect or be reflected many times **reverberation** *n*
WORD ORIGIN Latin *re-* again + *verberare* to beat

revere ❶ *vb* **-vering, -vered** to be in awe of and respect deeply
WORD ORIGIN Latin *revereri*

Revere *n* **Paul** 1735–1818, American patriot and silversmith, best known for his night ride on April 18, 1775, to

THESAURUS

5 = recur, come back, repeat, persist, revert, happen again, reappear, come and go, come again **9 = elect**, choose, pick, vote in ▷ *n* **11 = reappearance** **OPPOSITE:** departure
12, 13 = restoration, replacement, reinstatement, re-establishment **OPPOSITE:** removal
16 = recurrence, repetition, reappearance, reversion, persistence
17 = profit, interest, benefit, gain, income, advantage, revenue, yield, proceeds, takings, boot *(dialect)*
18 = statement, report, form, list, account, summary

revamp *vb* **= renovate**, restore, overhaul, refurbish, rehabilitate, do up *(informal)*, patch up, refit, repair, fix up *(informal, chiefly US & Canad)*, recondition, give a face-lift to

reveal *vb* **1 = make known**, disclose, give away, make public, tell, announce, publish, broadcast, leak, communicate, proclaim, betray, give out, let out, impart, divulge, let slip, let on, take the wraps off *(informal)*, blow wide open *(slang)*, get off your chest *(informal)* **OPPOSITE:** keep secret **2 = show**, display, bare, exhibit, unveil, uncover, manifest, unearth, unmask, lay bare, bring to light, expose to view **OPPOSITE:** hide

revel *vb* **2 = celebrate**, rave *(Brit slang)*, carouse, live it up *(informal)*, push the boat out *(Brit informal)*, whoop it up *(informal)*, make merry, paint the town red *(informal)*, go on a spree, roister ▷ *n* **3** *(pl)* **= merrymaking**, party, celebration, rave *(Brit slang)*, gala, spree, festivity, beano *(Brit slang)*, debauch, saturnalia, bacchanal, rave-up *(Brit slang)*, jollification, carousal, hooley *or* hoolie *(chiefly Irish & NZ)*, carouse

revelation *n* **1a = disclosure**, discovery, news, broadcast, exposé, announcement, publication, exposure, leak, uncovering, confession, divulgence
1b = exhibition, telling, communication, broadcasting, discovery, publication, exposure, leaking, unveiling, uncovering, manifestation, unearthing, giveaway, proclamation, exposition

revenge *n* **1 = retaliation**, satisfaction, vengeance, reprisal, retribution, vindictiveness, an eye for an eye, requital ▷ *vb* **3 = avenge**, repay, vindicate, pay (someone) back, take revenge for, requite, even the score for, get your own back for *(informal)*, make reprisal for, take an eye for an eye for

revenue *n* **1 = income**, interest, returns, profits, gain, rewards, yield, proceeds, receipts, takings **OPPOSITE:** expenditure

revere *vb* **= be in awe of**, respect, honour, worship, adore, reverence, exalt, look up to, defer to, venerate, have a high opinion of, put on a pedestal, think highly of **OPPOSITE:** despise

DICTIONARY

warn the Massachusetts colonists of the coming of the British troops

reverence *n* profound respect **reverential** *adj*

Reverence *n* **Your** *or* **His Reverence** a title sometimes used for a Roman Catholic priest

reverend *adj* **1** worthy of reverence **2** relating to or designating a clergyman ▷*n* **3** *informal* a clergyman

Reverend *adj* a title of respect for a clergyman

reverent *adj* feeling or expressing reverence

reverie *n* absent-minded daydream **WORD ORIGIN** Old French *resverie* wildness

revers (riv-**veer**) *n, pl* **-vers** the turned-back lining of part of a garment, such as the lapel or cuff **WORD ORIGIN** French

reverse ● *vb* **-versing, -versed 1** to turn or set in an opposite direction, order, or position **2** to change into something different or contrary: *the cabinet intends to reverse the trend of recent polls* **3** to move backwards or in an opposite direction: *as he started to reverse the car, the bomb exploded* **4** to run (machinery) in the opposite direction to normal **5** to turn inside out **6** *law* to revoke or set aside (a judgment or decree) **7 reverse the charges** to make a telephone call at the recipient's expense ▷*n* **8** the opposite or contrary of something **9** the back or rear side of something **10** a change to an opposite position, state, or direction **11** a change for the worse **12** the gear by which a motor vehicle can be made to go backwards **13** the side of a coin bearing a secondary design **14 in reverse** in an opposite or backward direction **15 the reverse of** not at all: *the result was the reverse of his expectations* ▷*adj* **16** opposite or contrary in direction, position, etc. **17** denoting the gear by which a motor vehicle can be made to go backwards **reversal** *n* **WORD ORIGIN** Latin *reversus* turned back

reversible *adj* **1** capable of being reversed: *the effect of the operation may not be reversible* **2** (of a garment) made so that either side may be used as the outer side

reversing lights *pl n* a pair of lights on the rear of a motor vehicle that go on when the vehicle is moving backwards

reversion *n* **1** a return to an earlier condition, practice, or belief **2** *biol* the return of individuals or organs to a more primitive condition or type **3** the rightful passing of property to the owner or designated heir

revert ● *vb* **1** to go back to a former state **2** *biol* (of individuals or organs) to return to a more primitive, earlier, or simpler condition or type **3** to come back to a subject **4** *property law* (of an estate) to return to its former owner **WORD ORIGIN** Latin *revertere*

review ● *n* **1** a critical assessment of a book, film, etc. **2** a publication containing such articles **3** a general survey or report: *the new curriculum is to be set up a year after the conclusions of the review are due* **4** a formal or official inspection **5** the act or an instance of reviewing **6** a second consideration; re-examination **7** a retrospective survey **8** *law* a re-examination of a case ▷*vb* **9** to hold or write a review of **10** to examine again: *the committee will review the ban in the summer* **11** to look back upon (a period of time or sequence of events): *he reviewed his achievements with pride* **12** to inspect formally or officially: *when he reviewed the troops they cheered him* **13** *law* to re-examine (a decision) judicially **WORD ORIGIN** Latin *re-* again + *videre* to see

reviewer ● *n* a person who writes reviews of books, films, etc.

revile *vb* **-viling, -viled** to be abusively scornful of: *his works were reviled and admired in equal measure* **WORD ORIGIN** Old French *reviler*

revise ● *vb* **-vising, -vised 1** to change or alter: *he grudgingly revised his opinion* **2** to prepare a new edition of (a previously printed work) **3** to read (something) several times in order to learn it in preparation for an examination **WORD ORIGIN** Latin *re-* again + *visere* to inspect

Revised Version *n* a revision of the Authorized Version of the Bible published between 1881 and 1885

revision ● *n* **1** the act or process of revising **2** a corrected or new version of a book, article, etc.

revisionism *n* **1** (in Marxist ideology) any dangerous departure from the true interpretation of Marx's teachings **2** the advocacy of revision of some political theory **revisionist** *n, adj*

revisory *adj* of or having the power of revision

revitalize *or* **-ise** *vb* **-izing, -ized** *or* **-ising, -ised** to make more lively or active

revival ● *n* **1** a reviving or being revived **2** a reawakening of religious

THESAURUS

reverse *vb* **1 = turn round**, turn over, turn upside down, upend **2 = transpose**, change, move, exchange, transfer, switch, shift, alter, swap, relocate, rearrange, invert, interchange, reorder **3 = go backwards**, retreat, back up, turn back, backtrack, move backwards, back **OPPOSITE:** go forward **6** *(law)* **= change**, alter, cancel, overturn, overthrow, set aside, undo, repeal, quash, revoke, overrule, retract, negate, rescind, invalidate, annul, obviate, countermand, declare null and void, overset, upset **OPPOSITE:** implement ▷*n* **8 = opposite**, contrary, converse, antithesis, inverse, contradiction **9, 13 = back**, rear, other side, wrong side, underside, flip side, verso **OPPOSITE:** front **11 = misfortune**, check, defeat, blow, failure, disappointment, setback, hardship, reversal, adversity, mishap, affliction, repulse, trial, misadventure, vicissitude

revert *vb* **1 = go back**, return, come back, resume, lapse, recur, relapse, regress, backslide, take up where you left off **4** *(property law)* **= return**

review *n* **1 = critique**, commentary, evaluation, critical assessment, study, notice, criticism, judgment **2 = magazine**, journal, periodical, zine *(informal)* **3 = survey**, report, study, analysis, examination, scrutiny, perusal **4 = inspection**, display, parade, procession, march past ▷*vb* **9 = assess**, write a critique of, study, judge, discuss, weigh, evaluate, criticize, read through, give your opinion of **10 = reconsider**, revise, rethink, run over, reassess, re-examine, re-evaluate, think over, take another look at, recapitulate, look at again, go over again **11 = look back on**, remember, recall, reflect on, summon up, recollect, call to mind **12 = inspect**, check, survey, examine, vet, check out *(informal)*, scrutinize, give (something *or* someone) the once-over *(informal)*

reviewer *n* **= critic**, judge, commentator, connoisseur, arbiter, essayist

revise *vb* **1 = change**, review, modify, reconsider, re-examine **2 = edit**, correct, alter, update, amend, rewrite, revamp, rework, redo, emend **3 = study**, go over, run through, cram *(informal)*, memorize, reread, swot up on *(Brit informal)*

revision *n* **1a = emendation**, editing, updating, correction, rewriting **1b = change**, review, amendment, modification, alteration, re-examination **1c = studying**, cramming *(informal)*, memorizing, swotting *(Brit informal)*, rereading, homework

revival *n* **1 = resurgence** **OPPOSITE:** decline **1, 4 = reawakening**, restoration, renaissance, renewal, awakening, resurrection, refreshment,

DICTIONARY

faith **3** a new production of a play that has not been recently performed **4** a renewed use or interest in: *there has been an Art Deco revival*

revivalism *n* a movement that seeks to revive religious faith **revivalist** *n, adj*

revive ❶ *vb* **-viving, -vived 1** to make or become lively or active again **2** to bring or be brought back to life, consciousness, or strength: *revived by a drop of whisky* **3** *theatre* to put on a new production of (an old play)
WORD ORIGIN Latin *re-* again + *vivere* to live

revivify *vb* **-fies, -fying, -fied** to give new life to **revivification** *n*

revoke *vb* **-voking, -voked 1** to take back or cancel (an agreement, will, etc.) **2** *cards* to break a rule by failing to follow suit when able to do so ▷ *n* **3** *cards* the act of revoking **revocation** *n*
WORD ORIGIN Latin *revocare* to call back

revolt ❶ *n* **1** a rebellion or uprising against authority **2** **in revolt** in the state of rebelling ▷ *vb* **3** to rise up in rebellion against authority **4** to cause to feel disgust
WORD ORIGIN French *révolter*

revolting ❶ *adj* horrible and disgusting

revolution ❶ *n* **1** the overthrow of a regime or political system by the governed **2** (in Marxist theory) the transition from one system of production in a society to the next **3** a far-reaching and drastic change **4 a** movement in or as if in a circle **b** one complete turn in a circle: *33 revolutions per minute*
WORD ORIGIN Latin *revolvere* to revolve

revolutionary ❶ *adj* **1** of or like a revolution **2** advocating or engaged in revolution **3** radically new or different: *they have designed revolutionary new materials to build power stations* ▷ *n, pl* **-aries 4** a person who advocates or engages in revolution

revolutionize *or* **-ise** *vb* **-izing, -ized** *or* **-ising, -ised** to bring about a radical change in

revolve ❶ *vb* **-volving, -volved 1** to move or cause to move around a centre **2** **revolve around** to be centred or focused upon: *the campaign revolves around one man* **3** to occur periodically or in cycles **4** to consider or be considered **revolvable** *adj*
WORD ORIGIN Latin *revolvere*

revolver *n* a pistol with a revolving cylinder that allows several shots to be fired without reloading

revolving door *n* a door with four leaves at right angles to each other, revolving about a vertical axis

revue *n* a theatrical entertainment with topical sketches and songs
WORD ORIGIN French

revulsion *n* a violent feeling of disgust
WORD ORIGIN Latin *revulsio* a pulling away

reward ❶ *n* **1** something given in return for a service **2** a sum of money offered for finding a criminal or missing property **3** something received in return for good or evil: *sacrifice provided its own reward* ▷ *vb* **4** to give something to (someone) for a service rendered
WORD ORIGIN Old French *rewarder* to regard

rewarding ❶ *adj* giving personal satisfaction: *my most professionally rewarding experience*

rewarewa (ray-wa-ray-wa) *n* a tall New Zealand tree with reddish wood
WORD ORIGIN Māori

rewind *vb* **-winding, -wound** to run (a tape or film) back to an earlier point in order to replay

rewire *vb* **-wiring, -wired** to provide (a house, engine, etc.) with new wiring

reword *vb* to alter the wording of

rework *vb* to improve or bring up to date: *they need to rework the system* **reworking** *n*

rewrite *vb* **-writing, -wrote, -written 1** to write again in a different way ▷ *n* **2** something rewritten

Rex *n* king: now used chiefly in documents and inscriptions
WORD ORIGIN Latin

Reynaud *n* **Paul** 1878–1966, French statesman: premier during the defeat of France by Germany (1940); later imprisoned by the Germans

Rf *chem* rutherfordium

RFC Rugby Football Club

RGN (in Britain, New Zealand, and Australia) Registered General Nurse

Rh 1 *chem* rhodium **2** ▸ see **Rh factor**

rhapsodize *or* **-dise** *vb* **-dizing, -dized** *or* **-dising, -dised** to speak or write with extravagant enthusiasm

rhapsody *n, pl* **-dies 1** *music* a freely structured and emotional piece of music **2** an expression of ecstatic enthusiasm **rhapsodic** *adj*
WORD ORIGIN Greek *rhaptein* to sew together + *ōidē* song

rhea (ree-a) *n* a large fast-running flightless bird of South America, similar to the ostrich

THESAURUS

quickening, rebirth, resuscitation, revitalization, recrudescence, reanimation, renascence, revivification

revive *vb* **1a = revitalize**, restore, rally, renew, renovate, rekindle, kick-start *(informal)*, breathe new life into, invigorate, reanimate **1b = refresh**, restore, comfort, cheer, renew, resurrect, rejuvenate, revivify **OPPOSITE:** exhaust
2a = bring round, awaken, animate, rouse, resuscitate, bring back to life
2b = come round, recover, quicken, spring up again

revolt *n* **1 = uprising**, rising, revolution, rebellion, mutiny, defection, insurrection, insurgency, putsch, sedition ▷ *vb* **4 = disgust**, offend, turn off *(informal)*, sicken, repel, repulse, nauseate, gross out *(US slang)*, shock, turn your stomach, make your flesh creep, give you the creeps *(informal)*

revolting *adj* **= disgusting**, shocking, offensive, appalling, nasty, foul, horrible, obscene, sickening, distasteful, horrid, repellent, obnoxious, repulsive, nauseating, repugnant, loathsome, abhorrent, abominable, nauseous, cringe-making *(Brit informal)*, noisome, yucky *or* yukky *(slang)*, yucko *(Austral slang)* **OPPOSITE:** delightful

revolution *n* **1 = revolt**, rising, coup, rebellion, uprising, mutiny, insurgency, coup d'état, putsch
3 = transformation, shift, innovation, upheaval, reformation, metamorphosis, sea change, drastic *or* radical change **4a, 4b = rotation**, turn, cycle, circle, wheel, spin, lap, circuit, orbit, whirl, gyration, round

revolutionary *adj* **1, 2 = rebel**, radical, extremist, subversive, insurgent, seditious, mutinous, insurrectionary **OPPOSITE:** reactionary
3 = innovative, new, different, novel, radical, fundamental, progressive, experimental, drastic, avant-garde, ground-breaking, thoroughgoing **OPPOSITE:** conventional
▷ *n* **4 = rebel**, insurgent, mutineer, insurrectionary, revolutionist, insurrectionist **OPPOSITE:** reactionary

revolve *vb* **1a = go round**, circle, orbit, gyrate **1b = rotate**, turn, wheel, spin, twist, whirl

reward *n* **2 = payment**, return, benefit, profit, gain, prize, wages, honour, compensation, bonus, premium, merit, repayment, bounty, remuneration, recompense, meed *(archaic)*, requital **OPPOSITE:** penalty
3 = punishment, desert, retribution, comeuppance *(slang)*, just deserts, requital ▷ *vb* **4 = compensate**, pay, honour, repay, recompense, requite, remunerate, make it worth your while **OPPOSITE:** penalize

rewarding *adj* **= satisfying**, fulfilling, gratifying, edifying, economic, pleasing, valuable, profitable, productive, worthwhile, beneficial, enriching, fruitful, advantageous, gainful, remunerative **OPPOSITE:** unrewarding

DICTIONARY

WORD ORIGIN after *Rhea*, mother of Zeus

Rhee *n* **Syngman** 1875–1965, Korean statesman, leader of the campaign for independence from Japan; first president of South Korea (1948–60). Popular unrest forced his resignation

rhenium *n chem* a silvery-white metallic element with a high melting point. Symbol: Re
WORD ORIGIN Latin *Rhenus* the Rhine

rheostat *n* a variable resistor in an electrical circuit, such as one used to dim lights **rheostatic** *adj*
WORD ORIGIN Greek *rheos* flow + *-statēs* stationary

rhesus factor (ree-suss) *n* ▸ see **Rh factor**

rhesus monkey *n* a small long-tailed monkey of S Asia
WORD ORIGIN Greek *Rhesos*, mythical Thracian king

rhetoric ❶ (ret-a-rik) *n* **1** the art of using speech or writing to persuade or influence **2** artificial or exaggerated language: *there's been no shortage of soaring rhetoric at this summit* **rhetorical** (rit-tor-ik-kl) *adj*
WORD ORIGIN Greek *rhētorikē (tekhnē)* (art) of rhetoric

rhetorical question *n* a question to which no answer is required, used for dramatic effect, for example *who knows?*

rheum (room) *n* a watery discharge from the eyes or nose **rheumy** *adj*
WORD ORIGIN Greek *rheuma* a flow

rheumatic *adj* **1** caused by or affected by rheumatism ▹ *n* **2** a person suffering from rheumatism **rheumatically** *adv*

rheumatic fever *n* a disease with inflammation and pain in the joints

rheumatics *n informal* rheumatism

rheumatism *n* any painful disorder of joints, muscles, or connective tissue
WORD ORIGIN Greek *rheuma* a flow

rheumatoid *adj* (of symptoms) resembling rheumatism

rheumatoid arthritis *n* a chronic disease causing painful swelling of the joints

Rh factor *n* an antigen commonly found in human blood: the terms **Rh positive** and **Rh negative** are used to indicate its presence or absence
WORD ORIGIN after the rhesus monkey, in which it was first discovered

rhinestone *n* an imitation diamond made of glass
WORD ORIGIN originally made at Strasbourg, on the Rhine

rhino *n, pl* **-nos** *or* **-no** a rhinoceros

rhinoceros *n, pl* **-oses** *or* **-os** a large plant-eating mammal of SE Asia and Africa with one or two horns on the nose and a very thick skin
WORD ORIGIN Greek *rhis* nose + *keras* horn

rhinovirus *n* any of various viruses that occur in the human respiratory tract and cause diseases, such as the common cold

rhizome *n* a thick horizontal underground stem whose buds develop into new plants
WORD ORIGIN Greek *rhiza* a root

rhodium *n chem* a hard silvery-white metallic element, used to harden platinum and palladium. Symbol: Rh
WORD ORIGIN Greek *rhodon* rose, from the pink colour of its compounds

rhododendron *n* an evergreen shrub with clusters of showy flowers
WORD ORIGIN Greek *rhodon* rose + *dendron* tree

rhombohedron (rom-boh-heed-ron) *n, pl* **-drons** *or* **-dra** (-dra) a six-sided prism whose sides are parallelograms
WORD ORIGIN RHOMBUS + Greek *-edron* -sided

rhomboid *n* **1** a parallelogram with adjacent sides of unequal length. It resembles a rectangle but does not have 90° angles ▹ *adj also* **rhomboidal** **2** having such a shape
WORD ORIGIN Greek *rhomboeidēs* shaped like a rhombus

rhombus (rom-buss) *n, pl* **-buses** *or* **-bi** (-bye) a parallelogram with sides of equal length but no right angles **rhombic** *adj*
WORD ORIGIN Greek *rhombos* something that spins

rhubarb *n* **1** a large-leaved plant with long green and red stalks which can be cooked and eaten **2** a related plant of central Asia, whose root can be dried and used as a laxative or astringent ▹ *interj, n* **3** the noise made by actors to simulate conversation, esp. by repeating the word *rhubarb*
WORD ORIGIN Old French *reubarbe*

rhyme ❶ *n* **1** sameness of the final sounds in lines of verse or in words **2** a word that is identical to another in its final sound: *'while' is a rhyme for 'mile'* **3** a piece of poetry with corresponding sounds at the ends of the lines **4** **rhyme or reason** sense or meaning ▹ *vb* **rhyming, rhymed** **5** (of a word) to form a rhyme with another word **6** to compose (verse) in a metrical structure
WORD ORIGIN Old French *rime;* spelling influenced by *rhythm*

rhymester *n* a mediocre poet

rhyming slang *n* slang in which a word is replaced by another word or phrase that rhymes with it, eg *apples and pears* meaning *stairs*

Rhys *n* **Jean** (**Ella Gwendolen Rees Williams**) ?1890–1979, Welsh novelist and short-story writer, born in Dominica. Her novels include *Voyage in the Dark* (1934), *Good Morning, Midnight* (1939), and *Wide Sargasso Sea* (1966)

rhythm ❶ *n* **1** any regular movement or beat: *the side-effects can cause changes in the rhythm of the heart beat* **2** any regular pattern that occurs over a period of time: *the seasonal rhythm of the agricultural year* **3** **a** the arrangement of the durations of and stress on the notes of a piece of music, usually laid out in regular groups (**bars**) of beats **b** any specific arrangement of such groupings: *waltz rhythm* **4** (in poetry) the arrangement of words to form a regular pattern of stresses **rhythmic** *or* **rhythmical** *adj* **rhythmically** *adv*
WORD ORIGIN Greek *rhuthmos*

rhythm and blues *n* a kind of popular music of Black American origin, derived from and influenced by the blues

rhythm method *n* a method of contraception in which intercourse is avoided at times when conception is most likely

RI Rhode Island

rialto *n, pl* **-tos** a market or exchange
WORD ORIGIN after the *Rialto*, the business centre of medieval Venice

rib[1] *n* **1** one of the curved bones forming the framework of the upper part of the body and attached to the spinal column **2** a cut of meat including one or more ribs **3** a curved supporting part, such as in the hull of a boat **4** one of a series of raised rows in knitted fabric ▹ *vb* **ribbing, ribbed** **5** to provide or support with ribs **6** to knit to form a rib pattern **ribbed** *adj*
WORD ORIGIN Old English *ribb*

rib[2] *vb* **ribbing, ribbed** *informal* to tease or ridicule **ribbing** *n*
WORD ORIGIN short for *rib-tickle*

RIBA Royal Institute of British Architects

ribald *adj* coarse or obscene in a

r

THESAURUS

rhetoric *n* **1 = oratory**, eloquence, public speaking, speech-making, elocution, declamation, speechifying, grandiloquence, spieling *(informal)*, whaikorero *(NZ)* **2 = hyperbole**, rant, hot air *(informal)*, pomposity, bombast, wordiness, verbosity, fustian, grandiloquence, magniloquence

rhyme *n* **3 = poem**, song, verse, ode

rhythm *n* **1, 3a = beat**, swing, accent, pulse, tempo, cadence, lilt **4 = metre**, time, measure *(Prosody)*

rich *adj* **1 = wealthy**, affluent, well-off, opulent, propertied, rolling *(slang)*,

DICTIONARY

humorous or mocking way
ribaldry *n*
WORD ORIGIN Old French *ribauld*
riband *or* **ribband** *n* a ribbon awarded for some achievement
Ribbentrop *n* **Joachim von** 1893–1946, German Nazi politician: foreign minister under Hitler (1938–45). He was hanged after conviction as a war criminal at Nuremberg
ribbing *n* **1** a pattern of ribs in knitted material **2** a framework or structure of ribs
ribbon *n* **1** a narrow strip of fine material used for trimming, tying, etc. **2** a long narrow strip of inked cloth or plastic used to produce print in a typewriter **3** a small strip of coloured cloth worn as a badge or as a symbol of an award **4** a long thin strip: *a ribbon of white water* **5** **ribbons** ragged strips or shreds: *his clothes were torn to ribbons; his credibility was shot to ribbons*
WORD ORIGIN Old French *riban*
ribbon development *n* the building of houses along a main road
ribbonwood *n* a small evergreen tree of New Zealand
ribcage *n* the bony structure formed by the ribs that encloses the lungs
Ribera *n* **José de** also called *Jusepe de Ribera*, Italian nickname *Lo Spagnoletto* (The Little Spaniard). 1591–1652, Spanish artist, living in Italy. His religious pictures often dwell on horrible suffering, presented in realistic detail
riboflavin (rye-boe-**flay**-vin) *n* a vitamin of the B complex that occurs in green vegetables, milk, fish, eggs, liver, and kidney: used as a yellow or orange food colouring (**E101**). Also called: **vitamin B$_2$**
WORD ORIGIN *ribose*, a sugar + Latin *flavus* yellow
ribonucleic acid *n* ▸ the full name of **RNA**
Ricci *n* **Matteo** 1552–1610, Italian Jesuit missionary and scholar, who introduced Christianity to China. He was later censured by the Church for allowing his converts to retain some of their ancient religious customs
rice *n* **1** the edible grain of an erect grass that grows on wet ground in warm climates ▷ *vb* **ricing, riced** **2** *US & Canad* to sieve (potatoes or other vegetables) to a coarse mashed consistency
WORD ORIGIN Greek *orūza*
Rice *n* **Elmer**, original name *Elmer Reizenstein*. 1892–1967, US dramatist. His plays include *The Adding Machine* (1923) and *Street Scene* (1929), which was made into a musical by Kurt Weill in 1947
rice paper *n* **1** a thin edible paper made from rice straw **2** a thin Chinese paper made from the rice-paper plant, the pith of which is flattened into sheets
rich ❶ *adj* **1** owning a lot of money or property **2** well supplied (with a desirable substance or quality): *a country rich with cultural interest* **3** having an abundance of natural resources, minerals, etc.: *a land rich in unexploited minerals* **4** producing abundantly: *the island is a blend of hilly moorland and rich farmland* **5** luxuriant or prolific: *the meadows rich with corn* **6** (of food) containing much fat or sugar **7** having a full-bodied flavour: *a gloriously rich Cabernet-dominated wine* **8** (of colour) intense or vivid: *her hair had a rich auburn tint* **9** (of sound or a voice) full or resonant **10** very amusing or ridiculous: *a rich joke* **11** (of a fuel-air mixture) containing a relatively high proportion of fuel
richness *n*
WORD ORIGIN Old English *rīce* (originally of people, with sense: great, mighty)
Rich *n* **1** **Adrienne** born 1929, US poet and feminist writer; her volumes of poetry include *Snapshots of a Daughter-in-Law* (1963) and *Diving Into the Wreck* (1973) **2** **Buddy**, real name *Bernard Rich*. 1917–87, US jazz drummer and band leader
Richard *n* **1** Sir **Cliff**, real name *Harry Rodger Webb*. born 1940, British pop singer. Film musicals include *The Young Ones* (1961) and *Summer Holiday* (1962) **2** **Maurice**, known as *Rocket*. (1821–2000); Canadian ice hockey player
Richards *n* **1** **I(vor) A(rmstrong)** 1893–1979, British literary critic and linguist, who, with C. K. Ogden, wrote *The Meaning of Meaning* (1923) and devised Basic English **2** Sir **Gordon**. 1904–86, British jockey **3** Sir **Viv**, full name *Isaac Vivian Alexander Richards*. born 1952, West Indian cricketer; captained the West Indies (1985–91)
Richardson *n* **1** **Dorothy M(iller)** 1873–1957, British novelist, a pioneer of stream-of-consciousness writing: author of the novel sequence *Pilgrimage* (14 vols, 1915–67) **2** **Henry Handel** pen name of *Ethel Florence Lindesay Richardson*, 1870–1946, Australian novelist; author of the trilogy *The Fortunes of Richard Mahony* (1917–29) **3** Sir **Owen Willans** 1879–1959, British physicist; a pioneer in the study of atomic physics: Nobel prize for physics 1928 **4** Sir **Ralph** (**David**) 1902–83, British stage and screen actor **5** **Samuel** 1689–1761, British novelist whose psychological insight and use of the epistolary form exerted a great influence on the development of the novel. His chief novels are *Pamela* (1740) and *Clarissa* (1747)
riches ❶ *pl n* valuable possessions or desirable substances: *the unexpected riches of Georgian culture*
Richler *n* **Mordecai** 1931–2001, Canadian novelist. His novels include *St Urbain's Horseman* (1971), *Solomon Gursky Was Here* (1990), and *Barney's Version* (1997)
richly ❶ *adv* **1** in a rich or elaborate manner: *the rooms are richly decorated with a variety of classical motifs* **2** fully and appropriately: *he left the field to a richly deserved standing ovation*
Richter *n* **1** **Burton** born 1931, US physicist: shared the 1976 Nobel prize for physics with Samuel Tring for discovering the subatomic particle known as the J/psi particle **2** **Johann Friedrich**, wrote under the name *Jean Paul*. 1763–1825, German romantic novelist. His works include *Hesperus* (1795) and *Titan* (1800–03) **3** **Sviatoslav** 1915–97, Ukrainian concert pianist
Richter scale *n* a scale for expressing the intensity of an earthquake, ranging from 0 to over 8
WORD ORIGIN after Charles *Richter*, seismologist
rick[1] *n* a large stack of hay or straw
WORD ORIGIN Old English *hrēac*
rick[2] *vb* **1** to wrench or sprain (a joint) ▷ *n* **2** a wrench or sprain of a joint
WORD ORIGIN variant of *wrick*
rickets *n* a disease of children, caused by a deficiency of vitamin D and characterized by softening of

THESAURUS

loaded *(slang)*, flush *(informal)*, prosperous, well-heeled *(informal)*, well-to-do, moneyed, filthy rich, stinking rich *(informal)*, made of money *(informal)*, minted *(Brit slang)* **OPPOSITE:** poor
2 = well-stocked, full, productive, ample, abundant, plentiful, copious, well-provided, well-supplied, plenteous **OPPOSITE:** scarce
4 = fruitful, productive, fertile, prolific, fecund **OPPOSITE:** barren
5 = abounding, full, luxurious, lush, abundant, exuberant, well-endowed
6, 7 = full-bodied, heavy, sweet, delicious, fatty, tasty, creamy, spicy, juicy, luscious, savoury, succulent, flavoursome, highly-flavoured **OPPOSITE:** bland
riches *pl n* **= wealth**, money, property, gold, assets, plenty, fortune, substance, treasure, abundance, richness, affluence, opulence, top whack *(informal)* **OPPOSITE:** poverty
richly *adv* **1 = elaborately**, lavishly, elegantly, splendidly, exquisitely, expensively, luxuriously, gorgeously, sumptuously, opulently, palatially
2 = fully, well, thoroughly, amply, appropriately, properly, suitably, in

DICTIONARY

developing bone, and hence bow legs
WORD ORIGIN origin unknown

rickety *adj* **1** likely to collapse or break: *a rickety wooden table* **2** resembling or afflicted with rickets **ricketiness** *n*

rickrack *or* **ricrac** *n* a zigzag braid used for trimming
WORD ORIGIN reduplication of RACK[1]

rickshaw *or* **ricksha** *n* **1** a small two-wheeled passenger vehicle pulled by one or two people, used in parts of Asia **2** a similar vehicle with three wheels, propelled by a person pedalling
WORD ORIGIN Japanese *jinrikisha*

ricochet (rik-osh-ay) *vb* **-cheting, -cheted** *or* **-chetting, -chetted 1** (of a bullet) to rebound from a surface ▹*n* **2** the motion or sound of a rebounding bullet
WORD ORIGIN French

Ricoeur *n* **Paul** 1913–2005, French philosopher, noted for his work on theories of interpretation. His books include *Philosophy of the Will* (3 vols, 1950–60), *Freud and Philosophy* (1965), and *The Living Metaphor* (1975)

ricotta *n* a soft white unsalted Italian cheese made from sheep's milk
WORD ORIGIN Italian

rid ⓣ *vb* **ridding, rid** *or* **ridded 1 rid of** to relieve (oneself) or make a place free of (something undesirable) **2 get rid of** to relieve or free oneself of (something undesirable)
WORD ORIGIN Old Norse *rythja*

riddance *n* **good riddance** relief at getting rid of someone or something

ridden *vb* **1** ▸ the past participle of **ride** ▹*adj* **2** afflicted or affected by the thing specified: *the police found three bullet-ridden bodies*

riddle[1] ⓣ *n* **1** a question, puzzle, or verse phrased so that ingenuity is required to find the answer or meaning **2** a puzzling person or thing ▹*vb* **-dling, -dled 3** to speak in riddles
WORD ORIGIN Old English *rǣdels(e)*

riddle[2] ⓣ *vb* **-dling, -dled 1** to pierce with many holes **2** to put through a sieve ▹*n* **3** a coarse sieve
WORD ORIGIN Old English *hriddel* a sieve

riddled *adj* **riddled with** full of (something undesirable): *riddled with mistakes*

ride ⓣ *vb* **riding, rode, ridden 1** to sit on and control the movements of (a horse or other animal) **2** to sit on and propel (a bicycle or motorcycle) **3** to travel on or in a vehicle: *he rides around in a chauffeur-driven Rolls-Royce* **4** to travel over: *they rode the countryside in search of shelter* **5** to travel through or be carried across (sea, sky, etc.): *the moon was riding high* **6** *US & Canad* to cause to be carried: *to ride someone out of town* **7** (of a vessel) to lie at anchor **8** to tyrannize over or dominate: *politicians must stop riding roughshod over voters' wishes* **9 be riding on** to be dependent on (something) for success: *a lot is riding on the profits of the film* **10** *informal* to continue undisturbed: *let it ride* **11 riding high** popular and successful ▹*n* **12** a journey on a bicycle, on horseback, or in a vehicle **13** transport in a vehicle: *most of us have been told not to accept rides from strangers* **14** the type of movement experienced in a vehicle: *a bumpy ride* **15** a path for riding on horseback **16 take for a ride** *informal* to cheat or deceive
WORD ORIGIN Old English *rīdan*

ride out *vb* to survive (a period of difficulty or danger) successfully

rider *n* **1** a person who rides **2** an extra clause or condition added to a document

ride up *vb* (of a garment) to move up from the proper position

ridge *n* **1** a long narrow raised land formation with sloping sides **2** a long narrow raised strip on a flat surface **3** the top of a roof where the two sloping sides meet **4** *meteorol* an elongated area of high pressure **ridged** *adj* **ridgy** *adj*
WORD ORIGIN Old English *hrycg*

ridgepole *n* **1** a timber along the ridge of a roof, to which the rafters are attached **2** the horizontal pole at the apex of a tent

ridicule ⓣ *n* **1** language or behaviour intended to humiliate or mock ▹*vb* **-culing, -culed 2** to make fun of or mock
WORD ORIGIN Latin *ridere* to laugh

ridiculous ⓣ *adj* worthy of or causing ridicule

riding[1] *n* the art or practice of horsemanship

riding[2] *n* **1 Riding** any of the three former administrative divisions of Yorkshire: North Riding, East Riding, and West Riding **2** *Canad* an electoral constituency
WORD ORIGIN Old English *thriding* a third

riding crop *n* a short whip with a handle at one end for opening gates

Ridley *n* **Nicholas** ?1500–55, English bishop, who helped to revise the liturgy under Edward VI. He was burnt at the stake for refusing to disavow his Protestant beliefs when Mary I assumed the throne

Rie *n* Dame **Lucie**, original name *Lucie Gomperz*. 1902–95, British potter, born in Austria

Riefenstahl *n* **Leni** 1902–2003, German photographer and film director, best known for her Nazi propaganda films, such as *Triumph of the Will* (1934)

Rienzi *or Italian* **Rienzo** *n* **Cola di** 1313–54, Italian radical political reformer in Rome

riesling *n* a medium-dry white wine
WORD ORIGIN from German

rife ⓣ *adj* **1** widespread or common **2 rife with** full of: *the media is rife with speculation*
WORD ORIGIN Old English *rīfe*

riff *n jazz, rock* a short series of chords
WORD ORIGIN probably from REFRAIN[2]

riffle *vb* **-fling, -fled 1** to flick through (papers or pages) quickly: *I riffled through the rest of the memos* ▹*n* **2** *US & Canad* **a** a rapid in a stream **b** a rocky shoal causing a rapid **c** a ripple on water **3** a riffling

THESAURUS

full measure

rid *vb* **1 = free**, clear, deliver, relieve, purge, lighten, unburden, disabuse, make free, disembarrass, disencumber, disburden
2 get rid of something *or* **someone = dispose of**, throw away *or* out, dispense with, dump, remove, eliminate, expel, unload, shake off, eject, do away with, jettison, weed out, see the back of, wipe from the face of the earth, give the bum's rush to *(slang)*

riddle[1] *n* **1 = puzzle**, problem, conundrum, teaser, poser, rebus, brain-teaser *(informal)*, Chinese puzzle **2 = enigma**, question, secret, mystery, puzzle, conundrum, teaser, problem

riddle[2] *vb* **1 = pierce**, pepper, puncture, perforate, honeycomb

ride *vb* **1 = control**, handle, sit on, manage **3 = travel**, be carried, be supported, be borne, go, move, sit, progress, journey ▹*n* **12, 13 = journey**, drive, trip, lift, spin *(informal)*, outing, whirl *(informal)*, jaunt

ridicule *n* **1 = mockery**, scorn, derision, laughter, irony, rib, taunting, sneer, satire, jeer, banter, sarcasm, chaff, gibe, raillery ▹*vb* **2 = laugh at**, mock, make fun of, make a fool of, humiliate, taunt, sneer at, parody, caricature, jeer at, scoff at, deride, send up *(Brit informal)*, lampoon, poke fun at, chaff, take the mickey out of *(informal)*, satirize, pooh-pooh, laugh out of court, make a monkey out of, make someone a laughing stock, laugh to scorn

ridiculous *adj* **= laughable**, stupid, incredible, silly, outrageous, absurd, foolish, unbelievable, hilarious, ludicrous, preposterous, farcical, comical, zany, nonsensical, derisory, inane, risible, contemptible, cockamamie *(slang, chiefly US)*
OPPOSITE: sensible

rife *adj* **1 = widespread**, abundant, plentiful, rampant, general, common, current, raging, universal,

r

DICTIONARY

WORD ORIGIN probably from *ruffle*

riffraff *n* worthless or disreputable people
WORD ORIGIN Old French *rif et raf*

rifle[1] *n* **1** a firearm having a long barrel with a spirally grooved interior, which gives the bullet a spinning motion and thus greater accuracy over a longer range **2 Rifles** a unit of soldiers equipped with rifles: *the Burma Rifles* ▷ *vb* **-fling, -fled 3** to cut spiral grooves inside the barrel of (a gun) **rifled** *adj*
WORD ORIGIN Old French *rifler* to scratch

rifle[2] ❶ *vb* **-fling, -fled 1** to search (a house or safe) and steal from it **2** to steal and carry off: *he rifled whatever valuables he could lay his hands on*
WORD ORIGIN Old French *rifler* to plunder, scratch

rift ❶ *n* **1** a break in friendly relations between people or groups of people **2** a gap or space made by splitting
WORD ORIGIN Old Norse

rift valley *n* a long narrow valley resulting from the subsidence of land between two faults

rig ❶ *vb* **rigging, rigged 1** to arrange in a dishonest way, for profit or advantage: *he claimed that the poll was rigged* **2** to set up or prepare (something) hastily ready for use **3** *naut* to equip (a vessel or mast) with (sails or rigging) ▷ *n* **4** an apparatus for drilling for oil and gas **5** *naut* the arrangement of the sails and masts of a vessel **6** apparatus or equipment **7** *informal* an outfit of clothes **8** *US, Canad & Austral* an articulated lorry ▸ See also **rig out, rig up**
WORD ORIGIN Scandinavian

-rigged *adj* (of a sailing vessel) having a rig of a certain kind: *a square-rigged ship*

rigging *n* the ropes and cables supporting a ship's masts and sails

right ❶ *adj* **1** morally or legally acceptable or correct: *his conduct seemed reasonable, even right* **2** correct or true: *the customer is always right* **3** appropriate, suitable, or proper: *there were problems involved in finding the right candidate* **4** most favourable or convenient: *she waited until the right moment to broach the subject* **5** in a satisfactory condition: *things are right again now* **6** accurate: *is that clock right?* **7** correct in opinion or judgment **8** sound in mind or body **9** of or on the side of something or someone that faces east when the front is turned towards the north **10** conservative or reactionary: *it was alleged he was an agent of the right wing* **11** *geom* formed by or containing a line or plane perpendicular to another line or plane: *a right angle* **12** of or on the side of cloth worn or facing outwards **13 in one's right mind** sane **14 she'll be right** *Austral & NZ informal* that's all right; not to worry **15 the right side of a** in favour with: *you'd better stay on the right side of him* **b** younger than: *he's still on the right side of fifty* **16 too right** *informal* an exclamation of agreement ▷ *adv* **17** correctly: *if we change the structure of local government we must do it right* **18** in the appropriate manner: *do it right next time!* **19** straight or directly: *let's go right to bed* **20** in the direction of the east from the point of view of a person or thing facing north **21** all the way: *he drove right up to the gate* **22** without delay: *I'll be right over* **23** exactly or precisely: *right here* **24** fittingly: *it serves him right* **25** to good or favourable advantage: *it all came out right in the end* ▷ *n* **26** a freedom or power that is morally or legally due to a person: *the defendant had an absolute right to a fair trial* **27** anything that accords with the principles of legal or moral justice **28 in the right** the state of being in accordance with reason or truth **29** the right side, direction, or part: *the right of the army* **30 the Right** the supporters or advocates of conservatism or reaction: *the rise of the far Right in France* **31** *boxing* a punch with the right hand **32 rights** *finance* the privilege of a company's shareholders to subscribe for new issues of the company's shares on advantageous terms **33 by right** *or* **rights** properly: *by rights he should have won* **34 in one's own right** having a claim or title oneself rather than through marriage or other connection **35 to rights** consistent with justice or orderly arrangement: *he put the matter to rights* ▷ *vb* **36** to bring or come back to a normal or correct state **37** to bring or come back to a vertical position: *he slipped and righted himself at once* **38** to compensate for or redress: *there is a wrong to be righted* **39** to make (something) accord with truth or facts ▷ *interj* **40** an expression of agreement or compliance
WORD ORIGIN Old English *riht*

right angle *n* **1** an angle of 90° or $\pi/2$ radians **2 at right angles** perpendicular or perpendicularly **right-angled** *adj*

right-angled triangle *n* a triangle with one angle which is a right angle

right away ❶ *adv* without delay

righteous ❶ (**rye**-chuss) *adj* **1** moral, just, or virtuous: *the lieutenant was a*

THESAURUS

frequent, prevailing, epidemic, prevalent, ubiquitous

rifle[2] *vb* **1, 2 = ransack**, rob, burgle, loot, strip, sack, gut, plunder, pillage, despoil

rift *n* **1 = breach**, difference, division, split, separation, falling out (*informal*), disagreement, quarrel, alienation, schism, estrangement **2 = split**, opening, space, crack, gap, break, fault, breach, fracture, flaw, cleavage, cleft, chink, crevice, fissure, cranny

rig *vb* **1 = fix**, doctor, engineer (*informal*), arrange, fake, manipulate, juggle, tamper with, fiddle with (*informal*), falsify, trump up, gerrymander **3** (*naut*) **= equip**, fit out, kit out, outfit, supply, turn out, provision, furnish, accoutre

right *adj* **1 = just**, good, fair, moral, proper, ethical, upright, honourable, honest, equitable, righteous, virtuous, lawful **OPPOSITE:** unfair **2, 7 = correct**, true, genuine, accurate, exact, precise, valid, authentic, satisfactory, spot-on (*Brit informal*), factual, on the money (*US*), unerring, admissible, dinkum (*Austral & NZ informal*), veracious, sound **OPPOSITE:** wrong **3 = proper**, done, becoming, seemly, fitting, fit, appropriate, suitable, desirable, comme il faut (*French*) **OPPOSITE:** inappropriate ▷ *adv* **17 = correctly**, truly, precisely, exactly, genuinely, accurately, factually, aright **OPPOSITE:** wrongly **18 = suitably**, fittingly, appropriately, properly, aptly, satisfactorily, befittingly **OPPOSITE:** improperly **19 = directly**, straight, precisely, exactly, unswervingly, without deviation, by the shortest route, in a beeline **19, 22 = straight**, directly, immediately, quickly, promptly, instantly, straightaway, without delay **OPPOSITE:** indirectly **23 = exactly**, squarely, precisely, bang, slap-bang (*informal*) ▷ *n* **26 = prerogative**, interest, business, power, claim, authority, title, due, freedom, licence, permission, liberty, privilege **27 = justice**, good, reason, truth, honour, equity, virtue, integrity, goodness, morality, fairness, legality, righteousness, propriety, rectitude, lawfulness, uprightness **OPPOSITE:** injustice ▷ *vb* **38 = rectify**, settle, fix, correct, repair, sort out, compensate for, straighten, redress, vindicate, put right

right away *adv* **= immediately**, now, directly, promptly, instantly, at once, right off, straightaway, without delay, without hesitation, straight off (*informal*), forthwith, pronto (*informal*), this instant, posthaste

righteous *adj* **1 = virtuous**, good, just, fair, moral, pure, ethical, upright, honourable, honest, equitable,

r

DICTIONARY

righteous cop **2** morally justifiable or right: *her eyes were blazing with righteous indignation* **righteousness** *n*
WORD ORIGIN Old English *rihtwīs*

rightful *adj* **1** in accordance with what is right **2** having a legally or morally just claim: *he is the rightful heir to her fortune* **3** held by virtue of a legal or just claim: *these moves will restore them to their rightful homes* **rightfully** *adv* **rightfulness** *n*

right-hand *adj* **1** of, on, or towards the right: *in the top right-hand corner* **2** for the right hand **3** **right-hand man** a person's most valuable assistant

right-handed *adj* **1** more adept with the right hand than with the left **2** made for or by the right hand **3** turning from left to right

rightist *adj* **1** of the political right or its principles ▷*n* **2** a supporter of the political right **rightism** *n*

rightly *adv* **1** in accordance with the true facts or justice **2** with good reason: *he was rightly praised for his constancy*

right-minded *or* **right-thinking** *adj* holding opinions or principles considered acceptable by the speaker

right of way *n, pl* **rights of way** **1** the right of one vehicle or ship to go before another **2** **a** the legal right of someone to pass over someone else's land **b** the path used by this right

right-on *adj informal* trendy and socially aware or relevant: *the judges were fed up with right-on comedy*

Right Reverend *adj* a title of respect for a bishop

rightward *adj* **1** situated on or directed towards the right ▷*adv also* **rightwards** **2** on or towards the right

right whale *n* a large grey or black whalebone whale with a large head
WORD ORIGIN origin unknown

right-wing *adj* **1** conservative or reactionary: *there's a very fast-growing right-wing feeling in our country* **2** belonging to the more conservative part of a political party: *a group of right-wing Labour MPs* ▷*n* **right wing** **3** *(often cap)* the more conservative or reactionary section, esp. of a political party: *the Right Wing of the Conservative Party* **4** *sport* **a** the right-hand side of the field of play **b** a player positioned in this area in certain games **right-winger** *n*

rigid ⊙ *adj* **1** inflexible or strict: *the talks will be general without a rigid agenda* **2** physically unyielding or stiff: *use only rigid plastic containers* **rigidity** *n* **rigidly** *adv*
WORD ORIGIN Latin *rigidus*

rigmarole *n* **1** a long complicated procedure **2** a set of incoherent or pointless statements
WORD ORIGIN earlier *ragman roll* a list

rigor mortis *n* the stiffness of joints and muscles of a dead body
WORD ORIGIN Latin: rigidity of death

rigorous ⊙ *adj* **1** harsh, strict, or severe: *rigorous enforcement of the libel laws* **2** severely accurate: *rigorous scientific testing*

rigour *or US* **rigor** *n* **1** a severe or cruel circumstance: *the rigours of forced labour* **2** strictness in judgment or conduct **3** harsh but just treatment
WORD ORIGIN Latin *rigor*

rig out *vb* **1** to dress: *I was rigged out in my usual green shell suit* **2** to equip: *his car is rigged out with gadgets* ▷*n* **rigout** **3** *informal* a person's clothing or costume

rig up *vb* to set up or build temporarily: *they rigged up a loudspeaker system*

rile *vb* **riling, riled** **1** to annoy or anger **2** *US & Canad* to stir up (a liquid)
WORD ORIGIN variant of *roil* to agitate

Riley¹ *n* **1 Bridget** (**Louise**) born 1931, British painter, best known for her black-and-white op art paintings of the 1960s **2 Gina** born 1961, Australian television actress and writer, best known for playing 'Kim' in the comedy series *Kath & Kim*

Riley² *n* **the life of Riley** a luxurious and carefree existence
WORD ORIGIN C20: origin unknown

rill *n* a small stream
WORD ORIGIN Low German *rille*

rim ⊙ *n* **1** the raised edge of an object **2** the outer part of a wheel to which the tyre is attached **rimless** *adj*
WORD ORIGIN Old English *rima*

rime¹ *literary n* **1** frost formed by the freezing of water droplets in fog onto solid objects ▷*vb* **riming, rimed** **2** to cover with rime or something resembling it **rimy** *adj*
WORD ORIGIN Old English *hrīm*

rime² *n, vb* **riming, rimed** *archaic* ▸same as **rhyme**

rind *n* a hard outer layer on fruits, bacon, or cheese
WORD ORIGIN Old English *rinde*

ring¹ ⊙ *vb* **ringing, rang, rung** **1** to give out a clear resonant sound, like that of a bell **2** to cause (a bell) to give out a ringing sound or (of a bell) to give out such a sound **3** *chiefly Brit & NZ* to call (a person) by telephone **4** **ring for** to call by means of a bell: *ring for the maid* **5** (of a building or place) to be filled with sound: *the church rang with singing* **6** (of the ears) to have the sensation of humming or ringing **7** *slang* to change the identity of (a stolen vehicle) by using the licence plate or serial number of another, usually disused, vehicle **8** **ring a bell** to bring something to the mind or memory: *the name doesn't ring a bell* **9** **ring down the curtain** **a** to lower the curtain at the end of a theatrical performance **b** **ring down the curtain on** to put an end to **10** **ring true** *or* **false** to give the impression of being true *or* false ▷*n* **11** the act of or a sound made by ringing **12** a sound produced by or sounding like a bell **13** *informal chiefly Brit & NZ* a telephone call **14** an inherent quality: *it has the ring of possibility to it* ▸See also **ring in, ring off**, etc.
WORD ORIGIN Old English *hringan*

ring² ⊙ *n* **1** a circular band of a precious metal worn on the finger **2** any object or mark that is circular in shape **3** a group of people or things standing or arranged in a circle: *a ring of standing stones* **4** a circular path or course: *crowds of people walking round in a ring* **5** a circular enclosure where circus acts perform or livestock is sold at a market **6** a square raised platform, marked off by ropes, in which contestants box or wrestle **7** a group of people, usually illegal, who control a specified market: *a drugs ring* **8** *chem* a closed loop of atoms in a molecule **9** one of the systems of circular bands orbiting the planets Saturn, Uranus, and Jupiter **10** **the ring** the

THESAURUS

law-abiding, squeaky-clean, blameless **OPPOSITE:** wicked

rigid *adj* **1a = strict**, set, fixed, exact, rigorous, stringent, austere, severe **OPPOSITE:** flexible **1b = inflexible**, harsh, stern, adamant, uncompromising, unrelenting, unyielding, intransigent, unbending, invariable, unalterable, undeviating **2 = stiff**, inflexible, inelastic **OPPOSITE:** pliable

rigorous *adj* **1 = strict**, hard, firm, demanding, challenging, tough, severe, exacting, harsh, stern, rigid, stringent, austere, inflexible **OPPOSITE:** soft

rim *n* **1 = edge**, lip, brim, flange

ring¹ *vb* **1, 2 = chime**, sound, toll, resound, resonate, reverberate, clang, peal **3** *(chiefly Brit & NZ)* **= phone**, call, telephone, buzz *(informal, chiefly Brit)* **5 = reverberate**, resound, resonate ▷*n* **11, 12 = chime**, knell, peal **13** *(chiefly Brit & NZ)* **= call**, phone call, buzz *(informal, chiefly Brit)*

ring² *n* **2, 3 = circle**, round, band, circuit, loop, hoop, halo **5, 6 = arena**, enclosure, circus, rink **7 = gang**, group, association, band, cell, combine, organization, circle, crew *(informal)*, knot, mob, syndicate, cartel, junta, clique, coterie, cabal ▷*vb* **13 = encircle**, surround, enclose, encompass, seal off, girdle, circumscribe, hem in, gird

rinse *vb* **1, 2 = wash**, clean, wet, dip,

r

DICTIONARY

sport of boxing **11 throw one's hat in the ring** to announce one's intention to be a candidate or contestant **12 run rings around** *informal* to outclass completely ▷ *vb* **ringing, ringed 13** to put a ring round **14** to mark (a bird) with a ring or clip for subsequent identification **15** to kill (a tree) by cutting the bark round the trunk **16** to fit a ring in the nose of (a bull, etc.) so that it can be led easily **ringed** *adj*
WORD ORIGIN Old English *hring*

ring binder *n* a loose-leaf binder with metal rings that can be opened to insert perforated paper

ringdove *n* a wood pigeon

ringer *n* **1** Also called: **dead ringer** a person or thing that is almost identical to another **2** *slang* a stolen vehicle the identity of which has been changed by the use of the licence plate or serial number of another, usually disused, vehicle

ring finger *n* the third finger, esp. of the left hand, on which a wedding ring is worn

ring in *vb* to report to someone by telephone

ringleader *n* a person who leads others in illegal or mischievous actions

ringlet *n* a lock of hair hanging down in a spiral curl **ringleted** *adj*

ring main *n* a domestic electrical supply in which outlet sockets are connected to the mains supply through a continuous closed circuit (**ring circuit**)

ringmaster *n* the master of ceremonies in a circus

ring off *vb chiefly Brit & NZ* to end a telephone conversation by replacing the receiver

ring out *vb* to send out a loud resounding noise: *I heard those shots ring out*

ring road *n* a main road that bypasses a town or town centre

ringside *n* **1** the row of seats nearest a boxing or wrestling ring ▷ *adj* **2** providing a close uninterrupted view: *a ringside seat for the election*

ringtail *n Austral* a possum with a curling tail used to grip branches while climbing

ringtone *n* a musical tune played by a mobile phone when it receives a call

ring up *vb* **1** to make a telephone call to **2** to record on a cash register **3 ring up the curtain a** to begin a theatrical performance **b ring up the curtain on** to make a start on

ringworm *n* a fungal infection of the skin producing itchy patches

rink *n* **1** a sheet of ice for skating on, usually indoors **2** an area for roller-skating on **3** a building for ice-skating or roller-skating **4 a** a strip of grass or ice on which a game of bowls or curling is played **b** the players on one side in a game of bowls or curling
WORD ORIGIN Old French *renc* row

rinkhals (rink-hals) *n, pl* **-hals** *or* **-halses** a highly venomous snake of Southern Africa capable of spitting its venom accurately at its victim's eyes
WORD ORIGIN Afrikaans

rink rat *n Canad slang* a youth who helps with odd chores at an ice-hockey rink in return for free admission to games

rinse ❶ *vb* **rinsing, rinsed 1** to remove soap or shampoo from (clothes, dishes, or hair) by washing it out with clean water **2** to wash lightly, esp. without using soap **3** to cleanse the mouth by swirling water or mouthwash in it and then spitting the liquid out **4** to give a light tint to (hair) ▷ *n* **5** the act or an instance of rinsing **6** *hairdressing* a liquid to tint hair: *a blue rinse*
WORD ORIGIN Old French *rincer*

rioja (ree-oh-ha) *n* a red or white Spanish wine with a vanilla bouquet and flavour
WORD ORIGIN *La Rioja*, area in central N Spain

riot ❶ *n* **1** a disturbance made by an unruly mob **2** *Brit, Austral & NZ* an occasion of lively enjoyment **3** a dazzling display: *the pansies provided the essential riot of colour* **4** *slang* a very amusing person or thing **5 read the riot act** to reprimand severely **6 run riot a** to behave without restraint **b** (of plants) to grow profusely ▷ *vb* **7** to take part in a riot **rioter** *n* **rioting** *n*
WORD ORIGIN Old French *riote* dispute

riotous *adj* **1** unrestrained and excessive: *riotous decadence* **2** unruly or rebellious **3** characterized by unrestrained merriment: *riotous celebration*

riot shield *n* a large shield used by police controlling crowds

rip ❶ *vb* **ripping, ripped 1** to tear or be torn violently or roughly **2** to remove hastily or roughly **3** *informal* to move violently or hurriedly **4 let rip** to act or speak without restraint ▷ *n* **5** a tear or split ▸ See also **rip off**
WORD ORIGIN origin unknown

RIP may he, she, *or* they rest in peace
WORD ORIGIN Latin *requiescat* or *requiescant in pace*

riparian (rip-pair-ee-an) *adj formal* of or on the bank of a river
WORD ORIGIN Latin *ripa* river bank

ripcord *n* a cord pulled to open a parachute from its pack

ripe ❶ *adj* **1** mature enough to be eaten or used: *a round ripe apple* **2** fully developed in mind or body **3** suitable: *wait until the time is ripe* **4 ripe for** ready or eager to (undertake or undergo an action): *China was ripe for revolution* **5 ripe old age** an elderly but healthy age
WORD ORIGIN Old English *rīpe*

ripen *vb* **1** to make or become ripe **2** to mature

Ripley *n* **George** 1802–80, US social reformer and transcendentalist: founder of the Brook Farm experiment in communal living in Massachusetts (1841)

rip off ❶ *slang vb* **1** to cheat by overcharging **2** to steal (something) ▷ *n* **rip-off 3** a grossly overpriced article **4** the act of stealing or cheating

riposte (rip-posst) *n* **1** a swift clever reply **2** *fencing* a counterattack made immediately after a successful parry ▷ *vb* **-posting, -posted 3** to make a riposte
WORD ORIGIN French

ripple *n* **1** a slight wave on the surface of water **2** a slight ruffling of a surface **3** a sound like water flowing gently in ripples: *a ripple of applause* **4** vanilla ice cream with stripes of another ice cream through it: *raspberry ripple* ▷ *vb* **-pling, -pled 5** to form ripples or flow with a waving motion **6** (of sounds) to rise and fall gently **rippling** *adj*
WORD ORIGIN origin unknown

rip-roaring *adj informal* boisterous and exciting

ripsaw *n* a handsaw for cutting along the grain of timber

r

THESAURUS

splash, cleanse, bathe, wash out ▷ *n* **5 = wash**, wetting, dip, splash, bath

riot *n* **1 = disturbance**, row, disorder, confusion, turmoil, quarrel, upheaval, fray, strife, uproar, turbulence, commotion, lawlessness, street fighting, tumult, donnybrook, mob violence **3 = display**, show, splash, flourish, extravaganza, profusion **4** *(slang)* **= laugh**, joke, scream *(informal)*, blast *(US slang)*, hoot *(informal)*, lark ▷ *vb* **7 = rampage**, take to the streets, run riot, go on the rampage, fight in the streets, raise an uproar

rip *vb* **1 = be torn**, tear, split, burst, be rent **1, 2 = tear**, cut, score, split, burst, rend, slash, hack, claw, slit, gash, lacerate ▷ *n* **5 = tear**, cut, hole, split, rent, slash, slit, cleavage, gash, laceration

ripe *adj* **1 = ripened**, seasoned, ready, mature, mellow, fully developed, fully grown **OPPOSITE:** unripe **3 = right**, suitable

rip off *n* **3** *(slang)* **= cheat**, con *(informal)*, scam *(slang)*, con trick *(informal)*, fraud, theft, sting *(informal)*, robbery, exploitation, swindle, daylight robbery *(informal)*

DICTIONARY

rise ❶ *vb* **rising, rose, risen 1** to get up from a lying, sitting, or kneeling position **2** to get out of bed, esp. to begin one's day: *she rises at 5 am every day to look after her horse* **3** to move from a lower to a higher position or place **4** to appear above the horizon: *as the sun rises higher the mist disappears* **5** to slope upwards: *the road crossed the valley then rose to a low ridge* **6** to increase in height or level: *the tide rose* **7** to swell up: *dough rises* **8** to increase in strength or degree: *frustration is rising amongst sections of the population* **9** to increase in amount or value: *living costs are rising at an annual rate of nine per cent* **10** *informal* to respond (to a challenge or remark) **11** to revolt: *the people rose against their oppressors* **12** (of a court or parliament) to adjourn **13** to be resurrected **14** to become erect or rigid: *the hairs on his neck rose in fear* **15** to originate: *that river rises in the mountains* **16** *angling* (of fish) to come to the surface of the water ▷ *n* **17** the act or an instance of rising **18** a piece of rising ground **19** an increase in wages **20** an increase in amount, cost, or quantity **21** an increase in height **22** an increase in status or position **23** an increase in degree or intensity **24** the vertical height of a step or of a flight of stairs **25 get** *or* **take a rise out of** *slang* to provoke an angry reaction from **26 give rise to** to cause the development of
WORD ORIGIN Old English *rīsan*

riser *n* **1** a person who rises from bed: *an early riser* **2** the vertical part of a step

risible (riz-zib-bl) *adj formal* ridiculous
WORD ORIGIN Latin *ridere* to laugh

rising *n* **1** a rebellion ▷ *adj* **2** increasing in rank or maturity

rising damp *n* seepage of moisture from the ground into the walls of buildings

risk ❶ *n* **1** the possibility of bringing about misfortune or loss **2** a person or thing considered as a potential hazard: *in parts of the world transfusions carry the risk of infection* **3 at risk** in a dangerous situation **4 take** *or* **run a risk** to act without regard to the danger involved ▷ *vb* **5** to act in spite of the possibility of (injury or loss): *if they clamp down they risk a revolution* **6** to expose to danger or loss **risky** *adj*
WORD ORIGIN French *risque*

risk assessment *n business* an analysis of the level of risk attached to a particular activity

risotto *n, pl* **-tos** a dish of rice cooked in stock with vegetables, meat, etc.
WORD ORIGIN Italian

risqué (risk-ay) *adj* making slightly rude references to sex: *risqué humour*
WORD ORIGIN French *risquer* to risk

rissole *n* a mixture of minced cooked meat coated in egg and breadcrumbs and fried
WORD ORIGIN French

ritardando *adj, adv* ▸ same as **rallentando**
WORD ORIGIN Italian

rite ❶ *n* **1** a formal act which forms part of a religious ceremony: *the rite of burial* **2** a custom that is carried out within a particular group: *the barbaric rites of public execution* **3** a particular body of such acts, esp. of a particular Christian Church: *the traditional Anglican rite*
WORD ORIGIN Latin *ritus*

rite of passage *n* a ceremony or event that marks an important change in a person's life

ritual ❶ *n* **1** a religious or other ceremony involving a series of fixed actions performed in a certain order **2** these ceremonies collectively: *people need ritual* **3** regular repeated action or behaviour **4** stereotyped activity or behaviour ▷ *adj* **5** of or like rituals **ritually** *adv*

ritualism *n* exaggerated emphasis on the importance of rites and ceremonies **ritualistic** *adj* **ritualistically** *adv*

ritzy *adj* **ritzier, ritziest** *slang* luxurious or elegant
WORD ORIGIN after the hotels established by César Ritz

rival ❶ *n* **1** a person or group that competes with another for the same object or in the same field **2** a person or thing that is considered the equal of another: *she is without rival in the field of physics* ▷ *adj* **3** in the position of a rival ▷ *vb* **-valling, -valled** *or US* **-valing, -valed 4** to be the equal or near equal of: *his inarticulateness was rivalled only by that of his brother* **5** to try to equal or surpass
WORD ORIGIN Latin *rivalis*, literally: one who shares the same brook

rivalry ❶ *n, pl* **-ries** active competition between people or groups

riven *adj old-fashioned* **1** split apart: *the party is riven by factions* **2** torn to shreds
WORD ORIGIN Old Norse *rīfa* to tear, rend

river ❶ *n* **1** a large natural stream of fresh water flowing along a definite course into the sea, a lake, or a larger river ▸ Related adjective: **fluvial 2** an abundant stream or flow: *rivers of blood*
WORD ORIGIN Old French *riviere*

Rivera *n* **Diego** 1886–1957, Mexican painter, noted for his monumental murals in public buildings, which are influenced by Aztec art and depict revolutionary themes

rivet (riv-vit) *n* **1** a short metal pin for fastening metal plates, with a head

r

THESAURUS

rise *vb* **1 = get up**, stand up, get to your feet **2 = arise**, surface, get out of bed, rise and shine **3 = go up**, climb, move up, ascend **OPPOSITE:** descend **5 = get steeper**, mount, climb, ascend, go uphill, slope upwards **OPPOSITE:** drop **6, 9 = increase**, mount, soar **OPPOSITE:** decrease **8 = grow**, go up, intensify **11 = rebel**, resist, revolt, mutiny, take up arms, mount the barricades ▷ *n* **18 = upward slope**, incline, elevation, ascent, hillock, rising ground, acclivity, kopje *or* koppie *(S African)* **19 = pay increase**, raise *(US)*, increment **20 = increase**, climb, upturn, upswing, advance, improvement, ascent, upsurge, upward turn **OPPOSITE:** decrease **22 = advancement**, progress, climb, promotion, aggrandizement **26 give rise to something = cause**, produce, effect, result in, provoke, bring about, bring on

risk *n* **1 = danger**, chance, possibility, speculation, uncertainty, hazard **2 = gamble**, chance, venture, speculation, leap in the dark ▷ *vb* **5 = stand a chance of 6 = dare**, endanger, jeopardize, imperil, venture, gamble, hazard, take a chance on, put in jeopardy, expose to danger

rite *n* **1, 2 = ceremony**, custom, ritual, act, service, form, practice, procedure, mystery, usage, formality, ceremonial, communion, ordinance, observance, sacrament, liturgy, solemnity

ritual *n* **1, 2, 3 = ceremony**, rite, ceremonial, sacrament, service, mystery, communion, observance, liturgy, solemnity ▷ *adj* **5 = ceremonial**, formal, conventional, routine, prescribed, stereotyped, customary, procedural, habitual, ceremonious

rival *n* **1 = opponent**, competitor, contender, challenger, contestant, adversary, antagonist, emulator **OPPOSITE:** supporter ▷ *adj* **3 = competing**, conflicting, opposed, opposing, competitive, emulating ▷ *vb* **4, 5 = compete with**, match, equal, oppose, compare with, contend, come up to, emulate, vie with, measure up to, be a match for, bear comparison with, seek to displace

rivalry *n* **= competition**, competitiveness, vying, opposition, struggle, conflict, contest, contention, duel, antagonism, emulation

river *n* **1 = stream**, brook, creek, beck, waterway, tributary, rivulet, watercourse, burn *(Scot)* **2 = flow**, rush, flood, spate, torrent

DICTIONARY

at one end, the other end being hammered flat after being put through holes in the plates ▷ *vb* **-eting, -eted 2** to join by riveting **3** to cause a person's attention to be fixed in fascination or horror: *their eyes riveted on the protesters* **riveter** *n*
WORD ORIGIN Old French *river* to fasten
riveting ❶ *adj* very interesting or exciting
rivulet *n* a small stream
WORD ORIGIN Latin *rivus* stream
Rizal[1] *n* another name for **Pasay**
Rizal[2] *n* **Jose** 1861–96, Philippine nationalist, executed by the Spanish during the Philippine revolution of 1896
Rizzio *or* **Riccio** *n* **David** ?1533–66, Italian musician and courtier who became the secretary and favourite of Mary, Queen of Scots. He was murdered at the instigation of a group of nobles, including Mary's husband, Darnley
RM 1 Royal Mail **2** Royal Marines **3** (in Canada) Rural Municipality **4** (in Canada) Regional Municipality
RMT (in Britain) (National Union of) Rail, Maritime and Transport (Workers)
Rn *chem* radon
RN 1 (in Canada and New Zealand) Registered Nurse **2** (in Britain) Royal Navy
RNA *n biochem* ribonucleic acid: any of a group of nucleic acids, present in all living cells, that play an essential role in the synthesis of proteins
RNLI (in Britain) Royal National Lifeboat Institution
RNZ Radio New Zealand
RNZAF Royal New Zealand Air Force
RNZN Royal New Zealand Navy
roach[1] *n, pl* **roaches** *or* **roach** a European freshwater food fish
WORD ORIGIN Old French *roche*
roach[2] *n chiefly US & Canad* a cockroach
Roach *n* **Hal**, full name *Harald Eugene Roach*. 1892–1992, US film producer, whose company produced numerous comedy films in the 1920s and 1930s, including those featuring Harold Lloyd and Laurel and Hardy
road ❶ *n* **1** a route, usually surfaced, used by travellers and vehicles to get from one place to another **2** a street **3** a way or course: *on the road to recovery* **4** *naut* ▸ same as **roadstead 5 one for the road** *informal* a last alcoholic drink before leaving **6 on the road** travelling about
WORD ORIGIN Old English *rād*
roadblock *n* a barrier set up across a road by the police or military, in order to stop and check vehicles
road hog *n informal* a selfish or aggressive driver
roadholding *n* the extent to which a vehicle is stable and does not skid on bends or wet roads
roadhouse *n* a pub or restaurant at the side of a road
roadie *n Brit, Austral & NZ informal* a person who transports and sets up equipment for a band
road metal *n* crushed rock or broken stone used in building roads
road rage *n* aggressive behaviour by a motorist in response to the actions of another road user
road show *n* **1** *radio* a live broadcast from a radio van taking a particular programme on a tour of the country **2** a group of entertainers on tour
roadside *n* **1** the edge of a road ▷ *adj* **2** by the edge or side of a road: *a roadside café*
roadstead *n naut* a partly sheltered anchorage
roadster *n* an open car with only two seats
road tax *n* (in Britain) a tax paid on vehicles used on the roads
road test *n* **1** a test of something, such as a vehicle in actual use ▷ *vb* **road-test 2** to test (a vehicle etc.) in actual use
roadway *n* the part of a road that is used by vehicles
roadworks *pl n* repairs to a road or cable under a road, esp. when they block part of the road
roadworthy *adj* (of a motor vehicle) mechanically sound **roadworthiness** *n*
roam ❶ *vb* to walk about with no fixed purpose or direction
WORD ORIGIN origin unknown
roan *adj* **1** (of a horse) having a brown or black coat sprinkled with white hairs ▷ *n* **2** a horse with such a coat
WORD ORIGIN Spanish *roano*
roar ❶ *vb* **1** (of lions and other animals) to make loud growling cries **2** to shout (something) with a loud deep cry: *'Don't do that!' he roared at me* **3** to make a very loud noise: *the engine roared* **4** to laugh in a loud hearty manner **5** (of a fire) to burn fiercely with a roaring sound ▷ *n* **6** a roaring noise: *there was a roar as the train came in* **7** a loud deep cry, uttered by a person or crowd, esp. in anger or triumph: *a roar of approval came from the crowd*
WORD ORIGIN Old English *rārian*
roaring *adj* **1 a roaring trade** a brisk and profitable business ▷ *adv* **2 roaring drunk** noisily or boisterously drunk
roast *vb* **1** to cook (food) by dry heat in an oven or over a fire **2** to brown or dry (coffee or nuts) by exposure to heat **3** to make or be extremely hot **4** *informal* to criticize severely ▷ *n* **5** a roasted joint of meat ▷ *adj* **6** cooked by roasting: *roast beef* **roaster** *n*
WORD ORIGIN Old French *rostir*
roasting *informal adj* **1** extremely hot ▷ *n* **2** severe criticism or scolding
rob ❶ *vb* **robbing, robbed 1** to take something from (a person or place) illegally **2** to deprive, esp. of something deserved: *I can't forgive him for robbing me of an Olympic gold* **robber** *n*
WORD ORIGIN Old French *rober*
Robbe-Grillet *n* **Alain** born 1922, French novelist and screenwriter. Author of *The Voyeur* (1955), *Jealousy* (1957), and *Djinn* (1981): he is one of the leading practitioners of the antinovel
robbery ❶ *n, pl* **-beries 1** *criminal law* the stealing of property from a person by using or threatening to use force **2** the act or an instance of robbing
Robbia *n* **1 Andrea della** 1435–1525, Florentine sculptor, best known for his polychrome reliefs and his statues of infants in swaddling clothes **2** his uncle, **Luca della** ?1400–82, Florentine sculptor, who perfected a technique of enamelling terra cotta for reliefs
Robbins *n* **Jerome** 1918–98, US ballet dancer and choreographer. He choreographed the musicals *The King and I* (1951) and *West Side Story* (1957)
robe ❶ *n* **1** a long loose flowing garment **2** a dressing gown or bathrobe ▷ *vb* **robing, robed 3** to put a robe on
WORD ORIGIN Old French
Robert II *n* 1316–90, king of Scotland (1371–90)

THESAURUS

riveting *adj* **= enthralling**, arresting, gripping, fascinating, absorbing, captivating, hypnotic, engrossing, spellbinding
road *n* **1, 2 = roadway**, street, highway, motorway, track, direction, route, path, lane, avenue, pathway, thoroughfare, course **3 = way**, path
roam *vb* **= wander**, walk, range, travel, drift, stroll, stray, ramble, prowl, meander, rove, stravaig (*Scot & Northern English dialect*), peregrinate
roar *vb* **2, 4 = cry**, shout, yell, howl, bellow, clamour, bawl, bay, vociferate ▷ *n* **7 = cry**, crash, shout, yell, howl, outcry, bellow, clamour
rob *vb* **1 = steal from**, hold up, rifle, mug (*informal*), stiff (*slang*) **2 = deprive**, strip, do out of (*informal*)
robbery *n* **1** (*criminal law*) **= burglary**, raid, hold-up, rip-off (*slang*), stick-up (*slang, chiefly US*), home invasion (*Austral & NZ*) **2 = theft**, stealing, fraud, steaming (*informal*), mugging (*informal*), plunder, swindle, pillage, embezzlement, larceny, depredation, filching, thievery, rapine, spoliation
robe *n* **1 = gown**, costume, vestment, habit

r

DICTIONARY

Robert III *n* ?1337–1406, king of Scotland (1390–1406), son of Robert II

Roberts *n* **1 Frederick Sleigh**, 1st Earl. 1832–1914, British field marshal. He was awarded the Victoria Cross (1858) for his service during the Indian Mutiny and was commander in chief (1899–1900) in the second Boer War **2 Julia** born 1967, US film actress; her films include *Pretty Woman* (1990), *Notting Hill* (1999), *Erin Brockovich* (2000), which earned her an Academy Award, and *Mona Lisa Smile* (2003)

Robertson *n* **George** (**Islay Macneill**), Baron. born 1946, Scottish Labour politician; secretary-general of NATO (1999–2003)

Robeson *n* **Paul** 1898–1976, US bass singer, actor, and leader in the Black civil rights movement

Robey *n* Sir **George**, original name *George Edward Wade*, known as *the prime minister of mirth*. 1869–1954, British music-hall comedian, who also appeared in films

robin *n* **1** Also called: **robin redbreast** a small Old World songbird with a brown back and an orange-red breast and face **2** a North American thrush similar to but larger than the Old World robin
WORD ORIGIN arbitrary use of name *Robin*

robot ⓣ *n* **1** a machine programmed to perform specific tasks in a human manner, esp. one with a human shape **2** a person of machine-like efficiency **3** *S African* a set of traffic lights **robotic** *adj*
WORD ORIGIN used in R.U.R., a play by a Czech writer, from Czech *robota* work

robotics *n* the science of designing, building, and using robots

Robson¹ *n* **Mount Robson** a mountain in SW Canada, in E British Columbia: the highest peak in the Canadian Rockies. Height: 3954 m (12 972 ft)

Robson² *n* **1** Sir **Bobby**, full name *Robert William*. 1933–2009, English footballer and manager of England (1982–90) **2 Bryan** born 1957, English footballer and manager: captain of England (1982–90) **3** Dame **Flora** 1902–84, English stage and film actress

robust ⓣ *adj* **1** very strong and healthy **2** sturdily built: *the new generation of robust lasers* **3** requiring or displaying physical strength: *robust tackles*
WORD ORIGIN Latin *robur* an oak, strength

roc *n* (in Arabian legend) a bird of enormous size and power
WORD ORIGIN Persian *rukh*

Rocard *n* **Michel** born 1930, French politician: prime minister of France (1988–91)

Rochester¹ *n* **1** a city in SE England, in Medway unitary authority, Kent, on the River Medway. Pop: 27 123 (2001) **2** a city in NW New York State, on Lake Ontario. Pop: 215 093 (2003 est) **3** a city in the US, in Minnesota: site of the Mayo Clinic. Pop: 92 507 (2003 est)

Rochester² *n* **2nd Earl of**, title of *John Wilmot*. 1647–80, English poet, wit, and libertine. His poems include satires, notably *A Satire against Mankind* (1675), love lyrics, and bawdy verse

rock¹ ⓣ *n* **1** *geol* the mass of mineral matter that makes up part of the earth's crust; stone **2** a large rugged mass of stone **3** *chiefly US, Canad, & Austral* a stone **4** a hard peppermint-flavoured sweet, usually in the shape of a long stick **5** a person or thing on which one can always depend: *your loyalty is a rock* **6** *slang* a precious jewel **7 on the rocks a** (of a marriage) about to end **b** (of an alcoholic drink) served with ice
WORD ORIGIN Old French *roche*

rock² ⓣ *vb* **1** to move from side to side or backwards and forwards **2** to shake or move (something) violently **3** to feel or cause to feel shock: *key events have rocked both countries* **4** to dance to or play rock music **5** *slang* to be very good ▷ *n* **6** Also called: **rock music** a style of pop music with a heavy beat **7** a rocking motion ▷ *adj* **8** of or relating to rock music
WORD ORIGIN Old English *roccian*

rockabilly *n* a fast style of White rock music which originated in the mid-1950s in the US South
WORD ORIGIN *rock and roll + hillbilly*

rock and roll *or* **rock'n'roll** *n* a type of pop music originating in the 1950s as a blend of rhythm and blues and country and western

rock bottom *n* the lowest possible level

rock cake *n* a small fruit cake with a rough surface

rock crystal *n* a pure transparent colourless quartz

rock dove *n* a common dove from which domestic and wild pigeons are descended

rocker *n* **1** a rocking chair **2** either of two curved supports on which a rocking chair stands **3** a rock music performer or fan **4 off one's rocker** *slang* crazy

rockery *n, pl* **-eries** a garden built of rocks and soil, for growing rock plants

rocket *n* **1** a self-propelling device, usually cylindrical, which produces thrust by expelling through a nozzle the gases produced by burning fuel, such as one used as a firework or distress signal **2** any vehicle propelled by a rocket engine, as a weapon or carrying a spacecraft **3** *informal* a severe reprimand: *my sister gave me a rocket for writing such dangerous nonsense* ▷ *vb* **-eting, -eted 4** to increase rapidly: *within six years their turnover had rocketed* **5** to attack with rockets
WORD ORIGIN Italian *rochetto* little distaff

rocketry *n* the science and technology of the design and operation of rockets

rock garden *n* a garden featuring rocks or rockeries

rocking chair *n* a chair set on curving supports so that the sitter may rock backwards and forwards

rocking horse *n* a toy horse mounted on a pair of rocking supports on which a child can rock to and fro

rock melon *n US, Austral, & NZ* ▸ same as **cantaloupe**

rock pool *n* a small pool between rocks on the seashore

rock salmon *n Brit* a former term for dogfish when used as a food

rock salt *n* common salt as a naturally occurring solid mineral

rock tripe *n Canad* any edible lichen that grows on rocks

Rockwell *n* **Norman** 1894–1978, US illustrator, noted esp. for magazine covers

rocky¹ ⓣ *adj* **rockier, rockiest** covered with rocks: *rocky and sandy shores*
rockiness *n*

rocky² ⓣ *adj* **rockier, rockiest** shaky or unstable: *a rocky relationship*
rockiness *n*

rococo (rok-**koe**-koe) *adj* **1** relating to an 18th-century style of architecture, decoration, and music characterized

THESAURUS

robot *n* **1 = machine**, automaton, android, mechanical man

robust *adj* **1, 2 = strong**, tough, powerful, athletic, well, sound, fit, healthy, strapping, hardy, rude, vigorous, rugged, muscular, sturdy, hale, stout, staunch, hearty, husky (*informal*), in good health, lusty, alive and kicking, fighting fit, sinewy, brawny, in fine fettle, thickset, fit as a fiddle (*informal*), able-bodied
OPPOSITE: weak

rock¹ *n* **2, 3 = stone**, boulder

rock² *vb* **3 = shock**, surprise, shake, stun, astonish, stagger, jar, astound, daze, dumbfound, set you back on your heels (*informal*)

rocky¹ *adj* **= rough**, rugged, stony, craggy, pebbly, boulder-strewn

rocky² *adj* **= unstable**, weak, uncertain, doubtful, shaky, unreliable, wobbly, rickety, unsteady, undependable

rod *n* **1 = stick**, bar, pole, shaft, switch,

DICTIONARY

by elaborate ornamentation **2** excessively elaborate in style
WORD ORIGIN French

rod ❶ *n* **1** a thin straight pole made of wood or metal **2** a cane used to beat people as a punishment **3** ▸ short for **fishing rod** **4** a type of cell in the retina, sensitive to dim light **rodlike** *adj*
WORD ORIGIN Old English *rodd*

Rodchenko *n* **Alexander (Mikhailovich)** 1891–1956, Soviet painter, sculptor, designer, and photographer, noted for his abstract geometrical style: a member of the constructivist movement

Roddick *n* **Anita** 1942–2007, British entrepreneur, founder (1976) of the Body Shop chain, selling natural beauty and health products

rode *vb* ▸ the past tense of **ride**

rodent *n* a small mammal with teeth specialized for gnawing, such as a rat, mouse, or squirrel **rodent-like** *adj*
WORD ORIGIN Latin *rodere* to gnaw

rodeo *n, pl* **-deos** a display of the skills of cowboys, including bareback riding
WORD ORIGIN Spanish

Rodgers *n* **Richard** 1902–79, US composer of musical comedies. He collaborated with the librettist Lorenz Hart on such musicals as *A Connecticut Yankee* (1927), *On Your Toes* (1936), and *Pal Joey* (1940). After Hart's death his librettist was Oscar Hammerstein II. Two of their musicals, *Oklahoma!* (1943) and *South Pacific* (1949), received the Pulitzer Prize

Rodney *n* **George Brydges**, 1st Baron Rodney. 1719–92, English admiral: captured Martinique (1762): defeated the Spanish at Cape St Vincent (1780) and the French under Admiral de Grasse off Dominica (1782), restoring British superiority in the Caribbean

rodomontade *n literary* boastful words or behaviour
WORD ORIGIN French

Rodrigo *n* **Joaquín** 1902–99, Spanish composer. His works include *Concierto de Aranjuez* (1940) for guitar and orchestra and *Concierto Pastorale* (1978)

roe[1] *n* the ovary and eggs of a female fish, sometimes eaten as food
WORD ORIGIN Middle Dutch *roge*

roe[2] *or* **roe deer** *n* a small graceful deer with short antlers
WORD ORIGIN Old English *rā(ha)*

Roeg *n* **Nic(olas)** born 1928, British film director and cinematographer. Films include *Walkabout* (1970), *Don't Look Now* (1972), *Insignificance* (1984), and *The Witches* (1990)

roentgen (**ront**-gan) *n* a unit measuring a radiation dose
WORD ORIGIN after the German physicist *Roentgen*, who discovered X-rays

Roethke *n* **Theodore** 1908–63, US poet, whose books include *Words for the Wind* (1957) and *The Far Field* (1964)

roger *interj* **1** (used in signalling) message received **2** an expression of agreement
WORD ORIGIN from the name *Roger*, representing R for *received*

Roger II *n* 1095–1154, Norman king of Siciliy (1130–54). His court was an intellectual centre for Muslim and Christian scholars

Roget *n* **Peter Mark** 1779–1869, English physician, who on retirement devised a *Thesaurus of English Words and Phrases* (1852), a classified list of synonyms

rogue ❶ *n* **1** a dishonest or unprincipled person **2** a mischievous person **3** a crop plant which is inferior, diseased, or of a different variety **4** an inferior or defective specimen ▹ *adj* **5** (of a wild animal) having a savage temper and living apart from the herd: *a rogue elephant* **6** inferior or defective: *rogue heroin* **roguish** *adj*
WORD ORIGIN origin unknown

roguery *n, pl* **-gueries** dishonest or immoral behaviour

rogues' gallery *n* a collection of photographs of known criminals kept by the police for identification purposes

Röhm *n* **Ernst** 1887–1934, German soldier, who organized (1921–34) Hitler's storm troops: murdered on Hitler's orders

ROI **1** Republic of Ireland **2** *finance* return on investment

roister *vb old-fashioned* to enjoy oneself noisily and boisterously **roisterer** *n*
WORD ORIGIN Old French *rustre* lout

Roland *n* the greatest of the legendary 12 peers (paladins, of whom Oliver was another) in attendance on Charlemagne; he died in battle at Roncesvalles (778 AD)

role ❶ *n* **1** a task or function: *their role in international relations* **2** an actor's part in a production
WORD ORIGIN French

role model *n* a person regarded by others, esp. younger people, as a good example to follow

Rolf *or* **Rolf the Ganger** *n* other names for **Rollo**

Rolfe *n* **Frederick William**, also known as *Baron Corvo*. 1860–1913, British novelist. His best-known work is *Hadrian the Seventh* (1904)

roll ❶ *vb* **1** to move along by turning over and over **2** to move along on wheels or rollers **3** to curl or make by curling into a ball or tube **4** to move along in an undulating movement **5** to rotate wholly or partially: *he would snort in derision, roll his eyes, and heave a deep sigh* **6** to spread out flat or smooth with a roller or rolling pin: *roll the pastry out thinly* **7** (of a ship or aircraft) to turn from side to side around the longitudinal axis **8** to operate or begin to operate: *the cameras continued to roll as she pulled up to the nightclub* **9** to make a continuous deep reverberating sound: *the thunder rolled* **10** to walk in a swaying manner: *the drunks came rolling home* **11** to appear like a series of waves: *mountain ranges rolling away in every direction* **12** to pass or elapse: *watching the time roll away* **13** (of animals) to turn onto the back and kick **14** to trill or cause to be trilled: *she rolled her r's* **15** to throw (dice) ▹ *n* **16** the act or an instance of rolling **17** anything rolled up into a tube: *a roll of paper towels* **18** a small cake of bread for one person **19** a flat pastry or cake rolled up with a meat, jam, or other filling **20** an official list or register of names: *the electoral roll; the voters' roll* **21** a complete rotation about its longitudinal axis by an aircraft **22** a continuous deep reverberating sound: *the roll of musketry* **23** a swaying or unsteady movement or gait **24** a rounded mass: *rolls of fat* **25** a very rapid beating of the sticks on a drum **26** **on a roll** *slang* experiencing continued good luck or success **27** **strike off the roll** to expel from

r

THESAURUS

crook, cane, birch, dowel **2 = staff**, baton, mace, wand, sceptre

rogue *n* **1 = scoundrel**, crook *(informal)*, villain, fraudster, sharper, fraud, cheat, devil, deceiver, charlatan, con man *(informal)*, swindler, knave *(archaic)*, ne'er-do-well, reprobate, scumbag *(slang)*, blackguard, mountebank, grifter *(slang, chiefly US & Canad)*, skelm *(S African)*, rorter *(Austral slang)*, wrong 'un *(slang)* **2 = scamp**, rascal, scally *(Northwest English dialect)*, rapscallion, nointer *(Austral slang)*

role *n* **1 = job**, part, position, post, task, duty, function, capacity **2 = part**, character, representation, portrayal, impersonation

roll *vb* **1 = turn**, wheel, spin, reel, go round, revolve, rotate, whirl, swivel, pivot, twirl, gyrate **2 = trundle**, go, move **4 = flow**, run, course, slide, glide, purl **6 = level**, even, press, spread, smooth, flatten **7 = toss**, rock, lurch, reel, tumble, sway, wallow, billow, swing, welter ▹ *n* **20 = register**, record, list, table, schedule, index, catalogue, directory, inventory, census, chronicle, scroll, roster, annals **21 = turn**, run, spin, rotation, cycle, wheel, revolution, reel, whirl, twirl, undulation, gyration **22 = rumble**, boom,

DICTIONARY

membership of a professional association ▸See also **roll in, roll on,** etc.

WORD ORIGIN Old French *roler*

Rolland *n* **Romain** 1866–1944, French novelist, dramatist, and essayist, known for his novels about a musical genius, *Jean-Christophe*, (1904–12): Nobel prize for literature 1915

roll call *n* the reading aloud of an official list of names, to check who is present

rolled gold *n* a metal, such as brass, coated with a thin layer of gold

roller *n* **1** a rotating cylinder used for smoothing, supporting a thing to be moved, spreading paint, etc. **2** a small tube around which hair may be wound in order to make it curly **3** a long heavy wave of the sea **4** a cylinder fitted on pivots, used to enable heavy objects to be easily moved

Rollerblade *n trademark* a type of roller skate in which the wheels are set in a single straight line under the boot

roller coaster *n* (at a funfair) a narrow railway with open carriages, sharp curves and steep slopes

roller skate *n* **1** a shoe with four small wheels that enable the wearer to glide swiftly over a floor ▹*vb* **roller-skate, -skating, -skated 2** to move on roller skates **roller skater** *n*

roller towel *n* **1** a towel with the two ends sewn together, hung on a roller **2** a towel wound inside a roller enabling a clean section to be pulled out when needed

rollicking *adj* boisterously carefree: *a rollicking read*

WORD ORIGIN origin unknown

roll in *vb* **1** to arrive in large numbers **2 be rolling in** *slang* to have plenty of (money etc.)

rolling *adj* **1** having gentle rising and falling slopes: *rolling hills* **2** (of a walk) slow and swaying **3** subject to regular review and updating: *a 10-year rolling programme* **4** progressing by stages or in succession: *a rolling campaign*

rolling mill *n* **1** a factory where metal ingots are passed between rollers to produce sheets or bars of the required shape **2** a machine with rollers for doing this

rolling pin *n* a cylinder with handles at both ends used for rolling pastry

rolling stock *n* the locomotives and coaches of a railway

rolling stone *n* a restless or wandering person

Rolling Stones *pl n* **the.** British rock group (formed 1962): comprising Mick Jagger, Keith Richards (born 1943; guitar, vocals), Brian Jones (1942–69; guitar), Charlie Watts (born 1941; drums), Bill Wyman (born 1936; bass guitar; now retired), and subsequently Mick Taylor (born 1948; guitar; with the group 1969–74) and Ron Wood (born 1947; guitar; with the group from 1975) ▸See also **Jagger**

Rollins *n* **Sonny**, original name *Theodore Walter Rollins*. born 1930, US jazz tenor saxophonist, noted for his improvisation

rollmop *n* a herring fillet rolled around onion slices and pickled

WORD ORIGIN German *rollen* to roll + *Mops* pug dog

rollneck *adj* (of a garment) having a high neck that is worn rolled over

Rollo *n* ?860–?930 AD, Norse war leader who received from Charles the Simple a fief that formed the basis of the duchy of Normandy. Also: **Rolf, Rolf the Ganger**

roll of honour *n* a list of those who have died in war for their country

roll on *interj* **1** used to express the wish that an eagerly anticipated event will come quickly: *roll on the next light-hearted romp* ▹*adj* **roll-on 2** (of a deodorant) applied by means of a revolving ball fitted into the neck of the container

roll-on/roll-off *adj* denoting a ship designed so that vehicles can be driven straight on and straight off

roll over *vb* **1** to overturn **2** to allow (a loan or prize) to continue in force for a further period ▹*n* **rollover 3** an instance of such a continuance of a loan or prize

roll-top *adj* (of a desk) having a slatted wooden panel that can be pulled down over the writing surface when not in use

roll up *vb* **1** to form into a cylindrical shape: *roll up a length of black material* **2** *informal* to arrive ▹*n* **roll-up 3** *Brit informal* a cigarette made by the smoker from loose tobacco and cigarette papers

roly-poly *adj* **1** plump or chubby ▹*n, pl* **-lies 2** *Brit* a strip of suet pastry spread with jam, rolled up, and baked or steamed

WORD ORIGIN probably from *roll*

ROM *n computers* read only memory: a storage device that holds data permanently and cannot be altered by the programmer

Romains *n* **Jules** pseudonym of *Louis Farigoule* 1885–1972, French poet, dramatist, and novelist. His works include the novel *Men of Good Will* (1932–46)

roman *adj* **1** in or relating to the vertical style of printing type used for most printed matter ▹*n* **2** roman type

WORD ORIGIN so called because the style of letters is that used in ancient Roman inscriptions

Roman *adj* **1** of Rome, a city in Italy, or its inhabitants in ancient or modern times **2** of Roman Catholicism or the Roman Catholic Church ▹*n* **3** a person from ancient or modern Rome

Roman alphabet *n* the alphabet evolved by the ancient Romans for writing Latin, used for writing most of the languages of W Europe, including English

Roman blind *n* a window blind which gathers into horizontal folds from the bottom when drawn up

Roman candle *n* a firework that produces a steady stream of coloured sparks

WORD ORIGIN it originated in Italy

Roman Catholic *adj* **1** of the Roman Catholic Church ▹*n* **2** a member of this Church **Roman Catholicism** *n*

Roman Catholic Church *n* the Christian Church over which the pope presides

romance ❶ *n* **1** a love affair: *a failed romance* **2** love, esp. romantic love idealized for its purity or beauty **3** a spirit of or inclination for adventure or mystery **4** a mysterious or sentimental quality **5** a story or film dealing with love, usually in an idealized way **6** a story or film dealing with events and characters remote from ordinary life **7** an extravagant, absurd, or fantastic account **8** a medieval narrative dealing with adventures of chivalrous heroes ▹*vb* **-mancing, -manced 9** to tell extravagant or improbable lies

WORD ORIGIN Old French *romans*

Romance *adj* of the languages derived from Latin, such as French, Spanish, and Italian

Romanesque *adj* of or in the style of architecture used in Europe from the 9th to the 12th century, characterized by rounded arches and massive walls

Romanian *adj* **1** of Romania ▹*n* **2** a person from Romania **3** the language of Romania

Roman nose *n* a nose with a high prominent bridge

THESAURUS

drumming, roar, thunder, grumble, resonance, growl, reverberation

romance *n* **1 = love affair**, relationship, affair, intrigue, attachment, liaison, amour, affair of the heart, affaire (du coeur) *(French)* **3 = excitement**, colour, charm, mystery, adventure, sentiment, glamour, fascination, nostalgia, exoticness **5 = story**, novel, tale, fantasy, legend, fiction, fairy tale, love story, melodrama, idyll, tear-jerker *(informal)*

romantic *adj* **1, 3 = loving**, tender, passionate, fond, sentimental,

DICTIONARY

Roman numerals *pl n* the letters used as numerals by the Romans, used occasionally today: I (= 1), V (= 5), X (= 10), L (= 50), C (= 100), D (= 500), and M (= 1000). VI = 6 (V + I) but IV = 4 (V – I)

romantic ❶ *adj* **1** of or dealing with love **2** idealistic but impractical: *a romantic notion* **3** evoking or given to thoughts and feelings of love: *romantic images* **4 Romantic** relating to a movement in European art, music, and literature in the late 18th and early 19th centuries, characterized by an emphasis on feeling and content rather than order and form ▷ *n* **5** a person who is idealistic or amorous **6** a person who likes or produces artistic works in the style of Romanticism **romantically** *adv*

romanticism *n* **1** idealistic but unrealistic thoughts and feelings **2 Romanticism** the spirit and style of the Romantic art, music, and literature of the late 18th and early 19th centuries **romanticist** *n*

romanticize *or* **-cise** *vb* **-cizing, -cized** *or* **-cising, -cised** to describe or regard (something or someone) in an unrealistic and idealized way: *the Victorian legacy of romanticizing family life*

Romany *n* **1** *pl* **-nies** a Gypsy **2** the language of the Gypsies
WORD ORIGIN Romany *romani* (adjective) Gypsy

Romberg *n* **Sigmund** 1887–1951, US composer of operettas, born in Hungary. He wrote *The Student Prince* (1924) and *The Desert Song* (1926)

Romeo *n, pl* **Romeos** an ardent male lover
WORD ORIGIN after the hero of Shakespeare's *Romeo and Juliet*

Romney *n* **George** 1734–1802, English painter, who painted more than 50 portraits of Lady Hamilton in various historical roles

romp ❶ *vb* **1** to play or run about wildly or joyfully **2 romp home** *or* **in** to win a race or other competition easily **3 romp through** to do (something) quickly and easily ▷ *n* **4** a noisy or boisterous game or prank
WORD ORIGIN probably from Old French *ramper* to crawl, climb

rompers *pl n* Also called: **romper suit** a one-piece baby garment combining trousers and a top

rondavel *n S African* a small circular building with a cone-shaped roof
WORD ORIGIN origin unknown

rondeau (ron-doe) *n, pl* **-deaux** (-doe) a poem consisting of 13 or 10 lines with the opening words of the first line used as a refrain
WORD ORIGIN Old French

rondo *n, pl* **-dos** a piece of music with a leading theme continually returned to: often forms the last movement of a sonata or concerto
WORD ORIGIN Italian

roo *n, pl* **roos** *Austral informal* a kangaroo

rood *n* **1** *Christianity* the Cross **2** a crucifix
WORD ORIGIN Old English *rōd*

rood screen *n* (in a church) a screen separating the nave from the choir

roof *n, pl* **roofs 1** a structure that covers or forms the top of a building **2** the top covering of a vehicle, oven, or other structure **3** the highest part of the mouth or a cave **4 hit** *or* **go through the roof** *informal* to get extremely angry **5 raise the roof** *informal* to be very noisy ▷ *vb* **6** to put a roof on
WORD ORIGIN Old English *hrōf*

roof garden *n* a garden on a flat roof of a building

roofing *n* material used to build a roof

roof rack *n* a rack for carrying luggage attached to the roof of a car

rooftree *n* ▸ same as **ridgepole**

rooibos (roy-boss) *n S African* a kind of tea made from the leaves of a South African wild shrub. Also called: **rooibos tea, bush tea**
WORD ORIGIN Afrikaans *rooi* red + *bos* bush

rooinek (roy-neck) *n S African* a contemptuous name for an Englishman
WORD ORIGIN Afrikaans *rooi* red + *nek* neck

rook[1] *n* **1** a large European black bird of the crow family ▷ *vb* **2** *old-fashioned, slang* to cheat or swindle
WORD ORIGIN Old English *hrōc*

rook[2] *n* a chessman that may move any number of unoccupied squares in a straight line, horizontally or vertically; castle
WORD ORIGIN Arabic *rukhkh*

rookery *n, pl* **-eries 1** a group of nesting rooks **2** a colony of penguins or seals

rookie *n informal* a newcomer without much experience
WORD ORIGIN changed from *recruit*

room ❶ *n* **1** an area within a building enclosed by a floor, a ceiling, and walls **2** the people present in a room: *the whole room was laughing* **3** unoccupied or unobstructed space: *there wasn't enough room* **4 room for** opportunity or scope for: *there was no room for acts of heroism* **5 rooms** lodgings ▷ *vb* **6** *US* to occupy or share a rented room: *I roomed with him for five years*
WORD ORIGIN Old English *rūm*

rooming house *n US* a house with self-contained furnished rooms or flats for renting

roommate *n* a person with whom one shares a room or apartment

room service *n* service in a hotel providing food and drinks in guests' rooms

roomy *adj* **roomier, roomiest** with plenty of space inside: *a roomy entrance hall* **roominess** *n*

Rooney *n* **Wayne** born 1985, English footballer; he played for Everton (2002–2004) and plays for Manchester United (from 2004) and England (from 2003)

roost *n* **1** a place where birds rest or sleep ▷ *vb* **2** to rest or sleep on a roost **3 come home to roost** to have unfavourable repercussions **4 rule the roost** to have authority over people in a particular place
WORD ORIGIN Old English *hrōst*

rooster *n* the male of the domestic fowl; a cock

root[1] ❶ *n* **1** the part of a plant that anchors the rest of the plant in the ground and absorbs water and mineral salts from the soil **2** a plant with an edible root, such as a carrot **3** *anat* the part of a tooth, hair, or nail that is below the skin **4 roots** a person's sense of belonging in a place, esp. the one in which he or she was brought up **5** source or origin **6** the essential part or nature of something: *the root of a problem* **7** *linguistics* the form of a word from which other words and forms are derived **8** *maths* a quantity that

r

THESAURUS

sloppy *(informal)*, amorous, mushy *(informal)*, soppy *(Brit informal)*, lovey-dovey, icky *(informal)*
OPPOSITE: unromantic
2 = idealistic, unrealistic, visionary, high-flown, impractical, dreamy, utopian, whimsical, quixotic, starry-eyed **OPPOSITE:** realistic
▷ *n* **5 = idealist**, romancer, visionary, dreamer, utopian, Don Quixote, sentimentalist

romp *vb* **1 = frolic**, sport, skip, have fun, revel, caper, cavort, frisk, gambol, make merry, rollick, roister, cut capers ▷ *n* **4 = frolic**, lark *(informal)*, caper

room *n* **1 = chamber**, office, apartment **3 = space**, area, territory, volume, capacity, extent, expanse, elbowroom

root[1] *n* **1 = stem**, tuber, rhizome, radix, radicle **4** *(pl)* **= sense of belonging**, origins, heritage, birthplace, home, family, cradle **5, 6 = source**, cause, heart, bottom, beginnings, base, seat, occasion, seed, foundation, origin, core, fundamental, essence, nucleus, starting point, germ, crux, nub, derivation, fountainhead, mainspring

root[2] *vb* **2** *(informal)* **= dig**, hunt, nose, poke, burrow, delve, ferret, pry, rummage, forage, rootle

DICTIONARY

when multiplied by itself a certain number of times equals a given quantity: *what is the cube root of a thousand?* **9** Also called: **solution** *maths* a number that when substituted for the variable satisfies a given equation **10** *Austral & NZ slang* sexual intercourse **11 root and branch** entirely or utterly ▸ Related adjective: **radical** *vb* **12** Also: **take root** to establish a root and begin to grow **13** Also: **take root** to become established or embedded **14** *Austral & NZ slang* to have sexual intercourse (with) ▸ See also **root out, roots**
WORD ORIGIN Old English *rōt*

root[2] *vb* **1** *Brit* to dig up the earth in search of food, using the snout: *dogs were rooting in the rushes for bones* **2** *informal* to search vigorously but unsystematically: *she was rooting around in her large untidy purse*
WORD ORIGIN Old English *wrōtan*

root canal *n* the passage in the root of a tooth through which its nerves and blood vessels enter

root crop *n* a crop, such as potato or turnip, cultivated for its roots

root for *vb informal* to give support to (a team or contestant)
WORD ORIGIN origin unknown

rootle *vb* **-ling, -led** *Brit* ▸ same as **root**[2]

rootless *adj* having no sense of belonging: *a rootless city dweller*

root mean square *n* the square root of the average of the squares of a set of numbers or quantities, for example *the root mean square of* 1, 2, *and* 4 *is* $\sqrt{[(1^2 + 2^2 + 4^2)/3]} = \sqrt{7}$

root out *vb* to get rid of completely: *a major drive to root out corruption*

roots *adj* (of popular music) going back to the origins of a style, esp. in being unpretentious: *roots reggae*

rootstock *n* ▸ same as **rhizome**

rope *n* **1** a fairly thick cord made of intertwined fibres or wire **2** a row of objects fastened to form a line: *a twenty-inch rope of pearls* **3 know the ropes** to have a thorough understanding of a particular activity **4 the rope a** a rope noose used for hanging someone **b** death by hanging ▹ *vb* **roping, roped 5** to tie with a rope **6 rope off** to enclose or divide with a rope
WORD ORIGIN Old English *rāp*

rope in *vb* to persuade to take part in some activity

ropey *or* **ropy** *adj* **ropier, ropiest** *Brit informal* **1** poor or unsatisfactory in quality: *a ropey performance* **2** slightly unwell **ropiness** *n*

Roquefort *n* a strong blue-veined cheese made from ewes' milk
WORD ORIGIN after *Roquefort*, village in S France

ro-ro *adj* (of a ferry) roll-on/roll-off

rorqual *n* a whalebone whale with a fin on the back
WORD ORIGIN Norwegian *rörhval*

Rorschach test (ror-shahk) *n psychol* a personality test consisting of a number of unstructured inkblots for interpretation
WORD ORIGIN after H. *Rorschach*, psychiatrist

rort *Austral informal n* **1** a dishonest scheme ▹ *vb* **2** to take unfair advantage of something

Rory O'Connor *n* Also called *Roderic*. ?1116–98, king of Connaught and last High King of Ireland

Rosa[1] *n* **Monte Rosa** a mountain between Italy and Switzerland: the highest in the Pennine Alps. Height: 4634 m (15 204 ft)

Rosa[2] *n* **Salvator** 1615–73, Italian artist, noted esp. for his romantic landscapes

rosaceous *adj* of or belonging to a family of plants typically having five-petalled flowers, which includes the rose, strawberry, and many fruit trees

rosary *n, pl* **-saries** *RC church* **1** a series of prayers counted on a string of beads **2** a string of beads used to count these prayers as they are recited
WORD ORIGIN Latin *rosarium* rose garden

rose[1] *n* **1** a shrub or climbing plant with prickly stems and fragrant flowers **2** the flower of any of these plants **3** a plant similar to this, such as the Christmas rose **4** a perforated cap fitted to a watering can or hose, causing the water to come out in a spray **5 bed of roses** a situation of comfort or ease ▹ *adj* **6** reddish-pink
WORD ORIGIN Latin *rosa*

rose[2] *vb* ▸ the past tense of **rise**

rosé (roe-zay) *n* a pink wine
WORD ORIGIN French

roseate (roe-zee-ate) *adj* **1** of the colour rose or pink **2** excessively optimistic

rosebay willowherb *n* a widespread perennial plant that has spikes of deep pink flowers

rosebud *n* a rose that has not yet fully opened

rose-coloured *adj* **1** reddish-pink **2 see through rose-coloured** *or* **rose-tinted glasses** *or* **spectacles** to view in an unrealistically optimistic light

rosehip *n* the berry-like fruit of a rose plant

rosella *n* a type of Australian parrot

rosemary *n, pl* **-maries** an aromatic European shrub widely cultivated for its grey-green evergreen leaves, which are used in cookery and perfumes
WORD ORIGIN Latin *ros* dew + *marinus* marine

Rosenberg *n* **1 Alfred** 1893–1946, German Nazi politician and writer, who devised much of the racial ideology of Nazism: hanged for war crimes **2 Isaac** 1890–1918, British poet and painter, best known for his poems about life in the trenches during World War I: died in action **3 Julius** 1918–53, US spy, who, with his wife **Ethel** (1914–53), was executed for passing information about nuclear weapons to the Russians

rosette *n* a rose-shaped decoration, esp. a circular bunch of ribbons

Rosewall *n* **Ken(neth)** born 1934, Australian tennis player: Australian champion 1953, 1955, and 1971–72; US champion 1956 and 1970

rose-water *n* scented water made by the distillation of rose petals

rose window *n* a circular window with spokes branching out from the centre to form a symmetrical roselike pattern

rosewood *n* a fragrant dark wood used to make furniture

Rosh Hashanah *or* **Rosh Hashana** *n* the festival celebrating the Jewish New Year
WORD ORIGIN Hebrew: beginning of the year

rosin (rozz-in) *n* **1** a translucent brittle substance produced from turpentine and used for treating the bows of stringed instruments ▹ *vb* **2** to apply rosin to
WORD ORIGIN variant of *resin*

ROSPA (in Britain) Royal Society for the Prevention of Accidents

Ross *n* **1 Diana** born 1944, US singer: lead vocalist (1961–69) with Motown group the Supremes, whose hits include "Baby Love" (1964). Her subsequent recordings include *Lady Sings the Blues* (film soundtrack, 1972), and *Chain Reaction* (1986) **2** Sir **James Clark** 1800–62, British naval officer; explorer of the Arctic and Antarctic. He located the north magnetic pole (1831) and discovered the Ross Sea during an Antarctic voyage (1839–43) **3** his uncle, Sir **John** 1777–1856, Scottish naval officer and Arctic explorer **4** Sir **Ronald** 1857–1932, English bacteriologist, who discovered the transmission of malaria by mosquitoes: Nobel prize for physiology or medicine 1902

THESAURUS

rope *n* **1 = cord**, line, cable, strand, hawser **3 know the ropes = be experienced**, know the score (*informal*), be knowledgeable, know what's what, be an old hand, know your way around, know where it's at (*slang*), know all the ins and outs

rosy *adj* **1 = glowing**, fresh, blooming, flushed, blushing, radiant, reddish,

DICTIONARY

Rossellini *n* **Roberto** 1906–77, Italian film director. His films include *Rome, Open City* (1945), *Paisà* (1946), and *L'Amore* (1948)

Rostand *n* **Edmond** 1868–1918, French playwright and poet in the romantic tradition; best known for his verse drama *Cyrano de Bergerac* (1897)

roster *n* **1** a list showing the order in which people are to perform a duty ▷*vb* **2** to place on a roster
WORD ORIGIN Dutch *rooster* grating or list

Rostropovich *n* **Mstislav Leopoldovich** 1927–2007, Soviet cellist, composer, and conductor; became a US citizen in 1978 after losing Soviet citizenship (restored in 1990)

rostrum *n, pl* **-trums** *or* **-tra** a platform or stage
WORD ORIGIN Latin: beak

rosy ❶ *adj* **rosier, rosiest 1** of the colour rose or pink: *rosy cheeks* **2** hopeful or promising: *the analysis revealed a far from rosy picture* **rosiness** *n*

rot ❶ *vb* **rotting, rotted 1** to decay or cause to decay **2** to deteriorate slowly, mentally and physically: I *thought he was either dead or rotting in a Chinese jail* ▷*n* **3** the process of rotting or the state of being rotten **4** something decomposed **5** ▸short for **dry rot 6** a plant or animal disease which causes decay of the tissues **7** nonsense
WORD ORIGIN Old English *rotian*

rota *n* a list of people who take it in turn to do a particular task
WORD ORIGIN Latin: a wheel

rotary *adj* **1** revolving **2** operating by rotation ▷*n, pl* **-ries 3** *US & Canad* a traffic roundabout

Rotary Club *n* a club that is part of **Rotary International**, an international association of professionals and businesspeople who raise money for charity **Rotarian** *n, adj*

rotate ❶ *vb* **-tating, -tated 1** to turn around a centre or pivot **2** to follow or cause to follow a set sequence **3** to regularly change the type of crop grown on a piece of land in order to preserve the fertility of the soil **rotation** *n* **rotational** *adj*
WORD ORIGIN Latin *rota* wheel

rotator cuff *n anat* the structure around the shoulder joint consisting of the capsule of the joint along with the tendons of the adjacent muscles

Rotavator *n trademark* a mechanical cultivator with rotary blades

Rotblat *n* See **Pugwash conferences**

rote *adj* **1** done by routine repetition: *rote learning* ▷*n* **2 by rote** by repetition: *we learned by rote*
WORD ORIGIN origin unknown

rotgut *n chiefly Brit facetious slang* alcoholic drink of inferior quality

Roth *n* **Philip** born 1933, US novelist. His works include *Goodbye, Columbus* (1959), *Portnoy's Complaint* (1969), *My Life as a Man* (1974), *Sabbath's Theater* (1995), *The Human Stain* (2000), and *The Plot Against America* (2004)

Rothermere *n* **Viscount** title of *Harold Sidney Harmsworth*. 1868–1940, British newspaper magnate

Rothko *n* **Mark.** 1903–70, US abstract expressionist painter, born in Russia

Rothschild *n* **1 Lionel Nathan**, Baron de Rothschild. 1809–79, British banker and first Jewish member of Parliament **2** his grandfather **Meyer Amschel** 1743–1812, German financier and founder of the Rothschild banking firm **3** his son, **Nathan Meyer**, Baron de Rothschild. 1777–1836, British banker, born in Germany

rotisserie *n* a rotating spit on which meat and poultry can be cooked
WORD ORIGIN French

rotor *n* **1** the rotating part of a machine or device, such as the revolving arm of the distributor of an internal-combustion engine **2** a rotating device with blades projecting from a hub which produces thrust to lift a helicopter

rotten ❶ *adj* **1** decomposing or decaying: *rotten vegetables* **2** breaking up through age or hard use: *the window frames are rotten* **3** *informal* very bad: *what rotten luck!* **4** morally corrupt: *this country's politics are rotten and out of date* **5** *informal* miserably unwell: *I had glandular fever and spent that year feeling rotten* **6** *informal* distressed and embarrassed: *I'm feeling rotten as a matter of fact, rotten and guilty* ▷*adv* **7** *informal* extremely; very much: *men fancy her rotten*
WORD ORIGIN Old Norse *rotinn*

rotter *n chiefly Brit old-fashioned slang* a despicable person

Rottweiler (rot-vile-er) *n* a large sturdy dog with a smooth black-and-tan coat and a docked tail
WORD ORIGIN *Rottweil*, German city where it was first bred

rotund (roe-**tund**) *adj* **1** round and plump **2** (of speech) pompous or grand **rotundity** *n* **rotundly** *adv*
WORD ORIGIN Latin *rotundus*

rotunda *n* a circular building or room, esp. with a dome
WORD ORIGIN Italian *rotonda*

Rouault *n* **Georges** 1871–1958, French expressionist artist. His work is deeply religious; it includes much stained glass

Roubiliac *or* **Roubillac** *n* **Louis-François** ?1695–1762, French sculptor: lived chiefly in England: his sculptures include the statue of Handel in Vauxhall Gardens (1737)

rouble *or* **ruble** (**roo**-bl) *n* the standard monetary unit of Russia and Tadzhikistan
WORD ORIGIN Russian *rubl*

roué (**roo**-ay) *n* a man who leads a sensual and immoral life
WORD ORIGIN French

rouge *n* **1** a red cosmetic for adding colour to the cheeks ▷*vb* **rouging, rouged 2** to apply rouge to
WORD ORIGIN French: red

Rouget de Lisle *n* **Claude Joseph** 1760–1836, French army officer: composer of the *Marseillaise* (1792), the French national anthem

THESAURUS

ruddy, healthy-looking, roseate, rubicund **OPPOSITE:** pale **2 = promising**, encouraging, bright, reassuring, optimistic, hopeful, sunny, cheerful, favourable, auspicious, rose-coloured, roseate **OPPOSITE:** gloomy

rot *vb* **1 = decay**, break down, spoil, corrupt, deteriorate, taint, perish, degenerate, fester, decompose, corrode, moulder, go bad, putrefy **2 = deteriorate**, decline, languish, degenerate, wither away, waste away ▷*n* **3 = decay**, disintegration, corrosion, decomposition, corruption, mould, blight, deterioration, canker, putrefaction, putrescence **7 = nonsense**, rubbish, drivel, twaddle, malarkey, pants *(slang)*, crap *(slang)*, garbage *(chiefly US)*, trash, bunk *(informal)*, hot air *(informal)*, tosh *(slang, chiefly Brit)*, pap, bilge *(informal)*, tripe *(informal)*, guff *(slang)*, moonshine, claptrap *(informal)*, hogwash, hokum *(slang, chiefly US & Canad)*, codswallop *(Brit slang)*, piffle *(informal)*, poppycock *(informal)*, balderdash, bosh *(informal)*, eyewash *(informal)*, stuff and nonsense, flapdoodle *(slang)*, tommyrot, horsefeathers *(US slang)*, bunkum *or* buncombe *(chiefly US)*, bizzo *(Austral slang)*, bull's wool *(Austral & NZ slang)* ▸*related adjective:* putrid

rotate *vb* **1 = revolve**, turn, wheel, spin, reel, go round, swivel, pivot, gyrate, pirouette **2 = follow in sequence**, switch, alternate, interchange, take turns

rotten *adj* **1 = decaying**, bad, rank, foul, corrupt, sour, stinking, tainted, perished, festering, decomposed, decomposing, mouldy, mouldering, fetid, putrid, putrescent, festy *(Austral slang)* **OPPOSITE:** fresh **2 = crumbling**, decayed, disintegrating, perished, corroded, unsound **4 = corrupt**, immoral, deceitful, untrustworthy, bent *(slang)*, crooked *(informal)*, vicious, degenerate, mercenary, treacherous, dishonest, disloyal, faithless, venal, dishonourable, perfidious **OPPOSITE:** honourable

DICTIONARY

rough ❶ *adj* **1** not smooth; uneven or irregular **2** not using enough care or gentleness **3** difficult or unpleasant: *tomorrow will be a rough day* **4** approximate: *a rough guess* **5** violent or stormy **6** troubled by violence or crime: *he lived in a rough area* **7** incomplete or basic: *a rough draft* **8** lacking refinement: *a rough shelter* **9** (of ground) covered with scrub or rubble **10** harsh or grating to the ear **11** harsh or sharp: *the rough interrogation of my father* **12** unfair: *rough luck* **13** *informal* ill: *Feeling rough? A good stiff drink will soon fix that!* **14** shaggy or hairy: *the rough wool of her sweater* **15** (of work etc.) requiring physical rather than mental effort: *wear gloves for any rough work* ▷ *vb* **16** to make rough **17 rough it** *informal* to live without the usual comforts of life ▷ *n* **18** rough ground **19** a sketch or preliminary piece of artwork **20** *informal* a violent person **21 in rough** in an unfinished or crude state **22 the rough** *golf* the part of the course beside the fairways where the grass is untrimmed **23** the unpleasant side of something: *you have to take the rough with the smooth* ▷ *adv* **24** roughly **25 sleep rough** to spend the night in the open without shelter ▸ See also **rough out, rough up** > **roughly** *adv*
WORD ORIGIN Old English *rūh*

roughage *n* the coarse indigestible constituents of food, which help digestion

rough-and-ready *adj* **1** hastily prepared but adequate for the purpose **2** (of a person) without formality or refinement

rough-and-tumble *n* **1** a playful fight **2** a disorderly situation

roughcast *n* **1** a mixture of plaster and small stones for outside walls ▷ *vb* **-casting, -cast 2** to put roughcast on (a wall)

rough diamond *n* **1** an unpolished diamond **2** a kind or trustworthy person whose manners are not good

roughen *vb* to make or become rough

rough-hewn *adj* roughly shaped or cut without being properly finished

roughhouse *n slang* rough or noisy behaviour

roughneck *n slang* **1** a violent person **2** a worker on an oil rig

rough out ❶ *vb* to prepare (a sketch or report) in preliminary form: *he offered to rough out some designs for the sets*

roughshod *adv* **ride roughshod over** to act with complete disregard for

rough up *vb informal* to beat up

roulette *n* a gambling game in which a ball is dropped onto a revolving wheel with numbered coloured slots
WORD ORIGIN French

round ❶ *adj* **1** having a flat circular shape, like a hoop **2** having the shape of a ball **3** curved; not angular **4** involving or using circular motion **5** complete **6** *maths* **a** forming or expressed by a whole number, with no fraction **b** expressed to the nearest ten, hundred, or thousand: *in round figures* ▷ *adv* **7** on all or most sides **8** on or outside the circumference or perimeter: *ponds which are steeply sided all round* **9** in rotation or revolution: *she swung round on me* **10** by a circuitous route: *a four-month cruise round the Mediterranean* **11** to all members of a group: *handing cigarettes round* **12** to a specific place: *the boys invited him round* **13 all year round** throughout the year ▷ *prep* **14** surrounding or encircling: *wrap your sash round the wound* **15** on all or most sides of: *the man turned in a circle, looking all round him* **16** on or outside the circumference or perimeter of **17** from place to place in: *a trip round the island in an ancient bus* **18** reached by making a partial circuit about: *just round the corner* **19** revolving about: *if you have two bodies in orbit, they orbit round their common centre of gravity* ▷ *vb* **20** to move round: *as he rounded the last corner, he raised a fist* ▷ *n* **21** a round shape or object **22** a session: *a round of talks* **23** a series: *the petty round of domestic matters* **24** a series of calls: *a paper round* **25 the daily round** the usual activities of a person's day **26** a playing of all the holes on a golf course **27** a stage of a competition: *the first round of the Portuguese Open* **28** one of a number of periods in a boxing or wrestling match **29** a single turn of play by each player in a card game **30** a number of drinks bought at one time for a group of people **31** a bullet or shell for a gun **32** a single discharge by a gun **33** *music* a part song in which the voices follow each other at equal intervals **34** circular movement **35 a** a single slice of bread **b** a serving of sandwiches made from two complete slices of bread **36** a general outburst: *a round of applause* **37 in the round a** in full detail **b** *theatre* with the audience all round the stage **38 go the rounds** (of information or infection) to be passed around from person to person ▸ See also **round down, round off**
WORD ORIGIN Old French *ront*

roundabout ❶ *n* **1** a road junction in which traffic moves in one direction around a central island **2** a revolving circular platform, often with seats, on which people ride for amusement ▷ *adj* **3** not straightforward: *the roundabout sea route; she thought of asking about it in a roundabout way* ▷ *adv, prep* **round about 4** approximately: *round about 1900*

round dance *n* **1** a dance in which the dancers form a circle **2** a ballroom dance, such as the waltz, in which couples revolve

round down *vb* to lower (a number) to the nearest whole number or ten, hundred, or thousand below it

roundel *n* **1** a circular identifying mark on military aircraft **2** a small circular object
WORD ORIGIN Old French *rondel*

r

THESAURUS

rough *adj* **1, 9 = uneven**, broken, rocky, rugged, irregular, jagged, bumpy, stony, craggy **OPPOSITE:** even
2 = ungracious, blunt, rude, coarse, bluff, curt, churlish, bearish, brusque, uncouth, unrefined, inconsiderate, impolite, loutish, untutored, discourteous, unpolished, indelicate, uncivil, uncultured, unceremonious, ill-bred, unmannerly, ill-mannered **OPPOSITE:** refined
3 = unpleasant, hard, difficult, tough, uncomfortable, drastic, unjust **OPPOSITE:** easy
4 = approximate, estimated **OPPOSITE:** exact
5 = stormy, wild, turbulent, agitated, choppy, tempestuous, inclement, squally **OPPOSITE:** calm
7 = basic, quick, raw, crude, unfinished, incomplete, hasty, imperfect, rudimentary, sketchy, cursory, shapeless, rough-and-ready, unrefined, formless, rough-hewn, untutored, unpolished **OPPOSITE:** complete
11 = harsh, tough, sharp, severe, nasty, cruel, rowdy, curt, unfeeling **OPPOSITE:** gentle
15 = boisterous, hard, tough, rugged, arduous ▷ *n* **19 = outline**, draft, mock-up, preliminary sketch, suggestion

rough out *vb* **= outline**, plan, draft, sketch, suggest, block out, delineate, adumbrate

round *adj* **1, 2, 3 = spherical**, rounded, bowed, curved, circular, cylindrical, bulbous, rotund, globular, curvilinear, ball-shaped, ring-shaped, disc-shaped, annular, discoid, orbicular ▷ *vb* **20 = go round**, circle, skirt, flank, bypass, encircle, turn, circumnavigate ▷ *n* **21 = sphere**, ball, band, ring, circle, disc, globe, orb **22, 23 = series**, session, cycle, sequence, succession, bout **24 = course**, turn, tour, circuit, beat, series, schedule, routine, compass, ambit **27 = stage**, turn, level, period, division, session, lap

roundabout *adj* **1, 2, 3 = indirect**, meandering, devious, tortuous, circuitous, evasive, discursive, circumlocutory **OPPOSITE:** direct

rouse[1] *vb* **1 = wake up**, call, wake,

DICTIONARY

little circle
roundelay *n* a song in which a line or phrase is repeated as a refrain **WORD ORIGIN** Old French *rondelet*
rounders *n Brit & NZ* a bat and ball game in which players run between posts after hitting the ball
Roundhead *n English history* a supporter of Parliament against Charles I during the Civil War **WORD ORIGIN** referring to their short-cut hair
roundhouse *n US & Canad* a circular building in which railway locomotives are serviced
roundly *adv* bluntly or thoroughly: *the Church roundly criticized the bill*
round off *vb* to complete agreeably or successfully: *our afternoon was rounded off with coffee and biscuits*
round on *vb* to attack or reply to (someone) with sudden irritation or anger
round robin *n* **1** a petition with the signatures in a circle to disguise the order of signing **2** a tournament in which each player plays against every other player
round-shouldered *adj* denoting poor posture with drooping shoulders and a slight forward bending of the back
round table *n* a meeting of people on equal terms for discussion
Round Table *n* **1** (in Arthurian legend) the table of King Arthur, shaped so that his knights could sit around as equals **2** one of an organization of clubs of young business and professional men who meet in order to further charitable work
round-the-clock *adj* throughout the day and night
round trip *n* a journey to a place and back again
round up *vb* **1** to gather together: *the police had rounded up a circle of drug users* **2** to raise (a number) to the nearest whole number or ten, hundred, or thousand above it ▷ *n* **roundup 3** a summary or discussion of news and information **4** the act of gathering together livestock or people
roundworm *n* a worm that is a common intestinal parasite of man
rouse[1] **T** *vb* **rousing, roused 1** to wake up **2** to provoke or excite: *his temper was roused and he had a gun* **3 rouse oneself** to become energetic **WORD ORIGIN** origin unknown
rouse[2] (rhymes with **mouse**) *vb* (foll. by *on*) *Austral* to scold or rebuke
rouseabout *n Austral & NZ* a labourer in a shearing shed
rousing **T** *adj* lively or vigorous: *a rousing speech*
roustabout *n* **1** an unskilled labourer on an oil rig **2** *Austral & NZ* ▸ another word for **rouseabout**
rout[1] **T** *n* **1** an overwhelming defeat **2** a disorderly retreat **3** a noisy rabble ▷ *vb* **4** to defeat and put to flight **WORD ORIGIN** Anglo-Norman *rute*
rout[2] *vb* **1** to find by searching **2** to drive out: *the dissidents had been routed out* **3** to dig (something) up **WORD ORIGIN** variant of ROOT[2]
route **T** *n* **1** the choice of roads taken to get to a place **2** a fixed path followed by buses, trains, etc. between two places **3** a chosen way or method: *the route to prosperity* ▷ *vb* **routeing, routed 4** to send by a particular route **WORD ORIGIN** Old French *rute*
routemarch *n mil* a long training march
router *n computers* a device that allows data to be moved efficiently between two points on a network
routine **T** *n* **1** a usual or regular method of procedure **2** the boring repetition of tasks: *mindless routine* **3** a set sequence of dance steps **4** *computers* a program or part of a program performing a specific function: *an input routine* ▷ *adj* **5** relating to or characteristic of routine **WORD ORIGIN** Old French *route* a customary way
roux (roo) *n* a cooked mixture of fat and flour used as a basis for sauces **WORD ORIGIN** French: brownish
rove *vb* **roving, roved 1** to wander about (a place) **2** (of the eyes) to look around **rover** *n* **WORD ORIGIN** probably from Old Norse
row[1] **T** (rhymes with **know**) *n* **1** an arrangement of people or things in a line: *a row of shops* **2** a line of seats in a cinema or theatre **3** *Brit* a street lined with identical houses **4** *maths* a horizontal line of numbers **5 in a row** in succession: *five championships in a row* **WORD ORIGIN** Old English *rāw, rǣw*
row[2] (rhymes with **know**) *vb* **1** to propel (a boat) by using oars **2** to carry (people or goods) in a rowing boat **3** to take part in the racing of rowing boats as a sport ▷ *n* **4** an act or spell of rowing **5** an excursion in a rowing boat **rowing** *n* **WORD ORIGIN** Old English *rōwan*
row[3] **T** (rhymes with **cow**) *informal n* **1** a noisy quarrel **2** a controversy or dispute: *the row over Europe* **3** a noisy disturbance: *go to the insurance offices and kick up a row about your money* **4** a reprimand ▷ *vb* **5** to quarrel noisily **WORD ORIGIN** origin unknown
rowan *n* a European tree with white flowers and red berries; mountain ash **WORD ORIGIN** Scandinavian
rowdy *adj* **-dier, -diest 1** rough, noisy, or disorderly ▷ *n, pl* **-dies 2** a person like this **rowdily** *adv* **WORD ORIGIN** origin unknown
Rowe *n* **Nicholas** 1674–1718, English dramatist, who produced the first critical edition of Shakespeare; poet laureate (1715–18). His plays include *Tamerlane* (1702) and *The Fair Penitent* (1703)
rowel (rhymes with **towel**) *n* a small

THESAURUS

awaken **2 = excite**, move, arouse, stir, disturb, provoke, anger, startle, animate, prod, exhilarate, get going, agitate, inflame, incite, whip up, galvanize, bestir
rousing *adj* **= lively**, moving, spirited, exciting, inspiring, stirring, stimulating, vigorous, brisk, exhilarating, inflammatory, electrifying **OPPOSITE:** dull
rout[1] *n* **1, 2 = defeat**, beating, hiding (*informal*), ruin, overthrow, thrashing, licking (*informal*), pasting (*slang*), shambles, debacle, drubbing, overwhelming defeat, headlong flight, disorderly retreat ▷ *vb* **4 = defeat**, beat, overthrow, thrash, stuff (*slang*), worst, destroy, chase, tank (*slang*), crush, scatter, conquer, lick (*informal*), dispel, drive off, overpower, clobber (*slang*), wipe the floor with (*informal*), cut to pieces, put to flight, drub, put to rout, throw back in confusion
route *n* **1, 3 = way**, course, road, direction, path, journey, passage, avenue, itinerary **2 = beat**, run, round, circuit
routine *n* **1 = procedure**, programme, way, order, practice, method, pattern, formula, custom, usage, wont, lockstep (*US & Canad*) ▷ *adj* **5 = usual**, standard, normal, customary, ordinary, familiar, typical, conventional, everyday, habitual, workaday, wonted **OPPOSITE:** unusual
row[1] *n* **1 = line**, bank, range, series, file, rank, string, column, sequence, queue, tier **5 in a row = consecutively**, running, in turn, one after the other, successively, in sequence
row[3] *n* **1, 2 = quarrel**, dispute, argument, squabble, tiff, trouble, controversy, scrap (*informal*), fuss, falling-out (*informal*), fray, brawl, fracas, altercation, slanging match (*Brit*), shouting match (*informal*), shindig (*informal*), ruction (*informal*), ruckus (*informal*), shindy (*informal*), bagarre (*French*) **3 = disturbance**, noise, racket, uproar, commotion, rumpus, tumult ▷ *vb* **5 = quarrel**, fight, argue, dispute, scrap (*informal*), brawl, squabble, spar, wrangle, go at it hammer and tongs

DICTIONARY

spiked wheel at the end of a spur **WORD ORIGIN** Old French *roel* a little wheel

rowing boat *n* a small pleasure boat propelled by oars. Usual US and Canad word: **rowboat**

Rowlandson *n* **Thomas** 1756–1827, English caricaturist, noted for the vigour of his attack on sordid aspects of contemporary society and on statesmen such as Napoleon

Rowley *n* **Thomas** ?1586–?1642, English dramatist, who collaborated with John Ford and Thomas Dekker on *The Witch of Edmonton* (1621) and with Thomas Middleton on *The Changeling* (1622)

rowlock (rol-luk) *n* a swivelling device attached to the top of the side of a boat that holds an oar in place

Roxas y Acuña *n* **Manuel** 1892–1948, Philippine statesman; first president of the Republic of the Philippines (1946–48)

royal ❶ *adj* **1** of or relating to a king or queen or a member of his or her family: *the royal yacht* **2 Royal** supported by or in the service of royalty: *the Royal Society of Medicine* **3** very grand: *royal treatment* ▹ *n* **4** *informal* a king or queen or a member of his or her family **royally** *adv* **WORD ORIGIN** Old French *roial*

Royal Air Force *n* the air force of the United Kingdom

royal-blue *adj* deep blue

royalist *n* **1** a supporter of a monarch or monarchy ▹ *adj* **2** of or relating to royalists **royalism** *n*

royal jelly *n* a substance secreted by worker bees and fed to all larvae when very young and to larvae destined to become queens throughout their growth

Royal Marines *pl n Brit* a corps of soldiers specially trained in amphibious warfare

Royal Navy *n* the navy of the United Kingdom

royalty *n, pl* **-ties 1** royal people **2** the rank or power of a king or queen **3** a percentage of the revenue from the sale of a book, performance of a work, use of a patented invention or of land, paid to the author, inventor, or owner

royal warrant *n* an authorization to a tradesman to supply goods to a royal household

Royce *n* **Josiah** 1855–1916, US philosopher of monistic idealism. In his ethical studies he emphasized the need for individual loyalty to the world community

RPI (in Britain) retail price index: a measure of the changes in the average level of retail prices of selected goods

rpm revolutions per minute

RR 1 Right Reverend **2** *US & Canad* rural route

RSA 1 Republic of South Africa **2** (in New Zealand) Returned Services Association **3** Royal Scottish Academy **4** Royal Society of Arts

RSI repetitive strain injury: pain in the arm caused by repeated awkward movements, such as in typing

RSM (in Britain) regimental sergeant major

RSPCA (in Britain) Royal Society for the Prevention of Cruelty to Animals

RSS Rich Site Summary *or* Really Simple Syndication: a way of allowing web users to receive updated information from selected websites on their browser

RSVP please reply **WORD ORIGIN** French *répondez s'il vous plaît*

RTA *Brit* road traffic accident

Rt Hon. Right Honourable: a title of respect for a Privy Councillor, certain peers, and the Lord Mayor or Lord Provost of certain cities

Ru *chem* ruthenium

RU486 *n* ▸ the technical name for **abortion pill**

rub ❶ *vb* **rubbing, rubbed 1** to apply pressure and friction to (something) with a circular or backwards-and-forwards movement **2** to move (something) with pressure along or against (a surface) **3** to clean, polish, or dry by rubbing **4** to spread with pressure, esp. so that it can be absorbed: *rub beeswax into all polishable surfaces* **5** to chafe or fray through rubbing **6** to mix (fat) into flour with the fingertips, as in making pastry **7 rub it in** to emphasize an unpleasant fact **8 rub up the wrong way** to annoy ▹ *n* **9** the act of rubbing **10 the rub** the obstacle or difficulty: *there's the rub* ▸ See also **rub along, rub down**, etc. **WORD ORIGIN** origin unknown

rub along *vb* **1** to have a friendly relationship **2** to continue in spite of difficulties

rubato *music n, pl* **-tos 1** flexibility of tempo in performance: *his playing brought much beautifully felt but never sentimental rubato to the music* ▹ *adj, adv* **2** to be played with a flexible tempo **WORD ORIGIN** Italian, literally: robbed

rubber[1] *n* **1** an elastic material obtained from the latex of certain plants, such as the rubber tree **2** a similar substance produced synthetically **3** a piece of rubber used for erasing something written **4** *US slang* a condom **5 rubbers** *US* rubber-coated waterproof overshoes ▹ *adj* **6** made of or producing rubber **rubbery** *adj* **WORD ORIGIN** the tree was so named because its product was used for rubbing out writing

rubber[2] *n* **1** *bridge, whist* a match of three games **2** a series of matches or games in various sports **WORD ORIGIN** origin unknown

rubber band *n* a continuous loop of thin rubber, used to hold papers together

rubberize *or* **-ise** *vb* **-izing, -ized** *or* **-ising, -ised** to coat or treat with rubber

rubberneck *slang vb* **1** to stare in a naive or foolish manner ▹ *n* **2** a person who stares inquisitively **3** a sightseer or tourist

rubber plant *n* **1** a large house plant with glossy leathery leaves **2** ▸ same as **rubber tree**

rubber stamp *n* **1** a device used for imprinting dates or signatures on forms or invoices **2** automatic authorization of something **3** a person or body that gives official approval to decisions taken elsewhere but has no real power ▹ *vb* **rubber-stamp 4** *informal* to approve automatically

rubber tree *n* a tropical tree cultivated for its latex, which is the major source of commercial rubber

rubbing *n* an impression taken of an

THESAURUS

royal *adj* **1 = regal**, kingly *or* queenly, princely, imperial, sovereign, monarchical, kinglike *or* queenlike **3 = splendid**, august, grand, impressive, superb, magnificent, superior, majestic, stately

rub *vb* **1 = stroke**, smooth, massage, caress, knead **3 = polish**, clean, shine, wipe, scour **5 = chafe**, scrape, grate, abrade ▹ *n* **9a = massage**, caress, kneading **9b = polish**, stroke, shine, wipe

rubbish *n* **1, 2 = waste**, refuse, scrap, junk *(informal)*, litter, debris, crap *(slang)*, garbage *(chiefly US)*, trash, lumber, offal, dross, dregs, flotsam and jetsam, grot *(slang)*, dreck *(slang, chiefly US)*, offscourings **3 = nonsense**, garbage *(chiefly US)*, drivel, malarkey, twaddle, pants *(slang)*, rot, crap *(slang)*, trash, hot air *(informal)*, tosh *(slang, chiefly Brit)*, pap, bilge *(informal)*, tripe *(informal)*, gibberish, guff *(slang)*, havers *(Scot)*, moonshine, claptrap *(informal)*, hogwash, hokum *(slang, chiefly US & Canad)*, codswallop *(Brit slang)*, piffle *(informal)*, poppycock *(informal)*, balderdash, bosh *(informal)*, wack *(US slang)*, eyewash *(informal)*, stuff and nonsense, flapdoodle *(slang)*, tommyrot, horsefeathers *(US slang)*, bunkum *or* buncombe *(chiefly US)*, bizzo *(Austral slang)*, bull's wool *(Austral & NZ slang)*

rude *adj* **1 = impolite**, insulting,

engraved or raised design by laying paper over it and rubbing with wax or charcoal

rubbish ⓘ *n* **1** discarded or waste matter **2** anything worthless or of poor quality: *the rubbish on television* **3** foolish words or speech ▹*vb* **4** *informal* to criticize **rubbishy** *adj*
WORD ORIGIN origin unknown

rubble *n* **1** debris from ruined buildings **2** pieces of broken stones or bricks
WORD ORIGIN origin unknown

Rubbra *n* **(Charles) Edmund** 1901–86, English composer of works in a traditional idiom

rub down *vb* **1** to prepare (a surface) for painting by rubbing it with sandpaper **2** to dry or clean (an animal or person) vigorously, esp. after exercise

rubella (roo-**bell**-a) *n* a mild contagious viral disease characterized by cough, sore throat, and skin rash. Also called: **German measles**
WORD ORIGIN Latin *rubellus* reddish

Rubicon (roo-bik-on) *n* **cross the Rubicon** to commit oneself to a course of action which cannot be altered
WORD ORIGIN a stream in N Italy: by leading his army across it, Julius Caesar caused civil war in Rome in 49 BC

rubicund (roo-bik-kund) *adj old-fashioned* of a reddish colour
WORD ORIGIN Latin *rubicundus*

rubidium (roo-**bid**-ee-um) *n chem* a soft highly reactive radioactive metallic element used in electronic valves, photocells, and special glass. Symbol: Rb
WORD ORIGIN Latin *rubidus* red

Rubinstein *n* **1 Anton Grigorevich** 1829–94, Russian composer and pianist **2 Artur** 1886–1982, US pianist, born in Poland

ruble *n* ▸same as **rouble**

Rublyov *or* **Rublev** *n* **Andrey** ?1370–1430, Russian icon painter. His masterpiece is *The Old Testament Trinity*

rub off *vb* **1** to remove or be removed by rubbing: *rub the skins off the hazelnuts* **2** to have an effect through close association: *glamour can rub off on you by association*

rub out *vb* **1** to remove or be removed with a rubber **2** *US slang* to murder

rubric (roo-brik) *n* **1** a set of rules of conduct or procedure, esp. one for the conduct of Christian church services **2** a title or heading in a book
WORD ORIGIN Latin *ruber* red

ruby *n, pl* **-bies** **1** a deep red transparent precious gemstone ▹*adj* **2** deep red **3** denoting a fortieth anniversary: *a ruby wedding*
WORD ORIGIN Latin *ruber* red

RUC Royal Ulster Constabulary: a former name for the Police Service of Northern Ireland

ruche *n* a strip of pleated or frilled lace or ribbon used to decorate clothes
WORD ORIGIN French, literally: beehive

ruck[1] *n* **1 the ruck** ordinary people, often in a crowd **2** *rugby* a loose scrum that forms around the ball when it is on the ground
WORD ORIGIN probably from Old Norse

ruck[2] *n* **1** a wrinkle or crease ▹*vb* **2** to wrinkle or crease: *the toe of his shoe had rucked up one corner of the pale rug*
WORD ORIGIN Scandinavian

rucksack *n Brit, Austral & S African* a large bag, with two straps, carried on the back
WORD ORIGIN from German

ruction *n informal* **1** an uproar **2 ructions** an unpleasant row
WORD ORIGIN origin unknown

rudder *n* **1** *naut* a vertical hinged piece that projects into the water at the stern, used to steer a boat **2** a vertical control surface attached to the rear of the fin used to steer an aircraft **rudderless** *adj*
WORD ORIGIN Old English *rōther*

ruddy *adj* **-dier, -diest** **1** (of the complexion) having a healthy reddish colour **2** red or pink: *a ruddy glow* ▹*adv, adj* **3** *informal* bloody: *too ruddy slow; I just went through the ruddy ceiling*
WORD ORIGIN Old English *rudig*

rude ⓘ *adj* **1** insulting or impolite **2** vulgar or obscene: *rude words* **3** unexpected and unpleasant: *we received a rude awakening* **4** roughly or crudely made: *the rude hovels* **5** robust or sturdy: *the very picture of rude health* **6** lacking refinement **rudely** *adv* **rudeness** *n*
WORD ORIGIN Latin *rudis*

rudiment *n* **1 rudiments a** the simplest and most basic stages of a subject: *the rudiments of painting* **b** a partially developed version of something: *the rudiments of a democratic society* **2** *biol* an organ or part that is incompletely developed or no longer functions **rudimentary** *adj*
WORD ORIGIN Latin *rudimentum*

Rudolf[1] *n* **Lake Rudolf** the former name (until 1979) of (Lake) **Turkana**

Rudolf[2] *or* **Rudolph** *n* 1858–89, archduke of Austria, son of emperor Franz Joseph: he and his mistress committed suicide at the royal hunting lodge in Mayerling

Rudolf I *or* **Rudolph I** *n* 1218–91, king of Germany (1273–91): founder of the Hapsburg dynasty based on the duchies of Styria and Austria

rue[1] ⓘ *vb* **ruing, rued** *literary* to feel regret for
WORD ORIGIN Old English *hrēowan*

rue[2] *n* an aromatic shrub with bitter evergreen leaves formerly used in medicine
WORD ORIGIN Greek *rhutē*

rueful *adj* feeling or expressing sorrow or regret: *a rueful smile* **ruefully** *adv*

ruff[1] *n* **1** a circular pleated or fluted cloth collar **2** a natural growth of long or coloured hair or feathers around the necks of certain animals or birds **3** a bird of the sandpiper family
WORD ORIGIN from *ruffle*

ruff[2] *n, vb cards* ▸same as **trump**[1] (senses 1, 2)
WORD ORIGIN Old French *roffle*

ruffian *n* a violent lawless person
WORD ORIGIN Old French *rufien*

ruffle ⓘ *vb* **-fling, -fled** **1** to disturb the smoothness of: *the wind was ruffling Dad's hair* **2** to annoy or irritate **3** (of a bird) to erect its feathers in anger or display **4** to flick cards or pages rapidly ▹*n* **5** a strip of pleated material used as a trim
WORD ORIGIN Germanic

r

THESAURUS

cheeky, abrupt, short, blunt, abusive, curt, churlish, disrespectful, brusque, offhand, impertinent, insolent, inconsiderate, peremptory, impudent, discourteous, uncivil, unmannerly, ill-mannered
OPPOSITE: polite
2 = vulgar, gross, crude
OPPOSITE: refined
3 = unpleasant, sharp, violent, sudden, harsh, startling, abrupt
4 = roughly-made, simple, rough, raw, crude, primitive, makeshift, rough-hewn, artless, inelegant, inartistic **OPPOSITE:** well-made
6 = uncivilized, low, rough, savage, ignorant, coarse, illiterate, uneducated, brutish, barbarous, scurrilous, boorish, uncouth, unrefined, loutish, untutored, graceless, ungracious, unpolished, oafish, uncultured

rue[1] *vb (literary)* **= regret**, mourn, grieve, lament, deplore, bemoan, repent, be sorry for, weep over, sorrow for, bewail, kick yourself for, reproach yourself for

ruffle *vb* **1 = disarrange**, disorder, wrinkle, mess up, rumple, tousle, derange, discompose, dishevel, muss (*US & Canad*) **2 = annoy**, worry, trouble, upset, confuse, stir, disturb, rattle (*informal*), irritate, put out, unsettle, shake up (*informal*), harass, hassle (*informal*), agitate, unnerve, disconcert, disquiet, nettle, vex, fluster, perturb, faze, peeve (*informal*), hack off (*informal*)
OPPOSITE: calm

DICTIONARY

rufous *adj* (of birds or animals) reddish-brown
WORD ORIGIN Latin *rufus*

rug *n* **1** a small carpet **2** a thick woollen blanket **3** *slang* a wig **4 pull the rug out from under** to betray or leave defenceless
WORD ORIGIN Scandinavian

rugby *or* **rugby football** *n* a form of football played with an oval ball in which the handling and carrying of the ball is permitted
WORD ORIGIN after the public school at *Rugby*, where it was first played

rugby league *n* a form of rugby played between teams of 13 players

rugby union *n* a form of rugby played between teams of 15 players

rugged ❶ (rug-gid) *adj* **1** rocky or steep: *the rugged mountains of Sicily's interior* **2** with an uneven or jagged surface **3** (of the face) strong-featured **4** rough, sturdy, or determined in character **5** (of equipment or machines) designed to withstand rough treatment or use in rough conditions
WORD ORIGIN probably from Old Norse

rugger *n chiefly Brit informal* rugby

rug rat *n informal* a young child not yet walking

ruin ❶ *vb* **1** to destroy or spoil completely: *the suit was ruined* **2** to cause (someone) to lose money: *the first war ruined him* ▹ *n* **3** the state of being destroyed or decayed **4** loss of wealth or position **5** a destroyed or decayed building or town **6** something that is severely damaged: *my heart was an aching ruin*
WORD ORIGIN Latin *ruina* a falling down

ruination *n* **1** the act of ruining or the state of being ruined **2** something that causes ruin

ruinous *adj* **1** causing ruin or destruction **2** more expensive than can reasonably be afforded: *ruinous rates of exchange* **ruinously** *adv*

Ruisdael *or* **Ruysdael** *n* **Jacob van** ?1628–82, Dutch landscape painter

rule ❶ *n* **1** a statement of what is allowed, for example in a game or procedure **2** a customary form or procedure: *he has his own rule: be firm, be clear, but never be rude* **3 the rule** the common order of things: *humanitarian gestures were more the exception than the rule* **4** the exercise of governmental authority or control: *the rule of President Marcos* **5** the period of time in which a monarch or government has power: *four decades of Communist rule* **6** a device with a straight edge for guiding or measuring: *a slide rule* **7** *printing* a long thin line or dash **8** *Christianity* a systematic body of laws and customs followed by members of a religious order **9** *law* an order by a court or judge **10 as a rule** usually ▹ *vb* **ruling, ruled 11** to govern (people or a political unit) **12** to be pre-eminent or superior **13** to be customary or prevalent: *chaos ruled as the scene turned into one of total confusion* **14** to decide authoritatively: *the judges ruled that men could be prosecuted for rape offences against their wives* **15** to mark with straight parallel lines or one straight line **16** to restrain or control
WORD ORIGIN Old French *riule*

rule of thumb *n* a rough and practical approach, based on experience, rather than theory

rule out *vb* **1** to dismiss from consideration **2** to make impossible

ruler ❶ *n* **1** a person who rules or commands **2** a strip of wood, metal, or plastic, with straight edges, used for measuring and drawing straight lines

ruling ❶ *adj* **1** controlling or exercising authority **2** predominant ▹ *n* **3** a decision of someone in authority

rum[1] *n* alcoholic drink made from sugar cane
WORD ORIGIN origin unknown

rum[2] *adj* **rummer, rummest** *Brit slang* strange or unusual
WORD ORIGIN origin unknown

Rumanian *adj, n* ▸ same as **Romanian**

rumba *n* **1** a rhythmic and syncopated dance of Cuban origin **2** music for this dance
WORD ORIGIN Spanish

rumble *vb* **-bling, -bled 1** to make or cause to make a deep echoing sound: *thunder rumbled overhead* **2** to move with such a sound: *a slow freight train rumbled past* **3** *Brit slang* to find out about (someone or something): *his real identity was rumbled* ▹ *n* **4** a deep resonant sound **5** *slang* a gang fight **rumbling** *adj, n*
WORD ORIGIN probably from Middle Dutch *rummelen*

rumbustious *adj* boisterous or unruly
WORD ORIGIN probably variant of *robustious*

THESAURUS

rugged *adj* **1, 2 = rocky**, broken, rough, craggy, difficult, ragged, stark, irregular, uneven, jagged, bumpy **OPPOSITE:** even
3 = strong-featured, lined, worn, weathered, wrinkled, furrowed, leathery, rough-hewn, weather-beaten **OPPOSITE:** delicate
4 = tough, strong, hardy, robust, vigorous, muscular, sturdy, hale, burly, husky *(informal)*, beefy *(informal)*, brawny **OPPOSITE:** delicate
5 = well-built, strong, tough, robust, sturdy

ruin *vb* **1a = destroy**, devastate, wreck, trash *(slang)*, break, total *(slang)*, defeat, smash, crush, overwhelm, shatter, overturn, overthrow, bring down, demolish, raze, lay waste, lay in ruins, wreak havoc upon, bring to ruin, bring to nothing, kennet *(Austral slang)*, jeff *(Austral slang)* **OPPOSITE:** create
1b = spoil, damage, mar, mess up, blow *(slang)*, injure, undo, screw up *(informal)*, botch, mangle, cock up *(Brit slang)*, disfigure, make a mess of, bodge *(informal)*, crool *or* cruel *(Austral slang)* **OPPOSITE:** improve
2 = bankrupt, break, impoverish, beggar, pauperize ▹ *n* **3a = disrepair**, decay, disintegration, ruination, wreckage **3b = destruction**, fall, the end, breakdown, damage, defeat, failure, crash, collapse, wreck, overthrow, undoing, havoc, Waterloo, downfall, devastation, dissolution, subversion, nemesis, crackup *(informal)* **OPPOSITE:** preservation
4 = bankruptcy, insolvency, destitution

rule *n* **1 = regulation**, order, law, ruling, guide, direction, guideline, decree, ordinance, dictum **4, 5 = government**, power, control, authority, influence, administration, direction, leadership, command, regime, empire, reign, sway, domination, jurisdiction, supremacy, mastery, dominion, ascendancy, mana *(NZ)*
10 as a rule = usually, generally, mainly, normally, on the whole, for the most part, ordinarily, customarily **11 = govern**, lead, control, manage, direct, guide, regulate, administer, oversee, preside over, have power over, reign over, command over, have charge of
12, 13 = be prevalent, prevail, predominate, hold sway, be customary, preponderate, obtain
14 = decree, find, decide, judge, establish, determine, settle, resolve, pronounce, lay down, adjudge

ruler *n* **1 = governor**, leader, lord, commander, controller, monarch, sovereign, head of state, potentate, crowned head, emperor *or* empress, king *or* queen, prince *or* princess
2 = measure, rule, yardstick, straight edge

ruling *adj* **1 = governing**, upper, reigning, controlling, leading, commanding, dominant, regnant
2 = predominant, dominant, prevailing, preponderant, chief, main, current, supreme, principal, prevalent, pre-eminent, regnant **OPPOSITE:** minor
▹ *n* **3 = decision**, finding, resolution, verdict, judgment, decree, adjudication, pronouncement

r

DICTIONARY

Rumford *n* **Count Rumford** ▸ See **Thompson** (sense 1)
ruminant *n* **1** a mammal that chews the cud, such as cattle, sheep, deer, goats, and camels ▹ *adj* **2** of ruminants **3** meditating or contemplating in a slow quiet way
ruminate *vb* **-nating, -nated 1** (of ruminants) to chew (the cud) **2** to meditate or ponder **rumination** *n* **ruminative** *adj*
WORD ORIGIN Latin *ruminare* to chew the cud
rummage *vb* **-maging, -maged 1** to search untidily ▹ *n* **2** an untidy search through a collection of things
WORD ORIGIN Old French *arrumage* to stow cargo
rummage sale *n US & Canad* a jumble sale
rummy *n* a card game based on collecting sets and sequences
WORD ORIGIN origin unknown
rumour ⊕ *or US* **rumor** *n* **1** information, often a mixture of truth and untruth, told by one person to another **2** gossip or common talk ▹ *vb* **3 be rumoured** to be circulated as a rumour: *he is rumoured to have at least 53 yachts*
WORD ORIGIN Latin *rumor*
rump *n* **1** a person's buttocks **2** the rear part of an animal's or bird's body **3** Also called: **rump steak** a cut of beef from the rump **4** a small core of members within a group who remain loyal to it: *the rump of the once-influential communist party*
WORD ORIGIN probably from Old Norse
rumple *vb* **-pling, -pled** to make or become crumpled or dishevelled
WORD ORIGIN Middle Dutch *rompelen*
rumpus *n, pl* **-puses** a noisy or confused commotion
WORD ORIGIN origin unknown
rumpy-pumpy *n informal* sexual intercourse
Rumsfeld *n* **Donald H** born 1932, US Republican politician and businessman: US Secretary of Defense (2001–06)
run ⊕ *vb* **running, ran, run 1** to move on foot at a rapid pace **2** to pass over (a distance or route) in running: *being a man isn't about running the fastest mile* **3** to take part in (a race): *I ran a decent race* **4** to carry out as if by running: *he is running errands for his big brother* **5** to flee **6** to travel somewhere in a vehicle **7** to give a lift to (someone) in a vehicle: *one wet day I ran her down to the service* **8** to drive or maintain and operate (a vehicle) **9** to travel regularly between places on a route: *trains running through the night* **10** to move or pass quickly: *he ran his hand across his forehead* **11** to function or cause to function: *run the video tape backwards* **12** to manage: *he ran a small hotel* **13** to continue in a particular direction or for a particular time or distance: *a road running alongside the Nile; a performing arts festival running in the city for six weeks* **14** *law* to have legal force or effect: *the club's lease runs out next May* **15** to be subjected to or affected by: *she ran a high risk of losing her hair* **16** to tend or incline: *he was of medium height and running to fat* **17** to recur persistently or be inherent: *the capacity for infidelity ran in the genes* **18** to flow or cause (liquids) to flow: *sweat ran down her face* **19** to dissolve and spread: *the soles of the shoes peeled off and the colours ran* **20** (of stitches) to unravel **21** to spread or circulate: *rumours ran around quickly* **22** to publish or be published in a newspaper or magazine: *our local newspaper ran a story on the appeal* **23** *chiefly US & Canad* to stand as a candidate for political or other office: *he has formally announced his decision to run for the office of President* **24** to get past or through: *the oil tanker was hit as it tried to run the blockade* **25** to smuggle (goods, esp. arms) **26** (of fish) to migrate upstream from the sea, esp. in order to spawn **27** *cricket* to score (a run or number of runs) by hitting the ball and running between the wickets ▹ *n* **28** the act or an instance of running: *he broke into a run* **29** a distance covered by running or a period of running: *it's a short run of about 20 kilometres* **30** a trip in a vehicle, esp. for pleasure: *our only treat is a run in the car to Dartmoor* **31** free and unrestricted access: *he had the run of the house* **32 a** a period of time during which a machine or computer operates **b** the amount of work performed in such a period **33** a continuous or sustained period: *a run of seven defeats* **34** a continuous sequence of performances: *the play had a long run* **35** *cards* a sequence of winning cards in one suit: *a run of spades* **36** type, class, or category: *he had nothing in common with the usual run of terrorists* **37** a continuous and urgent demand: *a run on the pound* **38** a series of unravelled stitches, esp. in tights **39** a steeply inclined course, esp. a snow-covered one used for skiing **40** an enclosure for domestic fowls or other animals: *the chicken run* **41** (esp. in Australia and New Zealand) a tract of land for grazing livestock **42** the migration of fish upstream in order to spawn **43** *music* a rapid scalelike passage of notes **44** *cricket* a score of one, normally achieved by both batsmen running from one end of the wicket to the other after one of them has hit the ball **45** *baseball* an instance of a batter touching all four bases safely, thereby scoring **46 a run for one's money** *informal* **a** a close competition **b** pleasure or success from an activity **47 in the long run** as an eventual outcome **48 on the run** escaping from arrest **49 the runs** *slang* diarrhoea ▸ See also **runabout, run across,** etc.
WORD ORIGIN Old English *runnen*
runabout *n* **1** a small car used for short journeys ▹ *vb* **run about 2** to move busily from place to place

r

THESAURUS

rumour *n* **1, 2 = story,** news, report, talk, word, whisper, buzz, gossip, dirt *(US slang)*, goss *(informal)*, hearsay, canard, tidings, scuttlebutt *(US slang)*, bush telegraph, bruit *(archaic)*
run *vb* **1 = race,** speed, rush, dash, hurry, career, barrel (along) *(informal, chiefly US & Canad)*, sprint, scramble, bolt, dart, gallop, hare *(Brit informal)*, jog, scud, hasten, scurry, stampede, scamper, leg it *(informal)*, lope, hie, hotfoot **OPPOSITE:** dawdle
3 = take part, compete **5 = flee,** escape, take off *(informal)*, depart, bolt, clear out, beat it *(slang)*, leg it *(informal)*, make off, abscond, decamp, take flight, do a runner *(slang)*, scarper *(Brit slang)*, slope off, cut and run *(informal)*, make a run for it, fly the coop *(US & Canad informal)*, beat a retreat, show a clean pair of heels, skedaddle *(informal)*, take a powder *(US & Canad slang)*, take it on the lam *(US & Canad slang)*, take to your heels **OPPOSITE:** stay
10 = pass, go, move, roll, slide, glide, skim **11a = go,** work, operate, perform, function, be in business, be in action, tick over **11b = work,** go, operate, function **12 = manage,** lead, direct, be in charge of, own, head, control, boss *(informal)*, operate, handle, conduct, look after, carry on, regulate, take care of, administer, oversee, supervise, mastermind, coordinate, superintend
13 = continue, go, stretch, last, reach, lie, range, extend, proceed
OPPOSITE: stop
18 = flow, pour, stream, cascade, go, move, issue, proceed, leak, spill, discharge, gush, spout, course
19 = melt, dissolve, liquefy, go soft, turn to liquid **22 = publish,** feature, display, print **23** *(chiefly US & Canad)* **= compete,** stand, contend, be a candidate, put yourself up for, take part, challenge **25 = smuggle,** deal in, traffic in, bootleg, ship, sneak ▹ *n* **28 = race,** rush, dash, sprint, gallop, jog, spurt **30 = ride,** drive, trip, lift, journey, spin *(informal)*, outing, excursion, jaunt, joy ride *(informal)*
33, 34 = sequence, period, stretch, spell, course, season, round, series, chain, cycle, string, passage, streak
40 = enclosure, pen, coop

DICTIONARY

run across *vb* to meet unexpectedly by chance

run along *vb* to go away

run away *vb* **1** to go away **2** to escape **3** (of a horse) to gallop away uncontrollably: *the horse ran away with him* **4 run away with a** to abscond or elope with: *I ran away with David* **b** to escape from the control of: *he let his imagination run away with him* **c** to win easily or be certain of victory in (a competition): *the Spaniards at one stage seemed to be running away with the match* ▷ *n* **runaway 5** a person or animal that runs away ▷ *adj* **runaway 6** no longer under control: *a runaway train* **7** (of a race or victory) easily won

Runcie *n* **Robert** (**Alexander Kennedy**), Baron. 1921–2000, Archbishop of Canterbury (1980–91)

run down ⓣ *vb* **1** to be rude about: *he is busy running us down and insulting other Europeans* **2** to reduce in number or size: *it should be possible to run down the existing hospitals almost entirely* **3** (of a device such as a clock or battery) to lose power gradually and cease to function **4** to hit and knock to the ground with a moving vehicle **5** to pursue and find or capture: *while I was there, Moscow ran me down, convinced I was ready to defect* ▷ *adj* **rundown 6** tired or ill **7** shabby or dilapidated ▷ *n* **rundown 8** a reduction in number or size **9** a brief review or summary

Rundstedt *n* **Karl Rudolf Gerd von** 1875–1953, German field marshal; directed the conquest of Poland and France in World War II; commander of the Western Front (1942–44); led the Ardennes counteroffensive (Dec 1944)

rune *n* **1** any of the characters of the earliest Germanic alphabet **2** an obscure piece of writing using mysterious symbols **runic** *adj*
WORD ORIGIN Old Norse *rūn* secret

Runeberg *n* **Johan Ludvig** 1804–77, Finnish poet, who wrote in Swedish. His works include the epic *King Fialar* (1844) and patriotic poems including the Finnish national anthem

rung¹ *n* **1** one of the bars forming the steps of a ladder **2** a crosspiece between the legs of a chair
WORD ORIGIN Old English *hrung*

rung² *vb* ▶ the past participle of **ring¹**

run-holder *n Austral & NZ* the owner or manager of a sheep or cattle station

run in *vb* **1** to run (an engine) gently, usually when it is new **2** *informal* to arrest ▷ *n* **run-in 3** *informal* an argument or quarrel **4** an approach to the end of an event: *the run-in for the championship*

run into *vb* **1** to be beset by: *the mission has run into difficulty* **2** to meet unexpectedly **3** to extend to: *businessmen denied losses running into the thousands* **4** to collide with

runnel *n literary* a small stream
WORD ORIGIN Old English *rynele*

runner ⓣ *n* **1** a competitor in a race **2** a messenger for a firm **3** a person involved in smuggling **4 a** either of the strips of metal or wood on which a sledge runs **b** the blade of an ice skate **5** *bot* a slender horizontal stem of a plant, such as the strawberry, that grows along the surface of the soil and produces new roots and shoots **6** a long strip of cloth used to decorate a table or as a rug **7** a roller or guide for a sliding component **8 do a runner** *slang* to run away to escape trouble or to avoid paying for something

runner bean *n* the edible pod and seeds of a type of climbing bean plant

runner-up *n, pl* **runners-up** a person who comes second in a competition

running ⓣ *adj* **1** maintained continuously: *a running battle* **2** without interruption: *for the third day running* **3 a** flowing: *rinse them under cold running water* **b** supplied through a tap: *there is no electricity, no running water, and no telephone* **4** operating: *running costs* **5** discharging pus: *a running sore* **6** accomplished at a run: *a running jump* **7** moving or slipping easily, as a rope or a knot ▷ *n* **8** the act of moving or flowing quickly **9** management or organization: *the running of the farm* **10** the operation or maintenance of a machine **11 in** *or* **out of the running** having *or* not having a good chance in a competition **12 make the running** to set the pace in a competition or race

running board *n* a board along the side of a vehicle, for help in stepping into it

running head *n printing* a heading printed at the top of every page of a book

running mate *n* **1** *US* a candidate for the lesser of two linked positions, esp. a candidate for the vice-presidency **2** a horse that pairs another in a team

running repairs *pl n* repairs that are done without greatly disrupting operations

runny *adj* **-nier, -niest 1** tending to flow: *a runny egg* **2** producing moisture: *a runny nose*

run off *vb* **1** to leave quickly **2 run off with a** to run away with in order to marry or live with **b** to steal **3** to produce (copies of a document) on a machine **4** to drain (liquid) or (of liquid) to be drained ▷ *n* **run-off 5** an extra race or contest to decide the winner after a tie **6** *NZ* grazing land for cattle

run-of-the-mill *adj* ordinary or average

run on *vb* to continue without interruption

run out *vb* **1** to use up or (of a supply) to be used up: *we soon ran out of gas* **2** to become invalid: *my passport has run out* **3 run out on** *informal* to desert or abandon **4** *cricket* to dismiss (a running batsman) by breaking the wicket with the ball while he is running between the wickets ▷ *n* **run-out 5** *cricket* dismissal of a batsman by running him out

run over *vb* **1** to knock down (a person) with a moving vehicle **2** to overflow **3** to examine hastily

runt *n* **1** the smallest and weakest young animal in a litter **2** an undersized or inferior person
WORD ORIGIN origin unknown

run through *vb* **1** to practise or rehearse **2** to pierce with a sword or other weapon ▷ *n* **run-through 3** a practice or rehearsal

run to *vb* **1** to reach an amount or size: *the testimony ran to a million words* **2** to be or have enough money for: *we do not run to these luxuries, I am afraid*

run up *vb* **1** to amass: *running up massive debts* **2** to make by sewing together quickly **3 run up against** to experience (difficulties) ▷ *n* **run-up 4** the time just before an event: *the run-up to the elections*

runway *n* a hard level roadway where aircraft take off and land

Runyon *n* (**Alfred**) **Damon** 1884–1946, US short-story writer, best known for his humorous tales about racy Broadway characters. His story

r

THESAURUS

run down *adj* **6 = exhausted**, weak, tired, drained, fatigued, weary, unhealthy, worn-out, debilitated, below par, under the weather (*informal*), enervated, out of condition, peaky OPPOSITE: fit **7 = dilapidated**, broken-down, shabby, worn-out, seedy, ramshackle, dingy, decrepit, tumbledown

runner *n* **1 = athlete**, miler, sprinter, harrier, jogger **2 = messenger**, courier, errand boy, dispatch bearer

running *adj* **1 = continuous**, constant, perpetual, uninterrupted, incessant, unceasing **2 = in succession**, together, unbroken, on the trot (*informal*) **3a = flowing**, moving, streaming, coursing ▷ *n* **9 = management**, control, administration, direction, conduct, charge, leadership, organization, regulation, supervision, coordination, superintendency **10 = working**, performance, operation, functioning, maintenance

collections include *Guys and Dolls* (1932), which became the basis of a musical (1950)

rupee *n* the standard monetary unit of a number of countries including India and Pakistan
WORD ORIGIN Hindi *rupaīyā*

Rupert[1] *n* **Prince** 1619–82, German-born nephew of Charles I: Royalist general during the Civil War (until 1646) and commander of the Royalist fleet (1648–50). After the Restoration he was an admiral of the English fleet in wars against the Dutch

Rupert[2] *n military derogatory, slang* a junior army officer

rupture ⊙ *n* **1** the act of breaking or the state of being broken **2** a breach of peaceful or friendly relations **3** *pathol* a hernia ▷ *vb* **-turing, -tured 4** to break or burst **5** to cause a breach in relations or friendship **6** to affect or be affected with a hernia
WORD ORIGIN Latin *rumpere* to burst forth

rural ⊙ *adj* in or of the countryside
WORD ORIGIN Latin *ruralis*

rural dean *n chiefly Brit* a clergyman with authority over a group of parishes

rural route *n US & Canad* a mail service or route in a rural area

Rurik *or* **Ryurik** *n* died 879 Varangian (Scandinavian Viking) leader who founded the Russian monarchy. He gained control over Novgorod (?862) and his dynasty, the **Rurikids**, ruled until 1598

ruse (**rooz**) *n* an action or plan intended to mislead someone
WORD ORIGIN Old French

rush[1] ⊙ *vb* **1** to move or do very quickly **2** to force (someone) to act hastily **3** to make a sudden attack upon (a person or place): *scores of pubescent girls rushed the stage* **4** to proceed or approach in a reckless manner **5** to come or flow quickly or suddenly: *the water rushed in, and the next instant the boat was swamped* ▷ *n* **6** a sudden quick or violent movement **7** a sudden demand or need **8** a sudden surge towards someone or something: *the gold rush* **9** a sudden surge of sensation **10** a sudden flow of air or liquid **11 rushes** (in film-making) the initial prints of a scene before editing ▷ *adj* **12** done with speed or urgency: *a rush job*
WORD ORIGIN Old French *ruser* to put to flight

rush[2] *n* a plant which grows in wet places and has a slender pithy stem **rushy** *adj*
WORD ORIGIN Old English *risce, rysce*

rush hour *n* a period at the beginning and end of the working day when large numbers of people are travelling to or from work

rush light *n* an old-fashioned candle made of rushes

rusk *n* a hard brown crisp biscuit, often used for feeding babies
WORD ORIGIN Spanish or Portuguese *rosca* screw, bread shaped in a twist

Rusk *n* (**David**) **Dean** 1909–94, US statesman: secretary of state (1961–69). He defended US military involvement in Vietnam and opposed recognition of communist China

russet *adj* **1** *literary* reddish-brown: *a disarray of russet curls* ▷ *n* **2** an apple with a rough reddish-brown skin
WORD ORIGIN Latin *russus*

Russian *adj* **1** of Russia ▷ *n* **2** a person from Russia **3** the official language of Russia and, formerly, of the Soviet Union

Russian doll *n* any of a set of hollow wooden figures, each of which splits in half to contain the next smallest figure, down to the smallest

Russian roulette *n* an act of bravado in which a person spins the cylinder of a revolver loaded with only one cartridge and presses the trigger with the barrel against his or her own head

rust ⊙ *n* **1** a reddish-brown oxide coating formed on iron or steel by the action of oxygen and moisture **2** a fungal disease of plants which produces a reddish-brown discoloration ▷ *adj* **3** reddish-brown ▷ *vb* **4** to become coated with a layer of rust **5** to deteriorate through lack of use: *my brain had rusted up*
WORD ORIGIN Old English *rūst*

rust belt *n* an area where heavy industry is in decline, esp. in the Midwest of the United States

rustic *adj* **1** of or resembling country people **2** of or living in the country **3** crude, awkward, or uncouth **4** made of untrimmed branches: *rustic furniture* ▷ *n* **5** a person from the country **rusticity** *n*
WORD ORIGIN Latin *rusticus*

rusticate *vb* **-cating, -cated 1** *Brit* to send (a student) down from university for a specified time as a punishment **2** to retire to the country **3** to make or become rustic
WORD ORIGIN Latin *rus* the country

rustle[1] *vb* **-tling, -tled 1** to make a low crisp whispering sound: *the leaves rustled in the breeze* ▷ *n* **2** this sound
WORD ORIGIN Old English *hrūxlian*

rustle[2] *vb* **-tling, -tled** *chiefly US & Canad* to steal (livestock) **rustler** *n*
WORD ORIGIN probably from RUSTLE[1] (in the sense: to move with a quiet sound)

rustle up *vb informal* to prepare or find at short notice: *Bob rustled up a meal*

rusty ⊙ *adj* **rustier, rustiest 1** affected by rust: *a rusty old freighter* **2** reddish-brown **3** out of practice in a skill or subject: *your skills may be a little rusty, but your past experience will more than make up for that* **rustily** *adv* **rustiness** *n*

rut[1] *n* **1** a groove or furrow in a soft road, caused by wheels **2** dull settled habits or way of living: *his career was in a rut*
WORD ORIGIN probably from French *route* road

rut[2] *n* **1** a recurrent period of sexual excitement in certain male ruminants ▷ *vb* **rutting, rutted 2** (of male ruminants) to be in a period of sexual excitement
WORD ORIGIN Old French *rut* noise, roar

rutabaga *n* ▸ the US and Canadian term for **swede**

ruthenium *n chem* a rare hard brittle white metallic element. Symbol: Ru
WORD ORIGIN Medieval Latin *Ruthenia* Russia, where it was discovered

rutherfordium *n chem* an artificially produced radioactive element. Symbol: Rf
WORD ORIGIN after E. *Rutherford*, physicist

ruthless ⊙ *adj* **1** feeling or showing no mercy **2** thorough and forceful,

r

THESAURUS

rupture *n* **1 = break**, tear, split, crack, rent, burst, breach, fracture, cleavage, cleft, fissure ▷ *vb* **4 = break**, separate, tear, split, crack, burst, rend, fracture, sever, puncture, cleave

rural *adj* **= agricultural**, country, agrarian, upcountry, agrestic

rush[1] *vb* **1 = hurry**, run, race, shoot, fly, career, speed, tear, dash, sprint, scramble, bolt, dart, hasten, scurry, stampede, lose no time, make short work of, burn rubber *(informal)*, make haste, hotfoot **OPPOSITE:** dawdle **3 = attack**, storm, capture, overcome, charge at, take by storm ▷ *n* **6 = dash**, charge, race, scramble, stampede, expedition, speed, dispatch **9 = surge**, flow, gush ▷ *adj* **12 = hasty**, fast, quick, hurried, emergency, prompt, rapid, urgent, swift, brisk, cursory, expeditious **OPPOSITE:** leisurely

rust *n* **1 = corrosion**, oxidation **2 = mildew**, must, mould, rot, blight ▷ *vb* **4 = corrode**, tarnish, oxidize

rusty *adj* **1 = corroded**, rusted, oxidized, rust-covered **2 = reddish-brown**, chestnut, reddish, russet, coppery, rust-coloured **3 = out of practice**, weak, impaired, sluggish, stale, deficient, not what it was, unpractised

ruthless *adj* **1, 2 = merciless**, hard, severe, fierce, harsh, cruel, savage, brutal, stern, relentless, adamant,

DICTIONARY

regardless of effect: *the ruthless pursuit of cost-effectiveness* **ruthlessly** *adv* **ruthlessness** *n*
WORD ORIGIN *ruth* pity

rutted *adj* (of a road) very uneven because of ruts

Ruyter *n* **Michiel Adriaanszoon de** 1607–76, Dutch admiral, noted for actions in the Anglo-Dutch wars in 1652–53, 1665–67, 1672, and 1673, when he prevented an Anglo-French invasion

RV Revised Version (of the Bible)

Ryder *n* **Susan**, Baroness Ryder of Warsaw. 1923–2000, British philanthropist; founder of the Sue Ryder Foundation for the Sick and Disabled, which is funded by a chain of charity shops: married to Leonard Cheshire

rye *n* **1** a tall grasslike cereal grown for its light brown grain **2** the grain of this plant **3** Also called: **rye whiskey** whisky distilled from rye **4** *US* ▸ short for **rye bread**
WORD ORIGIN Old English *ryge*

rye bread *n* bread made entirely or partly from rye flour

rye-grass *n* any of several grasses grown for fodder

Ryle *n* **1 Gilbert** 1900–76, British philosopher. His works include *The Concept of Mind* (1949) **2** Sir **Martin** 1918–84, British astronomer, noted for his research on radio astronomy: Astronomer Royal 1972–82; shared the Nobel prize for physics in 1974

THESAURUS

ferocious, callous, heartless, unrelenting, inhuman, inexorable, remorseless, barbarous, pitiless, unfeeling, hard-hearted, without pity, unmerciful, unpitying
OPPOSITE: merciful

r

Ss

s second (of time)

S 1 South(ern) **2** *chem* sulphur **3** *physics* siemens

-'s *suffix* **1** forming the possessive singular of nouns and some pronouns: *woman's; one's* **2** forming the possessive plural of nouns whose plurals do not end in *-s*: *children's* **3** forming the plural of numbers, letters, or symbols: *20's* **4** *informal* contraction of *is* or *has*: *it's over* **5** *informal* contraction of *us* with *let*: *let's go*

SA 1 Salvation Army **2** South Africa **3** South America **4** South Australia

SAA South African Airways

Saadi *n* ▸ a variant spelling of **Sadi**

Saarinen *n* **Eero** 1910–61, US architect, born in Finland. His works include the US Embassy, London (1960)

Sabatier *n* **Paul** 1854–1941, French chemist, who discovered a process for the hydrogenation of organic compounds: shared the Nobel prize for chemistry (1912)

Sabbath *n* **1** Saturday, observed by Jews as the day of worship and rest **2** Sunday, observed by Christians as the day of worship and rest
WORD ORIGIN Hebrew *shābath* to rest

sabbatical *adj* **1** denoting a period of leave granted at intervals to university teachers for rest, study, or travel: *a sabbatical year* ▹ *n* **2** a sabbatical period
WORD ORIGIN see SABBATH

SABC South African Broadcasting Corporation

Sabin *n* **Albert Bruce** 1906–93, US microbiologist, born in Poland. He developed the **Sabin vaccine** (1955), taken orally to immunize against poliomyelitis

sable *n, pl* **-bles** *or* **-ble 1** a marten of N Asia, N Europe, and America, with dark brown luxuriant fur **2** the highly valued fur of this animal, used to make coats and hats ▹ *adj* **3** dark brown-to-black
WORD ORIGIN Slavic

sable antelope *n* a large black African antelope with stout backward-curving horns

sabot (sab-oh) *n* a heavy wooden or wooden-soled shoe; clog
WORD ORIGIN French

sabotage ❶ *n* **1** the deliberate destruction or damage of equipment, for example by enemy agents or dissatisfied employees **2** deliberate obstruction of or damage to a cause or effort ▹ *vb* **-taging, -taged 3** to destroy or disrupt by sabotage
WORD ORIGIN French

saboteur *n* a person who commits sabotage
WORD ORIGIN French

sabre *or US* **saber** *n* **1** a heavy single-edged cavalry sword with a curved blade **2** a light sword used in fencing, with a narrow V-shaped blade
WORD ORIGIN German (dialect) *Sabel*

sac *n* a pouch or pouchlike part in an animal or plant
WORD ORIGIN Latin *saccus*

saccharin *n* an artificial sweetener
WORD ORIGIN Greek *sakkharon* sugar

saccharine *adj* **1** excessively sweet or sentimental: *saccharine ballads* **2** like or containing sugar or saccharin

Sacco *n* **Nicola** 1891–1927, US radical agitator, born in Italy. With Bartolomeo Vanzetti, he was executed for murder (1927) despite suspicions that their political opinions influenced the verdict: the case caused international protests

sacerdotal *adj formal* of priests or the priesthood
WORD ORIGIN Latin *sacerdos* priest

sachet *n* **1** a small sealed usually plastic envelope containing a small portion of a substance such as shampoo **2** a small soft bag of perfumed powder, placed in drawers to scent clothing
WORD ORIGIN French

Sachs *n* **1 Hans** (hans) 1494–1576, German master shoemaker and Meistersinger, portrayed by Wagner in *Die Meistersinger von Nürnberg* **2 Nelly** (**Leonie**) 1891–1970, German Jewish poet and dramatist, who escaped from Nazi Germany and settled in Sweden. Her works include *Eli: A Mystery Play of the Sufferings of Israel* (1951) and 'O the Chimneys', a poem about the Nazi extermination camps. Nobel prize for literature 1966 jointly with Shmuel Yosef Agnon

sack¹ ❶ *n* **1** a large bag made of coarse cloth or thick paper and used for carrying or storing goods **2** the amount contained in a sack **3 the sack** *informal* dismissal from employment **4** *slang* bed **5 hit the sack** *slang* to go to bed ▹ *vb* **6** *informal* to dismiss from employment
sacklike *adj*
WORD ORIGIN Greek *sakkos*

sack² ❶ *n* **1** the plundering of a captured town or city by an army or mob ▹ *vb* **2** to plunder and partially destroy (a town or city)
WORD ORIGIN French *mettre à sac* to put (loot) in a sack

sackbut *n* a medieval form of trombone
WORD ORIGIN French *saqueboute*

sackcloth *n* **1** ▸ same as **sacking 2** garments made of such cloth, worn formerly to indicate mourning **3 sackcloth and ashes** an exaggerated attempt to apologize or compensate for a mistake or wrongdoing

sacking *n* coarse cloth woven from flax, hemp, or jute, and used to make sacks

Sacks *n* Sir **Jonathan** (**Henry**) born 1948, British rabbi; Commonwealth chief rabbi from 1991; knighted 2005

Sackville *n* **Thomas,** 1st Earl of Dorset. 1536–1608, English poet, dramatist, and statesman. He collaborated with Thomas Norton on the early blank-verse tragedy *Gorboduc* (1561)

Sackville-West *n* **Victoria** (**Mary**), known as *Vita*. 1892–1962, British writer and gardener, whose works include the novel *The Edwardians* (1930) and the poem *The Land* (1931). She is also noted for the gardens at Sissinghurst Castle, Kent. Married to Harold Nicolson

sacrament *n* **1** a symbolic religious ceremony in the Christian Church, such as baptism or communion **2** Holy Communion **3** something regarded as sacred **sacramental** *adj*

THESAURUS

sabotage *n* **1 = damage**, destruction, wrecking, vandalism, deliberate damage ▹ *vb* **3 = damage**, destroy, wreck, undermine, disable, disrupt, cripple, subvert, incapacitate, vandalize, throw a spanner in the works *(Brit informal)*

sack¹ *n* **1 = bag**, pocket, poke *(Scot)*, sac, pouch, receptacle **3 the sack** *(informal)* **= dismissal**, discharge, the boot *(slang)*, the axe *(informal)*, the chop *(Brit slang)*, the push *(slang)*, the (old) heave-ho *(informal)*, termination of employment, the order of the boot *(slang)* ▹ *vb* **6** *(informal)* **= dismiss**, fire *(informal)*, axe *(informal)*, discharge, kick out *(informal)*, give (someone) the boot *(slang)*, give (someone) his marching orders, kiss off *(slang, chiefly US & Canad)*, give (someone) the push *(informal)*, give (someone) the bullet *(Brit slang)*, give (someone) his books *(informal)*, give (someone) the elbow, give (someone) his cards, kennet *(Austral slang)*, jeff *(Austral slang)*

sack² *n* **1 = plundering**, looting, pillage, waste, rape, ruin, destruction, ravage, plunder, devastation, depredation,

DICTIONARY

WORD ORIGIN Latin *sacrare* to consecrate

sacred ❶ *adj* **1** exclusively devoted to a god or gods; holy **2** connected with religion or intended for religious use: *sacred music* **3** regarded as too important to be changed or interfered with: *sacred principles of free speech* **4 sacred to** dedicated to: *the site is sacred to Vishnu*
WORD ORIGIN Latin *sacer* holy

sacred cow *n informal* a person, custom, belief, or institution regarded as being beyond criticism
WORD ORIGIN alluding to the Hindu belief that cattle are sacred

sacrifice ❶ *n* **1** a surrender of something of value in order to gain something more desirable or prevent some evil **2** a ritual killing of a person or animal as an offering to a god **3** a symbolic offering of something to a god **4** the person or animal killed or offered ▷ *vb* **-ficing, -ficed 5** to make a sacrifice (of) **6** *chess* to permit or force one's opponent to capture (a piece) as a tactical move **sacrificial** *adj*
WORD ORIGIN Latin *sacer* holy + *facere* to make

sacrilege *n* **1** the misuse of or disrespect shown to something sacred **2** disrespect for a person who is widely admired or a belief that is widely accepted: *it is a sacrilege to offend democracy* **sacrilegious** *adj*
WORD ORIGIN Latin *sacrilegus* temple robber

sacristan *n* a person in charge of the contents of a church; sexton
WORD ORIGIN Latin *sacer* holy

sacristy *n, pl* **-ties** a room attached to a church or chapel where the sacred objects are kept

sacrosanct *adj* regarded as too important to be criticized or changed: *weekend rest days were considered sacrosanct by staff* **sacrosanctity** *n*
WORD ORIGIN Latin *sacer* holy + *sanctus* hallowed

sacrum (say-krum) *n, pl* **-cra** *anat* the large wedge-shaped bone in the lower part of the back
WORD ORIGIN Latin *os sacrum* holy bone, because it was used in sacrifices

sad ❶ *adj* **sadder, saddest 1** feeling sorrow; unhappy **2** causing, suggesting, or expressing sorrow: *a sad story* **3** deplorably bad: *the garden was in a sad state* **4** regrettable: *it's rather sad he can't be with us* **5** *Brit informal* ridiculously pathetic: *a sad, boring little wimp* **6** *vb* **pack a sad** NZ *slang* to strongly express sadness or displeasure **sadly** *adv* **sadness** *n*
WORD ORIGIN Old English *sæd* weary

sadden ❶ *vb* to make (someone) sad

saddle ❶ *n* **1** a seat for a rider, usually made of leather, placed on a horse's back and secured under its belly **2** a similar seat on a bicycle, motorcycle, or tractor **3** a cut of meat, esp. mutton, consisting of both loins **4 in the saddle** in a position of control ▷ *vb* **-dling, -dled 5** to put a saddle on (a horse): *we saddled at dawn* **6 saddle with** to burden with (a responsibility): *he was also saddled with debt*
WORD ORIGIN Old English *sadol, sadul*

saddleback *n* **1** an animal with a marking resembling a saddle on its back **2** a hill with a concave outline at the top **saddle-backed** *adj*

saddlebag *n* a pouch or small bag attached to the saddle of a horse, bicycle, or motorcycle

saddle horse *n* a horse trained for riding only

saddler *n* a person who makes, deals in, or repairs saddles and other leather equipment for horses

saddlery *n, pl* **-dleries 1** saddles and harness for horses collectively **2** the work or place of work of a saddler

saddle soap *n* a soft soap used to preserve and clean leather

saddletree *n* the frame of a saddle

saddo *n Brit informal* a pathetic or socially inadequate person

Sadducee (sad-yew-see) *n judaism* a member of an ancient Jewish sect that denied the resurrection of the dead and accepted only the traditional written law

sadhu (sah-doo) *n* a Hindu wandering holy man
WORD ORIGIN Sanskrit

Sadi *or* **Saadi** *n* original name *Sheikh Muslih Addin* ?1184–1292, Persian poet. His best-known works are *Gulistan* (Flower Garden) and *Bostan* (Tree Garden), long moralistic poems in prose and verse

sadism (say-diz-zum) *n* the gaining of pleasure, esp. sexual pleasure, from infliction of suffering on another person **sadist** *n* **sadistic** *adj* **sadistically** *adv*
WORD ORIGIN after the Marquis de *Sade*, soldier & writer

sadomasochism *n* **1** the combination of sadistic and masochistic elements in one person, characterized by both submissive and aggressive periods in relationships with others **2** a sexual practice in which one partner adopts a masochistic role and the other a sadistic one **sadomasochist** *n* **sadomasochistic** *adj*

s.a.e. *Brit, Austral & NZ* stamped addressed envelope

safari *n, pl* **-ris** an overland expedition for hunting or observing animals, esp. in Africa
WORD ORIGIN Swahili: journey

safari park *n* an enclosed park in which wild animals are kept uncaged in the open and can be viewed by the public from cars or buses

safe ❶ *adj* **1** giving security or protection from harm: *a safe environment* **2** free from danger: *she*

S

THESAURUS

despoliation, rapine ▷ *vb* **2 = plunder**, loot, pillage, destroy, strip, rob, raid, ruin, devastate, spoil, rifle, demolish, ravage, lay waste, despoil, maraud, depredate *(rare)*

sacred *adj* **1 = holy**, hallowed, consecrated, blessed, divine, revered, venerable, sanctified
OPPOSITE: secular
2 = religious, holy, ecclesiastical, hallowed, venerated
OPPOSITE: unconsecrated
3 = inviolable, protected, sacrosanct, secure, hallowed, inalienable, invulnerable, inviolate, unalterable

sacrifice *n* **1 = surrender**, loss, giving up, resignation, rejection, waiver, abdication, renunciation, repudiation, forswearing, relinquishment, eschewal, self-denial **2 = offering**, immolation, oblation, hecatomb ▷ *vb* **5a = offer**, offer up, immolate **5b = give up**, abandon, relinquish, lose, surrender, let go, do without, renounce, forfeit, forego, say goodbye to

sad *adj* **1 = unhappy**, down, low, blue, depressed, gloomy, grieved, dismal, melancholy, sombre, glum, wistful, mournful, dejected, downcast, grief-stricken, tearful, lugubrious, pensive, disconsolate, doleful, heavy-hearted, down in the dumps *(informal)*, cheerless, lachrymose, woebegone, down in the mouth *(informal)*, low-spirited, triste *(archaic)*, sick at heart **OPPOSITE:** happy
2 = tragic, moving, upsetting, dark, sorry, depressing, disastrous, dismal, pathetic, poignant, harrowing, grievous, pitiful, calamitous, heart-rending, pitiable **3, 4 = deplorable**, bad, sorry, terrible, distressing, unfortunate, miserable, dismal, shabby, heartbreaking, regrettable, lamentable, wretched, to be deplored **OPPOSITE:** good

sadden *vb* **= upset**, depress, distress, grieve, desolate, cast down, bring tears to your eyes, make sad, dispirit, make your heart bleed, aggrieve, deject, cast a gloom upon

saddle *vb* **6 = burden**, load, lumber *(Brit informal)*, charge, tax, task, encumber

safe *adj* **1 = protected**, secure, in safety, impregnable, out of danger, safe and sound, in safe hands, out of harm's way, free from harm
OPPOSITE: endangered

DICTIONARY

doesn't feel safe **3** taking or involving no risks: *a safe bet* **4** not dangerous: *the beef is safe to eat* **5 on the safe side** as a precaution ▷ *n* **6** a strong metal container with a secure lock, for storing money or valuables
safely *adv*
WORD ORIGIN Old French *salf*

safe-conduct *n* **1** a document giving official permission to travel through a dangerous region, esp. in time of war **2** the protection given by such a document

safe-deposit *or* **safety-deposit** *n* a place or building with facilities for the safe storage of money and valuables

safeguard ❶ *vb* **1** to protect (something) from being harmed or destroyed ▷ *n* **2** a person or thing that ensures protection against danger or harm: *safeguards to prevent air collisions*

safekeeping *n* protection from theft or damage: *I put my money in a bank for safekeeping*

safe sex *or* **safer sex** *n* nonpenetrative sex, or intercourse using a condom, intended to prevent the spread of HIV

safety ❶ *n, pl* **-ties 1** the quality or state of being free from danger **2** shelter: *they swam to safety*

safety belt *n* ▸ same as **seat belt**

safety catch *n* a mechanism on a gun that prevents it from being fired accidentally

safety curtain *n* a fireproof curtain that can be lowered to separate the auditorium from the stage in a theatre to prevent the spread of a fire

safety lamp *n* a miner's oil lamp designed to prevent it from igniting combustible gas

safety match *n* a match that will light only when struck against a specially prepared surface

safety net *n* **1** a large net under a trapeze or high wire to catch performers if they fall **2** something that can be relied on for help in the event of difficulties: *the social security safety net*

safety pin *n* a pin bent back on itself so that it forms a spring, with the point shielded by a guard when closed

safety razor *n* a razor with a guard over the blade or blades to protect the skin from deep cuts

safety valve *n* **1** a valve in a boiler or machine that allows fluid or gases to escape at excess pressure **2** an outlet that allows one to express strong feelings without harming or offending other people: *sport acted as a safety valve for his pent-up frustrations*

safflower *n* a thistle-like plant with orange-yellow flowers, which yields a dye and an oil used in paints, medicines, and cooking
WORD ORIGIN Old French *saffleur*

saffron *n* **1** a type of crocus with purple or white flowers with orange stigmas **2** the dried orange-coloured stigmas of this plant, used for colouring or flavouring ▷ *adj* **3** orange-yellow
WORD ORIGIN Arabic *za'farān*

sag ❶ *vb* **sagging, sagged 1** to sink in the middle, under weight or pressure: *the bed sagged nearly to the floor* **2** (of courage or spirits) to weaken or tire **3** (of clothes) to hang loosely or unevenly **4** to fall in value: *the stock market sagged* ▷ *n* **5** the act or state of sagging **saggy** *adj*
WORD ORIGIN from Old Norse

saga ❶ (**sah**-ga) *n* **1** a medieval Scandinavian legend telling the adventures of a hero or a family **2** *informal* a long story or series of events: *the long-running saga of the hostage issue*
WORD ORIGIN Old Norse

sagacious *adj formal* wise or sensible
sagaciously *adv* **sagacity** *n*
WORD ORIGIN Latin *sagax*

Sagan *n* **1 Carl** (**Edward**) 1934–96, US astronomer and writer on scientific subjects; presenter of the television series *Cosmos* (1980) **2 Françoise** original name *Françoise Quoirez*. 1935–2004, French writer, best-known for the novels *Bonjour Tristesse* (1954) and *Aimez-vous Brahms?* (1959)

sage[1] ❶ *n* **1** a person, esp. an old man, regarded as being very wise ▷ *adj* **2** very wise or knowledgeable, esp. as the result of age or experience
WORD ORIGIN Latin *sapere* to be sensible

sage[2] *n* **1** a Mediterranean plant with grey-green leaves which are used in cooking for flavouring **2** ▸ short for **sagebrush**
WORD ORIGIN Latin *salvus* in good health (from its curative properties)

sagebrush *n* an aromatic plant of W North America, with silver-green leaves and large clusters of small white flowers

Sagittarius *n astrol* the ninth sign of the zodiac; the Archer
WORD ORIGIN Latin

sago *n* an edible starch from the powdered pith of the sago palm tree, used for puddings and as a thickening agent
WORD ORIGIN Malay *sāgū*

sahib *n* an Indian term of address equivalent to *sir*, formerly used as a mark of respect to a European man
WORD ORIGIN Urdu

said *adj* **1** named or mentioned already: *she had heard that the said lady was also a medium* ▷ *vb* **2** ▸ the past of **say**

Saigo Takamori *n* 1828–77, Japanese samurai, who led (1868) the coup that restored imperial government. In 1877 he reluctantly led a samurai rebellion, committing suicide when it failed

sail ❶ *n* **1** a sheet of canvas or other fabric, spread on rigging to catch the wind and move a ship over water **2** a voyage on such a ship: *a relaxing sail across the lake* **3** a ship or ships with sails: *to travel by sail* **4** one of the revolving arms of a windmill **5 set sail** to begin a voyage by water **6 under sail a** under way **b** with sail

S

THESAURUS

2 = all right, fine, intact, unscathed, unhurt, unharmed, undamaged, out of the woods, O.K. *or* okay *(informal)* **3 = risk-free**, sound, secure, certain, impregnable, riskless ▷ *n* **6 = strongbox**, vault, coffer, repository, deposit box, safe-deposit box

safeguard *vb* **1 = protect**, guard, defend, save, screen, secure, preserve, look after, shield, watch over, keep safe ▷ *n* **2 = protection**, security, defence, guard, shield, armour, aegis, bulwark, surety

safety *n* **1 = security**, protection, safeguards, assurance, precautions, immunity, safety measures, impregnability **OPPOSITE:** risk **2 = shelter**, haven, protection, cover, retreat, asylum, refuge, sanctuary

sag *vb* **1 = drop**, sink, slump, flop, droop, loll **2 = decline**, fall, slip, tire, slide, flag, slump, weaken, wilt, wane, cave in, droop **3 = droop**, bag, fall, drop, seat *(of a skirt, etc)*, settle, slump, dip, give way, bulge, swag, hang loosely, fall unevenly, sink

saga *n* **1 = epic**, story, tale, legend, adventure, romance, narrative, chronicle, yarn, fairy tale, folk tale, roman-fleuve *(French)* **2** *(informal)* **= carry-on** *(informal)*, to-do, performance *(informal)*, rigmarole, soap opera, pantomime *(informal)*

sage[1] *n* **1 = wise man**, philosopher, guru, authority, expert, master, elder, pundit, Solomon, mahatma, Nestor, savant, Solon, man of learning, tohunga *(NZ)* ▷ *adj* **2 = wise**, learned, intelligent, sensible, politic, acute, discerning, prudent, canny, judicious, perspicacious, sagacious, sapient

sail *n* **1 = sheet**, canvas ▷ *vb* **7 = go by water**, cruise, voyage, ride the waves, go by sea **8 = set sail**, embark, get under way, put to sea, put off, leave port, hoist sail, cast *or* weigh anchor **10 = pilot**, steer, navigate, captain, skipper **12 = glide**, sweep, float, shoot, fly, wing, soar, drift, skim, scud, skirr

DICTIONARY

hoisted ▷*vb* **7** to travel in a boat or ship: *to sail around the world* **8** to begin a voyage: *he hoped to sail at eleven* **9** (of a ship) to move over the water **10** to navigate (a ship): *she sailed the schooner up the channel* **11** to sail over: *he had already sailed the Pacific* **12** to move along smoothly **13 sail into** *informal* to make a violent attack on **14 sail through** to progress quickly or effortlessly: *the top seed sailed through to the second round*
WORD ORIGIN Old English *segl*

sailboard *n* a board with a mast and a single sail, used for windsurfing

sailcloth *n* **1** the fabric used for making sails **2** a canvas-like cloth used for clothing

sailfish *n, pl* **-fish** *or* **-fishes** a large tropical game fish, with a long sail-like fin on its back

sailor ⓣ *n* **1** any member of a ship's crew, esp. one below the rank of officer **2** a person considered as liable or not liable to seasickness: *a good sailor*

sainfoin (san-foin) *n* a Eurasian plant with pink flowers, widely grown as feed for grazing farm animals
WORD ORIGIN Medieval Latin *sanum faenum* wholesome hay

Sainsbury *n* **David John,** Baron born 1940, British businessman and politician, chief executive of the Sainsbury supermarket chain from 1992; science minister (1998–2006)

saint *n* **1** a person who after death is formally recognized by a Christian Church as deserving special honour because of having lived a very holy life **2** an exceptionally good person **sainthood** *n* **saintlike** *adj*
WORD ORIGIN Latin *sanctus* holy

Saint Bernard *n* a very large dog with a dense red-and-white coat, formerly used as a mountain-rescue dog

Sainte-Beuve *n* **Charles Augustin** 1804–69, French critic, best known for his collections of essays *Port Royal* (1840–59) and *Les Causeries du Lundi* (1851–62)

sainted *adj* **1** formally recognized by a Christian Church as a saint **2** having the qualities, such as patience and kindness, of a saint **3** hallowed or holy

Saint-Exupéry *n* **Antoine de** 1900–44, French novelist and aviator. His novels of aviation include *Vol de nuit* (1931) and *Terre des hommes* (1939). He also wrote the fairy tale *Le petit prince* (1943)

Saint-John Perse *n* ▸See **Perse**

Saint John's wort *n* a plant with yellow flowers

Saint-Just *n* **Louis Antoine Léon de** 1767–94, French Revolutionary leader and orator. A member of the Committee of Public Safety (1793–94), he was guillotined with Robespierre

Saint Leger *n* an annual horse race for three-year-old horses, run at Doncaster

saintly *adj* behaving in a very good, patient, or holy way **saintliness** *n*

Saint-Pierre[1] *n* usually abbreviated to **St-Pierre** a town on the coast of the French island of Martinique, destroyed by the eruption of Mont Pelée in 1902 with the loss of about 30 000 lives; later partly rebuilt

Saint-Pierre[2] *n* **Jacques Henri Bernardin de** 1737–1814, French author; his work, which was greatly influenced by the writings of Rousseau, includes *Voyage à l'Île de France* (1773), *Études de la nature* (1784, 1788), and *La chaumière indienne* (1791)

Saint-Saëns *n* **(Charles) Camille** (kamij) 1835–1921, French composer, pianist, and organist. His works include the symphonic poem *Danse Macabre* (1874), the opera *Samson and Delilah* (1877), the humorous orchestral suite *Carnival of Animals* (1886), five symphonies, and five piano concertos

Saintsbury *n* **George Edward Bateman** 1845–1933, British literary critic and historian; author of many works on English and French literature

Saint Vitus's dance *n* *pathol* ▸a nontechnical name for **chorea**

saithe *n* *Brit* a dark-coloured food fish found in northern seas
WORD ORIGIN Old Norse *seithr* coalfish

sake[1] ⓣ *n* **1 for someone's** *or* **one's own sake** for the benefit or interest of someone *or* oneself **2 for the sake of something** for the purpose of obtaining or achieving something **3 for its own sake** for the enjoyment obtained by doing something **4** used in various exclamations of annoyance, impatience, or urgency: *for God's sake*
WORD ORIGIN Old English *sacu* lawsuit (hence, a cause)

sake[2] *or* **saki** (sah-kee) *n* a Japanese alcoholic drink made from fermented rice
WORD ORIGIN Japanese

Sakharov *n* **Andrei** 1921–89, Soviet physicist and human-rights campaigner: Nobel peace prize 1975

salaam (sal-**ahm**) *n* **1** a Muslim greeting consisting of a deep bow with the right palm on the forehead **2** a greeting signifying peace ▷*vb* **3** to make a salaam (to)
WORD ORIGIN Arabic *salām* peace

salacious *adj* **1** having an excessive interest in sex **2** (of books, films, or jokes) concerned with sex in an unnecessarily detailed way **salaciousness** *n*
WORD ORIGIN Latin *salax* fond of leaping

salad *n* a dish of raw vegetables, often served with a dressing, eaten as a separate course or as part of a main course
WORD ORIGIN Old French *salade*

salad days *pl n* a period of youth and inexperience

salad dressing *n* a sauce for salad, such as oil and vinegar or mayonnaise

salamander *n* **1** a tailed amphibian which looks like a lizard **2** a mythical creature supposed to live in fire
WORD ORIGIN Greek *salamandra*

salami *n* a highly spiced sausage, usually flavoured with garlic
WORD ORIGIN Italian

salaried *adj* earning or providing a salary: *a salaried employee; a salaried position*

salary ⓣ *n, pl* **-ries** a fixed regular payment made by an employer, usually monthly, for professional or office work
WORD ORIGIN Latin *salarium* the sum given to Roman soldiers to buy salt

Salazar *n* **Antonio de Oliveira** 1889–1970, Portuguese statesman; dictator (1932–68)

sale ⓣ *n* **1** the exchange of goods or property for an agreed sum of money **2** the amount sold **3** an event at which goods are sold at reduced prices **4** an auction **5 sales** the department dealing with selling its company's products
WORD ORIGIN Old English *sala*

saleable *or US* **salable** *adj* fit for selling or capable of being sold **saleability** *or US* **salability** *n*

sale of work *n* a sale of articles, often handmade, the proceeds of which go to a charity

saleroom *n* *chiefly Brit* a room where objects are displayed for sale

S

THESAURUS

sailor *n* **1 = mariner**, marine, seaman, salt, tar *(informal)*, hearty *(informal)*, navigator, sea dog, seafarer, matelot *(slang, chiefly Brit)*, Jack Tar, seafaring man, lascar, leatherneck *(slang)*

sake[1] *n* **1 for someone's sake = in someone's interests**, to someone's advantage, on someone's account, for the benefit of, for the good of, for the welfare of, out of respect for, out of consideration for, out of regard for

salary *n* **= pay**, income, wage, fee, payment, wages, earnings, allowance, remuneration, recompense, stipend, emolument

sale *n* **1 = selling**, marketing, dealing, trading, transaction, disposal, vending **4 = auction**, fair, mart, bazaar

salt *n* **1 = seasoning**, sodium chloride,

DICTIONARY

by auction
salesgirl *n* a young woman who sells goods in a shop
salesman *n, pl* **-men** **1** a man who sells goods in a shop **2** ▸ short for **travelling salesman**
salesmanship *n* the technique of or skill in selling
salesperson *n, pl* **-people** *or* **-persons** a person who sells goods in a shop
sales pitch *or* **talk** *n* persuasive talk used by a salesperson in persuading a customer to buy something
saleswoman *n, pl* **-women** a woman who sells goods in a shop
saleyard *n Austral & NZ* an area with pens for holding animals before auction
salicylic acid (sal-liss-ill-ik) *n* a white crystalline substance used to make aspirin and as a fungicide
WORD ORIGIN Latin *salix* willow
salient (say-lee-ent) *adj* **1** (of points or facts) most important: *the salient points of his speech* ▹ *n* **2** *mil* a projection of the forward line of an army into enemy-held territory
WORD ORIGIN Latin *salire* to leap
Salieri *n* **Antonio** 1750–1825, Italian composer and conductor, who worked in Vienna (from 1766). The suggestion that he poisoned Mozart has no foundation
saline (say-line) *adj* **1** of or containing salt: *a saline flavour* **2** *med* of or relating to a saline: *a saline drip* ▹ *n* **3** *med* a solution of sodium chloride and water **salinity** *n*
WORD ORIGIN Latin *sal* salt
salinization *or* **-isation** *n* the process by which salts accumulate in undrained land, damaging its potential for plant growth
saliva (sal-lie-va) *n* the watery fluid secreted by glands in the mouth, which aids digestion **salivary** *adj*
WORD ORIGIN Latin
salivate *vb* **-vating, -vated** to produce saliva, esp. an excessive amount **salivation** *n*
Salk *n* **Jonas Edward** 1914–95, US virologist: developed an injected vaccine against poliomyelitis (1954)
sallee *n Austral* **1** a SE Australian eucalyptus with a pale grey bark **2** an acacia tree
sallow *adj* (of human skin) of an unhealthy pale or yellowish colour **sallowness** *n*
WORD ORIGIN Old English *salu*
Sallust *n* full name *Gaius Sallustius Crispus* 86–?34 BC, Roman historian and statesman, noted for his histories of the Catiline conspiracy and the Roman war against Jugurtha
sally *n, pl* **-lies** **1** a witty remark **2** a sudden brief attack by troops **3** an excursion ▹ *vb* **-lies, -lying, -lied** **4** **sally forth** **a** to set out on a journey **b** to set out in an energetic manner
WORD ORIGIN Latin *salire* to leap
salmon *n, pl* **-ons** *or* **-on** a large pink-fleshed fish which is highly valued for food and sport: salmon live in the sea but return to fresh water to spawn
WORD ORIGIN Latin *salmo*
Salmond *n* **Alex(ander Elliot Anderson)** born 1954, Scottish Nationalist politician; first minister of the Scottish Parliament from 2007
salmonella (sal-mon-ell-a) *n* a kind of bacteria that can cause food poisoning
WORD ORIGIN after Daniel E. *Salmon*, veterinary surgeon
salmon ladder *n* a series of steps designed to enable salmon to move upstream to their breeding grounds
salon *n* **1** a commercial establishment in which hairdressers or fashion designers carry on their business **2** an elegant room in a large house in which guests are received **3** an informal gathering, esp. in the 18th, 19th, and early 20th centuries, of major literary, artistic, and political figures in a fashionable household **4** an art exhibition
WORD ORIGIN French
saloon *n* **1** a two-door or four-door car with a fixed roof **2** a comfortable but more expensive bar in a pub or hotel **3** a large public room on a passenger ship **4** *chiefly US & Canad* a place where alcoholic drink is sold and consumed
WORD ORIGIN from *salon*
salsa *n* **1** a lively Puerto Rican dance **2** big-band music accompanying this dance
WORD ORIGIN Spanish, literally: sauce
salsify *n, pl* **-fies** a Mediterranean plant with a long white edible root
WORD ORIGIN Italian *sassefrica*
salt ❶ *n* **1** sodium chloride, a white crystalline substance, used for seasoning and preserving food **2** *chem* a crystalline solid compound formed from an acid by replacing its hydrogen with a metal **3** lively wit: *his humour added salt to the discussion* **4** **old salt** an experienced sailor **5** **rub salt into someone's wounds** to make an unpleasant situation even worse for someone **6** **salt of the earth** a person or people regarded as the finest of their kind **7** **take something with a pinch of salt** to refuse to believe something is completely true or accurate **8** **worth one's salt** worthy of one's pay; efficient ▹ *vb* **9** to season or preserve with salt **10** to scatter salt over (an iced road or path) to melt the ice ▹ *adj* **11** preserved in or tasting of salt: *salt beef* ▸ See also **salt away, salts** > **salted** *adj*
WORD ORIGIN Old English *sealt*
SALT Strategic Arms Limitation Talks *or* Treaty
salt away *vb* to hoard or save (money) for the future
saltbush *n* a shrub that grow in alkaline
saltcellar *n* a small container for salt used at the table
WORD ORIGIN changed from *salt saler; saler* from Old French *saliere* container for salt
saltire *n* **1** *heraldry* a diagonal cross on a shield **2** the national flag of Scotland, a white diagonal cross on a blue background
salt lick *n* **1** a place where wild animals go to lick salt deposits **2** a block of salt given to domestic animals to lick
saltpetre *or US* **saltpeter** *n* ▸ same as **potassium nitrate**
WORD ORIGIN Latin *sal petrae* salt of rock
salts *pl n* **1** *med* mineral salts used as a medicine **2** **like a dose of salts** *informal* very quickly
saltwater *adj* of or inhabiting salt water, esp. the sea: *saltwater fish*
salty *adj* **saltier, saltiest** **1** of, tasting of, or containing salt **2** (esp. of humour) sharp and witty **saltiness** *n*
salubrious *adj* favourable to health **salubrity** *n*
WORD ORIGIN Latin *salus* health
Saluki *n* a tall hound with a smooth coat and long fringes on the ears and tail
WORD ORIGIN from *Saluq*, ancient Arabian city
salutary *adj* **1** (of an experience) producing a beneficial result despite being unpleasant: *a salutary reminder* **2** promoting health
WORD ORIGIN Latin *salutaris* wholesome
salutation *n formal* a greeting by words or actions
WORD ORIGIN Latin *salutare* to greet
salute ❶ *vb* **-luting, -luted** **1** to greet with friendly words or gestures of respect, such as bowing **2** to acknowledge with praise: *the statement salutes the changes of the past year* **3** *mil* to pay formal respect to (someone) by raising the right hand to the forehead ▹ *n* **4** the act of saluting as a formal military gesture

THESAURUS

table salt, rock salt ▹ *adj* **11 = salty**, salted, saline, brackish, briny
salute *vb* **1 = greet**, welcome, acknowledge, address, kiss, hail, salaam, accost, pay your respects to, doff your cap to, mihi (NZ)
2 = honour, acknowledge, recognize, take your hat off to (*informal*), pay tribute *or* homage to

S

DICTIONARY

of respect **5** the act of firing guns as a military greeting of honour
WORD ORIGIN Latin *salutare* to greet

salvage ❶ *n* **1** the rescue of a ship or its cargo from loss at sea **2** the saving of any goods or property from destruction or waste **3** the goods or property so saved **4** compensation paid for the salvage of a ship or its cargo ▷*vb* **-vaging, -vaged 5** to save (goods or property) from shipwreck, destruction, or waste **6** to gain (something beneficial) from a failure: *it's too late to salvage anything from the whole dismal display*
salvageable *adj*
WORD ORIGIN Latin *salvare* to save

salvation ❶ *n* **1** the act of preserving someone or something from harm **2** a person or thing that preserves from harm **3** *Christianity* the fact or state of being saved from the influence or consequences of sin
WORD ORIGIN Latin *salvatus* saved

Salvation Army *n* a Christian body organized on military lines for working among the poor and spreading the Christian faith

salve *n* **1** an ointment for wounds **2** anything that heals or soothes ▷*vb* **salving, salved 3 salve one's conscience** to do something in order to feel less guilty
WORD ORIGIN Old English *sealf*

salver *n* a tray, usually a silver one, on which something is presented
WORD ORIGIN Spanish *salva* tray from which the king's taster sampled food

salvia *n* any small plant or shrub of the sage genus
WORD ORIGIN Latin

salvo *n, pl* **-vos** *or* **-voes 1** a simultaneous discharge of guns in battle or on a ceremonial occasion **2** an outburst of applause or questions
WORD ORIGIN Italian *salva*, from Latin *salve!* greetings!

sal volatile (sal vol-at-ill-ee) *n* a solution of ammonium carbonate, used as smelling salts
WORD ORIGIN New Latin: volatile salt

SAM surface-to-air missile

Samaritan *n* **1** ▸ short for **Good Samaritan 2** a member of a voluntary organization (**the Samaritans**) which offers counselling to people in despair, esp. by telephone

samarium *n chem* a silvery metallic element of the rare-earth series. Symbol: Sm
WORD ORIGIN after Col. von *Samarski*, Russian inspector of mines

samba *n, pl* **-bas 1** a lively Brazilian dance **2** music for this dance
WORD ORIGIN Portuguese

same ❶ *adj* (usually preceded by *the*) **1** being the very one: *she is wearing the same hat* **2** being the one previously referred to: *it causes problems for the same reason* **3** alike in kind or quantity: *the same age* **4** unchanged in character or nature: *his attitude is the same as ever* **5 all the same** *or* **just the same** nevertheless; even so **6 be all the same** to be a matter of indifference: *it was all the same to me* ▷*adv* **7** in the same way; similarly: *I felt much the same* ▷*n* **8 the same** something that is like something else in kind or quantity: *this is basically much more of the same* **sameness** *n*
WORD ORIGIN Old Norse *samr*

samizdat *n* (in the former Soviet Union) a system of secret printing and distribution of banned literature
WORD ORIGIN Russian

samosa *n* (in Indian cookery) a small fried triangular spiced meat or vegetable pasty. Also (in S Africa): **samoosa**
WORD ORIGIN Hindi

samovar *n* a Russian metal tea urn in which the water is heated by an inner container
WORD ORIGIN Russian

Samoyed *n* a dog with a thick white coat and a tightly curled tail
WORD ORIGIN Russian *Samoed*

sampan *n* a small flat-bottomed boat with oars, used esp. in China
WORD ORIGIN Chinese *san* three + *pan* board

samphire *n* a plant found on rocks by the seashore
WORD ORIGIN French *herbe de Saint Pierre* Saint Peter's herb

sample ❶ *n* **1** a small part of anything, taken as being representative of a whole ▷*vb* **-pling, -pled 2** to take a sample or samples of **3** *music* **a** to take a short extract from (one record) and mix it into a different backing track **b** to record (a sound) and feed it into a computerized synthesizer so that it can be reproduced at any pitch
sampling *n*
WORD ORIGIN Latin *exemplum*

sampler *n* **1** a piece of embroidery done to show the embroiderer's skill in using many different stitches **2** *music* a piece of electronic equipment used for sampling

Sampras *n* **Pete** born 1971, US tennis player: US singles champion (1990, 1993, 1995, 1996, 2002); Wimbledon singles champion (1993–95, 1997–2000)

Samson *n* a man of outstanding physical strength
WORD ORIGIN from the biblical character who was renowned for his strength

samurai *n, pl* **-rai** a member of the aristocratic warrior caste of feudal Japan
WORD ORIGIN Japanese

sanatorium *or US* **sanitarium** *n, pl* **-riums** *or* **-ria 1** an institution providing medical treatment and rest for invalids or convalescents **2** *Brit* a room in a boarding school where sick pupils may be treated
WORD ORIGIN Latin *sanare* to heal

sanctify *vb* **-fies, -fying, -fied 1** to make holy **2** to free from sin **3** to approve (an action or practice) as religiously binding: *she is trying to make amends for her marriage not being sanctified* **sanctification** *n*
WORD ORIGIN Latin *sanctus* holy + *facere* to make

sanctimonious *adj* pretending to be very religious and virtuous
WORD ORIGIN Latin *sanctimonia* sanctity

sanction ❶ *n* **1** permission granted by authority: *official sanction* **2** support or approval: *they could not exist without his sanction* **3** something that gives binding force to a law, such as a penalty for breaking it or a reward for obeying it **4 sanctions** coercive

S

THESAURUS

salvage *vb* **5 = save**, recover, rescue, restore, repair, get back, retrieve, redeem, glean, repossess, fetch back

salvation *n* **1 = saving**, rescue, recovery, restoration, salvage, redemption, deliverance **OPPOSITE:** ruin

same *adj* **1 = the very same**, very, one and the same, selfsame **2 = aforementioned**, aforesaid, selfsame **3 = identical**, similar, alike, equal, twin, equivalent, corresponding, comparable, duplicate, indistinguishable, interchangeable **OPPOSITE:** different **4 = unchanged**, consistent, constant, uniform, unaltered, unfailing, invariable, unvarying, changeless **OPPOSITE:** altered

sample *n* **1a = specimen**, example, model, pattern, instance, representative, indication, illustration, exemplification **1b = cross section**, test, sampling ▷*vb* **2 = test**, try, check out (*informal*), experience, taste, examine, evaluate, inspect, experiment with, appraise, partake of

sanction *n* **1, 2 = permission**, backing, support, authority, approval, allowance, confirmation, endorsement, countenance, ratification, authorization, approbation, O.K. *or* okay (*informal*), stamp *or* seal of approval **OPPOSITE:** ban **4** (*pl*) **= ban**, restriction, boycott, embargo, exclusion, penalty, deterrent, prohibition, coercive measures **OPPOSITE:** permission

DICTIONARY

measures, such as boycotts and trade embargoes, taken by one or more states against another guilty of violating international law ▷ *vb* **5** to officially approve of or allow: *they do not want to sanction direct payments* **6** to confirm or ratify
WORD ORIGIN Latin *sancire* to decree

sanctity *n* the quality of something considered so holy or important it must be respected totally: *the sanctity of the Sabbath; the sanctity of marriage*

sanctuary ❶ *n, pl* **-aries 1** a holy place, such as a consecrated building or shrine **2** the part of a church nearest the main altar **3** a place of refuge or protection for someone who is being chased or hunted **4** refuge or safety: *the sanctuary of your own home* **5** a place, protected by law, where animals can live and breed without interference
WORD ORIGIN Latin *sanctus* holy

sanctum *n, pl* **-tums** *or* **-ta 1** a sacred or holy place **2** a room or place of total privacy
WORD ORIGIN Latin

sand *n* **1** a powdery substance consisting of very small rock or mineral grains, found on the seashore and in deserts **2 sands** a large sandy area, esp. on the seashore or in a desert ▷ *vb* **3** to smooth or polish the surface of (something) with sandpaper or a sander **4** to fill with sand: *the channel sanded up*
WORD ORIGIN Old English

Sandage *n* **Allan Rex** born 1926, US astronomer, who discovered the first quasar (1961)

sandal *n* a light shoe consisting of a sole held on the foot by thongs or straps **sandalled** *or US* **sandaled** *adj*
WORD ORIGIN Greek *sandalon*

sandalwood *n* **1** the hard light-coloured wood of a S Asian or Australian tree, which is used for carving and for incense, and which yields an aromatic oil used in perfumes **2** a tree yielding this wood
WORD ORIGIN Sanskrit *candana*

sandbag *n* **1** a sack filled with sand used to make a temporary defence against gunfire or flood water ▷ *vb* **-bagging, -bagged 2** to protect or strengthen with sandbags

sandbank *or* **sand bar** *n* a bank of sand in a sea or river, that may be exposed at low tide

sandblast *n* **1** a jet of sand blown from a nozzle under air or steam pressure ▷ *vb* **2** to clean or decorate (a surface) with a sandblast **sandblaster** *n*

sandboy *n* **happy as a sandboy** very happy

Sandburg *n* **Carl** 1878–1967, US writer, noted esp. for his poetry, often written in free verse

sand castle *n* a model of a castle made from sand

sander *n* a power-driven tool for smoothing surfaces, removing layers of paint from walls, etc.

Sanderson *n* **Tessa** born 1956, British javelin-thrower

S & M *informal* sadomasochism

sandman *n, pl* **-men** (in folklore) a magical person supposed to put children to sleep by sprinkling sand in their eyes

sand martin *n* a small brown European songbird which nests in tunnels bored in sand or river banks

sandpaper *n* **1** a strong paper coated with sand or other abrasive material for smoothing or polishing a surface ▷ *vb* **2** to smooth or polish (a surface) with sandpaper

sandpiper *n* a wading shore bird with a long bill and slender legs

sandpit *n* a shallow pit or container holding sand for children to play in

Sandrocottus *n* ▸ the Greek name of **Chandragupta**

sandshoes *pl n* light canvas shoes with rubber soles

sandstone *n* a sedimentary rock consisting mainly of sand grains, much used in building

sandstorm *n* a strong wind that whips up clouds of sand, esp. in a desert

sandwich *n* **1** two or more slices of bread, usually buttered, with a layer of food between them ▷ *vb* **2** to place between two other things: *shops sandwiched between flats*
WORD ORIGIN after 4th Earl of *Sandwich*, who ate sandwiches rather than leave the gambling table for meals

sandwich board *n* one of two connected boards that are hung over the shoulders in front of and behind a person to display advertisements

sandwich course *n Brit* an educational course consisting of alternate periods of study and industrial work

sandy *adj* **sandier, sandiest 1** resembling, containing, or covered with sand **2** (of hair) reddish-yellow **sandiness** *n*

sane ❶ *adj* **1** having a normal healthy mind **2** sensible or well-judged: *sane advice*
WORD ORIGIN Latin *sanus* healthy

sang *vb* ▸ the past tense of **sing**

Sanger *n* **1 Frederick** born 1918, English biochemist, who determined the molecular structure of insulin: awarded two Nobel prizes for chemistry (1958; 1980) **2 Margaret** (**Higgins**) 1883–1966, US leader of the birth-control movement

sang-froid (sahng-**frwah**) *n* composure and calmness in a difficult situation
WORD ORIGIN French, literally: cold blood

sangoma (sang-**go**-ma) *n S African* a witch doctor
WORD ORIGIN Nguni (language group of southern Africa) *isangoma* a diviner

sangria *n* a Spanish drink of red wine, sugar, spices, and fruit
WORD ORIGIN Spanish: a bleeding

sanguinary *adj formal* **1** (of a battle or fight) involving much violence and bloodshed **2** (of a person) eager to see violence and bloodshed **3** of or stained with blood
WORD ORIGIN Latin *sanguinarius*

sanguine *adj* **1** cheerful and confident **2** (of the complexion) ruddy
WORD ORIGIN Latin *sanguineus* bloody

Sanhedrin (**san**-id-rin) *n judaism* the highest court and supreme council of the ancient Jewish nation

sanitary *adj* **1** promoting health by getting rid of dirt and germs **2** free from dirt or germs; hygienic
WORD ORIGIN Latin *sanitas* health

sanitary towel *or esp. US* **napkin** *n* a pad worn externally by women during menstruation to absorb the flow of blood

sanitation *n* **1** the use of sanitary measures to maintain public health **2** the drainage and disposal of sewage

sanitize *or* **-ise** *vb* **-izing, -ized** *or* **-ising, -ised** to omit unpleasant details to make (news) more acceptable

sanity *n* **1** the state of having a normal healthy mind **2** good sense or soundness of judgment
WORD ORIGIN Latin *sanitas* health

sank *vb* ▸ the past tense of **sink**

Sankara *n* 8th century AD, Hindu philosopher, the leading exponent of the Vedantic school: noted for his commentaries on the great Hindu texts

S

THESAURUS

▷ *vb* **5 = permit**, back, support, allow, approve, entitle, endorse, authorize, countenance, vouch for, lend your name to **OPPOSITE:** forbid

sanctuary *n* **3, 4 = protection**, shelter, refuge, haven, retreat, asylum **5 = reserve**, park, preserve, reservation, national park, tract, nature reserve, conservation area

sane *adj* **1 = rational**, normal, all there *(informal)*, lucid, of sound mind, compos mentis *(Latin)*, in your right mind, mentally sound, in possession of all your faculties **OPPOSITE:** insane **2 = sensible**, sound, reasonable, balanced, moderate, sober, judicious, level-headed, grounded **OPPOSITE:** foolish

DICTIONARY

Sankey *n* **Ira David** 1840–1908, US evangelist and hymnodist, noted for his revivalist campaigns in Britain and the US with D. L. Moody

Sanmicheli *n* **Michele** ?1484–1559, Italian mannerist architect

sans-culotte (sanz-kew-**lot**) *n* a revolutionary extremist
WORD ORIGIN French, literally: without knee breeches, because during the French Revolution the revolutionaries wore trousers

Sanskrit *n* the classical literary language of India, used since ancient times for religious purposes **Sanskritic** *adj*
WORD ORIGIN Sanskrit *samskrta* perfected

Santa Claus *n* the legendary patron saint of children, who brings presents to children on Christmas Eve, commonly identified with Saint Nicholas

Santa Cruz[1] *n* **1** a province of S Argentina, on the Atlantic: consists of a large part of Patagonia, with the forested foothills of the Andes in the west Capital: Río Gallegos. Pop: 206 897 (2000 est). Area: 243 940 sq km (94 186 sq miles) **2** a city in E Bolivia: the second largest town in Bolivia. Pop: 1 352 000 (2005 est) **3** ▸ another name for **Saint Croix**

Santa Cruz[2] *n* **Alvaro de Bazán** 1526–88, Spanish naval commander, who proposed, assembled, and prepared the Spanish Armada but died shortly before it sailed for England

Santayana *n* **George** 1863–1952, US philosopher, poet, and critic, born in Spain. His works include *The Life of Reason* (1905–06) and *The Realms of Being* (1927–40)

Santer *n* **Jacques** born 1937, Luxembourg politician: prime minister of Luxembourg (1984–95); president of the European Commission (1994–99)

Santos-Dumont *n* **Alberto** 1873–1932, Brazilian aeronaut, living in France. He constructed dirigibles and aircraft, including a monoplane (1909)

sap[1] ❶ *n* **1** a thin liquid that circulates in a plant, carrying food and water **2** *slang* a gullible person ▹*vb* **sapping, sapped 3** to drain of sap
WORD ORIGIN Old English *sæp*

sap[2] ❶ *vb* **sapping, sapped 1** to weaken or exhaust the strength or confidence of **2** to undermine (an enemy position) by digging saps ▹*n* **3** a deep and narrow trench used to approach or undermine an enemy position
WORD ORIGIN Italian *zappa* spade

sapient (**say**-pee-ent) *adj often used ironically* having great wisdom or sound judgment **sapience** *n*
WORD ORIGIN Latin *sapere* to taste, know

Sapir *n* **Edward** 1884–1939, US anthropologist and linguist, noted for his study of the ethnology and languages of North American Indians

sapling *n* a young tree

saponify *vb* **-fies, -fying, -fied** *chem* to convert (a fat) into a soap by treatment with alkali
saponification *n*
WORD ORIGIN Latin *sapo* soap

sapper *n* **1** a soldier who digs trenches **2** (in the British Army) a private of the Royal Engineers

Sapper *n* real name *Herman Cyril McNeile* 1888–1937, British novelist, author of the popular thriller *Bull-dog Drummond* (1920) and its sequels

sapphire *n* **1** a transparent blue precious stone ▹*adj* **2** deep blue
WORD ORIGIN Greek *sappheiros*

sappy *adj* **-pier, -piest** (of plants) full of sap

saprophyte *n biol* any plant, such as a fungus, that lives and feeds on dead organic matter
WORD ORIGIN Greek *sapros* rotten + *phuton* plant

sarabande *or* **saraband** *n* **1** a stately slow Spanish dance **2** music for this dance
WORD ORIGIN Spanish *zarabanda*

Saracen *n* **1** an Arab or Muslim who opposed the Crusades ▹*adj* **2** of the Saracens
WORD ORIGIN Late Greek *Sarakēnos*

Saramago *n* **José** born 1922, Portuguese novelist and writer; his works include the novel *O ano da morte de Ricardo Reis* (1984): Nobel prize for literature 1998

Sarandon *n* **Susan Abigail** born 1946, US film actress: her films include *Thelma and Louise* (1991), *Lorenzo's Oil* (1992), *The Client* (1994), *Dead Man Walking* (1996), and *Moonlight Mile* (2002)

Sarazen *n* **Gene,** original name *Eugenio Saraceni.* 1902–99, US golfer; won seven major tournaments between 1922 and 1935

sarcasm *n* **1** mocking or ironic language intended to insult someone **2** the use or tone of such language
WORD ORIGIN Greek *sarkazein* to rend the flesh

sarcastic *adj* **1** full of or showing sarcasm **2** tending to use sarcasm: *a sarcastic critic* **sarcastically** *adv*

sarcoma *n pathol* a malignant tumour beginning in connective tissue
WORD ORIGIN Greek *sarkōma* fleshy growth

sarcophagus (sahr-**koff**-a-guss) *n, pl* **-gi** (-guy) *or* **-guses** a stone or marble coffin or tomb, esp. one bearing sculpture or inscriptions
WORD ORIGIN Greek *sarkophagos* flesh-devouring

Sardanapalus *n* ▸ the Greek name of **Ashurbanipal**

sardine *n, pl* **-dines** *or* **-dine 1** a small fish of the herring family, often preserved in tightly packed tins **2 like sardines** very closely crowded together
WORD ORIGIN Latin *sardina*

sardonic *adj* (of behaviour) mocking or scornful **sardonically** *adv*
WORD ORIGIN Greek *sardonios*

sardonyx *n* a type of gemstone with alternating reddish-brown and white parallel bands
WORD ORIGIN Greek *sardonux*

Sardou *n* **Victorien** 1831–1908, French dramatist. His plays include *Fédora* (1882) and *La Tosca* (1887), the source of Puccini's opera

sargassum *n* a floating brown seaweed with long stringy fronds containing air sacs
WORD ORIGIN Portuguese *sargaço*

sarge *n informal* sergeant

Sargent *n* **1** Sir (**Harold**) **Malcolm** (**Watts**) 1895–1967, English conductor **2 John Singer** 1856–1925, US painter, esp. of society portraits; in London from 1885

Sargeson *n* **Frank** 1903–82, New Zealand short-story writer and novelist. His work includes the short-story collection *That Summer and Other Stories* (1946) and the novel *I Saw in my Dream* (1949)

Sargon II *n* died 705 BC, king of Assyria (722–705). He developed a policy of transporting conquered peoples to distant parts of his empire

Sargon of Akkad *n* 24th to 23rd century BC, semilegendary Mesopotamian ruler whose empire extended from the Gulf to the Mediterranean

THESAURUS

sap[1] *n* **1 = juice,** essence, vital fluid, secretion, lifeblood, plant fluid **2** *(slang)* **= fool,** jerk *(slang, chiefly US & Canad)*, idiot, noodle, wally *(slang)*, wet *(Brit informal)*, charlie *(Brit informal)*, drip *(informal)*, gull *(archaic)*, prat *(slang)*, plonker *(slang)*, noddy, twit *(informal)*, chump *(informal)*, oaf, simpleton, nitwit *(informal)*, ninny, nincompoop, dweeb *(US slang)*, wuss *(slang)*, Simple Simon, weenie *(US informal)*, muggins *(Brit slang)*, eejit *(Scot & Irish)*, dumb-ass *(slang)*, numpty *(Scot informal)*, doofus *(slang, chiefly US)*, nerd *or* nurd *(slang)*, numskull *or* numbskull, dorba *or* dorb *(Austral slang)*, bogan *(Austral slang)*

sap[2] *vb* **1 = weaken,** drain, undermine, rob, exhaust, bleed, erode, deplete, wear down, enervate, devitalize

S

DICTIONARY

sari *or* **saree** *n, pl* **-ris** *or* **-rees** the traditional dress of Hindu women, consisting of a very long piece of cloth swathed around the body with one end over the shoulder
WORD ORIGIN Hindi

sarking *n Scot, N English, Austral & NZ* flat planking supporting the roof cladding of a building
WORD ORIGIN Scots *sark* shirt

Sarkozy *n* **Nicolas** born 1955, French centre-right politician, president of France from 2007

sarky *adj* **-kier, -kiest** *informal* sarcastic

sarmie *n S African children's slang* a sandwich

sarnie *n S English informal* a sandwich

sarong *n* a garment worn by Malaysian men and women, consisting of a long piece of cloth tucked around the waist or under the armpits
WORD ORIGIN Malay

Sarpi *n* **Paolo**, real name *Pietro Soave Polano*. 1552–1623, Italian scholar, theologian, and patriot, who championed the Venetian republic in its dispute with Pope Paul V, arguing against papal absolutism and for the separation of church and state

Sarraute *n* **Nathalie** (natali) 1900–99, French novelist, noted as an exponent of the antinovel. Her novels include *Portrait of a Man Unknown* (1948), *Martereau* (1953), and *Ici* (1995)

SARS **1** severe acute respiratory syndrome; a severe and contagious viral infection of the lungs characterized by high fever, a dry cough, and breathing difficulties **2** South African Revenue Service

sarsaparilla *n* a nonalcoholic drink prepared from the roots of a tropical American climbing plant
WORD ORIGIN Spanish *sarzaparrilla*

Sarto *n* **Andrea del** 1486–1531, Florentine painter. His works include *The Nativity of the Virgin* (1514) in the church of Sant' Annunziata, Florence

sartorial *adj formal* of men's clothes or tailoring: *sartorial elegance*
WORD ORIGIN Latin *sartor* a tailor

SAS (in Britain) Special Air Service

sash¹ *n* a long piece of cloth worn around the waist or over one shoulder, usually as a symbol of rank
WORD ORIGIN Arabic *shāsh* muslin

sash² *n* **1** a frame that contains the panes of a window or door **2** a complete frame together with panes of glass
WORD ORIGIN French *châssis* a frame

sashay *vb informal* to move or walk in a casual or a showy manner: *the models sashayed down the catwalk*
WORD ORIGIN French *chassé* a gliding dance step

sash cord *n* a strong cord connecting a weight to the sliding half of a sash window

sashimi (sah-shee-mee) *n* a Japanese dish of thin fillets of raw fish
WORD ORIGIN Japanese *sashi* piercing + *mi* fish

sash window *n* a window consisting of two sashes placed one above the other so that the window can be opened by sliding one frame over the front of the other

Sask. Saskatchewan

sassafras *n* a tree of North America, with aromatic bark used medicinally and as a flavouring
WORD ORIGIN Spanish *sasafras*

Sassenach *n Scot & occasionally Irish* an English person
WORD ORIGIN Gaelic *Sassunach*

Sassoon *n* **1 Siegfried** (**Lorraine**) 1886–1967, British poet and novelist, best known for his poems of the horrors of war collected in *Counterattack* (1918) and *Satirical Poems* (1926). He also wrote a semi-fictitious autobiographical trilogy *The Memoirs of George Sherston* (1928–36) **2 Vidal** born 1928, British hair stylist: founder and chairman of Vidal Sassoon Inc.

sat *vb* ▸ the past of **sit**

Sat. Saturday

Satan *n* the Devil
WORD ORIGIN Hebrew: plotter

satanic ❶ *adj* **1** of Satan **2** supremely evil or wicked

Satanism *n* the worship of Satan **Satanist** *n, adj*

satchel *n* a small bag, usually with a shoulder strap
WORD ORIGIN Old French *sachel*

sate *vb* **sating, sated** to satisfy (a desire or appetite) fully
WORD ORIGIN Old English *sadian*

satellite *n* **1** a man-made device orbiting the earth or another planet, used in communications or to collect scientific information **2** a heavenly body orbiting a planet or star: *the earth is a satellite of the sun* **3** a country controlled by or dependent on a more powerful one ▹ *adj* **4** of, used in, or relating to the transmission of television signals from a satellite to the home: *satellite TV; a satellite dish*
WORD ORIGIN Latin *satelles* an attendant

satiate (say-she-ate) *vb* **-ating, -ated** to provide with more than enough, so as to disgust or weary: *enough cakes to satiate several children* **satiable** *adj* **satiation** *n*
WORD ORIGIN Latin *satiare*

Satie *n* **Erik** (**Alfred Leslie**) 1866–1925, French composer, noted for his eccentricity, experimentalism, and his direct and economical style. His music, including numerous piano pieces and several ballets, exercised a profound influence upon other composers, such as Debussy and Ravel

satiety (sat-tie-a-tee) *n formal* the feeling of having had too much

satin *n* **1** a fabric, usually made from silk or rayon, closely woven to give a smooth glossy surface on one side ▹ *adj* **2** like satin in texture: *satin polyurethane varnish* **satiny** *adj*
WORD ORIGIN Arabic *zaitūnī*

satinwood *n* **1** a hard wood with a satiny texture, used in fine furniture **2** the East Indian tree yielding this wood

satire ❶ *n* **1** the use of ridicule to expose incompetence, evil, or corruption **2** a play, novel, or poem containing satire **satirical** *adj*
WORD ORIGIN Latin *satira* a mixture

satirist *n* **1** a writer of satire **2** a person who uses satire

satirize *or* **-rise** *vb* **-rizing, -rized** *or* **-rising, -rised** to ridicule (a person or thing) by means of satire **satirization** *or* **-risation** *n*

satisfaction ❶ *n* **1** the pleasure obtained from the fulfilment of a desire **2** something that brings fulfilment: *craft workers get satisfaction from their work* **3** compensation or an apology for a wrong done: *consumers unable to get satisfaction from the gas board*

satisfactory ❶ *adj* **1** adequate or acceptable **2** giving satisfaction **satisfactorily** *adv*

S

THESAURUS

satanic *adj* **2 = evil**, demonic, hellish, black, malignant, wicked, inhuman, malevolent, devilish, infernal, fiendish, accursed, iniquitous, diabolic, demoniac, demoniacal
OPPOSITE: godly

satire *n* **1 = mockery**, wit, irony, ridicule, sarcasm **2 = parody**, mockery, caricature, send-up (*Brit informal*), spoof (*informal*), travesty, takeoff (*informal*), lampoon, skit, burlesque

satisfaction *n* **1 = fulfilment**, pleasure, achievement, joy, relish, glee, gratification, pride, complacency
OPPOSITE: dissatisfaction
2 = contentment, content, comfort, ease, pleasure, well-being, happiness, enjoyment, peace of mind, gratification, satiety, repletion, contentedness
OPPOSITE: discontent

satisfactory *adj* **1 = adequate**, acceptable, good enough, average, fair, all right, suitable, sufficient, competent, up to scratch, passable, up to standard, up to the mark
OPPOSITE: unsatisfactory

DICTIONARY

satisfy ❶ *vb* **-fies, -fying, -fied** **1** to fulfil the desires or needs of (a person): *his answer didn't satisfy me* **2** to provide sufficiently for (a need or desire): *to satisfy public demand* **3** to convince: *that trip did seem to satisfy her that he was dead* **4** to fulfil the requirements of: *unable to satisfy the conditions set by the commission* **satisfiable** *adj* **satisfying** *adj*
WORD ORIGIN Latin *satis* enough + *facere* to make

satnav *n* *motoring, informal* satellite navigation

Sato Eisaku *n* 1901–75, Japanese statesman: prime minister (1964–72). During his term of office Japan became a major economic power. He shared the Nobel peace prize (1974) for opposing the proliferation of nuclear weapons

satrap *n* (in ancient Persia) a provincial governor or subordinate ruler
WORD ORIGIN Old Persian *khshathrapāvan*, literally: protector of the land

SATs *Brit* standard assessment tasks

satsuma *n* a small loose-skinned variety of orange with easily separable segments
WORD ORIGIN *Satsuma*, former province of Japan

saturate ❶ *vb* **-rating, -rated** **1** to soak completely **2** to fill so completely that no more can be added: *saturating the area with their men* **3** *chem* to combine (a substance) or (of a substance) to be combined with the greatest possible amount of another substance
WORD ORIGIN Latin *saturare*

saturation *n* **1** the process or state that occurs when one substance is filled so full of another substance that no more can be added **2** *mil* the use of very heavy force, esp. bombing, against an area

saturation point *n* **1** the point at which the maximum amount of a substance has been absorbed **2** the point at which some capacity is at its fullest; limit: *the market is close to saturation point*

Saturday *n* the seventh day of the week
WORD ORIGIN Latin *Saturni dies* day of Saturn

Saturn *n* **1** the Roman god of agriculture and vegetation **2** the sixth planet from the sun, second largest in the solar system, around which revolve concentric rings

Saturnalia *n, pl* **-lia** *or* **-lias** **1** the ancient Roman festival of Saturn, renowned for its unrestrained revelry **2** **saturnalia** a wild party or orgy
WORD ORIGIN Latin *Saturnalis* relating to Saturn

saturnine *adj* having a gloomy temperament or appearance
WORD ORIGIN Latin *Saturnus* Saturn, from the gloomy influence attributed to the planet

satyr *n* **1** *Greek myth* a woodland god represented as having a man's body with the ears, horns, tail, and legs of a goat **2** a man who has strong sexual desires
WORD ORIGIN Greek *saturos*

sauce ❶ *n* **1** a liquid added to food to enhance its flavour **2** anything that adds interest or zest **3** *chiefly Brit informal* impudent language or behaviour
WORD ORIGIN Latin *salsus* salted

sauce boat *n* a boat-shaped container for serving sauce

saucepan *n* a metal pan with a long handle and often a lid, used for cooking food

saucer *n* **1** a small round dish on which a cup is set **2** something shaped like a saucer **saucerful** *n*
WORD ORIGIN Old French *saussier* container for sauce

saucy *adj* **saucier, sauciest** **1** cheeky or slightly rude in an amusing and light-hearted way **2** jaunty and boldly smart: *a saucy hat* **sauciness** *n*

Saud *n* full name *Saud ibn Abdul-Aziz* 1902–69, king of Saudi Arabia (1953–64); son of Ibn Saud. He was deposed by his brother Faisal

sauerkraut *n* a German dish of finely shredded pickled cabbage
WORD ORIGIN German *sauer* sour + *Kraut* cabbage

sault (soo) *n* *Canad* a waterfall or rapids
WORD ORIGIN French *saut* a leap

sauna *n* **1** a Finnish-style hot steam bath, usually followed by a cold plunge **2** the place in which such a bath is taken
WORD ORIGIN Finnish

Saunders *n* Dame **Cicely** 1918–2005, British philanthropist: founded St Christopher's Hospice in 1967 for the care of the terminally ill, upon which the modern hospice movement is modelled. Her books include *Living with Dying* (1983)

saunter *vb* **1** to walk in a leisurely manner; stroll ▷*n* **2** a leisurely pace or stroll
WORD ORIGIN origin unknown

saurian *adj* of or resembling a lizard
WORD ORIGIN Greek *sauros* lizard

sausage ❶ *n* **1** finely minced meat mixed with fat, cereal, and seasonings, in a tube-shaped casing **2** an object shaped like a sausage **3** **not a sausage** *informal* nothing at all
WORD ORIGIN Old French *saussiche*

sausage dog *n* *informal* ▸same as **dachshund**

sausage roll *n* a roll of sausage meat in pastry

sausage sizzle *n* *Austral & NZ* an event at which sausages are barbecued, often to raise money for a school or other organization

sauté (so-tay) *vb* **-téing** *or* **-téeing, -téed** **1** to fry (food) quickly in a little fat ▷*n* **2** a dish of sautéed food ▷*adj* **3** sautéed until lightly brown: *sauté potatoes*
WORD ORIGIN French: tossed

Sauternes (so-turn) *n* a sweet white wine produced in the southern Bordeaux district of France

savage ❶ *adj* **1** wild and untamed: *savage tigers* **2** fierce and cruel: *savage cries* **3** (of peoples) uncivilized or primitive: *savage tribes* **4** rude, crude, and violent: *savage behaviour on the terraces* **5** (of terrain) wild and uncultivated ▷*n* **6** a member of an uncivilized or primitive society **7** a

S

THESAURUS

satisfy *vb* **1 = content**, please, indulge, fill, feed, appease, gratify, pander to, assuage, pacify, quench, mollify, surfeit, satiate, slake, sate **OPPOSITE:** dissatisfy
3 = convince, persuade, assure, reassure, dispel (someone's) doubts, put (someone's) mind at rest **OPPOSITE:** dissuade
4 = comply with, meet, fulfil, answer, serve, fill, observe, obey, conform to **OPPOSITE:** fail to meet

saturate *vb* **1 = soak**, steep, drench, seep, imbue, douse, impregnate, suffuse, ret *(flax, etc)*, wet through, waterlog, souse, drouk *(Scot)*
2 = flood, overwhelm, swamp, overrun, deluge, glut

sauce *n* **1 = dressing**, dip, relish, condiment

sausage *n* **1 = banger**

savage *adj* **1 = wild**, fierce, ferocious, unbroken, feral, untamed, undomesticated **OPPOSITE:** tame
2, 4 = cruel, brutal, vicious, bloody, fierce, harsh, beastly, ruthless, ferocious, murderous, ravening, sadistic, inhuman, merciless, diabolical, brutish, devilish, bloodthirsty, barbarous, pitiless, bestial **OPPOSITE:** gentle
3 = primitive, undeveloped, uncultivated, uncivilized, in a state of nature, nonliterate
5 = uncultivated, rugged, unspoilt, uninhabited, waste, rough, uncivilized, unfrequented **OPPOSITE:** cultivated
▷*n* **7 = lout**, yob *(Brit slang)*, brute, bear, monster, beast, barbarian, fiend, yahoo, hoon *(Austral & NZ)*, yobbo *(Brit slang)*, roughneck *(slang)*, boor, cougan *(Austral slang)*, scozza *(Austral slang)*, bogan *(Austral slang)*
▷*vb* **8 = maul**, tear, claw, attack,

DICTIONARY

fierce or vicious person ▷ *vb* **-aging, -aged 8** to attack ferociously and wound: *savaged by a wild dog* **9** to criticize extremely severely: *savaged by the press for incompetence* **savagely** *adv*
WORD ORIGIN Latin *silvaticus* belonging to a wood

savagery *n, pl* **-ries** viciousness and cruelty

savannah *or* **savanna** *n* open grasslands, usually with scattered bushes or trees, in Africa
WORD ORIGIN Spanish *zavana*

savant *n* a very wise and knowledgeable man **savante** *fem n*
WORD ORIGIN French

save[1] ❶ *vb* **saving, saved 1** to rescue or preserve (a person or thing) from danger or harm **2** to avoid the spending, waste, or loss of (something): *an appeal on television for the public to save energy* **3** to set aside or reserve (money or goods) for future use: *I'm saving for a vintage Mercedes* **4** to treat with care so as to preserve **5** to prevent the necessity for: *a chance saved him from having to make up his mind* **6** *sport* to prevent (a goal) by stopping (a ball or puck) **7** *Christianity* to free (someone) from the influence or consequences of sin ▷ *n* **8** *sport* the act of saving a goal **9** *computers* an instruction to write information from the memory onto a tape or disk **savable** *or* **saveable** *adj* **saver** *n*
WORD ORIGIN Old French *salver*

save[2] *old-fashioned prep* **1** (often foll. by *for*) with the exception of: *the stage was empty save for a single chair* ▷ *conj* **2** but
WORD ORIGIN Middle English *sauf*

save as you earn *n* (in Britain) a savings scheme operated by the government, in which regular deposits are made into a savings account from a salary

saveloy *n Brit, Austral & NZ* a highly seasoned smoked sausage made from salted pork
WORD ORIGIN Italian *cervellato*

Savery *n* **Thomas** ?1650–1715, English engineer, who built (1698) the first practical steam engine, used to pump water from mines

Savigny *n* **Friedrich Karl von** 1779–1861, German legal scholar, who pioneered the historical approach to jurisprudence, emphasizing custom and precedent

saving ❶ *n* **1** preservation from destruction or danger **2** a reduction in the amount of time or money used **3 savings** money saved for future use ▷ *adj* **4** tending to rescue or preserve ▷ *prep* **5** with the exception of

saving grace *n* a good quality in a person that prevents him or her from being entirely bad or worthless

saviour ❶ *or US* **savior** *n* a person who rescues another person or a thing from danger or harm
WORD ORIGIN Church Latin *Salvator* the Saviour

Saviour ❶ *or US* **Savior** *n Christianity* Jesus Christ, regarded as the saviour of people from sin

Savitskaya *n* **Svetlana** born 1949, Soviet cosmonaut, the first woman to walk in space (1984). She was elected to the former Soviet parliament (1989)

savoir-faire (sav-wahr-**fair**) *n* the ability to say and do the right thing in any situation
WORD ORIGIN French

savory *n, pl* **-vories** an aromatic plant whose leaves are used in cooking
WORD ORIGIN Latin *satureia*

savour ❶ *or US* **savor** *vb* **1** to enjoy and appreciate (food or drink) slowly **2** to enjoy (a pleasure) for as long as possible: *an experience to be savoured* **3 savour of a** to have a suggestion of: *that could savour of ostentation* **b** to possess the taste or smell of: *the vegetables savoured of coriander* ▷ *n* **4** the taste or smell of something **5** a slight but distinctive quality or trace
WORD ORIGIN Latin *sapor* taste

savoury *or US* **savory** *adj* **1** salty or spicy: *savoury foods* **2** attractive to the sense of taste or smell **3** pleasant or acceptable: *one of the book's less savoury characters* ▷ *n, pl* **-ries 4** *chiefly Brit* a savoury dish served before or after a meal **savouriness** *or US* **savoriness** *n*

savoy *n* a cabbage with a compact head and wrinkled leaves
WORD ORIGIN after the *Savoy* region in France

savvy *slang vb* **-vies, -vying, -vied 1** to understand ▷ *n* **2** understanding or common sense ▷ *adj* **3** shrewd
WORD ORIGIN corruption of Spanish *sabe (usted)* (you) know

saw[1] *n* **1** a cutting tool with a toothed metal blade or edge, either operated by hand or powered by electricity ▷ *vb* **sawing, sawed; sawed** *or* **sawn 2** to cut with or as if with a saw **3** to form by sawing **4** to move (an object) from side to side as if moving a saw
WORD ORIGIN Old English *sagu*

saw[2] *vb* ▸ the past tense of **see[1]**

saw[3] *n old-fashioned* a wise saying or proverb
WORD ORIGIN Old English *sagu* a saying

saw doctor *n NZ* a sawmill specialist who sharpens and services saw blades

sawdust *n* particles of wood formed by sawing

sawfish *n, pl* **-fish** *or* **-fishes** a sharklike ray with a long toothed snout resembling a saw

sawhorse *n Austral & NZ* a structure for supporting wood that is being sawn

sawmill *n* a factory where timber is sawn into planks

sawn *vb* ▸ a past participle of **saw[1]**

sawn-off *or esp. US* **sawed-off** *adj* (of a shotgun) having the barrel cut short to make concealment of the weapon easier

saw-off *n Canad* **1** a deadlock or stalemate **2** a compromise

sawyer *n* a person who saws timber for a living

sax *n informal* ▸ short for **saxophone**

Saxe[1] *n* ▸ the French name for **Saxony**

Saxe[2] *n* **Hermann Maurice**, comte de Saxe. 1696–1750, French marshal born in Saxony: he distinguished himself in the War of the Austrian Succession (1740–48)

saxifrage *n* an alpine rock plant with small white, yellow, purple, or pink flowers
WORD ORIGIN Late Latin *saxifraga*, literally: rock breaker

THESAURUS

mangle, lacerate, mangulate *(Austral slang)*

save[1] *vb* **1 = rescue**, free, release, deliver, recover, get out, liberate, salvage, redeem, bail out, come to someone's rescue, set free, save the life of, extricate, save someone's bacon *(Brit informal)*
OPPOSITE: endanger
2 = keep, reserve, set aside, store, collect, gather, hold, hoard, hide away, lay by, put by, salt away, treasure up, keep up your sleeve *(informal)*, put aside for a rainy day
OPPOSITE: spend
3 = put aside, keep, reserve, collect, retain, set aside, amass, put by
4 = protect, keep, guard, preserve, look after, take care of, safeguard, salvage, conserve, keep safe

saving *n* **2 = economy**, discount, reduction, bargain, cut ▷ *pl n* **3 = nest egg**, fund, store, reserves, resources, fall-back, provision for a rainy day

saviour *or (US)* **savior** *n* **= rescuer**, deliverer, defender, guardian, salvation, protector, liberator, Good Samaritan, redeemer, preserver, knight in shining armour, friend in need

Saviour *or (US)* **Savior** *Christianity n* **= Christ**, Jesus, the Messiah, the Redeemer

savour *or (US)* **savor** *vb* **1 = enjoy**, appreciate, relish, delight in, revel in, partake of, drool over, luxuriate in, enjoy to the full, smack your lips over **2 = relish**, like, delight in, revel in, luxuriate in, gloat over ▷ *n* **4 = flavour**, taste, smell, relish, smack, zest, tang, zing *(informal)*, piquancy

S

DICTIONARY

Saxo Grammaticus *n* ?1150–?1220, Danish chronicler, noted for his *Gesta Danorum*, a history of Denmark down to 1185, written in Latin, which is partly historical and partly mythological, and contains the Hamlet (Amleth) legend

Saxon *n* **1** a member of a West Germanic people who raided and settled parts of Britain in the fifth and sixth centuries AD **2** any of the West Germanic dialects spoken by the ancient Saxons ▹*adj* **3** of the ancient Saxons or their language
WORD ORIGIN Late Latin *Saxon-, Saxo*

saxophone *n* a brass wind instrument with keys and a curved metal body **saxophonist** *n*
WORD ORIGIN after Adolphe *Sax*, who invented it

say ❶ *vb* **saying, said 1** to speak or utter **2** to express (an idea) in words: *I can't say what I feel* **3** to state (an opinion or fact) positively: *I say you are wrong* **4** to indicate or show: *the clock says ten to nine* **5** to recite: *to say grace* **6** to report or allege: *they say we shall have rain today* **7** to suppose as an example or possibility: *let us say that he is lying* **8** to convey by means of artistic expression: *what does the artist have to say in this picture?* **9** to make a case for: *there is much to be said for it* **10 go without saying** to be so obvious as to need no explanation **11 to say the least** at the very least ▹*adv* **12** approximately: *there were, say, 20 people present* **13** for example: *choose a number, say, four* ▹*n* **14** the right or chance to speak: *the opposition has hardly had a say in these affairs* **15** authority, esp. to influence a decision: *he has a lot of say*
WORD ORIGIN Old English *secgan*

SAYE (in Britain) save as you earn

Sayers *n* **Dorothy L(eigh)** 1893–1957, English detective-story writer

saying ❶ *n* a well-known phrase or sentence expressing a belief or a truth

Sb *chemistry* antimony
WORD ORIGIN New Latin *stibium*

Sc *chem* scandium

SC South Carolina

scab *n* **1** the dried crusty surface of a healing skin wound or sore **2** *disparaging* a person who refuses to support a trade union's actions, and continues to work during a strike **3** a contagious disease of sheep, caused by a mite **4** a fungal disease of plants ▹*vb* **scabbing, scabbed 5** to become covered with a scab **6** *disparaging* to work as a scab
WORD ORIGIN Old English *sceabb*

scabbard *n* a holder for a sword or dagger
WORD ORIGIN Middle English *scauberc*

scabby *adj* **-bier, -biest 1** *pathol* covered with scabs **2** *informal* mean or despicable **scabbiness** *n*

scabies (**skay**-beez) *n* a contagious skin infection caused by a mite, characterized by intense itching
WORD ORIGIN Latin *scabere* to scratch

scabious (**skay**-bee-uss) *n* a plant with showy blue, red, or whitish dome-shaped flower heads
WORD ORIGIN Medieval Latin *scabiosa herba* the scabies plant

scabrous (**skay**-bruss) *adj* **1** rough and scaly **2** indecent or crude: *scabrous stand-up comedy*
WORD ORIGIN Latin *scaber* rough

scaffold *n* **1** a temporary framework used to support workmen and materials during the construction or repair of a building **2** a raised wooden platform on which criminals are hanged; gallows
WORD ORIGIN Old French *eschaffaut*

scaffolding *n* **1** a scaffold or scaffolds **2** the building materials used to make scaffolds

scalar *maths n* **1** a quantity, such as time or temperature, that has magnitude but not direction ▹*adj* **2** having magnitude but not direction
WORD ORIGIN Latin *scala* ladder

scald *vb* **1** to burn with hot liquid or steam **2** to sterilize with boiling water **3** to heat (a liquid) almost to boiling point ▹*n* **4** a burn caused by scalding
WORD ORIGIN Late Latin *excaldare* to wash in warm water

scale[1] ❶ *n* **1** one of the thin flat overlapping plates covering the bodies of fishes and reptiles **2** a thin flat piece or flake **3** a coating which sometimes forms in kettles and hot-water pipes in areas where the water is hard **4** tartar formed on the teeth ▹*vb* **scaling, scaled 5** to remove the scales or coating from **6** to peel off in flakes or scales **7** to cover or become covered with scales **scaly** *adj*
WORD ORIGIN Old French *escale*

scale[2] *n* **1** (*often pl*) a machine or device for weighing **2** one of the pans of a balance **3 tip the scales** to have a decisive influence **4 tip the scales at** to amount in weight to
WORD ORIGIN Old Norse *skāl* bowl

scale[3] ❶ *n* **1** a sequence of marks at regular intervals, used as a reference in making measurements **2** a measuring instrument with such a scale **3** the ratio between the size of something real and that of a representation of it: *the map has a scale of 1:10 000* **4** a series of degrees or graded system of things: *the Western wage scale for the same work* **5** a relative degree or extent: *growing flowers on a very small scale* **6** *music* a sequence of notes taken in ascending or descending order, esp. within one octave **7** *maths* the notation of a given number system: *the decimal scale* ▹*vb* **scaling, scaled 8** to climb to the top of (an object or height): *the men scaled a wall* **9 scale up** *or* **down** to increase or reduce proportionately in size: *the design can easily be scaled up; after five days the search was scaled down*
WORD ORIGIN Latin *scala* ladder

scalene *adj maths* (of a triangle) having all sides of unequal length
WORD ORIGIN Greek *skalēnos*

Scaliger *n* **1 Joseph Justus** 1540–1609, French scholar, who revolutionized the study of ancient chronology by his work *De Emendatione temporum* (1583) **2** his father, **Julius Caesar** 1484–1558, Italian classical scholar, and writer on biology and medicine

scallion *n* a spring onion
WORD ORIGIN Anglo-French *scalun*

scallop *n* **1** an edible marine mollusc with two fluted fan-shaped shells **2** a single shell of this mollusc **3** one of a series of small curves along an edge **scalloping** *n*
WORD ORIGIN Old French *escalope* shell

scalloped *adj* decorated with small curves along the edge

scallywag *n informal* a badly behaved but likeable person; rascal
WORD ORIGIN origin unknown

THESAURUS

say *vb* **1 = speak**, utter, voice, express, pronounce, come out with (*informal*), put into words, give voice *or* utterance to **2 = state**, declare, remark, add, announce, maintain, mention, assert, affirm, asseverate **7 = suppose**, supposing, imagine, assume, presume **8 = suggest**, express, imply, communicate, disclose, give away, convey, divulge ▹*n* **14 = chance to speak**, vote, voice, crack (*informal*), opportunity to speak, turn to speak **15 = influence**, power, control, authority, weight, sway, clout (*informal*), predominance, mana (*NZ*)

saying *n* **= proverb**, maxim, adage, saw, slogan, gnome, dictum, axiom, aphorism, byword, apophthegm

scale[1] *n* **1, 2 = flake**, plate, layer, lamina

scale[3] *n* **1 = system of measurement**, register, measuring system, graduated system, calibration, calibrated system **3 = ratio**, proportion, relative size **4 = ranking**, ladder, spectrum, hierarchy, series, sequence, progression, pecking order (*informal*) **5 = degree**, size, range, spread, extent, dimensions, scope, magnitude, breadth ▹*vb* **8 = climb up**, mount, go up, ascend, surmount, scramble up, clamber up, escalade

DICTIONARY

scalp *n* **1** *anat* the skin and hair covering the top of the head **2** (formerly among Native Americans of N America) a part of this removed as a trophy from a slain enemy ▷*vb* **3** to cut the scalp from **4** *informal, chiefly US* to buy and resell so as to make a high or quick profit
WORD ORIGIN probably from Old Norse *skālpr* sheath

scalpel *n* a small surgical knife with a very sharp thin blade
WORD ORIGIN Latin *scalper* a knife

scam *n slang* a stratagem for gain; a swindle

scamp *n* a mischievous person, esp. a child
WORD ORIGIN probably from Middle Dutch *schampen* to decamp

scamper *vb* **1** to run about hurriedly or quickly ▷*n* **2** the act of scampering
WORD ORIGIN see SCAMP

scampi *n* large prawns, usually eaten fried in breadcrumbs
WORD ORIGIN Italian

scan ❶ *vb* **scanning, scanned 1** to scrutinize carefully **2** to glance over quickly **3** *prosody* to analyse (verse) by examining its rhythmic structure **4** *prosody* (of a line or verse) to be metrically correct **5** to examine or search (an area) by systematically moving a beam of light or electrons, or a radar or sonar beam over it **6** *med* to obtain an image of (a part of the body) by means of ultrasound or a scanner ▷*n* **7** an instance of scanning **8** *med* **a** the examination of part of the body by means of a scanner **b** the image produced by a scanner
WORD ORIGIN Latin *scandere* to climb

scandal ❶ *n* **1** a disgraceful action or event: *the chairman resigned after a loans scandal* **2** shame or outrage arising from a disgraceful action or event: *the figures were a national scandal* **3** malicious gossip

scandalous *adj* **scandalously** *adv*
WORD ORIGIN Greek *skandalon* a trap

scandalize *or* **-ise** *vb* **-izing, -ized** *or* **-ising, -ised** to shock or be shocked by improper behaviour

scandalmonger *n* a person who spreads or enjoys scandal or gossip

Scanderbeg *n* original name *George Castriota;* Turkish name *Iskender Bey* ?1403–68, Albanian patriot. He was an army commander for the sultan of Turkey until 1443, when he changed sides and drove the Turks from Albania

Scandinavian *adj* **1** of Scandinavia (Norway, Sweden, Denmark, and often Finland, Iceland, and the Faeroe Islands) ▷*n* **2** a person from Scandinavia **3** the northern group of Germanic languages, consisting of Swedish, Danish, Norwegian, Icelandic, and Faeroese

scandium *n chem* a rare silvery-white metallic element. Symbol: Sc
WORD ORIGIN Latin *Scandia* Scandinavia, where discovered

scanner *n* **1** an aerial or similar device designed to transmit or receive signals, esp. radar signals **2** a device used in medical diagnosis to obtain an image of an internal organ or part

scansion *n* the metrical scanning of verse

scant ❶ *adj* scarcely sufficient: *some issues will get scant attention*
WORD ORIGIN Old Norse *skamt* short

scanty *adj* **scantier, scantiest** barely sufficient or not sufficient **scantily** *adv* **scantiness** *n*

scapegoat ❶ *n* **1** a person made to bear the blame for others ▷*vb* **2** to make a scapegoat of
WORD ORIGIN *escape* + *goat*, coined to translate Biblical Hebrew *azāzēl*, probably goat for Azazel, mistakenly thought to mean 'goat that escapes'

scapula (skap-pew-la) *n, pl* **-lae** (-lee) ▸ the technical name for **shoulder blade**
WORD ORIGIN Late Latin: shoulder

scapular *adj* **1** *anat* of the scapula ▷*n* **2** a loose sleeveless garment worn by monks over their habits

scar[1] ❶ *n* **1** a mark left on the skin following the healing of a wound **2** a permanent effect on a person's character resulting from emotional distress **3** a mark on a plant where a leaf was formerly attached **4** a mark of damage ▷*vb* **scarring, scarred 5** to mark or become marked with a scar **6** to permanently effect or be permanently affected by mental trauma: *their divorce will scar those kids for life*
WORD ORIGIN Greek *eskhara* scab

scar[2] *n* a bare craggy rock formation
WORD ORIGIN Old Norse *sker* low reef

scarab *n* **1** the black dung-beetle, regarded by the ancient Egyptians as divine **2** an image or carving of this beetle
WORD ORIGIN Latin *scarabaeus*

scarce ❶ *adj* **1** insufficient to meet the demand: *scarce water resources* **2** not common; rarely found **3 make oneself scarce** *informal* to go away ▷*adv* **4** *archaic or literary* scarcely
WORD ORIGIN Old French *scars*

scarcely ❶ *adv* **1** hardly at all **2** *often used ironically* probably or definitely not: *that is scarcely justification for your actions*

scarcity *n, pl* **-ties** an inadequate supply

scare ❶ *vb* **scaring, scared 1** to frighten or be frightened **2 scare away** *or* **off** to drive away by frightening ▷*n* **3** a sudden attack of fear or alarm: *you gave me a scare* **4** a period of general fear or alarm: *the latest AIDS scare*
WORD ORIGIN Old Norse *skirra*

scarecrow *n* **1** an object, usually in the shape of a man, made out of sticks and old clothes, to scare birds away from crops **2** *informal* a raggedly dressed person

scaremonger *n* a person who starts

THESAURUS

scan *vb* **1 = survey**, search, investigate, sweep, con *(archaic)*, scour, scrutinize, take stock of, recce *(slang)* **2 = glance over**, skim, look over, eye, check, clock *(Brit slang)*, examine, check out *(informal)*, run over, eyeball *(slang)*, size up *(informal)*, get a load of *(informal)*, look someone up and down, run your eye over, take a dekko at *(Brit slang)*, surf *(computing)*

scandal *n* **1 = disgrace**, crime, offence, sin, embarrassment, wrongdoing, skeleton in the cupboard, dishonourable behaviour, discreditable behaviour **2a = shame**, offence, disgrace, stigma, infamy, opprobrium, obloquy **2b = outrage**, shame, insult, disgrace, injustice, crying shame **3 = gossip**, goss *(informal)*, talk, rumours, dirt, slander, tattle, dirty linen *(informal)*, calumny, backbiting, aspersion

scant *adj* **= inadequate**, insufficient, meagre, sparse, little, limited, bare, minimal, deficient, barely sufficient
OPPOSITE: adequate

scapegoat *n* **1 = fall guy**, whipping boy

scar[1] *n* **1 = mark**, injury, wound, trauma *(pathology)*, blemish, cicatrix **2 = trauma**, suffering, pain, strain, torture, disturbance, anguish ▷ *vb* **5 = mark**, disfigure, damage, brand, mar, mutilate, maim, blemish, deface, traumatize, disfeature

scarce *adj* **1 = in short supply**, wanting, insufficient, deficient, at a premium, thin on the ground
OPPOSITE: plentiful
2 = rare, few, unusual, uncommon, few and far between, infrequent, thin on the ground
OPPOSITE: common

scarcely *adv* **1 = hardly**, barely, only just, scarce *(archaic)* **2** *(often used ironically)* **= by no means**, hardly, not at all, definitely not, under no circumstances, on no account

scare *vb* **1 = frighten**, alarm, terrify, panic, shock, startle, intimidate, dismay, daunt, terrorize, put the wind up (someone) *(informal)*, give (someone) a fright, give (someone) a turn *(informal)*, affright *(archaic)* ▷ *n* **3 = fright**, shock, start **4 = panic**, hysteria

S

DICTIONARY

or spreads rumours of disaster to frighten people **scaremongering** *n*

scarf[1] *n, pl* **scarves** *or* **scarfs** a piece of material worn around the head, neck, or shoulders
WORD ORIGIN origin unknown

scarf[2] *n, pl* **scarfs** **1** a joint between two pieces of timber made by notching the ends and strapping or gluing the two pieces together ▷ *vb* **2** to join (two pieces of timber) by means of a scarf
WORD ORIGIN probably from Old Norse

Scarfe *n* **Gerald** born 1936, British cartoonist, famous for his scathing caricatures of politicians and celebrities

Scargill *n* **Arthur** born 1941, British trades union leader; president of the National Union of Mineworkers (1982–2002). He led the miners in a long and bitter strike (1984–85), but failed to prevent pit closures

scarify *vb* **-fies, -fying, -fied** **1** *surgery* to make slight incisions in (the skin) **2** *agriculture* to break up and loosen (topsoil) **3** to criticize without mercy **scarification** *n*
WORD ORIGIN Latin *scarifare* to scratch open

scarlatina *n* ▸ the technical name for **scarlet fever**
WORD ORIGIN Italian *scarlatto* scarlet

Scarlatti *n* **1** **Alessandro** ?1659–1725, Italian composer; regarded as the founder of modern opera **2** his son, (**Giuseppe**) **Domenico** 1685–1757, Italian composer and harpsichordist, in Portugal and Spain from 1720. He wrote over 550 single-movement sonatas for harpsichord, many of them exercises in virtuoso technique

scarlet *adj* bright red
WORD ORIGIN Old French *escarlate* fine cloth

scarlet fever *n* an acute contagious disease characterized by fever, a sore throat, and a red rash on the body

scarp *n* **1** a steep slope or ridge of rock **2** *fortifications* the side of a ditch cut nearest to a rampart
WORD ORIGIN Italian *scarpa*

scarper *vb chiefly Brit slang* to run away or escape
WORD ORIGIN origin unknown

Scarron *n* **Paul** 1610–60, French comic dramatist and novelist, noted particularly for his picaresque novel *Le Roman comique* (1651–57)

Scart *or* **SCART** *n electronics* a plug-and-socket system which carries pictures and sound, used in home entertainment systems

scarves *n* ▸ a plural of **scarf**[1]

scary ❶ *adj* **scarier, scariest** *informal* quite frightening

scat[1] *vb* **scatting, scatted** *informal* to go away in haste
WORD ORIGIN origin unknown

scat[2] *n* **1** a type of jazz singing using improvised vocal sounds instead of words ▷ *vb* **scatting, scatted** **2** to sing jazz in this way
WORD ORIGIN perhaps imitative

scathing *adj* harshly critical: *there was a scathing review of the play in the paper* **scathingly** *adv*
WORD ORIGIN Old Norse *skathi* harm

scatology *n* preoccupation with obscenity, esp. with references to excrement **scatological** *adj*
WORD ORIGIN Greek *skat-* excrement + -LOGY

scatter ❶ *vb* **1** to throw about in various directions: *scatter some oatmeal on top of the cake* **2** to separate and move in various directions; disperse: *the infantry were scattering* ▷ *n* **3** the act of scattering **4** a number of objects scattered about
WORD ORIGIN probably variant of *shatter*

scatterbrain *n* a person who is incapable of serious thought or concentration **scatterbrained** *adj*

scattershot *adj* wide-ranging but indiscriminate: *a scattershot approach to conservation*

scatty *adj* **-tier, -tiest** *informal* rather absent-minded **scattiness** *n*
WORD ORIGIN from *scatterbrained*

scavenge *vb* **-enging, -enged** to search for (anything usable) among discarded material

scavenger *n* **1** a person who collects things discarded by others **2** any animal that feeds on discarded or decaying matter
WORD ORIGIN Old French *escauwer* to scrutinize

SCE (in Scotland) Scottish Certificate of Education

scenario ❶ *n, pl* **-narios** **1** a summary of the plot and characters of a play or film **2** an imagined sequence of future events: *the likeliest scenario is another general election*
WORD ORIGIN Italian

scene ❶ *n* **1** the place where an action or event, real or imaginary, occurs **2** an incident or situation, real or imaginary, esp. as described or represented **3** a division of an act of a play, in which the setting is fixed and the action is continuous **4** *films* a shot or series of shots that constitutes a unit of the action **5** the backcloths or screens used to represent a location in a play or film set **6** the view of a place or landscape **7** a display of emotion or loss of temper in public: *you do not want to cause a scene* **8** *informal* a particular activity or aspect of life, and all the things associated with it: *the club scene* **9** **behind the scenes** **a** backstage **b** in secret or in private
WORD ORIGIN Greek *skēnē* tent, stage

scenery ❶ *n, pl* **-eries** **1** the natural features of a landscape **2** *theatre* the painted backcloths or screens used to represent a location in a theatre or studio

scenic ❶ *adj* **1** of or having beautiful natural scenery: *untouched scenic areas* **2** of the stage or stage scenery: *scenic artists*

scent ❶ *n* **1** a distinctive smell, esp. a pleasant one **2** a smell left in passing, by which a person or animal may be traced **3** a trail or series of clues by which something is followed: *he must have got on to the scent of the story through you* **4** perfume ▷ *vb* **5** to become aware of by

S

THESAURUS

scary *adj* *(informal)* **= frightening**, alarming, terrifying, shocking, chilling, horrifying, intimidating, horrendous, hairy *(slang)*, unnerving, spooky *(informal)*, creepy *(informal)*, hair-raising, spine-chilling, bloodcurdling

scatter *vb* **1 = throw about**, spread, sprinkle, strew, broadcast, shower, fling, litter, sow, diffuse, disseminate **OPPOSITE:** gather **2 = disperse**, separate, break up, dispel, disband, dissipate, disunite, put to flight **OPPOSITE:** assemble

scenario *n* **1 = story line**, résumé, outline, sketch, summary, rundown, synopsis **2 = situation**, sequence of events, chain of events, course of events, series of developments

scene *n* **1 = site**, place, setting, area, position, stage, situation, spot, whereabouts, locality **1, 5 = setting**, set, background, location, backdrop, mise en scène *(French)* **3 = act**, part, division, episode **6 = view**, prospect, panorama, vista, landscape, tableau, outlook **7 = fuss**, to-do, row, performance, upset, drama, exhibition, carry-on *(informal, chiefly Brit)*, confrontation, tantrum, commotion, hue and cry, display of emotion, hissy fit *(informal)* **8** *(informal)* **= world**, business, environment, preserve, arena, realm, domain, milieu, thing, field of interest

scenery *n* **1 = landscape**, view, surroundings, terrain, vista **2** *(theatre)* **= set**, setting, backdrop, flats, décor, stage set

scenic *adj* **1 = picturesque**, beautiful, spectacular, striking, grand, impressive, breathtaking, panoramic

scent *n* **1 = fragrance**, smell, perfume, bouquet, aroma, odour, niff *(Brit slang)*, redolence **2 = trail**, track, spoor ▷ *vb* **5 = smell**, sense, recognize, detect, sniff, discern, sniff out, nose out, get wind of *(informal)*, be on the track *or* trail of

sceptic *or (US)* **skeptic** *n* **1 = doubter**,

smelling **6** to suspect: *he scented the beginnings of irritation in the car* **7** to fill with odour or fragrance **scented** *adj*
WORD ORIGIN Old French *sentir* to sense

sceptic ❶ *or US* **skeptic** (skep-tik) *n* **1** a person who habitually doubts generally accepted beliefs **2** a person who doubts the truth of a religion **sceptical** *or US* **skeptical** *adj* **sceptically** *or US* **skeptically** *adv* **scepticism** *or US* **skepticism** *n*
WORD ORIGIN Greek *skeptikos* one who reflects upon

sceptre *or US* **scepter** *n* an ornamental rod symbolizing royal power **sceptred** *or US* **sceptered** *adj*
WORD ORIGIN Greek *skeptron* staff

Schadenfreude (shah-den-froy-da) *n* one person's delight in another's misfortune
WORD ORIGIN German *Schaden* harm + *Freude* joy

Schama *n* **Simon** (**Michael**) born 1945, British historian, art critic, and broadcaster, based in the US; his work includes *The Embarrassment of Riches* (1987), *Landscape and Memory* (1995), and the BBC television series *A History of Britain* (2000–02)

schedule ❶ *n* **1** a timed plan of procedure for a project **2** a list of details or items: *the schedule of priorities* **3** a timetable ▷*vb* **-uling, -uled 4** to plan and arrange (something) to happen at a certain time **5** to make a schedule or include in a schedule
WORD ORIGIN Latin *scheda* sheet of paper

Scheele *n* **Karl Wilhelm** 1742–86, Swedish chemist. He discovered oxygen, independently of Priestley, and many other substances

Schelling *n* **Friedrich Wilhelm Joseph von** 1775–1854, German philosopher. He expanded Fichte's idea that there is one reality, the infinite and absolute Ego, by regarding nature as an absolute being working towards self-consciousness. His works include *Ideas towards a Philosophy of Nature* (1797) and *System of Transcendental Idealism* (1800) **Schellingian** *adj*

schema *n, pl* **-mata** an outline of a plan or theory
WORD ORIGIN Greek: form

schematic *adj* presented as a diagram or plan **schematically** *adv*

schematize *or* **-tise** *vb* **-tizing, -tized** *or* **-tising, -tised** to form into or arrange in a systematic arrangement or plan

scheme ❶ *n* **1** a systematic plan for a course of action **2** a systematic arrangement of parts or features: *colour scheme* **3** a secret plot **4** a chart, diagram, or outline **5** a plan formally adopted by a government or organization: *a pension scheme* ▷*vb* **scheming, schemed 6** to plan in an underhand manner **schemer** *n* **scheming** *adj, n*
WORD ORIGIN Greek *skhēma* form

Schepisi *n* **Fred**, full name *Frederick Alan Schepisi*. born 1939, Australian film director. His films include *The Chant of Jimmie Blacksmith* (1978), *A Cry in the Dark* (1988) and *Last Orders* (2001)

scherzo (skairt-so) *n, pl* **-zos** a quick lively piece of music, often the second or third movement in a sonata or symphony
WORD ORIGIN Italian: joke

Schiaparelli *n* **1 Elsa** 1896–1973, Italian couturière, noted esp. for the dramatic colours of her designs **2 Giovanni Virginio** 1835–1910, Italian astronomer, who discovered the asteroid Hesperia (1861) and the so-called canals of Mars (1877)

Schiele *n* **Egon** 1890–1918, Austrian painter and draughtsman: a leading exponent of Austrian expressionism

Schiff *n* **Andras** born 1953, Hungarian concert pianist; became a British citizen in 2001

schilling *n* a former monetary unit of Austria
WORD ORIGIN from German: shilling

schism (skizz-um) *n* the division of a group, esp. a religious group, into opposing factions, due to differences in doctrine **schismatic** *adj*
WORD ORIGIN Greek *skhizein* to split

schist (skist) *n* a crystalline rock which splits into thin layers
WORD ORIGIN Greek *skhizein* to split

schistosomiasis (shiss-ta-so-my-a-siss) *n* ▸ same as **bilharzia**

schizo (skit-so) *offensive adj* **1** schizophrenic ▷*n, pl* **-os 2** a schizophrenic person

schizoid *adj* **1** *psychol* having a personality disorder characterized by extreme shyness and extreme sensitivity **2** *informal* characterized by conflicting or contradictory ideas or attitudes ▷*n* **3** a person who has a schizoid personality

schizophrenia *n* **1** a psychotic disorder characterized by withdrawal from reality, hallucinations, or emotional instability **2** *informal* behaviour that seems to be motivated by contradictory or conflicting principles **schizophrenic** *adj, n*
WORD ORIGIN Greek *skhizein* to split + *phrēn* mind

Schlegel *n* **1 August Wilhelm von** 1767–1845, German romantic critic and scholar, noted particularly for his translations of Shakespeare **2** his brother, **Friedrich von** 1772–1829, German philosopher and critic; a founder of the romantic movement in Germany

Schleiermacher *n* **Friedrich Ernst Daniel** 1768–1834, German Protestant theologian and philosopher. His works include *The Christian Faith* (1821–22)

Schlesinger *n* **John** (**Richard**) 1926–2003, British film and theatre director. Films include *Billy Liar* (1963), *Midnight Cowboy* (1969), *Sunday Bloody Sunday* (1971), and *Eye for an Eye* (1995)

Schlick *n* **Moritz** 1882–1936, German philosopher, working in Austria, who founded (1924) the Vienna Circle to develop the doctrine of logical positivism. His works include the *General Theory of Knowledge* (1918) and *Problems of Ethics* (1930)

schmaltz *n* excessive sentimentality, esp. in music **schmaltzy** *adj*
WORD ORIGIN Yiddish: melted fat

Schmidt *n* **Helmut** (**Heinrich Waldemar**) born 1918, German Social Democrat statesman; chancellor of West Germany (1974–82)

Schnabel *n* **Artur** 1882–1951, US pianist and composer, born in Austria

schnapps *n* a strong dry alcoholic drink distilled from potatoes
WORD ORIGIN German *Schnaps*

Schnittke *n* **Alfred** 1934–98, Russian composer: his works include four symphonies, four violin concertos, choral, chamber, and film music

schnitzel *n* a thin slice of meat, esp. veal
WORD ORIGIN German: cutlet

Schnitzler *n* **Arthur** 1862–1931, Austrian dramatist and novelist. His best-known works are *Anatol* (1893) a series of one-act plays, and *Reigen* (1900), both of which reveal his psychological insight and preoccupation with sexuality

scholar ❶ *n* **1** a person who studies an academic subject **2** a student who

THESAURUS

cynic, scoffer, disbeliever, Pyrrhonist **2 = agnostic**, doubter, unbeliever, doubting Thomas

schedule *n* **1, 3 = plan**, programme, agenda, calendar, timetable, itinerary, list of appointments ▷*vb* **4 = plan**, set up, book, programme, arrange, organize, timetable

scheme *n* **1 = plan**, programme, strategy, system, design, project, theory, proposal, device, tactics, course of action, contrivance **3 = plot**, dodge, ploy, ruse, game (*informal*), shift, intrigue, conspiracy, manoeuvre, machinations, subterfuge, stratagem ▷*vb* **6 = plot**, plan, intrigue, manoeuvre, conspire, contrive, collude, wheel and deal, machinate

scholar *n* **1 = intellectual**, academic, man of letters, bookworm, egghead

DICTIONARY

has a scholarship **3** a pupil
scholarly *adj*
WORD ORIGIN Latin *schola* school
scholarship ❶ *n* **1** academic achievement; learning gained by serious study **2** financial aid provided for a scholar because of academic merit
scholastic *adj* **1** of schools, scholars, or education **2** of or relating to scholasticism ▷*n* **3** a scholarly person **4** a disciple or adherent of scholasticism
WORD ORIGIN Greek *skholastikos* devoted to learning
scholasticism *n* the system of philosophy, theology, and teaching that dominated medieval Europe and was based on the writings of Aristotle
Schongauer *n* **Martin** ?1445–91, German painter and engraver
school[1] ❶ *n* **1** a place where children are educated **2** the staff and pupils of a school **3** a regular session of instruction in a school: *we stayed behind after school* **4** a faculty or department specializing in a particular subject: *the dental school* **5** a place or sphere of activity that instructs: *the school of hard knocks* **6** a group of artists, writers, or thinkers, linked by the same style, teachers, or methods **7** *informal* a group assembled for a common purpose, such as gambling: *a card school* ▷*vb* **8** to educate or train: *she schooled herself to be as ambitious as her sister*
WORD ORIGIN Greek *skholē* leisure spent in the pursuit of knowledge
school[2] *n* a group of sea-living animals that swim together, such as fish, whales, or dolphins
WORD ORIGIN Old English *scolu* shoal
schoolboy *n* a boy attending school
schooled *adj* **schooled in** trained or educated in: *well schooled in history*
schoolgirl *n* a girl attending school
schoolhouse *n* **1** a building used as a school **2** a house attached to a school
schoolie *n Austral informal* a schoolteacher or a high-school student
schoolies week *n Austral informal* a week of post-exam celebrations for students who have just completed their final year of high school
schooling *n* the education a person receives at school
schoolmarm *n informal* **1** a woman schoolteacher **2** a woman who is old-fashioned and easily shocked by bad language or references to sex
schoolmaster *or fem* **schoolmistress** *n* a person who teaches in or runs a school
schoolteacher *n* a person who teaches in a school
school year *n* **1** a twelve-month period, usually of three terms, during which pupils remain in the same class **2** the time during this period when the school is open
schooner *n* **1** a sailing ship with at least two masts, one at the back and one at the front **2** *Brit* a large glass for sherry **3** *US, Canad, Austral & NZ* a large glass for beer
WORD ORIGIN origin unknown
schottische *n* **1** a 19th-century German dance resembling a slow polka **2** music for this dance
WORD ORIGIN German *der schottische Tanz* the Scottish dance
Schreiner *n* **Olive** (**Emilie Albertina**) 1855–1920, South African novelist and feminist writer, whose works include the autobiographical *The Story of an African Farm* (1883) and *Women and Labour* (1911)
Schröder *n* **Gerhard** born 1944, German Social Democrat politician; chancellor of Germany from 1998–2005
Schrödinger *n* **Erwin** 1887–1961, Austrian physicist, who discovered the wave equation: shared the Nobel prize for physics 1933
Schuman *n* **1 Robert** 1886–1963, French statesman; prime minister (1947–48). He proposed (1950) pooling the coal and steel resources of W Europe **2 William** (**Howard**) 1910–91, US composer
schuss (**shooss**) *n skiing* a straight high-speed downhill run
WORD ORIGIN from German
Schuster *n* **Leon** born 1952, South African comedian and film maker. His films include *You Must Be Joking* (1986) and *Mr Bones* (2001)
Schütz *n* **Heinrich** 1585–1672, German composer, esp. of church music and madrigals
Schwann *n* **Theodor** 1810–82, German physiologist, who founded the theory that all animals consist of cells or cell products
Schwarzkopf *n* **1 Elisabeth** 1915–2006, Austro-British operatic soprano, born in Germany **2 Norman,** nicknamed *Stormin' Norman*. born 1934, US general. As head of Central Command, the US military district covering the Middle East, he became the victorious commander-in-chief of the US-led forces in the Gulf War (1991)
Schwitters *n* **Kurt** 1887–1948, German dadaist painter and poet, noted for his collages composed of discarded materials
sciatic *adj* **1** *anat* of the hip or the hipbone **2** of or afflicted with sciatica: *a sciatic injury*
WORD ORIGIN Greek *iskhia* hip joint
sciatica *n* severe pain in the large nerve in the back of the leg
science ❶ *n* **1** the study of the nature and behaviour of the physical universe, based on observation, experiment, and measurement **2** the knowledge obtained by these methods **3** any particular branch of this knowledge: *medical science* **4** any body of knowledge organized in a way resembling that of the physical sciences but concerned with other subjects: *political science*
WORD ORIGIN Latin *scientia* knowledge
science fiction *n* stories and films that make imaginative use of scientific knowledge or theories
science park *n* an area where scientific research and commercial development are carried on in cooperation
scientific ❶ *adj* **1** relating to science or a particular science: *scientific discovery* **2** done in a systematic way, using experiments or tests **scientifically** *adv*
scientist ❶ *n* a person who studies or practises a science
sci-fi *n* ▸short for **science fiction**
scimitar *n* a curved oriental sword
WORD ORIGIN probably from Persian *shimshīr*
scintilla (sin-**till**-a) *n* a very small amount; hint or trace
WORD ORIGIN Latin: a spark
scintillate *vb* **-lating, -lated** to give off (sparks); sparkle **scintillation** *n*
WORD ORIGIN Latin *scintilla* a spark
scintillating *adj* (of conversation or humour) very lively and amusing

S

THESAURUS

(informal), savant, bluestocking *(usually derogatory)*, acca *(Austral slang)* **3 = student**, pupil, learner, schoolboy *or* schoolgirl
scholarship *n* **1 = learning**, education, culture, knowledge, wisdom, accomplishments, attainments, lore, erudition, academic study, book-learning **2 = grant**, award, payment, exhibition, endowment, fellowship, bursary
school[1] *n* **1 = academy**, college, institution, institute, discipline, seminary, educational institution, centre of learning, alma mater **6 = group**, set, circle, following, class, faction, followers, disciples, sect, devotees, denomination, clique, adherents, schism ▷*vb* **8 = train**, prime, coach, prepare, discipline, educate, drill, tutor, instruct, verse, indoctrinate
science *n* **4 = discipline**, body of knowledge, branch of knowledge
scientific *adj* **2 = systematic**, accurate, exact, precise, controlled, mathematical
scientist *n* **= researcher**, inventor, boffin *(informal)*, technophile
scoff[1] *vb* **1 = scorn**, mock, laugh at,

DICTIONARY

scion (sy-on) *n* **1** a descendant or young member of a family **2** a shoot of a plant for grafting onto another plant
WORD ORIGIN Old French *cion*

scissors *pl n* a cutting instrument held in one hand, with two crossed blades pivoted so that they close together on what is to be cut
WORD ORIGIN Old French *cisoires*

sclera (skleer-a) *n biol* the tough white substance that forms the outer covering of the eyeball
WORD ORIGIN Greek *sklēros* hard

sclerosis (skleer-oh-siss) *n, pl* **-ses** (-seez) *pathol* an abnormal hardening or thickening of body tissues, esp. of the nervous system or the inner wall of arteries
WORD ORIGIN Greek *sklērōsis* a hardening

sclerotic (skleer-rot-ik) *adj* **1** of or relating to the sclera **2** of, relating to, or having sclerosis

scoff[1] *vb* **1** (often foll. by *at*) to speak in a scornful and mocking way about (something) ▹*n* **2** a mocking expression; jeer **scoffing** *adj, n*
WORD ORIGIN probably from Old Norse

scoff[2] *vb informal* to eat (food) fast and greedily
WORD ORIGIN variant of *scaff* food

Scofield *n* **(David) Paul** (1922–2008), English stage and film actor

scold *vb* **1** to find fault with or rebuke (a person) harshly **2** *old-fashioned* to use harsh or abusive language ▹*n* **3** a person, esp. a woman, who constantly scolds **scolding** *n*
WORD ORIGIN from Old Norse *skāld*

scollop *n, vb* ▸same as **scallop**

sconce *n* a bracket fixed to a wall for holding candles or lights
WORD ORIGIN Late Latin *absconsa* dark lantern

scone *n* a small plain cake baked in an oven or on a griddle
WORD ORIGIN Scots

scoop *n* **1** a spoonlike tool with a deep bowl, used for handling loose or soft materials such as flour or ice cream **2** the deep shovel of a mechanical digger **3** the amount taken up by a scoop **4** the act of scooping or dredging **5** a news story reported in one newspaper before all the others ▹*vb* **6** (often foll. by *up*) to take up and remove (something) with or as if with a scoop **7 scoop out** to hollow out with or as if with a scoop **8** to beat (rival newspapers) in reporting a news item **9** to win (a prize, a large sum of money, etc.)
WORD ORIGIN Germanic

scoot *vb* to leave or move quickly
WORD ORIGIN origin unknown

scooter *n* **1** a child's small cycle which is ridden by pushing the ground with one foot **2** a light motorcycle with a small engine

Scopas *n* 4th century BC, Greek sculptor and architect

scope *n* **1** opportunity for using abilities: *ample scope for creative work* **2** range of view or grasp: *that is outside my scope* **3** the area covered by an activity or topic: *the scope of his essay was vast*
WORD ORIGIN Greek *skopos* target

scorbutic (score-**byewt**-ik) *adj* of or having scurvy
WORD ORIGIN Medieval Latin *scorbutus*

scorch *vb* **1** to burn or become burnt slightly on the surface **2** to parch or shrivel from heat **3** *informal* to criticize harshly ▹*n* **4** a slight burn **5** a mark caused by the application of excessive heat **scorching** *adj*
WORD ORIGIN probably from Old Norse *skorpna* to shrivel up

scorcher *n informal* a very hot day

score *n* **1** the total number of points made by a side or individual in a game **2** the act of scoring a point or points: *there was no score and three minutes remained* **3 the score** *informal* the actual situation: *what's the score on this business?* **4** *old-fashioned* a group or set of twenty: *three score years and ten* **5 scores of** lots of: *we received scores of letters* **6** *music* a written version of a piece of music showing parts for each musician **7 a** the incidental music for a film or play **b** the songs and music for a stage or film musical **8** a mark or scratch **9** a record of money due: *what's the score for the drinks?* **10** an amount recorded as due **11** a reason: *some objections were made on the score of sentiment* **12** a grievance: *a score to settle* **13 over the score** *informal* excessive or unfair ▹*vb* **scoring, scored 14** to gain (a point or points) in a game or contest **15** to make a total score of **16** to keep a record of the score (of) **17** to be worth (a certain number of points) in a game: *red aces score twenty* **18** to make cuts or lines in or on **19** *slang* to purchase an illegal drug **20** *slang* to succeed in finding a sexual partner **21** to arrange (a piece of music) for specific instruments or voices **22** to write the music for (a film or play) **23** to achieve (success or an advantage): *your idea scored with the boss*
WORD ORIGIN Old English *scora*

scoreboard *n sport* a board for displaying the score of a game or match

scorecard *n* **1** a card on which scores are recorded in games such as golf **2** a card identifying the players in a sports match, esp. cricket

score off *vb* to make a clever or insulting reply to what someone has just said: *they spent the evening scoring off each other*

scorer *n* **1** a player of a sport who scores a goal, run, or point: *Ireland's record goal scorer has announced his retirement* **2** a person who keeps note of the score of a match or competition as it is being played

scoria (score-ee-a) *n* **1** *geol* a mass of solidified lava containing many cavities **2** refuse left after ore has been smelted
WORD ORIGIN Latin: dross

scorn *n* **1** open contempt for a person or thing ▹*vb* **2** to treat with

S

THESAURUS

ridicule, knock *(informal)*, taunt, despise, sneer, jeer, deride, slag (off) *(slang)*, flout, belittle, revile, make light of, poke fun at, twit, gibe, pooh-pooh, make sport of

scoff[2] *vb (informal)* **= gobble (up)**, wolf, devour, bolt, cram, put away, guzzle, gulp down, gorge yourself on, gollop, stuff yourself with, cram yourself on, make a pig of yourself on *(informal)*

scoop *n* **1 = ladle**, spoon, dipper **5 = exclusive**, exposé, coup, revelation, sensation, inside story **6 scoop something** *or* **someone up = gather up**, lift, pick up, take up, sweep up *or* away ▹*vb* **9 = win**, get, receive, land, gain, achieve, net, earn, pick up, bag *(informal)*, secure, collect, obtain, procure, come away with

scope *n* **1 = opportunity**, room, freedom, space, liberty, latitude, elbowroom, leeway **2, 3 = range**, capacity, reach, area, extent, outlook, orbit, span, sphere, ambit, purview, field of reference

scorch *vb* **1 = burn**, sear, char, roast, blister, wither, blacken, shrivel, parch, singe

score *vb* **14, 15 = gain**, win, achieve, make, get, net, bag, obtain, bring in, attain, amass, notch up *(informal)*, chalk up *(informal)* **18 = cut**, scratch, nick, mark, mar, slash, scrape, notch, graze, gouge, deface, indent, crosshatch **21, 22** *(music)* **= arrange**, set, orchestrate, adapt ▹*n* **1 = points**, result, total, outcome **6, 7a = composition**, soundtrack, arrangement, orchestration **12 = grievance**, wrong, injury, injustice, grudge, bone of contention, bone to pick ▹*pl n* **5 = lots**, loads, many, millions, gazillions *(informal)*, hundreds, hosts, crowds, masses, droves, an army, legions, swarms, multitudes, myriads, very many, a flock, a throng, a great number

scorn *n* **1 = contempt**, disdain, mockery, derision, despite, slight, sneer, sarcasm, disparagement, contumely, contemptuousness,

DICTIONARY

contempt: *she attacked the government for scorning her profession* **3** to refuse to have or do (something) because it is felt to be undesirable or wrong: *youths who scorn traditional morals* **scornful** *adj* **scornfully** *adv*
WORD ORIGIN Old French *escharnir*

Scorpio *n astrol* the eighth sign of the zodiac; the Scorpion
WORD ORIGIN Latin

scorpion *n* a small lobster-shaped animal with a sting at the end of a jointed tail
WORD ORIGIN Greek *skorpios*

Scot *n* a person from Scotland

Scot. **1** Scotland **2** Scottish

scotch *vb* **1** to put an end to: *she had scotched the idea of bingo in the church* **2** to wound without killing
WORD ORIGIN origin unknown

Scotch[1] *not standard adj* **1** ▸same as **Scottish** ▹*pl n* **2 the Scotch** the Scots

Scotch[2] *n* whisky distilled in Scotland from fermented malted barley

Scotch broth *n Brit* a thick soup made from mutton or beef stock, vegetables, and pearl barley

Scotch egg *n* a hard-boiled egg encased in sausage meat and breadcrumbs, and fried

Scotch mist *n* a heavy wet mist or drizzle

scot-free *adv, adj* without harm or punishment: *the real crooks got off scot-free*
WORD ORIGIN obsolete *scot* a tax

Scotland Yard *n* the headquarters of the police force of metropolitan London

Scots *adj* **1** of Scotland ▹*n* **2** any of the English dialects spoken or written in Scotland

Scotsman *or fem* **Scotswoman** *n, pl* **-men** *or* **-women** a person from Scotland

Scots pine *n* **1** a coniferous tree found in Europe and Asia, with needle-like leaves and brown cones **2** the wood of this tree

Scottish *adj* of Scotland

scoundrel *n old-fashioned* a person who cheats and deceives
WORD ORIGIN origin unknown

scour[1] ❶ *vb* **1** to clean or polish (a surface) by rubbing with something rough **2** to clear (a channel) by the force of water ▹*n* **3** the act of scouring **scourer** *n*
WORD ORIGIN Old French *escurer*

scour[2] ❶ *vb* **1** to search thoroughly and energetically: *he had scoured auction salerooms* **2** to move quickly over (land) in search or pursuit
WORD ORIGIN probably from Old Norse *skūr* shower

scourge *n* **1** a person who or thing that causes affliction or suffering **2** a whip formerly used for punishing people ▹*vb* **scourging, scourged 3** to cause severe suffering to **4** to whip
WORD ORIGIN Latin *excoriare* to whip

Scouse *Brit informal n* **1** Also called: **Scouser** a person from Liverpool **2** the Liverpool dialect ▹*adj* **3** of Liverpool, its people, or their dialect
WORD ORIGIN from *lobscouse* a sailor's stew

scout ❶ *n* **1** *mil* a person sent to find out the position of the enemy **2** ▸same as **talent scout 3** the act or an instance of scouting ▹*vb* **4** to examine or observe (something) in order to obtain information **5 scout about** *or* **around** to go in search of something
WORD ORIGIN Old French *ascouter* to listen to

Scout *or* **scout** *n* a member of the Scout Association, an organization for young people which aims to develop character and promote outdoor activities **Scouting** *n*

scow *n* an unpowered barge used for carrying freight
WORD ORIGIN Low German *schalde*

scowl *vb* **1** to have an angry or bad-tempered facial expression ▹*n* **2** an angry or bad-tempered facial expression
WORD ORIGIN probably from Old Norse

scrabble *vb* **-bling, -bled 1** to scrape at or grope for something with hands, feet, or claws: *scrabbling with his feet to find a foothold* **2** to move one's hands about in order to find something one cannot see: *scrabbling in her handbag for a comb*
WORD ORIGIN Middle Dutch *schrabbelen*

Scrabble *n trademark* a board game in which words are formed by placing letter tiles in a pattern similar to a crossword puzzle

scrag *n* **1** the thin end of a neck of veal or mutton **2** a thin or scrawny person or animal
WORD ORIGIN perhaps variant of *crag*

scraggy *adj* **-gier, -giest** unpleasantly thin and bony **scragginess** *n*

scram[1] *vb* **scramming, scrammed** *informal* to leave very quickly
WORD ORIGIN from *scramble*

scram[2] *n* **1** an emergency shutdown of a nuclear reactor ▹*vb* **scramming, scrammed 2** (of a nuclear reactor) to shut down or be shut down in an emergency
WORD ORIGIN perhaps from SCRAM[1]

scramble ❶ *vb* **-bling, -bled 1** to climb or crawl hurriedly by using the hands to aid movement **2** to go hurriedly or in a disorderly manner **3** to compete with others in a rough and undignified way: *spectators scrambled for the best seats* **4** to jumble together in a haphazard manner **5** to cook (eggs that have been whisked up with milk) in a pan **6** *mil* (of a crew or aircraft) to take off quickly in an emergency **7** to make (transmitted speech) unintelligible by the use of an electronic scrambler ▹*n* **8** the act of scrambling **9** a climb or trek over difficult ground **10** a rough and undignified struggle to gain possession of something **11** *mil* an immediate takeoff of crew or aircraft in an emergency **12** *Brit* a motorcycle race across rough open ground
WORD ORIGIN blend of SCRABBLE + RAMP

scrambler *n* an electronic device that makes broadcast or telephone messages unintelligible without a special receiver

scramjet *n* **a** a type of ramjet in which the forward motion of the craft forces oxygen to mix with fuel (usually hydrogen) at supersonic speeds within a duct in the engine **b** an aircraft powered by such an engine
WORD ORIGIN from s(*upersonic*) + c(*ombustion*) + RAMJET

scrap[1] ❶ *n* **1** a small piece of something larger; fragment **2** waste material or used articles, often

THESAURUS

scornfulness **OPPOSITE:** respect ▹*vb* **2, 3 = despise**, reject, disdain, slight, snub, shun, be above, spurn, rebuff, deride, flout, look down on, scoff at, make fun of, sneer at, hold in contempt, turn up your nose at *(informal)*, contemn, curl your lip at, consider beneath you
OPPOSITE: respect

scour[1] *vb* **1 = scrub**, clean, polish, rub, cleanse, buff, burnish, whiten, furbish, abrade

scour[2] *vb* **1 = search**, hunt, comb, ransack, forage, look high and low, go over with a fine-tooth comb

scout *n* **1** *(mil)* **= vanguard**, lookout, precursor, outrider, reconnoitrer, advance guard ▹*vb* **4 = reconnoitre**, investigate, check out, case *(slang)*, watch, survey, observe, spy, probe, recce *(slang)*, spy out, make a reconnaissance, see how the land lies

scramble *vb* **1 = struggle**, climb, clamber, push, crawl, swarm, scrabble, move with difficulty **3 = strive**, rush, contend, vie, run, push, hasten, jostle, jockey for position, make haste **4 = jumble**, mix up, muddle, shuffle, entangle, disarrange ▹*n* **8, 9 = clamber**, ascent **10 = race**, competition, struggle, rush, confusion, hustle, free-for-all *(informal)*, commotion, melee *or* mêlée

scrap[1] *n* **1 = piece**, fragment, bit, trace,

DICTIONARY

collected and reprocessed **3 scraps** pieces of leftover food ▹*vb* **scrapping, scrapped 4** to discard as useless
WORD ORIGIN Old Norse *skrap*

scrap² ❶ *informal n* **1** a fight or quarrel ▹*vb* **scrapping, scrapped 2** to quarrel or fight
WORD ORIGIN perhaps from *scrape*

scrapbook *n* a book of blank pages in which newspaper cuttings or pictures are stuck

scrape ❶ *vb* **scraping, scraped 1** to move (a rough or sharp object) across (a surface) **2** (often foll. by *away* or *off*) to remove (a layer) by rubbing **3** to produce a grating sound by rubbing against (something else) **4** to injure or damage by scraping: *he had scraped his knees* **5 scrimp and scrape** ▸see **scrimp** (sense 2) ▹*n* **6** the act or sound of scraping **7** a scraped place: *a scrape on the car door* **8** *informal* an awkward or embarrassing situation **9** *informal* a conflict or struggle **scraper** *n*
WORD ORIGIN Old English *scrapian*

scrape through *vb* to succeed in or survive with difficulty: *both teams had scraped through their semifinals*

scrape together *or* **up** *vb* to collect with difficulty: *he scraped together enough money to travel*

scrapheap *n* **on the scrapheap** (of people or things) no longer required: *I was tossed on the scrapheap at a very early age*

scrappy *adj* **-pier, -piest** badly organized or done: *a scrappy draft of a chapter of my thesis*

scratch ❶ *vb* **1** to mark or cut (the surface of something) with a rough or sharp instrument **2** (often foll. by *at* or *out* etc.) to tear or dig with the nails or claws **3** to scrape (the surface of the skin) with the nails to relieve itching **4** to rub against (the skin) causing a slight cut **5** to make or cause to make a grating sound **6** (sometimes foll. by *out*) to erase or cross out **7** to withdraw from a race or (in the US) an election ▹*n* **8** the act of scratching **9** a slight cut on a person's or an animal's body **10** a mark made by scratching **11** a slight grating sound **12 from scratch** *informal* from the very beginning **13 not up to scratch** *informal* not up to standard ▹*adj* **14** put together at short notice: *a scratch team* **15** *sport* with no handicap allowed: *a scratch golfer* **scratchy** *adj*
WORD ORIGIN Germanic

scratchcard *n* a ticket that reveals whether or not the holder is eligible for a prize when the surface is removed by scratching

scratching *n music* a sound produced when the record groove in contact with the stylus of a record player is moved back and forth by hand

scrawl *vb* **1** to write carelessly or hastily ▹*n* **2** careless or scribbled writing **scrawly** *adj*
WORD ORIGIN perhaps blend of SPRAWL + CRAWL

scrawny *adj* **scrawnier, scrawniest** very thin and bony **scrawniness** *n*
WORD ORIGIN dialect *scranny*

scream ❶ *vb* **1** to make a sharp piercing cry or sound because of fear or pain **2** (of a machine) to make a high-pitched noise **3** to laugh wildly **4** to utter with a scream: *he screamed abuse up into the sky* **5** to be unpleasantly conspicuous: *bad news screaming out from the headlines* ▹*n* **6** a sharp piercing cry or sound, esp. of fear or pain **7** *informal* a very funny person or thing
WORD ORIGIN Germanic

scree *n* a pile of rock fragments at the foot of a cliff or hill, often forming a sloping heap
WORD ORIGIN Old English *scrīthan* to slip

screech¹ *n* **1** a shrill or high-pitched sound or cry ▹*vb* **2** to utter a shrill cry **screechy** *adj*
WORD ORIGIN earlier *scritch*, imitative

screech² *n Canad* a dark rum
WORD ORIGIN origin unknown

screech owl *n* **1** *Brit* ▸same as **barn owl 2** a small North American barn owl

screed *n* a long tiresome speech or piece of writing
WORD ORIGIN probably from Old English *scrēade* shred

screen ❶ *n* **1** the blank surface of a television set, VDU, or radar receiver, on which a visible image is formed **2** the white surface on which films or slides are projected **3 the screen** the film industry or films collectively **4** a light movable frame, panel, or partition used to shelter, divide, or conceal **5** anything that shelters, protects, or conceals: *a screen of leaves blocking out the sun* **6** a frame containing a mesh that is used to keep out insects ▹*vb* **7** (sometimes foll. by *off*) to shelter, protect, or conceal with or as if with a screen **8** to test or check (an individual or group) so as to assess suitability for a task or to detect the presence of a disease or weapons: *women screened for breast cancer* **9** to show (a film) in the cinema or show (a programme) on television
WORD ORIGIN Old French *escren*

screenplay *n* the script for a film, including instructions for sets and camera work

screen process *n* a method of printing by forcing ink through a fine mesh of silk or nylon, some parts of which have been treated so as not to let the ink pass

screen saver *n computers* software that produces changing images on a monitor when the computer is

THESAURUS

S

grain, particle, portion, snatch, part, atom, remnant, crumb, mite, bite, mouthful, snippet, sliver, morsel, modicum, iota **2 = waste**, junk, off cuts ▹*pl n* **3 = leftovers**, remains, bits, scrapings, leavings ▹*vb* **4 = get rid of**, drop, abandon, shed, break up, ditch *(slang)*, junk *(informal)*, chuck *(informal)*, discard, write off, demolish, trash *(slang)*, dispense with, jettison, toss out, throw on the scrapheap, throw away *or* out
OPPOSITE: bring back

scrap² *(informal) n* **1 = fight**, battle, row, argument, dispute, set-to *(informal)*, disagreement, quarrel, brawl, squabble, wrangle, scuffle, tiff, dust-up *(informal)*, shindig *(informal)*, scrimmage, shindy *(informal)*, bagarre *(French)*, biffo *(Austral slang)* ▹*vb* **2 = fight**, argue, row, fall out *(informal)*, barney *(informal)*, squabble, spar, wrangle, bicker, have words, come to blows, have a shouting match *(informal)*

scrape *vb* **1 = rake**, sweep, drag, brush **2 = clean**, remove, scour **3 = grate**, grind, scratch, screech, squeak, rasp **4 = graze**, skin, scratch, bark, scuff, rub, abrade ▹*n* **8** *(informal)* **= predicament**, trouble, difficulty, spot *(informal)*, fix *(informal)*, mess, distress, dilemma, plight, tight spot, awkward situation, pretty pickle *(informal)*

scratch *vb* **1 = mark**, cut, score, damage, grate, graze, etch, lacerate, incise, make a mark on **2 = rub**, scrape, claw at ▹*n* **10 = mark**, scrape, graze, blemish, gash, laceration, claw mark **13 not up to scratch** *(informal)* **= inadequate**, unacceptable, unsatisfactory, incapable, insufficient, incompetent, not up to standard, not up to snuff *(informal)*

scream *vb* **1 = cry**, yell, shriek, screech, squeal, shrill, bawl, howl, holler *(informal)*, sing out ▹*n* **6 = cry**, yell, howl, wail, outcry, shriek, screech, yelp

screen *n* **4 = cover**, guard, shade, shelter, shield, hedge, partition, cloak, mantle, shroud, canopy, awning, concealment, room divider ▹*vb* **7a = cover**, hide, conceal, shade, mask, veil, cloak, shroud, shut out **7b = protect**, guard, shield, defend, shelter, safeguard **8 = investigate**, test, check, examine, scan **9 = broadcast**, show, put on, present, air, cable, beam, transmit, relay, televise, put on the air

DICTIONARY

operating but idle
screenshot *n* an image created by copying part or all of the display on a computer screen at a particular moment
screenwriter *n* a person who writes screenplays
screw ● *n* **1** a metal pin with a spiral ridge along its length, twisted into materials to fasten them together **2** a threaded cylindrical rod that engages with a similarly threaded cylindrical hole **3** a thread in a cylindrical hole corresponding with the one on the screw with which it is designed to engage **4** anything resembling a screw in shape **5** *slang* a prison guard **6** *taboo slang* an act of or partner in sexual intercourse **7 have a screw loose** *informal* to be insane **8 put the screws on** *slang* to use force on or threatening behaviour against ▹*vb* **9** to rotate (a screw or bolt) so as to drive it into or draw it out of a material **10** to twist or turn: *she screwed up the sheet of paper* **11** to attach or fasten with or as if with a screw or screws **12** *informal* to take advantage of, esp. illegally: *screwed by big business* **13** *informal* to distort or contort: *his face was screwed up in pain* **14** (often foll. by *out of*) *informal* to force out of; extort **15** *taboo slang* to have sexual intercourse (with) **16 have one's head screwed on the right way** *informal* to be sensible ▸See also **screw up**
WORD ORIGIN French *escroe*
screwball *slang chiefly US & Canad* *n* **1** an odd or eccentric person ▹*adj* **2** crazy or eccentric: *a screwball comedy*
screwdriver *n* **1** a tool used for turning screws, consisting of a long thin metal rod with a flattened tip that fits into a slot in the head of the screw **2** a drink consisting of orange juice and vodka
screw top *n* **1** a bottle top that screws onto the bottle, allowing the bottle to be resealed after use **2** a bottle with such a top
screw up *vb* **1** *informal* to mishandle or spoil (something): *that screws up all my arrangements* **2** to twist out of shape or distort **3 screw up one's courage** to force oneself to be brave
screwed-up *adj*
screwy *adj* **screwier, screwiest** *informal* crazy or eccentric
Scriabin *or* **Skryabin** *n* **Aleksandr Nikolayevich** 1872–1915, Russian composer, whose works came increasingly to express his theosophic beliefs. He wrote many piano works; his orchestral compositions include *Prometheus* (1911)
scribble ● *vb* **-bling, -bled** **1** to write or draw quickly and roughly **2** to make meaningless or illegible marks (on) ▹*n* **3** something written or drawn quickly or roughly **4** meaningless or illegible marks
scribbler *n* **scribbly** *adj*
WORD ORIGIN Latin *scribere* to write
scribe *n* **1** a person who made handwritten copies of manuscripts or documents before the invention of printing **2** *bible* a recognized scholar and teacher of the Jewish Law
WORD ORIGIN Latin *scriba* clerk
Scribe *n* **Augustin Eugène** 1791–1861, French author or coauthor of over 350 vaudevilles, comedies, and libretti for light opera
scrimmage *n* **1** a rough or disorderly struggle ▹*vb* **-maging, -maged** **2** to take part in a scrimmage
WORD ORIGIN earlier *scrimish*
scrimp *vb* **1** to be very sparing in the use of something: *they were scrimping by on the last of the potatoes* **2 scrimp and save** *or* **scrape** to spend as little money as possible
WORD ORIGIN Scots
scrip[1] *n* *finance* a certificate representing a claim to shares or stocks
WORD ORIGIN short for *subscription receipt*
scrip[2] *or* **script** *n* *informal* a medical prescription
WORD ORIGIN from PRESCRIPTION
script ● *n* **1** the text of a play, TV programme, or film for the use of performers **2** an alphabet or system of writing: *Cyrillic script* **3** a candidate's answer paper in an examination **4** handwriting **5** a typeface which looks like handwriting ▹*vb* **6** to write a script for
WORD ORIGIN Latin *scriptum* something written
scripture *n* the sacred writings of a religion **scriptural** *adj*
WORD ORIGIN Latin *scriptura* written material
Scripture ● *n* *Christianity* the Old and New Testaments
scriptwriter *n* a person who writes scripts, esp. for a film or TV programme **scriptwriting** *n*
scrofula *n* *no longer in technical use* tuberculosis of the lymphatic glands **scrofulous** *adj*
WORD ORIGIN Medieval Latin
scroggin *n* *NZ* a mixture of nuts and dried fruits
scroll *n* **1** a roll of parchment or paper, usually inscribed with writing **2** an ancient book in the form of a roll of parchment, papyrus, or paper **3** a decorative carving or moulding resembling a scroll ▹*vb* **4** *computers* to move (text) on a screen in order to view a section that cannot be fitted into a single display
WORD ORIGIN Middle English *scrowle*
Scrooge *n* a mean or miserly person
WORD ORIGIN after a character in Dickens' story *A Christmas Carol*
scrotum *n* the pouch of skin containing the testicles in most male mammals
WORD ORIGIN Latin
scrounge *vb* **scrounging, scrounged** *informal* to get (something) by asking for it rather than buying it or working for it **scrounger** *n*
WORD ORIGIN dialect *scrunge* to steal
scrub[1] ● *vb* **scrubbing, scrubbed** **1** to rub (something) hard in order to clean it **2** to remove (dirt) by rubbing with a brush and water **3 scrub up** (of a surgeon) to wash the hands and arms thoroughly before operating **4** *informal* to delete or cancel (an idea or plan) ▹*n* **5** the act of scrubbing
WORD ORIGIN Middle Low German *schrubben* or Middle Dutch *schrobben*
scrub[2] *n* **1** vegetation consisting of stunted trees or bushes growing in a dry area **2** an area of dry land covered with such vegetation ▹*adj* **3** stunted or inferior: *scrub pines*
WORD ORIGIN variant of *shrub*
scrubber *n* **1** *Austral & Brit offensive slang* a woman who has many sexual

S

THESAURUS

screw *n* **1 = nail**, pin, tack, rivet, fastener, spike ▹*vb* **10 = turn**, twist, tighten, work in **11 = fasten**, fix, attach, bolt, clamp, rivet **12** *(informal)* **= cheat**, do *(slang)*, rip (someone) off *(slang)*, skin *(slang)*, trick, con, stiff *(slang)*, sting *(informal)*, deceive, fleece, dupe, overcharge, rook *(slang)*, bamboozle *(informal)*, diddle *(informal)*, take (someone) for a ride *(informal)*, put one over on (someone) *(informal)*, pull a fast one (on someone) *(informal)*, take to the cleaners *(informal)*, sell a pup (to) *(slang)*, hornswoggle *(slang)* **14** *(informal)* *(often with* **out of***)* **= squeeze**, wring, extract, wrest, bleed someone of something
scribble *vb* **1 = scrawl**, write, jot, pen, scratch, doodle, dash off
script *n* **1 = text**, lines, words, book, copy, dialogue, manuscript, libretto **4 = handwriting**, writing, hand, letters, calligraphy, longhand, penmanship ▹*vb* **6 = write**, draft, compose, author
Scripture *n* *(Christianity)* **= The Bible**, The Word, The Gospels, The Scriptures, The Word of God, The Good Book, Holy Scripture, Holy Writ, Holy Bible, The Book of Books
scrub[1] *vb* **1 = scour**, clean, polish, rub, wash, cleanse, buff, exfoliate **4** *(informal)* **= cancel**, drop, give up, abandon, abolish, forget about, call

DICTIONARY

partners **2** a device that removes pollutants from the gases that are produced when coal is burned industrially

scrubby *adj* **-bier, -biest 1** (of land) rough, dry, and covered with scrub **2** (of plants) stunted **3** *Brit informal* shabby or untidy

scrubs *pl n* the hygienic clothing worn by surgeons and other operating-theatre staff during an operation

scruff[1] *n* the nape of the neck: *the sergeant had him by the scruff of the neck* **WORD ORIGIN** perhaps from Old Norse *skoft* hair

scruff[2] *n informal* a very untidy person

scruffy *adj* **scruffier, scruffiest** dirty and untidy in appearance

scrum *n* **1** *rugby* a formation in which players from each side form a tight pack and push against each other in an attempt to get the ball, which is thrown on the ground between them **2** *informal* a disorderly struggle ▷ *vb* **scrumming, scrummed 3** (usually foll. by *down*) *rugby* to form a scrum **WORD ORIGIN** from *scrummage*

scrum half *n rugby* a player who puts in the ball at scrums and tries to regain its possession in order to pass it to his team's backs

scrummage *n, vb* **-maging, -maged 1** *rugby* ▸ same as **scrum 2** ▸ same as **scrimmage** **WORD ORIGIN** variant of *scrimmage*

scrump *vb Brit dialect* to steal (apples) from an orchard or garden **WORD ORIGIN** variant of *scrimp*

scrumptious *adj informal* delicious or very attractive **WORD ORIGIN** probably changed from *sumptuous*

scrumpy *n Brit* a rough dry cider brewed in the West Country of England **WORD ORIGIN** dialect *scrump* withered apples

scrunch *vb* **1** to press or crush noisily or be pressed or crushed noisily ▷ *n* **2** the act or sound of scrunching: *the scrunch of tyres on gravel* **WORD ORIGIN** variant of *crunch*

scrunchie *n* a loop of elastic covered loosely with fabric, used to hold the hair in a ponytail

scruple *n* **1** a doubt or hesitation as to what is morally right in a certain situation: *he had no scruples about the drug trade* ▷ *vb* **-pling, -pled 2** to have doubts (about), esp. on moral grounds **WORD ORIGIN** Latin *scrupulus* a small weight

scrupulous *adj* **1** taking great care to do what is fair, honest, or morally right **2** very careful or precise: *scrupulous attention to detail* **scrupulously** *adv* **WORD ORIGIN** Latin *scrupulosus*

scrutinize *or* **-nise** *vb* **-nizing, -nized** *or* **-nising, -nised** to examine carefully or in minute detail

scrutiny ❶ *n, pl* **-nies 1** very careful study or observation **2** a searching look **WORD ORIGIN** Late Latin *scrutari* to search

scuba (skew-ba) *n* an apparatus used in skin diving, consisting of cylinders containing compressed air attached to a breathing apparatus **WORD ORIGIN** *s(elf-)c(ontained) u(nderwater) b(reathing) a(pparatus)*

scud *vb* **scudding, scudded 1** (esp. of clouds) to move along quickly **2** *naut* to run before a gale ▷ *n* **3** the act of scudding **4** spray, rain, or clouds driven by the wind **WORD ORIGIN** probably Scandinavian

scuff *vb* **1** to drag (the feet) while walking **2** to scrape (one's shoes) by doing so ▷ *n* **3** a mark caused by scuffing **4** the act or sound of scuffing **WORD ORIGIN** probably imitative

scuffle *vb* **-fling, -fled 1** to fight in a disorderly manner ▷ *n* **2** a short disorganized fight **3** a scuffling sound **WORD ORIGIN** Scandinavian

scull *n* **1** a single oar moved from side to side over the back of a boat **2** one of a pair of small oars, both of which are pulled by one oarsman **3** a racing boat rowed by one oarsman pulling two oars ▷ *vb* **4** to row (a boat) with a scull **sculler** *n* **WORD ORIGIN** origin unknown

scullery *n, pl* **-leries** *chiefly Brit* a small room where washing-up and other kitchen work is done **WORD ORIGIN** Anglo-Norman *squillerie*

scullion *n archaic* a servant employed to do the hard work in a kitchen **WORD ORIGIN** Old French *escouillon* cleaning cloth

sculpt *vb* ▸ same as **sculpture**

sculptor *or fem* **sculptress** *n* a person who makes sculptures

sculpture ❶ *n* **1** the art of making figures or designs in wood, plaster, stone, or metal **2** works or a work made in this way ▷ *vb* **-turing, -tured 3** to carve (a material) into figures or designs **4** to represent (a person or thing) in sculpture **5** to form or be formed in the manner of sculpture: *limestone sculptured by fast-flowing streams* **sculptural** *adj* **WORD ORIGIN** Latin *sculptura* a carving

scum *n* **1** a layer of impure or waste matter that forms on the surface of a liquid: *the build-up of soap scum* **2** a person or people regarded as worthless or criminal ▷ *vb* **scumming, scummed 3** to remove scum from **4** *rare* to form a layer of or become covered with scum **scummy** *adj* **WORD ORIGIN** Germanic

scumbag *n slang* an offensive or despicable person **WORD ORIGIN** perhaps from earlier US sense: condom

scungy (skun-jee) *adj* **scungier, scungiest** *Austral & NZ slang* miserable, sordid, or dirty **WORD ORIGIN** origin unknown

scunner *dialect chiefly Scot vb* **1** to produce a feeling of dislike in ▷ *n* **2 take a scunner to** to take a strong dislike to **3** a person or thing that is disliked **WORD ORIGIN** Scots *skunner*

scupper[1] *n naut* a drain or spout in a ship's side allowing water on the deck to flow overboard **WORD ORIGIN** origin unknown

scupper[2] *vb* **1** *Brit & NZ slang* to defeat or ruin: *a deliberate attempt to scupper the peace talks* **2** to sink (one's ship) deliberately **WORD ORIGIN** origin unknown

scurf *n* **1** ▸ same as **dandruff 2** any flaky or scaly matter sticking to or peeling off a surface **scurfy** *adj* **WORD ORIGIN** Old English

scurrilous *adj* untrue or unfair, insulting, and designed to damage a person's reputation: *scurrilous allegations* **scurrility** *n* **WORD ORIGIN** Latin *scurra* buffoon

scurry *vb* **-ries, -rying, -ried 1** to run quickly with short steps ▷ *n, pl* **-ries 2** a quick hurrying movement or the sound of this movement **3** a short shower of rain or snow **WORD ORIGIN** probably from *hurry-scurry*

scurvy *n* **1** a disease caused by a lack of vitamin C, resulting in weakness, spongy gums, and bleeding beneath the skin ▷ *adj* **-vier, -viest 2** *old-fashioned* deserving contempt **scurviness** *n* **WORD ORIGIN** from *scurf*

scut *n* the short tail of animals such as the deer and rabbit **WORD ORIGIN** probably from Old Norse

S

THESAURUS

off, delete, do away with, discontinue

scrutiny *n* **1 = examination**, study, investigation, search, inquiry, analysis, inspection, exploration, sifting, once-over (*informal*), perusal, close study

sculpture *n* **2 = statue**, figure, model, bust, effigy, figurine, statuette ▷ *vb* **3, 5 = carve**, form, cut, model, fashion, shape, mould, sculpt, chisel, hew, sculp

DICTIONARY

scuttle[1] *n* ▸same as **coal scuttle**
WORD ORIGIN Latin *scutella* bowl

scuttle[2] *vb* **-tling, -tled 1** to run with short quick steps ▹*n* **2** a hurried pace or run
WORD ORIGIN probably from *scud*

scuttle[3] *vb* **-tling, -tled 1** *naut* to cause (a ship) to sink by making holes in the sides or bottom **2** to ruin (hopes or plans) or have them ruined: *a new policy scuttled by popular resistance* ▹*n* **3** *naut* a small hatch in a ship's deck or side
WORD ORIGIN Spanish *escotilla* a small opening

Scylla (sill-a) *n* **1** (in classical mythology) a sea monster believed to drown sailors navigating the Straits of Messina **2 between Scylla and Charybdis** in an awkward situation in which avoidance of either of two dangers means exposure to the other

scythe *n* **1** a long-handled tool for cutting grass or grain, with a curved sharpened blade that is swung parallel to the ground ▹*vb* **scything, scythed 2** to cut (grass or grain) with a scythe
WORD ORIGIN Old English *sigthe*

SD South Dakota

SDI Strategic Defense Initiative

SDLP (in Northern Ireland) Social Democratic and Labour Party

Se *chem* selenium

SE southeast(ern)

sea ⊙ *n* **1 the sea** the mass of salt water that covers three-quarters of the earth's surface **2 a** one of the smaller areas of this: *the Irish Sea* **b** a large inland area of water: *the Caspian Sea* **3** the area on or close to the edge of the sea, esp. as a place where holidays are taken: *a day by the sea* **4** strong and uneven swirling movement of waves: *rough seas* **5** anything resembling the sea in size or movement: *a sea of red and yellow flags* **6 at sea a** on the ocean **b** in a state of confusion or uncertainty **7 go to sea** to become a sailor **8 put out to sea** to start a sea voyage
WORD ORIGIN Old English *sǣ*

sea anchor *n naut* a canvas-covered frame, dragged in the water behind a ship to slow it down or reduce drifting

sea anemone *n* a marine animal with a round body and rings of tentacles which trap food from the water

sea bird *n* a bird that lives on or near the sea

seaboard *n* land bordering on the sea

seaborgium *n chem* a synthetic element. Symbol: Sg
WORD ORIGIN after Glenn *Seaborg*, physicist and chemist

seaborne *adj* **1** carried on or by the sea **2** transported by ship: *seaborne reinforcements*

sea breeze *n* a breeze blowing inland from the sea

sea cow *n* **1** a whalelike mammal such as a dugong or manatee **2** *archaic* a walrus

sea dog *n* an experienced or old sailor

seafarer *n* **1** a traveller who goes by sea **2** a sailor

seafaring *adj* **1** travelling by sea **2** working as a sailor ▹*n* **3** the act of travelling by sea **4** the work of a sailor

seafood *n* edible saltwater fish or shellfish

seafront *n* a built-up area facing the sea

seagoing *adj* built for travelling on the sea

sea-green *adj* bluish-green

seagull *n* ▸same as **gull**

sea horse *n* a small marine fish with a horselike head, which swims upright

sea kale *n* a European coastal plant with broad fleshy leaves and asparagus-like shoots that can be eaten

seal[1] ⊙ *n* **1** a special design impressed on a piece of wax, lead, or paper, fixed to a letter or document as a mark of authentication **2** a stamp or signet ring engraved with a design to form such an impression **3** a substance placed over an envelope or container, so that it cannot be opened without the seal being broken **4** something that serves as an official confirmation of approval: *seal of approval* **5** any substance or device used to close an opening tightly **6 set the seal on** to confirm something: *the experience set the seal on their friendship* ▹*vb* **7** to close or secure with or as if with a seal: *once the manuscripts were sealed up, they were forgotten about* **8 seal off** to enclose or isolate (a place) completely **9** to close tightly so as to make airtight or watertight **10** to inject a compound around the edges of something to make it airtight or watertight **11** to attach a seal to or stamp with a seal **12** to finalize or authorize **13 seal one's fate** to make sure one dies or fails **14 seal one's lips** to promise not to reveal a secret **sealable** *adj*
WORD ORIGIN Latin *signum* a sign

seal[2] *n* **1** a fish-eating mammal with four flippers, which lives in the sea but comes ashore to breed **2** sealskin ▹*vb* **3** to hunt seals
WORD ORIGIN Old English *seolh*

sealant *n* any substance, such as wax, used for sealing, esp. to make airtight or watertight

sea legs *pl n informal* the ability to maintain one's balance on board ship and to avoid being seasick

sea level *n* the average level of the sea's surface in relation to the land

sealing wax *n* a hard material made of shellac and turpentine, which softens when heated and which is used to make a seal

sea lion *n* a type of large seal found in the Pacific Ocean

Sea Lord *n* (in Britain) a naval officer on the admiralty board of the Ministry of Defence

sealskin *n* the skin or prepared fur of a seal, used to make coats

seam ⊙ *n* **1** the line along which pieces of fabric are joined by stitching **2** a ridge or line made by joining two edges: *the seam between the old and the new buildings* **3** a long narrow layer of coal, marble, or ore formed between layers of other rocks **4** a mark or line like a seam, such as a wrinkle or scar ▹*adj* **5** *cricket* of a style of bowling in which the bowler uses the stitched seam round the ball in order to make it swing in flight and after touching the ground: *a seam bowler* ▹*vb* **6** to join together by or as if by a seam **7** to mark with furrows or wrinkles
WORD ORIGIN Old English *sēam*

seaman *n, pl* **-men 1** a man ranking below an officer in a navy **2** a sailor

seamanship *n* skill in navigating and operating a ship

seamer *or* **seam bowler** *n cricket* a fast bowler who makes the ball bounce on its seam so that it will change direction

THESAURUS

sea *n* **1 = ocean**, the deep, the waves, the drink *(informal)*, the briny *(informal)*, main **5 = mass**, lot, lots *(informal)*, army, host, crowd, collection, sheet, assembly, mob, congregation, legion, abundance, swarm, horde, multitude, myriad, throng, expanse, plethora, profusion, concourse, assemblage, vast number, great number **6b at sea = bewildered**, lost, confused, puzzled, uncertain, baffled, adrift, perplexed, disconcerted, at a loss, mystified, disoriented, bamboozled *(informal)*, flummoxed, at sixes and sevens

seal[1] *n* **4 = authentication**, stamp, confirmation, assurance, ratification, notification, insignia, imprimatur, attestation **5 = sealant**, sealer, adhesive ▹*vb* **12 = settle**, clinch, conclude, consummate, finalize, shake hands on *(informal)*

seam *n* **2 = joint**, closure, suture *(surgery)* **3 = layer**, vein, stratum, lode

sear *vb* **2 = wither**, burn, blight, brand, scorch, sizzle, shrivel, cauterize, desiccate, dry up *or* out

search *vb* **1, 3 = examine**, check,

S

DICTIONARY

Seami *n* ▸ a variant spelling of **Zeami**
seamless *adj* **1** (of a garment) without seams **2** continuous or flowing: *a seamless performance* **seamlessness** *n*
seamstress *n* a woman who sews, esp. professionally
seamy *adj* **seamier, seamiest** involving the sordid and unpleasant aspects of life, such as crime, prostitution, poverty, and violence **seaminess** *n*
seance *or* **séance** (say-onss) *n* a meeting at which a spiritualist attempts to communicate with the spirits of the dead
WORD ORIGIN French
seaplane *n* an aircraft that is designed to land on and take off from water
seaport *n* a town or city with a harbour for boats and ships
sear ❶ *vb* **1** to scorch or burn the surface of **2** to cause to wither
WORD ORIGIN Old English *sēarian* to become withered
search ❶ *vb* **1** to look through (a place) thoroughly in order to find someone or something **2** to examine (a person) for hidden objects **3** to look at or examine (something) closely: *I searched my heart for one good thing she had done* **4 search out** to find by searching **5** to make a search **6 search me** *informal* I don't know ▹ *n* **7** an attempt to find something by looking somewhere
WORD ORIGIN Old French *cerchier*
search engine *n computers* an internet service enabling users to search for items of interest
Search Engine Optimization *n* the process of improving a website's page ranking in a search engine
searching ❶ *adj* keen or thorough: *a searching analysis* **searchingly** *adv*
searchlight *n* **1** a light with a powerful beam that can be shone in any direction **2** the beam of light produced by this device
search warrant *n* a legal document allowing a policeman to enter and search premises
Searle *n* **Ronald** (**William Fordham**) born 1920, British cartoonist, best known as the creator of the schoolgirls of St Trinian's
seascape *n* a drawing, painting, or photograph of a scene at sea
Sea Scout *n* a member of the branch of the Scouts which gives training in seamanship
seashell *n* the empty shell of a marine mollusc
seashore *n* land bordering on the sea
seasick *adj* suffering from nausea and dizziness caused by the movement of a ship at sea **seasickness** *n*
seaside *n* an area, esp. a holiday resort, bordering on the sea
season ❶ *n* **1** one of the four divisions of the year (spring, summer, autumn, and winter), each of which has characteristic weather conditions **2** a period of the year characterized by particular conditions or activities: *the typhoon season; the football season* **3** the period during which any particular species of animal, bird, or fish is legally permitted to be caught or killed: *the deer season* **4** any definite or indefinite period: *the busy season* **5** any period during which a show or play is performed at one venue: *the show ran for three seasons* **6 in season a** (of game) permitted to be killed **b** (of fresh food) readily available **c** (of animals) ready to mate ▹ *vb* **7** to add herbs, salt, pepper, or spice to (food) in order to enhance the flavour **8** (in the preparation of timber) to dry and harden **9** to make experienced: *old men seasoned by living* **seasoned** *adj*
WORD ORIGIN Latin *satio* a sowing
seasonable *adj* **1** suitable for the season: *a seasonable Christmas snow scene* **2** coming or happening just at the right time: *seasonable advice*
seasonal *adj* of or depending on a certain season or seasons of the year: *seasonal employment* **seasonally** *adv*
seasoning ❶ *n* something that is added to food to enhance the flavour
season ticket *n* a ticket for a series of events or number of journeys, usually bought at a reduced rate
seat ❶ *n* **1** a piece of furniture designed for sitting on, such as a chair **2** the part of a chair or other piece of furniture on which one sits **3** a place to sit in a theatre, esp. one that requires a ticket: *there were two empty front-row seats at the pageant* **4** the buttocks **5** the part of a garment covering the buttocks **6** the part or surface on which an object rests **7** the place or centre in which something is based: *the seat of government* **8** *Brit* a country mansion **9** a membership or the right to membership of a legislative or administrative body: *a seat on the council* **10** *chiefly Brit* a parliamentary constituency **11** the manner in which a rider sits on a horse ▹ *vb* **12** to bring to or place on a seat **13** to provide seats for: *the dining hall seats 150 people* **14** to set firmly in place
WORD ORIGIN Old English *gesete*
seat belt *n* a strap attached to a car or aircraft seat, worn across the body to prevent a person being thrown forward in the event of a collision
seating *n* **1** seats which are provided somewhere, esp. in a public place: *the grandstand has seating for 10 000; hard plastic seating* ▹ *adj* **2** of or relating to the provision of places to sit: *the delegation leader complained about the seating arrangements*
sea urchin *n* a small sea animal with a round body enclosed in a spiny shell
seaward *adv also* **seawards 1** towards the sea ▹ *adj* **2** directed or moving towards the sea
seawater *n* salt water from the sea
seaweed *n* any plant growing in the sea or on the seashore
seaworthy *adj* (of a ship) in a fit condition for a sea voyage **seaworthiness** *n*
sebaceous *adj* of, like, or secreting fat
WORD ORIGIN Latin *sebum* tallow
sebaceous glands *pl n* the small glands in the skin that secrete oil into hair follicles and onto most of the body surface
Sebastian *n* **Saint** died ?288 AD, Christian martyr. According to tradition, he was first shot with arrows and then beaten to death. Feast day: Jan 20
sebum (see-bum) *n* the oily substance secreted by the sebaceous glands
WORD ORIGIN Latin: tallow
sec[1] *adj* (of wines) dry
WORD ORIGIN French

THESAURUS

investigate, explore, probe, inspect, comb, inquire, sift, scour, ferret, pry, ransack, forage, scrutinize, turn upside down, rummage through, frisk (*informal*), cast around, rifle through, leave no stone unturned, turn inside out, fossick (*Austral & NZ*), go over with a fine-tooth comb ▹ *n* **7 = hunt**, look, inquiry, investigation, examination, pursuit, quest, going-over (*informal*), inspection, exploration, scrutiny, rummage
searching *adj* **= keen**, sharp, probing, close, severe, intent, piercing, penetrating, thorough, quizzical
OPPOSITE: superficial
season *n* **2, 4 = period**, time, term, spell, time of year ▹ *vb* **7 = flavour**, salt, spice, lace, salt and pepper, enliven, pep up, leaven
seasoning *n* **= flavouring**, spice, salt and pepper, condiment
seat *n* **1 = chair**, bench, stall, throne, stool, pew, settle **7 = centre**, place, site, heart, capital, situation, source, station, location, headquarters, axis, cradle, hub **8** (*Brit*) **= mansion**, house, residence, abode, ancestral hall **9 = membership**, place, constituency, chair, incumbency ▹ *vb* **12 = sit**, place, settle, set, fix, deposit, locate, install **13 = hold**, take, accommodate, sit, contain, cater for,

S

DICTIONARY

sec² *n informal* a second (of time): *hang on a sec*
sec³ secant
sec. **1** second (of time) **2** secondary **3** secretary
secant (seek-ant) *n* **1** (in trigonometry) the ratio of the length of the hypotenuse to the length of the adjacent side in a right-angled triangle; the reciprocal of cosine **2** a straight line that intersects a curve
WORD ORIGIN Latin *secare* to cut
secateurs *pl n* a small pair of gardening shears for pruning
WORD ORIGIN French
secede *vb* **-ceding, -ceded** to make a formal withdrawal of membership from a political alliance, federation, or group: *it will secede from the federation within six months*
WORD ORIGIN Latin *se-* apart + *cedere* to go
secession *n* the act of seceding **secessionism** *n* **secessionist** *n, adj*
seclude *vb* **-cluding, -cluded** **1** to remove from contact with others **2** to shut off or screen from view
WORD ORIGIN Latin *secludere*
secluded *adj* **1** kept apart from the company of others: *a secluded private life* **2** private and sheltered: *a secluded cottage*
seclusion *n* the state of being secluded; privacy: *the seclusion of his winter retreat*
second¹ ❶ *adj* **1** coming directly after the first in order **2** rated, graded, or ranked between the first and third levels **3** alternate: *every second Saturday* **4** another of the same kind; additional: *a second chance* **5** resembling or comparable to a person or event from the past: *a second Virgin Mary* **6** of lesser importance or position; inferior **7** denoting the second lowest forward gear in a motor vehicle **8** *music* denoting a musical part, voice, or instrument subordinate to or lower in pitch than another (the first): *the second tenors* **9** **at second hand** by hearsay ▷*n* **10** a person or thing that is second **11** *Brit education* an honours degree of the second class **12** the second lowest forward gear in a motor vehicle **13** (in boxing or duelling) an attendant who looks after a boxer or duellist **14** **seconds** **a** *informal* a second helping of food or the second course of a meal **b** goods that are sold cheaply because they are slightly faulty ▷*vb* **15** to give aid or backing to **16** (in boxing or duelling) to act as second to (a boxer or duellist) **17** to express formal support for (a motion proposed in a meeting) ▷*adv* **18** Also: **secondly** in the second place
WORD ORIGIN Latin *secundus* next in order
second² ❶ *n* **1** the basic SI unit of time, equal to 1/60 of a minute **2** 1/60 of a minute of angle **3** a very short period of time
WORD ORIGIN Latin *pars minuta secunda* the second small part (a minute being the first small part of an hour)
second³ (sik-kond) *vb Brit & NZ* to transfer (a person) temporarily to another job **secondment** *n*
WORD ORIGIN French *en second* in second rank
secondary ❶ *adj* **1** below the first in rank or importance: *a secondary consideration* **2** coming next after the first: *secondary cancers* **3** derived from or depending on what is primary or first: *a secondary source* **4** of or relating to the education of people between the ages of 11 and 18 or, in New Zealand, between 13 and 18: *secondary education* **5** (of an industry) involving the manufacture of goods from raw materials ▷*n, pl* **-aries** **6** a person or thing that is secondary
secondary colour *n* a colour formed by mixing two primary colours
secondary picketing *n* the picketing by striking workers of the premises of a firm that supplies or distributes goods to or from their employer
second-best *adj* **1** next to the best ▷*adv* **second best** **2** **come off second best** *informal* to fail to win against someone ▷*n* **second best** **3** an inferior alternative
second chamber *n* the upper house of a two-chamber system of government
second childhood *n* the time in an old person's life when he or she starts to suffer from memory loss and confusion; senility
second class *n* **1** the class or grade next in value, rank, or quality to the first ▷*adj* **second-class** **2** of the class or grade next to the best in value, rank, or quality **3** shoddy or inferior **4** denoting the class of accommodation in a hotel or on a train, aircraft, or ship, lower in quality and price than first class **5** (of mail) sent by a cheaper type of postage and taking slightly longer to arrive than first-class mail ▷*adv* **6** by second-class mail, transport, etc.
Second Coming *n* the prophesied return of Christ to earth at the Last Judgment
second cousin *n* the child of one's parent's first cousin
second-degree burn *n* a burn in which blisters appear on the skin
second fiddle *n informal* a person who has a secondary status
second floor *n* the storey of a building immediately above the first and two floors up from the ground
second-hand ❶ *adj* **1** previously owned or used **2** not from an original source or one's own experience: *second-hand opinions* **3** dealing in or selling goods that are not new: *second-hand furniture shops* ▷*adv* **4** from a source of previously owned or used goods: *they preferred to buy second-hand* **5** not directly or from one's own experience: *his knowledge had been gleaned second-hand*
second hand *n* a pointer on the face of a watch or clock that indicates the seconds
second lieutenant *n* an officer holding the lowest commissioned rank in an army or navy
secondly ❶ *adv* ▸same as **second¹** (sense 18)
second nature *n* a habit or characteristic practised for so long that it seems to be part of one's character
second person *n* the form of a pronoun or verb used to refer to the person or people being addressed
second-rate *adj* **1** not of the highest quality; mediocre **2** second in importance or rank: *a second-rate citizen*
second sight *n* the supposed ability

THESAURUS

have room *or* capacity for
second¹ *adj* **1 = next**, following, succeeding, subsequent **4 = additional**, other, further, extra, alternative, repeated **6 = inferior**, secondary, subordinate, supporting, lower, lesser ▷*n* **13 = supporter**, assistant, aide, partner, colleague, associate, backer, helper, collaborator, henchman, right-hand man, cooperator ▷*vb* **15 = support**, back, endorse, forward, promote, approve, go along with, commend, give moral support to
second² *n* **3 = moment**, minute, instant, flash, tick (*Brit informal*), sec (*informal*), twinkling, split second, jiffy (*informal*), trice, twinkling of an eye, two shakes of a lamb's tail (*informal*), bat of an eye (*informal*)
secondary *adj* **1 = subordinate**, minor, lesser, lower, inferior, unimportant, second-rate **OPPOSITE:** main **2, 3 = resultant**, resulting, contingent, derived, derivative, indirect, second-hand, consequential **OPPOSITE:** original
second-hand *adj* **1 = used**, old, handed down, hand-me-down (*informal*), nearly new, reach-me-down (*informal*), preloved (*Austral slang*)
secondly *adv* **= next**, second, moreover, furthermore, also, in the second place
secrecy *n* **1a = confidentiality**, privacy **1b = privacy**, silence, retirement,

DICTIONARY

to foresee the future or see actions taking place elsewhere
second thoughts *pl n* a revised opinion or idea on a matter already considered
second wind *n* **1** the return of comfortable breathing following difficult or strenuous exercise **2** renewed ability to continue in an effort
secrecy ❶ *n, pl* **-cies 1** the state of being secret **2** the ability or tendency to keep things secret
secret ❶ *adj* **1** kept hidden or separate from the knowledge of all or all but a few others **2** secretive: *she had become a secret drinker* **3** operating without the knowledge of outsiders: *secret organizations* ▷*n* **4** something kept or to be kept hidden **5** something unrevealed; a mystery: *the secrets of nature* **6** an underlying explanation or reason: *the secret of great-looking hair* **7 in secret** without the knowledge of others **secretly** *adv*
WORD ORIGIN Latin *secretus* concealed
secret agent *n* a person employed by a government to find out the military and political secrets of other governments
secretaire (sek-rit-**air**) *n* ▸same as **escritoire**
secretariat *n* **1 a** an office responsible for the secretarial, clerical, and administrative affairs of a legislative body or international organization **b** the staff of such an office or department **2** the premises of a secretariat
WORD ORIGIN French
secretary *n, pl* **-taries 1** a person who handles correspondence, keeps records, and does general clerical work for an individual or organization **2** the official manager of the day-to-day business of a society, club, or committee **3** (in Britain) a senior civil servant who assists a government minister **4** (in the US) the head of a government administrative department **secretarial** *adj*
WORD ORIGIN Medieval Latin *secretarius* someone entrusted with secrets
secretary bird *n* a large long-legged African bird of prey
secretary-general *n, pl* **secretaries-general** the chief administrative official of a legislative body or international organization
secretary of state *n* **1** (in Britain) the head of a major government department **2** (in the US) the head of the government department in charge of foreign affairs
secrete[1] *vb* **-creting, -creted** (of a cell, organ, or gland) to produce and release (a substance) **secretory** (sik-**reet**-or-ee) *adj*
secrete[2] *vb* **-creting, -creted** to put in a hiding place
WORD ORIGIN variant of obsolete *secret* to hide away
secretion *n* **1** a substance that is released from a cell, organ, or gland **2** the process involved in producing and releasing such a substance
WORD ORIGIN Latin *secretio* a separation
secretive ❶ *adj* hiding feelings and intentions **secretively** *adv*
secret police *n* a police force that operates secretly to suppress opposition to the government
secret service *n* a government agency or department that conducts intelligence or counterintelligence operations
sect ❶ *n* **1** a subdivision of a larger religious or political group, esp. one regarded as extreme in its beliefs or practices **2** a group of people with a common interest or philosophy
WORD ORIGIN Latin *secta* faction
sectarian *adj* **1** of or belonging to a sect **2** narrow-minded as a result of supporting a particular sect ▷*n* **3** a member of a sect **sectarianism** *n*
section ❶ *n* **1** a part cut off or separated from the main body of something: *a non-smoking section* **2** a part or subdivision of a piece of writing or a book: *the business section* **3** a distinct part of a country or community: *the Arabic section* **4** *surgery* the act or process of cutting or separating by cutting **5** *geom* a plane surface formed by cutting through a solid **6** ▸short for **Caesarean section** **7** *NZ* a plot of land for building on **8** *Austral & NZ* a fare stage on a bus ▷*vb* **9** to cut or divide into sections **10** to commit (a mentally disturbed person) to a mental hospital
WORD ORIGIN Latin *secare* to cut
sectional *adj* **1** concerned with a particular area or group within a country or community, esp. to the exclusion of others: *narrow sectional interests* **2** made of sections **3** of a section
sector ❶ *n* **1** a part or subdivision, esp. of a society or an economy: *the public sector* **2** *geom* either portion of a circle bounded by two radii and the arc cut off by them **3** a portion into which an area is divided for military operations
WORD ORIGIN Latin: a cutter
secular ❶ *adj* **1** relating to worldly as opposed to sacred things **2** not connected with religion or the church **3** (of clerics) not bound by religious vows to a monastic or other order
WORD ORIGIN Late Latin *saecularis*
secularism *n* the belief that religion should have no place in civil affairs **secularist** *n, adj*
secularize *or* **-ise** *vb* **-izing, -ized** *or* **-ising, -ised** to change (something, such as education) so that it is no longer connected with religion or the Church **secularization** *or* **-isation** *n*
secure ❶ *adj* **1** free from danger or damage **2** free from fear, doubt, or

S

THESAURUS

solitude, seclusion **2 = mystery**, stealth, concealment, furtiveness, cloak and dagger, secretiveness, huggermugger *(archaic)*, clandestineness, covertness
secret *adj* **1a = undisclosed**, unknown, confidential, underground, undercover, unpublished, under wraps, unrevealed **1b = concealed**, hidden, disguised, covered, camouflaged, unseen
OPPOSITE: unconcealed
1c = mysterious, cryptic, abstruse, classified, esoteric, occult, clandestine, arcane, recondite, cabbalistic
OPPOSITE: straightforward
2 = secretive, reserved, withdrawn, close, deep, discreet, enigmatic, reticent, cagey *(informal)*, unforthcoming **OPPOSITE:** frank
3 = undercover, covert, furtive, shrouded, behind someone's back, conspiratorial, hush-hush *(informal)*, surreptitious, cloak-and-dagger, backstairs **OPPOSITE:** open
▷*n* **4 = private affair**, confidence, skeleton in the cupboard **7 in secret = secretly**, surreptitiously, slyly, behind closed doors, incognito, by stealth, in camera, huggermugger *(archaic)*
secretive *adj* **= reticent**, reserved, withdrawn, close, deep, enigmatic, cryptic, cagey *(informal)*, uncommunicative, unforthcoming, tight-lipped, playing your cards close to your chest, clamlike
OPPOSITE: open
sect *n* **1, 2 = group**, division, faction, party, school, camp, wing, denomination, school of thought, schism, splinter group
section *n* **1, 2 = part**, piece, portion, division, sample, slice, passage, component, segment, fragment, fraction, instalment, cross section, subdivision **3 = district**, area, region, sector, zone
sector *n* **1 = part**, division, category, stratum, subdivision **3 = area**, part, region, district, zone, quarter
secular *adj* **1, 2 = worldly**, state, lay, earthly, civil, temporal, profane, laic, nonspiritual, laical
OPPOSITE: religious
secure *adj* **1 = safe**, protected,

DICTIONARY

care **3** tightly locked or well protected **4** fixed or tied firmly in position **5** able to be relied on: *secure profits* ▷*vb* **-curing, -cured 6** to obtain: *to secure a change in German policy* **7** to make or become free from danger or fear **8** to make safe from loss, theft, or attack **9** to attach; make fast or firm **10** to guarantee (payment of a loan) by giving something as security **securely** *adv*
WORD ORIGIN Latin *securus* free from care

security ❶ *n, pl* **-ties 1** precautions taken to ensure against theft, espionage, or other danger **2** the state of being free from danger, damage, or worry **3** assured freedom from poverty: *the security of a weekly pay cheque* **4** a certificate of ownership, such as a share, stock, or bond **5** something given or pledged to guarantee payment of a loan

security risk *n* someone or something thought to be a threat to state security

sedan *n US, Canad, Austral & NZ* a saloon car
WORD ORIGIN origin unknown

sedan chair *n* an enclosed chair for one passenger, carried on poles by two bearers, commonly used in the 17th and 18th centuries

sedate[1] *adj* **1** quiet, calm, and dignified **2** slow or unhurried: *a sedate walk to the beach* **sedately** *adv*
WORD ORIGIN Latin *sedare* to soothe

sedate[2] *vb* **-dating, -dated** to calm down or make sleepy by giving a sedative drug to

sedation *n* **1** a state of calm, esp. when brought about by sedatives **2** the administration of a sedative

sedative *adj* **1** having a soothing or calming effect ▷*n* **2** *med* a sedative drug or agent that makes people sleep or calm down
WORD ORIGIN Latin *sedatus* assuaged

sedentary (**sed**-en-tree) *adj* **1** done sitting down and involving very little exercise: *a sedentary job* **2** tending to sit about without taking much exercise
WORD ORIGIN Latin *sedere* to sit

sedge *n* a coarse grasslike plant growing on wet ground **sedgy** *adj*
WORD ORIGIN Old English *secg*

sedge warbler *n* a European songbird living in marshy areas

Sedgwick *n* **Adam** 1785–1873, English geologist; played a major role in establishing parts of the geological time scale, esp. the Cambrian and Devonian periods

sediment ❶ *n* **1** matter that settles to the bottom of a liquid **2** material that has been deposited by water, ice, or wind **sedimentary** *adj*
WORD ORIGIN Latin *sedimentum* a settling

sedition *n* speech, writing, or behaviour intended to encourage rebellion or resistance against the government **seditionary** *n, adj* **seditious** *adj*
WORD ORIGIN Latin *seditio* discord

seduce ❶ *vb* **-ducing, -duced 1** to persuade to have sexual intercourse **2** to tempt into wrongdoing **seduction** *n*
WORD ORIGIN Latin *seducere* to lead apart

seductive ❶ *adj* **1** (of a woman) sexually attractive **2** very attractive or tempting: *a seductive argument* **seductively** *adv* **seductiveness** *n*

sedulous *adj* diligent or painstaking: *a sedulous concern with the achievements of western thought* **sedulously** *adv*
WORD ORIGIN Latin *sedulus*

sedum *n* a rock plant with thick clusters of white, yellow, or pink flowers
WORD ORIGIN Latin

see[1] ❶ *vb* **seeing, saw, seen 1** to look at or recognize with the eyes **2** to understand: *I explained the problem but he could not see it* **3** to perceive or be aware of: *she had never seen him so angry* **4** to view, watch, or attend: *we had barely seen a dozen movies in our lives* **5** to foresee: *they could see what their fate was to be* **6** to find out (a fact): *I was ringing to see whether you'd got it* **7** to make sure (of something) or take care (of something): *see that he is never in a position to do these things again; you must see to it* **8** to consider or decide: *see if you can come next week* **9** to have experience of: *he had seen active service in the revolution* **10** to meet or pay a visit to: *I see my specialist every three months* **11** to receive: *the Prime Minister will see the deputation now* **12** to frequent the company of: *we've been seeing each other since then* **13** to accompany: *she saw him to the door* **14** to refer to or look up: *see page 35* **15** (in gambling, esp. in poker) to match (another player's bet) or match the bet of (another player) by staking an equal sum **16 see fit** to consider it proper (to do something): *I did not see fit to send them home* **17 see you** *or* **see you later** *or* **be seeing you** an expression of farewell ▸See also **see about, see into**, etc.
WORD ORIGIN Old English *sēon*

see[2] *n* the diocese of a bishop or the place within it where his cathedral is situated
WORD ORIGIN Latin *sedes* a seat

THESAURUS

shielded, sheltered, immune, unassailable, impregnable
OPPOSITE: unprotected
2 = confident, sure, easy, certain, assured, reassured **OPPOSITE:** uneasy
4 = fast, firm, fixed, tight, stable, steady, fortified, fastened, dependable, immovable
OPPOSITE: insecure
▷ *vb* **6 = obtain**, get, acquire, land *(informal)*, score *(slang)*, gain, pick up, get hold of, come by, procure, make sure of, win possession of
OPPOSITE: lose
9 = attach, stick, fix, bind, pin, lash, glue, fasten, rivet **OPPOSITE:** detach

security *n* **1 = precautions**, defence, safeguards, guards, protection, surveillance, safety measures
2a = assurance, confidence, conviction, certainty, reliance, sureness, positiveness, ease of mind, freedom from doubt
OPPOSITE: insecurity
2b = protection, cover, safety, retreat, asylum, custody, refuge, sanctuary, immunity, preservation, safekeeping
OPPOSITE: vulnerability
5 = pledge, insurance, guarantee, hostage, collateral, pawn, gage, surety

sediment *n* **1 = dregs**, grounds, residue, lees, deposit, precipitate, settlings

seduce *vb* **1 = corrupt**, ruin *(archaic)*, betray, deprave, dishonour, debauch, deflower **2 = tempt**, attract, lure, entice, mislead, deceive, beguile, allure, decoy, ensnare, lead astray, inveigle

seductive *adj* **2 = tempting**, inviting, attractive, sexy *(informal)*, irresistible, siren, enticing, provocative, captivating, beguiling, alluring, bewitching, ravishing, flirtatious, come-to-bed *(informal)*, come-hither *(informal)*, hot *(informal)*

see[1] *vb* **1 = perceive**, note, spot, notice, mark, view, eye, check, regard, identify, sight, witness, clock *(Brit slang)*, observe, recognize, distinguish, glimpse, check out *(informal)*, make out, heed, discern, behold, eyeball *(slang)*, catch a glimpse of, catch sight of, espy, get a load of *(slang)*, descry, take a dekko at *(Brit slang)*, lay *or* clap eyes on *(informal)*
2 = understand, get, follow, realize, know, appreciate, take in, grasp, make out, catch on *(informal)*, comprehend, fathom, get the hang of *(informal)*, get the drift of **6 = find out**, learn, discover, determine, investigate, verify, ascertain, make inquiries **7 = make sure**, mind, ensure, guarantee, take care, make certain, see to it **8 = consider**, decide, judge, reflect, deliberate, mull over, think over, make up your mind, give some thought to **10 = meet**, encounter, come across, run into, happen on, bump into, run across, chance on **11 = speak to**, receive, interview, consult, confer with
12 = go out with, court, date *(informal*,

see about *vb* **1** to take care of: *I'll see about some coffee* **2** to investigate: *to see about a new car*

seed ⊙ *n* **1** *bot* the mature fertilized grain of a plant, containing an embryo ready for germination ▸ Related adjective: **seminal** **2** such seeds used for sowing **3** the source, beginning, or origin of anything: *the seeds of dissent* **4** *chiefly bible* descendants; offspring: *the seed of David* **5** *sport* a player ranked according to his or her ability **6 go** *or* **run to seed a** (of plants) to produce and shed seeds after flowering **b** to lose strength or usefulness ▹ *vb* **7** to plant (seeds) in (soil) **8** (of plants) to produce or shed seeds **9** to remove the seeds from (fruit or plants) **10** to scatter silver iodide in (clouds) in order to cause rain **11** to arrange (the draw of a tournament) so that outstanding teams or players will not meet in the early rounds **seedless** *adj*
WORD ORIGIN Old English *sǣd*

seedbed *n* **1** an area of soil prepared for the growing of seedlings before they are transplanted **2** the place where something develops: *a seedbed of immorality*

seedling *n* a plant produced from a seed, esp. a very young plant

seed pearl *n* a very small pearl

seed pod *n bot* a carpel or pistil enclosing the seeds of a plant, esp. a flowering plant

seedy *adj* **seedier, seediest 1** shabby in appearance: *a seedy cinema* **2** *informal* physically unwell **3** (of a plant) at the stage of producing seeds **seediness** *n*

Seeger *n* **Pete** born 1919 US folk singer and songwriter, noted for his protest songs, which include "We shall Overcome" (1960), "Where have all the Flowers gone?" (1961), "If I had a Hammer" (1962), and "Little Boxes" (1962)

seeing ⊙ *n* **1** the sense or faculty of sight ▹ *conj* **2** (often foll. by *that* or *as*) in light of the fact (that)

see into *vb* to discover the true nature of: *he could see into my intentions*

seek ⊙ *vb* **seeking, sought 1** to try to find by searching: *to seek employment* **2** to try to obtain: *to seek a diplomatic solution* **3** to try (to do something): *we seek to establish a stable relationship*
WORD ORIGIN Old English *sēcan*

seek out *vb* to search hard for and find (a specific person or thing): *you should seek out healthy role models*

seem ⊙ *vb* **1** to appear to the mind or eye; give the impression of: *the car seems to be running well* **2** to appear to be: *there seems no need for all this nonsense* **3** to have the impression: *I seem to remember you were there too*
WORD ORIGIN Old Norse *sōma* to be suitable

seeming *adj* apparent but not real: *his seeming willingness to participate* **seemingly** *adv*

seemly *adj* **-lier, -liest** *formal* proper or fitting

seen *vb* ▸ the past participle of **see**[1]

see off *vb* **1** to be present at the departure of (a person going on a journey): *your sisters came to see you off* **2** *informal* to cause to leave or depart, esp. by force

seep ⊙ *vb* to leak through slowly; ooze **seepage** *n*
WORD ORIGIN Old English *sīpian*

seer *n* a person who can supposedly see into the future

seersucker *n* a light cotton fabric with a slightly crinkled surface
WORD ORIGIN Hindi *śīr śakar*

seesaw *n* **1** a plank balanced in the middle so that two people seated on the ends can ride up and down by pushing on the ground with their feet **2** an up-and-down or back-and-forth movement ▹ *vb* **3** to move up and down or back and forth alternately
WORD ORIGIN reduplication of *saw*, alluding to the movement from side to side, as in sawing

seethe ⊙ *vb* **seething, seethed 1** to be in a state of extreme anger or indignation without publicly showing these feelings **2** (of a liquid) to boil or foam **seething** *adj*
WORD ORIGIN Old English *sēothan*

see through *vb* **1** to perceive the true nature of: *it was difficult to see through people* **2** to remain with until the end or completion: *not all of them saw it through* **3** to help out in a time of need or trouble: *he helped see her through her divorce* ▹ *adj* **see-through 4** (of clothing) made of thin cloth so that the wearer's body or underclothes are visible

Seferis *n* **George** pen name of *Georgios Seferiades* 1900–71, Greek poet and diplomat: Nobel prize for literature 1963

segment ⊙ *n* **1** one of several parts or sections into which an object is divided **2** *maths* **a** a part of a circle cut off by an intersecting line **b** a part of a sphere cut off by an intersecting plane or planes ▹ *vb* **3** to cut or divide into segments **segmental** *adj* **segmentation** *n*
WORD ORIGIN Latin *segmentum*

Segovia[1] *n* a town in central Spain: site of a Roman aqueduct, still in use, and the fortified palace of the kings of Castile (the Alcázar). Pop: 55 640 (2003 est)

Segovia[2] *n* **Andrés**, Marquis of Salobreña 1893–1987, Spanish classical guitarist

Segrè *n* **Emilio** 1905–89, US physicist, born in Italy, who was the first to produce an artificial element. He shared the Nobel prize for physics (1959) with Owen Chamberlain for their discovery (1955) of the antiproton

segregate ⊙ *vb* **-gating, -gated 1** to set apart from others or from the main group **2** to impose segregation on (a racial or minority group)
WORD ORIGIN Latin *se-* apart + *grex* a flock

segregation ⊙ *n* **1** the practice or policy of creating separate facilities

S

chiefly US), walk out with (*obsolete*), keep company with, go steady with (*informal*), consort *or* associate with, step out with (*informal*) **13 = accompany**, show, escort, lead, walk, attend, usher

seed *n* **1** (*bot*) **= grain**, pip, germ, kernel, egg, embryo, spore, ovum, egg cell, ovule **3a = beginning**, start, suspicion, germ, inkling **3b = origin**, source, nucleus **4** (*chiefly Bible*) **= offspring**, children, descendants, issue, race, successors, heirs, spawn, progeny, scions **6b go** *or* **run to seed = decline**, deteriorate, degenerate, decay, go downhill (*informal*), go to waste, go to pieces, let yourself go, go to pot, go to rack and ruin, retrogress

seeing *conj* **2 = since**, as, in view of the fact that, inasmuch as

seek *vb* **1 = look for**, pursue, search for, be after, hunt, go in search of, go in pursuit of, go gunning for, go in quest of **3 = try**, attempt, aim, strive, endeavour, essay, aspire to, have a go at (*informal*)

seem *vb* **1, 2 = appear**, give the impression of being, look, look to be, sound as if you are, look as if you are, look like you are, strike you as being, have the *or* every appearance of being

seep *vb* **= ooze**, well, leak, soak, bleed, weep, trickle, leach, exude, permeate, percolate

seethe *vb* **1 = be furious**, storm, rage, fume, simmer, be in a state (*informal*), see red (*informal*), be incensed, be livid, go ballistic (*slang, chiefly US*), foam at the mouth, be incandescent, get hot under the collar (*informal*), wig out (*slang*), breathe fire and slaughter **2 = boil**, bubble, foam, churn, fizz, ferment, froth

segment *n* **1 = section**, part, piece, division, slice, portion, wedge, compartment

segregate *vb* **1 = set apart**, divide, separate, isolate, single out, discriminate against, dissociate **OPPOSITE:** unite

segregation *n* **1, 2 = separation**,

DICTIONARY

within the same society for the use of a racial or minority group **2** the act of segregating **segregational** *adj* **segregationist** *n*

Seifert *n* **Jaroslav** 1901–86, Czech poet and journalist, noted esp. for poems dealing with the German occupation of Prague during World War II. Nobel prize for literature 1984

seigneur *n* a feudal lord, esp. in France **seigneurial** *adj*
WORD ORIGIN Old French

seine (sane) *n* **1** a large fishing net that hangs vertically in the water by means of floats at the top and weights at the bottom ▹*vb* **seining, seined 2** to catch (fish) using this net
WORD ORIGIN Old English *segne*

seismic *adj* relating to or caused by earthquakes
WORD ORIGIN Greek *seismos* earthquake

seismograph *n* an instrument that records the intensity and duration of earthquakes **seismographer** *n* **seismography** *n*
WORD ORIGIN Greek *seismos* earthquake + -GRAPH

seismology *n* the branch of geology concerned with the study of earthquakes **seismologist** *n*
WORD ORIGIN Greek *seismos* earthquake + -LOGY

seismometer *n* ▸same as **seismograph**

seize ❶ *vb* **seizing, seized 1** to take hold of forcibly or quickly; grab **2** to take immediate advantage of: *real journalists would have seized the opportunity* **3** to take legal possession of **4** (sometimes foll. by *on* or *upon*) to understand quickly: *she immediately seized his idea* **5** to affect or fill the mind of suddenly: *a wild frenzy seized her* **6** to take by force or capture: *the rebels seized a tank factory* **7** (often foll. by *up*) (of mechanical parts) to become jammed through overheating
WORD ORIGIN Old French *saisir*

seizure ❶ *n* **1** *pathol* a sudden violent attack of an illness, such as an epileptic convulsion **2** the act of seizing: *a seizure of drug traffickers' assets*

Selden *n* **John** 1584–1654, English antiquary and politician. As a member of Parliament, he was twice imprisoned for opposing the king

seldom ❶ *adv* rarely; not often
WORD ORIGIN Old English *seldon*

select ❶ *vb* **1** to choose (someone or something) in preference to another or others ▹*adj* **2** chosen in preference to others **3** restricted to a particular group; exclusive: *a select audience* **selector** *n*
WORD ORIGIN Latin *seligere* to sort

select committee *n* a small committee of Members of Parliament, set up to investigate and report on a specified matter

selection ❶ *n* **1** a selecting or being selected **2** a thing or number of things that have been selected **3** a range from which something may be selected: *a good selection of reasonably priced wines* **4** *biol* the process by which certain organisms or individuals are reproduced and survive in preference to others

selective ❶ *adj* **1** tending to choose carefully or characterized by careful choice: *they were selective in their reading* **2** of or characterized by selection **selectively** *adv* **selectivity** *n*

selenium *n chem* a nonmetallic element used in photocells, solar cells, and in xerography. Symbol: Se
WORD ORIGIN Greek *selēnē* moon

Seles *n* **Monica** born 1973, US tennis player, born in Yugoslavia: winner of the US Open (1991, 1992); stabbed while on court in an unprovoked attack

Seleucus I *n* surname *Nicator* ?358–280 BC, Macedonian general under Alexander the Great, who founded the Seleucid kingdom

self *n, pl* **selves 1** the distinct individuality or identity of a person or thing **2** a person's typical bodily make-up or personal characteristics: *back to my old self after the scare* **3** one's own welfare or interests: *he only thinks of self* **4** an individual's consciousness of his or her own identity or being ▹*pron* **5** *not standard* myself, yourself, himself, or herself: *setting goals for self and others*
WORD ORIGIN Old English

self- *combining form* **1** (used with many main words to mean) of oneself or itself: *self-defence* **2** (used with many main words to mean) by, to, in, due to, for, or from the self: *self-employed; self-respect* **3** (used with many main words to mean) automatic or automatically: *self-propelled*

self-abnegation *n* the denial of one's own interests in favour of the interests of others

self-absorption *n* preoccupation with oneself to the exclusion of others **self-absorbed** *adj*

self-abuse *n old-fashioned* masturbation

self-addressed *adj* addressed for return to the sender

self-aggrandizement *or* **self-aggrandisement** *n* the act of increasing one's own power, wealth, or importance

self-appointed *adj* having assumed authority without the agreement of others: *self-appointed moralists*

self-assertion *n* the act of putting forward one's own opinions or demanding one's rights, esp. in an aggressive or confident manner **self-assertive** *adj*

self-assurance *n* confidence in oneself, one's abilities, or one's judgment **self-assured** *adj*

self-catering *adj* (of accommodation) for tenants providing and preparing their own food

self-centred *or US* **self-centered** *adj* totally preoccupied with one's own concerns

self-certification *n* (in Britain) the completion of a form by a worker stating that his or her absence was due to sickness

self-coloured *or US* **self-colored** *adj* **1** having only a single and uniform colour: *a self-coloured tie* **2** (of cloth or wool) having the natural or original colour

self-confessed *adj* according to one's own admission: *a self-confessed addict*

self-confidence *n* confidence in oneself, one's abilities, or one's judgment **self-confident** *adj*

self-conscious *adj* embarrassed or ill at ease through being unduly aware of oneself as the object of the attention of others **self-consciously**

THESAURUS

discrimination, apartheid, isolation

seize *vb* **1 = grab**, grip, grasp, take, snatch, clutch, snap up, pluck, fasten, latch on to, lay hands on, catch *or* take hold of OPPOSITE: let go **6a = take by storm**, take over, acquire, occupy, conquer, annex, usurp **6b = capture**, catch, arrest, get, nail *(informal)*, grasp, collar *(informal)*, hijack, abduct, nab *(informal)*, apprehend, take captive OPPOSITE: release

seizure *n* **1** *(pathol)* **= attack**, fit, spasm, convulsion, paroxysm **2a = taking**, grabbing, annexation, confiscation, commandeering **2b = capture**, arrest, apprehension, abduction

seldom *adv* **= rarely**, occasionally, not often, infrequently, once in a blue moon *(informal)*, hardly ever, scarcely ever OPPOSITE: often

select *vb* **1 = choose**, take, pick, prefer, opt for, decide on, single out, adopt, single out, fix on, cherry-pick, settle upon OPPOSITE: reject ▹*adj* **2 = choice**, special, prime, picked, selected, excellent, rare, superior, first-class, posh *(informal, chiefly Brit)*, first-rate, hand-picked, top-notch *(informal)*, recherché OPPOSITE: ordinary **3 = exclusive**, elite, privileged, limited, cliquish OPPOSITE: indiscriminate

selection *n* **1 = choice**, choosing, pick, option, preference **2 = anthology**, collection, medley, choice, line-up, mixed bag *(informal)*,

S

DICTIONARY

adv **self-consciousness** *n*
self-contained *adj* **1** containing within itself all parts necessary for completeness **2** (of a flat) having its own kitchen, bathroom, and toilet not shared by others
self-control *n* the ability to control one's feelings, emotions, or reactions **self-controlled** *adj*
self-deception *or* **self-deceit** *n* the act or an instance of deceiving oneself
self-defence *or US* **self-defense** *n* **1** the act or skill of defending oneself against physical attack **2** the act of defending one's actions, ideas, or rights
self-denial *n* the repression or sacrifice of one's own desires **self-denying** *adj*
self-determination *n* **1** the ability to make a decision for oneself without influence from outside **2** the right of a nation or people to determine its own form of government **self-determined** *adj*
self-discipline *n* the act of controlling or power to control one's own feelings, desires, or behaviour **self-disciplined** *adj*
self-drive *adj* relating to a hired vehicle that is driven by the hirer
self-educated *adj* educated through one's own efforts without formal instruction
self-effacement *n* the act of making oneself or one's actions seem less important than they are because of modesty or timidity **self-effacing** *adj*
self-employed *adj* earning one's living in one's own business, rather than as the employee of another
self-esteem *n* respect for or a favourable opinion of oneself
self-evident *adj* so obvious that no proof or explanation is needed **self-evidently** *adv*
self-explanatory *adj* understandable without explanation
self-expression *n* the expression of one's own personality or feelings, esp. in the creative arts **self-expressive** *adj*
self-government *n* the government of a country, nation, or community by its own people **self-governing** *adj*
self-help *n* **1** the use of one's own abilities and resources to help oneself without relying on the assistance of others **2** the practice of solving one's problems within a group of people with similar problems
self-image *n* one's own idea of oneself or sense of one's worth
self-important *adj* having an unduly high opinion of one's own importance **self-importance** *n*
self-improvement *n* the improvement of one's position, skills, or education by one's own efforts
self-indulgent *adj* tending to allow oneself to have or do things that one enjoys **self-indulgence** *n*
self-interest *n* **1** one's personal interest or advantage **2** the pursuit of one's own interest **self-interested** *adj*
selfish ❶ *adj* **1** caring too much about oneself and not enough about others **2** (of behaviour or attitude) motivated by self-interest **selfishly** *adv* **selfishness** *n*
selfless *adj* putting other people's interests before one's own **selflessly** *adv* **selflessness** *n*
self-made *adj* having achieved wealth or status by one's own efforts
self-opinionated *adj* clinging stubbornly to one's own opinions
self-pity *n* pity for oneself, esp. when greatly exaggerated **self-pitying** *adj*
self-pollination *n bot* the transfer of pollen from the anthers to the stigma of the same flower
self-possessed *adj* having control of one's emotions or behaviour, esp. in difficult situations **self-possession** *n*
self-preservation *n* the instinctive behaviour that protects one from danger or injury
self-propelled *adj* **1** (of a vehicle) driven by its own engine rather than drawn by a locomotive, horse, etc. **2** (of a rocket launcher or artillery piece) mounted on a motor vehicle **self-propelling** *adj*
self-raising *adj* (of flour) having a raising agent, such as baking powder, already added
self-realization *or* **-isation** *n* the fulfilment of one's own potential or abilities
self-regard *n* **1** concern for one's own interest **2** proper esteem for oneself
self-reliance *n* reliance on oneself or one's own abilities **self-reliant** *adj*
self-reproach *n* the act of finding fault with or blaming oneself
self-respect *n* a feeling of confidence and pride in one's own abilities and worth **self-respecting** *adj*
self-restraint *n* control imposed by oneself on one's own feelings, desires, or actions
self-righteous *adj* thinking oneself more virtuous than others **self-righteousness** *n*
self-sacrifice *n* the giving up of one's own interests for the wellbeing of others **self-sacrificing** *adj*
selfsame *adj* the very same: *this was the selfsame woman I'd met on the train*
self-satisfied *adj* smug and complacently satisfied with oneself or one's own actions **self-satisfaction** *n*
self-sealing *adj* **1** (of an envelope) sealable by pressure alone **2** (of a tyre) automatically sealing small punctures
self-seeking *n* **1** the act or an instance of seeking one's own profit or interests ▷*adj* **2** inclined to promote only one's own profit or interests: *self-seeking politicians* **self-seeker** *n*
self-service *adj* **1** of or denoting a shop or restaurant where the customers serve themselves and then pay a cashier ▷*n* **2** the practice of serving oneself and then paying a cashier
self-serving *adj* continually seeking one's own advantage, esp. at the expense of others
self-starter *n* **1** an electric motor used to start an internal-combustion engine **2** a person who is strongly motivated and shows initiative at work
self-styled *adj* using a title or name that one has given oneself, esp. without right or justification; so-called: *the self-styled leader of the rebellion*
self-sufficient *adj* able to provide for or support oneself without the help of others **self-sufficiency** *n*
self-supporting *adj* **1** able to support or maintain oneself without the help of others **2** able to stand up or hold firm without support, props, or attachments
self-willed *adj* stubbornly determined to have one's own way, esp. at the expense of others
self-winding *adj* (of a wristwatch) having a mechanism which winds itself automatically
sell ❶ *vb* **selling, sold 1** to exchange (something) for money **2** to deal in (objects or property): *he sells used cars* **3** to give up or surrender for a price or reward: *to sell one's honour* **4 sell for** to have a specified price: *they sell for 10 pence each* **5** to promote the sale of (objects or property): *sex sells cigarettes* **6** to gain acceptance of: *he'll sell an idea to a producer* **7** to be in demand on the market: *his books did not sell well*

S

THESAURUS

potpourri, miscellany
selective *adj* **1 = particular**, discriminating, critical, careful, discerning, astute, discriminatory, tasteful, fastidious
OPPOSITE: indiscriminate
selfish *adj* **1, 2 = self-centred**, self-interested, greedy, mercenary, self-seeking, ungenerous, egoistic *or* egoistical, egotistic *or* egotistical, looking out for number one (*informal*) **OPPOSITE:** unselfish
sell *vb* **1 = trade**, dispose of, exchange, barter, put up for sale
OPPOSITE: buy

DICTIONARY

enough **8** **sell down the river** *informal* to betray **9** **sell oneself** **a** to convince someone else of one's potential or worth **b** to give up one's moral standards for a price or reward **10** **sell someone short** *informal* to undervalue someone ▷ *n* **11** the act or an instance of selling: *the hard sell* ▸ See also **sell off, sell out, sell up** > **seller** *n*

WORD ORIGIN Old English *sellan* to give, deliver

Sella *n* **Phillipe** French Rugby Union football player; played 111 internationals for France (1982–95)

sell-by date *n* **1** *Brit* the date printed on packaged food specifying the date after which the food should not be sold **2** **past one's sell-by date** beyond one's prime

Sellers *n* **Peter** 1925–80, English radio, stage, and film actor and comedian: noted for his gift of precise vocal mimicry, esp. in *The Goon Show* (with Spike Milligan and Harry Secombe; BBC Radio, 1952–60). His films include *I'm All Right, Jack* (1959), *The Millionairess* (1961), *The Pink Panther* (1963), *Dr Strangelove* (1964), and *Being There* (1979)

sell off *vb* to sell (remaining items) at reduced prices

Sellotape *n* **1** *trademark* a type of transparent adhesive tape ▷ *vb* **-taping, -taped** **2** to seal or stick using adhesive tape

sell out ❶ *vb* **1** **a** to dispose of (something) completely by selling **b** (of items for sale) to be bought up completely: *these tickets will sell out in minutes* **2** *informal* to abandon one's principles, standards, etc. **3** *informal* to betray in order to gain an advantage or benefit ▷ *n* **sellout** **4** *informal* a performance of a show etc. for which all tickets are sold **5** a commercial success **6** *informal* a betrayal

sell-through *adj* of the sale of prerecorded video cassettes, without their first being for hire only

sell up *vb chiefly Brit & Austral* to sell all one's goods or property

selvage *or* **selvedge** *n* a specially woven edge on a length of fabric to prevent it from unravelling **selvaged** *adj*

WORD ORIGIN SELF + EDGE

selves *n* ▸ the plural of **self**

Selznick *n* **David O(liver)** 1902–62, US film producer, who produced such films as *A Star is Born* (1937), *Gone with the Wind* (1939), and *A Farewell to Arms* (1957)

semantic *adj* **1** of or relating to the meanings of words **2** of or relating to semantics

WORD ORIGIN Greek *sēma* a sign

semantics *n* the branch of linguistics that deals with the study of meaning

semaphore *n* **1** a system of signalling by holding two flags in different positions to represent letters of the alphabet ▷ *vb* **-phoring, -phored** **2** to signal (information) by semaphore

WORD ORIGIN Greek *sēma* a signal + *-phoros* carrying

semblance *n* outward or superficial appearance: *some semblance of order had been established*

WORD ORIGIN Old French *sembler* to seem

semen *n* the thick whitish fluid containing spermatozoa that is produced by the male reproductive organs and ejaculated from the penis

WORD ORIGIN Latin: seed

semester *n* either of two divisions of the academic year

WORD ORIGIN Latin *semestris* half-yearly

semi *n Brit, Austral & S African informal* ▸ short for **semidetached** (sense 2)

semi- *prefix* **1** half: *semicircle* **2** partly or almost: *semiprofessional* **3** occurring twice in a specified period: *semiweekly*

WORD ORIGIN Latin

semiannual *adj* **1** occurring every half-year **2** lasting for half a year

semiarid *adj* denoting land that lies on the edges of a desert but has a slightly higher rainfall (above 300 mm) so that some farming is possible

semiautomatic *adj* **1** (of a firearm) self-loading but firing only one shot at each pull of the trigger ▷ *n* **2** a semiautomatic firearm

semibreve *n music* a note, now the longest in common use, with a time value that may be divided by any power of 2 to give all other notes

semicircle *n* **1** one half of a circle **2** anything having the shape or form of half a circle **semicircular** *adj*

semicolon *n* the punctuation mark (;) used to separate clauses or items in a list, or to indicate a pause longer than that of a comma and shorter than that of a full stop

semiconductor *n physics* a substance, such as silicon, which has an electrical conductivity that increases with temperature

semiconscious *adj* not fully conscious **semiconsciousness** *n*

semidetached *adj* **1** (of a house) joined to another house on one side by a common wall ▷ *n* **2** *Brit* a semidetached house: *the mock Georgian semidetached*

semifinal *n* the round before the final in a competition **semifinalist** *n*

seminal *adj* **1** highly original and influential: *seminal thinkers* **2** potentially capable of development **3** of semen: *seminal fluid* **4** *biol* of seed

WORD ORIGIN Latin *semen* seed

seminar *n* **1** a small group of students meeting regularly under the guidance of a tutor for study and discussion **2** one such meeting

WORD ORIGIN Latin *seminarium* a nursery garden

seminary *n, pl* **-naries** a college for the training of priests **seminarian** *n*

WORD ORIGIN Latin *seminarium* a nursery garden

semiotics *n* the study of human communication, esp. communication using signs and symbols **semiotic** *adj*

WORD ORIGIN Greek *sēmeion* a sign

semipermeable *adj* (of a cell membrane) allowing small molecules to pass through but not large ones

semiprecious *adj* (of certain stones) having less value than a precious stone

semiprofessional *adj* **1** (of a person) engaged in an activity or sport part time for pay **2** (of an activity or sport) engaged in by semiprofessional people ▷ *n* **3** a semiprofessional person

semiquaver *n music* a note having the time value of one-sixteenth of a semibreve

Semiramis *n* the legendary founder of Babylon and wife of Ninus, king of Assyria, which she ruled with great skill after his death

semirigid *adj* (of an airship) maintaining shape by means of a main supporting keel and internal gas pressure

semiskilled *adj* partly skilled or trained but not sufficiently so to perform specialized work

Semite *n* a member of the group of peoples who speak a Semitic language, such as the Jews and Arabs

WORD ORIGIN New Latin *semita* descendant of Shem, eldest of Noah's sons

Semitic *n* **1** a group of languages that includes Arabic, Hebrew, and Aramaic ▷ *adj* **2** of this group of languages **3** of any of the peoples speaking a Semitic language, esp. the Jews or the Arabs **4** ▸ same as **Jewish**

semitone *n* the smallest interval between two notes in Western

THESAURUS

2 = deal in, market, trade in, stock, handle, retail, hawk, merchandise, peddle, traffic in, vend, be in the business of **OPPOSITE:** buy

sell out *vb* **1a = run out of**, be out of stock of

send *vb* **1a = dispatch**, forward, direct, convey, consign, remit **3 = propel**, hurl, fling, shoot, fire,

DICTIONARY

music, represented on a piano by the difference in pitch between any two adjacent keys **semitonic** *adj*

semitrailer *n Austral* a large truck in two separate sections joined by a pivoted bar. Also called: **semi**

semitropical *adj* bordering on the tropics; nearly tropical **semitropics** *pl n*

semivowel *n phonetics* a vowel-like sound that acts like a consonant, such as the sound *w* in *well*

Semmelweis *n* **Ignaz Philipp** 1818–65, Hungarian obstetrician, who discovered the cause of puerperal infection and pioneered the use of antiseptics

semolina *n* the large hard grains of wheat left after flour has been milled, used for making puddings and pasta
WORD ORIGIN Italian *semolino*

Semtex *n* a pliable plastic explosive

SEN (in Britain) State Enrolled Nurse

Sen. *or* **sen.** 1 senate 2 senator 3 senior

senate *n* the main governing body at some universities
WORD ORIGIN Latin *senatus* council of the elders

Senate *n* the upper chamber of the legislatures of Australia, the US, Canada, and many other countries

senator *n* a member of a Senate **senatorial** *adj*

send ❶ *vb* **sending, sent** 1 to cause (a person or thing) to go or be taken or transmitted to another place: *send a cheque or postal order* 2 **send for** to dispatch a request or command for (someone or something): *she had sent for me* 3 to cause to go to a place or point: *the bullet sent him flying into the air* 4 to bring to a state or condition: *his schemes to send her mad* 5 to cause to happen or come: *the thunderstorm sent by the gods* 6 *old-fashioned, slang* to move to excitement or rapture: *this music really sends me* **sender** *n*
WORD ORIGIN Old English *sendan*

Sendak *n* **Maurice** (**Bernard**) born 1928, US artist, writer, and set designer, best known as an illustrator of children's books, including *Where the Wild Things Are* (1963), which he also wrote, *In the Night Kitchen* (1971), and *Nutcracker* (1984)

send down *vb* 1 *Brit* to expel from a university 2 *informal* to send to prison

sendoff ❶ *n* 1 *informal* a show of good wishes to a person about to set off on a journey or start a new career ▷ *vb* **send off** 2 to dispatch (something, such as a letter) 3 *sport* (of a referee) to dismiss (a player) from the field of play for some offence

send up ❶ *informal vb* 1 to make fun of by doing an imitation or parody ▷ *n* **send-up** 2 a parody or imitation

Seneca[1] *n* 1 (*pl* **-cas** *or* **-ca**) a member of a North American Indian people formerly living south of Lake Ontario; one of the Iroquois peoples 2 the language of this people, belonging to the Iroquoian family
WORD ORIGIN C19: from Dutch *Sennecaas* (plural), probably of Algonquian origin

Seneca[2] *n* 1 **Lucius Annaeus**, called *the Younger* ?4 BC–65 AD, Roman philosopher, statesman, and dramatist; tutor and adviser to Nero. He was implicated in a plot to murder Nero and committed suicide. His works include Stoical essays on ethical subjects and tragedies that had a considerable influence on Elizabethan drama 2 his father, **Marcus** or **Lucius Annaeus**, called *the Elder* or *the Rhetorician*. ?55 BC–?39 AD, Roman writer on oratory and history

Senefelder *n* (**Johan Nepomuk Franz**) **Aloys**. 1771–1834, German dramatist and engraver, born in Czechoslovakia, who invented (1796) lithography

senescent *adj formal* growing old **senescence** *n*
WORD ORIGIN Latin *senescere* to grow old

seneschal (sen-ish-al) *n history* a steward of the household of a medieval prince or nobleman
WORD ORIGIN Old French

Senghor *n* **Léopold Sédar** 1906–2001, Senegalese statesman and writer; president of Senegal (1960–80)

senile *adj* mentally or physically weak or infirm on account of old age **senility** *n*
WORD ORIGIN Latin *senex* an old man

senior ❶ *adj* 1 higher in rank or length of service 2 older in years: *senior citizens* 3 *education* of or designating more advanced or older pupils or students ▷ *n* 4 a senior person
WORD ORIGIN Latin: older

Senior *adj chiefly US* being older than someone of the same name: *Joe Yule Senior*

senior aircraftman *n* an ordinary rank in the Royal Air Force

senior citizen *n* an old person, esp. a pensioner

seniority *n, pl* **-ties** 1 the state of being senior 2 degree of power or importance in an organization from length of continuous service

senior service *n Brit* the Royal Navy

senna *n* 1 a tropical plant with yellow flowers and long pods 2 the dried leaves and pods of this plant, used as a laxative
WORD ORIGIN Arabic *sanā*

Senna *n* **Ayrton** 1960–94, Brazilian racing driver: world champion (1988, 1990, 1991)

Sennacherib *n* died 681 BC, king of Assyria (705–681); son of Sargon II. He invaded Judah twice, defeated Babylon, and rebuilt Nineveh

Sennett *n* **Mack,** original name *Michael Sinott*. 1884–1960, US film producer and director, born in Canada, who produced many silent comedy films featuring the Keystone Kops, Charlie Chaplin, and Harold Lloyd, for the Keystone Company

señor (sen-**nyor**) *n* a Spanish form of address equivalent to *sir* or *Mr*

señora (sen-**nyor**-a) *n* a Spanish form of address equivalent to *madam* or *Mrs*

señorita (sen-nyor-**ee**-ta) *n* a Spanish form of address equivalent to *madam* or *Miss*

sensation ❶ *n* 1 the power of feeling things physically: *I lose all sensation in my hands* 2 a physical feeling: *a burning sensation in the throat* 3 a general feeling or awareness: *a sensation of vague resentment* 4 a state of excitement: *imagine the sensation in Washington!* 5 an exciting person or thing: *you'll be a sensation*
WORD ORIGIN Late Latin *sensatus* endowed with feelings

sensational ❶ *adj* 1 causing intense feelings of shock, anger, or excitement: *sensational allegations* 2 *informal* extremely good: *the views are sensational* 3 of the senses or

S

THESAURUS

deliver, cast, let fly

sendoff *n* **1 = farewell**, departure, leave-taking, valediction, going-away party

send up (*Brit informal*) **1 = mock**, mimic, parody, spoof (*informal*), imitate, take off (*informal*), make fun of, lampoon, burlesque, take the mickey out of (*informal*), satirize

senior *adj* **1 = higher ranking**, superior
OPPOSITE: subordinate
2 = the elder, major (*Brit*)
OPPOSITE: junior

sensation *n* **1, 3 = feeling**, sense, impression, perception, awareness, consciousness **4 = excitement**, surprise, thrill, stir, scandal, furore, agitation, commotion

sensational *adj* **1a = amazing**, dramatic, thrilling, revealing, spectacular, eye-popping (*informal*), staggering, startling, horrifying, breathtaking, astounding, lurid, electrifying, hair-raising
OPPOSITE: dull
1b = shocking, scandalous, exciting, yellow (*of the press*), melodramatic, shock-horror (*facetious*), sensationalistic
OPPOSITE: unexciting
2 (*informal*) **= excellent**, brilliant, superb, mean (*slang*), topping (*Brit slang*), cracking (*Brit informal*), crucial

DICTIONARY

sensation **sensationally** *adv*

sensationalism *n* the deliberate use of sensational language or subject matter to arouse feelings of shock, anger, or excitement **sensationalist** *adj, n*

sense ⊕ *n* **1** any of the faculties (sight, hearing, touch, taste, and smell) by which the mind receives information about the external world or the state of the body **2** the ability to perceive **3** a feeling perceived through one of the senses: *a sense of warmth* **4** a mental perception or awareness: *a sense of security* **5** ability to make moral judgments: *a sense of honour* **6** (*usually pl*) sound practical judgment or intelligence: *a man lost his senses and killed his wife* **7** reason or purpose: *no sense in continuing* **8** general meaning: *he couldn't understand every word but he got the sense of what they were saying* **9** specific meaning; definition: *the three senses of the word* **10 make sense** to be understandable or practical ▷ *vb* **sensing, sensed 11** to perceive without the evidence of the senses: *he sensed that she was impressed* **12** to perceive through the senses
WORD ORIGIN Latin *sentire* to feel

senseless *adj* **1** having no meaning or purpose: *a senseless act of violence* **2** unconscious **senselessly** *adv* **senselessness** *n*

sense organ *n* a part of the body that receives stimuli and transmits them as sensations to the brain

sensibility ⊕ *n, pl* **-ties 1** (*often pl*) the ability to experience deep feelings **2** (*usually pl*) the tendency to be influenced or offended: *its sheer callousness offended her sensibilities* **3** the ability to perceive or feel

sensible ⊕ *adj* **1** having or showing good sense or judgment **2** (of clothing and footwear) practical and hard-wearing **3** capable of receiving sensation **4** capable of being perceived by the senses **5** perceptible to the mind **6** *literary* aware: *sensible of your kindness* **sensibly** *adv*
WORD ORIGIN Latin *sentire* to feel

sensitive ⊕ *adj* **1** easily hurt; tender **2** responsive to feelings and moods **3** responsive to external stimuli or impressions **4** easily offended or shocked **5** (of a subject or issue) liable to arouse controversy or strong feelings **6** (of an instrument) capable of registering small differences or changes in amounts **7** *photog* responding readily to light: *a sensitive emulsion* **8** *chiefly US* connected with matters affecting national security **sensitively** *adv* **sensitivity** *n*
WORD ORIGIN Latin *sentire* to feel

sensitize *or* **-tise** *vb* **-tizing, -tized** *or* **-tising, -tised** to make sensitive **sensitization** *or* **-tisation** *n*

sensor *n* a device that detects or measures a physical property, such as radiation

sensory *adj* relating to the physical senses

sensual ⊕ *adj* **1** giving pleasure to the body and senses rather than the mind: *soft sensual music* **2** having a strong liking for physical, esp. sexual, pleasures **3** of the body and senses rather than the mind or soul **sensualist** *n*
WORD ORIGIN Latin *sensus* feeling

sensuality *n* **1** the quality or state of being sensual **2** enjoyment of physical, esp. sexual, pleasures

sensuous *adj* **1** pleasing to the senses of the mind or body: *the sensuous rhythms of the drums* **2** (of a person) appreciating qualities perceived by the senses **sensuously** *adv*

sent *vb* ▸ the past of **send**

sentence ⊕ *n* **1** a sequence of words constituting a statement, question, or a command that begins with a capital letter and ends with a full stop when written down **2 a** the decision of a law court as to what punishment is passed on a convicted person **b** the punishment passed on a convicted person ▷ *vb* **-tencing, -tenced 3** to pronounce sentence on (a convicted person) in a law court **sentential** *adj*
WORD ORIGIN Latin *sententia* a way of thinking

sententious *adj formal* **1** trying to sound wise **2** making pompous remarks about morality **sententiously** *adv*
WORD ORIGIN Latin *sententiosus* full of meaning

sentient (sen-tee-ent, sen-shent) *adj* capable of perception and feeling **sentience** *n*
WORD ORIGIN Latin *sentiens* feeling

sentiment ⊕ *n* **1** a mental attitude based on a mixture of thoughts and

THESAURUS

(*slang*), impressive, smashing (*informal*), fabulous (*informal*), first class, marvellous, exceptional, mega (*slang*), sovereign, awesome (*slang*), def (*slang*), brill (*informal*), out of this world (*informal*), mind-blowing (*informal*), bodacious (*slang, chiefly US*), boffo (*slang*), jim-dandy (*slang*), chillin' (*US slang*), booshit (*Austral slang*), exo (*Austral slang*), sik (*Austral slang*), rad (*informal*), phat (*slang*), schmick (*Austral informal*), beaut (*informal*), barrie (*Scot slang*), belting (*Brit slang*), pearler (*Austral slang*), funky **OPPOSITE:** ordinary

sense *n* **1 = faculty**, sensibility **3, 4a = feeling**, impression, perception, awareness, consciousness, atmosphere, aura, intuition, premonition, presentiment **4b = understanding**, awareness, appreciation **6** (*usually pl*) **= intelligence**, reason, understanding, brains (*informal*), smarts (*slang, chiefly US*), judgment, discrimination, wisdom, wit(s), common sense, sanity, sharpness, tact, nous (*Brit slang*), cleverness, quickness, discernment, gumption (*Brit informal*), sagacity, clear-headedness, mother wit **OPPOSITE:** foolishness **8, 9 = meaning**, definition, interpretation, significance, message, import, substance, implication, drift, purport, nuance, gist, signification, denotation ▷ *vb* **11, 12 = perceive**, feel, understand, notice, pick up, suspect, realize, observe, appreciate, grasp, be aware of, divine, discern, just know, have a (funny) feeling (*informal*), get the impression, apprehend, have a hunch **OPPOSITE:** be unaware of

sensibility *n* **2** (*often pl*) **= feelings**, emotions, sentiments, susceptibilities, moral sense

sensible *adj* **1a = wise**, practical, prudent, shrewd, well-informed, judicious, well-advised **OPPOSITE:** foolish **1b = intelligent**, practical, reasonable, rational, sound, realistic, sober, discriminating, discreet, sage, shrewd, down-to-earth, matter-of-fact, prudent, sane, canny, judicious, far-sighted, sagacious, grounded **OPPOSITE:** senseless

sensitive *adj* **1 = delicate**, tender **2 = thoughtful**, kind, kindly, concerned, patient, attentive, tactful, unselfish **3 = susceptible**, responsive, reactive, easily affected **4 = touchy**, oversensitive, easily upset, easily offended, easily hurt, umbrageous (*rare*) **OPPOSITE:** insensitive **6 = precise**, fine, acute, keen, responsive, perceptive **OPPOSITE:** imprecise

sensual *adj* **2 = sexual**, sexy (*informal*), erotic, randy (*informal, chiefly Brit*), steamy (*informal*), raunchy (*slang*), lewd, lascivious, lustful, lecherous, libidinous, licentious, unchaste **3 = physical**, bodily, voluptuous, animal, luxurious, fleshly, carnal, epicurean, unspiritual

sentence *n* **2a = verdict**, order, ruling, decision, judgment, decree, pronouncement **2b = punishment**, prison term, condemnation ▷ *vb* **3a = condemn**, doom **3b = convict**, condemn, penalize, pass judgment on, mete out justice to

sentiment *n* (*often pl*) **2 = feeling**,

DICTIONARY

feelings: *anti-American sentiment* **2** *(often pl)* a thought, opinion, or attitude expressed in words: *his sentiments were echoed by subsequent speakers* **3** feelings such as tenderness, romance, and sadness, esp. when exaggerated: *a man without the softness of sentiment*
WORD ORIGIN Latin *sentire* to feel

sentimental ❶ *adj* **1** feeling or expressing tenderness, romance, or sadness to an exaggerated extent **2** appealing to the emotions, esp. to romantic feelings: *she kept the ring for sentimental reasons* **sentimentalism** *n* **sentimentalist** *n* **sentimentality** *n* **sentimentally** *adv*

sentimentalize *or* **-ise** *vb* **-izing, -ized** *or* **-ising, -ised** to make sentimental or behave sentimentally

sentimental value *n* the value of an article to a particular person because of the emotions it arouses

sentinel *n old-fashioned* a sentry
WORD ORIGIN Old French *sentinelle*

sentry *n, pl* **-tries** a soldier who keeps watch and guards a camp or building
WORD ORIGIN perhaps from obsolete *centrinel* sentinel

sentry box *n* a small shelter with an open front in which a sentry stands during bad weather

SEO search engine optimization

sepal *n bot* a leaflike division of the calyx of a flower
WORD ORIGIN New Latin *sepalum*

separable *adj* able to be separated

separate ❶ *vb* **-rating, -rated 1** to act as a barrier between: *the narrow stretch of water which separates Europe from Asia* **2** to part or be parted from a mass or group **3** to distinguish: *it's what separates the men from the boys* **4** to divide or be divided into component parts **5** to sever or be severed **6** (of a couple) to stop living together ▷ *adj* **7** existing or considered independently: *a separate issue* **8** set apart from the main body or mass **9** distinct or individual **separately** *adv* **separateness** *n* **separator** *n*
WORD ORIGIN Latin *separare*

separates *pl n Brit, Austral & NZ* clothes, such as skirts, blouses, and trousers, that only cover part of the body and are designed to be worn together or separately

separate school *n* (in certain Canadian provinces) a school for a large religious minority financed by provincial grants in addition to the education tax

separation ❶ *n* **1** the act of separating: *the separation of child from mother* **2** *family law* the living apart of a married couple without divorce **3** a mark, line, or object that separates one thing from another

separatist *n* a person who advocates the separation of his or her own group from an organization or country **separatism** *n*

sepia *adj* dark reddish-brown, like the colour of very old photographs
WORD ORIGIN Latin: a cuttlefish

sepoy *n* (formerly) an Indian soldier in the service of the British
WORD ORIGIN Urdu *sipāhī*

sepsis *n* poisoning caused by the presence of pus-forming bacteria in the body
WORD ORIGIN Greek: a rotting

sept *n* a clan, esp. in Ireland or Scotland
WORD ORIGIN perhaps variant of *sect*

Sept. September

September *n* the ninth month of the year
WORD ORIGIN Latin: the seventh (month)

septennial *adj* **1** occurring every seven years **2** lasting seven years
WORD ORIGIN Latin *septem* seven + *annus* a year

septet *n* **1** a group of seven performers **2** a piece of music for seven performers
WORD ORIGIN Latin *septem* seven

septic *adj* of or caused by harmful bacteria **septicity** *n*

septicaemia *or* **septicemia** (sep-tis-see-mee-a) *n* an infection of the blood which develops in a wound
WORD ORIGIN Greek *sēptos* decayed + *haima* blood

septic tank *n* a tank in which sewage is decomposed by the action of bacteria

septuagenarian *n* **1** a person who is between 70 and 79 years old ▷ *adj* **2** between 70 and 79 years old
WORD ORIGIN Latin *septuaginta* seventy

Septuagint (sept-yew-a-jint) *n* the ancient Greek version of the Old Testament, including the Apocrypha
WORD ORIGIN Latin *septuaginta* seventy

septum *n, pl* **-ta** *biol, anat* a dividing partition between two tissues or cavities, such as in the nose
WORD ORIGIN Latin *saeptum* wall

septuple *vb* **-pling, -pled 1** to multiply by seven ▷ *adj* **2** seven times as much or as many **3** consisting of seven parts ▷ *n* **4** a quantity or number seven times as great as another
WORD ORIGIN Latin *septem* seven

sepulchral (sip-pulk-ral) *adj* **1** gloomy and solemn, like a tomb or grave **2** of a sepulchre

sepulchre *or US* **sepulcher** (sep-pulk-er) *n* **1** a burial vault, tomb, or grave ▷ *vb* **-chring, -chred** *or US* **-chering, -chered 2** to bury in a sepulchre
WORD ORIGIN Latin *sepulcrum*

sepulture (sep-pult-cher) *n* the act of placing in a sepulchre

sequel ❶ *n* **1** a novel, play, or film that continues the story of an earlier one **2** anything that happens after or as a result of something else: *there was an amusing sequel to this incident*
WORD ORIGIN Latin *sequi* to follow

sequence ❶ *n* **1** an arrangement of two or more things in a successive order **2** the successive order of two or more things: *chronological sequence*

S

THESAURUS

thought, idea, view, opinion, attitude, belief, judgment, persuasion, way of thinking **3 = sentimentality**, emotion, tenderness, romanticism, sensibility, slush *(informal)*, emotionalism, tender feeling, mawkishness, soft-heartedness, overemotionalism

sentimental *adj* **1, 2 = romantic**, touching, emotional, tender, pathetic, nostalgic, sloppy *(informal)*, tearful, corny *(slang)*, impressionable, mushy *(informal)*, maudlin, simpering, weepy *(informal)*, slushy *(informal)*, mawkish, tear-jerking *(informal)*, drippy *(informal)*, schmaltzy *(slang)*, icky *(informal)*, gushy *(informal)*, soft-hearted, overemotional, dewy-eyed, three-hankie *(informal)*
OPPOSITE: unsentimental

separate *vb* **1 = divide**, detach, disconnect, come between, disentangle, keep apart, disjoin
OPPOSITE: combine
2 = come apart, split, break off, come away **OPPOSITE:** connect
3 = distinguish, mark, single out, set apart, make distinctive, set at variance *or* at odds **OPPOSITE:** link
5 = sever, disconnect, break apart, split in two, divide in two, uncouple, bifurcate **OPPOSITE:** join
6 = split up, part, divorce, break up, part company, get divorced, be estranged, go different ways
▷ *adj* **7 = unconnected**, individual, particular, divided, divorced, isolated, detached, disconnected, discrete, unattached, disjointed
OPPOSITE: connected
8, 9 = individual, independent, apart, distinct, autonomous
OPPOSITE: joined

separation *n* **1 = division**, break, segregation, detachment, severance, disengagement, dissociation, disconnection, disjunction, disunion, disconnect **2** *(family law)* **= split-up**, parting, split, divorce, break-up, farewell, rift, estrangement, leave-taking

sequel *n* **1 = follow-up**, continuation, development **2 = consequence**, result, outcome, conclusion, end, issue, payoff *(informal)*, upshot

sequence *n* **1 = succession**, course, series, order, chain, cycle,

DICTIONARY

3 an action or event that follows another or others **4** *maths* an ordered set of numbers or other quantities in one-to-one correspondence with the integers 1 to *n* **5** a section of a film forming a single uninterrupted episode ▷*vb* **6** to arrange in a sequence
WORD ORIGIN Latin *sequi* to follow
sequential *adj* happening in a fixed order or sequence
sequester *vb* **1** to seclude: *he could sequester himself in his own home* **2** *law* ▸same as **sequestrate**
WORD ORIGIN Late Latin *sequestrare* to surrender for safekeeping
sequestrate *vb* **-trating, -trated** *law* to confiscate (property) temporarily until creditors are satisfied or a court order is complied with **sequestration** *n* **sequestrator** *n*
sequin *n* a small piece of shiny metal foil used to decorate clothes **sequined** *adj*
WORD ORIGIN Italian *zecchino*
sequoia *n* a giant Californian coniferous tree
WORD ORIGIN after *Sequoya*, a Native American scholar
seraglio (sir-ah-lee-oh) *n, pl* **-raglios** **1** the part of a Muslim house or palace where the owner's wives live **2** a Turkish sultan's palace
WORD ORIGIN Italian *serraglio* animal cage
seraph *n, pl* **-aphim** *theol* a member of the highest order of angels **seraphic** *adj*
WORD ORIGIN from Hebrew
Serb *adj, n* ▸same as **Serbian**
Serbian *adj* **1** of Serbia ▷*n* **2** a person from Serbia **3** the dialect of Serbo-Croat spoken in Serbia
Serbo-Croat *or* **Serbo-Croatian** *n* **1** the chief official language of Serbia and Croatia ▷*adj* **2** of this language
serenade *n* **1** a piece of music played or sung to a woman by a lover **2** a piece of music suitable for this **3** an orchestral suite for a small ensemble ▷*vb* **-nading, -naded** **4** to sing or play a serenade to (someone)
WORD ORIGIN French
serendipity *n* the gift of making fortunate discoveries by accident
WORD ORIGIN from the fairy tale *The Three Princes of Serendip*, in which the heroes possess this gift
serene *adj* **1** peaceful or calm **2** (of the sky) clear or bright **serenely** *adv* **serenity** *n*
WORD ORIGIN Latin *serenus*
serf *n* (esp. in medieval Europe) a labourer who could not leave the land on which he worked **serfdom** *n*
WORD ORIGIN Latin *servus* a slave
serge *n* a strong fabric made of wool, cotton, silk, or rayon, used for clothing
WORD ORIGIN Old French *sarge*
sergeant *n* **1** a noncommissioned officer in the armed forces **2** (in Britain, S Africa, Australia, and NZ) a police officer ranking between constable and inspector
WORD ORIGIN Old French *sergent*
sergeant at arms *n* a parliamentary or court officer responsible for keeping order
sergeant major *n* a noncommissioned officer of the highest rank in the army
serial *n* **1** a story published or broadcast in instalments at regular intervals **2** a publication that is regularly issued and consecutively numbered ▷*adj* **3** of, in, or forming a series: *serial pregnancies* **4** published or presented as a serial **serially** *adv*
WORD ORIGIN Latin *series* series
serialize *or* **-ise** *vb* **-izing, -ized** *or* **-ising, -ised** to publish or present in the form of a serial **serialization** *or* **-isation** *n*
serial killer *n* a person who commits a number of murders
serial monogamy *n* the practice of having a number of long-term romantic or sexual partners in succession
serial number *n* any of the consecutive numbers given to objects in a series for identification
series ❶ *n, pl* **-ries** **1** a group or succession of related things **2** a set of radio or television programmes dealing with the same subject, esp. one having the same characters but different stories **3** *maths* the sum of a finite or infinite sequence of numbers or quantities **4** *electronics* an arrangement of two or more components connected in a circuit so that the same current flows in turn through each of them: *a number of resistors in series* **5** *geol* a set of layers that represent the rocks formed during an epoch
WORD ORIGIN Latin: a row
seriocomic (seer-ee-oh-kom-ik) *adj* mixing serious and comic elements
serious ❶ *adj* **1** giving cause for concern: *the situation is serious* **2** concerned with important matters: *there are some serious questions that need to be answered* **3** not cheerful; grave: *I am a serious person* **4** in earnest; sincere: *he believes we are serious* **5** requiring concentration: *a serious book* **6** *informal* impressive because of its substantial quantity or quality: *serious money* **seriously** *adv* **seriousness** *n*
WORD ORIGIN Latin *serius*
serjeant *n* ▸same as **sergeant**
Serlio *n* **Sebastiano** 1475–1554, Italian architect and painter, best known for his treatise *Complete Works on Architecture and Perspective* (1537–75), the first to set out the principles of classical architecture and to give rules for their application
sermon ❶ *n* **1** a speech on a religious or moral subject given by a clergyman as part of a church service **2** *disparaging* a serious talk on behaviour, morals, or duty, esp. a long and tedious one
WORD ORIGIN Latin *sermo* discourse
seropositive (seer-oh-poz-zit-iv) *adj* (of a person whose blood has been tested for a specific disease, such as AIDS) showing a significant level of serum antibodies, indicating the presence of the disease
serotonin (ser-roe-tone-in) *n biochem* a compound that occurs in the brain, intestines, and blood platelets and acts as a neurotransmitter
serous (seer-uss) *adj* of, containing, or like serum
serpent *n* **1** *literary* a snake **2** a devious person
WORD ORIGIN Latin *serpens* a creeping thing
serpentine[1] *adj* twisting like a snake
serpentine[2] *n* a soft green or brownish-red mineral
WORD ORIGIN so named from its snakelike patterns
serrated *adj* having a notched or sawlike edge **serration** *n*
WORD ORIGIN Latin *serratus* saw-shaped

THESAURUS

arrangement, procession, progression
series *n* **1 = sequence**, course, chain, succession, run, set, line, order, train, arrangement, string, progression **2 = drama**, serial, soap *(informal)*, sitcom *(informal)*, soap opera, soapie *or* soapie *(Austral slang)*, situation comedy
serious *adj* **1 = grave**, bad, critical, worrying, dangerous, acute, alarming, severe, extreme, grievous **2 = important**, crucial, urgent, pressing, difficult, worrying, deep, significant, grim, far-reaching, momentous, fateful, weighty, no laughing matter, of moment *or* consequence
OPPOSITE: unimportant
3 = solemn, earnest, grave, stern, sober, thoughtful, sedate, glum, staid, humourless, long-faced, pensive, unsmiling **OPPOSITE:** light-hearted
4 = sincere, determined, earnest, resolved, genuine, deliberate, honest, resolute, in earnest
OPPOSITE: insincere
5a = thoughtful, detailed, careful, deep, profound, in-depth **5b = deep**, sophisticated, highbrowed
sermon *n* **1 = homily**, address, exhortation

S

DICTIONARY

serried *adj literary* in close formation: *the serried ranks of fans* **WORD ORIGIN** Old French *serré* close-packed

Sertorius *n* **Quintus** ?123–72 BC, Roman soldier who fought with Marius in Gaul (102) and led an insurrection in Spain against Sulla until he was assassinated

serum (seer-um) *n* **1** the yellowish watery fluid left after blood has clotted **2** this fluid from the blood of immunized animals used for inoculation or vaccination **3** *physiol, zool* any clear watery animal fluid **WORD ORIGIN** Latin: whey

serval *n* a slender African wild cat with black-spotted tawny fur

servant ❶ *n* **1** a person employed to do household work for another person **2** a person or thing that is useful or provides a service: *a distinguished servant of this country* **WORD ORIGIN** Old French: serving

serve ❶ *vb* **serving, served** **1** to be of service to (a person, community, or cause); help **2** to perform an official duty or duties: *he served on several university committees* **3** to attend to (customers) in a shop **4** to provide (guests) with food or drink: *he served dinner guests German wine* **5** to provide (food or drink) for customers: *breakfast is served from 7 am* **6** to provide with something needed by the public: *the community served by the school* **7** to work as a servant for (a person) **8** to go through (a period of police or military service, apprenticeship, or imprisonment) **9** to meet the needs of: *they serve a purpose* **10** to perform a function: *the attacks only served to strengthen their resolve* **11** (of a male animal) to mate with (a female animal) **12** *tennis, squash, etc.* to put (the ball) into play **13** to deliver (a legal document) to (a person) **14** **serve someone right** *informal* to be what someone deserves, esp. for doing something stupid or wrong ▷*n* **15** *tennis, squash, etc.* ▸short for **service** (sense 12) **WORD ORIGIN** Latin *servus* a slave

server *n* **1** *computers* a computer or program that supplies data to other machines on a network **2** a person who serves

Servetus *n* **Michael,** Spanish name *Miguel Serveto.* 1511–53, Spanish theologian and physician. He was burnt at the stake by order of Calvin for denying the doctrine of the Trinity and the divinity of Christ

service ❶ *n* **1** an act of help or assistance **2** an organization or system that provides something needed by the public: *a consumer information service* **3** a department of public employment and its employees: *the diplomatic service* **4** the installation or maintenance of goods provided by a dealer after a sale **5** availability for use by the public: *the new plane could be in service within fifteen years* **6** a regular check made on a machine or vehicle in which parts are tested, cleaned, or replaced if worn **7** the serving of guests or customers: *service is included on the wine list* **8** one of the branches of the armed forces **9** the serving of food: *silver service* **10** a set of dishes, cups, and plates for use at table **11** a formal religious ceremony **12** *tennis, squash, etc.* **a** the act, manner, or right of serving the ball **b** the game in which a particular player serves: *she dropped only one point on her service* ▷*adj* **13** of or for the use of servants or employees: *a service elevator* **14** serving the public rather than producing goods: *service industries* ▷*vb* **-vicing, -viced** **15** to provide service or services to **16** to check and repair (a vehicle or machine) **17** (of a male animal) to mate with (a female animal) ▸See also **services** **WORD ORIGIN** Latin *servitium* condition of a slave

Service *n* **Robert (William)** 1874–1958, Canadian poet, born in England; noted for his ballad-like poems of gold-rush era Yukon, such as 'The Shooting of Dan McGrew'; his books include *Songs of a Sourdough* (1907)

serviceable *adj* **1** performing effectively: *serviceable boots* **2** able or ready to be used: *five remaining serviceable aircraft* **serviceability** *n*

service area *n* a place on a motorway with a garage, restaurants, and toilets

service charge *n* a percentage added to a bill in a hotel or restaurant to pay for service

service flat *n* a flat where domestic services are provided by the management

serviceman *n, pl* **-men** **1** a person in the armed services **2** a man employed to service and maintain equipment **servicewoman** *fem n*

service road *n Austral & Brit* a narrow road running parallel to a main road that provides access to houses and shops situated along its length

services *pl n* **1** work performed in a job: *the OBE for her services to the community* **2** **the services** the armed forces **3** a system of providing the public with something it needs, such as gas or water

service station *n* **1** a place that sells fuel, oil, and spare parts for motor vehicles **2** ▸same as **service area**

serviette *n* a table napkin **WORD ORIGIN** Old French

servile *adj* **1** too eager to obey people; fawning **2** of or suitable for a slave **servility** *n* **WORD ORIGIN** Latin *servus* slave

serving *n* a portion of food

servitor *n archaic* a servant or attendant

servitude *n formal* **1** slavery or bondage **2** the state or condition of being completely dominated **WORD ORIGIN** Latin *servus* a slave

servomechanism *n* a device which converts a small force into a larger force, used esp. in steering mechanisms

sesame (sess-am-ee) *n* a plant of the East Indies, grown for its seeds and oil, which are used in cooking **WORD ORIGIN** Greek

Sesostris I *n* 20th century BC, king of Egypt of the 12th dynasty. He conquered Nubia and brought ancient Egypt to the height of its prosperity. The funerary complex at Lisht was built during his reign

Sesshu *n* original family name *Oda,* also called *Toyo.* 1420–1506, Japanese landscape painter, who introduced the Chinese technique of ink painting on long scrolls to Japan

sessile *adj* **1** (of flowers or leaves) having no stalk **2** (of animals such as the barnacle) fixed in one position **WORD ORIGIN** Latin *sessilis* concerning sitting

session ❶ *n* **1** any period devoted to a particular activity **2** a meeting of a court, parliament, or council **3** a series or period of such meetings **4** a school or university term or year **sessional** *adj* **WORD ORIGIN** Latin *sessio* a sitting

S

THESAURUS

servant *n* **1 = attendant**, domestic, slave, maid, help, helper, retainer, menial, drudge, lackey, vassal, skivvy *(chiefly Brit)*, servitor *(archaic)*, varlet *(archaic)*, liegeman

serve *vb* **1 = work for**, help, aid, assist, be in the service of **4, 5 = present**, provide, supply, deliver, arrange, set out, distribute, dish up, purvey **8 = perform**, do, complete, go through, fulfil, pass, discharge **9 = be adequate**, do, suffice, answer, suit, content, satisfy, be good enough, be acceptable, fill the bill *(informal)*, answer the purpose

service *n* **2 = facility**, system, resource, utility, amenity **6 = check**, servicing, maintenance check **11 = ceremony**, worship, rite, function, observance ▷*vb* **16 = overhaul**, check, maintain, tune (up), repair, go over, fine tune, recondition

session *n* **2, 3 = meeting**, hearing, sitting, term, period, conference, congress, discussion, assembly, seminar, get-together *(informal)*

DICTIONARY

Sessions *n* **Roger** (**Huntington**) 1896–1985, US composer

sestet *n* **1** *prosody* the last six lines of a sonnet **2** ▸same as **sextet** (sense 1)
WORD ORIGIN Italian *sesto* sixth

set[1] ❶ *vb* **setting, set 1** to put in a specified position or state: *I set him free* **2 set to** *or* **on** to bring (something) into contact with (something else): *three prisoners set fire to their cells* **3** to put into order or make ready: *set the table* **4** to make or become firm or rigid: *before the eggs begin to set* **5** to put (a broken bone) or (of a broken bone) to be put into a normal position for healing **6** to adjust (a clock or other instrument) to a particular position **7** to arrange or establish: *to set a date for diplomatic talks; it set the standards of performance* **8** to prescribe or assign (a task or material for study): *the examiners have set 'Paradise Lost'* **9** to arrange (hair) while wet, so that it dries in position **10** to place a jewel in (a setting): *a ring set with diamonds* **11** to provide music for (a poem or other text to be sung) **12** *printing* **a** to arrange (type) for printing **b** to put (text) into type **13** to arrange (a stage or television studio) with scenery and props **14 set to** *or* **on** to value (something) at a specified price or worth: *he set a high price on his services* **15** (of the sun or moon) to disappear beneath the horizon **16** (of plants) to produce (fruits or seeds) or (of fruits or seeds) to develop **17** to place (a hen) on (eggs) to incubate them **18** (of a gun dog) to turn in the direction of game birds ▹*n* **19** the act of setting **20** a condition of firmness or hardness **21** manner of standing; posture: *the set of his shoulders* **22** the scenery and other props used in a play or film **23** ▸same as **sett** ▹*adj* **24** fixed or established by authority or agreement: *set hours of work* **25** rigid or inflexible: *she is set in her ways* **26** unmoving; fixed: *a set expression on his face* **27** conventional or stereotyped: *she made her apology in set phrases* **28 set in** (of a scene or story) represented as happening at a certain time or place: *a European film set in Africa* **29 set on** *or* **upon** determined to (do or achieve something): *why are you so set upon avoiding me?* **30** ready: *all set to go* **31** (of material for study) prescribed for students' preparation for an examination ▸See also **set about, set against**, etc.
WORD ORIGIN Old English *settan*

set[2] ❶ *n* **1** a number of objects or people grouped or belonging together: *a set of slides* **2** a group of people who associate with each other or have similar interests: *the tennis set* **3** *maths* a collection of numbers or objects that satisfy a given condition or share a property **4** a television or piece of radio equipment **5** the scenery and other props used in a dramatic production, film, etc. **6** *sport* a group of games or points in a match, of which the winner must win a certain number **7** a series of songs or tunes performed by a musician or group on a given occasion: *the front row spent the rest of the set craning their necks*
WORD ORIGIN Old French *sette*

set about *vb* **1** to start or begin **2** to attack

set against *vb* **1** to balance or compare **2** to cause to be unfriendly to: *the war set brother against brother*

set aside *vb* **1** to reserve for a special purpose **2** to discard or reject

set back ❶ *vb* **1** to delay or hinder **2** *informal* to cost (a person) a specified amount ▹*n* **setback 3** anything that delays progress

set down *vb* **1** to record in writing **2** *Brit* to allow (passengers) to get off a bus etc.

set forth *vb formal or archaic* **1** to state or present (an argument or facts) **2** to start out on a journey: *he set forth on foot*

set in *vb* **1** to begin and continue for some time: *decadence has set in* **2** to insert

set off *vb* **1** to start a journey **2** to cause (a person) to act or do something, such as laugh **3** to cause to explode **4** to act as a contrast to: *blue suits you, sets off the colour of your hair*

set on *or* **upon** *vb* to attack or cause to attack: *they set the dogs on him*

Seton *n* **Ernest Thompson** 1860–1946, US author and illustrator of animal books, born in England

set out *vb* **1** to present, arrange, or display **2** to give a full account of: *the policy was set out in an interview with the BBC* **3** to begin or embark on an undertaking, esp. a journey

set piece *n* **1** a work of literature, music, or art, intended to create an impressive effect **2** *football, hockey, etc.* an attacking move from a corner or free kick

set square *n* a thin flat piece of plastic or metal in the shape of a right-angled triangle, used in technical drawing

sett *or* **set** *n* **1** a badger's burrow **2** a small rectangular paving block made of stone
WORD ORIGIN variant of SET[1] (noun)

settee *n* a seat, for two or more people, with a back and usually with arms; couch
WORD ORIGIN from SETTLE[2]

setter *n* a large long-haired dog originally bred for hunting

set theory *n maths* the branch of mathematics concerned with the properties and interrelationships of sets

setting ❶ *n* **1** the surroundings in which something is set **2** the scenery, properties, or background used to create the location for a stage play or film **3** a piece of music written for the words of a text **4** the decorative metalwork in which a gem is set **5** the plates and cutlery for a single place at a table **6** one of the positions or levels to which the controls of a machine can be adjusted

settle[1] ❶ *vb* **-tling, -tled 1** to put in order: *he settled his affairs before he died*

S

THESAURUS

set[1] *vb* **1 = put**, place, lay, park (*informal*), position, rest, plant, station, stick, deposit, locate, lodge, situate, plump, plonk **3 = prepare**, lay, spread, arrange, make ready **4 = harden**, stiffen, condense, solidify, cake, thicken, crystallize, congeal, jell, gelatinize **7 = arrange**, decide (upon), settle, name, establish, determine, fix, schedule, appoint, specify, allocate, designate, ordain, fix up, agree upon **8 = assign**, give, allot, prescribe **15 = go down**, sink, dip, decline, disappear, vanish, subside ▹*n* **21 = position**, bearing, attitude, carriage, turn, fit, hang, posture **22 = scenery**, setting, scene, stage setting, stage set, mise-en-scène (*French*) ▹*adj* **24 = established**, planned, decided, agreed, usual, arranged, rigid, definite, inflexible, hard and fast, immovable **25 = strict**, firm, rigid, hardened, stubborn, entrenched, inflexible, hidebound
OPPOSITE: flexible
27 = conventional, stock, standard, traditional, formal, routine, artificial, stereotyped, rehearsed, hackneyed, unspontaneous

set[2] *n* **1 = series**, collection, assortment, kit, outfit, batch, compendium, assemblage, coordinated group, ensemble **2 = group**, company, crowd, circle, class, band, crew (*informal*), gang, outfit, faction, sect, posse (*informal*), clique, coterie, schism

setback *n* **3 = hold-up**, check, defeat, blow, upset, reverse, disappointment, hitch, misfortune, rebuff, whammy (*informal, chiefly US*), bummer (*slang*), bit of trouble

setting *n* **1, 2 = surroundings**, site, location, set, scene, surround, background, frame, context, perspective, backdrop, scenery, locale, mise en scène (*French*)

settle[1] *vb* **1 = resolve**, work out, put an end to, straighten out, set to rights **3 = land**, alight, descend, light, come to rest **4 = move to**, take up

DICTIONARY

2 to arrange or be arranged firmly or comfortably: *he settled into his own chair by the fire* **3** to come down to rest: *a bird settled on top of the hedge* **4** to establish or become established as a resident: *they eventually settled in Glasgow* **5** to establish or become established in a way of life or a job **6** to migrate to (a country) and form a community; colonize **7** to make or become quiet, calm, or stable **8** to cause (sediment) to sink to the bottom in a liquid or (of sediment) to sink thus **9** to subside: *the dust settled* **10** (sometimes foll. by *up*) to pay off (a bill or debt) **11** to decide or dispose of: *to settle an argument* **12** (often foll. by *on* or *upon*) to agree or fix: *they settled on an elementary code* **13** (usually foll. by *on* or *upon*) to give (a title or property) to a person by gift or legal deed: *he settled his property on his wife* **14** to decide (a legal dispute) by agreement without court action: *they settled out of court*
WORD ORIGIN Old English *setlan*

settle² *n* a long wooden bench with a high back and arms, sometimes having a storage space under the seat
WORD ORIGIN Old English *setl*

settle down *vb* **1** to make or become quiet and orderly **2 settle down to** to remove all distractions and concentrate on: *we settled down to a favourite movie* **3** to adopt an orderly and routine way of life, esp. after marriage

settle for *vb* to accept or agree to in spite of dissatisfaction

settlement *n* **1** an act of settling **2** a place newly settled; colony **3** subsidence of all or part of a building **4** an official agreement ending a dispute **5** *law* **a** an arrangement by which property is transferred to a person's possession **b** the deed transferring such property

settler ❶ *n* a person who settles in a new country or a colony

set to *vb* **1** to begin working **2** to start fighting ▷ *n* **set-to 3** *informal* a brief disagreement or fight

set-top box *n* a device which converts the signals from a digital television broadcast into a form which can be viewed on a standard television set

set up ❶ *vb* **1** to build or construct: *the soldiers had actually set up a munitions factory* **2** to put into a position of power or wealth **3** to begin or enable (someone) to begin (a new venture): *he set up a small shop* **4** to begin or produce: *to set up a nuclear chain reaction* **5** to establish: *Broad set up a world record* **6** *informal* to cause (a person) to be blamed or accused **7** to restore the health of: *a pub lunch set me up nicely* ▷ *n* **setup 8** *informal* the way in which anything is organized or arranged **9** *slang* an event the result of which is prearranged

seven *n* **1** the cardinal number that is the sum of one and six **2** a numeral, 7 or VII, representing this number **3** something representing or consisting of seven units ▷ *adj* **4** amounting to seven: *seven weeks* **seventh** *adj, n*
WORD ORIGIN Old English *seofon*

sevenfold *adj* **1** having seven times as many or as much **2** composed of seven parts ▷ *adv* **3** by seven times as many or as much

seven seas *pl n* *old-fashioned* all the oceans of the world

seventeen *n* **1** the cardinal number that is the sum of ten and seven **2** a numeral, 17 or XVII, representing this number **3** something representing or consisting of seventeen units ▷ *adj* **4** amounting to seventeen: *seventeen children* **seventeenth** *adj, n*

seventh heaven *n* a state of supreme happiness

seventy *n, pl* **-ties 1** the cardinal number that is the product of ten and seven **2** a numeral, 70 or LXX, representing this number **3** something representing or consisting of seventy units ▷ *adj* **4** amounting to seventy: *seventy countries* **seventieth** *adj, n*

sever ❶ *vb* **1** to cut right through or cut off (something): *it accidentally severed the electrical cable* **2** to break off (a tie or relationship) **severable** *adj* **severance** *n*
WORD ORIGIN Latin *separare* to separate

several ❶ *adj* **1** more than a few: *I spoke to several doctors* **2** *formal* various or separate: *the members with their several occupations* **3** *formal* distinct or different: *misfortune visited her three several times*
WORD ORIGIN Medieval Latin *separalis*

severally *adv* *formal* individually or separately: *the Western nations severally rather than jointly decided that they would have to act without Russia*

severance pay *n* compensation paid by a firm to an employee who has to leave because the job he or she was appointed to do no longer exists

severe ❶ *adj* **1** strict or harsh in the treatment of others: *a severe parent* **2** serious in appearance or manner: *a severe look; a severe hairdo* **3** very intense or unpleasant: *severe chest pains; the punishments are severe* **4** causing discomfort by its harshness: *severe frost* **5** hard to perform or accomplish: *a severe challenge* **severely** *adv* **severity** *n*
WORD ORIGIN Latin *severus*

Severus *n* **Lucius Septimius** 146–211 AD, Roman soldier and emperor (193–211). He waged war successfully against the Parthians (197–202) and spent his last years in Britain (208–211)

Sévigné *n* **Marquise de,** title of *Marie*

S

THESAURUS

residence in, live in, dwell in, inhabit, reside in, set up home in, put down roots in, make your home in **6 = colonize**, populate, people, pioneer **7 = calm**, quiet, relax, relieve, reassure, compose, soothe, lull, quell, allay, sedate, pacify, quieten, tranquillize
OPPOSITE: disturb
10 = pay, clear, square (up), discharge

settlement *n* **2 = colony**, community, outpost, peopling, hamlet, encampment, colonization, kainga *or* kaika (NZ) **4 = agreement**, arrangement, resolution, working out, conclusion, establishment, adjustment, confirmation, completion, disposition, termination

settler *n* **= colonist**, immigrant, pioneer, colonizer, frontiersman

setup *n* **8** *(informal)* **= arrangement**, system, structure, organization, conditions, circumstances, regime

sever *vb* **1 = cut**, separate, split, part, divide, rend, detach, disconnect, cleave, bisect, disunite, cut in two, sunder, disjoin **OPPOSITE:** join
2 = discontinue, terminate, break off, abandon, dissolve, put an end to, dissociate **OPPOSITE:** continue

several *adj* **2** *(formal)* **= various**, different, diverse, divers *(archaic)*, assorted, disparate, indefinite, sundry

severe *adj* **1 = strict**, hard, harsh, cruel, rigid, relentless, drastic, oppressive, austere, Draconian, unrelenting, inexorable, pitiless, unbending, iron-handed
OPPOSITE: lenient
2a = grim, serious, grave, cold, forbidding, stern, sober, disapproving, dour, unsmiling, flinty, strait-laced, tight-lipped
OPPOSITE: genial
2b = plain, simple, austere, classic, restrained, functional, Spartan, ascetic, unadorned, unfussy, unembellished, bare-bones
OPPOSITE: fancy
3 = serious, critical, terrible, desperate, alarming, extreme, awful, distressing, appalling, drastic, catastrophic, woeful, ruinous **3, 4 = acute**, extreme, intense, burning, violent, piercing, racking, searing, tormenting, exquisite, harrowing, unbearable, agonizing, insufferable, torturous, unendurable

DICTIONARY

de Rabutin-Chantal. 1626–96, French letter writer. Her correspondence with her daughter and others provides a vivid account of society during the reign of Louis XIV

Seville orange *n* a bitter orange used to make marmalade
WORD ORIGIN after *Seville* in Spain

Sèvres (sev-ra) *n* a kind of fine French porcelain
WORD ORIGIN after *Sèvres,* near Paris

sew ❶ *vb* **sewing, sewed; sewn** *or* **sewed 1** to join with thread repeatedly passed through with a needle **2** to attach, fasten, or close by sewing ▸See also **sew up**
WORD ORIGIN Old English *sēowan*

sewage *n* waste matter or excrement carried away in sewers or drains

sewage farm *n* a place where sewage is treated so that it can be used as manure or disposed of safely

Seward *n* **William Henry** 1801–72, US statesman; secretary of state (1861–69). He was a leading opponent of slavery and was responsible for the purchase of Alaska (1867)

sewer *n* a drain or pipe, usually underground, used to carry away surface water or sewage
WORD ORIGIN Old French *essever* to drain

sewerage *n* **1** a system of sewers **2** the removal of surface water or sewage by means of sewers

sewing *n* **1** a piece of fabric or an article, that is sewn or to be sewn **2** the act of fastening together (pieces of fabric, etc.) with needle and thread

sewing machine *n* a machine that sews material with a needle driven by an electric motor

sewn *vb* ▸a past participle of **sew**

sew up *vb* **1** to fasten or mend completely by sewing **2** *informal* to complete or negotiate successfully: *the deal was sewn up just before the deadline*

sex ❶ *n* **1** the state of being either male or female **2** either of the two categories, male or female, into which organisms are divided **3** sexual intercourse **4** feelings or behaviour connected with having sex or the desire to have sex **5** sexual matters in general ▹*adj* **6** of sexual matters: *sex education* **7** based on or resulting from the difference between the sexes: *sex discrimination* ▹*vb* **8** to find out the sex of (an animal)
WORD ORIGIN Latin *sexus*

sexagenarian *n* **1** a person who is between 60 and 69 years old ▹*adj* **2** between 60 and 69 years old
WORD ORIGIN Latin *sexaginta* sixty

sex appeal *n* sexual attractiveness

sex chromosome *n* either of the chromosomes that determine the sex of an animal

sexism *n* discrimination against the members of one sex, usually women **sexist** *n, adj*

sexless *adj* **1** neither male nor female **2** having no sexual desires **3** sexually unattractive

sex object *n* someone, esp. a woman, regarded only in terms of physical attractiveness and not as a person

sexology *n* the study of sexual behaviour in human beings **sexologist** *n*

sextant *n* an instrument used in navigation for measuring angular distance, for example between the sun and the horizon, to calculate the position of a ship or aircraft
WORD ORIGIN Latin *sextans* one sixth of a unit

sextet *n* **1** a group of six performers **2** a piece of music for six performers **3** a group of six people or things
WORD ORIGIN variant of *sestet*

sexton *n* a person employed to look after a church and its churchyard
WORD ORIGIN Medieval Latin *sacristanus* sacristan

sextuple *vb* **-pling, -pled 1** to multiply by six ▹*adj* **2** six times as much or as many **3** consisting of six parts ▹*n* **4** a quantity or number six times as great as another
WORD ORIGIN Latin *sextus* sixth

sextuplet *n* one of six children born at one birth

sexual ❶ *adj* **1** of or characterized by sex **2** (of reproduction) characterized by the union of male and female reproductive cells **3** of or relating to the differences between males and females **sexuality** *n* **sexually** *adv*

sexual harassment *n* the unwelcome directing of sexual remarks, looks, or advances, usually at a woman in the workplace

sexual intercourse *n* the sexual act in which the male's erect penis is inserted into the female's vagina, usually followed by the ejaculation of semen

sex up *vb informal* to make (something) more exciting

Sexwale *n* **Tokyo** full name *Mosima Gabriel Sexwale.* born 1953; South African political activist and businessman

sexy ❶ *adj* **sexier, sexiest** *informal* **1** sexually exciting or attractive: *a sexy voice* **2** interesting, exciting, or trendy: *a sexy project; a sexy new car* **sexiness** *n*

Seymour *n* **Jane** ?1509–37, third wife of Henry VIII of England; mother of Edward VI

SF *or* **sf** science fiction

SFA Scottish Football Association

SFO (in Britain) Serious Fraud Office

Sforza *n* **1** Count **Carlo** 1873–1952, Italian statesman; leader of the anti-Fascist opposition **2 Francesco** 1401–66, duke of Milan (1450–66) **3** his father **Giacomuzzo** or **Muzio,** original name *Attendolo.* 1369–1424, Italian condottiere and founder of the dynasty that ruled Milan (1450–1535) **4 Lodovico,** called *the Moor.* 1451–1508, duke of Milan (1494–1500), but effective ruler from 1480; patron of Leonardo da Vinci

Sg *chem* seaborgium

S. Glam South Glamorgan

Sgt. Sergeant

sh *interj* be quiet!

shabby ❶ *adj* **-bier, -biest 1** old and worn in appearance **2** wearing worn and dirty clothes **3** behaving in a mean or unfair way: *shabby manoeuvres* **shabbily** *adv* **shabbiness** *n*
WORD ORIGIN Old English *sceabb* scab

shack ❶ *n* **1** a roughly built hut ▹*vb* **2 shack up with** *slang* to live with (a lover)
WORD ORIGIN perhaps from dialect *shackly* ramshackle

shackle *n* **1** one of a pair of metal rings joined by a chain for securing someone's wrists or ankles **2 shackles** anything that confines or restricts freedom: *free from the shackles of its feudal past* **3** a metal loop or link closed by a bolt, used for securing ropes or chains ▹*vb* **-ling, -led 4** to fasten with shackles **5** to restrict or

S

THESAURUS

sew *vb* **2 = stitch,** tack, seam, hem

sex *n* **1, 2 = gender 3 = lovemaking,** sexual relations, copulation, the other *(informal),* screwing *(taboo slang),* intimacy, going to bed (with someone), shagging *(Brit taboo slang),* nookie *(slang),* fornication, coitus, rumpy-pumpy *(slang),* legover *(slang),* coition, rumpo *(slang)*

sexual *adj* **1 = carnal,** erotic, intimate, of the flesh, coital

sexy *adj* **1** *(informal)* **= erotic,** sensual, seductive, inviting, bedroom, provoking, arousing, naughty, provocative, sensuous, suggestive, voluptuous, slinky, titillating, flirtatious, come-hither *(informal),* kissable, beddable, hot *(informal)*

shabby *adj* **1 = rundown,** seedy, mean, neglected, dilapidated **1, 2 = tatty,** worn, ragged, scruffy, faded, frayed, worn-out, tattered, threadbare, down at heel, the worse for wear, having seen better days **OPPOSITE:** smart **3 = mean,** low, rotten *(informal),* cheap, dirty, shameful, low-down *(informal),* shoddy, unworthy, despicable, contemptible, scurvy, dishonourable, ignoble, ungentlemanly **OPPOSITE:** fair

shack *n* **1 = hut,** cabin, shanty, lean-to,

DICTIONARY

hamper: *an economy shackled by central control*
WORD ORIGIN Old English *sceacel*

shad *n, pl* **shad** *or* **shads** a herring-like food fish
WORD ORIGIN Old English *sceadd*

Shadbolt *n* **Maurice** 1932–2004, New Zealand novelist

shade ❶ *n* **1** relative darkness produced by blocking out sunlight **2** a place sheltered from the sun by trees, buildings, etc. **3** something used to provide a shield or protection from a direct source of light, such as a lamp shade **4** a shaded area in a painting or drawing **5** any of the different hues of a colour: *a much darker shade of grey* **6** a slight amount: *a shade of reluctance* **7** **put someone** *or* **something in the shade** to be so impressive as to make another person or thing seem unimportant by comparison **8** *literary* a ghost ▷ *vb* **shading, shaded** **9** to screen or protect from heat or light **10** to make darker or dimmer **11** to represent (a darker area) in (a painting or drawing), by graded areas of tone, lines, or dots **12** to change slightly or by degrees
WORD ORIGIN Old English *sceadu*

shades *pl n* **1** *slang* sunglasses **2** **shades of** a reminder of: *shades of Margaret Thatcher*

shading *n* the graded areas of tone, lines, or dots, indicating light and dark in a painting or drawing

shadow ❶ *n* **1** a dark image or shape cast on a surface when something stands between a light and the surface **2** a patch of shade **3** the dark portions of a picture **4** a hint or faint trace: *a shadow of a doubt* **5** a person less powerful or vigorous than his or her former self **6** a threatening influence: *news of the murder cast a shadow over the village* **7** a person who always accompanies another **8** a person who trails another in secret, such as a detective ▷ *adj* **9** *Austral & Brit* designating a member or members of the main opposition party in Parliament who would hold ministerial office if their party were in power: *the shadow chancellor* ▷ *vb* **10** to cast a shade or shadow over **11** to make dark or gloomy **12** to follow or trail secretly
WORD ORIGIN Old English *sceadwe*

shadow-box *vb boxing* to box against an imaginary opponent for practice **shadow-boxing** *n*

shadowy *adj* **1** (of a place) full of shadows; shady **2** faint or dark like a shadow: *a shadowy figure* **3** mysterious or not well known: *the shadowy world of espionage*

Shadwell *n* **Thomas** ?1642–92, English dramatist; poet laureate (1688–92). He was satirized by Dryden

shady ❶ *adj* **shadier, shadiest** **1** full of shade; shaded **2** giving or casting shade **3** *informal* of doubtful honesty or legality: *shady business dealings* **shadiness** *n*

Shaffer *n* Sir **Peter** born 1926, British dramatist. His plays include *The Royal Hunt of the Sun* (1964), *Equus* (1973), *Amadeus* (1979), and *The Gift of the Gorgon* (1992)

shaft ❶ *n* **1** **a** a spear or arrow **b** its long narrow stem **2** **shaft of wit** *or* **humour** a clever or amusing remark **3** a ray or streak of light **4** the long straight narrow handle of a tool or golf club **5** a revolving rod in a machine that transmits motion or power **6** one of the bars between which an animal is harnessed to a vehicle **7** *archit* the middle part of a column or pier, between the base and the capital **8** a vertical passageway through a building for a lift **9** a vertical passageway into a mine
WORD ORIGIN Old English *sceaft*

Shaftesbury *n* **1** **1st Earl of,** title of *Anthony Ashley Cooper.* 1621–83, English statesman, a major figure in the Whig opposition to Charles II **2** **7th Earl of,** title of *Anthony Ashley Cooper.* 1801–85, English evangelical churchman and social reformer. He promoted measures to improve conditions in mines (1842), factories (1833; 1847; 1850), and schools

shag[1] *n* **1** coarse shredded tobacco **2** a matted tangle of hair or wool ▷ *adj* **3** (of a carpet) having long thick woollen threads
WORD ORIGIN Old English *sceacga*

shag[2] *n* a kind of cormorant
WORD ORIGIN special use of SHAG[1] (with reference to its crest)

shag[3] *vb* **shagging, shagged** *Brit, Austral & NZ slang* **1** *taboo* to have sexual intercourse with (a person) **2** **shagged out** exhausted
WORD ORIGIN origin unknown

shaggy *adj* **-gier, -giest** **1** having or covered with rough unkempt fur, hair, or wool: *shaggy cattle* **2** rough and untidy **shagginess** *n*

shagreen *n* **1** the skin of a shark, used as an abrasive **2** a rough grainy leather made from certain animal hides
WORD ORIGIN French *chagrin*

shah *n* a ruler of certain Middle Eastern countries, esp. (formerly) Iran
WORD ORIGIN Persian: king

Shahn *n* **Ben** 1898–1969, US artist, born in Lithuania, best known as an exponent of social realism, especially in the series (1931–32) inspired by the executions of Sacco and Vanzetti

shake ❶ *vb* **shaking, shook, shaken** **1** to move up and down or back and forth with short quick movements **2** to be or make unsteady **3** (of a voice) to tremble because of anger or nervousness **4** to clasp or grasp (the hand) of (a person) in greeting or agreement: *they shook hands* **5** **shake on it** *informal* to shake hands in agreement or reconciliation **6** to wave vigorously and angrily: *he shook his fist* **7** (often foll. by *up*) to frighten or unsettle **8** to shock, disturb, or upset: *he was badly shaken but unharmed* **9** to undermine or weaken: *a team*

S

THESAURUS

dump *(informal)*, hovel, shiel *(Scot)*, shieling *(Scot)*, whare *(NZ)*

shade *n* **1, 2 = shadow**, screen, shadows, coolness, shadiness **3 = screen**, covering, cover, blind, curtain, shield, veil, canopy **5 = hue**, tone, colour, tint **6 = dash**, trace, hint, suggestion, suspicion, small amount, semblance **8** *(literary)* **= ghost**, spirit, shadow, phantom, spectre, manes, apparition, eidolon, kehua *(NZ)* ▷ *vb* **9 = cover**, protect, screen, hide, shield, conceal, obscure, veil, mute **10 = darken**, shadow, cloud, dim, cast a shadow over, shut out the light

shadow *n* **1 = silhouette**, shape, outline, profile **2 = shade**, dimness, darkness, gloom, cover, protection, shelter, dusk, obscurity, gloaming *(Scot poetic)*, gathering darkness ▷ *vb* **10, 11 = shade**, screen, shield, darken, overhang, cast a shadow over **12 = follow**, dog, tail *(informal)*, trail, stalk, spy on

shady *adj* **1, 2 = shaded**, cool, shadowy, dim, leafy, bowery, bosky *(literary)*, umbrageous **OPPOSITE:** sunny **3** *(informal)* **= crooked**, dodgy *(Brit, Austral & NZ informal)*, unethical, suspect, suspicious, dubious, slippery, questionable, unscrupulous, fishy *(informal)*, shifty, disreputable, untrustworthy, shonky *(Austral & NZ informal)* **OPPOSITE:** honest

shaft *n* **3 = ray**, beam, gleam, streak **4 = handle**, staff, pole, rod, stem, upright, baton, shank **9 = tunnel**, hole, passage, burrow, passageway, channel

shake *vb* **1 = jiggle**, agitate, joggle **2 = rock**, sway, shudder, wobble, waver, totter, oscillate **3 = tremble**, shiver, quake, shudder, quiver **6 = wave**, wield, flourish, brandish **8 = upset**, shock, frighten, disturb, distress, move, rattle *(informal)*, intimidate, unnerve, discompose, traumatize ▷ *n* **14 = vibration**, trembling, quaking, shock, jar, disturbance, jerk, shiver, shudder, jolt, tremor, agitation, convulsion, pulsation, jounce

DICTIONARY

whose morale had been badly shaken **10** *US & Canad informal* to get rid of **11** *music* to perform a trill on (a note) **12 shake one's head** to indicate disagreement or disapproval by moving the head from side to side ▷*n* **13** the act or an instance of shaking **14** a tremor or vibration **15 the shakes** *informal* a state of uncontrollable trembling **16** *informal* a very short period of time: *in half a shake* **17** *music* ▸ same as **trill** (sense 1) **18** ▸ short for **milk shake** ▸ See also **shake down, shake off, shake up**
WORD ORIGIN Old English *sceacan*

shake down *vb* **1** to go to bed, esp. in a makeshift bed ▷*n* **shakedown 2** a makeshift bed

shake off *vb* **1** to remove or get rid of: *I have been trying to shake off the stigma for some time* **2** to escape from; get away from: *they switched to a blue car in a bid to shake off reporters*

shaker *n* **1** a container used for shaking a powdered substance onto something: *a flour shaker* **2** a container in which the ingredients of alcoholic drinks are shaken together

Shakespearean *or* **Shakespearian** *adj* **1** of William Shakespeare, English dramatist and poet, or his works ▷*n* **2** a student of or specialist in Shakespeare's works

shake up *vb* **1** to mix by shaking **2** to reorganize drastically **3** *informal* to shock mentally or physically: *the thunderstorm really shook me up* ▷*n* **shake-up 4** *informal* a radical reorganization, such as the reorganization of employees in a company

shako (shack-oh) *n, pl* **shakos** a tall cylindrical peaked military hat with a plume
WORD ORIGIN Hungarian *csákó*

shaky ❶ *adj* **shakier, shakiest 1** weak and unsteady, esp. due to illness or shock **2** uncertain or doubtful: *their prospects are shaky* **3** tending to shake or tremble **shakily** *adv*

shale *n* a flaky sedimentary rock formed by compression of successive layers of clay
WORD ORIGIN Old English *scealu* shell

shall *vb, past* **should 1** (*with "I" or "we" as subject*) used as an auxiliary to make the future tense: *we shall see you tomorrow* **2** (*with "you", "he", "she", "it", "they", or a noun as subject*) **a** used as an auxiliary to indicate determination on the part of the speaker: *you shall pay for this!* **b** used as an auxiliary to indicate compulsion or obligation, now esp. in official documents **3** (*with "I" or "we" as subject*) used as an auxiliary in questions asking for advice or agreement: *what shall we do now?; shall I shut the door?*
WORD ORIGIN Old English *sceal*

shallot (shal-lot) *n* a small, onion-like plant used in cooking for flavouring
WORD ORIGIN Old French *eschaloigne*

shallow ❶ *adj* **1** having little depth **2** not involving sincere feelings or serious thought **3** (of breathing) consisting of short breaths ▷*n* **4** (*often pl*) a shallow place in a body of water **shallowness** *n*
WORD ORIGIN Middle English *shalow*

sham ❶ *n* **1** anything that is not genuine or is not what it appears to be **2** a person who pretends to be something other than he or she is ▷*adj* **3** not real or genuine ▷*vb* **shamming, shammed 4** to fake or feign (something); pretend: *he made a point of shamming nervousness*
WORD ORIGIN origin unknown

shaman (sham-man) *n* **1** a priest of shamanism **2** a medicine man or witch doctor of a similar religion
WORD ORIGIN Russian

shamanism (sham-man-iz-zum) *n* a religion of northern Asia, based on a belief in good and evil spirits who can be influenced or controlled only by the shamans **shamanist** *n, adj*

shamble *vb* **-bling, -bled 1** to walk or move along in an awkward shuffling way ▷*n* **2** an awkward or shuffling walk **shambling** *adj, n*
WORD ORIGIN perhaps from *shambles*, referring to legs of a meat vendor's table

shambles ❶ *n* **1** a disorderly or badly organized event or place: *the bathroom was a shambles* **2** *chiefly Brit* a butcher's slaughterhouse **3** *old-fashioned* any scene of great slaughter
WORD ORIGIN Middle English *shamble* table used by meat vendors

shambolic *adj informal* completely disorganized

shame ❶ *n* **1** a painful emotion resulting from an awareness of having done something wrong or foolish **2** capacity to feel such an emotion: *have they no shame?* **3** loss of respect; disgrace **4** a person or thing that causes this **5** a cause for regret or disappointment: *it's a shame to rush back* **6 put to shame** to show up as being inferior by comparison: *his essay put mine to shame* ▷*interj* **7** *S African informal* **a** an expression of sympathy **b** an expression of pleasure or endearment ▷*vb* **shaming, shamed 8** to cause to feel shame **9** to bring shame on **10** (often foll. by *into*) to force someone to do something by making him or her feel ashamed not to: *he was finally shamed into paying the bill*
WORD ORIGIN Old English *scamu*

shamefaced *adj* embarrassed or guilty **shamefacedly** *adv*
WORD ORIGIN earlier *shamefast*

shameful ❶ *adj* causing or deserving shame: *a shameful lack of concern* **shamefully** *adv*

shameless *adj* **1** having no sense of shame: *a shameless manipulator* **2** without decency or modesty: *a shameless attempt to stifle*

S

THESAURUS

shaky *adj* **1 = unstable**, weak, precarious, tottering, rickety OPPOSITE: stable **1, 3 = unsteady**, faint, trembling, faltering, wobbly, tremulous, quivery, all of a quiver *(informal)* **2 = uncertain**, suspect, dubious, questionable, unreliable, unsound, iffy *(informal)*, unsupported, undependable OPPOSITE: reliable

shallow *adj* **2 = superficial**, surface, empty, slight, foolish, idle, trivial, meaningless, flimsy, frivolous, skin-deep OPPOSITE: deep

sham *n* **1, 2 = fraud**, imitation, hoax, pretence, forgery, counterfeit, pretender, humbug, impostor, feint, pseud *(informal)*, wolf in sheep's clothing, imposture, phoney *or* phony *(informal)* OPPOSITE: the real thing ▷*adj* **3 = false**, artificial, bogus, pretended, mock, synthetic, imitation, simulated, pseudo *(informal)*, counterfeit, feigned, spurious, ersatz, pseud *(informal)*, phoney *or* phony *(informal)* OPPOSITE: real

shambles *n* **1a = chaos**, mess, disorder, confusion, muddle, havoc, anarchy, disarray, madhouse, disorganization **1b = mess**, state, jumble, untidiness

shame *n* **1 = embarrassment**, humiliation, chagrin, ignominy, compunction, mortification, loss of face, abashment OPPOSITE: shamelessness **3 = disgrace**, scandal, discredit, contempt, smear, degradation, disrepute, reproach, derision, dishonour, infamy, opprobrium, odium, ill repute, obloquy OPPOSITE: honour ▷*vb* **8 = embarrass**, disgrace, humiliate, humble, disconcert, mortify, take (someone) down a peg *(informal)*, abash OPPOSITE: make proud **9 = dishonour**, discredit, degrade, stain, smear, blot, debase, defile OPPOSITE: honour

shameful *adj* **= disgraceful**, outrageous, scandalous, mean, low, base, infamous, indecent, degrading, vile, wicked, atrocious, unworthy, reprehensible, ignominious, dastardly, unbecoming, dishonourable OPPOSITE: admirable

DICTIONARY

democracy **shamelessly** *adv*

Shamir *n* **Yitzhak** born 1915, Israeli statesman, born in Poland: prime minister (1983–84; 1986–92): foreign minister (1980–83; 1984–86)

shammy *n, pl* **-mies** *informal* a piece of chamois leather
WORD ORIGIN variant of *chamois*

shampoo *n* **1** a soapy liquid used to wash the hair **2** a similar liquid for washing carpets or upholstery **3** the process of shampooing ▹*vb* **-pooing, -pooed 4** to wash (the hair, carpets, or upholstery) with shampoo
WORD ORIGIN Hindi *chāmpo*

shamrock *n* a small clover-like plant with three round leaves on each stem: the national emblem of Ireland
WORD ORIGIN Irish Gaelic *seamrōg*

shandy *n, pl* **-dies** a drink made of beer and lemonade
WORD ORIGIN origin unknown

shanghai *slang vb* **-haiing, -haied 1** to force or trick (someone) into doing something **2** *history* to kidnap (a man) and force him to serve at sea **3** *Austral & NZ* to shoot with a catapult ▹*n* **4** *Austral & NZ* a catapult
WORD ORIGIN senses 1 and 2 after the city of *Shanghai*; senses 3 and 4 from Scots dialect *shangie, shangan* cleft stick

shank *n* **1** the part of the leg between the knee and the ankle **2** a cut of meat from the top part of an animal's shank **3** the long narrow part of a tool, key, spoon, etc.
WORD ORIGIN Old English *scanca*

Shankar *n* **Ravi** born 1920, Indian sitarist

Shankaracharya *or* **Shankara** *n* 9th century AD, Hindu philosopher and teacher; chief exponent of Vedanta philosophy

Shankly *n* **Bill** 1913–81, Scottish footballer and manager of Liverpool FC (1959–74)

shanks's pony *or US* **shanks's mare** *n informal* one's own legs as a means of transport
WORD ORIGIN from *shank*, the lower part of the leg

Shannon¹ *n* a river in the Republic of Ireland, rising in NW Co Cavan and flowing south to the Atlantic by an estuary 113 km (70 miles) long: the longest river in the Republic of Ireland. Length: 260 km (161 miles)

Shannon² *n* **Claude** (**Elwood**) 1916–2000, US mathematician, who first developed information theory

shan't shall not

shantung *n* a heavy Chinese silk with a knobbly surface
WORD ORIGIN after province of NE China

shanty¹ *n, pl* **-ties** a small rough hut; crude dwelling
WORD ORIGIN Canadian French *chantier* cabin built in a lumber camp

shanty² *or* **chanty** *n, pl* **-ties** a rhythmic song originally sung by sailors when working
WORD ORIGIN French *chanter* to sing

shantytown *n* a town of poor people living in shanties

shape ❶ *n* **1** the outward form of an object, produced by its outline **2** the figure or outline of the body of a person **3** organized or definite form: *to preserve the union in its present shape* **4** the specific form that anything takes on: *a gold locket in the shape of a heart* **5** pattern or mould **6** condition or state of efficiency: *in poor shape* **7 take shape** to assume a definite form ▹*vb* **shaping, shaped 8** (often foll. by *into* or *up*) to receive or cause to receive shape or form: *spinach shaped into a ball* **9** to mould into a particular pattern or form **10** to devise or develop: *to shape a system of free trade* ▸See also **shape up**
WORD ORIGIN Old English *gesceap*, literally: that which is created

shapeless *adj* **1** (of a person or object) lacking a pleasing shape: *a shapeless dress* **2** having no definite shape or form: *a shapeless mound*
shapelessness *n*

shapely *adj* **-lier, -liest** (esp. of a woman's body or legs) pleasing or attractive in shape **shapeliness** *n*

shape up *vb informal* **1** to progress or develop satisfactorily **2** to develop a definite or proper form **3** to start working efficiently or behaving properly: *shape up or face the sack*

Shapiro *n* **Jonathan** publishing as *Zapiro*. born 1958, South African political cartoonist

Shapley *n* **Harlow** 1885–1972, US astronomer, director of the Harvard College Observatory (1922–56): noted for his work on the size and structure of the galaxy

shard *n* a broken piece or fragment of pottery, glass, or metal
WORD ORIGIN Old English *sceard*

share¹ ❶ *n* **1** a part or portion of something that belongs to or is contributed by a person or group **2** (*often pl*) any of the equal parts into which the capital stock of a company is divided ▹*vb* **sharing, shared 3** (often foll. by *out*) to divide and distribute **4** to receive or contribute a portion of: *we shared a bottle of mineral water* **5** to join with another or others in the use of (something): *a programme about four women sharing a house* **6** to go through (a similar experience) as others: *we have all shared the nightmare of toothache* **7** to tell others about (something) **8** to have the same (beliefs or opinions) as others: *universal values shared by both east and west*
WORD ORIGIN Old English *scearu*

share² *n* ▸short for **ploughshare**
WORD ORIGIN Old English *scear*

shareholder *n* the owner of one or more shares in a company

share index *n* an index showing the movement of share prices

sharemilker *n* NZ a person who works on a dairy farm belonging to someone else and gets a share of the proceeds from the sale of the milk

sharia *n* the body of doctrines that regulate the lives of Muslims
WORD ORIGIN Arabic

shark *n* **1** a large, usually predatory fish with a long body, two dorsal fins, and rows of sharp teeth **2** *disparaging* a person who swindles or extorts money from other people
WORD ORIGIN origin unknown

sharkskin *n* a smooth glossy fabric used for sportswear

Sharon¹ *n* **Ariel** born 1928, Israeli soldier and politician; Likud prime minister (2001–06)

Sharon² *n* **Plain of Sharon** a plain in W Israel, between the Mediterranean and the hills of Samaria, extending from Haifa to Tel Aviv

sharp ❶ *adj* **1** having a keen cutting edge **2** tapering to an edge or point **3** involving a sudden change in direction: *a sharp bend on a road; a sharp rise in prices* **4** moving, acting, or reacting quickly: *sharp reflexes* **5** clearly defined: *a sharp contrast* **6** quick to notice or understand

S

THESAURUS

shape *n* **1, 2 = form**, profile, outline, lines, build, cut, figure, silhouette, configuration, contours **3 = appearance**, form, aspect, guise, likeness, semblance **5 = pattern**, model, frame, mould **6 = condition**, state, health, trim, kilter, fettle ▹*vb* **8, 9 = mould**, form, make, fashion, model, frame **10 = form**, make, produce, create, model, fashion, mould

share¹ *n* **1 = part**, portion, quota, ration, lot, cut (*informal*), due, division, contribution, proportion, allowance, whack (*informal*), allotment ▹*vb* **3 = divide**, split, distribute, assign, apportion, parcel out, divvy up (*informal*) **4 = go halves on**, go fifty-fifty on (*informal*), go Dutch on (*informal*)

sharp *adj* **1 = keen**, cutting, sharpened, honed, jagged, knife-edged, razor-sharp, serrated, knifelike **OPPOSITE:** blunt **3 = sudden**, marked, abrupt, extreme, distinct **OPPOSITE:** gradual **5 = clear**, distinct, clear-cut, well-defined, crisp **OPPOSITE:** indistinct **6 = quick-witted**, clever, astute,

DICTIONARY

things; keen-witted **7** clever in an underhand way: *sharp practices* **8** bitter or harsh: *a sharp response* **9** shrill or penetrating: *a sharp cry of horror* **10** having a bitter or sour taste **11** (of pain or cold) acute or biting: *a sharp gust of wind* **12** *music* **a** (of a note) raised in pitch by one semitone: F *sharp* **b** (of an instrument or voice) out of tune by being too high in pitch **13** *informal* neat and stylish: *a sharp dresser* ▹ *adv* **14** promptly **15** exactly: *at ten o'clock sharp* **16** *music* **a** higher than a standard pitch **b** out of tune by being too high in pitch: *she sings sharp* ▹ *n* **17** *music* **a** an accidental that raises the pitch of a note by one semitone. Symbol: ♯ **b** a note affected by this accidental **18** *informal* a cheat; a cardsharp **sharpish** *adj* **sharply** *adv* **sharpness** *n*
WORD ORIGIN Old English *scearp*

Sharp *n* **Cecil (James)** 1859–1924, British musician, best known for collecting, editing, and publishing English folk songs

sharpen ❶ *vb* to make or become sharp or sharper **sharpener** *n*

sharper *n* a person who cheats or swindles; fraud

sharpshooter *n* a skilled marksman

sharp-tongued *adj* very critical or sarcastic

sharp-witted *adj* very intelligent and perceptive

shat *vb taboo* ▸ a past tense and past participle of **shit**

shatter ❶ *vb* **1** to break suddenly into many small pieces **2** to damage badly or destroy: *to shatter American confidence* **3** to upset (someone) greatly: *the whole experience shattered me* **shattering** *adj*
WORD ORIGIN origin unknown

shattered ❶ *adj informal* **1** completely exhausted **2** badly upset: *he was shattered by the separation*

shave ❶ *vb* **shaving, shaved; shaved** *or* **shaven 1** to remove (the beard or hair) from (the face, head, or body) by using a razor or shaver **2** to remove thin slices from (wood or other material) with a sharp cutting tool **3** to touch (someone or something) lightly in passing ▹ *n* **4** the act or an instance of shaving **5** the removal of hair from a man's face by a razor **6** a tool for cutting off thin slices **7 close shave** *informal* a narrow escape
WORD ORIGIN Old English *sceafan*

shaver *n* **1** an electrically powered razor **2** *old-fashioned* a young boy

Shavian (**shave**-ee-an) *adj* **1** of or like George Bernard Shaw, Irish dramatist noted for his sharp wit, or his works ▹ *n* **2** an admirer of Shaw or his works

shaving *n* **1** a thin slice of something such as wood, which has been shaved off ▹ *adj* **2** used when shaving: *shaving foam*

shawl *n* a piece of woollen cloth worn over the head or shoulders by a woman or wrapped around a baby
WORD ORIGIN Persian *shāl*

Shays *n* **Daniel** ?1747–1825, American soldier and revolutionary leader of a rebellion of Massachusetts farmers against the US government (1786–87)

she *pron* **1** (refers to) the female person or animal previously mentioned or in question: *she is my sister* **2** (refers to) something regarded as female, such as a car, ship, or nation ▹ *n* **3** (refers to) a female person or animal
WORD ORIGIN Old English *sīe*

sheaf *n, pl* **sheaves 1** a bundle of papers tied together **2** a bundle of reaped corn tied together ▹ *vb* **3** to bind or tie into a sheaf
WORD ORIGIN Old English *scēaf*

shear *vb* **shearing, sheared** *or Austral & NZ sometimes* **shore; sheared** *or* **shorn 1** to remove (the fleece) of (a sheep) by cutting or clipping **2** to cut or cut through (something) with shears or a sharp instrument **3** *engineering* to cause (a part) to break or (of a part) to break through strain or twisting ▹ *n* **4** breakage caused through strain or twisting ▸ See also **shears** > **shearer** *n*
WORD ORIGIN Old English *sceran*

shearing shed *n Austral & NZ* a farm building with equipment for shearing sheep

shears *pl n* **a** large scissors, used for sheep shearing **b** a large scissor-like cutting tool with flat blades, used for cutting hedges

sheath *n, pl* **sheaths 1** a case or covering for the blade of a knife or sword **2** *biol* a structure that encloses or protects **3** *Brit, Austral & NZ* ▸ same as **condom 4** a close-fitting dress
WORD ORIGIN Old English *scēath*

sheathe *vb* **sheathing, sheathed 1** to insert (a knife or sword) into a sheath **2** to cover with a sheathe or sheathing

sheathing *n* any material used as an outer layer

sheaves *n* ▸ the plural of **sheaf**

shebeen *or* **shebean** *n Scot, Irish & S African* a place where alcoholic drink is sold illegally
WORD ORIGIN Irish Gaelic *sībīn* beer of poor quality

shed[1] ❶ *n* **1** a small, roughly made building used for storing garden tools, etc. **2** a large barnlike building used for various purposes at factories, train stations, etc.: *a locomotive shed*
WORD ORIGIN Old English *sced*

shed[2] ❶ *vb* **shedding, shed 1** to get rid of: *250 workers shed by the company* **2 shed tears** to cry **3 shed light on** to make (a problem or situation) easier to understand **4** to cast off (skin, hair, or leaves): *the trees were already beginning to shed their leaves* **5** to cause to flow off: *this coat sheds water* **6** to separate or divide (a group of sheep)
WORD ORIGIN Old English *sc(e)ādan*

sheen ❶ *n* a glistening brightness on the surface of something: *grass with a sheen of dew on it*
WORD ORIGIN Old English *sciēne*

Sheene *n* **Barry (Stephen Frank)**

S

THESAURUS

knowing, ready, quick, bright, alert, subtle, penetrating, apt, discerning, on the ball *(informal)*, perceptive, observant, long-headed
OPPOSITE: dim
8 = cutting, biting, severe, bitter, harsh, scathing, acrimonious, barbed, hurtful, sarcastic, sardonic, caustic, vitriolic, trenchant, mordant, mordacious, acerb
OPPOSITE: gentle
10 = sour, tart, pungent, hot, burning, acid, acerbic, acrid, piquant, acetic, vinegary, acerb
OPPOSITE: bland
11 = acute, violent, severe, intense, painful, shooting, distressing, stabbing, fierce, stinging, piercing, sore, excruciating, gut-wrenching
▹ *adv* **14, 15 = promptly**, precisely, exactly, on time, on the dot, punctually **OPPOSITE:** approximately

sharpen *vb* **= make sharp**, hone, whet, grind, edge, strop, put an edge on

shatter *vb* **1 = smash**, break, burst, split, crack, crush, explode, demolish, shiver, implode, pulverize, crush to smithereens **2 = destroy**, ruin, wreck, blast, disable, overturn, demolish, impair, blight, torpedo, bring to nought

shattered *adj (informal)* **1 = exhausted**, drained, worn out, spent, done in *(informal)*, all in *(slang)*, wiped out *(informal)*, weary, knackered *(slang)*, clapped out *(Brit, Austral & NZ informal)*, tired out, ready to drop, dog-tired *(informal)*, zonked *(slang)*, dead tired *(informal)*, dead beat *(informal)*, shagged out *(Brit slang)*, jiggered *(informal)* **2 = devastated**, crushed, upset, gutted *(slang)*

shave *vb* **1 = trim**, crop **2 = scrape**, plane, trim, shear, pare

shed[1] *n* **1 = hut**, shack, lean-to, outhouse, lockup, bothy *(chiefly Scot)*, whare *(NZ)*

shed[2] *vb* **4 = cast off**, discard, moult, slough off, exuviate **5 = drop**, spill, scatter

sheen *n* **= shine**, gleam, gloss, polish, brightness, lustre, burnish, patina, shininess

DICTIONARY

1950–2003, British racing motorcyclist: 500 cc. world champion (1976, 1977)
sheep *n, pl* **sheep 1** a cud-chewing mammal with a thick woolly coat, kept for its wool or meat ▸ Related adjective: **ovine 2** a timid person **3 like sheep** (of a group of people) allowing a single person to dictate their actions or beliefs **4 separate the sheep from the goats** to pick out the members of a group who are superior in some respects **sheeplike** *adj*
WORD ORIGIN Old English *scēap*
sheep-dip *n* **1** a liquid disinfectant and insecticide in which sheep are immersed **2** a deep trough containing such a liquid
sheepdog *n* **1** a dog used for herding sheep **2** a breed of dog reared originally for herding sheep
sheepfold *n* a pen or enclosure for sheep
sheepish *adj* embarrassed because of feeling foolish **sheepishly** *adv*
sheepshank *n* a knot made in a rope to shorten it temporarily
sheepskin *n* the skin of a sheep with the wool still attached, used to make clothing and rugs
sheer¹ ❶ *adj* **1** absolute; complete: *sheer amazement* **2** perpendicular; very steep: *the sheer rock face* **3** (of textiles) light, delicate, and see-through ▹ *adv* **4** steeply: *the cliff drops sheer to the sea*
WORD ORIGIN Old English *scīr*
sheer² *vb* **sheer off** *or* **away (from) a** to change course suddenly **b** to avoid an unpleasant person, thing, or topic
WORD ORIGIN origin unknown
sheet¹ ❶ *n* **1** a large rectangular piece of cloth used as an inner bed cover **2** a thin piece of material such as paper or glass, usually rectangular **3** a broad continuous surface or layer: *a sheet of ice* **4** a newspaper ▹ *vb* **5** to provide with, cover, or wrap in a sheet **6** (often foll. by *down*) to rain very heavily
WORD ORIGIN Old English *sciete*
sheet² *n naut* a line or rope for controlling the position of a sail
WORD ORIGIN Old English *scēata* corner of a sail
sheet anchor *n* **1** *naut* a large strong anchor for use in an emergency **2** a person or thing that can always be relied on
sheeting *n* any material from which sheets are made
sheet metal *n* metal formed into a thin sheet by rolling or hammering
sheet music *n* music printed on individual sheets of paper
sheikh *or* **sheik** (**shake**) *n* **a** the head of an Arab tribe, village, or family **b** (in Muslim communities) a religious leader **sheikhdom** *or* **sheikdom** *n*
WORD ORIGIN Arabic *shaykh* old man
sheila *n Austral & NZ old-fashioned informal* a girl or woman
WORD ORIGIN from the girl's name *Sheila*
shekel *n* **1** the monetary unit of Israel **2 shekels** *informal* money
WORD ORIGIN Hebrew *sheqel*
shelduck *or masc* **sheldrake** *n, pl* **-ducks, -duck** *or* **-drakes, -drake** a large brightly coloured wild duck of Europe and Asia
WORD ORIGIN probably from dialect *sheld* pied
shelf *n, pl* **shelves 1** a board fixed horizontally against a wall or in a cupboard, for holding things **2** a projecting layer of ice or rock on land or in the sea **3 off the shelf** (of products in shops) sold as standard **4 on the shelf** put aside or abandoned; used esp. of unmarried women considered to be past the age of marriage
WORD ORIGIN Old English *scylfe* ship's deck
shelf life *n* the length of time a packaged product will remain fresh or usable
shell ❶ *n* **1** the protective outer layer of an egg, fruit, or nut **2** the hard outer covering of an animal such as a crab or tortoise **3** any hard outer case **4** the external structure of a building, car, or ship, esp. one that is unfinished or gutted by fire **5** an explosive artillery projectile that can be fired from a large gun **6** a small-arms cartridge **7** *rowing* a very light narrow racing boat **8 come** *or* **bring out of one's shell** to become *or* help to become less shy and reserved ▹ *vb* **9** to remove the shell or husk from **10** to attack with artillery shells ▸ See also **shell out** > **shell-like** *adj*
WORD ORIGIN Old English *sciell*
she'll she will *or* she shall
shellac *n* **1** a yellowish resin used in varnishes and polishes **2** a varnish made by dissolving shellac in alcohol ▹ *vb* **-lacking, -lacked 3** to coat with shellac
WORD ORIGIN *shell* + *lac*
shellfish *n, pl* **-fish** *or* **-fishes** a sea-living animal, esp. one that can be eaten, having a shell
shell out ❶ *vb informal* to pay out or hand over (money)
shell shock *n* a nervous disorder characterized by anxiety and depression that occurs as a result of lengthy exposure to battle conditions **shell-shocked** *adj*
shell suit *n Brit* a lightweight tracksuit made of a waterproof nylon layer over a cotton layer
Shelta *n* a secret language based on Gaelic, used by some travelling people in Ireland and Britain
WORD ORIGIN origin unknown
shelter ❶ *n* **1** something that provides cover or protection from weather or danger **2** the protection given by such a cover ▹ *vb* **3** to take cover from bad weather **4** to provide with a place to live or a hiding place: *to shelter refugees*
WORD ORIGIN origin unknown
sheltered ❶ *adj* **1** protected from wind and rain **2** protected from unpleasant or upsetting experiences: *a sheltered childhood* **3** specially designed to provide a safe environment for the elderly, handicapped, or disabled: *sheltered housing*
shelve¹ ❶ *vb* **shelving, shelved 1** to put aside or postpone: *to shelve a project* **2** to place (something, such as a book) on a shelf **3** to provide with shelves: *to shelve a cupboard* **4** to

S

THESAURUS

sheer¹ *adj* **1 = total**, complete, absolute, utter, rank, pure, downright, unqualified, out-and-out, unadulterated, unmitigated, thoroughgoing, unalloyed, arrant **OPPOSITE:** moderate
2 = steep, abrupt, perpendicular, precipitous **OPPOSITE:** gradual
3 = fine, thin, transparent, see-through, gossamer, diaphanous, gauzy **OPPOSITE:** thick
sheet¹ *n* **2a = page**, leaf, folio, piece of paper **2b = plate**, piece, panel, slab, pane **3a = coat**, film, layer, membrane, surface, stratum, veneer, overlay, lamina **3b = expanse**, area, stretch, sweep, covering, blanket
shell *n* **1 = husk**, case, pod, shuck **2 = carapace**, armour **4 = frame**, structure, hull, framework, skeleton, chassis ▹ *vb* **10 = bomb**, barrage, bombard, attack, strike, blitz, strafe
shell out *vb (informal)* **= pay out**, fork out *(slang)*, expend, give, hand over, lay out *(informal)*, disburse, ante up *(informal, chiefly US)*
shelter *n* **1a = cover**, screen, awning, shiel *(Scot)* **1b = refuge**, haven, sanctuary, retreat, asylum **2 = protection**, safety, refuge, cover, security, defence, sanctuary ▹ *vb* **3, 4 = take shelter**, hide, seek refuge, take cover **4 = protect**, shield, harbour, safeguard, cover, hide, guard, defend, take in **OPPOSITE:** endanger
sheltered *adj* **1 = screened**, covered, protected, shielded, secluded **OPPOSITE:** exposed
2 = protected, screened, shielded, quiet, withdrawn, isolated, secluded, cloistered, reclusive, ensconced, hermitic, conventual
shelve¹ *vb* **1 = postpone**, put off, defer, table *(US)*, dismiss, freeze, suspend,

DICTIONARY

dismiss (someone) from active service
WORD ORIGIN from *shelves*, plural of *shelf*

shelve² *vb* **shelving, shelved** to slope away gradually
WORD ORIGIN origin unknown

shelves *n* ▸ the plural of **shelf**

shelving *n* **1** material for shelves **2** shelves collectively

shenanigans *pl n informal* **1** mischief or nonsense **2** trickery or deception
WORD ORIGIN origin unknown

Shepard *n* **1 Alan Bartlett, Jr** 1923–98, US naval officer; first US astronaut in space (1961) **2 Sam,** original name *Samuel Shepard Rogers.* born 1943, US dramatist, film actor, and director. His plays include *Chicago* (1966), *The Tooth of Crime* (1972), and *Buried Child* (1978): films as actor include *Days of Heaven* (1978) and *The Right Stuff* (1983); films as director include *Far North* (1989) and *Silent Tongue* (1994)

shepherd ❶ *n* **1** a person employed to tend sheep **2** *Christianity* a clergyman when considered as the moral and spiritual guide of the people in the parish ▹ *vb* **3** to guide or watch over (people) **shepherdess** *fem n*
WORD ORIGIN SHEEP + HERD

shepherd's pie *n* a baked dish of minced meat covered with mashed potato

Sheppard *n* **Jack** 1702–24, English criminal, whose daring escapes from prison were celebrated in many contemporary ballads and plays

Sher *n* Sir **Antony** born 1953, British actor and writer, born in South Africa

Sheraton *adj* denoting light and elegant furniture made by or in the style of Thomas Sheraton, English furniture maker

sherbet *n* **1** *Brit, Austral & NZ* a fruit-flavoured slightly fizzy powder, eaten as a sweet or used to make a drink **2** *US, Canad & S African* ▸ same as **sorbet**
WORD ORIGIN Turkish *şerbet*

sheriff *n* **1** (in the US) the chief elected law-enforcement officer in a county **2** (in Canada) a municipal officer who enforces court orders and escorts convicted criminals to prison **3** (in England and Wales) the chief executive officer of the Crown in a county, having chiefly ceremonial duties **4** (in Scotland) a judge in a sheriff court **5** (in Australia) an officer of the Supreme Court
WORD ORIGIN Old English *scīrgerēfa*

sheriff court *n* (in Scotland) a court having powers to try all but the most serious crimes and to deal with most civil actions

Sherpa *n, pl* **-pas** *or* **-pa** a member of a Tibetan people living on the southern slopes of the Himalayas

Sherriff *n* **R(obert) C(edric)** 1896–1975, British dramatist and film writer, best known for his play of World War I *Journey's End* (1928). His film scripts include *Goodbye Mr. Chips* (1936) and *The Dam Busters* (1955)

Sherrington *n* Sir **Charles Scott** 1857–1952, English physiologist, noted for his work on reflex action, published in *The Integrative Action of the Nervous System* (1906): shared the Nobel prize for physiology or medicine with Adrian (1932)

sherry *n, pl* **-ries** a pale or dark brown fortified wine, originally from southern Spain
WORD ORIGIN Spanish *Xeres*, now *Jerez*, in Spain

Sherwood *n* **Robert Emmet** 1896–1955, US dramatist. His plays include *The Petrified Forest* (1935), *Idiot's Delight* (1936), and *There shall be no Night* (1940)

Shetland pony *n* a very small sturdy breed of pony with a long shaggy mane and tail

Shevardnadze *n* **Eduard (Amvrosiyevich)** born 1928, Georgian statesman; president of Georgia (1992–2003); Soviet minister of foreign affairs (1985–91), who played an important part in arms negotiations with the US

shibboleth *n* **1** a slogan or catch phrase, usually considered outworn, that characterizes a particular party or sect: *the shibboleth of Western strategy* **2** a custom, phrase, or use of language that reliably distinguishes a member of one group or class from another
WORD ORIGIN word used in the Old Testament by the Gileadites as a test word for the Ephraimites, who could not pronounce *sh*

shickered *adj Austral & NZ old-fashioned slang* drunk
WORD ORIGIN Yiddish *shicker* liquor

shied *vb* ▸ the past of **shy¹** or **shy²**

shield ❶ *n* **1** a piece of defensive armour carried in the hand or on the arm to protect the body from blows or missiles **2** any person or thing that protects, hides, or defends: *a wind shield* **3** *heraldry* a representation of a shield used for displaying a coat of arms **4** anything that resembles a shield in shape, such as a trophy in a sports competition ▹ *vb* **5** to protect, hide, or defend (someone or something) from danger or harm: *an industry shielded from competition*
WORD ORIGIN Old English *scield*

Shields *n* **Carol (Ann)** 1935–2003, Canadian novelist and writer, born in the US; her novels include *Happenstance* (1980), *The Stone Diaries* (1995), and *Unless* (2002)

shift ❶ *vb* **1** to move from one place or position to another **2** to pass (blame or responsibility) onto someone else: *he was trying to shift the blame to me* **3** to change (gear) in a motor vehicle **4** to remove or be removed: *no detergent can shift these stains* **5** *US* to change for another or others **6** *slang* to move quickly ▹ *n* **7** the act or an instance of shifting **8 a** a group of workers who work during a specific period **b** the period of time worked by such a group **9** a method or scheme **10** a loose-fitting straight underskirt or dress
WORD ORIGIN Old English *sciftan*

shiftless *adj* lacking in ambition or initiative

shifty *adj* **shiftier, shiftiest** looking deceitful and not to be trusted **shiftiness** *n*

shillelagh (shil-lay-lee) *n* (in Ireland) a heavy club
WORD ORIGIN Irish Gaelic *sail* cudgel + *éille* thong

shilling *n* **1** a former British coin worth one twentieth of a pound, replaced by the 5p piece in 1970 **2** a former Australian coin, worth one twentieth of a pound **3** the standard monetary unit in several E African countries
WORD ORIGIN Old English *scilling*

shillyshally *vb* **-shallies, -shallying, -shallied** *informal* to be indecisive
WORD ORIGIN *shill I shall I*, reduplication of *shall I*

shim *n* **1** a thin strip of material placed between two close surfaces to fill a gap ▹ *vb* **shimming, shimmed 2** to fit or fill up with a shim
WORD ORIGIN origin unknown

S

THESAURUS

put aside, hold over, mothball, pigeonhole, lay aside, put on ice, put on the back burner *(informal)*, hold in abeyance, take a rain check on *(US & Canad informal)*

shepherd *n* **1 = drover**, stockman, herdsman, grazier ▹ *vb* **3 = guide**, conduct, steer, convoy, herd, marshal, usher

shield *n* **2 = protection**, cover, defence, screen, guard, ward *(archaic)*, shelter, safeguard, aegis, rampart, bulwark ▹ *vb* **5 = protect**, cover, screen, guard, defend, shelter, safeguard

shift *vb* **1a = move**, drift, move around, veer, budge, swerve, change position **1b = remove**, move, transfer, displace, relocate, rearrange, transpose, reposition ▹ *n* **7a = change**, switch, shifting, modification, alteration, displacement, about-turn, permutation, fluctuation **7b = move**, transfer, removal, veering, rearrangement

shimmer *vb* **1 = gleam**, twinkle, glimmer, dance, glisten, scintillate

DICTIONARY

shimmer ❶ *vb* **1** to shine with a faint unsteady light ▷*n* **2** a faint unsteady light **shimmering** *or* **shimmery** *adj*
WORD ORIGIN Old English *scimerian*
shin *n* **1** the front part of the lower leg **2** a cut of beef including the lower foreleg ▷*vb* **shinning, shinned** **3** **shin up** to climb (something, such as a rope or pole) by gripping with the hands or arms and the legs and hauling oneself up
WORD ORIGIN Old English *scinu*
shinbone *n* ▸ the nontechnical name for **tibia**
shindig *or* **shindy** *n, pl* **-digs** *or* **-dies** *slang* **1** a noisy party or dance **2** a quarrel or brawl
WORD ORIGIN variant of *shinty*
shine ❶ *vb* **shining, shone** **1** to give off or reflect light **2** to direct the light of (a lamp or torch): *I shone a torch at the ceiling* **3** *pt & pp* **shined** to make clean and bright by polishing: *they earned money by shining shoes* **4** to be very good at something: *she shone in most subjects; she shone at school* **5** to appear very bright and clear: *her hair shone like gold* ▷*n* **6** brightness or lustre **7** **take a shine to someone** *informal* to take a liking to someone
WORD ORIGIN Old English *scīnan*
shiner *n informal* a black eye
shingle¹ *n* **1** a thin rectangular tile laid with others in overlapping rows to cover a roof or a wall **2** a woman's short-cropped hairstyle ▷*vb* **-gling, -gled** **3** to cover (a roof or a wall) with shingles **4** to cut (the hair) in a short-cropped style
WORD ORIGIN Latin *scindere* to split
shingle² *n* coarse gravel found on beaches
WORD ORIGIN Scandinavian
shingles *n* a disease causing a rash of small blisters along a nerve
WORD ORIGIN Medieval Latin *cingulum* girdle
shingle slide *n NZ* the loose stones on a steep slope
Shinto *n* a Japanese religion in which ancestors and nature spirits are worshipped **Shintoism** *n* **Shintoist** *n, adj*
WORD ORIGIN Japanese: the way of the gods
shinty *n* **1** a game (of Scottish origin) like hockey but with taller goals **2** *pl* **-ties** the stick used in this game
WORD ORIGIN perhaps Scottish Gaelic *sinteag* a pace
shiny ❶ *adj* **shinier, shiniest** **1** bright and polished **2** (of clothes or material) worn to a smooth and glossy state by continual wear or rubbing
ship ❶ *n* **1** a large seagoing vessel with engines or sails **2** ▸ short for **airship** or **spaceship** **3** **when one's ship comes in** when one has become successful ▷*vb* **shipping, shipped** **4** to send or transport by any carrier, esp. a ship **5** *naut* to take in (water) over the side **6** to bring or go aboard a vessel: *to ship oars* **7** (often foll. by *off*) *informal* to send away: *they were shipped off to foreign countries* **8** to be hired to serve aboard a ship: *I shipped aboard a Liverpool liner*
WORD ORIGIN Old English *scip*
shipboard *adj* taking place or used aboard a ship: *a shipboard romance*
shipbuilder *n* a person or company that builds ships **shipbuilding** *n*
shipmate *n* a sailor who serves on the same ship as another
shipment *n* **1** goods shipped together as part of the same lot: *a shipment of arms* **2** the act of shipping cargo
shipper *n* a person or company that ships
shipping *n* **1** the business of transporting freight, esp. by ship **2** ships collectively: *all shipping should stay clear of the harbour*
shipshape *adj* **1** neat or orderly ▷*adv* **2** in a neat and orderly manner
shipwreck *n* **1** the destruction of a ship at sea **2** the remains of a wrecked ship **3** ruin or destruction: *the shipwreck of the old science* ▷*vb* **4** to wreck or destroy (a ship) **5** to bring to ruin or destruction
shipwright *n* someone, esp. a carpenter, who builds or repairs ships
shipyard *n* a place where ships are built and repaired
shire *n* **1** *Brit* a county **2** *Austral* a rural area with an elected council **3** **the Shires** the Midland counties of England
WORD ORIGIN Old English *scīr* office
shire horse *n* a large powerful breed of working horse
shirk *vb* to avoid doing (work or a duty); to be negligent: *no-one shirks when he's around* **shirker** *n*
WORD ORIGIN probably from German *Schurke* rogue
shirt *n* **1** an item of clothing worn on the upper part of the body, usually with a collar and sleeves and buttoning up the front **2** **keep your shirt on** *informal* keep your temper **3** **put one's shirt on something** *informal* to bet all one has on something
WORD ORIGIN Old English *scyrte*
shirt-lifter *n derogatory slang* a homosexual
shirtsleeve *n* **1** the sleeve of a shirt **2** **in one's shirtsleeves** not wearing a jacket
shirt-tail *n* the part of a shirt that extends below the waist
shirtwaister *or US* **shirtwaist** *n* a woman's dress with a tailored bodice resembling a shirt
shirty *adj* **shirtier, shirtiest** *slang* bad-tempered or annoyed
shish kebab *n* a dish of small pieces of meat and vegetables grilled on a skewer
WORD ORIGIN Turkish *şiş kebab*
shit *taboo vb* **shitting, shitted, shit** *or* **shat** **1** to defecate ▷*n* **2** faeces; excrement **3** *slang* rubbish; nonsense **4** *slang* a worthless person ▷*interj* **5** *slang* an exclamation of anger or disgust **shitty** *adj*
WORD ORIGIN Old English *scītan* to defecate
shiver¹ ❶ *vb* **1** to tremble from cold or fear ▷*n* **2** a tremble caused by cold or fear **3** **the shivers** a fit of shivering through fear or illness **shivering** *n, adj* **shivery** *adj*
WORD ORIGIN Middle English *chiveren*
shiver² *vb* **1** to break into fragments ▷*n* **2** a splintered piece
WORD ORIGIN Germanic
shoal¹ *n* **1** a large group of fish swimming together **2** a large group of people or things
WORD ORIGIN Old English *scolu*
shoal² *n* **1** a stretch of shallow water **2** a sandbank or rocky area, esp. one that can be seen at low water ▷*vb* **3** to make or become shallow
WORD ORIGIN Old English *sceald* shallow
shock¹ ❶ *vb* **1** to cause (someone) to experience extreme horror, disgust, or astonishment: *the similarity shocked me* **2** to cause a state of shock in (a person) ▷*n* **3** a sudden and violent

S

THESAURUS

▷*n* **2 = gleam**, glimmer, iridescence, unsteady light
shine *vb* **1 = gleam**, flash, beam, glow, sparkle, glitter, glare, shimmer, radiate, twinkle, glimmer, glisten, emit light, give off light, scintillate **3 = polish**, buff, burnish, brush, rub up **4 = be outstanding**, stand out, excel, star, be distinguished, steal the show, be conspicuous, be pre-eminent, stand out in a crowd ▷*n* **6a = polish**, gloss, sheen, glaze, lustre, patina **6b = brightness**, light, sparkle, radiance
shiny *adj* **1 = bright**, gleaming, glossy, glistening, polished, burnished, lustrous, satiny, sheeny, agleam
ship *n* **1 = vessel**, boat, craft
shiver¹ *vb* **1 = shudder**, shake, tremble, quake, quiver, palpitate ▷*n* **2 = tremble**, shudder, quiver, thrill, trembling, flutter, tremor, frisson *(French)*
shock¹ *vb* **1a = shake**, stun, stagger, jar, shake up *(informal)*, paralyse, numb, jolt, stupefy, shake out of your complacency **1b = horrify**, appal, disgust, outrage, offend, revolt, unsettle, sicken, agitate, disquiet, nauseate, raise someone's

DICTIONARY

blow or impact **4** **a** a sudden and violent emotional disturbance **b** something causing this **5** *pathol* a condition in which a person's blood cannot flow properly because of severe injury, burns, or fright **6** pain and muscular spasm caused by an electric current passing through a person's body **shocker** *n*
WORD ORIGIN Old French *choc*

shock[2] *n* **1** a number of grain sheaves set on end in a field to dry ▹*vb* **2** to set up (sheaves) in shocks
WORD ORIGIN probably Germanic

shock[3] *n* a thick bushy mass of hair
WORD ORIGIN origin unknown

shock absorber *n* any device designed to absorb mechanical shock, esp. one fitted to a motor vehicle to reduce the effects of travelling over bumpy surfaces

shocking ❶ *adj* **1** *informal* very bad or terrible: *a shocking match at Leicester* **2** causing dismay or disgust: *a shocking lack of concern* **3** **shocking pink** (of) a very bright shade of pink

Shockley *n* **William Bradfield** 1910–89, US physicist, born in Britain, who shared the Nobel prize for physics (1956) with John Bardeen and Walter Brattain for developing the transistor. He also held controversial views on the connection between race and intelligence

shockproof *adj* capable of absorbing shock without damage

shock tactics *pl n* the use of unexpected or unexpectedly forceful methods to carry out a plan

shock therapy *or* **treatment** *n* the treatment of certain mental conditions by passing an electric current through the patient's brain

shod *vb* ▸the past of **shoe**

shoddy *adj* **-dier, -diest** **1** made or done badly or carelessly: *shoddy goods* **2** of poor quality; shabby **shoddily** *adv* **shoddiness** *n*
WORD ORIGIN origin unknown

shoe *n* **1** one of a matching pair of coverings shaped to fit the foot, made of leather or other strong material and ending below the ankle **2** anything resembling a shoe in shape, function, or position **3** ▸short for **horseshoe** **4** **be in a person's shoes** *informal* to be in another person's situation ▹*vb* **shoeing, shod** **5** to fit (a horse) with horseshoes
WORD ORIGIN Old English *scōh*

shoehorn *n* a smooth curved piece of metal or plastic inserted at the heel of a shoe to ease the foot into it

shoelace *n* a cord for fastening shoes

shoemaker *n* a person who makes or repairs shoes or boots **shoemaking** *n*

shoestring *n* **1** ▸same as **shoelace** **2** *informal* a very small amount of money: *the theatre will be run on a shoestring*

shoetree *n* a long piece of metal, plastic, or wood, put into a shoe or boot to keep its shape

Sholem Aleichem *n* ▸See **Aleichem**

Sholes *n* **Christopher Latham** 1819–90, US inventor, who invented (1868) the typewriter and sold the patent to the Remington company (1873)

Sholokhov *n* **Mikhail Aleksandrovich** 1905–84, Soviet author, noted particularly for *And Quiet flows the Don* (1934) and *The Don flows Home to the Sea* (1940), describing the effect of the Revolution and civil war on the life of the Cossacks: Nobel prize for literature 1965

shone *vb* ▸a past of **shine**

shonky *adj* **-kier, -kiest** *Austral & NZ informal* unreliable or unsound

shoo *interj* **1** go away!: used to drive away unwanted or annoying animals or people ▹*vb* **shooing, shooed** **2** to drive away by crying 'shoo'
WORD ORIGIN imitative

shook *vb* ▸the past tense of **shake**

shoot ❶ *vb* **shooting, shot** **1** to hit, wound, or kill with a missile fired from a weapon **2** to fire (a missile or missiles) from a weapon **3** to fire (a weapon) **4** to hunt game with a gun for sport **5** to send out or be sent out quickly and aggressively: *he shot questions at her* **6** to move very rapidly: *the car shot forward* **7** to go or pass quickly over or through: *he was trying to shoot the white water* **8** to slide or push into or out of a fastening: *she shot the bolt quickly* **9** (of a plant) to sprout (a new growth) **10** to photograph or film **11** *sport* to hit or kick the ball at goal ▹*n* **12** the act of shooting **13** a new growth or sprout of a plant **14** *chiefly Brit* a meeting or party organized for hunting game with guns **15** an area where game can be hunted with guns **16** *informal* a photographic assignment: *a fashion shoot in New York*
WORD ORIGIN Old English *sceōtan*

shooter *n* **1** a person or thing that shoots **2** *slang* a gun

shooting gallery *n* a long narrow room where people practise shooting

shooting star *n* *informal* a meteor

shooting stick *n* a walking stick with a spike at one end and a folding seat at the other

shoot-out *n* **1** a gunfight **2** ▸short for **penalty shoot-out**

shoot up *vb* **1** to grow or increase rapidly: *crime rates have shot up; as my peers started to shoot up, I stopped growing* **2** *slang* to inject oneself with heroin or another strong drug

shop ❶ *n* **1** a place for the sale of goods and services **2** a place where a specified type of work is done; workshop: *a repair shop* **3** **all over the shop** *informal* scattered everywhere: *his papers were all over the shop* **4** **shut up shop** to close business at the end of the day or permanently **5** **talk shop** *informal* to discuss one's business or work on a social occasion ▹*vb* **shopping, shopped** **6** (often foll. by *for*) to visit a shop or shops in order to buy (goods) **7** *Brit, Austral & NZ slang* to inform on (someone), esp. to the police **shopper** *n*
WORD ORIGIN Old English *sceoppa* stall

shop around *vb* *informal* **1** to visit a number of shops or stores to compare goods and prices **2** to consider a number of possibilities before making a choice

shop assistant *n* a person who serves in a shop

shop floor *n* **1** the production area of a factory **2** workers, esp. factory workers, as opposed to management

S

THESAURUS

eyebrows, scandalize, gross out (*US slang*), traumatize, give (someone) a turn (*informal*) ▹*n* **3 = impact**, blow, jolt, clash, encounter, jarring, collision **4a = start**, scare, fright, turn, jolt **4a, 4b = upset**, blow, trauma, bombshell, turn (*informal*), distress, disturbance, consternation, whammy (*informal, chiefly US*), state of shock, rude awakening, bolt from the blue, prostration

shocking *adj* **1** (*informal*) **= terrible**, appalling, dreadful, bad, fearful, dire, horrendous, ghastly, from hell (*informal*), deplorable, abysmal, frightful, godawful (*slang*) **2 = appalling**, outrageous, disgraceful, offensive, distressing, disgusting, horrible, dreadful, horrifying, revolting, obscene, sickening, ghastly, hideous, monstrous, scandalous, disquieting, unspeakable, atrocious, repulsive, nauseating, odious, loathsome, abominable, stupefying, hellacious (*US slang*) **OPPOSITE:** wonderful

shoot *vb* **1 = open fire on**, blast (*slang*), hit, kill, bag, plug (*slang*), bring down, blow away (*slang, chiefly US*), zap (*slang*), pick off, pump full of lead (*slang*) **2 = fire**, launch, discharge, project, hurl, fling, propel, emit, let fly **6 = speed**, race, rush, charge, fly, spring, tear, flash, dash, barrel (along) (*informal, chiefly US & Canad*), bolt, streak, dart, whisk, whizz (*informal*), hurtle, scoot, burn rubber (*informal*) ▹*n* **13 = sprout**, branch, bud, twig, sprig, offshoot, scion, slip

shop *n* **1 = store**, market, supermarket, mart, boutique, emporium, hypermarket, dairy (*NZ*)

DICTIONARY

shopkeeper *n* a person who owns or manages a shop **shopkeeping** *n*
shoplifter *n* a customer who steals goods from a shop **shoplifting** *n*
shopping *n* **1** the act of going to shops and buying things **2** things that have been bought in shops
shopping centre *n* **1** a complex of stores, restaurants, and sometimes banks, usually under the same roof **2** the area of a town where most of the shops are situated
shopping list *n* **1** a written list of things to be bought when out shopping **2** any list of things desired or demanded: *a long shopping list of amendments to the treaty*
shopping mall *n* a large enclosed shopping centre
shopping plaza *n* a shopping centre, usually a small group of stores built as a strip
shopsoiled *adj* slightly dirty or faded, from being displayed in a shop
shop steward *n* a trade-union official elected by his or her fellow workers to be their representative in dealing with their employer
shoptalk *n* conversation about one's work, carried on outside working hours
shopwalker *n Brit* (esp. formerly) a person employed by a department store to assist sales personnel and help customers
shore[1] *n* **1** the land along the edge of a sea, lake, or wide river ▸ Related adjective: **littoral** **2** land, as opposed to water: *150 yards from shore* **3** **shores** a country: *foreign shores*
WORD ORIGIN probably from Middle Low German, Middle Dutch *schōre*
shore[2] *n* **1** a prop placed under or against something as a support ▹ *vb* **shoring, shored** **2** **shore up** **a** to prop up (an unsteady building or wall) with a strong support **b** to strengthen or support (something weak): *lower interest rates to shore up the economy*
WORD ORIGIN Middle Dutch *schōre*
shoreline *n* the edge of a sea, lake, or wide river
shorn *vb* ▸ a past participle of **shear**
short *adj* **1** of little length; not long **2** of little height; not tall **3** not lasting long **4** not enough: *the number of places laid at the table was short by four* **5** **short of** *or* **on** lacking in: *short of cash; short on detail* **6** concise: *a short book* **7** (of drinks) consisting chiefly of a spirit, such as whisky **8** (of someone's memory) lacking the ability to retain a lot of facts **9** (of a person's manner) abrupt and rather rude: *Kemp was short with her* **10** (of betting odds) almost even **11** *finance* **a** not possessing at the time of sale the stocks or commodities one sells **b** relating to such sales, which depend on falling prices for profit **12** *phonetics* (of a vowel) of relatively brief duration **13** (of pastry) crumbly in texture **14** **in short supply** scarce **15** **short and sweet** brief and to the point **16** **short for** a shortened form of ▹ *adv* **17** abruptly: *to stop short* **18** **be caught short** to have a sudden need to go to the toilet **19** **go short** not to have enough **20** **short of** except: *they want nothing short of his removal from power* ▹ *n* **21** a drink of spirits **22** a short film shown before the main feature in a cinema **23** ▸ same as **short circuit** **24** **for short** *informal* as a shortened form: *cystic fibrosis, CF for short* **25** **in short** briefly ▹ *vb* **26** to short-circuit ▸ See also **shorts**
> **shortness** *n*
WORD ORIGIN Old English *sceort*
shortage *n* not enough of something needed
shortbread *n* a rich crumbly biscuit made with butter
shortcake *n* **1** shortbread **2** a dessert made of layers of biscuit or cake filled with fruit and cream
short-change *vb* **-changing, -changed** **1** to give (someone) less than the correct change **2** *slang* to treat (someone), unfairly, esp. by giving less than is expected
short circuit *n* **1** a faulty or accidental connection in an electric circuit, which deflects current through a path of low resistance, usually causing the failure of the circuit ▹ *vb* **short-circuit** **2** to develop a short circuit **3** to bypass (a procedure): *she wrote to them direct and short-circuited the job agency* **4** to hinder or frustrate (a plan)
shortcoming *n* a fault or weakness
shortcrust pastry *n* a type of pastry with a crisp but crumbly texture
short cut *n* **1** a route that is shorter than the usual one **2** a way of saving time or effort
shorten *vb* to make or become short or shorter
shortening *n* butter or other fat, used in pastry to make it crumbly
shortfall *n* **1** failure to meet a requirement **2** the amount of such a failure; deficit
shorthand *n* a system of rapid writing using simple strokes and other symbols to represent words or phrases
short-handed *adj* (of a company or organization) lacking enough staff to do the required work
shorthand typist *n* a person skilled in the use of shorthand and in typing
shorthorn *n* a member of a breed of cattle with short horns
short list *n* **1** Also called (Scot): **short leet** a list of suitable candidates for a job or prize, from which the successful candidate will be selected ▹ *vb* **short-list** **2** to put (someone) on a short list
short-lived *adj* lasting only for a short time: *his authority was short-lived*
shortly *adv* **1** in a short time; soon **2** spoken in a cross and impatient manner
shorts *pl n* **1** trousers reaching the top of the thigh or partway to the knee **2** *chiefly US & Canad* men's underpants
short shrift *n* brief and unsympathetic treatment
short-sighted *adj* **1** unable to see faraway things clearly **2** not taking likely future developments into account: *a short-sighted approach to the problem* **short-sightedness** *n*
short-tempered *adj* easily angered

S

THESAURUS

shore[1] *n* **1 = beach**, coast, sands, strand *(poetic)*, lakeside, waterside, seaboard *(chiefly US)*, foreshore, seashore
short *adj* **1, 2 = small**, little, wee, squat, diminutive, petite, dumpy, knee high to a grasshopper, fubsy *(archaic, dialect)*, knee high to a gnat
OPPOSITE: tall
3 = brief, fleeting, short-term, short-lived, momentary
OPPOSITE: long
4 = scarce, wanting, low, missing, limited, lacking, tight, slim, inadequate, insufficient, slender, scant, meagre, sparse, deficient, scanty **OPPOSITE:** plentiful
6 = concise, brief, succinct, clipped, summary, compressed, curtailed, terse, laconic, pithy, abridged, compendious, sententious
OPPOSITE: lengthy
9 = abrupt, sharp, terse, curt, blunt, crusty, gruff, brusque, offhand, testy, impolite, discourteous, uncivil
OPPOSITE: polite
▹ *adv* **17 = abruptly**, suddenly, unaware, by surprise, without warning **OPPOSITE:** gradually
shortage *n* **= deficiency**, want, lack, failure, deficit, poverty, shortfall, inadequacy, scarcity, dearth, paucity, insufficiency
OPPOSITE: abundance
shortcoming *n* **= failing**, fault, weakness, defect, flaw, drawback, imperfection, frailty, foible, weak point
shorten *vb* **a = cut**, reduce, decrease, cut down, trim, diminish, dock, cut back, prune, lessen, curtail, abbreviate, truncate, abridge, downsize **OPPOSITE:** increase
b = turn up, trim
shortly *adv* **1 = soon**, presently, before long, anon *(archaic)*, in a little while, any minute now, erelong *(archaic, poetic)*

DICTIONARY

short-term *adj* of, for, or lasting a short time
short-termism *n* the tendency to concentrate on short-term gains, often at the expense of long-term success
short wave *n* a radio wave with a wavelength in the range 10–100 metres
short-winded *adj* tending to run out of breath easily
shot[1] ⓣ *n* **1** the act or an instance of firing a gun or rifle **2** *sport* the act or an instance of hitting, kicking, or throwing the ball **3** small round lead pellets used in shotguns **4** a person with specified skill in shooting: *my father was quite a good shot* **5** *informal* an attempt: *a second shot at writing a better treaty* **6** *informal* a guess **7 a** a single photograph **b** an uninterrupted sequence of film taken by a single camera **8** *informal* an injection of a vaccine or narcotic drug **9** *informal* a drink of spirits **10** the launching of a rocket or spacecraft to a specified destination: *a moon shot* **11** *sport* a heavy metal ball used in the shot put **12 like a shot** without hesitating **13 shot in the arm** *informal* something that brings back energy or confidence **14 shot in the dark** a wild guess
WORD ORIGIN Old English *scot*
shot[2] *vb* **1** ▸ the past of **shoot** ▹ *adj* **2** (of textiles) woven to give a changing colour effect **3** streaked with colour: *dark hair shot with streaks of grey*
shotgun *n* a gun for firing a charge of shot at short range
shot put *n* an athletic event in which contestants hurl a heavy metal ball called a shot as far as possible
shot-putter *n*
should *vb* ▸ the past tense of **shall**: used to indicate that an action is considered by the speaker to be obligatory (*you should go*) or to form the subjunctive mood (*I should like to see you; if I should die; should I be late, start without me*)
WORD ORIGIN Old English *sceolde*
shoulder ⓣ *n* **1** the part of the body where the arm, wing, or foreleg joins the trunk **2** a cut of meat including the upper part of the foreleg **3** the part of an item of clothing that covers the shoulder **4** the strip of unpaved land that borders a road **5 a shoulder to cry on** a person one turns to for sympathy with one's troubles **6 put one's shoulder to the wheel** *informal* to work very hard **7 rub shoulders with someone** *informal* to mix with someone socially **8 shoulder to shoulder a** side by side **b** working together ▹ *vb* **9** to accept (blame or responsibility) **10** to push with one's shoulder: *he shouldered his way through the crowd* **11** to lift or carry on one's shoulders **12 shoulder arms** *mil* to bring one's rifle vertically close to one's right side
WORD ORIGIN Old English *sculdor*
shoulder blade *n* either of two large flat triangular bones one on each side of the back part of the shoulder
shoulder strap *n* a strap worn over the shoulder to hold up an item of clothing or to support a bag
shouldn't should not
shout ⓣ *n* **1** a loud call or cry **2** *informal* one's turn to buy a round of drinks ▹ *vb* **3** to cry out loudly **4** *Austral & NZ informal* to treat (someone) to (something, such as a drink)
WORD ORIGIN probably from Old Norse *skūta* taunt
shout down ⓣ *vb* to silence (someone) by talking loudly
shove ⓣ *vb* **shoving, shoved 1** to give a violent push to **2** to push (one's way) roughly **3** *informal* to put (something) somewhere quickly and carelessly: *shove it into the boot* ▹ *n* **4** a rough push
WORD ORIGIN Old English *scūfan*
shovel ⓣ *n* **1** a tool for lifting or moving loose material, consisting of a broad blade attached to a large handle **2** a machine or part of a machine resembling a shovel in function ▹ *vb* **-elling, -elled** *or US* **-eling, -eled 3** to lift or move (loose material) with a shovel **4** to put away large quantities of (something) quickly: *shovelling food into their mouths*
WORD ORIGIN Old English *scofl*
shove off ⓣ *vb informal* to go away; depart
show ⓣ *vb* **showing, showed; shown** *or* **showed 1** to make, be, or become visible or noticeable: *to show an interest; excitement showed on everyone's face* **2** to present for inspection: *someone showed me the plans* **3** to demonstrate or prove: *evidence showed that this was the most economical way* **4** to instruct by demonstration: *she showed me how to feed the pullets* **5** to indicate: *the device shows changes in the pressure* **6** to behave towards (someone) in a particular way: *to show mercy* **7** to exhibit or display works of art, goods, etc.: *three artists are showing at the gallery* **8** to present (a film or play) or (of a film or play) to be presented **9** to guide or escort: *he offered to show me around* **10** *informal* to arrive ▹ *n* **11** a theatrical or other entertainment: *a magic show* **12** a display or exhibition: *a show of*

THESAURUS

shot[1] *n* **1 = discharge**, report, gunfire, crack, blast, explosion, bang **2** *(sport)* **= strike**, throw, lob **3 = ammunition**, bullet, slug, pellet, projectile, lead, ball **4 = marksman**, shooter, markswoman **5** *(informal)* **= attempt**, go *(informal)*, try, turn, chance, effort, opportunity, crack *(informal)*, essay, stab *(informal)*, endeavour
shoulder *vb* **9 = bear**, carry, take on, accept, assume, be responsible for, take upon yourself **10 = push**, thrust, elbow, shove, jostle, press
shout *n* **1 = cry**, call, yell, scream, roar, shriek, bellow ▹ *vb* **3 = cry (out)**, call (out), yell, scream, roar, shriek, bellow, bawl, holler *(informal)*, raise your voice
shout down *vb* **= drown out**, overwhelm, drown, silence
shove *vb* **1, 2 = push**, shoulder, thrust, elbow, drive, press, crowd, propel, jostle, impel ▹ *n* **4 = push**, knock, thrust, elbow, bump, nudge, jostle
shovel *vb* **3 = move**, scoop, dredge, shift, load, heap **4 = stuff**, spoon, ladle
shove off *vb (informal)* **= go away**, leave, clear off *(informal)*, depart, go to hell *(informal)*, push off *(informal)*, slope off, pack your bags *(informal)*, scram *(informal)*, get on your bike *(Brit slang)*, take yourself off, vamoose *(slang, chiefly US)*, sling your hook *(Brit slang)*, rack off *(Austral & NZ slang)*
show *vb* **1 = be visible**, be seen
OPPOSITE: be invisible
1, 3 = indicate, demonstrate, prove, reveal, display, evidence, point out, manifest, testify to, evince, flag up
OPPOSITE: disprove
2, 7 = display, exhibit, put on display, present, put on show, put before the public **4 = demonstrate**, describe, explain, teach, illustrate, instruct **5 = express**, display, reveal, indicate, register, demonstrate, disclose, manifest, divulge, make known, evince
OPPOSITE: hide
8 = broadcast, transmit, air, beam, relay, televise, put on the air, podcast **9 = guide**, lead, conduct, accompany, direct, steer, escort **10** *(informal)* **= turn up**, come, appear, arrive, attend, show up *(informal)*, put in *or* make an appearance **11a = programme**, broadcast, presentation, production **11b = entertainment**, performance, play, production, drama, musical, presentation, theatrical performance **12a = display**, view, sight, spectacle, array **12b = exhibition**, fair, display, parade, expo *(informal)*, exposition, pageant, pageantry **13a = appearance**,

DICTIONARY

paintings **13** something done to create an impression: *a show of indignation* **14** vain and conspicuous display: *it was nothing but mere show* **15** *slang, chiefly Brit* a thing or affair: *jolly good show* ▸See also **show off, show up**
WORD ORIGIN Old English *scēawian*

show business *n* the entertainment industry. Also (informal): **show biz**

showcase *n* **1** a setting in which something is displayed to best advantage: *a showcase for young opera singers* **2** a glass case used to display objects in a museum or shop

showdown ❶ *n informal* a major confrontation that settles a dispute

shower ❶ *n* **1 a** a kind of bathing in which a person stands upright and is sprayed with water from a nozzle **b** a device, room, or booth for such bathing **2** a brief period of rain, hail, sleet, or snow **3** a sudden fall of many small light objects: *a shower of loose gravel* **4** *Brit slang* a worthless or contemptible group of people **5** *US, Canad, Austral & NZ* a party held to honour and present gifts to a prospective bride or prospective mother ▹*vb* **6** to take a shower **7** to sprinkle with or as if with a shower: *the walkers were showered by volcanic ash* **8** to present (someone) with things liberally: *he showered her with presents* **showery** *adj*
WORD ORIGIN Old English *scūr*

showing *n* **1** a presentation, exhibition, or display **2** manner of presentation

showjumping *n* the sport of riding horses in competitions to demonstrate skill in jumping **showjumper** *n*

showman *n, pl* **-men** **1** a person skilled at presenting anything in an effective manner **2** a person who presents or produces a show **showmanship** *n*

shown *vb* ▸a past participle of **show**

show off ❶ *vb* **1** to exhibit or display (something) so as to invite admiration: *he was eager to show off his new car* **2** *informal* to flaunt skills, knowledge, or looks in order to attract attention or impress people ▹*n* **show-off** **3** *informal* a person who flaunts his or her skills, knowledge, or looks in order to attract attention or impress people

showpiece *n* **1** anything displayed or exhibited **2** something admired as a fine example of its type: *an orchestral showpiece*

showplace *n* a place visited for its beauty or interest

showroom *n* a room in which goods for sale, esp. cars or electrical or gas appliances, are on display

show up ❶ *vb* **1** to reveal or be revealed clearly **2** to expose the faults or defects of (someone or something) by comparison **3** *informal* to put (someone) to shame; embarrass **4** *informal* to arrive

showy *adj* **showier, showiest** **1** colourful, bright in appearance, and very noticeable, and perhaps rather vulgar: *showy jewellery* **2** making an imposing display **showily** *adv* **showiness** *n*

shrank *vb* ▸a past tense of **shrink**

shrapnel *n* **1** an artillery shell containing a number of small pellets or bullets which it is designed to scatter on explosion **2** fragments from this type of shell
WORD ORIGIN after H. *Shrapnel*, who invented it

shred ❶ *n* **1** a long narrow piece torn off something **2** a very small amount: *not a shred of truth* ▹*vb* **shredding, shredded** *or* **shred** **3** to tear into shreds **shredder** *n*
WORD ORIGIN Old English *scrēad*

shrew *n* **1** a small mouselike animal with a long snout **2** a bad-tempered nagging woman **shrewish** *adj*
WORD ORIGIN Old English *scrēawa*

shrewd ❶ *adj* intelligent and making good judgments **shrewdly** *adv* **shrewdness** *n*
WORD ORIGIN from *shrew* (obsolete verb) to curse, from *shrew*

shriek ❶ *n* **1** a high-pitched scream ▹*vb* **2** to utter (words or sounds) in a high-pitched tone
WORD ORIGIN probably from Old Norse *skrækja* to screech

shrift *n* ▸see **short shrift**
WORD ORIGIN Old English *scrift* penance

shrike *n* a bird with a heavy hooked bill, which kills small animals by dashing them on thorns
WORD ORIGIN Old English *scrīc* thrush

shrill *adj* **1** (of a sound) sharp and high-pitched ▹*vb* **2** to utter (words or sounds) in a shrill tone **shrillness** *n* **shrilly** *adv*
WORD ORIGIN origin unknown

shrimp *n* **1** a small edible shellfish with a long tail and a pair of pincers **2** *informal* a small person ▹*vb* **3** to fish for shrimps
WORD ORIGIN probably Germanic

shrine *n* **1** a place of worship associated with a sacred person or object **2** a container for sacred relics **3** the tomb of a saint or other holy person **4** a place that is visited and honoured because of its association with a famous person or event: *he'd come to worship at the shrine of Mozart*
WORD ORIGIN Latin *scrinium* bookcase

shrink ❶ *vb* **shrinking, shrank** *or* **shrunk; shrunk** *or* **shrunken** **1** to become or cause to become smaller, sometimes because of wetness, heat, or cold **2** **shrink from** **a** to withdraw or move away through fear: *they didn't shrink from danger* **b** to feel great reluctance (to perform a task or duty) ▹*n* **3** *slang* a psychiatrist
WORD ORIGIN Old English *scrincan*

shrinkage *n* **1** the fact of shrinking **2** the amount by which anything decreases in size, value, or weight

shrink-wrap *vb* **-wrapping, -wrapped** to package (a product) in a flexible

S

THESAURUS

display, pose, profession, parade, ostentation **13b = pretence**, appearance, semblance, illusion, pretext, likeness, affectation

showdown *n (informal)* **= confrontation**, crisis, clash, moment of truth, face-off *(slang)*

shower *n* **2 = deluge**, downpour ▹*vb* **7 = cover**, dust, spray, sprinkle **8 = inundate**, load, heap, lavish, pour, deluge

show off *vb* **1 = exhibit**, display, parade, advertise, demonstrate, spread out, flaunt **2** *(informal)* **= boast**, brag, blow your own trumpet, swagger, hot-dog *(chiefly US)*, strut your stuff *(chiefly US)*, make a spectacle of yourself ▹*n* **show-off** **3** *(informal)* **= exhibitionist**, boaster, swaggerer, hot dog *(chiefly US)*, poseur, egotist, braggart, braggadocio, peacock, figjam *(Austral slang)*

show up *vb* **1 = reveal**, expose, highlight, pinpoint, unmask, lay bare, put the spotlight on **3** *(informal)* **= embarrass**, shame, let down, mortify, put to shame, show in a bad light

shred *n* **1 = strip**, bit, piece, scrap, fragment, rag, ribbon, snippet, sliver, tatter **2 = particle**, trace, scrap, grain, atom, jot, whit, iota

shrewd *adj* **= astute**, clever, sharp, knowing, fly *(slang)*, keen, acute, smart, calculated, calculating, intelligent, discriminating, cunning, discerning, sly, canny, perceptive, wily, crafty, artful, far-sighted, far-seeing, long-headed, perspicacious, sagacious
OPPOSITE: naive

shriek *n* **1 = scream**, cry, yell, howl, wail, whoop, screech, squeal, holler ▹*vb* **2 = scream**, cry, yell, howl, wail, whoop, screech, squeal, holler

shrink *vb* **1 = decrease**, dwindle, lessen, grow *or* get smaller, contract, narrow, diminish, fall off, shorten, wrinkle, wither, drop off, deflate, shrivel, downsize
OPPOSITE: grow

DICTIONARY

plastic wrapping which shrinks about its contours to seal it

shrivel *vb* **-elling, -elled** *or US* **-eling, -eled** to become dry and withered
WORD ORIGIN probably Scandinavian

shroud ❶ *n* **1** a piece of cloth used to wrap a dead body **2** anything that hides things: *a shroud of smoke* ▷ *vb* **3** to hide or obscure (something): *shrouded in uncertainty; shrouded by smog*
WORD ORIGIN Old English *scrūd* garment

Shrove Tuesday *n* the day before Ash Wednesday
WORD ORIGIN Old English *scrīfan* to confess one's sins

shrub *n* a woody plant, smaller than a tree, with several stems instead of a trunk **shrubby** *adj*
WORD ORIGIN Old English *scrybb*

shrubbery *n, pl* **-beries 1** an area planted with shrubs **2** shrubs collectively

shrug *vb* **shrugging, shrugged 1** to draw up and drop (the shoulders) as a sign of indifference or doubt ▷ *n* **2** the action of shrugging
WORD ORIGIN origin unknown

shrug off *vb* **1** to treat (a matter) as unimportant **2** to get rid of (someone)

shrunk *vb* ▸ a past tense and past participle of **shrink**

shrunken *vb* **1** ▸ a past participle of **shrink** ▷ *adj* **2** reduced in size

shudder ❶ *vb* **1** to shake or tremble suddenly and violently from horror or fear **2** (of a machine) to shake violently ▷ *n* **3** a shiver of fear or horror
WORD ORIGIN Middle Low German *schōderen*

shuffle ❶ *vb* **-fling, -fled 1** to walk or move (the feet) with a slow dragging motion **2** to mix together in a jumbled mass: *the chairman shuffled his papers* **3** to mix up (playing cards) so as to change their order ▷ *n* **4** an instance of shuffling **5** a rearrangement: *a shuffle of top management* **6** a dance with short dragging movements of the feet
WORD ORIGIN probably from Low German *schüffeln*

shufti *n slang, chiefly Brit* a look; peep
WORD ORIGIN from Arabic

shun ❶ *vb* **shunning, shunned** to avoid deliberately
WORD ORIGIN Old English *scunian*

shunt *vb* **1** to move (objects or people) to a different position **2** *railways* to transfer (engines or carriages) from track to track ▷ *n* **3** the act of shunting **4** a railway point **5** *electronics* a conductor connected in parallel across a part of a circuit to divert a known fraction of the current **6** *informal* a collision where one vehicle runs into the back of another
WORD ORIGIN perhaps from Middle English *shunen* to shun

shush *interj* **1** be quiet! hush! ▷ *vb* **2** to quiet (someone) by saying 'shush'
WORD ORIGIN imitative

shut ❶ *vb* **shutting, shut 1** to move (something) so as to cover an opening: *shut the door* **2** to close (something) by bringing together the parts: *Ridley shut the folder* **3 shut up** to close or lock the doors of: *let's shut up the shop* **4 shut in** to confine or enclose **5 shut out** to prevent from entering **6** (of a shop or other establishment) to stop operating for the day: *the late-night rush after the pubs shut* ▷ *adj* **7** closed or fastened ▸ See also **shutdown, shut off**, etc.
WORD ORIGIN Old English *scyttan*

shutdown ❶ *n* **1** the closing of a factory, shop, or other business ▷ *vb* **shut down 2** to discontinue operations permanently

Shute *n* **Nevil**, real name *Nevil Shute Norway* 1899–1960, English novelist, in Australia after World War II: noted for his novels set in Australia, esp. *A Town like Alice* (1950) and *On the Beach* (1957)

shuteye *n slang* sleep

shut off *vb* **1** to cut off the flow or supply of **2** to turn off and stop working: *I shut off the car engine* **3** to isolate or separate: *ghettoes shut off from the rest of society*

shut out *vb* **1** to keep out or exclude **2** to conceal from sight: *blinds were drawn to shut out the sun*

shutter *n* **1** a hinged doorlike cover, usually one of a pair, for closing off a window **2 put up the shutters** to close business at the end of the day or permanently **3** *photog* a device in a camera that opens to allow light through the lens so as to expose the film when a photograph is taken ▷ *vb* **4** to close or equip with a shutter or shutters

shuttle ❶ *n* **1** a bus, train, or aircraft that makes frequent journeys between two places which are fairly near to each other **2** a bobbin-like device used in weaving to pass the weft thread between the warp threads **3** a small bobbin-like device used to hold the thread in a sewing machine ▷ *vb* **-tling, -tled 4** to travel back and forth
WORD ORIGIN Old English *scytel* dart, arrow

shuttlecock *n* a rounded piece of cork or plastic with feathers stuck in one end, struck to and fro in badminton

shut up *vb* **1** *informal* to stop talking or cause (someone) to stop talking: often used in commands **2** to confine or imprison (someone)

shy[1] ❶ *adj* **1** not at ease in the company of others **2** easily frightened; timid **3 shy of** cautious or wary of **4** reluctant or unwilling: *camera-shy; workshy* ▷ *vb* **shies, shying, shied 5** to move back or aside suddenly from fear: *with a terrified whinny the horse shied* **6 shy away from** to draw back from (doing something), through lack of confidence ▷ *n, pl* **shies 7** a sudden movement back or aside from fear **shyly** *adv* **shyness** *n*
WORD ORIGIN Old English *scēoh*

shy[2] *vb* **shies, shying, shied 1** to throw (something) ▷ *n, pl* **shies 2** a quick throw
WORD ORIGIN Germanic

Shylock *n* an unsympathetic and demanding person to whom one owes money
WORD ORIGIN after the heartless usurer in Shakespeare's *The Merchant of Venice*

S

THESAURUS

shroud *n* **1 = winding sheet**, grave clothes, cerecloth, cerement **2 = covering**, veil, mantle, screen, cloud, pall ▷ *vb* **3 = conceal**, cover, screen, hide, blanket, veil, cloak, swathe, envelop

shudder *vb* **1 = shiver**, shake, tremble, quake, quiver, convulse ▷ *n* **3 = shiver**, trembling, tremor, quiver, spasm, convulsion

shuffle *vb* **1a = shamble**, stagger, stumble, dodder **1b = scuffle**, drag, scrape, scuff **2 = rearrange**, jumble, mix, shift, disorder, disarrange, intermix

shun *vb* **= avoid**, steer clear of, keep away from, evade, eschew, shy away from, cold-shoulder, have no part in, fight shy of, give (someone *or* something) a wide berth, body-swerve *(Scot)*

shut *vb* **1 = close**, secure, fasten, bar, seal, slam, push to, draw to
OPPOSITE: open
▷ *adj* **7 = closed**, fastened, sealed, locked **OPPOSITE:** open

shut down *vb* **2 = stop work**, halt work, cease operating, close down, cease trading, discontinue

shuttle *vb* **4 = go back and forth**, commute, go to and fro, alternate, ply, shunt, seesaw

shy[1] *adj* **1 = timid**, self-conscious, bashful, reserved, retiring, nervous, modest, aw-shucks, shrinking, backward, coy, reticent, self-effacing, diffident, mousy
OPPOSITE: confident
2 = cautious, wary, hesitant, suspicious, reticent, distrustful, chary **OPPOSITE:** reckless
▷ *vb* **5 = recoil**, flinch, draw back, start, rear, buck, wince, swerve, balk, quail, take fright

DICTIONARY

si *n music* ▸same as **te**
Si *chem* silicon
SI ▸see **SI unit**
Siamese *n, pl* **-mese 1** ▸same as **Siamese cat** ▹*adj, n, pl* **-mese 2** ▸(formerly) same as **Thai**
Siamese cat *n* a breed of cat with cream fur, dark ears and face, and blue eyes
Siamese twins *pl n* twins born joined together at some part of the body
sibilant *adj* **1** having a hissing sound ▹*n* **2** *phonetics* a consonant, such as *s* or *z*, that is pronounced with a hissing sound
WORD ORIGIN Latin *sibilare* to hiss
sibling *n* a brother or sister
WORD ORIGIN Old English: a relative
sibyl *n* (in ancient Greece and Rome) a prophetess **sibylline** *adj*
WORD ORIGIN Greek *Sibulla*
sic[1] *adv* thus: inserted in brackets in a text to indicate that an odd spelling or reading is in fact what was written, even though it is or appears to be wrong
WORD ORIGIN Latin
sic[2] *vb* **sicking, sicked 1** to attack: used only in commands to a dog **2** to urge (a dog) to attack (someone)
WORD ORIGIN dialect variant of *seek*
sick ❶ *adj* **1** vomiting or likely to vomit **2** physically or mentally unwell **3** of or for ill people: *sick pay* **4** deeply affected with mental or spiritual distress: *sick at heart* **5** mentally disturbed **6** *informal* making fun of death, illness, or misfortune: *a sick joke* **7 sick of** *or* **sick and tired of** *informal* disgusted by or weary of: *I'm sick of this town* ▹*n, vb* **8** *informal* ▸same as **vomit**
WORD ORIGIN Old English *sēoc*
sickbay *n* a room for the treatment of sick people, for example on a ship
sicken ❶ *vb* **1** to make (someone) feel nauseated or disgusted **2 sicken for** to show symptoms of (an illness)
sickening ❶ *adj* **1** causing horror or disgust: *sickening scenes of violence* **2** *informal* extremely annoying **sickeningly** *adv*
Sickert *n* **Walter Richard** 1860–1942, British impressionist painter, esp. of scenes of London music halls
sickie *n informal* a day of sick leave from work
sickle *n* a tool for cutting grass and grain crops, with a curved blade and a short handle
WORD ORIGIN Old English *sicol*
sick leave *n* leave of absence from work through illness
sickly *adj* **-lier, -liest 1** weak and unhealthy **2** (of a person) looking pale and unwell: *sickly pallor* **3** unpleasant to smell, taste, or look at **4** showing excessive emotion in a weak and rather pathetic way: *a sickly tune* ▹*adv* **5** suggesting sickness: *sickly pale* **sickliness** *n*
sickness ❶ *n* **1** a particular illness or disease: *sleeping sickness* **2** the state of being ill or unhealthy: *absent from work due to sickness* **3** a feeling of queasiness in the stomach followed by vomiting
Siddons *n* **Sarah** 1755–1831, English tragedienne
side ❶ *n* **1** a line or surface that borders anything **2** *geom* a line forming part of the perimeter of a plane figure: *a square has four sides* **3** either of two parts into which an object, surface, or area can be divided: *the right side and the left side* **4** either of the two surfaces of a flat object: *write on both sides of the page* **5** the sloping part of a hill or bank **6** either the left or the right half of the body, esp. the area around the waist: *he took a nine millimetre bullet in the side* **7** the area immediately next to a person or thing: *at the side of my bed* **8** a place within an area identified by reference to a central point: *the south side of the island* **9** the area at the edge of something, as opposed to the centre: *the far side of the square* **10** aspect or part: *there is a positive side to truancy* **11** one of two or more contesting groups or teams: *the two sides will meet in the final* **12** a position held in opposition to another in a dispute **13** a line of descent through one parent: *a relative on his father's side* **14** *informal* a television channel **15** *Brit slang* conceit or cheek: *to put on side* **16 on one side** apart from the rest **17 on the side** in addition to a person's main work: *she did a little public speaking on the side* **18 side by side** close together **19 side by side with** beside or near to **20 take sides** to support one party in a dispute against another ▹*adj* **21** situated at the side: *the side entrance* **22** less important: *a side issue* ▹*vb* **siding, sided 23 side with** to support (one party in a dispute)
WORD ORIGIN Old English *sīde*
sideboard *n* a piece of furniture for a dining room, with drawers, cupboards, and shelves to hold tableware
sideboards *or esp. US & Canad* **sideburns** *pl n* a man's whiskers grown down either side of the face in front of the ears
sidecar *n* a small passenger car attached to the side of a motorcycle
side-effect *n* **1** a usually unwanted effect caused by a drug in addition to its intended one **2** any additional effect, usually an undesirable one: *the unforeseen side-effects of the end of the Cold War*
sidekick *n informal* a close friend or associate
sidelight *n* **1** *Brit* either of two small lights at the front of a motor vehicle **2** either of the two navigational lights used by ships at night
sideline *n* an extra job in addition to one's main job
sidelines *pl n* **1** *sport* **a** the lines that mark the side boundaries of a playing area **b** the area just outside the playing area, where substitute

S

THESAURUS

sick *adj* **1 = nauseous**, ill, queasy, nauseated, green about the gills (*informal*), qualmish **2 = unwell**, ill, poorly (*informal*), diseased, weak, crook (*Austral & NZ informal*), under par (*informal*), ailing, feeble, laid up (*informal*), under the weather (*informal*), indisposed, on the sick list (*informal*) **OPPOSITE:** well
6 (*informal*) **= morbid**, cruel, sadistic, black, macabre, ghoulish **7** (*informal*) **= tired**, bored, fed up, weary, jaded, blasé, satiated
sicken *vb* **1 = disgust**, revolt, nauseate, repel, gross out (*US slang*), turn your stomach, make your gorge rise
sickening *adj* **1 = disgusting**, revolting, vile, offensive, foul, distasteful, repulsive, nauseating, loathsome, nauseous, gut-wrenching, putrid, stomach-turning (*informal*), cringe-making (*Brit informal*), noisome, yucky *or* yukky (*slang*), yucko (*Austral slang*)
OPPOSITE: delightful
sickness *n* **1 = illness**, disorder, ailment, disease, complaint, bug (*informal*), affliction, malady, infirmity, indisposition, lurgy (*informal*) **3a = nausea**, queasiness **3b = vomiting**, nausea, upset stomach, throwing up (*informal*), puking (*slang*), retching, barfing (*US slang*)
side *n* **1, 7, 9 = border**, margin, boundary, verge, flank, rim, perimeter, periphery, edge
OPPOSITE: middle
4 = face, surface, facet **10 = aspect**, feature, angle, facet **11a = party**, camp, faction, cause **11b = team**, squad, crew, line-up **12 = point of view**, viewpoint, position, opinion, angle, slant, standpoint ▹*adj* **22 = subordinate**, minor, secondary, subsidiary, lesser, marginal, indirect, incidental, ancillary
OPPOSITE: main
23 side with someone = support, back, champion, agree with, stand up for, second, favour, defend, team up with (*informal*), go along with, befriend, join with, sympathize with, be loyal to, take the part of, associate yourself with, ally yourself with

DICTIONARY

players sit **2 on the sidelines a** only passively involved: *on the sidelines of the modern world* **b** waiting to join in an activity

sidelong *adj* **1** directed to the side; oblique ▹ *adv* **2** from the side; obliquely

sidereal (side-**eer**-ee-al) *adj* of or determined with reference to the stars: *the sidereal time*
WORD ORIGIN Latin *sidus* a star

side-saddle *n* **1** a riding saddle originally designed for women in skirts, allowing the rider to sit with both legs on the same side of the horse ▹ *adv* **2** on a side-saddle

sideshow *n* **1** an event or incident considered less important than another: *a mere sideshow compared to the war on the Russian front* **2** a small show or entertainment offered along with the main show at a circus or fair

side-splitting *adj* causing a great deal of laughter

sidestep *vb* **-stepping, -stepped 1** to step out of the way of (something) **2** to dodge (an issue) ▹ *n* **side step 3** a movement to one side, such as in dancing or boxing

sideswipe *n* **1** an unexpected criticism of someone or something while discussing another subject **2** a glancing blow along or from the side ▹ *vb* **-swiping, -swiped 3** to make a sideswipe

sidetrack *vb* to distract (someone) from a main subject

sidewalk ⊙ *n US & Canad* a raised space alongside a road, for pedestrians

sideways ⊙ *adv* **1** moving, facing, or inclining towards one side **2** from one side; obliquely **3** with one side forward ▹ *adj* **4** moving or directed to or from one side

side whiskers *pl n* ▸ same as **sideboards**

siding *n* a short stretch of railway track connected to a main line, used for loading and unloading freight and storing engines and carriages

sidle *vb* **-dling, -dled** to walk slowly and carefully, not wanting to be noticed
WORD ORIGIN obsolete *sideling* sideways

Sidney *or* **Sydney** *n* **1 Algernon** 1622–83, English Whig politician, beheaded for his supposed part in the Rye House Plot to assassinate Charles II and the future James II: author of *Discourses Concerning Government* (1689) **2** Sir **Philip** 1554–86, English poet, courtier, and soldier. His works include the pastoral romance *Arcadia* (1590), the sonnet sequence *Astrophel and Stella* (1591), and *The Defence of Poesie* (1595), one of the earliest works of literary criticism in English

SIDS sudden infant death syndrome; cot death

Siegbahn *n* **1 Kai** 1918–2007, Swedish physicist who worked on electron spectroscopy: Nobel prize for physics 1981 **2** his father, **Karl Manne Georg** 1886–1978, Swedish physicist, who discovered the M series in X-ray spectroscopy: Nobel prize for physics 1924

siege ⊙ *n* **1** a military operation carried out to capture a place by surrounding and blockading it **2** a similar operation carried out by police, for example to force people out of a place **3 lay siege to** to subject (a place) to a siege
WORD ORIGIN Old French *sege* a seat

siemens *n, pl* **siemens** the SI unit of electrical conductance
WORD ORIGIN after E. W. von *Siemens*, engineer

Siemens *n* **1 Ernst Werner von** 1816–92, German engineer, inventor, and pioneer in telegraphy. Among his inventions are the self-excited dynamo and an electrolytic refining process **2** his brother, Sir **William**, original name *Karl Wilhelm Siemens*. 1823–83, British engineer, born in Germany, who invented the open-hearth process for making steel

Sienkiewicz *n* **Henryk** 1846–1916, Polish novelist. His best-known works are *Quo Vadis?* (1896), set in Nero's Rome, and the war trilogy *With Fire and Sword* (1884), *The Deluge* (1886), and *Pan Michael* (1888), set in 17th-century Poland: Nobel prize for literature 1905

sienna *n* **1** a natural earth used as a reddish-brown or yellowish-brown pigment ▹ *adj* **2 burnt sienna** reddish-brown **3 raw sienna** yellowish-brown
WORD ORIGIN after *Siena*, Italian city

sierra *n* a range of mountains with jagged peaks in Spain or America
WORD ORIGIN Spanish, literally: saw

sies (siss) *interj S African informal* ▸ same as **sis**[2]

siesta *n* an afternoon nap, taken in hot countries
WORD ORIGIN Spanish

sieve (siv) *n* **1** a utensil with a mesh through which a substance is sifted or strained ▹ *vb* **sieving, sieved 2** to sift or strain through a sieve
WORD ORIGIN Old English *sife*

Sieyès *n* **Emmanuel Joseph**, called *Abbé Sieyès*. 1748–1836, French statesman, political theorist, and churchman, who became prominent during the Revolution following the publication of his pamphlet *Qu'est-ce que le tiers état?* (1789). He was instrumental in bringing Napoleon I to power (1799)

sift ⊙ *vb* **1** to sieve (a powdery substance) in order to remove the coarser particles **2** to examine (information or evidence) carefully to select what is important
WORD ORIGIN Old English *siftan*

sigh *vb* **1** to draw in and audibly let out a deep breath as an expression of sadness, tiredness, longing, or relief **2** to make a sound resembling this **3 sigh for** to long for **4** to say (something) with a sigh ▹ *n* **5** the act or sound of sighing
WORD ORIGIN Old English *sīcan*

sight ⊙ *n* **1** the ability to see; vision ▸ Related adjective: **visual 2** an instance of seeing **3** the range of vision: *the cemetery was out of sight* **4** anything that is seen **5** point of view; judgment: *nothing has changed in my sight* **6** *informal* anything unpleasant to see: *she looked a sight in the streetlamps* **7** a device for guiding the eye in aiming a gun or making an observation with an optical instrument **8** an aim or observation made with such a device **9 sights** anything worth seeing: *the great sights of Barcelona* **10 a sight** *informal* a great deal: *it's a sight warmer than in the hall* **11 a sight for sore eyes** a welcome sight **12 catch sight of** to glimpse **13 know someone by sight** to be able to recognize someone without having ever been introduced **14 lose sight of a** to be unable to see (something) any longer **b** to forget: *we lose sight of priorities* **15 on sight** as soon as someone or something is seen **16 set one's sights on** to have (a specified goal) in mind **17 sight unseen** without having seen the object concerned: *he would have taken*

THESAURUS

sidewalk *n* (*US & Canad*) = **pavement**, footpath (*Austral & NZ*)

sideways *adv* **1 = to the side**, laterally, crabwise **2 = indirectly**, obliquely ▹ *adj* **4 = sidelong**, side, slanted, oblique

siege *n* **1, 2 = blockade**, encirclement, besiegement

sift *vb* **1 = part**, filter, strain, separate, pan, bolt, riddle, sieve **2 = examine**, investigate, go through, research, screen, probe, analyse, work over, pore over, scrutinize

sight *n* **1 = vision**, eyes, eyesight, seeing, eye **3 = view**, field of vision, range of vision, eyeshot, viewing, ken, visibility **4 = spectacle**, show, scene, display, exhibition, vista, pageant **6** (*informal*) **= eyesore**, mess, spectacle, fright (*informal*), monstrosity, blot on the landscape (*informal*) ▹ *vb* **18 = spot**, see, observe, distinguish, perceive, make out, discern, behold

S

DICTIONARY

it sight unseen ▹*vb* **18** to see (someone or something) briefly or suddenly: *the two suspicious vessels were sighted* **19** to aim (a firearm) using the sight **WORD ORIGIN** Old English *sihth*

sighted *adj* not blind

sightless *adj* blind

sight-read *vb* **-reading, -read** to sing or play (music in a printed form) without previous preparation **sight-reading** *n*

sightscreen *n cricket* a large white screen placed near the boundary behind the bowler, which helps the batsman see the ball

sightseeing *n informal* visiting famous or interesting sights in a place **sightseer** *n*

Sigismund *n* 1368–1437, king of Hungary (1387–1437) and of Bohemia (1419–37); Holy Roman Emperor (1411–37). He helped to end the Great Schism in the Church; implicated in the death of Huss

Sigismund II *n* called *Sigismund Augustus* 1520–72, king of Poland (1548–72), who united Poland, Lithuania, and their dependencies by the Union of Lublin (1569)

sigma *n* **1** the 18th letter in the Greek alphabet (Σ, σ) **2** *maths* the symbol Σ, indicating summation

sign ❶ *n* **1** something that indicates a fact or condition that is not immediately or outwardly observable: *a sign of tension* **2** a gesture, mark, or symbol intended to convey an idea or information **3** a board or placard displayed in public and intended to advertise, inform, or warn **4** a conventional mark or symbol that has a specific meaning, for example £ for pounds **5** *maths* **a** any symbol used to indicate an operation: *a minus sign* **b** a symbol used to indicate whether a number or expression is positive or negative **6** a visible indication: *no sign of the enemy* **7** an omen **8** *med* any evidence of the presence of a disease or disorder **9** *astrol* ▸short for **sign of the zodiac** ▹*vb* **10** to write (one's name) on (a document or letter) to show its authenticity or one's agreement **11** to communicate using sign language **12** to make a sign to someone so as to convey an idea or information **13** to engage or be engaged by signing a contract: *he signed for another team* ▸See also **sign away, sign in,** etc. **WORD ORIGIN** Latin *signum*

Signac *n* **Paul** 1863–1935, French neoimpressionist painter, influenced by Seurat

signal ❶ *n* **1** any sign, gesture, sound, or action used to communicate information **2** anything that causes immediate action: *this is the signal for a detailed examination of the risk* **3 a** a variable voltage, current, or electromagnetic wave, by which information is conveyed through an electronic circuit **b** the information so conveyed ▹*adj* **4** *formal* very important: *a signal triumph for the government* ▹*vb* **-nalling, -nalled** or *US* **-naling, -naled 5** to communicate (information) by signal **signally** *adv* **WORD ORIGIN** Latin *signum* sign

signal box *n* a building from which railway signals are operated

signalman *n, pl* **-men** a railwayman in charge of the signals and points within a section

signatory (sig-na-tree) *n, pl* **-ries 1** a person, organization, or state that has signed a document such as a treaty ▹*adj* **2** having signed a document or treaty

signature *n* **1** a person's name written by himself or herself, used in signing something **2** a distinctive characteristic that identifies a person or animal **3** *music* a sign at the beginning of a piece to show key or time **4** *printing* a sheet of paper printed with several pages, which when folded becomes a section of a book **WORD ORIGIN** Latin *signare* to sign

signature tune *n* a piece of music used to introduce a particular television or radio programme

sign away *vb* to give up one's right to (something): *she will sign away all rights to these pictures*

signboard *n* a board carrying a sign or notice, often to advertise a business or product

signet *n* a small seal used to make documents official **WORD ORIGIN** Medieval Latin *signetum*

signet ring *n* a finger ring engraved with an initial or other emblem

significance ❶ *n* **1** the effect something is likely to have on other things: *an event of important significance in British history* **2** meaning: *the occult significance of the symbol*

significant ❶ *adj* **1** very important **2** having or expressing a meaning **significantly** *adv*

significant figures *pl n maths* **1** the figures of a number that express a magnitude to a specified degree of accuracy: *3.141 59 to four significant figures is 3.142* **2** the number of such figures: *3.142 has four significant figures*

signify ❶ *vb* **-fies, -fying, -fied 1** to indicate or suggest **2** to stand as a symbol or sign for: *a blue line on the map signified a river* **3** to be important **WORD ORIGIN** Latin *signum* a mark + *facere* to make

sign in *vb* **1** to sign a register on arrival at a place **2** to admit (a nonmember) to a club or institution as a guest by signing a register on his or her behalf

signing *n* a system of communication using hand and arm movements, such as one used by deaf people. Also called: **sign language**

sign off *vb* to announce the end of a radio or television programme

sign of the zodiac *n astrol* any of the 12 areas into which the zodiac is divided

sign on *vb* **1** *Austral & Brit* to register and report regularly at an unemployment-benefit office **2** to commit oneself to a job or activity by signing a form or contract

signor (see-nyor) *n* an Italian form of address equivalent to *sir* or *Mr*

signora (see-nyor-a) *n* an Italian form of address equivalent to *madam* or *Mrs*

Signorelli *n* **Luca** ?1441–1523, Italian painter, noted for his frescoes

S

THESAURUS

sign *n* **1, 6 = indication**, evidence, trace, mark, note, signal, suggestion, symptom, hint, proof, gesture, clue, token, manifestation, giveaway, vestige, spoor **2 = figure**, form, shape, outline **2, 4 = symbol**, mark, character, figure, device, representation, logo, badge, emblem, ensign, cipher **3 = notice**, board, warning, signpost, placard **7 = omen**, warning, portent, foreboding, presage, forewarning, writing on the wall, augury, auspice, wake-up call ▹*vb* **10 = autograph**, initial, inscribe, subscribe, set your hand to **12 = gesture**, indicate, signal, wave, beckon, gesticulate, use sign language

signal *n* **1 = sign**, gesture, indication, mark, note, evidence, expression, proof, token, indicator, manifestation **2 = cue**, sign, nod, prompting, go-ahead *(informal)*, reminder, green light

significance *n* **1 = importance**, import, consequence, matter, moment, weight, consideration, gravity, relevance, magnitude, impressiveness

significant *adj* **1 = important**, notable, serious, material, vital, critical, considerable, momentous, weighty, noteworthy **OPPOSITE:** insignificant **2 = meaningful**, expressive, eloquent, knowing, meaning, expressing, pregnant, indicative, suggestive **OPPOSITE:** meaningless

signify *vb* **1 = indicate**, show, mean, matter, suggest, announce, evidence, represent, express, imply, exhibit, communicate, intimate, stand for, proclaim, convey, be a sign of, symbolize, denote, connote, portend, betoken, flag up

DICTIONARY

Signoret *n* **Simone**, original name *Simone Kaminker* 1921–85, French stage and film actress, whose films include *La Ronde* (1950), *Casque d'Or* (1952), *Room at the Top* (1958), and *Ship of Fools* (1965): married the actor and singer Yves Montand (1921–91)

signorina (see-nyor-ee-na) *n* an Italian form of address equivalent to *madam* or *Miss*

sign out *vb* to sign a register to indicate that one is leaving a place

signpost *n* **1** a road sign displaying information, such as the distance to the next town **2** an indication as to how an event is likely to develop or advice on what course of action should be taken ▹ *vb* **3** to mark (the way) with signposts

sign up *vb* **1** to agree to do a job or course by signing a document **2 sign someone up** to hire (someone) officially to do a job **3** to enlist for military service

sik *adj Austral slang* excellent

Sikh (seek) *n* **1** a member of an Indian religion that teaches that there is only one God ▹ *adj* **2** of the Sikhs or their religious beliefs or customs **Sikhism** *n*
WORD ORIGIN Hindi: disciple

Sikorski *n* **Władysław** 1881–1943, Polish general and statesman: prime minister (1922–23) and prime minister of the Polish government in exile during World War II: died in an air crash

silage (sile-ij) *n* a fodder crop harvested while green and partially fermented in a silo

silence ❶ *n* **1** the state or quality of being silent **2** the absence of sound **3** refusal or failure to speak or communicate when expected: *he's broken his silence on the issue* ▹ *vb* **-lencing, -lenced 4** to cause (someone or something) to become silent **5** to put a stop to: *a way of silencing criticism*

silencer *n* any device designed to reduce noise, for example one fitted to the exhaust system of a motor vehicle or one fitted to the muzzle of a gun

silent ❶ *adj* **1** tending to speak very little **2** failing to speak or communicate when expected: *they remained silent as minutes passed* **3** producing no noise: *the silent room* **4** not spoken: *silent reproach* **5** (of a letter) used in the spelling of a word but not pronounced, such as the *k* in *know* **6** (of a film) having no soundtrack **silently** *adv*
WORD ORIGIN Latin *silere* to be quiet

silhouette ❶ *n* **1** the outline of a dark shape seen against a light background **2** an outline drawing, often a profile portrait, filled in with black ▹ *vb* **-etting, -etted 3** to show (something) in silhouette
WORD ORIGIN after E. de *Silhouette*, politician

silica *n* a hard glossy mineral, silicon dioxide, which occurs naturally as quartz and is used in the manufacture of glass
WORD ORIGIN Latin *silex* hard stone

silicate *n mineral* a compound of silicon, oxygen, and a metal

silicon *n* **1** *chem* a brittle non-metallic element: used in transistors, solar cells, and alloys. Symbol: Si ▹ *adj* **2** denoting an area of a country that contains much high-technology industry: *the Silicon Glen*
WORD ORIGIN from *silica*

silicon chip *n* ▸ same as **chip** (sense 3)

silicone *n chem* a tough synthetic material made from silicon and used in lubricants, paints, and resins

silicosis *n pathol* a lung disease caused by breathing in silica dust

silk *n* **1** the fine soft fibre produced by a silkworm **2** thread or fabric made from this fibre **3 silks** clothing made of this **4** *Brit* **a** the gown worn by a Queen's (or King's) Counsel **b** *informal* a Queen's (or King's) Counsel **c take silk** to become a Queen's (or King's) Counsel
WORD ORIGIN Old English *sioloc*

silken *adj* **1** made of silk **2** *literary* smooth and soft: *her silken hair*

silk-screen printing *n* ▸ same as **screen process**

silkworm *n* a caterpillar that spins a cocoon of silk

silky *adj* **silkier, silkiest 1** soft, smooth, and shiny **2** (of a voice or manner) smooth and elegant **silkiness** *n*

sill *n* **1** a shelf at the bottom of a window, either inside or outside a room **2** the lower horizontal part of a window or door frame
WORD ORIGIN Old English *syll*

Sillanpää *n* **Frans Eemil** 1888–1964, Finnish writer, noted for his novels *Meek Heritage* (1919) and *The Maid Silja* (1931): Nobel prize for literature 1939

Sillitoe *n* **Alan** born 1928, British novelist. His best-known works include *Saturday Night and Sunday Morning* (1958) and *The Loneliness of the Long Distance Runner* (1959)

Sills *n* **Beverley**, original name *Belle Silverman*. 1929–2007, US soprano: director of the New York City Opera (1979–89)

silly ❶ *adj* **-lier, -liest 1** behaving in a foolish or childish way **2** *old-fashioned* unable to think sensibly, as if from a blow **3** *cricket* (of a fielding position) near the batsman's wicket: *silly mid-off* ▹ *n, pl* **-lies 4** *informal* a foolish person **silliness** *n*
WORD ORIGIN Old English *sǣlig* (unattested) happy

silo *n, pl* **-los 1** an airtight pit or tower in which silage or grain is made and stored **2** an underground structure in which missile systems are sited for protection
WORD ORIGIN Spanish

Silone *n* **Ignazio** 1900–78, Italian writer, noted for his humanitarian socialistic novels, *Fontamara* (1933) and *Bread and Wine* (1937)

silt *n* **1** a fine sediment of mud or clay deposited by moving water ▹ *vb* **2 silt up** to fill or choke up with silt: *the channels have been silted up*
WORD ORIGIN probably Old Norse

Silurian (sile-yoor-ee-an) *adj geol* of the period of geological time about 425 million years ago, during which fishes first appeared
WORD ORIGIN after *Silures*, a Welsh tribe who opposed the Romans

silvan *adj* ▸ same as **sylvan**

silver *n* **1** a precious greyish-white metallic element: used in jewellery, tableware, and coins. Symbol: Ag **2** a coin or coins made of silver **3** any household articles made of silver **4** ▸ short for **silver medal** ▹ *adj* **5** greyish-white: *silver hair* **6** (of anniversaries) the 25th in a series: *Silver Jubilee; silver wedding* ▹ *vb* **7** to coat with silver or a silvery substance: *a*

S

THESAURUS

silence *n* **1, 2 = quiet**, peace, calm, hush, lull, stillness, quiescence, noiselessness **OPPOSITE:** noise **3 = reticence**, dumbness, taciturnity, speechlessness, muteness, uncommunicativeness **OPPOSITE:** speech ▹ *vb* **4 = quieten**, still, quiet, cut off, subdue, stifle, cut short, quell, muffle, deaden, strike dumb **OPPOSITE:** make louder

silent *adj* **1 = uncommunicative**, quiet, taciturn, tongue-tied, unspeaking, nonvocal, not talkative **2 = mute**, dumb, speechless, wordless, mum, struck dumb, voiceless, unspeaking **OPPOSITE:** noisy **3 = quiet**, still, hushed, soundless, noiseless, muted, stilly *(poetic)* **OPPOSITE:** loud

silhouette *n* **1 = outline**, form, shape, profile, delineation ▹ *vb* **3 = outline**, delineate, etch

silly *adj* **1a = stupid**, ridiculous, absurd, daft, inane, childish, immature, senseless, frivolous, preposterous, giddy, goofy *(informal)*, idiotic, dozy *(Brit informal)*, fatuous, witless, puerile, brainless, asinine, dumb-ass *(slang)*, dopy *(slang)* **OPPOSITE:** clever **1b = foolish**, stupid, unwise, inappropriate, rash, irresponsible, reckless, foolhardy, idiotic, thoughtless, imprudent, inadvisable **OPPOSITE:** sensible

company that silvers their own mirrors **8** to cause (something) to become silvery in colour: *the sun silvered the tarmac*
WORD ORIGIN Old English *siolfor*

silverbeet *n Austral & NZ* a beet of Australia and New Zealand with edible spinach-like leaves

silver birch *n* a tree with silvery-white peeling bark

Silverchair *pl n* Australian rock group (formed 1994): comprising Daniel Johns (born 1979; vocals, guitar), Ben Gillies (born 1979, drums) and Chris Joannou (born 1979, bass guitar); their albums include *Frogstomp* (1995) and *Young Modern* (2007)

silverfish *n, pl* **-fish** *or* **-fishes 1** a small wingless silver-coloured insect **2** a silver-coloured fish

silver goal *n soccer* (in certain competitions) a goal scored in a full half of extra time, counting as the winner if it is the only goal scored in the full half or full period of extra time

silver lining *n* a hopeful side of an otherwise desperate or unhappy situation

silver medal *n* a medal of silver awarded to a competitor who comes second in a contest or race

silver plate *n* **1** a thin layer of silver deposited on a base metal **2** articles, such as tableware, made of silver plate **silver-plate** *vb*

silver screen *n informal* films collectively or the film industry

silverside *n* a cut of beef from below the rump and above the leg

silversmith *n* a craftsman who makes or repairs items made of silver

silver thaw *n Canad* **1** a freezing rainstorm **2** ▸ same as **glitter** (sense 7)

silverware *n* items, such as tableware, made of or plated with silver

silvery *adj* **1** having the appearance or colour of silver: *her silvery eyes* **2** having a clear ringing sound: *a cascade of silvery notes*

silviculture *n* the cultivation of forest trees
WORD ORIGIN Latin *silva* woodland + CULTURE

sim *n* a computer game that simulates an activity such as flying or playing a sport

Si-ma Qian *or* **Ssu-ma Ch'ien** *n* ?145–?85 BC, Chinese historian, author of the *Shih-chi*, a history of China from earliest times to the 2nd century BC, usually considered the greatest historical work in Chinese

Simenon *n* **Georges** 1903–89, Belgian novelist. He wrote over two hundred novels, including the detective series featuring Maigret

Simeon Stylites *n* **Saint** ?390–459 AD, Syrian monk, first of the ascetics who lived on pillars. Feast day: Jan 5 or Sept 1

simian *adj* **1** of or resembling a monkey or ape ▹*n* **2** a monkey or ape
WORD ORIGIN Latin *simia* an ape

similar ❶ *adj* **1** alike but not identical **2** *geom* (of two or more figures) different in size or position, but with exactly the same shape **similarity** *n* **similarly** *adv*
WORD ORIGIN Latin *similis*

simile (sim-ill-ee) *n* a figure of speech that likens one thing to another of a different category, introduced by *as* or *like*
WORD ORIGIN Latin: something similar

similitude *n formal* likeness; similarity

simmer ❶ *vb* **1** to cook (food) gently at just below boiling point **2** (of violence or conflict) to threaten to break out: *revolt simmering among rural MPs* ▹*n* **3** the state of simmering
WORD ORIGIN perhaps imitative

simmer down ❶ *vb informal* to calm down after being angry

simnel cake *n Brit* a fruit cake with marzipan, traditionally eaten during Lent or at Easter
WORD ORIGIN Latin *simila* fine flour

Simon *n* **1** the original name of (Saint) **Peter** (sense 1) **2** *New Testament* **a** ▸ See **Simon Zelotes b** Also: **Simon the Tanner** a relative of Jesus, who may have been identical with Simon Zelotes (Matthew 13:55) **c** Also: **Simon the Tanner** a Christian of Joppa with whom Peter stayed (Acts of the Apostles 9:43) **3 John (Allsebrook)**, 1st Viscount Simon. 1873–1954, British statesman and lawyer. He was Liberal home secretary (1915–16) and, as a leader of the National Liberals, foreign secretary (1931–35), home secretary (1935–37), Chancellor of the Exchequer (1937–40), and Lord Chancellor (1940–45) **4 (Marvin) Neil** born 1927, US dramatist and librettist, whose plays include *Barefoot in the Park* (1963), *California Suite* (1976), *Biloxi Blues* (1985), *Lost in Yonkers* (1990), and *London Suite* (1995): many have been made into films **5 Paul** born 1942, US pop singer and songwriter. His albums include: with Art Garfunkel (born 1941), *The Sounds of Silence* (1966), and *Bridge over Troubled Water* (1970); and, solo, *Graceland* (1986), *The Rhythm of the Saints* (1990), and *You're The One* (2000)

Simonides *n* ?556–?468 BC, Greek lyric poet and epigrammatist, noted for his odes to victory

simony (sime-on-ee) *n Christianity* the practice of buying or selling Church benefits such as pardons
WORD ORIGIN after *Simon Magus*, a biblical sorcerer who tried to buy magical powers

simoom *n* a hot suffocating sand-laden desert wind
WORD ORIGIN Arabic *samūm* poisonous

simper *vb* **1** to smile in a silly and mannered way **2** to say (something) with a simper ▹*n* **3** a simpering smile **simpering** *adj*
WORD ORIGIN origin unknown

simple ❶ *adj* **1** easy to understand or do: *in simple English; simple exercises* **2** plain and not elaborate: *a simple red skirt; a simple answer* **3** not combined or complex: *simple diagnostic equipment* **4** leading an uncomplicated life: *I am a simple man myself* **5** sincere or frank: *a simple apology* **6** of humble background: *the simple country girl* **7** *informal* mentally retarded **8** straightforward: *a simple matter of choice* **9** *music* denoting a time where the number of beats per bar may be two, three, or four **simplicity** *n*
WORD ORIGIN Latin *simplex* plain

S

THESAURUS

similar *adj* **1 = alike**, uniform, resembling, corresponding, comparable, much the same, homogeneous, of a piece, homogenous, cut from the same cloth, congruous **OPPOSITE:** different

simmer *vb* **1 = bubble**, stew, boil gently, seethe, cook gently **2 = fume**, seethe, smoulder, burn, smart, rage, boil, be angry, see red *(informal)*, be tense, be agitated, be uptight *(informal)*

simmer down *vb (informal)* **= calm down**, grow quieter, control yourself, unwind *(informal)*, contain yourself, collect yourself, cool off *or* down, get down off your high horse *(informal)*

simple *adj* **1a = uncomplicated**, clear, plain, understandable, coherent, lucid, recognizable, unambiguous, comprehensible, intelligible, uninvolved **OPPOSITE:** complicated **1b = easy**, straightforward, not difficult, light, elementary, manageable, effortless, painless, uncomplicated, undemanding, easy-peasy *(slang)* **2 = plain**, natural, basic, classic, severe, Spartan, uncluttered, unadorned, unfussy, unembellished, bare-bones **OPPOSITE:** elaborate **3 = pure**, mere, sheer, unalloyed **4,5 = artless**, innocent, naive, natural, frank, green, sincere, simplistic, unaffected, childlike, unpretentious, unsophisticated, ingenuous, guileless **OPPOSITE:** sophisticated **6 = unpretentious**, modest, humble, homely, lowly, rustic, uncluttered, unfussy, unembellished **OPPOSITE:** fancy

DICTIONARY

simple fraction *n maths* a fraction in which the numerator and denominator are both whole numbers

simple fracture *n* a fracture in which the broken bone does not pierce the skin

simple interest *n finance* interest paid only on the original amount of a debt

simple-minded *adj* **1** (of people) naive and unsophisticated **2** (of opinions or explanations) not taking the complexity of an issue or subject into account **simple-mindedness** *n*

simple sentence *n* a sentence consisting of a single main clause

simpleton *n* a foolish or stupid person

simplify ❶ *vb* **-fies, -fying, -fied 1** to make (something) less complicated **2** *maths* to reduce (an equation or fraction) to its simplest form **simplification** *n*
WORD ORIGIN Latin *simplus* simple + *facere* to make

simplistic *adj* (of an opinion or interpretation) too simple or naive

simply ❶ *adv* **1** in a simple manner: *an interesting book, simply written* **2** merely; just: *he's simply too slow* **3** absolutely: *a simply enormous success*

Simpson *n* **1** Sir **James Young** 1811–70, Scottish obstetrician, who pioneered the use of chloroform as an anaesthetic **2 Wallis** (**Warfield**) ▸ See **Edward VIII**

simulate ❶ *vb* **-lating, -lated 1** to pretend to feel or perform (an emotion or action); imitate: *I tried to simulate anger* **2** to imitate the conditions of (a situation), as in carrying out an experiment: *we can then simulate global warming* **3** to have the appearance of: *the wood had been painted to simulate stone* **simulated** *adj* **simulation** *n*
WORD ORIGIN Latin *simulare* to copy

simulator *n* a device that simulates specific conditions for the purposes of research or training: *a flight simulator*

simultaneous ❶ *adj* occurring or existing at the same time **simultaneously** *adv* **simultaneity** *n*
WORD ORIGIN Latin *simul* at the same time

simultaneous equations *pl n maths* a set of equations that are all satisfied by the same values of the variables, the number of variables being equal to the number of equations

sin[1] ❶ *n* **1** the breaking of a religious or moral law **2** any offence against a principle or standard **3 live in sin** *old-fashioned, informal* (of an unmarried couple) to live together ▹ *vb* **sinning, sinned 4** to commit a sin **sinner** *n*
WORD ORIGIN Old English *synn*

sin[2] *maths* sine

SIN (in Canada) Social Insurance Number

sin bin *n slang* (in ice hockey etc.) the area in which players must sit for a specified period after committing a serious foul

since *prep* **1** during the period of time after: *one of their worst winters since 1945* ▹ *conj* **2** continuously from the time given: *they've been standing in line ever since she arrived* **3** for the reason that; because ▹ *adv* **4** from that time: *I have often been asked since*
WORD ORIGIN Old English *siththan*

sincere ❶ *adj* genuine and honest: *sincere concern* **sincerely** *adv* **sincerity** *n*
WORD ORIGIN Latin *sincerus*

Sinclair *n* **1** Sir **Clive** (**Marles**) born 1940, British electronics engineer, inventor, and entrepreneur, who produced such electronic goods as pocket calculators and some of the first home computers; however, the Sinclair C5, a small light electric vehicle for one person, proved a commercial failure **2 Upton** (**Beall**) 1878–1968, US novelist, whose *The Jungle* (1906) exposed the working and sanitary conditions of the Chicago meat-packing industry and prompted the passage of food inspection laws

sine *n* (in trigonometry) the ratio of the length of the opposite side to that of the hypotenuse in a right-angled triangle
WORD ORIGIN Latin *sinus* a bend

sinecure (sin-ee-cure) *n* a paid job that involves very little work or responsibility
WORD ORIGIN Latin *sine* without + *cura* care

sine die (sin-ay dee-ay) *adv* without fixing a day for future action or meeting
WORD ORIGIN Latin, literally: without a day

sine qua non (sin-ay kwah non) *n* an essential requirement
WORD ORIGIN Latin, literally: without which not

sinew *n* **1** *anat* a tough fibrous cord connecting muscle to bone **2** *literary* physical strength
WORD ORIGIN Old English *sinu, seonu*

sinewy *adj* lean and muscular

sinful *adj* **1** having committed or tending to commit sin: *I am a sinful man* **2** being a sin; wicked: *sinful acts*

sing ❶ *vb* **singing, sang, sung 1** to produce musical sounds with the voice **2** to perform (a song) **3** (of certain birds and insects) to make musical calls **4 sing of** to tell a story in song about: *the minstrels sang of courtly love* **5** to make a humming, ringing, or whistling sound: *the arrow sang past his ear* **6** (of one's ears) to be filled with a continuous ringing sound **7** to bring (someone) to a given state by singing: *I sang him to sleep* **8** *slang chiefly US* to act as an informer ▸ See also **sing out** › **singer** *n* **singing** *adj, n*
WORD ORIGIN Old English *singan*

sing. singular

singe *vb* **singeing, singed 1** to burn slightly without setting alight; scorch: *it singed his sheepskin* ▹ *n* **2** a slight burn
WORD ORIGIN Old English *sengan*

Singer *n* **1 Isaac Bashevis** 1904–91, US writer of Yiddish novels and short stories; born in Poland. His works include *Satan in Goray* (1935), *The Family Moscat* (1950), the autobiographical *In my Father's Court* (1966), and *The King*

S

THESAURUS

simplify *vb* **1 = make simpler**, facilitate, streamline, disentangle, dumb down, make intelligible, reduce to essentials, declutter

simply *adv* **1a = clearly**, straightforwardly, directly, plainly, intelligibly, unaffectedly **1b = plainly**, naturally, modestly, with restraint, unpretentiously, without any elaboration **2 = just**, only, merely, purely, solely **3a = totally**, really, completely, absolutely, altogether, wholly, utterly, unreservedly **3b = without doubt**, surely, certainly, definitely, unquestionably, undeniably, unmistakably, beyond question, beyond a shadow of (a) doubt

simulate *vb* **1 = pretend**, act, feign, affect, assume, put on, reproduce, imitate, sham, fabricate, counterfeit, make believe

simultaneous *adj* **= coinciding**, concurrent, contemporaneous, coincident, synchronous, happening at the same time

sin[1] *n* **1 = wickedness**, wrong, evil, crime, error, trespass, immorality, transgression, iniquity, sinfulness, unrighteousness, ungodliness **2 = crime**, offence, misdemeanour, error, wrongdoing, misdeed, transgression, act of evil, guilt ▹ *vb* **4 = transgress**, offend, lapse, err, trespass *(archaic)*, fall from grace, go astray, commit a sin, do wrong

sincere *adj* **= honest**, genuine, real, true, serious, natural, earnest, frank, open, straightforward, candid, unaffected, no-nonsense, heartfelt, upfront *(informal)*, bona fide, wholehearted, dinkum *(Austral & NZ informal)*, artless, guileless, unfeigned
OPPOSITE: false

sing *vb* **1, 2 = croon**, carol, chant, warble, yodel, pipe, vocalize **3 = trill**, chirp, warble, make melody

single *adj* **1 = one**, sole, lone, solitary,

of the Fields (1989): Nobel prize for literature 1978 **2 Isaac Merrit** 1811–75, US inventor, who originated and developed an improved chain-stitch sewing machine (1852)

Singhalese *n, pl* **-lese,** *adj* ▸same as **Sinhalese**

singing telegram *n* **1** a service by which a person is employed to present greetings to someone on a special occasion by singing **2** the greetings presented in this way **3** the person who presents the greetings

single ● *adj* **1** existing alone; solitary: *the cottage's single chimney* **2** distinct from others of the same kind: *every single housing society* **3** designed for one user: *a single room* **4** unmarried **5** even one: *there was not a single bathroom* **6** (of a flower) having only one circle of petals **7 single combat** a duel or fight involving two individuals ▹*n* **8** a hotel bedroom for one person **9** a gramophone record, CD, or cassette with a short recording of music on it **10** *cricket* a hit from which one run is scored **11 a** *Brit* a pound note or coin **b** *US & Canad* a dollar bill **12** a ticket valid for a one-way journey only ▹*vb* **-gling, -gled 13 single out** to select from a group of people or things: *the judge had singled him out for praise* ▸See also **singles**
WORD ORIGIN Old French *sengle*

single-breasted *adj* (of a jacket or coat) having the fronts overlapping only slightly and with one row of buttons

single cream *n Brit* cream which has a relatively low fat content and does not thicken when beaten

single-decker *n Brit informal* a bus with only one passenger deck

single entry *n* a book-keeping system in which all transactions are entered in one account only

single file *n* a line of people, one behind the other

single-handed *adj* **1** alone; unaided: *a single-handed raid on the enemy camp* ▹*adv* **2** unaided or working alone: *she had to take on the world single-handed*
single-handedly *adv*

single-minded *adj* having one purpose or aim only; dedicated **single-mindedly** *adv* **single-mindedness** *n*

single-parent family *n* a family consisting of one parent and his or her child or children living together, the other parent being dead or permanently absent

singles *pl n sport* a match played with one person on each side

singles bar *n* a bar that is a social meeting place for single people

singlet *n Brit & NZ* a man's sleeveless vest

single ticket *n* ▸same as **single** (sense 12)

singleton *n cards* the only card of a particular suit held by a player

singly ● *adv* one at a time; one by one

sing out *vb* to call out loudly

sing-song *n* **1** an informal group singing session ▹*adj* **2** (of a voice) having a repetitive rise and fall in tone

singular ● *adj* **1** *grammar* (of a word or form) denoting only one person or thing: *a singular noun* **2** remarkable; extraordinary: *one of the singular achievements* **3** unusual; odd: *a lovable but very singular old woman* ▹*n* **4** *grammar* the singular form of a word **singularity** *n* **singularly** *adv*
WORD ORIGIN Latin *singularis* single

Sinhalese *or* **Singhalese** *n* **1** *pl* **-lese** a member of a people living mainly in Sri Lanka **2** the language of this people ▹*adj* **3** of this people ▸See also **Sri Lankan**

sinister ● *adj* **1** threatening or suggesting evil or harm: *a sinister conspiracy* **2** *heraldry* of, on, or starting from the bearer's left side
WORD ORIGIN Latin: on the left-hand side, considered by Roman augurs to be the unlucky one

sink ● *vb* **sinking, sank, sunk** *or* **sunken 1** to submerge (in liquid) **2** to cause (a ship) to submerge by attacking it with bombs, torpedoes, etc. **3** to appear to descend towards or below the horizon **4** to make or become lower in amount or value: *sterling sank to a record low against the Deutschmark* **5** to move or fall into a lower position, esp. due to tiredness or weakness: *she sank back in her chair* **6 sink into** to pass into a lower state or condition, esp. an unpleasant one: *to sink into debt* **7** (of a voice) to become quieter **8** to become weaker in health **9** to dig (something sharp) into a solid object: *she sank her teeth into the steak* **10** *informal* to drink (a number of alcoholic drinks) **11** to dig, drill, or excavate (a hole or shaft) **12** to drive (a stake) into the ground **13 sink in** *or* **into** to invest (money) in (a venture) **14** *golf, snooker* to hit (the ball) into the hole or pocket: *he finally sank the shot for a bogey* ▹*n* **15** a fixed basin in a kitchen or bathroom, with a water supply and drainpipe ▹*adj* **16** *informal* (of a housing estate or school) deprived or having low standards of achievement
WORD ORIGIN Old English *sincan*

sinker *n* a weight attached to a fishing line or net to cause it to sink in water

sink in *vb* (of a fact) to become fully understood: *the euphoria started to wear off as the implications of it all sank in*

sinking fund *n* a fund set aside to repay a long-term debt

Sinn Féin (shin fane) *n* an Irish Republican political movement linked to the IRA
WORD ORIGIN Irish Gaelic: we ourselves

Sino- *combining form* Chinese: *Sino-European; Sinology*
WORD ORIGIN Late Latin *Sinae* the Chinese

Sinology (sine-ol-a-jee) *n* the study of Chinese history, language, and culture **Sinologist** *n*

sinuous *adj literary* **1** full of curves **2** having smooth twisting movements: *sinuous dances* **sinuosity** *n*
WORD ORIGIN Latin *sinuosus* winding

sinus (sine-uss) *n anat* a hollow space in bone, such as one in the skull opening into a nasal cavity
WORD ORIGIN Latin: a curve

sinusitis *n* inflammation of the

S

THESAURUS

only, only one, unique, singular **2 = individual**, particular, separate, distinct **3 = separate**, individual, exclusive, undivided, unshared **4 = unmarried**, free, unattached, a bachelor, unwed, a spinster **13 single something** *or* **someone out = pick**, choose, select, separate, distinguish, fix on, set apart, winnow, put on one side, pick on *or* out, flag up

singly *adv* **= one by one**, individually, one at a time, separately, one after the other

singular *adj* **1** *(grammar)* **= single**, individual **2 = remarkable**, unique, extraordinary, outstanding, exceptional, rare, notable, eminent, uncommon, conspicuous, prodigious, unparalleled, noteworthy **OPPOSITE:** ordinary **3 = unusual**, odd, strange, extraordinary, puzzling, curious, peculiar, eccentric, out-of-the-way, queer, oddball *(informal)*, atypical, wacko *(slang)*, outré, daggy *(Austral & NZ informal)* **OPPOSITE:** conventional

sinister *adj* **1 = threatening**, evil, menacing, forbidding, dire, ominous, malign, disquieting, malignant, malevolent, baleful, injurious, bodeful **OPPOSITE:** reassuring

sink *vb* **1 = go down**, founder, go under, submerge, capsize **4 = fall**, drop, decline, slip, plunge, plummet, subside, relapse, abate, retrogress **5 = slump**, drop, flop, collapse, droop **7 = drop**, fall **8 = decline**, die, fade, fail, flag, weaken, diminish, decrease, deteriorate, decay, worsen, dwindle, lessen, degenerate, depreciate, go downhill *(informal)* **OPPOSITE:** improve **11 = dig**, bore, drill, drive, lay, put down, excavate

DICTIONARY

membrane lining a sinus, esp. a nasal sinus

Sioux (soo) *n* **1** *pl* **Sioux** a member of a group of Native American peoples, formerly living over a wide area from Lake Michigan to the Rocky Mountains **2** any of the languages of these peoples

sip ❶ *vb* **sipping, sipped 1** to drink (a liquid) in small mouthfuls ▹*n* **2** an amount sipped **3** an instance of sipping
WORD ORIGIN probably from Low German *sippen*

siphon *or* **syphon** *n* **1** a tube which uses air pressure to draw liquid from a container **2** ▸same as **soda siphon** ▹*vb* **3 siphon off a** to draw (liquid) off through a siphon **b** to redirect (resources or money), esp. dishonestly, into other projects or bank accounts
WORD ORIGIN Greek

Siqueiros *n* **David Alfaro** 1896–1974, Mexican painter, noted for his murals expressing a revolutionary message

sir *n* a polite term of address for a man
WORD ORIGIN variant of SIRE

Sir *n* a title placed before the name of a knight or baronet: *Sir David Attenborough*

Siraj-ud-daula *n* ?1728–57, Indian leader who became the Great Mogul's deputy in Bengal (1756); opponent of English colonization. He captured Calcutta (1756) from the English and many of his prisoners suffocated in a crowded room that became known as the Black Hole of Calcutta. He was defeated (1757) by a group of Indian nobles in alliance with Robert Clive

sire *n* **1** a male parent of a horse or other domestic animal **2** *archaic* a respectful form of address used to a king ▹*vb* **siring, sired 3** to father
WORD ORIGIN Old French

siren *n* **1** a device that gives out a loud wailing sound as a warning or signal **2 Siren** *Greek myth* a sea nymph whose singing lured sailors to destruction on the rocks **3** a woman who is attractive but dangerous to men
WORD ORIGIN Greek *seirēn*

sirloin *n* a prime cut of beef from the upper part of the loin
WORD ORIGIN Old French *surlonge*

sirocco *n, pl* **-cos** a hot stifling wind blowing from N Africa into S Europe
WORD ORIGIN Italian

sis[1] *n informal* ▸short for **sister**

sis[2] *or* **sies** (siss) *interj S African informal* an exclamation of disgust
WORD ORIGIN Afrikaans

sisal (size-al) *n* a stiff fibre obtained from a Mexican plant and used for making rope
WORD ORIGIN after *Sisal*, a port in Mexico

siskin *n* a yellow-and-black finch
WORD ORIGIN Middle Dutch *sīseken*

Sisley *n* **Alfred** 1839–99, French painter, esp. of landscapes; one of the originators of impressionism

Sismondi *n* **Jean Charles Léonard Simonde de** 1773–1842, Swiss historian and economist. His *Histoire des républiques italiennes du moyen âge* (1807–18) contributed to the movement for Italian unification

sissy *or* **cissy** *n, pl* **-sies 1** an effeminate, weak, or cowardly person ▹*adj* **2** effeminate, weak, or cowardly
WORD ORIGIN from SIS[1]

sister *n* **1** a woman or girl having the same parents as another person **2** a female fellow member of a group, race, or profession **3** a female nurse in charge of a ward **4** *chiefly RC church* a nun ▹*adj* **5** of the same class, origin, or design, as another: *its sister paper*
WORD ORIGIN Old English *sweostor*

sisterhood *n* **1** the state of being sisters or like sisters **2** a religious group of women **3** a group of women united by a common interest or belief

sister-in-law *n, pl* **sisters-in-law 1** the sister of one's husband or wife **2** one's brother's wife

sisterly *adj* of or like a sister; affectionate

Siswati *n* a language of Swaziland

sit ❶ *vb* **sitting, sat 1** to rest one's body upright on the buttocks: *she had to sit on the ground* **2** to cause (someone) to rest in such a position: *they sat their grandfather in the shade* **3** (of an animal) to rest with the rear part of its body lowered to the ground **4** (of a bird) to perch or roost **5 sit on** (of a bird) to cover its eggs so as to hatch them **6** to be located: *the bank sits in the middle of the village* **7** to pose for a painting or photograph **8** to occupy a seat in some official capacity: *no police representatives will sit on the committee* **9** (of a parliament or court) to be in session **10** to remain unused: *his car sat in the garage* **11** (of clothes) to fit or hang in a certain way: *that dress sits well on you* **12** to take (an examination): *he's sitting his finals* **13** (*in combination*) to look after a specified person or thing for someone else: *is someone going to dog-sit for you?* **14 sit for** *chiefly Brit* to be a candidate for (a qualification): *he sat for a degree in medicine* **15 sit tight** *informal* **a** to wait patiently **b** to maintain one's position firmly ▸See also **sit back, sit down**, etc.
WORD ORIGIN Old English *sittan*

sitar *n* an Indian stringed musical instrument with a long neck and a rounded body
WORD ORIGIN Hindi

sit back *vb* to relax or be passive when action should be taken: *we can't just sit back and let this dreadful situation continue*

sitcom *n informal* (on television or radio) a comedy series involving the same characters in various everyday situations: *yet another unfunny sitcom set in Liverpool*

sit down *vb* **1** to adopt or cause (someone) to adopt a sitting position **2 sit down under** to suffer (insults or humiliations) without resistance ▹*n* **sit-down 3** a short rest sitting down ▹*adj* **sit-down 4** (of a meal) eaten while sitting down at a table

sit-down strike *n* a strike in which workers refuse to leave their place of employment until a settlement is reached

site ❶ *n* **1** the piece of ground where something was, is, or is intended to be located: *a building site; a car park is to be built on the site of a Roman fort* **2** ▸same as **website** ▹*vb* **siting, sited 3** to locate (something) on a specific site
WORD ORIGIN Latin *situs* position

Sithole *n* **Ndabaningi** 1920–2000, Zimbabwean clergyman and politician; leader of the Zimbabwe African National Union (1963–74). He was one of the negotiators of the internal settlement (1978) to pave the way for Black majority rule in Rhodesia (now Zimbabwe)

sit-in *n* **1** a protest in which the demonstrators sit in a public place and refuse to move ▹*vb* **sit in 2 sit in for** to stand in as a substitute for (someone) **3 sit in on** to be present at (a meeting) as an observer

sitka spruce *n* a tall North American spruce tree, now often grown in Britain
WORD ORIGIN after *Sitka*, a town in Alaska

sit on *vb informal* to delay action on: *they are sitting on their information*

THESAURUS

sip *vb* **1 = drink**, taste, sample, sup ▹*n* **2 = swallow**, mouthful, swig, drop, taste, thimbleful

sit *vb* **1 = take a seat**, perch, settle down, be seated, take the weight off your feet **2 = place**, set, put, position, rest, lay, settle, deposit, situate **8 = be a member of**, serve on, have a seat on, preside on **9 = convene**, meet, assemble, officiate, be in session

site *n* **1a = area**, ground, plot, patch, tract **1b = location**, place, setting, point, position, situation, spot, whereabouts, locus ▹*vb* **3 = locate**, put, place, set, position, establish, install, situate

situation *n* **1a = position**, state, case, condition, circumstances, equation,

DICTIONARY

sit out *vb* **1** to endure to the end: *just sit it out, and it will pass eventually* **2** to take no part in (a dance or game)

sitter *n* **1** a person posing for his or her portrait or photograph **2** ▸ same as **baby-sitter** **3** (*in combination*) a person who looks after a specified person or thing for someone else: *a house-sitter*

Sitter *n* **Willem de** 1872–1934, Dutch astronomer, who calculated the size of the universe and conceived of it as expanding

sitting *n* **1** a continuous period of being seated at some activity: *you may not be able to complete it in one sitting* **2** one of the times when a meal is served, when there is not enough space for everyone to eat at the same time: *the second sitting* **3** a period of posing for a painting or photograph **4** a meeting of an official body to conduct business ▹ *adj* **5** current: *a sitting member of Congress* **6** seated: *a sitting position*

sitting duck *n* *informal* a person or thing in a defenceless or vulnerable position

sitting room *n* a room in a house or flat where people sit and relax

sitting tenant *n* a tenant occupying a house or flat

situate *vb* **-ating, -ated** *formal* to place
WORD ORIGIN Late Latin *situare* to position

situation ❶ *n* **1 a** state of affairs **b** a complex or critical state of affairs **2** location and surroundings **3** social or financial circumstances **4** a position of employment

situation comedy *n* ▸ same as **sitcom**

sit up *vb* **1** to raise oneself from a lying position into a sitting one **2** to remain out of bed until a late hour **3** *informal* to become suddenly interested: *make the world sit up and take notice* ▹ *n* **sit-up 4** a physical exercise in which the body is brought into a sitting position from one of lying on the back

Sitwell *n* **1** Dame **Edith** 1887–1964, English poet and critic, noted esp. for her collection *Façade* (1922) **2** her brother, Sir **Osbert** 1892–1969, English writer, best known for his five autobiographical books (1944–50) **3** his brother, Sir **Sacheverell** 1897–1988, English poet and writer of books on art, architecture, music, and travel

SI unit *n* any of the units (metre, kilogram, second, ampere, kelvin, candela, mole, and those derived from them) adopted for international use under the Système International d'Unités, now employed for all scientific and most technical purposes

Siva *n* a Hindu god, the Destroyer

Sivaji *n* 1627–80, Indian king (1674–80), who led an uprising of Hindus against Muslim rule and founded the Masatha kingdom

six *n* **1** the cardinal number that is the sum of one and five **2** a numeral, 6 or VI, representing this number **3** something representing or consisting of six units **4** *cricket* a score of six runs, obtained by hitting the ball so that it crosses the boundary without bouncing **5 at sixes and sevens** in a state of confusion **6 knock someone for six** *informal* to upset or overwhelm someone completely **7 six of one and half a dozen of the other** a situation in which there is no real difference between the alternatives ▹ *adj* **8** amounting to six: *six days* **sixth** *adj, n*
WORD ORIGIN Old English *siex*

sixfold *adj* **1** having six times as many or as much **2** composed of six parts ▹ *adv* **3** by six times as many or as much

Six Nations Championship *n* *rugby union* an annual competition involving national sides representing England, France, Ireland, Italy, Scotland, and Wales

six-pack *n* *informal* **1** a package containing six units, esp. six cans of beer **2** a highly developed set of abdominal muscles in a man

sixpence *n* (formerly) a small British, Australian & New Zealand coin worth six old pennies, or 2½ pence

six-pointer *n* *informal* a football match between two teams in similar positions in the league table, which gains the winning team three points and denies the losing team three points

six-shooter *n* *US informal* a revolver that fires six shots without reloading

sixteen *n* **1** the cardinal number that is the sum of ten and six **2** a numeral, 16 or XVI, representing this number **3** something representing or consisting of sixteen units ▹ *adj* **4** amounting to sixteen: *sixteen years* **sixteenth** *adj, n*

sixth form *n* (in England and Wales) the most senior form in a secondary school, in which pupils over sixteen may take A levels or retake GCSEs **sixth-former** *n*

sixth sense *n* the supposed ability of knowing something instinctively without having any evidence for it

Sixtus IV *n* original name *Francesco della Rovere*. 1414–84, Italian ecclesiastic; pope (1471–84). Notorious for his nepotism and political intrigue, he was also a patron of the arts and commissioned the building (1473–81) of the Sistine Chapel

Sixtus V *n* original name *Felice Peretti* 1520–90, Italian ecclesiastic; pope (1585–90). He is noted for vigorous administrative reforms that contributed to the Counter-Reformation

sixty *n, pl* **-ties 1** the cardinal number that is the product of ten and six **2** a numeral, 60 or LX, representing this number **3** something representing or consisting of sixty units ▹ *adj* **4** amounting to sixty: *sixty seconds* **sixtieth** *adj, n*

sizable ❶ or **sizeable** *adj* quite large

size[1] ❶ *n* **1** the dimensions, amount, or extent of something **2** large dimensions, amount, or extent: *I was overwhelmed by the sheer size of the city* **3** one of a series of standard measurements for goods: *he takes size 11 shoes* **4** *informal* state of affairs as summarized: *that's about the size of it* ▹ *vb* **sizing, sized 5** to sort (things) according to size
WORD ORIGIN Old French *sise*

size[2] *n* **1** a thin gluey substance that is used as a sealer ▹ *vb* **sizing, sized 2** to treat (a surface) with size
WORD ORIGIN origin unknown

sized *adj* of a specified size: *average-sized*

size up ❶ *vb* *informal* to make an assessment of (a person or situation)

sizzle ❶ *vb* **-zling, -zled 1** to make a hissing sound like the sound of frying fat **2** *informal* to be very hot: *the city was sizzling in a hot summer spell* **3** *informal* to be very angry ▹ *n* **4** a hissing sound **sizzling** *adj*
WORD ORIGIN imitative

S

THESAURUS

plight, status quo, state of affairs, ball game (*informal*), kettle of fish (*informal*) **1a = scenario**, the picture (*informal*), the score (*informal*), state of affairs, lie of the land **2 = location**, place, setting, position, seat, site, spot, locality, locale

size[1] *n* **1 = dimensions**, extent, measurement(s), range, amount, mass, length, volume, capacity, proportions, bulk, width, magnitude, greatness, vastness, immensity, bigness, largeness, hugeness

sizeable or **sizable** *adj* **= large**, considerable, substantial, goodly, decent, respectable, tidy (*informal*), decent-sized, largish

size up *vb* (*informal*) **= assess**, evaluate, appraise, take stock of, eye up, get the measure of, get (something) taped (*Brit informal*)

sizzle *vb* **1 = hiss**, spit, crackle, sputter, fry, frizzle

DICTIONARY

sjambok (sham-bock) *S African* *n* **1** a whip or riding crop made of hide ▹ *vb* **-bokking, -bokked 2** to beat with a sjambok
WORD ORIGIN Malay *tjambok*

SK Saskatchewan

skanky *adj* **skankier, skankiest** *slang* **1** dirty or unattractive **2** promiscuous

skate[1] *n* **1** ▸ same as **ice skate** or **roller skate 2 get one's skates on** *informal* to hurry ▹ *vb* **skating, skated 3** to glide on or as if on skates **4 skate on thin ice** to place oneself in a dangerous situation **skater** *n* **skating** *n*
WORD ORIGIN Old French *éschasse* stilt

skate[2] *n, pl* **skate** *or* **skates** a large edible marine fish with a broad flat body
WORD ORIGIN Old Norse *skata*

skateboard *n* **1** a narrow board mounted on roller-skate wheels, usually ridden while standing up ▹ *vb* **2** to ride on a skateboard **skateboarding** *n*

skate round *or* **over** *vb* to avoid discussing or dealing with (a matter) fully: *friends and admirers skated round the question*

skean-dhu (skee-an-doo) *n* a dagger worn in the sock as part of Highland dress
WORD ORIGIN Gaelic *sgian* knife + *dhu* black

skedaddle *vb* **-dling, -dled** *informal* to run off hastily
WORD ORIGIN origin unknown

skein *n* **1** a length of yarn or thread wound in a loose coil **2** a flock of geese in flight
WORD ORIGIN Old French *escaigne*

skeleton *n* **1** the hard framework of bones that supports and protects the organs and muscles of the body **2** the essential framework of any structure: *a metal skeleton supporting the roof and floors* **3** *informal* an extremely thin person or animal **4** an outline consisting of bare essentials: *the mere skeleton of a script* **5** a small steel-frame sledge for racing down an ice-covered run **6** the sport of racing small steel-frame sledges down an ice-covered run **7 skeleton in the cupboard** *or* **closet** an embarrassing or scandalous fact from the past that is kept secret ▹ *adj* **8** reduced to a minimum: *a skeleton staff* **skeletal** *adj*
WORD ORIGIN Greek: something dried up

skeleton key *n* a key designed so that it can open many different locks

skelm *n* *S African informal* a villain or crook
WORD ORIGIN Afrikaans

Skelton *n* **John** ?1460–1529, English poet celebrated for his short rhyming lines using the rhythms of colloquial speech › **Skeltonic** *adj*

skeptic *n* *US & archaic* ▸ same as **sceptic**

skerry *n, pl* **-ries** *Scot* a rocky island or reef
WORD ORIGIN Old Norse *sker*

sketch ❶ *n* **1** a quick rough drawing **2** a brief descriptive piece of writing **3** a short funny piece of acting forming part of a show **4** any brief outline ▹ *vb* **5** to make a quick rough drawing (of) **6 sketch out** to make a brief description of: *they sketched out plans for the invasion*
WORD ORIGIN Greek *skhedios* unprepared

sketchbook *n* a book of blank pages for sketching on

sketchy *adj* **sketchier, sketchiest** giving only a rough or incomplete description **sketchily** *adv*

skew *adj* **1** having a slanting position ▹ *n* **2** a slanting position ▹ *vb* **3** to take or cause to take a slanting position: *our boat skewed off course* **4** to distort or misrepresent: *the takeover bid has skewed last month's figures*
WORD ORIGIN Old French *escuer* to shun

skewbald *adj* **1** marked with patches of white and another colour ▹ *n* **2** a horse with this marking
WORD ORIGIN origin unknown

skewed *adj* distorted or biased because of prejudice or lack of information: *a skewed conception of religion*

skewer *n* **1** a long pin for holding meat together during cooking ▹ *vb* **2** to fasten or pierce with or as if with a skewer
WORD ORIGIN probably from dialect *skiver*

skewwhiff *adj* *informal* crooked or slanting

ski *n, pl* **skis** *or* **ski 1** one of a pair of long runners that are used, fastened to boots, for gliding over snow ▹ *vb* **skiing, skied** *or* **ski'd 2** to travel on skis **skier** *n* **skiing** *n*
WORD ORIGIN Norwegian

skid *vb* **skidding, skidded 1** (of a vehicle or person) to slide sideways while in motion ▹ *n* **2** an instance of skidding
WORD ORIGIN origin unknown

skidoo *n, pl* **-doos** *Canad* ▸ same as **snowmobile**
WORD ORIGIN *Ski-Doo*, originally a trademark

skid row *n* *slang, chiefly US & Canad* a poor and neglected area of a city, inhabited by down-and-outs

skiff *n* a small narrow boat for one person
WORD ORIGIN French *esquif*

ski jump *n* a steep snow-covered slope ending in a horizontal ramp from which skiers compete to make the longest jump

skilful ❶ *or US* **skillful** *adj* having or showing skill **skilfully** *or US* **skillfully** *adv*

ski lift *n* a series of chairs hanging from a power-driven cable for carrying skiers up a slope

skill ❶ *n* **1** special ability or expertise enabling one to perform an activity very well **2** something, such as a trade, requiring special training or expertise **skilled** *adj*
WORD ORIGIN Old Norse *skil* distinction

skillet *n* **1** a small frying pan **2** *chiefly Brit* a long-handled cooking pot
WORD ORIGIN origin unknown

skim ❶ *vb* **skimming, skimmed 1** to remove floating material from the surface of (a liquid): *skim any impurities off the surface* **2** to glide smoothly over (a surface) **3** to throw (a flat stone) across a surface, so that it bounces: *two men skimmed stones on the surface of the sea* **4** (often foll. by *through*) to read (a piece of writing) quickly and without taking in the details
WORD ORIGIN Middle English *skimmen*

skimmed *or* **skim milk** *n* milk from which the cream has been removed

skimp *vb* **1** to be extremely sparing or supply (someone) sparingly **2** to do (something) carelessly or with inadequate materials
WORD ORIGIN perhaps a combination of SCANT + SCRIMP

skimpy *adj* **skimpier, skimpiest** inadequate in amount or size; scant

skin ❶ *n* **1** the tissue forming the outer covering of the body **2** a

THESAURUS

sketch *n* **1 = drawing**, design, draft, delineation ▹ *vb* **5 = draw**, paint, outline, represent, draft, portray, depict, delineate, rough out

skilful *or (US)* **skillful** *adj* **= expert**, skilled, masterly, trained, experienced, able, professional, quick, clever, practised, accomplished, handy, competent, apt, adept, proficient, adroit, dexterous **OPPOSITE:** clumsy

skill *n* **1 = expertise**, ability, proficiency, experience, art, technique, facility, talent, intelligence, craft, competence, readiness, accomplishment, knack, ingenuity, finesse, aptitude, dexterity, cleverness, quickness, adroitness, expertness, handiness, skilfulness **OPPOSITE:** clumsiness

skim *vb* **1 = remove**, separate, cream, take off **2 = glide**, fly, coast, sail, float, brush, dart **4** *(often foll. by* **through***)* **= scan**, glance, run your eye over, thumb *or* leaf through

skin *n* **3 = peel**, rind, husk, casing, outside, crust **4 = film**, coating, coat,

DICTIONARY

person's complexion: *sallow skin* **3** any outer layer or covering: *potato skin* **4** a thin solid layer on the surface of a liquid: *custard with a thick skin on it* **5** the outer covering of a furry animal, removed and prepared for use **6** a container for liquids, made from animal skin **7 by the skin of one's teeth** by a narrow margin **8 get under one's skin** *informal* to annoy one **9 no skin off one's nose** *informal* not a matter that concerns one **10 save one's skin** to save one from death or harm **11 skin and bone** extremely thin **12 thick** *or* **thin skin** an insensitive *or* sensitive nature ▷ *vb* **skinning, skinned 13** to remove the outer covering from (fruit, vegetables, dead animals, etc.) **14** to injure (a part of the body) by scraping some of the skin off: *I had skinned my knuckles* **15** *slang* to swindle **skinless** *adj*
WORD ORIGIN Old English *scinn*

skin-deep *adj* not of real importance; superficial: *beauty is only skin-deep*

skin diving *n* underwater swimming using only light breathing apparatus and without a special diving suit **skin-diver** *n*

skin flick *n slang* a pornographic film

skinflint *n* a very mean person
WORD ORIGIN referring to a person so greedy that he or she would skin (swindle) a flint

skin graft *n* a piece of skin removed from one part of the body and surgically grafted at the site of a severe burn or other injury

skinhead *n* **1** a member of a group of White youths, noted for their closely cropped hair, aggressive behaviour, and overt racism **2** a closely cropped hairstyle

skinny ❶ *adj* **-nier, -niest** extremely thin

skint *adj slang* without money, esp. only temporarily
WORD ORIGIN variant of *skinned*

skintight *adj* (of garments) fitting tightly over the body; clinging

skip[1] ❶ *vb* **skipping, skipped 1** to move lightly by hopping from one foot to the other **2** to jump over a skipping-rope **3** to cause (a stone) to skim over a surface or (of a stone) to move in this way **4** to pass over or miss out; omit: *I skipped a few paragraphs* **5 skip through** *informal* to read or deal with (something) quickly or without great effort or concentration **6 skip it!** *informal* it doesn't matter! **7** *informal* to miss deliberately: *she skipped the class* **8** *informal, chiefly US, Canad & Austral* to leave (a place) in a hurry: *he skipped town three years later* ▷ *n* **9** a skipping movement or action
WORD ORIGIN probably from Old Norse

skip[2] *n* **1** a large open container for transporting building materials or rubbish **2** a cage used as a lift in mines
WORD ORIGIN variant of *skep* a beehive

ski pants *pl n* stretch trousers, worn for skiing or leisure, which are kept taut by straps under the feet

skipper *n* **1** the captain of a ship or aircraft **2** the captain of a sporting team ▷ *vb* **3** to be the captain of
WORD ORIGIN Middle Low German, Middle Dutch *schipper* shipper

skipping *n* the act of jumping over a rope held either by the person jumping or by two other people, as a game or for exercise

skipping-rope *n* a rope that is held in the hands and swung round and down so that the holder or others can jump over it

skirl *Scot & N English dialect n* **1** the sound of bagpipes ▷ *vb* **2** (of bagpipes) to give out a shrill sound
WORD ORIGIN probably from Old Norse

skirmish *n* **1** a brief or minor fight or argument ▷ *vb* **2** to take part in a skirmish
WORD ORIGIN Old French *eskirmir*

skirt ❶ *n* **1** a woman's or girl's garment hanging from the waist **2** the part of a dress or coat below the waist **3** a circular hanging flap, for example round the base of a hovercraft **4** *Brit & NZ* a cut of beef from the flank **5 bit of skirt** *offensive slang* a girl or woman ▷ *vb* **6** to lie along or form the edge of (something): *a track skirting the foot of the mountain* **7** to go around the outer edge of (something): *we skirted the township* **8** to avoid dealing with (an issue): *I was skirting around the real issues*
WORD ORIGIN Old Norse *skyrta* shirt

skirting board *n* a narrow board round the bottom of an interior wall where it joins the floor

ski stick *or* **pole** *n* one of a pair of sharp pointed sticks used by skiers to gain speed and maintain balance

skit *n* a short funny or satirical sketch
WORD ORIGIN probably Scandinavian

skite *Austral & NZ vb* **1** to boast ▷ *n* **2** a boast

ski tow *n* a device for pulling skiers uphill, usually a motor-driven rope grasped by the skier while riding on his or her skis

skittish *adj* **1** playful or lively **2** (of a horse) excitable and easily frightened
WORD ORIGIN probably from Old Norse

skittle *n* **1** a bottle-shaped object used as a target in a game of skittles **2 skittles** a bowling game in which players knock over as many skittles as possible by rolling a wooden ball at them
WORD ORIGIN origin unknown

skive *vb* **skiving, skived** (often foll. by *off*) *Brit informal* to avoid work or responsibility **skiver** *n*
WORD ORIGIN origin unknown

skivvy *chiefly Brit, often disparaging n, pl* **-vies 1** a female servant who does menial work; drudge **2** *Austral & NZ* a garment resembling a sweater with long sleeves and a polo neck ▷ *vb* **-vies, -vying, -vied 3** to work as a skivvy
WORD ORIGIN origin unknown

skolly *or* **skollie** *n, pl* **-lies** *S African* a hooligan, usually one of a gang
WORD ORIGIN origin unknown

skookum ❶ *adj W Canad* strong or brave
WORD ORIGIN Chinook

Skryabin *n* ▸ a variant spelling of **Scriabin**

skua *n* a large predatory gull living in cold marine regions
WORD ORIGIN Faeroese *skūgvur*

skulduggery *or US* **skullduggery** *n informal* underhand dealing to achieve an aim
WORD ORIGIN origin unknown

skulk *vb* **1** to move stealthily, so as to avoid notice **2** to lie in hiding; lurk
WORD ORIGIN from Old Norse

skull *n* **1** the bony framework of the head **2** *informal* the head or mind: *that would have penetrated even your thick skull*
WORD ORIGIN probably from Old Norse

skull and crossbones *n* a picture of the human skull above two crossed bones, formerly on the pirate flag, now used as a warning of

S

THESAURUS

membrane **5 = hide**, fleece, pelt, fell, integument, tegument ▷ *vb* **13 = peel**, pare, hull **14 = scrape**, graze, bark, flay, excoriate, abrade

skinny *adj* **= thin**, lean, scrawny, skeletal, emaciated, twiggy, undernourished, skin-and-bone (*informal*), scraggy **OPPOSITE:** fat

skip[1] *vb* **1 = hop**, dance, bob, trip, bounce, caper, prance, cavort, frisk, gambol **4 = miss out**, omit, leave out, overlook, pass over, eschew, forgo, skim over, give (something) a miss

skirt *vb* **6 = border**, edge, lie alongside, line, fringe, flank **7 = go round**, bypass, walk round, circumvent **8 = avoid**, evade, steer clear of, sidestep, circumvent, detour, body-swerve (*Scot*)

skookum *adj* (*w Canad*) **= powerful**, influential, big, dominant, controlling, commanding, supreme, prevailing, sovereign, authoritative, puissant

DICTIONARY

danger or death
skullcap *n* a closely fitting brimless cap
skunk *n, pl* **skunks** *or* **skunk** **1** a mammal with a black-and-white coat and bushy tail, which gives out a foul-smelling fluid when attacked **2** *informal* an unpleasant or unfair person
WORD ORIGIN from a Native American language
sky ❶ *n, pl* **skies** **1** the upper atmosphere as seen from earth **2** **praise to the skies** praise rather excessively ▷*vb* **skies, skying, skied** **3** *informal* to hit (a ball) high in the air: *the blond-haired forward skied the ball high over the bar*
WORD ORIGIN Old Norse *skȳ* cloud
sky-blue *adj* bright clear blue
skydiving *n* the sport of jumping from an aircraft and falling freely or performing manoeuvres before opening the parachute **skydiver** *n*
sky-high *adj, adv* **1** very high: *most firms are no longer willing to pay sky-high prices* **2** **blow sky-high** to destroy completely
skyjack *vb* to hijack (an aircraft)
WORD ORIGIN SKY + HIJACK
skylark *n* **1** a lark that sings while soaring at a great height ▷*vb* **2** *old-fashioned* to play or frolic
skylight *n* a window placed in a roof or ceiling to let in daylight
skyline *n* **1** the line at which the earth and sky appear to meet **2** the outline of buildings, trees, or hills, seen against the sky
Skype *n trademark* a system that enables audiovisual communication over the internet
skyrocket *n* **1** ▸same as **rocket** (sense 1) ▷*vb* **2** *informal* to rise very quickly
skyscraper *n* a very tall building
skyward *adj* **1** towards the sky ▷*adv also* **skywards** **2** towards the sky
slab ❶ *n* **1** a broad flat thick piece of wood, stone, or other material **2** *informal* a package containing 24 cans of beer
WORD ORIGIN origin unknown
slack¹ ❶ *adj* **1** not tight, tense, or taut: *the slack jaw hung open* **2** careless in one's work **3** (esp. of water) moving slowly **4** (of trade) not busy ▷*n* **5** a part that is slack or hangs loose: *take up the slack* **6** a period of less busy activity ▷*vb* **7** to neglect one's duty or work in a lazy manner: *stop slacking, you pair!* **8** (often foll. by *off*) to loosen or slacken ▸See also **slacks** > **slackness** *n*
WORD ORIGIN Old English *slæc, sleac*
slack² *n* small pieces of coal with a high ash content
WORD ORIGIN probably Middle Low German *slecke*
slacken *vb* (often foll. by *off*) **1** to make or become looser **2** to make or become slower or less intense: *to slacken the pace of reform*
slacker *n* a person who evades work or duty; shirker
slacks *pl n old-fashioned* casual trousers
slag *n* **1** the waste material left after metal has been smelted **2** *Brit & NZ slang* a sexually immoral woman ▷*vb* **slagging, slagged** **3** *Brit, Austral & NZ slang* (often foll. by *off*) to criticize in an unpleasant way: *I don't think anyone can slag it off* **slagging** *n* **slaggy** *adj*
WORD ORIGIN Middle Low German *slagge*
slag heap *n* a pile of waste matter from metal smelting or coal mining
slain *vb* ▸the past participle of **slay**
slake *vb* **slaking, slaked** **1** *literary* to satisfy (thirst or desire) **2** to add water to (lime) to produce calcium hydroxide
WORD ORIGIN Old English *slacian*
slalom *n skiing, canoeing* a race over a winding course marked by artificial obstacles
WORD ORIGIN Norwegian
slam¹ ❶ *vb* **slamming, slammed** **1** to close violently and noisily **2** to throw (something or someone) down violently **3** *slang* to criticize harshly: *his new proposals were slammed by the opposition* **4** to strike with violent force: *he slammed the ball into the back of the net* ▷*n* **5** the act or noise of slamming
WORD ORIGIN Scandinavian
slam² *n* the winning of all (**grand slam**) or all but one (**little slam**) of the 13 tricks at bridge
WORD ORIGIN origin unknown
slam dunk *n* **1** *basketball* a scoring shot in which the player jumps up and forces the ball down through the basket **2** *informal* a task so easy that success in it is deemed a certainty ▷*vb* **slam-dunk** **3** *basketball* to jump up and force (a ball) through a basket
slammer *n* **the slammer** *slang* prison
slander *n* **1** *law* a false and damaging statement about a person **2** the crime of making such a statement ▷*vb* **3** to utter slander (about) **slanderous** *adj*
WORD ORIGIN Old French *escandle*
slang *n* **1** informal language not used in formal speech or writing and often restricted to a particular social group or profession ▷*vb* **2** to use insulting language to (someone) **slangy** *adj*
WORD ORIGIN origin unknown
slanging match *n* an angry quarrel in which people trade insults
slant ❶ *vb* **1** to lean at an angle; slope **2** to write or present (information) in a biased way ▷*n* **3** a sloping line or position **4** a point of view, esp. a biased one: *a right-wing slant on the story* **5** **on a** *or* **the slant** sloping ▷*adj* **6** oblique; sloping **slanting** *adj* **slantwise** *adv*
WORD ORIGIN Scandinavian
slap ❶ *n* **1** a sharp blow or smack with something flat, such as the open hand **2** the sound made by or as if by such a blow **3** **slap and tickle** *Brit old-fashioned informal* sexual play **4** **a slap in the face** an unexpected rejection or insult **5** **a slap on the back** congratulations ▷*vb* **slapping, slapped** **6** to strike sharply with something flat, such as the open hand **7** to bring (something) down forcefully: *he slapped down a fiver* **8** (usually foll. by *against*) to strike (something) with a slapping sound **9** *informal* to cover with quickly or carelessly: *she slapped on some make-up* **10** **slap on the back** to congratulate ▷*adv informal* **11** exactly: *slap in the middle* **12** **slap into** forcibly or abruptly into: *he ran slap into the guard*
WORD ORIGIN Low German *slapp*

THESAURUS

sky *n* **1 = heavens**, firmament, upper atmosphere, azure *(poetic)*, welkin *(archaic)*, vault of heaven, rangi *(NZ)*
slab *n* **1 = piece**, slice, lump, chunk, wedge, hunk, portion, nugget, wodge *(Brit informal)*
slack¹ *adj* **1a = limp**, relaxed, loose, lax, flaccid, not taut **1b = loose**, hanging, flapping, baggy **OPPOSITE:** taut **2 = negligent**, lazy, lax, idle, easy-going, inactive, tardy, slapdash, neglectful, slipshod, inattentive, remiss, asleep on the job *(informal)* **OPPOSITE:** strict **3, 4 = slow**, quiet, inactive, dull, sluggish, slow-moving **OPPOSITE:** busy ▷*vb* **7 = shirk**, idle, relax, flag, neglect, dodge, skive *(Brit slang)*, bob off *(Brit slang)*, bludge *(Austral & NZ informal)*
slam¹ *vb* **1 = bang**, crash, smash, thump, shut with a bang, shut noisily **2 = throw**, dash, hurl, fling
slant *vb* **1 = slope**, incline, tilt, list, bend, lean, heel, shelve, skew, cant, bevel, angle off **2 = bias**, colour, weight, twist, angle, distort ▷*n* **3 = slope**, incline, tilt, gradient, pitch, ramp, diagonal, camber, declination **4 = bias**, emphasis, prejudice, angle, leaning, point of view, viewpoint, one-sidedness
slap *n* **1 = smack**, blow, whack, wallop *(informal)*, bang, clout *(informal)*, cuff, swipe, spank ▷*vb* **6 = smack**, hit, strike, beat, bang, clap, clout *(informal)*, cuff, whack, swipe, spank, clobber *(slang)*, wallop *(informal)*, lay one on *(slang)*
slash *vb* **1, 2 = cut**, slit, gash, lacerate,

DICTIONARY

slap-bang *adv informal* **1** directly or exactly: *he's on holiday in LA and has run slap-bang into a famous face* **2** forcefully and abruptly: *he'd gone and run slap-bang into the watchman*
slapdash *adv* **1** carelessly or hastily ▷*adj* **2** careless or hasty
slap-happy *adj* **-pier, -piest** *informal* cheerfully careless
slaphead *n slang* a bald person
WORD ORIGIN from SLAP + HEAD
slapstick *n* rough and high-spirited comedy in which the characters behave childishly
slap-up *adj Brit informal* (esp. of meals) large and expensive
slash ❶ *vb* **1** to cut (a person or thing) with sharp sweeping strokes **2** to make large gashes in: *I slashed the tyres of his van* **3** to reduce drastically: *to slash costs* **4** to criticize harshly ▷*n* **5** a sharp sweeping stroke **6** a cut made by such a stroke **7** ▸same as **solidus** **8** *Brit slang* the act of urinating
WORD ORIGIN origin unknown
slasher *n Austral & NZ* a tool or tractor-drawn machine used for cutting scrub or undergrowth in the bush
slat *n* a narrow thin strip of wood or metal, such as used in a Venetian blind
WORD ORIGIN Old French *esclat* splinter
slate[1] *n* **1** a dark grey rock that can be easily split into thin layers and is used as a roofing material **2** a roofing tile of slate **3** (formerly) a writing tablet of slate **4** *chiefly US & Canad* a list of candidates in an election **5** **wipe the slate clean** forget about past mistakes or failures and start afresh **6** **on the slate** *Austral & Brit informal* on credit ▷*vb* **slating, slated** **7** to cover (a roof) with slates **8** *chiefly US* to plan or schedule: *another exercise is slated for tomorrow* **slaty** *adj*
WORD ORIGIN Old French *esclate* fragment
slate[2] ❶ *vb* **slating, slated** *informal, chiefly Brit & Austral* to criticize harshly: *the new series was slated by the critics* **slating** *n*
WORD ORIGIN probably from Old French *esclate* fragment
Slatkin *n* **Leonard** born 1944, US conductor; musical director of the St Louis Symphony Orchestra (1979–96) and of the National Symphony Orchestra from 1996
slattern *n old-fashioned* a dirty and untidy woman **slatternliness** *n* **slatternly** *adj*
WORD ORIGIN probably from dialect *slatter* to slop
slaughter ❶ *n* **1** the indiscriminate or brutal killing of large numbers of people **2** the savage killing of a person **3** the killing of animals for food ▷*vb* **4** to kill indiscriminately or in large numbers **5** to kill brutally **6** to kill (animals) for food **7** *informal* (in sport) to defeat easily
WORD ORIGIN Old English *sleaht*
slaughterhouse *n* a place where animals are killed for food
Slav *n* a member of any of the peoples of E Europe or the former Soviet Union who speak a Slavonic language
WORD ORIGIN Medieval Latin *Sclavus* a captive Slav
slave ❶ *n* **1** a person legally owned by another for whom he or she has to work without freedom, pay, or rights **2** a person under the domination of another or of some habit or influence: *a slave to party doctrine* **3** *informal* a badly-paid person doing menial tasks ▷*vb* **slaving, slaved** **4** (often foll. by *away* or *over*) to work very hard for little or no money
WORD ORIGIN Medieval Latin *Sclavus* a Slav (the Slavonic races were frequently conquered in the Middle Ages)
slave-driver *n* **1** a person who makes people work very hard **2** (esp. formerly) a person forcing slaves to work
slaver[1] (**slay**-ver) *n* **1** (esp. formerly) a dealer in slaves **2** *history* a ship used in the slave trade
slaver[2] (**slav**-ver) *vb* **1** to dribble saliva **2** (often foll. by *over*) to drool (over someone), making flattering remarks ▷*n* **3** saliva dribbling from the mouth **4** *informal* nonsense
WORD ORIGIN probably from Low German
slavery ❶ *n* **1** the state or condition of being a slave **2** the practice of owning slaves **3** hard work with little reward
slave trade *n* the buying and selling of slaves, esp. the transportation of Black Africans to America and the Caribbean from the 16th to the 19th centuries
slavish *adj* **1** of or like a slave **2** imitating or copying exactly without any originality: *a slavish adherence to the conventions of Italian opera* **slavishly** *adv*
Slavonic *or esp. US* **Slavic** *n* **1** a group of languages including Bulgarian, Russian, Polish, and Czech ▷*adj* **2** of this group of languages **3** of the people who speak these languages
slay ❶ *vb* **slaying, slew, slain** *archaic or literary* to kill, esp. violently **slayer** *n*
WORD ORIGIN Old English *slēan*
sleaze ❶ *n informal* behaviour in public life considered immoral, dishonest, or disreputable: *political sleaze*
sleazy *adj* **-zier, -ziest** dirty, rundown, and not respectable: *a sleazy hotel* **sleaziness** *n*
WORD ORIGIN origin unknown
sledge[1] *or esp. US & Canad* **sled** *n* **1** a vehicle mounted on runners, drawn by horses or dogs, for transporting people or goods over snow **2** a light wooden frame used, esp. by children, for sliding over snow ▷*vb* **sledging, sledged** **3** to travel by sledge
WORD ORIGIN Middle Dutch *sleedse*
sledge[2] *n* ▸short for **sledgehammer**
sledgehammer *n* **1** a large heavy hammer with a long handle, used for breaking rocks and concrete ▷*adj* **2** crushingly powerful: *the sledgehammer approach*

S

THESAURUS

score, rend, rip, hack **3 = reduce**, cut, decrease, drop, lower, moderate, diminish, cut down, lessen, curtail ▷*n* **6 = cut**, slit, gash, rent, rip, incision, laceration
slate[2] *vb (informal, chiefly Brit & Austral)* **= criticize**, blast, pan *(informal)*, slam *(slang)*, blame, roast *(informal)*, censure, rebuke, slang, scold, berate, castigate, rail against, tear into *(informal)*, lay into *(informal)*, pitch into *(informal)*, take to task, lambast(e), flame *(informal)*, excoriate, haul over the coals *(informal)*, tear (someone) off a strip *(informal)*, rap (someone's) knuckles
slaughter *n* **1, 2 = slaying**, killing, murder, massacre, holocaust, bloodshed, carnage, liquidation, extermination, butchery, blood bath ▷*vb* **4 = butcher**, kill, slay, destroy, massacre, exterminate **5 = kill**, murder, massacre, destroy, do in *(slang)*, execute, dispatch, assassinate, blow away *(slang, chiefly US)*, annihilate, bump off *(slang)*
slave *n* **1 = servant**, serf, vassal, bondsman, slavey *(Brit informal)*, varlet *(archaic)*, villein, bondservant **3** *(informal)* **= drudge**, skivvy *(chiefly Brit)*, scullion *(archaic)* ▷*vb* **4 = toil**, labour, grind *(informal)*, drudge, sweat, graft, slog, skivvy *(Brit)*, work your fingers to the bone
slavery *n* **1 = enslavement**, servitude, subjugation, captivity, bondage, thrall, serfdom, vassalage, thraldom
OPPOSITE: freedom
slay *vb* **a** *(archaic or literary)* **= kill**, destroy, slaughter, eliminate, massacre, butcher, dispatch, annihilate, exterminate **b = murder**, kill, assassinate, do in *(slang)*, eliminate, massacre, slaughter, do away with, exterminate, mow down, rub out *(US slang)*
sleaze *n (informal)* **= corruption**, fraud, dishonesty, fiddling *(informal)*, bribery, extortion, venality, shady dealings *(informal)*, crookedness *(informal)*, unscrupulousness

DICTIONARY

WORD ORIGIN Old English *slecg* a large hammer

sleek ❶ *adj* **1** smooth, shiny, and glossy: *sleek blond hair* **2** (of a person) elegantly dressed
WORD ORIGIN variant of *slick*

sleep ❶ *n* **1** a state of rest during which the eyes are closed, the muscles and nerves are relaxed, and the mind is unconscious **2** a period spent sleeping **3** the substance sometimes found in the corner of the eyes after sleep **4** a state of inactivity, like sleep **5** *poetic* death ▹ *vb* **sleeping, slept 6** to be in or as in the state of sleep **7** to be inactive or unaware: *their defence slept as we scored another try* **8** to have sleeping accommodation for (a certain number): *the villa sleeps ten* **9** *poetic* to be dead **10 sleep on it** to delay making a decision about (something) until the next day, in order to think about it ▸ See also **sleep around, sleep in,** etc.
WORD ORIGIN Old English *slǣpan*

sleep around *vb informal* to have many sexual partners

sleeper *n* **1** a railway sleeping car or compartment **2** one of the blocks supporting the rails on a railway track **3** a small plain gold ring worn in a pierced ear lobe to prevent the hole from closing up **4** *informal* a person or thing that achieves success after an initial period of obscurity

sleep in *vb* to sleep longer than usual

sleeping bag *n* a large well-padded bag for sleeping in, esp. outdoors

sleeping car *n* a railway carriage with small rooms containing beds for passengers to sleep in

sleeping partner *n* a partner in a business who shares in the financing but does not take part in its management

sleeping pill *n* a pill containing a drug that induces sleep

sleeping policeman *n Brit* a bump built across a road to prevent motorists from driving too fast

sleeping sickness *n* an infectious, usually fatal, African disease transmitted by the bite of the tsetse fly, causing fever and sluggishness

sleepless *adj* **1** (of a night) one during which one does not sleep **2** unable to sleep **3** *chiefly poetic* always active **sleeplessness** *n*

sleep off *vb informal* to get rid of by sleeping: *go home and sleep it off*

sleepout *n NZ* a small building for sleeping in

sleep out *vb* to sleep in the open air

sleepover *n* and occasion when a person stays overnight at a friend's house

sleep together *vb* to have sexual intercourse and, usually, spend the night together

sleepwalk *vb* to walk while asleep **sleepwalker** *n* **sleepwalking** *n*

sleep with *vb* to have sexual intercourse and, usually, spend the night with

sleepy ❶ *adj* **sleepier, sleepiest 1** tired and ready for sleep **2** (of a place) without activity or excitement: *a sleepy little town* **sleepily** *adv*

sleet *n* **1** partly melted falling snow or hail or (esp. US) partly frozen rain ▹ *vb* **2** to fall as sleet
WORD ORIGIN Germanic

sleeve *n* **1** the part of a garment covering the arm **2** a tubelike part which fits over or completely encloses another part **3** a flat cardboard container to protect a gramophone record **4 up one's sleeve** secretly ready: *he has a few more surprises up his sleeve* **sleeveless** *adj*
WORD ORIGIN Old English *slīefe, slēfe*

sleigh *n* **1** ▸ same as **sledge**[1] (sense 1) ▹ *vb* **2** to travel by sleigh
WORD ORIGIN Dutch *slee*

sleight (slite) *n old-fashioned* skill or cunning
WORD ORIGIN Old Norse *slǣgth*

sleight of hand *n* **1** the skilful use of the hands when performing magic tricks **2** the performance of such tricks

slender ❶ *adj* **1** (esp. of a person's figure) slim and graceful **2** of small width relative to length or height **3** small or inadequate in amount or size: *a slender advantage*
WORD ORIGIN origin unknown

slept *vb* ▸ the past of **sleep**

sleuth (rhymes with **tooth**) *n informal* a detective
WORD ORIGIN Old Norse *slōth* a trail

slew[1] *vb* ▸ the past tense of **slay**

slew[2] *or esp. US* **slue** *vb* **1** to slide or skid sideways: *the bus slewed across the road* ▹ *n* **2** the act of slewing
WORD ORIGIN origin unknown

slice ❶ *n* **1** a thin flat piece or wedge cut from something: *a slice of tomato* **2** a share or portion: *the biggest slice of their income* **3** a kitchen tool having a broad flat blade: *a fish slice* **4** *sport* a shot that causes the ball to go to one side, rather than straight ahead ▹ *vb* **slicing, sliced 5** to cut (something) into slices **6** (usually foll. by *through*) to cut through cleanly and effortlessly, with or as if with a knife **7** (usually foll. by *off, from* or *away*) to cut or be cut (from) a larger piece **8** *sport* to play (a ball) with a slice
WORD ORIGIN Old French *esclice* a piece split off

slick ❶ *adj* **1** (esp. of speech) easy and persuasive: *a slick answer* **2** skilfully devised or executed: *a slick marketing effort* **3** *informal, chiefly US & Canad* shrewd; sly **4** *informal* well-made and attractive, but superficial: *a slick publication* **5** *chiefly US & Canad* slippery ▹ *n* **6** a slippery area, esp. a patch of oil floating on water ▹ *vb* **7** to make smooth or shiny: *long hair slicked back with gel*
WORD ORIGIN probably from Old Norse

slide ❶ *vb* **sliding, slid 1** to move smoothly along a surface in continual contact with it: *doors that slide open* **2** to slip: *he slid on his back* **3** (usually foll. by *into, out of* or *away from*) to pass or move smoothly and quietly: *she slid out of her seat* **4** (usually foll. by *into*) to go (into a specified condition) gradually: *the republic will slide into political anarchy* **5** (of a currency) to lose value gradually **6 let slide** to allow to change to a worse state by neglect: *past chairmen have undoubtedly let things slide* ▹ *n* **7** the act or an instance of sliding **8** a small glass plate on which specimens are placed for study under a microscope **9** a photograph on a transparent base, mounted in a

THESAURUS

sleek *adj* **1 = glossy**, shiny, lustrous, smooth, silky, velvety, well-groomed **OPPOSITE:** shaggy

sleep *n* **1 = slumber(s)**, rest, nap, doze, kip (*Brit slang*), snooze (*informal*), repose, hibernation, siesta, dormancy, beauty sleep (*informal*), forty winks (*informal*), shuteye (*slang*), zizz (*Brit informal*) ▹ *vb* **6 = slumber**, drop off (*informal*), doze, kip (*Brit slang*), snooze (*informal*), snore, hibernate, nod off (*informal*), take a nap, catnap, drowse, go out like a light, take forty winks (*informal*), zizz (*Brit informal*), be in the land of Nod, rest in the arms of Morpheus

sleepy *adj* **1 = drowsy**, sluggish, lethargic, heavy, dull, inactive, somnolent, torpid **OPPOSITE:** wide-awake

slender *adj* **1 = slim**, narrow, slight, lean, svelte, willowy, sylphlike **OPPOSITE:** chubby **3 = meagre**, little, small, inadequate, insufficient, scant, scanty, inconsiderable **OPPOSITE:** large

slice *n* **1, 2 = piece**, segment, portion, wedge, sliver, helping, share, cut ▹ *vb* **5 = cut**, divide, carve, segment, sever, dissect, cleave, bisect

slick *adj* **1 = glib**, smooth, sophisticated, plausible, polished, specious, meretricious **2 = skilful**, deft, adroit, dextrous, dexterous, professional, polished **OPPOSITE:** clumsy ▹ *vb* **7 = smooth**, oil, grease, sleek, plaster down, make glossy, smarm down (*Brit informal*)

slide *vb* **1 = slip**, slither, glide, skim, coast, toboggan, glissade

frame, that can be viewed by means of a projector **10** a smooth surface, such as ice, for sliding on **11** a structure with a steep smooth slope for sliding down in playgrounds **12** *chiefly Brit* an ornamental clip to hold hair in place **13** the sliding curved tube of a trombone that is moved in and out to allow different notes to be played
WORD ORIGIN Old English *slīdan*

slide rule *n* a device formerly used to make mathematical calculations consisting of two strips, one sliding along a central groove in the other, each strip graduated in two or more logarithmic scales of numbers

slide show *n* **1** any display in the form of a series of static images, such as photographic transparencies on a slide projector or images on a computer screen ▷ *adj* **slide-show** **2** presented as a series of static images: *slide-show presentation*

sliding scale *n* a variable scale according to which things such as wages or prices alter in response to changes in other factors

slight ● *adj* **1** small in quantity or extent: *a slight improvement* **2** not very important or lacking in substance: *her political career was honourable but relatively slight* **3** slim and delicate ▷ *vb* **4** to insult (someone) by behaving rudely; snub ▷ *n* **5** an act of snubbing (someone) **slightly** *adv*
WORD ORIGIN Old Norse *slēttr* smooth

slim ● *adj* **slimmer, slimmest 1** (of a person) attractively thin **2** small in width relative to height or length: *a slim book* **3** poor; meagre: *a slim chance of progress* ▷ *vb* **slimming, slimmed 4** to make or become slim by diets and exercise **5** to reduce in size: *that would slim the overheads* **slimmer** *n* **slimming** *n*
WORD ORIGIN Dutch: crafty

Slim[1] *n* the E African name for **AIDS**
WORD ORIGIN from its wasting effects

Slim[2] *n* **William Joseph,** 1st Viscount 1891–1970, British field marshal, who commanded (1943–45) the 14th Army in the reconquest of Burma (now called Myanmar) from the Japanese; governor general of Australia (1953–60)

slime *n* **1** soft runny mud or any sticky substance esp. when disgusting or unpleasant **2** a thick, sticky substance produced by some fish, slugs, and fungi
WORD ORIGIN Old English *slīm*

slimy *adj* **slimier, slimiest 1** of, like, or covered with slime **2** pleasant and friendly in an insincere way

sling[1] ● *n* **1** *med* a wide piece of cloth suspended from the neck for supporting an injured hand or arm **2** a rope or strap by which something may be lifted **3** a simple weapon consisting of a strap tied to cords, in which a stone is whirled and then released ▷ *vb* **slinging, slung 4** *informal* to throw **5** to carry or hang loosely from or as if from a sling: *her shoulder bag was slung across her chest* **6** to hurl with or as if with a sling
WORD ORIGIN probably from Old Norse

sling[2] *n* a sweetened mixed drink with a spirit base: *gin sling*
WORD ORIGIN origin unknown

slingback *n* a shoe with a strap instead of a complete covering for the heel

sling off at *vb Austral & NZ informal* to mock and jeer

slink *vb* **slinking, slunk** to move or act in a quiet and secretive way from fear or guilt
WORD ORIGIN Old English *slincan*

slinky *adj* **slinkier, slinkiest** *informal* **1** (of clothes) figure-hugging **2** moving in an alluring way

slip[1] ● *vb* **slipping, slipped 1** to lose balance and slide unexpectedly: *he slipped on some leaves* **2** to let loose or be let loose: *the rope slipped from his fingers* **3** to move smoothly and easily: *small enough to slip into a pocket* **4** to place quickly or stealthily: *he slipped the pistol back into his holster* **5** to put on or take off easily or quickly: *we had slipped off our sandals* **6** to pass out of (the mind or memory) **7** to move or pass quickly and without being noticed: *we slipped out of the ballroom* **8** to make a mistake **9** to decline in health or mental ability **10** to become worse or lower: *sales had slipped below the level for June of last year* **11** to dislocate (a disc in the spine) **12** to pass (a stitch) from one needle to another without knitting it **13 let slip a** to allow to escape **b** to say unintentionally ▷ *n* **14** a slipping **15** a mistake or oversight: *one slip in concentration that cost us the game* **16** a woman's sleeveless undergarment, worn under a dress **17** ▸ same as **slipway 18** *cricket* a fielding position a little behind and to the offside of the wicketkeeper **19 give someone the slip** to escape from someone
▸ See also **slip up**
WORD ORIGIN Middle Low German or Dutch *slippen*

slip[2] *n* **1** a small piece of paper: *the registration slip* **2** a cutting taken from a plant **3** a young slim person: *a slip of a girl*
WORD ORIGIN probably Middle Low German, Middle Dutch *slippe* to cut

slip[3] *n* clay mixed with water to a thin paste, used for decorating or patching a ceramic piece
WORD ORIGIN Old English *slyppe* slime

slipe *n NZ* wool removed from the pelt of a slaughtered sheep by immersion in a chemical bath
WORD ORIGIN Middle English *slype* to skin

slipknot *n* a nooselike knot tied so that it will slip along the rope round which it is made

slip-on *adj* **1** (of a garment or shoe) without laces or buttons so as to be easily and quickly put on ▷ *n* **2** a slip-on garment or shoe

S

THESAURUS

slight *adj* **1, 2 = small**, minor, insignificant, negligible, weak, modest, trivial, superficial, feeble, trifling, meagre, unimportant, paltry, measly, insubstantial, scanty, inconsiderable **OPPOSITE:** large **3 = slim**, small, delicate, spare, fragile, lightly-built **OPPOSITE:** sturdy ▷ *vb* **4 = snub**, insult, ignore, rebuff, affront, neglect, put down, despise, scorn, disdain, disparage, cold-shoulder, treat with contempt, show disrespect for, give offence *or* umbrage to **OPPOSITE:** compliment ▷ *n* **5 = insult**, snub, affront, contempt, disregard, indifference, disdain, rebuff, disrespect, slap in the face (*informal*), inattention, discourtesy, (the) cold shoulder **OPPOSITE:** compliment

slim *adj* **1, 2 = slender**, slight, trim, thin, narrow, lean, svelte, willowy, sylphlike **OPPOSITE:** chubby **3 = slight**, remote, faint, distant, slender **OPPOSITE:** strong ▷ *vb* **4 = lose weight**, diet, get thinner, get into shape, slenderize (*chiefly US*) **OPPOSITE:** put on weight

sling[1] *vb* **4** (*informal*) **= throw**, cast, toss, hurl, fling, chuck (*informal*), lob (*informal*), heave, shy **5 = hang**, swing, suspend, string, drape, dangle

slip[1] *vb* **1 = fall**, trip (over), slide, skid, lose your balance, miss *or* lose your footing **2 = slide**, fall, drop, slither **7 = sneak**, creep, steal, insinuate yourself ▷ *n* **15 = mistake**, failure, error blunder, lapse, omission, boob (*Brit slang*), oversight, slip-up (*informal*), indiscretion, bloomer (*Brit informal*), faux pas, slip of the tongue, imprudence, barry *or* Barry Crocker (*Austral slang*) **19 give someone the slip = escape from**, get away from, evade, shake (someone) off, elude, lose (someone), flee, dodge, outwit, slip through someone's fingers

slippery *adj* **1 = smooth**, icy, greasy, glassy, slippy (*informal, dialect*), unsafe, lubricious (*rare*), skiddy (*informal*) **3 = untrustworthy**, tricky,

DICTIONARY

slipped disc *n pathol* a painful condition in which one of the discs which connects the bones of the spine becomes displaced and presses on a nerve

slipper *n* a light soft shoe for indoor wear **slippered** *adj*

slippery ❶ *adj* **1** liable or tending to cause objects to slip: *the road was slippery* **2** liable to slip from one's grasp: *a bar of slippery soap* **3** not to be trusted: *slippery politicians* **slipperiness** *n*

slippy *adj* **-pier, -piest** *informal or dialect* ▸ same as **slippery** (senses 1, 2) > **slippiness** *n*

slip road *n Brit* a short road connecting a motorway to another road

slipshod *adj* **1** (of an action) done in a careless way without attention to detail: *a slipshod piece of research* **2** (of a person's appearance) untidy and slovenly

slip-slop *n S African* ▸ same as **flip-flop**

slipstream *n* the stream of air forced backwards by an aircraft or car

slip up ❶ *informal vb* **1** to make a mistake ▹ *n* **slip-up 2** a mistake

slipway *n* a large ramp that slopes down from the shore into the water, on which a ship is built or repaired and from which it is launched

slit ❶ *n* **1** a long narrow cut or opening ▹ *vb* **slitting, slit 2** to make a straight long cut in (something)
WORD ORIGIN Old English *slītan* to slice

slither *vb* **1** to move or slide unsteadily, such as on a slippery surface **2** to move along the ground in a twisting way: *a snake slithered towards the tree* ▹ *n* **3** a slithering movement **slithery** *adj*
WORD ORIGIN Old English *slid(e)rian*

sliver (sliv-ver) *n* **1** a small thin piece that is cut or broken off lengthwise ▹ *vb* **2** to cut into slivers
WORD ORIGIN obsolete *sliven* to split

Sloan *n* **John** 1871–1951, US painter and etcher, a leading member of the group of realistic painters known as the Ash Can School. His pictures of city scenes include *McSorley's Bar* (1912) and *Backyards, Greenwich Village* (1914)

Sloane Ranger *n informal* (in Britain) a young upper-class woman having a home in London and in the country, characterized as wearing expensive informal clothes
WORD ORIGIN from *Sloane* Square, London + *Lone Ranger*, cowboy hero

slob *n informal* a lazy and untidy person **slobbish** *adj*
WORD ORIGIN Irish Gaelic *slab* mud

slobber *vb* **1** to dribble (liquid or saliva) from the mouth **2 slobber over** to behave in an excessively sentimental way towards (someone) ▹ *n* **3** liquid or saliva spilt from the mouth **slobbery** *adj*
WORD ORIGIN Middle Low German, Middle Dutch *slubberen*

slob ice *n Canad* sludgy masses of floating sea ice

sloe *n* **1** the small sour blue-black fruit of the blackthorn **2** ▸ same as **blackthorn**
WORD ORIGIN Old English *slāh*

sloe-eyed *adj* having dark almond-shaped eyes

slog *vb* **slogging, slogged 1** to work hard and steadily **2** to make one's way with difficulty: *we slogged our way through the snow* **3** to hit hard ▹ *n* **4** long exhausting work **5** a long and difficult walk: *a slog through heather and bracken* **6** a heavy blow
WORD ORIGIN origin unknown

slogan ❶ *n* a catchword or phrase used in politics or advertising
WORD ORIGIN Gaelic *sluagh-ghairm* war cry

sloop *n* a small sailing ship with a single mast
WORD ORIGIN Dutch *sloep*

slop *vb* **slopping, slopped 1** (often foll. by *about*) to splash or spill (liquid) **2 slop over** *informal, chiefly US & Canad* to be excessively sentimental ▹ *n* **3** a puddle of spilt liquid **4 slops** liquid refuse and waste food used to feed animals, esp. pigs **5** (*often pl*) *informal* liquid food
WORD ORIGIN Old English *-sloppe*

slope ❶ *n* **1** a stretch of ground where one end is higher than the other **2 slopes** hills or foothills **3** any slanting surface **4** the angle of such a slant ▹ *vb* **sloping, sloped 5** to slant or cause to slant **6** (esp. of natural features) to have one end or part higher than another: *the bank sloped sharply down to the river* **7 slope off** *or* **away** *informal* to go quietly and quickly in order to avoid something or someone **8 slope arms** *mil* (formerly) to hold (a rifle) in a sloping position against the shoulder
WORD ORIGIN origin unknown

slop out *vb* (of prisoners) to empty chamber pots and collect water

sloppy ❶ *adj* **-pier, -piest 1** *informal* careless or untidy: *sloppy workmanship* **2** *informal* excessively sentimental and romantic **3** wet; slushy **sloppily** *adv* **sloppiness** *n*

slosh *vb* **1** *informal* to throw or pour (liquid) carelessly **2** (often foll. by *about* or *around*) *informal* **a** to shake or stir (something) in a liquid **b** (of a person) to splash (around) in water or mud **3** (usually foll. by *about* or *around*) *informal* to shake (a container of liquid) or (of liquid in a container) to be shaken **4** *Brit slang* to deal a heavy blow to ▹ *n* **5** the sound of splashing liquid **6** slush **7** *Brit slang* a heavy blow **sloshy** *adj*
WORD ORIGIN variant of SLUSH

sloshed *adj slang, chiefly Brit & Austral* drunk

slot ❶ *n* **1** a narrow opening or groove, such as one in a vending machine for inserting a coin **2** *informal* a place in a series or scheme: *the late-night slot when people stop watching TV* ▹ *vb* **slotting, slotted 3** to make a slot or slots in **4** (usually foll. by *in* or *into*) to fit or be fitted into a slot: *I slotted my card into the machine*
WORD ORIGIN Old French *esclot* the depression of the breastbone

sloth (rhymes with **both**) *n* **1** a slow-moving shaggy-coated animal of Central and South America, which hangs upside down in trees by its long arms and feeds on vegetation **2** *formal* laziness, esp. regarding work
WORD ORIGIN Old English *slǣwth*

slothful *adj* lazy and unwilling to work

slot machine *n* a machine, esp. for vending food and cigarettes or featuring an electronic game on

THESAURUS

cunning, false, treacherous, dishonest, devious, crafty, evasive, sneaky, two-faced, shifty, foxy, duplicitous

slip up *vb (informal)* **= make a mistake**, go wrong, blunder, mistake, boob *(Brit slang)*, err, misjudge, miscalculate, drop a brick *or* clanger *(informal)*

slit *n* **1a = cut**, gash, incision, tear, rent, fissure **1b = opening**, split, crack, aperture, chink, space ▹ *vb* **2 = cut (open)**, rip, slash, knife, pierce, lance, gash, split open

slogan *n* **= catch phrase**, motto, jingle, rallying cry, tag-line, catchword, catchcry *(Austral)*

slope *n* **1, 4 = inclination**, rise, incline, tilt, descent, downgrade *(chiefly US)*, slant, ramp, gradient, brae *(Scot)*, scarp, declination, declivity ▹ *vb* **5, 6 = slant**, incline, drop away, fall, rise, pitch, lean, tilt
7 slope off *or* **away** *(informal)* **= slink away**, slip away, steal away, skulk, creep away, make yourself scarce

sloppy *adj (informal)* **1 = careless**, slovenly, slipshod, messy, clumsy, untidy, amateurish, hit-or-miss *(informal)*, inattentive
2 = sentimental, mushy *(informal)*, soppy *(Brit informal)*, slushy *(informal)*, wet *(Brit informal)*, gushing, banal, trite, mawkish, icky *(informal)*, overemotional, three-hankie *(informal)*

slot *n* **1 = opening**, hole, groove, vent, slit, aperture, channel **2** *(informal)* **= place**, time, space, spot, opening, position, window, vacancy, niche

DICTIONARY

which to gamble, worked by placing a coin in a slot

slouch *vb* **1** to sit, stand, or move with a drooping posture ▷*n* **2** a drooping posture **3** **be no slouch** *informal* be very good or talented: *he was no slouch himself as a negotiator*
WORD ORIGIN origin unknown

slouch hat *n* a soft hat with a brim that can be pulled down over the ears

slough[1] *n* **1** (rhymes with **now**) a swamp or marshy area **2** (rhymes with **blue**) *US & Canad* a large hole where water collects **3** despair or hopeless depression
WORD ORIGIN Old English *slōh*

slough[2] (**sluff**) *n* **1** any outer covering that is shed, such as the dead outer layer of the skin of a snake ▷*vb* **slough off** **2** to shed (an outer covering) or (of an outer covering) to be shed: *the dead cells would slough off* **3** to get rid of (something unwanted or unnecessary): *she tried hard to slough off her old personality*
WORD ORIGIN Germanic

Slovak *adj* **1** of Slovakia ▷*n* **2** a person from Slovakia **3** the language of Slovakia

sloven *n* a person who is always untidy or careless in appearance or behaviour
WORD ORIGIN origin unknown

Slovene *adj* **1** Also: **Slovenian** of Slovenia ▷*n* **2** a person from Slovenia **3** the language of Slovenia

slovenly *adj* **1** always unclean or untidy **2** negligent and careless: *to write in such a slovenly style* ▷*adv* **3** in a slovenly manner **slovenliness** *n*

slow ❶ *adj* **1** taking a longer time than is usual or expected **2** lacking speed: *slow movements* **3** adapted to or producing slow movement: *the slow lane* **4** (of a clock or watch) showing a time earlier than the correct time **5** not quick to understand: *slow on the uptake* **6** dull or uninteresting: *the play was very slow* **7** not easily aroused: *he is slow to anger* **8** (of business) not busy; slack **9** (of a fire or oven) giving off low heat **10** *photog* requiring a relatively long time of exposure: *a slow film* ▷*adv* **11** in a slow manner ▷*vb* **12** (often foll. by *up* or *down*) to decrease or cause to decrease in speed or activity **slowly** *adv*
WORD ORIGIN Old English *slāw* sluggish

slowcoach *n informal* a person who moves or works slowly

slow motion *n* **1** *films, television* action that is made to appear slower than normal by filming at a faster rate or by replaying a video recording more slowly ▷*adj* **slow-motion** **2** of or relating to such action **3** moving at considerably less than usual speed

slow virus *n* a type of virus that is present in the body for a long time before it becomes active or infectious

slowworm *n* a legless lizard with a brownish-grey snakelike body

sludge *n* **1** soft mud or snow **2** any muddy or slushy sediment **3** sewage **sludgy** *adj*
WORD ORIGIN probably related to SLUSH

slug[1] *n* a mollusc like a snail but without a shell
WORD ORIGIN probably from Old Norse

slug[2] *n* **1** a bullet **2** *printing* a line of type produced by a Linotype machine **3** *informal* a mouthful of alcoholic drink, esp. spirits: *he poured out a large slug of Scotch*
WORD ORIGIN probably from SLUG[1] (with allusion to the shape of the animal)

slug[3] *vb* **slugging, slugged** **1** *chiefly US & Canad* to hit very hard ▷*n* **2** *US & Canad* a heavy blow
WORD ORIGIN probably from SLUG[2] (bullet)

sluggard *n old-fashioned* a very lazy person
WORD ORIGIN Middle English *slogarde*

sluggish ❶ *adj* **1** lacking energy **2** moving or working at slower than the normal rate: *the sluggish waters of the canal*

sluice *n* **1** a channel that carries a rapid current of water, with a sluicegate to control the flow **2** the water controlled by a sluicegate **3** ▸same as **sluicegate** **4** *mining* a sloping trough for washing ore ▷*vb* **sluicing, sluiced** **5** to draw off or drain with a sluice **6** to wash with a stream of water **7** (often foll. by *away* or *out*) (of water) to run or flow from or as if from a sluice
WORD ORIGIN Old French *escluse*

sluicegate *n* a valve or gate fitted to a sluice to control the rate of flow of water

slum ❶ *n* **1** an overcrowded and badly maintained house **2** (*often pl*) a poor rundown overpopulated section of a city ▷*vb* **slumming, slummed** **3** to visit slums, esp. for curiosity **4** **slum it** to temporarily and deliberately experience poorer places or conditions **slummy** *adj*
WORD ORIGIN origin unknown

slumber *literary vb* **1** to sleep ▷*n* **2** sleep **slumbering** *adj*
WORD ORIGIN Old English *slūma*

slump ❶ *vb* **1** (of commercial activity or prices) to decline suddenly **2** to sink or fall heavily and suddenly: *she slumped back with exhaustion* ▷*n* **3** a severe decline in commercial activity or prices; depression **4** a sudden or marked decline or failure: *a slump in demand for oil*
WORD ORIGIN probably Scandinavian

slung *vb* ▸the past of **sling**[1]

slunk *vb* ▸the past of **slink**

slur ❶ *vb* **slurring, slurred** **1** to pronounce or say (words) unclearly **2** to make insulting remarks about **3** *music* to sing or play (successive notes) smoothly by moving from one to the other without a break **4** (often foll. by *over*) to treat hastily or carelessly ▷*n* **5** an insulting remark intended to damage someone's reputation **6** a slurring of words **7** *music* **a** a slurring of successive notes **b** the curved line ⁀ or ‿ indicating this
WORD ORIGIN probably from Middle Low German

slurp *informal vb* **1** to eat or drink

S

THESAURUS

▷*vb* **4 = fit**, slide, insert, put, place

slow *adj* **1 = prolonged**, time-consuming, protracted, long-drawn-out, lingering, gradual **2 = unhurried**, sluggish, leisurely, easy, measured, creeping, deliberate, lagging, lazy, plodding, slow-moving, loitering, ponderous, leaden, dawdling, laggard, lackadaisical, tortoise-like, sluggardly **OPPOSITE:** quick **5 = stupid**, dim, dense, thick, dull, dumb (*informal*), retarded, bovine, dozy (*Brit informal*), unresponsive, obtuse, slow on the uptake (*informal*), braindead (*informal*), dull-witted, blockish, slow-witted, intellectually handicapped (*Austral*) **OPPOSITE:** bright ▷*vb* **12a** (*often with* **up** *or* **down**) **= decelerate**, brake, lag **12b** (*often with* **up** *or* **down**) **= delay**, hold up, hinder, check, restrict, handicap, detain, curb, retard, rein in **OPPOSITE:** speed up

sluggish *adj* **1 = inactive**, slow, lethargic, listless, heavy, dull, lifeless, inert, slow-moving, unresponsive, phlegmatic, indolent, torpid, slothful **OPPOSITE:** energetic

slum *n* **1 = hovel**, ghetto, shanty

slump *vb* **1 = fall**, decline, sink, plunge, crash, collapse, slip, deteriorate, fall off, plummet, go downhill (*informal*) **OPPOSITE:** increase **2 = sag**, bend, hunch, droop, slouch, loll ▷*n* **3 = recession**, depression, stagnation, inactivity, hard *or* bad times **4 = fall**, drop, decline, crash, collapse, reverse, lapse, falling-off, downturn, depreciation, trough, meltdown (*informal*) **OPPOSITE:** increase

slur *n* **5 = insult**, stain, smear, stigma, disgrace, discredit, blot, affront, innuendo, calumny, insinuation, aspersion

DICTIONARY

(something) noisily ▷*n* **2** a slurping sound
WORD ORIGIN Middle Dutch *slorpen* to sip

slurry *n, pl* **-ries** a thin watery mixture of something such as cement or mud
WORD ORIGIN Middle English *slory*

slush *n* **1** any watery muddy substance, esp. melting snow **2** *informal* sloppily sentimental language or writing **slushy** *adj*
WORD ORIGIN origin unknown

slush fund *n* a fund for financing political or commercial corruption

slut *n offensive* a promiscuous woman **sluttish** *adj*
WORD ORIGIN origin unknown

Sluter *n* **Claus** ?1345–1406, Dutch sculptor, working in Burgundy, whose realism influenced many sculptors and painters in 15th-century Europe. He is best known for the portal sculptures and the *Well of Moses* in the Carthusian monastery at Champnol

sly ❶ *adj* **slyer, slyest** *or* **slier, sliest** **1** (of a person's remarks or gestures) indicating that he or she knows something of which other people may be unaware: *she had the feeling they were poking sly fun at her* **2** secretive and skilled at deception: *a sly trickster* **3** roguish: *sly comedy* ▷*n* **4 on the sly** secretively: *they were smoking on the sly behind the shed* **slyly** *adv*
WORD ORIGIN Old Norse *slœgr* clever

Sm *chem* samarium

smack¹ ❶ *vb* **1** to slap sharply **2** to strike loudly or to be struck loudly **3** to open and close (the lips) loudly to show pleasure or anticipation ▷*n* **4** a sharp loud slap, or the sound of such a slap **5** a loud kiss **6** a sharp sound made by the lips in enjoyment **7 smack in the eye** *informal* a snub or rejection ▷*adv informal* **8** directly; squarely: *smack in the middle* **9** sharply and unexpectedly: *he ran smack into one of the men*
WORD ORIGIN probably imitative

smack² *n* **1** a slight flavour or suggestion (of something): *the smack of loss of self-control* ▷*vb* **2 smack of a** to have a slight smell or flavour (of something) **b** to have a suggestion (of something): *it smacks of discrimination*
WORD ORIGIN Old English *smæc*

smack³ *n* ▸ a slang word for **heroin**
WORD ORIGIN perhaps from Yiddish *schmeck*

smack⁴ *n* a small single-masted fishing vessel
WORD ORIGIN Dutch *smak*

smacker *n slang* **1** a loud kiss **2** a pound note or dollar bill

small ❶ *adj* **1** not large in size or amount **2** of little importance or on a minor scale: *a small detail* **3** mean, ungenerous, or petty: *a small mind* **4** modest or humble: *small beginnings* **5 feel small** to be humiliated **6** (of a child or animal) young; not mature **7** unimportant or trivial: *a small matter* **8** (of a letter) written or printed in lower case rather as a capital ▷*adv* **9** into small pieces: *cut it small* ▷*n* **10** the small narrow part of the back **11 smalls** *informal, chiefly Brit* underwear **smallish** *adj* **smallness** *n*
WORD ORIGIN Old English *smæl*

small beer *n informal, chiefly Brit* people or things of no importance

small change *n* coins of low value

small fry *pl n* **1** people regarded as unimportant **2** young children

small goods *pl n Austral & NZ* meats bought from a delicatessen, such as sausages

smallholding *n* a piece of agricultural land smaller than a farm **smallholder** *n*

small hours *pl n* the early hours of the morning, after midnight and before dawn

small intestine *n anat* the narrow, longer part of the alimentary canal, in which digestion is completed

small-minded *adj* having narrow selfish attitudes; petty

smallpox *n* a contagious disease causing fever, a rash, and blisters which usually leave permanent scars

small print *n* details in a contract or document printed in small type, esp. when considered as containing important information that people may regret not reading

small-scale *adj* of limited size or scope

small screen *n* **the small screen** television, esp. in contrast to cinema: *despite his film success, he has achieved little on the small screen*

small talk *n* light conversation for social occasions

small-time *adj informal* operating on a limited scale; minor: *a small-time smuggler*

smarm *vb Brit informal* **1** to bring (oneself) into favour (with) **2** *old-fashioned* (often foll. by *down*) to flatten (the hair) with oil
WORD ORIGIN origin unknown

smarmy *adj* **smarmier, smarmiest** unpleasantly flattering or polite

smart ❶ *adj* **1** clean and neatly dressed **2** intelligent and shrewd **3** quick and witty in speech: *a smart talker* **4** (of places or events) fashionable; chic: *smart restaurants* **5** vigorous or brisk: *a smart pace* **6** causing a sharp stinging pain **7** (of a weapon) containing an electronic device which enables it to be guided to its target: *a smart bomb* ▷*vb* **8** to feel or cause a sharp stinging physical or mental pain: *I was still smarting from the insult* ▷*n* **9** a stinging pain or feeling ▷*adv* **10** in a smart manner ▸ See also **smarts** > **smartly** *adv* **smartness** *n*
WORD ORIGIN Old English *smeortan* be painful

Smart *n* **Christopher** 1722–71, British poet, author of *A Song to David* (1763) and *Jubilate Agno* (written 1758–63, published 1939). He was confined (1756–63) for religious mania and died in a debtors' prison

THESAURUS

sly *adj* **2 = cunning**, scheming, devious, secret, clever, subtle, tricky, covert, astute, wily, insidious, crafty, artful, furtive, conniving, Machiavellian, shifty, foxy, underhand, stealthy, guileful **OPPOSITE:** open **3 = roguish**, knowing, arch, mischievous, impish ▷*n* **4 on the sly = secretly**, privately, covertly, surreptitiously, under the counter *(informal)*, on the quiet, behind (someone's) back, like a thief in the night, underhandedly, on the q.t. *(informal)*

smack¹ *vb* **1 = slap**, hit, strike, pat, tap, sock *(slang)*, clap, cuff, swipe, box, spank **2 = drive**, hit, strike, thrust, impel ▷*n* **4 = slap**, blow, whack, clout *(informal)*, cuff, crack, swipe, spank, wallop *(informal)* ▷*adv* **8** *(informal)* **= directly**, right, straight, squarely, precisely, exactly, slap *(informal)*, plumb, point-blank

small *adj* **1 = little**, minute, tiny, slight, mini, miniature, minuscule, diminutive, petite, teeny, puny, pint-sized *(informal)*, pocket-sized, undersized, teeny-weeny, Lilliputian, teensy-weensy, pygmy *or* pigmy **OPPOSITE:** big **2, 7 = unimportant**, minor, trivial, insignificant, little, lesser, petty, trifling, negligible, paltry, piddling *(informal)* **OPPOSITE:** important **4 = modest**, small-scale, humble, unpretentious **OPPOSITE:** grand **6 = young**, little, growing up, junior, wee, juvenile, youthful, immature, unfledged, in the springtime of life

smart *adj* **1 = chic**, trim, neat, fashionable, stylish, fine, elegant, trendy *(Brit informal)*, spruce, snappy, natty *(informal)*, modish, well turned-out, schmick *(Austral informal)* **OPPOSITE:** scruffy **2 = clever**, bright, intelligent, quick, sharp, keen, acute, shrewd, apt, ingenious, astute, canny, quick-witted **OPPOSITE:** stupid **5 = brisk**, quick, lively, vigorous, spirited, cracking *(informal)*, spanking, jaunty ▷*vb* **8 = sting**, burn, tingle, pain, hurt, throb

DICTIONARY

smart alec *n informal* a person who thinks he or she is an expert on every subject; know-all
smart card *n* a plastic card with integrated circuits used for storing and processing computer data
smarten *vb* (usually foll. by *up*) to make or become smart
smarts *pl n slang, chiefly US* know-how, intelligence, or wits: *the street smarts of the old crooks*
smash ❶ *vb* **1** to break into pieces violently and noisily **2** (often foll. by *against*, *through* or *into*) to throw or crash (against) violently, causing shattering: *his head smashed against a window* **3** to hit or collide forcefully and suddenly **4** *racket sports* to hit (the ball) fast and powerfully with an overhead stroke **5** to defeat or destroy: *the police had smashed a major drug ring* ▹*n* **6** an act or sound of smashing **7** a violent collision of vehicles **8** *racket sports* a fast and powerful overhead stroke **9** *informal* a show, record or film which is very popular with the public ▹*adv* **10** with a smash
WORD ORIGIN probably imitative
smash-and-grab *adj informal* of a robbery in which a shop window is broken and the contents removed
smasher *n informal, chiefly Brit* a person or thing that is very attractive or outstanding
smashing ❶ *adj informal, chiefly Brit* excellent or first-rate
smash-up *informal n* **1** a bad collision or crash involving motor vehicles ▹*vb* **smash up 2** to damage to the point of complete destruction: *two men smashed up a bar*
smattering *n* a slight or superficial knowledge: *I knew a smattering of Russian*
smear ❶ *vb* **1** to spread with a greasy or sticky substance **2** to apply (a greasy or sticky substance) thickly **3** to rub so as to produce a smudge **4** to spread false and damaging rumours (about) ▹*n* **5** a dirty mark or smudge **6** a false but damaging rumour spread by a rival or enemy **7** *med* a small amount of a substance smeared onto a glass slide for examination under a microscope **smeary** *adj*
WORD ORIGIN Old English *smeoru* a smear
smear test *n med* ▸same as **Pap test**
smell ❶ *vb* **smelling, smelt** *or* **smelled 1** to perceive the scent of (a substance) with the nose **2** to have a specified kind of smell: *it smells fruity; your supper smells good* **3** (often foll. by *of*) to emit an odour (of): *the place smells of milk and babies* **4** to give off an unpleasant odour **5** (often foll. by *out*) to detect through instinct: *I smell trouble* **6** to use the sense of smell; sniff **7 smell of** to indicate or suggest: *anything that smells of devaluation* ▹*n* **8** the sense by which scents or odours are perceived ▸Related adjective: **olfactory 9** an odour or scent **10** the act of smelling
WORD ORIGIN origin unknown
smelling salts *pl n* a preparation containing crystals of ammonium carbonate, used to revive a person feeling faint
smelly *adj* **smellier, smelliest** having a nasty smell **smelliness** *n*
smelt[1] *vb* to extract (a metal) from (an ore) by heating
WORD ORIGIN Middle Low German, Middle Dutch *smelten*
smelt[2] *n, pl* **smelt** *or* **smelts** a small silvery food fish
WORD ORIGIN Old English *smylt*
smelt[3] *vb* ▸a past tense and past participle of **smell**
smelter *n* an industrial plant in which smelting is carried out
Smetana *n* **Bedřich** 1824–84, Czech composer, founder of his country's national school of music. His works include *My Fatherland* (1874–79), a cycle of six symphonic poems, and the opera *The Bartered Bride* (1866)
smile ❶ *n* **1** a facial expression in which the corners of the mouth are turned up, showing amusement or friendliness ▹*vb* **smiling, smiled 2** to give a smile **3 smile at a** to look at with a kindly expression **b** to look with amusement at **4 smile on** *or* **upon** to regard favourably: *fortune smiled on us today* **5** to express by a smile: *he smiled a comrade's greeting*
WORD ORIGIN probably from Old Norse
Smiles *n* **Samuel** 1812–1904, British writer: author of the didactic work *Self-Help* (1859)
smiley *adj* **1** cheerful **2** depicting a smile ▹*n* **3** a group of symbols depicting a smile, or other facial expression, used in e-mail
smirch *vb* **1** to disgrace **2** to dirty or soil ▹*n* **3** a disgrace **4** a smear or stain
WORD ORIGIN origin unknown
smirk *n* **1** a smug smile ▹*vb* **2** to give such a smile
WORD ORIGIN Old English *smearcian*
smite *vb* **smiting, smote; smitten** *or* **smit** *archaic, Bible* **1** to strike with a heavy blow **2** to affect severely: *hunger smites him again* **3** to burden with an affliction in order to punish: *God smote the enemies of the righteous* **4 smite on** to strike abruptly and with force: *the sun smote down on him*
WORD ORIGIN Old English *smītan*
smith *n* **1** a person who works in metal: *goldsmith* **2** ▸see **blacksmith**
WORD ORIGIN Old English
smithereens *pl n* shattered fragments
WORD ORIGIN Irish Gaelic *smidirīn*
smithy *n, pl* **smithies** the workshop of a blacksmith; forge
smitten *vb* **1** ▸a past participle of **smite** ▹*adj* **2** deeply affected by love (for)
smock *n* **1** a loose overall worn to protect the clothes **2** a loose blouselike garment worn by women **3** a loose protective overgarment decorated with smocking, worn

THESAURUS

smash *vb* **1a = break**, crush, shatter, crack, demolish, shiver, disintegrate, pulverize, crush to smithereens **1b = shatter**, break, disintegrate, split, crack, explode, splinter **3 = collide**, crash, meet head-on, clash, come into collision **5 = destroy**, ruin, wreck, total *(slang)*, defeat, overthrow, trash *(slang)*, lay waste ▹*n* **7 = collision**, crash, accident, pile-up *(informal)*, smash-up *(informal)*
smashing *adj (informal, chiefly Brit)* **= excellent**, mean *(slang)*, great *(informal)*, wonderful, topping *(Brit slang)*, brilliant *(informal)*, cracking *(Brit informal)*, crucial *(slang)*, superb, fantastic *(informal)*, magnificent, fabulous *(informal)*, first-class, marvellous, terrific *(informal)*, sensational *(informal)*, mega *(slang)*, sovereign, awesome *(slang)*, world-class, exhilarating, fab *(informal, chiefly Brit)*, super *(informal)*, first-rate, def *(slang)*, superlative, brill *(informal)*, stupendous, out of this world *(informal)*, bodacious *(slang, chiefly US)*, boffo *(slang)*, jim-dandy *(slang)*, chillin' *(US slang)*, booshit *(Austral slang)*, exo *(Austral slang)*, sik *(Austral slang)*, rad *(informal)*, phat *(slang)*, schmick *(Austral informal)*
OPPOSITE: awful
smear *vb* **1, 2 = spread over**, daub, rub on, cover, coat, plaster, bedaub **3 = smudge**, soil, dirty, stain, sully, besmirch, smirch **4 = slander**, tarnish, malign, vilify, blacken, sully, besmirch, traduce, calumniate, asperse, drag (someone's) name through the mud ▹*n* **5 = smudge**, daub, streak, blot, blotch, splotch, smirch **6 = slander**, libel, defamation, vilification, whispering campaign, calumny, mudslinging
smell *vb* **1 = sniff**, scent, get a whiff of, nose **4 = stink**, reek, pong *(Brit informal)*, hum *(slang)*, whiff *(Brit slang)*, stink to high heaven *(informal)*, niff *(Brit slang)*, be malodorous ▹*n* **9a = odour**, scent, fragrance, perfume, bouquet, aroma, whiff, niff *(Brit slang)*, redolence **9b = stink**, stench, reek, pong *(Brit informal)*, niff *(Brit slang)*, malodour, fetor
smile *n* **1 = grin**, beam, smirk ▹*vb* **2 = grin**, beam, smirk, twinkle, grin from ear to ear

S

DICTIONARY

formerly by farm workers ▷ *vb* **4** to gather (material) by sewing in a honeycomb pattern
WORD ORIGIN Old English *smocc*

smocking *n* ornamental needlework used to gather material

smog *n* a mixture of smoke and fog that occurs in some industrial areas **smoggy** *adj*
WORD ORIGIN SMOKE + FOG

smoke *n* **1** the cloudy mass that rises from something burning **2** the act of smoking tobacco **3** *informal* a cigarette or cigar **4 go up in smoke a** to come to nothing **b** to burn up vigorously ▷ *vb* **smoking, smoked 5** to give off smoke: *a smoking fireplace* **6 a** to draw the smoke of (burning tobacco) into the mouth and exhale it again **b** to do this habitually **7** to cure (meat, cheese, or fish) by treating with smoke
WORD ORIGIN Old English *smoca*

Smoke *n* **the Smoke** *informal* ▸ short for **Big Smoke**

smokeless *adj* having or producing little or no smoke: *smokeless fuel*

smokeless zone *n* an area where only smokeless fuels may be used

smoke out *vb* **1** to drive (a person or animal) out of a hiding place by filling it with smoke **2** to bring (someone) out of secrecy and into the open: *they smoked out the plotters*

smoker *n* **1** a person who habitually smokes tobacco **2** a train compartment where smoking is permitted

smoke screen *n* **1** something said or done to hide the truth **2** *mil* a cloud of smoke used to provide cover for manoeuvres

smokestack *n* a tall chimney that carries smoke away from a factory

smoko *or* **smokeho** (smoke-oh) *n, pl* **-kos** *or* **-hos** *Austral & NZ informal* **1** a short break from work for tea or a cigarette **2** refreshment taken during this break

smoky *adj* **smokier, smokiest 1** filled with or giving off smoke, sometimes excessively: *smoky coal or wood fires* **2** having the colour of smoke **3** having the taste or smell of smoke **4** made dirty or hazy by smoke **smokiness** *n*

Smollett *n* **Tobias George** 1721–71, Scottish novelist, whose picaresque satires include *Roderick Random* (1748), *Peregrine Pickle* (1751), and *Humphry Clinker* (1771)

smolt *n* a young salmon at the stage when it migrates from fresh water to the sea
WORD ORIGIN Scots

smooch *slang vb* **1** (of two people) to kiss and cuddle **2** *Brit* to dance very slowly with one's arms around another person or (of two people) to dance together in such a way ▷ *n* **3** the act of smooching
WORD ORIGIN dialect *smouch*, imitative

smoodge *or* **smooge** *vb* **smoodging, smoodged** *or* **smooging, smooged** *Austral & NZ* **1** ▸ same as **smooch** (sense 1) **2** to attempt to gain favour through flattery

smooth ❶ *adj* **1** having an even surface with no roughness, bumps, or holes **2** without obstructions or difficulties: *smooth progress towards an agreement* **3** without lumps: *a smooth paste* **4** free from jolts and bumps: *a smooth landing* **5** not harsh in taste; mellow: *an excellent smooth wine* **6** charming or persuasive but possibly insincere ▷ *adv* **7** in a smooth manner ▷ *vb* **8** (often foll. by *down*) to make or become even or without roughness **9** (often foll. by *out* or *away*) to remove in order to make smooth: *smoothing out the creases* **10** to make calm; soothe **11** to make easier: *Moscow smoothed the path to democracy* ▷ *n* **12** the smooth part of something **13** the act of smoothing **smoothly** *adv*
WORD ORIGIN Old English *smōth*

smoothie *n* **1** *slang* a man who is so confident, well-dressed, and charming that one is suspicious of his motives and doubts his honesty **2** a smooth thick drink made from fresh fruit and yoghurt, ice cream, or milk

smooth over *vb* to ease or gloss over: *their fears are now being smoothed over*

smooth-talking *adj* confident and persuasive but not necessarily honest or sincere

smorgasbord *n* a variety of savoury dishes served as hors d'oeuvres or as a buffet meal
WORD ORIGIN Swedish

smote *vb* ▸ the past tense of **smite**

smother ❶ *vb* **1** to extinguish (a fire) by covering so as to cut it off from the air **2** to suffocate **3** to surround or overwhelm (with): *she smothered him with her idea of affection* **4** to suppress or stifle: *he smothered an ironic chuckle* **5** to cover over thickly: *ice cream smothered with sauce*
WORD ORIGIN Old English *smorian* to suffocate

smoulder *or US* **smolder** *vb* **1** to burn slowly without flames, usually giving off smoke **2** (of emotions) to exist in a suppressed state without being released
WORD ORIGIN origin unknown

SMS short message system: used for sending data to mobile phones

smudge *vb* **smudging, smudged 1** to make or become smeared or soiled ▷ *n* **2** a smear or dirty mark **3** a blurred form or area: *the dull smudge of a ship* **smudgy** *adj*
WORD ORIGIN origin unknown

smug ❶ *adj* **smugger, smuggest** very pleased with oneself; self-satisfied **smugly** *adv* **smugness** *n*
WORD ORIGIN Germanic

smuggle *vb* **-gling, -gled 1** to import or export (goods that are prohibited or subject to taxation) secretly **2** (often foll. by *into* or *out of*) to bring or take secretly: *he was smuggled out of the country unnoticed* **smuggler** *n* **smuggling** *n*
WORD ORIGIN Low German *smukkelen*

smut *n* **1** stories, pictures, or jokes relating to sex or nudity **2** a speck of soot or a dark mark left by soot **3** a disease of cereals, in which black sooty masses cover the affected parts **smutty** *adj*
WORD ORIGIN Old English *smitte*

Smyth *n* Dame **Ethel** (**Mary**) 1858–1944, British composer, best known for her operas, such as *The Wreckers* (1906). She was imprisoned for supporting the suffragette movement

Sn *chem* tin
WORD ORIGIN New Latin *stannum*

snack ❶ *n* **1** a light quick meal eaten between or in place of main meals ▷ *vb* **2** to eat a snack
WORD ORIGIN probably from Middle Dutch *snacken*

snack bar *n* a place where light meals or snacks are sold

snaffle *n* **1** a mouthpiece for controlling a horse ▷ *vb* **-fling, -fled 2** *Brit, Austral & NZ informal* to steal or

S

THESAURUS

smooth *adj* **1a = even**, level, flat, plane, plain, flush, horizontal, unwrinkled **OPPOSITE:** uneven **1b = sleek**, polished, shiny, glossy, silky, velvety, glassy, mirror-like **OPPOSITE:** rough **2 = easy**, effortless, untroubled, well-ordered **4 = flowing**, steady, fluent, regular, uniform, rhythmic **5 = mellow**, pleasant, mild, soothing, bland, agreeable **6 = suave**, slick, persuasive, urbane, silky, glib, facile, ingratiating, debonair, unctuous, smarmy (*Brit informal*) ▷ *vb* **8, 9 = flatten**, level, press, plane, iron **11 = ease**, aid, assist, facilitate, pave the way, make easier, help along, iron out the difficulties of **OPPOSITE:** hinder

smother *vb* **1 = extinguish**, put out, stifle, snuff **2 = suffocate**, choke, strangle, stifle **4 = suppress**, stifle, repress, hide, conceal, muffle, keep back

smug *adj* **= self-satisfied**, superior, complacent, conceited, self-righteous, holier-than-thou, priggish, self-opinionated

snack *n* **1 = light meal**, bite, refreshment(s), nibble, titbit, bite to

DICTIONARY

take **3** to fit or control (a horse) with a snaffle
WORD ORIGIN origin unknown
snafu (snaf-foo) *chiefly mil slang n* **1** confusion or chaos regarded as the normal state ▹*adj* **2** confused or muddled up, as usual
WORD ORIGIN *s(ituation) n(ormal): a(ll) f(ucked) u(p)*
snag ❶ *n* **1** a small problem or difficulty: *one possible snag in his plans* **2** a sharp projecting point that may catch on things **3** a small hole in a fabric caused by a sharp object **4** a tree stump in a river bed that is a danger to navigation ▹*vb* **snagging, snagged 5** to tear or catch on a snag
WORD ORIGIN Scandinavian
snail *n* a slow-moving mollusc with a spiral shell
WORD ORIGIN Old English *snæg(e)l*
snail mail *informal n* **1** conventional post, as opposed to e-mail **2** the conventional postal system ▹*vb* **snail-mail 3** to send by the conventional postal system, rather than by e-mail
snail's pace *n* a very slow speed
snake ❶ *n* **1** a long scaly limbless reptile **2** Also: **snake in the grass** a person, esp. a colleague or friend, who secretly acts against one ▹*vb* **snaking, snaked 3** to glide or move in a winding course, like a snake
WORD ORIGIN Old English *snaca*
snakebite *n* **1** the bite of a snake **2** a drink of cider and lager
snake charmer *n* an entertainer who appears to hypnotize snakes by playing music
snakes and ladders *n* a board game in which players move counters along a series of squares by means of dice, going up the ladders to squares nearer the finish and down the snakes to squares nearer the start
snaky *adj* **snakier, snakiest 1** twisting or winding **2** treacherous
snap ❶ *vb* **snapping, snapped 1** to break suddenly, esp. with a sharp sound **2** to make or cause to make a sudden sharp cracking sound: *he snapped his fingers* **3** to move or close with a sudden sharp sound: *I snapped the lid shut* **4** to move in a sudden or abrupt way **5** to give way or collapse suddenly under strain: *one day someone's temper will snap* **6** to panic when a situation becomes too difficult to cope with: *he could snap at any moment* **7** (often foll. by *at* or *up*) to seize suddenly or quickly **8** (often foll. by *at*) (of animals) to bite at suddenly **9** to speak (words) sharply and angrily **10** to take a photograph of **11 snap one's fingers at** *informal* to defy or dismiss contemptuously **12 snap out of it** *informal* to recover quickly, esp. from depression or anger ▹*n* **13** the act of breaking suddenly or the sound of a sudden breakage **14** a sudden sharp sound **15** a clasp or fastener that closes with a snapping sound **16** a sudden grab or bite **17** a thin crisp biscuit: *brandy snaps* **18** *informal* an informal photograph taken with a simple camera **19** ▸see **cold snap 20** *Brit & NZ* a card game in which the word *snap* is called when two similar cards are turned up ▹*adj* **21** done on the spur of the moment: *snap judgments* ▹*adv* **22** with a snap ▹*interj* **23 a** *cards* the word called while playing snap **b** a cry used to draw attention to the similarity of two things ▸See also **snap up**
WORD ORIGIN Middle Dutch *snappen* to seize
snapdragon *n* a plant with spikes of colourful flowers that can open and shut like a mouth; antirrhinum
snap fastener *n* ▸same as **press stud**
snapper *n* a food fish of Australia and New Zealand with a pinkish body covered with blue spots
snappy *adj* **-pier, -piest 1** smart and fashionable: *snappy designs* **2** Also: **snappish** (of someone's behaviour) irritable, unfriendly, and cross **3** brisk or lively: *short snappy movements* **4 make it snappy** *slang* hurry up! **snappiness** *n*
snapshot *n* ▸same as **snap** (sense 18)
snap up ❶ *vb* to take advantage of eagerly and quickly: *the tickets have been snapped up*
snare¹ ❶ *n* **1** a trap for birds or small animals, usually a flexible loop that is drawn tight around the prey **2** anything that traps someone or something unawares ▹*vb* **snaring, snared 3** to catch in or as if in a snare
WORD ORIGIN Old English *sneare*
snare² *n music* a set of strings fitted against the lower head of a snare drum, which produces a rattling sound when the drum is beaten
WORD ORIGIN Middle Dutch *snaer* or Middle Low German *snare* string
snare drum *n music* a small drum fitted with a snare
snarl¹ *vb* **1** (of an animal) to growl fiercely with bared teeth **2** to speak or say (something) fiercely: *he snarled out a command to a subordinate* ▹*n* **3** a fierce growl or facial expression **4** the act of snarling
WORD ORIGIN Germanic
snarl² *n* **1** a complicated or confused state **2** a tangled mass ▹*vb* **3 snarl up** to become, be, or make tangled, confused or complicated: *the line became snarled up on the propeller; the postal service was snarled up at Christmas*
WORD ORIGIN from Old Norse
snarl-up *n informal* a confused, disorganized situation such as a traffic jam
snatch ❶ *vb* **1** to seize or grasp (something) suddenly: *she snatched the paper* **2** (usually foll. by *at*) to attempt to seize suddenly **3** to take hurriedly: *these players had snatched a few hours sleep* **4** to remove suddenly: *she snatched her hand away* ▹*n* **5** an act of snatching **6** a small piece or incomplete part: *snatches of song* **7** a brief spell: *snatches of sleep* **8** *slang chiefly US* an act of kidnapping **9** *Brit slang* a robbery: *a wages snatch*
WORD ORIGIN Middle English *snacchen*
snazzy *adj* **-zier, -ziest** *informal* (esp. of clothes) stylish and flashy
WORD ORIGIN origin unknown
Snead *n* **Sam(uel Jackson)** 1912–2002, US golfer; winner of seven major tournaments between 1938 and 1951
sneak ❶ *vb* **1** to move quietly, trying not be noticed **2** to behave in a cowardly or underhand manner **3** to bring, take, or put secretly: *we sneaked him over the border* **4** *informal chiefly Brit & NZ* (esp. in schools) to tell tales ▹*n* **5** a person who acts in an underhand or cowardly manner ▹*adj* **6** without warning: *a sneak attack* **sneaky** *adj*
WORD ORIGIN Old English *snícan* to creep

S

THESAURUS

eat, elevenses *(Brit informal)*
snag *n* **1 = difficulty,** hitch, problem, obstacle, catch, hazard, disadvantage, complication, drawback, inconvenience, downside, stumbling block, the rub ▹*vb* **5 = catch,** tear, rip, hole
snake *n* **1 = serpent**
snap *vb* **1 = break,** split, crack, separate, fracture, give way, come apart **2, 3 = pop,** click, crackle **8 = bite at,** bite, nip **9 = speak sharply,** bark, lash out at, flash, retort, snarl, growl, fly off the handle at *(informal)*, jump down (someone's) throat *(informal)* ▹*adj* **21 = instant,** immediate, sudden, abrupt, spur-of-the-moment, unpremeditated
snap up *vb* **= grab,** seize, take advantage of, swoop down on, pounce upon, avail yourself of
snare¹ *n* **1 = trap,** net, wire, gin, pitfall, noose, springe ▹*vb* **3 = trap,** catch, net, wire, seize, entrap, springe
snatch *vb* **1 = grab,** seize, wrench, wrest, take, grip, grasp, clutch, take hold of ▹*n* **6 = bit,** part, fragment, piece, spell, snippet, smattering
sneak *vb* **1 = slink,** slip, steal, pad, sidle, skulk **3 = slip,** smuggle, spirit ▹*n* **5 = informer,** grass *(Brit slang)*, betrayer, telltale, squealer *(slang)*, Judas, accuser, stool pigeon, snake in the grass, nark *(Brit, Austral & NZ slang)*, fizgig *(Austral slang)*

DICTIONARY

sneakers *pl n US, Canad, Austral & NZ* canvas shoes with rubber soles
sneaking Ⓣ *adj* **1** slight but nagging: *a sneaking suspicion* **2** secret: *a sneaking admiration* **3** acting in a cowardly and furtive way
sneak thief *n* a burglar who sneaks into houses through open doors and windows
sneer Ⓣ *n* **1** a facial expression showing distaste or contempt, typically with a curled upper lip **2** a remark showing distaste or contempt ▹*vb* **3** to make a facial expression of scorn or contempt **4** to say (something) in a scornful manner **sneering** *adj, n*
WORD ORIGIN origin unknown
sneeze *vb* **sneezing, sneezed** **1** to expel air from the nose suddenly and without control, esp. as the result of irritation in the nostrils ▹*n* **2** the act or sound of sneezing
WORD ORIGIN Old English *fnēosan* (unattested)
sneeze at *vb informal* to ignore or dismiss lightly: *the money's not to be sneezed at*
Snell *n* **Peter (George)** born 1938, New Zealand athlete; winner of three Olympic gold medals: for the 800 metres in 1960, and again in 1964, when he also won gold for the 1500 metres
snib *n Scot & NZ* the catch of a door or window
snick *n* **1** a small cut in something; notch **2** *cricket* a glancing blow off the edge of the bat ▹*vb* **3** to make a small cut or notch in (something) **4** *cricket* to hit (the ball) with a snick
WORD ORIGIN probably Scandinavian
snicker *n, vb chiefly US & Canad* ▸same as **snigger**
WORD ORIGIN probably imitative
snide *or* **snidey** *adj* (of comments) critical in an unfair and nasty way
WORD ORIGIN origin unknown
sniff Ⓣ *vb* **1** to inhale through the nose in short audible breaths **2** (often foll. by *at*) to smell by sniffing ▹*n* **3** the act or sound of sniffing **sniffer** *n*
WORD ORIGIN imitative
sniff at *vb* to express contempt or dislike for
sniffer dog *n* a police dog trained to locate drugs or explosives by smell
sniffle *vb* **-fling, -fled** **1** to sniff repeatedly when the nasal passages are blocked up ▹*n* **2** the act or sound of sniffling
sniffles *or* **snuffles** *pl n* **the sniffles** *informal* a cold in the head
sniff out *vb* to discover after some searching: *they eventually sniffed out a suitable Parliamentary seat for him*
sniffy *adj* **-fier, -fiest** *informal* contemptuous or scornful
snifter *n* **1** *informal* a small quantity of alcoholic drink **2** a pear-shaped brandy glass
WORD ORIGIN origin unknown
snig *vb* **snigging, snigged** *Austral & NZ* to drag (a felled log) by a chain or cable
WORD ORIGIN English dialect
snigger *n* **1** a quiet and disrespectful laugh kept to oneself ▹*vb* **2** to utter such a laugh
WORD ORIGIN variant of *snicker*
snip *vb* **snipping, snipped** **1** to cut with small quick strokes with scissors or shears ▹*n* **2** *informal, chiefly Brit* a bargain **3** the act or sound of snipping **4** a small piece snipped off **5** a small cut made by snipping
WORD ORIGIN Low German, Dutch *snippen*
snipe *n, pl* **snipe** *or* **snipes** **1** a wading bird with a long straight bill ▹*vb* **sniping, sniped** (often foll. by *at*) **2** to shoot (someone) from a place of hiding **3** (often foll. by *at*) to make critical remarks about **sniper** *n*
WORD ORIGIN Old Norse *snīpa*
snippet *n* a small scrap or fragment: *the odd snippet of knowledge*
snitch *slang vb* **1** to act as an informer **2** to steal small amounts ▹*n* **3** an informer
WORD ORIGIN origin unknown
snitchy *adj* **snitchier, snitchiest** *NZ informal* bad-tempered or irritable
snivel *vb* **-elling, -elled** *or US* **-eling, -eled** **1** to cry and sniff in a self-pitying way **2** to say (something) tearfully; whine **3** to have a runny nose ▹*n* **4** the act of snivelling
WORD ORIGIN Middle English *snivelen*
snob *n* **1** a person who tries to associate with those of higher social status and who hates those of a lower social status **2** a person who feels smugly superior with regard to his or her tastes or interests: *a cultural snob* **snobbery** *n* **snobbish** *adj*
WORD ORIGIN origin unknown
snoek **(snook)** *n* a South African edible marine fish
WORD ORIGIN Afrikaans, from Dutch: pike
snoep **(snoop)** *adj S African informal* mean or tight-fisted
WORD ORIGIN Afrikaans: greedy
snog *Brit, NZ & S African slang vb* **snogging, snogged** **1** to kiss and cuddle ▹*n* **2** the act of kissing and cuddling
WORD ORIGIN origin unknown
snood *n* a pouchlike hat loosely holding a woman's hair at the back
WORD ORIGIN Old English *snōd*
snook *n* **cock a snook at** *Brit* **a** to make a rude gesture at (someone) by putting one thumb to the nose with the fingers of the hand outstretched **b** to show contempt for (someone in authority) without fear of punishment
WORD ORIGIN origin unknown
snooker *n* **1** a game played on a billiard table with 15 red balls, six balls of other colours, and a white cue ball **2** a shot in which the cue ball is left in a position such that another ball blocks the target ball ▹*vb* **3** to leave (an opponent) in an unfavourable position by playing a snooker **4** to put someone in a position where he or she can do nothing
WORD ORIGIN origin unknown
snoop *informal vb* **1** (often foll. by *about* or *around*) to pry into the private business of others ▹*n* **2** the act of snooping **3** a person who snoops **snooper** *n* **snoopy** *adj*
WORD ORIGIN Dutch *snoepen* to eat furtively
snooty *adj* **snootier, snootiest** *informal* behaving as if superior to other people; snobbish
WORD ORIGIN from *snoot* nose
snooze *informal vb* **snoozing, snoozed** **1** to take a brief light sleep ▹*n* **2** a nap
WORD ORIGIN origin unknown
snore *vb* **snoring, snored** **1** to breathe with snorting sounds while asleep ▹*n* **2** the act or sound of snoring
WORD ORIGIN imitative
snorkel *n* **1** a tube allowing a swimmer to breathe while face down on the surface of the water **2** a device supplying air to a submarine when under water ▹*vb* **-kelling, -kelled** *or US* **-keling, -keled** **3** to swim with a snorkel
WORD ORIGIN German *Schnorchel*
Snorri Sturluson *n* 1179–1241, Icelandic historian and poet; author of *Younger* or *Prose Edda* (?1222), containing a collection of Norse myths and a treatise on poetry, and the *Heimskringla* sagas of the Norwegian kings from their mythological origins to the 12th century
snort *vb* **1** to exhale air noisily through the nostrils **2** to express contempt or annoyance by snorting **3** to say with a snort **4** *slang* to

THESAURUS

sneaking *adj* **1 = nagging**, worrying, persistent, niggling, uncomfortable **2 = secret**, private, hidden, suppressed, unexpressed, unvoiced, unavowed, unconfessed, undivulged
sneer *vb* **4 = say contemptuously**, snigger
sniff *vb* **1 = breathe in**, inhale, snuffle, snuff **2 = smell**, nose, breathe in, scent, get a whiff of
snub *vb* **1 = insult**, slight, put down, humiliate, cut *(informal)*, shame,

S

inhale a powdered drug through the nostrils ▷ *n* **5** a loud exhalation of air through the nostrils to express contempt or annoyance: *Clare gave a snort of disgust*
WORD ORIGIN Middle English *snorten*

snot *n usually considered vulgar* **1** mucus from the nose **2** *slang* an annoying or disgusting person
WORD ORIGIN Old English *gesnot*

snotty *adj* **-tier, -tiest** *considered vulgar* **1** dirty with nasal discharge **2** having a proud and superior attitude **3** *slang* contemptible; nasty **snottiness** *n*

snout *n* **1** the projecting nose and jaws of an animal **2** anything projecting like a snout: *the snout of a gun* **3** *slang* a person's nose
WORD ORIGIN Germanic

snow *n* **1** frozen vapour falling from the sky in flakes **2** a layer of snow on the ground **3** a falling of snow **4** *slang* cocaine ▷ *vb* **5** (*with "it" as subject*) to be the case that snow is falling: *it's snowing today* **6** to fall as or like snow **7** **be snowed in** *or* **up** *or* **over** to be covered by or confined with a heavy fall of snow **8** **be snowed under** to be overwhelmed, esp. with paperwork **snowy** *adj*
WORD ORIGIN Old English *snāw*

Snow *n* **C(harles) P(ercy)**, Baron 1905–80, British novelist and physicist. His novels include the series *Strangers and Brothers* (1949–70)

snowball *n* **1** snow pressed into a ball for throwing ▷ *vb* **2** to increase rapidly in size or importance: *production snowballed between 1950 and 1970* **3** to throw snowballs at

snowberry *n, pl* **-ries** a shrub grown for its white berries

snow-blind *adj* blinded for a short time by the intense reflection of sunlight from snow **snow blindness** *n*

snowboard *n* a shaped board, like a skateboard without wheels, on which a person stands to slide across the snow **snowboarding** *n*

snowbound *adj* shut in or blocked off by snow

snowcap *n* a cap of snow on top of a mountain **snowcapped** *adj*

Snowdon[1] *n* a mountain in NW Wales, in Gwynedd: the highest peak in Wales. Height: 1085 m (3560 ft). Welsh name: **Yr Wyddfa**

Snowdon[2] *n* **1st Earl of,** title of *Antony Armstrong-Jones* born 1930, British photographer, whose work includes television documentaries, photographic books, and the design of the Snowdon Aviary, London Zoo (1965). His marriage (1960–78) to Princess Margaret ended in divorce

snowdrift *n* a bank of deep snow driven together by the wind

snowdrop *n* a plant with small drooping white bell-shaped flowers

snowfall *n* **1** a fall of snow **2** *meteorol* the amount of snow that falls in a specified place and time

snowflake *n* a single crystal of snow

snow goose *n* a North American goose with white feathers and black wing tips

snow line *n* (on a mountain) the altitude above which there is permanent snow

snowman *n, pl* **-men** a figure like a person, made of packed snow

snowmobile *n* a motor vehicle for travelling on snow, esp. one with caterpillar tracks and front skis

snowplough *or esp. US* **snowplow** *n* a vehicle for clearing away snow

snowshoe *n* a racket-shaped frame with a network of thongs stretched across it, worn on the feet to make walking on snow less difficult

snowstorm *n* a storm with heavy snow

SNP Scottish National Party

Snr *or* **snr** senior

snub ❶ *vb* **snubbing, snubbed** **1** to insult (someone) deliberately ▷ *n* **2** a deliberately insulting act or remark ▷ *adj* **3** (of a nose) short and turned up
WORD ORIGIN Old Norse *snubba* to scold

snub-nosed *adj* having a short turned-up nose

snuff[1] *vb* **1** to inhale through the nose **2** (esp. of an animal) to examine by sniffing ▷ *n* **3** a sniff
WORD ORIGIN probably Middle Dutch *snuffen* to snuffle

snuff[2] *n* finely powdered tobacco for sniffing up the nostrils
WORD ORIGIN Dutch *snuf*

snuff[3] *vb* **1** (often foll. by *out*) to put out (a candle) **2** to cut off the charred part of (a candle wick) **3** (usually foll. by *out*) *informal* to put an end to **4** **snuff it** *Austral & Brit informal* to die ▷ *n* **5** the burned portion of the wick of a candle
WORD ORIGIN origin unknown

snuffbox *n* a small container for holding snuff

snuffle *vb* **-fling, -fled** **1** to breathe noisily or with difficulty **2** to say or speak through the nose **3** to cry and sniff in a self-pitying way ▷ *n* **4** an act or the sound of snuffling **snuffly** *adj*
WORD ORIGIN Low German or Dutch *snuffelen*

snug *adj* **snugger, snuggest** **1** comfortably warm and well protected; cosy: *safe and snug in their homes* **2** small but comfortable: *a snug office* **3** fitting closely and comfortably ▷ *n* **4** (in Britain and Ireland) a small room in a pub **snugly** *adv*
WORD ORIGIN Swedish *snygg* tidy

snuggery *n, pl* **-geries** a cosy and comfortable place or room

snuggle *vb* **-gling, -gled** to nestle into (a person or thing) for warmth or from affection
WORD ORIGIN from SNUG

so[1] ❶ *adv* **1** to such an extent: *the river is so dirty that it smells* **2** to the same extent as: *she is not so old as you* **3** extremely: *it's so lovely* **4** also: *I can speak Spanish and so can you* **5** thereupon: *and so we ended up in France* **6** in the state or manner expressed or implied: *they're happy and will remain so* **7** **and so on** *or* **forth** and continuing similarly **8** **or so** approximately: *fifty or so people came to see me* **9** **so be it** an expression of agreement or resignation **10** **so much** **a** a certain degree or amount (of) **b** a lot (of): *it's just so much nonsense* **11** **so much for** **a** no more need be said about **b** used to express contempt for something that has failed: *so much for all our plans* ▷ *conj* (often foll. by *that*) **12** in order (that): *to die so that you might live* **13** with the consequence (that): *he was late home, so that there was trouble* **14** **so as** in order (to): *to diet so as to lose weight* **15** *not standard* in consequence: *she wasn't needed, so she left* **16** **so what!** *informal* that is unimportant ▷ *pron* **17** used to substitute for a clause or sentence, which may be understood: *you'll stop because I said so* ▷ *adj* **18** true: *it can't be so* ▷ *interj* **19** an exclamation of surprise or triumph
WORD ORIGIN Old English *swā*

so[2] *n music* ▸ same as **soh**

soak ❶ *vb* **1** to put or lie in a liquid so as to become thoroughly wet **2** (usually foll. by *in* or *into*) (of a liquid) to penetrate or permeate **3** (usually foll. by *in* or *up*) to take in; absorb: *white clay soaks up excess oil* ▷ *n*

humble, rebuff, mortify, cold-shoulder, kick in the teeth (*slang*), give (someone) the cold shoulder, give (someone) the brush-off (*slang*), cut dead (*informal*) ▷ *n* **2 = insult**, put-down, humiliation, affront, slap in the face (*informal*), brush-off (*slang*)

so[1] *conj* **15** (*not standard*) **= therefore**, thus, hence, consequently, then, as a result, accordingly, for that reason, whence, thence, ergo

soak *vb* **1a = steep**, immerse, submerge, infuse, marinate (*cookery*), dunk, submerse **1b = wet**, damp, saturate, drench, douse, moisten, suffuse, wet through, waterlog, souse, drouk (*Scot*) **2 = penetrate**, pervade, permeate, enter, get in, infiltrate, diffuse, seep, suffuse, make inroads (into)
3 soak something up = absorb, suck

DICTIONARY

4 a soaking or being soaked 5 *slang* a person who drinks very heavily **soaking** *n, adj*
WORD ORIGIN Old English *sōcian*
so-and-so *n, pl* **so-and-sos** *informal* 1 a person whose name is not specified 2 *euphemistic* a person regarded as unpleasant; a name used in place of a swear word: *you're a dirty so-and-so*
Soane *n* Sir **John** 1753–1837, British architect. His work includes Dulwich College Art Gallery (1811–14) and his own house in Lincoln's Inn Fields, London (1812–13), which is now the Sir John Soane's Museum
soap *n* 1 a compound of alkali and fat, used with water as a cleaning agent 2 *informal* ▸short for **soap opera** ▹*vb* 3 to apply soap to
WORD ORIGIN Old English *sāpe*
soapbox *n* a crate used as a platform for making speeches
soap opera *n* an on-going television or radio serial about the daily lives of a group of people
WORD ORIGIN so called because manufacturers of soap were typical sponsors
soapstone *n* a soft mineral used for making table tops and ornaments
soapsuds *pl n* foam or lather produced when soap is mixed with water
soapy *adj* **soapier, soapiest** 1 containing or covered with soap: *a soapy liquid* 2 like soap in texture, smell, or taste: *the cheese had a soapy taste* 3 *slang* flattering or persuasive **soapiness** *n*
soar ⓣ *vb* 1 to rise or fly upwards into the air 2 (of a bird or aircraft) to glide while maintaining altitude 3 to rise or increase suddenly above the usual level: *television ratings soared*
WORD ORIGIN Old French *essorer*
Soares *n* **Mário** born 1924, Portuguese statesman; prime minister of Portugal (1976–77; 1978–80; 1983–86); president of Portugal (1986–96)
sob ⓣ *vb* **sobbing, sobbed** 1 to cry noisily, breathing in short gasps 2 to speak with sobs ▹*n* 3 the act or sound of sobbing
WORD ORIGIN probably from Low German
sober ⓣ *adj* 1 not drunk 2 tending to drink only moderate quantities of alcohol 3 serious and thoughtful: *a sober and serious fellow* 4 (of colours) plain and dull 5 free from exaggeration: *a fairly sober version of what happened* ▹*vb* 6 (usually foll. by *up*) to make or become less drunk **sobering** *adj*
WORD ORIGIN Latin *sobrius*
Sobers *n* Sir **Garfield St Auburn,** known as *Carry* born 1936, West Indian (Barbadian) cricketer; one of the finest all-rounders of all time
sobriety *n* the state of being sober
sobriquet *or* **soubriquet** (so-brik-ay) *n* a nickname
WORD ORIGIN French *soubriquet*
sob story *n* a tale of personal misfortune or bad luck intended to arouse sympathy
Soc. *or* **soc.** 1 socialist 2 society
soca (soak-a) *n* a mixture of soul and calypso music popular in the E Caribbean
so-called ⓣ *adj* called (in the speaker's opinion, wrongly) by that name: *so-called military experts*
soccer *n* a game in which two teams of eleven players try to kick or head a ball into their opponents' goal, only the goalkeeper on either side being allowed to touch the ball with his hands
WORD ORIGIN *Assoc(iation Football)*
sociable *adj* 1 friendly and enjoying other people's company 2 (of an occasion) providing the opportunity for relaxed and friendly companionship **sociability** *n* **sociably** *adv*
social ⓣ *adj* 1 living or preferring to live in a community rather than alone 2 of or relating to human society or organization 3 of the way people live and work together in groups: *social organization* 4 of or for companionship or communal activities: *social clubs* 5 of or engaged in social services: *a social worker* 6 relating to a certain class of society: *social misfits* 7 (of certain species of insects) living together in organized colonies: *social bees* ▹*n* 8 an informal gathering **socially** *adv*
WORD ORIGIN Latin *socius* a comrade
Social Charter *n* a proposed declaration of the rights, minimum wages, etc. of workers in the European Union
social climber *n* a person who tries to associate with people from a higher social class in the hope that he or she will be thought also to be upper-class
social contract *or* **compact** *n* an agreement among individuals to cooperate for greater security, which results in the loss of some personal liberties
social democrat *n* 1 a person who is in favour of a market or mixed economy but believes the State must play an active role in ensuring social justice and equality of opportunity 2 (formerly) a person who believed in the gradual transformation of capitalism into democratic socialism **social democracy** *n*
social exclusion *n sociol* the failure of society to provide certain people with those rights normally available to its members, such as employment, health care, education, etc.
social fund *n* (in Britain) a social security fund from which loans or payments may be made to people in cases of extreme need
social inclusion *n sociol* the provision of certain rights to all people in society, such as employment, health care, education, etc.
social intelligence *n* the ability to form rewarding relationships with other people
socialism *n* a political and economic theory or system in which the means of production, distribution, and exchange are owned by the community collectively, usually through the state **socialist** *n, adj*
socialite *n* a person who goes to many events attended by the rich, famous, and fashionable
socialize *or* **-ise** *vb* **-izing, -ized** *or* **-ising, -ised** 1 to meet others socially 2 to prepare for life in society 3 *chiefly US* to organize along socialist principles **socialization** *or* **-isation** *n*
social networking site *n* a website that allows subscribers to interact, esp. by forming online communities based around shared interests, experiences, etc.
social science *n* the systematic study of society and of human relationships within society **social scientist** *n*
social security *n* state provision for

S

THESAURUS

up, take in *or* up, drink in, assimilate
soar *vb* **1 = fly**, rise, wing, climb, ascend, fly up **OPPOSITE:** plunge **3a = rise**, increase, grow, mount, climb, go up, rocket, swell, escalate, shoot up **3b = tower**, rise, climb, go up
sob *vb* **1, 2 = cry**, weep, blubber, greet *(Scot)*, howl, bawl, snivel, shed tears, boohoo ▹*n* **3 = cry**, whimper, howl
sober *adj* **2 = abstinent**, temperate, abstemious, moderate, on the wagon *(informal)* **OPPOSITE:** drunk **3 = serious**, practical, realistic, sound, cool, calm, grave, reasonable, steady, composed, rational, solemn, lucid, sedate, staid, level-headed, dispassionate, unruffled, clear-headed, unexcited, grounded **OPPOSITE:** frivolous **4 = plain**, dark, sombre, quiet, severe, subdued, drab **OPPOSITE:** bright
so-called *adj* **= alleged**, supposed, professed, pretended, self-styled, ostensible, soi-disant *(French)*
social *adj* **1 = communal**, community, collective, group, public, general, common, societal **3 = organized**, gregarious ▹*n* **8 = get-together** *(informal)*, party, gathering, function,

DICTIONARY

the welfare of the elderly, unemployed, or sick, through pensions and other financial aid
social services *pl n* welfare services provided by local authorities or a state agency for people with particular social needs
social studies *n* the study of how people live and organize themselves in society
social welfare *n* **1** social services provided by a state for the benefit of its citizens **2** (in New Zealand) a government department concerned with pensions and benefits for the elderly, the sick, etc.
social work *n* social services that give help and advice to the poor, the elderly, and families with problems
social worker *n*
society ❶ *n, pl* **-ties** **1** human beings considered as a group **2** a group of people forming a single community with its own distinctive culture and institutions **3** the structure, culture, and institutions of such a group **4** an organized group of people sharing a common aim or interest: *a dramatic society* **5** the rich and fashionable class of society collectively **6** *old-fashioned* companionship: *I enjoy her society*
WORD ORIGIN Latin *societas*
Society of Friends *n* the Quakers
Society of Jesus *n* the religious order of the Jesuits
Socinus *n* **Faustus**, Italian name *Fausto Sozzini*, 1539–1604, and his uncle, **Laelius**, Italian name *Lelio Sozzini*, 1525–62, Italian Protestant theologians and reformers
socioeconomic *adj* of or involving economic and social factors
sociology *n* the study of the development, organization, functioning, and classification of human societies **sociological** *adj* **sociologist** *n*
sociopolitical *adj* of or involving political and social factors
sock[1] *n* **1** a cloth covering for the foot, reaching to between the ankle and knee and worn inside a shoe **2 pull one's socks up** *informal* to make a determined effort to improve **3 put a sock in it** *slang* be quiet!
WORD ORIGIN Greek *sukkhos* a light shoe
sock[2] *slang vb* **1** to hit hard ▷*n* **2** a hard blow
WORD ORIGIN origin unknown
socket *n* **1** a device into which an electric plug can be inserted in order to make a connection in a circuit **2** *anat* a bony hollow into which a part or structure fits: *the hip socket*
WORD ORIGIN Anglo-Norman *soket* a little ploughshare
Socratic *adj* of the Greek philosopher Socrates, or his teachings
Socratic method *n philosophy* the method of instruction used by Socrates, in which a series of questions and answers lead to a logical conclusion
sod[1] *n* **1** a piece of grass-covered surface soil; turf **2** *poetic* the ground
WORD ORIGIN Low German
sod[2] *slang, chiefly Brit n* **1** an unpleasant person **2** *jocular* a person, esp. an unlucky one: *the poor sod hasn't been out for weeks* **3 sod all** *slang* nothing ▷*interj* **4 sod it** an exclamation of annoyance
sodding *adj*
WORD ORIGIN from *sodomite*
soda *n* **1** a simple compound of sodium, such as sodium carbonate or sodium bicarbonate **2** ▸same as **soda water** **3** *US & Canad* a sweet fizzy drink
WORD ORIGIN perhaps from Arabic
soda bread *n* a type of bread raised with sodium bicarbonate
soda fountain *n US & Canad* **1** a counter that serves soft drinks and snacks **2** a device dispensing soda water
soda siphon *n* a sealed bottle containing soda water under pressure, which is forced up a tube when a lever is pressed
soda water *n* a fizzy drink made by charging water with carbon dioxide under pressure
sodden *adj* **1** soaking wet **2** (of someone's senses) dulled, esp. by excessive drinking
WORD ORIGIN *soden*, obsolete past participle of *seethe*
Soddy *n* **Frederick** 1877–1956, English chemist, whose work on radioactive disintegration led to the discovery of isotopes: Nobel prize for chemistry 1921
sodium *n chem* a very reactive soft silvery-white metallic element. Symbol: Na
WORD ORIGIN from SODA
sodium bicarbonate *n* a white soluble crystalline compound used in fizzy drinks, baking powder, and in medicine as an antacid
sodium carbonate *n* a colourless or white soluble crystalline compound used in the manufacture of glass, ceramics, soap, and paper, and as a cleansing agent
sodium chlorate *n* a colourless crystalline compound used as a bleaching agent, antiseptic, and weedkiller
sodium chloride *n* common table salt; a soluble colourless crystalline compound widely used as a seasoning and preservative for food and in the manufacture of chemicals, glass, and soap
sodium hydroxide *n* a white strongly alkaline solid used in the manufacture of rayon, paper, aluminium, and soap
sodomite *n* a person who practises sodomy
sodomy *n* anal intercourse committed by a man with another man or a woman
WORD ORIGIN after *Sodom*, Biblical city, noted for its depravity
Sod's Law *n informal* a humorous saying stating that if something can go wrong or turn out inconveniently it will
sofa ❶ *n* a long comfortable seat with back and arms for two or more people
WORD ORIGIN Arabic *suffah*
soft ❶ *adj* **1** easy to dent, shape, or cut: *soft material* **2** not hard; giving way easily under pressure: *a soft bed* **3** fine, smooth, or fluffy to the touch: *soft fur* **4** (of music or sounds) quiet and pleasing **5** (of light or colour) not excessively bright or harsh **6** (of a breeze or climate) temperate, mild, or pleasant **7** with smooth curves rather than sharp edges: *soft focus* **8** kind or lenient, often to excess

S

THESAURUS

do (*informal*), reception, bash (*informal*), social gathering
society *n* **1 = the community**, social order, people, the public, the population, humanity, civilization, mankind, the general public, the world at large **2 = culture**, community, population **4 = organization**, group, club, union, league, association, institute, circle, corporation, guild, fellowship, fraternity, brotherhood *or* sisterhood **5 = upper classes**, gentry, upper crust (*informal*), elite, the swells (*informal*), high society, the top drawer, polite society, the toffs (*Brit slang*), the smart set, beau monde, the nobs (*slang*), the country set, haut monde (*French*) **6** (*old-fashioned*) **= companionship**, company, fellowship, friendship, camaraderie
sofa *n* **= couch**, settee, divan, chaise longue, chesterfield, ottoman
soft *adj* **1 = pliable**, flexible, supple, malleable, plastic, elastic, tensile, ductile (*of a metal*), bendable, mouldable, impressible **2 = yielding**, flexible, pliable, cushioned, elastic, malleable, spongy, springy, cushiony **OPPOSITE:** hard **3 = velvety**, smooth, silky, furry, feathery, downy, fleecy, like a baby's bottom (*informal*) **OPPOSITE:** rough **4 = quiet**, low, gentle, sweet, whispered, soothing, murmured, muted, subdued, mellow, understated, melodious, mellifluous, dulcet, soft-toned **OPPOSITE:** loud

DICTIONARY

9 easy to influence or make demands on **10** *informal* feeble or silly; simple: *soft in the head* **11** not strong or able to endure hardship **12** (of a drug) nonaddictive **13** *informal* requiring little effort; easy: *a soft job* **14** *chem* (of water) relatively free of mineral salts and therefore easily able to make soap lather **15** loving and tender: *soft words* **16** *phonetics* denoting the consonants *c* and *g* when they are pronounced sibilantly, as in *cent* and *germ* **17 soft on a** lenient towards: *he was accused of being soft on criminals* **b** experiencing romantic love for ▹ *adv* **18** in a soft manner: *to speak soft* ▹ *interj* **19** *archaic* quiet! **softly** *adv*
WORD ORIGIN Old English *sōfte*

softball *n* a game similar to baseball, played using a larger softer ball

soft-boiled *adj* (of an egg) boiled for a short time so that the yolk is still soft

soft coal *n* ▸ same as **bituminous coal**

soft drink *n* a nonalcoholic drink

soften ❶ *vb* **1** to make or become soft or softer **2** to make or become more sympathetic and less critical: *the farmers softened their opposition to the legislation* **3** to lessen the severity or difficulty of: *foreign relief softened the hardship of a terrible winter* **softener** *n*

soft furnishings *pl n* curtains, hangings, rugs, and covers

softhearted *adj* kind and sympathetic

softie *or* **softy** *n, pl* **softies** *informal* a person who is easily hurt or upset

soft option *n* the easiest of a number of choices

soft palate *n* the fleshy part at the back of the roof of the mouth

soft-pedal *vb* **-alling, -alled** *or US* **-aling, -aled 1** to deliberately avoid emphasizing (something): *he was soft-pedalling the question of tax increases* ▹ *n* **soft pedal 2** a pedal on a piano that softens the tone

soft sell *n* a method of selling based on subtle suggestion and gentle persuasion

soft-soap *vb informal* to flatter (a person)

soft-spoken *adj* speaking or said with a soft gentle voice

soft touch *n informal* a person who is easily persuaded to perform favours for, or lend money to, other people

software *n computers* the programs used with a computer

softwood *n* the wood of coniferous trees

soggy *adj* **-gier, -giest 1** soaked with liquid: *a soggy running track* **2** moist and heavy: *a soggy sandwich*
sogginess *n*
WORD ORIGIN probably from dialect *sog* marsh

soh *n music* the fifth note of any ascending major scale

soigné *or fem* **soignée** (swah-nyay) *adj* neat, elegant, and well-dressed: *the soignée deputy editor of Vogue*
WORD ORIGIN French

soil[1] ❶ *n* **1** the top layer of the land surface of the earth **2** a specific type of this material: *sandy soil* **3** land, country, or region: *the first US side to lose on home soil*
WORD ORIGIN Latin *solium* a seat, confused with *solum* the ground

soil[2] ❶ *vb* **1** to make or become dirty or stained **2** to bring disgrace upon: *he's soiled our reputation* ▹ *n* **3** a soiled spot **4** refuse, manure, or excrement
WORD ORIGIN Old French *soillier*

soiree (swah-ray) *n* an evening social gathering
WORD ORIGIN French

sojourn (soj-urn) *literary n* **1** a short stay in a place ▹ *vb* **2** to stay temporarily: *he sojourned in Basle during a short illness*
WORD ORIGIN Old French *sojorner*

sol[1] *n music* ▸ same as **soh**

sol[2] *n chem* a liquid colloidal solution

solace (sol-iss) *n* **1** comfort in misery or disappointment: *it drove him to seek increasing solace in alcohol* **2** something that gives comfort or consolation: *his music was a solace to me during my illness* ▹ *vb* **-acing, -aced 3** to give comfort or cheer to (a person) in time of sorrow or distress
WORD ORIGIN Old French *solas*

Solana *or* **Solana Madariaga** *n* **Javier** born 1942, Spanish socialist politician; minister for foreign affairs (1992–95), secretary-general of NATO (1995–99), and EU high representative for foreign policy from 1999

solar *adj* **1** of the sun: *a solar eclipse* **2** operating by or using the energy of the sun: *solar cell*
WORD ORIGIN Latin *sol* the sun

solarium *n, pl* **-lariums** *or* **-laria** a place with beds equipped with ultraviolet lights used for giving people an artificial suntan
WORD ORIGIN Latin: a terrace

solar plexus *n* **1** *anat* a network of nerves behind the stomach **2** *not in technical use* the vulnerable part of the stomach beneath the diaphragm

solar system *n* the system containing the sun and the planets, comets, and asteroids that go round it

sold *vb* **1** ▸ the past of **sell** ▹ *adj* **2 sold on** *slang* enthusiastic and uncritical about

solder *n* **1** an alloy used for joining two metal surfaces by melting the alloy so that it forms a thin layer between the surfaces ▹ *vb* **2** to join or mend or be joined or mended with solder
WORD ORIGIN Latin *solidare* to strengthen

soldering iron *n* a hand tool with a copper tip that is heated and used to melt and apply solder

soldier ❶ *n* **1 a** a person who serves or has served in an army **b** a person who is not an officer in an army ▹ *vb* **2** to serve as a soldier **soldierly** *adj*
WORD ORIGIN Old French *soudier*

soldier of fortune *n* a man who seeks money or adventure as a soldier; mercenary

soldier on *vb* to continue one's efforts despite difficulties or pressure

sole[1] ❶ *adj* **1** being the only one; only **2** not shared; exclusive: *sole ownership*
WORD ORIGIN Latin *solus* alone

sole[2] *n* **1** the underside of the foot **2** the underside of a shoe **3** the lower surface of an object ▹ *vb* **soling, soled 4** to provide (a shoe) with a sole
WORD ORIGIN Latin *solea* sandal

sole[3] *n, pl* **sole** *or* **soles** an edible marine flatfish
WORD ORIGIN Latin *solea* a sandal

S

THESAURUS

5a = pale, light, subdued, pastel, pleasing, bland, mellow
OPPOSITE: bright
5b = dim, faint, dimmed
OPPOSITE: bright
6 = mild, delicate, caressing, temperate, balmy **8 = lenient**, easy-going, lax, liberal, weak, indulgent, permissive, spineless, boneless, overindulgent
OPPOSITE: harsh
13 *(informal)* **= easy**, comfortable, undemanding, cushy *(informal)*, easy-peasy *(slang)* **15 = kind**, tender, sentimental, compassionate, sensitive, gentle, pitying, sympathetic, tenderhearted, touchy-feely *(informal)*

soften *vb* **1 = melt**, tenderize
2 = lessen, moderate, diminish, temper, lower, relax, ease, calm, modify, cushion, soothe, subdue, alleviate, lighten, quell, muffle, allay, mitigate, abate, tone down, assuage

soil[1] *n* **1 = earth**, ground, clay, dust, dirt, loam **3 = territory**, country, land, region, turf *(US slang)*, terrain

soil[2] *vb* **1 = dirty**, foul, stain, smear, muddy, pollute, tarnish, spatter, sully, defile, besmirch, smirch, bedraggle, befoul, begrime
OPPOSITE: clean

soldier *n* **1a = fighter**, serviceman, trooper, warrior, Tommy *(Brit informal)*, GI *(US informal)*, military man, redcoat, enlisted man *(US)*, man-at-arms, squaddie *or* squaddy *(Brit slang)*

sole[1] *adj* **1, 2 = only**, one, single, individual, alone, exclusive, solitary, singular, one and only

DICTIONARY

(from the fish's shape)

sole charge school *n NZ* a country school with only one teacher

solecism (sol-iss-iz-zum) *n formal* **1** a minor grammatical mistake in speech or writing **2** an action considered not to be good manners **solecistic** *adj*
WORD ORIGIN Greek *soloikos* speaking incorrectly

solely ⓘ *adv* **1** only; completely: *an action intended solely to line his own pockets* **2** without others

solemn ⓘ *adj* **1** very serious; deeply sincere: *my solemn promise* **2** marked by ceremony or formality: *a solemn ritual* **3** serious or glum: *a solemn look on her face* **solemnly** *adv*
WORD ORIGIN Latin *sollemnis* appointed

solemnity *n, pl* **-ties 1** the state or quality of being solemn **2** a solemn ceremony or ritual

solemnize *or* **-nise** *vb* **-nizing, -nized** *or* **-nising, -nised 1** to celebrate or perform (a ceremony, esp. of marriage) **2** to make solemn or serious **solemnization** *or* **-nisation** *n*

solenoid (sole-in-oid) *n* a coil of wire, usually cylindrical, in which a magnetic field is set up by passing a current through it **solenoidal** *adj*
WORD ORIGIN French *solénoïde*

sol-fa *n* ▸ short for **tonic sol-fa**

solicit *vb* **1** *formal* to seek or request, esp. formally: *she was brushed aside when soliciting his support for the vote* **2** to approach a person with an offer of sex in return for money **solicitation** *n*
WORD ORIGIN Latin *sollicitare* to harass

solicitor *n Brit, Austral & NZ* a lawyer who advises clients on matters of law, draws up legal documents, and prepares cases for barristers

Solicitor General *n, pl* **Solicitors General** (in Britain) the law officer of the Crown ranking next to the Attorney General (in Scotland to the Lord Advocate) and acting as his assistant

solicitous *adj formal* **1** anxious about someone's welfare **2** eager **solicitousness** *n*
WORD ORIGIN Latin *sollicitus* anxious

solicitude *n formal* anxiety or concern for someone's welfare

solid ⓘ *adj* **1** (of a substance) in a physical state in which it resists changes in size and shape; not liquid or gaseous **2** consisting of matter all through; not hollow **3** of the same substance all through: *solid gold* **4** firm, strong, or substantial: *the solid door of a farmhouse* **5** proved or provable: *solid evidence* **6** law-abiding and respectable: *solid family men* **7** (of a meal or food) substantial **8** without interruption; continuous or unbroken: *solid bombardment* **9** financially sound: *a solid institution* **10** strongly united or established: *a solid marriage* **11** *geom* having or relating to three dimensions **12** adequate; sound, but not brilliant: *a solid career* **13** of a single uniform colour or tone ▷ *n* **14** *geom* a three-dimensional shape **15** a solid substance **solidity** *n* **solidly** *adv*
WORD ORIGIN Latin *solidus* firm

solidarity ⓘ *n, pl* **-ties** agreement in interests or aims among members of a group; total unity

solid geometry *n* the branch of geometry concerned with three-dimensional figures

solidify *vb* **-fies, -fying, -fied 1** to make or become solid or hard **2** to make or become strong or unlikely to change: *a move that solidified the allegiance of our followers* **solidification** *n*

solid-state *adj* (of an electronic device) using a semiconductor component, such as a transistor or silicon chip, in which current flow is through solid material, rather than a valve or mechanical part, in which current flow is through a vacuum

solidus *n, pl* **-di** a short oblique stroke used in text to separate items, such as *and/or*

soliloquize *or* **-quise** *vb* **-quizing, -quized** *or* **-quising, -quised** to say a soliloquy

soliloquy *n, pl* **-quies** a speech made by a person while alone, esp. in a play
WORD ORIGIN Latin *solus* sole + *loqui* to speak

solipsism *n philosophy* the doctrine that the self is the only thing known to exist **solipsist** *n*
WORD ORIGIN Latin *solus* alone + *ipse* self

solitaire *n* **1** a game played by one person, involving moving and taking pegs in a pegboard with the object of being left with only one **2** a gem, esp. a diamond, set alone in a ring **3** *chiefly US* patience (the card game)
WORD ORIGIN French

solitary ⓘ *adj* **1** experienced or performed alone: *a solitary dinner* **2** living a life of solitude: *a solitary child* **3** single; alone: *the solitary cigarette in the ashtray* **4** having few friends; lonely **5** (of a place) without people; empty ▷ *n, pl* **-taries 6** a person who lives on his or her own; hermit **7** *informal* ▸ short for **solitary confinement**: *I can't put him back in solitary* **solitariness** *n*
WORD ORIGIN Latin *solitarius*

solitary confinement *n* isolation of a prisoner in a special cell

solitude *n* the state of being alone

solo *n, pl* **-los 1** a piece of music or section of a piece of music for one performer: *a trumpet solo* **2** any performance by an individual without assistance ▷ *adj* **3** performed by an individual without assistance: *a solo dance* **4** Also: **solo whist** a card game in which each person plays on his or her own ▷ *adv* **5** by oneself; alone: *to fly solo across the Atlantic* **soloist** *n*
WORD ORIGIN Latin *solus* alone

Solomon *n* any person considered to be very wise
WORD ORIGIN after 10th-century BC king of Israel

Solomon's seal *n* a plant with greenish flowers and long waxy leaves

so long *interj* **1** *informal* farewell; goodbye ▷ *adv* **2** *S African slang* for the time being; meanwhile

solo parent *n NZ* a parent bringing up a child or children alone

solstice *n* either the shortest day of the year (**winter solstice**) or the

THESAURUS

solely *adv* **1, 2 = only**, completely, entirely, exclusively, alone, singly, merely, single-handedly

solemn *adj* **1, 3 = serious**, earnest, grave, sober, thoughtful, sedate, glum, staid, portentous
OPPOSITE: cheerful
2 = formal, august, grand, imposing, impressive, grave, majestic, dignified, ceremonial, stately, momentous, awe-inspiring, ceremonious **OPPOSITE:** informal

solid *adj* **2 = firm**, hard, compact, dense, massed, concrete
OPPOSITE: unsubstantial
4 = strong, stable, sturdy, sound, substantial, unshakable
OPPOSITE: unstable
5 = sound, real, reliable, good, genuine, dinkum *(Austral & NZ informal)* **OPPOSITE:** unsound
6 = reliable, decent, dependable, upstanding, serious, constant, sensible, worthy, upright, sober, law-abiding, trusty, level-headed, estimable **OPPOSITE:** unreliable

solidarity *n* **= unity**, harmony, unification, accord, stability, cohesion, team spirit, camaraderie, unanimity, soundness, concordance, esprit de corps, community of interest, singleness of purpose, like-mindedness, kotahitanga *(NZ)*

solitary *adj* **1 = lone**, alone **2, 4 = unsociable**, retiring, reclusive, unsocial, isolated, lonely, cloistered, lonesome, friendless, companionless
OPPOSITE: sociable
5 = isolated, remote, out-of-the-way, desolate, hidden, sequestered, unvisited, unfrequented
OPPOSITE: busy

DICTIONARY

longest day of the year (**summer solstice**)
WORD ORIGIN Latin *solstitium* the standing still of the sun

Solti *n* Sir **Georg** 1912–97, British conductor, born in Hungary

soluble *adj* **1** (of a substance) capable of being dissolved **2** (of a mystery or problem) capable of being solved
solubility *n*

solute *n chem* the substance in a solution that is dissolved
WORD ORIGIN Latin *solutus* free

solution ❶ *n* **1** a specific answer to or way of answering a problem **2** the act or process of solving a problem **3** *chem* a mixture of two or more substances in which the molecules or atoms of the substances are completely dispersed **4** the act or process of forming a solution **5** the state of being dissolved: *the sugar is held in solution*
WORD ORIGIN Latin *solutio* an unloosing

solve ❶ *vb* **solving, solved** to find the explanation for or solution to (a mystery or problem) **solvable** *adj*
WORD ORIGIN Latin *solvere* to loosen

solvent *adj* **1** having enough money to pay off one's debts **2** (of a liquid) capable of dissolving other substances ▹*n* **3** a liquid capable of dissolving other substances
solvency *n*
WORD ORIGIN Latin *solvens* releasing

solvent abuse *n* the deliberate inhaling of intoxicating fumes from certain solvents

Solyom *n* **Laszlo** born 1942, Hungarian politician, president of Hungary from 2005

somatic *adj* of or relating to the body as distinct from the mind: *somatic symptoms*
WORD ORIGIN Greek *sōma* the body

sombre ❶ *or US* **somber** *adj* **1** serious, sad, or gloomy: *a sombre message* **2** (of a place) dim or gloomy **3** (of colour or clothes) dull or dark **sombrely** *or US* **somberly** *adv*
WORD ORIGIN Latin *sub* beneath + *umbra* shade

sombrero *n, pl* **-ros** a wide-brimmed Mexican hat
WORD ORIGIN Spanish

some *adj* **1** unknown or unspecified: *some man called for you* **2** an unknown or unspecified quantity or number of: *I've got some money* **3 a** a considerable number or amount of: *he lived some years afterwards* **b** a little: *show some respect* **4** *informal* an impressive or remarkable: *that was some game!* ▹*pron* **5** certain unknown or unspecified people or things: *some can teach and others can't* **6** an unknown or unspecified quantity of something or number of people or things: *he will sell some in his pub* ▹*adv* **7** approximately: *some thirty pounds*
WORD ORIGIN Old English *sum*

somebody ❶ *pron* **1** some person; someone ▹*n, pl* **-bodies** **2** a person of great importance: *he was a somebody*

someday *adv* at some unspecified time in the future

somehow ❶ *adv* **1** in some unspecified way **2** for some unknown reason: *somehow I can't do it*

someone *pron* some person; somebody

someplace *adv US & Canad informal* ▸same as **somewhere**

somersault *n* **1** a leap or roll in which the head is placed on the ground and the trunk and legs are turned over it ▹*vb* **2** to perform a somersault
WORD ORIGIN Old French *soubresault*

Somerset[1] *n* a county of SW England, on the Bristol Channel: the Mendip Hills lie in the north and Exmoor in the west: the geographical and ceremonial county includes the unitary authorities of North Somerset and Bath and North East Somerset (both part of Avon county from 1975 until 1996): mainly agricultural (esp. dairying and fruit). Administrative centre: Taunton. Pop (excluding unitary authorities): 507 500 (2003 est). Area (excluding unitary authorities): 3452 sq km (1332 sq miles)

Somerset[2] *n* **1st Duke of,** title of *Edward Seymour*. ?1500–52, English statesman, protector of England (1547–49) during Edward VI's minority. He defeated the Scots (1547) and furthered the Protestant Reformation: executed

Somerville *n* **Mary,** original name *Mary Fairfax*. 1780–1872, British scientific writer, author of *Physical Geography* (1848) and other textbooks. Somerville College, Oxford, was named after her

something *pron* **1** an unspecified or unknown thing; some thing: *there was something wrong* **2** an unspecified or unknown amount: *something less than a hundred* **3** an impressive or important person, thing, or event: *isn't that something?* **4 something else** *slang, chiefly US* a remarkable person or thing ▹*adv* **5** to some degree; somewhat: *he looks something like me*

-something *n combining form* a person whose age can be approximately expressed by a specific decade: *twentysomethings*
WORD ORIGIN from the US television series *thirtysomething*

sometime *adv* **1** at some unspecified point of time ▹*adj* **2** former: *a sometime actress*

sometimes ❶ *adv* now and then; from time to time

someway *adv* in some unspecified manner

somewhat *adv* rather; a bit: *somewhat surprising*

somewhere *adv* **1** in, to, or at some unknown or unspecified place, point, or amount: *somewhere down south; somewhere between 35 and 45 per cent* **2 getting somewhere** *informal* making progress

somnambulism *n formal* the condition of walking in one's sleep
somnambulist *n*
WORD ORIGIN Latin *somnus* sleep + *ambulare* to walk

somnolent *adj formal* drowsy; sleepy
somnolence *n*
WORD ORIGIN Latin *somnus* sleep

son *n* **1** a male offspring **2** a form of address for a man or boy who is younger than the speaker **3** a male who comes from a certain place or one closely connected with a certain thing: *a good son of the church* ▸Related adjective: **filial**
WORD ORIGIN Old English *sunu*

Son *n Christianity* the second member of the Trinity, Jesus Christ

sonar *n* a device that locates objects by the reflection of sound waves:

THESAURUS

solution *n* **1, 2 = answer**, resolution, key, result, solving, explanation, unfolding, unravelling, clarification, explication, elucidation **3** *(chemistry)* **= mixture**, mix, compound, blend, suspension, solvent, emulsion

solve *vb* **= answer**, work out, resolve, explain, crack, interpret, unfold, clarify, clear up, unravel, decipher, expound, suss (out) *(slang)*, get to the bottom of, disentangle, elucidate

sombre *or (US)* **somber** *adj* **1 = gloomy**, sad, sober, grave, dismal, melancholy, mournful, lugubrious, joyless, funereal, doleful, sepulchral **OPPOSITE:** cheerful
2, 3 = dark, dull, gloomy, sober, drab **OPPOSITE:** bright

somebody *n* **2 = celebrity**, big name, public figure, name, star, heavyweight *(informal)*, notable, superstar, household name, dignitary, luminary, bigwig *(informal)*, celeb *(informal)*, big shot *(informal)*, personage, megastar *(informal)*, big wheel *(slang)*, big noise *(informal)*, big hitter *(informal)*, heavy hitter *(informal)*, person of note, V.I.P., someone **OPPOSITE:** nobody

somehow *adv* **1 = one way or another**, come what may, come hell or high water *(informal)*, by fair means or foul, by hook or (by) crook, by some means or other

sometimes *adv* **= occasionally**, at times, now and then, from time to time, on occasion, now and again, once in a while, every now and then, every so often, off and on

S

used in underwater navigation and target detection
WORD ORIGIN *so(und) na(vigation and) r(anging)*

sonata *n* a piece of classical music, usually in three or more movements, for piano or for another instrument with or without piano
WORD ORIGIN Italian

Sondheim *n* **Stephen (Joshua)** born 1930, US songwriter. He wrote the lyrics for *West Side Story* (1957), the score for *Company* (1971), and both for *A Little Night Music* (1973), *Into the Woods* (1987), and *Passion* (1994)

son et lumière (sonn ay **loom**-yair) *n* an entertainment staged at night at a famous building or historical site, at which its history is described by a speaker accompanied by lighting effects and music
WORD ORIGIN French, literally: sound and light

song ❶ *n* **1** a piece of music with words, composed for the voice **2** the tuneful call made by certain birds or insects **3** the act or process of singing: *he broke into song* **4 for a song** at a bargain price **5 make a song and dance** *informal* to make an unnecessary fuss
WORD ORIGIN Old English *sang*

songbird *n* any bird that has a musical call

songololo (song-gol-**loll**-o) *n, pl* **-los** *S African* a kind of millipede
WORD ORIGIN Nguni (language group of southern Africa) *ukusonga* to roll up

songstress *n* a female singer of popular songs

song thrush *n* a common thrush that repeats each note of its song

sonic *adj* of, involving, or producing sound
WORD ORIGIN Latin *sonus* sound

sonic barrier *n* ▸ same as **sound barrier**

sonic boom *n* a loud explosive sound caused by the shock wave of an aircraft travelling at supersonic speed

son-in-law *n, pl* **sons-in-law** the husband of one's daughter

sonnet *n prosody* a verse form consisting of 14 lines with a fixed rhyme scheme and rhythm pattern
WORD ORIGIN Old Provençal *sonet* a little poem

sonny *n* a familiar, often patronizing, term of address to a boy or man

sonorous *adj* **1** (of a sound) deep or rich **2** (of speech) using language that is unnecessarily complicated and difficult to understand; pompous **sonority** *n*
WORD ORIGIN Latin *sonor* a noise

Sontag *n* **Susan** 1933–2004, US intellectual and essayist, noted esp. for her writings on modern culture. Her works include 'Notes on Camp' (1964), 'Against Interpretation' (1968), *On Photography* (1977), *Illness as Metaphor* (1978), and the novel *The Volcano Lover* (1992)

soon ❶ *adv* **1** in or after a short time; before long **2 as soon as** at the very moment that: *as soon as he had closed the door* **3 as soon … as** used to indicate that the first alternative is slightly preferable to the second: *they'd just as soon die for him as live*
WORD ORIGIN Old English *sōna*

sooner *adv* **1** ▸ the comparative of **soon**: *I only wish I'd been back sooner* **2** rather; in preference: *he would sooner leave the party than break with me* **3 no sooner … than** immediately after or when: *no sooner had he spoken than the stench drifted up* **4 sooner or later** eventually

Soong *or* **Song** *n* an influential Chinese family, notably **Soong Ch'ing-ling** (1890–1981), who married **Sun Yat-sen** and became a vice-chairman of the People's Republic of China (1959); and **Soong Mei-ling** (1898-2003), who married **Chiang Kai-shek**

soot *n* a black powder formed by the incomplete burning of organic substances such as coal **sooty** *adj*
WORD ORIGIN Old English *sōt*

sooth *n* **in sooth** *archaic or poetic* in truth
WORD ORIGIN Old English *sōth*

soothe ❶ *vb* **soothing, soothed 1** to make (a worried or angry person) calm and relaxed **2** (of an ointment or cream) to relieve (pain) **soothing** *adj*
WORD ORIGIN Old English *sōthian* to prove

soothsayer *n* a person who makes predictions about the future; prophet

sop *n* **1** a small bribe or concession given or made to someone to keep them from causing trouble: *a sop to her conscience* **2** *informal* a stupid or weak person **3 sops** food soaked in a liquid before being eaten ▹ *vb* **sopping, sopped 4 sop up** to soak up or absorb (liquid)
WORD ORIGIN Old English *sopp*

Soper *n* **Donald (Oliver)**, Baron 1903–98, British Methodist minister and publicist, noted esp. for his pacifist convictions. His books include *All His Grace* (1953) and *Calling for Action* (1984)

Sophia *n* 1630–1714, electress of Hanover (1658–1714), in whom the Act of Settlement (1701) vested the English Crown. She was a granddaughter of James I of England and her son became George I of Great Britain and Ireland

sophism *n* an argument that seems reasonable but is actually false and misleading
WORD ORIGIN Greek *sophisma* ingenious trick

sophist *n* a person who uses clever but false arguments **sophistic** *adj*
WORD ORIGIN Greek *sophistēs* a wise man

sophisticate *vb* **-cating, -cated 1** to make (someone) less natural or innocent, such as by education **2** to make (a machine or method) more complex or refined ▹ *n* **3** a sophisticated person **sophistication** *n*
WORD ORIGIN Latin *sophisticus* sophistic

sophisticated ❶ *adj* **1** having or appealing to fashionable and refined tastes and habits: *a sophisticated restaurant* **2** intelligent, knowledgeable, or able to appreciate culture and the arts: *a sophisticated concert audience* **3** (of machines or methods) complex and using advanced technology

sophistry *n* **1** the practice of using arguments which seem clever but are actually false and misleading **2** *pl* **-ries** an instance of this

sophomore *n chiefly US & Canad* a second-year student at a secondary (high) school or college
WORD ORIGIN probably from earlier *sophum*, variant of *sophism*

soporific *adj* **1** causing sleep ▹ *n* **2** a drug that causes sleep
WORD ORIGIN Latin *sopor* sleep

sopping *adj* completely soaked; wet through. Also: **sopping wet**

soppy *adj* **-pier, -piest** *informal*

S

OPPOSITE: always

song *n* **1 = ballad**, air, tune, lay, strain, carol, lyric, chant, chorus, melody, anthem, number, hymn, psalm, shanty, pop song, ditty, canticle, canzonet, waiata (*NZ*)

soon *adv* **1 = before long**, shortly, in the near future, in a minute, anon (*archaic*), in a short time, in a little while, any minute now, betimes (*archaic*), in two shakes of a lamb's tail, erelong (*archaic, poetic*), in a couple of shakes

soothe *vb* **1 = calm**, still, quiet, hush, settle, calm down, appease, lull, mitigate, pacify, mollify, smooth down, tranquillize **OPPOSITE:** upset **2 = relieve**, ease, alleviate, dull, diminish, assuage **OPPOSITE:** irritate

sophisticated *adj* **2 = cultured**, refined, cultivated, worldly, cosmopolitan, urbane, jet-set, world-weary, citified, worldly-wise **OPPOSITE:** unsophisticated **3 = complex**, advanced, complicated, subtle, delicate, elaborate, refined, intricate, multifaceted, highly-

DICTIONARY

foolishly sentimental: *a soppy love song* **soppily** *adv*

soprano *n, pl* **-pranos 1** the highest adult female voice **2** the voice of a young boy before puberty **3** a singer with such a voice **4** the highest or second highest instrument in a family of instruments ▷ *adj* **5** denoting a musical instrument that is the highest or second highest pitched in its family: *the soprano saxophone* **6** of or relating to the highest female voice, or the voice of a young boy: *the part is quite possibly the most demanding soprano role Wagner ever wrote*
WORD ORIGIN Italian

Sopwith *n* Sir **Thomas Octave Murdoch** 1888–1989, British aircraft designer, who built the Sopwith Camel biplane used during World War I. He was chairman (1935–63) of the Hawker Siddeley Group, which developed the Hurricane fighter

sorbet (saw-bay) *n* a flavoured water ice
WORD ORIGIN French, from Arabic *sharbah* a drink

sorcerer *or fem* **sorceress** *n* a person who uses magic powers; a wizard
WORD ORIGIN Old French *sorcier*

sorcery *n, pl* **-ceries** witchcraft or magic
WORD ORIGIN Old French *sorcerie*

Sordello *n* born ?1200, Italian troubadour

sordid *adj* **1** dirty, depressing, and squalid: *a sordid backstreet in a slum area* **2** relating to sex in a crude or unpleasant way: *the sordid details of his affair* **3** involving immoral and selfish behaviour: *the sordid history of the slave trade*
WORD ORIGIN Latin *sordidus*

sore ⊕ *adj* **1** (of a wound, injury, etc.) painfully sensitive; tender **2** causing annoyance and resentment: *a sore point* **3** upset and angered: *she's still sore about last night* **4** *literary* urgent; pressing: *in sore need of firm government* ▷ *n* **5** a painful or sensitive wound or injury ▷ *adv* **6** **sore afraid** *archaic* greatly frightened
WORD ORIGIN Old English *sār*

Sorel *n* **Georges** (**Eugène**) 1847–1922, French social philosopher, who advocated revolutionary syndicalism and preached the creative role of violence and myth

sorely *adv* greatly: *sorely disappointed*

Sorenstam *n* **Annika** born 1970, Swedish golfer; winner of the US Women's Open (1995, 1996, 2006), the LPGA Championship (2003, 2004, 2005), and the British Women's Open (2003)

sorghum *n* a grass grown for grain and as a source of syrup
WORD ORIGIN Italian *sorgo*

sorority *n, pl* **-ties** *chiefly US* a society of female students
WORD ORIGIN Latin *soror* sister

sorrel *n* a plant with bitter-tasting leaves which are used in salads and sauces
WORD ORIGIN Old French *surele*

sorrow ⊕ *n* **1** deep sadness or regret, associated with death or sympathy for another's misfortune **2** a particular cause of this ▷ *vb* **3** *literary* to feel deep sadness (about death or another's misfortunes); mourn **sorrowful** *adj* **sorrowfully** *adv*
WORD ORIGIN Old English *sorg*

sorry ⊕ *adj* **-rier, -riest 1** (often foll. by *for* or *about*) feeling or expressing pity, sympathy, grief, or regret: *I'm sorry about this* **2** in bad mental or physical condition: *a sorry state* **3** poor: *a sorry performance* ▷ *interj* **4** an exclamation expressing apology or asking someone to repeat what he or she has said
WORD ORIGIN Old English *sārig*

sort ⊕ *n* **1** a class, group, or kind sharing certain characteristics or qualities **2** *informal* a type of character: *she was a good sort* **3** a more or less adequate example: *a sort of dream machine* **4** **of sorts** *or* **of a sort a** of a poorer quality: *she was wearing a uniform of sorts* **b** of a kind not quite as intended or desired: *it was a reward, of sorts, for my efforts* **5** **out of sorts** not in normal good health or temper **6** **sort of** as it were; rather: *I sort of quit; sort of insensitive* ▷ *vb* **7** to arrange (things or people) according to class or type **8** to put (something) into working order; fix **9** to arrange (computer information) by machine in an order the user finds convenient
WORD ORIGIN Latin *sors* fate

sort code *n* a sequence of numbers printed on a cheque or bank card identifying the branch holding the account

sortie *n* **1** a short or relatively short return trip **2** (of troops) a raid into enemy territory **3** an operational flight made by a military aircraft ▷ *vb* **-tieing, -tied 4** to make a sortie
WORD ORIGIN French

sort out *vb* **1** to find a solution to (a problem): *did they sort out the mess?* **2** to take or separate (things or people) from a larger group: *to sort out the wheat from the chaff* **3** to organize (things or people) into an orderly and disciplined group **4** **sort someone out** to deal with a person, especially an awkward one **5** *informal* to punish or tell off (someone)

SOS *n* **1** an international code signal of distress in which the letters SOS are repeatedly spelt out in Morse code **2** *informal* any call for help

so-so *informal adj* **1** neither good nor bad ▷ *adv* **2** in an average or indifferent way

sot *n* a person who is frequently drunk **sottish** *adj*
WORD ORIGIN Old English *sott*

Soto[1] *n* a Zen Buddhist school of Japan, characterized by the practice of sitting meditation leading to gradual enlightenment

Soto[2] *n* ▸ See **De Soto**

sotto voce (sot-toe voe-chay) *adv* with a soft voice
WORD ORIGIN Italian

sou *n* **1** a former French coin of low value **2** *old-fashioned* a very small amount of money: *the tax man never saw a sou from this income*
WORD ORIGIN French

soubrette (soo-brett) *n* a minor female role in comedy, often that of a pert maid

S

THESAURUS

developed **OPPOSITE:** simple

sore *adj* **1 = painful**, smarting, raw, tender, burning, angry, sensitive, irritated, inflamed, chafed, reddened **2 = annoying**, distressing, troublesome, harrowing, grievous **3 = annoyed**, cross, angry, pained, hurt, upset, stung, irritated, grieved, resentful, aggrieved, vexed, irked, peeved *(informal)*, tooshie *(Austral slang)*, hoha *(NZ)* **4** *(literary)* **= urgent**, desperate, extreme, dire, pressing, critical, acute

sorrow *n* **1 = grief**, sadness, woe, regret, distress, misery, mourning, anguish, unhappiness, heartache, heartbreak, affliction **OPPOSITE:** joy **2 = hardship**, trial, tribulation, affliction, worry, trouble, blow, woe, misfortune, bummer *(slang)* **OPPOSITE:** good fortune ▷ *vb* **3** *(literary)* **= grieve**, mourn, lament, weep, moan, be sad, bemoan, agonize, eat your heart out, bewail **OPPOSITE:** rejoice

sorry *adj* **1a = regretful**, apologetic, contrite, repentant, guilt-ridden, remorseful, penitent, shamefaced, conscience-stricken, in sackcloth and ashes, self-reproachful **OPPOSITE:** unapologetic **1b = sympathetic**, moved, full of pity, pitying, compassionate, commiserative **OPPOSITE:** unsympathetic **3 = wretched**, miserable, pathetic, mean, base, poor, sad, distressing, dismal, shabby, vile, paltry, pitiful, abject, deplorable, pitiable, piteous

sort *n* **1 = kind**, type, class, make, group, family, order, race, style, quality, character, nature, variety, brand, species, breed, category, stamp, description, denomination, genus, ilk ▷ *vb* **7 = arrange**, group, order, class, separate, file, rank, divide, grade, distribute, catalogue, classify, categorize, tabulate,

DICTIONARY

WORD ORIGIN French
soubriquet *n* ▸ same as **sobriquet**
soufflé (soo-flay) *n* a light fluffy dish made with beaten egg whites and other ingredients such as cheese or chocolate
WORD ORIGIN French
sough (rhymes with **now**) *vb literary* (of the wind) to make a sighing sound
WORD ORIGIN Old English *swōgan*
sought (sawt) *vb* ▸ the past of **seek**
souk (sook) *n* an open-air marketplace in Muslim countries
WORD ORIGIN Arabic *sūq*
soul ➊ *n* **1** the spiritual part of a person, regarded as the centre of personality, intellect, will, and emotions: believed by many to survive the body after death **2** the essential part or fundamental nature of anything: *the soul of contemporary America* **3** deep and sincere feelings: *you've got no soul* **4** Also called: **soul music** a type of Black music using blues and elements of jazz, gospel, and pop **5** a person regarded as a good example of some quality: *the soul of prudence* **6** a person: *there was hardly a soul there* **7 the life and soul** *informal* a person who is lively, entertaining, and fun to be with: *the life and soul of the campus*
WORD ORIGIN Old English *sāwol*
soul-destroying *adj* (of an occupation or situation) very boring and repetitive
soul food *n informal* food, such as chitterlings and yams, which is traditionally eaten by African-Americans
soulful *adj* expressing deep feelings: *a soulful performance of one of Tchaikovsky's songs*
soulless *adj* **1** lacking human qualities; mechanical: *soulless materialism* **2** (of a person) lacking in sensitivity or emotion
soul mate *n* a person with whom one gets along well because of having shared interests and experiences
soul-searching *n* deep examination of one's actions and feelings
Soult *n* **Nicolas Jean de Dieu** 1769–1851, French marshal under Napoleon I. Under Louis-Philippe he was minister of war (1830–34; 1840–44)
sound[1] ➊ *n* **1** anything that can be heard; noise **2** *physics* mechanical vibrations that travel in waves through the air, water, etc. **3** the sensation produced by such vibrations in the organs of hearing **4** the impression one has of something: *I didn't really like the sound of it* **5 sounds** *slang* music, esp. rock, jazz, or pop ▹ *vb* **6** to make or cause (an instrument, etc.) to make a sound **7** to announce (something) by a sound: *guns sound the end of the two minutes silence* **8** to make a noise with a certain quality: *her voice sounded shrill* **9** to suggest (a particular idea or quality): *his argument sounded false* **10** to pronounce (something) clearly: *to sound one's r's* ▸ See also **sound off**
WORD ORIGIN Latin *sonus*
sound[2] ➊ *adj* **1** free from damage, injury, or decay; in good condition **2** firm or substantial: *sound documentary evidence* **3** financially safe or stable: *a sound investment* **4** showing good judgment or reasoning; wise: *sound advice* **5** morally correct; honest **6** (of sleep) deep and uninterrupted **7** thorough: *a sound defeat* ▹ *adv* **8 sound asleep** in a deep sleep **soundly** *adv*
WORD ORIGIN Old English *sund*
sound[3] *vb* **1** to measure the depth of (a well, the sea, etc.) **2** *med* to examine (a part of the body) by tapping or with a stethoscope ▸ See also **sound out**
WORD ORIGIN Old French *sonder*
sound[4] *n* a channel between two larger areas of sea or between an island and the mainland
WORD ORIGIN Old English *sund*
soundalike *n* a person or thing that sounds like another, often well-known, person or thing
sound barrier *n* a sudden increase in the force of air against an aircraft flying at or above the speed of sound
sound bite *n* a short pithy sentence or phrase extracted from a longer speech for use on television or radio: *complicated political messages cannot be properly reduced to fifteen-second sound bites*
soundcard *n* a printed circuit board inserted into a computer, enabling the output and manipulation of sound
sound effects *pl n* sounds artificially produced to make a play, esp. a radio play, more realistic
sounding board *n* a person or group used to test a new idea or policy
soundings *pl n* **1** measurements of the depth of a river, lake, or sea **2** questions asked of someone in order to find out his or her opinion: *soundings among colleagues had revealed enthusiasm for the plan*
sound off *vb* to speak angrily or loudly
sound out *vb* to question (someone) in order to discover his or her opinion: *you might try sounding him out about his family*
soundproof *adj* **1** (of a room) built so that no sound can get in or out ▹ *vb* **2** to make (a room) soundproof
soundtrack *n* the recorded sound accompaniment to a film
sound wave *n* a wave that carries sound
Souness *n* **Graeme** born 1953, Scottish footballer and manager
soup *n* **1** a food made by cooking meat, fish, or vegetables in a stock **2 in the soup** *slang* in trouble or difficulties **soupy** *adj*
WORD ORIGIN Old French *soupe*
soupçon (soop-sonn) *n* a slight amount; dash
WORD ORIGIN French
souped-up *adj slang* (of a car, motorbike, or engine) adjusted so as to be faster or more powerful than normal
Souphanouvong *n* **Prince** 1902–95, Laotian statesman; president of Laos (1975–86)
soup kitchen *n* a place where food and drink are served to needy people
sour ➊ *adj* **1** having a sharp biting taste like the taste of lemon juice or vinegar **2** made acid or bad, such as when milk ferments **3** (of a person's mood) bad-tempered and unfriendly **4 go** *or* **turn sour** to become less

S

THESAURUS

systematize, put in order
soul *n* **1 = spirit**, essence, psyche, life, mind, reason, intellect, vital force, animating principle, wairua (*NZ*) **2, 5 = embodiment**, essence, incarnation, epitome, personification, quintessence, type **6 = person**, being, human, individual, body, creature, mortal, man *or* woman
sound[1] *n* **1 = noise**, racket, din, report, tone, resonance, hubbub, reverberation **4 = idea**, impression, implication(s), drift ▹ *vb* **6a = toll**, set off **6b = resound**, echo, go off, toll, set off, chime, resonate, reverberate, clang, peal **9 = seem**, seem to be, appear to be, give the impression of being, strike you as being
sound[2] *adj* **1 = fit**, healthy, robust, firm, perfect, intact, vigorous, hale, unhurt, undamaged, uninjured, unimpaired, hale and hearty **OPPOSITE:** frail **2 = sturdy**, strong, solid, stable, substantial, durable, stout, well-constructed **4 = sensible**, wise, reasonable, right, true, responsible, correct, proper, reliable, valid, orthodox, rational, logical, prudent, trustworthy, well-founded, level-headed, right-thinking, well-grounded, grounded **OPPOSITE:** irresponsible **6 = deep**, peaceful, unbroken, undisturbed, untroubled **OPPOSITE:** troubled
sour *adj* **1 = sharp**, acid, tart, bitter, unpleasant, pungent, acetic, acidulated, acerb **OPPOSITE:** sweet **2 = rancid**, turned, gone off, fermented, unsavoury, curdled,

DICTIONARY

enjoyable or happy: *the dream has turned sour* ▷*vb* **5** to make or become less enjoyable or friendly: *relations soured shortly after the war* **sourly** *adv*
WORD ORIGIN Old English *sūr*

source ❶ *n* **1** the origin or starting point: *the source of discontent among fishermen* **2** any person, book, or organization that provides information for a news report or for research **3** the area or spring where a river or stream begins ▷*vb* **4** to establish a supplier of (a product, etc.) **5** (foll. by *from*) to originate from
WORD ORIGIN Latin *surgere* to rise

source code *n computers* the original form of a computer program before it is converted into a machine-readable code

sour cream *n* cream soured by bacteria for use in cooking

sour grapes *n* the attitude of pretending to hate something because one cannot have it oneself

sourpuss *n informal* a person who is always gloomy, pessimistic, or bitter

souse *vb* **sousing, soused 1** to plunge (something) into water or other liquid **2** to drench **3** to steep or cook (food) in a marinade ▷*n* **4** the liquid used in pickling **5** the act or process of sousing
WORD ORIGIN Old French *sous*

soused *adj slang* drunk

soutane (soo-**tan**) *n RC church* a priest's robe
WORD ORIGIN French

south *n* **1** one of the four cardinal points of the compass, at 180° from north **2** the direction along a line of latitude towards the South Pole **3 the south** any area lying in or towards the south ▷*adj* **4** situated in, moving towards, or facing the south **5** (esp. of the wind) from the south ▷*adv* **6** in, to, or towards the south
WORD ORIGIN Old English *sūth*

South *n* **1 the South a** the southern part of England **b** (in the US) the Southern states that formed the Confederacy during the Civil War **c** the countries of the world that are not technically and economically advanced ▷*adj* **2** of or denoting the southern part of a country, area, etc.

South African *adj* **1** of the Republic of South Africa ▷*n* **2** a person from the Republic of South Africa

Southampton[1] *n* **1** a port in S England, in Southampton unitary authority, Hampshire on **Southampton Water** (an inlet of the English Channel): chief English passenger port; university (1952); shipyards and oil refinery. Pop: 234 224 (2001) **2** a unitary authority in S England, in Hampshire. Pop: 221 100 (2003 est). Area: 49 sq km (19 sq miles)

Southampton[2] *n* **3rd Earl of,** title of *Henry Wriothesley.* 1573–1624, English courtier and patron of Shakespeare, who dedicated *Venus and Adonis* (1593) and *The Rape of Lucrece* (1594) to him: sentenced to death (1601) for his part in the Essex rebellion but reprieved

southbound *adj* going towards the south

Southcott *n* **Joanna** 1750–1814, British religious fanatic, who claimed that she would give birth to the second Messiah

southeast *n* **1** the direction midway between south and east **2 the southeast** any area lying in or towards the southeast ▷*adj also* **southeastern 3** of or denoting that part of a country or area which lies in the southeast **4** situated in, moving towards, or facing the southeast **5** (esp. of the wind) from the southeast ▷*adv* **6** in, to, or towards the southeast
southeasterly *adj, adv, n*

Southeast *n* the southeast of Britain, esp. the London area

southeaster *n* a strong wind or storm from the southeast

southerly *adj* **1** of or in the south ▷*adv, adj* **2** towards the south **3** from the south: *light southerly winds*

southern *adj* **1** situated in or towards the south **2** facing or moving towards the south **3** (*sometimes cap*) of or characteristic of the south or South **southernmost** *adj*

Southerner *n* a person from the south of a country or area, esp. England or the US

southern hemisphere *n* that half of the globe lying south of the equator

southern lights *pl n* ▸same as **aurora australis**

southpaw *informal n* **1** any left-handed person, esp. a boxer ▷*adj* **2** left-handed

South Pole *n* the southernmost point on the earth's axis, at a latitude of 90°S, which has very low temperatures

South Seas *pl n* the seas south of the equator

southward *adj, adv also* **southwards 1** towards the south ▷*n* **2** the southward part or direction

Southwell *n* **Saint Robert** ?1561–95, English poet and Roman Catholic martyr, who was imprisoned, tortured, and executed for his Jesuit activities. His best known poem is 'The Burning Babe'

southwest *n* **1** the direction midway between west and south **2 the southwest** any area lying in or towards the southwest ▷*adj also* **southwestern 3** of or denoting that part of a country or area which lies in the southwest **4** situated in, moving towards, or facing the southwest **5** (esp. of the wind) from the southwest ▷*adv* **6** in, to, or towards the southwest
southwesterly *adj, adv, n*

Southwest *n* the southwestern part of Britain, esp. Cornwall, Devon, and Somerset

southwester *n* a strong wind or storm from the southwest

Soutine *n* **Chaim** 1893–1943, French expressionist painter, born in Russia; noted for his portraits and still lifes, esp. of animal carcasses

souvenir ❶ *n* an object that reminds one of a certain place, occasion, or person; memento
WORD ORIGIN French

sou'wester *n* **1** a seaman's hat with a broad brim that covers the back of the neck **2** ▸same as **southwester**
WORD ORIGIN a contraction of SOUTHWESTER

sovereign ❶ *n* **1** the Royal ruler of a country **2** a former British gold coin worth one pound sterling ▷*adj* **3** independent of outside authority; not governed by another country: *a sovereign nation* **4** supreme in rank or authority: *a sovereign queen* **5** *old-fashioned* excellent or outstanding: *a sovereign remedy for epilepsy*
WORD ORIGIN Old French *soverain*

sovereignty ❶ *n, pl* **-ties 1** the political power a nation has to govern itself **2** the position or authority of a sovereign

soviet *n* (in the former Soviet Union)

S

THESAURUS

unwholesome, gone bad, off
OPPOSITE: fresh
3 = bitter, cynical, crabbed, tart, discontented, grudging, acrimonious, embittered, disagreeable, churlish, ill-tempered, jaundiced, waspish, grouchy (*informal*), ungenerous, peevish, ill-natured **OPPOSITE:** good-natured

source *n* **1 = cause**, origin, derivation, beginning, author **2 = informant**, authority, documentation **3 = origin**, spring, fount, fountainhead, wellspring, rise

souvenir *n* **= keepsake**, token, reminder, relic, remembrancer (*archaic*), memento

sovereign *n* **1 = monarch**, ruler, king *or* queen, chief, shah, potentate, supreme ruler, emperor *or* empress, prince *or* princess, tsar *or* tsarina ▷*adj* **4 = supreme**, ruling, absolute, chief, royal, principal, dominant, imperial, unlimited, paramount, regal, predominant, monarchal, kingly *or* queenly **5** (*old-fashioned*) **= excellent**, efficient, efficacious, effectual

sovereignty *n* **2 = supreme power**, domination, supremacy, primacy, sway, ascendancy, kingship,

DICTIONARY

an elected government council at the local, regional, and national levels
WORD ORIGIN Russian *sovyet*

Soviet *adj* **1** of the former Soviet Union ▷*n* **2** a person from the former Soviet Union

sow[1] ❶ *vb* **sowing, sowed; sown** *or* **sowed 1** to scatter or plant (seed) in or on (the ground) so that it may grow: *sow sweet peas in pots; farmers sow their fields with fewer varieties* **2** to implant or introduce: *to sow confusion among the other members*
WORD ORIGIN Old English *sāwan*

sow[2] *n* a female adult pig
WORD ORIGIN Old English *sugu*

soya bean *or US & Canad* **soybean** *n* a plant whose bean is used for food and as a source of oil
WORD ORIGIN Japanese *shōyu*

Soyinka *n* **Wole** born 1934, Nigerian dramatist, novelist, poet, and literary critic. His works include the plays *The Strong Breed* (1963), *The Road* (1965), and *Kongi's Harvest* (1966), the novel *The Interpreters* (1965), and the political essays *The Burden of Memory, the Muse of Forgiveness* (1999); forced into exile by the military regime (1993–98). Nobel prize for literature 1986

soy sauce *n* a salty dark brown sauce made from fermented soya beans, used in Chinese cookery

sozzled *adj Brit, Austral & NZ informal* drunk
WORD ORIGIN origin unknown

spa *n* a mineral-water spring or a resort where such a spring is found
WORD ORIGIN after *Spa*, a watering place in Belgium

Spaak *n* **Paul Henri** 1899–1972, Belgian statesman, first socialist premier of Belgium (1937–38); a leading advocate of European unity, he was president of the consultative assembly of the Council of Europe (1949–51) and secretary-general of NATO (1957–61)

space ❶ *n* **1** the unlimited three-dimensional expanse in which all objects exist **2** an interval of distance or time between two points, objects, or events **3** a blank portion or area **4** unoccupied area or room: *barely enough space to walk around* **5** the region beyond the earth's atmosphere containing other planets, stars, and galaxies; the universe ▷*vb* **spacing, spaced 6** (often foll. by *out*) to place or arrange (things) at intervals or with spaces between them
WORD ORIGIN Latin *spatium*

space age *n* **1** the period in which the exploration of space has become possible ▷*adj* **space-age 2** very modern, futuristic, or using the latest technology: *a space-age helmet*

space-bar *n* a bar on a typewriter that is pressed in order to leave a space between words or letters

space capsule *n* the part of a spacecraft in which the crew live and work

spacecraft *n* a vehicle that can be used for travel in space

spaced-out *adj informal* vague and dreamy, as if influenced by drugs

Space Invaders *n trademark* a video game in which players try to defend themselves against attacking enemy spacecraft

spaceman *or fem* **spacewoman** *n, pl* **-men** *or fem* **-women** a person who travels in space

space probe *n* a small vehicle equipped to gather scientific information, normally transmitted back to earth by radio, about a planet or conditions in space

spaceship *n* (in science fiction) a spacecraft used for travel between planets and galaxies

space shuttle *n* a manned reusable spacecraft designed for making regular flights

space station *n* a large manned artificial satellite used as a base for scientific research in space and for people travelling in space

spacesuit *n* a sealed protective suit worn by astronauts

space-time *or* **space-time continuum** *n physics* the four-dimensional continuum having three space coordinates and one time coordinate that together completely specify the location of an object or an event

Spacey *n* **Kevin,** original name *Kevin Spacey Fowler*. born 1959, US actor; films include *Glengarry Glen Ross* (1992), *The Usual Suspects* (1995), *American Beauty* (1999), which earned him an Academy Award, *The Shipping News* (2001), and *Beyond the Sea* (2004); artistic director of Old Vic Theatre Company, London, from 2003

spacious ❶ *adj* having or providing a lot of space; roomy **spaciousness** *n*

spade[1] *n* **1** a tool for digging, with a flat steel blade and a long wooden handle **2 call a spade a spade** to speak plainly and frankly
WORD ORIGIN Old English *spadu*

spade[2] *n* **1 a spades** the suit of playing cards marked with a black leaf-shaped symbol **b** a card with one or more of these symbols on it **2** *offensive* a Black person **3 in spades** *informal* in plenty: *all you need is talent in spades*
WORD ORIGIN Italian *spada* sword, used as an emblem on playing cards

spadework *n* dull or routine work done as preparation for a project or activity

spadix (spade-ix) *n, pl* **spadices** (spade-ice-eez) *bot* a spike of small flowers on a fleshy stem
WORD ORIGIN Greek: torn-off frond

spaghetti *n* pasta in the form of long strings
WORD ORIGIN Italian

spaghetti junction *n* a junction between motorways with a large number of intersecting roads
WORD ORIGIN from the nickname of the Gravelly Hill Interchange, Birmingham

spaghetti western *n* a cowboy film made in Europe by an Italian director

spake *vb archaic* ▸a past tense of **speak**

Spallanzani *n* **Lazzaro.** 1729–99, Italian physiologist, noted esp. for his experimental studies of microorganisms and his work on animal reproduction and digestion

spam *vb* **spamming, spammed** *computers slang* to send unsolicited e-mail simultaneously to a number of newsgroups on the internet
WORD ORIGIN from the repeated use of the word *Spam* in a popular sketch from the British television show *Monty Python's Flying Circus*

Spam *n trademark* a cold meat made from pork and spices

span ❶ *n* **1** the interval or distance between two points, such as the ends of a bridge **2** the complete extent: *that span of time* **3** ▸short for **wingspan 4** a unit of length based on the width of a stretched hand, usually taken as nine inches (23 cms) ▷*vb* **spanning, spanned 5** to stretch or extend across, over, or around: *her career spanned fifty years; to span the Danube*
WORD ORIGIN Old English *spann*

S

THESAURUS

suzerainty, rangatiratanga (NZ)

sow[1] *vb* **1 = scatter**, plant, seed, lodge, implant, disseminate, broadcast, inseminate

space *n* **2 = period**, interval, time, while, span, duration, time frame, timeline **3 = blank**, gap, interval **4 = room**, volume, capacity, extent, margin, extension, scope, play, expanse, leeway, amplitude, spaciousness, elbowroom **5 = outer space**, the universe, the galaxy, the solar system, the cosmos

spacious *adj* **= roomy**, large, huge, broad, vast, extensive, ample, expansive, capacious, uncrowded, commodious, comfortable, sizable *or* sizeable **OPPOSITE:** limited

span *n* **1, 2a = period**, term, duration, spell **1, 2b = extent**, reach, spread, length, distance, stretch ▷*vb* **5 = extend across**, cross, bridge, cover, link, vault, traverse, range over, arch across

DICTIONARY

spangle *n* **1** a small piece of shiny material used as a decoration on clothes or hair; sequin ▷*vb* **-gling, -gled 2** to cover or decorate (something) with spangles
WORD ORIGIN Middle English *spange* clasp

Spaniard *n* a person from Spain

spaniel *n* a dog with long drooping ears and a silky coat
WORD ORIGIN Old French *espaigneul* Spanish (dog)

Spanish *adj* **1** of Spain ▷*n* **2** the official language of Spain, Mexico, and most countries of South and Central America ▷*pl n* **3 the Spanish** the people of Spain

Spanish fly *n* a beetle, the dried body of which is used in medicine

Spanish Main *n* **1** the N coast of South America **2** the Caribbean Sea, the S part of which was frequented by pirates

spank *vb* **1** to slap (someone) with the open hand, on the buttocks or legs ▷*n* **2** such a slap
WORD ORIGIN probably imitative

spanking[1] *n* a series of spanks, usually as a punishment for children

spanking[2] *adj* **1** *informal* outstandingly fine or smart: *spanking new uniforms* **2** very fast: *a spanking pace*

spanner *n* **1** a tool for gripping and turning a nut or bolt **2 throw a spanner in the works** *informal* to cause a problem that prevents things from running smoothly
WORD ORIGIN German *spannen* to stretch

spanspek *n S African* a cantaloupe melon
WORD ORIGIN Afrikaans

spar[1] *n* a pole used as a ship's mast, boom, or yard
WORD ORIGIN Old Norse *sperra* beam

spar[2] ⊕ *vb* **sparring, sparred 1** *boxing, martial arts* to fight using light blows for practice **2** to argue with someone ▷*n* **3** an argument
WORD ORIGIN Old English

spar[3] *n* a light-coloured, crystalline, easily split mineral
WORD ORIGIN Middle Low German

spare ⊕ *adj* **1** extra to what is needed: *there are some spare chairs at the back* **2** able to be used when needed: *a spare parking space* **3** (of a person) tall and thin **4** (of a style) plain and without unnecessary decoration or details; austere: *a spare but beautiful novel* **5** *Brit slang* frantic with anger or worry: *the boss went spare* ▷*n* **6** an extra thing kept in case it is needed ▷*vb* **sparing, spared 7** to stop from killing, punishing, or injuring (someone) **8** to protect (someone) from (something) unpleasant: *spare me the sermon* **9** to be able to afford or give: *can you spare me a moment to talk?* **10 not spare oneself** to try one's hardest **11 to spare** more than is required: *a few hours to spare*
WORD ORIGIN Old English *sparian*

spare part *n* a replacement piece of mechanical or electrical equipment kept in case the original component becomes damaged or worn

spareribs *pl n* a cut of pork ribs with most of the meat trimmed off

spare tyre *n* **1** an additional tyre kept in a motor vehicle in case of puncture **2** *slang* a roll of fat just above the waist

sparing ⊕ *adj* (sometimes foll. by *of*) economical (with): *she was mercifully sparing in her use of jargon* **sparingly** *adv*

spark ⊕ *n* **1** a fiery particle thrown out from a fire or caused by friction **2** a short flash of light followed by a sharp crackling noise, produced by a sudden electrical discharge through the air **3** a trace or hint: *a spark of goodwill* **4** liveliness, enthusiasm, or humour: *that spark in her eye* ▷*vb* **5** to give off sparks **6** to cause to start; trigger: *the incident sparked off an angry exchange*
WORD ORIGIN Old English *spearca*

Spark *n* Dame **Muriel** (**Sarah**) 1918–2006, British novelist and writer; her novels include *Memento Mori* (1959), *The Prime of Miss Jean Brodie* (1961), *The Takeover* (1976), *A Far Cry from Kensington* (1988), *Symposium* (1990), and *The Finishing School* (2004)

sparkie *n Brit, Austral & NZ informal* electrician

sparkle ⊕ *vb* **-kling, -kled 1** to glitter with many bright points of light **2** (of wine or mineral water) to be slightly fizzy **3** to be lively, witty, and intelligent ▷*n* **4** a small bright point of light **5** liveliness and wit **sparkling** *adj*
WORD ORIGIN Middle English *sparklen*

sparkler *n* **1** a type of hand-held firework that throws out sparks **2** *informal* a sparkling gem; esp. a diamond

spark plug *n* a device in an internal-combustion engine that ignites the fuel by producing an electric spark

sparring partner *n* **1** a person who practises with a boxer during training **2** a person with whom one has friendly arguments

sparrow *n* a very common small brown or grey bird which feeds on seeds and insects
WORD ORIGIN Old English *spearwa*

sparrowhawk *n* a small hawk which preys on smaller birds

sparse *adj* small in amount and spread out widely: *a sparse population* **sparsely** *adv*
WORD ORIGIN Latin *sparsus*

Spartan *adj* **1** of or relating to the ancient Greek city of Sparta **2** (of a way of life) strict or simple and with no luxuries: *Spartan accommodation* ▷*n* **3** a citizen of Sparta **4** a person who leads a strict or simple life without luxuries

spasm *n* **1** a sudden tightening of the muscles, over which one has no control **2** a sudden burst of activity or feeling: *a spasm of applause; sudden spasms of anger*
WORD ORIGIN Greek *spasmos* a cramp

spasmodic *adj* taking place in sudden short spells: *spasmodic bouts of illness* **spasmodically** *adv*

Spassky *n* **Boris** born 1937, Russian chess player; world champion (1969–72)

spastic *n* **1** a person who has cerebral palsy, and therefore has difficulty

S

THESAURUS

spar[2] *vb* **2 = argue**, row, squabble, dispute, scrap (*informal*), fall out (*informal*), spat (*US*), wrangle, skirmish, bicker, have a tiff

spare *adj* **1a = back-up**, reserve, second, extra, relief, emergency, additional, substitute, fall-back, auxiliary, in reserve **1b = extra**, surplus, leftover, over, free, odd, unwanted, in excess, unused, superfluous, supernumerary **OPPOSITE:** necessary
3 = thin, lean, slim, slender, slight, meagre, gaunt, wiry, lank **OPPOSITE:** plump
▷*vb* **7 = have mercy on**, pardon, have pity on, leave, release, excuse, let off (*informal*), go easy on (*informal*), be merciful to, grant pardon to, deal leniently with, refrain from hurting, save (from harm) **OPPOSITE:** show no mercy to
9 = afford, give, grant, do without, relinquish, part with, allow, bestow, dispense with, manage without, let someone have

sparing *adj* **= economical**, frugal, thrifty, saving, careful, prudent, cost-conscious, chary, money-conscious **OPPOSITE:** lavish

spark *n* **1 = flicker**, flash, gleam, glint, spit, flare, scintillation **3 = trace**, hint, scrap, atom, jot, vestige, scintilla ▷*vb* **6 = start**, stimulate, provoke, excite, inspire, stir, trigger (off), set off, animate, rouse, prod, precipitate, kick-start, set in motion, kindle, touch off

sparkle *vb* **1 = glitter**, flash, spark, shine, beam, glow, gleam, wink, shimmer, twinkle, dance, glint, glisten, glister (*archaic*), scintillate ▷*n* **4 = glitter**, flash, gleam, spark, dazzle, flicker, brilliance, twinkle, glint, radiance **5 = vivacity**, life, spirit, dash, zip (*informal*), vitality, animation, panache, gaiety, élan, brio, liveliness, vim (*slang*)

spate *n* **1 = series**, sequence, course,

DICTIONARY

controlling his or her muscles ▷ *adj* **2** affected by involuntary muscle contractions: *a spastic colon* **3** suffering from cerebral palsy
WORD ORIGIN Greek *spasmos* a cramp

spat[1] *n* a slight quarrel
WORD ORIGIN probably imitative

spat[2] *vb* ▸ a past of **spit[1]**

spate ❶ *n* **1** a large number of things happening within a period of time: *a spate of bombings* **2** a fast flow or outpouring: *an incomprehensible spate of words* **3** **in spate** *chiefly Brit* (of a river) flooded
WORD ORIGIN origin unknown

spathe *n bot* a large leaf that surrounds the base of a flower cluster
WORD ORIGIN Greek *spathē* a blade

spatial *adj* of or relating to size, area, or position: *spatial dimensions*
spatially *adv*

spats *pl n* cloth or leather coverings formerly worn by men over the ankle and instep
WORD ORIGIN obsolete *spatterdash* a long gaiter

spatter *vb* **1** to scatter or splash (a substance, esp. a liquid) in scattered drops: *spattering mud in all directions* **2** to sprinkle (an object or a surface) with a liquid ▷ *n* **3** the sound of spattering **4** something spattered, such as a spot or splash
WORD ORIGIN imitative

spatula *n* a utensil with a broad flat blade, used in cooking and by doctors
WORD ORIGIN Latin: a broad piece

spawn *n* **1** the jelly-like mass of eggs laid by fish, amphibians, or molluscs ▷ *vb* **2** (of fish, amphibians, or molluscs) to lay eggs **3** to cause (something) to be created: *the depressed economy spawned the riots*
WORD ORIGIN Anglo-Norman *espaundre*

spay *vb* to remove the ovaries from (a female animal)
WORD ORIGIN Old French *espeer* to cut with the sword

speak ❶ *vb* **speaking, spoke, spoken** **1** to say words; talk **2** to communicate or express (something) in words **3** to give a speech or lecture **4** to know how to talk in (a specified language): *I don't speak French* **5** **on speaking terms** on good terms; friendly **6** **so to speak** as it were **7** **speak one's mind** to express one's opinions honestly and plainly **8** **to speak of** of a significant nature: *no licensing laws to speak of*
WORD ORIGIN Old English *specan*

speakeasy *n, pl* **-easies** US a place where alcoholic drink was sold illegally during Prohibition

speaker ❶ *n* **1** a person who speaks, esp. someone making a speech **2** a person who speaks a particular language: *a fluent Tibetan and English speaker* **3** ▸ same as **loudspeaker**

Speaker *n* the official chairman of a law-making body

speak for *vb* **1** to speak on behalf of (other people) **2** **speak for itself** to be so obvious that no further comment is necessary: *his work on the convention speaks for itself* **3** **speak for yourself!** *informal* do not presume that other people agree with you!

speak up *or* **out** *vb* **1** to state one's beliefs bravely and firmly **2** to speak more loudly and clearly

spear[1] *n* **1** a weapon consisting of a long pole with a sharp point ▷ *vb* **2** to pierce (someone or something) with a spear or other pointed object: *she took her fork and speared an oyster from its shell*
WORD ORIGIN Old English *spere*

spear[2] *n* **1** a slender shoot, such as of grass **2** a single stalk of broccoli or asparagus
WORD ORIGIN probably variant of *spire*

spearhead ❶ *vb* **1** to lead (an attack or a campaign) ▷ *n* **2** the leading force in an attack or campaign

spearmint *n* a minty flavouring used for sweets and toothpaste, which comes from a purple-flowered plant

Spears *n* **Britney** born 1981, US pop singer; records include the single "Baby One More Time" (1998) and the album *Britney* (2001)

spec *n* **on spec** *informal* as a risk or gamble: *I still tend to buy on spec*

special ❶ *adj* **1** distinguished from or better than others of its kind: *a special occasion* **2** designed or reserved for a specific purpose: *special equipment* **3** not usual; different from normal: *a special case* **4** particular or primary: *a special interest in gifted children* **5** relating to the education of children with disabilities: *a special school* ▷ *n* **6** a product, TV programme, etc. which is only available or shown at a certain time: *a two-hour Christmas special live from Hollywood* **7** a meal, usually at a low price, in a bar or restaurant **8** ▸ short for **special constable** > **specially** *adv*
WORD ORIGIN Latin *specialis*

Special Branch *n* (in Britain and S Africa) the department of the police force that is concerned with political security

special constable *n* a person recruited for occasional police duties, such as in an emergency

special delivery *n* the delivery of a piece of mail outside the time of a scheduled delivery, for an extra fee

special effects *pl n films* techniques used in the production of scenes that cannot be achieved by normal methods: *the special effects and make-up are totally convincing*

specialist ❶ *n* **1** a person who is an expert in a particular activity or subject **2** a doctor who concentrates on treating one particular category of diseases or the diseases of one particular part of the body: *an eye specialist* ▷ *adj* **3** particular to or concentrating on one subject or activity: *a specialist comic shop*

speciality ❶ *or esp. US & Canad* **specialty** *n, pl* **-ties** **1** a special interest or skill **2** a service, product, or type of food specialized in

specialize *or* **-ise** *vb* **-izing, -ized** *or* **-ising, -ised** **1** (often foll. by *in*) to concentrate all one's efforts on studying a particular subject, occupation, or activity: *an expert who specializes in transport* **2** to modify

S

THESAURUS

chain, succession, run, train, string **2 = flood**, flow, torrent, rush, deluge, outpouring

speak *vb* **1a = talk**, say something **1b = converse**, talk, chat, discourse, confer, commune, exchange views, shoot the breeze *(slang, chiefly US & Canad)*, korero (NZ) **2 = articulate**, say, voice, pronounce, utter, tell, state, talk, express, communicate, make known, enunciate **3 = lecture**, talk, discourse, spout *(informal)*, make a speech, pontificate, give a speech, declaim, hold forth, spiel *(informal)*, address an audience, deliver an address, speechify

speaker *n* **1 = orator**, public speaker, lecturer, spokesperson, mouthpiece, spieler *(informal)*, word-spinner, spokesman *or* spokeswoman

spearhead *vb* **1 = lead**, head, pioneer, launch, set off, initiate, lead the way, set in motion, blaze the trail, be in the van, lay the first stone

special *adj* **1, 3 = exceptional**, important, significant, particular, unique, unusual, extraordinary, distinguished, memorable, gala, festive, uncommon, momentous, out of the ordinary, one in a million, red-letter, especial
OPPOSITE: ordinary
2 = specific, particular, distinctive, certain, individual, appropriate, characteristic, precise, peculiar, specialized, especial
OPPOSITE: general

specialist *n* **1 = expert**, authority, professional, master, consultant, guru, buff *(informal)*, whizz *(informal)*, connoisseur, boffin *(Brit informal)*, hotshot *(informal)*, wonk *(informal)*, maven (US), fundi *(S African)*

speciality *or (esp. US & Canad)* **specialty** *n* **1 = forte**, strength, special talent, métier, bag *(slang)*, claim to fame, pièce de résistance *(French)*, distinctive *or* distinguishing feature

DICTIONARY

(something) for a special use or purpose: *plants have evolved and specialized in every type of habitat* **specialization** *or* **-isation** *n*
special licence *n Brit* a licence allowing a marriage to take place without following all the usual legal procedures
specialty *n, pl* **-ties** *chiefly US & Canad* ▸ same as **speciality**
specie *n* coins as distinct from paper money
WORD ORIGIN Latin *in specie* in kind
species ⊙ *n, pl* **-cies** *biol* one of the groups into which a genus is divided, the members of which are able to interbreed
WORD ORIGIN Latin: appearance
specific ⊙ *adj* **1** particular or definite: *a specific area of economic policy* **2** precise and exact: *try and be more specific* ▹ *n* **3 specifics** particular qualities or aspects of something: *the specifics of the situation* **4** *med* any drug used to treat a particular disease **specifically** *adv* **specificity** *n*
WORD ORIGIN Latin *species* kind + *facere* to make
specification ⊙ *n* **1** a detailed description of features in the design of something: *engines built to racing specification* **2** a requirement or detail which is clearly stated: *the main specification was that a good degree was required* **3** the specifying of something
specific gravity *n physics* the ratio of the density of a substance to the density of water
specific heat capacity *n physics* the quantity of heat required to raise the temperature of unit mass of a substance by one degree centigrade
specify ⊙ *vb* **-fies, -fying, -fied** **1** to state or describe (something) clearly **2** to state (something) as a condition: *the rules specify the number of prisoners to be kept in each cell*
WORD ORIGIN Medieval Latin *specificare* to describe
specimen ⊙ *n* **1** an individual or part regarded as typical of its group or class **2** *med* a sample of tissue, blood, or urine taken for analysis **3** *informal* a person: *I'm quite a healthy specimen*
WORD ORIGIN Latin: mark, proof
specious (spee-shuss) *adj* apparently correct or true, but actually wrong or false
WORD ORIGIN Latin *species* outward appearance
speck *n* **1** a very small mark or spot **2** a small or tiny piece of something: *a speck of fluff*
WORD ORIGIN Old English *specca*
speckle *vb* **-ling, -led** **1** to mark (something) with speckles ▹ *n* **2** a small mark or spot, such as on the skin or on an egg **speckled** *adj*
WORD ORIGIN Middle Dutch *spekkel*
specs *pl n informal* ▸ short for **spectacles**
spectacle ⊙ *n* **1** a strange, interesting, or ridiculous scene **2** an impressive public show: *the opening ceremony of the Olympics was an impressive spectacle* **3 make a spectacle of oneself** to draw attention to oneself by behaving foolishly
WORD ORIGIN Latin *spectare* to watch
spectacles *pl n* a pair of glasses for correcting faulty vision
spectacular ⊙ *adj* **1** impressive, grand, or dramatic ▹ *n* **2** a spectacular show **spectacularly** *adv*
spectate *vb* **-tating, -tated** to be a spectator; watch
spectator ⊙ *n* a person viewing anything; onlooker
WORD ORIGIN Latin *spectare* to watch
spectator ion *n chem* an ion which is present in a mixture but plays no part in a reaction
Spector *n* **Phil** born 1940, US record producer and songwriter, noted for the densely orchestrated "Wall of Sound" in his work with groups such as the Ronettes and the Crystals; arrested on a murder charge in 2003
spectre ⊙ *or US* **specter** *n* **1** a ghost **2** an unpleasant or menacing vision in one's imagination: *the spectre of famine* **spectral** *adj*
WORD ORIGIN Latin *spectrum*
spectrometer (speck-**trom**-it-er) *n physics* an instrument for producing a spectrum, usually one in which wavelength, energy, or intensity can be measured
spectroscope *n physics* an instrument for forming or recording a spectrum by passing a light ray through a prism or grating
spectrum *n, pl* **-tra** **1** *physics* the distribution of colours produced when white light is dispersed by a prism or grating: violet, indigo, blue, green, yellow, orange, and red **2** *physics* the whole range of electromagnetic radiation with respect to its wavelength or frequency **3** a range or scale of anything such as opinions or emotions
WORD ORIGIN Latin: image
speculate ⊙ *vb* **-lating, -lated** **1** to form opinions about something, esp. its future consequences, based on the information available; conjecture: *it is too early to speculate about Jackie getting married* **2** to buy securities or property in the hope of selling them at a profit **speculation** *n* **speculative** *adj* **speculator** *n*
WORD ORIGIN Latin *speculari* to spy out
sped *vb* ▸ a past of **speed**
speech ⊙ *n* **1** the ability to speak: *the loss of speech* **2** spoken language: *Doran's lack of coherent speech* **3** a talk given to an audience: *a speech to parliament* **4** a person's manner of speaking: *her speech was extremely slow* **5** a national or regional language or dialect: *Canadian speech*
WORD ORIGIN Old English *spēc*

S

THESAURUS

species *n (biol)* **= kind**, sort, type, group, class, variety, breed, category, description, genus
specific *adj* **1 = particular**, special, characteristic, distinguishing, peculiar, definite, especial
OPPOSITE: general
2 = precise, exact, explicit, definite, limited, express, clear-cut, unequivocal, unambiguous
OPPOSITE: vague
specification *n* **2 = requirement**, detail, particular, stipulation, condition, qualification
specify *vb* **1, 2 = state**, designate, spell out, stipulate, name, detail, mention, indicate, define, cite, individualize, enumerate, itemize, be specific about, particularize
specimen *n* **1 = sample**, example, individual, model, type, pattern, instance, representative, exemplar, exemplification
spectacle *n* **1 = sight**, wonder, scene, phenomenon, curiosity, marvel, laughing stock **2 = show**, display, exhibition, event, performance, sight, parade, extravaganza, pageant
spectacular *adj* **1 = impressive**, striking, dramatic, stunning *(informal)*, marked, grand, remarkable, fantastic *(informal)*, magnificent, staggering, splendid, dazzling, sensational, breathtaking, eye-catching
OPPOSITE: unimpressive
▹ *n* **2 = show**, display, spectacle, extravaganza
spectator *n* **= onlooker**, observer, viewer, witness, looker-on, watcher, eyewitness, bystander, beholder
OPPOSITE: participant
spectre *or (US)* **specter** *n* **1 = ghost**, spirit, phantom, presence, vision, shadow, shade *(literary)*, apparition, wraith, kehua *(NZ)*
speculate *vb* **1 = conjecture**, consider, wonder, guess, contemplate, deliberate, muse, meditate, surmise, theorize, hypothesize, cogitate
2 = play the market
speech *n* **2 = communication**, talk, conversation, articulation, discussion, dialogue, intercourse
3 = talk, address, lecture, discourse, harangue, homily, oration, spiel *(informal)*, disquisition, whaikorero *(NZ)* **4 = diction**, pronunciation, articulation, delivery, fluency, inflection, intonation, elocution,

DICTIONARY

speech day *n* (in schools) an annual day on which prizes are presented and speeches are made by guest speakers

speechify *vb* **-fies, -fying, -fied** to make a dull or pompous speech

speechless *adj* **1** unable to speak for a short time because of great emotion or shock **2** unable to be expressed in words: *speechless disbelief*

speech therapy *n* the treatment of people with speech problems

speed ❶ *n* **1** the quality of acting or moving fast; swiftness **2** the rate at which something moves or happens **3** a gear ratio in a motor vehicle or bicycle: *five-speed gearbox* **4** *photog* a measure of the sensitivity to light of a particular type of film **5** *slang* amphetamine **6 at speed** quickly **7 up to speed a** operating at an acceptable level **b** in possession of all the necessary information ▹ *vb* **speeding, sped** *or* **speeded 8** to move or go somewhere quickly **9** to drive a motor vehicle faster than the legal limit ▸ See also **speed up**
WORD ORIGIN Old English *spēd* (originally: success)

speedboat *n* a high-speed motorboat

speed camera *n* a camera for photographing vehicles breaking the speed limit

speed limit *n* the maximum speed at which a vehicle may legally travel on a particular road

speedo *n, pl* **speedos** *informal* a speedometer

speedometer *n* a dial in a vehicle which shows the speed of travel

speed trap *n* a place on a road where the police check that passing vehicles are not being driven at an illegally high speed

speed up *vb* to accelerate or cause to accelerate

speedway *n* **1** the sport of racing on light powerful motorcycles round cinder tracks **2** *US, Canad & NZ* the track or stadium where such races are held

speedwell *n* a small blue or pinkish-white flower

speedy ❶ *adj* **speedier, speediest 1** done without delay **2** (of a vehicle) able to travel fast **speedily** *adv*

speleology *n* the scientific study of caves
WORD ORIGIN Latin *spelaeum* cave

spell[1] ❶ *vb* **spelling, spelt** *or* **spelled 1** to write or name in correct order the letters that make up (a word): *how do you spell that name?* **2** (of letters) to make up (a word): *c-a-t spells cat* **3** to indicate (a particular result): *share price slump spells disaster* ▸ See also **spell out**
WORD ORIGIN Old French *espeller*

spell[2] ❶ *n* **1** a sequence of words used to perform magic **2** the effect of a spell: *the wizard's spell was broken* **3 under someone's spell** fascinated by someone
WORD ORIGIN Old English *spell* speech

spell[3] ❶ *n* **1** a period of time of weather or activity: *the dry spell; a short spell in prison* **2** a period of duty after which one person or group relieves another **3** *Scot, Austral & NZ* a period of rest
WORD ORIGIN Old English *spelian* to take the place of

spellbinding *adj* so fascinating that nothing else can be thought of: *his spellbinding speeches*

spellbound *adj* completely fascinated; as if in a trance

spellchecker *n computers* a program that highlights any word in a word-processed document that is not recognized as being correctly spelt

spelling *n* **1** the way a word is spelt: *the British spelling of 'theatre'* **2** a person's ability to spell: *my spelling used to be excellent*

spell out *vb* **1** to make (something) as easy to understand as possible: *to spell out the implications* **2** to read with difficulty, working out each word letter by letter

spelt *vb* ▸ a past of **spell**[1]

Spence *n* Sir **Basil** (**Unwin**) 1907–76, Scottish architect, born in India; designed Coventry Cathedral (1951)

Spencer *n* **1 Herbert** 1820–1903, English philosopher, who applied evolutionary theory to the study of society, favouring laissez-faire doctrines **2** Sir **Stanley** 1891–1959, English painter, noted esp. for his paintings of Christ in a contemporary English setting

spend ❶ *vb* **spending, spent 1** to pay out (money) **2** to pass (time) in a specific way or place: *I spent a year in Budapest* **3** to concentrate (effort) on an activity: *a lot of energy was spent organizing the holiday* **4** to use up completely: *the hurricane spent its force* **spending** *n*
WORD ORIGIN Latin *expendere*

Spender *n* Sir **Stephen** 1909–95, English poet and critic, who played an important part in the left-wing literary movement of the 1930s. His works include *Journals 1939–83* (1985) and *Collected Poems* (1985)

spendthrift *n* **1** a person who spends money wastefully ▹ *adj* **2** of or like a spendthrift: *a spendthrift policy*

Spengler *n* **Oswald** 1880–1936, German philosopher of history, noted for *The Decline of the West* (1918–22), which argues that civilizations go through natural cycles of growth and decay

spent *vb* **1** ▸ the past of **spend** ▹ *adj* **2** used up or exhausted

Speranski *n* **Mikhail Mikhailovich** 1772–1839, Russian statesman, chief adviser (1807–12) to Alexander I. His greatest achievement was the codification of Russian law (begun 1826)

sperm *n* **1** *pl* **sperms** *or* **sperm** one of the male reproductive cells released in the semen during ejaculation **2** ▸ same as **semen**
WORD ORIGIN Greek *sperma*

spermaceti (sper-ma-set-ee) *n* a white waxy substance obtained from the sperm whale
WORD ORIGIN Medieval Latin *sperma ceti* whale's sperm

S

THESAURUS

enunciation **5 = language**, tongue, utterance, jargon, dialect, idiom, parlance, articulation, diction, lingo *(informal)*, enunciation

speed *n* **1 = swiftness**, rush, hurry, expedition, haste, rapidity, quickness, fleetness, celerity **OPPOSITE:** slowness **2 = rate**, pace, momentum, tempo, velocity ▹ *vb* **8 = race**, rush, hurry, zoom, career, bomb (along), tear, flash, belt (along) *(slang)*, barrel (along) *(informal, chiefly US & Canad)*, sprint, gallop, hasten, press on, quicken, lose no time, get a move on *(informal)*, burn rubber *(informal)*, bowl along, put your foot down *(informal)*, step on it *(informal)*, make haste, go hell for leather *(informal)*, exceed the speed limit, go like a bomb *(Brit & NZ informal)*, go like the wind, go like a bat out of hell **OPPOSITE:** crawl

speedy *adj* **1, 2 = quick**, fast, rapid, swift, express, winged, immediate, prompt, fleet, hurried, summary, precipitate, hasty, headlong, quickie *(informal)*, expeditious, fleet of foot, pdq *(slang)* **OPPOSITE:** slow

spell[1] *vb* **3 = indicate**, mean, signify, suggest, promise, point to, imply, amount to, herald, augur, presage, portend

spell[2] *n* **1 = incantation**, charm, sorcery, exorcism, abracadabra, witchery, conjuration, makutu (NZ) **2 = enchantment**, magic, fascination, glamour, allure, bewitchment

spell[3] *n* **1 = period**, time, term, stretch, turn, course, season, patch, interval, bout, stint

spend *vb* **1 = pay out**, fork out *(slang)*, expend, lay out, splash out *(Brit informal)*, shell out *(informal)*, disburse **OPPOSITE:** save **2 = pass**, fill, occupy, while away **4 = use up**, waste, squander, blow *(slang)*, empty, drain, exhaust, consume, run through, deplete, dissipate, fritter away **OPPOSITE:** save

DICTIONARY

spermatozoon (sper-ma-toe-zoe-on) *n, pl* **-zoa** ▸ same as **sperm** (sense 1)
WORD ORIGIN Greek *sperma* seed + *zōion* animal

spermicide *n* a substance, esp. a cream or jelly, that kills sperm, used as a means of contraception **spermicidal** *adj*
WORD ORIGIN SPERM + Latin *caedere* to kill

sperm oil *n* an oil obtained from the head of the sperm whale, used as a lubricant

sperm whale *n* a large whale which is hunted for spermaceti and ambergris
WORD ORIGIN short for SPERMACETI WHALE

spew *vb* **1** to vomit **2** to send or be sent out in a stream: *the hydrant spewed a tidal wave of water*
WORD ORIGIN Old English *spīwan*

SPF sun protection factor: an indicator of how a sun cream, lotion, etc. protects the skin from the harmful rays of the sun

sphagnum *n* a moss which is found in bogs and which decays to form peat
WORD ORIGIN Greek *sphagnos*

sphere ❶ *n* **1** *geom* a round solid figure in which every point on the surface is equally distant from the centre **2** an object having this shape, such as a planet **3** a particular field of activity **4** people of the same rank or with shared interests: *a humbler social sphere*
WORD ORIGIN Greek *sphaira*

spherical *adj* shaped like a sphere

spheroid *n geom* a solid figure that is almost but not exactly a sphere

sphincter *n anat* a ring of muscle surrounding the opening of a hollow organ and contracting to close it
WORD ORIGIN Greek *sphingein* to grip tightly

sphinx *n* **1** one of the huge statues built by the ancient Egyptians, with the body of a lion and the head of a man **2** a mysterious person

S

Sphinx *n* **1** the huge statue of a sphinx near the pyramids at El Gîza in Egypt **2** *Greek myth* a monster with a woman's head and a lion's body, who set a riddle for travellers, killing them when they failed to answer it. Oedipus answered the riddle and the Sphinx then killed herself
WORD ORIGIN Greek

spice ❶ *n* **1 a** an aromatic substance, such as ginger or cinnamon, used as flavouring **b** such substances collectively **2** something that makes life or an activity more exciting ▹ *vb* **spicing, spiced 3** to flavour (food) with spices **4** (often foll. by *up*) to add excitement or interest to (something): *they spiced their letters with pointed demands*
WORD ORIGIN Old French *espice*

spick-and-span *adj* very neat and clean
WORD ORIGIN obsolete *spick* spike + *span-new* absolutely new, like a freshly cut spike

spicy ❶ *adj* **spicier, spiciest 1** strongly flavoured with spices **2** *informal* slightly scandalous: *spicy new story lines*

spider *n* a small eight-legged creature, many species of which weave webs in which to trap insects for food **spidery** *adj*
WORD ORIGIN Old English *spīthra*

spider monkey *n* a tree-living monkey with very long legs, a long tail, and a small head

spiel *n* a prepared speech made to persuade someone to buy or do something
WORD ORIGIN German *Spiel* play

spigot *n* **1** a stopper for the vent hole of a cask **2** a wooden tap fitted to a cask
WORD ORIGIN probably from Latin *spica* a point

spike[1] ❶ *n* **1** a sharp-pointed metal object: *a high fence with iron spikes* **2** anything long and pointed: *a hedgehog bristling with spikes* **3** a long metal nail **4 spikes** sports shoes with metal spikes on the soles for greater grip ▹ *vb* **spiking, spiked 5** to secure or supply (something) with spikes: *spiked shoes* **6** to drive a spike or spikes into **7** to add alcohol to (a drink) **spiky** *adj*
WORD ORIGIN Middle English *spyk*

spike[2] *n bot* **1** an arrangement of flowers attached at the base to a long stem **2** an ear of grain
WORD ORIGIN Latin *spica* ear of corn

spikenard *n* **1** a fragrant Indian plant with rose-purple flowers **2** an ointment obtained from this plant
WORD ORIGIN Medieval Latin *spica nardi*

spill[1] ❶ *vb* **spilling, spilt** *or* **spilled 1** to pour from or as from a container by accident **2** (of large numbers of people) to come out of a place: *rival groups spilled out from the station* **3** to shed (blood) **4 spill the beans** *informal* to give away a secret ▹ *n* **5** *informal* a fall from a motorbike, bike, or horse, esp. in a competition **6** an amount of liquid spilt **spillage** *n*
WORD ORIGIN Old English *spillan* to destroy

spill[2] *n* a splinter of wood or strip of paper for lighting pipes or fires
WORD ORIGIN Germanic

Spillane *n* **Mickey**, original name *Frank Morrison Spillane*. 1918–2006, US detective-story writer, best known for his books featuring the detective Mike Hammer, for example *I, the Jury* (1947) and *The Twisted Thing* (1966)

spillikin *n Brit* a thin strip of wood, cardboard, or plastic used in spillikins

spillikins *n Brit* a game in which players try to pick each spillikin from a heap without moving the others

spin ❶ *vb* **spinning, spun 1** to revolve or cause to revolve quickly **2** to draw out and twist (fibres, such as silk or cotton) into thread **3** (of a spider or silkworm) to form (a web or cocoon) from a silky fibre that comes out of the body **4 spin a yarn** to tell an unlikely story **5** *sport* to throw, hit, or kick (a ball) so that it spins and changes direction or changes speed on bouncing **6** ▸ same as **spin-dry 7** to grow dizzy: *her head was spinning* **8** *informal* to present information in a way that creates a favourable impression ▹ *n* **9** a fast rotating motion **10** a flight manoeuvre in which an aircraft flies in a downward spiral **11** *sport* a spinning motion given to a ball **12** *informal* a short car drive taken for pleasure **13** *informal* the presenting of information in a way that creates a favourable impression ▸ See also **spin out** > **spinning** *n*
WORD ORIGIN Old English *spinnan*

spina bifida *n* a condition in which part of the spinal cord protrudes

THESAURUS

sphere *n* **2 = ball**, globe, orb, globule, circle **3 = field**, range, area, department, function, territory, capacity, province, patch, scope, turf *(US slang)*, realm, domain, compass, walk of life

spice *n* **1a = seasoning**, condiment **2 = excitement**, kick *(informal)*, zest, colour, pep, zip *(informal)*, tang, zap *(slang)*, gusto, zing *(informal)*, piquancy

spicy *adj* **1 = hot**, seasoned, pungent, aromatic, savoury, tangy, piquant, flavoursome **2** *(informal)* **= risqué**, racy, off-colour, ribald, hot *(informal)*, broad, improper, suggestive, unseemly, titillating, indelicate, indecorous

spike[1] *n* **1, 3 = point**, stake, spur, pin, nail, spine, barb, tine, prong ▹ *vb* **6 = impale**, spit, spear, stick

spill[1] *vb* **1a = shed**, scatter, discharge, throw off, disgorge, spill *or* run over **1b = slop**, flow, pour, run, overflow, slosh, splosh

spin *vb* **1 = revolve**, turn, rotate, wheel, twist, reel, whirl, twirl, gyrate, pirouette, birl *(Scot)* **7 = reel**, swim, whirl, be giddy, be in a whirl, grow dizzy ▹ *n* **9 = revolution**, roll, whirl, twist, gyration **12** *(informal)* **= drive**, ride, turn, hurl *(Scot)*, whirl, joy ride *(informal)*

through a gap in the backbone, sometimes causing paralysis
WORD ORIGIN New Latin: split spine
spinach *n* a dark green leafy vegetable
WORD ORIGIN Arabic *isfānākh*
spinal column *n* ▸ same as **spine** (sense 1)
spinal cord *n* the thick cord of nerve tissue within the spine, which connects the brain to the nerves of the body
spin bowler *n cricket* ▸ same as **spinner** (sense 1a)
spindle *n* **1** a rotating rod that acts as an axle **2** a rod with a notch in the top for drawing out, twisting and winding the thread in spinning
WORD ORIGIN Old English *spinel*
spindly *adj* **-dlier, -dliest** tall, thin, and frail
spin doctor *n informal* a person who provides a favourable slant to a news item or policy on behalf of a political personality or party
WORD ORIGIN from the spin given to a ball in sport to make it go in the desired direction
spindrift *n* spray blown up from the sea
WORD ORIGIN Scots variant of *spoondrift*, from *spoon* to scud + DRIFT
spin-dry *vb* **-dries, -drying, -dried** to dry (clothes) in a spin-dryer
spin-dryer *n* a device that removes water from washed clothes by spinning them in a perforated drum
spine ❶ *n* **1** the row of bony segments that surround and protect the spinal cord **2** the back of a book, record sleeve, or video-tape box **3** a sharp point on the body of an animal or on a plant **spinal** *adj*
WORD ORIGIN Latin *spina* thorn
spine-chiller *n* a frightening film or story **spine-chilling** *adj*
spineless *adj* **1** behaving in a cowardly way **2** (of an animal) having no spine
spinet *n* a small harpsichord
WORD ORIGIN Italian *spinetta*
spinifex *n* a coarse spiny Australian grass
spinnaker *n* a large triangular sail on a racing yacht
WORD ORIGIN probably from *spin*, but traditionally from Sphinx, the yacht that first used this type of sail
spinner *n* **1** *cricket* **a** a bowler who specializes in spinning the ball with his or her fingers to make it change direction when it bounces or strikes the batsman's bat **b** a ball that is bowled with a spinning motion **2** a small round object used in angling to attract fish to the bait by spinning in the water **3** a person who makes thread by spinning
spinneret *n* an organ through which silk threads come out of the body of a spider or insect
spinney *n chiefly Brit* a small wood: *the hollow tree in the spinney*
WORD ORIGIN Old French *espinei*
spinning jenny *n* an early type of spinning frame with several spindles
spinning wheel *n* a wheel-like machine for spinning at home, having one hand- or foot-operated spindle
spin-off *n* **1** a product or development that unexpectedly results from activities designed to achieve something else: *new energy sources could occur as a spin-off from the space effort* **2** a television series involving some of the characters from an earlier successful series
spin out ❶ *vb* **1** to take longer than necessary to do (something) **2** to make (money) last as long as possible
spinster *n* an unmarried woman **spinsterish** *adj*
WORD ORIGIN Middle English, in the sense a woman who spins
spiny *adj* **spinier, spiniest** (of animals or plants) covered with spines
spiracle (**spire**-a-kl) *n zool* a small blowhole for breathing through, such as that of a whale
WORD ORIGIN Latin *spiraculum* vent
spiraea *or esp. US* **spirea** (spire-**ee**-a) *n* a plant with small white or pink flowers
WORD ORIGIN Greek *speiraia*
spiral ❶ *n* **1** *geom* a plane curve formed by a point winding about a fixed point at an ever-increasing distance from it **2** something that follows a winding course or that has a twisting form **3** *econ* a continuous upward or downward movement in economic activity or prices ▹ *adj* **4** having the shape of a spiral: *a spiral staircase* ▹ *vb* **-ralling, -ralled** *or US* **-raling, -raled 5** to follow a spiral course or be in the shape of a spiral **6** to increase or decrease with steady acceleration: *oil prices continue to spiral* **spirally** *adv*
WORD ORIGIN Latin *spira* a coil
spire *n* the tall cone-shaped structure on the top of a church
WORD ORIGIN Old English *spīr* blade
spirit[1] ❶ *n* **1** the nonphysical aspect of a person concerned with profound thoughts and emotions **2** the nonphysical part of a person believed to live on after death **3** a shared feeling: *a spirit of fun and adventure* **4** mood or attitude: *fighting spirit* **5** a person's character or temperament: *the indomitable spirit of the Polish people* **6** liveliness shown in what a person does: *it has been undertaken with spirit* **7** the feelings that motivate someone to survive in difficult times or live according to his or her beliefs: *someone had broken his spirit* **8 spirits** an emotional state: *in good spirits* **9** the way in which something, such as a law or an agreement, was intended to be interpreted: *they acted against the spirit of the treaty* **10** a supernatural being, such as a ghost ▹ *vb* **-iting, -ited 11 spirit away** *or* **off** to carry (someone or something) off mysteriously or secretly
WORD ORIGIN Latin *spiritus* breath, spirit
spirit[2] *n* **1** (*usually pl*) distilled alcoholic liquor, such as whisky or gin **2** *chem* **a** a solution of ethanol obtained by distillation **b** the essence of a substance, extracted as a liquid by distillation **3** *pharmacol* a solution of a volatile oil in alcohol
WORD ORIGIN special use of SPIRIT[1]
spirited ❶ *adj* **1** showing liveliness or courage: *a spirited rendition of Schubert's ninth symphony; a spirited defence of the government's policy* **2** characterized by the mood as specified: *high-spirited; mean-spirited*
spirit gum *n* a solution of gum in ether, used to stick on false hair

S

THESAURUS

spine *n* **1 = backbone**, vertebrae, spinal column, vertebral column **3 = barb**, spur, needle, spike, ray, quill
spin out *vb* **1 = prolong**, extend, lengthen, draw out, drag out, delay, amplify, pad out, protract, prolongate
spiral *n* **1, 2 = coil**, helix, corkscrew, whorl, screw, curlicue ▹ *adj* **4 = coiled**, winding, corkscrew, circular, scrolled, whorled, helical, cochlear, voluted, cochleate (*biol*)
spirit[1] *n* **1 = soul**, life, psyche, essential being **2 = life force**, vital spark, breath, mauri (NZ) **3 = feeling**, atmosphere, character, feel, quality, tone, mood, flavour, tenor, ambience, vibes (*slang*) **4 = mood**, feelings, morale, humour, temper, tenor, disposition, state of mind, frame of mind **5 = attitude**, character, quality, humour, temper, outlook, temperament, complexion, disposition **6 = liveliness**, energy, vigour, life, force, fire, resolution, enterprise, enthusiasm, sparkle, warmth, animation, zest, mettle, ardour, earnestness, brio **9 = intention**, meaning, purpose, substance, intent, essence, purport, gist **10 = ghost**, phantom, spectre, vision, shadow, shade (*literary*), spook (*informal*), apparition, sprite, atua (NZ), kehua (NZ)
spirited *adj* **1 = lively**, vigorous, energetic, animated, game, active, bold, sparkling, have-a-go (*informal*), courageous, ardent, feisty (*informal, chiefly US & Canad*), plucky, high-

DICTIONARY

spirit lamp *n* a lamp that burns methylated or other spirits instead of oil

spirit level *n* a device for checking whether a surface is level, consisting of a block of wood or metal containing a tube partially filled with liquid set so that the air bubble in it rests between two marks on the tube when the block is level

spiritual ❶ *adj* **1** relating to a person's beliefs as opposed to his or her physical or material needs **2** relating to religious beliefs **3 one's spiritual home** the place where one feels one belongs ▷*n* **4** Also called: **Negro spiritual** a type of religious folk song originally sung by Black slaves in the American South **spirituality** *n* **spiritually** *adv*

spiritualism *n* the belief that the spirits of the dead can communicate with the living **spiritualist** *n*

spirituous *adj* containing alcohol

spirogyra (spire-oh-jire-a) *n* a green freshwater plant that floats on the surface of ponds and ditches
WORD ORIGIN Greek *speira* a coil + *guros* a circle

spit¹ ❶ *vb* **spitting, spat** *or* **spit 1** to force saliva out of one's mouth **2** to force (something) out of one's mouth: *he spat tobacco into an old coffee can* **3** (of a fire or hot fat) to throw out sparks or particles violently and explosively **4** to rain very lightly **5** (often foll. by *out*) to say (words) in a violent angry way **6** to show contempt or hatred by spitting **7 spit it out!** *informal* a command given to someone to say what is on his or her mind ▷*n* **8** ▸same as **spittle 9** *informal, chiefly Brit* ▸same as **spitting image**
WORD ORIGIN Old English *spittan*

spit² *n* **1** a pointed rod for skewering and roasting meat over a fire or in an oven **2** a long narrow strip of land jutting out into the sea
WORD ORIGIN Old English *spitu*

spit and polish *n informal* thorough cleaning and polishing

spite ❶ *n* **1** deliberate nastiness **2 in spite of** regardless of: *he loved them in spite of their shortcomings* ▷*vb* **spiting, spited 3** to annoy (someone) deliberately, out of spite: *it was to spite his father* **spiteful** *adj* **spitefully** *adv*
WORD ORIGIN variant of DESPITE

spitfire *n* a woman or girl who is easily angered

spitting image *n informal* a person who looks very like someone else
WORD ORIGIN from *spit* likeness

spittle *n* the fluid that is produced in the mouth; saliva
WORD ORIGIN Old English *spǣtl* saliva

spittoon *n* a bowl for people to spit into

spitz *n* a stockily built dog with a pointed face, erect ears, and a tightly curled tail
WORD ORIGIN from German

spiv *n Brit, Austral & NZ slang* a smartly dressed man who makes a living by underhand dealings; black marketeer
WORD ORIGIN dialect *spiving* smart

splash ❶ *vb* **1** to scatter (liquid) on (something) **2** to cause (liquid) to fall or (of liquid) to be scattered in drops **3** to display (a photograph or story) prominently in a newspaper ▷*n* **4** a splashing sound **5** an amount splashed **6** a patch (of colour or light) **7 make a splash** *informal* to attract a lot of attention **8** a small amount of liquid added to a drink
WORD ORIGIN alteration of *plash*

splashdown *n* **1** the landing of a spacecraft on water at the end of a flight ▷*vb* **splash down 2** (of a spacecraft) to make a splashdown

splash out *vb* to spend a lot of money on a treat or luxury: *she planned to splash out on a good holiday*

splatter *vb* **1** to splash (something or someone) with small blobs ▷*n* **2** a splash of liquid

splay *vb* to spread out, with ends spreading out in different directions: *her hair splayed over the pillow*
WORD ORIGIN short for DISPLAY

splayfooted *adj* ▸same as **flat-footed**

spleen *n* **1** a spongy organ near the stomach, which filters bacteria from the blood **2** spitefulness or bad temper: *we vent our spleen on drug barons*
WORD ORIGIN Greek *splēn*

spleenwort *n* a kind of fern that grows on walls

splendid ❶ *adj* **1** very good: *a splendid match* **2** beautiful or impressive: *a splendid palace* **splendidly** *adv*
WORD ORIGIN Latin *splendere* to shine

splendiferous *adj facetious, old-fashioned* grand in appearance
WORD ORIGIN Latin *splendor* radiance + *ferre* to bring

splendour ❶ *or US* **splendor** *n* **1** beauty or impressiveness **2 splendours** the impressive or beautiful features of something: *the splendours of the Emperor's Palace*

splenetic *adj literary* irritable or bad-tempered
WORD ORIGIN from SPLEEN

splice *vb* **splicing, spliced 1** to join up the trimmed ends of (two pieces of wire, film, or tape) with an adhesive material **2** to join (two ropes) by interweaving the ends **3 get spliced** *informal* to get married
WORD ORIGIN probably from Middle Dutch *splissen*

splint *n* a piece of wood used to support a broken bone
WORD ORIGIN Middle Low German *splinte*

splinter ❶ *n* **1** a small thin sharp piece broken off, esp. from wood ▷*vb* **2** to break or be broken into small sharp fragments
WORD ORIGIN Middle Dutch

splinter group *n* a number of

S

THESAURUS

spirited, sprightly, vivacious, spunky *(informal)*, mettlesome, (as) game as Ned Kelly *(Austral slang)*
OPPOSITE: lifeless

spiritual *adj* **1 = nonmaterial**, immaterial, incorporeal
OPPOSITE: material
2 = sacred, religious, holy, divine, ethereal, devotional, otherworldly

spit¹ *vb* **1, 2 = expectorate**, sputter

spite *n* **1 = malice**, malevolence, ill will, hate, hatred, gall, animosity, venom, spleen, pique, rancour, bitchiness *(slang)*, malignity, spitefulness **OPPOSITE:** kindness
2 in spite of = despite, regardless of, notwithstanding, in defiance of, (even) though ▷*vb* **3 = annoy**, hurt, injure, harm, provoke, offend, needle *(informal)*, put out, gall, nettle, vex, pique, discomfit, put someone's nose out of joint *(informal)*, hack someone off *(informal)* **OPPOSITE:** benefit

splash *vb* **1, 2 = scatter**, shower, spray, sprinkle, spread, wet, strew, squirt, spatter, slop, slosh *(informal)* ▷*n* **5 = dash**, touch, spattering, splodge **6 = spot**, burst, patch, stretch, spurt

splendid *adj* **1 = excellent**, wonderful, marvellous, mean *(slang)*, great *(informal)*, topping *(Brit slang)*, fine, cracking *(Brit informal)*, crucial *(slang)*, fantastic *(informal)*, first-class, glorious, mega *(slang)*, sovereign, awesome *(slang)*, def *(slang)*, brill *(informal)*, bodacious *(slang, chiefly US)*, boffo *(slang)*, chillin' *(US slang)*, booshit *(Austral slang)*, exo *(Austral slang)*, sik *(Austral slang)*, rad *(informal)*, phat *(slang)*, schmick *(Austral informal)*, beaut *(informal)*, barrie *(Scot slang)*, belting *(Brit slang)*, pearler *(Austral slang)* **OPPOSITE:** poor
2 = magnificent, grand, imposing, impressive, rich, superb, costly, gorgeous, dazzling, lavish, luxurious, sumptuous, ornate, resplendent, splendiferous *(facetious)*
OPPOSITE: squalid

splendour *or (US)* **splendor** *n* **1 = magnificence**, glory, grandeur, show, display, ceremony, luxury, spectacle, majesty, richness, nobility, pomp, opulence, solemnity, éclat, gorgeousness, sumptuousness, stateliness, resplendence, luxuriousness **OPPOSITE:** squalor

splinter *n* **1 = sliver**, fragment, chip, needle, shaving, flake, paring ▷*vb* **2 = shatter**, split, fracture, shiver,

DICTIONARY

members of an organization, who split from the main body and form an independent group of their own

split ❶ *vb* **splitting, split** **1** to break or cause (something) to break into separate pieces **2** to separate (a piece) or (of a piece) to be separated from (something) **3** (of a group) to separate into smaller groups, through disagreement: *the council is split over rent increases* **4** (often foll. by *up*) to divide (something) among two or more people **5** *slang* to leave a place **6** **split on** *slang* to betray; inform on: *he didn't tell tales or split on him* **7** **split one's sides** to laugh a great deal ▹ *n* **8** a gap or rift caused by splitting **9** a division in a group or the smaller group resulting from such a division **10** a dessert of sliced fruit and ice cream, covered with whipped cream and nuts: *banana split* ▹ *adj* **11** divided (especially in opinion, etc.) **12** having a split or splits: *split ends* ▸ See also **splits, split up**
WORD ORIGIN Middle Dutch *splitten*

split infinitive *n* (in English grammar) an infinitive used with another word between *to* and the verb, as in *to really finish it*. This is often thought to be incorrect

split-level *adj* (of a house or room) having the floor level of one part about half a storey above that of the other

split pea *n* a pea dried and split and used in soups or as a vegetable

split personality *n* **1** the tendency to change mood very quickly **2** a disorder in which a person's mind appears to have separated into two or more personalities

splits *n* (in gymnastics and dancing) the act of sitting with both legs outstretched, pointing in opposite directions, and at right angles to the body

split second *n* **1** an extremely short period of time; instant ▹ *adj* **split-second** **2** made in an extremely short time: *split-second timing*

splitting *adj* (of a headache) extremely painful

split up *vb* **1** to separate (something) into parts; divide **2** (of a couple) to end a relationship or marriage **3** (of a group of people) to go off in different directions ▹ *n* **split-up** **4** the act of separating

splodge *or US* **splotch** *n* **1** a large uneven spot or stain ▹ *vb* **splodging, splodged** **2** to mark (something) with a splodge or splodges
WORD ORIGIN alteration of earlier *splotch*

splurge *n* **1** a bout of spending money extravagantly ▹ *vb* **splurging, splurged** **2** (foll. by *on*) to spend (money) extravagantly: *they rushed out to splurge their pocket money on chocolate*
WORD ORIGIN origin unknown

splutter *vb* **1** to spit out (something) from the mouth when choking or laughing **2** to say (words) with spitting sounds when choking or in a rage **3** to throw out or to be thrown out explosively: *sparks spluttered from the fire* ▹ *n* **4** the act or noise of spluttering
WORD ORIGIN variant of SPUTTER

Spode *n* china or porcelain manufactured by the English potter Josiah Spode or his company

spoil ❶ *vb* **spoiling, spoilt** *or* **spoiled** **1** to make (something) less valuable, beautiful, or useful **2** to weaken the character of (a child) by giving it all it wants **3** (of oneself) to indulge one's desires: *go ahead and spoil yourself* **4** (of food) to become unfit for consumption **5** **be spoiling for** to have an aggressive urge for: *he is spoiling for a fight* ▸ See also **spoils**
WORD ORIGIN Latin *spolium* booty

spoilage *n* an amount of material that has been spoilt: *new ways to reduce spoilage*

spoiler *n* **1** a device fitted to an aircraft wing to increase drag and reduce lift **2** a similar device fitted to a car

spoils ❶ *pl n* **1** valuables seized during war **2** the rewards and benefits of having political power

spoilsport *n informal* a person who spoils the enjoyment of other people

spoke[1] *vb* ▸ the past tense of **speak**

spoke[2] *n* **1** a bar joining the centre of a wheel to the rim **2** **put a spoke in someone's wheel** *Brit & NZ* to create a difficulty for someone
WORD ORIGIN Old English *spāca*

spoken ❶ *vb* **1** ▸ the past participle of **speak** ▹ *adj* **2** said in speech: *spoken commands* **3** having speech as specified: *quiet-spoken* **4** **spoken for** engaged or reserved

spokesman ❶, **spokesperson** *or* **spokeswoman** *n, pl* **-men, -people** *or* **-women** a person chosen to speak on behalf of another person or group

spoliation *n* the act or an instance of plundering: *the spoliation of the countryside*
WORD ORIGIN Latin *spoliare* to plunder

spondee *n prosody* a metrical foot of two long syllables **spondaic** *adj*
WORD ORIGIN Greek *spondē* ritual offering of drink

sponge *n* **1** a sea animal with a porous absorbent elastic skeleton **2** the skeleton of a sponge, or a piece of artificial sponge, used for bathing or cleaning **3** a soft absorbent material like a sponge **4** Also called: **sponge cake** a light cake made of eggs, sugar, and flour **5** Also called: **sponge pudding** *Austral & Brit* a light steamed or baked spongy pudding **6** a rub with a wet sponge ▹ *vb* **sponging, sponged** **7** (often foll. by *down*) to clean (something) by rubbing it with a wet sponge **8** to remove (marks) by rubbing them with a wet sponge **9** (usually foll. by *off* or *on*) to get (something) from someone by taking advantage of his or her generosity: *stop sponging off the rest of us!* **spongy** *adj*
WORD ORIGIN Greek *spongia*

sponge bag *n* a small waterproof bag for holding toiletries when travelling

sponger *n informal, derogatory* a person

S

THESAURUS

disintegrate, break into fragments

split *vb* **1 = break**, crack, burst, snap, break up, open, give way, splinter, gape, come apart, come undone **2 = cut**, break, crack, snap, chop, cleave, hew **3a = divide**, separate, disunite, disrupt, disband, cleave, pull apart, set at odds, set at variance **3b = diverge**, separate, branch, fork, part, go separate ways **4 = share out**, divide, distribute, halve, allocate, partition, allot, carve up, dole out, apportion, slice up, parcel out, divvy up *(informal)* ▹ *n* **8 = crack**, tear, rip, damage, gap, rent, breach, slash, slit, fissure **9 = division**, break, breach, rift, difference, disruption, rupture, discord, divergence, schism, estrangement, dissension, disunion ▹ *adj* **11 = divided**, ambivalent, bisected **12 = broken**, cracked, snapped, fractured, splintered, ruptured, cleft

spoil *vb* **1 = ruin**, destroy, wreck, damage, total *(slang)*, blow *(slang)*, injure, upset, harm, mar, scar, undo, trash *(slang)*, impair, mess up, blemish, disfigure, debase, deface, put a damper on, crool *or* cruel *(Austral slang)* OPPOSITE: improve **2 = overindulge**, indulge, pamper, baby, cosset, coddle, spoon-feed, mollycoddle, kill with kindness OPPOSITE: deprive **3 = indulge**, treat, pamper, satisfy, gratify, pander to, regale **4 = go bad**, turn, go off *(Brit informal)*, rot, decay, decompose, curdle, mildew, addle, putrefy, become tainted

spoils *pl n* **1 = booty**, loot, plunder, gain, prizes, prey, pickings, pillage, swag *(slang)*, boodle *(slang, chiefly US)*, rapine

spoken *adj* **2 = verbal**, voiced, expressed, uttered, oral, said, told, unwritten, phonetic, by word of mouth, put into words, viva voce

spokesman, spokesperson *or* **spokeswoman** *n* **= speaker**, official, voice, spin doctor *(informal)*, mouthpiece

DICTIONARY

who lives off other people by continually taking advantage of their generosity
sponsor ❶ *n* **1** a person or group that promotes another person or group in an activity or the activity itself, either for profit or for charity **2** *chiefly US & Canad* a person or firm that pays the costs of a radio or television programme in return for advertising time **3** a person who presents and supports a proposal or suggestion **4** a person who makes certain promises on behalf of a person being baptized and takes responsibility for his or her Christian upbringing ▷*vb* **5** to act as a sponsor for (someone or something) **sponsored** *adj* **sponsorship** *n*
WORD ORIGIN Latin *spondere* to promise solemnly
spontaneous ❶ *adj* **1** not planned or arranged; impulsive: *a spontaneous celebration* **2** occurring through natural processes without outside influence: *a spontaneous explosion* **spontaneously** *adv* **spontaneity** *n*
WORD ORIGIN Latin *sponte* voluntarily
spontaneous combustion *n chem* the bursting into flame of a substance as a result of internal oxidation processes, without heat from an outside source
spoof *informal n* **1** an imitation of a film, TV programme, etc. that exaggerates in an amusing way the most memorable features of the original **2** a good-humoured trick or deception ▷*vb* **3** to fool (a person) with a trick or deception
WORD ORIGIN made-up word
spook *informal n* **1** a ghost **2** a strange and frightening person ▷*vb* **3** to frighten: *it was the wind that spooked her* **spooky** *adj*
WORD ORIGIN Dutch
spool *n* a cylinder around which film, thread, or tape can be wound
WORD ORIGIN Germanic
spoon *n* **1** a small shallow bowl attached to a handle, used for eating, stirring, or serving food **2 be born with a silver spoon in one's mouth** to be born into a very rich and respected family ▷*vb* **3** to scoop up (food or liquid) with a spoon **4** *old-fashioned slang* to kiss and cuddle
WORD ORIGIN Old English *spōn* splinter
spoonbill *n* a wading bird with a long flat bill
spoonerism *n* the accidental changing over of the first sounds of a pair of words, often with an amusing result, such as *hush my brat* for *brush my hat*
WORD ORIGIN after W. A. *Spooner*, clergyman
spoon-feed *vb* **-feeding, -fed 1** to feed (someone, usually a baby) using a spoon **2** to give (someone) too much help
spoor *n* the trail of an animal
WORD ORIGIN Afrikaans
sporadic *adj* happening at irregular intervals; intermittent: *sporadic bursts of gunfire* **sporadically** *adv*
WORD ORIGIN Greek *sporas* scattered
spore *n* a reproductive body, produced by nonflowering plants and bacteria, that develops into a new individual
WORD ORIGIN Greek *spora* a sowing
sporran *n* a large pouch worn hanging from a belt in front of the kilt in Scottish Highland dress
WORD ORIGIN Scottish Gaelic *sporan* purse
sport ❶ *n* **1** an activity for exercise, pleasure, or competition: *your favourite sport* **2** such activities collectively: *the minister for sport* **3** the enjoyment gained from a pastime: *just for the sport of it* **4** playful or good-humoured joking: *I only did it in sport* **5** *informal* a person who accepts defeat or teasing cheerfully **6 make sport of someone** to make fun of someone **7** an animal or plant that is very different from others of the same species, usually because of a mutation **8** *Austral & NZ informal* a term of address between males ▷*vb* **9** *informal* to wear proudly: *sporting a pair of bright yellow shorts* ▶See also **sports**
WORD ORIGIN variant of Middle English *disporten* to disport
sporting ❶ *adj* **1** of sport **2** behaving in a fair and decent way **3 a sporting chance** reasonable likelihood of happening: *a sporting chance of winning*
sportive *adj* playful or high-spirited
sports *adj* **1** of or used in sports: *a sports arena* ▷*n* **2** Also called: **sports day** *Brit* a meeting held at a school or college for competitions in athletic events
sports car *n* a fast car with a low body and usually seating only two people
sportscast *n US* a programme of sports news **sportscaster** *n*
sports jacket *n* a man's casual jacket, usually made of tweed. Also called: *US, Austral & NZ* **sports coat**
sportsman *n, pl* **-men 1** a man who plays sports **2** a person who plays by the rules, is fair, and accepts defeat with good humour **sportsman-like** *adj* **sportsmanship** *n*
sportsperson *n* a person who plays sports
sportswear *n* clothes worn for sport or outdoor leisure wear
sportswoman *n, pl* **-women** a woman who plays sports
sporty ❶ *adj* **sportier, sportiest 1** (of a person) interested in sport **2** (of clothes) suitable for sport **3** (of a car) small and fast **sportily** *adv* **sportiness** *n*
spot ❶ *n* **1** a small mark on a surface, which has a different colour or texture from its surroundings **2** a location: *a spot where they could sit* **3** a small mark or pimple on the skin **4** a feature of something that has the attribute mentioned: *the one bright spot in his whole day; the high spot of our trip* **5** *informal* a small amount: *a spot of bother* **6** *informal* an awkward situation: *I'm sometimes in a spot* **7** a part of a show, TV programme, etc. reserved for a specific performer or type of entertainment **8** ▶short for **spotlight** (sense 1) **9 in a tight spot** in a difficult situation **10 knock spots off someone** to be much better than someone **11 on the spot a** immediately: *he decided on the spot to fly down* **b** at the place in question: *the expert weapons man on the spot* **c** in an awkward situation: *the British*

THESAURUS

sponsor *n* **1 = backer**, patron, promoter, angel *(informal)*, guarantor ▷*vb* **5 = back**, fund, finance, promote, subsidize, patronize, put up the money for, lend your name to
spontaneous *adj* **1 = unplanned**, impromptu, unprompted, willing, free, natural, voluntary, instinctive, impulsive, unforced, unbidden, unconstrained, unpremeditated, extempore, uncompelled
OPPOSITE: planned
sport *n* **1, 2 = game**, exercise, recreation, play, entertainment, amusement, diversion, pastime, physical activity **4 = fun**, kidding *(informal)*, joking, teasing, ridicule, joshing *(slang, chiefly US & Canad)*, banter, frolic, jest, mirth, merriment, badinage, raillery ▷*vb* **9** *(informal)* **= wear**, display, flaunt, boast, exhibit, flourish, show off, vaunt
sporting *adj* **2 = fair**, sportsmanlike, game *(informal)*, gentlemanly
OPPOSITE: unfair
sporty *adj* **1 = athletic**, outdoor, energetic, hearty
spot *n* **1 = mark**, stain, speck, scar, flaw, taint, blot, smudge, blemish, daub, speckle, blotch, discoloration **2 = place**, situation, site, point, position, scene, location, locality **3 = pimple**, blackhead, pustule, zit *(slang)*, plook *(Scot)*, acne **6** *(informal)* **= predicament**, trouble, difficulty, mess, plight, hot water *(informal)*, quandary, tight spot ▷*vb* **13 = see**, observe, catch sight of, identify, sight, recognize, detect, make out, pick out, discern, behold *(archaic, literary)*, espy, descry **14 = mark**, stain, dot, soil, dirty, scar, taint, tarnish,

DICTIONARY

government will be put on the spot **12 soft spot** a special affection for someone: *a soft spot for older men* ▷ *vb* **spotting, spotted 13** to see (something or someone) suddenly **14** to put stains or spots on (something) **15** (of some fabrics) to be prone to marking by liquids: *silk spots easily* **16** to take note of (the numbers of trains or planes observed) **17** (of scouts, agents, etc.) to look out for (talented but unknown actors, sportspersons, etc.) **18** *Brit* to rain lightly
WORD ORIGIN from German

spot check *n* a quick unplanned inspection

spotless *adj* **1** perfectly clean **2** free from moral flaws: *a spotless reputation* **spotlessly** *adv*

spotlight ❶ *n* **1** a powerful light focused so as to light up a small area **2 the spotlight** the centre of attention: *the spotlight moved to the president* ▷ *vb* **-lighting, -lit** *or* **-lighted 3** to direct a spotlight on (something) **4** to focus attention on (something)

spot-on *adj informal* absolutely correct; very accurate: *they're spot-on in terms of style*

spotted ❶ *adj* **1** having a pattern of spots **2** marked with stains

spotted dick *n Brit* suet pudding containing dried fruit

spotter *n* a person whose hobby is watching for and noting numbers or types of trains or planes

spotty *adj* **-tier, -tiest 1** covered with spots or pimples **2** not consistent; irregular in quality: *a rather spotty performance* **spottiness** *n*

spouse ❶ *n* a person's partner in marriage
WORD ORIGIN Latin *sponsus, sponsa* betrothed man or woman

spout *vb* **1** (of a liquid or flames) to pour out in a stream or jet **2** *informal* to talk about (something) in a boring way or without much thought ▷ *n* **3** a projecting tube or lip for pouring liquids **4** a stream or jet of liquid: *a spout of steaming water* **5 up the spout** *slang* **a** ruined or lost: *the motor industry is up the spout* **b** pregnant
WORD ORIGIN Middle English *spouten*

spouting *n NZ* **a** a rainwater downpipe on the outside of a building **b** such pipes collectively

sprain *vb* **1** to injure (a joint) by a sudden twist ▷ *n* **2** this injury, which causes swelling and temporary disability
WORD ORIGIN origin unknown

sprang *vb* ▸ a past tense of **spring**

sprat *n* a small edible fish like a herring
WORD ORIGIN Old English *sprott*

sprawl ❶ *vb* **1** to sit or lie with one's arms and legs spread out **2** to spread out untidily over a large area: *the pulp mill sprawled over the narrow flats* ▷ *n* **3** the part of a city or town that has not been planned and spreads out untidily over a large area: *the huge Los Angeles sprawl* **sprawling** *adj*
WORD ORIGIN Old English *spreawlian*

spray[1] ❶ *n* **1** fine drops of a liquid **2 a** a liquid under pressure designed to be discharged in fine drops from an aerosol or atomizer: *hair spray* **b** the aerosol or atomizer itself **3** a number of small objects flying through the air: *a spray of bullets* ▷ *vb* **4** to scatter in fine drops **5** to squirt (a liquid) from an aerosol or atomizer **6** to cover with a spray: *spray the crops* **sprayer** *n*
WORD ORIGIN Middle Dutch *spräien*

spray[2] ❶ *n* **1** a sprig or branch with buds, leaves, flowers, or berries **2** an ornament or design like this
WORD ORIGIN Germanic

spray gun *n* a device for spraying fine drops of paint, etc.

spread ❶ *vb* **spreading, spread 1** to open out or unfold to the fullest width: *spread the material out* **2** to extend over a larger expanse: *the subsequent unrest spread countrywide* **3** to apply as a coating: *spread the paste evenly over your skin* **4** to be displayed to its fullest extent: *the shining bay spread out below* **5** to send or be sent out in all directions or to many people: *the news spread quickly; the sandflies that spread the disease* **6** to distribute or be distributed evenly: *we were advised to spread the workload over the whole year* **7 spread out** (of people) to increase the distance between one and other (to widen the scope of a search, for example) ▷ *n* **8** a spreading; distribution, dispersion, or expansion: *the spread of higher education* **9** *informal* a large meal **10** *informal* the wingspan of an aircraft or bird **11** *informal, chiefly US & Canad* a ranch or other large area of land **12** a soft food which can be spread: *cheese spread* **13** two facing pages in a book or magazine **14** a widening of the hips and waist: *middle-age spread*
WORD ORIGIN Old English *sprǣdan*

spread-eagled *adj* with arms and legs outstretched

spreadsheet *n* a computer program for manipulating figures, used for financial planning

spree *n* a session of overindulgence, usually in drinking or spending money
WORD ORIGIN Scots *spreath* plundered cattle

sprig *n* **1** a shoot, twig, or sprout **2** an ornamental device like this **3** *NZ* a stud on the sole of a soccer or rugby boot **sprigged** *adj*
WORD ORIGIN Germanic

sprightly *adj* **-lier, -liest** lively and active **sprightliness** *n*
WORD ORIGIN obsolete *spright*, variant of SPRITE

spring ❶ *vb* **springing, sprang** *or* **sprung; sprung 1** to jump suddenly upwards or forwards **2** to return or be returned into natural shape from a forced position by elasticity: *the coil sprang back* **3** to cause (something) to happen unexpectedly: *the national coach sprang a surprise* **4** (usually foll. by *from*) to originate; be descended: *this motivation springs from their inborn*

S

THESAURUS

blot, fleck, spatter, sully, speckle, besmirch, splodge, splotch, mottle, smirch

spotlight *n* **2 = attention**, limelight, public eye, interest, fame, notoriety, public attention ▷ *vb* **4 = highlight**, feature, draw attention to, focus attention on, accentuate, point up, give prominence to, throw into relief

spotted *adj* **1 = speckled**, dotted, flecked, pied, specked, mottled, dappled, polka-dot

spouse *n* **= partner**, mate, husband *or* wife, companion, consort, significant other *(US informal)*, better half *(humorous)*, her indoors *(Brit slang)*, helpmate

sprawl *vb* **1 = loll**, slump, lounge, flop, slouch

spray[1] *n* **1 = droplets**, moisture, fine mist, drizzle, spindrift, spoondrift **2b = aerosol**, sprinkler, atomizer ▷ *vb* **4 = scatter**, shower, sprinkle, diffuse

spray[2] *n* **1 = sprig**, floral arrangement, branch, bough, shoot, corsage

spread *vb* **1 = open (out)**, extend, stretch, unfold, sprawl, unfurl, fan out, unroll **2 = grow**, increase, develop, expand, widen, mushroom, escalate, proliferate, multiply, broaden **4 = extend**, open, stretch **5 = circulate**, publish, broadcast, advertise, distribute, scatter, proclaim, transmit, make public, publicize, propagate, disseminate, promulgate, make known, blazon, bruit **OPPOSITE:** suppress ▷ *n* **8 = increase**, development, advance, spreading, expansion, transmission, proliferation, advancement, escalation, diffusion, dissemination, dispersal, suffusion **10** *(informal)* **= extent**, reach, span, stretch, sweep, compass

spring *vb* **1 = jump**, bound, leap, bounce, hop, rebound, vault, recoil **4** *(usually foll. by* **from***)* **= originate**, come, derive, start, issue, grow, emerge, proceed, arise, stem, descend, be derived, emanate, be descended ▷ *n* **12 = flexibility**, give *(informal)*, bounce, resilience, elasticity, recoil, buoyancy, springiness, bounciness

DICTIONARY

curiosity; Truman sprang from ordinary people **5** (often foll. by *up*) to come into being or appear suddenly: *new courses will spring up* **6** to provide (something, such as a mattress) with springs **7** *informal* to arrange the escape of (someone) from prison ▹*n* **8** the season between winter and summer **9** a leap or jump **10** a coil which can be compressed, stretched, or bent and then return to its original shape when released **11** a natural pool forming the source of a stream **12** elasticity **springlike** *adj*
WORD ORIGIN Old English *springan*

spring balance *or esp. US* **spring scale** *n* a device that indicates the weight of an object by the extension of a spring to which the object is attached

springboard *n* **1** a flexible board used to gain height or momentum in diving or gymnastics **2** anything that makes it possible for an activity to begin: *the meeting acted as a springboard for future negotiations*

springbok *n, pl* **-bok** *or* **-boks 1** a S African antelope which moves in leaps **2** a person who has represented S Africa in a national sports team
WORD ORIGIN Afrikaans

spring chicken *n* **1** a young chicken, which is tender for cooking **2 he** *or* **she is no spring chicken** *informal* he or she is no longer young

spring-clean *vb* **1** to clean (a house) thoroughly, traditionally at the end of winter ▹*n* **2** an instance of this **spring-cleaning** *n*

spring onion *n* a small onion with a tiny bulb and long green leaves, eaten in salads

spring roll *n* an Oriental dish consisting of a savoury mixture rolled in a thin pancake and fried

spring tide *n* either of the two tides at or just after new moon and full moon: the greatest rise and fall in tidal level

springtime *n* the season of spring

springy *adj* **springier, springiest** (of an object) having the quality of returning to its original shape after being pressed or pulled **springiness** *n*

sprinkle ❶ *vb* **-kling, -kled 1** to scatter (liquid or powder) in tiny drops over (something) **2** to distribute over (something): *a dozen mud huts sprinkled around it* **sprinkler** *n*
WORD ORIGIN probably from Middle Dutch *sprenkelen*

sprinkling ❶ *n* a small quantity or amount: *a sprinkling of diamonds*

sprint ❶ *n* **1** *athletics* **a** a short race run at top speed **b** a fast run at the end of a longer race **2** any quick run ▹*vb* **3** to run or cycle a short distance at top speed **sprinter** *n*
WORD ORIGIN Scandinavian

sprit *n naut* a light pole set diagonally across a sail to extend it
WORD ORIGIN Old English *sprēot*

sprite *n* **1** (in folklore) a fairy or elf **2** an icon in a computer game which can be manoeuvred around the screen
WORD ORIGIN Latin *spiritus* spirit

spritsail *n naut* a sail mounted on a sprit

spritzer *n* a tall drink of wine and soda water
WORD ORIGIN German *spritzen* to splash

sprocket *n* **1** Also called: **sprocket wheel** a wheel with teeth on the rim, that drives or is driven by a chain **2** a cylindrical wheel with teeth on one or both rims for pulling film through a camera or projector
WORD ORIGIN origin unknown

sprout ❶ *vb* **1** (of a plant or seed) to produce (new leaves or shoots) **2** (often foll. by *up*) to begin to grow or develop ▹*n* **3** a new shoot or bud **4** ▸same as **Brussels sprout**
WORD ORIGIN Old English *sprūtan*

spruce[1] *n* **1** an evergreen pyramid-shaped tree with needle-like leaves **2** the light-coloured wood of this tree
WORD ORIGIN obsolete *Spruce* Prussia

spruce[2] *adj* neat and smart
WORD ORIGIN perhaps from *Spruce leather;* see SPRUCE[1]

spruce up *vb* **sprucing, spruced** to make neat and smart

sprung *vb* ▸a past tense and the past participle of **spring**

spry *adj* **spryer, spryest** *or* **sprier, spriest** active and lively; nimble
WORD ORIGIN origin unknown

spud *n informal* a potato
WORD ORIGIN obsolete *spudde* short knife

spume *n literary* **1** foam or froth on the sea ▹*vb* **spuming, spumed 2** (of the sea) to foam or froth
WORD ORIGIN Latin *spuma*

spun *vb* **1** ▸the past of **spin** ▹*adj* **2** made by spinning: *spun sugar; spun silk*

spunk *n* **1** *old-fashioned informal* courage or spirit **2** *chiefly Brit vulgar slang* semen **3** *Austral & NZ informal* a sexually attractive person, especially a male **spunky** *adj*
WORD ORIGIN Scottish Gaelic *spong* tinder, sponge

spur ❶ *n* **1** an incentive to get something done **2** a sharp spiked wheel on the heel of a rider's boot used to urge the horse on **3** a sharp horny part sticking out from a cock's leg **4** a ridge sticking out from a mountain side **5 on the spur of the moment** suddenly and without planning; on impulse **6 win one's spurs** to prove one's ability ▹*vb* **spurring, spurred 7** (often foll. by *on*) to encourage (someone)
WORD ORIGIN Old English *spura*

spurge *n* a plant with milky sap and small flowers
WORD ORIGIN Latin *expurgare* to cleanse

spurious *adj* not genuine or real
WORD ORIGIN Latin *spurius* of illegitimate birth

spurn ❶ *vb* to reject (a person or thing) with contempt
WORD ORIGIN Old English *spurnan*

spurt *vb* **1** to gush or cause (something) to gush out in a sudden powerful stream or jet **2** to make a sudden effort ▹*n* **3** a short burst of activity, speed, or energy **4** a sudden powerful stream or jet
WORD ORIGIN origin unknown

sputnik *n* a Russian artificial satellite
WORD ORIGIN Russian, literally: fellow traveller

sputter *vb, n* ▸same as **splutter**
WORD ORIGIN Dutch *sputteren,* imitative

sputum *n, pl* **-ta** saliva, usually mixed with mucus
WORD ORIGIN Latin

spy ❶ *n, pl* **spies 1** a person employed to find out secret information about

THESAURUS

sprinkle *vb* **1 = scatter**, dust, strew, pepper, shower, spray, powder, dredge

sprinkling *n* **= scattering**, dusting, scatter, few, dash, handful, sprinkle, smattering, admixture

sprint *vb* **3 = run**, race, shoot, tear, dash, barrel (along) *(informal, chiefly US & Canad)*, dart, hare *(Brit informal)*, whizz *(informal)*, scamper, hotfoot, go like a bomb *(Brit & NZ informal)*, put on a burst of speed, go at top speed

sprout *vb* **1 = germinate**, bud, shoot, push, spring, vegetate **2 = grow**, develop, blossom, ripen

spur *n* **1 = stimulus**, incentive, impetus, motive, impulse, inducement, incitement, kick up the backside *(informal)* **5 on the spur of the moment = on impulse**, without thinking, impulsively, on the spot, impromptu, unthinkingly, without planning, impetuously, unpremeditatedly ▹*vb* **7 = incite**, drive, prompt, press, urge, stimulate, animate, prod, prick, goad, impel

spurn *vb* **= reject**, slight, scorn, rebuff, put down, snub, disregard, despise, disdain, repulse, cold-shoulder, kick in the teeth *(slang)*, turn your nose up at *(informal)*, contemn *(formal)*
OPPOSITE: accept

spy *n* **1 = undercover agent**, secret agent, double agent, secret service agent, foreign agent, mole, fifth columnist, nark *(Brit, Austral & NZ*

S

DICTIONARY

other countries or organizations **2** a person who secretly keeps watch on others ▷*vb* **spies, spying, spied** **3** (foll. by *on*) to keep a secret watch on someone **4** to work as a spy **5** to catch sight of (someone or something); notice
WORD ORIGIN Old French *espier*
spyglass *n* a small telescope
spy out *vb* to discover (something) secretly
spyware *n computers* software surreptitiously installed in a computer via the internet to gather and transmit information about the user
sq. square
SQL *n* a computer programming language that is used for database management
WORD ORIGIN structured query language
Sqn. Ldr. squadron leader
squab *n, pl* **squabs** *or* **squab** a young bird yet to leave the nest
WORD ORIGIN probably Germanic
squabble ⓣ *vb* **-bling, -bled** **1** to quarrel over a small matter ▷*n* **2** a petty quarrel
WORD ORIGIN probably Scandinavian
squad ⓣ *n* **1** the smallest military formation, usually a dozen soldiers **2** any small group of people working together: *the fraud squad* **3** *sport* a number of players from which a team is to be selected
WORD ORIGIN Old French *esquade*
squadron *n* the basic unit of an air force
WORD ORIGIN Italian *squadrone* soldiers drawn up in square formation
squadron leader *n* a fairly senior commissioned officer in the air force; the rank above flight lieutenant
squalid *adj* **1** dirty, untidy, and in bad condition **2** unpleasant, selfish, and often dishonest: *this squalid affair*
WORD ORIGIN Latin *squalidus*
squall[1] *n* a sudden strong wind or short violent storm
WORD ORIGIN perhaps a special use of SQUALL[2]
squall[2] *vb* **1** to cry noisily; yell ▷*n* **2** a noisy cry or yell
WORD ORIGIN probably Scandinavian
squalor *n* **1** dirty, poor, and untidy physical conditions **2** the condition of being squalid
WORD ORIGIN Latin
squander ⓣ *vb* to waste (money or resources)
WORD ORIGIN origin unknown
square ⓣ *n* **1** a geometric figure with four equal sides and four right angles **2** anything of this shape **3** an open area in a town bordered by buildings or streets **4** *maths* the number produced when a number is multiplied by itself: *9 is the square of 3, written 3^2* **5** *informal* a person who is dull or unfashionable **6 go back to square one** to return to the start because of failure or lack of progress ▷*adj* **7** being a square in shape **8 a** having the same area as that of a square with sides of a specified length: *2,500 square metres of hillside* **b** denoting a square having a specified length on each side: *a cell of only four square metres* **9** straight or level: *I don't think that painting is square* **10** fair and honest: *a square deal* **11** *informal* dull or unfashionable **12** having all debts or accounts settled: *if I give you 50 pence, then we'll be square* **13 all square** on equal terms; even in score **14 square peg in a round hole** *informal* a misfit ▷*vb* **squaring, squared** **15** *maths* to multiply (a number or quantity) by itself **16** to position so as to be straight or level: *bravely he squared his shoulders* **17** to settle (a debt or account) **18** to level the score in (a game) **19** to be or cause to be consistent: *it would not have squared with her image* ▷*adj* **20** *informal* ▶same as **squarely** ▶See also **square off, square up**
WORD ORIGIN Old French *esquare*
square-bashing *n Brit mil slang* marching and other drill on a parade ground
square bracket *n* either of a pair of characters [ ], used to separate a section of writing or printing from the main text
square dance *n* a country dance in which the couples are arranged in squares
square leg *n cricket* a fielding position on the on side, at right angles to the batsman
squarely *adv* **1** directly; straight: *he looked her squarely in the eye* **2** in an honest and frank way: *you should face squarely anything that worries you*
square meal *n* a meal which is large enough to leave the eater feeling full: *we gave him his first square meal in days*
square off *vb* to stand up as if ready to start boxing or fighting
square-rigged *adj naut* having sails set at right angles to the keel
square root *n* a number that when multiplied by itself gives a given number: *the square roots of 4 are 2 and −2*
square up *vb* **1** to settle bills or debts **2 square up to** to prepare to confront (a problem or a person)
squash[1] ⓣ *vb* **1** to press or squeeze (something) so as to flatten it **2** to overcome (a difficult situation), often with force **3 squash in** *or* **into** to push or force (oneself or a thing) into a confined space **4** to humiliate (someone) with a sarcastic reply ▷*n* **5** *Austral & Brit* a drink made from fruit juice or fruit syrup diluted with water **6** a crowd of people in a confined space **7** Also called: **squash rackets** a game for two players played in an enclosed court with a small rubber ball and long-handled rackets
WORD ORIGIN Old French *esquasser*
squash[2] *n, pl* **squashes** *or* **squash** *chiefly US & Canad* a marrow-like vegetable
WORD ORIGIN from a Native American language
squashy *adj* **squashier, squashiest** soft and easily squashed
squat *vb* **squatting, squatted** **1** to crouch with the knees bent and the weight on the feet **2** *law* to occupy an unused building to which one has no legal right ▷*adj* **3** short and

S

THESAURUS

slang) ▷*vb* **5 = catch sight of**, see, spot, notice, sight, observe, glimpse, behold *(archaic, literary)*, set eyes on, espy, descry
squabble *vb* **1 = quarrel**, fight, argue, row, clash, dispute, scrap *(informal)*, fall out *(informal)*, brawl, spar, wrangle, bicker, have words, fight like cat and dog, go at it hammer and tongs ▷*n* **2 = quarrel**, fight, row, argument, dispute, set-to *(informal)*, scrap *(informal)*, disagreement, barney *(informal)*, spat *(US)*, difference of opinion, tiff, bagarre *(French)*
squad *n* **2 = team**, group, band, company, force, troop, crew, gang
squander *vb* **= waste**, spend, fritter away, blow *(slang)*, consume, scatter, run through, lavish, throw away, misuse, dissipate, expend, misspend, be prodigal with, frivol away, spend like water
OPPOSITE: save
square *adj* **10 = fair**, just, straight, genuine, decent, ethical, straightforward, upright, honest, equitable, upfront *(informal)*, on the level *(informal)*, kosher *(informal)*, dinkum *(Austral & NZ informal)*, above board, fair and square, on the up and up ▷*vb* **19 = agree**, match, fit, accord, correspond, tally, conform, reconcile, harmonize
squash[1] *vb* **1 = crush**, press, flatten, mash, pound, smash, distort, pulp, compress, stamp on, trample down **2 = suppress**, put down *(slang)*, quell, silence, sit on *(informal)*, crush, quash, annihilate **4 = embarrass**, put down, humiliate, shame, disgrace, degrade, mortify, debase, discomfit, take the wind out of someone's sails, put (someone) in his (*or* her) place, take down a peg *(informal)*

DICTIONARY

thick ▹*n* **4** a building occupied by squatters
WORD ORIGIN Old French *esquater*
squatter *n* an illegal occupier of an unused building
squaw *n offensive* a Native American woman of N America
WORD ORIGIN from a Native American language
squawk *n* **1** a loud harsh cry, esp. one made by a bird **2** *informal* a loud complaint ▹*vb* **3** to make a squawk
WORD ORIGIN imitative
squeak *n* **1** a short high-pitched cry or sound **2 a narrow squeak** *informal* a narrow escape or success ▹*vb* **3** to make a squeak **4 squeak through** *or* **by** to pass (an examination), but only just **squeaky** *adj* **squeakiness** *n*
WORD ORIGIN probably Scandinavian
squeaky clean *adj* **1** (of hair) washed so clean that wet strands squeak when rubbed **2** completely clean **3** *informal, derogatory* (of a person) cultivating a virtuous and wholesome image
squeal *n* **1** a long high-pitched yelp ▹*vb* **2** to make a squeal **3** *slang* to inform on someone to the police **4** *informal, chiefly Brit* to complain loudly **squealer** *n*
WORD ORIGIN Middle English *squelen*, imitative
squeamish *adj* easily shocked or upset by unpleasant sights or events
WORD ORIGIN Anglo-French *escoymous*
squeegee *n* a tool with a rubber blade used for wiping away excess water from a surface
WORD ORIGIN probably imitative
squeeze ❶ *vb* **squeezing, squeezed** **1** to grip or press (something) firmly **2** to crush or press (something) so as to extract (a liquid): *squeeze the tomato and strain the juice; freshly squeezed lemon juice* **3** to push (oneself or a thing) into a confined space **4** to hug (someone) closely **5** to obtain (something) by great effort or force: *to squeeze the last dollar out of every deal* ▹*n* **6** a squeezing **7** a hug **8** a crush of people in a confined space **9** *chiefly Brit & NZ* a restriction on borrowing made by a government to control price inflation **10** an amount extracted by squeezing: *a squeeze of lime* **11 put the squeeze on someone** *informal* to put pressure on someone in order to obtain something
WORD ORIGIN Old English *cwȳsan*
squelch *vb* **1** to make a wet sucking noise, such as by walking through mud **2** *informal* to silence (someone) with a sarcastic or wounding reply ▹*n* **3** a squelching sound **squelchy** *adj*
WORD ORIGIN imitative
squib *n* **1** a firework that burns with a hissing noise before exploding **2 damp squib** something expected to be exciting or successful but turning out to be a disappointment
WORD ORIGIN probably imitative of a light explosion
squid *n, pl* **squid** *or* **squids** a sea creature with ten tentacles and a long soft body
WORD ORIGIN origin unknown
squiffy *adj* **-fier, -fiest** *Brit informal* slightly drunk: *a bit squiffy*
WORD ORIGIN origin unknown
squiggle *n* a wavy line **squiggly** *adj*
WORD ORIGIN perhaps SQUIRM + WIGGLE
squill *n* a Mediterranean plant of the lily family
WORD ORIGIN Greek *skilla*
squint *vb* **1** to have eyes which face in different directions **2** to glance sideways ▹*n* **3** an eye disorder in which one or both eyes turn inwards or outwards from the nose **4** *informal* a quick look; glance: *take a squint at the map* ▹*adj* **5** *informal* not straight; crooked
WORD ORIGIN short for *asquint*
squire *n* **1** a country gentleman in England, usually the main landowner in a country community **2** *informal chiefly Brit* a term of address used by one man to another **3** *history* a knight's young attendant ▹*vb* **squiring, squired** **4** *old-fashioned* (of a man) to escort (a woman)
WORD ORIGIN Old French *esquier*
squirm *vb* **1** to wriggle **2** to feel embarrassed or guilty ▹*n* **3** a wriggling movement
WORD ORIGIN imitative
squirrel *n* a small bushy-tailed animal that lives in trees
WORD ORIGIN Greek *skiouros*, from *skia* shadow + *oura* tail
squirt *vb* **1** to force (a liquid) or (of a liquid) to be forced out of a narrow opening **2** to cover or spatter (a person or thing) with liquid in this way ▹*n* **3** a jet of liquid **4** a squirting **5** *informal* a small or insignificant person
WORD ORIGIN imitative
squish *vb* **1** to crush (something) with a soft squelching sound **2** to make a squelching sound ▹*n* **3** a soft squelching sound **squishy** *adj*
WORD ORIGIN imitative
Sr **1** (after a name) senior **2** Señor **3** *chem* strontium
Sri Lankan *adj* **1** of Sri Lanka ▹*n* **2** a person from Sri Lanka
SRN (formerly in Britain) State Registered Nurse
SS **1** an organization in the Nazi party that provided Hitler's bodyguard, security forces, and concentration-camp guards
WORD ORIGIN German *Schutzstaffel* protection squad **2** steamship
SSL *computers* secure sockets layer: a protocol for encrypting and transmitting sensitive data securely over the internet
Ssu-ma Ch'ien *n* ▸a variant transliteration of **Si-ma Qian**
St **1** Saint **2** Street
st. stone
stab ❶ *vb* **stabbing, stabbed** **1** to pierce with a sharp pointed instrument **2** (often foll. by *at*) to make a thrust (at); jab **3 stab someone in the back** to do harm to someone by betraying him or her ▹*n* **4** a stabbing **5** a sudden, usually unpleasant, sensation: *a stab of jealousy* **6** *informal* an attempt: *you've got to have a stab at it* **7 stab in the back** an act of betrayal that harms a person **stabbing** *n*
WORD ORIGIN Middle English *stabbe* stab wound
stability ❶ *n* the quality of being stable: *the security and stability of married life*
stabilize *or* **-lise** *vb* **-lizing, -lized** *or* **-lising, -lised** to make or become stable or more stable **stabilization** *or* **-lisation** *n*
stabilizer *or* **-liser** *n* **1** a device for stabilizing a child's bicycle, an aircraft, or a ship **2** a substance added to food to preserve its texture
stable[1] *n* **1** a building where horses are kept **2** an organization that breeds and trains racehorses **3** an organization that manages or trains

S

THESAURUS

squeeze *vb* **1a = press**, crush, squash, pinch **1b = clutch**, press, grip, crush, pinch, squash, nip, compress, wring **3 = cram**, press, crowd, force, stuff, pack, jam, thrust, ram, wedge, jostle **4 = hug**, embrace, cuddle, clasp, enfold, hold tight ▹*n* **6 = press**, grip, clasp, crush, pinch, squash, nip, wring **7 = hug**, embrace, cuddle, hold, clasp, handclasp **8 = crush**, jam, squash, press, crowd, congestion
stab *vb* **1 = pierce**, cut, gore, run through, stick, injure, wound, knife, thrust, spear, jab, puncture, bayonet, transfix, impale, spill blood ▹*n* **5 = twinge**, prick, pang, ache **6** *(informal)* **= attempt**, go *(informal)*, try, shot *(informal)*, crack *(informal)*, essay, endeavour
stability *n* **= firmness**, strength, soundness, durability, permanence, solidity, constancy, steadiness, steadfastness **OPPOSITE:** instability
stable[2] *adj* **1 = solid**, firm, secure, fixed, substantial, sturdy, durable, well-made, well-built, immovable, built to last **OPPOSITE:** unstable **2 = secure**, lasting, strong, sound, fast, sure, established, permanent,

DICTIONARY

several entertainers or athletes ▷ *vb* **-bling, -bled** **4** to put or keep (a horse) in a stable
WORD ORIGIN Latin *stabulum* shed

stable[2] ❶ *adj* **1** steady in position or balance; firm **2** lasting and not likely to experience any sudden changes: *a stable environment* **3** having a calm personality; not moody **4** *physics* (of an elementary particle) not subject to decay **5** *chem* (of a chemical compound) not easily decomposed
WORD ORIGIN Latin *stabilis* steady

staccato (stak-**ah**-toe) *adj* **1** *music* (of notes) short and separate **2** consisting of short abrupt sounds: *the staccato sound of high-heels on the stairs* ▷ *adv* **3** in a staccato manner
WORD ORIGIN Italian

stack ❶ *n* **1** a pile of things, one on top of the other **2** a large neat pile of hay or straw **3** **stacks** a large amount: *there's still stacks for us to do* **4** ▸ same as **chimney stack** or **smokestack** **5** an area in a computer memory for temporary storage ▷ *vb* **6** to place (things) in a stack **7** to load or fill (something) up with piles of objects: *Henry was watching her stack the dishwasher* **8** to control (a number of aircraft) waiting to land at an airport so that each flies at a different altitude
WORD ORIGIN Old Norse *stakkr* haystack

stack up *vb* to compare with someone or something else: *how does this stack up against what you have?*

stadium *n, pl* **-diums** *or* **-dia** a large sports arena with tiered rows of seats for spectators
WORD ORIGIN Greek *stadion*

Staël *n* **Madame de** full name *Baronne Anne Louise Germaine* (née *Necker*) *de Staël-Holstein* 1766–1817, French writer, whose works, esp. *De l'Allemagne* (1810), anticipated French romanticism

staff ❶ *n, pl for senses 1 and 2* **staffs;** *for senses 3 and 4* **staffs** *or* **staves** **1** the people employed in a company, school, or organization **2** *mil* the officers appointed to assist a commander **3** a stick with some special use, such as a walking stick or an emblem of authority **4** *music* a set of five horizontal lines on which music is written and which, along with a clef, indicates pitch ▷ *vb* **5** to provide (a company, school, or organization) with a staff
WORD ORIGIN Old English *stæf*

staff nurse *n* (in Britain) a qualified nurse ranking just below a sister or charge nurse

Stafford[1] *n* a market town in central England, administrative centre of Staffordshire. Pop: 63 681 (2001)

Stafford[2] *n* Sir **Edward William** 1819–1901, New Zealand statesman, born in Scotland: prime minister of New Zealand (1856–61; 1865–69; 1872)

Staffs Staffordshire

staff sergeant *n mil* a noncommissioned officer in an army or in the US Air Force or Marine Corps

stag *n* the adult male of a deer
WORD ORIGIN Old English *stagga*

stag beetle *n* a beetle with large branched jaws

stage ❶ *n* **1** a step or period of development, growth, or progress **2** the platform in a theatre where actors perform **3** **the stage** the theatre as a profession **4** the scene of an event or action **5** a part of a journey: *the last stage of his tour around France* **6** ▸ short for **stagecoach** **7** *Austral & Brit* a division of a bus route for which there is a fixed fare ▷ *vb* **staging, staged** **8** to present (a dramatic production) on stage: *to stage 'Hamlet'* **9** to organize and carry out (an event)
WORD ORIGIN Old French *estage* position

stagecoach *n* a large four-wheeled horse-drawn vehicle formerly used to carry passengers and mail on a regular route

stage direction *n* an instruction to an actor, written into the script of a play

stage door *n* a door at a theatre leading backstage

stage fright *n* feelings of fear and nervousness felt by a person about to appear in front of an audience

stagehand *n* a person who sets the stage and moves props in a theatre

stage-manage *vb* **-managing, -managed** to arrange (an event) from behind the scenes

stage manager *n* a person who supervises the stage arrangements of a production at a theatre

stage-struck *adj* having a great desire to act

stage whisper *n* **1** a loud whisper from an actor, intended to be heard by the audience **2** any loud whisper that is intended to be overheard

stagflation *n* inflation combined with stagnant or falling output and employment
WORD ORIGIN STAGNATION + INFLATION

stagger ❶ *vb* **1** to walk unsteadily **2** to amaze or shock (someone): *it staggered her that there was any liaison between them* **3** to arrange (events) so as not to happen at the same time: *staggered elections* ▷ *n* **4** a staggering
staggering *adj* **staggeringly** *adv*
WORD ORIGIN dialect *stacker*

staggers *n* a disease of horses and other domestic animals that causes staggering

staging *n* a temporary support used in building

stagnant *adj* **1** (of water) stale from not moving **2** unsuccessful or dull from lack of change or development
WORD ORIGIN Latin *stagnans*

stagnate *vb* **-nating, -nated** to become inactive or unchanging: *people in old age only stagnate when they have no interests* **stagnation** *n*

stag night *or* **party** *n* a party for men only, held for a man who is about to get married

stagy *or US* **stagey** *adj* **stagier, stagiest** too theatrical or dramatic

staid *adj* serious, rather dull, and old-fashioned in behaviour or appearance
WORD ORIGIN obsolete past participle of STAY

stain ❶ *vb* **1** to discolour (something) with marks that are not easily removed **2** to dye (something) with a lasting pigment ▷ *n* **3** a mark or discoloration that is not easily removed **4** an incident in someone's life that has damaged his or her reputation: *a stain on his character* **5** a liquid used to penetrate the surface of a material, such as wood, and colour it without

S

THESAURUS

constant, steady, enduring, reliable, abiding, durable, deep-rooted, well-founded, steadfast, immutable, unwavering, invariable, unalterable, unchangeable **OPPOSITE:** insecure **3** = **well-balanced**, balanced, sensible, reasonable, rational, mentally sound

stack *n* **1** = **pile**, heap, mountain, mass, load, cock, rick, clamp (*Brit agriculture*), mound ▷ *vb* **6** = **pile**, heap up, load, assemble, accumulate, amass, stockpile, bank up

staff *n* **1** = **workers**, employees, personnel, workforce, team, organization **3** = **stick**, pole, rod, prop, crook, cane, stave, wand, sceptre

stage *n* **1** = **step**, leg, phase, point, level, period, division, length, lap, juncture

stagger *vb* **1** = **totter**, reel, sway, falter, lurch, wobble, waver, teeter **2** = **astound**, amaze, stun, surprise, shock, shake, overwhelm, astonish, confound, take (someone) aback, bowl over (*informal*), stupefy, strike (someone) dumb, throw off balance, give (someone) a shock, dumbfound, nonplus, flabbergast (*informal*), take (someone's) breath away

stain *vb* **1** = **mark**, soil, discolour, dirty, tarnish, tinge, spot, blot, blemish, smirch **2** = **dye**, colour, tint ▷ *n* **3** = **mark**, spot, blot, blemish, discoloration, smirch **4** = **stigma**,

DICTIONARY

covering up the surface or grain
WORD ORIGIN Middle English *steynen*

stained glass *n* glass that has been coloured for artistic purposes

Stainer *n* Sir **John** 1840–1901, British composer and organist, noted for his sacred music, esp. the oratorio *The Crucifixion* (1887)

stainless steel *n* a type of steel that does not rust, as it contains large amounts of chromium

stair *n* **1** one step in a flight of stairs **2** a series of steps: *he fled down the back stair* ▸ See also **stairs**
WORD ORIGIN Old English *stǣger*

staircase *n* a flight of stairs, usually with a handrail or banisters

stairs *pl n* a flight of steps going from one level to another, usually indoors

stairway *n* a staircase

stairwell *n* a vertical shaft in a building that contains a staircase

stake[1] ❶ *n* **1** a stick or metal bar driven into the ground as part of a fence or as a support or marker **2** **be burned at the stake** to be executed by being tied to a stake in the centre of a pile of wood that is then set on fire ▹ *vb* **staking, staked 3** to lay (a claim) to land or rights **4** to support (something, such as a plant) with a stake
WORD ORIGIN Old English *staca* stake, post

stake[2] ❶ *n* **1** the money that a player must risk in order to take part in a gambling game or make a bet **2** an interest, usually financial, held in something: *a 50% stake in a new consortium* **3** **at stake** at risk **4** **stakes** **a** the money that a player has available for gambling **b** a prize in a race or contest **c** a horse race in which all owners of competing horses contribute to the prize ▹ *vb* **staking, staked 5** to risk (something, such as money) on a result **6** to give financial support to (a business)
WORD ORIGIN origin unknown

stakeholder *n* **1** a person or group not owning shares in an enterprise but having an interest in its operations, such as the employees, customers, or local community ▹ *adj* **2** relating to policies intended to allow people to participate in decisions made by enterprises in which they have a stake: *stakeholder economy*

stakeout *n* **1** *slang, chiefly US & Canad* a police surveillance of an area or house ▹ *vb* **stake out 2** *slang, chiefly US & Canad* to keep an area or house under surveillance **3** to surround (a piece of land) with stakes

stalactite *n* an icicle-shaped mass of calcium carbonate hanging from the roof of a cave: formed by continually dripping water
WORD ORIGIN Greek *stalaktos* dripping

stalagmite *n* a large pointed mass of calcium carbonate sticking up from the floor of a cave: formed by continually dripping water from a stalactite
WORD ORIGIN Greek *stalagmos* dripping

stale ❶ *adj* **1** (esp. of food) no longer fresh, having being kept too long **2** (of air) stagnant and having an unpleasant smell **3** lacking in enthusiasm or ideas through overwork or lack of variety **4** uninteresting from having been done or seen too many times: *such achievements now seem stale today* **5** no longer new: *her war had become stale news* **staleness** *n*
WORD ORIGIN probably from Old French *estale* motionless

stalemate *n* **1** a chess position in which any of a player's moves would place his king in check: in this position the game ends in a draw **2** a situation in which further action by two opposing forces is impossible or will not achieve anything; deadlock
WORD ORIGIN obsolete *stale* standing place + CHECKMATE

Stalinism *n* the policies associated with Joseph Stalin, general secretary of the Communist Party of the Soviet Union 1922–53, which resulted in rapid industrialization, state terror as a means of political control, and the abolition of collective leadership **Stalinist** *n, adj*

stalk[1] *n* **1** the main stem of a plant **2** a stem that joins a leaf or flower to the main stem of a plant
WORD ORIGIN probably from Old English *stalu* upright piece of wood

stalk[2] ❶ *vb* **1** to follow (an animal or person) quietly and secretly in order to catch or kill them **2** to pursue persistently and, sometimes, attack (a person with whom one is obsessed, often a celebrity) **3** to spread over (a place) in a menacing way: *danger stalked the streets* **4** to walk in an angry, arrogant, or stiff way **stalker** *n*
WORD ORIGIN Old English *bestealcian*

stalking-horse *n* something or someone used to hide a true purpose; pretext

stall[1] ❶ *n* **1** a small stand for the display and sale of goods **2** a compartment in a stable or shed for a single animal **3** any small room or compartment: *a shower stall* ▹ *vb* **4** to stop (a motor vehicle or its engine) or (of a motor vehicle or its engine) to stop, by incorrect use of the clutch or incorrect adjustment of the fuel mixture
WORD ORIGIN Old English *steall* a place for standing

stall[2] ❶ *vb* to employ delaying tactics towards (someone); be evasive
WORD ORIGIN Anglo-French *estale* bird used as a decoy

stallion *n* an uncastrated male horse, usually used for breeding
WORD ORIGIN Old French *estalon*

stalls *n* **1** the seats on the ground floor of a theatre or cinema **2** (in a church) a row of seats, divided by armrests or a small screen, for the choir or clergy

stalwart ❶ (**stawl**-wart) *adj* **1** strong and sturdy **2** loyal and reliable ▹ *n* **3** a hard-working and loyal supporter: *local party stalwarts*
WORD ORIGIN Old English *stǣlwirthe* serviceable

stamen *n* the part of a flower that produces pollen
WORD ORIGIN Latin: the warp in an upright loom

stamina ❶ *n* energy and strength sustained while performing an activity over a long time

THESAURUS

shame, disgrace, slur, reproach, blemish, dishonour, infamy, blot on the escutcheon **5 = dye**, colour, tint

stake[1] *n* **1 = pole**, post, spike, stick, pale, paling, picket, stave, palisade

stake[2] *n* **1 = bet**, ante, wager, chance, risk, venture, hazard **2 = interest**, share, involvement, claim, concern, investment ▹ *vb* **5 = bet**, gamble, wager, chance, risk, venture, hazard, jeopardize, imperil, put on the line

stale *adj* **1 = old**, hard, dry, decayed, fetid **OPPOSITE:** fresh **2 = musty**, stagnant, fusty **4 = unoriginal**, banal, trite, common, flat, stereotyped, commonplace, worn-out, antiquated, threadbare, old hat, insipid, hackneyed, overused, repetitious, platitudinous, cliché-ridden **OPPOSITE:** original

stalk[2] *vb* **1 = pursue**, follow, track, hunt, shadow, tail *(informal)*, haunt, creep up on

stall[1] *n* **1 = stand**, table, counter, booth, kiosk ▹ *vb* **4 = stop dead**, jam, seize up, catch, stick, stop short

stall[2] *vb* **= play for time**, delay, hedge, procrastinate, stonewall, beat about the bush *(informal)*, temporize, drag your feet

stalwart *adj* **1 = strong**, strapping, robust, athletic, vigorous, rugged, manly, hefty *(informal)*, muscular, sturdy, stout, husky *(informal)*, beefy *(informal)*, lusty, sinewy, brawny **OPPOSITE:** puny **2 = loyal**, faithful, strong, firm, true, constant, resolute, dependable, steadfast, true-blue, tried and true

stamina *n* **= staying power**, endurance, resilience, force, power, energy, strength, resistance, grit,

DICTIONARY

WORD ORIGIN Latin: the threads of life spun out by the Fates, hence energy

stammer ❶ *vb* **1** to speak or say (something) with involuntary pauses or repetition, as a result of a speech disorder or through fear or nervousness ▹*n* **2** a speech disorder characterized by involuntary repetitions and pauses

WORD ORIGIN Old English *stamerian*

stamp ❶ *n* **1** a printed paper label attached to a piece of mail to show that the required postage has been paid **2** a token issued by a shop or business after a purchase that can be saved and exchanged for other goods sold by that shop or business **3** the action or an act of stamping **4** an instrument for stamping a design or words **5** a design, device, or mark that has been stamped **6** a characteristic feature: *the stamp of inevitability* **7** *Brit informal* a national insurance contribution, formerly recorded by a stamp on an official card **8** type or class: *men of his stamp* ▹*vb* **9** (often foll. by *on*) to bring (one's foot) down heavily **10** to walk with heavy or noisy footsteps **11** to characterize: *a performance that stamped him as a star* **12 stamp on** to subdue or restrain: *all of which have stamped on dissent* **13** to impress or mark (a pattern or sign) on **14** to mark (something) with an official seal or device **15** to have a strong effect on: *a picture vividly stamped on memory* **16** to stick a stamp on (an envelope or parcel)

WORD ORIGIN probably from Old English *stampian*

stampede *n* **1** a sudden rush of frightened animals or of a crowd ▹*vb* **-peding, -peded 2** to run away in a stampede

WORD ORIGIN Spanish *estampar* to stamp

stamping ground *n* a favourite meeting place

stamp out ❶ *vb* **1** to put an end to (something) by force; suppress: *an attempt to stamp out democracy* **2** to put out by stamping: *I stamped out my cigarette*

stance ❶ *n* **1** an attitude towards a particular matter: *a tough stance in the trade talks* **2** the manner and position in which a person stands **3** *sport* the position taken when about to play the ball

WORD ORIGIN Latin *stare* to stand

stanch (stahnch) *vb* ▸same as **staunch²**

WORD ORIGIN Old French *estanchier*

stanchion *n* a vertical pole or bar used as a support

WORD ORIGIN Old French *estanchon*

stand ❶ *vb* **standing, stood 1** to be upright **2** to rise to an upright position **3** to place (something) upright **4** to be situated: *the property stands in a prime position* **5** to have a specified height when standing: *the structure stands sixty feet above the river* **6** to be in a specified position: *Turkey stands to gain handsomely* **7** to be in a specified state or condition: *how he stands in comparison to others* **8** to remain unchanged or valid: *the Conservatives were forced to let much of the legislation stand* **9 stand at** (of a score or an account) to be in the specified position: *now the total stands at nine* **10** to tolerate or bear: *Christopher can't stand him* **11** to survive: *stand the test of time* **12** (often foll. by *for*) to be a candidate: *to stand for president* **13** *informal* to buy: *to stand someone a drink* **14 stand a chance** to have a chance of succeeding **15 stand one's ground** to face a difficult situation bravely **16 stand trial** to be tried in a law court ▹*n* **17** a stall or counter selling goods: *the hot dog stand* **18** a structure at a sports ground where people can sit or stand **19** the act or an instance of standing **20** a firmly held opinion: *its firm stand on sanctions* **21** *US & Austral* a place in a law court where a witness stands **22** a rack on which coats and hats may be hung **23** a base, support, or piece of furniture in or on which articles may be held or stored: *a guitar stand* **24** an effort to defend oneself or one's beliefs against attack or criticism: *a last stand against superior forces* **25** *cricket* a long period at the wicket by two batsmen **26** ▸see **one-night stand** ▸See also **stand by, stand down**, etc.

WORD ORIGIN Old English *standan*

standard ❶ *n* **1** a level of quality: *cuisine of a high standard* **2** an accepted example of something against which others are judged or measured: *the work was good by any standard* **3** a moral principle of behaviour **4** a flag of a nation or cause **5** an upright pole or beam used as a support: *a lamp standard* **6** a song that has remained popular for many years ▹*adj* **7** of a usual, medium, or accepted kind: *a standard cost* **8** of recognized authority: *a standard reference book* **9** denoting pronunciations or grammar regarded as correct and acceptable by educated native speakers

WORD ORIGIN Old French *estandart* gathering place

standard assessment tasks *pl n* (in Britain) national standardized tests for assessing school pupils

standard-bearer *n* **1** a leader of a movement or party **2** a person who carries a flag in battle or in a march

Standard English *n linguistics* the style of English that is regarded as correct and acceptable by educated native speakers

standard gauge *n* **1** a railway track with a distance of 56½ inches (1.435 m) between the lines: used on most railways ▹*adj* **standard-gauge 2** denoting a railway with a standard gauge

THESAURUS

vigour, tenacity, power of endurance, indefatigability, lustiness

stammer *vb* **1 = stutter**, falter, splutter, pause, hesitate, hem and haw, stumble over your words

stamp *n* **5 = imprint**, mark, brand, cast, mould, signature, earmark, hallmark ▹*vb* **9 = trample**, step, tread, crush **11 = identify**, mark, brand, label, reveal, exhibit, betray, pronounce, show to be, categorize, typecast **13 = print**, mark, fix, impress, mould, imprint, engrave, inscribe

stamp out *vb* **1 = eliminate**, destroy, eradicate, crush, suppress, put down, put out, scotch, quell, extinguish, quench, extirpate

stance *n* **1 = attitude**, stand, position, viewpoint, standpoint **2 = posture**, carriage, bearing, deportment

stand *vb* **1 = be upright**, be erect, be vertical **2 = get to your feet**, rise, stand up, straighten up **3 = put**, place, position, set, mount **4 = be located**, be, sit, perch, nestle, be positioned, be sited, be perched, be situated *or* located **8 = be valid**, be in force, continue, stay, exist, prevail, remain valid **10a = tolerate**, bear, abide, suffer, stomach, endure, brook, hack *(slang)*, submit to, thole *(dialect)* **10b = take**, bear, handle, cope with, experience, sustain, endure, undergo, put up with *(informal)*, withstand, countenance **11 = resist**, endure, withstand, wear *(Brit slang)*, weather, undergo, defy, tolerate, stand up to, hold out against, stand firm against ▹*n* **17 = stall**, booth, kiosk, table **20 = position**, attitude, stance, opinion, determination, standpoint, firm stand

standard *n* **1 = level**, grade **2 = criterion**, measure, guideline, example, model, average, guide, pattern, sample, par, norm, gauge, benchmark, yardstick, touchstone **3 = principles**, ideals, morals, rule, ethics, canon, moral principles, code of honour **4 = flag**, banner, pennant, colours, ensign, pennon ▹*adj* **7 = usual**, normal, customary, set, stock, average, popular, basic, regular, typical, prevailing, orthodox, staple, one-size-fits-all **OPPOSITE:** unusual **8 = accepted**, official, established, classic, approved, recognized, definitive, authoritative **OPPOSITE:** unofficial

DICTIONARY

Standard Grade *n* **1** (in Scotland) an examination designed to test skills and application of knowledge, replacing the O Grade **2** a pass in an examination at this level

standardize *or* **-ise** *vb* **-izing, -ized** *or* **-ising, -ised** to make (things) standard: *to standardize the preparation process* **standardization** *or* **-isation** *n*

standard lamp *n* a tall electric lamp that has a shade and stands on a base

standard of living *n* the level of comfort and wealth of a person, group, or country

standard time *n* the official local time of a region or country determined by the distance from Greenwich of a line of longitude passing through the area

stand by *vb* **1** to be available and ready to act if needed: *stand by for firing* **2** to be present as an onlooker or without taking any action: *the military police stood by watching idly* **3** to be faithful to: *his wife will stand by him* ▹ *n* **stand-by 4** a person or thing that is ready for use or can be relied on in an emergency **5 on stand-by** ready for action or use ▹ *adj* **stand-by 6** not booked in advance but subject to availability: *stand-by planes*

stand down *vb* to resign or withdraw, often in favour of another

stand for *vb* **1** to represent: *AIDS stands for Acquired Immune Deficiency Syndrome* **2** to support and represent (an idea or a belief): *to stand for liberty and truth* **3** *informal* to tolerate or bear: *I won't stand for this!*

stand in Ⓣ *vb* **1** to act as a substitute: *she stood in for her father* ▹ *n* **stand-in 2** a person who acts as a substitute for another

standing Ⓣ *adj* **1** permanent, fixed, or lasting: *it was a standing joke* **2** used to stand in or on: *standing room only* **3** *athletics* (of a jump or the start of a race) begun from a standing position ▹ *n* **4** social or financial status or reputation: *her international standing* **5** duration: *a friendship of at least ten years' standing*

standing order *n* **1** an instruction to a bank to pay a fixed amount to a person or organization at regular intervals **2** a rule or order governing the procedure of an organization

Standish *n* **Myles** (or Miles) ?1584–1656, English military leader of the Pilgrim Fathers at Plymouth, New England

standoff *n* **1** *US & Canad* the act or an instance of standing off or apart **2** a deadlock or stalemate ▹ *vb* **stand off 3** to stay at a distance

standoffish *adj* behaving in a formal and unfriendly way

stand out *vb* **1** to be more impressive or important than others of the same kind: *his passing ability stood out in this game* **2** to be noticeable because of looking different: *her long fair hair made her stand out from the rest* **3** to refuse to agree or comply: *a hero who stood out against foreign domination*

standpipe *n chiefly Brit* a temporary vertical pipe installed in a street and supplying water when household water supplies are cut off

standpoint *n* a point of view from which a matter is considered

standstill *n* a complete stoppage or halt: *all traffic came to a standstill*

stand to *vb* **1** *mil* to take up positions in order to defend against attack **2 stand to reason** to be obvious or logical: *it stands to reason you will play better*

stand up Ⓣ *vb* **1** to rise to one's feet **2** *informal* to fail to keep a date with (a boyfriend or girlfriend): *sometimes he would stand me up* **3** to be accepted as satisfactory or true: *the decision would not stand up in court* **4 stand up for** to support or defend **5 stand up to a** to confront or resist (someone) bravely **b** to withstand and endure (something, such as criticism) ▹ *adj* **stand-up 6** (of a comedian) telling jokes alone to an audience **7** done while standing: *a stand-up breakfast* **8** (of a fight or row) angry and unrestrained ▹ *n* **9** stand-up comedy or a stand-up comedian

Stanford *n* Sir **Charles** (**Villiers**) 1852–1924, Anglo-Irish composer and conductor, who as a teacher at the Royal College of Music had much influence on the succeeding generation of composers: noted esp. for his church music, oratorios, and cantatas

Stanhope *n* **1 Charles**, 3rd Earl 1753–1816, British radical politician and scientist. His inventions included two calculating machines, a microscope lens, and a stereotyping machine **2** his grandfather, **James**, 1st Earl. 1673–1721, British soldier and statesman; George I's chief minister (1717–21). He fought under Marlborough in the War of the Spanish Succession (1701–14) and negotiated the Triple Alliance with France and Holland (1717)

Stanisław *or* **Stanislaus** *n* **Saint** 1030–79, the patron saint of Poland. As Bishop of Cracow (1072–79) he excommunicated King Bolesław II, who arranged his murder. Feast day: May 11

Stanisław II *n* surnamed *Poniatowski* 1732–98, the last king of Poland (1764–95), during whose reign Poland was repeatedly invaded and partitioned (1772, 1791, 1795) by its neighbours: abdicated

stank *vb* ▸ a past tense of **stink**

Stanley knife *n trademark* a type of knife with a thick metal handle with a short, very sharp, replaceable blade
WORD ORIGIN after F. T. *Stanley*, businessman

stanza *n prosody* a verse of a poem
WORD ORIGIN Italian: halting place

staphylococcus (staff-ill-oh-**kok**-uss) *n, pl* **-cocci** (-**kok**-eye) a bacterium occurring in clusters and including many species that cause disease
WORD ORIGIN Greek *staphulē* bunch of grapes + *kokkos* berry

staple[1] *n* **1** a short length of wire bent into a square U-shape, used to fasten papers or secure things ▹ *vb* **-pling, -pled 2** to secure (things) with staples
WORD ORIGIN Old English *stapol* prop

staple[2] Ⓣ *adj* **1** of prime importance; principal: *the staple diet of a country* ▹ *n* **2** something that forms a main part of the product, consumption, or trade of a region **3** a main constituent of anything: *the personal reflections which make up the staple of the book*
WORD ORIGIN Middle Dutch *stapel* warehouse

stapler *n* a device used to fasten things together with a staple

star Ⓣ *n* **1** a planet or meteor visible in the clear night sky as a point of light **2** a hot gaseous mass, such as the sun, that radiates energy as heat and light, or in some cases as radio waves and X-rays ▸ Related adjectives: **astral, sidereal, stellar 3 stars** ▸ same as **horoscope** (sense 1) **4** an emblem with five or more radiating points, often used as a symbol of rank or an award: *the RAC awarded the hotel three stars* **5** ▸ same as **asterisk**

S

THESAURUS

stand-in *n* **2 = substitute**, deputy, replacement, reserve, surrogate, understudy, locum, stopgap

standing *adj* **1 = permanent**, lasting, fixed, regular, repeated, perpetual ▹ *n* **4 = status**, position, station, footing, condition, credit, rank, reputation, eminence, estimation, repute **5 = duration**, existence, experience, continuance

stand up *vb* **4 stand up for = support**, champion, defend, uphold, side with, stick up for (*informal*), come to the defence of

staple[2] *adj* **1 = principal**, chief, main, key, basic, essential, primary, fundamental, predominant

star *n* **1, 2 = heavenly body**, sun, celestial body **6 = celebrity**, big name, celeb (*informal*), megastar (*informal*), name, draw, idol, luminary, leading man *or* lady, lead, hero *or* heroine, principal, main attraction ▹ *vb* **8 = play the lead**,

DICTIONARY

6 a famous person from the sports, acting, or music professions **7 see stars** to see flashes of light after a blow on the head ▹*vb* **starring, starred 8** to feature (an actor or actress) or (of an actor or actress) to be featured as a star: *he's starred in dozens of films* **9** to mark (something) with a star or stars
WORD ORIGIN Old English *steorra*
starboard *n* **1** the right side of an aeroplane or ship when facing forwards ▹*adj* **2** of or on the starboard
WORD ORIGIN Old English *stēorbord*, literally: steering side
starch *n* **1** a carbohydrate forming the main food element in bread, potatoes, and rice: in solution with water it is used to stiffen fabric **2** food containing a large amount of starch ▹*vb* **3** to stiffen (cloth) with starch
WORD ORIGIN Old English *sterced* stiffened
starchy *adj* **starchier, starchiest 1** of or containing starch **2** (of a person's behaviour) very formal and humourless
star-crossed *adj* (of lovers) destined to misfortune
stardom *n* the status of a star in the entertainment or sport world
stare ❶ *vb* **staring, stared 1** (often foll. by *at*) to look at for a long time **2 stare one in the face** to be glaringly obvious ▹*n* **3** a long fixed look
WORD ORIGIN Old English *starian*
starfish *n, pl* **-fish** *or* **-fishes** a star-shaped sea creature with a flat body and five limbs
star fruit *n* ▸same as **carambola**
stargazer *n informal* an astrologer
stargazing *n*
stark ❶ *adj* **1** harsh, unpleasant, and plain: *a stark choice* **2** grim, desolate, and lacking any beautiful features: *the stark landscapes* **3** utter; absolute: *in stark contrast* ▹*adv* **4** completely: *stark staring bonkers* **starkly** *adv* **starkness** *n*
WORD ORIGIN Old English *stearc* stiff
Stark *n* **1** Dame **Freya** (**Madeline**) 1893–1993, British traveller and writer, whose many books include *The Southern Gates of Arabia* (1936), *Beyond Euphrates* (1951), and *The Journey's Echo* (1963) **2 Johannes** 1874–1957, German physicist, who discovered the splitting of the lines of a spectrum when the source of light is subjected to a strong electrostatic field (**Stark effect**, 1913): Nobel prize for physics 1919
Starkey *n* **David** born 1945, British historian and broadcaster, noted for his books and television series on the Tudor period
stark-naked *adj* completely naked. Also (informal): **starkers**
WORD ORIGIN Middle English *stert naket*, literally: tail naked
starlet *n* a young actress who has the potential to become a star
starlight *n* the light that comes from the stars
starling *n* a common songbird with shiny blackish feathers and a short tail
WORD ORIGIN Old English *stærlinc*
Starling *n* **Ernest Henry** 1866–1927, British physiologist, who contributed greatly to the understanding of many bodily functions and with William Bayliss (1860–1924) discovered the hormone secretin (1902)
starlit *adj* lit by starlight
Star of David *n* a symbol of Judaism, consisting of a star formed by two interlaced equilateral triangles
Starr *n* **1** (**Myra**) **Belle** 1848–89, US outlaw, a famous rustler of horses and cattle **2 Ringo**, original name *Richard Starkey*. born 1940, British rock musician; drummer (1962–70) with the Beatles
starry *adj* **-rier, -riest 1** (of a sky or night) full of or lit by stars **2** of or like a star or stars: *a starry cast*
starry-eyed *adj* full of unrealistic hopes and dreams; naive
Stars and Stripes *n* the national flag of the United States of America
star sign *n astrol* the sign of the zodiac under which a person was born
Star-Spangled Banner *n* **1** the national anthem of the United States of America **2** ▸same as **Stars and Stripes**
star-studded *adj* featuring many well-known performers: *a star-studded premiere*
start ❶ *vb* **1** to begin (something or to do something); come or cause to come into being: *to start a war; this conflict started years ago* **2** to set or be set in motion: *he started the van* **3** to make a sudden involuntary movement from fright or surprise; jump **4** to establish; set up: *to start a state lottery* **5** to support (someone) in the first part of a career or activity **6** *Brit informal* to begin quarrelling or causing a disturbance: *don't start with me* **7 to start with** in the first place ▹*n* **8** the first part of something **9** the place or time at which something begins **10** a signal to begin, such as in a race **11** a lead or advantage, either in time or distance, in a competitive activity: *he had an hour's start on me* **12** a slight involuntary movement from fright or surprise: *I awoke with a start* **13** an opportunity to enter a career or begin a project **14 for a start** in the first place ▸See also **start off, start on**, etc.
WORD ORIGIN Old English *styrtan*
starter *n* **1** *chiefly Brit* the first course of a meal **2 for starters** *slang* in the first place **3** a device for starting an internal-combustion engine **4** a person who signals the start of a race **5** a competitor in a race or contest **6 under starter's orders** (of competitors in a race) waiting for the signal to start
startle ❶ *vb* **-tling, -tled** to slightly surprise or frighten someone
startling *adj*

S

THESAURUS

appear, feature, perform
stare *vb* **1 = gaze**, look, goggle, watch, gape, eyeball *(slang)*, ogle, gawp *(Brit slang)*, gawk, rubberneck *(slang)*
stark *adj* **1 = plain**, simple, harsh, basic, bare, grim, straightforward, blunt, bald **2a = austere**, severe, plain, bare, harsh, unadorned, bare-bones **2b = bleak**, grim, barren, hard, cold, depressing, dreary, desolate, forsaken, godforsaken, drear *(literary)* **3 = absolute**, pure, sheer, utter, downright, patent, consummate, palpable, out-and-out, flagrant, unmitigated, unalloyed, arrant ▹*adv* **4 = absolutely**, quite, completely, clean, entirely, altogether, wholly, utterly
start *vb* **1a = set about**, begin, proceed, embark upon, take the plunge *(informal)*, take the first step, make a beginning, put your hand to the plough *(informal)* **OPPOSITE:** stop
1b = begin, arise, originate, issue, appear, commence, get under way, come into being, come into existence, first see the light of day
OPPOSITE: end
2a = set in motion, initiate, instigate, open, trigger, kick off *(informal)*, originate, get going, engender, kick-start, get (something) off the ground *(informal)*, enter upon, get *or* set *or* start the ball rolling
OPPOSITE: stop
2b = start up, activate, get something going **OPPOSITE:** turn off
3 = jump, shy, jerk, twitch, flinch, recoil **4 = establish**, begin, found, father, create, launch, set up, introduce, institute, pioneer, initiate, inaugurate, lay the foundations of **OPPOSITE:** terminate ▹*n* **8, 9 = beginning**, outset, opening, birth, foundation, dawn, first step(s), onset, initiation, inauguration, inception, commencement, kickoff *(informal)*, opening move **OPPOSITE:** end
12 = jump, jerk, twitch, spasm, convulsion
startle *vb* **= surprise**, shock, alarm, frighten, scare, agitate, take (someone) aback, make (someone)

DICTIONARY

WORD ORIGIN Old English *steartlian* to kick, struggle

start off *vb* **1** to set out on a journey **2** to be or make the first step in (an activity): *beginners should start off with a walking programme* **3** to cause (a person) to do something, such as laugh

start on *vb Brit informal* to pick a quarrel with: *they started on me*

start out *vb* **1** to set out on a journey **2** to take the first steps in a career or on a course of action: *I started out as a beautician; it started out as a joke*

start up *vb* **1** to come or cause (something, such as a business) to come into being; found **2** to set (something) in motion: *she started up the car*

starve *vb* **starving, starved 1** to die from lack of food **2** to deliberately prevent (a person or animal) from having any food **3** *informal* to be very hungry: *we're both starving* **4 starve of** to deprive (someone) of something needed: *the heart is starved of oxygen* **5 starve into** to force someone into a specified state by starving: *an attempt to starve him into submission* **starvation** *n*

WORD ORIGIN Old English *steorfan* to die

Star Wars *n* (in the US) a proposed system of artificial satellites armed with lasers to destroy enemy missiles in space

stash *informal vb* **1** (often foll. by *away*) *informal* to store (money or valuables) in a secret place for safekeeping ▹ *n* **2** a secret store, usually of illegal drugs, or the place where this is hidden

WORD ORIGIN origin unknown

state ❶ *n* **1** the condition or circumstances of a person or thing **2** a sovereign political power or community **3** the territory of such a community **4** the sphere of power in such a community: *matters of state* **5** (*often cap*) one of a number of areas or communities having their own governments and forming a federation under a sovereign government, such as in the US or Australia **6** (*often cap*) the government, civil service, and armed forces **7 in a state** *informal* in an emotional or very worried condition **8 lie in state** (of a body) to be placed on public view before burial **9 state of affairs** circumstances or condition: *this wonderful state of affairs* **10** grand and luxurious lifestyle, as enjoyed by royalty, aristocrats, or the wealthy: *living in state* ▹ *adj* **11** controlled or financed by a state: *state ownership* **12** of or concerning the State: *state secrets* **13** involving ceremony: *a state visit* ▹ *vb* **stating, stated 14** to express (something) in words

WORD ORIGIN Latin *stare* to stand

State Enrolled Nurse *n* (in Britain) a nurse who has completed a two-year training course

statehouse *n NZ* a rented house built by the government

stateless *adj* not belonging to any country: *stateless refugees*

stately ❶ *adj* **-lier, -liest** having a dignified, impressive, and graceful appearance or manner: *the Rolls-Royce approached him at a stately speed* **stateliness** *n*

stately home *n Brit* a large old mansion, usually one open to the public

statement ❶ *n* **1** something stated, usually a formal prepared announcement or reply **2** *law* a declaration of matters of fact **3** an account prepared by a bank at regular intervals for a client to show all credits and debits and the balance at the end of the period **4** an account containing a summary of bills or invoices and showing the total amount due **5** the act of stating

state of the art *n* **1** the current level of knowledge and development achieved in a technology, science, or art ▹ *adj* **state-of-the-art 2** the most recent and therefore considered the best; up-to-the-minute: *state-of-the-art computers*

State Registered Nurse *n* (formerly in Britain) a nurse who has completed an extensive three-year training course

stateroom *n* **1** a private room on a ship **2** *chiefly Brit* a large room in a palace, etc. used on ceremonial occasions

States *pl n* **the States** *informal* the United States of America

state school *n* a school funded by the state, in which education is free

statesman *n, pl* **-men** an experienced and respected political leader **statesmanship** *n*

static *adj* **1** not active, changing, or moving; stationary **2** *physics* (of a weight, force, or pressure) acting but causing no movement **3** *physics* of forces that do not produce movement ▹ *n* **4** hissing or crackling or a speckled picture caused by interference in the reception of radio or television transmissions **5** electric sparks or crackling produced by friction

WORD ORIGIN Greek *statikos* causing to stand

static electricity *n* ▸ same as **static** (sense 5)

statics *n* the branch of mechanics concerned with the forces producing a state of equilibrium

statin *n med* any of several drugs that inhibit the production of cholesterol

station ❶ *n* **1** a place along a route or line at which a bus or train stops to pick up passengers or goods **2** the headquarters of an organization such as the police or fire service **3** a building with special equipment for some particular purpose: *power station; a filling station* **4** a television or radio channel **5** *mil* a place of duty **6** position in society: *he had ideas above his station* **7** *Austral & NZ* a large sheep or cattle farm **8** the place or position where a person is assigned to stand: *every man stood at his station* ▹ *vb* **9** to assign (someone) to a station

WORD ORIGIN Latin *statio* a standing still

stationary *adj* not moving: *a line of stationary traffic*

WORD ORIGIN Latin *stationarius*

stationer *n* a person or shop selling stationery

WORD ORIGIN Medieval Latin *stationarius* a person having a regular station, hence a shopkeeper

stationery *n* writing materials, such as paper, envelopes, and pens

stationmaster *n* the senior official in charge of a railway station

Stations of the Cross *pl n RC church*

THESAURUS

jump, give (someone) a turn (*informal*)

state *n* **1a = condition**, shape, state of affairs **1b = circumstances**, situation, position, case, pass, mode, plight, predicament **2, 3 = country**, nation, land, republic, territory, federation, commonwealth, kingdom, body politic **6** (*often cap*) **= government**, ministry, administration, executive, regime, powers-that-be **10 = ceremony**, glory, grandeur, splendour, dignity, majesty, pomp ▹ *vb* **14 = say**, report, declare, specify, put, present, explain, voice, express, assert, utter, articulate, affirm, expound, enumerate, propound, aver, asseverate

stately *adj* **= grand**, majestic, dignified, royal, august, imposing, impressive, elegant, imperial, noble, regal, solemn, lofty, pompous, ceremonious **OPPOSITE:** lowly

statement *n* **1 = announcement**, declaration, communication, explanation, communiqué, proclamation, utterance **2** (*law*) **= account**, report, testimony, evidence

station *n* **1 = railway station**, stop, stage, halt, terminal, train station, terminus **2 = headquarters**, base, depot **6 = position**, rank, status, standing, post, situation, grade, sphere **8 = post**, place, location, position, situation, seat ▹ *vb* **9 = assign**, post, locate, set, establish,

S

1 a series of 14 crosses with pictures or carvings, arranged around the walls of a church, to commemorate 14 stages in Christ's journey to Calvary 2 a series of 14 prayers relating to each of these stages

station wagon *n US, Austral & NZ* an estate car

statistic *n* a numerical fact collected and classified systematically **statistical** *adj* **statistically** *adv* **statistician** *n*

statistics *n* 1 the science dealing with the collection, classification, and interpretation of numerical information ▹*pl n* 2 numerical information which has been collected, classified, and interpreted **WORD ORIGIN** originally: science dealing with facts of a state, from New Latin *statisticus* concerning state affairs

Statius *n* **Publius Papinius** ?45–96 AD, Roman poet; author of the collection *Silvae* and of two epics, *Thebais* and the unfinished *Achilleis*

statuary *n* statues collectively

statue *n* a sculpture of a human or animal figure, usually life-size or larger **WORD ORIGIN** Latin *statuere* to set up

statuesque (stat-yoo-esk) *adj* (of a woman) tall and well-proportioned; like a classical statue

statuette *n* a small statue

stature ❶ *n* 1 height and size of a person 2 the reputation of a person or their achievements: *a batsman of international stature* 3 moral or intellectual distinction **WORD ORIGIN** Latin *stare* to stand

status ❶ *n* 1 a person's position in society 2 the esteem in which people hold a person: *priests feel they have lost some of their status in society* 3 the legal or official standing or classification of a person or country: *the status of refugees; Ireland's non-aligned status* 4 degree of importance **WORD ORIGIN** Latin: posture

status quo *n* the existing state of affairs **WORD ORIGIN** literally: the state in which

status symbol *n* a possession regarded as a mark of social position or wealth

statute *n* 1 a law made by a government and expressed in a formal document 2 a permanent rule made by a company or other institution **WORD ORIGIN** Latin *statuere* to set up, decree

statute law *n* 1 a law made by a government 2 such laws collectively

statutory *adj* 1 required or authorized by law 2 (of an offence) declared by law to be punishable

Stauffenberg *n* **Claus**, Graf von 1907–44, German army officer, who tried to assassinate Hitler (1944). He and his fellow conspirators were executed

staunch[1] ❶ *adj* strong and loyal: *a staunch supporter* **staunchly** *adv* **WORD ORIGIN** Old French *estanche*

staunch[2] *or* **stanch** *vb* to stop the flow of (blood) from someone's body

stave *n* 1 one of the long strips of wood joined together to form a barrel or bucket 2 a stick carried as a symbol of office 3 a verse of a poem 4 *music* ▸same as **staff** ▹*vb* **staving, stove** 5 **stave in** to burst a hole in something **WORD ORIGIN** from *staves*, plural of STAFF

stave off *vb* **staving, staved** to delay (something) for a short time: *to stave off political rebellion*

staves *n* ▸a plural of **staff** or **stave**

stay[1] ❶ *vb* 1 to continue or remain in a place, position, or condition: *to stay away; to stay inside* 2 to lodge as a guest or visitor temporarily: *we stay with friends* 3 *Scot & S African* to reside permanently; live 4 to endure (something testing or difficult): *you have stayed the course this long* ▹*n* 5 the period spent in one place 6 the postponement of an order of a court of law: *a stay of execution* **WORD ORIGIN** Old French *ester*

stay[2] *n* something that supports or steadies something, such as a prop or buttress **WORD ORIGIN** Old French *estaye*

stay[3] *n* a rope or chain supporting a ship's mast or funnel **WORD ORIGIN** Old English *stæg*

stay-at-home *adj* 1 (of a person) enjoying a quiet, settled, and unadventurous life ▹*n* 2 a stay-at-home person

staycation (stay-kay-shun) *n informal* a holiday in which leisure activities are pursued while staying at one's own home **WORD ORIGIN** from *stay*[1] + (VA)CATION

staying power *n* endurance to complete something undertaken; stamina

stays *pl n* old-fashioned corsets with bones in them

staysail *n* a sail fastened on a stay

STD 1 sexually transmitted disease 2 *Brit, Austral & S African* subscriber trunk dialling 3 *NZ* subscriber toll dialling

STD code *n Brit* a code preceding a local telephone number, allowing a caller to dial direct without the operator's help **WORD ORIGIN** *s(ubscriber) t(runk) d(ialling)*

stead *n* 1 **stand someone in good stead** to be useful to someone in the future 2 *rare* the function or position that should be taken by another: *I cannot let you rule in my stead* **WORD ORIGIN** Old English *stede*

Stead *n* **Christina** (**Ellen**) 1902–83, Australian novelist. Her works include *Seven Poor Men of Sydney* (1934), *The Man who Loved Children* (1940), and *Cotters' England* (1966)

steadfast *adj* dedicated and unwavering **steadfastly** *adv* **steadfastness** *n*

steady ❶ *adj* **steadier, steadiest** 1 firm and not shaking 2 without much change or variation: *we're on a steady course* 3 continuous: *a steady decline* 4 not easily excited; sober 5 regular; habitual: *the steady drinking of alcohol* ▹*vb* **steadies, steadying, steadied** 6 to make or become steady ▹*adv* 7 in a steady manner 8 **go steady** *informal* to date one person regularly ▹*n, pl* **steadies**

S

fix, install, garrison

stature *n* 1 = **height**, build, size 2 = **importance**, standing, prestige, size, rank, consequence, prominence, eminence, high station

status *n* 1 = **position**, rank, grade, degree 2 = **prestige**, standing, authority, influence, weight, reputation, honour, importance, consequence, fame, distinction, eminence, renown, mana (NZ) 3 = **state of play**, development, progress, condition, evolution, progression

staunch[1] *adj* = **loyal**, faithful, stalwart, sure, strong, firm, sound, true, constant, reliable, stout, resolute, dependable, trustworthy, trusty, steadfast, true-blue, immovable, tried and true

stay[1] *vb* 1 = **remain**, continue to be, linger, stand, stop, wait, settle, delay, halt, pause, hover, abide, hang around *(informal)*, reside, stay put, bide, loiter, hang in the air, tarry, put down roots, establish yourself **OPPOSITE:** go 1, 4 = **continue**, remain, go on, survive, endure 2 = **lodge**, visit, sojourn *(literary)*, put up at, be accommodated at ▹*n* 5 = **visit**, stop, holiday, stopover, sojourn *(literary)* 6 = **postponement**, delay, suspension, stopping, halt, pause, reprieve, remission, deferment

steady *adj* 1 = **stable**, fixed, secure, firm, safe, immovable, on an even keel **OPPOSITE:** unstable 2 = **regular**, established 3, 5 = **continuous**, even, regular, constant, consistent, persistent, rhythmic, unbroken, habitual, uninterrupted, incessant, ceaseless, unremitting, unwavering, nonstop, unvarying, unfaltering,

DICTIONARY

9 *informal* one's regular boyfriend or girlfriend ▹*interj* **10** a warning to keep calm or be careful **steadily** *adv* **steadiness** *n*
WORD ORIGIN from *stead*

steady state *n physics* the condition of a system when all or most changes or disturbances have been eliminated from it

steak *n* **1** a lean piece of beef for grilling or frying **2** a cut of beef for braising or stewing **3** a thick slice of pork, veal, or fish
WORD ORIGIN Old Norse *steik* roast

steakhouse *n* a restaurant that specializes in steaks

steal ⓘ *vb* **stealing, stole, stolen 1** to take (something) from someone without permission or unlawfully **2** to use (someone else's ideas or work) without acknowledgment **3** to move quietly and carefully, not wanting to be noticed: *my father stole up behind her* **4 steal the show** (of a performer) to draw the audience's attention to oneself and away from the other performers **5** to obtain or do (something) stealthily: *I stole a glance behind* ▹*n* **6** *US, Canad & NZ informal* something acquired easily or at little cost
WORD ORIGIN Old English *stelan*

stealth ⓘ *n* **1** moving carefully and quietly, so as to avoid being seen **2** cunning or underhand behaviour ▹*adj* **3** (of technology) able to render an aircraft almost invisible to radar **4** disguised or hidden **stealthy** *adj* **stealthily** *adv*
WORD ORIGIN Old English *stelan* to steal

stealth tax *n* an indirect tax, such as a tax on fuel or pension plans, esp. one of which people are unaware or one that is felt to be unfair

steam *n* **1** the vapour into which water changes when boiled **2** the mist formed when such vapour condenses in the atmosphere **3** *informal* power, energy, or speed **4 let off steam** *informal* to release pent-up energy or feelings **5 pick up steam** *informal* to gather momentum ▹*adj* **6** operated, heated, or powered by steam: *a steam train* ▹*vb* **7** to give off steam **8** (of a vehicle) to move by steam power **9** *informal* to proceed quickly and often forcefully **10** to cook (food) in steam **11** to treat (something) with steam, such as in cleaning or pressing clothes **12 steam open** *or* **off** to use steam in order to open or remove (something): *let me steam open this letter* ▸ See also **steam up**
WORD ORIGIN Old English *stēam*

steam engine *n* an engine worked by steam

steamer *n* **1** a boat or ship driven by steam engines **2** a container with holes in the bottom, used to cook food by steam

steam iron *n* an electric iron that uses steam to take creases out of clothes

steamroller *n* **1** a steam-powered vehicle with heavy rollers used for flattening road surfaces during road-making ▹*vb* **2** to make (someone) do what one wants by overpowering force

steamship *n* a ship powered by steam engines

steam up *vb* **1** to cover (windows or glasses) or (of windows or glasses) to become covered with steam **2 steamed up** *slang* excited or angry

steamy *adj* **steamier, steamiest 1** full of steam **2** *informal* (of books, films, etc.) erotic

steatite (stee-a-tite) *n* ▸ same as **soapstone**
WORD ORIGIN Greek *stear* fat

steed *n archaic or literary* a horse
WORD ORIGIN Old English *stēda* stallion

steel *n* **1** an alloy of iron and carbon, often with small quantities of other elements **2** a steel rod used for sharpening knives **3** courage and mental toughness ▹*vb* **4** to prepare (oneself) for coping with something unpleasant: *he had steeled himself to accept the fact* **steely** *adj*
WORD ORIGIN Old English *stēli*

Steel *n* **1 Danielle,** full name *Danielle Fernande Schüelein-Steel.* born 1950, US writer of romantic fiction **2** Baron **David** (**Martin Scott**). born 1938, British politician; leader of the Liberal Party (1976–88); Presiding Officer of the Scottish Parliament (1999–2003)

steel band *n music* a band of people playing on metal drums, popular in the West Indies

Steele *n* Sir **Richard** 1672–1729, British essayist and dramatist, born in Ireland; with Joseph Addison he was the chief contributor to the periodicals *The Tatler* (1709–11) and *The Spectator* (1711–12)

steel-grey *adj* dark bluish-grey

steel wool *n* a mass of fine steel fibres, used for cleaning metal surfaces

steelworks *n* a factory where steel is made **steelworker** *n*

Steen[1] *n* **Jan** 1626–79, Dutch genre painter

Steen[2] *n South African* **1** (in South Africa) the white grape variety known elsewhere as Chenin Blanc **2** any of the white wines made from this grape
WORD ORIGIN Afrikaans

steep[1] ⓘ *adj* **1** having a sharp slope **2** *informal* (of a fee, price, or demand) unreasonably high; excessive **steeply** *adv* **steepness** *n*
WORD ORIGIN Old English *stēap*

steep[2] ⓘ *vb* **1** to soak or be soaked in a liquid in order to soften or cleanse **2 steeped in** filled with: *an industry steeped in tradition*
WORD ORIGIN Old English *stēpan*

steepen *vb* to become or cause (something) to become steep or steeper

steeple *n* a tall ornamental tower on a church roof
WORD ORIGIN Old English *stēpel*

steeplechase *n* **1** a horse race over a course with fences to be jumped **2** a track race in which the runners have to leap hurdles and a water jump ▹*vb* **-chasing, -chased 3** to race in a steeplechase
WORD ORIGIN so called because it originally took place cross-country, with a church tower serving as a landmark for the riders in the race

steeplejack *n* a person who repairs steeples and chimneys

steer[1] ⓘ *vb* **1** to direct the course of (a

S

THESAURUS

unfluctuating **OPPOSITE:** irregular **4 = dependable**, sensible, reliable, balanced, settled, secure, calm, supportive, sober, staunch, serene, sedate, staid, steadfast, level-headed, serious-minded, imperturbable, equable, unchangeable, having both feet on the ground
OPPOSITE: undependable

steal *vb* **1 = take**, nick *(slang, chiefly Brit)*, pinch *(informal)*, lift *(informal)*, cabbage *(Brit slang)*, swipe *(slang)*, half-inch *(old-fashioned slang)*, heist *(US slang)*, embezzle, blag *(slang)*, pilfer, misappropriate, snitch *(slang)*, purloin, filch, prig *(Brit slang)*, shoplift, thieve, be light-fingered, peculate, walk *or* make off with **2 = copy**, take, plagiarize, appropriate, pinch *(informal)*, pirate, poach **3 = sneak**, slip, creep, flit, tiptoe, slink, insinuate yourself

stealth *n* **1, 2 = secrecy**, furtiveness, slyness, sneakiness, unobtrusiveness, stealthiness, surreptitiousness

steep[1] *adj* **1 = sheer**, precipitous, perpendicular, abrupt, headlong, vertical **OPPOSITE:** gradual **2** *(informal)* **= high**, excessive, exorbitant, extreme, stiff, unreasonable, overpriced, extortionate, uncalled-for
OPPOSITE: reasonable

steep[2] *vb* **1 = soak**, immerse, marinate *(cookery)*, damp, submerge, drench, moisten, macerate, souse, imbrue *(rare)*

steer[1] *vb* **1 = drive**, control, direct, handle, conduct, pilot, govern, be in the driver's seat **2 = direct**, lead, guide, conduct, escort, show in *or* out

vehicle or vessel) with a steering wheel or rudder **2** to direct the movements or course of (a person, conversation, or activity) **3** to follow (a specified course): *the Dutch government steered a middle course* **4 steer clear of** to avoid
WORD ORIGIN Old English *stīeran*

steer² *n* a castrated male ox or bull
WORD ORIGIN Old English *stēor*

steerage *n* **1** the cheapest accommodation on a passenger ship **2** steering

steering committee *n* a committee set up to prepare and arrange topics to be discussed, and the order of business, for a government, etc.

steering wheel *n* a wheel turned by the driver of a vehicle in order to change direction

steersman *n, pl* **-men** the person who steers a vessel

Stefan Dušan *n* 1308–55, king of Serbia (1331–55), who conquered Albania (1343) and large parts of the Byzantine empire, into which he introduced legal and administrative reforms

Stefansson *n* **Vilhjalmur** 1879–1962, Canadian explorer, noted for his books on the Inuit

Steffens *n* **(Joseph) Lincoln** 1866–1936, US political analyst, known for his exposure of political corruption

stein (stine) *n* an earthenware beer mug
WORD ORIGIN German *Stein*, literally: stone

Stein *n* **1 Gertrude** 1874–1946, US writer, resident in Paris (1903–1946). Her works include *Three Lives* (1908) and *The Autobiography of Alice B. Toklas* (1933) **2 Heinrich Friedrich Carl,** Baron Stein. 1757–1831, Prussian statesman, who contributed greatly to the modernization of Prussia and played a major role in the European coalition against Napoleon (1813–15) **3 Jock,** real name *John*. 1922–85, Scottish footballer and manager: managed Celtic (1965–78) and Scotland (1978–85)

Steiner *n* **Rudolf** 1861–1925, Austrian philosopher, founder of anthroposophy. He was particularly influential in education ▸ See also **anthroposophy**

Steinitz *n* **Wilhelm** 1836–1900, US chess player, born in Prague; world champion (1866–94)

Steinway *n* **Henry (Engelhard)**, original name *Heinrich Engelhardt Steinweg*. 1797–1871, US piano maker, born in Germany

stela (steal-a) *or* **stele** (steal-ee) *n, pl* **stelae** (steal-ee) *or* **steles** an upright stone slab or column decorated with figures or inscriptions, common in prehistoric times
WORD ORIGIN Greek *stēlē*

stellar *adj* **1** relating to the stars **2** *informal* outstanding or immense: *stellar profits*
WORD ORIGIN Latin *stella* star

stem¹ ❶ *n* **1** the long thin central part of a plant **2** a stalk that bears a flower, fruit, or leaf **3** the long slender part of anything, such as a wineglass **4** *linguistics* the form of a word that remains after removal of all inflectional endings ▹ *vb* **stemming, stemmed 5 stem from** originate from: *this tradition stems from pre-Christian times*
WORD ORIGIN Old English *stemn*

stem² ❶ *vb* **stemming, stemmed** to stop or hinder the spread of (something): *to stem the flow of firearms*
WORD ORIGIN Old Norse *stemma*

stem cell *n histology* an undifferentiated embryonic cell that gives rise to specialized cells, such as blood, bone, etc.

stemmed *adj* having a stem: *long-stemmed roses*

stench *n* a strong and very unpleasant smell
WORD ORIGIN Old English *stenc*

stencil *n* **1** a thin sheet with a cut-out pattern through which ink or paint passes to form the pattern on the surface below **2** a design or letters made in this way ▹ *vb* **-cilling, -cilled** *or US* **-ciling, -ciled 3** to make (a design or letters) with a stencil
WORD ORIGIN Old French *estenceler* to decorate brightly

Sten gun *n* a light sub-machine-gun
WORD ORIGIN *S & T* (initials of the inventors) + *-en*, as in *Bren gun*

stenographer *n US & Canad* a shorthand typist
WORD ORIGIN Greek *stenos* narrow + *graphein* to write

stent *n* a surgical implant used to keep an artery open

stentorian *adj* (of the voice) very loud: *a stentorian tone*
WORD ORIGIN after *Stentor*, a herald in Greek mythology

step ❶ *n* **1** the act of moving and setting down one's foot, such as when walking **2** the distance covered by such a movement **3** the sound made by such a movement **4** one of a sequence of foot movements that make up a dance **5** one of a sequence of actions taken in order to achieve a goal **6** a degree or rank in a series or scale **7** a flat surface for placing the foot on when going up or down **8** manner of walking: *he moved with a purposeful step* **9 steps a** a flight of stairs, usually out of doors **b** ▸ same as **stepladder** **10** a short easily travelled distance: *Mexico and Brazil were only a step away* **11 break step** to stop marching in step **12 in step a** marching or dancing in time or at the same pace as other people **b** *informal* in agreement: *in step with the West on this issue* **13 out of step a** not marching or dancing in time or at the same pace as other people **b** *informal* not in agreement: *out of step with the political mood* **14 step by step** gradually **15 take steps** to do what is necessary (to achieve something) **16 watch one's step a** *informal* to behave with caution **b** to walk carefully ▹ *vb* **stepping, stepped 17** to move by taking a step, such as in walking (often foll. by *on*) **18** to place or press the foot; tread **19** to walk a short distance: *please step this way* **20 step into** to enter (a situation) apparently without difficulty: *she stepped into a life of luxury* ▸ See also **step down, step in,** etc.
WORD ORIGIN Old English *stepe, stæpe*

Step *n* **1** a set of aerobic exercises which consists of stepping on and off a special box of adjustable height ▹ *adj* **2** denoting this type of exercise: *Step aerobics*

stepbrother *n* a son of one's stepmother or stepfather

stepchild *n, pl* **-children** a stepson or stepdaughter

stepdaughter *n* a daughter of one's husband or wife by an earlier relationship

step down *vb informal* to resign from a position

stepfather *n* a man who has married one's mother after the death or divorce of one's father

stephanotis (stef-fan-note-iss) *n* a tropical climbing shrub with sweet-smelling white flowers
WORD ORIGIN Greek: fit for a crown

step in ❶ *vb informal* to intervene (in a quarrel or difficult situation)

stepladder *n* a small folding portable

S

THESAURUS

stem¹ *n* **1, 2 = stalk**, branch, trunk, shoot, stock, axis, peduncle ▹ *vb* **5 stem from something = originate from**, be caused by, derive from, arise from, flow from, emanate from, develop from, be generated by, be brought about by, be bred by, issue forth from

stem² *vb* **= stop**, hold back, staunch, stay (*archaic*), check, contain, dam, curb, restrain, bring to a standstill, stanch

step *n* **2 = pace**, stride, footstep **3 = footfall 5 = move**, measure, action, means, act, proceeding, procedure, manoeuvre, deed, expedient **6a = stage**, point, phase **6b = level**, rank, remove, degree ▹ *vb* **17 = walk**, pace, tread, move

step in *vb (informal)* **= intervene**, take action, become involved, chip in

DICTIONARY

ladder with a supporting frame
stepmother *n* a woman who has married one's father after the death or divorce of one's mother
step on *vb* **1** to place or press one's foot on (something): *he stepped on the brakes* **2** *informal* to behave badly towards (a person in a less powerful position) **3 step on it** *informal* to go more quickly; hurry up
step out *vb* **1** to leave a room briefly **2** to walk quickly, taking long strides
step-parent *n* a stepfather or stepmother
steppes *pl n* wide grassy plains without trees
WORD ORIGIN Old Russian *step* lowland
stepping stone *n* **1** one of a series of stones acting as footrests for crossing a stream **2** a stage in a person's progress towards a goal: *it was a big stepping stone in his career*
stepsister *n* a daughter of one's stepmother or stepfather
stepson *n* a son of one's husband or wife by an earlier relationship
step up ❶ *vb* **1** *informal* to increase (something) by stages; accelerate **2 step up to the plate** *US & Canad* **a** *baseball* to move into batting position **b** to come forward and take responsibility for something
stereo *adj* **1** (of a sound system) using two or more separate microphones to feed two or more loudspeakers through separate channels ▷ *n, pl* **stereos 2** a music system in which sound is directed through two speakers **3** sound broadcast or played in stereo
stereophonic *adj* ▸ same as **stereo** (sense 1)
WORD ORIGIN Greek *stereos* solid + *phōnē* sound
stereoscopic *adj* having a three-dimensional effect: *stereoscopic vision*
stereotype ❶ *n* **1** a set of characteristics or a fixed idea considered to represent a particular kind of person **2** an idea or convention that has grown stale through fixed usage ▷ *vb* **-typing, -typed 3** to form a standard image or idea of (a type of person)
WORD ORIGIN Greek *stereos* solid + TYPE
sterile ❶ *adj* **1** free from germs **2** unable to produce offspring **3** (of plants) not producing or bearing seeds **4** lacking inspiration or energy; unproductive **sterility** *n*
WORD ORIGIN Latin *sterilis*
sterilize *or* **-lise** *vb* **-lizing, -lized** *or* **-lising, -lised** to make sterile **sterilization** *or* **-lisation** *n*
sterling ❶ *n* **1** British money: *sterling fell by almost a pfennig* ▷ *adj* **2** genuine and reliable: first-class: *he has a reputation for sterling honesty*
WORD ORIGIN probably Old English *steorra* star, referring to a small star on early Norman pennies
Sterling *n* **Peter** born 1960, Australian rugby league player
sterling silver *n* **1** an alloy containing at least 92.5 per cent of silver **2** articles made of sterling silver
stern[1] ❶ *adj* **1** strict and serious: *he's a very stern taskmaster* **2** difficult and often unpleasant: *the stern demands of the day* **3** (of a facial expression) severe and disapproving **sternly** *adv*
WORD ORIGIN Old English *styrne*
stern[2] *n* the rear part of a boat or ship
WORD ORIGIN Old Norse *stjórn* steering
Stern *n* **Isaac** 1920–2001, US concert violinist, born in (what is now) Ukraine
Sternberg *n* ▸ See **von Sternberg**
Sterne *n* **Laurence** 1713–68, English novelist, born in Ireland, author of *The Life and Opinions of Tristram Shandy, Gentleman* (1759–67) and *A Sentimental Journey through France and Italy* (1768)
sternum *n, pl* **-na** *or* **-nums** a long flat bone in the front of the body, to which the collarbone and most of the ribs are attached
WORD ORIGIN Greek *sternon*
steroid *n biochem* an organic compound containing a carbon ring system, such as sterols and many hormones
sterol *n biochem* a natural insoluble alcohol such as cholesterol and ergosterol
WORD ORIGIN shortened from *cholesterol, ergosterol*, etc.
stertorous *adj* (of breathing) laboured and noisy
WORD ORIGIN Latin *stertere* to snore
stet *vb* **stetting, stetted 1** used as an instruction to indicate to a printer that certain deleted matter is to be kept **2** to mark (matter) in this way
WORD ORIGIN Latin, literally: let it stand
stethoscope *n med* an instrument for listening to the sounds made inside the body, consisting of a hollow disc that transmits the sound through hollow tubes to earpieces
WORD ORIGIN Greek *stēthos* breast + *skopein* to look at
Stetson *n trademark* a felt hat with a broad brim and high crown, worn mainly by cowboys
WORD ORIGIN after John *Stetson*, American hat maker
stevedore *n chiefly US* a person employed to load or unload ships
WORD ORIGIN Spanish *estibador* a packer
Stevens *n* **1 Thaddeus** 1792–1868, US Radical Republican politician. An opponent of slavery, he supported Reconstruction and entered the resolution calling for the impeachment of President Andrew Johnson **2 Wallace** 1879–1955, US poet, whose books include the collections *Harmonium* (1923), *The Man with the Blue Guitar* (1937), and *Transport to Summer* (1947)
stew *n* **1** a dish of meat, fish, or other food, cooked slowly in a closed pot **2 in a stew** *informal* in a troubled or worried state ▷ *vb* **3** to cook by long slow simmering in a closed pot **4** *informal* (of a person) to be too hot **5** to cause (tea) to become bitter or (of tea) to become bitter through infusing for too long **6 stew in one's own juice** to suffer, without help, the results of one's actions
WORD ORIGIN Middle English *stuen* to take a very hot bath
steward *n* **1** a person who looks after passengers and serves meals on a ship or aircraft **2** an official who helps to supervise a public event, such as a race **3** a person who administers someone else's property **4** a person who manages the eating arrangements, staff, or service at a club or hotel **5** ▸ see **shop steward** ▷ *vb* **6** to act as a steward (of)
WORD ORIGIN Old English *stigweard* hall keeper
stewardess *n* a female steward on an aircraft or ship
stewed *adj* **1** (of food) cooked by stewing **2** *Brit* (of tea) bitter through having been left to infuse for too long **3** *slang* drunk
stick[1] ❶ *n* **1** a small thin branch of a tree **2 a** a long thin piece of wood **b** such a piece of wood shaped for a

S

THESAURUS

(*informal*), intercede, take a hand
step up *vb* **1 = increase**, boost, intensify, up, raise, accelerate, speed up, escalate, augment
stereotype *n* **1, 2 = formula**, cliché, pattern, mould, received idea ▷ *vb* **3 = categorize**, typecast, pigeonhole, dub, standardize, take to be, ghettoize, conventionalize
sterile *adj* **1 = germ-free**, antiseptic, sterilized, disinfected, aseptic **OPPOSITE:** unhygienic **2, 3 = barren**, infertile, unproductive, childless, infecund **OPPOSITE:** fertile
sterling *adj* **2 = excellent**, sound, fine, first-class, superlative
stern[1] *adj* **1, 2 = strict**, harsh, rigorous, hard, cruel, grim, rigid, relentless, drastic, authoritarian, austere, inflexible, unrelenting, unyielding, unsparing **OPPOSITE:** lenient **3 = severe**, serious, forbidding, steely, flinty **OPPOSITE:** friendly
stick[1] *n* **1 = twig**, branch, birch, offshoot **2a, 2b = cane**, staff, pole, rod, stake, switch, crook, baton, wand, sceptre **4** (*slang*) **= abuse**,

DICTIONARY

special purpose: *a walking stick; a hockey stick* **3** a piece of something shaped like a stick: *a stick of cinnamon* **4** *slang* verbal abuse, criticism: *they gave me a lot of stick* **5 the sticks** a country area considered backward or unsophisticated: *places out in the sticks* **6 sticks** pieces of furniture: *these few sticks are all I have* **7** *informal* a person: *not a bad old stick* **8 get hold of the stick wrong end of the stick** to misunderstand a situation or an explanation completely
WORD ORIGIN Old English *sticca*

stick² ❶ *vb* **sticking, stuck 1** to push (a pointed object) or (of a pointed object) to be pushed into another object **2** to fasten (something) in position by pins, nails, or glue: *she just stuck the label on* **3** to extend beyond something else; protrude: *he stuck his head out of the door* **4** *informal* to place (something) in a specified position: *stick it in the oven* **5** to fasten or be fastened by or as if by an adhesive **6** to come or be brought to a standstill: *stuck in a rut; two army lorries stuck behind us* **7** to remain for a long time: *the room that sticks in my mind the most* **8** *slang, chiefly Brit* to tolerate; abide: *you couldn't stick it for more than two days* **9 be stuck** *informal* to be at a loss for; to be baffled or puzzled: *I'm stuck; stuck for words* ▸ See also **stick around, stick by**, etc.
WORD ORIGIN Old English *stician*

stick around *vb informal* to remain in a place, often when waiting for something

stick by *vb* to remain faithful to: *she's stuck by me for sixty years*

sticker *n* a small piece of paper with a picture or writing on it that can be stuck to a surface

sticking plaster *n* a piece of adhesive material used for covering slight wounds

stick insect *n* a tropical insect with a long thin body and legs, which looks like a twig

stick-in-the-mud *n informal* a person who is unwilling to try anything new or do anything exciting

stickleback *n* a small fish with sharp spines along its back
WORD ORIGIN Old English *sticel* prick, sting + BACK

stickler *n* a person who insists on something: *a stickler for punctuality*

stick out ❶ *vb* **1** to (cause to) project from something else: *she stuck her tongue out at me* **2** *informal* to endure (something unpleasant): *she would stick it out for a year* **3 stick out a mile** *or* **like a sore thumb** *informal* to be very obvious **4 stick out for** to continue to demand (something), refusing to accept anything less

stick to *vb* **1** to adhere or cause (something) to adhere to: *the soil sticks to the blade* **2** to remain faithful to (a person, promise, or rule) **3** not to move away from: *stick to the agreement*

stick-up *n slang, chiefly US* a robbery at gunpoint; hold-up

stick up for ❶ *vb informal* to support or defend (oneself, another person, or a principle)

sticky ❶ *adj* **stickier, stickiest 1** covered with a substance that sticks to other things: *sticky little fingers* **2** intended to stick to a surface: *sticky labels* **3** *informal* difficult or painful: *a sticky meeting* **4** (of weather) unpleasantly warm and humid **stickiness** *n*

sticky wicket *n* **on a sticky wicket** *informal* in a difficult situation

Stieglitz *n* **Alfred** 1864–1946, US photographer, whose work helped to develop photography as an art: among his best photographs are those of his wife Georgia O'Keeffe. He was also well known as a promoter of modern art

stiff ❶ *adj* **1** firm and not easily bent **2** moving with pain or difficulty: *stiff and aching joints* **3** not moving easily: *the door is stiff* **4** difficult or severe: *a stiff challenge; stiff penalties* **5** formal and not relaxed **6** fairly firm in consistency; thick **7** powerful: *a stiff breeze* **8** (of a drink) containing a lot of alcohol ▹ *n* **9** *slang* a corpse ▹ *adv* **10** completely or utterly: *I was bored stiff* **stiffly** *adv* **stiffness** *n*
WORD ORIGIN Old English *stīf*

stiffen *vb* to make or become stiff or stiffer

stiff-necked *adj* proud and stubborn

stifle ❶ *vb* **-fling, -fled 1** to stop oneself from expressing (a yawn or cry) **2** to stop (something) from continuing: *the new leadership stifled all internal debate* **3** to feel discomfort and difficulty in breathing **4** to kill (someone) by preventing him or her from breathing
WORD ORIGIN probably from Old French *estouffer* to smother

stifling *adj* uncomfortably hot and stuffy

stigma ❶ *n, pl* **stigmas** *or* **stigmata 1** a mark of social disgrace: *a stigma attached to being redundant* **2** *bot* the part of a flower that receives pollen **3 stigmata** *Christianity* marks resembling the wounds of the crucified Christ, believed to appear on the bodies of certain people
WORD ORIGIN Greek: brand

stigmatize *or* **-tise** *vb* **-tizing, -tized** *or* **-tising, -tised** to regard as being shameful

stile *n* a set of steps in a wall or fence to allow people, but not animals, to pass over
WORD ORIGIN Old English *stigel*

stiletto *n, pl* **-tos 1** Also called: **spike heel, stiletto heel** a high narrow heel on a woman's shoe or a shoe with such a heel **2** a small dagger with a slender tapered blade
WORD ORIGIN Italian: little dagger

S

THESAURUS

criticism, flak *(informal)*, blame, knocking *(informal)*, hostility, slagging *(slang)*, denigration, critical remarks, fault-finding

stick² *vb* **1 = poke**, dig, stab, insert, thrust, pierce, penetrate, spear, prod, jab, transfix **2, 5 = fasten**, fix, bind, hold, bond, attach, hold on, glue, fuse, paste, adhere, affix **4** *(informal)* **= put**, place, set, position, drop, plant, store, lay, stuff, fix, deposit, install, plonk **5 = adhere**, cling, cleave, become joined, become cemented, become welded **7 = stay**, remain, linger, persist **8** *(slang, chiefly Brit)* **= tolerate**, take, stand, stomach, endure, hack *(slang)*, abide, bear up under

stick out *vb* **1 = protrude**, stand out, jut out, show, project, bulge, obtrude

stick up for *vb (informal)* **= defend**, support, champion, uphold, stand up for, take the part *or* side of

sticky *adj* **1 = gooey**, tacky *(informal)*, syrupy, viscous, glutinous, gummy, icky *(informal)*, gluey, clinging, claggy *(dialect)*, viscid **2 = adhesive**, gummed, adherent **3** *(informal)* **= difficult**, awkward, tricky, embarrassing, painful, nasty, delicate, unpleasant, discomforting, hairy *(slang)*, thorny, barro *(Austral slang)* **4 = humid**, close, sultry, oppressive, sweltering, clammy, muggy

stiff *adj* **1 = inflexible**, rigid, unyielding, hard, firm, tight, solid, tense, hardened, brittle, taut, solidified, unbending, inelastic
OPPOSITE: flexible
4a = severe, strict, harsh, hard, heavy, sharp, extreme, cruel, drastic, rigorous, stringent, oppressive, austere, inexorable, pitiless **4b = difficult**, hard, tough, exacting, formidable, trying, fatiguing, uphill, arduous, laborious **5 = formal**, constrained, forced, laboured, cold, mannered, wooden, artificial, uneasy, chilly, unnatural, austere, pompous, prim, stilted, starchy *(informal)*, punctilious, priggish, standoffish, ceremonious, unrelaxed
OPPOSITE: informal

stifle *vb* **1 = restrain**, suppress, repress, smother **2 = suppress**, repress, prevent, stop, check, silence, curb, restrain, cover up, gag, hush, smother, extinguish, muffle, choke back

stigma *n* **1 = disgrace**, shame, dishonour, mark, spot, brand, stain, slur, blot, reproach, imputation, smirch

DICTIONARY

Stilicho *n* **Flavius** ?365–408 AD, Roman general and statesman, born a Vandal. As the guardian of Emperor Theodosius' son Honorius, he was effective ruler of the Western Roman Empire (395–408), which he defended against the Visigoths

still[1] ⊕ *adv* **1** continuing now or in the future as in the past: *she still loved the theatre* **2** up to this or that time; yet **3** even or yet: *still more pressure on the government* **4** even then; nevertheless: *the baby has been fed and still cries* **5** quietly or without movement: *keep still* ▹ *adj* **6** motionless; stationary **7** undisturbed; silent and calm **8** (of a soft drink) not fizzy ▹ *n* **9** *poetic* silence or tranquillity: *the still of night* **10** a still photograph from a film ▹ *vb* **11** to make or become quiet or calm **12** to relieve or end: *Fowler stilled his conscience* **stillness** *n*
WORD ORIGIN Old English *stille*

still[2] *n* an apparatus for distilling spirits
WORD ORIGIN Latin *stilla* a drip

stillborn *adj* **1** (of a baby) dead at birth **2** (of an idea or plan) completely unsuccessful **stillbirth** *n*

still life *n, pl* **still lifes** **1** a painting or drawing of objects such as fruit or flowers **2** this kind of painting or drawing

still room *n Brit* **1** a room in which distilling is carried out **2** a room for storing food in a large house

stilt *n* **1** either of a pair of long poles with footrests for walking raised from the ground **2** a long post or column used with others to support a building above ground level
WORD ORIGIN Middle English *stilte*

stilted *adj* (of speech, writing, or behaviour) formal or pompous; not flowing continuously or naturally

Stilton *n trademark* a strong-flavoured blue-veined cheese
WORD ORIGIN named after *Stilton*, Cambridgeshire

Stilwell *n* **Joseph W**(**arren**), known as *Vinegar Joe* 1883–1946, US general, who was (1941–44) Chiang Kai-shek's chief of staff and commander of all US forces in China, Burma (Myanmar), and India

stimulant *n* **1** a drug, food, or drink that makes the body work faster, increases heart rate, and makes sleeping difficult **2** any stimulating thing ▹ *adj* **3** stimulating

stimulate ⊕ *vb* **-lating, -lated** **1** to encourage to start or progress further: *a cut in interest rates should help stimulate economic recovery* **2** to fill (a person) with ideas or enthusiasm: *books satisfy a part of the intellect that needs to be stimulated* **3** *physiol* to excite (a nerve or organ) with a stimulus **stimulation** *n*
WORD ORIGIN Latin *stimulare*

stimulating ⊕ *adj* **1** inspiring new ideas or enthusiasm **2** (of a physical activity) making one feel refreshed and energetic; invigorating

stimulus ⊕ (stim-myew-luss) *n, pl* **-li** (-lie) **1** something that acts as an incentive to (someone) **2** something, such as a drug or electrical impulse, that is capable of causing a response in a person or an animal
WORD ORIGIN Latin: a cattle goad

Stine *n* **R**(**obert**) **L**(**awrence**) born 1943, US writer, noted for his numerous bestselling horror novels for older children, esp. those in the *Goosebumps* and *Fear Street* series

sting ⊕ *vb* **stinging, stung** **1** (of certain animals and plants) to inflict a wound on (someone) by the injection of poison **2** to cause (someone) to feel a sharp physical pain: *her hand was stinging* **3** to offend or upset (someone) with a critical remark: *I was stung by what he said* **4** to provoke (a response) by angering: *the consulate would be stung into convulsive action* **5** *informal* to cheat (someone) by overcharging ▹ *n* **6** a skin wound caused by stinging **7** pain caused by or as if by a sting **8** a mental pain: *the sting of memory* **9** the sharp pointed organ of certain animals or plants used to inject poison **10** *slang* a deceptive trick **11** *slang* a trap set up by the police to entice a person to commit a crime, thereby producing evidence **stinging** *adj*
WORD ORIGIN Old English *stingan*

stinging nettle *n* ▸ same as **nettle** (sense 1)

stingray *n* a flat fish with a jagged whiplike tail capable of inflicting painful wounds

stingy *adj* **-gier, -giest** very mean **stinginess** *n*
WORD ORIGIN perhaps from *stinge*, dialect variant of STING

stink ⊕ *n* **1** a strong unpleasant smell **2 make** *or* **create** *or* **kick up a stink** *slang* to make a fuss ▹ *vb* **stinking, stank** *or* **stunk; stunk** **3** to give off a strong unpleasant smell **4** *slang* to be thoroughly bad or unpleasant: *the script stinks, the casting stinks* **stinky** *adj*
WORD ORIGIN Old English *stincan*

stink bomb *n* a small glass globe used by practical jokers: it releases a liquid with a strong unpleasant smell when broken

stinker *n slang* a difficult or very unpleasant person or thing

stinking *adj* **1** having a strong unpleasant smell **2** *informal* unpleasant or disgusting ▹ *adv* **3 stinking rich** *informal* very wealthy

stink out *vb* **1** to drive (people) away by a foul smell **2** *Brit & NZ* to cause (a place) to stink: *I won't have it stinking the car out!*

stint ⊕ *vb* **1** to be miserly with (something): *don't stint on paper napkins* ▹ *n* **2** a given amount of work
WORD ORIGIN Old English *styntan* to blunt

stipend (sty-pend) *n* a regular salary or allowance, esp. that paid to a member of the clergy **stipendiary** *adj*
WORD ORIGIN Latin *stipendium* tax

stipple *vb* **-pling, -pled** to draw, engrave, or paint (something) using dots or flecks
WORD ORIGIN Dutch *stippelen*

stipulate ⊕ *vb* **-lating, -lated** to specify (something) as a condition of an agreement **stipulation** *n*

S

THESAURUS

still[1] *adv* **4 = however**, but, yet, nevertheless, for all that, notwithstanding ▹ *adj* **6 = motionless**, stationary, at rest, calm, smooth, peaceful, serene, tranquil, lifeless, placid, undisturbed, inert, restful, unruffled, unstirring **OPPOSITE:** moving **7 = silent**, quiet, hushed, noiseless, stilly *(poetic)* **OPPOSITE:** noisy ▹ *vb* **11 = quieten**, calm, subdue, settle, quiet, silence, soothe, hush, alleviate, lull, tranquillize **OPPOSITE:** get louder

stimulate *vb* **1 = encourage**, inspire, prompt, fire, fan, urge, spur, provoke, turn on *(slang)*, arouse, animate, rouse, prod, quicken, inflame, incite, instigate, goad, whet, impel, foment, gee up

stimulating *adj* **1 = exciting**, inspiring, stirring, provoking, intriguing, rousing, provocative, exhilarating, thought-provoking, galvanic **OPPOSITE:** boring

stimulus *n* **1 = incentive**, spur, encouragement, impetus, provocation, inducement, goad, incitement, fillip, shot in the arm *(informal)*, clarion call, geeing-up

sting *vb* **1 = hurt**, burn, wound **2 = smart**, burn, pain, hurt, tingle

stink *n* **1 = stench**, pong *(Brit informal)*, foul smell, foulness, malodour, fetor, noisomeness ▹ *vb* **3 = reek**, pong *(Brit informal)*, whiff *(Brit slang)*, stink to high heaven *(informal)*, offend the nostrils

stint *vb* **1 = be mean**, hold back, be sparing, scrimp, skimp on, save, withhold, begrudge, economize, be frugal, be parsimonious, be mingy *(Brit informal)*, spoil the ship for a ha'porth of tar ▹ *n* **2 = term**, time, turn, bit, period, share, tour, shift, stretch, spell, quota, assignment

stipulate *vb* **= specify**, agree, require, promise, contract, settle, guarantee, engage, pledge, lay down, covenant, postulate, insist upon, lay down *or*

DICTIONARY

WORD ORIGIN Latin *stipulari*

stir[1] ❶ *vb* **stirring, stirred 1** to mix up (a liquid) by moving a spoon or stick around in it **2** to move slightly **3 stir from** to depart (from one's usual or preferred place) **4** to get up after sleeping **5** to excite or move (someone) emotionally **6** to move (oneself) quickly or vigorously; exert (oneself) **7** to wake up: *to stir someone from sleep* ▷ *n* **8** a stirring **9** a strong reaction, usually of excitement: *she created a stir wherever she went* ▸ See also **stir up**
WORD ORIGIN Old English *styrian*

stir[2] *n chiefly US slang* prison: *in stir*
WORD ORIGIN Romany *stariben* prison

stir-crazy *adj slang* mentally disturbed as a result of being in prison

stir-fry *vb* **-fries, -frying, -fried 1** to cook (food) quickly by stirring it in a wok or frying pan over a high heat ▷ *n, pl* **-fries 2** a dish cooked in this way

Stirling[1] *n* **1** a city in central Scotland, in Stirling council area on the River Forth: its castle was a regular residence of many Scottish monarchs between the 12th century and 1603. Pop: 32 673 (2001) **2** a council area of central Scotland, created from part of Central Region in 1996; includes most of the historical county of Stirlingshire: the Forth valley rises to the Grampian Mountains in the N. Administrative centre: Stirling. Pop: 86 370 (2003 est). Area: 2173 sq km (839 sq miles)

Stirling[2] *n* Sir **James** 1926–92, British architect; buildings include the Neue Staatsgalerie in Stuttgart (1977–84)

stirrer *n informal* a person who deliberately causes trouble

stirring *adj* causing emotion, excitement, and enthusiasm

stirrup *n* a metal loop attached to a saddle for supporting a rider's foot
WORD ORIGIN Old English *stig* step + *rāp* rope

stirrup cup *n chiefly Brit* a cup containing an alcoholic drink offered to riders before a fox hunt

stirrup pump *n* a hand-operated pump, the base of which is placed in a bucket of water: used in fighting fires

stir up *vb* **1** to cause (leaves or dust) to rise up and swirl around **2** to set (something) in motion: *that fact has stirred up resentment*

stitch *n* **1** a link made by drawing a thread through material with a needle **2** a loop of yarn formed around a needle or hook in knitting or crocheting **3** a particular kind of stitch **4** *informal* a link of thread joining the edges of a wound together **5** a sharp pain in the side caused by running or exercising **6 in stitches** *informal* laughing uncontrollably **7 not a stitch** *informal* no clothes at all ▷ *vb* **8** to sew or fasten (something) with stitches **stitching** *n*
WORD ORIGIN Old English *stice* sting

stitch up *vb* **1** to join by stitching **2** *slang* to incriminate by manufacturing evidence **3** *slang* to prearrange in a clandestine manner ▷ *n* **stitch-up 4** *slang* a matter that has been prearranged clandestinely

stoat *n* a small brown N European mammal related to the weasel: in winter it has a white coat and is then known as an ermine
WORD ORIGIN origin unknown

stock ❶ *n* **1** the total amount of goods kept on the premises of a shop or business **2** a supply of something stored for future use **3** *finance* **a** the money raised by a company through selling shares entitling their holders to dividends, partial ownership, and usually voting rights **b** the proportion of this money held by an individual shareholder **c** the shares of a specified company or industry **4** farm animals bred and kept for their meat, skins, etc. **5** the original type from which a particular race, family, or group is descended **6** the handle of a rifle, held by the firer against the shoulder **7** a liquid produced by simmering meat, fish, bones, or vegetables, and used to make soups and sauces **8** a kind of plant grown for its brightly coloured flowers **9** *old-fashioned* the degree of status a person has **10** ▸ see **laughing stock 11 in stock** stored on the premises or available for sale or use **12 out of stock** not immediately available for sale or use **13 take stock** to think carefully about a situation before making a decision ▷ *adj* **14** staple; standard: *stock sizes in clothes* **15** being a cliché; hackneyed: *the stock answer* ▷ *vb* **16** to keep (goods) for sale **17** to obtain a store of (something) for future use or sale: *to stock up on food* **18** to supply (a farm) with animals or (a lake or stream) with fish ▸ See also **stocks**
WORD ORIGIN Old English *stocc* tree trunk

stockade *n* an enclosure or barrier of large wooden posts
WORD ORIGIN Spanish *estacada*

stockbreeder *n* a person who breeds or rears farm animals

stockbroker *n* a person who buys and sells stocks and shares for customers and receives a percentage of their profits **stockbroking** *n*

stock car *n* a car that has been strengthened and modified for a form of racing in which the cars often collide

stock cube *n* a small solid cube made from dried meat or vegetables, used to add flavouring to stew, soup, etc.

stock exchange *n* **1 a** a highly organized market for the purchase and sale of stocks and shares, operated by professional stockbrokers and market makers according to fixed rules **b** a place where stocks and shares are traded **2** the prices or trading activity of a stock exchange: *the stock exchange has been rising*

stockholder *n* an owner of some of a company's stock

stockinette *n* a machine-knitted elastic fabric
WORD ORIGIN perhaps from *stocking-net*

stocking *n* a long piece of close-fitting nylon or knitted yarn covering the foot and part or all of a woman's leg
WORD ORIGIN dialect *stock* stocking

stockinged *adj* **in one's stockinged feet** wearing stockings, tights, or socks but no shoes

stocking stitch *n* alternate rows of plain and purl in knitting

stock in trade *n* a person's typical behaviour or usual work: *practicality is the farmer's stock in trade*

THESAURUS

impose conditions

stir[1] *vb* **1 = mix**, beat, agitate **5 = stimulate**, move, excite, fire, raise, touch, affect, urge, inspire, prompt, spur, thrill, provoke, arouse, awaken, animate, rouse, prod, quicken, inflame, incite, instigate, electrify, kindle **OPPOSITE:** inhibit ▷ *n* **9 = commotion**, to-do, excitement, activity, movement, disorder, fuss, disturbance, bustle, flurry, uproar, ferment, agitation, ado, tumult

stock *n* **1 = goods**, merchandise, wares, range, choice, variety, selection, commodities, array, assortment **2 = supply**, store, reserve, fund, reservoir, stockpile, hoard, cache **3** *(finance)* **a = property**, capital, assets, funds **3b, 3c = shares**, holdings, securities, investments, bonds, equities **4 = livestock**, cattle, beasts, domestic animals ▷ *adj* **14 = regular**, traditional, usual, basic, ordinary, conventional, staple, customary **15 = hackneyed**, standard, usual, set, routine, stereotyped, staple, commonplace, worn-out, banal, run-of-the-mill, trite, overused ▷ *vb* **16 = sell**, supply, handle, keep, trade in, deal in **18 = fill**, supply, provide with, provision, equip, furnish, fit out, kit out

S

DICTIONARY

stockist *n Brit commerce* a dealer who stocks a particular product
stock market *n* ▸ same as **stock exchange**
stockpile *vb* **-piling, -piled 1** to store a large quantity of (something) for future use ▹ *n* **2** a large store gathered for future use
stockpot *n Brit & NZ* a pot in which stock for soup is made
stockroom *n* a room in which a stock of goods is kept in a shop or factory
stock route *n Austral & NZ* a route designated for droving farm animals, so as to avoid traffic
stocks *pl n history* an instrument of punishment consisting of a heavy wooden frame with holes in which the feet, hands, or head of an offender were locked
stock-still *adv* absolutely still; motionlessly
stocktaking *n* **1** the counting and valuing of goods in a shop or business **2** a reassessment of a person's current situation and prospects
Stockwood *n* **(Arthur) Mervyn** 1913–95, British Anglican prelate; bishop of Southwark (1959–80)
stocky *adj* **stockier, stockiest** (of a person) short but well-built **stockily** *adv* **stockiness** *n*
stockyard *n* a large yard with pens or covered buildings where farm animals are sold
stodge *n Brit, Austral & NZ informal* heavy and filling starchy food
WORD ORIGIN perhaps blend of STUFF + *podge* a short plump person
stodgy *adj* **stodgier, stodgiest 1** (of food) full of starch and very filling **2** (of a person) dull, serious, or excessively formal **stodginess** *n*
WORD ORIGIN from STODGE
stoep (stoop) *n* (in South Africa) a verandah
WORD ORIGIN Afrikaans
stoic (stow-ik) *n* **1** a person who suffers great difficulties without showing his or her emotions ▹ *adj* **2** ▸ same as **stoical**
Stoic *n* **1** a member of the ancient Greek school of philosophy which believed that virtue and happiness could be achieved only by calmly accepting Fate ▹ *adj* **2** of or relating to the Stoics **Stoicism** *n*
WORD ORIGIN Greek *stoa* porch
stoical *adj* suffering great difficulties without showing one's feelings **stoically** *adv* **stoicism** (stow-iss-iz-zum) *n*
stoke *vb* **stoking, stoked 1** to feed and tend (a fire or furnace) **2** to excite or encourage (a strong emotion) in oneself or someone else
WORD ORIGIN from STOKER
stokehold *n naut* the hold for a ship's boilers; fire room
stoker *n* a person employed to tend a furnace on a ship or train powered by steam
WORD ORIGIN Dutch *stoken* to stoke
Stoker *n* **Bram,** original name *Abraham Stoker* 1847–1912, Irish novelist, author of *Dracula* (1897)
Stokowski *n* **Leopold** 1887–1977, US conductor, born in Britain. He did much to popularize classical music with orchestral transcriptions and film appearances, esp. in *Fantasia* (1940)
stole[1] *vb* ▸ the past tense of **steal**
stole[2] *n* a long scarf or shawl, worn by women
WORD ORIGIN Greek *stolē* clothing
stolen *vb* ▸ the past participle of **steal**
stolid *adj* showing little or no emotion or interest in anything **stolidity** *n* **stolidly** *adv*
WORD ORIGIN Latin *stolidus* dull
Stolypin *n* **Petr Arkadievich** 1863–1911, Russian conservative statesman: prime minister (1906–11). He instituted agrarian reforms but was ruthless in suppressing rebellion: assassinated
stoma (stow-ma) *n, pl* **stomata** (stow-ma-ta) **1** *bot* a pore in a plant leaf that controls the passage of gases into and out of the plant **2** *zool* a mouth or mouthlike part
WORD ORIGIN Greek: mouth
stomach ❶ *n* **1** an organ inside the body in which food is stored until it has been partially digested **2** the front of the body around the waist **3** desire or appetite: *he still has the stomach for a fight* ▹ *vb* **4** to put up with: *liberals could not stomach the rest of the package*
WORD ORIGIN Greek *stoma* mouth
stomachache *n* pain in the stomach, such as from indigestion. Also called: **stomach upset, upset stomach**
stomacher *n history* a decorative V-shaped panel of stiff material worn over the chest and stomach mainly by women
stomach pump *n med* a pump with a long tube used for removing the contents of a person's stomach, for instance after he or she has swallowed poison
stomp *vb* to tread or stamp heavily
WORD ORIGIN variant of STAMP
stompie *n S African slang* **1** a cigarette butt **2** a short man
WORD ORIGIN Afrikaans *stomp* stump
stone ❶ *n* **1** the hard nonmetallic material of which rocks are made **2** a small lump of rock **3** Also called: **gemstone** a precious or semiprecious stone that has been cut and polished **4** a piece of rock used for some particular purpose: *gravestone; millstone* **5** the hard central part of fruits such as the peach or date **6** *pl* **stone** *Brit* a unit of weight equal to 14 pounds or 6.350 kilograms **7** *pathol* a hard deposit formed in the kidney or bladder **8** **heart of stone** a hard or unemotional personality **9** **leave no stone unturned** to do everything possible to achieve something ▹ *adj* **10** made of stoneware: *the polished stone planter* ▹ *vb* **stoning, stoned 11** to throw stones at (someone), for example as a punishment **12** to remove the stones from (a fruit)
WORD ORIGIN Old English *stān*
Stone *n* **1 Oliver** born 1946, US film director and screenwriter: his films include *Platoon* (1986), *Born on the Fourth of July* (1989), *JFK* (1991), *Nixon* (1995), and *Alexander* (2004) **2 Sharon** born 1958, US film actress: her films include *Basic Instinct* (1991), *Casino* (1995), and *Cold Creek Manor* (2003)
Stone Age *n* a phase of human culture identified by the use of tools made of stone
stonechat *n* a songbird that has black feathers and a reddish-brown breast
WORD ORIGIN from its cry, which sounds like clattering pebbles
stone-cold *adj* **1** completely cold ▹ *adv* **2** **stone-cold sober** completely sober
stoned *adj slang* under the influence of drugs or alcohol
stone-deaf *adj* completely deaf
stone fruit *n* ▸ same as **drupe**
stoneground *adj* **1** (of flour) made by crushing grain between two large stones **2** made with stoneground flour: *stoneground wholemeal bread*
stonemason *n* a person who is skilled in preparing stone for building
Stones *pl n* **the.** ▸ See **Rolling Stones**
stone's throw *n* a short distance
stonewall *vb* **1** to deliberately prolong a discussion by being long-winded or evasive **2** *cricket* (of a batsman) to play defensively
stoneware *n* a hard type of pottery, fired at a very high temperature
stonewashed *adj* (of clothes or fabric) given a worn faded look by being washed with many small pieces of stone

THESAURUS

stomach *n* **1 = belly,** inside(s) *(informal),* gut *(informal),* abdomen, tummy *(informal),* puku (NZ) **2 = tummy,** pot, spare tyre *(informal),* paunch, breadbasket *(slang),* potbelly **3 = inclination,** taste, desire, appetite, relish, mind ▹ *vb* **4 = bear,** take, tolerate, suffer, endure, swallow, hack *(slang),* abide, put up with *(informal),* submit to, reconcile *or* resign yourself to
stone *n* **1 = masonry,** rock **2 = rock,**

S

DICTIONARY

stonework *n* any structure or part of a building made of stone
stonkered *adj NZ slang* completely exhausted or beaten; whacked
WORD ORIGIN from *stonker* to beat, of unknown origin
stony *or* **stoney** *adj* **stonier, stoniest** **1** (of ground) rough and covered with stones: *the stony path* **2** (of a face, voice, or attitude) unfriendly and unsympathetic **stonily** *adv*
stony-broke *adj slang* completely without money
stood *vb* ▸the past of **stand**
stooge *n* **1** an actor who feeds lines to a comedian or acts as the butt of his jokes **2** *slang* someone who is taken advantage of by someone in a superior position
WORD ORIGIN origin unknown
stool *n* **1** a seat with legs but no back **2** waste matter from the bowels
WORD ORIGIN Old English *stōl*
stool pigeon *n* an informer for the police
stoop[1] ❶ *vb* **1** to bend (the body) forward and downward **2** to stand or walk with head and shoulders habitually bent forward **3** **stoop to** to lower one's standards of behaviour; degrade oneself: *no real journalist would stoop to faking* ▹*n* **4** the act, position, or habit of stooping **stooping** *adj*
WORD ORIGIN Old English *stūpian*
stoop[2] *n US* an open porch or small platform with steps leading up to it at the entrance to a building
WORD ORIGIN Dutch *stoep*
stop ❶ *vb* **stopping, stopped** **1** to cease from doing (something); discontinue **2** to cause (something moving) to halt or (of something moving) to come to a halt **3** to prevent the continuance or completion of (something) **4** (often foll. by *from*) to prevent or restrain: *I stopped her from going on any further* **5** to keep back: *no agreement to stop arms supplies* **6** **stop up** to block or plug: *to stop up a pipe* **7** to stay or rest: *we stopped at a camp site for a change* **8** to instruct a bank not to honour (a cheque) **9** to deduct (money) from pay **10** *informal* to receive (a blow or hit) **11** *music* to alter the vibrating length of (a string on a violin, guitar, etc.) by pressing down on it at some point with the finger **12** **stop at nothing** to be prepared to do anything; be ruthless ▹*n* **13** prevention of movement or progress: *you can put a stop to it quite easily* **14** the act of stopping or the state of being stopped: *the car lurched to a stop* **15** a place where something halts or pauses: *a bus stop* **16** the act or an instance of blocking or obstructing **17** a device that prevents, limits, or ends the motion of a mechanism or moving part **18** *Brit* a full stop **19** *music* a knob on an organ that is operated to allow sets of pipes to sound **20** **pull out all the stops** to make a great effort
WORD ORIGIN Old English *stoppian* (unattested)
stopbank *n NZ* an embankment to prevent flooding
stopcock *n* a valve used to control or stop the flow of a fluid in a pipe
stopgap *n* a thing that serves as a substitute for a short time until replaced by something more suitable
stop off *vb* (often foll. by *at*) to halt and call somewhere on the way to another place
stopover *n* **1** a break in a journey ▹*vb* **stop over** **2** to make a stopover
stoppage *n* **1** the act of stopping something or the state of being stopped: *a heart stoppage* **2** a deduction of money, such as taxation, from pay **3** an organized stopping of work during industrial action
stoppage time *n chiefly Brit* ▸same as **injury time**
stopper *n* a plug for closing a bottle, pipe, etc.
stop press *n* news items inserted into a newspaper after the printing has been started
stopwatch *n* a watch which can be stopped instantly for exact timing of a sporting event
storage *n* **1** the act of storing or the state of being stored **2** space for storing **3** *computers* the process of storing information in a computer
storage device *n* a piece of computer equipment, such as a magnetic tape or a disk in or on which information can be stored
storage heater *n* an electric device that accumulates and radiates heat generated by cheap off-peak electricity
store ❶ *vb* **storing, stored** **1** to keep, set aside, or gather (things) for future use **2** to place furniture or other possessions in a warehouse for safekeeping **3** to supply or stock (certain goods) **4** *computers* to enter or keep (information) in a storage device ▹*n* **5** a shop (in Britain usually a large one) **6** a large supply or stock kept for future use **7** ▸short for **department store** **8** a storage place, such as a warehouse **9** *computers, chiefly Brit* ▸same as **memory** (sense 7) **10** **in store** about to happen; forthcoming: *you've got a treat in store* **11** **set great store by something** to value something as important ▸See also **stores**
WORD ORIGIN Old French *estor*
storehouse *n* **1** a building where goods are stored **2** a collection of things or ideas: *a storehouse of memories*
storeroom *n* a room in which things are stored
stores *pl n* supply or stock of food and other essentials for a journey
storey *or esp. US* **story** *n, pl* **-reys** *or* **-ries** a floor or level of a building
WORD ORIGIN Anglo-Latin *historia* picture, probably from the pictures on medieval windows
Storey *n* **David** (**Malcolm**) born 1933, British novelist and dramatist. His best-known works include the novels *This Sporting Life* (1960) and *A Serious Man* (1998) and the plays *In Celebration* (1969), *Home* (1970), and *Stages* (1992)

S

THESAURUS

pebble **5 = pip**, seed, pit, kernel
stoop[1] *vb* **1 = bend**, lean, bow, duck, descend, incline, kneel, crouch, squat **2 = hunch**, be bowed *or* round-shouldered ▹*n* **4 = slouch**, slump, droop, sag, bad posture, round-shoulderedness
stop *vb* **1a = quit**, cease, refrain, break off, put an end to, pack in *(Brit informal)*, discontinue, leave off, call it a day *(informal)*, desist, belay *(naut)*, bring *or* come to a halt *or* standstill **OPPOSITE:** start
1b = end, conclude, finish, be over, cut out *(informal)*, terminate, come to an end, peter out **OPPOSITE:** continue
1c = cease, shut down, discontinue, desist **OPPOSITE:** continue
2 = halt, pause, stall, draw up, pull up **OPPOSITE:** keep going
3 = prevent, suspend, cut short, close, break, check, bar, arrest, silence, frustrate, axe *(informal)*, interrupt, restrain, hold back, intercept, hinder, repress, impede, rein in, forestall, nip (something) in the bud **OPPOSITE:** facilitate
7 = stay, rest, put up, lodge, sojourn *(literary)*, tarry, break your journey ▹*n* **14 = halt**, standstill **15 = station**, stage, halt, destination, depot, termination, terminus
store *vb* **1a = put by**, save, hoard, keep, stock, husband, reserve, deposit, accumulate, garner, stockpile, put aside, stash *(informal)*, salt away, keep in reserve, put aside for a rainy day, lay by *or* in **1b = keep**, hold, preserve, maintain, retain, conserve **2 = put away**, put in storage, put in store, lock away ▹*n* **5 = shop**, outlet, department store, market, supermarket, mart, emporium, chain store, hypermarket **6 = supply**, stock, reserve, lot, fund, mine, plenty, provision, wealth, quantity, reservoir, abundance, accumulation, stockpile, hoard, plethora, cache **8 = repository**, warehouse, depot, storehouse, depository, storeroom

DICTIONARY

stork *n* a large wading bird with very long legs, a long bill, and white-and-black feathers
WORD ORIGIN Old English *storc*

storm ❶ *n* **1** a violent weather condition of strong winds, rain, hail, thunder, lightning, etc. **2** a violent disturbance or quarrel: *a storm of protest from the opposition* **3** (usually foll. by *of*) a heavy discharge of bullets or missiles **4** **take a place by storm** **a** to capture or overrun a place by a violent attack **b** to surprise people, but receive their praise, by being extremely successful at something ▷*vb* **5** to attack or capture (a place) suddenly and violently **6** to shout angrily **7** to move or rush violently or angrily: *she stormed into the study*
WORD ORIGIN Old English

storm centre *n* **1** the centre of a storm, where pressure is lowest **2** the centre of any disturbance or trouble

storm door *n* an additional door outside an ordinary door, providing extra protection against wind, cold, and rain

storm trooper *n* a member of the paramilitary wing of the Nazi Party

stormy ❶ *adj* **stormier, stormiest** **1** (of weather) violent with dark skies, heavy rain or snow, and strong winds **2** involving violent emotions: *a stormy affair*

stormy petrel *or* **storm petrel** *n* **1** a small sea bird with dark feathers and paler underparts **2** a person who brings trouble

story[1] ❶ *n, pl* **-ries** **1** a description of a chain of events told or written in prose or verse **2** Also called: **short story** a piece of fiction, shorter and usually less detailed than a novel **3** Also called: **story line** the plot of a book or film **4** a news report **5** the event or material for such a report **6** *informal* a lie
WORD ORIGIN Latin *historia*

story[2] *n, pl* **-ries** *chiefly US* ▸same as **storey**

storybook *n* **1** a book containing stories for children ▷*adj* **2** better or happier than in real life: *a storybook romance*

Stoss *n* **Viet** ?1445–1533, German Gothic sculptor and woodcarver. His masterpiece is the high altar in the Church of St Mary, Cracow (1477–89)

stoup *or* **stoop** (stoop) *n* a small basin in a church for holy water
WORD ORIGIN from Old Norse

stoush *Austral & NZ slang vb* **1** to hit or punch (someone) ▷*n* **2** fighting or violence
WORD ORIGIN origin unknown

stout ❶ *adj* **1** solidly built or fat **2** strong and sturdy: *stout footwear* **3** brave or determined: *we met unexpectedly stout resistance* ▷*n* **4** strong dark beer **stoutly** *adv*
WORD ORIGIN Old French *estout* bold

Stout *n* Sir **Robert** 1844–1930, New Zealand statesman, born in Scotland: prime minister of New Zealand (1884–87)

stouthearted *adj old-fashioned* determined or brave

stove[1] *n* **1** ▸same as **cooker** (sense 1) **2** any apparatus for heating, such as a kiln
WORD ORIGIN Old English *stofa* bathroom

stove[2] *vb* ▸a past tense and past participle of **stave**

stovepipe *n* a pipe that takes fumes and smoke away from a stove

stow *vb* (often foll. by *away*) to pack or store (something)
WORD ORIGIN Old English *stōwian* to keep

Stow *n* **John** 1525–1605, English antiquary, noted for his *Survey of London and Westminster* (1598; 1603)

stowage *n* **1** space, room, or a charge for stowing goods **2** the act of stowing

stowaway *n* **1** a person who hides aboard a ship or aircraft in order to travel free ▷*vb* **stow away** **2** to travel in such a way: *he stowed away on a ferry*

Stowe[1] *n* a mansion near Buckingham in N Buckinghamshire: built and decorated in the 17th and 18th centuries by Vanbrugh, Robert Adam, Grinling Gibbons, and William Kent; formerly the seat of the Dukes of Buckingham; fine landscaped gardens: now occupied by a public school

Stowe[2] *n* **Harriet Elizabeth Beecher** 1811–96, US writer, whose bestselling novel *Uncle Tom's Cabin* (1852) contributed to the antislavery cause

strabismus *n pathol* ▸same as **squint** (sense 3)
WORD ORIGIN Greek *strabismos*

Strabo *n* ?63 BC–?23 AD, Greek geographer and historian, noted for his *Geographica*

Strachey *n* (**Giles**) **Lytton** 1880–1932, English biographer and critic, best known for *Eminent Victorians* (1918) and *Queen Victoria* (1921)

straddle *vb* **-dling, -dled** **1** to have one leg or part on each side of (something) **2** *US & Canad informal* to be in favour of both sides of (an issue or argument)
WORD ORIGIN from *stride*

Stradivarius *n* a violin manufactured in Italy by Antonio Stradivari (?1644–1737) or his family

strafe *vb* **strafing, strafed** to machine-gun (an enemy) from the air
WORD ORIGIN German *strafen* to punish

Strafford *n* **Thomas Wentworth,** Earl of. 1593–1641, English statesman. As lord deputy of Ireland (1632–39) and a chief adviser to Charles I, he was a leading proponent of the king's absolutist rule. He was impeached by Parliament and executed

straggle *vb* **-gling, -gled** **1** to spread out in an untidy and rambling way: *the town straggled off to the east* **2** to linger behind or wander from a main line or part **straggler** *n* **straggly** *adj*
WORD ORIGIN origin unknown

straight ❶ *adj* **1** continuing in the same direction without bending; not curved or crooked **2** even, level, or upright **3** in keeping with the facts;

S

THESAURUS

storm *n* **1 = tempest**, blast, hurricane, gale, tornado, cyclone, blizzard, whirlwind, gust, squall **2 = outburst**, row, stir, outcry, furore, violence, anger, passion, outbreak, turmoil, disturbance, strife, clamour, agitation, commotion, rumpus, tumult, hubbub ▷*vb* **5 = attack**, charge, rush, assault, beset, assail, take by storm **6 = rage**, fume, rant, complain, thunder, rave, scold, bluster, go ballistic *(slang, chiefly US)*, fly off the handle *(informal)*, wig out *(slang)* **7 = rush**, stamp, flounce, fly, stalk, stomp *(informal)*

stormy *adj* **1a = wild**, rough, tempestuous, raging, dirty, foul, turbulent, windy, blustering, blustery, gusty, inclement, squally **1b = rough**, wild, turbulent, tempestuous, raging **2 = angry**, heated, fierce, passionate, fiery, impassioned, tumultuous

story[1] *n* **1 = anecdote**, account, tale, report, detail, relation **2 = tale**, romance, narrative, record, history, version, novel, legend, chronicle, yarn, recital, narration, urban myth, urban legend, fictional account **4 = report**, news, article, feature, scoop, news item

stout *adj* **1 = fat**, big, heavy, overweight, plump, bulky, substantial, burly, obese, fleshy, tubby, portly, rotund, corpulent, on the large *or* heavy side **OPPOSITE:** slim **2 = strong**, strapping, muscular, tough, substantial, athletic, hardy, robust, vigorous, sturdy, stalwart, husky *(informal)*, hulking, beefy *(informal)*, lusty, brawny, thickset, able-bodied **OPPOSITE:** puny **3 = brave**, bold, courageous, fearless, resolute, gallant, intrepid, valiant, plucky, doughty, indomitable, dauntless, lion-hearted, valorous **OPPOSITE:** timid

straight *adj* **1 = direct**, unswerving, undeviating **OPPOSITE:** indirect **2 = level**, even, right, square, true,

DICTIONARY

accurate **4** outright or candid: *a straight rejection* **5** in continuous succession **6** (of an alcoholic drink) undiluted **7** not wavy or curly: *straight hair* **8** in good order **9** (of a play or acting style) straightforward or serious **10** honest, respectable, or reliable **11** *slang* heterosexual **12** *slang* conventional in views, customs, or appearance **13** *informal* no longer owing or being owed something: *if you buy the next round we'll be straight* ▷ *adv* **14** in a straight line or direct course **15** immediately; at once: *get straight back here* **16** in a level or upright position: *he sat up straight* **17** continuously; uninterruptedly: *we waited for three hours straight* **18** (often foll. by *out*) frankly; candidly: *she asked me straight out* **19** **go straight** *informal* to reform after having been a criminal **20** **straight away** *or* **straightaway** at once ▷ *n* **21** a straight line, form, part, or position **22** *Brit* a straight part of a racetrack **23** *slang* a heterosexual person
WORD ORIGIN Old English *streccan* to stretch

straighten ❶ *vb* (sometimes foll. by *up* or *out*) **1** to make or become straight **2** to make (something) neat or tidy

straighten out *vb* to make (something) less complicated or confused

straight face *n* a serious facial expression which hides a desire to laugh **straight-faced** *adj*

straight fight *n* a contest between two candidates only

straightforward ❶ *adj* **1** (of a person) honest, frank, and open **2** (of a task) easy to do

straight man *n* an actor who acts as the butt of a comedian's jokes

strain¹ ❶ *n* **1** tension or tiredness resulting from overwork or worry **2** tension between people or organizations: *there are signs of strain between the economic superpowers* **3** an intense physical or mental effort **4** the damage resulting from excessive physical exertion **5** a great demand on the emotions, strength, or resources **6** a way of speaking: *he would have gone on in this strain for some time* **7** *physics* the change in dimension of a body caused by outside forces **8** **strains** *music* a theme, melody, or tune ▷ *vb* **9** to subject (someone) to mental tension or stress **10** to make an intense effort: *the rest were straining to follow the conversation* **11** to use (resources) to, or beyond, their limits **12** to injure or damage (oneself or a part of one's body) by overexertion: *he appeared to have strained a muscle* **13** to pour (a substance) through a sieve or filter **14** **strain at** to push, pull, or work with violent effort (on something) **15** to draw (something) taut or be drawn taut
WORD ORIGIN Latin *stringere* to bind tightly

strain² ❶ *n* **1** a group of animals or plants within a species or variety, distinguished by one or more minor characteristics **2** a trace or streak: *a strain of ruthlessness in their play*
WORD ORIGIN Old English *strēon*

strained ❶ *adj* **1** (of an action, expression, etc.) not natural or spontaneous **2** (of an atmosphere, relationship, etc.) not relaxed; tense

strainer *n* a sieve used for straining sauces, vegetables, or tea

strait ❶ *n* **1** (*often pl*) a narrow channel of the sea linking two larger areas of sea **2** **straits** a position of extreme difficulty: *in desperate straits*
WORD ORIGIN Old French *estreit* narrow

straitened *adj* **in straitened circumstances** not having much money

straitjacket *n* **1** a strong canvas jacket with long sleeves used to bind the arms of a violent person **2** anything which holds back or restricts development or freedom: *exporters are wrapped in a straitjacket of regulations*

strait-laced *or* **straight-laced** *adj* having a strict code of moral standards; puritanical

strand¹ *vb* **1** to leave or drive (ships or fish) ashore **2** to leave (someone) helpless, for example without

THESAURUS

smooth, in line, aligned, horizontal **OPPOSITE:** crooked
4 = frank, plain, straightforward, blunt, outright, honest, downright, candid, forthright, bold, point-blank, upfront *(informal)*, unqualified **OPPOSITE:** evasive
5 = successive, consecutive, continuous, through, running, solid, sustained, uninterrupted, nonstop, unrelieved **OPPOSITE:** discontinuous
6 = undiluted, pure, neat, unadulterated, unmixed **8 = in order**, organized, arranged, sorted out, neat, tidy, orderly, shipshape, put to rights **OPPOSITE:** untidy
10 = honest, just, fair, decent, reliable, respectable, upright, honourable, equitable, law-abiding, trustworthy, above board, fair and square **OPPOSITE:** dishonest
12 *(slang)* **= conventional**, conservative, orthodox, traditional, square *(informal)*, bourgeois, Pooterish **OPPOSITE:** fashionable
▷ *adv* **14 = directly**, precisely, exactly, as the crow flies, unswervingly, by the shortest route, in a beeline
15 = immediately, directly, promptly, instantly, at once, straight away, without delay, without hesitation, forthwith, unhesitatingly, before you could say Jack Robinson *(informal)*

straight away **20 = immediately**, now, at once, directly, instantly, on the spot, right away, there and then, this minute, straightway *(archaic)*, without more ado, without any delay

straighten *vb* **2 = neaten**, arrange, tidy (up), order, spruce up, smarten up, put in order, set *or* put to rights

straightforward *adj* **1 = honest**, open, direct, genuine, sincere, candid, truthful, forthright, upfront *(informal)*, dinkum *(Austral & NZ informal)*, above board, guileless **OPPOSITE:** devious
2 = simple, easy, uncomplicated, routine, elementary, clear-cut, undemanding, easy-peasy *(slang)* **OPPOSITE:** complicated

strain¹ *n* **1 = stress**, pressure, anxiety, difficulty, distress, nervous tension
3 = worry, effort, struggle, tension, hassle **OPPOSITE:** ease
4 = injury, wrench, sprain, pull, tension, tautness, tensity *(rare)*
5 = pressure, stress, difficulty, demands, burden, adversity ▷ *vb*
10 = strive, struggle, endeavour, labour, go for it *(informal)*, bend over backwards *(informal)*, go for broke *(slang)*, go all out for *(informal)*, bust a gut *(informal)*, give it your best shot *(informal)*, make an all-out effort *(informal)*, knock yourself out *(informal)*, do your damnedest *(informal)*, give it your all *(informal)*, break your back *or* neck *(informal)*, rupture yourself *(informal)* **OPPOSITE:** relax
11 = stretch, test, tax, overtax, push to the limit **13 = sieve**, filter, sift, screen, separate, riddle, purify

strain² *n* **1 = breed**, type, stock, family, race, blood, descent, pedigree, extraction, ancestry, lineage
2 = trace, suggestion, suspicion, tendency, streak, trait

strained *adj* **1 = forced**, put on, false, artificial, unnatural, laboured **OPPOSITE:** natural
2 = tense, difficult, uncomfortable, awkward, embarrassed, stiff, uneasy, constrained, self-conscious, unrelaxed **OPPOSITE:** relaxed

strait *n* **1** *(often pl)* **= channel**, sound, narrows, stretch of water, sea passage ▷ *pl n* **2 = difficulty**, crisis, mess, pass, hole *(slang)*, emergency, distress, dilemma, embarrassment, plight, hardship, uphill *(S African)*, predicament, extremity, perplexity, panic stations *(informal)*, pretty *or* fine kettle of fish *(informal)*

strand² *n* **1, 2 = filament**, fibre, thread, length, lock, string, twist, rope, wisp, tress

S

DICTIONARY

transport or money ▷ *n* **3** *chiefly poetic* a shore or beach
WORD ORIGIN Old English

strand² ❶ *n* **1** one of the individual fibres of string or wire that form a rope, cord, or cable **2** a single length of string, hair, wool, or wire **3** a string of pearls or beads **4** a part of something; element: *the many disparate strands of the Anglican Church*
WORD ORIGIN origin unknown

stranded ❶ *adj* stuck somewhere and unable to leave

strange ❶ *adj* **1** odd or unexpected **2** not known, seen, or experienced before; unfamiliar **3 strange to** inexperienced (in) or unaccustomed (to): *they are in some degree strange to it* **strangely** *adv* **strangeness** *n*
WORD ORIGIN Latin *extraneus* foreign

stranger ❶ *n* **1** any person whom one does not know **2** a person who is new to a particular place **3 stranger to** a person who is unfamiliar with or new to something: *Paul is no stranger to lavish spending*

strangle ❶ *vb* **-gling, -gled 1** to kill (someone) by pressing his or her windpipe; throttle **2** to prevent the growth or development of: *another attempt at strangling national identity* **3** to stifle (a voice, cry, or laugh) by swallowing suddenly: *the words were strangled by sobs* **strangler** *n*
WORD ORIGIN Greek *strangalē* a halter

stranglehold *n* **1** a wrestling hold in which a wrestler's arms are pressed against his opponent's windpipe **2** complete power or control over a person or situation

strangulate *vb* **-lating, -lated 1** *pathol* to constrict (a hollow organ or vessel) so as to stop the flow of air or blood through it: *a badly strangulated hernia* **2** ▸ same as **strangle** > **strangulation** *n*

strap ❶ *n* **1** a strip of strong flexible material used for carrying, lifting, fastening, or holding things in place **2** a loop of leather or rubber, hanging from the roof in a bus or train for standing passengers to hold on to **3** ▸ short for **shoulder strap 4 the strap** a beating with a strap as a punishment ▷ *vb* **strapping, strapped 5** to tie or bind (something) with a strap
WORD ORIGIN variant of STROP

straphanger *n informal* a passenger in a bus or train who has to travel standing and holding on to a strap

strapless *adj* (of women's clothes) without straps over the shoulders

strapped *adj* **strapped for** *slang* badly in need of: *strapped for cash*

strapping ❶ *adj* tall, strong, and healthy-looking: *a strapping young lad*
WORD ORIGIN from *strap* (in the archaic sense: to work vigorously)

strata *n* ▸ the plural of **stratum**

stratagem *n* a clever plan to deceive an enemy
WORD ORIGIN Greek *stratēgos* a general

strategic ❶ (strat-ee-jik) *adj* **1** planned to achieve an advantage; tactical **2** (of weapons, esp. missiles) directed against an enemy's homeland rather than used on a battlefield **strategically** *adv*

strategy ❶ *n, pl* **-gies 1** a long-term plan for success, such as in politics or business **2** the art of the planning and conduct of a war **strategist** *n*
WORD ORIGIN Greek *stratēgia* function of a general

strath *n Scot* a flat river valley
WORD ORIGIN Scottish & Irish Gaelic *srath*

strathspey *n* **1** a Scottish dance with gliding steps, slower than a reel **2** music for this dance
WORD ORIGIN after *Strathspey*, valley of the River Spey

stratified *adj* **1** (of rocks) formed in horizontal layers of different materials **2** *sociol* (of a society) divided into different classes or groups **stratification** *n*
WORD ORIGIN New Latin *stratificare* to form in layers

stratocumulus (strat-oh-kew-myew-luss) *n, pl* **-li** (-lie) *meteorol* an unbroken stretch of dark grey cloud

stratosphere *n* the atmospheric layer between about 15 and 50 km above the earth

stratum (strah-tum) *n, pl* **-ta** (-ta) **1** any of the distinct layers into which certain rocks are divided **2** a layer of ocean or atmosphere marked off naturally or decided arbitrarily by man **3** a social class
WORD ORIGIN Latin: something strewn

stratus (stray-tuss) *n, pl* **-ti** (-tie) a grey layer cloud
WORD ORIGIN Latin: strewn

Straus *n* **Oscar** 1870–1954, French composer, born in Austria, noted for such operettas as *Waltz Dream* (1907) and *The Chocolate Soldier* (1908)

straw *n* **1** dried stalks of threshed grain, such as wheat or barley **2** a single stalk of straw **3** a long thin hollow paper or plastic tube, used for sucking up liquids into the mouth **4 clutch at straws** to turn in desperation to something with little chance of success **5 draw the short straw** to be the person chosen to perform an unpleasant task ▷ *adj* **6** made of straw: *straw baskets*
WORD ORIGIN Old English *strēaw*

Straw *n* **Jack,** full name *John Whitaker Straw* born 1946, British Labour politician; Home Secretary (1997–2001); Foreign Secretary (2001–06); Lord Chancellor from 2007

strawberry *n, pl* **-ries** a sweet fleshy red fruit with small seeds on the outside
WORD ORIGIN Old English *strēawberige*

strawberry blonde *adj* **1** (of hair) reddish-blonde ▷ *n* **2** a woman with such hair

strawberry mark *n* a red birthmark

straw-coloured *adj* pale yellow: *straw-coloured hair*

straw poll *or* **vote** *n* an unofficial poll or vote taken to find out the opinion of a group or the public on some issue

Strawson *n* Sir **Peter** (**Frederick**) 1919–2006, British philosopher. His early work deals with the relationship between language and logic, his later work with metaphysics. His books include *The Bounds of Sense* (1966) and *Freedom and Resentment* (1974)

strawweight *n* a professional boxer weighing up to 105 pounds (47 kg).

S

THESAURUS

stranded *adj* **a = beached**, grounded, marooned, ashore, shipwrecked, aground, cast away **b = helpless**, abandoned, high and dry, left in the lurch

strange *adj* **1 = odd**, unusual, curious, weird, wonderful, rare, funny, extraordinary, remarkable, bizarre, fantastic, astonishing, marvellous, exceptional, peculiar, eccentric, abnormal, out-of-the-way, queer, irregular, rum *(Brit slang)*, uncommon, singular, perplexing, uncanny, mystifying, unheard-of, off-the-wall *(slang)*, oddball *(informal)*, unaccountable, left-field *(informal)*, outré, curiouser and curiouser, daggy *(Austral & NZ informal)*
OPPOSITE: ordinary
2 = unfamiliar, new, unknown, foreign, novel, alien, exotic, untried, unexplored, outside your experience
OPPOSITE: familiar

stranger *n* **1 = unknown person 2 = newcomer**, incomer, foreigner, guest, visitor, unknown, alien, new arrival, outlander

strangle *vb* **1 = throttle**, choke, asphyxiate, garrotte, strangulate, smother, suffocate **2 = suppress**, inhibit, subdue, stifle, gag, repress, overpower, quash, quell, quench

strap *n* **1 = tie**, thong, leash, belt

strapping *adj* **= well-built**, big, powerful, robust, hefty *(informal)*, sturdy, stalwart, burly, husky *(informal)*, hulking, beefy *(informal)*, brawny, well set-up

strategic *adj* **1 = tactical**, calculated, deliberate, planned, politic, diplomatic

strategy *n* **1 = plan**, approach,

DICTIONARY

Also called: **mini-flyweight**

stray ❶ *vb* **1** to wander away from the correct path or from a given area **2** to move away from the point or lose concentration **3** to fail to live up to certain moral standards: *her man had strayed* ▷ *n* **4** a domestic animal that has wandered away from its home **5** *old-fashioned* a lost or homeless child ▷ *adj* **6** (of a domestic animal) having wandered away from its home **7** random or separated from the main group of things of their kind: *stray bombs and rockets*
WORD ORIGIN Old French *estraier*

Strayhorn *n* **Billy,** full name *William Strayhorn.* 1915–67, US jazz composer and pianist, noted esp. for his association (1939–67) with Duke Ellington

streak ❶ *n* **1** a long thin stripe or trace of some contrasting colour **2** (of lightning) a sudden flash **3** a quality or characteristic: *a nasty streak* **4** a short stretch of good or bad luck: *a losing streak* **5** *informal* an instance of running naked through a public place ▷ *vb* **6** to mark (something) with a streak or streaks: *sweat streaking the grime of his face* **7** to move quickly in a straight line **8** *informal* to run naked through a public place **streaked** *or* **streaky** *adj* **streaker** *n*
WORD ORIGIN Old English *strica*

stream ❶ *n* **1** a small river **2** any steady flow of water or other liquid **3** something that resembles a stream in moving continuously in a line or particular direction: *the stream of traffic* **4** a fast and continuous flow of speech: *the constant stream of jargon* **5** *Brit, Austral & NZ* a class of school children grouped together because of similar ability ▷ *vb* **6** to pour in a continuous flow: *rain streamed down her cheeks* **7** (of a crowd of people or traffic or a herd of animals) to move in unbroken succession **8** to float freely or with a waving motion: *a flimsy pink dress that streamed out behind her* **9** *Brit & NZ* to group (school children) in streams **streaming** *n* **streamlet** *n*
WORD ORIGIN Old English *strēam*

streamer *n* **1** a long coiled ribbon of coloured paper that unrolls when tossed **2** a long narrow flag

streaming *n computers* a method of sending video or audio material over the internet so that the receiving system can process and play it almost simultaneously

streamline *vb* **-lining, -lined 1** to improve (something) by removing the parts that are least useful or profitable **2** to make (an aircraft, boat, or vehicle) less resistant to flowing air or water by improving its shape **streamlined** *adj*

Streep *n* **Meryl,** original name *Mary Louise Streep.* born 1949, US actress. Her films include *The Deerhunter* (1978), *Kramer vs Kramer* (1979), *The French Lieutenant's Woman* (1981), *Sophie's Choice* (1982), *Out of Africa* (1986), *Dancing at Lughnasa* (1999), and *The Hours* (2002)

street ❶ *n* **1** a public road that is usually lined with buildings, esp. in a town: *Sauchiehall Street* **2** the part of the road between the pavements, used by vehicles **3** the people living in a particular street **4 on the streets** homeless **5 right up one's street** *informal* just what one knows or likes best **6 streets ahead of** *informal* superior to or more advanced than
WORD ORIGIN Old English *strǣt*

streetcar *n US & Canad* a tram

street cred *or* **credibility** *n* a command of the styles, knowledge, etc. associated with urban youngsters who are respected by their contemporaries: *having children was the quickest way to lose your street cred*

street value *n* the price that would be paid for goods, esp. illegal ones such as drugs, by the final user: *cocaine with a street value of £2m was seized at Heathrow airport*

streetwalker *n* a prostitute who tries to find customers in the streets

streetwise *adj* knowing how to survive or succeed in poor and often criminal sections of big cities

Streicher *n* **Julius** 1885–1946, German Nazi journalist and politician, who spread anti-Semitic propaganda as editor of *Der Stürmer* (1923–45). He was hanged as a war criminal

Streisand *n* **Barbra** born 1942, US singer, actress, and film director: the films she has acted in include *Funny Girl* (1968) and *A Star is Born* (1976); her films as actress and director include *Yentl* (1983), *Prince of Tides* (1990), and *The Mirror has Two Faces* (1996)

strength ❶ *n* **1** the state or quality of being physically or mentally strong **2** the ability to withstand great force, stress, or pressure **3** something regarded as valuable or a source of power: *his chief strength is rocketry* **4** potency or effectiveness, such as of a drink or drug **5** power to convince: *the strength of this argument* **6** degree of intensity or concentration of colour, light, sound, or flavour: *a medium-strength cheese* **7** the total number of people in a group: *at full strength; 50 000 men below strength* **8 go from strength to strength** to have ever-increasing success **9 on the strength of** on the basis of or relying upon
WORD ORIGIN Old English *strengthu*

strengthen ❶ *vb* to become stronger or make (something) stronger

strenuous *adj* requiring or involving the use of great energy or effort **strenuously** *adv*
WORD ORIGIN Latin *strenuus* brisk

streptococcus (strep-toe-**kok**-uss) *n, pl* **-cocci** (-**kok**-eye) a bacterium occurring in chains and including many species that cause disease
WORD ORIGIN Greek *streptos* crooked + *kokkos* berry

S

THESAURUS

scheme, manoeuvring, grand design

stray *vb* **1a = wander**, roam, go astray, range, drift, meander, rove, straggle, lose your way, be abandoned *or* lost **1b = drift**, wander, roam, meander, rove **2 = digress**, diverge, deviate, ramble, get sidetracked, go off at a tangent, get off the point ▷ *adj* **6 = lost**, abandoned, homeless, roaming, vagrant **7 = random**, chance, freak, accidental, odd, scattered, erratic, scattershot

streak *n* **1, 3 = trace**, touch, element, strain, dash, vein ▷ *vb* **7 = speed**, fly, tear, sweep, flash, barrel (along) *(informal, chiefly US & Canad)*, whistle, sprint, dart, zoom, whizz *(informal)*, hurtle, burn rubber *(informal)*, move like greased lightning *(informal)*

stream *n* **1 = river**, brook, creek *(US)*, burn *(Scot)*, beck, tributary, bayou, rivulet, rill, freshet **2 = flow**, current, rush, run, course, drift, surge, tide, torrent, outpouring, tideway ▷ *vb* **6 = flow**, run, pour, course, issue, flood, shed, spill, emit, glide, cascade, gush, spout **7 = rush**, fly, speed, tear, flood, pour

street *n* **1 = road**, lane, avenue, terrace, row, boulevard, roadway, thoroughfare

strength *n* **1a = might**, muscle, brawn, sinew, brawniness **OPPOSITE:** weakness **1b = will**, spirit, resolution, resolve, courage, character, nerve, determination, pluck, stamina, grit, backbone, fortitude, toughness, tenacity, willpower, mettle, firmness, strength of character, steadfastness, moral fibre **2 = toughness**, soundness, robustness, sturdiness, stoutness **3 = strong point**, skill, asset, advantage, talent, forte, speciality, aptitude **OPPOSITE:** failing **4 = potency**, effectiveness, concentration, efficacy **6 = force**, power, intensity, energy, vehemence, intenseness **OPPOSITE:** weakness

strengthen *vb* **a = fortify**, encourage, harden, toughen, consolidate, stiffen, hearten, gee up, brace up, give new energy to **OPPOSITE:** weaken **b = reinforce**, support, confirm, establish, justify, enhance, intensify,

DICTIONARY

streptomycin *n med* an antibiotic used in the treatment of tuberculosis and other bacterial infections
WORD ORIGIN Greek *streptos* crooked + *mukēs* fungus

Stresemann *n* **Gustav** 1878–1929, German statesman; chancellor (1923) and foreign minister (1923–29) of the Weimar Republic. He gained (1926) Germany's admission to the League of Nations and shared the Nobel peace prize (1926) with Aristide Briand

stress ❶ *n* **1** mental, emotional, or physical strain or tension **2** special emphasis or significance **3** emphasis placed upon a syllable by pronouncing it more loudly than those that surround it **4** *physics* force producing a change in shape or volume ▷ *vb* **5** to give emphasis to (a point or subject): *she stressed how difficult it had been* **6** to pronounce (a word or syllable) more loudly than those surrounding it **stressful** *adj*
WORD ORIGIN shortened from *distress*

stressed-out *adj informal* suffering from anxiety or tension

stretch ❶ *vb* **1 stretch over** *or* **for** to extend or spread over (a specified distance): *the flood barrier stretches for several miles* **2** to draw out or extend (something) or to be drawn out or extended in length or area **3** to distort or lengthen (something) or to be distorted or lengthened permanently **4** to extend (the limbs or body), for example when one has just woken up **5** (often foll. by *out* or *forward, etc.*) to reach or hold out (a part of one's body) **6** to reach or suspend (a rope, etc.) from one place to another **7** to draw (something) tight; tighten **8** (usually foll. by *over*) to extend in time: *a dinner which stretched over three consecutive evenings* **9** to put a great strain upon (one's money or resources) **10** to make do with (limited resources): *the Walkers decided to stretch their budget* **11** to extend (someone) to the limit of his or her abilities **12** to extend (someone) to the limit of his or her tolerance **13 stretch a point** to make an exception not usually made ▷ *n* **14** the act of stretching **15** a large or continuous expanse or distance: *this stretch of desert* **16** extent in time **17** a term of imprisonment **18 at a stretch** *chiefly Brit & NZ* **a** with some difficulty; by making a special effort **b** at one time: *for hours at a stretch they had no conversation* ▷ *adj* **19** (of clothes) able to be stretched without permanently losing shape: *a stretch suit* **stretchy** *adj*
WORD ORIGIN Old English *streccan*

stretcher *n* a frame covered with canvas, on which an ill or injured person is carried

stretcher-bearer *n* a person who helps to carry a stretcher

strew *vb* **strewing, strewed, strewn** to scatter (things) over a surface
WORD ORIGIN Old English *streowian*

strewth *interj informal* an expression of surprise or alarm
WORD ORIGIN alteration of *God's truth*

stria (strye-a) *n, pl* **striae** (strye-ee) *geol* a scratch or groove on the surface of a rock crystal
WORD ORIGIN Latin: a groove

striation *n* **1** an arrangement or pattern of striae **2** ▸ same as **stria** > **striated** *adj*

stricken *adj* badly affected by disease, pain, grief, etc.: *flood-stricken areas*
WORD ORIGIN past participle of STRIKE

strict ❶ *adj* **1** severely correct in attention to behaviour or morality: *a strict disciplinarian* **2** following carefully and exactly a set of rules: *she is a strict vegetarian* **3** (of a rule or law) very precise and requiring total obedience: *a strict code of practice* **4** (of a meaning) exact: *this is not, in the strictest sense, a biography* **5** (of a punishment, etc.) harsh or severe **6** complete; absolute: *strict obedience* **strictly** *adv* **strictness** *n*
WORD ORIGIN Latin *strictus* drawn tight

stricture *n formal* a severe criticism
WORD ORIGIN Latin *strictura* contraction

stride *n* **1** a long step or pace **2** the length of such a step **3** a striding walk **4** progress or development: *he has made great strides in regaining his confidence* **5** a regular pace or rate of progress: *it put me off my stride* **6 take something in one's stride** to do something without difficulty or effort ▷ *vb* **striding, strode, stridden** **7** to walk with long steps or paces **8 stride over** *or* **across** to cross (over a space or an obstacle) with a stride
WORD ORIGIN Old English *strīdan*

strident *adj* **1** (of a voice or sound) loud and harsh **2** loud, persistent, and forceful: *a strident critic of the establishment* **stridency** *n*
WORD ORIGIN Latin *stridens*

strife ❶ *n* angry or violent struggle; conflict
WORD ORIGIN Old French *estrif*

strike ❶ *vb* **striking, struck** **1** (of employees) to stop work collectively as a protest against working conditions, low pay, etc. **2** to hit (someone) **3** to cause (something) to come into sudden or violent contact with something **4 strike at** to attack (someone or something) **5** to cause (a match) to light by friction **6** to sound (a specific note) on a musical

THESAURUS

S

bolster, substantiate, buttress, corroborate, give a boost to **c = bolster**, harden, reinforce, give a boost to **d = heighten**, intensify **e = make stronger**, build up, invigorate, restore, nourish, rejuvenate, give strength to **f = support**, brace, steel, reinforce, consolidate, harden, bolster, augment, buttress **g = become stronger**, intensify, heighten, gain strength

stress *n* **1 = strain**, pressure, worry, tension, burden, anxiety, trauma, oppression, hassle *(informal)*, nervous tension **2 = emphasis**, importance, significance, force, weight, urgency **3 = accent**, beat, emphasis, accentuation, ictus ▷ *vb* **5 = emphasize**, highlight, underline, repeat, draw attention to, dwell on, underscore, accentuate, point up, rub in, flag up, harp on, belabour **6 = place the emphasis on**, emphasize, give emphasis to, place the accent on, lay emphasis upon

stretch *vb* **1 = stretch over** *or* **for = extend**, cover, spread, reach, unfold, put forth, unroll **2, 3 = expand**, lengthen, be elastic, be stretchy **7 = pull**, distend, pull out of shape, strain, swell, tighten, rack, inflate, lengthen, draw out, elongate **8 = last**, continue, go on, extend, carry on, reach ▷ *n* **15 = expanse**, area, tract, spread, distance, sweep, extent **16 = period**, time, spell, stint, run, term, bit, space

strict *adj* **1 = stern**, firm, severe, harsh, authoritarian, austere, no-nonsense **4 = exact**, accurate, precise, close, true, particular, religious, faithful, meticulous, scrupulous **5 = severe**, harsh, stern, firm, rigid, rigorous, stringent, austere **OPPOSITE:** easy-going **6 = absolute**, complete, total, perfect, utter

strife *n* **= conflict**, battle, struggle, row, clash, clashes, contest, controversy, combat, warfare, rivalry, contention, quarrel, friction, squabbling, wrangling, bickering, animosity, discord, dissension

strike *vb* **1 = walk out**, take industrial action, down tools, revolt, mutiny **2 = hit**, smack, thump, pound, beat, box, knock, punch, hammer, deck *(slang)*, slap, sock *(slang)*, chin *(slang)*, buffet, clout *(informal)*, cuff, clump *(slang)*, swipe, clobber *(slang)*, smite, wallop *(informal)*, lambast(e), lay a finger on *(informal)*, lay one on *(slang)*, beat *or* knock seven bells out of *(informal)* **3a = collide with**, hit, run into, bump into, touch, smash into, come into contact with, knock into, be in collision with **3b = knock**, bang, smack, thump, beat, smite

DICTIONARY

instrument **7** (of a clock) to indicate (a time) by the sound of a bell **8** to affect (someone) deeply in a particular way: *he never struck me as the supportive type* **9** to enter the mind of: *a brilliant thought struck me* **10** (of a poisonous snake) to injure by biting **11** *pp* **struck** *or* **stricken** to change into (a different state): *struck blind* **12** to be noticed by; catch: *the heavy smell of incense struck my nostrils* **13** to arrive at (something) suddenly or unexpectedly: *to strike on a solution* **14** to afflict (someone) with a disease: *she has been struck down by breast cancer* **15** to discover a source of (gold, oil, etc.) **16** to reach (something) by agreement: *to strike a deal* **17** to take up (a posture or an attitude) **18** to take apart or pack up: *to strike camp* **19** to make (a coin) by stamping it **20 strike home** to achieve the desired effect **21 strike it rich** *informal* to have an unexpected financial success ▷*n* **22** a stopping of work, as a protest against working conditions, low pay, etc.: *a one-day strike* **23** an act or instance of striking **24** a military attack, esp. an air attack on a target on land or at sea: *a pre-emptive strike* **25** *baseball* a pitched ball swung at and missed by the batter **26** *tenpin bowling* the knocking down of all the pins with one bowl **27** the discovery of a source of gold, oil, etc. ▸See also **strike off, strike out, strike up**
WORD ORIGIN Old English *strīcan*

strikebreaker *n* a person who tries to make a strike fail by working or by taking the place of those on strike

strike off *vb* to remove the name of (a doctor or lawyer who has done something wrong) from an official register, preventing him or her from practising again

strike out *vb* **1** to score out (something written) **2** to start out or begin: *I'm going to strike out for town*

strike pay *n* money paid to strikers by a trade union

striker *n* **1** a person who is on strike **2** *soccer* an attacking player

strike up *vb* **1** to begin (a conversation or friendship) **2** (of a band or an orchestra) to begin to play (a tune)

striking *adj* **1** attracting attention; impressive: *her striking appearance* **2** very noticeable: *a striking difference* **strikingly** *adv*

Strimmer *n trademark* an electrical tool for trimming the edges of lawns

Strine *n* a humorous transliteration of Australian pronunciation, as in *Gloria Soame* for *glorious home*
WORD ORIGIN a jocular rendering of the Australian pronunciation of *Australian*

string *n* **1** thin cord or twine used for tying, hanging, or binding things **2** a group of objects threaded on a single strand: *a string of pearls* **3** a series of things or events: *a string of wins* **4** a tightly stretched wire or cord on a musical instrument, such as the guitar, violin, or piano, that produces sound when vibrated **5 the strings** *music* **a** violins, violas, cellos, and double basses collectively **b** the section of an orchestra consisting of such instruments **6** a group of characters that can be treated as a unit by a computer program **7 with no strings attached** (of an offer) without complications or conditions **8 pull strings** *informal* to use one's power or influence, esp. secretly or unofficially ▷*adj* **9** composed of stringlike strands woven in a large mesh: *a string bag* ▷*vb* **stringing, strung 10** to hang or stretch (something) from one point to another **11** to provide (something) with a string or strings **12** to thread (beads) on a string **13** to extend in a line or series: *towns strung out along the valley* **stringlike** *adj*
WORD ORIGIN Old English *streng*

string along *vb informal* **1 string along with** to accompany: *I'll string along with you* **2** to deceive (someone) over a period of time: *she had only been stringing him along*

string bean *n* ▸same as **runner bean**

string course *n archit* an ornamental projecting band along a wall

stringed *adj* (of musical instruments) having strings

stringent (strin-jent) *adj* requiring strict attention to rules or detail: *all have particularly stringent environmental laws* **stringency** *n*
WORD ORIGIN Latin *stringere* to bind

stringer *n* **1** *archit* a long horizontal timber beam that connects upright posts **2** a journalist employed by a newspaper on a part-time basis to cover a particular town or area

string quartet *n music* **1** a group of musicians consisting of two violins, one viola, and one cello **2** a piece of music composed for such a group

string up *vb informal* to kill (a person) by hanging

stringy *adj* **stringier, stringiest 1** thin and rough: *stringy hair* **2** (of meat or other food) tough and fibrous

stringy-bark *n* an Australian eucalyptus with a fibrous bark

strip[1] *vb* **stripping, stripped 1** to take (the covering or clothes) off (oneself, another person, or thing) **2 a** to undress completely **b** to perform a striptease **3** to empty (a building) of all furniture **4** to take something away from (someone): *they were stripped of their possessions* **5** to remove (paint) from (a surface or furniture): *she stripped the plaster from the kitchen walls* **6** (often foll. by *down*) to dismantle (an engine or a mechanism) into individual parts ▷*n* **7** the act or an instance of undressing or of performing a striptease
WORD ORIGIN Old English *bestrīepan* to plunder

strip[2] *n* **1** a long narrow piece of something **2** ▸short for **airstrip** **3** *Brit, Austral & NZ* the clothes a sports team plays in
WORD ORIGIN Middle Dutch *strīpe* stripe

strip cartoon *n* a sequence of drawings in a newspaper or magazine, telling an amusing story or an adventure

strip club *n* a club in which striptease performances take place

stripe[1] *n* **1** a long band of colour that differs from the surrounding material **2** a chevron or band worn on a uniform to indicate rank ▷*vb* **striping, striped 3** to mark (something) with stripes **striped, stripy** *or* **stripey** *adj*
WORD ORIGIN probably from Middle Dutch *strīpe*

stripe[2] *n* a stroke from a whip, rod, or cane
WORD ORIGIN from Middle Low German *strippe*

S

THESAURUS

8a = seem to, appear to, look to, give the impression to **8b = move**, touch, impress, hit, affect, overcome, stir, disturb, perturb, make an impact on **9 = occur to**, hit, come to, register *(informal)*, come to the mind of, dawn on *or* upon **14 = affect**, move, hit, touch, devastate, overwhelm, leave a mark on, make an impact *or* impression on ▷*n* **22 = walkout**, industrial action, mutiny, revolt

striking *adj* **1, 2 = impressive**, dramatic, stunning *(informal)*, wonderful, extraordinary, outstanding, astonishing, memorable, dazzling, noticeable, conspicuous, drop-dead *(slang)*, out of the ordinary, forcible, jaw-dropping, eye-popping *(informal)*
OPPOSITE: unimpressive

string *n* **1 = cord**, yarn, twine, strand, fibre, thread **3a = series**, line, row, file, sequence, queue, succession, procession **3b = sequence**, run, series, chain, succession, streak

stringent *adj* **= strict**, tough, rigorous, demanding, binding, tight, severe, exacting, rigid, inflexible
OPPOSITE: lax

strip[1] *vb* **1, 2a = undress**, disrobe, unclothe, uncover yourself **4 = plunder**, rob, loot, empty, sack, deprive, ransack, pillage, divest, denude

strip[2] *n* **1 = piece**, shred, bit, band, slip, belt, tongue, ribbon, fillet, swathe

DICTIONARY

strip lighting *n* a method of electric lighting that uses fluorescent lamps in long glass tubes

stripling *n* a teenage boy or young man

stripper *n* **1** a person who performs a striptease **2** a tool or liquid for removing paint or varnish

strip-search *vb* **1** (of police, customs officials, etc.) to strip (a prisoner or suspect) naked to search him or her for drugs or smuggled goods ▷*n* **2** a search that involves stripping a person naked

striptease *n* an entertainment in which a person gradually undresses to music

strive ⊤ *vb* **striving, strove, striven** to make a great effort: *to strive for a peaceful settlement*
WORD ORIGIN Old French *estriver*

strobe *n* ▸short for **strobe lighting** or **stroboscope**

strobe lighting *n* a flashing beam of very bright light produced by a perforated disc rotating in front of a light source

stroboscope *n* an instrument producing a very bright flashing light which makes moving people appear stationary
WORD ORIGIN Greek *strobos* a whirling + *skopein* to look at

strode *vb* ▸the past tense of **stride**

Stroessner *n* **Alfredo** 1912–2006, Paraguayan soldier and politician; president (1954–89): deposed in a military coup

stroganoff *n* a dish of sliced beef cooked with onions and mushrooms, served in a sour-cream sauce. Also called: **beef stroganoff**
WORD ORIGIN after Count *Stroganoff*, Russian diplomat

Stroheim *n* ▸See **von Stroheim**

stroke ⊤ *vb* **stroking, stroked 1** to touch or brush lightly or gently ▷*n* **2** a light touch or caress with the fingers **3** *pathol* rupture of a blood vessel in the brain resulting in loss of consciousness, often followed by paralysis and damage to speech **4** a blow, knock, or hit **5** an action or occurrence of the kind specified: *a fantastic stroke of luck; a stroke of intuition* **6 a** the striking of a clock **b** the hour registered by this: *at the stroke of twelve* **7** a mark made by a pen or paintbrush **8** ▸same as **solidus**: used esp. when dictating or reading aloud **9** the hitting of the ball in sports such as golf or cricket **10** any one of the repeated movements used by a swimmer **11** a particular style of swimming, such as the crawl **12** a single pull on the oars in rowing **13 at a stroke** with one action **14 not a stroke (of work)** no work at all
WORD ORIGIN Old English *strācian*

stroll ⊤ *vb* **1** to walk about in a leisurely manner ▷*n* **2** a leisurely walk
WORD ORIGIN probably from dialect German *strollen*

stroller *n US & Canad* a chair-shaped carriage for a baby

strong ⊤ *adj* **stronger, strongest 1** having physical power **2** not easily broken or injured; solid or robust **3** great in degree or intensity; not faint or feeble: *a strong voice; a strong smell of explosive* **4** (of arguments) supported by evidence; convincing **5** concentrated; not weak or diluted **6** having a powerful taste or smell: *strong perfume* **7** (of language) using swear words **8** (of a person) self-confident: *a strong personality* **9** committed or fervent: *a strong believer in free trade* **10** important or having a lot of power or influence: *a strong left-wing tendency within the university* **11** very competent at a particular activity: *they sent a very strong team to the Olympics* **12** containing or having a specified number: *the 700-strong workforce* **13** (of an accent) distinct and indicating where the speaker comes from **14** (of a relationship) stable and likely to last **15** having an extreme or drastic effect: *strong discipline* **16** (of a colour) very bright and intense **17** (of a wind, current, or earthquake) moving fast or intensely **18** (of an economy, an industry, a currency, etc.) growing, successful, or increasing in value ▷*adv* **19 come on strong** *informal* **a** to show blatantly that one is sexually attracted to someone **b** to make a forceful or exaggerated impression **20 going strong** *informal* working or performing well; thriving **strongly** *adv*
WORD ORIGIN Old English *strang*

strong-arm *adj informal* involving physical force or violence: *strong-arm tactics*

strongbox *n* a box in which valuables are locked for safety

strong drink *n* alcoholic drink

stronghold ⊤ *n* **1** an area in which a particular belief is shared by many people: *a Labour stronghold* **2** a place that is well defended; fortress

strong-minded *adj* not easily persuaded to change beliefs or opinions

strong point *n* something at which one is very good: *diplomacy wasn't his strong point*

strongroom *n* a specially designed room in which valuables are locked for safety

strontium *n chem* a soft silvery-white metallic element: the radioactive isotope **strontium-90** is used in nuclear power sources and is a hazardous nuclear fallout product. Symbol: Sr
WORD ORIGIN after *Strontian*, in Scotland, where discovered

strop *n* a leather strap for sharpening razors
WORD ORIGIN Greek *strophos* cord

stroppy *adj* **-pier, -piest** *informal* bad-tempered or deliberately awkward
WORD ORIGIN from *obstreperous*

S

THESAURUS

strive *vb* **= try**, labour, struggle, fight, attempt, compete, strain, contend, endeavour, go for it *(informal)*, try hard, toil, make every effort, go all out *(informal)*, bend over backwards *(informal)*, do your best, go for broke *(slang)*, leave no stone unturned, bust a gut *(informal)*, do all you can, give it your best shot *(informal)*, jump through hoops *(informal)*, break your neck *(informal)*, exert yourself, make an all-out effort *(informal)*, knock yourself out *(informal)*, do your utmost, do your damnedest *(informal)*, give it your all *(informal)*, rupture yourself *(informal)*

stroke *vb* **1 = caress**, rub, fondle, pat, pet ▷*n* **3** *(pathology)* **= apoplexy**, fit, seizure, attack, shock, collapse **4 = blow**, hit, knock, pat, rap, thump, swipe

stroll *vb* **1 = walk**, ramble, amble, wander, promenade, saunter, stooge *(slang)*, take a turn, toddle, make your way, mooch *(slang)*, mosey *(informal)*, stretch your legs ▷*n* **2 = walk**, promenade, turn, airing, constitutional, excursion, ramble, breath of air

strong *adj* **1 = powerful**, muscular, tough, capable, athletic, strapping, hardy, sturdy, stout, stalwart, burly, beefy *(informal)*, virile, Herculean, sinewy, brawny **OPPOSITE:** weak **2 = durable**, substantial, sturdy, reinforced, heavy-duty, well-built, well-armed, hard-wearing, well-protected, on a firm foundation **OPPOSITE:** flimsy **9a = keen**, deep, acute, eager, fervent, zealous, vehement **9b = intense**, deep, passionate, ardent, fierce, profound, forceful, fervent, deep-rooted, vehement, fervid **9c = staunch**, firm, keen, dedicated, fierce, ardent, eager, enthusiastic, passionate, fervent **13 = distinct**, marked, clear, unmistakable **OPPOSITE:** slight **15 = extreme**, radical, drastic, strict, harsh, rigid, forceful, uncompromising, Draconian, unbending **16 = bright**, brilliant, dazzling, loud, bold, stark, glaring **OPPOSITE:** dull

stronghold *n* **1, 2 = bastion**, fortress, bulwark, fastness

DICTIONARY

strove *vb* ▸ the past tense of **strive**

struck *vb* ▸ a past of **strike**

structural *adj* **1** of or having structure or a structure **2** of or forming part of the structure of a building **3** *chem* of or involving the arrangement of atoms in molecules: *a structural formula* **structurally** *adv*

structuralism *n* an approach to social sciences and to literature which sees changes in the subject as caused and organized by a hidden set of universal rules **structuralist** *n, adj*

structure ❶ *n* **1** something that has been built or organized **2** the way the individual parts of something are made, built, or organized into a whole **3** the pattern of interrelationships within an organization, society, etc. **4** an organized method of working, thinking, or behaving **5** *chem* the arrangement of atoms in a molecule of a chemical compound **6** *geol* the way in which a rock is made up of its component parts ▹ *vb* **-turing, -tured** **7** to arrange (something) into an organized system or pattern: *a structured school curriculum*
WORD ORIGIN Latin *structura*

strudel *n* a thin sheet of filled dough rolled up and baked: *apple strudel*
WORD ORIGIN from German

struggle ❶ *vb* **-gling, -gled** **1** to work or strive: *the old regime struggled for power; he struggled to keep the conversation flowing* **2** to move about violently in an attempt to escape from something restricting **3** to fight with someone, often for possession of something **4** to go or progress with difficulty **5** **struggle on** to manage to do (something) with difficulty ▹ *n* **6** something requiring a lot of exertion or effort to achieve **7** a fight or battle **8** **the struggle** *S African* the concerted opposition to apartheid **struggling** *adj*
WORD ORIGIN origin unknown

strum *vb* **strumming, strummed** **1** to play (a stringed instrument) by sweeping the thumb or a plectrum across the strings **2** to play (a tune) in this way
WORD ORIGIN probably imitative

strumpet *n archaic* a prostitute or promiscuous woman
WORD ORIGIN origin unknown

strung *vb* ▸ the past of **string**

strung up *adj informal* tense or nervous: *you sound a bit strung up*

strut ❶ *vb* **strutting, strutted** **1** to walk in a stiff proud way with head high and shoulders back; swagger ▹ *n* **2** a piece of wood or metal that forms part of the framework of a structure
WORD ORIGIN Old English *strūtian* to stand stiffly

Struve *n* **Otto** 1897–1963, US astronomer, born in Russia, noted for his work in stellar spectroscopy and his discovery (1937) of interstellar hydrogen

strychnine (strik-neen) *n* a very poisonous drug formerly used in small quantities as a stimulant
WORD ORIGIN Greek *strukhnos* nightshade

Stuart *adj* of or relating to the royal house that ruled Scotland from 1371 to 1714 and England from 1603 to 1714

stub *n* **1** a short piece remaining after something has been used: *a cigarette stub* **2** the section of a ticket or cheque which the purchaser keeps as a receipt ▹ *vb* **stubbing, stubbed** **3** to strike (one's toe or foot) painfully against a hard surface **4** **stub out** to put out (a cigarette or cigar) by pressing the end against a surface
WORD ORIGIN Old English *stubb*

stubble *n* **1** the short stalks left in a field where a crop has been harvested **2** the short bristly hair on the chin of a man who has not shaved for a while **stubbly** *adj*
WORD ORIGIN Old French *estuble*

stubble-jumper *n Canad slang* a prairie grain farmer

stubborn ❶ *adj* **1** refusing to agree or give in **2** persistent and determined **3** difficult to handle, treat, or overcome: *the most stubborn dandruff* **stubbornly** *adv* **stubbornness** *n*
WORD ORIGIN origin unknown

Stubbs *n* **George** 1724–1806, English painter, noted esp. for his pictures of horses

stubby *adj* **-bier, -biest** short and broad

STUC Scottish Trades Union Congress

stucco *n* **1** plaster used for coating or decorating outside walls ▹ *vb* **-coing, -coed** **2** to apply stucco to (a building)
WORD ORIGIN Italian

stuck ❶ *vb* **1** ▸ the past of **stick²** ▹ *adj* **2** *informal* baffled by a problem or unable to find an answer to a question **3** **be stuck on** *slang* to feel a strong attraction to; be infatuated with **4** **get stuck in** *informal* to perform a task with determination

stuck-up *adj informal* proud or snobbish

stud¹ *n* **1** a small piece of metal attached to a surface for decoration **2** a fastener consisting of two discs at either end of a short bar, usually used with clothes **3** one of several small round objects attached to the sole of a football boot to give better grip ▹ *vb* **studding, studded** **4** to decorate or cover (something) with or as if with studs: *apartment houses studded with satellite dishes*
WORD ORIGIN Old English *studu*

stud² *n* **1** a male animal, esp. a stallion kept for breeding **2** Also: **stud farm** a place where animals are bred **3** the state of being kept for breeding purposes **4** *slang* a virile or sexually active man
WORD ORIGIN Old English *stōd*

student ❶ *n* **1** a person following a course of study in a school, college, or university **2** a person who makes a thorough study of a subject: *a keen student of opinion polls*
WORD ORIGIN Latin *studens* diligent

studied ❶ *adj* carefully practised or

S

THESAURUS

structure *n* **1 = building**, construction, erection, edifice, pile **2 = arrangement**, form, make-up, make, design, organization, construction, fabric, formation, configuration, conformation, interrelation of parts ▹ *vb* **7 = arrange**, organize, design, shape, build up, assemble, put together

struggle *vb* **1 = strive**, labour, toil, work, strain, go for it *(informal)*, make every effort, go all out *(informal)*, bend over backwards *(informal)*, go for broke *(slang)*, bust a gut *(informal)*, give it your best shot *(informal)*, break your neck *(informal)*, exert yourself, make an all-out effort *(informal)*, work like a Trojan, knock yourself out *(informal)*, do your damnedest *(informal)*, give it your all *(informal)*, rupture yourself *(informal)* **3 = fight**, battle, wrestle, grapple, compete, contend, scuffle, lock horns ▹ *n* **7 = fight**, battle, conflict, clash, contest, encounter, brush, combat, hostilities, strife, skirmish, tussle, biffo *(Austral slang)*

strut *vb* **1 = swagger**, parade, stalk, peacock, prance

stubborn *adj* **1, 2 = obstinate**, dogged, inflexible, fixed, persistent, intractable, wilful, tenacious, recalcitrant, unyielding, headstrong, unmanageable, unbending, obdurate, stiff-necked, unshakeable, self-willed, refractory, pig-headed, bull-headed, mulish, cross-grained, contumacious **OPPOSITE:** compliant

stuck *adj* **2** *(informal)* **= baffled**, stumped, at a loss, beaten, nonplussed, at a standstill, bereft of ideas, up against a brick wall *(informal)*, at your wits' end

student *n* **1a = undergraduate**, scholar **1b = pupil**, scholar, schoolchild, schoolboy *or* schoolgirl **2 = learner**, observer, trainee, apprentice, disciple

studied *adj* **= planned**, calculated, deliberate, conscious, intentional, wilful, purposeful, premeditated, well-considered
OPPOSITE: unplanned

DICTIONARY

planned: *studied calm*
studio ❶ *n, pl* **-dios** 1 a room in which an artist, photographer, or musician works 2 a room used to record television or radio programmes or to make films or records 3 **studios** the premises of a radio, television, record, or film company
WORD ORIGIN Italian
studio couch *n* a backless couch that can be converted into a double bed
studio flat *n Brit* a flat with one main room and, usually, a small kitchen and bathroom. Also called: **studio apartment**
studious (styoo-dee-uss) *adj* 1 serious, thoughtful, and hard-working 2 precise, careful, or deliberate **studiously** *adv*
WORD ORIGIN Latin *studiosus* devoted to
study ❶ *vb* **studies, studying, studied** 1 to be engaged in the learning or understanding of (a subject) 2 to investigate or examine (something) by observation and research 3 to look at (something or someone) closely; scrutinize ▷ *n, pl* **studies** 4 the act or process of studying 5 a room used for studying, reading, or writing 6 (*often pl*) work relating to a particular area of learning: *environmental studies* 7 an investigation and analysis of a particular subject 8 a paper or book produced as a result of study 9 a work of art, such as a drawing, done for practice or in preparation for another work 10 a musical composition designed to develop playing technique
WORD ORIGIN Latin *studium* zeal
stuff ❶ *n* 1 substance or material 2 any collection of unnamed things 3 the raw material of something 4 subject matter, skill, etc.: *this journalist knew his stuff* 5 woollen fabric 6 **do one's stuff** *informal* to do what is expected of one ▷ *vb* 7 to pack or fill (something) completely; cram 8 to force, shove, or squeeze (something somewhere): *I stuffed it in my briefcase* 9 to fill (food such as poultry or tomatoes) with a seasoned mixture 10 to fill (a dead animal's skin) with material so as to restore the shape of the live animal 11 *slang* to frustrate or defeat 12 **get stuffed!** *Brit, Austral & NZ slang* an exclamation of anger or annoyance with someone 13 **stuff oneself** *or* **one's face** to eat a large amount of food
WORD ORIGIN Old French *estoffe*
stuffed shirt *n informal* a pompous or old-fashioned person
stuffed-up *adj* having the passages of one's nose blocked with mucus
stuffing ❶ *n* 1 a mixture of ingredients with which poultry or meat is stuffed before cooking 2 the material used to fill and give shape to soft toys, pillows, furniture, etc.; padding
stuffy *adj* **-ier, -iest** 1 lacking fresh air 2 old-fashioned and very formal: *an image of stuffy tradition* **stuffiness** *n*
stultify *vb* **-fies, -fying, -fied** to dull (the mind) by boring routine **stultifying** *adj*
WORD ORIGIN Latin *stultus* stupid + *facere* to make
stumble ❶ *vb* **-bling, -bled** 1 to trip and almost fall while walking or running 2 to walk in an unsteady or unsure way 3 to make mistakes or hesitate in speech 4 **stumble across** *or* **on** *or* **upon** to encounter or discover (someone or something) by accident ▷ *n* 5 an act of stumbling
WORD ORIGIN Middle English *stomble*
stumbling block *n* any obstacle that prevents something from taking place or progressing
stump ❶ *n* 1 the base of a tree trunk left standing after the tree has been cut down or has fallen 2 the part of something, such as a tooth or limb, that remains after a larger part has been removed 3 *cricket* any of three upright wooden sticks that, with two bails laid across them, form a wicket ▷ *vb* 4 to baffle or confuse (someone) 5 *cricket* to dismiss (a batsman) by breaking his wicket with the ball 6 *chiefly US & Canad* to campaign or canvass (an area), by political speech-making 7 to walk with heavy steps; trudge
WORD ORIGIN Middle Low German
stump up *vb Brit informal* to give (the money required)
stumpy *adj* **stumpier, stumpiest** short and thick like a stump; stubby
stun ❶ *vb* **stunning, stunned** 1 to shock or astonish (someone) so that he or she is unable to speak or act 2 (of a heavy blow or fall) to make (a person or an animal) unconscious
WORD ORIGIN Old French *estoner* to daze
stung *vb* ▸ the past of **sting**
stunk *vb* ▸ a past of **stink**
stunner *n Brit, Austral & NZ informal* a person or thing of great beauty
stunning ❶ *adj informal* very attractive or impressive **stunningly** *adv*
stunt[1] *vb* to prevent or slow down (the growth or development of a plant, animal, or person) **stunted** *adj*
WORD ORIGIN Old English: foolish
stunt[2] ❶ *n* 1 an acrobatic or

THESAURUS

studio *n* 1 = **workshop**, shop, workroom, atelier
study *vb* 1 = **learn**, cram (*informal*), swot (up) (*Brit informal*), read up, hammer away at, bone up on (*informal*), burn the midnight oil, mug up (*Brit slang*) 2 = **contemplate**, read, examine, consider, go into, con (*archaic*), pore over, apply yourself (to) 3 = **examine**, survey, look at, scrutinize, peruse ▷ *n* 4 = **learning**, lessons, school work, academic work, reading, research, cramming (*informal*), swotting (*Brit informal*), book work 7 = **examination**, investigation, analysis, consideration, inspection, scrutiny, contemplation, perusal, cogitation 8 = **piece of research**, survey, report, paper, review, article, inquiry, investigation
stuff *n* 2 = **things**, gear, possessions, effects, materials, equipment, objects, tackle, kit, junk, luggage, belongings, trappings, bits and pieces, paraphernalia, clobber (*Brit slang*), impedimenta, goods and chattels 3 = **substance**, material, essence, matter, staple, pith, quintessence ▷ *vb* 7 = **cram**, fill, pack, load, crowd 8 = **shove**, force, push, squeeze, jam, ram, wedge, compress, stow
stuffing *n* 2 = **wadding**, filling, packing, quilting, kapok
stumble *vb* 1 = **trip**, fall, slip, reel, stagger, falter, flounder, lurch, come a cropper (*informal*), lose your balance, blunder about 2 = **totter**, reel, stagger, blunder, falter, lurch, wobble, teeter 4 **stumble across** *or* **on** *or* **upon something** *or* **someone** = **discover**, find, come across, encounter, run across, chance upon, happen upon, light upon, blunder upon
stump *n* 2 = **tail end**, end, remnant, remainder ▷ *vb* 4 = **baffle**, confuse, puzzle, snooker, foil, bewilder, confound, perplex, mystify, outwit, stymie, flummox, bring (someone) up short, dumbfound, nonplus
stun *vb* 1 = **overcome**, shock, amaze, confuse, astonish, stagger, bewilder, astound, overpower, confound, stupefy, strike (someone) dumb, knock (someone) for six (*informal*), dumbfound, flabbergast (*informal*), hit (someone) like a ton of bricks (*informal*), take (someone's) breath away 2 = **daze**, knock out, stupefy, numb, benumb
stunning *adj* (*informal*) = **wonderful**, beautiful, impressive, great (*informal*), striking, brilliant, dramatic, lovely, remarkable, smashing (*informal*), heavenly, devastating (*informal*), spectacular, marvellous, splendid, gorgeous, dazzling, sensational (*informal*), drop-dead (*slang*), ravishing, out of this world (*informal*), jaw-dropping, eye-popping (*informal*)
OPPOSITE: unimpressive
stunt[2] *n* 2 = **feat**, act, trick, exploit, deed, tour de force (*French*)

DICTIONARY

dangerous piece of action in a film or television programme **2** anything spectacular or unusual done to gain publicity ▷ *adj* **3** of or relating to acrobatic or dangerous pieces of action in films or television programmes: *a stunt man*
WORD ORIGIN origin unknown

stupefaction *n* the state of being unable to think clearly because of tiredness or boredom

stupefy *vb* **-pefies, -pefying, -pefied** **1** to make (someone) feel so bored and tired that he or she is unable to think clearly **2** to confuse or astound (someone) **stupefying** *adj*
WORD ORIGIN Old French *stupefier*

stupendous *adj* very large or impressive **stupendously** *adv*
WORD ORIGIN Latin *stupere* to be amazed

stupid ❶ *adj* **1** lacking in common sense or intelligence **2** trivial, silly, or childish: *we got into a stupid quarrel* **3** unable to think clearly; dazed: *stupid with tiredness* **stupidity** *n* **stupidly** *adv*
WORD ORIGIN Latin *stupidus*

stupor *n* a state of near unconsciousness in which a person is unable to behave normally or think clearly
WORD ORIGIN Latin

sturdy ❶ *adj* **-dier, -diest** **1** (of a person) healthy, strong, and unlikely to tire or become injured **2** (of a piece of furniture, shoes, etc.) strongly built or made **sturdily** *adv*
WORD ORIGIN Old French *estordi* dazed

sturgeon *n* a bony fish from which caviar is obtained
WORD ORIGIN Old French *estourgeon*

Sturt *n* **Charles** 1795–1869, English explorer, who led three expeditions (1828–29; 1829; 1844–45) into the Australian interior, discovering the Darling River (1828)

stutter *vb* **1** to speak (a word or phrase) with involuntary repetition of initial consonants ▷ *n* **2** the tendency to involuntarily repeat initial consonants while speaking **stuttering** *n*
WORD ORIGIN Middle English *stutten*

Stuyvesant *n* **Peter** ?1610–72, Dutch colonial administrator of New Netherland (later New York) (1646–64)

sty *n, pl* **sties** a pen in which pigs are kept
WORD ORIGIN Old English *stīg*

stye *or* **sty** *n, pl* **styes** *or* **sties** inflammation of a gland at the base of an eyelash
WORD ORIGIN Old English *stīgend* swelling + *ye* eye

Stygian (stij-jee-an) *adj chiefly literary* dark or gloomy
WORD ORIGIN after the *Styx*, a river in Hades

style ❶ *n* **1** a form of appearance, design, or production: *I like that style of dress* **2** the way in which something is done: *a new style of command* **3** elegance or refinement of manners and dress: *he has bags of style* **4** a distinctive manner of expression in words, music, painting, etc.: *a painting in the Expressionist style* **5** popular fashion in dress and looks: *the old ones had gone out of style* **6** a fashionable or showy way of life: *the newly rich could dine in style* **7** the particular kind of spelling, punctuation, and design followed in a book, journal, or publishing house **8** *bot* the stemlike part of a flower that bears the stigma ▷ *vb* **styling, styled** **9** to design, shape, or tailor: *neatly styled hair* **10** to name or call: *Walsh, who styled himself the Memory Man*
WORD ORIGIN Latin *stilus* writing implement

styling mousse *n* a light foam applied to the hair before styling in order to hold the style

stylish ❶ *adj* smart, fashionable, and attracting attention **stylishly** *adv*

stylist *n* **1** a hairdresser who styles hair **2** a person who performs, writes, or acts with great attention to the particular style he or she employs

stylistic *adj* of the techniques used in creating or performing a work of art: *there are many stylistic problems facing the performers of Baroque music* **stylistically** *adv*

stylized *or* **-ised** *adj* conforming to an established stylistic form

stylus *n* a needle-like device in the pick-up arm of a record player that rests in the groove in the record and picks up the sound signals
WORD ORIGIN Latin *stilus* writing implement

stymie *vb* **-mieing, -mied** **1** to hinder or foil (someone): *the President was stymied by a reluctant Congress* ▷ *n, pl* **-mies** **2** *golf* (formerly) a situation in which an opponent's ball is blocking the line between the hole and the ball about to be played
WORD ORIGIN origin unknown

styptic *adj* **1** used to stop bleeding: *a styptic pencil* ▷ *n* **2** a styptic drug
WORD ORIGIN Greek *stuphein* to contract

Suárez *n* **Francisco de** 1548–1617, Spanish theologian, considered the leading scholastic philosopher after Aquinas and the principal Jesuit theologian. His works include *Disputationes Metaphysicae* (1597) and *De Legibus* (1612)

suave (swahv) *adj* (esp. of a man) smooth, confident, and sophisticated **suavely** *adv*
WORD ORIGIN Latin *suavis* sweet

sub *n* **1** ▸ short for **subeditor, submarine, subscription** or **substitute** **2** *Brit informal* an advance payment of wages or salary. Formal

THESAURUS

S

stupid *adj* **1 = unintelligent**, thick, dumb (*informal*), simple, slow, dull, dim, dense, sluggish, deficient, crass, gullible, simple-minded, dozy (*Brit informal*), witless, stolid, dopey (*informal*), moronic, obtuse, brainless, cretinous, half-witted, slow on the uptake (*informal*), braindead (*informal*), dumb-ass (*slang*), doltish, dead from the neck up, thickheaded, slow-witted, Boeotian, thick as mince (*Scot informal*), woodenheaded (*informal*) **OPPOSITE:** intelligent **2 = silly**, foolish, daft (*informal*), rash, trivial, ludicrous, meaningless, irresponsible, pointless, futile, senseless, mindless, laughable, short-sighted, ill-advised, idiotic, fatuous, nonsensical, half-baked (*informal*), inane, crackpot (*informal*), unthinking, puerile, unintelligent, asinine, imbecilic, crackbrained **OPPOSITE:** sensible **3 = senseless**, dazed, groggy, punch-drunk, insensate, semiconscious, into a daze

sturdy *adj* **1 = robust**, hardy, vigorous, powerful, athletic, muscular, stalwart, staunch, hearty, lusty, brawny, thickset **OPPOSITE:** puny **2 = substantial**, secure, solid, durable, well-made, well-built, built to last **OPPOSITE:** flimsy

style *n* **1a = design**, form, cut **1b = type**, sort, kind, spirit, pattern, variety, appearance, tone, strain, category, characteristic, genre, tenor **2 = manner**, way, method, approach, technique, custom, mode **3 = elegance**, taste, chic, flair, polish, grace, dash, sophistication, refinement, panache, élan, cosmopolitanism, savoir-faire, smartness, urbanity, stylishness, bon ton (*French*), fashionableness, dressiness (*informal*) **5 = fashion**, trend, mode, vogue, rage **6 = luxury**, ease, comfort, elegance, grandeur, affluence, gracious living ▷ *vb* **9 = design**, cut, tailor, fashion, shape, arrange, adapt **10 = call**, name, term, address, label, entitle, dub, designate, christen, denominate

stylish *adj* **= smart**, chic, polished, fashionable, trendy (*Brit informal*), classy (*slang*), in fashion, snappy, in vogue, dapper, natty (*informal*), snazzy (*informal*), modish, well turned-out, dressy (*informal*), à la mode, voguish, schmick (*Austral informal*), bling (*slang*), funky **OPPOSITE:** scruffy

DICTIONARY

term: **subsistence allowance** ▷ *vb* **subbing, subbed 3** to act as a substitute

sub- *or before r* **sur-** *prefix* **1** situated under or beneath: *subterranean* **2** secondary in rank; subordinate: *sublieutenant* **3** falling short of; less than or imperfectly: *subarctic; subhuman* **4** forming a subdivision or less important part: *subcommittee*
WORD ORIGIN Latin

subaltern *n* a British army officer below the rank of captain
WORD ORIGIN Latin *sub-* under + *alter* another

subaqua *adj* of or relating to underwater sport: *subaqua swimming*

subatomic *adj physics* of, relating to, or being one of the particles making up an atom

subcommittee *n* a small committee consisting of members of a larger committee and which is set up to look into a particular matter

subconscious *adj* **1** happening or existing without one's awareness ▷ *n* **2** *psychol* the part of the mind that contains memories and motives of which one is not aware but which can influence one's behaviour **subconsciously** *adv*

subcontinent *n* a large land mass that is a distinct part of a continent, such as India is of Asia

subcontract *n* **1** a secondary contract by which the main contractor for a job puts work out to another company ▷ *vb* **2** to let out (work) on a subcontract **subcontractor** *n*

subculture *n* a group of people within a society or class with a distinct pattern of behaviour, beliefs, and attitudes

subcutaneous (sub-cute-ayn-ee-uss) *adj med* beneath the skin

subdivide *vb* **-viding, -vided** to divide (a part of something) into smaller parts **subdivision** *n*

subdue ❶ *vb* **-duing, -dued 1** to overcome and bring (a person or people) under control by persuasion or force **2** to make (feelings, colour, or lighting) less intense
WORD ORIGIN Latin *subducere* to remove

subeditor *n* a person who checks and edits text for a newspaper or other publication

subgroup *n* a small group that is part of a larger group

subheading *n* the heading of a subdivision of a piece of writing

subhuman *adj* lacking the intelligence or decency expected of a human being

subject ❶ *n* **1** the person, thing, or topic being dealt with or discussed **2** any branch of learning considered as a course of study **3** a person, object, idea, or scene portrayed in a work of art **4** *grammar* a word or phrase that represents the person or thing performing the action of the verb in a sentence; for example, *the cat* in the sentence *The cat catches mice* **5** a person or thing that undergoes an experiment or treatment **6** a person under the rule of a monarch or government: *Zambian subjects* ▷ *adj* **7** being under the rule or a monarch or government: *a subject race* **8 subject to a** showing a tendency towards: *they are expensive and subject to over-runs in cost and time* **b** exposed or vulnerable to: *subject to ridicule* **c** conditional upon: *pay is subject to negotiation* ▷ *adv* **9 subject to** under the condition that something takes place: *my visit was agreed subject to certain conditions* ▷ *vb* (sub-**ject**) **10 subject to a** to cause (someone) to experience (something unpleasant): *they were subjected to beatings* **b** to bring under the control or authority (of): *to subject a soldier to discipline* **subjection** *n*
WORD ORIGIN Latin *subjectus* brought under

subjective ❶ *adj* **1** of or based on a person's emotions or prejudices ▷ *n* **2** *grammar* the grammatical case in certain languages that identifies the subject of a verb **subjectively** *adv*

sub judice (sub joo-diss-ee) *adj* before a court of law: *he declined to comment on the case saying it was sub judice*
WORD ORIGIN Latin

subjugate *vb* **-gating, -gated** to bring (a group of people) under one's control **subjugation** *n*
WORD ORIGIN Latin *sub-* under + *jugum* yoke

subjunctive *grammar adj* **1** denoting a mood of verbs used when the content of the clause is being doubted, supposed, or feared true, for example *were* in the sentence *I'd be careful if I were you* ▷ *n* **2** the subjunctive mood
WORD ORIGIN Latin *subjungere* to add to

sublet *vb* **-letting, -let** to rent out (property which one is renting from someone else)

sublieutenant *n* a junior officer in a navy

sublimate *vb* **-mating, -mated** *psychol* to direct the energy of (a strong desire, esp. a sexual one) into activities that are socially more acceptable **sublimation** *n*
WORD ORIGIN Latin *sublimare* to elevate

sublime ❶ *adj* **1** causing deep emotions and feelings of wonder or joy **2** without equal; supreme **3** of great moral, artistic, or spiritual value ▷ *n* **4 the sublime** something that is sublime ▷ *vb* **-liming, -limed 5** *chem, physics* to change directly from a solid to a vapour without first melting **sublimely** *adv*
WORD ORIGIN Latin *sublimis* lofty

subliminal *adj* resulting from or relating to mental processes of which the individual is not aware: *the subliminal message*
WORD ORIGIN Latin *sub* below + *limen* threshold

sub-machine-gun *n* a portable automatic or semiautomatic gun with a short barrel

submarine *n* **1** a vessel which can operate below the surface of the sea ▷ *adj* **2** existing or located below the surface of the sea: *submarine cables* **submariner** *n*

submerge ❶ *vb* **-merging, -merged 1** to put or go below the surface of water or another liquid **2** to involve totally: *she submerged herself in her work* **submersion** *n*
WORD ORIGIN Latin *submergere*

submersible *adj* **1** capable of operating under water ▷ *n* **2** a small vessel designed to operate under water

submission ❶ *n* **1** an act or instance of capitulation **2** the act of

THESAURUS

subdue *vb* **1 = overcome**, defeat, master, break, control, discipline, crush, humble, put down, conquer, tame, overpower, overrun, trample, quell, triumph over, get the better of, vanquish, beat down, get under control, get the upper hand over, gain ascendancy over **2 = moderate**, control, check, suppress, soften, repress, mellow, tone down, quieten down **OPPOSITE:** arouse

subject *n* **1 = topic**, question, issue, matter, point, business, affair, object, theme, substance, subject matter, field of inquiry *or* reference **6a = citizen**, resident, native, inhabitant, national **6b = dependant**, subordinate, vassal, liegeman ▷ *vb* **10 subject to b = put through**, expose, submit, lay open, make liable

subjective *adj* **1 = personal**, emotional, prejudiced, biased, instinctive, intuitive, idiosyncratic, nonobjective **OPPOSITE:** objective

sublime *adj* **1, 3 = noble**, magnificent, glorious, high, great, grand, imposing, elevated, eminent, majestic, lofty, exalted, transcendent **OPPOSITE:** lowly

submerge *vb* **1a = immerse**, plunge, dip, duck, dunk **1b = sink**, plunge, go under water **2 = overwhelm**, swamp, engulf, overload, inundate, deluge, snow under, overburden

submission *n* **1 = surrender**, yielding, giving in, cave-in (*informal*), capitulation, acquiescence **2 = presentation**, submitting,

S

submitting (something) **3** something submitted, such as a proposal **4** the state in which someone has to accept the control of another person

submissive *adj* showing quiet obedience **submissively** *adv* **submissiveness** *n*

submit ⊙ *vb* **-mitting, -mitted 1** to accept the will of another person or a superior force **2** to send (an application or proposal) to someone for judgment or consideration **3** to be voluntarily subjected (to medical or psychiatric treatment) **WORD ORIGIN** Latin *submittere* to place under

subnormal *adj* **1** less than the normal: *subnormal white blood cells* **2** *no longer in technical use* having a lower than average intelligence ▷*n* **3** *no longer in technical use* a subnormal person

subordinate ⊙ *adj* **1** of lesser rank or importance ▷*n* **2** a person or thing that is of lesser rank or importance ▷*vb* **-nating, -nated 3** (usually foll. by *to*) to regard (something) as less important than another: *the army's interests were subordinated to those of the air force* **subordination** *n* **WORD ORIGIN** Latin *sub-* lower + *ordo* rank

subordinate clause *n grammar* a clause that functions as an adjective, an adverb, or a noun rather than one that functions as a sentence in its own right

suborn *vb formal* to bribe or incite (a person) to commit a wrongful act **WORD ORIGIN** Latin *subornare*

subplot *n* a secondary plot in a novel, play, or film

subpoena (sub-**pee**-na) *n* **1** a legal document requiring a person to appear before a court of law at a specified time ▷*vb* **-naing, -naed 2** to summon (someone) with a subpoena **WORD ORIGIN** Latin: under penalty

sub-post office *n* (in Britain) a post office which is run by a self-employed agent for the Post Office

subprime *adj* **1** (of a loan) made to a borrower with a poor credit rating: *subprime mortgage* ▷*n* **2** such a loan

sub rosa (sub **rose**-a) *adv literary* in secret **WORD ORIGIN** Latin, literally: under the rose; in ancient times a rose was hung over a table as a mark of secrecy

subroutine *n* a section of a computer program that is stored only once but can be used at several different points in the program

subscribe ⊙ *vb* **-scribing, -scribed 1** (usually foll. by *to*) to pay (money) as a contribution (to a charity, for a magazine, etc.) at regular intervals **2 subscribe to** to give support or approval to: *I do not subscribe to this view* **subscriber** *n* **WORD ORIGIN** Latin *subscribere* to write underneath

subscript *printing adj* **1** (of a character) written or printed below the line ▷*n* **2** a subscript character

subscription ⊙ *n* **1** a payment for issues of a publication over a specified period of time **2** money paid or promised, such as to a charity, or the fund raised in this way **3** *Brit, Austral & NZ* the membership fees paid to a society **4** an advance order for a new product

subsection *n* any of the smaller parts into which a section may be divided

subsequent ⊙ *adj* occurring after; succeeding **subsequently** *adv* **WORD ORIGIN** Latin *subsequens*

subservient *adj* **1** overeager to carry out someone else's wishes **2** of less importance or rank: *the subservient role of women in society* **subservience** *n* **WORD ORIGIN** Latin *subserviens*

subset *n* a mathematical set contained within a larger set

subside ⊙ *vb* **-siding, -sided 1** to become less loud, excited, or violent **2** to sink to a lower level **3** (of the surface of the earth) to cave in; collapse **subsidence** *n* **WORD ORIGIN** Latin *subsidere* to settle down

subsidiarity *n* the principle of taking political decisions at the lowest practical level

subsidiary ⊙ *n, pl* **-aries 1** Also called: **subsidiary company** a company which is at least half owned by another company **2** a person or thing that is of lesser importance ▷*adj* **3** of lesser importance; subordinate **WORD ORIGIN** Latin *subsidiarius* supporting

subsidize *or* **-dise** *vb* **-dizing, -dized** *or* **-dising, -dised** to aid or support (an industry, a person, a public service, or a venture) with money

subsidy ⊙ *n, pl* **-dies 1** financial aid supplied by a government, for example to industry, or for public welfare **2** any financial aid, grant, or contribution **WORD ORIGIN** Latin *subsidium* assistance

subsist *vb* **subsist on** to manage to live: *to subsist on a diet of sausage rolls* **subsistence** *n* **WORD ORIGIN** Latin *subsistere* to stand firm

subsistence farming *n* a type of farming in which most of the produce is consumed by the farmer and his family

subsoil *n* the layer of soil beneath the surface soil

subsonic *adj* being or moving at a speed below that of sound

substance ⊙ *n* **1** the basic matter of which a thing consists **2** a specific type of matter with definite or fairly definite chemical composition: *a fatty substance* **3** the essential meaning of a speech, thought, or written article **4** important or meaningful quality: *the only evidence of substance against him* **5** material

handing in, entry, tendering **4 = compliance**, obedience, submissiveness, meekness, resignation, deference, passivity, docility, tractability, unassertiveness

submit *vb* **1 = surrender**, yield, give in, agree, bend, bow, endure, tolerate, comply, put up with *(informal)*, succumb, defer, stoop, cave in *(informal)*, capitulate, accede, acquiesce, toe the line, knuckle under, resign yourself, lay down arms, hoist the white flag, throw in the sponge **2 = present**, hand in, tender, put forward, table, commit, refer, proffer

subordinate *adj* **1 = inferior**, lesser, lower, junior, subject, minor, secondary, dependent, subservient **OPPOSITE:** superior ▷*n* **2 = inferior**, junior, assistant, aide, second, attendant, dependant, underling, subaltern **OPPOSITE:** superior

subscribe to *vb* **1 = contribute to**, give to, donate to, chip in to *(informal)* **2 = support**, agree with, advocate, consent to, endorse, countenance, acquiesce with

subscription *n* **3** *(Brit, Austral & NZ)* **= membership fee**, charge, dues, annual payment

subsequent *adj* **= following**, later, succeeding, after, successive, ensuing, consequent **OPPOSITE:** previous

subside *vb* **1 = decrease**, diminish, lessen, ease, moderate, dwindle, wane, recede, ebb, abate, let up, peter out, slacken, melt away, quieten, level off, de-escalate **OPPOSITE:** increase **3 = collapse**, sink, cave in, drop, lower, settle

subsidiary *adj* **3 = secondary**, lesser, subordinate, minor, supplementary, auxiliary, supplemental, contributory, ancillary, subservient **OPPOSITE:** main

subsidy *n* **1, 2 = aid**, help, support, grant, contribution, assistance, allowance, financial aid, stipend, subvention

substance *n* **1 = material**, body, stuff, element, fabric, texture **3 = meaning**, main point, gist, matter, subject, theme, import,

DICTIONARY

possessions or wealth: *a woman of substance* **6 in substance** with regard to the most important points
WORD ORIGIN Latin *substantia*
substandard *adj* below an established or required standard
substantial ❶ *adj* **1** of a considerable size or value: *a substantial amount of money* **2** (of food or a meal) large and filling **3** solid or strong: *substantial brick pillars* **4** *formal* available to the senses; real: *substantial evidence* **5** of or relating to the basic material substance of a thing **substantially** *adv*
substantiate *vb* **-ating, -ated** to establish (a story) as genuine **substantiation** *n*
substantive *n* **1** *grammar* a noun or pronoun used in place of a noun ▹ *adj* **2** having importance or significance: *substantive negotiations between management and staff* **3** of or being the essential element of a thing
WORD ORIGIN Latin *substare* to stand beneath
substitute ❶ *vb* **-tuting, -tuted** **1** (often foll. by *for*) to take the place of or put in place of another person or thing **2** *chem* to replace (an atom or group in a molecule) with (another atom or group) ▹ *n* **3** a person or thing that takes the place of another, such as a player who takes the place of a team-mate **substitution** *n*
WORD ORIGIN Latin *substituere*
substitution reaction *n chem* the replacing of an atom or group in a molecule by another atom or group
substrate *n biol* the substance upon which an enzyme acts
WORD ORIGIN Latin *substratus* strewn beneath
substructure *n* **1** a structure that forms a part of anything **2** a structure that forms a foundation or framework for a building
subsume *vb* **-suming, -sumed** *formal* to include (something) under a larger classification or group: *an attempt to subsume fascism and communism under a general concept of totalitarianism*
WORD ORIGIN Latin *sub-* under + *sumere* to take
subtenant *n* a person who rents property from a tenant **subtenancy** *n*
subtend *vb geom* to be opposite (an angle or side)
WORD ORIGIN Latin *subtendere* to extend beneath
subterfuge *n* a trick or deception used to achieve an objective
WORD ORIGIN Latin *subterfugere* to escape by stealth
subterranean *adj* **1** found or operating below the surface of the earth **2** existing or working in a concealed or mysterious way: *the resistance movement worked largely by subterranean methods*
WORD ORIGIN Latin *sub* beneath + *terra* earth
subtext *n* **1** an underlying theme in a piece of writing **2** a message which is not stated directly but can be inferred
subtitle *n* **1 subtitles** *films* a written translation at the bottom of the picture in a film with foreign dialogue **2** a secondary title given to a book or play ▹ *vb* **-tling, -tled** **3** to provide subtitles for (a film) or a subtitle for (a book or play)
subtle ❶ *adj* **1** not immediately obvious: *a subtle change in his views* **2** (of a colour, taste, or smell) delicate or faint: *the subtle aroma* **3** using shrewd and indirect methods to achieve an objective **4** having or requiring the ability to make fine distinctions: *a subtle argument* **subtly** *adv*
WORD ORIGIN Latin *subtilis* finely woven
subtlety ❶ *n* **1** *pl* **-ties** a fine distinction **2** the state or quality of being subtle
subtract *vb* **1** *maths* to take (one number or quantity) away from another **2** to remove (a part of something) from the whole **subtraction** *n*
WORD ORIGIN Latin *subtrahere* to draw away from beneath
subtropical *adj* of the region lying between the tropics and temperate lands
suburb *n* a residential district on the outskirts of a city or town
WORD ORIGIN Latin *sub-* close to + *urbs* a city
suburban *adj* **1** of, in, or inhabiting a suburb **2** *mildly disparaging* conventional and unexciting
suburbanite *n* a person who lives in a suburb
suburbia *n* suburbs or the people living in them considered as a distinct community or class in society
subvention *n formal* a grant or subsidy, for example one from a government
WORD ORIGIN Late Latin *subventio* assistance
subversion *n* the act or an instance of attempting to weaken or overthrow a government or an institution
subversive ❶ *adj* **1** intended or intending to weaken or overthrow a government or an institution ▹ *n* **2** a person engaged in subversive activities
subvert *vb* to bring about the downfall of (something existing by a system of law, such as a government)
WORD ORIGIN Latin *subvertere* to overturn
subway *n* **1** *Austral & Brit* an underground passage for pedestrians to cross a road or railway **2** an underground railway
subzero *adj* lower than zero: *subzero temperatures*
succeed ❶ *vb* **1** to achieve an aim **2** to turn out satisfactorily: *Grandfather's plan succeeded* **3** to do well in a specified field: *how to succeed in show*

S

THESAURUS

significance, essence, pith, burden, sum and substance **4 = importance**, significance, concreteness **5 = wealth**, means, property, assets, resources, estate, affluence
substantial *adj* **1 = big**, significant, considerable, goodly, large, important, generous, worthwhile, tidy *(informal)*, ample, sizable *or* sizeable **OPPOSITE:** small
substitute *vb* **1 = replace**, exchange, swap, change, switch, commute, interchange ▹ *n* **3 = replacement**, reserve, equivalent, surrogate, deputy, relief, representative, sub, temporary, stand-by, makeshift, proxy, temp *(informal)*, expedient, locum, depute *(Scot)*, stopgap, locum tenens
subtle *adj* **1, 2 = faint**, slight, implied, delicate, indirect, understated, insinuated **OPPOSITE:** obvious **2 = muted**, soft, subdued, low-key, toned down **3 = crafty**, cunning, sly, designing, scheming, intriguing, shrewd, ingenious, astute, devious, wily, artful, Machiavellian **OPPOSITE:** straightforward **4 = fine**, minute, narrow, tenuous, hair-splitting
subtlety *n* **1 = fine point**, refinement, nicety, sophistication, delicacy, intricacy, discernment **2 = skill**, acumen, astuteness, ingenuity, guile, cleverness, deviousness, sagacity, acuteness, craftiness, artfulness, slyness, wiliness
subversive *adj* **1 = seditious**, inflammatory, incendiary, underground, undermining, destructive, overthrowing, riotous, insurrectionary, treasonous, perversive ▹ *n* **2 = dissident**, terrorist, saboteur, insurrectionary, quisling, fifth columnist, deviationist, seditionary, seditionist
succeed *vb* **1 = triumph**, win, prevail **2 = work out**, work, be successful, come off *(informal)*, do the trick *(informal)*, turn out well, go like a bomb *(Brit & NZ informal)*, go down a bomb *(informal, chiefly Brit)*, do the business *(informal)* **3 = make it** *(informal)*, do well, be successful, arrive *(informal)*, triumph, thrive, flourish, make good, prosper, cut it *(informal)*, make the grade *(informal)*,

DICTIONARY

biz **4** to come next in order after (someone or something): *the first shock had been succeeded by a different kind of gloom* **5** to take over (a position) from (someone): *Henry VIII succeeded to the throne in 1509; he will be succeeded as president by his deputy* **succeeding** *adj*
WORD ORIGIN Latin *succedere* to follow after

success ⊙ *n* **1** the achievement of something attempted **2** the attainment of wealth, fame, or position **3** a person or thing that is successful
WORD ORIGIN Latin *successus* an outcome

successful ⊙ *adj* **1** having a favourable outcome **2** having attained fame, wealth, or position **successfully** *adv*

succession ⊙ *n* **1** a number of people or things following one another in order **2** the act or right by which one person succeeds another in a position **3 in succession** one after another: *the third time in succession*

successive ⊙ *adj* following another or others without interruption: *eleven successive victories* **successively** *adv*

successor *n* a person or thing that follows another, esp. a person who takes over another's job or position

succinct *adj* brief and clear: *a succinct answer to this question* **succinctly** *adv*
WORD ORIGIN Latin *succinctus*

succour *or US* **succor** *n* **1** help in time of difficulty ▷*vb* **2** to give aid to (someone in time of difficulty)
WORD ORIGIN Latin *succurrere* to hurry to help

succubus *n, pl* **-bi** a female demon fabled to have sex with sleeping men
WORD ORIGIN Latin *succubare* to lie beneath

succulent *adj* **1** (of food) juicy and delicious **2** (of plants) having thick fleshy leaves or stems ▷*n* **3** a plant that can exist in very dry conditions by using water stored in its fleshy tissues **succulence** *n*
WORD ORIGIN Latin *sucus* juice

succumb ⊙ *vb* **succumb to a** to give way to the force of or desire for (something) **b** to die of (a disease)
WORD ORIGIN Latin *succumbere*

such *adj* **1** of the sort specified or understood: *such places* **2** so great or so much: *such a mess* ▷*adv* **3** extremely: *such a powerful friend* ▷*pron* **4** a person or thing of the sort specified or understood: *such is the law of the land; fruitcakes and puddings and such* **5 as such** in itself or themselves: *the Nordic countries are not lifting sanctions as such* **6 such as** for example: *other socialist groups, such as the Fabians*
WORD ORIGIN Old English *swilc*

such and such *adj* **1** specific, but not known or named: *such and such a percentage* ▷*n* **2** a specific, but not known or named, person or thing: *you have not taken such and such into account*

suchlike *n* **1** such or similar things: *shampoos, talcs, and suchlike* ▷*adj* **2** of such a kind; similar: *astrology and suchlike nonsense*

suck ⊙ *vb* **1** to draw (a liquid) into the mouth through pursed lips **2** to take (something) into the mouth and moisten, dissolve, or roll it around with the tongue: *suck a mint* **3** to extract liquid from (a solid food): *he sat sucking orange segments* **4** to draw in (fluid) as if by sucking: *the mussel sucks in water* **5** to drink milk from (a mother's breast); suckle **6** (often foll. by *down* or *in, etc.*) to draw (a thing or person somewhere) with a powerful force **7** *slang* to be contemptible or disgusting ▷*n* **8** a sucking
WORD ORIGIN Old English *sūcan*

sucker *n* **1** *slang* a person who is easily deceived or swindled **2** *slang* a person who cannot resist something: *he's a sucker for fast cars* **3** *zool* a part of the body of certain animals that is used for sucking or sticking to a surface **4** a rubber cup-shaped device attached to objects allowing them to stick to a surface by suction **5** *bot* a strong shoot coming from a mature plant's root or the base of its main stem

suck into *vb* to draw (someone) into (a situation) by using a powerful pressure or inducement: *to be sucked into a guerrilla war*

suckle *vb* **-ling, -led** to give (a baby or young animal) milk from the breast or udder or (of a baby or young animal) to suck milk from its mother's breast or udder

suckling *n* a baby or young animal that is still sucking milk from its mother's breast or udder

Suckling *n* Sir **John** 1609–42, English Cavalier poet and dramatist

suck up to *vb informal* to flatter (a person in authority) in order to get something, such as praise or promotion

sucrose (soo-kroze) *n chem* sugar
WORD ORIGIN French *sucre* sugar

suction *n* **1** the act or process of sucking **2** the force produced by drawing air out of a space to make a vacuum that will suck in a substance from another space
WORD ORIGIN Latin *sugere* to suck

Sudanese *adj* **1** of the Sudan ▷*n, pl* **-nese 2** a person from the Sudan

sudden ⊙ *adj* **1** occurring or performed quickly and without warning ▷*n* **2 all of a sudden** without warning; unexpectedly **suddenly** *adv* **suddenness** *n*
WORD ORIGIN Latin *subitus* unexpected

sudden death *n sport* an extra period of play to decide the winner of a tied competition: the first player or team to go into the lead is the winner

sudden infant death syndrome *n* ▸same as **cot death**

sudoku (soo-**doh**-koo) *n* a logic puzzle involving the insertion of numbers so that none is repeated in the same row, column, or internal square of a larger square
WORD ORIGIN from Japanese

sudorific (syoo-dor-if-ik) *adj*

S

THESAURUS

get to the top, crack it *(informal)*, hit the jackpot *(informal)*, bring home the bacon *(informal)*, make your mark *(informal)*, gain your end, carry all before you, do all right for yourself
OPPOSITE: fail
4 = follow, come after, follow after, replace, be subsequent to, supervene
OPPOSITE: precede
5 = take over from, replace, assume the office of, fill (someone's) boots, step into (someone's) boots

success *n* **1 = victory**, triumph, positive result, favourable outcome
OPPOSITE: failure
2 = prosperity, fortune, luck, fame, eminence, ascendancy **3a = hit** *(informal)*, winner, smash *(informal)*, triumph, sensation, wow *(slang)*, best seller, market leader, smash hit *(informal)* **OPPOSITE:** flop *(informal)*
3b = big name, star, hit *(informal)*, somebody, celebrity, sensation, megastar *(informal)*, V.I.P.
OPPOSITE: nobody

successful *adj* **1 = triumphant**, victorious, lucky, fortunate
2a = thriving, profitable, productive, paying, effective, rewarding, booming, efficient, flourishing, unbeaten, lucrative, favourable, fruitful, efficacious, moneymaking
OPPOSITE: unprofitable
2b = top, prosperous, acknowledged, wealthy, out in front *(informal)*, going places, at the top of the tree

succession *n* **1 = series**, run, sequence, course, order, train, flow, chain, cycle, procession, continuation, progression
2 = taking over, assumption, inheritance, elevation, accession, entering upon

successive *adj* **= consecutive**, following, succeeding, in a row, in succession, sequent

succumb *vb* **succumb to** *(with* **to***)* **= catch**, fall victim to, fall ill with

suck *vb* **1 = drink**, sip, draw **6 = take**, draw, pull, extract

sudden *adj* **1 = quick**, rapid, unexpected, swift, hurried, abrupt, hasty, impulsive, unforeseen
OPPOSITE: gradual

DICTIONARY

1 causing sweating ▷*n* **2** a drug that causes sweating
WORD ORIGIN Latin *sudor* sweat + *facere* to make

suds *pl n* the bubbles on the surface of water in which soap or detergent has been dissolved; lather
WORD ORIGIN probably from Middle Dutch *sudse* marsh

sue *vb* **suing, sued** to start legal proceedings (against): *we want to sue the council; he sued for custody of the three children*
WORD ORIGIN Latin *sequi* to follow

Sue *n* **Eugène** original name *Marie-Joseph Sue* 1804–57, French novelist, whose works, notably *Les mystères de Paris* (1842–43) and *Le juif errant* (1844–45), were among the first to reflect the impact of the industrial revolution on France

suede *n* a leather with a fine velvet-like surface on one side
WORD ORIGIN French *gants de Suède*, literally: gloves from Sweden

suet *n* a hard fat obtained from sheep and cattle and used for making pastry and puddings
WORD ORIGIN Old French *seu*

Suetonius *n* full name *Gaius Suetonius Tranquillus*. 75–150 AD, Roman biographer and historian, whose chief works were *Concerning Illustrious Men* and *The Lives of the Caesars* (from Julius Caesar to Domitian)

suffer *vb* **1** to undergo or be subjected to (physical pain or mental distress) **2 suffer from** to be badly affected by (an illness): *he was suffering from depression* **3** to become worse in quality; deteriorate: *his work suffered during their divorce* **4** to tolerate: *he suffers no fools* **5** to be set at a disadvantage: *the strongest of them suffers by comparison* **sufferer** *n* **suffering** *n*
WORD ORIGIN Latin *sufferre*

sufferance *n* **on sufferance** tolerated with reluctance: *I was there on sufferance and all knew it*

suffice (suf-fice) *vb* **-ficing, -ficed 1** to be enough or satisfactory for a purpose **2 suffice it to say ...** it is enough to say ...: *suffice it to say that AIDS is on the increase*
WORD ORIGIN Latin *sufficere*

sufficiency *n, pl* **-cies** an adequate amount

sufficient *adj* enough to meet a need or purpose; adequate **sufficiently** *adv*
WORD ORIGIN Latin *sufficiens*

suffix *grammar n* **1** a letter or letters added to the end of a word to form another word, such as *-s* and *-ness* in *dogs* and *softness* ▷*vb* **2** to add (a letter or letters) to the end of a word to form another word
WORD ORIGIN Latin *suffixus* fastened below

suffocate *vb* **-cating, -cated 1** to kill or die through lack of oxygen, such as by blockage of the air passage **2** to feel uncomfortable from heat and lack of air **suffocating** *adj* **suffocation** *n*
WORD ORIGIN Latin *suffocare*

suffragan *n* a bishop appointed to assist an archbishop
WORD ORIGIN Medieval Latin *suffragium* assistance

suffrage *n* the right to vote in public elections
WORD ORIGIN Latin *suffragium*

suffragette *n* (in Britain at the beginning of the 20th century) a woman who campaigned militantly for women to be given the right to vote in public elections

suffragist *n* (in Britain at the beginning of the 20th century) a person who campaigned for women to be given the right to vote in public elections

suffuse *vb* **-fusing, -fused** to spread through or over (something): *the dawn suffused the sky with a cold grey wash* **suffusion** *n*
WORD ORIGIN Latin *suffusus* overspread with

sugar *n* **1** a sweet carbohydrate, usually in the form of white or brown crystals, which is found in many plants and is used to sweeten food and drinks **2** *informal chiefly US & Canad* a term of affection ▷*vb* **3** to add sugar to (food or drink) to make it sweet **4** to cover with sugar: *sugared almonds* **5 sugar the pill** to make something unpleasant more tolerable by adding something pleasant **sugared** *adj*
WORD ORIGIN Old French *çucre*, from Sanskrit *śarkarā*

Sugar *n* Sir **Alan** (**Michael**) born 1947, British electronics entrepreneur; chairman of Amstrad from 1968

sugar beet *n* a beet grown for the sugar obtained from its roots

sugar cane *n* a tropical grass grown for the sugar obtained from its tall stout canes

sugar daddy *n* an elderly man who gives a young woman money and gifts in return for her company

sugar glider *n* a common phalanger that glides from tree to tree feeding on insects and nectar

sugaring off *n Canad* the boiling down of maple sap to produce sugar, traditionally a social event in early spring

sugar loaf *n* a large cone-shaped mass of hard refined sugar

sugar maple *n* a North American maple tree, grown as a source of sugar, which is extracted from the sap

sugary *adj* **1** of, like, or containing sugar: *sugary snacks* **2** (of behaviour or language) very pleasant but probably not sincere: *sugary sentiment* **sugariness** *n*

Suger *n* 1081–1151, French ecclesiastic and statesman, who acted as adviser to Louis VI and regent (1147–49) to Louis VII. As abbot of Saint-Denis (1122–51) he influenced the development of Gothic architecture

suggest *vb* **1** to put forward (a plan or an idea) for consideration: *he didn't suggest a meeting* **2** to bring (a person or thing) to the mind by the association of ideas: *a man whose very name suggests blandness* **3** to give a hint of: *her grey eyes suggesting a livelier mood than usual*
WORD ORIGIN Latin *suggerere* to bring up

suggestible *adj* easily influenced by other people's ideas

suggestion *n* **1** something that is suggested **2** a hint or indication: *the entire castle gave no suggestion of period* **3** *psychol* the process whereby the presentation of an idea to a receptive individual leads to the acceptance of that idea

suggestive *adj* **1** (of remarks or

THESAURUS

sue *vb* **= take (someone) to court**, prosecute, bring an action against (someone), charge, summon, indict, have the law on (someone) *(informal)*, prefer charges against (someone), institute legal proceedings against (someone)

suffer *vb* **1a = be in pain**, hurt, ache, be racked, have a bad time, go through a lot *(informal)*, go through the mill *(informal)*, feel wretched
1b = undergo, experience, sustain, feel, bear, go through, endure
4 = tolerate, stand, put up with *(informal)*, support, bear, endure, hack *(Brit informal)*, abide

suffice *vb* **1 = be enough**, do, be sufficient, be adequate, answer, serve, content, satisfy, fill the bill *(informal)*, meet requirements

sufficient *adj* **= adequate**, enough, ample, satisfactory, enow *(archaic)*
OPPOSITE: insufficient

suggest *vb* **1 = recommend**, propose, advise, move, advocate, prescribe, put forward, offer a suggestion
2 = bring to mind, evoke, remind you of, connote, make you think of, put you in mind of **3a = indicate**, lead you to believe **3b = hint at**, imply, insinuate, intimate, get at, drive at *(informal)*

suggestion *n* **1 = recommendation**, proposal, proposition, plan, motion
2 = hint, implication, insinuation, intimation

DICTIONARY

gestures) causing people to think of sex **2 suggestive of** communicating a hint of

suicidal *adj* **1** wanting to commit suicide **2** likely to lead to danger or death: *a suicidal attempt to rescue her son* **3** likely to destroy one's own career or future: *it would be suicidal for them to ignore public opinion*

suicide *n* **1** the act of killing oneself deliberately: *he tried to commit suicide* **2** a person who kills himself or herself intentionally **3** the self-inflicted ruin of one's own career or future: *such a cut would be political suicide*
WORD ORIGIN Latin *sui* of oneself + *caedere* to kill

suicide bomber *n* a terrorist who carries out a bomb attack, knowing that he or she will be killed in the explosion

suit ❶ *n* **1** a set of clothes of the same material designed to be worn together, usually a jacket with matching trousers or skirt **2** an outfit worn for a specific purpose: *a diving suit* **3** a legal action taken against someone; lawsuit **4** any of the four types of card in a pack of playing cards: spades, hearts, diamonds, or clubs **5** *slang* a business executive or white-collar worker **6 follow suit** to act in the same way as someone else **7 strong suit** *or* **strongest suit** something one excels in ▹*vb* **8** to be fit or appropriate for: *that colour suits you* **9** to be acceptable to (someone) **10 suit oneself** to do what one wants without considering other people **suited** *adj*
WORD ORIGIN Old French *sieute* set of things

suitable ❶ *adj* appropriate for a particular function or occasion; proper **suitability** *n* **suitably** *adv*

suitcase *n* a large portable travelling case for clothing

suite ❶ *n* **1** a set of connected rooms in a hotel **2** a matching set of furniture, for example two armchairs and a settee **3** *music* a composition of several movements in the same key
WORD ORIGIN French

suitor *n* **1** *old-fashioned* a man who wants to marry a woman **2** *law* a person who starts legal proceedings against someone; plaintiff
WORD ORIGIN Latin *secutor* follower

Sukarnoputri *n* **Megawati** born 1949, Indonesian politician; president of Indonesia (2001–04): daughter of Achmed Sukarno

Sukkoth (sook-oat) *n* an eight-day Jewish harvest festival, commemorating the period when the Israelites lived in the wilderness

sulk *vb* **1** to be silent and moody as a way of showing anger or resentment: *I went home and sulked for two days* ▹*n* **2** a mood in which one shows anger or resentment by being silent and moody: *he was just in a sulk*

sulky *adj* **sulkier, sulkiest** moody or silent because of anger or resentment **sulkily** *adv* **sulkiness** *n*
WORD ORIGIN perhaps from obsolete *sulke* sluggish

Sulla *n* full name *Lucius Cornelius Sulla Felix*. 138–78 BC, Roman general and dictator (82–79). He introduced reforms to strengthen the power of the Senate

sullen *adj* unwilling to talk or be sociable; sulky **sullenly** *adv* **sullenness** *n*
WORD ORIGIN Latin *solus* alone

Sullivan *n* **1** Sir **Arthur** (**Seymour**) 1842–1900, English composer who wrote operettas, such as *H.M.S. Pinafore* (1878) and *The Mikado* (1885), with W. S. Gilbert as librettist **2 Louis** (**Henri**). 1856–1924, US pioneer of modern architecture: he coined the slogan "form follows function"

sully *vb* **-lies, -lying, -lied 1** to ruin (someone's reputation) **2** to spoil or make dirty: *the stream had been sullied by the smelter's pollution*
WORD ORIGIN probably from French *souiller* to soil

Sully *n* **Maximilien de Béthune**, Duc de Sully. 1559–1641, French statesman; minister of Henry IV. He helped restore the finances of France after the Wars of Religion

Sully-Prudhomme *n* **René François Armand** 1839–1907, French poet: Nobel prize for literature 1901

sulpha *or US* **sulfa drug** *n pharmacol* any of a group of sulphonamides that prevent the growth of bacteria: used to treat bacterial infections

sulphate *or US* **sulfate** *n chem* a salt or ester of sulphuric acid

sulphide *or US* **sulfide** *n chem* a compound of sulphur with another element

sulphite *or US* **sulfite** *n chem* any salt or ester of sulphurous acid

sulphonamide *or US* **sulfonamide** (sulf-on-a-mide) *n pharmacol* any of a class of organic compounds that prevent the growth of bacteria

sulphur *or US* **sulfur** *n chem* a light yellow, highly inflammable, nonmetallic element used in the production of sulphuric acid, in the vulcanization of rubber, and in medicine. Symbol: S **sulphuric** *or US* **sulfuric** *adj*
WORD ORIGIN Latin *sulfur*

sulphur dioxide *n chem* a strong-smelling colourless soluble gas, used in the manufacture of sulphuric acid and in the preservation of foodstuffs

sulphureous *or US* **sulfureous** (sulf-yoor-ee-uss) *adj* ▸same as **sulphurous** (sense 1)

sulphuric acid *n chem* a colourless dense oily corrosive liquid used in the manufacture of fertilizers and explosives

sulphurize *or* **-rise** *or US* **sulfurize** (sulf-yoor-rise) *vb* **-rizing, -rized** *or* **-rising, -rised** *chem* to combine with or treat (something) with sulphur or a sulphur compound

sulphurous *or US* **sulfurous** *adj chem* **1** of or resembling sulphur **2** containing sulphur, esp. with a valence of four

sultan *n* the sovereign of a Muslim country
WORD ORIGIN Arabic: rule

sultana *n* **1** the dried fruit of a small white seedless grape **2** a sultan's wife, mother, daughter, or concubine
WORD ORIGIN Italian

sultanate *n* **1** the territory ruled by a sultan **2** the office or rank of a sultan

sultry *adj* **-trier, -triest 1** (of weather or climate) very hot and humid **2** suggesting hidden passion: *a sultry brunette*
WORD ORIGIN obsolete *sulter* to swelter

sum ❶ *n* **1** the result of the addition of numbers or quantities **2** one or more columns or rows of numbers to be added, subtracted, multiplied, or divided **3** a quantity of money: *they can win enormous sums* **4 in sum** as a summary; in short: *in sum, it's been a bad week for the government* ▹*adj* **5** complete or final: *the sum total* ▹*vb* **summing, summed 6** ▸see **sum up**
WORD ORIGIN Latin *summa* the top, sum

S

THESAURUS

suit *n* **2 = outfit**, costume, ensemble, dress, clothing, habit **3 = lawsuit**, case, trial, proceeding, cause, action, prosecution, industrial tribunal ▹*vb* **8 = agree with**, become, match, go with, correspond with, conform to, befit, harmonize with **9 = be acceptable to**, please, satisfy, do, answer, gratify

suitable *adj* **a = appropriate**, right, fitting, fit, suited, acceptable, becoming, satisfactory, apt, befitting **OPPOSITE:** inappropriate **b = seemly**, fitting, becoming, due, proper, correct **OPPOSITE:** unseemly

suite *n* **1 = rooms**, apartment, set of rooms, living quarters

sum *n* **1 = total**, aggregate, entirety, sum total **2 = calculation**, figures, arithmetic, problem, numbers, reckonings, mathematics, maths (*Brit informal*), tally, math (*US informal*), arithmetical problem **3 = amount**, quantity, volume

DICTIONARY

summarize ❶ *or* **-rise** *vb* **-rizing, -rized** *or* **-rising, -rised** to give a short account of (something)
summary ❶ *n, pl* **-maries 1** a brief account giving the main points of something ▷ *adj* **2** performed quickly, without formality or attention to details: *a summary judgment* **summarily** *adv*
WORD ORIGIN Latin *summarium*
summation *n* **1** a summary of what has just been done or said **2** the process of working out a sum; addition **3** the result of such a process
summer *n* **1** the warmest season of the year, between spring and autumn **2** *literary* a time of youth, success, or happiness **summery** *adj*
WORD ORIGIN Old English *sumor*
summerhouse *n* a small building in a garden, used for shade in the summer
summer school *n* an academic course held during the summer
summer solstice *n* the time at which the sun is at its northernmost point in the sky (southernmost point in the S hemisphere), appearing at noon at its highest altitude above the horizon. It occurs about June 21 (December 22 in the S hemisphere)
summertime *n* the period or season of summer
summing-up *n* **1** a summary of the main points of an argument, speech, or piece of writing **2** concluding statements made by a judge to the jury before they retire to consider their verdict
summit ❶ *n* **1** the highest point or part of a mountain or hill **2** the highest possible degree or state; peak or climax: *the summit of success* **3** a meeting of heads of governments or other high officials
WORD ORIGIN Old French *somet*
summon ❶ *vb* **1** to order (someone) to come **2** to send for (someone) to appear in court **3** to call upon (someone) to do something: *the authorities had summoned the relatives to be available* **4** to convene (a meeting) **5** (often foll. by *up*) to call into action (one's strength, courage, etc.); muster
WORD ORIGIN Latin *summonere* to give a discreet reminder
summons *n, pl* **-monses 1** a call or an order to attend a specified place at a specified time **2** an official order requiring a person to attend court, either to answer a charge or to give evidence ▷ *vb* **3** to order (someone) to appear in court: *three others had been summonsed for questioning*
sumo *n* the national style of wrestling of Japan, in which two contestants of great height and weight attempt to force each other out of the ring
WORD ORIGIN Japanese
sump *n* **1** a container in an internal-combustion engine into which oil can drain **2** ▸ same as **cesspool 3** *mining* a hollow at the bottom of a shaft where water collects
WORD ORIGIN Middle Dutch *somp* marsh
sumptuary *adj* controlling expenditure or extravagant use of resources
WORD ORIGIN Latin *sumptuarius* concerning expense
sumptuous ❶ *adj* magnificent and very expensive; splendid: *sumptuous decoration*
WORD ORIGIN Latin *sumptuosus* costly
sum up *vb* **1** to give a short account of (the main points of an argument, speech, or piece of writing) **2** to form a quick opinion of: *how well you have summed me up!*
sun *n* **1** the star that is the source of heat and light for the planets in the solar system ▸ Related adjective: **solar 2** any star around which a system of planets revolves **3** the heat and light received from the sun; sunshine **4 catch the sun** to become slightly suntanned **5 under the sun** on earth; at all: *there are no free lunches under the sun* ▷ *vb* **sunning, sunned 6 sun oneself** to lie, sit, or walk in the sunshine on a warm day **sunless** *adj*
WORD ORIGIN Old English *sunne*
Sun. Sunday
sunbathe *vb* **-bathing, -bathed** to lie or sit in the sunshine, in order to get a suntan **sunbather** *n* **sunbathing** *n*
sunbeam *n* a ray of sunlight
sun block *n* a chemical applied to exposed skin to block out all or almost all of the ultraviolet rays of the sun
sunburn *n* painful reddening of the skin caused by overexposure to the sun **sunburnt** *or* **sunburned** *adj*
sun cream *n* a cream applied to exposed skin to reduce the effect of the ultraviolet rays of the sun
sundae *n* ice cream topped with a sweet sauce, nuts, whipped cream, and fruit
WORD ORIGIN origin unknown
Sunday *n* the first day of the week and the Christian day of worship
WORD ORIGIN Old English *sunnandæg* day of the sun
Sunday best *n* a person's best clothes, sometimes regarded as those most suitable for wearing at church
Sunday school *n* a school for teaching children about Christianity, usually held in a church hall on Sunday
sundial *n* a device used for telling the time during the hours of sunlight, consisting of a pointer that casts a shadow onto a surface marked in hours
sundown *n US* sunset
sundries *pl n* several things of various sorts
sundry *adj* **1** several or various; miscellaneous ▷ *pron* **2 all and sundry** everybody
WORD ORIGIN Old English *syndrig* separate
sunfish *n, pl* **-fish** *or* **-fishes** a large sea fish with a rounded body
sunflower *n* **1** a very tall plant with large yellow flowers **2 sunflower seed oil** the oil extracted from sunflower seeds, used as a salad oil and in margarine
sung *vb* ▸ the past participle of **sing**
sunglasses *pl n* glasses with darkened lenses that protect the eyes from bright sunlight
sun-god *n* the sun considered as a god
sunk *vb* ▸ a past participle of **sink**
sunken *vb* **1** ▸ a past participle of **sink** ▷ *adj* **2** (of a person's cheeks, eyes, or chest) curving inward due to old age or bad health **3** situated at a lower level than the surrounding or usual one: *the sunken garden* **4** situated under water; submerged: *sunken ships*
sun lamp *n* a lamp that gives off ultraviolet rays, used for muscular therapy or for giving people an artificial suntan
sunlight *n* the light that comes from

S

THESAURUS

summarize *vb* **= sum up**, recap, review, outline, condense, encapsulate, epitomize, abridge, précis, recapitulate, give a rundown of, put in a nutshell, give the main points of
summary *n* **1 = synopsis**, résumé, précis, recapitulation, review, outline, extract, essence, abstract, summing-up, digest, epitome, rundown, compendium, abridgment
summit *n* **1 = peak**, top, tip, pinnacle, apex, head, crown, crest
OPPOSITE: base
2 = height, pinnacle, culmination, peak, high point, zenith, acme, crowning point OPPOSITE: depths
summon *vb* **1, 3 = send for**, call, bid, invite, rally, assemble, convene, call together, convoke **5** *(often with* **up***)* **= gather**, muster, draw on, invoke, mobilize, call into action
sumptuous *adj* **= luxurious**, rich, grand, expensive, superb, magnificent, costly, splendid, posh *(informal, chiefly Brit)*, gorgeous, lavish, extravagant, plush *(informal)*, opulent, palatial, ritzy *(slang)*, de luxe, splendiferous *(facetious)*
OPPOSITE: plain

DICTIONARY

the sun **sunlit** *adj*
sun lounge *or US* **sun parlor** *n* a room with large windows designed to receive as much sunlight as possible
sunny ❶ *adj* **-nier, -niest 1** full of or lit up by sunshine **2** cheerful and happy
sunrise *n* **1** the daily appearance of the sun above the horizon **2** the time at which the sun rises
sunrise industry *n* any of the fast-developing high-technology industries, such as electronics
sunroof *n* a panel in the roof of a car that may be opened to let in air or sunshine
sunset ❶ *n* **1** the daily disappearance of the sun below the horizon **2** the time at which the sun sets
sunshade *n* anything used to shade people from the sun, such as a parasol or awning
sunshine *n* **1** the light and warmth from the sun **2** *Brit* a light-hearted term of address
sunspot *n* **1** *informal* a sunny holiday resort **2** a dark cool patch on the surface of the sun **3** *Austral* a small area of skin damage caused by exposure to the sun
sunstroke *n* a condition caused by spending too much time exposed to intensely hot sunlight and producing high fever and sometimes loss of consciousness
suntan *n* a brownish colouring of the skin caused by exposure to the sun or a sun lamp **suntanned** *adj*
sun-up *n US & Austral* sunrise
Sun Yat-sen *n* 1866–1925, Chinese statesman, who was instrumental in the overthrow of the Manchu dynasty and was the first president of the Republic of China (1911). He reorganized the Kuomintang
sup[1] *vb* **supping, supped 1** to take (liquid) by swallowing a little at a time ▷ *n* **2** a sip
WORD ORIGIN Old English *sūpan*
sup[2] *vb* **supping, supped** *archaic* to have supper
WORD ORIGIN Old French *soper*
super *informal adj* **1** very good or very nice: *they had a super holiday* ▷ *n Austral & NZ* **2** superannuation **3** superphosphate
WORD ORIGIN Latin: above
super- *prefix* **1** above or over: *superscript* **2** outstanding: *superstar* **3** of greater size, extent, or quality: *supermarket*
WORD ORIGIN Latin
superabundant *adj* existing in very large numbers or amount **superabundance** *n*
superannuated *adj* **1** discharged with a pension, owing to age or illness **2** too old to be useful; obsolete
WORD ORIGIN Medieval Latin *superannatus* aged more than one year
superannuation *n* **a** a regular payment made by an employee into a pension fund **b** the pension finally paid
superb ❶ *adj* extremely good or impressive **superbly** *adv*
WORD ORIGIN Latin *superbus* distinguished
Super Bowl *n American football* the championship game held annually between the best team of the American Football Conference and that of the National Football Conference
superbug *n informal* a bacterium resistant to antibiotics
supercharge *vb* **-charging, -charged 1** to increase the power of (an internal-combustion engine) with a supercharger **2** to charge (the atmosphere, a remark, etc.) with an excess amount of (tension, emotion, etc.) **3** to apply pressure to (a fluid); pressurize
supercharger *n* a device that increases the power of an internal-combustion engine by forcing extra air into it
supercilious *adj* behaving in a superior and arrogant manner **superciliously** *adv* **superciliousness** *n*
WORD ORIGIN Latin *supercilium* eyebrow
superconductivity *n physics* the ability of certain substances to conduct electric current with almost no resistance at very low temperatures **superconducting** *adj* **superconductor** *n*
supercontinent *n* a huge landmass thought to have existed in the geological past and to have split into smaller landmasses and formed the present continents
superego *n, pl* **-egos** *psychoanal* that part of the unconscious mind that governs a person's ideas concerning what is right and wrong
supererogation *n* the act of doing more work than is required
WORD ORIGIN Latin *supererogare* to spend over and above
superficial ❶ *adj* **1** not careful or thorough: *a superficial analysis* **2** only outwardly apparent rather than genuine or actual: *those are merely superficial differences* **3** (of a person) lacking deep emotions or serious interests; shallow **4** of, near, or forming the surface: *the gash was superficial* **superficiality** *n* **superficially** *adv*
WORD ORIGIN Late Latin *superficialis*
superfluous (soo-per-flew-uss) *adj* more than is sufficient or required **superfluity** *n*
WORD ORIGIN Latin *superfluus* overflowing
superglue *n* an extremely strong and quick-drying glue
supergrass *n Brit, Austral & NZ* an informer who names a large number of people as terrorists or criminals, esp. one who gives this information in order to avoid being put on trial
super heavyweight *n* an amateur boxer weighing over 201 pounds (91 kg)
superhuman *adj* beyond normal human ability or experience: *a superhuman effort*
superimpose *vb* **-posing, -posed** to set or place (something) on or over something else
superintend *vb* to supervise (a person or an activity)
WORD ORIGIN Latin *super-* above + *intendere* to give attention to
superintendent ❶ *n* **1** a senior police officer **2** a person who directs and manages an organization or office

THESAURUS

sunny *adj* **1 = bright**, clear, fine, brilliant, radiant, luminous, sunlit, summery, unclouded, sunshiny, without a cloud in the sky
OPPOSITE: dull
2 = cheerful, happy, cheery, smiling, beaming, pleasant, optimistic, buoyant, joyful, genial, chirpy *(informal)*, blithe, light-hearted
OPPOSITE: gloomy
sunset *n* **1, 2 = nightfall**, dusk, sundown, eventide, gloaming *(Scot poetic)*, close of (the) day
superb *adj* **a = splendid**, excellent, magnificent, topping *(Brit slang)*, fine, choice, grand, superior, divine, marvellous, gorgeous, mega *(slang)*, awesome *(slang)*, world-class, exquisite, breathtaking, first-rate, superlative, unrivalled, brill *(informal)*, bodacious *(slang, chiefly US)*, boffo *(slang)*, splendiferous *(facetious)*, of the first water, chillin' *(US slang)*, booshit *(Austral slang)*, exo *(Austral slang)*, sik *(Austral slang)*, rad *(informal)*, phat *(slang)*, schmick *(Austral informal)*
OPPOSITE: inferior
b = magnificent, superior, marvellous, exquisite, breathtaking, admirable, superlative, unrivalled, splendiferous *(facetious)*
OPPOSITE: terrible
superficial *adj* **1 = hasty**, cursory, perfunctory, passing, nodding, hurried, casual, sketchy, facile, desultory, slapdash, inattentive
OPPOSITE: thorough
3 = shallow, frivolous, empty-headed, empty, silly, lightweight, trivial **OPPOSITE:** serious
4 = slight, surface, external, cosmetic, on the surface, exterior, peripheral, skin-deep
OPPOSITE: profound
superintendent *n* **2 = supervisor**,

DICTIONARY

superior ❶ *adj* **1** greater in quality, quantity, or usefulness **2** higher in rank, position, or status: *he was reprimanded by a superior officer* **3** believing oneself to be better than others **4** of very high quality or respectability: *superior merchandise* **5** *formal* placed higher up: *damage to the superior surface of the wing* **6** *printing* (of a character) written or printed above the line ▷ *n* **7** a person of greater rank or status **8** ▸ see **mother superior** > **superiority** *n*
WORD ORIGIN Latin *superus* placed above

superlative (soo-per-lat-iv) *adj* **1** of outstanding quality; supreme **2** *grammar* denoting the form of an adjective or adverb that expresses the highest degree of quality ▷ *n* **3** the highest quality **4** *grammar* the superlative form of an adjective or adverb
WORD ORIGIN Old French *superlatif*

superman *n, pl* **-men** any man with great physical or mental powers

supermarket *n* a large self-service shop selling food and household goods

supermodel *n* a famous and highly-paid fashion model

supernatural ❶ *adj* **1** of or relating to things that cannot be explained by science, such as clairvoyance, ghosts, etc. ▷ *n* **2 the supernatural** forces, occurrences, and beings that cannot be explained by science

supernova *n, pl* **-vae** *or* **-vas** a star that explodes and, for a few days, becomes one hundred million times brighter than the sun

supernumerary *adj* **1** exceeding the required or regular number; extra **2** employed as a substitute or assistant ▷ *n, pl* **-aries 3** a person or thing that exceeds the required or regular number **4** a substitute or assistant **5** an actor who has no lines to say
WORD ORIGIN Latin *super-* above + *numerus* number

superphosphate *n* a chemical fertilizer, esp. one made by treating rock phosphate with sulphuric acid

superpower *n* a country of very great military and economic power, such as the US

superscript *printing adj* **1** (of a character) written or printed above the line ▷ *n* **2** a superscript character

supersede *vb* **-seding, -seded 1** to take the place of (something old-fashioned or less appropriate): *cavalry was superseded by armoured vehicles* **2** to replace (someone) in function or office
WORD ORIGIN Latin *supersedere* to sit above

supersize *adj also* **supersized 1** larger than standard size ▷ *vb* **-sizes, -sizing, -sized 2** to increase the size of (something, such as a standard portion of food)

supersonic *adj* being, having, or capable of a speed greater than the speed of sound

superstar *n* an extremely popular and famous entertainer or sportsperson **superstardom** *n*

superstate *n* a large state, esp. one created from a federation of states

superstition *n* **1** irrational belief in magic and the powers that supposedly bring good luck or bad luck **2** a belief or practice based on this **superstitious** *adj*
WORD ORIGIN Latin *superstitio*

superstore *n* a large supermarket

superstructure *n* **1** any structure or concept built on something else **2** *naut* any structure above the main deck of a ship

supertanker *n* a very large fast tanker

supertax *n* an extra tax on incomes above a certain level

Super Twelve *n* an annual international southern hemisphere Rugby Union tournament between professional club sides from South Africa, Australia, and New Zealand

supervene *vb* **-vening, -vened** to happen as an unexpected development **supervention** *n*
WORD ORIGIN Latin *supervenire* to come upon

supervise ❶ *vb* **-vising, -vised 1** to direct the performance or operation of (an activity or a process) **2** to watch over (people) so as to ensure appropriate behaviour **supervision** *n* **supervisor** *n* **supervisory** *adj*
WORD ORIGIN Latin *super-* over + *videre* to see

supine (soo-pine) *adj formal* lying on one's back
WORD ORIGIN Latin *supinus*

supper *n* **1** an evening meal **2** a late evening snack
WORD ORIGIN Old French *soper*

Suppiluliumas I *n* king of the Hittites (?1375–?1335 BC); founder of the Hittite empire

supplant *vb* to take the place of (someone or something)
WORD ORIGIN Latin *supplantare* to trip up

supple *adj* **1** (of a person) moving and bending easily and gracefully **2** (of a material or object) soft and bending easily without breaking **suppleness** *n*
WORD ORIGIN Latin *supplex* bowed

supplement ❶ *n* **1** an addition designed to make something more adequate **2** a magazine distributed free with a newspaper **3** a section added to a publication to supply further information or correct errors **4** (of money) an additional payment to obtain special services ▷ *vb* **5** to provide an addition to (something), esp. in order to make up for an inadequacy: *a Saturday job to supplement her grant* **supplementary** *adj*
WORD ORIGIN Latin *supplementum*

supplicant *n formal* a person who makes a humble request
WORD ORIGIN Latin *supplicans* beseeching

supplication *n formal* a humble request for help
WORD ORIGIN Latin *supplicare* to beg

S

THESAURUS

director, manager, chief, governor, inspector, administrator, conductor, controller, overseer

superior *adj* **1 = better**, higher, greater, grander, preferred, prevailing, paramount, surpassing, more advanced, predominant, unrivalled, more extensive, more skilful, more expert, a cut above *(informal)*, streets ahead *(informal)*, running rings around *(informal)* **OPPOSITE:** inferior **3 = supercilious**, patronizing, condescending, haughty, disdainful, lordly, lofty, airy, pretentious, stuck-up *(informal)*, snobbish, on your high horse *(informal)* **4 = first-class**, excellent, first-rate, good, fine, choice, exclusive, distinguished, exceptional, world-class, good quality, admirable, high-class, high-calibre, de luxe, of the first order, booshit *(Austral slang)*, exo *(Austral slang)*, sik *(Austral slang)*, rad *(informal)*, phat *(slang)*, schmick *(Austral informal)* **OPPOSITE:** average ▷ *n* **7 = boss**, senior, director, manager, chief *(informal)*, principal, supervisor, baas *(S African)*, sherang *(Austral & NZ)* **OPPOSITE:** subordinate

supernatural *adj* **1 = paranormal**, mysterious, unearthly, uncanny, dark, hidden, ghostly, psychic, phantom, abnormal, mystic, miraculous, unnatural, occult, spectral, preternatural, supranatural

supervise *vb* **1 = oversee**, run, manage, control, direct, handle, conduct, look after, be responsible for, administer, inspect, preside over, keep an eye on, be on duty at, superintend, have *or* be in charge of **2 = observe**, guide, monitor, oversee, keep an eye on

supplement *n* **2 = pull-out**, insert, magazine section, added feature **3 = appendix**, sequel, add-on, complement, postscript, addendum, codicil **4 = addition**, extra, surcharge ▷ *vb* **5 = add to**, reinforce, complement, augment, extend, top up, fill out

supply *vb* **1a = provide**, give, furnish, produce, stock, store, grant, afford,

DICTIONARY

on one's knees

supply ❶ *vb* **-plies, -plying, -plied** **1** to provide with something required: *Nigeria may supply them with oil* ▷ *n, pl* **-plies** **2** the act of providing something **3** an amount available for use; stock: *electricity supply* **4** **supplies** food and equipment needed for a trip or military campaign **5** *econ* the amount of a commodity that producers are willing and able to offer for sale at a specified price: *supply and demand* **6** a person who acts as a temporary substitute ▷ *adj* **7** acting as a temporary substitute: *supply teachers* **supplier** *n*
WORD ORIGIN Latin *supplere* to complete

support ❶ *vb* **1** to carry the weight of (a thing or person) **2** to provide the necessities of life for (a family or person) **3** to give practical or emotional help to (someone) **4** to give approval to (a cause, idea, or political party) **5** to take an active interest in and be loyal to (a particular football or other sport team) **6** to establish the truthfulness or accuracy of (a theory or statement) by providing new facts **7** to speak in a debate in favour of (a motion) **8** (in a concert) to perform earlier than (the main attraction) **9** *films, theatre* to play a less important role to (the leading actor or actress) ▷ *n* **10** the act of supporting or the condition of being supported **11** a thing that bears the weight of an object from below **12** a person who gives someone practical or emotional help **13** the means of providing the necessities of life for a family or person **14** a band or entertainer not topping the bill **supportive** *adj*
WORD ORIGIN Latin *supportare* to bring

supporter ❶ *n* a person who supports a sports team, politician, etc.

suppose ❶ *vb* **-posing, -posed** **1** to presume (something) to be true without certain knowledge: *I suppose it will be in the papers* **2** to consider (something) as a possible suggestion for the sake of discussion: *suppose you're arrested on a misdemeanour* **3** (of a theory) to depend on the truth or existence of: *this scenario supposes that he would do so*
WORD ORIGIN Latin *supponere* to substitute

supposed ❶ *adj* **1** **supposed to** expected to: *spies aren't supposed to be nice* **2** presumed to be true without certain knowledge; doubtful: *the supposed wonders of drug therapy* **supposedly** *adv*

supposition *n* **1** an idea or a statement believed or assumed to be true **2** the act of supposing: *much of it is based on supposition*

suppositious *adj* deduced from an idea or statement believed or assumed to be true; hypothetical

suppository *n, pl* **-ries** *med* a medicine in solid form that is inserted into the vagina or rectum and left to dissolve
WORD ORIGIN Latin *suppositus* placed beneath

suppress ❶ *vb* **1** to put an end to (something) by physical or legal force **2** to prevent the circulation or publication of (information or books) **3** to hold (an emotion or a response) in check; restrain: *he could barely suppress a groan* **4** *electronics* to reduce or eliminate (interference) in a circuit **suppression** *n*
WORD ORIGIN Latin *suppressus* held down

suppressant *n* a drug that suppresses an action: *a cough suppressant*

suppurate *vb* **-rating, -rated** *pathol* (of a wound or sore) to produce or leak pus
WORD ORIGIN Latin *suppurare*

supremacy ❶ *n* **1** supreme power; dominance **2** the state or quality of being superior

supreme ❶ *adj* **1** of highest status or power: *the Supreme Council* **2** of highest quality or importance: *a supreme player* **3** greatest in degree; extreme: *supreme happiness* **supremely** *adv*
WORD ORIGIN Latin *supremus* highest

THESAURUS

contribute, yield, come up with, outfit, endow, purvey, victual
1b = furnish, provide, equip, endow ▷ *n* **3 = store**, fund, stock, source, reserve, quantity, reservoir, stockpile, hoard, cache ▷ *pl n* **4 = provisions**, necessities, stores, food, materials, items, equipment, rations, foodstuff, provender

support *vb* **1 = bear**, hold up, carry, sustain, prop (up), reinforce, hold, brace, uphold, bolster, underpin, shore up, buttress **2 = provide for**, maintain, look after, keep, fund, finance, sustain, foster, take care of, subsidize **OPPOSITE:** live off
3 = help, back, champion, second, aid, forward, encourage, defend, promote, take (someone's) part, strengthen, assist, advocate, uphold, side with, go along with, stand up for, espouse, stand behind, hold (someone's) hand, stick up for *(informal)*, succour, buoy up, boost (someone's) morale, take up the cudgels for, be a source of strength to **OPPOSITE:** oppose
6 = bear out, confirm, verify, substantiate, corroborate, document, endorse, attest to, authenticate, lend credence to **OPPOSITE:** refute
▷ *n* **10a = furtherance**, backing, promotion, championship, approval, assistance, encouragement, espousal
10b = help, protection, comfort, friendship, assistance, blessing, loyalty, patronage, moral support, succour **OPPOSITE:** opposition
11 = prop, post, foundation, back, lining, stay, shore, brace, pillar, underpinning, stanchion, stiffener, abutment **12 = supporter**, prop, mainstay, tower of strength, second, stay, backer, backbone, comforter **OPPOSITE:** antagonist
13 = upkeep, maintenance, keep, livelihood, subsistence, sustenance

supporter *n* **= follower**, fan, advocate, friend, champion, ally, defender, sponsor, patron, helper, protagonist, adherent, henchman, apologist, upholder, well-wisher **OPPOSITE:** opponent

suppose *vb* **1 = think**, imagine, expect, judge, assume, guess *(informal, chiefly US & Canad)*, calculate *(US dialect)*, presume, take for granted, infer, conjecture, surmise, dare say, opine, presuppose, take as read
2 = imagine, believe, consider, conclude, fancy, conceive, conjecture, postulate, hypothesize

supposed *adj* **2 = presumed**, alleged, professed, reputed, accepted, assumed, rumoured, hypothetical, putative, presupposed

suppress *vb* **1a = stamp out**, stop, check, crush, conquer, overthrow, subdue, put an end to, overpower, quash, crack down on, quell, extinguish, clamp down on, snuff out, quench, beat down, trample on, drive underground
OPPOSITE: encourage
1b = check, inhibit, subdue, stop, quell, quench **3 = restrain**, cover up, withhold, stifle, contain, silence, conceal, curb, repress, smother, keep secret, muffle, muzzle, hold in check, hold in *or* back

supremacy *n* **1, 2 = domination**, dominance, ascendancy, sovereignty, sway, lordship, mastery, dominion, primacy, pre-eminence, predominance, supreme power, absolute rule, paramountcy

supreme *adj* **1 = paramount**, surpassing, superlative, prevailing, sovereign, predominant, incomparable, mother of all *(informal)*, unsurpassed, matchless
OPPOSITE: least
2 = chief, leading, principal, first, highest, head, top, prime, cardinal, foremost, pre-eminent, peerless
OPPOSITE: lowest
3 = ultimate, highest, greatest, utmost, final, crowning, extreme, culminating

DICTIONARY

supremo ⓘ *n, pl* **-mos** *informal* a person in overall authority
sur-[1] *prefix* over; above; beyond: *surcharge; surrealism*
WORD ORIGIN Old French
sur-[2] *prefix* ▸ see **sub-**
surcharge *n* **1** a charge in addition to the usual payment or tax **2** an excessive sum charged, often unlawfully ▹ *vb* **-charging, -charged** **3** to charge (someone) an additional sum or tax **4** to overcharge (someone) for something
surd *maths n* **1** an irrational number ▹ *adj* **2** of or relating to a surd
WORD ORIGIN Latin *surdus* muffled
sure ⓘ *adj* **1** free from doubt or uncertainty (in regard to a belief): *she was sure that she was still at home; I am sure he didn't mean it* **2** **sure of** having no doubt, such as of the occurrence of a future state or event: *sure of winning the point* **3** reliable or accurate: *a sure sign of dry rot* **4** bound inevitably (to be or do something); certain: *his aggressive style is sure to please the American fans* **5** **sure of** *or* **about** happy to put one's trust in (someone): *I'm still not quite sure about her* **6** **sure of oneself** confident in one's own abilities and opinions **7** not open to doubt: *sure proof* **8** bound to be or occur; inevitable: *victory is sure* **9** physically secure: *a sure footing* **10** **be sure** (usually foll. by *to* or *and*) be careful or certain (to do something): *be sure to label each jar* **11** **for sure** without a doubt **12** **make sure** to make certain: *make sure there is no-one in the car* **13** **sure enough** *informal* in fact: *sure enough, this is happening* **14** **to be sure** it has to be acknowledged; admittedly ▹ *adv* **15** *informal, chiefly US & Canad* without question; certainly: *it sure is bad news* ▹ *interj* **16** *informal* willingly; yes **sureness** *n*
WORD ORIGIN Old French *seur*
sure-fire *adj informal* certain to succeed: *a sure-fire cure*
sure-footed *adj* **1** unlikely to fall, slip, or stumble **2** unlikely to make a mistake
surely ⓘ *adv* **1** am I not right in thinking that? I am sure that: *surely you can see that?* **2** without doubt: *without support they will surely fail* **3** **slowly but surely** gradually but noticeably ▹ *interj* **4** *chiefly US & Canad* willingly; yes
surety *n, pl* **-ties** **1** a person who takes legal responsibility for the fulfilment of another's debt or obligation **2** security given as a guarantee that an obligation will be met
WORD ORIGIN Latin *securitas* security
surf *n* **1** foam caused by waves breaking on the shore or on a reef ▹ *vb* **2** to take part in surfing **3** to move rapidly through a particular medium: *surfing the internet* **4** *informal* to be carried on top of something: *that guy's surfing the audience* **surfer** *n*
WORD ORIGIN probably variant of *sough*
surface ⓘ *n* **1** the outside or top of an object **2** the size of such an area **3** material covering the surface of an object **4** the outward appearance as opposed to the real or hidden nature of something: *on the surface the idea seems attractive* **5** *geom* **a** the complete boundary of a solid figure **b** something that has length and breadth but no thickness **6** the uppermost level of the land or sea **7** **come to the surface** to become apparent after being hidden ▹ *vb* **-facing, -faced** **8** to become apparent or widely known **9** to rise to the surface of water **10** to give (an area) a particular kind of surface **11** *informal* to get up out of bed
WORD ORIGIN French
surface tension *n physics* a property of liquids, caused by molecular forces, that leads to the apparent presence of a surface film and to rising and falling in contact with solids
surfboard *n* a long narrow board used in surfing
surfeit *n formal* **1** an excessive amount **2** excessive eating or drinking **3** an uncomfortably full or sickened feeling caused by eating or drinking too much
WORD ORIGIN French *sourfait*
surfing *n* the sport of riding towards shore on the crest of a wave by standing or lying on a surfboard
surge ⓘ *n* **1** a sudden powerful increase: *a surge in spending* **2** a strong rolling movement of the sea **3** a heavy rolling motion or sound: *a great surge of people* ▹ *vb* **surging, surged** **4** to move forward strongly and suddenly **5** to increase quickly and strongly **6** (of the sea) to rise or roll with a heavy swelling motion
WORD ORIGIN Latin *surgere* to rise
surgeon *n* a medical doctor who specializes in surgery
surgery *n, pl* **-geries** **1** medical treatment in which a person's body is cut open by a surgeon in order to treat or remove the problem part **2** *Brit* a place where, or time when, a doctor or dentist can be consulted **3** *Brit* a time when an MP or councillor can be consulted
WORD ORIGIN Greek *kheir* hand + *ergon* work
surgical *adj* **1** involving or used in surgery **2** (of an action) performed with extreme precision: *a surgical air attack* **surgically** *adv*
surgical spirit *n* methylated spirit used medically for cleaning wounds and sterilizing equipment
surly *adj* **-lier, -liest** bad-tempered and rude
WORD ORIGIN from obsolete *sirly* haughty
surmise *vb* **-mising, -mised** **1** to guess (something) from incomplete or uncertain evidence ▹ *n* **2** a conclusion based on incomplete or uncertain evidence
WORD ORIGIN Old French *surmettre* to accuse
surmount *vb* **1** to overcome (a problem) **2** to be situated on top of (something): *the island is surmounted by a huge black castle* **surmountable** *adj*
WORD ORIGIN Old French *surmonter*
surname *n* a family name as opposed to a first or Christian name

S

THESAURUS

supremo *n (informal)* = **head**, leader, boss *(informal)*, director, master, governor, commander, principal, ruler, baas *(S African)*
sure *adj* **1** = **certain**, positive, clear, decided, convinced, persuaded, confident, satisfied, assured, definite, free from doubt **OPPOSITE:** uncertain **3** = **reliable**, accurate, dependable, effective, precise, honest, unmistakable, undoubted, undeniable, trustworthy, never-failing, trusty, foolproof, infallible, indisputable, sure-fire *(informal)*, unerring, well-proven, unfailing, tried and true **OPPOSITE:** unreliable **4, 8** = **inevitable**, guaranteed, bound, assured, in the bag *(slang)*, inescapable, irrevocable, ineluctable, nailed-on *(slang)* **OPPOSITE:** unsure
surely *adv* **1** = **it must be the case that**, assuredly **2** = **undoubtedly**, certainly, definitely, inevitably, doubtless, for certain, without doubt, unquestionably, inexorably, come what may, without fail, indubitably, doubtlessly, beyond the shadow of a doubt
surface *n* **1** = **covering**, face, exterior, side, top, skin, plane, facet, veneer **4** = **façade**, outward appearance ▹ *vb* **8** = **appear**, emerge, arise, come to light, crop up *(informal)*, transpire, materialize **9** = **emerge**, come up, come to the surface
surge *n* **1** = **rush**, flood, upsurge, sudden increase, uprush **2a** = **flow**, wave, rush, roller, breaker, gush, upsurge, outpouring, uprush **2b** = **tide**, roll, rolling, swell, swirling, billowing **3** = **rush**, wave, storm, outburst, torrent, eruption ▹ *vb* **4a** = **rush**, pour, stream, rise, swell, spill, swarm, seethe, gush, well forth **4b** = **sweep**, rush, storm **6** = **roll**, rush, billow, heave, swirl, eddy, undulate

DICTIONARY

WORD ORIGIN Old French *sur-* over + *nom* name

surpass ❶ *vb* **1** to be greater in extent than or superior in achievement to (something or someone) **2 surpass oneself** *or* **expectations** to go beyond the limit of what was expected
WORD ORIGIN French *surpasser*

surplice *n* a loose knee-length garment with wide sleeves, worn by clergymen and choristers
WORD ORIGIN Old French *sourpelis*

surplus ❶ *n* **1** a quantity or amount left over in excess of what is required **2** *accounting* an excess of income over spending ▷ *adj* **3** being in excess; extra: *surplus to requirements*
WORD ORIGIN Old French

surprise ❶ *n* **1** the act of taking someone unawares: *the element of surprise* **2** a sudden or unexpected event, gift, etc.: *this is a nice surprise* **3** the feeling of being surprised; astonishment: *to our great surprise* **4 take someone by surprise** to capture someone unexpectedly or catch someone unprepared ▷ *adj* **5** causing surprise: *a surprise attack* ▷ *vb* **-prising, -prised 6** to cause (someone) to feel amazement or wonder **7** to come upon or discover (someone) unexpectedly or suddenly **8** to capture or attack (someone) suddenly and without warning **9 surprise into** to provoke (someone) to unintended action by a trick or deception **surprised** *adj* **surprising** *adj* **surprisingly** *adv*
WORD ORIGIN Old French *surprendre* to overtake

surreal *adj* very strange or dreamlike; bizarre

surrealism *n* a movement in art and literature in the 1920s, involving the combination of images that would not normally be found together, as if in a dream **surrealist** *n, adj* **surrealistic** *adj*
WORD ORIGIN French *surréalisme*

surrender ❶ *vb* **1** to give oneself up physically to an enemy after defeat **2** to give (something) up to another, under pressure or on demand: *the rebels surrendered their arms* **3** to give (something) up voluntarily to another: *he was surrendering his own chance for the championship* **4** to give in to a temptation or an influence ▷ *n* **5** the act or instance of surrendering
WORD ORIGIN Old French *surrendre*

surreptitious *adj* done in secret or without permission: *surreptitious moments of bliss* **surreptitiously** *adv*
WORD ORIGIN Latin *surrepticius* furtive

Surrey[1] *n* a county of SE England, on the River Thames: urban in the northeast; crossed from east to west by the North Downs and drained by tributaries of the Thames. Administrative centre: Kingston upon Thames. Pop: 1 064 600 (2003 est). Area: 1679 sq km (648 sq miles)

Surrey[2] *n* **Earl of,** title of *Henry Howard.* ?1517–47, English courtier and poet; one of the first in England to write sonnets. He was beheaded for high treason

surrogate *n* **1** a person or thing acting as a substitute ▷ *adj* **2** acting as a substitute: *a surrogate father*
WORD ORIGIN Latin *surrogare* to substitute

surrogate mother *n* a woman who gives birth to a child on behalf of a couple who cannot have a baby themselves, usually by artificial insemination **surrogate motherhood** *or* **surrogacy** *n*

surround ❶ *vb* **1** to encircle or enclose (something or someone) **2** to exist around (someone or something): *the family members who surround him* ▷ *n* **3** *chiefly Brit* a border, such as the area of uncovered floor between the walls of a room and the carpet **surrounding** *adj*
WORD ORIGIN Old French *suronder*

surroundings ❶ *pl n* the area and environment around a person, place, or thing

surtax *n* an extra tax on incomes above a certain level

Surtees *n* **1 John** born 1934, British racing motorcyclist and motor-racing driver. He was motorcycling world champion (1956, 1958–60) and world champion motor-racing driver (1964), the only man to have been world champion in both sports **2 Robert Smith** 1803–64, British journalist and novelist, who satirized the sporting life of the English gentry in such works as *Jorrocks's Jaunts and Jollities* (1838)

surveillance ❶ *n* close observation of a person suspected of being a spy or a criminal
WORD ORIGIN French

survey ❶ *vb* **1** to view or consider (something) as a whole: *she surveyed her purchases anxiously* **2** to make a detailed map of (an area of land) by measuring or calculating distances and height **3** *Brit* to inspect (a building) to assess its condition and value **4** to make a detailed investigation of the behaviour, opinions, etc. of (a group of people) ▷ *n* **5** a detailed investigation of the behaviour, opinions, etc. of a group of people **6** the act of making a detailed map of an area of land by measuring or calculating distance and height **7** *Brit* an inspection of a building to assess its condition and value **surveying** *n* **surveyor** *n*
WORD ORIGIN French *surveoir*

THESAURUS

S

surpass *vb* **1 = outdo**, top, beat, best, cap *(informal)*, exceed, eclipse, overshadow, excel, transcend, outstrip, outshine, tower above, go one better than *(informal)*, put in the shade

surplus *n* **1 = excess**, surfeit, superabundance, superfluity
OPPOSITE: shortage
▷ *adj* **3 = extra**, spare, excess, remaining, odd, in excess, left over, unused, superfluous
OPPOSITE: insufficient

surprise *n* **2 = shock**, start, revelation, jolt, bombshell, eye-opener *(informal)*, bolt from the blue, turn-up for the books *(informal)*
3 = amazement, astonishment, wonder, incredulity, stupefaction
▷ *vb* **6 = amaze**, astonish, astound, stun, startle, stagger, disconcert, take aback, bowl over *(informal)*, leave open-mouthed, nonplus, flabbergast *(informal)*, take (someone's) breath away **7, 8 = catch unawares** *or* **off-guard**, catch napping, catch on the hop *(informal)*, burst in on, spring upon, catch in the act *or* red-handed, come down on like a bolt from the blue

surrender *vb* **1, 4 = give in**, yield, submit, give way, quit, succumb, cave in *(informal)*, capitulate, throw in the towel, lay down arms, give yourself up, show the white flag
OPPOSITE: resist
2, 3 = give up, abandon, relinquish, resign, yield, concede, part with, renounce, waive, forgo, cede, deliver up ▷ *n* **5 = submission**, yielding, cave-in *(informal)*, capitulation, resignation, renunciation, relinquishment

surround *vb* **1 = enclose**, ring, encircle, encompass, envelop, close in on, fence in, girdle, hem in, environ, enwreath

surroundings *pl n* **= environment**, setting, background, location, neighbourhood, milieu, environs

surveillance *n* **= observation**, watch, scrutiny, supervision, control, care, direction, inspection, vigilance, superintendence

survey *vb* **1 = look over**, view, scan, examine, observe, contemplate, supervise, inspect, eyeball *(slang)*, scrutinize, size up, take stock of, eye up, recce *(slang)*, reconnoitre
2 = measure, estimate, prospect, assess, appraise, triangulate
4 = interview, question, poll, study, research, investigate, sample, canvass ▷ *n* **5 = poll**, study, research, review, inquiry, investigation, opinion poll, questionnaire, census
7 *(Brit)* **= valuation**, estimate, assessment, appraisal

DICTIONARY

survival *n* **1** the condition of having survived something **2** a person or thing that continues to exist in the present despite being from an earlier time, such as a custom ▷ *adj* **3** of, relating to, or assisting the act of surviving: *survival suits*

survive ❶ *vb* **-viving, -vived 1 a** to continue to live or exist **b** to continue to live or exist after (a passage of time or a difficult or dangerous experience) **2** to live after the death of (another)
survivor *n*
WORD ORIGIN Old French *sourvivre*

Susanna *n Apocrypha* **1** the wife of Joachim, who was condemned to death for adultery because of a false accusation, but saved by Daniel's sagacity **2** the book of the Apocrypha containing this story

susceptibility *n, pl* **-ties 1** the quality or condition of being easily affected or influenced by something **2 susceptibilities** emotional feelings

susceptible ❶ *adj* **1 susceptible to a** giving in easily to: *susceptible to political pressure* **b** vulnerable to (a disease or injury): *susceptible to pneumonia* **2** easily affected emotionally; impressionable
WORD ORIGIN Late Latin *susceptibilis*

sushi (soo-shee) *n* a Japanese dish consisting of small cakes of cold rice with a topping of raw fish
WORD ORIGIN Japanese

suspect ❶ *vb* **1** to believe (someone) to be guilty without having any proof **2** to think (something) to be false or doubtful: *he suspected her intent* **3** to believe (something) to be the case; think probable: *I suspect he had another reason* ▷ *n* **4** a person who is believed guilty of a specified offence ▷ *adj* **5** not to be trusted or relied upon: *her commitment to the cause has always been suspect*
WORD ORIGIN Latin *suspicere* to mistrust

suspend ❶ *vb* **1** to hang (something) from a high place **2** to cause (something) to remain floating or hanging: *a huge orange sun suspended above the horizon* **3** to cause (something) to stop temporarily: *the discussions have been suspended* **4** to remove (someone) temporarily from a job or position, usually as a punishment
WORD ORIGIN Latin *suspendere*

suspended animation *n* a state in which the body's functions are slowed down to a minimum for a period of time, such as by freezing or hibernation

suspended sentence *n* a sentence of imprisonment that is not served by an offender unless he or she commits a further offence during a specified time

suspender belt *n* a belt with suspenders hanging from it for holding up women's stockings

suspenders *pl n* **1 a** elastic straps attached to a belt or corset, with fasteners for holding up women's stockings **b** similar fasteners attached to garters for holding up men's socks **2** *US & Canad* also called (Brit): **braces** a pair of straps worn over the shoulders for holding up the trousers

suspense *n* **1** a state of anxiety or uncertainty: *Sue and I stared at each other in suspense* **2** excitement felt at the approach of the climax of a book, film, or play: *action and suspense abound in this thriller* **suspenseful** *adj*
WORD ORIGIN Medieval Latin *suspensum* delay

suspension ❶ *n* **1** the delaying or stopping temporarily of something: *the suspension of the talks* **2** temporary removal from a job or position, usually as a punishment **3** the act of suspending or the state of being suspended **4** a system of springs and shock absorbers that supports the body of a vehicle **5** a device, usually a wire or spring, that suspends or supports something, such as the pendulum of a clock **6** *chem* a mixture in which fine solid or liquid particles are suspended in a fluid

suspension bridge *n* a bridge suspended from cables that hang between two towers and are secured at both ends

suspicion ❶ *n* **1** the act or an instance of suspecting; belief without sure proof that something is wrong **2** a feeling of mistrust **3** a slight trace: *the merest suspicion of a threat* **4 above suspicion** not possibly guilty of anything, through having a good reputation **5 under suspicion** suspected of doing something wrong
WORD ORIGIN Latin *suspicio* distrust

suspicious ❶ *adj* **1** causing one to suspect something is wrong: *suspicious activities* **2** unwilling to trust: *I'm suspicious of his motives*
suspiciously *adv*

suss out *vb Brit, Austral & NZ slang* to work out (a situation or a person's character), using one's intuition
WORD ORIGIN from *suspect*

sustain ❶ *vb* **1** to maintain or continue for a period of time: *I managed to sustain a conversation* **2** to keep up the strength or energy of (someone): *one mouthful of water to sustain him; the merest drop of comfort to sustain me* **3** to suffer (an injury or loss): *he sustained a spinal injury* **4** to support (something) from below **5** to support or agree with (a decision or statement): *objection sustained*
sustained *adj*
WORD ORIGIN Latin *sustinere* to hold up

S

THESAURUS

survive *vb* **1a = remain alive**, live, pull through, last, exist, live on, endure, hold out, subsist, keep body and soul together *(informal)*, be extant, fight for your life, keep your head above water **1a = continue**, last, live on, pull through **2 = live longer than**, outlive, outlast

susceptible *adj* **2 = responsive**, sensitive, receptive, alive to, impressionable, easily moved, suggestible OPPOSITE: unresponsive

suspect *vb* **2 = distrust**, doubt, mistrust, smell a rat *(informal)*, harbour suspicions about, have your doubts about OPPOSITE: trust **3 = believe**, feel, guess, consider, suppose, conclude, fancy, speculate, conjecture, surmise, hazard a guess, have a sneaking suspicion, think probable OPPOSITE: know ▷ *adj* **5 = dubious**, doubtful, dodgy *(Brit, Austral & NZ informal)*, questionable, fishy *(informal)*, iffy *(informal)*, open to suspicion, shonky *(Austral & NZ informal)* OPPOSITE: innocent

suspend *vb* **1, 2 = hang**, attach, dangle, swing, append **3 = postpone**, delay, put off, arrest, cease, interrupt, shelve, withhold, defer, adjourn, hold off, cut short, discontinue, lay aside, put in cold storage OPPOSITE: continue

suspension *n* **1 = postponement**, delay, break, stay, breaking off, interruption, moratorium, respite, remission, adjournment, abeyance, deferment, discontinuation, disbarment

suspicion *n* **1 = idea**, notion, hunch, guess, impression, conjecture, surmise, gut feeling *(informal)*, supposition **2 = distrust**, scepticism, mistrust, doubt, misgiving, qualm, lack of confidence, wariness, bad vibes *(slang)*, dubiety, chariness **3 = trace**, touch, hint, shadow, suggestion, strain, shade, streak, tinge, glimmer, soupçon *(French)*

suspicious *adj* **1 = suspect**, dubious, questionable, funny, doubtful, dodgy *(Brit, Austral & NZ informal)*, queer, irregular, shady *(informal)*, fishy *(informal)*, of doubtful honesty, open to doubt *or* misconstruction, shonky *(Austral & NZ informal)* OPPOSITE: beyond suspicion **2 = distrustful**, suspecting, sceptical, doubtful, apprehensive, leery *(slang)*, mistrustful, unbelieving, wary OPPOSITE: trusting

sustain *vb* **1 = maintain**, continue, keep up, prolong, keep going, keep alive, protract **2a = help**, aid, comfort, foster, assist, relieve,

DICTIONARY

sustainable *adj* **1** capable of being sustained **2** (of economic development or energy sources) capable of being maintained at a steady level without exhausting natural resources or causing ecological damage: *sustainable development*
sustained-release *adj* (of a pill or tablet) coated with a chemical substance that controls the dosage released into a patient's system
sustenance *n* means of maintaining health or life; food and drink
Sutcliffe *n* **Herbert** 1894–1978, English cricketer, who played for Yorkshire; scorer of 149 centuries and 1000 runs in a season 24 times
suture (soo-tcher) *n surgery* a stitch made with catgut or silk thread, to join the edges of a wound together
WORD ORIGIN Latin *suere* to sew
SUV sport (*or* sports) utility vehicle: a high-powered car with four-wheel drive, originally designed for off-road use
Suvorov *n* **Aleksandr Vasilyevich** 1729–1800, Russian field marshal, who fought successfully against the Turks (1787–91), the Poles (1794), and the French in Italy (1798–99)
suzerain *n* **1** a state or sovereign that has some degree of control over a dependent state **2** (formerly) a person who had power over many people **suzerainty** *n*
WORD ORIGIN French
svelte *adj* attractively or gracefully slim; slender
WORD ORIGIN French
Svevo *n* **Italo**, original name *Ettore Schmitz.* 1861–1928, Italian novelist and short-story writer, best known for the novel *Confessions of Zeno* (1923)
SW **1** southwest(ern) **2** short wave
swab *n* **1** *med* a small piece of cotton wool used for applying medication or cleansing a wound ▷*vb* **swabbing, swabbed** **2** to clean or apply medication to (a wound) with a swab **3** to clean (the deck of a ship) with a mop
WORD ORIGIN probably from Middle Dutch *swabbe* mop
swaddle *vb* **-dling, -dled** to wrap (a baby) in swaddling clothes
WORD ORIGIN Old English *swæthel* swaddling clothes
swaddling clothes *pl n* long strips of cloth formerly wrapped round a newborn baby
swag *n* **1** *slang* stolen property **2** *Austral & NZ informal* (formerly) a swagman's pack containing personal belongings
WORD ORIGIN probably Scandinavian
swagger *vb* **1** to walk or behave in an arrogant manner ▷*n* **2** an arrogant walk or manner
WORD ORIGIN probably from *swag*
swagger stick *n* a short cane carried by army officers
swagman *n, pl* **-men** *Austral & NZ informal* a labourer who carries his personal possessions in a pack while looking for work
Swahili (swah-heel-ee) *n* a language of E Africa that is an official language of Kenya and Tanzania
WORD ORIGIN Arabic *sawāhil* coasts
swain *n archaic or poetic* **1** a male lover or admirer **2** a young man from the countryside
WORD ORIGIN Old English *swān* swineherd
swallow[1] ❶ *vb* **1** to pass (food, drink, etc.) through the mouth and gullet to the stomach **2** *informal* to believe (something) trustingly: *I was supposed to swallow the lie* **3** not to show: *I believe they should swallow their pride* **4** to make a gulping movement in the throat, such as when nervous **5** to put up with (an insult) without answering back **6** **be swallowed up** to be taken into and made a part of something: *the old centre was being swallowed up by new estates* ▷*n* **7** the act of swallowing **8** the amount swallowed at any single time; mouthful
WORD ORIGIN Old English *swelgan*
swallow[2] *n* a small migratory bird with long pointed wings and a forked tail
WORD ORIGIN Old English *swealwe*
swallow dive *n* a dive in which the legs are kept straight and the arms outstretched while in the air, with entry into the water made headfirst
swallowtail *n* **1** a butterfly with a long tail-like part on each hind wing **2** the forked tail of a swallow or similar bird
swam *vb* ▸ the past tense of **swim**
swami (swah-mee) *n* a Hindu religious teacher
WORD ORIGIN Hindi *svāmī*
swamp ❶ *n* **1** an area of permanently waterlogged land; bog ▷*vb* **2** *naut* to cause (a boat) to sink or fill with water **3** to overwhelm (a person or place) with more than can be dealt with or accommodated **swampy** *adj*
WORD ORIGIN probably from Middle Dutch *somp*
swan *n* **1** a large, usually white, water bird with a long neck ▷*vb* **swanning, swanned** **2** **swan around** *or* **about** *informal* to wander about without purpose, but with an air of superiority
WORD ORIGIN Old English
Swan[1] *n* a river in SW Western Australia, rising as the Avon northeast of Narrogin and flowing northwest and west to the Indian Ocean below Perth. Length: about 240 km (150 miles)
Swan[2] *n* Sir **Joseph Wilson** 1828–1914, English physicist and chemist, who developed the incandescent electric light (1880) independently of Edison
swank *informal vb* **1** to show off or boast ▷*n* **2** showing off or boasting **swanky** *adj*
WORD ORIGIN origin unknown
swanndri (swan-dry) *n trademark, NZ* a weatherproof woollen shirt or jacket. Also called: **swannie**
swan song *n* the last public act of a person before retirement or death
swap ❶ *or* **swop** *vb* **swapping, swapped** **1** to exchange (something) for something else ▷*n* **2** an exchange
WORD ORIGIN originally, to shake hands on a bargain, strike: probably imitative
SWAPO *or* **Swapo** South-West Africa People's Organization
sward *n* a stretch of turf or grass
WORD ORIGIN Old English *sweard* skin
swarm[1] ❶ *n* **1** a group of bees, led by a queen, that has left the hive to make a new home **2** a large mass of insects or other small animals **3** a moving mass of people ▷*vb* **4** to move quickly and in large numbers **5** to be overrun: *the place is swarming with cops*
WORD ORIGIN Old English *swearm*
swarm[2] *vb* **swarm up** to climb (a ladder or rope) by gripping it with the hands and feet: *the boys swarmed up the rigging*
WORD ORIGIN origin unknown

S

THESAURUS

nurture **2b = keep alive**, nourish, provide for **3 = suffer**, experience, undergo, feel, bear, endure, withstand, bear up under **4 = support**, carry, bear, keep up, uphold, keep from falling
swallow[1] *vb* **1a = eat**, down (*informal*), consume, devour, absorb, swig (*informal*), swill, wash down, ingest **1b = gulp**, drink
swamp *n* **1 = bog**, marsh, quagmire, moss (*Scot & Northern English dialect*), slough, fen, mire, morass, everglade(s) (*US*), pakihi (*NZ*), muskeg (*Canad*) ▷*vb* **2** (*nautical*) **= flood**, engulf, submerge, inundate, deluge **3 = overload**, overwhelm, inundate, besiege, beset, snow under
swap *or* **swop** *vb* **1 = exchange**, trade, switch, traffic, interchange, barter
swarm[1] *n* **2, 3 = multitude**, crowd, mass, army, host, drove, flock, herd, horde, myriad, throng, shoal, concourse, bevy ▷*vb* **4 = crowd**, flock, throng, mass, stream, congregate **5 = teem**, crawl, be alive, abound, bristle, be overrun, be infested

DICTIONARY

swarthy *adj* **swarthier, swarthiest** having a dark complexion
WORD ORIGIN obsolete *swarty*

swash (swosh) *n* the rush of water up a beach following each break of the waves
WORD ORIGIN probably imitative

swashbuckling *adj* having the exciting manner or behaviour of pirates, esp. those depicted in films **swashbuckler** *n*
WORD ORIGIN obsolete *swash* to make the noise of a sword striking a shield + *buckler* shield

swastika *n* **1** a primitive religious symbol in the shape of a Greek cross with the ends of the arms bent at right angles **2** this symbol with clockwise arms as the emblem of Nazi Germany
WORD ORIGIN Sanskrit *svastika*

swat *vb* **swatting, swatted 1** to hit sharply: *swatting the ball with confidence* ▹*n* **2** a sharp blow
WORD ORIGIN dialect variant of *squat*

swatch *n* **1** a sample of cloth **2** a collection of such samples
WORD ORIGIN origin unknown

swath (swawth) *n* ▸same as **swathe**
WORD ORIGIN Old English *swæth*

swathe ➊ *vb* **swathing, swathed 1** to wrap a bandage, garment, or piece of cloth around (a person or part of the body) ▹*n* **2** a long strip of cloth wrapped around something **3** the width of one sweep of a scythe or of the blade of a mowing machine **4** the strip cut in one sweep **5** the quantity of cut crops left in one sweep **6** a long narrow strip of land
WORD ORIGIN Old English *swathian*

sway ➊ *vb* **1** to swing to and fro: *red poppies swayed in the faint breeze* **2** to lean to one side and then the other: *entire rows swayed in time* **3** to be unable to decide between two or more opinions **4** to influence (someone) in his or her opinion or judgment ▹*n* **5** power or influence **6** a swinging or leaning movement **7 hold sway** to have power or influence
WORD ORIGIN probably from Old Norse *sveigja* to bend

swear ➊ *vb* **swearing, swore, sworn 1** to use words considered obscene or blasphemous **2** to promise solemnly on oath; vow: *Sally and Peter swore to love and cherish each other* **3 swear by** to have complete confidence in (something) **4** to state (something) earnestly: *I swear he was all right* **5** to give evidence on oath in a law court
WORD ORIGIN Old English *swerian*

swear in *vb* to make (someone) take an oath when taking up an official position or entering the witness box to give evidence in court: *a new federal president was sworn in*

swear off *vb* to promise to give up: *I lived with memories of the gooey sundaes I've sworn off*

swearword *n* a word considered rude or blasphemous

sweat ➊ *n* **1** the salty liquid that comes out of the skin's pores during strenuous activity in excessive heat or when afraid **2** the state or condition of sweating: *he worked up a sweat* **3** *slang* hard work or effort: *climbing to the crest of Ward Hill was a sweat* **4 in a sweat** *informal* in a state of worry **5 no sweat** *slang* no problem ▹*vb* **sweating, sweat** *or* **sweated 6** to have sweat come through the skin's pores, as a result of strenuous activity, excessive heat, nervousness, or fear **7** *informal* to suffer anxiety or distress **8 sweat blood** *informal* **a** to work very hard **b** to be filled with anxiety ▸See also **sweats** > **sweaty** *adj*
WORD ORIGIN Old English *swǣtan*

sweatband *n* a piece of cloth tied around the forehead or around the wrist to absorb sweat during strenuous physical activity

sweater *n* a warm knitted piece of clothing covering the upper part of the body

sweat lodge *n* (among native N American peoples) a structure in which water is poured onto hot stones to make the occupants sweat for religious or medicinal purposes

sweat off *vb informal* to get rid of (weight) by doing exercises

sweat out *vb* **sweat it out** *informal* to endure an unpleasant situation for a time, hoping for an improvement

sweats *pl n* sweatshirts and sweat suit trousers collectively

sweatshirt *n* a long-sleeved casual top made of knitted cotton or cotton mixture

sweatshop *n* a workshop where employees work long hours in poor conditions for low pay

sweat suit *n* a suit worn by athletes for training, consisting of a sweatshirt and trousers made of the same material

swede *n* a round root vegetable with a purplish-brown skin and yellow flesh
WORD ORIGIN introduced from Sweden in the 18th century

Swede *n* a person from Sweden

Swedish *adj* **1** of Sweden ▹*n* **2** the language of Sweden

Sweelinck *n* **Jan Pieterszoon** 1562–1621, Dutch composer and organist, whose organ works are important for being the first to incorporate independent parts for the pedals

sweep ➊ *vb* **sweeping, swept 1** to clean (a floor or chimney) with a brush **2** (often foll. by *up*) to remove or collect (dirt or rubbish) with a brush **3** to move smoothly and quickly: *the car swept into the drive* **4** to spread rapidly across or through (a place): *the wave of democracy that had swept through Eastern Europe* **5** to move in a proud and majestic fashion: *the boss himself swept into the hall* **6** to direct (one's eyes, line of fire, etc.) over (a place or target) **7 sweep away** *or* **off** to overwhelm (someone) emotionally: *I've been swept away by my fears* **8** to brush or lightly touch (a surface): *the dress swept along the ground* **9** to clear away or get rid of (something) suddenly or forcefully: *these doubts were quickly swept aside; bridges have been swept away by the floods* **10** to stretch out gracefully or majestically, esp. in a wide circle: *the hills swept down into the green valley* **11** to win overwhelmingly in an election: *the umbrella party which swept these elections* **12 sweep the board** to win every event or prize in a contest ▹*n* **13** the act or an instance of sweeping **14** a swift or steady movement: *the wide sweep of the shoulders* **15** a wide expanse: *the whole sweep of the bay* **16** any curving line or contour, such

S

THESAURUS

swathe *vb* **1 = wrap**, drape, envelop, bind, lap, fold, bandage, cloak, shroud, swaddle, furl, sheathe, enfold, bundle up, muffle up, enwrap

sway *vb* **1, 2 = move from side to side**, rock, wave, roll, swing, bend, lean, incline, lurch, oscillate, move to and fro **4 = influence**, control, direct, affect, guide, dominate, persuade, govern, win over, induce, prevail on ▹*n* **5 = power**, control, influence, government, rule, authority, command, sovereignty, jurisdiction, clout *(informal)*, dominion, predominance, ascendency

swear *vb* **1 = curse**, cuss *(informal)*, blaspheme, turn the air blue *(informal)*, be foul-mouthed, take the Lord's name in vain, utter profanities, imprecate **2, 5 = vow**, promise, take an oath, warrant, testify, depose, attest, avow, give your word, state under oath, pledge yourself **4 = declare**, assert, affirm, swear blind, asseverate

sweat *n* **1 = perspiration**, moisture, dampness ▹*vb* **6 = perspire**, swelter, break out in a sweat, exude moisture, glow **7** *(informal)* **= worry**, fret, agonize, lose sleep over, be on tenterhooks, torture yourself, be on pins and needles *(informal)*

sweep *vb* **1 = brush**, clean **2 = clear**, remove, brush, clean **3 = sail**, pass, fly, tear, zoom, glide, skim, scud, hurtle ▹*n* **14 = movement**, move, swing, stroke, gesture **15 = extent**, range, span, stretch, scope, compass

as a driveway **17** ▸ short for **sweepstake 18** *chiefly Brit* ▸ same as **chimney sweep 19 make a clean sweep** to win an overwhelming victory
WORD ORIGIN Middle English *swepen*

sweeper *n* **1** a device used to sweep carpets, consisting of a long handle attached to a revolving brush **2** *soccer* a defensive player usually positioned in front of the goalkeeper

sweeping ⊙ *adj* **1** affecting many people to a great extent: *sweeping financial reforms* **2** (of a statement) making general assumptions about an issue without considering the details **3** decisive or overwhelming: *to suffer sweeping losses* **4** taking in a wide area: *a sweeping view of the area*

sweepstake *or esp. US* **sweepstakes** *n* **1** a lottery in which the stakes of the participants make up the prize **2** a horse race involving such a lottery
WORD ORIGIN originally referring to someone who *sweeps* or takes all the stakes in a game

sweet ⊙ *adj* **1** tasting of or like sugar **2** kind and charming: *that was really sweet of you* **3** attractive and delightful: *a sweet child* **4** (of a sound) pleasant and tuneful: *sweet music* **5** (of wine) having a high sugar content; not dry **6** fresh, clear, and clean: *sweet water; sweet air* **7 sweet on someone** fond of or infatuated with someone ▹ *n* **8** *Brit, Austral & NZ* a shaped piece of confectionery consisting mainly of sugar **9** *Brit, Austral & NZ* a dessert **sweetly** *adv* **sweetness** *n*
WORD ORIGIN Old English *swēte*

Sweet *n* **Henry** 1845–1912, English philologist; a pioneer of modern phonetics. His books include *A History of English Sounds* (1874)

sweet-and-sour *adj* (of food) cooked in a sauce made from sugar and vinegar and other ingredients

sweetbread *n* the meat obtained from the pancreas of a calf or lamb

sweetbrier *n* a wild rose with sweet-smelling leaves and pink flowers

sweet corn *n* **1** a kind of maize with sweet yellow kernels, eaten as a vegetable when young **2** the sweet kernels removed from the maize cob, cooked as a vegetable

sweeten *vb* **1** to make (food or drink) sweet or sweeter **2** to be nice to (someone) in order to ensure cooperation **3** to make (an offer or a proposal) more acceptable

sweetener *n* **1** a sweetening agent that does not contain sugar **2** *Brit, Austral & NZ slang* an inducement offered to someone in order to persuade them to accept an offer or business deal

sweetheart ⊙ *n* **1** an affectionate name to call someone **2** *old-fashioned* one's boyfriend or girlfriend **3** *informal* a lovable or generous person

sweetie *n* *informal* **1** an affectionate name to call someone **2** *Brit & NZ* ▸ same as **sweet** (sense 8) **3** *chiefly Brit* a lovable or generous person

sweetmeat *n* *old-fashioned* a small delicacy preserved in sugar

sweet pea *n* a climbing plant with sweet-smelling pastel-coloured flowers

sweet pepper *n* the large bell-shaped fruit of the pepper plant, which is eaten unripe (**green pepper**) or ripe (**red pepper**) as a vegetable

sweet potato *n* a root vegetable, grown in the tropics, with pinkish-brown skin and yellow flesh

sweet spot *n* *sport* the centre area of a racquet, club, etc. from which the cleanest shots are made

sweet-talk *informal* *vb* **1** to persuade (someone) by flattery: *I thought I could sweet-talk you into teaching me* ▹ *n* **sweet talk 2** insincere flattery intended to persuade

sweet tooth *n* a strong liking for sweet foods

sweet william *n* a garden plant with clusters of white, pink, red, or purple flowers

swell ⊙ *vb* **swelling, swelled; swollen** *or* **swelled 1** (of a part of the body) to grow in size as a result of injury or infection: *his face swelled and became pale* **2** to increase in size as a result of being filled with air or liquid: *a balloon swells if you force in more air* **3** to grow or cause (something) to grow in size, numbers, amount, or degree: *Israel's population is swelling* **4** (of an emotion) to become more intense: *his anger swelled within him* **5** (of the seas) to rise in waves **6** (of a sound) to become gradually louder and then die away ▹ *n* **7** the waving movement of the surface of the open sea **8** an increase in size, numbers, amount, or degree **9** a bulge **10** *old-fashioned informal* a person who is wealthy, upper class, and fashionably dressed **11** *music* an increase in sound followed by an immediate dying away ▹ *adj* **12** *slang, chiefly US* excellent or fine
WORD ORIGIN Old English *swellan*

swelling ⊙ *n* an enlargement of a part of the body as the result of injury or infection

swelter *vb* **1** to feel uncomfortable under extreme heat ▹ *n* **2** a hot and uncomfortable condition: *they left the city swelter for the beach*
WORD ORIGIN Old English *sweltan* to die

sweltering *adj* uncomfortably hot: *a sweltering summer*

swept *vb* ▸ the past of **sweep**

swerve *vb* **swerving, swerved 1** to turn aside from a course sharply or suddenly ▹ *n* **2** the act of swerving
WORD ORIGIN Old English *sweorfan* to scour

Sweyn *n* known as *Sweyn Forkbeard* died 1014, king of Denmark (?986–1014). He conquered England, forcing Ethelred II to flee (1013); father of Canute

THESAURUS

sweeping *adj* **1 = wide-ranging**, global, comprehensive, wide, broad, radical, extensive, all-inclusive, all-embracing, overarching, thoroughgoing **OPPOSITE:** limited **2 = indiscriminate**, blanket, across-the-board, wholesale, exaggerated, overstated, unqualified, overdrawn

sweet *adj* **1 = sugary**, sweetened, cloying, honeyed, saccharine, syrupy, icky (*informal*), treacly **OPPOSITE:** sour **2 = charming**, kind, gentle, tender, affectionate, agreeable, amiable, sweet-tempered **OPPOSITE:** nasty **3 = delightful**, appealing, cute, taking, winning, fair, beautiful, attractive, engaging, lovable, winsome, cutesy (*informal, chiefly US*), likable *or* likeable **OPPOSITE:** unpleasant **4 = melodious**, musical, harmonious, soft, mellow, silvery, tuneful, dulcet, sweet-sounding, euphonious, silver-toned, euphonic **OPPOSITE:** harsh **6 = fresh**, clean, pure, wholesome ▹ *n* **8** (*Brit, Austral & NZ*) **= confectionery**, candy (*US*), sweetie, lolly (*Austral & NZ*), sweetmeat, bonbon **9** (*Brit, Austral & NZ*) **= dessert**, pudding, afters (*Brit informal*), sweet course

sweetheart *n* **1 = dearest**, beloved, sweet, angel, treasure, honey, dear, sweetie (*informal*) **2** (*old-fashioned*) **= love**, boyfriend *or* girlfriend, beloved, lover, steady (*informal*), flame (*informal*), darling, follower (*obsolete*), valentine, admirer, suitor, beau, swain (*archaic*), truelove, leman (*archaic*), inamorata *or* inamorato

swell *vb* **1, 2 = expand**, increase, grow, rise, extend, balloon, belly, enlarge, bulge, protrude, well up, billow, fatten, dilate, puff up, round out, be inflated, become larger, distend, bloat, tumefy, become bloated *or* distended **OPPOSITE:** shrink **3, 4 = increase**, rise, grow, mount, expand, accelerate, escalate, multiply, grow larger **OPPOSITE:** decrease ▹ *n* **7 = wave**, rise, surge, billow

swelling *n* **= enlargement**, lump, puffiness, bump, blister, bulge, inflammation, dilation, protuberance, distension, tumescence

DICTIONARY

swift ❶ *adj* **1** moving or able to move quickly; fast **2** happening or performed quickly or suddenly: *a swift glance this way* **3** **swift to** prompt to (do something): *swift to retaliate* ▷ *n* **4** a small fast-flying insect-eating bird with long wings **swiftly** *adv* **swiftness** *n*
WORD ORIGIN Old English

swig *informal n* **1** a large swallow or deep drink, esp. from a bottle ▷ *vb* **swigging, swigged 2** to drink (some liquid) in large swallows, esp. from a bottle
WORD ORIGIN origin unknown

swill *vb* **1** to drink large quantities of (an alcoholic drink) **2** (often foll. by *out*) *chiefly Brit & NZ* to rinse (something) in large amounts of water ▷ *n* **3** a liquid mixture containing waste food, fed to pigs **4** a deep drink, esp. of beer
WORD ORIGIN Old English *swilian* to wash out

swim *vb* **swimming, swam, swum 1** to move along in water by movements of the arms and legs, or (in the case of fish) tail and fins **2** to cover (a stretch of water) in this way: *the first person to swim the Atlantic* **3** to float on a liquid: *flies swimming on the milk* **4** to be affected by dizziness: *his head was swimming* **5** (of the objects in someone's vision) to appear to spin or move around: *the faces of the nurses swam around her* **6** (often foll. by *in* or *with*) to be covered or flooded with liquid: *a steak swimming in gravy* ▷ *n* **7** the act, an instance, or a period of swimming **8** **in the swim** *informal* fashionable or active in social or political activities **swimmer** *n* **swimming** *n*
WORD ORIGIN Old English *swimman*

swimming bath *n* an indoor swimming pool

swimming costume *or* **bathing costume** *n chiefly Brit, Austral & NZ* ▶ same as **swimsuit**

swimmingly *adv* successfully, effortlessly, or well: *everything went swimmingly*

swimming pool *n* a large hole in the ground, tiled and filled with water for swimming in

swimsuit *n* a woman's swimming garment that leaves the arms and legs bare

Swinburne *n* **Algernon Charles** 1837–1909, English lyric poet and critic

swindle *vb* **-dling, -dled 1** to cheat (someone) out of money **2** to obtain (money) from someone by fraud ▷ *n* **3** an instance of cheating someone out of money **swindler** *n*
WORD ORIGIN German *schwindeln*

swine *n* **1** a mean or unpleasant person **2** *pl* **swine** ▶ same as **pig** ▷ **swinish** *adj*
WORD ORIGIN Old English *swīn*

swine flu *n* a form of influenza occurring in swine caused by a virus capable of spreading to humans

swing ❶ *vb* **swinging, swung 1** to move backwards and forwards; sway **2** to pivot or cause (something) to pivot from a fixed point such as a hinge: *the door swung open* **3** to wave (a weapon, etc.) in a sweeping motion **4** to move in a sweeping curve: *the headlights swung along the street* **5** to alter one's opinion or mood suddenly **6** to hang so as to be able to turn freely **7** *old-fashioned slang* to be hanged: *you'll swing for this!* **8** *informal* to manipulate or influence successfully: *it may help to swing the election* **9** (often foll. by *at*) to hit out with a sweeping motion **10** *old-fashioned* to play (music) in the style of swing **11** *old-fashioned slang* to be lively and modern ▷ *n* **12** the act of swinging **13** a sweeping stroke or punch **14** a seat hanging from two chains or ropes on which a person may swing back and forth **15** popular dance music played by big bands in the 1930s and 1940s **16** *informal* the normal pace at which an activity, such as work, happens: *I'm into the swing of things now* **17** a sudden or extreme change, for example in some business activity or voting pattern **18** **go with a swing** to go well; be successful **19** **in full swing** at the height of activity
WORD ORIGIN Old English *swingan*

swing bridge *n* a bridge that can be swung open to let ships pass through

swing by *vb informal* to go somewhere to pay a visit

swingeing (swin-jing) *adj chiefly Brit* severe or causing hardship: *swingeing spending cuts*

Swinney *n* **John** (**Ramsay**) born 1964, Scottish politician; leader of the Scottish National Party (2000–04)

swipe *vb* **swiping, swiped 1** *informal* to try to hit (someone or something) with a sweeping blow: *he swiped at a boy who ran forward* **2** *slang* to steal (something) **3** to pass (a credit or debit card) through a machine which electronically interprets the information stored in the card ▷ *n* **4** *informal* a hard blow
WORD ORIGIN origin unknown

swirl ❶ *vb* **1** to turn round and round with a twisting motion ▷ *n* **2** a twisting or spinning motion **3** a twisting shape **swirling** *adj*
WORD ORIGIN probably from Dutch *zwirrelen*

swish *vb* **1** to move with or cause (something) to make a whistling or hissing sound ▷ *n* **2** a hissing or rustling sound or movement: *she turned with a swish of her skirt* ▷ *adj* **3** *informal, chiefly Brit, Austral & NZ* smart and fashionable
WORD ORIGIN imitative

Swiss *adj* **1** of Switzerland ▷ *n, pl* **Swiss** **2** a person from Switzerland

Swiss ball *n* a very large inflatable ball made of strong elastic rubber, used for physical exercise and physiotherapy

swiss roll *n* a sponge cake spread with jam or cream and rolled up

switch ❶ *n* **1** a device for opening or closing an electric circuit **2** a sudden quick change **3** an exchange or swap **4** a flexible rod or twig, used for punishment **5** *US & Canad* a pair of movable rails for diverting moving trains from one track to another ▷ *vb* **6** to change quickly and suddenly **7** to exchange (places) or swap (something for something else) **8** *chiefly US & Canad* to transfer (rolling stock) from one railway track to another **9** ▶ see **switch off, switch on**
WORD ORIGIN probably from Middle Dutch *swijch* twig

switchback *n* a steep mountain road, railway, or track which rises and falls sharply many times

switchboard *n* the place in a telephone exchange or office building where telephone calls are connected

switch off *vb* **1** to cause (a device) to stop operating by moving a switch or lever: *she switched off the television* **2** *informal* to become bored and stop paying attention: *when the conversation turned to house prices I switched off*

switch on *vb* **1** to cause (a device) to

THESAURUS

swift *adj* **1 = fast**, quick, rapid, flying, express, winged, sudden, fleet, hurried, speedy, spanking, nimble, quickie (*informal*), nippy (*Brit informal*), fleet-footed, pdq (*slang*)
OPPOSITE: slow
2 = quick, immediate, prompt, rapid, instant, abrupt, ready, expeditious

swing *vb* **1 = sway**, rock, wave, veer, vibrate, oscillate, move back and forth, move to and fro **3 = brandish**, wave, shake, flourish, wield, dangle **4 = turn**, veer, swivel, twist, curve, rotate, pivot, turn on your heel **6 = hang**, dangle, be suspended, suspend, move back and forth **9 = hit out**, strike, swipe, lash out at, slap ▷ *n* **12 = swaying**, sway

swirl *vb* **1 = whirl**, churn, spin, twist, boil, surge, agitate, eddy, twirl

switch *n* **1 = control**, button, lever, on/off device **2 = change**, shift, transition, conversion, reversal, alteration, about-turn, change of direction ▷ *vb* **6 = change**, shift, convert, divert, deviate, change course **7 = exchange**, trade, swap,

DICTIONARY

operate by moving a switch or lever **2** *informal* to produce (a certain type of behaviour or emotion) suddenly or automatically: *she was good at switching on the charm*

swither *Scot vb* **1** to hesitate or be indecisive ▷*n* **2** a state of hesitation or uncertainty
WORD ORIGIN origin unknown

swivel *vb* **-elling, -elled** *or US* **-eling, -eled 1** to turn on or swing round on a central point ▷*n* **2** a coupling device which allows an attached object to turn freely
WORD ORIGIN Old English *swīfan* to turn

swivel chair *n* a chair whose seat is joined to the legs by a swivel, enabling it to be spun round

swizz *n Brit, NZ & S African informal* a swindle or disappointment
WORD ORIGIN origin unknown

swizzle stick *n* a small stick used to stir cocktails

swollen ● *vb* **1** ▸a past participle of **swell** ▷*adj* **2** enlarged by swelling

swoon *vb* **1** *literary* to faint because of shock or strong emotion **2** to be deeply affected by passion for (someone): *you've swooned over a string of rotten men* ▷*n* **3** *literary* a faint **swooning** *adj*
WORD ORIGIN Old English *geswōgen* insensible

swoop ● *vb* **1** (usually foll. by *down*) to move quickly through the air in a downward curve: *an owl swooped down from its perch* **2** (usually foll. by *on*) to move suddenly and quickly towards (a place) in order to attack, arrest, or question the people inside: *nine police cars and vans swooped on the premises* ▷*n* **3** the act of swooping
WORD ORIGIN Old English *swāpan* to sweep

swoosh *vb* **1** to make a swirling or rustling sound when moving or pouring out ▷*n* **2** a swirling or rustling sound or movement
WORD ORIGIN imitative

swop *vb* **swopping, swopped,** *n* ▸same as **swap**

sword *n* **1** a weapon with a long sharp blade and a short handle **2 the sword a** military power **b** death; destruction: *we will put them to the sword* **3 cross swords** to have a disagreement with someone
WORD ORIGIN Old English *sweord*

sword dance *n* a dance in which the performer dances over swords on the ground

swordfish *n, pl* **-fish** *or* **-fishes** a large fish with a very long upper jaw that resembles a sword

Sword of Damocles (**dam**-a-kleez) *n* a disaster that is about to take place
WORD ORIGIN after a flattering courtier forced by Dionysius, tyrant of ancient Syracuse, to sit under a sword suspended by a hair

swordplay *n* the action or art of fighting with a sword

swordsman *n, pl* **-men** a person who is skilled in the use of a sword **swordsmanship** *n*

swordstick *n* a hollow walking stick that contains a short sword

swore *vb* ▸the past tense of **swear**

sworn *vb* **1** ▸the past participle of **swear** ▷*adj* **2** bound by or as if by an oath: *a sworn enemy*

swot[1] *informal vb* **swotting, swotted 1** (often foll. by *up*) to study (a subject) very hard, esp. for an exam; cram ▷*n* **2** a person who works or studies hard
WORD ORIGIN variant of *sweat*

swot[2] *vb* **swotting, swotted,** *n* ▸same as **swat**

swum *vb* ▸the past participle of **swim**

swung *vb* ▸the past of **swing**

Syal *n* **Meera** born 1964, British actress and writer of Punjabi origin, who appeared in the TV comedy series *Goodness Gracious Me* (1998) and *The Kumars at No. 42* (2001–06); her screenplays include *Bhaji on the Beach* (1993)

sybarite (**sib**-bar-ite) *n* **1** a lover of luxury and pleasure ▷*adj* **2** luxurious or sensuous **sybaritic** *adj*
WORD ORIGIN after *Sybaris*, ancient Greek colony in S Italy, famed for its luxury

sycamore *n* **1** a tree with five-pointed leaves and two-winged fruits **2** *US & Canad* an American plane tree
WORD ORIGIN Latin *sycomorus*

sycophant *n* a person who uses flattery to win favour from people with power or influence **sycophancy** *n* **sycophantic** *adj*
WORD ORIGIN Greek *sukophantēs*

Sydney[1] *n* **1** a port in SE Australia, capital of New South Wales, on an inlet of the S Pacific: the largest city in Australia and the first British settlement, established as a penal colony in 1788; developed rapidly after 1820 with the discovery of gold in its hinterland; large wool market; three universities. Pop: 3 502 301 (2001) **2** a port in SE Canada, in Nova Scotia on NE Cape Breton Island: capital of Cape Breton Island until 1820, when the island united administratively with Nova Scotia. Pop: 32 286 (2006)

Sydney[2] *n* a variant spelling of (Sir Philip) **Sidney**

syllabic *adj* of or relating to syllables

syllabify *vb* **-fies, -fying, -fied** to divide (a word) into syllables **syllabification** *n*

syllable *n* **1** a part of a word which is pronounced as a unit, which contains a single vowel sound, and which may or may not contain consonants: for example, 'paper' has two syllables **2** the least mention: *without a syllable about what went on* **3 in words of one syllable** simply and plainly
WORD ORIGIN Greek *sullabē*

syllabub *n Austral & Brit* a dessert made from milk or cream beaten with sugar, wine, and lemon juice
WORD ORIGIN origin unknown

syllabus (**sill**-lab-buss) *n, pl* **-buses** *or* **-bi** (-bye) **a** the subjects studied for a particular course **b** a list of these subjects
WORD ORIGIN Late Latin

syllogism *n* a form of reasoning consisting of two premises and a conclusion, for example *some temples are in ruins; all ruins are fascinating; so some temples are fascinating* **syllogistic** *adj*
WORD ORIGIN Greek *sullogismos*

sylph *n* **1** a slender graceful girl or young woman **2** an imaginary creature believed to live in the air **sylphlike** *adj*
WORD ORIGIN New Latin *sylphus*

sylvan *or* **silvan** *adj chiefly poetic* of or consisting of woods or forests
WORD ORIGIN Latin *silva* forest

Sylvester II *n* original name *Gerbert of Aurillac. c.* 940–1003 AD, French ecclesiastic and scholar; pope (999–1003): noted for his achievements in mathematics and astronomy

symbiosis *n* **1** *biol* a close association of two different animal or plant species living together to their mutual benefit **2** a similar relationship between different individuals or groups: *the symbiosis of the coal and railway industries* **symbiotic** *adj*
WORD ORIGIN Greek: a living together

symbol ● *n* **1** something that represents or stands for something else, usually an object used to represent something abstract **2** a letter, figure, or sign used in mathematics, music, etc. to represent a quantity, operation, function, etc.
WORD ORIGIN Greek *sumbolon* sign

S

THESAURUS

replace, substitute, rearrange, interchange

swollen *adj* **2 = enlarged**, bloated, puffy, inflamed, puffed up, distended, tumescent, oedematous, dropsical, tumid, edematous

swoop *vb* **1 = drop**, plunge, dive, sweep, descend, plummet, pounce, stoop **2 = pounce**, attack, charge, rush, descend

symbol *n* **1 = metaphor**, image, sign, representation, token **2 = representation**, sign, figure, mark, type, image, token, logo, badge, emblem, glyph

DICTIONARY

symbolic ⓣ *adj* **1** of or relating to a symbol or symbols **2** being a symbol of something **symbolically** *adv*

symbolism *n* **1** the representation of something by the use of symbols **2** an art movement involving the use of symbols to express mystical or abstract ideas **symbolist** *adj, n*

symbolize *or* **-ise** *vb* **-izing, -ized** *or* **-ising, -ised 1** to be a symbol of (something) **2** to represent with a symbol **symbolization** *or* **-isation** *n*

symmetry *n, pl* **-tries 1** the state of having two halves that are mirror images of each other **2** beauty resulting from a balanced arrangement of parts **symmetrical** *adj* **symmetrically** *adv*
WORD ORIGIN Greek *summetria* proportion

Symonds *n* **John Addington** 1840–93, English writer, noted for his *Renaissance in Italy* (1875–86) and for studies of homosexuality

Symons *n* **Arthur** 1865–1945, English poet and critic, who helped to introduce the French symbolists to England

sympathetic ⓣ *adj* **1** feeling or showing kindness and understanding **2** (of a person) likeable and appealing: *the film's only sympathetic character* **3 sympathetic to** showing agreement with or willing to lend support to: *sympathetic to the movement* **sympathetically** *adv*

sympathize *or* **-thise** *vb* **-thizing, -thized** *or* **-thising, -thised** ▪ **sympathize with a** to feel or express sympathy for: *I sympathized with this fear* **b** to agree with or support: *Pitt sympathized with these objectives* **sympathizer** *or* **-thiser** *n*

sympathy ⓣ *n, pl* **-thies 1** (often foll. by *for*) understanding of other people's problems; compassion **2 sympathy with** agreement with someone's feelings or interests: *we have every sympathy with how she felt* **3** (*often pl*) feelings of loyalty or support for an idea or a cause: *was this where her sympathies lay?* **4** mutual affection or understanding between two people or a person and an animal
WORD ORIGIN Greek *sympatheia*

symphony *n, pl* **-nies 1** a large-scale orchestral composition with several movements **2** an orchestral movement in a vocal work such as an oratorio **3** ▸ short for **symphony orchestra 4** anything that has a pleasing arrangement of colours or shapes: *the garden was a symphony of coloured bunting* **symphonic** *adj*
WORD ORIGIN Greek *sun-* together + *phōnē* sound

symphony orchestra *n music* a large orchestra that performs symphonies

symposium *n, pl* **-sia** *or* **-siums 1** a conference at which experts or academics discuss a particular subject **2** a collection of essays on a particular subject
WORD ORIGIN Greek *sumposion* a drinking party

symptom ⓣ *n* **1** *med* a sign indicating the presence of an illness or disease **2** anything that is taken as an indication that something is wrong: *a growing symptom of grave social injustice* **symptomatic** *adj*
WORD ORIGIN Greek *sumptōma* chance

synagogue *n* a building for Jewish religious services and religious instruction
WORD ORIGIN Greek *sunagōgē* a gathering

synapse *n anat* a gap where nerve impulses pass between two nerve cells
WORD ORIGIN Greek *sunapsis* junction

sync *or* **synch** *films, television, computers informal vb* **1** to synchronize ▹ *n* **2** synchronization: *the film and sound are in sync*

synchromesh *adj* **1** (of a gearbox) having a system of clutches that synchronizes the speeds of the gearwheels before they engage ▹ *n* **2** a gear system having these features
WORD ORIGIN *synchronized mesh*

synchronism *n* the quality or condition of occurrence at the same time or rate

synchronize *or* **-nise** *vb* **-nizing, -nized** *or* **-nising, -nised 1** (of two or more people) to perform (an action) at the same time: *a synchronized withdrawal of Allied forces* **2** to cause (two or more clocks or watches) to show the same time **3** *films* to match (the soundtrack and the action of a film) precisely **synchronization** *or* **-nisation** *n*

synchronous *adj* occurring at the same time and rate **synchrony** *n*
WORD ORIGIN Greek *sun-* together + *khronos* time

syncline *n geol* a downward slope of stratified rock in which the layers dip towards each other from either side

syncopate *vb* **-pating, -pated** *music* to stress the weak beats in (a rhythm or a piece of music) instead of the strong beats **syncopation** *n*
WORD ORIGIN Medieval Latin *syncopare* to omit a letter or syllable

syncope (**sing**-kop-ee) *n* **1** *med* a faint **2** *linguistics* the omission of sounds or letters from the middle of a word, as in *ne'er* for *never*
WORD ORIGIN Greek *sunkopē* a cutting off

syndic *n Brit* a business or legal agent of some universities or other institutions
WORD ORIGIN Greek *sundikos* defendant's advocate

syndicalism *n* a movement advocating seizure of economic and political power by the industrial working class by means of industrial action, esp. general strikes **syndicalist** *n*

syndicate *n* **1** a group of people or firms organized to undertake a joint project **2** an association of individuals who control organized crime **3** a news agency that sells articles and photographs to a number of newspapers for simultaneous publication ▹ *vb* **-cating, -cated 4** to sell (articles and photographs) to several newspapers for simultaneous publication **5** to form a syndicate of (people) **syndication** *n*
WORD ORIGIN Old French *syndicat*

syndrome *n* **1** *med* a combination of signs and symptoms that indicate a particular disease **2** a set of characteristics indicating the existence of a particular condition or problem
WORD ORIGIN Greek *sundromē*, literally: a running together

synecdoche (sin-**neck**-dock-ee) *n* a figure of speech in which a part is substituted for a whole or a whole for a part, as in *50 head of cattle* for *50 cows*
WORD ORIGIN Greek *sunekdokhē*

synergy *n* the potential ability for individuals or groups to be more successful working together than on their own
WORD ORIGIN Greek *sunergos*

Synge *n* **John Millington** 1871–1909,

S

THESAURUS

symbolic *adj* **1 = representative**, figurative **2 = representative**, token, emblematic, allegorical

sympathetic *adj* **1 = caring**, kind, understanding, concerned, feeling, interested, kindly, warm, tender, pitying, supportive, responsive, affectionate, compassionate, commiserating, warm-hearted, condoling **OPPOSITE:** uncaring

sympathy *n* **1 = compassion**, understanding, pity, empathy, tenderness, condolence(s), thoughtfulness, commiseration, aroha (*NZ*) **OPPOSITE:** indifference **4 = affinity**, agreement, rapport, union, harmony, warmth, correspondence, fellow feeling, congeniality **OPPOSITE:** opposition

symptom *n* **1** (*medical*) **= sign**, mark, indication, warning **2 = manifestation**, sign, indication, mark, evidence, expression, proof, token

Irish playwright. His plays, marked by vivid colloquial Irish speech, include *Riders to the Sea* (1904) and *The Playboy of the Western World*, produced amidst uproar at the Abbey Theatre, Dublin, in 1907

synod *n* a special church council which meets regularly to discuss church affairs
WORD ORIGIN Greek *sunodos*

synonym *n* a word that means the same as another word, such as *bucket* and *pail*
WORD ORIGIN Greek *sun-* together + *onoma* name

synonymous *adj* **1** (often foll. by *with*) having the same meaning (as) **2** (foll. by *with*) closely associated (with): *a family whose name had been synonymous with fine jewellery*

synopsis (sin-op-siss) *n, pl* **-ses** (-seez) a brief review or outline of a subject; summary: *they have sent me a monthly synopsis of the plot*
WORD ORIGIN Greek *sunopsis*

synoptic *adj* **1** of or relating to a synopsis **2** *bible* of or relating to the Gospels of Matthew, Mark, and Luke **synoptically** *adv*

synovia (sine-oh-vee-a) *n med* a clear thick fluid that lubricates the body joints **synovial** *adj*
WORD ORIGIN New Latin

syntax *n* the grammatical rules of a language and the way in which words are arranged to form phrases and sentences **syntactic** *or* **syntactical** *adj*
WORD ORIGIN Greek *suntassein* to put in order

synthesis (sinth-iss-siss) *n, pl* **-ses** (-seez) **1** the process of combining objects or ideas into a complex whole **2** the combination produced by such a process **3** *chem* the process of producing a compound by one or more chemical reactions, usually from simpler starting materials
WORD ORIGIN Greek *sunthesis*

synthesize *or* **-sise** *vb* **-sizing, -sized** *or* **-sising, -sised** **1** to combine (objects or ideas) into a complex whole **2** to produce (a compound) by synthesis

synthesizer *n* a keyboard instrument in which speech, music, or other sounds are produced electronically

synthetic ❶ *adj* **1** (of a substance or material) made artificially by chemical reaction **2** not sincere or genuine: *synthetic compassion* ▹*n* **3** a synthetic substance or material **synthetically** *adv*
WORD ORIGIN Greek *sunthetikos* expert in putting together

syphilis *n* a sexually transmitted disease that causes sores on the genitals and eventually on other parts of the body **syphilitic** *adj*
WORD ORIGIN *Syphilis*, hero of a 16th-century Latin poem

syphon *n, vb* ▸same as **siphon**

Syrian *adj* **1** of Syria ▹*n* **2** a person from Syria

syringa *n* ▸same as **mock orange** or **lilac**
WORD ORIGIN Greek *surinx* tube (its hollow stems were used for pipes)

syringe *n* **1** *med* a device used for withdrawing or injecting fluids, consisting of a hollow cylinder of glass or plastic, a tightly fitting piston, and a hollow needle ▹*vb* **-ringing, -ringed** **2** to wash out, inject, or spray with a syringe: *a harmless blue dye is syringed into the uterus*
WORD ORIGIN Greek *surinx* tube

syrup *n* **1** a solution of sugar dissolved in water and often flavoured with fruit juice: used for sweetening fruit, etc. **2** a thick sweet liquid food made from sugar or molasses: *maple syrup* **3** a liquid medicine containing a sugar solution: *cough syrup*
WORD ORIGIN Arabic *sharāb* a drink

syrupy *adj* **1** (of a liquid) thick or sweet **2** excessively sentimental: *a soundtrack of syrupy violins*

system ❶ *n* **1** a method or set of methods for doing or organizing something: *a new system of production or distribution* **2** orderliness or routine; an ordered manner: *there is no system in his work* **3** the manner in which an institution or aspect of society has been arranged: *the Scottish legal system* **4** **the system** the government and state regarded as exploiting, restricting, and repressing individuals **5** the manner in which the parts of something fit or function together; structure: *disruption of the earth's weather system* **6** any scheme or set of rules used to classify, explain, or calculate: *the Newtonian system of physics* **7** a network of communications, transportation, or distribution **8** *biol* an animal considered as a whole **9** *biol* a set of organs or structures that together perform some function: *the immune system* **10** one's physical or mental constitution: *the intrusion of the ME virus into my system; to get the hate out of my system* **11** an assembly of electronic or mechanical parts forming a self-contained unit: *an alarm system*
WORD ORIGIN Greek *sustēma*

systematic ❶ *adj* following a fixed plan and done in an efficient and methodical way: *a systematic approach to teaching* **systematically** *adv*

systematize *or* **-tise** *vb* **-tizing, -tized** *or* **-tising, -tised** to arrange (information) in a system **systematization** *or* **-tisation** *n*

systemic *adj biol* (of a poison, disease, etc.) affecting the entire animal or body **systemically** *adv*

systems analysis *n* the analysis of the requirements of a task and the expression of these in a form that enables a computer to perform the task **systems analyst** *n*

systole (siss-tol-ee) *n physiol* contraction of the heart, during which blood is pumped into the arteries **systolic** *adj*
WORD ORIGIN Greek *sustolē*

Szell *n* **George** 1897–1970, US conductor, born in Hungary

Szent-Györgyi *n* **Albert (von Nagyrapolt)** 1893–1986, US biochemist, born in Hungary, who isolated ascorbic acid and identified it as vitamin C. Nobel prize for physiology or medicine 1937

Szilard *n* **Leo** 1898–1964, US physicist, born in Hungary, who originated the idea of a self-sustaining nuclear chain reaction (1934). He worked on the atomic bomb during World War II but later pressed for the international control of nuclear weapons

Szymanowski *n* **Karol** 1882–1937, Polish composer, whose works include the opera *King Roger* (1926), two violin concertos, symphonies, piano music, and songs

Szymborska *n* **Wisława** born 1923, Polish poet and writer: Nobel prize for literature 1996

S

THESAURUS

synthetic *adj* **1 = artificial**, manufactured, fake, man-made, mock, simulated, sham, pseudo (*informal*), ersatz **OPPOSITE:** real

system *n* **1 = method**, practice, technique, procedure, routine, theory, usage, methodology, frame of reference, modus operandi, fixed order **6 = arrangement**, structure, organization, scheme, combination, classification, coordination, setup (*informal*)

systematic *adj* **= methodical**, organized, efficient, precise, orderly, standardized, businesslike, well-ordered, systematized **OPPOSITE:** unmethodical

Tt

DICTIONARY

t *or* **T** *n, pl* **t's, T's** *or* **Ts 1** the 20th letter of the English alphabet **2 to a T a** in every detail: *that's her to a T* **b** perfectly: *that dress suits you to a T*

t tonne(s)

T 1 *chem* tritium **2** tera-

t. 1 temperature **2** ton(s)

ta *interj Brit, Austral & NZ informal* thank you

WORD ORIGIN imitative of baby talk

Ta *chem* tantalum

TA (in Britain) Territorial Army

tab¹ *n* **1** a small flap of material, esp. one on a garment for decoration or for fastening to a button **2** any similar flap, such as a piece of paper attached to a file for identification **3** *chiefly US & Canad* a bill, esp. for a meal or drinks **4 keep tabs on** *informal* to keep a watchful eye on

WORD ORIGIN origin unknown

tab² *n* ▸ short for **tabulator**

TAB (in New Zealand) Totalisator Agency Board

tabard *n* **1** a sleeveless jacket, esp. one worn by a medieval knight over his armour **2** a short coat bearing the coat of arms of the sovereign, worn by a herald

WORD ORIGIN Old French *tabart*

Tabari *n* **Muhammad ibn Jarir al-** 838–923 AD, Arab scholar, whose works include a history of the world from the Creation to 915 AD and a commentary on the Koran

Tabasco *n trademark* a very hot red sauce made from peppers

tabby *n, pl* **-bies 1** a cat whose fur has dark stripes or wavy markings on a lighter background ▹ *adj* **2** having dark stripes or wavy markings on a lighter background

WORD ORIGIN from the girl's name *Tabitha*, influenced by *tabby*, old kind of striped silk

tabernacle *n* **1 the Tabernacle** *bible* the portable sanctuary in which the ancient Israelites carried the Ark of the Covenant **2** any place of Christian worship that is not called a church **3** *RC church* a receptacle in which the Blessed Sacrament is kept

WORD ORIGIN Latin *tabernaculum* a tent

tabla *n, pl* **-bla** *or* **-blas** one of a pair of Indian drums played with the hands

WORD ORIGIN Hindi, from Arabic: drum

table ⓣ *n* **1** a piece of furniture consisting of a flat top supported by legs: *a coffee table* **2** a set of facts or figures arranged in rows and columns: *a league table* **3** a group of people sitting round a table for a meal, game, etc.: *the whole table laughed* **4** *formal* the food provided at a meal or in a particular house: *he keeps a good table* **5 turn the tables** to cause a complete reversal of circumstances ▹ *vb* **-bling, -bled 6** *Austral & Brit* to submit (a motion) for discussion by a meeting **7** *US* to suspend discussion of (a proposal) indefinitely

WORD ORIGIN Latin *tabula* a writing tablet

tableau (tab-loh) *n, pl* **-leaux** (-loh) a silent motionless group of people arranged to represent a scene from history, legend, or literature

WORD ORIGIN French

tablecloth *n* a cloth for covering the top of a table, esp. during meals

table d'hôte (tah-bla **dote**) *adj* **1** (of a meal) consisting of a set number of courses with a limited choice of dishes offered at a fixed price ▹ *n, pl* **tables d'hôte** (tah-bla **dote**) **2** a table d'hôte meal or menu

WORD ORIGIN French: the host's table

table football *n Brit* a game based on soccer, played on a table with sets of miniature human figures mounted on rods allowing them to be tilted or spun to strike the ball.. US & Canad name: **foosball**

tableland *n* a flat area of high ground; plateau

table licence *n Brit* a licence permitting the sale of alcohol with meals only

tablespoon *n* **1** a spoon, larger than a dessertspoon, used for serving food **2** Also called: **tablespoonful** the amount contained in such a spoon **3** a unit of capacity used in cooking, equal to half a fluid ounce

tablet *n* **1** a pill consisting of a compressed medicinal substance **2** a flattish cake of some substance, such as soap **3** a slab of stone, wood, etc. used for writing on before the invention of paper **4** an inscribed piece of stone, wood, etc. that is fixed to a wall as a memorial: *a tablet in memory of those who died*

WORD ORIGIN Latin *tabula* a board

table tennis *n* a game resembling a miniature form of tennis played on a table with bats and a small light ball

table wine *n* **1** fairly cheap wine for everyday drinking with meals **2** ordinary wine, as opposed to fortified wine such as sherry or port

tabloid *n* a newspaper with fairly small pages, usually with many photographs and a concise and often sensational style

WORD ORIGIN from *tablet*

taboo ⓣ *or* **tabu** *n, pl* **-boos** *or* **-bus 1** a restriction or prohibition resulting from social or other conventions **2** a ritual prohibition, esp. of something that is considered holy or unclean ▹ *adj* **3** forbidden or disapproved-of: *a taboo subject*

WORD ORIGIN Tongan *tapu*

tabor *n* a small drum used esp. in the Middle Ages, struck with one hand while the other held a pipe

WORD ORIGIN Old French *tabour*

tabular *adj* arranged in parallel columns so as to form a table

WORD ORIGIN Latin *tabula* a board

tabulate *vb* **-lating, -lated** to arrange (information) in rows and columns **tabulation** *n*

tabulator *n* a key on a typewriter or word processor that sets stops so that data can be arranged and presented in columns

tachograph *n* a device that measures the speed of a vehicle and the distance that it covers, and produces a record (**tachogram**) of its readings

WORD ORIGIN Greek *takhos* speed + -GRAPH

tachometer *n* a device for measuring speed, esp. that of a revolving shaft

WORD ORIGIN Greek *takhos* speed + -METER

tacit (tass-it) *adj* understood or implied without actually being stated: *tacit support*

WORD ORIGIN Latin *tacitus* silent

taciturn (tass-it-turn) *adj* habitually silent, reserved, or uncommunicative **taciturnity** *n*

WORD ORIGIN Latin *tacere* to be silent

Tacitus *n* **Publius Cornelius** ?55–?120 AD, Roman historian and orator, famous as a prose stylist. His works include the *Histories*, dealing with the period 68–96, and the *Annals*, dealing with the period 14–68

THESAURUS

table *n* **1 = counter**, bench, stand, board, surface, slab, work surface **2 = list**, chart, tabulation, record, roll, index, register, digest, diagram, inventory, graph, synopsis, itemization ▹ *vb* **6** *(Brit)* **= submit**, propose, put forward, move, suggest, enter, file, lodge, moot

taboo *or* **tabu** *n* **1, 2 = prohibition**, ban, restriction, disapproval, anathema, interdict, proscription, tapu *(NZ)* ▹ *adj* **3 = forbidden**, banned, prohibited, ruled out, not allowed, unacceptable, outlawed, unthinkable, not permitted, disapproved of, anathema, off limits, frowned on, proscribed, beyond the pale, unmentionable

DICTIONARY

tack[1] ⓘ *n* **1** a short sharp-pointed nail with a large flat head **2** *Brit & NZ* a long loose temporary stitch used in dressmaking ▷ *vb* **3** to fasten (something) with a tack or tacks: *the carpet needs to be tacked down* **4** *Brit & NZ* to sew (something) with long loose temporary stitches ▸ See also **tack on**
WORD ORIGIN Middle English *tak* fastening, nail

tack[2] *n* **1** *naut* the course of a boat sailing obliquely into the wind, expressed in terms of the side of the boat against which the wind is blowing: *on the port tack* **2** a course of action or a policy: *telling her to get off my back hadn't worked, so I took a different tack* ▷ *vb* **3** *naut* to steer (a boat) on a zigzag course, so as to make progress against the wind
WORD ORIGIN from *tack* rope used to secure a sail

tack[3] *n* riding harness for horses, including saddles and bridles
WORD ORIGIN from *tackle*

tackies *or* **takkies** *pl n, sing* **tacky** *S African informal* tennis shoes or plimsolls
WORD ORIGIN origin unknown

tackle ⓘ *vb* **-ling, -led** **1** to deal with (a problem or task) in a determined way **2** to confront (someone) about something: *I intend to tackle both management and union on this issue* **3** to attack and fight (a person or animal) **4** *sport* to attempt to get the ball away from (an opposing player) ▷ *n* **5** *sport* an attempt to get the ball away from an opposing player **6** the equipment required for a particular sport or occupation: *fishing tackle* **7** a set of ropes and pulleys for lifting heavy weights **8** *naut* the ropes and other rigging aboard a ship
WORD ORIGIN Middle English

tack on ⓘ *vb* to attach or add (something) to something that is already complete: *an elegant mansion with a modern extension tacked on at the back*

tack room *n* a room in a stable building in which bridles, saddles, etc. are kept

tacky[1] *adj* **tackier, tackiest** slightly sticky **tackiness** *n*
WORD ORIGIN earlier *tack* stickiness

tacky[2] *adj* **tackier, tackiest** *informal* **1** vulgar and tasteless: *tacky commercialism* **2** shabby or shoddy: *tacky streets* **tackiness** *n*
WORD ORIGIN origin unknown

taco (tah-koh) *n, pl* **tacos** *Mexican cookery* a tortilla folded into a roll with a filling and usually fried
WORD ORIGIN from Mexican Spanish, from Spanish: literally, a bite to eat

tact *n* **1** a sense of the best and most considerate way to deal with people so as not to upset them **2** skill in handling difficult situations **tactful** *adj* **tactfully** *adv* **tactless** *adj* **tactlessly** *adv* **tactlessness** *n*
WORD ORIGIN Latin *tactus* a touching

tactic ⓘ *n* a move or method used to achieve an aim or task: *he has perfected dissent as a tactic to further his career.* ▸ See also **tactics**

tactical ⓘ *adj* **1** of or employing tactics: *a tactical advantage* **2** (of missiles, bombing, etc.) for use in limited military operations **tactically** *adv*

tactical voting *n* (in an election) the practice of voting for a candidate or party one would not normally support in an attempt to prevent an even less acceptable candidate or party being elected

tactics ⓘ *n* **1** *mil* the science of the detailed direction of forces in battle to achieve an aim or task ▷ *pl n* **2** the plans and methods used to achieve a particular short-term aim **tactician** *n*
WORD ORIGIN Greek *tassein* to arrange

tactile *adj* of or having a sense of touch: *the tactile sense*
WORD ORIGIN Latin *tactilis*

tadpole *n* the aquatic larva of a frog or toad, which develops from a limbless tailed form with external gills into a form with internal gills, limbs, and a reduced tail
WORD ORIGIN Middle English *tadde* toad + *pol* head

TAFE (in Australia) Technical and Further Education

taffeta *n* a thin shiny silk or rayon fabric used esp. for women's clothes
WORD ORIGIN Persian *tāftah* spun

taffrail *n naut* a rail at the back of a ship or boat
WORD ORIGIN Dutch *taffereel* panel

tag[1] ⓘ *n* **1** a piece of paper, leather, etc. for attaching to something as a mark or label: *the price tag* **2** a point of metal or plastic at the end of a cord or lace **3** a brief trite quotation **4** an electronic device worn by a prisoner under house arrest so that his or her movements can be monitored **5** *slang* a graffito consisting of a nickname or personal symbol ▷ *vb* **tagging, tagged** **6** to mark with a tag ▸ See also **tag along, tag on**
WORD ORIGIN origin unknown

tag[2] *n* **1** a children's game in which one player chases the others in an attempt to touch one of them, who will then become the chaser ▷ *vb* **tagging, tagged** **2** to catch and touch (another child) in the game of tag. Also: **tig**
WORD ORIGIN origin unknown

Tagalog (tag-**gah**-log) *n* a language spoken in the Philippines

tag along *vb* to accompany someone, esp. when uninvited: *I tagged along behind the gang*

tag end *n* the last part of something: *at the tag end of the Ice Age*

tagetes (taj-**eat**-eez) *n, pl* **-tes** any of a genus of plants with yellow or orange flowers, including the French and African marigolds
WORD ORIGIN Latin *Tages*, a god of ancient Etruria

tagliatelle (tal-yat-**tell**-ee) *n* a form of pasta made in narrow strips
WORD ORIGIN Italian

Taglioni *n* **Marie** 1804–84, Italian ballet dancer, whose romantic style greatly influenced ballet in the 19th century

tag on *vb* to add at the end of something: *a throwaway remark, tagged on at the end of a casual conversation*

Tagore *n* **Rabindranath** 1861–1941, Indian poet and philosopher. His verse collections, written in Bengali and English, include *Gitanjali* (1910; 1912): Nobel prize for literature 1913

tahini (tah-**hee**-nee) *n* a paste made from ground sesame seeds, used esp. in Middle Eastern cookery
WORD ORIGIN from Arabic

t'ai chi (tie **chee**) *n* a Chinese system

THESAURUS

OPPOSITE: permitted

tack[1] *n* **1 = nail**, pin, stud, staple, rivet, drawing pin, thumbtack (*US*), tintack ▷ *vb* **3 = fasten**, fix, attach, pin, nail, staple, affix

tackle *vb* **1a = deal with**, take on, set about, wade into, get stuck into (*informal*), sink your teeth into, apply yourself to, come *or* get to grips with, step up to the plate (*informal*) **1b = undertake**, deal with, attempt, try, begin, essay, engage in, embark upon, get stuck into (*informal*), turn your hand to, have a go *or* stab at (*informal*) **4** (*sport*) **= intercept**, block, bring down, stop, challenge ▷ *n* **5** (*sport*) **= block**, stop, challenge **7 = rig**, rigging, apparatus

tack on *vb* **= append**, add, attach, tag, annex

tactic *n* **= policy**, approach, course, way, means, move, line, scheme, plans, method, trick, device, manoeuvre, tack, ploy, stratagem

tactical *adj* **1 = strategic**, politic, shrewd, smart, diplomatic, clever, cunning, skilful, artful, foxy, adroit
OPPOSITE: impolitic

tactics *pl n* **2 = strategy**, campaigning, manoeuvres, generalship

tag[1] *n* **1 = label**, tab, sticker, note, ticket, slip, flag, identification, marker, flap, docket ▷ *vb* **6 = label**, mark, flag, ticket, identify, earmark

DICTIONARY

of exercises and self-defence characterized by slow rhythmic movements
WORD ORIGIN Chinese *t'ai chi ch'uan* great art of boxing

taiga (tie-ga) *n* the belt of coniferous forest extending across much of subarctic North America, Europe, and Asia

taikonaut *n* an astronaut from the People's Republic of China
WORD ORIGIN from Cantonese *taikon(g)* cosmos

tail[1] ⊕ *n* **1** the rear part of an animal's body, usually forming a long thin flexible part attached to the trunk ▸ Related adjective: **caudal** **2** any long thin part projecting or hanging from the back or end of something: *the waiter produced menus from beneath the tail of his coat* **3** the last part: *the tail of the procession* **4** the rear part of an aircraft **5** *astron* the luminous stream of gas and dust particles driven from the head of a comet when it is close to the sun **6** *informal* a person employed to follow and spy upon another **7 turn tail** to run away **8 with one's tail between one's legs** completely defeated and demoralized ▹*adj* **9** at the back: *tail feathers* ▹*vb* **10** *informal* to follow (someone) stealthily ▸ See also **tail off, tails** > **tailless** *adj*
WORD ORIGIN Old English *tægel*

tail[2] *n law* the limitation of an estate or interest to a person and his or her descendants
WORD ORIGIN Old French *taille* a division

tailback *n Brit* a queue of traffic stretching back from an obstruction

tailboard *n* a removable or hinged rear board on a lorry or trailer

tail coat *n* a man's black coat which stops at the hips at the front and has a long back split into two below the waist

tailgate *n* **1** ▸ same as **tailboard** **2** a door at the rear of a hatchback vehicle ▹*vb* **3** to drive very close behind (a vehicle) **tailgater** *n*

tail-light *or* **tail lamp** *n* ▸ same as **rear light**

tail off *or* **away** *vb* **1** to decrease gradually: *orders tailed off* **2** (of someone's voice) to become gradually quieter and then silent

tailor ⊕ *n* **1** a person who makes, repairs, or alters outer garments, esp. menswear ▸ Related adjective: **sartorial** *vb* **2** to cut or style (a garment) to satisfy specific requirements **3** to adapt (something) so as to make it suitable: *activities are tailored to participants' capabilities* **tailored** *adj*
WORD ORIGIN Old French *taillier* to cut

tailorbird *n* a tropical Asian warbler that builds a nest by sewing together large leaves using plant fibres

tailor-made *adj* **1** (of clothing) made by a tailor to fit exactly **2** perfect for a particular purpose: *I'm tailor-made for the role*

tailpiece *n* **1** a piece added at the end of something, for example a report **2** a decorative design at the end of a chapter in a book **3** a piece of wood to which the strings of a stringed musical instrument are attached at its lower end

tailpipe *n* a pipe from which exhaust gases are discharged, esp. in a motor vehicle

tailplane *n* a small horizontal wing at the tail of an aircraft to help keep it stable

tails *pl n* **1** *informal* ▸ same as **tail coat** ▹*interj, adv* **2** with the side of a coin uppermost that does not have a portrait of a head on it

tailspin *n* **1** *aeronautics* ▸ same as **spin** (sense 10) **2** *informal* a state of confusion or panic

tailwind *n* a wind blowing from behind an aircraft or vehicle

Taine *n* **Hippolyte Adolphe** 1828–93, French literary critic and historian. He applied determinist criteria to the study of literature, art, history, and psychology, regarding them as products of environment and race. His works include *Histoire de la littérature anglaise* (1863–64) and *Les Origines de la France contemporaine* (1875–93)

taint ⊕ *vb* **1** to spoil or contaminate by an undesirable quality: *tainted by corruption* ▹*n* **2** a defect or flaw **3** a trace of contamination or infection **tainted** *adj*
WORD ORIGIN Old French *teindre* to dye

taipan *n* a large poisonous Australian snake
WORD ORIGIN Aboriginal

take ⊕ *vb* **taking, took, taken** **1** to remove from a place, usually by grasping with the hand: *he took a fifty-dollar note from his wallet* **2** to accompany or escort: *he took me home* **3** to use as a means of transport: *we took a taxi* **4** to conduct or lead: *that road takes you to Preston* **5** to obtain possession of (something), often dishonestly: *they had taken everything most precious to us* **6** to seize or capture: *her husband had been taken by the rebels* **7** (in games such as chess or cards) to win or capture (a piece, trick, etc.) **8** to choose or select (something to use or buy): *I'll take the green one, please* **9** to put an end to: *he took his own life* **10** to require (time, resources, or ability): *this would have taken years to set up* **11** to use as a particular case: *take a friend of mine for example* **12** to find and make use of (a seat, flat, etc.) **13** to accept the duties of: *the legitimate government will take office* **14** to receive in a specified way: *my mother took it calmly* **15** to receive and make use of: *she took the opportunity to splash her heated face* **16** to eat or drink: *all food substances are toxic if taken in excess* **17** to perform (an action, esp. a beneficial one): *she took a deep breath* **18** to accept (something that is offered or given): *she took a job as a waitress* **19** to put into effect: *taking military action* **20** to make (a photograph) **21** to write down or copy: *taking notes* **22** to work at or study: *taking painting lessons* **23** to do or sit (a test, exam, etc.) **24** to begin to

t

THESAURUS

tail[1] *n* **1 = extremity**, appendage, brush, rear end, hindquarters, hind part, empennage **2, 5** *(astronomy)* **= train**, end, trail, tailpiece ▹*vb* **7 turn tail = run away**, flee, run off, escape, take off *(informal)*, retreat, make off, hook it *(slang)*, run for it *(informal)*, scarper *(Brit slang)*, cut and run, show a clean pair of heels, skedaddle *(informal)*, take to your heels **10** *(informal)* **= follow**, track, shadow, trail, stalk, keep an eye on, dog the footsteps of

tailor *n* **1 = outfitter**, couturier, dressmaker, seamstress, clothier, costumier, garment maker ▹*vb* **3 = adapt**, adjust, modify, cut, style, fit, fashion, shape, suit, convert, alter, accommodate, mould, customize

taint *vb* **1 = spoil**, ruin, contaminate, damage, soil, dirty, poison, foul, infect, stain, corrupt, smear, muddy, pollute, blight, tarnish, blot, blemish, sully, defile, adulterate, besmirch, vitiate, smirch **OPPOSITE:** purify

take *vb* **1 = remove**, draw, pull, fish, withdraw, extract, abstract **2 = accompany**, lead, bring, guide, conduct, escort, convoy, usher **5 = steal**, nick *(slang, chiefly Brit)*, appropriate, pocket, pinch *(informal)*, carry off, swipe *(slang)*, run off with, blag *(slang)*, walk off with, misappropriate, cart off *(slang)*, purloin, filch, help yourself to, gain possession of **OPPOSITE:** return **6 = capture**, arrest, seize, abduct, take into custody, ensnare, entrap, lay hold of **OPPOSITE:** release **10 = require**, need, involve, demand, call for, entail, necessitate **27 = tolerate**, stand, bear, suffer, weather, go through, brave, stomach, endure, undergo, swallow, brook, hack *(slang)*, abide, put up with *(informal)*, withstand, submit to, countenance, pocket, thole *(Scot)* **OPPOSITE:** avoid **29 = have room for**, hold, contain,

DICTIONARY

experience or feel: *he took an interest in psychoanalysis* **25** to accept (responsibility, blame, or credit) **26** to accept as valid: *I take your point* **27** to stand up to or endure: *I can't take this harassment any more* **28** to wear a particular size of shoes or clothes: *what size of shoes do you take?* **29** to have a capacity of or room for: *the Concert Hall can take about 2500 people* **30** to ascertain by measuring: *she comes after breakfast to take her pulse and temperature* **31** to subtract or deduct: *take seven from eleven* **32** to aim or direct: *he took a few steps towards the door* **33** (of a shop, club, etc.) to make (a specified amount of money) from sales, tickets, etc.: *films that take no money at the box office* **34** to have or produce the intended effect: *the dye hasn't taken on your shoes* **35** (of seedlings) to start growing successfully **36** **take account of** *or* **take into account** ▸see **account** (sense 9) **37** **take advantage of** ▸see **advantage** (sense 4) **38** **take care** ▸see **care** (sense 10) **39** **take care of** ▸see **care** (sense 11) **40** **take it** to assume or believe: *I take it that means they don't want to leave* **41** **take part in** ▸see **part** (sense 17) **42** **take place** ▸see **place** (sense 20) **43** **take upon oneself** to assume the right or duty (to do something) **44** **take your time** use as much time as you need ▹*n* **45** *films, music* one of a series of recordings from which the best will be selected **46** *informal chiefly US* a version or interpretation: *Minnelli's bleak take on the story* ▸See also **take after, take against**, etc.

WORD ORIGIN Old English *tacan*

take after *vb* to resemble in appearance or character: *he takes after his grandfather*

take against *vb informal* to start to dislike, esp. for no good reason: *I took against her right from the start*

take apart *vb* **1** to separate (something) into its component parts: *once I'd taken the clock apart I couldn't fit the bits together again* **2** *informal* to criticize severely

take away *vb* **1** to remove or subtract: *the lymph glands are taken away and examined under a microscope* **2** to detract from or lessen the value of (something): *the fact that he beat his wife doesn't take away from his merits as a writer* ▹*prep* **3** minus: *six take away two is four* ▹*adj* **takeaway** **4** *Brit, Austral, & NZ* sold for consumption away from the premises: *takeaway food* ▹*n* **takeaway** *Brit, Austral, & NZ* **5** a shop or restaurant that sells such food **6** a meal sold for consumption away from the premises

take back *vb* **1** to retract or withdraw (something said or promised): *I take back what I said about him* **2** to regain possession of **3** to return for exchange or a refund: *shopkeepers are often reluctant to take back unsatisfactory goods* **4** to accept (someone) back into one's home, affections, etc.: *I'll only take you back if you promise to behave* **5** to remind (one) of the past: *this takes me back to my childhood*

take down *vb* **1** to record in writing **2** to dismantle or remove **3** to reduce (someone) in power or arrogance: *I do think he needed taking down a peg or two*

take for ❶ *vb informal* to consider or suppose to be, esp. mistakenly: *what kind of mug do you take me for?*

take-home pay *n* the remainder of one's pay after income tax and other compulsory deductions have been made

take in *vb* **1** to understand: *I was too tired to take in all of what was being said* **2** *informal* to cheat or deceive: *don't be taken in by his charming manner* **3** to include: *this tour takes in the romance and history of Salzburg, Vienna, and Munich* **4** to receive into one's house: *his widowed mother lived by taking in boarders* **5** to make (clothing) smaller by altering the seams **6** to go to: *taking in a movie*

taken *vb* **1** ▸the past participle of **take** ▹*adj* **2** **taken with** enthusiastically impressed by

take off ❶ *vb* **1** to remove (a garment) **2** (of an aircraft) to become airborne **3** *informal* to set out on a journey: *taking off for the Highlands* **4** *informal* to become successful or popular: *the record took off after being used in a film* **5** to deduct (an amount) from a price or total **6** to withdraw or put an end to: *the bus service has been taken off because of lack of demand* **7** *informal* to mimic (someone) ▹*n* **takeoff** **8** the act or process of making an aircraft airborne **9** *informal* an act of mimicry

take on *vb* **1** to employ or hire **2** to assume or acquire: *his eyes took on a strange intensity* **3** to agree to do: *he took on the job of treasurer* **4** to compete against: *we must take on our foreign competitors*

take out *vb* **1** to remove (something) from a place: *she took a comb out of her bag* **2** to obtain: *she took out American citizenship in 1937* **3** to escort or go out with (someone) on a social trip: *can I take you out for a meal some time?* **4** *informal* to kill, destroy, or maim: *most of the enemy's air defences have been taken out* **5** **take it** *or* **a lot out of** *informal* to sap the energy or vitality of **6** **take it out on** *informal* to vent one's anger on ▹*adj, n* **takeout** **7** *chiefly US & Canad* ▸same as **takeaway** (senses 4, 5, 6)

take over *vb* **1** to gain control or management of **2** to become responsible for (a job) after another person has stopped doing it: *I'll take over the driving if you want a break* **3** **take over from** to become more successful or important than (something), and eventually replace it: *CDs have more or less taken over from records* ▹*n* **takeover** **4** the act of gaining control of a company by buying its shares **5** the act of seizing and taking control of something: *the rebel takeover in Ethiopia*

taker *n* a person who agrees to take something that is offered: *there's only one sweet left – any takers?*

take to *vb* **1** to form a liking for **2** to start using or doing (something) as a habit: *I took to studying the published records of his life*

take up *vb* **1** to occupy or fill (space or time): *looking after the baby takes up most of my time* **2** to adopt the study, practice, or activity of: *I took up architecture* **3** to shorten (a garment) **4** to accept (an offer): *I'd like to take up your offer of help* **5** **take up on** **a** to accept what is offered by (someone): *I might just take you up on that offer* **b** to discuss (something) further with (someone): *I'd like to take you up on that last point* **6** **take up with** **a** to discuss (an issue) with (someone): *take up the matter with the District Council more seriously* **b** to begin to be friendly and spend time with (someone): *he's already taken up with the woman he would marry*

taking *adj* charming, fascinating, or intriguing

takings *pl n* receipts; earnings

Talabani *n* **Jalal** born 1933, Iraqi politician, a Kurd, president of Iraq from 2005

talaq *or* **talak** *n* a form of divorce under Islamic law in which the husband repudiates the marriage by saying 'talaq' three times

WORD ORIGIN Arabic

talc *or* **talcum** *n* **1** ▸same as **talcum powder** **2** a soft mineral, consisting of magnesium silicate, used in the manufacture of ceramics, paints, and talcum powder

WORD ORIGIN Persian *talk*

THESAURUS

accommodate, accept

take for *(informal)* *vb* **= regard as**, see as, believe to be, consider to be, think of as, deem to be, perceive to be, hold to be, judge to be, reckon to be, presume to be, look on as

take off *(informal)* *vb* **7 = parody**, imitate, mimic, mock, ridicule, ape, caricature, send up *(Brit informal)*, spoof *(informal)*, travesty, impersonate, lampoon, burlesque, satirize

takeover *n* **4, 5 = merger**, coup, change of leadership, incorporation

DICTIONARY

talcum powder *n* a powder made of purified talc, usually scented, used to dry or perfume the body

tale ❶ *n* **1** a report, account, or story: *everyone had their own tale to tell about the flood* **2** a malicious piece of gossip **3 tell tales a** to tell fanciful lies **b** to report malicious stories or trivial complaints, esp. to someone in authority **4 tell a tale** to reveal something important **5 tell its own tale** to be self-evident
WORD ORIGIN Old English *talu*

talent ❶ *n* **1** a natural ability to do something well: *the boy has a real talent for writing* **2** a person or people with such ability: *he is the major talent in Italian fashion* **3** *informal* attractive members of the opposite sex collectively: *there's always lots of talent in that pub* **4** any of various ancient units of weight and money
talented *adj*
WORD ORIGIN Greek *talanton* unit of money

talent scout *n* a person whose occupation is the search for talented people, such as sportsmen or performers, for work as professionals

Taliesin *n* 6th century AD, Welsh bard; supposed author of 12 heroic poems in the *Book of Taliesin*

talisman *n, pl* **-mans** a stone or other small object, usually inscribed or carved, believed to protect the wearer from evil influences
talismanic *adj*
WORD ORIGIN Medieval Greek *telesma* ritual

talk ❶ *vb* **1** to express one's thoughts or feelings by means of spoken words **2** to exchange ideas or opinions about something: *they were talking about where they would go on holiday* **3** to give voice to; utter: *he was talking rubbish* **4** to discuss: *the political leaders were talking peace* **5** to reveal information: *she was ready to talk* **6** to be able to speak (a language or style) in conversation: *the ferry was full of people talking French* **7** to spread rumours or gossip **8** to be effective or persuasive: *money talks* **9** to get into a particular condition or state of mind by talking: *I had talked myself hoarse* **10 now you're talking** *informal* at last you're saying something agreeable **11 you can** *or* **can't talk** *informal* you are in no position to comment or criticize ▷*n* **12** a speech or lecture: *a talk on local government reform* **13** an exchange of ideas or thoughts: *we had a talk about our holiday plans* **14** idle chatter, gossip, or rumour **15** (*often pl*) a conference, discussion, or negotiation ▸See also **talk back, talk down**, etc. **talker** *n*
WORD ORIGIN Middle English *talkien*

talkative *adj* given to talking a great deal

talkback *n NZ* a broadcast in which telephone comments or questions from the public are transmitted live

talk back *vb* to answer (someone) rudely or cheekily

talk down *vb* **1 talk down to** to speak to (someone) in a patronizing manner **2** to give instructions to (an aircraft) by radio to enable it to land

talkie *n informal* an early film with a soundtrack

Talking Book *n trademark* a recording of a book, designed to be used by the blind

talking head *n* (on television) a person, shown only from the shoulders up, who speaks without illustrative material

talking point *n* something that causes discussion or argument: *his appointment as manager was a major talking point in football circles*

talking-to ❶ *n informal* a scolding or telling-off

talk into *vb* to persuade (someone) to do something by talking to him or her: *don't let anyone talk you into buying things you don't want*

talk out *vb* **1** to resolve (a problem) by talking: *we won't reach a compromise unless we can talk out our differences* **2** *Brit* to block (a bill) in parliament by discussing it for so long that there is no time to vote on it **3 talk out of** to dissuade (someone) from doing something by talking to him or her

talk round *vb* **1** to persuade (someone) to agree with one's opinion or suggestion: *he didn't want to go, but I talked him round* **2** to discuss (a subject) without coming to a conclusion

tall ❶ *adj* **1** of greater than average height **2** having a specified height: *five feet tall*
WORD ORIGIN Middle English

tallboy *n Brit* a high chest of drawers made in two sections placed one on top of the other

Tallis *n* **Thomas** ?1505–85, English composer and organist; noted for his music for the Anglican liturgy

tall order *n informal* a difficult or unreasonable request

tallow *n* a hard fatty animal fat used in making soap and candles

tall poppy syndrome *n Austral & NZ informal* a tendency to disparage any person who is conspicuously successful

tall ship *n* a large square-rigged sailing ship

tall story *n informal* an unlikely and probably untrue tale

tally ❶ *vb* **-lies, -lying, -lied 1** to agree with or be consistent with something else: *this description didn't seem to me to tally with what we saw* **2** to keep score ▷*n, pl* **-lies 3** any record of debit, credit, the score in a game, etc. **4** an identifying label or mark **5** a stick used (esp. formerly) as a record of the amount of a debt according to the notches cut in it
WORD ORIGIN Latin *talea* a stick

tally-ho *interj* the cry of a participant at a hunt when the quarry is sighted

Talmud *n judaism* the primary source of Jewish religious law **Talmudic** *adj* **Talmudist** *n*
WORD ORIGIN Hebrew *talmūdh* instruction

talon *n* a sharply hooked claw, such as that of a bird of prey
WORD ORIGIN Latin *talus* ankle

tamarillo *n, pl* **-los** a shrub with a red oval edible fruit

tamarind *n* a tropical evergreen tree with fruit whose acid pulp is used as

THESAURUS

tale *n* **1 = story**, narrative, anecdote, account, relation, novel, legend, fiction, romance, saga, short story, yarn (*informal*), fable, narration, conte (*French*), spiel (*informal*), urban myth, urban legend

talent *n* **1 = ability**, gift, aptitude, power, skill, facility, capacity, bent, genius, expertise, faculty, endowment, forte, flair, knack

talk *vb* **1 = speak**, chat, chatter, converse, communicate, rap (*slang*), articulate, witter (*informal*), gab (*informal*), express yourself, prattle, natter, shoot the breeze (*US slang*), prate, run off at the mouth (*slang*), earbash (*Austral & NZ slang*) **2, 4 = discuss**, confer, hold discussions, negotiate, palaver, parley, confabulate, have a confab (*informal*), chew the rag *or* fat (*slang*), korero (*NZ*) **5 = inform**, shop (*slang, chiefly Brit*), grass (*Brit slang*), sing (*slang, chiefly US*), squeal (*slang*), squeak (*informal*), tell all, spill the beans (*informal*), give the game away, blab, let the cat out of the bag, reveal information, spill your guts (*slang*) ▷*n* **12 = speech**, lecture, presentation, report, address, seminar, discourse, sermon, symposium, dissertation, harangue, oration, disquisition, whaikorero (*NZ*)

talking-to *n* (*informal*) **= reprimand**, lecture, rebuke, scolding, row, criticism, wigging (*Brit slang*), slating (*informal*), reproach, ticking-off (*informal*), dressing-down (*informal*), telling-off (*informal*), reproof, rap on the knuckles **OPPOSITE:** praise

tall *adj* **1a = lofty**, big, giant, long-legged, lanky, leggy **1b = high**, towering, soaring, steep, elevated, lofty **OPPOSITE:** short

tally *vb* **1 = agree**, match, accord, fit, suit, square, parallel, coincide, correspond, conform, concur, harmonize **OPPOSITE:** disagree

a food and to make beverages and medicines
WORD ORIGIN Arabic *tamr hindī* Indian date

tamarisk *n* a tree or shrub of the Mediterranean region and S Asia, with scalelike leaves, slender branches, and feathery flower clusters
WORD ORIGIN Latin *tamarix*

Tambo *n* **Oliver** 1917–93, South African politician; president (1977–91) of the African National Congress. He was arrested (1956) with Nelson Mandela but released (1957)

tambour *n* an embroidery frame, consisting of two hoops over which the fabric is stretched while being worked
WORD ORIGIN French

tambourine *n music* a percussion instrument consisting of a single drum skin stretched over a circular wooden frame with pairs of metal discs that jingle when it is struck or shaken
WORD ORIGIN from Old French

tame ❶ *adj* **1 a** (of an animal) changed by humans from a wild state into a domesticated state **b** (of an animal) not afraid of or aggressive towards humans **2** (of a person) tending to do what one is told without questioning or criticizing it **3** mild and unexciting: *the love scenes are fairly tame by modern standards* ▹*vb* **taming, tamed 4** to make (an animal) tame; domesticate **5** to bring under control; make less extreme or dangerous: *many previously deadly diseases have been tamed by antibiotics*
WORD ORIGIN Old English *tam*

Tamil *n* **1** *pl* **-ils** *or* **-il** a member of a people of S India and Sri Lanka **2** the language of the Tamils ▹*adj* **3** of the Tamils

tam-o'-shanter *n* a Scottish brimless woollen cap with a bobble in the centre
WORD ORIGIN after the hero of Burns's poem *Tam o' Shanter*

tamp *vb* to force or pack (something) down by tapping it several times: *he tamped the bowl of his pipe*
WORD ORIGIN probably from obsolete *tampin* plug for gun's muzzle

tamper *vb* (foll. by *with*) **1** to interfere or meddle with without permission: *someone has been tampering with the locks* **2** to attempt to influence someone, esp. by bribery: *an attempt to tamper with the jury*
WORD ORIGIN alteration of *temper* (verb)

tampon *n* an absorbent plug of cotton wool inserted into the vagina during menstruation
WORD ORIGIN French

tan[1] *n* **1** a brown coloration of the skin caused by exposure to ultraviolet rays, esp. those of the sun ▹*vb* **tanning, tanned 2** (of a person or his or her skin) to go brown after exposure to ultraviolet rays **3** to convert (a skin or hide) into leather by treating it with a tanning agent **4** *slang* to beat or flog ▹*adj* **5** yellowish-brown
WORD ORIGIN Medieval Latin *tannare*

tan[2] *maths* tangent

Tancred *n* died 1112, Norman hero of the First Crusade, who played a prominent part in the capture of Jerusalem (1099)

tandem *n* **1** a bicycle with two sets of pedals and two saddles, arranged one behind the other for two riders **2 in tandem** together or in conjunction: *the two drugs work in tandem to combat the disease* ▹*adv* **3** one behind the other: *Jim and Ruth arrived, riding tandem*
WORD ORIGIN Latin *tandem* at length

tandoor *n* a type of Indian clay oven
WORD ORIGIN Urdu

tandoori *adj* cooked in a tandoor: *tandoori chicken*

tang *n* **1** a strong sharp taste or smell: *we could already smell the tang of the distant sea* **2** a trace or hint of something: *there was a tang of cloves in the apple pie* **3** the pointed end of a tool, such as a knife or chisel, which fits into the handle **tangy** *adj*
WORD ORIGIN Old Norse *tangi* point

tangata whenua (**tang**-ah-tah **fen**-noo-ah) *pl n* NZ **1** the original Polynesian settlers in New Zealand **2** descendants of the original Polynesian settlers
WORD ORIGIN Māori: people of the land

Tange *n* **Kenzo** 1913–2005, Japanese architect. His buildings include the Kurashiki city hall (1960) and St Mary's Cathedral in Tokyo (1962–64)

tangent *n* **1** a line, curve, or plane that touches another curve or surface at one point but does not cross it **2** (in trigonometry) the ratio of the length of the opposite side to that of the adjacent side of a right-angled triangle **3 go off at a tangent** suddenly take a completely different line of thought or action ▹*adj* **4** of or involving a tangent **5** touching at a single point
WORD ORIGIN Latin *linea tangens* the touching line

tangential *adj* **1** only having an indirect or superficial relevance: *Hitler's vegetarianism only has a tangential link with the policies of the Nazis* **2** of or being a tangent: *a street tangential to the market square* **tangentially** *adv*

tangerine *n* **1** the small orange-like fruit, with a sweet juicy flesh, of an Asian tree ▹*adj* **2** reddish-orange
WORD ORIGIN *Tangier*, a port in Morocco

tangi (**tang**-ee) *n* NZ **1** a Māori funeral ceremony **2** *informal* a lamentation

tangible ❶ *adj* **1** able to be touched; material or physical **2** real or substantial: *tangible results* **tangibility** *n* **tangibly** *adv*
WORD ORIGIN Latin *tangere* to touch

tangle ❶ *n* **1** a confused or complicated mass of things, such as hair or fibres, knotted or coiled together: *a tangle of wires* **2** a complicated problem or situation ▹*vb* **-gling, -gled 3** to twist (things, such as hair or fibres) together in a confused mass **4** to come into conflict: *the last thing she wanted was to tangle with the police* **5** to catch or trap in a net, ropes, etc.: *the string of the kite had got tangled in the branches* **tangled** *adj*
WORD ORIGIN Middle English *tangilen*

t

THESAURUS

▹*n* **3 = record**, score, total, count, reckoning, running total

tame *adj* **1a, 1b = domesticated**, unafraid, docile, broken, gentle, fearless, obedient, amenable, tractable, used to human contact **OPPOSITE:** wild
2 = submissive, meek, compliant, subdued, manageable, obedient, docile, spiritless, unresisting **OPPOSITE:** stubborn
3 = unexciting, boring, dull, bland, tedious, flat, tiresome, lifeless, prosaic, uninspiring, humdrum, uninteresting, insipid, vapid, wearisome **OPPOSITE:** exciting
▹*vb* **4 = domesticate**, train, break in, gentle, pacify, house-train, make tame **OPPOSITE:** make fiercer
5 = subdue, suppress, master, discipline, curb, humble, conquer, repress, bridle, enslave, subjugate, bring to heel, break the spirit of **OPPOSITE:** arouse

tangible *adj* **1, 2 = definite**, real, positive, solid, material, physical, actual, substantial, objective, concrete, evident, manifest, palpable, discernible, tactile, perceptible, corporeal, touchable **OPPOSITE:** intangible

tangle *n* **1 = knot**, mass, twist, web, jungle, mat, coil, snarl, mesh, ravel, entanglement **2 = mess**, jam, fix (*informal*), confusion, complication, maze, mix-up, shambles, labyrinth, entanglement, imbroglio ▹*vb*
3 = twist, knot, mat, coil, snarl, mesh, entangle, interlock, kink, interweave, ravel, interlace, enmesh, intertwist **OPPOSITE:** disentangle
4 tangle with someone = come into conflict with, come up against, cross swords with, dispute with, contend with, contest with, lock horns with

DICTIONARY

tango *n, pl* **-gos 1** a Latin-American dance characterized by long gliding steps and sudden pauses **2** music for this dance ▹*vb* **-going, -goed 3** to perform this dance
WORD ORIGIN American Spanish

Tanguy *n* **Yves** (iv) 1900–55, US surrealist painter, born in France

taniwha (tun-ee-fah) *n NZ* a mythical Māori monster that lives in rivers and lakes
WORD ORIGIN Māori

Tanizaki Jun-ichiro *n* 1886–1965, Japanese novelist, whose works, such as *Some Prefer Nettles* (1929) and *The Makioka Sisters* (1943–48), reflect the tension between Western values and Japanese traditions

tank *n* **1** a large container for storing liquids or gases **2** an armoured combat vehicle moving on tracks and armed with guns **3** Also called: **tankful** the quantity contained in a tank
WORD ORIGIN Gujarati (language of W India) *tānkh* artificial lake

tankard *n* a large one-handled beer-mug, sometimes fitted with a hinged lid
WORD ORIGIN Middle English

tanked up *adj slang chiefly Brit* very drunk

tanker *n* a ship or lorry for carrying liquid in bulk: *an oil tanker*

tank farming *n* ▸same as **hydroponics** > **tank farmer** *n*

tannery *n, pl* **-neries** a place or building where skins and hides are tanned

Tannhäuser *n* 13th-century German minnesinger, commonly identified with a legendary knight who sought papal absolution after years spent in revelry with Venus. The legend forms the basis of an opera by Wagner

tannic *adj* of, containing, or produced from tannin or tannic acid

tannie (tun-nee) *n S African* a title of respect used to refer to an elderly woman
WORD ORIGIN Afrikaans, literally: aunt

tannin *n* a yellowish compound found in many plants, such as tea and grapes, and used in tanning and dyeing. Also called: **tannic acid**

Tannoy *n trademark, Brit* a type of public-address system

tansy *n, pl* **-sies** a plant with yellow flowers in flat-topped clusters
WORD ORIGIN Greek *athanasia* immortality

tantalize *or* **-lise** *vb* **-lizing, -lized** *or* **-lising, -lised** to tease or make frustrated, for example by tormenting (someone) with the sight of something that he or she wants but cannot have **tantalizing** *or* **-lising** *adj* **tantalizingly** *or* **-lisingly** *adv*
WORD ORIGIN after *Tantalus*, a mythological king condemned to stand in water that receded when he tried to drink it and under fruit that moved away when he reached for it

tantalum *n chem* a hard greyish-white metallic element that resists corrosion. Symbol: Ta
WORD ORIGIN after *Tantalus* (see TANTALIZE), from the metal's incapacity to absorb acids

tantalus *n Brit* a case in which bottles of wine and spirits may be locked with their contents tantalizingly visible

tantamount *adj* **tantamount to** equivalent in effect to: *the raid was tantamount to a declaration of war*
WORD ORIGIN Anglo-French *tant amunter* to amount to as much

tantrum ⓣ *n* a childish outburst of bad temper
WORD ORIGIN origin unknown

Taoiseach (tee-shack) *n* the Prime Minister of the Irish Republic

Taoism (rhymes with **Maoism**) *n* a Chinese system of religion and philosophy advocating a simple honest life and noninterference with the course of natural events
Taoist *n, adj*

tap[1] ⓣ *vb* **tapping, tapped 1** to knock lightly and usually repeatedly: *she tapped gently on the door* **2** to make a rhythmic sound with the hands or feet by lightly and repeatedly hitting a surface with them: *he was tapping one foot to the music* ▹*n* **3** a light blow or knock, or the sound made by it **4** the metal piece attached to the toe or heel of a shoe used for tap-dancing **5** ▸same as **tap-dancing**
WORD ORIGIN Middle English *tappen*

tap[2] ⓣ *n* **1** *Brit, Austral & NZ* a valve by which the flow of a liquid or gas from a pipe can be controlled ▸Usual US word **faucet 2** a stopper to plug a cask or barrel **3** a concealed listening or recording device connected to a telephone **4** *med* the withdrawal of fluid from a bodily cavity: *a spinal tap* **5 on tap a** *informal* ready for use **b** (of drinks) on draught rather than in bottles ▹*vb* **tapping, tapped 6** to listen in on (a telephone conversation) secretly by making an illegal connection **7** to obtain something useful or desirable from (something): *a new way of tapping the sun's energy* **8** to withdraw liquid from (something) as if through a tap: *to tap a cask of wine* **9** to cut into (a tree) and draw off sap from it **10** *Brit, Austral & NZ informal* to obtain (money or information) from (someone) **11** *informal* to make an illicit attempt to recruit (a player or employee bound by an existing contract)
WORD ORIGIN Old English *tæppa*

tapas (tap-ass) *pl n* (in Spanish cookery) light snacks or appetizers, usually eaten with drinks
WORD ORIGIN Spanish *tapa* cover, lid

tap-dancing *n* a style of dancing in which the performer wears shoes with metal plates at the heels and toes that make a rhythmic sound on the stage as he or she dances
tap-dancer *n* **tap dance** *n*

tape ⓣ *n* **1** a long thin strip of cotton or linen used for tying or fastening: *a parcel tied with pink tape* **2 a** ▸short for **magnetic tape b** a spool or cassette containing magnetic tape, and used for recording or playing sound or video signals: *he put a tape into his stereo* **c** the music, speech, or pictures which have been recorded on a particular cassette or spool of magnetic tape **3** a narrow strip of plastic which has one side coated with an adhesive substance and is used to stick paper, etc. together: *sticky tape* **4** a string stretched across the track at the end of a race course **5** ▸short for **tape measure** ▹*vb* **taping, taped 6** Also: **tape-record** to record (speech, music, etc.) on magnetic tape **7** to bind or fasten with tape **8 have a person** *or* **situation taped** *Austral & Brit informal* to have full understanding and control of a person *or* situation
WORD ORIGIN Old English *tæppe*

tape deck *n* **1** the part of a tape recorder which supports the spools or cassettes, and contains the motor and the playback, recording, and erasing heads **2** the unit in a hi-fi system which fulfils the same function

tape drive *n* a machine for storing or transferring information from a computer onto tape

tape measure *n* a tape or length of metal marked off in centimetres or inches, used for measuring

taper *vb* **1** to become narrower

THESAURUS

tantrum *n* **= outburst**, temper, hysterics, fit, storm, paddy (*Brit informal*), wax (*informal, chiefly Brit*), flare-up, paroxysm, bate (*Brit slang*), ill humour, foulie (*Austral slang*), hissy fit (*informal*), strop (*Brit informal*)

tap[1] *vb* **1, 2 = knock**, strike, pat, rap, beat, touch, drum ▹*n* **3 = knock**, pat, rap, beat, touch, drumming, light blow

tap[2] *n* **1 = valve**, spout, faucet (*US & Canad*), spigot, stopcock ▹*vb* **6 = listen in on**, monitor, bug (*informal*), spy on, eavesdrop on, wiretap

tape *n* **1 = binding**, strip, band, string, ribbon ▹*vb* **6 = record**, video, tape-record, make a recording of **7** (*sometimes with* **up**) **= bind**, secure,

DICTIONARY

towards one end **2 taper off** to become gradually less: *treatment should be tapered off gradually* ▷ *n* **3** a long thin fast-burning candle **4** a narrowing
WORD ORIGIN Old English *tapor*

tape recorder *n* an electrical device used for recording and reproducing sounds on magnetic tape

tape recording *n* **1** the act of recording sounds on magnetic tape **2** the magnetic tape used for this: *a tape recording of the interview* **3** the sounds so recorded

tapestry *n, pl* **-tries 1** a heavy woven fabric, often in the form of a picture, used for wall hangings or furnishings **2** ▸ same as **needlepoint** (sense 1) **3** a colourful and complicated situation that is made up of many different kinds of things: *the rich tapestry of Hindustani music*
WORD ORIGIN Old French *tapisserie* carpeting

tapeworm *n* a long flat parasitic worm that inhabits the intestines of vertebrates, including man

tapioca *n* a beadlike starch made from cassava root, used in puddings
WORD ORIGIN S American Indian *tipioca* pressed-out juice

tapir (**tape**-er) *n* a piglike mammal of South and Central America and SE Asia, with a long snout, three-toed hind legs, and four-toed forelegs
WORD ORIGIN S American Indian *tapiira*

tappet *n* a short steel rod in an engine which moves up and down transferring movement from one part of the machine to another
WORD ORIGIN from TAP[1]

taproom *n old-fashioned* the public bar in a hotel or pub

taproot *n* the main root of plants such as the dandelion, which grows straight down and bears smaller lateral roots

tar[1] *n* **1** a dark sticky substance obtained by distilling organic matter such as coal, wood, or peat **2** ▸ same as **coal tar** ▷ *vb* **tarring, tarred 3** to coat with tar **4 tar and feather** to cover (someone) with tar and feathers as a punishment **5 tarred with the same brush** having, or regarded as having, the same faults **tarry** *adj*
WORD ORIGIN Old English *teoru*

tar[2] *n informal* a seaman
WORD ORIGIN short for *tarpaulin*

tarakihi (tarr-a-kee-hee) *or* **terakihi** (terr-a-kee-hee) *n* a common edible sea fish of New Zealand waters
WORD ORIGIN Māori

taramasalata *n* a creamy pale pink pâté, made from the eggs of fish, esp. smoked cod's roe, and served as an hors d'oeuvre
WORD ORIGIN Modern Greek

tarantella *n* **1** a peasant dance from S Italy **2** music for this dance
WORD ORIGIN Italian

tarantula *n* **1** a large hairy spider of tropical America with a poisonous bite **2** a large hairy spider of S Europe
WORD ORIGIN Medieval Latin

tarboosh *n* a felt or cloth brimless cap, usually red and often with a silk tassel, formerly worn by Muslim men
WORD ORIGIN Arabic *tarbūsh*

tardy *adj* **-dier, -diest 1** occurring later than it is expected to or than it should: *he spent the weekend writing tardy thank-you letters* **2** slow in progress, growth, etc.: *we made tardy progress across the ice* **tardily** *adv* **tardiness** *n*
WORD ORIGIN Latin *tardus* slow

tare[1] *n* **1** the weight of the wrapping or container in which goods are packed **2** the weight of a vehicle without its cargo or passengers
WORD ORIGIN Arabic *tarhah* something discarded

tare[2] *n* **1** any of various vetch plants of Eurasia and N Africa **2** *bible* a weed, thought to be the darnel
WORD ORIGIN origin unknown

target ● *n* **1** the object or person that a weapon, ball, etc. is aimed at: *the station was an easy target for an air attack* **2** an object at which an archer or marksman aims, usually a round flat surface marked with circles **3** a fixed goal or objective: *our sales figures are well below target* **4** a person or thing at which criticism or ridicule is directed: *the Chancellor has been the target of much of the criticism* ▷ *vb* **-geting, -geted 5** to direct: *an advertising campaign targeted at gay men* **6** to aim (a missile)
WORD ORIGIN Old French *targette* a little shield

tariff ● *n* **1 a** a tax levied by a government on imports or occasionally exports **b** a list of such taxes **2** a list of fixed prices, for example in a hotel **3** *chiefly Brit* a method of charging for services such as gas and electricity by setting a price per unit
WORD ORIGIN Arabic *ta'rīfa* to inform

Tarkington *n* (**Newton**) **Booth** 1869–1946, US novelist. His works include the historical romance *Monsieur Beaucaire* (1900), tales of the Middle West, such as *The Magnificent Ambersons* (1918) and *Alice Adams* (1921), and the series featuring the character Penrod

Tarkovsky *n* **Andrei** 1932–86, Soviet film director, whose films include *Andrei Rublev* (1966), *Solaris* (1971), *Nostalgia* (1983), and *The Sacrifice* (1986)

Tarmac *n* **1** *trademark* a paving material made of crushed stone bound with a mixture of tar and bitumen, used for a road or airport runway **2 the tarmac** the area of an airport where planes wait and take off or land: *we had to wait for an hour on the tarmac* ▷ *vb* **tarmac, -macking, -macked 3** to apply Tarmac to (a surface)
WORD ORIGIN TAR + MAC(ADAM)

tarn *n chiefly Brit* a small mountain lake
WORD ORIGIN from Old Norse

tarnish ● *vb* **1** (of a metal) to become stained or less bright, esp. by exposure to air or moisture **2** to damage or taint: *the affair could tarnish the reputation of the prime minister* ▷ *n* **3** a tarnished condition, surface, or film on a surface **tarnished** *adj*
WORD ORIGIN Old French *ternir* to make dull

taro *n, pl* **-ros** a plant with a large edible rootstock
WORD ORIGIN Tahitian & Polynesian

tarot (**tarr**-oh) *n* **1** a special pack of cards, now used mainly for fortune-telling **2** a card in a tarot pack with a distinctive symbolic design
WORD ORIGIN French

tarpaulin *n* **1** a heavy waterproof canvas coated with tar, wax, or paint **2** a sheet of this canvas, used as a waterproof covering
WORD ORIGIN probably from TAR[1] + PALL[1]

tarragon *n* a European herb with narrow leaves, which are used as seasoning in cooking
WORD ORIGIN Old French *targon*

tarry *vb* **-ries, -rying, -ried** *old-fashioned* **1** to delay or linger: *I have no plans to tarry longer than necessary* **2** to stay briefly: *most people tarried only a few hours before moving on*
WORD ORIGIN origin unknown

tarsal *anat adj* **1** of the tarsus or tarsi ▷ *n* **2** a tarsal bone

tarseal *n NZ* **1** the bitumen surface of a road **2 the tarseal** the main highway

THESAURUS

stick, seal, wrap

target *n* **1, 2 = mark**, goal, bull's-eye **3 = goal**, aim, objective, end, mark, object, intention, ambition, Holy Grail *(informal)* **4 = victim**, butt, prey, quarry, scapegoat

tariff *n* **1a = tax**, rate, duty, toll, levy, excise, impost, assessment **2 = price list**, charges, schedule

tarnish *vb* **1 = stain**, dull, discolour, spot, soil, dim, rust, darken, blot, blemish, befoul, lose lustre *or* shine
OPPOSITE: brighten
2 = damage, taint, blacken, sully, drag through the mud, smirch
OPPOSITE: enhance
▷ *n* **3 = stain**, taint, discoloration, spot, rust, blot, blemish

DICTIONARY

tarsier *n* a small nocturnal primate of the E Indies, which has very large eyes

tarsus *n, pl* **-si** **1** the bones of the ankle and heel collectively **2** the corresponding part in other mammals and in amphibians and reptiles
WORD ORIGIN Greek *tarsos* flat surface, instep

tart[1] ❶ *n* **1** a pastry case, often having no top crust, with a sweet filling, such as jam or custard **2** *chiefly US* a small open pie with a fruit filling
WORD ORIGIN Old French *tarte*

tart[2] ❶ *adj* **1** (of a flavour) sour or bitter **2** sharp and hurtful: *he made a rather tart comment* **tartly** *adv* **tartness** *n*
WORD ORIGIN Old English *teart* rough

tart[3] ❶ *n informal* a sexually provocative or promiscuous woman: *you look like a tart.* ▸See also **tart up**
WORD ORIGIN from *sweetheart*

tartan *n* **1** a design of straight lines, crossing at right angles to give a chequered appearance, esp. one associated with a Scottish clan **2** a fabric with this design
WORD ORIGIN origin unknown

tartar[1] *n* **1** a hard deposit on the teeth **2** a brownish-red substance deposited in a cask during the fermentation of wine
WORD ORIGIN Medieval Greek *tartaron*

tartar[2] *n* a fearsome or formidable person
WORD ORIGIN from *Tartar*

Tartar *or* **Tatar** *n* **1** a member of a Mongoloid people who established a powerful state in central Asia in the 13th century, now scattered throughout Russia and central Asia ▹*adj* **2** of the Tartars
WORD ORIGIN Persian *Tātār*

tartaric *adj* of or derived from tartar or tartaric acid

tartaric acid *n* a colourless crystalline acid which is found in many fruits

tartar sauce *n* a mayonnaise sauce mixed with chopped herbs and capers, served with seafood

tartine *n* an open sandwich, esp. one with a rich or elaborate topping
WORD ORIGIN French

tartrazine (tar-traz-zeen) *n* an artificial yellow dye used as a food additive

tart up *vb Brit informal* **1** to decorate in a cheap and flashy way: *the shops were tarted up for Christmas* **2** to try to make (oneself) look smart and attractive

Tarzan *n informal, often ironic* a man with great physical strength, agility, and virility
WORD ORIGIN after the hero of stories by E. R. Burroughs

task ❶ *n* **1** a specific piece of work required to be done **2** an unpleasant or difficult job or duty **3 take to task** to criticize or rebuke
WORD ORIGIN Old French *tasche*

taskbar *n* a row of selectable buttons and icons typically running along the bottom of a computer screen, displaying information such as the names of running programs

task force *n* **1** a temporary grouping of military units formed to undertake a specific mission **2** any organization set up to carry out a continuing task

taskmaster *n* a person who enforces hard or continuous work

Tasmanian devil *n* a small flesh-eating marsupial of Tasmania

Tass *n* (formerly) the principal news agency of the Soviet Union

tassel *n* a tuft of loose threads secured by a knot or knob, used to decorate a cushion, piece of clothing, etc.
WORD ORIGIN Old French

Tasso *n* **Torquato** 1544–95, Italian poet, noted for his pastoral idyll *Aminta* (1573) and for *Jerusalem Delivered* (1581), dealing with the First Crusade

taste ❶ *n* **1** the sense by which the flavour of a substance is distinguished by the taste buds **2** the sensation experienced by means of the taste buds **3** a small amount eaten, sipped, or tried on the tongue **4** a brief experience of something: *a taste of the planter's life* **5** a liking for something: *a taste for puns* **6** the ability to appreciate what is beautiful and excellent: *she's got very good taste in clothes* **7** a person's typical preferences as displayed by what they choose to buy, enjoy, etc.: *the film was good but a bit violent for my taste* **8** the quality of not being offensive or bad-mannered: *that remark was in rather poor taste* ▹*vb* **tasting, tasted** **9** to distinguish the taste of (a substance) by means of the taste buds: *I've got a stinking cold and can't taste anything* **10** to take a small amount of (a food or liquid) into the mouth, esp. in order to test the flavour **11** to have a flavour or taste as specified: *the pizza tastes delicious* **12** to have a brief experience of (something): *they have tasted democracy and they won't let go*
WORD ORIGIN Old French *taster*

taste bud *n* any of the cells on the surface of the tongue, by means of which the sensation of taste is experienced

tasteful *adj* having or showing good social or aesthetic taste: *tasteful decor* **tastefully** *adv*

tasteless *adj* **1** lacking in flavour: *the canteen serves cold, tasteless pizzas* **2** lacking social or aesthetic taste: *a room full of tasteless ornaments; a tasteless remark* **tastelessly** *adv* **tastelessness** *n*

taster *n* **1** a person employed to test the quality of food or drink by tasting it **2** a sample of something intended to indicate what the entire thing is like: *the entrance hall was filled with flowers, giving a taster of the splendours in the main exhibition*

tasty ❶ *adj* **tastier, tastiest** having

t

THESAURUS

tart[1] *n* **1 = pie**, pastry, pasty, tartlet, patty

tart[2] *adj* **1 = sharp**, acid, sour, bitter, pungent, tangy, astringent, piquant, vinegary, acidulous, acerb
OPPOSITE: sweet

tart[3] *n (informal)* **= slut**, prostitute, hooker *(US slang)*, whore, slag *(Brit slang)*, call girl, working girl *(facetious, slang)*, harlot, streetwalker, loose woman, fallen woman, scrubber *(Brit & Austral slang)*, strumpet, trollop, floozy *(slang)*, woman of easy virtue, fille de joie *(French)*, hornbag *(Austral slang)*

task *n* **1 = job**, duty, assignment, work, business, charge, labour, exercise, mission, employment, enterprise, undertaking, occupation, chore, toil **3 take someone to task = criticize**, blame, blast, lecture, carpet *(informal)*, censure, rebuke, reprimand, reproach, scold, tear into *(informal)*, tell off *(informal)*, diss *(slang, chiefly US)*, read the riot act to, reprove, upbraid, lambast(e), bawl out *(informal)*, chew out *(US & Canad informal)*, tear (someone) off a strip *(Brit informal)*, give a rocket to *(Brit & NZ informal)*

taste *n* **2 = flavour**, savour, relish, smack, tang **OPPOSITE:** blandness **3 = bit**, bite, drop, swallow, sip, mouthful, touch, sample, dash, nip, spoonful, morsel, titbit, soupçon *(French)* **5 = liking**, preference, penchant, fondness, partiality, desire, fancy, leaning, bent, appetite, relish, inclination, palate, predilection **OPPOSITE:** dislike **6 = refinement**, style, judgment, culture, polish, grace, discrimination, perception, appreciation, elegance, sophistication, cultivation, discernment **OPPOSITE:** lack of judgment ▹*vb* **9 = distinguish**, perceive, discern, differentiate **10 = sample**, try, test, relish, sip, savour, nibble **11** *(often with* **of***)* **= have a flavour of**, smack of, savour of **12 = experience**, know, undergo, partake of, feel, encounter, meet with, come up against, have knowledge of
OPPOSITE: miss

tasty *adj* **= delicious**, luscious,

DICTIONARY

a pleasant flavour

tat *n Brit* tatty or tasteless articles

ta-ta *interj chiefly Brit informal* goodbye
WORD ORIGIN origin unknown

Tatar *n, adj* ▸ same as **Tartar**

Tate *n* **1** (**John Orley**) **Allen** 1899–1979, US poet and critic **2** Sir **Henry** 1819–99, British sugar refiner and philanthropist; founder of the Tate Gallery **3** **Nahum** 1652–1715, British poet, dramatist, and hymn-writer, born in Ireland: poet laureate (1692–1715). He is best known for writing a version of *King Lear* with a happy ending

tater *n Brit dialect* a potato

Tati *n* **Jacques**, real name *Jacques Tatischeff*. 1908–82, French film director, pantomimist, and comic actor, creator of the character Monsieur Hulot

tattered *adj* **1** ragged or torn: *a tattered old book* **2** wearing ragged or torn clothing: *the tattered refugees*

tatters *pl n* **1** torn ragged clothing **2** **in tatters** **a** (of clothing) torn in several places **b** (of an argument, plan, etc.) completely destroyed

tatting *n* **1** an intricate type of lace made by looping a thread of cotton or linen with a hand shuttle **2** the work of producing this
WORD ORIGIN origin unknown

tattle *vb* **-tling, -tled** **1** to gossip or chatter ▹ *n* **2** gossip or chatter **tattler** *n*
WORD ORIGIN Middle Dutch *tatelen*

tattletale ❶ *n chiefly US & Canad* a scandalmonger or gossip

tattoo¹ *n, pl* **-toos** **1** a picture or design made on someone's body by pricking small holes in the skin and filling them with indelible dye ▹ *vb* **-tooing, -tooed** **2** to make pictures or designs on (a person's skin) by pricking and staining it with indelible colours **tattooed** *adj* **tattooist** *n*
WORD ORIGIN Tahitian *tatau*

tattoo² *n, pl* **-toos** **1** (formerly) a signal by drum or bugle ordering soldiers to return to their quarters **2** a military display or pageant **3** any drumming or tapping
WORD ORIGIN Dutch *taptoe*

tatty *adj* **-tier, -tiest** worn out, shabby, or unkempt
WORD ORIGIN Scots

Tatum *n* **1** **Art,** full name *Arthur Tatum*. 1910–56, US jazz pianist **2** **Edward Lawrie** 1909–75, US biochemist, who showed how genes regulate biochemical processes in an organism and demonstrated that bacteria reproduce sexually; Nobel prize for physiology or medicine (1958) with Beadle and Lederberg

taught *vb* ▸ the past of **teach**

taunt ❶ *vb* **1** to tease or provoke (someone) with jeering remarks ▹ *n* **2** a jeering remark **taunting** *adj*
WORD ORIGIN French *tant pour tant* like for like

Taurus *n astrol* the second sign of the zodiac; the Bull
WORD ORIGIN Latin

taut *adj* **1** stretched tight: *the cable must be taut* **2** showing nervous strain: *he was looking taut and anxious* **3** (of a film or piece of writing) having no unnecessary or irrelevant details: *a taut thriller*
WORD ORIGIN Middle English *tought*

tauten *vb* to make or become taut

tautology *n, pl* **-gies** the use of words which merely repeat something already stated, as in *reverse back* **tautological** *or* **tautologous** *adj*
WORD ORIGIN Greek *tautologia*

Tavener *n* Sir **John** (**Kenneth**) born 1944, British composer, whose works include the cantata *The Whale* (1966), the opera *Thérèse* (1979), and the choral work *The Last Discourse* (1998); many of his later works are inspired by the liturgy of the Russian Orthodox Church

tavern ❶ *n* **1** *old-fashioned* a pub **2** *US, Canad, Austral & NZ* a place licensed for the sale and consumption of alcoholic drink
WORD ORIGIN Latin *taberna* hut

Taverner *n* **John** ?1495–1545, English composer, esp. of church music; best known for the mass *Western Wynde*, based on a secular song

tawdry *adj* **-drier, -driest** cheap, showy, and of poor quality: *tawdry Christmas decorations*
WORD ORIGIN Middle English *seynt Audries lace*, finery sold at the fair of St Audrey

Tawney *n* **R**(**ichard**) **H**(**enry**) 1880–1962, British economic historian, born in India. His chief works are *The Acquisitive Society* (1920), *Religion and the Rise of Capitalism* (1926), and *Equality* (1931)

tawny *adj* brown to brownish-orange
WORD ORIGIN Old French *tané*

tawny owl *n* a European owl having a reddish-brown plumage and a round head

tawse *n Scot* a leather strap with one end cut into thongs, formerly used by schoolteachers to hit children who had misbehaved
WORD ORIGIN probably plural of obsolete *taw* strip of leather

tax ❶ *n* **1** a compulsory payment to a government to raise revenue, levied on income, property, or goods and services ▹ *vb* **2** to levy a tax on (people, companies, etc.) **3** to make heavy demands on: *the task taxed his ingenuity and patience* **4** **tax someone with** to accuse someone of: *he was taxed with parochialism and meanness* **taxable** *adj* **taxing** *adj*
WORD ORIGIN Latin *taxare* to appraise

taxation *n* the levying of taxes or the condition of being taxed

tax avoidance *n* reduction of tax liability by lawful methods

tax-deductible *adj* legally deductible from income or wealth before tax assessment

tax disc *n* (in Britain) a small disc of paper which must be displayed on a vehicle to show that the tax due on it for that year has been paid

tax evasion *n* reduction of tax liability by illegal methods

tax-free *adj* not needing to have tax paid on it: *a tax-free lump sum*

tax haven *n* a country or state having a lower rate of taxation than elsewhere

taxi *n, pl* **taxis** **1** Also called: **cab, taxicab** a car that may be hired, along with its driver, to carry passengers to any specified destination ▹ *vb* **taxiing, taxied** **2** (of an aircraft) to move along the ground, esp. before takeoff and after landing
WORD ORIGIN *taximeter cab*

taxidermy *n* the art of preparing, stuffing, and mounting animal skins so that they have a lifelike

THESAURUS

palatable, delectable, good-tasting, savoury, full-flavoured, yummy *(slang)*, flavoursome, scrumptious *(informal)*, appetizing, toothsome, flavourful, sapid, lekker *(S African slang)*, yummo *(Austral slang)*
OPPOSITE: bland

tattletale *n (chiefly US & Canad)* = **gossip**, busybody, babbler, prattler, chatterbox *(informal)*, blether, chatterer, bigmouth *(slang)*, scandalmonger, gossipmonger

taunt *vb* **1** = **jeer**, mock, tease, ridicule, provoke, insult, torment, sneer, deride, revile, twit, guy *(informal)*, gibe ▹ *n* **2** = **jeer**, dig, insult, ridicule, cut, teasing, provocation, barb, derision, sarcasm, gibe

tavern *n* **1** = **inn**, bar, pub *(informal, chiefly Brit)*, public house, watering hole *(facetious, slang)*, boozer *(Brit, Austral & NZ informal)*, beer parlour *(Canad)*, beverage room *(Canad)*, hostelry, alehouse *(archaic)*, taproom

tax *n* **1** = **charge**, rate, duty, toll, levy, tariff, excise, contribution, assessment, customs, tribute, imposition, tithe, impost ▹ *vb* **2** = **charge**, impose a tax on, levy a tax on, rate, demand, assess, extract, exact, tithe **3** = **strain**, push, stretch, try, test, task, load, burden, drain, exhaust, weaken, weary, put pressure on, sap, wear out, weigh heavily on, overburden, make heavy demands on, enervate

DICTIONARY

appearance **taxidermist** *n*
WORD ORIGIN Greek *taxis* arrangement + *derma* skin

taximeter *n* a meter fitted to a taxi to register the fare, based on the length of the journey

taxi rank *n* a place where taxis wait to be hired

taxman *n, pl* **-men 1** a collector of taxes **2** *informal* a tax-collecting body personified: *he was convicted of conspiring to cheat the taxman*

taxonomy *n* **1** the branch of biology concerned with the classification of plants and animals into groups based on their similarities and differences **2** the science or practice of classification **taxonomic** *adj* **taxonomist** *n*
WORD ORIGIN Greek *taxis* order + *nomia* law

taxpayer *n* a person or organization that pays taxes

tax relief *n* a reduction in the amount of tax a person or company has to pay

tax return *n* a declaration of personal income used as a basis for assessing an individual's liability for taxation

tax year *n* a period of twelve months used by a government as a basis for calculating taxes

Tb *chem* terbium

TB tuberculosis

tba *or* **TBA** to be arranged

tbc *or* **TBC** to be confirmed

T-bone steak *n* a large choice steak cut from the sirloin of beef, containing a T-shaped bone

tbs. *or* **tbsp.** tablespoon(ful)

Tc *chem* technetium

te *n music* (in tonic sol-fa) the seventh note of any ascending major scale

Te *chem* tellurium

tea *n* **1 a** a drink made by infusing the dried chopped leaves of an Asian shrub in boiling water: *would you like a cup of tea?* **b** the dried chopped leaves of an Asian shrub used to make this drink: *could you get some tea at the grocer's?* **c** the Asian shrub on which these leaves grow **2** *Brit, Austral, & NZ* the main evening meal **3** *chiefly Brit* a light meal eaten in mid-afternoon, usually consisting of tea and cakes, sometimes with sandwiches **4** a drink like tea made from other plants: *mint tea*
WORD ORIGIN Ancient Chinese *d'a*

tea bag *n* a small bag containing tea leaves, infused in boiling water to make tea

teacake *n chiefly Brit* a flat bun, usually eaten toasted and buttered

teach ❶ *vb* **teaching, taught 1** to tell or show (someone) how to do something **2** to give instruction or lessons in (a subject) to (students) **3** to cause to learn or understand: *life has taught me to seize the day* **4 teach someone a lesson** to warn or punish someone: *a bully has to be taught a lesson* **teachable** *adj*
WORD ORIGIN Old English *tǣcan*

Teach *n* **Edward,** known as *Blackbeard.* died 1718, English pirate, active in the West Indies and on the Atlantic coast of North America

teacher ❶ *n* a person whose job is to teach others, esp. children

tea chest *n* a large light wooden box used for exporting tea or storing things in

teaching *n* **1** the art or profession of a teacher **2 teachings** the ideas and principles taught by a person, school of thought, etc.: *the teachings of the Catholic Church*

teaching hospital *n* a hospital attached to a medical school, in which students are taught and given supervised practical experience

tea cloth *n* ▸ same as **tea towel**

tea cosy *n* a covering for a teapot to keep the contents hot

teacup *n* **1** a cup out of which tea may be drunk **2** Also called: **teacupful** the amount a teacup will hold

teahouse *n* a restaurant, esp. in Japan or China, where tea and light refreshments are served

teak *n* the hard yellowish-brown wood of an East Indian tree, used for furniture making
WORD ORIGIN Malayalam (a language of S India) *tēkka*

teal *n, pl* **teals** *or* **teal** a small freshwater duck related to the mallard
WORD ORIGIN Middle English *tele*

tea leaves *pl n, sing* **tea leaf** the dried and shredded leaves of the tea shrub, esp. those left behind in a cup or teapot after tea has been made and drunk

team ❶ *n* **1** a group of players forming one of the sides in a sporting contest **2** a group of people organized to work together: *a team of scientists* **3** two or more animals working together: *a sledge pulled by a team of dogs* ▹ *vb* **4 team up with** to join with (someone) in order to work together **5 team with** to match (something) with something else: *navy skirts teamed with various coloured blouses*
WORD ORIGIN Old English *tēam* offspring

team-mate *n* a fellow member of a team

team spirit *n* willingness to cooperate as part of a team

teamster *n* **1** *US & Canad* a truck driver **2** (formerly) a driver of a team of horses

teamwork *n* the cooperative work done by a team

teapot *n* a container with a lid, spout, and handle, in which tea is made and from which it is served

tear[1] ❶ *n* **1** Also called: **teardrop** a drop of salty fluid appearing in and falling from the eye ▸ Related adjectives: **lacrimal, lachrymal, lacrymal 2 in tears** weeping
WORD ORIGIN Old English *tēar*

tear[2] ❶ *vb* **tearing, tore, torn 1** to rip a hole in (something): *I tore my jumper on a nail* **2** to pull apart or to pieces: *eagles have powerful beaks for tearing flesh* **3** to hurry or rush **4** to remove or take by force: *the sacred things torn from the temples of Inca worshippers* **5 tear at someone's heartstrings** to cause someone distress or anguish **6** to injure (a muscle or ligament) by moving or twisting it violently ▹ *n* **7** a hole or split ▸ See also **tear away, tear down, tear into**
WORD ORIGIN Old English *teran*

tear away *vb* **1** to persuade (oneself or someone else) to leave: *she stood and watched, unable to tear herself away from the room* ▹ *n* **tearaway 2** *Brit* a wild or unruly person

tear down *vb* to destroy or demolish: *it will be cheaper to tear down the old house and build a new one than to repair it*

tear duct *n* a short tube in the inner corner of the eyelid, through which tears drain into the nose

tearful *adj* weeping or about to weep **tearfully** *adv*

tear gas *n* a gas that stings the eyes and causes temporary blindness, used in warfare and to control riots

tearing *adj* very urgent: *I had been in a tearing hurry to leave the camp*

tear into *vb informal* to attack vigorously and damagingly

THESAURUS

teach *vb* **1** *(often with* **how***)* **= show,** train, demonstrate **2 = instruct,** train, coach, school, direct, advise, inform, discipline, educate, drill, tutor, enlighten, impart, instil, inculcate, edify, give lessons in

teacher *n* **= instructor,** coach, tutor, don, guide, professor, trainer, lecturer, guru, mentor, educator, handler, schoolteacher, pedagogue, dominie *(Scot)*, master *or* mistress, schoolmaster *or* schoolmistress

team *n* **1 = side,** squad, troupe **2 = group,** company, set, body, band, crew, gang, line-up, bunch, posse *(informal)*

tear[1] *pl n* **2 in tears = weeping,** crying, sobbing, whimpering, blubbering, visibly moved

tear[2] *vb* **1 = rip,** split, rend, shred, rupture, sunder **2 = pull apart,** claw, lacerate, sever, mutilate, mangle, mangulate *(Austral slang)* **3 = rush,** run, charge, race, shoot, fly, career, speed, belt *(slang)*, dash, hurry, barrel (along) *(informal, chiefly US & Canad)*, sprint, bolt, dart, gallop, zoom, burn

DICTIONARY

tear-jerker *n informal* an excessively sentimental film or book
tearoom *n* **1** *chiefly Brit* a restaurant where tea and light refreshments are served **2** *NZ* a room in a school or university where hot drinks are served
tease ❶ *vb* **teasing, teased 1** to make fun of (someone) in a provocative and often playful manner **2** to arouse sexual desire in (someone) with no intention of satisfying it **3** to raise the nap of (a fabric) with a teasel ▷*n* **4** a person who teases **5** a piece of teasing behaviour **teasing** *adj*
WORD ORIGIN Old English *tǣsan*
teasel, teazel *or* **teazle** *n* **1** a plant of Eurasia and N Africa, with prickly heads of yellow or purple flowers **2** the dried flower head of a teasel, used, esp. formerly, for raising the nap of cloth
WORD ORIGIN Old English *tǣsel*
tease out *vb* **1** to comb (hair, flax, or wool) so as to remove any tangles **2** to extract information with difficulty: *it's not easy to tease out the differences between anxiety and depression*
teaser *n* **1** a difficult question **2** a preliminary advertisement in a campaign that makes people curious to know what product is being advertised
teaspoon *n* **1** a small spoon used for stirring tea or coffee **2** Also called: **teaspoonful** the amount contained in such a spoon **3** a unit of capacity used in cooking etc. equal to 5 ml
teat *n* **1** the nipple of a breast or udder **2** something resembling a teat such as the rubber mouthpiece of a feeding bottle
WORD ORIGIN Old French *tete*
tea towel *or* **tea cloth** *n* a towel for drying dishes
tea tree *n* a tree of Australia and New Zealand that yields an oil used as an antiseptic
tech *n informal* a technical college
tech. 1 technical **2** technology
techie *or* **techy** *informal n* **1** a person who is skilled in the use of technological devices, such as computers ▷*adj* **2** of, relating to, or skilled in the use of such devices
technetium (tek-**neesh**-ee-um) *n chem* a silvery-grey metallic element, produced artificially, esp. by the fission of uranium. Symbol: Tc
WORD ORIGIN Greek *tekhnētos* man-made
technical ❶ *adj* **1** of or specializing in industrial, practical, or mechanical arts and applied sciences: *a technical school* **2** skilled in practical activities rather than abstract thinking **3** relating to a particular field of activity: *technical jargon* **4** according to the letter of the law: *a last-minute penalty awarded to the Irish for a technical offence* **5** showing technique: *technical perfection* **technically** *adv*
technical college *n Austral & Brit* an institution for further education that provides courses in art and technical subjects
technical drawing *n* drawing done by a draughtsman with compasses, T-squares, etc.
technicality *n, pl* **-ties 1** a petty formal point arising from a strict interpretation of the law or a set of rules: *the case was dismissed on a legal technicality* **2** a detail of the method used to do something: *the technicalities of making a recording*
technical knockout *n boxing* a judgment of a knockout given when a boxer is, in the referee's opinion, too badly beaten to continue without risk of serious injury
technician *n* a person skilled in a particular technical field: *oil technicians*
Technicolor *n trademark* a process of producing colour film for the cinema by superimposing synchronized films of the same scene, each having a different colour filter
technikon *n S African* a technical college
technique ❶ *n* **1** a method or skill used for a particular task: *modern management techniques* **2** proficiency in a practical or mechanical skill: *he lacks the technique to be a good player*
WORD ORIGIN Greek *tekhnē* skill
techno *n* a type of very fast disco music, using electronic sounds and having a strong technological influence
techno- *combining form* of or relating to technology: *technocrat*
WORD ORIGIN Greek *tekhnē* skill
technocracy *n, pl* **-cies** government by scientists, engineers, and other experts **technocrat** *n* **technocratic** *adj*
WORD ORIGIN Greek *tekhnē* skill + *kratos* power
technology *n, pl* **-gies 1** the application of practical or mechanical sciences to industry or commerce **2** the scientific methods or devices used in a particular field: *the latest aircraft technology* **technological** *adj* **technologist** *n*
WORD ORIGIN Greek *tekhnologia* systematic treatment
technophile *n* **1** a person who is enthusiastic about technology ▷*adj* **2** enthusiastic about technology
technophobia *n* fear of using technological devices, such as computers **technophobe** *n* **technophobic** *adj*
tectonics *n geol* the study of the earth's crust and the forces that produce changes in it
WORD ORIGIN Greek *tektōn* a builder
Tecumseh *n* ?1768–1813, American Indian chief of the Shawnee tribe. He attempted to unite western Indian tribes against the White people, but was defeated at Tippecanoe (1811). He was killed while fighting for the British in the War of 1812
ted[1] *vb* **tedding, tedded** to shake out (hay), so as to dry it
WORD ORIGIN Old Norse *tethja*
ted[2] *n Brit informal* ▸short for **teddy boy**
Tedder *n* **Arthur William,** 1st Baron Tedder of Glenguin. 1890–1967, British marshal of the Royal Air Force; deputy commander under Eisenhower of the Allied Expeditionary Force (1944–45)
teddy[1] *n, pl* **-dies** ▸short for **teddy bear**
teddy[2] *n, pl* **-dies** a woman's one-piece undergarment incorporating a camisole top and French knickers
WORD ORIGIN origin unknown
teddy bear *n* a stuffed toy bear
WORD ORIGIN after *Teddy* (Theodore) Roosevelt, US president
teddy boy *n* (in Britain, esp. in the mid-1950s) a youth who wore mock Edwardian fashions
WORD ORIGIN *Teddy*, from *Edward*
Te Deum (tee **dee**-um) *n Christianity* an ancient Latin hymn beginning Te Deum Laudamus (we praise thee, O God)
tedious ❶ *adj* boring and uninteresting **tediously** *adv* **tediousness** *n*

t

THESAURUS

rubber *(informal)* ▷*n* **7 = hole**, split, rip, run, rent, snag, rupture
tease *vb* **1 = mock**, bait, wind up *(Brit slang)*, worry, bother, provoke, annoy, needle *(informal)*, plague *(informal)*, rag, rib *(informal)*, torment, ridicule, taunt, aggravate *(informal)*, badger, pester, vex, goad, bedevil, take the mickey out of *(informal)*, twit, chaff, guy *(informal)*, gibe, pull someone's leg *(informal)*, make fun of **2 = tantalize**, lead on, flirt with, titillate
technical *adj* **2 = scientific**, technological, skilled, specialist, specialized, hi-tech *or* high-tech
technique *n* **1 = method**, way, system, approach, means, course, style, fashion, manner, procedure, mode, MO, modus operandi **2 = skill**, art, performance, craft, touch, know-how *(informal)*, facility, delivery, execution, knack, artistry, craftsmanship, proficiency, adroitness
tedious *adj* **= boring**, dull, dreary, monotonous, tiring, annoying, fatiguing, drab, banal, tiresome,

DICTIONARY

tedium *n* the state of being bored or the quality of being boring: *the tedium of a nine-to-five white-collar job*
WORD ORIGIN Latin *taedium*

tee *n* **1** a support for a golf ball, usually a small wooden or plastic peg, used when teeing off **2** an area on a golf course from which the first stroke of a hole is made **3** a mark used as a target in certain games such as curling and quoits ▸See also **tee off**
WORD ORIGIN origin unknown

tee-hee *or* **te-hee** *interj* an exclamation of mocking laughter
WORD ORIGIN imitative

teem[1] *vb* **teem with** to have a great number of: *the woods were teeming with snakes and bears*
WORD ORIGIN Old English *tēman* to produce offspring

teem[2] *vb* (of rain) to pour down in torrents
WORD ORIGIN Old Norse *tœma*

teen *adj informal* ▸same as **teenage**

teenage *adj* **1** (of a person) aged between 13 and 19 **2** typical of or designed for people aged between 13 and 19: *teenage fashions*

teenager ❶ *n* a person between the ages of 13 and 19

teens *pl n* **1** the years of a person's life between the ages of 13 and 19 **2** all the numbers that end in *-teen*

teeny *adj* **-nier, -niest** *informal* extremely small
WORD ORIGIN variant of *tiny*

teenybopper *n old-fashioned slang* a young teenager, usually a girl, who is a keen follower of fashion and pop music
WORD ORIGIN *teeny* teenage + *-bopper* someone who bops

tee off *vb* **teeing, teed** *golf* to hit (the ball) from a tee at the start of a hole

teepee *n* ▸same as **tepee**

teeter *vb* to wobble or move unsteadily
WORD ORIGIN Middle English *titeren*

teeth *n* **1** ▸the plural of **tooth** **2** the power to produce a desired effect: *resolution 672 had no teeth* **3 armed to the teeth** very heavily armed **4 get one's teeth into** to become engrossed in **5 in the teeth of** in spite of: *trying to run a business in the teeth of the recession*

teethe *vb* **teething, teethed** (of a baby) to grow his or her first teeth

teething ring *n* a hard ring on which babies may bite while teething

teething troubles *pl n* problems arising during the early stages of a project

teetotal *adj* never drinking alcohol **teetotaller** *n*
WORD ORIGIN reduplication of *t* + *total*

TEFL Teaching of English as a Foreign Language

Teflon *n trademark* a substance used for nonstick coatings on saucepans etc.

te-hee *interj* ▸same as **tee-hee**

Teilhard de Chardin *n* **Pierre** 1881–1955, French Jesuit priest, palaeontologist, and philosopher. *The Phenomenon of Man* (1938–40), uses scientific evolution to prove the existence of God

Te Kanawa *n* Dame **Kiri** born 1944, New Zealand operatic soprano

tel. telephone

tele- *combining form* **1** at or over a distance: *telecommunications* **2** television: *telegenic* **3** via telephone or television: *teleconference*
WORD ORIGIN Greek *tele* far

telecast *vb* **-casting, -cast** *or* **-casted** **1** to broadcast by television ▹*n* **2** a television broadcast **telecaster** *n*

telecommunications *n* communications using electronic equipment, such as telephones, radio, and television

telecommuting *n* ▸same as **teleworking**

telegram *n* (formerly) a message transmitted by telegraph

telegraph *n* **1** (formerly) a system by which information could be transmitted over a distance, using electrical signals sent along a cable ▹*vb* **2** (formerly) to send (a message) by telegraph **3** to give advance notice of (something), esp. unintentionally: *the twist in the plot was telegraphed long in advance* **4** *Canad informal* to cast (a vote) illegally by impersonating a registered voter **telegraphist** *n* **telegraphic** *adj*

telegraphy *n* (formerly) the science or use of a telegraph

telekinesis *n* movement of a body by thought or willpower, without the application of a physical force **telekinetic** *adj*

Telemann *n* **Georg Philipp** 1681–1767, German composer, noted for his prolific output

telemetry *n* the use of electronic devices to record or measure a distant event and transmit the data to a receiver **telemetric** *adj*

teleology *n* **1** *philosophy* the doctrine that there is evidence of purpose or design in the universe **2** *biol* the belief that natural phenomena have a predetermined purpose and are not determined by mechanical laws **teleological** *adj* **teleologist** *n*
WORD ORIGIN Greek *telos* end + -LOGY

telepathy *n* the direct communication of thoughts and feelings between minds without the need to use normal means such as speech, writing, or touch **telepathic** *adj* **telepathically** *adv*
WORD ORIGIN Greek *tele* far + *pathos* suffering

telephone ❶ *n* **1** a piece of equipment for transmitting speech, consisting of a microphone and receiver mounted on a handset: *the telephone was ringing* **2** the worldwide system of communications using telephones: *reports came in by telephone* ▹*vb* **-phoning, -phoned** **3** to call or talk to (a person) by telephone ▹*adj* **4** of or using a telephone: *a telephone call* **telephonic** *adj*
WORD ORIGIN Greek *tele* far + *phōnē* voice

telephone box *n* an enclosure from which a paid telephone call can be made

telephone directory *n* a book listing the names, addresses, and telephone numbers of subscribers in a particular area

telephonist *n* a person who operates a telephone switchboard

telephony *n* a system of telecommunications for the transmission of speech or other sounds

telephoto lens *n* a lens fitted to a camera to produce a magnified image of a distant object

teleprinter *n Brit* an apparatus, similar to a typewriter, by which typed messages are sent and received by wire

Teleprompter *n trademark* a device for displaying a script under a television camera, so that a speaker can read it while appearing to look at the camera

telesales *n* the selling of a commodity or service by telephone

telescope ❶ *n* **1** an optical instrument for making distant objects appear closer by use of a

THESAURUS

lifeless, prosaic, laborious, humdrum, uninteresting, long-drawn-out, mind-numbing, irksome, unexciting, soporific, ho-hum *(informal)*, vapid, wearisome, deadly dull, prosy, dreich *(Scot)*
OPPOSITE: exciting

teenager *n* **= youth**, minor, adolescent, juvenile, girl, boy

telephone *n* **1 = phone**, blower *(informal)*, mobile, mobile phone *or (informal)* moby, cellphone *or* cellular phone *(US)*, handset, dog and bone *(slang)* ▹*vb* **3 = call**, phone, ring *(chiefly Brit)*, buzz *(informal)*, dial, call up, give someone a call, give someone a ring *(informal, chiefly Brit)*, give someone a buzz *(informal)*, give someone a bell *(Brit slang)*, put a call through to, give someone a tinkle *(Brit informal)*, get on the blower to *(informal)*

telescope *n* **1 = glass**, scope *(informal)*, spyglass ▹*vb* **3 = shorten**, contract,

DICTIONARY

combination of lenses **2** ▸ see **radio telescope** ▹ *vb* **-scoping, -scoped** **3** to shorten (something) while still keeping the important parts: *a hundred years of change has been telescoped into five years* **telescopic** *adj*
WORD ORIGIN New Latin *telescopium* far-seeing instrument

telescopic sight *n* a sight on a rifle, etc. consisting of a telescope, used for aiming at distant objects

teletext *n* a Videotex service in which information is broadcast by a television station and received on a specially equipped television set

Teletext *n trademark* (in Britain) the ITV teletext service

Teletype *n trademark* a type of teleprinter

televangelist *n US* an evangelical preacher who appears regularly on television, preaching the gospel and appealing for donations from viewers
WORD ORIGIN *tele(vision)* + *(e)vangelist*

televise *vb* **-vising, -vised** to show (a programme or event) on television

television ❶ *n* **1** the system or process of producing a moving image with accompanying sound on a distant screen **2** Also called: **television set** a device for receiving broadcast signals and converting them into sound and pictures **3** the content of television programmes: *some people think that television is too violent nowadays* ▹ *adj* **4** of or relating to television: *a television interview* **televisual** *adj*

teleworking *n* the use of home computers, telephones, etc. to enable a person to work from home while maintaining contact with colleagues or customers **teleworker** *n*

telex *n* **1** an international communication service which sends messages by teleprinter **2** a teleprinter used in such a service **3** a message sent by telex ▹ *vb* **4** to transmit (a message) by telex
WORD ORIGIN *tel(eprinter) ex(change)*

Telford[1] *n* a town in W central England, in Telford and Wrekin unitary authority, Shropshire: designated a new town in 1963. Pop: 138 241 (2001)

Telford[2] *n* **Thomas** 1757–1834, Scottish civil engineer, known esp. for his roads and such bridges as the Menai suspension bridge (1825)

tell ❶ *vb* **telling, told** **1** to make known in words; notify: *I told her what had happened* **2** to order or instruct (someone to do something): *he had been told to wait in the lobby* **3** to give an account (of an event or situation): *the President had been told of the developments* **4** to communicate by words: *he was woken at 5 am to be told the news* **5** to discover, distinguish, or discern: *she could tell that he was not sorry* **6** to have or produce an impact or effect: *the pressure had begun to tell on him* **7** *informal* to reveal secrets or gossip **8** **tell the time** to read the time from a clock **9** **you're telling me** *slang* I know that very well
WORD ORIGIN Old English *tellan*

tell apart *vb* to distinguish between: *they're different colours, otherwise how would you tell them apart?*

teller *n* **1** a narrator **2** a bank cashier **3** a person appointed to count votes

Teller *n* **Edward** 1908–2003, US nuclear physicist, born in Hungary: a major contributor to the development of the hydrogen bomb (1952)

telling ❶ *adj* having a marked effect or impact: *to inflict telling damage on the enemy*

tell off ❶ *vb informal* to reprimand or scold (someone) **telling-off** *n*

telltale *n* **1** a person who tells tales about others ▹ *adj* **2** giving away information: *examining the hands for telltale signs of age*

tellurian *adj* of the earth
WORD ORIGIN Latin *tellus* the earth

tellurium *n chem* a brittle silvery-white nonmetallic element. Symbol: Te
WORD ORIGIN Latin *tellus* the earth

telly *n, pl* **-lies** *informal* ▸ short for **television**

telomere *n genetics* either of the ends of a chromosome
WORD ORIGIN Greek *telos* end + *meros* part

temazepam (ti-maz-i-pam) *n* (*sometimes cap*) a sedative in the form of a gel-like capsule, which is taken orally or melted and injected by drug users

temerity (tim-merr-it-tee) *n* boldness or audacity
WORD ORIGIN Latin *temere* at random

temp *Brit informal n* **1** a person, esp. a secretary, employed on a temporary basis ▹ *vb* **2** to work as a temp

temp. **1** temperature **2** temporary

temper ❶ *n* **1** a sudden outburst of anger: *she stormed out in a temper* **2** a tendency to have sudden outbursts of anger: *you've got a temper all right* **3** a mental condition of moderation and calm: *he lost his temper* **4** a person's frame of mind: *he was in a bad temper* ▹ *vb* **5** to modify so as to make less extreme or more acceptable: *past militancy has been tempered with compassion and caring* **6** to reduce the brittleness of (a hardened metal) by reheating it and allowing it to cool **7** *music* to adjust the frequency differences between the notes of a scale on (a keyboard instrument)
WORD ORIGIN Latin *temperare* to mix

tempera *n* a painting medium for powdered pigments, consisting

THESAURUS

compress, cut, trim, shrink, tighten, condense, abbreviate, abridge, capsulize **OPPOSITE:** lengthen

television *n* **2 = TV**, telly (*Brit informal*), small screen (*informal*), the box (*Brit informal*), receiver, the tube (*slang*), TV set, gogglebox (*Brit slang*), idiot box (*slang*)

tell *vb* **1 = inform**, notify, make aware, say to, state to, warn, reveal to, express to, brief, advise, disclose to, proclaim to, fill in, speak about to, confess to, impart, alert to, divulge, announce to, acquaint with, communicate to, mention to, make known to, apprise, utter to, get off your chest (*informal*), let know, flag up **2 = instruct**, order, command, direct, bid, enjoin **3 = describe**, relate, recount, report, portray, depict, chronicle, rehearse, narrate, give an account of **5 = distinguish**, discriminate, discern, differentiate, identify **6 = have** *or* **take effect**, register, weigh, have force, count, take its toll, carry weight, make its presence felt

telling *adj* **= effective**, significant, considerable, marked, striking, powerful, solid, impressive, influential, decisive, potent, forceful, weighty, forcible, trenchant, effectual
OPPOSITE: unimportant

tell someone off *vb* **= reprimand**, rebuke, scold, lecture, carpet (*informal*), censure, reproach, berate, chide, tear into (*informal*), read the riot act to, reprove, upbraid, take to task, tick off (*informal*), bawl out (*informal*), chew out (*US & Canad informal*), tear off a strip (*Brit informal*), give a piece of your mind to, haul over the coals (*informal*), give a rocket to (*Brit & NZ informal*)

temper *n* **1 = rage**, fury, bad mood, passion, paddy (*Brit informal*), wax (*informal, chiefly Brit*), tantrum, bate (*Brit slang*), fit of pique, foulie (*Austral slang*), hissy fit (*informal*), strop (*Brit informal*) **2 = irritability**, anger, irascibility, passion, resentment, irritation, annoyance, petulance, surliness, ill humour, peevishness, hot-headedness **OPPOSITE:** good humour
3 = self-control, composure, cool (*slang*), calm, good humour, tranquillity, coolness, calmness, equanimity **OPPOSITE:** anger
4 = frame of mind, character, nature, attitude, mind, mood, constitution, humour, vein, temperament, tenor, disposition ▹ *vb* **5 = moderate**, restrain, tone down, calm, soften, soothe, lessen, allay, mitigate, abate,

DICTIONARY

usually of egg yolk and water
WORD ORIGIN Italian *temperare* to mingle

temperament *n* a person's character or disposition
WORD ORIGIN Latin *temperamentum* a mixing

temperamental *adj* **1** (of a person) tending to be moody and have sudden outbursts of anger **2** *informal* working erratically and inconsistently; unreliable: *the temperamental microphone* **3** of or relating to a person's temperament: *we discussed temperamental and developmental differences* **temperamentally** *adv*

temperance *n* **1** restraint or moderation, esp. in yielding to one's appetites or desires **2** abstinence from alcoholic drink
WORD ORIGIN Latin *temperare* to regulate

temperate *adj* **1** of a climate which is never extremely hot or extremely cold **2** mild or moderate in quality or character: *try to be more temperate in your statements*
WORD ORIGIN Latin *temperatus*

Temperate Zone *n* those parts of the earth's surface lying between the Arctic Circle and the tropic of Cancer and between the Antarctic Circle and the tropic of Capricorn

temperature *n* **1** the hotness or coldness of something, as measured on a scale that has one or more fixed reference points **2** *informal* an abnormally high body temperature **3** the strength of feeling among a group of people: *his remarks are likely to raise the political temperature considerably*
WORD ORIGIN Latin *temperatura* proportion

tempest *n literary* a violent wind or storm
WORD ORIGIN Latin *tempestas*

tempestuous *adj* **1** violent or stormy **2** extremely emotional or passionate: *a tempestuous relationship* **tempestuously** *adv*

template *n* a wood or metal pattern, used to help cut out shapes accurately
WORD ORIGIN from *temple* a part in a loom that keeps the cloth stretched

temple[1] *n* a building or place used for the worship of a god or gods
WORD ORIGIN Latin *templum*

temple[2] *n* the region on each side of the head in front of the ear and above the cheek bone
WORD ORIGIN Latin *tempus*

tempo (tem-po) *n, pl* **-pi** (-pee) *or* **-pos** **1** rate or pace: *the slow tempo of change in an overwhelmingly rural country* **2** the speed at which a piece of music is played or meant to be played
WORD ORIGIN Italian

temporal[1] *adj* **1** of or relating to time **2** of secular as opposed to spiritual or religious affairs: *in the Middle Ages the Pope had temporal as well as spiritual power* **3** not permanent or eternal: *a temporal view of drugs as the No. 1 social problem*
WORD ORIGIN Latin *tempus* time

temporal[2] *adj anat* of or near the temple or temples

temporal bone *n* either of two compound bones forming the sides of the skull

temporary *adj* lasting only for a short time; not permanent: *temporary accommodation* **temporarily** *adv*
WORD ORIGIN Latin *temporarius*

temporize *or* **-rise** *vb* **-rizing, -rized** *or* **-rising, -rised** **1** to delay, act evasively, or protract a negotiation in order to gain time or avoid making a decision: *'Well,' I temporized, 'I'll have to ask your mother'* **2** to adapt oneself to circumstances, as by temporary or apparent agreement
WORD ORIGIN Latin *tempus* time

tempt *vb* **1** to entice (someone) to do something, esp. something morally wrong or unwise: *can I tempt you to have another whisky?* **2** to allure or attract: *she was tempted by the glamour of a modelling career* **3 be tempted** to want to do something while knowing it would be wrong or inappropriate to do so: *many youngsters are tempted to experiment with drugs* **4 tempt fate** *or* **providence** to take foolish or unnecessary risks **tempter** *n* **temptress** *fem n*
WORD ORIGIN Latin *temptare* to test

temptation *n* **1** the act of tempting or the state of being tempted **2** a person or thing that tempts

tempting *adj* attractive or inviting: *it's tempting to say I told you so* **temptingly** *adv*

ten *n* **1** the cardinal number that is the sum of one and nine **2** a numeral, 10 or X, representing this number **3** something representing or consisting of ten units ▷ *adj* **4** amounting to ten: *ten years* **tenth** *adj, n*
WORD ORIGIN Old English *tēn*

tenable *adj* **1** able to be upheld or maintained: *a tenable strategy* **2** (of a job) intended to be held by a person for a particular length of time: *the post will be tenable for three years in the first instance* **tenability** *n* **tenably** *adv*
WORD ORIGIN Latin *tenere* to hold

tenacious *adj* **1** holding firmly: *a tenacious grasp* **2** stubborn or persistent: *tenacious support* **tenaciously** *adv* **tenacity** *n*
WORD ORIGIN Latin *tenere* to hold

tenancy *n, pl* **-cies** **1** the temporary possession or use of lands or property owned by somebody else, in return for payment **2** the period of holding or occupying such property

tenant *n* **1** a person who pays rent for the use of land or property **2** any holder or occupant
WORD ORIGIN Old French: one who is holding

tenant farmer *n* a person who farms land rented from somebody else

tenantry *n old-fashioned* tenants collectively

tench *n* a European freshwater game fish of the carp family
WORD ORIGIN Old French *tenche*

Ten Commandments *pl n bible* the commandments given by God to Moses on Mount Sinai, summarizing the basic obligations of people towards God and their fellow humans

tend[1] *vb* to be inclined (to take a particular kind of action or to be in a particular condition) as a rule: *she tends to be rather absent-minded*

t

THESAURUS

assuage, mollify, soft-pedal *(informal)*, palliate, admix **OPPOSITE:** intensify **6 = strengthen**, harden, toughen, anneal **OPPOSITE:** soften

temperament *n* **= nature**, character, personality, quality, spirit, make-up, soul, constitution, bent, stamp, humour, tendencies, tendency, temper, outlook, complexion, disposition, frame of mind, mettle, cast of mind

temple[1] *n* **= shrine**, church, sanctuary, holy place, place of worship, house of God

temporary *adj* **a = impermanent**, passing, transitory, brief, fleeting, interim, short-lived, fugitive, transient, momentary, ephemeral, evanescent, pro tem, here today and gone tomorrow, pro tempore *(Latin)*, fugacious **OPPOSITE:** permanent **b = short-term**, acting, interim, supply, stand-in, fill-in, caretaker, provisional, stopgap

tempt *vb* **1 = entice**, lure, lead on, invite, woo, seduce, coax, decoy, inveigle **OPPOSITE:** discourage **2 = attract**, draw, appeal to, allure, whet the appetite of, make your mouth water

temptation *n* **1 = enticement**, lure, inducement, pull, come-on *(informal)*, invitation, bait, coaxing, snare, seduction, decoy, allurement, tantalization

tempting *adj* **= inviting**, enticing, seductive, alluring, attractive, mouthwatering, appetizing **OPPOSITE:** uninviting

tenant *n* **1, 2 = leaseholder**, resident, renter, occupant, holder, inhabitant, occupier, lodger, boarder, lessee

tend[1] *vb* **= be inclined**, be likely, be liable, have a tendency, be apt, be prone, trend, lean, incline, be biased,

DICTIONARY

WORD ORIGIN Latin *tendere* to stretch
tend² ❶ *vb* **1** to take care of: *it is she who tends his wounds* **2 tend to** to attend to: *excuse me, I have to tend to the other guests*
WORD ORIGIN variant of *attend*
tendency ❶ *n, pl* **-cies 1** an inclination to act in a particular way **2** the general course or drift of something **3** a faction, esp. within a political party
WORD ORIGIN Latin *tendere* to stretch
tendentious *adj* expressing a particular viewpoint or opinion, esp. a controversial one, in very strong terms: *a somewhat tendentious reading of French history* **tendentiously** *adv*
tender¹ ❶ *adj* **1** (of cooked food) having softened and become easy to chew or cut **2** gentle and kind: *tender loving care* **3** vulnerable or sensitive: *at the tender age of 9* **4** painful when touched: *his wrist was swollen and tender* **tenderly** *adv* **tenderness** *n*
WORD ORIGIN Old French *tendre*
tender² ❶ *vb* **1** to present or offer: *he tendered his resignation* **2** to make a formal offer or estimate for a job or contract: *contractors tendering for government work* ▹*n* **3** a formal offer to supply specified goods or services at a stated cost or rate: *the government invited tenders to run television and radio services* **tenderer** *n* **tendering** *n*
WORD ORIGIN Latin *tendere* to extend
tender³ *n* **1** a small boat that brings supplies to larger vessels in a port **2** a wagon attached to the rear of a steam locomotive that carries the fuel and water
WORD ORIGIN variant of *attender*
tenderfoot *n, pl* **-foots** *or* **-feet** a newcomer to a particular activity
tenderize *or* **-ise** *vb* **-izing, -ized** *or* **-ising, -ised** to make (meat) tender, by pounding it or adding a substance to break down the fibres **tenderizer** *or* **-iser** *n*
tenderloin *n* a tender cut of pork from between the sirloin and ribs
tendon *n* a band of tough tissue that attaches a muscle to a bone
WORD ORIGIN Medieval Latin *tendo*
tendril *n* a threadlike leaf or stem by which a climbing plant attaches itself to a support
WORD ORIGIN probably from Old French *tendron*
Tendulkar *n* **Sachin** (**Ramesh**) born 1973, Indian cricketer; captain of India (1996–2000)
tenement *n* a large building divided into several different flats
WORD ORIGIN Latin *tenere* to hold
tenet (ten-nit) *n* a principle on which a belief or doctrine is based
WORD ORIGIN Latin, literally: he (it) holds
tenfold *adj* **1** having ten times as many or as much **2** composed of ten parts ▹*adv* **3** by ten times as many or as much
ten-gallon hat *n* (in the US) a cowboy's broad-brimmed felt hat with a very high crown
Teniers *n* **David**, called *the Elder*, 1582–1649, and his son **David,** called *the Younger*, 1610–90, Flemish painters
tenner *n Brit, Austral & NZ informal* **1** a ten-pound or ten-dollar note **2** the sum of ten pounds or ten dollars: *it's worth a tenner at least*
Tenniel *n* Sir **John** 1820–1914, English caricaturist, noted for his illustrations to Lewis Carroll's *Alice* books and for his political cartoons in *Punch* (1851–1901)
tennis *n* a game played between two players or pairs of players who use a racket to hit a ball to and fro over a net on a rectangular court ▸See also **lawn tennis, real tennis, table tennis**
WORD ORIGIN probably from Anglo-French *tenetz* hold!
tennis elbow *n* inflammation of the elbow, typically caused by exertion in playing tennis
tenon *n* a projecting end of a piece of wood, formed to fit into a corresponding slot in another piece
WORD ORIGIN Old French
tenor *n* **1 a** the second highest male voice, between alto and baritone **b** a singer with such a voice **c** a saxophone, horn, or other musical instrument between the alto and baritone or bass **2** a general meaning or character: *it was clear from the tenor of the meeting that the chairman's actions are very unpopular* ▹*adj* **3** denoting a musical instrument between alto and baritone: *a tenor saxophone* **4** of or relating to the second highest male voice: *his voice lacks the range needed for the tenor role*
WORD ORIGIN Old French *tenour*
tenpin bowling *n* a game in which players try to knock over ten skittles by rolling a ball at them
tense¹ ❶ *adj* **1** having, showing, or causing mental or emotional strain: *the tense atmosphere* **2** stretched tight: *tense muscles* ▹*vb* **tensing, tensed 3** Also: **tense up** to make or become tense **tensely** *adv* **tenseness** *n*
WORD ORIGIN Latin *tensus* taut
tense² *n grammar* the form of a verb that indicates whether the action referred to in the sentence is located in the past, the present, or the future: *'ate' is the past tense of 'to eat'*
WORD ORIGIN Old French *tens* time
tensile *adj* of or relating to tension or being stretched: *The posts were linked by high tensile wire.*
tensile strength *n* a measure of the ability of a material to withstand lengthwise stress, expressed as the greatest stress that the material can stand without breaking: *the addition of linseed oil improved the tensile strength of the cricket bat*
tension ❶ *n* **1** a situation or condition of hostility, suspense, or uneasiness: *a renewed state of tension between old enemies* **2** mental or emotional strain: *nervous tension* **3** a force that

THESAURUS

be disposed, gravitate, have a leaning, have an inclination
tend² *vb* **1a = take care of**, look after, care for, keep, watch, serve, protect, feed, handle, attend, guard, nurse, see to, nurture, minister to, cater for, keep an eye on, wait on, watch over
OPPOSITE: neglect
1b = maintain, take care of, nurture, cultivate, manage **OPPOSITE:** neglect
tendency *n* **1 = inclination**, leaning, bent, liability, readiness, disposition, penchant, propensity, susceptibility, predisposition, predilection, proclivity, partiality, proneness
tender¹ *adj* **2 = gentle**, loving, kind, caring, warm, sympathetic, fond, sentimental, humane, affectionate, compassionate, benevolent, considerate, merciful, amorous, warm-hearted, tenderhearted, softhearted, touchy-feely *(informal)*
OPPOSITE: harsh
3 = vulnerable, young, sensitive, new, green, raw, youthful, inexperienced, immature, callow, impressionable, unripe, wet behind the ears *(informal)*
OPPOSITE: experienced
4 = sensitive, painful, sore, smarting, raw, bruised, irritated, aching, inflamed
tender² *vb* **1 = offer**, present, submit, give, suggest, propose, extend, volunteer, hand in, put forward, proffer ▹*n* **3 = offer**, bid, estimate, proposal, suggestion, submission, proffer
tense¹ *adj* **1a = strained**, uneasy, stressful, fraught, charged, difficult, worrying, exciting, uncomfortable, knife-edge, nail-biting, nerve-racking **1b = nervous**, wound up *(informal)*, edgy, strained, wired *(slang)*, anxious, under pressure, restless, apprehensive, jittery *(informal)*, uptight *(informal)*, on edge, jumpy, twitchy *(informal)*, overwrought, strung up *(informal)*, on tenterhooks, fidgety, keyed up, antsy *(informal)*, wrought up, adrenalized
OPPOSITE: calm
2 = rigid, strained, taut, stretched, tight **OPPOSITE:** relaxed
▹*vb* **3 = tighten**, strain, brace, tauten, stretch, flex, stiffen **OPPOSITE:** relax
tension *n* **1 = friction**, hostility, unease, antagonism, antipathy, enmity, ill feeling **1, 2 = strain**, stress, nervousness, pressure, anxiety,

DICTIONARY

stretches or the state or degree of being stretched tight: *keep tension on the line until the fish comes within range of the net* **4** *physics* a force that tends to produce an elongation of a body or structure **5** *physics* voltage, electromotive force, or potential difference
WORD ORIGIN Latin *tensio*

tent *n* **1** a portable shelter made of canvas or other fabric supported on poles, stretched out, and fastened to the ground by pegs and ropes **2** ▸see **oxygen tent**
WORD ORIGIN Old French *tente*

tentacle *n* **1** a flexible organ that grows near the mouth in many invertebrates and is used for feeding, grasping, etc. **2 tentacles** the unseen methods by which an organization or idea, esp. a sinister one, influences people and events: *the tentacles of the secret police* **tentacled** *adj*
WORD ORIGIN Latin *tentare* to feel

tentative ⓘ *adj* **1** provisional or unconfirmed: *a tentative agreement* **2** hesitant, uncertain, or cautious: *their rather tentative approach* **tentatively** *adv* **tentativeness** *n*
WORD ORIGIN Latin *tentare* to test

tenterhooks *pl n* **on tenterhooks** in a state of tension or suspense
WORD ORIGIN Latin *tentus* stretched + HOOK

tenth *adj, n* ▸see **ten**

tenuous *adj* insignificant or flimsy: *there is only the most tenuous evidence for it* **tenuously** *adv*
WORD ORIGIN Latin *tenuis*

tenure *n* **1** the holding of an office or position **2** the length of time an office or position lasts **3** the holding of a teaching position at a university on a permanent basis **4** the legal right to live in a place or to use land or buildings for a period of time
WORD ORIGIN Latin *tenere* to hold

tepee *or* **teepee** (tee-pee) *n* a cone-shaped tent of animal skins, formerly used by American Indians
WORD ORIGIN Sioux *tīpī*

tepid *adj* **1** slightly warm **2** lacking enthusiasm: *tepid applause* **tepidity** *n* **tepidly** *adv*
WORD ORIGIN Latin *tepidus*

tequila *n* a Mexican alcoholic spirit distilled from the agave plant
WORD ORIGIN after *Tequila*, district in Mexico

tera- *combining form* denoting one million million (10^{12}): *terameter*
WORD ORIGIN Greek *teras* monster

teratology (terr-a-**tol**-a-jee) *n* the branch of medicine concerned with the development of physical abnormalities during the fetal or early embryonic stage
WORD ORIGIN Greek *teras* monster + -LOGY

Te Rauparaha *n* ?1768–1849, Māori warrior chief, head of the Ngāti Toa tribe and signatory to the **Treaty of Waitangi**; noted for his cunning and his prowess in battle, he is also credited with composing "Ka Mate", the All Blacks' usual pre-match haka

terbium *n chem* a soft silvery-grey element of the lanthanide series of metals Symbol: Tb
WORD ORIGIN after *Ytterby*, Sweden, where discovered

Ter Borch *or* **Terborch** *n* **Gerard** 1617–81, Dutch genre and portrait painter

Terbrugghen *n* **Hendrik** 1588–1629, Dutch painter of the Utrecht school, who specialized in religious subjects, for example the *Incredulity of St Thomas* and the *Calling of St Matthew*

tercentenary *or* **tercentennial** *adj* **1** marking a 300th anniversary ▹*n, pl* **-tenaries** *or* **-tennials** **2** a 300th anniversary
WORD ORIGIN Latin *ter* three times + CENTENARY

teredo (ter-**ree**-doh) *n, pl* **-dos** *or* **-dines** (-din-eez) a marine mollusc that bores into and destroys submerged timber
WORD ORIGIN Greek *terēdōn* wood-boring worm

Terence *n* Latin name *Publius Terentius Afer* ?190–159 BC, Roman comic dramatist. His six comedies, *Andria, Hecyra, Heauton Timoroumenos, Eunuchus, Phormio*, and *Adelphoe*, are based on Greek originals by Menander

Terfel *n* **Bryn,** real name *Bryn Terfel Jones*. born 1965, Welsh bass baritone

tergiversate (tur-jiv-verse-ate) *vb* **-sating, -sated** *formal* **1** to be evasive or ambiguous **2** to change sides or loyalties **tergiversation** *n* **tergiversator** *n*
WORD ORIGIN Latin *tergiversari* to turn one's back

term ⓘ *n* **1** a word or expression, esp. one used in a specialized field of knowledge: *he coined the term 'inferiority complex'* **2** a period of time: *a four-year prison term* **3** one of the periods of the year when a school, university, or college is open or a lawcourt holds sessions **4** the period of pregnancy when childbirth is imminent **5** *maths* any distinct quantity making up a fraction or proportion, or contained in a sequence, series, etc. **6** *logic* any of the three subjects or predicates occurring in a syllogism **7 full term** the end of a specific period of time: *the agony of carrying the child to full term* ▹*vb* **8** to name, call, or describe as being: *social workers tend to be termed lefties* ▸See also **terms**
WORD ORIGIN Latin *terminus* end

termagant *n literary* an unpleasant, aggressive, and overbearing woman
WORD ORIGIN earlier *Tervagaunt*, after an arrogant character in medieval mystery plays

terminable *adj* capable of being terminated: *his terminable interest in the property* **terminability** *n*

terminal ⓘ *adj* **1** (of an illness) ending in death **2** situated at an end, terminus, or boundary: *the terminal joints of the fingers* **3** *informal* extreme or severe: *terminal boredom* ▹*n* **4** a place where vehicles, passengers, or goods begin or end a journey: *the ferry terminal* **5** a point at which current enters or leaves an electrical device **6** *computers* a device, usually a keyboard and a visual display unit, having input/output links with a computer **terminally** *adv*
WORD ORIGIN Latin *terminus* end

terminal velocity *n physics* the maximum velocity reached by a body falling under gravity through a liquid or gas, esp. the atmosphere

terminate ⓘ *vb* **-nating, -nated** **1** to bring or come to an end: *his flying career was terminated by this crash* **2** to put an end to (a pregnancy) by inducing an abortion **3** (of the route of a train, bus, etc.) to stop at a particular place and not go any further: *this train terminates at Leicester* **termination** *n*

THESAURUS

unease, apprehension, suspense, restlessness, the jitters (*informal*), edginess OPPOSITE: calmness **3 = rigidity**, tightness, stiffness, pressure, stress, stretching, straining, tautness

tentative *adj* **1 = unconfirmed**, provisional, indefinite, test, trial, pilot, preliminary, experimental, unsettled, speculative, pencilled in, exploratory, to be confirmed, TBC, conjectural OPPOSITE: confirmed **2 = hesitant**, cautious, uncertain, doubtful, backward, faltering, unsure, timid, undecided, diffident, iffy (*informal*) OPPOSITE: confident

term *n* **1 = word**, name, expression, title, label, phrase, denomination, designation, appellation, locution **2 = period**, time, spell, while, season, space, interval, span, duration, incumbency ▹*vb* **8 = call**, name, label, style, entitle, tag, dub, designate, describe as, denominate

terminal *adj* **1 = fatal**, deadly, lethal, killing, mortal, incurable, inoperable, untreatable **2 = final**, last, closing, finishing, concluding, ultimate, terminating OPPOSITE: initial ▹*n* **4 = terminus**, station, depot, end of the line

terminate *vb* **1a = end**, stop, conclude, finish, complete, axe (*informal*), cut off, wind up, put an end to, discontinue, pull the plug on (*informal*), belay (*nautical*), bring *or*

DICTIONARY

word origin Latin *terminare* to set boundaries
terminology *n, pl* **-gies** the specialized words and expressions relating to a particular subject **terminological** *adj* **terminologist** *n*
terminus (term-in-nuss) *n, pl* **-ni** (-nye) *or* **-nuses** the station or town at one end of a railway line or bus route: *Vienna's Westbahnhof is the terminus for trains to France*
word origin Latin: end
termite *n* a whitish antlike insect of warm and tropical regions that destroys timber
word origin New Latin *termites* white ants
terms *pl n* **1** the actual language or mode of presentation used: *the test is carried out in plain non-engineering terms* **2** the conditions of an agreement **3** mutual relationship or standing of a specified nature: *he is on first-name terms with many of the directors* **4 come to terms with** to learn to accept (an unpleasant or difficult situation) **5 in terms of** as expressed by; with regard to: *he is the best cricketer we have got in fact in terms of pure ability*
tern *n* a gull-like sea bird with a forked tail and long narrow wings
word origin Old Norse *therna*
ternary *adj* **1** consisting of three items or groups of three items **2** *maths* (of a number system) to the base three
word origin Latin *ternarius*
Terpsichore (turp-sick-or-ee) *n Greek myth* the Muse of dance
Terpsichorean (turp-sick-or-ee-an) *adj often used facetiously* of or relating to dancing
word origin from *Terpsichore*, the Muse of dance in Greek mythology
Terr. **1** terrace **2** territory
terrace *n* **1** a row of houses, usually identical and joined together by common dividing walls, or the street onto which they face **2** a paved area alongside a building **3** a horizontal flat area of ground, often one of a series in a slope **4 the terraces** *or* **terracing** *Brit & NZ* a tiered area in a stadium where spectators stand ▷*vb* **-racing, -raced 5** to make into terraces
word origin Latin *terra* earth
terraced house *n Brit* a house that is part of a terrace
terracotta *n* **1** a hard unglazed brownish-red earthenware used for pottery ▷*adj* **2** made of terracotta **3** brownish-orange
word origin Italian, literally: baked earth
terra firma *n* the ground, as opposed to the sea
word origin Latin
terraforming *n* planetary engineering designed to enhance the capacity of an extraterrestrial planetary environment to sustain life
word origin Latin *terra* earth
terrain ⓘ *n* an area of ground, esp. with reference to its physical character: *mountainous terrain*
word origin Latin *terra* earth
terra incognita (terr-a in-**kog**-nit-a) *n* an unexplored region
word origin Latin
terrapin *n* a small turtle-like reptile of N America that lives in fresh water and on land
word origin from a Native American language
terrarium *n* **1** an enclosed area or container where small land animals are kept **2** a glass container in which plants are grown
word origin Latin *terra* earth
terrazzo *n, pl* **-zos** a floor made by setting marble chips into a layer of mortar and polishing the surface
word origin Italian: terrace
terrestrial ⓘ *adj* **1** of the planet earth **2** of the land as opposed to the sea or air **3** (of animals and plants) living or growing on the land **4** *television* denoting or using a signal sent over land from a transmitter on land, rather than by satellite
word origin Latin *terra* earth
terrible ⓘ *adj* **1** very serious or extreme: *war is a terrible thing* **2** *informal* very bad, unpleasant, or unsatisfactory: *terrible books* **3** causing fear **terribly** *adv*
word origin Latin *terribilis*
terrier *n* any of several small active breeds of dog, originally trained to hunt animals living underground
word origin Old French *chien terrier* earth dog
terrific ⓘ *adj* **1** very great or intense: *a terrific blow on the head* **2** *informal* very good; excellent: *a terrific book* **terrifically** *adv*
word origin Latin *terrere* to frighten
terrify ⓘ *vb* **-fies, -fying, -fied** to frighten greatly **terrified** *adj* **terrifying** *adj* **terrifyingly** *adv*
word origin Latin *terrificare*
terrine (terr-**reen**) *n* **1** an oval earthenware cooking dish with a tightly fitting lid **2** the food cooked or served in such a dish, esp. pâté
word origin earlier form of *tureen*
territorial *adj* **1** of or relating to a territory or territories **2** of or concerned with the ownership and control of an area of land or water: *a territorial dispute* **3** (of an animal or bird) establishing and defending an area which it will not let other animals or birds into: *the baboon is a territorial species* **4** of or relating to a territorial army **territorially** *adv* **territoriality** *n*
Territorial *n* a member of a Territorial Army
Territorial Army *n* (in Britain) a reserve army whose members are not full-time soldiers but undergo military training in their spare time so that they can be called upon in an emergency
territorial waters *pl n* the part of the sea near to a country's coast, which

THESAURUS

come to an end **opposite:** begin **1b = cease**, end, close, finish, run out, expire, lapse **2 = abort**, end
terrain *n* **= ground**, country, land, landscape, topography, going
terrestrial *adj* **1 = earthly**, worldly, global, mundane, sublunary, tellurian, terrene
terrible *adj* **1 = serious**, desperate, severe, extreme, bad, dangerous, insufferable **opposite:** mild **1, 3 = awful**, shocking, appalling, terrifying, horrible, dreadful, horrifying, dread, dreaded, fearful, horrendous, monstrous, harrowing, gruesome, horrid, unspeakable, frightful, hellacious *(US slang)* **2** *(informal)* **= bad**, awful, dreadful, beastly *(informal)*, dire, abysmal, abhorrent, poor, offensive, foul, unpleasant, revolting, rotten *(informal)*, obscene, hideous, vile, from hell *(informal)*, obnoxious, repulsive, frightful, odious, hateful, loathsome, godawful *(slang)* **opposite:** wonderful
terrific *adj* **1 = intense**, great, huge, terrible, enormous, severe, extreme, awful, tremendous, fierce, harsh, excessive, dreadful, horrific, fearful, awesome, gigantic, monstrous **2** *(informal)* **= excellent**, great *(informal)*, wonderful, mean *(slang)*, topping *(Brit slang)*, fine, brilliant, very good, cracking *(Brit informal)*, amazing, outstanding, smashing *(informal)*, superb, fantastic *(informal)*, ace *(informal)*, magnificent, fabulous *(informal)*, marvellous, sensational *(informal)*, sovereign, awesome *(slang)*, breathtaking, super *(informal)*, brill *(informal)*, stupendous, bodacious *(slang, chiefly US)*, boffo *(slang)*, jim-dandy *(slang)*, chillin' *(US slang)*, booshit *(Austral slang)*, exo *(Austral slang)*, sik *(Austral slang)*, ka pai *(NZ)*, rad *(informal)*, phat *(slang)*, schmick *(Austral informal)*, beaut *(informal)*, barrie *(Scot slang)*, belting *(Brit slang)*, pearler *(Austral slang)* **opposite:** awful
terrify *vb* **= frighten**, scare, petrify, alarm, intimidate, terrorize, scare to death, put the fear of God into, make your hair stand on end, fill with terror, make your flesh creep, make your blood run cold, frighten out of your wits

t

DICTIONARY

is under the control of the government of that country

territory ❶ *n, pl* **-ries** **1** any tract of land; district: *mountainous territory* **2** the geographical area under the control of a particular government: *the islands are Japanese territory* **3** an area inhabited and defended by a particular animal or pair of animals **4** an area of knowledge or experience: *all this is familiar territory to readers of her recent novels* **5** a country or region under the control of a foreign country: *a French Overseas Territory* **6** a region of a country, esp. of a federal state, that enjoys less autonomy and a lower status than most constituent parts of the state
WORD ORIGIN Latin *territorium* land surrounding a town

terror ❶ *n* **1** very great fear, panic, or dread **2** a person or thing that inspires great dread **3** *Brit, Austral & NZ informal* a troublesome person, esp. a child
WORD ORIGIN Latin

terrorism *n* the systematic use of violence and intimidation to achieve political ends **terrorist** *n, adj*

terrorize *or* **-ise** *vb* **-izing, -ized** *or* **-ising, -ised** **1** to control or force (someone) to do something by violence, fear, threats, etc.: *he was terrorized into withdrawing his accusations* **2** to make (someone) very frightened **terrorization** *or* **-isation** *n* **terrorizer** *or* **-iser** *n*

terry *n* a fabric covered on both sides with small uncut loops, used for towelling and nappies
WORD ORIGIN origin unknown

Terry *n* **1** Dame **Ellen** 1847–1928, British actress, noted for her Shakespearean roles opposite Sir Henry Irving and for her correspondence with George Bernard Shaw **2** **(John) Quinlan** born 1937, British architect, noted for his works in neoclassical style, such as the Richmond riverside project (1984)

terse *adj* **1** neatly brief and concise **2** curt or abrupt **tersely** *adv* **terseness** *n*
WORD ORIGIN Latin *tersus* precise

tertiary (tur-shar-ee) *adj* **1** third in degree, order, etc. **2** (of education) at university or college level **3** (of an industry) involving services, such as transport and financial services, as opposed to manufacture
WORD ORIGIN Latin *tertius*

Tertiary *adj geol* of the period of geological time lasting from about 65 million years ago to 600 000 years ago

Tertullian *n* Latin name *Quintus Septimius Florens Tertullianus*. ?160–?220 AD, Carthaginian Christian theologian, who wrote in Latin rather than Greek and originated much of Christian terminology

Terylene *n trademark* a synthetic polyester fibre or fabric

TESL Teaching of English as a Second Language

tessellated *adj* paved or inlaid with a mosaic of small tiles
WORD ORIGIN Latin *tessellatus* checked

tessera *n, pl* **-serae** a small square tile used in mosaics
WORD ORIGIN Latin

test[1] ❶ *vb* **1** to try (something) out to ascertain its worth, safety, or endurance: *the company has never tested its products on animals* **2** to carry out an examination on (a substance, material, or system) in order to discover whether a particular substance, component, or feature is present: *baby foods are regularly tested for pesticides* **3** to put under severe strain: *the long delay tested my patience* **4** to achieve a result in a test which indicates the presence or absence of something: *he tested positive for cocaine* ▷ *n* **5** a method, practice, or examination designed to test a person or thing **6** a series of questions or problems designed to test a specific skill or knowledge: *a spelling test* **7** a chemical reaction or physical procedure for testing the composition or other qualities of a substance **8** *sport* ▸ short for **Test match** **9** **put to the test** to use (something) in order to gauge its usefulness or effectiveness **testable** *adj* **testing** *adj*
WORD ORIGIN Latin *testum* earthen vessel

test[2] *n* the hard outer covering of certain invertebrates
WORD ORIGIN Latin *testa* shell

testa (tess-ta) *n, pl* **-tae** (-tee) the hard outer layer of a seed
WORD ORIGIN Latin: shell

testaceous (test-ay-shuss) *adj biol* of or having a hard continuous shell
WORD ORIGIN Latin *testacens*, from TESTA

testament ❶ *n* **1** something which provides proof of a fact about someone or something: *the size of the audience was an immediate testament to his appeal* **2** *law* a formal statement of how a person wants his or her property to be disposed of after his or her death: *last will and testament* **testamentary** *adj*
WORD ORIGIN Latin *testis* a witness

Testament *n* either of the two main parts of the Bible, the Old Testament or the New Testament

testate *law adj* **1** having left a legally valid will at death ▷ *n* **2** a person who dies and leaves a legally valid will **testacy** *n*
WORD ORIGIN Latin *testari* to make a will

testator (test-tay-tor) *or fem* **testatrix** (test-tay-triks) *n law* a person who has made a will, esp. one who has died testate

test card *n* a complex pattern used to test the characteristics of a television transmission system

test case *n* a legal action that serves as a precedent in deciding similar succeeding cases

testicle *n* either of the two male reproductive glands, in most mammals enclosed within the scrotum, that produce spermatozoa
WORD ORIGIN Latin *testis* a witness (to masculinity)

testify ❶ *vb* **-fies, -fying, -fied** **1** *law* to declare or give evidence under oath, esp. in court **2** **testify to** to be evidence of: *a piece of paper testifying to their educational qualifications*
WORD ORIGIN Latin *testis* witness

testimonial *n* **1** a recommendation of the character or worth of a person or thing **2** a tribute given for services or achievements ▷ *adj* **3** of a testimony or testimonial: *a testimonial match*

testimony ❶ *n, pl* **-nies** **1** a declaration of truth or fact **2** *law* evidence given by a witness, esp. in

THESAURUS

territory *n* **1, 2 = district**, area, land, region, state, country, sector, zone, province, patch, turf *(US slang)*, domain, terrain, tract, bailiwick

terror *n* **1 = fear**, alarm, dread, fright, panic, anxiety, intimidation, fear and trembling **2 = nightmare**, monster, bogeyman, devil, fiend, bugbear, scourge

test[1] *vb* **1 = check**, try, investigate, assess, research, prove, analyse, experiment with, try out, verify, assay, put something to the proof, put something to the test ▷ *n* **5, 6 = examination**, paper, assessment, evaluation **7 = trial**, research, check, investigation, attempt, analysis, assessment, proof, examination, evaluation, acid test

testament *n* **1 = proof**, evidence, testimony, witness, demonstration, tribute, attestation, exemplification **2** *(law)* **= will**, last wishes

testify *vb* **1 = bear witness**, state, swear, certify, declare, witness, assert, affirm, depose *(law)*, attest, corroborate, vouch, evince, give testimony, asseverate
OPPOSITE: disprove

testimony *n* **1, 2** *(law)* **= evidence**, information, statement, witness, profession, declaration, confirmation, submission, affirmation, affidavit, deposition, corroboration, avowal,

DICTIONARY

court under oath **3** evidence proving or supporting something: *that they are still talking is a testimony to their 20-year friendship*
WORD ORIGIN Latin *testimonium*

testis *n, pl* **-tes** ▸ same as **testicle**

Test match *n* (in various sports, esp. cricket) an international match, esp. one of a series

testosterone *n* a steroid male sex hormone secreted by the testes

test paper *n* **1** the question sheet of a test **2** *chem* paper impregnated with an indicator for use in chemical tests

test pilot *n* a pilot who flies aircraft of new design to test their performance in the air

test tube *n* a cylindrical round-bottomed glass tube open at one end, which is used in scientific experiments

test-tube baby *n* **1** a fetus that has developed from an ovum fertilized in an artificial womb **2** a baby conceived by artificial insemination

testy *adj* **-tier, -tiest** irritable or touchy **testily** *adv* **testiness** *n*
WORD ORIGIN Anglo-Norman *testif* headstrong

tetanus *n* an acute infectious disease in which toxins released from a bacterium cause muscular spasms and convulsions
WORD ORIGIN Greek *tetanos*

tetchy *adj* **tetchier, tetchiest** cross, irritable, or touchy **tetchily** *adv* **tetchiness** *n*
WORD ORIGIN probably from obsolete *tetch* defect

tête-à-tête *n, pl* **-têtes** *or* **-tête** **1** a private conversation between two people ▹ *adv* **2** together in private: *they dined tête-à-tête*
WORD ORIGIN French, literally: head to head

tether *n* **1** a rope or chain for tying an animal to a fence, post, etc. so that it cannot move away from a particular place **2 at the end of one's tether** at the limit of one's patience or endurance ▹ *vb* **3** to tie with a tether
WORD ORIGIN Old Norse *tjōthr*

tetra- *combining form* four: *tetrapod*

tetrad *n* a group or series of four
WORD ORIGIN Greek *tetras*

tetraethyl lead *n* a colourless oily insoluble liquid used in petrol to prevent knocking

tetragon *n* a shape with four angles and four sides **tetragonal** *adj*
WORD ORIGIN Greek *tetragōnon*

tetrahedron (tet-ra-**heed**-ron) *n, pl* **-drons** *or* **-dra** a solid figure with four triangular plane faces **tetrahedral** *adj*
WORD ORIGIN Late Greek *tetraedron*

tetralogy *n, pl* **-gies** a series of four related books, dramas, operas, etc.
WORD ORIGIN Greek *tetralogia*

tetrameter (tet-**tram**-it-er) *n* **1** *prosody* a line of verse consisting of four metrical feet **2** verse consisting of such lines
WORD ORIGIN Greek *tetra-* four + METER

Tetrazzini *n* **Luisa** 1871–1940, Italian coloratura soprano

Tetzel *or* **Tezel** *n* **Johann** ?1465–1519, German Dominican monk. His preaching on papal indulgences provoked Luther's 95 theses at Wittenberg (1517)

Teuton (tew-tun) *n* **1** a member of an ancient Germanic people of N Europe **2** a member of any people speaking a Germanic language, esp. a German ▹ *adj* **3** Teutonic
WORD ORIGIN Latin *Teutoni* the Teutons

Teutonic (tew-**tonn**-ik) *adj* **1** characteristic of or relating to the Germans **2** of the ancient Teutons

Tevez *n* **Carlos (Alberto)** born 1984, Argentinian footballer; plays for Argentina and Manchester City (from 2009)

Tex-Mex *adj* **1** combining elements of Texan and Mexican culture ▹ *n* **2** Tex-Mex music or cooking

text ⊕ *n* **1** the main body of a printed or written work as distinct from items such as notes or illustrations **2** any written material, such as words displayed on a visual display unit **3** the written version of the words of a speech, broadcast or recording: *an advance text of the remarks the president will deliver tonight* **4** a short passage of the Bible used as a starting point for a sermon **5** a book required as part of a course of study: *shelves full of sociology texts* ▹ *vb* **6** to send (a text message) by mobile phone **7** to contact (a person) by means of a text message
WORD ORIGIN Latin *texere* to compose

textbook *n* **1** a book of facts about a subject used by someone who is studying that subject ▹ *adj* **2** perfect or exemplary: *a textbook example of an emergency descent*

textile *n* **1** any fabric or cloth, esp. a woven one ▹ *adj* **2** of or relating to fabrics or their production: *the world textile market*
WORD ORIGIN Latin *textilis* woven

text message *n* **1** a message sent in text form, esp. by means of a mobile phone **2** a message appearing on a computer screen **text messaging** *n*

textual *adj* of, based on, or relating to, a text or texts **textually** *adv*

texture ⊕ *n* **1** the structure, appearance, and feel of a substance: *curtains of many textures and colours* **2** the overall sound of a piece of music, resulting from the way the different instrumental parts in it are combined: *a big orchestra weaving rich textures* ▹ *vb* **-turing, -tured** **3** to give a distinctive texture to (something) **textural** *adj*
WORD ORIGIN Latin *texere* to weave

Tezel *n* a variant spelling of (Johann) **Tetzel**

TGV *n* (in France) a high-speed passenger train
WORD ORIGIN French *train à grande vitesse*

TGWU (in Britain) Transport and General Workers Union

Th *chem* thorium

Thai *adj* **1** of Thailand ▹ *n* **2** *pl* **Thais** *or* **Thai** a person from Thailand **3** the main language of Thailand

Thaïs *n* 4th-century BC Athenian courtesan; mistress of Alexander the Great

Thales *n* ?624–?546 BC, Greek philosopher, mathematician, and astronomer, born in Miletus. He held that water was the origin of all things and he predicted the solar eclipse of May 28, 585 BC

Thalia *n Greek myth* the Muse of comedy

thalidomide (thal-**lid**-oh-mide) *n* a drug formerly used as a sedative and hypnotic but withdrawn from use when found to cause abnormalities in developing fetuses
WORD ORIGIN *thali(mi)do(glutari)mide*

thallium *n chem* a soft highly toxic white metallic element. Symbol: Tl
WORD ORIGIN Greek *thallos* a green shoot; from the green line in its spectrum

than *conj, prep* **1** used to introduce the second element of a comparison, the first element of which expresses difference: *men are less observant than women and children* **2** used to state a number, quantity, or value in approximate terms by contrasting it with another number, quantity, or value: *temperatures lower than 25 degrees* **3** used after the adverbs *rather* and *sooner* to introduce a rejected alternative: *fruit is examined by hand, rather than by machine*
WORD ORIGIN Old English *thanne*

thane *n* **1** (in Anglo-Saxon England) a nobleman who held land from the king or from a superior nobleman in

THESAURUS

attestation **3 = proof,** evidence, demonstration, indication, support, manifestation, verification, corroboration

text *n* **1 = contents,** words, content, wording, body, matter, subject matter, main body **2 = words,** wording **3 = transcript,** script

texture *n* **1 = feel,** quality, character, consistency, structure, surface, constitution, fabric, tissue, grain, weave, composition

t

DICTIONARY

return for certain services **2** (in medieval Scotland) a person of rank holding land from the king
WORD ORIGIN Old English *thegn*

thank ❶ *vb* **1** to convey feelings of gratitude to: *he thanked the nursing staff for saving his life* **2** to hold responsible: *he has his father to thank for his familiarity with the film world* **3 thank you** a polite response or expression of gratitude **4 thank goodness** *or* **thank heavens** *or* **thank God** an exclamation of relief
WORD ORIGIN Old English *thancian*

thankful *adj* grateful and appreciative **thankfully** *adv*

thankless *adj* unrewarding or unappreciated: *she took on the thankless task of organizing the office Xmas lunch* **thanklessly** *adv* **thanklessness** *n*

thanks ❶ *pl n* **1** an expression of appreciation or gratitude **2 thanks to** because of: *the birth went very smoothly, thanks to the help of the GHQ medical officer* ▷ *interj* **3** *informal* an exclamation expressing gratitude

thanksgiving *n* a formal public expression of thanks to God

Thanksgiving Day *n* (in North America) an annual holiday celebrated on the fourth Thursday of November in the United States and on the second Monday of October in Canada

Thant *n* **U** 1909–74, Burmese diplomat; secretary-general of the United Nations (1962–71)

Tharp *n* **Twyla** born 1941, US choreographer, whose work fuses classical ballet with modern dance

that *adj* **1** used preceding a noun that has been mentioned or is already familiar: *he'd have to give up on that idea* **2** used preceding a noun that denotes something more remote: *that book on the top shelf* ▷ *pron* **3** used to denote something already mentioned or understood: *that's right* **4** used to denote a more remote person or thing: *is that him over there?* **5** used to introduce a restrictive relative clause: *a problem that has to be overcome* **6 and all that** *or* **and that** *informal* and similar or related things: *import cutting and all that* **7 that is a** to be precise **b** in other words **8 that's that** there is no more to be said or done ▷ *conj* **9** used to introduce a noun clause: *he denied that the country was suffering from famine* **10** used, usually after *so*, to introduce a clause of purpose: *he turns his face away from her so that she shall not see his tears* **11** used to introduce a clause of result: *a scene so sickening and horrible that it is impossible to describe it* ▷ *adv* **12** Also: **all that** *informal* very or particularly: *the fines imposed have not been that large*
WORD ORIGIN Old English *thæt*

thatch *n* **1** Also called: **thatching** a roofing material that consists of straw or reeds **2** a roof made of such a material **3** a mass of thick untidy hair on someone's head ▷ *vb* **4** to cover with thatch **thatched** *adj* **thatcher** *n*
WORD ORIGIN Old English *theccan* to cover

thaw ❶ *vb* **1** to melt or cause to melt: *snow thawing in the gutter* **2** (of frozen food) to become or cause to become unfrozen; defrost **3** (of weather) to be warm enough to cause ice or snow to melt: *it's not freezing, it's thawing again* **4** to become more relaxed or friendly: *only with Llewelyn did he thaw, let his defences down* ▷ *n* **5** the act or process of thawing **6** a spell of relatively warm weather, causing snow or ice to melt
WORD ORIGIN Old English *thawian*

THC tetrahydrocannabidinol: the active ingredient in cannabis which gives it its narcotic effect

the[1] *adj (definite article)* **1** used preceding a noun that has been previously specified or is a matter of common knowledge: *those involved in the search* **2** used to indicate a particular person or object: *the man called Frank turned to look at it* **3** used preceding certain nouns associated with one's culture, society, or community: *to comply with the law* **4** used preceding an adjective that is functioning as a collective noun: *the unemployed* **5** used preceding titles and certain proper nouns: *the Middle East* **6** used preceding an adjective or noun in certain names or titles: *Alexander the Great* **7** used preceding a noun to make it refer to its class as a whole: *cultivation of the coca plant* **8** used instead of *my, your, her*, etc. with parts of the body: *swelling of tissues in the brain* **9** the best or most remarkable: *it's THE place in town for good Mexican food*
WORD ORIGIN Old English *thē*

the[2] *adv* used in front of each of two things which are being compared to show how they increase or decrease in relation to each other: *the smaller the baby, the lower its chances of survival*
WORD ORIGIN Old English *thē, thȳ*

theatre *or US* **theater** *n* **1** a building designed for the performance of plays, operas, etc. **2** a large room or hall with tiered seats for an audience: *a lecture theatre* **3** a room in a hospital equipped for surgical operations **4 the theatre** drama and acting in general **5** a region in which a war or conflict takes place: *a potential theatre of war close to Russian borders* **6** *US, Austral, & NZ* ▸ same as **cinema** (sense 1)
WORD ORIGIN Greek *theatron*

theatrical ❶ *adj* **1** of or relating to the theatre or dramatic performances **2** exaggerated and affected in manner or behaviour **theatricality** *n* **theatrically** *adv*

theatricals *pl n* dramatic performances, esp. as given by amateurs

thee *pron old-fashioned* ▸ the objective form of **thou**[1]

theft ❶ *n* **1** the act or an instance of stealing: *he reported the theft of his passport* **2** the crime of stealing: *he had a number of convictions for theft*
WORD ORIGIN Old English *thēofth*

Theiler *n* **Max** 1899–1972, US virologist, born in South Africa, who developed a vaccine against yellow fever. Nobel prize for physiology or medicine 1951

their *adj* of or associated with them: *owning their own land; two girls on their way to school*
WORD ORIGIN Old Norse *theira*

theirs *pron* **1** something or someone belonging to or associated with them: *it was his fault, not theirs* **2 of theirs** belonging to them

theism (thee-iz-zum) *n* **1** belief in one God as the creator of everything in the universe **2** belief in the existence of a God or gods **theist** *n, adj* **theistic** *adj*
WORD ORIGIN Greek *theos* god

them *pron (objective)* refers to things or people other than the speaker or people addressed: *I want you to give this to them*
WORD ORIGIN Old English *thǣm*

theme ❶ *n* **1** the main idea or topic in a discussion or lecture **2** (in literature, music, or art) an idea,

t

THESAURUS

thank *vb* **1 = say thank you to**, express gratitude to, show gratitude to, show your appreciation to

thanks *pl n* **1 = gratitude**, appreciation, thanksgiving, credit, recognition, acknowledgment, gratefulness
2 thanks to = because of, through, due to, as a result of, owing to, by reason of

thaw *vb* **1, 2 = melt**, dissolve, soften, defrost, warm, liquefy, unfreeze **OPPOSITE:** freeze

theatrical *adj* **1 = dramatic**, stage, Thespian, dramaturgical
2 = exaggerated, dramatic, melodramatic, histrionic, affected, camp *(informal)*, mannered, artificial, overdone, unreal, pompous, stilted, showy, ostentatious, hammy *(informal)*, ceremonious, stagy, actorly *or* actressy **OPPOSITE:** natural

theft *n* **1, 2 = stealing**, robbery, thieving, fraud, rip-off *(slang)*, swindling, embezzlement, pilfering, larceny, purloining, thievery

image, or motif, repeated or developed throughout a work or throughout an artist's career **3** *music* a group of notes forming a recognizable melodic unit, used as the basis of part or all of a composition **4** a short essay, esp. one set as an exercise for a student **thematic** *adj* **thematically** *adv*
WORD ORIGIN Greek *thema*

theme park *n* an area planned as a leisure attraction in which all the displays and activities are based on a particular theme, story, or idea: *a Wild West theme park*

theme tune *or* **theme song** *n* a tune or song used to introduce or identify a television or radio programme or performer

Themistocles *n* ?527–?460 BC, Athenian statesman, who was responsible for the Athenian victory against the Persians at Salamis (480). He was ostracized in 470

themselves *pron* **1 a** the reflexive form of *they* or *them*: *two men barricaded themselves into a cell* **b** used for emphasis: *among the targets were police officers themselves* **2** their normal or usual selves: *they don't seem themselves these days*

then *adv* **1** at that time: *he was then at the height of his sporting career* **2** after that: *let's eat first and then we can explore the town* **3** in that case: *then why did he work for you?* ▷ *pron* **4** that time: *since then the list of grievances has steadily grown* ▷ *adj* **5** existing or functioning at that time: *the then Defence Minister*
WORD ORIGIN Old English *thænne, thanne*

thence *adv formal* **1** from that place: *the train went south into Switzerland, and thence on to Italy* **2** for that reason; therefore
WORD ORIGIN Middle English *thannes*

thenceforth *or* **thenceforward** *adv formal* from that time on

theocracy *n, pl* **-cies 1** government by a god or by priests **2** a community under such government **theocrat** *n* **theocratic** *adj* **theocratically** *adv*
WORD ORIGIN Greek *theos* god + *kratos* power

Theocritus *n* ?310–?250 BC, Greek poet, born in Syracuse. He wrote the first pastoral poems in Greek literature and was closely imitated by Virgil > **Theocritan** *or* **Theocritean** *adj, n*

theodolite (thee-odd-oh-lite) *n* an instrument used in surveying for measuring horizontal and vertical angles
WORD ORIGIN origin unknown

Theodora *n* ?500–548 AD, Byzantine empress; wife and counsellor of Justinian I

Theodorakis *n* **Mikis** born 1925, Greek composer, who wrote the music for the film *Zorba the Greek* (1965): imprisoned (1967–70) for his opposition to the Greek military government

Theodore I *n* called *Lascaris*. ?1175–1222, Byzantine ruler, who founded a Byzantine state in exile at Nicaea after Constantinople fell to the Crusaders (1204)

Theodoric *or* **Theoderic** *n* called *the Great*. ?454–526 AD, king of the Ostrogoths and founder of the Ostrogothic kingdom in Italy after his murder of Odoacer (493)

Theodosius I *n* called *the Great*. ?346–395 AD, Roman emperor of the Eastern Roman Empire (379–95) and of the Western Roman Empire (392–95)

theologian *n* a person versed in the study of theology

theology *n, pl* **-gies 1** the systematic study of religions and religious beliefs **2** a specific system, form, or branch of this study: *Muslim theology* **theological** *adj* **theologically** *adv*
WORD ORIGIN Greek *theos* god + **-logy**

Theophilus[1] *n* a conspicuous crater in the SE quadrant of the moon, 100 kilometres in diameter
WORD ORIGIN after **THEOPHILUS**[2]

Theophilus[2] *n* died 842 AD, Byzantine emperor (829–42); a patron of learning and supporter of iconoclasm

Theophrastus *n* ?372–?287 BC, Greek Peripatetic philosopher, noted esp. for his *Characters*, a collection of sketches of moral types

theorem *n* a proposition, esp. in maths, that can be proved by reasoning from the basic principles of a subject
WORD ORIGIN Greek *theōrein* to view

theoretical ❶ *or* **theoretic** *adj* **1** based on or concerned with the ideas and abstract principles relating to a particular subject rather than its practical uses: *theoretical physics* **2** existing in theory but perhaps not in reality: *the secret service is under the theoretical control of the government* **theoretically** *adv*

theoretician *n* a person who develops or studies the theory of a subject rather than its practical aspects

theorize *or* **-rise** *vb* **-rizing, -rized** *or* **-rising, -rised** to produce or use theories; speculate **theorist** *n*

theory ❶ *n, pl* **-ries 1** a set of ideas, based on evidence and careful reasoning, which offers an explanation of how something works or why something happens, but has not been completely proved: *the theory of cosmology* **2** the ideas and abstract knowledge relating to something: *political theory* **3** an idea or opinion: *it's only a theory, admittedly, but I think it's worth pursuing* **4 in theory** in an ideal or hypothetical situation: *in theory, the tax is supposed to limit inflation*
WORD ORIGIN Greek *theōria* a sight

theosophy *n* a religious or philosophical system claiming to be based on an intuitive insight into the divine nature **theosophical** *adj* **theosophist** *n*
WORD ORIGIN Greek *theos* god + *sophia* wisdom

therapeutic ❶ (ther-rap-pew-tik) *adj* of or relating to the treatment and cure of disease **therapeutically** *adv*
WORD ORIGIN Greek *therapeuein* to minister to

therapeutics *n* the branch of medicine concerned with the treatment of disease

therapy ❶ *n, pl* **-pies** the treatment of physical, mental, or social disorders or disease **therapist** *n*
WORD ORIGIN Greek *therapeia* attendance

there *adv* **1** in, at, or to that place or position: *he won't be there* **2** in that respect: *you're right there* **3 there and then** immediately and without delay: *he walked out there and then* ▷ *adj* **4 not all there** *informal* mentally defective or silly ▷ *pron* **5** that place: *to return from there* **6** used as a grammatical subject when the true subject follows the verb, esp. the verb 'to be': *there are no children in the house* **7 so there!** an exclamation, used esp. by children, that usually follows a declaration of refusal or defiance: *you can't come, so there!* **8 there you are** *or* **go a** an expression used when handing a person something **b** an

t

THESAURUS

theme *n* **1 = subject**, idea, topic, matter, argument, text, burden, essence, thesis, subject matter, keynote, gist **2 = motif**, leitmotif, recurrent image, unifying idea

theoretical *or* **theoretic** *adj* **1 = abstract**, pure, speculative, ideal, impractical **OPPOSITE:** practical **2 = hypothetical**, academic, notional, unproven, conjectural, postulatory

theory *n* **3 = belief**, feeling, speculation, assumption, guess, hunch, presumption, conjecture, surmise, supposition

therapeutic *adj* **= beneficial**, healing, restorative, good, corrective, remedial, salutary, curative, salubrious, ameliorative, analeptic, sanative **OPPOSITE:** harmful

therapy *n* **= remedy**, treatment, cure, healing, method of healing, remedial treatment

DICTIONARY

exclamation of satisfaction or vindication ▹ *interj* **9** an expression of sympathy, for example when consoling a child: *there, there, pet!*
WORD ORIGIN Old English *thǣr*

thereabouts *or US* **thereabout** *adv* near that place, time, amount, etc.: *meet me at three o'clock or thereabouts; Methuselah lived 900 years or thereabouts*

thereafter *adv formal* from that time onwards

thereby *adv formal* by that means or consequently

therefore ❶ *adv* for that reason: *the training is long, and therefore expensive*

therein *adv formal* in or into that place or thing

thereof *adv formal* of or concerning that or it

Theresa *n* See **Teresa** (sense 1)

Thérèse de Lisieux *n* **Saint,** known as *the Little Flower of Jesus*. 1873–97, French Carmelite nun, noted for her autobiography, *The Story of a Soul* (1897). Feast day: Oct 3

thereto *adv formal* **1** to that or it **2** Also: **thereunto** in addition to that

thereupon *adv formal* immediately after that; at that point

therm *n Brit* a unit of heat equal to $1.055\,056 \times 10^8$ joules
WORD ORIGIN Greek *thermē* heat

thermal *adj* **1** of, caused by, or generating heat **2** hot or warm: *thermal springs* **3** (of garments) specially made so as to have exceptional heat-retaining qualities: *thermal underwear* ▹ *n* **4** a column of rising air caused by uneven heating of the land surface, and used by gliders and birds to gain height

thermionic valve *or esp. US & Canad* **thermionic tube** *n* an electronic valve in which electrons are emitted from a heated rather than a cold cathode

thermistor (therm-**mist**-or) *n physics* a metal-oxide rod whose resistance falls as temperature rises, used in electronic circuits and as a thermometer

thermocouple *n* a device for measuring temperature, consisting of a pair of wires of different metals joined at both ends

thermodynamics *n* the branch of physical science concerned with the relationship between heat and other forms of energy

thermoelectric *or* **thermoelectrical** *adj* of or relating to the conversion of heat energy to electrical energy

thermometer *n* an instrument used to measure temperature, esp. one in which a thin column of liquid, such as mercury, expands and contracts within a sealed tube marked with a temperature scale

thermonuclear *adj* **1** (of a nuclear reaction) involving a nuclear fusion reaction of a type which occurs at very high temperatures **2** (of a weapon) giving off energy as the result of a thermonuclear reaction **3** involving thermonuclear weapons

thermoplastic *adj* **1** (of a material, esp. a synthetic plastic) becoming soft when heated and rehardening on cooling ▹ *n* **2** a synthetic plastic or resin, such as polystyrene

Thermos *or* **Thermos flask** *n trademark* a type of stoppered vacuum flask used to preserve the temperature of its contents

thermosetting *adj* (of a material, esp. a synthetic plastic) hardening permanently after one application of heat and pressure

thermostat *n* a device which automatically regulates the temperature of central heating, an oven, etc. by switching it off or on when it reaches or drops below a particular temperature
thermostatic *adj* **thermostatically** *adv*

Theron *n* **Charlize** born 1975, South African film actress; her films include *The Cider House Rules* (1999) and *Monster* (2003), which earned her an Oscar

Theroux *n* **Paul** (**Edward**). born 1941, US novelist and travel writer. His novels include *Picture Palace* (1978), *The Mosquito Coast* (1981), and *My Other Life* (1996); travel writings include *The Great Railway Bazaar* (1975)

thesaurus (thiss-**sore**-uss) *n, pl* **-ruses** *or* **-ri** a book containing lists of synonyms and related words
WORD ORIGIN Greek *thēsauros* a treasury

these *adj, pron* ▸ the plural of **this**

Thesiger *n* **Wilfred** (**Patrick**). 1910–2003, British writer, who explored the Empty Quarter of Arabia (1945–50) and lived with the Iraqi marsh Arabs (1950–58). His books include *Arabian Sands* (1958), *The Marsh Arabs* (1964), and *My Kenya Days* (1994)

thesis ❶ (**theess**-siss) *n, pl* **-ses** (-seez) **1** a written work resulting from original research, esp. one submitted for a higher degree in a university **2** an opinion supported by reasoned argument: *it is the author's thesis that Britain has yet to come to terms with the loss of its Empire* **3** *logic* an unproved statement put forward as a premise in an argument
WORD ORIGIN Greek: a placing

Thespian *n* **1** *often facetious* an actor or actress ▹ *adj* **2** of or relating to drama and the theatre
WORD ORIGIN after *Thespis*, a Greek poet

they *pron* (*subjective*) **1** refers to people or things other than the speaker or people addressed: *they both giggled* **2** refers to people in general: *they say he beats his wife* **3** *informal* refers to an individual person, whose sex is either not known or not regarded as important: *someone could have a nasty accident if they tripped over that*
WORD ORIGIN Old Norse *their*

thiamine *or* **thiamin** *n* vitamin B_1, a vitamin found in the outer coat of rice and other grains, a deficiency of which leads to nervous disorders and to beriberi
WORD ORIGIN Greek *theion* sulphur + VITAMIN

thick ❶ *adj* **1** having a relatively great distance between opposite surfaces: *thick slices* **2** having a specified distance between opposite surfaces: *fifty metres thick* **3** having a dense consistency: *thick fog* **4** consisting of a lot of things grouped closely together: *thick forest* **5** (of clothes) made of heavy cloth or wool: *a thick jumper* **6** *informal* stupid, slow, or insensitive **7** (of an accent) very noticeable: *each word was pronounced in a thick Dutch accent* **8** Also: **thick as thieves** *informal* very friendly **9** **a bit**

THESAURUS

therefore *adv* **= consequently,** so, thus, as a result, hence, accordingly, for that reason, whence, thence, ergo

thesis *n* **1 = dissertation,** paper, treatise, essay, composition, monograph, disquisition **2 = proposition,** theory, hypothesis, idea, view, opinion, proposal, contention, line of argument

thick *adj* **1 = bulky,** broad, big, large, fat, solid, substantial, hefty, plump, sturdy, stout, chunky, stocky, meaty, beefy, thickset **OPPOSITE:** thin **2 = wide,** across, deep, broad, in extent *or* diameter **3a = dense,** close, heavy, deep, compact, impenetrable, lush **3b = opaque,** heavy, dense, impenetrable **3c = viscous,** concentrated, stiff, condensed, clotted, coagulated, gelatinous, semi-solid, viscid **OPPOSITE:** runny **4 = crowded,** full, packed, covered, filled, bursting, jammed, crawling, choked, crammed, swarming, abundant, bristling, brimming, overflowing, seething, thronged, teeming, congested, replete, chock-full, bursting at the seams, chock-a-block **OPPOSITE:** empty **5 = heavy,** heavyweight, dense, chunky, bulky, woolly **6 = stupid,** slow, dull, dense, insensitive, dozy (*Brit informal*), dopey (*informal*), moronic, obtuse, brainless, blockheaded, braindead (*informal*), dumb-ass (*informal*), thickheaded, dim-witted (*informal*), slow-witted **OPPOSITE:** clever **8** (*informal*) **= friendly,** close, intimate,

DICTIONARY

thick *Brit informal* unfair or unreasonable: *£2 an hour, that's a bit thick!* **10** **thick with a** covered with a lot of: *glass panels thick with dust* **b** (of a voice) throaty and hard to make out: *his voice was thick with emotion* ▹ *adv* **11** in order to produce something thick: *the machine sliced the potatoes too thick* **12** **lay it on thick** *informal* **a** to exaggerate a story **b** to flatter someone excessively **13** **thick and fast** quickly and in large numbers: *theories were flying thick and fast* ▹ *n* **14** **the thick** the most intense or active part: *in the thick of the fighting* **15** **through thick and thin** in good times and bad **thickly** *adv*
WORD ORIGIN Old English *thicce*

thicken ❶ *vb* **1** to make or become thick or thicker **2** to become more complicated: *the plot thickens* **thickener** *n*

thickening *n* **1** something added to a liquid to thicken it **2** a thickened part or piece

thicket *n* a dense growth of small trees or shrubs
WORD ORIGIN Old English *thiccet*

thickhead *n slang* a stupid or ignorant person **thickheaded** *adj*

thickie *n slang* ▸ same as **thicko**

thickness *n* **1** the state or quality of being thick **2** the dimension through an object, as opposed to length or width **3** a layer: *several thicknesses of brown paper*

thicko *n, pl* **thickos** *or* **thickoes** *Brit slang* a slow-witted unintelligent person

thickset *adj* **1** stocky in build **2** planted or placed close together

thick-skinned *adj* insensitive to criticism or hints; not easily upset

thief ❶ *n, pl* **thieves** a person who steals something from another **thievish** *adj*
WORD ORIGIN Old English *thēof*

Thiers *n* **Louis Adolphe**. 1797–1877, French statesman and historian. After the Franco-Prussian war, he suppressed the Paris Commune and became first president of the Third Republic (1871–73). His policies made possible the paying off of the war indemnity exacted by Germany

thieve *vb* **thieving, thieved** to steal other people's possessions **thieving** *adj*
WORD ORIGIN Old English *thēofian*

thigh *n* the part of the human leg between the hip and the knee
WORD ORIGIN Old English *thēh*

thighbone *n* ▸ same as **femur**

thimble *n* a small metal or plastic cap used to protect the end of the finger from the needle when sewing
WORD ORIGIN Old English *thȳmel* thumbstall

thin ❶ *adj* **thinner, thinnest** **1** having a relatively small distance between opposite surfaces: *a thin mattress* **2** much narrower than it is long: *push a thin stick up the pipe in order to clear it* **3** (of a person or animal) having no excess body fat **4** made up of only a few, widely separated, people or things: *thin hair* **5** not dense: *a thin film of dust* **6** unconvincing because badly thought out or badly presented: *the evidence against him was extremely thin* **7** (of a voice) high-pitched and not very loud: *a thin squeaky voice* ▹ *adv* **8** in order to produce something thin: *roll the dough very thin* ▹ *vb* **thinning, thinned** **9** to make or become thin or sparse **thinly** *adv* **thinness** *n*
WORD ORIGIN Old English *thynne*

thin client *n computers* a computer on a network where most functions are carried out on a central server

thine *old-fashioned adj* **1** (*preceding a vowel*) of or associated with you (thou): *if thine eye offend thee, pluck it out!* ▹ *pron* **2** something belonging to you (thou): *the victory shall be thine*
WORD ORIGIN Old English *thīn*

thing ❶ *n* **1** any physical object that is not alive: *there are very few jobs left where people actually make things* **2** an object, fact, circumstance, or concept considered as being a separate entity: *that would be a terrible thing to do* **3** an object or entity that cannot or need not be precisely named: *squares and circles and things* **4** *informal* a person or animal: *pretty little thing, isn't she?* **5** a possession, article of clothing, etc.: *have you brought your swimming things?* **6** *informal* a preoccupation or obsession: *they have this thing about policemen* **7** **do one's own thing** to engage in an activity or mode of behaviour satisfying to one's personality **8** **make a thing of** to exaggerate the importance of **9** **the thing** the latest fashion
WORD ORIGIN Old English: assembly

thingumabob *or* **thingamabob** *n informal* a person or thing the name of which is unknown, temporarily forgotten, or deliberately overlooked. Also: **thingumajig, thingamajig, thingummy**

think ❶ *vb* **thinking, thought** **1** to consider, judge, or believe: *I think that it is scandalous* **2** to make use of the mind, for example in order to make a decision: *I'll need to think about what I'm going to do* **3** to engage in conscious thought: *that made me think* **4** to be considerate enough or remember (to do something): *no other company had thought to bring high tech down to the user* **5** **think much** *or* **a lot of** to have a favourable opinion of: *I don't think much of the new design* **6** **think of a** to remember or recollect: *I couldn't think of your surname* **b** to conceive of or formulate: *for a long time he couldn't think of a response* **7** **think twice** to consider something carefully before making a decision ▹ *n* **8** *informal* a careful open-minded assessment: *she had a long hard think* **thinker** *n*
WORD ORIGIN Old English *thencan*

THESAURUS

familiar, pally (*informal*), devoted, well in (*informal*), confidential, inseparable, on good terms, chummy (*informal*), hand in glove, buddy-buddy (*slang, chiefly US & Canad*), palsy-walsy (*informal*), matey or maty (*Brit informal*)
OPPOSITE: unfriendly

thicken *vb* **1 = set**, condense, congeal, cake, gel, clot, jell, coagulate, inspissate (*archaic*) **OPPOSITE:** thin

thief *n* **= robber**, crook (*informal*), burglar, stealer, bandit, plunderer, mugger (*informal*), shoplifter, embezzler, pickpocket, pilferer, swindler, purloiner, housebreaker, footpad (*archaic*), cracksman (*slang*), larcenist

thin *adj* **2 = narrow**, fine, attenuate, attenuated, threadlike
OPPOSITE: thick
3 = slim, spare, lean, slight, slender, skinny, light, meagre, skeletal, bony, lanky, emaciated, spindly, underweight, scrawny, lank, undernourished, skin and bone, scraggy, thin as a rake **OPPOSITE:** fat
4 = wispy, thinning, sparse, scarce, scanty **5 = fine**, delicate, flimsy, sheer, transparent, see-through, translucent, skimpy, gossamer, diaphanous, filmy, unsubstantial
OPPOSITE: thick
6 = unconvincing, inadequate, feeble, poor, weak, slight, shallow, insufficient, superficial, lame, scant, flimsy, scanty, unsubstantial
OPPOSITE: convincing

thing *n* **5a** (*often plural*) **= possessions**, stuff, gear, belongings, goods, effects, clothes, luggage, baggage, bits and pieces, paraphernalia, clobber (*Brit slang*), odds and ends, chattels, impedimenta
5b = equipment, gear, tool, stuff, tackle, implement, kit, apparatus, utensil, accoutrement **6** (*informal*) **= obsession**, liking, preoccupation, mania, quirk, fetish, fixation, soft spot, predilection, idée fixe (*French*)

think *vb* **1a = believe**, hold that, be of the opinion, conclude, esteem, conceive, be of the view **1b = judge**, consider, estimate, reckon, deem, regard as **2, 3 = ponder**, reflect, contemplate, deliberate, brood, meditate, ruminate, cogitate, rack your brains, be lost in thought, cerebrate

DICTIONARY

thinking ❶ *n* **1** opinion or judgment: *contrary to all fashionable thinking* **2** the process of thought ▹*adj* **3** using intelligent thought: *the thinking man's sport*
think over *vb* to ponder or consider
think-tank *n informal* a group of experts employed to study specific problems
think up ❶ *vb* to invent or devise
thinner *n* a solvent, such as turpentine, added to paint or varnish to dilute it
thin-skinned *adj* sensitive to criticism or hints; easily upset
third *adj* **1** of or being number three in a series **2** rated, graded, or ranked below the second level **3** denoting the third from lowest forward gear in a motor vehicle ▹*n* **4** one of three equal parts of something **5** the fraction equal to one divided by three (⅓) **6** the third from lowest forward gear in a motor vehicle **7** *Brit* an honours degree of the third and usually the lowest class **8** *music* the interval between one note and the note four semitones (**major third**) or three semitones (**minor third**) higher or lower than it ▹*adv* **9** Also: **thirdly** in the third place
WORD ORIGIN Old English *thirda*
third class *n* **1** the class or grade next in value, rank, or quality to the second ▹*adj* **third-class** **2** of the class or grade next in value, rank, or quality to the second
third degree *n informal* torture or bullying, esp. as used to extort confessions or information
third-degree burn *n* a burn in which both the surface and the underlying layers of the skin are destroyed
third man *n cricket* a fielding position on the off side, near the boundary behind the batsman's wicket
third party *n* **1** a person who is involved in an event, legal proceeding, agreement, or other transaction only by chance or indirectly ▹*adj* **third-party** **2** *insurance* providing protection against liability caused by accidental injury or death of other people: *third-party cover*
third person *n* the form of a pronoun or verb used to refer to something or someone other than the speaker or the person or people being addressed
third-rate *adj* mediocre or inferior
Third Reich *n* ▸see **Reich**
Third World *n* the developing countries of Africa, Asia, and Latin America collectively
thirst ❶ *n* **1** a desire to drink, accompanied by a feeling of dryness in the mouth and throat **2** a craving or yearning: *a thirst for knowledge* ▹*vb* **3** to feel a thirst
WORD ORIGIN Old English *thurst*
thirsty *adj* **thirstier, thirstiest** **1** feeling a desire to drink **2** causing thirst: *morris dancing is thirsty work* **3** **thirsty for** feeling an eager desire for: *thirsty for information* **thirstily** *adv*
thirteen *n* **1** the cardinal number that is the sum of ten and three **2** a numeral, 13 or XIII, representing this number **3** something representing or consisting of thirteen units ▹*adj* **4** amounting to thirteen: *thirteen people* **thirteenth** *adj, n*
thirty *n, pl* **-ties** **1** the cardinal number that is the product of ten and three **2** a numeral, 30 or XXX, representing this number **3** something representing or consisting of thirty units ▹*adj* **4** amounting to thirty: *thirty miles* **thirtieth** *adj, n*
Thirty-nine Articles *pl n* a set of formulas defining the doctrinal position of the Church of England
this *adj* **1** used preceding a noun referring to something or someone that is closer: *on this side of the Channel* **2** used preceding a noun that has just been mentioned or is understood: *this text has two chief goals* **3** used to refer to something about to be mentioned: *NPR's Anne Garrels has this report* **4** used to refer to the present time or occasion: *this week's edition of the newspaper* **5** *informal* used instead of *a* or *the* in telling a story: *see, it's about this bird who fancies you* ▹*pron* **6** used to denote a person or thing that is relatively close: *black coral like this* **7** used to denote something already mentioned or understood: *this didn't seem fair to me* **8** used to denote something about to be mentioned: *just say this: collect Standish from the top of the fire escape* **9** the present time or occasion: *after this it was impossible to talk to him about his feelings* **10** **this and that** various unspecified and trivial events or facts
WORD ORIGIN Old English *thes, thēos, this* (masculine, feminine, and neuter singular)
thistle *n* a plant with prickly-edged leaves, dense flower heads, and feathery hairs on the seeds **thistly** *adj*
WORD ORIGIN Old English *thīstel*
thistledown *n* the mass of feathery plumed seeds produced by a thistle
thither *adv formal* to or towards that place
WORD ORIGIN Old English *thider*
tho' *or* **tho** *conj, adv US or poetic* ▸same as **though**
thole[1] *or* **tholepin** *n* one of a pair of wooden pins set upright in the gunwale on either side of a rowing boat to serve as a fulcrum in rowing
WORD ORIGIN Old English *tholl*
thole[2] *vb* **tholing, tholed** *Scot & N English* to bear or put up with
Thomas of Erceldoune *n* called *Thomas the Rhymer.* ?1220–?97, Scottish seer and poet; reputed author of a poem on the Tristan legend
Thomas of Woodstock *n* 1355–97, youngest son of Edward III, who led opposition to his nephew Richard II (1386–89); arrested in 1397, he died in prison
Thompson *n* **1 Benjamin,** Count Rumford. 1753–1814, Anglo-American physicist, noted for his work on the nature of heat **2 Daley.** born 1958, British athlete: Olympic decathlon champion (1980, 1984) **3 Emma.** born 1959, British actress: her films include *Howards End* (1991), *Sense and Sensibility* (1996; also wrote screenplay), *Primary Colors* (1998), and *Love Actually* (2003) **4 Flora (Jane).** 1876–1947, British writer, author of the autobiographical *Lark Rise to Candleford* (1945) **5 Francis.** 1859–1907, British poet, best known for the mystical poem *The Hound of Heaven* (1893)
Thomson *n* **1** Sir **George Paget,** son of Joseph John Thomson. 1892–1975, British physicist, who discovered (1927) the diffraction of electrons by crystals: shared the Nobel prize for physics 1937 **2 James.** 1700–48, Scottish poet. He anticipated the romantics' feeling for nature in *The Seasons* (1726–30) **3 James,** pen name *B.V.* 1834–82, British poet, born in Scotland, noted esp. for *The City of Dreadful Night* (1874), reflecting man's isolation and despair **4** Sir **Joseph John.** 1856–1940, British physicist. He discovered the electron (1897) and his work on the nature of positive rays led to the discovery of isotopes: Nobel prize for physics 1906 **5 Roy,** 1st Baron Thomson of Fleet. 1894–

t

THESAURUS

thinking *n* **1, 2 = reasoning,** thoughts, philosophy, idea, view, position, theory, opinion, conclusions, assessment, judgment, outlook, conjecture ▹*adj* **3 = thoughtful,** intelligent, cultured, reasoning, sophisticated, rational, philosophical, reflective, contemplative, meditative, ratiocinative
think up *vb* **= devise,** create, imagine, manufacture, come up with, invent, contrive, improvise, visualize, concoct, dream up, trump up
thirst *n* **1 = dryness,** thirstiness, drought, craving to drink **2 = craving,** hunger, appetite, longing, desire, passion, yen *(informal)*, ache, lust, yearning, eagerness, hankering, keenness **OPPOSITE:** aversion

DICTIONARY

1976, British newspaper proprietor, born in Canada **6 Virgil.** 1896–1989, US composer, music critic, and conductor, whose works include two operas, *Four Saints in Three Acts* (1928) and *The Mother of Us All* (1947), piano sonatas, a cello concerto, songs, and film music **7** ▸ Sir **William.** See (1st Baron) **Kelvin**

thong *n* **1** a thin strip of leather or other material **2** *Austral, US, & Canad* ▸ same as **flip-flop 3** a skimpy article of beachwear consisting of thin strips of leather or cloth attached to a piece of material that covers the genitals while leaving the buttocks bare
WORD ORIGIN Old English *thwang*

Thor *n Norse myth* the god of thunder

thorax (thaw-racks) *n, pl* **thoraxes** *or* **thoraces** (thaw-rass-seez) **1** the part of the human body enclosed by the ribs **2** the part of an insect's body between the head and abdomen **thoracic** *adj*
WORD ORIGIN Greek: breastplate, chest

Thoreau *n* **Henry David.** 1817–62, US writer, noted esp. for *Walden, or Life in the Woods* (1854), an account of his experiment in living in solitude. A powerful social critic, his essay *Civil Disobedience* (1849) influenced such dissenters as Gandhi

thorium *n chem* a silvery-white radioactive metallic element. It is used in electronic equipment and as a nuclear power source. Symbol: Th
WORD ORIGIN after *Thor*, Norse god of thunder

thorn ⊕ *n* **1** a sharp pointed woody projection from a stem or leaf **2** any of various trees or shrubs having thorns, esp. the hawthorn **3 a thorn in one's side** *or* **flesh** a source of irritation: *he was sufficiently bright at school to become a thorn in the side of his maths teacher* **thornless** *adj*
WORD ORIGIN Old English

Thornhill *n* Sir **James.** 1675–1734, English baroque painter. He is best known for decorating the Painted Hall, Greenwich Hospital (1708–27) and the interior of the dome of St Paul's Cathedral (1715–17)

thorny *adj* **thornier, thorniest** **1** covered with thorns **2** difficult or unpleasant: *a thorny issue*

thorough ⊕ *adj* **1** carried out completely and carefully: *he needs a thorough checkup by the doctor* **2** (of a person) painstakingly careful: *he is very thorough if rather unimaginative* **3** great in extent or degree; utter: *a thorough disgrace* **thoroughly** *adv* **thoroughness** *n*
WORD ORIGIN Old English *thurh* through

thoroughbred *adj* **1** obtained through successive generations of selective breeding: *thoroughbred horses* ▹ *n* **2** a pedigree animal, esp. a horse

thoroughfare *n* a way through from one place to another: *the great thoroughfare from the Castle to the Palace of Holyrood*

thoroughgoing *adj* **1** extremely thorough **2** absolute or complete: *a thoroughgoing hatred*

Thorpe *n* **1 Ian.** born 1982, Australian swimmer; won three gold medals at the 2000 Olympic Games, six gold medals at the 2002 Commonwealth Games, and two gold medals at the 2004 Olympic Games. **2 James Francis.** 1888–1953, American football player and athlete: Olympic pentathlon and decathlon champion (1912) **3 Jeremy.** born 1929, British politician; leader of the Liberal party (1967–76)

Thorvaldsen *n* **Bertel.** 1770–1844, Danish neoclassical sculptor

those *adj, pron* ▸ the plural of **that**
WORD ORIGIN Old English *thās*, plural of *this*

thou[1] *pron old-fashioned* ▸ same as **you**: used when talking to one person
WORD ORIGIN Old English *thū*

thou[2] *n, pl* **thou** *informal* **1** one thousandth of an inch **2** a thousand

though ⊕ *conj* **1** despite the fact that: *he was smiling with relief and happiness though the tears still flowed down his cheeks* ▹ *adv* **2** nevertheless or however: *he can't dance – he sings well, though*
WORD ORIGIN Old English *thēah*

thought ⊕ *vb* **1** ▸ the past of **think** ▹ *n* **2** the act or process of thinking **3** a concept or idea **4** ideas typical of a particular time or place: *the development of Western intellectual thought* **5** detailed consideration: *he appeared to give some sort of thought to the question* **6** an intention, hope, or reason for doing something: *his first thought was to call the guard and have the man arrested*
WORD ORIGIN Old English *thōht*

thoughtful ⊕ *adj* **1** considerate in the treatment of other people **2** showing careful thought: *a thoughtful and scholarly book* **3** quiet, serious, and deep in thought **thoughtfully** *adv* **thoughtfulness** *n*

thoughtless *adj* not considerate of the feelings of other people **thoughtlessly** *adv* **thoughtlessness** *n*

thousand *n, pl* **-sands** *or* **-sand** **1** the cardinal number that is the product of ten and one hundred **2** a numeral, 1000 or 10^3, representing this number **3** a very large but unspecified number: *thousands of bees swarmed out of the hive* **4** something representing or consisting of 1000 units ▹ *adj* **5** amounting to a thousand: *a thousand members* **thousandth** *adj, n*
WORD ORIGIN Old English *thūsend*

Thrale *n* **Hester Lynch,** known as *Mrs Thrale* or (later) *Mrs Piozzi* (née *Salusbury*). 1741–1821, English writer of memoirs, noted for her friendship with Dr Johnson. Her works include *Anecdotes of the late Samuel Johnson* (1786) and *Letters to and from the late Samuel Johnson* (1788)

thrall *n* the state of being completely in the power of, or spellbound by, a person or thing: *he was held in thrall by her almost supernatural beauty*
WORD ORIGIN Old English *thrǣl* slave

thrash ⊕ *vb* **1** to beat (someone), esp. with a stick or whip **2** to defeat

t

THESAURUS

thorn *n* **1 = prickle**, spike, spine, barb

thorough *adj* **1, 3 = comprehensive**, full, complete, sweeping, intensive, in-depth, exhaustive, all-inclusive, all-embracing, leaving no stone unturned **OPPOSITE:** cursory **2 = careful**, conscientious, painstaking, efficient, meticulous, exhaustive, scrupulous, assiduous **OPPOSITE:** careless **3 = complete**, total, absolute, utter, perfect, entire, pure, sheer, outright, downright, unqualified, out-and-out, unmitigated, arrant, deep-dyed *(usually derogatory)* **OPPOSITE:** partial

though *conj* **1 = although**, while, even if, despite the fact that, allowing, granted, even though, albeit, notwithstanding, even supposing, tho' *(US poetic)* ▹ *adv* **2 = nevertheless**, still, however, yet, nonetheless, all the same, for all that, notwithstanding

thought *n* **2 = thinking**, consideration, reflection, deliberation, regard, musing, meditation, contemplation, introspection, rumination, navel-gazing *(slang)*, cogitation, brainwork, cerebration **3 = opinion**, view, belief, idea, thinking, concept, conclusion, assessment, notion, conviction, judgment, conception, conjecture, estimation **5 = consideration**, study, attention, care, regard, scrutiny, heed **6a = intention**, plan, idea, design, aim, purpose, object, notion **6b = hope**, expectation, dream, prospect, aspiration, anticipation

thoughtful *adj* **1 = considerate**, kind, caring, kindly, helpful, attentive, unselfish, solicitous **OPPOSITE:** inconsiderate **3 = reflective**, pensive, contemplative, meditative, thinking, serious, musing, wistful, introspective, rapt, studious, lost in thought, deliberative, ruminative, in a brown study **OPPOSITE:** shallow

thrash *vb* **1 = beat**, wallop, whip, hide *(informal)*, belt *(informal)*, leather, tan

DICTIONARY

totally: *the All Blacks thrashed England 24-3* **3** to move about in a wild manner: *his legs stuck and he fell sideways, thrashing about wildly* **4** ▸ same as **thresh** ▹ *n* **5** *informal* a party ▸ See also **thrash out**
WORD ORIGIN Old English *therscan*

thrashing ❶ *n* a severe beating

thrash out ❶ *vb* to discuss (a problem or difficulty) fully in order to come to an agreement or decision about it: *we must arrange a meeting to thrash out the details of the scheme*

thread ❶ *n* **1** a fine strand or fibre of some material **2** a fine cord of twisted yarns, esp. of cotton, used in sewing or weaving **3** something acting as the continuous link or theme of a whole: *the thread of the story* **4** the spiral ridge on a screw, bolt, or nut **5** a very small amount (of something): *there was a thread of nervousness in his voice* **6** a very thin seam of coal or vein of ore ▹ *pl n* **threads 7** *chiefly US slang* clothes ▹ *vb* **8** to pass thread through the eye of (a needle) before sewing with it **9** to string together: *plastic beads threaded on lengths of nylon line* **10** to make (one's way) through a crowd of people or group of objects: *she threaded and pushed her way through the crowds* **threadlike** *adj*
WORD ORIGIN Old English *thrǣd*

threadbare *adj* **1** (of cloth, clothing, or a carpet) having the nap worn off so that the threads are exposed **2** having been used or expressed so often as to be no longer interesting: *threadbare ideas* **3** wearing shabby worn-out clothes

threadworm *n* a small threadlike worm that is a parasite of humans

threat ❶ *n* **1** a declaration of an intention to inflict harm: *they carried out their threat to kill the hostages* **2** a strong possibility of something dangerous or unpleasant happening: *the wet weather will bring a threat of flooding* **3** a person or thing that is regarded as dangerous and likely to inflict harm: *unemployment is a serious threat to the social order*
WORD ORIGIN Old English *thrēat*

threaten ❶ *vb* **1** to express a threat to (someone): *he threatened John with the sack* **2** to be a threat to: *he was worried about anything that might threaten the health of his child* **3** to be a menacing indication of (something): *the early summer threatened drought* **threatening** *adj* **threateningly** *adv*

three *n* **1** the cardinal number that is the sum of one and two **2** a numeral, 3 or III, representing this number **3** something representing or consisting of three units ▹ *adj* **4** amounting to three: *three days*
WORD ORIGIN Old English *thrēo*

three-decker *n* **1** a warship with guns on three decks **2** anything that has three levels, layers, or tiers

three-dimensional *or* **3-D** *adj* **1** having three dimensions **2** lifelike or realistic: *all the characters are three-dimensional*

threefold *adj* **1** having three times as many or as much **2** composed of three parts ▹ *adv* **3** by three times as many or as much

three-legged race *n* a race in which pairs of competitors run with their adjacent legs tied together

three-ply *adj* made of three thicknesses, layers, or strands

three-point turn *n* a complete turn of a motor vehicle using forward and reverse gears alternately, and completed after only three movements

three-quarter *adj* **1** amounting to three out of four equal parts of something **2** being three quarters of the normal length: *a three-quarter-length coat* ▹ *n* **3** *rugby* any of the four players between the fullback and the halfbacks

three Rs *pl n* reading, writing, and arithmetic regarded as the three fundamental skills to be taught in primary schools
WORD ORIGIN humorous spelling of *reading, 'riting, and 'rithmetic*

threescore *adj archaic* sixty

threesome *n* a group of three people

threnody *n, pl* **threnodies** *formal* a lament for the dead **threnodic** *adj* **threnodist** *n*
WORD ORIGIN Greek *thrēnōidia*

thresh *vb* **1** to beat (stalks of ripe corn, rice, etc.), either with a hand tool or by machine to separate the grain from the husks and straw **2 thresh about** to toss and turn
WORD ORIGIN Old English *therscan*

thresher *n* any of a genus of large sharks occurring in tropical and temperate seas. They have a very long whiplike tail

threshold ❶ *n* **1** the lower horizontal part of an entrance or doorway, esp. one made of stone or hardwood **2** any doorway or entrance: *he had never been over the threshold of a pub before* **3** the starting point of an experience, event, or venture: *she was on the threshold of a glorious career* **4** the point at which something begins to take effect or be noticeable: *the threshold for basic rate tax; he has a low boredom threshold*
WORD ORIGIN Old English *therscold*

threw *vb* ▸ the past tense of **throw**

thrice *adv literary* **1** three times: *twice or thrice in a lifetime* **2** three times as big, much, etc.: *his vegetables are thrice the size of mine*
WORD ORIGIN Old English *thrīwa, thrīga*

thrift ❶ *n* **1** wisdom and caution with money **2** a low-growing plant of Europe, W Asia, and North America, with narrow leaves and round heads of pink or white flowers **thriftless** *adj*
WORD ORIGIN Old Norse: success

thrifty *adj* **thriftier, thriftiest** not wasteful with money **thriftily** *adv* **thriftiness** *n*

t

THESAURUS

(slang), cane, lick *(informal)*, paste *(slang)*, birch, flog, scourge, spank, clobber *(slang)*, lambast(e), flagellate, horsewhip, give someone a (good) hiding *(informal)*, drub, take a stick to, beat *or* knock seven bells out of *(informal)* **2 = defeat**, beat, hammer *(informal)*, stuff *(slang)*, tank *(slang)*, crush, overwhelm, slaughter *(informal)*, lick *(informal)*, paste *(slang)*, rout, maul, trounce, clobber *(slang)*, run rings around *(informal)*, wipe the floor with *(informal)*, make mincemeat of *(informal)*, blow someone out of the water *(slang)*, drub, beat someone hollow *(Brit informal)* **3 = thresh**, flail, jerk, plunge, toss, squirm, writhe, heave, toss and turn

thrashing *n* **= beating**, hiding *(informal)*, belting *(informal)*, whipping, tanning *(slang)*, lashing, caning, pasting *(slang)*, flogging, drubbing, chastisement

thrash out *vb* **= settle**, resolve, discuss, debate, solve, argue out, have out, talk over

thread *n* **1, 2 = strand**, fibre, yarn, filament, line, string, cotton, twine **3 = theme**, motif, train of thought, course, direction, strain, plot, drift, tenor, story line ▹ *vb* **10 = move**, pass, inch, ease, thrust, meander, squeeze through, pick your way

threat *n* **1 = threatening remark**, menace, commination, intimidatory remark **3 = danger**, risk, hazard, menace, peril

threaten *vb* **1 = intimidate**, bully, menace, terrorize, warn, cow, lean on *(slang)*, pressurize, browbeat, make threats to **OPPOSITE:** defend **2 = endanger**, jeopardize, put at risk, imperil, put in jeopardy, put on the line **OPPOSITE:** protect **3 = be imminent**, hang over, be in the air, loom, be in the offing, hang over someone's head, impend

threshold *n* **1, 2 = entrance**, doorway, door, doorstep, sill, doorsill **3 = start**, beginning, opening, dawn, verge, brink, outset, starting point, inception **OPPOSITE:** end **4 = limit**, margin, starting point, minimum

thrift *n* **1 = economy**, prudence, frugality, saving, parsimony,

DICTIONARY

thrill ❶ *n* **1** a sudden sensation of excitement and pleasure: *he felt a thrill of excitement* **2** a situation producing such a sensation: *all the thrills of rafting the meandering Dordogne* **3** a sudden trembling sensation caused by fear or emotional shock ▹ *vb* **4** to feel or cause to feel a thrill **5** to vibrate or quiver **thrilling** *adj*
WORD ORIGIN Old English *thȳrlian* to pierce

thriller *n* a book, film, or play depicting crime, mystery, or espionage in an atmosphere of excitement and suspense

thrips *n, pl* **thrips** a small slender-bodied insect with piercing mouthparts that feeds on plant sap
WORD ORIGIN Greek: woodworm

thrive ❶ *vb* **thriving; thrived** *or* **throve; thrived** *or* **thriven 1** to do well; be successful: *Munich has thrived as a centre of European commerce* **2** to grow strongly and vigorously: *the vine can thrive in the most unlikely soils*
WORD ORIGIN Old Norse *thrīfask* to grasp for oneself

thro' *or* **thro** *prep, adv informal* ▸ same as **through**

throat *n* **1** the passage from the mouth and nose to the stomach and lungs **2** the front part of the neck **3 at each other's throats** quarrelling or fighting with each other **4 cut one's own throat** to bring about one's own ruin **5 cut someone's throat** to kill someone **6 ram** *or* **force something down someone's throat** to insist that someone listen to or accept something **7 stick in one's throat** to be hard to accept: *his arrogance really sticks in my throat*
WORD ORIGIN Old English *throtu*

throaty *adj* **throatier, throatiest 1** hoarse and suggestive of a sore throat: *a throaty 40 fags-a-day bark* **2** deep, husky, or guttural: *she gives a deliciously throaty laugh*

throb ❶ *vb* **throbbing, throbbed 1** to pulsate or beat repeatedly, esp. with abnormally strong force: *her eardrums were throbbing with pain* **2** (of engines, drums, etc.) to have a strong rhythmic vibration or beat ▹ *n* **3** the act or sensation of throbbing: *he felt a throb of fear; the throb of the engines* **throbbing** *adj, n*
WORD ORIGIN imitative

Throckmorton *or* **Throgmorton** *n* **Francis.** 1554–84, English conspirator, who with French and Spanish support plotted (1583) to depose Elizabeth I in favour of Mary, Queen of Scots: executed

throes *pl n* **1** violent pangs, pain, or convulsions: *an animal in its death throes* **2 in the throes of** struggling to cope with (something difficult or disruptive): *in the throes of a civil war*
WORD ORIGIN Old English *thrāwu* threat

thrombosis (throm-**boh**-siss) *n, pl* **-ses** (-seez) coagulation of the blood in the heart or in a blood vessel, forming a blood clot **thrombotic** (throm-**bot**-ik) *adj*
WORD ORIGIN Greek: curdling

throne *n* **1** the ceremonial seat occupied by a monarch or bishop on occasions of state **2** the rank or power of a monarch: *she came to the throne after her father was murdered*
WORD ORIGIN Greek *thronos*

throng ❶ *n* **1** a great number of people or things crowded together ▹ *vb* **2** to gather in or fill (a place) in large numbers: *streets thronged with shoppers*
WORD ORIGIN Old English *gethrang*

throstle *n poetic* a song thrush
WORD ORIGIN Old English

throttle ❶ *n* **1** a device that controls the fuel-and-air mixture entering an engine ▹ *vb* **-tling, -tled 2** to kill or injure (someone) by squeezing his or her throat **3** to suppress or censor: *the government is trying to throttle dissent*
WORD ORIGIN Middle English *throtel* throat

throttle back *vb* to reduce the speed of a vehicle or aircraft by reducing the quantity of fuel entering the engine: *throttling back the engine failed to bring the plane under control*

through ❶ *prep* **1** going in at one side and coming out at the other side of: *he drove through the West of the city* **2** occupying or visiting several points scattered around in (an area): *a journey through the Scottish Highlands* **3** as a result of: *diminished responsibility through temporary insanity* **4** during: *driving for five hours through the night* **5** for all of (a period): *it rained all through that summer* **6** *chiefly US* up to and including: *from Monday through Saturday* ▹ *adj* **7** finished: *I'm through with history* **8** having completed a specified amount of an activity: *he tried to stop the investigation halfway through* **9** (on a telephone line) connected **10** no longer able to function successfully in some specified capacity: *they are through, they haven't got a chance* **11** (of a train, plane flight, etc.) going directly to a place, so that passengers do not have to change: *the first ever through train between Singapore and Bangkok* ▹ *adv* **12** through a thing, place, or period of time: *the script gives up around halfway through* **13** extremely or absolutely: *I'm soaked through* **14 through and through** to the greatest possible extent: *the boards are rotten through and through*
WORD ORIGIN Old English *thurh*

throughout ❶ *prep* **1** through the whole of (a place or a period of time): *radio stations throughout the UK* ▹ *adv* **2** through the whole of a place or a period of time: *I led both races throughout*

THESAURUS

carefulness, good husbandry, thriftiness **OPPOSITE:** extravagance

thrill *n* **1 = pleasure**, charge *(slang)*, kick *(informal)*, glow, sensation, buzz *(slang)*, high, stimulation, tingle, titillation, flush of excitement **OPPOSITE:** tedium ▹ *vb* **4 = excite**, stimulate, arouse, move, send *(slang)*, stir, flush, tingle, electrify, titillate, give someone a kick

thrive *vb* **1, 2 = prosper**, do well, flourish, increase, grow, develop, advance, succeed, get on, boom, bloom, wax, burgeon, grow rich **OPPOSITE:** decline

throb *vb* **1 = pulsate**, pound, beat, pulse, thump, palpitate **2 = vibrate**, pulse, resonate, pulsate, reverberate, shake, judder *(informal)* ▹ *n* **3a = pulse**, pounding, beat, thump, thumping, pulsating, palpitation **3b = vibration**, pulse, throbbing, resonance, reverberation, judder *(informal)*, pulsation

throng *n* **1 = crowd**, mob, horde, press, host, pack, mass, crush, jam, congregation, swarm, multitude, concourse, assemblage ▹ *vb* **2a = crowd**, flock, congregate, troop, bunch, herd, cram, converge, hem in, mill around, swarm around **OPPOSITE:** disperse **2b = pack**, fill, crowd, press, jam

throttle *vb* **2 = strangle**, choke, garrotte, strangulate

through *prep* **1 = via**, by way of, by, between, past, in and out of, from end to end of, from one side to the other of **3a = because of**, by way of, by means of, by virtue of, with the assistance of, as a consequence *or* result of **3b = using**, via, by way of, by means of, by virtue of, with the assistance of **4, 5 = during**, throughout, in the middle of, for the duration of, in ▹ **14 through and through = completely**, totally, fully, thoroughly, entirely, altogether, wholly, utterly, to the core, unreservedly

throughout *prep* **1a = right through**, all through, everywhere in, for the duration of, during the whole of, through the whole of, from end to end of **1b = all over**, all through, everywhere in, through the whole of, over the length and breadth of ▹ *adv* **2a = from start to finish**, right through, the whole time, all the time, from the start, all through, from beginning to end **2b = all through**, right through, in every nook and cranny

t

DICTIONARY

throughput *n* the amount of material processed in a given period, esp. by a computer

throve *vb* ▸ a past tense of **thrive**

throw ❶ *vb* **throwing, threw, thrown** **1** to hurl (something) through the air, esp. with a rapid motion of the arm **2** to put or move suddenly, carelessly, or violently: *she threw her arms round his neck* **3** to bring into a specified state or condition, esp. suddenly: *the invasion threw the region into turmoil* **4** to move (a switch or lever) so as to engage or disengage a mechanism **5** to cause (someone) to fall: *I'm riding the horse that threw me* **6 a** to tip (dice) out onto a flat surface **b** to obtain (a specified number) in this way: *one throws a 3 and the other throws a 5* **7** to shape (clay) on a potter's wheel **8** to give (a party) **9** *informal* to confuse or disconcert: *the question threw me* **10** to direct or cast (a look, light, etc.): *the lamp threw a shadow on the ceiling* **11** to project (the voice) so as to make it appear to come from somewhere else **12** *informal* to lose (a contest) deliberately **13 throw a punch** to strike, or attempt to strike, someone with one's fist **14 throw oneself at** to behave in a way which makes it clear that one is trying to win the affection of (someone) **15 throw oneself into** to involve oneself enthusiastically in **16 throw oneself on** to rely entirely upon (someone's goodwill, etc.): *the president threw himself on the mercy of the American people* ▹ *n* **17** the act or an instance of throwing **18** the distance thrown: *a throw of 90 metres* **19** (in sports such as wrestling or judo) a move which causes one's opponent to fall to the floor **20** a decorative blanket or cover **21 a throw** each: *we drank our way through a couple of bottles of claret at £12.50 a throw* ▸ See also **throwaway, throwback**, etc.
WORD ORIGIN Old English *thrāwan* to turn, torment

throwaway *adj* **1** said or done incidentally: *a throwaway line* **2** designed to be discarded after use: *throwaway cups* ▹ *vb* **throw away 3** to get rid of or discard: *try to recycle glass bottles instead of simply throwing them away* **4** to fail to make good use of: *she threw away the chance of a brilliant career when she got married*

throwback *n* **1** a person or thing that is like something that existed or was common long ago: *his ideas were a throwback to old colonial attitudes* ▹ *vb* **throw back 2** to remind someone of (something he or she said or did previously) in order to upset him or her: *he threw back at me everything I'd said the week before*

throw in *vb* **1** to add at no additional cost: *he'd got good at bargaining them down, making them throw in variations for free* **2** to contribute (a remark) in a discussion **3 throw in the towel** *informal* to give in; accept defeat ▹ *n* **throw-in 4** *soccer, etc.* the act of putting the ball back into play when it has gone over one of the sidelines, by throwing it over one's head with both hands

throw off *vb* **1** to take off (clothing) hurriedly **2** *literary* to free oneself of: *Vietnamese farmers threw off their dependency on European seed potatoes*

throw out *vb* **1** to discard or reject: *the court threw out the case* **2** to expel or dismiss, esp. forcibly: *her parents threw her out when they discovered she was pregnant*

throw over *vb old-fashioned* to leave or reject (a lover)

throw together *vb* **1** to assemble (something) hurriedly **2** (of a set of circumstances) to cause (people) to meet and get to know each other

throw up *vb* **1** *informal* to vomit **2** to give up or abandon: *he would threaten to throw up his job* **3** to construct (a building or structure) hastily **4** to produce: *these links are throwing up fresh opportunities*

thru *prep, adv, adj chiefly US* ▸ same as **through**

thrum *vb* **thrumming, thrummed** **1** to strum rhythmically but without expression on (a musical instrument) **2** to make a low beating or humming sound: *the air conditioner thrummed* ▹ *n* **3** a repetitive strumming
WORD ORIGIN imitative

thrush[1] *n* any of a large group of songbirds, esp. one having a brown plumage with a spotted breast, such as the mistle thrush and song thrush
WORD ORIGIN Old English *thrȳsce*

thrush[2] *n* **1** a fungal disease, esp. of infants, in which whitish spots form on the mouth, throat, and lips **2** a genital infection caused by the same fungus
WORD ORIGIN origin unknown

thrust ❶ *vb* **thrusting, thrust 1** to push (someone or something) with force: *he took him by the arm and thrust him towards the door* **2** to force (someone) into some condition or situation: *the unemployed have been thrust into the front line of politics* **3** to force (one's way) through a crowd, forest, etc.: *Edward thrust his way towards them* **4** to stick out or up: *she thrust out her lower lip* ▹ *n* **5** a forceful drive, push, stab, or lunge: *the thrust of his spear* **6** a force, esp. one that produces motion **7** the propulsive force produced by the pressure of air and gas forced out of a jet engine or rocket engine **8** the essential or most forceful part: *the main thrust of the report* **9** *physics* a continuous pressure exerted by one part of an object against another **10** *informal* intellectual or emotional drive; forcefulness: *thanks to the ingenuity and enterprising thrust of this company*
WORD ORIGIN Old Norse *thrȳsta*

thrusting *adj* ambitious and having great drive: *a thrusting young executive*

Thucydides *n* ?460–?395 BC, Greek historian and politician, distinguished for his *History of the Peloponnesian War* > **Thucydidean** *adj*

thud *n* **1** a dull heavy sound **2** a blow or fall that causes such a sound ▹ *vb* **thudding, thudded 3** to make or cause to make such a sound
WORD ORIGIN Old English *thyddan* to strike

thug ❶ *n* a tough and violent man, esp. a criminal **thuggery** *n* **thuggish** *adj*
WORD ORIGIN Hindi *thag* thief

thulium *n chem* a silvery-grey element of the lanthanide series. Symbol: Tm
WORD ORIGIN after *Thule*, a region thought by ancient geographers to be northernmost in the world

thumb *n* **1** the short thick finger of the hand set apart from the others **2** the part of a glove shaped to fit the thumb **3 all thumbs** very clumsy **4 thumbs down** an indication of refusal or disapproval **5 thumbs up** an indication of encouragement or approval **6 under someone's thumb** completely under someone else's control ▹ *vb* **7** to touch, mark, or move with the thumb: *he thumbed the volume switch to maximum* **8** to attempt to obtain (a lift in a motor vehicle) by

t

THESAURUS

throw *vb* **1 = hurl**, toss, fling, send, project, launch, cast, pitch, shy, chuck *(informal)*, propel, sling, lob *(informal)*, heave, put **2 = toss**, fling, chuck *(informal)*, cast, hurl, sling, heave, put **9** *(informal)* **= confuse**, baffle, faze, astonish, confound, unnerve, disconcert, perturb, throw you out, throw you off, dumbfound, discompose, put you off your stroke, throw you off your stride, unsettle ▹ *n* **17 = toss**, pitch, fling, put, cast, shy, sling, lob *(informal)*, heave

thrust *vb* **1 = push**, force, shove, drive, press, plunge, jam, butt, ram, poke, propel, prod, impel ▹ *n* **5a = stab**, pierce, lunge **5b = push**, shove, poke, prod **6 = momentum**, impetus, drive, motive power, motive force, propulsive force

thug *n* **= ruffian**, hooligan, tough, heavy *(slang)*, killer, murderer, robber, gangster, assassin, bandit, mugger *(informal)*, cut-throat, bully

DICTIONARY

signalling with the thumb: *he thumbed a lift to the station* **9 thumb one's nose at** to behave in a way that shows one's contempt or disregard for: *her mother had always thumbed her nose at convention* **10 thumb through** to flip the pages of (a book or magazine) in order to glance at the contents
WORD ORIGIN Old English *thūma*

thumb index *n* a series of notches cut into the fore-edge of a book to facilitate quick reference

thumbnail *n* **1** the nail of the thumb ▷*adj* **2** concise and brief: *a thumbnail sketch*

thumbscrew *n* (formerly) an instrument of torture that pinches or crushes the thumbs

thumbtack *n* ▸the US and Canadian term for **drawing pin**

thump ❶ *n* **1** the sound of something heavy hitting a comparatively soft surface **2** a heavy blow with the hand ▷*vb* **3** to place (something) on or bang against (something) with a loud dull sound: *thumping the table is aggressive* **4** to hit or punch (someone): *stop that at once or I'll thump you!* **5** to throb or beat violently: *he could feel his heart thumping*
WORD ORIGIN imitative

thumping *adj slang* huge or excessive: *a thumping majority*

thunder ❶ *n* **1** a loud cracking or deep rumbling noise caused by the rapid expansion of atmospheric gases that are suddenly heated by lightning **2** any loud booming sound: *the thunder of heavy gunfire* **3 steal someone's thunder** to lessen the effect of someone's idea or action by anticipating it ▷*vb* **4** to make a loud noise like thunder: *an explosion thundered through the shaft* **5** to speak in a loud, angry manner: *'Get out of here this instant!' he thundered* **6** to move fast, heavily, and noisily: *a lorry thundered by* **thundery** *adj*
WORD ORIGIN Old English *thunor*

thunderbolt *n* **1** a flash of lightning accompanying thunder **2** something sudden and unexpected: *his career has been no thunderbolt* **3** *myth* a weapon thrown to earth by certain gods **4** *sport* a very fast-moving shot or serve

thunderclap *n* **1** a loud outburst of thunder **2** something as violent or unexpected as a clap of thunder

thundercloud *n* a large dark electrically charged cloud associated with thunderstorms

thundering *old-fashioned slang adj* **1** extreme: *a thundering disgrace* ▷*adv* **2** extremely: *thundering good music*

thunderous *adj* **1** resembling thunder in loudness: *thunderous applause* **2** threatening or angry: *a thunderous scowl*

thunderstorm *n* a storm with thunder and lightning and usually heavy rain or hail

thunderstruck *adj* amazed or shocked

thurible (**thyoor**-rib-bl) *n* ▸same as **censer**
WORD ORIGIN Latin *turibulum*

Thurs. Thursday

Thursday *n* the fifth day of the week
WORD ORIGIN Old English *Thursdæg* Thor's day

thus ❶ *adv* **1** as a result or consequence: *the platforms provided a new floor and thus improved and enlarged the premises* **2** in this manner: *I sat thus for nearly half an hour* **3** to such a degree: *the competition has been almost bereft of surprise thus far*
WORD ORIGIN Old English

Thutmose I *n* died *c.* 1500 BC, king of Egypt of the 18th dynasty, who extended his territory in Nubia and Syria and enlarged the Temple of Amon at Karnak

Thutmose III *n* died *c.* 1450 BC, king of Egypt of the 18th dynasty, who completed the conquest of Syria and dominated the Middle East. He was also a patron of the arts and a famous athlete

thwack *vb* **1** to beat with something flat ▷*n* **2 a** a blow with something flat **b** the sound made by it
WORD ORIGIN imitative

thwart ❶ *vb* **1** to prevent or foil: *they inflicted such severe losses that they thwarted the invasion* ▷*n* **2** the seat across a boat where the rower sits
WORD ORIGIN Old Norse *thvert* across

thy *adj old-fashioned* belonging to or associated in some way with you (thou): *love thy neighbour*
WORD ORIGIN variant of *thine*

thyme (**time**) *n* a small shrub with white, pink, or red flowers and scented leaves used for seasoning food
WORD ORIGIN Greek *thumon*

thymol *n* a white crystalline substance obtained from thyme, used as a fungicide and an antiseptic

thymus (**thigh**-muss) *n, pl* **-muses** *or* **-mi** (-my) *anat* a small gland situated near the base of the neck
WORD ORIGIN Greek *thumos* sweetbread

thyroid *anat adj* **1** of or relating to the thyroid gland **2** of or relating to the largest cartilage of the larynx, which forms the Adam's apple in men ▷*n* **3** the thyroid gland
WORD ORIGIN Greek *thureos* oblong shield

thyroid gland *n anat* an endocrine gland that secretes hormones that control metabolism and body growth

thyself *pron old-fashioned* ▸the reflexive form of **thou**[1]

ti *n music* ▸same as **te**

Ti *chem* titanium

tiara *n* **1** a semicircular jewelled headdress worn by some women on formal occasions **2** the triple-tiered crown sometimes worn by the pope
WORD ORIGIN Greek

tibia (**tib**-ee-a) *n, pl* **tibiae** (**tib**-ee-ee) *or* **tibias** the inner and thicker of the two bones of the human leg below the knee; shinbone **tibial** *adj*
WORD ORIGIN Latin: leg, pipe

Tibullus *n* **Albius**. ?54–?19 BC, Roman elegiac poet

tic *n* a spasmodic muscular twitch
WORD ORIGIN French

tick[1] ❶ *n* **1** a mark (✓) used to check off or indicate the correctness of something **2** a recurrent metallic tapping or clicking sound, such as that made by a clock **3** *informal* a moment or instant: *won't be a tick* ▷*vb* **4** to mark or check with a tick **5** to produce a recurrent tapping sound or indicate by such a sound: *the clock*

t

THESAURUS

boy, bruiser *(informal)*, tsotsi *(S African)*

thump *n* **1 = thud**, crash, bang, clunk, thwack **2 = blow**, knock, punch, rap, smack, clout *(informal)*, whack, swipe, wallop *(informal)* ▷*vb* **4 = strike**, hit, punch, pound, beat, knock, deck *(slang)*, batter, rap, chin *(slang)*, smack, thrash, clout *(informal)*, whack, swipe, clobber *(slang)*, wallop *(informal)*, lambast(e), belabour, lay one on *(slang)*, beat *or* knock seven bells out of *(informal)*

thunder *n* **2 = rumble**, crash, crashing, boom, booming, explosion, rumbling, pealing, detonation, cracking ▷*vb* **4 = rumble**, crash, blast, boom, explode, roar, clap, resound, detonate, reverberate, crack, peal **5 = shout**, roar, yell, bark, bellow, declaim

thus *adv* **1 = therefore**, so, hence, consequently, accordingly, for this reason, ergo, on that account **2 = in this way**, so, like this, as follows, like so, in this manner, in this fashion, to such a degree

thwart *vb* **1 = frustrate**, stop, foil, check, defeat, prevent, oppose, snooker, baffle, hinder, obstruct, impede, balk, outwit, stymie, cook someone's goose *(informal)*, put a spoke in someone's wheel *(informal)*
OPPOSITE: assist

tick[1] *n* **1 = check mark**, mark, line, stroke, dash **2 = click**, tap, tapping, clicking, clack, ticktock **3** *(informal)* **= moment**, second, minute, shake *(informal)*, flash, instant, sec *(informal)*, twinkling, split second, jiffy *(informal)*, trice, half a mo *(informal)*, two shakes of a lamb's tail *(informal)*, bat of an eye *(informal)* ▷*vb* **4 = mark**,

DICTIONARY

ticked away **6 what makes someone tick** *informal* the basic motivation of a person ▸ See also **tick off, tick over**
WORD ORIGIN Low German *tikk* touch

tick[2] *n* a small parasitic creature typically living on the skin of warm-blooded animals and feeding on the blood and tissues of their hosts: *a sheep tick*
WORD ORIGIN Old English *ticca*

tick[3] *n Brit & NZ informal* account or credit: *a spending spree that was financed on tick*
WORD ORIGIN from *ticket*

ticker *n slang* the heart

ticker tape *n* (formerly) a continuous paper tape on which current stock quotations were printed by machine

ticket ❶ *n* **1** a printed piece of paper or cardboard showing that the holder is entitled to certain rights, such as travel on a train or bus or entry to a place of public entertainment **2** a label or tag attached to an article showing information such as its price and size **3** an official notification of a parking or traffic offence **4** the declared policy of a political party **5 that's (just) the ticket** *informal* that's the right or appropriate thing ▹ *vb* **-eting, -eted** **6** to issue or attach a ticket or tickets to
WORD ORIGIN Old French *etiquet*

tickets *pl n S African informal* death or ruin; the end

ticking *n* a strong cotton fabric, often striped, used esp. for mattress and pillow covers
WORD ORIGIN probably from Middle Dutch *tīke*

tickle *vb* **-ling, -led** **1** to touch or stroke (someone), so as to produce laughter or a twitching sensation **2** to itch or tingle **3** to amuse or please **4 tickled pink** *or* **to death** *informal* greatly pleased **5 tickle someone's fancy** to appeal to or amuse someone ▹ *n* **6** a sensation of light stroking or itching: *a tickle in the throat* **7** the act of tickling **8** *Canad* (in the Atlantic Provinces) a narrow strait

WORD ORIGIN Middle English *titelen*

ticklish *adj* **1** sensitive to being tickled **2** delicate or difficult: *a ticklish problem*

tick off *vb* **1** to mark with a tick, esp. to show that an item on a list has been dealt with **2** *informal* to reprimand or scold (someone)
ticking-off *n*

tick over *vb* **1** (of an engine) to run at low speed with the transmission disengaged **2** to run smoothly without any major changes: *the business is just ticking over*

ticktack *n Austral & Brit* a system of sign language, mainly using the hands, by which bookmakers transmit their odds to each other at race courses

ticktock *n* a ticking sound made by a clock

tidal *adj* **1** (of a river, lake, or sea) having tides **2** of or relating to tides: *a tidal surge*

tidal wave *n* **1** *not in technical use* ▸ same as **tsunami** **2** an unusually large incoming wave, often caused by high winds and spring tides **3** a forceful and widespread movement in public opinion, action, etc.: *a tidal wave of scandals and embezzlement*

tiddler *n informal* **1** a very small fish, esp. a stickleback **2** a small child
WORD ORIGIN perhaps from TIDDLY[1]

tiddly[1] *adj* **-dlier, -dliest** *Brit* very small
WORD ORIGIN childish variant of *little*

tiddly[2] *adj* **-dlier, -dliest** *informal chiefly Brit* slightly drunk
WORD ORIGIN origin unknown

tiddlywinks *n* a game in which players try to flick discs of plastic into a cup
WORD ORIGIN origin unknown

tide ❶ *n* **1** the alternate rise and fall of sea level caused by the gravitational pull of the sun and moon **2** the current caused by these changes in level: *I got caught by the tide and almost drowned* **3** a widespread tendency or movement: *the rising tide of nationalism* **4** *literary or old-fashioned* a season or time: *Yuletide*
WORD ORIGIN Old English *tīd* time

tideline *n* the mark or line left by the tide when it retreats from its highest point

tidemark *n* **1** a mark left by the highest or lowest point of a tide **2** *chiefly Brit & NZ* a line of dirt left round a bath after the water has been drained away **3** *informal chiefly Brit* a dirty mark on the skin, indicating the extent to which someone has washed

tide over *vb* **tiding, tided** to help (someone) to get through a period of difficulty or distress: *they need some form of Social Security to tide them over*

tidings *pl n* information or news
WORD ORIGIN Old English *tīdung*

tidy ❶ *adj* **-dier, -diest** **1** neat and orderly **2** *Brit, Austral & NZ informal* quite large: *a tidy sum of money* ▹ *vb* **-dies, -dying, -died** **3** to put (things) in their proper place; make neat: *I've tidied up the toys under the bed* ▹ *n, pl* **-dies** **4** a small container for odds and ends **tidily** *adv* **tidiness** *n*
WORD ORIGIN (originally: timely, excellent) from *tide*

tie ❶ *vb* **tying, tied** **1** to fasten or be fastened with string, rope, etc.: *a parcel tied with string* **2** to make a knot or bow in (something): *hang on while I tie my laces* **3** to restrict or limit: *they had children and were consequently tied to the school holidays* **4** to equal the score of a competitor or fellow candidate: *three players tied for second place* ▹ *n* **5** a long narrow piece of material worn, esp. by men, under the collar of a shirt, tied in a knot close to the throat with the ends hanging down the front **6** a bond or link: *he still has close ties to the town where he grew up* **7** a string, wire, etc. with which something is tied **8** *Brit sport* a match in a knockout competition: *whoever wins the tie will play Australia in the semifinals* **9 a** a result in a match or competition in which the scores or times of some of the competitors are the same: *a tie for second place* **b** the match or competition in which the scores or results are equal **10** a regular commitment that limits a person's freedom: *it's a bit of a tie having*

t

THESAURUS

indicate, mark off, check off, choose, select **5 = click**, tap, clack, ticktock

ticket *n* **1 = voucher**, pass, coupon, card, slip, certificate, token, chit **2 = label**, tag, marker, sticker, card, slip, tab, docket

tide *n* **1, 2 = current**, flow, stream, course, ebb, undertow, tideway **3 = course**, direction, trend, current, movement, tendency, drift

tidy *adj* **1a = neat**, orderly, ordered, clean, trim, systematic, spruce, businesslike, well-kept, well-ordered, shipshape, spick-and-span, trig *(archaic, dialect)*, in apple-pie order *(informal)* **OPPOSITE:** untidy **1b = organized**, neat, fastidious, methodical, smart, efficient, spruce, businesslike, well-groomed, well turned out **2** *(informal)* **= considerable**, large, substantial, good, goodly, fair, healthy, generous, handsome, respectable, ample, largish, sizable *or* sizeable **OPPOSITE:** small ▹ *vb* **3 = neaten**, straighten, put in order, order, clean, groom, spruce up, put to rights, put in trim **OPPOSITE:** disorder

tie *vb* **1a = fasten**, bind, join, unite, link, connect, attach, knot, truss, interlace **OPPOSITE:** unfasten **1b = tether**, secure, rope, moor, lash, make fast **3 = restrict**, limit, confine, hold, bind, restrain, hamper, hinder **OPPOSITE:** free **4 = draw**, be even, be level, be neck and neck, match, equal ▹ *n* **6 = bond**, relationship, connection, duty, commitment, obligation, liaison, allegiance, affinity, affiliation, kinship **7 = fastening**, binding, link, band, bond, joint, connection, string, rope, knot, cord, fetter, ligature **9a, 9b = draw**, dead heat,

DICTIONARY

to visit him every day **11** something which supports or links parts of a structure **12** *US & Canad* a sleeper on a railway track **13** *music* a curved line connecting two notes of the same pitch indicating that the sound is to be prolonged for their joint time value ▸ See also **tie in, tie up**
WORD ORIGIN Old English *tīgan*

tie-break *or* **tie-breaker** *n* an extra game or question that decides the result of a contest that has ended in a draw

Tieck *n* **Ludwig.** 1773–1853, German romantic writer, noted esp. for his fairy tales

tied *adj Brit* **1** (of a public house) allowed to sell beer from only one particular brewery **2** (of a house) rented out to the tenant for as long as he or she is employed by the owner

tie-dye, tie-dyed *or* **tie and dye** *adj* (of a garment or fabric) dyed in a pattern by tying sections of the cloth together so that they will not absorb the dye: *a tie-dye T-shirt*

tie in *vb* **1** to have or cause to have a close link or connection: *there's no evidence to tie this killing in with the murder of Mrs McGowan* ▹ *n* **tie-in 2** a link or connection **3** a book or other product that is linked with a film or TV programme

tiepin *n* an ornamental pin used to pin the two ends of a tie to a shirt

Tiepolo *n* **Giovanni Battista.** 1696–1770, Italian rococo painter, esp. of frescoes as in the Residenz at Würzburg

tier ❶ *n* one of a set of rows placed one above and behind the other, such as theatre seats
WORD ORIGIN Old French *tire*

tie up *vb* **1** to bind (someone or something) securely with string or rope **2** to moor (a vessel) **3** to commit (money etc.) so that it is unavailable for other uses: *people don't want to tie up their savings for a long period* ▹ *n* **tie-up 4** a link or connection

tiff *n* a minor quarrel
WORD ORIGIN origin unknown

Tiffany[1] *n* **Louis Comfort.** 1848–1933, US glass-maker and Art-Nouveau craftsman, best known for creating the Favrile style of stained glass

Tiffany[2] *n, pl* **-nies** another name for **Chantilly** (sense 2)

tiffin *n* (in India) a light meal, esp. at midday
WORD ORIGIN probably from obsolete *tiff* to sip

tiger *n* **1** a large Asian mammal of the cat family which has a tawny yellow coat with black stripes **2** a dynamic, forceful, or cruel person **3** a country, esp. in E Asia, that is achieving rapid economic growth
WORD ORIGIN Greek *tigris*

tiger lily *n* a lily of China and Japan with black-spotted orange flowers

tiger moth *n* a moth with conspicuously striped and spotted wings

tiger snake *n* a highly venomous brown-and-yellow Australian snake

tight ❶ *adj* **1** stretched or drawn taut: *loosening-up of tight muscles* **2** closely fitting: *wearing a jacket that was too tight for him* **3** made, fixed, or closed firmly and securely: *a tight band* **4** constructed so as to prevent the passage of water, air, etc.: *watertight; airtight* **5** cramped and allowing very little room for movement: *they squeezed him into the tight space* **6** unyielding or stringent: *tight security* **7** (of a situation) difficult or dangerous **8** allowing only the minimum time or money for doing something: *we have been working to a tight schedule* **9** *Brit, Austral & NZ informal* mean or miserly **10** (of a match or game) very close or even **11** *informal* drunk **12** (of a corner or turn) turning through a large angle in a short distance: *the boat skidded round in a tight turn* ▹ *adv* **13** in a close, firm, or secure way: *they held each other tight* **tightly** *adv* **tightness** *n*
WORD ORIGIN Old Norse *thēttr* of close texture

tighten ❶ *vb* to make or become tight or tighter

tight-fisted *adj* unwilling to spend money; mean

tightknit *adj* closely integrated: *a tightknit community*

tight-lipped *adj* **1** unwilling to give any information; secretive: *the Minister remained tight-lipped when it came to answering the press's questions* **2** with the lips pressed tightly together, as through anger: *tight-lipped determination*

tightrope *n* a rope stretched taut on which acrobats perform

tights *pl n* a one-piece clinging garment covering the body from the waist to the feet, worn by women and also by acrobats, dancers, etc.

Tiglath-pileser I *n* king of Assyria (?1116–?1093 BC), who extended his kingdom to the upper Euphrates and defeated the king of Babylonia

Tiglath-pileser III *n* known as *Pulu.* died ?727 BC, king of Assyria (745–727), who greatly extended his empire, subjugating Syria and Palestine

tigress *n* **1** a female tiger **2** a fierce, cruel, or passionate woman

tike *n* ▸ same as **tyke**

tiki (tee-kee) *n* a Māori greenstone neck ornament in the form of a fetus
WORD ORIGIN Māori

tikka *adj Indian cookery* (of meat) marinated in spices and then dry-roasted: *chicken tikka*

Tilak *n* **Bal Gangadhar,** also called *Lokamanya.* 1856–1920, Indian nationalist leader, educationalist, and scholar, who founded (1914) the Indian Home Rule League

tilde *n* a mark (˜) used in some languages to indicate that the letter over which it is placed is pronounced in a certain way, as in Spanish *señor*
WORD ORIGIN Spanish

Tilden *n* **Bill,** full name *William Tatem Tilden,* known as *Big Bill.* 1893–1953, US tennis player: won the US singles championship (1920–25, 1929) and the British singles championship (1920–21, 1930)

tile *n* **1** a thin piece of ceramic, plastic, etc. used with others to cover a surface, such as a floor or wall **2** a rectangular block used as a playing piece in mah jong and other games **3 on the tiles** *informal* out having a good time and drinking a lot ▹ *vb* **tiling, tiled 4** to cover (a surface) with tiles **tiled** *adj* **tiler** *n*
WORD ORIGIN Latin *tegula*

tiling *n* **1** tiles collectively **2** something made of or surfaced with tiles

t

THESAURUS

deadlock, stalemate

tier *n* **= row,** bank, layer, line, order, level, series, file, rank, storey, stratum, echelon

tight *adj* **1 = taut,** stretched, tense, rigid, stiff **OPPOSITE:** slack
2 = close-fitting, narrow, cramped, snug, constricted, close
OPPOSITE: loose
3 = secure, firm, fast, fixed
9 *(informal)* **= miserly,** mean, stingy, close, sparing, grasping, parsimonious, niggardly, penurious, tightfisted **OPPOSITE:** generous
10 = close, even, well-matched, near, hard-fought, evenly-balanced
OPPOSITE: uneven
11 *(informal)* **= drunk,** intoxicated, flying *(slang),* bombed *(slang),* stoned *(slang),* wasted *(slang),* smashed *(slang),* steaming *(slang),* wrecked *(slang),* out of it *(slang),* plastered *(slang),* blitzed *(slang),* lit up *(slang),* stewed *(slang),* pickled *(informal),* bladdered *(slang),* under the influence *(informal),* tipsy, legless *(informal),* paralytic *(informal),* sozzled *(informal),* steamboats *(Scot slang),* tiddly *(slang, chiefly Brit),* half cut *(Brit slang),* zonked *(slang),* blotto *(slang),* inebriated, out to it *(Austral & NZ slang),* three sheets to the wind *(slang),* in your cups, half seas over *(Brit informal),* bevvied *(dialect),* pie-eyed *(slang)*
OPPOSITE: sober

tighten *vb* **= close,** narrow, strengthen, squeeze, harden, constrict **OPPOSITE:** slacken

DICTIONARY

till[1] *conj, prep* ▸ same as **until**
WORD ORIGIN Old English *til*

till[2] ❶ *vb* to cultivate (land) for the raising of crops: *a constant round of sowing, tilling and harvesting* **tillable** *adj* **tiller** *n*
WORD ORIGIN Old English *tilian* to try, obtain

till[3] ❶ *n* a box or drawer into which money taken from customers is put, now usually part of a cash register
WORD ORIGIN origin unknown

tillage *n* **1** the act, process, or art of tilling **2** tilled land

tiller *n naut* a handle used to turn the rudder when steering a boat
WORD ORIGIN Anglo-French *teiler* beam of a loom

Tilley *n* **Vesta**, original name *Matilda Alice Powles*. 1864–1952, British music-hall entertainer, best known as a male impersonator

Tillich *n* **Paul Johannes.** 1886–1965, US Protestant theologian and philosopher, born in Germany. His works include *The Courage to Be* (1952) and *Systematic Theology* (1951–63)

Tilly *n* Count **Johan Tserclaes von.** 1559–1632, Flemish soldier, who commanded the army of The Catholic League (1618–32) and the imperial forces (1630–32) in the Thirty Years' War

tilt ❶ *vb* **1** to move into a sloping position with one end or side higher than the other: *Dave tilted his chair back on two legs* **2** to move (part of the body) slightly upwards or to the side: *Marie tilted her head back* **3** to become more influenced by a particular idea or group: *the party is tilting more and more to the right* **4** to compete against someone in a jousting contest ▹ *n* **5** a slope or angle: *a tilt to one side* **6** the act of tilting **7 a** a jousting contest, esp. in medieval Europe **b** a thrust with a lance delivered during a medieval tournament **8** an attempt to win a contest: *a tilt at the world title* **9 at full tilt** at full speed or force
WORD ORIGIN Old English *tealtian*

tilth *n* **1** the tilling of land **2** the condition of land that has been tilled

timber ❶ *n* **1** wood as a building material **2** trees collectively **3** a wooden beam in the frame of a house, boat, etc. ▹ *adj* **4** made out of timber: *timber houses* **5** of or involved in the production or sale of wood as a building material: *a timber merchant* **timbered** *adj* **timbering** *n*
WORD ORIGIN Old English

Timberlake *n* **Justin.** born 1981, US pop singer; a member of the boy band NSYNC, he later found success with the bestselling solo album *Justified* (2002)

timber limit *n Canad* **1** the area to which rights of cutting timber, granted by a government licence, are limited **2** ▸ same as **timber line**

timber line *n* the geographical limit beyond which trees will not grow

timbre (**tam**-bra) *n* the distinctive quality of sound produced by a particular voice or musical instrument
WORD ORIGIN French

timbrel *n chiefly biblical* a tambourine
WORD ORIGIN Old French

Timbuktu *or* **Timbuctoo** (tim-buck-**too**) *n* any distant or outlandish place: *we could run our office from Timbuktu as long as there was a good fax line*
WORD ORIGIN after *Timbuktu*, town in Africa

time ❶ *n* **1** the past, present, and future regarded as a continuous whole ▸ Related adjective: **temporal** **2** *physics* a quantity measuring duration, measured with reference to the rotation of the earth or from the vibrations of certain atoms **3** a specific point in time expressed in hours and minutes: *what time are you going?* **4** a system of reckoning for expressing time: *the deadline is 5:00 Eastern Time today* **5** an unspecified interval; a while: *some recover for a time and then relapse* **6** an instance or occasion: *when was the last time you saw it?* **7** a sufficient interval or period: *I need time to think* **8** an occasion or period of specified quality: *they'd had a lovely time* **9** a suitable moment: *the time has come to make peace* **10** a period or point marked by specific attributes or events: *in Victorian times* **11** *Brit* the time at which licensed premises are required by law to stop selling alcoholic drinks **12** the rate of pay for work done in normal working hours: *you get double time for working on a Sunday* **13 a** the system of combining beats in music into successive groupings by which the rhythm of the music is established **b** a specific system having a specific number of beats in each grouping or bar: *duple time* **14 against time** in an effort to complete something in a limited period **15 ahead of time** before the deadline **16 at one time a** once or formerly **b** simultaneously **17 at the same time a** simultaneously **b** nevertheless or however **18 at times** sometimes **19 beat time** to indicate the tempo of a piece of music by waving a baton, hand, etc. **20 do time** *informal* to serve a term in jail **21 for the time being** for the moment; temporarily **22 from time to time** at intervals; occasionally **23 have no time for** to have no patience with **24 in no time** very quickly **25 in one's own time a** outside paid working hours **b** at the speed of one's choice **26 in time a** early or at the appointed time: *he made it to the hospital in time for the baby's arrival* **b** eventually: *in time, the children of intelligent parents will come to dominate* **c** *music* at a correct metrical or rhythmic pulse **27 make time** to find an opportunity **28 on time** at the expected or scheduled time **29 pass the time** to occupy oneself when there is nothing else to do: *they pass their time watching game shows on television* **30 pass the time of day** to have a short casual conversation (with someone) **31 time and again** frequently **32 time of one's life** a memorably enjoyable time **33 time out of mind** from long before anyone can remember ▹ *vb* **timing, timed** **34** to measure the speed or duration of: *my Porsche was timed at 128 mph* **35** to set a time for: *the attack was timed for 6 am* **36** to do (something) at a suitable time: *her entry could not have been better timed* ▹ *adj* **37** operating automatically at or for a set time: *an electrical time switch* ▹ *interj* **38** the word called out by a publican signalling that it is closing time ▸ See also **times**
WORD ORIGIN Old English *tīma*

time and a half *n* a rate of pay one and a half times the normal rate, often offered for overtime work

time-and-motion study *n* the analysis of work procedures to work out the most efficient methods of operation

time bomb *n* **1** a bomb containing a timing mechanism that is set so that the bomb will explode at a

THESAURUS

till[2] *vb* **= cultivate**, dig, plough, work, turn over

till[3] *n* **= cash register**, cash box, cash drawer

tilt *vb* **1 = slant**, tip, slope, list, lean, heel, incline, cant ▹ *n* **5 = slope**, angle, inclination, list, pitch, incline, slant, cant, camber, gradient **7a** *(medieval history)* **= joust**, fight, tournament, lists, clash, set-to *(informal)*, encounter, combat, duel, tourney

timber *n* **2 = wood**, logs **3 = beams**, boards, planks

time *n* **5,7 = period**, while, term, season, space, stretch, spell, phase, interval, span, period of time, stint, duration, length of time, time frame, timeline **6, 9 = occasion**, point, moment, stage, instance, point in time, juncture **10 = age**, days, era, year, date, generation, duration, epoch, chronology, aeon **13a, 13b = tempo**, beat, rhythm, measure, metre ▹ *vb* **35, 36 = schedule**, set, plan, book, programme, set up, fix, arrange, line

t

DICTIONARY

specified time **2** something that will have a large, often damaging, effect at a later date: *the decline of the manufacturing industry is a political time bomb*

time capsule *n* a container holding articles representative of the current age, buried for discovery in the future

time clock *n* a clock with a device for recording the time of arrival or departure of an employee

time-consuming *adj* taking up a great deal of time

time exposure *n* a photograph produced by exposing film for a relatively long period, usually a few seconds

time-honoured *adj* having been used or done for a long time and established by custom

timekeeper *n* **1** a person or thing that keeps or records time, for instance at a sporting event **2** an employee with a record of punctuality as specified: *a poor timekeeper* **timekeeping** *n*

time lag *n* a gap or delay between one event and a related event that happens after it: *the time lag between the development and the marketing of new products*

timeless ❶ *adj* **1** unaffected by time or by changes in fashion, society, etc.: *the timeless appeal of tailored wool jackets* **2** eternal and everlasting: *the timeless universal reality behind all religions* **timelessness** *n*

timely ❶ *adj* **-lier, -liest,** *adv* at the right or an appropriate time

time-out *n* **1** *sport chiefly US, Canad & Austral* an interruption in play during which players rest, discuss tactics, etc. **2 take time out** to take a break from a job or activity

timepiece *n* a device, such as a clock or watch, which measures and indicates time

timer *n* a device for measuring time, esp. a switch or regulator that causes a mechanism to operate at a specific time

times *prep* multiplied by: *ten times four is forty*

timescale *n* the period of time within which events occur or are due to occur

time-served *adj* having successfully completed an apprenticeship or period of training: *a time-served electrician*

timeserver *n* a person who changes his or her views in order to gain support or favour

time sharing *n* **1** a system of part ownership of a property for use as a holiday home whereby each participant owns the property for a particular period every year **2** a system by which users at different terminals of a computer can communicate with it at the same time

time signature *n music* a sign, usually consisting of two figures placed after the key signature, that indicates the number and length of beats in the bar

timetable ❶ *n* **1** a plan of the times when a job or activity should be done: *the timetable for the Royal Visit* **2** a list of departure and arrival times of trains or buses: *a timetable hung on the wall beside the ticket office* **3** a plan of the times when different subjects or classes are taught in a school or college: *a heavy timetable of lectures and practical classes* ▷ *vb* **-tabling, -tabled** **4** to set a time when a particular thing should be done: *the meeting is timetabled for 3 o'clock*

time value *n music* the duration of a note relative to other notes in a composition and considered in relation to the basic tempo

time warp *n* an imagined distortion of the progress of time, so that, for instance, events from the past seem to be happening in the present

timeworn *adj* **1** showing the adverse effects of overlong use or of old age: *a timeworn café* **2** having been used so often as to be no longer interesting: *a timeworn cliché*

time zone *n* a region throughout which the same standard time is used

timid *adj* **1** lacking courage or self-confidence: *a timid youth* **2** indicating shyness or fear: *a timid and embarrassed smile* **timidity** *n* **timidly** *adv*
WORD ORIGIN Latin *timere* to fear

timing *n* the ability to judge when to do or say something so as to make the best effect, for instance in the theatre, in playing an instrument, or in hitting a ball in sport

timorous (tim-mor-uss) *adj literary* lacking courage or self-confidence: *a reclusive timorous creature* **timorously** *adv*
WORD ORIGIN Latin *timor* fear

Timoshenko *n* **Semyon Konstantinovich.** 1895–1970, Soviet general in World War II

timpani *or* **tympani** (tim-pan-ee) *pl n* a set of kettledrums **timpanist** *or* **tympanist** *n*
WORD ORIGIN Italian

tin *n* **1** a soft silvery-white metallic element. Symbol: Sn **2** a sealed airtight metal container used for preserving and storing food or drink: *a cupboard full of packets and tins* **3** any metal container: *a tin of paint* **4** the contents of a tin **5** *Brit, Austral, & NZ* galvanized iron, used to make roofs ▷ *vb* **tinning, tinned** **6** to put (food) into tins
WORD ORIGIN Old English

Tinbergen *n* **1 Jan.** 1903–94, Dutch economist, noted for his work on econometrics. He shared (1969) the first Nobel prize for economics with Ragnar Frisch **2** his brother, **Nikolaas.** 1907–88, British zoologist, born in the Netherlands; studied animal behaviour, esp. instincts, and was one of the founders of ethology; Nobel prize for physiology or medicine 1973

tin can *n* a metal food container

tincture *n* a medicine consisting of a small amount of a drug dissolved in alcohol
WORD ORIGIN Latin *tinctura* a dyeing

tinder *n* dry wood or other easily-burning material used to start a fire **tindery** *adj*
WORD ORIGIN Old English *tynder*

tinderbox *n* (formerly) a small box for tinder, esp. one fitted with a flint and steel which could be used to make a spark

tine *n* a slender prong of a fork or a deer's antler **tined** *adj*
WORD ORIGIN Old English *tind*

tinfoil *n* a paper-thin sheet of metal, used for wrapping foodstuffs

ting *n* a high metallic sound such as that made by a small bell
WORD ORIGIN imitative

Ting *n* **Samuel Chao Chung.** born 1936, US physicist, who discovered the J/psi particle independently of Burton Richter, with whom he shared (1976) the Nobel prize for physics

ting-a-ling *n* the sound of a small bell

tinge ❶ *n* **1** a slight tint or colouring: *his skin had an unhealthy greyish tinge* **2** a very small amount: *both goals had a tinge of fortune* ▷ *vb* **tingeing** *or* **tinging,**

THESAURUS

up, organize, timetable, slate *(US)*, fix up, prearrange

timeless *adj* **1, 2 = eternal,** lasting, permanent, enduring, abiding, immortal, everlasting, ceaseless, immutable, indestructible, undying, ageless, imperishable, deathless, changeless **OPPOSITE:** temporary

timely *adj* **= opportune,** appropriate, well-timed, prompt, suitable, convenient, at the right time, judicious, punctual, propitious, seasonable **OPPOSITE:** untimely

timetable *n* **1 = schedule,** programme, agenda, list, diary, calendar, order of the day **3 = syllabus,** course, curriculum, programme, teaching programme

tinge *n* **1 = tint,** colour, shade, cast, wash, stain, dye, tincture **2 = trace,** bit, drop, touch, suggestion, dash, pinch, smack, sprinkling, smattering, soupçon *(French)* ▷ *vb* **3 = tint,** colour, shade, stain, dye

DICTIONARY

tinged 3 to colour or tint faintly: *the sunset tinged the lake with pink* 4 **tinged with** having a small amount of a particular quality: *the victory was tinged with sadness*
WORD ORIGIN Latin *tingere* to colour
tingle *vb* **-gling, -gled** 1 to feel a mild prickling or stinging sensation, as from cold or excitement ▷ *n* 2 a mild prickling or stinging feeling **tingling** *adj* **tingly** *adj*
WORD ORIGIN probably a variant of *tinkle*
tin god *n* a self-important person
tinker ❶ *n* 1 (esp. formerly) a travelling mender of pots and pans 2 *Scot & Irish* a Gypsy 3 a mischievous child ▷ *vb* 4 **tinker with** to try to repair or improve (something) by making lots of minor adjustments
WORD ORIGIN origin unknown
tinker's damn *or* **cuss** *n* **not give a tinker's damn** *or* **cuss** *slang* not to care at all
tinkle *vb* **-kling, -kled** 1 to ring with a high tinny sound like a small bell ▷ *n* 2 a high clear ringing sound 3 *Brit informal* a telephone call **tinkly** *adj*
WORD ORIGIN imitative
tinned *adj* (of food) preserved by being sealed in a tin
tinny[1] *adj* **-nier, -niest** 1 (of a sound) high, thin, and metallic: *the tinny sound of a transistor radio* 2 cheap or shoddy: *a tinny East European car*
tinny[2] *adj* **-nier, -niest** *Austral & NZ slang* lucky
tin-opener *n* a small tool for opening tins
Tin Pan Alley *n* the popular music industry, esp. the more commercial aspects of it
tin plate *n* thin steel sheet coated with a layer of tin to protect it from corrosion
tinpot *adj informal* worthless or unimportant: *a tinpot dictator*
tinsel *n* 1 a decoration consisting of a piece of metallic thread with thin strips of metal foil attached along its length 2 anything cheap, showy, and gaudy: *all their tinsel and show counts for nothing* ▷ *adj* 3 made of or decorated with tinsel 4 cheap, showy, and gaudy **tinselly** *adj*
WORD ORIGIN Latin *scintilla* a spark
Tinseltown *n informal* Hollywood, the centre of the US film industry
tinsmith *n* a person who works with tin or tin plate
tint ❶ *n* 1 a shade of a colour, esp. a pale one: *his eyes had a yellow tint* 2 a colour that is softened by the addition of white: *a room decorated in pastel tints* 3 a dye for the hair ▷ *vb* 4 to give a tint to (something, such as hair)
WORD ORIGIN Latin *tingere* to colour
tintinnabulation *n* the ringing or pealing of bells
WORD ORIGIN Latin *tintinnare* to tinkle
Tintoretto *n* **Il** (il). original name *Jacopo Robusti*. 1518–94, Italian painter of the Venetian school. His works include *Susanna bathing* (?1550) and the fresco cycle in the Scuola di San Rocco, Venice (from 1564)
tiny ❶ *adj* **tinier, tiniest** very small
WORD ORIGIN origin unknown
tip[1] ❶ *n* 1 a narrow or pointed end of something: *the northern tip of Japan* 2 a small piece attached to the end or bottom of something: *boot tips keep boots from getting scuffed* ▷ *vb* **tipping, tipped** 3 to make or form a tip on: *the long strips that hang down are tipped with silver cones* **tipped** *adj*
WORD ORIGIN Old Norse *typpi*
tip[2] ❶ *n* 1 an amount of money given to someone, such as a waiter, in return for service 2 a helpful hint or warning: *here are some sensible tips to help you avoid sunburn* 3 a piece of inside information, esp. in betting or investing ▷ *vb* **tipping, tipped** 4 to give a tip to
WORD ORIGIN origin unknown
tip[3] ❶ *vb* **tipping, tipped** 1 to tilt: *he tipped back his chair* 2 **tip over** to tilt so as to overturn or fall: *the box tipped over and the clothes in it spilled out* 3 *Brit* to dump (rubbish) 4 to pour out (the contents of a container): *he tipped the water from the basin down the sink* ▷ *n* 5 a rubbish dump
WORD ORIGIN origin unknown
tip-off *n* 1 a warning or hint, esp. one given confidentially and based on inside information ▷ *vb* **tip off** 2 to give a hint or warning to: *the police had been tipped off about the robbery*
tippet *n* a scarflike piece of fur, often made from a whole animal skin, worn, esp. formerly, round a woman's shoulders
WORD ORIGIN probably from TIP[1]
Tippett *n* Sir **Michael.** 1905–98, English composer, whose works include the oratorio *A Child of Our Time* (1941) and the operas *The Midsummer Marriage* (1952), *King Priam* (1961), *The Knot Garden* (1970), *The Ice Break* (1976), and *New Year* (1989)
tipple *vb* **-pling, -pled** 1 to drink alcohol regularly, esp. in small quantities ▷ *n* 2 an alcoholic drink **tippler** *n*
WORD ORIGIN origin unknown
tipstaff *n* 1 a court official 2 a metal-tipped staff formerly used as a symbol of office
tipster *n* a person who sells tips to people betting on horse races or speculating on the stock market
tipsy *adj* **-sier, -siest** slightly drunk **tipsiness** *n*
WORD ORIGIN from TIP[3]
tiptoe *vb* **-toeing, -toed** 1 to walk quietly with the heels off the ground ▷ *n* 2 **on tiptoe** on the tips of the toes or on the ball of the foot and the toes: *I stood on tiptoe*
tiptop *adj, adv* of the highest quality or condition
tip-up *adj* able to be turned upwards around a hinge or pivot: *tip-up seats*
Tipu Sahib *or* **Tippoo Sahib** *n* ?1750–99, sultan of Mysore (1782–99): killed fighting the British
TIR International Road Transport
WORD ORIGIN French *Transports Internationaux Routiers*
tirade *n* a long angry speech or denunciation
WORD ORIGIN French
tire[1] ❶ *vb* **tiring, tired** 1 to reduce the energy of, as by exertion: *she could still do things that would tire women half her age* 2 to become wearied or bored: *he simply stopped talking when he tired of my questions* **tiring** *adj*
WORD ORIGIN Old English *tēorian*
tire[2] *n US* ▸ same as **tyre**

THESAURUS

tinker *vb* 4 = **meddle**, play, toy, monkey, potter, fiddle *(informal)*, dabble, mess about, muck about *(Brit slang)*
tint *n* 1 = **shade**, colour, tone, hue, cast 3 = **dye**, wash, stain, rinse, tinge, tincture ▷ *vb* 4 = **dye**, colour, stain, rinse, tinge, tincture
tiny *adj* = **small**, little, minute, slight, mini, wee, miniature, trifling, insignificant, negligible, microscopic, diminutive, petite, puny, pint-sized *(informal)*, infinitesimal, teeny-weeny, Lilliputian, dwarfish, teensy-weensy, pygmy *or* pigmy OPPOSITE: huge
tip[1] *n* 1 = **end**, point, head, extremity, sharp end, nib, prong ▷ *vb* 3 = **cap**, top, crown, surmount, finish
tip[2] *n* 1 = **gratuity**, gift, reward, present, sweetener *(informal)*, perquisite, baksheesh, pourboire *(French)* 2, 3 = **hint**, suggestion, piece of information, piece of advice, gen *(Brit informal)*, pointer, piece of inside information, heads up *(US & Canad)* ▷ *vb* 4 = **reward**, remunerate, give a tip to, sweeten *(informal)*
tip[3] *vb* 3 *(Brit)* = **dump**, empty, ditch *(slang)*, unload, pour out 4 = **pour**, drop, empty, dump, drain, spill, discharge, unload, jettison, offload, slop *(informal)*, slosh *(informal)*, decant ▷ *n* 5 *(Brit)* = **dump**, midden, rubbish heap, refuse heap
tire[1] *vb* 1 = **exhaust**, drain, fatigue, weary, fag *(informal)*, whack *(Brit informal)*, wear out, wear down, take it out of *(informal)*, knacker *(slang)*, enervate OPPOSITE: refresh 2 = **flag**, become tired, fail, droop

DICTIONARY

tired ❶ *adj* 1 weary or exhausted: *they were tired after their long journey* 2 bored with or no longer interested in something: *I'm tired of staying in watching TV every night* 3 having been used so often as to be no longer interesting: *you haven't fallen for that tired old line, have you?* **tiredness** *n*

tireless *adj* energetic and determined: *a tireless worker for charity* **tirelessly** *adv*

tiresome *adj* boring and irritating

Tirpitz *n* **Alfred von.** 1849–1930, German admiral: as secretary of state for the Imperial Navy (1897–1916), he created the modern German navy, which challenged British supremacy at sea

Tirso de Molina *n* See **de Molina**

'tis *poetic or dialect* it is

Tissot *n* **James Joseph Jacques.** 1836–1902, French painter and etcher, best known for scenes of fashionable Victorian life painted in England

tissue *n* 1 a group of cells in an animal or plant with a similar structure and function: *muscular tissue forms 42% of the body tissue* 2 a thin piece of soft absorbent paper used as a disposable handkerchief, towel, etc. 3 ▸short for **tissue paper** 4 an interwoven series: *a tissue of lies*
WORD ORIGIN Old French *tissu* woven cloth

tissue paper *n* very thin soft delicate paper used esp. to wrap breakable goods

tit[1] *n* any of various small European songbirds, such as the bluetit, that feed on insects and seeds
WORD ORIGIN Middle English *tite* little

tit[2] *n* 1 *slang* a female breast 2 a teat or nipple
WORD ORIGIN Old English *titt*

titan *n* a person of great strength, importance, or size: *one of the titans of the computer industry*
WORD ORIGIN after the *Titans*, a family of gods in Greek mythology

titanic *adj* having or requiring colossal strength: *a titanic struggle*

titanium *n chem* a strong white metallic element used in the manufacture of strong lightweight alloys, esp. aircraft parts. Symbol: Ti
WORD ORIGIN from *titan*

titbit *or esp. US* **tidbit** *n* 1 a tasty small piece of food 2 a pleasing scrap of scandal: *an interesting titbit of gossip*
WORD ORIGIN origin unknown

titfer *n old-fashioned Brit slang* a hat
WORD ORIGIN rhyming slang *tit for tat*

tit-for-tat *adj* done in return or retaliation for a similar act: *a spate of tit-for-tat killings*
WORD ORIGIN earlier *tip for tap*

tithe *n* 1 one tenth of one's income or produce paid to the church as a tax 2 a tenth or very small part of anything: *he had accomplished only a tithe of his great dream* ▷*vb* **tithing, tithed** 3 to demand a tithe from 4 to pay a tithe or tithes **tithable** *adj*
WORD ORIGIN Old English *teogotha*

tithe barn *n* a large barn where, formerly, the agricultural tithe of a parish was stored

Titian (tish-un) *adj* (of hair) reddish-yellow
WORD ORIGIN from *Titian*, Italian painter, because he often used this hair colour in his paintings

titillate *vb* **-lating, -lated** to arouse or excite pleasurably, esp. in a sexual way **titillating** *adj* **titillation** *n*
WORD ORIGIN Latin *titillare*

titivate *vb* **-vating, -vated** to make smarter or neater **titivation** *n*
WORD ORIGIN perhaps from *tidy* + *cultivate*

title ❶ *n* 1 the distinctive name of a book, film, record, etc.: *his first album bore the title 'Safe as Milk'* 2 a descriptive name or heading of a section of a book, speech, etc. 3 a book or periodical: *publishers were averaging a total of 500 new titles annually* 4 a name or epithet signifying rank, office, or function: *the job bears the title Assistant Divisional Administrator* 5 a formal designation, such as *Mrs* or *Dr* 6 *sport* a championship: *the Italians have won the title* 7 *law* the legal right to possession of property
WORD ORIGIN Latin *titulus*

titled *adj* having a title such as 'Lady' or 'Sir' which indicates a high social rank

title deed *n* a document containing evidence of a person's legal right or title to property, esp. a house or land

titleholder *n* a person who holds a title, esp. a sporting championship

title page *n* the page in a book that gives the title, author, publisher, etc.

title role *n* the role of the character after whom a play or film is named

titmouse *n, pl* **-mice** ▸same as **tit**[1]
WORD ORIGIN Middle English *tite* little + MOUSE

titrate (tite-rate) *vb* **-trating, -trated** *chem* to measure the volume or concentration of (a solution) by titration
WORD ORIGIN French *titrer*

titration *n chem* an operation in which a measured amount of one solution is added to a known quantity of another solution until the reaction between the two is complete. If the concentration of one solution is known, that of the other can be calculated

titter *vb* 1 to snigger, esp. derisively or in a suppressed way ▷*n* 2 a suppressed laugh or snigger
WORD ORIGIN imitative

tittle *n* a very small amount: *it doesn't matter one jot or tittle what you think*
WORD ORIGIN Latin *titulus* title

tittle-tattle *n* 1 idle chat or gossip ▷*vb* **-tattling, -tattled** 2 to chatter or gossip

tittup *vb* **-tupping, -tupped** *or US* **-tuping, -tuped** 1 to prance or frolic ▷*n* 2 a caper
WORD ORIGIN probably imitative

titular *adj* 1 in name only: *titular head of state* 2 of or having a title

Tizard *n* Sir **Henry (Thomas).** 1885–1959, British chemist and scientific administrator, who specialized in the military application of science and backed the development of radar

tizzy *n, pl* **-zies** *informal* a state of confusion or excitement
WORD ORIGIN origin unknown

T-junction *n* a junction where one road joins another at right angles but does not cross it

Tl *chem* thallium

Tm *chem* thulium

TN Tennessee

TNT *n* 2,4,6-trinitrotoluene: a type of powerful explosive

to *prep* 1 used to indicate the destination of the subject or object of an action: *he went to the theatre* 2 used to introduce the indirect object of a verb: *talk to him* 3 used to introduce the infinitive of a verb: *I'm going to lie down* 4 as far as or until: *from September 11 to October 25* 5 used to indicate that two things have an

THESAURUS

tired *adj* 1 = **exhausted**, fatigued, weary, spent, done in *(informal)*, flagging, all in *(slang)*, drained, sleepy, fagged *(informal)*, whacked *(Brit informal)*, worn out, drooping, knackered *(slang)*, drowsy, clapped out *(Brit, Austral & NZ informal)*, enervated, ready to drop, dog-tired *(informal)*, zonked *(slang)*, dead beat *(informal)*, tuckered out *(Austral & NZ informal)*, asleep *or* dead on your feet *(informal)* OPPOSITE: energetic
2 = **bored**, fed up, weary, sick, annoyed, irritated, exasperated, irked, hoha *(NZ)*
OPPOSITE: enthusiastic about
3 = **hackneyed**, stale, well-worn, old, stock, familiar, conventional, corny *(slang)*, threadbare, trite, clichéd, outworn OPPOSITE: original

title *n* 4, 5 = **name**, designation, epithet, term, handle *(slang)*, nickname, denomination, pseudonym, appellation, sobriquet, nom de plume, moniker *or* monicker *(slang)* 6 *(sport)* = **championship**, trophy, laurels, bays, crown, honour 7 *(law)* = **ownership**, right, claim, privilege, entitlement, tenure, prerogative, freehold

DICTIONARY

equivalent value: *there are 16 ounces to the pound* **6** against or onto: *I put my ear to the door* **7** before the hour of: *17 minutes to midnight* **8** accompanied by: *dancing to a live band* **9** as compared with: *four goals to nil* **10** used to indicate a resulting condition: *burnt to death* **11** working for or employed by: *Chaplain to the Nigerian Chaplaincy in Britain* **12** in commemoration of: *a memorial to the victims of the disaster* ▷ *adv* **13** towards a closed position: *push the door to*
WORD ORIGIN Old English *tō*

toad *n* **1** an amphibian which resembles a frog, but has a warty skin and spends more time on dry land **2** a loathsome person
WORD ORIGIN Old English *tādige*

toadflax *n* a plant with narrow leaves and yellow-orange flowers

toad-in-the-hole *n* a traditional British dish made of sausages baked in a batter

toadstool *n* any of various poisonous funguses consisting of a caplike top on a stem

toady *n, pl* **toadies 1** a person who flatters and ingratiates himself or herself in a fawning way: *a spineless political toady* ▷ *vb* **toadies, toadying, toadied 2** to fawn on and flatter (someone) **toadyism** *n*
WORD ORIGIN shortened from *toadeater*, originally a quack's assistant who pretended to eat toads, hence a flatterer

to and fro *adv, adj also* **to-and-fro 1** back and forth: *he moved his head to and fro as if dodging blows* **2** from one place to another then back again: *the ferry sailed to and fro across the river* **toing and froing** *n*

toast¹ ⓣ *n* **1** sliced bread browned by exposure to heat ▷ *vb* **2** to brown (bread) under a grill or over a fire **3** to warm or be warmed: *toasting his feet at the fire*
WORD ORIGIN Latin *tostus* parched

toast² ⓣ *n* **1** a proposal of health or success given to a person or thing and marked by people raising glasses and drinking together **2** a person or thing that is honoured: *his success made him the toast of the British film industry* ▷ *vb* **3** to propose or drink a toast to (a person or thing)
WORD ORIGIN from the spiced toast formerly put in wine

toaster *n* an electrical device for toasting bread

toastmaster *n* a person who introduces speakers and proposes toasts at public dinners

tobacco *n, pl* **-cos** *or* **-coes** an American plant with large leaves which are dried for smoking, or chewing, or made into snuff
WORD ORIGIN Spanish *tabaco*

tobacconist *n Austral & Brit* a person or shop that sells tobacco, cigarettes, pipes, etc.

-to-be *adj* about to be; future: *the bride-to-be*

Tobey *n* **Mark.** 1890–1976, US painter. Influenced by Chinese calligraphy, he devised a style of improvisatory abstract painting called "white writing"

toboggan *n* **1** a long narrow sledge used for sliding over snow and ice ▷ *vb* **2** to ride on a toboggan
WORD ORIGIN from a Native American language

toby *n, pl* **-bies** *Scot & NZ* a water stopcock at the boundary of a street and house section
WORD ORIGIN origin unknown

toby jug *n chiefly Brit* a beer mug or jug in the form of a stout seated man wearing a three-cornered hat and smoking a pipe
WORD ORIGIN from the name *Tobias*

toccata (tok-**kah**-ta) *n* a piece of fast music for the organ, harpsichord, or piano, usually in a rhythmically free style
WORD ORIGIN Italian

Toc H *n* a society formed after World War I to encourage Christian comradeship
WORD ORIGIN from initials of *Talbot House*, Poperinge, Belgium, its original headquarters

Tocqueville *n* **Alexis Charles Henri Maurice Clérel de.** 1805–59, French politician and political writer. His chief works are *De la Démocratie en Amérique* (1835–40) and *L'Ancien régime et la révolution* (1856)

tocsin *n* **1** a warning signal **2** an alarm bell
WORD ORIGIN French

tod *n* **on one's tod** *Brit slang* by oneself; alone
WORD ORIGIN rhyming slang *Tod Sloan/alone*

today *n* **1** this day, as distinct from yesterday or tomorrow **2** the present age: *in today's world* ▷ *adv* **3** during or on this day: *I hope you're feeling better today* **4** nowadays: *this is one of the most reliable cars available today*
WORD ORIGIN Old English *tō dæge*, literally: on this day

Todd *n* Baron **Alexander Robertus.** 1907–97, Scottish chemist, noted for his research into the structure of nucleic acids: Nobel prize for chemistry 1957

toddle *vb* **-dling, -dled 1** to walk with short unsteady steps, like a young child **2 toddle off** *jocular* to depart: *he toddled off to bed* ▷ *n* **3** the act or an instance of walking with short unsteady steps
WORD ORIGIN origin unknown

toddler *n* a young child who has only just learned how to walk

toddy *n, pl* **-dies** a drink made from spirits, esp. whisky, hot water, sugar, and usually lemon juice
WORD ORIGIN Hindi *tārī* juice of the palmyra palm

to-do *n, pl* **-dos** *Brit, Austral & NZ* a commotion, fuss, or quarrel

toe *n* **1** any one of the digits of the foot **2** the part of a shoe or sock covering the toes **3 on one's toes** alert **4 tread on someone's toes** to offend a person, esp. by trespassing on his or her field of responsibility ▷ *vb* **toeing, toed 5** to touch or kick with the toe **6 toe the line** to conform to expected attitudes or standards
WORD ORIGIN Old English *tā*

toecap *n* a reinforced covering for the toe of a boot or shoe

toehold *n* **1** a small space on a rock, mountain, etc. which can be used to support the toe of the foot in climbing **2** any means of gaining access or advantage: *the French car industry has lost its last toehold in America*

toenail *n* a thin hard clear plate covering part of the upper surface of the end of each toe

toerag *n Brit slang* a contemptible or despicable person

toff *n Brit slang* a well-dressed or upper-class person
WORD ORIGIN perhaps from *tuft*, nickname for a titled student at Oxford University wearing a cap with a gold tassel

toffee *n* **1** a sticky chewy sweet made by boiling sugar with water and butter **2 can't (do something) for toffee** *informal* is not competent or talented at (doing something): *she couldn't dance for toffee*
WORD ORIGIN earlier *taffy*

toffee-apple *n* an apple fixed on a stick and coated with a thin layer of toffee

toffee-nosed *adj slang* snobbish or conceited

tofu *n* a food with a soft cheeselike consistency made from unfermented soya-bean curd
WORD ORIGIN Japanese

tog *n* a unit for measuring the insulating power of duvets

toga (**toe**-ga) *n* a garment worn by

THESAURUS

toast¹ *vb* **2 = brown**, grill, crisp, roast **3 = warm (up)**, heat (up), thaw, bring back to life

toast² *n* **1 = tribute**, drink, compliment, salute, health, pledge, salutation **2 = favourite**, celebrity, darling, talk, pet, focus of attention, hero *or* heroine, blue-eyed boy *or* girl (*Brit informal*) ▷ *vb* **3 = drink to**, honour, pledge to, salute, drink (to) the health of

together *adv* **1 = collectively**, jointly,

t

DICTIONARY

citizens of ancient Rome, consisting of a piece of cloth draped around the body **togaed** *adj*
WORD ORIGIN Latin

together ❶ *adv* **1** with cooperation between people or organizations: *we started a company together* **2** in or into contact with each other: *he clasped his hands together* **3** in or into one place: *the family gets together to talk* **4** at the same time: *'Disgusting,' said Julie and Alice together* **5** considered collectively: *the properties together were worth more as a unit* **6** *old-fashioned* continuously: *working for eight hours together* **7 together with** in addition to ▷ *adj* **8** *informal* self-possessed, competent, and well-organized
WORD ORIGIN Old English *tōgædere*

togetherness *n* a feeling of closeness to and affection for other people

togged up *adj informal* dressed up in smart clothes. Also: **togged out**

toggle *n* **1** a bar-shaped button inserted through a loop for fastening coats etc. **2** *computers* a key on a keyboard which, when pressed, will turn a function or feature on if it is currently off, and turn it off if it is currently on **3** ▸ short for **toggle switch** (sense 1)
WORD ORIGIN origin unknown

toggle switch *n* **1** an electric switch with a projecting lever that is moved in a particular way to open or close a circuit **2** ▸ same as **toggle** (sense 2)

Toghril Beg *n* ?990–1063 AD, Sultan of Turkey (1055–63), who founded the Seljuq dynasty and conquered Baghdad (1055)

Togliatti[1] *n* a city in W central Russia, on the Volga River: automobile industry: renamed in honour of Palmiro Togliatti. Pop: 718 000 (2005 est). Former name (until 1964): **Stavropol**. Russian name: **Tolyatti**

Togliatti[2] *n* **Palmiro**. 1893–1964, Italian politician; leader of the Italian Communist Party (1926–64). After Mussolini's fall he became a minister (1944) and vice premier (1945)

Togo[1] *n* a republic in West Africa, on the Gulf of Guinea: became French Togoland (a League of Nations mandate) after the division of German Togoland in 1922; independent since 1960. Official language: French. Religion: animist majority. Currency: franc. Capital: Lomé. Pop: 5 017 000 (2004 est). Area: 56 700 sq km (20 900 sq miles)

Togo[2] *n* Marquis **Heihachiro**. 1847–1934, Japanese admiral, who commanded the Japanese fleet in the war with Russia (1904–05)

togs *pl n* **1** *Brit, Austral & NZ informal* clothes **2** *Austral, NZ & Irish* a swimming costume
WORD ORIGIN probably from *toga*

toheroa (toe-a-**roe**-a) *n* a large edible mollusc of New Zealand with a distinctive flavour
WORD ORIGIN Māori

tohunga (**toe**-hung-a) *n NZ* a Māori priest
WORD ORIGIN Māori

toil ❶ *n* **1** hard or exhausting work: *hours of toil beneath the Catalan sun* ▷ *vb* **2** to work hard: *workers toiling in the fields to produce tea for westerners to drink* **3** to move slowly and with difficulty, for instance because of exhaustion or the steepness of a slope: *Joanna toiled up the steps to the church*
WORD ORIGIN Anglo-French *toiler* to struggle

toilet ❶ *n* **1 a** a bowl fitted with a water-flushing device and connected to a drain, for receiving and disposing of urine and faeces **b** a room with such a fitment **2** *old-fashioned* the act of dressing and preparing oneself
WORD ORIGIN French *toilette* dress

toilet paper *n* thin absorbent paper used for cleaning oneself after defecation or urination

toilet roll *n* a long strip of toilet paper wound around a cardboard tube

toiletry *n, pl* **-ries** an object or cosmetic used in making up, dressing, etc.

toilette (twah-**let**) *n* ▸ same as **toilet** (sense 2)
WORD ORIGIN French

toilet water *n* liquid perfume lighter than cologne

toilsome *adj literary* requiring hard work: *a most toilsome job*

token ❶ *n* **1** a symbol, sign, or indication of something: *as a token of respect* **2** a gift voucher that can be used as payment for goods of a specified value **3** a metal or plastic disc, such as a substitute for currency for use in a slot machine **4 by the same token** in the same way as something mentioned previously ▷ *adj* **5** intended to create an impression but having no real importance: *as a token gesture of goodwill*
WORD ORIGIN Old English *tācen*

tokenism *n* the practice of making only a token effort or doing no more than the minimum, esp. in order to comply with a law **tokenist** *adj*

token strike *n* a brief stoppage of work intended to convey strength of feeling on a disputed issue

Tokugawa Iyeyasu *n* See **Iyeyasu**

told *vb* ▸ the past of **tell**

tolerable *adj* **1** able to be put up with; bearable **2** *informal* fairly good **tolerably** *adv*

tolerance ❶ *n* **1** the quality of accepting other people's rights to their own opinions, beliefs, or

THESAURUS

closely, as one, with each other, in conjunction, side by side, mutually, hand in hand, as a group, in partnership, in concert, in unison, shoulder to shoulder, cheek by jowl, in cooperation, in a body, hand in glove **OPPOSITE:** separately
4 = at the same time, simultaneously, in unison, as one, (all) at once, en masse, concurrently, contemporaneously, with one accord, at one fell swoop ▷ *adj*
8 *(informal)* **= self-possessed**, calm, composed, well-balanced, cool, stable, well-organized, well-adjusted, grounded

toil *n* **1 = hard work**, industry, labour, effort, pains, application, sweat, graft *(informal)*, slog, exertion, drudgery, travail, donkey-work, elbow grease *(informal)*, blood, sweat and tears *(informal)*
OPPOSITE: idleness
▷ *vb* **2 = labour**, work, struggle, strive, grind *(informal)*, sweat *(informal)*, slave, graft *(informal)*, go for it *(informal)*, slog, grub, bend over backwards *(informal)*, drudge, go for broke *(slang)*, push yourself, bust a gut *(informal)*, give it your best shot *(informal)*, break your neck *(informal)*, work like a dog, make an all-out effort *(informal)*, work like a Trojan, knock yourself out *(informal)*, do your damnedest *(informal)*, give it your all *(informal)*, work your fingers to the bone, rupture yourself *(informal)*
3 = struggle, trek, slog, trudge, push yourself, fight your way, drag yourself, footslog

toilet *n* **1a, 1b = lavatory**, bathroom, loo *(Brit informal)*, bog *(slang)*, gents *or* ladies, can *(US & Canad slang)*, john *(slang, chiefly US & Canad)*, head(s) *(nautical) (slang)*, throne *(informal)*, closet, privy, cloakroom *(Brit)*, urinal, latrine, washroom, powder room, ablutions *(military) (informal)*, dunny *(Austral & NZ old-fashioned, informal)*, water closet, khazi *(slang)*, pissoir *(French)*, little boy's room *or* little girl's room *(informal)*, (public) convenience, W.C., bogger *(Austral slang)*, brasco *(Austral slang)*
1b = bathroom, washroom, gents *or* ladies *(Brit informal)*, privy, outhouse, latrine, powder room, water closet, pissoir *(French)*, ladies' room, little boy's *or* little girl's room, W.C.

token *n* **1 = symbol**, mark, sign, note, evidence, earnest, index, expression, demonstration, proof, indication, clue, representation, badge, manifestation ▷ *adj* **5 = nominal**, symbolic, minimal, hollow, superficial, perfunctory

tolerance *n* **1 = broad-mindedness**, charity, sympathy, patience, indulgence, forbearance,

t

DICTIONARY

actions **2** capacity to endure something, esp. pain or hardship **3** the ability of a substance to withstand heat, stress, etc. without damage **4** *med* the capacity to endure the effects of a continued or increasing dose of a drug, poison, etc. **5** an acceptable degree of variation in a measurement or value: *the bodywork of the car is precision-engineered with a tolerance of 0.01 millimetres*

tolerant ➊ *adj* **1** accepting of the beliefs, actions, etc. of other people **2 tolerant of** able to withstand (heat, stress, etc.) without damage

tolerate ➊ *vb* **-ating, -ated 1** to allow something to exist or happen, even although one does not approve of it: *you must learn to tolerate opinions other than your own* **2** to put up with (someone or something): *he found the pain hard to tolerate* **toleration** *n*
WORD ORIGIN Latin *tolerare* to sustain

toll¹ ➊ *vb* **1** to ring (a bell) slowly and regularly **2** to announce by tolling: *the bells tolled the Queen's death* ▷ *n* **3** the slow regular ringing of a bell
WORD ORIGIN origin unknown

toll² ➊ *n* **1** a charge for the use of certain roads and bridges: *the Skye bridge toll* **2** loss or damage from a disaster: *the annual death toll on the roads is about 4500* **3 take a** *or* **its toll** to have a severe and damaging effect: *the continued stress had taken a toll on her health*
WORD ORIGIN Old English *toln*

Toller *n* **Ernst.** 1893–1939, German dramatist and revolutionary, noted particularly for his expressionist plays, esp. *Masse Mensch* (1921)

tollgate *n* a gate across a toll road or bridge at which travellers must pay

tolu (tol-loo) *n* a sweet-smelling balsam obtained from a South American tree, used in medicine and perfume
WORD ORIGIN after *Santiago de Tolu*, Colombia

toluene *n* a flammable liquid obtained from petroleum and coal tar and used as a solvent and in the manufacture of dyes, explosives, etc.
WORD ORIGIN previously obtained from tolu

tom *n* **1** a male cat ▷ *adj* **2** (of an animal) male: *a tom turkey*
WORD ORIGIN from *Thomas*

tomahawk *n* a fighting axe used by the Native Americans of N America
WORD ORIGIN from a Native American language

tomato *n, pl* **-toes 1** a red fleshy juicy fruit with many edible seeds, eaten in salads, as a vegetable, etc. **2** the plant, originally from South America, on which this fruit grows
WORD ORIGIN S American Indian *tomatl*

tomb ➊ *n* **1** a place for the burial of a corpse **2** a monument over a grave **3 the tomb** *poetic* death
WORD ORIGIN Greek *tumbos*

Tombaugh *n* **Clyde William.** 1906–97, US astronomer, who discovered (1930) the dwarf planet Pluto

tombola *n Brit* a type of lottery, in which tickets are drawn from a revolving drum
WORD ORIGIN Italian

tomboy *n* a girl who behaves or dresses like a boy

tombstone *n* a gravestone

tome *n* a large heavy book
WORD ORIGIN Greek *tomos* a slice

tomfoolery *n* foolish behaviour

Tommy *n, pl* **-mies** *Brit, old-fashioned informal* a private in the British Army
WORD ORIGIN originally *Thomas Atkins*, name used in specimen copies of official forms

Tommy gun *n* a type of light sub-machine-gun
WORD ORIGIN in full *Thompson sub-machine-gun*, from the name of the manufacturer

tommyrot *n old-fashioned, informal* utter nonsense

tomorrow *n* **1** the day after today: *tomorrow's meeting has been cancelled* **2** the future: *the struggle to build a better tomorrow* ▷ *adv* **3** on the day after today: *the festival starts tomorrow* **4** at some time in the future: *they live today as millions more will live tomorrow*
WORD ORIGIN Old English *tō morgenne*

tomtit *n Brit* a small European bird that eats insects and seeds

tom-tom *n* a long narrow drum beaten with the hands
WORD ORIGIN Hindi *tamtam*

ton¹ *n* **1** *Brit* a unit of weight equal to 2240 pounds or 1016.046 kilograms **2** *US & Canad* a unit of weight equal to 2000 pounds or 907.184 kilograms **3** ▸ see **metric ton 4 come down on someone like a ton of bricks** to scold someone very severely ▷ *adv* **5 tons** a lot: *I've got tons of things to do before going on holiday*
WORD ORIGIN variant of *tun*

ton² *n slang chiefly Brit* a hundred miles per hour
WORD ORIGIN special use of TON¹

tonal *adj* **1** *music* written in a key **2** of or relating to tone or tonality

tonality *n, pl* **-ties 1** *music* the presence of a musical key in a composition **2** the overall scheme of colours and tones in a painting

tone ➊ *n* **1** sound with reference to its pitch, timbre, or volume **2** *US & Canad* ▸ same as **note** (sense 6) **3** *music* an interval of two semitones, such as that between doh and ray in tonic sol-fa **4** the quality or character of a sound: *her tone was angry* **5** general aspect, quality, or style: *the tone of the conversation made him queasy* **6** high quality or style: *my car with its patches of rust lowered the tone of the neighbourhood* **7** the quality of a given colour, as modified by mixture with white or black; shade or tint **8** *physiol* the natural firmness of the tissues and normal functioning of bodily organs in health ▷ *vb* **toning, toned 9** to be of a matching or similar tone **10** to give a tone to or correct the tone of **toneless** *adj* **tonelessly** *adv*
WORD ORIGIN Greek *tonos*

Tone *n* **(Theobald) Wolfe.** 1763–98, Irish nationalist, who founded (1791)

t

THESAURUS

permissiveness, magnanimity, open-mindedness, sufferance, lenity **OPPOSITE:** intolerance **2 = endurance**, resistance, stamina, fortitude, resilience, toughness, staying power, hardness, hardiness **4 = resistance**, immunity, resilience, non-susceptibility

tolerant *adj* **1 = broad-minded**, understanding, sympathetic, open-minded, patient, fair, soft, catholic, charitable, indulgent, easy-going, long-suffering, lax, lenient, permissive, magnanimous, free and easy, forbearing, kind-hearted, unprejudiced, complaisant, latitudinarian, unbigoted, easy-oasy *(slang)* **OPPOSITE:** intolerant

tolerate *vb* **1 = allow**, accept, permit, sanction, take, receive, admit, brook, indulge, put up with *(informal)*, condone, countenance, turn a blind eye to, wink at **OPPOSITE:** forbid **2 = endure**, stand, suffer, bear, take, stomach, undergo, swallow, hack *(slang)*, abide, put up with *(informal)*, submit to, thole *(Scot)*

toll¹ *vb* **1 = ring**, sound, strike, chime, knell, clang, peal ▷ *n* **3 = ringing**, ring, tolling, chime, knell, clang, peal

toll² *n* **1 = charge**, tax, fee, duty, rate, demand, payment, assessment, customs, tribute, levy, tariff, impost **2 = damage**, cost, loss, roll, penalty, sum, number, roster, inroad

tomb *n* **1 = grave**, vault, crypt, mausoleum, sarcophagus, catacomb, sepulchre, burial chamber

tone *n* **1 = pitch**, stress, volume, accent, force, strength, emphasis, inflection, intonation, timbre, modulation, tonality **1, 4 = volume**, timbre, tonality **5 = character**, style, approach, feel, air, effect, note, quality, spirit, attitude, aspect, frame, manner, mood, drift, grain, temper, vein, tenor **7 = colour**, cast, shade, tint, tinge, hue ▷ *vb* **9 = harmonize**, match, blend, suit,

DICTIONARY

the Society of United Irishmen and led (1798) French military forces to Ireland. He was captured and sentenced to death but committed suicide

tone-deaf *adj* unable to distinguish subtle differences in musical pitch

tone down *vb* to moderate in tone: *I sensed some reserve in his manner, so I toned down my enthusiasm*

tone poem *n music* an extended orchestral composition based on nonmusical material, such as a work of literature or a fairy tale

toner *n* **1** a cosmetic applied to the skin to reduce oiliness **2** a powdered chemical that forms the image produced by a photocopier

tone up *vb* to make or become more vigorous, healthy, etc.: *muscle tissue can be toned up*

tong *n* (formerly) a secret society of Chinese Americans
WORD ORIGIN Chinese (Cantonese) *t'ong* meeting place

tongs *pl n* a tool for grasping or lifting, consisting of two long metal or wooden arms, joined with a hinge or flexible metal strip at one end
WORD ORIGIN Old English *tange*

tongue ❶ *n* **1** a movable mass of muscular tissue attached to the floor of the mouth, used for tasting, eating, and speaking **2** a language, dialect, or idiom: *the Scots tongue* **3** the ability to speak: *taken aback, she could not find her tongue* **4** a manner of speaking: *a sharp tongue* **5** the tongue of certain animals used as food **6** a narrow strip of something that extends outwards: *a narrow tongue of flame* **7** a flap of leather on a shoe **8** the clapper of a bell **9** a projecting strip along an edge of a board that is made to fit a groove in another board **10 hold one's tongue** to keep quiet **11 on the tip of one's tongue** about to come to mind **12 with (one's) tongue in one's cheek** with insincere or ironical intent
WORD ORIGIN Old English *tunge*

tongue-tie *n* a congenital condition in which movement of the tongue is limited as the result of the fold of skin under the tongue extending too close to the front of the tongue

tongue-tied *adj* speechless, esp. with embarrassment or shyness

tongue twister *n* a sentence or phrase that is difficult to say clearly and quickly, such as *the sixth sick sheikh's sixth sheep's sick*

tonguing *n* a technique of playing a wind instrument by obstructing and uncovering the air passage through the lips with the tongue

tonic ❶ *n* **1** a medicine that improves the functioning of the body or increases the feeling of wellbeing **2** anything that enlivens or strengthens: *his dry humour was a stimulating tonic* **3** Also called: **tonic water** a carbonated beverage containing quinine and often mixed with alcoholic drinks: *gin and tonic* **4** *music* the first note of a major or minor scale and the tonal centre of a piece composed in a particular key ▷ *adj* **5** having an invigorating or refreshing effect: *a tonic bath* **6** *music* of the first note of a major or minor scale
WORD ORIGIN Greek *tonikos* concerning tone

tonic sol-fa *n* a method of teaching music, by which syllables are used as names for the notes of the major scale in any key

tonight *n* **1** the night or evening of this present day: *tonight's programme examines the rise of poverty in the 1990s* ▷ *adv* **2** in or during the night or evening of this day: *I want to go out dancing tonight*
WORD ORIGIN Old English *tōniht*

toning table *n* an exercise table, parts of which move mechanically to exercise specific parts of the body of the person lying on it

tonnage *n* **1** the capacity of a merchant ship expressed in tons **2** the weight of the cargo of a merchant ship **3** the total amount of shipping of a port or nation

tonne (tunn) *n* a unit of mass equal to 1000 kg or 2204.6 pounds
WORD ORIGIN French

tonsil *n* either of two small oval lumps of spongy tissue situated one on each side of the back of the mouth **tonsillar** *adj*
WORD ORIGIN Latin *tonsillae* tonsils

tonsillectomy *n, pl* **-mies** surgical removal of the tonsils
WORD ORIGIN TONSIL + Greek *tomē* a cutting

tonsillitis *n* inflammation of the tonsils, causing a sore throat and fever

tonsorial *adj often facetious* of a barber or his trade
WORD ORIGIN Latin *tondere* to shave

tonsure *n* **1 a** (in certain religions and monastic orders) the shaving of the head or the crown of the head only **b** the part of the head left bare by such shaving ▷ *vb* **-suring, -sured 2** to shave the head of **tonsured** *adj*
WORD ORIGIN Latin *tonsura* a clipping

too ❶ *adv* **1** as well or also: *I'll miss you, too* **2** in or to an excessive degree: *it's too noisy in here* **3** extremely: *you're too kind* **4** *US, Canad & Austral informal* used to emphasize contradiction of a negative statement: *You didn't! – I did too!*
WORD ORIGIN Old English *tō*

took *vb* ▸ the past tense of **take**

Tooke *n* **John Horne,** original name *John Horne.* 1736–1812, British radical, who founded (1771) the Constitutional Society to press for parliamentary reform: acquitted (1794) of high treason. He also wrote the philological treatise *The Diversions of Purley* (1786)

tool ❶ *n* **1 a** an implement, such as a hammer, saw, or spade, that is used by hand to help do a particular type of work **b** a power-driven instrument: *machine tool* **2** the cutting part of such an instrument **3** a person used to perform dishonourable or unpleasant tasks for another: *the government is acting as a tool of big business* **4** any object, skill, etc. used for a particular task or in a particular job: *a skilled therapist can use photographs as tools* ▷ *vb* **5** to work, cut, or form (something) with a tool
WORD ORIGIN Old English *tōl*

toolbar *n* a row or column of buttons displayed on a computer screen, allowing the user to select a variety of functions

tool-maker *n* a person who specializes in the production or reconditioning of machine tools **tool-making** *n*

tool-pusher *n* a person who supervises drilling operations on an oil rig

toonie *or* **twonie** *n Canad informal* a Canadian two-dollar coin

toot *n* **1** a short hooting sound ▷ *vb* **2** to give or cause to give a short blast, hoot, or whistle: *motorists tooted their car horns*
WORD ORIGIN imitative

tooth *n, pl* **teeth 1** one of the bonelike projections in the jaws of most vertebrates that are used for biting,

THESAURUS

go well with

tongue *n* **2 = language**, speech, vernacular, talk, dialect, idiom, parlance, lingo *(informal)*, patois, argot

tonic *n* **1, 2 = stimulant**, boost, bracer *(informal)*, refresher, cordial, pick-me-up *(informal)*, fillip, shot in the arm *(informal)*, restorative, livener, analeptic, roborant

too *adv* **1 = also**, as well, further, in addition, moreover, besides, likewise, to boot, into the bargain **2 = excessively**, very, extremely, overly, unduly, unreasonably, inordinately, exorbitantly, immoderately, over-

tool *n* **1a = implement**, device, appliance, apparatus, machine, instrument, gadget, utensil, contraption, contrivance **3 = puppet**, creature, pawn, dupe, stooge *(slang)*, jackal, minion, lackey, flunkey, hireling, cat's-paw

DICTIONARY

tearing, or chewing **2** one of the sharp projections on the edge of a comb, saw, zip, etc. **3** **long in the tooth** old or ageing **4** **a sweet tooth** a liking for sweet food **5** **tooth and nail** with great vigour and determination: *the union would oppose compulsory redundancies tooth and nail* ▸ See also **teeth**
WORD ORIGIN Old English *tōth*

toothache *n* a pain in or near a tooth

toothbrush *n* a small brush with a long handle, for cleaning the teeth

toothless *adj* **1** having no teeth **2** having no real power: *the proposed Commission will not be as toothless as scoffers suggest*

toothpaste *n* a paste used for cleaning the teeth, applied with a toothbrush

toothpick *n* a small wooden or plastic stick used for extracting pieces of food from between the teeth

tooth powder *n* a powder used for cleaning the teeth, applied with a toothbrush

toothsome *adj* delicious or appetizing in appearance, flavour, or smell

toothy *adj* **toothier, toothiest** having or showing numerous, large, or prominent teeth: *a toothy grin*

tootle *vb* **-tling, -tled** **1** to hoot softly or repeatedly ▹ *n* **2** a soft hoot or series of hoots

top[1] Ⓣ *n* **1** the highest point or part of anything: *the top of the stairs* **2** the most important or successful position: *at the top of the agenda* **3** a lid or cap that fits on to one end of something, esp. to close it: *he unscrewed the top from a quart of ale* **4** the highest degree or point: *the two people at the top of the Party* **5** the most important person or people in an organization: *the top of the military establishment* **6** the loudest or highest pitch: *she cheered and sang at the top of her voice* **7** a garment, esp. for a woman, that extends from the shoulders to the waist or hips **8** the part of a plant that is above ground: *nettle tops* **9** ▸ same as **top gear** **10** **off the top of one's head** without previous preparation or careful thought **11** **on top of** **a** in addition to: *the average member of staff will get 25% on top of salary* **b** *informal* in complete control of: *we're on top of our costs and expenses and looking for other opportunities* **12** **over the top** **a** lacking restraint or a sense of proportion: *you went over the top when you called her a religious maniac* **b** *mil* over the edge of a trench ▹ *adj* **13** at, of, or being the top: *men still hold most of the top jobs in industry* ▹ *vb* **topping, topped** **14** to put on top of (something): *top your salad with a mild dressing* **15** to reach or pass the top of **16** to be at the top of: *her biggest hit topped the charts for six weeks* **17** to exceed or surpass: *his estimated fortune tops £2 billion* **18** **top and tail** **a** to trim off the ends of (fruit or vegetables) before cooking **b** to wash only a baby's face and bottom ▸ See also **top off, top out, tops**, etc.
WORD ORIGIN Old English *topp*

top[2] *n* **1** a toy that is spun on its pointed base **2** **sleep like a top** to sleep very soundly
WORD ORIGIN Old English

topaz (toe-pazz) *n* a hard glassy yellow, pink, or colourless mineral used in making jewellery
WORD ORIGIN Greek *topazos*

top brass *pl n* the most important or high-ranking officials or leaders

topcoat *n* **1** an overcoat **2** a final coat of paint applied to a surface

top dog *n informal* the leader or chief of a group

top drawer *n old-fashioned, informal* people of the highest social standing

top dressing *n* a layer of fertilizer or manure spread on the surface of land **top-dress** *vb*

tope[1] *vb* **toping, toped** to drink (alcohol), usually in large quantities **toper** *n*
WORD ORIGIN perhaps from French *toper* to take a bet

tope[2] *n* a small grey shark of European coastal waters
WORD ORIGIN origin unknown

topee *or* **topi** (toe-pee) *n* ▸ same as **pith helmet**
WORD ORIGIN Hindi *topī* hat

top-flight *adj* of very high quality

topgallant *n* **1** a mast or sail above a topmast ▹ *adj* **2** of or relating to a topgallant

top gear *n* the highest forward ratio of a gearbox in a motor vehicle

top hat *n* a man's hat with a tall cylindrical crown and narrow brim, now only worn for some formal occasions

top-heavy *adj* unstable through being overloaded at the top

topiary (tope-yar-ee) *n* **1** the art of trimming trees or bushes into artificial decorative shapes **2** trees or bushes trimmed into decorative shapes ▹ *adj* **3** of or relating to topiary **topiarist** *n*
WORD ORIGIN Latin *topia* decorative garden work

topic Ⓣ *n* a subject of a speech, book, conversation, etc.
WORD ORIGIN Greek *topos* place

topical Ⓣ *adj* of or relating to current affairs **topicality** *n* **topically** *adv*

topknot *n* a crest, tuft, decorative bow, etc. on the top of the head

topless *adj* of or relating to women wearing costumes that do not cover the breasts: *topless bars*

top-level *adj* of, involving, or by those with the highest level of influence or ability: *a top-level meeting*

topmast *n* the mast next above a lower mast on a sailing vessel

topmost *adj* at or nearest the top

top-notch *adj informal* excellent or superb: *top-notch entertainment*

top off *vb* to finish or complete, esp. with some decisive action

topography *n, pl* **-phies** **1** the surface features of a region, such as its hills, valleys, or rivers: *the islands are fragile, with a topography constantly changed by wind and wave* **2** the study or description of such surface features **3** the representation of these features on a map **topographer** *n* **topographical** *adj*
WORD ORIGIN Greek *topos* a place + -GRAPHY

topology *n* a branch of geometry describing the properties of a figure that are unaffected by continuous distortion **topological** *adj*
WORD ORIGIN Greek *topos* a place + -LOGY

Topolski *n* **Feliks.** 1907–89, British painter, born in Poland; best known for his sketches and murals, esp. for

THESAURUS

top[1] *n* **1 = peak**, summit, head, crown, height, ridge, brow, crest, high point, pinnacle, culmination, meridian, zenith, apex, apogee, acme, vertex **OPPOSITE:** bottom **2 = first place**, head, peak, lead, highest rank, high point **3 = lid**, cover, cap, cork, plug, stopper, bung ▹ *adj* **13a = highest**, upper, loftiest, furthest up, uppermost, topmost **13b = leading**, best, first, highest, greatest, lead, head, prime, finest, crowning, crack (*informal*), elite, superior, dominant, foremost, pre-eminent **OPPOSITE:** lowest **13c = chief**, most important, principal, most powerful, highest, lead, head, ruling, leading, main, commanding, prominent, notable, sovereign, eminent, high-ranking, illustrious **13d = prime**, best, select, first-class, capital, quality, choice, excellent, premier, superb, elite, superior, top-class, A1 (*informal*), top-quality, first-rate, top-notch (*informal*), grade A, top-grade ▹ *vb* **14 = cover**, coat, garnish, finish, crown, cap, overspread **16 = lead**, head, command, be at the top of, be first in **17 = surpass**, better, beat, improve on, cap, exceed, best, eclipse, go beyond, excel, transcend, outstrip, outdo, outshine **OPPOSITE:** not be as good as

topic *n* **= subject**, point, question, issue, matter, theme, text, thesis, subject matter

topical *adj* **= current**, popular, contemporary, up-to-date, up-to-

DICTIONARY

Memoir of the Century (1975–89) painted on viaduct arches on London's South Bank
top out *vb* to place the highest stone on (a building)
topper *n informal* a top hat
topping *n* a sauce or garnish for food
topple ⊕ *vb* **-pling, -pled** 1 to fall over or cause (something) to fall over, esp. from a height: *he staggered back against the railing and toppled over into the river* 2 to overthrow or oust: *few believe the scandal will topple the government*
WORD ORIGIN from TOP[1] (verb)
tops *slang n* 1 **the tops** a person or thing of top quality ▹*adj* 2 excellent: *Pacino's no-holds-barred performance is tops*
topsail *n* a square sail carried on a yard set on a topmast
top-secret *adj* (of military or government information) classified as needing the highest level of secrecy and security
topside *n* a lean cut of beef from the thigh containing no bone
topsoil *n* the surface layer of soil
topsy-turvy *adj* 1 upside down 2 in a state of confusion ▹*adv* 3 in a topsy-turvy manner
WORD ORIGIN probably *top* + obsolete *tervy* to turn upside down
top up *vb* 1 to refill (a container), usually to the brim: *I topped up his glass* 2 to add to (an amount) in order to make it sufficient: *the grant can be topped up by a student loan* ▹*n* **top-up** 3 another serving of a drink in the glass that was used for the first one: *anyone want a top-up?* ▹*adj* **top-up** 4 serving to top something up: *a top-up loan*
toque (toke) *n* 1 a woman's small round brimless hat 2 *Canad* ▸same as **tuque** (sense 2)
WORD ORIGIN French
tor *n chiefly Brit* a high hill, esp. a bare rocky one
WORD ORIGIN Old English *torr*
Torah *n* the whole body of traditional Jewish teaching, including the Oral Law
WORD ORIGIN Hebrew: precept
torch *n* 1 a small portable electric lamp powered by batteries 2 a wooden shaft dipped in wax or tallow and set alight 3 anything regarded as a source of enlightenment, guidance, etc.: *a torch of hope* 4 **carry a torch for** to be in love with (someone), esp. unrequitedly ▹*vb* 5 *informal* to deliberately set (a building) on fire
WORD ORIGIN Old French *torche* handful of twisted straw
tore *vb* ▸the past tense of **tear²**
toreador (torr-ee-a-dor) *n* a bullfighter, esp. one on horseback
WORD ORIGIN Spanish
torero (tor-air-oh) *n, pl* **-ros** a bullfighter, esp. one on foot
WORD ORIGIN Spanish
torment ⊕ *vb* 1 to cause (someone) great pain or suffering 2 to tease or pester (a person or animal) in an annoying or cruel way ▹*n* 3 physical or mental pain 4 a source of pain or suffering **tormentor** *n*
WORD ORIGIN Latin *tormentum*
tormentil *n* a creeping plant with yellow four-petalled flowers
WORD ORIGIN Old French *tormentille*
torn ⊕ *vb* 1 ▸the past participle of **tear²** ▹*adj* 2 split or cut 3 divided or undecided, as in preference: *torn between two lovers*
tornado ⊕ *n, pl* **-dos** *or* **-does** a rapidly whirling column of air, usually characterized by a dark funnel-shaped cloud causing damage along its path
WORD ORIGIN Spanish *tronada* thunderstorm
torpedo *n, pl* **-does** 1 a cylindrical self-propelled weapon carrying explosives that is launched from aircraft, ships, or submarines and follows an underwater path to hit its target ▹*vb* **-doing, -doed** 2 to attack or hit (a ship) with one or a number of torpedoes 3 to destroy or wreck: *the Prime Minister warned his party against torpedoing the bill*
WORD ORIGIN Latin: crampfish (whose electric discharges can cause numbness)
torpedo boat *n* (formerly) a small high-speed warship for torpedo attacks
torpid *adj* 1 sluggish or dull: *he has a rather torpid intellect* 2 (of a hibernating animal) dormant
WORD ORIGIN Latin *torpere* to be numb
torpor *n* drowsiness and apathy
torque (tork) *n* 1 a force that causes rotation around a central point such as an axle 2 an ancient Celtic necklace or armband made of twisted metal
WORD ORIGIN Latin *torques* necklace + *torquere* to twist
torr *n, pl* **torr** a unit of pressure equal to one millimetre of mercury (133.3 newtons per square metre)
WORD ORIGIN after E. *Torricelli*, physicist
torrent *n* 1 a fast or violent stream, esp. of water 2 a rapid flow of questions, abuse, etc.
WORD ORIGIN Latin *torrens*
torrential *adj* (of rain) very heavy
torrid *adj* 1 (of weather) so hot and dry as to parch or scorch 2 (of land) arid or parched 3 highly charged emotionally: *a torrid affair*
WORD ORIGIN Latin *torrere* to scorch
torsion *n* the twisting of a part by equal forces being applied at both ends but in opposite directions **torsional** *adj*
WORD ORIGIN Latin *torquere* to twist
torso *n, pl* **-sos** 1 the trunk of the human body 2 a statue of a nude human trunk, esp. without the head or limbs
WORD ORIGIN Italian: stalk, stump
tort *n law* a civil wrong or injury, for which an action for damages may be brought
WORD ORIGIN Latin *torquere* to twist
Tortelier *n* **Paul.** 1914–90, French cellist and composer
tortilla *n Mexican cookery* a kind of thin pancake made from corn meal
WORD ORIGIN Spanish: little cake
tortoise *n* a land reptile with a heavy dome-shaped shell into which it can withdraw its head and legs
WORD ORIGIN Medieval Latin *tortuca*
tortoiseshell *n* 1 the horny yellow-and-brown mottled shell of a sea turtle, used for making ornaments and jewellery 2 a domestic cat with black, cream, and brownish markings 3 a butterfly which has orange-brown wings with black markings ▹*adj* 4 made of tortoiseshell
tortuous *adj* 1 twisted or winding: *a tortuous route* 2 devious or cunning: *months of tortuous negotiations*
torture ⊕ *vb* **-turing, -tured** 1 to cause (someone) extreme physical pain, esp. to extract information,

t

THESAURUS

the-minute, newsworthy
topple *vb* **1a = fall over**, fall, collapse, tumble, overturn, capsize, totter, tip over, keel over, overbalance, fall headlong **1b = knock over**, upset, knock down, tip over **2 = overthrow**, overturn, bring down, oust, unseat, bring low
torment *vb* **1 = torture**, pain, distress, afflict, rack, harrow, crucify, agonize, excruciate OPPOSITE: comfort **2 = tease**, annoy, worry, trouble, bother, provoke, devil (*informal*), harry, plague, irritate, hound, harass, hassle (*informal*), aggravate (*informal*), persecute, pester, vex, bedevil, chivvy, give someone grief (*Brit & S African*), lead someone a merry dance (*Brit informal*) ▹*n* **3 = suffering**, distress, misery, pain, hell, torture, agony, anguish OPPOSITE: bliss
torn *adj* **2 = cut**, split, rent, ripped, ragged, slit, lacerated **3 = undecided**, divided, uncertain, split, unsure, wavering, vacillating, in two minds (*informal*), irresolute
tornado *n* **= whirlwind**, storm, hurricane, gale, cyclone, typhoon, tempest, squall, twister (*US informal*), windstorm
torture *vb* **1 = torment**, abuse, persecute, afflict, martyr, scourge,

DICTIONARY

etc.: *suspects were regularly tortured and murdered by the secret police* **2** to cause (someone) mental anguish ▷ *n* **3** physical or mental anguish **4** the practice of torturing a person **5** something which causes great mental distress: *she was going through the torture of a collapsing marriage* **tortured** *adj* **torturer** *n* **torturous** *adj*
WORD ORIGIN Latin *torquere* to twist

Torvill and Dean *n* two British ice dancers, **Jayne Torvill,** born 1957, and **Christopher Dean,** born 1958. They won the world championships in 1981–84, the European championships in 1981–82, 1984, and 1994, and the gold medal in the 1984 Olympic Games

Tory *n, pl* **-ries 1** a member or supporter of the Conservative Party in Great Britain or Canada **2** *history* a member of the English political party that supported the Church and Crown and traditional political structures and opposed the Whigs ▷ *adj* **3** of or relating to a Tory or Tories **Toryism** *n*
WORD ORIGIN Irish *tōraidhe* outlaw

tosa (toe-za) *n* a large reddish dog, originally bred for fighting
WORD ORIGIN after a province on the Japanese island of Shikoku

Toscanini *n* **Arturo.** 1867–1957, Italian conductor; musical director of La Scala, Milan, and of the NBC symphony orchestra (1937–57) in New York

toss ❶ *vb* **1** to throw (something) lightly **2** to fling or be flung about, esp. in a violent way: *the salty sea breeze tossing the branches of the palms* **3** to coat (food) with a dressing by gentle stirring or mixing: *her technique for tossing Caesar salad* **4** (of a horse) to throw (its rider) **5** to move (one's head) suddenly backwards, as in impatience **6** to throw up (a coin) to decide between alternatives by guessing which side will land uppermost **7 toss and turn** to be restless when trying to sleep ▷ *n* **8** the act or an instance of tossing **9** the act of deciding between alternatives by throwing up a coin and guessing which side will land uppermost: *Essex won the toss and decided to bat first* **10 argue the toss** to waste time and energy arguing about an unimportant point **11 not give a toss** *informal* not to care at all
WORD ORIGIN Scandinavian

toss off *vb* **1** to do or produce (something) quickly and easily: *the tales my sister tossed off so lightly over the dusting* **2** to finish (a drink) in one swallow

toss up *vb* **1** to spin (a coin) in the air in order to decide between alternatives by guessing which side will land uppermost ▷ *n* **toss-up 2** an instance of tossing up a coin **3** *informal* an even chance or risk: *if it's a toss-up for a top position, he gives it to the woman*

Tostig *n* died 1066, earl of Northumbria (1055–65), brother of King Harold II. He joined the Norwegian forces that invaded England in 1066 and died at Stamford Bridge

tot ❶ *n* **1** a very young child **2** a small drink of spirits
WORD ORIGIN origin unknown

total ❶ *n* **1** the whole, esp. regarded as the sum of a number of parts **2 in total** overall: *the company employs over 700 people in total* ▷ *adj* **3** complete: *a total ban on alcohol* **4** being or related to a total: *the total number of deaths* ▷ *vb* **-talling, -talled** *or US* **-taling, -taled 5** to amount to: *the firm's losses totalled more than $2 billion* **6** to add up: *purchases are totalled with a pencil and a notepad* **totally** *adv*
WORD ORIGIN Latin *totus* all

totalitarian *adj* **1** of a political system in which there is only one party, which allows no opposition and attempts to control everything: *a totalitarian state* ▷ *n* **2** a person who is in favour of totalitarian policies **totalitarianism** *n*

totality *n, pl* **-ties 1** the whole amount **2** the state of being total

totalizator, totalizer *or* **totalisator, totaliser** *n* a machine to operate a system of betting on a racecourse in which money is paid out to the winners in proportion to their stakes

tote[1] *vb* **toting, toted** *informal* **1** to carry or wear (a gun) **2** to haul or carry
WORD ORIGIN origin unknown

tote[2] *n* **the tote** *trademark* ▸ short for **totalizator**

tote bag *n* a large handbag or shopping bag

totem *n* **1** (esp. among Native Americans) an object or animal symbolizing a clan or family **2** a representation of such an object **totemic** *adj* **totemism** *n*
WORD ORIGIN from a Native American language

totem pole *n* a pole carved or painted with totemic figures set up by certain North American Indians as a tribal symbol

totter *vb* **1** to move in an unsteady manner **2** to sway or shake as if about to fall **3** to be failing, unstable, or precarious: *the world was tottering on the edge of war*
WORD ORIGIN origin unknown

tot up *vb* **totting, totted** to add (numbers) together: *I'll just tot up what you owe me*
WORD ORIGIN from *total*

toucan *n* a tropical American fruit-eating bird with a large brightly coloured bill
WORD ORIGIN Portuguese *tucano*

touch ❶ *vb* **1** to cause or permit a part of the body to come into contact with (someone or something): *the baking tin is too hot to touch* **2** to tap, feel, or strike (someone or something): *he touched me on the shoulder* **3** to come or bring (something) into contact with

THESAURUS

molest, crucify, mistreat, ill-treat, maltreat, put on the rack
OPPOSITE: comfort
2 = distress, torment, worry, trouble, pain, rack, afflict, harrow, agonize, give someone grief *(Brit & S African)*, inflict anguish on ▷ *n* **3 = agony**, suffering, misery, anguish, hell, distress, torment, heartbreak
OPPOSITE: bliss
4 = ill-treatment, abuse, torment, persecution, martyrdom, maltreatment, harsh treatment

toss *vb* **1 = throw**, pitch, hurl, fling, project, launch, cast, shy, chuck *(informal)*, flip, propel, sling, lob *(informal)* **3 = shake**, turn, mix, stir, tumble, agitate, jiggle **7 = thrash (about)**, twitch, wriggle, squirm, writhe ▷ *n* **8 = throw**, cast, pitch, shy, fling, lob *(informal)*

tot *n* **1 = infant**, child, baby, toddler, mite, wean *(Scot)*, little one, sprog *(slang)*, munchkin *(informal, chiefly US)*, rug rat *(slang)*, littlie *(Austral informal)*, ankle-biter *(Austral slang)*, tacker *(Austral slang)* **2 = measure**, shot *(informal)*, finger, nip, slug, dram, snifter *(informal)*, toothful

total *n* **1 = sum**, mass, entirety, grand total, whole, amount, aggregate, totality, full amount, sum total
OPPOSITE: part
▷ *adj* **3 = complete**, absolute, utter, whole, perfect, entire, sheer, outright, all-out, thorough, unconditional, downright, undisputed, consummate, unqualified, out-and-out, undivided, overarching, unmitigated, thoroughgoing, arrant, deep-dyed *(usually derogatory)*
OPPOSITE: partial
▷ *vb* **5 = amount to**, make, come to, reach, equal, run to, number, add up to, correspond to, work out as, mount up to, tot up to **6 = add up**, work out, sum up, compute, reckon, tot up
OPPOSITE: subtract

touch *vb* **1 = come into contact**, meet, contact, border, brush, come together, graze, adjoin, converge, be in contact, abut, impinge upon **2 = feel**, handle, finger, stroke, brush, make contact with, graze, caress, fondle, lay a finger on, palpate **2, 3 = tap**, hit, strike, push, pat

(something else): *the plane's wheels touched the runway* **4** to move or disturb by handling: *we shouldn't touch anything before the police arrive* **5** to have an effect on: *millions of people's lives had been touched by the music of the Beatles* **6** to produce an emotional response in: *the painful truth of it touched her* **7** to eat or drink: *she hardly ever touched alcohol* **8** to compare to in quality or attainment; equal or match: *nothing can touch them for scope and detail* **9** *Brit, Austral & NZ slang* to ask (someone) for a loan or gift of money **10** to fondle in a sexual manner: *I wouldn't let him touch me unless I was in the mood* **11** to strike, harm, or molest: *I never touched him!* **12** **touch on** *or* **upon** to allude to briefly or in passing: *these two issues may be touched upon during the talks* ▹ *n* **13** the sense by which the texture and other qualities of objects can be experienced when they come in contact with a part of the body surface, esp. the tips of the fingers ▸ Related adjective: **tactile** **14** the feel or texture of an object as perceived by this sense: *she enjoyed the touch of the damp grass on her feet* **15** the act or an instance of something coming into contact with the body: *he remembered the touch of her hand* **16** a gentle push, tap, or caress: *the switch takes only the merest touch to operate* **17** a small amount; trace: *a touch of luxury* **18** a particular manner or style of doing something: *his songs always reveal his keen melodic touch* **19** a detail of some work: *final touches were now being put to the plans* **20** a slight attack: *a touch of dysentery* **21** (in sports such as football or rugby) the area outside the lines marking the side of the pitch: *he kicked the ball into touch* **22** the technique of fingering a keyboard instrument **23** **a touch** slightly or marginally: *it's nice, but a touch expensive* **24** **in touch** **a** regularly speaking to, writing to, or visiting someone **b** having up-to-date knowledge or understanding of a situation or trend **25** **lose touch** **a** to gradually stop speaking to, writing to, or visiting someone **b** to stop having up-to-date knowledge or understanding of a situation or trend **26** **out of touch** **a** no longer speaking to, writing to, or visiting someone **b** no longer having up-to-date knowledge or understanding of a situation or trend ▸ See also **touchdown, touch off, touch up**

WORD ORIGIN Old French *tochier*

touch and go ❶ *adj* risky or critical: *it was touch and go whether the mission would succeed*

touchdown *n* **1** the moment at which a landing aircraft or spacecraft comes into contact with the landing surface **2** *American football* a scoring move in which an attacking player takes the ball into the area behind his opponents' goal ▹ *vb* **touch down** **3** (of an aircraft or spacecraft) to land

touché (too-shay) *interj* **1** an acknowledgment that a remark or witty reply has been effective **2** an acknowledgment of a scoring hit in fencing

WORD ORIGIN French, literally: touched

touched *adj* **1** moved to sympathy or emotion: *I was touched by her understanding* **2** slightly mad: *she's a bit touched*

touching ❶ *adj* **1** arousing tender feelings ▹ *prep* **2** relating to or concerning: *she might talk about matters touching both of them*

touch judge *n* one of the two linesmen in rugby

touchline *n* either of the lines marking the side of the playing area in certain games, such as rugby

touch off *vb* to cause (a disturbance, violence, etc.) to begin: *the death of a teenager in police custody touched off a night of riots*

touchpaper *n* a fuse of dark blue paper on a firework

touchstone *n* a standard by which judgment is made: *this restaurant is the touchstone for genuine Italian cookery in Leeds*

touch-type *vb* **-typing, -typed** to type without looking at the keyboard **touch-typist** *n*

touch up *vb* to enhance, renovate, or falsify (a picture) by adding extra touches to it

touchwood *n* something, esp. dry wood, used as tinder

WORD ORIGIN *touch* (in the sense: to kindle)

touchy *adj* **touchier, touchiest** **1** easily upset or irritated: *he is a touchy and quick-tempered man* **2** requiring careful and tactful handling: *a touchy subject* **touchiness** *n*

touchy-feely *adj informal, sometimes offensive* sensitive and caring

tough ❶ *adj* **1** strong and difficult to break, cut, or tear: *this fabric is tough and water-resistant* **2** (of meat or other food) difficult to cut and chew; not tender **3** physically or mentally strong and able to cope with hardship: *a tough uncompromising woman, unwilling to take no for an answer* **4** rough or violent: *a tough and ruthless mercenary* **5** strict and firm: *the country's tough drugs laws* **6** difficult or troublesome to do or deal with: *a tough task* **7** **tough luck!** *informal* an expression of lack of sympathy for someone else's problems ▹ *n* **8** a rough, vicious, or violent person ▹ *vb* **9** **tough it out** *informal* to endure a difficult situation until it improves: *criticism of his performance has reinforced his desire to tough it out* **toughness** *n*

WORD ORIGIN Old English *tōh*

5 = affect, mark, involve, strike, get to *(informal)*, influence, inspire, impress, get through to, have an effect on, make an impression on **6 = move**, upset, stir, disturb, melt, soften, tug at someone's heartstrings *(often facetious)*, leave an impression on **7 = consume**, take, drink, eat, partake of **8 = match**, rival, equal, compare with, parallel, come up to, come near, be on a par with, be a match for, hold a candle to *(informal)*, be in the same league as **12 touch on** *or* **upon something** **= refer to**, cover, raise, deal with, mention, bring in, speak of, hint at, allude to, broach, make allusions to ▹ *n* **13 = feeling**, feel, handling, physical contact, palpation, tactility **16 = contact**, push, stroke, brush, press, tap, poke, nudge, prod, caress, fondling **17 = bit**, spot, trace, drop, taste, suggestion, hint, dash, suspicion, pinch, smack, small amount, tinge, whiff, jot, speck, smattering, intimation, tincture **18 = style**, approach, method, technique, way, manner, characteristic, trademark, handiwork

touch and go *adj* **= risky**, close, near, dangerous, critical, tricky, sticky *(informal)*, hazardous, hairy *(slang)*, precarious, perilous, nerve-racking, parlous

touching *adj* **1 = moving**, affecting, sad, stirring, tender, melting, pathetic, poignant, heartbreaking, emotive, pitiful, pitiable, piteous

tough *adj* **1 = resilient**, hard, resistant, durable, strong, firm, solid, stiff, rigid, rugged, sturdy, inflexible, cohesive, tenacious, leathery, hard-wearing, robust **OPPOSITE:** fragile **3a = strong**, determined, aggressive, high-powered, feisty *(informal, chiefly US & Canad)*, hard-nosed *(informal)*, self-confident, unyielding, hard as nails, two-fisted, self-assertive, badass *(slang, chiefly US)* **OPPOSITE:** weak **3b = hardy**, strong, seasoned, fit, strapping, hardened, vigorous, sturdy, stout, stalwart, resilient, brawny, hard as nails **4 = violent**, rough, vicious, ruthless, pugnacious, hard-bitten, ruffianly, two-fisted **5 = strict**, severe, stern, hard, firm, exacting, adamant, resolute, draconian, intractable, inflexible, merciless, unforgiving, unyielding, unbending **OPPOSITE:** lenient

DICTIONARY

toughen *vb* to make or become tough or tougher

toupee (too-pay) *n* a hairpiece worn by men to cover a bald place
WORD ORIGIN French *toupet* forelock

tour ⊕ *n* **1** an extended journey visiting places of interest along the route **2** a trip, by a band, theatre company, etc. to perform in several places **3** an overseas trip made by a cricket team, rugby team, etc. to play in several places **4** *mil* a period of service, esp. in one place: *the regiment has served several tours in Northern Ireland* ▹ *vb* **5** to make a tour of (a place)
WORD ORIGIN Old French: a turn

tour de force *n, pl* **tours de force** a masterly or brilliant stroke or achievement
WORD ORIGIN French, literally: feat of skill or strength

Touré *n* (**Ahmed**) **Sékou** 1922–84, president of the Republic of Guinea (1958–84)

tourism *n* tourist travel, esp. when regarded as an industry

tourist ⊕ *n* **1** a person who travels for pleasure, usually sightseeing and staying in hotels **2** a member of a sports team which is visiting a country to play a series of matches: *the tourists were bowled out for 135* **3** the lowest class of accommodation on a passenger ship ▹ *adj* **4** of or relating to tourists or tourism: *a popular tourist attraction* **5** of the lowest class of accommodation on a passenger ship or aircraft

touristy *adj informal, often disparaging* full of tourists or tourist attractions

tourmaline *n* a hard crystalline mineral used in jewellery and electrical equipment
WORD ORIGIN German *Turmalin*

tournament ⊕ *n* **1** a sporting competition in which contestants play a series of games to determine an overall winner **2** Also: **tourney** *medieval history* a contest in which mounted knights fought for a prize
WORD ORIGIN Old French *torneiement*

tournedos (tour-ned-doh) *n, pl* **-dos** (-doze) a thick round steak of beef
WORD ORIGIN French

Tourneur *n* **Cyril** ?1575–1626, English dramatist; author of *The Atheist's Tragedy* (1611) and, reputedly, of *The Revenger's Tragedy* (1607)

tourniquet (tour-nick-kay) *n med* a strip of cloth tied tightly round an arm or leg to stop bleeding from an artery
WORD ORIGIN French

tourtière (tour-tee-air) *n Canad* a type of meat pie

tousle (rhymes with **arousal**) *vb* **-sling, -sled** to make (hair or clothes) ruffled and untidy **tousled** *adj*
WORD ORIGIN Low German *tūsen* to shake

tout (rhymes with **shout**) *vb* **1** to seek (business, customers, etc.) or try to sell (goods), esp. in a persistent or direct manner: *he went from door to door touting for business* **2** to put forward or recommend (a person or thing) as a good or suitable example or candidate: *the plant was once touted as a showcase factory* ▹ *n* **3** a person who sells tickets for a heavily booked event at inflated prices
WORD ORIGIN Old English *tӯtan* to peep

tow[1] ⊕ *vb* **1** to pull or drag (a vehicle), esp. by means of a rope or cable ▹ *n* **2** the act or an instance of towing **3 in tow** *informal* in one's company or one's charge or under one's influence: *she had an older man in tow* **4 on tow** (of a vehicle) being towed
WORD ORIGIN Old English *togian*

tow[2] *n* fibres of hemp, flax, jute, etc. prepared for spinning
WORD ORIGIN Old English *tōw*

towards ⊕ *or US* **toward** *prep* **1** in the direction of: *towards the lake* **2** with regard to: *hostility towards the President* **3** as a contribution to: *the profits will go towards three projects* **4** just before: *towards evening*

towbar *n* a rigid metal bar attached to the back of a vehicle, from which a trailer or caravan can be towed

towel *n* **1** a piece of absorbent cloth or paper used for drying things **2 throw in the towel** ▸ see **throw in** (sense 3) ▹ *vb* **-elling, -elled** *or US* **-eling, -eled 3** to dry or wipe with a towel
WORD ORIGIN Old French *toaille*

towelling *or US* **toweling** *n* a soft, fairly thick fabric used to make towels and dressing gowns

tower ⊕ *n* **1** a tall, usually square or circular structure, sometimes part of a larger building and usually built for a specific purpose **2 tower of strength** a person who supports or comforts someone else at a time of difficulty ▹ *vb* **3 tower over** to be much taller than: *sheer walls of limestone towered over us*
WORD ORIGIN Latin *turris*

tower block *n Brit* a very tall building divided into flats or offices

towering *adj* **1** very tall **2** very impressive or important: *his towering presence on stage* **3** very intense: *in a towering rage*

towheaded *adj* having blonde or yellowish hair
WORD ORIGIN *tow* flax

town *n* **1** a large group of houses, shops, factories, etc. smaller than a city and larger than a village ▸ Related adjective: **urban 2** the nearest town or the chief town of an area: *people from town rarely went out to the farm* **3** the central area of a town where most of the shops and offices are: *we're going to a pub in town tonight* **4** the people of a town: *the town is split over the plans for a bypass* **5** built-up areas in general, as opposed to the countryside: *migration from the country to the town* **6 go to town** to make a supreme or unrestricted effort **7 on the town** visiting nightclubs, restaurants, etc.: *we'd a night on the town to celebrate her promotion*
WORD ORIGIN Old English *tūn* village

town clerk *n* (currently in Australia and in Britain until 1974) the chief administrative officer of a town

town crier *n* (formerly) a person employed to make public announcements in the streets

Townes *n* **Charles Hard** born 1915, US physicist, noted for his research in quantum electronics leading to the invention of the maser and the laser; shared the Nobel prize for physics in 1964

town hall *n* a large building in a town often containing the council offices and a hall for public meetings

town house *n* **1** a terraced house in an urban area, esp. an up-market one **2** a person's town residence as distinct from his or her country residence

townie *or* **townee** *n chiefly Brit informal, often disparaging* a resident in a town,

THESAURUS

6 = hard, difficult, exhausting, troublesome, uphill, strenuous, arduous, thorny, laborious, irksome ▹ *n* **8 = ruffian**, heavy *(slang)*, rough *(informal)*, bully, thug, hooligan, brute, rowdy, bravo, bully boy, bruiser *(informal)*, roughneck *(slang)*, tsotsi *(S African)*

tour *n* **1 = journey**, expedition, excursion, trip, progress, outing, jaunt, junket, peregrination ▹ *vb* **5a = travel round**, holiday in, travel through, journey round, trek round, go on a trip through **5b = visit**, explore, go round, inspect, walk round, drive round, sightsee

tourist *n* **1 = traveller**, journeyer, voyager, tripper, globetrotter, holiday-maker, sightseer, excursionist

tournament *n* **1 = competition**, meeting, match, event, series, contest

tow[1] *vb* **1 = drag**, draw, pull, trail, haul, tug, yank, hale, trawl, lug

towards *prep* **1 = in the direction of**, to, for, on the way to, on the road to, en route for **2 = regarding**, about, concerning, respecting, in relation to, with regard to, with respect to, apropos

tower *n* **1 = column**, pillar, turret, belfry, steeple, obelisk

DICTIONARY

esp. as distinct from country dwellers
town planning *n* the comprehensive planning of the physical and social development of a town
Townshend *n* **1 Charles,** 2nd Viscount, nicknamed *Turnip Townshend.* 1674–1738, English politician and agriculturist **2 Pete** born 1945, British rock guitarist, singer, and songwriter: member of the Who from 1964 and composer of much of their material
township *n* **1** a small town **2** (in South Africa) a planned urban settlement of black people or people of mixed racial descent **3** (in the US and Canada) a small unit of local government, often consisting of a town and the area surrounding it **4** (in Canada) a land-survey area, usually 36 square miles (93 square kilometres)
townsman *n, pl* **-men** an inhabitant of a town **townswoman** *fem n*
townspeople *or* **townsfolk** *pl n* the people who live in a town
towpath *n* a path beside a canal or river, formerly used by horses pulling barges
towrope *n* a rope or cable used for towing a vehicle or vessel
toxaemia *or US* **toxemia** (tox-seem-ya) *n* **1** a form of blood poisoning caused by toxins released by bacteria at a wound or other site of infection **2** a condition in pregnant women characterized by high blood pressure **toxaemic** *or US* **toxemic** *adj*
WORD ORIGIN Latin *toxicum* poison + *haima* blood
toxic ❶ *adj* **1** poisonous: *toxic fumes* **2** caused by poison: *toxic effects* **toxicity** *n*
WORD ORIGIN Greek *toxikon (pharmakon)* (poison) used on arrows
toxicology *n* the branch of science concerned with poisons and their effects **toxicological** *adj* **toxicologist** *n*
toxin *n* **1** any of various poisonous substances produced by microorganisms and causing certain diseases **2** any other poisonous substance of plant or animal origin
toy ❶ *n* **1** an object designed for children to play with, such as a doll or model car **2** an object that adults use for entertainment rather than for a serious purpose: *I do use my computer: it's not just a toy* ▷ *adj* **3** being an imitation or model of something for children to play with: *a toy aeroplane* **4** (of a dog) of a variety much smaller than is normal for that breed: *a toy poodle*
WORD ORIGIN origin unknown
toy boy *n* the much younger male lover of an older woman
Toynbee *n* **1 Arnold** 1852–83, British economist and social reformer, after whom **Toynbee Hall**, a residential settlement in East London, is named **2** his nephew, **Arnold Joseph**. 1889–1975, British historian. In his chief work, *A Study of History* (1934–61), he attempted to analyse the principles determining the rise and fall of civilizations
toy-toy *or* **toyi-toyi** *S African n* **1** a dance expressing defiance and protest ▷ *vb* **2** to dance in this way
WORD ORIGIN origin uncertain
toy with *vb* **1** to consider an idea without being serious about it or being able to decide about it: *I've been toying with the idea of setting up my own firm* **2** to keep moving (an object) about with one's fingers, esp. when thinking about something else: *Jessica sat toying with her glass*
trace ❶ *vb* **tracing, traced 1** to locate or work out (the cause or source of something): *he traced the trouble to a faulty connection* **2** to find (something or someone that was missing): *the police were unable to trace her missing husband* **3** to discover or describe the progress or development of (something): *throughout the 19th century we can trace the development of more complex machinery* **4** to copy (a design, map, etc.) by putting a piece of transparent paper over it and following the lines which show through the paper with a pencil **5** to make the outline of (a shape or pattern): *his index finger was tracing circles on the arm of the chair* ▷ *n* **6** a mark, footprint, or other sign that shows that a person, animal, or thing has been in a particular place: *the police could find no trace of the missing van* **7** an amount of something so small that it is barely noticeable: I *detected a trace of jealousy in her voice* **8** a remnant of something: *traces of an Iron-Age fort remain visible* **9** a pattern made on a screen or a piece of paper by a device that is measuring or detecting something: *a baffling radar trace* **traceable** *adj*
WORD ORIGIN French *tracier*
trace element *n* a chemical element that occurs in very small amounts in soil, water, etc. and is essential for healthy growth
tracer *n* **1** a projectile that can be observed when in flight by the burning of chemical substances in its base **2** *med* an element or other substance introduced into the body to study metabolic processes
tracer bullet *n* a round of small-arms ammunition containing a tracer
tracery *n, pl* **-eries 1** a pattern of interlacing lines, esp. one in a stained glass window **2** any fine lacy pattern resembling this
traces *pl n* **1** the two side straps that connect a horse's harness to the vehicle being pulled **2 kick over the traces** to escape or defy control
WORD ORIGIN Old French *trait*
trachea (track-kee-a) *n, pl* **-cheae** (-kee-ee) *anat, zool* the tube that carries inhaled air from the throat to the lungs
WORD ORIGIN Greek
tracheotomy (track-ee-ot-a-mee) *n, pl* **-mies** surgical incision into the trachea, as performed when the air passage has been blocked
WORD ORIGIN TRACHEA + Greek *tomē* a cutting
trachoma (track-oh-ma) *n* a chronic contagious disease of the eye characterized by inflammation of the inner surface of the lids and the formation of scar tissue
WORD ORIGIN Greek *trakhōma* roughness
tracing *n* **1** a copy of something, such as a map, made by tracing **2** a line traced by a recording instrument
track ❶ *n* **1** a rough road or path: *a farm track* **2** the mark or trail left by something that has passed by: *the fox didn't leave any tracks* **3** a rail or pair of parallel rails on which a vehicle, such as a train, runs **4** a course for running or racing on: *a running track* **5** a separate song or piece of music on a record, tape, or CD: *Dolphy switches back to bass clarinet for the final track* **6** a course of action, thought, etc.: *I don't think you're on the right track at all* **7** an endless band on the wheels of a tank, bulldozer, etc. to enable it to move across rough ground **8 keep**

t

THESAURUS

toxic *adj* **1, 2 = poisonous**, deadly, lethal, harmful, pernicious, noxious, septic, pestilential, baneful *(archaic)*
OPPOSITE: harmless
toy *n* **1 = plaything**, game, doll
trace *vb* **1 = search for**, follow, seek out, track, determine, pursue, unearth, ascertain, hunt down **2 = find**, track (down), discover, trail, detect, unearth, hunt down, ferret out, locate **3 = outline**, chart, sketch, draw, map out, depict, mark out, delineate **4 = copy**, map, draft, outline, sketch, reproduce, draw over *n* **6 = track**, trail, footstep, path, slot, footprint, spoor, footmark **7 = bit**, drop, touch, shadow, suggestion, hint, dash, suspicion, tinge, trifle, whiff, jot, tincture, iota **8 = remnant**, remains, sign, record, mark, evidence, indication, token, relic, vestige
track *n* **1 = path**, way, road, route, trail, pathway, footpath **3 = line**, rail, tramline ▷ *vb* **10 = follow**, pursue, chase, trace, tail *(informal)*, dog, shadow, trail, stalk, hunt down,

DICTIONARY

or **lose track of** to follow *or* fail to follow the course or progress of **9 off the beaten track** in an isolated location: *the village where she lives is a bit off the beaten track* ▷ *vb* **10** to follow the trail of (a person or animal) **11** to follow the flight path of (a satellite etc.) by picking up signals transmitted or reflected by it **12** *films* to follow (a moving object) while filming ▸ See also **tracks** > **tracker** *n*
WORD ORIGIN Old French *trac*

track down ❶ *vb* to find (someone or something) by tracking or pursuing

tracker dog *n* a dog specially trained to search for missing people

track event *n* a competition in athletics, such as sprinting, that takes place on a running track

track record *n informal* the past record of the accomplishments and failures of a person or organization

tracks *pl n* **1** marks, such as footprints, left by someone or something that has passed **2 in one's tracks** on the very spot where one is standing: *those words stopped her in her tracks* **3 make tracks** to leave or depart: *it was time to start making tracks*

track shoe *n* a light running shoe fitted with steel spikes for better grip

tracksuit *n* a warm loose-fitting suit worn by athletes etc. esp. during training

tract[1] ❶ *n* **1** a large area, esp. of land: *an extensive tract of moorland* **2** *anat* a system of organs or glands that has a particular function: *the urinary tract*
WORD ORIGIN Latin *tractus* a stretching out

tract[2] ❶ *n* a pamphlet, esp. a religious one
WORD ORIGIN Latin *tractatus*

tractable *adj formal* easy to control, manage, or deal with: *he could easily manage his tractable and worshipping younger brother* **tractability** *n*
WORD ORIGIN Latin *tractare* to manage

traction *n* **1** pulling, esp. by engine power: *the increased use of electric traction* **2** *med* the application of a steady pull on an injured limb using a system of weights and pulleys or splints: *he was in traction for weeks following the accident* **3** the grip that the wheels of a vehicle have on the ground: *four-wheel drive gives much better traction in wet or icy conditions*
WORD ORIGIN Latin *tractus* dragged

traction engine *n* a heavy steam-powered vehicle used, esp. formerly, for drawing heavy loads along roads or over rough ground

tractor *n* a motor vehicle with large rear wheels, used to pull heavy loads, esp. farm machinery
WORD ORIGIN Late Latin: one who pulls

trade ❶ *n* **1** the buying and selling of goods and services **2** a person's job, esp. a craft requiring skill: *he's a plumber by trade* **3** the people and practices of an industry, craft, or business **4** amount of custom or commercial dealings: *a brisk trade in second-hand weapons* **5** a specified market or business: *the wool trade* **6 trades** the trade winds ▷ *vb* **trading, traded 7** to buy and sell (goods) **8** to exchange: *he traded a job in New York for a life as a cowboy* **9** to engage in trade **10** to deal or do business (with) **tradable** *or* **tradeable** *adj* **trader** *n* **trading** *n*
WORD ORIGIN Low German: track, hence a regular business

trade-in *n* **1** a used article given in part payment for the purchase of a new article ▷ *vb* **trade in 2** to give (a used article) as part payment for a new article

trademark *n* **1 a** the name or other symbol used by a manufacturer to distinguish his or her products from those of competitors **b Registered Trademark** one that is officially registered and legally protected **2** any distinctive sign or mark of a person or thing: *the designer bars which have become the trademark of the city*

trade name *n* **1** the name used by a trade to refer to a product or range of products **2** the name under which a commercial enterprise operates in business

trade-off *n* an exchange, esp. as a compromise: *there is often a trade-off between manpower costs and computer costs*

trade on *vb* to exploit or take advantage of: *a demanding woman who traded on her poor health to get her own way*

Tradescant *n* **1 John** 1570–1638, English botanist and gardener to Charles I. He introduced many plants from overseas into Britain **2** his son, **John** 1608–62, English naturalist and gardener, who continued his father's work

tradescantia (trad-dess-**kan**-shee-a) *n* a widely cultivated plant with striped leaves
WORD ORIGIN after John *Tradescant*, botanist

trade secret *n* a secret formula, technique, or process known and used to advantage by only one manufacturer

tradesman *n, pl* **-men 1** a skilled worker, such as an electrician or painter **2** a shopkeeper
tradeswoman *fem n*

Trades Union Congress *n* (in Britain and South Africa) the major association of trade unions, which includes all the larger unions

trade union *or* **trades union** *n* a society of workers formed to protect and improve their working conditions, pay, etc. **trade unionism** *or* **trades unionism** *n* **trade unionist** *or* **trades unionist** *n*

trade wind *n* a wind blowing steadily towards the equator either from the northeast in the N hemisphere or the southeast in the S hemisphere

trading estate *n chiefly Brit* a large area in which a number of commercial or industrial firms are situated

tradition ❶ *n* **1** the handing down from generation to generation of customs, beliefs, etc. **2** the unwritten body of beliefs, customs, etc. handed down from generation to generation **3** a custom or practice of long standing **4 in the tradition of** having many features similar to those of a person or thing in the past: *a thriller writer in the tradition of Chandler*
WORD ORIGIN Latin *traditio* a handing down

traditional ❶ *adj* of, relating to, or being a tradition **traditionally** *adv*

traditionalist *n* a person who supports established customs or beliefs **traditionalism** *n*

traduce *vb* **-ducing, -duced** *formal* to speak badly of (someone)

THESAURUS

follow the trail of

track down *vb* **= find**, catch, capture, apprehend, discover, expose, trace, unearth, dig up, hunt down, sniff out, bring to light, ferret out, run to earth *or* ground

tract[1] *n* **1 = area**, lot, region, estate, district, stretch, quarter, territory, extent, zone, plot, expanse

tract[2] *n* **= treatise**, essay, leaflet, brochure, booklet, pamphlet, dissertation, monograph, homily, disquisition, tractate

trade *n* **1, 4 = commerce**, business, transactions, buying and selling, dealing, exchange, traffic, truck, barter **2, 5 = job**, employment, calling, business, line, skill, craft, profession, occupation, pursuit, line of work, métier, avocation ▷ *vb* **7, 10 = deal**, do business, buy and sell, exchange, traffic, truck, bargain, peddle, barter, transact, cut a deal, have dealings **8 = exchange**, switch, swap, barter **9 = operate**, run, deal, do business

tradition *n* **1, 2 = customs**, institution, ritual, folklore, lore, praxis, tikanga *(NZ)* **3 = established practice**, custom, convention, habit, ritual, unwritten law

traditional *adj* **= old-fashioned**, old, established, conventional, fixed, usual, transmitted, accustomed, customary, ancestral, long-established, unwritten, time-

DICTIONARY

traducement *n* **traducer** *n*
WORD ORIGIN Latin *traducere* to lead over, disgrace

traffic ❶ *n* **1** the vehicles travelling on roads **2** the movement of vehicles or people in a particular place or for a particular purpose: *air traffic* **3** trade, esp. of an illicit kind: *drug traffic* **4** the exchange of ideas between people or organizations: *a lively traffic in ideas* ▹ *vb* **-ficking, -ficked 5** to carry on trade or business, esp. of an illicit kind: *he confessed to trafficking in gold and ivory* **trafficker** *n*
WORD ORIGIN Old French *trafique*

traffic island *n* a raised area in the middle of a road designed as a guide for traffic flow and to provide a stopping place for pedestrians crossing

traffic jam *n* a number of vehicles so obstructed that they can scarcely move

traffic light *n* one of a set of coloured lights placed at a junction to control the flow of traffic

traffic warden *n Brit* a person employed to supervise road traffic and report traffic offences

tragedian (traj-**jee**-dee-an) *or fem* **tragedienne** (traj-jee-dee-**enn**) *n* **1** an actor who specializes in tragic roles **2** a writer of tragedy

tragedy ❶ *n, pl* **-dies 1** a shocking or sad event **2** a serious play, film, or opera in which the main character is destroyed by a combination of a personal failing and adverse circumstances
WORD ORIGIN Greek *tragōidia*

tragic ❶ *adj* **1** sad and distressing because it involves death or suffering: *she was blinded in a tragic accident* **2** of or like a tragedy: *a tragic hero* **3** sad or mournful: *a tragic melody* **tragically** *adv*

tragicomedy *n, pl* **-dies** a play or other written work having both comic and tragic elements **tragicomic** *adj*

Traherne *n* **Thomas**. 1637–74, English mystical prose writer and poet. His prose works include *Centuries of Meditations*, which was discovered in manuscript in 1896 and published in 1908

trail ❶ *n* **1** a rough path across open country or through a forest **2** a route along a series of roads or paths that has been specially planned to let people see or do particular things: *a nature trail through the woods* **3** a print, mark, or scent left by a person, animal, or object: *a trail of blood was found down three flights of stairs* **4** something that trails behind: *a vapour trail* **5** a sequence of results from an event: *a trail of mishaps* ▹ *vb* **6** to drag or stream along the ground or through the air behind someone or something: *part of her sari trailed behind her on the floor* **7** to lag behind (a person or thing): *Max had arrived as well, trailing behind the others* **8** to follow or hunt (an animal or person), usually secretly, by following the marks or tracks he, she, or it has made: *the police had trailed him the length and breadth of the country* **9** to be falling behind in a race, match or competition: *they trailed 2-1 at half-time* **10** to move wearily or slowly: *we spent the afternoon trailing round the shops*
WORD ORIGIN Old French *trailler* to tow

trail away *or* **off** *vb* to become fainter, quieter, or weaker: *his voice trailed away*

trailblazer *n* a pioneer in a particular field **trailblazing** *adj, n*

trailer *n* **1** a road vehicle, usually two-wheeled, towed by a motor vehicle and used for carrying goods, transporting boats, etc.: *ahead of us was a tractor, drawing a trailer laden with dung* **2** the rear section of an articulated lorry **3** an extract or series of extracts from a film, TV, or radio programme, used to advertise it **4** *US & Canad* ▸ same as **caravan** (sense 1)

trailer trash *n derogatory* poor people living in trailer parks in the US

trailing *adj* (of a plant) having a long stem which spreads over the ground or hangs loosely: *trailing ivy*

train ❶ *vb* **1** to instruct (someone) in a skill: *soldiers are trained to obey orders unquestioningly* **2** to learn the skills needed to do a particular job or activity: *she was training to be a computer programmer* **3** to do exercises and prepare for a specific purpose: *he was training for a marathon* **4** to focus on or aim at (something): *the warship kept its guns trained on the trawler* **5** to discipline (an animal) to obey commands or perform tricks **6** to tie or prune (a plant) so that it grows in a particular way: *he had trained the roses to grow up the wall* ▹ *n* **7** a line of railway coaches or wagons coupled together and drawn by a engine **8** a sequence or series: *following an earlier train of thought* **9** the long back section of a dress that trails along the floor **10 in its train** as a consequence: *economic mismanagement brought unemployment and inflation in its train* **11 in train** actually happening or being done: *the programme of reforms set in train by the new government* ▹ *adj* **12** of or by a train: *the long train journey North*
WORD ORIGIN Old French *trahiner*

trainbearer *n* an attendant who holds up the train of a dignitary's robe or bride's gown

trainee *n* **1** a person undergoing training ▹ *adj* **2** (of a person) undergoing training: *a trainee journalist*

trainer ❶ *n* **1** a person who coaches a person or team in a sport **2** a person who trains racehorses **3** an aircraft used for training pilots **4** *Brit* a flat-soled sports shoe of the style used by athletes when training

training *n* the process of bringing a

THESAURUS

honoured **OPPOSITE:** revolutionary

traffic *n* **1, 2 = transport**, movement, vehicles, transportation, freight, coming and going **3 = trade**, dealing, commerce, buying and selling, business, exchange, truck, dealings, peddling, barter, doings ▹ *vb* **5** *(often with* **in***)* **= trade**, market, deal, exchange, truck, bargain, do business, buy and sell, peddle, barter, cut a deal, have dealings, have transactions

tragedy *n* **1 = disaster**, catastrophe, misfortune, adversity, calamity, affliction, whammy *(informal, chiefly US)*, bummer *(slang)*, grievous blow **OPPOSITE:** fortune

tragic *adj* **1 = distressing**, shocking, sad, awful, appalling, fatal, deadly, unfortunate, disastrous, dreadful, dire, catastrophic, grievous, woeful, lamentable, ruinous, calamitous, wretched, ill-starred, ill-fated **OPPOSITE:** fortunate **3 = sad**, miserable, dismal, pathetic, heartbreaking, anguished, mournful, heart-rending, sorrowful, doleful, pitiable **OPPOSITE:** happy

trail *n* **1 = path**, track, route, way, course, road, pathway, footpath, beaten track **3 = tracks**, path, mark, marks, wake, trace, scent, footsteps, footprints, spoor **4 = wake**, stream, tail, slipstream ▹ *vb* **6 = drag**, draw, pull, sweep, stream, haul, tow, dangle, droop **7, 10 = lag**, follow, drift, wander, linger, trudge, fall behind, plod, meander, amble, loiter, straggle, traipse *(informal)*, dawdle, hang back, tag along *(informal)*, bring up the rear, drag yourself **8 = follow**, track, chase, pursue, dog, hunt, shadow, trace, tail *(informal)*, hound, stalk, keep an eye on, keep tabs on *(informal)*, run to ground

train *vb* **1 = instruct**, school, prepare, improve, coach, teach, guide, discipline, rear, educate, drill, tutor, rehearse **3 = exercise**, prepare, work out, practise, do exercise, get into shape **4 = aim**, point, level, position, direct, focus, sight, line up, turn on, fix on, zero in, bring to bear ▹ *n* **8 = sequence**, series, chain, string, set, course, order, cycle, trail, succession, progression, concatenation

trainer *n* **1 = coach**, manager, guide, adviser, tutor, instructor, counsellor, guru, handler

t

DICTIONARY

person to an agreed standard of proficiency by practice and instruction

training shoe *n* ▸ same as **trainer** (sense 4)

train spotter *n Brit* **1** a person who collects the numbers of railway locomotives **2** *informal* a person who is obsessed with trivial details, esp. of a subject generally considered uninteresting

traipse *informal vb* **traipsing, traipsed** **1** to walk heavily or tiredly ▹*n* **2** a long or tiring walk
WORD ORIGIN origin unknown

trait ⊕ *n* a characteristic feature or quality of a person or thing
WORD ORIGIN French

traitor ⊕ *n* a person who betrays friends, country, a cause, etc. **traitorous** *adj* **traitress** *fem n*
WORD ORIGIN Latin *tradere* to hand over

trajectory *n, pl* **-ries** the path described by an object moving in air or space, esp. the curved path of a projectile
WORD ORIGIN Latin *trajectus* cast over

Trakl *n* **Georg** 1887–1914, Austrian poet, noted for his expressionist style: died of a drug overdose while serving as a medical officer in World War I

tram *n* an electrically driven public transport vehicle that runs on rails laid into the road and takes its power from an overhead cable
WORD ORIGIN probably from Low German *traam* beam

tramlines *pl n* **1** the tracks on which a tram runs **2** the outer markings along the sides of a tennis or badminton court

trammel *vb* **-elling, -elled** *or US* **-eling, -eled** **1** to hinder or restrict: *trammelled by family responsibilities* ▹*n* **2 trammels** things that hinder or restrict someone: *the trammels of social respectability*
WORD ORIGIN Old French *tramail* three-mesh net

tramp ⊕ *vb* **1** to walk long and far; hike **2** to walk heavily or firmly across or through (a place): *she tramped slowly up the beach* ▹*n* **3** a homeless person who travels about on foot, living by begging or doing casual work **4** a long hard walk; hike: *we went for a long tramp over the downs* **5** the sound of heavy regular footsteps: *we could hear the tramp of the marching soldiers* **6** a small cargo ship that does not run on a regular schedule **7** *US, Canad, Austral & NZ slang* a promiscuous woman
WORD ORIGIN probably from Middle Low German *trampen*

tramping *n NZ* the leisure activity of walking in the bush **tramper** *n*

trample ⊕ *vb* **-pling, -pled** **1** Also: **trample on** to tread on and crush: *three children were trampled to death when the crowd panicked and ran* **2 trample on** to treat (a person or his or her rights or feelings) with disregard or contempt
WORD ORIGIN from *tramp*

trampoline *n* **1** a tough canvas sheet suspended by springs or cords from a frame, which acrobats, gymnasts, etc. bounce on ▹*vb* **-lining, -lined** **2** to exercise on a trampoline
WORD ORIGIN Italian *trampolino*

trance ⊕ *n* **1** a hypnotic state resembling sleep in which a person is unable to move or act of his or her own will **2** a dazed or stunned state
WORD ORIGIN Latin *transire* to go over

tranche (**trahnsh**) *n* an instalment or portion, esp. of a loan or share issue: *the new shares will be offered in four tranches around the world*

trannie *or* **tranny** *n, pl* **-nies** *informal chiefly Brit* a transistor radio

tranquil *adj* calm, peaceful, or quiet **tranquilly** *adv*
WORD ORIGIN Latin *tranquillus*

tranquillity *or US sometimes* **tranquility** *n* a state of calmness or peace

tranquillize, -lise *or US* **tranquilize** *vb* **-lizing, -lized** *or* **-lising, -lised** **1** to make or become calm or calmer **2** to give (someone) a drug to make them calm or calmer **tranquillization, -lisation** *or US* **tranquilization** *n* **tranquillizing, -lising** *or US* **tranquilizing** *adj*

tranquillizer, -liser *or US* **tranquilizer** *n* a drug that calms someone suffering from anxiety, tension, etc.

trans. **1** transitive **2** translated

trans- *prefix* **1** across, beyond, crossing, or on the other side of: *transnational* **2** changing thoroughly: *transliterate*
WORD ORIGIN Latin

transact *vb* to do, conduct, or negotiate (a business deal)
WORD ORIGIN Latin *transigere* to drive through

transaction ⊕ *n* **1** something that is transacted, esp. a business deal **2 transactions** the records of the proceedings of a society etc.: *an article on land use in the Niagara area taken from the 'Transactions of the Royal Canadian Institute'*

transalpine *adj* beyond the Alps, esp. as viewed from Italy

transatlantic *adj* **1** on or from the other side of the Atlantic **2** crossing the Atlantic

transceiver *n* a device which transmits and receives radio or electronic signals
WORD ORIGIN *trans(mitter)* + *(re)ceiver*

transcend ⊕ *vb* **1** to go above or beyond what is expected or normal: *a vital party issue that transcends traditional party loyalties* **2** to overcome or be superior to: *to transcend all difficulties*
WORD ORIGIN Latin *transcendere* to climb over

transcendent *adj* **1** above or beyond what is expected or normal **2** *theol* (of God) having existence outside the created world **transcendence** *n*

transcendental *adj* **1** above or beyond what is expected or normal **2** *philosophy* based on intuition or innate belief rather than experience **3** supernatural or mystical **transcendentally** *adv*

transcendentalism *n* any system of philosophy that seeks to discover the nature of reality by examining the processes of thought rather than the things thought about, or that emphasizes intuition as a means to knowledge **transcendentalist** *n, adj*

Transcendental Meditation *n* a technique (trademarked in the US), based on Hindu traditions, for relaxing and refreshing the mind and body through the silent repetition of a special formula of words

transcribe *vb* **-scribing, -scribed** **1** to write, type, or print out (a text) fully

t

THESAURUS

trait *n* = **characteristic**, feature, quality, attribute, quirk, peculiarity, mannerism, idiosyncrasy, lineament

traitor *n* = **betrayer**, deserter, turncoat, deceiver, informer, renegade, defector, Judas, double-crosser *(informal)*, quisling, apostate, miscreant, fifth columnist, snake in the grass *(informal)*, back-stabber, fizgig *(Austral slang)*
OPPOSITE: loyalist

tramp *vb* **1** = **hike**, walk, trek, roam, march, range, ramble, slog, rove, yomp, footslog **1, 2** = **trudge**, march, stamp, stump, toil, plod, traipse *(informal)*, walk heavily ▹*n* **3** = **vagrant**, bum *(informal)*, derelict, drifter, down-and-out, hobo *(chiefly US)*, vagabond, bag lady *(chiefly US)*, dosser *(Brit slang)*, derro *(Austral slang)* **4** = **hike**, march, trek, ramble, slog **5** = **tread**, stamp, footstep, footfall

trample *vb* **1** *(often with* **on**, **upon**, *or* **over**) = **stamp**, crush, squash, tread, flatten, run over, walk over

trance *n* **1, 2** = **daze**, dream, spell, ecstasy, muse, abstraction, rapture, reverie, stupor, unconsciousness, hypnotic state

transaction *n* **1** = **deal**, matter, affair, negotiation, business, action, event, proceeding, enterprise, bargain, coup, undertaking, deed, occurrence

transcend *vb* **1, 2** = **surpass**, exceed, go beyond, rise above, leave behind, eclipse, excel, outstrip, outdo,

DICTIONARY

from a speech or notes **2** to make an electrical recording of (a programme or speech) for a later broadcast **3** *music* to rewrite (a piece of music) for an instrument other than that originally intended **transcriber** *n*
WORD ORIGIN Latin *transcribere*

transcript ❶ *n* **1** a written, typed, or printed copy made by transcribing **2** *chiefly US & Canad* an official record of a student's school progress

transcription *n* **1** the act of transcribing **2** something transcribed

transducer *n* any device, such as a microphone or electric motor, that converts one form of energy into another
WORD ORIGIN Latin *transducere* to lead across

transect *n biol* a sample strip of land used to monitor plant distribution and animal populations within a given area

transept *n* either of the two shorter wings of a cross-shaped church
WORD ORIGIN Latin *trans-* across + *saeptum* enclosure

transfer ❶ *vb* **-ferring, -ferred 1** to change or move from one thing, person, place, etc. to another: *he was transferred from prison to hospital* **2** to move (money or property) from the control of one person or organization to that of another: *the money has been transferred into your account* **3** (of a football club) to sell or release (a player) to another club: *he was transferred to Juventus for a world record fee* **4** to move (a drawing or design) from one surface to another ▷ *n* **5** the act, process, or system of transferring, or the state of being transferred **6** a person or thing that transfers or is transferred **7** a design or drawing that is transferred from one surface to another **8** the moving of (money or property) from the control of one person or organization to that of another **transferable** *or* **transferrable** *adj* **transference** *n*
WORD ORIGIN Latin *trans* across + *ferre* to carry

transfer station *n NZ* a depot where rubbish is sorted for recycling

transfiguration *n* a transfiguring or being transfigured

Transfiguration *n* **1** *new testament* the change in the appearance of Christ on the mountain **2** the Church festival held in commemoration of this on August 6

transfigure *vb* **-uring, -ured 1** to change or cause to change in appearance **2** to become or cause to become more exalted
WORD ORIGIN Latin *trans-* beyond + *figura* appearance

transfix *vb* **-fixing, -fixed** *or* **-fixt 1** to make (someone) motionless, esp. with horror or shock: *they stood transfixed and revolted by what they saw* **2** to pierce (a person or animal) through with a pointed object: *the Pharaoh is shown transfixing enemies with arrows from a moving chariot*
WORD ORIGIN Latin *transfigere* to pierce through

transform ❶ *vb* **1** to change completely in form or function: *the last forty years have seen the country transformed from a peasant economy to a major industrial power* **2** to change so as to make better or more attractive: *most religions claim to be able to transform people's lives* **3** to convert (one form of energy) to another **4** *maths* to change the form of (an equation, expression, etc.) without changing its value **5** to change (an alternating current or voltage) using a transformer
WORD ORIGIN Latin *transformare*

transformation ❶ *n* **1** a change or alteration, esp. a radical one **2** the act of transforming or the state of being transformed **3** *S African* a political slogan for demographic change in the power struggle

transformer *n* a device that transfers an alternating current from one circuit to one or more other circuits, usually with a change of voltage

transfuse *vb* **-fusing, -fused 1** to inject (blood or other fluid) into a blood vessel **2** *literary* to transmit or instil
WORD ORIGIN Latin *transfundere* to pour out

transfusion *n* **1** the injection of blood, blood plasma, etc. into the blood vessels of a patient **2** the act of transferring something: *a transfusion of new funds*

transgenic *adj* (of an animal or plant) containing genetic material artificially transferred from another species

transgress *vb formal* **1** to break (a law or rule) **2** to overstep (a limit): *he had never before been known to transgress the very slowest of walks* **transgression** *n* **transgressor** *n*
WORD ORIGIN Latin *trans* beyond + *gradi* to step

transient *adj* **1** lasting for a short time only: *she had a number of transient relationships with fellow students* **2** (of a person) not remaining in a place for a long time: *the transient population of the inner city* ▷ *n* **3** a transient person or thing **transience** *n*
WORD ORIGIN Latin *transiens* going over

transistor *n* **1** a semiconductor device used to amplify and control electric currents **2** *informal* a small portable radio containing transistors
WORD ORIGIN *transfer* + *resistor*

transistorized *or* **-ised** *adj* (of an electronic device) using transistors

transit ❶ *n* **1** the moving or carrying of goods or people from one place to another **2** a route or means of transport: *transit by road* **3** *astron* the apparent passage of a celestial body across the meridian **4 in transit** while travelling or being taken from one place to another: *in transit the fruit can be damaged* ▷ *adj* **5** indicating a place or building where people wait or goods are kept between different stages of a journey: *a transit lounge for passengers who are changing planes*
WORD ORIGIN Latin *transitus* a going over

transit camp *n* a camp in which refugees, soldiers, etc. live temporarily

transition ❶ *n* **1** the process of changing from one state or stage to another: *the transition from dictatorship to democracy* **2** *music* a movement from one key to another **transitional** *adj*

t

THESAURUS

outshine, overstep, go above, leave in the shade *(informal)*, outrival, outvie

transcript *n* **1 = copy**, record, note, summary, notes, version, carbon, log, translation, manuscript, reproduction, duplicate, transcription, carbon copy, transliteration, written version

transfer *vb* **1 = move**, carry, remove, transport, shift, transplant, displace, relocate, transpose, change ▷ *n* **5 = transference**, move, removal, handover, change, shift, transmission, translation, displacement, relocation, transposition

transform *vb* **1 = change**, convert, alter, translate, reconstruct, metamorphose, transmute, renew, transmogrify *(humorous)* **2 = make over**, overhaul, revamp, remake, renovate, remodel, revolutionize, redo, transfigure, restyle

transformation *n* **1, 2a = change**, conversion, alteration, metamorphosis, transmutation, renewal, transmogrification *(humorous)* **1, 2b = revolution**, radical change, sea change, revolutionary change, transfiguration

transit *n* **1 = movement**, transfer, transport, passage, travel, crossing, motion, transportation, carriage, shipment, traverse, conveyance, portage

transition *n* **1 = change**, passing, development, shift, passage, conversion, evolution, transit, upheaval, alteration, progression, flux, metamorphosis, changeover, transmutation, metastasis

DICTIONARY

WORD ORIGIN Latin *transitio* a going over

transition element *or* **metal** *n chem* any element belonging to one of three series of elements with atomic numbers between 21 and 30, 39 and 48, and 57 and 80 (**transition series**). They tend to have more than one valency and to form complexes

transitive *adj grammar* denoting a verb that requires a direct object: *'to find' is a transitive verb*

transitory *adj* lasting only for a short time

translate ⓣ *vb* **-lating, -lated 1 a** to change (something spoken or written in one language) into another **b** to be capable of being changed from one language into another: *puns do not translate well* **2** to express (something) in a different way, for instance by using a different measurement system or less technical language: *the temperature is 30° Celsius, or if we translate into Fahrenheit, 86°* **3** to transform or convert, for instance by putting an idea into practice: *cheap crops translate into lower feed prices* **4** to interpret the significance of (a gesture, action, etc.): *I gave him what I hoped would be translated as a thoughtful look* **5** to act as a translator: *I had to translate for a party of visiting Greeks* **translatable** *adj* **translator** *n*

WORD ORIGIN Latin *translatus* carried over

translation ⓣ *n* **1** a piece of writing or speech that has been translated into another language **2** the act of translating something **3** the expression of something in a different way or form: *the book's plot was radically altered during its translation to film* **4** *maths* a transformation in which the origin of a coordinate system is moved to another position so that each axis retains the same direction **translational** *adj*

transliterate *vb* **-ating, -ated** to write or spell (a word etc.) into corresponding letters of another alphabet **transliteration** *n*

WORD ORIGIN Latin *trans-* across + *littera* letter

translucent *adj* allowing light to pass through, but not transparent **translucency** *or* **translucence** *n*

WORD ORIGIN Latin *translucere* to shine through

transmigrate *vb* **-grating, -grated** (of a soul) to pass from one body into another at death **transmigration** *n*

transmission ⓣ *n* **1** the sending or passing of something, such as a message or disease from one place or person to another **2** something that is transmitted, esp. a radio or television broadcast **3** a system of shafts and gears that transmits power from the engine to the driving wheels of a motor vehicle

transmit ⓣ *vb* **-mitting, -mitted 1** to pass (something, such as a message or disease) from one place or person to another **2 a** to send out (signals) by means of radio waves **b** to broadcast (a radio or television programme) **3** to allow the passage of (particles, energy, etc.): *water transmits sound better than air* **4** to transfer (a force, motion, etc.) from one part of a mechanical system to another: *the chain of the bike transmits the motion of the pedals to the rear wheel* **transmittable** *adj*

WORD ORIGIN Latin *transmittere* to send across

transmitter *n* **1** a piece of equipment used for broadcasting radio or television programmes **2** a person or thing that transmits something

transmogrify *vb* **-fies, -fying, -fied** *jocular* to change or transform (someone or something) into a different shape or appearance, esp. a grotesque or bizarre one **transmogrification** *n*

WORD ORIGIN origin unknown

transmute *vb* **-muting, -muted** to change the form or nature of: *self-contempt is transmuted into hatred of others* **transmutation** *n*

WORD ORIGIN Latin *transmutare* to shift

transom *n* **1** a horizontal bar across a window **2** a horizontal bar that separates a door from a window over it

WORD ORIGIN Old French *traversin*

transparency *n, pl* **-cies 1** the state of being transparent **2** a positive photograph on transparent film, usually mounted in a frame or between glass plates, which can be viewed with the use of a slide projector

transparent ⓣ *adj* **1** able to be seen through; clear **2** easy to understand or recognize; obvious: *transparent honesty* **transparently** *adv*

WORD ORIGIN Latin *trans-* through + *parere* to appear

transpire *vb* **-spiring, -spired 1** to come to light; become known **2** *not standard* to happen or occur **3** *physiol* to give off (water or vapour) through the pores of the skin, etc. **4** (of plants) to lose (water vapour) through the stomata **transpiration** *n*

WORD ORIGIN Latin *trans-* through + *spirare* to breathe

transplant ⓣ *vb* **1** *surgery* to transfer (an organ or tissue) from one part of the body or from one person to another **2** to remove or transfer (esp. a plant) from one place to another ▷*n* **3** *surgery* **a** the procedure involved in transferring an organ or tissue **b** the organ or tissue transplanted **transplantation** *n*

transponder *n* a type of radio or radar transmitter-receiver that transmits signals automatically when it receives predetermined signals

WORD ORIGIN *transmitter + responder*

transport ⓣ *vb* **1** to carry or move (people or goods) from one place to another, esp. over some distance **2** *history* to exile (a criminal) to a penal colony **3** to have a strong emotional effect on: *transported by joy*

THESAURUS

translate *vb* **1a = render**, put, change, convert, interpret, decode, transcribe, construe, paraphrase, decipher, transliterate

translation *n* **1 = interpretation**, version, rendering, gloss, rendition, decoding, transcription, paraphrase, transliteration

transmission *n* **1a = transfer**, spread, spreading, communication, passing on, circulation, dispatch, relaying, mediation, imparting, diffusion, transference, dissemination, conveyance, channeling **1b = broadcasting**, showing, putting out, relaying, sending **2 = programme**, broadcast, show, production, telecast, podcast

transmit *vb* **1 = pass on**, carry, spread, communicate, take, send, forward, bear, transfer, transport, hand on, convey, dispatch, hand down, diffuse, remit, impart, disseminate **2a, 2b = broadcast**, put on the air, televise, relay, send, air, radio, send out, disseminate, beam out, podcast

transparent *adj* **1 = clear**, sheer, see-through, lucid, translucent, crystal clear, crystalline, limpid, lucent, diaphanous, gauzy, filmy, pellucid **OPPOSITE:** opaque **2 = obvious**, plain, apparent, visible, bold, patent, evident, distinct, explicit, easy, understandable, manifest, recognizable, unambiguous, undisguised, as plain as the nose on your face *(informal)*, perspicuous **OPPOSITE:** uncertain

transplant *vb* **1** *(surgery)* **= implant**, transfer, graft **2 = transfer**, take, bring, carry, remove, transport, shift, convey, fetch, displace, relocate, uproot

transport *vb* **1 = convey**, take, run, move, bring, send, carry, bear, remove, ship, transfer, deliver, conduct, shift, ferry, haul, fetch **2 = exile**, banish, deport, sentence to transportation **3 = enrapture**, move, delight, entrance, enchant, carry away, captivate, electrify, ravish, spellbind ▷*n* **4 = vehicle**, wheels *(informal)*, transportation, conveyance **4, 7 = transference**, carrying,

DICTIONARY

▷*n* **4** the business or system of transporting goods or people: *public transport* **5** *Brit* freight vehicles generally **6** a vehicle used to transport troops **7** a transporting or being transported **8** ecstasy or rapture: *transports of delight* **transportable** *adj*
WORD ORIGIN Latin *trans-* across + *portare* to carry

transportation *n* **1** a means or system of transporting **2** the act of transporting or the state of being transported **3** *history* deportation to a penal colony

transport café *n Brit* an inexpensive eating place on a main road, used mainly by long-distance lorry drivers

transporter *n* a large vehicle used for carrying cars from the factory to garages for sale

transpose *vb* **-posing, -posed 1** to change the order of (letters, words, or sentences) **2** *music* to play (notes, music, etc.) in a different key **3** *maths* to move (a term) from one side of an equation to the other with a corresponding reversal in sign: *transposing* 3 *in* $x-3=6$ *gives* $x=6+3$ **transposition** *n*
WORD ORIGIN Old French *transposer*

transsexual *or* **transexual** *n* **1** a person who believes that his or her true identity is of the opposite sex **2** a person who has had medical treatment to alter his or her sexual characteristics to those of the opposite sex

transship *vb* **-shipping, -shipped** to transfer or be transferred from one ship or vehicle to another **transshipment** *n*

transubstantiation *n Christianity* the doctrine that the bread and wine consecrated in Communion changes into the substance of Christ's body and blood
WORD ORIGIN Latin *trans-* over + *substantia* substance

transuranic (tranz-yoor-**ran**-ik) *adj chem* (of an element) having an atomic number greater than that of uranium

transverse *adj* crossing from side to side: *the transverse arches in the main hall of the college*
WORD ORIGIN Latin *transvertere* to turn across

transvestite *n* a person, esp. a man, who seeks sexual pleasure from wearing clothes of the opposite sex **transvestism** *n*
WORD ORIGIN Latin *trans-* across + *vestitus* clothed

trap ❶ *n* **1** a device or hole in which something, esp. an animal, is caught: *a fox trap* **2** a plan for tricking a person into being caught unawares **3** a situation from which it is difficult to escape: *caught in the poverty trap* **4** a bend in a pipe that contains standing water to prevent the passage of gases **5** a boxlike stall in which greyhounds are enclosed before the start of a race **6** a device that hurls clay pigeons into the air to be fired at **7** ▸see **trap door 8** a light two-wheeled carriage: *a pony and trap* **9** *Brit, Austral & NZ slang* the mouth: *shut your trap!* ▷*vb* **trapping, trapped 10** to catch (an animal) in a trap **11** to catch (someone) by a trick: *the police trapped the drug dealers by posing as potential customers* **12** to hold or confine in an unpleasant situation from which it is difficult to escape: *trapped in the rubble of collapsed buildings* ▸See also **trap out**
WORD ORIGIN Old English *træppe*

trap door *n* a hinged door in a ceiling, floor, or stage

trap-door spider *n* a spider that builds a silk-lined hole in the ground closed by a hinged door of earth and silk

trapeze *n* a horizontal bar suspended from two ropes, used by circus acrobats
WORD ORIGIN French

trapezium *n, pl* **-ziums** *or* **-zia 1** a quadrilateral having two parallel sides of unequal length **2** *chiefly US & Canad* a quadrilateral having neither pair of sides parallel **trapezial** *adj*
WORD ORIGIN Greek *trapeza* table

trapezoid (**trap**-piz-zoid) *n* **1** a quadrilateral having neither pair of sides parallel **2** *US & Canad* ▸same as **trapezium** (sense 1)
WORD ORIGIN Greek *trapeza* table

trap out *vb* **trapping, trapped** to dress or adorn
WORD ORIGIN Old French *drap* cloth

trapper *n* a person who traps animals, esp. for their furs or skins

trappings *pl n* **1** the accessories that symbolize a condition, office, etc.: *the trappings of power* **2** ceremonial harness for a horse or other animal
WORD ORIGIN probably from Old French *drap* cloth

Trappist *n* a member of an order of Christian monks who follow a rule of strict silence

trash ❶ *n* **1** foolish ideas or talk; nonsense **2** *US, Canad, NZ & S African* unwanted objects; rubbish **3** *chiefly US, Canad & NZ* a worthless person or group of people ▷*vb* **4** *slang* to attack or destroy maliciously: *we've never trashed a hotel room* **trashy** *adj*
WORD ORIGIN origin unknown

trattoria (trat-or-**ee**-a) *n* an Italian restaurant
WORD ORIGIN Italian

trauma ❶ (**traw**-ma) *n* **1** *psychol* an emotional shock that may have long-lasting effects **2** *pathol* any bodily injury or wound **traumatic** *adj* **traumatically** *adv* **traumatize** *or* **-ise** *vb*
WORD ORIGIN Greek: a wound

travail *n literary* painful or exceptionally hard work
WORD ORIGIN Old French *travaillier*

travel ❶ *vb* **-elling, -elled** *or US* **-eling, -eled 1** to go or move from one place to another **2** to go or journey through or across (an area, region,

THESAURUS

shipping, delivery, distribution, removal, transportation, carriage, shipment, freight, haulage, conveyance, freightage **8** *(often plural)* **= ecstasy**, delight, heaven, happiness, bliss, euphoria, rapture, enchantment, cloud nine *(informal)*, seventh heaven, ravishment
OPPOSITE: despondency

trap *n* **1 = snare**, net, booby trap, gin, toils *(old-fashioned)*, pitfall, noose, springe **2a = ambush**, set-up *(informal)*, device, lure, bait, honey trap, ambuscade *(old-fashioned)* **2b = trick**, set-up *(informal)*, deception, ploy, ruse, artifice, trickery, subterfuge, stratagem, wile, device ▷*vb* **10 = catch**, snare, ensnare, entrap, take, corner, bag, lay hold of, enmesh, lay a trap for, run to earth *or* ground **11a = trick**, fool, cheat, lure, seduce, deceive, dupe, beguile, gull, cajole, ensnare, hoodwink, wheedle, inveigle **11b = capture**, catch, arrest, seize, take, lift *(slang)*, secure, nail *(informal)*, collar *(informal)*, nab *(informal)*, apprehend, take prisoner, take into custody

trash *n* **1 = nonsense**, rubbish, garbage *(informal)*, rot, pants *(slang)*, crap *(slang)*, hot air *(informal)*, tosh *(slang, chiefly Brit)*, pap, bilge *(informal)*, drivel, twaddle, tripe *(informal)*, guff *(slang)*, moonshine, hogwash, malarkey, hokum *(slang, chiefly US & Canad)*, piffle *(informal)*, poppycock *(informal)*, inanity, balderdash, bosh *(informal)*, eyewash *(informal)*, kak *(S African taboo, slang)*, trumpery, tommyrot, foolish talk, horsefeathers *(US slang)*, bunkum *or* buncombe *(chiefly US)*, bizzo *(Austral slang)*, bull's wool *(Austral & NZ slang)*
OPPOSITE: sense
2 *(chiefly US & Canad)* **= litter**, refuse, waste, rubbish, sweepings, junk *(informal)*, garbage, dross, dregs, dreck *(slang, chiefly US)*, offscourings

trauma *n* **1 = shock**, suffering, worry, pain, stress, upset, strain, torture, distress, misery, disturbance, ordeal, anguish, upheaval, jolt **2** *(pathology)* **= injury**, damage, hurt, wound, agony

travel *vb* **1, 2 = go**, journey, proceed, make a journey, move, walk, cross, tour, progress, wander, trek, voyage,

DICTIONARY

etc.): *Margaret travelled widely when she was in New Zealand* **3** to go at a specified speed or for a specified distance: *the car was travelling at 30 mph* **4** to go from place to place as a salesman **5** (of perishable goods) to withstand a journey: *not all wines travel well* **6** (of light or sound) to be transmitted or carried from one place to another: *sound travels a long distance in these conditions* **7** (of a machine or part) to move in a fixed path **8** *informal* (of a vehicle) to move rapidly ▷*n* **9** the act or a means of travelling: *air travel has changed the way people live* **10** a tour or journey: *his travels took him to Dublin* **11** the distance moved by a mechanical part, such as the stroke of a piston
WORD ORIGIN Old French *travaillier* to travail

travel agency *n* an agency that arranges flights, hotel accommodation, etc. for tourists **travel agent** *n*

traveller ❶ *or US* **traveler** *n* **1** a person who travels, esp. habitually **2** a travelling salesman **3** a Gypsy

traveller's cheque *n* a cheque sold by a bank, travel agency, etc. which the buyer signs on purchase and can cash abroad by re-signing it

travelling salesman *n* a salesman who travels within an assigned area in order to sell goods or get orders for the company he or she represents

travelogue *or US* **travelog** *n* a film or lecture on travels and travelling

travel sickness *n* nausea or vomiting caused by riding in a car or other moving vehicle **travel-sick** *adj*

Traven *n* **B(en)**, original name *Albert Otto Max Feige*. ?1882–1969, US novelist, born in Germany and living in Mexico from 1920, who kept his identity secret. His novels, originally written in German, include *The Treasure of Sierra Madre* (1934)

Travers *n* **Ben(jamin)** 1886–1980, British dramatist, best known for such farces as *Rookery Nook* (1926), *Thark* (1927), and *Plunder* (1928)

traverse *vb* **-ersing, -ersed 1** to move over or back and forth over; cross: *he once traversed San Francisco harbour in a balloon* **2** to reach across **3** to walk, climb, or ski diagonally up or down a slope ▷*n* **4** something being or lying across, such as a crossbar **5** the act or an instance of traversing or crossing **6** a path or road across ▷*adj* **7** being or lying across **traversal** *n*
WORD ORIGIN Latin *transversus* turned across

travesty *n, pl* **-ties 1** a grotesque imitation or mockery: *a travesty of justice* ▷*vb* **-ties, -tying, -tied 2** to make or be a travesty of
WORD ORIGIN French *travesti* disguised

travois (trav-voy) *n, pl* **-vois** (-voyz) *Canad* a sled used for dragging logs
WORD ORIGIN Canadian French

trawl *n* **1** a large net, usually in the shape of a sock or bag, dragged at deep levels behind a fishing boat ▷*vb* **2** to fish using such a net
WORD ORIGIN Middle Dutch *traghelen* to drag

trawler *n* a ship used for trawling

tray *n* **1** a flat board of wood, plastic, or metal, usually with a rim, on which things can be carried **2** an open receptacle for office correspondence
WORD ORIGIN Old English *trieg*

TRC *n* (in South Africa) Truth and Reconciliation Commission: a commission which encourages people who committed human rights abuses or acts of terror during the apartheid era to reveal the truth about their crimes in return for immunity from prosecution

treacherous *adj* **1** disloyal and untrustworthy: *he was cruel, treacherous, and unscrupulous* **2** unreliable or dangerous, esp. because of sudden changes: *the tides here can be very treacherous* **treacherously** *adv*

treachery *n, pl* **-eries** the act or an instance of wilful betrayal
WORD ORIGIN Old French *trecherie*

treacle *n* a thick dark syrup obtained during the refining of sugar **treacly** *adj*
WORD ORIGIN Latin *theriaca* antidote to poison

tread ❶ *vb* **treading, trod; trodden** *or* **trod 1** to set one's foot down on or in something: *he trod on some dog's dirt* **2** to crush or squash by treading (on): *treading on a biscuit* **3** to walk along (a path or road) **4 tread carefully** *or* **warily** to proceed in a delicate or tactful manner **5 tread water** to stay afloat in an upright position by moving the legs in a walking motion ▷*n* **6** a way of walking or the sound of walking: *he walked, with a heavy tread, up the stairs* **7** the top surface of a step in a staircase **8** the pattern of grooves in the outer surface of a tyre that helps it grip the road **9** the part of a shoe that is generally in contact with the ground
WORD ORIGIN Old English *tredan*

treadle (tred-dl) *n* a lever operated by the foot to turn a wheel
WORD ORIGIN Old English *tredan* to tread

treadmill *n* **1** (formerly) an apparatus turned by the weight of men or animals climbing steps on a revolving cylinder or wheel **2** a dreary routine: *they are chained to the treadmill of a job* **3** an exercise machine that consists of a continuous moving belt on which to walk or jog

treason ❶ *n* **1** betrayal of one's sovereign or country, esp. by attempting to overthrow the government **2** any treachery or betrayal **treasonable** *adj* **treasonous** *adj*
WORD ORIGIN Latin *traditio* a handing over

treasure ❶ *n* **1** a collection of wealth, esp. in the form of money, precious metals, or gems **2** a valuable painting, ornament, or other object: *the museum has many art treasures* **3** *informal* a person who is highly valued: *she can turn her hand to anything, she's a perfect treasure* ▷*vb* **-uring, -ured 4** to cherish (someone or something)
WORD ORIGIN Greek *thēsauros*

treasure hunt *n* a game in which players act upon successive clues to find a hidden prize

treasurer *n* a person appointed to look after the funds of a society or other organization

treasure-trove *n law* any articles, such as coins or valuable objects found hidden and without any evidence of ownership
WORD ORIGIN Anglo-French *tresor trové* treasure found

treasury ❶ *n, pl* **-uries 1** a storage place for treasure **2** the revenues or

THESAURUS

roam, ramble, traverse, rove, take a trip, make your way, wend your way ▷*n* **10** *(usually plural)* **= journey**, wandering, expedition, globetrotting, walk, tour, touring, movement, trip, passage, voyage, excursion, ramble, peregrination

traveller *n* **1 = voyager**, tourist, passenger, journeyer, explorer, hiker, tripper, globetrotter, holiday-maker, wayfarer, excursionist

tread *vb* **1, 3 = step**, walk, march, pace, stamp, stride, hike, tramp, trudge, plod ▷*n* **6 = step**, walk, pace, stride, footstep, gait, footfall

treason *n* **1, 2 = disloyalty**, mutiny, treachery, subversion, disaffection, duplicity, sedition, perfidy, lese-majesty, traitorousness
OPPOSITE: loyalty

treasure *n* **1 = riches**, money, gold, fortune, wealth, valuables, jewels, funds, cash **3 = angel**, darling, find, star *(informal)*, prize, pearl, something else *(informal)*, jewel, gem, paragon, one in a million *(informal)*, one of a kind *(informal)*, nonpareil ▷*vb* **4 = prize**, value, worship, esteem, adore, cherish, revere, venerate, hold dear, love, idolize, set great store by, dote upon, place great value on

treasury *n* **1 = storehouse**, bank, store, vault, hoard, cache, repository funds of a government or organization

Treasury *n* (in various countries) the government department in charge of finance

treat ❶ *vb* **1** to deal with or regard in a certain manner: *her love for a man who treats her abominably* **2** to attempt to cure or lessen the symptoms of (an illness or injury or a person suffering from it): *the drug is prescribed to treat asthma* **3** to subject to a chemical or industrial process: *the wood should be treated with a preservative* **4** to provide (someone) with something as a treat: *I'll treat you to an ice cream* **5 treat of** to deal with (something) in writing or speaking: *this book treats of a most abstruse subject* ▷ *n* **6** a celebration, entertainment, gift, or meal given for or to someone and paid for by someone else **7** any delightful surprise or specially pleasant occasion **treatable** *adj*
WORD ORIGIN Old French *tretier*

treatise (treat-izz) *n* a formal piece of writing that deals systematically with a particular subject
WORD ORIGIN Anglo-French *tretiz*

treatment ❶ *n* **1** the medical or surgical care given to a patient **2** a way of handling a person or thing: *the party has had unfair treatment in the press*

treaty ❶ *n, pl* **-ties 1** a formal written agreement between two or more states, such as an alliance or trade arrangement: *the Treaty of Rome established the Common Market* **2** an agreement between two parties concerning the purchase of property
WORD ORIGIN Old French *traité*

treble *adj* **1** three times as much or as many **2** of or denoting a soprano voice or part or a high-pitched instrument **3** of the highest range of musical notes: *these loudspeakers give excellent treble reproduction* ▷ *n* **4** a soprano voice or part or a high-pitched instrument ▷ *vb* **-bling, -bled 5** to make or become three times as much or as many: *sales have trebled in three years* **trebly** *adv*
WORD ORIGIN Latin *triplus* threefold

treble chance *n Brit* a method of betting in football pools in which the chances of winning are related to the number of draws and the number of home and away wins forecast by the competitor

treble clef *n music* the clef that establishes G a fifth above middle C as being on the second line of the staff

tree *n* **1** any large woody perennial plant with a distinct trunk and usually having leaves and branches ▸ Related adjective: **arboreal 2** ▸ see **family tree, shoetree, saddletree 3 at the top of the tree** in the highest position of a profession **treeless** *adj*
WORD ORIGIN Old English *trēow*

Tree *n* Sir **Herbert Beerbohm**. 1853–1917, English actor and theatre manager; half-brother of Sir Max Beerbohm. He was noted for his lavish productions of Shakespeare

tree creeper *n* a small songbird of the N hemisphere that creeps up trees to feed on insects

tree diagram *n maths* a branching diagram showing the probability of various events

tree fern *n* any of numerous large tropical ferns with a trunklike stem

tree kangaroo *n* a tree-living kangaroo of New Guinea and N Australia

tree line *n* ▸ same as **timber line**

tree-lined *adj* (of a road) having trees on either side of it: *a pleasant tree-lined avenue in Bristol*

tree surgery *n* the treatment of damaged trees by filling cavities, applying braces, etc. **tree surgeon** *n*

tree tomato *n* ▸ same as **tamarillo**

treetop *n* the highest part of a tree, where the leaves and branches are: *monkeys swung through the treetops*

trefoil (tref-foil) *n* **1** a plant, such as clover, with leaves divided into three smaller leaves **2** *archit* a carved ornament with a shape like such leaves **trefoiled** *adj*
WORD ORIGIN Latin *trifolium* three-leaved herb

Treitschke *n* **Heinrich von**. 1834–96, German historian, noted for his highly nationalistic views

trek ❶ *n* **1** a long and often difficult journey, esp. on foot **2** *S African* a journey or stage of a journey, esp. a migration by ox wagon ▷ *vb* **trekking, trekked 3** to make a trek
WORD ORIGIN Afrikaans

trellis *n* a frame made of vertical and horizontal strips of wood, esp. one used to support climbing plants **trelliswork** *n*
WORD ORIGIN Old French *treliz* fabric of open texture

tremble ❶ *vb* **-bling, -bled 1** to shake with short slight movements: *her hands trembled uncontrollably; he felt the ground trembling beneath him* **2** to experience fear or anxiety: *his parents trembled with apprehension about his future* **3** (of the voice) to sound uncertain or unsteady, for instance through pain or emotion ▷ *n* **4** the act or an instance of trembling **trembling** *adj*
WORD ORIGIN Latin *tremere*

tremendous ❶ *adj* **1** very large or impressive: *a tremendous amount of money* **2** very exciting or unusual: *a tremendous feeling of elation* **3** very good or pleasing: *my wife has given me tremendous support* **tremendously** *adv*
WORD ORIGIN Latin *tremendus* terrible

treat *vb* **1 = behave towards**, deal with, handle, act towards, use, consider, serve, manage, regard, look upon **2 = take care of**, minister to, attend to, give medical treatment to, doctor *(informal)*, nurse, care for, medicate, prescribe medicine for, apply treatment to **4** *(often with* **to***)* **= provide**, give, buy, stand *(informal)*, pay for, entertain, feast, lay on, regale, wine and dine, take out for, foot *or* pay the bill ▷ *n* **6 = entertainment**, party, surprise, gift, celebration, feast, outing, excursion, banquet, refreshment **7 = pleasure**, delight, joy, thrill, satisfaction, enjoyment, gratification, source of pleasure, fun

treatment *n* **1a = care**, medical care, nursing, medicine, surgery, therapy, healing, medication, therapeutics, ministrations **1b = cure**, remedy, medication, medicine **2** *(often with* **of***)* **= handling**, dealings with, behaviour towards, conduct towards, management, reception, usage, manipulation, action towards

treaty *n* **1, 2 = agreement**, pact, contract, bond, alliance, bargain, convention, compact, covenant, entente, concordat

trek *n* **1a = slog**, tramp, long haul, footslog **1b = journey**, hike, expedition, safari, march, odyssey ▷ *vb* **3a = journey**, march, range, hike, roam, tramp, rove, go walkabout *(Austral)* **3b = trudge**, plod, traipse *(informal)*, footslog, slog

tremble *vb* **1 = shake**, shiver, quake, shudder, quiver, teeter, totter, quake in your boots, shake in your boots *or* shoes **1, 3 = vibrate**, rock, shake, quake, wobble, oscillate ▷ *n* **4 = shake**, shiver, quake, shudder, wobble, tremor, quiver, vibration, oscillation

tremendous *adj* **1 = huge**, great, towering, vast, enormous, terrific, formidable, immense, awesome, titanic, gigantic, monstrous, mammoth, colossal, whopping *(informal)*, stellar *(informal)*, prodigious, stupendous, gargantuan **OPPOSITE:** tiny
3 = excellent, great, wonderful, brilliant, mean *(slang)*, topping *(Brit slang)*, cracking *(Brit informal)*, amazing, extraordinary, fantastic *(informal)*, ace *(informal)*, incredible, fabulous *(informal)*, marvellous, exceptional, terrific *(informal)*, sensational *(informal)*, sovereign, awesome *(slang)*, super *(informal)*, brill *(informal)*, bodacious *(slang, chiefly US)*, boffo *(slang)*, jim-dandy *(slang)*, chillin' *(US slang)*, booshit *(Austral*

DICTIONARY

tremolo *n, pl* **-los** *music* **1** (in playing the violin or other stringed instrument) the rapid repetition of a note or notes to produce a trembling effect **2** (in singing) a fluctuation in pitch
WORD ORIGIN Italian: quavering

tremor *n* **1** an involuntary shudder or vibration: *the slight tremor of excitement* **2** a minor earthquake
WORD ORIGIN Latin

tremulous *adj literary* trembling, as from fear or excitement: *I managed a tremulous smile* **tremulously** *adv*
WORD ORIGIN Latin *tremere* to shake

trench ➊ *n* **1** a long narrow ditch in the ground, such as one for laying a pipe in **2** a long deep ditch used by soldiers for protection in a war: *my grandfather fought in the trenches in the First World War* ▷ *adj* **3** of or involving military trenches: *trench warfare*
WORD ORIGIN Old French *trenche* something cut

trenchant *adj* **1** keen or incisive: *a trenchant screenplay* **2** vigorous and effective: *the prime minister's trenchant adoption of this issue* **trenchancy** *n*
WORD ORIGIN Old French: cutting

Trenchard *n* **Hugh Montague**, 1st Viscount. 1873–1956, British air marshal, who as chief of air staff (1918, 1919–27) and marshal of the RAF (1927–29) established the RAF as a fully independent service. As commissioner of the Metropolitan Police (1931–35) he founded the police college at Hendon

trench coat *n* a belted raincoat similar in style to a military officer's coat

trencher *n history* a wooden board on which food was served or cut
WORD ORIGIN Old French *trencheoir*

trencherman *n, pl* **-men** a person who enjoys food; hearty eater

trench warfare *n* a type of warfare in which opposing armies face each other in entrenched positions

trend ➊ *n* **1** general tendency or direction: *an accelerating trend towards the use of mobile phones* **2** fashionable style: *she set a trend for wearing lingerie as outer garments* ▷ *vb* **3** to take a certain trend
WORD ORIGIN Old English *trendan* to turn

trendsetter *n* a person or thing that creates, or may create, a new fashion **trendsetting** *adj*

trendy ➊ *informal adj* **trendier, trendiest 1** consciously fashionable: *a flat in Glasgow's trendy West End* ▷ *n, pl* **trendies 2** a trendy person: *a media trendy* **trendily** *adv* **trendiness** *n*

trepidation *n formal* a state of fear or anxiety
WORD ORIGIN Latin *trepidatio*

trespass *vb* **1** to go onto somebody else's property without permission ▷ *n* **2** the act or an instance of trespassing **3** *old-fashioned* a sin or wrongdoing **trespasser** *n*
WORD ORIGIN Old French *trespas* a passage

trespass on *or* **upon** *vb formal* to take unfair advantage of (someone's friendship, patience, etc.): *I won't trespass upon your hospitality any longer*

tresses *pl n* a woman's long flowing hair
WORD ORIGIN Old French *trece*

trestle *n* **1** a support for one end of a table or beam, consisting of two rectangular frameworks or sets of legs which are joined at the top but not the bottom **2** Also called: **trestle table** a table consisting of a board supported by a trestle at each end
WORD ORIGIN Old French *trestel*

Tretchikoff *n* **Vladimir** 1913–2006, South African painter, born in Russia, known for his kitsch appeal, especially for his much-reproduced *Chinese Girl* (1950; also known as *The Green Lady*)

trevally (trih-**val**-lee) *n, pl* **-lies** *Austral & NZ* any of various food and game fishes
WORD ORIGIN probably alteration of *cavalla*, species of tropical fish

Trevelyan *n* **1 George Macaulay** 1876–1962, British historian, noted for his *English Social History* (1944) **2** his father, Sir **George Otto** 1838–1928, British historian and biographer. His works include a biography of his uncle Lord Macaulay (1876)

Trevino *n* **Lee** born 1939, US professional golfer: winner of the US Open Championship (1968; 1971) and the British Open Championship (1971; 1972)

Trevithick *n* **Richard** 1771–1833, British engineer, who built the first steam-driven passenger carriage (1801) and the first locomotive to run on smooth wheels on smooth rails (1804)

Trevor *n* **William**, real name William Trevor Cox. born 1928, Irish novelist and short-story writer. His novels include *The Old Boys* (1964), *The Children of Dynmouth* (1977), *Felicia's Journey* (1994), and *The Story of Lucy Gault* (2002)

trews *pl n chiefly Brit* close-fitting trousers of tartan cloth
WORD ORIGIN Scottish Gaelic *triubhas*

tri- *combining form* **1** three or thrice: *trilingual* **2** occurring every three: *triweekly*
WORD ORIGIN Latin *tres*

triad *n* **1** a group of three **2** *music* a three-note chord consisting of a note and the third and fifth above it **triadic** *adj*
WORD ORIGIN Greek *trias*

Triad *n* a Chinese secret society involved in criminal activities, such as drug trafficking

trial ➊ *n* **1** *law* an investigation of a case in front of a judge to decide whether a person is innocent or guilty of a crime by questioning him or her and considering the evidence **2** the act or an instance of trying or proving; test or experiment: *the new drug is undergoing clinical trials* **3** an annoying or frustrating person or thing: *young children can be a great trial at times* **4** a motorcycling competition in which the skills of the riders are tested over rough ground **5 trials** a sporting competition for individual people or animals: *horse trials* **6 on trial a** undergoing trial, esp. before a court of law **b** being tested, for example before a commitment to purchase: *I only have the car out on trial* ▷ *adj* **7** on a temporary basis while being tried out or tested: *a trial run* ▷ *vb* **trialling, trialled 8** to test or make experimental use of: *the idea has been trialled in several schools*
WORD ORIGIN Anglo-French *trier* to try

trial and error *n* a method of discovery based on practical experiment and experience rather than on theory: *raising her children has been a matter of trial and error*

trial balance *n book-keeping* a statement of all the debit and credit

THESAURUS

slang), exo (*Austral slang*), sik (*Austral slang*), rad (*informal*), phat (*slang*), schmick (*Austral informal*), beaut (*informal*), barrie (*Scot slang*), belting (*Brit slang*), pearler (*Austral slang*)
OPPOSITE: terrible

trench *n* **1, 2 = ditch**, cut, channel, drain, pit, waterway, gutter, trough, furrow, excavation, earthwork, fosse, entrenchment

trend *n* **1 = tendency**, swing, drift, inclination, current, direction, flow, leaning, bias **2 = fashion**, craze, fad (*informal*), mode, look, thing, style, rage, vogue, mania

trendy *adj* **1 = fashionable**, in (*slang*), now (*informal*), latest, with it (*informal*), flash (*informal*), stylish, in fashion, in vogue, up to the minute, modish, voguish, schmick (*Austral informal*), funky

trial *n* **1** (*law*) **= hearing**, case, court case, inquiry, contest, tribunal, lawsuit, appeal, litigation, industrial tribunal, court martial, legal proceedings, judicial proceedings, judicial examination **2 = test**, testing, experiment, evaluation, check, examination, audition, assay, dry run (*informal*), assessment, proof, probation, appraisal, try-out, test-run, pilot study, dummy run

DICTIONARY

balances in the double-entry ledger

triallist *or* **trialist** *n* **1** a person who takes part in a competition **2** *sport* a person who takes part in a preliminary match or heat held to determine selection for a team or event

triangle *n* **1** a geometric figure with three sides and three angles **2** any object shaped like a triangle: *a triangle of streets running up from the river* **3** *music* a percussion instrument that consists of a metal bar bent into a triangular shape, played by striking it with a metal stick **4** any situation involving three people or points of view: *a torrid sex triangle* **triangular** *adj*
WORD ORIGIN TRI- + Latin *angulus* corner

triangulate *vb* **-lating, -lated** to survey (an area) by dividing it into triangles

triangulation *n* a method of surveying in which an area is divided into triangles, one side (the base line) and all angles of which are measured and the lengths of the other lines calculated by trigonometry

Triassic *adj* *geol* of the period of geological time about 230 million years ago
WORD ORIGIN Latin *trias* triad

triathlon *n* an athletic contest in which each athlete competes in three different events: swimming, cycling, and running **triathlete** *n*
WORD ORIGIN TRI- + Greek *athlon* contest

tribalism *n* loyalty to a tribe, esp. as opposed to a modern political entity such as a state

tribe ❶ *n* **1** a group of families or clans believed to have a common ancestor **2** *informal* a group of people who do the same type of thing: *a tribe of German yachtsmen* **tribal** *adj*
WORD ORIGIN Latin *tribus*

tribesman *n, pl* **-men** a member of a tribe

tribulation *n* great distress: *the tribulations of a deserted wife*
WORD ORIGIN Latin *tribulare* to afflict

tribunal ❶ *n* **1** a special court or committee that is appointed to deal with a particular problem: *an industrial tribunal investigating allegations of unfair dismissal* **2** a court of justice
WORD ORIGIN Latin *tribunus* tribune

tribune *n* **1** a person who upholds public rights **2** (in ancient Rome) an officer elected by the plebs to protect their interests
WORD ORIGIN Latin *tribunus*

tributary *n, pl* **-taries 1** a stream or river that flows into a larger one: *Frankfurt lies on the River Main, a tributary of the Rhine* **2** a person, nation, or people that pays tribute ▷ *adj* **3** (of a stream or river) flowing into a larger stream **4** paying tribute: *Egypt was formerly a tributary province of the Turkish Empire*

tribute ❶ *n* **1** something given, done, or said as a mark of respect or admiration **2** a payment by one ruler or state to another, usually as an acknowledgment of submission **3** something that shows the merits of a particular quality of a person or thing: *the car's low fuel consumption is a tribute to the quality of its engine*
WORD ORIGIN Latin *tributum*

trice *n* **in a trice** in a moment: *she was back in a trice*
WORD ORIGIN originally, at one tug, from *trice* to haul up

triceps *n* the muscle at the back of the upper arm
WORD ORIGIN Latin

trichology (trick-ol-a-jee) *n* the branch of medicine concerned with the hair and its diseases **trichologist** *n*
WORD ORIGIN Greek *thrix* hair

trichromatic *or* **trichromic** *adj* **1** having or involving three colours **2** of or having normal colour vision **trichromatism** *n*

trick ❶ *n* **1** a deceitful or cunning action or plan: *she was willing to use any dirty trick to get what she wanted* **2** a joke or prank: *he loves playing tricks on his sister* **3** a clever way of doing something, learned from experience: *an old campers' trick is to use three thin blankets rather than one thick one* **4** an illusory or magical feat or device **5** a simple feat learned by an animal or person **6** a deceptive illusion: *a trick of the light* **7** a habit or mannerism: *she had a trick of saying 'oh dear'* **8** *cards* a batch of cards played in turn and won by the person playing the highest card **9** **do the trick** *informal* to produce the desired result **10** **how's tricks?** *slang* how are you? ▷ *vb* **11** to defraud, deceive, or cheat (someone) **trickery** *n*
WORD ORIGIN Old French *trique*

trickle ❶ *vb* **-ling, -led 1** to flow or cause to flow in a thin stream or drops: *tears trickled down her cheeks* **2** to move slowly or in small groups: *voters trickled to the polls* ▷ *n* **3** a thin, irregular, or slow flow of something: *a trickle of blood*
WORD ORIGIN probably imitative

trickle-down *adj* of the theory that granting concessions like tax cuts to the rich will benefit all levels of society by stimulating the economy

trick out *vb* to dress up: *tricked out in chauffeur's rig*

trickster *n* a person who deceives or plays tricks

tricky ❶ *adj* **trickier, trickiest 1** involving snags or difficulties: *a tricky task* **2** needing careful handling: *a tricky situation* **3** sly or wily: *a tricky customer* **trickily** *adv* **trickiness** *n*

tricolour *or US* **tricolor** (trick-kol-lor) *n* a flag with three equal stripes in different colours, esp. the French or Irish national flags

tricycle *n* a three-wheeled cycle **tricyclist** *n*

trident *n* a three-pronged spear
WORD ORIGIN Latin *tridens* three-pronged

THESAURUS

t

tribe *n* **1 = race**, ethnic group, people, family, class, stock, house, division, blood, seed *(chiefly biblical)*, sept, gens, clan, caste, dynasty, hapu (NZ), iwi (NZ)

tribunal *n* **1, 2 = hearing**, court, trial, bar, bench, industrial tribunal, judgment seat, judicial examination

tribute *n* **1 = accolade**, testimonial, eulogy, recognition, respect, gift, honour, praise, esteem, applause, compliment, gratitude, acknowledgment, commendation, panegyric, encomium, laudation **OPPOSITE:** criticism

trick *n* **1 = deception**, trap, fraud, con *(slang)*, sting *(informal)*, manoeuvre, dodge, ploy, scam *(slang)*, imposition, gimmick, device, hoax, deceit, swindle, ruse, artifice, subterfuge, canard, feint, stratagem, wile, imposture, fastie *(Austral slang)* **2 = joke**, put-on *(slang)*, gag *(informal)*, stunt, spoof *(informal)*, caper, prank, frolic, practical joke, antic, jape, leg-pull *(Brit informal)*, cantrip *(Scot)* **3 = secret**, skill, device, knack, art, hang *(informal)*, technique, know-how *(informal)*, gift, command, craft, expertise **4 = sleight of hand**, device, feat, stunt, juggle, legerdemain **7 = mannerism**, habit, characteristic, trait, quirk, peculiarity, foible, idiosyncrasy, practice, crotchet ▷ *vb* **11 = deceive**, trap, have someone on, take someone in *(informal)*, fool, cheat, con *(informal)*, kid *(informal)*, stiff *(slang)*, sting *(informal)*, mislead, hoax, defraud, dupe, gull *(archaic)*, delude, swindle, impose upon, bamboozle *(informal)*, hoodwink, put one over on *(informal)*, pull the wool over someone's eyes, pull a fast one on *(informal)*, scam *(slang)*

trickle *vb* **1 = dribble**, run, drop, stream, creep, crawl, drip, ooze, seep, exude, percolate ▷ *n* **3 = dribble**, drip, seepage, thin stream

tricky *adj* **1, 2 = difficult**, sensitive, complicated, delicate, risky, sticky *(informal)*, hairy *(informal)*, problematic, thorny, touch-and-go, knotty, dicey *(informal)*, ticklish **OPPOSITE:** simple **3 = crafty**, scheming, subtle, cunning, slippery, sly, deceptive, devious, wily, artful, foxy, deceitful **OPPOSITE:** open

DICTIONARY

tried *vb* ▸ the past of **try**
triennial *adj* occurring every three years **triennially** *adv*
WORD ORIGIN TRI- + Latin *annus* year
trier *n* a person or thing that tries
trifle[1] *n* **1** a thing of little or no value or significance **2** *Brit, Austral & NZ* a cold dessert made of sponge cake spread with jam or fruit, soaked in sherry, covered with custard and cream **3 a trifle** to a small extent or degree; slightly: *he is a trifle eccentric*
WORD ORIGIN Old French *trufle* mockery
trifle[2] *vb* **trifling, trifled** ▪ **trifle with** to treat (a person or his or her feelings) with disdain or disregard
trifling *adj* insignificant, petty, or frivolous: *a trifling misunderstanding*
trig. trigonometry
trigger *n* **1** a small lever that releases a catch on a gun or machine **2** any event that sets a course of action in motion: *his murder was the trigger for a night of rioting* ▹ *vb* **3** Also: **trigger off** to set (an action or process) in motion: *various factors can trigger off a migraine*
WORD ORIGIN Dutch *trekker*
trigger-happy *adj informal* too ready or willing to use guns or violence: *trigger-happy border guards*
trigonometry *n* the branch of mathematics concerned with the relations of sides and angles of triangles, which is used in surveying, navigation, etc.
WORD ORIGIN Greek *trigōnon* triangle
trig point *n* a point on a hilltop etc. used for triangulation by a surveyor
trike *n informal* a tricycle
trilateral *adj* having three sides
trilby *n, pl* **-bies** a man's soft felt hat with an indented crown
WORD ORIGIN after *Trilby*, the heroine of a novel by George Du Maurier
trill *n* **1** *music* a rapid alternation between a note and the note above it **2** a shrill warbling sound made by some birds: *the canary's high trills* ▹ *vb* **3** (of a bird) to make a shrill warbling sound **4** (of a person) to talk or laugh in a high-pitched musical voice
WORD ORIGIN Italian *trillo*
Trilling *n* **Lionel** 1905–75, US literary critic, whose works include *The Liberal Imagination* (1950) and *Sincerity and Authenticity* (1974)
trillion *n* **-lions** *or* **-lion** **1** the number represented as one followed by twelve zeros (10^{12}); a million million **2** (in Britain, originally) the number represented as one followed by eighteen zeros (10^{18}); a million million million ▹ *adj* **3** amounting to a trillion: *a trillion dollars* **trillionth** *n, adj*
WORD ORIGIN French
trillium *n* a plant of Asia and North America that has three leaves at the top of the stem with a single white, pink, or purple three-petalled flower
WORD ORIGIN New Latin
trilobite (**trile**-oh-bite) *n* a small prehistoric marine arthropod, found as a fossil
WORD ORIGIN Greek *trilobos* having three lobes
trilogy (**trill**-a-jee) *n, pl* **-gies** a series of three books, plays, etc. which form a related group but are each complete works in themselves
WORD ORIGIN Greek *trilogia*
trim *adj* **trimmer, trimmest** **1** neat and spruce in appearance: *trim lace curtains* **2** attractively slim: *his body was trim and athletic* ▹ *vb* **trimming, trimmed** **3** to make (something) neater by cutting it slightly without changing its basic shape: *his white beard was neatly trimmed* **4** to adorn or decorate (something, such as a garment) with lace, ribbons, etc.: *a cotton camisole neatly trimmed with lace* **5 a** to adjust the balance of (a ship or aircraft) by shifting cargo etc. **b** to adjust (a ship's sails) to take advantage of the wind **6** to reduce or lower the size of: *the company has trimmed its pretax profits forecast by $2.3 million* **7** to alter (a plan or policy) by removing parts which seem unnecessary or unpopular: *the government would rather trim its policies than lose the election* **8 trim off** *or* **away** to cut so as to remove: *trim off most of the fat before cooking the meat* ▹ *n* **9** a decoration or adornment: *a black suit with scarlet trim* **10** the upholstery and decorative facings of a car's interior **11** good physical condition: *he had always kept himself in trim* **12** a haircut that neatens but does not alter the existing hairstyle
WORD ORIGIN Old English *trymman* to strengthen
trimaran (**trime**-a-ran) *n* a boat with one smaller hull on each side of the main hull
WORD ORIGIN *tri-* + *(cata)maran*
Trimble *n* (**William**) **David** born 1944, Northern Irish politician; leader of the Ulster Unionist party (1995–2005), First Minister of Northern Ireland (1998–2001); Nobel peace prize jointly with John Hume in 1998
trimming *n* **1** an extra piece added to a garment for decoration: *a pink nightie with lace trimming* **2 trimmings** usual or traditional accompaniments: *bacon and eggs with all the trimmings*
Trinitarian *n* **1** a person who believes in the doctrine of the Trinity ▹ *adj* **2** of or relating to the Trinity **Trinitarianism** *n*
trinitrotoluene *n* ▸ the full name for **TNT**
trinity *n, pl* **-ties** a group of three people or things
WORD ORIGIN Latin *trinus* triple
Trinity *n Christianity* the union of three persons, the Father, Son, and Holy Spirit, in one God
trinket *n* a small or worthless ornament or piece of jewellery
WORD ORIGIN origin unknown
trio *n, pl* **trios** **1** a group of three people or things **2** a group of three instrumentalists or singers **3** a piece of music for three performers
WORD ORIGIN Italian

t

THESAURUS

trifle[1] *n* **1 = knick-knack**, nothing, toy, plaything, bauble, triviality, bagatelle, gewgaw
trifling *adj* **= insignificant**, small, tiny, empty, slight, silly, shallow, petty, idle, trivial, worthless, negligible, unimportant, frivolous, paltry, minuscule, puny, measly, piddling *(informal)*, inconsiderable, valueless, nickel-and-dime *(US slang)*, footling *(informal)*
OPPOSITE: significant
trigger *vb* **3 = bring about**, start, cause, produce, generate, prompt, provoke, set off, activate, give rise to, elicit, spark off, set in motion
OPPOSITE: prevent
trim *adj* **1 = neat**, nice, smart, compact, tidy, orderly, spruce, dapper, natty *(informal)*, well-groomed, well-ordered, well turned-out, shipshape, spick-and-span, trig *(archaic, dialect)*, soigné *or* soignée OPPOSITE: untidy **2 = slender**, fit, slim, sleek, streamlined, shapely, svelte, willowy, lissom ▹ *vb* **3 = cut**, crop, clip, dock, shave, barber, tidy, prune, shear, pare, lop, even up, neaten **4 = decorate**, dress, array, adorn, embroider, garnish, ornament, embellish, deck out, bedeck, beautify, trick out ▹ *n* **9 = decoration**, edging, border, piping, trimming, fringe, garnish, frill, embellishment, adornment, ornamentation **11 = condition**, form, health, shape *(informal)*, repair, fitness, wellness, order, fettle **12 = cut**, crop, trimming, clipping, shave, pruning, shearing, tidying up
trimming *n* **1 = decoration**, edging, border, piping, fringe, garnish, braid, frill, festoon, embellishment, adornment, ornamentation ▹ *pl n* **2 = extras**, accessories, garnish, ornaments, accompaniments, frills, trappings, paraphernalia, appurtenances
trinity *n* **= threesome**, triple, trio, trilogy, triplet, triad, triumvirate, triptych, trine, triune
trio *n* **1 = threesome**, triple, trinity, trilogy, triplet, triad, triumvirate,

DICTIONARY

trip ❶ *n* **1** a journey to a place and back, esp. for pleasure: *they took a coach trip round the island* **2** a false step; stumble **3** the act of causing someone to stumble or fall by catching his or her foot with one's own **4** *informal* a hallucinogenic drug experience **5** a catch on a mechanism that acts as a switch ▷ *vb* **tripping, tripped 6** Also: **trip up** to stumble or cause (someone) to stumble **7** Also: **trip up** to trap or catch (someone) in a mistake **8** to walk lightly and quickly, with a dancelike motion: *I could see Amelia tripping along beside him* **9** *informal* to experience the effects of a hallucinogenic drug
WORD ORIGIN Old French *triper* to tread

tripartite *adj* involving or composed of three people or parts **tripartism** *n*

tripe *n* **1** the stomach lining of a cow or pig used as a food **2** *Brit, Austral & NZ informal* nonsense or rubbish
WORD ORIGIN Old French

Tripitaka (trip-**it**-**tah**-ka) *n* the three collections of books making up the Buddhist scriptures
WORD ORIGIN Pali (an ancient language of India) *tri* three + *pitaka* basket

triple ❶ *adj* **1** made up of three parts or things: *a triple murder* **2** (of musical time or rhythm) having three beats in each bar **3** three times as great or as much: *a triple brandy* ▷ *vb* **-pling, -pled 4** to make or become three times as much or as many: *the company has tripled its sales over the past five years* ▷ *n* **5** something that is, or contains, three times as much as normal **6** a group of three **triply** *adv*
WORD ORIGIN Latin *triplus*

triple jump *n* an athletic event in which the competitor has to perform a hop, a step, and a jump in a continuous movement

triple point *n chem* the temperature and pressure at which a substance can exist as a solid, liquid, and gas

triplet *n* **1** one of three children born at one birth **2** a group of three musical notes played in the time that two would normally take **3** a group or set of three similar things

triplicate *adj* **1** triple ▷ *vb* **-cating, -cated 2** to multiply or be multiplied by three ▷ *n* **3 in triplicate** written out three times: *my request to interview the commander had to be made in triplicate* **triplication** *n*
WORD ORIGIN Latin *triplicare* to triple

tripod (**tripe**-pod) *n* **1** a three-legged stand to which a camera can be attached to hold it steady **2** a three-legged stool, table, etc.
WORD ORIGIN TRI- + Greek *pous* a foot

tripos (**tripe**-poss) *n Brit* the final honours degree examinations at Cambridge University
WORD ORIGIN Latin *tripus* tripod

tripper *n chiefly Brit* a tourist

triptych (**trip**-tick) *n* a set of three pictures or panels, usually hinged together and often used as an altarpiece
WORD ORIGIN TRI- + Greek *ptux* plate

trireme (**try**-ream) *n* an ancient Greek warship with three rows of oars on each side
WORD ORIGIN TRI- + Latin *remus* oar

trismus *n pathol* the state of being unable to open the mouth because of sustained contractions of the jaw muscles, caused by tetanus. Nontechnical name: **lockjaw**
WORD ORIGIN Greek *trismos* a grinding

triste (**treest**) *adj old-fashioned* sad
WORD ORIGIN French

trite *adj* (of a remark or idea) commonplace and unoriginal
WORD ORIGIN Latin *tritus* worn down

tritium *n* a radioactive isotope of hydrogen. Symbol: T or ^{3}H
WORD ORIGIN Greek *tritos* third

triumph ❶ *n* **1** the feeling of great happiness resulting from a victory or major achievement **2** an outstanding success, achievement, or victory: *the concert was a musical triumph* **3** (in ancient Rome) a procession held in honour of a victorious general ▷ *vb* **4** to gain control or success: *triumphing over adversity* **5** to rejoice over a victory **triumphal** *adj*
WORD ORIGIN Latin *triumphus*

triumphant ❶ *adj* **1** feeling or displaying triumph: *her smile was triumphant* **2** celebrating a victory or success: *the general's triumphant tour round the city* **triumphantly** *adv*

triumvir (try-**umm**-vir) *n* (esp. in ancient Rome) a member of a triumvirate
WORD ORIGIN Latin

triumvirate (try-**umm**-vir-rit) *n* **1** a group of three people in joint control of something: *the triumvirate of great orchestras which dominates classical music in Europe* **2** (in ancient Rome) a board of three officials jointly responsible for some task

trivalent *adj chem* **1** having a valency of three **2** having three valencies **trivalency** *n*

trivet (**triv**-vit) *n* **1** a three-legged stand for holding a pot, kettle, etc. over a fire **2** a short metal stand on which hot dishes are placed on a table
WORD ORIGIN Old English *trefet*

trivia *n* petty and unimportant things or details

trivial ❶ *adj* of little importance: *a trivial matter* **triviality** *n* **trivially** *adv*
WORD ORIGIN Latin *trivialis* common

trivialize *or* **-ise** *vb* **-izing, -ized** *or* **-ising, -ised** to make (something) seem less important or complex than it is

trochee (**troke**-ee) *n prosody* a metrical foot of one long and one short syllable **trochaic** *adj*
WORD ORIGIN Greek *trekhein* to run

THESAURUS

triptych, trine, triune

trip *n* **1 = journey**, outing, excursion, day out, run, drive, travel, tour, spin *(informal)*, expedition, voyage, ramble, foray, jaunt, errand, junket *(informal)* **2 = stumble**, fall, slip, blunder, false move, misstep, false step ▷ *vb* **6** *(often with* **up***)* **= stumble**, fall, fall over, slip, tumble, topple, stagger, misstep, lose your balance, make a false move, lose your footing, take a spill
7 trip someone up = catch out, trap, confuse, unsettle, disconcert, throw you off, wrongfoot, put you off your stride **8 = skip**, dance, spring, hop, caper, flit, frisk, gambol, tread lightly

triple *adj* **1 = three-way**, threefold, tripartite **3 = treble**, three times, three times as much as ▷ *vb* **4 = treble**, triplicate, increase threefold

triumph *n* **1 = joy**, pride, happiness, rejoicing, elation, jubilation, exultation **2 = success**, victory, accomplishment, mastery, hit *(informal)*, achievement, smash *(informal)*, coup, sensation, feat, conquest, attainment, smash hit *(informal)*, tour de force *(French)*, walkover *(informal)*, feather in your cap, smasheroo *(slang)*
OPPOSITE: failure
▷ *vb* **4** *(often with* **over***)* **= succeed**, win, overcome, prevail, best, dominate, overwhelm, thrive, flourish, subdue, prosper, get the better of, vanquish, come out on top *(informal)*, carry the day, take the honours **OPPOSITE:** fail
5 = rejoice, celebrate, glory, revel, swagger, drool, gloat, exult, jubilate, crow

triumphant *adj* **1 = victorious**, winning, successful, dominant, conquering, undefeated
OPPOSITE: defeated
2 = celebratory, rejoicing, jubilant, triumphal, proud, glorious, swaggering, elated, exultant, boastful, cock-a-hoop

trivial *adj* **= unimportant**, little, small, minor, slight, everyday, petty, meaningless, commonplace, worthless, trifling, insignificant, negligible, frivolous, paltry, incidental, puny, inconsequential, trite, inconsiderable, valueless, nickel-and-dime *(US slang)*
OPPOSITE: important

t

DICTIONARY

trod *vb* ▸ the past tense and a past participle of **tread**

trodden *vb* ▸ a past participle of **tread**

troglodyte *n* a person who lives in a cave
WORD ORIGIN Greek *trōglodutēs* one who enters caves

troika *n* **1** a Russian coach or sleigh drawn by three horses abreast **2** a group of three people in authority: *a troika of European foreign ministers*
WORD ORIGIN Russian

Trojan *adj* **1** of ancient Troy or its people ▹ *n* **2** a person from ancient Troy **3** a hard-working person

Trojan Horse *n* **1** *Greek myth* the huge wooden hollow figure of a horse used by the Greeks to enter Troy **2** a trap or trick intended to undermine an enemy

troll[1] *n* (in Scandinavian folklore) a supernatural dwarf or giant that dwells in a cave or mountain
WORD ORIGIN Old Norse: demon

troll[2] *vb angling* to fish by dragging a lure through the water
WORD ORIGIN Old French *troller* to run about

troll[3] *internet n* **1** a person who posts deliberately inflammatory messages on an internet discussion board ▹ *vb* **2** to post such a message

trolley *n* **1** a small table on casters used for carrying food or drink **2** a wheeled cart or stand used for moving heavy items, such as shopping in a supermarket or luggage at a railway station **3** *Brit* ▸ see **trolley bus** **4** *US & Canad* ▸ see **trolley car** **5** a device, such as a wheel that collects the current from an overhead wire, to drive the motor of an electric vehicle **6** *Austral & Brit* a low truck running on rails, used in factories, mines, etc.
WORD ORIGIN probably from TROLL[2]

trolley bus *n* a bus powered by electricity from two overhead wires but not running on rails

trolley car *n US & Canad* ▸ same as **tram**

trollop *n derogatory* a promiscuous or slovenly woman
WORD ORIGIN origin unknown

trombone *n* a brass musical instrument with a sliding tube which is moved in or out to alter the note played **trombonist** *n*
WORD ORIGIN Italian

Tromp *n* **1 Cornelius** (**Martenszoon**) 1629–91, Dutch admiral, who fought during the 2nd and 3rd Anglo-Dutch Wars **2** his father, **Maarten** (**Harpertszoon**). 1598–1653, Dutch admiral, who fought in the 1st Anglo-Dutch War: killed in action

trompe l'oeil (tromp **luh**-ee) *n, pl* **trompe l'oeils** (tromp **luh**-ee) **1** a painting etc. giving a convincing illusion that the objects represented are real **2** an effect of this kind
WORD ORIGIN French, literally: deception of the eye

troop ⓘ *n* **1** a large group: *a troop of dogs* **2 troops** soldiers: *troops have been maintaining an unusually high profile* **3** a subdivision of a cavalry or armoured regiment **4** a large group of Scouts made up of several patrols ▹ *vb* **5** to move in a crowd: *we trooped into the room after her* **6** *mil chiefly Brit & Austral* to parade (a flag or banner) ceremonially: *trooping the colour*
WORD ORIGIN French *troupe*

trooper *n* **1** a soldier in a cavalry regiment **2** *US & Austral* a mounted policeman **3** *US* a state policeman **4** a cavalry horse **5** *informal chiefly Brit* a troopship

troopship *n* a ship used to transport military personnel

trope *n* a word or expression used in a figurative sense
WORD ORIGIN Greek *tropos* style, turn

trophy ⓘ *n, pl* **-phies** **1** a cup, shield, etc. given as a prize **2** a memento of success, esp. one taken in war or hunting: *stuffed animal heads and other hunting trophies* ▹ *adj* **3** *informal* regarded as a highly desirable symbol of wealth or success: *a trophy wife*
WORD ORIGIN Greek *tropaion*

tropic *n* **1** either of the lines of latitude at about 23½°N (**tropic of Cancer**) and 23½°S (**tropic of Capricorn**) of the equator **2 the tropics** that part of the earth's surface between the tropics of Cancer and Capricorn: *the intense heat and humidity of the tropics*
WORD ORIGIN Greek *tropos* a turn; from the belief that the sun turned back at the solstices

tropical ⓘ *adj* belonging to, typical of, or located in, the tropics: *tropical rainforests* **tropically** *adv*

tropism *n* the tendency of a plant or animal to turn or curve in response to an external stimulus
WORD ORIGIN Greek *tropos* a turn

troposphere *n* the lowest layer of the earth's atmosphere, about 18 kilometres (11 miles) thick at the equator to about 6 km (4 miles) at the Poles
WORD ORIGIN Greek *tropos* a turn + SPHERE

trot ⓘ *vb* **trotting, trotted** **1** (of a horse) to move in a manner faster than a walk but slower than a gallop, in which diagonally opposite legs come down together **2** (of a person) to move fairly quickly, with small quick steps ▹ *n* **3** a medium-paced gait of a horse, in which diagonally opposite legs come down together **4** a steady brisk pace **5 on the trot** *informal* one after the other: *ten years on the trot* **6 the trots** *slang* diarrhoea
WORD ORIGIN Old French

Trot *n chiefly Brit informal* a follower of Trotsky

troth (rhymes with **growth**) *n archaic* **1** a pledge of fidelity, esp. a betrothal **2 in troth** truly
WORD ORIGIN Old English *trēowth*

trot out *vb informal* to repeat (old information or ideas) without fresh thought: *the government trots out the same excuse every time*

Trotskyist *or* **Trotskyite** *adj* **1** of the theories of Leon Trotsky (1879–1940), Russian Communist, which call for a worldwide revolution by the proletariat ▹ *n* **2** a supporter of Trotsky or his theories **Trotskyism** *n*

trotter *n* **1** the foot of a pig **2** a horse that is specially trained to trot fast

troubadour (troo-bad-oor) *n* a travelling poet and singer in S France or N Italy from the 11th to the 13th century who wrote chiefly on courtly love
WORD ORIGIN French

trouble ⓘ *n* **1** difficulties or problems: *I'd trouble finding somewhere to park* **2** a cause of distress, disturbance, or pain: *we must be sensitive to the troubles of other people* **3** disease or a problem with one's health: *ear trouble* **4** a state

THESAURUS

troop *n* **1 = group**, company, team, body, unit, band, crowd, pack, squad, gathering, crew *(informal)*, drove, gang, bunch *(informal)*, flock, herd, contingent, swarm, horde, multitude, throng, posse *(informal)*, bevy, assemblage **2** *(pl)* **= soldiers**, men, armed forces, servicemen, fighting men, military, army, soldiery ▹ *vb* **5 = flock**, march, crowd, stream, parade, swarm, throng, traipse *(informal)*

trophy *n* **1 = prize**, cup, award, bays, laurels **2 = souvenir**, spoils, relic, memento, booty, keepsake

tropical *adj* **= hot**, stifling, lush, steamy, humid, torrid, sultry, sweltering **OPPOSITE:** cold

trot *vb* **2 = run**, jog, scamper, lope, go briskly, canter ▹ *n* **4 = run**, jog, lope, brisk pace, canter

trouble *n* **1 = bother**, problems, concern, worry, stress, difficulty *(informal)*, anxiety, distress, grief *(Brit & S African)*, irritation, hassle *(informal)*, strife, inconvenience, unease, disquiet, annoyance, agitation, commotion, unpleasantness, vexation **2** *(often plural)* **= distress**, problem, suffering, worry, pain, anxiety, grief, torment, hardship, sorrow, woe, irritation, hassle *(informal)*, misfortune, heartache, disquiet, annoyance, agitation, tribulation, bummer *(slang)*, vexation **OPPOSITE:** pleasure

DICTIONARY

of disorder, ill-feeling, or unrest: *the police had orders to intervene at the first sign of trouble* **5** effort or exertion to do something: *they didn't even take the trouble to see the film before banning it* **6** a personal weakness or cause of annoyance: *his trouble is that he's constitutionally jealous* **7** **in trouble** **a** likely to be punished for something one has done: *in trouble with the public prosecutor* **b** pregnant when not married **8** **more trouble than it's worth** involving a lot of time or effort for very little reward: *making your own pasta is more trouble than it's worth* ▷ *vb* **-bling, -bled** **9** to cause trouble to **10** to make an effort or exert oneself: *he dismissed the letters as forgeries without troubling to examine them* **11** to cause inconvenience or discomfort to: *sorry to trouble you!* **troubled** *adj*
WORD ORIGIN Old French *troubler*

troublemaker *n* a person who causes trouble, esp. between people **troublemaking** *adj, n*

troubleshooter *n* a person employed to locate and deal with faults or problems **troubleshooting** *n, adj*

troublesome Ⓣ *adj* causing trouble

trouble spot *n* a place where there is frequent fighting or violence: *the Balkans have long been one of the major European trouble spots*

troublous *adj literary* unsettled or agitated

trough Ⓣ (troff) *n* **1** a long open container, esp. one for animals' food or water **2** a narrow channel between two waves or ridges **3** a low point in a pattern that has regular high and low points: *the trough of the slump in pupil numbers was in 1985* **4** *meteorol* a long narrow area of low pressure **5** a narrow channel or gutter
WORD ORIGIN Old English *trōh*

trounce *vb* **trouncing, trounced** to defeat (someone) utterly
WORD ORIGIN origin unknown

troupe (troop) *n* a company of actors or other performers
WORD ORIGIN French

trouper *n* **1** a member of a troupe **2** an experienced person: *Bette plays a showbiz trouper*

trouser *adj* **1** of or relating to trousers: *trouser legs* ▷ *vb* **2** *Brit slang* to take (something, esp. money), often surreptitiously or unlawfully

trousers *pl n* a garment that covers the body from the waist to the ankles or knees with a separate tube-shaped section for each leg
WORD ORIGIN Scottish Gaelic *triubhas* trews

trousseau (troo-so) *n, pl* **-seaux** (-so) the clothes, linen, and other possessions collected by a bride for her marriage
WORD ORIGIN Old French

trout *n, pl* **trout** *or* **trouts** any of various game fishes related to the salmon and found chiefly in fresh water in northern regions
WORD ORIGIN Old English *trūht*

trove *n* ▸ see **treasure-trove**

trowel *n* **1** a hand tool resembling a small spade with a curved blade, used by gardeners for lifting plants, etc. **2** a similar tool with a flat metal blade, used for spreading cement or plaster on a surface
WORD ORIGIN Latin *trulla* a scoop

troy weight *or* **troy** *n* a system of weights used for precious metals and gemstones in which one pound equals twelve ounces
WORD ORIGIN after the city of *Troyes*, France, where first used

truant *n* **1** a pupil who stays away from school without permission **2** **play truant** to stay away from school without permission ▷ *adj* **3** being or relating to a truant: *a truant schoolkid* **truancy** *n*
WORD ORIGIN Old French: vagabond

truce Ⓣ *n* a temporary agreement to stop fighting or quarrelling
WORD ORIGIN plural of Old English *trēow* pledge

truck[1] *n* **1** *Brit* a railway wagon for carrying freight **2** a large motor vehicle for transporting heavy loads **3** any wheeled vehicle used to move goods ▷ *vb* **4** *chiefly US* to transport goods in a truck
WORD ORIGIN perhaps from *truckle* a small wheel

truck[2] *n* **1** *history* the payment of wages in goods rather than in money **2** **have no truck with** to refuse to be involved with: *the opposition will have no truck with the planned cut in pensions*
WORD ORIGIN Old French *troquer* (unattested) to barter

trucker *n* a long-distance lorry driver

truckie *n Austral & NZ informal* a truck driver

truckle *vb* **-ling, -led** to yield weakly or give in: *he accused the government of truckling to the right-wing press*
WORD ORIGIN from obsolete *truckle* to sleep in a truckle bed

truckle bed *n chiefly Brit* a low bed on wheels, stored under a larger bed

truculent (truck-yew-lent) *adj* defiantly aggressive or bad-tempered **truculence** *n* **truculently** *adv*
WORD ORIGIN Latin *trux* fierce

trudge *vb* **trudging, trudged** **1** to walk or plod heavily or wearily ▷ *n* **2** a long tiring walk
WORD ORIGIN origin unknown

true Ⓣ *adj* **truer, truest** **1** in accordance with the truth or facts; factual: *not all of the stories about her are true* **2** real or genuine: *he didn't want to reveal his true feelings* **3** faithful and loyal: *a true friend* **4** accurate or precise: *he looked through the telescopic sight until he was convinced his aim was*

THESAURUS

3 = ailment, disease, failure, complaint, upset, illness, disorder, disability, defect, malfunction **4 = disorder**, fighting, row, conflict, bother, grief *(Brit & S African)*, unrest, disturbance, to-do *(informal)*, discontent, dissatisfaction, furore, uproar, scuffling, discord, fracas, commotion, rumpus, breach of the peace, tumult, affray *(law)*, brouhaha, ructions, hullabaloo *(informal)*, kerfuffle *(Brit informal)*, hoo-ha *(informal)*, biffo *(Austral slang)*, boilover *(Austral)* **OPPOSITE:** peace **5 = effort**, work, thought, care, labour, struggle, pains, bother, hassle *(informal)*, inconvenience, exertion **OPPOSITE:** convenience ▷ *vb* **9 = bother**, worry, upset, disturb, distress, annoy, plague, grieve, torment, harass, hassle *(informal)*, afflict, pain, fret, agitate, sadden, perplex, disconcert, disquiet, pester, vex, perturb, faze, give someone grief *(Brit & S African)*, discompose, put or get someone's back up, hack you off *(informal)* **OPPOSITE:** please **10 = take pains**, take the time, make an effort, go to the effort of, exert yourself **OPPOSITE:** avoid **11a = afflict**, hurt, bother, cause discomfort to, pain, grieve **11b = inconvenience**, disturb, burden, put out, impose upon, discommode, incommode **OPPOSITE:** relieve

troublesome *adj* **a = bothersome**, trying, taxing, demanding, difficult, worrying, upsetting, annoying, irritating, tricky, harassing, oppressive, arduous, tiresome, inconvenient, laborious, burdensome, hard, worrisome, irksome, wearisome, vexatious, importunate, pestilential, plaguy *(informal)* **OPPOSITE:** simple **b = disorderly**, violent, turbulent, rebellious, unruly, rowdy, recalcitrant, undisciplined, uncooperative, refractory, insubordinate **OPPOSITE:** well-behaved

trough *n* **1 = manger**, crib, water trough

truce *n* **= ceasefire**, break, stay, rest, peace, treaty, interval, moratorium, respite, lull, cessation, let-up *(informal)*, armistice, intermission, cessation of hostilities

true *adj* **1 = correct**, right, accurate, exact, precise, valid, legitimate, factual, truthful, veritable, bona fide, veracious **OPPOSITE:** false **2 = actual**, real, natural, pure,

DICTIONARY

true **5** (of a compass bearing) according to the earth's geographical rather than magnetic poles: *true north* **6 come true** to actually happen: *fortunately his gloomy prediction didn't come true* ▷ *n* **7 in** *or* **out of true** in *or* not in correct alignment ▷ *adv* **8** truthfully or rightly: *I'd like to move to Edinburgh, true, but I'd need to get a job there first*
WORD ORIGIN Old English *trīewe*

true-blue *adj* **1** staunchly loyal ▷ *n* **true blue 2** *chiefly Brit & Austral* a staunch royalist or Conservative

true-life *adj* taken directly from reality: *true-life TV horror stories*

truelove *n* the person that one loves

Trueman *n* **Freddy**, full name *Frederick Sewards Trueman*. 1931–2006, English cricketer, a fast bowler for Yorkshire and England

true north *n* the direction from any point along a meridian towards the North Pole

Truffaut *n* **François** 1932–84, French film director of the New Wave. His films include *Les Quatre cents coups* (1959), *Jules et Jim* (1961), *Baisers volés* (1968), and *Le Dernier Métro* (1980)

truffle *n* **1** a round fungus which grows underground and is regarded as a delicacy **2** Also called: **rum truffle** a sweet flavoured with chocolate or rum
WORD ORIGIN French *truffe*

trug *n Brit* a long shallow basket for carrying garden tools, flowers, etc.
WORD ORIGIN perhaps variant of *trough*

truism *n* a statement that is clearly true and well known

Trujillo[1] *n* a city in NW Peru: founded 1535; university (1824); centre of a district producing rice and sugar cane. Pop: 686 000 (2005 est)

Trujillo[2] *n* **Rafael** (**Léonidas**), original name *Rafael Léonidas Trujillo Molina*. 1891–1961, Dominican dictator, who governed the Dominican Republic (1930–61) with the help of a powerful police force: assassinated

truly ❶ *adv* **1** in a true, just, or faithful manner **2** really: *a truly awful poem*

trump[1] *n* **1** ▸ same as **trump card** ▷ *vb* **2** *cards* to beat a card by playing a card which belongs to a suit which outranks it **3** to outdo or surpass: *she trumped his news by announcing that she had been picked for the Olympic team* ▸ See also **trumps**
WORD ORIGIN variant of *triumph*

trump[2] *n archaic or literary* **1** a trumpet or the sound produced by one **2 the last trump** the final trumpet call on the Day of Judgment
WORD ORIGIN Old French *trompe*

trump card *n* **1** any card from the suit that ranks higher than any other suit in one particular game **2** an advantage, weapon, etc. that is kept in reserve until needed: *the President hoped to use his experience of foreign affairs as a trump card in the election*. Also called: **trump**

trumped up *adj* (of charges, excuses, etc.) made up in order to deceive

trumpery *n, pl* **-eries 1** something useless or worthless ▷ *adj* **2** useless or worthless
WORD ORIGIN Old French *tromperie* deceit

trumpet ❶ *n* **1** a valved brass musical instrument consisting of a narrow tube ending in a flare **2** a loud sound such as that of a trumpet: *the elephant gave a loud trumpet* **3 blow one's own trumpet** to boast about one's own skills or good qualities ▷ *vb* **-peting, -peted 4** to proclaim or state forcefully: *almost every one of the party's loudly trumpeted election claims is untrue* **5** (of an elephant) to make a loud cry **trumpeter** *n*
WORD ORIGIN Old French *trompette*

trumps *pl n* **1** *cards* any one of the four suits that outranks all the other suits for the duration of a deal or game **2 turn up trumps** (of a person) to bring about a happy or successful conclusion, esp. unexpectedly

truncate *vb* **-cating, -cated** to shorten by cutting **truncated** *adj* **truncation** *n*
WORD ORIGIN Latin *truncare*

truncheon *n chiefly Brit* a small club, esp. one carried by a policeman
WORD ORIGIN Old French *tronchon* stump

trundle *vb* **-dling, -dled** to move heavily on or as if on wheels: *a bus trundled along the drive*
WORD ORIGIN Old English *tryndel* circular or spherical object

trundle bed *n US, Canad & NZ* a low bed on wheels, stored under a larger bed

trundler *n* **1** *NZ* a golf or shopping trolley **2** a child's pushchair

trunk ❶ *n* **1** the main stem of a tree **2** a large strong case or box used to contain clothes when travelling and for storage **3** a person's body excluding the head, neck, and limbs; torso **4** the long nose of an elephant **5** *US* the boot of a car ▸ See also **trunks**
WORD ORIGIN Latin *truncus*

trunk call *n chiefly Brit & Austral* a long-distance telephone call

trunk line *n* **1** a direct link between two distant telephone exchanges or switchboards **2** the main route or routes on a railway

trunk road *n Brit* a main road, esp. one maintained by the central government

trunks *pl n* shorts worn by a man for swimming

truss *vb* **1** to tie or bind (someone) up **2** to bind the wings and legs of (a fowl) before cooking ▷ *n* **3** *med* a device for holding a hernia in place **4** a framework of wood or metal used to support a roof, bridge, etc. **5** a cluster of flowers or fruit growing at the end of a single stalk
WORD ORIGIN Old French *trousse*

trust ❶ *vb* **1** to believe that (someone) is honest and means no harm: *my father warned me never to trust strangers* **2** to feel that (something) is safe and reliable: *I don't trust those new gadgets* **3** to entrust (someone) with important information or valuables: *she's not somebody I would trust with this sort of secret* **4** to believe that (someone) is likely to do something safely and reliably: *I wouldn't trust anyone else to look after my child properly* **5** to believe (a story, account, etc.)

t

THESAURUS

genuine, proper, authentic, dinkum (*Austral & NZ informal*) **3 = faithful**, loyal, devoted, dedicated, firm, fast, constant, pure, steady, reliable, upright, sincere, honourable, honest, staunch, trustworthy, trusty, dutiful, true-blue, unswerving
OPPOSITE: unfaithful
4 = exact, perfect, correct, accurate, proper, precise, spot-on (*Brit informal*), on target, unerring
OPPOSITE: inaccurate

truly *adv* **1 = faithfully**, firmly, constantly, steadily, honestly, sincerely, staunchly, dutifully, loyally, honourably, devotedly, with all your heart, with dedication, with devotion, confirmedly
2a = genuinely, really, correctly, truthfully, rightly, in fact, precisely, exactly, legitimately, accurately, in reality, in truth, beyond doubt, without a doubt, authentically, beyond question, factually, in actuality, veritably, veraciously
OPPOSITE: falsely
2b = really, very, greatly, indeed, seriously (*informal*), extremely, to be sure, exceptionally, verily

trumpet *n* **1 = horn**, clarion, bugle ▷ *vb* **4 = proclaim**, advertise, extol, tout (*informal*), announce, publish, broadcast, crack up (*informal*), sound loudly, shout from the rooftops, noise abroad
OPPOSITE: keep secret

trunk *n* **1 = stem**, stock, stalk, bole **2 = chest**, case, box, crate, bin, suitcase, locker, coffer, casket, portmanteau, kist (*Scot & Northern English dialect*) **3 = body**, torso **4 = snout**, nose, proboscis

trust *vb* **1, 2, 4, 5 = believe in**, have faith in, depend on, count on, bank on, lean on, rely upon, swear by, take at face value, take as gospel, place reliance on, place your trust in, pin your faith on, place *or* have

DICTIONARY

6 to expect, hope, or suppose: *I trust you've made your brother welcome here* ▷ *n* **7** confidence in the truth, worth, reliability, etc. of a person or thing; faith: *he knew that his father had great trust in him* **8** the obligation of someone in a responsible position: *he was in a position of trust as her substitute father* **9 a** a legal arrangement whereby one person looks after property, money, etc. on another's behalf **b** property that is the subject of such an arrangement **10** (in Britain) a self-governing hospital, group of hospitals, or other body that operates as an independent commercial unit within the National Health Service **11** *chiefly US & Canad* a group of companies joined together to control the market for any commodity ▷ *adj* **12** of or relating to a trust or trusts: *trust status*
WORD ORIGIN Old Norse *traust* help, support, confidence

trustee *n* **1** a person who administers property on someone else's behalf **2** a member of a board that manages the affairs of an institution or organization

trustful ❶ *or* **trusting** *adj* characterized by a readiness to trust others **trustfully** *or* **trustingly** *adv*

trust fund *n* money, securities, etc. held in trust

trustworthy *adj* (of a person) honest, reliable, or dependable

trusty *adj* **trustier, trustiest** **1** faithful or reliable: *his trusty steed* ▷ *n, pl* **trusties** **2** a trustworthy convict to whom special privileges are granted

truth ❶ *n* **1** the quality of being true, genuine, or factual: *there is no truth in the allegations* **2** something that is true: *he finally learned the truth about his parents' marriage* **3** a proven or verified fact, principle, etc.: *some profound truths about biology have come to light*
WORD ORIGIN Old English *trīewth*

truthful *adj* **1** telling the truth; honest **2** true; based on facts: *a truthful answer* **truthfully** *adv* **truthfulness** *n*

try ❶ *vb* **tries, trying, tried** **1** to make an effort or attempt: *you must try to understand* **2** to sample or test (something) to see how enjoyable, good, or useful it is: *I tried smoking once but didn't like it* **3** to put strain or stress on (someone's patience) **4** to give pain, affliction, or vexation to: *sometimes when I've been sorely tried, my temper gets a little out of hand* **5 a** to investigate (a case) in a court of law **b** to hear evidence in order to determine the guilt or innocence of (a person) ▷ *n, pl* **tries** **6** an attempt or effort **7** *rugby* a score made by placing the ball down behind the opposing team's goal line
WORD ORIGIN Old French *trier* to sort

trying ❶ *adj* upsetting, difficult, or annoying

try on *vb* **1** to put on (a garment) to find out whether it fits **2 try it on** *informal* to attempt to deceive or fool someone ▷ *n* **try-on** **3** *Brit informal* something done to test out a person's tolerance etc.

try out *vb* **1** to test (something), esp. to find out how good it is ▷ *n* **tryout** **2** *chiefly US & Canad* a trial or test, for example of an athlete or actor

trysail *n* a small fore-and-aft sail set on a sailing vessel to help keep her head to the wind in a storm

tryst *n archaic or literary* **1** an arrangement to meet, esp. secretly **2** a meeting, esp. a secret one with a lover, or the place where such a meeting takes place
WORD ORIGIN Old French *triste* lookout post

tsar *or* **czar** (zahr) *n* (until 1917) the emperor of Russia. Also: **tzar** > **tsarist** *or* **czarist** *n*
WORD ORIGIN Russian, ultimately from CAESAR

tsarevitch *or* **czarevitch** (**zahr**-rev-itch) *n* the eldest son of a Russian tsar

tsarina *or* **czarina** (zahr-**een**-a) *n* the wife of a Russian tsar

tsetse fly *or* **tzetze fly** (**tset**-see) *n* a bloodsucking African fly whose bite transmits disease, esp. sleeping sickness
WORD ORIGIN Tswana (language of southern Africa) *tse tse*

T-shirt *or* **tee-shirt** *n* a short-sleeved casual shirt or top
WORD ORIGIN T-shape formed when laid flat

Tshombe *n* **Moise** 1919–69, Congolese statesman. He led the secession of Katanga (1960) from the newly independent Congo; forced into exile (1963) but returned (1964–65) as premier of the Congo; died in exile

Tsiolkovski *n* **Konstantin Eduardovich** 1857–1935, Russian aeronautical engineer, a pioneer of rocket and space research. His work on liquid-fuelled rockets anticipated the ideas of Robert Goddard

tsotsi (**tsot**-see) *n S African* a Black street thug or gang member
WORD ORIGIN perhaps from Nguni (language group of southern Africa) *tsotsa* to dress flashily

tsp. teaspoon

T-square *n* a T-shaped ruler used for drawing horizontal lines and to support set squares when drawing vertical and inclined lines

tsunami *n* a large, often destructive, sea wave, usually caused by an earthquake under the sea
WORD ORIGIN Japanese

Tsvangirai *n* **Morgan** born 1952, Zimbabwean trade unionist and politician; leader of the Movement for Democratic Change, the main opposition party to President Mugabe's Zanu-PF since 1999

Tsvetaeva *n* **Marina (Ivanovna)** 1892–1941, Russian poet. Opposed to

THESAURUS

confidence in **OPPOSITE:** distrust **3 = entrust**, commit, assign, confide, consign, put into the hands of, allow to look after, hand over, turn over, sign over, delegate **6 = expect**, believe, hope, suppose, assume, guess *(informal)*, take it, presume, surmise, think likely
▷ *n* **7 = confidence**, credit, belief, faith, expectation, conviction, assurance, certainty, reliance, credence, certitude
OPPOSITE: distrust

trustful *or* **trusting** *adj* **= unsuspecting**, simple, innocent, optimistic, naive, confiding, gullible, unwary, unguarded, credulous, unsuspicious
OPPOSITE: suspicious

truth *n* **1a = reality**, fact(s), real life, actuality **OPPOSITE:** unreality **1b = truthfulness**, fact, accuracy, honesty, precision, validity, legitimacy, authenticity, correctness, sincerity, verity, candour, veracity, rightness, genuineness, exactness, factuality, factualness
OPPOSITE: inaccuracy

try *vb* **1 = attempt**, seek, aim, undertake, essay, strive, struggle, endeavour, have a go, go for it *(informal)*, make an effort, have a shot *(informal)*, have a crack *(informal)*, bend over backwards *(informal)*, do your best, go for broke *(slang)*, make an attempt, move heaven and earth, bust a gut *(informal)*, give it your best shot *(informal)*, have a stab *(informal)*, break your neck *(informal)*, exert yourself, make an all-out effort *(informal)*, knock yourself out *(informal)*, have a whack *(informal)*, do your damnedest *(informal)*, give it your all *(informal)*, rupture yourself *(informal)* **2 = experiment with**, try out, put to the test, test, taste, examine, investigate, sample, evaluate, check out, inspect, appraise ▷ *n* **6 = attempt**, go *(informal)*, shot *(informal)*, effort, crack *(informal)*, essay, stab *(informal)*, bash *(informal)*, endeavour, whack *(informal)*

trying *adj* **= annoying**, hard, taxing, difficult, tough, upsetting, irritating, fatiguing, stressful, aggravating *(informal)*, troublesome, exasperating, arduous, tiresome, vexing, irksome, wearisome, bothersome
OPPOSITE: straightforward

t

DICTIONARY

the Revolution, she left Russia (1922) and lived in Paris: when she returned (1939) her husband was shot and she committed suicide

TT **1** teetotal **2** teetotaller **3** tuberculin-tested

tuatara (too-ah-**tah**-rah) *n* a large lizard-like New Zealand reptile
WORD ORIGIN Māori *tua* back + *tara* spine

tub *n* **1** a low wide, usually round container **2** a small plastic or cardboard container for ice cream etc. **3** *chiefly US* ▸ same as **bath** (sense 1) **4** Also called: **tubful** the amount a tub will hold **5** a slow and uncomfortable boat or ship
WORD ORIGIN Middle Dutch *tubbe*

tuba (**tube**-a) *n* a low-pitched brass musical instrument with valves
WORD ORIGIN Latin

tubby *adj* **-bier, -biest** (of a person) fat and short **tubbiness** *n*

tube *n* **1** a long hollow cylindrical object, used for the passage of fluids or as a container **2** a flexible cylinder of soft metal or plastic closed with a cap, used to hold substances such as toothpaste **3** *anat* any hollow cylindrical structure: *the Fallopian tubes* **4** **the tube** *Brit* the underground railway system in London **5** *electronics* ▸ see **cathode-ray tube** **6** *slang chiefly US* a television set **tubeless** *adj*
WORD ORIGIN Latin *tubus*

tuber (**tube**-er) *n* a fleshy underground root of a plant such as a potato
WORD ORIGIN Latin: hump

tubercle (**tube**-er-kl) *n* **1** a small rounded swelling **2** any abnormal hard swelling, esp. one characteristic of tuberculosis
WORD ORIGIN Latin *tuberculum* a little swelling

tubercular (tube-**berk**-yew-lar) *or* **tuberculous** *adj* **1** of or symptomatic of tuberculosis **2** of or relating to a tubercle

tuberculin (tube-**berk**-yew-lin) *n* a sterile liquid prepared from cultures of the tubercle bacillus and used in the diagnosis of tuberculosis

tuberculin-tested *adj* (of milk) produced by cows that have been certified as free of tuberculosis

tuberculosis (tube-berk-yew-**lohss**-iss) *n* an infectious disease characterized by the formation of tubercles, esp. in the lungs

tuberous (**tube**-er-uss) *adj* (of plants) forming, bearing, or resembling a tuber or tubers

tubing (**tube**-ing) *n* **1** a length of tube **2** a system of tubes

Tubman *n* **William Vacanarat Shadrach** 1895–1971, Liberian statesman; president of Liberia (1944–71)

tub-thumper *n* a noisy or ranting public speaker **tub-thumping** *adj, n*

tubular (**tube**-yew-lar) *adj* **1** having the shape of a tube or tubes **2** of or relating to a tube or tubing

tubule (**tube**-yewl) *n* any small tubular structure, esp. in an animal or plant

TUC (in Britain and South Africa) Trades Union Congress

tuck ❶ *vb* **1** to push or fold into a small space or between two surfaces: *she tucked the letter into her handbag* **2** to thrust the loose ends or sides of (something) into a confining space, so as to make it neat and secure: *he tucked his shirt back into his trousers* **3** to make a tuck or tucks in (a garment) ▹ *n* **4** a pleat or fold in a part of a garment, usually stitched down **5** *Brit informal* food, esp. cakes and sweets
WORD ORIGIN Old English *tūcian* to torment

Tuck *n* See **Friar Tuck**

tuck away *vb informal* **1** to eat (a large amount of food) **2** to store (something) in a safe place: *we knew he had some money tucked away somewhere* **3** to have a quiet, rarely disturbed or visited location: *the chapel is tucked away in a side street*

tucker *n* **1** a detachable yoke of lace, linen, etc. formerly worn over the breast of a low-cut dress **2** *Austral & NZ informal* food **3** **one's best bib and tucker** *informal* one's best clothes

tuckered *adj* **tuckered out** *informal chiefly US & Canad* exhausted

tuck in *vb* **1** to put (someone) to bed and make him or her snug **2** to thrust the loose ends or sides of (something) into a confining space: *tuck in the bedclothes* **3** *informal* to eat, esp. heartily

tuck shop *n chiefly Brit* a shop in or near a school, where cakes and sweets are sold

Tudor *adj* **1** of or in the reign of the English royal house ruling from 1485 to 1603 **2** denoting a style of architecture characterized by half-timbered houses: *a Tudor cottage*

Tues. Tuesday

Tuesday *n* the third day of the week
WORD ORIGIN Old English *tīwesdæg* day of Tyr, Norse god

tufa (**tew**-fa) *n* a porous rock formed of calcium carbonate deposited from springs
WORD ORIGIN Italian *tufo*

tuff *n geol* a porous rock formed from volcanic dust or ash
WORD ORIGIN Old French *tuf*

tuffet *n* a small mound or low seat
WORD ORIGIN from *tuft*

tuft *n* a bunch of feathers, grass, hair, threads, etc. held together at the base **tufted** *adj* **tufty** *adj*
WORD ORIGIN probably from Old French *tufe*

Tu Fu *n* a variant transliteration of the Chinese name for **Du Fu**

tug ❶ *vb* **tugging, tugged** **1** to pull or drag with a sharp or powerful movement: *she tugged at my arm* **2** to tow (a ship or boat) by means of a tug ▹ *n* **3** a strong pull or jerk **4** Also called: **tugboat** a boat with a powerful engine, used for towing barges, ships, etc.
WORD ORIGIN Middle English *tuggen*

tug-of-love *n* a conflict over the custody of a child between divorced parents or between the child's natural parents and its foster or adoptive parents

tug-of-war *n* **1** a contest in which two people or teams pull opposite ends of a rope in an attempt to drag the opposition over a central line **2** any hard struggle between two people or two groups

tuition ❶ *n* **1** instruction, esp. that received individually or in a small group **2** the payment for instruction, esp. in colleges or universities
WORD ORIGIN Latin *tueri* to watch over

tuktu *n Canad* ▸ another name for **caribou**

tuk-tuk *n* (in Thailand) a three-wheeled motor vehicle used as a taxi

tulip *n* **1** a plant which produces bright cup-shaped flowers in spring **2** the flower or bulb
WORD ORIGIN Turkish *tülbend* turban

tulip tree *n* a North American tree with tulip-shaped greenish-yellow flowers and long conelike fruits

Tull *n* **Jethro** 1674–1741, English agriculturalist, who invented the seed drill

tulle (**tewl**) *n* a fine net fabric of silk, rayon, etc. used to make evening dresses
WORD ORIGIN French

tumble ❶ *vb* **-bling, -bled** **1** to fall or cause to fall, esp. awkwardly or

THESAURUS

tuck *vb* **1, 2 = push**, stick, stuff, slip, ease, insert, pop *(informal)* ▹ *n* **4 = fold**, gather, pleat, pinch **5** *(Brit informal)* **= food**, eats *(slang)*, tack *(informal)*, scoff *(slang)*, grub *(slang)*, kai *(NZ informal)*, nosh *(slang)*, victuals, comestibles, nosebag *(slang)*, vittles *(obsolete, dialect)*

tug *vb* **1a = pull**, drag, pluck, jerk, yank, wrench, lug **1b = drag**, pull, haul, tow, lug, heave, draw ▹ *n* **3 = pull**, jerk, yank, wrench, drag, haul, tow, traction, heave

tuition *n* **1 = training**, schooling, education, teaching, lessons, instruction, tutoring, tutelage

tumble *vb* **1 = fall**, drop, topple, plummet, roll, pitch, toss, stumble,

t

DICTIONARY

violently: *chairs tumbled over* **2** to roll or twist, esp. in playing: *they rolled and tumbled as wild beasts* **3** to decrease in value suddenly: *interest rates tumbled* **4** to move in a quick and uncontrolled manner: *the crowd tumbled down the stairs* **5** to disturb, rumple, or toss around: *she was all tumbled by the fall* **6** to perform leaps or somersaults ▹ *n* **7** a fall, esp. an awkward or violent one: *he took a tumble down the stairs* **8** a somersault **tumbled** *adj*
WORD ORIGIN Old English *tumbian* dance, jump

tumbledown *adj* (of a building) falling to pieces; dilapidated

tumble dryer *or* **drier** *n* an electrically-operated machine that dries wet laundry by rotating it in warmed air inside a metal drum

tumbler *n* **1 a** a flat-bottomed drinking glass with no handle or stem **b** the amount a tumbler will hold **2** a person who performs somersaults and other acrobatic feats **3** a part of the mechanism of a lock

tumble to *vb* to understand or become aware of: *how did he tumble to this?*

tumbril *n* a farm cart that tilts backwards to empty its load, which was used to take condemned prisoners to the guillotine during the French Revolution
WORD ORIGIN Old French *tumberel*

tumescent (tew-**mess**-ent) *adj* swollen or becoming swollen

tumid (**tew**-mid) *adj rare* **1** (of an organ or part of the body) enlarged or swollen **2** pompous or fulsome in style: *a tumid tome* **tumidity** *n*
WORD ORIGIN Latin *tumere* to swell

tummy *n, pl* **-mies** ▸ an informal or childish word for **stomach**

tumour ❶ *or US* **tumor** (**tew**-mer) *n pathol* **a** any abnormal swelling **b** a mass of tissue formed by a new growth of cells **tumorous** *adj*
WORD ORIGIN Latin *tumere* to swell

tumult (**tew**-mult) *n* **1** a loud confused noise, such as one produced by a crowd **2** a state of confusion and excitement: *a tumult of emotions*
WORD ORIGIN Latin *tumultus*

tumultuous (tew-**mull**-tew-uss) *adj* **1** exciting, confused, or turbulent: *this week's tumultuous events* **2** unruly, noisy, or excited: *a tumultuous welcome*

tumulus (**tew**-myew-luss) *n, pl* **-li** (-lie) *archaeol no longer in technical usage* a burial mound
WORD ORIGIN Latin: a hillock

tun *n* a large beer cask
WORD ORIGIN Old English *tunne*

tuna (**tune**-a) *n, pl* **-na** *or* **-nas** **1** a large marine spiny-finned fish **2** the flesh of this fish, often tinned for food
WORD ORIGIN American Spanish

tundra *n* a vast treeless Arctic region with permanently frozen subsoil
WORD ORIGIN Russian

tune ❶ *n* **1** a melody, esp. one for which harmony is not essential **2** the correct musical pitch: *many of the notes are out of tune* **3 call the tune** to be in control of the proceedings **4 change one's tune** to alter one's attitude or tone of speech **5 in** *or* **out of tune with** in *or* not in agreement or sympathy with: *in tune with public opinion* **6 to the tune of** *informal* to the amount or extent of ▹ *vb* **tuning, tuned** **7** to adjust (a musical instrument) so each string, key, etc. produces the right note **8** to make small adjustments to (an engine, machine, etc.) to obtain the proper or desired performance **9** to adjust (a radio or television) to receive a particular station or programme: *the radio was tuned to the local station* **tuner** *n*
WORD ORIGIN variant of *tone*

tuneful *adj* having a pleasant tune **tunefully** *adv*

tune in *vb* **1** to adjust (a radio or television) to receive (a station or programme) **2 tuned in to** *slang* aware of or knowledgeable about: *tuned in to European cinema*

tuneless *adj* having no melody or tune

tune up *vb* **1** to adjust (a musical instrument) to a particular pitch **2** to adjust the engine of a car, etc. to improve its performance

tungsten *n chem* a hard greyish-white metallic element. Symbol: W
WORD ORIGIN Swedish *tung* heavy + *sten* stone

tunic *n* **1** a close-fitting jacket forming part of some uniforms **2** a loose-fitting knee-length garment
WORD ORIGIN Latin *tunica*

tuning fork *n* a two-pronged metal fork that when struck produces a pure note of constant specified pitch

tunnel ❶ *n* **1** an underground passageway, esp. one for trains or cars **2** any passage or channel through or under something: *the carpal tunnel* ▹ *vb* **-nelling, -nelled** *or US* **-neling, -neled** **3** to make one's way through or under (something) by digging a tunnel: *ten men succeeded in tunnelling out of the prisoner-of-war camp* **4** to dig a tunnel (through or under something): *the idea of tunnelling under the English Channel has been around for a long time*
WORD ORIGIN Old French *tonel* cask

tunnel vision *n* **1** a condition in which a person is unable to see things that are not straight in front **2** narrowness of viewpoint resulting from concentration on only one aspect of a subject or situation

Tunney *n* **Gene**, original name *James Joseph Tunney*. 1897–1978, US boxer; world heavyweight champion (1926–28)

tunny *n, pl* **-nies** *or* **-ny** ▸ same as **tuna**
WORD ORIGIN Latin *thunnus*

tup *n chiefly Brit* a male sheep
WORD ORIGIN origin unknown

tupik (**too**-pick) *n* a tent of seal or caribou skin used for shelter by the Inuit in summer
WORD ORIGIN Inuktitut *tupiq*

Tupolev *n* **Andrei Nikolaievich** 1888–1972, Soviet aircraft designer, who designed the first supersonic passenger aircraft, the TU-144 (tested 1969). He also designed supersonic bombers and the TU-104, one of the first passenger jet aircraft (1955)

tuppence *n Brit* ▸ same as **twopence** > **tuppenny** *adj*

tuque (rhymes with **fluke**) *n Canad* **1** a knitted cap with a long tapering end **2** a close-fitting knitted hat often with a tassel or pompom
WORD ORIGIN Canadian French

turban *n* **1** a head-covering worn by a Muslim, Hindu, or Sikh man, consisting of a long piece of cloth wound round the head **2** any head-covering resembling this **turbaned** *adj*
WORD ORIGIN Turkish *tülbend*

turbid *adj literary* (of water or air) full of mud or dirt, and frequently swirling around: *the turbid stream of the Loire* **turbidity** *n*
WORD ORIGIN Latin *turbare* to agitate

turbine *n* a machine in which power is produced by a stream of water, air, etc. that pushes the blades of a wheel and causes it to rotate
WORD ORIGIN Latin *turbo* whirlwind

turbocharger *n* a device that increases the power of an internal-combustion engine by using the exhaust gases to drive a turbine **turbocharged** *adj*

THESAURUS

flop, trip up, fall head over heels, fall headlong, fall end over end ▹ *n* **7 = fall**, drop, roll, trip, collapse, plunge, spill, toss, stumble, flop, headlong fall

tumour *n* **b = growth**, cancer, swelling, lump, carcinoma *(pathology)*, sarcoma *(medical)*, neoplasm *(medical)*

tune *n* **1 = melody**, air, song, theme, strain(s), motif, jingle, ditty, melody line **2 = harmony**, pitch, euphony ▹ *vb* **7 = tune up**, adjust, bring into harmony **8 = regulate**, adapt, modulate, harmonize, attune, pitch

tunnel *n* **1, 2 = passage**, underpass, passageway, subway, channel, hole, shaft ▹ *vb* **3, 4 = dig**, dig your way,

DICTIONARY

turbofan *n* a type of engine in which a large fan driven by a turbine forces air rearwards to increase the propulsive thrust

turbojet *n* **1** a gas turbine in which the exhaust gases provide the propulsive thrust to drive an aircraft **2** an aircraft powered by turbojet engines

turboprop *n* an aircraft propulsion unit where the propeller is driven by a gas turbine

turbot *n, pl* **-bot** *or* **-bots** a European flatfish, highly valued as a food fish
WORD ORIGIN Old French *tourbot*

turbulence *n* **1** a state or condition of confusion, movement, or agitation **2** *meteorol* instability in the atmosphere causing gusty air currents

turbulent ● *adj* **1** involving a lot of sudden changes and conflicting elements: *the city has had a turbulent history* **2** (of people) wild and unruly: *a harsh mountain land inhabited by a score of turbulent tribes* **3** (of water or air) full of violent unpredictable currents: *the turbulent ocean*
WORD ORIGIN Latin *turba* confusion

turd *n taboo* **1** a piece of excrement **2** *slang* a contemptible person
WORD ORIGIN Old English *tord*

tureen *n* a large deep dish with a lid, used for serving soups
WORD ORIGIN French *terrine* earthenware vessel

Turenne *n* **Vicomte de**, title of *Henri de la Tour d'Auvergne*. 1611–75, French marshal. He commanded armies during the Thirty Years' War and the wars of the Fronde

turf ● *n, pl* **turfs** *or* **turves** **1** a layer of thick even grass with roots and soil attached: *a short turf rich in wild flowers* **2** a piece cut from this layer: *we spent the afternoon digging turves* **3** *informal* **a** the area where a person lives and feels at home: *my boyhood turf of east Cork* **b** a person's area of knowledge or influence: *when Kate is at work, she's on her own turf* **4 the turf a** a track where horse races are run **b** horse racing as a sport or industry **5** ▸ same as **peat** ▹*vb* **6** to cover (an area of ground) with pieces of turf
WORD ORIGIN Old English

turf accountant *n Brit* ▸ same as **bookmaker**

turf out *vb informal* to throw (someone or something) out: *the residents fear a new landlord might push up rents and turf them out of their homes*

turgid (tur-jid) *adj* **1** (of language) pompous, boring, and hard to understand **2** (of water or mud) unpleasantly thick and brown
turgidity *n*
WORD ORIGIN Latin *turgere* to swell

Turgot *n* **Anne Robert Jacques** 1727–81, French economist and statesman. As controller general of finances (1774–76), he attempted to abolish feudal privileges, incurring the hostility of the aristocracy and his final dismissal

Turishcheva *n* **Ludmilla** born 1952, Soviet gymnast: world champion 1970, 1972 (at the Olympic Games), and 1974

Turk *n* a person from Turkey

turkey *n, pl* **-keys** *or* **-key** **1** a large bird of North America bred for its meat **2** *informal chiefly US & Canad* something, esp. a theatrical production, that fails **3 cold turkey** *slang* a method of curing drug addiction by abrupt withdrawal of all doses **4 talk turkey** *informal chiefly US & Canad* to discuss, esp. business, frankly and practically
WORD ORIGIN used at first of the African guinea fowl (because it was brought through Turkish territory), later applied by mistake to the American bird

Turkic *n* a family of Asian languages including Turkish and Azerbaijani

Turkish *adj* **1** of Turkey ▹*n* **2** the language of Turkey

Turkish bath *n* **1** a type of bath in which the bather sweats freely in hot dry air, is then washed, often massaged, and has a cold plunge or shower **2 Turkish baths** an establishment for such baths

Turkish coffee *n* very strong black coffee

Turkish delight *n* a jelly-like sweet flavoured with flower essences, usually cut into cubes and covered in icing sugar

turmeric *n* **1** a tropical Asian plant with yellow flowers and an aromatic underground stem **2** a yellow spice obtained from the root of this plant
WORD ORIGIN Old French *terre merite* meritorious earth

turmoil ● *n* disorder, agitation, or confusion: *a period of political turmoil and uncertainty*
WORD ORIGIN origin unknown

turn ● *vb* **1** to move to face in another direction **2** to rotate or move round **3** to operate (a switch, key, etc.) by twisting it **4** to aim or point (something) in a particular direction: *they turned their guns on the crowd* **5** to change in course or direction: *the van turned right into Victoria Road* **6** (of a road, river, etc.) to have a bend or curve in it **7** to perform or do (something) with a rotating movement: *a small boy was turning somersaults* **8** to change so as to become: *he turned pale* **9** to reach, pass, or progress beyond in age, time, etc.: *she had just turned fourteen* **10** to find (a particular page) in a book: *turn to page 78* **11** to look at the other side of: *turning the pages of a book* **12** to shape (wood, metal, etc.) on a lathe **13** (of leaves) to change colour in autumn **14** to make or become sour: *the milk is starting to turn* **15** to affect or be affected with nausea or giddiness: *that would turn the strongest stomach* **16** (of the tide) to start coming in or going out **17 turn against** to stop liking (something or someone one previously liked): *people turned against her because she became so dictatorial* **18 turn into** to become or change into: *my mother turned our house into four apartments* **19 turn loose** to set (an animal or a person) free **20 turn someone's head** to affect someone mentally or emotionally **21 turn to a** to direct or apply (one's attention

t

THESAURUS

burrow, mine, bore, drill, excavate

turbulent *adj* **3 = stormy**, rough, raging, tempestuous, boiling, disordered, furious, unsettled, foaming, unstable, agitated, tumultuous, choppy, blustery
OPPOSITE: calm

turf *n* **1 = grass**, green, sward **2 = sod**, divot, clod **4b the turf = horse-racing**, the flat, racecourse, racetrack, racing

turmoil *n* **= confusion**, trouble, violence, row, noise, stir, disorder, chaos, disturbance, upheaval, bustle, flurry, strife, disarray, uproar, turbulence, ferment, agitation, commotion, pandemonium, bedlam, tumult, hubbub, brouhaha
OPPOSITE: peace

turn *vb* **1** *(sometimes with* **round***)* **= change course**, swing round, wheel round, veer, move, return, go back, switch, shift, reverse, swerve, change position **2 = rotate**, spin, go round (and round), revolve, roll, circle, wheel, twist, spiral, whirl, swivel, pivot, twirl, gyrate, go round in circles, move in a circle **8** *(with* **into***)* **= change**, transform, fashion, shape, convert, alter, adapt, mould, remodel, form, mutate, refit, metamorphose, transmute, transfigure **12 = shape**, form, fashion, cast, frame, construct, execute, mould, make **14a = go bad**, go off *(Brit informal)*, curdle, go sour, become rancid **14b = make rancid**, spoil, sour, taint **22, 24 = change of direction**, bend, curve, change of course, shift, departure, deviation **26 = opportunity**, go, spell, shot *(informal)*, time, try, round, chance, period, shift, crack *(informal)*, succession, fling, stint, whack *(informal)* **27 = direction**, course, tack, swing, tendency, drift, bias **32 = deed**, service, act, action, favour, gesture

DICTIONARY

or thoughts) to **b** to stop doing or using one thing and start doing or using (another): *I turned to photography from writing* **c** to appeal or apply to (someone) for help, advice, etc. ▷ *n* **22** the act of turning **23** a movement of complete or partial rotation: *a turn of the dial* **24** a change of direction or position **25** ▸ same as **turning** (sense 1) **26** the right or opportunity to do something in an agreed order or succession: *it was her turn to play next* **27** a change in something that is happening or being done: *events took an unhappy turn* **28** a period of action, work, etc. **29** a short walk, ride, or excursion **30** natural inclination: *a liberal turn of mind* **31** distinctive form or style: *she'd a nice turn of phrase* **32** a deed that helps or hinders someone: *I'm trying to do you a good turn* **33** a twist, bend, or distortion in shape **34** a slight attack of an illness: *she's just having one of her turns* **35** *music* a melodic ornament that alternates the main note with the notes above and below it, beginning with the note above, in a variety of sequences **36** a short theatrical act: *tonight's star turn* **37** *informal* a shock or surprise: *you gave me rather a turn* **38** **done to a turn** *informal* cooked perfectly **39** **turn and turn about** one after another; alternately ▸ See also **turn down, turn in**, etc. **turner** *n*
WORD ORIGIN Old English *tyrnan*

turnaround *or* **turnabout** *n* a complete change or reversal: *a prompt economic turnaround*

turncoat *n* a person who deserts one cause or party to join an opposing one

turn down *vb* **1** to reduce (the volume, brightness, or temperature of something): *turn the heat down* **2** to reject or refuse: *the invitation was turned down* **3** to fold down (sheets, etc.)

turn in ❶ *vb informal* **1** to go to bed for the night **2** to hand in: *turning in my essay* **3** to hand (a suspect or criminal) over to the police: *his own brother turned him in*

turning ❶ *n* **1** a road, river, or path that turns off the main way **2** the point where such a way turns off **3** the process of turning objects on a lathe

turning circle *n* the smallest circle in which a vehicle can turn

turning point ❶ *n* a moment when a decisive change occurs

turnip *n* a vegetable with a large yellow or white edible root
WORD ORIGIN Latin *napus*

turnkey *n old-fashioned* a jailer

turn off ❶ *vb* **1** to leave (a road or path): *turning off the main road* **2** (of a road or path) to lead away from (another road or path): *a main street with alleys twisting and turning off it* **3** to cause (something) to stop operating by turning a knob, pushing a button, etc. **4** *informal* to cause disgust or disinterest in (someone): *keeping kids from getting turned off by mathematics* ▷ *n* **turn-off 5** a road or other way branching off from the main thoroughfare **6** *informal* a person or thing that causes dislike

turn on ❶ *vb* **1** to cause (something) to operate by turning a knob, pushing a button, etc.: *turn on the radio, please* **2** to attack (someone), esp. without warning: *the Labrador turned on me* **3** *informal* to produce suddenly or automatically: *turning on that bland smile* **4** *slang* to arouse emotionally or sexually **5** to depend or hinge on: *the match turned on three double faults by Sampras* ▷ *n* **turn-on 6** *slang* a person or thing that causes emotional or sexual arousal

turn out ❶ *vb* **1** to cause (something, esp. a light) to stop operating by moving a switch **2** to produce or create: *turning out two hits a year* **3** to force (someone) out of a place or position: *turned out of office* **4** to empty the contents of (something): *the police ordered him to turn out his pockets* **5** to be discovered or found (to be or do something): *he turned out to be a Finn* **6** to end up or result: *how interesting to see how it all turned out!* **7** to dress and groom: *she is always very well turned out* **8** to assemble or gather: *crowds turned out to see him* **9** **turn out for** *informal* to make an appearance, esp. in a sporting competition: *he was asked to turn out for Liverpool* ▷ *n* **turnout 10** a number of people attending an event: *there has been a high turnout of voters in elections in Bulgaria* **11** the quantity or amount produced

turn over ❶ *vb* **1** to change position, esp. so as to reverse top and bottom **2** to shift position, for instance by rolling onto one's side: *he turned over and went straight to sleep* **3** to consider carefully: *as I walked, I turned her story over* **4** to give (something) to someone who has a right to it or to the authorities: *the police ordered him to turn over the files to them* **5** (of an engine) to start or function correctly: *when he pressed the starter button, the engine turned over at once* **6** *slang* to rob: *the house had been turned over while they were out* ▷ *n* **turnover 7 a** the amount of business done by a company during a specified period **b** the rate at which stock in trade is sold and replenished **8** a small pastry case filled with fruit or jam: *an apple turnover* **9** the number of workers employed by a firm in a given period to replace those who have left

turnpike *n* **1** *history* a barrier across a road to prevent vehicles or pedestrians passing until a charge (toll) had been paid **2** *US* a motorway for use of which a toll is charged
WORD ORIGIN *turn* + *pike* a spike

turnstile *n* a mechanical barrier with arms that are turned to admit one person at a time

turntable *n* **1** the circular platform in a record player that rotates the record while it is being played **2** a circular platform used for turning locomotives and cars

turn up *vb* **1** to arrive or appear: *few people turned up* **2** to find or discover or be found or discovered: *a medical checkup has only turned up a sinus infection* **3** to increase the flow, volume, etc. of: *he turned up the radio* ▷ *n* **turn-up 4** *Brit* the turned-up fold at the bottom of some trouser legs **5** **a turn-up for the books** *informal* an unexpected happening

turpentine *n* **1** a strong-smelling colourless oil distilled from the resin of some coniferous trees, and used for thinning paint, for cleaning, and in medicine **2** a semisolid mixture of resin and oil obtained from various conifers, which is the main source of commercial turpentine **3** *not in technical usage* any one of a number of thinners for paints and varnishes, consisting of fractions of petroleum
WORD ORIGIN Latin *terebinthina*

turpitude *n formal* depravity or wickedness: *newspapers owned by*

THESAURUS

turn in *vb* **2 = hand in**, return, deliver, give back, give up, hand over, submit, surrender, tender

turning *n* **1 = bend**, turn, curve **2 = turn-off**, turn, junction, crossroads, side road, exit

turning point *n* **= crossroads**, critical moment, decisive moment, change, crisis, crux, moment of truth, point of no return, moment of decision, climacteric, tipping point

turn off *vb* **3 = switch off**, turn out, put out, stop, kill, cut out, shut down, unplug, flick off

turn on *vb* **1 = switch on**, put on, activate, start, start up, ignite, kick-start, set in motion, energize **4** *(slang)* **= arouse**, attract, excite, thrill, stimulate, please, press someone's buttons *(slang)*, work someone up, titillate, ring someone's bell *(US slang)*, arouse someone's desire

turnout *n* **10 = attendance**, crowd, audience, gate, assembly, congregation, number, throng, assemblage

turnover *n* **7a = output**, business, production, flow, volume, yield, productivity, outturn *(rare)*

t

DICTIONARY

proprietors whose moral turpitude far exceeded anything chronicled in their pages **WORD ORIGIN** Latin *turpitudo* ugliness

turps *n* ▸ short for **turpentine** (senses 1, 3)

turquoise *adj* **1** greenish-blue ▹ *n* **2** a greenish-blue precious stone **WORD ORIGIN** Old French *turqueise* Turkish (stone)

turret *n* **1** a small tower that projects from the wall of a building, esp. a castle **2** (on a tank or warship) a rotating structure on which guns are mounted **3** (on a machine tool) a turret-like steel structure with tools projecting from it that can be rotated to bring each tool to bear on the work **turreted** *adj* **WORD ORIGIN** Latin *turris* tower

turtle *n* **1** an aquatic reptile with a flattened shell enclosing the body and flipper-like limbs adapted for swimming **2 turn turtle** (of a boat) to capsize **WORD ORIGIN** French *tortue* tortoise

turtledove *n* an Old World dove noted for its soft cooing and devotion to its mate **WORD ORIGIN** Old English *turtla*

turtleneck *n* a round high close-fitting neck on a sweater or a sweater with such a neck

Tuscan *adj* of a style of classical architecture characterized by unfluted columns **WORD ORIGIN** from *Tuscany*, a region in central Italy

tusk *n* a long pointed tooth in the elephant, walrus, and certain other mammals **tusked** *adj* **WORD ORIGIN** Old English *tūsc*

tussle *n* **1** an energetic fight, struggle, or argument: *she resigned following a protracted boardroom tussle* ▹ *vb* **-sling, -sled 2** to fight or struggle energetically **WORD ORIGIN** Middle English *tusen* to pull

tussock *n* a dense tuft of grass or other vegetation **tussocky** *adj* **WORD ORIGIN** origin unknown

tut *interj, n, vb* **tutting, tutted** ▸ short for **tut-tut**

tutelage (tew-till-lij) *n formal* **1** instruction or guidance, esp. by a tutor **2** the state of being supervised by a guardian or tutor **WORD ORIGIN** Latin *tueri* to watch over

tutelary (tew-till-lar-ee) *adj literary* **1** having the role of guardian or protector **2** of a guardian

tutor ❶ *n* **1** a teacher, usually one instructing individual pupils **2** (at a college or university) a member of staff responsible for the teaching and supervision of a certain number of students ▹ *vb* **3** to act as a tutor to (someone) **tutorship** *n* **WORD ORIGIN** Latin: a watcher

tutorial *n* **1** a period of intensive tuition given by a tutor to an individual student or to a small group of students ▹ *adj* **2** of or relating to a tutor

tutti *adj, adv music* to be performed by the whole orchestra, choir, etc. **WORD ORIGIN** Italian

tutti-frutti *n, pl* **-fruttis** an ice cream or other sweet food containing small pieces of candied or fresh fruits **WORD ORIGIN** Italian, literally: all the fruits

tut-tut *interj* **1** an exclamation of mild reprimand, disapproval, or surprise ▹ *vb* **-tutting, -tutted 2** to express disapproval by the exclamation of 'tut-tut' ▹ *n* **3** the act of tut-tutting: *his bright red tennis shorts provoked a few tut-tuts from the traditionalists*

tutu *n* a very short skirt worn by ballerinas, made of projecting layers of stiffened material **WORD ORIGIN** French

Tutuola *n* **Amos** 1920–97, Nigerian writer: his books include *The Palm-Wine Drinkard* (1952) and *Pauper, Brawler and Slanderer* (1987)

tuxedo *n, pl* **-dos** a dinner jacket **WORD ORIGIN** after a country club in *Tuxedo Park*, New York

TV television

TVEI *Brit* technical and vocational educational initiative: a national educational scheme in which pupils gain practical experience in technology and industry, often through work placement

twaddle *n* **1** silly, trivial, or pretentious talk or writing ▹ *vb* **-dling, -dled 2** to talk or write in a silly or pretentious way **WORD ORIGIN** earlier *twattle*

twain *adj, n archaic* two **WORD ORIGIN** Old English *twēgen*

twang *n* **1** a sharp ringing sound produced by or as if by the plucking of a taut string **2** a strongly nasal quality in a person's speech: *a high-pitched Texas twang* ▹ *vb* **3** to make or cause to make a twang: *a bunch of angels twanging harps* **twangy** *adj* **WORD ORIGIN** imitative

twat *n Brit, Austral & NZ taboo slang* **1** the female genitals **2** a foolish person **WORD ORIGIN** origin unknown

tweak *vb* **1** to twist or pinch with a sharp or sudden movement: *she tweaked his ear* **2** *informal* to make a minor alteration ▹ *n* **3** the act of tweaking **4** *informal* a minor alteration **WORD ORIGIN** Old English *twiccian*

twee *adj informal* excessively sentimental, sweet, or pretty **WORD ORIGIN** from *tweet*, affected pronunciation of *sweet*

tweed *n* **1** a thick woollen cloth produced originally in Scotland **2 tweeds** a suit made of tweed **WORD ORIGIN** probably from *tweel*, Scots variant of *twill*

Tweedsmuir *n* **Baron Tweedsmuir** the title of Scottish novelist John Buchan ▸ See **Buchan**

tweedy *adj* **tweedier, tweediest 1** of, made of, or resembling tweed **2** showing a fondness for a hearty outdoor life, often associated with wearers of tweeds

tweet *interj* **1** an imitation of the thin chirping sound made by small birds ▹ *vb* **2** to make this sound **3** to write a short message on the Twitter website ▹ *n* **4** a thin chirping sound **5** a short message posted on the Twitter website **WORD ORIGIN** imitative

tweeter *n* a loudspeaker used in high-fidelity systems for the reproduction of high audio frequencies

tweezers *pl n* a small pincer-like tool used for tasks such as handling small objects or plucking out hairs **WORD ORIGIN** obsolete *tweeze* case of instruments

twelfth *adj* **1** of or being number twelve in a series ▹ *n* **2** number twelve in a series **3** one of twelve equal parts of something

Twelfth Day *n* January 6, the twelfth day after Christmas and the feast of the Epiphany

twelfth man *n* a reserve player in a cricket team

Twelfth Night *n* **a** the evening of January 5, the eve of Twelfth Day **b** the evening of Twelfth Day itself

twelve *n* **1** the cardinal number that is the sum of ten and two **2** a numeral, 12 or XII, representing this number **3** something representing or consisting of twelve units ▹ *adj* **4** amounting to twelve: *twelve months* **WORD ORIGIN** Old English *twelf*

twelvemonth *n archaic chiefly Brit* a year

twelve-tone *adj* of or denoting the type of serial music which uses as its musical material a sequence of notes containing all 12 semitones of the chromatic scale

twenty *n, pl* **-ties 1** the cardinal number that is the product of ten and two **2** a numeral, 20 or XX,

t

THESAURUS

9 = movement, replacement, coming and going, change

tutor *n* **1 = teacher**, coach, instructor, educator, guide, governor, guardian, lecturer, guru, mentor, preceptor, master *or* mistress, schoolmaster *or* schoolmistress ▹ *vb* **3 = teach**, educate, school, train, coach, guide, discipline, lecture,

DICTIONARY

representing this number **3** something representing or consisting of twenty units ▷ *adj* **4** amounting to twenty: *twenty minutes* **twentieth** *adj, n*

Twenty20 *n* form of one-day cricket in which each side bats for twenty overs

twenty-four-seven *or* **24/7** *adv informal* constantly or all the time: *consultants would no longer be available 24/7*
WORD ORIGIN from twenty-four hours a day, seven days a week

twerp *or* **twirp** *n informal* a silly, stupid, or contemptible person
WORD ORIGIN origin unknown

twice *adv* **1** two times; on two occasions or in two cases: *I've met her only twice* **2** double in degree or quantity: *twice as big*
WORD ORIGIN Old English *twiwa*

twiddle *vb* **-dling, -dled 1** to twirl or fiddle, often in an idle way: *twiddling the knobs of a radio* **2 twiddle one's thumbs a** to rotate one's thumbs around one another, when bored or impatient **b** to be bored, with nothing to do ▷ *n* **3** an unnecessary decoration, esp. a curly one
WORD ORIGIN probably *twirl* + *fiddle*

twig[1] **T** *n* a small branch or shoot of a tree **twiggy** *adj*
WORD ORIGIN Old English *twigge*

twig[2] *vb* **twigging, twigged** *informal* to realize or understand: *I should have twigged it earlier*
WORD ORIGIN origin unknown

twilight **T** *n* **1** the soft dim light that occurs when the sun is just below the horizon after sunset **2** the period in which this light occurs: *soon after twilight we started marching again* **3** a period in which strength, importance, etc. is gradually declining: *the twilight of his political career* ▷ *adj* **4** of or relating to the period towards the end of the day: *the twilight shift* **5** of or being a period of decline: *he spent most of his twilight years working on a history of France* **6** denoting irregularity and obscurity: *a twilight existence* **twilit** *adj*
WORD ORIGIN Old English *twi-* half + LIGHT

twilight zone *n* any indefinite or intermediate condition or area: *the twilight zone between sleep and wakefulness*

twill *n* a fabric woven to produce an effect of parallel diagonal lines or ribs in the cloth
WORD ORIGIN Old English *twilic* having a double thread

twin **T** *n* **1** one of a pair of people or animals conceived at the same time **2** one of a pair of people or things that are identical or very similar ▷ *vb* **twinning, twinned 3** to pair or be paired together
WORD ORIGIN Old English *twinn*

twin bed *n* one of a pair of matching single beds

twin-bedded *adj* (of a room in a hotel etc.) containing two single beds

twine *n* **1** string or cord made by twisting fibres together ▷ *vb* **twining, twined 2** to twist or wind together: *she twined the flowers into a garland* **3 twine round** *or* **around** to twist or wind around: *she twined her arms around her neck*
WORD ORIGIN Old English *twīn*

twin-engined *adj* (of an aeroplane) having two engines

twinge *n* **1** a sudden brief darting or stabbing pain **2** a sharp emotional pang: *a twinge of conscience*
WORD ORIGIN Old English *twengan* to pinch

twinkle **T** *vb* **-kling, -kled 1** to shine brightly and intermittently; sparkle **2** (of the eyes) to sparkle, esp. with amusement or delight ▷ *n* **3** a flickering brightness; sparkle
WORD ORIGIN Old English *twinclian*

twinkling *n* **in the twinkling of an eye** in a very short time

twinset *n* a matching jumper and cardigan

twin town *n* a town that has cultural and social links with a foreign town: *Nuremberg is one of Glasgow's twin towns*

twirl *vb* **1** to move around rapidly and repeatedly in a circle **2** to twist, wind, or twiddle, often idly: *twirling the glass in her hand* ▷ *n* **3** a whirl or twist **4** a written flourish
WORD ORIGIN origin unknown

twist **T** *vb* **1** to turn one end or part while the other end or parts remain still or turn in the opposite direction: *never twist or wring woollen garments* **2** to distort or be distorted **3** to wind or twine: *the wire had been twisted twice* **4** to force or be forced out of the natural form or position: *I twisted my knee* **5** to change the meaning of; distort: *he'd twisted the truth to make himself look good* **6** to revolve or rotate: *he twisted the switch to turn the radio off* **7** to wrench with a turning action: *he twisted the wheel sharply* **8** to follow a winding course: *the road twisted as it climbed* **9** to dance the twist **10 twist someone's arm** to persuade or coerce someone ▷ *n* **11** the act of twisting: *she gave a dainty little twist to her parasol* **12** something formed by or as if by twisting: *there's a twist in the cable* **13** a decisive change of direction, aim, meaning, or character: *the latest revelations give a new twist to the company's boardroom wranglings* **14** an unexpected development in a story, play, or film **15** a bend: *a twist of the mountain road* **16** a distortion of the original shape or form **17** a jerky pull, wrench, or turn **18 the twist** a dance popular in the 1960s, in which dancers vigorously twist the hips **19 round the twist** *slang* mad or eccentric **twisty** *adj*
WORD ORIGIN Old English

twisted *adj* (of a person) cruel or perverted

twister *n Brit* a swindling or dishonest person

twit[1] *vb* **twitting, twitted** *Brit* to poke fun at (someone)
WORD ORIGIN Old English *ætwītan*

twit[2] *n informal* a foolish or stupid person
WORD ORIGIN from TWIT[1]

twitch **T** *vb* **1** (of a person or part of a person's body) to move in a jerky spasmodic way: *his left eyelid twitched involuntarily* **2** to pull (something) with a quick jerky movement: *she twitched the curtains shut* ▷ *n* **3** a sharp jerking movement, esp. one caused by a nervous condition
WORD ORIGIN Old English *twiccian* to pluck

twitcher *n Brit informal* a bird-watcher who tries to spot as many rare varieties as possible

twitchy *adj* **twitchier, twitchiest** nervous, worried, and ill-at-ease: *he*

THESAURUS

drill, instruct, edify, direct

twig[1] *n* **= branch**, stick, sprig, offshoot, shoot, spray, withe

twilight *n* **1 = half-light**, gloom, dimness, semi-darkness **2 = dusk**, evening, sunset, early evening, nightfall, sundown, gloaming *(Scot poetic)*, close of day, evo *(Austral slang)*
OPPOSITE: dawn

twin *n* **1, 2 = double**, counterpart, mate, match, fellow, clone, duplicate, lookalike, likeness, ringer *(slang)*, corollary ▷ *vb* **3 = pair**, match, join, couple, link, yoke

twinkle *vb* **1, 2 = sparkle**, flash, shine, glitter, gleam, blink, flicker, wink, shimmer, glint, glisten, scintillate, coruscate ▷ *n* **3 = sparkle**, light, flash, spark, shine, glittering, gleam, blink, flicker, wink, shimmer, glimmer, glistening, scintillation, coruscation

twist *vb* **1 = coil**, curl, wind, plait, wrap, screw, twirl **2 = distort**, screw up, contort, mangle, mangulate *(Austral slang)* **OPPOSITE:** straighten **3 = intertwine**, wind, weave, braid, interweave, plait, entwine, twine, wreathe, interlace ▷ *n* **11, 17 = wind**, turn, spin, swivel, twirl **13 = development**, emphasis, variation, slant **14 = surprise**, change, turn, development, revelation **15 = curve**, turn, bend, loop, arc, kink, zigzag, convolution, dog-leg, undulation

twitch *vb* **1 = jerk**, blink, flutter, jump, squirm **2 = pull (at)**, snatch (at), tug (at), pluck (at), yank (at) ▷ *n* **3 = jerk**,

t

DICTIONARY

was twitchy with anticipation

twitter *vb* **1** (esp. of a bird) to utter a succession of chirping sounds **2** to talk rapidly and nervously in a high-pitched voice: *novelists who twittered about how much they admired him* **3** to write a short message on the Twitter website ▹*n* **4** the act or sound of twittering **5 Twitter** *trademark* a website where people can post short messages about their current activities **6 in a twitter** in a state of nervous excitement **twitterer** *n* **twittering** *n* **twittery** *adj*
WORD ORIGIN imitative

two *n* **1** the cardinal number that is the sum of one and one **2** a numeral, 2 or II, representing this number **3** something representing or consisting of two units **4 in two** in or into two parts: *cut the cake in two and take a bit each* **5 put two and two together** to reach an obvious conclusion by considering the evidence available **6 that makes two of us** the same applies to me ▹*adj* **7** amounting to two: *two years*
WORD ORIGIN Old English *twā*

twoccing *or* **twocking** *n Brit slang* the act of breaking into a motor vehicle and driving it away **twoccer** *or* **twocker** *n*
WORD ORIGIN from *T(aking) W(ithout) O(wner's) C(onsent)*, the legal offence

two-dimensional *adj* **1** having two dimensions **2** somewhat lacking in depth or complexity: *a modern audience is unable to tolerate two-dimensional characters*

two-edged *adj* **1** (of a remark) having both a favourable and an unfavourable interpretation, such as *she looks nice when she smiles* **2** (of a knife, saw, etc.) having two cutting edges

two-faced *adj* deceitful or hypocritical: *he's a two-faced liar and opportunist*

twofold *adj* **1** having twice as many or as much **2** composed of two parts ▹*adv* **3** by twice as many or as much

two-four *n Canad informal* a box containing 24 bottles of beer

two-handed *adj* **1** requiring the use of both hands **2** requiring the participation of two people: *a two-handed transatlantic yacht race*

twopence *or* **tuppence** (tup-pence) *n Brit* **1** the sum of two pennies **2** the slightest amount: *I don't care twopence who your father is*

twopenny *or* **tuppenny** (tup-pen-ee) *adj chiefly Brit* **1** cheap or tawdry **2** worth or costing two pence **3 not care a twopenny damn** to not care at all

two-piece *adj* **1** consisting of two separate parts, usually matching, such as a woman's suit or swimsuit ▹*n* **2** such an outfit

two-ply *adj* made of two thicknesses, layers, or strands

two-sided *adj* **1** having two sides: *two-sided paper* **2** having two aspects or interpretations: *an ambivalent two-sided event*

twosome *n* a group of two people

two-step *n* **1** an old-time dance in duple time: *the next dance was the Military Two-Step* **2** music for this dance

two-stroke *adj* of an internal-combustion engine whose piston makes two strokes for every explosion

Two Thousand Guineas *n* **the Two Thousand Guineas** an annual horse race for three-year-olds, run at Newmarket

two-time *vb* **-timing, -timed** *informal* to deceive (a lover) by having an affair with someone else **two-timer** *n*

two-way *adj* **1** moving in, or allowing movement in, two opposite directions: *two-way traffic* **2** involving mutual involvement or cooperation: *two-way communication* **3** (of a radio or transmitter) capable of both transmission and reception of messages

TX Texas

tycoon ❶ *n* a businessman of great wealth and power
WORD ORIGIN Japanese *taikun* great ruler

tyke *or* **tike** *n* **1** *Brit, Austral & NZ informal* a small or cheeky child **2** *Brit dialect* a rough ill-mannered person
WORD ORIGIN Old Norse *tīk* bitch

Tylor *n* Sir **Edward Burnett** 1832–1917, British anthropologist; first professor of anthropology at Oxford (1896). His *Primitive Culture* (1871) became a standard work

tympani *pl n* ▸ same as **timpani**

tympanic membrane *n anat* the thin membrane separating the external ear from the middle ear; eardrum

tympanum *n, pl* **-nums** *or* **-na 1** *anat* **a** the cavity of the middle ear **b** ▸ same as **tympanic membrane 2** *archit* the recessed space between the arch and the lintel above a door **tympanic** *adj*
WORD ORIGIN Greek *tumpanon* drum

Tyndall *n* **John** 1820–93, Irish physicist, noted for his work on the radiation of heat by gases, the transmission of sound through the atmosphere, and the scattering of light

Tynwald (tin-wold) *n* the Parliament of the Isle of Man
WORD ORIGIN Old Norse *thing* assembly + *vollr* field

type ❶ *n* **1** a kind, class, or category of things, all of which have something in common **2** a subdivision of a particular class; sort: *it is more alcoholic than most wines of this type* **3** the general characteristics distinguishing a particular group: *the old-fashioned type of nanny* **4** *informal* a person, esp. of a specified kind: *a seagoing type* **5** a block with a raised character on it used for printing **6** text printed from type; print ▹*vb* **typing, typed 7** to write using a typewriter or word processor **8** to be a symbol of or typify **9** to decide the type of; classify
WORD ORIGIN Greek *tupos* image

typecast *vb* **-casting, -cast** to cast (an actor or actress) in the same kind of role continually

typeface *n* the size and style of printing used in a book, magazine, etc.

typescript *n* any typewritten document

typeset *vb* **-setting, -set** *printing* to set (text for printing) in type

typesetter *n* a person who sets type; compositor

typewriter *n* a machine which prints a letter or other character when the appropriate key is pressed

typewritten *adj* typed on a typewriter or word processor

typhoid *pathol n* **1** ▸ short for **typhoid fever** ▹*adj* **2** of or relating to typhoid fever: *typhoid vaccines*

typhoid fever *n* an acute infectious disease characterized by high fever, spots, abdominal pain, etc. It is spread by contaminated food or water

typhoon *n* a violent tropical storm, esp. one in the China Seas or W Pacific
WORD ORIGIN Chinese *tai fung* great wind

typhus *n* an acute infectious disease transmitted by lice or mites and characterized by high fever, skin rash, and severe headache
WORD ORIGIN Greek *tuphos* fever

typical ❶ *adj* **1** being or serving as a representative example of a

t

THESAURUS

tic, spasm, twinge, jump, blink, flutter, tremor

tycoon *n* **= magnate**, capitalist, baron, industrialist, financier, fat cat *(slang, chiefly US)*, mogul, captain of industry, potentate, wealthy businessman, big cheese *(slang, old-fashioned)*, plutocrat, big noise *(informal)*, merchant prince

type *n* **1, 2, 3 = kind**, sort, class, variety, group, form, order, style, species, breed, strain, category, stamp, kidney, genre, classification, ilk, subdivision

typical *adj* **1a = archetypal**, standard, model, normal, classic, stock, essential, representative, usual, conventional, regular, characteristic,

DICTIONARY

particular type; characteristic: *a typical working day* **2** considered to be an example of some undesirable trait: *it was typical that he should start talking almost before he was inside the room* **typically** *adv*
WORD ORIGIN Greek *tupos* image

typify *vb* **-fies, -fying, -fied 1** to be typical of or characterize: *the beers made here typify all that is best about the independent brewing sector* **2** to symbolize or represent: *a number of dissident intellectuals, typified by Andrei Sakharov*

typing *n* **1** the work or activity of using a typewriter or word processor **2** the skill of using a typewriter quickly and accurately

typist *n* a person who types letters, reports, etc. esp. for a living

typo *n, pl* **-pos** *informal* a typographical error

typography *n* **1** the art or craft of printing **2** the style or quality of printing and layout in a book, magazine, etc. **typographical** *adj* **typographically** *adv*

tyrannical *adj* of or like a tyrant; unjust and oppressive

tyrannize *or* **-ise** *vb* **-nizing, -nized** *or* **-nising, -nised** to rule or exercise power (over) in a cruel or oppressive manner: *he dominated and tyrannized his younger brother*

tyrannosaurus (tirr-ran-oh-**sore**-uss) *or* **tyrannosaur** *n* a large two-footed flesh-eating dinosaur common in North America in Cretaceous times
WORD ORIGIN Greek *turannos* tyrant + *sauros* lizard

tyranny ❶ *n, pl* **-nies 1 a** government by a tyrant **b** oppressive and unjust government by more than one person **2** the condition or state of being dominated or controlled by something that makes unpleasant or harsh demands: *the tyranny of fashion drives many women to diet although they are not overweight* **tyrannous** *adj*

tyrant *n* **1** a person who governs oppressively, unjustly, and arbitrarily **2** any person who exercises authority in a tyrannical manner: *a domestic tyrant*
WORD ORIGIN Greek *turannos*

tyre *or US* **tire** *n* a ring of rubber, usually filled with air but sometimes solid, fitted round the rim of a wheel of a road vehicle to grip the road
WORD ORIGIN earlier *tire*, probably archaic variant of *attire*

tyro *n, pl* **-ros** a novice or beginner
WORD ORIGIN Latin *tiro* recruit

tzar *n* ▸ same as **tsar**

Tzara *n* **Tristan,** original name *Samuel Rosenstock*. 1896–1963, French poet and essayist, born in Romania, best known as the founder of Dada: author of *The Approximate Man* (1931)

tzatziki (tsat-see-kee) *n* a Greek dip made from yogurt, chopped cucumber, and mint
WORD ORIGIN Modern Greek

tzetze fly *n* ▸ same as **tsetse fly**

THESAURUS

orthodox, indicative, illustrative, archetypical, stereotypical
OPPOSITE: unusual
1b = average, normal, usual, conventional, routine, regular, orthodox, predictable, run-of-the-mill, bog-standard *(Brit & Irish slang)*
2 = characteristic, in keeping, in character, true to type

tyranny *n* **1b = oppression**, cruelty, dictatorship, authoritarianism, reign of terror, despotism, autocracy, absolutism, coercion, high-handedness, harsh discipline, unreasonableness, imperiousness, peremptoriness **OPPOSITE:** liberality

Uu

DICTIONARY

U 1 (in Britain) universal (used to describe a film certified as suitable for viewing by anyone) 2 *chem* uranium ▷ *adj* 3 *Brit informal* (of language or behaviour) characteristic of the upper class
UB40 *n* 1 (in Britain) a registration card issued to an unemployed person 2 *informal* (in Britain) a person registered as unemployed
ubiquitous ⓘ (yew-**bik**-wit-uss) *adj* being or seeming to be everywhere at once **ubiquity** *n*
WORD ORIGIN Latin *ubique* everywhere
U-boat *n* a German submarine
WORD ORIGIN German *Unterseeboot* undersea boat
Ubuntu *n S African* humanity or fellow feeling; kindness
WORD ORIGIN Nguni (language group of southern Africa)
uc *printing* upper case
UCAS (in Britain) Universities and Colleges Admissions Service
UCCA (formerly, in Britain) Universities Central Council on Admissions
Uccello *n* **Paolo** 1397–1475, Florentine painter noted esp. for three paintings of *The Battle of San Romano, 1432* (1456–60)
UCW (in Britain) Union of Communications Workers
Udall *or* **Uvedale** *n* **Nicholas** ?1505–56, English dramatist, whose comedy *Ralph Roister Doister* (?1553), modelled on Terence and Plautus, is the earliest known English comedy
udder *n* the large baglike milk-producing gland of cows, sheep, or goats, with two or more teats
WORD ORIGIN Old English *ūder*
UDI Unilateral Declaration of Independence
UEFA Union of European Football Associations
UFO unidentified flying object
ugh (uhh) *interj* an exclamation of disgust, annoyance, or dislike
UGLI *n, pl* **-LIS** *or* **-LIES** *trademark* a yellow citrus fruit: a cross between a tangerine, grapefruit, and orange
WORD ORIGIN probably an alteration of *ugly*, from its wrinkled skin
ugly ⓘ *adj* **uglier, ugliest** 1 so unattractive as to be unpleasant to look at 2 very unpleasant and involving violence or aggression: *an ugly incident in which one man was stabbed* 3 repulsive or displeasing: *ugly rumours* 4 bad-tempered or sullen: *an ugly mood* **ugliness** *n*
WORD ORIGIN Old Norse *uggligr* dreadful
ugly duckling *n* a person or thing, initially ugly or unpromising, that becomes beautiful or admirable
WORD ORIGIN from *The Ugly Duckling* by Hans Christian Andersen
UHF *radio* ultrahigh frequency
Uhland *n* **Johann Ludwig** 1787–1862, German romantic poet, esp. of lyrics and ballads
UHT ultra-heat-treated (milk or cream)
UK United Kingdom
ukase (yew-**kaze**) *n* (in imperial Russia) a decree from the tsar
WORD ORIGIN Russian *ukaz*
Ukrainian *adj* 1 of Ukraine ▷ *n* 2 a person from Ukraine 3 the language of Ukraine
ukulele *or* **ukelele** (yew-kal-**lay**-lee) *n* a small four-stringed guitar
WORD ORIGIN Hawaiian, literally: jumping flea
Ulanova *n* **Galina** (**Sergeyevna**) 1910–98, Russian ballet dancer, who performed with the Leningrad Kirov ballet (1928–44) and the Moscow Bolshoi Ballet (1944–62)
Ulbricht *n* **Walter** 1893-1973, East German statesman; largely responsible for the establishment and development of East German communism
ulcer ⓘ *n* an open sore on the surface of the skin or a mucous membrane
WORD ORIGIN Latin *ulcus*
ulcerated *adj* made or becoming ulcerous **ulceration** *n*
ulcerous *adj* of, like, or characterized by ulcers
Ulfilas, Ulfila, *or* **Wulfila** *n* ?311–?382 AD, Christian bishop of the Goths who translated the Bible from Greek into Gothic
ulna *n, pl* **-nae** *or* **-nas** the inner and longer of the two bones of the human forearm or of the forelimb in other vertebrates **ulnar** *adj*
WORD ORIGIN Latin: elbow
Ulpian *n* Latin name *Domitius Ulpianus* died ?228 AD, Roman jurist, born in Phoenicia
ulster *n* a man's heavy double-breasted overcoat
WORD ORIGIN *Ulster*, the northernmost province of Ireland
Ulsterman *or fem* **Ulsterwoman** *n, pl* **-men** *or* **-women** a person from Ulster
ult. ultimo
ulterior (ult-**ear**-ee-or) *adj* (of an aim, reason, etc.) concealed or hidden: *an ulterior motive*
WORD ORIGIN Latin: further
ultimate ⓘ *adj* 1 final in a series or process: *predictions about the ultimate destination of modern art* 2 highest, supreme, or unchallengeable: *he has the ultimate power to dismiss the Prime Minister* 3 fundamental or essential: *a believer in the ultimate goodness of man* 4 most extreme: *genocide is the ultimate abuse of human rights* 5 final or total: *she should be able to estimate the ultimate cost* ▷ *n* 6 **the ultimate in** the best example of: *the ultimate in luxury holidays* **ultimately** *adv*
WORD ORIGIN Latin *ultimus* last, distant
ultimatum (ult-im-**may**-tum) *n* a final warning to someone that they must agree to certain conditions or requirements, or else action will be taken against them: *Britain declared war after the Nazis rejected the ultimatum to withdraw from Poland*
ultimo *adv* in or during the previous month. It is rare except when abbreviated to ult. in formal correspondence: *your communication of the 1st ultimo*
WORD ORIGIN Latin: on the last
ultra *n* a person who has extreme or immoderate beliefs or opinions
WORD ORIGIN Latin: beyond
ultra- *prefix* 1 beyond a specified extent, range, or limit: *ultrasonic* 2 extremely: *ultraleftist*
WORD ORIGIN Latin
ultraconservative *adj* 1 highly

THESAURUS

ubiquitous *adj* = **ever-present**, pervasive, omnipresent, all-over, everywhere, universal
ugly *adj* 1 = **unattractive**, homely (*chiefly US*), plain, unsightly, unlovely, unprepossessing, not much to look at, no oil painting (*informal*), ill-favoured, hard-featured, hard-favoured OPPOSITE: beautiful
2, 3 = **unpleasant**, shocking, terrible, offensive, nasty, disgusting, revolting, obscene, hideous, monstrous, vile, distasteful, horrid, repulsive, frightful, objectionable, disagreeable, repugnant
OPPOSITE: pleasant
4 = **bad-tempered**, nasty, sullen, surly, threatening, dangerous, angry, forbidding, menacing, sinister, ominous, malevolent, spiteful, baleful, bodeful OPPOSITE: good-natured
ulcer *n* = **sore**, abscess, gathering, peptic ulcer, gumboil
ultimate *adj* 1 = **final**, eventual, conclusive, last, end, furthest, extreme, terminal, decisive
2 = **supreme**, highest, greatest, maximum, paramount, most significant, superlative, topmost

DICTIONARY

reactionary ▷*n* 2 a reactionary person

ultrahigh frequency *n* a radio frequency between 3000 and 300 megahertz

ultramarine *n* 1 a blue pigment originally made from lapis lazuli ▷*adj* 2 vivid blue
WORD ORIGIN Latin *ultra* beyond + *mare* sea; because the lapis lazuli from which the pigment was made was imported from Asia

ultramodern *adj* extremely modern

ultramontane *adj* 1 on the other side of the mountains, usually the Alps, from the speaker or writer 2 of a movement in the Roman Catholic Church which favours supreme papal authority ▷*n* 3 a person from beyond the Alps 4 a member of the ultramontane party of the Roman Catholic Church

ultrasonic *adj* of or producing sound waves with higher frequencies than humans can hear **ultrasonically** *adv*

ultrasonics *n* the branch of physics concerned with ultrasonic waves

ultrasound *n* ultrasonic waves, used in echo sounding, medical diagnosis, and therapy

ultrasound scan *n* an examination of an internal bodily structure by the use of ultrasonic waves, esp. for diagnosing abnormality in a fetus

ultraviolet *n* 1 the part of the electromagnetic spectrum with wavelengths shorter than light but longer than X-rays ▷*adj* 2 of or consisting of radiation lying in the ultraviolet: *ultraviolet light*

ultra vires (ult-ra vire-eez) *adv, adj* beyond the legal power of a person or organization
WORD ORIGIN Latin, literally: beyond strength

ululate (yewl-yew-late) *vb literary* **-lating, -lated** to howl or wail **ululation** *n*
WORD ORIGIN Latin *ululare*

Umar *n* a variant transliteration of the Arabic name for **Omar**

Umar Tal *n* ?1797–1864, African religious and military leader, who created a Muslim empire in W Africa

umbel *n* a type of compound flower in which the flowers arise from the same point in the main stem and have stalks of the same length, to give a cluster with the youngest flowers at the centre **umbellate** *adj*
WORD ORIGIN Latin *umbella* a sunshade

umbelliferous *adj* of or denoting a plant with flowers in umbels, such as fennel, parsley, carrot, or parsnip
WORD ORIGIN Latin *umbella* a sunshade + *ferre* to bear

umber *n* 1 a type of dark brown earth containing ferric oxide (rust) ▷*adj* 2 dark brown to reddish-brown
WORD ORIGIN French *(terre d')ombre* or Italian *(terra di) ombra* shadow (earth)

Umberto I *n* 1844–1900, king of Italy (1878–1900); son of Victor Emmanuel II: assassinated at Monza

Umberto II *n* 1904–83, the last king of Italy (1946), following the abdication of his father Victor Emmanuel III: abdicated when a referendum supported the abolition of the monarchy

umbilical (um-bill-ik-kl) *adj* of or like the navel or the umbilical cord

umbilical cord *n* the long flexible cordlike structure that connects a fetus to the placenta

umbilicus (um-bill-ik-kuss) *n anat* the navel
WORD ORIGIN Latin: navel, centre

umbra *n, pl* **-brae** *or* **-bras** a shadow, usually the shadow cast by the moon onto the earth during a solar eclipse
WORD ORIGIN Latin: shade

umbrage *n* **take umbrage** to take offence
WORD ORIGIN Latin *umbra* shade

umbrella *n* 1 a portable device used for protection against rain, consisting of a light canopy supported on a collapsible metal frame mounted on a central rod 2 a single organization, idea, etc. that contains or covers many different organizations or ideas 3 anything that has the effect of a protective screen or general cover: *under the umbrella of the Helsinki security conference* ▷*adj* 4 containing or covering many different organizations, ideas, etc.: *an umbrella group of nationalists and anti-communists* **umbrella-like** *adj*
WORD ORIGIN Italian *ombrella*, from *ombra* shade

UMF *n trademark* a standard for the level of antibacterial agent possessed by manuka honey

umiak, oomiak *or* **oomiac** (oo-mee-ak) *n* a large open boat made of stretched skins, used by Inuit
WORD ORIGIN Inuktitut

umlaut (oom-lout) *n* 1 the mark (¨) placed over a vowel, esp. in German, indicating change in its sound 2 (esp. in Germanic languages) the change of a vowel brought about by the influence of a vowel in the next syllable
WORD ORIGIN German, from *um* around + *Laut* sound

umlungu (oom-loong-goo) *n S African* a White man: used esp. as a term of address
WORD ORIGIN Nguni (language group of southern Africa)

umpire ❶ *n* 1 an official who ensures that the people taking part in a game follow the rules; referee ▷*vb* **-piring, -pired** 2 to act as umpire in a game
WORD ORIGIN Old French *nomper* not one of a pair

umpteen *adj informal* very many: *the centre of umpteen scandals* **umpteenth** *n, adj*
WORD ORIGIN *umpty* a great deal + *-teen* ten

UN United Nations

un-[1] *prefix (freely used with adjectives, participles, and their derivative adverbs and nouns: less frequently used with certain other nouns)* not; contrary to; opposite of: *uncertain; untidiness; unbelief; untruth*
WORD ORIGIN Old English *on-, un-*

un-[2] *prefix forming verbs* 1 denoting reversal of an action or state: *uncover; untie* 2 denoting removal from, release, or deprivation: *unharness*
WORD ORIGIN Old English *un-, on-*

unabashed *adj* not ashamed or embarrassed

unabated *adv* without any reduction in force: *the storm continued unabated*

unable ❶ *adj* **unable to** not having the power, ability, or authority to; not able to

unabridged *adj* (of a book or text) complete and not shortened or condensed

unacceptable *adj* too bad to be accepted; intolerable

unaccompanied *adj* 1 not having anyone with one: *unaccompanied female travellers should take care* 2 (of singing or a musical instrument) not being accompanied by musical instruments

unaccountable *adj* 1 without any sensible explanation: *for some unaccountable reason I got on the wrong bus* 2 not having to justify or answer for one's actions to other people: *the secret service remains unaccountable to the public* **unaccountably** *adv*

unaccounted *adj* **unaccounted for** unable to be found or traced: *four people were killed in the floods, and eleven remain unaccounted for*

unaccustomed *adj* 1 **unaccustomed to** not used to: *unaccustomed to such behaviour* 2 not familiar: *moments of unaccustomed freedom*

unacknowledged *adj* 1 ignored or not accepted as true or existing 2 not officially recognized as being important

U

THESAURUS

4 = **worst**, greatest, utmost, extreme

umpire *n* 1 = **referee**, judge, ref *(informal)*, arbiter, arbitrator, moderator, adjudicator, umpie *(Austral slang)* ▷*vb* 2 = **referee**, judge, adjudicate, arbitrate, call *(sport)*, moderate, mediate

unable *adj (with* **to***)* = **incapable**, inadequate, powerless, unfit, unfitted, not able, impotent, not up to, unqualified, ineffectual, not equal to OPPOSITE: able

DICTIONARY

unacquainted *adj* **unacquainted with** not knowing about; unfamiliar with

unadopted *adj Brit* (of a road) not maintained by a local authority

unadorned *adj* not decorated; plain

unadulterated *adj* **1** completely pure, with nothing added: *fresh unadulterated spring water* **2** (of an emotion) not mixed with anything else: *a look of unadulterated terror*

unadventurous *adj* not taking chances or trying anything new

unaffected[1] *adj* unpretentious, natural, or sincere

unaffected[2] *adj* not influenced or changed

unafraid *adj* not frightened or nervous

unaided *adv* without any help or assistance; independently: *he could not walk unaided for months after the accident*

unalienable *adj law* ▸ same as **inalienable**

unalike *adj* not similar; different

unalloyed *adj literary* not spoiled by being mixed with anything else

unalterable *adj* not able to be changed

unambiguous *adj* having a clear meaning which can only be interpreted in one way

un-American *adj* **1** not in accordance with the aims, ideals, or customs of the US **2** against the interests of the US **un-Americanism** *n*

Unamuno *n* **Miguel de** 1864–1936, Spanish philosopher and writer

unanimous ❶ (yew-nan-im-uss) *adj* **1** in complete agreement **2** characterized by complete agreement: *unanimous approval* **unanimity** *n* **unanimously** *adv*
WORD ORIGIN Latin *unus* one + *animus* mind

unannounced *adv* without warning: *she turned up unannounced*

unanswerable *adj* **1** having no possible answer **2** so obviously correct that disagreement is impossible

unappealing *adj* unpleasant or off-putting

unappetizing *adj* tasting, looking, or smelling unpleasant to eat

unappreciated *adj* not given the respect or recognition that is deserved

unapproachable *adj* discouraging friendliness; aloof

unarguable *adj* so obviously correct that disagreement is impossible

unarmed ❶ *adj* **1** not carrying any weapons: *they were shooting unarmed peasants* **2** not using any weapons: *unarmed combat*

unashamed *adj* not embarrassed, esp. when doing something some people might find offensive: *unashamed greed* **unashamedly** *adv*

unasked *adv* **1** without being asked to do something: *he opened the door unasked* ▹ *adj* **2** (of a question) not asked, although sometimes implied

unassailable *adj* not able to be destroyed or overcome: *an unassailable lead*

unassisted *adj* without help from anyone else

unassuming *adj* modest or unpretentious

unattached *adj* **1** not connected with any specific body or group **2** not engaged or married

unattainable *adj* not able to be achieved; impossible

unattended *adj* not being watched or looked after: *unattended baggage*

unattractive *adj* not attractive or appealing

unauthorized *or* **-ised** *adj* done or made without official permission

unavailable *adj* not able to be met, obtained, or contacted

unavailing *adj* useless or futile

unavoidable *adj* unable to be avoided or prevented **unavoidably** *adv*

unaware ❶ *adj* **1** not aware or conscious: *unaware of my surroundings* ▹ *adv* **2** *not standard* ▸ same as **unawares**

unawares *adv* **1** by surprise: *death had taken him unawares* **2** without knowing: *had he passed her, all unawares?*

unbalanced *adj* **1** lacking balance **2** mentally deranged **3** biased; one-sided: *his unbalanced summing-up*

unbearable ❶ *adj* not able to be endured **unbearably** *adv*

unbeatable *adj* not able to be bettered

unbecoming *adj* **1** unattractive or unsuitable: *unbecoming garments* **2** not proper or appropriate to a person or position: *acts unbecoming of university students*

unbeknown *adv* (foll. by *to*) without the knowledge of (a person): *unbeknown to her family she had acquired modern ways*. Also (*esp. Brit*): **unbeknownst**
WORD ORIGIN archaic *beknown* known

unbelievable *adj* **1** too unlikely to be believed **2** extremely impressive; marvellous **3** *informal* terrible or shocking **unbelievably** *adv*

unbeliever *n* a person who does not believe in a religion

unbend *vb* **-bending, -bent** to become less strict or more informal in one's attitudes or behaviour

unbending *adj* rigid or inflexible: *an unbending routine*

unbiased *adj* not having or showing prejudice or favouritism; impartial

unbidden *adj literary* not ordered or asked; voluntary or spontaneous: *unbidden thoughts came into Catherine's mind*

unbind *vb* **-binding, -bound** **1** to set free from bonds or chains **2** to unfasten or untie

unblemished *adj* not spoiled or tarnished: *smooth unblemished skins*

unblinking *adj* looking at something without blinking

unblock *vb* to remove a blockage from; clear or free

unblushing *adj* immodest or shameless

unbolt *vb* to unfasten a bolt of a door

unborn ❶ *adj* not yet born

unbosom *vb* to relieve oneself of secrets or feelings by telling someone
WORD ORIGIN UN-[2] + *bosom* (in the sense: centre of the emotions)

unbounded *adj* having no boundaries or limits

unbowed *adj* not giving in or submitting: *the battered but as yet unbowed general secretary*

unbreakable *adj* not able to be broken; indestructible

unbridled *adj* (of feelings or behaviour) not restrained or controlled in any way: *unbridled passion*

unbroken *adj* **1** complete or whole **2** continuous: *I slept for eight unbroken hours* **3** not disturbed or upset: *an unbroken night* **4** (of a record) not improved upon **5** (of animals, esp. horses) not tamed

unburden *vb* to relieve one's mind or oneself of a worry or trouble by telling someone about it

uncalled-for *adj* unnecessary or

THESAURUS

unanimous *adj* **1 = agreed**, united, in agreement, agreeing, at one, harmonious, like-minded, concordant, of one mind, of the same mind, in complete accord **OPPOSITE:** divided
2 = united, common, concerted, solid, consistent, harmonious, undivided, congruent, concordant, unopposed **OPPOSITE:** split

unarmed *adj* **1 = defenceless**, helpless, unprotected, without arms, unarmoured, weaponless **OPPOSITE:** armed

unaware *adj* **1 = ignorant**, unconscious, oblivious, in the dark (*informal*), unsuspecting, uninformed, unknowing, heedless, unenlightened, unmindful, not in the loop (*informal*), incognizant **OPPOSITE:** aware

unbearable *adj* **= intolerable**, insufferable, unendurable, too much (*informal*), unacceptable, oppressive, insupportable **OPPOSITE:** tolerable

unborn *adj* **= expected**, awaited, embryonic, in utero (*Latin*)

U

DICTIONARY

unwarranted: *uncalled-for comments*
uncanny *adj* **1** weird or mysterious: *an uncanny silence* **2** beyond what is normal: *an uncanny eye for detail* **uncannily** *adv* **uncanniness** *n*
uncared-for *adj* not cared for; neglected
uncaring *adj* showing no concern for other people's suffering and hardship
unceasing *adj* continuing without a break; never stopping
unceremonious *adj* **1** relaxed and informal: *she greeted him with unceremonious friendliness* **2** abrupt or rude: *the answer was an unceremonious 'no'* **unceremoniously** *adv*
uncertain ❶ *adj* **1** not able to be accurately known or predicted: *an uncertain future* **2** not definitely decided: *they are uncertain about the date* **3** not to be depended upon: *an uncertain career* **4** changeable: *an uncertain sky* **uncertainty** *n*
unchallenged *adj, adv* done or accepted without being challenged: *seventy years of unchallenged rule; her decisions went unchallenged*
unchangeable *adj* not able to be altered
unchanged *adj* remaining the same
uncharacteristic *adj* not typical **uncharacteristically** *adv*
uncharitable *adj* unkind or harsh **uncharitably** *adv*
uncharted *adj* **1** (of an area of sea or land) not having had a map made of it, esp. because it is unexplored **2** unknown or unfamiliar: *a whole uncharted universe of emotions*
unchecked *adj* **1** not prevented from continuing or growing: *unchecked population growth* **2** not examined or inspected ▹*adv* **3** without being stopped or hindered: *the virus could spread unchecked* **4** without being examined or inspected: *the drugs passed unchecked through airport security*
unchristian *or* **un-Christian** *adj* not in accordance with Christian principles
uncial (un-see-al) *adj* **1** of or written in letters that resemble modern capitals, as used in Greek and Latin manuscripts of the third to ninth centuries ▹*n* **2** an uncial letter or manuscript
WORD ORIGIN Late Latin *unciales litterae* letters an inch long
uncivil *adj* impolite, rude or bad-mannered **uncivilly** *adv*
uncivilized *or* **-ised** *adj* **1** (of a tribe or people) not yet civilized **2** lacking culture or sophistication
unclassified *adj* **1** not arranged in any specific order or grouping **2** (of official information) not secret
uncle *n* **1** a brother of one's father or mother **2** the husband of one's aunt **3** a child's term of address for a male friend of its parents **4** *slang* a pawnbroker
WORD ORIGIN Latin *avunculus*
unclean *adj* lacking moral, spiritual, or physical cleanliness
unclear *adj* confusing or hard to understand
Uncle Sam *n* a personification of the government of the United States
WORD ORIGIN apparently a humorous interpretation of the letters stamped on army supply boxes during the War of 1812: US
Uncle Tom *n informal, offensive* a Black person whose behaviour towards White people is regarded as servile
WORD ORIGIN from *Uncle Tom's Cabin* by H. B. Stowe
unclothed *adj* not wearing any clothes; naked
uncluttered *adj* not containing anything unnecessary; austere and simple
uncoil *vb* to unwind or untwist
uncomfortable ❶ *adj* **1** not physically relaxed: *he was forced to sit in an uncomfortable cross-legged position* **2** not comfortable to be in or use: *an uncomfortable chair* **3** causing discomfort or unease: *the uncomfortable truth* **uncomfortably** *adv*
uncommitted *adj* not bound to a specific opinion, course of action, or cause
uncommon ❶ *adj* **1** not happening or encountered often **2** in excess of what is normal: *an uncommon amount of powder*
uncommonly *adv* **1** in an unusual manner or degree **2** extremely: *an uncommonly good humour*
uncommunicative *adj* disinclined to talk or give information
uncomplaining *adj* doing or tolerating something unpleasant or difficult without complaint: *uncomplaining devotion*
uncomplicated *adj* simple and straightforward
uncomplimentary *adj* not expressing respect or praise; insulting
uncomprehending *adj* not understanding what is happening or what has been said
uncompromising ❶ *adj* not prepared to compromise; inflexible **uncompromisingly** *adv*
unconcealed *adj* not hidden or disguised: *a look of unconcealed hatred*
unconcern *n* apathy or indifference
unconcerned *adj* **1** not interested in something and not wanting to become involved **2** not worried or troubled **unconcernedly** (un-kon-sern-id-lee) *adv*
unconditional ❶ *adj* without conditions or limitations: *an unconditional ceasefire* **unconditionally** *adv*
unconfirmed *adj* not yet proved to be true: *unconfirmed reports of a major accident*
uncongenial *adj* (of a place or condition) unpleasant and unfriendly
unconnected *adj* not linked to each other: *a series of unconnected incidents*
unconscionable *adj* **1** unscrupulous or unprincipled: *an unconscionable charmer* **2** excessive in amount or degree: *unconscionable number of social obligations*
unconscious ❶ *adj* **1** unable to notice or respond to things which one would normally be aware of through the senses; insensible or comatose **2** not aware of one's actions or behaviour: *unconscious of his failure* **3** not realized or intended: *unconscious*

THESAURUS

uncertain *adj* **2 = unsure**, undecided, at a loss, vague, unclear, doubtful, dubious, ambivalent, hazy, hesitant, vacillating, in two minds, undetermined, irresolute **OPPOSITE:** sure
uncomfortable *adj* **2 = painful**, awkward, irritating, hard, rough, troublesome, disagreeable, causing discomfort **3 = uneasy**, troubled, disturbed, embarrassed, distressed, awkward, out of place, self-conscious, disquieted, ill at ease, discomfited, like a fish out of water **OPPOSITE:** comfortable
uncommon *adj* **1 = rare**, unusual, odd, novel, strange, bizarre, curious, peculiar, unfamiliar, scarce, queer, singular, few and far between, out of the ordinary, infrequent, thin on the ground **OPPOSITE:** common **2 = extraordinary**, rare, remarkable, special, outstanding, superior, distinctive, exceptional, unprecedented, notable, singular, unparalleled, noteworthy, inimitable, incomparable **OPPOSITE:** ordinary
uncompromising *adj* **= inflexible**, strict, rigid, decided, firm, tough, stubborn, hardline, die-hard, inexorable, steadfast, unyielding, obstinate, intransigent, unbending, obdurate, stiff-necked
unconditional *adj* **= absolute**, full, complete, total, positive, entire, utter, explicit, outright, unlimited, downright, unqualified, unrestricted, out-and-out, plenary, categorical, unreserved **OPPOSITE:** qualified
unconscious *adj* **1 = senseless**, knocked out, out cold *(informal)*, out, stunned, numb, dazed, blacked out *(informal)*, in a coma, comatose, stupefied, asleep, out for the count *(informal)*, insensible, dead to the world *(informal)* **OPPOSITE:** awake

DICTIONARY

duplicity **4** coming from or produced by the unconscious: *unconscious mental processes* ▷ *n* **5** *psychoanal* the part of the mind containing instincts, impulses, and ideas that are not available for direct examination **unconsciously** *adv* **unconsciousness** *n*

unconstitutional *adj* forbidden by the rules or laws which state how an organization or country must function

uncontrollable *adj* **1** unable to be restrained or prevented: *a fit of uncontrollable giggles* **2** (of a person) wild and unmanageable in behaviour: *he became violent and uncontrollable* **uncontrollably** *adv*

unconventional *adj* not conforming to accepted rules or standards

unconvinced *adj* not certain that something is true or right: *I remained unconvinced by his arguments*

unconvincing *adj* (of a reason, argument, etc.) not good enough to convince people that something is true or right

uncooked *adj* raw

uncooperative *adj* not willing to help other people with what they are trying to do

uncoordinated *adj* **1** not joining or functioning together properly to form a whole **2** (of a person) not able to control his or her movements properly; clumsy

uncork *vb* to remove the cork from a bottle

uncorroborated *adj* not supported by other evidence or proof

uncountable *adj* existing in such large numbers that it is impossible to say how many there are: *uncountable millions*

uncouple *vb* **-pling, -pled** to disconnect or become disconnected

uncouth *adj* lacking in good manners, refinement, or grace
WORD ORIGIN Old English *un-* not + *cūth* familiar

uncover ➊ *vb* **1** to remove the cover or top from **2** to reveal or disclose: *they have uncovered a plot to overthrow the government* **uncovered** *adj*

uncritical *adj* not making a judgment about the merits or morality of something

uncrowned *adj* **1** having the powers, but not the title, of royalty **2** (of a king or queen) not yet crowned

unction *n* **1** *chiefly RC & Eastern Churches* the act of anointing with oil in sacramental ceremonies **2** oily charm **3** an ointment **4** anything soothing
WORD ORIGIN Latin *unguere* to anoint

unctuous *adj* pretending to be kind and concerned but obviously not sincere
WORD ORIGIN Latin *unctum* ointment

uncultured *adj* not knowing much about art, literature, etc.

uncut *adj* **1** not shortened or censored **2** not cut **3** (of precious stones) not having shaped and polished surfaces

undamaged *adj* not spoilt or damaged; intact

undaunted *adj* not put off, discouraged, or beaten

undeceive *vb* **-ceiving, -ceived** to reveal the truth to someone previously misled or deceived

undecided *adj* **1** not having made up one's mind **2** (of an issue or problem) not agreed or decided upon

undeclared *adj* not acknowledged for tax purposes

undemanding *adj* not difficult to do or deal with: *an undemanding task*

undemonstrative *adj* not showing emotions openly or easily

undeniable *adj* **1** unquestionably true **2** of unquestionable excellence: *of undeniable character* **undeniably** *adv*

under ➊ *prep* **1** directly below; on, to, or beneath the underside or base of: *under the bed* **2** less than: *in just under an hour* **3** lower in rank than: *under a general* **4** subject to the supervision, control, or influence of: *under communism for 45 years* **5** in or subject to certain circumstances or conditions: *the bridge is still under construction; under battle conditions* **6** in (a specified category): *he had filed Kafka's 'The Trial' under crime stories* **7** known by: *under their own names* **8** planted with: *a field under corn* **9** powered by: *under sail* ▷ *adv* **10** below; to a position underneath
WORD ORIGIN Old English

under- *prefix* **1** below or beneath: *underarm; underground* **2** insufficient or insufficiently: *underemployed* **3** of lesser importance or lower rank: *undersecretary* **4** indicating secrecy or deception: *underhand*

underachieve *vb* **-achieving, -achieved** to fail to achieve a performance appropriate to one's age or talents **underachiever** *n*

underactive *adj* less active than is normal or desirable: *an underactive thyroid gland*

underage *adj* below the required or standard age, usually below the legal age for voting or drinking: *underage sex*

underarm *adj* **1** *sport* denoting a style of throwing, bowling, or serving in which the hand is swung below shoulder level **2** below the arm ▷ *adv* **3** in an underarm style

underbelly *n, pl* **-lies** **1** the part of an animal's belly nearest the ground **2** a vulnerable or unprotected part, aspect, or region

underbrush *n Austral, US, & Canad* ▸ same as **undergrowth**

undercarriage *n* **1** the wheels, shock absorbers, and struts that support an aircraft on the ground and enable it to take off and land **2** the framework supporting the body of a vehicle

undercharge *vb* **-charging, -charged** to charge too little for something

underclass *n* a class beneath the usual social scale consisting of the most disadvantaged people, such as the long-term unemployed

underclothes *pl n* ▸ same as **underwear**. Also called: **underclothing**

undercoat *n* **1** a coat of paint applied before the top coat **2** *zool* a layer of soft fur beneath the outer fur of animals such as the otter ▷ *vb* **3** to apply an undercoat to a surface

undercook *vb* to cook for too short a time or at too low a temperature

undercover ➊ *adj* done or acting in secret: *an undercover investigation*

undercurrent *n* **1** a current that is not apparent at the surface **2** an underlying opinion or emotion

undercut *vb* **-cutting, -cut** **1** to charge less than a competitor in order to obtain trade **2** to undermine or render less effective:

THESAURUS

2 = unaware, ignorant, oblivious, unsuspecting, lost to, blind to, in ignorance, unknowing
OPPOSITE: aware
3 = unintentional, unwitting, unintended, inadvertent, accidental, unpremeditated
OPPOSITE: intentional

uncover *vb* **1 = open**, unveil, unwrap, show, strip, expose, bare, lay bare, lift the lid, lay open **2 = reveal**, find, discover, expose, encounter, turn up, detect, disclose, unveil, come across, unearth, dig up, divulge, chance on, root out, unmask, lay bare, make known, blow the whistle on *(informal)*, bring to light, smoke out, take the wraps off, blow wide open *(slang)*, stumble on *or* across
OPPOSITE: conceal

under *prep* **1 = below**, beneath, underneath, on the bottom of
OPPOSITE: over
3 = subordinate to, subject to, reporting to, directed by, governed by, inferior to, secondary to, subservient to, junior to ▷ *adv*
10 = below, down, beneath, downward, to the bottom
OPPOSITE: up

undercover *adj* **= secret**, covert, clandestine, private, hidden, intelligence, underground, spy, concealed, confidential, hush-hush *(informal)*, surreptitious
OPPOSITE: open

u

DICTIONARY

the latest fighting undercuts diplomatic attempts to find a peaceful solution **3** to cut away the under part of something
underdeveloped *adj* **1** immature or undersized **2** (of a country or its economy) lacking the finance, industries, and organization necessary to advance
underdog ❶ *n* a person or team in a weak or underprivileged position
underdone *adj* insufficiently or lightly cooked
underemployed *adj* not fully or adequately employed
underestimate ❶ *vb* **-mating, -mated** **1** to make too low an estimate of: *the trust had underestimated the cost of work* **2** to not be aware or take account of the full abilities or potential of: *the police had underestimated him* ▷ *n* **3** too low an estimate **underestimation** *n*
underexpose *vb* **-posing, -posed** *photog* to expose (a film, plate, or paper) for too short a time or with insufficient light **underexposure** *n*
underfed *adj* not getting enough food to be healthy
underfelt *n* thick felt laid under a carpet to increase insulation
underfoot *adv* **1** underneath the feet; on the ground **2 trample** *or* **crush underfoot a** to damage or destroy by stepping on **b** to treat with contempt
undergarment *n* a garment worn under clothes
undergo ❶ *vb* **-going, -went, -gone** to experience, endure, or sustain: *he underwent a three-hour operation*
WORD ORIGIN Old English *undergān*
undergraduate *n* a person studying in a university for a first degree
underground ❶ *adv* **1** below ground level: *moles digging underground* **2** secretly: *several political parties had to operate underground for many years* ▷ *adj* **3** beneath the ground: *an underground bunker* **4** secret; clandestine: *an underground organization* **5** (of art, film, music, etc.) avant-garde, experimental, or subversive ▷ *n* **6** a movement dedicated to overthrowing a government or occupation forces **7** (often preceded by *the*) an electric passenger railway operated in underground tunnels
undergrowth *n* small trees and bushes growing beneath taller trees in a wood or forest
underhand *adj also* **underhanded** **1** sly, deceitful, and secretive **2** *sport* ▸ same as **underarm** ▷ *adv* **3** in an underhand manner or style
underinsured *adj* not insured for enough money to cover the replacement value of the goods covered
underlay *n* felt or rubber laid under a carpet to increase insulation and resilience
underlie *vb* **-lying, -lay, -lain** **1** to lie or be placed under **2** to be the foundation, cause, or basis of: *the basic unity which underlies all religion*
underline ❶ *vb* **-lining, -lined** **1** to put a line under **2** to emphasize
underling *n derogatory* a subordinate
underlying ❶ *adj* **1** not obvious but detectable: *the deeper and underlying aim of her travels* **2** fundamental; basic: *an underlying belief* **3** lying under: *the underlying layers of the skin*
undermanned *adj* not having enough staff to function properly
undermentioned *adj* mentioned below or later
undermine ❶ *vb* **-mining, -mined** **1** to weaken gradually or insidiously: *morphia had undermined his grasp of reality* **2** (of the sea or wind) to wear away the base of cliffs
underneath *prep* **1** under or beneath: *a table underneath an olive tree* ▷ *adv* **2** under or beneath: *the chest of drawers was scratched underneath* ▷ *adj* **3** lower ▷ *n* **4** a lower part or surface
WORD ORIGIN Old English *underneothan*
undernourished *adj* lacking the food needed for health and growth **undernourishment** *n*
underpaid *adj* not paid as much as the job deserves
underpants *pl n* a man's undergarment covering the body from the waist or hips to the thighs
underpass *n* **1** a section of a road that passes under another road or a railway line **2** a subway for pedestrians
underpay *vb* **-paying, -paid** to pay someone insufficiently **underpayment** *n*
underpin *vb* **-pinning, -pinned** **1** to give strength or support to: *the principles that underpin his political convictions* **2** to support from beneath with a prop: *to underpin a wall* **underpinning** *n*
underplay *vb* to achieve (an effect) by deliberate lack of emphasis
underprivileged *adj* **1** lacking the rights and advantages of other members of society; deprived ▷ *n* **2 the underprivileged** underprivileged people regarded as a group
underrate *vb* **-rating, -rated** to not be aware or take account of the full abilities or potential of **underrated** *adj*
underscore *vb* **-scoring, -scored** ▸ same as **underline**
undersea *adj, adv* below the surface of the sea
underseal *n* **1** a special coating applied to the underside of a motor vehicle to prevent corrosion ▷ *vb* **2** to apply such a coating to a motor vehicle
undersecretary *n, pl* **-taries** a senior civil servant or junior minister in a government department
undersell *vb* **-selling, -sold** to sell at a price lower than that of another seller
undersexed *adj* having weaker sexual urges than is considered normal
undershirt *n US & Canad* an undergarment covering the body from the shoulders to the hips
undershoot *vb* **-shooting, -shot** *aviation* to land an aircraft short of a runway
underside *n* the bottom or lower surface
undersigned *n* **the undersigned** the person or people who have signed at the foot of a document, statement, or letter
undersized *adj* smaller than normal
underskirt *n* a skirtlike garment worn under a skirt or dress; petticoat
understaffed *adj* not having enough staff to function properly

U

THESAURUS

underdog *n* **= weaker party**, victim, loser, little fellow *(informal)*, outsider, fall guy *(informal)*
underestimate *vb* **1 = underrate**, undervalue, belittle, sell short *(informal)*, not do justice to, rate too low, set no store by, hold cheap, think too little of **OPPOSITE:** overrate **2 = undervalue**, understate, underrate, diminish, play down, minimize, downgrade, miscalculate, trivialize, rate too low, underemphasize, hold cheap, misprize **OPPOSITE:** overestimate
undergo *vb* **= experience**, go through, be subjected to, stand, suffer, bear, weather, sustain, endure, withstand, submit to
underground *adj* **3 = subterranean**, basement, lower-level, sunken, covered, buried, below the surface, below ground, subterrestrial **4 = secret**, undercover, covert, hidden, guerrilla, revolutionary, concealed, confidential, dissident, closet, subversive, clandestine, renegade, insurgent, hush-hush *(informal)*, surreptitious, cloak-and-dagger, hugger-mugger, insurrectionist, hole-and-corner, radical
underline *vb* **1 = underscore**, mark, italicize, rule a line under **2 = emphasize**, stress, highlight, bring home, accentuate, point up, give emphasis to, call *or* draw attention to **OPPOSITE:** minimize
underlying *adj* **2 = fundamental**, basic, essential, root, prime, primary, radical, elementary, intrinsic, basal
undermine *vb* **1 = weaken**, sabotage, subvert, compromise, disable,

DICTIONARY

understand ❶ *vb* **-standing, -stood** **1** to know and comprehend the nature or meaning of: *I understand what you are saying* **2** to know what is happening or why it is happening: *in order to understand the problems that can occur* **3** to assume, infer, or believe: *I understand he is based in this town* **4** to know how to translate or read: *don't you understand Russian?* **5** to be sympathetic to or compatible with: *she needed him to understand her completely* **understandable** *adj* **understandably** *adv*
WORD ORIGIN Old English *understandan*

understanding ❶ *n* **1** the ability to learn, judge, or make decisions **2** personal opinion or interpretation of a subject: *my understanding of what he said* **3** a mutual agreement, usually an informal or private one ▷*adj* **4** kind, sympathetic, or tolerant towards people

understate *vb* **-stating, -stated** **1** to describe or portray something in restrained terms, often to obtain an ironic effect **2** to state that something, such as a number, is less than it is **understatement** *n*

understood *vb* **1** ▸the past of **understand** ▷*adj* **2** implied or inferred **3** taken for granted

understudy *n, pl* **-studies** **1** an actor who studies a part so as to be able to replace the usual actor if necessary **2** anyone who is trained to take the place of another if necessary ▷*vb* **-studies, -studying, -studied** **3** to act as an understudy to

undertake ❶ *vb* **-taking, -took, -taken** **1** to agree to or commit oneself to something or to do something: *I undertook the worst job in gardening* **2** to promise to do something

undertaker *n* a person whose job is to look after the bodies of people who have died and to organize funerals

undertaking ❶ *n* **1** a task or enterprise **2** an agreement to do something **3** *informal* the practice of overtaking on an inner lane a vehicle which is travelling in an outer lane

undertone *n* **1** a quiet tone of voice **2** something which suggests an underlying quality or feeling: *an undertone of anger*

undertow *n* a strong undercurrent flowing in a different direction from the surface current, such as in the sea

undervalue *vb* **-valuing, -valued** to value a person or thing at less than the true worth or importance

underwater *adj* **1** situated, occurring, or for use under the surface of the sea, a lake, or a river ▷*adv* **2** beneath the surface of the sea, a lake, or a river

under way *adj* **1** in progress; taking place: *this test is already under way* **2** *naut* in motion in the direction headed

underwear ❶ *n* clothing worn under other garments, usually next to the skin

underweight *adj* weighing less than is average, expected, or healthy

underwent *vb* ▸the past tense of **undergo**

Underwood *n* **Rory** born 1963, British Rugby Union football player; played for England (1984–99), becoming Britain's most capped player

underworld ❶ *n* **1** criminals and their associates **2** *Greek and Roman myth* the regions below the earth's surface regarded as the abode of the dead

underwrite ❶ *vb* **-writing, -wrote, -written** **1** to accept financial responsibility for a commercial project or enterprise **2** to sign and issue an insurance policy, thus accepting liability **3** to support **underwriter** *n*

undeserved *adj* not earned or deserved

undesirable ❶ *adj* **1** not desirable or pleasant; objectionable ▷*n* **2** a person considered undesirable

undetected *adj* not having been discovered: *an undetected cancer*

undeterred *adj* not put off or dissuaded

undeveloped *adj* **1** not yet mature or adult **2** (of land) not built on or used for commercial or agricultural purposes

undies *pl n* *Brit, Austral & NZ informal* women's underwear

undignified *adj* foolish or embarrassing

undiluted *adj* **1** (of a liquid) not having any water added to it; concentrated **2** not mixed with any other feeling or quality: *undiluted hatred*

undiminished *adj* not lessened or decreased: *his admiration for her remained undiminished*

undine (un-dean) *n* a female water spirit
WORD ORIGIN Latin *unda* a wave

undisciplined *adj* behaving badly, with a lack of self-control

undisguised *adj* shown openly; not

THESAURUS

debilitate **OPPOSITE:** reinforce

understand *vb* **1, 2 = comprehend**, get, take in, perceive, grasp, know, see, follow, realize, recognize, appreciate, be aware of, penetrate, make out, discern, twig (*Brit informal*), fathom, savvy (*slang*), apprehend, conceive of, suss (*Brit informal*), get to the bottom of, get the hang of (*informal*), tumble to (*informal*), catch on to (*informal*), cotton on to (*informal*), make head or tail of (*informal*), get your head round **3 = believe**, hear, learn, gather, think, see, suppose, notice, assume, take it, conclude, fancy, presume, be informed, infer, surmise, hear tell, draw the inference

understanding *n* **1 = perception**, knowledge, grasp, sense, know-how (*informal*), intelligence, judgment, awareness, appreciation, insight, skill, penetration, mastery, comprehension, familiarity with, discernment, proficiency **OPPOSITE:** ignorance **2 = belief**, view, opinion, impression, interpretation, feeling, idea, conclusion, notion, conviction, judgment, assumption, point of view, perception, suspicion, viewpoint, hunch, way of thinking, estimation, supposition, sneaking suspicion, funny feeling **3 = agreement**, deal, promise, arrangement, accord, contract, bond, pledge, bargain, pact, compact, concord, gentlemen's agreement **OPPOSITE:** disagreement ▷*adj* **4 = sympathetic**, kind, compassionate, considerate, kindly, accepting, patient, sensitive, forgiving, discerning, tolerant, responsive, perceptive, forbearing **OPPOSITE:** unsympathetic

undertake *vb* **1, 2 = agree**, promise, contract, guarantee, engage, pledge, covenant, commit yourself, take upon yourself

undertaking *n* **1 = task**, business, operation, project, game, attempt, effort, affair, venture, enterprise, endeavour **2 = promise**, commitment, pledge, word, vow, assurance, word of honour, solemn word

underwear *n* **= underclothes**, lingerie, undies (*informal*), smalls (*informal*), undergarments, unmentionables (*humorous*), underclothing, underthings, underlinen, broekies (*S African informal*), underdaks (*Austral slang*)

underworld *n* **1 = criminals**, gangsters, organized crime, gangland (*informal*), criminal element **2 = nether world**, hell, Hades, the inferno, nether regions, infernal region, abode of the dead

underwrite *vb* **1 = finance**, back, fund, guarantee, sponsor, insure, ratify, subsidize, bankroll (*US informal*), provide security, provide capital for

undesirable *adj* **1 = unwanted**, unwelcome, disagreeable, objectionable, offensive, disliked, unacceptable, dreaded, unpopular, unsuitable, out of place, unattractive, distasteful, unsavoury, obnoxious, repugnant, unpleasing, unwished-for **OPPOSITE:** desirable

DICTIONARY

concealed: *undisguised curiosity*
undismayed *adj* not upset about something; undaunted
undisputed *adj* unquestionably true or accurately described: *Mao became undisputed leader of China*
undistinguished *adj* not particularly good or bad; mediocre
undisturbed *adj* **1** quiet and peaceful: *an undisturbed village* **2** uninterrupted: *three hours' undisturbed work* **3** not touched, moved, or used by anyone: *the wreck has lain undisturbed for centuries*
undivided *adj* **1** total and whole-hearted: *her undivided attention* **2** not separated into different parts or groups
undo *vb* **-doing, -did, -done** **1** to open, unwrap or untie **2** to reverse the effects of: *all the work of the congress would be undone* **3** to cause the downfall of
undoing *n* **1** ruin; downfall **2** the cause of someone's downfall: *his confidence was his undoing*
undone[1] *adj* not done or completed; unfinished
undone[2] *adj* **1** ruined; destroyed **2** unfastened; untied
undoubted *adj* beyond doubt; certain or indisputable **undoubtedly** *adv*
undreamed *or* **undreamt** *adj* (often foll. by *of*) not thought of or imagined
undress *vb* **1** to take off the clothes of oneself or another ▷*n* **2** **in a state of undress** naked or nearly naked **3** informal or ordinary working clothes or uniform **undressed** *adj*
Undset *n* **Sigrid** 1882–1949, Norwegian novelist, best known for her trilogy *Kristin Lavransdatter* (1920–22): Nobel prize for literature 1928
undue *adj* greater than is reasonable; excessive: *undue attention*
undulate *vb* **-lating, -lated** **1** to move gently and slowly from side to side or up and down **2** to have a wavy shape or appearance **undulation** *n*
WORD ORIGIN Latin *unda* a wave
unduly *adv* excessively
undying *adj* never ending; eternal
unearned *adj* **1** not deserved **2** not yet earned
unearned income *n* income from property or investments rather than work
unearth *vb* **1** to discover by searching **2** to dig up out of the earth
unearthly *adj* **1** strange, unnatural, or eerie: *unearthly beauty* **2** ridiculous or unreasonable: *the unearthly hour of seven in the morning* **unearthliness** *n*
unease *n* **1** anxiety or nervousness: *my unease grew when she was not back by midnight* **2** dissatisfaction or tension: *unease about the government's handling of the affair*
uneasy *adj* **1** (of a person) anxious or apprehensive **2** (of a condition) precarious or insecure: *an uneasy peace* **3** (of a thought or feeling) disquieting **uneasily** *adv* **uneasiness** *n*
uneatable *adj* (of food) so rotten or unattractive as to be unfit to eat
uneconomic *adj* not producing enough profit
uneconomical *adj* not economical; wasteful
uneducated *adj* not educated well or at all
unemotional *adj* (of a person) not displaying any emotion
unemployable *adj* unable or unfit to keep a job
unemployed *adj* **1** without paid employment; out of work **2** not being used; idle ▷*pl n* **3** people who are out of work: *the long-term unemployed*
unemployment *n* **1** the condition of being unemployed **2** the number of unemployed workers: *unemployment rose again last month*
unemployment benefit *n* (formerly, in the British National Insurance scheme, and currently, in New Zealand) a regular payment to an unemployed person
unencumbered *adj* not hindered or held back: *unencumbered by the responsibilities of childcare*
unending *adj* not showing any signs of ever stopping
unendurable *adj* too unpleasant to bear
unenthusiastic *adj* not keen about or interested in (something) **unenthusiastically** *adv*
unenviable *adj* (of a task) so difficult, dangerous, or unpleasant that one is glad not to have to do it oneself: *the unenviable task of phoning the parents of the dead child*
unequal *adj* **1** not equal in quantity, size, rank, or value **2** **unequal to** inadequate for: *he felt unequal to the job* **3** not offering all people or groups the same opportunities and privileges: *the unequal distribution of wealth* **4** (of a contest) having competitors of different ability **unequally** *adv*
unequalled *or US* **unequaled** *adj* greater, better, or more extreme than anything else of the same kind
unequivocal *adj* completely clear in meaning; unambiguous **unequivocally** *adv*
unerring *adj* never mistaken; consistently accurate
UNESCO United Nations Educational, Scientific, and Cultural Organization
unethical *adj* morally wrong
uneven *adj* **1** (of a surface) not level or flat **2** not consistent in quality: *an uneven performance* **3** not parallel, straight, or horizontal **4** not fairly matched: *the uneven battle*
uneventful *adj* ordinary, routine, or quiet **uneventfully** *adv*
unexampled *adj* without precedent
unexceptionable *adj* not likely to be criticized or objected to
unexceptional *adj* usual, ordinary, or normal
unexciting *adj* slightly dull and boring
unexpected *adj* surprising or unforeseen **unexpectedly** *adv*
unexplained *adj* strange or unclear because the reason for it is not known
unexpurgated *adj* (of a piece of writing) not censored by having allegedly offensive passages removed
unfailing *adj* continuous or reliable: *his unfailing enthusiasm* **unfailingly** *adv*

THESAURUS

undo *vb* **1 = open**, unfasten, loose, loosen, unlock, unwrap, untie, disengage, unbutton, disentangle, unstrap, unclasp **2 = reverse**, cancel, offset, wipe out, neutralize, invalidate, annul, nullify **3 = ruin**, defeat, destroy, wreck, shatter, upset, mar, undermine, overturn, quash, subvert, bring to naught
undone[1] *adj* **= unfinished**, left, outstanding, not done, neglected, omitted, incomplete, passed over, unfulfilled, not completed, unperformed, unattended to
OPPOSITE: finished
unearth *vb* **1 = discover**, find, reveal, expose, turn up, uncover, bring to light, ferret out, root up **2 = dig up**, excavate, exhume, dredge up, disinter
unearthly *adj* **1 = eerie**, strange, supernatural, ghostly, weird, phantom, uncanny, spooky *(informal)*, nightmarish, spectral, eldritch *(poetic)*, preternatural
uneasy *adj* **1 = anxious**, worried, troubled, upset, wired *(slang)*, nervous, disturbed, uncomfortable, unsettled, impatient, restless, agitated, apprehensive, edgy, jittery *(informal)*, perturbed, on edge, ill at ease, restive, twitchy *(informal)*, like a fish out of water, antsy *(informal)*, discomposed
OPPOSITE: relaxed
2 = precarious, strained, uncomfortable, tense, awkward, unstable, shaky, insecure, constrained
unemployed *adj* **1 = out of work**, redundant, laid off, jobless, idle, on the dole *(Brit informal)*, out of a job, workless, resting *(of an actor)*
OPPOSITE: working

DICTIONARY

unfair ❶ *adj* **1** unequal or unjust **2** dishonest or unethical **unfairly** *adv* **unfairness** *n*

unfaithful *adj* **1** having sex with someone other than one's regular partner **2** not true to a promise or vow **unfaithfulness** *n*

unfamiliar *adj* **1** not known; strange: *an unfamiliar American accent* **2 unfamiliar with** not acquainted with: *anyone who is unfamiliar with the language* **unfamiliarity** *n*

unfashionable *adj* not popular or in vogue

unfasten *vb* to undo, untie, or open or become undone, untied, or opened

unfathomable *adj* too strange or complicated to be understood: *pugs exert a powerful, unfathomable hold over their owners*

unfavourable *or US* **unfavorable** *adj* **1** making a successful or positive outcome unlikely: *unfavourable weather conditions* **2** disapproving: *an unfavourable opinion* **unfavourably** *or US* **unfavorably** *adv*

unfeeling *adj* without sympathy; callous

unfettered *adj* not limited or controlled: *unfettered competition*

unfinished *adj* **1** incomplete or imperfect **2** (of paint) without an applied finish

unfit ❶ *adj* **1** unqualified for or incapable of a particular role or task: *an unfit mother; he was unfit to drive* **2** unsuitable: *this meat is unfit for human consumption* **3** in poor physical condition

unfitted *adj* unsuitable: *unused to and unfitted for any form of manual labour*

unflappable *adj informal* (of a person) not easily upset **unflappability** *n*

unfledged *adj* **1** (of a young bird) not having developed adult feathers **2** immature and inexperienced

unflinching *adj* not shrinking from danger or difficulty

unfold ❶ *vb* **1** to open or spread out from a folded state **2** to reveal or be revealed: *a terrible truth unfolds* **3** to develop or be developed: *the novel unfolds through their recollections*

unfollow *vb* to choose to no longer receive someone's updates on the Twitter website

unforeseen *adj* surprising because not expected

unforgettable *adj* making such a strong impression that it is impossible to forget **unforgettably** *adv*

unforgivable *adj* too bad or cruel to be excused

unforgiving *adj* **1** unwilling to forgive other people's mistakes or wrongdoings **2** (of a machine) allowing little or no opportunity for mistakes to be corrected **3** harsh: *an unforgiving and desolate landscape*

unformed *adj* in an early stage of development; not fully developed or thought out

unforthcoming *adj* not inclined to speak, explain, or communicate

unfortunate ❶ *adj* **1** caused or accompanied by bad luck: *an unfortunate coincidence* **2** having bad luck: *my unfortunate daughter* **3** regrettable or unsuitable: *an unfortunate choice of phrase* ▷ *n* **4** an unlucky person **unfortunately** *adv*

unfounded *adj* (of ideas, fears, or allegations) not based on facts or evidence

unfreeze *vb* **-freezing, -froze, -frozen** **1** to thaw or cause to thaw **2** to relax restrictions or controls on (trade, the transfer of money, etc.): *Congress is considering unfreezing US aid to Jordan*

unfriend *or* **defriend** *vb* to choose to no longer be friends with someone on the social networking site Facebook

unfriendly *adj* **-lier, -liest** not friendly; hostile

unfrock *vb* to deprive (a person in holy orders) of the status of a priest

unfulfilled *adj* not satisfied

unfurl *vb* to unroll or spread out (an umbrella, flag, or sail) or (of an umbrella, flag, or sail) to be unrolled or spread out

unfurnished *adj* not containing any furniture

ungainly *adj* **-lier, -liest** lacking grace when moving **ungainliness** *n*

WORD ORIGIN dialect *gainly* graceful

Ungaretti *n* **Giuseppe** 1888–1970, Italian poet, best known for his collection of war poems *Allegria di naufragi* (1919)

ungenerous *adj* **1** mean or overly thrifty **2** (of a remark or thought) unfair or harsh

ungodly *adj* **-lier, -liest** **1** wicked or sinful **2** *informal* unreasonable or outrageous: *at this ungodly hour* **ungodliness** *n*

ungovernable *adj* **1** (of an emotion) not able to be controlled or restrained: *an ungovernable rage* **2** (of a country or area) not able to be effectively governed, esp. because of unrest or violence: *years of religious conflict had made much of the island ungovernable*

ungracious *adj* not polite or friendly, esp. when being offered praise or thanks

ungrammatical *adj* not following the rules of grammar

ungrateful *adj* not showing or offering thanks for a favour or compliment

unguarded *adj* **1** unprotected **2** open or frank: *one unguarded briefing* **3** incautious or careless: *an unguarded moment*

unguent (ung-gwent) *n literary* an ointment

WORD ORIGIN Latin *unguere* to anoint

ungulate (ung-gyew-lit) *n* a hoofed mammal

WORD ORIGIN Latin *ungula* hoof

unhallowed *adj* **1** not consecrated or holy: *unhallowed ground* **2** sinful or wicked

unhand *vb old-fashioned or literary* to release from one's grasp

unhappy ❶ *adj* **-pier, -piest** **1** sad or depressed **2** unfortunate or wretched **unhappily** *adv* **unhappiness** *n*

THESAURUS

unfair *adj* **1 = biased**, prejudiced, unjust, one-sided, partial, partisan, arbitrary, discriminatory, bigoted, inequitable **2 = unscrupulous**, crooked *(informal)*, dishonest, unethical, wrongful, unprincipled, dishonourable, unsporting
OPPOSITE: ethical

unfit *adj* **1 = incapable**, inadequate, incompetent, no good, useless, not up to, unprepared, ineligible, unqualified, untrained, ill-equipped, not equal, not cut out
OPPOSITE: capable
2 = unsuitable, inadequate, inappropriate, useless, not fit, not designed, unsuited, ill-adapted
OPPOSITE: suitable
3 = out of shape, feeble, unhealthy, debilitated, flabby, decrepit, in poor condition, out of trim, out of kilter
OPPOSITE: healthy

unfold *vb* **1 = open**, spread out, undo, expand, flatten, straighten, stretch out, unfurl, unwrap, unroll
2 = reveal, tell, present, show, describe, explain, illustrate, disclose, uncover, clarify, divulge, narrate, make known

unfortunate *adj* **1 = disastrous**, calamitous, inopportune, adverse, untimely, unfavourable, untoward, ruinous, ill-starred, infelicitous, ill-fated **OPPOSITE:** opportune
2 = unlucky, poor, unhappy, doomed, cursed, hopeless, unsuccessful, hapless, luckless, out of luck, wretched, star-crossed, unprosperous **OPPOSITE:** fortunate
3 = regrettable, deplorable, lamentable, inappropriate, unsuitable, ill-advised, unbecoming
OPPOSITE: becoming

unhappy *adj* **1 = sad**, depressed, miserable, down, low, blue, gloomy, melancholy, mournful, dejected, despondent, dispirited, downcast, long-faced, sorrowful, disconsolate, crestfallen, down in the dumps *(informal)* **OPPOSITE:** happy
2 = unlucky, unfortunate, hapless, luckless, cursed, wretched, ill-omened, ill-fated
OPPOSITE: fortunate

unharmed *adj* not hurt or damaged in any way

unhealthy ❶ *adj* **-healthier, -healthiest 1** likely to cause illness or poor health: *unhealthy foods such as hamburger and chips* **2** not very fit or well **3** caused by or looking as if caused by poor health: *a thin unhealthy look about him* **4** morbid or unwholesome: *an unhealthy interest in computer fraud* **unhealthiness** *n*

unheard *adj* not listened to; unheeded: *all my warnings went unheard*

unheard-of *adj* **1** without precedent: *an unheard-of phenomenon* **2** highly offensive: *unheard-of behaviour*

unheeded *adj* noticed but ignored: *their protests went unheeded*

unhelpful *adj* doing nothing to improve a situation

unheralded *adj* not announced beforehand

unhindered *adj* **1** not prevented or obstructed: *unhindered access* ▹ *adv* **2** without being prevented or obstructed: *he was able to go about his work unhindered*

unhinge *vb* **-hinging, -hinged** to make a person mentally deranged or unbalanced **unhinged** *adj*

unholy *adj* **-lier, -liest 1** immoral or wicked **2** *informal* outrageous or unnatural: *this unholy mess* **unholiness** *n*

unhook *vb* **1** to unfasten the hooks of a garment **2** to remove something from a hook

unhurried *adj* done at a leisurely pace, without any rush or anxiety

unhurt *adj* not injured in an accident, attack, etc.

unhygienic *adj* dirty and likely to cause disease or infection

uni *n Brit, Austral & NZ informal* ▸ short for **university**

uni- *combining form* of, consisting of, or having only one: *unilateral*
WORD ORIGIN Latin *unus* one

unicameral *adj* of or having a single legislative chamber: *Denmark's unicameral parliament, known as the Folketing*

UNICEF United Nations Children's Fund

unicellular *adj* (of organisms) consisting of a single cell

Unicode *n computers* a character set for all languages

unicorn *n* a legendary creature resembling a white horse with one horn growing from its forehead
WORD ORIGIN Latin *unus* one + *cornu* a horn

unicycle *n* a one-wheeled vehicle driven by pedals, used in a circus **unicyclist** *n*

unidentified *adj* **1** not able to be recognized; unknown: *unidentified gunmen* **2** anonymous or unnamed: *the house of an unidentified Scottish businessman* **unidentifiable** *adj*

uniform ❶ *n* **1** a special identifying set of clothes for the members of an organization, such as soldiers ▹ *adj* **2** regular and even throughout: *the mixture must be beaten to a uniform consistency* **3** alike or like: *uniform green metal filing cabinets* **uniformity** *n* **uniformly** *adv*
WORD ORIGIN Latin *unus* one + *forma* shape

unify ❶ *vb* **-fies, -fying, -fied** to make or become one; unite **unification** *n*
WORD ORIGIN Latin *unus* one + *facere* to make

unilateral *adj* made or done by only one person or group: *unilateral action* **unilateralism** *n*

unilingual *adj* **1** of or relating to only one language **2** *chiefly Canad* knowing only one language ▹ *n* **3** *chiefly Canad* a person who knows only one language

unimaginable *adj* so unusual, great, or extreme that it is difficult to imagine or understand: *the unimaginable vastness of space*

unimaginative *adj* not having or showing much imagination

unimpeachable *adj* completely honest and reliable

unimpeded *adj* not stopped or disrupted by anything

unimportant *adj* trivial or insignificant

uninhabitable *adj* not able to support human life: *an uninhabitable wasteland*

uninhabited *adj* having no people living in or on it: *an uninhabited island*

uninhibited *adj* behaving freely and naturally, without worrying what other people will think

uninitiated *pl n* **the uninitiated** people who have no special knowledge or experience: *no easy way for the uninitiated to find out what the internet can do*

uninspired *adj* not particularly good or exciting

uninspiring *adj* not likely to make people interested or excited

unintelligible *adj* impossible to make out or understand; incomprehensible: *an unintelligible London accent*

unintended *adj* (of an action or its consequences) not planned or intended: *sometimes drugs have unintended side-effects*

unintentional *adj* (of an action) not done deliberately; accidental: *unintentional discrimination* **unintentionally** *adv*

uninterested *adj* having or showing no interest in someone or something

uninteresting *adj* boring or dull

uninterrupted *adj* continuous, with no breaks or interruptions: *uninterrupted applause*

uninvited *adj* **1** not having been asked: *uninvited guests* ▹ *adv* **2** without having been asked: *he sat down uninvited on the side of the bed*

union ❶ *n* **1** the act of merging two or more things to become one, or the state of being merged in such a way **2** ▸ short for **trade union 3** an association of individuals or groups for a common purpose: *the Scripture Union* **4 a** an association or society: *the Students' union* **b** the buildings of such an organization **5** marriage or sexual intercourse **6** *maths* a set containing all the members of two given sets **7** (in 19th-century England) a workhouse maintained by a number of parishes ▹ *adj* **8** of a trade union
WORD ORIGIN Latin *unus* one

unionism *n* **1** the principles of trade unions **2** adherence to the principles of trade unions **unionist** *n, adj*

Unionist *n* a supporter of union between Britain and Northern Ireland

unionize *or* **-ise** *vb* **-izing, -ized** *or* **-ising, -ised** to organize workers into a trade union **unionization** *or* **-isation** *n*

Union Jack *or* **Union flag** *n* the

U

THESAURUS

unhealthy *adj* **1 = harmful**, detrimental, unwholesome, noxious, deleterious, insanitary, noisome, insalubrious **OPPOSITE:** beneficial
2a = sick, sickly, unwell, poorly (*informal*), weak, delicate, crook (*Austral & NZ informal*), ailing, frail, feeble, invalid, unsound, infirm, in poor health **OPPOSITE:** well
2b = weak, unsound, ailing **OPPOSITE:** strong

uniform *n* **1a = regalia**, suit, livery, colours, habit, regimentals **1b = outfit**, dress, costume, attire, gear (*informal*), get-up (*informal*), ensemble, garb ▹ *adj* **2 = consistent**, unvarying, similar, even, same, matching, regular, constant, equivalent, identical, homogeneous, unchanging, equable, undeviating **OPPOSITE:** varying
3 = alike, similar, identical, like, same, equal, selfsame

unify *vb* **= unite**, join, combine, merge, consolidate, bring together, fuse, confederate, amalgamate, federate **OPPOSITE:** divide

union *n* **1 = joining**, uniting, unification, combination, coalition, merger, mixture, blend, merging, integration, conjunction, fusion, synthesis, amalgamating, amalgam, amalgamation **3 = alliance**, league, association, coalition, federation, confederation, confederacy, Bund

DICTIONARY

national flag of the United Kingdom, combining the crosses of Saint George, Saint Andrew, and Saint Patrick

unique ⊙ (yew-neek) *adj* **1** being the only one of a particular type **2 unique to** concerning or belonging to a particular person, thing, or group: *certain dishes are unique to this restaurant* **3** without equal or like **4** *informal* remarkable **uniquely** *adv*
WORD ORIGIN Latin *unicus* unparalleled

unisex *adj* (of clothing, a hairstyle, or hairdressers) designed for both sexes

unisexual *adj* **1** of one sex only **2** (of an organism) having either male or female reproductive organs but not both

unison *n* **1 in unison** at the same time as another person or other people: *smiling and nodding in unison* **2** (usually preceded by *in*) complete agreement: *to act in unison* **3** *music* a style, technique, or passage in which all the performers sing or play the same notes at the same time
WORD ORIGIN Latin *unus* one + *sonus* sound

UNISON *n* a British trade union consisting mainly of council and hospital workers

unit ⊙ *n* **1** a single undivided entity or whole **2** a group or individual regarded as a basic element of a larger whole: *the clan was the basic unit of Highland society* **3** a mechanical part or small device that does a particular job: *a waste disposal unit* **4** a team of people that performs a specific function, and often also their buildings and equipment: *a combat unit* **5** a standard amount of a physical quantity, such as length or energy, used to express magnitudes of that quantity: *the year as a unit of time* **6** *maths* the digit or position immediately to the left of the decimal point **7** a piece of furniture designed to be fitted with other similar pieces: *bedroom units* **8** NZ a self-propelled railcar **9** *Austral & NZ* ▸ short for **home unit**
WORD ORIGIN from *unity*

Unitarian *n* **1** a person who believes that God is one being and rejects the Trinity ▹ *adj* **2** of Unitarians or Unitarianism **Unitarianism** *n*

unitary *adj* **1** consisting of a single undivided whole: *a unitary state* **2** of a unit or units

unit cost *n* the actual cost of producing one article

unite ⊙ *vb* **uniting, united 1** to make or become an integrated whole: *conception occurs when a sperm unites with the egg* **2** to form an association or alliance: *the opposition parties united to fight against privatization* **3** to possess (a combination of qualities) at the same time: *he manages to unite charm and ruthlessness*
WORD ORIGIN Latin *unus* one

united *adj* **1** produced by two or more people or things in combination: *a united effort* **2** in agreement: *we are united in our opposition to these proposals* **3** in association or alliance

United Kingdom *n* a kingdom of NW Europe, consisting of the island of Great Britain together with Northern Ireland

United Nations *n* an international organization of independent states, formed to promote peace and international security

unit price *n* the price charged per unit

unit trust *n Austral & Brit* an investment trust that issues units for public sale and invests the money in many different businesses

unity ⊙ *n, pl* **-ties 1** the state of being one **2** mutual agreement: *unity of intention* **3** the state of being a single thing that is composed of separate parts, organizations, etc.: *moves towards church unity* **4** *maths* the number or numeral one
WORD ORIGIN Latin *unus* one

Univ. University

univalent *adj chem* ▸ same as **monovalent**

universal ⊙ *adj* **1** of or relating to everyone in the world or everyone in a particular place or society: *the introduction of universal primary education* **2** of, relating to, or affecting the entire world or universe: *the universal laws of physics* **3** true and relevant at all times and in all situations: *there may be no single universal solution* ▹ *n* **4** something which exists or is true in all places and all situations: *universals such as beauty and justice*
universality *n* **universally** *adv*

universal joint *or* **coupling** *n* a form of coupling between two rotating shafts allowing freedom of movement in all directions

universe ⊙ *n* **1** the whole of all existing matter, energy, and space **2** the world
WORD ORIGIN Latin *universum* the whole world

university *n, pl* **-ties 1** an institution of higher education with authority to award degrees **2** the buildings, members, staff, or campus of a university
WORD ORIGIN Medieval Latin *universitas* group of scholars

Unix (yew-nicks) *n trademark* an operating system found on many types of computer

unjust *adj* not fair or just

unjustifiable *adj* inexcusably wrong or unfair

unjustified *adj* not necessary or reasonable

unkempt *adj* **1** (of the hair) uncombed or dishevelled **2** untidy or slovenly: *an unkempt appearance*
WORD ORIGIN Old English *uncembed*, from *cemban* to comb

unkind *adj* unsympathetic or cruel **unkindly** *adv* **unkindness** *n*

unknowing *adj* unaware or ignorant: *unknowing victims of fraud*

unknown ⊙ *adj* **1** not known, understood, or recognized **2** not famous: *a young and then unknown actor* **3 unknown quantity** a person or thing whose action or effect is

THESAURUS

unique *adj* **1 = distinct**, special, exclusive, peculiar, only, single, lone, solitary, one and only, sui generis **3 = unparalleled**, unrivalled, incomparable, inimitable, unmatched, peerless, unequalled, matchless, without equal, nonpareil, unexampled

unit *n* **1 = entity**, whole, item, feature, piece, portion, module **2 = part**, section, segment, class, element, component, constituent, tutorial **4 = section**, company, group, force, detail, division, cell, squad, crew, outfit, faction, corps, brigade, regiment, battalion, legion, contingent, squadron, garrison, detachment, platoon **5 = measure**, quantity, measurement

unite *vb* **1, 3 = join**, link, combine, couple, marry, wed, blend, incorporate, merge, consolidate, unify, fuse, amalgamate, coalesce, meld **OPPOSITE:** separate **2 = cooperate**, ally, join forces, league, band, associate, pool, collaborate, confederate, pull together, join together, close ranks, club together **OPPOSITE:** split

unity *n* **1 = wholeness**, integrity, oneness, union, unification, entity, singleness, undividedness **OPPOSITE:** disunity **2 = agreement**, accord, consensus, peace, harmony, solidarity, unison, assent, unanimity, concord, concurrence **OPPOSITE:** disagreement **3 = union**, unification, coalition, federation, integration, confederation, amalgamation

universal *adj* **1 = widespread**, general, common, whole, total, entire, catholic, unlimited, ecumenical, omnipresent, all-embracing, overarching, one-size-fits-all **2 = global**, worldwide, international, pandemic

universe *n* **1 = cosmos**, space, creation, everything, nature, heavens, the natural world, macrocosm, all existence

unknown *adj* **1a = strange**, new, undiscovered, uncharted,

u

DICTIONARY

unknown or unpredictable ▷ *n* **4** an unknown person, quantity, or thing ▷ *adv* **5 unknown to someone** without someone being aware: *unknown to him, the starboard engine had dropped off*

unlawful *adj* not permitted by law; illegal

unleaded *adj* (of petrol) containing less tetraethyl lead, in order to reduce environmental pollution

unlearn *vb* **-learning, -learned** *or* **-learnt** to try to forget something learnt or to discard accumulated knowledge

unlearned (un-lurn-id) *adj* ignorant or uneducated

unlearnt *or* **unlearned** *adj* **1** denoting knowledge or skills innately present rather than learnt **2** not learnt or taken notice of: *unlearnt lessons*

unleash *vb* to set loose or cause (something bad): *to unleash war*

unleavened (un-lev-vend) *adj* (of bread) made without yeast or leavening

unless *conj* except under the circumstances that; except on the condition that: *you can't get in unless you can prove you're over eighteen*

unlettered *adj* uneducated or illiterate

unlike ❶ *adj* **1** not similar; different ▷ *prep* **2** not like or typical of: *unlike his brother, he could not control his weight* **unlikeness** *n*

unlikely ❶ *adj* not likely; improbable **unlikeliness** *n*

unlimited *adj* **1** apparently endless: *there was unlimited coffee* **2** not restricted or limited: *unlimited access to the rest of the palace*

unlisted *adj* **1** not entered on a list **2** (of securities) not quoted on a stock exchange **3** *Austral, US & Canad* not listed in a telephone directory by request

unlit *adj* **1** (of a fire, cigarette, etc.) not lit and therefore not burning **2** (of a road) not having any streetlights switched on

unload ❶ *vb* **1** to remove cargo from a ship, lorry, or plane **2** to express worries or problems by telling someone about them **3** to remove the ammunition from a gun

unlock *vb* **1** to unfasten a lock or door **2** to release or let loose: *the revelation unlocked a flood of tears*

unlooked-for *adj* unexpected or unforeseen

unloose *or* **unloosen** *vb* **-loosing, -loosed** *or* **-loosening, -loosened** to set free or release

unlovable *adj* too unpleasant or unattractive to be loved

unloved *adj* not loved by anyone

unlovely *adj* unpleasant in appearance or character

unlucky *adj* **1** having bad luck or misfortune: *an unlucky man* **2** caused by bad luck or misfortune: *an unlucky coincidence* **3** regarded as likely to bring about bad luck: *an unlucky number* **unluckily** *adv*

unmade *adj* **1** (of a bed) with the bedclothes not smoothed and tidied **2** (of a road) not surfaced with tarmac **3** not yet made

unmake *vb* **-making, -made** to undo or destroy

unman *vb* **-manning, -manned 1** to cause to lose courage or nerve **2** to make effeminate

unmanageable *adj* difficult to use, deal with, or control, esp. because it is too big

unmanly *adj* **1** not masculine or virile **2** cowardly or dishonourable

unmanned *adj* **1** having no personnel or crew: *the border posts were unmanned* **2** (of an aircraft or spacecraft) operated by automatic or remote control

unmannerly *adj* lacking manners; discourteous **unmannerliness** *n*

unmarked *adj* **1** having no signs of damage or injury **2** not having any identifying signs or markings: *an unmarked police car*

unmarried *adj* not married

unmask *vb* **1** to remove the mask or disguise from **2** to expose or reveal the true nature or character of

unmatched *adj* **1** not equalled or surpassed: *his pace is unmatched by any other modern player* **2** not coordinated or forming a set with anything else: *three unmatched chairs*

unmentionable *adj* unsuitable as a topic of conversation

unmercifully *adv* excessively and relentlessly: *the young boy is hounded unmercifully*

unmistakable *or* **unmistakeable** *adj* clear or unambiguous **unmistakably** *or* **unmistakeably** *adv*

unmitigated *adj* **1** not reduced or lessened in severity or intensity **2** total and complete: *unmitigated boredom*

unmolested *adv* without disturbance or interference: *the enemy aircraft passed overhead unmolested*

unmoved *adj* not affected by emotion; indifferent

unmoving *adj* still and motionless

unmusical *adj* **1** (of a person) unable to appreciate or play music **2** (of a sound) harsh and unpleasant

unnamed *adj* **1** not mentioned by name; anonymous: *an unnamed government spokesman* **2** not known or described clearly enough to be named: *unnamed fears*

unnatural ❶ *adj* **1** strange and slightly frightening because it is not usual; abnormal: *an unnatural silence* **2** not in accordance with accepted standards of behaviour: *an unnatural relationship* **3** affected or forced: *a determined smile which seemed unnatural* **4** inhuman or monstrous: *unnatural evils* **unnaturally** *adv*

unnecessary *adj* not essential, or more than is essential **unnecessarily** *adv*

unnerve *vb* **-nerving, -nerved** to cause to lose courage, confidence, or self-control: *he unnerves me* **unnerving** *adj*

unnoticed *adj* without being seen or noticed

unnumbered *adj* **1** countless; too many to count **2** not counted or given a number

UNO United Nations Organization

unobtainable *adj* impossible to get

unobtrusive *adj* not drawing attention to oneself or itself; inconspicuous

unoccupied *adj* **1** (of a building) without occupants **2** unemployed or

U

THESAURUS

unexplored, virgin, remote, alien, exotic, outlandish, unmapped, untravelled, beyond your ken **1b = unidentified**, mysterious, anonymous, unnamed, nameless, incognito **2 = obscure**, little known, minor, humble, unfamiliar, insignificant, lowly, unimportant, unheard-of, unsung, inconsequential, undistinguished, unrenowned **OPPOSITE:** famous

unlike *prep* **2a = different from**, dissimilar to, not resembling, far from, not like, distinct from, incompatible with, unrelated to, distant from, unequal to, far apart from, divergent from, not similar to, as different as chalk and cheese from (*informal*) **OPPOSITE:** similar to **2b = contrasted with**, not like, in contradiction to, in contrast with *or* to, as opposed to, differently from, opposite to

unlikely *adj* **= improbable**, doubtful, remote, slight, faint, not likely, unimaginable **OPPOSITE:** probable

unload *vb* **1 = empty**, clear, unpack, dump, discharge, off-load, disburden, unlade **2 = unburden**, relieve, lighten, disburden

unnatural *adj* **1 = abnormal**, odd, strange, unusual, extraordinary, bizarre, perverted, queer, irregular, perverse, supernatural, uncanny, outlandish, unaccountable, anomalous, freakish, aberrant **OPPOSITE:** normal **3 = false**, forced, artificial, studied, laboured, affected, assumed, mannered, strained, stiff, theatrical, contrived, self-conscious, feigned, stilted, insincere, factitious, stagy, phoney *or* phony (*informal*) **OPPOSITE:** genuine

DICTIONARY

idle **3** (of an area or country) not overrun by foreign troops
unofficial *adj* **1** not authorized or approved by the relevant organization or person: *an unofficial strike* **2** not confirmed officially: *unofficial reports of the minister's resignation*
unorganized *or* **-nised** *adj* **1** not arranged into an organized system or structure **2** (of workers) not unionized
unorthodox *adj* **1** (of ideas, methods, etc.) unconventional and not generally accepted **2** (of a person) not conventional in beliefs, behaviour, etc.
unpack *vb* **1** to remove the packed contents of a case **2** to take something out of a packed container
unpaid *adj* **1** without a salary or wage: *unpaid overtime* **2** still to be paid: *unpaid bills*
unpalatable *adj* **1** (of food) unpleasant to taste **2** (of a fact, idea, etc.) unpleasant and hard to accept
unparalleled *adj* not equalled; supreme
unpardonable *adj* unforgivably wrong or rude
unparliamentary *adj* not consistent with parliamentary procedure or practice
unperson *n* a person whose existence is officially denied or ignored
unpick *vb* to undo the stitches of a piece of sewing
unpin *vb* **-pinning, -pinned 1** to remove a pin or pins from **2** to unfasten by removing pins
unplanned *adj* not intentional or deliberate
unplayable *adj sport* **1** (of a ball) thrown too fast or too skilfully to be hit **2** (of a pitch or course) too badly affected by rain or frost to be used
unpleasant ⓘ *adj* not pleasant or agreeable **unpleasantly** *adv* **unpleasantness** *n*
unplug *vb* **-plugging, -plugged** to disconnect a piece of electrical equipment by taking the plug out of the socket
unplugged *adj* using acoustic rather than electric instruments: *an unplugged version of the song*
unplumbed *adj* **1** not measured **2** not understood in depth
unpolished *adj* **1** not polished **2** not elegant or refined
unpopular *adj* generally disliked or disapproved of **unpopularity** *n*
unpractised *or US* **unpracticed** *adj* not experienced or skilled: *an unpractised surgical technique*
unprecedented *adj* never having happened before: *an unprecedented decision*
unpredictable *adj* not easy to predict or foresee
unprejudiced *adj* free from bias; impartial
unprepared *adj* surprised or put at a disadvantage by something because you are not ready to deal with it
unprepossessing *adj* not very attractive or appealing
unpretentious *adj* modest, unassuming, and down-to-earth
unprincipled *adj* lacking moral principles; unscrupulous
unprintable *adj* unsuitable for printing for reasons of obscenity, libel, or indecency
unproductive *adj* not producing any worthwhile results: *unproductive talks*
unprofessional *adj* not behaving according to the standards expected of a member of a particular profession
unprofitable *adj* **1** not making a profit **2** not producing any worthwhile results: *an unprofitable line of thinking*
unpromising *adj* not likely to turn out well
unprompted *adj* doing without being urged by anyone else; spontaneous
unpronounceable *adj* (of a name or word) too difficult to say
unprotected *adj* not defended or protected from harm
unprovoked *adj* carried out without any cause or reason: *an unprovoked attack*
unpunished *adj* without suffering or resulting in a penalty: *the guilty must not go unpunished; such crimes should not remain unpunished*
unputdownable *adj* (of a book, usually a novel) so gripping that one wants to read it at one sitting
unqualified *adj* **1** lacking the necessary qualifications **2** having no conditions or limitations: *an unqualified denial* **3** total or complete: *unqualified admiration*
unquestionable *adj* not to be doubted; indisputable **unquestionably** *adv*
unquestioned *adj* accepted by everyone without doubt or disagreement: *an engineer of unquestioned genius*
unquestioning *adj* accepting a belief or order without thinking about or doubting it in any way: *unquestioning obedience* **unquestioningly** *adv*
unquiet *adj chiefly literary* anxious or uneasy
unquote *interj* an expression used to indicate the end of a quotation that was introduced with the word 'quote'
unravel ⓘ *vb* **-elling, -elled** *or US* **-eling, -eled 1** to separate something knitted or woven into individual strands **2** to become separated into individual strands **3** to explain or solve: *we unravelled the secrets*
unreactive *adj* (of a substance) not readily partaking in chemical reactions
unread *adj* **1** (of a book or article) not yet read **2** (of a person) having read little
unreadable *adj* **1** unable to be read or deciphered; illegible **2** too difficult or dull to read
unreal *adj* **1** existing only in the imagination or giving the impression of doing so: *an unreal quality* **2** insincere or artificial **unreality** *n*
unrealistic *adj* **1** not accepting the facts of a situation and not dealing with them in a practical way: *he had unrealistic expectations of his son* **2** not true to life: *an unrealistic portrayal of Scottish life* **unrealistically** *adv*
unreasonable *adj* **1** unfair and excessive: *an unreasonable request* **2** refusing to listen to reason **unreasonably** *adv*
unreasoning *adj* not controlled by reason; irrational
unrecognizable *or* **-isable** *adj* changed or damaged so much that it is hard to recognize
unrecognized *or* **-ised** *adj* not properly identified or acknowledged: *her talents went unrecognized during her lifetime*
unregenerate *adj* unrepentant or unreformed
unrelated *adj* not connected with each other: *a series of unrelated mishaps*
unrelenting *adj* **1** refusing to relent or take pity **2** not diminishing in determination, effort, or force
unreliable *adj* not able to be trusted or relied on
unremitting *adj* never slackening or stopping
unrepentant *adj* not ashamed of one's beliefs or actions

U

THESAURUS

unpleasant *adj* **a = nasty**, bad, horrid, distressing, annoying, irritating, miserable, troublesome, distasteful, obnoxious, unpalatable, displeasing, repulsive, objectionable, disagreeable, abhorrent, irksome, unlovely, execrable **OPPOSITE:** nice **b = obnoxious**, disagreeable, vicious, malicious, rude, mean, cruel, poisonous, unattractive, unfriendly, vindictive, venomous, mean-spirited, inconsiderate, impolite, unloveable, ill-natured, unlikable *or* unlikeable **OPPOSITE:** likable *or* likeable
unravel *vb* **1 = undo**, separate, disentangle, free, unwind, extricate, straighten out, untangle, unknot **3 = solve**, explain, work out, resolve, interpret, figure out *(informal)*, make out, clear up, suss (out) *(slang)*, get to

DICTIONARY

unrequited *adj* (of love) not returned
unreserved *adj* **1** complete and without holding back any doubts: *unreserved support* **2** open and forthcoming in manner **3** not booked or not able to be booked: *all the seats are unreserved* **unreservedly** (un-riz-**zerv**-id-lee) *adv*
unresolved *adj* not satisfactorily solved or concluded: *the mystery of her death remains unresolved*
unresponsive *adj* not reacting or responding
unrest ⓣ *n* **1** a rebellious state of discontent **2** an uneasy or troubled state
unrestrained *adj* not controlled or limited: *the unrestrained use of state power*
unrestricted *adj* not limited by any laws or rules
unrewarding *adj* not giving any satisfaction
unrighteous *adj* sinful or wicked
unripe *adj* not fully matured
unrivalled *or US* **unrivaled** *adj* having no equal; matchless
unroll *vb* **1** to open out or unwind: *I unrolled the map* **2** (of a series of events or period of time) to happen or be revealed or remembered one after the other
unruffled *adj* **1** calm and unperturbed **2** smooth and still: *unruffled ponds*
unruly *adj* **-lier, -liest** difficult to control or organize; disobedient or undisciplined **unruliness** *n*
unsaddle *vb* **-dling, -dled 1** to remove the saddle from a horse **2** to cause to fall or dismount from a horse
unsafe *adj* **1** dangerous **2** (of a criminal conviction) based on inadequate or false evidence
unsaid *adj* not said or expressed
unsaleable *adj* unable to be sold
unsatisfactory *adj* not good enough
unsaturated *adj* **1** *chem* (of an organic compound) containing a double or triple bond and therefore capable of combining with other substances **2** (of a fat, esp. a vegetable fat) containing a high proportion of fatty acids with double bonds
unsavoury *or US* **unsavory** *adj* objectionable or distasteful: *an unsavoury divorce*
unscathed *adj* not harmed or injured
unscheduled *adj* not planned or intended
unscramble *vb* **-bling, -bled 1** to sort out something confused or disorderly **2** to restore a scrambled message to an intelligible form **unscrambler** *n*
unscrew *vb* **1** to loosen a screw or lid by turning it **2** to unfasten something by removing the screws which fasten it: *the mirror had been unscrewed and removed*
unscripted *adj* spoken without a previously prepared text
unscrupulous *adj* prepared to act in a dishonest or immoral manner
unseasonable *adj* **1** (of the weather) inappropriate for the season **2** inappropriate or unusual for the time of year: *an unseasonable dip in the sea*
unseat *vb* **1** to throw or displace from a seat or saddle **2** to depose from office or position
unseeded *adj* (of a player in a sport) not given a top player's position in the opening rounds of a tournament
unseeing *adj* not noticing or looking at anything: *staring with unseeing eyes*
unseemly *adj* not according to expected standards of behaviour **unseemliness** *n*
unseen *adj* **1** hidden or invisible: *an unseen organist was practising* **2** mysterious or supernatural: *unseen powers* ▷ *adv* **3** without being seen; unnoticed: *the thief entered unseen* ▷ *n* **4** a passage which is given to students for translation without them having seen it in advance
unselfish *adj* concerned about other people's wishes and needs rather than one's own **unselfishly** *adv* **unselfishness** *n*
unsettle *vb* **-tling, -tled 1** to change or become changed from a fixed or settled condition **2** to confuse or agitate a person or the mind
unsettled ⓣ *adj* **1** lacking order or stability: *an unsettled time* **2** disturbed and restless: *your child will feel unsettled and insecure* **3** constantly changing or moving from place to place: *his wandering unsettled life* **4** (of an argument or dispute) not resolved **5** (of a debt or bill) not yet paid
unshakable *or* **unshakeable** *adj* (of beliefs) utterly firm and unwavering
unshaken *adj* (of faith or feelings) not having been weakened
unshaven *adj* (of a man who does not have a beard) having stubble on his chin because he has not shaved recently
unsheathe *vb* **-sheathing, -sheathed** to pull a weapon from a sheath
unshockable *adj* not likely to be upset by anything seen, heard, or read
unsightly *adj* unpleasant to look at; ugly **unsightliness** *n*
unsigned *adj* (of a letter etc.) anonymous
unskilled *adj* not having or requiring any special skill or training
unsociable *adj* (of a person) not fond of the company of other people
unsocial *adj* **1** not fond of the company of other people **2** (of the hours of work of a job) falling outside the normal working day
unsolicited *adj* given or sent without being asked for: *unsolicited advice; unsolicited junk mail*
unsophisticated *adj* **1** (of a person) lacking experience or worldly wisdom **2** lacking refinement or complexity: *unsophisticated fighter aircraft*
unsound *adj* **1** unhealthy or unstable: *of unsound mind* **2** based on faulty ideas: *unsound judgment* **3** not firm: *unsound foundations* **4** not financially reliable: *his business plan was unsound*
unsparing *adj* **1** very generous; lavish **2** harsh or severe **unsparingly** *adv*
unspeakable *adj* **1** incapable of expression in words: *unspeakable gratitude* **2** indescribably bad or evil: *unspeakable atrocities* **unspeakably** *adv*
unspoiled *adj* **1** not damaged or harmed **2** (of a place) attractive and not having changed for a long time
unspoken *adj* not openly expressed: *unspoken fears; an unspoken agreement*
unsporting *adj* not following the principles of fair play
unstable ⓣ *adj* **1** not firmly fixed and likely to wobble or fall: *an unstable pile of books* **2** likely to change suddenly and create difficulties or danger: *the unstable political climate* **3** (of a person) having abrupt changes of mood or behaviour **4** *chem, physics* readily decomposing
unsteady *adj* **1** not securely fixed: *unsteady metal posts* **2** (of a manner of walking, standing, or holding) shaky or staggering **unsteadily** *adv* **unsteadiness** *n*

U

THESAURUS

the bottom of, get straight, puzzle out
unrest *n* **1 = discontent**, rebellion, dissatisfaction, protest, turmoil, upheaval, strife, agitation, discord, disaffection, sedition, tumult, dissension **OPPOSITE:** peace
unsettled *adj* **1 = unstable**, shaky, insecure, disorderly, unsteady **2 = restless**, tense, uneasy, troubled, shaken, confused, wired *(slang)*, disturbed, anxious, agitated, unnerved, flustered, perturbed, on edge, restive, adrenalized **3 = inconstant**, changing, unpredictable, variable, uncertain, changeable
unstable *adj* **1 = insecure**, shaky, precarious, unsettled, wobbly, tottering, rickety, unsteady, not fixed **2 = changeable**, volatile, unpredictable, variable, fluctuating, unsteady, fitful, inconstant **OPPOSITE:** constant **3 = unpredictable**, irrational, erratic, inconsistent, unreliable, temperamental, capricious, changeable, untrustworthy, vacillating **OPPOSITE:** level-headed

DICTIONARY

unstinting *adj* generous and gladly given: *unstinting praise*
unstoppable *adj* impossible to prevent from continuing or developing
unstrap *vb* **-strapping, -strapped** to undo the straps fastening (something) in position
unstructured *adj* without formal or systematic organization
unstuck *adj* **1** freed from being stuck, glued, or fastened **2 come unstuck** to suffer failure or disaster
unstudied *adj* natural or spontaneous: *her unstudied elegance and grace*
unsubstantial *adj* **1** lacking weight or firmness **2** having no material existence
unsubstantiated *adj* not yet confirmed or proved to be true: *unsubstantiated rumours*
unsuccessful *adj* not achieving success
unsuitable *adj* not right or appropriate for a particular purpose
unsuited *adj* **1** not appropriate for a particular task or situation: *a likeable man unsuited to a military career* **2** (of a couple) having different personalities or tastes and unlikely to form a lasting relationship: *they are totally unsuited to each other*
unsung *adj* not appreciated or honoured: *an unsung hero*
unsure *adj* **1** lacking assurance or self-confidence **2** uncertain or undecided: *he was unsure who was really in charge*
unsurpassed *adj* better or greater than anything else of its kind
unsuspected *adj* **1** not known to exist: *an unsuspected talent* **2** not under suspicion
unsuspecting *adj* having no idea of what is happening or about to happen
unsweetened *adj* having no sugar or other sweetener added
unswerving *adj* not turning aside; constant
unsympathetic *adj* **1** not feeling or showing sympathy **2** unpleasant and unlikeable **3** (foll. by *to*) opposed or hostile to
untamed *adj* not brought under human control; wild: *an untamed wilderness*
untangle *vb* **-gling, -gled** to free from tangles or confusion
untapped *adj* not yet used or exploited: *untapped mineral reserves*
untaught *adj* **1** without training or education **2** acquired without instruction
untenable *adj* (of a theory, idea, etc.) impossible to defend in an argument
unthinkable ● *adj* **1** so shocking or unpleasant that one cannot believe it to be true **2** unimaginable or inconceivable
unthinking *adj* **1** thoughtless and inconsiderate **2** done or happening without careful consideration: *an unthinking reflex* **unthinkingly** *adv*
untidy *adj* **-dier, -diest** not neat; messy and disordered **untidily** *adv* **untidiness** *n*
untie *vb* **-tying, -tied** to unfasten or free something that is tied
until ● *conj* **1** up to a time that: *he lifted the wire until it was taut* **2** before (a time or event): *until the present crisis, they weren't allowed into the country* ▷ *prep* **3** (often preceded by *up*) in or throughout the period before: *up until then I'd never thought about having kids* **4** before: *Baker does not get to Israel until Sunday*
WORD ORIGIN earlier *untill*
untimely *adj* **1** occurring before the expected or normal time: *his untimely death* **2** inappropriate to the occasion or time: *an untimely idea to raise at the United Nations* **untimeliness** *n*
unto *prep archaic* to
WORD ORIGIN from Old Norse
untold ● *adj* **1** incapable of description: *untold misery* **2** incalculably great in number or quantity: *untold millions* **3** not told
untouchable *adj* **1** above criticism, suspicion or punishment **2** unable to be touched ▷ *n* **3** a member of the lowest class in India, whose touch was formerly regarded as defiling to the four main castes
untouched *adj* **1** not changed, moved, or affected: *a sleepy backwater untouched by mass tourism* **2** not injured or harmed: *the Cathedral survived the war untouched* **3** (of food or drink) not eaten or consumed **4** emotionally unaffected: *he was untouched by the news of his uncle's death*
untoward *adj* **1** causing misfortune or annoyance **2** unfavourable: *untoward reactions* **3** out of the ordinary; out of the way: *nothing untoward had happened*
untrained *adj* without formal or adequate training or education
untrammelled *or US* **untrammeled** *adj* able to act freely and without restrictions
untried *adj* **1** not yet used, done, or tested **2** (of a prisoner) not yet put on trial
untroubled *adj* calm and unworried
untrue ● *adj* **1** incorrect or false **2** disloyal or unfaithful
untrustworthy *adj* unreliable and not able to be trusted
untruth *n* a statement that is not true; lie
untruthful *adj* **1** (of a person) given to lying **2** (of a statement) not true **untruthfully** *adv*
untutored *adj* **1** without formal education **2** lacking sophistication or refinement
unusable *adj* not in good enough condition to be used
unused *adj* **1** not being or never having been used **2** (foll. by *to*) not accustomed to
unusual ● *adj* uncommon or extraordinary **unusually** *adv*
unutterable *adj* incapable of being expressed in words **unutterably** *adv*
unvarnished *adj* not elaborated upon; plain: *an unvarnished account of literary life*
unvarying *adj* always staying the same; unchanging
unveil *vb* **1** to ceremonially remove the cover from a new picture, statue, plaque, etc. **2** to make public a secret **3** to remove the veil from one's own

THESAURUS

unthinkable *adj* **1 = impossible**, out of the question, inconceivable, unlikely, not on *(informal)*, absurd, unreasonable, improbable, preposterous, illogical **2 = inconceivable**, incredible, unbelievable, unimaginable, beyond belief, beyond the bounds of possibility
until *conj* **1 = till**, up to, up till, up to the time, as late as **2 = before**, up to, prior to, in advance of, previous to ▷ *prep* **3 = till**, up to, up till, up to the time, as late as **4 = before**, up to, prior to, in advance of, previous to, pre-
untold *adj* **1 = indescribable**, unthinkable, unimaginable, unspeakable, undreamed of, unutterable, inexpressible **2 = countless**, incalculable, innumerable, myriad, numberless, uncounted, uncountable, unnumbered, measureless
untrue *adj* **1 = false**, lying, wrong, mistaken, misleading, incorrect, inaccurate, sham, dishonest, deceptive, spurious, erroneous, fallacious, untruthful **OPPOSITE:** true **2 = unfaithful**, disloyal, deceitful, treacherous, two-faced, faithless, false, untrustworthy, perfidious, forsworn, traitorous, inconstant **OPPOSITE:** faithful
unusual *adj* **a = rare**, odd, strange, extraordinary, different, surprising, novel, bizarre, unexpected, curious, weird *(informal)*, unfamiliar, abnormal, queer, phenomenal, uncommon, out of the ordinary, left-field *(informal)*, unwonted **OPPOSITE:** common **b = extraordinary**, unique, remarkable, exceptional, notable, phenomenal, uncommon, singular, unconventional, out of the ordinary, atypical **OPPOSITE:** average

DICTIONARY

or another person's face

unveiling *n* **1** a ceremony involving the removal of a veil covering a statue **2** the presentation of something for the first time

unvoiced *adj* **1** not expressed or spoken **2** *phonetics* voiceless

unwaged *adj* (of a person) not having a paid job

unwanted *adj* not wanted or welcome

unwarranted *adj* not justified or necessary

unwary *adj* not careful or cautious and therefore likely to be harmed **unwarily** *adv* **unwariness** *n*

unwavering *adj* (of a feeling or attitude) remaining firm and never weakening

unwelcome *adj* unpleasant and unwanted

unwell *adj* not healthy; ill

unwept *adj* not wept for or lamented

unwholesome *adj* **1** harmful to the body or mind: *unwholesome food* **2** morally harmful: *unwholesome dreams* **3** unhealthy-looking **4** (of food) of inferior quality

unwieldy *adj* too heavy, large, or awkward to be easily handled

unwilling *adj* **1** reluctant **2** done or said with reluctance **unwillingly** *adv* **unwillingness** *n*

unwind *vb* **-winding, -wound 1** to slacken, undo, or unravel: *Paul started to unwind the bandage* **2** to relax after a busy or tense time: *we go out to unwind after work*

unwise *adj* foolish; not sensible **unwisely** *adv*

unwitting *adj* **1** not intentional **2** not knowing or conscious **unwittingly** *adv* **WORD ORIGIN** Old English *unwitende*

unwonted *adj* out of the ordinary; unusual

unworkable *adj* impractical and certain to fail: *unworkable proposals for reform*

unworldly *adj* **1** not concerned with material values or pursuits **2** lacking sophistication; naive

unworn *adj* **1** not having deteriorated through use or age **2** (of a garment) never having been worn

unworried *adj* not bothered or perturbed

unworthy *adj* **1** not deserving or meriting: *a person deemed unworthy of membership* **2** (often foll. by *of*) beneath the level considered befitting (to): *unworthy of a prime minister* **3** lacking merit or value **unworthiness** *n*

unwrap *vb* **-wrapping, -wrapped** to remove the wrapping from something or (of something wrapped) to have the covering removed

unwritten *adj* **1** not printed or in writing **2** operating only through custom: *an unwritten code of conduct*

unyielding *adj* remaining firm and determined

unzip *vb* **-zipping, -zipped** to unfasten the zip of a garment or (of a zip or a garment with a zip) to become unfastened

up *prep* **1** indicating movement to a higher position: *go up the stairs* **2** at a higher or further level or position in or on: *a shop up the road* ▷ *adv* **3** to an upward, higher, or erect position: *the men straightened up from their digging* **4** indicating readiness for an activity: *up and about* **5** indicating intensity or completion of an action: *he tore up the cheque* **6** to the place referred to or where the speaker is: *a man came up to me* **7 a** to a more important place: *up to the city* **b** to a more northerly place: *pensioners who were going up to Norway* **c** to or at university **8** above the horizon: *the sun came up* **9** appearing for trial: *up before the judge* **10** having gained: *ten pounds up on the deal* **11** higher in price: *beer has gone up again* **12 all up with someone** *informal* over for or hopeless for someone **13 something's up** *informal* something strange is happening **14 up against** having to cope with: *look what we're up against now* **15 up for** being a candidate or applicant for: *he's up for the job* **16 up to a** occupied with; scheming: *she's up to no good* **b** dependent upon: *the decision is up to you* **c** equal to or capable of: *are you up to playing in the final?* **d** as far as: *up to his neck in mud* **e** as many as: *up to two years' credit* **f** comparable with: *not up to my usual standard* **17 what's up?** *informal* **a** what is the matter? **b** what is happening? ▷ *adj* **18** of a high or higher position **19** out of bed: *aren't you up yet?* **20** (of a period of time) over or completed: *the examiner announced that their time was up* **21** of or relating to a train going to a more important place: *the up platform* ▷ *vb* **upping, upped 22** to increase or raise **23 up and** *informal* to do something suddenly: *he upped and left her* ▷ *n* **24** a high point: *when the ups come along you have to enjoy them* **25 on the up and up a** *Brit* trustworthy or honest **b** *Brit, Austral & NZ* on an upward trend: *our firm's on the up and up* **WORD ORIGIN** Old English *upp*

up-and-coming *adj* likely to be successful in the future; promising

upbeat ⊕ *adj* **1** *informal* cheerful and optimistic: *the upbeat atmosphere of a thriving metropolis* ▷ *n* **2** *music* **a** an unaccented beat **b** the upward gesture of a conductor's baton indicating this

upbraid *vb* to scold or reproach **WORD ORIGIN** Old English *upbrēdan*

upbringing ⊕ *n* the education of a person during his or her formative years

upcoming *adj* coming soon: *the upcoming election*

upcountry *adj* **1** of or from the interior of a country ▷ *adv* **2** towards or in the interior of a country

update ⊕ *vb* **-dating, -dated 1** to bring up to date **2** inform; relay the most recent information to

upend *vb* to turn or set or become turned or set on end

upfront *adj* **1** open and frank **2** (of money) paid at the beginning of a business arrangement ▷ *adv* **up front 3** at the front; (in sport) in attack: *Liverpool's strikers dominated up front* **4** at the beginning of a business arrangement; in advance: *we charge up front*

upgrade ⊕ *vb* **-grading, -graded 1** to promote a person or job to a higher rank **2** to raise in value, importance, or esteem

Upham *n* **Charles (Hazlitt)** 1908–94, New Zealand soldier; hero of World War II and one of only three people to have been awarded the Victoria Cross twice

upheaval ⊕ *n* a strong, sudden, or violent disturbance

uphill ⊕ *adj* **1** sloping or leading upwards **2** requiring a great deal of effort: *an uphill struggle* ▷ *adv* **3** up a slope ▷ *n* **4** *S African* a difficulty

THESAURUS

upbeat *adj* **1** *(informal)* = **cheerful**, positive, optimistic, promising, encouraging, looking up, hopeful, favourable, rosy, buoyant, heartening, cheery, forward-looking

upbringing *n* = **education**, training, breeding, rearing, care, raising, tending, bringing-up, nurture, cultivation

update *vb* **1** = **bring up to date**, improve, correct, renew, revise, upgrade, amend, overhaul, streamline, modernize, rebrand

upgrade *vb* **1** = **promote**, raise, advance, boost, move up, elevate, kick upstairs *(informal)*, give promotion to **OPPOSITE:** demote **2** = **improve**, better, update, reform, add to, enhance, refurbish, renovate, remodel, make better, modernize, spruce up, ameliorate

upheaval *n* = **disturbance**, revolution, disorder, turmoil, overthrow, disruption, eruption, cataclysm, violent change

uphill *adj* **1** = **ascending**, rising, upward, mounting, climbing **OPPOSITE:** descending **2** = **arduous**, hard, taxing, difficult, tough, exhausting, punishing,

DICTIONARY

uphold ❶ *vb* **-holding, -held 1** to maintain or defend against opposition **2** to give moral support to **upholder** *n*

upholster *vb* to fit chairs or sofas with padding, springs, and covering **upholstered** *adj* **upholsterer** *n*

upholstery *n* the padding, springs, and covering of a chair or sofa

upkeep *n* **1** the act or process of keeping something in good repair **2** the cost of maintenance

upland *adj* of or in an area of high or relatively high ground: *an upland wilderness*

uplands *pl n* an area of high or relatively high ground: *the uplands of Nepal*

uplift ❶ *vb* **1** to raise or lift up **2** to raise morally or spiritually **3** *Scot* to collect or pick up ▷*n* **4** the act or process of bettering moral, social, or cultural conditions ▷*adj* **5** (of a bra) designed to lift and support the breasts **uplifting** *adj*

upload *vb* to transfer(data or a program) from one computer's memory into that of another

upmarket *adj* expensive and of superior quality

upon *prep* **1** on **2** up and on: *they climbed upon his lap for comfort*
WORD ORIGIN *up + on*

upper ❶ *adj* **1** higher or highest in physical position, wealth, rank, or status **2 Upper** *geol* denoting the late part of a period or formation: *Upper Cretaceous* ▷*n* **3** the part of a shoe above the sole **4 on one's uppers** *Brit, Austral & NZ* very poor; penniless

upper-case *adj* denoting capital letters as used in printed or typed matter

upper class ❶ *n* **1** the highest social class; aristocracy ▷*adj* **upper-class 2** of the upper class

upper crust *n Brit, Austral & NZ informal* the upper class

uppercut *n* a short swinging upward punch delivered to the chin

upper hand *n* the position of control: *the hardliners have gained the upper hand*

Upper House *n* the smaller and less representative chamber of a two-chamber parliament, for example the House of Lords or a Senate

uppermost *adj* **1** highest in position, power, or importance ▷*adv* **2** in or into the highest place or position

uppish *adj Brit informal* uppity

uppity *adj informal* snobbish, arrogant, or presumptuous
WORD ORIGIN *up* + fanciful ending

upright ❶ *adj* **1** vertical or erect **2** honest or just ▷*adv* **3** vertically or in an erect position ▷*n* **4** a vertical support, such as a post **5** ▶short for **upright piano 6** the state of being vertical **uprightness** *n*

upright piano *n* a piano which has a rectangular vertical case

uprising ❶ *n* a revolt or rebellion

up-river *adj, adv* nearer the source of a river: *we sailed slowly up-river; the village of Juffure, four days up-river*

uproar ❶ *n* **1** a commotion or disturbance characterized by loud noise and confusion **2** angry public criticism or debates: *the decision to close the railway led to an uproar*

uproarious *adj* **1** very funny **2** (of laughter) loud and boisterous

uproot *vb* **1** to pull up by or as if by the roots **2** to displace (a person or people) from their native or usual surroundings **3** to remove or destroy utterly: *we must uproot all remnants of feudalism*

ups and downs *pl n* alternating periods of good and bad luck or high and low spirits

upscale *informal adj* (**up**-skale) **1** of or for the upper end of an economic or social scale; upmarket ▷*vb* (up-**skale**), **-scaling, -scaled 2** to increase the scale of

upset ❶ *adj* **1** emotionally or physically disturbed or distressed ▷*vb* **-setting, -set 2** to turn or tip over **3** to disrupt the normal state or progress of: *bad weather upset their plans* **4** to disturb mentally or emotionally **5** to make physically ill: *it still seems to upset my stomach* ▷*n* **6** an unexpected defeat or reversal, as in a contest or plans **7** a disturbance or disorder of the emotions, mind, or body **upsetting** *adj*

upset price *n chiefly Scot, US, & Canad* the lowest price acceptable for something that is for sale by auction, usually a house

upshot *n* the final result or conclusion; outcome
WORD ORIGIN *up + shot*

upside down ❶ *adj* **1** with the bottom where the top would normally be; inverted **2** *informal* confused or jumbled ▷*adv* **3** in an inverted fashion **4** in a chaotic manner or into a chaotic state: *recent events have*

THESAURUS

gruelling, strenuous, laborious, wearisome, Sisyphean

uphold *vb* **1 = confirm**, support, sustain, endorse, approve, justify, hold to, ratify, vindicate, validate **2 = support**, back, defend, aid, champion, encourage, maintain, promote, sustain, advocate, stand by, stick up for *(informal)*

uplift *vb* **2 = improve**, better, raise, advance, inspire, upgrade, refine, cultivate, civilize, ameliorate, edify ▷*n* **4 = improvement**, enlightenment, advancement, cultivation, refinement, enhancement, enrichment, betterment, edification

upper *adj* **1a = topmost**, top **OPPOSITE:** bottom **1b = higher**, high **OPPOSITE:** lower **1c = superior**, senior, higher-level, greater, top, important, chief, most important, elevated, eminent, higher-ranking **OPPOSITE:** inferior

upper class *adj* **2 = aristocratic**, upper-class, noble, high-class, patrician, top-drawer, blue-blooded, highborn

upright *adj* **1 = vertical**, straight, standing up, erect, on end, perpendicular, bolt upright **OPPOSITE:** horizontal **2 = honest**, good, principled, just, true, faithful, ethical, straightforward, honourable, righteous, conscientious, virtuous, trustworthy, high-minded, above board, incorruptible, unimpeachable **OPPOSITE:** dishonourable

uprising *n* **= rebellion**, rising, revolution, outbreak, revolt, disturbance, upheaval, mutiny, insurrection, putsch, insurgence

uproar *n* **1 = commotion**, noise, racket, riot, confusion, turmoil, brawl, mayhem, clamour, din, turbulence, pandemonium, rumpus, hubbub, hurly-burly, brouhaha, ruction *(informal)*, hullabaloo, ruckus *(informal)*, bagarre *(French)* **2 = protest**, outrage, complaint, objection, fuss, stink *(informal)*, outcry, furore, hue and cry

upset *adj* **1a = distressed**, shaken, disturbed, worried, troubled, hurt, bothered, confused, unhappy, gutted *(Brit informal)*, put out, dismayed, choked *(informal)*, grieved, frantic, hassled *(informal)*, agitated, ruffled, cut up *(informal)*, disconcerted, disquieted, overwrought, discomposed **1b = sick**, queasy, bad, poorly *(informal)*, ill, gippy *(slang)* ▷*vb* **2 = tip over**, overturn, capsize, knock over, spill, topple over **3 = mess up**, spoil, disturb, change, confuse, disorder, unsettle, mix up, disorganize, turn topsy-turvy, put out of order, throw into disorder **4 = distress**, trouble, disturb, worry, alarm, bother, dismay, grieve, hassle *(informal)*, agitate, ruffle, unnerve, disconcert, disquiet, fluster, perturb, faze, throw someone off balance, give someone grief *(Brit & S African)*, discompose ▷*n* **6 = reversal**, surprise, shake-up *(informal)*, defeat, sudden change **7 = illness**, complaint, disorder, bug *(informal)*, disturbance, sickness, malady, queasiness, indisposition

upside down *or* **upside-down** *adj* **1 = inverted**, overturned, upturned, on its head, bottom up, wrong side

turned many people's lives upside down **WORD ORIGIN** by folk etymology, from *upsodown*

upsides *adv informal chiefly Brit* (foll. by *with*) equal or level with, as through revenge

upstage *adv* **1** on, at, or to the rear of the stage ▷*adj* **2** at the back half of the stage ▷*vb* **-staging, -staged 3** to move upstage of another actor, forcing him or her to turn away from the audience **4** *informal* to draw attention to oneself and away from someone else

upstairs *adv* **1** to or on an upper floor of a building **2** *informal* to or into a higher rank or office ▷*n* **3** an upper floor ▷*adj* **4** situated on an upper floor: *an upstairs bedroom*

upstanding *adj* **1** of good character **2** upright and vigorous in build

upstart *n* a person who has risen suddenly to a position of power and behaves arrogantly

upstream *adv, adj* in or towards the higher part of a stream; against the current

upsurge *n* a rapid rise or swell

upswing *n* **1** *econ* a recovery period in the trade cycle **2** any increase or improvement

upsy-daisy *or* **upsadaisy** *interj* an expression of reassurance, usually used to a child, e.g. when it stumbles or is being lifted up **WORD ORIGIN** originally *up-a-daisy*

uptake *n* **1 quick** *or* **slow on the uptake** *informal* quick *or* slow to understand or learn **2** the use or consumption of something by a machine or part of the body: *the uptake of oxygen into the blood*

upthrust *n* **1** an upward push **2** *geol* a violent upheaval of the earth's surface

uptight *adj informal* **1** nervously tense, irritable, or angry **2** unable to express one's feelings

up-to-date ● *adj* modern or fashionable: *an up-to-date kitchen*

up-to-the-minute *adj* the latest or most modern possible: *up-to-the-minute news about what's on in town*

uptown *US & Canad adj, adv* **1** towards, in, or relating to some part of a town that is away from the centre ▷*n* **2** such a part of town, esp. a residential part

upturn *n* **1** an upward trend or improvement ▷*vb* **2** to turn or cause to turn over or upside down

UPVC unplasticized polyvinyl chloride

upward *adj* **1** directed or moving towards a higher place or level ▷*adv also* **upwards 2** from a lower to a higher place, level, or condition **3 upward** *or* **upwards of** more than (the stated figure): *a crowd estimated at upward of one hundred thousand people*

upward mobility *n* movement from a lower to a higher economic and social status

upwind *adv* **1** into or against the wind **2** towards or on the side where the wind is blowing ▷*adj* **3** going against the wind **4** on the windward side

Urania *n Greek myth* the Muse of astronomy

uranium (yew-**rain**-ee-um) *n chem* a radioactive silvery-white metallic element of the actinide series. It is used chiefly as a source of nuclear energy by fission of the radioisotope **uranium 235**. Symbol: U **WORD ORIGIN** from *Uranus*, from the fact that the element was discovered soon after the planet

Uranus *n* **1** *Greek myth* a god; the personification of the sky **2** the seventh planet from the sun **WORD ORIGIN** Greek *Ouranos* heaven

urban ● *adj* **1** of or living in a city or town **2** relating to modern pop music of African-American origin, such as hip-hop **WORD ORIGIN** Latin *urbs* city

urbane *adj* polite, elegant, and sophisticated in manner **WORD ORIGIN** Latin *urbanus* of the town

Urban II *n* original name *Odo* or *Udo*. ?1042–99, French ecclesiastic; pope (1088–99). He inaugurated the First Crusade at the Council of Clermont (1095)

urbanity *n* the quality of being urbane

urbanize *or* **-ise** *vb* **-izing, -ized** *or* **-ising, -ised** to make a rural area more industrialized and urban **urbanization** *or* **-isation** *n*

Urban VI *n* original name *Bartolomeo Prignano* ?1318–89, Italian ecclesiastic; pope (1378–89). His policies led to the election of an antipope by the French cardinals, thus beginning the Great Schism in the West

Urban VIII *n* original name *Maffeo Barberini* 1568–1644, Italian ecclesiastic; pope (1623–44) during the Thirty Years' War, in which he supported Richelieu against the Hapsburgs

urchin *n* **1** a mischievous child **2** ▸see **sea urchin** **WORD ORIGIN** Latin *ericius* hedgehog

Urdu (**oor**-doo) *n* an Indic language of the Indo-European family which is an official language of Pakistan and is also spoken in India **WORD ORIGIN** Hindustani *(zabāni) urdū* (language of the) camp

urea (yew-**ree**-a) *n* a white soluble crystalline compound found in urine **WORD ORIGIN** Greek *ouron* urine

ureter (yew-**reet**-er) *n* the tube that carries urine from the kidney to the bladder **WORD ORIGIN** Greek *ourein* to urinate

urethra (yew-**reeth**-ra) *n* the tube that in most mammals carries urine from the bladder out of the body **WORD ORIGIN** Greek *ourein* to urinate

urethritis (yew-rith-**rite**-iss) *n* inflammation of the urethra causing a discharge and painful urination **urethritic** *adj*

Urey *n* **Harold Clayton** 1893–1981, US chemist, who discovered the heavy isotope of hydrogen, deuterium (1932), and worked on methods of separating uranium isotopes: Nobel prize for chemistry 1934

Urfé *n* **Honoré d'** 1568–1625, French writer, whose pastoral *L'Astrée* (1607–27) is considered the first French novel

urge ● *n* **1** a strong impulse, inner drive, or yearning ▷*vb* **urging, urged 2** to plead with or press someone to do something: *he urged his readers to do the same* **3** to advocate earnestly and persistently: *I have long urged this change* **4** (often foll. by *on*) to force or hasten onwards: *something very powerful urged him on* **WORD ORIGIN** Latin *urgere*

urgent ● *adj* **1** requiring speedy action or attention: *an urgent inquiry*

THESAURUS

up **2** *(informal)* = **confused**, disordered, chaotic, muddled, jumbled, in disarray, in chaos, topsy-turvy, in confusion, higgledy-piggledy *(informal)*, in disorder ▷*adv* **3, 4** = **wrong side up**, bottom up, on its head

up-to-date *adj* = **modern**, fashionable, trendy *(Brit informal)*, in, newest, now *(informal)*, happening *(informal)*, current, with it *(informal)*, stylish, in vogue, all the rage, up-to-the-minute, having your finger on the pulse **OPPOSITE:** out-of-date

urban *adj* **1** = **civic**, city, town, metropolitan, municipal, dorp *(S African)*, inner-city

urge *n* **1** = **impulse**, longing, wish, desire, fancy, drive, yen *(informal)*, hunger, appetite, craving, yearning, itch *(informal)*, thirst, compulsion, hankering **OPPOSITE:** reluctance ▷*vb* **2** = **beg**, appeal to, exhort, press, prompt, plead, put pressure on, lean on, solicit, goad, implore, enjoin, beseech, pressurize, entreat, twist someone's arm *(informal)*, put the heat on *(informal)*, put the screws on *(informal)* **3** = **advocate**, suggest, recommend, advise, back, support, champion, counsel, insist on, endorse, push for **OPPOSITE:** discourage

urgent *adj* **1** = **crucial**, desperate, pressing, great, important, crying,

DICTIONARY

2 earnest and forceful: *she heard loud urgent voices in the corridor* **urgency** *n* **urgently** *adv*
WORD ORIGIN Latin *urgere* to urge

uric (yew-rik) *adj* of or derived from urine

uric acid *n* a white odourless crystalline acid present in the blood and urine

urinal *n* 1 a sanitary fitting, used by men for urination 2 a room containing urinals

urinary *adj anat* of urine or the organs that secrete and pass urine

urinary bladder *n* a membranous sac that can expand in which urine excreted from the kidneys is stored

urinate *vb* **-nating, -nated** to excrete urine **urination** *n*

urine *n* the pale yellow fluid excreted by the kidneys, containing waste products from the blood. It is stored in the bladder and discharged through the urethra
WORD ORIGIN Latin *urina*

urinogenital (yew-rin-oh-jen-it-al) *adj* ▸ same as **urogenital**

URL uniform resource locator: a standardized address of a location on the internet

urn *n* 1 a vaselike container, usually with a foot and a rounded body 2 a vase used as a container for the ashes of the dead 3 a large metal container, with a tap, used for making and holding tea or coffee
WORD ORIGIN Latin *urna*

urogenital (yew-roh-**jen**-it-al) *or* **urinogenital** *adj* of the urinary and genital organs and their functions. Also: **genitourinary**

urology (yew-**rol**-a-jee) *n* the branch of medicine concerned with the urinary system and its diseases

Urquhart *n* Sir **Thomas** 1611–60, Scottish author and translator of Rabelais' *Gargantua* and *Pantagruel* (1653; 1693)

ursine *adj* of or like a bear
WORD ORIGIN Latin *ursus* a bear

us *pron* (*objective*) 1 refers to the speaker or writer and another person or other people: *the bond between us* 2 refers to all people or people in general: *this table shows us the tides* 3 *informal* me: *give us a kiss!* 4 *formal* ▸ same as **me**: used by monarchs
WORD ORIGIN Old English *ūs*

US *or* **U.S.** United States

USA *or* **U.S.A.** United States of America

usable *adj* able to be used **usability** *n*

usage ⓘ *n* 1 regular or constant use: *a move to reduce pesticide usage* 2 the way in which a word is actually used in a language 3 a particular meaning or use that a word can have
WORD ORIGIN Latin *usus* a use

USB Universal Serial Bus: a standard for connection sockets on computers and other electronic equipment

USB drive *n computers* a small portable data storage device with a USB connection

use ⓘ *vb* **using, used** 1 to put into service or action; employ for a given purpose: *use a garden fork to mix them together* 2 to choose or employ regularly: *what sort of toothpaste do you use?* 3 to take advantage of; exploit: *I used Jason and he used me* 4 to consume or expend: *a manufacturing plant uses 1000 tonnes of steel a month* ▹ *n* 5 the act or fact of using or being used: *large-scale use of pesticides* 6 the ability or permission to use 7 need or opportunity to use: *the Colombian government had no use for them* 8 usefulness or advantage: *there is no use in complaining* 9 the purpose for which something is used 10 **have no use for** a to have no need of b to have a contemptuous dislike for 11 **make use of** a to employ; use b to exploit (a person) ▸ See also **use up** ▹ **user** *n*
WORD ORIGIN Latin *usus* having used

use-by date *n* the date on packaged food after which it should not be sold

used ⓘ *adj* second-hand: *it was a used car*

used to ⓘ *adj* 1 accustomed to: *I am used to being a medical guinea pig* ▹ *vb* 2 used as an auxiliary to express habitual or accustomed actions or states taking place in the past but not continuing to be the case in the present: *he used to vanish into his studio for days*

useful ⓘ *adj* 1 able to be used advantageously or for several purposes 2 *informal* commendable or capable: *a useful hurdler* **usefully** *adv* **usefulness** *n*

useless ⓘ *adj* 1 having no practical use 2 *informal* ineffectual, weak, or stupid: *I'm useless at most things* **uselessly** *adv* **uselessness** *n*

Usenet *n computers* a vast collection of newsgroups that follow agreed naming, maintaining, and distribution practices

user-friendly *adj* easy to familiarize oneself with, understand, and use

username *n computers* a name that someone uses for identification purposes when logging onto a computer or certain computer applications

use up *vb* to finish a supply of something completely

U-shaped valley *n* a steep-sided valley caused by glacial erosion

usher ⓘ *n* 1 an official who shows people to their seats, as in a church 2 a person who acts as doorkeeper in a court of law ▹ *vb* 3 to conduct or escort 4 (foll. by *in*) to happen immediately before something or cause it to happen; herald: *the French Revolution ushered in a new age*
WORD ORIGIN Old French *huissier* doorkeeper

THESAURUS

critical, immediate, acute, grave, instant, compelling, imperative, top-priority, now or never, exigent, not to be delayed
OPPOSITE: unimportant

usage *n* 1 = **use**, operation, employment, running, control, management, treatment, handling

use *vb* 1 = **employ**, utilize, make use of, work, apply, operate, exercise, practise, resort to, exert, wield, ply, put to use, bring into play, find a use for, avail yourself of, turn to account 3 = **take advantage of**, exploit, manipulate, abuse, milk, profit from, impose on, misuse, make use of, cash in on (*informal*), walk all over (*informal*), take liberties with 4 (*sometimes with* **up**) = **consume**, go through, exhaust, spend, waste, get through, run through, deplete, dissipate, expend, fritter away ▹ *n* 5 = **usage**, employment, utilization, operation, application 7, 9 = **purpose**, call, need, end, point, cause, reason, occasion, object, necessity 8 = **good**, point, help, service, value, benefit, profit, worth, advantage, utility, mileage (*informal*), avail, usefulness

used *adj* = **second-hand**, worn, not new, cast-off, hand-me-down (*informal*), nearly new, shopsoiled, reach-me-down (*informal*), preloved (*Austral slang*) OPPOSITE: new

used to *adj* 1 = **accustomed to**, familiar with, in the habit of, given to, at home in, attuned to, tolerant of, wont to, inured to, hardened to, habituated to

useful *adj* 1 = **helpful**, effective, valuable, practical, of use, profitable, of service, worthwhile, beneficial, of help, fruitful, advantageous, all-purpose, salutary, general-purpose, serviceable
OPPOSITE: useless

useless *adj* 1 = **pointless**, hopeless, futile, vain, idle, profitless
OPPOSITE: worthwhile
2a = **worthless**, of no use, valueless, pants (*slang*), ineffective, impractical, fruitless, unproductive, ineffectual, unworkable, disadvantageous, unavailing, bootless, unsuitable
OPPOSITE: useful
2b (*informal*) = **inept**, no good, hopeless, weak, stupid, pants (*slang*), incompetent, ineffectual

usher *n* 1, 2 = **attendant**, guide, doorman, usherette, escort, doorkeeper ▹ *vb* 3 = **escort**, lead,

DICTIONARY

Usher *n* a variant spelling of (James) **Ussher**
usherette *n* a woman assistant in a cinema, who shows people to their seats
Usman dan Fodio *n* 1754–1817, African mystic and revolutionary leader, who created a Muslim state in Nigeria
USP *marketing* unique selling proposition (*or* point)
Ussher *or* **Usher** *n* **James** 1581–1656, Irish prelate and scholar. His system of biblical chronology, which dated the creation at 4004 BC, was for long accepted
USSR Union of Soviet Socialist Republics: a former state in E Europe and N Asia, covering the area now composed of Russia, Ukraine, Kazakhstan and a number of smaller states
Ustinov *n* Sir **Peter** (**Alexander**) 1921–2004, British stage and film actor, director, dramatist, and raconteur
usual ❶ *adj* **1** of the most normal, frequent, or regular type: *the usual assortment of stories* ▷ *n* **2** ordinary or commonplace events: *the dirt was nothing out of the usual* **3** **as usual** as happens normally **4** **the usual** *informal* the habitual or usual drink **usually** *adv*
WORD ORIGIN Latin *usus* use
usurp (yewz-**zurp**) *vb* to seize a position or power without authority **usurpation** *n* **usurper** *n*
WORD ORIGIN Latin *usurpare* to take into use
usury (**yewz**-yoor-ree) *n, pl* **-ries** *old-fashioned* **1** the practice of loaning money at an exorbitant rate of interest **2** an unlawfully high rate of interest **usurer** *n*
WORD ORIGIN Latin *usura* usage
UT Utah
Utagawa Kuniyoshi *n* original name *Igusa Magosabwo* 1797–1861, Japanese painter and printmaker of the ukiyo-e school, best known for his prints of warriors and landscapes
Utamaro *n* **Kitagawa**, original name *Kitagawa Nebsuyoshi*. 1753–1806, Japanese master of wood-block prints, of the ukiyo-e school; noted esp. for his portraits of women
ute *n Austral & NZ informal* a utility truck
utensil *n* a tool or container for practical use: *cooking utensils*
WORD ORIGIN Latin *utensilia* necessaries
uterine *adj* of or affecting the womb
uterus (**yew**-ter-russ) *n, pl* **uteri** (**yew**-ter-rye) *anat* a hollow muscular organ in the pelvic cavity of female mammals, which houses the developing fetus; womb
WORD ORIGIN Latin
U Thant *n* See **Thant**
Uthman *n* died 656 AD, third caliph of Islam, who established an authoritative version of the Koran
utilidor (yew-**till**-lid-or) *n Canad* above-ground insulated casing for pipes carrying water, sewerage and electricity in permafrost regions
WORD ORIGIN *utility* + *-dor*, from Greek *dōron* gift
utilitarian *adj* **1** useful rather than beautiful **2** of utilitarianism ▷ *n* **3** an advocate of utilitarianism
utilitarianism *n ethics* the doctrine that the right thing to do is that which brings about the greatest good for the greatest number
utility ❶ *n, pl* **-ties** **1** usefulness **2** something useful **3** a public service, such as water or electricity ▷ *adj* **4** designed for use rather than beauty: *utility fabrics*
WORD ORIGIN Latin *utilitas* usefulness, from *uti* to use
utility room *n* a room with equipment for domestic work like washing and ironing
utility truck *n Austral & NZ* a small truck with an open body and low sides
utilize ❶ *or* **-lise** *vb* **-lizing, -lized** *or* **-lising, -lised** to make practical or worthwhile use of **utilization** *or* **-lisation** *n*
utmost ❶ *adj* **1** of the greatest possible degree or amount: *the utmost seriousness* **2** at the furthest limit: *the utmost point* ▷ *n* **3** the greatest possible degree or amount: *I was doing my utmost to comply*
WORD ORIGIN Old English *ūtemest*
Utopia (yew-**tope**-ee-a) *n* any real or imaginary society, place, or state considered to be perfect or ideal **Utopian** *adj*
WORD ORIGIN coined by Sir Thomas More in 1516 as the title of his book that described an imaginary island representing the perfect society, literally: no place, from Greek *ou* not + *topos* a place
Utrillo *n* **Maurice** 1883–1955, French painter, noted for his Parisian street scenes
utter[1] ❶ *vb* **1** to express something in sounds or words: *she hadn't uttered a single word* **2** *criminal law* to put counterfeit money or forged cheques into circulation
WORD ORIGIN Middle Dutch *ūteren* to make known
utter[2] ❶ *adj* total or absolute: *utter amazement* **utterly** *adv*
WORD ORIGIN Old English *ūtera* outer
utterance *n* **1** something expressed in speech or writing **2** the expression in words of ideas, thoughts, or feelings
uttermost *adj, n* ▸ same as **utmost**
U-turn *n* **1** a turn, made by a vehicle, in the shape of a U, resulting in a reversal of direction **2** a complete change in policy
Utzon *n* **Jørn** 1918–2008, Danish architect known primarily for his unique design for the Sydney Opera House (1966)
UV ultraviolet
UV-A *or* **UVA** *n* ultraviolet radiation with a range of 320-380 nanometres
UV-B *or* **UVB** *n* ultraviolet radiation with a range of 280-320 nanometres
Uvedale *n* a variant of (Nicholas) **Udall**
uvula (**yew**-view-la) *n* the small fleshy part of the soft palate that hangs in the back of the throat **uvular** *adj*
WORD ORIGIN Medieval Latin, literally: a little grape
uxorious (ux-**or**-ee-uss) *adj* excessively fond of or dependent on one's wife
WORD ORIGIN Latin *uxor* wife
Uys *n* **Pieter-Dirk** born 1945, South African comedian and satirist, noted for creating the female character Evita Bezuidenhout

U

THESAURUS

direct, guide, conduct, pilot, steer, show
usual *adj* **1** = **normal**, customary, regular, expected, general, common, stock, standard, fixed, ordinary, familiar, typical, constant, routine, everyday, accustomed, habitual, bog-standard (*Brit & Irish slang*), wonted **OPPOSITE:** unusual
utility *n* **1** = **usefulness**, use, point, benefit, service, profit, fitness, convenience, mileage (*informal*), avail, practicality, efficacy, advantageousness, serviceableness
utilize *vb* = **use**, employ, deploy, take advantage of, resort to, make the most of, make use of, put to use, bring into play, have recourse to, avail yourself of, turn to account
utmost *adj* **1** = **greatest**, highest, maximum, supreme, extreme, paramount, pre-eminent **2** = **farthest**, extreme, last, final, outermost, uttermost, farthermost ▷ *n* **3** = **best**, greatest, maximum, most, highest, hardest
utter[1] *vb* **1** = **say**, state, speak, voice, express, deliver, declare, mouth, breathe, pronounce, articulate, enunciate, put into words, verbalize, vocalize
utter[2] *adj* = **absolute**, complete, total, perfect, positive, pure, sheer, stark, outright, all-out, thorough, downright, real, consummate, veritable, unqualified, out-and-out, unadulterated, unmitigated, thoroughgoing, arrant, deep-dyed (*usually derogatory*)

Vv

DICTIONARY

V 1 *chem* vanadium 2 volt 3 the Roman numeral for five

v. 1 verb 2 verse 3 versus 4 volume

VA Virginia

vac *n Brit informal* ▸ short for **vacation**

vacancy *n, pl* **-cies** 1 an unoccupied job or position: *he had heard of a vacancy for a librarian* 2 an unoccupied room in a hotel or guesthouse: *the last hotel we tried had a vacancy* 3 the state of being unoccupied

vacant *adj* 1 (of a toilet, room, etc.) unoccupied or not being used: *I sat down in a vacant chair* 2 (of a job or position) unfilled at the present time 3 having or suggesting a lack of interest or understanding: *he sat there staring at me with a vacant look* 4 (of a period of time) not set aside for any particular activity: *two slots in his programme have been left vacant*
vacantly *adv*
WORD ORIGIN Latin *vacare* to be empty

vacate *vb* **-cating, -cated** 1 to cause (something) to be empty by leaving: *do you wish us to vacate the room?* 2 to give up (a job or position)

vacation *n* 1 *Brit & S African* a time of the year when the universities or law courts are closed 2 *US, Canad & Austral* ▸ same as **holiday** (sense 2)
WORD ORIGIN Latin *vacatio* freedom

vaccinate *vb* **-nating, -nated** to inject (someone) with a vaccine in order to protect them against a disease: *children vaccinated against meningitis*
vaccination *n*

vaccine *n* 1 *med* a substance made from the germs that cause a disease which is given to people to prevent them getting the disease 2 *computers* a piece of software that detects and removes computer viruses from a system
WORD ORIGIN Latin *variolae vaccinae* cowpox (source of the first smallpox vaccine), from *vacca* a cow

vacillate (vass-ill-late) *vb* **-lating, -lated** to keep changing one's mind or opinions about something: *he vacillated between republican and monarchist sentiments* **vacillation** *n*
WORD ORIGIN Latin *vacillare* to sway

vacuity *n* an absence of intelligent thought or ideas: *I suggested to one of his advisers that his vacuity was a handicap in these debates*

vacuous *adj* 1 lacking in intelligent ideas 2 showing no sign of intelligence or understanding: *her smile was vacuous but without malice*
WORD ORIGIN Latin *vacuus* empty

vacuum *n, pl* **vacuums** *or* **vacua** 1 a space which contains no air or other gas 2 a vacant place or position that needs to be filled by someone or something else: *the army moved in to fill the power vacuum* 3 ▸ short for **vacuum cleaner** ▹ *vb* 4 to clean (something) with a vacuum cleaner
WORD ORIGIN Latin *vacuus* empty

vacuum cleaner *n* an electric machine which sucks up dust and dirt from carpets and upholstery
vacuum cleaning *n*

vacuum flask *n* a double-walled flask with a vacuum between the walls that keeps drinks hot or cold

vacuum-packed *adj* (of food) packed in an airtight container in order to preserve freshness

vacuum tube *or* **valve** *n* ▸ same as **valve** (sense 3)

vade mecum (vah-dee **make**-um) *n* a handbook carried for immediate use when needed
WORD ORIGIN Latin, literally: go with me

vagabond *n* a person who travels from place to place and has no fixed home or job
WORD ORIGIN Latin *vagari* to roam

vagary (vaig-a-ree) *n, pl* **-garies** an unpredictable change in a situation or in someone's behaviour: *I was unused to the vagaries of the retailer's world*
WORD ORIGIN probably from Latin *vagari* to roam

vagina (vaj-**jine**-a) *n* the passage in most female mammals that extends from the neck of the womb to the external genitals **vaginal** *adj*
WORD ORIGIN Latin: sheath

vagrant (vaig-rant) *n* 1 a person who moves from place to place and has no regular home or job ▹ *adj* 2 wandering about **vagrancy** *n*
WORD ORIGIN probably from Old French *waucrant*

vague *adj* 1 not expressed or explained clearly: *he thought of his instructions, so vague and imprecise* 2 deliberately withholding information: *he was rather vague about the whole deal* 3 (of a sound or shape) unable to be heard or seen clearly: *he heard some vague sound from downstairs* 4 (of a person) not concentrating or thinking clearly: *she was mumbling to herself in a vague way* 5 not clearly established or known: *it was a vague rumour which would fade away and be forgotten* **vaguely** *adv* **vagueness** *n*
WORD ORIGIN Latin *vagus* wandering

vain *adj* 1 excessively proud of one's appearance or achievements 2 senseless or unsuccessful: *he made a vain attempt to lighten the atmosphere* ▹ *n*

THESAURUS

vacancy *n* 1 = **opening**, job, post, place, position, role, situation, opportunity, slot, berth *(informal)*, niche, job opportunity, vacant position, situation vacant 2 = **room**, space, available accommodation, unoccupied room

vacant *adj* 1 = **empty**, free, available, abandoned, deserted, to let, for sale, on the market, void, up for grabs, disengaged, uninhabited, unoccupied, not in use, unfilled, untenanted **OPPOSITE:** occupied
2 = **unfilled**, unoccupied
OPPOSITE: taken
3 = **blank**, vague, dreamy, dreaming, empty, abstracted, idle, thoughtless, vacuous, inane, expressionless, unthinking, absent-minded, incurious, ditzy *or* ditsy *(slang)*
OPPOSITE: thoughtful

vacuum *n* 1 = **emptiness**, space, void, gap, empty space, nothingness, vacuity 2 = **gap**, lack, absence, space, deficiency, void

vague *adj* 1 = **unclear**, indefinite, hazy, confused, loose, uncertain, doubtful, unsure, superficial, incomplete, woolly, imperfect, sketchy, cursory **OPPOSITE:** clear
2 = **imprecise**, unspecified, generalized, rough, loose, ambiguous, hazy, equivocal, ill-defined, non-specific, inexact, obfuscatory, inexplicit 3 = **indistinct**, blurred, unclear, dim, fuzzy, unknown, obscure, faint, shadowy, indefinite, misty, hazy, indistinguishable, amorphous, indeterminate, bleary, nebulous, out of focus, ill-defined, indiscernible
OPPOSITE: distinct
4 = **absent-minded**, absorbed, abstracted, distracted, unaware, musing, vacant, preoccupied, bemused, oblivious, dreamy, daydreaming, faraway, unthinking, heedless, inattentive, unheeding

vain *adj* 1 = **conceited**, narcissistic, proud, arrogant, inflated, swaggering, stuck-up *(informal)*, cocky, swanky *(informal)*, ostentatious, egotistical, self-important, overweening, vainglorious, swollen-headed *(informal)*, pleased with yourself, bigheaded *(informal)*, peacockish
OPPOSITE: modest
2 = **futile**, useless, pointless, unsuccessful, empty, hollow, idle, trivial, worthless, trifling, senseless, unimportant, fruitless, unproductive, abortive, unprofitable, time-wasting, unavailing, nugatory
OPPOSITE: successful

DICTIONARY

3 in vain without achieving the desired effects or results: *the old man searched in vain for his son* **vainly** *adv*
WORD ORIGIN Latin *vanus*

vainglorious *adj* boastful or proud: *his vainglorious posturing had earned him numerous powerful enemies*

Vajpayee *n* **A**(**tal**) **B**(**ihari**) born 1926, Indian politician; prime minister of India (1996, 1998–2004)

valance (val-lenss) *n* a short piece of decorative material hung round the edge of a bed or above a window
WORD ORIGIN perhaps after *Valence* in SE France

Valdemar I *n* a variant spelling of **Waldemar I**

Valdemar II *n* See **Waldemar II**

Valdemar IV *n* See **Waldemar IV**

Valdivia[1] *n* a port in S Chile, on the **Valdivia River** about 19 km (12 miles) from the Pacific: developed chiefly by German settlers in the 1850s; university (1954). Pop: 136 000 (2005 est)

Valdivia[2] *n* **Pedro de** ?1500–54, Spanish soldier; conqueror of Chile

vale *n literary* a valley
WORD ORIGIN Latin *vallis* valley

valediction (val-lid-**dik**-shun) *n* a farewell speech **valedictory** *adj*
WORD ORIGIN Latin *vale* farewell + *dicere* to say

valence (vale-enss) *n chem* the ability of atoms and chemical groups to form compounds

valency *or esp. US & Canad* **valence** *n, pl* **-cies** *or* **-ces** *chem* the number of atoms of hydrogen that an atom or chemical group is able to combine with in forming compounds
WORD ORIGIN Latin *valere* to be strong

Valens *n* ?328–378 AD, emperor of the Eastern Roman Empire (364–378); appointed by his elder brother Valentinian I, emperor of the Western Empire

valentine *n* **1** a card sent, often anonymously, as an expression of love on Saint Valentine's Day, February 14 **2** the person to whom one sends such a card
WORD ORIGIN after Saint *Valentine*

Valentinian I *or* **Valentinianus I** *n* 321–375 AD, emperor of the Western Roman Empire (364–375); appointed his brother Valens to rule the Eastern Empire

Valentinian II *or* **Valentinianus II** *n* 371–392 AD, emperor of the Western Roman Empire (375–392), reigning jointly with his half brother Gratian until 383

Valentinian III *or* **Valentinianus III** *n* ?419–455 AD, emperor of the Western Roman Empire (425–455). His government lost Africa to the Vandals. With Pope Leo I he issued (444) an edict giving the bishop of Rome supremacy over the provincial churches

valerian *n* a plant with small white or pinkish flowers and a medicinal root
WORD ORIGIN Medieval Latin *valeriana (herba)* (herb) of Valerius

Valerian *n* Latin name *Publius Licinius Valerianus.* died 260 AD, Roman emperor (253–260): renewed persecution of the Christians; defeated by the Persians

Valéry *n* **Paul** 1871–1945, French poet and essayist, influenced by the symbolists, esp. Mallarmé. He wrote lyric poetry, rich in imagery, as in *La Jeune Parque* (1917) and *Album de vers anciens 1890–1900* (1920)

valet *n* **1** a male servant employed to look after another man ▷ *vb* **-eting, -eted 2** to act as a valet (for) **3** to clean the bodywork and interior of (a car) as a professional service
WORD ORIGIN Old French *vaslet* page

valeta *or* **veleta** (vel-lee-ta) *n* an old-time dance in triple time
WORD ORIGIN Spanish *veleta* weather vane

valetudinarian (val-lit-yew-din-**air**-ee-an) *n* **1** a person who is chronically sick **2** a person who continually worries about his or her health **valetudinarianism** *n*
WORD ORIGIN Latin *valetudo* state of health

Valhalla *n Norse myth* the great hall of Odin where warriors who die as heroes in battle dwell eternally
WORD ORIGIN Old Norse *valr* slain warriors + *höll* hall

valiant *adj* very brave: *it was a valiant attempt to rescue the struggling victim* **valiantly** *adv*
WORD ORIGIN Latin *valere* to be strong

valid ❶ *adj* **1** based on sound reasoning: *I think that's a very valid question* **2** legally acceptable: *she must produce a valid driving licence* **3** important or serious enough to say or do: *religious broadcasting has a valid purpose* **validity** *n*
WORD ORIGIN Latin *validus* robust

validate *vb* **-dating, -dated 1** to prove (a claim or statement) to be true or correct **2** to give legal force or official confirmation to **validation** *n*

valise (val-leez) *n old-fashioned* a small suitcase
WORD ORIGIN Italian *valigia*

Valium *n trademark* a drug used as a tranquillizer

Valkyrie (val-keer-ee) *n Norse myth* any of the beautiful maidens who take the dead heroes to Valhalla
WORD ORIGIN Old Norse *valr* slain warriors + *kyrja* chooser

Valla *n* **Lorenzo** 1405–57, Italian humanist scholar. His writings include *De voluptate* (1431), a philosophical dialogue on pleasure

Valle-Inclán *n* **Rámon María del** 1866–1936, Spanish novelist and dramatist. His works include the novel *Tirano Banderas* (1926) and the satirical play *Don Friolera's Horns* (1925)

Vallejo *n* **César** (**Abraham**) 1892–1938, Peruvian poet, living in France and Spain from 1923: noted for his experimental style in such works as *Trilce* (1922)

valley ❶ *n* a long stretch of land between hills, often with a river flowing through it
WORD ORIGIN Latin *vallis*

Valois[1] *n* a historic region and former duchy of N France

Valois[2] *n* a royal house of France, ruling from 1328 to 1589

Valois[3] *n* See **de Valois**

valour *or US* **valor** *n literary* great bravery, esp. in battle **valorous** *adj*
WORD ORIGIN Latin *valere* to be strong

valuable ❶ *adj* **1** worth a large amount of money: *his house was furnished with valuable antique furniture* **2** of great use or importance: *the investigations will provide valuable information* ▷ *n* **3 valuables** valuable articles of personal property, such as jewellery

valuation *n* **1** a formal assessment of how much something is worth: *they will arrange a valuation on your house* **2** the price arrived at by the process of valuing

value ❶ *n* **1** the desirability of something, often in terms of its

V

THESAURUS

valid *adj* **1 = sound**, good, reasonable, just, telling, powerful, convincing, substantial, acceptable, sensible, rational, logical, viable, credible, sustainable, plausible, conclusive, weighty, well-founded, cogent, well-grounded **OPPOSITE:** unfounded **2 = legal**, official, legitimate, correct, genuine, proper, in effect, authentic, in force, lawful, bona fide, legally binding, signed and sealed **OPPOSITE:** invalid

valley *n* **= hollow**, dale, glen, vale, depression, dell, dingle, strath *(Scot)*, cwm *(Welsh)*, coomb

valuable *adj* **1 = precious**, expensive, costly, dear, high-priced, priceless, irreplaceable **OPPOSITE:** worthless **2 = useful**, important, profitable, worthwhile, beneficial, valued, helpful, worthy, of use, of help, invaluable, serviceable, worth its weight in gold **OPPOSITE:** useless ▷ *pl n* **3 = treasures**, prized possessions, precious items, heirlooms, personal effects, costly articles

value *n* **1 = importance**, use, benefit, worth, merit, point, help, service, sense, profit, advantage,

DICTIONARY

usefulness or exchangeability **2** an amount of money considered to be a fair exchange for something: *50 kilos of cocaine with a high street value* **3** something worth the money it cost: *the set meal was value for money* **4 values** the moral principles and beliefs of a person or group **5** *maths* a particular number or quantity represented by a figure or symbol **6** *music* ▸short for **time value** ▹*vb* **-uing, -ued 7** (with *at*) to assess the worth or desirability of (something) **8** to hold (someone or something) in high regard **valued** *adj* **valueless** *adj* **valuer** *n*
WORD ORIGIN Latin *valere* to be worth

value-added tax *n Brit & S African* ▸see **VAT**

value judgment *n* a personal opinion about something based on an individual's beliefs and not on facts which can be checked or proved

valve *n* **1** a part attached to a pipe or tube which controls the flow of gas or liquid **2** *anat* a small flap in a hollow organ, such as the heart, that controls the flow and direction of blood **3** a closed tube through which electrons move in a vacuum **4** *zool* one of the hinged shells of an oyster or clam **5** *music* a device on some brass instruments by which the effective length of the tube may be varied
WORD ORIGIN Latin *valva* a folding door

valvular *adj* of or relating to valves: *valvular heart disease*

vamoose *vb* **-moosing, -moosed** *slang chiefly US* to leave a place hurriedly
WORD ORIGIN Spanish *vamos* let's go

vamp[1] *informal n* **1** a sexually attractive woman who seduces men ▹*vb* **2** (of a woman) to seduce (a man)
WORD ORIGIN short for *vampire*

vamp[2] *vb* **vamp up** to make (a story, piece of music, etc.) seem new by inventing additional parts
WORD ORIGIN Old French *avantpié* the front part of a shoe

vampire *n* (in European folklore) a corpse that rises nightly from its grave to drink the blood of living people
WORD ORIGIN from Magyar

vampire bat *n* a bat of Central and South America that feeds on the blood of birds and mammals

van[1] *n* **1** a road vehicle with a roof and no side windows used to transport goods **2** *Brit* a closed railway wagon used to transport luggage, goods, or mail
WORD ORIGIN shortened from *caravan*

van[2] *n* ▸short for **vanguard**

vanadium *n chem* a silvery-white metallic element used to toughen steel. Symbol: V
WORD ORIGIN Old Norse *Vanadīs*, epithet of the goddess Freya

Van Allen belt *n* either of two belts of charged particles which surround the Earth
WORD ORIGIN after J. A. *Van Allen*, physicist

Vancouver[1] *n* **1 Vancouver Island** an island of SW Canada, off the SW coast of British Columbia: separated from the Canadian mainland by the Strait of Georgia and Queen Charlotte Sound, and from the US mainland by Juan de Fuca Strait; the largest island off the W coast of North America. Chief town: Victoria. Pop: 706 243 (2001). Area: 32 137 sq km (12 408 sq miles) **2** a city in SW Canada, in SW British Columbia: Canada's chief Pacific port, named after Captain George Vancouver: university (1908). Pop: 545 671 (2001) **3 Mount Vancouver** a mountain on the border between Canada and Alaska, in the St Elias Mountains. Height: 4785 m (15 700 ft)

Vancouver[2] *n* Captain **George** 1757–98, English navigator, noted for his exploration of the Pacific coast of North America (1792–94)

vandal *n* someone who deliberately causes damage to personal or public property **vandalism** *n*
WORD ORIGIN from the name of a Germanic tribe of the 3rd and 4th centuries AD

vandalize *or* **-ise** *vb* **-izing, -ized** *or* **-ising, -ised** to cause damage to (personal or public property) deliberately

Vanderbilt *n* **Cornelius,** known as *Commodore Vanderbilt*. 1794–1877, US steamship and railway magnate and philanthropist

Van der Hum *n S African* a liqueur made from tangerines
WORD ORIGIN origin uncertain but possibly derived from the humorous uncertainty of the name, equivalent of *whatshisname*

Van der Post *n* Sir **Laurens (Jan)** 1906–96, South African writer and traveller. His works include the travel books *Venture to the Interior* (1952), *The Lost World of the Kalahari* (1958), and *Testament to the Bushmen* (1984) and the novels *The Hunter and the Whale* (1967) and *The Admiral's Baby* (1996)

van der Waals *n* **Johannes Diderik** 1837–1923, Dutch physicist, noted for his research on the equations of states of gases and liquids: Nobel prize for physics in 1910

van der Weyden *n* **Rogier** ?1400–64, Flemish painter, esp. of religious works and portraits

van de Velde *n* **1 Adriaen** 1636–72, Dutch painter of landscapes with animals and figures **2** his uncle, **Esaias** ?1591–1630, Dutch landscape and genre painter, noted for such works as *The Winter Scene* (1623) **3 Henry** 1863–1957, Belgian architect and designer, who introduced the British Arts and Crafts movement to the Continent and helped to develop the Art Nouveau style **4 Willem,** known as *the Elder:* father of Adriaen van de Velde. 1611–93, Dutch marine painter, working in England as court painter to Charles II **5** his son, **Willem,** known as *the Younger*. 1633–1707, Dutch marine painter, working in England as court painter to Charles II

Vandyke beard *n* a short pointed beard
WORD ORIGIN after Sir Anthony *Van Dyck*, Flemish painter

vane *n* **1** one of the blades forming part of the wheel of a windmill, a screw propeller, etc. **2** ▸short for **weather vane**
WORD ORIGIN Old English *fana*

Vane *n* Sir **Henry,** known as *Sir Harry Vane*. 1613–62, English Puritan statesman and colonial administrator; governor of Massachusetts (1636–37). He was executed for high treason after the Restoration

van Eyck *n* **Jan** died 1441, Flemish painter; founder of the Flemish school of painting. His most famous work is the altarpiece *The Adoration of the Lamb*, in Ghent, in which he may have been assisted by his brother **Hubert**, died ?1426

vanguard *n* **1** the leading division or units of an army **2** the most advanced group or position in scientific research, a movement, etc.: *a distinguished architect in the vanguard of his profession*

THESAURUS

utility, significance, effectiveness, mileage *(informal)*, practicality, usefulness, efficacy, desirability, serviceableness
OPPOSITE: worthlessness
2 = cost, price, worth, rate, equivalent, market price, face value, asking price, selling price, monetary worth ▹*pl n* **4 = principles,** morals, ethics, mores, standards of behaviour, code of behaviour, (moral) standards ▹*vb* **7** *(with* **at***)* **= evaluate,** price, estimate, rate, cost, survey, assess, set at, appraise, put a price on **8 = appreciate,** rate, prize, regard highly, respect, admire, treasure, esteem, cherish, think much of, hold dear, have a high opinion of, set store by, hold in high regard *or* esteem
OPPOSITE: undervalue

V

DICTIONARY

WORD ORIGIN Old French *avant-garde* advance guard

vanilla *n* **1** a flavouring for food such as ice cream, which comes from the pods of a tropical plant **2** a flavouring extract prepared from the beans of this plant and used in cooking ▷ *adj* **3** flavoured with vanilla: *vanilla essence* **4** *slang* ordinary or conventional: *a vanilla kind of guy*
WORD ORIGIN Spanish *vainilla* pod

vanish ❶ *vb* **1** to disappear suddenly: *the choppers vanished from radar screens at dawn yesterday* **2** to cease to exist: *the old landmarks had vanished*
WORD ORIGIN Latin *evanescere* to evaporate

vanishing cream *n old-fashioned* a cosmetic cream that is colourless once applied

vanishing point *n* the point in the distance where parallel lines appear to meet

vanity ❶ *n* **1** a feeling of pride about one's appearance or ability **2** *pl* **-ties** something about which one is vain: *it's one of my vanities that I can guess scents*
WORD ORIGIN Latin *vanitas* emptiness

vanity case *n* a small bag for holding cosmetics

vanity unit *n* a hand basin built into a surface, usually with a cupboard below it

vanquish *vb literary* to defeat (someone) in a battle, contest, or argument
WORD ORIGIN Latin *vincere*

Vansittart *n* **Robert Gilbert,** 1st Baron Vansittart of Denham. 1881–1957, British diplomat and writer; a fierce opponent of Nazi Germany and of Communism

vantage *n* a state, position, or opportunity offering advantage
WORD ORIGIN Old French *avantage* advantage

vantage point *n* a position that gives one an overall view of a scene or situation

van't Hoff *n* **Jacobus Hendricus** 1852–1911, Dutch physical chemist: founded stereochemistry with his theory of the asymmetric carbon atom; the first to apply thermodynamics to chemical reactions: Nobel prize for chemistry 1901

Vanzetti *n* **Bartolomeo** 1888–1927, US radical agitator, born in Italy: executed with Sacco in a case that had worldwide political repercussions

vapid *adj* dull and uninteresting: *their publications were vapid and amateurish* **vapidity** *n*
WORD ORIGIN Latin *vapidus*

vapor *n US* ▸ same as **vapour**

vaporize *or* **-ise** *vb* **-izing, -ized** *or* **-ising, -ised** (of a liquid or solid) to change into vapour **vaporization** *or* **-isation** *n*

vaporous *adj* resembling or full of vapour

vapour *or US* **vapor** *n* **1** a mass of tiny drops of water or other liquids in the air, which appear as a mist **2** the gaseous form of a substance that is usually a liquid or a solid **3 the vapours** *old-fashioned* a feeling of faintness, dizziness, and depression
WORD ORIGIN Latin *vapor*

Vardhamana *n* See **Mahavira**

Vardon *n* **Harry** 1870–1937, British golfer

Varèse *n* **Edgar(d)** 1883–1965, US composer, born in France. His works, which combine extreme dissonance with complex rhythms and the use of electronic techniques, include *Ionisation* (1931) and *Poème électronique* (1958)

Vargas *n* **Getúlio Dornelles** 1883–1954, Brazilian statesman; president (1930–45; 1951–54)

Vargas Llosa *n* **(Jorge) Mario (Pedro)** born 1936, Peruvian novelist, writer, and political figure. His novels include *The City and the Dogs* (1963), *Conversation in the Cathedral* (1969), *The Storyteller* (1990), and *The Notebok of Don Rigoberto* (1998). In 1990 he stood unsuccessfully for the presidency of Peru

variable ❶ *adj* **1** likely to change at any time: *variable weather* **2** *maths* having a range of possible values ▷ *n* **3** something that is subject to variation **4** *maths* an expression that can be assigned any of a set of values **variability** *n* **variably** *adv*
WORD ORIGIN Latin *variare* to diversify

variance *n* **at variance** not in agreement: *the real record is at variance with the public record*

variant ❶ *adj* **1** differing from a standard or type: *variant spellings* ▷ *n* **2** something that differs from a standard or type

variation ❶ *n* **1** something presented in a slightly different form: *his books are all variations on a basic theme* **2** a change in level, amount, or quantity: *there was a variation in the figures* **3** *music* the repetition of a simple tune with the addition of new harmonies or a change in rhythm: *Variations on a Hussar's Song*

varicoloured *or US* **varicolored** *adj* having many colours

varicose *adj* of or resulting from varicose veins: *a varicose ulcer*
WORD ORIGIN Latin *varix* a swollen vein

varicose veins *pl n* veins, usually in the legs, which have become knotted, swollen, and sometimes painful

varied ❶ *adj* of different types, sizes, or quantities: *these young men and women would be of varied backgrounds*

variegated *adj* having patches or streaks of different colours: *variegated holly* **variegation** *n*

variety ❶ *n, pl* **-ties 1** the state of being diverse or various **2** different things of the same kind: *I'm cooking the mince with a variety of vegetables* **3** a particular type of something in the same general category: *this variety of pear is extremely juicy* **4** *taxonomy* a race whose distinct characters do not justify classification as a separate species **5** a type of entertainment

THESAURUS

vanish *vb* **1 = disappear**, become invisible, be lost to sight, dissolve, evaporate, fade away, melt away, disappear from sight, exit, evanesce **OPPOSITE:** appear
2 = die out, disappear, pass away, end, fade, dwindle, cease to exist, become extinct, disappear from the face of the earth

vanity *n* **1 = pride**, arrogance, conceit, airs, showing off *(informal)*, pretension, narcissism, egotism, self-love, ostentation, vainglory, self-admiration, affected ways, bigheadedness *(informal)*, conceitedness, swollen-headedness *(informal)* **OPPOSITE:** modesty

variable *adj* **1 = changeable**, unstable, fluctuating, shifting, flexible, wavering, uneven, fickle, temperamental, mercurial, capricious, unsteady, protean, vacillating, fitful, mutable, inconstant, chameleonic **OPPOSITE:** constant

variant *adj* **1 = different**, alternative, modified, derived, exceptional, divergent ▷ *n* **2 = variation**, form, version, development, alternative, adaptation, revision, modification, permutation, transfiguration, aberration, derived form

variation *n* **1 = alternative**, variety, modification, departure, innovation, variant **2 = variety**, change, deviation, difference, diversity, diversion, novelty, alteration, discrepancy, diversification, departure from the norm, break in routine **OPPOSITE:** uniformity

varied *adj* **= different**, mixed, various, diverse, assorted, miscellaneous, sundry, motley, manifold, heterogeneous **OPPOSITE:** unvarying

variety *n* **1 = diversity**, change, variation, difference, diversification, heterogeneity, many-sidedness, multifariousness **OPPOSITE:** uniformity
2 = range, selection, assortment, mix, collection, line-up, mixture,

V

DICTIONARY

consisting of short unrelated acts, such as singing, dancing, and comedy
WORD ORIGIN Latin *varietas*
varifocal *adj* of a lens that is gradated to permit any length of vision between near and distant
varifocals *pl n* a pair of spectacles with varifocal lenses
various ❶ *adj* **1** several different: *there are various possible answers to this question* **2** of different kinds: *the causes of high blood pressure are various and complicated* **variously** *adv*
WORD ORIGIN Latin *varius* changing
varlet *n old-fashioned* **1** a menial servant **2** a rascal
WORD ORIGIN Old French *vaslet*
varmint *n informal* an irritating or obnoxious person or animal
WORD ORIGIN dialect variant of *varmin* vermin
varnish ❶ *n* **1** a liquid painted onto a surface to give it a hard glossy finish **2** a smooth surface, coated with or as if with varnish **3** an artificial, superficial, or deceptively pleasing manner or appearance: *those who aspired to become civil servants acquired a varnish of university education* **4** *chiefly Brit* ▸ short for **nail varnish** ▹ *vb* **5** to apply varnish to **6** to try to make (something unpleasant) appear more attractive: *when did we start equivocating, camouflaging, varnishing the truth?*
WORD ORIGIN Old French *vernis*
Varro *n* **Marcus Terentius** 116–27 BC, Roman scholar and satirist
varsity *n, pl* **-ties** *old-fashioned & informal* ▸ short for **university**
vary ❶ *vb* **varies, varying, varied 1** to change in appearance, character, or form **2** to be different or cause to be different: *the age of appearance of underarm and body hair varies greatly from person to person* **3** to give variety to: *you can vary the type of exercise you do* **4** to change in accordance with another variable: *an individual's calorie requirement varies with age, sex, and physical activity* **varying** *adj*
WORD ORIGIN Latin *varius* changing
vas *n, pl* **vasa** *anat, zool* a vessel or tube that carries a fluid
WORD ORIGIN Latin: vessel
Vasarely *n* **Victor** 1908–97, French painter, born in Hungary; a leading exponent of Pop art
Vasari *n* **Giorgio** 1511–74, Italian architect, painter, and art historian, noted for his *Lives of the Most Excellent Italian Architects, Painters, and Sculptors* (1550; 1568), a principal source for the history of Italian Renaissance art
vascular *adj biol, anat* of or relating to the vessels that conduct and circulate body fluids such as blood or sap
WORD ORIGIN Latin *vas* vessel
vas deferens *n, pl* **vasa deferentia** *anat* either of the two ducts that convey sperm from the testicles to the penis
WORD ORIGIN Latin *vas* vessel + *deferens* carrying away
vase *n* a glass or pottery jar used as an ornament or for holding cut flowers
WORD ORIGIN Latin *vas* vessel
vasectomy *n, pl* **-mies** surgical removal of all or part of the vas deferens as a method of contraception
WORD ORIGIN VAS + Greek *tomē* a cutting
Vaseline *n trademark* petroleum jelly, used as an ointment or a lubricant
vassal *n* **1** (in feudal society) a man who gave military service to a lord in return for protection and often land **2** a person, nation, or state dominated by another **vassalage** *n*
WORD ORIGIN Medieval Latin *vassus* servant
vast ❶ *adj* unusually large in size, degree, or number **vastly** *adv* **vastness** *n*
WORD ORIGIN Latin *vastus* deserted
vat *n* a large container for holding or storing liquids
WORD ORIGIN Old English *fæt*
VAT (in Britain and S Africa) value-added tax: a tax levied on the difference between the cost of materials and the selling price of a commodity or service
Vatican *n* **1** the Pope's palace, in Rome **2** the authority of the Pope
WORD ORIGIN Latin *Vaticanus (mons)* Vatican (hill)
Vauban *n* **Sébastien Le Prestre de** 1633–1707, French military engineer and marshal, who greatly developed the science of fortification and devised novel siege tactics using a series of parallel trenches
vaudeville *n* variety entertainment consisting of short acts such as song-and-dance routines and comic turns
WORD ORIGIN French
Vaughan *n* **1 Henry** 1622–95, Welsh mystic poet, best known for his *Silex Scintillans* (1650; 1655) **2** Dame **Janet (Maria)** 1899–1993, British physician and university official: helped set up Britain's first National Blood Transfusion Service (1939): after World War II, became Britain's expert on the effects of radiation on humans; Principal of Somerville College, Oxford (1945–67) **3 Sarah (Lois)** 1924–90, US jazz vocalist and pianist, noted esp. for her skill in vocal improvisation
vault[1] ❶ *n* **1** a secure room where money and other valuables are stored safely **2** an underground burial chamber **3** an arched structure that forms a roof or ceiling **4** a cellar for storing wine
WORD ORIGIN Old French *voute, voulte*
vault[2] ❶ *vb* **1** to jump over (something) by resting one's hands on it or by using a long pole ▹ *n* **2** the act of vaulting **vaulter** *n*
WORD ORIGIN Italian *voltare* to turn
vaulted *adj* being or having an arched roof: *an atmospheric vaulted dining room*
vaulting[1] *n* the arrangement of ceiling vaults in a building
vaulting[2] *adj* excessively confident: *a vaulting ambition for the highest political office*
vaunt *vb* **1** to describe or display (one's success or possessions) boastfully ▹ *n* **2** a boast **vaunted** *adj*
WORD ORIGIN Latin *vanus* vain
Vavilov *n* **Nikolai Ivanovich** 1887–?1943, Soviet plant geneticist, noted for his research into the origins of cultivated plants. His findings were regarded as contrary to official ideology and he was arrested (1940), dying in a labour camp
vb verb

V

THESAURUS

array, cross section, medley, multiplicity, mixed bag *(informal)*, miscellany, motley collection, intermixture **3 = type**, sort, kind, make, order, class, brand, species, breed, strain, category
various *adj* **1 = many**, numerous, countless, several, abundant, innumerable, sundry, manifold, profuse **2 = different**, assorted, miscellaneous, varied, differing, distinct, diverse, divers *(archaic)*, diversified, disparate, sundry, heterogeneous **OPPOSITE:** similar
varnish *n* **1 = lacquer**, polish, glaze, japan, gloss, shellac ▹ *vb* **5 = lacquer**, polish, glaze, japan, gloss, shellac
vary *vb* **2 = differ**, be different, be dissimilar, disagree, diverge, be unlike **3 = alternate**, mix, diversify, reorder, intermix, bring variety to, permutate, variegate **4 = change**, shift, swing, transform, alter, fluctuate, oscillate, see-saw
vast *adj* **= huge**, massive, enormous, great, wide, sweeping, extensive, tremendous, immense, mega *(slang)*, unlimited, gigantic, astronomical, monumental, monstrous, mammoth, colossal, never-ending, prodigious, limitless, boundless, voluminous, immeasurable, unbounded, elephantine, ginormous *(informal)*, vasty *(archaic)*, measureless, illimitable, humongous *or* humungous *(US slang)* **OPPOSITE:** tiny
vault[1] *n* **1 = strongroom**, repository, depository **2 = crypt**, tomb, catacomb, cellar, mausoleum, charnel house, undercroft
vault[2] *vb* **1 = jump**, spring, leap, clear, bound, hurdle

DICTIONARY

VC **1** Vice Chancellor **2** Victoria Cross **3** *history* Vietcong: the Communist-led guerrilla force of South Vietnam
V-chip *n* a device within a television set that allows the set to be programmed not to receive transmissions that have been classified as containing sex, violence, or obscene language
vCJD variant Creutzfeldt-Jakob disease
VCR video cassette recorder
VD venereal disease
VDU visual display unit
veal *n* the meat from a calf, used as food
WORD ORIGIN Latin *vitulus* calf
Veblen *n* **Thorstein** 1857–1929, US economist and social scientist, noted for his analysis of social and economic institutions. His works include *The Theory of the Leisure Class* (1899) and *The Theory of Business Enterprise* (1904)
vector *n* **1** *maths* a variable quantity, such as force, that has magnitude and direction **2** *pathol* an animal, usually an insect, that carries a disease-producing microorganism from person to person
WORD ORIGIN Latin: carrier
Veda (vay-da) *n* any or all of the most ancient sacred writings of Hinduism **Vedic** *adj*
WORD ORIGIN Sanskrit: knowledge
veer ❶ *vb* **1** to change direction suddenly: *the plane veered off the runway and careered through the perimeter fence* **2** to change from one position or opinion to another: *her feelings veered from tenderness to sudden spurts of genuine love* ▷ *n* **3** a change of course or direction
WORD ORIGIN Old French *virer*
veg *n informal* a vegetable or vegetables
Vega[1] *n* the brightest star in the constellation Lyra and one of the most conspicuous in the N hemisphere. It is part of an optical double star having a faint companion. Distance: 25.3 light years; spectral type: AoV
WORD ORIGIN C17: from Medieval Latin, from Arabic *(al nasr) al wāqi*, literally: the falling (vulture), that is, the constellation Lyra
Vega[2] *n* See **Lope de Vega**
vegan (vee-gan) *n* a person who does not eat meat, fish, or any animal products such as cheese, butter, etc.
vegeburger *or* **veggieburger** *n* a flat cake of chopped vegetables or pulses that is grilled or fried and served in a roll
vegetable *n* **1** a plant, such as potato or cauliflower, with parts that are used as food **2** *informal* someone who is unable to move or think, as a result of brain damage ▷ *adj* **3** of or like plants or vegetables
WORD ORIGIN Late Latin *vegetabilis* animating
vegetable marrow *n* a long green vegetable which can be cooked and eaten
vegetable oil *n* any of a group of oils that are obtained from plants
vegetal *adj* of or relating to plant life
vegetarian *n* **1** a person who does not eat meat or fish ▷ *adj* **2** excluding meat and fish: *a vegetarian diet* **vegetarianism** *n*
vegetate *vb* **-tating, -tated** to live in a dull and boring way with no mental stimulation
vegetation *n* plant life as a whole
vegetative *adj* **1** of or relating to plant life or plant growth **2** (of reproduction) characterized by asexual processes
veggie *informal n* **1** a vegetable **2** a vegetarian ▷ *adj* **3** vegetarian: *a veggie cookbook*
veggieburger *n* ▸ same as **vegeburger**
vehement *adj* **1** expressing strong feelings or opinions **2** (of actions or gestures) performed with great force or energy **vehemence** *n* **vehemently** *adv*
WORD ORIGIN Latin *vehemens* ardent
vehicle ❶ *n* **1** a machine such as a bus or car for transporting people or goods **2** something used to achieve a particular purpose or as a means of expression: *the newspaper was a vehicle for explaining government policies* **3** *pharmacol* an inactive substance mixed with the active ingredient in a medicine **4** a liquid, such as oil, in which a pigment is mixed before it is applied to a surface **vehicular** *adj*
WORD ORIGIN Latin *vehere* to carry
veil ❶ *n* **1** a piece of thin cloth, usually as part of a hat or headdress, used to cover a woman's face **2** something that conceals the truth: *a veil of secrecy* **3 take the veil** to become a nun ▷ *vb* **4** to cover or conceal with or as if with a veil
WORD ORIGIN Latin *velum* a covering
Veil *n* **Simone (Annie)** born 1927, French stateswoman; president of the European Parliament (1979–82): a survivor of Nazi concentration camps
veiled ❶ *adj* (of a comment or remark) presented in a disguised form: *it was a thinly veiled criticism*
vein ❶ *n* **1** any of the tubes that carry blood to the heart **2** a thin line in a leaf or in an insect's wing **3** a clearly defined layer of ore or mineral in rock **4** an irregular streak of colour in marble, wood, or cheese **5** a distinctive trait or quality in speech or writing: *critics have exposed a strong vein of moralism in the poem* **6** a temporary mood: *we're in a very humorous vein tonight* **veined** *adj*
WORD ORIGIN Latin *vena*
Velcro *n trademark* a type of fastening consisting of one piece of fabric with tiny hooked threads and another with a coarse surface that sticks to it
veld *or* **veldt** *n* the open country of South Africa including landscapes which are grassy, bushy, or thinly forested
WORD ORIGIN Afrikaans: field
Velde *n* See **van de Velde**
veldskoen, velskoen (felt-skoon) *n S African* a sturdy ankle boot
WORD ORIGIN Afrikaans
veleta *n* ▸ same as **valeta**
vellum *n* **1** a fine calf, kid, or lamb parchment **2** a strong good-quality paper that resembles vellum
WORD ORIGIN Old French *velin* of a calf
velocipede (vel-loss-sip-peed) *n* an early form of bicycle
WORD ORIGIN Latin *velox* swift + *pes* foot
velocity ❶ (vel-loss-it-ee) *n, pl* **-ties** the speed at which something is moving in a particular direction
WORD ORIGIN Latin *velox* swift
velour *or* **velours** (vel-loor) *n* a silk or cotton cloth similar to velvet
WORD ORIGIN Latin *villus* shaggy hair
velouté (vuh-loo-tay) *n* a rich white sauce made from stock, eggs, and cream
WORD ORIGIN French, literally: velvety

THESAURUS

veer *vb* **1 = change direction**, turn, swerve, shift, sheer, tack, be deflected, change course
vehicle *n* **1 = conveyance**, machine, motor vehicle, means of transport **2 = medium**, means, channel, mechanism, organ, apparatus, means of expression
veil *n* **1 = mask**, cover, shroud, film, shade, curtain, cloak **2a = screen**, mask, disguise, blind **2b = film**, cover, curtain, cloak, shroud ▷ *vb* **4 = cover**, screen, hide, mask, shield, disguise, conceal, obscure, dim, cloak, mantle **OPPOSITE:** reveal
veiled *adj* **= disguised**, implied, hinted at, covert, masked, concealed, suppressed
vein *n* **1 = blood vessel** **3 = seam**, layer, stratum, course, current, bed, deposit, streak, stripe, lode **6 = mood**, style, spirit, way, turn, note, key, character, attitude, atmosphere, tone, manner, bent, stamp, humour, tendency, mode, temper, temperament, tenor, inclination, disposition, frame of mind
velocity *n* **= speed**, pace, rapidity, quickness, swiftness, fleetness, celerity

DICTIONARY

velskoen *n* ▸ same as **veldskoen**

velvet *n* **1** a fabric with a thick close soft pile on one side **2** the furry covering of the newly formed antlers of a deer ▹ *adj* **3** made of velvet **4** soft or smooth like velvet **5 an iron fist** *or* **hand in a velvet glove** determination concealed by a gentle manner **velvety** *adj*
WORD ORIGIN Old French, from Latin *villus* shaggy hair

velveteen *n* a cotton fabric that resembles velvet

venal (vee-nal) *adj* **1** willing to accept bribes in return for acting dishonestly: *venal politicians* **2** associated with corruption or bribery: *venal greed* **venality** *n*
WORD ORIGIN Latin *venum* sale

vend *vb* to sell (goods)
WORD ORIGIN Latin *vendere* to sell

Venda *n* **1** *pl* **-da** *or* **-das** a member of a Negroid people of southern Africa, living chiefly in NE South Africa **2** the language of this people

vendetta *n* **1** a long-lasting quarrel between people or organizations in which they attempt to harm each other: *it's an inexplicable vendetta against the firm and its directors* **2** a private feud between families in which members of one family kill members of the other family in revenge for earlier murders
WORD ORIGIN Italian

vending machine *n* a machine that automatically dispenses food, drinks, or cigarettes when money is inserted

Vendôme *n* **Louis Joseph de** 1654–1712, French marshal, noted for his command during the War of the Spanish Succession (1701–14)

vendor *n* **1** a person who sells goods such as newspapers or hamburgers from a stall or cart **2** *chiefly law* a person who sells property

veneer *n* **1** a thin layer of wood or plastic used to cover the surface of something made of cheaper material **2** a deceptive but convincing appearance: *nobody penetrated his veneer of modest charm*
WORD ORIGIN Old French *fournir* to furnish

venerable *adj* **1** (of a person) entitled to respect because of great age or wisdom **2** (of an object) impressive because it is old or important historically **3** *RC church* a title given to a dead person who is going to be declared a saint **4** *Church of England* a title given to an archdeacon
WORD ORIGIN Latin *venerari* to venerate

venerate *vb* **-ating, -ated** to hold (someone) in deep respect **venerator** *n*
WORD ORIGIN Latin *venerari*

veneration *n* a feeling of awe or great respect: *George Gershwin is worthy of the veneration accorded his classical counterparts*

venereal (vin-ear-ee-al) *adj* **1** transmitted by sexual intercourse: *venereal infections* **2** of the genitals: *venereal warts*
WORD ORIGIN Latin *venus* sexual love

venereal disease *n* a disease, such as syphilis, transmitted by sexual intercourse

Venetian *adj* **1** of Venice, a port in NE Italy ▹ *n* **2** a person from Venice

Venetian blind *n* a window blind made of thin horizontal slats

vengeance ❶ *n* **1** the act of killing, injuring, or harming someone for revenge **2 with a vengeance** to a much greater extent or with much greater force than expected: *my career was beginning to take off with a vengeance*
WORD ORIGIN Old French, from Latin *vindicare* to punish

vengeful *adj* wanting revenge

venial (veen-ee-al) *adj* easily excused or forgiven: *venial sins*
WORD ORIGIN Latin *venia* forgiveness

venison *n* the flesh of a deer, used as food
WORD ORIGIN Old French *venaison*

Venizélos *n* **Eleuthérios** 1864–1936, Greek statesman, who greatly extended Greek territory: prime minister (1910–15; 1917–20; 1924; 1928–32; 1933)

Venn diagram *n* *maths* a drawing which uses circles to show the relationships between different sets
WORD ORIGIN after John Venn, logician

venom *n* **1** a feeling of great bitterness or anger towards someone **2** the poison that certain snakes and scorpions inject when they bite or sting **venomous** *adj* **venomously** *adv*
WORD ORIGIN Latin *venenum* poison, love potion

venous (vee-nuss) *adj* of or relating to veins
WORD ORIGIN Latin *vena* vein

vent¹ ❶ *n* **1** a small opening in something through which fresh air can enter and fumes can be released **2** the shaft of a volcano through which lava and gases erupt **3** the anal opening of a bird or other small animal **4 give vent to** to release (an emotion) in an outburst: *she gave vent to her misery and loneliness* ▹ *vb* **5** to release or express freely: *consumers vented their anger on the group by boycotting its products* **6** to make vents in
WORD ORIGIN Old French *esventer* to blow out

vent² *n* a vertical slit in the lower hem of a jacket
WORD ORIGIN Latin *findere* to cleave

Venter *n* **(John) Craig** born 1946, US biologist: founder of the Institute for Genomic Research (1992) whose work contributed greatly to the mapping of the human genome

ventilate *vb* **-lating, -lated 1** to let fresh air into (a room or building) **2** to discuss (ideas or feelings) openly: *ultra-rightists ventilated anti-Semitic sentiments* **ventilation** *n*
WORD ORIGIN Latin *ventilare* to fan

ventilator *n* an opening or device, such as a fan, used to let fresh air into a room or building

ventral *adj* relating to the front part of the body **ventrally** *adv*
WORD ORIGIN Latin *venter* abdomen

ventricle *n* *anat* **1** a chamber of the heart that pumps blood to the arteries **2** any one of the four main cavities of the brain **ventricular** *adj*
WORD ORIGIN Latin *ventriculus*

ventriloquism *n* the ability to speak without moving the lips so that the words appear to come from another person or from another part of the room **ventriloquist** *n*
WORD ORIGIN Latin *venter* belly + *loqui* to speak

Ventris *n* **Michael George Francis** 1922–56, English architect and scholar, who deciphered the Linear B script, identifying it as an early form of Mycenaean Greek

venture ❶ *n* **1** a project or activity that is risky or of uncertain outcome **2** a business operation in which there is the risk of loss as well as the opportunity for profit ▹ *vb* **-turing, -tured 3** to do something that involves risk or danger: *I thought it wise to venture into foreign trade* **4** to dare to express (an opinion) **5** to go to an

THESAURUS

vengeance *n* **1 = revenge**, retaliation, reprisal, retribution, avenging, an eye for an eye, settling of scores, requital, lex talionis
OPPOSITE: forgiveness

vent¹ *n* **1 = outlet**, opening, hole, split, aperture, duct, orifice ▹ *vb* **5 = express**, release, voice, air, empty, discharge, utter, emit, come out with, pour out, give vent to, give expression to OPPOSITE: hold back

venture *n* **1 = undertaking**, project, enterprise, chance, campaign, risk, operation, activity, scheme, task, mission, speculation, gamble, adventure, exploit, pursuit, fling, hazard, crusade, endeavour ▹ *vb* **4 = put forward**, offer, suggest, present, air, table, advance, propose, volunteer, submit, bring up, postulate, proffer, broach, posit, moot, propound, dare to say **5 = go**, travel, journey, set out, wander, stray, plunge into, rove, set forth **6 = dare**, presume, have the courage to, be brave enough, hazard, go out on a limb *(informal)*, take the liberty,

DICTIONARY

unknown or dangerous place **6** to dare (to do something): *you have asked me so often to come to your place that I ventured to drop in* **venturer** *n*
WORD ORIGIN variant of *adventure*
venture capital *n* money provided for investment in new commercial enterprises **venture capitalist** *n*
Venture Scout *or* **Venturer** *n* a member of the senior branch of the Scouts
venturesome *adj* willing to take risks
Venturi *n* **Robert** born 1925, US architect, a pioneer of the postmodernist style. His writings include *Complexity and Contradiction in Architecture* (1966)
venue *n* a place where an organized gathering, such as a concert or a sporting event, is held
WORD ORIGIN Latin *venire* to come
Venus *n* **1** the Roman goddess of love **2** the planet second nearest to the sun
Venus's flytrap *or* **Venus flytrap** *n* a plant that traps and digests insects between hinged leaves
veracious *adj* habitually truthful
WORD ORIGIN Latin *verus* true
veracity *n* **1** habitual truthfulness **2** accuracy
verandah *or* **veranda** *n* **1** an open porch attached to a house **2** *NZ* a continuous overhead canopy outside shops that gives shelter to pedestrians
WORD ORIGIN Portuguese *varanda* railing
verb *n* a word that is used to indicate the occurrence or performance of an action or the existence of a state, for example *run, make,* or *do*
WORD ORIGIN Latin *verbum* word
verbal ❶ *adj* **1** of or relating to words: *verbal skills* **2** spoken rather than written: *a verbal agreement* **3** *grammar* of or relating to a verb **verbally** *adv*
verbalism *n* an exaggerated emphasis on the importance of words
verbalize *or* **-ise** *vb* **-izing, -ized** *or* **-ising, -ised** to express (an idea or feeling) in words
verbal noun *n grammar* a noun derived from a verb, for example *smoking* in the sentence *smoking is bad for you*
verbatim (verb-**bait**-im) *adv* **1** using exactly the same words: *I'll repeat it verbatim* ▷ *adj* **2** using exactly the same words: *a verbatim account*
WORD ORIGIN Medieval Latin: word by word
verbena *n* a plant with red, white, or purple sweet-smelling flowers
WORD ORIGIN Latin: sacred bough used by the priest in religious acts
verbiage *n* the excessive use of words
WORD ORIGIN Latin *verbum* word
verbose (verb-**bohss**) *adj* using more words than is necessary **verbosity** *n*
Vercingetorix *n* died ?45 BC, Gallic chieftain and hero, executed for leading a revolt against the Romans under Julius Caesar (52 BC)
verdant *adj literary* covered with green vegetation
WORD ORIGIN from Latin *viridis* green
verdict ❶ *n* **1** the decision made by a jury about the guilt or innocence of a defendant **2** an opinion formed after examining the facts
WORD ORIGIN Latin *vere dictum* truly spoken
verdigris (**ver**-dig-reess) *n* a green or bluish coating which forms on copper, brass, or bronze that has been exposed to damp
WORD ORIGIN Old French *vert de Grice* green of Greece
verdure *n literary* flourishing green vegetation
WORD ORIGIN from Latin *viridis* green
verge[1] ❶ *n* **1** a grass border along a road **2 on the verge of** having almost reached (a point or condition) **3** an edge or rim ▷ *vb* **verging, verged 4 verge on** to be near to: *she was verging on hysteria*
WORD ORIGIN Latin *virga* rod
verge[2] *vb* **verging, verged** to move in a specified direction: *verging towards the Irish Sea*
WORD ORIGIN Latin *vergere*
verger *n chiefly Church of England* **1** a church official who acts as caretaker **2** an official who carries the rod of office before a bishop or dean in ceremonies and processions
WORD ORIGIN Latin *virga* rod, twig
Verhaeren *n* **Émile** 1855–1916, Belgian poet, writing in French. His works include the collections *Les Flamandes* (1883), *Les Soirs* (1887), and *Les Visages de la Vie* (1899)
verify ❶ *vb* **-fies, -fying, -fied 1** to check the truth of (something) by investigation **2** to prove (something) to be true **verifiable** *adj* **verification** *n*
WORD ORIGIN Latin *verus* true + *facere* to make
verily *adv literary* truly: *for verily, this was their destiny*
WORD ORIGIN from *very*
verisimilitude *n* the appearance of truth or reality
WORD ORIGIN Latin *verus* true + *similitudo* similitude
veritable *adj* rightly called; real: *a veritable mine of information* **veritably** *adv*
verity *n, pl* **-ties** a true statement or principle
WORD ORIGIN Latin *verus* true
vermicelli (ver-me-**chell**-ee) *n* **1** very fine strands of pasta, used in soups **2** tiny chocolate strands used as a topping for cakes or ice cream
WORD ORIGIN Italian: little worms
vermiform *adj* shaped like a worm
vermiform appendix *n anat* ▸ same as **appendix**
vermilion *adj* **1** orange-red ▷ *n* **2** mercuric sulphide, used as an orange-red pigment; cinnabar
WORD ORIGIN Late Latin *vermiculus* insect from which red dye was prepared
vermin *pl n* **1** small animals collectively, such as insects and rodents, that spread disease and damage crops **2** unpleasant people **verminous** *adj*
WORD ORIGIN Latin *vermis* worm
vermouth (**ver**-muth) *n* a wine flavoured with herbs
WORD ORIGIN German *Wermut* wormwood
vernacular (ver-**nak**-yew-lar) *n* **1** the commonly spoken language or dialect of a particular people or place ▷ *adj* **2** in or using the vernacular
WORD ORIGIN Latin *vernaculus* belonging to a household slave
vernal *adj* of or occurring in spring **vernally** *adv*
WORD ORIGIN Latin *ver* spring
vernier (**ver**-nee-er) *n* a small movable scale in certain measuring instruments such as theodolites, used to obtain a fractional reading of one of the divisions on the main scale
WORD ORIGIN after Paul *Vernier*, mathematician
Veronese *n* **Paolo**, original name *Paolo Cagliari* or *Caliari*. 1528–88, Italian painter of the Venetian school. His works include *The Marriage at Cana* (1563) and *The Feast of the Levi* (1573)

THESAURUS

stick your neck out *(informal)*, go so far as, make so bold as, have the temerity *or* effrontery *or* nerve
verbal *adj* **2 = spoken**, oral, word-of-mouth, unwritten
verdict *n* **1, 2 = decision**, finding, judgment, opinion, sentence, conclusion, conviction, adjudication, pronouncement
verge[1] *n* **3** *(Brit)* **= border**, edge, margin, limit, extreme, lip, boundary, threshold, roadside, brim **4** (foll. by *on*) **= come near to**, approach, border on, resemble, incline to, be similar to, touch on, be more or less, be tantamount to, tend towards, be not far from, incline towards
verify *vb* **1 = check**, confirm, make sure, examine, monitor, check out *(informal)*, inspect **2 = confirm**, prove, substantiate, support, validate, bear out, attest, corroborate, attest to, authenticate **OPPOSITE:** disprove

DICTIONARY

veronica *n* a plant with small blue, pink, or white flowers
WORD ORIGIN perhaps from the name *Veronica*

Verrazano *or* **Verrazzano** *n* **Giovanni da** ?1485–?1528, Florentine navigator; the first European to sight what was to become New York (1524)

Verrocchio *n* **Andrea del** 1435–88, Italian sculptor, painter, and goldsmith of the Florentine school: noted esp. for the equestrian statue of Bartolommeo Colleoni in Venice

verruca (ver-**roo**-ka) *n pathol* a wart, usually on the sole of the foot
WORD ORIGIN Latin: wart

Versace *n* **1 Donatella** born 1955, Italian fashion designer and businesswoman; creative director of the Versace group from 1997 **2** her brother, **Gianni** 1946–97, Italian fashion designer

versatile ⊤ *adj* having many different skills or uses **versatility** *n*
WORD ORIGIN Latin *versare* to turn

verse *n* **1** a division of a poem or song **2** poetry as distinct from prose **3** one of the short sections into which chapters of the books of the Bible are divided **4** a poem
WORD ORIGIN Latin *versus* furrow, literally: a turning (of the plough)

versed ⊤ *adj* **versed in** knowledgeable about or skilled in

versify *vb* **-fies, -fying, -fied 1** to put (something) into verse **2** to write in verse **versification** *n* **versifier** *n*
WORD ORIGIN Latin *versus* verse + *facere* to make

version ⊤ *n* **1** a form of something, such as a piece of writing, with some differences from other forms **2** an account of something from a certain point of view: *so far there's been no official version of the incident* **3** an adaptation, for example of a book or play into a film
WORD ORIGIN Latin *vertere* to turn

verso *n, pl* **-sos 1** the left-hand page of a book **2** the back of a sheet of printed paper
WORD ORIGIN New Latin *verso (folio)* (the leaf) having been turned

versus *prep* **1** (in a sporting competition or lawsuit) against **2** in opposition to or in contrast with: *man versus machine*
WORD ORIGIN Latin: turned (in the direction of), opposite

vertebra (**ver**-tib-bra) *n, pl* **-brae** (-bree) one of the bony segments of the spinal column **vertebral** *adj*
WORD ORIGIN Latin

vertebrate *n* **1** an animal with a backbone, such as a fish, amphibian, reptile, bird, or mammal ▷ *adj* **2** having a backbone

vertex (**ver**-tex) *n, pl* **-tices** (-tiss-seez) **1** the highest point **2** *maths* **a** the point on a geometric figure where the sides form an angle **b** the highest point of a triangle
WORD ORIGIN Latin: top

vertical ⊤ *adj* **1** at right angles to the horizon: *the vertical cliff* **2** straight up and down: *a vertical cut* **3** *econ* of or relating to associated or consecutive, though not identical, stages of industrial activity: *the purchase of a chain of travel agents by a leading tour operator will increase vertical integration in the holiday industry* ▷ *n* **4** a vertical line or direction **vertically** *adv*
WORD ORIGIN from Latin *vertex* top, pole of the sky

vertiginous *adj* producing dizziness

vertigo *n pathol* a sensation of dizziness felt because one's balance is disturbed, sometimes experienced when looking down from a high place
WORD ORIGIN Latin: a whirling round

vervain *n* a plant with long slender spikes of purple, blue, or white flowers
WORD ORIGIN Latin *verbena* sacred bough

verve *n* great enthusiasm or liveliness
WORD ORIGIN Latin *verba* words, chatter

very ⊤ *adv* **1** used to add emphasis to adjectives and adverbs that are able to be graded: *I'm very happy; he'll be home very soon* ▷ *adj* **2** used with nouns to give emphasis or exaggerated intensity: *the very end of his visit; the very thing I need*
WORD ORIGIN Old French *verai* true

very high frequency *n* a radio-frequency band lying between 30 and 300 megahertz

Very light *n* a coloured flare for signalling at night
WORD ORIGIN after Edward W. *Very*, naval ordnance officer

Vesalius *n* **Andreas** 1514–64, Flemish anatomist, whose *De Humani Corporis fabrica* (1543) formed the basis of modern anatomical research and medicine

vesicle *n biol* **1** a small sac or cavity, esp. one filled with fluid **2** a blister
WORD ORIGIN Latin *vesica* bladder, sac

vespers *n* an evening service in some Christian churches
WORD ORIGIN Latin *vesper* the evening star

vessel ⊤ *n* **1** a ship or large boat **2** an object used as a container for liquid **3** *biol* a tubular structure in animals and plants that carries body fluids, such as blood and sap
WORD ORIGIN Latin *vas*

vest ⊤ *n* **1** *Brit* an undergarment covering the top half of the body **2** *Austral, US, & Canad* a waistcoat ▷ *vb* **3 vest in** to settle (power or property) on: *by the power vested in me, I pronounce you man and wife* **4 vest with** to bestow on: *the sponsorship has vested these matches with a new interest*
WORD ORIGIN Latin *vestis* clothing

vestal *adj* **1** chaste or pure ▷ *n* **2** a chaste woman

THESAURUS

versatile *adj* **a = adaptable**, flexible, all-round, resourceful, protean, multifaceted, many-sided, all-singing, all-dancing **OPPOSITE:** unadaptable **b = all-purpose**, handy, functional, variable, adjustable, all-singing, all-dancing **OPPOSITE:** limited

versed *adj (with* **in***)* **= knowledgeable**, experienced, skilled, seasoned, qualified, familiar, practised, accomplished, competent, acquainted, well-informed, proficient, well up *(informal)*, conversant **OPPOSITE:** ignorant

version *n* **1 = form**, variety, variant, sort, kind, class, design, style, model, type, brand, genre **2 = account**, report, side, description, record, reading, story, view, understanding, history, statement, analysis, take *(informal, chiefly US)*, construction, tale, impression, explanation, interpretation, rendering, narrative, chronicle, rendition, narration, construal **3 = adaptation**, edition, interpretation, form, reading, copy, rendering, translation, reproduction, portrayal

vertical *adj* **1, 2 = upright**, sheer, perpendicular, straight (up and down), erect, plumb, on end, precipitous, vertiginous, bolt upright **OPPOSITE:** horizontal

very *adv* **1 = extremely**, highly, greatly, really, deeply, particularly, seriously *(informal)*, truly, absolutely, terribly, remarkably, unusually, jolly *(Brit)*, wonderfully, profoundly, decidedly, awfully *(informal)*, acutely, exceedingly, excessively, noticeably, eminently, superlatively, uncommonly, surpassingly ▷ *adj* **2a = exact**, actual, precise, same, real, express, identical, unqualified, selfsame **2b = ideal**, perfect, right, fitting, appropriate, suitable, spot on *(Brit informal)*, apt, just the job *(Brit informal)*

vessel *n* **1 = ship**, boat, craft, barque *(poetic)* **2 = container**, receptacle, can, bowl, tank, pot, drum, barrel, butt, vat, bin, jar, basin, tub, jug, pitcher, urn, canister, repository, cask

vest *vb* **3** (foll. by *in, usually passive)* **= place**, invest, entrust, settle, lodge, confer, endow, bestow, consign, put in the hands of, be devolved upon **4** (foll. by *with, usually passive)* **= endow with**, furnish with, entrust with,

DICTIONARY

WORD ORIGIN Latin *Vestalis* virgin priestess of the goddess Vesta
vestal virgin *n* (in ancient Rome) one of the virgin priestesses dedicated to the goddess Vesta and to maintaining the sacred fire in her temple
vested *adj property law* having an existing right to the immediate or future possession of property
vested interest *n* **1** a strong personal interest someone has in a matter because he or she might benefit from it **2** *property law* an existing right to the immediate or future possession of property
vestibule *n* a small entrance hall
WORD ORIGIN Latin *vestibulum*
vestige (vest-ij) *n* **1** a small amount or trace **2** *biol* an organ or part that is a small nonfunctional remnant of a functional organ in an ancestor
WORD ORIGIN Latin *vestigium* track
vestigial (vest-ij-ee-al) *adj* remaining after a larger or more important thing has gone: *a strong seam of vestigial belief*
vestments *pl n* **1** ceremonial clothes worn by the clergy at religious services **2** robes that show authority or rank
WORD ORIGIN Latin *vestire* to clothe
vestry *n, pl* **-tries** a room in a church used as an office by the priest or minister
WORD ORIGIN probably Old French *vestiarie* wardrobe
vet[1] ⓣ *n* **1** ▸ short for **veterinary surgeon** ▹ *vb* **vetting, vetted 2** to make a careful check of (a person or document) for suitability: *guests have to be vetted and vouched for*
vet[2] *n US, Canad, Austral & NZ* ▸ short for **veteran**
vetch *n* **1** a climbing plant with blue or purple flowers **2** the beanlike fruit of the vetch, used as fodder
WORD ORIGIN Latin *vicia*
veteran ⓣ *n* **1** a person who has given long service in some capacity **2** a soldier who has seen a lot of active service **3** a person who has served in the military forces ▹ *adj* **4** long-serving: *the veteran American politician*
WORD ORIGIN Latin *vetus* old
veteran car *n Austral & Brit* a car built before 1919, esp. before 1905
veterinarian *n US, Canad & Austral* a veterinary surgeon
veterinary *adj* relating to veterinary science
WORD ORIGIN Latin *veterinae* draught animals
veterinary medicine *or* **science** *n* the branch of medicine concerned with the treatment of animals
veterinary surgeon *n Brit* a person qualified to practise veterinary medicine
veto ⓣ (vee-toe) *n, pl* **-toes 1** the power to prevent legislation or action proposed by others: *no single state has a veto* **2** the exercise of this power ▹ *vb* **-toing, -toed 3** to refuse consent to (a proposal, such as a government bill) **4** to prohibit or forbid: *the Sports Minister vetoed the appointments*
WORD ORIGIN Latin: I forbid
vex *vb* to cause (someone) to feel annoyance or irritation **vexing** *adj* **vexation** *n*
WORD ORIGIN Latin *vexare* to jolt (in carrying)
vexatious *adj* vexing
vexed *adj* **1** annoyed and puzzled **2** much debated: *the vexed question of pay*
VHF *or* **vhf** *radio* very high frequency
VHS Video Home System: a video cassette recorder system using half-inch magnetic tape
VI Vancouver Island
via *prep* **1** by way of; through: *he fled to London via Crete* **2** by means of: *working from home and keeping in touch with office life via a video link-up*
WORD ORIGIN Latin
viable ⓣ *adj* **1** able to be put into practice: *the party has failed to propose a viable alternative* **2** (of seeds or eggs) capable of growth **3** (of a fetus) sufficiently developed to survive outside the uterus **viability** *n*
WORD ORIGIN Latin *vita* life
viaduct *n* a bridge for carrying a road or railway across a valley
WORD ORIGIN Latin *via* way + *ducere* to bring
Viagra *n trademark* a drug that allows increased blood flow into the penis, used to treat impotence in men
vial *n* ▸ same as **phial**
WORD ORIGIN Greek *phialē* a bowl
viands *pl n old-fashioned* food
WORD ORIGIN Latin *vivenda* things to be lived on
viaticum *n, pl* **-ca** *or* **-cums** *Christianity* Holy Communion given to a person dying or in danger of death
WORD ORIGIN Latin *viaticus* belonging to a journey
vibes *pl n informal* **1** the emotional reactions between people **2** the atmosphere of a place **3** ▸ short for **vibraphone**
vibrant ⓣ (vibe-rant) *adj* **1** full of energy and enthusiasm **2** (of a voice) rich and full of emotion **3** (of a colour) strong and bright **vibrancy** *n*
WORD ORIGIN Latin *vibrare* to agitate
vibraphone *n* a musical instrument with metal bars that resonate electronically when hit
vibrate *vb* **-brating, -brated 1** to move backwards and forwards rapidly **2** to have or produce a quivering or echoing sound **3** *physics* to undergo or cause to undergo vibration **vibratory** *adj*
WORD ORIGIN Latin *vibrare*
vibration *n* **1** a vibrating **2** *physics* **a** a periodic motion about an equilibrium position, such as in the production of sound **b** a single cycle of such a motion
vibrato *n, pl* **-tos** *music* a slight rapid fluctuation in the pitch of a note
vibrator *n* a device for producing a vibratory motion, used for massage or as a sex aid
viburnum (vie-burn-um) *n* a subtropical shrub with white flowers and berry-like fruits
WORD ORIGIN Latin
Vic. Victoria (Australian state)
vicar *n* **1** *Church of England* a priest who is in charge of a parish **2** *RC church* a church officer acting as deputy to a bishop **vicarial** *adj*
WORD ORIGIN Latin *vicarius* a deputy
vicarage *n* the house where a vicar lives
vicar apostolic *n RC church*

THESAURUS

empower with, authorize with
vet[1] *n* **1 = veterinary surgeon,** veterinarian *(US)*, animal doctor ▹ *vb* **2 = check,** examine, investigate, check out, review, scan, look over, appraise, scrutinize, size up *(informal)*, give the once-over *(informal)*, pass under review
veteran *n* **1 = old hand,** master, pro *(informal)*, old-timer, past master, trouper, warhorse *(informal)*, old stager **OPPOSITE:** novice ▹ *adj* **4 = long-serving,** seasoned, experienced, old, established, expert, qualified, mature, practised, hardened, adept, proficient, well trained, battle-scarred, worldly-wise
veto *n* **1, 2 = ban,** dismissal, rejection, vetoing, boycott, embargo, prohibiting, prohibition, suppression, knock-back *(informal)*, interdict, declination, preclusion, nonconsent **OPPOSITE:** ratification ▹ *vb* **3, 4 = ban,** block, reject, rule out, kill *(informal)*, negative, turn down, forbid, boycott, prohibit, disallow, put a stop to, refuse permission to, interdict, give the thumbs down to, put the kibosh on *(slang)* **OPPOSITE:** pass
viable *adj* **1 = workable,** practical, feasible, suitable, realistic, operational, applicable, usable, practicable, serviceable, operable, within the bounds of possibility **OPPOSITE:** unworkable
vibrant *adj* **1 = energetic,** dynamic, sparkling, vivid, spirited, storming, alive, sensitive, colourful, vigorous, animated, responsive, electrifying, vivacious, full of pep *(informal)* **3 = vivid,** bright, brilliant, intense,

DICTIONARY

a clergyman with authority in missionary countries

vicar general *n, pl* **vicars general** an official appointed to assist the bishop in his administrative duties

vicarious (vik-air-ee-uss) *adj* **1** felt indirectly by imagining what another person experiences: *vicarious satisfaction* **2** undergone or done as the substitute for another: *vicarious adventures* **3** delegated: *vicarious power* **vicariously** *adv*
WORD ORIGIN Latin *vicarius* substituted

Vicar of Christ *n RC church* the Pope as Christ's representative on earth

vice[1] ❶ *n* **1** an immoral or evil habit or action: *greed is only one of their vices* **2** a habit regarded as a weakness in someone's character: *one of his few vices is cigars* **3** criminal activities involving sex, drugs, or gambling
WORD ORIGIN Latin *vitium* a defect

vice[2] *or US* **vise** *n* a tool with a pair of jaws for holding an object while work is done on it
WORD ORIGIN Latin *vitis* vine, plant with spiralling tendrils

vice[3] *adj* serving in the place of; being next in importance to: *the vice chairman*
WORD ORIGIN Latin *vicis* interchange

vice admiral *n* a senior commissioned officer in certain navies

vice chancellor *n* the chief executive or administrator at a number of universities

vicegerent *n* a person appointed to exercise all or some of the authority of another
WORD ORIGIN VICE[3] + Latin *gerere* to manage

Vicente *n* **Gil** ?1465–?1536, Portuguese dramatist, noted for his court entertainments, religious dramas, and comedies

vice president *n* an officer ranking immediately below a president and serving as his or her deputy **vice-presidency** *n*

viceregal *adj* **1** of a viceroy **2** *chiefly Austral & NZ* of a governor or governor general

viceroy *n* a governor of a colony or country who represents the monarch
WORD ORIGIN VICE[3] + French *roi* king

vice squad *n* a police division responsible for the enforcement of gaming and prostitution laws

vice versa ❶ *adv* the other way round: *there were attacks on northerners by southerners and vice versa*
WORD ORIGIN Latin: relations being reversed

Vichy water (vee-shee) *n* a natural mineral water from Vichy in France which is supposed to be good for the health

vicinity (viss-in-it-ee) *n* the area immediately surrounding a place
WORD ORIGIN Latin *vicinus* neighbouring

vicious ❶ *adj* **1** cruel or violent: *vicious attacks* **2** forceful or ferocious: *she gave the chair a vicious jerk* **3** intended to cause hurt or distress: *vicious letters* **4** (of an animal) fierce or hostile **viciously** *adv* **viciousness** *n*
WORD ORIGIN Latin *vitiosus* full of faults

vicious circle *n* a situation in which an attempt to resolve one problem creates new problems that recreate the original one

vicissitudes (viss-iss-it-yewds) *pl n* changes in circumstance or fortune
WORD ORIGIN Latin *vicis* change

Vicky *n* professional name of *Victor Weisz*. 1913–66, British left-wing political cartoonist, born in Germany

Vico *n* **Giovanni Battista** 1668–1744, Italian philosopher. In *Scienza Nuova* (1721) he postulated that civilizations rise and fall in evolutionary cycles, making use of myths, poetry, and linguistics as historical evidence

victim ❶ *n* **1** a person or thing that suffers harm or death **2** a person who is tricked or swindled **3** a living person or animal sacrificed in a religious rite
WORD ORIGIN Latin *victima*

victimize *or* **-ise** *vb* **-izing, -ized** *or* **-ising, -ised** to punish or discriminate against (someone) selectively or unfairly **victimization** *or* **-isation** *n*

victor ❶ *n* **1** a person or nation that has defeated an enemy in war **2** the winner of a contest or struggle
WORD ORIGIN Latin, from *vincere* to conquer

Victor Emmanuel II *n* 1820–78, king of Sardinia-Piedmont (1849–78) and first king of Italy from 1861

Victor Emmanuel III *n* 1869–1947, last king of Italy (1900–46): dominated after 1922 by Mussolini, whom he appointed as premier; abdicated

victoria *n* **1** a large sweet red-and-yellow plum **2** a light four-wheeled horse-drawn carriage with a folding hood
WORD ORIGIN after Queen *Victoria*

Victoria Cross *n* the highest decoration for bravery in battle awarded to the British and Commonwealth armed forces

Victorian *adj* **1** of or in the reign of Queen Victoria of Great Britain and Ireland (1837–1901) **2** characterized by prudery or hypocrisy **3** of or relating to Victoria (the state or any of the cities) ▷ *n* **4** a person who lived during the reign of Queen Victoria **5** an inhabitant of Victoria (the state or any of the cities)

Victoriana *pl n* objects of the Victorian period

victorious ❶ *adj* **1** having defeated an enemy or opponent: *the victorious allies* **2** of or characterized by victory: *a victorious smile*

victory ❶ *n, pl* **-ries** **1** the winning of a war or battle **2** success attained in a contest or struggle
WORD ORIGIN Latin *victoria*

victual *vb* **-ualling, -ualled** *or US* **-ualing, -ualed** *old-fashioned* to supply with or obtain victuals **victualler** *or US* **-ualer** *n*
WORD ORIGIN Latin *victus* sustenance

victuals (vit-tals) *pl n old-fashioned* food and drink

vicuna (vik-kew-na) *n* **1** a S American mammal like the llama **2** the fine cloth made from its wool
WORD ORIGIN Spanish

Vidal *n* **Gore** born 1925, US novelist and essayist. His novels include *Julian* (1964), *Myra Breckinridge* (1968), *Burr* (1974), *Lincoln* (1984), and *The Season of Conflict* (1996)

vide (vie-dee) see: used to direct a reader to a specified place in a text or in another book

THESAURUS

clear, rich, glowing, colourful, highly-coloured

vice[1] *n* **1, 2 = fault**, failing, weakness, limitation, defect, deficiency, flaw, shortcoming, blemish, imperfection, frailty, foible, weak point, infirmity **OPPOSITE:** good point
3 = wickedness, evil, corruption, sin, depravity, immorality, iniquity, profligacy, degeneracy, venality, turpitude, evildoing **OPPOSITE:** virtue

vice versa *adv* **= the other way round**, conversely, in reverse, contrariwise

vicious *adj* **1, 4 = savage**, brutal, violent, bad, dangerous, foul, cruel, ferocious, monstrous, vile, atrocious, diabolical, heinous, abhorrent, barbarous, fiendish **OPPOSITE:** gentle
3 = malicious, vindictive, spiteful, mean, cruel, venomous, bitchy *(informal)*, defamatory, rancorous, backbiting, slanderous
OPPOSITE: complimentary

victim *n* **1 = casualty**, sufferer, injured party, fatality **OPPOSITE:** survivor

victor *n* **1, 2 = winner**, champion, conqueror, first, champ *(informal)*, vanquisher, top dog *(informal)*, prizewinner, conquering hero
OPPOSITE: loser

victorious *adj* **1 = winning**, successful, triumphant, first, champion, conquering, vanquishing, prizewinning **OPPOSITE:** losing

victory *n* **1, 2 = win**, success, triumph, the prize, superiority, conquest, laurels, mastery, walkover *(informal)*
OPPOSITE: defeat

DICTIONARY

WORD ORIGIN Latin
videlicet (vid-deal-ee-set) *adv* namely: used to specify items
WORD ORIGIN Latin
video *n, pl* **-os 1** the recording and showing of films and events using a television set, video tapes, and a video recorder **2** ▸ short for **video cassette 3** ▸ short for **video cassette recorder** ▹ *vb* **videoing, videoed 4** to record (a television programme or an event) on video ▹ *adj* **5** relating to or used in producing televised images
WORD ORIGIN Latin *videre* to see
video cassette *n* a cassette containing video tape
video cassette recorder *n* a device for recording and playing back television programmes and films
video game *n* a game that can be played by using an electronic control to move symbols on the screen of a visual display unit
video nasty *n* a film, usually specially made for video, that is explicitly horrific and pornographic
videophone *n* a communications device by which people can both see and speak to each other
video recorder *n* ▸ short for **video cassette recorder**
video tape *n* **1** magnetic tape used mainly for recording the video-frequency signals of a television programme or film ▹ *vb* **video-tape, -taping, -taped 2** to record (a film or programme) on video tape
Videotex *n trademark* ▸ same as **Viewdata**
videotext *n* a means of providing a written or graphical representation of computerized information on a television screen
vie ❶ *vb* **vying, vied** (with *with* or *for*) to compete (with someone): *the sisters vied with each other to care for her*
WORD ORIGIN probably Old French *envier* to challenge
Vietnamese *adj* **1** of Vietnam ▹ *n* **2** *pl* **-ese** a person from Vietnam **3** the language of Vietnam
view ❶ *n* **1** opinion, judgment, or belief: *in my view that doesn't really work* **2** an understanding of or outlook on something: *a specific view of human history* **3** everything that can be seen from a particular place or in a particular direction: *there was a beautiful view from the window* **4** vision or sight, esp. range of vision: *as they turned into the drive, the house came into view* **5** a picture of a scene **6** the act of seeing or observing **7 in view of** taking into consideration **8 on view** exhibited to the public **9 take a dim** *or* **poor view of** to regard (something) unfavourably **10 with a view to** with the intention of ▹ *vb* **11** to consider in a specified manner: *they viewed the visit with hardly disguised apprehension* **12** to examine or inspect (a house or flat) carefully with a view to buying it **13** to look at **14** to watch (television)
WORD ORIGIN Latin *videre* to see
Viewdata *n trademark* a videotext service linking users to a computer by telephone, enabling shopping, ticket booking, etc. to be done from home
viewer ❶ *n* **1** a person who views something, esp. television **2** a hand-held device for looking at photographic slides
viewfinder *n* a device on a camera that lets the user see what will be included in the photograph
viewpoint *n* **1** a person's attitude towards something **2** a place from which one gets a good view
Vigée-Lebrun *n* **(Marie Louise) Élisabeth** 1755–1842, French painter, noted for her portraits of women
vigil (vij-ill) *n* **1** a night-time period of staying awake to look after a sick person, pray, etc. **2** *RC church, Church of England* the eve of certain major festivals
WORD ORIGIN Latin: alert
vigilance *n* careful attention
vigilance committee *n* (in the US) a self-appointed body of citizens organized to maintain order
vigilant *adj* on the watch for trouble or danger
WORD ORIGIN Latin *vigilare* to be watchful
vigilante (vij-ill-ant-ee) *n* a person who takes it upon himself or herself to enforce the law
WORD ORIGIN Spanish, from Latin *vigilare* to keep watch
vignette (vin-yet) *n* **1** a short description of the typical features of something **2** a small decorative illustration in a book **3** a photograph or drawing with edges that are shaded off
WORD ORIGIN French, literally: little vine (frequently used to embellish a text)
Vignola *n* **Giacomo Barozzi da** 1507–73, Italian architect, whose cruciform design for Il Gesù, Rome, greatly influenced later Church architecture
Vigny *n* **Alfred Victor de** 1797–1863, French romantic poet, novelist, and dramatist, noted for his pessimistic lyric verse *Poèmes antiques et modernes* (1826) and *Les Destinées* (1864), the novel *Cinq-Mars* (1826), and the play *Chatterton* (1835)
vigorous ❶ *adj* **1** having physical or mental energy **2** displaying or performed with vigour: *vigorous exercise* **vigorously** *adv*
vigour *or US* **vigor** ❶ *n* **1** physical or mental energy: *the vigour of his invective astonished MPs* **2** strong healthy growth
WORD ORIGIN Latin *vigor*
Viking *n* any of the Scandinavians who raided by sea most of N and W Europe from the 8th to the 11th centuries
WORD ORIGIN Old Norse *víkingr*
vile ❶ *adj* **1** morally wicked: *a vile regime* **2** disgusting: *the vile smell of the man* **3** unpleasant or bad: *I had a vile day at work* **vilely** *adv* **vileness** *n*
WORD ORIGIN Latin *vilis* cheap
vilify (vill-if-fie) *vb* **-fies, -fying, -fied**

THESAURUS

vie *vb* (*with* **with** *or* **for**) **= compete**, struggle, contend, contest, strive, be rivals, match yourself against
view *n* **1 = opinion**, thought, idea, belief, thinking, feeling, attitude, reckoning, impression, notion, conviction, judgment, point of view, sentiment, viewpoint, persuasion, way of thinking, standpoint **3 = scene**, picture, sight, prospect, aspect, perspective, landscape, outlook, spectacle, panorama, vista **4 = vision**, sight, visibility, perspective, eyeshot, range *or* field of vision ▹ *vb* **11 = regard**, see, consider, judge, perceive, treat, estimate, reckon, deem, look on, adjudge, think about *or* of
viewer *n* **1 = watcher**, observer, spectator, onlooker, couch potato (*informal*), TV watcher, one of an audience
vigorous *adj* **1a = spirited**, lively, energetic, active, intense, dynamic, sparkling, animated, forceful, feisty (*informal*), spanking, high-spirited, sprightly, vivacious, forcible, effervescent, full of energy, zippy (*informal*), spunky (*informal*) **OPPOSITE:** lethargic **1b = strong**, powerful, robust, sound, healthy, vital, lively, flourishing, hardy, hale, hearty, lusty, virile, alive and kicking, red-blooded, fighting fit, full of energy, full of beans (*informal*), hale and hearty, fit as a fiddle (*informal*) **OPPOSITE:** weak **2 = strenuous**, energetic, arduous, hard, taxing, active, intense, exhausting, rigorous, brisk
vigour *or* (*US*) **vigor** *n* **1 = energy**, might, force, vitality, power, activity, spirit, strength, snap (*informal*), punch (*informal*), dash, pep, zip (*informal*), animation, verve, gusto, dynamism, oomph (*informal*), brio, robustness, liveliness, vim (*slang*), forcefulness **OPPOSITE:** weakness
vile *adj* **1 = wicked**, base, evil, mean, bad, low, shocking, appalling, ugly, corrupt, miserable, vicious, humiliating, perverted, coarse, degrading, worthless, disgraceful, vulgar, degenerate, abject, sinful,

DICTIONARY

to speak very badly of (someone) **vilification** *n*
WORD ORIGIN Latin *vilis* worthless + *facere* to make

villa *n* **1** a large house with gardens **2** *Brit* a house rented to holiday-makers
WORD ORIGIN Latin: a farmhouse

village *n* **1** a small group of houses in a country area **2** the inhabitants of such a community **villager** *n*
WORD ORIGIN Latin *villa* a farmhouse

villain ❶ *n* **1** a wicked or evil person **2** the main wicked character in a novel or play
WORD ORIGIN Late Latin *villanus* worker on a country estate

villainous *adj* of or like a villain

villainy *n, pl* **-lainies** evil or vicious behaviour

Villa-Lobos *n* **Heitor** 1887–1959, Brazilian composer, much of whose work is based on Brazilian folk tunes

Villars *n* **Claude Louis Hector de** 1653–1734, French marshal, distinguished for his command in the War of the Spanish Succession (1701–14)

villein (vill-an) *n* (in medieval Europe) a peasant who was directly subject to his lord, to whom he paid dues and services in return for his land **villeinage** *n*
WORD ORIGIN see VILLAIN

Villeneuve *n* **Pierre Charles Jean Baptiste Silvestre de** 1763–1806, French admiral, defeated by Nelson at the Battle of Trafalgar (1805)

Villiers de l'Isle Adam *n* **August, Comte de** 1838–89, French poet and dramatist; pioneer of the symbolist movement. His works include *Contes cruels* (1883) and the play *Axel* (1885)

Villon *n* **1 François** born 1431, French poet. His poems, such as those in *Le Petit testament* (?1456) and *Le Grand testament* (1461), are mostly ballades and rondeaux, verse forms that he revitalized. He was banished in 1463, after which nothing more was heard of him **2 Jacques**, real name *Gaston Duchamp*. 1875–1963, French cubist painter and engraver

villus *n, pl* **villi** *zool, anat* **1** any of the numerous finger-like projections of the mucous membrane lining the small intestine of many vertebrates **2** any of the finger-like projections formed in the placenta of mammals
WORD ORIGIN from Latin: shaggy hair

vim *n informal* vigour and energy
WORD ORIGIN Latin *vis* force

vinaigrette *n* salad dressing made from oil and vinegar with seasonings
WORD ORIGIN French

Vincent de Paul *n* **Saint** ?1581–1660, French Roman Catholic priest, who founded two charitable orders, the Lazarists (1625) and the Sisters of Charity (1634). Feast day: Sept 27

vindaloo *n, pl* **-loos** a type of very hot Indian curry
WORD ORIGIN perhaps from Portuguese *vin d'alho* wine and garlic sauce

vindicate ❶ *vb* **-cating, -cated 1** to clear (someone) of guilt or suspicion **2** to provide justification for: *the arrests may vindicate the strong-arm tactics* **vindication** *n*
WORD ORIGIN Latin *vindex* claimant

vindictive *adj* **1** maliciously seeking revenge **2** characterized by spite or ill will **vindictively** *adv* **vindictiveness** *n*
WORD ORIGIN Latin *vindicare* to avenge

vine *n* **1** a plant, such as the grapevine, with long flexible stems that climb by clinging to a support **2** the stem of such a plant **viny** *adj*
WORD ORIGIN Latin *vinea* vineyard

vinegar *n* **1** a sour-tasting liquid made by fermentation of beer, wine, or cider, used for salad dressing or for pickling **2** bad temper or spitefulness: *the vinegar in her pen is often a welcome seasoning to duller news* **vinegary** *adj*
WORD ORIGIN French *vin* wine + *aigre* sour

vineyard (vinn-yard) *n* an area of land where grapes are grown
WORD ORIGIN Old English *wīngeard*

vingt-et-un (van-tay-uhn) *n* ▸ same as **pontoon**[2]
WORD ORIGIN French, literally: twenty-one

viniculture *n* the process or business of growing grapes and making wine **viniculturist** *n*
WORD ORIGIN Latin *vinum* wine + CULTURE

vino (vee-noh) *n, pl* **-nos** *informal* wine
WORD ORIGIN Spanish or Italian: wine

vinous (vine-uss) *adj* of or characteristic of wine
WORD ORIGIN Latin *vinum* wine

vintage ❶ *n* **1** the wine obtained from a particular harvest of grapes **2** the harvest from which such a wine is obtained **3** a time of origin: *an open-necked shirt of uncertain vintage* ▹ *adj* **4** (of wine) of an outstandingly good year **5** representative of the best and most typical: *a vintage Saint Laurent dress*
WORD ORIGIN Latin *vindemia*

vintage car *n* a car built between 1919 and 1930

vintner *n* a wine merchant
WORD ORIGIN Latin *vinetum* vineyard

vinyl (vine-ill) *n* **1** any of various strong plastics made by the polymerization of vinyl compounds, such as PVC **2** conventional records made of vinyl as opposed to compact discs ▹ *adj* **3** *chem* of or containing the monovalent group of atoms CH_2CH–: *vinyl chloride* **4** of or made of vinyl: *vinyl tiles*
WORD ORIGIN Latin *vinum* wine

viol (vie-oll) *n* a stringed musical instrument that preceded the violin
WORD ORIGIN Old Provençal *viola*

viola[1] (vee-oh-la) *n* a bowed stringed instrument of the violin family, slightly larger and lower in pitch than the violin
WORD ORIGIN Italian

viola[2] (vie-ol-la) *n* a variety of pansy
WORD ORIGIN Latin: violet

viola da gamba (vee-oh-la da gam-ba) *n* the second largest and lowest member of the viol family
WORD ORIGIN Italian, literally: viol for the leg

violate ❶ *vb* **-lating, -lated 1** to break (a law or agreement): *he violated export laws* **2** to disturb rudely or improperly: *these men who were violating her privacy* **3** to treat (a sacred place) disrespectfully **4** to rape **violation** *n* **violator** *n*
WORD ORIGIN Latin *violare* to do violence to

violence ❶ *n* **1** the use of physical

V

THESAURUS

despicable, depraved, debased, loathsome, contemptible, impure, wretched, nefarious, ignoble **OPPOSITE:** honourable
2 = disgusting, foul, revolting, offensive, nasty, obscene, sickening, horrid, repellent, repulsive, noxious, nauseating, repugnant, loathsome, yucky *or* yukky *(slang)*, yucko *(Austral slang)* **OPPOSITE:** pleasant

villain *n* **1 = evildoer**, criminal, rogue, profligate, scoundrel, wretch, libertine, knave *(archaic)*, reprobate, miscreant, malefactor, blackguard, rapscallion, caitiff *(archaic)*, wrong 'un *(Austral slang)* **2 = baddy** *(informal)*, antihero **OPPOSITE:** hero

vindicate *vb* **1 = clear**, acquit, exonerate, absolve, let off the hook, exculpate, free from blame **OPPOSITE:** condemn
2 = support, uphold, ratify, defend, excuse, justify, substantiate

vintage *n* **1, 2** *(of a wine)* **= harvest**, year, crop, yield ▹ *adj* **4** *(of a wine)* **= high-quality**, best, prime, quality, choice, select, rare, superior
5 = classic, old, veteran, historic, heritage, enduring, antique, timeless, old-world, age-old, ageless

violate *vb* **1 = break**, infringe, disobey, transgress, ignore, defy, disregard, flout, rebel against, contravene, fly in the face of, overstep, not comply with, take no notice of, encroach upon, pay no heed to, infract

DICTIONARY

force, usually intended to cause injury or destruction **2** great force or strength in action, feeling, or expression
WORD ORIGIN Latin *violentus* violent
violent ◑ *adj* **1** using or involving physical force with the intention of causing injury or destruction: *violent clashes with government supporters* **2** very intense: *I took a violent dislike to him* **3** sudden and forceful: *a violent explosion* **violently** *adv*
violet *n* **1** a plant with bluish-purple flowers ▹ *adj* **2** bluish-purple
WORD ORIGIN Latin *viola*
violin *n* a musical instrument, the highest member of the violin family, with four strings played with a bow
WORD ORIGIN Italian *violino* a little viola
violinist *n* a person who plays the violin
violist (vee-oh-list) *n* a person who plays the viola
Viollet-le-Duc *n* **Eugène Emmanuel** 1814–79, French architect and leader of the Gothic Revival in France, noted for his dictionary of French architecture (1854–68) and for his restoration of medieval buildings
violoncello (vie-oll-on-chell-oh) *n, pl* **-los** ▸ same as **cello**
WORD ORIGIN Italian
VIP ◑ very important person
viper *n* a type of poisonous snake
WORD ORIGIN Latin *vipera*
virago (vir-rah-go) *n, pl* **-goes** *or* **-gos** an aggressive woman
WORD ORIGIN Latin: a manlike maiden
viral (vie-ral) *adj* of or caused by a virus
Virchow *n* **Rudolf Ludwig Karl**. 1821–1902, German pathologist, who is considered the founder of modern (cellular) pathology
Viren *n* **Lasse** born 1949, Finnish distance runner: winner of the 5000 metres and the 10 000 metres in the 1972 and 1976 Olympic Games
virgin ◑ *n* **1** a person, esp. a woman, who has never had sexual intercourse **2** a person who is inexperienced in a specified field: *a ski virgin* ▹ *adj* **3** not having had sexual intercourse **4** fresh and unused: *he found a scrap of virgin paper in a sea of memoranda* **5** not yet cultivated, explored, or exploited by people: *virgin territory*
WORD ORIGIN Latin *virgo*
Virgin *n* **1** **the Virgin** ▸ same as **Virgin Mary** **2** a statue or picture of the Virgin Mary
virginal[1] *adj* **1** like a virgin **2** extremely pure or fresh
virginal[2] *n* an early keyboard instrument like a small harpsichord
WORD ORIGIN probably Latin *virginalis* virginal, perhaps because it was played largely by young ladies
Virgin Birth *n Christianity* the doctrine that Jesus Christ was conceived solely by the direct intervention of the Holy Spirit so that Mary remained a virgin
Virginia creeper *n* a climbing plant with leaves that turn red in autumn
virginity *n* the condition or fact of being a virgin
Virgin Mary *n* **the Virgin Mary** *Christianity* Mary, the mother of Christ
Virgin Queen *n* **the Virgin Queen** another name for Queen Elizabeth I of England ▸ See **Elizabeth I**
Virgo *n astrol* the sixth sign of the zodiac; the Virgin
WORD ORIGIN Latin
virile *adj* **1** having the traditional male characteristics of physical strength and a high sex drive **2** forceful and energetic: *a virile Highland fling* **virility** *n*
WORD ORIGIN Latin *virilis* manly
virology *n* the branch of medicine concerned with the study of viruses **virological** *adj*
virtual ◑ *adj* **1** having the effect but not the appearance or form of: *the investigation has now come to a virtual standstill* **2** *computers* designed so as to extend the potential of a finite system beyond its immediate limits: *virtual memory* **3** of or relating to virtual reality
WORD ORIGIN Latin *virtus* virtue
virtually ◑ *adv* almost or nearly: *he is virtually a prisoner in his own palace*
virtual reality *n* a computer-generated environment that seems real to the user
virtue ◑ *n* **1** moral goodness **2** a positive moral quality: *the virtue of humility* **3** an advantage or benefit: *the added virtue of being harmless* **4** chastity, esp. in women **5** **by virtue of** by reason of; because of: *they escaped execution by virtue of their high rank*
WORD ORIGIN Latin *virtus* manliness, courage
virtuoso *n, pl* **-si** *or* **-sos** **1** a person with exceptional musical skill **2** a person with exceptional skill in any area ▹ *adj* **3** showing exceptional

THESAURUS

OPPOSITE: obey
2 = invade, infringe on, disturb, upset, shatter, disrupt, impinge on, encroach on, intrude on, trespass on, obtrude on **3 = desecrate**, profane, defile, abuse, outrage, pollute, deface, dishonour, vandalize, treat with disrespect, befoul **OPPOSITE:** honour **4 = rape**, molest, sexually assault, ravish, abuse, assault, interfere with, sexually abuse, indecently assault, force yourself on
violence *n* **1 = brutality**, bloodshed, savagery, fighting, terrorism, frenzy, thuggery, destructiveness, bestiality, strong-arm tactics *(informal)*, rough handling, bloodthirstiness, murderousness **2a = force**, power, strength, might, ferocity, brute force, fierceness, forcefulness, powerfulness **2b = intensity**, passion, fury, force, cruelty, severity, fervour, sharpness, harshness, vehemence
violent *adj* **1a = brutal**, aggressive, savage, wild, rough, fierce, bullying, cruel, vicious, destructive, ruthless, murderous, maddened, berserk, merciless, bloodthirsty, homicidal, pitiless, hot-headed, thuggish, maniacal, hot-tempered
OPPOSITE: gentle
1b = sharp, hard, powerful, forceful, strong, fierce, fatal, savage, deadly, brutal, vicious, lethal, hefty, ferocious, death-dealing
2a = passionate, intense, extreme, strong, wild, consuming, uncontrollable, vehement, unrestrained, tempestuous, ungovernable **2b = fiery**, raging, fierce, flaming, furious, passionate, peppery, ungovernable
VIP *n* **= celebrity**, big name, public figure, star, somebody, lion, notable, luminary, bigwig *(informal)*, leading light *(informal)*, big shot *(informal)*, personage, big noise *(informal)*, big hitter *(informal)*, heavy hitter *(informal)*, man *or* woman of the hour
virgin *n* **1 = maiden**, maid *(archaic)*, damsel *(archaic)*, girl *(archaic)*, celibate, vestal, virgo intacta ▹ *adj* **3 = pure**, maidenly, chaste, immaculate, virginal, unsullied, vestal, uncorrupted, undefiled
OPPOSITE: corrupted
virtual *adj* **1 = practical**, near, essential, implied, indirect, implicit, tacit, near enough, unacknowledged, in all but name
virtually *adv* **= practically**, almost, nearly, in effect, in essence, as good as, to all intents and purposes, in all but name, for all practical purposes, effectually
virtue *n* **1 = goodness**, honour, integrity, worth, dignity, excellence, morality, honesty, decency, respectability, nobility, righteousness, propriety, probity, rectitude, worthiness, high-mindedness, incorruptibility, uprightness, virtuousness, ethicalness **OPPOSITE:** vice **2 = merit**, strength, asset, plus *(informal)*, attribute, good quality, good point, strong point
OPPOSITE: failing
3 = advantage, benefit, merit, credit, usefulness, efficacy

DICTIONARY

skill or brilliance: *a virtuoso performance* **virtuosity** *n*
WORD ORIGIN Italian: skilled

virtuous *adj* **1** morally good **2** (of a woman) chaste **virtuously** *adv*

virulent (vir-yew-lent) *adj* **1** extremely bitter or hostile **2 a** (of a microorganism) very infectious **b** (of a disease) having a violent effect **3** extremely poisonous or harmful: *the most virulent poison known to man* **virulence** *n*
WORD ORIGIN Latin *virulentus* full of poison

virus *n* **1** a microorganism that is smaller than a bacterium and can cause disease in humans, animals, or plants **2** *informal* a disease caused by a virus **3** *computers* an unsanctioned and self-replicating program which, when activated, corrupts a computer's data and disables its operating system
WORD ORIGIN Latin: slime, poisonous liquid

visa *n* an official stamp in a passport permitting its holder to travel into or through the country of the government issuing it
WORD ORIGIN Latin: things seen

visage (viz-zij) *n chiefly literary* **1** face **2** appearance
WORD ORIGIN Latin *visus* appearance

vis-à-vis (veez-ah-vee) *prep* in relation to
WORD ORIGIN French: face-to-face

viscera (viss-er-a) *pl n anat* the large internal organs of the body collectively
WORD ORIGIN Latin: entrails

visceral *adj* **1** of or affecting the viscera **2** instinctive rather than rational: *visceral hatred of the neighbours*

viscid (viss-id) *adj* sticky
WORD ORIGIN Latin *viscum* mistletoe, birdlime

Visconti *n* **1** the ruling family of Milan from 1277 to 1447 **2 Luchino,** real name *Luchino Visconti de Modrone.* 1906–76, Italian stage and film director, whose neorealist films include *Ossessione* (1942). His other films include *The Leopard* (1963), *Death in Venice* (1970), and *The Innocents* (1976)

viscose *n* **1** a sticky solution obtained by dissolving cellulose **2** rayon made from this material
WORD ORIGIN Latin *viscum* birdlime

viscosity *n, pl* **-ties** **1** the state of being viscous **2** *physics* the extent to which a fluid resists a tendency to flow

viscount (vie-count) *n* (in the British Isles) a nobleman ranking below an earl and above a baron **viscountcy** *n*
WORD ORIGIN Old French *visconte*

viscountess (vie-count-iss) *n* **1** a woman holding the rank of viscount **2** the wife or widow of a viscount

viscous *adj* (of liquids) thick and sticky

vise *n US* ▸ same as **vice²**

Vishinsky *n* a variant spelling of (Andrei Yanuaryevich) **Vyshinsky**

Vishnu *n* a Hindu god, the Preserver

visibility *n* **1** the range or clarity of vision: *visibility was good, despite rain* **2** the condition of being visible

visible Ⓣ *adj* **1** able to be seen **2** able to be perceived by the mind: *a visible and flagrant act of aggression* **visibly** *adv*
WORD ORIGIN Latin *visibilis*

vision Ⓣ *n* **1** the ability to see **2** a vivid mental image produced by the imagination: *I kept having visions of him being tortured* **3** a hallucination caused by divine inspiration, madness, or drugs: *visions of God* **4** great perception of future developments: *what he had instead of charisma was vision* **5** the image on a television screen **6** a person or thing of extraordinary beauty
WORD ORIGIN Latin *visio* sight, from *videre* to see

visionary Ⓣ *adj* **1** showing foresight: *a visionary statesman* **2** idealistic but impractical **3** given to having visions **4** of or like visions ▹ *n, pl* **-aries** **5** a visionary person

visit Ⓣ *vb* **-iting, -ited** **1** to go or come to see (a person or place) **2** to stay with (someone) as a guest **3** *old-fashioned* (of a disease or disaster) to afflict **4 visit on** *or* **upon** to inflict (punishment) on **5 visit with** *US informal* to chat with (someone) ▹ *n* **6** the act or an instance of visiting **7** a professional or official call **8** a stay as a guest
WORD ORIGIN Latin *visitare* to go to see

visitant *n* **1** a ghost or apparition **2** a migratory bird temporarily resting in a particular region

visitation *n* **1** an official visit or inspection **2** a punishment or reward from heaven **3** an appearance of a supernatural being

Visitation *n* **a** the visit made by the Virgin Mary to her cousin Elizabeth (Luke 1: 39–56) **b** the Church festival commemorating this, held on July 2

visiting hours *pl n* the times when visitors are allowed to see someone in a hospital or other institution: *many prisoners' wives complain about the short visiting hours*

visitor Ⓣ *n* a person who visits a person or place

visitor's passport *n* a British passport, valid for one year, that grants access to some countries, usually for a restricted period

visor (vize-or) *n* **1** a transparent flap on a helmet that can be pulled down to protect the face **2** a small movable screen attached above the windscreen in a vehicle, used as protection against the glare of the sun **3** a peak on a cap
WORD ORIGIN Old French *vis* face

vista Ⓣ *n* **1** an extensive view **2** a wide range of possibilities or future

THESAURUS

visible *adj* **1, 2 = perceptible,** noticeable, observable, clear, obvious, plain, apparent, bold, patent, to be seen, evident, manifest, in sight, in view, conspicuous, unmistakable, palpable, discernible, salient, detectable, not hidden, distinguishable, unconcealed, perceivable, discoverable, anywhere to be seen **OPPOSITE:** invisible

vision *n* **1 = sight,** seeing, eyesight, view, eyes, perception **2 = image,** idea, dream, plans, hopes, prospect, ideal, concept, fancy, fantasy, conception, delusion, daydream, reverie, flight of fancy, mental picture, pipe dream, imago *(psychoanalysis)*, castle in the air, fanciful notion **3 = hallucination,** illusion, apparition, revelation, ghost, phantom, delusion, spectre, mirage, wraith, chimera, phantasm, eidolon **4 = foresight,** imagination, perception, insight, awareness, inspiration, innovation, creativity, intuition, penetration, inventiveness, shrewdness, discernment, prescience, perceptiveness, farsightedness, breadth of view

visionary *adj* **2 = idealistic,** romantic, unrealistic, utopian, dreaming, speculative, impractical, dreamy, unworkable, quixotic, starry-eyed, with your head in the clouds **OPPOSITE:** realistic **3 = prophetic,** mystical, divinatory, predictive, oracular, sibylline, mantic, vatic *(rare)*, fatidic *(rare)* ▹ *n* **5a = idealist,** romantic, dreamer, daydreamer, utopian, enthusiast *(archaic)*, theorist, zealot, Don Quixote **OPPOSITE:** realist **5b = prophet,** diviner, mystic, seer, soothsayer, sibyl, scryer, spaewife *(Scot)*

visit *vb* **1a = call on,** go to see, drop in on *(informal)*, stop by, look up, call in on, pop in on *(informal)*, pay a call on, go see *(US)*, swing by *(informal)* **1b = stay in,** see, tour, explore, take in *(informal)*, holiday in, go to see, stop by, spend time in, vacation in *(US)*, stop over in **2 = stay at,** stay with, spend time with, pay a visit to, be the guest of ▹ *n* **6 = call,** social call **8 = trip,** stop, stay, break, tour, holiday, vacation *(informal)*, stopover, sojourn

visitor *n* **= guest,** caller, company, visitant, manu(w)hiri *(NZ)*

vista *n* **1 = view,** scene, prospect, landscape, panorama, perspective

DICTIONARY

events: *the vista of opportunity*
WORD ORIGIN Italian
visual ⓘ *adj* **1** done by or used in seeing **2** capable of being seen **visually** *adv*
WORD ORIGIN Latin *visus* sight
visual aids *pl n* objects to be looked at that help the viewer to understand or remember something
visual display unit *n computers* a device with a screen for displaying data held in a computer
visualize *or* **-ise** *vb* **-izing, -ized** *or* **-ising, -ised** to form a mental image of (something not at that moment visible) **visualization** *or* **-isation** *n*
vital ⓘ *adj* **1** essential or highly important: *marriage isn't such a vital part of his life* **2** energetic or lively: *the epitome of vital youthful manhood* **3** necessary to maintain life: *the vital organs* ▷ *n* **4 vitals** the bodily organs, such as the brain and heart, that are necessary to maintain life **vitally** *adv*
WORD ORIGIN Latin *vita* life
vitality ⓘ *n* physical or mental energy
vitalize *or* **-ise** *vb* **-izing, -ized** *or* **-ising, -ised** to fill with life or vitality **vitalization** *or* **-isation** *n*
vital statistics *pl n* **1** population statistics, such as the numbers of births, marriages, and deaths **2** *informal* the measurements of a woman's bust, waist, and hips
vitamin *n* one of a group of substances that occur naturally in certain foods and are essential for normal health and growth
WORD ORIGIN from Latin *vita* life + AMINE
vitiate (vish-ee-ate) *vb* **-ating, -ated** **1** to spoil or weaken the effectiveness of (something) **2** to destroy the legal effect of (a contract) **vitiation** *n*
WORD ORIGIN Latin *vitiare* to injure
viticulture *n* the cultivation of grapevines
WORD ORIGIN Latin *vitis* vine
Vitoria[1] *n* a city in NE Spain: scene of Wellington's decisive victory (1813) over Napoleon's forces in the Peninsular War. Pop: 223 257 (2003 est). Official name (including the Basque name): **Vitoria-Gasteiz**
Vitoria[2] *n* **Francisco de** ?1486–1546, Spanish theologian, sometimes considered the father of international law. He criticized Spanish colonial policy in the New World and argued that war was only defensible in certain strictly defined circumstances
vitreous *adj* **1** of or like glass **2** of or relating to the vitreous humour
WORD ORIGIN Latin *vitrum* glass
vitreous humour *or* **body** *n* a transparent gelatinous substance that fills the eyeball between the lens and the retina
vitrify *vb* **-fies, -fying, -fied** to change into glass or a glassy substance **vitrification** *n*
vitriol *n* **1** language expressing bitterness and hatred **2** sulphuric acid
WORD ORIGIN Latin *vitrum* glass, referring to the glossy appearance of the sulphates
vitriolic *adj* (of language) severely bitter or harsh
vituperative (vite-tyew-pra-tiv) *adj* bitterly abusive **vituperation** *n*
WORD ORIGIN Latin *vituperare* to blame
viva[1] *interj* long live (a specified person or thing)
WORD ORIGIN Italian, literally: may (he) live!
viva[2] *Brit n* **1** an examination in the form of an interview ▷ *vb* **vivaing, vivaed** **2** to examine (a candidate) in a spoken interview
WORD ORIGIN from VIVA VOCE
vivace (viv-vah-chee) *adj music* to be performed in a lively manner
WORD ORIGIN Italian
vivacious *adj* full of energy and enthusiasm
WORD ORIGIN Latin *vivax* lively
vivacity *n* the quality of being vivacious
vivarium *n, pl* **-iums** *or* **-ia** a place where live animals are kept under natural conditions
WORD ORIGIN Latin *vivus* alive
viva voce (vive-a voh-chee) *adv, adj* **1** by word of mouth ▷ *n* **2** ▸ same as **viva**[2] (sense 1)
WORD ORIGIN Medieval Latin, literally: with living voice
Vivekananda *n* original name *Narendranath Datta* 1862–1902, Indian Hindu religious teacher. A disciple of Ramakrishna, he introduced Vedantism to the West
vivid ⓘ *adj* **1** very bright: *a vivid blue sky* **2** very clear and detailed: *vivid memories* **3** easily forming lifelike images: *a vivid imagination* **vividly** *adv* **vividness** *n*
WORD ORIGIN Latin *vividus* animated
vivify *vb* **-fies, -fying, -fied** **1** to bring to life **2** to make more vivid or striking
WORD ORIGIN Latin *vivus* alive + *facere* to make
viviparous (viv-vip-a-russ) *adj* giving birth to living offspring, as most mammals do
WORD ORIGIN Latin *vivus* alive + *parere* to bring forth
vivisection *n* the performing of experiments on living animals, involving cutting into or dissecting the body **vivisectionist** *n*
WORD ORIGIN Latin *vivus* living + *sectio* a cutting
vixen *n* **1** a female fox **2** *Brit, Austral & NZ informal* a spiteful woman
WORD ORIGIN related to Old English *fyxe*, feminine of *fox*
viz *adv* namely: used to specify items: *I had only one object, viz, to beat the Germans*
WORD ORIGIN abbreviated from Latin *videlicet* namely
vizier (viz-zeer) *n* a high official in certain Muslim countries
WORD ORIGIN Turkish *vezīr*
vizor *n* ▸ same as **visor**
Vladimir[1] *n* a city in W central Russia: capital of the principality of Vladimir until the court transferred to Moscow in 1328. Pop: 310 000 (2005 est)
Vladimir[2] *n* **Saint,** called *the Great*. ?956–1015, grand prince of Kiev (980–1015); first Christian ruler of Russia. Feast day: July 15
VLF *or* **vlf** *radio* very low frequency
V neck *n* **a** a neck on a garment that comes down to a point, like the letter V **b** a sweater with a neck like this **V-neck** *or* **V-necked** *adj*
vocab *n* ▸ short for **vocabulary**
vocable *n linguistics* a word regarded simply as a sequence of letters or spoken sounds
WORD ORIGIN Latin *vocare* to call
vocabulary ⓘ *n, pl* **-laries** **1** all the words that a person knows **2** all the

V

THESAURUS

visual *adj* **1 = optical**, optic, ocular **2 = observable**, visible, perceptible, discernible **OPPOSITE:** imperceptible
vital *adj* **1 = essential**, important, necessary, key, basic, significant, critical, radical, crucial, fundamental, urgent, decisive, cardinal, imperative, indispensable, requisite, life-or-death, must-have **OPPOSITE:** unnecessary **2 = lively**, vigorous, energetic, spirited, dynamic, animated, vibrant, forceful, sparky, vivacious, full of beans *(informal)*, zestful, full of the joy of living **OPPOSITE:** lethargic
vitality *n* **= energy**, vivacity, sparkle, go *(informal)*, life, strength, pep, stamina, animation, vigour, exuberance, brio, robustness, liveliness, vim *(slang)*, lustiness, vivaciousness **OPPOSITE:** lethargy
vivid *adj* **1 = bright**, brilliant, intense, clear, rich, glowing, colourful, highly-coloured **OPPOSITE:** dull **2 = clear**, detailed, realistic, telling, moving, strong, affecting, arresting, powerful, sharp, dramatic, stirring, stimulating, haunting, graphic, distinct, lively, memorable, unforgettable, evocative, lucid, lifelike, true to life, sharply-etched **OPPOSITE:** vague
vocabulary *n* **1, 2 = language**, words, lexicon, word stock, word hoard **4 = wordbook**, dictionary, glossary, lexicon

DICTIONARY

words contained in a language **3** the specialist terms used in a given subject **4** a list of words in another language with their translations **5** a range of symbols or techniques as used in any of the arts or crafts: *the building's vocabulary of materials, textures, and tones*
WORD ORIGIN Latin *vocabulum* vocable

vocal *adj* **1** of or relating to the voice: *vocal pitch* **2** expressing one's opinions clearly and openly: *a vocal minority with racist views* ▹*n* **3 vocals** the singing part of a piece of jazz or pop music **vocally** *adv*
WORD ORIGIN Latin *vox* voice

vocal cords *pl n* either of two pairs of membranous folds in the larynx, of which the lower pair can be made to vibrate and produce sound by forcing air from the lungs over them

vocalist *n* a singer with a pop group

vocalize *or* **-ise** *vb* **-izing, -ized** *or* **-ising, -ised 1** to express with or use the voice **2** to make vocal or articulate: *vocalize your discontent* **3** *phonetics* to articulate (a speech sound) with voice **vocalization** *or* **-isation** *n*

vocation *n* **1** a specified profession or trade **2 a** a special urge to a particular calling or career, esp. a religious one **b** such a calling or career
WORD ORIGIN Latin *vocare* to call

vocational *adj* directed towards a particular profession or trade: *vocational training*

vocative *n grammar* a grammatical case used in some languages when addressing a person or thing
WORD ORIGIN Latin *vocare* to call

vociferate *vb* **-ating, -ated** to exclaim or cry out about (something) noisily **vociferation** *n*
WORD ORIGIN Latin *vox* voice + *ferre* to bear

vociferous *adj* loud and forceful: *a vociferous minority* **vociferously** *adv*

VOD video on demand: an interactive TV system that allows the viewer to select content and view it at a time of his or her own choosing

vodka *n* a clear alcoholic spirit originating in Russia, made from potatoes or grain
WORD ORIGIN Russian

voetsak *or* **voetsek** (foot-sak) *interj S African, offensive informal* an expression of dismissal or rejection
WORD ORIGIN Afrikaans, from Dutch *voort se ek* forward, I say, commonly applied to animals

Vogel *n* Sir **Julius** 1835–99, New Zealand statesman; prime minister of New Zealand (1873–75; 1876)

Vogelweide *n* See **Walther von der Vogelweide**

Vogts *n* **Hans-Hubert,** known as *Berti.* born 1946, German footballer and coach; played for Germany (1967–79); coach of Germany (1990–98) and Scotland (2002–04)

vogue *n* **1** the popular style at a given time **2 in vogue** fashionable ▹*adj* **3** fashionable: *a vogue word* **voguish** *adj*
WORD ORIGIN French

voice *n* **1** the sound made by the vibration of the vocal cords, esp. when modified by the tongue and mouth **2** a distinctive tone of the speech sounds characteristic of a particular person: *he can recognize her voice* **3** the ability to speak or sing: *he had at last found his voice* **4** the condition or quality of a person's voice: *her voice was kind* **5** the musical sound of a singing voice: *what I have is a good voice and a great love of lyrics* **6** the expression of feeling or opinion: *there was a chorus of dissenting voices* **7** a right to express an opinion: *the party should now move towards a system which will give every member an equal voice* **8** *grammar* a category of the verb that expresses whether it is active or passive **9** *phonetics* the sound characterizing the articulation of several speech sounds, that is produced when the vocal cords are vibrated by the breath **10 with one voice** unanimously ▹*vb* **voicing, voiced 11** to express verbally: *anyone with an objection has a chance to voice it* **12** to articulate (a speech sound) with voice
WORD ORIGIN Latin *vox*

voiced *adj phonetics* articulated with accompanying vibration of the vocal cords, for example 'b' in English

voiceless *adj* **1** without a voice **2** *phonetics* articulated without accompanying vibration of the vocal cords, for example 'p' in English

voice mail *n* an electronic system for the transfer and storage of telephone messages, which can then be dealt with by the user at his or her convenience

voice-over *n* the voice of an unseen commentator heard during a film

void *n* **1** a feeling or condition of loneliness or deprivation **2** an empty space or area ▹*adj* **3** having no official value or authority, because the terms have been broken or have not been fulfilled: *the race was declared void and rerun* **4** *old-fashioned or literary* empty: *behold, the tomb is void!* **5 void of** devoid of or without: *the fact of being punished becomes void of all moral significance* ▹*vb* **6** to make ineffective or invalid **7** to empty **8** to discharge the contents of (the bowels or bladder)
WORD ORIGIN Latin *vacare* to be empty

voile (voyl) *n* a light semitransparent dress fabric
WORD ORIGIN French: veil

voip *n informal* voice-over internet protocol: a system for converting analogue signals to digital so that telephone calls may be made over the internet

vol. volume

volatile (voll-a-tile) *adj* **1** (of circumstances) liable to sudden change **2** (of people) liable to sudden changes of mood and behaviour **3** (of a substance) changing quickly from a solid or liquid form to a vapour **volatility** *n*
WORD ORIGIN Latin *volare* to fly

volatilize *or* **-lise** *vb* **-lizing, -lized** *or*

THESAURUS

vocal *adj* **1 = spoken**, voiced, uttered, oral, said, articulate, articulated, put into words **2 = outspoken**, frank, blunt, forthright, strident, vociferous, noisy, articulate, expressive, eloquent, plain-spoken, clamorous, free-spoken
OPPOSITE: quiet

vocation *n* **1 = profession**, calling, job, business, office, trade, role, post, career, mission, employment, pursuit, life work, métier

vogue *n* **1 = fashion**, trend, craze, style, the latest, the thing *(informal)*, mode, last word, the rage, passing fancy, dernier cri *(French)*

voice *n* **1 = tone**, sound, language, articulation, power of speech **3 = utterance**, expression, words, airing, vocalization, verbalization **6 = opinion**, will, feeling, wish, desire **7 = say**, part, view, decision, vote, comment, input ▹*vb* **11 = express**, say, declare, air, raise, table, reveal, mention, mouth, assert, pronounce, utter, articulate, come out with *(informal)*, divulge, ventilate, enunciate, put into words, vocalize, give expression *or* utterance to

void *n* **1 = gap**, space, lack, want, hole, blank, emptiness **2 = emptiness**, space, vacuum, oblivion, blankness, nullity, vacuity ▹*adj* **3 = invalid**, null and void, inoperative, useless, ineffective, worthless, ineffectual, unenforceable, nonviable ▹*vb* **6 = invalidate**, nullify, cancel, withdraw, reverse, undo, repeal, quash, revoke, disallow, retract, repudiate, negate, rescind, annul, abrogate, countermand, render invalid, abnegate

volatile *adj* **1 = changeable**, shifting, variable, unsettled, unstable, explosive, unreliable, unsteady, inconstant **OPPOSITE:** stable **2 = temperamental**, erratic, mercurial, up and down *(informal)*, fickle, whimsical, giddy, flighty, over-emotional, inconstant

V

DICTIONARY

-lising, -lised to change from a solid or liquid to a vapour **volatilization** *or* **-lisation** *n*
vol-au-vent (voll-oh-von) *n* a very light puff pastry case with a savoury filling
WORD ORIGIN French, literally: flight in the wind
volcanic *adj* **1** of or relating to volcanoes: *volcanic ash* **2** displaying sudden violence or anger: *their boisterous and often volcanic behaviour*
volcano *n, pl* **-noes** *or* **-nos** **1** an opening in the earth's crust from which molten lava, ashes, dust, and gases are ejected from below the earth's surface **2** a mountain formed from volcanic material ejected from a vent
WORD ORIGIN Italian, from Latin *Volcanus* Vulcan, Roman god of fire
vole *n* a small rodent with a stocky body and a short tail
WORD ORIGIN short for *volemouse*, from Old Norse *vollr* field + *mus* mouse
volition *n* **1** the ability to decide things for oneself **2 of one's own volition** through one's own choice **volitional** *adj*
WORD ORIGIN Latin *volo* I will
volley ❶ *n* **1** the simultaneous firing of several weapons **2** the bullets fired **3** a burst of questions or critical comments **4** *sport* a stroke or kick at a moving ball before it hits the ground ▷ *vb* **5** to fire (weapons) in a volley **6** *sport* to hit or kick (a moving ball) before it hits the ground
WORD ORIGIN French *volée* a flight
volleyball *n* a game in which two teams hit a large ball backwards and forwards over a high net with their hands
volt *n* the SI unit of electric potential; the potential difference between two points on a conductor carrying a current of 1 ampere, when the power dissipated between these points is 1 watt
WORD ORIGIN after Count Alessandro *Volta*, physicist
voltage *n* an electromotive force or potential difference expressed in volts
voltaic *adj* ▸ same as **galvanic** (sense 1)
volte-face (volt-fass) *n, pl* **volte-face** a reversal of opinion
WORD ORIGIN Italian *volta* turn + *faccia* face
voltmeter *n* an instrument for measuring voltage
voluble *adj* talking easily and at length **volubility** *n* **volubly** *adv*
WORD ORIGIN Latin *volubilis* turning readily
volume ❶ *n* **1** the magnitude of the three-dimensional space enclosed within or occupied by something **2** an amount or total: *the volume of trade between the two countries; the volume of military traffic* **3** loudness of sound **4** the control on a radio etc. for adjusting the loudness of sound **5** a book: *a slim volume* **6** one of several books that make up a series **7** a set of issues of a magazine over a specified period
WORD ORIGIN Latin *volumen* a roll
volumetric *adj* of or using measurement by volume: *a simple volumetric measurement*
voluminous *adj* **1** (of clothes) large and roomy **2** (of writings) extensive and detailed
voluntary ❶ *adj* **1** done or undertaken by free choice: *voluntary repatriation* **2** done or maintained without payment: *voluntary work* **3** (of muscles) having their action controlled by the will ▷ *n, pl* **-taries** **4** *music* a composition, usually for organ, played at the beginning or end of a church service **voluntarily** *adv*
WORD ORIGIN Latin *voluntarius*
volunteer ❶ *n* **1** a person who offers voluntarily to do something **2** a person who freely undertakes military service ▷ *vb* **3** to offer (oneself or one's services) by choice and without being forced **4** to enlist voluntarily for military service **5** to give (information) willingly **6** to offer the services of (another person)
voluptuary *n, pl* **-aries** a person devoted to luxury and sensual pleasures
WORD ORIGIN Latin *voluptas* pleasure
voluptuous *adj* **1** (of a woman) sexually alluring because of the fullness of her figure **2** pleasing to the senses: *voluptuous yellow peaches* **voluptuously** *adv* **voluptuousness** *n*
volute *n* a spiral or twisting shape or object, such as a carved spiral scroll on an Ionic capital
WORD ORIGIN Latin *volvere* to roll up
vomit ❶ *vb* **-iting, -ited** **1** to eject (the contents of the stomach) through the mouth **2** to eject or be ejected forcefully ▷ *n* **3** the partly digested food and drink ejected in vomiting
WORD ORIGIN Latin *vomitare* to vomit repeatedly
Vondel *n* **Joost van den** 1587–1679, Dutch poet and dramatist, author of the Biblical plays *Lucifer* (1654), *Adam in Exile* (1664), and *Noah* (1667)
von Laue *n* See **Laue**
Vonnegut *n* **Kurt** 1922–2007, US novelist. His works include *Cat's Cradle* (1963), *Slaughterhouse Five* (1969), *Galapagos* (1985), *Hocus Pocus* (1990), and *Timequake* (1997)
von Neumann *n* **John** 1903–57, US mathematician, born in Hungary. He formulated game theory and contributed to the development of the atomic bomb and to the development of the stored-program computer (**von Neumann machine**)
von Rundstedt *n* See **Rundstedt**
von Sternberg *n* **Joseph**, real name *Jonas Sternberg*. 1894–1969, US film director, born in Austria, whose films include *The Blue Angel* (1930), *Blonde Venus* (1932), *The Scarlet Empress* (1934), and the unfinished *I, Claudius* (1937)
von Stroheim *n* **Erich**, real name *Hans Erich Maria Stroheim von Nordenwall*. 1885–1957, US film director and actor, born in Austria, whose films include *Foolish Wives* (1921) and *Greed* (1923)
voodoo *n* **1** a religion involving ancestor worship and witchcraft, practised by Black people in the West

THESAURUS

OPPOSITE: calm
volley *n* **1 = barrage**, blast, burst, explosion, shower, hail, discharge, bombardment, salvo, fusillade, cannonade
volume *n* **1 = capacity**, size, mass, extent, proportions, dimensions, bulk, measurements, magnitude, compass, largeness, cubic content **2 = amount**, quantity, level, body, total, measure, degree, mass, proportion, bulk, aggregate **3 = loudness**, sound, amplification **5, 6 = book**, work, title, opus, publication, manual, tome, treatise, almanac, compendium
voluntary *adj* **1a = intentional**, intended, deliberate, planned, studied, purposed, calculated, wilful, done on purpose
OPPOSITE: unintentional
1b = optional, discretionary, up to the individual, open, unforced, unconstrained, unenforced, at your discretion, discretional, open to choice, uncompelled
OPPOSITE: obligatory
2 = unpaid, volunteer, free, willing, honorary, gratuitous, pro bono *(law)*
volunteer *vb* **3 = offer**, step forward, offer your services, propose, let yourself in for *(informal)*, need no invitation, present your services, proffer your services, put yourself at someone's disposal
OPPOSITE: refuse
vomit *vb* **1a = be sick**, throw up *(informal)*, spew, chuck *(Austral & NZ informal)*, heave *(slang)*, puke *(slang)*, retch, barf *(US slang)*, chunder *(slang, chiefly Austral)*, belch forth, upchuck *(US slang)*, do a technicolour yawn, toss your cookies *(US slang)* **1b** *(often with* **up***)* **= bring up**, throw up, regurgitate, chuck (up) *(slang, chiefly US)*, emit *(informal)*, eject, puke *(slang)*, disgorge, sick up *(informal)*, spew out *or* up

DICTIONARY

Indies, esp. in Haiti ▷ *adj* **2** of or relating to voodoo: *a voodoo curse*
WORD ORIGIN from West African

voorkamer (foor-kahm-er) *n S African* the front room of a house
WORD ORIGIN Afrikaans

voracious *adj* **1** eating or craving great quantities of food **2** very eager or insatiable in some activity: *a voracious collector* **voraciously** *adv* **voracity** *n*
WORD ORIGIN Latin *vorare* to devour

Voroshilov *n* **Kliment Yefremovich** 1881–1969, Soviet military leader; president of the Soviet Union (1953–60)

vortex (vor-tex) *n, pl* **-tices** (-tiss-seez) **1** a whirling mass or motion, such as a whirlpool or whirlwind **2** a situation which draws people into it against their will: *the vortex of other people's problems* **vortical** *adj*
WORD ORIGIN Latin: a whirlpool

votary *n, pl* **-ries 1** *RC church, Eastern Churches* a person who has dedicated himself or herself to religion by taking vows **2** a person devoted to a cause **votaress** *fem n*
WORD ORIGIN Latin *votum* a vow

vote ❶ *n* **1** a choice made by a participant in a shared decision, esp. in electing a candidate **2** the right to vote **3** the total number of votes cast **4** the opinion of a group of people as determined by voting: *the draft should be put to the vote at a meeting of the Council* **5** a body of votes or voters collectively: *the youth vote* ▷ *vb* **voting, voted 6** to make a choice by vote **7** to authorize or allow by voting: *the organizing committee voted itself controversial new powers* **8** to declare oneself as being (something or in favour of something) by voting: *I've always voted Labour* **9** *informal* to declare by common opinion: *he was voted hotelier of the year for the third time*
WORD ORIGIN Latin *votum* a solemn promise

vote down *vb* to decide against or defeat in a vote: *a proposed British resolution was voted down*

voter *n* a person who can or does vote

votive *adj* done or given to fulfil a vow
WORD ORIGIN Latin *votivus* promised by a vow

V

vouch *vb* **vouch for a** to give personal assurance about: *I can vouch for the man, he's a relative by marriage* **b** to give supporting evidence for or be proof of: *his presence alone vouches for the political nature of the trip*
WORD ORIGIN Latin *vocare* to call

voucher ❶ *n* **1** a ticket or card used instead of money to buy specified goods: *a gift voucher* **2** a document recording a financial transaction
WORD ORIGIN Old French *vo(u)cher* to summon

vouchsafe *vb* **-safing, -safed 1** *old-fashioned* to give or grant: *she has powers vouchsafed to few* **2** to offer assurances about; guarantee: *he absolutely vouchsafed your integrity*
WORD ORIGIN *vouch* + *safe*

vow ❶ *n* **1** a solemn and binding promise **2 take vows** to enter a religious order and commit oneself to its rule of life by the vows of poverty, chastity, and obedience ▷ *vb* **3** to promise or decide solemnly: *she vowed to fight on; I solemnly vowed that some day I would return to live in Europe*
WORD ORIGIN Latin *votum*

vowel *n* **a** a voiced speech sound made with the mouth open and the stream of breath unobstructed by the tongue, teeth, or lips, for example *a* or *e* **b** a letter representing this
WORD ORIGIN Latin *vocalis (littera)*, from *vox* voice

vox pop *n Brit* interviews with members of the public on a radio or television programme

vox populi *n* public opinion
WORD ORIGIN Latin: the voice of the people

voyage ❶ *n* **1** a long journey by sea or in space ▷ *vb* **-aging, -aged 2** to go on a voyage: *in this story he voyages to Ireland* **voyager** *n*
WORD ORIGIN Latin *viaticum* provision for travelling

voyageur (voy-ahzh-ur) *n* **1** formerly a French or Métis canoeman who transported furs from trading posts in the North American interior **2** (in Canada) a woodsman, guide, trapper, boatman, or explorer, esp. in the North
WORD ORIGIN French: voyager

voyeur *n* a person who obtains sexual pleasure from watching people undressing or having sexual intercourse **voyeurism** *n* **voyeuristic** *adj*
WORD ORIGIN French, literally: one who sees

Voysey *n* **Charles** (**Francis Annesley**) 1857–1941, British architect and designer of furniture, fittings, and decor

Voznesensky *n* **Andrei** (**Andreievich**) born 1933, Russian poet, noted for his experimental style

VPL *jocular* visible panty line

VPN virtual private network: a network that uses the internet to transfer information using secure methods

VR virtual reality

Vries *n* See **De Vries**

vrou (froh) *n S African* an Afrikaner woman, esp. a married woman
WORD ORIGIN Afrikaans

vs versus

VSA (in New Zealand) Voluntary Service Abroad

V-sign *n* **1** (in Britain and Australia) an offensive gesture made by sticking up the index and middle fingers with the palm of the hand inwards **2** a similar gesture with the palm outwards meaning victory or peace

VSO (in Britain) Voluntary Service Overseas

VSOP very special (*or* superior) old pale: used of brandy or port

VT Vermont

VTOL vertical takeoff and landing

VTR video tape recorder

Vuillard *n* **Jean Édouard** 1868–1940, French painter and lithographer

Vulcan *n* the Roman god of fire

vulcanite *n* a hard black rubber produced by vulcanizing natural rubber with sulphur

vulcanize *or* **-ise** *vb* **-izing, -ized** *or* **-ising, -ised** to treat (rubber) with sulphur under heat and pressure to improve elasticity and strength **vulcanization** *or* **-isation** *n*
WORD ORIGIN after *Vulcan*, Roman god of fire

vulgar ❶ *adj* **1** showing lack of good taste, decency, or refinement: *vulgar tabloid sensationalism* **2** denoting a form of a language spoken by the ordinary people, rather than the literary form **vulgarly** *adv*
WORD ORIGIN Latin *vulgus* the common people

vulgar fraction *n* ▸ same as **simple fraction**

vulgarian *n* a vulgar person, usually one who is rich

vulgarism *n* a coarse or obscene

THESAURUS

vote *n* **1 = poll**, election, ballot, referendum, popular vote, plebiscite, straw poll, show of hands ▷ *vb* **6 = cast your vote**, go to the polls, mark your ballot paper

voucher *n* **1 = ticket**, token, coupon, pass, slip, chit, chitty (*Brit informal*), docket

vow *n* **1 = promise**, commitment, pledge, oath, profession, troth (*archaic*), avowal ▷ *vb* **3 = promise**, pledge, swear, commit, engage, affirm, avow, bind yourself, undertake solemnly

voyage *n* **1 = journey**, travels, trip, passage, expedition, crossing, sail, cruise, excursion ▷ *vb* **2 = travel**, journey, tour, cruise, steam, take a trip, go on an expedition

vulgar *adj* **1a = tasteless**, common, flashy, low, gross, nasty, gaudy, tawdry, cheap and nasty, common as muck **OPPOSITE:** tasteful **1b = crude**, dirty, rude, low, blue, nasty, naughty, coarse, indecent, improper, suggestive, tasteless, risqué, off colour, ribald, indelicate,

DICTIONARY

word or phrase
vulgarity *n, pl* **-ties 1** the condition of being vulgar **2** a vulgar action or phrase
vulgarize *or* **-ise** *vb* **-izing, -ized** *or* **-ising, -ised 1** to make vulgar **2** to make (something little known or difficult to understand) popular **vulgarization** *or* **-isation** *n*
Vulgar Latin *n* any of the dialects of Latin spoken in the Roman Empire other than classical Latin
Vulgate *n* the fourth-century Latin version of the Bible
vulnerable ⓣ *adj* **1** able to be physically or emotionally hurt **2** easily influenced or tempted **3** *mil* exposed to attack **4** financially weak and likely to fail: *this company could be vulnerable in a prolonged economic slump* **5** *bridge* (of a side that has won one game towards rubber) subject to increased bonuses or penalties **vulnerability** *n*
WORD ORIGIN Latin *vulnus* a wound
vulpine *adj* **1** of or like a fox **2** clever and cunning
WORD ORIGIN Latin *vulpes* fox
vulture *n* **1** a very large bird of prey that feeds on flesh of dead animals **2** a person who profits from the misfortune and weakness of others
WORD ORIGIN Latin *vultur*
vulva *n* the external genitals of human females
WORD ORIGIN Latin: covering, womb, matrix
vuvuzela *n S African* an elongated plastic instrument that football fans blow to make a loud trumpeting noise
WORD ORIGIN from Zulu
vying *vb* ▸ the present participle of **vie**
Vyshinsky *or* **Vishinsky** *n* **Andrei Yanuaryevich** 1883–1954, Soviet jurist, statesman, and diplomat; foreign minister (1949–53). He was public prosecutor (1935–38) at the trials held to purge Stalin's rivals and was the Soviet representative at the United Nations (1945–49; 1953–54)

THESAURUS

indecorous **1c = uncouth**, boorish, unrefined, impolite, ill-bred, unmannerly **OPPOSITE:** refined
vulnerable *adj* **1 = susceptible**, helpless, unprotected, defenceless, exposed, weak, sensitive, tender, unguarded, thin-skinned **OPPOSITE:** immune
3 (*military*) **= exposed**, open, unprotected, defenceless, accessible, wide open, open to attack, assailable **OPPOSITE:** well-protected

V

Ww

w *cricket* **a** wicket **b** wide

W **1** *chem* tungsten
WORD ORIGIN German *Wolfram*
2 watt **3** West(ern)

WA **1** Washington (state) **2** Western Australia

Wace *n* **Robert** born ?1100, Anglo-Norman poet; author of the *Roman de Brut* and *Roman de Rou*

wacko *chiefly US & Canad informal adj* **1** mad or eccentric ▷ *n, pl* **wackos** **2** a mad or eccentric person
WORD ORIGIN from WACKY

wacky *adj* **wackier, wackiest** *slang* odd, eccentric, or crazy: *a wacky idea*
wackiness *n*
WORD ORIGIN dialect: a fool

wad *n* **1** a small mass of soft material, such as cotton wool, used for packing or stuffing **2** a roll or bundle of banknotes or papers
WORD ORIGIN Late Latin *wadda*

wadding *n* a soft material used for padding or stuffing

Waddington *n* **C(onrad) H(all)** 1905–75, British embryologist and geneticist: author of *Principles of Embryology* (1956) and *The Ethical Animal* (1960)

waddle ⓣ *vb* **-dling, -dled** **1** to walk with short steps, rocking slightly from side to side ▷ *n* **2** a swaying walk
WORD ORIGIN from *wade*

waddy *n, pl* **-dies** a heavy wooden club used by Australian Aborigines

wade ⓣ *vb* **wading, waded** **1** to walk slowly and with difficulty through water or mud **2** **wade in** *or* **into** to begin doing (something) in an energetic way: *wading into the fray* **3** **wade through** to proceed with difficulty through: *a stack of literature to wade through*
WORD ORIGIN Old English *wadan*

Wade *n* **(Sarah) Virginia** born 1945, British tennis player: Wimbledon champion 1977

wader *n* a long-legged bird, such as the heron or stork, that lives near water and feeds on fish. Also called: **wading bird**

waders *pl n* long waterproof boots which completely cover the legs, worn by anglers for standing in water

wadi (wod-dee) *n, pl* **-dies** a river in N Africa or Arabia, which is dry except in the rainy season
WORD ORIGIN Arabic

wafer *n* **1** a thin crisp sweetened biscuit, often served with ice cream **2** *Christianity* a round thin piece of unleavened bread used at Communion **3** *electronics* a small thin slice of germanium or silicon that is separated into numerous individual components or circuits
WORD ORIGIN Old French *waufre*

wafer-thin *adj* very thin: *wafer-thin meat*

waffle[1] *n* a square crisp pancake with a gridlike pattern
WORD ORIGIN Dutch *wafel*

waffle[2] *informal chiefly Brit, Austral & NZ vb* **-fling, -fled** **1** to speak or write in a vague and wordy manner ▷ *n* **2** vague and wordy speech or writing
WORD ORIGIN origin unknown

waft *vb* **1** to move gently through the air as if being carried by the wind: *the scent of summer flowers gently wafting through my window* ▷ *n* **2** a scent carried on the air
WORD ORIGIN Middle Dutch *wachter* guard

wag[1] ⓣ *vb* **wagging, wagged** **1** to move rapidly and repeatedly from side to side or up and down: *Franklin wagged his tail* ▷ *n* **2** an instance of wagging
WORD ORIGIN Old English *wagian*

wag[2] *n old-fashioned* a humorous or witty person **waggish** *adj*
WORD ORIGIN origin unknown

Wag *n informal* the wife or girlfriend of a famous sportsperson

wage ⓣ *n* **1** Also: **wages** the money paid in return for a person's work, esp. when paid weekly or daily rather than monthly: *a campaign for higher wages* ▷ *vb* **waging, waged** **2** to engage in (a campaign or war)
WORD ORIGIN Old French *wagier* to pledge

wager *n* **1** a bet on the outcome of an event or activity ▷ *vb* **2** to bet (something, esp. money) on the outcome of an event or activity
WORD ORIGIN Old French *wagier* to pledge

waggle *vb* **-gling, -gled** to move with a rapid shaking or wobbling motion
WORD ORIGIN from WAG[1]

Wagner-Jauregg *n* **Julius** 1857–1940, Austrian psychiatrist and neurologist; a pioneer of the use of fever therapy in the treatment of mental disorders. Nobel prize for physiology or medicine 1927

wagon *or* **waggon** *n* **1** a four-wheeled vehicle used for carrying heavy loads, sometimes pulled by a horse or tractor **2** an open railway freight truck **3** a lorry **4** **on the wagon** *informal* abstaining from alcoholic drink **wagoner** *or* **waggoner** *n*
WORD ORIGIN Dutch *wagen*

wagtail *n* a small songbird of Eurasia and Africa with a very long tail that wags up and down when it walks

Wagyu (wag-yoo) *n* **1** any of several Japanese breeds of beef cattle, raised to produce Kobe beef **2** ▶ another name for **Kobe beef**

wahine (wah-hee-nay) *n NZ* a Māori woman, esp. a wife
WORD ORIGIN Māori

wahoo *n* a large food and game fish of tropical seas

waif *n* a person, esp. a child, who is, or who looks as if he or she might be, homeless or neglected
WORD ORIGIN Anglo-Norman

wail ⓣ *vb* **1** to utter a prolonged high-pitched cry of pain or sorrow ▷ *n* **2** a prolonged high-pitched cry of pain or sorrow **wailing** *n, adj*
WORD ORIGIN from Old Norse

wain *n poetic* a farm cart
WORD ORIGIN Old English *wægn*

Wain *n* **John (Barrington)** 1925–94, British novelist, poet, and critic. His novels include *Hurry on Down* (1953), *Strike the Father Dead* (1962), and *Young Shoulders* (1982)

wainscot *n* a wooden covering on the lower half of the walls of a room. Also: **wainscoting**
WORD ORIGIN Middle Low German *wagenschot*

Wainwright *n* **1** **Loudon** born 1946, US rock singer and songwriter. His albums include *Loudon Wainwright III* (1970), *Fame and Wealth* (1983), *Grown Man* (1995) and *Strange Weirdos* (2007) **2** his daughter, **Martha** born 1976, US rock singer and songwriter. Her

THESAURUS

waddle *vb* **1 = shuffle**, shamble, totter, toddle, rock, stagger, sway, wobble

wade *vb* **1a = paddle**, splash, splash about, slop **1b = walk through**, cross, ford, pass through, go across, travel across, make your way across

wag[1] *vb* **1a = wave**, shake, swing, waggle, stir, sway, flutter, waver, quiver, vibrate, wiggle, oscillate **1b = waggle**, wave, shake, flourish, brandish, wobble, wiggle **1c = shake**, bob, nod ▷ *n* **2a = wave**, shake, swing, toss, sway, flutter, waver, quiver, vibration, wiggle, oscillation, waggle **2b = nod**, bob, shake

wage *n* **1** *(often plural)* **= payment**, pay, earnings, remuneration, fee, reward, compensation, income, allowance, recompense, stipend, emolument ▷ *vb* **2 = engage in**, conduct, pursue, carry on, undertake, practise, prosecute, proceed with

wail *vb* **1 = cry**, weep, grieve, lament, keen, greet *(Scot archaic)*, howl, whine, deplore, bemoan, bawl, bewail, yowl, ululate ▷ *n* **2 = cry**, moan, sob, howl, keening, lament,

DICTIONARY

recordings include the album *Martha Wainwright* (2005) **3** his son, **Rufus** born 1973, US rock singer and songwriter. His albums include *Want One* (2003), *Want Two* (2004) and *Release the Stars* (2007)

waist *n* **1** *anat* the narrow part of the body between the ribs and the hips **2** the part of a garment covering the waist
WORD ORIGIN origin unknown

waistband *n* a band of material sewn on to the waist of a garment to strengthen it

waistcoat *n* a sleeveless upper garment which buttons up the front and is usually worn by men over a shirt and under a jacket

waistline *n* **1** an imaginary line around the body at the narrowest part of the waist **2** the place where the upper and lower part of a garment are joined together

wait ⊕ *vb* **1** to stay in one place or remain inactive in expectation of something: *the delegates have to wait for a reply* **2** to be temporarily delayed: *the celebrations can wait* **3** (of a thing) to be ready or be in store: *waiting for her on the library table was the latest Jilly Cooper novel* ▷*n* **4** the act or a period of waiting **5 lie in wait for a** to prepare an ambush for **b** to be ready or be in store for ▸See also **wait on, wait up**
WORD ORIGIN Old French *waitier*

Waitangi Day *n* February 6, the national day of New Zealand commemorating the Treaty Of Waitangi in 1840

Waite *n* **Terry,** full name *Terence Hardy Waite.* born 1939, British special envoy to the Archbishop of Canterbury, who negotiated the release of Western hostages held in the Middle East before being taken hostage himself (1987–91) in Lebanon

waiter ⊕ *n* a man who serves people with food and drink in a restaurant

waiting game *n* **play a waiting game** to postpone taking action or making a decision in order to gain an advantage

waiting list *n* a list of people waiting for something that is not immediately available: *a long waiting list for heart surgery*

waiting room *n* a room in which people can wait, for example at a railway station or doctor's surgery

wait on *vb* **1** to serve (people) with food and drink in a restaurant **2** to look after the needs of: *they were waited on by a manservant* ▷*interj* **3** NZ stop! hold on!. Also (for senses 1, 2): **wait upon**

waitress ⊕ *n* **1** a woman who serves people with food and drink in a restaurant ▷*vb* **2** to work as a waitress

wait up *vb* to delay going to bed in order to wait for someone or something: *when he's late, she waits up for him*

Waitz *n* **Greta** born 1953, Norwegian long-distance runner and former marathon world champion

waive ⊕ *vb* **waiving, waived** to refrain from enforcing or claiming (a rule or right)
WORD ORIGIN Old French *weyver*

waiver *n* the act or an instance of voluntarily giving up a claim or right

Wajda *n* **Andrei** or **Andrzej** born 1926, Polish film director. His films include *Ashes and Diamonds* (1958), *The Wedding* (1972), *Man of Iron* (1980), *Danton* (1982), and *Miss Nobody* (1997)

waka *n* NZ a Māori canoe

wake[1] ⊕ *vb* **waking, woke, woken** **1** Also: **wake up** to become conscious again or bring (someone) to consciousness again after a sleep **2 wake up** to make (someone) more alert after a period of inactivity **3 wake up to** to become aware of: *the world did not wake up to this tragedy until many people had died* **4 waking hours** the time when a person is awake: *he often used his waking hours to write music* ▷*n* **5** a watch or vigil held over the body of a dead person during the night before burial
WORD ORIGIN Old English *wacian*

wake[2] ⊕ *n* **1** the track left by a ship moving through water **2 in the wake of** following soon after: *the arrests come in the wake of the assassination*
WORD ORIGIN Scandinavian

wakeful *adj* **1** unable to sleep **2** without sleep: *wakeful nights* **3** alert: *wakeful readiness* **wakefulness** *n*

waken *vb* to become conscious again or bring (someone) to consciousness again after a sleep

Waksman *n* **Selman Abraham** 1888–1973, US microbiologist, born in Russia. He discovered streptomycin: Nobel prize for physiology or medicine 1952

Walcott *n* **1 Derek** (**Alton**) born 1930, St Lucian poet and playwright, whose works include the poetry collections *In a Green Night* (1962) and *The Bounty* (1997), the play *The Dream on Monkey Mountain* (1967), and the long poem *Omeros* (1990): Nobel prize for literature 1992 **2 Jersey Joe,** real name *Arnold Raymond Cream.* 1914–94, US boxer: world heavyweight champion 1951–52

Waldemar I *or* **Valdemar I** *n* known as *Waldemar the Great.* 1131–82, king of Denmark (1157–82). He conquered the Wends (1169), increased the territory of Denmark, and established the hereditary rule of his line

Waldemar II *or* **Valdemar II** *n* known as *Waldemar the Victorious.* 1170–1241, king of Denmark (1202–41); son of Waldemar I. He extended the Danish empire, conquering much of Estonia (1219)

Waldemar IV *or* **Valdemar IV** *n* surnamed *Atterdag.* ?1320–75, king of Denmark (1340–75), who reunited the Danish territories but was defeated (1368) by a coalition of his Baltic neighbours

Waldheim *n* **Kurt** 1918–2007, Austrian diplomat; secretary-general of the United Nations (1972–81); president of Austria (1986–92)

Waldstein *n* a variant of (Albrecht Wenzel Eusebius von) **Wallenstein**

Waley *n* **Arthur** real name *Arthur Schloss.* 1889–1966, English orientalist, best known for his translations of Chinese poetry

THESAURUS

bawl, lamentation, yowl, ululation

wait *vb* **1a = stay**, remain, stop, pause, rest, delay, linger, hover, hang around *(informal)*, dally, loiter, tarry
OPPOSITE: go
1b = stand by, delay, hold on *(informal)*, hold back, wait in the wings, mark time, hang fire, bide your time, kick your heels, cool your heels **2 = be postponed**, be suspended, be delayed, be put off, be put back, be deferred, be put on hold *(informal)*, be shelved, be tabled, be held over, be put on ice *(informal)*, be put on the back burner *(informal)* ▷*n* **4 = delay**, gap, pause, interval, stay, rest, halt, hold-up, lull, stoppage, hindrance, hiatus, entr'acte

waiter *n* **= attendant**, server, flunkey, steward, servant

waitress *n* **1 = attendant**, server, stewardess, servant

waive *vb* **a = give up**, relinquish, renounce, forsake, drop, abandon, resign, yield, surrender, set aside, dispense with, cede, forgo
OPPOSITE: claim
b = disregard, ignore, discount, overlook, set aside, pass over, dispense with, brush aside, turn a blind eye to, forgo

wake[1] *vb* **1a** (also with **up**) **= awake**, stir, awaken, come to, arise, get up, rouse, get out of bed, waken, bestir, rouse from sleep, bestir yourself
OPPOSITE: fall asleep
1b = awaken, arouse, rouse, waken, rouse someone from sleep ▷*n* **5 = vigil**, watch, funeral, deathwatch, tangi (NZ)

wake[2] *n* **1 = slipstream**, wash, trail, backwash, train, track, waves, path **2 in the wake of = in the aftermath of**, following, because of, as a result of, on account of, as a consequence of

DICTIONARY

walk ❶ *vb* **1** to move on foot at a moderate rate with at least one foot always on the ground **2** to pass through, on, or over on foot: *to walk a short distance* **3** to walk somewhere with (a person or a dog) **4 walking on air** very happy and excited **5 walk the streets** to wander about, esp. when looking for work or when homeless ▷ *n* **6** a short journey on foot, usually for pleasure **7** the action of walking rather than running **8** a manner of walking: *a proud slow walk* **9** a place or route for walking **10 walk of life** social position or profession: *people from all walks of life were drawn to her* ▸ See also **walk into, walk out**, etc. **walker** *n*
WORD ORIGIN Old English *wealcan*

walkabout *n* **1** an occasion when royalty, politicians, or other celebrities walk among and meet the public **2 go walkabout** *Austral* **a** to wander through the bush as a nomad **b** *informal* to be lost or misplaced **c** *informal* to lose one's concentration

Walker *n* **1 Alice (Malsenior)** born 1944, US writer: her works include *In Love and Trouble: Stories of Black Women* (1973) and the novels *Meridian* (1976), *The Color Purple* (1982), and *Possessing the Secret of Joy* (1992) **2 John** born 1952, New Zealand middle-distance runner, the first athlete to run one hundred sub-four-minute miles

walkie-talkie *n* a small combined radio transmitter and receiver that can be carried around by one person

walking stick *n* a stick or cane carried in the hand to assist walking

walk into *vb* to encounter unexpectedly: *the troop reinforcements had walked into a trap*

Walkman *n trademark* a small portable cassette player with headphones

walk-on *adj* (of a part in a film or play) small and not involving speaking

walk out *vb* **1** to leave suddenly and without explanation, usually in anger **2** (of workers) to go on strike **3 walk out on** *informal* to abandon or desert ▷ *n* **walkout 4** a strike by workers

walkover *n* **1** *informal* an easy victory ▷ *vb* **walk over 2** to mistreat or bully; take advantage of: *if you don't make your mark early, people will walk all over you*

walkway *n* **1** a path designed for use by pedestrians **2** a passage or pathway between two buildings

wall ❶ *n* **1** a vertical structure made of stone, brick, or wood, with a length and height much greater than its thickness, used to enclose, divide, or support ▸ Related adjective: **mural 2** anything that suggests a wall in function or effect: *a wall of elm trees; a wall of suspicion* **3** *anat* any lining or membrane that encloses a bodily cavity or structure: *cell walls* **4 drive someone up the wall** *slang* to make someone angry or irritated **5 go to the wall** *informal* to be financially ruined **6 have one's back to the wall** *informal* to be in a very difficult situation, with no obvious way out of it ▷ *vb* **7** to surround or enclose (an area) with a wall **8 wall in** *or* **up** to enclose (someone or something) completely in a room or place **walled** *adj*
WORD ORIGIN Old English *weall*

wallaby *n, pl* **-bies** a marsupial of Australia and New Guinea that resembles a small kangaroo
WORD ORIGIN Aboriginal *wolabā*

wallah (**woll**-a) *n informal* a person involved with or in charge of a specified thing: *rickshaw wallahs*
WORD ORIGIN Hindi *-wālā*

wallaroo *n* a large stocky Australian kangaroo of rocky regions

wall bars *pl n* a series of horizontal bars attached to a wall and used in gymnastics

Wallenberg *n* **Raoul** 1912–?, Swedish diplomat, who helped (1944–45) thousands of Hungarian Jews to escape from the Nazis. After his arrest (1945) by the Soviets nothing is certainly known of him, despite claims that he is still alive he is presumed to have died in prison

Wallenstein *or* **Waldstein** *n* **Albrecht Wenzel Eusebius von**, duke of Friedland and Mecklenburg, prince of Sagan. 1583–1634, German general and statesman, born in Bohemia. As leader of the Hapsburg forces in the Thirty Years' War he won many successes until his defeat at Lützen (1632) by Gustavus Adolphus

Waller *n* **1 Edmund** 1606–87, English poet and politician, famous for his poem "Go, Lovely Rose" **2 Fats**, real name *Thomas Waller*. 1904–43, US jazz pianist and singer

wallet ❶ *n* a small folding case, usually of leather, for holding paper money and credit cards
WORD ORIGIN Germanic

walleye *n* a fish with large staring eyes

walleyed *adj* having eyes with an abnormal amount of white showing because of a squint
WORD ORIGIN Old Norse *vagleygr*

wallflower *n* **1** a plant grown for its clusters of yellow, orange, red, or purple fragrant flowers **2** *informal* a woman who does not join in the dancing at a party or dance because she has no partner

Wallis[1] *n* the German name for **Valais**

Wallis[2] *n* Sir **Barnes (Neville)** 1887–1979, English aeronautical engineer. He designed the airship R100, the Wellesley and Wellington bombers, and the bouncing bomb (1943), which was used to destroy the Ruhr dams during World War II

Walloon (wol-**loon**) *n* **1** a French-speaking person from S Belgium or the neighbouring part of France **2** the French dialect of Belgium ▷ *adj* **3** of the Walloons
WORD ORIGIN Germanic

wallop *informal vb* **1** to hit hard ▷ *n* **2** a hard blow
WORD ORIGIN Old French *waloper* to gallop

walloping *informal n* **1** a severe physical beating ▷ *adj* **2** large or great: *a walloping amount of sodium*

wallow *vb* **1** to indulge oneself in some emotion: *they wallow in self-pity* **2** to lie or roll about in mud or water for pleasure ▷ *n* **3** the act or an instance of wallowing **4** a muddy place where animals wallow
WORD ORIGIN Old English *wealwian* to roll (in mud)

wallpaper *n* **1** a printed or embossed paper for covering the walls of a room ▷ *vb* **2** to cover (walls) with wallpaper

THESAURUS

W

walk *vb* **1 = travel on foot**, go on foot, hoof it *(slang)*, foot it, go by shanks's pony *(informal)* **2 = stride**, wander, stroll, trudge, go, move, step, march, advance, pace, trek, hike, tread, ramble, tramp, promenade, amble, saunter, take a turn, traipse *(informal)*, toddle, make your way, mosey *(informal)*, plod on, perambulate, footslog **3 = escort**, take, see, show, partner, guide, conduct, accompany, shepherd, convoy, usher, chaperon ▷ *n* **6 = stroll**, hike, ramble, tramp, turn, march, constitutional, trek, outing, trudge, promenade, amble, saunter, traipse *(informal)*, breath of air, perambulation **8 = gait**, manner of walking, step, bearing, pace, stride, carriage, tread **9 = path**, pathway, footpath, track, way, road, lane, trail, avenue, pavement, alley, aisle, sidewalk *(chiefly US)*, walkway *(chiefly US)*, promenade, towpath, esplanade, footway, berm *(NZ)* **10 walk of life = area**, calling, business, line, course, trade, class, field, career, rank, employment, province, profession, occupation, arena, sphere, realm, domain, caste, vocation, line of work, métier

wall *n* **1 = partition**, divider, room divider, screen, panel, barrier, enclosure **2 = barrier**, obstacle, barricade, obstruction, check, bar, block, fence, impediment, hindrance

wallet *n* **= purse**, pocketbook, notecase, pouch, case, holder, moneybag

wall-to-wall *adj* (of carpeting) completely covering a floor

wally *n, pl* **-lies** *Brit slang* a stupid or foolish person
WORD ORIGIN from the name *Walter*

walnut *n* **1** an edible nut with a hard, wrinkled, light brown shell **2** a tree on which walnuts grow **3** the light brown wood of a walnut tree, used for making furniture
WORD ORIGIN Old English *walh-hnutu* foreign nut

walrus *n, pl* **-ruses** *or* **-rus** a mammal of cold northern seas, with two tusks that hang down from the upper jaw, tough thick skin, and coarse whiskers
WORD ORIGIN Dutch: whale horse

Walsh *n* **Courtney** (**Andrew**) born 1962, Jamaican cricketer; a fast bowler, he took 519 test match wickets

Walsingham[1] *n* a village in E England, in Norfolk: remains of a medieval priory; site of the shrine of Our Lady of Walsingham

Walsingham[2] *n* Sir **Francis** ?1530–90, English statesman. As secretary of state (1573–90) to Elizabeth I he developed a system of domestic and foreign espionage and uncovered several plots against the Queen

Walter *n* **1 Bruno**, real name *Bruno Walter Schlesinger.* 1876–1962, US conductor, born in Germany: famous for his performances of Haydn, Mozart, and Mahler **2 John** 1739–1812, English publisher; founded *The Daily Universal Register* (1785), which in 1788 became *The Times*

Walther von der Vogelweide *n* ?1170–?1230, German minnesinger, noted for his lyric verse on political and moral themes

waltz *n* **1** a ballroom dance in triple time in which couples spin round as they progress round the room **2** music for this dance ▷ *vb* **3** to dance a waltz **4** *informal* to move in a relaxed and confident way: *he waltzed over to her table to say hello*
WORD ORIGIN German *Walzer*

wampum (wom-pum) *n* (formerly) money used by Native Americans of N America, made of shells strung or woven together
WORD ORIGIN Native American *wampompeag*

wan (rhymes with **swan**) *adj* **wanner, wannest** very pale, as a result of illness or unhappiness **wanly** *adv*
WORD ORIGIN Old English *wann* dark

WAN *computers* wide area network

wand *n* **1** a rod used by a magician when performing a trick or by a fairy when casting a spell **2** a hand-held electronic device which is pointed at or passed over an item to read the data stored there
WORD ORIGIN Old Norse *vöndr*

wander ❶ *vb* **1** to walk about in a place without any definite purpose or destination **2** (often foll. by *off*) to leave a place where one is supposed to stay: *kids wander off* **3** (of the mind) to lose concentration ▷ *n* **4** the act or an instance of wandering **wanderer** *n* **wandering** *adj, n*
WORD ORIGIN Old English *wandrian*

wanderlust *n* a great desire to travel

wane ❶ *vb* **waning, waned 1** to decrease gradually in size, strength, or power: *the influence of the extremists is waning* **2** (of the moon) to show a gradually decreasing area of brightness from full moon until new moon ▷ *n* **3 on the wane** decreasing in size, strength, or power: *his fame was on the wane* **waning** *adj*
WORD ORIGIN Old English *wanian*

Wang An Shi *or* **Wang An-shih** *n* 1021–86, Chinese statesman and writer: remembered for his economic reforms, known as the New Policies (1069–76)

Wang Jing Wei *or* **Wang Ching-wei** *n* 1883–1944, Chinese politician. A leading revolutionary, he struggled (1927–32) with Chiang Kai-shek for control of the Kuomintang. During World War II he was head of a Japanese puppet government in Nanjing

wangle *vb* **-gling, -gled** *informal* to get (something) by cunning or devious methods: *I've wangled you both an invitation*
WORD ORIGIN origin unknown

wanigan (wonn-ig-an) *n Canad* **1** a watertight box or chest used by canoeists or lumberjacks to hold provisions **2** a sled or boat for carrying camping supplies
WORD ORIGIN from a Native American language

wank *taboo slang vb* **1** (of a man) to masturbate ▷ *n* **2** an instance of masturbating
WORD ORIGIN origin unknown

wanker *n taboo slang* a worthless or stupid person

wannabe *or* **wannabee** *adj* **1** wanting to be, or be like, a particular person or thing: *a wannabe actress* ▷ *n* **2** a person who wants to be, or be like, a particular person or thing

want ❶ *vb* **1** to feel a need or longing for: *I want a job* **2** to wish or desire (to do something): *we did not want to get involved* **3** *Brit, Austral & NZ* to have need of or require (doing or being something): *what will you do when it wants cleaning?* **4** *informal* should or ought (to do something): *the last person you want to hire is someone who is desperate for a job* **5 want for** to be lacking or deficient in: *they were convinced I was wealthy and wanted for nothing* ▷ *n* **6** something that is needed, desired, or lacked: *attempts to satisfy a number of wants* **7** a lack, shortage, or absence: *for want of opportunity* **8 in want of** needing or lacking: *the Chinese peasant farmer may be in want of a roof, a job, a doctor nearby*
WORD ORIGIN Old Norse *vanta* to be deficient

wanted *adj* being searched for by the police in connection with a crime that has been committed

wanting ❶ *adj* **1** lacking: *I would be wanting in charity if I did not explain the terms* **2** not meeting requirements or expectations: *she compares herself to her sister and finds herself wanting*

wanton *adj* **1** without motive,

THESAURUS

wander *vb* **1 = roam**, walk, drift, stroll, range, cruise, stray, ramble, prowl, meander, rove, straggle, traipse *(informal)*, mooch around *(slang)*, stravaig *(Scot & Northern English dialect)*, knock about *or* around, peregrinate ▷ *n* **4 = excursion**, turn, walk, stroll, cruise, ramble, meander, promenade, traipse *(informal)*, mosey *(informal)*, peregrination

wane *vb* **1 = decline**, flag, weaken, diminish, fall, fail, drop, sink, fade, decrease, dim, dwindle, wither, lessen, subside, ebb, wind down, die out, fade away, abate, draw to a close, atrophy, taper off **OPPOSITE:** grow **2 = diminish**, decrease, dwindle **OPPOSITE:** wax

want *vb* **1a = wish for**, desire, fancy, long for, crave, covet, hope for, yearn for, thirst for, hunger for, pine for, hanker after, set your heart on, feel a need for, have a yen for *(informal)*, have a fancy for, eat your heart out over, would give your eyeteeth for **OPPOSITE:** have **1b = desire**, fancy, long for, crave, wish for, yearn for, thirst for, hanker after, burn for **3 = need**, demand, require, call for, have need of, stand in need of **4 = should**, need, must, ought **5 = lack**, need, require, be short of, miss, be deficient in, be without, fall short in ▷ *n* **6 = wish**, will, need, demand, desire, requirement, fancy, yen *(informal)*, longing, hunger, necessity, appetite, craving, yearning, thirst, whim, hankering **7 = lack**, need, absence, shortage, deficiency, famine, default, shortfall, inadequacy, scarcity, dearth, paucity, shortness, insufficiency, non-existence, scantiness **OPPOSITE:** abundance

wanting *adj* **1 = lacking**, missing, absent, incomplete, needing, short, shy **OPPOSITE:** complete **2 = deficient**, poor, disappointing, inadequate, pathetic, inferior, insufficient, faulty, not good enough, defective, patchy, imperfect,

DICTIONARY

provocation, or justification: *sheer wanton destruction* **2** (of a person) maliciously and unnecessarily cruel **3** *old-fashioned* (of a woman) sexually unrestrained or immodest ▷*n* **4** *old-fashioned* a sexually unrestrained or immodest woman
WORD ORIGIN Middle English *wantowen* unruly

WAP *n* Wireless Application Protocol: a system that allows mobile phone users to access the internet and other information services

wapiti (wop-pit-tee) *n, pl* **-tis** a large North American deer, now also found in New Zealand
WORD ORIGIN from a Native American language

war ● *n* **1** open armed conflict between two or more countries or groups: *this international situation led to war* **2** a particular armed conflict: *the American war in Vietnam* **3** any conflict or contest: *a trade war* **4 have been in the wars** *informal* to look as if one has been in a fight ▷*adj* **5** relating to war or a war: *the war effort; a war correspondent* ▷*vb* **warring, warred** **6** to conduct a war **warring** *adj*
WORD ORIGIN Old Northern French *werre*

waratah *n* an Australian shrub with crimson flowers

Warbeck *n* **Perkin** ?1474–99, Flemish impostor, pretender to the English throne. Professing to be Richard, Duke of York, he led an unsuccessful rising against Henry VII (1497) and was later executed

warble *vb* **-bling, -bled** to sing in a high-pitched trilling voice
WORD ORIGIN Old French *werbler*

warbler *n* any of various small songbirds

Warburg *n* **Otto (Heinrich)** 1883–1970, German biochemist and physiologist: Nobel prize for physiology or medicine (1931) for his work on respiratory enzymes

war crime *n* a crime committed in wartime in violation of the accepted customs, such as ill-treatment of prisoners **war criminal** *n*

war cry *n* **1** a rallying cry used by combatants in battle **2** a slogan used to rally support for a cause

ward ● *n* **1** a room in a hospital for patients requiring similar kinds of care: *the maternity ward* **2** one of the districts into which a town, parish, or other area is divided for administration or elections **3** Also called: **ward of court** *law* a person, esp. a child whose parents are dead, who is placed under the control or protection of a guardian or of a court ▸See also **ward off** > **wardship** *n*
WORD ORIGIN Old English *weard* protector

-ward *suffix* **1** (*forming adjectives*) indicating direction towards: *a backward step* **2** (*forming adverbs*) *chiefly US & Canad* ▸same as **-wards**
WORD ORIGIN Old English *-weard*

warden ● *n* **1** a person who is in charge of a building, such as a youth hostel, and its occupants **2** a public official who is responsible for the enforcement of certain regulations: *a game warden* **3** *Brit* the chief officer in charge of a prison
WORD ORIGIN Old French *wardein*

warder *or fem* **wardress** *n* *chiefly Brit* a prison officer
WORD ORIGIN Old French *warder* to guard

ward off *vb* to prevent (something unpleasant) from happening or from causing harm: *to ward off the pangs of hunger; to ward off cancer cells*

wardrobe ● *n* **1** a tall cupboard, with a rail or hooks on which to hang clothes **2** the total collection of articles of clothing belonging to one person: *your autumn wardrobe* **3** the collection of costumes belonging to a theatre or theatrical company
WORD ORIGIN Old French *warder* to guard + *robe* robe

wardrobe mistress *n* the woman in charge of the costumes in a theatre or theatrical company **wardrobe master** *masc n*

wardroom *n* the quarters assigned to the officers of a warship, apart from the captain

-wards *or* **-ward** *suffix forming adverbs* indicating direction towards: *a step backwards*
WORD ORIGIN Old English *-weardes*

ware *n* articles of the same kind or material: *crystal ware.* ▸See also **wares**
WORD ORIGIN Old English *waru*

warehouse ● *n* a place where goods are stored prior to their sale or distribution

wares ● *pl n* goods for sale

warfare ● *n* **1** the act of conducting a war **2** a violent or intense conflict of any kind: *class warfare*

war game *n* **1** a tactical exercise for training military commanders, in which no military units are actually deployed **2** a game in which model soldiers are used to create battles in order to study tactics

warhead *n* the front section of a missile or projectile that contains explosives

warhorse *n* **1** (formerly) a horse used in battle **2** *informal* a veteran soldier or politician

warlike *adj* **1** of or relating to war: *warlike stores and equipment* **2** hostile and eager to have a war: *a warlike nation*

warlock *n* a man who practises black magic
WORD ORIGIN Old English *wǣrloga* oath breaker

Warlock *n* **Peter,** real name *Philip Arnold Heseltine* 1894–1930, British composer and scholar of early English music. His works include song cycles, such as *The Curlew* (1920–22), and the *Capriol Suite* (1926) for strings

warlord *n* a military leader of a nation or part of a nation

THESAURUS

sketchy, unsound, substandard, leaving much to be desired, not much cop (*Brit slang*), not up to par, not up to expectations, bodger *or* bodgie (*Austral slang*)
OPPOSITE: adequate

war *n* **1 = conflict**, drive, attack, fighting, fight, operation, battle, movement, push, struggle, clash, combat, offensive, hostilities, hostility, warfare, expedition, crusade, strife, bloodshed, jihad, enmity, armed conflict
OPPOSITE: peace
2, 3 = campaign, drive, attack, operation, movement, push, mission, offensive, crusade ▷*vb* **6 = fight**, battle, clash, wage war, campaign, struggle, combat, contend, go to war, do battle, make war, take up arms, bear arms, cross swords, conduct a war, engage in hostilities, carry on hostilities **OPPOSITE:** make peace

ward *n* **1 = room**, department, unit, quarter, division, section, apartment, cubicle **2 = district**, constituency, area, division, zone, parish, precinct **3 = dependant**, charge, pupil, minor, protégé

warden *n* **1 = steward**, guardian, administrator, superintendent, caretaker, curator, warder, custodian, watchman, janitor **2 = ranger**, keeper, guardian, protector, custodian, official **3** (*Brit*) **= governor**, head, leader, director, manager, chief, executive, boss (*informal*), commander, ruler, controller, overseer, baas (*S African*)

wardrobe *n* **1 = clothes cupboard**, cupboard, closet (*US*), clothes-press, cabinet **2 = clothes**, outfit, apparel, clobber (*Brit slang*), attire, collection of clothes

warehouse *n* **= store**, depot, storehouse, repository, depository, stockroom

wares *pl n* **= goods**, produce, stock, products, stuff, commodities, merchandise, lines

warfare *n* **1, 2 = war**, fighting, campaigning, battle, struggle, conflict, combat, hostilities, strife, bloodshed, jihad, armed struggle, discord, enmity, armed conflict, clash of arms, passage of arms
OPPOSITE: peace

DICTIONARY

warm ❶ *adj* **1** feeling or having a moderate degree of heat **2** giving heat: *warm clothing* **3** (of colours) predominantly red or yellow in tone **4** kindly or affectionate: *warm embraces* **5** *informal* near to finding a hidden object or guessing facts, for example in a children's game ▷*vb* **6** to make warm **7 warm to a** to become fonder of: *I warmed to him when he defended me* **b** to become more excited or enthusiastic about: *he had warmed to his theme* ▸ See also **warm up** > **warmly** *adv* **warmness** *n*
WORD ORIGIN Old English *wearm*

warm-blooded *adj* **1** (of an animal, such as a mammal or a bird) having a constant body temperature, usually higher than the surrounding temperature **2** having a passionate nature **warm-bloodedness** *n*

warm-down *n* light exercises performed to aid recovery from strenuous physical activity

war memorial *n* a monument to people who have died in a war, esp. local people

warm front *n meteorol* the boundary between a warm air mass and the cold air it is replacing

warm-hearted *adj* kind, affectionate, or sympathetic

warming pan *n* a long-handled pan filled with hot coals, formerly pulled over the sheets to warm a bed

warmonger *n* a person who encourages warlike ideas or advocates war **warmongering** *n*

warmth ❶ *n* **1** the state of being warm **2** affection or cordiality: *the warmth of their friendship*

warm up *vb* **1** to make or become warm or warmer **2** to prepare for a race, sporting contest, or exercise routine by doing gentle exercises immediately beforehand **3** (of an engine or machine) to be started and left running until the working temperature is reached **4** to become more lively: *wait until things warm up* **5** to reheat (food that has already been cooked) ▷*n* **warm-up 6** a preparatory exercise routine

warn ❶ *vb* **1** to make (someone) aware of a possible danger or problem **2** to inform (someone) in advance: *you'd better warn your girlfriend that you'll be working at the weekend* **3 warn off** to advise (someone) to go away or not to do something
WORD ORIGIN Old English *wearnian*

Warne *n* **Shane** (**Keith**) born 1969, Australian cricketer, played for Australia (1991–2007), taking 708 test wickets

warning ❶ *n* **1** a hint, threat, or advance notice of a possible danger or problem **2** advice not to do something ▷*adj* **3** giving or serving as a warning: *warning signs* **warningly** *adv*

warp ❶ *vb* **1** (esp. of wooden objects) to be twisted out of shape, for example by heat or damp **2** to distort or influence in a negative way: *love warps judgment* ▷*n* **3** a fault or an irregularity in the shape or surface of an object **4** a fault or deviation in someone's character **5** ▸ see **time warp 6** the yarns arranged lengthways on a loom through which the weft yarns are woven **warped** *adj*
WORD ORIGIN Old English *wearp* a throw

war paint *n* **1** paint applied to the face and body by certain North American Indians before battle **2** *informal* cosmetics

warpath *n* **on the warpath a** preparing to engage in battle **b** *informal* angry and looking for a fight or conflict

warrant ❶ *n* **1** an official authorization for some action or decision: *Scotland Yard today issued a warrant for the arrest of this man* **2** a document that certifies or guarantees something, such as a receipt or licence ▷*vb* **3** to make necessary: *we've no hard evidence to warrant a murder investigation*
WORD ORIGIN Old French *guarant*

warrant officer *n* an officer in certain armed services with a rank between those of commissioned and noncommissioned officers

Warrant of Fitness *n NZ* a six-monthly certificate required for a motor vehicle certifying that it is mechanically sound

warrantor *n* a person or company that provides a warranty

warranty ❶ *n, pl* **-ties** a guarantee or assurance that goods meet a specified standard or that the facts in a legal document are as stated
WORD ORIGIN Anglo-French *warantie*

warren *n* **1** a series of interconnected underground tunnels in which rabbits live **2** an overcrowded building or area of a city with many narrow passages or streets: *a mountainous concrete warren of apartments*
WORD ORIGIN Anglo-French *warenne*

Warren[1] *n* a city in the US, in SE Michigan, northeast of Detroit. Pop: 136 016 (2003 est)

Warren[2] *n* **Earl** 1891–1974, US lawyer; chief justice of the US (1953–69). He chaired the commission that investigated the murder of President Kennedy

warrigal *Austral n* **1** a dingo ▷*adj* **2** wild

THESAURUS

warm *adj* **1a = balmy**, mild, temperate, pleasant, fine, bright, sunny, agreeable, sultry, summery, moderately hot **OPPOSITE:** cool **1b = cosy**, snug, toasty *(informal)*, comfortable, homely, comfy *(informal)* **1c = moderately hot**, heated **OPPOSITE:** cool **2 = thermal**, winter, thick, chunky, woolly **OPPOSITE:** cool **3 = mellow**, relaxing, pleasant, agreeable, restful **4 = affable**, kindly, friendly, affectionate, loving, happy, tender, pleasant, cheerful, hearty, good-humoured, amiable, amicable, cordial, sociable, genial, congenial, hospitable, approachable, amorous, good-natured, likable *or* likeable **OPPOSITE:** unfriendly **5** *(informal)* **= near**, close, hot, near to the truth ▷*vb* **6 = warm up**, heat, thaw (out), heat up **OPPOSITE:** cool down

warmth *n* **1 = heat**, snugness, warmness, comfort, homeliness, hotness **OPPOSITE:** coolness **2 = affection**, feeling, love, goodwill, kindness, tenderness, friendliness, cheerfulness, amity, cordiality, affability, kindliness, heartiness, amorousness, hospitableness, fondness **OPPOSITE:** hostility

warn *vb* **1, 2 = notify**, tell, remind, inform, alert, tip off, give notice, make someone aware, forewarn, apprise, give fair warning

warning *n* **1a = notice**, notification, word, sign, threat, tip, signal, alarm, announcement, hint, alert, tip-off *(informal)*, heads up *(US & Canad)* **1b = omen**, sign, forecast, indication, token, prediction, prophecy, premonition, foreboding, portent, presage, augury, foretoken, rahui *(NZ)* **2 = caution**, information, advice, injunction, notification, caveat, word to the wise

warp *vb* **1a = distort**, bend, twist, buckle, deform, disfigure, contort, misshape, malform **1b = become distorted**, bend, twist, contort, become deformed, become misshapen **2 = pervert**, twist, corrupt, degrade, deprave, debase, desecrate, debauch, lead astray ▷*n* **3 = twist**, turn, bend, defect, flaw, distortion, deviation, quirk, imperfection, kink, contortion, deformation

warrant *n* **1 = authorization**, permit, licence, permission, security, authority, commission, sanction, pledge, warranty, carte blanche ▷*vb* **3 = call for**, demand, require, merit, rate, commission, earn, deserve, permit, sanction, excuse, justify, license, authorize, entail, necessitate, be worthy of, give ground for

warranty *n* **= guarantee**, promise, contract, bond, pledge, certificate, assurance, covenant

DICTIONARY

warrior ⊕ *n* a person who is engaged in or experienced in war
WORD ORIGIN Old French *werreieor*

warship *n* a ship designed for naval warfare

wart *n* **1** a firm abnormal growth on the skin caused by a virus **2 warts and all** including faults: *she loves him warts and all* **warty** *adj*
WORD ORIGIN Old English *weart(e)*

warthog *n* a wild African pig with heavy tusks, wartlike lumps on the face, and a mane of coarse hair

wartime *n* **1** a time of war ▹*adj* **2** of or in a time of war: *the wartime coalition*

Warton *n* **1 Joseph** 1722–1800, British poet and critic, noted for his poem *The Enthusiast* (1744) and his *Essay on the Writings and Genius of Pope* (1756) **2** his brother **Thomas** 1728–90, poet laureate (1785–90); author of the poem *The Pleasures of Melancholy* (1747) and the first *History of English Poetry* (1774–81)

wary ⊕ (ware-ree) *adj* **warier, wariest** cautious or on one's guard: *be wary of hitchhikers* **warily** *adv* **wariness** *n*
WORD ORIGIN Old English *wær* aware, careful

was *vb* (*with "I", "he", "she", "it", or a singular noun as subject*) ▸the past tense of **be**
WORD ORIGIN Old English *wæs*

wash ⊕ *vb* **1** to clean (oneself, part of one's body, or a thing) with soap or detergent and water **2** (of a garment or fabric) to be capable of being washed without damage or loss of colour **3** to move or be moved in a particular direction by water: *houses may be washed away in floods* **4** (of waves) to flow or sweep against or over (a surface or object), often with a lapping sound **5** *informal* to be acceptable or believable: *the masculine pride argument won't wash now when so many women go out to work* ▹*n* **6** the act or process of washing **7** all the clothes etc. to be washed together on one occasion **8** a thin layer of paint or ink: *a pale wash of blue* **9** the disturbance in the air or water produced at the rear of an aircraft, boat, or other moving object: *we were hit by the wash of a large vessel* **10 come out in the wash** *informal* to become known or apparent in the course of time ▸See also **wash down, wash out, wash up** > **washable** *adj*
WORD ORIGIN Old English *wæscan, waxan*

Wash. Washington (state)

washbasin *n* a small sink in a bathroom, used for washing the face and hands. Also: **wash-hand basin**

wash down *vb* **1** to have a drink with or after (food or medicine): *a large steak, washed down with coffee* **2** to wash from top to bottom: *she washed down the staircase*

washed out *adj* **1** exhausted and lacking in energy **2** faded or colourless

washed up *adj informal* no longer as successful or important as previously: *she stands discredited, her career probably washed up*

washer *n* **1** a flat ring of rubber, felt, or metal used to provide a seal under a nut or bolt or in a tap or valve **2** *informal* a washing machine **3** a person who washes things, esp. as a job: *chief cook and bottle washer* **4** *Austral* a small piece of towelling cloth used to wash the face

washerwoman *n, pl* **-women** a woman who washes clothes as a job

washing *n* all the clothes etc. to be washed together on one occasion

washing machine *n* a machine for washing clothes and bed linen in

washing soda *n* crystalline sodium carbonate, used as a cleansing agent

washing-up *n* the act of washing used dishes and cutlery after a meal

wash out *vb* **1** Also: **wash off** to remove or be removed by washing: *the rain washes the red dye out of the cap* **2** to wash the inside of (a container) ▹*n* **washout 3** *informal* a total failure or disaster **4** NZ a part of a road or railway washed away by floodwaters

washroom *n US & Canad* a toilet

washstand *n* a piece of furniture designed to hold a basin for washing the face and hands in

wash up *vb* **1** to wash used dishes and cutlery after a meal **2** *US & Canad* to wash one's face and hands

washy *adj* **washier, washiest** **1** overdiluted or weak **2** lacking intensity of colour: *a washy blend of pale brown and pale grey*

Wasim Akram *n* **Chaudhry** born 1966, Pakistani cricketer; captain of Pakistan 1993–94, 1995–2000

wasn't was not

wasp *n* a common stinging insect with a slender black-and-yellow striped body
WORD ORIGIN Old English *wæsp*

Wasp *or* **WASP** (in the US and Canada) White Anglo-Saxon Protestant: a person descended from N European, usually Protestant stock, forming a group often considered to be the most dominant and privileged in N American society

waspish *adj* bad-tempered or spiteful: *waspish comments*

wasp waist *n* a very narrow waist **wasp-waisted** *adj*

wassail *n* **1** (formerly) a toast drunk to a person during festivities **2** a festivity involving a lot of drinking **3** hot spiced beer or mulled wine drunk at such a festivity ▹*vb* **4 go wassailing** to go from house to house singing carols at Christmas
WORD ORIGIN Old Norse *ves heill* be in good health

wastage *n* **1** the act of wasting something or the state of being wasted: *wastage of raw materials* **2** reduction in the size of a workforce by retirement, redundancy, etc.

waste ⊕ *vb* **wasting, wasted** **1** to use up thoughtlessly, carelessly, or unsuccessfully **2** to fail to take advantage of: *let's not waste an opportunity to see the children* **3 be wasted on** to be too good for; not be

THESAURUS

warrior *n* **= soldier**, combatant, fighter, gladiator, champion, brave, trooper, military man, fighting man, man-at-arms

wary *adj* **a = suspicious**, sceptical, mistrustful, suspecting, guarded, apprehensive, cagey (*informal*), leery (*slang*), distrustful, on your guard, chary, heedful **b = watchful**, careful, alert, cautious, prudent, attentive, vigilant, circumspect, heedful
OPPOSITE: careless

wash *vb* **1a = clean**, scrub, sponge, rinse, scour, cleanse **1b = launder**, clean, wet, rinse, dry-clean, moisten **1c = rinse**, clean, scrub, lather **1d = bathe**, bath, shower, take a bath *or* shower, clean yourself, soak, sponge, douse, freshen up, lave (*archaic*), soap, scrub yourself down **5** (*informal*) (*used in negative constructions*)**= be plausible**, stand up, hold up, pass muster, hold water, stick, carry weight, be convincing, bear scrutiny ▹*n* **6a = laundering**, cleaning, clean, cleansing **6b = bathe**, bath, shower, dip, soak, scrub, shampoo, rinse, ablution **8 = coat**, film, covering, layer, screen, coating, stain, overlay, suffusion **9a = backwash**, slipstream, path, trail, train, track, waves, aftermath **9b = splash**, roll, flow, sweep, surge, swell, rise and fall, ebb and flow, undulation

waste *vb* **1, 2 = squander**, throw away, blow (*slang*), run through, lavish, misuse, dissipate, fritter away, frivol away (*informal*) **OPPOSITE:** save **4** (**foll. by away**) **= decline**, dwindle, wither, perish, sink, fade, crumble, decay, wane, ebb, wear out, atrophy ▹*n* **5 = squandering**, misuse, loss, expenditure, extravagance, frittering away, lost opportunity, dissipation, wastefulness, misapplication, prodigality, unthriftiness **OPPOSITE:** saving **7 = rubbish**, refuse, debris, sweepings, scrap, litter, garbage, trash, leftovers, offal, dross, dregs, leavings, offscourings **9** (*usually plural*) **= desert**, wilds, wilderness, void, solitude, wasteland

W

DICTIONARY

appreciated by: *fine brandy is wasted on you* **4 waste away** to lose one's strength or health: *wasting away from unrequited love* ▷ *n* **5** the act of wasting something or the state of being wasted: *a waste of time* **6** something that is left over because it is in excess of requirements **7** rubbish: *toxic waste* **8** *physiol* matter discharged from the body as faeces or urine **9 wastes** a region that is wild or uncultivated ▷ *adj* **10** rejected as being useless, unwanted, or worthless: *waste products* **11** not cultivated or productive: *waste ground* **12** *physiol* discharged from the body as faeces or urine: *waste matter* **13 lay waste** *or* **lay waste to** to devastate or destroy: *the Bikini atoll, laid waste by nuclear tests*
WORD ORIGIN Latin *vastare* to lay waste

wasted *adj* **1** unnecessary or unfruitful: *wasted effort* **2** pale, thin, and unhealthy: *the hunched shoulders and the wasted appearance of his body*

wasteful *adj* causing waste: *wasteful expenditure* **wastefully** *adv*

wasteland *n* **1** a barren or desolate area of land **2** something that is considered spiritually, intellectually, or aesthetically barren: *the TV wasteland*

wastepaper basket *n* a container for paper discarded after use

waster *n informal* a lazy or worthless person

wasting *adj* reducing the vitality and strength of the body: *a pernicious wasting illness*

wastrel *n literary* a lazy or worthless person

watap (wat-**tahp**) *n* a stringy thread made by Native Americans from the roots of conifers
WORD ORIGIN from a Native American language

watch ❶ *vb* **1** to look at or observe closely and attentively **2** to look after (a child or a pet) **3** to maintain a careful interest in or control over: *it reminds me to watch my diet* **4 watch for** to be keenly alert to or cautious about: *the vigilant night watchman hired to watch for thieves* **5 watch it!** be careful! ▷ *n* **6** a small portable timepiece worn strapped to the wrist or in a waistcoat pocket **7** the act or an instance of watching **8** *naut* any of the periods, usually of four hours, during which part of a ship's crew are on duty **9 keep a close watch on** to maintain a careful interest in or control over: *he keeps a close watch on party opinion* **10 keep watch** to be keenly alert to danger; keep guard **11 on the watch** on the lookout ▸ See also **watch out, watch over** > **watcher** *n*
WORD ORIGIN Old English *wæccan*

watchable *adj* interesting, enjoyable, or entertaining: *watchable films*

watchdog ❶ *n* **1** a dog kept to guard property **2** a person or group that acts as a guard against inefficiency or illegality

watchful *adj* **1** carefully observing everything that happens **2 under the watchful eye of** being closely observed by **watchfully** *adv* **watchfulness** *n*

watchmaker *n* a person who makes or mends watches and clocks

watchman *n, pl* **-men** a man employed to guard buildings or property

watch-night service *n* **a** (in Protestant churches) a service held on the night of December 24, to mark the arrival of Christmas Day **b** (in Protestant churches) a service held on the night of December 31, to mark the passing of the old year

watch out *vb* to be careful or on one's guard

watch over *vb* to look after or supervise: *her main ambition is still to watch over the family*

watchstrap *n* a strap attached to a watch for fastening it round the wrist. Also called (US and Canad): **watchband**

watchtower *n* a tower on which a sentry keeps watch

watchword *n* a slogan or motto: *quality, not quantity, is the watchword*

water ❶ *n* **1** a clear colourless tasteless liquid that is essential for plant and animal life, that falls as rain, and forms seas, rivers, and lakes ▸ Related adjectives: **aquatic, aqueous 2** (*often pl*) any area of this liquid, such as a sea, river, or lake **3** the surface of such an area of water: *four-fifths of an iceberg's mass lie below water* **4** the level of the tide: *at high water* **5** *physiol* **a** any fluid discharged from the body, such as sweat, urine, or tears **b** the fluid surrounding a fetus in the womb **6 hold water** (of an argument or idea) to be believable or reasonable **7 of the first water** of the highest quality or the most extreme degree: *he's a scoundrel of the first water* **8 pass water** to urinate **9 water under the bridge** events that are past and done with ▷ *vb* **10** to moisten or soak with water: *keep greenhouse plants well watered* **11** to give (an animal) water to drink **12** (of the eyes) to fill with tears: *our eyes were watering from the fumes* **13** (of the mouth) to fill with saliva in anticipation of food ▸ See also **water down** > **waterless** *adj*
WORD ORIGIN Old English *wæter*

water bed *n* a waterproof mattress filled with water

water biscuit *n* a thin crisp unsweetened biscuit, usually eaten with butter or cheese

water buffalo *n* a large black oxlike draught animal of S Asia, with long backward-curving horns

water cannon *n* a machine that pumps a jet of water through a nozzle at high pressure, used to disperse crowds

water chestnut *n* the edible tuber of a Chinese plant, used in Oriental cookery

water closet *n old-fashioned* a toilet. Abbrev: **WC**

watercolour *or US* **watercolor** *n* **1** a kind of paint that is applied with water rather than oil **2** a painting done in watercolours

water-cooled *adj* (of an engine) kept from overheating by a flow of water circulating in a casing

watercourse *n* the channel or bed of a river or stream

watercress *n* a plant that grows in ponds and streams, with strong-tasting leaves that are used in salads and as a garnish

water cycle *n geol* the circulation of the earth's water, in which water from the sea evaporates, forms

THESAURUS

▷ *adj* **10 = unwanted**, useless, worthless, unused, leftover, superfluous, unusable, supernumerary **OPPOSITE:** necessary **11 = uncultivated**, wild, bare, barren, empty, devastated, dismal, dreary, desolate, unproductive, uninhabited **OPPOSITE:** cultivated

watch *vb* **1a = look at**, observe, regard, eye, see, mark, view, note, check, clock (*Brit slang*), stare at, contemplate, check out (*informal*), look on, gaze at, pay attention to, eyeball (*slang*), peer at, leer at, get a load of (*informal*), feast your eyes on, take a butcher's at (*Brit informal*), take a dekko at (*Brit slang*) **1b = spy on**, follow, track, monitor, keep an eye on, stake out, keep tabs on (*informal*), keep watch on, keep under observation, keep under surveillance **2 = guard**, keep, mind, protect, tend, look after, shelter, take care of, safeguard, superintend ▷ *n* **6 = wristwatch**, timepiece, pocket watch, clock, chronometer **7 = guard**, eye, attention, supervision, surveillance, notice, observation, inspection, vigil, lookout, vigilance

watchdog *n* **1 = guard dog 2 = guardian**, monitor, inspector, protector, custodian, scrutineer

water *n* **1, 5b = liquid**, aqua, Adam's ale *or* wine, H_2O, wai (*NZ*) **2** (*often plural*) **= sea**, main, waves, ocean, depths, briny ▷ *vb* **10 = sprinkle**, spray, soak, irrigate, damp, hose, dampen, drench, douse, moisten, souse, fertigate (*Austral*) **12 = get wet**, cry, weep, become wet, exude water

W

DICTIONARY

clouds, falls as rain or snow, and returns to the sea by rivers
water diviner *n* a person who can locate the presence of water underground with a divining rod
water down *vb* **1** to weaken (a drink or food) with water **2** to make (a story, plan, or proposal) weaker and less controversial **watered-down** *adj*
waterfall ❶ *n* a cascade of falling water where there is a vertical or almost vertical step in a river
waterfowl *n, pl* **-fowl** a bird that swims on water, such as a duck or swan
waterfront *n* the area of a town or city next to an area of water, such as a harbour or dockyard
waterhole *n* a pond or pool in a desert or other dry area, used by animals as a drinking place
Waterhouse *n* **1 Alfred** 1830–1905, British architect; a leader of the Gothic Revival. His buildings include Manchester Town Hall (1868) and the Natural History Museum, London (1881) **2 George Marsden** 1824–1906, New Zealand statesman, born in England: prime minister of New Zealand (1872–73) **3 Keith** (**Spencer**) born 1929, British novelist, dramatist, and journalist: best known for the novel *Billy Liar* (1959) and his collaborations with the dramatist Willis Hall (1929–2005)
water ice *n* ice cream made from frozen fruit-flavoured syrup
watering can *n* a container with a handle and a spout with a perforated nozzle, used to sprinkle water over plants
watering hole *n facetious slang* a pub
watering place *n* **1** a place where people or animals can find drinking water **2** *Brit* a spa or seaside resort
water jump *n* a ditch or brook over which athletes or horses must jump in a steeplechase
water level *n* **1** the level reached by the surface of an area of water **2** ▸ same as **water line**
water lily *n* a plant with large leaves and showy flowers that float on the surface of an area of water
water line *n* the level to which a ship's hull will be immersed when afloat
waterlogged *adj* **1** saturated with water: *waterlogged meadows* **2** (of a boat) having taken in so much water as to be likely to sink
water main *n* a principal supply pipe in an arrangement of pipes for distributing water to houses and other buildings
watermark *n* **1** a mark impressed on paper during manufacture, visible when the paper is held up to the light **2** a line marking the level reached by an area of water
water meadow *n* a meadow that remains fertile by being periodically flooded by a stream
watermelon *n* a large round melon with a hard green rind and sweet watery reddish flesh
water pistol *n* a toy pistol that squirts a stream of water
water polo *n* a game played in water by two teams of seven swimmers in which each side tries to throw a ball into the opponents' goal
water power *n* the power of flowing or falling water to drive machinery or generate electricity
waterproof *adj* **1** not allowing water to pass through: *waterproof trousers* ▹ *n* **2** *chiefly Brit* a waterproof garment, such as a raincoat ▹ *vb* **3** to make waterproof: *the bridge is having its deck waterproofed*
water rat *n* ▸ same as **water vole**
water rate *n* a charge made for the public supply of water
water-resistant *adj* (of a fabric or garment) having a finish that resists the absorption of water
Waters *n* **Muddy,** real name *McKinley Morganfield.* 1915–83, US blues guitarist, singer, and songwriter. His songs include "Rollin' Stone" (1948) and "Got my Mojo Working" (1954)
watershed *n* **1** the dividing line between two adjacent river systems, such as a ridge **2** an important period or factor that serves as a dividing line: *a watershed in history*
waterside *n* the area of land beside a river or lake
watersider *n NZ* a person employed to load and unload ships
water-ski *n* **1** a type of ski used for gliding over water ▹ *vb* **-skiing, -skied** *or* **-ski'd 2** to ride over water on water-skis while holding a rope towed by a speedboat **water-skier** *n* **water-skiing** *n*
water softener *n* a device or substance that removes the minerals that make water hard
waterspout *n* a tornado occurring over water, which forms a column of water and mist
water table *n* the level below which the ground is saturated with water
watertight *adj* **1** not letting water through: *watertight compartments* **2** without loopholes or weak points: *a watertight system*
water tower *n* a storage tank mounted on a tower so that water can be distributed at a steady pressure
water vapour *n* water in a gaseous state, esp. when due to evaporation at a temperature below the boiling point
water vole *n* a small ratlike animal that can swim and lives on the banks of streams and ponds
waterway *n* a river, canal, or other navigable channel used as a means of travel or transport
water wheel *n* a large wheel with vanes set across its rim, which is turned by flowing water to drive machinery
water wings *pl n* an inflatable rubber device shaped like a pair of wings, which is placed under the arms of a person learning to swim
waterworks *n* **1** an establishment for storing, purifying, and distributing water for community supply ▹ *pl n* **2** *informal chiefly Brit euphemistic* the urinary system **3 turn on the waterworks** *informal* to begin to cry deliberately, in order to attract attention or gain sympathy
watery *adj* **1** of, like, or containing water: *a watery discharge* **2** (of eyes) filled with tears **3** insipid, thin, or weak: *a watery sun had appeared*
Watson-Watt *n* Sir **Robert Alexander** 1892–1973, Scottish physicist, who played a leading role in the development of radar
watt (wott) *n* the SI unit of power, equal to the power dissipated by a current of 1 ampere flowing across a potential difference of 1 volt
WORD ORIGIN after J. *Watt*, engineer
wattage *n* the amount of electrical power, expressed in watts, that an appliance uses or generates
Watteau *n* **Jean-Antoine** 1684–1721, French painter, esp. of *fêtes champêtres*
wattle (wott-tl) *n* **1** a frame of rods or stakes interwoven with twigs or branches used to make fences **2** a loose fold of brightly coloured skin hanging from the throat of certain birds and lizards **3** an Australian acacia tree with dense golden, yellow, or cream flowers ▹ *adj* **4** made of, formed by, or covered with wattle: *a wattle fence*
WORD ORIGIN Old English *watol*
wattle and daub *n* a building material consisting of interwoven twigs plastered with a mixture of clay and water
Watts *n* **1 George Frederick** 1817–1904, English painter and sculptor, noted esp. for his painting *Hope* (1886) and his sculpture *Physical Energy* (1904) in Kensington Gardens, London **2 Isaac** 1674–1748, English hymn-writer
wave ❶ *vb* **waving, waved 1** to move (one's hand) to and fro as a greeting **2** to direct (someone) to move in a

W

THESAURUS

waterfall *n* **= cascade**, fall, cataract, chute, linn *(Scot)*, force *(Northern English dialect)*
wave *vb* **1 = signal**, sign, gesture, gesticulate **2 = guide**, point, direct, indicate, signal, motion, gesture,

DICTIONARY

particular direction by waving: I *waved him on* **3** to hold (something) up and move it from side to side in order to attract attention **4** to move freely to and fro: *flowers waving in the wind* ▷ *n* **5** one of a sequence of ridges or undulations that moves across the surface of the sea or a lake **6** a curve in the hair **7** a sudden rise in the frequency or intensity of something: *a wave of sympathy* **8** a widespread movement that advances in a body: *a new wave of refugees* **9** a prolonged spell of some particular type of weather: *a heat wave* **10** the act or an instance of waving **11** *physics* an energy-carrying disturbance travelling through a medium or space by a series of vibrations without any overall movement of matter **12** **make waves** to cause trouble
WORD ORIGIN Old English *wafian*

waveband *n* a range of wavelengths or frequencies used for a particular type of radio transmission

wave down *vb* to signal to (the driver of a vehicle) to stop

wavelength *n* **1** *physics* the distance between two points of the same phase in consecutive cycles of a wave **2** the wavelength of the carrier wave used by a particular broadcasting station **3** **on the same wavelength** *informal* having similar views, feelings, or thoughts

Wavell *n* **Archibald** (**Percival**), 1st Earl. 1883–1950, British field marshal. During World War II he was commander in chief in the Middle East (1939–41), defeating the Italians in N Africa. He was commander in chief in India (1941–43) and viceroy of India (1943–47)

waver ❶ *vb* **1** to hesitate between possibilities; be indecisive **2** to swing from one thing to another: *she wavered between annoyance and civility* **3** (of a voice or stare) to become unsteady **4** to move back and forth or one way and another: *the barrel of the gun began to waver* **wavering** *adj*
WORD ORIGIN Old Norse *vafra* to flicker

wavey *n Canad* a snow goose or other wild goose
WORD ORIGIN from a Native American language

wavy *adj* **wavier, waviest** having curves: *wavy hair; a wavy line*

wax[1] *n* **1** a solid fatty or oily substance used for making candles and polish, which softens and melts when heated **2** ▸ short for **beeswax** or **sealing wax** **3** *physiol* a brownish-yellow waxy substance secreted by glands in the ear ▷ *vb* **4** to coat or polish with wax **waxed** *adj* **waxy** *adj*
WORD ORIGIN Old English *weax*

wax[2] ❶ *vb* **1** to increase gradually in size, strength, or power: *trading has waxed and waned with the economic cycle* **2** (of the moon) to show a gradually increasing area of brightness from new moon until full moon **3** to become: *he waxed eloquent on the disadvantages of marriage*
WORD ORIGIN Old English *weaxan*

waxed paper *or* **wax paper** *n* paper treated or coated with wax or paraffin to make it waterproof

waxen *adj* **1** resembling wax in colour or texture: *his face is waxen and pale* **2** made of, treated with, or covered with wax: *a waxen image*

waxeye *n* a small New Zealand bird with a white circle round its eye

waxwork *n* a life-size lifelike wax figure of a famous person

waxworks *n* a museum or exhibition of wax figures

way ❶ *n* **1** a manner, method, or means: *a new way of life; a tactful way of finding out* **2** a characteristic style or manner: *we are all special in our own way* **3** **ways** habits or customs: *he had a liking for British ways* **4** an aspect or detail of something: *the tourist industry is in many ways a success story* **5** a choice or option, for example in a vote: *he thought it could go either way* **6** a route or direction: *the shortest way home* **7** a journey: *you could buy a magazine to read on the way* **8** distance: *they are a long way from Paris* **9** space or room for movement or activity: *you won't be in his way* **10** **by the way** incidentally: *by the way, I've decided to leave* **11** **by way of** **a** serving as: *by way of explanation* **b** by the route of: *I went by way of my family home* **12** **get one's own way** to have things exactly as one wants them to be **13** **give way** **a** to collapse or break **b** to yield or concede: *I tried to make him understand but he did not give way an inch* **14** **give way to** **a** to be replaced by: *my first feelings of dismay have given way to comparative complacency* **b** to show (an emotion) unrestrainedly **c** to slow down or stop when driving to let (another driver) pass **15** **go out of one's way** to take considerable trouble: *he had gone out of his way to reassure me* **16** **have it both ways** to enjoy two things that would normally be mutually exclusive **17** **in a bad way** *informal* in a poor state of health or a poor financial state **18** **in a way** in some respects **19** **in no way** not at all **20** **make one's way** to proceed or go: *he decided to make his way back in the dark* **21** **on the way out** *informal* becoming unfashionable **22** **out of the way** **a** removed or dealt with so as to be no longer a hindrance **b** remote **23** **under way** having started moving or making progress ▷ *adv* **24** *informal* far or by far: *that is way out of line*
WORD ORIGIN Old English *weg*

waybill *n* a document stating the nature, origin, and destination of goods being transported

wayfarer *n old-fashioned* a traveller

waylay *vb* **-laying, -laid** **1** to lie in wait for and attack **2** to intercept (someone) unexpectedly

way-out *adj old-fashioned, informal* extremely unconventional

waypoint *n* the co-ordinates of a specific location as defined by a GPS

ways and means *pl n* **1** the methods and resources for accomplishing something **2** the money and the methods of raising the money needed for the functioning of a political unit

wayside *adj* **1** *old-fashioned* situated by the side of a road: *wayside shrines* ▷ *n* **2** **fall by the wayside** to be unsuccessful or stop being successful: *thousands of new diets are*

THESAURUS

nod, beckon, point in the direction **3 = brandish**, swing, flourish, wield, wag, move something to and fro, shake **4 = flutter**, flap, stir, waver, shake, swing, sway, ripple, wag, quiver, undulate, oscillate, move to and fro ▷ *n* **5 = ripple**, breaker, sea surf, swell, ridge, roller, comber, billow **7 = outbreak**, trend, rash, upsurge, sweep, flood, tendency, surge, ground swell **8 = stream**, flood, surge, spate, current, movement, flow, rush, tide, torrent, deluge, upsurge **10 = gesture**, sign, signal, indication, gesticulation

waver *vb* **1, 2 = hesitate**, dither *(chiefly Brit)*, vacillate, be irresolute, falter, fluctuate, seesaw, blow hot and cold *(informal)*, be indecisive, hum and haw, be unable to decide, shillyshally *(informal)*, be unable to make up your mind, swither *(Scot)*
OPPOSITE: be decisive
4 = flicker, wave, shake, vary, reel, weave, sway, tremble, wobble, fluctuate, quiver, undulate, totter

wax[2] *vb* **1 = increase**, rise, grow, develop, mount, expand, swell, enlarge, fill out, magnify, get bigger, dilate, become larger **OPPOSITE:** wane **2 = become fuller**, become larger, enlarge, get bigger

way *n* **1 = method**, means, system, process, approach, practice, scheme, technique, manner, plan, procedure, mode, course of action **2 = manner**, style, fashion, mode **3** *(often plural)* **= custom**, manner, habit, idiosyncrasy, style, practice, nature, conduct, personality, characteristic, trait, usage, wont, tikanga (NZ) **6 = route**, direction, course, road, path **7 = journey**, approach, advance, progress, passage **8 = distance**, length, stretch, journey, trail

DICTIONARY

dreamed up yearly – many fall by the wayside

wayward ⓘ *adj* erratic, selfish, or stubborn **waywardness** *n*
WORD ORIGIN AWAY + -WARD

Wb *physics* weber

WC *or* **wc** *n* a toilet

we *pron (used as the subject of a verb)* **1** the speaker or writer and another person or other people: *we arrived in Calais* **2** all people or people in general: *it's an unfair world we live in* **3** *formal* ▸ same as **I**: used by monarchs and editors
WORD ORIGIN Old English *wē*

weak ⓘ *adj* **1** lacking in physical or mental strength **2** (of a part of the body) not functioning as well as is normal: *a weak heart* **3** liable to collapse or break: *weak bridges* **4** lacking in importance, influence, or strength: *a weak government* **5** (of a currency or shares) falling in price or characterized by falling prices **6** lacking in moral strength; easily influenced **7** not convincing: *weak arguments* **8** lacking strength or power: *his voice was weak* **9** not having a strong flavour: *weak coffee* **weakly** *adv*
WORD ORIGIN Old English *wāc* soft

weaken ⓘ *vb* to become or make weak or weaker

weak-kneed *adj informal* lacking strength, courage, or resolution

weakling *n* a person who is lacking in physical or mental strength

weak-minded *adj* **1** lacking willpower **2** of low intelligence; foolish

weakness ⓘ *n* **1** the state of being weak **2** a failing in a person's character: *his weakness is his impetuosity* **3** a self-indulgent liking: *a weakness for gin*

weal¹ *n* a raised mark on the skin produced by a blow
WORD ORIGIN from Old English *walu* ridge

weal² *n old-fashioned* prosperity or wellbeing: *the public weal*
WORD ORIGIN Old English *wela*

wealth ⓘ *n* **1** the state of being rich **2** a large amount of money and valuable material possessions: *redistribution of wealth* **3** a great amount or number: *a wealth of detail*
WORD ORIGIN Middle English *welthe*

wealthy ⓘ *adj* **wealthier, wealthiest** **1** having a large amount of money and valuable material possessions **2** **wealthy in** having a great amount or number of: *a continent exceptionally wealthy in minerals*

wean *vb* **1** to start giving (a baby or young mammal) food other than its mother's milk **2** to cause (oneself or someone else) to give up a former habit: *they are unable to wean themselves from the tobacco habit* **weaning** *n*
WORD ORIGIN Old English *wenian* to accustom

weapon *n* **1** an object used in fighting, such as a knife or gun **2** anything used to get the better of an opponent: *having a sense of humour is a weapon of self-defence*
WORD ORIGIN Old English *wǣpen*

weaponry *n* weapons regarded collectively

wear ⓘ *vb* **wearing, wore, worn** **1** to carry or have (a garment or jewellery) on one's body as clothing or ornament **2** to have (a particular facial expression): *she wore a scowl of frank antagonism* **3** to style (the hair) in a particular way: *she wears her hair in a braid* **4** to deteriorate or cause to deteriorate by constant use or action **5** *informal* to accept: *he won't be given a top job – the Party wouldn't wear it* **6** **wear thin** to lessen or become weaker: *his patience began to wear thin* **7** **wear well** to remain in good condition for a long time ▹ *n* **8** clothes that are suitable for a particular time or purpose: *evening wear; beach wear* **9** deterioration from constant or normal use **10** the quality of resisting the effects of constant use ▸ See also **wear down, wear off, wear out** > **wearable** *adj* **wearer** *n*
WORD ORIGIN Old English *werian*

wear and tear *n* damage or loss resulting from ordinary use

wear down *vb* **1** to make shorter by long or constant wearing or rubbing: *the back of his heels were worn down* **2** to overcome gradually by persistent effort: *to wear down the enemy*

THESAURUS

wayward *adj* **= erratic**, unruly, wilful, unmanageable, disobedient, contrary, unpredictable, stubborn, perverse, rebellious, fickle, intractable, capricious, obstinate, headstrong, changeable, flighty, incorrigible, obdurate, ungovernable, self-willed, refractory, insubordinate, undependable, inconstant, mulish, cross-grained, contumacious, froward *(archaic)* **OPPOSITE:** obedient

weak *adj* **1 = feeble**, exhausted, frail, debilitated, spent, wasted, weakly, tender, delicate, faint, fragile, shaky, sickly, languid, puny, decrepit, unsteady, infirm, anaemic, effete, enervated **OPPOSITE:** strong **3 = fragile**, brittle, flimsy, unsound, fine, delicate, frail, dainty, breakable **4 = unsafe**, exposed, vulnerable, helpless, wide open, unprotected, untenable, defenceless, unguarded **OPPOSITE:** secure **7 = unconvincing**, unsatisfactory, lame, invalid, flimsy, inconclusive, pathetic **OPPOSITE:** convincing **9 = tasteless**, thin, diluted, watery, runny, insipid, wishy-washy *(informal)*, under-strength, milk-and-water, waterish **OPPOSITE:** strong

weaken *vb* **a = reduce**, undermine, moderate, diminish, temper, impair, lessen, sap, mitigate, invalidate, soften up, take the edge off **OPPOSITE:** boost **b = wane**, fail, diminish, dwindle, lower, flag, fade, give way, lessen, abate, droop, ease up **OPPOSITE:** grow **c = sap the strength of**, tire, exhaust, debilitate, depress, disable, cripple, incapacitate, enfeeble, enervate **OPPOSITE:** strengthen

weakness *n* **1a = frailty**, fatigue, exhaustion, fragility, infirmity, debility, feebleness, faintness, decrepitude, enervation **OPPOSITE:** strength **1b = powerlessness**, vulnerability, impotence, meekness, irresolution, spinelessness, ineffectuality, timorousness, cravenness, cowardliness **2 = failing**, fault, defect, deficiency, flaw, shortcoming, blemish, imperfection, Achilles' heel, chink in your armour, lack **OPPOSITE:** strong point **3 = liking**, appetite, penchant, soft spot, passion, inclination, fondness, predilection, proclivity, partiality, proneness **OPPOSITE:** aversion

wealth *n* **1 = riches**, fortune, prosperity, affluence, goods, means, money, funds, property, cash, resources, substance, possessions, big money, big bucks *(informal, chiefly US)*, opulence, megabucks *(US & Canad slang)*, lucre, pelf **OPPOSITE:** poverty **2 = property**, funds, capital, estate, assets, fortune, possessions **3 = abundance**, store, plenty, richness, bounty, profusion, fullness, cornucopia, plenitude, copiousness **OPPOSITE:** lack

wealthy *adj* **1 = rich**, prosperous, affluent, well-off, loaded *(slang)*, comfortable, flush *(informal)*, in the money *(informal)*, opulent, well-heeled *(informal)*, well-to-do, moneyed, quids in *(slang)*, filthy rich, rolling in it *(slang)*, on Easy Street *(informal)*, stinking rich *(slang)*, made of money *(informal)*, minted *(Brit slang)* **OPPOSITE:** poor

wear *vb* **1 = be dressed in**, have on, dress in, be clothed in, carry, sport *(informal)*, bear, put on, clothe yourself in **2 = show**, present, bear, display, assume, put on, exhibit **4 = deteriorate**, fray, wear thin, become threadbare ▹ *n* **8 = clothes**, things, dress, gear *(informal)*, attire, habit, outfit, costume, threads *(slang)*, garments, apparel, garb, raiments **9 = damage**, wear and tear, use, erosion, friction, deterioration, depreciation, attrition, corrosion, abrasion **OPPOSITE:** repair

DICTIONARY

wearing ⊕ *adj* causing exhaustion and sometimes irritation
wearisome *adj* causing fatigue and irritation
wear off *vb* to have a gradual decrease in effect or intensity: *the cocaine injection was beginning to wear off*
wear out *vb* **1** to make or become unfit for use through wear: *my red trousers are worn out* **2** *informal* to exhaust: *the afternoon's races and games had worn him out*
weary ⊕ *adj* **-rier, -riest 1** very tired; lacking energy **2** caused by or suggestive of weariness: *he managed a weary smile* **3** causing exhaustion: *a long weary struggle* **4 weary of** discontented or bored with: *he was weary of the war* ▹ *vb* **-ries, -rying, -ried 5** to make weary **6 weary of** to become discontented or bored with: *he seems to have wearied of her possessiveness* **wearily** *adv* **weariness** *n* **wearying** *adj*
WORD ORIGIN Old English *wērig*
weasel *n, pl* **-sels** *or* **-sel** a small meat-eating mammal with reddish-brown fur, a long body and neck, and short legs
WORD ORIGIN Old English *wesle*
weather ⊕ *n* **1** the day-to-day atmospheric conditions, such as temperature, cloudiness, and rainfall, affecting a specific place **2 make heavy weather of** *informal* to carry out (a task) with great difficulty or needless effort **3 under the weather** *informal* feeling slightly ill ▹ *vb* **4** to undergo or cause to undergo changes, such as discoloration, due to the action of the weather **5** to come safely through (a storm, problem, or difficulty)
WORD ORIGIN Old English *weder*
weather-beaten *adj* **1** tanned by exposure to the weather: *a crumpled weather-beaten face* **2** worn or damaged as a result of exposure to the weather
weatherboard *n* a timber board that is fixed with others in overlapping horizontal rows to form an exterior cladding on a wall or roof **weatherboarded** *adj*
weathercock *n* a weather vane in the shape of a cock
weather eye *n* **keep a weather eye on** to keep a careful watch on: *keep a weather eye on your symptoms*
weathering *n* the breakdown of rocks by the action of the weather
weatherman *n, pl* **-men** a man who forecasts the weather on radio or television **weather girl** *fem n*
weatherproof *adj* able to withstand exposure to weather without deterioration: *a weatherproof roof*
weather vane *n* a metal object on a roof that indicates the direction in which the wind is blowing
weave ⊕ *vb* **weaving, wove** *or* **weaved, woven** *or* **weaved 1** to form (a fabric) by interlacing yarn on a loom **2** to make (a garment or a blanket) by this process **3** to construct (a basket or fence) by interlacing cane or twigs **4** to compose (a story or plan) by combining separate elements into a whole **5** to move from side to side while going forward: *to weave in and out of lanes* **6 get weaving** *informal* to hurry ▹ *n* **7** the structure or pattern of a woven fabric: *the rough weave of the cloth* **weaver** *n* **weaving** *n*
WORD ORIGIN Old English *wefan*
web ⊕ *n* **1** a mesh of fine tough threads built by a spider to trap insects **2** anything that is intricately formed or complex: *a web of relationships* **3** a membrane connecting the toes of some water birds and water-dwelling animals such as frogs **4 the web** (*often cap*) ▸ short for **World Wide Web** ▹ *adj* **5** of or situated on the World Wide Web: *a web server; web pages* **webbed** *adj*
WORD ORIGIN Old English *webb*
web address *n* ▸ another name for **URL**
Webb *n* **1** Sir **Aston** 1849–1930, British architect. His work includes the Victoria and Albert Museum (1909), the Victoria Memorial (1911), and Admiralty Arch (1911) **2 Mary** (**Gladys**) 1881–1927, British novelist, remembered for her novels of rustic life, notably *Precious Bane* (1924) **3 Sidney** (**James**), Baron Passfield 1859–1947, British economist, social historian, and Fabian socialist. He and his wife (**Martha**) **Beatrice** (née *Potter*), 1858–1943, British writer on social and economic problems, collaborated in *The History of Trade Unionism* (1894) and *English Local Government* (1906–29), helped found the London School of Economics (1895), and started the *New Statesman* (1913)
webbing *n* a strong fabric that is woven in strips and used under springs in upholstery or for straps
webcam *n* a camera that transmits still or moving images over the internet
webcast *n* a broadcast of an event over the internet
weber (vay-ber) *n* the SI unit of magnetic flux (the strength of a magnetic field over a given area)
WORD ORIGIN after W. E. *Weber*, physicist
Webern *n* **Anton von.** 1883–1945, Austrian composer; pupil of Schoenberg, whose twelve-tone technique he adopted. His works include those for chamber ensemble, such as *Five Pieces for Orchestra* (1911–13)
web-footed *or* **web-toed** *adj* (of certain animals or birds) having webbed feet that aid swimming
weblog *n* a person's online journal
webmail *n* an e-mail system that allows account holders to access mail via an internet site rather than by downloading it onto a computer
website *n* a group of connected pages on the World Wide Web containing information on a particular subject
Web 2.0 *n* the internet viewed as a medium in which interactive experience plays a more important role than simply accessing information
wed ⊕ *vb* **wedding, wedded** *or* **wed**

THESAURUS

wearing *adj* **= tiresome**, trying, taxing, tiring, exhausting, fatiguing, oppressive, exasperating, irksome, wearisome
OPPOSITE: refreshing
weary *adj* **1 = tired**, exhausted, drained, worn out, spent, done in (*informal*), flagging, all in (*slang*), fatigued, wearied, sleepy, fagged (*informal*), whacked (*Brit informal*), jaded, drooping, knackered (*slang*), drowsy, clapped out (*Austral & NZ informal*), enervated, ready to drop, dog-tired (*informal*), zonked (*slang*), dead beat (*informal*), asleep *or* dead on your feet (*informal*)
OPPOSITE: energetic
3 = tiring, taxing, wearing, arduous, tiresome, laborious, irksome, wearisome, enervative
OPPOSITE: refreshing
▹ *vb* **6** (with *of*) **= grow tired**, tire, sicken, have had enough, become bored
weather *n* **1 = climate**, conditions, temperature, forecast, outlook, meteorological conditions, elements
▹ *vb* **5 = withstand**, stand, suffer, survive, overcome, resist, brave, endure, come through, get through, rise above, live through, ride out, make it through (*informal*), surmount, pull through, stick it out (*informal*), bear up against
OPPOSITE: surrender to
weave *vb* **1 = knit**, twist, intertwine, plait, unite, introduce, blend, incorporate, merge, mat, fuse, braid, entwine, intermingle, interlace
4 = create, tell, recount, narrate, make, build, relate, make up, spin, construct, invent, put together, unfold, contrive, fabricate
5 = zigzag, wind, move in and out, crisscross, weave your way
web *n* **1 = cobweb**, spider's web
2 = tangle, series, network, mass, chain, knot, maze, toils, nexus
wed *vb* **1a = get married to**, espouse, get hitched to (*slang*), be united to, plight your troth to (*old-fashioned*), get

DICTIONARY

1 *old-fashioned* to take (a person) as a husband or wife; marry **2** to unite closely: *to wed folklore and magic*
WORD ORIGIN Old English *weddian*

Wed. Wednesday

wedded *adj* **1** of marriage: *wedded bliss* **2** firmly in support of an idea or institution: *wedded to the virtues of capitalism*

wedding ⊕ *n* **1** a marriage ceremony **2** a special wedding anniversary, esp. the 25th (**silver wedding**) or 50th (**golden wedding**)

wedding breakfast *n* the meal usually served after a wedding ceremony or just before the bride and bridegroom leave for their honeymoon

wedding cake *n* a rich iced fruit cake, with one, two, or more tiers, which is served at a wedding reception

wedding ring *n* a plain ring, usually made of a precious metal, worn to indicate that one is married

Wedekind *n* **Frank** 1864–1918, German dramatist, whose plays, such as *The Awakening of Spring* (1891) and *Pandora's Box* (1904), bitterly satirize the sexual repressiveness of society

wedge ⊕ *n* **1** a block of solid material, esp. wood or metal, that is shaped like a narrow V in cross section and can be pushed or driven between two objects or parts of an object in order to split or secure them **2** a slice shaped like a wedge: *a wedge of quiche* **3** *golf* a club with a wedge-shaped face, used for bunker or pitch shots **4** **drive a wedge between** to cause a split between (people or groups) **5** **the thin end of the wedge** anything unimportant in itself that implies the start of something much larger ▷ *vb* **wedging, wedged 6** to secure (something) with a wedge **7** to squeeze into a narrow space: *a book wedged between the bed and the table*
WORD ORIGIN Old English *wecg*

wedge-tailed eagle *n* a large brown Australian eagle with a wedge-shaped tail

Wedgwood *n trademark* a type of fine pottery with applied decoration in white on a coloured background
WORD ORIGIN after Josiah *Wedgwood*, potter

wedlock *n* **1** the state of being married **2** **born out of wedlock** born when one's parents are not legally married
WORD ORIGIN Old English *wedlāc*

Wednesday *n* the fourth day of the week
WORD ORIGIN Old English *Wōdnes dæg* Woden's day

wee[1] *adj Brit, Austral & NZ* small or short
WORD ORIGIN Old English *wǣg* weight

wee[2] *informal n* **1** an instance of urinating ▷ *vb* **weeing, weed 2** to urinate. Also: **wee-wee**
WORD ORIGIN origin unknown

weed *n* **1** any plant that grows wild and profusely, esp. among cultivated plants **2** *slang* **a** marijuana **b** **the weed** *or* **the evil weed** tobacco **3** *informal* a thin weak person ▷ *vb* **4** to remove weeds from (a garden)
WORD ORIGIN Old English *wēod*

weedkiller *n* a chemical or hormonal substance used to kill weeds

weed out *vb* to separate out, remove, or eliminate (an unwanted element): *to weed out the thugs*

weedy *adj* **weedier, weediest 1** *informal* thin or weak: *sick and weedy children* **2** full of weeds: *weedy patches of garden*

week *n* **1** a period of seven consecutive days, esp. one beginning with Sunday **2** a period of seven consecutive days from a specified day: *a week from today* **3** the period of time within a week that is spent at work
WORD ORIGIN Old English *wice, wicu*

weekday *n* any day of the week other than Saturday or Sunday

weekend *n* Saturday and Sunday

weekly *adj* **1** happening once a week or every week: *a weekly column* **2** determined or calculated by the week: *weekly earnings* ▷ *adv* **3** once a week or every week: *report to the police weekly* ▷ *n, pl* **-lies 4** a newspaper or magazine issued every week

Weelkes *n* **Thomas** ?1575–1623, English composer of madrigals

weeny *adj* **-nier, -niest** *informal* very small; tiny
WORD ORIGIN from WEE[1]

weep ⊕ *vb* **weeping, wept 1** to shed tears; cry **2** to ooze liquid: *the skin cracked and wept; the label is weeping black ink in the rain* ▷ *n* **3** a spell of weeping: *together we had a good weep*
WORD ORIGIN Old English *wēpan*

weeping willow *n* a willow tree with graceful drooping branches

weepy *informal adj* **weepier, weepiest 1** liable or tending to weep ▷ *n, pl* **weepies 2** a sentimental film or book

weevil *n* a beetle with a long snout that feeds on plants
WORD ORIGIN Old English *wifel*

wee-wee *n, vb* **-weeing, -weed** *informal chiefly Brit* ▸ same as **wee**[2]

weft *n* the yarns woven across the width of the fabric through the lengthways warp yarns
WORD ORIGIN Old English

Wegener *n* **Alfred** 1880–1930, German meteorologist: regarded as the originator of the theory of continental drift

weigh ⊕ *vb* **1** to have weight as specified: *the tree weighs nearly three tons* **2** to measure the weight of **3** to consider carefully: *the President now has to weigh his options* **4** to be influential: *the authorities did not enter my mind or weigh with me* **5** **weigh anchor** to raise a ship's anchor **6** **weigh out** to measure out by weight ▸ See also **weigh down, weigh in**, etc.
WORD ORIGIN Old English *wegan*

weighbridge *n* a machine for weighing vehicles by means of a metal plate set into a road

weigh down *vb* **1** (of a heavy load) to impede the movements of **2** (of a problem or difficulty) to worry (someone) a great deal

weigh in *vb* **1** (of a boxer or jockey) to be weighed to check that one is of the correct weight for the contest **2** *informal* to contribute to a discussion or conversation: *he weighed in with a few sharp comments* ▷ *n* **weigh-in 3** *sport* the occasion of checking the competitors' weight before a boxing match or a horse race

weigh on *vb* to be oppressive or burdensome to: *the expectations that weigh so heavily on diplomats' wives*

THESAURUS

spliced to (*informal*), take as your husband *or* wife **OPPOSITE:** divorce **1b = get married**, marry, be united, tie the knot (*informal*), take the plunge (*informal*), get hitched (*slang*), get spliced (*informal*), become man and wife, plight your troth (*old-fashioned*) **OPPOSITE:** divorce **2 = unite**, combine, bring together, amalgamate, join, link, marry, ally, connect, blend, integrate, merge, unify, make one, fuse, weld, interweave, yoke, coalesce, commingle **OPPOSITE:** divide

wedding *n* **1 = marriage**, nuptials, wedding ceremony, marriage ceremony, marriage service, wedding service, nuptial rite, espousals

wedge *n* **1, 2 = block**, segment, lump, chunk, triangle, slab, hunk, chock, wodge (*Brit informal*) ▷ *vb* **7 = squeeze**, force, lodge, jam, crowd, block, stuff, pack, thrust, ram, cram, stow

weep *vb* **1 = cry**, shed tears, sob, whimper, complain, keen, greet (*Scot*), moan, mourn, grieve, lament, whinge (*informal*), blubber, snivel, ululate, blub (*slang*), boohoo **OPPOSITE:** rejoice

weigh *vb* **1 = have a weight of**, tip the scales at (*informal*) **3 = consider**, study, examine, contemplate, evaluate, ponder, mull over, think over, eye up, reflect upon, give thought to, meditate upon, deliberate upon **4 = matter**, carry weight, cut any ice (*informal*), impress, tell, count, have influence, be influential

W

DICTIONARY

weight ⓣ *n* **1** the heaviness of an object, substance, or person **2** *physics* the vertical force experienced by a mass as a result of gravitation **3 a** a system of units used to express weight: *metric weight* **b** a unit used to measure weight: *the kilogram is the weight used in the metric system* **4 a** an object of known heaviness used for weighing objects, substances, or people **b** an object of known heaviness used in weight training or weightlifting to strengthen the muscles **5** any heavy load: *with a weight of fish on their backs* **6** force, importance, or influence: *they want their words to carry weight* **7** an oppressive force: *the weight of expectation* **8 pull one's weight** *informal* to do one's full share of a task **9 throw one's weight about** *informal* to act in an aggressive authoritarian manner ▷ *vb* **10** (often with *down*) to add weight to; make heavier **11** to slant (a system) so that it favours one side rather than another
WORD ORIGIN Old English *wiht*

weighting *n Brit* an allowance paid to compensate for higher living costs: *salary includes Inner London weighting*

weightless *adj* **1** seeming to have very little weight or no weight at all **2** seeming not to be affected by gravity, as in the case of astronauts in an orbiting spacecraft **weightlessness** *n*

weightlifting *n* the sport of lifting barbells of specified weights in a prescribed manner **weightlifter** *n*

weight training *n* physical exercise using light or heavy weights in order to strengthen the muscles

weighty *adj* **weightier, weightiest** **1** important or serious: *weighty matters* **2** very heavy

weigh up *vb* to make an assessment of (a person or situation)

Weil *n* **Simone** 1909–43, French philosopher and mystic, whose works include *Waiting for God* (1951), *The Need for Roots* (1952), and *Notebooks* (1956)

Weill *n* **Kurt** 1900–50, German composer, in the US from 1935. He wrote the music for Brecht's *The Rise and Fall of the City of Mahagonny* (1927) and *The Threepenny Opera* (1928)

Weinberg *n* **Steven** born 1933, US physicist, who shared the Nobel prize for physics (1979) with Sheldon Glashow and Abdus Salam for his role in formulating the electroweak theory

weir *n* **1** a low dam that is built across a river to divert the water or control its flow **2** a fencelike trap built across a stream for catching fish in
WORD ORIGIN Old English *wer*

Weir *n* **1 Judith** born 1954, Scottish composer, noted esp. for her opera *A Night at the Chinese Opera* (1987) **2 Peter** born 1944, Australian film director; his films include *Dead Poets Society* (1989), *The Truman Show* (1998), and *Master and Commander* (2003)

weird ⓣ *adj* **1** strange or bizarre **2** suggestive of the supernatural; uncanny **weirdly** *adv* **weirdness** *n*
WORD ORIGIN Old English *(ge)wyrd* destiny

weirdo *n, pl* **-dos** *informal* a person who behaves in a bizarre or eccentric manner

Weissmuller *n* **John Peter,** known as *Johnny*. 1904–84, US swimmer and film actor, who won Olympic gold medals in 1924 and 1928 and played the title role in the early Tarzan films

Weizmann *n* **Chaim** 1874–1952, Israeli statesman, born in Russia. As a leading Zionist, he was largely responsible for securing the Balfour Declaration (1917); first president of Israel (1949–52)

welch *vb* ▸ same as **welsh**

welcome ⓣ *vb* **-coming, -comed** **1** to greet the arrival of (a guest) cordially **2** to receive or accept (something) gladly: *I would welcome a chance to speak to him* ▷ *n* **3** the act of greeting or receiving someone or something in a specified manner: *the President was given a warm welcome* ▷ *adj* **4** gladly received or admitted: *I wouldn't want to stay where I'm not welcome* **5** encouraged or invited: *you are welcome to join us at one of our social events* **6** bringing pleasure: *a welcome change* **7 you're welcome** an expression used to acknowledge someone's thanks **welcoming** *adj*
WORD ORIGIN Old English *wilcuma*

weld ⓣ *vb* **1** to join (two pieces of metal or plastic) by softening with heat and hammering or by fusion **2** to unite closely: *the diverse ethnic groups had been welded together by the anti-Fascist cause* ▷ *n* **3** a joint formed by welding **welder** *n*
WORD ORIGIN obsolete *well* to melt, weld

Weld *n* Sir **Frederick Aloysius** 1823–91, New Zealand statesman, born in England: prime minister of New Zealand (1864–65)

Weldon *n* **Fay** born 1931, British novelist and writer. Her novels include *Praxis* (1978), *Life and Loves of a She-Devil* (1984), *Big Women* (1998), and *Rhode Island Blues* (2003)

welfare ⓣ *n* **1** health, happiness, prosperity, and general wellbeing **2** financial and other assistance given, usually by the government, to people in need
WORD ORIGIN WEL(L)[1] + FARE

welfare state *n* a system in which the government undertakes responsibility for the wellbeing of its population, through unemployment insurance, old age pensions, and other social-security measures

THESAURUS

weight *n* **1 = heaviness,** mass, burden, poundage, pressure, load, gravity, tonnage, heft *(informal)*, avoirdupois **6 = importance,** force, power, moment, value, authority, influence, bottom, impact, import, muscle, consequence, substance, consideration, emphasis, significance, sway, clout *(informal)*, leverage, efficacy, mana (NZ), persuasiveness ▷ *vb* **10** *(often with* **down***)* **= load,** ballast, make heavier **11 = bias,** load, slant, unbalance

weird *adj* **1 = bizarre,** odd, strange, unusual, queer, grotesque, unnatural, creepy *(informal)*, outlandish, freakish **OPPOSITE:** ordinary **2 = strange,** odd, unusual, bizarre, ghostly, mysterious, queer, unearthly, eerie, grotesque, supernatural, unnatural, far-out *(slang)*, uncanny, spooky *(informal)*, creepy *(informal)*, eldritch *(poetic)* **OPPOSITE:** normal

welcome *vb* **1 = greet,** meet, receive, embrace, hail, usher in, say hello to, roll out the red carpet for, offer hospitality to, receive with open arms, bid welcome, karanga (NZ), mihi (NZ) **OPPOSITE:** reject **2 = accept gladly,** appreciate, embrace, approve of, be pleased by, give the thumbs up to *(informal)*, be glad about, express pleasure *or* satisfaction at ▷ *n* **3 = greeting,** welcoming, entertainment, reception, acceptance, hail, hospitality, salutation **OPPOSITE:** rejection ▷ *adj* **4 = wanted,** at home, invited **OPPOSITE:** unwanted **5 = free,** invited **6 = pleasing,** wanted, accepted, appreciated, acceptable, pleasant, desirable, refreshing, delightful, gratifying, agreeable, pleasurable, gladly received **OPPOSITE:** unpleasant

weld *vb* **1 = join,** link, bond, bind, connect, cement, fuse, solder, braze **2 = unite,** combine, blend, consolidate, unify, fuse, meld

welfare *n* **1 = wellbeing,** good, interest, health, security, benefit, success, profit, safety, protection, fortune, comfort, happiness, prosperity, prosperousness **2 = state benefit,** support, benefits, pensions, dole *(slang)*, social security, unemployment benefit, state benefits, pogey *(Canad)*

DICTIONARY

well[1] ⊕ *adv* **better, best** **1** satisfactorily or pleasingly: *well proportioned* **2** skilfully: *I played well for the last six holes* **3** thoroughly: *make sure the chicken is well cooked* **4** comfortably or prosperously: *he has lived well from his various nautical exploits* **5** suitably or fittingly: *you can't very well refuse* **6** intimately: *darling Robert, I know him so well* **7** favourably: *it will go down very well with all the people who support him* **8** by a considerable margin: *well over half; she left well before tea* **9** very likely: *the claim may well be true* **10** *informal* extremely: *well cool* **11 all very well** used ironically to express discontent or annoyance: *that's all very well, but I'm left to pick up the pieces* **12 as well a** in addition **b** with equal effect: used to express indifference or reluctance: *I might as well go out* **13 as well as** in addition to **14 just as well** fortunate or appropriate: *it's just as well I didn't spend all my money* ▷ *adj* **15** in good health: *I'm not feeling well* **16** satisfactory or acceptable: *all was well in the aircraft* ▷ *interj* **17 a** an expression of surprise, indignation, or reproof: *well, what a cheek!* **b** an expression of anticipation in waiting for an answer or remark: *well, what do you think?*
WORD ORIGIN Old English *wel*

well[2] ⊕ *n* **1** a hole or shaft bored into the earth to tap a supply of water, oil, or gas **2** an open shaft through the floors of a building, used for a staircase ▷ *vb* **3** to flow upwards or outwards: *tears welled up into my eyes*
WORD ORIGIN Old English *wella*

we'll we will *or* we shall

well-advised *adj* prudent or sensible: *you would be well-advised to cooperate with me*

well-appointed *adj* (of a room or building) equipped or furnished to a high standard

well-balanced *adj* sensible and emotionally stable

well-behaved *adj* having good manners; not causing trouble or mischief

well-being *n* the state of being contented and healthy: *a sense of well-being*

well-born *adj* belonging to a noble or upper-class family

well-bred *adj* having good manners; polite

well-built *adj* strong and well-proportioned

well-connected *adj* having influential or important relatives or friends

well-disposed *adj* inclined to be sympathetic, kindly, or friendly towards a person or idea

well-done *adj* **1** made or accomplished satisfactorily **2** (of food, esp. meat) cooked very thoroughly

Wellesley *n* **1 Arthur** See (1st Duke of) **Wellington 2** his brother, **Richard Colley,** Marquis Wellesley. 1760–1842, British administrator. As governor general of Bengal (1797–1805) he consolidated British power in India

Wellesz *n* **Egon** 1885–1974, British composer, born in Austria

well-founded *adj* having a sound basis in fact: *a well-founded fear of persecution*

well-groomed *adj* having a smart tidy appearance

well-grounded *adj* having a sound basis in fact: *well-grounded suspicions*

wellhead *n* **1** the source of a well or stream **2** a source, fountainhead, or origin

well-heeled *adj informal* wealthy

wellies *pl n Brit, NZ & Austral informal* Wellington boots

well-informed *adj* knowing a lot about a great variety of subjects or about one particular subject

Wellington boots *or* **wellingtons** *pl n* long rubber boots, worn in wet or muddy conditions
WORD ORIGIN after the 1st Duke of *Wellington*, soldier and statesman

well-intentioned *adj* having good or kindly intentions, usually with unfortunate results

well-known *adj* widely known; famous

well-meaning *adj* having or indicating good intentions, usually with unfortunate results

well-nigh *adv* almost: *a well-nigh impossible task*

well-off *adj* **1** moderately wealthy **2** in a fortunate position: *some people don't know when they are well-off*

well-preserved *adj* not showing signs of ageing: *amazingly well-preserved for a man of 70*

well-read *adj* having read and learned a lot

well-rounded *adj* **1** desirably varied: *his well-rounded team* **2** rounded in shape or well developed: *a voluptuous well-rounded lady*

well-spoken *adj* having a clear, articulate, and socially acceptable accent and way of speaking

wellspring *n* a source of abundant supply: *the wellspring of truth*

well-thought-of *adj* liked and respected

well-to-do *adj* moderately wealthy

well-versed *adj* knowing a lot about a particular subject

well-wisher *n* a person who shows benevolence or sympathy towards a person or cause

well-worn *adj* **1** (of a word or phrase) having lost its meaning or force through being overused **2** having been used so much as to show signs of wear: *well-worn leather*

welly *n* **1** *informal* ▶ same as **Wellington boot 2** *Brit slang* energy or commitment: *give it some welly!*

welsh *or* **welch** *vb* **welsh on** to fail to pay (a debt) or fulfil (an obligation)
WORD ORIGIN origin unknown

Welsh *adj* **1** of Wales ▷ *n* **2** a Celtic language spoken in some parts of Wales ▷ *pl n* **3 the Welsh** the people of Wales

THESAURUS

well[1] *adv* **1 = satisfactorily**, nicely, smoothly, successfully, capitally, pleasantly, happily, famously *(informal)*, splendidly, agreeably, like nobody's business *(informal)*, in a satisfactory manner **OPPOSITE:** badly **2 = skilfully**, expertly, adeptly, with skill, professionally, correctly, properly, effectively, efficiently, adequately, admirably, ably, conscientiously, proficiently **OPPOSITE:** badly **3 = thoroughly**, completely, fully, carefully, effectively, efficiently, rigorously **4 = prosperously**, comfortably, splendidly, in comfort, in (the lap of) luxury, flourishingly, without hardship **5 = decently**, right, kindly, fittingly, fairly, easily, correctly, properly, readily, politely, suitably, generously, justly, in all fairness, genially, civilly, hospitably **OPPOSITE:** unfairly **6 = intimately**, closely, completely, deeply, fully, personally, profoundly **OPPOSITE:** slightly **7 = favourably**, highly, kindly, warmly, enthusiastically, graciously, approvingly, admiringly, with admiration, appreciatively, with praise, glowingly, with approbation **OPPOSITE:** unfavourably **8 = considerably**, easily, very much, significantly, substantially, markedly **9 = possibly**, probably, certainly, reasonably, conceivably, justifiably **10** *(informal)* **= fully**, highly, greatly, completely, amply, very much, thoroughly, considerably, sufficiently, substantially, heartily, abundantly ▷ *adj* **15 = healthy**, strong, sound, fit, blooming, robust, hale, hearty, in good health, alive and kicking, fighting fit *(informal)*, in fine fettle, up to par, fit as a fiddle, able-bodied, in good condition **OPPOSITE:** ill **16 = satisfactory**, good, right, fine, happy, fitting, pleasing, bright, useful, lucky, proper, thriving, flourishing, profitable, fortunate **OPPOSITE:** unsatisfactory

well[2] *n* **1 = hole**, bore, pit, shaft ▷ *vb* **3 = flow**, trickle, seep, run, issue, spring, pour, jet, burst, stream, surge, discharge, trickle, gush, ooze, seep, exude, spurt, spout

DICTIONARY

WORD ORIGIN Old English *Wēlisc*, *Wǣlisc*

Welshman *or fem* **Welshwoman** *n, pl* **-men** *or* **-women** a person from Wales

Welsh rarebit *n* melted cheese, sometimes mixed with milk or seasonings, served on hot toast. Also called: **Welsh rabbit**

welt *n* **1** a raised mark on the skin produced by a blow **2** a raised or strengthened seam in a garment
WORD ORIGIN origin unknown

welter *n* a confused mass or jumble: *a welter of facts*
WORD ORIGIN Middle Low German, Middle Dutch *weltern*

welterweight *n* a professional boxer weighing up to 147 pounds (66.5 kg) or an amateur boxer weighing up to 67 kg

Welty *n* **Eudora** 1909–2001, US novelist and short-story writer, noted for her depiction of life in the Mississippi delta. Her novels include *Delta Wedding* (1946) and *The Optimist's Daughter* (1972)

wen *n pathol* a cyst on the scalp
WORD ORIGIN Old English *wenn*

wench *n old-fashioned* **1** *facetious* a girl or young woman **2** a prostitute or female servant
WORD ORIGIN Old English *wencel* child

wend *vb* to make (one's way) in a particular direction: *it's time to wend our way back home*
WORD ORIGIN Old English *wendan*

Wendy house *n* a small toy house for a child to play in
WORD ORIGIN after *Wendy*, the girl in J. M. Barrie's play *Peter Pan*

wensleydale *n* a white cheese with a flaky texture
WORD ORIGIN after *Wensleydale*, North Yorkshire

went *vb* ▸ the past tense of **go**

wept *vb* ▸ the past of **weep**

were *vb* ▸ the form of the past tense of **be**: used after *we, you, they*, or a plural noun, or as a subjunctive in conditional sentences
WORD ORIGIN Old English *wēron*, *wǣron*

we're we are

weren't were not

werewolf *n, pl* **-wolves** (in folklore) a person who can turn into a wolf
WORD ORIGIN Old English *wer* man + *wulf* wolf

Werfel *n* **Franz** 1890–1945, Austro-Hungarian poet, novelist, and dramatist of the German expressionist movement. His novels include *The Forty Days of Musa Dagh* (1933) and *The Song of Bernadette* (1941)

Wergeland *n* **Henrik Arnold** 1808–45, Norwegian poet and nationalist, remembered for his lyric and narrative verse

Werner *n* **1 Abraham Gottlieb** 1749–1817, German geologist. He emphasized the importance of field and laboratory observation for understanding the earth **2 Alfred** 1866–1919, Swiss chemist, born in Germany. He developed a coordination theory of the valency of inorganic complexes: Nobel prize for chemistry 1913

Wesker *n* **Arnold** born 1932, British dramatist, whose plays include *Roots* (1959), *Chips With Everything* (1962), *The Merchant* (1976), *Caritas* (1981), and *Break My Heart* (1997)

Wessex[1] *n* **1** an Anglo-Saxon kingdom in S and SW England that became the most powerful English kingdom by the 10th century A.D **2 a** (in Thomas Hardy's works) the southwestern counties of England, esp. Dorset **b** (*as modifier*): *Wessex Poems*

Wessex[2] *n* **Earl of Wessex** ▸ See **Edward** (sense 2)

west *n* **1** one of the four cardinal points of the compass, at 270° clockwise from north; the direction along a line of latitude towards the sunset **2 the west** any area lying in or towards the west ▹ *adj* **3** situated in, moving towards, or facing the west **4** (esp. of the wind) from the west ▹ *adv* **5** in, to, or towards the west
WORD ORIGIN Old English

West[1] *n* **the West 1** the western part of the world contrasted historically and culturally with the East or Orient; the Occident **2** (formerly) the non-Communist countries of Europe and America contrasted with the Communist states of the East ▸ Compare **East** (sense 2) **3** (in the US) **a** that part of the US lying approximately to the west of the Mississippi **b** (during the Colonial period) the region outside the 13 colonies, lying mainly to the west of the Alleghenies **4** (in the ancient and medieval world) the Western Roman Empire and, later, the Holy Roman Empire ▹ *adj* **5 a** of or denoting the western part of a specified country, area, etc. **b** (*as part of a name*): *the West Coast*

West[2] *n* **1 Benjamin** 1738–1820, US painter, in England from 1763 **2 Kanye**, born 1977, US rap singer and producer; his albums include *The College Dropout* (2004) and *Graduation* (2007) **3 Mae** 1892–1980, US film actress **4 Nathanael**, real name *Nathan Weinstein*. 1903–40, US novelist: author of *Miss Lonely-Hearts* (1933) and *The Day of the Locust* (1939) **5** Dame **Rebecca**, real name *Cicily Isabel Andrews* (*née Fairfield*). 1892–1983, British journalist, novelist, and critic

westbound *adj* going towards the west

Westenra *n* **Hayley** (**Dee**) born 1987, New Zealand singer, known for the purity of her voice in many musical genres

westerly *adj* **1** of or in the west ▹ *adv, adj* **2** towards the west **3** from the west: *a westerly wind*

western *adj* **1** situated in or towards the west **2** facing or moving towards the west **3** (*sometimes cap*) of or characteristic of the west or West ▹ *n* **4** a film or book about cowboys in the western states of the US in the 19th century **westernmost** *adj*

Western *adj* (esp. formerly) of or characteristic of the Americas and the parts of Europe not under Communist rule

Westerner *n* a person from the west of a country or region

western hemisphere *n* the half of the globe that contains the Americas

westernize *or* **-ise** *vb* **-izing, -ized** *or* **-ising, -ised** to influence or make familiar with the customs or practices of the West
westernization *or* **-isation** *n*

West Indian *adj* **1** of the West Indies ▹ *n* **2** a person from the West Indies

Westminster *n* the British Houses of Parliament

westward *adj, adv also* **westwards** **1** towards the west ▹ *n* **2** the westward part or direction

Westwood *n* **Vivienne** (**Isabel**) born 1941, British fashion designer: noted for her punk designs of the late 1970s

wet ❶ *adj* **wetter, wettest** **1** moistened, covered, or soaked with water or some other liquid **2** not yet dry or solid: *wet paint* **3** rainy: *the weather was cold and wet* **4** *Brit & NZ informal* feeble or foolish **5 wet**

W

THESAURUS

wet *adj* **1 = damp**, soaked, soaking, dripping, saturated, moist, drenched, watery, soggy, sodden, waterlogged, moistened, dank, sopping, aqueous, wringing wet **OPPOSITE:** dry
3 = rainy, damp, drizzly, showery, raining, pouring, drizzling, misty, teeming, humid, dank, clammy **OPPOSITE:** sunny
4 (*Brit & NZ informal*) **= feeble**, soft, weak, silly, foolish, ineffectual, weedy (*informal*), spineless, effete, boneless, timorous, namby-pamby, irresolute, wussy (*slang*), nerdy *or* nurdy (*slang*) ▹ *n* **6 = rain**, rains, damp, drizzle, wet weather, rainy season, rainy weather, damp weather **OPPOSITE:** fine weather ▹ *vb* **9 = moisten**, spray, damp, dampen, water, dip, splash, soak, steep, sprinkle, saturate, drench, douse, irrigate, humidify, fertigate (*Austral*) **OPPOSITE:** dry

DICTIONARY

behind the ears *informal* immature or inexperienced ▷*n* **6** rainy weather **7** *Brit informal* a feeble or foolish person **8** *Brit informal* a Conservative politician who supports moderate policies ▷*vb* **wetting, wet** *or* **wetted 9** to make wet: *wet the brush before applying the paint* **10** to urinate in (one's clothes or bed) **11 wet oneself** to urinate in one's clothes **wetly** *adv* **wetness** *n*
WORD ORIGIN Old English *wǣt*

wet blanket *n informal* a person whose low spirits or lack of enthusiasm have a depressing effect on others

wet dream *n* an erotic dream accompanied by an emission of semen

wether *n* a male sheep, esp. a castrated one
WORD ORIGIN Old English

wetland *n* an area of marshy land

wet nurse *n* (esp. formerly) a woman hired to breast-feed another woman's baby

wet room *n* a type of waterproofed room with a drain in the floor often serving as an open-plan shower

wet suit *n* a close-fitting rubber suit used by skin-divers and yachtsmen to retain body heat

Weygand *n* **Maxime** 1867–1965, French general; as commander in chief of the Allied armies in France (1940) he advised the French Government to surrender to Germany

Weyl *n* **Hermann** 1885–1955, US mathematician, born in Germany; noted for his work on group theory and the mathematics of relativity

W. Glam West Glamorgan

whack ⓣ *vb* **1** to hit hard: *that lad whacked him over the head with a bottle* **2** (usually foll. by *in* or *on*) *informal* to put something onto or into (something else) with force or abandon: *whack on some sunscreen* ▷*n* **3** a hard blow or the sound of one: *a whack with a blunt instrument* **4** *informal* a share: *he took his whack of that money* **5 have a whack** to make an attempt **6 out of whack** *informal* out of order or out of condition: *my body is just a little out of whack*
WORD ORIGIN imitative

whacked *adj informal* completely exhausted

whacking *n* **1** *old-fashioned* a severe beating ▷*adv* **2** *Brit, Austral & NZ informal* extremely: *a whacking great elm*

whale *n* **1** a very large fishlike sea mammal that breathes through a blowhole on the top of its head **2 have a whale of a time** *informal* to enjoy oneself very much
WORD ORIGIN Old English *hwæl*

whalebone *n* a thin strip of a horny material that hangs from the upper jaw of some whales, formerly used for stiffening corsets

whalebone whale *n* any whale with a double blowhole and strips of whalebone between the jaws instead of teeth, including the right whale and the blue whale

whaler *n* **1** a ship used for hunting whales **2** a person whose job is to hunt whales

whaling *n* the activity of hunting and killing whales for food or oil

wham *interj informal* an expression indicating suddenness or forcefulness: *suddenly, wham! you are caught up right in the middle of it*
WORD ORIGIN imitative

whammy *n, pl* **-mies** *informal* a devastating setback: *the double whammy of drugs and divorce*

wharepuni (for-rep-poon-ee) *n NZ* (in a Māori community) a tall carved building used as a guesthouse
WORD ORIGIN Māori

wharf ⓣ *n, pl* **wharves** *or* **wharfs** a platform along the side of a waterfront for docking, loading, and unloading ships
WORD ORIGIN Old English *hwearf*

wharfie *n Austral & NZ* a dock labourer

Wharton *n* **Edith** (**Newbold**). 1862–1937, US novelist; author of *The House of Mirth* (1905) and *Ethan Frome* (1911)

what *pron* **1** used in requesting further information about the identity or categorization of something: *what was he wearing?; I knew what would happen* **2** the person, thing, people, or things that: *all was not what it seemed* **3** used in exclamations to add emphasis: *what a creep!* **4 what for?** for what reason? **5 what have you** other similar or related things: *qualifications, interests, profession, what have you* ▷*adj* **6** used with a noun in requesting further information about the identity or categorization of something: *what difference can it make now?* **7** to any degree or in any amount: *they provided what financial support they could*
WORD ORIGIN Old English *hwæt*

whatever *pron* **1** everything or anything that: *I can handle whatever comes up* **2** no matter what: *whatever you do, keep your temper* **3** *informal* other similar or related things: *a block of wood, rock, or whatever* **4** an intensive form of *what*, used in questions: *whatever gave you that impression?* ▷*adj* **5** an intensive form of *what*: *I can take whatever actions I deem necessary* **6** at all: *there is no foundation whatever for such opinions*

whatnot *n informal* other similar or related things: *groceries, wines, and whatnot*

whatsoever *adj* at all: used for emphasis after a noun phrase that uses words such as *none* or *any*: *there is nothing whatsoever wrong with your heart; it can be used at any time and under any circumstances whatsoever*

wheat *n* **1** a kind of grain used in making flour and pasta **2** the plant from which this grain is obtained
WORD ORIGIN Old English *hwǣte*

wheatear *n* a small northern songbird with a white rump
WORD ORIGIN from *white* + *arse*

wheaten *adj* made from the grain or flour of wheat: *wheaten bread*

wheat germ *n* the vitamin-rich middle part of a grain of wheat

wheatmeal *n* a brown flour intermediate between white flour and wholemeal flour

wheedle *vb* **-dling, -dled 1** to try to persuade (someone) by coaxing or flattery: *wheedling you into giving them their way* **2** to obtain (something) in this way: *she wheedled money out of him* **wheedling** *adj, n*
WORD ORIGIN origin unknown

wheel ⓣ *n* **1** a circular object mounted on a shaft around which it can turn, fixed under vehicles to enable them to move **2** anything like a wheel in shape or function: *the steering wheel; a spinning wheel* **3** something that is repeated in cycles: *the wheel of fashion would turn, and the clothes would be back in style* **4 at** *or* **behind the wheel** driving a vehicle ▷*vb* **5** to push (a bicycle, wheelchair, or pram) along **6** to turn in a circle **7 wheel and deal** to operate shrewdly and sometimes unscrupulously in order to advance one's own interests **8 wheel round** to change direction or turn round suddenly ▸ See also **wheels**
WORD ORIGIN Old English *hwēol, hweowol*

wheelbarrow *n* a shallow open box for carrying small loads, with a

W

THESAURUS

whack *vb* **1 = strike**, hit, beat, box, belt (*informal*), deck (*slang*), bang, rap, slap, bash (*informal*), sock (*slang*), chin (*slang*), smack, thrash, thump, buffet, clout (*informal*), slug, cuff, swipe, clobber (*slang*), wallop (*informal*), thwack, lambast(e), lay one on (*slang*), beat *or* knock seven bells out of (*informal*) ▷*n* **3 = blow**, hit, box, stroke, belt (*informal*), bang, rap, slap, bash (*informal*), sock (*slang*), smack, thump, buffet, clout (*informal*), slug, cuff, swipe, wallop (*informal*), wham, thwack **4** (*informal*) **= share**, part, cut (*informal*), bit, portion, quota, allotment

wharf *n* **= dock**, pier, berth, quay, jetty, landing stage

wheel *n* **1, 2 = disc**, ring, hoop ▷*vb* **5 = push**, trundle, roll **6 = turn**, swing, spin, revolve, rotate,

DICTIONARY

wheel at the front and two handles
wheelbase *n* the distance between the front and back axles of a motor vehicle
wheelchair *n* a special chair on large wheels, for use by people who cannot walk properly
wheel clamp *n* a device fixed onto one wheel of an illegally parked car to prevent the car being driven off
Wheeler *n* **1 John Archibald** 1911–2008, US physicist, noted for his work on nuclear fission and the development (1949–51) of the hydrogen bomb, also for his work on unified field theory **2** Sir (**Robert Eric**) **Mortimer** 1890–1976, Scottish archaeologist, who did much to increase public interest in archaeology. He is noted esp. for his excavations at Mohenjo-Daro and Harappa in the Indus Valley and at Maiden Castle in Dorset
wheelhouse *n* an enclosed structure on the bridge of a ship from which it is steered
wheelie *n* a manoeuvre on a cycle or skateboard in which the front wheel or wheels are raised off the ground
wheelie bin *n Brit, Austral & NZ* a large container for household rubbish, mounted on wheels so that it can be moved more easily
wheeling and dealing *n* shrewd and sometimes unscrupulous moves made in order to advance one's own interests **wheeler-dealer** *n*
wheels *pl n* **1** *informal* a car **2** the main force and mechanism of an organization or system: *the wheels of the economy* **3 wheels within wheels** a series of intricately connected events or plots
wheelwright *n* a person whose job is to make and mend wheels
wheeze *vb* **wheezing, wheezed 1** to breathe with a rasping or whistling sound ▷*n* **2** a wheezing breath or sound **3** *Brit old-fashioned slang* a trick or plan: *a glorious tax wheeze* **wheezy** *adj*
WORD ORIGIN probably from Old Norse *hvǣsa* to hiss
whelk *n* an edible sea creature with a strong snail-like shell
WORD ORIGIN Old English *weoloc*
whelp *n* **1** a young wolf or dog **2** *offensive* a youth ▷*vb* **3** (of an animal) to give birth
WORD ORIGIN Old English *hwelp*
when *adv* **1** at what time?: *when are they leaving?* ▷*conj* **2** at the time at which: *he was twenty when the war started* **3** although: *he drives when he could walk* **4** considering the fact that: *how did you pass the exam when you hadn't studied for it?* ▷*pron* **5** at which time: *she's at the age when girls get interested in boys*
WORD ORIGIN Old English *hwanne, hwænne*
whence *conj old-fashioned or poetic* from what place, cause, or origin: *he would then ask them whence they came*
WORD ORIGIN Middle English *whannes*
whenever *conj* **1** at every or any time that: *the filly was trained to stop whenever a jockey used a whip* ▷*adv* **2** no matter when: *I am eager to come whenever you suggest* **3** *informal* at an unknown or unspecified time: *the 16th, 17th, or whenever* **4** an intensive form of *when*, used in questions: *if we can't exercise restraint now, whenever can we?*
where *adv* **1** in, at, or to what place, point, or position?: *where are we going?; I know where he found it* ▷*pron* **2** in, at, or to which place: *he found a sandwich bar where he could get a snack* ▷*conj* **3** in the place at which: *he should have stayed where he was doing well*
WORD ORIGIN Old English *hwǣr*
whereabouts ⓘ *pl n* **1** the place, esp. the approximate place, where a person or thing is: *the whereabouts of the president are unknown* ▷*adv* **2** approximately where: *whereabouts will you go?*
whereas *conj* but by contrast: *she was crazy about him, whereas for him it was just another affair*
whereby *pron* by or because of which: *the process whereby pests become resistant to pesticides*
wherefore *n* **1 the whys and wherefores** the reasons or explanation: *the whys and wherefores of the war* ▷*conj* **2** *old-fashioned or formal* for which reason
wherein *old-fashioned or formal adv* **1** in what place or respect?: *wherein lies the truth?* ▷*pron* **2** in which place or thing: *the mirror wherein he had been gazing*
whereof *old-fashioned or formal adv* **1** of what or which person or thing? ▷*pron* **2** of which person or thing: *I know whereof I speak*
whereupon *conj* at which point: *they sentenced him to death, whereupon he fainted*
wherever *pron* **1** at, in, or to every place or point which: *I got a wonderful reception wherever I went* ▷*conj* **2** in, to, or at whatever place: *wherever they went, the conditions were harsh* ▷*adv* **3** no matter where: *we're going to find him, wherever he is* **4** *informal* at, in, or to an unknown or unspecified place: *the jungles of Borneo or wherever* **5** an intensive form of *where*, used in questions: *wherever have you been?*
wherewithal *n* **the wherewithal** the necessary funds, resources, or equipment: *the wherewithal for making chemical weapons*
whet *vb* **whetting, whetted 1 whet someone's appetite** to increase someone's desire for or interest in something: *she gave him just enough information to whet his appetite* **2** *old-fashioned* to sharpen (a knife or other tool)
WORD ORIGIN Old English *hwettan*
whether *conj* **1** used to introduce an indirect question: *he asked him whether he had seen the hunter* **2** used to introduce a clause expressing doubt or choice: *you are entitled to the assistance of a lawyer, whether or not you can afford one; we learn from experience, whether good or bad*
WORD ORIGIN Old English *hwæther*
whetstone *n* a stone used for sharpening knives or other tools
whew *interj* an exclamation of relief, surprise, disbelief, or weariness
whey (**way**) *n* the watery liquid that separates from the curd when milk is clotted, for example in making cheese
WORD ORIGIN Old English *hwǣg*
which *adj* **1** used with a noun in requesting that the particular thing being referred to is further identified or distinguished: *which way had he gone?; a questionnaire to find out which shops local consumers use* **2** any out of several: *you have to choose which goods and services you want* ▷*pron* **3** used in requesting that the particular thing being referred to is further identified or distinguished: *which of these occupations would be suitable for you?* **4** used in relative clauses referring to a thing rather than a person: *a discovery which could have lasting effects* **5** and that: *her books were all over the dining table, which meant we had to eat in the kitchen*
WORD ORIGIN Old English *hwelc*
whichever *adj* **1** any out of several: *choose whichever line you feel more comfortable with* **2** no matter which: *whichever bridge you take, pause mid-stream for a look up and down the river* ▷*pron* **3** any one or ones out of several: *delete whichever is inapplicable* **4** no matter which one or ones: *whichever you choose, you must be consistent throughout*
whiff ⓘ *n* **1** a passing odour: *I got a whiff of her perfume* **2** a trace or hint: *the first whiff of jealousy*
WORD ORIGIN imitative
Whig *n* **1** a member of a British political party of the 18th–19th centuries that sought limited political and social reform and provided the core of the Liberal Party ▷*adj* **2** of or relating to Whigs

W

THESAURUS

whirl, swivel
whereabouts *pl n* **1 = position**, situation, site, location
whiff *n* **1 = smell**, hint, scent, sniff, aroma, odour, draught, niff (*Brit slang*)

DICTIONARY

Whiggism *n*
WORD ORIGIN probably from *whiggamore*, one of a group of 17th-century Scottish rebels

while *conj* **1** at the same time that: *anti-inflammatory remedies may be used to alleviate the condition while background factors are investigated* **2** at some point during the time that: *her father had died while she was gone* **3** although or whereas: *while she tossed and turned, he fell into a dreamless sleep* ▹*n* **4** a period of time: *I'd like to stay a while*
WORD ORIGIN Old English *hwīl*

while away *vb* **whiling, whiled** to pass (time) idly but pleasantly

whilst *conj chiefly Brit* ▸same as **while**

whim ⓘ *n* a sudden, passing, and often fanciful idea
WORD ORIGIN origin unknown

whimper *vb* **1** to cry, complain, or say (something) in a whining plaintive way ▹*n* **2** a soft plaintive whine
WORD ORIGIN imitative

whimsical *adj* unusual, playful, and fanciful: *a whimsical story* **whimsically** *adv*

whimsy *n* **1** *pl* **-sies** a fanciful or playful idea: *they thought sparing the rod a foolish whimsy* **2** capricious or playful behaviour: *sudden flights of whimsy*
WORD ORIGIN from *whim*

whin *n chiefly Brit* ▸same as **gorse**
WORD ORIGIN from Old Norse

whine ⓘ *n* **1** a long high-pitched plaintive cry or moan **2** a peevish complaint ▹*vb* **whining, whined** **3** to whinge or complain **4** to issue a long high-pitched moan **whiner** *n* **whining** *adj, n*
WORD ORIGIN Old English *hwīnan*

whinge *Brit, Austral & NZ informal vb* **whingeing, whinged** **1** to complain in a moaning manner ▹*n* **2** a complaint **whinger** *n*
WORD ORIGIN Old English *hwinsian* to whine

whinny *vb* **-nies, -nying, -nied** **1** (of a horse) to neigh softly or gently ▹*n, pl* **-nies** **2** a gentle or low-pitched neigh
WORD ORIGIN imitative

whip ⓘ *n* **1** a piece of leather or rope attached at one end to a stiff handle, used for hitting people or animals **2 a** a member of a political party who is responsible for urging members to attend Parliament to vote on an important issue **b** a notice sent to members of a political party by the whip, urging them to attend Parliament to vote in a particular way on an important issue **3** a dessert made from egg whites or cream beaten stiff: *raspberry whip* ▹*vb* **whipping, whipped** **4** to hit with a whip **5** to hit sharply: *strands of hair whipped across her cheeks* **6** *informal* to move or go quickly and suddenly: *machine-gun bullets whipped past him* **7** to beat (cream or eggs) with a whisk or fork until frothy or stiff **8** to rouse (someone) into a particular condition: *politicians and businessmen have whipped themselves into a panic about never-ending recession* **9** *informal* to steal (something) ▸See also **whip out, whip-round, whip up** > **whipping** *n*
WORD ORIGIN perhaps from Middle Dutch *wippen* to swing

whip bird *n Austral* a bird with a whistle ending in a whipcrack note

whip hand *n* **the whip hand** an advantage or dominating position: *buyers have the whip hand over estate agents*

whiplash *n* **1** a quick lash of a whip **2** ▸short for **whiplash injury**

whiplash injury *n* an injury to the neck resulting from the head being suddenly thrust forward and then snapped back, for example in a car crash

whip out *or* **off** *vb* to take (something) out or off quickly and suddenly: *she whipped off her glasses*

whipper-in *n, pl* **whippers-in** a huntsman's assistant who manages the hounds

whippersnapper *n old-fashioned* a young impertinent overconfident person

whippet *n* a small slender dog similar to a greyhound
WORD ORIGIN perhaps based on *whip it!* move quickly!

whipping boy *n* a person who is expected to take the blame for other people's mistakes or incompetence

whip-round *n informal* an impromptu collection of money

whipstock *n* the handle of a whip

whip up *vb* **1** to excite or arouse: *to get people all whipped up about something; to whip up enthusiasm* **2** *informal* to prepare quickly: *she had whipped up a rich sauce*

whir *n, vb* **whirring, whirred** ▸same as **whirr**

whirl ⓘ *vb* **1** to spin or turn round very fast **2** to seem to spin from dizziness or confusion: *my mind whirled with half-formed thoughts* ▹*n* **3** the act or an instance of whirling: *he grasps her by the waist and gives her a whirl* **4** a round of intense activity: *the social whirl of Paris* **5** a confused state: *my thoughts are in a whirl* **6** **give something a whirl** *informal* to try something new
WORD ORIGIN Old Norse *hvirfla* to turn about

whirligig *n* **1** a spinning toy, such as a top **2** ▸same as **merry-go-round** **3** anything that whirls

whirlpool *n* a powerful circular current of water, into which objects floating nearby are drawn

whirlwind *n* **1** a column of air whirling violently upwards in a spiral ▹*adj* **2** done or happening much more quickly than usual: *a whirlwind tour of France*

whirr *or* **whir** *n* **1** a prolonged soft whizz or buzz: *the whirr of the fax machine* ▹*vb* **whirring, whirred** **2** to produce a prolonged soft whizz or buzz **whirring** *n, adj*
WORD ORIGIN probably from Old Norse

whisk ⓘ *vb* **1** to move or take somewhere swiftly: *I was whisked away in a police car* **2** to brush away lightly: *the waiter whisked the crumbs away with a*

THESAURUS

whim *n* **= impulse**, sudden notion, caprice, fancy, sport, urge, notion, humour, freak, craze, fad *(informal)*, quirk, conceit, vagary, whimsy, passing thought, crotchet

whine *n* **1 = cry**, moan, sob, wail, whimper, plaintive cry **2 = complaint**, moan, grumble, grouse, gripe *(informal)*, whinge *(informal)*, grouch *(informal)*, beef *(slang)* ▹*vb* **3 = complain**, grumble, gripe *(informal)*, whinge *(informal)*, moan, cry, beef *(slang)*, carp, sob, wail, grouse, whimper, bleat, grizzle *(informal, chiefly Brit)*, grouch *(informal)*, bellyache *(slang)*, kvetch *(US slang)* **4 = cry**, sob, wail, whimper, sniffle, snivel, moan

whip *n* **1 = lash**, cane, birch, switch, crop, scourge, thong, rawhide, riding crop, horsewhip, bullwhip, knout, cat-o'-nine-tails ▹*vb* **4 = lash**, cane, flog, beat, switch, leather, punish, strap, tan *(slang)*, thrash, lick *(informal)*, birch, scourge, spank, castigate, lambast(e), flagellate, give a hiding *(informal)* **6** *(informal)* **= dash**, shoot, fly, tear, rush, dive, dart, whisk, flit **7 = whisk**, beat, mix vigorously, stir vigorously **8 = incite**, drive, push, urge, stir, spur, provoke, compel, hound, prod, work up, get going, agitate, prick, inflame, instigate, goad, foment

whirl *vb* **1a = spin**, turn, circle, wheel, twist, reel, rotate, pivot, twirl **1b = rotate**, roll, twist, revolve, swirl, twirl, gyrate, pirouette **2 = feel dizzy**, swim, spin, reel, go round ▹*n* **3 = revolution**, turn, roll, circle, wheel, spin, twist, reel, swirl, rotation, twirl, pirouette, gyration, birl *(Scot)* **4 = bustle**, round, series, succession, flurry, merry-go-round **5a = confusion**, daze, dither *(chiefly Brit)*, giddiness **5b = tumult**, spin, stir, agitation, commotion, hurly-burly

whisk *vb* **2 = flick**, whip, sweep, brush, wipe, twitch **3 = beat**, mix vigorously, stir vigorously, whip, fluff up ▹*n* **4 = flick**, sweep, brush, whip, wipe **5 = beater**, mixer, blender

DICTIONARY

napkin **3** to beat (cream or eggs) with a whisk or fork until frothy or stiff ▷ *n* **4** the act or an instance of whisking: *a whisk of a scaly tail* **5** a utensil for beating cream or eggs until frothy or stiff
WORD ORIGIN Old Norse *visk* wisp

whisker *n* **1** any of the long stiff hairs that grow out from the sides of the mouth of a cat or other mammal **2** any of the hairs growing on a man's face, esp. on the cheeks or chin **3 by a whisker** by a very small distance or amount: *we missed him by a whisker* **whiskered** *or* **whiskery** *adj*
WORD ORIGIN Old Norse *visk* wisp

whiskey *n* Irish or American whisky

whisky *n, pl* **-kies** a strong alcoholic drink made by distilling fermented cereals, esp. in Scotland
WORD ORIGIN Scottish Gaelic *uisge beatha* water of life

whisky-jack *n Canad* ▸ same as **Canada jay**

whisper ❶ *vb* **1** to speak or say (something) very softly, using the breath instead of the vocal cords **2** to make a low soft rustling sound: *the leaves whispered* ▷ *n* **3** a low soft voice: *her voice sank to a whisper* **4** *informal* a rumour: *I just picked up a whisper on this killing* **5** a low soft rustling sound: *a whisper of breeze in the shrubbery* **whispered** *adj*
WORD ORIGIN Old English *hwisprian*

whist *n* a card game for two pairs of players
WORD ORIGIN perhaps from *whisk*, referring to the whisking up of the tricks

whist drive *n* a social gathering where whist is played

whistle *vb* **-tling, -tled 1** to produce a shrill sound by forcing breath between pursed lips **2** to produce (a tune) by making a series of such sounds **3** to signal (to) by whistling or blowing a whistle: *the doorman whistled a cruising cab* **4** to move with a whistling sound: *a shell whistled through the upper air* **5** (of a kettle or train) to produce a shrill sound caused by steam being forced through a small opening **6** (of a bird) to give a shrill cry **7 whistle in the dark** to try to keep up one's confidence in spite of being afraid ▷ *n* **8** the act or sound of whistling: *he gave a whistle of astonishment* **9** a metal instrument that is blown down its end to produce a tune, signal, or alarm: *he played the tin whistle; the referee's whistle* **10** a device in a kettle or a train that makes a shrill sound by means of steam under pressure **11 blow the whistle on** *informal* to reveal and put a stop to (wrongdoing or a wrongdoer): *to blow the whistle on corrupt top-level officials* **12 wet one's whistle** *informal* to have a drink
WORD ORIGIN Old English *hwistlian*

whistle-blower *n informal* a person who informs on someone or puts a stop to something

whistle for *vb informal* to expect in vain: *he could whistle for his vote in the future*

whistle-stop *adj* denoting a tour, esp. a campaign tour by a political candidate, in which short stops are made at many different places

whit *n* **not a whit** not at all: *it does not matter a whit*
WORD ORIGIN probably variant of obsolete *wight* a person

Whit *n* **1** ▸ short for **Whitsuntide** ▷ *adj* **2** of Whitsuntide: *Whit Monday*

Whitaker *n* **1** Sir **Frederick** 1812–91, New Zealand statesman, born in England: prime minister of New Zealand (1863–64; 1882–83) **2 Forrest (Steven)**, born 1961, US actor and film director; his films include (as actor) *Ghost Dog* (1999) and *The Last King of Scotland* (2006); (as director) *Waiting to Exhale* (1995)

Whitbread *n* **Fatima** born 1961, British javelin thrower

white ❶ *adj* **1** having no hue, owing to the reflection of all or almost all light; of the colour of snow **2** pale, because of illness, fear, shock, or another emotion: *white with rage* **3** (of hair) having lost its colour, usually from age **4** (of coffee or tea) with milk or cream **5** (of wine) made from pale grapes or from black grapes separated from their skins **6** denoting flour, or bread made from flour, that has had part of the grain removed ▷ *n* **7** the lightest colour; the colour of snow **8** the clear fluid that surrounds the yolk of an egg **9** *anat* the white part of the eyeball **10** anything white, such as white paint or white clothing: *a room decorated all in white* ▸ See also **whites** > **whiteness** *n* **whitish** *adj*
WORD ORIGIN Old English *hwīt*

White¹ *n* **1** a person, esp. one of European ancestry, from a human population having light pigmentation of the skin ▷ *adj* **2** denoting or relating to a White person or White people

White² *n* **1 Gilbert** 1720–93, English clergyman and naturalist, noted for his *Natural History and Antiquities of Selborne* (1789) **2 Jimmy** born 1962, British snooker player **3 Marco Pierre** born 1961, British chef and restaurateur **4 Patrick (Victor Martindale)** 1912–90, Australian novelist: his works include *Voss* (1957), *The Eye of the Storm* (1973), and *A Fringe of Leaves* (1976): Nobel prize for literature 1973 **5 T(erence) H(anbury)** 1906–64, British novelist: author of the Arthurian sequence *The Once and Future King* (1939–58) **6 Willard (Wentworth)** born 1946, British operatic bass, born in Jamaica

whitebait *n* **1** the young of herrings, sprats, or pilchards, cooked and eaten whole **2** any of various small silvery fishes of Australia and New Zealand and of North American coastal regions of the Pacific

white blood cell *n* ▸ same as **leucocyte**

whitecaps *pl n* waves with white broken crests

white-collar ❶ *adj* denoting workers employed in professional and clerical occupations

white dwarf *n* a small, faint, very dense star

white elephant *n* a possession that is unwanted by its owner

white feather *n* a symbol of cowardice

Whitefield *n* **George** 1714–70, English Methodist preacher, who separated from the Wesleys (?1741) because of his Calvinistic views

white fish *n* a sea fish with white flesh that is used for food, such as cod or haddock

white flag *n* a signal of surrender or to request a truce

whitefly *n, pl* **-flies** a tiny whitish insect that is harmful to greenhouse plants

White Friar *n* a Carmelite friar

white gold *n* a white lustrous hard-wearing alloy containing gold together with platinum or other metals, used in jewellery

white goods *pl n* large household appliances, such as refrigerators and cookers

THESAURUS

whisper *vb* **1 = murmur**, breathe, mutter, mumble, purr, speak in hushed tones, say softly, say sotto voce, utter under the breath
OPPOSITE: shout
2 = rustle, sigh, moan, murmur, hiss, swish, sough, susurrate *(literary)* ▷ *n* **3 = murmur**, mutter, mumble, undertone, low voice, soft voice, hushed tone **4** *(informal)* **= rumour**, report, word, story, hint, buzz, gossip, dirt *(US slang)*, goss *(informal)*, innuendo, insinuation, scuttlebutt *(US slang)* **5 = rustle**, sigh, sighing, murmur, hiss, swish, soughing, susurration *or* susurrus *(literary)*

white *adj* **2 = pale**, grey, ghastly, wan, pasty, bloodless, pallid, ashen, waxen, like death warmed up *(informal)*, wheyfaced

white-collar *adj* **= clerical**, office, executive, professional, salaried, nonmanual

DICTIONARY

Whitehead *n* **Alfred North** 1861–1947, English mathematician and philosopher, who collaborated with Bertrand Russell in writing *Principia Mathematica* (1910–13), and developed a holistic philosophy of science, chiefly in *Process and Reality* (1929)

white heat *n* **1** intense heat that produces a white light **2** *informal* a state of intense emotion: *the white heat of hate*

white hope *n informal* a person who is expected to accomplish a great deal: *the great white hope of Polish cinema*

white horses *pl n* ▸ same as **whitecaps**

white-hot *adj* **1** at such a high temperature that white light is produced **2** *informal* in a state of intense emotion: *white-hot agony*

White House *n* the US president and the executive branch of the US government: *the White House reviewed the report*
WORD ORIGIN after the official home of the US president in Washington DC

Whitelaw *n* **William** (**Stephen Ian**), 1st Viscount Whitelaw of Penrith. 1918–99, British Conservative politician; Home Secretary (1979–83); leader of the House of Lords (1983–88)

Whiteley *n* **Brett** 1939–1992, Australian artist, who travelled widely in Europe and Asia; his works include landscapes, nudes, and portraits

white lie *n* a small lie, usually told to avoid hurting someone's feelings

white light *n* light that contains all the wavelengths of the visible spectrum, as in sunlight

white matter *n* the whitish tissue of the brain and spinal cord, consisting mainly of nerve fibres

white meat *n* meat, such as chicken or pork, that is light in colour when cooked

whiten *vb* to make or become white or whiter **whitener** *n* **whitening** *n*

white noise *n* noise that has a wide range of frequencies of uniform intensity

whiteout *n* an atmospheric condition in which blizzards or low clouds make it very difficult to see

white paper *n* an official government report which sets out the government's policy on a specific matter

white pepper *n* a hot seasoning made from the seeds of the pepper plant with the husks removed

White Russian *adj* **1** (formerly) of Byelorussia, an administrative division of the W Soviet Union: now Belarus ▹*n* **2** (formerly) a person from Byelorussia **3** (formerly) the language of Byelorussia

whites *pl n* white clothes, as worn for playing cricket

white sauce *n* a thick sauce made from flour, butter, seasonings, and milk or stock

white slave *n* a girl or woman forced or sold into prostitution **white slavery** *n*

white spirit *n* a colourless liquid obtained from petroleum and used as a substitute for turpentine

White supremacy *n* the theory or belief that White people are superior to people of other races **White supremacist** *n, adj*

white tie *n* **1** a white bow tie worn as part of a man's formal evening dress ▹*adj* **white-tie** **2** denoting an occasion when formal evening dress should be worn: *tickets for the white-tie Shelley Ball*

white trash *n* poor White people living in the United States, esp. in the South

whitewash *n* **1** a mixture of lime or chalk in water, for whitening walls and other surfaces **2** an attempt to conceal the unpleasant truth: *the report was a whitewash* ▹*vb* **3** to cover with whitewash **4** to conceal the unpleasant truth about **whitewashed** *adj*

whitewood *n* a light-coloured wood often prepared for staining

Whitgift *n* **John** ?1530–1604, English churchman; as archbishop of Canterbury (1583–1604) he tried to curb the influence of Puritanism

whither *conj old-fashioned or poetic* to what place or for what purpose: *they knew not whither they went*
WORD ORIGIN Old English *hwider, hwæder*

whiting (white-ing) *n* **1** a white-fleshed food fish of European seas **2** *Austral* any of several marine food fishes

whitlow *n* an inflamed sore on the end of a finger or toe
WORD ORIGIN originally *white + flaw*

Whitney[1] *n* **Mount Whitney** a mountain in E California: the highest peak in the Sierra Nevada Mountains and in continental US (excluding Alaska). Height: 4418 m (14 495 ft)

Whitney[2] *n* **1 Eli** 1765–1825, US inventor of a mechanical cotton gin (1793) and pioneer manufacturer of interchangeable parts **2 William Dwight** 1827–94, US philologist, noted esp. for his *Sanskrit Grammar* (1879)

Whitsun *n* **1** ▸ short for **Whitsuntide** ▹*adj* **2** of Whit Sunday or Whitsuntide

Whit Sunday *n* the seventh Sunday after Easter
WORD ORIGIN Old English *hwīta sunnandæg* white Sunday

Whitsuntide *n* the week that begins with Whit Sunday

Whittier *n* **John Greenleaf** 1807–92, US poet and humanitarian: a leading campaigner in the antislavery movement. His poems include *Snow-Bound* (1866)

whittle ⓣ *vb* **-tling, -tled** **1** to make (an object) by cutting or shaving pieces from (a piece of wood) with a small knife **2** **whittle down** *or* **away** to reduce in size or effectiveness gradually: *my self-confidence had been whittled away to almost nothing*
WORD ORIGIN Old English *thwītan* to cut

whizz *or* **whiz** *vb* **whizzing, whizzed** **1** to move with a loud humming or buzzing sound: *the bullets whizzed overhead* **2** *informal* to move or go quickly: *the wind surfers fairly whizzed along the water* ▹*n, pl* **whizzes** **3** a loud humming or buzzing sound **4** *informal* a person who is extremely good at something: *he's a whizz on finance* **5** *slang* amphetamine
WORD ORIGIN imitative

whizz kid *or* **whiz kid** *n informal* a person who is outstandingly able and successful for his or her age

who *pron* **1** which person: *who are you?; he didn't know who had started it* **2** used at the beginning of a relative clause referring to a person or people already mentioned: *he is a man who can effect change*
WORD ORIGIN Old English *hwā*

WHO World Health Organization

whoa *interj* a command used to stop horses or to slow down someone who is moving or talking too fast

whodunnit *or* **whodunit** (hoo-**dun**-nit) *n informal* a novel, play, or film about the solving of a murder mystery

whoever *pron* **1** the person or people who: *whoever bought it for you has to make the claim* **2** no matter who: *I pity him, whoever he is* **3** *informal* other similar or related people or person: *your best friend, your neighbours, or whoever* **4** an intensive form of *who*, used in questions: *whoever thought of such a thing?*

whole ⓣ *adj* **1** constituting or referring to all of something: *I'd spent*

W

THESAURUS

whittle *vb* **1 = carve**, cut, hew, shape, trim, shave, pare
2 (foll. by **down** or **away**) **= undermine**, reduce, destroy, consume, erode, eat away, wear away, cut down, cut, decrease, prune, scale down

whole *adj* **1 = complete**, full, total, entire, integral, uncut, undivided, unabridged, unexpurgated, uncondensed **OPPOSITE:** partial
2 = undamaged, intact, unscathed,

my whole allowance by Saturday afternoon **2** unbroken or undamaged ▹*adv* **3** in an undivided or unbroken piece: *truffles are cooked whole* **4** *informal* completely or entirely: *a whole new theory of treatment* ▹*n* **5** all there is of a thing: *the whole of my salary* **6** a collection of parts viewed together as a unit: *taking Great Britain as a whole* **7 on the whole a** taking all things into consideration: *on the whole he has worked about one year out of twelve* **b** in general: *on the whole they were not successful* **wholeness** *n*
WORD ORIGIN Old English *hāl*

wholefood *n* **1** food that has been refined or processed as little as possible ▹*adj* **2** of or relating to wholefood: *a wholefood diet*

wholehearted *adj* done or given with total sincerity or enthusiasm: *wholehearted support* **wholeheartedly** *adv*

wholemeal *adj Austral & Brit* **1** (of flour) made from the entire wheat kernel **2** made from wholemeal flour: *wholemeal bread*

whole number *n maths* a number that does not contain a fraction, such as 0, 1, or 2

wholesale ❶ *n* **1** the business of selling goods in large quantities and at lower prices to retailers for resale **2** relating to such business: *wholesale prices* **3** extensive or indiscriminate: *the wholesale destruction of forests* ▹*adv* **4** by or through the wholesale business: *we buy beef wholesale* **5** extensively or indiscriminately: *buffalo were slaughtered wholesale* **wholesaler** *n*

wholesome *adj* **1** physically beneficial: *wholesome food* **2** morally beneficial: *a wholesome attitude of the mind*
WORD ORIGIN from *whole* healthy

whole-wheat *adj US & Canad* ▸same as **wholemeal**

wholly ❶ *adv* completely or totally

whom *pron* the objective form of *who*: *whom will you tell?; he was devoted to his wife, whom he married in 1960*
WORD ORIGIN Old English *hwām*

whomever *pron* the objective form of *whoever*: *this law limits an employer's right to employ whomever he wants*

whoop *vb* **1** to cry out in excitement or joy **2 whoop it up** *informal* to indulge in a noisy celebration ▹*n* **3** a loud cry of excitement or joy
WORD ORIGIN imitative

whoopee *old-fashioned informal interj* **1** an exclamation of joy or excitement ▹*n* **2 make whoopee a** to indulge in a noisy celebration **b** to make love

whooping cough *n* an acute infectious disease mainly affecting children, that causes coughing spasms ending with a shrill crowing sound on breathing in

whoops *interj* an exclamation of mild surprise or of apology

whopper *n informal* **1** an unusually large or impressive example of something: *Deauville's beach is a whopper* **2** a big lie

whopping *informal adj* **1** unusually large: *a whopping 40 per cent* ▹*adv* **2** extremely: *it's a whopping great gamble*

whore ❶ (hore) *n* a prostitute or promiscuous woman: often a term of abuse
WORD ORIGIN Old English *hōre*

whorehouse *n informal* a brothel

Whorf *n* **Benjamin Lee** 1897–1943, US linguist, who argued that human language determines perception ▸See also **Sapir-Whorf hypothesis**

whorl *n* **1** *bot* a circular arrangement of leaves or flowers round the stem of a plant **2** *zool* a single turn in a spiral shell **3** anything shaped like a coil
WORD ORIGIN probably variant of *whirl*

who's who is *or* who has

whose *pron* **1** of whom? belonging to whom?: used in direct and indirect questions: *whose idea was it?; I wondered whose it was* **2** of whom or of which: used as a relative pronoun: *Gran had sympathy for anybody whose life had gone wrong*
WORD ORIGIN Old English *hwæs*, genitive of *hwā* who + *hwæt* what

whosoever *pron old-fashioned or formal* ▸same as **whoever**

why *adv* **1** for what reason?: *why did he marry her?; she avoided asking him why he was there* ▹*pron* **2** for or because of which: *you can think of all kinds of reasons why you should not believe it* ▹*n, pl* **whys 3 the whys and wherefores** ▸see **wherefore** (sense 1) ▹*interj* **4** an exclamation of surprise, indignation, or impatience: *why, I listen to you on the radio twice a week*
WORD ORIGIN Old English *hwȳ, hwī*

WI 1 Wisconsin **2** *Brit & NZ* Women's Institute

wick *n* **1** a cord through the middle of a candle, through which the fuel reaches the flame **2 get on someone's wick** *Austral & Brit slang* to annoy someone
WORD ORIGIN Old English *wēoce*

wicked *adj* **1** morally bad: *the wicked queen in 'Snow White'* **2** playfully mischievous or roguish: *let's be wicked and go skinny-dipping* **3** dangerous or unpleasant: *there was a wicked cut over his eye* **4** *slang* very good **wickedly** *adv* **wickedness** *n*
WORD ORIGIN Old English *wicca* sorcerer, *wicce* witch

wicker *adj* made of wickerwork: *a wicker chair*
WORD ORIGIN from Old Norse

wickerwork *n* a material consisting of slender flexible twigs woven together

wicket *n cricket* **1** either of two sets of three stumps stuck in the ground with two wooden bails resting on top, at which the batsman stands **2** the playing space between these **3** the act or instance of a batsman being got out
WORD ORIGIN Old French *wiket*

wicketkeeper *n cricket* the fielder positioned directly behind the wicket

wicking *adj* acting to move moisture by capillary action from the inside to the surface: *wicking fabric*

wide ❶ *adj* **1** having a great extent from side to side: *the wide main street* **2** having a specified extent from side to side: *three metres wide* **3** covering or including many different things: *a wide range of services* **4** covering a large

THESAURUS

unbroken, good, sound, perfect, mint, untouched, flawless, unhurt, faultless, unharmed, in one piece, uninjured, inviolate, unimpaired, unmutilated **OPPOSITE:** damaged ▹*n* **6 = unit**, body, piece, object, combination, unity, entity, ensemble, entirety, fullness, totality **OPPOSITE:** part

wholesale *adj* **3 = extensive**, total, mass, sweeping, broad, comprehensive, wide-ranging, blanket, outright, far-reaching, indiscriminate, all-inclusive **OPPOSITE:** limited ▹*adv* **5 = extensively**, comprehensively, across the board, all at once, indiscriminately, without exception, on a large scale

wholly *adv* **= completely**, totally, perfectly, fully, entirely, comprehensively, altogether, thoroughly, utterly, heart and soul, one hundred per cent *(informal)*, in every respect **OPPOSITE:** partly

whore *n* **= prostitute**, hooker *(US slang)*, tart *(informal)*, streetwalker, tom *(Brit slang)*, brass *(slang)*, slag *(Brit slang)*, hustler *(US & Canad slang)*, call girl, courtesan, working girl *(facetious, slang)*, harlot, loose woman, fallen woman, scrubber *(Brit & Austral slang)*, strumpet, trollop, lady of the night, cocotte, woman of easy virtue, demimondaine, woman of ill repute, fille de joie *(French)*, demirep *(rare)*

wide *adj* **1 = spacious**, broad, extensive, ample, roomy, commodious **OPPOSITE:** confined **3 = broad**, comprehensive, extensive, wide-ranging, large, catholic, expanded, sweeping, vast, immense, ample, inclusive, expansive, exhaustive, encyclopedic, far-ranging, compendious

DICTIONARY

distance or extent: *the proposal was voted down by a wide margin* **5** (of eyes) opened fully ▷ *adv* **6** to a large or full extent: *he swung the door wide* **7** **far and wide** ▸ see **far** (sense 7) ▷ *n* **8** *cricket* a ball bowled outside the batsman's reach, which scores a run for the batting side **widely** *adv*
WORD ORIGIN Old English *wīd*

wide-angle lens *n* a lens on a camera which can cover a wider angle of view than an ordinary lens

wide-awake *adj* fully awake

wide-eyed *adj* **1** innocent or naive **2** surprised or frightened: *wide-eyed astonishment* ▷ *adv* **3** in a frightened, surprised, or excited manner: *they looked at me wide-eyed*

widen ⊙ *vb* to make or become wide or wider

wide open *adj* **1** open to the full extent: *the main door was wide open* **2** exposed or vulnerable: *he was leaving himself wide open to problems*

wide-ranging *adj* covering or including many different things or subjects: *a wide-ranging review*

widespread ⊙ *adj* affecting an extensive area or a large number of people: *widespread damage; widespread public support*

widgeon *n* ▸ same as **wigeon**

widget *n* **1** *informal* any small device, the name of which is unknown or forgotten **2** a small device in a beer can which, when the can is opened, releases nitrogen gas into the beer, giving it a head **3** a small computer program that can be installed on and executed from the desktop of a personal computer
WORD ORIGIN changed from GADGET

widow *n* a woman whose husband has died and who has not remarried **widowhood** *n*
WORD ORIGIN Old English *widewe*

widowed *adj* denoting a person, usually a woman, whose spouse has died and who has not remarried

widower *n* a man whose wife has died and who has not remarried

widow's weeds *pl n old-fashioned* the black mourning clothes traditionally worn by a widow
WORD ORIGIN from Old English *wǣd* a band worn in mourning

width ⊙ *n* **1** the extent or measurement of something from side to side **2** the distance across a rectangular swimming bath, as opposed to its length

Wieland[1] *n* the German name for **Wayland**

Wieland[2] *n* **Christoph Martin** 1733–1813, German writer, noted esp. for his verse epic *Oberon* (1780)

wield ⊙ *vb* **1** to handle or use (a weapon or tool) **2** to exert or maintain (power or influence)
WORD ORIGIN Old English *wieldan, wealdan*

Wien[1] *n* the German name for **Vienna**

Wien[2] *n* **Wilhelm** 1864–1928, German physicist, who studied black-body radiation: Nobel prize for physics 1911

Wiener *n* **Norbert** 1894–1964, US mathematician, who developed the concept of cybernetics

Wiesel *n* **Elie** born 1928, US human rights campaigner: noted esp. for his documentaries of wartime atrocities against the Jews; Nobel peace prize 1986

wife ⊙ *n, pl* **wives** the woman to whom a man is married **wifely** *adj*
WORD ORIGIN Old English *wīf*

Wi-Fi *n computers* a system of wireless access to the internet

wig *n* an artificial head of hair
WORD ORIGIN from *periwig*

wigeon *or* **widgeon** *n* a wild marshland duck
WORD ORIGIN origin unknown

wigging *n Brit old-fashioned slang* a reprimand
WORD ORIGIN origin unknown

wiggle *vb* **-gling, -gled** **1** to move with jerky movements from side to side or up and down: *she wiggled her toes in the cool water* ▷ *n* **2** a wiggling movement or walk
WORD ORIGIN Middle Low German, Middle Dutch *wiggelen*

Wigner *n* **Eugene Paul** 1902–95, US physicist, born in Hungary. He is noted for his contributions to nuclear physics: shared the Nobel prize for physics 1963

wigwam *n* a Native American's tent, made of animal skins
WORD ORIGIN Native American *wīkwām*

wiki *computers n* **1** a website, or page within one, whose content can be edited freely by anyone with access to a web browser ▷ *adj* **2** of or relating to the software which facilitates such open editing: *wiki technology*
WORD ORIGIN from Hawaiian *wiki-wiki* quick

wilco *interj* an expression in signalling and telecommunications, indicating that a message just received will be complied with
WORD ORIGIN abbreviation for *I will comply*

wild ⊙ *adj* **1** (of animals or birds) living in natural surroundings; not domesticated or tame **2** (of plants) growing in a natural state; not cultivated **3** uninhabited and desolate: *wild country* **4** living in a savage or uncivilized way: *a wild mountain man* **5** lacking restraint or control: *a wild party* **6** stormy or violent: *a wild windy October morning* **7** in a state of extreme emotional intensity: *wild with excitement* **8** without reason or substance: *wild accusations* **9** **wild about** *informal* very enthusiastic about: *his colleagues aren't all that wild about him* ▷ *adv* **10** **run wild** to behave without restraint: *she was allowed to run completely wild* ▷ *n* **11** **the wild** a free natural state of living:

THESAURUS

OPPOSITE: restricted
4 = large, broad, vast, immense
5 = expanded, dilated, fully open, distended **OPPOSITE:** shut
▷ *adv* **6 = fully**, completely, right out, as far as possible, to the furthest extent **OPPOSITE:** partly

widen *vb* **a = broaden**, expand, enlarge, dilate, spread, extend, stretch, open wide, open out *or* up **OPPOSITE:** narrow
b = get wider, spread, extend, expand, broaden, open wide, open out *or* up **OPPOSITE:** narrow

widespread *adj* **= common**, general, popular, sweeping, broad, extensive, universal, epidemic, wholesale, far-reaching, prevalent, rife, pervasive, far-flung **OPPOSITE:** limited

width *n* **1 = breadth**, extent, span, wideness, reach, range, measure, scope, diameter, compass, thickness, girth

wield *vb* **1 = brandish**, flourish, manipulate, swing, use, manage, handle, employ, ply **2 = exert**, hold, maintain, exercise, have, control, manage, apply, command, possess, make use of, utilize, put to use, be possessed of, have at your disposal

wife *n* **= spouse**, woman *(informal)*, partner, mate, bride, old woman *(informal)*, old lady *(informal)*, little woman *(informal)*, significant other *(US informal)*, better half *(humorous)*, her indoors *(Brit slang)*, helpmate, helpmeet, (the) missis *or* missus *(informal)*, vrou *(S African)*, wahine *(NZ)*, wifey *(informal)*

wild *adj* **1 = untamed**, fierce, savage, ferocious, unbroken, feral, undomesticated, free, warrigal *(Austral literary)* **OPPOSITE:** tame
2 = uncultivated, natural, native, indigenous **OPPOSITE:** cultivated
4 = uncivilized, fierce, savage, primitive, rude, ferocious, barbaric, brutish, barbarous
OPPOSITE: civilized
5 = uncontrolled, violent, rough, disorderly, noisy, chaotic, turbulent, wayward, unruly, rowdy, boisterous, lawless, unfettered, unbridled, riotous, unrestrained, unmanageable, impetuous, undisciplined, ungovernable, self-willed, uproarious
OPPOSITE: calm
6 = stormy, violent, rough, intense,

DICTIONARY

creatures of the wild **12 the wilds** a desolate or uninhabited region: *the wilds of Africa* **wildly** *adv* **wildness** *n*
WORD ORIGIN Old English *wilde*

Wild *n* **Jonathan** ?1682–1725, British criminal, who organized a network of thieves, highwaymen, etc., while also working as an informer: said to have sent over a hundred men to the gallows before being hanged himself

wild card *n* **1** *sport* a player or team that is allowed to take part in a competition despite not having met the normal qualifying requirements **2** *computers* a character that can be substituted for any other in a file

wildcat *n, pl* **-cats** *or* **-cat 1** a wild European cat that looks like a domesticated cat but is larger and has a bushy tail **2** *informal* a quick-tempered person ▹*adj* **3** *chiefly* US risky and financially unsound: *a wildcat operation*

wildcat strike *n* a strike begun by workers spontaneously or without union approval

wildebeest *n, pl* **-beests** *or* **-beest** ▸ same as **gnu**
WORD ORIGIN Afrikaans

Wilder *n* **1 Billy,** real name *Samuel Wilder.* 1906–2002, US film director and screenwriter, born in Austria. His films include *Double Indemnity* (1944), *The Lost Weekend* (1945), *Sunset Boulevard* (1950), *The Seven Year Itch* (1955), *Some Like it Hot* (1959), *The Apartment* (1960), and *Buddy Buddy* (1981) **2 Thornton** 1897–1975 US novelist and dramatist. His works include the novel *The Bridge of San Luis Rey* (1927) and the play *The Skin of Our Teeth* (1942)

wilderness ❶ *n* **1** a wild uninhabited uncultivated region **2** a confused mass or tangle: *a wilderness of long grass and wild flowers* **3** a state of being no longer in a prominent position: *a long spell in the political wilderness*
WORD ORIGIN Old English *wildēornes,* from *wildēor* wild beast

wildfire *n* **spread like wildfire** to spread very quickly or uncontrollably

wild flower *n* any flowering plant that grows in an uncultivated state

wildfowl *pl n* wild birds, such as grouse and pheasants, that are hunted for sport or food

wild-goose chase *n* a search that has little or no chance of success

Wilding *n* (**Frederick**) **Anthony** 1883–1915, New Zealand tennis player; Wimbledon singles champion (1910–1913) and doubles champion (1907–08, 1910, 1913)

wildlife *n* wild animals and plants collectively

wild rice *n* the dark-coloured edible grain of a North American grass that grows on wet ground

Wild West *n* the western US during its settlement, esp. with reference to its lawlessness

wiles *pl n* artful or seductive tricks or ploys
WORD ORIGIN from Old Norse *vēl* craft

Wilfrid *n* **Saint** 634–709 AD, English churchman; bishop of York (?663–?703). At the Synod of Whitby (664) he argued successfully that Celtic practices should be replaced by Roman ones in the English Church. Feast day: Oct 12

wilful *or US* **willful** *adj* **1** determined to do things in one's own way: *a wilful and insubordinate child* **2** deliberate and intentional: *wilful misconduct* **wilfully** *adv*

Wilhelmina I *n* 1880–1962, queen of the Netherlands from 1890 until her abdication (1948) in favour of her daughter Juliana

Wilkes *n* **1 Charles** 1798–1877, US explorer of Antarctica **2 John** 1727–97, English politician, who was expelled from the House of Commons and outlawed for writing scurrilous articles about the government. He became a champion of parliamentary reform

Wilkins *n* **1** Sir **George Hubert** 1888–1958, Australian polar explorer and aviator **2 Maurice Hugh Frederick** 1916–2004, British biochemist, born in New Zealand. With Crick and Watson, he shared the Nobel prize 1962 for his work on the structure of DNA

Wilkinson *n* **Jonny** born 1979, English Rugby Union player; he scored the last-minute drop goal that won England victory in the final of the 2003 World Cup

will[1] *vb, past* **would 1** used as an auxiliary to make the future tense: *he will go on trial on October 7* **2** to express resolution: *they will not consider giving up territories* **3** to express a polite request: *will you please calm Mummy and Daddy down* **4** to express ability: *many essential oils will protect clothing from moths* **5** to express probability or expectation: *his followers will be relieved to hear that* **6** to express customary practice: *boys will be boys!* **7** to express desire: *go in very small steps, if you will*
WORD ORIGIN Old English *willan*

will[2] ❶ *n* **1** a strong determination: *a fierce will to survive* **2** desire or wish: *a referendum to determine the will of the people* **3** a document setting out a person's wishes regarding the disposal of his or her property after death **4 at will** when and as one chooses: *customers can withdraw money at will* ▹*vb* **willing, willed 5** to try to make (something) happen by wishing very hard for it: *she willed herself not to cry* **6** to wish or desire: *if he wills it, we will meet again* **7** to leave (property) in one's will: *the farm had been willed to her*
WORD ORIGIN Old English *willa*

William *n* **1** known as *William the Lion.* ?1143–1214, king of Scotland (1165–1214) **2 Prince** born 1982, first son of Prince Charles and Diana, Princess of Wales

William of Malmesbury *n* ?1090–?1143, English monk and chronicler, whose *Gesta regum Anglorum* and *Historia novella* are valuable sources for English history to 1142

Williams *n* **1 Hank,** real name *Hiram Williams.* 1923–53, US country singer and songwriter. His songs (all 1948–52) include "Jambalaya", "Your Cheatin' Heart", and "Why Don't you Love me (like you Used to Do?)" **2 John** born 1941, Australian classical guitarist, living in Britain **3 John** (**Towner**) born 1932, US composer of film music; his scores include those for *Jaws* (1975), *Star Wars* (1977), *E.T.* (1982), *Schindler's List* (1993), and *Harry Potter and the Philosopher's Stone* (2001) **4** ▸ **Ralph Vaughan** See (Ralph) **Vaughan Williams 5 Raymond** (**Henry**) 1921–88, British literary critic and novelist, noted esp. for such works as *Culture and Society* (1958) and *The Long Revolution* (1961), which offer a socialist analysis of the relationship between society and culture **6 Robbie,** full name *Robert Peter Williams.* born 1974, British pop

THESAURUS

raging, furious, howling, choppy, tempestuous, blustery **7 = excited**, mad (*informal*), crazy (*informal*), eager, nuts (*slang*), enthusiastic, raving, frantic, daft (*informal*), frenzied, hysterical, avid, potty (*Brit informal*), delirious, agog
OPPOSITE: unenthusiastic
12 the wilds = wilderness, desert, wasteland, middle of nowhere (*informal*), backwoods, back of beyond (*informal*), uninhabited area

wilderness *n* **1 = wilds**, waste, desert, wasteland, uncultivated region

will[2] *n* **1 = determination**, drive, aim, purpose, commitment, resolution, resolve, intention, spine, backbone, tenacity, willpower, single-mindedness, doggedness, firmness of purpose **2a = wish**, mind, desire, pleasure, intention, fancy, preference, inclination **2b = decree**, wish, desire, command, dictate, ordinance **3 = testament**, declaration, bequest(s), last wishes, last will and testament ▹*vb* **6 = wish**, want, choose, prefer, desire, elect, opt, see fit **7 = bequeath**, give, leave, transfer, gift, hand on, pass on, confer, hand down, settle on

DICTIONARY

singer and songwriter. A member of Take That (1990–95), he later found success with "Angels" (1997) and the albums *Life Thru a Lens* (1997), *Swing When You're Winning* (2001), and *Escapology* (2002) **7 Robin (McLaurim)** born 1951, US film actor and comedian; films include *Good Morning, Vietnam* (1987), *Dead Poets' Society* (1989), *Mrs Doubtfire* (1993), and *Insomnia* (2002) **8 Rowan (Douglas)** born 1950, Archbishop of Canterbury from 2002; formerly Archbishop of Wales (2000–02) **9 Serena** born 1981, US tennis player: Wimbledon champion 2002–03; US champion 1999, 2002 **10 Tennessee,** real name *Thomas Lanier Williams*. 1911–83, US dramatist. His plays include *The Glass Menagerie* (1944), *A Streetcar Named Desire* (1947), *Cat on a Hot Tin Roof* (1955), and *Night of the Iguana* (1961) **11 Venus** born 1980, US tennis player, sister of Serena Williams: Wimbledon champion 2000, 2001, 2005, 2007; US champion 2000–01 **12 William Carlos** 1883–1963, US poet, who formulated the poetic concept "no ideas but in things". His works include *Paterson* (1946–58), which explores the daily life of a man living in a modern city, and the prose work *In the American Grain* (1925)

Williamson *n* **1 David** born 1942, Australian dramatist. His plays include *Don's Party* (1971), *Emerald City* (1987) and *Brilliant Lies* (1993) **2 Henry** 1895–1977, British novelist, best known for *Tarka the Otter* (1927) and other animal stories **3 Malcolm** 1931–2003, Australian composer, living in Britain: Master of the Queen's Music since 1975. His works include operas and music for children

willies *pl n* **give someone the willies** *slang* to make someone nervous or frightened
WORD ORIGIN origin unknown

willing ❶ *adj* **1** favourably disposed or inclined: *I'm willing to hear what you have to say* **2** keen and obliging: *willing volunteers* **willingly** *adv* **willingness** *n*

Willis *n* **1 Norman (David)** born 1933, British trade union leader; general secretary of the Trades Union Congress (1984–93) **2 Ted** Baron Willis of Chislehurst. 1918–92, British author. His works include the play *Hot Summer Night* (1959) and the novel *Death May Surprise Us* (1974)

will-o'-the-wisp *n* **1** someone or something that is elusive or deceptively alluring: *their freedom was just a will-o'-the-wisp* **2** a pale light that is sometimes seen over marshy ground at night
WORD ORIGIN *Will*, short for *William* + *wisp* twist of hay burning as a torch

willow *n* a tree that grows near water, with thin flexible branches used in weaving baskets and wood used for making cricket bats
WORD ORIGIN Old English *welig*

willowherb *n* a plant with narrow leaves and purplish flowers

willow pattern *n* a pattern in blue on white china, depicting a Chinese landscape with a willow tree, river, bridge, and figures

willowy *adj* slender and graceful

willpower *n* strong self-disciplined determination to do something

Wills *n* **1 Helen Newington,** married name *Helen Wills Moody Roark*. 1905–98, US tennis player. She was Wimbledon singles champion eight times between 1927 and 1938. She also won the US title seven times and the French title four times **2 William John** 1834–61, English explorer: Robert Burke's deputy in an expedition on which both men died after crossing Australia from north to south for the first time

willy *n, pl* **-lies** *Brit, Austral & NZ informal* ▸a childish or jocular word for **penis**

willy-nilly *adv* **1** in a haphazard fashion; indiscriminately: *spending taxpayers' money willy-nilly* **2** whether desired or not
WORD ORIGIN Old English *wile hē, nyle hē* will he or will he not

willy wagtail *n Austral* black-and-white flycatcher

willy-willy *n Austral* a small tropical dust storm
WORD ORIGIN from a native Australian language

wilt ❶ *vb* **1** (of a flower or plant) to become limp or drooping **2** (of a person) to lose strength or confidence
WORD ORIGIN perhaps from obsolete *wilk* to wither

Wilts Wiltshire

wily *adj* **wilier, wiliest** sly or crafty

wimp *informal n* **1** a feeble ineffective person ▹*vb* **2 wimp out of** to fail to do (something) through lack of courage **wimpish** *or* **wimpy** *adj*
WORD ORIGIN origin unknown

WIMP *computers* windows, icons, menus (or mice), pointers: denoting a type of user-friendly screen display used on small computers

wimple *n* a piece of cloth draped round the head to frame the face, worn by women in the Middle Ages and now by some nuns
WORD ORIGIN Old English *wimpel*

win ❶ *vb* **winning, won 1** to achieve first place in (a competition or race) **2** to gain (a prize or first place) in a competition or race **3** to gain victory in (a battle, argument, or struggle) **4** to gain (sympathy, approval, or support) ▹*n* **5** *informal* a success, victory, or triumph: *three consecutive wins* ▸See also **win over** >**winnable** *adj*
WORD ORIGIN Old English *winnan*

wince ❶ *vb* **wincing, winced 1** to draw back slightly, as if in sudden pain ▹*n* **2** the act of wincing
WORD ORIGIN Old French *wencier, guenchir* to avoid

winch *n* **1** a lifting or hauling device consisting of a rope or chain wound round a barrel or drum ▹*vb* **2** to haul or lift using a winch: *two men were winched to safety by a helicopter*
WORD ORIGIN Old English *wince* pulley

Winckelmann *n* **Johann Joachim** 1717–68, German archaeologist and art historian; one of the founders of neoclassicism

wind[1] ❶ *n* **1** a current of air moving across the earth's surface **2** a trend or force: *the chill wind of change* **3** the power to breathe normally, esp. during or after physical exercise: *if you feel tired during the exercise, persevere – you'll soon get a second wind* **4** gas in

THESAURUS

willing *adj* **1 = inclined**, prepared, happy, pleased, content, in favour, consenting, disposed, favourable, agreeable, in the mood, compliant, amenable, desirous, so-minded, nothing loath **OPPOSITE:** unwilling **2 = ready**, game *(informal)*, eager, enthusiastic **OPPOSITE:** reluctant

wilt *vb* **1 = droop**, wither, sag, shrivel, become limp *or* flaccid **2 = weaken**, sag, languish, droop

win *vb* **1, 3 = be victorious in**, succeed in, prevail in, come first in, finish first in, be the victor in, gain victory in, achieve first place in **OPPOSITE:** lose **2, 4 = gain**, get, receive, land, catch, achieve, net, earn, pick up, bag *(informal)*, secure, collect, obtain, acquire, accomplish, attain, procure, come away with **OPPOSITE:** forfeit ▹*n* **5** *(informal)* **= victory**, success, triumph, conquest **OPPOSITE:** defeat

wince *vb* **1 = flinch**, start, shrink, cringe, quail, recoil, cower, draw back, blench ▹*n* **2 = flinch**, start, cringe

wind[1] *n* **1 = air**, blast, breath, hurricane, breeze, draught, gust, zephyr, air-current, current of air **3 = breath**, puff, respiration **4 = flatulence**, gas, flatus **5** *(informal)* **= nonsense**, talk, boasting, hot air, babble, bluster, humbug, twaddle *(informal)*, gab *(informal)*, verbalizing, blather, codswallop *(informal)*, eyewash *(informal)*, idle talk, empty talk, bizzo *(Austral slang)*, bull's wool *(Austral & NZ slang)* **7 get wind of = hear about**, learn of, find out about, become aware of, be told about, be informed of, be made

DICTIONARY

the stomach or intestines **5** *informal* foolish or empty talk: *political language is designed to give an appearance of solidity to pure wind* **6 break wind** to release intestinal gas through the anus **7 get wind of** *informal* to find out about: *the media finally got wind of her disappearance* ▷ *adj* **8** *music* of or relating to wind instruments: *the wind section* ▷ *vb* **winding, winded 9** to cause (someone) to be short of breath: *he fell with a thud that left him winded* **10** to cause (a baby) to bring up wind after feeding **windless** *adj*
WORD ORIGIN Old English

wind² ❶ *vb* **winding, wound 1** to twist (something flexible) round some object: *a sweatband was wound round his head* **2** to tighten the spring of (a clock or watch) by turning a key or knob **3** to follow a twisting course: *a narrow path wound through the shrubbery* ▸ See also **wind down, wind up** ▷ **winding** *adj, n*
WORD ORIGIN Old English *windan*

windbag *n slang* a person who talks a lot but says little of interest

windblown *adj* blown about by the wind: *windblown hair*

windbreak *n* a fence or a line of trees that gives protection from the wind by breaking its force

windcheater *n chiefly Brit* a warm jacket with a close-fitting knitted neck, cuffs, and waistband

wind chill *n* the serious chilling effect of wind and low temperature

wind down *vb* **1** to move downwards by turning a handle: *he wound down the rear window* **2** (of a clock or watch) to slow down before stopping completely **3** to relax after a stressful or tiring time: *I have not had a chance to wind down from a busy day* **4** to diminish gradually: *trading wound down for the day*

winded *adj* temporarily out of breath after physical exercise or a blow to the stomach

windfall ❶ *n* **1** a piece of unexpected good fortune, esp. financial gain **2** a fruit blown off a tree by the wind

windfall tax *n* a tax levied on profits made from the privatization of public utilities

wind farm *n* a large group of wind-driven generators for electricity supply

wind gauge *n* ▸ same as **anemometer**

winding sheet *n* a sheet in which a dead person is wrapped before being buried

wind instrument *n* a musical instrument, such as a flute, that is played by having air blown into it

windjammer *n history* a large merchant sailing ship

windlass *n* a machine for lifting heavy objects by winding a rope or chain round a barrel or drum driven by a motor
WORD ORIGIN Old Norse *vindās*

windmill *n* **1** a building containing machinery for grinding corn or for pumping, driven by sails that are turned by the wind **2** *Brit* a toy consisting of a stick with plastic vanes attached, which revolve in the wind

window *n* **1** an opening in a building or a vehicle containing glass within a framework, which lets in light and enables people to see in or out **2** the display area behind a glass window in a shop **3** a transparent area in an envelope which reveals the address on the letter inside **4** an area on a computer screen that can be manipulated separately from the rest of the display area, for example so that two or more files can be displayed at the same time **5** a period of unbooked time in a diary or schedule
WORD ORIGIN Old Norse *vindauga* wind eye

window box *n* a long narrow box, placed on a windowsill, in which plants are grown

window-dressing *n* **1** the art of arranging goods in shop windows in such a way as to attract customers **2** an attempt to make something seem better than it is by stressing only its attractive features: *do you think that the president's calling for an investigation is window-dressing, or do you think he actually means to do something?* **window-dresser** *n*

windowpane *n* a sheet of glass in a window

window seat *n* **1** a seat below a window **2** a seat beside a window in a bus, train, or aircraft

window-shopping *n* looking at goods in shop windows without intending to buy anything

windowsill *n* a shelf at the bottom of a window, either inside or outside a room

windpipe *n* ▸ a nontechnical name for **trachea**

windscreen *n Brit, Austral & NZ* the sheet of glass that forms the front window of a motor vehicle

windscreen wiper *n Brit, Austral & NZ* an electrically operated blade with a rubber edge that wipes a windscreen clear of rain

windshield *n US & Canad* the sheet of glass that forms the front window of a motor vehicle

windshield wiper *n US & Canad* an electrically operated blade with a rubber edge that wipes a windshield clear of rain

windsock *n* a cloth cone mounted on a mast, used esp. at airports to indicate the direction of the wind

Windsor¹ *n* **1** a town in S England, in Windsor and Maidenhead unitary authority, Berkshire, on the River Thames, linked by bridge with Eton: site of **Windsor Castle**, residence of English monarchs since its founding by William the Conqueror; **Old Windsor**, royal residence in the time of Edward the Confessor, is 3 km (2 miles) southeast. Pop: 26 747 (2001 est). Official name: **New Windsor 2** a city in SE Canada, in S Ontario on the Detroit River opposite Detroit: motor-vehicle manufacturing; university (1963). Pop: 208 402 (2001)

Windsor² *n* **1** the official name of the British royal family from 1917 **2 Duke of Windsor** ▸ the title, from 1937, of **Edward VIII**

windsurfing *n* the sport of riding on water using a surfboard steered and propelled by an attached sail **windsurfer** *n*

windswept *adj* **1** exposed to the wind: *the vast windswept plains* **2** blown about by the wind: *his hair was looking a bit windswept*

wind tunnel *n* a chamber through which a stream of air is forced, in order to test the effects of wind on aircraft

wind up ❶ *vb* **1** to bring to a conclusion: *we want to wind this conflict up as quickly as possible* **2** *informal* to dissolve (a company) and divide its assets among creditors **3** to tighten the spring of (a clockwork mechanism) by turning a key or knob **4** to move (a car window) upwards by turning a handle **5** *informal* to end up: *to wind up in the hospital* **6** *informal* to make nervous or tense: *as crisis after crisis broke, I became increasingly wound up* **7** *Brit, Austral & NZ slang* to tease or annoy: *that really used to wind my old man up something rotten* ▷ *adj* **wind-up 8** operated by clockwork: *a wind-up toy* ▷ *n* **wind-up 9** a light-hearted hoax **10** the finish

windward *chiefly naut adj* **1** of or in the direction from which the wind blows ▷ *n* **2** the windward direction ▷ *adv* **3** towards the wind

W

THESAURUS

aware of, hear tell of, have brought to your notice, hear on the grape vine *(informal)*

wind² *vb* **1 = wrap**, twist, reel, curl, loop, coil, twine, furl, wreathe **3 = meander**, turn, bend, twist, curve, snake, ramble, twist and turn, deviate, zigzag

windfall *n* **1 = godsend**, find, jackpot, bonanza, stroke of luck, manna from heaven, pot of gold at the end of the rainbow **OPPOSITE:** misfortune

wind up *(informal)* **5 = end up**, be left, find yourself, finish up, fetch up *(informal)*, land up, end your days

DICTIONARY

windy ❶ *adj* **windier, windiest** **1** denoting a time or conditions in which there is a strong wind: *a windy day* **2** exposed to the wind: *the windy graveyard* **3** long-winded or pompous: *his speeches are long and windy* **4** *old-fashioned slang* frightened

wine *n* **1 a** an alcoholic drink produced by the fermenting of grapes with water and sugar **b** an alcoholic drink produced in this way from other fruits or flowers: *dandelion wine* ▹ *adj* **2** dark purplish-red ▹ *vb* **wining, wined 3 wine and dine** to entertain (someone) with wine and fine food
WORD ORIGIN Latin *vinum*

wine bar *n* a bar that specializes in serving wine and usually food

wine box *n* a cubic carton containing wine, with a tap for dispensing

wine cellar *n* **1** a cellar where wine is stored **2** the stock of wines stored there

wineglass *n* a glass for wine, usually with a small bowl on a stem with a flared base

Winehouse *n* **Amy (Jade)** born 1983, English rock singer and songwriter; her albums include *Frank* (2003) and *Back to Black* (2006)

wing ❶ *n* **1** one of the limbs or organs of a bird, bat, or insect that are used for flying **2** one of the two winglike supporting parts of an aircraft **3** a projecting part of a building: *converting the unused east wing into a suitable habitation* **4** a faction or group within a political party or other organization: *the youth wing of the African National Congress* **5** *Brit* the part of a car body surrounding the wheels **6** *sport* **a** either of the two sides of the pitch near the touchline **b** ▸ same as **winger 7 wings** *theatre* the space offstage to the right or left of the acting area **8 in the wings** ready to step in when needed **9 on the wing** flying **10 spread one's wings** to make fuller use of one's abilities by trying new experiences: *he increasingly spread his wings abroad* **11 take someone under one's wing** to look after someone **12 take wing** to fly away ▹ *vb* **13** to fly: *a lone bird winging its way from the island* **14** to move through the air: *sending a shower of loose gravel winging towards the house* **15** to shoot or wound in the wing or arm **16** to provide with wings **winged** *adj* **wingless** *adj*
WORD ORIGIN Old Norse *vængr*

Wingate *n* **Orde (Charles)** 1903–44, British soldier. During World War II he organized the Chindits in Burma (Myanmar) to disrupt Japanese communications. He died in an air crash

wing chair *n* an easy chair with side pieces extending forward from a high back

wing commander *n* a middle-ranking commissioned officer in an air force

winger *n* *sport* a player positioned on a wing

wing nut *n* **1** a threaded nut with two flat projections which allow it to be turned by the thumb and forefinger **2** a foolish or insane person

wingspan *n* the distance between the wing tips of a bird, insect, bat, or aircraft

wink ❶ *vb* **1** to close and open one eye quickly as a signal **2** (of a light) to shine brightly and intermittently; twinkle ▹ *n* **3** the act or an instance of winking, esp. as a signal **4** a twinkling of light **5** *informal* the smallest amount of sleep: *I didn't sleep a wink last night* **6 tip someone the wink** *Brit, Austral & NZ informal* to give someone a hint or warning
WORD ORIGIN Old English *wincian*

Winkelried *n* **Arnold von** died ?1386, Swiss hero of the battle of Sempach (1386) against the Austrians

winkle *n* **1** an edible shellfish with a spirally coiled shell ▹ *vb* **-kling, -kled 2 winkle out** *informal chiefly Brit* **a** to obtain (information) from someone who is not willing to provide it: *try to winkle the real problem out of them* **b** to coax or force out: *he somehow managed to winkle him out of his room*

winkle-pickers *pl n* *old-fashioned* shoes with very pointed narrow toes

winner ❶ *n* **1** a person or thing that wins **2** *informal* a person or thing that seems sure to be successful

winning ❶ *adj* **1** gaining victory: *the winning side* **2** charming or attractive: *her winning smiles*

winnings ❶ *pl n* the money won in a competition or in gambling

winnow *vb* **1** to separate (grain) from (chaff) by a current of air **2** (often foll. by *out*) to separate out (an unwanted element): *the committee will need to winnow out the nonsense*
WORD ORIGIN Old English *windwian*

wino (wine-oh) *n, pl* **winos** *informal* a destitute person who habitually drinks cheap wine

win over ❶ *vb* to gain the support or consent of: *his robust performance won over his critics*

Winslet *n* **Kate** born 1975, British film actress; her films include *Sense and Sensibility* (1995), *Titanic* (1997), *Iris* (2001), and *Little Children* (2006)

winsome *adj* *literary* charming or attractive: *a winsome smile*
WORD ORIGIN Old English *wynsum*

Winstanley *n* **Gerrard** ?1609–60, English radical; leader of the Diggers (1649–50) and author of the pamphlet *The Law of Freedom in a Platform* (1652)

Winston *n* **Robert (Maurice Lipson)**, Baron. born 1940, British obstetrician and gynaecologist, noted for his work on human infertility treatment; also a well-known broadcaster

winter *n* **1** the coldest season of the year, between autumn and spring ▹ *vb* **2** to spend the winter in a specified place: *wintering in Rome*
WORD ORIGIN Old English

wintergreen *n* an evergreen shrub from which is obtained a pleasant-smelling oil that is used medicinally and for flavouring

winter solstice *n* the time, about December 22, at which the sun is at its southernmost point in the sky

winter sports *pl n* sports held on snow or ice, such as skiing and skating

wintertime *n* the period or season of winter

Winthrop *n* **1 John** 1588–1649, English lawyer and colonist, first governor of the Massachusetts Bay colony: the leading figure among the Puritan settlers of New England **2** his son, **John** 1606–76, English lawyer and

THESAURUS

windy *adj* **1 = breezy**, wild, stormy, boisterous, blustering, windswept, tempestuous, blustery, gusty, inclement, squally, blowy
OPPOSITE: calm

wing *n* **4 = faction**, grouping, group, set, side, arm, section, camp, branch, circle, lobby, segment, caucus, clique, coterie, schism, cabal ▹ *vb* **13 = fly**, soar, glide, take wing **15 = wound**, hit, nick, clip, graze

wink *vb* **1 = blink**, bat, flutter, nictate, nictitate **2 = twinkle**, flash, shine, sparkle, gleam, shimmer, glimmer ▹ *n* **3 = blink**, flutter, nictation, nictitation

winner *n* **1 = victor**, first, champion, master, champ *(informal)*, conqueror, vanquisher, prizewinner, conquering hero **OPPOSITE:** loser

winning *adj* **1 = victorious**, first, top, successful, unbeaten, conquering, triumphant, undefeated, vanquishing, top-scoring, unvanquished **2 = charming**, taking, pleasing, sweet, attractive, engaging, lovely, fascinating, fetching, delightful, cute, disarming, enchanting, endearing, captivating, amiable, alluring, bewitching, delectable, winsome, prepossessing, likable *or* likeable
OPPOSITE: unpleasant

winnings = spoils, profits, gains, prize, proceeds, takings, booty

win over = convince, influence, attract, persuade, convert, charm, sway, disarm, allure, prevail upon, bring *or* talk round

DICTIONARY

colonist; a founder of Agawan (now Ipswich), Massachusetts; governor of Connecticut

Winton *n* **Tim**, full name *Timothy John Winton*, born 1960. Australian writer. His novels include *Cloudstreet* (1992), *The Riders* (1995) and *Dirt Music* (2002)

wintry *adj* **-trier, -triest 1** of or characteristic of winter: *a cold wintry day* **2** cold or unfriendly: *a wintry smile*

win-win *adj* guaranteeing a favourable outcome for everyone involved: *a win-win situation for NATO*

wipe ❶ *vb* **wiping, wiped 1** to rub (a surface or object) lightly with a cloth or the hand, in order to remove dirt or liquid from it **2** to remove by wiping: *she made a futile attempt to wipe away her tears* **3** to erase a recording from (a video or audio tape) ▷*n* **4** the act or an instance of wiping: *a quick wipe*
WORD ORIGIN Old English *wīpian*

wipe out ❶ *vb* to destroy or get rid of completely: *a hail storm wipes out a wheat crop in five minutes*

wiper *n* ▸short for **windscreen wiper**

wire *n* **1** a slender flexible strand of metal **2** a length of this used to carry electric current in a circuit **3** a long continuous piece of wire or cable connecting points in a telephone or telegraph system **4** *old-fashioned informal* a telegram ▷*vb* **wiring, wired 5** to fasten with wire **6** to equip (an electrical system, circuit, or component) with wires **7** *informal* to send a telegram to **8** to send by telegraph: *they wired the money for a train ticket*
WORD ORIGIN Old English *wīr*

wired *adj* **1** *slang* excitable or edgy, usually from stimulant intake: *I don't want coffee, I'm wired enough as it is* **2** using computers to send and receive information, esp. via the internet

wire-haired *adj* (of a dog) having a rough wiry coat

wireless *n* **1** *old-fashioned* ▸same as **radio** ▷*adj* **2** *computers* communicating without connecting wires: *wireless application protocol*

wire netting *n* a net made of wire, used for fencing

wiretapping *n* the practice of making a connection to a telegraph or telephone wire in order to obtain information secretly

wireworm *n* a destructive wormlike beetle larva

wiring *n* the network of wires used in an electrical system, device, or circuit

wiry *adj* **wirier, wiriest 1** (of a person) slim but strong **2** coarse and stiff: *wiry grass*

Wisden *n* **John** 1826–84, English cricketer; publisher of *Wisden Cricketers' Almanack*, which first appeared in 1864

wisdom ❶ *n* **1** the ability to use one's experience and knowledge to make sensible decisions or judgments **2** accumulated knowledge or learning: *the wisdom of Asia and of Africa*
WORD ORIGIN Old English *wīsdōm*

wisdom tooth *n* any of the four molar teeth, one at the back of each side of the jaw, that are the last of the permanent teeth to come through

wise[1] ❶ *adj* **1** possessing or showing wisdom: *a wise move* **2 none the wiser** knowing no more than before: *I left the conference none the wiser* **3 wise to** *informal* aware of or informed about: *they'll get wise to our system; he put him wise to the rumour* **wisely** *adv*
WORD ORIGIN Old English *wīs*

wise[2] *n old-fashioned* way, manner, or respect: *in no wise*
WORD ORIGIN Old English *wīse* manner

-wise *adv suffix* **1** indicating direction or manner: *crabwise* **2** with reference to: *moneywise*
WORD ORIGIN Old English *-wisan*

wiseacre *n* a person who wishes to seem wise
WORD ORIGIN Middle Dutch *wijsseggher* soothsayer

wisecrack *informal n* **1** a clever, amusing, sometimes unkind, remark ▷*vb* **2** to make such remarks **wisecracking** *adj*

wise guy *n informal* a person who likes to give the impression of knowing more than other people

Wiseman *n* **Nicholas Patrick Stephen** 1802–65, British cardinal; first Roman Catholic archbishop of Westminster (1850–65)

wise up *vb* **wising, wised** *slang* (often foll. by *to*) to become aware (of) or informed (about)

wish ❶ *vb* **1** to want or desire (something impossible or improbable): *he wished he'd kept quiet* **2** to desire or prefer to be or do something: *the next person who wished to speak* **3** to feel or express a hope concerning the welfare, health, or success of: *we wished him well* **4** to greet as specified: *I wished her a Merry Christmas* ▷*n* **5** a desire, often for something impossible or improbable: *a desperate wish to succeed as a professional artist* **6** something desired or wished for: *your wishes will come true* **7** the expression of a hope for someone's welfare, health, or success: *give him our best wishes*
WORD ORIGIN Old English *wȳscan*

wishbone *n* the V-shaped bone above the breastbone of a chicken or turkey

wishful *adj* desirous or longing: *she seemed wishful of prolonging the discussion*

wishful thinking *n* an interpretation of the facts as one would like them to be, rather than as they are: *was it wishful thinking, or had the enemy lost heart?*

wish list *n* a list of things desired by a person or organization: *the government's wish list*

wish on *vb* to want (something unpleasant) to be experienced by: *I wouldn't wish that wretched childhood on anyone*

wishy-washy *adj informal* lacking in character, force, or colour

wisp *n* **1** a thin, delicate, or filmy piece or streak: *little wisps of cloud* **2** a small untidy bundle, tuft, or strand: *a wisp of hair* **3** a slight trace: *a wisp of a smile*
WORD ORIGIN origin unknown

wispy *adj* **wispier, wispiest** thin, fine, or delicate: *grey wispy hair*

wisteria *n* a climbing plant with large drooping clusters of blue, purple, or white flowers

THESAURUS

wipe *vb* **1 = clean**, dry, polish, brush, dust, rub, sponge, mop, swab **2 = erase**, remove, take off, get rid of, take away, rub off, efface, clean off, sponge off ▷*n* **4 = rub**, clean, polish, brush, lick, sponge, mop, swab

wipe out = destroy, eliminate, take out *(slang)*, massacre, slaughter, erase, eradicate, blow away *(slang, chiefly US)*, obliterate, liquidate *(informal)*, annihilate, efface, exterminate, expunge, extirpate, wipe from the face of the earth *(informal)*, kill to the last man, kennet *(Austral slang)*, jeff *(Austral slang)*

wisdom *n* **1 = understanding**, learning, knowledge, intelligence, smarts *(slang, chiefly US)*, judgment, insight, enlightenment, penetration, comprehension, foresight, erudition, discernment, sagacity, sound judgment, sapience **OPPOSITE:** foolishness

wise[1] *adj* **1a = sage**, knowing, understanding, aware, informed, clever, intelligent, sensible, enlightened, shrewd, discerning, perceptive, well-informed, erudite, sagacious, sapient, clued-up *(informal)*, grounded **OPPOSITE:** foolish **1b = sensible**, sound, politic, informed, reasonable, clever, intelligent, rational, logical, shrewd, prudent, judicious, well-advised **OPPOSITE:** unwise

wish *vb* **2 = want**, feel, choose, please, desire, think fit ▷*n* **5 = desire**, liking, want, longing, hope, urge, intention, fancy *(informal)*, ambition, yen *(informal)*, hunger, aspiration, craving, lust, yearning, inclination, itch *(informal)*, thirst, whim, hankering **OPPOSITE:** aversion

DICTIONARY

WORD ORIGIN after Caspar *Wistar*, anatomist

wistful *adj* sadly wishing for something lost or unobtainable
wistfully *adv* **wistfulness** *n*

wit[1] ❶ *n* **1** the ability to use words or ideas in a clever, amusing, and imaginative way **2** a person possessing this ability **3** practical intelligence: *do credit me with some wit* ▸ See also **wits**
WORD ORIGIN Old English *witt*

wit[2] *vb* **to wit** (used to introduce a statement or explanation) that is to say; namely
WORD ORIGIN Old English *witan*

witblits (vit-blits) *n S African* an illegally distilled strong alcoholic drink
WORD ORIGIN Afrikaans *wit* white + *blits* lightning

witch ❶ *n* **1** (in former times) a woman believed to possess evil magic powers **2** a person who practises magic or sorcery, esp. black magic **3** an ugly or wicked old woman
WORD ORIGIN Old English *wicce*

witchcraft ❶ *n* the use of magic, esp. for evil purposes

witch doctor *n* a man in certain tribal societies who is believed to possess magical powers, which can be used to cure sickness or to harm people

witchetty grub *n* a wood-boring edible Australian caterpillar

witch hazel *n* a medicinal solution made from the bark and leaves of a N American shrub, which is put on the skin to treat bruises and inflammation

witch-hunt *n* a rigorous campaign to expose and discredit people considered to hold unorthodox views on the pretext of safeguarding the public welfare

with *prep* **1** accompanying; in the company of: *the captain called to the sergeant to come with him* **2** using; by means of: *unlocking the padlock with a key* **3** possessing or having: *a woman with black hair; the patient with angina* **4** concerning or regarding: *be gentle with me* **5** in a manner characterized by: *I know you will handle it with discretion* **6** as a result of: *his voice was hoarse with nervousness* **7** following the line of thought of: *are you with me so far?* **8** having the same opinions as; supporting: *are you with us or against us?*
WORD ORIGIN Old English

withdraw ❶ *vb* **-drawing, -drew, -drawn 1** to take out or remove: *he withdrew an envelope from his pocket* **2** to remove (money) from a bank account or savings account **3** to leave one place to go to another, usually quieter, place: *he withdrew into his bedroom* **4** (of troops) to leave or be pulled back from the battleground **5** to take back (a statement) formally **6 withdraw from** to give up: *they withdrew from the competition*
WORD ORIGIN *with*, in the sense: away from

withdrawal ❶ *n* **1** the act or an instance of withdrawing **2** the period that a drug addict goes through after stopping using drugs, during which he or she may experience symptoms such as tremors, sweating, and vomiting ▹ *adj* **3** of or relating to withdrawal from an addictive drug: *withdrawal symptoms*

withdrawn ❶ *vb* **1** ▸ the past participle of **withdraw** ▹ *adj* **2** extremely reserved or shy

wither ❶ *vb* **1** to make or become dried up or shrivelled: *the leaves had withered but not fallen* **2** to fade or waste: *deprived of the nerve supply the muscles wither* **3** to humiliate (someone) with a scornful look or remark **withered** *adj*
WORD ORIGIN probably variant of *weather* (verb)

withering ❶ *adj* (of a look or remark) extremely scornful

withers *pl n* the highest part of the back of a horse, between the shoulders
WORD ORIGIN earlier *widersones*

withhold ❶ *vb* **-holding, -held** to keep back (information or money)

within *prep* **1** in or inside: *within the hospital grounds* **2** before (a period of time) has passed: *within a month* **3** not beyond: *within the confines of a low budget; he positioned a low table within her reach* ▹ *adv* **4** *formal* inside or internally: *a glimpse of what was hidden within*

without *prep* **1** not accompanied by: *I can't imagine going through life without him* **2** not using: *our Jeep drove without lights* **3** not possessing or having: *four months without a job; a lot of them came across the border without shoes* **4** in a manner showing a lack of: *without reverence* **5** while not or after not: *she sat without speaking for some while* ▹ *adv* **6** *formal* outside: *seated on the graveyard without*

withstand ❶ *vb* **-standing, -stood** to resist or endure successfully: *our ability to withstand stress*

witless *adj* **1** *formal* lacking intelligence or sense **2 scared witless** extremely frightened

witness ❶ *n* **1** a person who has seen or can give first-hand evidence of some event: *the only witness to a killing* **2** a person who gives evidence in a

THESAURUS

wit[1] *n* **1 = humour**, fun, quips, banter, puns, pleasantry, repartee, wordplay, levity, witticisms, badinage, jocularity, facetiousness, drollery, raillery, waggishness, wittiness
OPPOSITE: seriousness
2 = humorist, card *(informal)*, comedian, wag, joker, dag *(NZ informal)*, punster, epigrammatist
3 = cleverness, mind, reason, understanding, sense, brains, smarts *(slang, chiefly US)*, judgment, perception, wisdom, insight, common sense, intellect, comprehension, ingenuity, acumen, nous *(Brit slang)*, discernment, practical intelligence
OPPOSITE: stupidity

witch *n* **1 = enchantress**, magician, hag, crone, occultist, sorceress, Wiccan, necromancer

witchcraft *n* **= magic**, spell, witching, voodoo, the occult, wizardry, black magic, enchantment, occultism, sorcery, incantation, Wicca, the black art, witchery, necromancy, sortilege, makutu *(NZ)*

withdraw *vb* **1 = remove**, pull, take off, pull out, extract, take away, pull back, draw out, draw back **2 = take out**, extract, draw out

withdrawal *n* **1 = removal**, ending, stopping, taking away, abolition, elimination, cancellation, termination, extraction, discontinuation

withdrawn *adj* **2 = uncommunicative**, reserved, retiring, quiet, silent, distant, shy, shrinking, detached, aloof, taciturn, introverted, timorous, unforthcoming
OPPOSITE: outgoing

wither *vb* **1 = wilt**, dry, decline, shrink, decay, disintegrate, perish, languish, droop, shrivel, desiccate
OPPOSITE: flourish
2a = waste, decline, shrink, shrivel, atrophy **2b = fade**, decline, wane, perish **OPPOSITE:** increase

withering *adj* **= scornful**, blasting, devastating, humiliating, snubbing, blighting, hurtful, mortifying

withhold *vb* **a = keep secret**, keep, refuse, hide, reserve, retain, sit on *(informal)*, conceal, suppress, hold back, keep back **OPPOSITE:** reveal
b = hold back, check, resist, suppress, restrain, repress, keep back
OPPOSITE: release

withstand *vb* **= resist**, take, face, suffer, bear, weather, oppose, take on, cope with, brave, confront, combat, endure, defy, tolerate, put up with *(informal)*, thwart, stand up to, hold off, grapple with, hold out against, stand firm against
OPPOSITE: give in to

witness *n* **1 = observer**, viewer, spectator, looker-on, watcher, onlooker, eyewitness, bystander, beholder **2 = testifier**, deponent, attestant ▹ *vb* **6 = see**, mark, view,

DICTIONARY

court of law: *a witness for the defence* **3** a person who confirms the genuineness of a document or signature by adding his or her own signature **4** evidence proving or supporting something: *the Church of England, that historic witness to the power of the Christian faith* **5 bear witness to** to be evidence or proof of: *the high turn-out bore witness to the popularity of the contest* ▹*vb* **6** to see, be present at, or know at first hand: *I have witnessed many motor-racing accidents* **7** to be the scene or setting of: *the 1970s witnessed an enormous increase in international lending* **8** to confirm the genuineness of (a document or signature) by adding one's own signature **9 witness to** *formal* to confirm: *our aim is to witness to the fact of the empty tomb*
WORD ORIGIN Old English *witnes*

witness box *or esp. US* **witness stand** *n* the place in a court of law where witnesses stand to give evidence

wits *pl n* **1** the ability to think and act quickly: *when he was sober his wits were razor-sharp* **2 at one's wits' end** at a loss to know what to do **3 have one's wits about one** to be able to think and act quickly **4 live by** *or* **on one's wits** to gain a livelihood by craftiness rather than by hard work **5 scared out of one's wits** extremely frightened

Witt *n* See **de Witt**

Witte *n* **Sergei Yulievich** 1849–1915, Russian statesman; prime minister (1905–06). As minister of finance (1892–1903) he tried to modernize the Russian economy

witter *vb chiefly Brit informal* to chatter or babble pointlessly or at unnecessary length
WORD ORIGIN origin unknown

witticism *n* a witty remark

wittingly *adv* intentionally and knowingly

witty ❶ *adj* **-tier, -tiest** clever and amusing **wittily** *adv*

wives *n* ▸the plural of **wife**

wizard ❶ *n* **1** a man in fairy tales who has magic powers **2** a person who is outstandingly gifted in some specified field: *a financial wizard*
WORD ORIGIN from *wise*

wizardry *n* **1** magic or sorcery **2** outstanding skill or accomplishment in some specified field: *technological wizardry*

wizened (wiz-zend) *adj* shrivelled, wrinkled, or dried up with age

Władysław II *n* original name *Jogaila*. ?1351–1434, grand duke of Lithuania (1377–1401) and king of Poland (1386–1434). He united Lithuania and Poland and founded the Jagiellon dynasty

Władysław IV *n* 1595–1648, king of Poland (1632–48)

WMD *n* weapon(s) of mass destruction

woad *n* a blue dye obtained from a European plant, used by the ancient Britons as a body dye
WORD ORIGIN Old English *wād*

wobbegong *n* an Australian shark with brown-and-white skin

wobble ❶ *vb* **-bling, -bled 1** to move or sway unsteadily **2** to shake: *she was having difficulty in controlling her voice, which wobbled about* ▹*n* **3** a wobbling movement or sound
WORD ORIGIN Low German *wabbeln*

wobbly *adj* **-blier, -bliest 1** unsteady **2** trembling ▹*n* **3 throw a wobbly** *slang* to become suddenly angry or upset

wodge *n informal* a thick lump or chunk: *my wodge of Kleenex was a sodden ball*
WORD ORIGIN from *wedge*

woe ❶ *n* **1** *literary* intense grief **2 woes** misfortunes or problems: *economic woes* **3 woe betide someone** someone will or would experience misfortune: *woe betide anyone who got in his way*
WORD ORIGIN Old English *wā, wǣ*

woebegone *adj* sad in appearance
WORD ORIGIN *woe* + obsolete *bego* to surround

woeful *adj* **1** extremely sad **2** pitiful or deplorable: *a woeful lack of understanding* **woefully** *adv*

Woffington *n* **Peg**, full name *Margaret Woffington*. ?1714–60, Irish actress

Wöhler *n* **Friedrich** 1800–82, German chemist, who proved that organic compounds could be synthesized from inorganic compounds

wok *n* a large bowl-shaped metal Chinese cooking pot, used for stir-frying
WORD ORIGIN Chinese (Cantonese)

woke *vb* ▸the past tense of **wake¹**

woken *vb* ▸the past participle of **wake¹**

wold *n* a large area of high open rolling country
WORD ORIGIN Old English *weald* wood

wolf *n, pl* **wolves 1** a predatory doglike wild animal which hunts in packs **2** *old-fashioned informal* a man who habitually tries to seduce women **3 cry wolf** to give false alarms repeatedly: *if you cry wolf too often, people will take no notice* ▹*vb* **4 wolf down** to eat quickly or greedily: *they will wolf down kidneys but refuse tongue*
WORD ORIGIN Old English *wulf*

Wolf *n* **1 Friedrich August** 1759–1824, German classical scholar, who suggested that the Homeric poems, esp. the *Iliad*, are products of an oral tradition **2 Hugo** 1860–1903, Austrian composer, esp. of songs, including the *Italienisches Liederbuch* and the *Spanisches Liederbuch* **3 Howlin'** ▸See **Howlin' Wolf**

Wolfensohn *n* **James D.**, known as *Jim*. born 1933, US businessman and international official, born in Australia; president of the International Bank for Reconstruction and Development (the World Bank) (1995–2005)

Wolf-Ferrari *n* **Ermanno** 1876–1948, Italian composer born of a German father, in Germany from 1909. His works, mainly in a lyrical style, include operas, such as *The Jewels of the Madonna* (1911) and *Susanna's Secret* (1909)

wolfhound *n* a very large dog, formerly used to hunt wolves

Wolfit *n* Sir **Donald** 1902–68, English stage actor and manager

Wolfram von Eschenbach *n* died ?1220, German poet: author of the epic *Parzival*, incorporating the story of the Grail

wolf whistle *n* **1** a whistle produced by a man to express admiration of a woman's appearance ▹*vb* **wolf-whistle, -whistling, -whistled 2** to produce such a whistle

Wollstonecraft *n* **Mary** 1759–97, British feminist and writer, author

THESAURUS

watch, note, notice, attend, observe, perceive, look on, be present at, behold *(archaic, literary)*
8 = countersign, sign, endorse, validate

witty *adj* **= humorous**, gay, original, brilliant, funny, clever, amusing, lively, sparkling, ingenious, fanciful, whimsical, droll, piquant, facetious, jocular, epigrammatic, waggish
OPPOSITE: dull

wizard *n* **1 = magician**, witch, shaman, sorcerer, occultist, magus, conjuror, warlock, mage *(archaic)*, enchanter, necromancer, thaumaturge *(rare)*, tohunga *(NZ)*

wobble *vb* **1 = shake**, rock, sway, tremble, quake, waver, teeter, totter, seesaw **2 = tremble**, shake, vibrate ▹*n* **3a = unsteadiness**, shake, tremble, quaking **3b = unsteadiness**, shake, tremor, vibration

woe *n* **1** *(literary)* **= misery**, suffering, trouble, pain, disaster, depression, distress, grief, agony, gloom, sadness, hardship, sorrow, anguish, misfortune, unhappiness, heartache, heartbreak, adversity, dejection, wretchedness
OPPOSITE: happiness
2 *(pl)* **= problem**, trouble, trial, burden, grief, misery, curse, hardship, sorrow, misfortune, heartache, heartbreak, affliction, tribulation

DICTIONARY

of *A Vindication of the Rights of Women* (1792); wife of William Godwin and mother of Mary Shelley

Wolseley *n* **Garnet Joseph,** 1st Viscount 1833–1913, British field marshal, noted for his army reforms

wolverine *n* a large meat-eating mammal of Eurasia and North America with very thick dark fur
WORD ORIGIN earlier *wolvering*, from *wolf*

wolves *n* ▸ the plural of **wolf**

woman ❶ *n, pl* **women** **1** an adult female human being **2** adult female human beings collectively: *the very image of woman pared of the trappings of 'femininity'* **3** an adult female human being with qualities associated with the female, such as tenderness or maternalism: *she's more woman than you know* **4** a female servant or domestic help **5** *informal* a wife or girlfriend ▹ *adj* **6** female: *a woman doctor*
WORD ORIGIN Old English *wīfmann*

womanhood *n* **1** the state of being a woman: *young girls approaching womanhood* **2** women collectively: *Asian womanhood*

womanish *adj* (of a man) looking or behaving like a woman

womanizer *or* **-iser** *n* a man who has casual affairs with many women

womanizing *or* **-ising** *n* (of a man) the practice of indulging in casual affairs with women

womankind *n* all women considered as a group

womanly ❶ *adj* possessing qualities generally regarded as typical of, or appropriate to, a woman

womb *n* ▸ the nontechnical name for **uterus**
WORD ORIGIN Old English *wamb*

wombat *n* a furry heavily-built plant-eating Australian marsupial
WORD ORIGIN Aboriginal

women *n* ▸ the plural of **woman**

womenfolk *pl n* **1** women collectively **2** a group of women, esp. the female members of one's family

Women's Liberation *n* a movement promoting the removal of inequalities based upon the assumption that men are superior to women. Also called: **women's lib**

won *vb* ▸ the past of **win**

wonder ❶ *vb* **1** to think about something with curiosity or doubt: *I wonder why she did that* **2** to be amazed: *I did wonder at her leaving valuable china on the shelves* ▹ *n* **3** something that causes surprise or awe: *it's a wonder she isn't speechless with fright* **4** the feeling of surprise or awe caused by something strange: *the wonder of travel* **5** **do** *or* **work wonders** to achieve spectacularly good results **6** **no** *or* **small wonder** it is not surprising: *no wonder you're going broke* ▹ *adj* **7** causing surprise or awe because of spectacular results achieved: *a new wonder drug for treating migraine*
wonderingly *adv* **wonderment** *n*
WORD ORIGIN Old English *wundor*

Wonder *n* **Stevie** real name *Steveland Judkins Morris*. born 1950, US Motown singer, songwriter, and multi-instrumentalist. His recordings include *Up-Tight* (1966), *Superstition* (1972), *Innervisions* (1973), *Songs in the Key of Life* (1976), and *I Just Called to Say I Love You* (1985)

wonderful ❶ *adj* **1** extremely fine; excellent: *I've been offered a wonderful job* **2** causing surprise, amazement, or awe: *a strange and wonderful phenomenon*
wonderfully *adv*

wonderland *n* **1** an imaginary land of marvels or wonders **2** an actual place of great or strange beauty: *the apartment was a wonderland of design and colour*

wondrous *adj old-fashioned or literary* causing surprise or awe; marvellous

wonky *adj* **-kier, -kiest** *Brit, Austral & NZ slang* **1** shaky or unsteady: *wonky wheelbarrows; wonky knees* **2** insecure or unreliable: *his marriage is looking a bit wonky*
WORD ORIGIN dialect *wanky*

wont (rhymes with **don't**) *old-fashioned adj* **1** accustomed: *most murderers, his police friends were wont to say, were male* ▹ *n* **2** a usual practice: *she waded straight in, as was her wont*
WORD ORIGIN Old English *gewunod*

won't will not

woo ❶ *vb* **wooing, wooed** **1** to coax or urge: *it will woo people back into the kitchen* **2** *old-fashioned* to attempt to gain the love of (a woman) **wooing** *n*
WORD ORIGIN Old English *wōgian*

wood ❶ *n* **1** the hard fibrous substance beneath the bark in trees and shrubs, which is used in building and carpentry and as fuel ▸ Related adjective: **ligneous** **2** an area of trees growing together that is smaller than a forest: *a track leading into a wood* ▸ Related adjective: **sylvan** **3** *golf* a long-shafted club with a wooden head ▹ *adj* **4** made of, using, or for use with wood: *wood fires* ▸ See also **woods**
WORD ORIGIN Old English *widu, wudu*

Wood *n* **1** Mrs **Henry**, married name of *Ellen Price*. 1814–87, British novelist, noted esp. for the melodramatic novel *East Lynne* (1861) **2** Sir **Henry** (**Joseph**) 1869–1944, English conductor, who founded the Promenade Concerts in London **3** **John,** known as *the Elder*. 1707–54, British architect and town planner, working mainly in Bath, where he designed the North and South Parades (1728) and the Circus (1754) **4** his son, **John**, known as *the Younger*. 1727–82, British architect: designed the Royal Crescent (1767–71) and the

THESAURUS

woman *n* **1 = lady**, girl, miss, female, bird *(slang)*, dame *(slang)*, ho *(US derogatory, slang)*, sheila *(Austral & NZ informal)*, vrou *(S African)*, maiden *(archaic)*, chick *(slang)*, maid *(archaic)*, gal *(slang)*, lass, lassie *(informal)*, wench *(facetious)*, adult female, she, charlie *(Austral slang)*, chook *(Austral slang)*, wahine *(NZ)* **OPPOSITE:** man

womanly *adj* **= feminine**, motherly, female, warm, tender, matronly, ladylike

wonder *vb* **1 = think**, question, doubt, puzzle, speculate, query, ponder, inquire, ask yourself, meditate, be curious, conjecture, be inquisitive **2 = be amazed**, stare, marvel, be astonished, gape, boggle, be awed, be flabbergasted *(informal)*, gawk, be dumbstruck, stand amazed ▹ *n* **3 = phenomenon**, sight, miracle, spectacle, curiosity, marvel, prodigy, rarity, portent, wonderment, nonpareil **4 = amazement**, surprise, curiosity, admiration, awe, fascination, astonishment, bewilderment, wonderment, stupefaction

wonderful *adj* **1 = excellent**, mean *(slang)*, great *(informal)*, topping *(Brit slang)*, brilliant, cracking *(Brit informal)*, outstanding, smashing *(informal)*, superb, fantastic *(informal)*, tremendous, ace *(informal)*, magnificent, fabulous *(informal)*, marvellous, terrific, sensational *(informal)*, sovereign, awesome *(slang)*, admirable, super *(informal)*, brill *(informal)*, stupendous, out of this world *(informal)*, tiptop, bodacious *(slang, chiefly US)*, boffo *(slang)*, jim-dandy *(slang)*, chillin' *(US slang)*, booshit *(Austral slang)*, exo *(Austral slang)*, sik *(Austral slang)*, rad *(informal)*, phat *(slang)*, schmick *(Austral informal)* **OPPOSITE:** terrible **2 = remarkable**, surprising, odd, strange, amazing, extraordinary, fantastic, incredible, astonishing, staggering, eye-popping *(informal)*, marvellous, startling, peculiar, awesome, phenomenal, astounding, miraculous, unheard-of, wondrous *(archaic, literary)*, awe-inspiring, jaw-dropping **OPPOSITE:** ordinary

woo *vb* **2** *(old-fashioned)* **= court**, chase, pursue, spark *(rare)*, importune, seek to win, pay court to, seek the hand of, set your cap at *(old-fashioned)*, pay your addresses to, pay suit to, press your suit with

wood *n* **1a = timber**, planks, planking, lumber *(US)* **1b = firewood**, fuel, logs, kindling **2 = woodland**, trees, forest, grove, hurst *(archaic)*, thicket, copse, coppice, bushland

DICTIONARY

Assembly Rooms (1769–71), Bath **5 Ralph** 1715–72, British potter, working in Staffordshire, who made the first toby jug (1762)

wood alcohol *n* ▸ same as **methanol**

woodbine *n* a wild honeysuckle with sweet-smelling yellow flowers

woodcarving *n* **1** a work of art produced by carving wood **2** the act or craft of carving wood

woodcock *n* a large game bird with a long straight bill

woodcut *n* a print made from a block of wood with a design cut into it

woodcutter *n* a person who cuts down trees or chops wood

wooded ❶ *adj* covered with woods or trees

wooden ❶ *adj* **1** made of wood **2** lacking spirit or animation: *the man's expression became wooden* **woodenly** *adv*

wooden spoon *n* a booby prize, esp. in sporting contests

woodland *n* **1** land that is mostly covered with woods or trees ▷ *adj* **2** living in woods: *woodland birds*

woodlouse *n, pl* **-lice** a very small grey creature with many legs that lives in damp places

woodpecker *n* a bird with a strong beak with which it bores into trees for insects

wood pulp *n* pulp made from wood fibre, used to make paper

woodruff *n* a plant with small sweet-smelling white flowers and sweet-smelling leaves
WORD ORIGIN Old English *wudurofe*

woods *pl n* closely packed trees forming a forest or wood

woodsman *n, pl* **-men** a person who lives in a wood or who is skilled at woodwork or carving

Woodville *n* **Elizabeth** ?1437–92, wife of Edward IV of England and mother of Edward V

Woodward *n* **1** Sir **Clive** born 1956, English Rugby Union player and subsequently (1997–2004) coach of the England team that won the Rugby World Cup in 2003. **2 R**(**obert**) **B**(**urns**) 1917–79, US chemist. For his work on the synthesis of quinine, strychnine, cholesterol, and other organic compounds he won the Nobel prize for chemistry 1965

woodwind *music adj* **1** of or denoting a type of wind instrument, such as the oboe ▷ *n* **2** the woodwind instruments of an orchestra

woodwork *n* **1** the parts of a room or house that are made of wood, such as the doors and window frames: *stark white walls and blue woodwork* **2** the art or craft of making objects from wood **3 crawl out of the woodwork** to appear suddenly and in large numbers: *intellectuals and environmentalists crawled out of the woodwork*

woodworm *n* **1** a beetle larva that bores into wooden furniture or beams **2** the damage caused to wood by these larvae

woody *adj* **woodier, woodiest 1** (of a plant) having a very hard stem **2** (of an area) covered with woods or trees

woof[1] *n* ▸ same as **weft**
WORD ORIGIN Old English *ōwef*

woof[2] *n* an imitation of the bark of a dog

woofer *n* a loudspeaker used in high-fidelity systems for the reproduction of low audio frequencies

wool ❶ *n* **1** the soft curly hair of sheep and some other animals **2** yarn spun from this, used in weaving and knitting **3** cloth made from this yarn **4 pull the wool over someone's eyes** to deceive someone
WORD ORIGIN Old English *wull*

woolgathering *n* idle or absent-minded daydreaming

Woollcott *n* **Alexander** 1887–1943, US writer and critic. His collected essays include *Shouts and Murmurs* (1922)

woollen *or US* **woolen** *adj* **1** made of wool or of a mixture of wool and another material **2** relating to wool: *woollen mills* ▷ *n* **3 woollens** woollen clothes, esp. knitted ones

Woolley *n* Sir (**Charles**) **Leonard** 1880–1960, British archaeologist, noted for his excavations at Ur in Mesopotamia (1922–34)

woolly *or US* **wooly** *adj* **-lier, -liest 1** made of or like wool **2** confused or indistinct: *woolly ideas* ▷ *n, pl* **-lies 3** a woollen garment, such as a sweater

woolshed *n Austral & NZ* a large building in which sheep shearing takes place

Woolworth *n* **Frank Winfield** 1852–1919, US merchant; founder of an international chain of department stores selling inexpensive goods

woomera *n* a notched stick used by Australian Aborigines to aid the propulsion of a spear

Wootton *n* **Barbara** (**Frances**), Baroness of Abinger. 1897–1988, English economist, educationalist, social scientist, and criminologist

woozy *adj* **woozier, wooziest** *informal* feeling slightly dizzy
WORD ORIGIN origin unknown

wop-wops *pl n NZ informal* remote rural areas

Worcester sauce (wooss-ter) *or* **Worcestershire sauce** *n* a sharp-tasting sauce, made from soy sauce, vinegar, and spices

Worcs Worcestershire

word ❶ *n* **1** the smallest single meaningful unit of speech or writing ▸ Related adjective: **lexical 2** a brief conversation: *I would like a word with you* **3** a brief statement: *a word of warning* **4** news or information: *let me know if you get word of my wife* **5** a solemn promise: *he had given his word as a rabbi* **6** a command or order: *he had only to say the word and they'd hang him* **7** *computers* a set of bits used to store, transmit, or operate upon an item of information in a computer **8 by word of mouth** by spoken rather than by written means: *their reputation spreads by word of mouth* **9 in a word** briefly or in short: *in a word, we've won* **10 my word!** Also: **upon my word!** *old-fashioned* an exclamation of surprise or amazement **11 take someone at his** *or* **her word** to accept that someone really means what he or she says: *they're willing to take him at his word when he says he'll change* **12 take someone's word for it** to believe what someone says **13 the last word** the closing remark of a conversation or argument, often regarded as settling an issue **14 the last word in** the finest example of: *the last word in comfort* **15 word for word** using exactly the same words: *he repeated almost word for word what had been said* **16 word of honour** a solemn promise ▷ *vb* **17** to state in words: *the questions*

THESAURUS

wooded *adj* **= tree-covered**, forested, timbered, woody, sylvan (*poetic*), tree-clad

wooden *adj* **1 = made of wood**, timber, woody, of wood, ligneous **2 = expressionless**, empty, dull, blank, vacant, lifeless, deadpan, colourless, glassy, unresponsive, unemotional, emotionless, spiritless

wool *n* **1 = fleece**, hair, coat **2 = yarn**

word *n* **1 = term**, name, expression, designation, appellation (*formal*), locution, vocable **2 = chat**, tête-à-tête, talk, discussion, consultation, chitchat, brief conversation, colloquy, confabulation, confab (*informal*), heart-to-heart, powwow (*informal*) **3 = comment**, remark, expression, declaration, utterance, brief statement **4 = message**, news, latest (*informal*), report, information, account, notice, advice, communication, intelligence, bulletin, dispatch, gen (*Brit informal*), communiqué, intimation, tidings, heads up (*US & Canad*) **5 = promise**, guarantee, pledge, undertaking, vow, assurance, oath, parole, word of honour, solemn oath, solemn word **6 = command**, will, order, go-ahead (*informal*), decree, bidding, mandate, commandment, edict, ukase (*rare*) ▷ *vb* **17 = express**, say, state, put,

DICTIONARY

have to be carefully worded ▸ See also **words**
WORD ORIGIN Old English

Word *n* **the Word** the message and teachings contained in the Bible

-word *n combining form (preceded by 'the' and an initial letter)* a euphemistic way of referring to a word by its first letter because it is considered to be unmentionable by the user: *the c-word, meaning cancer*

word game *n* any game involving the discovery, formation, or alteration of a word or words

wording ⊕ *n* the way in which words are used to express something: *the exact wording of the regulation has still not been worked out*

word-perfect *adj* able to repeat from memory the exact words of a text one has learned

word processing *n* the storage and organization of text by electronic means, esp. for business purposes

word processor *n* an electronic machine for word processing, consisting of a keyboard, a VDU incorporating a microprocessor, and a printer

words *pl n* **1** the text of a song, as opposed to the music **2** the text of an actor's part **3 have words** to have an argument or disagreement **4 in other words** expressing the same idea in a different, more understandable, way **5 put into words** to express in speech or writing: *she was reluctant to put her thoughts into words*

wordy *adj* **wordier, wordiest** using too many words, esp. long words: *wordy explanations*

wore *vb* ▸ the past tense of **wear**

work ⊕ *n* **1** physical or mental effort directed to doing or making something **2** paid employment at a job, trade, or profession **3** duties or tasks: *I had to delegate as much work as I could* **4** something done or made as a result of effort: *a work by a major artist* **5** the place where a person is employed: *accidents at work* **6** *physics old-fashioned* the transfer of energy occurring when a force is applied to move a body **7 at work** working or in action: *the social forces at work in society* ▹ *adj* **8** of or for work: *work experience* ▹ *vb* **9** to do work; labour: *no-one worked harder than Arnold* **10** to be employed: *she worked as a waitress* **11** to make (a person or animal) labour **12** to operate (a machine or a piece of equipment) **13** (of a machine or a piece of equipment) to function, esp. effectively: *he doesn't have to know how things work* **14** (of a plan or system) to be successful **15** to cultivate (land) **16** to move gradually into a specific condition or position: *he picked up the shovel, worked it under the ice, and levered* **17** to make (one's way) with effort: *he worked his way to the top* **18** *informal* to manipulate to one's own advantage: *they could see an angle and they'd know how to work it* ▸ See also **work off, works,** etc.
WORD ORIGIN Old English *weorc*

workable *adj* **1** able to operate efficiently: *a workable solution* **2** able to be used: *a workable mine*

workaday *adj* commonplace or ordinary: *workaday surroundings*

workaholic *n* a person who is obsessed with work

workbench *n* a heavy table at which a craftsman or mechanic works

worker ⊕ *n* **1** a person who works in a specified way: *a hard worker* **2** a person who works at a specific job: *a government worker* **3** an employee, as opposed to an employer **4** a sterile female bee, ant, or wasp, that works for the colony

work ethic *n* a belief in the moral value of work

workforce *n* **1** the total number of workers employed by a company **2** the total number of people available for work: *the local workforce*

workhorse *n* a person or thing that does a lot of work, esp. dull or routine work: *this plane is the workhorse of most short-haul airlines*

workhouse *n* (formerly, in England) a public institution where very poor people did work in return for food and accommodation

working *adj* **1** having a job: *the working mother* **2** concerned with, used in, or suitable for work: *working conditions* **3** capable of being operated or used: *a working mechanism* ▹ *n* **4** a part of a mine or quarry that is or has been used **5 workings** the way that something works: *the workings of the human brain*

working capital *n* the amount of capital that a business has available to meet the day-to-day cash requirements of its operations

working class *n* **1** the social group that consists of people who earn wages, esp. as manual workers ▹ *adj* **working-class 2** of or relating to the working class: *a working-class neighbourhood*

working day *or esp. US & Canad* **workday** *n* **1** a day when people normally go to work: *the last working day of the week* **2** the part of the day allocated to work: *the long working day of twelve to fourteen hours*

working party *n* a committee established to investigate a problem

workload *n* the amount of work to be done, esp. in a specified period: *a heavy workload*

workman ⊕ *n, pl* **-men** a man who is employed to do manual work

workmanlike *adj* skilfully done: *a neat workmanlike job*

workmanship *n* the degree of skill with which an object is made: *shoddy workmanship*

workmate *n informal* a person who works with another person; fellow worker

work of art *n* **1** a piece of fine art, such as a painting or sculpture **2** an object or a piece of work that has been exceptionally skilfully made or produced: *the doll was truly a work of art*

work off *vb* to get rid of, usually by effort: *he went along to the tennis club and worked off his pique there*

work on *vb* to try to persuade or influence (someone)

work out *vb* **1** to solve, find out, or plan by reasoning or calculation: *working out a new budget* **2** to happen in a particular way: *he decided to wait and see how things worked out* **3** to be

THESAURUS

phrase, utter, couch, formulate

wording *n* **= phraseology**, words, language, phrasing, terminology, choice of words, mode of expression

work *n* **1 = effort**, industry, labour, grind *(informal)*, sweat, toil, slog, exertion, drudgery, travail *(literary)*, elbow grease *(facetious)*
OPPOSITE: leisure
2 = employment, calling, business, job, line, office, trade, duty, craft, profession, occupation, pursuit, livelihood, métier **OPPOSITE:** play
3 = task, jobs, projects, commissions, duties, assignments, chores, yakka *(Austral & NZ informal)* **4 = creation**, performance, piece, production, opus, achievement, composition, oeuvre *(French)*, handiwork ▹ *vb*
9 = labour, sweat, slave, toil, slog (away), drudge, peg away, exert yourself, break your back
OPPOSITE: relax
10 = be employed, do business, have a job, earn a living, be in work, hold down a job **12 = operate**, use, move, control, drive, manage, direct, handle, manipulate, wield, ply
13 = function, go, run, operate, perform, be in working order
OPPOSITE: be out of order
14 = succeed, work out, pay off *(informal)*, be successful, be effective, do the trick *(informal)*, do the business *(informal)*, get results, turn out well, have the desired result, go as planned, do the business *(informal)*
15 = cultivate, farm, dig, till, plough

worker *n* **2 = employee**, hand, labourer, workman, craftsman, artisan, tradesman, wage earner, proletarian, working man *or* working woman

workman *n* **= labourer**, hand, worker, employee, mechanic, operative,

W

successful or satisfactory: *the dates never worked out* **4** to take part in physical exercise **5** **work out at** to be calculated at (a certain amount): *the return on capital works out at 15 per cent* ▷ *n* **workout** **6** a session of physical exercise for training or to keep fit

work over *vb slang* to give (someone) a severe beating: *whoever worked her over did a thorough job*

works ❶ *n* **1** a place where something is manufactured: *a chemical works* ▷ *pl n* **2** the sum total of a writer's or artist's achievements considered together: *the works of Goethe* **3** **the works** *slang* everything associated with a particular subject or thing: *traditional Indian music, sitars, the works*

worksheet *n* a sheet of paper containing exercises to be completed by a student

workshop ❶ *n* **1** a room or building where manufacturing or other manual work is carried on **2** a group of people engaged in intensive study or work in a creative or practical field: *a writers' workshop*

workshy *adj* not inclined to work; lazy

work station *n* **1** an area in an office where one person works **2** *computers* a component of an electronic office system consisting of a VDU and keyboard

worktable *n* a table at which writing, sewing, or other work may be done

worktop *n* a surface in a kitchen, usually the top of a fitted kitchen unit, which is used for food preparation. Also: **work surface**

work-to-rule *n* a form of industrial action in which employees keep strictly to their employers' rules, with the result of reducing the work rate

work up *vb* **1** to make angry, excited, or upset: *he worked himself up into a rage* **2** to build up or develop: *I'd worked up a thirst* **3** to work on (something) in order to improve it: *there was enough material to be worked up into something publishable* **4** **work one's way up** to make progress: *he worked his way up in the catering trade* **5** **work up to** to develop gradually towards: *the fete worked up to a climax around lunch time*

world ❶ *n* **1** the earth as a planet **2** the human race; people generally: *providing food for the world* **3** any planet or moon, esp. one that might be inhabited **4** a particular group of countries or period of history, or its inhabitants: *the Arab world; the post-Cold War world* **5** an area, sphere, or realm considered as a complete environment: *the art world; the world of nature* **6** the total circumstances and experience of a person that make up his or her life: *there may not ever be a place for us in your world* **7** **bring into the world** to deliver or give birth to (a baby) **8** **come into the world** to be born **9** **for all the world** exactly or very much: *they looked for all the world like a pair of newly-weds* **10** **in the world** used to emphasize a statement: *she didn't have a worry in the world* **11** **man** *or* **woman of the world** a man *or* woman who is experienced in social or public life **12** **worlds apart** very different from each other: *this man and I are worlds apart* ▷ *adj* **13** of or concerning the entire world: *the world championship*

WORD ORIGIN Old English *w(e)orold*

world-class *adj* being as good as anyone else in the world in a particular field: *he has the makings of a world-class batsman*

World Cup *n* an international competition held between national teams in various sports, most notably association football

worldly ❶ *adj* **-lier, -liest** **1** not spiritual; earthly or temporal: *as a simple monk he had no interest in politics and other worldly affairs* **2** of or relating to material things: *all his worldly goods* **3** wise in the ways of the world; sophisticated: *a suave, worldly, charming Frenchman* **worldliness** *n*

worldly-wise *adj* wise in the ways of the world; sophisticated

world music *n* popular music of a variety of ethnic origins and styles

world-shaking *adj* of enormous significance; momentous: *world-shaking events*

World War I *n* the war (1914–18) between the Allies (principally France, Russia, Britain, Italy, Australia, Canada, and the US) and the Central Powers (principally Germany, Austria-Hungary, and Turkey). Also: **First World War**

World War II *n* the war (1939–45) between the Allies (Britain, France, Australia, Canada, the US, and the Soviet Union) and the Axis (Germany, Italy, and Japan). Also: **Second World War**

world-weary *adj* no longer finding pleasure in life

worldwide *adj* applying or extending throughout the world

World Wide Web *n computers* a vast network of hypertext files, stored on computers throughout the world, that can provide a computer user with information on a huge variety of subjects

worm *n* **1** a small invertebrate animal with a long thin body and no limbs **2** an insect larva that looks like a worm **3** a despicable or weak person **4** a slight trace: *a worm of doubt* **5** a shaft on which a spiral thread has been cut, for example in a gear arrangement in which such a shaft drives a toothed wheel **6** *computers* a type of virus ▷ *vb* **7** to rid (an animal) of worms in its intestines **8** **worm one's way** **a** to go or move slowly and with difficulty: *I had to worm my way out sideways from the bench* **b** to get oneself into a certain situation or position gradually: *worming your way into my good books* **9** **worm out of** to obtain (information) from someone who is not willing to provide it: *it took me weeks to worm the facts out of him* ▸ See also **worms**

WORD ORIGIN Old English *wyrm*

WORM *n computers* write once read many (times): an optical disk which enables users to store their own data

wormcast *n* a coil of earth or sand that has been excreted by a burrowing worm

worm-eaten *adj* eaten into by worms: *worm-eaten beams*

wormhole *n* a hole made by a worm in timber, plants, or fruit

worms *n* a disease caused by parasitic worms living in the intestines

wormwood *n* a plant from which a bitter oil formerly used in making absinthe is obtained

WORD ORIGIN Old English *wormōd, wermōd*

wormy *adj* **wormier, wormiest** infested with or eaten by worms

worn ❶ *vb* **1** ▸ the past participle of **wear** ▷ *adj* **2** showing signs of long use or wear: *the worn soles of his boots* **3** looking tired and ill: *that worn pain-creased face*

THESAURUS

craftsman, artisan, tradesman, journeyman, artificer *(rare)*

works *pl n* **1 = factory**, shop, plant, mill, workshop **2 = writings**, productions, output, canon, oeuvre *(French)*

workshop *n* **1a = factory**, works, shop, plant, mill **1b = workroom**, studio, atelier

world *n* **1 = earth**, planet, globe, earthly sphere **2 = mankind**, man, men, everyone, the public, everybody, humanity, human race, humankind, the race of man **5 = sphere**, system, area, field, environment, province, kingdom, realm, domain

worldly *adj* **1 = earthly**, lay, physical, fleshly, secular, mundane, terrestrial, temporal, carnal, profane, sublunary **OPPOSITE:** spiritual **3 = worldly-wise**, knowing, experienced, politic, sophisticated, cosmopolitan, urbane, blasé, well versed in the ways of the world **OPPOSITE:** naive

worn *adj* **2 = ragged**, shiny, frayed, shabby, tattered, tatty, threadbare, the worse for wear

DICTIONARY

worn-out *adj* **1** worn or used until threadbare, valueless, or useless **2** completely exhausted: *worn-out by their exertions*

worried ❶ *adj* concerned and anxious about things that may happen **worriedly** *adv*

worrisome *adj old-fashioned* causing worry

worry ❶ *vb* **-ries, -rying, -ried 1** to be or cause to be anxious or uneasy **2** to annoy or bother: *don't worry yourself with the details* **3** (of a dog) to frighten (sheep or other animals) by chasing and trying to bite them **4 worry away at** to struggle with or work on (a problem) ▹ *n, pl* **-ries 5** a state or feeling of anxiety: *he was beside himself with worry* **6** a cause for anxiety: *having a premature baby is much less of a worry these days* **worrier** *n*
WORD ORIGIN Old English *wyrgan*

worry beads *pl n* a string of beads that supposedly relieves nervous tension when fingered or played with

worrying *adj* causing concern and anxiety

worse *adj* **1** ▸ the comparative of **bad 2 none the worse for** not harmed by (adverse events or circumstances) **3 the worse for wear** *informal* in a poor condition; not at one's best: *returning the worse for wear from the pub* ▹ *n* **4 for the worse** into a worse condition: *taking a turn for the worse* ▹ *adv* **5** ▸ the comparative of **badly 6 worse off** in a worse condition, esp. financially
WORD ORIGIN Old English *wiersa*

worsen ❶ *vb* to make or become worse **worsening** *adj, n*

worship ❶ *vb* **-shipping, -shipped** *or US* **-shiping, -shiped 1** to show profound religious devotion to (one's god), for example by praying **2** to have intense love and admiration for (a person) ▹ *n* **3** religious adoration or devotion **4** formal expression of religious adoration, for example by praying **5** intense love or devotion to a person **worshipper** *n*
WORD ORIGIN Old English *weorthscipe*

Worship *n* **Your** *or* **His** *or* **Her Worship** *chiefly Brit* a title for a mayor or magistrate

worshipful *adj* feeling or showing reverence or adoration

worst *adj, adv* **1** ▸ the superlative of **bad** or **badly** ▹ *n* **2** the least good or the most terrible person, thing, or part: *the worst is yet to come* **3 at one's worst** in the worst condition or aspect of a thing or person: *the British male is at his worst in July and August* **4 at worst** in the least favourable interpretation or conditions: *all the questions should ideally be answered 'no', or at worst 'sometimes'* ▹ *vb* **5** *old-fashioned* to defeat or beat
WORD ORIGIN Old English *wierrest*

worsted (wooss-tid) *n* a close-textured woollen fabric used to make jackets and trousers
WORD ORIGIN after *Worstead*, a district in Norfolk

worth ❶ *prep* **1** having a value of: *the fire destroyed property worth $200 million* **2** worthy of; meriting or justifying: *if a job is worth doing, it's worth doing well* **3 worth one's weight in gold** extremely useful or helpful; very highly valued **4 worth one's while** worthy of spending one's time or effort on something: *they needed a wage of at least £140 a week to make it worth their while returning to work* ▹ *n* **5** monetary value: *the corporation's net worth* **6** high quality; value: *the submarine proved its military worth during the Second World War* **7** the amount of something that can be bought for a specified price: *$10 billion worth of property*
WORD ORIGIN Old English *weorth*

Worth *n* **Charles Frederick** 1825–95, English couturier, who founded Parisian *haute couture*

worthless ❶ *adj* **1** without value or usefulness: *worthless junk bonds* **2** without merit: *he sees himself as a worthless creature* **worthlessness** *n*

worthwhile ❶ *adj* sufficiently important, rewarding, or valuable to justify spending time or effort on it

worthy ❶ *adj* **-thier, -thiest 1** deserving of admiration or respect: *motives which were less than worthy* **2 worthy of** deserving of: *he would practise extra hard to be worthy of such an honour* ▹ *n, pl* **-thies 3** *often facetious* an important person **worthily** *adv* **worthiness** *n*

Wotton *n* Sir **Henry** 1568–1639, English poet and diplomat

would *vb* **1** ▸ used as an auxiliary to form the past tense or subjunctive

THESAURUS

worried *adj* **= anxious**, concerned, troubled, upset, afraid, bothered, frightened, wired *(slang)*, nervous, disturbed, distressed, tense, distracted, uneasy, fearful, tormented, distraught, apprehensive, perturbed, on edge, ill at ease, overwrought, fretful, hot and bothered, unquiet, antsy *(informal)* **OPPOSITE:** unworried

worry *vb* **1 = be anxious**, be concerned, be worried, obsess, brood, fret, agonize, feel uneasy, get in a lather *(informal)*, get in a sweat *(informal)*, get in a tizzy *(informal)*, get overwrought **OPPOSITE:** be unconcerned
2 = trouble, upset, harry, bother, disturb, distress, annoy, plague, irritate, tease, unsettle, torment, harass, hassle *(informal)*, badger, hector, disquiet, pester, vex, perturb, tantalize, importune, make anxious **OPPOSITE:** soothe
▹ *n* **5 = anxiety**, concern, care, fear, trouble, misery, disturbance, torment, woe, irritation, unease, apprehension, misgiving, annoyance, trepidation, perplexity, vexation **OPPOSITE:** peace of mind
6 = problem, care, trouble, trial, bother, plague, pest, torment, irritation, hassle *(informal)*, annoyance, vexation

worsen *vb* **a = deteriorate**, decline, sink, decay, get worse, degenerate, go downhill *(informal)*, go from bad to worse, take a turn for the worse, retrogress **OPPOSITE:** improve
b = aggravate, damage, exacerbate, make worse **OPPOSITE:** improve

worship *vb* **1 = revere**, praise, respect, honour, adore, glorify, reverence, exalt, laud, pray to, venerate, deify, adulate **OPPOSITE:** dishonour
2 = love, adore, idolize, put on a pedestal **OPPOSITE:** despise
▹ *n* **3, 5 = reverence**, praise, love, regard, respect, honour, glory, prayer(s), devotion, homage, adulation, adoration, admiration, exaltation, glorification, deification, laudation

worth *n* **5 = value**, price, rate, cost, estimate, valuation **OPPOSITE:** worthlessness
6a = merit, value, quality, importance, desert(s), virtue, excellence, goodness, estimation, worthiness **OPPOSITE:** unworthiness
6b = usefulness, value, benefit, quality, importance, utility, excellence, goodness **OPPOSITE:** uselessness

worthless *adj* **1a = valueless**, poor, miserable, trivial, trifling, paltry, trashy, measly, wretched, two a penny *(informal)*, rubbishy, poxy *(slang)*, nickel-and-dime *(US slang)*, wanky *(taboo, slang)*, a dime a dozen, nugatory, negligible **OPPOSITE:** valuable
1b = useless, meaningless, pointless, futile, no use, insignificant, unimportant, ineffectual, unusable, unavailing, not much cop *(Brit slang)*, inutile, not worth a hill of beans *(chiefly US)*, negligible, pants *(slang)* **OPPOSITE:** useful
2 = good-for-nothing, base, abandoned, useless, vile, abject, despicable, depraved, contemptible, ignoble **OPPOSITE:** honourable

worthwhile *adj* **= useful**, good, valuable, helpful, worthy, profitable, productive, beneficial, meaningful, constructive, justifiable, expedient, gainful **OPPOSITE:** useless

worthy *adj* **1 = praiseworthy**, good, excellent, deserving, valuable, decent, reliable, worthwhile,

W

mood of **will**[1]: *he asked if she would marry him; that would be delightful* **2** to express a polite offer or request: *would you like some lunch?* **3** to describe a habitual past action: *sometimes at lunch time I would choose a painting to go and see*

would-be ❶ *adj* wanting or pretending to be: *would-be brides*

wouldn't would not

wound[1] ❶ *n* **1** an injury to the body such as a cut or a gunshot injury **2** an injury to one's feelings or reputation ▷*vb* **3** to cause an injury to the body or feelings of **wounding** *adj*
WORD ORIGIN Old English *wund*

wound[2] *vb* ▸the past of **wind**[2]

wove *vb* ▸a past tense of **weave**

woven *vb* ▸a past participle of **weave**

wow *interj* **1** an exclamation of admiration or amazement ▷*n* **2** *slang* a person or thing that is amazingly successful: *he would be an absolute wow on the chat shows* ▷*vb* **3** *slang* to be a great success with: *the new Disney film wowed festival audiences*
WORD ORIGIN Scots

wowser *n Austral & NZ slang* **1** a fanatically puritanical person **2** a teetotaller
WORD ORIGIN dialect *wow* to complain

Wozniak *n* **Steve**, full name *Stephan Gary Wozniak*. born 1950, US computer scientist and executive: co-founder (with Steve Jobs, 1976) of Apple Inc

wp word processor

WPC (in Britain) woman police constable

wpm words per minute

WRAC (in Britain) Women's Royal Army Corps

wrack[1] *n* ▸same as **rack**[2]
WORD ORIGIN Old English *wræc* persecution

wrack[2] *n* seaweed that is floating in the sea or has been washed ashore
WORD ORIGIN probably from Middle Dutch *wrak* wreckage

WRAF (in Britain) Women's Royal Air Force

wraith *n literary* a ghost **wraithlike** *adj*
WORD ORIGIN Scots

wrangle ❶ *vb* **-gling, -gled** **1** to argue noisily or angrily ▷*n* **2** a noisy or angry argument
WORD ORIGIN Low German *wrangeln*

wrap ❶ *vb* **wrapping, wrapped** **1** to fold a covering round (something) and fasten it securely: *a small package wrapped in brown paper* **2** to fold or wind (something) round a person or thing: *she wrapped a handkerchief around her bleeding palm* **3** to fold, wind, or coil: *she wrapped her arms around her mother* **4** to complete the filming of (a motion picture or television programme) ▷*n* **5** *old-fashioned* a garment worn wrapped round the shoulders **6** (in the filming of a motion picture or television programme) the end of a day's filming or the completion of filming **7** a type of sandwich consisting of filling rolled up in a flour tortilla **8** *Brit slang* a small packet of an illegal drug in powder form: *a wrap of heroin* **9** **keep something under wraps** to keep something secret
WORD ORIGIN origin unknown

wraparound *adj* **1** (of a skirt) designed to be worn wrapped round the body **2** extending in a curve from the front round to the sides: *wraparound shades*

wrap party *n* a party held by cast and crew to celebrate the completion of filming of a motion picture or television programme

wrapper *n* a paper, foil, or plastic cover in which a product is wrapped: *a single sweet wrapper*

wrapping *n* a piece of paper, foil, or other material used to wrap something in

wrap up *vb* **1** to fold paper, cloth, or other material round (something) **2** to put warm clothes on: *remember to wrap up warmly on cold or windy days* **3** *informal* to finish or settle: *he will need 60 to 90 days to wrap up his current business dealings* **4** *slang* to stop talking **5** **wrapped up in** giving all one's attention to: *wrapped up in her new baby*

wrasse *n* a brightly coloured sea fish
WORD ORIGIN Cornish *wrach*

wrath ❶ (roth) *n old-fashioned or literary* intense anger **wrathful** *adj*
WORD ORIGIN Old English *wrǣththu*

wreak *vb* **1** **wreak havoc** to cause chaos or damage: *this Australian sun will wreak havoc with your complexions* **2** **wreak vengeance on** to take revenge on
WORD ORIGIN Old English *wrecan*

wreath *n, pl* **wreaths** **1** a ring of flowers or leaves, placed on a grave as a memorial or worn on the head as a garland or a mark of honour **2** anything circular or spiral: *a wreath of smoke*
WORD ORIGIN Old English *writha*

wreathe *vb* **wreathing, wreathed** *literary* **1** **wreathed in** **a** surrounded by: *wreathed in pipe smoke* **b** surrounded by a ring of: *wreathed in geraniums* **2** **wreathed in smiles** smiling broadly

wreck ❶ *vb* **1** to break, spoil, or destroy completely **2** to cause the accidental sinking or destruction of (a ship) at sea ▷*n* **3** something that has been destroyed or badly damaged, such as a crashed car or aircraft **4** a ship that has been sunk or destroyed at sea **5** a person in a poor mental or physical state
WORD ORIGIN from Old Norse

wreckage *n* the remains of something that has been destroyed or badly damaged, such as a crashed car or aircraft

wrecker *n* **1** a person who destroys or badly damages something: *a marriage*

respectable, upright, admirable, honourable, honest, righteous, reputable, virtuous, dependable, commendable, creditable, laudable, meritorious, estimable
OPPOSITE: disreputable

would-be *adj* = **budding**, potential, so-called, professed, dormant, self-styled, latent, wannabe (*informal*), unfulfilled, undeveloped, self-appointed, unrealized, manqué, soi-disant (*French*), quasi-

wound[1] *n* **1** = **injury**, cut, damage, hurt, harm, slash, trauma (*pathology*), gash, lesion, laceration **2** = **trauma**, injury, shock, pain, offence, slight, torture, distress, insult, grief, torment, anguish, heartbreak, pang, sense of loss ▷*vb* **3a** = **injure**, cut, hit, damage, wing, hurt, harm, slash, pierce, irritate, gash, lacerate **3b** = **offend**, shock, pain, hurt, distress, annoy, sting, grieve, mortify, cut to the quick, hurt the feelings of, traumatize

wrangle *vb* **1** = **argue**, fight, row, dispute, scrap, disagree, fall out (*informal*), contend, quarrel, brawl, squabble, spar, bicker, have words, altercate ▷*n* **2** = **argument**, row, clash, dispute, contest, set-to (*informal*), controversy, falling-out (*informal*), quarrel, brawl, barney (*informal*), squabble, bickering, tiff, altercation, slanging match (*Brit*), angry exchange, argy-bargy (*Brit informal*), bagarre (*French*)

wrap *vb* **1a** = **cover**, surround, fold, enclose, roll up, cloak, shroud, swathe, muffle, envelop, encase, sheathe, enfold, bundle up
OPPOSITE: uncover
1b = **pack**, package, parcel (up), tie up, gift-wrap **OPPOSITE:** unpack
2, 3 = **bind**, wind, fold, swathe
OPPOSITE: unwind
▷*n* **5** (*old-fashioned*) = **cloak**, cape, stole, mantle, shawl

wrath (*old-fashioned or literary*) *n* = **anger**, passion, rage, temper, fury, resentment, irritation, indignation, ire, displeasure, exasperation, choler
OPPOSITE: satisfaction

wreck *vb* **1a** = **destroy**, break, total (*slang*), smash, ruin, devastate, mar, shatter, spoil, demolish, sabotage, trash (*slang*), ravage, dash to pieces, kennet (*Austral slang*), jeff (*Austral slang*) **OPPOSITE:** build
1b = **spoil**, blow (*slang*), ruin, devastate, shatter, undo, screw up (*informal*), cock up (*Brit slang*), play

DICTIONARY

wrecker **2** (formerly) a person who lured ships on to the rocks in order to plunder them **3** *chiefly US, Canad & NZ* a person whose job is to demolish buildings or dismantle cars **4** *US & Canad* a breakdown van

wreckers *pl n* NZ a business which sells material from demolished cars or buildings

wren *n* a very small brown songbird
WORD ORIGIN Old English *wrenna*

Wren *n informal* (formerly, in Britain and certain other nations) a member of the former Women's Royal Naval Service
WORD ORIGIN from abbreviation *WRNS*

wrench ❶ *vb* **1** to twist or pull (something) violently, for example to remove it from something to which it is attached: *he grabbed the cable and wrenched it out of the wall socket* **2** to move or twist away with a sudden violent effort: *she wrenched free of his embrace* **3** to injure (a limb or joint) by a sudden twist ▷*n* **4** a violent twist or pull **5** an injury to a limb or joint, caused by twisting it **6** a feeling of sadness experienced on leaving a person or place: *it would be a wrench to leave Essex after all these years* **7** a spanner with adjustable jaws
WORD ORIGIN Old English *wrencan*

wrest *vb* **1** to take (something) away from someone with a violent pull or twist **2** to seize forcibly by violent or unlawful means: *she must begin to wrest control of the army and the police*
WORD ORIGIN Old English *wrǣstan*

wrestle ❶ *vb* **-tling, -tled 1** to fight (someone) by grappling and trying to throw or pin him or her to the ground, often as a sport **2 wrestle with** to struggle hard with (a person, problem, or thing): *I wrestled with my conscience* **wrestler** *n*
WORD ORIGIN Old English *wrǣstlian*

wrestling *n* a sport in which each contestant tries to overcome the other either by throwing or pinning him or her to the ground or by forcing a submission

wretch *n old-fashioned* **1** a despicable person **2** a person pitied for his or her misfortune
WORD ORIGIN Old English *wrecca*

wretched (**retch**-id) *adj* **1** in poor or pitiful circumstances: *a vast wretched slum* **2** feeling very unhappy **3** of poor quality: *the wretched state of the cabbages* **4** *informal* undesirable or displeasing: *what a wretched muddle* **wretchedly** *adv* **wretchedness** *n*

wriggle *vb* **-gling, -gled 1** to twist and turn with quick movements: *he wriggled on the hard seat* **2** to move along by twisting and turning **3 wriggle out of** to avoid (doing something that one does not want to do): *he wriggled out of donating blood* ▷*n* **4** a wriggling movement or action
WORD ORIGIN Middle Low German *wriggeln*

wring *vb* **wringing, wrung 1** Also: **wring out** to squeeze water from (a cloth or clothing) by twisting it tightly **2** to twist (a neck) violently **3** to clasp and twist (one's hands) in anguish **4** to grip (someone's hand) vigorously in greeting **5** to obtain by forceful means: *to wring concessions from the army* **6 wring someone's heart** to make someone feel sorrow or pity
WORD ORIGIN Old English *wringan*

wringer *n* ▸same as **mangle**[2] (sense 1)

wringing *adv* **wringing wet** extremely wet

wrinkle ❶ *n* **1** a slight ridge in the smoothness of a surface, such as a crease in the skin as a result of age ▷*vb* **-kling, -kled 2** to develop or cause to develop wrinkles **wrinkled** *or* **wrinkly** *adj*
WORD ORIGIN Old English *wrinclian* to wind around

wrist *n* **1** the joint between the forearm and the hand **2** the part of a sleeve that covers the wrist
WORD ORIGIN Old English

wristwatch *n* a watch worn strapped round the wrist

writ ❶ *n* a formal legal document ordering a person to do or not to do something
WORD ORIGIN Old English

write ❶ *vb* **writing, wrote, written 1** to draw or mark (words, letters, or numbers) on paper or a blackboard with a pen, pencil, or chalk **2** to describe or record (something) in writing: *he began to write his memoirs* **3** to be an author: *he still taught writing, but he didn't write* **4** to write a letter to or correspond regularly with someone: *don't forget to write!* **5** *informal chiefly US & Canad* to write a letter to (someone): *I wrote him several times* **6** to say or communicate in a letter or a book: *in a recent letter a friend wrote that everything costs more in Russia now* **7** to fill in the details for (a cheque or document) **8** *computers* to record (data) in a storage device **9 write down** to record in writing: *write it down if you find it too embarrassing to talk about*
WORD ORIGIN Old English *wrītan*

write off *vb* **1** *accounting* to cancel (a bad debt) from the accounts **2** to dismiss from consideration: *he wrote her off as a tense woman* **3** to send a written request (for something): *he wrote off for leaflets on the subject* **4** *informal* to damage (a vehicle) beyond repair ▷*n* **write-off 5** *informal* a vehicle that is damaged beyond repair

write out *vb* **1** to put into writing or reproduce in full form in writing **2** to remove (a character) from a television or radio series: *another actress is to be written out of the BBC soap*

writer ❶ *n* **1** a person whose job is writing; author **2** the person who has written something specified: *the writer of this letter is pretty dangerous*

write up *vb* **1** to describe fully, complete, or bring up to date in writing: *she would write up her diary in bed* ▷*n* **write-up 2** a published account of something, such as a review in a newspaper or magazine: *I see the Herald didn't give you a very good write-up*

writhe *vb* **writhing, writhed** to twist or squirm in pain: *writhing in agony*
WORD ORIGIN Old English *wrīthan*

writing ❶ *n* **1** something that has been written: *the writing on the outer flap was faint* **2** written form:

THESAURUS

havoc with, crool *or* cruel (*Austral slang*) **OPPOSITE:** save ▷*n* **4 = shipwreck**, derelict, hulk, sunken vessel

wrench *vb* **1 = twist**, force, pull, tear, rip, tug, jerk, yank, wring, wrest **3 = sprain**, strain, rick, distort ▷*n* **4 = twist**, pull, rip, tug, jerk, yank **5 = sprain**, strain, twist **6 = blow**, shock, pain, ache, upheaval, uprooting, pang **7 = spanner**, adjustable spanner, shifting spanner

wrestle *vb* **1 = fight**, battle, struggle, combat, contend, strive, grapple, tussle, scuffle

wrinkle *n* **1a = line**, fold, crease, furrow, pucker, crow's-foot, corrugation **1b = crease**, gather, fold, crumple, furrow, rumple, pucker, crinkle, corrugation ▷*vb* **2 = crease**, line, gather, fold, crumple, ruck, furrow, rumple, pucker, crinkle, corrugate **OPPOSITE:** smooth

writ *n* **= summons**, document, decree, indictment, court order, subpoena, arraignment

write *vb* **1 = record**, copy, scribble, take down, inscribe, set down, transcribe, jot down, put in writing, commit to paper, indite, put down in black and white **2 = compose**, create, author, draft, pen, draw up **4 = correspond**, get in touch, keep in touch, write a letter, drop a line, drop a note, e-mail

writer *n* **1 = author**, novelist, hack, columnist, scribbler, scribe, essayist, penman, wordsmith, man of letters, penpusher, littérateur, penny-a-liner (*rare*) ▸See: **dramatist poetry**

writing *n* **3 = script**, hand, print, printing, fist (*informal*), scribble, handwriting, scrawl, calligraphy, longhand, penmanship, chirography

W

DICTIONARY

permission in writing **3** ▸ short for **handwriting** **4** a kind or style of writing: *creative writing* **5** the work of a writer: *Wilde never mentioned chess in his writing*

written *vb* **1** ▸ the past participle of **write** ▹ *adj* **2** recorded in writing: *written permission*

WRNS (in Britain, formerly) Women's Royal Naval Service

wrong ❶ *adj* **1** not correct or accurate: *the wrong answers* **2** acting or judging in error; mistaken: *do correct me if I'm wrong* **3** not in accordance with correct or conventional rules or standards; immoral: *this group argues that even gently slapping a child is wrong* **4** not intended or appropriate: *I ordered the wrong things; you've picked the wrong time to ask such questions* **5** being a problem or trouble: *come on, I know when something's wrong* **6** not functioning properly: *there's something wrong with the temperature sensor* **7** denoting the side of cloth that is worn facing inwards ▹ *adv* **8** in a wrong manner: *I guessed wrong* **9** **get someone wrong** to misunderstand someone: *don't get me wrong, I'm not making threats* **10** **get something wrong** to make a mistake about something: *he had got his body language wrong* **11** **go wrong** **a** to turn out badly or not as intended **b** to make a mistake **c** (of a machine) to stop functioning properly: *pilots must be able to react instantly if the automatic equipment suddenly goes wrong* ▹ *n* **12** something bad, immoral, or unjust: *how can such a wrong be redressed?* **13** **in the wrong** mistaken or guilty ▹ *vb* **14** to treat (someone) unjustly **15** to think or speak unfairly of (someone) **wrongly** *adv*
WORD ORIGIN Old English *wrang* injustice

wrongdoing *n* immoral or illegal behaviour **wrongdoer** *n*

wrong-foot *vb* **1** *sport* to play a shot in such a way as to catch (an opponent) off-balance: *he constantly wrong-footed his opponent with fine passing* **2** to gain an advantage over (someone) by doing something unexpected: *China wrong-footed Vietnam by supporting the peace plan*

wrongful *adj* unjust or illegal: *wrongful imprisonment* **wrongfully** *adv*

wrong-headed *adj* constantly and stubbornly wrong in judgment

wrote *vb* ▸ the past tense of **write**

wroth *adj old-fashioned or literary* angry
WORD ORIGIN Old English *wrāth*

wrought (rawt) *vb* **1** *old-fashioned* ▸ a past of **work** ▹ *adj* **2** *metallurgy* shaped by hammering or beating: *wrought copper and brass*

wrought iron *n* a pure form of iron with a low carbon content, often used for decorative work

wrung *vb* ▸ the past of **wring**

WRVS (in Britain) Women's Royal Voluntary Service

wry *adj* **wrier, wriest** *or* **wryer, wryest** **1** drily humorous; sardonic: *wry amusement* **2** (of a facial expression) produced by twisting one's features to denote amusement or displeasure: *a small wry smile twisted the corner of his mouth* **wryly** *adv*
WORD ORIGIN Old English *wrīgian* to turn

wrybill *n* a New Zealand plover whose bill is bent to one side enabling it to search for food beneath stones

wryneck *n* a woodpecker that has a habit of twisting its neck round

wt. weight

WTO World Trade Organization

Wu[1] *n* **Harry,** real name *Wu Hongda.* born 1937, Chinese dissident and human-rights campaigner, a US citizen from 1994: held in labour camps (1960–79); exiled to the US in 1985 but returned secretly to document forced labour in Chinese prisons

Wu[2] *n* a group of dialects of Chinese spoken around the Yangtze delta

Wu Di *or* **Wu Ti** *n* 156 BC–86 BC, Chinese emperor (140–86) of the Han dynasty, who greatly extended the Chinese empire and made Confucianism the state religion

Wu Hou *n* 625–705 AD Chinese empress (655–705) of the Tang dynasty

Wulfila *n* same as **Ulfilas**

Wundt *n* **Wilhelm Max** 1832–1920, German experimental psychologist

wuss (woos) *or* **wussy** *n, pl* **wusses** *or* **wussies** *slang chiefly US* a feeble or effeminate person
WORD ORIGIN perhaps from PUSSY[1]

Wu Ti *n* See **Wu Di**

WV West Virginia

WWI World War One

WWII World War Two

WWW World Wide Web

WY Wyoming

Wyatt *n* **1 James** 1746–1813, British architect; a pioneer of the Gothic Revival **2** Sir **Thomas** ?1503–42, English poet at the court of Henry VIII

wych-elm *or* **witch-elm** *n* a Eurasian elm with long pointed leaves
WORD ORIGIN Old English *wice*

Wycherley *n* **William** ?1640–1716, English dramatist. His Restoration comedies include *The Country Wife* (1675) and *The Plain Dealer* (1676)

Wykeham *n* **William of** 1324–1404, English prelate and statesman, who founded New College, Oxford, and Winchester College: chancellor of England (1367–71; 1389–91); bishop of Winchester (1367–1404)

Wyndham *n* **John,** pseudonym of *John Wyndham Parkes Lucas Beynon Harris.* 1903–69, British writer of science fiction novels and stories. His works include *The Day of the Triffids* (1951), *The Kraken Wakes* (1953), and *The Midwich Cuckoos* (1957)

Wynette *n* **Tammy,** original name *Virginia Wynette Pugh.* 1942–98, US country singer; her bestselling records include "Your Good Girl's Gonna Go Bad" (1967) and "Stand By Your Man" (1969)

Wyn Jones *n* **Ieuan** born 1949, Welsh politician; leader of Plaid Cymru from 2000

WYSIWYG *n, adj computers* what you see is what you get: referring to what is displayed on the screen being the same as what will be printed out

THESAURUS

wrong *adj* **1, 2 = incorrect**, mistaken, false, faulty, inaccurate, untrue, erroneous, off target, unsound, in error, wide of the mark, fallacious, off base (*US & Canad informal*), off beam (*informal*), way off beam (*informal*) **3 = bad**, criminal, illegal, evil, unfair, crooked, unlawful, illicit, immoral, unjust, dishonest, wicked, sinful, unethical, wrongful, under-the-table, reprehensible, dishonourable, iniquitous, not cricket (*informal*), felonious, blameworthy **OPPOSITE:** moral **4 = inappropriate**, incorrect, unfitting, unsuitable, unhappy, not done, unacceptable, undesirable, improper, unconventional, incongruous, unseemly, unbecoming, indecorous, inapt, infelicitous, malapropos **OPPOSITE:** correct **5 = amiss**, faulty, unsatisfactory, not right, defective, awry **6 = defective**, not working, faulty, out of order, awry, askew, out of commission ▹ *adv* **8 = incorrectly**, badly, wrongly, mistakenly, erroneously, inaccurately **OPPOSITE:** correctly ▹ *n* **12 = offence**, injury, crime, abuse, error, sin, injustice, grievance, infringement, trespass, misdeed, transgression, infraction, bad *or* evil deed **OPPOSITE:** good deed ▹ *vb* **14 = mistreat**, abuse, hurt, injure, harm, cheat, take advantage of, discredit, oppress, malign, misrepresent, dump on (*slang, chiefly US*), impose upon, dishonour, ill-treat, maltreat, ill-use **OPPOSITE:** treat well

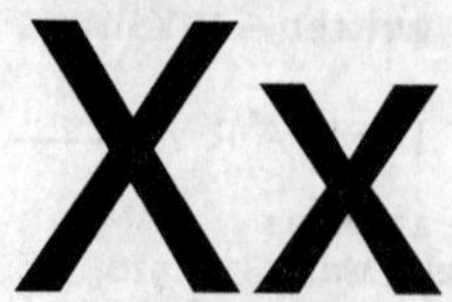

DICTIONARY

x *maths* **1** (along with *y* and *z*) an unknown quantity **2** the multiplication symbol

X 1 indicating an error, a choice, or a kiss **2** indicating an unknown, unspecified, or variable factor, person, or thing: *Miss X* **3** the Roman numeral for ten **4** (formerly) indicating a film that may not be publicly shown to anyone under 18: since 1982 replaced by symbol 18

X-chromosome *n* the sex chromosome that occurs in pairs in the females of many animals, including humans, and as one of a pair with the Y-chromosome in males

Xe *chem* xenon

Xenakis *n* **Yannis.** 1922–2001, Greek composer and musical theorist, born in Romania: later a French citizen. He was noted for his use of computers in composition: his works include *ST/10-1, 080262* (1962) and *Dox-orkh* (1991)

Xenocrates *n* ?396–314 BC, Greek Platonic philosopher ▸ **Xenocratic** *adj*

xenon *n chem* a colourless odourless gas found in minute quantities in the air. Symbol: Xe
WORD ORIGIN Greek: something strange

Xenophanes *n* ?570–?480 BC, Greek philosopher and poet, noted for his monotheism and regarded as a founder of the Eleatic school

xenophobia (zen-oh-fobe-ee-a) *n* hatred or fear of foreigners or strangers **xenophobic** *adj*
WORD ORIGIN Greek *xenos* foreign + *phobos* fear

Xenophon *n* 431–?355 BC, Greek general and historian; a disciple of Socrates. He accompanied Cyrus the Younger against Artaxerxes II and, after Cyrus' death at Cunaxa (401), he led his army of 10 000 Greek soldiers to the Black Sea, an expedition described in his *Anabasis*. His other works include *Hellenica*, a history of Greece, and the *Memorabilia, Apology*, and *Symposium*, which contain recollections of Socrates

xerography (zeer-og-ra-fee) *n* a photocopying process in which an image of the written or printed material is electrically charged on a surface and attracts oppositely charged dry ink particles which are then fixed by heating
xerographic *adj*
WORD ORIGIN Greek *xēros* dry + -GRAPHY

Xerox (zeer-ox) *n trademark* **1** a machine for copying printed material **2** a copy made by a Xerox machine ▹ *vb* **3** to produce a copy of (a document) using such a machine

Xhosa (kawss-a) *n* **1** *pl* **-sa** *or* **-sas** a member of a Black people living in the Republic of South Africa **2** the language of this people **Xhosan** *adj*

Xia Gui *or* **Hsia Kuei** *n* ?1180–1230, Chinese landscape painter of the Sung dynasty; noted for his misty mountain landscapes in ink monochrome

Ximenes *or* **Ximenez** *n* See **Jiménez de Cisneros**

Xmas (eks-mass) *n informal* ▸ short for **Christmas**
WORD ORIGIN from the Greek letter *chi* (X), first letter of *Khristos* Christ

XML extensible markup language: a computer language used in text formatting

X-rated *adj* **1** (formerly, in Britain) (of a film) considered suitable for viewing by adults only **2** *informal* involving bad language, violence, or sex: *an X-rated conversation*

X-ray ❶ *or* **x-ray** *n* **1** a stream of electromagnetic radiation of short wavelength that can pass through some solid materials **2** a picture produced by exposing photographic film to X-rays: used in medicine as a diagnostic aid, since parts of the body, such as bones, absorb X-rays and so appear as opaque areas on the picture ▹ *vb* **3** to photograph, treat, or examine using X-rays

X-ray diffraction *n physics* the scattering of X-rays on contact with matter, resulting in changes in radiation intensity, which is used for studying atomic structure

Xuan-tong *n* the Pinyin transliteration of the title as emperor of China of (Henry) **Pu-yi**

Xuan Zang *or* **Hsüan-tsang** *n* 602–664 AD, Chinese Buddhist monk, who travelled to India to study the Buddhist scriptures, many of which he translated into Chinese: noted also for his account of his travels

Xuan Zong *or* **Hsüan-tsung** *n* 685–762 AD, Chinese emperor (712–56) of the Tang dynasty

Xun Zi *or* **Hsün-tzu** *n* original name *Hsun Kuang*. c. 300 BC–c. 230 BC, Chinese philosopher, who systematized Confucian teaching

xylem (zile-em) *n bot* a plant tissue that conducts water and mineral salts from the roots to all other parts
WORD ORIGIN Greek *xulon* wood

xylene (zile-lean) *n chem* a hydrocarbon existing in three isomeric forms, all three being colourless flammable volatile liquids used as solvents and in the manufacture of synthetic resins, dyes, and insecticides
WORD ORIGIN Greek *xulon* wood

xylitol *n chem* an artificial sweetener produced from xylose and used esp. in chewing gum

xylophone (zile-oh-fone) *n music* a percussion instrument consisting of a set of wooden bars played with hammers **xylophonist** *n*
WORD ORIGIN Greek *xulon* wood

xylose *n* a white crystalline sugar derived from wood and straw

THESAURUS

X-ray *n* **2 = radiograph,** x-ray image

Yy

DICTIONARY

y *maths* (along with *x* and *z*) an unknown quantity
Y **1** an unknown, unspecified, or variable factor, number, person, or thing **2** *chem* yttrium
Y2K *n informal* name for the year 2000 AD (esp. referring to the millennium bug)
ya *interj S African* yes
yabby *n, pl* **-bies** *Austral* **1** a small freshwater crayfish **2** a marine prawn used as bait
WORD ORIGIN from a native Australian language
yacht (yott) *n* **1** a large boat with sails or an engine, used for racing or pleasure cruising ▷*vb* **2** to sail or cruise in a yacht **yachting** *n, adj*
WORD ORIGIN obsolete Dutch *jaghte*
yachtsman *or fem* **yachtswoman** *n, pl* **-men** *or* **-women** a person who sails a yacht
yack *n, vb* ▸same as **yak²**
yah *interj* **1** *informal* ▸same as **yes** **2** an exclamation of derision or disgust
yahoo *n, pl* **-hoos** a crude, brutish, or obscenely coarse person
WORD ORIGIN after the brutish creatures in *Gulliver's Travels*
yahweh *or* **yahveh** *n bible* a personal name of god
WORD ORIGIN Hebrew YHVH, with conjectural vowels
yak¹ *n* a Tibetan ox with long shaggy hair
WORD ORIGIN Tibetan *gyag*
yak² *slang n* **1** noisy, continuous, and trivial talk ▷*vb* **yakking, yakked** **2** to talk continuously about unimportant matters
WORD ORIGIN imitative
yakka *n Austral & NZ informal* work
WORD ORIGIN from a native Australian language
Yale lock *n trademark* a type of cylinder lock using a flat serrated key
WORD ORIGIN after L. *Yale*, inventor
yam *n* **1** a twining plant of tropical and subtropical regions, cultivated for its starchy roots which are eaten as a vegetable **2** the sweet potato
WORD ORIGIN Portuguese *inhame*
Yamagata *n* Prince **Aritomo** 1838–1922, Japanese soldier and politician. As war minister (1873) and chief of staff (1878), he modernized Japan's military system. He was premier of Japan (1889–93; 1898)
Yamani *n* Sheikh **Ahmed Zaki** born 1930, Saudi Arabian politician; minister of petroleum and mineral resources (1962–86)
Yamasaki *n* **Minoru** 1912–86, US architect. His buildings include St Louis Airport, Missouri (1953–55) and the World Trade Center, New York (1970–77)
Yamashita *n* **Tomoyuki** 1885–1946, Japanese general. He commanded Japanese forces in the Malayan campaign in World War II and took Singapore (1942); captured (1945) and hanged
yammer *informal vb* **1** to whine in a complaining manner ▷*n* **2** a yammering sound **3** nonsense or jabber
WORD ORIGIN Old English *geōmrian* to grumble
Yang *n* ▸see **Yin and Yang**
Yang¹ *n* See **Yin and Yang**
Yang² *n* **Chen Ning** born 1922, US physicist, born in China: with Tsung-Dao Lee, he disproved the physical principle known as the conservation of parity and shared the Nobel prize for physics (1957)
yank ⓘ *vb* **1** to pull (someone or something) with a sharp movement: *I yanked myself out of the water* ▷*n* **2** a sudden pull or jerk
WORD ORIGIN origin unknown
Yank *n slang* a person from the United States
Yankee *n* **1** *slang* ▸same as **Yank** **2** a person from the Northern United States ▷*adj* **3** of or characteristic of Yankees
WORD ORIGIN perhaps from Dutch *Jan Kees* John Cheese, nickname for English colonists
yap *vb* **yapping, yapped** **1** to bark with a high-pitched sound **2** *informal* to talk at length in an annoying or stupid way ▷*n* **3** a high-pitched bark **4** *slang* annoying or stupid speech **yappy** *adj*
WORD ORIGIN imitative
yarborough *n bridge, whist* a hand in which no card is higher than nine
WORD ORIGIN supposedly after the second earl of *Yarborough*, said to have bet a thousand to one against its occurrence
yard¹ *n* **1** a unit of length equal to 3 feet (0.9144 metre) **2** *naut* a spar slung across a ship's mast to extend the sail
WORD ORIGIN Old English *gierd* rod, twig
yard² *n* **1** a piece of enclosed ground, often adjoining or surrounded by a building or buildings **2** an enclosed or open area where a particular type of work is done: *a shipbuilding yard* **3** *Austral, US, & Canad* the garden of a house **4** *US & Canad* the winter pasture of deer, moose, and similar animals
WORD ORIGIN Old English *geard*
Yard *n* **the Yard** *Brit informal* ▸short for **Scotland Yard**
yardarm *n naut* the outer end of a ship's yard
yardstick *n* **1** a measure or standard used for comparison: *there's no yardstick for judging a problem of this sort* **2** a graduated measuring stick one yard long
yarmulke (yar-mull-ka) *n* a skullcap worn by Jewish men
WORD ORIGIN Yiddish
yarn ⓘ *n* **1** a continuous twisted strand of natural or synthetic fibres, used for knitting or making cloth **2** *informal* a long involved story **3** **spin a yarn** *informal* to tell such a story
WORD ORIGIN Old English *gearn*
yarrow *n* a wild plant with flat clusters of white flowers
WORD ORIGIN Old English *gearwe*
yashmak *n* a veil worn by a Muslim woman to cover her face in public
WORD ORIGIN Arabic
yaw *vb* **1** (of an aircraft or ship) to turn to one side or from side to side while moving ▷*n* **2** the act or movement of yawing
WORD ORIGIN origin unknown
yawl *n* **1** a two-masted sailing boat **2** a ship's small boat
WORD ORIGIN Dutch *jol* or Middle Low German *jolle*
yawn *vb* **1** to open one's mouth wide and take in air deeply, often when sleepy or bored **2** to be open wide as if threatening to engulf someone or something: *the doorway yawned blackly open at the end of the hall* ▷*n* **3** the act or an instance of yawning **yawning** *adj*
WORD ORIGIN Old English *geonian*
yaws *n* an infectious disease of tropical climates characterized by red skin eruptions
WORD ORIGIN Carib
Yb *chem* ytterbium
Y-chromosome *n* the sex chromosome that occurs as one of a pair with the X-chromosome in the males of many animals, including humans
yd yard (measure)
YDT Yukon Daylight Time
ye¹ (yee) *pron old-fashioned or dialect* you
WORD ORIGIN Old English *gē*

THESAURUS

yank *vb* **1 = pull**, tug, jerk, seize, snatch, pluck, hitch, wrench ▷*n* **2 = pull**, tug, jerk, snatch, hitch, wrench, tweak
yarn *n* **1 = thread**, fibre, cotton, wool **2** *(informal)* **= story**, tale, anecdote, account, narrative, fable, reminiscence, urban myth, tall story, urban legend, cock-and-bull story *(informal)*

DICTIONARY

ye² *adj (definite article) old-fashioned or jocular* the: *ye olde Rose and Crown pub* **WORD ORIGIN** a misinterpretation of *the*, written with the old letter thorn (þ), representing *th*

yea *interj* **1** *old-fashioned* yes ▹*adv* **2** *old-fashioned or literary* indeed or truly: *they wandered about the church, yea, even unto the altar* **WORD ORIGIN** Old English *gēa*

yeah *interj informal* ▸same as **yes**

year *n* **1** the time taken for the earth to make one revolution around the sun, about 365 days **2** the twelve months from January 1 to December 31 **3** a period of twelve months from any specified date **4** a specific period of time, usually occupying a definite part or parts of a twelve-month period, used for some particular activity: *the financial year* **5** a group of people who have started an academic course at the same time **6 year in, year out** regularly or monotonously, over a long period **7 years a** a long time: *the legal case could take years to resolve* **b** age, usually old age: *a man of his years* **WORD ORIGIN** Old English *gēar*

yearbook *n* a reference book published once a year containing details of events of the previous year

yearling *n* an animal that is between one and two years old

yearly ❶ *adj* **1** occurring, done, or appearing once a year or every year **2** lasting or valid for a year: *the yearly cycle* ▹*adv* **3** once a year

yearn ❶ *vb* **1** (often with *for*) to have an intense desire or longing: *he often yearned for life in a country town* **2** to feel tenderness or affection: *I yearn for you* **yearning** *n, adj* **WORD ORIGIN** Old English *giernan*

yeast *n* a yellowish fungus used in fermenting alcoholic drinks and in raising dough for bread **yeasty** *adj* **WORD ORIGIN** Old English *giest*

yebo *interj S African informal* yes **WORD ORIGIN** Zulu *yebo* yes, I agree

yell ❶ *vb* **1** to shout, scream, or cheer in a loud or piercing way ▹*n* **2** a loud piercing cry of pain, anger, or fear **WORD ORIGIN** Old English *giellan*

yellow ❶ *n* **1** the colour of a lemon or an egg yolk **2** anything yellow, such as yellow clothing or yellow paint: *painted in yellow* ▹*adj* **3** of the colour yellow; of the colour of a lemon or an egg yolk **4** *informal* cowardly or afraid **5** having a yellowish complexion ▹*vb* **6** to make or become yellow or yellower **yellowish** *or* **yellowy** *adj* **WORD ORIGIN** Old English *geolu*

yellow-belly *n, pl* **-bellies** *slang* a coward **yellow-bellied** *adj*

yellow card *n soccer* a piece of yellow pasteboard raised by a referee to indicate that a player has been booked for a serious violation of the rules

yellow fever *n* an acute infectious tropical disease causing fever and jaundice, caused by certain mosquitoes

yellowfin tuna *n* a large marine food fish of tropical and subtropical waters

yellowhammer *n* a European songbird with a yellowish head and body **WORD ORIGIN** origin unknown

Yellow Pages *pl n trademark* a telephone directory that lists businesses under the headings of the type of business or service they provide

yellow streak *n informal* a cowardly or weak trait

yelp *vb* **1** to utter a sharp or high-pitched cry of pain ▹*n* **2** a sharp or high-pitched cry of pain **WORD ORIGIN** Old English *gielpan* to boast

yen¹ *n, pl* **yen** the standard monetary unit of Japan **WORD ORIGIN** Japanese *en*

yen² ❶ *informal n* **1** a longing or desire ▹*vb* **yenning, yenned 2** to have a longing **WORD ORIGIN** perhaps from Chinese *yän* a craving

yeoman (yo-man) *n, pl* **-men** *history* a farmer owning and farming his own land **WORD ORIGIN** perhaps from *yongman* young man

yeoman of the guard *n* a member of the ceremonial bodyguard (**Yeomen of the Guard**) of the British monarch

yeomanry *n* **1** yeomen collectively **2** (in Britain) a former volunteer cavalry force

yep *interj informal* ▸same as **yes**

yes *interj* **1** used to express consent, agreement, or approval, or to answer when one is addressed **2** used to signal someone to speak or keep speaking, enter a room, or do something ▹*n* **3** an answer or vote of *yes* **4** a person who answers or votes *yes* **WORD ORIGIN** Old English *gēse*

yes man *n* a person who always agrees with his or her superior in order to gain favour

yesterday *n* **1** the day before today **2** the recent past ▹*adv* **3** on or during the day before today **4** in the recent past

yesteryear *formal or literary n* **1** last year or the past in general ▹*adv* **2** during last year or the past in general

yet ❶ *conj* **1** nevertheless or still: *I'm too tired to work, yet I have to go on* ▹*adv* **2** up until then or now: *this may be her most rewarding book yet* **3** still: *yet more work to do* **4** now (as contrasted with later): *not ready for that yet* **5** eventually in spite of everything: *I'll break your spirit yet!* **6 as yet** up until then or now **WORD ORIGIN** Old English *gīeta*

yeti *n* ▸same as **abominable snowman** **WORD ORIGIN** Tibetan

Yevtushenko *n* **Yevgeny Aleksandrovich** born 1933, Russian poet. His often outspoken poetry includes *Babi Yar* (1962), *Bratsk Station* (1966), and *Farewell to Red Banner* (1992)

yew *n* an evergreen tree with needle-like leaves, red berries, and fine-grained elastic wood **WORD ORIGIN** Old English *īw*

Y-fronts *pl n trademark* men's or boys' underpants that have a front opening within an inverted Y shape

YHA (in Britain) Youth Hostels Association

yid *n slang, offensive* a Jew **WORD ORIGIN** probably from *Yiddish*

Yiddish *n* **1** a language derived from High German, spoken by Jews in Europe and elsewhere by Jewish emigrants, and usually written in the Hebrew alphabet ▹*adj* **2** of this language **WORD ORIGIN** German *jüdisch* Jewish

THESAURUS

yearly *adj* **1 = annual**, each year, every year, once a year ▹*adv* **3 = annually**, every year, by the year, once a year, per annum

yearn *vb* **1** *(often with* **for***)* **= long**, desire, pine, pant, hunger, ache, lust, crave, covet, itch, languish, hanker after, have a yen for *(informal)*, eat your heart out over, set your heart upon, suspire *(archaic, poetic)*, would give your eyeteeth for

yell *vb* **1 = scream**, shout, cry out, howl, call out, wail, shriek, screech, squeal, bawl, holler *(informal)*, yelp, call at the top of your voice **OPPOSITE:** whisper ▹*n* **2 = scream**, cry, shout, roar, howl, shriek, whoop, screech, squeal, holler *(informal)*, yelp, yowl **OPPOSITE:** whisper

yellow *n* **1 = lemon**, gold, amber

yen² *n* **1 = longing**, desire, craving, yearning, passion, hunger, ache, itch, thirst, hankering

yet *conj* **1 = nevertheless**, still, however, for all that, notwithstanding, just the same, be that as it may ▹*adv* **2 = so far**, until now, up to now, still, as yet, even now, thus far, up till now, up to the present time **3 = still**, further, in addition, as well, moreover, besides, to boot, additionally, over and above, into the bargain **4 = now**, right now, just now, so soon, already

DICTIONARY

yield ◐ *vb* **1** to produce or bear **2** to give as a return: *some of his policies have yielded large savings* **3** to give up control of; surrender **4** to give way, submit, or surrender, through force or persuasion: *the players finally yielded to the weather* **5** to agree (to): *governments too weak to say no repeatedly yielded to petitions for charters* **6** to grant or allow: *to yield right of way* ▷ *n* **7** the amount produced
WORD ORIGIN Old English *gieldan*

yielding ◐ *adj* **1** compliant or submissive **2** soft or flexible: *he landed on a yielding surface rather than rock or board*

Yin and Yang *n* two complementary principles of Chinese philosophy: Yin is negative, dark, and feminine, Yang is positive, bright, and masculine
WORD ORIGIN Chinese *yin* dark + *yang* bright

yippee *interj* an exclamation of joy, pleasure, or anticipation

YMCA Young Men's Christian Association

yo *interj* an expression used as a greeting or to attract someone's attention
WORD ORIGIN origin unknown

yob ◐ *or* **yobbo** *n, pl* **yobs** *or* **yobbos** *Brit, Austral & NZ slang* a bad-mannered aggressive youth
yobbish *adj*
WORD ORIGIN perhaps back slang for *boy*

yodel *vb* **-delling, -delled** *or US* **-deling, -deled** **1** to sing with abrupt changes back and forth between the normal voice and falsetto, as in folk songs of the Swiss Alps ▷ *n* **2** the act or sound of yodelling **yodeller** *or US* **yodeler** *n*
WORD ORIGIN German *jodeln* (imitative)

yoga *n* **1** a Hindu system of philosophy aiming at spiritual, mental, and physical wellbeing by means of deep meditation, prescribed postures, and controlled breathing **2** a system of exercising involving such meditation, postures, and breathing
WORD ORIGIN Sanskrit: a yoking

yogi *n* a person who practises or is a master of yoga

yogurt *or* **yoghurt** *n* a slightly sour custard-like food made from milk curdled by bacteria, often sweetened and flavoured with fruit
WORD ORIGIN Turkish

yoke *n, pl* **yokes** *or* **yoke** **1** a wooden frame with a bar put across the necks of two animals to hold them together so that they can be worked as a team **2** a pair of animals joined by a yoke **3** a frame fitting over a person's shoulders for carrying buckets **4** an oppressive force or burden: *people are still suffering under the yoke of slavery* **5** a fitted part of a garment to which a fuller part is attached ▷ *vb* **yoking, yoked** **6** to put a yoke on **7** to unite or link
WORD ORIGIN Old English *geoc*

yokel *n disparaging* a person who lives in the country, esp. one who appears simple and old-fashioned
WORD ORIGIN perhaps from dialect *yokel* green woodpecker

yolk *n* the yellow part in the middle of an egg that provides food for the developing embryo
WORD ORIGIN Old English *geoloca*

Yom Kippur *n* an annual Jewish holiday celebrated as a day of fasting, with prayers of penitence
WORD ORIGIN Hebrew *yōm* day + *kippūr* atonement

yon *adj* **1** *chiefly Scot & N English dialect* that: *yon dog* ▷ *adv* **2** yonder: *he flicked glances hither and yon* ▷ *pron* **3** that person or thing: *yon was a pretty sight*
WORD ORIGIN Old English *geon*

yonder *adv* **1** over there ▷ *adj* **2** situated over there: *a tree at yonder waterfall*
WORD ORIGIN Old English *geond*

Yonge *n* **Charlotte M(ary)** 1823–1901, British novelist, whose works reflect the religious ideals of the Oxford Movement. Her best-known book is *The Heir of Redclyffe* (1853)

Yong Lo *or* **Yung-Lo** *n* 1360–1424, Chinese emperor (1404–24) of the Ming dynasty. He moved the capital from Nanjing to Peking (now Beijing), which he rebuilt. Also called: *Ch'eng Tsu*

yonks *pl n informal* a very long time: *he must have been planning this for yonks*
WORD ORIGIN origin unknown

yoo-hoo *interj* a call to attract a person's attention

yore *n* **of yore** a long time ago: *in days of yore*
WORD ORIGIN Old English *geāra*

yorker *n cricket* a ball bowled so as to pitch just under or just beyond the bat
WORD ORIGIN probably after the Yorkshire County Cricket Club

Yorkist *English history n* **1** a supporter of the royal House of York, esp. during the Wars of the Roses ▷ *adj* **2** of or relating to the supporters or members of the House of York

Yorks. Yorkshire

Yorkshire pudding *n* a baked pudding made from a batter of flour, eggs, and milk, often served with roast beef
WORD ORIGIN from *Yorkshire*, county in NE England

you *pron* **1** (refers to) the person or people addressed: *can I get you a drink?* **2** (refers to) an unspecified person or people in general: *stick to British goods and you can't go wrong* ▷ *n* **3** *informal* the personality of the person being addressed: *that hat isn't really you*
WORD ORIGIN Old English *ēow*

you'd you had *or* you would

you'll you will *or* you shall

young ◐ *adj* **1** having lived or existed for a relatively short time **2** having qualities associated with youth: *their innovative approach and young attitude appealed to him* **3** of or relating to youth: *he'd been a terrorist himself in France in his young days* **4** of a group representing the younger members of a larger organization: *Young Conservatives* ▷ *n* **5** young people in general: *that never seems very important to the young* **6** offspring, esp. young animals: *a deer suckling her young*
youngish *adj*
WORD ORIGIN Old English *geong*

Younghusband *n* Sir **Francis Edward** 1863–1942, British explorer, mainly of N India and Tibet. He used military force to compel the Dalai Lama to sign (1904) a trade agreement with Britain

THESAURUS

yield *vb* **1, 2 = produce**, give, provide, pay, return, supply, bear, net, earn, afford, generate, bring in, furnish, bring forth **OPPOSITE:** use up
3 = relinquish, resign, hand over, surrender, turn over, part with, make over, cede, give over, bequeath, abdicate, deliver up **OPPOSITE:** retain
4 = bow, submit, give in, surrender, give way, succumb, cave in *(informal)*, capitulate, knuckle under, resign yourself ▷ *n* **7a = produce**, crop, harvest, output **7b = profit**, return, income, revenue, earnings, takings **OPPOSITE:** loss

yielding *adj* **1 = submissive**, obedient, compliant, docile, easy, flexible, accommodating, pliant, tractable, acquiescent, biddable **OPPOSITE:** obstinate
2 = soft, pliable, springy, elastic, resilient, supple, spongy, unresisting, quaggy

yob *or* **yobbo** *(Brit, Austral & NZ slang) n* **= thug**, hooligan, lout, heavy *(slang)*, tough, rough *(informal)*, rowdy, yahoo, hoon *(Austral & NZ slang)*, hoodlum, ruffian, roughneck *(slang)*, tsotsi *(S African)*, cougan *(Austral slang)*, scozza *(Austral slang)*, bogan *(Austral slang)*

young *adj* **1a = immature**, juvenile, youthful, little, growing, green, junior, infant, adolescent, callow, unfledged, in the springtime of life **OPPOSITE:** old
1b = early, new, undeveloped, fledgling, newish, not far advanced **OPPOSITE:** advanced
▷ *n* **6 = offspring**, baby, litter, family, issue, brood, little onesy, progeny **OPPOSITE:** parent

DICTIONARY

youngster ❶ *n* a young person
your *adj* **1** of, belonging to, or associated with you: *ask your doctor to make the necessary calls* **2** of, belonging to, or associated with an unspecified person or people in general: *it is not right to take another baby to replace your own* **3** *informal* used to indicate all things or people of a certain type: *these characters are not your average housebreakers*
WORD ORIGIN Old English *ēower*
Yourcenar *n* **Marguerite,** original name *Marguerite de Crayencour*. 1903–87, French novelist and writer, in the US from 1939; noted for her historical novels, esp. *Mémoires d'Hadrien* (1952)
you're you are
yours *pron* **1** something belonging to you: *my reputation is better than yours* **2** your family: *a blessed Christmas to you and yours* **3** used in closing phrases at the end of a letter: *yours sincerely; yours faithfully* **4 of yours** belonging to you: *that husband of yours*
yourself *pron, pl* **-selves 1 a** the reflexive form of *you* **b** used for emphasis: *you've stated publicly that you yourself use drugs* **2** your normal self: *you're not yourself today*
yours truly *pron informal* I or me
WORD ORIGIN from the closing phrase of letters
youth ❶ *n* **1** the period between childhood and maturity **2** the quality or condition of being young, immature, or inexperienced: *his youth told against him in the contest* **3** a young man or boy **4** young people collectively: *there is still hope for today's youth* **5** the freshness, vigour, or vitality associated with being young
WORD ORIGIN Old English *geogoth*
youth club *n* a club that provides leisure activities for young people
youthful ❶ *adj* **1** vigorous or active: *the intermediate section was won by a youthful grandmother* **2** of, relating to, possessing, or associated with youth: *youthful good looks* **youthfully** *adv* **youthfulness** *n*
youth hostel *n* an inexpensive lodging place for young people travelling cheaply
YouTube *n* a website on which subscribers can post video files
you've you have
yowl *vb* **1** to produce a loud mournful wail or cry ▷*n* **2** a wail or howl
WORD ORIGIN Old Norse *gaula*
yo-yo *n, pl* **-yos 1** a toy consisting of a spool attached to a string, the end of which is held while it is repeatedly spun out and reeled in ▷*vb* **yo-yoing, yo-yoed 2** to change repeatedly from one position to another
WORD ORIGIN originally a trademark for this type of toy
Ypsilanti, Hypsilantis, *or* **Hypsilantes** *n* **1 Alexander** 1792–1828, Greek patriot, who led an unsuccessful revolt against the Turks (1821) **2** his brother, **Demetrios** 1793–1832, Greek revolutionary leader; commander in chief of Greek forces (1828–30) during the war of independence
yrs 1 years **2** yours
YST Yukon Standard Time
YT Yukon Territory
YTS (in Britain) Youth Training Scheme
ytterbium (it-terb-ee-um) *n chem* a soft silvery element that is used to improve the mechanical properties of steel. Symbol: Yb
WORD ORIGIN after *Ytterby*, Swedish quarry where discovered
yttrium (it-ree-um) *n chem* a silvery metallic element used in various alloys and in lasers. Symbol: Y
WORD ORIGIN see YTTERBIUM
yuan *n, pl* **-an** the standard monetary unit of the People's Republic of China
WORD ORIGIN Chinese *yüan* round object
Yuan Shi Kai *n* 1859–1916, Chinese general and statesman: first president (1912–16) of the Chinese republic
yucca *n* a tropical plant with spiky leaves and white flowers
WORD ORIGIN from a Native American language
yucky *or* **yukky** *adj* **yuckier, yuckiest** *or* **yukkier, yukkiest** *slang* disgusting or nasty
WORD ORIGIN from *yuck*, exclamation of disgust
Yugoslav *adj* **1** of the former Yugoslavia ▷*n* **2** a person from the former Yugoslavia
Yukawa *n* **Hideki.** 1907–81, Japanese nuclear physicist, who predicted (1935) the existence of mesons: Nobel prize for physics 1949
Yule *n literary or old-fashioned* Christmas or the Christmas season: *Yuletide*
WORD ORIGIN Old English *geōla*, originally a pagan feast lasting 12 days
yummy *slang adj* **-mier, -miest 1** delicious or attractive: *yummy sauces* ▷*interj* **2** Also: **yum-yum** an exclamation indicating pleasure or delight, as in anticipation of delicious food
WORD ORIGIN *yum-yum* (imitative)
Yung-lo *n* a variant transliteration of the Chinese name for **Yong Lo**
yuppie *n* **1** a young highly-paid professional person, esp. one who has a fashionable way of life ▷*adj* **2** typical of or reflecting the values of yuppies: *a yuppie accessory*
WORD ORIGIN *y(oung) u(rban)* or *u(pwardly mobile) p(rofessional)*
yuppify *vb* **-fies, -fying, -fied** to make yuppie in nature: *Mount Pleasant was being yuppified* **yuppification** *n*
YWCA Young Women's Christian Association

THESAURUS

youngster *n* = **youth**, girl, boy, kid *(informal)*, lad, teenager, juvenile, cub, young person, lass, young adult, pup *(informal, chiefly Brit)*, urchin, teenybopper *(slang)*, young shaver *(informal)*, young 'un *(informal)*
youth *n* **1 = immaturity**, adolescence, early life, young days, boyhood *or* girlhood, salad days, juvenescence **OPPOSITE:** old age **3 = boy**, lad, youngster, kid *(informal)*, teenager, young man, adolescent, teen *(informal)*, stripling, young shaver *(informal)* **OPPOSITE:** adult
youthful *adj* **2 = young**, juvenile, childish, immature, boyish, pubescent, girlish, puerile **OPPOSITE:** elderly

Zz

DICTIONARY

z *or* **Z** *n, pl* **z's, Z's** *or* **Zs** **1** the 26th and last letter of the English alphabet **2 from A to Z** ▸ see **a** (sense 3)
z *maths* (along with *x* and *y*) an unknown quantity
Z *chem* atomic number
zabaglione (zab-al-**lyoh**-nee) *n* a dessert made of egg yolks, sugar, and wine, whipped together
WORD ORIGIN Italian
Zaghlul *n* **Saad** 1857–1927, Egyptian nationalist politician; prime minister (1924)
Zahir-ud-din Muhammad *n* the original name of **Baber**
Zamyatin *n* **Yevgenii Ivanovich** 1884–1937, Russian novelist and writer, in Paris from 1931, whose works include satirical studies of provincial life in Russia and England, where he worked during World War I, and the dystopian novel *We* (1924)
zany (**zane**-ee) *adj* **zanier, zaniest** comical in an endearing way
WORD ORIGIN Italian dialect *Zanni*, nickname for *Giovanni* John; traditional name for a clown
zap *vb* **zapping, zapped** *slang* **1** to kill, esp. by shooting **2** to change television channels rapidly by remote control **3** to move quickly
WORD ORIGIN imitative
Zappa *n* **Frank** 1940–93, US rock musician, songwriter, and experimental composer: founder and only permanent member of the Mothers of Invention. His recordings include *Freak Out* (1966), *Hot Rats* (1969), and *Sheik Yerbouti* (1979)
Zatlers *n* **Valdis** born 1955, Latvian politician, president of Latvia from 2007
Zátopek *n* **Emil** 1922–2000, Czech runner; winner of the 5000 and 10 000 metres and the marathon at the 1952 Olympic Games in Helsinki
zeal ❶ *n* great enthusiasm or eagerness, esp. for a religious movement
WORD ORIGIN Greek *zēlos*
zealot (**zel**-lot) *n* a fanatic or an extreme enthusiast **zealotry** *n*
zealous (**zel**-luss) *adj* extremely eager or enthusiastic **zealously** *adv*
Zeami *or* **Seami** *n* **Motokiyo** 1363–1443, Japanese dramatist, regarded as the greatest figure in the history of No drama
zebra *n, pl* **-ras** *or* **-ra** a black-and-white striped African animal of the horse family
WORD ORIGIN Old Spanish: wild ass
zebra crossing *n Brit* a pedestrian crossing marked by broad black and white stripes: once on the crossing the pedestrian has right of way
zebu (**zee**-boo) *n* a domesticated ox of Africa and Asia, with a humped back and long horns
WORD ORIGIN French
zed *n* the British and New Zealand spoken form of the letter *z*
zee *n* the US spoken form of the letter *z*
Zeffirelli *n* **Franco** born 1923, Italian stage and film director and designer, noted esp. for his work in opera
Zeitgeist (**tsite**-guyst) *n* the spirit or general outlook of a specific time or period
WORD ORIGIN German, literally: time spirit
Zellweger *n* **Renée** (**Kathleen**) born 1969, US film actress, best known for her performances in *Nurse Betty* (2000), *Bridget Jones's Diary* (2001) and its sequel *Bridget Jones and the Edge of Reason* (2004), and *Chicago* (2002)
Zemlinsky *n* **Alexander** 1871–1942, Austrian composer, living in the US from 1938. His works include the operas *Es war einmal* (1900) and *Eine florentische Tragödie* (1917) and the *Lyric Symphony* (1923)
Zen *n* a Japanese form of Buddhism that concentrates on learning through meditation and intuition
Zend-Avesta *n* the Zoroastrian scriptures (the **Avesta**), together with the traditional interpretive commentary known as the **Zend**
zenith *n* **1** the point in the sky directly above an observer **2** the highest or most successful point of anything: *he was at the zenith of his military career* **zenithal** *adj*
WORD ORIGIN Arabic *samt arrās* path over one's head
Zenobia *n* 3rd century AD, queen of Palmyra (?267–272), who was captured by the Roman emperor Aurelian
Zeno of Elea *n* ?490–?430 BC, Greek Eleatic philosopher; disciple of Parmenides. He defended the belief that motion and change are illusions in a series of paradoxical arguments, of which the best known is that of Achilles and the tortoise
zephyr (**zef**-fer) *n* a soft gentle breeze
WORD ORIGIN Greek *zephuros* the west wind
Zeppelin *n* a large cylindrical rigid German airship of the early 20th century
WORD ORIGIN after Count von *Zeppelin*, its designer
zero ❶ *n, pl* **-ros** *or* **-roes** **1** the cardinal number between +1 and −1 **2** the symbol, 0, representing this number **3** the line or point on a scale of measurement from which the graduations commence **4** the lowest point or degree: *my credibility is down to zero* **5** nothing or nil **6** the temperature, pressure, etc. that registers a reading of zero on a scale ▸ *adj* **7** amounting to zero: *zero inflation* **8** *meteorol* (of visibility) limited to a very short distance ▸ *vb* **-roing, -roed** **9** to adjust (an instrument or scale) so as to read zero
WORD ORIGIN Arabic *sifr* empty
zero gravity *n* the state of weightlessness
zero hour *n* **1** *mil* the time set for the start of an operation **2** *informal* a critical time, usually at the beginning of an action
zero in on *vb* **1** to aim a weapon at (a target) **2** to concentrate one's attention on
zero-rated *adj* denoting goods on which the buyer pays no value-added tax
zest *n* **1** invigorating or keen excitement or enjoyment: *he has a zest for life and a quick intellect* **2** added interest, flavour, or charm: *he said that she would provide a new zest for his government* **3** the peel of an orange or lemon, used as flavouring **zestful** *adj*
WORD ORIGIN French *zeste*
Zeta-Jones *n* **Catherine**, original name *Catherine Jones*. born 1969, Welsh actress, who made her name in the TV series *The Darling Buds of May* (1991) before starring in the films *Traffic* (2000), *Chicago* (2002), and *Smoke and Mirrors* (2004). She is married to the US actor Michael Douglas
Zeus *n Greek myth* the ruler of the gods
Zeuxis *n* late 5th century BC, Greek painter, noted for the verisimilitude of his works
Zhivkov *n* **Todor** 1911–98, Bulgarian statesman and party leader; prime minister (1962–71); president (1971–89)
Zhou En Lai *n* the Pinyin

THESAURUS

zeal *n* **= enthusiasm**, passion, zest, fire, spirit, warmth, devotion, verve, fervour, eagerness, gusto, militancy, fanaticism, ardour, earnestness, keenness, fervency
OPPOSITE: apathy
zero *n* **1 = nought**, nothing, nil, naught, cipher **4 = rock bottom**, the bottom, an all-time low, a nadir, as low as you can get, the lowest point *or* ebb

DICTIONARY

transliteration of the Chinese name for **Chou En-lai**

Zhuangzi *or* **Chuang-tzu** *n* ?369–286 BC, Chinese philosopher, who greatly influenced Chinese religion through the book of Taoist philosophy that bears his name

Zhu De *n* the Pinyin transliteration of the Chinese name for **Chu Teh**

Zhukov *n* **Georgi Konstantinovich** 1896–1974, Soviet marshal. In World War II, he led the offensives that broke the sieges of Stalingrad and Leningrad (1942–43) and later captured Warsaw and Berlin; minister of defence (1955–57)

Zia ul Haq *n* **Mohammed** 1924–88, Pakistani general: president of Pakistan (1978–88), following the overthrow (1977) of Z. A. Bhutto by a military coup. He was killed in an air crash, possibly through sabotage

Zidane *n* **Zinedine** born 1972, French football player, known as *Zizou*; scored two goals in the 1998 World Cup final

Ziegfeld *n* **Florenz** 1869–1932, US theatrical producer, noted for his series of extravagant revues (1907–31), known as the Ziegfeld Follies

ziggurat *n* (in ancient Mesopotamia) a temple in the shape of a pyramid
WORD ORIGIN Assyrian *ziqqurati* summit

zigzag *n* **1** a line or course having sharp turns in alternating directions ▷ *adj* **2** formed in or proceeding in a zigzag ▷ *adv* **3** in a zigzag manner ▷ *vb* **-zagging, -zagged 4** to move in a zigzag
WORD ORIGIN German *zickzack*

zilch *n informal* nothing
WORD ORIGIN origin unknown

Zille *n* **Helen** born 1951, South African politician and journalist: mayor of Cape Town from 2006 and leader of the Democratic Alliance party from 2007

zillion *n, pl* **-lions** *or* **-lion** *(often pl) informal* an extremely large but unspecified number: *there are zillions of beautiful spots to visit*
WORD ORIGIN after *million*

Zimmer *n trademark* a tubular frame with rubber feet, used as a support to help disabled or infirm people walk

zinc *n chem* a brittle bluish-white metallic element that is used in alloys such as brass, to form a protective coating on metals, and in battery electrodes. Symbol: Zn
WORD ORIGIN German *Zink*

zinc ointment *n* a medicinal ointment consisting of zinc oxide, petroleum jelly, and paraffin

zinc oxide *n chem, pharmacol* a white insoluble powder used as a pigment and in making zinc ointment

zing *n* **1** *informal* the quality in something that makes it lively or interesting **2** a short high-pitched buzzing sound, like the sound of a bullet or vibrating string
WORD ORIGIN imitative

zinnia *n* a plant of tropical and subtropical America, with solitary heads of brightly coloured flowers
WORD ORIGIN after J. G. *Zinn*, botanist

Zinoviev *n* **Grigori Yevseevich,** original name *Ovsel Gershon Aronov Radomyslsky*. 1883–1936, Soviet politician; chairman of the Comintern (1919–26) executed for supposed complicity in the murder of Kirov. He was the supposed author of the forged 'Zinoviev letter' urging British Communists to revolt, publication of which helped to defeat (1924) the first Labour Government

Zinzendorf *n* Count **Nikolaus Ludwig von** 1700–60, German religious reformer, who organized the Moravian Church

Zion *n* **1** the hill on which the city of Jerusalem stands **2 a** the modern Jewish nation **b** Israel as the national home of the Jewish people **3** *Christianity* heaven

Zionism *n* a political movement for the establishment and support of a national homeland for Jews in what is now Israel **Zionist** *n, adj*

zip ❶ *n* **1** Also called: **zip fastener** a fastener with two parallel rows of metal or plastic teeth, one on either side of a closure, which are interlocked by a sliding tab **2** *informal* energy or vigour **3** a short sharp whizzing sound, like the sound of a passing bullet ▷ *vb* **zipping, zipped 4** (often foll. by *up*) to fasten with a zip **5** to move with a sharp whizzing sound: *bullets zipped and ricocheted all around us* **6** to hurry or rush
WORD ORIGIN imitative

zip code *n* ▸ the US equivalent of **postcode**
WORD ORIGIN *z(one) i(mprovement) p(lan)*

zipper *n US & Canad* ▸ same as **zip** (sense 1)

zippy *adj* **-pier, -piest** *informal* full of energy

zircon *n mineral* a hard mineral consisting of zirconium silicate, used as a gemstone and in industry
WORD ORIGIN German *Zirkon*

zirconium *n chem* a greyish-white metallic element, occurring chiefly in zircon, that is exceptionally corrosion-resistant. Symbol: Zr

Ziska *or Czech* **Žižka** *n* **Jan** ?1370–1424, Bohemian soldier, who successfully led the Hussite rebellion (1420–24) against emperor Sigismund

zit *n slang* a spot or pimple

zither *n* a musical instrument consisting of numerous strings stretched over a flat box and plucked to produce notes **zitherist** *n*
WORD ORIGIN Greek *kithara*

Zi Xi *or* **Tz'u-hsi** *n* 1835–1908, Chinese empress dowager, who as regent for her son Tong Zhi and her nephew Guang Xu dominated Chinese politics from 1861 to 1908. Her reactionary policies were instrumental in the fall of imperial China

zloty *n, pl* **-tys** *or* **-ty** the standard monetary unit of Poland
WORD ORIGIN Polish: golden

Zn *chem* zinc

zodiac *n* **1** an imaginary belt in the sky within which the sun, moon, and planets appear to move, and which is divided into 12 equal areas called **signs of the zodiac,** each named after the constellation which once lay in it **2** *astrol* a diagram, usually circular, representing this belt **zodiacal** *adj*
WORD ORIGIN Greek *zōidion* animal sign, from *zōion* animal

Zoffany *n* **John** or **Johann** ?1733–1810, British painter, esp. of portraits; born in Germany

Zog I *n* 1895–1961, king of Albania (1928–39), formerly prime minister (1922–24) and president (1925–28). He allowed Albania to become dominated by Fascist Italy and fled into exile when Mussolini invaded (1939)

zombie *or* **zombi** *n, pl* **-bies** *or* **-bis 1** a person who appears to be lifeless, apathetic, or totally lacking in independent judgment **2** a corpse brought to life by witchcraft
WORD ORIGIN W African *zumbi* good-luck fetish

zone ❶ *n* **1** a region, area, or section characterized by some distinctive feature or quality: *a demilitarized zone* **2** *geog* one of the divisions of the earth's surface according to temperature **3** a section on a transport route **4** *maths* a portion of a sphere between two parallel lines

THESAURUS

Z

zip *n* **2** *(informal)* **= energy**, go *(informal)*, life, drive, spirit, punch *(informal)*, pep, sparkle, vitality, vigour, verve, zest, gusto, get-up-and-go *(informal)*, oomph *(informal)*, brio, zing *(informal)*, liveliness, vim *(slang)*, pizzazz *or* pizazz *(informal)* **OPPOSITE:** lethargy ▷ *vb* **5, 6 = speed**, shoot, fly, tear, rush, flash, dash, hurry, barrel (along) *(informal, chiefly US & Canad)*, buzz, streak, hare *(Brit informal)*, zoom, whizz *(informal)*, hurtle, pelt, burn rubber *(informal)*

zone *n* **1 = area**, region, section, sector, district, territory, belt, sphere, tract

DICTIONARY

intersecting the sphere **5** NZ a catchment area for a specific school ▷*vb* **zoning, zoned 6** to divide (a place) into zones for different uses or activities **zonal** *adj* **zoning** *n*
WORD ORIGIN Greek *zōnē* girdle

zonked *adj Brit, Austral & NZ slang* **1** highly intoxicated with drugs or alcohol **2** exhausted
WORD ORIGIN imitative

zoo *n, pl* **zoos** a place where live animals are kept, studied, bred, and exhibited to the public
WORD ORIGIN from *zoological garden*

zooid (zoh-oid) *n* **1** any independent animal body, such as an individual of a coral colony **2** a cell or body, produced by an organism and capable of independent motion, such as a gamete
WORD ORIGIN Greek *zōion* animal

zool. 1 zoological **2** zoology

zoological garden *n* ▸the formal term for **zoo**

zoology *n* the study of animals, including their classification, structure, physiology, and history **zoological** *adj* **zoologist** *n*
WORD ORIGIN Greek *zōion* animal + -LOGY

zoom ❶ *vb* **1** to move very rapidly: *the first rocket zoomed into the sky* **2** to increase or rise rapidly: *stocks zoomed on the American exchange* **3** to move with or make a continuous buzzing or humming sound ▷*n* **4** the sound or act of zooming **5** a zoom lens
WORD ORIGIN imitative

zoom in *or* **out** *vb photog, films, television* to increase or decrease rapidly the magnification of the image of a distant object by means of a zoom lens

zoom lens *n* a lens system that can make the details of a picture larger or smaller while keeping the picture in focus

zoophyte (zoh-a-fite) *n* any animal resembling a plant, such as a sea anemone
WORD ORIGIN Greek *zōion* animal + *phuton* plant

Zorn *n* **Anders Leonhard** 1860–1920, Swedish painter and etcher, esp. of impressionist portraits and landscapes

Zoroastrianism (zorr-oh-**ass**-tree-an-iz-zum) *or* **Zoroastrism** *n* the religion founded by the ancient Persian prophet Zoroaster, based on the concept of a continuous struggle between good and evil **Zoroastrian** *adj*

Zorrilla y Moral *n* **José** 1817–93, Spanish poet and dramatist, noted for his romantic plays based on national legends, esp. *Don Juan Tenorio* (1844)

zounds *interj old-fashioned* a mild oath indicating surprise or indignation
WORD ORIGIN euphemistic shortening of *God's wounds*

Zr *chem* zirconium

Zsigmondy *n* **Richard Adolf** 1865–1929, German chemist, born in Austria, noted for his work on colloidal particles and, with H. Siedentopf, his introduction (1903) of the ultramicroscope: Nobel prize for chemistry 1925

zucchetto (tsoo-**ket**-toe) *n, pl* **-tos** *RC church* a small round skullcap worn by clergymen and varying in colour according to the rank of the wearer
WORD ORIGIN Italian

zucchini (zoo-**keen**-ee) *n, pl* **-ni** *or* **-nis** *chiefly US, Canad, & Austral* a courgette
WORD ORIGIN Italian

Zuckerman *n* **Solly**, Baron 1904–93, British zoologist, born in South Africa; chief scientific adviser (1964–71) to the British Government. His books include *The Social Life of Monkeys* (1932) and the autobiography *From Apes to Warlords* (1978)

Zukerman *n* **Pinchas** born 1948, Israeli violinist

Zulu *n* **1** *pl* **-lus** *or* **-lu** a member of a tall Black people of Southern Africa **2** the language of this people

Zurbarán *n* **Francisco de** 1598–1664, Spanish Baroque painter, esp. of religious subjects

Zweig *n* **1 Arnold** 1887–1968, German novelist, famous for his realistic war novel *The Case of Sergeant Grischa* (1927) **2 Stefan** 1881–1942, Austrian novelist, dramatist, essayist, and poet

Zwicky *n* **Fritz** 1898–1974, Swiss astronomer and physicist, working in the US from 1925; noted for his study of supernovae

Zworykin *n* **Vladimir Kosma** 1889–1982, US physicist and television pioneer, born in Russia. He developed the first practical television camera

zygote *n* the cell resulting from the union of an ovum and a spermatozoon
WORD ORIGIN Greek *zugōtos* yoked

THESAURUS

zoom *vb* **1 = speed**, shoot, fly, tear, rush, flash, dash, barrel (along) (*informal, chiefly US & Canad*), buzz, streak, hare (*Brit informal*), zip (*informal*), whizz (*informal*), hurtle, pelt, burn rubber (*informal*)